CHILDREN'S CORE COLLECTION

TWENTY-FIRST EDITION

CORE COLLECTION SERIES

**FORMERLY
STANDARD CATALOG SERIES**

CHRISTI SHOWMAN FARRAR, GENERAL EDITOR

**CHILDREN'S CORE COLLECTION
MIDDLE AND JUNIOR HIGH CORE COLLECTION
SENIOR HIGH CORE COLLECTION
PUBLIC LIBRARY CORE COLLECTION: NONFICTION
PUBLIC LIBRARY CORE COLLECTION: FICTION**

CHILDREN'S
CORE COLLECTION

TWENTY-FIRST EDITION

EDITED BY

EVE-MARIE MILLER

LIZA OLDHAM

AND

CHRISTI SHOWMAN FARRAR

H. W. Wilson
A Division of EBSCO Information Services
Ipswich, Massachusetts
2014

GREY HOUSE PUBLISHING

ISBN 978-0-8242-1239-1

Abridged Dewey Decimal Classification and Relative Index, Edition 15 is © 2004-2012 OCLC Online Computer Library Center, Inc. Used with Permission. DDC, Dewey, Dewey Decimal Classification, and WebDewey are registered trademarks of OCLC.

Children's Core Collection, 2014, published by Grey House Publishing, Inc., Amenia, NY, under exclusive license from EBSCO Infomation Systems, Inc.

A catalog record for this title is available from the Library of Congress.

PRINTED IN CANADA

CONTENTS

CONTENTS

PREFACE

CHILDREN'S CORE COLLECTION is a comprehensive list of fiction and nonfiction books recommended for children from preschool through grade six, together with professional aids for librarians and library media specialists. The Core Collections are also available in electronic format via EBSCO*host*, updated weekly.

What's new in this Edition?

A new feature is the identification of titles that are considered "most highly recommended". These titles constitute a short list of the essential books in a given category or on a given subject. There are often a number of recommended titles on a single subject, such as biographies of Abraham Lincoln, and the Short List designation helps a user who wants only one or two. A star (★) at the start of an entry indicates that a book is a "most highly recommended" title.

This edition includes more than 17,000 book titles, over 6,000 more than the 20th edition. Of these 17,000 titles, over 4,000 titles are new since the 20th edition. There are broad revisions in the areas of computers, math, the sciences, and the arts.

This is the first edition of the CHILDREN'S CORE COLLECTION published under EBSCO Information Services. As such, users may notice some formatting and indexing changes that reflect differences in book processing procedures and the merging of two bodies of metadata. These changes include, but are not limited to, the move of the E section to before Fiction. As with any transition, there have been adjustments and challenges, but EBSCO is committed to the CHILDREN'S CORE COLLECTION, and to all of the titles in the Core Collections line. EBSCO invites feedback from Core Collections customers at corecollections@ebsco.com.

Scope

All books listed are published in the United States, or published in Canada or the United Kingdom and distributed in the United States. All titles were available for purchase at the time of printing.

The Core Collection excludes the following: non-English-language materials, with the exception of bilingual materials, dictionaries, and similar items; textbooks; and books about individual computer programs or versions of programs, and other topics that quickly become outdated.

Preparation

Books included in this edition were selected by experienced librarians representing public library systems and school libraries across the United States who also act as a committee of advisors on library policy and trends. The names of participating librarians and their affiliations are listed in the Acknowledgments.

Organization

The Core Collection is organized into two parts: the Classified Collection; and an Author, Title, and Subject Index.

Part 1. Classified Collection. This is arranged according to the Dewey Decimal Classification. Within classes, arrangement is by main entry, with complete bibliographical and cataloging information given for each book. The classified arrangement, along with the descriptive and critical annotations, provides a useful guide to book selection. Entries include such information as price and ISBN to facilitate acquisitions.

Part 2. Author, Title, and Subject Index. This is a comprehensive key to the Classified List with entries for authors, titles, and subjects.

ACKNOWLEDGMENTS

H. W. Wilson and EBSCO Information Services express special gratitude to the following librarians who both advised the company in editorial matters and assisted in the selection and weeding of titles for this Core Collection:

Advisory Board

Betty Carter
Texas Woman's University
Denton, Texas

Gail de Vos
University of Alberta
Edmonton, Alberta, Canada

Pam Spencer Holley
Library Consultant
Hallwood, Virginia

Angela Leeper
University of Richmond
Richmond, Virginia

John Peters
Children's Literature Specialist
Bronx, New York

Emily Tragert
Noble and Greenough School
Dedham, Massachusetts

Linda Ward-Callaghan
Joliet Public Library
Joliet, Illinois

The following EBSCO librarians and contributors were instrumental in the creation of this collection:

Julie Corsaro
Jennifer Sawtelle
Kendal Spires
Gabriela Toth
Brittany Wylde

DIRECTIONS FOR USE OF THE
CORE COLLECTION

USES OF THE COLLECTION

CHILDREN'S CORE COLLECTION is designed to serve a number of purposes:

As an aid in purchasing. The Core Collection is designed to assist in the selection and ordering of titles. Annotations and grade level designations are provided for each title along with information concerning the publisher, ISBN, price, and availability. Since Part 1, Classified Collection, is arranged according to the Dewey Decimal Classification, the Core Collection may be used to identify parts of the library collection that should be updated or strengthened. In evaluating the suitability of a work each library will want to consider the special character of the school and community it serves.

As an aid in user service. Every title in this Core Collection is a recommended work of its kind and can be given with confidence to a user who expresses a need based on topic, genre, etc. Reference work and user service are further aided by information about grade level, sequels, and companion volumes; by the descriptive and critical annotations; and by the series and subject headings in the Index. In addition, the Index includes entries under names of illustrators and series.

As an aid in curriculum support. The classification, subject indexing, annotations, and grade level designations are helpful in identifying materials appropriate for classroom use.

As an aid in collection maintenance. Information about titles available on a subject facilitates decisions to rebind, replace, or discard items. If a book has been deleted from the Core Collection in this edition because it is no longer in print, that deletion is not intended as a sign that the book is no longer valuable or that it should necessarily be weeded from the collection.

As an aid in professional development. The Core Collection is useful in courses that deal with children's literature and book selection, especially in the creation of bibliographies and reading lists.

ORGANIZATION

The Core Collection consists of two parts: a Classified Collection, and an Author, Title, and Subject Index.

Part 1. Classified Collection

The Classified Collection is arranged with nonfiction books first, classified according to the Dewey Decimal Classification in numerical order from 000 to 999. Individual biographies are classed at 92 and follow the 920s (collective biography). Three sections follow nonfiction: Easy Books (E), consisting chiefly of picture books of interest to children from preschool to grade three; Fiction (Fic); and Story Collections (S C). The information supplied for each book includes bibliographic description, suggested subject headings, an annotation, and frequently, an evaluation from a quote source.

An Outline of Classification, which serves as a table of contents for the Classified Collection, is reproduced below. It should be noted that many topics can be classified in more than one discipline. If a particular title is not found where it might be expected, the Index should be consulted to determine if it is classified elsewhere.

Within classes, works are arranged alphabetically under main entry, usually the author. Works of individual biography are arranged alphabetically under the biography's subject.

Each listing consists of a full bibliographical description. Prices, which are always subject to change, have been obtained from the publisher, when available, and are as current as possible. Entries include recommended subject headings derived from the *Sears List of Subject Headings,* a suggested classification number from the *Abridged Dewey Decimal Classification and Relative Index,* a brief description of the contents, and, whenever possible, an evaluation from a quoted source. The following is an example of a typical entry and a description of its components:

★**Silverstein, Alvin**
Wildfires; the science behind raging infernos; [by] Alvin and Virginia Silverstein and Laura Silverstein Nunn. Enslow Publishers 2010 48p il map (The science behind natural disasters) lib bdg $23.95
Grades: 4 5 6   **634.9**
1. Wildfires
ISBN 978-0-7660-2973-6 (lib bdg); 0-7660-2973-5 (lib bdg)
LC 2004-13282
"Examines the science behind wildfires, including what causes them, the different types of wildfires, their devastating effects, and how to stay safe during a wildfire" Publisher's note
"Scientific explanations are accompanied by plentiful color diagrams that will help students to grasp causes and effect.... Photos...are effective, and are sometimes turning into helpful, lively diagrams by the addition of such features as wind-direction arrows." SLJ
Includes glossary and bibliographical references

The star at the start of the entry indicates this is a "most highly recommended" title. The name of the author, Alvin Silverstein, is given in conformity with *Anglo-American Cataloguing Rules,* 2nd edition, 2002 revision. The title of the book is *Wildfires; the science behind raging infernos.* The book was published by Enslow Publishers in 2010.

The book has 48 pages and contains illustrations. It is published in the "The science behind natural disasters" series, in a library binding, and sells for $23.95. (Prices given were current when the Collection went to press.) The book is recommended for any of the following grade levels: 4 5 6.

At the end of the last line of type in the body entry is the figure 634.9 in bold face type. This is the classification number derived from the fifteenth edition of the *Abridged Dewey Decimal Classification.* The number 634.9 is the classification number for "Forestry".

The numbered term "1. Wildfires" is a recommended subject heading for this book based on *Sears List of Subject Headings.*

The ISBN (International Standard Book Number) is included to facilitate ordering. The Library of Congress control number is provided when available.

Following are three notes supplying additional information about the book. The first is a description of the book's content. The second is a critical note from *School Library Journal.* Such annotations are useful in evaluating books for selection and in determining which of several books on the same subject is best suited for the individual reader. The final note describes special features, in this case a glossary and a bibliography. Notes are also made to describe sequels and companion volumes, editions available, awards, and publication history.

Part 2. Author, Title, and Subject Index

The Index is a single alphabetical list of all the books entered in the Core Collection. Each book is entered under author; title (if distinctive); and subject. The classification number, displayed in boldface type, is the key to the location of the main entry for the book in the Classified Collection.

Appropriate added entries are made for joint authors and editors. "See" references are made from forms of names or subjects that are not used as headings. "See also" references are made to related or more specific headings.

The following are examples of Index entries for the book cited above:

Author	**Silverstein, Alvin** Wildfires	**634.9**
Title	**Wildfires;** the science behind raging infernos	**634.9**
Subject	**Wildfires** Silverstein, A. Wildfires	**634.9**
Publisher's series	**The science behind natural disasters** [series] Silverstein, A. Wildfires	**634.9**
Joint authors	**Silverstein, Virginia B.** (jt. auth) Silverstein, A. Wildfires	**634.9**

Standards Used

Anglo-American Cataloguing Rules, 2nd ed., 2002 revision, 2005 update. Chicago: American Library Association, 2005.

Dewey, Melvil. *Abridged Dewey Decimal Classification and Relative Index.* 15th ed. Edited by Joan S. Mitchell, et al. Dublin, Ohio: OCLC, 2012.

McCarthy, Susan and Joseph Miller, eds. *Sears List of Subject Headings.* 20th ed. New York: The H. W. Wilson Company, 2010.

This index is an alphabetical list of all the books entered in the Core Collection. Each book is entered under author, title (if distinctive), and subject. The classification number, displayed in boldface type, is the key to the location of the main entry for the book in the Core Collection.

Appropriate added entries are made for joint authors and editors. "See" references are made from forms of names or subject that are not used as headings. "See also" references are made to related and/or more specific headings.

The following are examples of index entries for the book cited above:

Author	Silverstein, Alvin	
	Wildfires	634.9
Title	Wildfires : the science behind raging infernos	634.9
Subject	Wildfires	
	Silverstein, Wildfires	634.9
Publisher series	The science behind natural disasters [series]	
	Silverstein, A. Wildfires	634.9
Joint author	Silverstein, Virginia B.	
	(joint) Silverstein, A. Wildfires	634.9

Standards Used

Index to Chicago Citation Index, 3rd ed., 2002 rev. ed., 2005 update. Chicago: American Library Association, 2005.

Hawes, Kevin Alex, and Francesca DeFranco. Classification and Reference Index, 5th ed. Edited by Joan S. Mitchell et al. Dublin, Ohio: OCLC, 2013.

McGraw, Susan, and Joseph Miller, eds. Sears List of Subject Headings, 20th ed. New York: The H.W. Wilson Company, 2010.

OUTLINE OF CLASSIFICATION

Reproduced below is the Second Summary of the Dewey Decimal Classification.* As Part 1 of this Core Collection is arranged according to this classification, the outline will serve as a table of contents for it. Please note, however, that the inclusion of this outline is not to be considered a substitute for consulting the Dewey Decimal Classification itself.

* Reproduced from Edition 15 of the Abridged Dewey Decimal Classification and Relative Index, published in 2012, by permission of OCLC Online Computer Library Center, Inc., owner of copyright.

OUTLINE OF CLASSIFICATION

Reproduced below is the Second Summary of the Dewey Decimal Classification. As Part 1 of this Core Collection is arranged according to this classification, this outline will serve as a table of contents for it. Please note, however, that the inclusion of this outline is not to be considered a substitute for consulting the Dewey Decimal Classification itself.

000 Computer science, knowledge & systems
010 Bibliographies
020 Library & information sciences
030 Encyclopedias & books of facts
040 [Unassigned]
050 Magazines, journals & serials
060 Associations, organizations & museums
070 News media, journalism & publishing
080 Quotations
090 Manuscripts & rare books

100 Philosophy
110 Metaphysics
120 Epistemology
130 Parapsychology & occultism
140 Philosophical schools of thought
150 Psychology
160 Logic
170 Ethics
180 Ancient, medieval & eastern philosophy
190 Modern western philosophy

200 Religion
210 Philosophy & theory of religion
220 The Bible
230 Christianity & Christian theology
240 Christian practice & observance
250 Christian pastoral practice & religious orders
260 Christian organization, social work & worship
270 History of Christianity
280 Christian denominations
290 Other religions

300 Social sciences, sociology & anthropology
310 Statistics
320 Political science
330 Economics
340 Law
350 Public administration & military science
360 Social problems & social services
370 Education
380 Commerce, communications & transportation
390 Customs, etiquette & folklore

400 Language
410 Linguistics
420 English & Old English languages
430 German & related languages
440 French & related languages
450 Italian, Romanian & related languages
460 Spanish & Portuguese languages
470 Latin & Italic languages
480 Classical & modern Greek languages
490 Other languages

500 Science
510 Mathematics
520 Astronomy
530 Physics
540 Chemistry
550 Earth sciences & geology
560 Fossils & prehistoric life
570 Life sciences; biology
580 Plants (Botany)
590 Animals (Zoology)

600 Technology
610 Medicine & health
620 Engineering
630 Agriculture
640 Home & family management
650 Management & public relations
660 Chemical engineering
670 Manufacturing
680 Manufacture for specific uses
690 Building & construction

700 Arts
710 Landscaping & area planning
720 Architecture
730 Sculpture, ceramics & metalwork
740 Drawing & decorative arts
750 Painting
760 Graphic arts
770 Photography & computer art
780 Music
790 Sports, games & entertainment

800 Literature, rhetoric & criticism
810 American literature in English
820 English & Old English literatures
830 German & related literatures
840 French & related literatures
850 Italian, Romanian & related literatures
860 Spanish & Portuguese literatures
870 Latin & Italic literatures
880 Classical & modern Greek literatures
890 Other literatures

900 History
910 Geography & travel
920 Biography & genealogy
930 History of ancient world (to ca. 499)
940 History of Europe
950 History of Asia
960 History of Africa
970 History of North America
980 History of South America
990 History of other areas

Reproduced from Edition 15 of the Abridged Dewey Decimal Classification and Relative Index, published in 2012, by permission of OCLC Online Computer Library Center, Inc., owner of copyright.

CHILDREN'S CORE COLLECTION
TWENTY-FIRST EDITION
CLASSIFIED COLLECTION

000   COMPUTER SCIENCE, KNOWLEDGE & SYSTEMS

001.4   Research; statistical methods

Besel, Jennifer M.

Lions and tigers and graphs! oh my! Capstone Press 2011 24p il (First facts. Data mania) lib bdg $23.99

Grades: 3 4 5 6 **001.4**

1. Mathematics 2. Graphic methods

ISBN 978-1-4296-4527-0; 1-4296-4527-X

LC 2010000549

"Information is presented in a few pages in a clear, concise manner. The definitions provided for words will help readers learn the [subject]. This is an excellent introduction to elementary statistics and statistical analysis." Libr Media Connect

Includes glossary and bibliographical references

Cefrey, Holly

★ **Researching** people, places, and events. Rosen Central 2010 48p il (Digital and information literacy) lib bdg $26.50

Grades: 5 6 7 8 **001.4**

1. Research 2. Report writing 3. Internet research

ISBN 978-1-4358-5317-1 lib bdg; 1-4358-5317-2 lib bdg

LC 2008-46785

Describes researching people, places, and events on the Internet, including using primary and secondary sources, evaluating source material, and avoiding plagiarism

"Colorful photos, diagrams, and sidebars and [a] lively [text creates an] appealing, user-friendly [presentation].... . Students and teachers will find [this title] useful in keeping up-to-date on and utilizing online resources and today's technology in a rapidly changing digital world." SLJ

Includes glossary and bibliographical references

Gaines, Ann

Ace your Internet research; [by] Ann Graham Gaines. Enslow Publishers 2009 48p il (Ace it! information literacy) lib bdg $23.93

Grades: 3 4 5 **001.4**

1. Internet research 2. Internet searching

ISBN 978-0-7660-3392-4 lib bdg; 0-7660-3392-9 lib bdg

LC 2008032351

"Readers will learn what the internet is, and how to do effective research while staying safe online" Publisher's note

Includes bibliographical references

Jakubiak, David J.

A **smart** kid's guide to doing Internet research. PowerKids Press 2009 24p il (Kids online) lib bdg $21.25; pa $8.25

Grades: 3 4 5 6 **001.4**

1. Internet research

ISBN 978-1-4042-8116-5 lib bdg; 1-4042-8116-9 lib bdg; 978-1-4358-3352-4 pa; 1-4358-3352-X pa

LC 2009002879

In this title "readers are shown how to read URL tags, use browsers, and develop search-term strings. Readers are told that Wikipedia is not reliable because anybody can add to it.... [This is a] worthwhile [purchase] for ... updating collections in this area." SLJ

Includes glossary

Randolph, Ryan P.

New research techniques; getting the most out of search engine tools. [by] Ryan Randolph. Rosen Central 2011 48p il (Digital and information literacy) lib bdg $27.95; pa $11.75

Grades: 5 6 7 8 **001.4**

1. Internet resources 2. Internet searching 3. Web search engines

ISBN 978-1-4488-1321-6 lib bdg; 1-4488-1321-2 lib bdg; 978-1-4488-2292-8 pa; 1-4488-2292-0 pa

LC 2010016912

Explains new research techniques and tools that are available for online searching. Among the topics covered are browser tools and search engine toolbars, browser add-ons, Web mashups, e-mail and text alerts, RSS feeds and readers, Boolean operators, and refining research results.

"Color illustrations, large fonts, clearly defined subheadings, and easy to read content encourage access to copious information.... Teachers and librarians should find this ... to be a highly versatile teaching tool." Libr Media Connect

Includes glossary and bibliographical references

001.9   Controversial knowledge

Allen, Judy

★ **Unexplained**. Kingfisher 2006 144p il $19.95

Grades: 5 6 7 8 **001.9**

1. Parapsychology 2. Curiosities and wonders

ISBN 978-0-7534-5950-8; 0-7534-5950-7

This addresses such topics as ghosts, psychic phenomena, superstitions, mysterious natural phenomena, alleged monsters, disappearances, secrets and mysteries of ancient history, and possible extraterrestrials.

"A seamless combination of absorbing fact-filled text and stunning visuals in an investigation of mysteries that continue to baffle, tantalize, and spark endless debate." SLJ

Includes glossary

Allman, Toney

Are extraterrestrials a threat to mankind? Reference-Point Press 2011 il $28.95 (Extraterrestrial life)

Grades: 5 6 7 8   **001.9**

1. Extraterrestrial beings

ISBN 1-60152-170-7; 978-1-60152-170-5

LC 2010046621

This "captures the subject's inherent allure, while maintaining a serious . . . tone. Kids . . . will . . . learn about the compounds necessary for life and their availability on other planets, the microbial threat of extraterrestrial life, and communication with other life forms. The solid text also includes theories about what (and who) might be out there. . . . The book's computer-generated illustrations . . . take advantage of its subject with a couple of images of scary ETs. . . . [This is a] well-sourced volume." Booklist

Includes bibliographical references

Arnosky, Jim

Monster hunt; exploring mysterious creatures with Jim Arnosky. Disney/Hyperion 2011 32p il $16.99

Grades: 2 3 4 5   **001.9**

1. Monsters

ISBN 978-1-4231-3028-4; 1-4231-3028-6

"Arnosky invites readers to join him on a cryptozoology adventure. . . . He compares legends to fact and asks if, for example, sharks could be the documented carcharodon from 13 millennia ago, or if the Loch Ness Monster might be a plesiosaur, thought extinct for 100 million years. The expansive format is appealing. A third of each full-page spread features accessible text, while two-thirds are given over to a painting of the subject. . . . This offers many opportunities for readers to speculate about these intriguing mysteries." Booklist

Bardhan-Quallen, Sudipta

The **real** monsters; written by Sudipta Bardhan-Quallen; illustrated by Josh Cochran. Sterling 2008 88p il (Mysteries unwrapped) pa $5.95

Grades: 5 6 7 8   **001.9**

1. Ghosts 2. Monsters

ISBN 978-1-4027-3776-3 pa; 1-4027-3776-9 pa

LC 2009275635

Investigates whether ghosts, werewolves, vampires, mummies, zombies and other such monsters exist

The book has "an ample number of clear black-and-white and full-color photographs and illustrations. . . . Perfect for libraries that need a boost or an update to their scary-story collections." SLJ

Includes bibliographical references

Emmer, Rick

Kraken; fact or fiction? Chelsea House 2010 108p il lib bdg $35.00

Grades: 5 6 7 8   **001.9**

1. Squids

ISBN 978-0-7910-9780-9

LC 2009011467

Describes the sea monster known as the kraken, presents evidence of the existence of giant squids and their relatives, and discusses how the kraken is portrayed historically and in popular culture.

Erickson, Justin

Alien abductions. Bellwether Media 2011 24p il (Torque: The unexplained) lib bdg $15.95

Grades: 3 4 5 6   **001.9**

1. Extraterrestrial beings

ISBN 978-1-60014-582-7; 1-60014-582-5

LC 2010034773

This book explores the history of alien abduction stories, some of the commonly reported themes, and whether or not the stories could be true.

"Designed for struggling readers, this . . . combines accessible writing, dynamic illustrations, and [a] high-interest [topic]. [A] snazzy [cover] and an abundance of glossy, full-color illustrations provide appeal. . . . The writing is succinct but informative." SLJ

Includes glossary and bibliographical references

Gee, Joshua

★ **Encyclopedia** horrifica; the terrifying truth! about vampires, ghosts, monsters, and more. Scholastic Inc. 2007 129p il $14.99

Grades: 4 5 6 7   **001.9**

1. Ghosts 2. Monsters 3. Vampires

ISBN 978-0-439-92255-5; 0-439-92255-0

LC 2007061733

A visual reference contains true stories of such creatures as vampires, aliens, werewolves, and ghosts, accompanied by photographic evidence, eyewitness accounts, and original interviews.

"Each topic is replete with color illustrations and photos and is accompanied by a light, readable text that tries to separate fact from fiction." Voice Youth Advocates

Includes bibliographical references

Halls, Kelly Milner

In search of Sasquatch; an exercise in zoological evidence. Houghton Mifflin Books for Children 2011 47p il map $16.99

Grades: 4 5 6   **001.9**

1. Animals 2. Sasquatch

ISBN 978-0-547-25761-7; 0-547-25761-9

LC 2011005785

"This book does a fair job of presenting the evidence for Sasquatch through stories of people who have dedicated their lives to finding the cryptid. Evidence for its existence might leave many kids unconvinced, but they will likely be entertained anyway. Black-and-white and muted color illustrations and photos of people, lush forests, clues, and Sasquatch itself are scattered throughout." SLJ

★ **Tales** of the cryptids; mysterious creatures that may or may not exist. by Kelly Milner Halls, Rick Spears, Roxyanne Young; [illustrated by Rick Spears] Darby Creek 2006 72p il map $18.95

Grades: 4 5 6 7   **001.9**

1. Monsters

ISBN 1-58196-049-2

This considers the existance of creatures such as Bigfoot, the Loch Ness Monster, Marozi of Kenya, the Orangpendek of Sumatra, and the Thylacine of Tasmania.

"The conversational text makes for fun reading, and a plethora of pictures . . . will prove enticing." SLJ

Helstrom, Kraig

Crop circles. Bellwether Media 2011 24p il (Torque: The unexplained) lib bdg $15.95

Grades: 3 4 5 6   **001.9**

1. Crop circles

ISBN 978-1-60014-583-4; 1-60014-583-3

LC 2010034776

This title explores the history of crop circles and looks into whether or not some could be of alien origin.

"Designed for struggling readers, this . . . combines accessible writing, dynamic illustrations, and [a] high-interest [topic]. [A] snazzy [cover] and an abundance of glossy, full-color illustrations provide appeal. . . . The writing is succinct but informative." SLJ

Includes glossary and bibliographical references

Kallen, Stuart A.

Crop circles. ReferencePoint Press 2010 104p il (The mysterious & unknown) $25.95

Grades: 4 5 6 7   **001.9**

1. Crop circles

ISBN 978-1-60152-103-3; 1-60152-103-0

LC 2009034368

In an attempt to explain the phenomenon of crop circles, "Kallen reaches back to a 1678 account of a 'mowing devil' before considering numerous potential culprits: plasma vortexes, psychokenesis, UFOs, the military, and even wallabies stoned on opium. Equal time is spent between cereologists (those who study these formations) and plain old hoaxsters—and both are equally interesting." Booklist

Includes bibliographical references

Matthews, Rupert

Disappearances. QEB Pub. 2010 32p il map (Unexplained) lib bdg $28.50

Grades: 4 5 6 7   **001.9**

1. Parapsychology 2. Missing persons

ISBN 978-1-59566-855-4; 1-59566-855-1

LC 2010014190

This discusses some mysterious disappearances such as the lost colony of Roanoke, the Mary Celeste, disappearances on Mt. Everest, vanishing lighthousemen, and the Maya.

"This well-written and thoughtfully designed [book] features [an] engrossing [topic]. . . . Though the pages are profusely illustrated with large, well-reproduced photographs and drawings, the layout is not cluttered. This [book] just might inspire kids to seek out more in-depth materials." SLJ

Includes glossary and bibliographical references

Strange animals. QEB Pub. 2011 30p il (Unexplained) lib bdg $28.50

Grades: 4 5 6 7   **001.9**

1. Monsters

ISBN 978-1-59566-856-1; 1-59566-856-X

LC 2010017915

This discusses the possible existance of cryptids such as Bigfoot, the Loch Ness monster, the Bunyip, sea monsters, the Orang Pendek, and the Marozi.

"This well-written and thoughtfully designed [book] features [an] engrossing [topic]. . . . Though the pages are profusely illustrated with large, well-reproduced photographs and drawings, the layout is not cluttered. This [book] just might inspire kids to seek out more in-depth materials." SLJ

Includes glossary and bibliographical references

Michels, Troy

Atlantis. Bellwether Media 2011 24p il (Torque: The unexplained) lib bdg $15.95

Grades: 3 4 5 6   **001.9**

1. Atlantis

ISBN 978-1-60014-585-8; 1-60014-585-X

This book explores the story of Atlantis and the debate about the existence of this ancient civilization.

"Designed for struggling readers, this . . . combines accessible writing, dynamic illustrations, and [a] high-interest [topic]. [A] snazzy [cover] and an abundance of glossy, full-color illustrations provide appeal. . . . The writing is succinct but informative." SLJ

Includes glossary and bibliographical references

Nardo, Don

Martians; by Don Nardo. KidHaven Press 2008 48p il (Monsters) lib bdg $26.20

Grades: 4 5 6 7   **001.9**

1. Popular culture 2. Extraterrestrial beings

ISBN 978-0-7377-3639-7 lib bdg; 0-7377-3639-9 lib bdg

LC 2007-30616

"Nardo walks readers through everything from early astronautical observations of the Red Planet to Martians in the movies and on television. His writing is clear, informative and often humorous." SLJ

Includes glossary and bibliographical references

004 Computer science; computer programming, programs, data; special computer methods

Snedden, Robert

Who invented the computer? Arcturus Pub. 2011 46p il (Breakthroughs in science and technology) lib bdg $32.80

Grades: 5 6 7 8   **004**

1. Computers -- History

ISBN 978-1-84837-678-6; 1-84837-678-2

LC 2010011017

This is "divided into easy to read short chapters with large, colorful photographs and graphics on every page. . . . The added inserts provide additional information to engage readers and help them connect with the scientific details." Libr Media Connect

Includes glossary and bibliographical references

Wilkinson, Colin

Mobile platforms; getting information on the go. Rosen Pub. 2011 48p il (Digital and information literacy) lib bdg $26.50; pa $11.75

Grades: 5 6 7 8   **004**

1. Cellular telephones 2. Wireless communication

systems

ISBN 978-1-4488-1320-9 lib bdg; 1-4488-1320-4 lib bdg; 978-1-4488-2291-1 pa; 1-4488-2291-2 pa

LC 2010023682

Though this "title is a broad overview of a sometimes-complex subject, the detail is significant. . . . Touches of blue enhance the clean design. . . . [This] offers very current explanations of smart phones and apps, with plenty of information that will be new even to tech-savvy kids." Booklist

Includes bibliographical references

004.6   Interfacing and communications

Cornwall, Phyllis

Online etiquette and safety. Cherry Lake Pub. 2010 32p il (Super smart information strategies) lib bdg $27.07

Grades: 3 4 5 6   **004.6**

1. Etiquette 2. Internet -- Social aspects 3. Internet -- Security measures

ISBN 978-1-60279-956-1 lib bdg; 1-60279-956-3 lib bdg

LC 2010002023

This "teaches valuable lessons on why it's important to be responsible online citizens despite the misleading anonymity of the Web and offers tips on how to deal with cyberbullies and other online dangers." Booklist

Includes bibliographical references

Grayson, Robert

Managing your digital footprint. Rosen Central 2011 48p il (Digital and information literacy) lib bdg $26.50; pa $11.75

Grades: 5 6 7 8   **004.6**

1. Internet 2. Etiquette 3. Right of privacy

ISBN 978-1-4488-1319-3 lib bdg; 1-4488-1319-0 lib bdg; 978-1-4488-2290-4 pa; 1-4488-2290-4 pa

LC 2010025746

Though this "title is a broad overview of a sometimes-complex subject, the detail is significant. . . . Touches of blue enhance the clean design. . . . [This] discusses the permanence of impulsively posted material online, contrasting it with more retro forms of self-expression, such as keeping a paper diary." Booklist

Includes bibliographical references

Jakubiak, David J.

★ A **smart** kid's guide to avoiding online predators. PowerKids Press 2009 24p il (Kids online) lib bdg $21.25; pa $8.95

Grades: 3 4 5 6   **004.6**

1. Safety education 2. Internet and children 3. Internet -- Security measures

ISBN 978-1-4042-8117-2 lib bdg; 1-4042-8117-7 lib bdg; 978-1-4358-3354-8 pa; 1-4358-3354-6 pa

LC 2009004343

In this title "the focus is on treating the Internet as you would any other public place: avoiding strangers and telling someone if you see or read something you are uncomfortable with. . . . [This is a] worthwhile [purchase] for teaching online safety and updating collections in this area." SLJ

Includes glossary

004.67   Wide-area networks

Brasch, Nicolas

The **Internet**; Nicolas Brasch. Smart Apple Media 2011 32 p. col. ill., map (library) $28.50

Grades: 5 6 7 8   **004.67**

1. Internet

ISBN 159920567X; 9781599205670

LC 2009054445

Brasch "provides much worthwhile information. He discusses recent history and current tools and suggests where this know-how might be headed in the near future. He differentiates between the Internet and the World Wide Web; clarifies how search engines, web pages, blogs, and e-mail work; explains instant messaging, tweeting, and voice-over Internet protocol (VOIP); and distinguishes between Web 2.0 and Web 3.0 technology. . . . Topics are discussed in heavily illustrated double-page spreads containing numerous sidebars, web links, definitions, and diagrams. . . . The text reads smoothly, and pages have a clean, inviting look." Booklist

005   Computer programming, programs, data

Orr, Tamra

★ **Creating** multimedia presentations. Rosen Central 2010 48p il (Digital and information literacy) lib bdg $26.50

Grades: 5 6 7 8   **005**

1. Multimedia 2. Presentation software

ISBN 978-1-4358-5319-5 lib bdg; 1-4358-5319-9 lib bdg

LC 2008-54736

Describes how to create a multimedia presentation, including adding graphs, images, sounds, and video, and how to integrate these elements to form an informative presentation

"Colorful photos, diagrams, and sidebars and [a lively text creates an] appealing, user-friendly [presentation]. . . . Students and teachers will find [this title] useful in keeping up-to-date on and utilizing online resources and today's technology in a rapidly changing digital world." SLJ

Includes glossary and bibliographical references

005.8   Data security

Jakubiak, David J.

A **smart** kid's guide to Internet privacy. PowerKids Press 2009 24p il (Kids online) lib bdg $21.25; pa $8.25

Grades: 3 4 5 6   **005.8**

1. Computer crimes 2. Right of privacy 3. Internet and children 4. Internet -- Security measures

ISBN 978-1-4042-8118-9 lib bdg; 1-4042-8118-5 lib bdg; 978-1-4358-3356-2 pa; 1-4358-3356-2 pa

LC 2009005369

This title "is straightforward about not sharing information without parental permission and also gives support and suggestions in case something does happen. . . . [A] worthwhile [purchase] for teaching online safety and updating collections in this area." SLJ

Includes glossary and bibliographical references

006.7   Multimedia systems

Fontichiaro, Kristin

Podcasting 101. Cherry Lake Pub. 2010 32p il (Super smart information strategies) lib bdg $27.07

Grades: 3 4 5 6   **006.7**

1. Podcasting

ISBN 978-1-60279-953-0 lib bdg; 1-60279-953-9 lib bdg

LC 2010004533

"A knockout resource for media-fair projects, Podcasting 101 doles out page after page of useful information, from the equipment required to content ideas for those who might need a creative spark to tips for structuring and adding effects to a successful podcast." Booklist

Includes bibliographical references

Mills, J. Elizabeth

Creating content; maximizing wikis, widgets, blogs, and more. Rosen Central 2011 48p il (Digital and information literacy) lib bdg $27.95; pa $11.75

Grades: Adult Professional   **006.7**

1. Web 2.0 2. Internet and teenagers 3. User generated content 4. Internet -- Safety measures

ISBN 978-1-4488-1322-3 lib bdg; 1-4488-1322-0 lib bdg; 978-1-4488-2293-5 pa; 1-4488-2293-9 pa

LC 2010026860

Describes the ways that users may generate Internet content, including blogs, Wikipedia, social networks, and sites for posting photographs and videos, and discusses Internet dangers and such activities to avoid as copyright violations.

"Color illustrations, large fonts, clearly defined subheadings, and easy to read content encourage access to copious information. . . . Teachers and librarians should find this . . . to be a highly versatile teaching tool." Libr Media Connect

Includes glossary and bibliographical references

Rainie, Lee

Networked; the new social operating system. Lee Rainie and Barry Wellman. MIT Press 2012 xiii, 358 p.p ill.

Grades: Adult   **006.7**

1. Online social networks 2. Interpersonal relations 3. Internet -- Social aspects 4. Social networks

ISBN 0262017199; 9780262017190

LC 2011038146

This book "outline[s] the 'triple revolution'" in human communication: "the rise of social networking, the capacity of the Internet to empower individuals, and the always-on connectivity of mobile devices." The authors "examine how the move to networked individualism has expanded personal relationships . . . transformed work into less hierarchical, more team-driven enterprises; encouraged individuals to create and share content; and changed the way people obtain information." (Publisher's note)

Includes bibliographical references and index.

Rowell, Rebecca

YouTube; the company and its founders. ABDO Pub. Co. 2011 112p il (Technology pioneers) lib bdg $32.44

Grades: 5 6 7 8   **006.7**

1. Internet

ISBN 978-1-61714-813-2 lib bdg; 1-61714-813-X lib bdg; 978-1-61758-971-3 e-book

LC 2010043379

This is an introduction to YouTube and its founders.

"Written in a clear, linear fashion, this series offers vivid, well-researched details about the development of technological advancements considered essential in today's society. . . . Readers who are interested in technology and inventions will be thoroughly engrossed." SLJ

Includes glossary and bibliographical references

Selfridge, Benjamin

A teen's guide to creating Web pages and blogs; [by] Benjamin Selfridge, Peter Selfridge, and Jennifer Osburn. Prufrock Press 2009 148p il pa $16.95

Grades: 5 6 7 8 9 10   **006.7**

1. Weblogs 2. Internet and teenagers 3. Web sites -- Design

ISBN 978-1-59363-345-5; 1-59363-345-9

LC 2008-40044

First published 2004 by Zephyr Press with title: Kid's guide to creating Web pages for home and school

"This guide begins with basic step-by-step information about HTML, fonts, images, lists, and tables. . . . The book's last half introduces more advanced techniques, such as JavaScript, functions, loops, and applications like Flash and Instant Messenger. . . . Illustrated, with references and a glossary, this attractive paperback has lots of practical content." Voice Youth Advocates

Includes glossary and bibliographical references

Truesdell, Ann

Wonderful wikis; by Ann Truesdell. Cherry Lake Publishing 2013 32 p. (Information explorer) (library) $28.50; (paperback) $14.21

Grades: 4 5 6 7   **006.7**

1. Wikis (Computer science) -- Juvenile literature

ISBN 1610804805; 9781610804806; 9781610806541

LC 2012001758

This juvenile nonfiction book, by Ann Truesdell, as part of the publisher's "Explorer Library" series, presents a profile and guidelines for school children to make use of wikis online for educational purposes. Topics addressed include definitions of what a wiki is, how to contribute to them properly, and what ways they are most useful.

Includes bibliographical references and index

Woog, Adam

YouTube. Norwood House Press 2008 48p il (A great idea) lib bdg $25.27

Grades: 3 4 5 6   **006.7**

1. Internet

ISBN 978-1-59953-198-4 lib bdg; 1-59953-198-4 lib bdg

LC 2008010724

This "offers a fresh topic and handles it extremely well. . . . Woog's account is interesting and informative and written in simple yet uncondescending prose that's spot-on for the intended audience. . . . The attractive design features full-color photographs, while fast facts appear throughout the narrative in eye-catching sidebars." Booklist

Includes glossary and bibliographical references

011.6 General bibliographies and catalogs of works for young people and people with disabilities; for specific types of libraries

East, Kathy

★ Across cultures; a guide to multicultural literature for children. Libraries Unlimited 2007 342p il (Children's and young adult literature reference series) $55

Grades: Adult Professional   **011.6**
1. Reference books 2. Multiculturalism -- Bibliography 3. Children's literature -- Bibliography
ISBN 978-1-59158-336-3; 1-59158-336-5

LC 2007013573

This is "user-friendly and extremely helpful both in terms of the choices and the descriptions." SLJ

Includes bibliographical references

Fichtelberg, Susan

★ Primary genreflecting; a guide to picture books and easy readers. [by] Susan Fichtelberg and Bridget Dealy Volz. Libraries Unlimited 2010 375p (Genreflecting advisory series) $48

Grades: Adult Professional   **011.6**
1. Picture books for children 2. Children's literature -- Bibliography 3. Picture books for children -- Bibliography
ISBN 1-56308-907-6; 978-1-56308-907-7

LC 2010036578

This "covers picture books and easy readers for children ages three to eight. . . . Fichtelberg and Volz . . . organize 2,500 annotated titles by theme. Most titles are positively reviewed and award-winning books published between 1999 and 2009. . . . Succinct descriptions of plot and style of illustration accompany bibliographic information, awards won, and grade level." Booklist

Includes bibliographical references

Freeman, Judy

★ Books kids will sit still for 3; a read-aloud guide. [by] Judy Freeman; Catherine Barr, series editor. Libraries Unlimited 2006 915p il (Children's and young adult literature reference series) $70; pa $55

Grades: Adult Professional   **011.6**
1. Best books 2. Reference books 3. Children's literature -- Bibliography
ISBN 1-59158-163-X; 1-59158-164-8 pa

First published 1984 by Alleyside with title: Books kids will sit still for

"This excellent resource will be a favorite with teachers who need assistance finding quality children's literature, and it will also aid librarians and media specialists." SLJ

Gillespie, John Thomas

The children's and young adult literature handbook; a research and reference guide. Libraries Unlimited 2005 393p (Children's and young adult literature reference series) $55

Grades: Adult Professional   **011.6**
1. Reference books 2. Children's literature 3. Young adult literature 4. Children's literature -- Bibliography 5. Young adult literature -- Bibliography 6. Children's literature -- History and criticism 7. Young adult

literature -- History and criticism
ISBN 1-56308-949-1

"This reference should meet the needs of librarians, teachers, and scholars." Choice

Matthew, Kathryn I.

Neal-Schuman guide to recommended children's books and media for use with every elementary subject; by Kathryn I. Matthew and Joy L. Lowe. 2nd ed; Neal-Schuman Publishers 2010 356p pa $75

Grades: Adult Professional   **011.6**
1. Best books 2 Children -- Books and reading 3. Audiovisual materials -- Catalogs 4. Children's literature -- Bibliography
ISBN 978-1-55570-688-3; 1-55570-688-6

LC 2010014082

First published 2002

"Listing more than 1,000 books, videos, software, CDs, and Web sites up through early 2010, this book offers elementary (and middle-school) librarians a wonderful collection-development and collaboration tool. Each chapter covers one elementary subject area. . . . The chapters are broken down into narrower topics; each section covers the book and media choices plus ideas for exploring many of the resources listed. Each chapter begins with relevant national standards and ends with teacher resources and references including books, professional organizations, and Web sites. The annotated listings are arranged by grade level from pre–K up through middle school and include full bibliographic information." Booklist

Includes bibliographical references

Meese, Ruth Lyn

Family matters; adoption and foster care in children's literature. Libraries Unlimited 2010 147p pa $35

Grades: Adult Professional   **011.6**
1. Adoption -- Fiction 2. Adoption in literature 3. Adoption -- Bibliography 4. Foster children -- Fiction 5. Foster home care -- Bibliography 6. Children's literature -- Bibliography
ISBN 978-1-59158-782-8 pa; 1-59158-782-4 pa

LC 2009040750

"Meese's goal is to help adults, particularly educators, select high-quality children's books about adoption and foster care and to raise awareness about the unique issues that adoptees often face. . . . Charts, Venn diagrams, and extensive annotations supplement the annotated list of books for children in kindergarten through grade eight. Meese explains her rationale for choosing these books so that readers have the tools to evaluate other selections." SLJ

Includes bibliographical references

Polette, Nancy

Find someone who; introducing 200 favorite picture books. [by] Nancy Polette. Libraries Unlimited 2006 205p pa $35

Grades: Adult Professional   **011.6**
1. Reference books 2. Children -- Books and reading 3. Picture books for children -- Bibliography
ISBN 1-59158-465-5 pa; 978-1-59158-465-0 pa

LC 2006027318

"Polette shows a new way to present well-known picture books to preschoolers and primary-grade students. A one-paragraph booktalk introduces the story and is followed by

10 questions based upon the characters or situations. Children are instructed to find someone in their group who can relate to a portion of the story. . . . The book will be useful for quick, spur-of-the-moment planning as well as for quality lesson plans in working with ESL groups." SLJ

Reid, Rob

Reid's read-alouds; selections for children and teens. American Library Association 2009 xiii, 121p pa $45
Grades: Adult Professional 011.6
1. Books and reading 2. Children's literature -- Bibliography 3. Young adult literature -- Bibliography
ISBN 978-0-8389-0980-5 pa; 0-8389-0980-9 pa
LC 2008045376

"Reid has collected 200 titles published between 2000 and 2008 that have both readability and general kid appeal. The titles are organized alphabetically by author, and the book includes subject and age-level indexes. Each selection has a cursory summary, grade-level range, and a suggestion for a 10-minute read-aloud, which either provides an introduction to the main characters or a glimpse into the story. . . . This last part is what makes the book so useful." SLJ

Includes bibliographical references

Reid's read-alouds 2; modern day classics from C.S. Lewis to Lemony Snicket. American Library Association 2011 160p
Grades: Adult Professional 011.6
1. Books and reading 2. Children's literature -- Bibliography 3. Young adult literature -- Bibliography
ISBN 0-8389-1072-6; 978-0-8389-1072-6
LC 2010028985

"The very successful first edition of Reid's Read-Alouds (ALA, 2009) profiled children's and young adult books published between the years 2000 and 2008. This companion volume showcases 200 strong titles that were published from 1950 to 1999. Reid offers a variety of genres and age levels, and a good balance between male and female protagonists. . . . The focus is on books that are great to read to groups of young people. Each entry includes a brief plot summary, suggested grade level, and Reid's signature '10 Minute Selections,' which are engaging episodes from the books that can be read in one sitting. These alone make the book a valuable resource." SLJ

Includes bibliographical references

Safford, Barbara Ripp

Guide to reference materials for school library media centers; 6th ed; Libraries Unlimited 2010 236p $60
Grades: Adult Professional 011.6
1. Instructional materials centers 2. Children's reference books 3. School libraries -- Catalogs 4. Reference books -- Bibliography
ISBN 978-1-59158-277-9; 1-59158-277-6
LC 2009-51190

First edition by Christine Gehrt Wynar published 1973 with title: Guide to reference books for school media centers

"This volume has been updated to include web-based reference offerings as well as listings of older sources, provided that their content is still valid. . . . This title profiles resources recommended for use by school librarians for collection management, readers' advisory, teaching, general reference materials, the social sciences and humanities, and science and technology. This volume is an excellent starting point for new school librarians, as well as for those who are building a library from scratch." SLJ

Includes bibliographical references

Schon, Isabel

Recommended books in Spanish for children and young adults, 2004-2008. Scarecrow Press 2009 414p $55
Grades: Adult Professional 011.6
1. Reference books 2. Children's literature, Spanish 3. Young adult literature, Spanish 4. Spanish literature -- Bibliography 5. Children's literature -- Bibliography 6. Young adult literature -- Bibliography 7. Children's literature, Spanish American 8. Young adult literature, Spanish American 9. Latin American literature -- Bibliography 10. Children's literature -- Translations into Spanish 11. Young adult literature -- Translations into Spanish
ISBN 978-0-8108-6386-6; 0-8108-6386-3
LC 2008-33390

"Schon evaluates 1231 reference books, fiction, and nonfiction. . . . Entries are arranged alphabetically by author and include a grade level for each book. . . . Schon examines and recommends materials based on the quality of the Spanish language, literary appeal, and the versatility of the translators, paying special attention to the effective use of Peninsular Spanish or the Spanish from the Americas. This annotated bibliography will help selectors in public libraries and media centers to develop existing Spanish-language collections." SLJ

Spiegel, Carol

Book by book; an annotated guide to young people's literature with peacemaking and conflict resolution themes. Educators for Social Responsibility 2010 186p pa $35
Grades: Adult Professional 011.6
1. Young adult literature 2. Peace -- Bibliography 3. Peace -- Juvenile literature 4. Conflict management -- Bibliography 5. Children's literature -- Bibliography 6. Young adult literature -- Bibliography 7. Conflict management -- Juvenile literature
ISBN 978-0-942349-93-1 pa; 0-942349-93-8 pa

"More than 900 books for preschool through high school have been organized by title into two sections, picture and chapter books; described; and assigned behavioral headings. Thematic clusters include making connections, emotional literacy, caring and effective communication, cultural competence and social responsibility, and conflict management and responsible decision making. . . . Useful especially in elementary and middle schools where character education is part of the curriculum without the explicit mandate." SLJ

011.62 Works for young people

Hearne, Betsy Gould

Choosing books for children; a commonsense guide. [by] Betsy Hearne with Deborah Stevenson. 3rd ed; University of Ill. Press 1999 229p il hardcover o.p. pa $21
Grades: Adult Professional 011.62
1. Reference books 2. Books and reading 3. Children's literature 4. Children's literature -- Bibliography 5. Children -- Books and reading -- United States 6.

Children's literature, English -- Bibliography
ISBN 0-252-02516-4; 0-252-06928-5 pa

LC 99-6144

First published 1981 by Delacorte Press

"The focus is on books since 1950; the 14 chapter-opening illustrations mainly represent books of the last decade. Chapters divide books by age and genre; one chapter considers the value of controversial books while another affectionately revisits classics." Publ Wkly

016 Bibliographies and catalogs of works on specific subjects

Al-Hazza, Tami Craft

Books about the Middle East; selecting and using them with children and adolescents. [by] Tami Craft Al-Hazza and Katherine T. Bucher. Linworth Pub. 2008 168p pa $39.95

Grades: Adult Professional   016
1. Reference books   2. Children's literature -- Bibliography 3. Young adult literature -- Bibliography
ISBN 978-1-58683-285-8; 1-58683-285-9

LC 2007-40149

"This book examines the body of literature about the diverse groups of people who inhabit the Middle East, and it also explores a variety of ways in which this literature can be used. . . . It fills a huge gap and should not be overlooked. This powerhouse book will be tremendously helpful to media specialists, educators, and public librarians." Voice Youth Advocates

Includes bibliographical references

Child Study Children's Book Committee at Bank Street

The **best** children's books of the year; selected by the Children's Book Committee at Bank Street College of Education. Teacher's College Press

Grades: Adult Professional   016
1. Reference books   2. Children's literature -- Bibliography
First published 1998

"This is a comprehensive annotated book list for children, aged infant–14." Publisher's note

Crew, Hilary S.

Women engaged in war in literature for youth; a guide to resources for children and young adults. Scarecrow Press 2007 303p (Literature for youth) pa $51

Grades: Adult Professional   016
1. Women soldiers 2. Reference books 3. Young adult literature 4. Women and war 5. War -- Bibliography 6. Women -- Bibliography 7. Children's literature -- Bibliography 8. Young adult literature -- Bibliography
ISBN 978-0-8108-4929-7; 0-8108-4929-1

LC 2006-101112

"Crew's guide to print and online sources documents women's roles in wars over the centuries and throughout the world, divided by time periods. . . . This is a great addition for libraries looking for a way to move Women's Studies beyond the month of March." SLJ

Includes bibliographical references

Garcha, Rajinder

The **world** of Islam in literature for youth; a selective annotated bibliography for K-12. [by] Rajinder Garcha, Patricia Yates Russell. Scarecrow Press 2006 xx, 221p (Literature for youth) pa $35

Grades: Adult Professional   016
1. Best books 2. Reference books 3. Children's literature 4. Young adult literature -- Bibliography 5. Islam in literature 6. Islam -- Bibliography 7. Islam -- Juvenile literature 8. Children's literature -- Bibliography
ISBN 978-0-8108-5488-8; 0-8108-5488-0

LC 2005-26645

"This highly useful bibliography fills a conspicuous gap in a much-needed cultural area." Voice Youth Advocates

Includes bibliographical references

Hall, Susan

★ **Using** picture storybooks to teach literary devices; recommended books for children and young adults. Libraries Unlimited 2007 282p (Using picture books to teach) pa $42

Grades: Adult Professional   016
1. Children's literature 2. Literature -- Study and teaching
ISBN 978-1-59158-493-3 pa; 1-59158-493-0 pa

"This fourth volume of the series, . . . gives teachers and librarians the . . . tool to teach literary devices in grades K–12. With this volume, the author has added: colloquialism; counterpoint; solecism; archetype; and others to the list of devices. The entries have been reorganized to include all the information under the book listing itself. Each entry includes an annotation, a listing of curricular tie-ins for the book and the art style used, and a listing and explanation of all the literary devices taught by that title." Publisher's note

Includes bibliographic references

Thomas, Rebecca L.

★ **Popular** series fiction for K-6 readers; a reading and selection guide. [by] Rebecca L. Thomas and Catherine Barr. 2nd ed; Libraries Unlimited 2008 1002p (Children's and young adult literature reference series) $65

Grades: Adult Professional   016
1. Reference books 2. Children -- Books and reading 3. Children's literature -- Series 4. Children's literature -- Bibliography
ISBN 978-1-59158-659-3; 1-59158-659-3

LC 2008-38124

First published 2004

"Using standard review sources and bibliographies as well as author, publisher, bookseller, and library Web sites, the authors have identified nearly 2,200 in-print series appropriate for K–6 readers. . . . Entries are arranged by the series title and contain author, most recent publisher, grade level, notation for availability of accelerated-reader resources, genre, a descriptive three to five-sentence annotation, and a list of individual titles in the series, arranged by publication date. Following the entries are author, title, and genre/subject indexes as well as appendixes that list books for boys, girls, and reluctant readers. . . . [This is] essential as reference and selection tools in all school, public, and academic libraries." Booklist

Includes bibliographical references

Walter, Virginia A.

★ **War** & peace; a guide to literature and new media, grades 4-8. [by] Virginia A. Walter. Libraries Unlimited 2007 276p (Children's and young adult literature reference series) pa $40

Grades: Adult Professional   **016**

1. Reference books 2. War -- Bibliography 3. Peace -- Bibliography 4. War -- Juvenile literature 5. Children's literature -- Bibliography 6. Young adult literature -- Bibliography

ISBN 1-59158-271-7 pa; 978-1-59158-271-7 pa

LC 2006030671

"Walter addresses the issue of war—and peace—by examining the information needs of children and how we as professionals can meet them. . . . The bulk of the book is the annotated listing of resources that is divided topically. . . . The well-annotated bibliography includes books, DVDs, Web sites, and CDs, as well as suggestions for using the materials. . . . This book should be a 'must purchase.'" SLJ

Includes bibliographical references

Wesson, Lindsey Patrick

Green reads; best environmental resources for youth, K-12. Libraries Unlimited 2009 219p (Children's and young adult literature reference series) $50

Grades: Adult Professional   **016**

1. Reference books 2. Children's literature 3. Young adult literature 4. Ecology -- Juvenile literature 5. Environmental protection -- Bibliography 6. Environmental protection -- Juvenile literature 7. Conservation of natural resources -- Bibliography

ISBN 978-1-59158-834-4; 1-59158-834-0

LC 2009-17353

"This well-organized bibliography offers 450 annotated resources that can be integrated into the classroom to introduce students to environmental concepts. The five chapters focus on global warming, pollution, the Earth's resources, recycling, and conservation. Subchapters follow a uniform organization, including fiction; DVDs and CDs; nonfiction; seminal works, which are labeled 'Recycled Favorites'; and a storytime lesson plan with a variety of activities including songs and tactile learning activities. . . . This reference will delight educators and professionals interested in making students aware of environmental issues and to help youngsters rediscover the outside and natural worlds around them." SLJ

Includes bibliographical references

020   Library and information sciences

Fontichiaro, Kristin

Go straight to the source. Cherry Lake Pub. 2010 32p il (Super smart information strategies) lib bdg $27.07

Grades: 3 4 5 6   **020**

1. Research 2. Information resources 3. History -- Sources

ISBN 978-1-60279-640-9 lib bdg; 1-60279-640-8 lib bdg

LC 2009028057

"The appealing layout includes manageable paragraphs, a variety of engaging illustrations, and examples that clearly guide readers through each topic. . . . [This] provides an excellent introduction to primary sources and will create enthusiasm in readers for examining old photographs and ads." SLJ

Includes glossary and bibliographical references

Gaines, Ann

Master the library and media center; [by] Ann Graham Gaines. Enslow Publishers, Inc. 2009 48p il (Ace it! information literacy) lib bdg $23.93

Grades: 3 4 5   **020**

1. Research 2. Libraries 3. Information literacy 4. Information resources 5. Instructional materials centers

ISBN 978-0-7660-3393-1 lib bdg; 0-7660-3393-7 lib bdg

LC 2008024886

"Readers will learn about both the regular and electronic research materials available at the library" Publisher's note

Includes bibliographical references

Kenney, Karen Latchana

Librarians at work; by Karen L. Kenney; illustrated by Brian Caleb Dumm; content consultant, Judith Stepan-Norris. Magic Wagon 2010 32p il (Meet your community workers!) lib bdg $18.95

Grades: K 1 2 3   **020**

1. Librarians 2. Vocational guidance

ISBN 978-1-60270-649-1 lib bdg; 1-60270-649-2 lib bdg

LC 2009-2386

This book about librarians has "an uncluttered layout and consistent organization. . . . Chapter headings such as 'Problems on the Job,' 'Technology at Work,' and 'Special Skills and Training' make it easy to pinpoint specific information." SLJ

Includes glossary

Pinborough, Jan

Miss Moore thought otherwise; the story of the lady who made libraries for children. by Jan Pinborough; illustrated by Debby Atwell. Houghton Mifflin Harcourt 2013 40 p. (reinforced) $16.99

Grades: 1 2 3 4 5   **020**

1. Librarians 2. Children's libraries 3. Children's libraries -- United States -- History -- Juvenile literature 4. Children's librarians -- United States -- Biography -- Juvenile literature

ISBN 054747105X; 9780547471051

LC 2012018092

This book is a biography of "children's advocate and librarian [Anne Carroll] Moore (1871-1961), celebrated for her pioneering work in making libraries and library services accessible to (and fun for) kids." Author Jan Pinborough "has selected highlights from Moore's life—her belief in letting children touch and borrow books, her ascent to the head of children's services for the New York Public Library—and streamlined them." (Publishers Weekly)

Includes bibliographical references

021   Relationships of libraries, archives, information centers

York, Sherry

Booktalking authentic multicultural literature; fiction and history for young readers. Linworth Pub. 2009 112p pa $39.95

Grades: Adult Professional   **021**

1. Book talks 2. Young adult literature 3. Multicultural education 4. Multiculturalism in literature 5. Youth -- Books and reading 6. Ethnic groups in literature 7. Teenagers -- Books and reading 8. Multiculturalism -- Bibliography 9. Ethnic groups -- Juvenile literature 10. American literature -- Minority authors 11. Multiculturalism -- Juvenile literature

ISBN 978-1-58683-300-8 pa; 1-58683-300-6 pa

LC 200843798

This title "highlights 101 contemporary books by a variety of U.S. authors. Arranged alphabetically by title, entries include the cultural background of author, illustrator, and translator; their Web sites when available; reading and interest levels; genre; related titles; and the single-paragraph booktalk itself. Over 20 ethnic groups are represented. . . . Librarians will find this book helpful in expanding their collections to reflect our global society." SLJ

021.2   Relationships with the community

Langemack, Chapple

★ The **author** event primer; how to plan, execute and enjoy author events. Libraries Unlimited 2007 188p pa $35

Grades: Adult Professional   **021.2**

1. Authors 2. Libraries and community 3. Author-library relations 4. Program planning -- Handbooks, manuals, etc.

ISBN 978-1-59158-302-8 pa; 1-59158-302-0 pa

LC 2006032405

"Langemack gives practical guidance that will be useful to experienced and novice planners on how to host an author event. She covers everything, from reasons for having author visits to carrying off 'the really big do,' with humor and experience. The text is supplemented with charts; sample event proposals, fact sheets, letters, forms, and emails. . . . This book will be an invaluable source." Libr Media Connect

Includes bibliographical references

Squires, Tasha

Library partnerships; making connections between school and public libraries. Information Today, Inc. 2009 203p pa $39.50

Grades: Adult Professional   **021.2**

1. Public libraries 2. School libraries 3. Library cooperation 4. Libraries and schools 5. Libraries and students

ISBN 978-1-57387-362-8; 1-57387-362-4

LC 2008-51647

"Squires's confident advice can get beleaguered librarians through . . . difficulties and into mutually productive partnerships." Voice Youth Advocates

Includes bibliographical references

021.7   Promotion of libraries, archives, information centers

Cole, Sonja

Booktalking around the world; great global reads for ages 9-14. Libraries Unlimited 2010 155p pa $35

Grades: Adult Professional   **021.7**

1. Book talks 2. Children's literature 3. Ethnology -- Juvenile literature 4. World history -- Juvenile literature 5. Children's literature -- Bibliography

ISBN 1-59884-613-2 pa; 978-1-59884-613-3 pa; 978-1-59884-614-0 ebook

LC 2010036580

"In this authoritative and highly readable text, [Cole] presents booktalks and reading lists of interest to children. The titles chosen are set in Africa, Asia, Europe, the Americas, Australia, New Zealand and the South Pacific Islands, and the Arctic and Antarctic. Each booktalk contains an enticing description of the book, bibliographic information, interest and reading levels, and awards. Those that have videos available are noted." SLJ

Includes bibliographical references

Imhoff, Kathleen R.

★ **Library** contests; a how-to-do-it manual. [by] Kathleen R.T. Imhoff, Ruthie Maslin. Neal-Schuman Publishers 2007 182p il (How-to-do-it manuals for librarians) pa $55

Grades: Adult Professional   **021.7**

1. Contests 2. Libraries and community 3. Advertising -- Libraries 4. Libraries -- Public relations

ISBN 1-55570-559-6 pa; 978-1-55570-559-6 pa

LC 2006-33177

"This comprehensive book covers planning, implementing, and evaluating contests of all kinds, for all kinds of libraries. It addresses setting budgets and schedules, choosing prizes and judges, establishing rules, promoting the contest, and evaluating it once it is over. . . . The authors . . . cover potential negatives as well as positives in plain language. . . . The illustrations are informative." SLJ

Includes bibliographical references

Keane, Nancy J.

★ The **tech**-savvy booktalker; a guide for 21st-century educators. [by] Nancy J. Keane and Terence W. Cavanaugh. Libraries Unlimited 2009 162p il pa $35

Grades: Adult Professional   **021.7**

1. Book talks 2. Information technology

ISBN 978-1-59158-637-1 pa; 1-59158-637-2 pa

LC 2008-38988

"Keane offers a way to enhance booktalks with technology and to invite students to explore new ways to talk about books using Web 2.0 tools. The volume is divided into 11 chapters from booktalking concepts to more advanced uses of technology including scanners, digital cameras, computer software, and audio recording. Also included are chapters on software programs such as PowerPoint and iMovie as well as Internet sites such as YouTube and Amazon. The sequence of chapters is designed to allow easy access to information for both novice and experienced computer users. . . . This excellent resource shows ways to use existing technology to augment booktalks and to expand the experience beyond the classroom." SLJ

Includes bibliographical references

Phillips, Susan P.

Great displays for your library step by step. McFarland & Co. 2008 234p il pa $45

Grades: Adult Professional **021.7**

1. Libraries -- Exhibitions

ISBN 978-0-7864-3164-9; 0-7864-3164-4

LC 2007-47450

"Phillips' enthusiasm, creativity, and breadth of personal interests are evident throughout this book. . . . This text will inspire readers to locate and showcase the treasures in their own collections." SLJ

Includes bibliographical references

Skaggs, Gayle

Look, it's books! marketing your library with displays and promotions. [by] Gayle Skaggs. McFarland & Co. 2008 188p il pa $45

Grades: Adult Professional **021.7**

1. School libraries 2. Books and reading 3. Libraries -- Exhibitions

ISBN 978-0-7864-3132-8 pa; 0-7864-3132-6 pa

LC 2007049517

"A good basic resource for anyone needing ideas to promote reading to elementary students." Booklist

025.04   Information storage and retrieval systems

Bell, Suzanne S.

Librarian's guide to online searching; 2nd ed.; Libraries Unlimited, an imprint of ABC-CLIO, LLC 2012 286 p. il (paperback) $55

Grades: Adult Professional **025.04**

1. Internet searching 2. Librarians -- Training of

ISBN 9781610690355; 1610690354

LC 200835924

First published 2006

This book, the second edition by Suzanne S. Bell, looks at online searching and "covers everything from Boolean searching to using specific topic-based databases. Bell also includes a variety of screen captures from many of the databases she discusses. . . . The final chapter guides librarians in how to use the searching knowledge they have in order to teach others." (Voice of Youth Advocates)

This "online searching guide will be invaluable to anyone starting out or looking for a refresher course on this topic. In clear concise language, the author covers everything from Boolean searching to using specific topic-based databases. . . . This easy-to-use manual, written with just a touch of humor and not a drop of condescension, is sure to be embraced by librarians of all skill levels." Voice Youth Advocates

Includes bibliographical references

Jaeger, Paul T.

Public libraries and internet service roles; measuring and maximizing Internet services. [by] Charles R. McClure and Paul T. Jaeger. American Library Association 2009 112p il map $65

Grades: Adult Professional **025.04**

1. Internet 2. Public libraries 3. Libraries and the Internet 4. Internet -- Public libraries 5. Librarianship -- Social aspects 6. Public libraries -- Social aspects 7. Public libraries -- Aims and objectives

ISBN 978-0-8389-3576-7; 0-8389-3576-1

LC 2008-26622

The authors "summarize the existing research on the meanings of social roles and expectations of public libraries and the results of studies detailing those roles and expectations in relation to the Internet. . . . Their book raises our awareness of some very critical issues and is required reading for anyone who cares about public libraries." Booklist

Includes bibliographical references

Pascaretti, Vicki

Team up online; by Vicki Pascaretti and Sara Wilkie. Cherry Lake Pub. 2010 32p il (Super smart information strategies) lib bdg $27.07

Grades: 3 4 5 6 **025.04**

1. Internet research 2. Wikis (Computer science)

ISBN 978-1-60279-644-7 lib bdg; 1-60279-644-0 lib bdg

LC 2009027082

"The appealing layout includes manageable paragraphs, a variety of engaging illustrations, and examples that clearly guide readers through each topic. . . . [This] introduces collaboration by using a garden analogy: plant, dig, garden, and ponder. It also insists on adequate privacy safeguards and discusses online tools such as wikis that will help students work together." SLJ

Includes glossary and bibliographical references

Porterfield, Jason

★ **Conducting** basic and advanced searches. Rosen Central 2010 48p il (Digital and information literacy) lib bdg $26.50

Grades: 5 6 7 8 **025.04**

1. Internet resources 2. Internet searching

ISBN 978-1-4358-5316-4 lib bdg; 1-4358-5316-4 lib bdg

LC 2008-46783

Describes how to conduct both basic and advanced searches on the Internet, from the basics of online search engines, boolean search terms, and evaluating the content of search results

"Colorful photos, diagrams, and sidebars and [a] lively [text creates an] appealing, user-friendly [presentation]. . . . Students and teachers will find [this title] useful in keeping up-to-date on and utilizing online resources and today's technology in a rapidly changing digital world." SLJ

Includes glossary and bibliographical references

Rabbat, Suzy

Find your way online. Cherry Lake Pub. 2010 32p il (Super smart information strategies) lib bdg $27.07

Grades: 3 4 5 6 **025.04**

1. Internet searching

ISBN 978-1-60279-639-3 lib bdg; 1-60279-639-4 lib bdg

LC 2009024549

"The appealing layout includes manageable paragraphs, a variety of engaging illustrations, and examples that clearly guide readers through each topic. . . . [This] begins with keywords, narrowing the search, and search engines. Then it shows students how to 'drill down' using subject directories and databases." SLJ

Scheeren, William O.

Technology for the school librarian; theory and practice. Libraries Unlimited 2010 223p il $50

Grades: Adult Professional   025.04

1. School libraries 2. Digital libraries 3. Information technology 4. Libraries -- Special collections

ISBN 978-1-59158-900-6; 1-59158-900-2

LC 2009-51922

"This title provides information on the practical aspects of technology in the school library as well as the theoretical framework to spark continued learning. Sharing actual case studies as well as practical tips on technology implentation and terminology, this title will be a valuable resource to any school librarian." Libr Media Connect

Includes bibliographical references

Truesdell, Ann

Find the right site. Cherry Lake Pub. 2010 32p il (Super smart information strategies) lib bdg $27.07

Grades: 3 4 5 6   025.04

1. Internet searching

ISBN 978-1-60279-638-6 lib bdg; 1-60279-638-6 lib bdg

LC 2009027083

"The appealing layout includes manageable paragraphs, a variety of engaging illustrations, and examples that clearly guide readers through each topic. . . . [This] is an excellent introduction to Web site evaluation and related pitfalls." SLJ

Includes glossary and bibliographical references

025.1 Administration

Anderson, Cynthia

Write grants, get money; [by] Cynthia Anderson and Kathi Knop. 2nd ed.; Linworth Pub. 2008 128p pa $44.95

Grades: Adult Professional   025.1

1. Grants-in-aid

ISBN 978-1-58683-303-9 pa; 1-58683-303-0 pa

LC 2008-22038

First published 2002

"This practical, grant writing manual will prove invaluable to both novice and experienced grant writers. Written clearly and concisely, this title outlines the grant writing process step by step, from generating ideas to the nuts and bolts of writing an effective proposal. . . . Multiple appendices provide a plethora of supplemental information such as resources on grant writing, Web sites, awards and contests, listservs for media specialists, and a sample grant proposal format. . . . This book makes grant writing as simple as its title." Libr Media Connect

Includes glossary and bibliographical references

Curzon, Susan Carol

Managing change; a how-to-do-it manual for librarians. rev ed.; Neal-Schuman Publishers 2005 129p (How-to-do-it manuals for librarians) pa $55

Grades: Adult Professional   025.1

1. Planning, Library 2. Libraries -- Administration

3. Personnel -- Administration 4. Libraries -- Human resource management 5. Administration -- Handbooks, manuals, etc.

ISBN 1-55570-553-7

LC 2005-22846

First published 1989

"The real-world approach makes the book a valuable addition to the professional collection." Booklist

Includes bibliographical references

Farmer, Lesley S. Johnson

Neal-Schuman technology management handbook for school library media centers; by Lesley S. Johnson Farmer and Marc E. McPhee. Neal-Schuman Publishers 2010 289p il pa $59.95

Grades: Adult Professional   025.1

1. School libraries 2. Instructional materials centers

ISBN 978-1-55570-659-3; 1-55570-659-2

LC 2010-9301

"This informative, well-researched text is perfect for those in the early stages of integrating technology into their programs. The first chapter begins with an overview of the impact technology has had on society and defines technology and its role in the library, including past, present, and possible future changes, as well as managerial roles of the librarian. Other chapters examine planning for management, assessing, researching, developing a technology plan, acquiring all types of tech resources, and managing the physical space to accommodate equipment and networking." SLJ

Includes bibliographical references

The **frugal** librarian; thriving in tough economic times. edited by Carol Smallwood. American Library Association 2011 277p il

Grades: Adult Professional   025.1

1. Library finance 2. Libraries and community 3. Libraries -- United States

ISBN 0-8389-1075-0; 978-0-8389-1075-7

LC 2010034317

"The thirty-four chapters in Smallwood's collection address a myriad of issues faced by libraries and librarians when times get tough and money is tight. Written by practicing librarians from academic, public, and school libraries, the concise essays are easy to read, sometimes personal, and highly practical. . . . This issue is certainly timely, but in reality, sound management and creative budgeting never vanish from the library environment. The table of contents and descriptive title chapters, coupled with the index, allow for ease of use for the browser. This inexpensive volume from ALA will be particularly helpful to public and academic librarians." Voice Youth Advocates

Includes bibliographical references

Fullner, Sheryl Kindle

The **shoestring** library. Linworth Publishing 2010 139p il pa $30

Grades: Adult Professional   025.1

1. Library finance

ISBN 978-1-58683-520-0 pa; 1-58683-520-3 pa

LC 2010-718

"Every librarian will find plenty of new ideas, insights, and inspiration from the wealth of suggestions found here." Libr Media Connect

Independent school libraries; perspectives on excellence. Dorcas Hand, editor. Libraries Unlimited 2010 369p il (Libraries Unlimited professional guides in school librarianship) pa $45

Grades: Adult Professional **025.1**

1. Private schools 2. School libraries

ISBN 978-1-59158-803-0 pa; 1-59158-803-0 pa; 978-1-59158-812-2 ebook

LC 2010-14567

"Twenty-one essays by prominent independent school librarians both address the current state of independent school librarianship in the United States and offer suggestions for the future. Pieces cover the library's role in the school, statistical comparisons, staffing, advocacy, assessment, technology, information commons, collaboration, college preparation, programming, traditions, collection development, minors' rights, budgeting, facilities, accreditation, and disaster planning. . . . Librarians from all schools will find a wealth of information here." Voice Youth Advocates

Includes bibliographical references

Lushington, Nolan

★ **Libraries** designed for kids. Neal-Schuman Publishers 2008 173p il pa $85

Grades: Adult Professional **025.1**

1. Children's libraries 2. Young adults' libraries 3. Libraries -- Administration

ISBN 978-1-55570-631-9

LC 2008-32537

"Lushington's guide will be invaluable to librarians and boards of trustees as they consider renovating, expanding, or creating new service areas for children and teens. . . . Lushington guides the planning team through creating the library program utilizing demographics and community input, which will help with determining the size of the facility. However, the largest sections of the book focus on design considerations to both enhance the user's experience and to most efficiently organize and supervise the collection and facility." SLJ

Includes bibliographical references

MacDonell, Colleen

★ **Essential** documents for school libraries; 2nd ed.; Linworth 2010 xxiv, 156p il $50

Grades: Adult Professional **025.1**

1. Libraries -- Administration

ISBN 978-1-58683-400-5

LC 2010-21241

First published 2004

"Each chapter begins with why the documents are needed, followed by practical advice for writing the documents, and examples of how the documents make an effective change in the library media program." Libr Media Connect [review of 2004 edition]

Includes bibliographical references

Martin, Barbara Stein

★ **Fundamentals** of school library media management; a how-to-do-it manual. [by] Barbara Stein Martin and Marco Zannier. Neal-Schuman Publishers 2009 172p il (How-to-do-it manuals for librarians) pa $59.95

Grades: Adult Professional **025.1**

1. Instructional materials centers 2. School libraries -- Administration 3. Administration -- Handbooks, manuals, etc.

ISBN 978-1-55570-656-2; 1-55570-656-8

LC 2009-7930

This book "contains useful information to help school librarians manage a myriad of tasks and roles. . . . [The authors] have created a book that is helpful, accessible, and full of down-to-earth, concrete examples." Booklist

Includes bibliographical references

★ **School** library management; [edited by] Judi Repman and Gail Dickinson. 6th ed.; Linworth Pub. 2007 200p il pa $44.95

Grades: Adult Professional **025.1**

1. School libraries 2. Libraries -- Administration

ISBN 978-1-58683-296-4; 1-58683-296-4

LC 2006-103468

First published 1987 with title: School library management notebook

"This collection of more than 35 articles written for Library Media Connection from 2003 to 2006 is a virtual treasure trove for library media specialists. . . . The book covers the very practical everyday issues such as scheduling and overdues, and also provides invaluable information on data gathering, facilities planning, professional development, the role of the library in the world of standardized testing, the technological future of libraries, and much more." SLJ

Includes bibliographical references

Tips and other bright ideas for elementary school libraries. Volume 4 Kate Vande Brake, editor. Linworth 2010 134p Volume 4 pa $35

Grades: Adult Professional **025.1**

1. Elementary school libraries 2. Libraries -- Administration

ISBN 978-1-58683-416-6 pa; 1-58683-416-9 pa; 978-1-58683-417-3 ebook

LC 2010011049

This title includes "fun and informative management advice from fellow librarians. All of it has been taken from 2006-2009 Library Media Connection magazine. . . . [The introduction] reviews some of the many jobs and responsibilities in a librarian's day. Section one includes management hints to help maximize effectiveness, followed by sections on working with students, teaching skills, . . . working with teachers, technology, reading promotion, public relations, and working with helpers." SLJ

025.2 Acquisitions and collection development

Baumbach, Donna

★ **Less** is more; a practical guide to weeding school library collections. American Library Association 2006 194p il pa $32

Grades: Adult Professional **025.2**

1. Libraries -- Collection development 2. Discarding of books, periodicals, etc. 3. School libraries -- Collection development

ISBN 978-0-8389-0919-5; 0-8389-0919-1

LC 2006-7490

"This outstanding, easy-to-use guide makes weeding realistic and achievable. . . . This is an indispensable resource for every school library." Booklist

Includes bibliographical references

Brenner, Robin E.

★ **Understanding** manga and anime. Libraries Unlimited 2007 335p il pa $40

Grades: Adult Professional   **025.2**

1. Anime 2. Manga -- Study and teaching 3. Libraries -- Collection development 4. Libraries -- Special collections -- Graphic novels

ISBN 978-1-59158-332-5; 1-59158-332-2

LC 2007-9773

The author "provides thorough explanations of manga and anime vocabulary, potential censorship issues because of cultural disparities, and typical Manga conventions. . . . No professional collection could possibly be complete without this all-inclusive and exceptional work." Voice Youth Advocates

Fagan, Bryan D.

Comic book collections for libraries; [by] Bryan D. Fagan and Jody Condit Fagan; foreword by Stan Sakai; cover art by Derek Steed. Libraries Unlimited 2011 162p pa $45; e-book $45

Grades: Adult Professional   **025.2**

1. Graphic novels 2. Comic books, strips, etc. 3. Graphic novels -- Bibliography 4. Graphic novels -- History and criticism 5. Comic books, strips, etc. -- Bibliography 6. Comic books, strips, etc. -- History and criticism 7. Libraries -- Special collections -- Graphic novels

ISBN 978-1-59884-511-2 pa; 1-59884-511-X pa; 978-1-59884-512-9 e-book

LC 2010052532

"Armed with this book, librarian should feel confident about knowledgeably creating and maintaining a successful comic-book collection." SLJ

Includes bibliographical references

Franklin, Patricia

School library collection development; just the basics. Claire Gatrell Stephens and Patricia Franklin. Libraries Unlimited 2012 x, 71 p.p ill. (Just the basics) (paperback) $35

Grades: Adult Professional   **025.2**

1. School libraries 2. Libraries -- Collection development 3. Collection management (Libraries) -- United States 4. School libraries -- Collection development -- United States

ISBN 1598849433; 9781598849431

LC 2012016990

This book, by Claire Gatrell Stephens and Patricia Franklin, discusses collection development for school librarians. This volume offers a "manual that explains the fundamentals of purchasing, developing, and managing a collection. Containing information useful to anyone from a paraprofessional working under the guidance of a certified school librarian to a newcomer to the field to a certified media specialist, this book covers all of the basics through best practices." (Publisher's note)

Gallaway, Beth

★ **Game** on! gaming at the library. Neal-Schuman Publishers 2009 306p il pa $55

Grades: Adult Professional   **025.2**

1. Video games 2. Video games and children 3. Video games and teenagers 4. Multimedia library services 5. Electronic games -- Collections 6. Libraries -- Special collections

ISBN 978-1-55570-595-4; 1-55570-595-2

LC 2009-14110

"An essential guide for any librarian who plans on embracing the video-game phenomenon, or at the very least, understanding it. . . . [The chapters] are well organized and contain an abundance of practical information. The sections on selection, collection, and circulation of video games include relevant advice on policy, cataloging, marketing, storage, and displays. . . . The annotated list of video games for a core collection is wonderful for selection purposes." SLJ

Includes bibliographical references

Goldsmith, Francisca

The **readers'** advisory guide to graphic novels. American Library Association 2010 124p (ALA readers' advisory series) pa $45

Grades: Adult Professional   **025.2**

1. Graphic novels 2. Graphic novels -- Bibliography 3. Libraries -- Special collections -- Graphic novels

ISBN 978-0-8389-1008-5; 0-8389-1008-4

LC 2009-25239

"After dispelling the two main myths that ghettoize graphic novels—they are just for adolescents and they are far less complex than texts without pictures—Goldsmith emphasizes that GNs are a format and not a genre. She suggests active and passive ways to offer readers' advisory (RA) from face-to-face encounters with patrons to book displays and book groups and offers guidance on helping established GN readers to find new titles they might enjoy. . . . All in all it is a valuable and quite readable resource that belongs in every library's professional collection." Voice Youth Advocates

Includes glossary and bibliographical references

Graphic novels beyond the basics; insights and issues for libraries. Martha Cornog and Timothy Perper, editors. Libraries Unlimited 2009 xxx, 281p il pa $45

Grades: Adult Professional   **025.2**

1. Graphic novels -- History and criticism 2. Comic books, strips, etc. -- History and criticism 3. Libraries -- Special collections -- Graphic novels

ISBN 978-1-59158-478-0; 1-59158-478-7

LC 2009-16189

Editors Cornog and Perper have collected essays by experts Robin Brenner, Francisca Goldsmith, Trina Robbins, Michael R. Lavin, Gilles Poitras, Lorena O'English, Michael Niederhausen, Erin Byrne, and Cornog herself, all about graphic novels in libraries. Topics covered range from the appeal of superheroes to manga, the appeal of comics to women and girls, anime, independent comics, dealing with challenges to the material, and more. Appendices provide resource information on African American-interest graphic novels, Latino-Interest graphic novels, LGBT-interest graphic novels, religious-themed graphic novels, a bibliography of books about graphic novels in libraries, and online resources.

"Whether you are serious about the genre, interested in the history, or looking for ammunition, this book should be on your shelf. The wealth of knowledge and research that went into these essays is impressive, and reading this book will put you on the road to becoming an expert." Libr Media Connect

Includes bibliographical references

Herald, Nathan

Graphic novels for young readers; a genre guide for ages 4-14. Libraries Unlimited 2011 188p (Genreflecting advisory series) $40

Grades: Adult Professional   **025.2**
1. Graphic novels 2. Children's literature 3. Graphic novels -- Bibliography
ISBN 1-59884-395-8; 978-1-59884-395-8

         LC 2010044947

"Librarians looking to beef up their graphic-novel collections will do well to get their hands on this valuable volume. The annotated entries are laid out in eight chapters organized by major genre, and from action and adventure to educational. Within chapters, the titles, 600 in all, are arranged alphabetically into popular subgenres such as superheroes, mythology, sports, and many more. . . . The intended audience for each title is clear, with bold icons providing an age range. Herald's writing style lends personality to what could easily be a dry overview. . . . A thorough, well-organized, one-stop shop for quality graphic novels." SLJ

Includes bibliographical references

★ **Intellectual** freedom manual; 8th ed; American Library Association 2010 xxii, 439 p.p

Grades: Adult Professional   **025.2**
1. Intellectual freedom -- United States -- Handbooks, manuals, etc. 2. Libraries -- Censorship -- United States -- Handbooks, manuals, etc.
ISBN 0838935907; 9780838935903

         LC 2010016157

"All libraries should have a copy of this book to use when writing or revising policies; indispensable." Libr J

Mayer, Brian

Libraries got game; aligned learning through modern board games. [by] Brian Mayer and Christopher Harris. American Library Association 2010 134p il pa $45

Grades: Adult Professional   **025.2**
1. Board games 2. Libraries -- Special collections
ISBN 978-0-8389-1009-2; 0-8389-1009-2

         LC 2009-26839

"This is a valuable resource for K-12 librarians interested in building curriculum-aligned 'designer' game collections. The authors . . . explain how specific games enhance language-arts, social-studies, and math units, and build literacy skills. The two chapters devoted to promoting and justifying the inclusion of games in the library are well documented and a wonderful source to have to convince skeptical administrators. Suggestions for building a core collection, which highlights top recommended games for elementary school, middle school, and high school; a list of game publishers; a list of games discussed; and a glossary of terminology are included." SLJ

Includes bibliographical references

Scales, Pat R.

★ **Protecting** intellectual freedom in your school library; scenarios from the front lines. [by] Pat R. Scales for the Office for Intellectual Freedom. American Library Association 2009 148p (Intellectual freedom front lines) pa $55

Grades: Adult Professional   **025.2**
1. School libraries 2. Intellectual freedom
ISBN 978-0-8389-3581-1; 0-8389-3581-8

         LC 2008-39893

"Scales uses court opinions, federal and state laws, and ALA documents to offer solutions for responding to infringements. A broad range of potential scenarios—from challenges to materials in both the library and the classroom, the legality of film rating systems, using computerized reading programs as selection tools and labeling books by reading levels, policies for interlibrary loans and reserves to confidentiality of children's and teens' circulation records—are covered. . . . This resource should be in every school library's professional collection." Voice Youth Advocates

Includes bibliographical references

Serchay, David S.

★ The **librarian's** guide to graphic novels for children and tweens. Neal-Schuman Publishers 2008 272p pa $55

Grades: Adult Professional   **025.2**
1. Graphic novels 2. Children -- Books and reading 3. Libraries -- Special collections -- Graphic novels
ISBN 978-1-55570-626-5 pa; 1-55570-626-5 pa

         LC 2008-6487

This book provides a brief history of graphic novels, describes genres, discusses manga, gives librarians reasons to include graphic novels in library collections and in school curricula. It also discusses some of the major comic book publishers in the U.S., suggests how to purchase graphic novels, and how to process, catalog, and shelve them, and also how to use them in programming. Several lengthy appendices provide annotated lists of titles that are suitable for children and tween readers, online resources for purchasing, reviews, and news, and additional, comics-related books.

"An insightful introduction to this format as well as an effective selection tool, this guide is highly recommended." Booklist

Includes bibliographical references

025.3   Bibliographic analysis and control

★ **Cataloging** correctly for kids; an introduction to the tools. edited by Sheila S. Intner, Joanna F. Fountain, and Jean Weihs. 5th ed.; Association for Library Collections and Technical Services, American Library Association 2011 224p pa $55

Grades: Adult Professional   **025.3**
1. Cataloging 2. Reference books 3. Children's literature -- Cataloging
ISBN 978-0-8389-3589-7 pa; 0-8389-3589-3 pa

         LC 2010012945

First published 1989 by the Cataloging for Children's Materials Committee

Among the topics discussed are: guidelines for standardized cataloging for children; how children search; using AACR2 and MARC 21; copy cataloging; using RDA;

Sears List of Subject Headings; LC Children's headings; sources for Dewey numbers; cataloging nonbook materials; authority control; how the CIP program helps children; cataloging for kids in the academic library; cataloging for non-English-speaking children and preliterate children; automating the children's catalog; vendors of cataloging for children's materials.

Includes bibliographical references

Oliver, Chris

★ **Introducing** RDA; a guide to the basics. Chris Oliver. American Library Association 2010 vii, 117 p.p ill. (paperback) $45

Grades: Adult Professional   025.3
1. Cataloging 2. Resource description & access -- Handbooks, manuals, etc. 3. Cataloging/Standards 4. Descriptive cataloging/Standards
ISBN 083893594X; 9780838935941

LC 2010021719

This book looks at Resource Description and Access (RDA), the cataloging standard that's replacing Anglo-American Cataloguing Rules (AACR). "Through numerous examples, [Chris] Oliver compares and contrasts RDA and AACR. He also discusses RDA background and its connection to the Functional Requirements for Bibliographic Records (FRBR) and Functional Requirements for Authority Data (FRAD) models and international standards." This is "a useful guide that provides a clear explanation of what RDA is all about. . . . Highly recommended for novice and experienced catalogers." Libr J

Includes bibliographical references (p. 105-109) and index.

025.4   Subject analysis and control

Donovan, Sandra, 1967-

Bob the Alien discovers the Dewey decimal system; by Sandy Donovan; illustrated by Martin Haake. Picture Window 2010 24p il (In the library) lib bdg $25.32

Grades: 2 3 4   025.4
1. Bibliographic instruction 2. Dewey Decimal Classification
ISBN 978-1-4048-5757-5 lib bdg; 1-4048-5757-5 lib bdg

Bob is from planet Plainold, where they have just discovered spiders. But planet Plainold doesn't have books, so Bob has traveled to Earth to find books about spiders. Join Allison Wonderland as she teaches Bob how to use the Dewey Decimal System to find books about spiders.

"What is wonderful about this . . . is that key terms and phrases are enlarged and placed in bold letters to stress their importance. . . . [This is a] vital resource for teaching library skills. All elementary librarians will appreciate the innovative way the author and illustrator combine their talents to create an exciting way to share specifics about libraries and books." Libr Media Connect

Bored Bella learns about fiction and nonfiction; by Sandy Donovan; illustrated by Leeza Hernandez. Picture Window 2010 24p il (In the library) lib bdg $25.32

Grades: 2 3 4   025.4
1. Library classification 2. Bibliographic instruction
ISBN 978-1-4048-5758-2 lib bdg; 1-4048-5758-3 lib bdg

Bored Bella thinks books are boring. When his class takes a trip to the library, Bella isn't thrilled. Join Ms. Paige Turner as she introduces fiction and nonfiction books to Bella and her class.

"What is wonderful about this . . . is that key terms and phrases are enlarged and placed in bold letters to stress their importance. . . . [This is a] vital resource for teaching library skills. All elementary librarians will appreciate the innovative way the author and illustrator combine their talents to create an exciting way to share specifics about libraries and books." Libr Media Connect

Includes glossary

★ **Sears** list of subject headings; Joseph Miller, editor; Susan McCarthy, associate editor. 20th ed; H.W. Wilson Co. 2010 liii, 847p $150

Grades: Adult Professional   025.4
1. Reference books 2. Subject headings
ISBN 978-0-8242-1105-9; 0-8242-1105-7

LC 2010-5731

First published 1923 with title: List of subject headings for small libraries, by Minnie Earl Sears

"The Sears List of Subject Headings delivers a core list of key headings, together with patterns and examples to guide the cataloger in creating additional headings as required. It features: agreement with the Dewey Decimal Classification system to ensure that subject headings conform with library standards; [a] thesaurus-like format; accompanying list of canceled and replacement headings; and legends within the list that identify earlier forms of headings; scope notes accompanying . . . headings where clarification of the specialized use of a term may be required." Publisher's note

Includes bibliographical references

025.5   Services for users

American Association of School Librarians

Standards for the 21st-century learner in action. American Association of School Librarians 2009 120p pa $39

Grades: Adult Professional   025.5
1. Information literacy 2. Libraries -- Standards
ISBN 978-0-8389-8507-6 pa; 0-8389-8507-6 pa

"Standards in Action attempts to expand upon AASL's Standards for the 21st Century Learner by providing benchmarks and action examples. The original document was a nine-page brochure that outlined nine common beliefs, four learning standards, four strands, and indicators under each strand. It was an excellent starting point, but the addition of benchmarks at grades two, five, eight, ten, and twelve helps flesh out the original vision. . . . School libraries should own a copy of this professional, which has a role within any program." Voice Youth Advocates

Includes glossary and bibliographical references

Gaines, Ann

Ace your research paper; [by] Ann Graham Gaines. Enslow Publishers 2009 48p il (Ace it! information literacy) lib bdg $23.93

Grades: 3 4 5 **025.5**
1. Research 2. Report writing 3. English language -- Composition and exercises
ISBN 978-0-7660-3390-0 lib bdg; 0-7660-3390-2 lib bdg
LC 2008024884
"Readers will learn how to research, take notes, write, and revise their research papers" Publisher's note
Includes glossary and bibliographical references

Grassian, Esther S.
★ **Information** literacy instruction; theory and practice. [by] Esther S. Grassian and Joan R. Kaplowitz. 2nd ed; Neal-Schuman Publishers 2009 xxvii, 412p pa $75
Grades: Adult Professional **025.5**
1. Information literacy 2. Information literacy -- Study and teaching 3. Information retrieval -- Study and teaching 4. Bibliographic instruction -- College and university students
ISBN 978-155570-666-1; 1-55570-666-5
LC 2009-23647
First published 2001
This "is designed for anyone involved in the creation and management of information literacy programming. Sixteen well-written chapters, organized into five sections, provide both theory and practical applications, with the emphasis on the practical. . . . Several extras appear in the accompanying CD-ROM. . . . A timely, thorough, and endlessly useful must-have title for librarians, teaching librarians, and library schools." Booklist
Includes bibliographical references

Harper, Meghan
Reference sources and services for youth. Neal-Schuman Publishers 2011 307p $65
Grades: Adult Professional **025.5**
1. School libraries 2. Children's libraries 3. Young adults' libraries 4. Reference services (Libraries)
ISBN 978-1-55570-641-8; 1-55570-641-X
LC 2011004987
"The concept of school and public library collaboration is thoroughly explored in this excellent volume on providing reference services. The chapter on information literacy includes web links with information about standards, models, instruction and assessment, rubrics, web quests, graphic organizers, evaluation tools, and assessment. Additional chapters provide a discussion of online resources, government resources for youth, evaluation and marketing reference services, and managing them." SLJ
Includes bibliographical references

Intner, Carol F.
Homework help from the library; in person and online. American Library Association 2011 202p il pa $47
Grades: Adult Professional **025.5**
1. Homework 2. Library resources 3. Libraries and students
ISBN 978-0-8389-1046-7; 0-8389-1046-7
LC 2010042096
"Building on the concept that information services and education converge with homework help, the author sketches in the history of youth services and current learning theories. She offers practical suggestions for needs assessment and determining a guiding philosophy. Speaking to the public librarian, Intner outlines the points to consider in designing a homework help program and training staff. Possible workshop topics include an overview of student needs and available resources, creating a comfortable and inviting space, considering the needs of different ages, understanding youth culture, and responding to various learning styles. . . . Youth librarians will want this comprehensive and practical guide within easy reach. " Voice Youth Advocates
Includes bibliographical references

Lanning, Scott
Essential reference services for today's school media specialists; [by] Scott Lanning and John Bryner. 2nd ed.; Libraries Unlimited 2010 141p il pa $45
Grades: Adult Professional **025.5**
1. School libraries 2. Reference services (Libraries)
ISBN 978-1-59158-883-2; 1-59158-883-9
LC 2009-39375
"The content focuses on core reference skills, electronic resources, and leadership. The first few chapters discuss information literacy, evaluation of resources, the role of print resources, and the reference interview. These are followed by chapters on the library catalog, electronic resources, and the Web as a reference tool. Finally, there are several chapters dealing with the teacher-librarians' instructional and leadership roles. The authors use a very accessible tone while providing the basics." Booklist
Includes bibliographical references

Peck, Penny
Readers' advisory for children and 'tweens. Libraries Unlimited 2010 190p pa $36
Grades: Adult Professional **025.5**
1. Children's libraries 2. Children's literature 3. Young adult literature 4. Children -- Books and reading 5. Children's literature -- Bibliography
ISBN 978-1-59884-387-3 pa; 1-59884-387-7 pa
LC 2010002589
"Written for novices, this useful guide will provide many valuable suggestions to library staff unfamiliar with the literature and how to go about recommending it to their young patrons and their caregivers. The first two chapters define readers' advisory and describe how to provide it successfully. The next few chapters are divided into age categories. . . The concluding chapters are divided by type of literature. . . . All of the chapters include helpful booklists and websites, which are great collection development tools as well. There are some tips on promoting books. . . . This title is a valuable resource." SLJ
Includes bibliographical references

Wichman, Emily T.
Librarian's guide to passive programming; easy and affordable activities for all ages. Emily T. Wichman. Libraries Unlimited Inc. 2012 xvii, 152 p.p ill. (pbk.: acid-free paper) $40
Grades: Professional **025.5**
1. Librarians 2. Library finance 3. Library services
ISBN 159884895X; 9781598848953; 9781598848960
LC 2011045419
In her book, author Emily T. Wichman discusses library budget cuts, and how "librarians are seeking new ways to stretch their programming dollars and maximize staff resources. Passive programming allows libraries to inexpen-

sively showcase their services while inviting visitors of all ages to enjoy the value that libraries bring to the community." (Publisher's note)

Includes bibliographical references and index.

027 General libraries, archives, information centers

Sawa, Maureen

The **library** book; the story of libraries from camels to computers. illustrated by Bill Slavin. Tundra Books 2006 72p il $18.95

Grades: 3 4 5 6   027

1. Libraries

ISBN 0-88776-698-6

"This information-packed picture book is an excellent tribute to libraries around the world, describing the development of libraries from ancient times to today. . . . The picture-book format, filled with earth-toned illustrations, adds appeal. . . . The book is also filled with interesting sidebars and highlighted sections of information." Voice Youth Advocates

Includes bibliographical references

Trumble, Kelly

The **Library** of Alexandria; illustrated by Robina MacIntyre Marshall. Clarion Bks. 2003 72p il maps $17

Grades: 5 6 7 8   027

1. Ancient civilization

ISBN 0-395-75832-7

LC 2003-150

An introduction to the largest and most famous library in the ancient world, discussing its construction in Alexandria, Egypt, its vast collections, rivalry with the Pergamum Library, famous scholars, and destruction by fire.

This is a "well-organized and thorough resource." SLJ

Includes glossary and bibliographical references

027.4 Public libraries

King, M. G.

Librarian on the roof! a true story. illustrated by Stephen Gilpin. Albert Whitman 2010 un il $16.95

Grades: K 1 2 3   027.4

1. Libraries 2. Librarians

ISBN 978-0-8075-4512-6; 0-8075-4512-0

"King's writing is clear and often witty, and she does a credible job of capturing Laurell's determined and forthright personality, as well as the drama and excitement of this unusual approach to fund-raising. Gilpin's hand-drawn, vibrantly colored cartoon illustrations enliven the story." SLJ

027.6 Libraries for special groups and organizations

Alire, Camila

★ **Serving** Latino communities; a how-to-do-it manual for librarians. [by] Camila Alire, Jacqueline Ayala. 2nd ed; Neal-Schuman Publishers 2007 229p il (How-to-do-it manuals for librarians) pa $59.95

Grades: Adult Professional   027.6

1. Libraries and Hispanic Americans 2. Public libraries -- Services to Hispanic Americans

ISBN 978-1-55570-606-7; 1-55570-606-1

LC 2007-7783

First published 1998

"The information covered helps library staff understand the needs of their library's Latino community; develop successful programs and services; obtain funding for projects and programs; prepare staff to work more effectively with Latinos; establish partnerships with relevant external agencies and organizations; improve collection development; and perform effective outreach and public relations. . . . There are few resources widely available on this topic and none as complete." Libr Media Connect

Includes bibliographical references

Diamant-Cohen, Betsy

Early literacy programming en Espanol; Mother Goose on the Loose programs for bilingual learners. Neal-Schuman Publishers 2010 xxii, 177p il pa $65

Grades: Adult Professional   027.6

1. Nursery rhymes 2. Bilingual education 3. Children's libraries

ISBN 978-1-55570-691-3; 1-55570-691-6

LC 2009049594

"Diamant-Cohen has developed this manual to encourage librarians to present Spanish-language MGOL programs. . . . The author proposes recruiting community partners fluent in Spanish who will be trained by the children's librarian and will copresent the sessions. Five parts cover the basics on how to run the program successfully. The manual is complemented with illustrations that can be replicated and used as flannel-board figures; bibliographies, worksheets, and a CD with instructions; nursery rhymes in English and Spanish; and graphics and templates of documents. This volume is infused with enthusiasm to serve the children of Spanish-speakers. It will not only help English-speaking librarians, but also the bilingual ones to present and enjoy MGOL." SLJ

Includes bibliographical references

Feinberg, Sandra

The **family**-centered library handbook; Sandra Feinberg . . . [et al.] Neal-Schuman Publishers 2007 xv, 324p il pa $65

Grades: Adult Professional   027.6

1. Children's libraries 2. Children's library services 3. Library-community relations 4. Reading -- Parent participation 5. Libraries -- Services to families 6. Public libraries -- Services to parents 7. Libraries -- Services to preschool children

ISBN 978-1-55570-541-1 pa; 1-55570-541-3 pa

LC 2006102709

"This volume encourages libraries to increase services to children and those who care for these children, make programming developmentally appropriate, incorporate early intervention and primary prevention strategies, build relationships with family service professionals, and make children's library spaces inviting. . . . This highly organized handbook provides a wealth of information for libraries wanting to enhance their children's programming." Booklist

Includes bibliographical references

MacMillan, Kathy

A **box** full of tales; easy ways to share library resources through story boxes. American Library Association 2008 222p pa $45

Grades: Adult Professional   **027.6**

1. Storytelling 2. Children's stories 3. Library cooperation 4. Children's libraries 5. Children's libraries -- Activity programs 6. Children's library services -- Activity projects

ISBN 978-0-8389-0960-7 pa; 0-8389-0960-4 pa

LC 2007-48794

"The author, a veteran librarian and storyteller, here offers up the story box model of program resource sharing pioneered at Maryland's Carroll County Library System. Story boxes contain all the resources necessary to conduct a theme-based story time session; the boxes are created by children's librarians to be shared with other librarians at different locations within a system. . . . Even children's librarians who don't work in multibranch systems will find this guide extremely valuable for its theme-based program outlines, whether or not they choose to create story boxes. Strongly recommended for public libraries." Libr J

Includes bibliographical references

027.62   Libraries for specific age groups

Bauer, Caroline Feller

Leading kids to books through crafts. American Lib. Assn. 2000 145p (Mighty easy motivators) pa $30

Grades: Adult Professional   **027.62**

1. Handicraft 2. Reference books 3. Books and reading 4. Children's libraries 5. Children's literature 6. Book talks -- United States 7. Handicraft -- United States 8. Children -- Books and reading 9. Children's reading -- Projects 10. Creative activities and seat work 11. Children's literature -- Bibliography 12. Children's libraries -- Activity programs -- United States 13. Children -- Reading -- Study and teaching -- Activities and projects

ISBN 0-8389-0769-5

LC 99-41387

"Bauer gives basic, practical information on presenting programs that introduce preschool and primary-grade youngsters to stories and poems and demonstrates related crafts that are easy to prepare and execute." SLJ

Leading kids to books through magic; illustrated by Richard Laurent. American Lib. Assn. 1996 128p il (Mighty easy motivators) pa $35

Grades: Adult Professional   **027.62**

1. Book talks 2. Magic tricks 3. Reference books 4. Books and reading 5. Children's libraries 6. Children's literature 7. Children's literature -- Bibliography 8. Children's library services -- Activity projects

ISBN 978-0-8389-0684-2 pa; 0-8389-0684-2 pa

LC 95-53049

The author's "concise yet thorough directions accompanied by Richard Laurent's delightful line drawings make this book a useful tool for teachers and librarians looking for ways to promote children's enthusiasm for reading." J Youth Serv Libr

Includes bibliographical references

Leading kids to books through puppets; illustrated by Richard Laurent. American Lib. Assn. 1997 156p il (Mighty easy motivators) pa $35

Grades: Adult Professional   **027.62**

1. Reference books 2. Books and reading 3. Children's libraries 4. Children's literature 5. Puppets and puppet plays 6. Puppets 7. Children's literature -- Bibliography 8. Children's library services -- Activity projects

ISBN 978-0-8389-0706-1 pa; 0-8389-0706-7 pa

LC 97-1357

"Even the most reluctant performer will be encouraged by this practical, concise, easy-to-use book." SLJ

Includes bibliographical references

Benton, Gail

Ready-to-go storytimes; fingerplays, scripts, patterns, music, and more. [by] Gail Benton, Trisha Waichulaitis. Neal-Schuman 2003 239p il pa $65

Grades: Adult Professional   **027.62**

1. Storytelling 2. Children's libraries

ISBN 978-1-55570-449-0 pa; 1-55570-449-2 pa

LC 2002-5806

"This resource is excellent for beginning librarians and teachers and for any professionals who seek new ideas to freshen up their repertoires." Booklist

Includes bibliographical references

Bird, Elizabeth

Children's literature gems; choosing and using them in your library career. American Library Association 2009 125p pa $45

Grades: Adult Professional   **027.62**

1. Book selection 2. Children's libraries 3. Children's literature 4. Children -- Books and reading 5. Children's literature -- Bibliography

ISBN 978-0-8389-0995-9 pa; 0-8389-0995-7 pa

LC 2009003079

"Bird writes in a chatty tone reminiscent of her popular blog, A Fuse #8 Production, and her love of children's literature shines through on every page. This slim volume is not meant to be an in-depth textbook, but rather a brief overview of the field and an introduction to the stars of children's literature. . . . Highlighted boxes throughout feature questions and answers from seasoned professionals on how they handle various parts of their collections and aspects of their work. Readers who are new to the field may find this a comforting basic guide to managing their collections. " SLJ

Includes bibliographical references

Bromann, Jennifer

More storytime action! 2,000+ more ideas for making 500+ picture books interactive. Neal-Schuman Publishers 2009 326p pa $55

Grades: Adult Professional   **027.62**

1. Storytelling 2. Children's libraries 3. Children's literature 4. Picture books for children 5. Picture books for children -- Bibliography 7. Children's library services -- Activity projects

ISBN 978-1-55570-675-3 pa; 1-55570-675-4 pa

LC 2009031724

"Bromann presents more than 2,000 activities related to more than 500 picture books published since 2003. Beginning chapters cover 10 elements of interactive stories; storytelling, including how to select and prepare stories; and how to select books for interactive storytimes, identifying clues found in reviews. . . . The final chapter lists the more than 500 books alphabetically by author with bibliographic information, summary, and storytime activities. . . . For librarians looking to hold the attention of their youngest patrons or to spice up storytime, this title will be a welcome resource." Booklist

Includes bibliographical references

Cerny, Rosanne

★ **Outstanding** library service to children; putting the core competencies to work. [by] Rosanne Cerny, Penny Markey, and Amanda Williams. American Library Association 2006 94p pa $25

Grades: Adult Professional   **027.62**
1. Children's libraries
ISBN 978-0-8389-0922-5 pa; 0-8389-0922-1 pa
"This slim volume should be required reading for all future children's services librarians." Booklist
Includes bibliographical references

Children's services; partnerships for success. edited by Betsy Diamant-Cohen. American Library Association 2010 126p il (ALA public library handbook series) pa $50

Grades: Adult Professional   **027.62**
1. Children's libraries 2. Libraries and schools 3. Libraries and community
ISBN 978-0-8389-1044-3 pa; 0-8389-1044-0 pa
LC 2009045788
"Diamant-Cohen has created a valuable resource by providing practical examples of successful partnerships between libraries of various sizes and community organizations. Concrete scenarios include successful partnerships with law enforcement agencies, recreation departments, academic institutions, children's museums, cultural institutions, churches that attract mainly immigrant populations, businesses, and other agencies." SLJ
Includes bibliographical references

Cullum, Carolyn N.

★ The **storytime** sourcebook II; [a compendium of 3500+ new ideas and resources for storytellers] Neal-Schuman Publishers 2007 489p pa $75

Grades: Adult Professional   **027.62**
1. Storytelling 2. Children's libraries
ISBN 978-1-55570-589-3 pa; 1-55570-589-8 pa
LC 2006-35096
First published 1990 with title: The storytime sourcebook
"Each of the 146 themed programs, designed for children ages two to eight, appears on two facing pages that include appropriate calendar tie-ins, videos, books, music, movements, crafts, activities, and songs. . . . [The author] presents clear and simple directions for crafts and activities, quick and uncomplicated for librarians to prepare, and easy for children to follow. . . . This sourcebook is an essential purchase for libraries serving this audience." SLJ
Includes bibliographical references

De las Casas, Dianne

Tell along tales! playing with participation stories. illustrated by Soleil Lisette. Libraries Unlimited 2011 125p il pa $30

Grades: Adult Professional   **027.62**
1. Storytelling 2. Children's libraries
ISBN 978-1-59884-635-5; 1-59884-635-3
LC 2011000335
"In five chapters chock-full of storyteller tips and ideas, de las Casas explains various types of participation models from call-and-response to directed role-playing and covers how to direct questions to the group. She offers valuable clues for warming up an audience and for settling boisterous children back down. . . . The main body of the book contains the author's choices of suitable stories from around the world with suggested age levels and pointers for leaders. . . . Both novice and veteran storytellers will benefit from the myriad suggestions offered here." SLJ
Includes bibliographical references

Diamant-Cohen, Betsy

Crash course in library services to preschool children. Libraries Unlimited 2010 137p pa $30

Grades: Adult Professional   **027.62**
1. Children's libraries
ISBN 978-1-59884-688-1 pa; 1-59884-688-4 pa
LC 2010024071
"This book presents 10 chapters to quickly immerse the librarian working with preschoolers into the field. An overview of children's services to preschoolers in public libraries is followed by chapters on programming, books, collections, reader's advisory and reference, and the children's room. . . . All librarians who deal with preschoolers, whether experienced public librarians or new school media specialist, will benefit from the ideas, concepts, and guidance provided here." SLJ
Includes bibliographical references

Dixon, Tiara

The **sound** of storytime; [by] Tiara Dixon and Paula Blough. Neal-Schuman Publishers 2006 206p il pa $65

Grades: Adult Professional   **027.62**
1. Storytelling 2. Reference books 3. Children's libraries 4. Children's literature -- Bibliography
ISBN 978-1-55570-552-7 pa; 1-55570-552-9 pa
LC 2006001299
"This book takes the traditional storytime for early childhood and adds singing and simple instruments such as bells and rhythm sticks. Forty-two lesson plans centered around specific books are given in detail, with song suggestions and lists of additional appropriate books. Simple crafts complete each program. The inclusion of a CD-ROM with Ellison die cuts and original lyrics matched to commonly known songs such as 'Three Blind Mice' adds to the lessons." Booklist
Includes bibliographical references

Ernst, Linda L.

Baby rhyming time; [by] Linda L. Ernst. Neal-Schuman Publishers 2008 235p il pa $59.95

Grades: Adult Professional   **027.62**
1. Children's libraries
ISBN 978-1-55570-540-4 pa; 1-55570-540-5 pa
LC 2007043246

"This useful resource provides background, logistics, and a wealth of practical ideas for programs. Ernst describes brain development and language acquisition clearly, with quotes and references for support. She does a good job of tying the science to infant/toddler growth and explaining the librarian's important role in sharing the information with caregivers. She discusses broader factors to consider when planning baby-time programs, including community, facilities, staffing, and potential partnerships." SLJ

Includes bibliographical references

Fasick, Adele M.

Managing children's services in the public library; [by] Adele M. Fasick and Leslie E. Holt. 3rd ed; Libraries Unlimited 2008 248p bibl il tab pa $45

Grades: Adult Professional   **027.62**

1. Public libraries 2. Children's libraries 3. Children -- Books and reading 4. Children's library services -- Administration

ISBN 978-1-59158-412-4 pa; 1-59158-412-4 pa

LC 2007032759

First published 1991

"Excellent support for newbies and as a basis for professional development." Booklist

Includes bibliographical references

Fiore, Carole D.

Fiore's summer library reading program handbook. Neal-Schuman Publishers 2005 xxiii, 312p pa $65

Grades: Adult Professional   **027.62**

1. Books and reading 2. Children's libraries 3. Children's reading -- Projects 4. Young adults' reading -- Projects 5. Children -- Reading -- Study and teaching -- Activities and projects 6. Young adults -- Reading -- Study and teaching -- Activities and projects

ISBN 1-55570-513-8

LC 2004-31104

"This research-laden handbook . . . serves as a 'comprehensive program-planning and implementation tool' for public libraries seeking to revamp, revise, or develop a summer library reading program. . . . This is an invaluable resource, both for its concrete guidance and its abstract exploration of the meaning of summer library programs." Bull Cent Child Books

Includes bibliographical references

Follos, Alison M. G.

★ **Reviving** reading; school library programming, author visits, and books that rock! [by] Alison M. G. Follos; foreword by Jack Gantos. Libraries Unlimited 2006 xx, 143p bibl pa $32

Grades: Adult Professional   **027.62**

1. Books and reading 2. Children's libraries 3. Young adults' libraries 4. School libraries -- Activity projects 5. School libraries -- Relations with teachers and curriculum

ISBN 1-59158-356-X

LC 2006017616

This is an "idea-packed manual on innovative literacy programs for elementary, middle, and high-school students. . . . Three sections address why, how, and what needs to be done to instill lifelong reading habits in children and young adults. . . . This realistic and reasonable guide is recommend-

ed for school and public library professional collections." Booklist

Includes bibliographical references

Harker, Christa

★ **Library** research with emergent readers; meeting standards through collaboration. [by] Christa Harker and Dorette Putonti. Linworth Books 2008 112p il pa $39.95

Grades: Adult Professional   **027.62**

1. Research 2. School libraries 3. Information literacy

ISBN 978-1-58683-288-9 pa; 1-58683-288-3 pa

LC 2007042179

This "is an all-encompassing look at the needs of emergent readers along with examples of standards-based library research projects. Definitely a great resource for those serving kindergarten or first-grade classrooms." Booklist

Includes bibliographical references

Kirker, Christine

Multicultural storytime magic; Kathy MacMillan and Christine Kirker. American Library Association 2012 241 p. $47

Grades: Professional   **027.62**

1. Storytelling 2. Multicultural education 3. Children's libraries -- Activity programs 4. Storytelling -- United States

ISBN 0838911420; 9780838911426

LC 2011043434

"Authors [Kathy] MacMillan and [Christine] Kirker offer a . . . paradigm for multicultural programs, one in which diversity is woven into any and every storytime, no matter what the topic. Arranged thematically around dozens of popular storytime themes, the authors . . . offer . . . book recommendations, fingerplays, and other activities that can be integrated into existing storytimes." (Publisher's note)

Includes bibliographical references and indexes

LibrarySparks: library lessons. Upstart Bks. 2011 200p $17.95

Grades: Adult Professional   **027.62**

1. Books and reading 2. Children's libraries 3. Bibliographic instruction

ISBN 1-60213-052-3; 978-1-60213-052-4

"Compiled from the first six volumes of the magazine LibrarySparks, this book contains 24 lessons by librarians and educators attuned to the interests, needs, and learning styles of youngsters from kindergarten through fifth grade. . . . Students are challenged to access information in a variety of formats. This fine collection will provide rich and rewarding lessons all year long." SLJ

Lowe, Joy L.

Puppet magic; [by] Joy L. Lowe and Kathryn I. Matthew. Neal-Schuman Publishers 2008 173p il pa $45

Grades: Adult Professional   **027.62**

1. Storytelling 2. Children's libraries 3. Puppets and puppet plays

ISBN 978-1-55570-599-2 pa; 1-55570-599-5 pa

LC 2007024108

"Adults who are looking for a quick, unfussy way to present stories, songs, and rhymes to children will find enough material in Puppet Magic to launch them into a timeless art form. . . . Lowe and Matthew's title gives beginners just enough material and easy puppets—made primarily from socks, felt, and paper plates—to get them started without much of an investment of time or effort. . . . Photos, patterns, online resources, and a good resource list are included." SLJ

Includes bibliographical references

MacDonald, Margaret Read

Look back and see; twenty lively tales for gentle tellers. illustrations by Roxane Murphy. Wilson, H.W. 1991 178p il $60

Grades: Adult Professional   **027.62**
1. Folklore 2. Storytelling 3. Children's library services -- Activity projects 4. Libraries -- Services to children -- Activities and projects
ISBN 978-0-8242-0810-3; 0-8242-0810-3

LC 91-2539

The author presents twenty non-violent folktales from around the world, with background notes and suggestions for storytelling uses

"Delightfully varied in mood, the tales range from silly and rowdy to contemplative and touching. . . . MacDonald's useful, informative, and entertaining notes follow each story. . . . The notes alone are worth the price of the book." J Youth Serv Libr

Includes bibliographical references

★ **When** the lights go out; twenty scary tales to tell. illustrations by Roxane Murphy. Wilson, H.W. 1988 176p il $70

Grades: Adult Professional   **027.62**
1. Folklore 2. Storytelling 3. Horror fiction 4. Folk literature 5. Children's library services -- Activity projects
ISBN 0-8242-0770-X

LC 88-14197

"Divided into six sections—Not Too Scary, Scary in the Dark, Gross Stuff, Jump Tales, Tales to Act Out, and Tales to Draw or Stir Up—the selections will be especially useful around Halloween, although, as the author points out, the book can be used year round. Following each inclusion are helpful notes on telling the stories and a section that gives sources on origins and variants. Murphy's decorative drawings introduce chapters and are scattered throughout the text. Several concluding chapters list bibliographies and provide other helpful information." Booklist

Includes bibliographical references

MacMillan, Kathy

Storytime magic; 400 fingerplays, flannelboards, and other activities. [by] Kathy MacMillan and Christine Kirker. American Library Association 2009 139p il pa $45

Grades: Adult Professional   **027.62**
1. Storytelling 2. Children's libraries 3. Children's literature 4. Picture books for children
ISBN 978-0-8389-0977-5 pa; 0-8389-0977-9 pa

LC 2008030266

"Both new and veteran storytellers will appreciate this book. Sixteen chapters are arranged by themes such as 'All About Me,' 'Animals,' and 'Holidays.' Whenever a flannelboard idea is listed, a thumbnail pen-and-ink sketch of the necessary pieces is included next to a Web icon. Readers can then proceed to an ALA Web page to view the actual-sized

pattern. An appendix gives further instruction on how to use other props or costumes along with a story." SLJ

Includes bibliographical references

Marino, Jane

★ **Babies** in the library! Scarecrow Press 2003 149p hardcover o.p. pa $32

Grades: Adult Professional   **027.62**
1. Children's libraries 2. Libraries and infants -- United States 3. Libraries and toddlers -- United States 4. Libraries and caregivers -- United States 5. Children's libraries -- Activity programs -- United States
ISBN 0-8108-4576-8; 0-8108-6044-9 pa

LC 2002-12022

The author presents "arguments for holding library programs specifically geared toward babies. Organizing and presenting her ideas in a thoughtful and philosophical manner, she addresses many relevant topics: making babies feel comfortable in the library, creating programs for prewalkers and walkers, handling registration, and offering suggestions for planning and executing programs. She also includes various activities that introduce books, rhymes, puppets, and other tools that enhance language skills." SLJ

Includes bibliographical references

Nichols, Judy

Storytimes for two-year-olds; [by] Judy Nichols; illustrated by Lori D. Sears. 3rd ed; American Library Association 2007 252p bibl il pa $40

Grades: Adult Professional   **027.62**
1. Storytelling 2. Children's libraries 3. Children's library services -- Activity projects
ISBN 0-8389-0925-6 pa; 978-0-8389-0925-6 pa

LC 2006023915

First published 1987

This outlines techniques for creating library programs for two-year-olds using books, rhymes, songs, fingerplays, puppets, and crafts on such themes as farms, animals, seasons, and bedtimes.

"The variety of programs, the diverse and excellent book selections, and the other program components . . . make this book useful for librarians, nursery-school teachers, and homeschoolers." Booklist

Includes bibliographical references

Pavon, Ana-Elba

★ **25** Latino craft projects; [by] Ana-Elba Pavon, Diana Borrego. American Library Association 2003 80p il (Celebrating culture in your library) pa $35

Grades: Adult Professional   **027.62**
1. Handicraft 2. Children's libraries 3. Hispanic Americans -- Social life and customs 4. Children's libraries -- Services to Hispanic Americans 5. Children's libraries -- Activity programs -- United States 6. Multicultural education -- Activity programs -- United States
ISBN 978-0-8389-0833-4 pa; 0-8389-0833-0 pa

LC 2002-5750

Following a "chapter on planning, the projects are organized around important Latino holidays and are inspired by artesenias (Latino folk art). . . . For each celebration, there is a suggested program for preschoolers, after-schooler, and families; each program incorporates the craft with songs, poems, and books. Activities include making piñatas, paper flowers, sweet tamales, and salsa." SLJ

Includes glossary and bibliographical references

Peck, Penny

Crash course in storytime fundamentals. Libraries Unlimited 2009 154p (Crash course) pa $30

Grades: Adult Professional   **027.62**

    1. Storytelling 2. Children's libraries

    ISBN 978-1-59158-715-6 pa; 1-59158-715-8 pa

                  LC 2008031234

"Practical and concise, this well-organized and readable guide is for inexperienced staff members who are not necessarily children's librarians. . . . The 75 themed storytimes include different types of books and Web sites and sources for songs, musical instruments, fingerplays, games, puppets, and crafts. The author discusses best times and settings for programs; special issues, such as children's and parents' behavior; selection and training of volunteers; the 'registration' question, and more." SLJ

Includes bibliographical references

Reid, Rob

More family storytimes; twenty-four creative programs for all ages. American Library Association 2009 181p pa $45

Grades: Adult Professional   **027.62**

    1. Storytelling 2. Children's libraries 3. Picture books for children

    ISBN 978-0-8389-0973-7

                  LC 2008015377

"This volume contains 24 programs, each lasting 30 minutes, that promote learning readiness and reading skills. . . . Clearly presented and easy to follow, this is an excellent resource for librarians who want to come up with winning story hours that have broad appeal." Booklist

Includes bibliographical references

Shake & shout; 16 noisy, lively story programs. Upstart Books 2008 110p il pa $17.95

Grades: Adult Professional   **027.62**

    1. Dance 2. Songs 3. Storytelling 4. Children's libraries 5. Children -- Books and reading

    ISBN 978-1-60213-006-7 pa; 1-60213-006-X pa

                  LC 2009535346

"This book centers on the idea of using one song as the jumping-off point for a thematic storytime. Each program features two to three picture books that support the theme, along with one or two movement activities. There's also a 'backup picture book' listed as well as more related songs. . . . The featured songs are listed within the programs, where recordings can be found, and are also printed at the end of the chapter with suggested guitar chords. The themes run the gamut from seasonal, to various animals and their environments, to pretend activities and emotions. This volume will spark creativity and imagination." SLJ

Includes bibliographical references

★ **What's** black and white and Reid all over? something hilarious happened at the library. Rob Reid. American Library Association 2012 xii, 175 p.p (softbound) $45

Grades: Professional   **027.62**

    1. Storytelling 2. Humorous fiction 3. Children's libraries 4. Storytelling -- United States 5. Wit and humor, Juvenile -- Bibliography 6. Children's libraries -- Activity programs -- United States

    ISBN 0838911471; 9780838911471

                  LC 2011043233

This book presents "10 humorous story programs -- five aimed at preschoolers and five for school-aged children. . . . Each one provides read-aloud suggestions and movement activities. There are also . . . storytelling tips that include everything from how to hold the book to what props to use. . . . Reid also includes an additional list of titles that can be substituted, jokes, call-and-response chants, short storybooks, songs, and musical activities." (School Library Journal)

"Those new to interactive book talking will appreciate his instructions for hamming up particular titles. Seasoned users will be grateful for the flexibility Reid provides to tailor programs to the tastes, time slots, and collection at hand." VOYA

Includes bibliographical references and index

Sierra, Judy

The **flannel** board storytelling book; 2nd ed rev & expanded; Wilson, H.W. 1997 241p il music $65

Grades: Adult Professional   **027.62**

    1. Storytelling 2. Children's libraries

    ISBN 978-0-8242-0932-2; 0-8242-0932-X

                  LC 97-15107

First published 1987

"Fifty stories, poems, and songs and over three hundred patterns are included for presenting stories to children in a flannel board medium, including classic children's stories, nursery rhymes, folk tales, and songs. . . . Sierra's experience telling stories with children is reflected throughout her book." J Youth Serv Libr

Sima, Judy

Raising voices; creating youth storytelling groups and troupes. [by] Judy Sima, Kevin Cordi. Libraries Unlimited 2003 xxviii, 241p pa $32.50

Grades: Adult Professional   **027.62**

    1. Storytelling 2. Children's stories

    ISBN 1-56308-919-X

                  LC 2003-47631

This offers a "blueprint for beginning and sustaining a successful group or troupe of storytellers from grades 4 to 12. . . . The book includes reproducible forms that will save a lot of work and lists of valuable resources. . . . Raising Voices is the complete, and essential, handbook for this special group of storytellers." SLJ

Includes bibliographical references

Simpson, Martha Seif

★ **Bringing** classes into the public library; a handbook for librarians. [by] Martha Seif Simpson and Lucretia I. Duwel. McFarland & Co. 2007 175p il pa $45

Grades: Adult Professional   **027.62**

    1. Public libraries 2. Children's libraries 3. Libraries and schools 4. Young adults' libraries

    ISBN 978-0-7864-2806-9 pa; 0-7864-2806-6 pa

                  LC 2006037527

"This handbook articulates the reasons and defines a strategy for promoting a program of class visits to the public library, and provides . . . instructions and . . . templates to assist librarians in initiating an organized program of class visits." Publisher's note

Soltan, Rita

Summer reading renaissance; an interactive exhibits approach. [by] Rita Soltan; illustrations by Jill Reichenbach Fill. Libraries Unlimited 2008 248p il pa $45

Grades: Adult Professional   027.62

1. Children's literature 2. Reading promotion 3. Children -- Books and reading 4. Children's reading -- Projects

ISBN 978-1-59158-572-5 pa; 1-59158-572-4 pa

LC 2008025702

"A children's librarian explores a new mode of summer-reading programming through an innovative, family-oriented series utilizing hands-on approaches for a six- to eight-week period, as done in many museums.... Well organized, with detailed directions and ideas, the book is good for any librarian working with children from beginning readers to sixth grade." Booklist

Includes bibliographical references

Totten, Kathryn

Family literacy storytimes; readymade storytimes suitable for the whole family. Neal-Schuman Publishers 2009 168p pa $59.95

Grades: Adult Professional   027.62

1. Storytelling 2. Books and reading 3. Children's libraries 4. Children's literature 5. Picture books for children

ISBN 978-1-55570-671-5 pa; 1-55570-671-1 pa

LC 2009027770

"Part I explains the basics of family literacy storytimes and how to meet the needs of adults and children in this format. Special attention is given to working with low-income families who are struggling with, or are new to, the English language. The author suggests that, with an adjustment in focus, storytimes can provide a language-learning environment for parents as well as children. Part II gives detailed planning ideas and 25 ready-to-use themed programs. Other chapters include music (with original songs), nursery rhymes, stories, and action rhymes, all with reproducible illustrations." SLJ

Includes bibliographical references

Walter, Virginia A.

Twenty-first-century kids, twenty-first-century librarians. American Library Association 2010 104p pa $45

Grades: Adult Professional   027.62

1. Librarians 2. Children's libraries 3. Young adults' libraries

ISBN 978-0-8389-1007-8 pa; 0-8389-1007-6 pa

LC 2009016972

"This volume more than updates Walter's 2001 Children and Libraries; it revisits the nature of children, addressing social changes and encouraging a new generation of children's librarians. Chapter 1 provides a fine history about U.S. library services to children, primarily in public libraries. Subsequent chapters detail six enduring core values of children's library services and add two emerging themes: the need for information (and information literacy) and collaboration. Walter's main contribution lies in her description of five models of children relative to the library: as reader, as a child of the information age, as a community member, as global, and as an empowered person. Another chapter fo-

cuses on management principals. ... Walter's core values are worth reading and implementing." Booklist

Includes bibliographical references

Weissman, Annie

Do tell! storytelling for you and your students. Linworth Pub. 2002 86p il pa $36.95

Grades: Adult Professional   027.62

1. Storytelling 2. Children's libraries

ISBN 1-58683-074-0

LC 2002-32969

"This concise beginner's guide encourages school librarians and teachers to incorporate storytelling into the elementary curriculum. It discusses how to select a story; how to learn it; and how to present it, including voice, pace, dialects, facial expressions, sound effects, and audience participation. ... Proverbs, myths, fables, and folktales, all in the public domain and selected with beginning storytellers in mind, make this a handy one-volume source." SLJ

Includes bibliographical references

027.8   School libraries

Adams, Helen R.

★ **Ensuring** intellectual freedom and access to information in the school library media program. Libraries Unlimited 2008 xxi, 254p il map pa $40

Grades: Adult Professional   027.8

1. Censorship 2. School libraries 3. Freedom of information

ISBN 978-1-59158-539-8; 1-59158-539-2

LC 2008-16753

This is "an extremely helpful guide for dealing with intellectual-freedom and information-access issues. In chapters geared to school situations and covering topics including selection of resources, the First Amendment, privacy, challenges to resources, the Internet, and access for students with disabilities, Adams offers background on the topic and bulleted lists of strategies for dealing with the issue.... This is a book that every school librarian needs to keep handy and share with administrators, colleagues, and parents." Booklist

Includes bibliographical references

Bishop, Kay

The **collection** program in schools; concepts, practices, and information sources. 4th ed. Libraries Unlimited 2007 xx, 269p il (Library and information science text series) pa $50; $65

Grades: Adult Professional   027.8

1. School libraries 2. Libraries -- Collection development 3. School libraries -- Collection development 4. Children's literature -- Bibliography of bibliographies 5. Young adult literature -- Bibliography of bibliographies

ISBN 1-59158-360-8 pa; 1-59158-583-X; 978-1-59158-360-8 pa; 978-1-59158-583-1

LC 2007-9005

First published 1988 under the authorship of Phyllis J. Van Orden

"Media specialists who read this book will be renewed in their quest for excellence in their collections. ... The book covers A-Z: Acquisitions, Evaluation, Ethical Issues,

Inventory, Procedure Manual, Selection, Special Groups of Students, Weeding, etc. . . . This is a must purchase for every school library media center." Libr Media Connect

Includes bibliographical references

Bush, Gail

Tales out of the school library; developing professional dispositions. [by] Gail Bush and Jami Biles Jones; foreword by Theodore R. Sizer. Libraries Unlimited 2010 135p il pa $40

Grades: Adult Professional   **027.8**

    1. Librarians 2. School libraries

    ISBN 978-1-59158-832-0; 1-59158-832-4

               LC 2009-46648

This book "answers the question, how should school librarians conduct themselves in their teaching, communicating, and leading roles in light of the AASL Standards for the 21st-Century Learner? In addition, what factors make an exemplary school librarian who will not only inspire students, but also nurture needed dispositions in them? . . . Readers are introduced to three fictional, yet very realistic school librarians in a series of thought-provoking vignettes that focus on instructional strategies, information literacy, assessment, literacy and reading, diversity, intellectual freedom, communication, advocacy, collaboration, resiliency, leadership, and professional ethics. Each chapter connects to the AASL standards and includes follow-up and discussion questions. All school librarians aiming to become reflective practitioners who model professional dispositions should read this unique book." SLJ

Includes bibliographical references

Buzzeo, Toni

Collaborating to meet standards: teacher/librarian partnerships for K-6; [by] Toni Buzzeo. 2nd ed.; Linworth Pub. 2007 246p pa $39.95

Grades: Adult Professional   **027.8**

    1. School libraries

    ISBN 1-58683-302-2 pa; 978-1-58683-302-2 pa

               LC 2007015406

First published 2002

This "addresses the assessment-driven educational environment of the No Child Left Behind Act. In the first section, Buzzeo focuses on the benefits of an involved school librarian to the educational process and how best to achieve this collaboration. She includes a template for collaborative planning and instruction. Sample lessons for specific grades from librarians around the United States complete the book. Practical suggestions and examples from school librarians across the country appear in separate text boxes. . . . Buzzeo gives worthwhile advice." SLJ

Includes bibliographical references

The **collaboration** handbook. Linworth Pub. 2008 132p il pa $42.95

Grades: Adult Professional   **027.8**

    1. School libraries

    ISBN 978-1-58683-298-8 pa; 1-58683-298-0 pa

               LC 2008-18119

"In this succinct guide, Buzzeo paints a picture of how media specialists can use instructional collaboration to transform a media program and increase student achievement. . . . Those new to the field will appreciate the step-by-step approach to increasing collaboration, while experienced

media specialists will likely benefit most from the chapters on data-driven collaboration and assessment. The book concludes with a substantial amount of information on how to overcome common barriers to collaboration, the role of advocacy, and the importance of integrating new technologies into collaborative projects." SLJ

Includes bibliographical references

Doll, Carol Ann

The **resilient** school library; [by] Carol A. Doll and Beth Doll. Libraries Unlimited 2010 123p il pa $40

Grades: Adult Professional   **027.8**

    1. School libraries 2. Academic achievement

    ISBN 978-1-59158-639-5; 1-59158-639-9

               LC 2010-21570

"The premise of the research provided in this informative text is that school library media specialists have the opportunity to play a major role in promoting resiliency through library programming and services for at-risk students. . . . The content of this comprehensive and interesting text provides examples; a planning template to follow; and supplementary graphs, charts, and tables." SLJ

Includes bibliographical references

Downs, Elizabeth

★ The **school** library media specialist's policy & procedure writer. Neal-Schuman Publishers 2009 195p pa $75

Grades: Adult Professional   **027.8**

    1. School libraries 2. School libraries -- Administration

    3. School libraries -- Policy statements

    ISBN 978-1-55570-621-0; 1-55570-621-5

               LC 2009-35177

"School library media specialists who need policies or procedures will surely find what they are looking for in this thorough book. Downs lays the foundation by describing necessary forms and policies for a school library media center, then provides a variety of examples and templates. The book includes mission statements, goals and objectives, budgeting, facilities use, circulation, collection development, disaster management, weeding, copyright, ILL, ethics, and accessibility policies." SLJ

Erikson, Rolf

Designing a school library media center for the future; [by] Rolf Erikson and Carolyn Markuson. 2nd ed; American Library Association 2007 117p il pa $45

Grades: Adult Professional   **027.8**

    1. School libraries -- Design and construction 2. Architecture and building -- School libraries 3. Instructional materials centers -- Design and construction

    ISBN 978-0-8389-0945-4; 0-8389-0945-0

               LC 2006-37644

First published 2000

"The first chapter offers an overview of the various steps involved in any project. Succeeding chapters cover technology planning, space allocations, furniture and placement, lighting and acoustics, ADA requirements, specifications, and bids." Booklist

Includes bibliographical references

Farmer, Lesley S. Johnson

★ **Collaborating** with administrators and educational support staff; [by] Lesley S. J. Farmer. Neal-Schuman Publishers 2007 217p (Best practices for school library media professionals) pa $65

Grades: Adult Professional **027.8**

1. School libraries 2. Instructional materials centers 3. Schools -- Administration 4. School management and organization 5. School libraries -- Relations with teachers and curriculum 6. School libraries -- Relations with principals and superintendents

ISBN 978-1-55570-572-5; 1-55570-572-3

LC 2006-11171

"Farmer begins by exploring how schools work, the role of the library media specialist, and the background on collaboration. She then discusses, in some depth, how to work with different levels of administrators and key service personnel, such as technology directors, reading specialists, special-education educators, pupil services personnel, and physical health and co-curricular personnel. Farmer concludes with ways of measuring the impact of collaboration and improving literacy, and provides suggestions for becoming a collaborative leader. This book is a must for school districts and a school library media specialists' personal collections." SLJ

Includes bibliographical references

Grimes, Sharon

★ **Reading** is our business; how libraries can foster reading comprehension. American Library Association 2006 155p il pa $35

Grades: Adult Professional **027.8**

1. School libraries 2. Books and reading 3. Reading comprehension 4. School libraries -- Activity projects 5. Children's reading -- Educational aspects 6. Children -- Reading -- Educational aspects

ISBN 0-8389-0912-4

LC 2005028263

Grimes "led a school-wide research study with classroom teachers to transform the reading program at Lansdowne Elementary School in Baltimore. The study resulted in dramatic and measurable gains in student reading achievement. This book can be used as a toolkit to duplicate those results. Grimes's work is informed by solid educational research in the field of reading comprehension. The text is lively and clearly written, accessible to teachers and librarians." SLJ

Includes bibliographical references

Harada, Violet H.

Assessing for learning; librarians and teachers as partners. [by] Violet H. Harada and Joan M. Yoshina. 2nd ed.; Libraries Unlimited 2010 242p il pa $45

Grades: Adult Professional **027.8**

1. School libraries 2. Instructional materials centers

ISBN 978-1-59884-470-2; 1-59884-470-9

First published 2055 with title: Assessing learning

"Using assessment tools familiar to the classroom teacher, the authors show how to use them in the library setting. Starting with the challenges that face 21st century schools, the rationale for schools as learning organizations is laid out. The tools for assessment are the main points of this title and include checklists, rubrics, rating scales, conferences, logs, personal correspondence, exit passes, graphic organizers, and student portfolios. . . . The tools for better instruction and assessment of learning need to be used by all educators,

and this title provides examples and models for all librarians." Libr Media Connect

Includes bibliographical references

Hughes-Hassell, Sandra

★ **School** reform and the school library media specialist; [by] Sandra Hughes-Hassell and Violet H. Harada. Libraries Unlimited 2007 xxiii, 204p il (Principles and practice series) pa $40

Grades: Adult Professional **027.8**

1. School libraries 2. Educational change 3. School libraries -- Relations with teachers and curriculum

ISBN 978-1-59158-427-8; 1-59158-427-2

LC 2007-16437

"This volume covers critical issues impacting school libraries today and offers practical solutions to meet these challenges. Written by leaders in the field such as Pam Berger, Carol Gordon, Barbara Stripling, and Ross Todd, the articles expound on implications of No Child Left Behind legislation, 21st-century literacy requirements, population diversity, and professional growth. . . . This volume will empower current and future school librarians as they embrace its guidelines." SLJ

Johnson, Doug

School libraries head for the edge; rants, recommendations, and reflections. Linworth Pub. 2010 196p pa $35

Grades: Adult Professional **027.8**

1. School libraries

ISBN 978-1-58683-392-3; 1-58683-392-8

LC 2009-22053

"Eighty long-running 'Head for the Edge' columns in Library Media Connection and its predecessor, Technology Connection, are collected here, in topical clusters dealing with professional issues relevant to both veterans and newbies. . . . The columns are reflective, conversational, and characteristically humorous. . . . Chapters end with quotes, questions, and self-evaluative reflection that readers will be inspired to mirror. For all practitioners." SLJ

Morris, Betty J.

★ **Administering** the school library media center; 5th ed.; Libraries Unlimited 2010 580p il $75; pa $60

Grades: Adult Professional **027.8**

1. School libraries 2. Instructional materials centers

ISBN 978-1-59158-685-2; 1-59158-685-2; 978-1-59158-689-0 pa; 1-59158-689-5 pa

LC 2010015939

First published 1973 under the authorship of John T. Gillespie and Diana L. Spirt with title: Creating a school media program

"This updated edition provides a comprehensive and current examination of the multiple and varied jobs media specialists do to manage today's school library media centers. . . . Sample job description statements, media center budgets, and budget justification tools are thorough and valuable references. Morris addresses the proactive and visible leadership role that today's media specialists must take on to remain viable and support student learning. . . . The title supports concepts on current standards. It is a forward thinking text for new or future library media specialists and a realistic, functional reference for practitioners." Libr Media Connect

Includes bibliographical references

Ray, Virginia Lawrence

School wide book events; how to make them happen. [by] Virginia Lawrence Ray. Libraries Unlimited 2003 133p pa $28

Grades: Adult Professional 027.8

1. School libraries 2. Books and reading 3. Reading promotion 4. Children -- Books and reading 5. School libraries -- Activity programs 6. Language arts (Elementary) -- Activity programs

ISBN 978-1-59158-038-6 pa; 1-59158-038-2 pa

LC 2003-47724

"The author's intent is to present ideas on how to celebrate reading across grade levels and curriculum, involving teachers, administration, faculty, and students both in preparation and actual activities. She proposes that school libraries have a Book Event for the whole school. . . . All events require simple resources and are easy to follow even for school systems with extremely limited budgets." SLJ

Includes bibliographical references

Schuckett, Sandy

Political advocacy for school librarians; you have the power! Linworth Pub. 2004 128p pa $39.95

Grades: Adult Professional 027.8

1. Lobbying 2. School libraries 3. Libraries and community

ISBN 1-58683-158-5

LC 2004-4869

"Schuckett motivates and explicitly details an exciting 'how-to' of political lobbying at all levels—from the school site and local board all the way to the national level. . . . School librarians need political clout, and Schuckett shows us how to get it." SLJ

Includes bibliographical references

Stephens, Claire Gatrell

Library 101; a handbook for the school library media specialist. [by] Claire Gatrell Stephens and Patricia Franklin. Libraries Unlimited 2007 233p il pa $35

Grades: Adult Professional 027.8

1. School libraries 2. Instructional materials centers 3. Procedure manuals 4. Libraries -- Handbooks, manuals, etc.

ISBN 978-1-59158-324-0; 1-59158-324-1

LC 2007-18420

"This handbook provides information for brand-new and inexperienced librarians preparing for a first job in a school library media center. Articles are divided into four subcategories covering day-to-day operations (library organization, circulation policies, media management, scheduling, staffing, and media center arrangement); collaboration with teachers; collection development and management; and equipment." Booklist

Includes bibliographical references

028 Reading and use of other information media

Ellis, Sarah

From reader to writer; teaching writing through classic children's books. Douglas & McIntyre 2000 176p hardcover o.p. pa $14.95

Grades: Adult Professional 028

1. Poets 2. Artists 3. Authors 4. Novelists 5. Dramatists 6. Librarians 7. Theologians 8. Illustrators 9. Mathematicians 10. Creative writing 11. Children's literature 12. Editors 13. Essayists 14. Linguists 15. Satirists 16. Biographers 17. Philologists 18. Travel writers 19. Fantasy writers 20. Literary critics 21. Children's authors 22. Nonfiction writers 23. Writers on science 24. Short story writers 25. Young adult authors 26. Science fiction writers 27. Children -- Books and reading 28. Rhetoric -- Study and teaching 29. Children's literature -- Study and teaching

ISBN 0-88899-372-2; 0-88899-440-0 pa

The author discusses the work of seventeen British, Canadian and American authors of children's literature. "With each classic book, there's a 'sneak preview' (i.e., booktalk), a suggested read-aloud, exercises to help students and adult writers find their own stories, and a short annotated bibliography of related children's books." Booklist

028.1 Reviews

Baxter, Kathleen A.

★ From cover to cover; evaluating and reviewing children's books. rev ed.; Collins 2010 229p $14.99

Grades: Adult Professional 028.1

1. Books -- Reviews 2. Children's literature -- History and criticism

ISBN 978-0-06-077757-9; 0-06-077757-5

First published 1997

The author addresses the distinctions between evaluation and review, and what makes a good children's book. She discusses categories of children's books including nonfiction; traditional literature (folktales, myths, legends, etc.); poetry, verse, rhymes, and songs; picture books; easy readers and transitional books; and fiction. She then describes the process of writing a review.

This is a "very complete resource that will continue to be the venerable reference tool and required reading for education and library-science students, youth librarians, teachers, and anyone else interested in kids, reading, and children's literature." SLJ

Blass, Rosanne J.

Celebrate with books; booktalks for holidays and other occasions. [by] Rosanne J. Blass. Libraries Unlimited 2005 226p pa $35

Grades: Adult Professional 028.1

1. Holidays 2. Book talks 3. Reference books 4. Children's literature 5. Holidays -- Bibliography 6. Children's literature -- Bibliography 7. Children's library services -- Activity projects 8. Libraries -- Services to children -- Activities and projects

ISBN 1-59158-076-5

"This collection of booktalks for children in kindergarten through sixth grade emphasizes picture books, chapter books, and poetry published from 2000 to 2004. The volume begins with general holidays celebrated by cultures around the world . . . and then takes a month-by-month approach. Additional year-round celebrations . . . are appended. For each observation, at least two selections are suggested and include a complete citation, genre, age level, culture (where appropriate), summary, the booktalk itself, and a learning extension. . . . A great aid for collection development and for thematic planning." SLJ

Naidoo, Jamie Campbell

★ **Rainbow** family collections; selecting and using children's books with lesbian, gay, bisexual, transgender, and queer content. Jamie Campbell Naidoo. Libraries Unlimited, an imprint of ABC-CLIO, LLC 2012 xvii, 260 p.p ill. (hardback) $50

Grades: Professional **028.1**

1. Libraries and sexual minorities 2. Sexual minorities in literature 3. Libraries and sexual minorities -- United States 4. Libraries -- Special collections -- Sexual minorities 5. Sexual minorities -- Juvenile literature -- Bibliography 6. Children's libraries -- Collection development -- United States 7. Children's libraries -- Services to minorities -- United States 8. Children of sexual minority parents -- Books and reading -- United States

ISBN 1598849603; 9781598849608

LC 2012008362

This book by Jamie Campbell Naidoo "highlight[s] titles for children from infancy to age 11" featuring lesbian, gay, bisexual, transgender, and queer content. It "supplies a synopsis of the title's content, lists awards it has received, cites professional reviews, and provides suggestions for librarians considering acquisition. The book also provides a brief historical overview of LGBTQ children's literature along with the major book awards for this genre." (Publisher's note)

Includes bibliographical references and index

028.5 Reading and use of other information media by young people

Allyn, Pam

What to read when; the books and stories to read with your child, and all the best times to read them. Avery 2009 318p pa $16.95

Grades: Adult Professional **028.5**

1. Children -- Books and reading

ISBN 978-1-58333-334-1

LC 2008-54501

The author "provides many ways to promote a love of reading to children and offers top-ten lists of reasons to read to kids that incorporate practical, easy-to-use tips to encourage literacy from a young age. . . . This is an indispensable guide to choosing age-appropriate books for children. Allyn provides a list of more than 300 titles on 50 themes including such issues as adoption, feelings about school, sharing, and coping with illness. This valuable resource for children's librarians, educators, and parents is highly recommended." Libr J

Baxter, Kathleen A.

Gotcha again for guys! more nonfiction books to get boys excited about reading. [by] Kathleen A. Baxter and Marcia Agness Kochel. Libraries Unlimited 2010 248p il pa $35

Grades: Adult Professional **028.5**

1. Book talks 2. Children's literature 3. Boys -- Books and reading 4. Boys -- Juvenile literature 5. Children's

literature -- Bibliography

ISBN 978-1-59884-376-7 pa; 1-59884-376-1 pa; 978-1-59884-377-4 e-book

LC 2010036577

This "highlights books published mainly between 2007 and 2009. Twelve chapters cover themes such as sports, animals, gross/disgusting stuff, mysteries/disasters, and machines. Each one features anywhere from a few to two dozen ready-to-use booktalks, most aimed at grades 3-8, along with extensive bibliographies (not annotated) of other titles that have received good reviews in Booklist, Horn Book Guide, and School Library Journal. New to this volume are enlightening interviews with male authors such as Kadir Nelson, Nic Bishop, and Seymour Simon, whose books are featured in the text. The introduction also lists ideas for promoting books to boys in public libraries and school media centers." SLJ

Includes bibliographical references

Gotcha good! nonfiction books to get kids excited about reading. [by] Kathleen A. Baxter and Marcia Agness Kochel. Libraries Unlimited 2008 259p pa $35

Grades: Adult Professional **028.5**

1. Books and reading 2. Children's literature 3. Children's literature -- Bibliography 4. Young adult literature -- Bibliography

ISBN 978-1-59158-654-8 pa; 1-59158-654-2 pa

LC 2008010350

"In addition to annotations for over 1000 nonfiction titles, [the authors] profile eight prolific authors and provide fun top-10 features for the various subjects covered. . . . The titles chosen are truly high quality, relevant, and up-to-date, with suggested ages provided, most ranging from grades three through eight. . . . A must-have for all librarians who want to get kids excited about nonfiction." SLJ

Includes bibliographical references

Bishop, Rudine Sims

Free within ourselves; the development of African American children's literature. Heinemann/Greenwood 2007 295p bibl il $65; pa $22

Grades: Adult Professional **028.5**

1. African Americans in literature 2. Children -- Books and reading 3. Blacks in literature -- History 4. Children's literature -- History 5. African Americans -- Juvenile literature 6. Children's literature -- History and criticism 7. Children's literature, American -- African American authors 8. American literature -- African American authors -- History and criticism

ISBN 978-0-325-07135-0 Heinemann; 978-0-313-34093-2 pa Greenwood

LC 2007000612

"Bishop traces the evolution of fiction written for black children and by black authors and illustrators within the context of African-American social and literary history. . . . Her writing is precise and engaging, and it really comes alive when presenting primary-source material. . . . Librarians as well as teachers will be enriched by this work." SLJ

Includes bibliographical references

Brooks, Wanda M.

Embracing, evaluating, and examining African American children's and young adult literature; edited by Wanda

M. Brooks, Jonda C. McNair; foreword by Rudine Sims Bishop. Scarecrow Press 2008 251p pa $45

Grades: Adult Professional **028.5**

1. African Americans in literature 2. Children -- Books and reading 3. Children's literature -- History and criticism 4. Young adult literature -- History and criticism 5. American literature -- African American authors -- History and criticism

ISBN 978-0-8108-6027-8 pa; 0-8108-6027-9 pa

LC 2007025703

"Brooks and McNair have compiled 12 scholarly studies about the use of books by and about African-American children and young adults in classrooms across the United States. Selections include a detailed textual analysis of the work of Arna Bontemps and Langston Hughes; a sociolinguistic perspective on readers' response to books containing African-American Vernacular English; and a detailed study of the books used as classroom read-alouds by teachers in rural schools, which found that only three percent were about African Americans. While each study is complete in and of itself, the text as a whole gives a broad picture of what is currently being done in this field, both in K-12 classrooms and college classes that emphasize children's literature." SLJ

Includes bibliographical references

Casement, Rose

Black history in the pages of children's literature. Scarecrow Press 2008 317p pa $55

Grades: Adult Professional **028.5**

1. Children's literature 2. African Americans in literature 3. Children's literature -- Bibliography 4. African Americans -- Juvenile literature 5. Children's literature -- History and criticism

ISBN 978-0-8108-5843-5 pa; 0-8108-5843-6 pa

LC 2007018137

"Casement has organized her book along a time line from the initial presence of Africans in America before colonization to the present day. Each chapter begins with a brief description of important historical events that have often been left out of our history books. This is followed by an annotated bibliography that includes excerpts from each title and a description of the content. Books listed are primarily straight nonfiction but some fantasy, realistic fiction, biography, and poetry are included. The final two chapters address criteria for selecting children's literature for classroom use and introduce several talented African-American writers and illustrators. Putting this eminently accessible book into the hands of teachers should greatly increase the use of accurate books about African Americans and help to identify and pass on a more truthful historical picture than most of us were given in school." SLJ

Includes bibliographical references

Cox Clark, Ruth E.

Tantalizing tidbits for middle schoolers; quick booktalks for the busy middle school and jr. high library media specialist. [by] Ruth E. Cox Clark. Linworth Pub. 2005 140p pa $36.95

Grades: Adult Professional **028.5**

1. Book talks 2. Books and reading 3. Children's literature -- Bibliography 4. Young adult literature -- Bibliography

ISBN 1-58683-195-X

LC 2005013159

"In the first sections, the author provides information on annual recommended reading lists and children's book awards and describes different booktalking techniques. Section 5, the heart of the book, offers 75 booktalk examples. For each, the author provides bibliographic information, subjects and genres, references to pertinent reading lists and awards, and interest levels. This information is followed by a brief annotation, a booktalk, a page reference for an excerpt to read, a curriculum connection, and a list of similar books. A list of themes and an index of the books and authors mentioned conclude the volume, which is highly recommended for librarians, teachers, and students." Booklist

Diamant-Cohen, Betsy

Booktalking bonanza; ten ready-to-use multimedia sessions for the busy librarian. American Library Association 2009 240p il pa $40

Grades: Adult Professional **028.5**

1. Book talks 2. Books and reading 3. Children's literature

ISBN 978-0-8389-0965-2; 0-8389-0965-5

LC 2008-15371

"This volume is a collection of scripts for multimedia-enriched booktalks. After an introductory chapter that explains the reasoning for this approach, 10 scripts are outlined. Books, music, video, and Web sites are included for each one. The programs are geared toward elementary-aged children, although suggestions for adapting them for a middle or high school audience are included." SLJ

Includes bibliographical references

Embracing, evaluating, and examining African American children's and young adult literature; edited by Wanda M. Brooks, Jonda C. McNair; foreword by Rudine Sims Bishop. Scarecrow Press 2008 251p pa $45

Grades: Adult Professional **028.5**

1. African Americans in literature 2. Children -- Books and reading 3. Children's literature -- History and criticism 4. Young adult literature -- History and criticism 5. American literature -- African American authors -- History and criticism

ISBN 978-0-8108-6027-8 pa; 0-8108-6027-9 pa

LC 2007025703

"Brooks and McNair have compiled 12 scholarly studies about the use of books by and about African-American children and young adults in classrooms across the United States. Selections include a detailed textual analysis of the work of Arna Bontemps and Langston Hughes; a sociolinguistic perspective on readers' response to books containing African-American Vernacular English; and a detailed study of the books used as classroom read-alouds by teachers in rural schools, which found that only three percent were about African Americans. While each study is complete in and of itself, the text as a whole gives a broad picture of what is currently being done in this field, both in K-12 classrooms and college classes that emphasize children's literature." SLJ

Includes bibliographical references

Feinberg, Barbara

Welcome to Lizard Motel; children, stories, and the mystery of making things up: a memoir. Beacon Press 2004 256p $20

Grades: Adult Professional **028.5**

1. Imagination 2. Imagination in children 3. Children --

Books and reading 4. Young adult literature, American
ISBN 0-8070-7144-7

LC 2004-710

"Feinberg, who's spent years working with children in
a creativity workshop she designed, has the independence
and experience to raise important questions. Her critique .
. . should stir some much-needed controversy." Publ Wkly

Includes bibliographical references

Gilmore, Barry

★ **Speaking** volumes; how to get students discussing
books, and much more. Heinemann 2006 128p pa $17.95
Grades: Adult Professional   **028.5**
1. Books and reading
ISBN 978-0-325-00915-5 pa; 0-325-00915-5 pa

LC 2005-28371

"Gilmore provides practical, hands-on methods to involve students in oral and written classroom conversations
that encourage reflection and ultimately polished, coherent expression. . . . Both new and seasoned discussion
leaders will want a copy for repeated reference." Voice
Youth Advocates

Includes bibliographical references

Gilton, Donna L.

Multicultural and ethnic children's literature in the
United States; [by] Donna L. Gilton. Scarecrow Press 2007
236p pa $45
Grades: Adult Professional   **028.5**
1. Multiculturalism 2. Children's literature 3.
Minorities in literature 4. Ethnic groups -- Juvenile
literature 5. Children's literature -- History and criticism
ISBN 978-0-8108-5672-1 pa; 0-8108-5672-7 pa

LC 2007006391

"Gilton writes with authority, clarity, and conviction,
presenting a strong rationale for the necessity for teachers
to use multicultural literature whether or not their schools
and/or classrooms have diverse populations. . . . The author
offers a wealth of information. . . . She gives a history of
multicultural literature in the U.S. . . . Gilton addresses current issues. . . . There is ample information on how to find the
best books that appropriately represent a variety of cultures.
Finally, Gilton looks closely at groups that are growing in
the U.S." SLJ

Includes bibliographical references

Handbook of research on children's and young adult literature; edited by Shelby A. Wolf . . . [et al.] Routledge
2010 555p $295; pa $119.95
Grades: Adult Professional   **028.5**
1. Children's literature -- History and criticism 2.
Young adult literature -- History and criticism
ISBN 978-0-415-96505-7; 0-415-96505-5; 978-0-415-
96506-4 pa; 0-415-96506-3 pa; 978-0-203-84354-3
e-book

LC 2010-16339

"The book examines readers, texts, and cultural contexts
of children's literature and across the three intersecting disciplines of Education, English, and Library and Information
Science, in an effort to model a multidisciplinary approach
to children's literature research. Thirty-seven scholarly articles, by figures such as Eliza Dresang, Rudine Sims Bishop,
and Roderick McGillis . . . are counterpointed by responses
that often provide more personal perspectives, including in-

sights from noted authors such as Lois Lowry, M. T. Anderson, and Markus Zusak." Bull Cent Child Books

Herb, Steven

Connecting fathers, children, and reading; a how-to-do
it manual for librarians. [by] Steven Herb, Sara Willoughby-
Herb. Neal-Schuman 2001 196p (How-to-do-it manuals
for librarians) pa $45
Grades: Adult Professional   **028.5**
1. Fathers 2. Books and reading
ISBN 1-55570-390-9

LC 2001-18315

This "book looks at both the importance and effect of
father involvement in children's reading. . . . Case studies,
anecdotes, and interesting sidebars abound in this well-organized, well-written source. . . . An extensive bibliography
includes more than 450 children's books about fathers and
fathering." SLJ

Keane, Nancy J.

101 great, ready-to-use book lists for children; Nancy J.
Keane. Libraries Unlimited, an imprint of ABC-CLIO, LLC
2012 xiv, 246 p.p $45
Grades: Adult Professional   **028.5**
1. Best books 2. Children -- Books and reading 3.
Children's literature -- Bibliography
ISBN 1610690834; 9781610690836

LC 2011051429

Includes bibliographical references and index

Kitain, Sandra

Shelf-esteem; [by] Sandra Kitain. Neal-Schuman Publishers 2008 183p pa $49.95
Grades: Adult Professional   **028.5**
1. Book talks 2. Reference books 3. Books and
reading 4. Children's libraries 5. Children's literature
-- Bibliography
ISBN 978-1-55570-568-8 pa; 1-55570-568-5 pa

LC 2007034737

"Kitain offers an array of books that 'help children relate
to their personal lives and individual challenges.' Chapters
are based on themes including but not limited to friendship,
courage, emotions, moving, new siblings, physical challenges, and bullies. Tough subjects like alcoholism, illness and
death, and homelessness are also included. . . . The quality
and variety of texts are excellent. The remaining chapters
of the book explore working with community partners. This
text is highly recommended for all librarians, teachers, caregivers, and parents of younger readers." SLJ

Includes bibliographical references

Knowles, Elizabeth

Boys and literacy; practical strategies for librarians,
teachers, and parents. [by] Elizabeth Knowles and Martha
Smith. Libraries Unlimited 2005 xxi, 164p il pa $35
Grades: Adult Professional   **028.5**
1. Reading interests 2. Boys -- Books and reading 3.
Children's literature -- Bibliography 4. Young adult
literature -- Bibliography
ISBN 1-59158-212-1

"Boys don't seem to like to read. . . . This book briefly
explores the research about this situation, outlines strategies
to reverse this trend, and lists books within genres that boys
enjoy reading. . . . The best part of the book is the author

section. . . . For each author covered, there is a complete list of books, contact information, . . . and Web sites. . . . This is a wonderful resource for teachers and parents to begin working on improving literacy with boys." Booklist

Larson, Jeanette C.

Bringing mysteries alive for children and young adults; [by] Jeanette Larson. Linworth Pub. 2004 134p il pa $39.95

Grades: Adult Professional   028.5
   1. Mystery fiction 2. Interdisciplinary approach in education 3. Children -- Books and reading 4. Activity programs in education 5. Teenagers -- Books and reading 6. Children's literature in series 7. Children's literature -- Bibliography 8. Children's libraries -- Activity programs 9. Teenagers -- Books and reading -- United States 10. Detective and mystery stories -- Study and teaching
   ISBN 1-58683-012-0
                                        LC 2003-22064
"The book has excellent ideas for beginning as well as seasoned professionals." SLJ
   Includes bibliographical references

Latrobe, Kathy Howard

The **children's** literature dictionary; definitions, resources, and teaching activities. [by] Kathy Latrobe, Carolyn S. Brodie, Maureen White. Neal-Schuman 2002 282p pa $59.95

Grades: Adult Professional   028.5
   1. Reference books 2. Children's literature -- Dictionaries
   ISBN 1-55570-424-7
                                        LC 2001-44434
"The first section is an alphabetical dictionary of 325 terms found in reviews, lesson plans, and other resources. Definitions of terms contain meanings and examples from popular children's literature and activities related to the term. The activities descriptions provide a starting point for teaching or demonstrating the term. This reference book supports resources and materials that librarians or teachers should have in their collection." Book Rep

Lerer, Seth

★ **Children's** literature; a reader's history, from Aesop to Harry Potter. University of Chicago Press 2008 385p il

Grades: Adult Professional   028.5
   1. Books and reading 2. Children's literature -- History and criticism
   ISBN 0-226-47300-7; 978-0-226-47300-0
                                        LC 2007046708
The author sets out to "chart the makings of the Western literary imagination from Aesop's fables to Mother Goose, from Alice's Adventures in Wonderland to Peter Pan, from Where the Wild Things Are to Harry Potter. Lerer here explores the iconic books, ancient and contemporary alike, that have forged a lifelong love of literature in young readers during their formative years. Along the way, Lerer also looks at the changing environments of family life and human growth, schooling and scholarship, and publishing and politics in which children found themselves changed by the books they read." (Publisher's note) Index.
   "This work presents a true critical history of [children's literature], from Aesop to the present. Scholarly, erudite, and

all but exhaustive, it is also entertaining and accessible. . . . [Lerer] asks important questions about writers' intentions and readers' reactions, about why some texts endure and others do not, about the influence of science and religion on children's literature, and even about the impact of libraries and literary prizes upon the genre." Libr J
   Includes bibliographical references

Lukenbill, W. Bernard

Biography in the lives of youth; culture, society, and information. Libraries Unlimited 2006 251p il pa $45
Grades: Adult Professional   028.5
   1. Biography 2. Children's libraries 3. Young adults' libraries 4. Children -- Books and reading 5. Teenagers -- Books and reading 6. Biography -- Juvenile literature 7. Children's literature -- Non-fiction 8. School libraries -- Activity projects 9. Children's reading -- Psychological aspects 10. Children -- Reading -- Psychological aspects 11. Young adults' reading -- Psychological aspects 12. Young adults -- Reading -- Psychological aspects
   ISBN 1-59158-284-9
                                        LC 2006007466
"Reflecting on the different and varied uses of biography depending on the age, interests, and developmental needs of students, Lukenbill breaks the genre down into the different types of biographies and how they have changed over time. He includes author and literature suggestions throughout the text and concludes with an extensive bibliography of selection aids, including books and periodicals, for locating recommended titles." SLJ
   Includes bibliographical references

Marks, Diana F.

Children's book award handbook. Libraries Unlimited 2006 412p bibl il tab pa $40
Grades: Adult Professional   028.5
   1. Children's literature 2. Young adult literature 3. Children's reading -- Projects 4. Children's literature -- Awards 5. Young adult literature -- Awards 6. Young adults' reading -- Projects 7. Young adults' literature -- Awards 8. Children -- Reading -- Study and teaching -- Activities and projects 9. Young adults -- Reading -- Study and teaching -- Activities and projects
   ISBN 1-59158-304-7
The author "has compiled a valuable resource that will be much appreciated by teachers and school librarians. Her handbook provides details on the history and origins of 24 major children's book awards from the Jane Addams Book Award to the Charlotte Zolotow Award and includes lesson plans and student activity sheets for 21 of them." Libr J

McDaniel, Deanna

Gentle reads; great books to warm hearts and lift spirits, grades 5-9. [by] Deanna J. McDaniel. Libraries Unlimited 2008 318p (Children's and young adult literature reference series) $45
Grades: Adult Professional   028.5
   1. Young adult literature 2. Conduct of life -- Fiction 3. Children's literature -- Bibliography 4. Young adult literature -- Bibliography
   ISBN 978-1-59158-491-9
                                        LC 2008018878

This includes "500 recommended titles. Here readers will find books with divorce, drug use, attempted suicides, and more but they all meet the criteria the author has set by being either inspiring, heartwarming, or in some way uplifting. . . . Arranged by genres, the entries include full bibliographic information, an annotation, and a description of why the book fits the 'gentle criteria.'" SLJ

Includes bibliographical references

Hey! listen to this; stories to read aloud. edited by Jim Trelease. Viking 1992 414p hardcover o.p. pa $15
Grades: Adult Professional   028.5
  1. Authors   2. Books and reading   3. Literature -- Collections
ISBN 0-14-014653-9 pa
                   LC 91-37668
"Divided into categories such as 'Animal Tales,' 'Children of Courage,' or 'Classic Tales,' the forty-eight selections cover a wide spectrum from folktales to fantasy, classics to contemporary stories. More than half are complete stories, while the remainder are one or two chapters from longer books. Trelease skillfully weaves his choices into a cohesive whole. Beyond merely categorizing them, he refers to other authors or stories in the discussions that precede and follow each story." J Youth Serv Libr

Includes bibliographical references

Nespeca, Sue McCleaf
  Picture books plus; 100 extension activities in art, drama, music, math, and science. [by] Sue McCleaf Nespeca, Joan B. Reeve. American Lib. Assn. 2003 133p il pa $38
Grades: Adult Professional   028.5
  1. Books and reading   2. Picture books for children   3. School children -- Books and reading   4. Education, Elementary -- Activity programs   5. Picture books for children -- Educational aspects
ISBN 0-8389-0840-3
                 LC 2002-11822
"This book is intended for use by teachers, librarians, and others working with children in preschool through grade three and features extension activities for use with a variety of materials. . . . Each chapter includes titles with annotations, 20 activities, and a list of resource books that will introduce readers to further activities. . . . Librarians and teachers will find many useful ideas here." Booklist

Includes bibliographical references

Reid, Rob
  ★ **Cool** story programs for the school-age crowd. American Library Association 2004 181p il pa $32
Grades: Adult Professional   028.5
  1. Books and reading   2. Children's literature   3. Children -- Books and reading   4. Children's reading -- Projects   5. Reading (Elementary) -- Activity programs   6. Children -- Reading -- Study and teaching -- Activities and projects   7. Children's literature -- Study and teaching (Elementary) -- Activity programs
ISBN 0-8389-0887-X
                 LC 2004-9933
This offers plans for story programs which incorporate poetry, picture books, chapter book excerpts, and short stories
"Eighteen well-developed plans with wacky themes that kids will love will bring literature to life with a minimum

of stress for public librarians, teachers, and school media specialists. . . . A useful book with surefire suggestions for winning programs." SLJ

Includes bibliographical references

Saccardi, Marianne
  Books that teach kids to write; [by] Marianne C. Saccardi. Libraries Unlimited 2011 150p pa $30; e-book $30
Grades: Adult Professional   028.5
  1. Creative writing   2. Books and reading   3. Children's literature   4. Literature -- Study and teaching
ISBN 978-1-59884-451-1 pa; 978-1-59884-452-8 e-book
                 LC 2011001866
"Divided into sections such as 'Making Stories Unique,' 'Creating Memorable Characters,' and 'Putting Passion and Voice into Nonfiction Writing,' this book gives countless recommendations for teaching various skills. Saccardi offers short, annotated summaries of mentor texts and describes how they can be used to model good writing techniques. . . . After reading this resource, educators will have a long wish list of materials to purchase." SLJ

Includes bibliographical references

Sullivan, Michael
  ★ **Connecting** boys with books 2; closing the reading gap. American Library Association 2009 119p il pa $40
Grades: Adult Professional   028.5
  1. School libraries   2. Children's libraries   3. Young adults' libraries   4. Reading promotion   5. Boys -- Books and reading   6. Reading -- Sex differences   7. Teenage boys -- Books and reading   8. Children's libraries -- Activity programs   9. Young adults' libraries -- Activity programs
ISBN 978-0-8389-0979-9 pa; 0-8389-0979-5 pa
                 LC 2008-34925
"A must-read for all librarians and media specialists." SLJ

Includes bibliographical references (p. 105-110)

  Serving boys through readers' advisory. American Library Association 2010 152p (ALA readers' advisory series) pa $48
Grades: Adult Professional   028.5
  1. Children's literature   2. Reference services (Libraries)   3. Boys -- Books and reading   4. Boys -- Juvenile literature
ISBN 978-0-8389-1022-1; 0-8389-1022-X
                 LC 2009-26841
"This volume was created to give a general direction when helping most boys select books. . . . Sullivan challenges us to throw out our preconceived notions about how to conduct such an interview. Methods of performing indirect readers' advisory with parents and teachers are included. The excellent booktalks for elementary, middle school, and high school boys alone make this a worthwhile purchase." SLJ

Includes bibliographical references

Temple, Charles A.
  Children's books in children's hands; an introduction to their literature. [by] Charles Temple, Miriam Martinez, Junko Yokota; with contributions by Evelyn B. Freeman. 4th ed.; Pearson Allyn & Bacon 2010 572p pa $137.40

Grades: Adult Professional **028.5**
1. Books and reading 2. Children's literature -- History and criticism
ISBN 978-0-1370-7403-7 pa; 0-1370-7403-4 pa
LC 2010018237
First published 1998
The authors focus on creating an understanding of how literature works and how children respond to literature, they provide a wide range of good books to use with children, and they suggest ways to guide children into books and help them enjoy the experience.
Includes bibliographical references

Trelease, Jim
★ The **read**-aloud handbook; 6th ed.; Penguin Books 2006 xxvi, 340p il pa $15
Grades: Adult Professional **028.5**
1. Books and reading 2. Children's literature 3. Picture books for children 4. Children's literature -- Bibliography
ISBN 0-14-303739-0
LC 2006-41773
First published 1982
This handbook explains the importance of reading aloud to children, offers guidance on how to set up a read-aloud atmosphere in the home or classroom and suggests 1,500 titles for reading aloud.
Includes bibliographical references

Vardell, Sylvia M.
Children's literature in action; a librarian's guide. Libraries Unlimited 2008 323p (Library and information science text series) $65; pa $50
Grades: Adult Professional **028.5**
1. Children's literature 2. Children -- Books and reading 3. Children's literature -- History and criticism 4. Children's library services -- Activity projects
ISBN 978-1-59158-657-9; 1-59158-657-7; 978-1-59158-557-2 pa; 1-59158-557-2 pa
LC 2007038012
"This excellent introduction to children's literature and its various genres and forms offers many activities and practical applications. Each chapter includes 'Action' components that highlight literature, authors, specific book titles, or history. . . . It also includes evaluation criteria, writing reviews, collection development of various genres, awards, and other programs of merit as well as additional information in numerous bibliographies and lists of recommended reading and Web sites." SLJ
Includes bibliographical references

Yolen, Jane
Touch magic; fantasy, faerie & folklore in the literature of childhood. Expanded ed; August House 2000 128p pa $11.95
Grades: Adult Professional **028.5**
1. Folklore 2. Fantasy in children 3. Folklore and children 4. Children's stories -- Psychological aspects 5. Children's literature -- History and criticism
ISBN 0-87483-591-7
LC 00-27565
First published 1981 by Philomel Bks.
The author provides perspectives on reading, appreciating, and preserving fantasy and folklore for children. Among

topics discussed are the morality of fairy tales, the definition of story, and the theme of time travel
Includes bibliographical references

Zbaracki, Matthew D.
Best books for boys; a resource for educators. foreward by Jon Scieszka. Libraries Unlimited 2008 189p il (Children's and young adult literature reference series)
Grades: Adult Professional **028.5**
1. Best books 2. Children's literature 3. Young adult literature 4. Reading interests 5. Boys -- Books and reading 6. Boys -- Juvenile literature 7. Children's literature -- Bibliography 8. Young adult literature -- Bibliography
ISBN 1-59158-599-6; 978-1-59158-599-2
LC 2007-51065
"Good source notes guide readers to additional writings on the topic and speak to the author's significant research in his field. Nicely indexed by author, title, and subject, this [is an] easy-to-navigate resource." Voice Youth Advocates
Includes bibliographical references

028.7 Use of books and other information media as sources of information

Callison, Daniel
★ The **blue** book on information age inquiry, instruction and literacy; [by] Daniel Callison and Leslie Preddy. Libraries Unlimited 2006 643p il pa $45
Grades: Adult Professional **028.7**
1. Information literacy 2. Bibliographic instruction 3. Media literacy -- Study and teaching 4. Information literacy -- Study and teaching
ISBN 978-1-59158-325-7; 1-59158-325-X
LC 2006-23645
A revised edition of Key Words, Concepts and Methods for Information Age Instruction, published 2003 by LMS Associates
"Part 1 introduces the concepts of information inquiry, providing foundational documents and exploring search and use models, information literacy, standards, the instructional role of library media specialists, online inquiry learning, and resource management. Part 2 offers concrete examples of inquiry applied to the middle-school student research process and supplies reproducible pages for classroom use. Part 3 discusses and defines 51 key terms. Entries here are several pages in length and include citations and references. Indispensable for all school media specialists, this book will also appeal to other readers, who will be impressed by its well-organized design, thoroughness, and practicality." Booklist
Includes bibliographical references

030 General encyclopedic works

Anderson, Jennifer Joline
Wikipedia; the company and its founders. ABDO Pub. Co. 2011 112p il (Technology pioneers) lib bdg $34.22

Grades: 5 6 7 8 **030**
1. Electronic encyclopedias 2. Wikis (Computer science)
ISBN 978-1-61714-812-5 lib bdg; 1-61714-812-1 lib
bdg; 978-1-61758-970-6 e-book

LC 2010037886

This is an introduction to Wikipedia and its founders.

"Written in a clear, linear fashion, this series offers vivid,
well-researched details about the development of technological advancements considered essential in today's society. .
. . Readers who are interested in technology and inventions
will be thoroughly engrossed." SLJ

Includes glossary and bibliographical references

031 General encyclopedic works in specific languages and language families

DK Publishing, Inc.
DK children's illustrated encyclopedia; 7th ed.; DK
Pub. 2010 600p il map $34.99
Grades: 4 5 6 7 **031**
1. Encyclopedias and dictionaries
ISBN 978-0-7566-5759-8; 0-7566-5759-8

LC 2010279636

First published 1991 with title: Random House children's
encyclopedia; a revised edition of Dorling Kindersley's children's illustrated encyclopedia 6th ed. published 2006

A highly illustrated one-volume encyclopedia containing
entries ranging from Abolitionist movement to Zoos.

"This handsome revision features more than 3000 photographs, maps, time lines, and illustrations. . . . The attractive
format encourages browsing." SLJ

The **Kingfisher** children's encyclopedia. Kingfisher 2012
480 p. (hardcover) $29.99
Grades: 3 4 5 6 7 8 **031**
1. Picture books for children 2. Encyclopedias and
dictionaries
ISBN 075346814X; 9780753468142

The entries in this updated children's encyclopedia
"range from one to four pages in length each, feature full-
color illustrations and photos and subheadings in a large,
easy-to-read font and sidebars and fact boxes of thought-
provoking information." Topics include "continents and
countries, technology, transportation, animal and plant life,
religion, and space." (School Library Journal)

Turner, Tracey
World of the weird. Firefly Books 2009 144p il
$14.95
Grades: 5 6 7 8 **031**
1. Curiosities and wonders
ISBN 978-1-55407-481-5; 1-55407-481-9

"A first-rate browsing item, from the bicycle-riding frog
on the front cover to the recipe for chocolate-covered crickets at the end. . . . Turner presents barrages of snippets on
extreme sports ('chessboxing'), uncommon maladies ('exploding head syndrome'), oddball festivals, bizarre beliefs
('Eating stolen bacon is a cure for constipation.' Do tell!),
strange creatures real or otherwise, supernatural phenomena
and . . . more. . . . Illustrated with photos that are often startling but never gory or gross, this compact page-turner will

light up the imaginations of motivated young readers and
jaded nonreaders alike." Kirkus

Wilkes, Angela
My world of discovery. Kingfisher 2007 192p il
$14.95
Grades: 3 4 5 6 **031**
1. Reference books 2. Encyclopedias and dictionaries
3. Science -- Juvenile literature
ISBN 0-7534-5931-0

This "is an excellent resource for a young person de-
veloping an interest in a diverse number of science topics.
Many colorful, clear illustrations accompany the text. . . .
The text is easy to read and follow." Sci Books Films

The **World** Book Encyclopedia. World Book, Inc. 2013 22
p. col. ill. (hardcover) $1,422
Grades: 4 5 6 7 8 9 10 11 12 Adult **031**
1. Curiosities and wonders 2. Encyclopedias and
dictionaries
ISBN 0716601133; 9780716601135

LC 2012024690

This 2013 encyclopedia "engages more than 4,000
scholars and experts as contributors, reviewers, and consultants" and includes "more than 25,000 . . . photographs and
illustrations." The "22-volume World Book Encyclopedia
set includes thousands of articles covering" a variety of topics including "Pixar Animation Studios, rhythm and blues,
National September 11 Memorial and Museum, magnetism,
Adélie penguin, prime number," and the Cold War. (Publisher's note)

★ The **World** Book encyclopedia. World Book, Inc. 2010
22v il map set $1,044
Grades: 4 5 6 7 8 9 10 11 12 Adult **031**
1. Reference books 2. Encyclopedias and dictionaries
ISBN 978-0-7166-0110-4

LC 2009-29267

First published 1917-1918 by Field Enterprises.
Frequently revised

"A 22-volume, highly illustrated, A-Z general encyclopedia for all ages, featuring sections on how to use World
Book, other research aids, pronunciation key, a student
guide to better writing, speaking, and research skills, and
comprehensive index." Publisher's note

Includes bibliographical references

031.02 Books of miscellaneous facts

Aronson, Marc
For boys only; the biggest, baddest book ever. [by]
Marc Aronson [and] H.P. Newquist. Feiwel and Friends
2007 157p il map $14.95
Grades: 4 5 6 7 **031.02**
1. Boys 2. Curiosities and wonders 3. Boys -- Juvenile
literature
ISBN 978-0-312-37706-9; 0-312-37706-1

LC 2007-32847

"In a tone both light and humorous, Newquist and Aronson aim to please by assembling a tantalizing miscellany—
codes, puzzles, best lists, brief history and science facts,

instructions for making fake blood and playing Ultimate Frisbee. . . . This offers lots of good fun." Booklist

Buchanan, Andrea J.

The **daring** book for girls; [by] Andrea J. Buchanan, Miriam Peskowitz; illustrations by Alexis Seabrook. Collins 2007 279p il map $24.95

Grades: 4 5 6 7   **031.02**

1. Girls 2. Amusements 3. Recreation 4. Curiosities and wonders

ISBN 978-0-06-147257-2

          LC 2007031986

"In the introduction, the authors invite girls to explore their world . . . and they deliver a resource that will help them to do just that. The pages that follow are filled with interesting activities to try and important facts they may not know, but are sure to keep them busy for hours. The authors cover everything from making a lemon-powered clock to the history of writing and cursive, from how to paddle a canoe to the Periodic Table of the Elements in clear, thoughtful language that readers of all ages are sure to embrace." SLJ

Farndon, John

Do not open; written by John Farndon. DK Publishing 2007 256p il $24.99

Grades: 4 5 6 7   **031.02**

1. Curiosities and wonders

ISBN 978-0-7566-3205-2; 0-7566-3205-6

          LC 2007300131

This encyclopedic tome catalogues "the mysterious and unusual. . . . Flaps, foldout pages and varied styles of illustration—from photomontage to digital cartoons and more conventional line art—keep the book visually fresh and ably complement the subject matter. . . . Taking in everything from weird weather like St. Elmo's fire and raining frogs to possible locations of Atlantis, the book incites curiosity—and expansively rewards it." Publ Wkly

Iggulden, Conn

The **dangerous** book for boys; [by] Conn Iggulden, Hal Iggulden. Collins 2007 270p il map $24.95

Grades: 4 5 6 7   **031.02**

1. Boys 2. Amusements 3. Recreation 4. Curiosities and wonders 5. Fathers and sons 6. Handbooks, vademecums, etc.

ISBN 0-06-124358-2; 978-0-06-124358-5

          LC 2006-491918

"This eclectic collection addresses the undeniable boy-appeal of certain facts and activities. Dozens of short chapters, in fairly random order, cover a wide range of topics in conversational prose. Simple instructions for coin tricks and paper airplanes alternate with excerpts from history such as Famous Battles and facts about ancient wonders of the world and astronomy. . . . Tongue-in-cheek humor emerges throughout." SLJ

Kane, Joseph Nathan

★ **Famous** first facts; a record of first happenings, discoveries, and inventions in American history. [by] Joseph Nathan Kane, Steven Anzovin, & Janet Podell. 6th ed.; Wilson, H.W. 2006 1307p il $185

Grades: 5 6 7 8 9 10 11 12 Adult   **031.02**

1. Reference books 2. Encyclopedias and dictionaries

ISBN 978-0-8242-1065-6; 0-8242-1065-4

          LC 2006-3096

First published 1933

Over 7500 entries cover first occurences in American history, organized into 16 chapters each divided into sections. Sections are alphabetically organized, and individual entries are organized chronologically within each section. Includes five indexes: subject index, index by years, index by days, index to personal names, and geographical index

"Besides serving as an essential ready-reference source, the book is also fun to read out loud to colleagues—when was bubble gum first manufactured in the U.S.? When was the spray can introduced?" Booklist

Masoff, Joy

Oh, yuck! the encyclopedia of everything nasty. illustrated by Terry Sirrell. Workman 2000 212p il pa $14.95

Grades: 4 5 6 7   **031.02**

1. Curiosities and wonders

ISBN 0-7611-0771-1

          LC 99-43603

An alphabetical collection of articles about disgusting things, from acne, ants, and bacteria to worms, x-periments, and zits

"Amusing cartoons and well-chosen, black-and-white photographs with humorous captions support the text. . . . This delightful volume will be enjoyed by fans of grossness everywhere." SLJ

Includes bibliographical references

Murrie, Matthew

While You Were Sleeping; Fun Facts That Happen at Night. by Steve Murrie and Matthew Murrie; illustrated by Tom Bloom. Turtleback Books 2012 224 p. col. ill. (paperback) $9.99; (prebind) $20.85

Grades: 2 3 4   **031.02**

1. Night -- Juvenile literature 2. Sleep -- Juvenile literature

ISBN 0545430283; 0606267468; 9780545430289; 9780606267465

This book "provides general observations about internal biological processes associated with sleep, nocturnal animals, nighttime jobs, and wee-hours activities—interleaved with minidisquisitions on earthquakes, Mount Rushmore, bamboo, comets, space probes, the largest Lego tower every constructed, and an array of other subjects." (Booklist)

Ripley, Catherine

How? the most awesome question and answer book about nature, animals, people, places, and you! by Catherine Ripley; illustrated by Scot Ritchie. Owlkids Books 2012 192 p. col. ill. (hardcover) $19.95

Grades: 1 2 3   **031.02**

1. Shells 2. Hamsters 3. Questions and answers 4. Children's questions and answers

ISBN 1926973240; 9781926973241

          LC 2012405052

Author Catherine Ripley uses humor to answer questions about how everyday subjects work for children. In "question-and-answer format, . . . [the questions] include how batter turns into cake and how birthday candles stay on fire, why hamsters run on wheels and why they stuff their cheeks with food, why you hear the sea in a seashell and why the ocean is salty." (Kirkus Reviews)

Shields, Amy

Little kids first big book of why. National Geographic 2011 127p (National geographic little kids) $14.95

Grades: K 1 2 3   **031.02**

1. Science 2. Curiosities and wonders

ISBN 978-1-4263-0793-5; 1-4263-0793-4

"Young readers will find clear answers to a variety of basic science, nature, technology, and human body questions in this random but potentially useful volume. . . . Crisp photographs illustrate the information, including brief explanations behind everything from curly hair to blue skies to purring cats to why planes fly." Horn Book Guide

Thomas, Keltie

Planet Earth News presents: super humans. Maple Tree Press 2006 64p il $19.95; pa $9.95

Grades: 3 4 5 6   **031.02**

1. Curiosities and wonders 2. Human beings -- Juvenile literature 3. Civilization -- History -- Juvenile literature

ISBN 978-1-897066-51-5; 1-897066-51-1; 978-1-897066-52-2 pa; 1-897066-52-X pa

This "is a high-energy account of all things human that manages to include fun factoids about subject material ranging from biology and history to engineering and linguistics. . . . Each turn of the page gives us a landscape strewn with multiple brightly colored illustrations and up to eight blurbs covering subjects pulled from every direction." Sci Books Films

★ The World almanac for kids. World Almanac il maps

Grades: 4 5 6 7   **031.02**

1. Almanacs 2. Reference books

Annual. First published 1995 for 1996

This volume contains information on animals, art, religion, sports, books, law, language, science and computers. Includes a section of full-color maps and flags. Illustrated throughout with pictures, diagrams, and charts

050   General serial publications

Botzakis, Stergios

Pretty in print; questioning magazines. by Stergios Botzakis. Fact Finders 2007 32p il (Media literacy) lib bdg $22.60; pa $7.95

Grades: 4 5 6 7   **050**

1. Periodicals 2. Publishers and publishing

ISBN 978-0-7368-6764-1 lib bdg; 0-7368-6764-3 lib bdg; 978-0-7368-7860-9 pa; 0-7368-7860-2 pa

LC 2006021443

This is "written in a breezy style and [has] plenty of popping colors and photos. . . . Useful and attractive." SLJ

Includes bibliographical references

051   General serial publications in specific languages and language families

Hopkins, Lee Bennett 1938-

★ **Days** to celebrate; a full year of poetry, people, holidays, history, fascinating facts, and more. written and edited by Lee Bennett Hopkins; illustrated by Stephen Alcorn. Greenwillow Books 2005 112p il $17.99; lib bdg $18.89

Grades: 3 4 5   **051**

1. Almanacs 2. Holidays 3. Reference books 4. Almanacs, Children's 5. Poetry -- Collections

ISBN 0-06-000765-6; 0-06-000766-4 lib bdg

LC 2003-49288

"The writers represented include Robert Frost, Langston Hughes, Richard Wilbur, and Gwendolyn Brooks. Alcorn's large, vibrant, whimsical artwork perfectly enhances the prose and verse to make this book a delight to the eye and the ear." SLJ

069   Museology (Museum science)

Korrell, Emily B.

Awesome adventures at the Smithsonian; the official kids guide to the Smithsonian Institution. Emily B. Korrell. Smithsonian Books 2013 127 p. ill. (chiefly col.) (paperback) $14.95

Grades: 4 5 6   **069.097**

1. Museums -- Guidebooks 2. Smithsonian Institution -- Juvenile literature 3. Science museums -- Washington (D.C.) -- Guidebooks -- Juvenile literature

ISBN 1588343499; 9781588343499

LC 2012029119

This "guide offers children ages 8-12 years a way to navigate the Smithsonian. Engaging maps, photographs, and illustrations present the main museum halls along with puzzles, games, mad libs, and pages for journal entries, drawings, and superlatives that will help get kids ready for their big trip to the nation's capital and keep them focused and attentive as they navigate the world's largest museum complex that is the Smithsonian Institution." (Publisher's note)

Mark, Jan

The **museum** book; a guide to strange and wonderful collections. written by Jan Mark; illustrated by Richard Holland. Candlewick Press 2007 54p il $15

Grades: 3 4 5 6   **069**

1. Museums

ISBN 978-0-7636-3370-7; 0-7636-3370-4

LC 2006-49055

Explains what a museum is, and what fascinating things you might find there.

This "tome will launch readers on a leisurely and edifying journey of discovery. . . . Holland . . . jolts readers . . . with his mixed-media collages, which sparingly employ color and liberally combine to look like Victorian engravings, pencil sketches, Gorey-like figures, and photos of various locales." Publ Wkly

070.4 Journalism

Sullivan, George
Journalists at risk; reporting America's wars. [by] George Sullivan. Twenty-First Century Books 2006 128p il (People's history) lib bdg $26.60
Grades: 5 6 7 8   **070.4**
1. War 2. Journalism
ISBN 0-7613-2745-2

LC 2003015855

Discusses the role of reporters during war time, including the risks they take and the censorship they face, and how their jobs have changed with each conflict since the Civil War.

"As a case study in the fluidity of First Amendment rights in wartime, it's thought-provoking reading." Booklist
Includes bibliographical references

070.5 Publishing

Donovan, Sandra, 1967-
★ Pingpong Perry experiences how a book is made; by Sandy Donovan; illustrated by Martin Haake. Picture Window 2010 24p il (In the library) lib bdg $25.32
Grades: 1 2 3   **070.5**
1. Publishers and publishing
ISBN 978-1-4048-5759-9 lib bdg; 1-4048-5759-1 lib bdg

This volume "surprises and amuses with every page, while also neatly explaining the publishing process. . . . On the first page, Perry (digitally illustrated in an angular, retro-cool style) is clutching his own book: Perry's Practical Guide to the Pizza Picks of Popular Pingpong Players. Donovan then backtracks to relate Perry's meteoric transformation into publishing royalty. . . . The editing process, complete with a sample of a copyedited page, is admirably realistic, as is the portrayal of the savvy professional women Perry encounters at every turn." Booklist

Neuburger, Emily K.
Golden legacy; how Golden Books won children's hearts, changed publishing forever, and became an American icon along the way. Golden Books 2007 245p il $40
Grades: Adult Professional   **070.5**
1. Publishers and publishing 2. Publishers and publishing -- United States 3. Children's literature -- History and criticism 4. Children's literature -- Publishing -- United States -- History -- 20th century
ISBN 978-0-375-82996-3; 0-375-82996-2

LC 2006-939312

Presents a history of Golden Books, discussing how it was founded in the midst of World War II providing quality books at inexpensive prices and used innovative writers and marketing techniques to establish itself as a highly successful publishing firm

This is a "lavishly illustrated, handsomely designed volume. . . . The author unearths some startling facts. . . . The highly readable narrative is documented with thorough and detailed footnotes. . . . This winning combination of nostalgia and clear-eyed, meticulously researched history breaks new ground." SLJ

★ Minders of make-believe; idealists, entrepreneurs, and the shaping of American children's literature. Houghton Mifflin Co. 2008 402p $28
Grades: Adult Professional   **070.5**
1. Children -- Books and reading -- History 2. Children's literature -- History and criticism 3. Children's literature -- Publishing -- United States -- History -- 20th century
ISBN 978-0-395-67407-9; 0-395-67407-7

LC 2008-00589

"Marcus' approach and tone are always, and irresistibly, well informed, sensible, and intelligent. . . . It is hard to imagine any issue that he has overlooked, and the resulting book is, in word, indispensable." Booklist
Includes bibliographical references

★ Side by side; five favorite picture-book teams go to work. Walker & Co. 2001 64p il $22.95; lib bdg $23.85
Grades: 4 5 6 7   **070.5**
1. Illustrators 2. Picture books for children 3. Picture books 4. Authors, American 5. Children's literature -- Authorship -- Juvenile literature 6. Children's literature -- Illustrations -- Juvenile literature 7. Illustrators -- United States -- Biography -- Juvenile literature 8. Authors, American -- 20th century -- Biography -- Juvenile literature 9. Picture books for children -- Publishing -- United States -- Juvenile literature
ISBN 0-8027-8778-9; 0-8027-8779-7 lib bdg

LC 2001-26344

This "volume introduces five sets of collaborators in the field of picture books: Arthur Yorinks and Richard Egielski, Alice and Martin Provensen, Julius Lester and Jerry Pinkney, Joanna Cole and Bruce Degen, and Jon Scieszka, Lane Smith, and Molly Leach. Each chapter discusses how the writer and artist (and in Leach's case, designer) got together, and highlights their collaboration during various projects, as well as providing a wealth of interesting details about these creative individuals and their books. The clearly reproduced illustrations, many in color, include photographs, sketches for book illustrations, and finished art." Booklist
Includes glossary and bibliographical references

Wickings, Ruth
Pop-up; everything you need to know to create your own pop-up book. paper engineering by Ruth Wickings; illustrated by Frances Castle. Candlewick Press 2010 un il $19.99
Grades: 3 4 5 6   **070.5**
1. Toy and movable books 2. Pop-up books
ISBN 978-0-7636-5056-8; 0-7636-5056-0

LC 2010-05488

"First outlining the basic building blocks of pop-up engineering (types of folds, mechanics like noisemakers and spirals), the book then uses the example of a pop-up robot to demonstrate how such components work together. The remaining sections offer four illustrated scenes, into which punch-put elements can be incorporated. . . . Completing the pop-ups will be tricky for younger readers (the difficulty level increases with each project) but the end result should be as gratifying as it is illuminating." Publ Wkly

081 General collections in specific languages and language families

Hudson, Wade

★ **Powerful** words; more than 200 years of extraordinary writing by African Americans. illustrated by Sean Qualls; foreword by Marian Wright Edelman. Scholastic Nonfiction 2004 178p il $19.95

Grades: 5 6 7 8 **081**

1. Quotations 2. African Americans 3. Speeches, addresses, etc 4. African Americans -- History 5. African Americans -- Biography 6. American literature -- African American authors 7. African Americans -- Biography -- Juvenile literature 8. African Americans -- Quotations -- Juvenile literature 9. African Americans -- History -- Sources -- Juvenile literature 10. Speeches, addresses, etc., American -- African American authors -- Juvenile literature

ISBN 0-439-40969-1

LC 2003-42792

A collection of speeches and writings by African Americans, with commentary about the time period in which each person lived, information about the speaker/writer, and public response to the words.

"Short enough to hold attention, the selections . . . are also long enough to show the writers' tone and style. Many sensitive full-page portraits are included. . . . This well-designed volume will be an excellent addition to many library collections." Booklist

Includes bibliographical references

098 Prohibited works, forgeries, hoaxes

Scales, Pat R.

Teaching banned books; 12 guides for young readers. American Library Association 2001 134p pa $28

Grades: Adult Professional **098**

1. School libraries 2. Books -- Censorship 3. Children's literature -- Study and teaching

ISBN 0-8389-0807-1

LC 01-22340

"Scales knows her material inside out. She also knows how to inspire others to take up this cause and gives them an effective handbook to do just that." Booklist

Includes bibliographical references

100 PHILOSOPHY

100 Philosophy, parapsychology and occultism, psychology

Law, Stephen

Really, really big questions; about the weird, the wonderful, and everything else. illustrated by Nishant Choksi. Kingfisher 2009 62p il $16.99

Grades: 5 6 7 8 **100**

1. Philosophy

ISBN 978-0-7534-6309-3; 0-7534-6309-1

An introduction to philosophy which uses clear analogies to explore some of life's biggest moral and scientific questions, including the origins of the universe and the meaning of life

"Through a combination of vibrant colors; hip, retro illustrations; and interesting quotes, Law has produced a stimulating work for young minds that is sure to spark conversation and, of course, more questions." SLJ

133.1 Apparitions

Everett, J. H.

Haunted histories; creepy castles, dark dungeons, and powerful palaces. J. H. Everett and Marilyn Scott-Waters. 1st ed. Henry Holt and Company 2012 160 p. (hardcover) $14.99; (paperback) $5.99

Grades: 4 5 6 **133.1**

1. Castles 2. Torture 3. Historic sites 4. Ghosts -- Juvenile literature 5. Haunted places -- Juvenile literature

ISBN 0805089713; 9780805089714; 9781250027269

LC 2011033495

In this book, authors J.H. Everett and Marilyn Scott-Waters focus on "Virgil Dante, youngest Master Ghostorian in London," ghosts, and his raven, Thor, as they "tour history with the assistance of a cursed pocket watch and look in on castles, dungeons, palaces and graveyards. . . . The usual suspects get the eye: The Tower of London and the Bastille figure prominently, but there are also lesser-known nests of nastiness like Himeji Castle in Japan and Castle Neuschwanstein in Bavaria." (Kirkus Reviews)

Gudgeon, Christopher

Ghost trackers; the unreal world of ghosts, ghost-hunting, and the paranormal. by Chris Gudgeon; foreword by Joe MacLeod. Tundra Books 2010 75p il pa $14.95

Grades: 4 5 6 7 **133.1**

1. Ghosts 2. Parapsychology

ISBN 978-0-88776-950-4; 0-88776-950-0

"Gudgeon thoroughly discusses all things ghostly. Chapters take on the history of sightings, scientists and paranormal research, haunted places around the world, and ghost tracking. . . . Side boxes offer other assorted information, and photographs and illustrations, some quite eerie, are sprinkled throughout. The writing is clear and the subject is presented in an evenhanded manner." SLJ

Hawes, Jason

Ghost hunt; chilling tales of the unknown. [by] Jason Hawes & Grant Wilson; with Cameron Dokey. Little Brown & Co. 2010 218p il $16.99

Grades: 4 5 6 7 8 9 **133.1**

1. Ghosts

ISBN 978-0-316-09959-2; 0-316-09959-7

"This collection of stories is based on case files from The [Atlantic] Paranormal Society, TAPS, founded by Hawes and Wilson. Each of the eight selections describes the sightings and paranormal activity from the perspective of the observer, then describes how members of TAPS researched, set up equipment, and discovered explanations for what happened. . . . The stories have enough elements of the unknown to make them spine-tingling, but they are more mystery than horror. . . . The easy-to-read format and subject matter will keep even the most reluctant of readers interested." SLJ

Ghost hunt 2; more chilling tales of the unknown. by Jason Hawes and Grant Wilson; with Cameron Dokey. Little Brown & Co. 2011 297p il $16.99

Grades: 4 5 6 7 8   **133.1**

1. Ghosts

ISBN 978-0-316-09958-5; 0-316-09958-9

"From ghostly spirits roaming Alcatraz to glowing red eyes in the woods, The Atlantic Paranormal Society (aka the popular reality television series Ghost Hunters) is back with a compilation of even more chilling and terrifying tales. Selections include a restless spirit terrorizing a house-sitting victim through her dreams, ghosts reappearing in the O.K. Corral in Tombstone, AZ, and a saddened ghost revisiting a lighthouse where her family was eradicated long ago." SLJ

Matthews, Rupert

Ghosts and spirits. QEB Pub. 2011 32p il (Unexplained) lib bdg $28.50

Grades: 4 5 6 7   **133.1**

1. Ghosts 2. Apparitions

ISBN 978-1-59566-857-8; 1-59566-857-8

LC 2010014205

This discusses stories about ghosts and poltergeists.

"This well-written and thoughtfully designed [book] features [an] engrossing [topic]. . . . Though the pages are profusely illustrated with large, well-reproduced photographs and drawings, the layout is not cluttered. This [book] just might inspire kids to seek out more in-depth materials." SLJ

Includes glossary

Stefoff, Rebecca

Ghosts and spirits; [by] Rebecca Stefoff. Marshall Cavendish Benchmark 2007 94p il (Secrets of the supernatural) lib bdg $32.79

Grades: 5 6 7 8   **133.1**

1. Ghosts

ISBN 978-0-7614-2634-9 lib bdg; 0-7614-2634-5 lib bdg

LC 2006031652

This is a history of beliefs in ghosts and spirits throughout the world, including haunted houses, spiritualism, hauxes, and investigations into paranormal phenomena.

"Nearly every other page has an illustration. . . . The text is accessible." Libr Media Connect

Includes glossary and bibliographical references

Wetzel, Charles

Haunted U.S.A. written by Charles Wetzel; illustrated by Josh Cochran. Sterling 2008 86p il (Mysteries unwrapped) pa $5.95

Grades: 5 6 7 8   **133.1**

1. Ghosts

ISBN 978-1-4027-3735-0 pa; 1-4027-3735-1 pa

LC 2007045905

"Wetzel tells stories of haunted America from the White House to Hollywood. Although some of the places and people mentioned, such as the Amityville house and Rudolph Valentino, might be unfamiliar to younger readers, the selections are still good ghost stories. . . . [The book has] an ample number of clear black-and-white and full-color photographs

and illustrations. . . . Perfect for libraries that need a boost or an update to their scary-story collections." SLJ

Includes bibliographical references

133.3   Divinatory arts

Doft, Tony

Nostradamus. Bellwether Media 2011 24p il (Torque: The unexplained) lib bdg $15.95

Grades: 3 4 5 6   **133.3**

1. Physicians 2. Prophecies 3. Astrologers 4. Futurologists

ISBN 978-1-60014-584-1; 1-60014-584-1

LC 2010034777

This considers the life and predictions of Nostradamus, who died in 1566.

"Designed for struggling readers, this . . . combines accessible writing, dynamic illustrations, and [a] high-interest [topic]. [A] snazzy [cover] and an abundance of glossy, full-color illustrations provide appeal. . . . The writing is succinct but informative." SLJ

Includes bibliographical references

Stefoff, Rebecca

Prophets and prophecy; [by] Rebecca Stefoff. Marshall Cavendish Benchmark 2007 79p il (Secrets of the supernatural) lib bdg $32.79

Grades: 5 6 7 8   **133.3**

1. Prophets 2. Prophecies

ISBN 978-0-7614-2638-7 lib bdg; 0-7614-2638-8 lib bdg

LC 2007008779

This is a history of prophecy and fortune-telling from ancient times to the present, discussing such topics as tarot cards, the Oracle of Delphi, astrology, fate, Nostradamus, Jean Dixon, omens, and the I Ching.

"Nearly every other page has an illustration. . . . The text is accessible." Libr Media Connect

Includes glossary and bibliographical references

133.4   Demonology and witchcraft

Hill, Douglas

Witches & magic-makers; written by Douglas Hill; photographed by Alex Wilson. Dorling Kindersley 2000 61p il (DK eyewitness books) $15.99; lib bdg $19.99

Grades: 4 5 6 7   **133.4**

1. Magic 2. Witchcraft

ISBN 0-7894-5878-0; 0-7894-6619-8 lib bdg

First published 1997 by Knopf

This book on "witchcraft, shamanism, and mysticism . . . introduces magical charms, talismans, and amulets from around the world. . . . This title gives a colorful overview of the topic." [review of 1997 edition]

Hirschmann, Kris

Demons. ReferencePoint Press 2011 80p il (Monsters and mythical creatures) $26.95

Grades: 5 6 7 8   **133.4**
1. Demonology
ISBN 978-1-60152-147-7; 1-60152-147-2
LC 2010029905

"Beginning with an introduction that explains the origins of the devilish creatures, the book discusses demon-like entities throughout cultures and religions. . . . The book's visuals, which include contemporary photos of ceremonies and artists' rendering of demons, can be quite startling. Excellent sidebars . . . cover topics such as the number of exorcists in the Catholic Church." Booklist

Includes bibliographical references

Jackson, Shirley
The **witchcraft** of Salem Village. Random House 1987 146p hardcover o.p. pa $5.99
Grades: 4 5 6 7   **133.4**
1. Witchcraft
ISBN 0-394-89176-7 pa
LC 87-4543

A reissue of the title first published 1956
"A simple, chilling account of the witchcraft trials of 1692 and '93 when, because of testimony given by a group of little girls, twenty persons were executed as witches and others died in jail. There is good introductory background and though the story's subject is by nature horrifying the book does not play on the emotions. . . . It presents a difficult theme lucidly and without condescension." Horn Book

Kerns, Ann
Wizards and witches. Lerner Publications 2010 48p il (Fantasy chronicles) lib bdg $27.93
Grades: 4 5 6 7   **133.4**
1. Witches
ISBN 978-0-8225-9983-8 lib bdg; 0-8225-9983-X lib bdg
LC 2008050757

"The explanations and history behind . . . witches [and wizards] . . . will provide satisfaction for readers who want to know more about these familiar characters from myth, fantasy, and folk and fairy tales. Brief and concise." SLJ

Includes bibliographical references

Roach, Marilynne K.
In the days of the Salem witchcraft trials. Houghton Mifflin 1996 92p il map hardcover o.p. pa $5.95
Grades: 4 5 6 7   **133.4**
1. Witchcraft 2. Trials -- Juvenile literature 3. Salem (Mass.) -- History -- Juvenile literature
ISBN 0-395-69704-2; 0-618-39196-7 pa
LC 94-32383

"After discussing the Salem Witchcraft trials in one short chapter, this attractive volume explores the social history of the times to show the context that made such events possible. Topics include the law and punishment, magic, social status, clothing, food, household goods, occupations, recreation, common activities, government, and the political troubles leading to widespread tension and unrest. Readers will come away with a much fuller picture of who lived in Salem and how they lived. Small ink drawings decorate the pages." Booklist

Includes bibliographical references

133.5   Astrology

Young, Ed
Cat and Rat; the legend of the Chinese zodiac. Holt & Co. 1995 un il $15.95; pa $6.95
Grades: K 1 2 3   **133.5**
1. Zodiac 2. Cats -- Folklore 3. Rats -- Folklore 4. Folklore -- China 5. Zodiac -- Juvenile literature 6. Chinese New Year -- Juvenile literature 7. Folklore -- China -- Juvenile literature
ISBN 0-8050-2977-X; 0-8050-6049-9 pa
LC 94-49147

"Young tells the story in lively, spare prose. . . . His charcoal and pastel drawings on dark blue and buff rice paper are elegant and full of action." SLJ

152.1   Sensory perception

Cobb, Vicki
How to really fool yourself; illusions for all your senses. illustrated by Jessica Wolk-Stanley. Wiley 1999 120p il pa $12.95
Grades: 5 6 7 8   **152.1**
1. Perception 2. Optical illusions 3. Senses and sensation 4. Perception -- Juvenile literature 5. Optical illusions -- Juvenile literature 6. Senses and sensation -- Juvenile literature
ISBN 0-471-31592-3
LC 98-27723

A newly illustrated edition of the title first published 1981 by Lippincott
"The book begins with an explanation of perception and explores many different sensory aspects of it through experiments, definitions of important terms (italicized), background information and how illusions affect us in everyday life." SLJ

152.14   Visual perception

Banyai, Istvan
Zoom. Viking 1995 un il $16.99; pa $6.99
Grades: K 1 2 3   **152.14**
1. Stories without words 2. Perception -- Juvenile literature
ISBN 0-670-85804-8; 0-14-055774-1 pa
LC 94-33181

A wordless picture book presents a series of scenes, each one from farther away, showing, for example, a girl playing with toys which is actually a picture on a magazine cover, which is part of a sign on a bus, and so on
"If the concept is not wholly new, the execution is superior. Readers are in for a perpetually surprising—and even philosophical—adventure." Publ Wkly

Brocket, Jane
Spotty, stripy, swirly; what are patterns? [written and photographed by Jane Brocket] Millbrook Press 2012 31 p. (Jane brocket's clever concepts)
Grades: PreK K 1 2   **152.14**
1. Color 2. Pattern perception 3. Pattern perception

-- Juvenile literature
ISBN 9780761346135

LC 2011022179

This illustrated children's book, a part of Jane Brocket's Clever Concepts Series, "examines patterns from almost every conceivable angle. There are patterns determined sometimes by shape, sometimes by color, sometimes by object. They run the gamut from simple to quite complex. There are man-made patterns such as brickwork or quilts, and patterns that occur in nature, such as geranium leaves." (School Libr J) "[Brocket's] up-close photos show a wide array of objects with their own distinctive patterns, from fabrics and architectural elements to food and plants. . . . [S]he delves into the reasons for patterns. They help us identify plants, stay organized, decorate and plan, but, most of all, they are pleasing to the eye." (Kirkus)

Simon, Seymour

★ **Now** you see it, now you don't; the amazing world of optical illusions. drawings by Constance Ftera. rev ed; Morrow Junior Bks. 1998 64p il $17.99

Grades: 4 5 6 7   **152.14**

1. Optical illusions
ISBN 0-688-16152-9

LC 97-49855

First published 1976 by FourWinds Press with title: The optical illusion book

The author explains optical illusions involving lines and spaces, changeable figures, depth and distance, brightness and contrast, and color

"One of the clearest and most interesting discussions of optical illusions ever written for children." Booklist

Includes bibliographical references

Vry, Silke

Trick of the eye; art and illusion. Prestel 2010 89p il $14.95

Grades: 4 5 6   **152.14**

1. Art appreciation 2. Optical illusions
ISBN 978-3-7913-7026-2; 3-7913-7026-X

"From the Parthenon to the Mona Lisa to the Op-Art of the 1960s, images and text reveal the many ways our eyes play tricks on us. Perception of size and color is discussed using standard optical illusions, but this book includes much more. Anecdotes, such as the story of dueling Greek painters Zeuxis and Parrhasius, and unique reproductions, like portraits with altered facial features, lend excitement. The author has taken an interactive approach, filling the pages with questions, puzzles, and project ideas. . . . Text explains the images, which are large and clear. The broad range of styles represented and the fun of the interactive approach will no doubt appeal to young art lovers and curious kids alike." SLJ

Wick, Walter

★ **Walter** Wick's optical tricks; by Walter Wick. 10th anniversary edition; Cartwheel Books 2008 43p il $14.99

Grades: 4 5 6 7   **152.14**

1. Optical illusions
ISBN 978-0-439-85520-4; 0-439-85520-9
First published 1998

Presents a series of optical illusions and explains what is seen.

The author "has produced a stunning picture book of optical illusions. With crystal-clear photographs, he creates a series of scenes that fool the eye and the brain." Booklist [review of 1998 ed.]

152.4   Emotions

Aliki

★ **Feelings**. Greenwillow Bks. 1984 32p il $16; pa $5.95

Grades: K 1 2 3   **152.4**

1. Emotions
ISBN 0-688-03831-X; 0-688-06518-X pa

LC 84-4098

"Small pen-and-ink cartoons with vivid coloring depict boys and girls interacting and experiencing the full range of feelings which evolve in everyday settings. This creative, unique book would be ideal for parent/child interaction or use by elementary teachers in language arts classes. Children will enjoy the comic book 'frame' format." Child Book Rev Serv

Freymann, Saxton

★ **How** are you peeling? foods with moods. [by] Saxton Freymann and Joost Elffers. Scholastic 1999 un il $16.95; pa $6.99

Grades: PreK K 1 2 3   **152.4**

1. Emotions 2. Emotions -- Juvenile literature 3. Vegetable carving -- Juvenile literature
ISBN 0-439-10431-9; 0-439-59841-9 pa

LC 99-18162

Brief text and photographs of carvings made from vegetables introduce the world of emotions by presenting leading questions such as "Are you feeling angry?"

"Kids will find the inherent silliness irresistible and be drawn in by the book's visual appeal: the colors are strong, the photography is excellent, and the expressions . . . . are surprisingly masterful." Booklist

Graves, Sue

But why can't I? written by Sue Graves; illustrated by Desideria Guicciardini. Free Spirit Pub. 2011 25p il (Our emotions and behavior)

Grades: PreK K 1   **152.4**

1. Etiquette 2. Conduct of life
ISBN 1-57542-376-6; 978-1-57542-376-0

LC 2011001563

This book joins Noah and his babysitter, Jenny, who shows him how rules help keep people safe, healthy, and happy.

"Short sentences and [a] simple [plotline] create [an] excellent [lead-in] to talking about making good decisions what faced with new and difficult emotions. . . . The color cartoon illustrations help make the concepts easy to grasp. . . . Discussion questions are included in the back matter." SLJ

I'm not happy; written by Sue Graves; illustrated by Desideria Guicciardini. Free Spirit Pub. 2011 25p il (Our emotions and behavior)

Grades: PreK K 1   **152.4**

1. Kindness 2. Happiness
ISBN 1-57542-373-1; 978-1-57542-373-9

LC 2011001565

Ben helps cheer up his friends and shows how kids can turn sadness into smiles.

"Short sentences and [a] simple [plotline] create [an] excellent [lead-in] to talking about making good decisions when faced with new and difficult emotions. . . . The color cartoon illustrations help make the concepts easy to grasp. . . . Discussion questions are included in the back matter." SLJ

Not fair, won't share; written by Sue Graves; illustrated by Desideria Guicciardini. Free Spirit Pub. 2011 25p il (Our emotions and behavior)

Grades: PreK K 1   **152.4**
1. Conduct of life 2. Interpersonal relations
ISBN 1-57542-375-8; 978-1-57542-375-3
LC 2011001566

When Nora, Dan, and Henry have trouble sharing at school, they all end up feeling mad. With the help of their teacher, the friends learn that when kids get frustrated, there are ways to calm down, share, and play fairly.

"Short sentences and [a] simple [plotline] create [an] excellent [lead-in] to talking about making good decisions when faced with new and difficult emotions. . . . The color cartoon illustrations help make the concepts easy to grasp. . . . Discussion questions are included in the back matter." SLJ

Who feels scared? written by Sue Graves; illustrated by Desideria Guicciardini. Free Spirit Pub. 2011 25p il (Our emotions and behavior) $12.99

Grades: PreK K 1   **152.4**
1. Fear
ISBN 978-1-57542-374-6; 1-57542-374-X
LC 2011001626

Everybody feels afraid sometimes—like Jack and his friends Ravi and Kevin when they have a sleepover. This book shows children that they can cope with their fears and be brave.

"Short sentences and [a] simple [plotline] create [an] excellent [lead-in] to talking about making good decisions when faced with new and difficult emotions. . . . The color cartoon illustrations help make the concepts easy to grasp. . . . Discussion questions are included in the back matter." SLJ

153.4   Thought, thinking, reasoning, intuition, value, judgment

Watanabe, Ken
No problem! an easy guide to getting what you want. illustrated by Elwood H. Smith; adapted by Sarah L. Thomson. Viking 2010 70p il $16.99; pa $9.99

Grades: 4 5 6   **153.4**
1. Problem solving
ISBN 978-0-670-01203-9; 0-670-01203-3; 978-0-670-01254-1 pa; 0-670-01254-8 pa

Adaptation of: Problem solving 101, published 2009 for adults

"This little gem explains how to approach intimidating goals or jobs by breaking them down into simple tasks. Realistic scenarios such as finding money for a big purchase or choosing a high school are approached with data-driven evaluation tools. The author defines the steps involved along with terms such as hypotheses, logic trees, matrixes, and evaluation charts." SLJ

153.7   Perceptual processes

Hillman, Ben
How big is it? a big book all about bigness. Scholastic 2007 47p il $14.99

Grades: 3 4 5   **153.7**
1. Size
ISBN 0-439-91808-1; 978-0-439-91808-4
LC 2006050609

"This oversize picture book . . . presents 22 giant creatures, objects, and plants, prehistoric and contemporary. On each double-page spread there is a panel of chatty information next to a huge, unframed color picture, which uses digitally blended images to show comparative size. . . . These clear, astonishing pictures [are] both a magnet to browsers as well as a device to demonstrate gradations of bigness." Booklist

Miller, Margaret
★ **Big** and little. Greenwillow Bks. 1998 un il $15.99

Grades: PreK   **153.7**
1. Size 2. Size judgement -- Pictorial works -- Juvenile literature 3. Size perception -- Pictorial works -- Juvenile literature
ISBN 0-688-14748-8
LC 97-17242

Photographs and easy text introduce the concepts of size and opposites

"This book uses cheerful, clear color photos of active toddlers to teach basic concepts." Booklist

155.45   Exceptional children; children by social and economic levels, by ethnic or national group

Fonseca, Christine
101 success secrets for gifted kids; the ultimate guide. Prufrock Press 2011 xi, 191p pa $14.95

Grades: 4 5 6 7 8   **155.45**
1. Gifted children
ISBN 978-1-59363-544-2; 1-59363-544-3
LC 2011004912

"Fonseca explains what it means to be labeled 'gifted,' how to cope in school, and how to interact with friends and family. Information is delivered in a friendly, conversational manner with firsthand advice from gifted kids and their parents. The myriad tips include how to deal with stress, how to complete homework assignments effectively, how to be respectful of others, how to accept oneself, and even how to deal with bullies. All are incredibly useful." SLJ

Includes bibliographical references

Gerstein, Mordicai
★ **The wild** boy; based on the true story of the Wild Boy of Aveyron. Foster Bks. 1998 39p il hardcover o.p. pa $6.95

Grades: K 1 2 3   **155.45**
1. Wild children 2. Feral children -- Juvenile literature
ISBN 0-374-38431-2; 0-374-48396-5 pa
LC 97-37246

Relates the story of a boy who grew up wild in the forests of France and was captured in 1800, studied and cared for and named Victor, but who never learned to speak

"Gerstein's prose finds power in its simplicity and emotional resonance in its declarative understatement. . . . The narrative strength and energy of the illustrations expand the inherent drama of Victor's situation. Together, Gerstein's text and pictures work to create an unforgettable story." Booklist

155.9   Environmental psychology

Brown, Laurene Krasny

When dinosaurs die; a guide to understanding death. [by] Laurie Krasny Brown and Marc Brown. Little, Brown 1996 32p il hardcover o.p. pa $5.95

Grades: K 1 2 3   155.9

1. Death 2. Bereavement 3. Death -- Psychological aspects -- Juvenile literature

ISBN 0-316-10917-7; 0-316-11955-5 pa

LC 95-14511

"The text explains the inevitability of death, various reasons for death (including old age, sickness, accident, and suicide), and the difference between death and sleep; it then goes on to examine feelings about death and ways, both individual and cultural, of dealing with the loss of loved ones. . . . The simple watercolor illustrations help to make some scary situations more approachable. Quiet, respectful, and unthreatening, this will probably become a primary-grades standard on the subject." Bull Cent Child Books

Includes glossary

Krementz, Jill

How it feels when a parent dies. Knopf 1981 110p il hardcover o.p. pa $16

Grades: 4 5 6 7   155.9

1. Death 2. Bereavement

ISBN 0-394-75854-4 pa

LC 80-8808

This book is "a hopeful tribute to the healing power sustained by young survivors, who are competently interviewed and photographed in their widely varied reactions and situations. The subjects range in age from 7 to 16 and cope with a variety of deaths by suicide, accident, and illness. Adults helping children through a hard time will better understand their charges' problems through the honest opinions expressed here, and young readers might feel less alone." Booklist

Murphy, Patricia J.

Death; [by] Patricia J. Murphy. Heinemann Library 2008 32p il (Tough topics) lib bdg $25.36; pa $7.99

Grades: PreK K 1 2 3   155.9

1. Death 2. Bereavement

ISBN 978-1-4034-9778-9 lib bdg; 978-1-4034-9783-3 pa

LC 2007007230

The author "discusses what death is, how it can happen, how it affects people, funerals and memories, and different ways of coping with such loss. . . . The two-page chapters include full-color photos and two paragraphs of text that are frank yet sensitive in their approach." SLJ

Includes glossary and bibliographical references

Raschka, Christopher

The purple balloon; [by] Chris Raschka. Schwartz & Wade Books 2007 un il $16.99; lib bdg $19.99

Grades: PreK K 1 2   155.9

1. Death 2. Terminally ill

ISBN 978-0-375-84146-0; 0-375-84146-6; 978-0-375-94259-4 lib bdg; 0-375-94259-9 lib bdg

LC 2006-23725

"Dying is the subject of this sensitive and somber book intended for terminally ill children and their families and friends. . . . The focus is first on how support from those around us can help 'make dying not so hard' for an older person. The same case is then made for a child who faces death. . . . The illustrations are appropriately subdued, with balloons as the characters, all of them given loving and supportive faces and postures. . . . The book ends with suggestions on how to help a friend who is terminally ill." Booklist

Simons, Rae

Survival skills; how to handle life's catastrophes. Mason Crest Publishers 2009 128p il (Survivors: ordinary people, extraordinary circumstances) lib bdg $24.95

Grades: 5 6 7 8   155.9

1. Life skills 2. Survival skills

ISBN 978-1-4222-0456-6 lib bdg; 1-4222-0456-1 lib bdg

LC 2008-50320

"Begins with a brief and accessible discussion of the psychology of stress and its role in adolescence, and offers twelve pieces of advice for overcoming difficult experiences and catastrophes. . . . [This book features] important, and sometimes complex, information in an easy-to-read format, offering high gloss photographs, marginal glossary notes, concept definitions, a bibliography, and further reading reccommendations." Voice Youth Advocates

Includes glossary and bibliographical references

158   Applied psychology

Andrews, Linda Wasmer

Meditation; [by] Linda Wasmer Andrews. F. Watts 2004 79p (Life balance) $19.50; pa $6.95

Grades: 5 6 7 8   158

1. Meditation 2. Meditation -- Juvenile literature

ISBN 0-531-12219-0; 0-531-16609-0 pa

LC 2003-7153

"Andrews emphasizes that meditation is not a flaky practice, or a particularly religious one, but one that's designed to reduce stress and help individuals manage their lives. Four chapters explain the why and how of meditating. . . . [This offers] solid, easy-to-understand information" SLJ

Includes bibliographical references

Burstein, John

I said no! refusal skills. Crabtree Pub. Co. 2010 32p il (Slim Goodbody's life skills 101) lib bdg $26.60; pa $8.95

Grades: 1 2 3 4 5   158

1. Peer pressure 2. Decision making 3. Risk-taking (Psychology)

ISBN 978-0-7787-4789-5 lib bdg; 0-7787-4789-1 lib bdg; 978-0-7787-4805-2 pa; 0-7787-4805-7 pa

LC 2009022850

In this book children are taught to understand when and why they need to say "no," and how to refuse and still keep their friends

This book offers "clear and simple advice for children and [provides] adults with springboards for discussion and role-playing. [It has] appealing color photographs of a variety of types of kids, . . . opening scenarios, concrete coping suggestions, and solid reasoning." SLJ

Includes bibliographical references

Crist, James J.

What to do when you're sad & lonely; a guide for kids. [by] James J. Crist. Free Spirit Pub. 2006 124p il pa $9.95

Grades: 4 5 6 7   158
    1. Solitude 2. Depression (Psychology)
    ISBN 978-1-57542-189-6 pa; 1-57542-189-5 pa
                                                 LC 2005021794

"Advising his audience to read this book and work through negative feelings with an adult, Crist describes sad and lonely feelings, distinguishes them from more serious conditions such as depression, and then suggests 'Blues Busters' and ways to ask for help. . . . Crist's clear explanations and simple techniques . . . are relevant for both children and adults." Voice Youth Advocates

Includes bibliographical references

What to do when you're scared & worried; a guide for kids. [by] James Crist. Free Spirit Pub. 2004 128p il pa $9.95

Grades: 4 5 6 7   158
    1. Fear 2. Worry
    ISBN 1-57542-153-4

"Part one deals with normal anxiety, offering detailed steps for developing 10 coping mechanisms. Expert help is needed to deal with the more serious problems discussed in Part two (e.g., phobias, separation anxiety, obsessive-compulsive disorder). Throughout, the author provides information, case histories, and coping skills in a manner that is both reassuring and encouraging. . . . Illustrations lighten the tone of the subject matter." SLJ

Includes bibliographical references

Fox, Annie

Real friends vs. the other kind. Free Spirit Pub. 2009 90p il pa $9.99

Grades: 5 6 7 8   158
    1. Friendship 2. Interpersonal relations
    ISBN 1-57542-319-7 pa; 978-1-57542-319-7 pa
                                                 LC 2008031368

"Jack, Abby, Mateo, Jen, Chris, and Michelle are the middle school students of various ethnicities who take readers through this slim, interactive guide. Chapters cover such topics as friendship dilemmas, so-called friends, when friendships aren't working, crushes, and making new friends. Each chapter opens with a scene played out by the students in cartoon panels. Next, bits of text, along with a multitude of side boxes, address the topic at hand. . . . Lists of questions are offered, along with the answers. There's a lot packed into this colorful title that falls somewhere between self-help and peer advice." SLJ

McIntyre, Thomas

The behavior survival guide for kids; how to make good choices and stay out of trouble. [by] Thomas McIntyre. Free Spirit Pub. 2003 167p pa $14.95

Grades: 5 6 7 8   158
    1. Conduct of life 2. Interpersonal relations 3. Problem children
    ISBN 1-57542-132-1
                                                 LC 2003-4565

"The author provides skills and activities to learn and practice so that new behaviors can replace those that have resulted in getting students into trouble. . . . Those motivated to make better choices for how they behave in school or with friends and family will find much to help them." Voice Youth Advocates

Moss, Wendy

Being me; a kid's guide to boosting confidence and self-esteem. by Wendy L. Moss. Magination Press 2010 112p il $14.95; pa $9.95

Grades: 5 6 7 8   158
    1. Self-esteem 2. Self-confidence
    ISBN 978-1-4338-0883-8; 1-4338-0883-8; 978-1-4338-0884-5 pa; 1-4338-0884-6 pa
                                                 LC 2010014384

"Moss encourages her young audience to concentrate on two areas: focusing on inner self-esteem and building social confidence. Through procedure and practice . . . Moss reminds kids that real confidence doesn't come from being the smartest, prettiest, or the most popular one in the room but from the comfort one has with him- or herself. . . . Moss' offering gives great tips for the truly interested." Booklist

Rogers, Fred

Making friends; photographs by Jim Judkis. Putnam 1987 un il hardcover o.p. pa $6.99

Grades: PreK K 1   158
    1. Friendship
    ISBN 0-698-11409-4 pa
                                                 LC 86-12353

"From its opening lines ('When people like each other and like to do things together, they're friends. Can you think of someone who's your friend?'), Rogers's inimitable voice reaches out to his small readers with understanding and reassurance. He describes the pleasures of friendship as well as potential problem areas. . . . Judkis's large color photos capture the range of emotions Rogers writes about." Publ Wkly

Seuss, Dr., 1904-1991

Oh, the places you'll go! Random House 1990 un il $17; lib bdg $20.99

Grades: PreK K 1 2   158
    1. Stories in rhyme 2. Success -- Juvenile literature
    ISBN 0-679-80527-3; 0-679-90527-8 lib bdg
                                                 LC 89-36892

Advice in rhyme for proceeding in life; weathering fear, loneliness, and confusion; and being in charge of your actions

"The combination of the lively text and wacky, offbeat pictures will delight both children and their parents." Child Book Rev Serv

158.2 Interpersonal relations

Brown, Laurene Krasny

How to be a friend; a guide to making friends and keeping them. [by] Laurie Krasny Brown and Marc Brown. Little, Brown 1998 31p il $15.99; pa $6.99

Grades: K 1 2 3   **158.2**

1. Friendship 2. Friendship in children -- Juvenile literature

ISBN 0-316-10913-4; 0-316-11153-8 pa

LC 97-10179

Dinosaur characters illustrate the value of friends, how to make friends, and how to be and not to be a good friend

"Dialogue balloons personalize, enrich, and add humor to the main text.... How to Be a Friend will be very useful to parents, teachers, and other caregivers of young children." Horn Book

170 Ethics (Moral philosophy)

MacGregor, Cynthia

Think for yourself; a kid's guide to solving life's dilemmas and other sticky problems. by Cynthia MacGregor; illustrator: Paula Becker. 2nd ed.; Lobster Press 2008 142p il pa $14.95

Grades: 3 4 5 6   **170**

1. Ethics 2. Conduct of life

ISBN 978-1-897073-90-2 pa; 1-897073-90-9 pa

First published 2003

This book "presents 53 real-life dilemmas that 21st century children might face. Topics range from cyberbullying, chat rooms, and online porn to situations with friends, family and adults.... Each dilemma is ... followed by three questions.... The questions encourage readers to examine why the predicaments are dilemmas, to analyze possible solutions, and to arrive at acceptable decisions.... This indispensible book is recommended for school and public library collections." Libr Media Connect

Parker, Victoria

Making choices; [by] Vic Parker. Heinemann Library 2010 32p il (Exploring citizenship) $25.36; pa $7.99

Grades: 1 2 3 4   **170**

1. Decision making 2. Choice (Psychology)

ISBN 978-1-4329-3317-3; 1-4329-3317-5; 978-1-4329-3325-8 pa; 1-4329-3325-6 pa

LC 2008-55310

This describes the different choices and decisions people have to make every day and why it is important to think for yourself, what to do if you are bullied, and how to make the right choices for your health.

"The text presents a multitude of realistic situations to which young children will relate. There are 'Think About It' fact boxes and checklists that aid in understanding and that will spark discussion. All are filled with captioned, color photographs that relate to the text. The information is relevant and current.... Strongly consider this." Libr Media Connect

Includes glossary and bibliographical references

172 Applied ethics

Halperin, Wendy Anderson

Peace; Wendy Anderson Halperin. Atheneum Books for Young Readers 2013 40 p. $16.99

Grades: K 1 2   **172**

1. Picture books for children 2. Peace -- Juvenile literature 3. Taoism -- Juvenile literature

ISBN 0689825528; 9780689825521; 9781442467873

LC 2012030589

This picture book, by Wendy Anderson Halperin, offers a "compilation of ... illustrations and wisely chosen words [which] reveals the heart of where peace truly must originate: within ourselves. ... Intricate artwork, with tiny, precisely rendered details of life across the globe, complements ... text that includes quotations from famous peacemakers." (Publisher's note)

174 Occupational ethics

Hartman, Eve

Science ethics and controversies; [by] Eve Hartman and Wendy Meshbesher. Raintree 2009 48p il (Sci-hi: life science) $31.43; pa $8.99

Grades: 5 6 7 8   **174**

1. Science -- Ethical aspects

ISBN 978-1-4109-3330-0; 1-4109-3330-X; 978-1-4109-3338-6 pa; 1-4109-3338-5 pa

LC 2009003475

In this introduction to science ethics and controversies "clear language, embedded definitions, and interesting examples illustrate abstract concepts through both text and well-chosen photographs. ... [It] discusses topics such as global warming and animal research, and their implications for decision-making by scientists, policy makers, and voters. Because so many issues are raised in this book, it will be especially useful as a research starter in both science and social-studies classes.... [The] book also includes suggested activities to test ideas as well as a thorough glossary and a Webliography." SLJ

Includes glossary and bibliographical references

175 Ethics of recreation, leisure, public performances, communication

Barraclough, Sue

Fair play. Heinemann Library 2010 32p il (Exploring citizenship) $25.36; pa $7.99

Grades: 1 2 3 4   **175**

1. Respect 2. Sportsmanship

ISBN 978-1-4329-3313-5; 1-4329-3313-2; 978-1-4329-3321-0 pa; 1-4329-3321-3 pa

LC 2008-55301

"The text presents a multitude of realistic situations to which young children will relate. There are 'Think About It' fact boxes and checklists that aid in understanding and that will spark discussion. All are filled with captioned, color photographs that relate to the text. The information is relevant and current. ... Strongly consider this." Libr Media Connect

Includes glossary and bibliographical references

177 Ethics of social relations

Barraclough, Sue

Sharing. Heinemann Library 2010 32p il (Exploring citizenship) $25.36; pa $7.99
Grades: 1 2 3 4   177
   1. Kindness 2. Etiquette
   ISBN 978-1-4329-3312-8; 1-4329-3312-4; 978-1-
   4329-3320-3 pa; 1-4329-3320-5 pa
                                        LC 2008-55300
   "The text presents a multitude of realistic situations to which young children will relate. There are 'Think About It' fact boxes and checklists that aid in understanding and that will spark discussion. All are filled with captioned, color photographs that relate to the text. The information is relevant and current. . . . Strongly consider this." Libr Media Connect
   Includes glossary and bibliographical references

Parker, Victoria

Good relationships. Heinemann Library 2008 32p il (Exploring citizenship) $25.36; pa $7.99
Grades: 1 2 3 4   177
   1. Interpersonal relations
   ISBN 978-1-4329-3316-6; 1-4329-3316-7; 978-1-
   4329-3324-1 pa; 1-4329-3324-8 pa
                                        LC 2008-55306
   This describes how important it is to get along with the people around us and what can happen when people do not try to listen to or understand each other.
   "The text presents a multitude of realistic situations to which young children will relate. There are 'Think About It' fact boxes and checklists that aid in understanding and that will spark discussion. All are filled with captioned, color photographs that relate to the text. The information is relevant and current. . . . Strongly consider this." Libr Media Connect
   Includes glossary and bibliographical references

Pryor, Kimberley Jane

Cooperation; by Kimberley Jane Pryor. Marshall Cavendish Benchmark 2008 32p il (Values) lib bdg $19.95
Grades: 1 2 3   177
   1. Cooperation 2. Conduct of life
   ISBN 978-0-7614-3124-4 lib bdg; 0-7614-3124-1
   lib bdg
                                        LC 2008001617
   In this book "cooperation is described as following instructions, sharing, and solving problems. [This] value is considered in a direct manner, which makes the [book] useful for the younger part of the age range, while the [title] will provide springboards for discussion among the older children. The brief [text is] accompanied by attractive, captioned color photographs." SLJ

Honesty; by Kimberley Jane Pryor. Marshall Cavendish Benchmark 2008 32p il (Values) lib bdg $19.95
Grades: 1 2 3   177
   1. Honesty 2. Conduct of life
   ISBN 978-0-7614-3125-1 lib bdg; 0-7614-3125-X
   lib bdg
                                        LC 2008001673
   This "well-executed [book provides a] simple [definition] of [honesty], examples of how it can be demonstrated,

and a breakdown of the behavior into individual actions. . . . . The brief [text is] accompanied by attractive, captioned color photographs." SLJ

Kindness; by Kimberley Jane Pryor. Marshall Cavendish Benchmark 2008 32p il (Values) lib bdg $19.95
Grades: 1 2 3   177
   1. Kindness 2. Conduct of life
   ISBN 978-0-7614-3126-8 lib bdg; 0-7614-3126-8
   lib bdg
                                        LC 2008001661
   This "begins with a bulleted explanation of the word 'values.'. . . The rest of the text describes [kindness]. . . . The author then goes on to discuss examples of behaviors and emotions such as being kind to family and friends, feeling sympathy, and caring. The accompanying color photographs, showing children that appear to be unposed, are age-appropriate, culturally diverse, and complement the [narrative]." SLJ

Respect; by Kimberley Jane Pryor. Marshall Cavendish Benchmark 2008 32p il (Values) lib bdg $19.95
Grades: 1 2 3   177
   1. Respect 2. Conduct of life
   ISBN 978-0-7614-3128-2 lib bdg; 0-7614-3128-4
   lib bdg
                                        LC 2008001669
   This "begins with a bulleted explanation of the word 'values.' . . . The rest of the text describes [respect]. . . . The author then goes on to discuss examples of behaviors and emotions such as being kind to family and friends, feeling sympathy, and caring. The accompanying color photographs, showing children that appear to be unposed, are age-appropriate, culturally diverse, and complement the [narrative]." SLJ

Tolerance; by Kimberley Jane Pryor. Marshall Cavendish Benchmark 2008 32p il (Values) lib bdg $19.95
Grades: 1 2 3   177
   1. Toleration 2. Conduct of life
   ISBN 978-0-7614-3129-9 lib bdg; 0-7614-3129-2
   lib bdg
                                        LC 2008001672
   This "begins with a bulleted explanation of the word 'values.' . . . The rest of the text describes [tolerance]. . . . The author then goes on to discuss examples of behaviors and emotions such as being kind to family and friends, feeling sympathy, and caring. The accompanying color photographs, showing children that appear to be unposed, are age-appropriate, culturally diverse, and complement the [narrative]." SLJ

Verdick, Elizabeth

Words are not for hurting; illustrated by Marieka Heinlen. Free Spirit Pub. 2004 33p il pa $11.95; bd bk $7.95
Grades: K 1 2   177
   1. Etiquette 2. Conversation 3. Interpersonal relations
   4. Etiquette for children and teenagers
   ISBN 1-57542-156-9 pa; 1-57542-155-0 bd bk
                                        LC 2003-21273
   Encourages toddlers and preschoolers to express themselves using helpful, not hurtful, words. Includes a note for parents and caregivers

"The brightly colored drawings, which bring the minimal text to life, are especially effective at showing the range of emotions children experience when they hear unkind language. An excellent resource for sharing at home and at preschools." Booklist

179 Other ethical norms

Barraclough, Sue
Honesty. Heinemann Library 2010 32p il (Exploring citizenship) $25.36; pa $7.99
Grades: 1 2 3 4   179
1. Honesty 2. Citizenship
ISBN 978-1-4329-3311-1; 1-4329-3311-6; 978-1-4329-3319-7 pa; 1-4329-3319-1 pa
LC 2008-55297
"The text presents a multitude of realistic situations to which young children will relate. There are 'Think About It' fact boxes and checklists that aid in understanding and that will spark discussion. All are filled with captioned, color photographs that relate to the text. The information is relevant and current. . . . Strongly consider this." Libr Media Connect
Includes glossary and bibliographical references

Belanger, Jeff
What it's like; to climb Mount Everest, blast off into space, survive a tornado, and other extraordinary stories. Sterling Pub. Co. 2010 136p il pa $9.95
Grades: 5 6 7 8   179
1. Courage 2. Anecdotes 3. Adventure and adventurers
ISBN 978-1-4027-6711-1; 1-4027-6711-0
LC 2009040875
"This illustrated collection presents short, first-person accounts of high-octane adventures—and, in some cases, personal disasters—by the people who actually experienced them. . . . The stories are told in present-tense, straightforward language, filled in with many pertinent and fascinating details. . . . The exciting action and the entries' short length will draw reluctant readers, as will the many color photographs, which are imaginatively laid out. This attractive package will be an easy sell." Booklist

Burstein, John
Can we get along? dealing with differences. Crabtree Pub. Company 2010 32p il (Slim Goodbody's life skills 101) lib bdg $26.60; pa $8.95
Grades: 1 2 3 4 5   179
1. Toleration
ISBN 978-0-7787-4788-8 lib bdg; 0-7787-4788-3 lib bdg; 978-0-7787-4804-5 pa; 0-7787-4804-9 pa
LC 2009023634
This book helps students understand the need and importance for tolerance, and the steps they can take to increase peace in their lives and in the world.
These books offer "clear and simple advice for children and [provides] adults with springboards for discussion and roleplaying. All have appealing color photographs of a variety of types of kids, . . . opening scenarios, concrete coping suggestions, and solid reasoning." SLJ
Includes bibliographical references

Obama, Barack, 1961-
Of thee I sing; a letter to my daughters. illustrated by Loren Long. Alfred A. Knopf 2010 un il $17.99; lib bdg $20.99
Grades: 1 2 3 4   179
1. Conduct of life 2. Heroes and heroines
ISBN 0-375-83527-X; 0-375-93527-4 lib bdg; 978-0-375-83527-8; 978-0-375-93527-5 lib bdg
"In characteristically measured prose, the 44th President introduces 13 American icons and heroes as exemplars of personal virtues, from Georgia O'Keeffe (creativity) and Jackie Robinson (courage) to Helen Keller (strength) and Cesar Chavez (inspiration). . . . Long's superb technical gifts and gentle sense of humor shine in the pictures. . . . [This offers] thought-provoking choices and commentary. . . . This [is a] stately outing." SLJ

Parker, Victoria
Acting responsibly; [by] Vic Parker. Heinemann Library 2010 32p il (Exploring citizenship) $25.36; pa $7.99
Grades: 1 2 3 4   179
1. Responsibility
ISBN 978-1-4329-3315-9; 1-4329-3315-9; 978-1-4329-3323-4 pa; 1-4329-3323-X pa
LC 2008-55305
This describes how and why to behave in a responsible way
"The text presents a multitude of realistic situations to which young children will relate. There are 'Think About It' fact boxes and checklists that aid in understanding and that will spark discussion. All are filled with captioned, color photographs that relate to the text. The information is relevant and current. . . . Strongly consider this." Libr Media Connection
Includes glossary and bibliographical references

Pryor, Kimberley Jane
Courage; by Kimberley Jane Pryor. Marshall Cavendish Benchmark 2008 32p il (Values) lib bdg $19.95
Grades: 1 2 3   179
1. Courage 2. Conduct of life
ISBN 978-0-7614-3131-2 lib bdg; 0-7614-3131-4 lib bdg
LC 2008001662
This "well-executed [book provides a] simple [definition] of [courage], examples of how it can be demonstrated, and a breakdown of the behavior into individual actions. . . . The brief [text is] accompanied by attractive, captioned color photographs." SLJ

183 Sophistic, Socratic, related Greek philosophies

Jun Lim
Socrates; the public conscience of Golden Age Athens. by Jun Lim. 1st ed. Rosen Pub. 2006 112 p. col. ill., col. map (library) $34.60
Grades: 5 6 7 8   183
1. Philosophers -- Juvenile literature
ISBN 1404205640; 9781404205642
LC 2005012259

This book by Jun Lim is part of the Library of Greek Philosophers series and looks at Socrates. "This series introduces students to the great philosophers and mathematicians who helped shape the intellectual world in modern times." Examples are given "of the kinds of knowledge these men taught to their students. The early years, travels, and education of each man are told, and the contributions to society are detailed in the context of the times." (Library Media Connection)

Includes bibliographical references (p. 107-108) and index.

200 RELIGION

200 Religion

Ajmera, Maya

Faith; [by] Maya Ajmera, Magda Nakassis, and Cynthia Pon. Charlesbridge 2009 un il lib bdg $16.95; pa $7.95
Grades: 1 2 3   **200**

1. Religion 2. Religions
ISBN 978-1-58089-177-6 lib bdg; 1-58089-177-2 lib bdg; 978-1-58089-178-3 pa; 1-58089-178-0 pa
LC 2008008282

This "explores through full-color photographs the many ways in which the world celebrates and practices religious belief, highlighting the common threads—praying and meditating, chants and songs, holy books, cleansing, holy places, holidays and festivals, important events, dress, food and drink, and helping others. Spare text accompanies the pictures of children and identifies the specific religion and practices. . . . The excellent photographs are clear and colorful and invite careful observation." SLJ

Buller, Laura

A **faith** like mine; a celebration of the world's religions . . , seen through the eyes of children. DK Pub. 2005 80p il maps $19.99
Grades: 4 5 6 7   **200**

1. Religions
ISBN 0-7566-1177-6

"Buller introduces Hinduism, Islam, Judaism, Christianity, Buddhism, and Sikhism through the eyes of children. . . . The amount of information is adequate and straightforward and focuses on aspects of the religion that would appeal to children. The clear, vibrant photographs are especially inviting." SLJ

Osborne, Mary Pope

★ **One** world, many religions; the ways we worship. Knopf 1996 86p il map $19.95
Grades: 4 5 6 7   **200**

1. Religions
ISBN 0-679-83930-5
LC 96-836

"The presentation is notable for its respect to each group, succinctness, and clarity. . . . The artful, full-page, color and black-and-white photographs tell much of the story." SLJ

Includes glossary and bibliographical references

What do you believe? religion and faith in the world today. DK Pub. 2011 96p il map $16.99
Grades: 4 5 6 7   **200**

1. Religions 2. Philosophy
ISBN 978-0-7566-7228-7; 0-7566-7228-7

"This extensive guidebook covers the beliefs and history of the world's major religions. Focusing in particular on Buddhism, Christianity, Hinduism, Islam, Judaism, and Sikhism, the book also explores atheism and agnosticism, indigenous belief systems, East Asian religions, philosophy, and morality. . . . The graphically bold format—which mixes photographs, cartoons, and sidebars—will keep kids' attention, whether they are seeking truth, knowledge, or more to ponder." Publ Wkly

201 Specific aspects of religion

Hamilton, Virginia

★ **In** the beginning; creation stories from around the world; told by Virginia Hamilton; illustrated by Barry Moser. Harcourt Brace Jovanovich 1988 161p il hardcover o.p. pa $20
Grades: 5 6 7 8   **201**

1. Creation 2. Mythology
ISBN 0-15-238740-4; 0-15-238742-0 pa
LC 88-6211

A Newbery Medal honor book, 1989

"Hamilton has gathered 25 creation myths from various cultures and retold them in language true to the original. Images from the tales are captured in Moser's 42 full-page illustrations, tantalizing oil paintings that are rich with somber colors and striking compositions. Included in the collection are the familiar stories (biblical creation stories, Greek and Roman myths), and some that are not so familiar (tales from the Australian aborigines, various African and native American tribes, as well as from countries like Russia, China, and Iceland). At the end of each tale, Hamilton provides a brief commentary on the story's origin and originators." Booklist

Includes bibliographical references

Reinhart, Matthew

Gods & heroes; [by] Matthew Reinhart and Robert Sabuda. Candlewick Press 2010 un il (Encyclopedia mythologica) $29.99
Grades: K 1 2 3   **201**

1. Mythology 2. Gods and goddesses 3. Pop-up books
ISBN 978-0-7636-3171-0; 0-7636-3171-X
LC 2009-15140

This is "a global tour of gods and other deities. Multiple stories unfold on each page within layered tableaus in miniature booklets, like treasures to be unveiled. . . . A fun and engaging assemblage that seamlessly marries its form and content." Publ Wkly

204 Religious experience, life, practice

Pelham, Sophie

Food and faith; [by] Susan Reuben and Sophie Pelham. Frances Lincoln Children's Books 2011 45 p. ill. $18.99

Grades: 3 4 5   204
1. Food 2. Religions 3. Religious holidays
ISBN 1845079868; 9781845079864

Author Susan Reuben presents a cookbook for "people of various ethnic backgrounds [and religious celebrations] . . . [The book discusses] the Jewish Shabbat, as well as Chanukah, Rosh Hashanah, Yom Kippur, Purim and Passover, [in addition to] the Muslim Eid ul Fitr . . . and Christingle . . . Recipes for one representative dish per religion are included, [such as] Hinduism and Sikhism." (Kirkus)

220   Bible

Brown, Alan
The **Bible** and Christianity; by Alan Brown. Smart Apple Media 2003 30p il (Sacred texts) $27.10
Grades: 5 6 7 8   220
1. Christianity 2. Bible (as subject)
ISBN 1-58340-243-8

LC 2003-41645
Explains how the Old and New Testaments came to be part of the Bible used by Christians and discusses some of the important messages found in the holy scriptures.

"Colorful strips of symbolic patterns adorn the pages and accent the informative text boxes. . . . The clear captioned . . . illustrations (photos and historical art) provide additional background." Horn Book Guide

Includes glossary

220.5   Modern versions and translations

The **Bible**: Authorized King James Version; with an introduction and notes by Robert Carroll and Stephen Prickett. Oxford University Press 2008 lxxiv, 1039, 248, 445p il map (Oxford world's classics) pa $18.95
Grades: 5 6 7 8 9 10 11 12 Adult   220.5
ISBN 978-0-19-953594-1

LC 2008-273825
This Oxford World's Classics version first published 1997.
The authorized or King James Version originally published 1611.
Includes bibliographical references

The **Holy** Bible; containing the Old and New Testaments with the Apocryphal/Deuterocanonical books: New Revised Standard Version. Oxford University Press 1989 xxi, 996, 298, 284p map $29.99
Grades: 5 6 7 8 9 10 11 12 Adult   220.5
ISBN 0-19-528330-9; 978-0-19-528330-3

LC 90-222105
"Intended for public reading, congregational worship, private study, instruction, and meditation, it attempts to be as literal as possible while following standard American English usage, avoids colloquialism, and prefers simple, direct terms and phrases." Sheehy. Guide to Ref Books. 10th edition. suppl

220.8   Nonreligious subjects treated in Bible

Animals of the Bible; a picture book by Dorothy P. Lathrop; with text selected by Helen Dean Fish from the King James Bible. Harper & Row 1987 65p il $17.95; lib bdg $18.89
Grades: 1 2 3 4   220.8
1. Animals 2. Bible--Natural history
ISBN 0-397-31536-8; 0-397-30047-6 lib bdg
A reissue of the title first published 1937 by Lippincott
Awarded the Caldecott Medal, 1938

"Dorothy Lathrop's love and understanding of animals, the sensitiveness and joy with which she draws them, make her the ideal artist for such a volume. It is more than a beautiful picture book, for she has studied the fauna and flora of Bible lands until each animal and bird, each flower and tree, is true to natural history." NY Times Book Rev

220.9   Geography, history, chronology, persons of Bible lands in Bible times

Barnes, Trevor
The **Kingfisher** children's illustrated Bible; illustrated by Vanessa Card . . . [et al.] 2011 256p il map $14.99
Grades: 3 4 5 6   220.9
1. Bible stories
ISBN 978-0-7534-6490-8; 0-7534-6490-X
"In the straightforward style of a practiced storyteller, Barnes recreates the ancient world of the Israelites peopled by patriarchs, prophets, kings, the Messiah, and his disciples. Beginning with Creation and concluding the first portion of the book with a selection of psalms and proverbs, he pays homage to key Old Testament figures. . . . The second section focuses on the New Testament stories of Jesus' life and teachings and the spread of Christianity. . . . The one to two-page stories flow together seamlessly from Genesis to Revelation. Each entry includes a citation to the corresponding scripture passages and is complemented by illustrations replete with historically correct cultural details. A supplementary reference section featuring commentary, maps, and captioned photographs puts the sacred stories in historical and geographical context." SLJ

Brown, Laaren
The **Children's** illustrated Jewish Bible; retold by Laaren Brown & Lenny Hort; illustrated by Eric Thomas. rev ed; DK Pub. 2007 192p il map $19.99
Grades: 1 2 3 4 5 6   220.9
1. Bible stories
ISBN 978-0-7566-2665-5
"This is indeed a Jewish Bible, written by Jewish authors, and successful in its inclusion of many popular stories retold in a lively, child-friendly style. Realistic and colorful pencil-drawn illustrations add to the telling, and as a treat for curious minds, the small photographs on the sidebars are really interesting." SLJ

De Paola, Tomie
★ **Tomie** dePaola's book of Bible stories. Putnam 1989 127p il $24.99; pa $12.99

Grades: 2 3 4 5 **220.9**
1. Bible stories
ISBN 0-399-21690-1; 0-698-11923-1 pa

LC 88-26468

"A collection of 17 stories from the Old Testament, 15 from the New Testament, and 4 psalms. The text is from the New International Version. . . . De Paola uses the text as written with some abridgement to make the stories an appropriate length. Done in his typical style, the illustrations feature stylized people and objects. . . . There are several illustrations for each story, many of which are full page, and most make dramatic use of color. The large format enhances the impact of the pictures." SLJ

Delval, Marie-Helene
The **Bible** for young children; [illustrated by] Götting. Eerdmans Books for Young Readers 2010 88p il $16.50
Grades: K 1 2 3 **220.9**
1. Bible stories
ISBN 978-0-8028-5383-7; 0-8028-5383-8

LC 2010005164

Original French edition 2002

"This introduction to the Christian Bible uses simple format that is accessible both to younger children and new readers. Forty Bible stories are retold with just a few sentences for each story or incident. . . . The text is set in large type on the left-hand pages against an attractive corresponding illustration on the right-hand pages. The paintings used for the illustrations use a variety of perspectives and a palette of deep shades that suggests an ancient setting. The clear and simple format provides an accessible introduction to major stories and characters in the Bible." Kirkus
Includes bibliographical references

Graham, Lorenz B.
How God fix Jonah; by Lorenz Graham; illustrated by Ashley Bryan; foreword by W.E.B. Du Bois; new foreword by Effie Lee Morris. Boyds Mills Press 2000 156p il $17.95
Grades: 4 5 6 7 **220.9**
1. Bible stories 2. Folklore -- West Africa
ISBN 1-56397-698-6

A newly illustrated edition of the title first published 1946 by Reynal & Hitchcock

"Ashley Bryan's magnificent black-and-white woodblock illustrations lend an added power and dignity to the text of this most unusual and captivating book." Horn Book Guide

Lottridge, Celia Barker
Stories from Adam and Eve to Ezekiel; retold from the Bible. by Celia Barker Lottridge; illustrated by Gary Clement. Douglas & McIntyre/Groundwood 2004 192p il $24.95
Grades: 4 5 6 7 **220.9**
1. Bible stories
ISBN 0-88899-490-7

"Lottridge uses her storyteller's ear to bring ancient stories from the Hebrew Bible to a young audience, tailoring them to make them more age appropriate. . . . The numerous, well-drawn ink-and-watercolor illustrations are reminiscent of Warwick Hutton's work. Some pictures . . . are quite spectacular." Booklist

Osborne, Mary Pope
The **Random** House book of Bible stories; by Mary Pope Osborne and Natalie Pope Boyce; illustrated by Michael Welply. Random House 2009 165p il $24.99; lib bdg $27.99
Grades: 2 3 4 5 **220.9**
1. Bible stories
ISBN 978-0-375-82281-0; 0-375-82281-X; 978-0-375-92281-7 lib bdg; 0-375-92281-4 lib bdg

LC 2007047308

"The retellers do a credible job of adapting more than 50 Old and New Testament selections in sequential order. Each story is related in language that evokes biblical storytelling, giving the collection the feel of a real Bible with the accessibility of a shared read-aloud. . . . Welply's realistic illustrations . . . will help readers contextualize the place and time." SLJ

Pirotta, Saviour
Children's stories from the Bible; stories retold. color art by Anne Yvonne Gilbert; monochrome art by Ian Andrew. Templar Books 2009 292p il map $19.99
Grades: 4 5 6 **220.9**
1. Bible stories
ISBN 978-0-7636-4551-9; 0-7636-4551-6

LC 2008944069

Recounts over seventy stories from the Bible, including "The Walls of Jericho," "The Prodigal Son," "Jesus and the Children," and "Rahab and the Spies"

Pirotta "adds, for example, kid-friendly details about the weather on the day Mary and Joseph travel to Bethlehem, and he resolves each story with a tidy ending. Softly textured illustrations enhance the mood of the tales." Horn Book Guide

Watts, Murray
The **Bible** for children from Good Books; retold by Murray Watts; illustrated by Helen Cann. Good Bks. (Pa.) 2002 352p il map $23.99
Grades: 3 4 5 6 **220.9**
1. Bible stories
ISBN 1-56148-362-1

LC 2002-20243

A collection of approximately two hundred and fifty illustrated stories from the Old and New Testaments, retold for children

"Watts' retellings from the Old and New Testaments are vivid and evocative. . . . The handsome pictures and decorated borders employ a rich palette of colors and patterns, giving the book a contemporary look." Booklist

221.9 Geography, history, chronology, persons of Old Testament lands in Old Testament times

Hanft, Joshua E.
Miracles of the Bible; by Josh Hanft; illustrated by Seymour Chwast. Blue Apple Books 2007 un il $16.95
Grades: K 1 2 **221.9**
1. Miracles 2. Bible stories
ISBN 978-1-59354-617-5; 1-59354-617-3

LC 2007007093

This retells "such familiar Bible stories as 'Daniel in the Lion's Den' and 'Jonah and the Fish' and 'Noah's Ark.' He also includes such dramatic episodes as the parting of the Red Sea and the conquests of Samson and David. . . . It's Chwast's full-page-and-more compositions, rendered in creamy, pastel-toned ink-and-watercolor that stand out—literally. A number of these illustrations, in Chwast's signature comics-influenced style, appear on foldout pages that boldly expand the scene, vertically or horizontally. Children will likely flock to this hands-on reading experience." Publ Wkly

Sasso, Sandy Eisenberg

But God remembered; stories of women from creation to the promised land. illustrated by Bethanne Andersen. Jewish Lights Pub. 1995 31p il $16.95

Grades: 3 4 5   **221.9**

1. Bible stories 2. Women in the Bible
ISBN 1-879045-43-5

LC 95-3591

"Although part of the pleasure of the book lies in its strong feminist voice, Sasso also tells good stories; and these will have even more value for the discussions they can generate. Andersen's evocative paintings are beautiful additions to this carefully designed book." Booklist

Ward, Elaine M.

Old Testament women; [by] Elaine Ward. Enchanted Lion 2004 32p il (Art revelations) $18.95

Grades: 5 6 7 8   **221.9**

1. Bible stories 2. Women in the Bible
ISBN 1-59270-011-X

These Old Testament stories about women include "explanatory paragraphs, sidebars, and captions by the author. Art masterpieces . . . illustrate each story. . . . The captions provide background on the artist and the significance of each painting or mosaic. . . . The 18 women . . . include Rachel, Leah, Ruth, and Bathsheba. . . . Bosch, Botticelli, and Poussin are among the painters whose work appears here. . . . Visually stunning." SLJ

222   Historical books of Old Testament

Feiler, Bruce S.

★ **Walking** the Bible; an illustrated journey for kids through the greatest stories ever told. by Bruce Feiler; illustrated by Sasha Meret. HarperCollinsPublishers 2004 108p il map $16.99; lib bdg $17.89

Grades: 5 6 7 8   **222**

1. Authors 2. Journalists 3. Bible (as subject) 4. Travel writers
ISBN 0-06-051117-6; 0-06-051118-4 lib bdg

LC 2003-15861

The author describes his journey through places mentioned in the Old Testament

"In this version of his adult book with the same title (Morrow, 2001), Feiler largely succeeds in slimming rather than dumbing down his account of his trip across the 10,000-mile setting of the earliest Bible stories. The author's unpretentious . . . tone and astute pacing help make the volume accessible, and his sincerity is palpable." SLJ

Fischer, Chuck

★ **In** the beginning: the art of Genesis; a pop-up book. by Chuck Fischer. Little, Brown 2008 un il $35

Grades: 5 6 7 8   **222**

1. Bible stories 2. Religious art 3. Pop-up books
ISBN 978-0-316-11842-2; 0-316-11842-7

LC 2007045411

Fischer "presents an impressive, three-dimensional view of the Book of Genesis. . . . Fischer and his collaborators offer a Garden of Eden scene executed in an artistic style that recalls ancient tile work; a huge Noah's Ark landed atop a mountain; and a Tower of Babel impressively high. . . . The text, more commentary than story, is hidden in inset mini-books and is accompanied by reproductions of biblical masterpieces. . . . This book becomes more amazing as the pages are turned." Booklist

Hodges, Margaret

★ **Moses**; illustrated by Barry Moser. Harcourt, Inc. 2006 un il $16

Grades: 3 4 5   **222**

1. Prophets 2. Bible stories 3. Biblical characters 4. Biography, Individual -- Juvenile literature
ISBN 978-0-15-200946-5; 0-15-200946-9

Retells the story of Moses, from his birth and trip in a boat of bulrushes to his bringing of the Ten Commandments down from Mount Sinai.

"The venerable story of Moses gets a brisk yet compelling treatment by Hodges. . . . The book is beautiful to page through, with cream-colored pages and the bordered watercolors in Moser's signature style." Booklist

Jules, Jacqueline

Abraham's search for God; by Jacqueline Jules; illustrated by Natascia Ugliano. Kar-Ben Pub. 2007 un il lib bdg $17.95

Grades: K 1 2 3   **222**

1. God 2. Prophets 3. Biblical characters
ISBN 978-1-58013-243-5 lib bdg; 1-58013-243-X lib bdg

LC 2006027429

"Jules retells a midrash (a legend based on biblical text) in which the youthful Abraham discovers the concept of monotheism. Rejecting worship of unresponsive idols, Abraham spends time outdoors where he senses an unseen hand directing the movements of the moon, sun, storm, and rainbow. He concludes that 'God is everywhere. God is in everything. God is something we know with our hearts.' . . . The energetic pastel illustrations are cheerful and warm. . . . This simply told tale is an excellent introduction to the concept of monotheism, and would be a great discussion starter for talking about God." SLJ

Includes bibliographical references

Benjamin and the silver goblet; illustrated by Natascia Ugliano. Kar-Ben Pub. 2009 un il $17.95; pa $8.95

Grades: K 1 2 3   **222**

1. Bible stories
ISBN 978-0-8225-8757-6; 0-8225-8757-2; 978-0-8225-8758-3 pa; 0-8225-8758-0 pa

LC 2007048344

"When Jacob's sons arrive home from their travels in Egypt, they tell their father that one brother is being held as a hostage by the governor, who demands that they return with the youngest brother, Benjamin. The child, aching to see the world, is only too happy to oblige, though Jacob fears that he will lose this son the way he lost his eldest, Joseph, years before.... Well paced and well told, this familiar story makes itself fresh with a folkloric feel and a satisfying ending. Ugliano's heavily textured, colorful pastel illustrations ably support and extend the text." Kirkus

Miriam in the desert; illustrated by Natascia Ugliano. Kar-Ben Pub. 2010 un il lib bdg $17.95; pa $8.95
Grades: K 1 2 3   **222**
1. Bible stories 2. Biblical characters
ISBN 978-0-7613-4494-0 lib bdg; 0-7613-4494-2 lib bdg; 978-0-7613-4496-4 pa; 0-7613-4496-9 pa
LC 2009001874
"Miriam, Moses's sister, is featured in [this book] ... , offering encouragement and guidance to the Israelites as they continue their seemingly endless thirst- and hunger-filled journey through the desert following their escape from Egypt. . . . Deeply colored pastel-and-acrylic double-page paintings effectively portray a legendary biblical setting in a guileless and unsophisticated style. . . . They effectively match the original and simple dialogue-driven text." Kirkus

Sarah laughs; by Jacqueline Jules; illustrated by Natascia Ugliano. Kar-Ben Pub. 2008 32p il $17.95; pa $8.95
Grades: K 1 2 3   **222**
1. Prophets 2. Bible stories 3. Biblical characters
ISBN 978-0-8225-7216-9; 0-8225-7216-8; 978-0-8225-9934-0 pa; 0-8225-9934-1 pa
LC 2006039738
"Through poetic language and sweeping illustrations, this picture book tells the story of the biblical patriarch and matriarch Abraham and Sarah from Sarah's point of view. . . Sarah is portrayed as graceful, loving, and faithful. However, her sadness about remaining childless through the years has made her lose her bright laughter. With the birth of Isaac, when she is gray-haired and wrinkled, she finally laughs again.... This lovely retelling deserves a place on the shelves of any library that collects religious materials." SLJ
Includes bibliographical references

Kimmel, Eric A.
★ The **story** of Esther; retold by Eric A. Kimmel; illustrated by Jill Weber. Holiday House 2010 un il $16.95
Grades: K 1 2   **222**
1. Purim 2. Queens 3. Bible stories 4. Biblical characters
ISBN 978-0-8234-2223-4; 0-8234-2223-2
LC 2008048490
"Kimmel and Weber turn their considerable talents to the Book of Esther and its corresponding Jewish holiday.... As always, Kimmel is an effortless storyteller, his learnedness leavened with an expert sense of pacing for young audiences—even the book's longer passages feel like they're exactly the right length. In vibrant mixed-media paintings, Weber proves once again that she's an excellent match for this unflashy master." Publ Wkly

Koralek, Jenny
The **coat** of many colors; illustrated by Pauline Baynes. Eerdmans Books for Young Readers 2004 un il $16

Grades: K 1 2 3   **222**
1. Bible stories 2. Biblical characters
ISBN 0-8028-5277-7
LC 2004-6575
This "retelling of the story from the Book of Genesis highlights the key events in the life of Joseph ... and explores timeless themes of sibling rivalry and the power of forgiveness. . . . Baynes enhances the straightforward text with atmospheric illustrations rendered in muted desert shades.... This appealing rendition of a well-known tale is perfect for reading aloud." SLJ

The **story** of Queen Esther; written by Jenny Koralek; illustrated by Grizelda Holderness. Eerdmans Books for Young Readers 2008 un il $17.50
Grades: K 1 2 3   **222**
1. Queens 2. Bible stories 3. Biblical characters
ISBN 978-0-8028-5348-6; 0-8028-5348-X
LC 2008017713
This is a "retelling of the biblical story of the Jewish queen of ancient Persia who saved her people from the plotting of the king's evil vizier, Haman.... The Jewish holiday of Purim, which commemorates the story of Queen Esther, is mentioned on the final spread. . . . The illustrations are the highlight of the book. Stylized, dreamy pastel spreads sing with deep color.... The dignified pictures support the solemn tone of the text." SLJ

Manushkin, Fran
Miriam's cup; a Passover story. illustrated by Bob Dacey. Scholastic 1998 un il hardcover o.p. pa $6.99
Grades: K 1 2 3   **222**
1. Passover 2. Bible stories 3. Biblical characters 4. Seder -- Juvenile literature
ISBN 0-590-67720-9; 0-439-81111-2 pa
LC 96-2480
A Jewish mother preparing for Passover tells her young children, the story of Miriam, the Biblical woman who prophesied the birth of Moses
"The text and the lush double-spread watercolors, which are painted to reflect a child's perspective, are framed on a papyrus background. Each illustration bursts with movement, immersing readers and pre-readers alike in the sequence and drama of the story." Booklist
Includes bibliographical references

Paterson, Katherine
The **angel** and the donkey; retold by Katherine Paterson; illustrated by Alexander Koshkin. Clarion Bks. 1996 34p il $15.95; pa $5.95
Grades: 3 4 5   **222**
1. Bible stories 2. Biblical characters
ISBN 0-395-68969-4; 0-618-37840-5 pa
LC 94-22430
"This faithful, graceful retelling is embellished with many equally graceful watercolor, tempera, and gouache paintings executed in a detailed and realistic manner." SLJ

Ray, Jane
Adam and Eve and the Garden of Eden; written and illustrated by Jane Ray. Eerdmans Books for Young Readers 2005 un il $17

Grades: K 1 2 3 **222**
1. Bible stories 2. Biblical characters
ISBN 0-8028-5278-5

LC 2004-6804

"Adam and Eve live harmoniously with the animals that have been named by the first man, until Eve is tempted by the serpent. In rich prose, the author describes the garden in lyrical detail. The descriptive passages are complemented by exquisite illustrations that lend a mystical aura to the narrative." SLJ

Sasso, Sandy Eisenberg
Cain & Abel; finding the fruits of peace. illustrated by Joani Keller Rothenberg. Jewish Lights Pub. 2001 32p il $16.95
Grades: K 1 2 3 **222**
1. Bible stories 2. Biblical characters
ISBN 1-58023-123-3

LC 2001-2206

Retells the story of two brothers who, after years of sharing everything, become angry enough to lose control and bring violence into the world

"In this simple yet effective book, Sasso leads children to think not only about how the brothers' personal relationship failed but also about the story's connection to today's violence. The eye-catching, folk-art-style illustrations, with thick swathes of color and inventive background designs, make as strong a statement as the text." Booklist

Spier, Peter
★ **Noah's** ark; illustrated by Peter Spier. Doubleday 1977 un il $16.95; pa $7.99
Grades: K 1 2 **222**
1. Noah's ark 2. Bible stories
ISBN 0-385-09473-6; 0-440-49693-8 pa

LC 76-43630

Awarded the Caldecott Medal, 1978

"A seventeenth-century Dutch poem, 'The Flood' by Jacobus Revius, opens the otherwise almost wordless book. Skillfully translated by the artist and set in a readable, appropriately archaic type, the artlessly reverent verses add an unexpected dimension to the full-color pictures. Peter Spier's characteristic panoramas are marvels of minute detail, activity, vitality, and humor." Horn Book

Stewig, John W.
The **animals** watched; by John Warren Stewig; illustrated by Rosanne Litzinger. Holiday House 2007 un il $16.95
Grades: K 1 2 **222**
1. Alphabet 2. Noah's ark
ISBN 978-0-8234-1906-7; 0-8234-1906-1

LC 2006004784

"A simple account of the story of Noah's ark. The language is easy enough for young children to understand, but remains true to the basics of the Genesis text. . . . In alphabetical order from aardvarks to jaguars to zebras, animals tell a part of the tale. . . . The appealing illustrations are done in pencil, watercolor, gouache, and colored pencil." SLJ

Wolf, Gita
The **Enduring** Ark; by Gita Wolf; illustrated by Joydeb Chitrakar. Pgw 2013 34 p. ill. (hardcover) $21.95

Grades: 1 2 3 4 **222**
1. Toy and movable books 2. Noah's Ark
ISBN 9380340184; 9789380340180

This children's book, by Gita Wolf, illustrated by Joydeb Chitrakar, offers an "Indian version of the Biblical tale [of the Flood and Noah's Ark, which] . . . leads the reader from a deluge of water to a rainbow of hope. A book that can be leafed through in the traditional way or unfolded out as an accordion." (Publisher's note)

223   Poetic books of Old Testament

Delval, Marie-Helene
Psalms for young children; by Marie-Helene Delval; illustrated by Arno. Eerdmans Books for Young Readers 2008 un il $16
Grades: K 1 2 3 **223**
1. Bible 2. Old Testament
ISBN 978-0-8028-5322-6; 0-8028-5322-6

LC 2006031831

"Each psalm expresses feelings familiar to children: fear and uncertainty, comfort and contentment, amazement and gratitude. The sacred songs, paraphrased in simple, child-friendly language, celebrate the beautiful world, which is protected by God's all-encompassing love, and provide a sense of reassurance. . . . Organized in numerical order, the selections are printed in a large, readable font. . . . The magical paintings feature exotic settings, bold outlines, and rich hues. They are filled with images of children and the natural world." SLJ

Lindbergh, Reeve
On morning wings; adapted from Psalm 139 by Reeve Lindbergh; illustrated by Holly Meade. Candlewick Press 2002 un il $15.99
Grades: K 1 2 3 **223**
1. God 2. Children's poetry, English
ISBN 0-7636-1106-9

LC 2001-58169

'On morning wings' was previously published in the anthology In every tiny grain of sand: a child's book of prayers and praise, collected by Reeve Lindbergh, published by Candlewick Press, 2000

Retells, in simple words, a psalm of God's knowledge of and love for each of us

"Meade's visual story line shows four children spending an idyllic summer day together outdoors. The striking use of light, reflected in water or filtered by campfire, conveys the natural reverence of the text with seeming spontaneity." Publ Wkly

Moser, Barry
Psalm 23; illustrated by Barry Moser. Zonderkidz 2008 un il $14.99
Grades: K 1 2 **223**
1. Bible 2. Old Testament
ISBN 978-0-310-71085-1; 0-310-71085-5

LC 2006027616

"In a two-page introduction, Moser invites readers to see the venerable poem through a new prism: that of a boy tending goats and sheep on a Caribbean island such as Antigua, where the author-illustrator has spent much time. While watching the island animals, Moser says he has often recited the psalm, which he writes here in simple words. . . . Moser strives to accentuate mood and nature, and the paintings in this book . . . highlight the feeling that as God watches over us, we watch over those in our charge." Booklist

★ **To** every thing there is a season; verses from Ecclesiastes. illustrations by Leo and Diane Dillon. Blue Sky Press (NY) 1998 un il $16.95
Grades: 4 5 6 7 8   **223**
   1. Bible -- Pictorial works
   ISBN 0-590-47887-7
                                               LC 97-35124
Presents that selection from Ecclesiastes which relates that everything in life has its own time and season
   "The Dillons compellingly convey the relevance of the Ecclesiastes verse throughout history, via a stunning array of artwork that embraces motifs from cultures the world over." Publ Wkly

226   Gospels and Acts

Warren, Rick
   The **Lord's** prayer; [illustrated by] Richard Jesse Watson; commentary by Rick Warren. Zonderkidz 2011 un il (Master illustrator series) $16.99
Grades: PreK K 1 2   **226**
   1. Prayer
   ISBN 978-0-310-71086-8; 0-310-71086-3
                                               LC 2009037508
   "With vibrant illustrations featuring children of all ages and nationalities, Watson illuminates the message of love and worship contained within the lines of the King James Version of The Lord's Prayer. Each spread focuses on a single line, which is printed in elegant font and incorporated into the painting. Images of animals and the sun recur throughout the book. Some of the pictures are painted in rich colors while others appear to be shadowy, gray pencil sketches. . . . Warren explains the meaning behind the words Jesus taught his disciples with line-by-line commentary, teaching young readers the value of prayer. The artist also offers a reflection on what this prayer means to him. This lovely picture book is a fine choice to help parents introduce the practice of prayer into their children's daily lives." SLJ

230   Christianity

Nardo, Don
   Christianity. Compass Point Books 2010 48p il map (World religions) lib bdg $27.99
Grades: 5 6 7 8   **230**
   1. Christianity
   ISBN 978-0-7565-4237-5 lib bdg; 0-7565-4237-5 lib bdg
                                               LC 2009-15811
   "The colorful, attractive layout includes high-quality reproductions of photographs, maps, and paintings. Students who are new to religious studies, as well as those doing reports, will find that this . . . meets their needs." SLJ
   Includes glossary and bibliographical references

Self, David
   ★ **Christianity**; [by] David Self. World Almanac Library 2005 48p il map (Religions of the world) lib bdg $30
Grades: 5 6 7 8   **230**
   1. Christianity
   ISBN 0-8368-5866-2
                                               LC 2005041712
This is a summary of the Christian religion including history, beliefs, worship, festivals, practice, and current disagreements.
   "Wonderfully colorful in images, language, and fact. . . . [This is] enumerated with full-color photographs on every page, charts, maps, and tables." SLJ
   Includes bibliographical references

231   Christian doctrinal theology

Delval, Marie-Helene
   Images of God for young children; illustrated by Barbara Nascimbeni. Eerdmans Books for Young Readers 2011 88p il $16.50
Grades: K 1 2 3   **231**
   1. God
   ISBN 978-0-8028-5391-2; 0-8028-5391-9
   This "sets out to explain the concept of God to children in creative, often metaphorical ways. . . . The explanatory text is written in a thoughtful, calm voice with a comforting view of God as kind, loving and all-encompassing. This modern point of view is complemented by Nascimbeni's bright, imaginative illustrations on the right-hand pages, using children and images from nature painted in a cheery surrealistically childlike style." Kirkus

Fitch, Florence Mary
   A **book** about God; illustrated by Henri Sorensen. Lothrop, Lee & Shepard Bks. 1998 24p il hardcover o.p. lib bdg $15.93
Grades: K 1 2 3   **231**
   1. God 2. Nature -- Religious aspects -- Juvenile literature
   ISBN 0-688-16128-6; 0-688-16129-4 lib bdg
                                               LC 97-48682
A newly illustrated edition of the title first published 1953
   The "text explains how people can understand God's nature by observing the world he created. Fitch describes the ways that characteristics of the sun, air, trees, mountains, and oceans reflect the character of God. Proponents of many faiths will embrace this book's message." Horn Book Guide

231.7   Relation to the world

De Paola, Tomie
   ★ **Let** the whole earth sing praise. G. P. Putnam's Sons 2011 un il $15.99
Grades: PreK K 1   **231.7**
   1. Creation
   ISBN 978-0-399-25478-9; 0-399-25478-1
                                               LC 2010011565
   "In this small-format book, dePaola masterfully pairs simple words and resonant images. Rendered in acrylics and

inspired by the folk art of the Otomi people from Puebla, Mexico, the pictures offer primitive depictions of natural phenomena. . . . Based on two pieces of Old Testament scripture—the Canticle of the Three Young Men from the Book of Daniel and Psalm 148—dePaola's narrative bids specific creatures and forces of nature to give praise, before issuing a cumulative call-out: 'Let everything in heaven and on earth bless and praise God.' The very largeness of the loose, hand-lettered text, which appears in all caps, amplifies the message, while the joy that emanates from the cheerful spreads confirms its value." Publ Wkly

Tutu, Desmond

God's dream; by Archbishop Desmond Tutu and Douglas Carton Adams; illustrated by LeUyen Pham. Candlewick Press 2008 un il $16.99

Grades: PreK K   231.7
1. God 2. Peace 3. Multiculturalism
ISBN 978-0-7636-3388-2; 0-7636-3388-7

"In a series of energetic scenes, a multicultural cast of toddlers follow God's dreams about people caring, sharing . . . and playing together. Adding a touch of drama is the elemental scene in which two kids get in a fight. . . . The large, digitally enhanced pictures, alive with color and pattern, make clear the hurt, anger, and regret. Finally, the two fighters make up, and they join a big circle of laughing kids. . . . Praying together are Muslims, Jews, Buddhists, Christians, and more." Booklist

232.9   Family and life of Jesus

★ **Christmas** is here; words from the King James Bible; illustrated by Lauren Castillo. Simon & Schuster 2010 un il $12.99

Grades: PreK K 1 2   232.9
1. Christmas
ISBN 978-1-4424-0822-7; 1-4424-0822-7

"This touching interpretation of the Christmas story wordlessly follows a modern-day family as they journey through a snowy town in the evening to view a live Nativity scene. . . . The setting shifts in time and place to Bethlehem of long ago, accompanied by the traditional words from the King James Bible, before returning to the contemporary setting. Gorgeous watercolor illustrations in a subdued palette of twilight grays set off the falling snowflakes in the modern scenes, while the biblical scenes are brilliantly lit by starlight. Castillo's smudgy style infuses all with wonder." Kirkus

Crossley-Holland, Kevin

★ **How** many miles to Bethlehem? illustrated by Peter Malone. Arthur A. Levine Books 2004 un il $16.95

Grades: K 1 2 3   232.9
1. Christmas
ISBN 0-439-67642-8

LC 2003-28079

This is a telling of the Nativity story, told from the perspectives of Mary, the innkeeper, the ox, the donkey, the shepherds, the Wise Men, King Herod, the child, the lamb, and the angels.

"The language is both colloquial and lyrical. . . . Malone's illustrations are reminiscent of early Renaissance

and medieval Eastern art in their wealth of detail and color. . . . The paintings evoke both sumptuous glory and a serene stillness." SLJ

Demi

★ **Jesus**; written and illustrated by Demi. Margaret K. McElderry Books 2005 un il $19.95

Grades: 3 4 5 6   232.9
1. Jesus Christ
ISBN 0-689-86905-3

LC 2004-12854

"Brilliantly colored artwork and text based on the King James version of the Bible tell the story of the life of Jesus, beginning with the prophesies and the annunciation and ending with his ascension into Heaven. Demi's paintings are full of bright, intricate patterns, and bold touches of gold produce a feeling of awe and splendor." SLJ

Jones, Sally Lloyd

Little one, we knew you'd come; by Sally Lloyd-Jones; illustrated by Jackie Morris. Little, Brown 2006 un il $16.99

Grades: PreK K 1 2   232.9
ISBN 978-0-316-52391-2; 0-316-52391-7

LC 2005024661

"Although the illustrations depicting Mary and Joseph's arrival in Bethlehem and the birth of Baby Jesus make clear that this is a Christmas story, the simple text sings a universal hymn of anticipation and love from a parent to a child. . . . The sumptuous watercolor and gold-leaf illustrations, bordered with cherries, peacock feathers, flowers, and stars, portray an arid yet animal-filled landscape enlivened by the gloriously bedecked angels and kings." SLJ

Lottridge, Celia Barker

Stories from the life of Jesus; retold from the Bible by Celia Barker Lottridge; illustrated by Linda Wolfsgruber. Doulgas & McIntyre 2004 140p il $24.95

Grades: 4 5 6 7   232.9
1. Bible stories
ISBN 0-88899-497-4

A retelling of selected events from the life of Christ based on biblical accounts

This is an "exceptional collection. . . . Each story is retold in three or four pages of clear, concise prose that is meant to be read aloud. . . . Each selection is enhanced by dramatic and atmospheric, mixed-media illustrations that are executed in warm earth tones." SLJ

Menotti, Gian Carlo

Amahl and the night visitors; illustrated by Michèle Lemieux. Morrow 1986 64p il $21

Grades: 2 3 4   232.9
1. Magi -- Fiction 2. Christmas stories
ISBN 0-688-05426-9

LC 84-27196

Relates how a crippled young shepherd comes to accompany the three Kings on their way to pay hommage to the newborn Jesus

"Some of the pictures, which are dominated by reddish brown, have rich tension and composition, as in the one of Amahl's mother contemplating theft, or in the portrait of Melchior describing the Christ child. . . . There is a great deal to look at, and the story, popular since the opera's 1951 debut, has sentimental appeal, humor, and some command-ing moments." Bull Cent Child Books

Paterson, Katherine

★ The **light** of the world; the life of Jesus for children. [by] Katherine Paterson; [illustrated by] François Roca. Arthur A. Levine Books 2008 un il $17.99
Grades: K 1 2 3   **232.9**
  1. Jesus Christ
  ISBN 978-0-545-01172-3; 0-545-01172-8
             LC 2007-06811

"The incisive text . . . deftly moves through the story of Jesus' life and death, and also highlights several of the best-known parables. . . . Roca presents . . . close-ups of the various people surrounding Jesus and . . . handsome landscapes that give import to events." Booklist

Skevington, Andrea

The **story** of Jesus; illustrated by Angelo Ruta. Lion Children's 2009 127p il $16.95
Grades: 2 3 4 5   **232.9**
  1. Bible stories
  ISBN 978-0-7459-4982-6; 0-7459-4982-7
             LC 2008278094

"Skevington's collection of key New Testament stories chronicles the life of Jesus beginning with his birth in a humble stable in Bethlehem and concluding with the feast of Pentecost when the Holy Spirit descends upon the disciples. Retelling stories from all four gospels, the author fictionalizes the scripture passages, adding dialogue and cultural details to enliven the characters and the setting. . . . Explanatory margin notes supplement the stories, and the neatly drawn illustrations portray Jesus and his followers in a palette of soft pastels." SLJ

Slegers, Liesbet

The **child** in the manger. Clavis Pub. 2010 un il $15.95
Grades: PreK K 1   **232.9**
  ISBN 978-1-60537-084-2; 1-60537-084-3

"This is a short version of the Nativity story, told in simple language that very young children can understand. . . . The cheerful, colorful paintings, rendered in primary colors with bold outlines, feature childlike animals and smiley-faced Biblical people. This is a fine choice for sharing with toddlers and preschoolers one-on-one, as well as in a religious preschool storytime." SLJ

Spirin, Gennady

★ **Jesus**; his life in verses from the King James Holy Bible. art by Gennady Spirin. Marshall Cavendish Children 2010 un il $21
Grades: 5 6 7 8   **232.9**
  1. Jesus Christ
  ISBN 978-0-7614-5630-8; 0-7614-5630-9
             LC 2009005956

"In an unusual project, a tempera painting by Spirin has been digitally dissected to create individual images for this picture book that portrays 13 events from the life of Jesus. . . . Details from the larger work illustrate key moments—including the Annunciation, Jesus' baptism, and the raising of Lazarus, among others—beside passages from the King James Bible (Jesus' words are printed in red). The result is

an elegant, large-format volume that offers a reverent and arresting visual interpretation of biblical events." Publ Wkly

The **story** of Christmas; from the King James Bible. illustrations by Pamela Dalton. Handprint Books 2011 un il $17.99
Grades: 1 2 3   **232.9**
  ISBN 978-1-4521-0470-6; 1-4521-0470-0
             LC 2011025407

"Delicate paper-cut illustrations provide a lovely, solemn backdrop to the King James Bible's account of the Nativity story. . . . As shepherds, wise men, and angels gather to honor the birth of Jesus, Dalton sets her tableaus against black backgrounds, which both focus attention on the story's major players and make logical sense given the nocturnal setting of much of the story's events. The iconic nature of Dalton's scenes is ideally suited to the traditional Biblical translation used." Publ Wkly

Wildsmith, Brian

Jesus. Eerdmans Bks. for Young Readers 2000 un il $20
Grades: K 1 2 3   **232.9**
  ISBN 0-8028-5212-2
             LC 00-55126

"Wildsmith's pictures are framed in windowlike arches, set against backgrounds of pure colors. As with his other works, gold embellishments add majesty." Booklist

Williams, Sophy

The **first** Christmas; a changing picture book. Templar Books 2010 un il $12.99
Grades: PreK K 1 2   **232.9**
  ISBN 978-0-7636-5013-1; 0-7636-5013-7
             LC 2010004644

"This lovely presentation of the Nativity story includes four 'changing-pictures,' which are created by overlaying two images divided into vertical slats. In this case, the images change when a flap is opened. Williams's pastel illustrations are both luminous and child-centric, conveying a sense of mystery, awe, and gentle humor." SLJ

232.91   Mary, mother of Jesus

Bernier-Grand, Carmen T.

Our Lady of Guadalupe; retold by Carmen T. Bernier-Grand; illustrated by Tonya Engel. 1st ed. Marshall Cavendish Children 2012 31 p. ill. (hardcover) $17.99
Grades: 1 2 3   **232.91**
  1. Aztecs -- Folklore 2. Religious biography 3. Guadalupe, Our Lady of -- Juvenile literature
  ISBN 9780761461357; 9780761461371
             LC 2011016398

Author Carmen Bernier-Grand "describes the Aztec Juan Diego's three encounters with the Virgin Mary on Tepeyac Hill, near Tlatelolco (now Mexico City). Mary requests that Juan Diego tell the local bishop to build her a shrine on the hill . . . [and he] carries a sign from the Virgin to the bishop: roses in December. . . . The author concludes the tale with details on the significance of the shrine, the origins of the name 'Our Lady of Guadalupe' and other relevant historical facts and dates." (Kirkus Reivews)

Córdova, Amy, 1953-

Talking Eagle and the Lady of Roses; the story of Juan Diego and Our Lady of Guadalupe. illustrated by Amy Córdova; written by Amy Córdova, with Eugene Gollogly. SteinerBooks 2010 un il

Grades: K 1 2   **232.91**

1. Christian saints

ISBN 0-88010-719-7; 978-0-88010-719-8

LC 2010032329

This "story tells of the appearance of Our Lady of Guadalupe to an indigenous healer, Talking Eagle, who had converted to Catholicism, becoming Juan Diego. . . . Rendered in dazzling jewel tones, Córdova's drawings possess a quiet radiance." Publ Wkly

Demi

Mary; written and illustrated by Demi. Margaret K. McElderry Books 2006 un il $19.95

Grades: 3 4 5 6   **232.91**

1. Saints

ISBN 0-689-87692-0; 978-0-689-87692-9

LC 2005005844

"Demi begins her story before Mary is born, when her parents, Anna and Joachim, learn that their prayers have been heard, and that they will have a child whom they will dedicate to the service of the Lord. . . . The words simply serve as a backdrop for the glorious artwork. . . . Along with her familiar beautiful borders and diminutive characters, she incorporates many Jewish and Christian symbols that tie the religions together." SLJ

242   Devotional literature

Billingsley, Mary

The **life** of Jesus; an illustrated rosary. written and illustrated by Mary Billingsley; foreword by Benedict J. Groeschel. Eerdmans Books for Young Readers 2010 56p il $19.99

Grades: 3 4 5 6   **242**

1. Prayer

ISBN 978-0-8028-5362-2; 0-8028-5362-5

"Billingsley has divided this book according to the four 'Mysteries' that are emblematic of Christ's life—'Joyful,' 'Luminous,' 'Sorrowful,' and 'Glorious,' and then into subsections about each of its five parts. The book is remarkable in the accessibility it offers to readers of all ages. The introductory page provides visual instruction—a painting of a rosary with labels and arrows indicating which beads are meant for each prayer—followed by the prayers themselves. . . . Billingsley's unusual technique is what stands out; she has created 'shrines' of everyday objects, flowers, puppets, children's toys arranged in a vignette, and then reproduced them in gouache. The overall effect is child-friendly but also intensely emotionally evocative." SLJ

Brooks, Jeremy

Let there be peace; prayers from around the world. illustrated by Jude Daly. Frances Lincoln 2009 un il $16.95

Grades: PreK K 1 2 3   **242**

1. Peace 2. Prayers

ISBN 978-1-8450-7530-9; 1-8450-7530-7

"This picture-book collection of prayers sends universal messages of peace and global unity. Brooks . . . has pulled from diverse religious traditions. . . . Almost all of the selections are simple, immediate, and rhythmic. . . . Daly's delicately rendered, brightly hued paintings greatly increase the impact of the words. . . . Children of many backgrounds will be stirred by these prayers." Booklist

A **child's** book of prayers; collected and illustrated by Juli Kangas. Dial Books for Young Readers 2007 un il $12.99

Grades: PreK K   **242**

1. Prayers

ISBN 978-0-8037-3054-0; 0-8037-3054-3

LC 2006017595

"Simple meditations, both familiar and less well known, are presented along with warmhearted illustrations for the purpose of exposing children to the spiritual benefits of prayer. The well-chosen selections begin at the start of the day and follow different youngsters and their families through school, meals, and other typical pursuits, offering prayers of blessing, thanksgiving, or praise suited to each endeavor. The pencil, watercolor, and oil-wash artwork skillfully depicts the charismatic characters, who hale from a variety of ethnic backgrounds and live in both city and rural settings." SLJ

Field, Rachel

Prayer for a child; pictures by Elizabeth Orton Jones. Diamond anniversary ed; Simon & Schuster Books for Young Readers 2004 un il $10.95

Grades: K 1 2   **242**

1. Prayers 2. Bedtime prayers 3. Children -- Prayerbooks and devotions -- English

ISBN 0-689-87356-5

LC 2004-5259

A reissue of the title first published 1944 by Macmillan

Awarded the Caldecott Medal, 1945

"The complete prayer, written in rhymed couplets, appears on the first page; then a few lines per page accompany serene illustrations of a girl in tender moments—stargazing out a window or smiling up at her parents. . . . This lovely book lends itself to nightly repetition (a reference to Jesus tags it for a Christian audience)." Publ Wkly

Goble, Paul

Song of creation; written and illustrated by Paul Goble. Eerdmans Books for Young Readers 2004 un il $16

Grades: K 1 2 3   **242**

1. Prayers 2. Creation 3. Creation -- Prayer-books and devotions -- English 4. Christian children -- Prayerbooks and devotions -- English

ISBN 0-8028-5271-8

LC 2004-6576

"In striking graphic compositions, Goble creates magical, yet concrete, scenes of birds, beasts, fish, and more, conveying a personal and a universal reverence for and connection to nature. A beautiful, praiseworthy volume that does, indeed, sing." Booklist

Jordan, Deloris

Baby blessings; a prayer for the day you are born. illustrated by James E. Ransome. Simon & Schuster Books for Young Readers 2010 un il $16.99

Grades: PreK K   **242**
1. Prayers
ISBN 978-1-4169-5362-3; 1-4169-5362-0
LC 2008017131
Jordan "offers a colloquial prayer to greet the newborn child, offers advice, and gives reassurance of family love and support as well as God's blessings. . . . Ransome's handsome . . . oil paintings follow an African American child growing from infancy to the start of kindergarten under the watchful eyes of his loving parents. . . . Tenderly portraying a child growing up within a warmhearted family, this appealing picture book clearly expresses the faith, love, and hopes that surround him." Booklist

My first prayers. Albert Whitman 2009 un il $16.95
Grades: K 1 2   **242**
1. Prayers
ISBN 978-1-84507-535-4; 1-84507-535-8
"Brooks has collected prayers from a variety of nations including Poland, South Africa, the United States, and France, as well as several from his native England. The book features prayers of thanks, requests for guidance, blessings, and bedtime prayers. . . . Young readers will appreciate Brooks's gentle message of acceptance and inclusiveness." SLJ

Piper, Sophie
I can say a prayer; illustrated by Emily Bolam. IPG/Lion 2011 un il $12.99
Grades: PreK   **242**
1. Prayers
ISBN 978-0-7459-6233-7; 0-7459-6233-5
"This collection of 12 rhyming prayers for the young child is accompanied by simple pen, ink, and watercolor illustrations that are right up preschoolers' alleys. Some of the prayers are original and some are familiar, such as the Lord's Prayer. A few are accompanied by verses from the Bible that serve to introduce that particular prayer. The prayers include familiar preschool concepts like counting, sharing, and making music. The bright, smiley illustrations, meanwhile, depict children going about their everyday activities. . . . This book does its job and does it well." Booklist

Prayers for a better world; [illustrated by] Mique Moriuchi. Lion Children's 2010 63p il $9.99
Grades: 1 2 3   **242**
1. Prayers 2. Religious poetry
ISBN 978-0-7459-6929-9; 0-7459-6929-1
"This brightly colored little book offers 38 short prayers in verse that reflect on the earth, its animals and plants, and living in harmony with other people and with nature. Most are original . . . while a few of the entries are attributed to other poets. The verses are lyrical and thought-provoking but still accessible to a young audience. . . . Moriuchi's naive artwork illustrates children and the natural world in joyful, colorful, and occasionally playful collages of painted papers." Booklist

Rivett, Rachel
I imagine; a child's book of prayers. illustrated by Mique Moriushi. Lion/Trafalgar 2011 il $12.99
Grades: PreK K 1   **242**
1. Prayers
ISBN 978-0-7459-6208-5; 0-7459-6208-4

"An unusual, whimsical collection of 12 short prayers offers an imaginative approach with a patterned text and creative responses from the children narrating the prayers. Each prayer follows a similar pattern, describing a particular circumstance or challenge familiar to young children ('if life is stormy'), followed by the child narrator's imagined action ('I imagine I'm a tree, tossed and tumbled in the wind'). In alternating spreads, there is also a comforting response from God ('you show me how my roots are getting stronger'). . . . Moriuchi's pleasing collage illustrations of chubby-cheeked children incorporate textured papers, fabrics and snippets of print along with painted elements. . . . The light, soothing atmosphere created by the well-matched prayers and illustrations is deceptively simple, effectively conveying powerful images and a strong sense of comfort." Kirkus

Rock, Lois
A **child's** first book of prayers; illustrated by Alison Jay. IPG/Lion 2012 il $12.99
Grades: K 1 2 3 4   **242**
1. Prayers
ISBN 978-0-7459-4474-6; 0-7459-4474-4
First published 2002 in the United Kingdom
"With its portable size, thick binding, comforting illustrations, and more than 150 prayers, this book is an appealing package. . . . The book's strength is that has something for everyone. The table of contents provides a quick guide, offering chapters like 'This Fragile World' and 'Prayers for Sad Times.' . . . The often attributed prayers, some of which rhyme, run the gamut from aspirational to celebratory to comforting and are uniformly short. . . . Jay's omnipresent soft watercolors add a further peacefulness." Booklist

A **world** of prayers; illustrated by Elena Gomez. Eerdmans Books for Young Readers 2006 un il $16
Grades: 1 2 3 4   **242**
1. Prayers
ISBN 0-8028-5285-8
LC 2004017482
"A collection of 26 prayers assembled under the headings, Prayers for the Morning, Mealtime Graces, Prayers for Nighttime, and Blessings. A brief introduction and comments at the beginning of each chapter reflect on the place of prayer in our lives. Written in simple, easy-to-read language, the entreaties are recited by children in a variety of lands. . . . Dreamlike, decorative paintings that reflect the various cultures greatly enhance the selections and emphasize the books message of inclusiveness." SLJ

263   Days, times, places of religious observance

Fisher, Aileen Lucia
The **story** of Easter; by Aileen Fisher; illustrated by Stefano Vitale. HarperCollins Pubs. 1997 un il hardcover o.p. pa $5.95
Grades: 3 4 5   **263**
1. Easter
ISBN 0-06-027296-1; 0-06-443490-7 pa
LC 96-17395
A newly illustrated edition of Easter published 1968 by Crowell

"This book begins with the story of Jesus' crucifixion and resurrection, but focuses on the origins of various Easter and vernal equinox traditions, with an emphasis on the history of egg decorating. . . . The folk-art illustrations are defined by strong black outlines, simple shapes, and natural colors." Horn Book Guide

264 Public worship

Alexander, Cecil Frances

★ **All** things bright and beautiful; based on the hymn by Cecil F. Alexander. Atheneum Books for Young Readers 2010 un il $16.99

Grades: PreK K 1 2 3   **264**
1. Hymns 2. Religious poetry
ISBN 978-1-4169-8939-4; 1-4169-8939-0
       LC 2009032628

Bryan "interprets Cecil F. Alexander's 19th century hymn with cut-paper art defined by swirling geometrical shapes in neon hues, contributing to a pervasively jubilant atmosphere. Every spread is a riot of colors, movement, and natural splendors." Publ Wkly

Granfield, Linda

Out of slavery; the journey to Amazing Grace. illustrated by Janet Wilson. Tundra Books 2009 un il map $15.95

Grades: 4 5 6 7   **264**
1. Hymns 2. Clergy 3. Slave trade
ISBN 978-0-88776-915-3; 0-88776-915-2
       LC 2009502001

First published 1997 with title: Amazing Grace

This story of the hymn Amazing Grace "and its writer is beautifully written, evocative, and heart-wrenching. With an emphasis on John Newton and his years as a slave trader, Granfield shares how the events in his life led him to become an abolitionist, a pastor, and a writer of hymns. . . . Quotations from Newton's own writings are peppered throughout. Full-color, full-page illustrations add grandeur and appeal to the story. Rich in texture and color, the artwork is somber in tone and content." SLJ

266 Missions

Perritano, John

Spanish missions. Children's Press 2010 48p il map (True book) lib bdg $35; pa $6.95

Grades: 3 4 5   **266**
1. Native Americans 2. Missions 3. Spaniards -- United States
ISBN 978-0-531-20575-4 lib bdg; 0-531-20575-4 lib bdg; 978-0-531-21238-7 pa; 0-531-21238-6 pa
       LC 2009017742

This "takes a look at the Christianity-fueled Spanish side of New World colonization. Beginning with a pithy account that delves into the conquer-and-cash-in strategy of Spanish exploration, it then nicely outlines what missions are . . . . who built them . . . and why they were built. . . . With an evenhanded tone, Perritano also touches on important Spanish priests, . . . native revolts, and various missions in what is

now Mexico and the southwestern U.S. . . . The colorful, amply illustrated design make for an accessible read." Booklist

Includes glossary and bibliographical references

270 History, geographic treatment, biography of Christianity; Church history; Christian denominations and sects

Demi

The **legend** of Saint Nicholas. Margaret K. McElderry Bks. 2003 un il $19.95

Grades: 3 4 5 6   **270**
1. Saints 2. Bishops 3. Santa Claus 4. Christian saints
ISBN 0-689-84681-9
       LC 2002-8426

Recounts pivotal events in the history and life of Saint Nicholas, including how he came to be associated with Christmas and Santa Claus

"The gilded paintings are full of absorbing . . . details. . . . The greatest strength of this book is its straightforward, affectionate depiction of a person who, by his deep love for the young and the needy, embodies the spirit of Christmas." SLJ

270.1 Historical periods

Sabuda, Robert

Saint Valentine; retold and illustrated by Robert Sabuda. Atheneum Pubs. 1992 un il $16.95; pa $5.99

Grades: 1 2 3   **270.1**
1. Saints 2. Christian saints 3. Christian legends -- Juvenile literature
ISBN 0-689-31762-X; 0-689-82429-7 pa
       LC 91-25012

Recounts an incident in the life of St. Valentine, a physician who lived some 200 years after Christ, in which he treated a small child for blindness

"The fluid, straightforward retelling of the legend is accompanied by evocative, mosaiclike illustrations created from colored cut paper. Varying sizes of illustrations, careful page placement, and effective use of white space create the impression of the large-scale period mosaics. A fine melding of text and art." SLJ

271 Religious congregations and orders in church history

Kennedy, Robert Francis

Saint Francis of Assisi; a life of joy. written by Robert F. Kennedy, Jr.; illustrated by Dennis Nolan. Hyperion Books for Children 2004 31p il $18.99

Grades: 2 3 4   **271**
1. Saints 2. Christian saints 3. Writers on religion
ISBN 0-7868-1875-1
       LC 2003-60420

"The book paints Francis in glowing terms . . . weaving together the major threads of his life: his early kindness to beggars in his family's fabric shop; his call to and ultimate rejection of a military career; his estrangement from his wealthy father; and his ministry to lepers, the impoverished, and animals. . . . Nolan's oil paintings render realistic figures in carefully staged scenes." SLJ

Norris, Kathleen

★ The **holy** twins: Benedict and Scholastica; written by Kathleen Norris; illustrated by Tomie De Paola. Putnam 2001 un il $16.99

Grades: 3 4 5   **271**

1. Monks 2. Saints 3. Christian saints 4. Writers on religion 5. Christian saints -- Italy -- Biography -- Juvenile literature

ISBN 0-399-23424-1

LC 00-40294

"This fictionalized biography of Saints Benedict and Scholastica, twins who lived in sixth-century Italy, is told in a lively, authoritative manner. . . . dePaola's elegant, stylized artwork seems particularly well suited to the eternal quality of religious subjects. The framed spreads are painted in soft, warm acrylics on tea-stained watercolor paper, which gives the semblance of an old manuscript." SLJ

Visconti, Guido

Clare and Francis; text by Guido Visconti, inspired by the biographies and written works of the two saints of Assisi collected in the Franciscan Sources. Eerdmans Books for Young Readers 2004 un il $20

Grades: 4 5 6 7   **271**

1. Nuns 2. Saints 3. Christian saints 4. Writers on religion 5. Assisi (Italy) -- Biography -- Juvenile literature

ISBN 0-8028-5269-6

LC 2003-13441

Reviews the lives and works of two members of Assisi society, Francis and Clare, who renounced their wealth and founded religious orders dedicated to relying on God and living in peace, poverty, and humility.

"The familiar story of Francis (and to a lesser extent, Clare) is beautifully treated in this book, with luminous iconic artwork and a text that is both down-to-earth and stroking the stars." Booklist

282   Roman Catholic Church

Hawker, Frances

Christianity in Mexico; written by Frances Hawker and Noemi Paz; photography by Bruce Campbell. Crabtree Pub. Co. 2010 32p il (Families and their faiths) lib bdg $26.60; pa $8.95

Grades: 3 4 5   **282**

1. Catholics

ISBN 978-0-7787-5007-9 lib bdg; 0-7787-5007-8 lib bdg; 978-0-7787-5024-6 pa; 0-7787-5024-8 pa

LC 2009-14157

This "book introduces a child who practices [Christianity]. . . . Provides a solid introduction without overwhelming readers with complex regional variations in practices and beliefs. . . . Words and phrases that are unique to the faith appear in bold font and are defined at greater length in the glossary." SLJ

Includes glossary

282.092   Cardinals (Clergy)

Schmidt, Gary D.

Martin de Porres; the rose in the desert. written by Gary D. Schmidt; illustrated by David Diaz. Clarion Books 2012 32 p. col. ill. (reinforced) $16.99

Grades: 1 2 3   **282.092**

1. Picture books for children 2. Christian saints -- Biography

ISBN 0547612184; 9780547612188

LC 2011025721

Pura Belpré Illustrator Award (2013)

This children's picture book offers a biography of the Catholic saint Martin de Porres. The "illegitimate son of a former slave and a Spanish conquistador in 1579 in Lima, Peru," he "was the first black saint of the Americas." Author Gary Schmidt focuses on the saint's "extreme humility . . . emphasizing his humble servitude and great empathy." (School Library Journal)

289.3   Latter-Day Saints (Mormons)

Bial, Raymond

Nauvoo; Mormon city on the Mississippi River. [by] Raymond Bial. Houghton Mifflin Co. 2006 44p il map $17

Grades: 5 6 7 8   **289.3**

1. Mormons 2. Church of Jesus Christ of Latter-day Saints

ISBN 978-0-618-39685-6; 0-618-39685-3

LC 2005027528

"Bial introduces readers to a city that was established by the Church of Jesus Christ of Latter Day Saints in 1839. . . . This effectively written account provides a sympathetic but balanced introduction to Mormon beliefs. . . . Excellent color photographs grace almost every page." SLJ

George, Charles

What makes me a Mormon? by Charles George. KidHaven Press 2004 48p il map (What makes me a--?) $27

Grades: 3 4 5   **289.3**

1. Mormons 2. Church of Jesus Christ of Latter-day Saints

ISBN 978-0-7377-3083-8; 0-7377-3083-8

LC 2004-13636

This describes Morman origins, beliefs, practices, and holidays

"Presenting information about religion objectively for younger audiences poses a difficult challenge, but [this title does] an excellent job of it." Booklist

Includes bibliographical references

289.6   Society of Friends (Quakers)

Woog, Adam

What makes me a Quaker? by Adam Woog. KidHaven Press 2004 48p il (What makes me a--?) $27

Grades: 3 4 5   **289.6**

1. Society of Friends

ISBN 978-0-7377-3082-1; 0-7377-3082-X

LC 2004-13096

This explains Quakerism's origins, beliefs, practices, and future

"Presenting information about religion objectively for younger readers poses a difficult challenge, but [this title does] an excellent job of it." Booklist

Includes glossary and bibliographical references

289.7 Mennonite churches

Bial, Raymond

Amish home. Houghton Mifflin 1993 40p il hardcover o.p. pa $5.95

Grades: 3 4 5   **289.7**

1. Amish

ISBN 0-395-59504-5; 0-395-72021-4 pa

LC 92-4406

Text and photographs depict the way of life of the Amish

The full-color photos depict "cozy kitchens, lovingly tended gardens, prized horses, and rolling landscapes. As well as being informative, these photographs create a mood through which readers enter another lifestyle." SLJ

Includes bibliographical references

292 Classical religion (Greek and Roman religion)

Aliki

★ The **gods** and goddesses of Olympus; written and illustrated by Aliki. HarperCollins Pubs. 1994 48p il $16; pa $6.95

Grades: 2 3 4 5   **292**

1. Classical mythology 2. Gods and goddesses -- Juvenile literature

ISBN 0-06-023530-6; 0-06-446189-0 pa

LC 93-17834

"This large-format book provides a quick, brightly illustrated introduction to the ancient Greek gods and goddesses." Booklist

Bryant, Megan E.

Oh my gods! a look-it-up guide to the gods of mythology. Franklin Watts 2009 128p il map (Mythlopedia) lib bdg $39; pa $13.95

Grades: 4 5 6 7   **292**

1. Gods and goddesses 2. Classical mythology

ISBN 978-1-60631-026-7 lib bdg; 1-60631-026-7 lib bdg; 978-1-60631-058-8 pa; 1-60631-058-5 pa

LC 2009-17169

Presents a guide to Greek mythology, providing profiles of gods and goddesses along with information on monsters, heroes, and the underworld.

"The book is organized around entries on major gods and titans, each with vital stats and a Top 10 Things to Know about Me, followed by a few highlights from their lore and sidebars that delve into their cultural relevance. Illustrations abound, from embellished stock images to original cartoons, and the pastel-heavy color scheme may entice readers otherwise resistant to the grays and ivories that tend to dominate classicism." Booklist

Includes glossary and bibliographical references

She's all that! a look-it-up guide to the goddesses of mythology. Franklin Watts 2009 128p il map (Mythlopedia) lib bdg $39; pa $13.95

Grades: 4 5 6 7   **292**

1. Gods and goddesses 2. Classical mythology

ISBN 978-1-60631-027-4 lib bdg; 1-60631-027-5 lib bdg; 978-1-60631-059-5 pa; 1-60631-059-3 pa

LC 2009-17168

Presents a guide to Greek mythology, providing profiles of goddesses and the myths surrounding them.

This "spices things up with sassy artwork, a pastel color scheme, and an OMG sensibility. . . . Aside from the heaps of information coming from all angles on just about every page, . . . [this] book also contains a decent family tree, a rudimentary star chart, and lists of further reading. . . . For kids unconvinced that anything so old and gray could have any bearing on their lives, . . . [this provides] a feisty . . . guide to the many cultural references lingering from antiquity." Booklist

Includes glossary and bibliographical references

Clayton, Sally Pomme

★ **Persephone**; a journey from winter to spring. by Sally Pomme Clayton; illustrated by Virginia Lee. Eerdmans Books for Young Readers 2009 un il $18

Grades: 2 3 4   **292**

1. Persephone (Greek deity)

ISBN 978-0-8028-5349-3; 0-8028-5349-8

LC 2008018391

"Approaching the Greek myth of Persephone with the respect that a good storyteller holds for a great story, Clayton retells the tale with drama and grace. The mixed-media artwork creates a series of scenes defined by sweeping lines, broad views, and restrained use of color." Booklist

Curlee, Lynn

Mythological creatures; a classical bestiary: tales of strange beings, fabulous creatures, fearsome beasts, & hideous monsters from ancient Greek mythology. Atheneum Books for Young Readers 2008 35p il $17.99

Grades: 3 4 5   **292**

1. Mythical animals 2. Classical mythology

ISBN 978-1-4169-1453-2; 1-4169-1453-6

LC 2006-16980

"A preponderance of these sixteen fabulous beasts are half human (or, like Pan, minor deities). Most are monstrous in behavior as well as body; only the purely animal Pegasus and Phoenix possess some sort of nobility. Confining each within a broad, sober border, Curlee depicts all as classically statuesque. . . . Staightforward and clean, the accompanying text outlines without dramatization what these mythical beings were and their role in Greek lore. . . . The book is an eye-catching introduction to the world of ancient myth." Horn Book

Karas, G. Brian

★ **Young** Zeus. Scholastic Press 2010 un il $17.99

Grades: 2 3 4 5   **292**

1. Zeus (Greek deity) 2. Classical mythology 3. Mythology, Greek -- Juvenile literature 4. Zeus (Greek deity) -- Juvenile literature

ISBN 978-0-439-72806-5; 0-439-72806-1

LC 2009-10148

Karas "opens this spirited embellishment of Zeus's little-documented boyhood with an author's note explaining that he drew form early accounts of the Greek gods and 'true to the nature of myths, imagined the rest.' . . . But Kara's imagination serves him well in making Zeus a relatable character. . . . Droll dialogue and asides mitigate the tale's dark undertones [and] . . . energetic, airy gouache and pencil cartoons playfully skew scale and also keep the tone light." Publ Wkly

Kimmel, Eric A.

★ The **McElderry** book of Greek myths; [by] Eric A. Kimmel; illustrated by Pep Montserrat. M.K. McElderry Books 2008 96p il $21.99
Grades: K 1 2 3   **292**
   1. Classical mythology
   ISBN 1-4169-1534-6; 978-1-4169-1534-8
              LC 2005031010

In this collection of retellings of Greek myths "Kimmel uses spare, direct language and lots of exciting action. . . . Montserrat's stylish computer-generated artwork picks up on ancient Greek design motifs and creates memorable characters from the mythical archetypes." Booklist

Lupton, Hugh

The **adventures** of Odysseus; [by] Hugh Lupton and Daniel Morden; [illustrated by] Christina Balit. Barefoot Books 2006 un il $19.99
Grades: 3 4 5 6   **292**
   1. Classical mythology 2. Odysseus (Greek mythology)
   ISBN 1-84148-800-3
              LC 2005032532

This "book retells Homer's epic of Odysseus' perilous journey home in a immediate, fast-paced narrative. . . . The text is beautifully framed with crisp, brightly colored, mosaic-style illustrations of the heroes and monsters, rendered in watercolor, gouache, and gold ink." Booklist

Mayer, Marianna

★ **Pegasus**; as told by Marianna Mayer; illustrated by K. Y. Craft. Morrow Junior Bks. 1998 un il $17.99
Grades: 4 5 6   **292**
   1. Classical mythology 2. Pegasus (Greek mythology)
   ISBN 0-688-13382-7; 0-688-13383-5 lib bdg
              LC 96-32442

Retells how Bellerophon, son of the King of Corinth, secures the help of the winged horse Pegasus in order to fight the monstrous Chimera

"Dark, painterly illustrations set in gold frames heighten the mysticism in this lyrical interpretation of the Greek myth." Horn Book Guide

McCaughrean, Geraldine

★ **Hercules**; retold by Geraldine McCaughrean. Cricket Books 2005 142p il (Heroes) $16.95
Grades: 5 6 7 8   **292**
   1. Classical mythology 2. Hercules (Legendary character)
   ISBN 978-0-8126-2737-4; 0-8126-2737-7
              LC 2005004524
First published 2003 by Oxford University Press

This is a retelling of the twelve labors of Hercules including his battles with the Cretan Bull, the many-headed Hydra, the Nemean Lion, and the three-headed guardian of hell, Cerberus.

"This volume does a creditable job of making Hercules a dimensional character whose struggles against fate and the vindictiveness of the gods arouse readers' sympathy. . . . McCaughrean enlivens the familiar story with arresting imagery." SLJ

★ **Odysseus**; retold by Geraldine McCaughrean. Cricket Books 2004 148p il (Heroes) $16.95
Grades: 5 6 7 8   **292**
   1. Classical mythology 2. Odysseus (Greek mythology)
   ISBN 978-0-8126-2721-3; 0-8126-2721-0
              LC 2004-10734

"With mounting suspense, wild action, and simple, rhythmic prose, this dramatic retelling of Homer's classic makes a gripping read-aloud as well as an exciting introduction to the story." Booklist

★ **Perseus**; retold by Geraldine McCaughrean. Cricket Books 2005 118p il (Heroes) $16.95
Grades: 5 6 7 8   **292**
   1. Classical mythology 2. Perseus (Greek mythology)
   ISBN 978-0-8126-2735-0; 0-8126-2735-0

This "makes a thrilling read-aloud. . . . McCaughrean blends the colloquial and contemporary into the heroic quest." Booklist

Osborne, Mary Pope

Favorite Greek myths; retold by Mary Pope Osborne; illustrated by Troy Howell. Scholastic 1989 81p il lib bdg $18.95
Grades: 3 4 5 6   **292**
   1. Classical mythology
   ISBN 0-590-41338-4
              LC 87-32332

Retells twelve tales from Greek mythology, including the stories of King Midas, Echo and Narcissus, the Golden Apples, and Cupid and Psyche

"Osborne's retellings are both lively and descriptive, while Howell's full-color, often iridescent illustrations set the scene and mood at the start of each tale." Publ Wkly
   Includes glossary and bibliographical references

Otfinoski, Steven

All in the family; a look-it-up guide to the in-laws, outlaws, and offspring of mythology. F. Watts 2009 128p il (Mythlopedia) lib bdg $39; pa $13.95
Grades: 4 5 6 7   **292**
   1. Classical mythology
   ISBN 978-1-60631-025-0 lib bdg; 1-60631-025-9 lib bdg; 978-1-60631-057-1 pa; 1-60631-057-7 pa
              LC 2009-20999

"Jam-packed with trivia, brief profiles, god and goddess relationships, stories, 'Top 10 Things to Know About Me' facts, and entertaining illustrations, this title explores 20 heroes and mortals of classic Greek mythology. The selections include the well-known Achilles, Heracles, Odysseus, and Pandora and the more obscure Meleager, Orion, Atalanta, and Bellerophon; each one is given lively treatment. . . . The lighthearted style and humorous collage and cartoon illustrations may draw even the most reluctant of readers. " SLJ
   Includes glossary and bibliographical references

Rylant, Cynthia

The **beautiful** stories of life; six Greek myths, retold. illustrated by Carson Ellis. Harcourt 2009 71p il $16
Grades: 5 6 7 8 **292**
    1. Classical mythology 2. Young adult literature -- Works 3. Mythology, Greek -- Juvenile literature
    ISBN 978-0-15-206184-5; 0-15-206184-3
                        LC 2007-34808

"Rylant retells the stories of Pandora, Persephone, Orpheus, Pygmalion, Narcissus, and Psyche in this trim, handsome book. Written in a modern style with an old-fashioned feel, the selections sit well with other titles in the genre. . . . Accompanied by full-page black-and-white illustrations and sprinkled with decorations, the whole package is nicely done." SLJ

Steer, Dugald

The **mythology** handbook; a course in ancient Greek myths. by Hestia Evans; edited by Dugald A. Steer and Clint Twist. Candlewick Press 2009 71p il map $12.99
Grades: 4 5 6 7 **292**
    1. Classical mythology
    ISBN 978-0-7636-4291-4

"This follow-up to Mythology (Candlewick, 2007) again uses the voice of a fictional 19th-century scholar. Here, Lady Hestia Evans offers a guide to elements of Greek myth for her two children, providing information in 'lessons' . . . with exercises based on each topic. Some of the activities encourage students to do further research . . . while others suggest that they draw new monsters, write hymns with the Muses' help, or design a new pentathlon for the Olympics. Mazes and a word search (using Greek letters) are also included. . . . The activities are engaging, and the illustrations of creatures and maps of the ancient world will add to the knowledge of even more experienced myth fans." SLJ

Townsend, Michael

Michael Townsend's amazing Greek myths of wonder and blunders. Dial Books for Young Readers 2010 160p il $14.99
Grades: 4 5 6 7 **292**
    1. Greek mythology -- Graphic novels
    ISBN 978-0-8037-3308-4; 0-8037-3308-9

"Ten familiar myths—the stories of Pandora, Arachne, Midas, Perseus, and others—are embellished with humor, the gory parts glossed over, and served up in blazing color for fans of either comic books or Percy Jackson, or both. . . . Conversational, up-to-date language and broad jokes help to make the stories accessible and coordinate well with the simple, cartoon illustration style." SLJ

Turnbull, Ann

★ **Greek** myths; retold by Ann Turnbull; illustrated by Sarah Young. Candlewick Press 2011 165p il **292**
Grades: 5 6 7 8 9 10 **292**
    1. Classical mythology 2. Mythology, Greek -- Juvenile literature
    ISBN 0-7636-5111-7; 978-0-7636-5111-4
                        LC 2010-39178

Turnbull divides sixteen Greek myths "under three headings: Earth, the Heavens, and the Underworld; Monsters and Heroes; Gods and Mortals. . . . Grades five to ten." (Bull Cent Child Books)

"Sixteen Greek myths . . . are retold here with stylistic grace well matched to beautiful visual presentation. . . . Turnbull narrates with . . . vibrancy. . . . Sarah Young's mixed-media artwork—regal, yet sensuous compositions in richly textured earthtones touch[ed] with gold—is sufficiently representational to assist younger readers with context clues, and sufficiently elegant and sophisticated to satisfy seasoned readers." Bull Cent Child Books

292.1 Specific elements

Craft, Marie

★ **Cupid** and Psyche; as told by M. Charlotte Craft; illustrated by K. Y. Craft. Morrow Junior Bks. 1996 un il $16
Grades: 4 5 6 7 **292.1**
    1. Eros (Greek deity) 2. Classical mythology 3. Psyche (Greek deity)
    ISBN 0-688-13163-8
                        LC 95-14895

"In this Greek myth, Cupid falls in love with Psyche and treats her royally but does not reveal himself. When Psyche tries to discover his identity, Cupid leaves her, but she wins him back by accomplishing three difficult tasks. Recalling an earlier artistic era, the occasionally ornate romantic paintings—some of them quite dramatic—feature detailed landscapes and beautiful figures in flowing drapery." Horn Book Guide

293 Germanic religion

Fisher, Leonard Everett

Gods and goddesses of the ancient Norse. Holiday House 2001 un il $16.95
Grades: 3 4 5 6 **293**
    1. Norse mythology
    ISBN 0-8234-1569-4
                        LC 00-32040

In this guide each "double-page spread is devoted to one or two of the major gods or goddesses, accompanied by a succinct description that includes significant characteristics and responsibilities. A pronunciation guide and family tree are appended." Horn Book Guide

Includes bibliographical references

Lunge-Larsen, Lise

The **adventures** of Thor the Thunder God; retold by Lise Lunge-Larsen; illustrated by Jim Madsen. Houghton Mifflin 2007 76p il $19.95
Grades: 3 4 5 6 **293**
    1. Norse mythology
    ISBN 0-618-47301-7; 978-0-618-47301-4
                        LC 2004015765

"Madsen's . . . majestic digitally rendered illustrations bring the tales to life, echoing their humor. . . . These retellings offer an accessible and engaging doorway into the world of Norse mythology." Publ Wkly

294   Religions of Indic origin

Ollhoff, Jim
   Indian mythology. ABDO Pub. 2012 32 p. il map
(The world of mythology) lib bdg $27.07
Grades: 5 6 7 8   **294**
   1. Hinduism   2. Indic mythology
   ISBN 978-1-61714-722-7; 1-61714-722-2
                         LC 2010041628
'This book offers information about Indian mythology,
answering questions such as "Who is Devi? What is Gane-
sha? Why are myths so important in our lives? Myths are
a rich source of history. People use them to make sense of
our world. Even before myths were written down, people
told and retold the stories of the gods and goddesses of their
homeland. Readers of Indian Mythology will learn the history of myths, as well as their deeper meaning." (Publisher's
note) The book "introduces Brahma, Vishnu, Shiva, Kali,
and other Hindu gods and goddesses while also discussing
how the deities often took on different forms called avatars."
(Booklist)
   "Ollhoff writes in a clear and engaging fashion, presenting complex issues in a way that will be easy for youngsters
to grasp. . . . The photographs and reproductions of art tie
directly to the [text]." SLJ

294.3   Buddhism

Chodzin, Sherab
   The **wisdom** of the crows and other Buddhist tales; re-
told by Sherab Chödzin & Alexandra Kohn; illustrated by
Marie Cameron. Tricycle Press 1998 80p il pa $16.95
Grades: 4 5 6 7   **294.3**
   1. Buddhism
   ISBN 1-883672-68-6
                         LC 97-30441
First published 1997 in the United Kingdom with title:
The Barefoot book of Buddhist tales
   A collection of thirteen retold Buddhist tales from all
over Asia, illustrating various aspects of Buddhist thought
   "Folktale lovers will find much to like here. Marie Cam-
eron's clear, fresh watercolors, incorporating Asian artistic
motifs and bordered with waves and origami, are handsome-
ly rendered." Booklist
   Includes bibliographical references

Demi
   ★ **Buddha**. Holt & Co. 1996 un il $21.95
Grades: 4 5 6   **294.3**
   1. Philosophers   2. Buddhist leaders   3. Buddhism --
Juvenile literature
   ISBN 0-8050-4203-2
                         LC 95-16906
Demi "uses clear, uncomplicated storytelling to pres-
ent complex philosophical concepts. . . . The gilded il-
lustrations (based, according to the jacket, on 'Indian,
Chinese, Japanese, Burmese, and Indonesian paintings,
sculptures, and sutra illustrations') are delicate, yet the
colors and composition are bold, with central figures and
action cascading beyond the careful borders." Bull Cent
Child Books

   Buddha stories. Holt & Co. 1997 un il $21.95
Grades: 3 4 5 6   **294.3**
   1. Fables   2. Jataka stories   3. Buddhist legends --
Juvenile literature
   ISBN 0-8050-4886-3
                         LC 96-31253
This "is a picture-book collection of eleven Jataka tales
retold in a formal yet straightforward style. . . . An author's
note gives the source of the tales as well as the historical basis for the design concept behind the elegantly sophisticated
artwork. Both text and illustrations are done in gold ink on
deep indigo paper, resulting in a striking visual impact." Bull
Cent Child Books

   ★ The **Dalai** Lama; a biography of the Tibetan spiritual and political leader. Henry Holt & Co. 1998 un il
$18.95
Grades: 4 5 6 7   **294.3**
   1. Buddhism   2. Buddhist leaders   3. Political leaders   4.
Nobel laureates for peace   5. Dalai Lamas -- Biography
-- Juvenile literature
   ISBN 0-8050-5443-X
                         LC 97-30654
In this biography of the Buddhist spiritual leader, Demi
"uses straightforward prose and fluid, eastern-influenced
art—small pen-and-ink and watercolor images with fine, intricate detail. . . . Told with respect and devotion, this is an
inspirational picture-book biography." Horn Book

Ganeri, Anita
   ★ **Buddhism**; [by] Anita Ganeri. World Almanac Library 2006 48p il map (Religions of the world) lib bdg
$30.60
Grades: 5 6 7 8   **294.3**
   1. Buddhism
   ISBN 0-8368-5865-4
                        LC 2005041708
The author "presents a survey of Buddhist history, beliefs, sacred texts, festivals, and lifecycle events. . . . There
is discussion of the art and folk literature associated with the
religious tradition. Colorful photographs, illustrations, and
art reproductions appear throughout." SLJ
   Includes bibliographical references

George, Charles
   What makes me a Buddhist? by Charles George. Kid-
Haven Press 2004 48p il (What makes me a--?) $23.70
Grades: 3 4 5   **294.3**
   1. Buddhism
   ISBN 0-7377-2269-X
                        LC 2003-24344
This describes the beliefs, origins, practices, holidays
and future of Buddhism.
   "An attractive, colorful design is the background for a
map and numerous color photographs and diagrams. But
best of all is the straightforward organization and the clarity
of the text." Booklist
   Includes bibliographical references

Hawker, Frances
   Buddhism in Thailand; written by Frances Hawker
and Sunantha Phusomsai; photography by Bruce Campbell.
Crabtree Pub. Co. 2009 32p il map (Families and their
faiths) lib bdg $26.60; pa $8.95

Grades: 3 4 5 **294.3**
1. Buddhism
ISBN 978-0-7787-5006-2 lib bdg; 0-7787-5006-X lib bdg; 978-0-7787-5023-9 pa; 0-7787-5023-X pa
LC 2009-14156
This "book introduces a child who practices [Buddhism]. . . . Provides a solid introduction without overwhelming readers with complex regional variations in practices and beliefs. . . . Words and phrases that are unique to the faith appear in bold font and are defined at greater length in the glossary." SLJ
Includes glossary

Nardo, Don
Buddhism. Compass Point Books 2009 48p il map (World religions) lib bdg $27.99
Grades: 5 6 7 8 **294.3**
1. Buddhism
ISBN 978-0-7565-4236-8 lib bdg; 0-7565-4236-7 lib bdg
LC 2009-11453
"The colorful, attractive layout includes high-quality reproductions of photographs, maps, and paintings. Students who are new to religious studies, as well as those doing reports, will find that this . . . meets their needs." SLJ
Includes glossary and bibliographical references

294.5 Hinduism

Ganeri, Anita
The **Ramayana** and Hinduism. Smart Apple Media 2003 30p il (Sacred texts) $27.10
Grades: 5 6 7 8 9 **294.5**
1. Hinduism
ISBN 1-58340-242-X
LC 2003-42352
Explains the history and practices of the religion of Hinduism, especially as revealed through its sacred book, the Ramayana

George, Charles
What makes me a Hindu? by Charles George. KidHaven Press 2004 48p il map (What makes me a--?) $27
Grades: 3 4 5 **294.5**
1. Hinduism 2. Hinduism -- Juvenile literature
ISBN 978-0-7377-2267-3; 0-7377-2267-3
LC 2003-24346
This describes Hindu origins, beliefs, practices, and holidays
"Presenting information about religion objectively for younger audiences poses a difficult challenge, but [this title does] an excellent job of it." Booklist
Includes bibliographical references

Hawker, Frances
Hinduism in Bali; written by Frances Hawker and Putu Resi; photography by Bruce Campbell. Crabtree Pub. Company 2009 32p il (Families and their faiths) lib bdg $26.60; pa $8.95

Grades: 3 4 5 **294.5**
1. Hinduism
ISBN 978-0-7787-5008-6 lib bdg; 0-7787-5008-6 lib bdg; 978-0-7787-5008-6 pa; 0-7787-5008-6 pa
LC 2009-14297
This "book introduces a child who practices [Hinduism]. . . . Provides a solid introduction without overwhelming readers with complex regional variations in practices and beliefs. . . . Words and phrases that are unique to the faith appear in bold font and are defined at greater length in the glossary," SLJ
Includes glossary

Heiligman, Deborah
★ **Celebrate** Diwali; [by] Deborah Heiligman; consultant, Dr. Vasudha Narayanan. National Geographic 2006 32p il map (Holidays around the world) $15.95; lib bdg $23.90
Grades: K 1 2 3 **294.5**
1. Divali
ISBN 0-7922-5922-X; 0-7922-5923-8 lib bdg
LC 2006003426
This "focuses on the Hindu celebration in India but mentions observance by the Sikh and Jain faiths and also show customs in four other countries. . . . Each spread features up to three high-quality color photographs." SLJ

Jani, Mahendra
What you will see inside a Hindu temple; [by] Mahendra Jani and Vandana Jani; with photographs by Neirah Bhargava and Vijay Dave. Skylight Paths 2005 32p il (What you will see inside) $17.99
Grades: 3 4 5 6 **294.5**
1. Hinduism
ISBN 978-1-59473-116-7; 1-59473-116-0
"This introduces the beliefs and practices of the Hindu religion. The book opens with a traditional Sanskrit word of greeting . . . setting the respectful, inviting tone of the text, which leads readers into a temple. The book explains what can be seen there and discusses Hindu beliefs, worship practices, scriptures, celebrations, blessing ceremonies, and family shrines in homes. A typical double-page spread includes one large color photograph and a few small ones illustrating several paragraphs of clear, concise text." Booklist

Plum-Ucci, Carol
Celebrate Diwali; [by] Carol Plum-Ucci. Enslow Publishers 2008 128p il map (Celebrate holidays) $31.93
Grades: 5 6 7 8 **294.5**
1. Divali
ISBN 978-0-7660-2778-7; 0-7660-2778-3
LC 2006028106
This describes the history, cultural significance, customs, symbols and celebrations around the world of the Hindu holiday of Diwali.
"Captioned photographs, maps, drawings, and sidebars combine with accessible text to present a thorough discussion of [Diwali]. . . . This . . . is a useful resource." Horn Book Guide
Includes glossary and bibliographical references

Rasamandala Das
★ **Hinduism**. World Almanac Library 2006 48p il map (Religions of the world) $30.60

Grades: 5 6 7 8 **294.5**
1. Hinduism
ISBN 0-8368-5867-0

Hinduism is "explored in an accessible introductory manner, including information on [its] history, teachings, religious practices, culture and lifestyle, and the [faith's role] in today's global society. Vibrant full-color photographs are appropriately placed within the [text]. Ideal for . . . school reports or for general interest." SLJ

Includes bibliographical references

294.6 Sikhism

Hawker, Frances
Sikhism in India; written by Frances Hawker and Mohini Kaur Bhatia; photography by Bruce Campbell. Crabtree Pub. Company 2009 32p il (Families and their faiths) lib bdg $26.60; pa $8.95
Grades: 3 4 5 **294.6**
1. Sikhs 2. Sikhism
ISBN 978-0-7787-5011-6 lib bdg; 0-7787-5011-6 lib bdg; 978-0-7787-5028-4 pa; 0-7787-5028-0 pa
LC 2009-14160

This "book introduces a child who practices [Sikhism]. . . . Provides a solid introduction without overwhelming readers with complex regional variations in practices and beliefs. . . . Words and phrases that are unique to the faith appear in bold font and are defined at greater length in the glossary." SLJ

Includes glossary

296 Judaism

Hawker, Frances
Judaism in Israel; written by Frances Hawker and Daniel Taub; photography by Bruce Campbell. Crabtree Pub. 2010 32p il (Families and their faiths) lib bdg $26.60; pa $8.95
Grades: 3 4 5 **296**
1. Judaism
ISBN 978-0-7787-5010-9 lib bdg; 0-7787-5010-8 lib bdg; 978-0-7787-5027-7 pa; 0-7787-5027-2 pa
LC 2009-14159

This "book introduces a child who practices [Judaism]. . . . Provides a solid introduction without overwhelming readers with complex regional variations in practices and beliefs. . . . Words and phrases that are unique to the faith appear in bold font and are defined at greater length in the glossary." SLJ

Includes glossary

Keene, Michael
★ **Judaism**; [by] Michael Keene. World Almanac Library 2006 48p il map (Religions of the world) lib bdg $30.60
Grades: 5 6 7 8 **296**
1. Judaism
ISBN 0-8368-5869-7
LC 2005041734

This "volume presents fundamental beliefs and faith foundations, current status and practices of [Judaism] around the globe, and a time line of historically significant events. . . . The [book is] enumerated with full-color photographs on every page, charts, maps, and tables. . . . [This title] will enhance the education of diverse populations." SLJ

Includes bibliographical references

Rosinsky, Natalie M.
Judaism. Compass Point Books 2009 48p il map (World religions) lib bdg $27.99
Grades: 5 6 7 8 **296**
1. Judaism
ISBN 978-0-7565-4240-5 lib bdg; 0-7565-4240-5 lib bdg
LC 2009-15813

"The colorful, attractive layout includes high-quality reproductions of photographs, maps, and paintings. Students who are new to religious studies, as well as those doing reports, will find that this . . . meets their needs." SLJ

Includes glossary and bibliographical references

296.1 Sources

Chaikin, Miriam
Angels sweep the desert floor; Bible legends about Moses in the wilderness. illustrated by Alexander Koshkin. Clarion Bks. 2002 102p il $19
Grades: 4 5 6 7 **296.1**
1. Prophets 2. Bible stories 3. Jewish legends 4. Angels -- Fiction 5. Biblical characters
ISBN 0-395-97825-4
LC 2001-47501

A collection of eighteen stories based on the Bible which tell how angels respond to God's commands to ease the way for Moses and the Israelites as they cross the wilderness after being freed from slavery in Egypt

"The full-page watercolor, tempera, and gouache illustrations have a fanciful formality that complements the narrative. Capable of exciting the creative, as well as the spiritual imagination, these wonderful stories make great read-alouds." SLJ

Includes bibliographical references

Heiman, Diane
It's a-- it's a-- it's a mitzvah! Diane Heiman and Liz Suneby; Illustrations by Laurel Molk. Jewish Lights Publishing 2012 32 p. $18.99
Grades: PreK K 1 2 **296.1**
1. Judaism -- Juvenile fiction 2. Kindness -- Juvenile fiction 3. Judaism -- Customs and practices -- Juvenile fiction 4. Commandments (Judaism) -- Juvenile literature
ISBN 1580235093; 9781580235099
LC 2012003703

This book by Liz Suneby and Diane Heiman, illustrated by Laurel Molk, is an "introduction to the joys of doing mitzvoth. Join Mitzvah Meerkat and friends as they introduce children to the everyday kindnesses that mark the beginning of . . . a lifetime commitment to 'tikkun olam' (repairing the world). . . . Children engage with Jewish wisdom as they share in welcoming new friends, forgiving mistakes, respecting elders, sharing food with the hungry, and much, much more." (Publisher's note)

Pinsker, Marlee

In the days of sand and stars; illustrated by François Thisdale. Tundra Books 2006 87p il $22.95

Grades: 5 6 7 8   **296.1**

1. Bible stories 2. Jewish legends 3. Women in the Bible

ISBN 978-0-88776-724-1; 0-88776-724-9

This is a collection of stories from the Midrash about women including Eve, Naamah, Sarai, Sarah, Rebecca, Leah, Rachel, Dina, and Yocheved.

"Pinsker works like a musician, playing with words instead of notes, but the result is just as lilting and lyrical. The stories are matched by unusual illustrations. Thisdale blends traditional artwork with digital technology. Pieces of photographs mix with ancient elements, giving the pictures a fresh, compelling look." Booklist

296.4   Traditions, rites, public services

Balsley, Tilda

Maccabee! the story of Hanukkah. illustrated by David Harrington. Kar-Ben Pub. 2010 un il lib bdg $17.95; pa $7.95

Grades: K 1 2 3   **296.4**

1. Hanukkah 2. Stories in rhyme

ISBN 978-0-7613-4507-7 lib bdg; 0-7613-4507-8 lib bdg; 978-0-7613-4508-4 pa; 0-7613-4508-6 pa

LC 2009001877

Judah and his small army of Maccabees fight to free Jerusalem from the cruel King Antiochus in this rhyming version of the Hanukkah story.

"Balsley's rhythmic narration includes basic characterization and dialogue for the key players to make the story come alive. Bold opaque paintings of brave, bearded men with flowing hair . . . provide a cinematic view of this legend of heroism and determination." Kirkus

Bernhard, Durga Yael

Around the world in one Shabbat; Jewish people celebrate the Sabbath together. [by] Durga Yael Bernhard. Jewish Lights Pub. 2011 32p il $18.99

Grades: K 1 2 3   **296.4**

1. Jews 2. Sabbath

ISBN 978-1-58023-433-7; 1-58023-433-X

LC 2010041803

"Bernhard uses a global, child-centric approach to explore traditions and rituals that accompany the Sabbath. Each spread tells the story of a different child; in Buenos Aires, Alicia awakens from a nap and helps her sister braid challah, while in Istanbul Leyla joins her brother and parents around the table. . . . As Bernhard moves from France and Canada to Ethiopia and Thailand, warm, genial paintings add to an overall sense of serenity and community. The lyricism of the vignettes belies just how much information Bernhard packs into the book—it's an excellent resource." Publ Wkly

Chaikin, Miriam

★ Menorahs, mezuzas, and other Jewish symbols; illustrated by Erika Weihs. Clarion Bks. 1990 102p il $17; pa $5.95

Grades: 5 6 7 8   **296.4**

1. Jewish art and symbolism 2. Judaism -- Customs and practices 3. Judaism -- Customs and practices -- Juvenile literature

ISBN 0-89919-856-2; 0-618-37835-9 pa

LC 89-77719

Explains the history and significance of many Jewish symbols, such as the Shield of David, the menorah, and the mezuza, and discusses holiday symbols and rituals

"Embellished with bibliographical references as well as Weihs' simple yet elegant and wonderfully dramatic scratchboard illustrations, this smoothly woven patchwork of history and culture is a fine introduction that will attract browsers and be useful for children investigating the subject of symbolism in school." Booklist

Cooper, Ilene

★ Jewish holidays all year round; a family treasury. written by Ilene Cooper; illustrations by Elivia Savadier; captions by Josh Feinberg; in association with the Jewish Museum, New York. Abrams 2002 80p il $19.95

Grades: 4 5 6 7   **296.4**

1. Handicraft 2. Jewish cooking 3. Jewish holidays 4. Fasts and feasts -- Judaism

ISBN 0-8109-0550-7

LC 2001-56741

As the author "explores the history and significance of the holidays and festivals of the Jewish year, she . . . links these to traditions and rituals. . . . Instructions for holiday activities (crafts, recipes, etc.) are also included. . . . Savadier's vignettes, mostly of busy, happy people, underscore the liveliness of Jewish faith." Publ Wkly

Includes bibliographical references

Fishman, Cathy

On Hanukkah; by Cathy Goldberg Fishman; illustrated by Melanie W. Hall. Atheneum Bks. for Young Readers 1998 un il $16

Grades: K 1 2 3   **296.4**

1. Hanukkah 2. Hanukkah -- Juvenile literature

ISBN 0-689-80643-4

LC 96-44696

"Fishman and Hall focus on a family's celebration of a Jewish holiday. The writing is simple and direct, yet the coverage is ample. . . . The fanciful, mixed-media paintings feature strong texturing and glowing, gilt-edged colors." Booklist

On Rosh Hashanah and Yom Kippur; by Cathy Goldberg Fishman; illustrated by Melanie W. Hall. Atheneum Bks. for Young Readers 1997 un il hardcover o.p. pa $5.99

Grades: K 1 2 3   **296.4**

1. Yom Kippur 2. Rosh ha-Shanah

ISBN 0-689-80526-8; 0-689-83892-1 pa

LC 96-23258

"Fishman explores and explains the traditions associated with the Jewish High Holidays. She focuses mainly on Rosh Hashanah . . . and in a quiet, almost reverent way uses the voice of a little girl to make readers party to a family's celebrations. . . . Hall's beautiful, rosy, expressionistic pictures are a fine complement to Fishman's text. They capture the warm glow of a family celebrating together." Booklist

On Sukkot and Simchat Torah; [by] Cathy Goldberg Fishman; illustrations by Melanie W. Hall. Kar-Ben Pub. 2006 un il lib bdg $17.95

Grades: K 1 2 3   **296.4**
1. Sukkot 2. Simchath Torah
ISBN 1-58013-165-4

LC 2001022789

"Readers watch a family get ready for the Sukkot by building a small shelter, a sukkah . . . In evocative prose, Fishman not only explains the holiday but also captures the joyous mood that infuses it. . . . She also captures the celebratory feel of Simchat Torah, complete with the marching and singing that take place as the Torah is carried around the synagogue. The lively text is matched by Hall's stirring artwork, in shades of blue, green, gold, and orange, which is ethereal yet full of sweet, everyday detail." Booklist

Had gadya; a Passover song. paintings by Seymour Chwast; afterword by Michael Strassfeld. Roaring Brook Press 2005 un il $16.95; pa $7.95

Grades: K 1 2 3   **296.4**
1. Songs 2. Passover 3. Children's songs, Jewish
ISBN 1-59643-033-8; 1-59643-298-5 pa

LC 2003-17831

"The bright, acrylic folk-art paintings express the rhythm of the chant. . . . The book, complete with musical notation and Hebrew and English words, is bound to add to the pleasure of the seder." Booklist

Hanft, Josh
The **miracles** of Passover; [by] Josh Hanft; illustrated by Seymour Chwast. Blue Apple Books 2007 un il $15.95
Grades: PreK K 1 2   **296.4**
1. Passover
ISBN 978-1-59354-600-7; 1-59354-600-9

LC 2006031585

"The story of Moses, Pharaoh, the 10 plagues, and the crossing of the Red Sea is explained in child-friendly language with additional information included about the traditions of the Seder. What distinguishes this book from others of its kind is the overall excellence of the colorful artwork." SLJ

Heiligman, Deborah
★ **Celebrate** Hanukkah; [by] Deborah Heiligman; consultant, Shira Stern. National Geographic 2006 32p il (Holidays around the world) $15.95; lib bdg $23.90
Grades: K 1 2 3   **296.4**
1. Hanukkah
ISBN 0-7922-5924-6; 0-7922-5925-4 lib bdg

LC 2005032427

This "introduces children to the Jewish Festival of Lights. Heiligman recounts the holiday's history and origins and describes how it is celebrated today. . . . The main text is succinct and appropriate for reading aloud. . . . Decorating the pages are sumerous crisp, full-color photos." Booklist
Includes glossary and bibliographical references

★ **Celebrate** Passover; [by] Deborah Heiligman. National Geographic 2007 32p il (Holidays around the world) $15.95; lib bdg $23.90

Grades: K 1 2 3   **296.4**
1. Passover
ISBN 978-1-4263-0018-9; 978-1-4263-00196 lib bdg

LC 2006020676

This "begins with a short recitation of the Passover story and then moves directly into how the holiday is celebrated. . . . A concluding essay by a rabbi offers thoughts on the meaning of the holiday. The clean format evokes the spring holiday, but the book's visual emphasis is also on Jewish communities in Africa, Asia, the Middle East, and elsewhere." Booklist
Includes bibliographical references

★ **Celebrate** Rosh Hashanah and Yom Kippur; [by] Deborah Heiligman; consultant, Shira Stern. National Geographic 2007 31p il (Holidays around the world) $15.95; lib bdg $23.90
Grades: K 1 2 3   **296.4**
1. Yom Kippur 2. Rosh ha-Shanah
ISBN 978-1-4263-0076-9; 978-1-4263-0077-6 lib bdg

LC 2006100317

"Lush color photographs show the diversity of the celebrants and bring an immediacy to these observances. Clear, simple [text provides] history and background information, descriptions of customs, and basic analyses of each celebration's deeper meaning. . . . Exemplary back matter includes quick facts and extra information to provide context. There is even a map showing where all of the fascinating photos were taken." SLJ
Includes glossary and bibliographical references

Heller, Esther Susan
Menorah under the sea; photographs by David Ginsburg. Kar-Ben Pub. 2009 29p il lib bdg $17.95
Grades: K 1 2 3   **296.4**
1. Hanukkah 2. Marine biology
ISBN 978-0-8225-7386-9 lib bdg; 0-8225-7386-5 lib bdg

LC 2007043175

Describes how, while studying sea urchins in Antarctica, marine biologist David Ginsburg celebrated Hanukkah by creating his own menorah on the sea floor
"The vibrant color photography and surprising thematic juxtaposition—readers will learn as much about urchins as about the holiday—makes this a memorable selection, even for readers who don't celebrate Hanukkah." Publ Wkly

Hoffman, Lawrence A.
What you will see inside a synagogue; [by] Lawrence Hoffman and Ron Wolfson; with photographs by Bill Aron. SkyLight Paths 2004 31p il (What you will see inside--) $17.99
Grades: 3 4 5 6   **296.4**
1. Judaism
ISBN 1-59473-012-1

LC 2004-11178

"This book provides a warm and thorough welcome to the center of Jewish life. . . . Numerous clear color photos and pronunciation guides for Hebrew words are included. . . . An excellent overview." SLJ

Hoyt-Goldsmith, Diane

★ **Celebrating** Hanukkah; photographs by Lawrence Migdale. Holiday House 1996 31p il hardcover o.p. pa $6.95

Grades: 3 4 5   **296.4**

    1. Hanukkah

    ISBN 0-8234-1252-0; 0-8234-1411-6 pa

                     LC 96-5110

The photographs "are warm and inviting, with Migdale catching celebrations at home, at school, and in the synagogue. . . . The text is equally fine, well organized and rich in detail but also friendly." Booklist

    Includes glossary

★ **Celebrating** Passover; photographs by Lawrence Migdale. Holiday House 2000 32p il lib bdg $16.95

Grades: 3 4 5   **296.4**

    1. Seder 2. Passover

    ISBN 0-8234-1420-5

                    LC 99-49006

Uses one family's celebration of Passover to describe the religious significance, traditions, customs, and symbols of this Jewish holiday

"An attractive and useful choice for the holiday shelf; recipes, songs, and a glossary are a bonus." Booklist

Kimmel, Eric A.

The **Chanukkah** guest; illustrated by Giora Carmi. Holiday House 1990 un il $15.95; pa $6.95

Grades: K 1 2 3   **296.4**

    1. Jews -- Fiction 2. Bears -- Fiction 3. Hanukkah -- Fiction

    ISBN 0-8234-0788-8; 0-8234-0978-3 pa

                    LC 89-20073

On the first night of Chanukkah, Old Bear wanders into Bubba Brayna's house and receives a delicious helping of potato latkes when she mistakes him for the rabbi

"In this comical story, Kimmel captures the kindness of an old woman and the innocence of a hungry bear in an unusual visit. Carmi's airy pastel illustrations shade the tale with a golden glow appropriate for the Festival of Lights." Publ Wkly

★ **Wonders** and miracles; a Passover companion. illustrated with art spanning three thousand years; written and compiled by Eric A. Kimmel. Scholastic Press 2004 136p il $18.95

Grades: 4 5 6 7   **296.4**

    1. Passover

    ISBN 0-439-07175-5

                    LC 2002-4732

Presents the steps performed in a traditional Passover Seder, plus stories, songs, poetry, and pictures that celebrate the historical significance of this holiday to Jews all over the world.

"The marvelous selection of art—paintings, photographs, artifacts, and illustrations from historical Haggadahs—illuminates each step in the service. . . . Both the presentation of information and the overall design attest to the careful and loving attention given to every detail. This inviting, handsome, and informative compendium should find a place of honor in every library." SLJ

    Includes bibliographical references

Lehman-Wilzig, Tami

Hanukkah around the world; by Tami Lehman-Wilzig; illustrated by Vicki Wehrman. Kar-Ben Pub. 2009 48p il map $16.95

Grades: 2 3 4 5   **296.4**

    1. Hanukkah

    ISBN 978-0-8225-8761-3; 0-8225-8761-0

                  LC 2008031196

"This tour of Hanukkah includes information on its historical significance and the ways in which it is celebrated in places like New York City, Turin, Sydney and Warsaw. After an introductory section about the history, terminology and customs associated with the holiday, the book features a story of a child living in each city." Publ Wkly

Melmed, Laura Krauss

Eight winter nights; a family Hanukkah book. illustrated by Elisabeth Schlossberg. Chronicle Books 2010 un il $16.99

Grades: PreK K 1   **296.4**

    1. Hanukkah

    ISBN 978-0-8118-5552-5; 0-8118-5552-X

                  LC 2009019574

Short verses describe symbols, foods, and family fun associated with the festival of Hanukkah. Includes facts about the history and traditions.

"The verse and illustrations work well together. . . . Created with pencil and pastels, the illustrations use plenty of curved lines and deep, warm colors to depict the celebrations in this lively, amiable household." Booklist

Metter, Bert

Bar mitzvah, bat mitzvah; the ceremony, the party, and how the day came to be. by Bert Metter; illustrated by Joan Reilly. Clarion Books 2007 un il $16; pa $5.95

Grades: 4 5 6 7   **296.4**

    1. Bar mitzvah 2. Bat mitzvah

    ISBN 978-0-618-76772-4; 0-618-76772-X; 978-0-618-76773-1 pa; 0-618-76773-8 pa

                  LC 2006032942

The author "describes a typical ceremony and explains how this custom began for boys during the Middle Ages and how it was adapted for girls beginning in 1922. He also discusses the recent custom of adult bar and bat mitzvahs and celebratory parties. The writing is clear and concise; ink illustrations . . . help break up the text." Booklist

    Includes bibliographical references

Podwal, Mark H.

Built by angels; the story of the old-new synagogue. by Mark Podwal. Harcourt Children's Books 2009 un il $16

Grades: 1 2 3 4   **296.4**

    1. Synagogues 2. Jews -- Czech Republic

    ISBN 978-0-15-206678-9; 0-15-206678-0

                  LC 2007052091

"Legend, history and spiritual significance intertwine in Podwal's illustrated free-verse poem paying homage to Prague's Altneuschul, or Old-New Synagogue, which is the oldest in Europe, dating back to 1270, and is treasured for its early Gothic architecture. . . . Childlike yet abstract drawings in acrylic, gouache and colored pencil-dominated by a combination of reds . . . delineate the building's history as a haven for worship throughout the centuries. . . . A beautiful,

Impressionistic introduction to a portion of Judaic lore and a European architectural marvel." Kirkus

★ A **sweet** year; a taste of the Jewish holidays. [by] Mark Podwal. Doubleday Bks. for Young Readers 2003 un il hardcover o.p. lib bdg $14.99

Grades: K 1 2 3 **296.4**
1. Food 2. Jewish holidays 3. Food -- Religious aspects 4. Fasts and feasts -- Judaism 5. Judaism -- Customs and practices 6. Fasts and feasts -- Judaism -- Juvenile literature 7. Food -- Religious aspects -- Judaism -- Juvenile literature
ISBN 0-385-74637-7; 0-385-90869-5 lib bdg
LC 2002-155442

Pictures and easy-to-read text introduce Jewish holidays, focusing on the foods associated with each

This offers "beautifully crafted poetic text and symbolic paintings in gouache and acrylics." SLJ

Includes bibliographical references

Schecter, Ellen
★ The **family** Haggadah; illustrated by Neil Waldman. Viking 1999 66p il music pa $13.99

Grades: 4 5 6 7 **296.4**
1. Passover
ISBN 0-670-88341-7
LC 98-28597

"Although really intended for parents to use with their children at a family Passover seder, this attractive book may also be useful to children wanting to plan their own model celebration." Booklist

The **story** of Hanukkah; illustrated by Jill Weber. Holiday House 2011 un il $14.95

Grades: PreK K 1 2 **296.4**
1. Hanukkah 2. Hanukkah stories
ISBN 978-0-8234-2295-1; 0-8234-2295-X

This retells the Hanukkah story of the Maccabees and the miracle that took place in the Temple in Jerusalem. Includes a recipe for latkes and directions for playing dreidel.

"The events commemorated in the holiday of Hanukkah are retold simply for young ears. . . . Weber's full-spread color illustrations, with an emphasis on traditional holiday blue, convey the epic scope of the story." Publ Wkly

Walker, Robert
Bar and bat mitzvahs; Robert Walker. Crabtree Pub. Co. 2012 32 p. (reinforced library binding: alk. paper) $26.60

Grades: 1 2 3 **296.4**
1. Bar mitzvah 2. Bat mitzvah
ISBN 0778740862; 0778740919; 1427178453; 1427179603; 9780778740865; 9780778740919; 9781427178459; 9781427179609
LC 2012004070

This book looks at bar and bat mitzvahs. Chapters explore themes including the "history of the ceremony," "the Sabbath," "important religious texts," "the Hebrew language," and how "girls get their own day." The post-ceremony reception and party is also considered. (WorldCat)

Includes bibliographical references and index

Woog, Adam
What makes me a Jew? Kidhaven Press 2004 48p il (What makes me a-- ?) $23.70

Grades: 3 4 5 **296.4**
1. Judaism
ISBN 0-7377-2266-5
LC 2003-20951

This describes Jewish origins, beliefs, practices, foods, and holidays.

"Presenting information about religion objectively for younger audiences poses a difficult challenge, but [this title does] and excellent job of it." Booklist

Includes bibliographical references

Ziefert, Harriet
★ **Hanukkah** haiku; [by] Harriet Ziefert; paintings by Karla Gudeon. Blue Apple Books 2008 un il $16.95

Grades: PreK K 1 **296.4**
1. Haiku 2. Hanukkah
ISBN 978-1-934706-33-6; 1-934706-33-7
LC 2008005877

"Combining festive illustrations and a playful format, this title uses haiku to celebrate the eight nights of Hanukkah. . . . Each turn of the stepped pages brings fresh excitement as another lit candle and verse are revealed. Illustrations have a lovely folkloric quality in which Chagall-like figures, surrounded by richly colored flowers and stars, float across a fibrous tan background." SLJ

Passover; celebrating now, remembering then. paintings by Karla Gudeon. Blue Apple Books 2010 un il $17.99

Grades: PreK K 1 2 3 **296.4**
1. Passover
ISBN 978-1-60905-020-7; 1-60905-020-7

"Ziefert provides a simplified adaptation of Exodus, a description of holiday preparations, and a concise Haggadah, or service for this ritual meal. Throughout, Ziefert contrasts current practice . . . with ancient origins. . . . On every page, Gudeon's Chagall-like paintings exhibit a folkloric style. . . . This title is one that families with young children will appreciate and want to own." Booklist

297 Islam, Babism, Bahai Faith

Barnard, Bryn
★ The **genius** of Islam; how Muslims made the modern world. Alfred A. Knopf 2011 37p il map $17.99; lib bdg $20.99

Grades: 4 5 6 7 **297**
1. Islamic civilization 2. Islam -- History
ISBN 978-0-375-84072-2; 0-375-84072-9; 978-0-375-94072-9 lib bdg; 0-375-94072-3 lib bdg
LC 2010-12777

This is a "concise and eloquent exploration of the far-reaching influence of Islam over the centuries. Each spread is devoted to a different subject (writing, Arabic numerals, architecture, astronomy, agriculture), while captioned spot art homes in on specific inventions and innovations (the zither, the astrolabe, advanced medical knowledge)." Publ Wkly

Includes bibliographical references

Cooper, Alison

Facts about Islam. Rosen Central 2010 45p il map (World religions) lib bdg $26.50

Grades: 3 4 5 6   **297**

1. Islam

ISBN 978-1-61532-322-7 lib bdg; 1-61532-322-8 lib bdg

LC 2009052445

"This book describes who Muslims are, the beginning of Islam, beliefs and leaders, the Qur'an, Sunna, family life, worship, the Islamic calendar, Hajj, festivals, and how the religion spread. . . . Colorful photographs, maps, and illustrations appear on every chapter spread, and the language is easy to understand, making this a useful resource for children." SLJ

Includes glossary and bibliographical references

Demi

★ **Muhammad**; written and illustrated by Demi. Margaret K. McElderry Bks. 2003 un il $19.95

Grades: 4 5 6 7   **297**

1. Islam 2. Prophets 3. Islamic leaders 4. Writers on religion

ISBN 0-689-85264-9

LC 2002-2985

"With dramatic scenes extending past the borders of the intricately patterned frames, the art will be a continual source of interest for young people. . . . [An] excellent retelling of the Prophet's life that combines beauty and scholarship." Booklist

Includes bibliographical references

Hawker, Frances

Islam in Turkey; written by Frances Hawker and Leyla Alicavusoglu; photography by Bruce Campbell. Crabtree Pub. Company 2010 32p il (Families and their faiths) lib bdg $26.60; pa $8.95

Grades: 3 4 5   **297**

1. Islam

ISBN 978-0-7787-5009-3 lib bdg; 0-7787-5009-4 lib bdg; 978-0-7787-5026-0 pa; 0-7787-5026-4 pa

LC 2009-14158

This "book introduces a child who practices [Islam]. . . . Provides a solid introduction without overwhelming readers with complex regional variations in practices and beliefs. . . . Words and phrases that are unique to the faith appear in bold font and are defined at greater length in the glossary." SLJ

Includes glossary

Raatma, Lucia

Islam. Compass Point Books 2010 48p il map (World religions) lib bdg $27.99

Grades: 5 6 7 8   **297**

1. Islam

ISBN 978-0-7565-4239-9 lib bdg; 0-7565-4239-1 lib bdg

LC 2009-15812

"The colorful, attractive layout includes high-quality reproductions of photographs, maps, and paintings. Students who are new to religious studies, as well as those doing reports, will find that this . . . meets their needs." SLJ

Includes glossary and bibliographical references

297.09   History, geographic treatment, biography

Whiting, Jim

The **role** of religion in the early Islamic world; Jim Whiting. Crabtree Pub. Company 2012 48 p. (Life in the early islamic world) (reinforced library binding: alk. paper) $30.60

Grades: 4 5 6   **297.09**

1. Islam -- History 2. Picture books for children

ISBN 0778721698; 9780778721697; 9780778721765; 9781427195623; 9781427198419

LC 2012000075

This book looks at the role of religion in the early Islamic world. "Information is presented in concise chapters. . . . The main texts are supplemented with blue boxes of information, subsections, and many . . . reproductions, maps, and paintings. Each book contains time lines and short biographies of important historical figures." (School Library Journal)

297.3   Islamic worship

Brown, Tricia

Salaam; a Muslim American boy's story. Henry Holt 2006 un il $17.95

Grades: K 1 2 3   **297.3**

1. Islam 2. Muslims

ISBN 978-0-8050-6538-1; 0-8050-6538-5

LC 2005013147

"A gentle and informative look at a Muslim-American boy and the way he practices his faith. The book does a good job of explaining each of the Five Pillars of Islam. . . . Good-quality black-and-white photos enhance the presentation and effectively show the warmth of Imran's family life." SLJ

Includes glossary

Bullard, Lisa

Rashad's Ramadan and Eid al-Fitr; by Lisa Bullard; illustrated by Holli Conger. Millbrook Press 2012 24 p. col. ill. (lib. bdg.: alk. paper) $23.93; (ebook) $35.93; (paperback) $6.95

Grades: 1 2 3   **297.3**

1. Muslims 2. Islamic holidays 3. Picture books for children 4. Ramadan -- Juvenile literature 5. Id al-Fitr -- Juvenile literature

ISBN 0761350799; 9780761350798; 9780761388425; 9780761385837

LC 2011024545

Author Lisa Bullard's book focuses on Muslim holidays and celebrations. "For Muslims, Ramadan is a time for fasting, prayer, and thinking of others. Rashad tries to be good all month. When it's time for Eid al-Fitr, he feasts and plays! Find out how people celebrate this special time of year. Learn the history behind the days people celebrate in the Holidays and Special Days series, part of the Cloverleaf Books collection." (Publisher's note)

Dickmann, Nancy

Ramadan and Id-ul-Fitr. Heinemann Library 2010 24p il (Holidays and festivals) $21.50; pa $5.99

Grades: PreK K 1   297.3
    1. Islam 2. Ramadan 3. Id al-Adha
    ISBN 978-1-4329-4049-2; 1-4329-4049-X; 978-1-
    4329-4068-3 pa; 1-4329-4068-6 pa
                      LC 2009054305
This is a "clear introduction to Islam's holy month. . . . Large photos dominate the top two-thirds of each page, while a single line of large-print text delivers information. . . . Even lesser known to Americans is the celebration of Id-ul-Fitr at the end of Ramadan, and it is here where the book's photographs are particularly effective." Booklist
    Includes bibliographical references

Douglass, Susan L.
    ★ **Ramadan**; illustrations by Jeni Reeves. Carolrhoda Books 2004 48p il (On my own holidays) lib bdg $23.93; pa $4.95
Grades: 1 2 3   297.3
    1. Islam 2. Ramadan 3. Holidays 4. Id al-Adha 5. Id al-Fitr 6. Islam -- Customs and practices
    ISBN 0-87614-932-8 lib bdg; 1-57505-584-8 pa
                      LC 2002-6781
An introduction to Islamic observances during the month of Ramadan and the subsequent festival of Eid-al-Fitr
    "Reeves's abundant, framed illustrations in pastel colors provide detailed windows on the observance. . . . An easy-to-read, well-organized introduction." SLJ

Heiligman, Deborah
    ★ **Celebrate** Ramadan & Eid al-Fitr; [by] Deborah Heiligman; consultant, Neguin Yavari. National Geographic 2006 31p il map (Holidays around the world) $15.95; lib bdg $23.90
Grades: K 1 2 3   297.3
    1. Islam 2. Ramadan 3. Id al-Adha
    ISBN 0-7922-5926-2; 0-7922-5927-0 lib bdg
                      LC 2006008889
"Heiligman offers a simple, accessible introduction to the traditions of this solemn month and its concluding festival. Numerous clear, expressive photos feature captions that describe the experiences of children from varying countries and cultures and how they observe Ramadan." Publ Wkly
    Includes glossary and bibliographical references

Hoyt-Goldsmith, Diane
    ★ **Celebrating** Ramadan; Ramadan al-mu'azzam. photographs by Lawrence Migdale. Holiday House 2001 32p il map $16.95
Grades: 3 4 5   297.3
    1. Islam 2. Ramadan 3. Fasts and feasts -- Islam
    ISBN 0-8234-1581-3
                      LC 2001-16643
"This picture book for older readers follows devout muslim Ibraheem, a fourth-grader living in New Jersey, through the holy month of Ramadan. . . . This is a sensitive introduction to Ramadan; the quality of the photographs and the eloquent text make the book the one of the best introductions in recent memory." Booklist

Jeffrey, Laura S.
    Celebrate Ramadan; [by] Laura S. Jeffrey. Enslow Publishers 2007 112p il (Celebrate holidays) lib bdg $31.93

Grades: 5 6 7 8   297.3
    1. Islam 2. Ramadan 3. Id al-Adha
    ISBN 978-0-7660-2774-9 lib bdg; 0-7660-2774-0 lib bdg
                      LC 2006028107
"This book opens by introducing a contemporary Muslim, Bushra, who celebrated Ramadan as a girl growing up in England [and] later immigrated to the United States. . . . An informative chapter surveys the history, beliefs, and practices of Islam. . . . The remainder of the book offers a detailed discussion of Ramadan, prayer, and spiritual awareness, and of l'Id al Fitr. . . . Punctuated by sidebars and illustrated with color photos, this clearly written book offers a good overview of how the holidays of Islam are celebrated." Booklist
    Includes glossary and bibliographical references

Khan, Aisha Karen
    What you will see inside a mosque; photographs by Aaron Pepis. Skylight Paths Pub. 2003 31p il (What you will see inside--) $16.95; pa $8.99
Grades: 3 4 5 6   297.3
    1. Islam 2. Mosques
    ISBN 1-893361-60-8; 1-594732-57-4 pa
                    LC 2002-153436
Describes what happens inside a mosque and introduces the Muslim faith
    This is an "excellent introduction. . . . Full-page photographs are supplemented by smaller photos with informative captions." SLJ

MacMillan, Dianne M.
    Ramadan and Id al-Fitr; [by] Dianne M. MacMillan. rev and updated ed.; Enslow Elementary 2008 48p il map (Best holiday books) $23.93
Grades: 2 3 4   297.3
    1. Islam 2. Ramadan 3. Id al-Adha
    ISBN 978-0-7660-3045-9; 0-7660-3045-8
                    LC 2007002425
First published 1994
This describes the history of the Muslim holidays of Ramadan and Id al-Fitr and how they are celebrated in the United States
    "The well-written [text] aptly [describes] the traditions and customs and capture the flavor of the [holidays]. The open, spacious format makes the [book] accessible, and the full-color and black-and-white photos lend interest." SLJ
    Includes glossary and bibliographical references

Marchant, Kerena
    Id-ul-Fitr. Millbrook Press 1998 32p il (Festivals) lib bdg $21.90
Grades: 3 4 5   297.3
    1. Islam 2. Holidays 3. Id al-Fitr 4. Fasts and feasts -- Islam
    ISBN 0-7613-0963-2
                    LC 97-46035
Looks at some of the ways Muslims around the world celebrate the joyous festival of Id-ul-Fitr
    Includes bibliographical references

Murray, Julie
    Ramadan. ABDO Pub. Company 2011 24p il (Holidays) $25.26

Grades: 2 3 4 **297.3**
1. Ramadan
ISBN 978-1-61783-041-9; 1-61783-041-0
LC 2011002287

"This short, concise introduction is simple enough for the target audience, and it is accurate. Each two-page chapter introduces an aspect of Ramadan that is rooted in religious practices that are common to all Muslims: Sunnis and Shi'ites, Salafis and Sufis, liberals and conservatives. Each spread has a large, full-color picture. The publisher's website provides further reading with links to additional, credible Internet resources. This title succeeds where others have been undermined by cultural bias. An excellent addition." SLJ

Petrini, Catherine M.
★ **What** makes me a Muslim? [by] Catherine M. Petrini. KidHaven Press 2005 48p il map (What makes me a-- ?) $27
Grades: 3 4 5 **297.3**
1. Islam
ISBN 978-0-7377-2265-9; 0-7377-2265-7
LC 2004014526

"This overview explains what Islam is, where it came from, and how it has spread over time. Petrini provides a look at the background, beliefs, practices, holidays, and challenges of the religion today. . . . The full-color photographs and religious paintings throughout the book are as informative as they are appealing." SLJ
Includes bibliographical references

Whitman, Sylvia
Under the Ramadan moon; [by] Sylvia Whitman; illustrated by Sue Williams. A. Whitman & Co. 2008 un il $15.99
Grades: PreK K 1 2 **297.3**
1. Ramadan
ISBN 978-0-8075-8304-3; 0-8075-8304-9
LC 2008001307

"This delightful picture book describes the month-long Muslim observance of Ramadan by a modern family. . . . The images of the waxing, full, and waning moon progress along with the spare, lyrical text. Practices such as fasting, speaking kind words, giving to the poor, decorating with bright lights, and praying all take place, 'under the moon, under the Ramadan moon.' Williams uses soft, luminous pastels in richly textured, detailed spreads." SLJ

299   Religions not provided for elsewhere

Fisher, Leonard Everett
★ The **gods** and goddesses of ancient China. Holiday House 2003 un il $16.95
Grades: 3 4 5 6 **299**
1. Gods and goddesses 2. Gods, Chinese -- Juvenile literature 3. Goddesses, Chinese -- Juvenile literature
LC 2002-68802

"Beginning with an introduction that mentions Qin Shi Huangdi, China's First Supreme Emperor, Fisher offers very brief historical and cultural background to China's deities. . . . Profiles of 17 gods and goddesses follow, each one presented on a double-page spread that includes a roughly brushed portrait opposite a few paragraphs summarizing the figure's corresponding legend. . . . Fisher combines concise, accessible language, colorful art, and exciting stories about figures that aren't often covered in books for youth." Booklist
Includes bibliographical references

Kramer, Ann
Egyptian myth; a treasury of legends, art, and history. M. E. Sharpe 2008 96p il map (The world of mythology) $35.95
Grades: 5 6 7 8 **299**
1. Egyptian art 2. Egyptian mythology
ISBN 978-0-7656-8105-8; 0-7656-8105-6
LC 2007005876

This "handsomely designed [book is] illustrated with works of art from the culture. [It] is a well-organized presentation that includes information and tales about the gods and the pharoahs as well as magical stories and legends, providing an excellent introduction to this fascinating culture." SLJ
Includes glossary and bibliographical references

Williams, Marcia
Ancient Egypt; tales of gods and pharaohs. Candlewick Press 2011 un il $16.99
Grades: 4 5 6 **299**
1. Egyptian mythology
ISBN 978-0-7636-5308-8; 0-7636-5308-X
LC 2010040745

"The highpoints of Egyptian mythology—creation, the divinity of Ra, the death of Osiris, and the vengeance of his son Horus—as well as the stories of four great pharaohs—are presented in this lighthearted picture book/graphic novel. . . . This book makes them all seem like fun. Williams utilizes a beautiful, sun-soaked palette of gold, turquoise, lapis, jade, and carnelian lifted right off a sarcophagus. . . . Expressive postures, smiling faces, and playful interactions among them keep readers scouring the pages for every little joke. . . . Each figure in this book . . . fairly leaps off the page in order to grab readers' attention." SLJ

299.5   Religions of East and Southeast Asian origin

Demi
★ The **legend** of Lao Tzu and the Tao te ching. Margaret K. McElderry Books 2007 un il $21.99
Grades: 4 5 6 7 **299.5**
1. Taoism 2. Philosophers 3. Taoism -- Juvenile literature
ISBN 1-4169-1206-1; 978-1-4169-1206-4
LC 2005029695

"This is the legend of Lao Tzu . . . who may or may not have founded Taoism, one of the greatest religions of the world. Demi's elegant picture-book introduction to the legendary Chinese philosopher . . . combines nuggets of his purported life with 20 verses from the Tao Te Ching. . . . The narrative and graceful paintings are contained in a gold circular frame on each parchment shaded page." SLJ

Levin, Judith

Japanese mythology; [by] Judith Levin. The Rosen Pub. Group 2008 64p il map (Mythology around the world) $29.95

Grades: 5 6 7 8   **299.5**

1. Shinto 2. Buddhism 3. Japanese mythology

ISBN 978-1-4042-0736-3; 1-4042-0736-8

            LC 2005035279

This "presents not only an introduction to Shinto and Buddhist beliefs, but also Japanese history and mythology in general. . . . The most remarkable part of [this book] . . . is the respect [it shows] for the mythological customs, treating them throughout with the same care that writers of books on major religions might offer. The illustrations show both ancient and modern incarnations of the deities and heroes." SLJ

Includes glossary and bibliographical references

299.7   Religions of North American native origin

Swamp, Jake

Giving thanks; a Native American good morning message. by Chief Jake Swamp; illustrated by Erwin Printup, Jr. Lee & Low Bks. 1995 un il $16.95; pa $6.95

Grades: K 1 2 3   **299.7**

1. Human ecology 2. Mohawk Indians 3. Native Americans 4. Prayers -- Juvenile literature

ISBN 1-880000-15-6; 1-880000-54-7 pa

            LC 94-5955

"Its simple, timeless language bears witness to the Native American reverence for the natural world and sense of unity with all living things. . . . The gifts of the earth . . . are richly depicted in paintings of wildlife and bountiful harvests." Publ Wkly

300   SOCIAL SCIENCES, SOCIOLOGY & ANTHROPOLOGY

302.23   Media (Means of communication)

Marcovitz, Hal

Bias in the media. Lucent Books 2010 112p il (Hot topics) lib bdg $32.45

Grades: 5 6 7 8   **302.23**

1. Journalism 2. Mass media

ISBN 978-1-4205-0224-4 lib bdg; 1-4205-0224-7 lib bdg

            LC 2009048285

"Young researchers are ill-equipped to judge the integrity of media, much less distinguish between conservative or liberal points of view. Marcovitz's thorough text not only gives them an in-depth look at bias in the news, but also leaves them with knowledge that will help them discern such slants in the future. . . . This text needs to be introduced to kids, perhaps in the context of a current-events class. Discussion questions are included. A comprehensive, useful book." SLJ

Includes bibliographical references

Milich, Zoran

City signs. Kids Can Press 2002 un il $15.95; pa $6.95

Grades: PreK K 1 2   **302.23**

1. Signs and signboards

ISBN 1-55337-003-1; 1-55337-748-6 pa

"Milich took to the streets with his camera, looking for printed words found in various outdoor environments. The 30 photographs here demonstrate that even children who can't yet read a book understand many of the words they see around them. The quality of the pictures is very good. They are nicely composed, clear, and often colorful." Booklist

302.3   Social interaction within groups

Burstein, John

Why are you picking on me? dealing with bullies. Crabtree Pub. Company 2009 32p il (Slim Goodbody's life skills 101) lib bdg $26.60; pa $8.95

Grades: 1 2 3 4 5   **302.3**

1. Bullies

ISBN 978-0-7787-4792-5 lib bdg; 0-7787-4792-1 lib bdg; 978-0-7787-4808-3 pa; 0-7787-4808-1 pa

            LC 2009022427

This book about dealing with bullies offers "clear and simple advice for children and [provides] adults with springboards for discussion and roleplaying. All have appealing color photographs of a variety of types of kids, . . . opening scenarios, concrete coping suggestions, and solid reasoning." SLJ

Includes bibliographical references

Ellis, Deborah

★ **We** want you to know; kids talk about bullying. Coteau Books 2010 120p il $19.95; pa $15.95

Grades: 5 6 7 8 9 10   **302.3**

1. Bullies 2. Bullying -- Juvenile literature

ISBN 978-1-55050-417-0; 1-55050-417-7; 978-1-55050-463-7 pa; 1-55050-463-0

"As part of her work with an anti-bullying campaign in her local Canadian community, Ellis interviewed young people between the ages of 9 and 19 about their experiences. In honest, straightforward prose, she shares their stories, many as targets and some as perpetrators or bystanders. . . . Each story is written from the first-person point of view, some with real names and photos, providing an intimacy and immediacy that are critical with these kinds of issues. Readers will find at least one or two stories they can relate to, and educators should be able to use many of the narratives to jumpstart conversation." SLJ

Includes bibliographical references

Fox, Debbie

★ **Good-bye** bully machine; written by Debbie Fox and Allan L. Beane; illustrated by Debbie Fox. Free Spirit Pub. 2009 39p il pa $8.95; $12.99

Grades: K 1 2 3 4 5   **302.3**

1. Bullies

ISBN 978-1-57542-321-0 pa; 1-57542-321-9 pa; 978-1-57542-326-5; 1-57542-326-X

            LC 2008-41025

Kids learn what bullying is, why it hurts, and what they can do to end it with this fresh, compelling book including contemporary collage art, lively layout, and straightforward text.

"The authors provide tips for dealing with negative behaviors and encourage readers to take a stand against bullying and unplug the bully machine. Fox's enticing, edgy, collage artwork will draw readers in. . . . This offering will be a great discussion springboard for teachers and counselors." SLJ

Golus, Carrie

Take a stand! what you can do about bullying. illustrated by Jack Desrocher. Lerner Publications Co. 2009 64p il (Health zone) lib bdg $30.60 **302.3**
1. Bullies
ISBN 978-0-8225-7554-2; 0-8225-7554-X
LC 2007-49659

This offers advice about stopping bullying.

"The format is beyond lively, with lots of color, cartoons, and an informal writing style, but it manages to present sometimes frightening material in a non-threatening and browsable way." Booklist

Includes glossary and bibliographical references

Jakubiak, David J.

A **smart** kid's guide to online bullying. PowerKids Press 2009 24p il (Kids online) lib bdg $21.25; pa $8.95
Grades: 3 4 5 6 **302.3**
1. Bullies 2. Safety education 3. Internet -- Security measures
ISBN 978-1-4042-8114-1 lib bdg; 978-1-4358-3348-7 pa
LC 2009000695

This describes how to identify bullies online, how to deal with them, and how to avoid becoming a bully.

"This . . . is easy to read, has vibrant photos on each page, and offers Tips. Additional links can be found at the publisher's portal, which is regularly updated." Libr Media Connect

Includes glossary

Kevorkian, Meline

★ **101** facts about bullying; what everyone should know. [by] Meline Kevorkian and Robin D'Antona. Rowman & Littlefield Pub. 2008 148p $32.95
Grades: Adult Professional **302.3**
1. Bullies
ISBN 978-1-57886-849-0; 1-57886-849-1

"A user-friendly, accessible, and well-organized resource. . . . The format will lend itself well to group discussions and give teachers and others who work with young people a solid basis upon which to explore the issues surrounding this prevalent problem." SLJ

Lusted, Marcia Amidon

Social networking: MySpace, Facebook, & Twitter. ABDO Pub. Co. 2011 112p il (Technology pioneers) lib bdg $34.22
Grades: 5 6 7 8 **302.3**
1. Online social networks
ISBN 978-1-61714-811-8 lib bdg; 1-61714-811-3 lib bdg; 978-1-61758-969-0 e-book
LC 2010037885

This is an introduction to social networking sites, MySpace, Facebook, and Twitter.

"Written in a clear, linear fashion, this series offers vivid, well-researched details about the development of technological advancements considered essential in today's society. . . . Readers who are interested in technology and inventions will be thoroughly engrossed." SLJ

Includes glossary and bibliographical references

Lutz, Lisa

How to negotiate everything; David Spellman with Lisa Lutz; illustrated by Jaime Temairik. Simon & Schuster Books for Young Readers 2012 32 p. (hardcover) $16.99
Grades: K 1 2 3 **302.3**
1. Wit and humor 2. Negotiation -- Juvenile literature
ISBN 144245119X; 9781442451193
LC 2011038386

This humorous juvenile picture book, by Lisa Lutz, illustrated by Jaime Temairik, "teaches you how to get everything you want. . . . Through several simple steps, you will learn the best way to ask for what you want, how to ask for more of what you want, and the importance of not overreaching. With helpful illustrations and a complete glossary, there is no end to what these skills can get you." (Publisher's note)

Shapiro, Ouisie

Bullying and me; schoolyard stories. illustrated by Steven Vote. Albert Whitman & Company 2010 un il $16.99
Grades: 4 5 6 7 **302.3**
1. Bullies
ISBN 978-0-8075-0921-0; 0-8075-0921-3
LC 2010000754

"Thirteen individuals, including some adults, who have been bullied at school share their painful experiences. . . . Vote's full-color portraits sensitively depict the faces at the receiving end of abuse. . . . An educational psychologist specifically addresses each individual's dilemma, but the book's strength lies in the honestly conveyed through the personal stories." Publ Wkly

Includes glossary and bibliographical references

302.302   Computer applications

Schwartz, Heather E.

Safe social networking; by Heather E. Schwartz. Capstone Press 2013 32 p. col. ill. (Fact finders. Tech safety smarts) (library) $26.65
Grades: 4 5 6 7 **302.302**
1. Online social networks 2. Internet -- Security measures 3. Social networking -- Juvenile literature
ISBN 1429699434; 9781429699433; 9781620658024
LC 2012026027

This children's resource book, by Heather E. Schwartz, is part of the publisher's "Fact Finders" series, providing guidance for young children to safely use and navigate online social media. "If a strange person asks to be your online friend, do you know what to do? . . . This book is here to help! Learn tech-savvy ways to keep your social networking sites safe sites without taking away all the fun!" (Publisher's note)

Includes bibliographical references (p. 31) and index.

303.3 Coordination and control

Barraclough, Sue

Leadership. Heinemann Library 2009 32p il (Exploring Citizenship) $25.36; pa $7.99

Grades: 1 2 3 4   **303.3**

1. Leadership

ISBN 978-1-4329-3314-2; 1-4329-3314-0; 978-1-4329-3322-7 pa; 1-4329-3322-1 pa

LC 2008-55302

"The text presents a multitude of realistic situations to which young children will relate. There are 'Think About It' fact boxes and checklists that aid in understanding and that will spark discussion. All are filled with captioned, color photographs that relate to the text. The information is relevant and current. . . . Strongly consider this." Libr Media Connect

Includes glossary and bibliographical references

303.4 Social change

Solway, Andrew

Communication; the impact of science and technology. Gareth Stevens Pub. 2010 64p il (Pros and cons) lib bdg $35

Grades: 5 6 7 8   **303.4**

1. Communication 2. Telecommunication 3. Information technology

ISBN 978-1-4339-1986-2 lib bdg; 1-4339-1986-9 lib bdg

LC 2009-12435

An "active layout that features color photographs, maps, graphs or charts on every spread, this . . . [book] has much to offer. . . . It conveniently outlines the range of views . . . helping students to learn how to view both sides of [the] issue[s]." SLJ

Includes glossary and bibliographical references

303.48 Causes of change

Scandiffio, Laura

People who said no; courage against oppression. Laura Scandiffio. Annick Press 2012 168 p. $24.95

Grades: 5 6 7   **303.48**

1. Demonstrations 2. Protest movements 3. Civil disobedience 4. Resistance to government

ISBN 1554513839; 9781554513833

This book, by Laura Scandiffio, profiles activists who broke the law to protest injustices. "Sometimes it's okay to ignore the rules or break the law. . . . This . . . book features people who did just that: Sophie and Hans Scholl . . . and Andrei Sakharov. . . . Also included are Helen Suzman, . . . Aung San Suu Kyi, . . . and the people of Egypt, who recently brought down the repressive government of Hosni Mubarak." (Publisher's note)

303.6 Conflict and conflict resolution

Ellis, Deborah

Off to war; voices of soldiers' children. Groundwood Books/House of Anansi Press 2008 175p il $15.95; pa $9.95

Grades: 5 6 7 8   **303.6**

1. Children and war 2. Iraq War, 2003-2011 3. Children of military personnel -- Juvenile literature

ISBN 978-0-88899-894-1; 0-88899-894-5; 978-0-88899-895-8 pa; 0-88899-895-3 pa

The wars in Iraq and Afghanistan have impacted the children of soldiers—men and women who have been called away from their families to fight in a faraway war. In their own words, some of these children describe how their experience has marked and shaped their lives

"Accessible and utterly readable. . . . The book is an excellent resource for opening discussions about the current events." SLJ

Includes glossary and bibliographical references

Engle, Dawn

PeaceJam; a billion simple acts of peace. written by Ivan Suvanjieff and Dawn Gifford Engle. Puffin Books 2008 194p il pa $16.99

Grades: 5 6 7 8 9   **303.6**

1. Peace 2. Youth

ISBN 978-0-14-241234-3 pa; 0-14-241234-1 pa

LC 2008-24865

"This visually impressive and well-organized book would work well as a reference tool, how-to handbook, or promotional device for classroom altruistic activities or civil service clubs. Each stand-alone chapter uses a Noble Peace Laureate as the catalyst for a particular crisis, introduces the reader to a courageous young person who has been inspired to help with a specific problem, and ends with a list of ten very 'doable' suggestions of ways that every concerned citizen can help. The resources listed in the back of the book are extensive and current. An excellent addition to the text is a snappy thirty-minute DVD that could serve as a book talk, review tool or promotional device." Voice Youth Advocates

Gilley, Jeremy

★ **Peace** one day; illustrated by Karen Blessen. Putnam 2005 48p il $16.99 **303.6**

1. Peace 2. Pacifists 3. Motion picture directors 4. Peace -- Juvenile literature

ISBN 0-399-24330-5

LC 2004-20475

The author "tells how he persuaded world leaders to establish World Peace Day. . . . His personal account of filming the consequences of war in several countries . . . draws attention to the issue, as do his accounts of meeting with world leaders. . . . Most powerful are the double-page collage illustrations . . . which blend some of Gilley's film images of kids caught up in war and portraits of world peace leaders with colored pencil drawings, posters, and even news headlines. [This offers] passionate prose and stirring images." Booklist

304.2 Human ecology

McCarthy, Pat

Friends of the earth; a history of American environmentalism. Pat McCarthy. 1st ed. Chicago Review Press 2012 132 p. ill. (paperback) $16.95

Grades: 3 4 5   **304.2**

1. Environmentalists 2. Environmental movement --
United States 3. Environmentalism -- United States
-- History -- Juvenile literature 4. Environmentalists
-- United States -- History -- Juvenile literature 5.
Environmental protection -- United States -- History --
Juvenile literature

ISBN 1569767181; 9781569767184

LC 2012039334

This book provides "10 profiles of American naturalists and environmentalists" that "offer a broad overview of the movement's past highlights." Also included are "photos, sidebars, resource lists, and a quick closing survey of current environmental issues." Figures mentioned include John Muir, Henry David Thoreau, and Rachel Carson. (Booklist)

Urrutia, María Cristina

Who will save my planet? Maria Cristina Urrutia. Tundra Books of Northern New York 2012 32 p. (hardcover) $10.95

Grades: 3 4 5   **304.2**

1. Human influence on nature

ISBN 177049281X; 9781770492813

LC 2011923291

This book by Maria Cristina Urrutia "uses striking photos to show the impact of humans on the environment. . . . On every spread we are shown a treasure that nature has given us beside a picture of how we've abused that treasure. We see a beautiful forest glade beside a devastated patch of burned-out wood, a gorgeous green parrot beside a dull-feathered caged bird, a sparkling waterfall beside a garbage-clogged river." (Publisher's note)

304.6 Population

Barber, Nicola

Coping with population growth; Nicola Barber. Raintree 2011 48 p. col. ill.

Grades: 4 5 6 7   **304.6**

1. Population 2. Population -- Environmental aspects
-- Juvenile literature

ISBN 9781410942968; 9781410943033

LC 2010052702

"Barber examines the pressures exerted on the environment and global resources due to population growth... Color photographs add interest, and helpful diagrams effectively convey statistical concepts." Horn Book

Includes bibliographical references (p. 46-47) and index

304.8 Movement of people

Andryszewski, Tricia

Walking the earth; a history of human migration. [by] Tricia Andryszewski. Twenty-First Century Books 2007 80p il map lib bdg $27.23

Grades: 5 6 7 8   **304.8**

1. Population 2. Prehistoric peoples 3. Immigration
and emigration

ISBN 978-0-7613-3458-3 lib bdg; 0-7613-3458-0
lib bdg

LC 2005033430

"Copious sepia-toned visuals, including drawings, photographs, maps, and charts, create an attractive and accessible presentation of complex material." SLJ

Includes bibliographical references

Ellis Island Oral History Project

★ **I** was dreaming to come to America; memories from the Ellis Island Oral History Project. selected and illustrated by Veronica Lawlor; foreword by Rudolph W. Giuliani. Viking 1995 38p il hardcover o.p. pa $6.99

Grades: 4 5 6 7   **304.8**

1. Immigrants -- Biography -- Juvenile literature

ISBN 0-670-86164-2; 0-14-055622-2 pa

LC 95-1281

In their own words, coupled with hand-painted collage illustrations, immigrants recall their arrival in the United States. Includes brief biographies and facts about the Ellis Island Oral History Project

"There is a flavor of Chagall in the peasant figures dancing above the ship or hopping ashore near the turreted towers of the huge building on Ellis Island. The elegant rendering offers a timeless view of this significant journey that is at once personal and universal." Horn Book

Kenney, Karen Latchana

Ellis Island; illustrated by Judith A. Hunt. Magic Wagon 2011 32p il (Our nation's pride) lib bdg $28.50

Grades: 2 3 4   **304.8**

ISBN 978-1-61641-150-3; 1-61641-150-3

LC 2010013995

"The author describes how the existing island was built up and expanded to accomodate the station to process immigrants coming into the United States and the various buildings that were constructed. . . . The full-color artwork not only explains the text but also gives almost photographic rendering of the [topic]." SLJ

Ollhoff, Jim

Exploring immigration. ABDO Pub. Co. 2011 32p il (Your family tree) $18.95

Grades: 4 5 6 7   **304.8**

1. Genealogy 2. Immigrants

ISBN 978-1-61613-463-1; 1-61613-463-1

LC 2009050807

This book about immigration is "great . . . for kids interested in genealogy. [It does] a wonderful job of presenting the fundamentals of genealogical research in a clear and exciting manner. . . . Understanding and properly using primary documents is stressed throughout. . . . [An] attractive, spacious [layout]; full-color, sharp images; clearly labeled diagrams; and scattered maps add information and appeal." SLJ

Includes glossary

Walker, Paul Robert

A nation of immigrants. Kingfisher 2012 32 p.

Grades: 2 3 4 5 6   **304.8**

1. United States -- History 2. Immigrants -- United

States
ISBN 0753466716; 0753467135; 9780753466711; 9780753467138

This book, part of the "All About America" series, "covers the role immigration played in the development of the United States." Features include "text, . . . illustrations, a one-paragraph introduction on the contents page that summarizes the scope of the book, and translation of period costs to current dollar values. . . . Each spread is busy with illustrations, engravings, and photos, all with captions." (School Library Journal)

305.23 Young people

Asael, Anthony
★ **Children** of the world; how we live, learn, and play in poems, drawings, and photographs. [by] Anthony Asael [and] Stéphanie Rabemiafara. Rizzoli/Universe 2011 416p il $29.95
Grades: 3 4 5 6   **305.23**
1. Children
ISBN 978-0-7893-2267-8; 0-7893-2267-6

"This captivating volume, ambitious in scope and remarkable in execution, combines striking candid photographs of children from 192 nations with poems and artwork from children in each nation. Organized by country, the volume also includes details about language, diet, and local activities. . . . Asael and Rabemiafara deliver a powerful kaleidoscope of young voices, diverse yet united." Publ Wkly

★ **Come** and play; snapshots of our world's children having fun; poems by children; edited by Ayana Lowe; photographs from the Magnum Collection. Bloomsbury 2008 un il $16.95
Grades: K 1 2 3   **305.23**
1. Play 2. Children -- Pictorial works
ISBN 978-1-59990-245-6; 1-59990-245-1
LC 2007039970

"Beautiful, clear photos by top professional photographers show children across the world at play. Each full-page picture is placed opposite a few simple lines of free verse, which are based on 'word-riffs' by students in the editor's New York City grade-school classes. . . . The images reflect the kids' individuality and connections, and their anger, hurt, joy, and loneliness—which will spark discussion and more 'word-riffs.'" Booklist

Freedman, Russell
★ **Children** of the Great Depression. Clarion Books 2005 118p il lib bdg $20
Grades: 4 5 6 7   **305.23**
1. Great Depression, 1929-1939 2. Children -- United States 3. Depressions -- 1929 -- Juvenile literature
ISBN 0-618-44630-3
LC 2005-06506

"This stirring photo-essay combines . . . unforgettable personal details with a clear historical overview of the period and black-and-white photos by Dorothea Lange, Walker Evans, and many others." Booklist

Kerley, Barbara
★ **One** world, one day. National Geographic 2009 un il map $17.95; lib bdg $26.90
Grades: PreK K 1 2   **305.23**
1. Children -- Pictorial works
ISBN 978-1-4263-0460-6; 1-4263-0460-9; 978-1-4263-0461-3 lib bdg; 1-4263-0461-7 lib bdg
LC 2008-29315

"An arresting, eye-opening compilation." Publ Wkly

Kindersley, Anabel
★ **Children** just like me; by Barnabas & Anabel Kindersley. Dorling Kindersley 1995 79p il maps $19.95
Grades: 3 4 5 6   **305.23**
1. Children -- Pictorial works 2. Children -- Juvenile literature 3. Documentary photography -- Juvenile literature
ISBN 0-7894-0201-7
LC 95-10199

"A delightful, attractive look at children from around the world. . . . This book is factual, respectful, and insightful. It provides just the right balance of information and visual interest for the intended audience." SLJ

Konrad, Marla Stewart
I like to play. Tundra Books 2010 un il (World vision early readers) $12.95
Grades: PreK K   **305.23**
1. Play
ISBN 978-0-88776-998-6; 0-88776-998-5

This features color photographs of children around the world engaged in play.

This book's "simple, sharp aesthetic will capture the imagination of a good number of children." Booklist

Pinkney, Sandra L.
★ **Shades** of black; a celebration of our children. photographs by Myles C. Pinkney. Scholastic 2000 un il $14.95; bd bk $6.99
Grades: PreK K 1   **305.23**
1. African Americans 2. Afro-Americans
ISBN 0-439-14892-8; 0-439-80251-2 bd bk
LC 99-86593

Photographs and text celebrate the beauty and diversity of African American children

"Wonderful, clear, full-color photographs of youngsters illustrate a poetic, vivid text that describes a range of skin and eye colors and hair textures." SLJ

Smith, David J.
This child, every child; a book about the world's children. written by David J. Smith; illustrated by Shelagh Armstrong. Kids Can Press 2011 36p il (CitizenKid) $18.95
Grades: 4 5 6 7   **305.23**
1. Children
ISBN 978-1-55453-466-1; 1-55453-466-6

This title "takes a global look at the lives of contemporary children. Balancing statistics with fictional profiles of kids, Smith's concise narrative focuses on such topics as families, homes, health, work, war, and play. Each spread contains accessible summaries of articles from 1989's United Nations Convention on the Rights of the Child, underscoring the disparity between many children's lives and that document's vision and goals. . . . Rendered in acrylics with digital textures, Armstrong's gauzy paintings sometimes span multiple cultures in a single illustration . . . reinforcing the universal nature of children's needs." Publ Wkly

UNICEF
A **Life** like mine. DK Pub. 2002 127p il maps hardcover o.p. pa $12.99
Grades: 3 4 5 6   **305.23**
1. Children 2. Children's rights 3. Children -- Cross-cultural studies -- Juvenile literature 4. Children's rights -- Cross-cultural studies -- Juvenile literature
ISBN 0-7894-8859-0; 0-7566-1803-7 pa
LC 2002-11197
Looks at what life is like for children of different countries and how each child can fulfill his or her hopes and ambitions no matter how little or much their human rights are infringed
"This book gives the reader a remarkable look at the lives of children around the world. . . . The text is varied within each page and is written in language easy for a child to understand. The photographs are dispersed throughout all pages and enhance the meaning of the text." Libr Media Connect

Wilson, Janet
One peace; true stories of young activists. written and illustrated by Janet Wilson. Orca Book Publishers 2008 43p il $19.95
Grades: 4 5 6 7   **305.23**
1. Peace 2. Children and war 3. Pacifists -- Juvenile literature
ISBN 978-1-55143-892-4; 1-55143-892-5
"The stories of young people who have been refugees from war, injured by land mines, or learned about the consequences of violence through other means are interspersed with children's poems, quotes, artwork, and photographs. The brief, powerful accounts document how these children ages 8 to 15 worked for or became symbols of peace." SLJ

305.4 Women

Bingham, Jane
Women at war; the progressive era, World War I and women's suffrage, 1900-1920. Chelsea House 2011 il (A cultural history of women in America) $35
Grades: 5 6 7 8   **305.4**
1. World War, 1914-1918 2. Women -- Employment 3. Women -- Social conditions 4. Women -- United States -- History
ISBN 978-1-6041-3932-7; 1-6041-3932-3
LC 2010044828
An "eye-catching [layout] with good use of color, photographs, and informative sidebars, many of which use primary-source quotations, are the highlights of [this] appealing [volume]. . . . After a succinct overview of contemporary events, the chapters describe women's lives at home, at work, in education, in politics, in the arts, and their role in the general culture. . . . [This book] explores the changing role of women during the Progressive Era, the impact of World War I on their lives, and the struggle for voting rights." SLJ
Includes glossary and bibliographical references

Carosella, Melissa
Founding mothers; women who shaped America. Teacher Created Materials 2011 il (Primary source readers: focus on women in U.S. history)
Grades: 3 4 5 6   **305.4**
1. Women -- United States -- History
ISBN 143331505X; 978-1-43331505-3
"This introduction to influential women in early American history begins with the colonial period and closes with the Civil War. . . . The clear text is enhanced with archival illustrations and sidebars that highlight notable items about the women discussed in the narrative. A glossary, an index, and two suggested extension activities conclude this informative book." Booklist

Coster, Patience
A **new** deal for women; the expanding roles of women, 1938-1960. Chelsea House 2011 il (A cultural history of women in America) $35
Grades: 5 6 7 8   **305.4**
1. Feminism 2. Women -- Social conditions 3. Women -- United States -- History
ISBN 978-1-6041-3934-1; 1-6041-3934-X
LC 2010045959
An "eye-catching [layout] with good use of color, photographs, and informative sidebars, many of which use primary-source quotations, are the highlights of [this] appealing [volume]. . . . After a succinct overview of contemporary events, the chapters describe women's lives at home, at work, in education, in politics, in the arts, and their role in the general culture. . . . New opportunities for women were a part of the New Deal and World War II and together changed American culture—these topics are explored [this] volume covering the years 1938-1960." SLJ
Includes glossary and bibliographical references

Gorman, Jacqueline Laks
The **modern** feminist movement; sisters under the skin, 1961-1979. Chelsea House 2011 il (A cultural history of women in America) $35
Grades: 5 6 7 8   **305.4**
1. Feminism 2. Women -- Social conditions 3. Women -- United States -- History
ISBN 978-1-6041-3935-8; 1-6041-3935-8
LC 2010045990
An "eye-catching [layout] with good use of color, photographs, and informative sidebars, many of which use primary-source quotations, are the highlights of [this] appealing [volume]. . . . After a succinct overview of contemporary events, the chapters describe women's lives at home, at work, in education, in politics, in the arts, and their role in the general culture. . . . [This book] delves into the years of protest and quest for equal rights." SLJ
Includes glossary and bibliographical references

Heinemann, Sue
★ The **New** York Public Library amazing women in American history; a book of answers for kids. Wiley 1998 192p (New York Public Library answer books for kids series) pa $12.95
Grades: 5 6 7 8   **305.4**
1. Women -- United States -- History
ISBN 0-471-19216-3
LC 97-18465

Consists of short answers to questions about the roles and achievements of women in America from prehistory to the end of the twentieth century

"The text is succinct, easy to read, and informative. . . . Pertinent black-and-white photos appear throughout." SLJ

Includes glossary and bibliographical references

Stearman, Kaye

Women of today; contemporary issues and conflicts, 1980-present. [by] Kaye Stearman and Patience Coster. Chelsea House 2011 il (A cultural history of women in America) $35

Grades: 5 6 7 8   **305.4**

1. Feminism 2. Women -- United States 3. Women -- Social conditions

ISBN 978-1-6041-3936-5; 1-6041-3936-6

LC 2010046014

An "eye-catching [layout] with good use of color, photographs, and informative sidebars, many of which use primary-source quotations, are the highlights of [this] appealing [volume]. . . . After a succinct overview of contemporary events, the chapters describe women's lives at home, at work, in education, in politics, in the arts, and their role in the general culture. . . . [This book] highlights women's achievements, including U.S. Supreme Court justices, Speaker of the U.S. House of Representatives, and presidential candidates." SLJ

Includes glossary and bibliographical references

305.5 People by social and economic levels

Adler, David A., 1947-

A **picture** book of Harriet Tubman; illustrated by Samuel Byrd. Holiday House 1992 un il $17.95; pa $6.95

Grades: 1 2 3   **305.5**

1. Abolitionists 2. Underground railroad 3. African American women 4. African American women -- Biography 5. Underground Railroad -- Juvenile literature 6. Slavery -- United States -- Juvenile literature

ISBN 0-8234-0926-0; 0-8234-1065-X pa

LC 91-19628

Biography of the black woman who escaped from slavery to become famous as a conductor on the Underground Railroad

This book features "brief, easy-to-read text. . . . Byrd's appealing, colorful illustrations convey the quiet dignity of a brave heroine." Booklist

A **picture** book of Sojourner Truth; illustrated by Gershom Griffith. Holiday House 1994 un il $17.95; pa $6.95

Grades: 1 2 3   **305.5**

1. Feminism 2. Abolitionists 3. African American women 4. Memoirists 5. African American women -- Biography

ISBN 0-8234-1072-2; 0-8234-1262-8 pa

LC 93-7478

An introduction to the life of the woman born into slavery who became a well-known abolitionist and crusader for the rights of African Americans in the United States

The author "portrays his subject in a realistic manner, discussing slavery and other issues in an easy-to-read style. The quotes, while undocumented, are simple enough for the target audience and help to place events in context. Excellent-quality watercolor illustrations capture the action and provide effective representations and details of the time period." SLJ

Horn, Geoffrey M.

Sojourner Truth; speaking up for freedom. by Geoffrey Michael Horn. Crabtree Pub. Co. 2010 64 p. ill. (some col.) (pbk.: alk. paper) $10.95

Grades: 4 5 6 7 8   **305.5**

1. Abolitionists -- United States -- Biography -- Juvenile literature 2. African American women -- Biography -- Juvenile literature 3. African American abolitionists -- Biography -- Juvenile literature 4. Social reformers -- United States -- Biography -- Juvenile literature

ISBN 0778748405; 9780778748243; 9780778748403

LC 2009022428

This children's picture book by Geoffrey M. Horn in the Voices for Freedom: Abolitionist Views series looks at abolitionist Sojourner Truth. It "relates and details Truth's life and times, from her often-brutal treatment as a slave, named Isabella at birth, to her freedom, religious influences, and self-determination . . . and path to outspoken, sometimes provocative, and influential traveling speaker on a mission to raise awareness of and support for abolitionism."

"Combining accessible, lively prose and abundant visuals, this title . . . offers an engaging, informative introduction to the early advocate for the rights of African Americans and women." Booklist

Schroeder, Alan

Minty: a story of young Harriet Tubman; pictures by Jerry Pinkney. Dial Bks. for Young Readers 1996 un il hardcover o.p. pa $6.99

Grades: 1 2 3 4   **305.5**

1. Abolitionists 2. Slavery -- Fiction

ISBN 0-8037-1888-8; 0-14-056196-X pa

LC 95-23499

Coretta Scott King Award for illustration

Pinkney's "paintings, done in pencil, colored-pencils, and watercolor, use light and shadow to great effect. . . . This is a dramatic story that will hold listeners' interest and may lead them to biographical material." SLJ

305.8 Ethnic and national groups

Bolden, Tonya

Tell all the children our story; memories and mementos of being young and Black in America. Abrams 2001 128p il $24.95

Grades: 5 6 7 8   **305.8**

1. Race relations 2. African Americans 3. African American children 4. African Americans -- History 5. African American children -- History 6. African American children -- Social conditions

ISBN 0-8109-4496-0

LC 2001-1353

"This compilation of the African American experience, from colonial times through the twentieth century, reads and looks like a family scrapbook. . . . Photographs, excerpts from diaries and memoirs, and reproductions of artwork by black artists such as Charles Altson beautifully bring the story of each generation to life. Bolden vibrantly delivers her historical message through a contemporary perspective." Booklist

Includes bibliographical references

Cha, Dia

★ **Dia's** story cloth; written by Dia Cha; stitched by Chue and Nhia Thao Cha. Lee & Low Bks. 1996 un il $15.95; pa $6.95

Grades: 3 4 5   **305.8**

1. Hmong (Asian people) 2. Embroidery -- Juvenile literature 3. Asian Americans -- Juvenile literature

ISBN 1-880000-34-2; 1-880000-63-6 pa

LC 95-41465

The story cloth made for her by her aunt and uncle chronicles the life of the author and her family in their native Laos and their eventual emigration to the United States

"An interesting and unusual title that resists neat categorization. . . . Part autobiography, part history, part description of a changing culture adapting life and art to new circumstances, the book serves as a brief introduction to the Hmong people." SLJ

Includes bibliographical references

Haskins, James

★ The **rise** of Jim Crow; by James Haskins and Kathleen Benson; with Virginia Schomp. Marshall Cavendish Benchmark 2008 80p il (Drama of African-American history) lib bdg $23.95

Grades: 5 6 7 8   **305.8**

1. African Americans -- History 2. African Americans -- Segregation

ISBN 978-0-7614-2640-0

"Provides a history of the decades of poverty, oppression, and terror that African Americans suffered under the system of segregation in the United States, from the end of the Reconstruction era through the early decades of the twentieth century." Publisher's note

Includes glossary and bibliographical references

Hernandez, Roger E.

1898 to World War II. Marshall Cavendish Benchmark 2009 78p il (Hispanic America) lib bdg $34.21

Grades: 4 5 6 7   **305.8**

1. Hispanic Americans -- History

ISBN 978-0-7614-4176-2 lib bdg; 0-7614-4176-X lib bdg

LC 2008041140

"Provides comprehensive information on the history of the Spanish coming to the United States, focusing on the time from 1898 to the start of World War II." Publisher's note

Includes glossary and bibliographical references

Keedle, Jayne

Americans from the Caribbean and Central America. Marshall Cavendish Benchmark 2009 80p il map (New Americans) lib bdg $35.64

Grades: 5 6 7 8   **305.8**

1. Caribbean Americans 2. Central American

Americans 3. Immigrants -- United States

ISBN 978-0-7614-4302-5 lib bdg; 0-7614-4302-9 lib bdg

LC 2009003171

This title looks at Caribbean and Central American "communities in America today, detailing earlier generations of immigrants and current arrivals who are making new lives, changing the American culture, and looking to the future. [The] title includes many full-color photos, maps, and charts. . . . The [book does] a good job of helping readers to understand the differences between undocumented and documented immigrants and describe the citizenship process. The topics of racism, stereotypes, and other issues related to integration into American society are sensitively covered." SLJ

Includes glossary and bibliographical references

Mexican Americans. Marshall Cavendish Benchmark 2009 80p il map (New Americans) lib bdg $35.64

Grades: 5 6 7 8   **305.8**

1. Mexican Americans 2. Immigrants -- United States

ISBN 978-0-7614-4307-0 lib bdg; 0-7614-4307-X lib bdg

LC 2008052101

This describes the history of Mexican Americans

"Consistent in content, and providing a mix of facts and personal accounts, this . . . will be [a] . . . very useful addition to the collection." Libr Media Collect

Includes glossary and bibliographical references

West African Americans. Marshall Cavendish Benchmark 2009 80p il map (New Americans) lib bdg $35.64

Grades: 5 6 7 8   **305.8**

1. African Americans 2. Africans -- United States 3. Immigrants -- United States

ISBN 978-0-7614-4313-1 lib bdg; 0-7614-4313-4 lib bdg

LC 2008055753

This title looks at West African "communities in America today, detailing earlier generations of immigrants and current arrivals who are making new lives, changing the American culture, and looking to the future. [The] title includes many full-color photos, maps, and charts. . . . [The book does] a good job of helping readers to understand the differences between undocumented and documented immigrants and describe the citizenship process. The topics of racism, stereotypes, and other issues related to integration into American society are sensitively covered." SLJ

Includes glossary and bibliographical references

Lester, Julius

★ **Let's** talk about race; illustrated by Karen Barbour. HarperCollinsPublishers 2005 un il $15.99; lib bdg $16.89

Grades: K 1 2 3   **305.8**

1. Racism 2. Prejudices 3. Racism -- Juvenile literature 4. Prejudices -- Juvenile literature 5. Race awareness -- Juvenile literature

ISBN 0-06-028596-6; 0-06-028598-2 lib bdg

LC 2002-10979

This "picture book introduces race as just one of many chapters in a person's story. . . . Throughout the narrative, [the author] asks questions that young readers can answer, creating a dialogue about who they are and encouraging them to tell their own tales. He also discusses 'stories' that are not always true, pointing out that we create prejudice by perceiving ourselves as better than others. . . . The pairing of text and dazzling artwork is flawless." SLJ

Masoff, Joy

★ The **African** American story; the events that shaped our nation--and the people that changed our lives. Five Ponds 2007 95p il map $26.50
Grades: 4 5 6 7   **305.8**
1. African Americans -- History
ISBN 978-0-9727156-9-0

This "covers the history of the African people in America from the 1400s to the present. Historical photographs, archival documents, maps, and a fact-filled time line provide a visually stimulating introduction to the subject. . . . Masoff provides a tremendous amount of material in an exciting, appealing title that is useful for browsing, introductory lessons, quick reference, and beginning research." SLJ

Includes bibliographical references

Myers, Walter Dean, 1937-

★ **Now** is your time! the African-American struggle for freedom. HarperCollins Pubs. 1991 292p il hardcover o.p. pa $14.99
Grades: 6 7 8 9   **305.8**
1. African Americans -- History
ISBN 0-06-446120-3 pa

LC 91-314

Coretta Scott King Award for text

A history of the African-American struggle for freedom and equality, beginning with the capture of Africans in 1619, continuing through the American Revolution, the Civil War, and into contemporary times

"Myers's unique episodic approach makes this history a compelling exploration of the African-American experience. . . . This fascinating book will engender pride in heritage for young African Americans and provide insight into American history for all of us." Horn Book

Includes bibliographical references

Nelson, Kadir

★ **Heart** and soul; words and paintings by Kadir Nelson. Balzer + Bray 2011 108p. col. ill. $19.99; lib bdg $20.89
Grades: 3 4 5 6   **305.8**
1. African Americans -- History
ISBN 978-0-06-173074-0; 0-06-173074-2; 978-0-06-173076-4 lib bdg; 0-06-173076-9 lib bdg

LC 2010046236

Coretta Scott King Award (Authors) (2012)

"Nelson knits together the nation's proudest moments with its most shameful, taking on the whole of African-American history, from Revolutionary-era slavery up to the election of Barack Obama. He handles this vast subject with easy grace. . . . In jaw-dropping portraits, Nelson paints heroes like Frederick Douglass and Joe Louis, conferring equal dignity on the slaves, workers, soldiers, and students. . . . A tremendous achievement." Publ Wkly

Include bibliographical references (p. 104) and index.

Park, Ken

Americans from India and other South Asian countries. Marshall Cavendish Benchmark 2009 80p il map (New Americans) lib bdg $35.64

Grades: 5 6 7 8   **305.8**
1. Asian Americans 2. Immigrants -- United States 3. East Indians -- United States
ISBN 978-0-7614-4305-6 lib bdg; 0-7614-4305-3 lib bdg

LC 2009002599

This title looks at Indian and other South Asian "communities in America today, detailing earlier generations of immigrants and current arrivals who are making new lives, changing the American culture, and looking to the future. [The] title includes many full-color photos, maps, and charts.. . . The [book does] a good job of helping readers to understand the differences between undocumented and documented immigrants and describe the citizenship process. The topics of racism, stereotypes, and other issues related to integration into American society are sensitively covered." SLJ

Includes glossary and bibliographical references

Petrillo, Valerie

★ A **kid's** guide to Latino history; more than 70 activities. Chicago Review Press 2009 214p il pa $14.95
Grades: 4 5 6 7   **305.8**
1. Hispanic Americans -- History
ISBN 978-1-55652-771-5 pa; 1-55652-771-3 pa

LC 2008040433

"This big, lively overview examines the history of Latinos in the U.S. . . . The chatty, informative text, presented in readable, spacious layouts, will draw kids with lots of fun, illustrated instructions for related activities. . . . The accessible facts and the individual portraits of notable authors, athletes, entertainers, and politicians portray Latinos' rich contribution to U.S. heritage, and kids will want to talk about the well-presented issues." Booklist

Includes bibliographical references

Rappaport, Doreen

★ **Free** at last! stories and songs of Emancipation. illustrated by Shane W. Evans. Candlewick Press 2004 63p il $19.99; pa $7.99
Grades: 3 4 5 6   **305.8**
1. African Americans -- History 2. African Americans -- Civil rights 3. Southern States -- Race relations -- Miscellanea -- Juvenile literature 4. African Americans -- History -- 1863-1877 -- Miscellanea -- Juvenile literature
ISBN 0-7636-1440-8; 0-7636-3147-7 pa

LC 2003-43853

"Stories, poems, and songs about events from the Emancipation Proclamation of 1863 through the Brown v. Board of Education decision of 1954 are perfectly matched with vibrant oil paintings. The result is a glorious tribute to the lives of African-American heroes and heroines." SLJ

Reynolds, Jan

Only the mountains do not move; a Maasai story of culture and conservation. Lee & Low Books 2011 40p il $18.95; pa $9.95
Grades: 2 3 4   **305.8**
1. Agriculture
ISBN 978-1-60060-333-4; 1-60060-333-5; 978-1-60060-844-5 pa; 1-60060-844-2 pa

LC 2010050879

"With many clear color photos and an appended glossary with pronunciation, this is an excellent addition to classroom units on Africa today." Booklist

Schomp, Virginia
Marching toward freedom; by Virginia Schomp. Marshall Cavendish Benchmark 2008 80p il (Drama of African-American history) lib bdg $23.95
Grades: 5 6 7 8   305.8
1. African Americans -- History
ISBN 978-0-7614-2643-1
"Explores the period between 1929 and 1954 in African-American history, when the 'New Negro' emerged, proud of his or her racial heritage and determined to topple the barriers to black advancement." Publisher's note
Includes glossary and bibliographical references

Slade, Suzanne
Climbing Lincoln's steps; the African American journey. illustrated by Colin Bootman. Albert Whitman 2010 un il $16.99
Grades: 2 3 4 5   305.8
1. African Americans -- Civil rights
ISBN 978-0-8075-1204-3; 0-8075-1204-4
LC 2010004962
"This attractive, accessible title uses the Lincoln Memorial as a vehicle to outline the history of the Civil Rights Movement from the Emancipation Proclamation to Dr. King's 'I Have a Dream' speech to the 2008 presidential election. Other pivotal moments include world-renowned singer Marian Anderson's 1939 performance at the memorial when she was barred from singing at Constitution Hall. . . . Bootman's realistic watercolor spreads are striking." SLJ

Stefoff, Rebecca, 1951-
A **different** mirror for young people; a history of multicultural America. by Ronald Takaki; adapted by Rebecca Stefoff. Seven Stories Press 2012 vi, 377 p.p ill. (paperback: alk. paper) $18.95; (hardcover: alk. paper) $40.00; (ebook) $18.95
Grades: 7 8 9 10   305.8
1. Letters 2. Multiculturalism 3. United States -- History 4. Minorities -- United States -- History -- Juvenile literature 5. Cultural pluralism -- United States -- History -- Juvenile literature
ISBN 1609804163; 9781609804169; 9781609804848; 9781609804176
LC 2012017004
Through studies of "American ethnic history . . . multicultural studies . . . and diversity" author Ronald Takaki "brings ethnic history alive through the words of people, including teenagers, who recorded their experiences in letters, diaries, and poems." The book "offers a rich and rewarding 'people's view' perspective on the American story." (Publisher's note)
Includes bibliographical references and index.

Thomas, William David
Korean Americans. Marshall Cavendish Benchmark 2009 80p il (New Americans) lib bdg $35.64

Grades: 5 6 7 8   305.8
1. Korean Americans 2. Immigrants -- United States
ISBN 978-0-7614-4306-3 lib bdg; 0-7614-4306-1 lib bdg
LC 2008054846
This describes the history of Korean Americans
"Consistent in content, and providing a mix of facts, and personal accounts, this . . . will be [a] . . . very useful addition to the collection." Libr Media Connect
Includes glossary and bibliographical references

Wachtel, Alan
Southeast Asian Americans. Marshall Cavendish Benchmark 2009 80p il map (New Americans) lib bdg $35.64
Grades: 5 6 7 8   305.8
1. Asian Americans 2. Immigrants -- United States
ISBN 978-0-7614-4312-4 lib bdg; 0-7614-4312-6 lib bdg
LC 2008055752
This title looks at Southeast Asian "communities in America today, detailing earlier generations of immigrants and current arrivals who are making new lives, changing the American culture, and looking to the future. [The] title includes many full-color photos, maps, and charts. . . . The books [does] a good job of helping readers to understand the differences between undocumented and documented immigrants and describe the citizenship process. The topics of racism, stereotypes, and other issues related to integration into American society are sensitively covered." SLJ
Includes glossary and bibliographical references

Weiss, Gail Garfinkel
Americans from Russia and Eastern Europe. Marshall Cavendish Benchmark 2009 80p il (New Americans) lib bdg $35.64
Grades: 5 6 7 8   305.8
1. Russian Americans 2. East European Americans 3. Immigrants -- United States
ISBN 978-0-7614-4310-0 lib bdg; 0-7614-4310-X lib bdg
LC 2008046350
This title looks at Russian and Eastern European "communities in America today, detailing earlier generations of immigrants and current arrivals who are making new lives, changing the American culture, and looking to the future. [The] title includes many full-color photos, maps, and charts. . . . The [book does] a good job of helping readers to understand the differences between undocumented and documented immigrants and describe the citizenship process. The topics of racism, stereotypes, and other issues related to integration into American society are sensitively covered." SLJ
Includes glossary and bibliographical references

305.896   Africans and people of African descent

King, Martin Luther
★ **I** have a dream; foreword by Coretta Scott King; paintings by fifteen Coretta Scott King Award and Honor Book artists, Ashley Bryan . . . [et al.] Scholastic 1997 40p il $16.95

Grades: K 1 2 3   **305.896**
1. Illustration of books 2. African Americans -- Civil
rights
ISBN 0-590-20516-1
LC 95-45189
"Martin Luther King, Jr.'s classic speech is creatively illustrated by 15 Coretta Scott King Award-winning artists.
Signed statements from the artists explain the emotions they
were trying to capture and why and how they used certain
colors and tones. . . . From cover to cover this is a beautiful
book." SLJ

306.3   Economic institutions

Lester, Julius
★ **From** slave ship to freedom road; paintings by Rod
Brown. Dial Bks. 1998 40p il hardcover o.p. pa $6.99
Grades: 5 6 7 8   **306.3**
1. Slavery -- United States 2. Afro-Americans -- Social
conditions -- Juvenile literature 3. Slavery -- United
States -- History -- Juvenile literature 4. Slavery --
United States -- Pictorial works -- Juvenile literature
ISBN 0-8037-1893-4; 0-14-056669-4 pa
LC 96-44422
"Lester's impassioned questions grow from his visceral
response to Brown's narrative paintings. . . . The combina-
tion of history, art, and commentary demands interaction."
Booklist

306.76   Sexual orientation, transgenderism, intersexuality

Seba, Jaime
Gallup guides for youth facing persistent prejudice; by
Jaime Seba. Mason Crest Publishers 2013 64 p. col. ill.,
photographs (library) $22.95
Grades: 5 6 7 8   **306.76**
1. LGBT people -- Civil rights 2. Homophobia --
Juvenile literature 3. Gay youth -- United States --
Juvenile literature 4. Homophobia -- United States --
Juvenile literature 5. Sexual minorities -- Civil rights
-- United States -- Juvenile literature
ISBN 1422224678; 9781422224670
LC 2012017108
This book by Jaime Seba on the LGBT community "discusses the history of prejudice toward this group, the laws
that protect people against discrimination-and what you can
do to fight the prejudice you find in the world." (Publisher's
note) As part of the "Gallup Guides for Youth Facing Persistent Prejudice" series, it "emphasiz[es] recent violence and
other problems, such as bullying and depression, which are,
unfortunately, still routine for many LGBT youth." (Booklist)
Includes bibliographical references (p. 62) and index.

306.8   Marriage and family

Ajmera, Maya
Our grandparents; a global album. [by] Maya Ajmera,
Sheila Kinkade, Cynthia Pon; with a foreword by Archbishop Desmond Tutu. Charlesbridge 2010 un il $16.95
Grades: PreK K 1 2   **306.8**
1. Grandparents
ISBN 978-1-57091-458-4; 1-57091-458-3
LC 2009005494
"Clear, colorful photographs show the two generations
engaged in a variety of activities and invite careful observation. The pictures are clearly labeled with the name of
the families' countries and highlight common threads, e.g.,
'listening,' in Tibet, India, Mexico, and USA. Spare text defines the actions represented. The book concludes with 'Five
Things to Do with Your Grandparents.'" SLJ

Crist, James J.
Siblings; you're stuck with each other so stick together.
by James J. Crist & Elizabeth Verdick; illustrated by Steve
Mark. Free Spirit Pub. 2010 118p il (Laugh & learn) pa
$8.95
Grades: 3 4 5 6   **306.8**
1. Siblings
ISBN 978-1-57542-336-4 pa; 1-57542-336-7 pa
"Starting with the wry subtitle and the colorful cover cartoon of two fuming kids standing back to back, this lively title uses accessible humor to approach sibling-related topics,
such as birth order, privacy, jealousy, bullying, and bonding.
The authors discuss each subject in a child-centered, casual,
and humorous tone. . . . The book's open design and interactive features, such as quick checklists and quizzes, help
make this a great choice for kids and grownups to talk and
laugh about together." Booklist
Includes bibliographical references

Guillain, Charlotte
A **new** brother or sister. Heinemann Library 2011 24p
il (Growing up) lib bdg $22; pa $6.49
Grades: PreK K 1 2   **306.8**
1. Infants 2. Siblings
ISBN 978-1-4329-4803-0 lib bdg; 1-4329-4803-2 lib
bdg; 978-1-4329-4813-9 pa; 1-4329-4813-X pa
LC 2010024197
Brief text and photographs explain what happens when
a new baby joins your family, the special care babies need,
and how you can help take care of your new brother or sister.
Includes bibliographical references

Hoffman, Mary
★ The **great** big book of families; pictures by Ros
Asquith. Dial Books for Young Readers 2011 un il $16.99
Grades: PreK K 1 2   **306.8**
1. Family 2. Family -- Juvenile literature 3. Single-
parent families -- Juvenile literature
ISBN 978-0-8037-3516-3; 0-8037-3516-2
LC 2010-12141
"In matter-of-fact prose and genial pen-and-ink drawings, Hoffman and Asquith reassure readers [that] . . . there's
no one right way to be a family. What sets their survey of
familyhood apart . . . is the collaborators' expansive take on
demographics. They cover not only a wide range of parental
and domestic arrangements, but also schooling, homes, con-

sumerism, employment—or lack of it—and psychographics. . . . Asquith's spreads have a lively, encyclopedic feel, with whimsical themed borders." Publ Wkly

Konrad, Marla Stewart

Grand. Tundra Books 2010 un il (World vision early readers) $12.95

Grades: PreK K   306.8

   1. Grandparents

   ISBN 978-0-88776-997-9; 0-88776-997-7

This features color photographs of children around the world engaged in activities with their grandparents.

This book's "simple, sharp aesthetic will capture the imagination of a good number of children." Booklist

Mom and me. Tundra Books 2009 un il (World vision early readers) $12.95

Grades: PreK K   306.8

   1. Mother-child relationship 2. Mother and child -- Juvenile literature

   ISBN 978-0-88776-866-8; 0-88776-866-0

"A spare easy-to-read text combined with high-quality, full-color photographs highlights youngsters and mothers throughout the world involved in universal activities such as bathing, feeding, and providing comfort and support. Each spread demonstrates strong emotions and provides evidence of the woman's love and pride in her child. The vivid photos present a variety of settings, including many different cultures, and draw viewers into the pages." SLJ

Sheldon, Annette

★ **Big** sister now; a story about me and our new baby. written by Annette Sheldon; illustrated by Karen Maizel. Magination Press 2006 32p il $14.95; pa $8.95

Grades: PreK   306.8

   1. Infants 2. Siblings

   ISBN 1-59147-243-1; 1-59147-244-X pa

                     LC 2005005839

"Among the flood of titles about older siblings and new babies, this book, published under the auspices of the American Psychological Association, stands out for its appealing illustrations and direct story, which wraps a clear, comforting message. . . . An appended section offers parents solid ideas for helping a child adjust to a new baby." Booklist

306.874 Parent-child relationship

Joosse, Barbara M.

★ **Mama,** do you love me? illustrated by Barbara Lavallee. Chronicle Bks. 1991 un il $15.99; bd bk $6.99

Grades: PreK K   306.874

   1. Inuit -- Fiction 2. Love -- Juvenile literature 3. Mother-daughter relationship -- Fiction 4. Parent and child -- Juvenile literature

   ISBN 978-0-87701-759-2; 0-87701-759-X; 978-0-8118-2131-5 bd bk; 0-8118-2131-5 bd bk

                     LC 90-1863

"A young girl asks how much her mother loves her, even when she is naughty, and receives warm, reassuring answers. The twist on this familiar theme is that the two are Inuits, and the text and pictures draw on their unique culture. . . . Two pages of back matter define and explain the functions

of various terms in Inuit life past and present. Charming, vibrant watercolor illustrations expand the simple rhythmic text, adding to the characters' personalities and to the cultural information." SLJ

Thomas, Pat

This is my family: a first look at same sex parents; by Pat Thomas. 1st ed. Barron's Educational Series, Inc. 2012 29 p. ill. (A first look at) (paperback) $7.99

Grades: K 1 2   306.874

   1. Same-sex marriage -- Juvenile fiction 2. Children of gay parents -- Juvenile fiction 3. Families -- Juvenile literature 4. Gay parents -- Juvenile literature 5. Children of gay parents -- Juvenile literature 6. Gay fathers -- Family relationships -- Juvenile literature 7. Lesbian mothers -- Family relationships -- Juvenile literature

   ISBN 1438001878; 9781438001876

                     LC 2012940639

This book by Pat Thomas is part of the "A First Look At" series, which "encourages kids of preschool through early school age to understand and overcome problems that might trouble them in social and family relationships." It "takes a child's point of view in its discussion of same-sex marriage. Its message is intended both for children of gay or lesbian parents, as well as for the kids and parents of the children's friends and playmates." (Publisher's note)

Includes bibliographical references (p. 29).

306.875 Sibling relationships

Cole, Joanna

★ **The new** baby at your house; photographs by Margaret Miller. rev ed; Morrow Junior Bks. 1998 un il hardcover o.p. pa $6.99

Grades: K 1 2 3   306.875

   1. Infants 2. Siblings 3. Infants -- Care -- Pictorial works -- Juvenile literature 4. Sibling rivalry -- Pictorial works -- Juvenile literature 5. Infants -- Growth -- Pictorial works -- Juvenile literature 6. Brothers and sisters -- Pictorial works -- Juvenile literature

   ISBN 0-688-13897-7; 0-688-13898-5 lib bdg; 0-688-16698-9 pa

                     LC 97-29267

A revised and newly illustrated edition of the title first published 1985

Describes the activities and changes involved in having a new baby in the house and the feelings experienced by the older brothers and sisters

"Miller captures many intimate and touching moments with her pictures. . . . There is a good balance of families from varied ethnic backgrounds. . . . This book opens with a clear and precise note to parents that gives honest, practical advice." SLJ

Includes bibliographical references

306.89   Separation and divorce

Brown, Laurene Krasny

★ **Dinosaurs** divorce; a guide for changing families. [by] Laurene Krasny Brown and Marc Brown. Atlantic Monthly Press 1986 31p il $15.95; pa $7.95

Grades: K 1 2 3   **306.89**

1. Divorce

ISBN 0-316-11248-8; 0-316-10996-7 pa

                 LC 86-1079

Text and illustrations of dinosaur characters introduce aspects of divorce such as its causes and effects, living with a single parent, spending holidays in two separate households, and adjusting to a stepparent

"The picture-book, almost comic-book, format, the touches of humor, and the distancing effect of the dinosaurs as surrogate humans may make the book accessible to young or extremely anxious children. A thoughtful, useful book." Horn Book

Holyoke, Nancy

A **smart** girl's guide to her parents' divorce; how to land on your feet when your world turns upside down. illustrated by Scott Nash. American Girl Pub. 2009 120p il pa $9.95

Grades: 3 4 5   **306.89**

1. Divorce 2. Children of divorced parents

ISBN 978-1-59369-488-3 pa; 1-59369-488-1 pa

"Short chapters illustrated with bright cartoon drawings cover many important concerns and offer explanations of the divorce process. Topics range from how to deal with negative emotions, family changes, and new living arrangements, to tougher issues such as violence and financial troubles. The text has a compassionate tone, and sprinkled throughout are answers to questions that readers might have as well as snippets of advice from girls who have found what works for them." SLJ

Murphy, Patricia J.

Divorce and separation; [by] Patricia J Murphy. Heinemann Library 2008 32p il (Tough topics) $25.36; pa $7.99

Grades: 1 2 3   **306.89**

1. Divorce

ISBN 978-1-4034-9775-8; 1-4034-9775-3; 978-1-4034-9780-2 pa; 1-4034-9780-X pa

             LC 2007005347

"Murphy addresses these emotionally charged topics in a basic and direct manner. The book defines the terms and explains the differences between separation and divorce. It also covers various emotions and feelings that are often associated with them. The writing is frank yet sensitive enough in its approach and the accompanying full-color photographs effectively illustrate the text. A solid introduction to a tough topic." SLJ

Includes bibliographical references

306.9   Institutions pertaining to death

Thornhill, Jan

I found a dead bird; the kids' guide to the cycle of life & death. Maple Tree Press 2006 64p il $21.95; pa $9.95

Grades: 4 5 6   **306.9**

1. Death 2. Bereavement 3. Life cycles (Biology) -- Juvenile literature

ISBN 1-897066-70-8; 1-897066-71-6 pa

Explores the cycle of life and death, and how the process is necessary in nature, while also commenting on how death effects people personally, and the skills they use to cope with such a trauma when it occurs.

"This straightforward, no holds barred approach to the subject will captivate children. Chock-full of color photographs, the well-designed book contains boxes with tidbits of information on a wide variety of topics, such as death of a species, human destruction, plant decomposition, trapped in time, and learning from death." SLJ

307   Communities

Ajmera, Maya

Be my neighbor; [by] Maya Ajmera & John D. Ivanko. Shakti for Children, Charlesbridge 2004 un il $15.95; pa $6.95

Grades: K 1 2   **307**

1. Community life

ISBN 1-57091-504-0; 1-57091-685-3 pa

            LC 2003-21230

A simple introduction to the characteristics of a neighborhood

"This beautifully crafted book explores the concept of community, using well-chosen words from the late Mr. Rogers as a starting point. . . . Illustrated with bright, beautiful full-color photos of children around the world, the gorgeous spreads are organized by themes." SLJ

307.7   Specific kinds of communities

Kent, Peter

Peter Kent's city across time. Kingfisher 2010 48p $16.99

Grades: 4 5 6   **307.7**

1. Cities and towns -- Growth

ISBN 978-0-7534-6400-7; 0-7534-6400-4

"Kent offers a quick tour of modern civilization as seen through the archaeological lens of an imagined European city in this detail-rich picture book. Beginning in the Stone Age, each spread uses the same vantage point to show a cutaway snapshot of what the landscape and city would look like in each era. . . . It's a winning format, and Kent knows how to provide the mini-dramas . . . that make it such a fun, flip back-and-forth experience." Booklist

Includes glossary

320   Political science (Politics and government)

Giesecke, Ernestine

National government; 2nd ed; Heinemann Library 2010 32p il map (Kids' guide to government) $29.29; pa $7.99

Grades: 3 4 5 **320**

1. United States -- Politics and government
ISBN 978-1-4329-2708-0; 1-4329-2708-6; 978-1-4329-2713-4 pa; 1-4329-2713-2 pa
First published 2000

Introduces the purpose and function of national government, the significance of the Constitution, the three branches of government, how the government raises money, and how a bill becomes a law

"This . . . would be a great asset. . . . Students will learn about a different, but related government every two pages. The font is large and easy to read. The photos, diagrams, charts, maps, and illustrations supplement the text well." Libr Media Connect

Includes glossary

320.3   Comparative government

Giesecke, Ernestine
Governments around the world; 2nd ed; Heinemann Library 2010 32p il map (Kids' guide to government) $29.29; pa $7.99
Grades: 3 4 5 **320.3**

1. Comparative government
ISBN 978-1-4329-2705-9; 1-4329-2705-1; 978-1-4329-2710-3 pa; 1-4329-2710-8 pa
First published 2000

Introduces the concept of government, exploring various types of systems, including democracy, communism, and socialism, and presenting international organizations such as the UN and NATO

"This . . . would be a great asset. . . . Students will learn about a different, but related government every two pages. The font is large and easy to read. The photos, diagrams, charts, maps, and illustrations supplement the text well." Libr Media Connect

Includes glossary and bibliographical references

Who's in charge? how governments make the world go round. foreword by Andrew Marr; [editors, Alexander Cox, Deborah Lock, Fleur Star; US editor, Margaret Parrish] DK 2010 96p il $16.99
Grades: 3 4 5 6 **320.3**

1. Political science
ISBN 978-0-7566-6278-3; 0-7566-6278-8
LC 2010280417

Introduces politicians and how laws are made, what happens in government and how the reader can get involved.

"The book explains ideas like democracy, monarchy, communism, and capitalism in a way that is accessible to children. Information is presented with DK's signature bright, colorful graphics. . . . This book is a timely and useful addition." Libr Media Connect

Includes glossary

320.4   Structure and functions of government

Wyatt, Valerie
How to build your own country; written by Valerie Wyatt; illustrated by Fred Rix. Kids Can Press 2009 40p il (CitizenKid) $17.95

Grades: 3 4 5 **320.4**

1. Citizenship 2. Political science 3. Civics -- Juvenile literature 4. Citizenship -- Juvenile literature
ISBN 978-1-55453-310-7; 1-55453-310-4

"This unique, odd, and informative book offers a guide for readers to create their own personal countries. Everything from finding unclaimed land and coming up with a name . . . to holding elections and serving one's citizens is covered. Despite the silliness, useful information is given, teaching readers about the value of diplomacy and how actual governments function." Horn Book Guide

Includes glossary

320.8   Local government

Giesecke, Ernestine
Local government; 2nd ed; Heinemann Library 2009 32p il map (Kids' guide to government) $29.29; pa $7.99
Grades: 3 4 5 **320.8**

1. Local government
ISBN 978-1-4329-2706-6; 1-4329-2706-X; 978-1-4329-2711-0 pa; 1-4329-2711-6 pa
First published 2000

Introduces the purpose and function of local governments, explores the three branches of government at the city and county level, and presents the relationships between city and suburban governments and between various governments and schools

"This . . . would be a great asset. . . . Students will learn about a different, but related government every two pages. The font is large and easy to read. The photos, diagrams, charts, maps, and illustrations supplement the text well." Libr Media Connect

Includes glossary

322.4   Political action groups

Schwartz, Heather E.
Political activism; how you can make a difference. by Heather E. Schwartz. Capstone Press 2009 32p il (Take action) lib bdg $19.99
Grades: 3 4 5 6 **322.4**

1. Lobbying 2. Social action 3. Political activists
ISBN 978-1-4296-2799-3 lib bdg; 1-4296-2799-9 lib bdg

LC 2008026939

"Whether the issue is animal rights, global warming, or student representation in government, this lively hands-on title . . . combines personal profiles of activist teens with the politics of what they are fighting for, and includes realistic advice about how to do research, set goals, ask questions, and take one step at a time to reach those in power. The open, attractive design will draw readers with color photos of young activists." Booklist

Includes bibliographical references

323   Civil and political rights

Amnesty International

★ **We** are all born free. Frances Lincoln Children's Books 2008 un il $19.95

Grades: K 1 2 3   **323**

1. Human rights

ISBN 978-1-84507-650-4; 1-84507-650-8

A commemorative edition of the Universal Declaration of Human Rights as adopted in 1948 by the United Nations General Assembly offers insight into the world's shared views about the rights of all people.

"Amnesty International has taken the 30 articles that comprise the Declaration and simplified them in such a way that they are clear to elementary school students. Each right is illustrated by an international array of well-known artists . . . [including] Bob Graham, . . . Alan Lee, . . . John Burningham, Niki Daly, Polly Dunbar, Jessica Souhami, and Satoshi Kitamura. This is an important book, best shared with children in a setting where discussion of both the rights and the illustrations is encouraged." SLJ

Marzollo, Jean

★ **Happy** birthday, Martin Luther King; illustrated by J. Brian Pinkney. Scholastic 1993 un il $15.95; pa $6.99

Grades: K 1 2 3   **323**

1. Clergy 2. Nonfiction writers 3. Civil rights activists 4. Nobel laureates for peace 5. African Americans -- Biography 6. African Americans -- Civil rights

ISBN 0-590-44065-9; 0-439-78224-4 pa

LC 91-42137

"This very easy biography of Martin Luther King is distinguished by its succinct explanations of King's achievements. . . . The narrative of King's life is smooth and accessible. Pinkney's scratchboard paintings are fluidly drawn, warm, and dignified." Bull Cent Child Books

National Geographic Society (U.S.)

★ **Every** human has rights; a photographic declaration for kids. based on the United Nations Universal Declaration of Human Rights; with poetry from the ePals community; foreword by Mary Robinson. National Geographic 2009 30p il $26.90

Grades: 4 5 6 7 8   **323**

1. Human rights

ISBN 978-1-4263-0511-5; 1-4263-0511-7

"On the sixtieth anniversary of the Universal Declaration of Human Rights, this full-color photo-essay combines prize-winning poems by young people with beautiful photographs from all over the world. . . . The stirring pictures will stimulate classroom discussion about the declaration, which is quoted in full at the back." Booklist

Thomas, William David

What are citizens' basic rights? [by] William David Thomas. Gareth Stevens Pub. 2008 32p il (My American government) lib bdg $23.93; pa $8.95

Grades: 3 4 5   **323**

1. Civil rights

ISBN 978-0-8368-8861-4 lib bdg; 0-8368-8861-8 lib bdg; 978-0-8368-8866-9 pa; 0-8368-8866-9 pa

LC 2007032425

This describes the basic legal rights of United States citizens

This book has "an accessible format and clear writing. . . . Black-and-white and full-color vintage and more recent photographs appear throughout." SLJ

Includes glossary and bibliographical references

323.092

King, Martin Luther, Jr., 1929-1968

I have a dream; Martin Luther King, Jr.; illustrated by Kadir Nelson. 1st ed. Schwartz & Wade Books 2012 40 p. il. (some col.) $18.99

Grades: K 1 2 3 4 5   **323.092**

1. Freedom 2. Equality 3. Speeches 4. Picture books for children 5. African Americans -- Civil rights -- Juvenile literature 6. Civil rights movements -- United States -- History -- Juvenile literature

ISBN 0375858873; 9780375858871; 9780375958878

LC 2011044259

Coretta Scott King Illustrator Honor Book (2013)

This children's book celebrates Civil Rights activist Martin Luther King, Jr. "On August 28, 1963, on the steps of the Lincoln Memorial during the March on Washington, Martin Luther King [Jr.] gave one of the most powerful and memorable speeches in our nation's history. His words [are] paired with Caldecott Honor winner Kadir Nelson's . . . paintings" for this book. (Publisher's note)

Pinkney, Andrea Davis

Martin and Mahalia; his words, her song. by Andrea Davis Pinkney; illustrated by Brian Pinkney. 1st ed. Little, Brown and Co. 2013 40 p. ill. (reinforced) $17.99

Grades: 1 2 3 4   **323.092**

1. Picture books for children 2. African Americans -- Civil rights -- History -- 20th century -- Juvenile literature 3. Civil rights movements -- United States -- History -- 20th century -- Juvenile literture

ISBN 0316070130; 9780316070133

LC 2012005499

This children's picture book weaves together "the stories of two giants of the American civil rights movement," Martin Luther King, Jr. and Mahalia Jackson. "At first the stories are distinct, with alternating, dedicated spreads tracing the individuals' paths as gospel preacher and singer until they meet and combine forces at the Montgomery bus boycott in 1955 and forge a collaboration that takes them through Martin's most famous speech, at the Lincoln Memorial." (Booklist)

323.1   Civil and political rights of nondominant groups

Aretha, David

Sit-ins and freedom rides. Morgan Reynolds Pub. 2009 128p il lib bdg $28.95

Grades: 5 6 7 8   **323.1**

1. African Americans -- Civil rights

ISBN 978-1-59935-098-1 lib bdg; 1-59935-098-X lib bdg

LC 2008039600

"Aretha opens with an introduction to the four college students who orchestrated the famous sit-in at Woolworth's

in Greensboro, NC, in 1960. He follows that with chapters that describe slavery, Reconstruction, and Jim Crow in terms of how they set the stage for the resistance efforts. . . . [The book] offers insight into to workings of the protests at the grassroots level. Individual anecdotes interspersed though-out the detailed narrative provide personal and effective accounts that go beyond mere facts. Black-and-white and some color photographs appear on almost every page." SLJ
Includes bibliographical references

Bausum, Ann

Freedom Riders; John Lewis and Jim Zwerg on the front lines of the civil rights movement. by Ann Bausum; forewords by Freedom Riders Congressman John Lewis and Jim Zwerg. National Geographic 2006 79p il por $18.95; lib bdg $28.90
Grades: 5 6 7 8   323.1
1. Members of Congress 2. Civil rights activists 3. African Americans -- Civil rights
ISBN 0-7922-4173-8; 0-7922-4174-6 lib bdg
LC 2005012947
"Bausum's narrative style, fresh, engrossing, and at times heart-stopping, brings the story of the turbulent and often violent dismantling of segregated travel alive in vivid detail. The language, presentation of material, and pacing will draw readers in and keep them captivated." SLJ
Includes bibliographical references

Brimner, Larry Dane, 1949-

★ **Birmingham** Sunday. Calkins Creek 2010 48p il
Grades: 5 6 7 8   323.1
1. Bombings 2. Hate crimes 3. Racism -- Juvenile literature 4. African Americans -- Civil rights 5. Hate crimes -- Birmingham (Ala.) -- Juvenile literature 6. African Americans -- Civil rights -- Juvenile literature 7. Bombings -- Alabama -- Birmingham -- Juvenile literature
ISBN 1590786130; 9781590786130
LC 2009035716
This book describes the bombing of the Sixteenth Street Church in 1963 by Ku Klux Klan members, which killed four girls, and discusses how the event contributed to the civil rights movement. "Grades five to eight." (Bull Cent Child Books)
"This moving photo-essay covers much more than just an account of the Birmingham, Alabama, Baptist Church bombing that killed four young girls in 1963. The detailed text, illustrated with black-and-white photos on every spacious double-page spread, sets the shocking assassination of the children within a general overview of both the racist segregation of the times and the struggle against it." Booklist

Freedman, Russell

★ **Freedom** walkers; the story of the Montgomery bus boycott. Holiday House 2006 114p il $18.95
Grades: 4 5 6 7   323.1
1. Clergy 2. Historians 3. College teachers 4. Nonfiction writers 5. Civil rights activists 6. Nobel laureates for peace 7. Boycotts -- Juvenile literature 8. African Americans -- Civil rights 9. Civil rights movements -- Alabama -- Montgomery -- Juvenile literature
ISBN 978-0-8234-2031-5; 0-8234-2031-0
LC 2006-41148

This account of the Montgomery bus boycott of 1955 focuses on Jo Ann Robinson, Claudette Colvin, Rosa Parks, Martin Luther King, and other participants.
This offers "expertly paced text, balanced but im-passioned. . . . The narrative arc is compelling; well-captioned black-and-white photographs enhance the impact." Horn Book
Includes bibliographical references

Holland, Leslie J.

Dr. Martin Luther King Jr.'s I have a dream speech in translation; what it really means. Capstone Press 2009 32p il (Fact finders. Kids' translations) lib bdg $23.99; pa $7.95
Grades: 3 4 5   323.1
1. Clergy 2. American speeches 3. Nonfiction writers 4. Civil rights activists 5. Nobel laureates for peace 6. African Americans -- Civil rights
ISBN 978-1-4296-2793-1 lib bdg; 1-4296-2793-X lib bdg; 978-1-4296-3449-6 pa; 1-4296-3449-9 pa
LC 2008-32867
"Presents Dr. Martin Luther King Jr.'s speech and explains its meaning using everyday language. Describes the events that led to the speech and its significance through history." Publisher's note
Includes glossary and bibliographical references

Hynson, Colin

The **civil** rights movement. Arcturus 2010 48p il (Timelines) lib bdg $34.25
Grades: 5 6 7 8   323.1
1. African Americans -- Civil rights
ISBN 978-1-84837-638-0 lib bdg; 1-84837-638-3 lib bdg
LC 2009051261
"This title offers a succinct overview of the civil rights movement in the U.S., beginning with the country's first-ever Civil Rights Act, signed by Congress in 1866. The picture-book-sized format is dynamic: each neatly laid-out spread combines short, informative paragraphs with a time line of landmark dates; well-chosen boxed quotes and archival images; and cross-referenced notes that link to related spreads and help students synthesize the events into a bigger historical picture." Booklist
Includes glossary and bibliographical references

Kittinger, Jo S.

Rosa's bus; illustrated by Steven Walker. Boyds Mills Press 2010 un il $17.95
Grades: 1 2 3 4   323.1
1. Buses 2. Civil rights activists 3. African Americans -- Civil rights
ISBN 978-1-59078-722-9; 1-59078-722-6
LC 2010005091
"In an inventive approach, this handsome picture book frames the biography of Rosa Parks with the story of the bus on which she famously refused to give up her seat to a white passenger. . . . The free-verse narrative and dramatic oil paintings tell the larger story of discrimination in daily life." Booklist
Includes bibliographical references

McClaurin, Irma

★ The **civil** rights movement; by Irma McClaurin. Marshall Cavendish Benchmark 2008 80p il (Drama of African-American history) lib bdg $23.95

Grades: 5 6 7 8   **323.1**

1. African Americans -- Civil rights

ISBN 978-0-7614-2642-4

"Covers the struggle of African Americans to gain their civil rights, from Brown v. Board of Education in 1954 through the turbulent Sixties." Publisher's note

McWhorter, Diane

★ A **dream** of freedom; the Civil Rights Movement from 1954 to 1968. foreword by Reverend Fred Shuttlesworth. Scholastic Nonfiction 2004 160p il $19.95

Grades: 5 6 7 8   **323.1**

1. African Americans -- Civil rights

ISBN 0-439-57678-4

The author discusses "the national civil rights movement from Brown v. the Board of Education to the assassination of Martin Luther King Jr. . . . This account is both factual and personal. She discusses her feelings as a white child in the South, and she focuses in on the many ways in which both white and black children were involved in the movement. . . . The breadth and depth of McWhorter's book is exemplary." Booklist

Pinkney, Andrea Davis

★ **Sit-**in; how four friends stood up by sitting down. [by] Andrea Davis Pinkney and Brian Pinkney. Little, Brown and Company 2010 un il $16.99

Grades: K 1 2 3   **323.1**

1. African Americans -- Civil rights   2. Civil rights movements -- Juvenile literature   3. African Americans -- Civil rights -- Juvenile literature

ISBN 0-316-07016-5; 978-0-316-07016-4

LC 2009-19470

Flora Stieglitz Straus Award for Nonficton 2011

"This picture book is a celebration of the 50th anniversary of the . . . Woolworth's lunch counter sit-in, when four college students staged a peaceful protest." (Publisher's note) "Grades three to five." (Bull Cent Child Books)

"This compelling picture book is based on the historic sit-in 50 years ago by four college students who tried to integrate a Woolworth's lunch counter in Greensboro, North Carolina. Food-related wordplay adds layers to free verse. . . At the core of the exciting narrative are scenes that show the difficulty of facing hatred. . . . Even young children will grasp the powerful, elemental, and historic story." Booklist

Rappaport, Doreen

★ **Nobody** gonna turn me 'round; stories and songs of the civil rights movement. illustrated by Shane W. Evans. Candlewick Press 2006 63p il $19.99

Grades: 3 4 5 6   **323.1**

1. African Americans -- Civil rights   3. Civil rights movements -- Juvenile literature   4. African Americans -- Civil rights -- Juvenile literature

ISBN 0-7636-1927-2; 978-0-7636-1927-5

LC 2005-53184

"Rappaport draws on songs, poems, memories, letters, court testimony, and first-person accounts to provide a moving portrayal of the experiences of African Americans from the 1955 Montgomery Bus Boycott to the Voting Rights Act

in July 1965. . . . Evans's earth-toned oil paintings enhance the stories with images that are by turns poignant, sad, hurtful, resigned, determined, hopeful, and triumphant." SLJ

Includes bibliographical references

Shelton, Paula Young

★ **Child** of the civil rights movement; illustrated by Raul Colón. Schwartz & Wade Books 2010 un il $17.99; lib bdg $20.99

Grades: K 1 2 3   **323.1**

1. Clergy 2. Mayors 3. Members of Congress 4. Civil rights activists 5. United Nations officials 6. African Americans -- Civil rights

ISBN 978-0-375-84314-3; 0-375-84314-0; 978-0-375-95414-6 lib bdg; 0-375-95414-7 lib bdg

LC 2008045855

The daughter of Andrew Young recalls her memories of her father and other African American civil rights activists, including Martin Luther King Jr., Dorothy Cotton and Ralph Abernathy, and the march from Selma to Montgomery Alabama.

"Colón's . . . soft-focus art features his customarily rich textural backdrop of speckles, scratches, and waves. Both contributors evoke the drama and emotion of the times . . . and a triumphal sense of community and family." Publ Wkly

Includes bibliographical references

Watkins, Angela Farris

My Uncle Martin's words of love for America; Martin Luther King Jr.'s niece tells how he made a difference. by Angela Farris Watkins, PhD; Illustrated by Eric Velasquez. Abrams Books for Young Readers 2011 40p il

Grades: 2 3 4   **323.1**

1. Clergy 2. Nonfiction writers 3. Civil rights activists 4. Nobel laureates for peace 5. African Americans -- Civil rights

ISBN 1-4197-0022-7; 978-1-4197-0022-4

LC 2011003888

"Explaining Jim Crow laws and the Civil Rights movement to a very young audience is not easy, but Watkins and Velasquez rise to the challenge with grace and warmth. Using a childlike voice, Martin Luther King Jr.'s niece simply and clearly emphasizes themes of love, nonviolence, freedom and equality. The repetitive text instills the message 'people listened, and things changed' and focuses on the positive. While the prejudice and violence of segregation is broached, . . . the intensity and extent of that violence is omitted. . . . Though picture books about Dr. King by his family members and others abound, this stands out for its graceful, age-appropriate treatment of the Movement." Kirkus

Includes bibliographical references

Weatherford, Carole Boston

★ The **beatitudes**; from slavery to civil rights. written by Carole Boston Weatherford; illustrated by Tim Ladwig. Eerdmans Books for Young Readers 2010 un il $16.99

Grades: 1 2 3 4   **323.1**

1. African Americans -- History 2. African Americans -- Civil rights 3. Civil rights movements -- Juvenile literature 4. Slavery -- United States -- Juvenile literature 5. African Americans -- Civil rights -- History -- Juvenile literature

ISBN 978-0-8028-5352-3; 0-8028-5352-8

"Using the Beatitudes of blessings found in the Sermon on the Mount as an underpinning, Weatherford . . . highlights the faith that bolstered the African American struggle for freedom and civil rights. . . . The words serve as a refrain to puncuate Ladwig's elegant watercolors and lend a dreamlike quality to the stirring depictions." Booklist

323.3   Civil and political rights of other social groups

Serres, Alain
I have the right to be a child; author, Alain Serres; illustrator, Aurélia Fronty; translator, Helen Mixter. Groundwood Books 2012 48 p.
Grades: 3 4 5 6 7   **323.3**
1. Treaties 2. Human rights 3. Children -- Civil rights
ISBN 1554981492; 9781554981496

In this children's book, "a young narrator describes what it means to be a child with rights -- from the right to food, water and shelter, to the right to go to school, to the right to be free from violence, to the right to breathe clean air, and much more. The book emphasizes that these rights belong to every child on the planet. . . . A brief afterword explains that the rights outlined in the book come from the Convention on the Rights of the Child." (Publisher's note)

323.6   Citizenship and related topics

Raum, Elizabeth
The **Pledge** of Allegiance in translation; what it really means. by Elizabeth Raum. Capstone Press 2009 32p il map (Fact finders. Kids' translations) lib bdg $23.93; pa $7.95
Grades: 3 4 5   **323.6**
ISBN 978-1-4296-1931-8 lib bdg; 1-4296-1931-7 lib bdg; 978-1-4296-2846-4 pa; 1-4296-2846-4 pa
LC 2007-51304

Provides "a nearly line-by-line translation that makes . . . the written word accessible and meaningful." SLJ

Includes glossary and bibliographical references

323.609

Raatma, Lucia
Citizenship; by Lucia Raatma. Children's Press 2012 64 p. ill. (chiefly col.), col. map (Cornerstones of freedom) (library) $30; (paperback) $8.95
Grades: 4 5 6   **323.609**
1. Citizenship -- United States -- Juvenile literature
ISBN 0329917374; 0531230643; 0531281647; 9780329917371; 9780531230640; 9780531281642
LC 2011031340

This book on citizenship by Lucia Raatma "covers everything from basic facts about naturalization to debates over hot issues such as gun control." It is part of the "Cornerstones of Freedom" series for students in grades 4 to 6. Included are "a two-page map of 'What Happened Where?'; a two-page epilogue; glossary-style identifications of significant people; a page of primary sources; a bibliography of books; a glossary; and an index plus author bio." (Booklist)

Includes bibliographical references (p. 61) and index.

324   The political process

Steele, Philip
Vote. DK Pub. 2008 72p il (Eyewitness books) $15.99
Grades: 4 5 6 7 8   **324**
1. Elections
ISBN 978-0-7566-3382-0; 0-7566-3382-6

"Engaging visual material and a wealth of assorted facts trace the history of voting and its impact on human rights, politics, and other related areas. The first half moves chronologically from ancient Greece to modern times, with current information into the 21st century. Later sections look at political structures, election logistics, and even nongovernmental elections (including trade unions, the Oscars, and Britain's Pop Idol). Several high-quality photographs and reproductions appear on each spread. . . . The book does a nice job of pulling together an impressive array of topics, events, and ideas within the broad concept of global suffrage. The book comes with a poster-size wall chart and a clip-art CD with downloadable images of many of the illustrations." SLJ

Stier, Catherine
★ **If** I ran for president; illustrated by Lynne Avril. Albert Whitman & Co. 2007 un il $16.99; pa $6.99
Grades: 1 2 3   **324**
1. Presidents -- United States -- Election
ISBN 978-0-8075-3543-1; 0-8075-3543-5; 978-0-8075-3544-5 pa; 0-8075-3544-3 pa

"This title is a step above the usual election books, both in content and entertainment value. . . . The lively cartoons cheerfully clarify the action and reinforce the concepts." SLJ

324.6   Election systems and procedures; suffrage

Fritz, Jean
You want women to vote, Lizzie Stanton? illustrated by DyAnne DiSalvo-Ryan. Putnam 1995 88p il $16.99; pa $5.99
Grades: 2 3 4   **324.6**
1. Feminism 2. Suffragists 3. Women -- Suffrage
ISBN 0-399-22786-5; 0-698-11764-6 pa
LC 94-30018

This is a biography of the 19th century feminist and advocate of women's suffrage

"With remarkable clarity, sensitivity, and momentum, Fritz has captured—but never imprisoned [Stanton's] spirit in an accessible, fascinating portrait." Horn Book

Includes bibliographical references

Hollihan, Kerrie Logan
Rightfully ours; how women won the vote: 21 activities. Kerrie Logan Hollihan. 1st ed. Chicago Review Press 2012 xiii, 130 p.p ill. (some col.) (paperback) $16.95
Grades: 4 5 6 7 8   **324.6**
1. Women -- Suffrage 2. Women -- United States -- History 3. Suffragists -- United States -- History -- Juvenile literature 4. Women's rights -- United States

-- History -- Juvenile literature 5. Women's rights -- Study and teaching -- Activity programs -- United States 6. Women -- Suffrage -- Study and teaching -- Activity programs -- United States

ISBN 1883052890; 9781883052898

LC 2012006044

This book is an "account of the struggle for women's suffrage. The first three chapters focus on notable activists Lucy Stone, Elizabeth Cady Stanton, and Susan B. Anthony. [Kerrie Logan] Hollihan recounts how this battle was inexorably tied to the antislavery movement and the role played by women of color in both movements, including Harriett Tubman, Sojourner Truth, and Ida Wells-Barnett." (School Library Journal)

Includes bibliographical references (p. 121-124) and index

Van Rynbach, Iris

The **taxing** case of the cows; a true story about suffrage. by Iris Van Rynbach and Pegi Deitz Shea; illustrated by Emily Arnold McCully. Clarion Books 2010 32p il $16.99

Grades: 1 2 3   324.6

1. Cattle 2. Taxation 3. Suffragists 4. Women -- Suffrage 5. Women -- Suffrage -- Juvenile literature

ISBN 978-0-547-23631-5; 0-547-23631-X

"This title introduces the little-known story of two elderly sisters, Abby and Julia Smith, who fought against the taxation levied upon them as nonvoting citizens in nineteenth-century Connecticut. . . . The sisters' beloved cows became pawns in the arguments, used as collateral and bargaining chips by both sides. . . . McCully's watercolor illustrations of the historical scenes enhance this account of a pivotal event in women's long struggle for equality." Booklist

Wallner, Alexandra

Susan B. Anthony; by Alexandra Wallner. Holiday House 2011 32 p. col. ill. (hardcover) $16.95

Grades: K 1 2 3   324.6

1. Women -- Suffrage 2. Picture books for children 3. Women's rights -- United States -- Juvenile literature 4. Feminists -- United States -- Biography -- Juvenile literature 5. Suffragists -- United States -- Biography -- Juvenile literature

ISBN 0823419533; 9780823419531

LC 2009017815

This "picture-book biography focuses on America's foremost champion for women's rights," Susan B. Anthony. It covers her life, "from her strict upbringing in Massachusetts to her death after 58 years of working for reform, and her passionate role in the women's-suffrage movement." (School Library Journal)

Includes bibliographical references

324.9 History and geographic treatment of elections

Christelow, Eileen

★ **Vote!** Clarion 2003 47p il $16

Grades: K 1 2 3   324.9

1. Politics 2. Elections

ISBN 0-618-24754-8

LC 2002-152288

Using a campaign for mayor as an example, shows the steps involved in an election, from the candidate's speeches and rallies, to the voting booth where every vote counts, to the announcement of the winner

"It's hard to imagine a more accessible introduction to voting. The words are straightforward, the art whimsical and creative, and two darling dogs provide color commentary on the action." Booklist

Includes glossary

325 International migration and colonization

Bial, Raymond

Ellis Island; coming to the land of liberty. Houghton Mifflin Books for Children 2009 56p il $18

Grades: 4 5 6 7   325

1. Ellis Island Immigration Station 2. United States -- Immigration and emigration

ISBN 978-0-618-99943-9; 0-618-99943-4

LC 2008-36794

"Bial examines the history of the famed immigration station. . . . He looks at the socio-historical roots of the mass exodus to America and provides a detailed look at the immigrant experience from ship to shore, with Ellis Island in between. Primary-source quotes and period photos pair eloquently with the modern narrative voice and color photographs of the museum exhibits. . . . The generously sized period photos and Bial's museum shots tell a vivid and poignant tale." SLJ

Includes bibliographical references

Freedman, Russell

★ **Immigrant** kids. Dutton 1980 72p il hardcover o.p. pa $8.99

Grades: 4 5 6 7   325

1. City and town life 2. Children of immigrants

ISBN 0-14-037594-5 pa

LC 79-20060

The author has "assembled an interesting collection of old photographs for a book that gives a broad view of the experiences of immigrant children in an urban environment. The text is divided into such areas as the journey to America, schools, play, work (much of it illegal), and home life. Photographs are carefully placed in relation to textual references, and the text itself is enlivened by quotations from the reminiscences of several people about their first days in the United States as child immigrants. Large, clear print and an index add to the book's usefulness." Horn Book

Levine, Ellen

★ . . . if your name was changed at Ellis Island; illustrated by Wayne Parmenter. Scholastic 1993 80p il hardcover o.p. pa $6.99

Grades: 3 4 5   325

1. Immigrants -- United States 2. Ellis Island (N.J. & N.Y.)

ISBN 0-590-43829-8 pa

LC 92-27940

Describes, in question and answer format, the great migration of immigrants to New York's Ellis Island, from the 1880s to 1914. Features quotes from children and adults who passed through the station

The author "writes in a clear, direct style that's packed with information and lively case histories. . . . There are many illustrations, sometimes full-page, sometimes small, in acrylic earth colors . . . they are an attractive part of a clear and accessible design." Booklist

Maestro, Betsy

★ **Coming** to America: the story of immigration; illustrated by Susannah Ryan. Scholastic 1996 un il $15.95
Grades: K 1 2 3   **325**
  1. Immigrants -- United States
  ISBN 0-590-44151-5

                   LC 94-31110

"In an introductory look at immigration, all inhabitants of the United States are considered immigrants or descendants of immigrants, whether they crossed the land bridge from Asia, came across the oceans voluntarily, or were brought as slaves. The clear, simple text and bright, animated illustrations convey excitement and adventure as well as hardship and loss." Horn Book Guide

Sandler, Martin W.

Island of hope; the story of Ellis Island and the journey to America. Scholastic Nonfiction 2004 144p il $18.95
Grades: 5 6 7 8   **325**
  1. Immigrants -- United States   2. Ellis Island (N.J. & N.Y.)
  ISBN 0-439-53082-2

                   LC 2003-54448

Relates the story of immigration to America through the voices and stories of those who passed through Ellis Island, from its opening in 1892 to the release of the last detainee in 1954.

"This engagingly written, inspirational account will give children, particularly immigrants or descendants of immigrants, some sharp insight into the trials and triumphs of their predecessors." Booklist

Includes bibliographical references

Solway, Andrew

Graphing immigration. Raintree 2010 32p il (Real world data) $28.21; pa $7.99
Grades: 4 5 6 7   **325**
  1. Statistics   2. Graphic methods 3. Immigrants -- United States
  ISBN 978-1-4329-2617-5; 1-4329-2617-9; 978-1-4329-2626-7 pa; 1-4329-2626-8 pa

                   LC 2009001185

"A line graph in [this] title shows the estimated number of illegal immigrants in the U.S. from 1980 to 2005. Arguments about costs and benefits of all kinds of immigrants include a pie chart that shows where immigrants in the U.S. come from and pairs thoughts on why people migrate with a discussion of costs and benefits. . . . The clear design, with lots of full-color photos and sidebars, will encourage browsers as much as the up-to-date examples and the clear directions for remaining 'chart smart.'" Booklist

Includes glossary and bibliographical references

Staton, Hilarie

Ellis Island. Chelsea Clubhouse 2009 48p il (Symbols of American freedom) $30
Grades: 3 4 5   **325**
  1. Immigrants -- United States   2. Ellis Island (N.J. & N.Y.)
  ISBN 978-1-60413-519-0; 1-60413-519-0

                   LC 2009-12067

This book about Ellis Island Immigration Station "provides nearly as much information as a guided tour by a park ranger. [It begins] with the story of how the place came to be, and where it fits into U.S. history. Information boxes offer additional background and some surprising facts, such as the stages an immigrant would pass through at Ellis Island. . . . The final chapter shows the landmark today and includes maps and photographs of the visitors' center and some of the things individuals might see or do while visiting the site. Much information is packed into [this] slim [book]. Excellent . . . for state reports or to complement U.S. history units." SLJ

Includes glossary

326   Slavery and emancipation

Bial, Raymond

The **Underground** Railroad. Houghton Mifflin 1995 48p il map hardcover o.p. pa $6.95
Grades: 4 5 6 7   **326**
  1. Underground railroad 2. Slavery -- United States 3. Slaves -- Juvenile literature
  ISBN 0-395-69937-1; 0-395-97915-3 pa

                   LC 94-19614

"Although the text covers ground often trodden by other works on this popular subject, Bial's shots of places and things which now appear tidy and innocent conjure spirits of desperate freedom-seekers as handily as do more detailed narratives." Bull Cent Child Books

Includes bibliographical references

Hamilton, Virginia

★ **Many** thousand gone; African Americans from slavery to freedom. illustrated by Leo and Diane Dillon. Knopf 1993 151p il hardcover o.p. pa $12.95
Grades: 5 6 7 8   **326**
  1. Underground railroad 2. Slavery -- United States
  ISBN 0-394-92873-3; 0-679-87936-6 pa

                   LC 89-19988

In this book the author tells "the story of slavery through a series of dramatic biographical vignettes. . . . Her book includes such famous historical figures as Frederick Douglass, Sojourner Truth and Harriet Tubman. She also presents some more obscure individuals. . . . All of these profiles drive home the sickening realities of slavery in a personal way. . . . These are powerful stories eloquently told." N Y Times Book Rev

Includes bibliographical references

Haskins, James

Get on board: the story of the Underground Railroad. Scholastic 1993 152p il map hardcover o.p. pa $4.50
Grades: 5 6 7 8   **326**
  1. Slaves 2. Abolitionists 3. Underground railroad 4.

Slavery -- United States
ISBN 0-590-45419-6; 0-590-45418-8 pa

LC 92-13247

"Weaving together poignant personal stories and carefully researched historical data, Haskins has produced a stirring account of the founding and the workings of the Underground Railroad." Publ Wkly

Includes bibliographical references

Heinrichs, Ann

★ The **Underground** Railroad. Compass Point Bks. 2001 48p il map (We the people) lib bdg $21.26

Grades: 2 3 4   **326**

1. Fugitive slaves 2. Underground railroad 3. Slavery -- United States 4. Fugitive slaves -- United States -- History -- 19th century -- Juvenile literature

ISBN 0-7565-0102-4

LC 00-11020

This book briefly describes the Underground Railroad, slavery, and important abolitionists in the U.S.

"Short chapters, succinct text, large print, and well-chosen illustrations make this book a good starting point for young readers embarking on a study of the topic." SLJ

Includes glossary and bibliographical references

Lester, Julius

★ **To** be a slave; paintings by Tom Feelings. 30th anniversary ed; Dial Bks. 1998 160p il hardcover o.p. pa $6.99

Grades: 6 7 8 9   **326**

1. Slaves 2. Slave trade 3. Slavery -- United States 4. Slaves -- United States -- Biography 5. Slaves -- United States -- Quotations 6. Slaves -- United States -- Social conditions

ISBN 0-8037-2347-4; 0-14-131001-4 pa

LC 98-5213

A reissue of the title first published 1968

"Through the words of the slave, interwoven with strongly sympathetic commentary, the reader learns what it is to be another man's property; how the slave feels about himself; and how he feels about others. Every aspect of slavery, regardless of how grim, has been painfully and unrelentingly described." Read Ladders for Hum Relat. 6th edition

Includes bibliographical references

McKissack, Patricia C.

Rebels against slavery; by Patricia C. McKissack and Fredrick McKissack. Scholastic 1996 181p il $15.95

Grades: 5 6 7 8   **326**

1. Slavery -- United States 2. Slaves -- Juvenile literature

ISBN 0-590-45735-7

LC 94-41089

A Coretta Scott King honor book for text, 1997

The authors "explore slave revolts and the men and women who led them, weaving a tale of courage and defiance in the face of tremendous odds. Readers learn not only about Nat Turner and Denmark Vesey, but also about Cato, Gabriel Prosser, the maroons, and the relationship between escaped slaves and Seminole Indians. The activities of abolitionists are described as well. The authors' careful research, sensitivity, and evenhanded style reveal a sad, yet inspiring story of the will to be free." SLJ

Sharp, S. Pearl

The **slave** trade and the middle passage; by S. Pearl Sharp with Virginia Schomp. Marshall Cavendish Benchmark 2007 70p il map (Drama of African-American history) lib bdg $34.21

Grades: 5 6 7 8   **326**

1. Slavery 2. Slave trade

ISBN 978-0-7614-2176-4 lib bdg; 0-7614-2176-9 lib bdg

LC 2006005321

"Traces the history of the transatlantic slave trade and the development of slavery in the New World." Publisher's note

Includes glossary and bibliographical references

327   International relations

Deedy, Carmen Agra

14 cows for America; [by] Carmen Agra Deedy in collaboration with Wilson Kimeli Naiyomah; illustrated by Thomas Gonzalez. Peachtree 2009 un il $17.95

Grades: K 1 2 3   **327**

1. Authors 2. Masai (African people) 3. September 11 terrorist attacks, 2001 4. Children's authors 5. September 11 terrorist attacks, 2001 -- Juvenile literature

ISBN 978-1-56145-490-7; 1-56145-490-7

"A native of Kenya, Naiyomah was in New York City on September 11, 2001. In his and Deedy's . . . lyrical account, he returns to his homeland and tells the members of his Maasai tribe the story that had 'burned a hole in his heart.' . . . Featuring luminous images . . . Gonzalez's pastel, colored pencil and airbrush paintings appear almost three-dimensional in their realism. A moving tale of compassion and generosity." Publ Wkly

327.1   Foreign policy and specific topics in international relations

Kerley, Barbara

A **little** peace; by Barbara Kerley; with a note by Richard H. Solomon. National Geographic 2007 un il $16.95; lib bdg $25.90

Grades: 1 2 3 4   **327.1**

1. Peace

ISBN 978-1-4263-0086-8; 1-4263-0086-7; 978-1-4263-0087-5 lib bdg; 1-4263-0087-5 lib bdg

LC 2006026367

Juxtaposes photographs from around the world with a simple message about our responsibilities for making and keeping peace on the planet.

This is a "simple, beautiful photo-essay. . . . The colorful pictures are supported by limited, yet powerful text, illustrating how each person can work to achieve peace." SLJ

Includes bibliographical references

327.12   Espionage and subversion

Earnest, Peter

The **real** spy's guide to becoming a spy; by Peter Earnest and Suzanne Harper, in association with the Spy Museum. Abrams Books for Young Readers 2009 144p il $16.95

Grades: 4 5 6 7   **327.12**
1. Spies 2. Espionage 3. Intelligence service 4. Spies -- Juvenile literature
ISBN 978-0-8109-8329-8; 0-8109-8329-X
LC 2009-00518

"This guide, written by the executive director of the International Spy Museum, gives readers a glimpse at how spies work. Along with descriptions of the different types of intelligence officers and agencies and the tasks they perform, the text includes brief stories of spies in action." Horn Book Guide

Gilbert, Adrian
Secret agents. Firefly 2009 32p il (Spy files) pa $6.95

Grades: 3 4 5 6   **327.12**
1. Spies 2. Secret service
ISBN 978-1-55407-574-4; 1-55407-574-2
First published 2008 in the United Kingdom

Discusses American, British, and Russian spies and secret agents, and the history of espionage. Includes profiles of famous spies and double agents.

The text's "short paragraphs and great pictures are combined in a collage style that will draw readers quickly through the information. Useful for reports and browsing." SLJ

Includes glossary

Spy school. Firefly 2009 32p il (Spy files) pa $6.95
Grades: 3 4 5 6   **327.12**
1. Spies 2. Espionage
ISBN 978-1-55407-575-1 pa; 1-55407-575-0 pa

"Gilbert reveals how spies are recruited and trained, discussing methods of disguise, surveillance, interrogation, evasion, and escape. . . . The [text's] short paragraphs and great pictures are combined in a collage style that will draw readers quickly through the information. Useful for reports and browsing." SLJ

Includes glossary

Janeczko, Paul B.
The dark game; true spy stories. Candlewick Press 2010 248p il $16.99

Grades: 5 6 7 8   **327.12**
1. Espionage
ISBN 978-0-7636-2915-1; 0-7636-2915-4

"From Benedict Arnold and Mata Hari to the lesser-known Elizabeth Van Lew and Juan Pujol, Janeczko delves into [spies'] stories with delicious detail, drawing readers into a world of intrigue and danger. Did you ever wonder why invisible ink works? How a code breaker deciphers a message? Or whether dentistry could affect a secret agent's success? The answers to these questions and more can be found here. Each chapter covers a historical era and chronicles the maturation of spying, while primary-source photographs are interspersed throughout, lending an authentic feel to each section." SLJ

Mitchell, Susan K.
Spies and lies; famous and infamous spies. Enslow Publishers 2011 48p il (The secret world of spies) lib bdg $23.93

Grades: 4 5 6   **327.12**
1. Spies 2. Espionage
ISBN 978-0-7660-3713-7
LC 2010044126

Includes glosssary and bibliographical references

Spies, double agents, and traitors. Enslow Publishers 2011 48p il (The secret world of spies) lib bdg $23.93
Grades: 4 5 6   **327.12**
1. Spies 2. Espionage
ISBN 978-0-7660-3711-3
LC 2010006178

Discusses double agents and traitors throughout history, such as Benedict Arnold, Dusan Popov, Kim Philby, and Robert Hanssen, and includes information on becoming a spy catcher (counterintelligence agent).

Includes glossary bibliographical references

Spy gizmos and gadgets. Enslow Publishers 2011 48p il (The secret world of spies) lib bdg $23.93
Grades: 4 5 6   **327.12**
1. Espionage 2. Electronic surveillance
ISBN 978-0-7660-3710-6
LC 2010006177

Discusses different gadgets used by spies, such as invisible ink, hidden cameras, small guns made to look like ordinary objects, and bugs, and includes career information.

Includes glossary and bibliographical references

★ Spyology; the complete book of spycraft. Candlewick Press 2008 un il $22.99
Grades: 3 4 5 6   **327.12**
1. Spies 2. Espionage
ISBN 978-0-7636-4048-4; 0-7636-4048-4

This "poses as a collection of items assembled in 1958 and stored in national archives, now declassified under the 'fifty-year rule.' Agent K, a British spy, is tracking down the evil international Operation Codex, using his mission to ground a training manual for spies. Readers can match wits with Agent K as they pick up clues." Publ Wkly

328 The legislative process

Hamilton, John
How a bill becomes a law; [by] John Hamilton. ABDO Pub. Co. 2004 32p il (Government in action!) lib bdg $15.95

Grades: 3 4 5   **328**
1. Law 2. Legislation
ISBN 1-59197-646-4
LC 2003-69305

This describes the steps in passing a federal law in the United States

This "book has an interesting assortment of vintage and recent color photos, all well captioned, and is logically arranged." SLJ

Obama, Barack, 1961-
Change has come; an artist celebrates our American spirit. the drawings of Kadir Nelson; with the words of Barack Obama. Simon & Schuster 2009 un il $12.99

Grades: 1 2 3   **328**

1. Presidents -- United States -- Election -- 2008
ISBN 978-1-4169-8955-4; 1-4169-8955-2

"Weaving Obama's words with his own extraordinary graphite drawings, Nelson has created a moving celebration of the election of our 44th president." SLJ

330   Economics

Hlinka, Michael

Follow Your Money; Who Gets It, Who Spends It, Where Does It Go? by Kevin Sylvester and Michael Hlinka; illustrated by Kevin Sylvester. Annick Press 2013 56 p. col. ill. (paperback) $14.95; (hardcover) $24.95
Grades: 5 6 7 8   **330**

1. Pricing 2. Money -- Juvenile literature
ISBN 1554514800; 1554514819; 9781554514809; 9781554514816

This book by Kevin Sylvester and Michael Hlinka answers the questions "what happens to your money after you hand it to the cashier? Who actually pockets it or puts it into the bank? Was the price you paid fair? Why do things cost what they do? Kids will also discover the trail their money takes through advertising, banks [and] charitable giving. [It is an] introduction to the . . .people and companies that we influence and are influenced by when we pay for a product or service." (Publisher's note)

330.9   Economic situation and conditions

Heinrichs, Ann

★ The **great** recession. Children's Press 2011 il (Cornerstones of freedom) lib bdg $30; pa $8.95
Grades: 4 5 6 7   **330.9**

1. Recessions 2. Financial crises 3. Economic policy -- United States
ISBN 978-0-531-25035-8 lib bdg; 0-531-25035-0 lib bdg; 978-0-531-26560-4 pa; 0-531-26560-9 pa
               LC 2011010824

This "offers simplified but not simplistic explanations of the current great recession's course and immediate causes. The . . . design has . . . visually stimulating pages that combine big color photos, boxed side essays, and blocks of large text with bright-red headers and highlights. In simple language and a judicious, matter-of-fact tone, Heinrichs describes the origins and growth of the housing bubble and the trade in mortgage-backed securities that magnified the effects of its eventual collapse; summarizes the federal government's palliative measures; surveys the effects of hard times on general patterns of living and spending; and notes the creation of a 'Generation R,' for whom high unemployment and financial insecurity are likely to become ways of life." Booklist

Includes bibliographical references

Mooney, Carla

The **Industrial** Revolution; investigate how science and technology changed the world with 25 projects. illustrated by Jen Vaughn. Nomad Press 2011 120p il (Build it yourself) $21.95; pa $15.95

Grades: 4 5 6 7   **330.9**

1. Industrial revolution
ISBN 978-1-936313-81-5; 1-936313-81-2; 978-1936313-80-8; 1-936313-80-4 pa

This "gives on overview of the era known as the Industrial Revolution as well as the consequences, good and bad, of each new development upon the average citizen. Topics covered include the transformation of textiles from homespun to manufactured, the birth of labor unions, advances in transportation and communication, the inventions of Thomas Edison, and brief profiles of 'Captains of Industry,' such as Carnegie, Vanderbilt, and Rockefeller. Each chapter ends with enticing projects related to the topic. . . . The crisp, clear format, featuring ample black-and-white sketches and diagrams and pleasingly arranged type in a large font, is in sync with the straightforward text." Booklist

Staton, Hilarie N.

The **Industrial** Revolution. Kingfisher 2012 32 p. ill. (some col.), col. maps
Grades: 3 4 5 6   **330.9**

1. Industrial revolution 2. United States -- History
ISBN 0753466708; 0753467127; 9780753466704; 9780753467121

This book is a "survey of the growth of industries in this country from the Colonial period to the post–World War II era." Also included are "narrative-overview blocks, boxed side observations and . . . captions" with "contemporary prints or . . . photos." Other "entries in the All About America series deal . . . with 'Explorers, Trappers, and Pioneers,' 'A Nation of Immigrants' and 'Stagecoaches and Railroads.'" (Kirkus)

Includes bibliographical references (p. 31) and index.

331.1   Labor force and market

Lynette, Rachel

What to do when your parent is out of work. PowerKids Press 2010 24p il (Let's work it out) lib bdg $21.25; pa $8.25
Grades: 2 3 4   **331.1**

1. Unemployed
ISBN 978-1-4358-9338-2 lib bdg; 1-4358-9338-7 lib bdg; 978-1-4358-9764-9 pa; 1-4358-9764-1 pa
               LC 2009-23067

A guide to unemployment, what it is, what it may mean for your family, and how you can help.

"Full-page color photographs appear opposite the [narrative], depicting multicultural children, parents, grandparents, social workers, and others, whose demeanors match the hopeful tone of the [title]. This . . . will help promote empathy and understanding for the plight of others and is a key purchase." SLJ

Includes glossary

331.3   Labor force by personal attributes

Bartoletti, Susan Campbell

★ **Growing** up in coal country. Houghton Mifflin 1996 127p il $17; pa $7.95

Grades: 5 6 7 8 **331.3**

1. Child labor 2. Coal mines and mining 3. Immigrants -- Juvenile literature 4. Coal miners -- Juvenile literature 5. Coal mines and mining -- Juvenile literature 6. Pennsylvania -- History -- Juvenile literature

ISBN 0-395-77847-6; 0-395-97914-5 pa

LC 96-3142

This is an "account of working and living conditions in Pennsylvania coal towns. The first half of the volume . . . {describes} various duties in the mines, from jobs performed by the youngest boys to the tasks of adult miners, while the second half describes the company village, common customs and recreational activities, and the accidents and diseases that frequently beset the workers. Preceding each chapter and within the text {are} quotes from personal interviews with miners, as well as taped interviews and transcripts." (Horn Book) Bibliography. "Grade five and up." (Booklist)

"With compelling black-and-white photographs of children at work in the coal mines of northeastern Pennsylvania about 100 years ago, this handsome, spacious photo-essay will draw browsers as well as students doing research on labor and immigrant history." Booklist

Includes bibliographical references

Freedman, Russell

★ **Kids** at work; Lewis Hine and the crusade against child labor. with photographs by Lewis Hine. Clarion Bks. 1994 104p il $20; pa $9.95

Grades: 5 6 7 8 **331.3**

1. Child labor 2. Photographers 3. Children -- Employment -- Juvenile literature 4. Labor -- United States -- Juvenile literature 5. Documentary photography -- Juvenile literature

ISBN 0-395-58703-4; 0-395-79726-8 pa

LC 93-5989

Freedman "does an outstanding job of integrating historical photographs with meticulously researched and highly readable prose." Publ Wkly

Includes bibliographical references

331.4 Women workers

Colman, Penny

★ **Rosie** the riveter; women working on the home front in World War II. Crown 1995 120p il hardcover o.p. pa $10.99

Grades: 5 6 7 8 **331.4**

1. Women -- Employment 2. World War, 1939-1945 -- United States 3. Women -- Employment -- Juvenile literature 4. World War, 1939-1945 -- Women -- Juvenile literature 5. World War, 1939-1945 -- War work -- Juvenile literature 6. World War, 1939-1945 -- United States -- Juvenile literature

ISBN 0-517-59790-X; 0-517-88567-0 pa

LC 94-3614

"A thoughtfully prepared look at women's history and wartime society, this dynamic book is characterized by extensive research." Horn Book

Includes bibliographical references

Warren, Sarah

Dolores Huerta; a hero to migrant workers. by Sarah E. Warren; illustrated by Robert Casilla. Marshall Cavendish Children 2012 32 p. (hardcover) $17.99

Grades: 3 4 5 **331.4**

1. Labor unions 2. Migrant labor 3. Women political activists 4. Mexican American women -- Biography -- Juvenile literature 5. Women labor leaders -- United States -- Biography -- Juvenile literature 6. Mexican American women labor union members -- Biography -- Juvenile literature 7. Migrant agricultural laborers -- Labor unions -- United States -- History -- Juvenile literature 8. Mexican American migrant agricultural laborers -- Labor unions -- Organizing -- History -- Juvenile literature

ISBN 0761461078; 9780761461074; 9780761461081

LC 2011016403

This picture-book, by Sarah E. Warren, "chronicles the campaigns of the Latina activist who advocated for the rights of agricultural laborers in 1960s and '70s California. . . . Each double-page spread begins with 'Dolores is a . . . ' and adds a noun that embodies an aspect of her advocacy. . . . An appended timeline offers expanded details of Huerta's personal life and her collaboration with Cesar and Richard Chavez." (Bulletin of the Center for Children's Books)

"While the book alone will work with younger children, the backmatter makes this title an exceptional resource for both Hispanic Heritage and Woman's History months. A welcome title for children and educators alike." Kirkus

331.7 Labor by industry and occupation

Coulter, Laurie

★ **Cowboys** and coffin makers; one hundred 19th-century jobs you might have feared or fancied. by Laurie Coulter; art by Martha Newbigging. Annick Press 2007 96p il $25.95; pa $16.95

Grades: 3 4 5 6 **331.7**

1. Occupations 2. World history -- 19th century

ISBN 978-1-55451-068-9; 1-55451-068-6; 978-1-55451-067-2 pa; 1-55451-067-8 pa

"Short job descriptions, usually one or two per page, are written in an entertaining style and grouped according to headings. . . . The author considers a variety of economic and social classes, from robber barons to forced laborers and slaves, and acknowledges how locations affect available occupations. . . . Bright watercolor, cartoon-style illustrations accompany each job description." SLJ

Hopkinson, Deborah

★ **Up** before daybreak; cotton and people in America. Scholastic Nonfiction 2005 120p il $18.99

Grades: 5 6 7 8 **331.7**

1. Cotton 2. Working class 3. Textile industry 4. Textile industry -- History 5. Cotton trade -- Juvenile literature 6. Cotton growing -- Juvenile literature 7. Cotton picking -- Juvenile literature 8. Slavery -- United States -- Juvenile literature

ISBN 0-439-63901-8

LC 2005-8128

"From the industrial revolution to the 1950s demise of the Lowell cotton mills, Hopkinson discusses the history and sociology of king cotton, frequently emphasizing the children who labored under slave masters, endured dead-end mill jobs, or helped sharecropping parents claw out a living. . . . Stories of real people . . . sharply focus the dramatic history, as do arresting archival photos of stern youngsters manipulating hoes, cotton sags, or bobbins." Booklist

Hord, Colleen
My safe community. Rourke 2011 il (Little world social studies)
Grades: K 1 2 3   **331.7**
1. Occupations
ISBN 1-61741-795-5; 1-61741-997-4 pa; 978-1-61741-795-5 lib bdg; 978-1-61741-997-3 pa
This "introduces various community workers such as the mayor, police, or sanitation workers. . . . The [book has] minimal text but still [manages] to impart basic information and even raise questions. The full-page color photographs that face the text pages are crisp." Booklist

Miller, Margaret
★ Guess who? Greenwillow Bks. 1994 un il $16.99
Grades: PreK   **331.7**
1. Occupations 2. Concepts -- Juvenile literature
ISBN 0-688-12783-5
                                                   LC 93-26704
A child is asked who delivers the mail, gives haircuts, flies an airplane, and performs other important tasks. Each question has several different answers from which to choose
"Gender and ethnic representation are deftly handled. The author's sharp, clear full-color photographs are well composed, and her use of cropped photos and white space alternating with bled photos is an effective tool for involving youngsters." SLJ

Tsiang, Sarah
Warriors and wailers; one hundred ancient Chinese jobs you might have relished or reviled. Annick Press 2012 96 p.
Grades: 4 5 6   **331.7**
1. China -- History -- Juvenile literature 2. Occupations -- History -- Juvenile literature 3. Professions -- History -- Juvenile literature
ISBN 155451391X; 9781554513918
This book, by Sarah Tsiang, is part of the "Jobs in History" series. "China was one of the most advanced societies in the ancient world. Whether in medicine, the arts, or education, the Chinese far outpaced the Europeans. Although most people were peasants, society included a myriad of other jobs. . . . Other jobs included wailer, . . . noodle maker, . . . or Shaolin warrior monk." (Publisher's note)

331.702   Choice of vocation

Loy, Jessica
When I grow up; a young person's guide to interesting & unusual occupations. Jessica Loy. Holt 2008 37 p. $16.95
Grades: 4 5 6   **331.702**
1. Vocational guidance -- Juvenile literature
ISBN 0805077170; 9780805077179
                                               LC 2007938930

This juvenile book, by Jessica Loy, explores fourteen unusual professional careers. "What do you want to be when you grow up? Consider all your options. How about being a game designer. . . .? Or, if you like chocolate, you could become a chocolatier. . . . The choices are endless. So come read about . . . unusual and satisfying work. . . . Maybe some of these career paths will inspire ideas of your own." (Publisher's note)
Includes bibliographical references

Zephaniah, Benjamin, 1958-
When I Grow Up; poems by Benjamin Zephaniah; photographs by Prodeepta Das. Pgw 2012 32 p. $17.99
Grades: 1 2 3 4 5   **331.702**
1. Occupations 2. Vocational guidance
ISBN 1847800599; 9781847800596
This book by Benjamin Zephaniah "takes an alternative look at 12 occupations and the people who fill them. Its aim is to open up children's imaginations to the possibility that there are many more roles open to them than they may think. It . . . depict[s] . . .broad-ranging examples of unusual people doing unusual jobs, such as Sikh lollipop man, a female clown and a black British Space Scientist." (Publisher's note)

331.8   Labor unions, labor-management bargaining and disputes

Brill, Marlene Targ
Annie Shapiro and the clothing workers' strike; illustrated by Jamel Akib. Millbrook Press 2010 48p il (History speaks: picture books plus reader's theater) lib bdg $27.93; pa $9.95
Grades: 2 3 4   **331.8**
1. Strikes 2. Labor unions 3. Readers' theater 4. Clothing industry 5. Labor leaders
ISBN 978-1-58013-672-3 lib bdg; 1-58013-672-9 lib bdg; 978-0-7613-6132-9 pa; 0-7613-6132-4 pa
                                               LC 2009051812
"This partly fictionalized picture-book story is followed by an eight-page script for reader's theater. In 1910, Hannah 'Annie' Shapiro, a teenage Russian immigrant, led a walkout in Chicago to protest pay cuts and poor conditions in the clothing factory where she worked. . . . Dramatic double-page spreads in deep shades of red and brown focus on Annie as they show the confrontations. . . . After the story, an author's note fills in more historical facts, and a reader's theater section features roles for Annie, two narrators, and two additional readers and includes practical notes about costumes, props, and performance." Booklist
Includes bibliographical references

331.892   Strikes

Bartoletti, Susan Campbell
★ Kids on strike! Houghton Mifflin 1999 208p il $20; pa $8.95
Grades: 5 6 7 8   **331.892**
1. Strikes 2. Child labor 3. Labor leaders 4. Child labor -- History 5. Child labor -- United States -- History

-- Juvenile literature

ISBN 0-395-88892-1; 0-618-36923-6 pa

LC 98-50575

Describes the conditions and treatment that drove workers, including many children, to various strikes, from the mill workers strikes in 1828 and 1836 and the coal strikes at the turn of the century to the work of Mother Jones on behalf of child workers

"This well-researched and well-illustrated account creates a vivid portrait of the working conditions of many American children in the 19th and early 20th centuries." SLJ

Includes bibliographical references

Markel, Michelle

★ **Brave** girl; Clara and the Shirtwaist Makers' Strike of 1909. written by Michelle Markel; pictures by Melissa Sweet. Balzer + Bray 2013 32 p. (hardcover bdg.) $17.99

Grades: K 1 2 3 4   **331.892**

1. Picture books for children 2. Strikes -- United States -- History 3. Shirtwaist Makers' Strike, New York, N.Y., 1909 -- Juvenile literature 4. Women clothing workers -- New York (State) -- New York -- Juvenile literature 5. Women in the labor movement -- New York (State) -- New York -- Juvenile literature

ISBN 0061804428; 9780061804427

LC 2012025439

This children's picture book offers a biography of Clara Lemlich, early 20th-century union organizer. "She not only worked to support her family in a factory that made women's clothing, but read and studied at night. When the male workers talked about a strike to protest their fearsome working conditions," Clara "called for a general strike. She was arrested 17 times and beaten, but the strike won the right to unionize for workers in many factories." (Kirkus Reviews)

332.024   Personal finance

Bochner, Rose

The **new** totally awesome money book for kids (and their parents) [by] Arthur Bochner & Rose Bochner; foreword by Adriane G. Berg. 3rd ed., rev & updated.; Newmarket Press 2007 189p il pa $9.95

Grades: 4 5 6 7   **332.024**

1. Personal finance

ISBN 978-1-55704-738-0

LC 2006038930

First published 1993 with title: The totally awesome money book for kids (and their parents)

An introduction to money for kids including the basics of saving, investing, working, and taxes.

"Using an easy and comfortable style that young people will find unthreatening, the book presents a wealth of information. . . . The cute illustrations are also fun." Voice Youth Advocates

Includes bibliographical references

Chatzky, Jean

Not your parents' money book; making, saving, and spending your own money. [by Jean Sherman Chatzky]; illustrated by Erwin Haya. Simon & Schuster Books for Young Readers 2010 162p il pa $12.99

Grades: 5 6 7 8   **332.024**

1. Money 2. Personal finance

ISBN 978-1-4169-9472-5 pa; 1-4169-9472-6 pa

LC 2010008840

"Written in a light, somewhat jocular tone and sprinkled with amusing but eye-opening and conversation-starting quotes from 12, 13, and 14-year-olds, this book is sure to hold readers' attention. The content includes how you get money, via allowances and jobs, and notes the difference between cash-only and paychecks. Tracking typical teen expenditures, both long-term and short, is juxtaposed against keeping money in checking, savings, and money-market accounts. . . . Chatzky's presentation is engaging. . . . Cartoons appear on almost every page, adding humor and some additional material." SLJ

Includes bibliographical references

Hall, Alvin

★ **Show** me the money; [by] Alvin Hall. DK 2008 96p il $15.99

Grades: 4 5 6   **332.024**

1. Money 2. Personal finance

ISBN 978-0-7566-3762-0; 0-7566-3762-7

"Four main sections cover the history of money, expenses/income, the basics of economics, and the world of work and business. Brief profiles of eight wealthy entrepreneurs and their paths to prosperity and eight significant economists and their theories are included. The lively writing features real-life examples that will be meaningful to students and is presented in a balanced, nonjudgmental style that encourages them to decide for themselves among the various ideas concerning economic policies. . . . Color photos and graphics excel at conveying the concepts presented and represent diversity well." SLJ

Includes glossary

Hall, Margaret

Your allowance; [2nd ed]; Heinemann Library 2008 32p il (Earning, saving, spending) $25.36; pa $7.99

Grades: 3 4 5   **332.024**

1. Personal finance

ISBN 978-1-4034-9817-5; 1-4034-9817-2; 978-1-4034-9822-9 pa; 1-4034-9822-9 pa

LC 2007015113

First published 2000

Offers young people information on how to manage the money they have, providing advice on spending, saving, and donating money to help others

Includes bibliographical references

Holyoke, Nancy

★ **A smart** girl's guide to money; how to make it, save it, and spend it. illustrated by Ali Douglass. Pleasant Co. 2006 95p il pa $9.95

Grades: 4 5 6 7   **332.024**

1. Personal finance

ISBN 1-59369-103-3

This "offers advice on earning, saving, and spending money. Holyoke addresses topics such as feelings about money, launching a business, becoming a smart shopper, and investing. . . . The text is upbeat and informal. . . . This book is an engaging introduction to personal economics." Booklist

Hord, Colleen

Need it or want it? Rourke 2011 il (Little world social studies) $22.79; pa $7.95

Grades: K 1 2 3　　　　332.024

1. Personal finance

ISBN 978-1-61741-793-1; 1-61741-793-9; 978-1-61741-995-9 pa; 1-61741-995-8 pa

This book "brings up the provocative question of whether you desire something because it will be useful or just because it will be fun. Examples of both are given, and a page reminds readers they can give back to their communities by donating needed goods. The [book has] minimal text but still [manages] to impart basic information and even raise questions. The full-page color photographs that face the text pages are crisp." Booklist

Larson, Jennifer S.

Do I need it? or do I want it? making budget choices. Lerner 2010 32p il (Exploring economics) lib bdg $25.26; pa $7.95

Grades: K 1 2　　　　332.024

1. Personal finance

ISBN 978-0-7613-3914-4 lib bdg; 0-7613-3914-0 lib bdg; 978-0-7613-5664-6 pa; 0-7613-5664-9 pa

An introduction to budgeting that explains how to make a budget and stick to it, how to decide if something is a need or a want, why it is important to have a budget, and how to save and spend money wisely.

"Clear, age-appropriate language explains new concepts well. . . . The [book's] layout is interesting and fresh, and each page features a large, well-chosen photograph with a boxed caption." SLJ

What can you do with money? earning, spending, and saving. Lerner Pub. 2010 32p il (Exploring economics) lib bdg $25.26; pa $7.95

Grades: K 1 2　　　　332.024

1. Personal finance

ISBN 978-0-7613-3910-6 lib bdg; 0-7613-3910-8 lib bdg; 978-0-7613-5666-0 pa; 0-7613-5666-5 pa

Provides an introduction to earning, spending, and saving and discusses goods, services, and how people choose what to buy.

"Clear, age-appropriate language explains new concepts well. . . . The [book's] layout is interesting and fresh, and each page features a large, well-chosen photograph with a boxed caption." SLJ

Lynette, Rachel

What to do when your family has to cut costs. PowerKids Press 2010 24p il (Let's work it out) lib bdg $21.25; pa $8.25

Grades: 2 3 4　　　　332.024

1. Personal finance

ISBN 978-1-4358-9340-5 lib bdg; 1-4358-9340-9 lib bdg; 978-1-4358-9768-7 pa; 1-4358-9768-4 pa

LC 2009-23737

Learn about prioritizing needs over wants and ways to be cost-conscious and frugal.

"Full-page color photographs appear opposite the [narrative], depicting multicultural children, parents, grandparents, social workers, and others, whose demeanors match the hopeful tone of the [title]. This . . . will help promote

empathy and understanding for the plight of others and is a key purchase." SLJ

Includes glossary

What to do when your family is in debt. PowerKids Press 2010 24p il (Let's work it out) lib bdg $21.25; pa $8.25

Grades: 2 3 4　　　　332.024

1. Debt 2. Consumer credit

ISBN 978-1-4358-9341-2 lib bdg; 1-4358-9341-7 lib bdg; 978-1-4358-9770-0 pa; 1-4358-9770-6 pa

A guide to debt, what it is, what it may mean for your family, and how you can help.

"Full-page color photographs appear opposite the [narrative], depicting multicultural children, parents, grandparents, social workers, and others, whose demeanors match the hopeful tone of the [title]. This . . . will help promote empathy and understanding for the plight of others and is a key purchase." SLJ

Includes glossary

Mitten, Ellen K.

Goods or services? Ellen K. Mitten. Rourke 2011 24 p. col. ill. (library) $22.79; $15.95; (paperback) $7.95

Grades: K 1 2 3　　　　332.024

1. Personal finance

ISBN 9781617417917; 9781612367095; 9781617419935

LC 2011924836

In this book "the concept of different ways to use money is introduced, with pages showing how you can buy something, like an apple, or have a service provided to you, like getting a haircut. Readers are told families must make choices about how to spend their money. . . . The [book has] minimal text but still [manages] to impart basic information and even raise questions. The full-page color photographs that face the text pages are crisp." Booklist

Includes bibliographical references and index.

Morrison, Jessica

Saving. Weigl Publishers 2009 32p il (Everyday economics) lib bdg $26; pa $9.95

Grades: 5 6 7　　　　332.024

1. Saving and investment

ISBN 978-1-60596-647-2 lib bdg; 1-60596-647-9 lib bdg; 978-1-60596-648-9 pa; 1-60596-648-7 pa

LC 2009018567

This "informative [book introduces savings in] U.S. economic theory and practices using everyday language and real-life examples. [It] includes history, a brief annotated chronology, sidebar and intext explanations of terminology, and helpful diagrams. . . . With brief paragraphs; large, captioned photographs; ample margins; and well-organized graphics, the [book's] design makes economics accessible without sacrificing content. . . . [This is] easy to navigate and full of solid information and interesting facts." SLJ

Includes glossary

Roderick, Stacey

Centsibility; the Planet Girl guide to money. [by] Stacey Roderick and Ellen Warwick; illustrated by Monika Melnychuk. Kids Can Press 2008 80p il (Planet girl) $12.95

Grades: 5 6 7 8 **332.024**
1. Personal finance
ISBN 978-1-55453-208-7

"This book presents handy methods for managing money. . . . Chapters are broken down into subsections . . . which are peppered with quizzes and craft projects to keep readers engaged. . . . The book's sound advice is both practical and approachable." Horn Book Guide

Schwartz, David M.
If you made a million; pictures by Steven Kellogg. Lothrop, Lee & Shepard Bks. 1989 un il hardcover o.p. pa $6.99
Grades: PreK K 1 2 3 **332.024**
1. Personal finance 2. Money -- Juvenile literature 3. Personal finance -- Juvenile literature
ISBN 0-688-07017-5; 0-688-13634-6 pa
LC 88-12819

"The concepts of banks and banking . . . are all explained with absurd and humorous examples involving Ferris wheels, ogres, and rhinoceroses. . . . The best advice of all is 'Enjoying your work is more important than money,' Steven Kellogg's splendidly funny illustrations contain a troupe of two cats, one dog, numerous kids, a unicorn, and the wonderful magician Marvelosissimo." Horn Book

Wiseman, Blaine
Budgeting. Weigl Publishers 2009 32p il (Everyday economics) lib bdg $26; pa $9.95
Grades: 5 6 7 **332.024**
1. Budget
ISBN 978-1-60596-643-4 lib bdg; 1-60596-643-6 lib bdg; 978-1-60596-644-1 pa; 1-60596-644-4 pa
LC 2009018439

This "informative [book introduces budgeting in] U.S. economic theory and practices using everyday language and real-life examples. [It] includes history, a brief annotated chronology, sidebar and intext explanations of terminology, and helpful diagrams. . . . With brief paragraphs; large, captioned photographs; ample margins; and well-organized graphics, the [book's] design makes economics accessible without sacrificing content. . . . [This is] easy to navigate and full of solid information and interesting facts." SLJ

Includes glossary

332.4 Money

Adler, David A., 1947-
★ **Money** madness; by David A. Adler; illustrated by Edward Miller. Holiday House 2009 un il $16.95
Grades: PreK K 1 2 **332.4**
1. Money
ISBN 978-0-8234-1474-1; 0-8234-1474-4
LC 2008004223

"This brightly illustrated picture book introduces the concept of money, first by looking at its development as an alternative to bartering and then by explaining the many forms of money, from primitive rocks, feathers, and metal lumps to the familiar coins and paper bills to alternatives such as checks, credit cards, and digital forms of payment. Adler does a particularly good job explaining the inconvenience of bartering through child-friendly examples. . . . Us-

ing flat colors and stylized designs, Miller's upbeat digital artwork helps to clarify points made in the text, while adding occasional bits of visual humor. Photos of coins and bills are incorporated where appropriate." Booklist

Callery, Sean
Money matters. QEB Pub. 2010 48p il lib bdg $28.50
Grades: 2 3 4 **332.4**
1. Money
ISBN 978-1-59566-729-8; 1-59566-729-6
LC 2010001156

Find out all the facts about the way we use money, from the history of currency to number crunching and penny saving.

"Primary students looking for a clear, concise introduction to money, its many related topics, including taxes, budgets, savings, earnings, and history, will find everything they need in this title. . . . The text is succinct. There are plenty of photos, pictures, and charts, and an occasional money challenge for readers to try." Libr Media Connect

Cleary, Brian P., 1959-
A **dollar,** a penny, how much and how many? by Brian P. Cleary; illustrated by Brian Gable. Millbrook Press 2012 31 p. col. ill. (Math is Categorical) (reinforced) $16.95
Grades: K 1 2 **332.4**
1. Money -- Juvenile literature 2. Mathematics -- Juvenile literature 3. Coins -- Juvenile literature
ISBN 0822578824; 9780822578826
LC 2011045864

This nonfiction children's book was written by Brian P. Cleary. "In rhyming text young readers are introduced to the world of currency and coins, and more subtly, to the economic concepts of value and compensation. In this new series called 'Math is CATegorical,' the popular cats from the 'Words are CATegorical' series show how to combine bills and coins of various denominations in order to pay for goods and services." (Children's Literature)

Cribb, Joe
★ **Money**; written by Joe Cribb. rev ed; DK Pub. 2005 72p il (DK eyewitness books) lib bdg $15.99
Grades: 4 5 6 7 **332.4**
1. Money
ISBN 0-7566-1389-2
First published 1990 by Knopf

Examines, in text and photographs, the symbolic and material meaning of money, from shekels, shells, and beads to gold, silver, checks, and credit cards. Also discusses how coins and banknotes are made, the value of money during wartime, and how to collect coins

Forest, Christopher
The **dollar** bill in translation; what it really means. Capstone Press 2009 32p il (Fact finders. Kids' translations) lib bdg $23.99; pa $7.95
Grades: 3 4 5 **332.4**
1. Money 2. Dollar 3. Paper money 4. Signs and symbols
ISBN 978-1-4296-2794-8 lib bdg; 1-4296-2794-8 lib bdg; 978-1-4296-3448-9 pa; 1-4296-3448-0 pa
LC 2008-28981

"Presents the dollar bill and explains its meaning and symbolism using everyday language. Describes the events that led to the creation of currency and its significance through history." Publisher's note

Includes glossary and bibliographical references

Larson, Jennifer S.

What is money, anyway? why dollars and coins have value. Lerner Pub. 2010 32p il (Exploring economics) lib bdg $25.26

Grades: K 1 2　　　　　　　　　　　**332.4**

1. Money

ISBN 978-0-7613-3915-1 lib bdg; 0-7613-3915-9 lib bdg

An introduction to money that discusses what it is made of, the values of coins and bills, how it is used, and other related topics.

"Clear, age-appropriate language explains new concepts well. . . . The [book's] layout is interesting and fresh, and each page features a large, well-chosen photograph with a boxed caption." SLJ

Leedy, Loreen

★ Follow the money! written and illustrated by Loreen Leedy. Holiday House 2002 un il $16.95; pa $6.95

Grades: K 1 2 3　　　　　　　　　　**332.4**

1. Coins 2. Money 3. Money -- United States

ISBN 0-8234-1587-2; 0-8234-1794-8 pa

LC 2001-39418

A quarter describes all the ways it is used from the time it is minted until it is taken back to a bank

"Leedy includes a good deal of information, while keeping the book light, energetic, and entertaining." Booklist

Includes glossary

Orr, Tamra

Coins and other currency; a kid's guide to coin collecting. by Tamra Orr. Mitchell Lane Publishers 2009 48p il map (Money matters: a kid's guide to money) lib bdg $29.95

Grades: 4 5 6　　　　　　　　　　　**332.4**

1. Coins 2. Money

ISBN 978-1-58415-640-6 lib bdg; 1-58415-640-6 lib bdg

LC 2008-2262

"Photos feature multigenerational and diverse subjects and illustrate related locations and historical figures, while graphs and sidebars enhance the [text]. Well-documented and informative." SLJ

Includes glossary and bibliographical references

Robinson, Elizabeth Keeler

Making cents; by Elizabeth Keeler Robinson; illustrated by Bob McMahon. Tricycle Press 2008 un il $14.95

Grades: K 1 2　　　　　　　　　　　**332.4**

1. Money 2. Arithmetic

ISBN 978-1-58246-214-1

LC 2007018197

"This book introduces American coins and paper money in a clear and entertaining way. A group of children from a variety of ethnic backgrounds is hard at work earning money, saving, and planning for a neighborhood clubhouse. Readers see the purchasing power of the different coins and bills in terms of nails, screws, marking pencils, sandpaper, and other building supplies. They also view different ways that coins can be combined to equal a nickel, dime, quarter,

dollar, etc. . . . The text is well paced, and the layout is attractive. . . . The colorful . . . computer-generated cartoons have child appeal." SLJ

332.6　Investment

Minden, Cecilia

Investing; making your money work for you. Cherry Lake Pub. 2008 32p il (Real world math: personal finance) lib bdg $25.26

Grades: 3 4 5 6　　　　　　　　　　**332.6**

1. Investments 2. Personal finance

ISBN 978-1-60279-003-2 lib bdg; 1-60279-003-5 lib bdg

LC 2007005917

This "examines the importance of short-term and long-term savings and explains the pros and cons of savings accounts, certificates of deposit, government bonds, and stocks. Engaging full-color photographs on every page feature diverse children and families, and plenty of white space." SLJ

Includes bibliographical references

Morrison, Jessica

Investing. Weigl Publishers 2009 32p il (Everyday economics) lib bdg $26; pa $9.95

Grades: 5 6 7　　　　　　　　　　　**332.6**

1. Investments

ISBN 978-1-60596-649-6 lib bdg; 1-60596-649-5 lib bdg; 978-1-60596-650-2 pa; 1-60596-650-9 pa

LC 2009018568

This explains the advantages of investing money, how to read a stock report, interest, and the types of investments provided by different companies.

This "informative [book introduces] U.S. economic theory and practices using everyday language and real-life examples. . . . [This is] easy to navigate and full of solid information and interesting facts." SLJ

Includes glossary

332.7　Credit

Hall, Margaret

Credit cards and checks; [by] Margaret Hall. 2nd ed.; Heinemann Library 2008 32p il (Earning, saving, spending) lib bdg $28.21; pa $7.99

Grades: 1 2 3　　　　　　　　　　　**332.7**

1. Debit cards 2. Credit cards 3. Personal finance

ISBN 978-1-4034-9816-8 lib bdg; 978-1-4034-9821-2 pa

LC 2007015150

First published 2000

This offers an overview of spending money without using cash, including details on credit, checkbooks, debt and interest.

"Illustrated with sharp, clear photographs, each spread presents a different concept in a logical procession. The author uses simple sentences, highlighting important words." SLJ

Includes glossary and bibliographical references

Tomljanovic, Tatiana

Borrowing. Weigl Pubs. 2009 32p il (Everyday economics) lib bdg $26; pa $9.95

Grades: 5 6 7   332.7

1. Credit

ISBN 978-1-60596-645-8 lib bdg; 1-60596-645-2 lib bdg; 978-1-60596-646-5 pa; 1-60596-646-0 pa

LC 2009018444

This "informative [book introduces borrowing in] U.S. economic theory and practices using everyday language and real-life examples. [It] includes history, a brief annotated chronology, sidebar and intext explanations of terminology, and helpful diagrams. . . . With brief paragraphs; large, captioned photographs; ample margins; and well-organized graphics, the [book's] design makes economics accessible without sacrificing content. . . . [This is] easy to navigate and full of solid information and interesting facts." SLJ

Includes glossary

333.7   Natural resources and energy

Gazlay, Suzy

Managing green spaces; careers in wilderness and wildlife management. Crabtree 2010 64p il (Green-collar careers) lib bdg $30.60; pa $10.95

Grades: 4 5 6 7   333.7

1. Wildlife 2. Wilderness areas 3. Vocational guidance 4. Disaster relief -- Juvenile literature 5. Conservation of natural resources -- Juvenile literature 6. Environmental protection -- Vocational guidance -- Juvenile literature

ISBN 978-0-7787-4855-7 lib bdg; 0-7787-4855-3 lib bdg; 978-0-7787-4866-3 pa; 0-7787-4866-9 pa

LC 2009-28145

"Passions often lead to professions, as this upbeat title . . . shows. . . . There is inevitable overlap among the categories: government-run parks and forestry, outdoor adventure, science, and wildlife sanctuaries. The browsable format, combining many crisp color photos with blocks of narrative texts and sidebars featuring specific ecoprofessionals, will easily lead students through the survey of nature-focused careers." Booklist

333.72   Conservation and protection

Bailey, Jacqui

What's the point of being green? [illustrated by Jan McCafferty] Barron's Educational Series 2010 96p il map pa $12.99

Grades: 4 5 6 7   333.72

1. Environmental movement 2. Environmental protection

ISBN 978-0-7641-4427-1 pa; 0-7641-4427-8 pa

"This colorful book outlines in lively, conversational prose the reasons that kids should be concerned about the future of our planet. Each short chapter covers different environmental challenges and discusses ways that children can work toward improving the situation. . . . A cartoon teen appears on each page and directly addresses readers. There are also ample color photos and diagrams. The layout is dynamic with text and illustrations placed at odd angles and in

a variety of bold fonts. Kids will find this book incredibly informational, fun to read, and full of great ideas." SLJ

Includes bibliographical references

Black, Jess

A year in the life of Bindi; Australia's Favorite Wildlife Warrior. Random House Australia 2012 95 p.

Grades: 4 5 6   333.72

1. Wildlife -- Juvenile literature

ISBN 1864718382; 9781864718386

This book gives "the inside scoop on how Bindi Irwin, daughter of Steve Irwin the Crocodile Hunter, spends her time. Appearing on 'Oprah' in Sydney one day, helping out at the Australia Zoo Wildlife Hospital the next, spending weeks croc tagging in the Cape York Peninsula--she's an Australian girl with a life like no other." (Publisher's note)

Bullard, Lisa

Earth Day every day; illustrated by Xiao Xin. Millbrook Press 2011 24p col. ill. (Planet protectors) lib bdg $23.93

Grades: K 1 2 3   333.72

1. Earth Day 2. Environmental protection

ISBN 978-0-7613-6109-1; 0-7613-6109-X

LC 2010053466

On Earth Day Trina plants trees with her class. She forms an Earth Day club with her friends and explains what can you do to make every day Earth Day.

"The bright colors used in the illustrations . . . will attract young readers to the environmental science content. . . . [The] facts are written in child-friendly language and the information should be attainable by young children. . . . [This book] will raise the environmental awareness of young children." Sci Books Films

Dell, Pamela

Protecting the planet; environmental activism. Compass Point Books 2010 64p il (Green generation) lib bdg $31.99; pa $6.95

Grades: 5 6 7 8 9   333.72

1. Environmental movement 2. Environmental protection

ISBN 978-0-7565-4248-1 lib bdg; 0-7565-4248-0 lib bdg; 978-0-7565-4295-5 pa; 0-7565-4295-2 pa

LC 2009-8782

"The cover design, layout, and graphics feel hip and of the moment. The clear writing is easy to understand and includes many concrete examples of environmentally friendly practices. . . . [A] good choice[s] for both leisure reading and reports." SLJ

Includes glossary and bibliographical references

Fuoco, Gina Dal

Earth. Compass Point Books 2009 40p il (Mission: science) lib bdg $26.60

Grades: 4 5 6   333.72

ISBN 978-0-7565-4070-8 lib bdg; 0-7565-4070-4 lib bdg

LC 2008-37575

Discusses the basic parts systems (atmosphere, hydrosphere, and geosphere) of Earth and how important it is to protect Earth's resources

Includes glossary

Hewitt, Sally

Your local environment. Crabtree Pub. Co. 2009 32p
il (Green team) lib bdg $26.60; pa $8.95

Grades: 3 4 5 6 **333.72**

1. Environmental protection

ISBN 978-0-7787-4100-8 lib bdg; 0-7787-4100-1 lib
bdg; 978-0-7787-4107-7 pa; 0-7787-4107-9 pa

LC 2008023292

This offers suggestions for improving local environments, such as keeping schools and playgrounds clean and tidy, planning and creating gardens, attracting wildlife, controlling litter, planting trees, and maintaining parks

"The color graphics and layouts are highly appealing and will definitely be attractive to young readers. . . . This . . . is an excellent resource for school libraries, science teachers, and community sponsors." Libr Media Connect

Hirsch, Rebecca E.

Protecting our natural resources; by Rebecca Hirsch.
Cherry Lake Pub. 2010 32p il (Save the planet) lib bdg
$27.07

Grades: 3 4 5 6 **333.72**

1. Conservation of natural resources

ISBN 978-1-60279-661-4 lib bdg; 1-60279-661-0
lib bdg

LC 2009-38097

Explains what natural resources are, how they are being exploited, and what should be done to protect them

"At the beginning of . . . [the] book, readers are given a mission and advised to be alert to the facts provided so that they can successfully answer the questions at the end. . . . Children are made to feel part of the process; suggestions for how they can become involved abound." SLJ

Includes glossary and bibliographical references

Kelsey, Elin

★ **Not** your typical book about the environment; illustrated by Clayton Hammer. Owlkids 2010 64p il $22.95;
pa $10.95

Grades: 4 5 6 7 **333.72**

1. Environmental protection 2. Ecology -- Juvenile literature 3. Sustainable living -- Juvenile literature

ISBN 978-1-897349-79-3; 1-897349-79-3; 978-1-897349-84-7 pa; 1-897349-84-X pa

Written to allay children's fears about the environment, this book shows how smart technologies, innovative ideas, and a growing commitment to alternative lifestyles are exploding around the world, creating a future that will be brighter than we sometimes might think. Includes profiles of unexpected personalities.

"Imaginative, comic-booklike illustrations add to a lively layout that will keep readers moving from one paragraph to the next, and funny wordplay prevents the facts from becoming overwhelming or dry. . . . This hilarious, information-packed work is an excellent addition." SLJ

Kriesberg, Daniel A.

Think green, take action; books and activities for kids.
illustrated by Kathleen A. Price. Libraries Unlimited 2010
136p il pa $30; e-book $30

Grades: Adult Professional **333.72**

1. Children's literature 2. Environmental sciences
-- Study and teaching 3. Environmental sciences --

Juvenile literature

ISBN 978-1-59884-378-1 pa; 1-59884-378-8 pa;
978-1-59884-379-8 e-book

LC 2010014409

"A resource for teaching environmental understanding and activism through stewardship, this book outlines teaching strategies for ages 6-10, provides resources for understanding environmental concerns for ages 10-13, and promotes action and growth for ages 13+. Chapters focus on local ecology, endangered species, resource depletion, and pollution. Extensive annotated bibliographies of both recent and older fiction and nonfiction selections . . . supplement the activities." SLJ

Includes bibliographical references

McKay, Kim

True green kids; 100 things you can do to save the planet. [by] Kim McKay and Jenny Bonnin. National Geographic 2008 143p il $15.95

Grades: 4 5 6 7 **333.72**

1. Environmental protection 2. Environmentalism --
Juvenile literature 3. Recycling (Waste, etc.) -- Juvenile literature 4. Environmental responsibility -- Juvenile literature 5. Conservation of natural resources --
Juvenile literature

ISBN 978-1-4263-0442-2; 1-4263-0442-0

Presents an overview of global warming and describes 100 simple ways to be more environmentally friendly in the bedroom, in the house, at school, and on vacation.

"Accompanied by attractive, up-to-date pictures in a lively design, the one hundred suggestions are direct . . . and generally practical." Horn Book Guide

Includes glossary

Parr, Todd

The **Earth** book. Little, Brown Books for Young Readers 2010 un il $15.99

Grades: PreK K 1 **333.72**

1. Environmental protection

ISBN 978-0-316-04265-9; 0-316-04265-X

LC 2008047562

"With illustrations that look as though they might have been done by enthusiastic children themselves, Parr's book offers first-person advice about ways to take care of the earth. . . . The strong appeal comes from the simple artwork done in Parr's signature style, which features pure colors, objects and people outlined in thick black ink, and kids whose round faces are comprised of two dots for eyes and upturned lines for mouths. Young children will get a kick out of the vivid art." Booklist

Raatma, Lucia

Green living; no action too small. Compass Point Books 2009 64p il (Green generation) lib bdg $31.99;
pa $6.95

Grades: 5 6 7 8 9 **333.72**

1. Environmental movement 2. Environmental protection

ISBN 978-0-7565-4245-0 lib bdg; 0-7565-4245-6 lib bdg; 978-0-7565-4293-1 pa; 0-7565-4293-6 pa

LC 2009-8779

Shows children how can they make a difference. From fighting global warming to protecting wildlife, this book contains the information young environmentalists need to change the world

"The cover design, layout, and graphics feel hip and of the moment. The clear writing is easy to understand and includes many concrete examples of environmentally friendly practices. . . . [A] good [choice] for both leisure reading and reports." SLJ

Includes glossary and bibliographical references

★ **Recycle** this book; 100 top children's book authors tell you how to go green. edited by Dan Gutman. Yearling 2009 267p pa $5.99

Grades: 5 6 7 8   **333.72**
1. Authors 2. Recycling 3. Environmental protection
ISBN 978-0-385-73721-0 pa; 0-385-73721-1 pa
LC 2008-10800

"This lively collection of brief essays (and a poem) by 100 outstanding children's and young adult authors teaches through example. Each selection highlights a small step (or steps) taken by the writer toward a greener Earth. . . . The essays also provide insight into the lives and thoughts of many familiar and beloved authors such as Laurie Halse Anderson, Ralph Fletcher, Gary Schmidt, Lois Lowry, Susan Patron, and Rick Riordan. Several pages of Web sites offer a starting point for action and information. Highly useful for classroom and family discussions and science-project ideas." SLJ

Reilly, Kathleen M.
Planet Earth; 25 environmental projects you can build yourself. Nomad Press 2008 122p il (Projects you can build yourself) $21.95; pa $14.95

Grades: 4 5 6 7   **333.72**
1. Science projects 2. Environmental sciences 3. Environmental education -- Juvenile literature 4. Recycling (Waste, etc.) -- Juvenile literature
ISBN 978-1-934670-05-7; 1-934670-05-7; 978-1-934670-04-0 pa; 1-934670-04-9 pa

"Both comprehensive and approachable, this title . . . combines explanations of science concepts and environmental issues with hands-on projects. . . . Elementary- and middle-school students will find the succinct overview of the facts very useful, and they'll welcome the clearly presented projects." Booklist

Ride, Sally K.
Mission: save the planet; things you can do to help fight global warming. [by] Sally Ride and Tam O'Shaughnessy; illustrated by Andrew Arnold. Roaring Brook Press 2009 61p il (Sally Ride science) pa $7.99

Grades: 5 6 7 8   **333.72**
1. Environmental protection 2. Global warming -- Juvenile literature 3. Climatic changes -- Juvenile literature
ISBN 978-159643-379-3 pa; 1-59643-379-5 pa
LC 2009-29254

"The first chapter in this slim volume discusses our energy use, dependence on fossil fuels, and the environmental impact of these practices. The remaining chapters are packed with facts and suggestions on reducing our carbon footprint. . . . The authors' background in science education is evident, as the writing style is clear, precise, and kid-friendly. Black-and-white cartoon illustrations provide excellent visuals for many of the recommendations." SLJ

Rohmer, Harriet
★ **Heroes** of the environment; true stories of people who are helping to protect our planet. illustrated by Julie McLaughlin. Chronicle Books 2009 109p il map $16.99

Grades: 4 5 6   **333.72**
1. Environmentalists
ISBN 978-0-8118-6779-5; 0-8118-6779-X
LC 2009004366

"Engaging graphics and clear writing combine to provide a compelling reading experience." Sci Books Films

Sirett, Dawn
Love your world; how to take care of the plants, the animals, and the planet. written by Dawn Sirett; illustrations by Rachael Parfitt; special photography by Howard Shooter and Dave King. Dorling Kindersley Pub. 2009 un il pa $8.99

Grades: K 1 2 3   **333.72**
1. Environmental protection
ISBN 978-0-7566-4590-8 pa; 0-7566-4590-5 pa

"This is a vivid, cheerful introduction to going green." SLJ

Smalley, Carol Parenzan
Green changes you can make around your home. Mitchell Lane Publishers 2010 47p il (Tell your parents) lib bdg $21.50

Grades: 4 5 6 7   **333.72**
1. Environmental movement 2. Environmental protection
ISBN 978-1-58415-764-9 lib bdg; 1-58415-764-X lib bdg
LC 2009-4527

This book that explains how to be environmentally friendly "offers numerous facts and statistics, all of which are cited. . . . Chapters cover present-day issues and . . . are interspersed with full-color photographs and short 'Did You Know' trivia boxes. . . . Back matter includes detailed resource lists and 'Try This!' experiments." SLJ

Includes glossary and bibliographical references

Try this at home; planet-friendly projects for kids. Jackie Farquhar, D.I.Y. editor. Owlkids 2009 93p il pa $10.95

Grades: 5 6 7 8   **333.72**
1. Environmental protection 2. Environmental education -- Juvenile literature ISBN 978-2-89579-192-8 pa; 2-89579-192-9 pa

"Many of these projects are unique or innovative, featuring ideas like growing your own pizza ingredients and making a foosball game out of recycled corks, clothespins, and plastic fruit baskets. One of the best projects provides tips on making sure a bike is road ready, offering advice on checking the cables, gears, and oiling the chain. The book also includes sections designed to increase environmental awareness, including information on carbon footprint and 'eco all-stars.' Interactive elements, like a game board, should appeal to children. Illustrations are hip collages of full-color photographs and cartoons." SLJ

Includes bibliographical references

Walsh, Melanie
★ **10** things I can do to help my world. Candlewick Press 2008 un il $15.99

Grades: PreK K 1   **333.72**

1. Waste minimization 2. Environmentalism -- Juvenile literature 3. Energy conservation -- Juvenile literature 4. Recycling (Waste, etc.) -- Juvenile literature
ISBN 978-0-7636-4144-3; 0-7636-4144-8

LC 2007051888

"A thoroughly successful presentation on how even small changes in lifestyle can make a big difference. On each spread, a large and colorful acrylic painting is accompanied by a sturdy die-cut flap and eco-friendly tips. Each suggestion opens with 'I,' followed by a verb, such as 'remember,' 'try,' and 'always.' The sentence is completed under the flap, along with a reason why the tip is conservation friendly. The recommendations are those that children can easily relate to, such as turning off the water while brushing your teeth, . . . using both sides of the paper, recycling, etc. Visually appealing and effective in its presentation, this title will serve as an introduction to environmental studies." SLJ

Wilson, Janet

★ **Our** earth; how kids are saving the planet. written and illustrated by Janet Wilson. Second Story Press 2010 un il $18.95

Grades: 2 3 4 5   **333.72**

1. Environmentalists
ISBN 978-1-897187-84-5; 1-897187-84-X

"Packed with inspiring, true-life stories on every spread, this collective biography introduces contemporary kids around the world who have made remarkable efforts to help protect the earth. . . . The spreads combine both paintings and photos of the young activists with brief, lively descriptions of their environmental work, including web links when available so that readers can learn more." Booklist

333.78   Recreational and wilderness areas

McHugh, Erin

National Parks; A Kid's Guide to America's Parks, Monuments and Landmarks. Erin McHugh; Art by Neal Aspinall, Doug Leen, and Brian Maebius. Black Dog & Leventhal Publishers 2012 128 p. col. ill., col. map (hbk.) $19.95; (hbk.) $19.95

Grades: 4 5 6   **333.78**

1. National parks and reserves -- United States
ISBN 157912884X; 9781579128845

This book, "arranged alphabetically by state . . . tours more than 75 U.S. parks, monuments, and landmarks, from the rocky shores of Maine's Acadia National Park to the ancient redwood groves of Northern California. Also included is a removable, fold-out collector map to house" the commemorative quarters from the America the Beautiful series. (Publisher's note)

333.79   Energy

Bailey, Gerry

Out of energy. Gareth Stevens 2011 48p il (Planet SOS) lib bdg $31.95; pa $14.05

Grades: 4 5 6   **333.79**

1. Energy resources 2. Renewable energy resources
ISBN 978-1-4339-4978-4 lib bdg; 1-4339-4978-4 lib bdg; 978-1-4339-4979-1 pa; 1-4339-4979-2 pa

LC 2010032889

This book "has separate chapters on fossil fuels, renewable energy, nuclear energy, and more. The many large, colorful photos will engage readers and assist them in understanding the important concepts introduced." SLJ

Includes glossary

Brezina, Corona

Jobs in sustainable energy. Rosen Pub. 2010 80p il (Green careers) lib bdg $30

Grades: 5 6 7 8   **333.79**

1. Vocational guidance 2. Renewable energy resources
ISBN 978-1-4358-3569-6 lib bdg; 1-4358-3569-7 lib bdg

LC 2009021855

This "well-conceived [introduction focuses] on various jobs in [sustainable energy], the education and experience required, and expected earnings. The [book is] well organized, making it easy to gain an overview of the major aspects of the work. . . . [This book] will make [a] good [addition] to career collections. Photographs from the field and website and contact information for professional organizations add value." SLJ

Includes glossary and bibliographical references

Bullard, Lisa

Go easy on energy; illustrated by Wes Thomas. Millbrook Press 2011 24p il (Planet protectors)

Grades: K 1 2 3   **333.79**

1. Energy conservation
ISBN 0-7613-6107-3; 978-0-7613-6107-7

LC 2010053302

A boy named Tyler shows how we can use energy wisely.

"The bright colors used in the illustrations . . . . will attract young readers to the environmental science content. . . . [The] facts are written in child-friendly language and the information should be attainable by young children. . . . [This book] will raise the environmental awareness of young children." Sci Book Films

Includes bibliographical references

Caduto, Michael J.

★ **Catch** the wind, harness the sun; 22 super-charged science projects for kids. Storey Pub. 2011 223p il $26.95; pa $16.95

Grades: 5 6 7 8   **333.79**

1. Energy conservation 2. Renewable energy resources 3. Science -- Experiments
ISBN 978-1-60342-971-9; 1-60342-971-9; 978-1-60342-794-4 pa; 1-60342-794-5 pa; 1603427945 pa; 1603429719; 9781603427944 pa; 9781603429719

LC 2010051169

"The eco-themed activities that Caduto lays out here are only the beginning, as he embeds them in short but clear explanations of relevant scientific facts, profiles of young eco-activitists, provocative follow-up questions, photos and cartoon spot art aplenty, folktales, and other enhancements." Booklist

Farrell, Courtney

Using alternative energies. Cherry Lake Pub. 2010 32p il (Save the planet) lib bdg $27.07

Grades: 3 4 5 6 **333.79**

1. Renewable energy resources
ISBN 978-1-60279-663-8 lib bdg; 1-60279-663-7 lib bdg

Examines the climate change and the problems caused by the use of traditional fossil fuels, and looks at alternatives such wind, solar, and hydroelectric energy

"At the beginning of . . . [the] book, readers are given a mission and advised to be alert to the facts provided so that they can successfully answer the questions at the end. . . . Children are made to feel part of the process; suggestions for how they can become involved abound." SLJ

Includes glossary and bibliographical references

Gaarder-Juntti, Oona

What in the world is green energy? ABDO Pub. Company 2010 24p il (Going green) lib bdg $24.21

Grades: 1 2 3 4 **333.79**

1. Renewable energy resources
ISBN 978-1-61613-191-3 lib bdg; 1-61613-191-8 lib bdg

LC 2010004320

"The lively layout design, featuring colorful headings, short paragraphs, and attractive photographs, has a scrapbook-like quality. . . . [The title explains] how all our choices require energy and resources, and encourage readers to make changes in their lifestyles. . . . [This] . . . will inspire and empower readers to make a difference." SLJ

Includes glossary and bibliographical references

Guillain, Charlotte

Saving energy; [by] Charlotte Guillain. Heinemann Library 2008 24p il (Help the environment) $21.70; pa $5.99

Grades: PreK K 1 2 **333.79**

1. Energy conservation
ISBN 978-1-4329-0887-4; 1-4329-0887-1; 978-1-4329-0893-5 pa; 1-4329-0893-6 pa

LC 2007-41172

This describes ways to save energy.

"A great jumping-off point for a broader discussion of environmentalism. . . . The bright, vibrant photographs will grab readers' attention as they reinforce the simple sentences." Libr Media Connect

Includes glossary

Hewitt, Sally

Using energy. Crabtree Pub. Co. 2009 32p il (Green team) $26.60; pa $8.95

Grades: 3 4 5 6 **333.79**

1. Energy resources 2. Energy conservation
ISBN 978-0-7787-4096-4; 0-7787-4096-X; 978-0-7787-4103-9 pa; 0-7787-4103-6 pa

LC 2008023288

"The color graphics and layouts are highly appealing and will definitely be attractive to young readers. . . . This . . . is an excellent resource for school libraries, science teachers, and community sponsors." Libr Media Connect

Leedy, Loreen

The shocking truth about energy; written and illustrated by Loreen Leedy. Holiday House 2010 32p il $17.95

Grades: 1 2 3 **333.79**

1. Energy resources
ISBN 978-0-8234-2220-3; 0-8234-2220-8

An imaginary bolt of pure energy named Erg introduces the nature of energy, offers tips on how to use energy sensibly, and shows different ways energy can be harnessed.

"Leedy's experience selecting facts that are most relevant and engaging for young readers is evident, and the information is eminently digestible. The design moves from energetic to near-frenetic. Her brightly colored mixed-media illustrations are filled with animated appliances, bursts of information, and decorated fonts." Booklist

Ollhoff, Jim

Geothermal, biomass, and hydrogen. ABDO Pub. 2010 32p il (Future energy) lib bdg $18.95

Grades: 3 4 5 6 **333.79**

1. Renewable energy resources
ISBN 978-1-60453-937-0 lib bdg; 1-60453-937-2 lib bdg

Discusses the advantages and disadvantages of alternative energy sources and the promise of harnessing other renewable energy sources, such as hydrogen fuel cells, geothermal power, and biomass.

"Liberally filled with bright photographs, the text provides examples with accurate data and narrative. . . . Inquiring readers will find this . . . valuable." Libr Media Connect

Includes glossary

Nuclear energy. ABDO Pub. 2010 32p il (Future energy) lib bdg $18.95

Grades: 3 4 5 6 **333.79**

1. Nuclear energy 2. Nuclear engineering 3. Nuclear power plants
ISBN 978-1-60453-936-3; 1-60453-936-4

Discusses fusion energy and the possible future of nuclear power.

"Liberally filled with bright photographs, the text provides examples with accurate data and narrative. . . . Inquiring readers will find this . . . valuable." Libr Media Connect

Includes glossary

Solar power. ABDO Pub. 2010 32p il (Future energy) lib bdg $18.95

Grades: 3 4 5 6 **333.79**

1. Solar energy
ISBN 978-1-60453-938-7; 1-60453-938-0

Discusses the history and the possible future of solar power.

"Liberally filled with bright photographs, the text provides examples with accurate data and narrative. . . . Inquiring readers will find this . . . valuable." Libr Media Connect

Includes glossary

World in crisis. ABDO Pub. 2010 32p il (Future energy) lib bdg $18.95

Grades: 3 4 5 6 **333.79**

1. Energy policy 2. Energy resources
ISBN 978-1-60453-940-0; 1-60453-940-2

Discusses what can be done and the possible future of energy.

"Liberally filled with bright photographs, the text provides examples with accurate data and narrative. . . . Inquiring readers will find this . . . . valuable." Libr Media Connect

Includes glossary

Rau, Dana Meachen

Alternative energy beyond fossil fuels. Compass Point Books 2010 64p il (Green generation) lib bdg $31.99; pa $6.95

Grades: 5 6 7 8 9   **333.79**

1. Energy resources 2. Renewable energy resources 3. Fossil fuels -- Juvenile literature 4. Power resources -- Juvenile literature

ISBN 978-0-7565-4247-4 lib bdg; 0-7565-4247-2 lib bdg; 978-0-7565-4289-4 pa; 0-7565-4289-8 pa

LC 2009-08778

"This great little book introduces the topics of fossil fuel usage, the limited nature of fossil fuels, and alternative energy options. It is particularly praiseworthy for its refreshingly objective, but still enthusiastic, presentations on solar, wind, geothermal, hydro, and biomass energy. . . . Interesting, well-written, and appropriately illustrated, the book is entertaining enough for general reading, but factual enough for use as a science text." Sci Books Films

Includes glossary and bibliographical references

Slade, Suzanne

What can we do about the energy crisis? PowerKids Press 2010 24p il (Protecting our planet) lib bdg $21.25; pa $8

Grades: 2 3 4   **333.79**

1. Energy resources 2. Energy development

ISBN 978-1-4042-8081-6 lib bdg; 1-4042-8081-2 lib bdg; 978-1-4358-2481-2 pa; 1-4358-2481-4 pa

LC 2008-51935

This book provides "straightforward information . . . complemented by full-page, color photographs. . . . Links for further information . . . are housed at the publisher's Web site (which allows feedback so that readers can suggest more sites)." SLJ

Includes glossary

Solway, Andrew

Renewable energy sources. Raintree 2010 48p il (Sci-hi: Earth and space science) lib bdg $31.43; pa $8.99

Grades: 4 5 6 7   **333.79**

1. Renewable energy resources

ISBN 978-1-4109-3351-5 lib bdg; 1-4109-3351-2 lib bdg; 978-1-4109-3361-4 pa; 1-4109-3361-X pa

LC 2009-3535

"Multiple colorful sidebars and large and small diagrams and photographs will help students to grasp the fundamentals being discussed, and the easy but interesting science experiments will act as further reinforcements." SLJ

Includes glossary and bibliographical references

Vogel, Julia

Power up! Learn about energy; illustrated by Jane Yamada. The Child's World 2010 24p il (Science definitions) lib bdg $22.79

Grades: PreK K 1 2   **333.79**

1. Energy resources

ISBN 978-1-60253-512-1; 1-60253-512-4

LC 2010010980

This book about energy is "attractive and succinct. . . . Large, eye-catching photos cover the recto of each spread. . . . Varying, jewel-toned accents are used in headings, highlighted glossary terms, and in a sidebar on each spread." SLJ

Includes glossary

Weakland, Mark

Onion juice, poop, and other surprising sources of alternative energy. Capstone Press 2010 32p il (Fact finders. Nasty (but useful!) science) lib bdg $25.99

Grades: 3 4 5   **333.79**

1. Biomass energy 2. Renewable energy resources

ISBN 978-1-4296-4536-2; 1-4296-4536-9

This informative guide also explains "relevant chemical processes, medical rationales, and ecological functions in reasonably specific detail. . . . A list of relevant web resources is maintained on the publisher's page." SLJ

Includes glossary and bibliographical references

333.8 Subsurface resources

Hartman, Eve

Fossil fuels; [by] Eve Hartman and Wendy Meshbesher. Raintree 2010 48p il map (Sci-hi: Earth and space science) lib bdg $31.43; pa $8.99

Grades: 4 5 6 7   **333.8**

1. Coal 2. Oils and fats

ISBN 978-1-4109-3350-8 lib bdg; 1-4109-3350-4 lib bdg; 978-1-4109-3360-7 pa; 1-4109-3360-1 pa

LC 2009-3548

"Multiple colorful sidebars and large and small diagrams and photographs will help students to grasp the fundamentals being discussed, and the easy but interesting science experiments will act as further reinforcements." SLJ

Includes glossary and bibliographical references

Ollhoff, Jim

Fossil fuels. ABDO Pub. 2010 32p il (Future energy) lib bdg $18.95

Grades: 3 4 5 6   **333.8**

1. Fuel 2. Energy resources

ISBN 978-1-60453-935-6; 1-60453-935-6

LC 2009-29857

Discusses how coal is mined and burned and the possible future of fossil fuels.

"Liberally filled with bright photographs, the text provides examples with accurate data and narrative. . . . Inquiring readers will find this . . . valuable." Libr Media Connect

Includes glossary

White, Nancy

Using Earth's underground heat. Bearport Pub. 2009 32p il (Going green) lib bdg $25.27

Grades: 4 5 6 7   **333.8**

1. Geothermal resources

ISBN 978-1-59716-963-9 lib bdg; 1-59716-963-3 lib bdg

LC 2009-15119

"Color photographs (most full page) and a few diagrams accompany the informative text[s]. . . . Overall, the [book] .

.. is user-friendly and covers topics that are not easily found elsewhere." SLJ

Includes glossary and bibliographical references

333.9 Other natural resources

Dobson, Clive

Wind power; 20 projects to make with paper. Firefly Books 2010 96p il $24.95; pa $12.95

Grades: 5 6 7 8   **333.9**

1. Wind power 2. Paper crafts

ISBN 978-1-55407-659-8; 1-55407-659-5; 978-1-55407-749-6 pa; 1-55407-749-4 pa

"In this informative craft book, a celebration of wind and of innovative efforts to harness its energy, Dobson describes the geometric and aerodynamic principles behind windmills, sails, and wind turbines, then implements these concepts via 20 paper projects, ranging from a two-blade pinwheel to a dramatic 'Squirrel Cage' turbine. . . . Readers should gain a more palpable understanding of the subject matter by building and watching the graceful compositions function." Publ Wkly

Drummond, Allan

★ Energy island; how one community harnessed the wind and changed their world. Farrar, Straus and Giroux 2011 un il $16.99

Grades: K 1 2 3   **333.9**

1. Wind power 2. Renewable energy resources

ISBN 978-0-374-32184-0; 0-374-32184-1

This is an "account of how the residents of a Danish island made large and small changes to switch to renewable energy sources. . . . Now people from around the world come to Samsø to learn about ways to harness renewable energy and reduce carbon emissions. Informative sidebars supply information on global warming, renewable and nonrenewable energy, and conservation. What is most remarkable about this island . . . is how ordinary people achieved an extraordinary 140 percent reduction in carbon emissions in just 10 years. The illustrations further personalize the story with energy of their own as they bring Samsø and its residents to life." SLJ

Includes bibliographical references

Ollhoff, Jim

Wind and water. ABDO Pub. 2010 32p il (Future energy) lib bdg $18.95

Grades: 3 4 5 6   **333.9**

1. Wind power 2. Water power

ISBN 978-1-60453-939-4; 1-60453-939-9

Discusses the possible future of energy from wind and water.

"Liberally filled with bright photographs, the text provides examples with accurate data and narrative. . . . Inquiring readers will find this . . . valuable." Libr Media Connect

Includes glossary

333.91 Water and lands adjoining bodies of water

Bullard, Lisa

Watch over our water; illustrated by Xiao Xin. Millbrook Press 2011 il (Planet protectors) lib bdg $23.93

Grades: K 1 2 3   **333.91**

1. Water 2. Water pollution

ISBN 978-0-7613-6106-0; 0-7613-6106-5

                 LC 2010053299

A girl named Trina shows how to care for Earth's water.

"The bright colors used in the illustrations . . . will attract young readers to the environmental science content. . . . [The] facts are written in child-friendly language and the information should be attainable by young children. . . . [This book] will raise the environmental awareness of young children." Sci Books Films

333.95 Biological resources

Arnosky, Jim

★ Crinkleroot's guide to giving back to nature; by Jim Arnosky. G.P. Putnam's Sons 2012 48 p. $17.99

Grades: K 1 2   **333.95**

1. Hermits -- Juvenile fiction 2. Nature -- Juvenile literature 3. Nature conservation -- Juvenile literature

ISBN 0399255206; 9780399255205

                 LC 2011028758

This children's nature book, by Jim Arnosky, shows "[f]orest-dweller Crinkleroot . . . lead[ing] 21st-century readers outdoors, urging them to appreciate and give back to nature. Arnosky's bearded guide [was] inspired by 19th-century naturalist John Burroughs. . . . In this . . . title, the author focuses on things children can do on their own for their environment." (Kirkus)

Guerive, Gaelle

Extraordinary endangered animals; by Sandrine Silhol & Gaëlle Guérive; illustrated by Marie Doucedame. Abrams 2011 il $24.95

Grades: 5 6 7 8   **333.95**

1. Endangered species

ISBN 978-1-4197-0034-7; 1-4197-0034-0

"Detailed, large-scale photographs and intricate drawings depict 35 endangered species from around the globe, including the California condor, the sea otter, the golden lion tamarin, and the sawfish. Silhol and Guérive describe the habitat, behavior, and endangered status of each animal, while sidebars place each in human context, implicating our role in their endangerment. . . . Honest but not downbeat, this informative collection encourages readers to take action before these species disappear." Publ Wkly

Guillain, Charlotte

Caring for nature; [by] Charlotte Guillain. Heinemann Library 2008 24p il (Help the environment) $21.70; pa $5.99

Grades: PreK K 1 2   **333.95**

1. Nature conservation

ISBN 978-1-4329-0889-8; 1-4329-0889-8; 978-1-4329-0895-9 pa; 1-4329-0895-2 pa

                 LC 2007-41174

This book is "a great jumping–off point for a broader discussion of environmentalism. . . . The bright, vibrant photographs will grab readers' attention as they reinforce the simple sentences." Libr Media Connect

Includes glossary

Morgan, Sally

Animal rescue. Cherrytree Books 2011 30p il (Helping our planet) lib bdg $28.50

Grades: 1 2 3   **333.95**

1. Endangered species 2. Wildlife conservation

ISBN 978-1-84234-606-8; 1-84234-606-7

LC 2010000035

This book "addresses how and why animals become endangered and what can be done. . . . The [book features] large, full-color photos with one or two paragraphs of large-print text per page. 'Find Out More' boxes scattered throughout give additional facts with related websites and 'You Choose' boxes ask students questions regarding important choices they can make. . . . [This] well-designed [book] will be useful for reports and general interest." SLJ

Includes glossary

Reptiles and amphibians; edited by Tim Harris. Brown Bear Books 2012 64 p. (library binding) $35.65

Grades: 5 6 7 8   **333.95**

1. Reptiles 2. Amphibians 3. Endangered species 4. Rare reptiles -- Juvenile literature 5. Rare amphibians -- Juvenile literature

ISBN 1936333368; 9781936333363

LC 2010053968

This book "profiles a global sampling of reptiles and amphibians in various degrees of endangerment . . . . Twenty-one species are described in . . . detail that includes information on their classification, distribution, physical characteristics, habitat, diet, and reproduction." The book is part of "the 'Facts at Your Fingertips: Endangered Animals' series, which profiles various groups of endangered species from all parts of the planet." (National Science Teachers Association)

Includes bibliographical references and index

Salmansohn, Pete, 1947-

Saving birds; heroes around the world. [by] Pete Salmansohn and Stephen W. Kress. Tilbury House 2003 39p il $16.95; pa $7.95

Grades: 5 6 7 8   **333.95**

1. Endangered species 2. Wildlife conservation 3. Birds -- Protection

ISBN 0-88448-237-5; 0-88448-276-6 pa

LC 2002-6710

Profiles adults and children working in six habitats around the world to save wild birds, some of which are on the brink of extinction.

"As a teaching aid, this volume is an exceptional supplement. The six articles relating the heroic rescue of the endangered birds are accurate and enhanced by appropriate color photographs." Sci Books Films

Sheehan, Sean

Endangered species; by Sean Sheehan. Gareth Stevens Pub. 2009 48p il map (What if we do nothing?) lib bdg $31

Grades: 5 6 7 8   **333.95**

1. Endangered species

ISBN 978-1-4339-0086-0 lib bdg; 1-4339-0086-6 lib bdg

LC 2008029167

"Using intelligent, focused text; an open design; vivid photos; and excellent maps, [this] book demands attention." Booklist

Includes bibliographical references

338.7 Business enterprises

Buckley, A. M.

Pixar; the company and its founders. ABDO Pub. Co. 2011 112p il (Technology pioneers) lib bdg $34.22

Grades: 5 6 7 8   **338.7**

1. Animated films 2. Computer animation

ISBN 978-1-61714-810-1 lib bdg; 1-61714-810-5 lib bdg; 978-1-61758-968-3 e-book

LC 2010044831

An introduction to Pixar Animation Studios and its founders.

"Written in a clear, linear fashion, this series offers vivid, well-researched details about the development of technological advancements considered essential in today's society. . . . Readers who are interested in technology and inventions will be thoroughly engrossed." SLJ

Includes glossary and bibliographical references

Firestone, Mary

Nintendo; the company and its founders. ABDO Pub. Co. 2011 112p il (Technology pioneers) lib bdg $34.22

Grades: 5 6 7 8   **338.7**

1. Video games

ISBN 978-1-61714-809-5 lib bdg; 1-61714-809-1 lib bdg; 978-1-61758-967-6 e-book

LC 2010044664

This is an introduction to the Nintendo video game company and its founders.

"Written in a clear, linear fashion, this series offers vivid, well-researched details about the development of technological advancements considered essential in today's society. . . . Readers who are interested in technology and inventions will be thoroughly engrossed." SLJ

Includes glossary and bibliographical references

Gitlin, Marty

EBay; the company and its founder. ABDO Pub. Co. 2011 112p il (Technology pioneers) lib bdg $34.22

Grades: 5 6 7 8   **338.7**

1. Auctions 2. Executives 3. Businesspeople 4. Internet marketing 5. Software engineers 6. Internet executives

ISBN 978-1-61714-807-1 lib bdg; 1-61714-807-5 lib bdg; 978-1-61758-965-2 e-book

LC 2010044663

This is an introduction to eBay internet auction site and its founder, Pierre Omidyar.

"Written in a clear, linear fashion, this series offers vivid, well-researched details about the development of technological advancements considered essential in today's society. . .

. . Readers who are interested in technology and inventions will be thoroughly engrossed." SLJ

Includes glossary and bibliographical references

Hamen, Susan E.

Google; the company and its founders. ABDO Pub. Co. 2011 112p il (Technology pioneers) lib bdg $34.22

Grades: 5 6 7 8   **338.7**

1. Computer industry 2. Web search engines 3. Computer scientists 4. Internet executives 5. Information technology executives

ISBN 978-1-61714-808-8; 1-61714-808-3

LC 2010037884

This book about Google and its founders "provides a compact, direct, well-researched, and relevant explanation of how Sergey Brin, Larry Page, and their brand have changed the world. . . . This title presents just the right amount of background on the two men . . . before it moves into more thorough explorations of how the founders' creation has grown far beyond providing basic Web searching. . . . Dynamically designed with clear and colorful photographs, sidebars, and wide margins, this is at once a dual biography, Internet history, and business primer." Booklist

Includes bibliographical references

342 Branches of law; laws, regulations, cases; law of specific jurisdictions, areas, socioeconomic regions

Cheney, Lynne V.

We the people; the story of our Constitution. by Lynne Cheney; illustrated by Greg Harlin. Simon & Schuster Books for Young Readers 2008 30p il pbk. $7.99

Grades: 3 4 5   **342**

1. Constitutional history -- United States

ISBN 9781442444225

LC 2008-8871

In May 1787 delegates from across the country-including George Washington, James Madison, and Benjamin Franklin-gathered in Philadelphia and, meeting over the course of a sweltering summer, created a new framework for governing: the Constitution of the United States

This book is written "in clear, cogent prose. . . . The vocabulary is rich, and the author incorporates fascinating details. . . . [It is illustrated with] Harlin's impressive artwork, described as being done in 'various water media.' The sweep of these realistic paintings across the pages highlights the drama of each situation, and the artist makes remarkable use of perspective." SLJ

Includes bibliographical references

Fritz, Jean

★ Shh! we're writing the Constitution; illustrated by Tomie dePaola. Putnam 1987 64p il $15.99; pa $5.99

Grades: 2 3 4   **342**

1. Constitutional history -- United States

ISBN 0-399-21403-8; 0-698-11624-0 pa

LC 86-22528

"Jean Fritz gives a vivid, vibrant picture of the 1787 Constitutional Convention. The wonderful, full-color illustrations are a perfect match for the captivating text." Child Book Rev Serv

Krull, Kathleen

A **kid's** guide to America's Bill of Rights; curfews, censorship, and the 100-pound giant. illustrated by Anna DiVito. Avon Bks. 1999 226p il $15.99

Grades: 4 5 6 7   **342**

1. Civil rights 2. Constitutional amendments -- United States

ISBN 0-380-97497-5

LC 99-17324

"After describing how the first 10 amendments came to be added to the Constitution, the book considers each one from a historical point of view, examining Supreme Court cases and famous challenges, and explaining in what ways each amendment applies to children and teenagers. Anna DiVito's cartoonlike drawings add a visually appealing touch." Booklist

Includes bibliographical references

Leavitt, Amie Jane

The **Bill** of Rights in translation; what it really means. by Amie Jane Leavitt. Capstone Press 2009 32p il (Fact finders. Kids' translations) lib bdg $23.93; pa $7.95

Grades: 3 4 5   **342**

1. Civil rights

ISBN 978-1-4296-1928-8 lib bdg; 1-4296-1928-7 lib bdg; 978-1-4296-2843-3 pa; 1-4296-2843-X pa

LC 2007-51307

Provides "a nearly line-by-line translation that makes . . . the written word accessible and meaningful." SLJ

Includes glossary and bibliographical references

Maestro, Betsy

A **more** perfect union; the story of our Constitution. illustrated by Giulio Maestro. Lothrop, Lee & Shepard Bks. 1987 48p il hardcover o.p. pa $7.99

Grades: 2 3 4   **342**

1. Constitutional history -- United States

ISBN 0-688-10192-5 pa

LC 87-4083

"A simple, straightforward account using an oversize format with full-color illustration throughout. There is an excellent, fact-filled addenda that also includes the Preamble, chronologies and summaries of the Articles of the Constitution, the Bill of Rights, the Amendments and the Connecticut Compromise. This fine book places important events in historical context." Publ Wkly

Mortensen, Lori

★ **Writing** the U.S. Constitution; illustrated by Siri Weber Feeney. Picture Window Books 2010 32p il (Our American story) lib bdg $23.99

Grades: 2 3 4   **342**

1. Constitutional history

ISBN 978-1-4048-5540-3 lib bdg; 1-4048-5540-8 lib bdg

LC 2009-6895

Discusses the history of the writing of the United States Constitution

This title is "illustrated with well-executed, full-page, color illustrations, maps, and photos. . . . [It has] accurate, clearly written information that students can use for either leisure reading or reports." SLJ

Includes glossary and bibliographical references

Thomas, William David

What is a constitution? [by] William David Thomas. Gareth Stevens Pub. 2008 32p il (My American government) lib bdg $23.93; pa $8.95

Grades: 3 4 5   **342**

    1. Democracy 2. Constitutions

    ISBN 978-0-8368-8863-8 lib bdg; 0-8368-8863-4 lib bdg; 978-0-8368-8868-3 pa; 0-8368-8868-5 pa

                     LC 2007027281

This describes the United States constitution as well as the constitutions of state governments.

This book has "an accessible format and clear writing. . . . Black-and-white and full-color vintage and more recent photographs appear throughout." SLJ

Includes glossary and bibliographical references

344   Labor, social service, education, cultural law

Chmara, Theresa

    ★ Privacy and confidentiality issues; a guide for libraries and their lawyers. American Library Association 2009 98p pa $40

Grades: Adult Professional   **344**

    1. Library services 2. Right of privacy 3. Libraries -- Law and legislation

    ISBN 978-0-8389-0970-6; 0-8389-0970-1

                     LC 2008-34902

"This slim title is a must read. Chmara, a First Amendment attorney and litigation expert, clarifies privacy and confidentiality issues such as requests or subpoenas for patron-use records (both book and Internet), hostile-work-environment issues, state and federal privacy and confidentiality statutes, and minors' First Amendment rights and rights to privacy." Booklist

Includes bibliographical references

345   Criminal law

Coleman, Wim

    Racism on trial; From the Medgar Evers murder case to 'Ghosts of Mississippi' [by] Wim Coleman and Pat Perrin. Enslow Publishers 2009 112p il lib bdg $31.93

Grades: 5 6 7 8   **345**

    1. Lynching 2. Trials (Homicide) 3. Murderers 4. White supremacists 5. Civil rights activists

    ISBN 978-0-7660-3059-6; 0-7660-3059-8

                     LC 2008-21483

"Examines the Byron De La Beckwith murder trials, including the mistrials and his eventual conviction, key figures in the case, and the inspiration for the movie Ghosts of Mississippi." Publisher's note

346   Private law

Butler, Rebecca P.

    Copyright for teachers & librarians in the 21st century. Neal-Schuman Publishers 2011 274p il pa $70

Grades: Adult Professional   **346**

    1. Copyright 2. Fair use (Copyright)

    ISBN 978-1-55570-738-5

                     LC 2011012600

First published 2004 with title: Copyright for teachers and librarians

"Library educator Rebecca Butler explains fair use, public domain, documentation and licenses, permissions, violations and penalties, policies and ethics codes, citations, creation and ownership, how to register copyrights, and gives tips for staying out of trouble." Publisher's note

Includes bibliographical references

Popek, Emily

    Copyright and digital ethics. Rosen Central 2011 48p il (Digital and information literacy) lib bdg $26.50; pa $11.75

Grades: 5 6 7 8   **346**

    1. Ethics 2. Internet 3. Copyright

    ISBN 978-1-4488-1323-0 lib bdg; 1-4488-1323-9; 978-1-4488-2294-2 pa; 1-4488-2294-7 pa

                     LC 2010027018

Though this "title is a broad overview of a sometimes-complex subject, the detail is significant. . . . Touches of blue enhance the clean design. . . . [This] explains concepts like fair use and tries to persuade readers of the damage done by digital piracy and plagiarism." Booklist

Includes bibliographical references

346.04   Property

Crews, Kenneth D.

    Copyright law for librarians and educators; creative strategies and practical solutions. with contributions from Dwayne K. Buttler . . . [et al.] 2nd ed; American Library Association 2012 xii, 192 p.p ill. (alk. paper) $57

Grades: Adult Professional   **346.04**

    1. Copyright 2. Sound recordings 3. Fair use (Copyright) 4. Copyright -- United States 5. Teachers -- United States -- Handbooks, manuals, etc 6. Librarians -- United States -- Handbooks, manuals, etc

    ISBN 0838910920; 9780838910924

                     LC 2011027604

First published 2000 with title: Copyright essentials for librarians and educators

Author Kenneth D. Crews' book "allows readers to get up to speed on current interpretations of the Digital Millennium Copyright Act from a librarian-educator viewpoint." It also "draws on cutting-edge case law in 18 discrete areas of copyright, including specialized and controversial music and sound recording issues. [This guide offers] information professionals . . . the tools they need to take control of their rights and responsibilities as copyright owners and users." (Publisher's note)

The author "addresses 18 areas of copyright in 5 parts. He begins with the scope of protectable works as well as works without copyright protection. Next, he discusses the rights of ownership, including duration and exceptions. He then explains fair use and its related guidelines. Part 4 focuses on the TEACH Act, Section 108, and responsibilities and liabilities. Lastly, Crews examines special issues such as the Digital Millennium Copyright Act." Booklist

Includes bibliographical references and index.

Russell, Carrie

Complete copyright for K-12 librarians and educators; Carrie Russell. American Library Association 2012 xi, 173 p.p ill. (chiefly col.) (alk. paper) $50

Grades: Professional **346.04**

1. Copyright 2. Fair use (Copyright) 3. Copyright -- United States 4. Fair use (Copyright) -- United States 5. Librarians -- Legal status, laws, etc. -- United States 6. School libraries -- Law and legislation -- United States
ISBN 0838910831; 9780838910832

LC 2012016674

This book by Carrie Russell "is designed as a resource for educators, offering guidance for providing material to students while carefully observing copyright law. The book offers detailed advice on distinctive issues of intellectual property in the school setting; explores scenarios often encountered by educators . . . and precisely defines 'fair use,' by showing readers exactly what's possible within the law." (Education Digest)

Includes bibliographical references and index

347 Procedure and courts

Adler, David A., 1947-

A **picture** book of Thurgood Marshall; illustrated by Robert Casilla. Holiday House 1997 un il $16.95; pa $6.95

Grades: 1 2 3 **347**

1. Judges 2. Lawyers 3. Solicitors general 4. Civil rights activists 5. Supreme Court justices 6. African Americans -- Biography
ISBN 0-8234-1308-X; 0-823-41506-6 pa

LC 96-37248

Follows the life of the first African American to serve as a judge on the United States Supreme Court

"Adler presents the high points of Marshall's life with enough detail to humanize the man. . . . Sensitive line-and-watercolor illustrations on every page add warmth to the story as they define people and settings." Booklist

352.13 Administration of subordinate jurisdictions

Giesecke, Ernestine

State government; Rev. and updated; Heinemann Library 2010 32p il map (Kids' guide to government) $29.29; pa $7.99

Grades: 3 4 5 **352.13**

1. State governments
ISBN 978-1-4329-2707-3; 1-4329-2707-8; 978-1-4329-2712-7 pa; 1-4329-2712-4 pa
First published 2000

Introduces the purpose and function of state government, the function of the three branches, how states raise money, how state government operates, and how a bill becomes a state law.

"This . . . would be a great asset. . . . Students will learn about a different, but related government every two pages. The font is large and easy to read. The photos, diagrams, charts, maps, and illustrations supplement the text well." Libr Media Connect

Includes glossary

352.23 Chief executives

Obama, Barack, 1961-

Our enduring spirit; President Barack Obama's first words to America. with illustrations by Greg Ruth. Harper 2009 un il $17.99; lib bdg $18.89

Grades: 2 3 4 5 6 **352.23**

1. Lawyers 2. Presidents 3. Senators 4. State legislators 5. Nobel laureates for peace 6. Presidents -- United States -- Inaugural addresses
ISBN 978-0-06-183455-4; 0-06-183455-6; 978-0-06-183456-1 lib bdg; 0-06-183456-4 lib bdg

LC 2009014361

"The selected excerpts from Obama's speech (also printed in its entirety at the end of the book) only obliquely note the nation's current crises, but make ample use of Obama's numerous historical references. . . . Dramatic washes of color are juxtaposed with Ruth's inky paintings of the president and of Americans past and present, as strong brush-strokes define their subjects while creating a tangible sense of movement. With the book's emphasis on common values and backgrounds, readers are likely to come away with a sense of pride, hope and belonging, while recognizing that freedom doesn't come without work." Publ Wkly

355 Military science

Chapman, Caroline

Battles & weapons: exploring history through art; [by] Caroline Chapman. Two-Can 2007 64p il (Picture that!) $19.95

Grades: 5 6 7 8 **355**

1. War in art 2. Military history 3. Military art and science
ISBN 978-1-58728-588-2

LC 2006033229

"High quality reproductions of paintings, murals, sculptures, and artifacts show military customs and equipment over the centuries. . . . The lively, informative text creates a 'you are there' sense that will engage even reluctant readers." SLJ

Includes bibliographical references

Murrell, Deborah Jane

Greek warrior; by Deborah Murrell. QEB Pub. 2010 32p il map (QEB warriors) lib bdg $28.50

Grades: 4 5 6 7 **355**

1. Military art and science -- History
ISBN 978-1-59566-759-5 lib bdg; 1-59566-759-8 lib bdg

LC 2009-3542

"Bold, comprehensible type and full-color and black-and-white illustrations; reproductions; and photographs will make this offering a hit with its target audience, including reluctant readers." SLJ

Includes glossary

Park, Louise

The **Japanese** samurai; [by] Louise Park and Timothy Love. Marshall Cavendish Benchmark 2010 32p il map (Ancient and medieval people) lib bdg $28.50

Grades: 4 5 6   **355**

   1. Samurai 2. Military art and science -- History
   ISBN 978-0-7614-4448-0 lib bdg; 0-7614-4448-3 lib bdg

                    LC 2009-3573

This title has "a simple and elegant design with the proper balance of quality writing and quantity of information. . . . Handy time lines, well-chosen photos of ruins and artifacts, quality illustrations, inset 'Quick Facts', and 'What You Should Know About' features will grab reluctant readers and captivate even those with short attention spans." SLJ

Includes glossary

The **Pharaohs'** armies; by Louise Park and Timothy Love. Marshall Cavendish Benchmark 2009 32p il map (Ancient and medieval people) lib bdg $28.50

Grades: 4 5 6   **355**

   1. Military art and science -- History
   ISBN 978-0-7614-4451-0 lib bdg; 0-7614-4451-3 lib bdg

This title has "a simple and elegant design with the proper balance of quality writing and quantity of information. . . . Handy time lines, well-chosen photos of ruins and artifacts, quality illustrations, inset 'Quick Facts', and 'What You Should Know About' features will grab reluctant readers and captivate even those with short attention spans." SLJ

Includes glossary

Solway, Andrew

Graphing war and conflict. Raintree 2010 32p il (Real world data) $28.21; pa $7.99

Grades: 4 5 6 7   **355**

   1. Graphic methods 2. Military history
   ISBN 978-1-4329-2620-5; 1-4329-2620-9; 978-1-4329-2629-8 pa; 1-4329-2629-2 pa

                   LC 2009001188

This "uses graphs and charts to talk about global conflicts between 1990 and 2005, from guerilla warfare and civil war to nuclear attacks, with a special section on terrorism, including 9/11 and suicide bombers. . . . The clear design, with lots of full-color photos and sidebars, will encourage browsers as much as the up-to-date examples and the clear directions for remaining 'chart smart.'" Booklist

Includes glossary and bibliographical references

Souter, Janet

War in Afghanistan and Iraq; the daily life of the men and women serving in Afghanistan and Iraq. [by] Janet Souter and Gerry Souter. Carlton Books 2011 47p il map $16.95

Grades: 2 3 4   **355**

   1. Afghan War, 2001- 2. Iraq War, 2003-2011
   ISBN 978-1-84732-895-3; 1-84732-895-4

"An overview of these wartorn countries' physical and religious make-ups leads to the review of current political instability in the region. The discussion of combat tech-niques illustrates America's military power, though a nod to numerous international organizations (from NATO to ISAF) conveys the global scope. Double-page spreads address the perceived catalysts for conflict and the United States' accompanying responses (including Osama Bin Laden's recent death). . . . Despite its slimness, a remarkably effective and timely treatment." Kirkus

Inlcudes glossary

355.02   War and warfare

Benoit, Peter

The **nuclear** age; by Peter Benoit. Children's Press 2012 64 p. ill. (chiefly col.), col. map (library) $30.00; (paperback) $8.95

Grades: 4 5 6   **355.02**

   1. Nuclear energy -- History -- Juvenile literature 2. Nuclear weapons -- History -- Juvenile literature 3. Nuclear energy -- History
   ISBN 0531230627; 0531281620; 9780531230626; 9780531281628

                   LC 2011031341

This book by Peter Benoit, part of the "Cornerstones of Freedom" series, "offers comprehensive coverage of all concepts related to the nuclear age beginning in the late 1800s through current times. . . . Four chapters highlight issues that emerge--birth of the new age, cold war, atom's legacy and human dilemma." Topics include "the atomic bomb, [Adolf] Hitler versus allies, international competitions, precautions, peaceful pursuits and cleaner sources of energy." (Children's Literature)

Includes bibliographical references (p. 61) and index.

355.1   Military life and customs

Biden, Jill

Don't forget, God bless our troops; Jill Biden; illustrated by Raúl Colón. Simon & Schuster Books for Young Readers 2012 40 p. (hbk.) $16.99

Grades: K 1 2   **355.1**

   1. Children and war 2. Afghan War, 2001- 3. Father-daughter relationship 4. Children of military personnel -- United States -- Juvenile literature 5. Families of military personnel -- United States -- Juvenile literature 6. Soldiers -- Family relationships -- United States -- Juvenile literature
   ISBN 144245735X; 1442457376; 9781442457355; 9781442457379

                   LC 2012008493

In the book by author Jill Biden, "when her father leaves for a year of being at war, Natalie knows that she will miss him. Natalie is proud of her father but there is nothing to stop her from wishing he was home. Some things do help her feel better. Natalie works with her Nana to send her dad and the other service men and women cookies and treats they have made. Natalie, her mom, and brother can see and talk to Dad over the computer, and the kindness of friends at school and at church help her feel supported and loved. But there is nothing like the day when her Dad comes home at last." (Publisher's note)

Includes bibliographical references.

355.4   Military operations

Durman, Laura

Siege; by Laura Durman. Arcturus Pub. 2012 32 p. col. ill. (library) $28.50

Grades: 4 5 6   **355.4**

1. Middle Ages 2. Military art and science 3. Sieges -- Juvenile literature 4. Castles -- Juvenile literature

ISBN 1848585624; 9781848585621

LC 2011051446

This book by Laura Durman is part of the Knights and Castles series and looks at sieges. In "two-page spreads filled with photos, staged reenactments, diagrams, and line drawings, Durman . . . outlines how both sides prepared and fared in a siege. Chapters on castle defense, defense tactics, and personal protection" are included as is an "in-depth look at the precision and force at work with such siege machines as the trebuchet, mangonel, battering ram, and belfry." (Children's Literature)

Includes bibliographical references (p. 31) and index.

Grayson, Robert

Military. Marshall Cavendish Benchmark 2010 62p il (Working animals) lib bdg $28.50

Grades: 4 5 6 7   **355.4**

1. Animals -- War use

ISBN 978-1-60870-164-3 lib bdg; 1-60870-164-6 lib bdg

"Describes animals, including elephants, dogs, horses, mules, sea lions, dolphins, rats, and homing pigeons, which provide valuable service to the military." Publisher's note

Includes glossary and bibliographical references

Patent, Dorothy Hinshaw

Dogs on duty; soldiers' best friends on the battlefield and beyond. by Dorothy Hinshaw Patent. Walker & Co. 2012 48 p. (hardcover) $16.99

Grades: 3 4 5 6   **355.4**

1. Working dogs 2. Dogs -- War use

ISBN 0802728456; 9780802728456

LC 2012004457

Author Dorothy Hinshaw Patent reports that "nine thousand dogs served in World War II, . . . four thousand dogs served in Vietnam, and hundreds died in combat. . . . [She] sketches the history of dogs in war from ancient times to World Wars I and II and on to modern wars--Vietnam, Iraq and Afghanistan. It's dogs' 'super senses' of sight, sound and smell, and their capacity to bond with soldiers that make them so useful in military theaters. They uncovered hidden tunnels in Vietnam, find dangerous land mines in Afghan villages, and locate weapons, explosives and drugs at home and abroad." (Kirkus Reviews)

"The straightforward text and color photographs celebrate the bonds between dogs and handlers that are so crucial in modern warfare. A sure hit with dog lovers everywhere." Kirkus

355.8   Military equipment and supplies (Matériel)

Byam, Michele

Arms & armor; written by Michéle Byam. rev ed; DK Pub. 2004 72p il (DK eyewitness books) $15.99

Grades: 4 5 6 7   **355.8**

1. Armor 2. Weapons

ISBN 0-7566-0654-3

LC 2004-558979

First published 1988 by Knopf

A photo essay examining the design, construction, and uses of hand weapons and armor from a Stone Age axe to the revolvers and rifles of the Wild West

358.4   Air forces and warfare

Schwartz, Heather E.

Women of the U.S. Air Force; aiming high. Capstone Press 2011 32p (Women in the U.S. Armed Forces) lib bdg $26.65

Grades: 4 5 6 7   **358.4**

1. Women air pilots 2. Women in the armed forces

ISBN 978-1-4296-5449-4; 1-4296-5449-X

LC 2010040749

Describes the past, present, and future of women in the U.S. Air Force.

The book has "a snappy design and eye-catching photographs, and the [text is] written with struggling readers in mind. The content is engaging, the material is worthy, and the [package is] attractive." SLJ

Includes glossary and bibliographical references

359   Sea forces and warfare

Llanas, Sheila Griffin

Women of the U.S. Navy; making waves. Capstone Press 2011 32p il (Women in the U. S. Armed Forces) lib bdg $26.65

Grades: 4 5 6 7   **359**

1. Sailors 2. Women in the armed forces

ISBN 978-1-4296-5448-7; 1-4296-5448-1

LC 2010040801

This book explains "how women's roles in the U.S. [Navy] have evolved over the years. [The] volume starts with an account of one specific servicewoman and then delves into her branch's history. [The book has] a snappy design and eye-catching photographs, and the [text is] written with struggling readers in mind. The content is engaging, the material is worthy, and the [package is] attractive." SLJ

Includes glossary and bibliographical references

361.2   Social action

Olien, Rebecca

Kids care! 75 ways to make a difference for people, animals & the environment. [by] Rebecca Olien; illustrations by Michael Kline. Williamson Books 2007 128p il (Williamson kids can! book) $16.99; pa $12.99

Grades: 3 4 5 6   **361.2**
  1. Social action 2. Interpersonal relations
  ISBN 978-0-8249-6793-2; 0-8249-6793-3; 978-0-
  8249-6792-5 pa; 0-8249-6792-5 pa
                                    LC 2006036186
"This book is filled with ideas that children can implement in order to make a positive impact on the world around
them. It is divided into five sections: people, pets, wildlife,
environment, and kids joining together. . . . Throughout, material is neatly organized and the book has plenty of factual
insets; color cartoon illustrations appear on every spread. . .
. This is an excellent resource." SLJ
  Includes bibliographical references

361.3 Social work

O'Neal, Claire
  Volunteering in your school. Mitchell Lane Publishers 2011 47p (How to help: a guide to giving back) lib
bdg $29.95
Grades: 4 5 6   **361.3**
  1. Volunteer work
  ISBN 978-1-58415-920-9; 1-58415-920-0
                                    LC 2010011982
This suggests ways in which young people can volunteer
to do such tasks as participating in a clean-up day, setting
up a recycling center, or planting a garden to enhance and
contribute to the school community.
  This "well-organized [book] will encourage children
to contribute to the world around them. [The] title is filled
with examples of volunteer opportunities that can be accomplished with some adult involvement and supervision to
guide, steer, and maintain focus so that youngsters will have
varied and successful experiences." SLJ
  Includes bibliographical references

  Ways to help in your community. Mitchell Lane 2010
47p il (How to help: a guide to giving back) lib bdg $29.95
Grades: 4 5 6   **361.3**
  1. Community life 2. Volunteer work
  ISBN 978-1-58415-921-6 lib bdg; 1-58415-921-9
  lib bdg
This "well-organized [book] will encourage children
to contribute to the world around them. [The] title is filled
with examples of volunteer opportunities that can be accomplished with some adult involvement and supervision to
guide, steer, and maintain focus so that youngsters will have
varied and successful experiences. . . . [The book] offers specific examples and steps for making a neighborhood safer,
organizing yard sales, spending time with an elderly person,
helping at a soup kitchen, or offering to do storyhours at a
library." SLJ
  Includes bibliographical references

361.7 Private action

Reusser, Kayleen
  Celebrities giving back. Mitchell Lane Publishers
2011 47p (How to help: a guide to giving back) lib bdg
$29.95

Grades: 4 5 6   **361.7**
  1. Charities 2. Celebrities 3. Philanthropists
  ISBN 978-1-58415-922-3 lib bdg; 1-58415-922-7
  lib bdg
                                    LC 2010014904
"Reusser writes about 17 people, including Bono and
his interest in eliminating world hunger and poverty, President Carter's dreams of building homes for the homeless,
and charitable works by Rihanna, Shakira, Tony Hawk, and
others." SLJ
  Includes bibliographical references

Shoveller, Herb
  Ryan and Jimmy; and the well in Africa that brought
them together. Kids Can Press 2006 55p il $16.95; pa
$9.95
Grades: 3 4 5 6   **361.7**
  1. Wells 2. Children 3. Social action 4. International
cooperation 5. Humanitarians
  ISBN 978-1-55337-967-6; 1-55337-967-5; 978-1-
  55453-271-1 pa; 1-55453-271-X pa
This is an account of the a Canadian boy named Ryan
Hreljac, whose efforts helped provide clean drinking water
to a village in Uganda, and who befriended and ultimately
rescued a boy named Akana Jimmy from Ugandan rebels
  "Clearly written and illustrated with full-color family
photographs set against colorful backgrounds, this story is
both personal and representative of the many people living
in developing countries, the individuals working against all
odds to help them, and the power of young people to make
a difference." SLJ

362.1 People with illnesses and disabilities

Barber, Nicola
  Going to the hospital. PowerKids Press 2009 24p il
(The big day!) lib bdg $21.25; pa $8.25
Grades: PreK K 1   **362.1**
  1. Hospitals 2. Medical care
  ISBN 978-1-4358-2840-7 lib bdg; 1-4358-2840-2 lib
  bdg; 978-1-4358-2896-4 pa; 1-4358-2896-8 pa
                                    LC 2008025812
"Children in kindergarten will enjoy [this book] as a
read-aloud] . . . while those at the end of first grade will
be able to read [it] independently. The writing is straightforward and reassuring, and the content provides a realistic
view of what youngsters might experience in [a hospital]. . . .
[The book] discusses sickness, admission and surroundings,
fasting for surgery, and blood tests." SLJ
  Includes bibliographical references

Fleischman, John
  ★ **Phineas** Gage: a gruesome but true story about brain
science. Houghton Mifflin 2002 86p il $16; pa $8.95
Grades: 5 6 7 8 9   **362.1**
  1. Railroad workers 2. Brain -- Wounds and injuries 3.
Brain damage -- Complications 4. Personality disorders
-- Etiology 5. Brain damage -- Patients -- United States
-- Biography
  ISBN 0-618-05252-6; 0-618-49478-2 pa
                                    LC 2001-39253

"The author deftly introduces readers to a diverse range of relevant scientific history as well as more specific beliefs that influenced the medical establishment's understanding of Gage, then goes on to examine subsequent neurological discoveries that have changed and enhanced our understanding of Gage's fate. The book's present-tense narrative is inviting and intimate, and the text is crisp and lucid." Bull Cent Child Books

Includes glossary and bibliographical references

Parker, Victoria

Going to the hospital; [by] Vic Parker. Heinemann Library 2011 24p il (Growing up) lib bdg $22; pa $6.49

Grades: PreK K 1 2   362.1

1. Hospitals 2. Medical care

ISBN 978-1-4329-4797-2 lib bdg; 1-4329-4797-4 lib bdg; 978-1-4329-4807-8 pa; 1-4329-4807-5 pa

LC 2010024191

This describes the experience of being a patient in a hospital.

Includes bibliographical references

362.18   Emergency services

Shepherd, Jodie

A day with paramedics; by Jodie Shepherd. Children's Press 2013 32 p. (pbk.) $5.95

Grades: K 1 2   362.18

1. Emergency medical technicians 2. Emergency medical services -- Juvenile literature

ISBN 0531289540; 9780531289549; 9780531292549

LC 2012013358

This book describes the job of paramedics. "In four short chapters dominated by photos of stretchers, oxygen masks, and neck braces . . . and a couple lines of text, [Jodie] Shepherd . . . list[s] where you find paramedics (football games, fairs) and establish[es] their professionalism: "They work quickly and calmly.' After stating that paramedics sometimes restart hearts or lungs, we go inside the ambulance . . . before wrapping up with some odder means of rescue (skis and helicopters)." (Booklist)

362.29   Substance abuse

Gottfried, Ted

Marijuana; by Ted Gottfried with Lisa Harkrader. Marshall Cavendish Benchmark 2010 32p il (Drug facts) $19.95

Grades: 4 5 6 7   362.29

1. Marijuana

ISBN 978-0-7614-4351-3; 0-7614-4351-7

LC 2008-52761

"Provides clear explanations about effects, followed by diagrams of the body to clarify the specific organs/body systems that suffer the most damage. . . . An excellent starting point." SLJ

Includes glossary

LeVert, Suzanne

Ecstasy; by Suzanne LeVert with Jeff Hendricks. Marshall Cavendish Benchmark 2010 32p il (Drug facts) $19.95

Grades: 4 5 6 7   362.29

1. Drug abuse 2. Designer drugs 3. Ecstasy (Drug)

ISBN 978-0-7614-4349-0; 0-7614-4349-5

LC 2008-52753

"Provides clear explanations about effects, followed by diagrams of the body to clarify the specific organs/body systems that suffer the most damage. . . . An excellent starting point." SLJ

Includes glossary

Steroids; by Suzanne LeVert with Jim Whiting. Marshall Cavendish Benchmark 2010 32p il (Drug facts) $19.95

Grades: 4 5 6 7   362.29

1. Steroids 2. Sports -- Corrupt practices

ISBN 978-0-7614-4352-0; 0-7614-4352-5

LC 2008-52752

"Provides clear explanations about effects, followed by diagrams of the body to clarify the specific organs/body systems that suffer the most damage. . . . An excellent starting point." SLJ

Includes glossary

Menhard, Francha Roffe

The facts about inhalants; by Francha Roffe Menhard with Laura Purdie Salas. Marshall Cavendish Benchmark 2010 32p il (Drug facts) $19.95

Grades: 4 5 6 7   362.29

1. Inhalant abuse

ISBN 978-0-7614-4350-6; 0-7614-4350-9

LC 2008-52739

"Provides clear explanations about effects, followed by diagrams of the body to clarify the specific organs/body systems that suffer the most damage. . . . An excellent starting point." SLJ

Includes glossary

Schaefer, Adam

Steroids; [by] A.R. Schaefer. Cherry Lake Pub. 2009 32p il (Health at risk) lib bdg $27.07

Grades: 4 5 6 7   362.29

1. Steroids 2. Athletes -- Drug use

ISBN 978-1-60279-287-6 lib bdg; 1-60279-287-9 lib bdg

LC 2008017502

This describes how steroids affect the body and what sports groups are doing to halt their use.

"Great for reports or reluctant readers." Booklist

Includes bibliographical references

362.292   Alcohol

Bjornlund, Lydia D.

Alcohol; [by] Lydia Bjornlund. Cherry Lake Pub. 2009 32p il (Health at risk) lib bdg $27.07

Grades: 4 5 6 7   **362.292**
1. Alcohol 2. Alcoholism
ISBN 978-1-60279-280-7 lib bdg; 1-60279-280-1
lib bdg
    LC 2008017495
This describes the effects of alcohol, the dangers of driving drunk, how to get help, and how to make good choices.
"Great for reports or reluctant readers." Booklist
Includes bibliographical references

Gottfried, Ted
Alcohol; by Ted Gottfried with Katherine Follett. Marshall Cavendish Benchmark 2010 32p il (Drug facts) $19.95
Grades: 4 5 6 7   **362.292**
1. Alcoholism 2. Drinking of alcoholic beverages 3. Alcohol -- Physiological effect
ISBN 978-0-7614-4348-3; 0-7614-4348-7
    LC 2008-52751
"Provides clear explanations about effects, followed by diagrams of the body to clarify the specific organs/body systems that suffer the most damage. . . . An excellent starting point." SLJ
Includes glossary

362.4   People with physical disabilities

Bozzo, Linda
Guide dog heroes. Enslow Publishers 2010 48p il (Amazing working dogs with American Humane) lib bdg $23.93
Grades: 2 3 4   **362.4**
1. Guide dogs
ISBN 978-0-7660-3198-2; 0-7660-3198-5
This describes the work of guide dogs, the breeds that are best suited to the job, the training required, the tasks the dogs perform, and what happens to them after they retire.
"Full-color photos, some full page, appear throughout. [This book is] clearly written in a personable style, with plenty of anecdotal and factual information, which makes [it] suitable for report writing and enjoyable for general reading." SLJ
Includes glossary and bibliographical references

Service dog heroes. Enslow Publishers 2010 48p il (Amazing working dogs with American Humane) lib bdg $23.93
Grades: 2 3 4   **362.4**
1. Working dogs 2. Animals and the handicapped
ISBN 978-0-7660-3199-9; 0-7660-3199-3
This describes the work of service dogs who help people with disabilities, the breeds that are best suited to the work, the training required, the tasks the dogs perform, and what happens to them after they retire.
"Full-color photos, some full page, appear throughout. [This book is] clearly written in a personable style, with plenty of anecdotal and factual information, which makes [it] suitable for report writing and enjoyable for general reading." SLJ
Includes glossary and bibliographical references

Goldish, Meish
Prison puppies. Bearport Pub. 2011 32p il (Dog heroes) lib bdg $25.27
Grades: 3 4 5   **362.4**
1. Prisoners 2. Animals and the handicapped
ISBN 978-1-61772-151-9; 1-61772-151-4
    LC 2010037154
In this book, "readers learn about the 'Puppies Behind Bars' program, where inmates train dogs for careers as service animals. While the future work duties of the dogs are evident, the real story here is how they give the inmates an opportunity to contribute to society in a positive way. . . . [This book is] engaging not just because the content is so compelling, but also because the [author has] highlighted specific dogs currently working in [this field]. The use of real names and full-color photographs on every page, many contributed by the individuals who work with these dogs, makes reading [this book] a personal experience. . . . [An] excellent [introduction] to [this] new [development] in service-dog training." SLJ
Includes glossary and bibliographical references

Hoffman, Mary Ann
Helping dogs. Gareth Stevens Pub. 2011 24p il (Working dogs) lib bdg $22.60; pa $8.15
Grades: 2 3 4   **362.4**
1. Animals and the handicapped
ISBN 978-1-4339-4651-6 lib bdg; 1-4339-4651-3 lib bdg; 978-1-4339-4652-3 pa; 1-4339-4652-1 pa
    LC 2010035242
This describes helping "dogs and the training they receive. The short chapters, complemented by numerous color photographs, provide examples of particular breeds that do [this] job and show how their characteristics are suited for the tasks. The charts provided are especially helpful, covering commands and more specific tasks. There is enough information to make the [text] feel fresh. . . . A solid choice for readers looking for more than cute pictures." SLJ

Hopkinson, Deborah
Annie and Helen; by Deborah Hopkinson; illustrated by Raul Colón. Schwartz & Wade Books 2012 48 p. $17.99
Grades: 2 3 4 5   **362.4**
1. Reading 2. Female friendship 3. Deafblind women -- United States -- Biography -- Juvenile literature
ISBN 0375857060; 9780375857065; 9780375957062
    LC 2010031443
Author Deborah Hopkinson presents a picture-book biography on Helen Keller. "Focusing on the relationship between Helen and her teacher, Annie Sullivan, the book is interspersed with excerpts of Annie's letters home, written as she struggled with her angry, wild pupil. But slowly, with devotion and determination, Annie teaches Helen finger spelling and braille, letters, and sentences. As Helen comes to understand language and starts to communicate, she connects for the first time with her family and the world around her." (Publisher's note)
Includes bibliographical references.

Lambert, Joseph
The Center for Cartoon Studies presents Annie Sullivan and the trials of Helen Keller; by Joseph Lambert; with an introduction by TK. Disney Hyperion Books 2012 96 p.

Grades: 5 6 7   **362.4**
1. Women authors -- Biography 2. Handicapped --
Graphic novels 3. Female friendship -- Graphic novels
4. Graphic novels 5. Women -- United States -- History
6. Women -- United States -- Biography 7. Female
friendship -- United States -- History
ISBN 9781423113362

LC 2011036324

This nonfiction graphic novel about Annie Sullivan and
Helen Keller "focuses on the trials both Annie and Helen
struggle with in their lives," particularly the incident when
Helen was accused of plagiarism in her story 'The Frost
King' and interrogated at the Perkins Institution. "Helen's
perspective is . . . communicated in dialogue-free black panels in which she is represented as only a gray silhouette" by
author/illustrator Joseph Lambert. (Kirkus)

Martin, Claudia
    Helpers. Marshall Cavendish Benchmark 2010 64p il
(Working animals) lib bdg $28.50
Grades: 4 5 6 7   **362.4**
    1. Animals and the handicapped
    ISBN 978-1-60870-163-6 lib bdg; 1-60870-163-8
lib bdg

"Attractively designed and packed with information. . .
. The composition of each page is attractively set up with
well-selected and reproduced stock and historical photos."
SLJ

Patent, Dorothy Hinshaw
    ★ The **right** dog for the job; Ira's path from service
dog to guide dog. photographs by William Muñoz. Walker
& Co. 2004 un il $16.95
Grades: 2 3 4   **362.4**
    1. Guide dogs 2. Animals and the handicapped 3.
    Animals -- Training
    ISBN 0-8027-8914-5

LC 2003-65785

This "photo-essay follows a puppy from his training to
become a service dog to becoming a guide dog. . . . . The
author . . . manages to slip in an extraordinary amount of
information about the raising and training of guide dogs. . . .
Myriad full-color photographs that will capture kids' interest
accompany the text." SLJ

Rappaport, Doreen, 1939-
    ★ **Helen's** big world; the life of Helen Keller. written
by Doreen Rappaport; illustrated by Matt Tavares. Disney/
Hyperion Books 2012 48 p. $17.99
Grades: K 1 2 3 4   **362.4**
    1. Disabilities 2. Picture books for children 3.
    Deafblind women -- United States -- Biography --
    Juvenile literature 4. Deafblind people -- United States
    -- Biography -- Juvenile literature
    ISBN 078680890X; 9780786808908

LC 2011053516

In this children's picture-book biography of Helen
Keller, author Doreen Rappaport and illustrator Matt Tavares begin "when Keller was a healthy baby . . . and end . . .
with her death at 87, when she had long been a national icon
and social activist." Her teacher Annie Sullivan is featured
throughout the book, which "conveys . . . both the catastrophic nature of Helen's disabilities and the steely will that
raged to be unleashed." (Publishers Weekly)
    Includes bibliographical references.

362.5   Poor people

Lynette, Rachel
    What to do when your family loses its home. PowerKids
Press 2010 24p il (Let's work it out) lib bdg $21.25; pa
$8.25
Grades: 2 3 4   **362.5**
    1. Homeless persons
    ISBN 978-1-4358-9339-9 lib bdg; 1-4358-9339-5 lib
    bdg; 978-1-4358-9766-3 pa; 1-4358-9766-8 pa

"Full-page color photographs appear opposite the [nar-
rative], depicting multicultural children, parents, grandparents, social workers, and others, whose demeanors match
the hopeful tone of the [title]. This . . . . will help promote
empathy and understanding for the plight of others and is a
key purchase." SLJ
    Includes glossary

Mason, Paul, 1967-
    Poverty; [by] Paul Mason. Heinemann Library 2006
48p il map (Planet under pressure) lib bdg $31.43
Grades: 4 5 6 7   **362.5**
    1. Poverty
    ISBN 1-4034-7743-4

LC 2005017166

"Mason presents common factors for poverty worldwide, such as lack of money and education, as well as natural disasters. He also addresses the effects of outsourcing
jobs from wealthier countries to poorer ones and how poverty affects environment. The book should make the global
situation clearer. [This has] numerous quality color visuals,
and sidebars. Up-to-date and informative." SLJ
    Includes bibliographical references

362.7   Young people

Krementz, Jill
    How it feels to be adopted. Knopf 1982 107p il hard-
cover o.p. pa $15
Grades: 4 5 6 7   **362.7**
    1. Adoption
    ISBN 0-394-75853-6 pa

LC 82-48011

This "is an important contribution to literature on adoption and the question of searching for biological parents."
SLJ
    Includes bibliographical references

Lynette, Rachel
    What to do when your family is on welfare. PowerKids
Press 2010 24p il (Let's work it out) lib bdg $21.25; pa
$8.25
Grades: 2 3 4   **362.7**
    1. Public welfare
    ISBN 978-1-4358-9337-5 lib bdg; 1-4358-9337-9 lib
    bdg; 978-1-4358-9762-5 pa; 1-4358-9762-5 pa

LC 2009-19863

"Full-page color photographs appear opposite the [narrative], depicting multicultural children, parents, grandparents, social workers, and others, whose demeanors match the hopeful tone of the [title]. This . . . will help promote empathy and understanding for the plight of others and is a key purchase." SLJ

Includes glossary

Parr, Todd

We belong together; a book about adoption and families. Little, Brown 2007 32p il $15.99

Grades: PreK K   362.7

1. Family 2. Adoption

ISBN 0-316-01668-3

"Parr illustrates the rewards of family ties in this heartfelt, supportive book geared toward adopted children and their parents. In each double-page spread, Parr completes the phrase 'We belong together because . . .' with poignant explanations that touch upon basic, tangible needs . . . as well as emotional ones. . . . Cheerful, friendly artwork, with thickly outlined forms and characters and a bold rainbow palette, inclusively depicts an array of children and families—including one with a single parent and one with two dads." Booklist

Rotner, Shelley

I'm adopted! by Shelley Rotner and Sheila M. Kelly; photographs by Shelley Rotner. Holiday House 2011 un il $16.95

Grades: PreK K 1   362.7

1. Adoption

ISBN 978-0-8234-2294-4; 0-8234-2294-1

LC 2010029561

"This introduction to adoption for very young children stands out in its clear, accessible approach to [the] topic. . . . Engaging, full-color photos portray kids and parents of varying ethnicities and families of varying compositions. The process of adoption is explained in simple language that children understand. . . . Both domestic and international adoption are addressed, making this suitable for all kinds of adoptive families. The photo album-like design . . . adds to the appeal." Kirkus

Saul, Laya

Ways to help disadvantaged youth. Mitchell Lane Publishers 2011 47p (How to help: a guide to giving back) lib bdg $29.95

Grades: 4 5 6   362.7

1. Poor 2. Social action

ISBN 978-1-58415-918-6; 1-58415-918-9

LC 2010006536

This "well-organized [book] will encourage children to contribute to the world around them. [This] title is filled with examples of volunteer opportunities that can be accomplished with some adult involvement and supervision to guide, steer, and maintain focus so that youngsters will have varied and successful experiences. . . . [The book] suggests tutoring, having a toy or food drive, etc." SLJ

Includes bibliographical references

Stewart, Sheila

A **house** between homes; kids in the foster care system. by Sheila Stewart and Camden Flath. Mason Crest Publish-

ers 2010 48p il (Kids have troubles too) lib bdg $19.95; pa $7.95

Grades: 3 4 5 6   362.7

1. Foster home care

ISBN 978-1-4222-1692-7 lib bdg; 1-4222-1692-6 lib bdg; 978-1-4222-1905-8 pa; 1-4222-1905-4 pa

LC 2010012756

"The prose is respectable in its dialogue, character development, and pacing... This series will be well placed in a school media center, as well as in any institution that serves high-risk children." SLJ

Includes bibliographical references

362.73   Institutional and related services

Warren, Andrea

★ We rode the orphan trains. Houghton Mifflin 2001 132p il $18; pa $8.95

Grades: 4 5 6 7   362.73

1. Orphans 2. Orphan trains

ISBN 0-618-11712-1; 0-618-11712-1 pa

LC 00-47279

"This is powerful nonfiction for classroom and personal reading and for discussion." Booklist

Includes bibliographical references

362.82   Families

Stewart, Sheila

When Daddy hit Mommy; by Sheila Stewart and Rae Simons. Mason Crest Publishers 2011 48p il (Kids have troubles too) lib bdg $19.95; pa $7.95

Grades: 3 4 5   362.82

1. Child abuse 2. Domestic violence

ISBN 978-1-4222-1696-5 lib bdg; 1-4222-1696-9 lib bdg; 978-1-4222-1909-6 pa; 1-4222-1909-7 pa

LC 2010029346

Includes bibliographical references

363.1   Public safety programs

Aronson, Marc

★ Trapped; how the world rescued 33 miners from 2,000 feet below the Chilean desert. Atheneum 2011 144p il

Grades: 4 5 6 7   363.1

1. Rescue work 2. Gold mines and mining 3. Copper mines and mining 4. San José Mine Accident, Chile, 2010 -- Juvenile literature

ISBN 1-4169-1397-1; 978-1-4169-1397-9

LC 2011000777

This title is about thirty-three miners trapped in a copper-gold mine in San Jose, Chile and how experts from around the world, from drillers, to astronauts, to submarine specialists, came together to make their remarkable rescue possible.

This is "a riveting, in-depth recounting of the events that held the world rapt. . . . Twelve short chapters with photos and diagrams keep the story well-paced." Publ Wkly

Includes bibliographical references

Benoit, Peter
The **Hindenburg** disaster. Children's Press 2011 48p
il map (True book) lib bdg $28
Grades: 3 4 5   **363.1**
1. Airships 2. Aircraft accidents
ISBN 978-0-531-20626-3 lib bdg; 0-531-20626-2 lib
bdg; 978-0-531-29025-5 pa; 0-531-29025-5 pa
                                          LC 2010045931
This describes how the Hindenburg blimp crashed and
burned in New Jersey on May 6, 1937.
"Benoit provides unbiased information that is on target
for the intended audience. . . . The photographs and reproductions enhance the [text]. . . . [This book is] well-conceived." SLJ
Includes bibliographical references

Nuclear meltdowns. Children's Press 2011 48p il
(True book: disasters) lib bdg $28; pa $6.99
Grades: 3 4 5   **363.1**
1. Chernobyl Nuclear Accident, Chernobyl, Ukraine,
1986 2. Nuclear power plants -- Security measures
ISBN 978-0-531-25422-6 lib bdg; 0-531-25422-4;
978-0-531-26627-4 pa; 0-531-26627-3 pa
                                          LC 2011007142
This describes nuclear power plant accidents at Three
Mile Island, Chernobyl, and in Japan.
This is "thoughtfully designed. . . . The information . . .
is right on target: concise, accurate, and thorough. . . . The
photographs . . . are especially effective at putting a human
face on large-scale devastation." Booklist
Includes glossary and bibliographical references

363.11 Occupational and industrial hazards

Scott, Elaine
★ **Buried** alive! how 33 miners survived 69 days deep
under the Chilean desert. Elaine Scott. Houghton Mifflin Harcourt 2012 80 p. col. ill., col. maps (hardcover)
$17.99; (ebook) $17.99
Grades: 4 5 6 7 8   **363.11**
1. Miners 2. Disasters 3. Industrial accidents 4.
San José Mine Accident, Chile, 2010 5. Mine rescue
work -- Chile -- Copiapó Region 6. San José Mine
Accident, Chile, 2010 -- Juvenile literature 7. Gold
mines and mining -- Accidents -- Chile -- Copiapó
Region 8. Copper mines and mining -- Accidents --
Chile -- Copiapó Region 9. Mine rescue work -- Chile
-- Copiapó Region -- Juvenile literature 10. Gold mines
and mining -- Accidents -- Chile -- Copiapó Region
-- Juvenile literature 11. Copper mines and mining
-- Accidents -- Chile -- Copiapó Region -- Juvenile
literature
ISBN 0547707789; 9780547707785; 9780547691787
                                          LC 2011025945
Author Elaine Scott chronicles the events that took place
"[o]n August 5, 2010, [when] a copper mine in Chile col-
lapsed, trapping 33 miners nearly half a mile underground
. . . [The author] describes the choices the miners' strong
leader advised that prolonged their survival long enough to
be rescued and the creative solutions that effected that rescue. They drilled through over 2,000 feet of especially hard
rock, delivered supplies to the trapped men through a tiny

bore hole and then invented a way to carry the men, one at a
time, to the surface in a very small capsule." (Kirkus)
Includes bibliographical references (p. 78) and index.

363.12 Transportation hazards

Verstraete, Larry
Surviving the Hindenburg; by Larry Verstraete; illus-
trated by David Geister. Sleeping Bear Press 2012 32 p.
col. ill.
Grades: 2 3 4   **363.12**
1. Airships 2. Aeronautics -- Juvenile literature 3.
Aircraft accidents -- Juvenile literature 4. Hindenburg
(Airship) -- Juvenile literature 5. Cabin boys -- Germany
-- Biography -- Juvenile literature 6. Airships --
Germany -- History -- 20th century -- Juvenile literature
7. Survival -- New Jersey -- History -- 20th century --
Juvenile literature 8. Aircraft accident victims -- New
Jersey -- Biography -- Juvenile literature 9. Aircraft
accidents -- New Jersey -- History -- 20th century --
Juvenile literature
ISBN 1585367877; 9781585367870
                                          LC 2011027879
This historical story, by Larry Verstraete and David
Geister, relates the story of the German airship "Hindenburg." "On May 6, 1937, the . . . airship . . . exploded. . . .
62 survived, including Werner Franz, the ship's 14-year-old
cabin boy. . . . Verstrate recounts young Werner's story. . . .
Through Werner's memories young readers will explore the
inner workings of the giant airship . . . and hold their breath
during Werner's terrifying escape from the fiery devastation." (Publisher's note)

363.2 Police services

Arroyo, Sheri L.
How crime fighters use math; math curriculum consultant: Rhea A. Stewart. Chelsea Clubhouse 2010 32p il
(Math in the real world) lib bdg $28
Grades: 4 5 6   **363.2**
1. Mathematics 2. Vocational guidance 3. Criminal
investigation
ISBN 978-1-60413-602-9 lib bdg; 1-60413-602-2
lib bdg
                                          LC 2009-23330
"The layout for [this] slim [title] is bright and colorful
with a photograph and a 'You Do the Math' problem to solve
and large, easy-to-read text on every spread. An answer key
is included in the back matter, along with a page detailing
the career choices and the educational requirements. [It]
touches on crime-scene grids, the importance of shoe prints
in tracking a criminal, cracking secret codes, and more. . . .
[This title] would be useful to supplement lessons on mathematics. [It] will also appeal to students wanting to learn
more about math as it relates to specific careers." SLJ
Includes glossary and bibliographical references

Bozzo, Linda
Police dog heroes. Enslow Publishers 2010 48p il
(Amazing working dogs with American Humane) lib bdg
$23.93

Grades: 2 3 4 **363.2**

1. Working dogs 2. Animals in police work

ISBN 978-0-7660-3197-5; 0-7660-3197-7

LC 2008048017

"Full-color photos, some full page, appear throughout. [This book is] clearly written in a personable style, with plenty of anecdotal and factual information, which makes [it] suitable for report writing and enjoyable for general reading." SLJ

Includes glossary and bibliographical references

Graham, Ian

Forensic technology. Smart Apple Media 2011 il (New technology) lib bdg $34.25

Grades: 4 5 6 7 **363.2**

1. Forensic sciences 2. Criminal investigation

ISBN 978-1-599-20532-8; 1-599-20532-7

LC 2010044238

Describes the technology used by forensic scientists to gather and analyze evidence from crime scenes.

This "offers a fine overview for reports, and its attractive design may also entice middle-grade readers to learn more." Booklist

Hoffman, Mary Ann

Police dogs. Gareth Stevens Pub. 2011 24p il (Working dogs) lib bdg $22.60; pa $8.15

Grades: 2 3 4 **363.2**

1. Dogs

ISBN 978-1-4339-4659-2 lib bdg; 1-4339-4659-9 lib bdg; 978-1-4339-4660-8 pa; 1-4339-4660-2 pa

LC 2010035244

This describes police "dogs and the training they receive. The short chapters, complemented by numerous color photographs, provide examples of particular breeds that do [this] job and show how their characteristics are suited for the tasks. The charts provided are especially helpful, covering commands and more specific tasks. There is enough information to make the [text] feel fresh. . . . A solid choice for readers looking for more than cute pictures." SLJ

Jackson, Donna M.

★ The **wildlife** detectives; how forensic scientists fight crimes against nature. by Donna M. Jackson; photographs by Wendy Shattil and Bob Rozinski. Houghton Mifflin 2000 47p il $16

Grades: 4 5 6 7 **363.2**

1. Game protection 2. Forensic sciences 3. Wildlife conservation -- Juvenile literature 4. Poaching -- Prevention -- Juvenile literature

ISBN 0-395-86976-5

LC 99-34857

Describes how the wildlife detectives at the National Fish and Wildlife Forensics Laboratory in Ashland, Oregon, analyze clues to catch and convict people responsible for crimes against animals

This book features "a smoothly written text that unfolds almost like a mystery novel. . . . Engaging full-color photographs help clarify the text and will appeal to browsers. A list of follow-up suggestions and a glossary of terms are appended. A book that will be welcomed by mystery fans and anyone who cares about animals." Booklist

Kenney, Karen Latchana

Police officers at work; by Karen L. Kenney; illustrated by Brian Caleb Dumm; content consultant: Judith Stepan-Norris. Magic Wagon 2009 32p il (Meet your community workers!) lib bdg $18.95

Grades: K 1 2 3 **363.2**

1. Police 2. Vocational guidance

ISBN 978-1-60270-652-1 lib bdg; 1-60270-652-2 lib bdg

LC 2009-2391

This book about police officers has "an uncluttered layout and consistent organization. . . . Chapter headings such as 'Problems on the Job,' and 'Technology at Work,' and 'Special Skills and Training' make it easy to pinpoint specific information." SLJ

Includes glossary

Mezzanotte, Jim

Police. Marshall Cavendish Benchmark 2010 64p il (Working animals) lib bdg $28.50

Grades: 4 5 6 7 **363.2**

1. Animals in police work

ISBN 978-1-60870-166-7 lib bdg; 1-60870-166-2 lib bdg

LC 2010007006

Describes animals, such as dogs and horses, which work with police in such areas as search-and-rescue, tracking criminals, and sniffing out explosives

"Attractively designed and packed with information. . . . The composition of each page is attractively set up with well-selected and reproduced stock and historical photos." SLJ

Perritano, John

Science beats crime. Marshall Cavendish Benchmark 2010 48p il (Cool science) lib bdg $28.50

Grades: 5 6 7 8 **363.2**

1. Forensic sciences 2. Criminal investigation

ISBN 978-1-60870-078-3 lib bdg; 1-60870-078-X lib bdg

LC 2009053774

"Perritano briefly traces the history of forensic science, . . . discusses different subspecialities, such as toxicology and forensic anthropology, and then gets into the good stuff— fingerprinting, DNA profiling, ballistics, splatter patterns, even a gross-out spread of how studying maggots can determine time of death. Interspersed throughout are real-life case studies. . . . This solid, amply illustrated, and easy-reading introduction to forensic science ends with a look at the future of the field." Booklist

Includes glossary and bibliographical references

Spilsbury, Richard

Counterfeit! stopping fakes and forgeries. Enslow Publishers 2009 48p il (Solve that crime!) lib bdg $23.93

Grades: 5 6 7 8 **363.2**

1. Fraud 2. Forgery

ISBN 978-0-7660-3378-8 lib bdg; 0-7660-3378-3 lib bdg

LC 2008-33310

This "title boasts in-depth information, sidebars detailing events of true crime, and activities that will increase understanding. . . . Photographs are colorful, well-captioned, and related to the text." SLJ

Includes glossary and bibliographical references

Townsend, John
   Famous forensic cases. Amicus 2011 il (Amazing crime scene science) $19.95
Grades: 4 5 6 7   **363.2**
   1. Forensic sciences 2. Criminal investigation
   ISBN 978-1-60753-169-2; 1-60753-169-0
   In this book "readers will find a straight presentation of fascinating information. Loosely organized by era, the book opens with a history of fingerprinting . . . which focuses on the 1920s and 1930s. Other topics include hair science in the 1950s, voiceprints in the 1970s, and recent advancements in DNA forensics. Scatter throughout are case studies. . . . This entry features an eye-catching layout, plenty of sidebars, and well-chosen photos. . . . Kids will go for this one." Booklist

363.25 Detection of crime (Criminal investigation)

MacLeod, Elizabeth
   Bones Never Lie; How Forensics Helps Solve History's Mysteries. Elizabeth MacLeod. Firefly Books Ltd 2013 iv, 156 p.p (hardcover) $24.95
Grades: 4 5 6 7 8   **363.25**
   1. Forensic sciences -- Encyclopedias
   ISBN 1554514835; 9781554514830
   This children's book, by Elizabeth MacLeod, explores how through "forensics--the scientific way of examining physical evidence--we now know what killed Napoleon and whether Anastasia survived the massacre of the Russian royal family. Seven intriguing stories about historical royal figures whose demise was suspicious, and hard scientific facts about crime-solving techniques make each event seem like an episode of CSI rather than a history lesson." (Publisher's note)
   "In real life, forensics can be slow and tedious, but MacLeod invests these high-profile deaths with considerable vim and drama. A good selection of staged and archival photographs and artwork accompany the stories. A fully fleshed and crisply told story of forensics at its romantic best." Kirkus

363.28 Services of special kinds of security and law enforcement agencies

Butts, Ed
   Bodyguards! from gladiators to the secret service. Annick Press 2012 121 p. $24.95
Grades: 3 4 5   **363.28**
   1. Bodyguards 2. Gladiators 3. Guard animals 4. Secret service
   ISBN 1554514371; 9781554514373
   This book "includes all the information you need to become a bodyguard" as well as facts about the bodyguards of the Egyptian pharaoh and animals with hearing that makes them good alert systems. "Aside from ancient Egyptian priests and animals, other types of bodyguards mentioned include, among others, the Vatican's Swiss Guard, Abraham

Lincoln's tippling police guard and Elvis' Memphis Mafia." (Kirkus)

363.3 Other aspects of public safety

Nolan, Janet
   ★ The **firehouse** light; illustrations by Marie Lafrance. Tricycle Press 2010 un il lib bdg $18.95; $15.99
Grades: K 1 2 3   **363.3**
   1. Electric lamps 2. Fire departments
   ISBN 978-1-58246-346-9 lib bdg; 1-58246-346-8 lib bdg; 978-1-58246-298-1; 1-58246-298-4
                                          LC 2009-7964
   The true story of a lightbulb in a firehouse located in Livermore, California, that has stayed lit for more than one hundred years.
   "The narrative successfully knits firefighting and history into a fast dash through the twentieth century. . . . Flat, folk-style acrylic illustrations feature fluid, sinewy human figures amid a variety of vintage fire trucks." Booklist

363.34 Disasters

Bailey, Gerry
   Fragile planet. Gareth Stevens Pub. 2011 48p il map (Planet SOS) lib bdg $31.95; pa $14.05
Grades: 4 5 6   **363.34**
   1. Natural disasters
   ISBN 978-1-4339-4974-6 lib bdg; 1-4339-4974-1 lib bdg; 978-1-4339-4975-3 pa; 1-4339-4975-X pa
                                          LC 2010032886
   This "well-designed [book]. . . . discusses natural events and disasters, such as avalanches, earthquakes, floods, hurricanes, lightning, volcanoes, and windstorms. . . . The many large, colorful photos will engage readers and assist them in understanding the important concepts introduced." SLJ
   Includes glossary

Fradin, Judith Bloom
   ★ **Droughts**; [by] Judy & Dennis Fradin. National Geographic 2008 48p il map (Witness to disaster) $16.95; lib bdg $20.90
Grades: 4 5 6 7   **363.34**
   1. Droughts
   ISBN 978-1-4263-0339-5; 1-4263-0339-4; 978-1-4263-0340-1 lib bdg; 1-4263-0340-8 lib bdg
                                          LC 2008020424
   "This book examines the lessons from the Dust Bowl droughts for farmers, including the importance of topsoil. The history of droughts around the world compares impacts on a wide variety of societies. The final chapter looks at the latest tools and technologies developed to help us survive future droughts." Publisher's note
   Includes glossary and bibliographical references

   Hurricane Katrina; [by] Judith Bloom Fradin, Dennis Brindell Fradin. Marshall Cavendish Benchmark 2009 47p il map (Turning points in U.S. history) lib bdg $21.95

Grades: 3 4 5   **363.34**
1. Hurricane Katrina, 2005
ISBN 978-0-7614-4261-5 lib bdg; 0-7614-4261-8
lib bdg

LC 2008038268

This book provides "accurate, nonsensationalized information in [a] well-organized, clearly written, and politically neutral [text]. The photos are crisp, and, due to the subject matter, heartrending." SLJ
Includes glossary and bibliographical references

Garbe, Suzanne
The **Worst** wildfires of all time; by Suzanne Garbe. Capstone Press 2013 32 p. ill. (chiefly col.), col. maps (library) $27.32
Grades: 4 5 6 7   **363.34**
1. Wildfires -- Juvenile literature 2. Natural disasters -- Juvenile literature
ISBN 1429684186; 9781429684187

LC 2011053150

This book by Suzanne Garbe is part of the Epic Disasters series and looks at the worst wildfires of all time. "These uncontrolled fires can strike in the blink of an eye and spread just as quickly. Put out the flames and read about the worst wildfires in history." The series allows readers to "witness the destructive power of hurricanes, earthquakes, and more." (Publisher's note)
Includes bibliographical references and index.

Karwoski, Gail
Tsunami; the true story of an April Fools' Day disaster. [by] Gail Langer Karwoski; illustrated by John MacDonald. Darby Creek Pub. 2006 64p il $17.95
Grades: 4 5 6 7   **363.34**
1. Tsunamis 2. Hawaii -- History
ISBN 1-58196-044-1

The author "opens with a description of the tsunami waves that struck the northern coast of the Hawaiian Islands in 1946, destroying a school and sweeping many children and adults out to sea. The book goes on to provide broader information about tsunamis, from scientific understanding of how they occur to ongoing efforts at early warning systems. . . . Clearly written and informative." Booklist

Langley, Andrew
Hurricanes, tsunamis, and other natural disasters; [by] Andrew Langley. Kingfisher 2006 63p il map (Kingfisher knowledge) $12.95
Grades: 5 6 7 8   **363.34**
1. Natural disasters
ISBN 978-0-7534-5975-1; 0-7534-5975-2

LC 2005027200

This briefly describes such natural disasters as hurricanes, tsunamis, avalanches, brush fires, earthquakes, floods, tornadoes, drought and famine, pandemics, with many color illustrations and maps
"This book presents a high-interest topic in an attractively designed format that features colorful, eye-catching graphics and a solidly written text." Booklist
Includes glossary and bibliographical references

Markle, Sandra
★ **Rescues!** Millbrook Press 2006 88p il map lib bdg $25.26

Grades: 4 5 6 7   **363.34**
1. Rescue work 2. Survival after airplane accidents, shipwrecks, etc.
ISBN 978-0-8225-3413-6 lib bdg; 0-8225-3413-4
lib bdg

LC 2005-09707

"From the collapse of a Pennsylvania coal mine in 2002 to the tsunami that struck 11 countries in 2004 to Hurricane Katrina in 2005, the 11 disasters Markle describes are straight from news headlines. In this full-color photo-essay, she uses individual experiences of rescue and survival to bring each drama close." Booklist
Includes bibliographical references

Meyer, Susan
Adapting to flooding and rising sea levels; Susan Meyer. 1st ed. Rosen Central 2012 64 p. col. ill., col. maps (Science to the rescue: Adapting to climate change) (library) $31.95
Grades: 4 5 6   **363.34**
1. Sea level 2. Climate change 3. Global warming 4. Floods 5. Climatic changes 6. Sea level -- Climatic factors
ISBN 1448868475; 9781448868476

LC 2011045624

This book is part of the Science to the Rescue: Adapting to Climate Change series. It "focuses on the devastation to coastal regions worldwide caused by storms and global warming and how those issues are being addressed in various countries. A succinct explanation of the reasons for global warming and the rising sea level is followed by a section on the methods of adaptation . . . and a rundown of the current research being conducted." (Booklist)
Includes bibliographical references and index

Miller, Mara
Hurricane Katrina strikes the Gulf Coast; disaster & survival. [by] Mara Miller. Enslow Publishers 2006 48p il map (Deadly disasters) $23.93
Grades: 4 5 6 7   **363.34**
1. Hurricanes 2. Rescue work 3. Hurricane Katrina, 2005
ISBN 0-7660-2803-8

LC 2005030989

"Miller begins with an account of the development of Hurricane Katrina as it struck Florida and then threatened the Gulf Coast. She discusses the subsequent flooding of New Orleans, the damage it caused, rescue and recovery attempts, and planning for the aftermath of future hurricanes. The author includes a clear scientific description of hurricanes, defining key terms. Color photos and graphics help explain concepts such as the structure of a hurricane, Katrina's path, and the conditions endured by the victims." SLJ
Includes glossary and bibliographical references

Reilly, Kathleen M.
Natural disasters; investigate Earth's most destructive forces. by Kathleen M. Reilly; illustrated by Tom Casteel. Nomad Press 2012 121 p. (paperback) $15.95
Grades: 4 5 6 7   **363.34**
1. Weather -- Juvenile literature 2. Natural disasters -- Juvenile literature
ISBN 1619301466; 9781619301467

In this book, "spiraling winds, surging waters, eruptions, blazing forests, and chilling snows are discussed." Topics include "the MMS Scale and the Enhanced Fujita Scale." In addition to an "explanation of each type of phenomenon, safety tips, historical incidences, pen-and-ink line drawings, and correlative projects using simple materials are included." (School Library Journal)

Rusch, Elizabeth

Eruption! volcanoes and the science of saving lives. text by Elizabeth Rusch; illustrated by Tom Uhlman. Houghton Mifflin Harcourt 2013 76 p. col. ill. (hardcover) $18.99

Grades: 5 6 7 8   363.34
 1. Disaster response and recovery 2. Volcanoes -- Juvenile literature 3. Natural disasters -- Juvenile literature
 ISBN 0547503504; 9780547503509
                                           LC 2012034055
This book by Elizabeth Rusch contains "photographs and sidebars [which] reveals the perilous . . . life-saving work of an international volcano crisis team (VDAP) and the sleeping giants they study, from Colombia to the Philippines, from Chile to Indonesia. [It presents an] stunning account of volcanologists Andy Lockhart, John Pallister, and their group of scientists who risk their lives, investigating deadly volcanoes that remain constant threats to people around the world." (Publisher's note)

Includes bibliographical references (pages 74-75) and index.

Saul, Laya

Ways to help after a natural disaster; by Laya Saul. Mitchell Lane Publishers 2011 47 p. col. ill. (library) $29.95

Grades: 4 5 6   363.34
 1. Volunteer work 2. Disaster relief
 ISBN 1584159170; 9781584159179
                                           LC 2010006538
"This focuses on various activities in which children can participate to help families be prepared in the event of a natural disaster or in its aftermath, when citizens experience the devastating results. The brief sections on teaching preparedness include advice for putting together supply kits and a sample list for collecting emergency numbers. The bulk of the information is sound, practical, commonsense recommendations. . . . Included are simple measures, such as offering emotional support, as well as those that are more complicated, such as organizing drives for collecting blood or food and clothing. The design is inviting, with text appealingly laid out and offset by blocks of color." Booklist

Includes bibliographical references and index.

Somervill, Barbara A.

Graphing natural disasters. Heinemann Library 2010 32p il (Real world data) $28.21; pa $7.99

Grades: 5 6 7 8   363.34
 1. Graphic methods 2. Natural disasters
 ISBN 978-1-4329-2622-9; 1-4329-2622-5; 978-1-4329-2631-1 pa; 1-4329-2631-4 pa
                                           LC 2009001290
This describes natural disasters such as tornadoes and volcanic eruptions using graphs and charts.

The book is "colorful, easy to read, and well designed." SLJ

Includes glossary and bibliographical references

363.6   Public utilities and related services

Brown, Cynthia Light

Discover National Monuments, National Parks; natural wonders. illustrated by Blair Shedd. Nomad Press 2009 106p il (Discover your world) pa $19.95

Grades: 5 6 7 8   363.6
 1. National parks and reserves
 ISBN 978-1-9346702-8-6 pa; 1-9346702-8-6 pa
"With an inviting, browsable design and a chatty style, this large-sized volume . . . covers 15 national monuments and parks in the U.S. that celebrate and protect natural phenomena . . . The science will excite readers, with detailed explanations of tectonic plates, radiometric dating, and dendrochronology." Booklist

Burgan, Michael

Not a drop to drink; water for a thirsty world. Peter H. Gleick, consultant. National Geographic 2008 64p il map (National Geographic investigates) $17.95

Grades: 4 5 6 7   363.6
 1. Water 2. Water supply 3. Climatic changes -- Juvenile literature
 ISBN 978-1-4263-0360-9; 1-4263-0360-2
Explores the important connections between human activity and the water cycle and shows how researchers are working to understand such issues as how climate change affects water supplies and how the oceans can help solve the water crisis.

Hollyer, Beatrice

★ Our world of water; children and water around the world. foreword by Zadie Smith. Henry Holt and Co. 2009 47p il map $16.99

Grades: 3 4 5   363.6
 1. Water 2. Water supply
 ISBN 978-0-8050-8941-7; 0-8050-8941-1
                                           LC 2008040596
"Seven and eight-year-olds share what water means to them by revealing their everyday uses of it. An opening spread introduces the children and their countries—Peru, Ethiopia, Mauritania, Tajikistan, Bangladesh, and the United States—on an outline world map. Locations vary from mountaintop to seaside and from scarcity to abundance. . . . There is no order to the countries and the text is matter-of-fact, leaving readers to draw their own conclusions about the subjects' varying circumstances. Several full-color, captioned photos appear on each spread. . . . Questions will inevitably arise from this revealing look at the status of water in the world." SLJ

Includes bibliographical references

Kerley, Barbara

A cool drink of water. National Geographic Soc. 2002 un il map $16.95; pa $7.95

Grades: K 1 2 3   363.6
 1. Water 2. Water supply 3. Drinking water 4. Water

conservation 5. Water use
ISBN 0-7922-6723-0; 0-7922-5489-9 pa
LC 2001-2479

Depicts people around the world collecting, chilling, and drinking water

"Children will be entranced by the beautiful images of a basic substance that connects us all. Excellent for cross-cultural discussions." Booklist

363.7   Environmental problems

Aitken, Stephen

Earth's fever; written and illustrated by Stephen Aitken. Magic Wagon 2011 il (Climate change) $28.50
Grades: K 1 2 3   **363.7**
1. **Greenhouse effect** 2. Climate -- Environmental aspects
ISBN 1-61641-670-X; 978-1-61641-670-6
LC 2011001872

This "strikes a perfect balance for young readers. Aitken presents scientific facts straightforwardly and offers practical, age-appropriate suggestions for environmentally friendly activities. . . . The earnest cartoon illustrations . . . are generally helpful." Booklist

Albee, Sarah

★ **Poop** happened! a history of the world from the bottom up. illustrated by Robert Leighton. Walker 2010 170p il lib bdg $20.89; pa $15.99
Grades: 4 5 6 7   **363.7**
1. Feces 2. Toilets 3. Sanitation 4. Refuse and refuse disposal 5. Sanitation -- Juvenile literature 6. Refuse and refuse disposal -- Juvenile literature
ISBN 978-0-8027-9825-1 lib bdg; 0-8027-9825-X lib bdg; 978-0-8027-2077-1 pa; 0-8027-2077-3 pa

"Albee deposits a heaping history of human sanitation—or rather lack thereof— and its effects. . . . She pumps out a steady stream of comments on the miasmic effects of urbanization, waste disposal, and the roles of (not) bathing in ancient Greece, Rome, medieval Europe, . . . and the 'Reeking Renaissance.' She then digs into the gradual adoption of better practices in the nineteenth century. . . . The cartoon illustrations feature sludgy green highlights." Booklist

Barnham, Kay

★ **Recycle**; [by] Kay Barnham. Crabtree Pub. 2008 32p il (Environment action!) lib bdg $22.60; pa $7.95
Grades: K 1 2 3   **363.7**
1. Recycling
ISBN 978-0-7787-3659-2 lib bdg; 0-7787-3659-8 lib bdg; 978-0-7787-3669-1 pa; 0-7787-3669-5 pa
LC 2007030000

This book "exposes young children to concepts that can truly make a difference. . . . [The book has] plenty of colorful, relevant, and interesting glossy color photographs." Sci Books Films

Includes glossary

Barraclough, Sue

Reusing things; by Sue Barraclough. Sea to Sea Publications 2008 30p il (Making a difference) lib bdg $27.10

Grades: 1 2 3   **363.7**
1. Recycling 2. Environmental protection
ISBN 978-1-59771-109-8 lib bdg; 1-59771-109-8 lib bdg
LC 2006051277

This suggests ways in which people can reduce waste by reusing paper or junk, repairing or repainting old items, borrowing or giving away things, and buying or using second-hand things.

This features "clear, concise information that is simple to read and understand, alternating between giving simple facts and dispersing helpful hints and suggestions. The full-color photographs are crisp and attractive." SLJ

Benoit, Peter

The **BP** oil spill. Children's Press 2011 48p il map (True book) lib bdg $28; pa $6.95
Grades: 3 4 5   **363.7**
1. Gulf of Mexico oil spill, 2010
ISBN 978-0-531-20630-0 lib bdg; 0-531-20630-0 lib bdg; 978-0-531-28999-0 pa; 0-531-28999-0 pa
LC 2010045927

Photographs, maps, time lines, and text describe the events surrounding the 2010 British Petroleum oil spill in the Gulf of Mexico.

"Benoit provides unbiased information that is on target for the intended audience. . . . The photos are realistic and well chosen to show that current events can be examined as critically as historical events." SLJ

Includes bibliographical references

Bridges, Andrew

Clean air. Roaring Brook Press 2009 40p il (Sally Ride science) pa $7.99
Grades: 5 6 7 8   **363.7**
1. Air pollution 2. Greenhouse effect
ISBN 978-1-59643-576-6 pa; 1-59643-576-3 pa

This is a "well-written, engaging book. . . . The [book's] best feature is the conversational tone that simply and clearly conveys important, and sometimes complicated, scientific concepts. Illustrations and layout are well done, and include colorful photographs and charts. Excellent." SLJ

Bullard, Lisa

Power up to fight pollution; illustrated by Wes Thomas. Lerner 2011 24p il (Planet protectors) lib bdg $23.93
Grades: K 1 2 3   **363.7**
1. Pollution 2. Environmental protection
ISBN 978-0-7613-6108-4; 0-7613-6108-1
LC 2010048862

A boy named Tyler shows what makes Earth's land, air, and water dirty and ways to clean up our world.

"The bright colors used in the illustrations . . . will attract young readers to the environmental science content. . . . [The] facts are written in child-friendly language and the information should be attainable by young children. . . . [This book] will raise the environmental awareness of young children." Sci Books Films

Includes bibliographical references

Cherry, Lynne

★ **How** we know what we know about our changing climate; scientists and kids explore global warming. by

Lynne Cherry and Gary Braasch; with a foreword by David Sobel. Dawn Publications 2008 66p il $18.95; pa $11.95
Grades: 4 5 6 7   363.7
   1. Greenhouse effect 2. Climate -- Environmental aspects 3. Earth sciences -- Juvenile literature 4. Global warming -- Juvenile literature 5. Climatic changes -- Juvenile literature
   ISBN 978-1-58469-103-7; 0-1-58469-103-4; 978-1-58469-130-3 pa; 1-58469-130-1 pa
                LC 2007-37255
"The can-do emphasis helps to make the topic less depressing, and the intriguing color photographs are thoughtful and upbeat." Booklist

Cole, Joanna
   The **magic** school bus and the climate challenge; illustrated by Bruce Degen. Scholastic 2010 37p il $16.99
Grades: 2 3 4   363.7
   1. Environmental protection 2. Greenhouse effect 3. Climate -- Environmental aspects
   ISBN 978-0-590-10826-3; 0-590-10826-3
"Ms. Frizzle and her class challenge readers to go green. After traveling in their bus-plane and showing in storyboard style example after example of the Earth's changing climate, Ms. Frizzle, reluctant traveler Arnold, new South Korean classmate Joon, and the gang ride sun rays to the Earth, and then get back on the bus as those rays (and riders) get caught by heat-trapping gases." SLJ

David, Laurie
   ★ The **down**-to-earth guide to global warming; [by] Laurie David and Cambria Gordon. Orchard Books 2007 112p il map pa $15.99
Grades: 4 5 6 7   363.7
   1. Greenhouse effect 2. Climate -- Environmental aspects 3. Global warming -- Juvenile literature
   ISBN 978-0-439-02494-5 pa; 0-439-02494-3 pa
                LC 2006-35705
The authors "put forth the basics on global warming, climate change, and how readers can green up the environment. They temper the book's often troubling subject matter with kid-friendly humor, some celebrity shout-outs, and explanations of the scientific underpinnings. An amply illustrated layout, featuring attention-grabbing sidebars, dramatic photos, and diagrams, will sustain reader interest." Booklist
   Includes bibliographical references

Davies, Nicola, 1958-
   Gaia warriors; urgent; the fight is on! with an afterword by James Lovelock. Candlewick Press 2011 192p il $14.99
Grades: 5 6 7 8   363.7
   1. Gaia hypothesis 2. Environmental protection 3. Greenhouse effect 4. Climate -- Environmental aspects
   ISBN 978-0-7636-4808-4; 0-7636-4808-6
                LC 2010-40126
This "offers a dynamic overview of global warming's causes and concerns. Davies . . . devotes half the book to exciting profiles of individuals . . . who are working to slow climate change. . . . They include scientists, rock musicians, food distributors, architects, and youth organizers, and their broad variety reinforces the sense that every creative individual effort matters. Highly browsable layouts combine color

photos and quotes printed in varied, eye-catching fonts. . . . [This has a] humorous, conversational tone." Booklist
   Includes glossary

Delano, Marfe Ferguson
   ★ **Earth** in the hot seat; bulletins from a warming world. National Geographic 2009 63p il (Preserve our planet) $19.95; lib bdg $28.90
Grades: 5 6 7 8   363.7
   1. Greenhouse effect 2. Climate -- Environmental aspects 3. Global warming -- Juvenile literature 4. Climatic changes -- Juvenile literature 5. Greenhouse effect, Atmospheric -- Juvenile literature 6. Conservation of natural resources -- Juvenile literature
   ISBN 978-1-4263-0434-7; 1-4263-0434-X; 978-1-4263-0435-4 lib bdg; 1-4263-0435-8 lib bdg
                LC 2008029317
"This book lays out . . . the evidence for global warming and the part that human activity plays in it. Five chapters lay out the signs and evidences of a warming world. . . . Subsequent chapters of the book are devoted to what humankind can expect in a warming world and steps that must be taken to avert catastrophe for humans and the planet. . . . The illustrative photos are fully up to National Geographic high standards. This [is a] fine book, reasonably priced and carefully researched." Voice Youth Advocates
   Includes bibliographical references

Farrell, Courtney
   Keeping water clean. Cherry Lake Pub. 2010 32p il (Save the planet) lib bdg $27.04
Grades: 3 4 5 6   363.7
   1. Water pollution
   ISBN 978-1-60279-659-1 lib bdg; 1-60279-659-9 lib bdg
Teaches young readers the importance of unpolluted water, and describes how to keep water clean by using gray water processes, conserving drinking water, and reducing overall pollution
"At the beginning of . . . [the] book, readers are given a mission and advised to be alert to the facts provided so that they can successfully answer the questions at the end. . . . Children are made to feel part of the process; suggestions for how they can become involved abound." SLJ
   Includes glossary and bibliographical references

Geiger, Beth
   Clean water. Roaring Brook Press 2009 40p il (Sally Ride science) pa $7.99
Grades: 5 6 7 8   363.7
   1. Water supply 2. Water pollution
   ISBN 978-1-59643-577-3 pa; 1-59643-577-1 pa
This is a "well-written, engaging book. . . . The [book']s best feature is the conversational tone that simply and clearly conveys important, and sometimes complicated, scientific concepts. Illustrations and layout are well done, and include colorful photographs and charts. Excellent." SLJ

Gore, Al, 1948-
   ★ An **inconvenient** truth; the crisis of global warming. adapted for young readers by Jane O'Connor. rev ed.; Viking 2007 191p il map $23; pa $16
Grades: 5 6 7 8   363.7
   1. Greenhouse effect 2. Climate -- Environmental

aspects

ISBN 978-0-670-06271-3; 978-0-670-06272-0 pa

Adapted from the title for adults published 2006 by Rodale Press

This explains what global warming is, what causes it, and explains how to take action to stop this crisis.

This is illustrated with "easy-to-grasp graphics and revealing before-and-after photos. . . . O'Connor rephrases Gore's arguments in briefer, simpler language without compromising their flow." SLJ

Guiberson, Brenda Z.

★ **Earth** feeling the heat; illustrated by Chad Wallace. Henry Holt and Company 2010 un il map $16.99

Grades: K 1 2 3   **363.7**

1. Animals 2. Greenhouse effect 3. Climate -- Environmental aspects

ISBN 978-0-8050-7719-3; 0-8050-7719-7

LC 2009012219

"This handsome picture book shows the threat of global warming, one creature at a time. . . . On each double-page spread, the detailed oil paintings pair with rhythmic text. . . . An accompanying world map shows the habitat of each creature and emphasizes the sense of global connections among living beings, while a final page features detailed suggestions for kids to practice conservation in their daily lives." Booklist

Hanel, Rachael

Climate fever; stopping global warming. Compass Point Books 2010 64p il (Green generation) lib bdg $31.99; pa $6.95

Grades: 5 6 7 8 9   **363.7**

1. Greenhouse effect 2. Climate -- Environmental aspects

ISBN 978-0-7565-4246-7 lib bdg; 0-7565-4246-4 lib bdg; 978-0-7565-4291-7 pa; 0-7565-4291-X pa

LC 2009-11448

"The cover design, layout, and graphics feel hip and of the moment. The clear writing is easy to understand and includes many concrete examples of environmentally friendly practices. . . . [A] good choice[s] for both leisure reading and reports." SLJ

Includes glossary and bibliographical references

Jakab, Cheryl

Waste management. Marshall Cavendish Benchmark 2010 32p il map (Environment in focus) lib bdg $28.50

Grades: 4 5 6   **363.7**

1. Refuse and refuse disposal

ISBN 978-1-60870-093-6; 1-60870-093-3

"The layout gives each topic the look of a file folder, with the first spread going to a case-study problem and the second going to a 'Toward a Sustainable Future' case-study solution. . . . Photos bring home the heartbreaking litter, human-waste treatment plants, etc." Booklist

Includes glossary

Jakubiak, David J.

What can we do about acid rain? PowerKids Press 2011 24p il (Protecting our planet) lib bdg $21.25; pa $8.25

Grades: 2 3 4   **363.7**

1. Acid rain

ISBN 9781448849840 lib bdg; 9781448851164 pa

LC 2010053329

This explains how acid rain forms, how it affects the environment, and what can be done about it.

"Every spread has a full-page, thoughtfully captioned color photograph. . . . School and public libraries will want [this title] to round out collections or as [an update] to replace older books." SLJ

Includes glossary and bibliographical references

What can we do about nuclear waste? PowerKids Press 2011 24p il (Protecting our planet) lib bdg $21.25; pa $8.25

Grades: 2 3 4   **363.7**

1. Nuclear engineering 2. Radioactive waste disposal

ISBN 978-1-4488-4983-3 lib bdg; 978-1-4488-5114-0 pa

LC 2010052216

This describes nuclear waste, how nuclear energy is used, how nuclear waste is stored, and how it affects the environment.

Includes glossary

What can we do about oil spills and ocean pollution? PowerKids Press 2011 24p il (Protecting our planet) lib bdg $21.25; pa $8.25

Grades: 2 3 4   **363.7**

1. Oil spills 2. Marine pollution

ISBN 978-1-4488-4982-6 lib bdg; 978-1-4488-5112-6 pa

LC 2010047319

This explains the importance of oceans, how they can be polluted, and the damage caused by oil spills.

Includes glossary

What can we do about ozone loss? PowerKids Press 2011 24p il (Protecting our planet) lib bdg $21.25; pa $8.25

Grades: 2 3 4   **363.7**

1. Pollution 2. Ozone layer 3. Greenhouse effect

ISBN 978-1-4488-4985-7 lib bdg; 978-1-4488-5118-8 pa

LC 2011000156

This explains the depletion of the ozone layer and its affect on the environment.

Includes glossary

Landau, Elaine

★ **Oil** spill! disaster in the Gulf of Mexico. Millbrook Press 2011 32p il lib bdg $25.26

Grades: 3 4 5   **363.7**

1. Oil spills 2. Gulf of Mexico oil spill, 2010

ISBN 978-0-7613-7485-5; 0-7613-7485-X

LC 2010029390

"Landau documents the mind-boggling scope of the 2010 oil spill in the Gulf of Mexico, and the urgent progression of measures taken to contain the calamity. . . . Throughout, Landau applies the clearsighted, nonalarmist tone of a veteran science writer but still manages to infuse the narrative with nearly the same urgency as an edge-of-your-seat disaster flick. Diagrams and photos present a revealing look at the fascinating science and technology behind deep-sea drilling and complex, one-step-forward/two steps back cleanup efforts." Booklist

Includes glossary and bibliographical references

Martin, Laura C.

Recycled crafts box; [by] Laura C. Martin. Storey Publishing 2004 88p il $19.95; pa $10.95

Grades: 3 4 5 6   **363.7**

1. Recycling 2. Handicraft

ISBN 1-58017-523-6; 1-58017-522-8 pa

LC 2003-16703

Discusses recycling and provides information and instructions for making art projects from a variety of recycled materials

"Illustrated with cheerful cartoon drawings and color photos of the finished projects, and bolstered by many resource lists, this is a surprisingly attractive, substantive offering." Booklist

Metz, Lorijo

What can we do about global warming? Rosen Pub. Group 2010 24p il (Protecting our planet) lib bdg $21.25; pa $8

Grades: 2 3 4   **363.7**

1. Environmental protection 2. Greenhouse effect 3. Climate -- Environmental aspects

ISBN 978-1-4042-8079-3 lib bdg; 1-4042-8079-0 lib bdg; 978-1-4358-2479-9 pa; 1-4358-2479-2 pa

LC 2008-50766

This book provides "straightforward information . . . complemented by full-page, color photographs. . . . Links for further information . . . are housed at the publisher's Web site (which allows feedback so that readers can suggest more sites)." SLJ

Includes glossary

What can we do about trash and recycling? PowerKids Press 2010 24p il (Protecting our planet) lib bdg $21.25; pa $8

Grades: 2 3 4   **363.7**

1. Recycling

ISBN 978-1-4042-8082-3 lib bdg; 1-4042-8082-0 lib bdg; 978-1-4358-2483-6 pa; 1-4358-2483-0 pa

LC 2008-53812

This book provides "straightforward information . . . complemented by full-page, color photographs. . . . Links for further information . . . are housed at the publisher's Web site (which allows feedback so that readers can suggest more sites)." SLJ

Includes glossary

Minden, Cecilia

Reduce, reuse, and recycle. Cherry Lake Pub. 2010 32p il (Save the planet) lib bdg $27.07

Grades: 3 4 5 6   **363.7**

1. Recycling 2. Waste minimization 3. Conservation of natural resources

ISBN 978-1-60279-662-1 lib bdg; 1-60279-662-9 lib bdg

Presents tips for how to reduce the amount of garbage thrown away, from buying items that have less packaging at the store to precycling and making art from trash

"At the beginning of . . . [the] book, readers are given a mission and advised to be alert to the facts provided so that they can successfully answer the questions at the end. . . . Children are made to feel part of the process; suggestions for how they can become involved abound." SLJ

Includes glossary and bibliographical references

Morgan, Sally

Pollution. Cherrytree Books 2011 30p il (Helping our planet) lib bdg $28.50

Grades: 1 2 3   **363.7**

1. Pollution

ISBN 978-1-84234-607-5; 1-84234-607-5

LC 2010000036

This book "discusses activities that are harming the planet and how individuals can prevent or minimize their effects. . . . The [book features] large, full-color photos with one or two paragraphs of large-print text per page. 'Find Out More' boxes scattered throughout give additional facts with related websites and 'You Choose' boxes ask students questions regarding important choices they can make. . . . [This] well-designed [book] will be useful for reports and general interest." SLJ

Includes glossary

Waste and recycling. Cherrytree Books 2010 30p il (Helping our planet) lib bdg $28.50

Grades: 1 2 3   **363.7**

1. Recycling 2. Refuse and refuse disposal

ISBN 978-1-84234-608-2

LC 2010000037

This book "suggests how discarded items can be reduced, reused, and recycled. The [book features] large, full-color photos with one or two paragraphs of large-print text per page. 'Find Out More' boxes scattered throughout give additional facts with related websites and 'You Choose' boxes ask students questions regarding important choices they can make. . . . [This] well-designed [book] will be useful for reports and general interest." SLJ

Includes glossary

Morris, Neil

★ **Global** warming. World Almanac Library 2007 48p il (What if we do nothing?) lib bdg $22.95; pa $11.95

Grades: 5 6 7 8   **363.7**

1. Greenhouse effect 2. Climate -- Environmental aspects

ISBN 978-0-8368-7755-7 lib bdg; 0-8368-7755-1 lib bdg; 978-0-8368-155-4 pa; 0-8368-8155-9 pa

LC 2006-30444

This "boasts an attractive format, with large pages that allow room for pictures, excellent charts and graphs, as well as a thoughtful, clear discussion of the topic." Booklist

Includes bibliographical references

Nardo, Don

Climate crisis; the science of global warming. by Don Nardo. Compass Point Books 2009 47p il map (Headline science) lib bdg $27.93; pa $7.95

Grades: 5 6 7   **363.7**

1. Greenhouse effect 2. Climate -- Environmental aspects

ISBN 978-0-7565-3571-1 lib bdg; 0-7565-3571-9 lib bdg; 978-0-7565-3948-1 pa; 0-7565-3948-X pa

LC 2008-7259

"Color photos and graphics provide visual information; a timeline is helpful to find fast facts, and the Facthound Web site provides students with additional information." Libr Media Connect

Includes glossary and bibliographical references

Oil spill; disaster. Scholastic Press 2010 31p il pa $5.99
Grades: 4 5 6 7 8 **363.7**
1. Oil spills 2. Gulf of Mexico oil spill, 2010
ISBN 978-0-545-31776-4; 0-545-31776-2

Explores the immediate and future consequences of the Gulf of Mexico oil spill in April 2010, when the offshore oil rig Deepwater Horizon exploded, causing major environmental and economical damage along the Gulf coast of the United States.

"While text and color photographs convey the extent of the devastation to the Gulf, the book also highlights some innovative attempts to clean up oil spills and profiles two middle school students, who researched cleaning up oil in their own neighborhood." Publ Wkly

Parker, Steve, 1952-
Population. QEB Pub. 2010 32p il (QEB changes in . . .) lib bdg $28.50
Grades: 3 4 5 6 **363.7**
1. Human ecology 2. Human influence on nature
ISBN 978-1-59566-774-8 lib bdg; 1-59566-774-1 lib bdg

LC 2008-56070

"The information is presented in brief paragraphs and sidebars. Suggestions for kids to help improve the planet are sprinkled throughout. . . . Students will enjoy this appealing layout and the information can spark further research on the topic[s]. . . . Either digitally or on paper, students could make fantastic presentations using a similar design." Libr Media Connect

Includes glossary

Potts, Aiden
The **smash!** smash! truck; recycling as you've never heard it before. by Professor Potts. David Fickling Books 2009 un il $16.99; lib bdg $19.99
Grades: PreK K 1 2 **363.7**
1. Recycling
ISBN 978-0-385-75143-8; 0-385-75143-5; 978-0-385-75144-5 lib bdg; 0-385-75144-3 lib bdg

Rapp, Valerie
Protecting Earth's air quality; by Valerie Rapp. Lerner Publications 2009 72p il map (Saving our living Earth) lib bdg $30.60
Grades: 5 6 7 8 **363.7**
1. Air pollution
ISBN 978-0-8225-7558-0 lib bdg; 0-8225-7558-2 lib bdg

LC 2008-907

"Provides a thorough, interesting discussion of multiple aspects of [protecting Earth's air quality], including historical origins, the current situation, and potential solutions. . . . Photos from around the world accompany discussions. . . . [This is a] solid choice to replace outdated books." SLJ

Includes glossary and bibliographical references

Rockwell, Anne F.
★ **Why** are the ice caps melting? the dangers of global warming. by Anne Rockwell; illustrated by Paul Meisel. HarperCollins 2006 33p il (Let's-read-and-find-out science) $15.99; pa $4.99
Grades: K 1 2 3 **363.7**
1. Greenhouse effect 2. Climate -- Environmental aspects 3. Global warming -- Juvenile literature 4. Greenhouse effect, Atmospheric -- Juvenile literature

LC 2005-17972

Tells about the greenhouse effect, recycling, and what you can do to help fight global warming

"The information is detailed, but not overwhelming. . . . Colorful illustrations provide details that support the [text]." SLJ

Royston, Angela
Global warming. Heinemann 2008 32p il (Protect our planet) lib bdg $25.36; pa $7.99
Grades: 1 2 3 **363.7**
1. Greenhouse effect 2. Climate -- Environmental aspects
ISBN 978-1-4329-0924-6 lib bdg; 1-4329-0924-X lib bdg; 978-1-4329-0930-7 pa; 1-4329-0930-4 pa

This is a "very basic introduction to some of the causes and effects of global warming. . . . [The author] discusses extreme weather, changing climates, melting ice caps, alternative sources of energy . . . and low-carbon living. Young readers will come away not frightened, but understanding why they should be concerned." Booklist

Includes glossary and bibliographical references

Silverstein, Alvin
Smog, oil spills, sewage, and more; the yucky pollution book. by Alvin Silverstein, Virginia Silverstein, and Laura Silverstein Nunn; illustrated by Gerald Kelley. Enslow Publishers 2010 48p il (Yucky science) lib bdg $23.93
Grades: 3 4 5 6 **363.7**
1. Pollution 2. Environmental protection
ISBN 978-0-7660-3313-9 lib bdg; 0-7660-3313-9 lib bdg

LC 2009021274

"With conversational prose and zany, retro-gross illustrations, . . . [this volume provides] a painless intro to . . . pollution. Filthy air, polluted water, . . . nonbiodegradable landfills, asbestos, greenhouse gases, and the scourge of 'cow farts' are all here. . . . Kelley's art . . . is a perfect fit for the material, and 'Yikes!' sidebars keep things gregariously gross." Booklist

Simon, Seymour
★ **Global** warming. Collins 2010 31p il $17.99; lib bdg $18.89
Grades: 3 4 5 **363.7**
1. Greenhouse effect 2. Climate -- Environmental aspects 3. Global warming -- Juvenile literature
ISBN 978-0-06-114250-5; 0-06-114250-6; 978-0-06-114251-2 lib bdg; 0-06-114251-4 lib bdg

LC 2009001265

This takes "on the timely matter of climate change. Informative and noncondescending, this boils down large, complex issues into understandable concepts, even as it covers the range of current understanding on how we are impacting the planet. . . . Thoughtfully chosen full-page photos complement and reflect the text." Booklist

Includes glossary, bibliographical references and index

Wells, Robert E.
  Polar bear, why is your world melting? Albert Whitman & Co. 2008 un il $16.99; pa $6.99

Grades: 1 2 3 4   **363.7**
  1. Ice 2. Greenhouse effect 3. Global warming -- Juvenile literature 4. Environmental protection -- Juvenile literature
  ISBN 978-0-8075-6598-8; 0-8075-6598-9; 978-0-8075-6599-5 pa; 0-8075-6599-7 pa

                                                       LC 2008-01308

"Two children sail in a red research vessel through the pages of this clear and simple explanation of global warming. Colorful, cartoon drawings show the youngsters rescuing a mother polar bear and her two cubs by hauling them onto their boat. Then, beginning with an explanation of the sun's effect on the Earth's atmosphere, they pursue the reasons that the Arctic ice is melting. Without oversimplifying, Wells makes the large concepts of the Greenhouse Effect and the sources of CO2 understandable for young children. . . . An excellent introduction to the topic." SLJ

363.738   Pollutants

Arnold, Caroline
  A **warmer** world; from polar bears to butterflies, how global warming is changing lives. Caroline Arnold; illustrated by Jamie Hogan. Charlesbridge 2012 31 p.

Grades: 3 4 5   **363.738**
  1. Ecology 2. Wildlife 3. Climate change 4. Global warming 5. Adaptation (Biology)
  ISBN 9781580892667

                                                       LC 2011000811

The focus of this book is how "[a] warmer world is the new reality for many animals and plants . . . and how they are reacting to climbing temperatures. . . . [Caroline] Arnold looks at the . . . impact of melting ice on polar bears and at the broadening range of Edith's checkerspot butterflies. . . . The speed of this change is leaving many species unable to adapt, and as many as a million species are feared to face extinction. A few might actually benefit from a wider habitable range, but often at a cost to other species. Combining general information on rising seas, melting ice caps, and warmer water with specific emphasis on individual animals such as loggerhead turtles, marmots, penguins, and walruses, this book offers students the opportunity to examine a natural world in flux." (School Libr J)

364   Criminology

Somervill, Barbara A.
  Graphing crime. Raintree 2010 32p il (Real world data) $28.21; pa $7.99

Grades: 4 5 6 7   **364**
  1. Crime 2. Statistics 3. Graphic methods
  ISBN 978-1-4329-2623-6; 1-4329-2623-3; 978-1-4329-2632-8 pa; 1-4329-2632-2 pa

                                                       LC 2009001292

This "discusses juvenile offenders, drug money, terrorism, and more, and teaches readers how to evaluate statistics in the various charts, such as the difference between crimes committed and crimes reported, or between total numbers and rate per population. . . . The clear design, with lots of full-color photos and sidebars, will encourage browsers as much as the up-to-date examples and the clear directions for remaining 'chart smart.'" Booklist

Includes glossary and bibliographical references

364.15   Offenses against the person

Schroeder, Andreas
  Robbers! true stories of the world's most notorious thieves. by Andreas Schroeder, illustrated by Remy Simard. Annick Press 2012 166 p. $21.95

Grades: 4 5 6   **364.15**
  1. Picture books for children 2. Crime -- Juvenile literature 3. Thieves -- Juvenile literature
  ISBN 155451441X; 9781554514410

This juvenile book, by Andreas Schroeder, illustrated by Remy Simard, offers true stories of historical thieves. In it accounts are given for "eight cunning master thieves, including master-of-disguise Willie Sutton, who robbed banks in costume, . . . D. B. Cooper, who hijacked a plane, demanded $200,000, and parachuted to safety, . . . [and] London's Great Train Robbers, who held up a moving train to pull off one of the largest ever hauls of banknotes." (Publisher's note)

364.16   Offenses against property

Guillain, Charlotte
  Great art thefts; by Charlotte Guillain. Capstone Raintree 2013 48 p. col. ill. (library) $29.33; (paperback) $8.99

Grades: 5 6 7 8   **364.16**
  1. Theft -- History 2. Art thefts -- Juvenile literature
  ISBN 1410949583; 9781410949516; 9781410949585
                                                       LC 2012012759

This book by Charlotte Guillain, part of the Treasure Hunters series, looks at art thefts. "After . . . introductions that lay foundations so children will understand why thieves might want to steal art or treasure hunters take such risks, each volume contains chapters that follow the discovery and/or quests for objects such as 'Roman Riches' or locations such as the legendary city of Troy." (School Library Journal)

Includes bibliographical references and index.

368.3   Old-age insurance and insurance against death, illness, injury

Lynette, Rachel
  What to do when your family can't afford healthcare. PowerKids Press 2010 24p il (Let's work it out) $21.25; pa $8.25

Grades: 2 3 4   **368.3**
  1. Medicaid 2. Health insurance
  ISBN 978-1-4358-9342-9; 1-4358-9342-5; 978-1-4358-9772-4 pa; 1-4358-9772-2 pa

This book explains what healthcare and insurance are and why they are so crucial. It also explains the many different low-cost insurance options that are available so that every family can get the care they need.

"Full-page color photographs appear opposite the [narrative], depicting multicultural children, parents, grandparents, social workers, and others, whose demeanors match the hopeful tone of the [title]. This . . . will help promote empathy and understanding for the plight of others and is a key purchase." SLJ

Includes glossary

369.463 Girl Scouts and Girl Guides

Corey, Shana

Here come the Girl Scouts! by Shana Corey; illustrated by Hadley Hooper. Scholastic Press 2012 40 p.
Grades: 2 3 4   369.463
1. Girl Scouts -- History 2. Women -- United States -- Biography
ISBN 0545342783; 9780545342780
LC 2011008690
This book, a "celebration of the life of [Juliette] Low, founder of the Girl Scouts, reveals a gutsy, active girl growing up in Savannah, Ga., at a time when 'proper young ladies were supposed to be dainty and delicate.' Low craved 'adventure and excitement,' and, as an adult, she traveled extensively and decided that she 'wanted to be useful, to make a difference in the world.' . . . [S]he launched the Girl Scouts and, at an inaugural meeting, told the girls what to expect: 'They'd hike and camp and swim! They'd do good deeds. They'd learn to tie knots and survive in the wilderness and even save lives!' [Shana Corey] . . . conveys Low's gumption and optimism, and . . . quotations from the first Girl Scout handbook impart . . . tenets for living and scouting." (Publishers Weekly)

Includes bibliographical references

Wadsworth, Ginger

★ First Girl Scout; Ginger Wadsworth. Clarion Books 2012 xiii, 210p ill. $17.99
Grades: 7 8 9 10 11 12   369.463
1. Biography 2. Girl Scouts 3. Philanthropists 4. Scout leaders
ISBN 978-0-547-24394-8; 0-547-24394-4
LC 2011009642
This book offers a biography of the founder of the Girl Scouts organization. "Juliette (Daisy) Gordon Low [who] was a . . . woman with ideas that were ahead of her time. She witnessed important eras in U.S. history, from the Civil War and Reconstruction to westward expansion to post–World War I. And she made history by founding the first national organization to bring girls from all backgrounds into the out-of-doors. Daisy created controversy by encouraging them to prepare not only for traditional homemaking but also for roles as professional women—in the arts, sciences, and business—and for active citizenship outside the home. Her group also welcomed girls with disabilities at a time when they were usually excluded." (Publisher's note)

"This well-documented biography introduces readers to the founder of the Girl Scouts. . . . Low's personality really comes to life through the details in the narrative. Wadsworth

shows readers that this remarkable woman was a skilled leader and hostess in spite of having suffered severe hearing loss that made conversation difficult. . . . The attractive book design features chapter headings that look like Girl Scout badges, and most spreads include period photos or reproductions of primary-source documents. Exemplary nonfiction." SLJ

Includes bibliographical references (p. 201-204) and index.

370.1 Philosophy and theory, education for specific objectives, educational psychology

Barker, Dan

Maybe right, maybe wrong; a guide for young thinkers. by Dan Barker; illustrated by Brian Strassburg. Prometheus Bks. 1992 76p il pa $17.98
Grades: 4 5 6   370.1
1. Human rights 2. Conduct of life 3. Moral education
ISBN 978-0-87975-731-1 pa; 0-87975-731-0 pa
LC 92-416
Discusses learning right from wrong, stressing such aspects as the difference between rules and principles and the importance of an individual's rights

370.71 Education

McKeown, Rosalyn

Into the classroom; a practical guide for starting student teaching. Rosalyn McKeown. University of Tennessee Press 2011 xv, 165 p.p (pbk.) $14.95
Grades: Adult Professional   370.71
1. Teaching 2. Student teaching
ISBN 1572338164; 9781572338166
LC 2011011282
This book offers suggestions to those "just starting out in a secondary school classroom. . . . After exploring the pitfalls of inexperience and providing . . . guidance on maintaining order in the classroom, [Rosalyn] McKeown focuses on teaching skills. She advises readers on writing objectives and lesson plans, creating interesting ways to start and end class, introducing variety into the classroom, lecturing, asking meaningful questions, and using visual aids." (Amazon.com)

Includes bibliographical references and index.

370.9 History, geographic treatment, biography

Aillaud, Cindy Lou

★ Recess at 20 below. Alaska Northwest Books 2005 un il hardcover o.p. pa $8.95
Grades: K 1 2 3   370.9
1. Schools -- Alaska
ISBN 0-88240-604-3; 0-88240-609-4 pa
"Aillaud, who wrote the text and took the photos here, teaches elementary physical education in Delta Junction, Alaska, a town at the end of the Alaska Highway, above the Arctic Circle. By focusing on one school activity—outdoor recess . . . she demonstrates how cold things get and how

kids deal with it and still have plenty of fun. . . . Twenty-five color photographs capture marvelous details." Booklist

Ruurs, Margriet

My school in the rain forest; how children attend school around the world. Boyds Mills Press 2009 31p il map $17.95

Grades: 1 2 3 4 5   **370.9**

1. Schools 2. Students

ISBN 978-1-59078-601-7; 1-59078-601-7

LC 2009000366

"The book introduces 13 schools, including home schools in Australia and the U.S., a floating school on a Cambodian lake, a village school in Guatemala, a monastery school in Myanmar, and one operated by a global charity. Each double-page spread includes several paragraphs of text, four color photos, and fact box with information about the country, a drawing of its flag, and a map. . . . The book as a whole gives a good sense of the vastly different educational experiences of children around the world." Booklist

370.92   Education biography

Asim, Jabari

★ Fifty cents and a dream; by Jabari Asim; illustrated by Bryan Collier. Little, Brown and Co. 2012 48 p. $16.99

Grades: 2 3 4   **370.92**

1. Biography 2. United States -- History 3. Education -- United States -- History 4. African Americans -- Biography -- Juvenile literature 5. Educators -- United States -- Biography -- Juvenile literature

ISBN 0316086576; 9780316086578

LC 2012007265

Author Jabari Asim tells the story of Booker T. Washington. "Born into slavery, young Booker T. Washington could only dream of learning to read and write. After emancipation, Booker began a five-hundred-mile journey, mostly on foot, to Hampton Institute, taking his first of many steps towards a college degree. When he arrived, he had just fifty cents in his pocket and a dream about to come true." (Publisher's note)

McKissack, Fredrick, 1939-2013

Mary McLeod Bethune; woman of courage. Patricia and Frederick McKissack. Enslow Publishers 2013 24 p. (Famous African Americans) (library) $21.26

Grades: 1 2 3   **370.92**

1. African American women 2. African Americans -- Education 3. Teachers -- United States -- Biography -- Juvenile literature

ISBN 0766041034; 9780766041035

LC 2012007620

This book, part of the Famous African Americans series, looks at Mary McLeod Bethune. She was "her parents' fifteenth child but the first born free. Determined to read the family Bible, she went to school, then college, and then, with just $1.50 in her pocket, opened the first school for black girls in Daytona Beach, Florida." (Booklist)

371   Schools and their activities; special education

Guillain, Charlotte

My first day at a new school. Heinemann Library 2011 24p il (Growing up) lib bdg $22; pa $6.49

Grades: PreK K 1 2   **371**

1. Schools

ISBN 978-1-4329-4796-5 lib bdg; 1-4329-4796-6 lib bdg; 978-1-4329-4806-1 pa; 1-4329-4806-7 pa

LC 2010024189

This book examines a "common, often scary [event] in children's lives and [guides] readers through [it] step-by-step. The [author discusses] the who, what, and why of [the] experience. . . . By confronting . . . fears head-on, children will feel 'in the know' and be prepared to experience [this first]. The text—two sentences per page in a large font and placed on white space—is accompanied by large color photos of children, families, and adults of a variety of ethnic backgrounds. [The] volume includes boldface vocabulary words, a picture glossary, and dos and don'ts." SLJ

Includes glossary and bibliographical references

Hughes, Susan

Off to class; incredible and unusual schools around the world. Owlkids Books 2011 64p il map $22.95; pa $12.95

Grades: 2 3 4 5   **371**

1. Schools 2. Students

ISBN 978-1-926818-85-6; 1-926818-85-7; 978-1-926818-86-3 pa; 1-926818-86-5 pa

"This book examines innovative schools around the world, the educators who brought them about, and the students who attend them. The book has three chapters. 'Working with the Environment' features boat schools, rainforest schools, and tent schools; 'No School? No Way!,' focuses on educational opportunities for disenfranchised populations; and 'One Size Doesn't Fit All' is about unconventional programs in nontraditional settings. Each spread is devoted to one school, with five to seven paragraphs of text, vivid full-color photographs, and a map indicating its general area of the world. The strong emphasis on humanitarianism will move, excite, and inspire those reading about Hurricane Katrina survivors planting gardens, homeless children in India hearing stories on a train platform, and Maasai girls going to school instead of being sold into marriage." SLJ

Mara, Wil

The schoolmaster. Marshall Cavendish Benchmark 2010 48p il (Colonial people) lib bdg $29.93

Grades: 3 4 5 6   **371**

1. Teachers 2. Schools -- United States -- History

ISBN 978-0-7614-4801-3; 0-7614-4801-2

This describes the life of a colonial schoolmaster and his importance to the community, as well as everyday life, responsibilities, and social practices during that time.

"The type font, just slightly larger than usual, makes the text very visually appealing. . . . [The] book is liberally illustrated with artwork dating from the colonial period . . . [and] information boxes offer supplemental material." Libr Media Connect

Includes glossary and bibliographical references

371.1   Schools and their activities

Harada, Violet H.

Inquiry learning through librarian-teacher partnerships; [by] Violet H. Harada and Joan M. Yoshina. Linworth Pub. 2004 172p il pa $39.95

Grades: Adult Professional   **371.1**

1. Teaching teams 2. School libraries 3. Questioning 4. Curriculum planning -- United States

ISBN 1-58683-134-8

LC 2004-662

"The authors describe what happens in an inquiry-based classroom and library media center and show teachers/librarians how to develop a curriculum that incorporates essential questions and important habits of mind, all aligned with content standards. . . . The volume contains everything a teacher-librarian team would need to create, teach, research, and assess major interdisciplinary units." SLJ

Includes bibliographical references

Houston, Gloria

My great-aunt Arizona; illustrated by Susan Condie Lamb. HarperCollins Pubs. 1992 un il $15.99; pa $6.99

Grades: K 1 2 3   **371.1**

1. Teachers 2. Biography, Individual -- Juvenile literature

ISBN 0-06-022606-4; 0-06-022607-2 lib bdg; 0-06-443374-9 pa

LC 90-44112

"The pleasant, conversational rhythm of the prose, the unobtrusive use of repetition, and the ability to sum up the unique quality of a life in a few telling phrases give the writing its substance. . . . Sunny and lively, the watercolor paintings have a naive quality that suits the story well." Booklist

Kenney, Karen Latchana

Teachers at work; by Karen L. Kenney; illustrated by Brian Caleb Dumm; content consultant, Judith Stepan-Norris. Magic Wagon 2009 32p il (Meet your community workers!) lib bdg $18.95

Grades: K 1 2 3   **371.1**

1. Teachers 2. Vocational guidance

ISBN 978-1-60270-653-8 lib bdg; 1-60270-653-0 lib bdg

LC 2009-2395

This book about teachers has "an uncluttered layout and consistent organization. . . . Chapter headings such as 'Problems on the Job,' and 'Technology at Work,' and 'Special Skills and Training' make it easy to pinpoint specific information." SLJ

Includes glossary

371.3   Methods of instruction and study

Crane, Beverley E.

Using WEB 2.0 tools in the K-12 classroom. Neal-Schuman Publishers 2009 189p il

Grades: Adult Professional   **371.3**

1. Web 2.0 2. Internet in education 3. Education -- Curricula

ISBN 1-55570-653-3; 978-1-55570-653-1

LC 2008-46167

"This excellent resource should be widely appealing to teachers, librarians, and school media specialists." Voice Youth Advocates

Includes glossary and bibliographical references

Fox, Janet S.

Get organized without losing it; by Janet S. Fox; edited by Pamela Espeland. Free Spirit Pub. 2006 105p il (Laugh & learn) pa $8.95

Grades: 5 6 7 8   **371.3**

1. Life skills 2. Study skills 3. Time management

ISBN 978-1-57542-193-3 pa; 1-57542-193-3 pa

LC 2005032809

"In this handbook for students, Fox uses humor to provide practical, easy-to-follow ideas for organizing desks, backpacks, and lockers; managing time for homework and after school activities; planning long-term projects; and taking better notes. . . . Fox writes in a conversational style. . . . Humorous illustrations complement the text." Voice Youth Advocates

Includes bibliographical references

Green, Julie

Write it down. Cherry Lake Pub. 2010 32p il (Super smart information strategies) lib bdg $27.07

Grades: 3 4 5 6   **371.3**

1. Note-taking

ISBN 978-1-60279-645-4 lib bdg; 1-60279-645-9 lib bdg

LC 2009024741

"The appealing layout includes manageable paragraphs, a variety of engaging illustrations, and examples that clearly guide readers through each topic. . . . Effective note taking and highlighting are the focus of [this book], but the book also suggests using sticky notes and creating diagrams and charts." SLJ

Includes glossary and bibliographical references

Kraus, Jeanne

Annie's plan; taking charge of schoolwork and homework. written by Jeanne Kraus; illustrated by Charles Beyl. Magination Press 2007 47p il $14.95; pa $8.95

Grades: 2 3 4 5   **371.3**

1. Homework 2. Study skills 3. Attention deficit disorder

ISBN 978-1-59147-481-4; 1-59147-481-7; 978-1-59147-482-1 pa; 1-59147-482-5 pa

LC 2006009948

"Annie is smart but she just can't stay focused on anything so she is always behind in class. With the help of her parents and teacher, she learns how to organize her work and is given other tips for completing her assignments. The book offers 10 easy-to-follow steps that begin with a clean, organized desk at school and a quiet, organized work space at home, and end with a signed reward contract. . . . Comical color illustrations and a conversational tone explain that a youngster with ADHD is neither dumb nor an incurable behavioral problem. . . . An extensive note for adults is included. This is an excellent resource for school libraries, professional collections, and parenting collections, and a great shared read for parent and child." SLJ

November, Alan C.

Empowering students with technology; 2nd ed.; Corwin Press 2010 115p il pa $25.95

Grades: Adult Professional **371.3**

1. Internet in education 2. Computer-assisted instruction

ISBN 978-1-4129-7425-7; 1-4129-7425-9

LC 2009-43649

First published 2001 by Skylight Professional Development

"Discusses the relationship of technology to today's learning environment and the potential for technology to encourage students to learn collaboratively. This . . . edition emphasizes current topics such as information literacy, global connectivity, and the educational applications of utilities such as digital cameras and cell phones. The book's usefulness is as a reasource for teachers and librarians to consult in creating, planning, and assisting with school projects in all subjects." Libr Media Connect

Includes bibliographical references

Richardson, Will

Blogs, wikis, podcasts, and other powerful Web tools for classrooms; 3rd ed.; Corwin 2010 171p il pa $31.95

Grades: Adult Professional **371.3**

1. Weblogs 2. Podcasting 3. Internet in education 4. Online social networks 5. Wikis (Computer science) 6. Teaching -- Aids and devices

ISBN 978-1-4129-7747-0; 1-4129-7747-9

LC 2009-51376

First published 2006

"The book is well-written and comprehensive. The author's engaging writing style will instill confidence in readers that they will be able to easily integrate the same technologies with the same results in their classrooms. Readers will not want to stop reading this eye-opening and inspirational book. It is jam-packed with proven ideas, and individuals, especially educators, will want to try out these technologies." Libr Media Connect

Includes bibliographical references

Teehan, Kay

Wikis; the educator's power tool. Linworth 2010 78p il pa $30

Grades: Adult Professional **371.3**

1. Internet in education 2. Electronic encyclopedias 3. Wikis (Computer science) 4. Computer-assisted instruction

ISBN 978-1-58683-530-9 pa; 1-58683-530-0 pa; 978-1-58683-531-6 e-book; 1-58683-531-9 e-book

LC 2010020285

"This book breaks down three types of wikis: library wikis, which are usually content and link-to-content focused; reciprocal wikis, which are collaborative in nature; and student-produced wikis that are developed to share projects and research. . . . There is also a wiki to complement the guidelines in the book. This is a simple to use quick-start guide and a great resource for school technology teachers and librarians." Libr Media Connect

Includes bibliographical references

371.5 School discipline and related activities

Beaudoin, Marie-Nathalie

Responding to the culture of bullying and disrespect; new perspectives on collaboration, compassion, and responsibility. [by] Marie-Nathalie Beaudoin, Maureen Taylor. rev 2nd ed.; Corwin Press 2009 281p il $76.95; pa $36.95

Grades: Adult Professional **371.5**

1. Bullies 2. School discipline

ISBN 978-1-4129-6853-9; 1-4129-6853-4; 978-1-4129-6854-6 pa; 1-4129-6854-2 pa

LC 2008-55933

First published 2004 with title: Breaking the culture of bullying and disrespect

"This profound resource explores the behaviors that cultivate a culture of bullying and disrespect. . . . Concrete solutions to issues are offered, and the authors make sure to load this title with practical suggestions for affecting change. They delve into ways to work directly with young people to better address their concerns. . . . This purchase is essential for any educator, counselor, or parent. It should be a staple of the school library reference collection because the information provided should be used daily. It will be a title that can be referenced for years to come and will help with adults struggling to overcome bullying." Voice Youth Advocates

Includes glossary and bibliographical references

★ **Bully;** an action plan for teachers and parents to combat the bullying crisis. edited by Lee Hirsch and Cynthia Lowen; with Dina Santorelli. Perseus Books Group 2012 viii, 295 p.p ill. $15.99

Grades: Adult Professional **371.5**

1. Bullies 2. Bullying 3. Bullying -- Prevention 4. Cyberbullying -- Prevention 5. Bullying in schools -- Prevention

ISBN 1602861846; 1602861854; 9781602861848; 9781602861855

LC 2012289039

"This companion book to the documentary film Bully was edited by filmmaker [Lee]Hirsch and writer/producer [Cynthia] Lowen, with contributing chapters by a number of celebrities, authors, experts, government officials, and educators. Part homage to the film, part resource, the book interweaves the stories of children who have been bullied with practical information and advice for parents and other readers." (Publishers Weekly)

Includes bibliographical references (p. 281-289) and index

Bott, C. J.

More bullies in more books. Scarecrow Press 2009 197p il pa $35

Grades: Adult Professional **371.5**

1. Bullies 2. Reference books 3. Bullying in schools 4. Children's literature -- Bibliography 5. Young adult literature -- Bibliography

ISBN 978-0-8108-6654-6 pa; 0-8108-6654-4 pa

LC 2009-923

This "offers more than 350 annotated titles published since 2000 to create awareness of the many types of harassment and bullying. . . . Although the text is written for educators and librarians for use in classroom settings, the information is equally helpful for parents, caregivers, and public librarians." SLJ

Includes bibliographical references

Myers, Jill J.

Responding to cyber bullying; an action tool for school leaders. [by] Jill J. Myers, Donna S. McCaw, Leaunda S. Hemphill. Corwin Press 2011 195p pa $33.95

Grades: Adult Professional **371.5**

1. Bullies 2. Cyberbullying 3. School violence

ISBN 978-1-4129-9484-2; 1-4129-9484-5

LC 2010040679

"The book's introduction addresses the nature of 'digital generation' students. The problem of cyberbullying is introduced in light of the generational reality. The book covers decisions made to resolve real-life situations, practical principles about censorship, and the capacity and limitations of school authority, Included is a matrix that serves as a decision-making tool for administration. This resource is a healthy blend of the theoretical and practical." Libr Media Connect

Includes bibliographical references

371.6 Physical plant; materials management

Gaarder-Juntti, Oona

What in the world is a green school? ABDO Pub. Company 2011 24p il (Going green) lib bdg $24.21

Grades: 1 2 3 4 **371.6**

1. School buildings 2. Environmental protection

ISBN 978-1-61613-190-6 lib bdg; 1-61613-190-X lib bdg

LC 2010004324

"The lively layout design, featuring colorful headings, short paragraphs, and attractive photographs, has a scrapbook-like quality. . . . [The title explains] how all our choices require energy and resources, and encourage readers to make changes in their lifestyles. . . . [This] . . . will inspire and empower readers to make a difference." SLJ

Includes glossary and bibliographical references

371.7 Student welfare

Curtis, Andrea

What's for lunch? How schoolchildren eat around the world. Andrea Curtis; Yvonne Duivenvoorden. Red Deer Press 2012 40 p. $12.95

Grades: 3 4 5 **371.7**

1. School children -- Food

ISBN 0889954828; 9780889954823

This book by Andrea Curtis and Yvonne Duivenvoorden "reveals the variety and inequality to be found in the food consumed by young people in typical school lunches from thirteen countries around the world, including Japan, Kenya, Russia, United States, Canada, Mexico, Brazil and Afghanistan. In some countries, the meals are nutritious and well-balanced. In others they barely satisfy basic nutrition standards." (Publisher's note)

371.82 Specific groups of students; schools for specific groups of students

Marx, Trish

Kindergarten day USA and China; a flip-me-over book. by Trish Marx and Ellen B. Senisi. Charlesbridge 2010 un il $16.95; pa $7.95

Grades: PreK K 1 **371.82**

1. Kindergarten 2. Schools -- China 3. Schools -- United States

ISBN 978-1-58089-219-3; 1-58089-219-1; 978-1-58089-220-9 pa; 1-58089-220-5 pa

"Half of this book narrates a day at a kindergarten in Schenectady, NY; when flipped, it details a day with Chinese children in Beijing. Although there are some differences between the two classes, the book focuses on illustrating their similarities. . . . Large, bright photographs and a limited number of words per page make this a good choice for storytime." SLJ

Mortenson, Greg

★ **Listen** to the wind; the story of Dr. Greg and Three Cups of Tea. by Greg Mortenson and Susan L. Roth; collages by Susan L. Roth. Dial Books for Young Readers 2009 un il $16.99

Grades: K 1 2 3 **371.82**

1. Humanitarian intervention 2. Mountaineers 3. Humanitarians 4. Schools -- Pakistan 5. Humanitarian assistance -- Juvenile literature

ISBN 978-0-8037-3058-8; 0-8037-3058-6

LC 2008-12268

Roth "pairs the words with her signature mixed-media collage work . . . using scraps of cloth along with a variety of papers. Her work has a welcoming, tactile dimension." Publ Wkly

Includes bibliographical references

Three cups of tea; one man's mission to promote peace--one school at a time. [by] Greg Mortenson and David Oliver Relin; adapted for young readers by Sarah Thomson. Dial Books for Young Readers 2009 209p il $16.99; pa $8.99

Grades: 4 5 6 7 **371.82**

1. Humanitarian intervention 2. Mountaineers 3. Humanitarians 4. Schools -- Pakistan 5. Schools -- Afghanistan

ISBN 978-0-8037-3392-3; 0-8037-3392-5; 978-0-14-241412-5 pa; 0-14-241412-3 pa

Based on Three cups of tea: one man's mission to fight terrorism and build nations one school at a time, published 2006 by Viking for adults

"In 1993, while climbing one of the world's most difficult peaks, Mortenson became lost and ill, and eventually found aid in the tiny Pakistani village of Korphe. He vowed to repay his generous hosts by building a school; his efforts have grown into the Central Asia Institute. . . . Retold for middle readers, the story remains inspirational and compelling. . . . Illustrated throughout with b&w photos, it also contains two eight-page insets of color photos." Publ Wkly

UNICEF

A **school** like mine; a unique celebration of schools around the world. DK 2007 79p il map $19.99

Grades: 3 4 5 6 **371.82**

1. Schools 2. Children

ISBN 978-0-7566-2913-7; 0-7566-2913-6

LC 2007298451

Introduces children from around the world and discuss-es where they live, how they play, and what their schools are like

Winter, Jeanette

★ **Nasreen's** secret school; a true story from Afghani-stan. Beach Lane Books 2009 un il $16.99

Grades: 2 3 4 **371.82**

1. Girls -- Education 2. Schools -- Afghanistan 3. Women -- Education -- Afghanistan -- Juvenile literature

ISBN 978-1-4169-9437-4; 1-4169-9437-8

LC 2009-08285

"This story begins with an author's note that succinctly explains the drastic changes that occurred when the Taliban came to power in Afghanistan in 1996. The focus is primar-ily on the regime's impact on women, who were no longer allowed to attend school or leave home without a male chap-erone, and had to cover their heads and bodies with a burqa. After Nasreen's parents disappeared, the child neither spoke nor smiled. Her grandmother, the story's narrator, took her to a secret school, where she slowly discovered a world of art, literature, and history obscured by the harsh prohibitions of the Taliban. . . . Winter manages to achieve that delicate bal-ance that is respectful of the seriousness of the experience, yet presents it in a way that is appropriate for young chil-dren. Winter's acrylic paintings make effective use of color. . . . This is an important book that makes events in a faraway place immediate and real." SLJ

Includes bibliographical references

371.9 Special education

Lauren, Jill

That's like me! stories about amazing people with learning differences. foreword by Jerry Pinkney. Star Bright Books 2009 un il $17.95; pa $7.95

Grades: 3 4 5 **371.9**

1. Learning disabilities

ISBN 978-1-59572-207-2; 1-59572-207-6; 978-1-59572-208-9 pa; 1-59572-208-4 pa

LC 2009028647

"This colorful book spotlights people of different ages, backgrounds, and interests who have coped with learning disabilities and succeeded in their chosen fields. . . . Each entry includes several photos showing the person at different ages. A good resource for encouraging children with learn-ing disabilities." Booklist

Includes bibliographical references

Stanley, Jerry

★ **Children** of the Dust Bowl; the true story of the school at Weedpatch Camp. Crown 1992 85p il map hard-cover o.p. $9.95

Grades: 5 6 7 8 **371.9**

1. Migrant labor 2. Great Depression, 1929-1939 3. Education -- Social aspects

ISBN 0-517-88094-6; 0-517-58782-3 pa

LC 92-393

Describes the plight of the migrant workers who traveled from the Dust Bowl to California during the Depression and were forced to live in a federal labor camp and discusses the school that was built for their children

"Stanley's text is a compelling document. . . . The story is inspiring and disturbing, and Stanley has recorded the de-tails with passion and dignity." Booklist

Includes bibliographical references

371.91 Students with physical disabilities

Hauser, Peter C.

★ **How** deaf children learn; what parents and teachers need to know. Marc Marschark Peter C. Hauser. Oxford University Press 2012 156 p. $26.50

Grades: Adult Professional **371.91**

1. Teaching 2. Deaf children 3. Elementary education 4. Deaf -- Education 5. Deaf -- Means of communication

ISBN 0195389751; 9780195389753

LC 2011012553

This book is "about teaching deaf children. Written pri-marily for parents and teachers of deaf or hard-of-hearing children, this work covers general information about their education, gives insights into their cognitive development, and provides steps to their school success. The authors also discuss issues such as the value of cochlear implants and the debate over signing vs. speaking." (Library Journal)

Includes bibliographical references.

372 Specific levels of education

Barber, Nicola

First day of school. PowerKids Press 2009 24p il (The big day!) lib bdg $21.25; pa $8.25

Grades: PreK K 1 **372**

1. Schools

ISBN 978-1-4358-2839-1 lib bdg; 1-4358-2839-9 lib bdg; 978-1-4358-2895-7 pa; 1-4358-2895-X pa

LC 2008025816

"Children in kindergarten will enjoy [this book] as [a read-aloud] . . . while those at the end of first grade will be able to read [it] independently. The writing is straight-forward and reassuring, and the content provides a realistic view of what youngsters might experience in [school]. . . .The author discusses the activities of a typical day as well as feelings of sadness or loneliness that may occur." SLJ

Includes bibliographical references

Brooks-Young, Susan

Teaching with the tools kids really use; learning with Web and mobile technologies. Corwin 2010 137p pa $26.95

Grades: Adult Professional **372**

1. Web 2.0 2. Teachers -- Training

ISBN 978-1-4129-7275-8 pa; 1-4129-7275-2 pa

LC 2009-43856

"In this book, we see how technology can be used, but we also see the reponsibility of the educator to make sure it is done appropriately, so 21st-century skills are addressed. The author addresses technologies and applications, and also discusses their ethical uses and how to think ahead to make adjustments for the future. . . . This book will be incredibly useful for those who are unsure about Web 2.0 tools, want to explore their possibilities, and would like to educate themselves further about usage in their own schools." Libr Media Connect

Includes bibliographical references

Carlow, Regina

Exploring the connection between children's literature and music. Libraries Unlimited 2008 124p il pa $30

Grades: Adult Professional   **372**

1. Children's poetry 2. Music in libraries 3. Music -- Study and teaching 4. Children's literature -- Bibliography 5. Children's library services -- Activity projects

ISBN 978-1-59158-439-1 pa; 1-59158-439-6 pa

LC 2007-40134

"Carlow sees music as part of developmental human activity and issues a plea to introduce it as direct participation. . . . This collection of methods and lessons encourages adults to broaden the possibilities of interacting with music, thereby using it to introduce young children to language, literature, and culture. Text is divided into chapters on singing and other ways to be musical. . . . The succeeding chapters are devoted to specific grade levels. . . . Each chapter includes an explanation of methods appropriate for the age group, followed by numerous lesson ideas for classrooms. The organization of this book makes it a solid addition to enhance curriculum materials." SLJ

Includes bibliographical references

Gates, Pamela

Cultural Journeys; Multicultural Literature for Elementary and Middle School Students. Rowman & Littlefield Pub Inc 2010 258 p. (paperback) $29.95

Grades: Adult Professional   **372**

1. Best books 2. Multicultural literature

ISBN 144220687X; 9781442206878

This book looks at multicultural literature for elementary and middle school students. The first chapter asks "the question of 'why.' Why use multicultural literature? . . . The 'why' is further developed as the chapter continues with a definition of multicultural literature." The seventh chapter looks at "works that challenge stereotypes and go beyond the common one-dimensional diversity theme." (Alberta Journal of Educational Research)

Libresco, Andrea S.

Every book is a social studies book; how to meet standards with picture books, K-6. [by] Andrea S. Libresco, Jeannette Balantic, and Jonie C. Kipling. Libraries Unlimited 2011 269p il pa $30

Grades: Adult Professional   **372**

1. Social sciences -- Study and teaching

ISBN 978-1-59884-520-4; 1-59884-520-9

LC 2010053649

"Based on observations and instructional surveys, the authors theorize that consistent social studies instruction no longer occurs due to the time requirements of reading and math instruction. They recommend teaching reading and social studies concurrently by using trade picture books. Each of the national standards' thematic strands is featured along with essential questions to frame classroom discussion. Three representative titles are featured for each theme, fol-

lowed by social studies concepts and supporting discussion questions. Thoughtful hands-on, student-centered activities are provided for each title as well as reproducibles, study sheets, and graphic organizers." Libr Media Connect

Includes bibliographical references

Lukenbill, W. Bernard

Health information in a changing world; practical approaches for teachers, schools, and school librarians. [by] W. Bernard Lukenbill and Barbara Froling Immroth. Libraries Unlimited 2010 244p il $45

Grades: Adult Professional   **372**

1. Health education 2. Youth -- Health and hygiene 3. Health -- Information services

ISBN 978-1-59884-398-9; 1-59884-398-2

LC 2010-7505

"This is quite an impressive book and a real treasure for any professional involved with health education, whether for the classroom, public health, or personal counseling." Voice Youth Advocates

Includes bibliographical references

MacDonell, Colleen

Thematic inquiry through fiction and nonfiction, PreK to grade 6. Linworth Pub. 2009 121p il pa $44.95

Grades: Adult Professional   **372**

1. Active learning 2. Education -- Curricula

ISBN 978-1-58683-350-3 pa; 1-58683-350-2 pa

LC 2008-33365

"This is an excellent guide for classroom teachers and school media specialists interested in adding inquiry-based collaborative lessons to their repertoire." Libr Media Connect

Includes bibliographical references

Mackey, Bonnie

A **librarian's** guide to cultivating an elementary school garden; [by] Bonnie Mackey and Jennifer Mackey Stewart. Linworth Pub. 2009 124p il pa $39.95

Grades: Adult Professional   **372**

1. Gardening 2. School libraries -- Activity projects

ISBN 978-1-58683-328-2 pa; 1-58683-328-6 pa

LC 2008-34963

"Its unusual topic makes this book a standout." Libr Media Connect

Includes bibliographical references

372.21 Preschool education

Howe, James

★ **When** you go to kindergarten; text by James Howe; photographs by Betsy Imershein. rev & updated ed; Morrow Junior Bks. 1994 un il hardcover o.p. pa $6.99

Grades: PreK K   **372.21**

1. Kindergarten 2. Kindergarten -- Juvenile literature

ISBN 0-688-12912-9; 0-688-14387-3 pa

LC 93-48152

First published 1986 by Knopf

"The author tells youngsters what school might look like and how they might get there, and describes some of the possible activities. . . . Multicultural children are welcomed and taught by both male and female teachers. Smiling, busy kids engaged in many activities portray school as an exciting, interesting, and happy place." SLJ

372.4 Reading

Hutchins, Darcy J.

Family reading night; [by] Darcy J. Hutchins, Marsha D. Greenfeld, Joyce L. Epstein. Eye on Education 2008 126p il pa $29.95

Grades: Adult Professional **372.4**

  1. Reading 2. Family literacy programs

  ISBN 978-1-59667-063-1 pa; 1-59667-063-0 pa

LC 2007034492

"This guide presents clear examples of how to plan and implement thematic, monthly programs to help engage families with elementary-age children in literacy activities that they can do together. . . . This title would be an excellent tool for any school librarian, educator, or administrator working to devise a successful and strategically planned school-wide family reading program." SLJ

Moreillon, Judi

Collaborative strategies for teaching reading comprehension; maximizing your impact. [by] Judi Moreillon. American Library Association 2007 170p il $38

Grades: Adult Professional **372.4**

  1. Reading comprehension

  ISBN 978-0-8389-0929-4; 0-8389-0929-9

LC 2006036132

This "begins by emphasizing the importance of collaboration between classroom teachers and teacher-librarians. . . . The bulk of the book focuses on seven reading comprehension strategies and how to teach them. . . . Overall this book is a cut above other 'how-to' books with its plethora of suggestions and resources for teachers and librarians." Voice Youth Advocates

  Includes glossary and bibliographical references

372.5 The arts

Press, Judy

  ★ **Around**-the-world art & activities; visiting the 7 continents through craft fun. illustrations by Betsy Day. Williamson 2001 128p il (Williamson Little Hands book) pa $12.95

Grades: K 1 2 **372.5**

  1. Handicraft 2. Activity programs in education -- Juvenile literature 3. Handicraft -- Study and teaching -- Juvenile literature 4. Multiculural education -- Activity programs -- Juvenile literature

  ISBN 1-88559-345-7

LC 00-60030

"North American totem poles, Hawaiian leis, Aboriginal bark painting, Japanese dolls in kimonos, Korean drums, egg-carton camels, Masai beaded necklaces, nesting Russian dolls, and South American gaucho belts are among the projects. While the ideas will not be new to veteran crafters, they are basic and solid for the intended audience." SLJ

372.6 Language arts (Communication skills)

Bauer, Caroline Feller

  ★ **Caroline** Feller Bauer's new handbook for storytellers; with stories, poems, magic, and more. illustrations by Lynn Gates Bredeson. American Library Association 1993 550p il hardcover o.p. pa $45

Grades: Adult Professional **372.6**

  1. Storytelling

  ISBN 0-8389-0664-8 pa

LC 93-14959

First published 1977 with title: Handbook for storytellers

Bauer's introduction "incorporates a broad variety of media and props into the storytelling process. . . . Beginners and veterans alike can benefit from this practical approach to program planning and promotion, story selection and preparation, and activities extending various themes or occasions." Bull Cent Child Books

  Includes bibliographical references

Briggs, Diane

Preschool favorites; 35 storytimes kids love. [by] Diane Briggs; illustrated by Thomas Briggs. American Library Association 2007 227p bibl il pa $40

Grades: Adult Professional **372.6**

  1. Storytelling 2. Children's literature 3. Picture books for children 4. Children's library services -- Activity projects

  ISBN 0-8389-0938-8 pa; 978-0-8389-0938-6 pa

LC 2006103159

"This book presents suggestions and resources for a variety of themes, from 'Animal Oddballs' to 'A Woggle of Witches.' Each session includes a variety of books and activities per topic. . . . Several fingerplays and folk rhymes per theme come with clear instructions for accompanying motions. . . . A useful discography provides sources for musical selections. Each theme also incorporates a flannel board poem, story, or song, with simple reproducible patterns and instructions on how to present them. . . . The thematic groupings and quantity of ideas should be useful to beginners and some experienced presenters looking to freshen up their programs." SLJ

  Includes bibliographical references

Toddler storytimes II; [by] Diane Briggs; illustrations by Thomas Briggs. Scarecrow Press 2008 165p il pa $45

Grades: Adult Professional **372.6**

  1. Storytelling

  ISBN 978-0-8108-6057-5 pa; 0-8108-6057-0 pa

LC 2008006243

"With 25 theme-based chapters, this is a handy resource. Each theme includes book recommendations, often 10 or more, with a nice mixture of classic and newer titles, and a suggestion to choose two or three per session. Words and instructions for fingerplays, rhymes, and songs are provided, while a discography provides melody sources for all songs. Each theme includes a flannel-board activity, complete with reproducible patterns and brief directions on how to present the story or song on the board." SLJ

  Includes discography and bibliographical references

Cavanaugh, Terence W.

Bookmapping; lit trips and beyond. [by] Terence W. Cavanaugh, Jerome Burg. International Society for Technology in Education 2011 228p il pa $34.95

Grades: Adult Professional   **372.6**

1. Audiovisual education 2. Literature -- Study and teaching 3. Maps -- Study and teaching -- Activities and projects

ISBN 978-1-56484-283-1; 1-56484-283-5

LC 2010051664

This book "provides ideas on how teachers can use elements from different disciplines in their own classrooms. . . Other information includes using Google Earth, sources for images, Bing maps, information on creating your own bookmaps, instruction for bookmaps done individually and in cooperation with another teacher's class or classes, how to set up mapping in the classroom, and exploring existing bookmaps available on the Web. . . . This book should be in the professional collection of every middle and high school library, preferably in every classroom." Voice Youth Advocates

Includes bibliographical references

Chatton, Barbara

Using poetry across the curriculum; learning to love language. 2nd ed; Libraries Unlimited 2010 241p pa $40

Grades: Adult Professional   **372.6**

1. Poetry -- Study and teaching

ISBN 978-1-59158-697-5; 1-59158-697-6

LC 2009-36711

First published 1993

"With the emphasis in most schools on improving literacy, fluency, and reading and writing test scores, this book is extremely valuable. Sections are divided into various curricula areas. Each section begins with the national standards for that discipline, then a few paragraphs explain how the poetry in the extensive listing can be used. . . . Because all teachers must incorporate writing into their teaching, having relevant poetry for their curriculum and ideas on how to use it, will make this book popular." Libr Media Connect

Includes bibliographical references

Greene, Ellin

Storytelling: art & technique; [by] Ellin Greene and Janice Del Negro. 4th ed.; Libraries Unlimited 2010 xxvii, 455p il $55

Grades: Adult Professional   **372.6**

1. Storytelling

ISBN 978-1-59158-600-5; 1-59158-600-3

First published 1977 by Bowker under the authorship of Augusta Baker and Ellin Greene

"The fourth edition of this storytelling standby includes a wealth of updated and new materials." Bull Cent Child Books

Includes bibliographical references

Heitman, Jane

★ **Once** upon a time; fairy tales in the library and language arts. [by] Jane Heitman. Linworth Pub. 2007 132p pa $36.95

Grades: Adult Professional   **372.6**

1. Reading 2. Fairy tales 3. Language arts

ISBN 1-58683-231-X pa; 978-1-58683-231-X pa

LC 2007006890

"Heitman presents a well-organized and comprehensive look at how fairy tales can be infused into the curriculum. . . . The book includes ways in which various lessons can be adapted for special and English-language learners, as well as numerous templates for writing, speaking, and listening activities. . . . This excellent resource deserves a place in most professional collections." SLJ

Includes bibliographical references

Hostmeyer, Phyllis

Storytelling and QAR strategies; [by] Phyllis Hostmeyer and Marilyn Adele Kinsella. Libraries Unlimited 2010 123p pa $30

Grades: Adult Professional   **372.6**

1. Storytelling

ISBN 978-1-59884-494-8 pa; 1-59884-494-6 pa; 978-1-59884-495-5 e-book

LC 2010036576

"The authors, both storytellers with backgrounds in education and library work, present 18 stories based on six aspects of character development. These selections, which include folktales, fables, and myths, are just right for youngsters in third through eighth grades. Each one is followed by telling tips, a story path, and questions using the QAR (Question-Answer Relationships) model." SLJ

Includes bibliographical references

MacDonald, Margaret Read

Shake-it-up tales! stories to sing, dance, drum, and act out. August House 2000 174p il music $24.95; pa $14.95

Grades: Adult Professional   **372.6**

1. Folklore 2. Storytelling 3. Tales 4. Storytelling -- United States 5. Activity programs in education -- United States

ISBN 0-87483-590-9; 0-87483-570-4 pa

LC 00-36228

This is a collection of "participation tales from different cultures. Each of the 20 stories is easy to learn and MacDonald provides wonderful ideas on how to inspire elementary-aged children to join in and become part of the storytelling tradition." SLJ

Includes bibliographical references

Miller, Donalyn

★ The **book** whisperer; awakening the inner reader in every child. [by] Donalyn Miller; foreword by Jeff Anderson. Jossey-Bass 2009 227p

Grades: Adult Professional   **372.6**

1. Books and reading

ISBN 978-0-4703-7227-2; 0-4703-7227-3

LC 2008055666

Donalyn Miller's approach to reading promotion "is simple yet provocative: affirm the reader in every student, allow students to choose their own books, carve out extra reading time, model authentic reading behaviors, discard time-worn reading assignments such as book reports and comprehension worksheets, and develop a classroom library filled with high-interest books. . . . Miller provides many tips for teachers and parents and includes a useful list of ultimate reading suggestions picked by her students. This outstanding contribution to the literature is highly recommended." Libr J

Includes bibliographical references

Roth, Rita

The **story** road to literacy; [by] Rita Roth. Teacher Ideas Press 2006 176p il pa $30

Grades: Adult Professional   **372.6**

1. Immigrants 2. Language arts 3. Children of immigrants 4. English language -- Study and teaching 5. Children's reading -- Educational aspects 6. Children -- Reading -- Educational aspects

ISBN 1-59158-323-3

LC 2005030835

"Roth advances the idea that using traditional literature with students who are learning English will help them acquire critical communication skills while tying unfamiliar new places to familiar elements of their own heritages. The author provides practical, ready-to-use lesson plans, story samples, and suggested activities." SLJ

Includes bibliographical references

Sawyer, Ruth

The **way** of the storyteller. Viking 1962 360p il hardcover o.p. pa $16

Grades: Adult Professional   **372.6**

1. Storytelling 2. Literature -- Collections

ISBN 0-14-004436-1 pa

First published 1942

"This is not primarily a book on how to tell stories; it is rather the whole philosophy of story telling as a creative art. From her own rich experience the author writes inspiringly of the background, experience, creative imagination, technique and selection essential to this art. A part of the book is devoted to a few well-loved stories with suggestions and comments." Booklist

Includes bibliographical references

Spaulding, Amy E.

The **art** of storytelling; telling truths through telling stories. Scarecrow Press, Inc. 2011 210p $49.95

Grades: Adult Professional   **372.6**

1. Storytelling

ISBN 978-0-8108-7776-4; 0-8108-7776-7; 978-0-8108-7777-1 ebook

LC 2010039697

"Spaulding's passion for storytelling is evident as she shares the skills she has learned over the years. . . . She offers practical advice on selecting and learning stories, matching the story to the audience, and avoiding common performance pitfalls. . . . The presentation is conversational, filled with personal insights, interesting quotes, and thorough documentation." SLJ

Includes bibliographical references

372.63   Spelling and handwriting

Cunha, Stephen F.

How to ace the National Geographic Bee; official study guide. by Stephen F. Cunha. 4th ed. National Geographic 2012 127 p. ill., maps (library) $18.90; (paperback) $9.95

Grades: 4 5 6 7 8   **372.63**

1. Maps 2. Geography 3. Examinations -- Study guides 4. Contests 5. Geography -- Competitions 6. School contests -- United States -- Juvenile literature 7. Geography -- Competitions -- United States -- Juvenile

literature

ISBN 1426309856; 1426309864; 9781426309854; 9781426309861

LC 2012419185

This book "is a study guide to prepare the reader for test questions in geographic trivia. . . . The book then separates into six distinct chapters. It begins with defining geography and giving the reader an overall understanding of how the bee is conducted. Chapter 3 . . . defines the various types of maps and how they should be interpreted and also explains map features and landforms." (Voice of Youth Advocates)

Includes bibliographical references (p. 109-117).

372.64   Literature appreciation

MacDonald, Margaret Read

★ The **storyteller's** start-up book; finding, learning, performing, and using folktales including twelve tellable tales. August House 1993 215p $26.95; pa $14.95

Grades: Adult Professional   **372.64**

1. Folklore 2. Storytelling 3. Storytelling -- Handbooks, manuals, etc.

ISBN 0-87483-304-3; 0-87483-305-1 pa

LC 93-1580

The author's advice on storytelling "covers the practical ground, from selection, learning (in one hour!), performance, and setting to classroom applications. . . . A dozen texts of proven success follow, with performance tips and source notes. Equally valuable are the selected and annotated bibliographies appended to every chapter." Libr J

Includes bibliographical references

Pellowski, Anne

★ The **storytelling** handbook; a young people's collection of unusual tales and helpful hints on how to tell them. illustrated by Martha Stoberock. Simon & Schuster Bks. for Young Readers 1995 129p il hardcover o.p. pa $7.99

Grades: Adult Professional   **372.64**

1. Storytelling 2. Storytelling -- Juvenile literature

ISBN 0-689-80311-7; 978-1-4169-7598-4 pa; 1-4169-7598-5 pa

LC 95-2991

This work "addresses the young person who wants to tell stories in a public setting. It is similar in format to many adult books on storytelling how-tos, with sections on getting started and selecting and preparing stories, as well as a selection of sample tales. Pellowski's notes are extensive and will be very useful to novices looking for ways to research stories." Booklist

Includes bibliographical references

372.66   Drama (Theater)

Bany-Winters, Lisa

On stage; theater games and activities for kids. Lisa Bany-Winters. Chicago Review Press 2012 227 p. il (pbk.) $16.95

Grades: 3 4 5   **372.66**

1. Children's plays 2. Educational games 3. Drama in

education 4. Play 5. Children's plays, American
ISBN 1613740735; 9781613740736

LC 2012012741

This book, by Lisa Bany-Winters, is a theater teaching
resource for young actors, offering "more than 125 theater
games that spark creativity, boost confidence, and encourage
collaboration. They'll learn all about how to make a stage
performance great with improvisational games, . . . they'll
make puppets, discover makeup secrets, and design and
build a set." (Publisher's note)

Includes bibliographical references

Champlin, Connie

  ★ **Storytelling** with puppets; 2nd ed; American Library Association 1998 249p il pa $35

Grades: Adult Professional   **372.66**

  1. Storytelling 2. Puppets and puppet plays 3. Puppets
4. Puppet theater in education

ISBN 0-8389-0709-1

LC 97-24810

First published 1985 under the authorship of Connie
Champlin and Nancy Renfro

This book covers "such topics as puppet types and
styles, developing a puppet collection, participatory storytelling, and presentation formats. . . . A very useful choice
for professional shelves in both school and public libraries."
Booklist

Includes bibliographical references

372.7   Mathematics

Long, Ethan

  ★ The **Wing** Wing brothers math spectacular! Ethan
Long. Holiday House 2012 32 p. (hardcover) $15.95

Grades: PreK K 1 2   **372.7**

  1. Vaudeville -- Fiction 2. Mathematics -- Juvenile
literature 3. Numeration -- Study and teaching (Primary)
4. Numbers, Natural -- Study and teaching (Primary)

ISBN 0823423204; 9780823423200

LC 2011018256

The protagonists of this children's picture book, "Wilber,
Wendell, Willy, Walter, and Woody really know how to put
on a show. Five hilarious ducks juggle pies . . . spin plates . .
. and show off their magic box. . . . Their slapstick routine is
also a math lesson. They introduce the concepts greater than,
less than, and equal to as well as addition and subtraction."
(Publisher's note)

"[Long's] humorous illustrations—black pencil outlines
with digital color that are reminiscent of Mo Willems' pigeon—will keep kids riveted with the birds' fantastically expressive faces. This is how learning math should be—painless, comical and, yes, spectacular." Kirkus

Long, Lynette

  Measurement mania; games and activities that make
math easy and fun. Wiley 2001 122p il (Magical math)
pa $12.95

Grades: 3 4 5 6   **372.7**

  1. Measurement

ISBN 0-471-36980-2

LC 00-43383

In this introduction to measurement "the activities range
from using hands and feet to measure distance to making
a sundial. . . . [This book provides] valuable activities and
games to help children learn about the concepts." SLJ

VanCleave, Janice Pratt, 1942-

  Janice VanCleave's play and find out about math; easy
activities for young children. Wiley 1998 122p il $29.95;
pa $12.95

Grades: K 1 2   **372.7**

  1. Mathematics 2. Mathematics -- Juvenile literature

ISBN 0-471-12937-2; 0-471-12938-0 pa

LC 96-53002

"Fifty simple activities that involve basic arithmetic such
as using one's fingers to do simple addition and subtraction. .
. . Most procedures are between four and eight steps and are
clearly written and accompanied by pencil drawings." SLJ

372.89   History and geography

Panchyk, Richard

  New York City history for kids; from New Amsterdam
to the Big Apple, with 21 activities. Richard Panchyk. Chicago Review Press 2012 134 p. $16.95

Grades: 4 5 6   **372.89**

  1. Picture books for children 2. Historic buildings
-- New York (N.Y.) 3. New York (N.Y.) -- History --
Juvenile literature

ISBN 1883052939; 9781883052935

LC 2012029893

"In this . . . 400-year history [of New York City, by Richard Panchyk,] kids will read about Peter Stuyvesant and the
enterprising Dutch colonists, follow the . . . patriots as they
rebel against the British during the American Revolution, .
. . journey through the notorious Five Points slum with its
tenements and street vendors, and soar to new heights with
the Empire State Building and New York City's other . . .
skyscrapers." (Publisher's note)

  Includes bibliographical references and index

373.1   Organization and activities in secondary education

Glasser, Debbie

  New kid, new scene; a guide to moving and switching
schools. by Debbie Glasser and Emily Schenck. Magination Press 2012 112p il $14.95; pa 9.95

Grades: 5 6 7 8   **373.1**

  1. Moving 2. Students

ISBN 978-1-4338-1039-8; 1-4338-1039-5; 978-1-
4338-1038-1 pa; 1-4338-1038-7 pa

LC 2011013608

"Students making the transition to new schools, new
communities, or new homes will always experience a bit of
anxiety, and this self-help book offers practical advice on
how to make those changes smoother. The ideas and suggestions are sound and practical. . . . The eye-catching layout
will keep students flipping through the pages." SLJ

375 Curricula

Bishop, Kay

Connecting libraries with classrooms; the curricular roles of the media specialist. 2nd. ed.; Linworth 2011 122p pa $45

Grades: Adult Professional   **375**

1. Librarians 2. School libraries 3. Instructional materials centers

ISBN 978-1-59884-599-0; 1-59884-599-3

LC 2010051623

This book provides an . . . exploration of the topics that are currently relevant in K-12 curricula, including the school librarian's role in dealing with these issues, collaborating with teachers, and connecting to classrooms.

"Kay Bishop's book covers a wide range of topics and issues within the school library field. . . . Collaborative planning between classroom teacher, principal, students, and the community is also addressed. This material will be a welcome addition to the Library Media Specialist's arsenal of resources to stay current and involved." Libr Media Connect

Includes bibliographical references

379 Public policy issues in education

Morrison, Toni

Remember; the journey to school integration. Houghton Mifflin Co. 2004 78p il $18

Grades: 3 4 5   **379**

1. School integration 2. Discrimination in education 3. African Americans -- Education 4. School integration -- United States -- Juvenile literature 5. Discrimination in education -- United States -- Juvenile literature

ISBN 978-0-618-39740-2; 0-618-39740-X

LC 2003-22884

Historical real photo/portraits combined with simple factual statement from the point of view of African American children tells the history of the school integration in this country

"The provocative, candid images and conversational text should spark questions and discussion, a respect for past sacrifices, and inspiration for facing future challenges." SLJ

Walker, Paul Robert

★ **Remember** Little Rock; the time, the people, the stories. by Paul Robert Walker. National Geographic 2008 61p il map $17.95; lib bdg $27.90

Grades: 5 6 7 8 9   **379**

1. School integration 2. Segregation in education 3. African Americans -- Education

ISBN 978-1-4263-0402-6; 1-4263-0402-1; 978-1-4263-0403-3 lib bdg; 1-4263-0403-X lib bdg

LC 2008-24959

"The story of the battle to integrate Central High School in 1957 Little Rock, Arkansas, is presented through photographs and firsthand accounts from those who were there. . . . The multitude of eyewitness accounts, the poignant photographs, and the contextual background make this text a must-have addition to any classroom or library." Voice Youth Advocates

Includes bibliographical references

381 Commerce (Trade)

Freese, Susan M.

Craigslist; the company and its founder. ABDO Pub. Co. 2011 112p il (Technology pioneers) lib bdg $34.22

Grades: 5 6 7 8   **381**

1. Advertising 2. Businessmen 3. Internet marketing 4. Online social networks 5. Webmasters 6. Software engineers

ISBN 978-1-61714-806-4 lib bdg; 1-61714-806-7 lib bdg; 978-1-61758-964-5 e-book

LC 2010042448

This is an introduction to Craigslist and its founder, Craig Newmark.

"Written in a clear, linear fashion, this series offers vivid, well-researched details about the development of technological advancements considered essential in today's society. . . . Readers who are interested in technology and inventions will be thoroughly engrossed." SLJ

Includes glossary and bibliographical references

Krull, Kathleen

Supermarket; illustrated by Melanie Hope Greenberg. Holiday House 2001 un il $16.95

Grades: K 1 2 3   **381**

1. Supermarkets 2. Supermarkets -- United States -- Juvenile literature

ISBN 0-8234-1546-5

LC 99-88042

Explains modern supermarkets and how they work, discussing how they organize, display, and keep track of the items they sell

"Written in a clear and lively style. . . . Best of all, however, are the vibrant double-page gouache cartoon-style pictures using flat, decorative forms." SLJ

Lanz, Helen

Shopping choices; Helen Lanz. Sea-to-Sea Publications 2012 30 p. col. ill. (Go green) (library) $28.50

Grades: 3 4 5   **381**

1. Commerce -- Environmental aspects 2. Consumers -- Environmental aspects 3. Shopping -- Juvenile literature 4. Sustainable living -- Juvenile literature

ISBN 159771304X; 9781597713047

LC 2011005509

This entry in the Go Green series "reminds readers that all goods come from a finite supply of natural resources." It looks at "where products come from and how commerce contributes to global warming and impacts forests, while also suggesting solutions like frequenting thrift stores, purchasing products made from recycled materials, and identifying items approved by the Forest Stewardship Council." (Booklist)

Larson, Jennifer S.

Who's buying? Who's selling? understanding consumers and producers. Lerner Pub. 2010 32p il (Exploring economics) lib bdg $25.26; pa $7.95

Grades: K 1 2   **381**

1. Commerce

ISBN 978-0-7613-3912-0 lib bdg; 0-7613-3912-4 lib bdg; 978-0-7613-5665-3 pa; 0-7613-5665-3 pa

Photographs and simple text introduce young readers to how people buy and sell goods.

"Clear, age-appropriate language explains new concepts well. . . . The [book's] layout is interesting and fresh, and each page features a large, well-chosen photograph with a boxed caption." SLJ

Lassieur, Allison

Trade and commerce in the early Islamic world; Allison Lassieur. Crabtree Pub. Company 2012 48 p. (Life in the early Islamic world) (reinforced library binding: alk. paper) $30.60

Grades: 4 5 6   **381**

1. Commerce 2. Islam -- History

ISBN 0778721728; 9780778721727; 9780778721796; 9781427195654; 9781427198426

LC 2012000078

This book is part of a series where "each book covers a particular aspect of life in the early Islamic world. . . . The main texts are supplemented with blue boxes of information, subsections, and many . . . reproductions, maps, and paintings. Each book contains time lines and short biographies of important historical figures." (School Library Journal)

McClure, Nikki

★ **To** market, to market. Abrams Books for Young Readers 2011 un il $17.95

Grades: K 1 2 3   **381**

1. Food 2. Markets 3. Farm produce

ISBN 0-8109-9738-X; 978-0-8109-9738-7

LC 2010032946

"As a mother and son meander through the Olympia, WA, market, a full-page illustration shows them at a farmer's table while the facing page names the food sold there and briefly introduces the person who grows it. On the next page the farmer is illustrated at work and several paragraphs of elegant prose describe each process, ending with a simple 'thank you.' In this way, youngsters learn about apple-tree grafting and pruning, growing kale, beekeeping, smoking fish, baking, making batik napkins, and the art of cheese-making. . . . McClure's mysterious and beautiful images are cut from black paper with an X-Acto knife; the lacelike result is scanned and colored. McClure's art and life intersect in this stirring tribute to the connections among nature, people, and the food that nourishes them." SLJ

383 Communications and transportation

Brown, Craig McFarland

★ **Mule** train mail. Charlesbridge Pub. 2009 un il lib bdg $16.95; pa $7.95

Grades: 1 2 3   **383**

1. Postal service -- West (U.S.) 2. Muleteers -- Juvenile literature 3. Postal service -- Juvenile literature 4. Havasupai Indians -- Juvenile literature

ISBN 978-1-58089-187-5 lib bdg; 1-58089-187-X lib bdg; 978-1-58089-188-2 pa; 1-58089-188-8 pa

LC 2008007252

"Brown relates the daily trip made by Anthony the Postman from the top of the Grand Canyon to the village of Supai far below on the canyon floor. . . . An author's note gives additional details that children will appreciate. . . . He also describes the expedition he made with Anthony Paya, lead muleteer, to appreciate firsthand the journey and the rigors of the landscape. Brown's wonderful pastel and colored pencil illustrations are a testament to the time he spent on the trail. . . . A fascinating and informative addition." SLJ

Kay, Verla

Whatever happened to the Pony Express? illustrated by Kimberley Bulcken Root & Barry Root. G. P. Putnam's Sons 2010 un il $16.99

Grades: K 1 2 3   **383**

1. Pony express 2. Postal service

ISBN 978-0-399-24483-4; 0-399-24483-2

"Through a series of letters between a brother and sister, Kay examines changes in mail delivery during the time period 1851-1870. . . . The rhymed text flows well. . . . While the brief phrases provide the larger historical context, the illustrations, rendered in pencil, ink, gouache, and watercolor, are crucial in developing the personal drama of the siblings and their families. . . . Libraries will want to accept delivery of this attractive and informative package." SLJ

Kenney, Karen Latchana

Mail carriers at work; by Karen L. Kenney; illustrated by Brian Caleb Dumm; content consultant: Judith Stepan-Norris. Magic Wagon 2009 32p il (Meet your community!) lib bdg $18.95

Grades: K 1 2 3   **383**

1. Letter carriers 2. Vocational guidance

ISBN 978-1-60270-650-7 lib bdg; 1-60270-650-6 lib bdg

LC 2009-2398

This book about mail carriers has "an uncluttered layout and consistent organization. . . . Chapter headings such as 'Problems on the Job,' and 'Technology at Work,' and 'Special Skills and Training' make it easy to pinpoint specific information." SLJ

Includes glossary

Spradlin, Michael P.

Off like the wind! the first ride of the pony express. illustrated by Layne Johnson. Walker Books for Young Readers 2010 un il map $17.99; lib bdg $18.89

Grades: 3 4 5   **383**

1. Pony express 2. Postal service

ISBN 978-0-8027-9652-3; 0-8027-9652-4; 978-0-8027-9653-0 lib bdg; 0-8027-9653-2 lib bdg

LC 2009-10827

"Basing his book, as much as possible, on scanty historical records . . . Spradlin re-creates the Pony Express' first rides east from Sacramento and west from St. Joseph, Missouri—naming riders and horses when he can, and providing a composite of various Express riders' adventures. Johnson heightens the drama with evocative full-bleed oils." Booklist

Includes bibliographical references

Thompson, Gare

Riding with the mail; the story of the Pony Express. by Gare Thompson. National Geographic 2007 40p il map (National Geographic history chapters) lib bdg $17.90

Grades: 2 3 4   **383**

1. Pony express

ISBN 978-1-4263-0192-6 lib bdg; 1-4263-0192-8 lib bdg

LC 2007007897

"After an introduction sets the historical scene, this engaging volume provides a comprehensive introduction to the rise and fall of America's first postal service, the Pony Express.... Archival photographs, ... maps, and ... sidebars extend the text." Horn Book Guide

384.55 Television

Hirschmann, Kris
HDTV; high definition television. Norwood House Press 2010 48p il (A great idea) lib bdg $25.27
Grades: 3 4 5 6   **384.55**
1. High definition television
ISBN 978-1-59953-379-7 lib bdg; 1-59953-379-0 lib bdg
LC 2010008699
This "book is peppered with clear, current photographs, useful websites, and [a] complete [index]. Students do not need prior knowledge to appreciate [this] worthy [title]." SLJ
Includes glossary and bibliographical references

385 Railroad transportation

Curlee, Lynn
★ **Trains**. Atheneum Books for Young Readers 2009 40p il $19.99
Grades: 4 5 6   **385**
1. Railroads -- History
ISBN 978-1-4169-4848-3; 1-4169-4848-1
LC 2007-40425
"Curlee illuminates ... trains ... with stunning, clean-lined illustrations and informative narration. He opens with a romantic reminiscence about the mighty engines that rumbled through his North Carolina hometown. ... Launching into a chronological account of the evolution of the 'iron horse,' subsequent pages highlight major developments in (mostly American) railroad history, from the first steam engines to run on rails to the high-speed trains of Europe and Asia. Flatly styled and employing limited color palettes, several of Curlee's acrylic paintings will impress and awe readers." Publ Wkly

Floca, Brian
Locomotive; written and illustrated by Brian Floca. Atheneum Books for Young Readers 2013 64 p. ill. (hardcover) $17.99
Grades: K 1 2 3 4 5   **385**
1. Picture books for children 2. Locomotives -- Juvenile literature 3. Railroads -- United States -- History -- 19th century -- Juvenile literature
ISBN 1416994157; 9781416994152; 9781442485228
LC 2012042295
In this children's picture book, Brian Richard Floca "invites readers to join a family—mother, daughter and son—on one of the first passenger trips from Omaha to Sacramento after the meeting of the Union Pacific and the Central Pacific in May 1869. ... Floca visually documents the trip, vignettes illustrating the train's equipment as well as such ... details as toilet and sleeping conditions." (Kirkus Reviews)

Halpern, Monica
★ **Railroad** fever; building the Transcontinental Railroad, 1830-1870. [by] Monica Halpern. National Geographic 2004 40p il map (Crossroads America) $21.90; pa $12.95
Grades: 4 5 6   **385**
1. Frontier and pioneer life 2. Railroads -- History
ISBN 0-7922-6767-2; 0-7922-6767-2 pa
LC 2003-17858
Presents a history of the building of the transcontinental railroad and its effects on American life
"This is a first-choice purchase for its visually appealing presentation and its succinct yet thorough treatment of the topic." SLJ
Includes glossary

McMahon, Peter
Ultimate trains. Kids Can Press 2010 40p il (Machines of the future) $16.95
Grades: 4 5 6 7   **385**
1. Railroads 2. Science -- Experiments
ISBN 978-1-55453-366-4; 1-55453-366-X
"In simple engaging text and illustrations, McMahon and Mora present a brief history of [railroads]. Integral to the book are five experiments children can create. ... Each experiment ties in well with a particular type of train, features clear instructions, and offers safety precautions." Booklist
Includes glossary

Murphy, Jim
Across America on an emigrant train. Clarion Bks. 1993 150p il hardcover o.p. pa $10.95
Grades: 5 6 7 8   **385**
1. Poets 2. Authors 3. Novelists 4. Authors, Scottish 5. Essayists 6. Travel writers 7. Short story writers 8. Railroads -- History 9. Railroads -- United States -- Juvenile literature 10. United States -- Description -- Juvenile literature 11. United States -- Immigration and emigration -- Juvenile literature
ISBN 0-395-63390-7; 0-395-76483-1 pa
LC 92-38650
"Murphy presents a forthright and thoroughly engrossing history of the transcontinental railway, with entries from Robert Louis Stevenson's 1879 journal as he rode cross country. It's also an inviting introduction to Stevenson, with a romance in the bargain." SLJ
Includes bibliographical references

Perritano, John
The **transcontinental** railroad. Children's Press 2010 48p il map (True book) lib bdg $26; pa $6.95
Grades: 3 4 5   **385**
1. Railroads -- History
ISBN 978-0-531-20585-3 lib bdg; 978-0-531-21248-6 pa
LC 2009014185
This introduction to the history of the transcontinental railroads provides "elementary readers with clear explanations, maps, illustrations, time lines, and engaging reproductions of primary resources. [This] volume contains eye-catching quick facts; illustrations and photographs are representational of regional Native Americans, pioneers, and

explorers. This is ideal material for reports on the Westward expansion." SLJ

Includes bibliographical references

Simon, Seymour

★ **Seymour** Simon's book of trains. HarperCollins Pubs. 2002 un il $16.99; lib bdg $17.89; pa $6.99
Grades: K 1 2 3   **385**
1. Railroads 2. Railroads -- Trains
ISBN 0-06-028475-7; 0-06-028476-5 lib bdg; 0-06-446223-4 pa

LC 2001-24020

"Each double-page spread in this picture book sets a dramatic close-up photo of a moving train opposite a few sentences about the train's source of power (steam, diesel, electric) and how it works. The full-color, close-up pictures by a number of photographers will grab even young pre-schoolers. . . . The astonishing facts will interest older train buffs." Booklist

Steele, Phillip W.

Legendary journeys: trains. Kingfisher 2010 30p $19.99
Grades: 3 4 5   **385**
1. Railroads -- History
ISBN 978-0-7534-6465-6; 0-7534-6465-9

"The squat, wide format of this book is already well-suited to its subject matter, and it becomes even more so when its trick is revealed: five pages pull out, almost tripling the scenes' width and unveiling additional railroad cars. Steele provides an informative chronology of locomotive history from the advent of steam power to the rise of luxury trains." Publ Wkly

Zimmermann, Karl R.

★ **All** aboard! passenger trains around the world. [by] Karl Zimmermann; photography by the author. Boyds Mills Press 2006 48p il $19.95
Grades: 5 6 7 8   **385**
1. Railroads 2. Railroads -- Passenger-cars -- Juvenile literature
ISBN 1-59078-325-5

LC 2005-24990

Zimmermann "has traveled by train across six continents, and his beautiful, big color photos appear on every double-page spread of this enthusiastic account, which blends history, geography, business, and engineering with his personal focus." Booklist

★ **Steam** locomotives; whistling, chugging, smoking iron horses of the past. Boyds Mills Press 2004 48p il $19.95
Grades: 4 5 6 7   **385**
1. Locomotives 2. Steam engines
ISBN 1-59078-165-1

"In this photo-essay, Zimmermann shares his excitement for steam locomotives with young readers, tracing the development of the early engines and their impact on the history of the U.S. He includes a clear explanation . . . of how a steam engine works. The photographs, some archival and some from the present day, are excellent. . . . The engaging text clearly imparts the author's enthusiasm and love for the subject." SLJ

Includes glossary

386   Inland waterway and ferry transportation

Harness, Cheryl

★ The **amazing** impossible Erie Canal. Macmillan Bks. for Young Readers 1995 un il map hardcover o.p. pa $5.99
Grades: 3 4 5   **386**
1. Erie Canal (N.Y.) -- Juvenile literature
ISBN 0-02-742641-6; 0-689-82584-6 pa

LC 94-11114

"Harness has done a wonderful job of making the history and construction of the Erie Canal come alive. . . . The narrative is matched with illustrations that cover each page." SLJ

Includes bibliographical references

Kendall, Martha E.

The **Erie** Canal; by Martha E. Kendall. National Geographic 2008 128p il $18.95; lib bdg $28.90
Grades: 4 5 6   **386**
1. Erie Canal (N.Y.)
ISBN 978-1-4263-0022-6; 978-1-4263-0023-3 lib bdg

LC 2007029386

"This handsomely packaged introduction to our country's first great public works project pairs plenty of period prints and photos to a fluidly written account of the canal's origins, construction, uses and the folklore surrounding it." Booklist

387.1   Ports

House, Katherine L.

Lighthouses for kids; history, science, and lore with 21 activities. [by] Katherine L. House. Chicago Review Press 2008 118p il pa $14.95
Grades: 4 5 6 7 8   **387.1**
1. Lighthouses
ISBN 978-1-55652-720-3 pa; 1-55652-720-9 pa

LC 2007-27093

"This book is noteworthy for the way in which the activities are related to the information in the text. . . . Readers learn about the challenges of building . . . [lighthouses], inventions to make them more reliable, and how lighthouses function as historical relics today." SLJ

Includes glossary and bibliographical references

387.2   Ships

Barton, Byron

★ **Boats**. Crowell 1986 un il lib bdg $16.89; bd bk $6.99
Grades: K 1   **387.2**
1. Ships 2. Boats and boating
ISBN 0-690-04536-0 lib bdg; 0-694-01165-7 bd bk

LC 85-47900

Depicts a variety of boats and a cruise ship docking and unloading passengers

"Thick black outlines contain vivid colors . . . clean lines, bright hues, and undemanding text." Booklist

Floca, Brian

★ **Lightship**. Atheneum Books for Young Readers 2007 un il $16.99

Grades: K 1 2   **387.2**

1. Lightships

ISBN 978-1-4169-2436-4; 1-4169-2436-1

LC 2005-28028

"Lightships—floating lighthouses—were retired in 1983, but they live on in Floca's handsome picture book, which uses simple words and repeated phrases to emphasize the vessels' purpose and uniqueness as well as their day-to-day operation. . . . Some pictures include elements of humor, while other scenes are notable for their quiet beauty." Booklist

Lavery, Brian

Legendary journeys: ships; illustrated Sebastian Quigley. Kingfisher 2011 il $19.99

Grades: 3 4 5   **387.2**

1. Ships

ISBN 978-0-7534-6681-0; 0-7534-6681-3

"Compelling details and interactive effects appear throughout this guide to ships. . . . Recreations of Greek triremes, Viking longships, and the Titanic, among others, are enhanced by slide-out pages that double (or more) the spreads' width, providing a sense of the boats' scale. Flaps reveal cross-sections of ships' interiors, while depictions of naval, cargo, and other commercial vessels emphasize our continued reliance on ships. A thorough and well-constructed guide for boat fanatics." Publ Wkly

Zimmermann, Karl R.

★ **Ocean** liners; crossing and cruising the seven seas. photographs by the author. Boyds Mills Press 2008 48p il $17.95

Grades: 5 6 7 8   **387.2**

1. Ocean liners 2. Ocean travel

ISBN 978-1-59078-552-2; 1-59078-552-5

LC 2007049323

This is "a comprehensive overview of ships from sail to steam to diesel, from the important modes of transportation to the modern resorts at sea. The information is organized in chapters about the history and development of the ships, the star ships of the Atlantic crossings and the conversion to modern cruising. . . . All is accompanied by photographs taken over the years by the author and supplemented by historic drawings, photos and documents. . . . A fascinating voyage." Kirkus

Includes glossary

387.7   Air transportation

Barton, Byron

★ **Airplanes**. Crowell 1986 un il lib bdg $15.89

Grades: PreK K 1   **387.7**

1. Airplanes

ISBN 0-690-04532-8

LC 85-47899

Brief text and illustrations present a variety of airplanes and what they do, "as well as some of the usual scenes surrounding each (e.g., workers checking a passenger plane). Brightly colored illustrations outlined in heavy black convey

a bold and simple first impression, yet they portray a good number of accurate details that preschoolers find so fascinating." SLJ

★ **Airport**. Crowell 1982 un il lib bdg $18.89; pa $6.99

Grades: PreK K 1   **387.7**

1. Airports 2. Airplanes

ISBN 0-690-04169-1 lib bdg; 0-06-443145-2 pa

LC 79-7816

"In a brightly illustrated book, the author/artist captures the hustle and bustle of passenger traffic from arrival at the terminal to take off." Kobrin Letter

Parker, Steve

By air. Marshall Cavendish Benchmark 2011 il (Future transport)

Grades: 4 5 6   **387.7**

1. Aeronautics 2. Forecasting

ISBN 1608707776; 9781608707775

LC 2011000998

"Beginning with a speculative illustration featuring people of the future traveling through the air in carlike personal jets, this title . . . offers a fascinating look at prototypes for all sorts of aircraft, from small planes to passenger airliners to lighter-than-air vehicles. . . . The various possibilities for future aircraft are covered in double-page spreads that are well laid out and easy to digest. Illustrated with plenty of striking, digitally enhanced color pictures, this will probably be of equal interest to those doing reports and browsers." Booklist

Includes bibliographical references

Parker, Steve, 1952-

My first trip on an airplane. Heinemann Library 2011 24p il (Growing up) lib bdg $22; pa $6.49

Grades: PreK K 1 2   **387.7**

1. Airports 2. Airplanes 3. Aeronautics

ISBN 978-1-4329-4801-6 lib bdg; 1-4329-4801-6 lib bdg; 978-1-4329-4811-5 pa; 1-4329-4811-3 pa

LC 2010024195

This book examines a "common, often scary [event] in children's lives and [guides] readers through [it] step-by-step. The [author discusses] the who, what, and why of [the] experience . . . [including] what happens before and during a flight. . . . By confronting . . . fears head-on, children will feel 'in the know' and be prepared to experience [this first]. The text—two sentences per page in a large font and placed on white space—is accompanied by large color photos of children, families, and adults of a variety of ethnic backgrounds. [The] volume includes boldface vocabulary words, a picture glossary, and dos and don'ts." SLJ

Includes glossary and bibliographical references

388   Transportation

Flatt, Lizann

Let's go! the story of getting from there to here. [by] Lizann Flatt; illustrated by Scot Ritchie. Maple Tree 2007 un il $16.95

Grades: K 1 2   **388**
1. Transportation
ISBN 978-1-897349-02-1; 1-897349-02-5

"A breezy picture book introduction to modes of North American transportation from foot power to space vehicle. The book is rich in descriptive language and follows a logical time line. . . . Vivid, double-page spreads of artwork, rendered in rainbow colors, provide added details." SLJ

Gaarder-Juntti, Oona
What in the world is green transportation? ABDO Pub. Company 2011 24p il (Going green) lib bdg $24.21
Grades: 1 2 3 4   **388**
1. Transportation -- Environmental aspects
ISBN 978-1-61613-193-7 lib bdg; 1-61613-193-4 lib bdg

LC 2010004310

"The lively layout design, featuring colorful headings, short paragraphs, and attractive photographs, has a scrapbook-like quality. . . . [The title explains] how all our choices require energy and resources, and encourage readers to make changes in their lifestyles. . . . [This] . . . will inspire and empower readers to make a difference." SLJ
Includes glossary and bibliographical references

Konrad, Marla Stewart
Getting there. Tundra Books 2009 un il (World vision early readers) $12.95
Grades: PreK K   **388**
1. Transportation
ISBN 978-0-88776-867-5; 0-88776-867-9

"This book depicts an ordinary aspect of every child's life—getting from one place to another. . . . What makes it extraordinary are the images that depict the journey: a child in Africa sitting on his mother's shoulders, for example, or a little girl riding a yak to her destination. Each spread includes an easy, large-font sentence or phrase, but it is the stunning color photographs that tell the richer story. Sure to spark questions, observations, and awe." SLJ

Mulder, Michelle
Pedal it! how bicycles are changing the world. Michelle Mulder. Orca Book Publishers 2013 48 p. (Footprints) (hardcover) $19.95
Grades: 3 4 5 6 7 8   **388**
1. Cycling 2. Bicycles
ISBN 1459802195; 9781459802193

LC 2012953464

This book, by Michelle Mulder, "celebrates the humble bicycle--from the very first boneshakers to the sleek racing bikes of today, from handlebars to spokes to gear sprockets--and shows you why and how bikes can make the world a better place. Not only can bikes be used to power computers and generators, they can also reduce pollution, promote wellness and get a package across a crowded city--fast!" (Publisher's note)

Wooldridge, Connie Nordhielm
Just fine the way they are; from dirt roads to rail roads to interstates. illustrated by Richard Walz. Calkins Creek 2011 un il $17.95
Grades: 2 3 4 5   **388**
1. Roads 2. Transportation
ISBN 978-1-59078-710-6; 1-59078-710-2

"Wooldridge's picture book traces the development of the National Road in the United States. . . . Wooldridge interjects the public's positive and negative opinions regarding the road's development and describes how the inventions of the steam engine and automobile influenced changes in the highway, which ultimately became Route 40 and crossed the country. As the story winds down, Wooldridge raises the problem of air pollution. Her folksy, conversational writing style incorporates flavorful language. . . . Muscular horses, changing modes of transportation, and caricatured people populate the bright artwork." SLJ
Includes bibliographical references

388.4   Local transportation

Miller, Heather
★ **Subway** ride; illustrated by Sue Rama. Charlesbridge 2009 un il lib bdg $15.95
Grades: PreK K 1   **388.4**
1. Subways
ISBN 978-1-58089-111-0 lib bdg; 1-58089-111-X lib bdg

LC 2008-7249

"Take a ride on subway trains all around the world. Beginning in Cairo, a multicultural group of children rides the trains in ten cities, zigzagging from stop to stop around the globe. . . . Vivid colors and blurred lines evoke a bustling cheer. Cleverly composed to suggest both depth and action, the pictures tell most of the story. . . . The offbeat idea is deftly handled and should trigger further study." Kirkus

389   Metrology and standardization

Adler, David A., 1947-
Time zones; illustrated by Edward Miller. Holiday House 2010 31p il map $16.95
Grades: 3 4 5   **389**
1. Time
ISBN 978-0-8234-2201-2; 0-8234-2201-1

LC 2009007733

"Adler offers a simple but thorough explanation of time zones and why people experience different parts of the day simultaneously depending on their location around the globe. Illustrations of an astronaut and his robot dog provide a perspective from high above Earth, which helps readers visualize the way sunlight reaches different parts of the planet as it rotates. . . . Numerous maps and diagrams help visualize these abstract boundaries, including the international date line in the Pacific. . . . Adler explains the impact of daylight savings time and includes a simple experiment for readers to see for themselves how noon and midnight occur simultaneously on opposite sides of the globe." SLJ

Bernhard, Durga
While you are sleeping; a lift-the-flap book of time around the world. Charlesbridge 2011 un il map $14.95
Grades: PreK K 1 2 3   **389**
1. Time
ISBN 978-1-57091-473-7; 1-57091-473-7

LC 2010007589

"A clever design allows readers to travel the world, one page turn at a time. . . . The illustrations show an Alaskan child curled up in bed with a parent at 10 p.m., facing a map of Africa, Nigeria highlighted, with an inset gatefold. A flip reveals a young Nigerian girl at 9 a.m. Turning the page reveals that same Nigerian girl opposite a Japanese child . . . and so on until the circular tale returns to Alaska. Teachers will appreciate Bernhard's incorporation of 12- and 24-hour digital clocks, as well as the analog clock hiding under each gatefold. The final page is a map of the world delineated by time zone and includes thumbnails from each highlighted country. A small text block explains the reason for the time zones and tells how they work. Gorgeous illustrations combine beautiful colors with a glimpse of life in other countries." Kirkus

Murphy, Stuart J.

Mighty Maddie; comparing weights. illustrated by Bernice Lum. HarperCollins Publishers 2004 31p il (MathStart) hardcover o.p. pa $4.99

Grades: K 1 2   389

1. Cleanliness 2. Measurement 3. Orderliness 4. Weights and measures 5. Weight (Physics) -- Measurement

ISBN 0-06-053159-2; 0-06-053161-4 pa

LC 2003-17610

As Maddie cleans up her room, she learns how to compare the weights of various objects

"Childlike line drawings with bright colors give readers a sense of action. This appealing book has uses beyond the math concept, and offers messages about family life, self-image, and responsibility." SLJ

391 Customs

Bliss, John

Preening, painting, and piercing; body art. Raintree 2010 32p il (Culture in action) lib bdg $29

Grades: 5 6 7 8   391

1. Body art 2. Cosmetics 3. Tattooing 4. Theatrical makeup

ISBN 978-1-4109-3924-1; 1-4109-3924-1

LC 2009051182

"This book covers different looks achieved through makeup, body painting, tattoos, and piercing. Photographs, advertisements, paintings, and artifacts show a variety of cultures and time periods and help readers see the huge changes in the fashion of physical appearance. . . . The author does a good job of explaining that some cultures have negative stereotypes of tattooed people being criminals and some piercing can be dangerous to people with allergies. Fun activities are included. . . . This book . . . is well written and has few biases." SLJ

Includes glossary and bibliographical references

DeCarufel, Laura

Learn to speak fashion; a guide to creating, showcasing, and promoting your style. DeCarufel, Laura. Owlkids Books, Inc. 2012 96 p. (hardcover) $22.95

Grades: 4 5 6   391

1. Fashion -- Juvenile literature 2. Fashion -- Handbooks, manuals, etc. 3. Clothing and dress -- Juvenile literature ISBN 1926973372; 9781926973371

LC 2011941966

Author Laura deCarufel "takes preteen readers with her on the 'clothes + art = fashion' formula. She starts with finding one's own style and continues with learning to see: using visual curiosity to examine design, pattern, color and so on to find what inspires. Window shopping, building a wardrobe, preparing a sketchbook and learning to sew are all part of the plan. She gives advice about runway shows, models, fashion shoots, stylists and so on." (Kirkus)

Jaber, Pamela

When royals wore ruffles; a funny & fashionable alphabet! written by Chesley McLaren and Pamela Jaber; illustrated by Chesley McLaren. Schwartz & Wade Books 2009 un il $16.99; lib bdg $19.99

Grades: K 1 2 3   391

1. Alphabet 2. Fashion -- History 3. Clothing and dress -- History

ISBN 978-0-375-85166-7; 0-375-85166-6; 978-0-375-95166-4 lib bdg; 0-375-95166-0 lib bdg

LC 2008017374

McLaren and "Jaber cover the fashion waterfront, enlightening readers on both history . . . and the less tangible aspects of glamour. . . . The commentary is smart and accessible. . . . Witty as the writing may be, the illustrations are irresistible. Like the best fashion, the lines and colors feel effortlessly right." Publ Wkly

Krull, Kathleen

★ Big wig; a little history of hair. illustrated by Peter Malone. Arthur A. Levine Books 2011 un il $18.99

Grades: 3 4 5 6   391

1. Hair 2. Fashion

ISBN 978-0-439-67640-3; 0-439-67640-1

LC 2010031005

"Krull delivers a fascinating and quite funny 'history' of humankind's relationship with hair, from furry prehistory to the advent of punk style. . . . Equally wonderful are Malone's gouache illustrations, rife with humor." Publ Wkly

Includes bibliographical references

Morris, Ann

Hats, hats, hats; photographs by Ken Heyman. Lothrop, Lee & Shepard Bks. 1989 un il $16; pa $4.95

Grades: PreK K 1   391

1. Hats

ISBN 0-688-06338-1; 0-688-12274-4 pa

LC 88-26676

This book introduces a variety of hats worn around the world

"The vivid color photographs, one or two per page, show people engaged in lively activities while . . . wearing their hats. Each picture offers a strong ethnic identity or a thought-provoking human interaction, with captions of only a few words in large print. An unusual index . . . gives background information about the pictures, citing the countries of origin and a few facts about each . . . kind of hat." SLJ

Shoes, shoes, shoes. Lothrop, Lee & Shepard Bks. 1995 32p il hardcover o.p. pa $4.95

Grades: PreK K 1   391
1. Shoes
ISBN 0-688-13666-4; 0-688-16166-9 pa

LC 94-46649

"Morris gives a world-tour of shoes . . . in [a] picture book illustrated by various photographers. In rhyming text, she talks about shoes for all kinds of activities. . . . [The] book includes a map and a photograph key of the places visited." Bull Cent Child Books

Platt, Richard
They wore what?! the weird history of fashion and beauty. [by] Richard Platt. Two-Can 2007 48p il $16.95; pa $9.95
Grades: 4 5 6   391
1. Personal appearance 2. Fashion -- History
ISBN 978-1-58728-582-0; 1-58728-582-7; 978-1-58728-584-4 pa; 1-58728-584-3 pa

LC 2006039159

Published in the United Kingdom with title: Would you believe in 1500, platform shoes were outlawed?

"Busy, colorful pages recount the historical, social, and political sides of clothing, hair, hats, and shoes, from legal and moral issues such as wearing fur to dangerous practices like cinched waists and bound feet. . . . Ever-fluctuating ideas of beauty and body image are also explored." Horn Book Guide

Includes glossary and bibliographical references

Rowland-Warne, L.
Costume; written by L. Rowland-Warne; [special photography, Liz McAulay] Dorling Kindersley 2000 63p il (DK eyewitness books) $15.99; lib bdg $19.99
Grades: 4 5 6 7   391
1. Costume 2. Clothing and dress 3. Fashion -- History
ISBN 0-7894-5586-2; 0-7894-6584-1 lib bdg
First published 1992 by Knopf

Photographs and text document the history and meaning of clothing, from loincloths to modern children's clothes

Swain, Ruth Freeman
Underwear; what we wear under there. by Ruth Freeman Swain; illustrated by John O'Brien. Holiday House 2008 32p il $16.95
Grades: 2 3 4 5   391
1. Underwear 2. Fashion -- History
ISBN 978-0-8234-1920-3; 0-8234-1920-7

LC 2008-4041

"Swain packs a lot of detail into the text as she quickly and chronologically progresses through a discussion of different types of underwear throughout the ages and how it has accommodated people's lifestyles. Children will find a multitude of interesting historical tidbits. . . . The winsome, imaginative illustrations vary in size and are rendered in watercolor over ink." SLJ

392   Customs of life cycle and domestic life

Laroche, Giles
★ If you lived here; houses of the world. Houghton Mifflin Harcourt 2011 un il $16.99

Grades: K 1 2 3   392
1. Houses
ISBN 978-0-547-23892-0; 0-547-23892-4

LC 2010044361

"Laroche applies his signature bas-relief cut-paper collage technique to sixteen different dwellings that illustrate the range of places that people call home. . . . Each . . . is introduced with a paragraph that begins with the phrase 'If you lived here,' enticing the reader to imagine how it might be. . . . For young readers, these profiles not only provide glimpses into the lives of people who might live very differently from us but also expand and broaden their worldview." Horn Book

Lauber, Patricia
★ What you never knew about beds, bedrooms, and pajamas; illustrated by John Manders. Simon & Schuster Books for Young Readers 2007 un il (Around-the-house history) $16.95
Grades: 2 3 4   392
1. Sleeping customs 2. Beds -- Juvenile literature 3. Sleepwear -- Juvenile literature
ISBN 0-689-85211-8

LC 2004-20654

"Focusing on sleeping customs through the ages, Lauber begins with the Stone Age and moves up to the 1700s, but includes some more contemporary facts as well. . . . Manders's engaging artwork varies between full-page and spot illustrations. The humorous asides from characters in the comic-style pictures will entertain youngsters." SLJ

Includes bibliographical references

393   Death customs

Carney, Elizabeth
Mummies. National Geographic 2009 31p il (National Geographic readers) lib bdg $11.90; pa $3.99
Grades: 1 2 3   393
1. Mummies
ISBN 978-1-4263-0529-0 lib bdg; 1-4263-0529-X lib bdg; 978-1-4263-0528-3 pa; 1-4263-0528-1 pa

LC 2009-3630

"In challenging but readable text for early independent readers, Carney highlights mummies discovered all over the world. Details such as a 2,300-year-old vegetable soup in one mummy's stomach and another's still-soft hair and skin raise the bar on an already high-interest topic. Photographs don't shy away from showing human remains." Horn Book Guide

Deem, James M.
★ Bodies from the ice; melting glaciers and the recovery of the past. Houghton Mifflin 2008 58p il map $17
Grades: 5 6 7 8 9 10   393
1. Mummies 2. Glaciers 3. Glaciers -- Juvenile literature 4. Young adult literature -- Works 5. Ice mummies -- Juvenile literature
ISBN 978-0-618-80045-2; 0-618-80045-X

LC 2008-01868

A Sibert Medal honor book, 2009

This describes the discovery of human remains preserved in glaciers in the Alps, the Andes, The Himalayas, and other places around the world and what can be learned from them

"Full-color photographs, reproductions, and maps are clearly captioned; grand images of glaciated mountain peaks span entire pages, and detailed pictures of recovered objects . . . are presented. . . . [This] is a fantastic resource. Deem superbly weaves diverse geographical settings, time periods, and climate issues into a readable work that reveals the increasing interdisciplinary dimensions of the sciences." SLJ

Includes bibliographical references

Halls, Kelly Milner
Mysteries of the mummy kids. Darby Creek Pub. 2007 72p il map $18.95
Grades: 4 5 6 7   393
1. Mummies 2. Human remains (Archæology) -- Juvenile literature

"Halls presents an eerily fascinating exploration of mummified children and teens found in South and North America, Europe, and Asia. . . . The writing style is plain yet absorbing, presenting scientific and historical information in simple terms." Voice Youth Advocates

Includes bibliographical references

Knapp, Ron
Mummy secrets uncovered. Enslow Publishers 2011 48p il (Bizarre science) lib bdg $23.93
Grades: 5 6 7 8   393
1. Mummies
ISBN 978-0-7660-3670-3; 0-7660-3670-7
                                              LC 2010000976
First published 1996 with title: Mummies
This describes mummies such as the Iceman found in the Italian Alps in 1991, King Tut of Egypt, the people of Pompeii killed by the eruption of Mount Vesuvius, Tollund Man found in Denmark in 1950, and the Ice Maiden found in the Siberian Steppes.

"Aimed at reluctant readers, [this title is] sure to disgust and delight in equal measure. . . . [The title] will pique interest and get kids lining up at the reference desk looking for more. The text is complemented by illustrations and magnified photos of things that you would hope never to see." SLJ

Includes glossary and bibliographical references

Markle, Sandra
★ **Outside** and inside mummies. Walker & Co. 2005 40p il $17.95; lib bdg $18.85
Grades: 4 5 6 7   393
1. Mummies 2. Mummies -- Juvenile literature
ISBN 0-8027-8966-8; 0-8027-8967-6 lib bdg
                                              LC 2004-66128
"Markle explores a global smorgasbord of mummy varieties, both those created by human procedures and those caused by nature. Crisp (if gruesome) color photos accompany the readable, informative text, which discusses not only the mummification process, but also the cutting-edge technologies used by forensic anthropologists and others to study the mummies themselves." SLJ

Includes glossary

Rau, Dana Meachen
Mummies. Marshall Cavendish Benchmark 2010 24p il (Surprising science) lib bdg $22.79

Grades: 2 3 4   393
1. Mummies
ISBN 978-0-7614-4869-3; 0-7614-4869-1
                                              LC 2009053761
"Colorfully illustrated with photographs on each page, this . . . will be well received by elementary students and educators." Libr Media Connect

Includes glossary and bibliographical references

Robson, David
The **mummy**. ReferencePoint Press 2011 il (Monsters and mythical creatures) $27.95
Grades: 6 7 8 9   393
1. Mummies
ISBN 978-1-60152-182-8; 1-60152-182-0
                                              LC 2011022437
This is "an ideal starting point for young researchers interested in the weird, mysterious, and paranormal. Using fleet, descriptive prose to communicate the impressively researched (and sourced) information, [this] medium-length [work manages] to rope in just about everything, from folklore to history to pop culture. . . . The Mummy begins with the seminal 1932 Boris Karloff film before backtracking into the worldwide 'mummy lust' that began with the 1922 discovery of King Tut's tomb and and the subsequent curses and legends. . . . The illustrations are fine and varied, the sidebars always illuminating, and the back matter robust." Booklist

Includes bibliographical references

Sloan, Christopher
Mummies. National Geographic 2010 48p il (National Geographic Kids) $17.95; lib bdg $26.90
Grades: 4 5 6 7   393
1. Mummies
ISBN 978-1-4263-0695-2; 1-4263-0695-4; 978-1-4263-0696-9 lib bdg; 1-4263-0696-2 lib bdg
                                              LC 2010-08498
"A gratifyingly grisly album of choice photos accompanies Sloan's lucid, informative text as he describes not only the mummification processes but also individual mummies produced whether by intent or by chance. From the dried Beauty of Krorän in China to the bundled Lady of Cao in a Peruvian pyramid or the familiar Boy King Tut in Egypt, a global variety is offered to fascinated readers. . . . [This is a] well-written, heavily illustrated glimpse into the world of after-death preservation, either by accident or design." SLJ

Includes glossary and bibliographical references

394 General customs

Gibbons, Gail
★ **Knights** in shining armor. Little, Brown 1995 un il hardcover o.p. pa $7.99
Grades: K 1 2 3   394
1. Medieval civilization 2. Knights and knighthood
3. Armor -- Juvenile literature 4. Chivalry -- Juvenile literature
ISBN 0-316-30948-6 lib bdg; 0-316-30038-1 pa
                                              LC 94-35525
The author "covers tournaments, chivalry, and what happened when a bad knight was caught. Legendary knights

such as Sir Gawain and the knights of the Round Table are briefly described, as is St. George and the dragon, and Gibbons also discusses present-day knights. The watercolor-and-ink pictures are some of Gibbons' liveliest and most attractive." Booklist

394.1 Eating, drinking; using drugs

Ancona, George
Come and eat. Charlesbridge 2011 il $16.95; pa $7.95
Grades: K 1 2 **394.1**
1. Eating customs
ISBN 158089366X; 1580893678; 9781580893664; 9781580893671
LC 2010033632
"This introduces food customs around the world for younger children. As focused on culture as on food, the brief, chatty text discusses the varied ways foods are eaten. . . . The clean design features full-color photos." Booklist

Augustin, Byron
The food of Mexico. Marshall Cavendish Benchmark 2011 il (Flavors of the world) $21.95
Grades: 4 5 6 7 **394.1**
1. Mexican cooking 2. Festivals -- Mexico
ISBN 978-1-6087-0237-4
LC 2010013830
Includes bibliographical references

Ichord, Loretta Frances
★ Double cheeseburgers, quiche, and vegetarian burritos; American cooking from the 1920s through today. by Loretta Frances Ichord; illustrated by Jan Davey Ellis. Millbrook Press 2007 63p il (Cooking through time) lib bdg $25.26
Grades: 3 4 5 6 **394.1**
1. Cooking 2. Eating customs 3. Food habits -- Juvenile literature 4. Cookery, American -- Juvenile literature
ISBN 978-0-8225-5969-6 lib bdg; 0-8225-5969-2 lib bdg
LC 2005-24535
"Each chapter, illustrated with lighthearted drawings, presents a quick, cogent overview of an American eating trend—from the first processed foods through TV dinners, fast food, the mainstreaming of organic foods, and more—ending with the influential fad diets of the 1990s. The examples are clear and lively, and relevant recipes close each chapter." Booklist
Includes bibliographical references

Kras, Sara Louise
The food of Italy. Marshall Cavendish Benchmark 2011 il (Flavors of the world) $21.95
Grades: 4 5 6 7 **394.1**
1. Italian cooking 2. Festivals -- Italy
ISBN 978-1-6087-0236-7
LC 2010021542
This explores the culture, traditions, and festivals of Italy through its food.
Includes bibliographical references

Kummer, Patricia K.
The food of Thailand. Marshall Cavendish Benchmark 2011 il (Flavors of the world) $21.95
Grades: 4 5 6 7 **394.1**
1. Thai cooking 2. Festivals -- Thailand
ISBN 978-1-6087-0238-1
LC 2010023508
This explores the culture, traditions, and festivals of Thailand through its food.
Includes bibliographical references

Lauber, Patricia
★ What you never knew about fingers, forks, & chopsticks; illustrated by John Manders. Simon & Schuster Bks. for Young Readers 1999 un il (Around-the-house history) $16
Grades: 2 3 4 **394.1**
1. Tableware 2. Eating customs 3. Table etiquette
ISBN 0-689-80479-2
LC 97-17041
Describes changes in eating customs throughout the centuries and the origins of table manners
"A delicious blend of humor and fascinating facts. . . . The lively, linear drawings incorporate amusing asides in dialogue balloons that will entertain readers as the text enlightens them about the subject." SLJ
Includes bibliographical references

Mogren, Molly
Andrew Zimmern's field guide to exceptionally weird, wild, & wonderful foods; an intrepid eater's digest. by Andrew Zimmern. 1st ed. Feiwel & Friends 2012 197 p. ill. (paperback) $14.99; (hardcover) $19.99
Grades: 5 6 7 **394.1**
1. Food 2. Cooking
ISBN 0312606613; 125001929X; 9780312606619; 9781250019295
LC 2012289475
This book is a "guide to world cuisine." The authors Andrew Zimmern and Molly Mogren "focus on 40 unusual foodstuffs including cockroaches, guinea pigs, headcheese, lutefisk, turducken, and Twinkies. Recipes, interviews, and a great many facts . . . lead to . . . digressions, including suggestions on how to survive a zombie outbreak . . . and a time line of popular dances, following a discussion of eating 'dancing' (live) shrimp." (Publishers Weekly)

Orr, Tamra
The food of Greece; [by] Tamra B. Orr. Marshall Cavendish Benchmark 2011 il (Flavors of the world) $21.95
Grades: 4 5 6 7 **394.1**
1. Greek cooking 2. Festivals -- Greece 3. Greece -- Social life and customs
ISBN 978-1-6087-0235-0; 978-1-6087-0688-4 e-book
LC 2010035820
This explores the culture, traditions, and festivals of Greece through its food.
Includes bibliographical references

Orr, Tamra B.
The food of China; [by] Tamra B. Orr. Marshall Cavendish Benchmark 2011 il (Flavors of the world)

Grades: 4 5 6 7 **394.1**

1. Chinese cooking 2. Festivals -- China
ISBN 1-608-70234-0; 978-1-608-70234-3; 978-1-608-70687-7 e-book

LC 2010039293

This explores the culture, traditions, and festivals of China through its food.

"Numerous high-quality, close-up color photos of outdoor vegetable markets, food in various stages of preparation, and families gathering around the table will keep readers engaged (and hungry) throughout the accessible and enlightening food tour." Booklist

Includes bibliographical references

Silverstein, Alvin

Chocolate ants, maggot cheese, and more; the yucky food book. by Alvin and Virginia Silverstein and Laura Silverstein Nunn; illustrated by Gerald Kelley. Enslow Publishers 2010 48p il (Yucky science) lib bdg $23.93
Grades: 4 5 6 7 **394.1**

1. Eating customs
ISBN 978-0-7660-3315-3 lib bdg; 0-7660-3315-5 lib bdg

LC 2009012283

"Written in an engaging and conversational style and full of revolting descriptions and entertaining cartoon illustrations . . . [this is] sure to turn even the strongest stomach. An introduction . . . puts 'yucky' in perspective, reminding kids that our world is diverse and that everyone has a different definition of repulsive." SLJ

Includes glossary and bibliographical references

394.2   Special occasions

Ancona, George

Powwow; photographs and text by George Ancona. Harcourt Brace Jovanovich 1993 un il hardcover o.p. pa $10
Grades: 3 4 5 6 **394.2**

1. Native Americans -- Rites and ceremonies 2. Indians of North America -- Dances -- Juvenile literature
ISBN 0-15-263268-9; 0-15-263269-7 pa

LC 92-15912

A photo essay on the pan-Indian celebration called a powwow, this particular one being held on the Crow Reservation in Montana

The book is "illustrated with well-placed, full-color photos that clearly reflect the text. . . . An exquisite kaleidoscope of Native American music, customs, and crafts." SLJ

Johnston, Tony

Day of the Dead; illustrated by Jeanette Winter. Harcourt Brace & Co. 1997 un il hardcover o.p. pa $6
Grades: PreK K 1 2 **394.2**

1. All Souls' Day -- Fiction 2. All Souls' Day -- Juvenile literature 3. Mexico -- Social life and customs -- Juvenile literature
ISBN 0-15-222863-2; 0-15-202446-8 pa

LC 96-2276

Describes a Mexican family preparing for and celebrating the Day of the Dead

"Spanish phrases are a natural part of the storytelling as the children ask questions about the cooking and preparations. . . . Winter's brilliantly colored, acrylic illustratons in folk-art style express the magic realism that is part of the ceremony under the stars." Booklist

394.26   Holidays

Chocolate, Debbi

My first Kwanzaa book; illustrated by Cal Massey. Scholastic 1992 un il hardcover o.p. pa $5.99
Grades: K 1 2 **394.26**

1. Kwanzaa 2. African Americans -- Social life and customs
ISBN 0-590-45762-4; 0-439-12926-5 pa

LC 92-1200

Introduces Kwanzaa, the holiday in which Afro-Americans celebrate their cultural heritage

"The book effectively conveys the spirit of the holiday through the text and the acrylic paint and colored-pencil illustrations, all outlined in a thin line of earthy brown." SLJ

Includes glossary

Craats, Rennay

Columbus Day; American celebrations. AV2 by Weigl Pubs. 2011 24p il (American celebrations) lib bdg $27.13; pa $11.95
Grades: 3 4 5 **394.26**

1. Explorers 2. Columbus Day
ISBN 978-1-60596-775-2 lib bdg; 1-60596-6775-0 lib bdg; 978-1-60596-933-6 pa; 1-60596-933-8 pa; 978-1-60596-940-4 e-book

LC 2009050986

First published 2004

This book about Columbus Day "is well positioned to plug holes in school units on holidays, with [a] punchy, informative [entry] on the past and present [history] of [the holiday]. The colorful [layout features] an ever-shifting mix of period and modern photographs, while sidebars keep things from settling too comfortably into the organizing structure, which is: . . . introduction, history, key personalities, celebrations, symbols, and activities." Booklist

Demi

Happy, happy Chinese New Year! Crown Pubs. 2003 un il $8.95
Grades: K 1 2 3 **394.26**

1. Chinese New Year
ISBN 0-375-82642-4

LC 2003-43469

First published in different form 1997 with title: Happy New Year! Kung-Hsi Fa-ts'ai!

Examines the customs, traditions, food, and lore associated with the celebration of Chinese New Year

Farmer, Jacqueline

O Christmas tree; its history and holiday traditions. illustrated by Joanne Friar. Charlesbridge 2010 un il lib bdg $16.95; pa $7.95

Grades: 1 2 3 4   **394.26**
1. Christmas trees
ISBN 978-1-58089-238-4 lib bdg; 1-58089-238-8 lib
bdg; 978-1-58089-239-1 pa; 1-58089-239-6 pa
LC 2009027788
"This slender but informative book traces the roots and
history of the Christmas tree through pagan and Christian
practices over thousands of years. . . . Then the focus shifts
to Christmas tree agriculture in North America: the varieties
of trees grown, the stages of growing them, and the challenges of tree farming. . . . The clearly written text shows
respect for its audience by introducing some stories . . . as
legends rather than history. . . . Colorful gouache paintings
brighten the presentation and provide visual information that
complements the text." Booklist
Includes bibliographical references

Foran, Jill
Martin Luther King, Jr. Day; American celebrations.
AV2 by Weigl Pubs. 2011 24p il (American celebrations)
lib bdg $27.13; pa $11.95
Grades: 3 4 5   **394.26**
1. Clergy 2. Martin Luther King Day 3. Nonfiction
writers 4. Civil rights activists 5. Nobel laureates for
peace
ISBN 978-1-60596-772-1 lib bdg; 1-60596-772-6 lib
bdg; 978-1-60596-779-0 pa; 1-60596-779-3 pa; 978-
1-60596-937-4 e-book
LC 2009050988
First published 2004
This book about Martin Luther King Day "is well positioned to plug holes in school units on holidays, with [a]
punchy, informative [entry] on the past and present histories
of [the holiday]. The colorful [layout features] an ever-shifting mix of period and modern photographs, while sidebars
keep things from settling too comfortably into the organizing structure: . . . introduction, history, key personalities,
celebrations, symbols, and activities." Booklist

Gibbons, Gail
Easter. Holiday House 1989 un il lib bdg $16.95;
pa $6.95
Grades: K 1 2 3   **394.26**
1. Easter
ISBN 0-8234-0737-3 lib bdg; 0-8234-0866-3 pa
LC 88-23292
Examines the background, significance, symbols, and
traditions of Easter
Gibbons "simplifies complex beliefs and traditions in
a straightforward way, though transitions are occasionally
abrupt. Pleasing watercolors outlined in black ink illustrate
the text." Booklist

Groundhog day! shadow or no shadow? by Gail Gibbons. Holiday House 2007 32p il $16.95
Grades: K 1 2 3   **394.26**
1. Marmots 2. Groundhog Day
ISBN 978-0-8234-2003-2; 0-8234-2003-5
LC 2006003456
"A look at some fascinating facts about this red-letter
day, presented in Gibbons's signature style. Readers will
learn about the traditions that led to the big celebration now
held each year on February 2nd in Punxsutawney, PA. The
author includes tidbits about the groundhog's diet, habitat,

burrows, newborns/kits and looks at past cultures that de-
pended on hibernating animals to help them determine the
arrival of spring." SLJ

Halloween is-- Holiday House 2002 un il $16.95;
pa $6.95
Grades: K 1 2 3   **394.26**
1. Holidays 2. Halloween
ISBN 0-8234-1758-1; 0-8234-1797-2 pa
LC 2001-59429
Describes the origins and history of Halloween traditions and festivities from ancient times to the present day
"The new version of Gibbons' Halloween (1984) features a larger format, new illustrations, and a revised and
slightly longer text as well as the new title. . . . Libraries with
multiple copies of the earlier book will still find this version useful when the holiday rush is on, and given a choice,
children will reach for this bigger, brighter, new edition."
Booklist

St. Patrick's Day. Holiday House 1994 un il lib bdg
$16.95; pa $6.95
Grades: K 1 2 3   **394.26**
1. Saint Patrick's Day
ISBN 0-8234-1119-2 lib bdg; 0-8234-1173-7 pa
LC 93-29570
"A basic introduction to the holiday—how it began, the
life and works of St. Patrick, and the various ways in which
the day is celebrated. The text is clear and concise, and the
pages are full of information. Gibbons's simple, clean, full-
page watercolor-and-ink illustrations flow logically from
one to the next." SLJ

Hamilton, Lynn
Presidents' Day; American celebrations. AV2 by
Weigl Pubs. 2011 24p il (American celebrations) lib bdg
$27.13; pa $11.95
Grades: 3 4 5   **394.26**
1. Presidents' Day 2. Presidents -- United States
ISBN 978-1-60596-773-8 lib bdg; 1-60596-773-4 lib
bdg; 978-1-60596-931-2 pa; 1-60596-931-1 pa; 978-
1-60596-938-1 e-book
LC 2009050991
First published 2004
This book about Presidents' Day "is well positioned to
plug holes in school units on holidays, with [a] punchy, informative [entry] on the past and present histories of [the
holiday]. The colorful [layout features] an ever-shifting mix
of period and modern photographs, while sidebars keep
things from settling too comfortably into the organizing
structure: . . . introduction, history, key personalities, celebrations, symbols, and activities. . . . With its fascinating
account of the frequently renamed and repositioned holiday,
Presidents' Day is a series standout and expands the idea of
'symbols' to include not just Mount Rushmore but also U.S.
currency." Booklist

Heiligman, Deborah
★ **Celebrate** Christmas; [by] Deborah Heiligman;
consultant, Reverend Father Nathan J.A. Humphrey. National Geographic 2007 31p il (Holidays around the
world) $15.95; lib bdg $23.90

Grades: K 1 2 3 **394.26**
1. Christmas
ISBN 978-1-4263-0122-3; 978-1-4263-0123-0 lib bdg
LC 2007012659

"Brief text accompanies captivating and colorful photographs that demonstrate customs around the world. The use of bonfires and candles, Nativity plays, Advent wreaths, Three Kings Day, and Yule logs are among the topics touched upon. . . . A solid addition." SLJ

Includes glossary and bibliographical references

★ **Celebrate** Halloween; [by] Deborah Heiligman; consultant, Jack Santino. National Geographic Society 2007 31p il (Holidays around the world) $15.95; lib bdg $23.90
Grades: K 1 2 3 **394.26**
1. Halloween
ISBN 978-1-4263-0120-9; 978-1-4263-0121-6 lib bdg
LC 2007003121

In this introduction to Halloween "children will recognize familiar customs, such as carving pumpkins, dressing up, and hanging decorations, explained in simple, yet satisfying, text. The holiday is made accessible and inviting. . . . Lovely, well-captioned color photographs feature children around the world joyfully taking part in festivities." SLJ

Includes glossary and bibliographical references

★ **Celebrate** Independence Day; [by] Deborah Heiligman; consultant, Matthew Dennis. National Geographic 2007 31p il map (Holidays around the world) $15.95; lib bdg $23.90
Grades: K 1 2 3 **394.26**
1. Fourth of July
ISBN 978-1-4263-0074-5; 978-1-4263-0075-2 lib bdg
LC 2006100316

"Heiligman captures the festiveness of Independence Day, also reminding readers of its origin and relevence. . . . Her writing is clear and easy to read. . . . Plentiful photographs depict varied community celebrations." Horn Book Guide

Includes glossary and bibliographical references

★ **Celebrate** Thanksgiving; [by] Deborah Heiligman; consultant, Elizabeth Pleck. National Geographic 2006 32p il map (Holidays around the world) $15.95; lib bdg $23.90
Grades: K 1 2 3 **394.26**
1. Thanksgiving Day
ISBN 0-7922-5928-9; 0-7922-5929-7 lib bdg
LC 2006008685

This briefly describes the history of Thanksgiving Day and how it is celebrated.

Includes glossary and bibliographical references

Hoyt-Goldsmith, Diane
★ **Cinco** de Mayo; celebrating the traditions of Mexico. by Diane Hoyt-Goldsmith; photographs by Lawrence Migdale. Holiday House 2007 30p il $16.95
Grades: 3 4 5 **394.26**
1. Cinco de Mayo
ISBN 978-0-8234-2107-7; 0-8234-2107-4
LC 2006101433

"This colorful photo-essay introduces Rosie, whose family celebrates their Mexican American traditions in California. After discussing Benito Juárez, the history of Cinco

de Mayo, and three major waves of immigration from Mexico, Hoyt-Goldsmith presents elements of Rosie's heritage such as food, language, and mariachi music. . . . The clearly written text and the many fine, color photos provide readers with information as well as glimpses of the life in Rosie's community." Booklist

Includes glossary

★ **Three** Kings Day; a celebration at Christmastime. photographs by Lawrence Migdale. Holiday House 2004 30p il map $16.95
Grades: 3 4 5 **394.26**
1. Epiphany 2. Puerto Ricans -- United States
ISBN 0-8234-1839-1
LC 2003-67625

This "photo-essay introduces Three Kings Day, or Dia de los Tres Reyes, and shows the celebration as experienced by a 10-year-old girl in New York's Puerto Rican community. . . . The clearly written text conveys a good deal of information in a lively, accessible manner. The many photographs capture the joyful spirit of the holiday." Booklist

Includes glossary

Jango-Cohen, Judith
Chinese New Year; illustrations by Jason Chin. Carolrhoda Books 2005 48p il (On my own holidays) lib bdg $23.93; pa $5.95
Grades: 1 2 3 **394.26**
1. Chinese New Year
ISBN 1-57505-653-4 lib bdg; 1-57505-763-8 pa
LC 2004-4472

This "book describes the celebration of Chinese New Year. . . . Among the topics discussed are the Chinese zodiac, traditional symbols of the new year, family feasts and traditions for the holiday, and community activities, such as parades. . . . Clearly written, informative, and child-centered without talking down to children, this provides a good introduction to the holiday." Booklist

Jeffrey, Laura S.
Celebrate Martin Luther King, Jr., Day; [by] Laura S. Jeffrey. Enslow 2006 104p il (Celebrate holidays) lib bdg $31.93
Grades: 5 6 7 8 **394.26**
1. Clergy 2. Martin Luther King Day 3. Nonfiction writers 4. Civil rights activists 5. Nobel laureates for peace 6. African Americans -- Civil rights
ISBN 0-7660-2492-X
LC 2005028110

This offers a brief introduction to the life of Martin Luther King and the Civil Rights movement in the United States and how Martin Luther King Day became a holiday and is celebrated.

Includes glossary and bibliographical references

Celebrate Tet; [by] Laura S. Jeffrey. Enslow Publishers 2008 104p il map (Celebrate holidays) lib bdg $31.93
Grades: 5 6 7 8 **394.26**
1. Vietnamese New Year
ISBN 978-0-7660-2775-6 lib bdg; 0-7660-2775-9 lib bdg
LC 2006031922

"Captioned photographs, maps, drawings, and sidebars combine with an accessible text to present a thorough discussion of the Vietnamese New Year celebration. Jeffrey discusses the holiday's legendary origins and ancient traditions along with people's modern-day observances." Horn Book Guide

Includes glossary and bibliographical references

Jones, Lynda

Kids around the world celebrate! the best feasts and festivals from many lands. Wiley 1999 124p il pa $12.95
Grades: 4 5 6   **394.26**
1. Holidays 2. Festivals
ISBN 0-471-34527-X

LC 99-14639

Introduces a variety of festivals celebrated around the world. Includes recipes and hands-on activities to give a taste of what it is like to be part of a feast or ceremony in another country

Lankford, Mary D.

★ **Christmas** around the world; illustrated by Karen Dugan. Morrow Junior Bks. 1995 47p il map hardcover o.p. pa $5.95
Grades: 3 4 5   **394.26**
1. Christmas
ISBN 0-688-12166-7; 0-688-12167-5 lib bdg; 0-688-16323-8 pa

LC 93-38566

This book "looks at the rich diversity of Christmas traditions found in 12 distinctly different cultures. A small amount of pertinent background information serves as an introduction to each entry, but the majority of the text discusses the special ways each culture celebrates the holiday. The book's attractive layout effectively uses repetition of color and theme, with each double-page spread of text and art surrounded by a decorative border. . . . The book features a small selection of craft activities. . . . A helpful pronunciation guide, and an interesting selection of Christmas superstitions." Booklist

Includes bibliographical references

Lewis, Anne Margaret

What am I? Halloween; illustrated by Tom Mills. Albert Whitman 2011 un il $9.99
Grades: PreK   **394.26**
1. Halloween
ISBN 978-0-8075-8959-5; 0-8075-8959-4

LC 2010049643

"When looking for a simple yet entertaining introduction to Halloween for the very youngest readers, search no further. . . . A friendly witch, pumpkin to carve, funny bat, silly scarecrow, hooting owl, happy monster, black cat, dancing skeleton, busy spider and trick-or-treater are all included in this easy interactive guessing game. . . . This nonthreatening approach will surely satisfy those who wish to avoid the scary or creepy Halloween offerings that abound. A solid introduction for toddlers." Kirkus

MacMillan, Dianne M.

Diwali--Hindu festival of lights; [by] Dianne M. MacMillan. rev and updated ed.; Enslow Elementary 2008 48p il (Best holiday books) lib bdg $23.93

Grades: 2 3 4   **394.26**
1. Divali 2. Hindu holidays
ISBN 978-0-7660-3060-2 lib bdg; 0-7660-3060-1 lib bdg

LC 2007002420

First published 1997

This describes the history of the Hindu festival of Diwali and how it is celebrated in the United States

Includes glossary and bibliographical references

Mattern, Joanne

Celebrate Christmas; [by] Joanne Mattern. Enslow Publishers 2007 112p il (Celebrate holidays) lib bdg $31.93
Grades: 5 6 7 8   **394.26**
1. Christmas
ISBN 978-0-7660-2776-3 lib bdg; 0-7660-2776-7 lib bdg

LC 2006025258

The author "devotes several pages to the origins of Christmas, first as a pagan holiday, then as a celebration of Jesus' birth, and its evolution into the holiday as it is observed today. Symbols of Christmas, important people, and traditions from around the world are explored, and there is a fair amount of discussion about the commercialization of the holiday. . . . Full-color photos and reproductions appear throughout. There is plenty here for reports." SLJ

Includes glossary and bibliographical references

Celebrate Cinco de Mayo; [by] Joanne Mattern. Enslow Pub. 2006 104p il map (Celebrate holidays) lib bdg $31.93
Grades: 5 6 7 8   **394.26**
1. Cinco de Mayo
ISBN 0-7660-2579-9

LC 2005028107

This describes the history of Cinco de Mayo and how it is celebrated.

Includes glossary and bibliographical references

Nelson, Vaunda Micheaux

★ **Juneteenth**; by Vaunda Micheaux Nelson and Drew Nelson; illustrations by Mark Schroder. Millbrook Press 2006 48p il (On my own holidays) lib bdg $23.93
Grades: 2 3 4   **394.26**
1. Juneteenth 2. African Americans -- Social life and customs
ISBN 978-1-57505-876-4 lib bdg; 1-57505-876-6 lib bdg

LC 2005-15334

This is an introduction to the holiday "which celebrates the belated arrival of emancipation news to Texas slaves on June 19, 1865. . . . [This] offers a solid introduction to the holiday for independent readers or for presenting to small groups." Booklist

Otto, Carolyn

★ **Celebrate** Chinese New Year; [by] Carolyn Otto; consultant, Haiwang Yuan. National Geographic 2008 32p il (Holidays around the world) $15.95; lib bdg $23.90

Grades: K 1 2 3 **394.26**
1. Chinese New Year
ISBN 978-1-4263-0381-4; 1-4263-0381-5; 978-1-
4263-0382-1 lib bdg; 1-4263-0382-3 lib bdg
LC 2008024678
"Vivid, colorful photographs of fireworks, lion dancers, and food fill the pages of this introduction to Chinese
New Year. The concise but informative narrative notes when
the event occurs, cites a few of the countries where it is observed, and explains the reasons behind the customs and
symbols, especially those traditions involving children. The
well-captioned pictures capture the intense excitement and
raucous exuberance of the festivities." Booklist
Includes glossary and bibliographical references

★ **Celebrate** Cinco de Mayo; [by] Carolyn Otto; consultant, Jose M. Alamillo. National Geographic 2008 32p
il map (Holidays around the world) $15.95; lib bdg $23.90
Grades: K 1 2 3 **394.26**
1. Cinco de Mayo
ISBN 978-1-4263-0215-2; 1-4263-0215-0; 978-1-
4263-0216-9 lib bdg; 1-4263-0216-9 lib bdg
This "combines a clear, read-aloud-friendly text with
big, beautiful color photos. After introducing Cinco de
Mayo's 1862 origins, Otto shows and tells how the celebration has become an annual, joyous festival of Mexican culture, both north and south of the border. . . . Excellent back
matter includes bibliography, recipes, a glossary and an informative afterword." Booklist

★ **Celebrate** Kwanzaa; [by] Carolyn Otto; consultant,
Keith A. Mayes. National Geographic 2007 32p il (Holi-
days around the world) $15.95; lib bdg $23.90
Grades: K 1 2 3 **394.26**
1. Kwanzaa 2. African Americans -- Social life and
customs
ISBN 978-1-4263-0319-7; 978-1-4263-0320-3 lib bdg
LC 2007041221
This describes the history of the African American holi-
day of Kwanzaa and how it is celebrated and includes a craft
activity and a recipe.
Includes glossary and bibliographical references

★ **Celebrate** Valentine's Day; [by] Carolyn Otto; consultant, Jack Santino. National Geographic 2008 32p il
map (Holidays around the world) $15.95; lib bdg $23.90
Grades: K 1 2 3 **394.26**
1. Valentine's Day
ISBN 978-1-4263-0213-8; 1-4263-0213-4; 978-1-
4263-0214-5 lib bdg; 1-4263-0214-2 lib bdg
LC 2007033764
This describes how Valentine's Day is celebrated and
includes a game and a recipe
Includes glossary and bibliographical references

Pfeffer, Wendy
The **longest** day; celebrating the summer solstice. illustrated by Linda Bleck. Dutton Children's Books 2010
un il $17.99
Grades: K 1 2 3 **394.26**
1. Summer 2. Summer solstice
ISBN 978-0-525-42237-2; 0-525-42237-4
"Science, myth and custom merge into a celebratory introduction to the Summer Solstice. . . . Bleck's sprightly,

colorful illustrations offer a visual celebration as they faithfully track the text. A comfortable, multidimensional investigation of the Summer Solstice that transcends time and
place." Kirkus

A **new** beginning; celebrating the spring equinox. illustrated by Linda Bleck. Dutton Children's Books 2008
un il $17.99
Grades: K 1 2 3 **394.26**
1. Spring 2. Vernal equinox 3. Spring festivals --
Juvenile literature
ISBN 978-0-525-47874-4; 0-525-47874-4
LC 2007-18123
This "covers the spring equinox and how people mark
its passage in the northern hemisphere. . . . [It includes]
five multicultural activities. The free-verse text is clear and
simple, and the colorful illustrations blanket every page with
celebrants clad in traditional, festive clothing." Booklist
Includes bibliographical references

The **shortest** day; celebrating the winter solstice. illustrated by Jesse Reisch. Dutton Children's Books 2003
un il $16.99
Grades: K 1 2 3 **394.26**
1. Winter solstice
ISBN 0-525-46968-0
LC 2003-40811
Describes how and why daylight grows shorter as winter
approaches, the effect of shorter days on animals and people,
and how the winter solstice has been celebrated throughout
history. Includes activities
This uses "clear, concise language. . . . Pfeffer uses an
easy, comfortable tone for conveying the basic information. .
. . Reisch's realistic craypas illustrations provide serviceable
interpretations of the author's ideas." SLJ

Rissman, Rebecca
Martin Luther King, Jr. Day. Heinemann Library 2011
24p il (Holidays and festivals) $21.50; pa $5.99
Grades: PreK K **394.26**
1. Clergy 2. Martin Luther King Day 3. Nonfiction
writers 4. Civil rights activists 5. Nobel laureates for
peace 6. African Americans -- Civil rights
ISBN 978-1-4329-4055-3; 1-4329-4055-4; 978-1-
4329-4074-4 pa; 1-4329-4074-0 pa
LC 2009052855
This introduction to Martin Luther King Day offers
"large pictures on the top three-fourths of the page and a
simple line or two of text below. . . . Pictures of segregation—in particular, a 'For Colored Only' water fountain—
still retain their power to shock and will compel children
to ask questions. Rissman uses five very short chapters to
take the youngest readers through some simple facts about
slavery . . . before touching on King's life. . . . This is . . . a
fine introduction." Booklist
Includes bibliographical references

Simonds, Nina
★ **Moonbeams,** dumplings & dragon boats; a treasury
of Chinese holiday tales, activities & recipes. [by] Nina Simonds, Leslie Swartz, & the Children's Museum of Boston;
illustrated by Meilo So. Harcourt 2002 74p il $20
Grades: 4 5 6 7 **394.26**
1. Handicraft 2. Chinese cooking 3. Chinese New

Year 4. Tales -- China 5. Folklore -- China 6. Holidays -- China 7. Festivals -- China 8. Festivals -- China -- Juvenile literature

ISBN 0-15-201983-9

LC 2001-4280

Presents background information, related tales, and activities for celebrating five Chinese festivals—Chinese New Year, the Lantern Festival, Qing Ming, the Dragon Boat Festival, and the Moon Festival

"The ample white space surrounding the text is filled with small, whimsical watercolor illustrations. . . . [This] is a useful, visually appealing addition to any holiday collection." SLJ

Includes bibliographical references

Tait, Leia

Cinco de Mayo. AV2 by Weigl Pubs. 2011 24p il (American celebrations) lib bdg $27.13; pa $8.95

Grades: 3 4 5   **394.26**

1. Cinco de Mayo 2. Mexican Americans -- Social life and customs

ISBN 978-1-6059-6776-9 lib bdg; 1-60596-776-9 lib bdg; 978-1-60596-934-3 pa; 1-60496-934-6 pa

LC 2009050985

This book about Cinco de Mayo "is well positioned to plug holes in school units on holidays, with [a] punchy, informative [entry] on the past and present [history] of [the holiday]. The colorful [layout features] an ever-shifting mix of period and modern photographs, while sidebars keep things from settling too comfortably into the organizing structure: . . . introduction, history, key personalities, celebrations, symbols, and activities. . . . Cinco de Mayo does an admirable job explaining this all-too-infrequently-explained holiday." Booklist

Tokunbo, Dimitrea

The **sound** of Kwanzaa; illustrated by Lisa Cohen. Scholastic Press 2009 un il $16.99

Grades: PreK K 1 2   **394.26**

1. Kwanzaa 2. African Americans -- Social life and customs

ISBN 978-0-545-01865-4; 0-545-01865-X

LC 2007025916

"This picture book provides readers with an introduction to Kwanzaa's seven principles. . . . Rhythmic text includes the definitions, pronunciations, and significances of the principles. Uncluttered, vibrantly colored illustrations extend the meanings of each of the seven candles of Kwanzaa." Horn Book Guide

Includes bibliographical references

Waters, Kate

Lion dancer: Ernie Wan's Chinese New Year; by Kate Waters and Madeline Slovenz-Low; photographs by Martha Cooper. Scholastic 1990 un il hardcover o.p. pa $4.99

Grades: K 1 2 3   **394.26**

1. Chinese New Year 2. Chinese Americans -- Social life and customs

ISBN 0-590-43047-5 pa

LC 89-6423

Describes six-year-old Ernie Wan's preparations, at home and in school, for the Chinese New Year celebrations and his first public performance of the lion dance

"While some of the pictures look posed, the marvelously colorful photographs successfully capture Ernie's pride and anticipation as he is dressed in his gorgeous costume and the excitement and swirling movement of the subsequent parade. Illustrations of a Chinese lunar calendar and a Chinese horoscope are extra dividends in a useful and appealing book." Horn Book

394.264   Thanksgiving

Grace, Catherine O'Neill

★ **1621**; a new look at Thanksgiving. [by] Catherine O'Neill Grace and Margaret M. Bruchac with Plimoth Plantation; photographs by Sisse Brimberg and Cotton Coulson. National Geographic Soc. 2001 47p il map $17.95; pa $7.95

Grades: 3 4 5   **394.264**

1. Thanksgiving Day 2. Wampanoag Indians 3. Pilgrims (New England colonists) 4. Thanksgiving Day -- History

ISBN 0-7922-7027-4; 0-7922-6139-1 pa

LC 2001-124

This is a "pictorial presentation of the reenactment of the first Thanksgiving, held at Plimoth Plantation museum in October, 2000. Countering the prevailing, traditional story of the first Thanksgiving . . . this lushly illustrated photoessay presents a more measured, balanced, and historically accurate version of the three-day harvest celebration in 1621." SLJ

Includes bibliographical references

395   Etiquette (Manners)

Aliki

★ **Manners**. Greenwillow Bks. 1990 un il $16; lib bdg $15.93; pa $5.95

Grades: K 1 2 3   **395**

1. Etiquette

ISBN 0-688-09198-9; 0-688-09199-7 lib bdg; 0-688-04579-0 pa

LC 89-34622

The author discusses etiquette and good manners

"Aliki makes manners accessible to children through colorful cartoon-style illustrations. . . . Her lively primer sparkles with examples of the proper and the poor." Booklist

Joslin, Sesyle

★ **What** do you do, dear? pictures by Maurice Sendak. Harper & Row 1985 un il hardcover o.p. pa $6.95

Grades: PreK K 1 2   **395**

1. Etiquette

ISBN 0-06-443113-4 pa

LC 84-43139

First published 1961 by Addison-Wesley

A "wonderful spoof on manners in a hilarious picturebook made for laughing aloud." Child Study Assoc of Am

★ **What** do you say, dear? pictures by Maurice Sendak. Harper & Row 1986 un il lib bdg $15.89; pa $5.95

Grades: PreK K 1 2   **395**
1. Etiquette
ISBN 0-06-023074-6 lib bdg; 0-06-443112-6 pa
LC 84-43140

First published 1958 by Addison-Wesley
A Caldecott Medal honor book, 1959
"A rollicking introduction to manners for the very young. A series of delightfully absurd situations—being introduced to a baby elephant, bumping into a crocodile, being rescued from a dragon—are posed and appropriately answered. The illustrations are among Sendak's best—and funniest." Bull Cent Child Books

Post, Peggy
Emily Post's The guide to good manners for kids; by Peggy Post & Cindy Post Senning. HarperCollins 2004 144p il $15.99; lib bdg $16.89
Grades: 4 5 6 7   **395**
1. Etiquette
ISBN 0-06-057196-9; 0-06-057197-7 lib bdg
LC 2003-26426

This offers advice on etiquette at home, at school, and other places, including letter writing and on-line communication, table manners, phone answering, and behavior at social gatherings, and public places.
"The writing is clear, friendly, and sometimes clever. . . . The advice is consistently practical and simple." SLJ

Emily Post's table manners for kids. Collins 2009 96p $15.99
Grades: 4 5 6 7   **395**
1. Etiquette
ISBN 978-0-06-111709-1; 0-06-111709-9
LC 2008010655

"This deceptively slim guide teems with advice about everything from meal courses to table settings, from the art of conversation to dining out. The tone is measured and mildly proscriptive, offset by Bjorkman's amusing cartoons. . . . A strength: the excellent troubleshooting for specific concerns, such as eating fondue and using chopsticks." Kirkus

Emily's everyday manners; [by] Peggy Post and Cindy Post Senning; illustrated by Steve Bjorkman. HarperCollins 2006 un il $16.99; lib bdg $17.89
Grades: PreK K 1 2   **395**
1. Etiquette 2. Etiquette for children and teenagers
ISBN 0-06-076174-1; 0-06-076177-6 lib bdg
"Cheerful illustrations set the upbeat (and updated) tone for this introduction to manners. A succinct running text introduces young Emily and her neighbor Ethan and comments on how and why they use manners as well as how etiquette can differ according to the time and place." Booklist
Other titles in this series are:
Emily's magic words (2007)
Emily's Christmas gifts (2008)
Emily's sharing and caring book (2008)
Emily's out and about book (2009)
Emily's new friend (2010)

Verdick, Elizabeth
Don't behave like you live in a cave. Free Spirit Pub. 2010 120p il (Laugh & learn) pa $8.95

Grades: 4 5 6   **395**
1. Etiquette 2. Child psychology
ISBN 978-1-57542-353-1 pa; 1-57542-353-7 pa
LC 2010010441

Explains how children can make smarter, more positive choices about how they behave at home and at school and, as a result, stay out of trouble, feel good about themselves, and get along better with family, friends, and teachers.
"Not only are the antics of a cartoon Cave Boy and Cave Girl used to represent bad behavior throughout the book, but they are also part of the infusion of humor that makes the tone light, accessible, and soapbox free. Verdick keeps the dialogue conversational." SLJ

★ Manners mash-up: a goofy guide to good behavior; story and pictures. featuring Tedd Arnold [et al.] Dial Books for Young Readers 2010 un il $16.99
Grades: 2 3 4 5   **395**
1. Etiquette 2. Etiquette for children and teenagers
ISBN 0-8037-3480-8; 978-0-8037-3480-7
LC 2010-11882

This "picture-book look at manners showcases the . . . [work] of fourteen illustrators, each of whom get a spread to explore a particular area of behavior. . . . Grades two to four." (Bull Cent Child Books)
"This follow-up to Why Did the Chicken Cross the Road? (2006) and Knock Knock (2007) rounds up 14 of the usual suspects—the most gifted illustrators working today—and gives them one spread to explain the hows and whys of etiquette. . . . The results are top-notch." Publ Wkly

395.2   Etiquette for stages in life cycle

Hoyt-Goldsmith, Diane
★ Celebrating a Quinceanera; a Latina's 15th birthday celebration. photographs by Lawrence Migdale. Holiday House 2002 30p il $16.95
Grades: 3 4 5   **395.2**
1. Quinceanera (Social custom) 2. Mexican Americans -- Social life and customs
ISBN 0-8234-1693-3
LC 2001-59424

Describes the customs and traditions connected with the celebration of a Mexican-American girl's fifteenth birthday, marking her coming of age
This offers "eye-catching, full-color photos. . . . The clearly written, engaging text conveys both the social and religious significance of the event." SLJ

398   Folklore

Beeler, Selby B.
Throw your tooth on the roof; tooth traditions from around the world. illustrated by G. Brian Karas. Houghton Mifflin 1998 un il $16; pa $6.95
Grades: K 1 2 3   **398**
1. Teeth -- Folklore
ISBN 0-395-89108-6; 0-618-15238-5 pa
LC 97-46042

Consists of brief statements relating what children from around the world do with a tooth that has fallen out. Includes facts about teeth

"This book will be an eye-opener for young Americans who may have assumed that the Tooth Fairy holds a worldwide visa." Publ Wkly

Berk, Ariel

Secret history of mermaids and creatures of the deep; or the Liber Aquaticum. written and collected by Ari Berk, magister and scribe; illuminated by Wayne Anderson, Gary Chalk, Matt Dangler, Virginia Lee. Candlewick Press 2009 un il $16.99

Grades: 4 5 6   398

1. Mermaids and mermen

ISBN 978-0-7636-4515-1; 0-7636-4515-X

"This volume details merfolk from tales and mythologies around the world. A wide variety of creatures, their customs, and habitats are touched on. The often ornately scripted text is accompanied by intricate illustrations and numerous foldouts." Horn Book Guide

Harpur, James

Mythical creatures; illustrated by Stuart Martin. Barron's 2009 un il $22.99

Grades: 3 4 5   398

1. Mythical animals

ISBN 978-0-7641-6204-6; 0-7641-6204-7

"Mythical creatures like the Minotaur, the kraken and the selkies are featured in this sturdy, encyclopedia-style book. There are plenty of unique components: a pull-tab box addresses how to tell if a unicorn is real or not. . . . and an impressive pop-up 'Arabian Phoenix' spreads its red wings and opens its beak above a roaring fire. . . . [This] will give fantasy fans food for thought." Publ Wkly

Kallen, Stuart A.

Werewolves. Reference Point Press 2010 104p il (The mysterious & unknown) $25.95

Grades: 4 5 6 7   398

1. Werewolves

ISBN 978-1-60152-097-5; 1-60152-097-2

Describes the history and lore surrounding the topic of werewolves, examining how the shape-shifting beast has been feared by various cultures around the world, and its continuing influence on popular culture

This is "surprisingly exhaustive. . . . Breakout summaries and quotes enliven the layout. . . . There is . . . plenty of creepy stuff to scrutinize." Booklist

Includes bibliographical references

The **sphinx**; part of the Monsters and mythical creatures series. by Stuart A. Kallen. ReferencePoint Press 2012 80 p. ill. (chiefly col.) (hardback) $27.95

Grades: 4 5 6 7 8   398

1. Sphinxes (Mythology) 2. Sphinxes (Mythology) -- Juvenile literature

ISBN 1601522223; 9781601522221

LC 2011026636

This book, part of the "Monsters and Mythical Creatures" series, looks at the "history . . . [and] associated mythology" of the Sphinx. (School Library Journal) It "reveals the significant symbolic role this creature has played in human civilization from ancient Egypt through classical

Greece and the Renaissance into the twenty-first century. . . . The ancient mythical creature has been an inspiration for artists, writers, architects, scholars, and theologians for millennia." (Publisher's note)

"Children will get a well-rounded look at the featured subjects and how they have evolved into the creatures that still fascinate many today.—" SLJ

Includes bibliographical references and index

Kelly, Sophia

What a beast! a look-it-up guide to the monsters and mutants of mythology. Scholastic 2010 128p il map (Mythlopedia) lib bdg $39; pa $13.95

Grades: 4 5 6 7   398

1. Monsters 2. Classical mythology

ISBN 978-1-60631-028-1 lib bdg; 1-60631-028-3 lib bdg; 978-1-60631-060-1 pa; 1-60631-060-7 pa

LC 2009-20998

Describes some of the creatures and monsters in Greek mythology.

This "spices things up with sassy artwork, a pastel color scheme, and an OMG sensibility. . . . [This title is] loaded with information on the inspired methods with which various nasty creatures could put an end to bothersome heroes. Aside from the heaps of information coming from all angles on just about every page, . . . [the] book also contains a decent family tree, a rudimentary star chart, and lists of further reading. . . . For kids unconvinced that anything so old and gray could have any bearing on their lives, . . . [this book provides] a feisty . . . guide to the many cultural references lingering from antiquity." Booklist

Includes glossary and bibliographical references

Knudsen, Shannon

Fairies and elves. Lerner 2010 48p il (Fantasy chronicles) lib bdg $27.93

Grades: 4 5 6 7   398

1. Fairies

ISBN 978-0-8225-9979-1 lib bdg; 0-8225-9979-1 lib bdg

LC 2008050207

"The explanations and history behind . . . fairies [and elves] . . . will provide satisfaction for readers who want to know more about these familiar characters from myth, fantasy, and folk and fairy tales. Brief and concise." SLJ

Includes bibliographical references

Fantastical creatures and magical beasts. Lerner Publications 2010 48p il (Fantasy chronicles) lib bdg $27.93

Grades: 4 5 6 7   398

1. Mythical animals

ISBN 978-0-8225-9987-6 lib bdg; 0-8225-9987-2 lib bdg

LC 2009004794

This describes mythical beasts such as dragons, unicorns, Hydra, Medusa, the labyrinth, and basilisks

"The explanations and history behind well-known fantastical creatures . . . will provide satisfaction for readers who want to know more about these familiar characters from myth, fantasy, and folk and fairy tales. Brief and concise." SLJ

Includes bibliographical references

Losure, Mary

The **Fairy** Ring, or, Elsie and Frances Fool the World; Mary Losure. Candlewick Press 2012 184 p. ill.

Grades: 5 6 7 8   **398**

1. Deception 2. Fairies -- Juvenile literature 3. Fairies -- England -- Juvenile literature
ISBN 9780763656706; 0763656704

     LC 2011046081

This book offers explores an event that occurred "[t]owards the end of World War I, [when] two girls in Yorkshire took photographs that purported to capture the fairies they regularly saw, and these pictures . . . became a national sensation when . . . Sir Arthur Conan Doyle . . . championed them as authentic. . . . [The] book . . . conveys the widening of the ripples from the event and . . . the impulses behind the creation of the photographs." (Bulletin of the Center for Children's Books)

Ogburn, Jacqueline K.

A **dignity** of dragons; collective nouns for magical beasts. by Jacqueline K. Ogburn, Nicoletta Ceccoli; illustrated by Nicoletta Ceccoli. Houghton Mifflin Books for Children 2010 un il $16

Grades: 2 3 4   **398**

1. Mythical animals
ISBN 978-0-618-86254-2; 0-618-86254-4

"Gorgeous mixed-media illustrations complement dozens of inventive collective nouns. . . . These creative descriptions comprise the only text in the book. A four-page glossary defines each fantastic creature and identifies the culture(s) of its origin. Ceccoli has created a stylized and luminous fantasyland energetically inhabited by Ogburn's enchanting bestiary. Fans of mythology and fantasy as well as budding lexophiles will savor this sophisticated picture book." SLJ

Regan, Sally

The **vampire** book. DK Pub. 2009 93p il $19.99

Grades: 5 6 7 8   **398**

1. Vampires
ISBN 978-0-7566-5551-8; 0-7566-5551-X

"This guide covers the origins and evolution of vampires throughout history, giving a worldwide perspective on legends, mythology, and lore, from African tales of terror to blood-drinking witches of Southeast Asia. It also covers vampires in literature, film, and television. . . . The vivid colors in the often full-page art leap from the pages, and the bold font demands attention." SLJ

Reinhart, Matthew

★ **Dragons** & Monsters; [by] Matthew Reinhart and Robert Sabuda. Candlewick Press 2011 un il (Encyclopedia mythologica)

Grades: K 1 2 3   **398**

1. Dragons 2. Monsters 3. Pop-up books
ISBN 0-7636-3173-6; 978-0-7636-3173-4

     LC 2010015485

"The pop-up book veterans continue to push the envelope in this addition to the Encyclopedia Mythologica series, with infamous figures like Medusa . . . joining more general creatures such as dragons, sea monsters, and vampires. Minibooks and sidebars profile less recognizable monsters—the golem, sharklike 'taniwha,' and 'wendigo,' known to Algonquian tribes. . . . Once again, Reinhart and

Sabuda have created an offering distinguished by clever details, superb execution, and a sense of wonder."

"The pop-up book veterans continue to push the envelope in this addition to the Encyclopedia Mythologica series, with infamous figures like Medusa . . . joining more general creatures such as dragons, sea monsters, and vampires. Minibooks and sidebars profile less recognizable monsters—the golem, sharklike 'taniwha,' and 'wendigo,' known to Algonquian tribes. . . . Once again, Reinhart and Sabuda have created an offering distinguished by clever details, superb execution, and a sense of wonder." Publ Wkly

★ **Fairies** and magical creatures; [by] Matthew Reinhart and Robert Sabuda. Candlewick Press 2008 un il (Encyclopedia mythologica) $27.99

Grades: K 1 2 3   **398**

1. Fairies 2. Mythical animals 3. Pop-up books
ISBN 978-0-7636-3172-7; 0-7636-3172-8

This pop-up book depicts and describes such magical creatures as Shakespeare's fairy queen Titania, hobgoblins, trolls, a humanoid magical tree, brownies, Pegasus, satyrs, Serbian enchanted birds, and merfolk.

"A dramatic pop-up towers over each spread, surrounded by flaps and corner gatefolds that open up more surprises. . . . The paper engineering consistently enhances the text. . . . The emphasis on global legends as well as a palette heavy on blues, purples and reds widen the audience way past the girly-girl set." Publ Wkly

Scieszka, Jon

★ The **Stinky** Cheese Man and other fairly stupid tales; [by Jon Scieszka & Lane Smith] Viking 1992 un il $17.99

Grades: 2 3 4 5   **398**

1. Fairy tales 2. Short stories
ISBN 0-670-84487-X

     LC 91-48194

A Caldecott Medal honor book, 1993

"The picture-book set will probably recognize the stories enough to know that what's going on isn't what's 'supposed' to happen. But The Stinky Cheese Man isn't a book for little ones. It will take older children (that's teens along with 10s) to follow the disordered story lines and appreciate the narrative's dry wit, wordplay, and wacky, sophomoric jokes. . . . Smith's New Wave art is an intricate part of the whole, extending as well as reinforcing the narrative; the pictures are every bit as comically insolent and deliberately clever as the words." Booklist

★ The **true** story of the 3 little pigs; pictures by Lane Smith. Viking Kestrel 1989 un il $16.99; pa $7.99

Grades: K 1 2 3 4   **398**

1. Pigs -- Fiction 2. Wolves -- Fiction
ISBN 0-670-82759-2; 0-14-054451-8 pa

     LC 89-8953

The wolf gives his own outlandish version of what really happened when he tangled with the three little pigs

"The 'excited and funky' illustrations match the hilarious revisionist text to a standard story." N Y Times Book Rev

Sierra, Judy

The **gruesome** guide to world monsters; illustrated by Henrik Drescher. Candlewick Press 2005 63p il $18.99

Grades: 5 6 7 8   **398**
1. Folklore 2. Monsters
ISBN 0-7636-1727-X

LC 2004-57470

This presents "brief introductions to dozens of ugly customers from world folklore. . . . [The author] offers wonderfully provocative warnings against creatures as diverse as the giant skunk Aniwye, the bloodsucking bat Mansusopsop, and Bloody Mary, an evil specter who lives on the other side of mirrors." SLJ

Thong, Roseanne
Wish; wishing traditions around the world. illustrated by Elisa Kleven. Chronicle Books 2008 un il $16.99
Grades: K 1 2 3   **398**
1. Wishes
ISBN 978-0-8118-5716-1

LC 2007038299

"'The many ways to make a wish wherever home may be' come in for lighthearted yet respectful exploration in this attractive square-format book. Thong . . . entices readers with consistently well-rhymed verses . . . following up each with a brief description of a national custom. . . . Rendered in Kleven's . . . kaleidoscopic style, many of the full-bleed spreads nearly shimmer. . . . Endnotes include more information along with an invitation to find 15 lucky symbols hidden in the pictures." Publ Wkly

398.2   Folk literature

Aardema, Verna
★ **Borreguita** and the coyote; a tale from Ayutla, Mexico. retold by Verna Aardema; illustrated by Petra Mathers. Knopf 1991 un il hardcover o.p. pa $6.99
Grades: K 1 2 3   **398.2**
1. Coyote (Legendary character) 2. Sheep -- Folklore
3. Folklore -- Mexico
ISBN 0-679-88936-1 pa

LC 90-33302

A little lamb uses her clever wiles to keep a coyote from eating her up
This folk tale "is energetically told and comfortably packed with many recognizable motifs. Mathers enlarges upon the humorous elements of the story in her boldly colored paintings. . . . Aardema and Mathers are felicitously paired in a tale of trickery rewarded that begs to be read aloud." Horn Book
Includes glossary

★ **Bringing** the rain to Kapiti Plain; a Nandi tale. retold by Verna Aardema; pictures by Beatriz Vidal. Dial Bks. for Young Readers 1981 un il $16.99; pa $5.99
Grades: K 1 2 3   **398.2**
1. Stories in rhyme 2. Folklore -- Africa 3. Droughts -- Folklore
ISBN 0-8037-0809-2; 0-8037-0904-8 pa

LC 80-25886

"Effective both in the rhythm of its metered storytelling and in the brilliance of its stylized paintings, the panoramic picture book quickly engages both eye and ear." Horn Book

Rabbit makes a monkey of lion; a Swahili tale. retold by Verna Aardema; pictures by Jerry Pinkney. Dial Bks. for Young Readers 1989 un il hardcover o.p. pa $5.99
Grades: K 1 2 3   **398.2**
1. Animals -- Folklore 2. Folklore -- Zanzibar
ISBN 0-14-054593-X pa

LC 86-11523

Text adapted from The hare and the lion, published 1901 in Zanzibar tales
With the help of his friends Bush-rat and Turtle, smart and nimble Rabbit makes a fool of the mighty but slow-witted king of the forest
"Aardema's version of the tale reinforces the amusing trickster qualities of rascally Rabbit, making it a sure-fire choice for sharing with groups of children, who will instantly root for her success. Pinkney's lovely watercolor and pencil paintings in hues of green, brown, and gold fill the pages with lush scenes which evoke the East African setting." Horn Book

Who's in Rabbit's house? a Masai tale. retold by Verna Aardema; pictures by Leo and Diane Dillon. Dial Bks. for Young Readers 1977 un il hardcover o.p. pa $6.99
Grades: K 1 2 3   **398.2**
1. Animals -- Folklore 2. Folklore -- East Africa 3. Masai (African people) -- Folklore
ISBN 0-14-054724-X pa

LC 77-71514

This "tale relates the attempts of Rabbit to regain possession of her house after it is taken over by an intruder. Rabbit's friends offer suggestions on how to solve the problem, but the solution comes from 'an unexpected source.' The story, adapted from the Masai tale 'The Long One,' uses repetition of key phrases to produce a rhythmic read-aloud text. The Dillons skillfully present their artistry in a vivid, colorful and impressive manner which contributes to the story and sets the tone." Child Book Rev Serv

★ **Why** mosquitoes buzz in people's ears; a West African tale retold. pictures by Leo and Diane Dillon. Dial Bks. for Young Readers 1975 un il $16.99; pa $6.99
Grades: K 1 2 3   **398.2**
1. Animals -- Folklore 2. Mosquitoes -- Folklore 3. Folklore -- West Africa
ISBN 0-8037-6089-2; 0-14-054905-6 pa
Awarded the Caldecott Medal, 1976
"Stunning full-color illustrations—watercolor sprayed with air gun, overlayed with pastel, cut out and repasted—give an eye-catching abstract effect and tell the story with humor and power." SLJ

Alley, Zoe B.
★ **There's** a princess in the palace; pictures by R.W. Alley. Roaring Brook Press 2010 34p il $19.99
Grades: 1 2 3 4   **398.2**
1. Fairy tales 2. Graphic novels 3. Humorous graphic novels 4. Folklore -- Graphic novels 5. Princesses -- Graphic novels
ISBN 978-1-59643-471-4; 1-59643-471-6
"Within a graphic-novel format, the tales of Cinderella, Sleeping Beauty, Snow White, the Frog Prince and the Princess and the Pea develop familial and hilarious interconnec-

tions while retaining the stories' traditional structures. . . . Smartly hysterical." Kirkus

★ **There's** a wolf at the door; pictures by R. W. Alley. Roaring Brook Press 2008 40p il $19.95

Grades: K 1 2 3   **398.2**

1. Graphic novels 2. Humorous graphic novels 3. Folklore -- Juvenile literature 4. Wolves -- Folklore -- Graphic novels

ISBN 978-1-59643-275-8; 1-59643-275-6

LC 2007-44025

As his plans are spoiled over and over again, the wolf keeps trying to find his dinner, in this retelling of five well-known stories and fables.

This is a "hilarious romp. . . . Illustrated with softly colored pen-and-ink drawings, these five stories meld seamlessly together. The text is full of puns, alliteration, and occasional rhymes." SLJ

Andrews, Jan

Rude stories; illustrations by Francis Blake. Tundra Books 2010 87p il $19.95

Grades: 3 4 5   **398.2**

1. Folklore

ISBN 978-0-88776-921-4; 0-88776-921-7

"Andrews has added her own special touches to a collection of humorous, traditional tales from cultures around the world. The rudeness in the stories takes different forms: in an original tale, two sisters compete in a belching contest. In a Swahili tale, a girl known for her kindness finally speaks her mind to her family, and in another from Japan, a man receives a magical fan from a goblin. Its special power? Waving it will increase or decrease the size of someone's bottom. . . . A selection of witty, original poems is interspersed among the stories. . . . The selections have the flavor of the oral tradition. Blake's colorful spot art and occasional full-page illustrations are a perfect match for the irreverent humor." SLJ

Includes bibliographical references

Stories at the door; [retold] by Jan Andrews; illustrations by Francis Blake. Tundra Books 2007 79p il $18.95

Grades: 2 3 4   **398.2**

1. Folklore

ISBN 978-0-88776-811-8; 0-88776-811-3

This is a "collection of six folktales from around the world. Selections include a Scandinavian story, . . . an amusing Palestinian tale, . . . and an Indian story. . . . Andrews contributes a short poem before each selection and retells the stories in simple language. . . . With humor running through them like a bright thread, the lively stories are well matched by Blake's jaunty, colorful, and often comical line-and-wash artwork." Booklist

Includes bibliographical references

★ **When** apples grew noses and white horses flew; tales of Ti-Jean. illustrations by Dušan Petričić. Groundwood Books/House of Anansi Press 2011 67p il $16.95

Grades: 2 3 4 5   **398.2**

1. Folklore -- Canada

ISBN 978-0-88899-952-8; 0-88899-952-6

This is a retelling of three stories featuring "Quebec's traditional folktale hero, Ti-Jean. He's an endearing character who is both wise and foolish, and though he does find

himself in hard situations (often of his own making), in the end, he somehow manages to do what needs to be done. In 'Ti-Jean and the Princess of Tomboso,' he outwits a greedy princess; in 'Ti-Jean the Marble Player,' he gets the best of a pint-sized scoundrel; and in 'How Ti-Jean Became a Fiddler,' he turns the tables on a too-clever-for-her-own-good seigneur's daughter, and finds true love in the process." (Publisher's note) "Ages seven to ten." (Quill Quire)

"Ti-Jean, the cheerful, hapless, ultimately triumphant stripling of French-Canadian folklore . . . makes a winning appearance in three tales of European origin lightly transposed to a New World setting. . . . These zesty, well-paced texts virtually read themselves. . . . Sly Petričić drawings underpin the fun throughout." Horn Book

Arabian nights

The **Arabian** nights entertainments; selected and edited by Andrew Lang; with numerous illustrations by H. J. Ford. Dover Publs. 1969 424p il pa $9.95

Grades: 5 6 7 8   **398.2**

1. Fairy tales 2. Arabs -- Folklore

ISBN 0-486-22289-6

First published 1898 in the United Kingdom

"A collection of popular tales assembled over many centuries, and well known in Europe from the 18th cent. It contains the stories of 'Aladdin, Alibaba, and Sindbad the sailor.' . . . The framing story in which the tales are set concerns Scheherazade, who is determined to delay her royal husband's plan of killing her—he has taken to murdering his wives because the first was unfaithful to him—by telling him a story every evening. She leaves each evening's tale incomplete until the next day, so that he has to spare her life in order to hear its conclusion. He is so entertained that he finally abandons his murderous plan." Oxford Companion to Child Lit

Aylesworth, Jim

Goldilocks and the three bears; retold by Jim Aylesworth; illustrated by Barbara McClintock. Scholastic Press 2003 un il $15.95

Grades: K 1 2 3   **398.2**

1. Ravens 2. Folklore 3. Prisoners 4. Jacobites 5. Bears -- Folklore

ISBN 0-439-39545-3

LC 2002-15964

A little girl walking in the woods finds the house of the three bears and helps herself to their belongings

"Aylesworth's text is faithful to the traditional elements of the original, juicing up the plot with folksy, conversational asides. . . . The artist's watercolor, sepia ink, and gouache illustrations are pastel and dainty yet full of life and action." SLJ

★ The **mitten**; retold by Jim Aylesworth; illustrated by Barbara McClintock. Scholastic Press 2009 un il $16.99

Grades: PreK K 1 2   **398.2**

1. Winter -- Folklore 2. Animals -- Folklore 3. Folklore -- Ukraine 4. Folklore -- Juvenile literature

ISBN 978-0-439-92544-0; 0-439-92544-4

LC 2006-37115

A retelling of the traditional tale of how a boy's lost mitten becomes a refuge from the cold for an increasing number of animals.

"Aylesworth's polished story together with McClintock's energetic pictures prove that The Mitten can hold one more. Aylesworth's text shows its storytelling roots with its perfect pacing, precisely chosen details, and most of all its particapatory repetition." Horn Book

The **tale** of Tricky Fox; a New England trickster tale. retold by Jim Aylesworth; illustrated by Barbara McClintock. Scholastic Press 2001 un il $15.95
Grades: K 1 2 3   **398.2**
1. Foxes 2. Tricksters 3. Foxes -- Folklore 4. Folklore -- New England
ISBN 0-439-09543-3
LC 00-35773
Tricky Fox uses his sack to trick everyone he meets into giving him ever more valuable items
"The romping good humor of the story is carried by the old-fashioned illustrations in sepia tones." SLJ

Badoe, Adwoa
The **pot** of wisdom: Ananse stories; pictures by Baba Wagué Diakité. Douglas & McIntyre 2001 63p il hardcover o.p. pa $12.95
Grades: 3 4 5 6   **398.2**
1. Anansi (Legendary character) 2. Folklore -- West Africa
ISBN 0-88899-429-X; 0-88899-869-4 pa
"Badoe remembers hearing these trickster stories in her youth in Ghana, and she retells them with the freshness and verve of the spoken word. . . . Each tale is illustrated with a brilliantly colored polychrome tile by Diakite, the Mali-born illustrator. The tiles employ strong black linear motifs and sun-and-earth colors: gold, orange, brown, blue, lemon." Booklist

Barrager, Brigette
The **twelve** dancing princesses; written and illustrated by Brigette Barrager. Chronicle Books 2011 un il $16.99
Grades: K 1 2 3   **398.2**
1. Fairy tales 2. Folklore -- Germany
ISBN 978-0-8118-7696-4; 0-8118-7696-9
LC 2010011580
A retelling of the Grimm brothers' tale of twelve princesses who dance secretly all night long and how their secret is eventually discovered.
"With art resembling that of animated film and several graceful dance scenes, this story could easily be set to a sound track. The plot is true to that told by the Grimms, and nice bits of dialogue and observations by Pip thread easily through the narrative, bringing the characters to life." SLJ

Bateman, Teresa
The **Frog** with the Big Mouth; retold by Teresa Bateman; illustrated by Will Terry. Albert Whitman & Co. 2008 un il $16.99
Grades: K 1 2   **398.2**
1. Frogs -- Folklore 2. Folklore -- South America 3. Rain forest animals -- Folklore
ISBN 978-0-8075-2621-7; 0-8075-2621-5
LC 2007052157
An Argentine wide-mouthed frog sets out through the rain forest to brag about his fly-eating abilities and encounters a toco toucan, a coati, a capybara, and a jaguar. Includes a note about the animals.

"Terry's shiny, verdant rain forest capably offsets myriad greens with shadows of lavender, an electric-blue beetle, and wine-red berries. The spreads swirl with movement and beckon forward via fluid lines. . . . This is an inventive version of a long-favored tale." SLJ

Baynes, Pauline
Questionable creatures; a bestiary. [by] Pauline Baynes. Eerdmans Books for Young Readers 2006 47p il $18
Grades: 4 5 6 7   **398.2**
1. Bestiaries 2. Mythical animals
ISBN 978-0-8028-5284-7; 0-8028-5284-X
LC 2005033658
"Baynes introduces readers to the creatures and myths found in medieval bestiaries and explains how the books were made and how they were viewed by the general public. The rest of the volume details the commonly held beliefs that both peasants and scholars embraced about specific animals. . . . Baynes's detailed gouache and colored-pencil illustrations . . . are done in the style of medieval illuminations. . . . The artist shows great respect for the early bestiary creators while also giving the stories relevance for modern readers." SLJ
Includes bibliographical references

Bell, Anthea
The **porridge** pot; 1854 by the Brothers Carl and Theodor Colshorn; retold from the German by Anthea Bell; pictures by Claudia Carls. Minedition 2007 un il $16.99
Grades: 2 3 4 5   **398.2**
1. Fairy tales 2. Folklore -- Germany
ISBN 978-0-698-40073-3
"A starving miller chases his porridge pot-toting wife into the woods, followed by their young daughter. The daughter loses her parents and her shoe, but is befriended by an eccentric-looking old woman who . . . directs her to her destiny as wife of the kingdom's prince. . . . Carls uses an amalgamation of computer-enhanced images and paintings to create an oddly textured folktale world. Claymation figures parade with Meer cats and ostriches in outlandish costumes. . . . and hyperrealistic, imagination-stretching details." Booklist

Berger, Barbara
All the way to Lhasa; a tale from Tibet. retelling & art by Barbara Helen Berger. Philomel Bks. 2002 un il $17.99
Grades: K 1 2 3   **398.2**
1. Yak -- Fiction 2. Folklore -- Tibet 3. Folklore -- Tibet (China)
ISBN 0-399-23387-3
LC 2001-54560
A boy and his yak persevere along the difficult way to the holy city of Lhasa and succeed where others fail
"Berger distills the pilgrim's quest into a simply told, evocative tale. . . . Berger's paint-and-pencil illustrations are gloriously colored and filled with subtle details borrowed from Tibetan Buddhism." Booklist

Berner, Rotraut Susanne
Definitely not for little ones; some very Grimm fairytale comics. translated by Shelley Tanaka. House of Anansi Press 2009 un il $18.95

Grades: 4 5 6 **398.2**

1. Authors 2. Folklore 3. Fairy tales 4. Folklorists 5. Philologists 6. Short story writers 7. Folklore -- Germany -- Juvenile literature

ISBN 978-0-88899-957-3; 0-88899-957-7

"In a comic book format, Berner retells the Brothers Grimm tales of the Frog Prince, Mother Holle, Tom Thumb, Rapunzel, Jorinda & Jorindel, Lucky Hans, Hans the Hedgehog, and Little Red Cap, using a humorous, breezy and somewhat ironic tone. . . . Older elementary-school readers who like sneaky humor, slightly violent demises of villains, and humorous takes on familiar tales will enjoy these comics. . . . Tanaka's translation lets the narration and dialogue flow seamlessly." Booklist

Blackstone, Stella

Storytime; first tales for sharing. told by Stella Blackstone; illustrated by Anne Wilson. Barefoot Books 2005 94p il $19.99; pa $12.99

Grades: K 1 **398.2**

1. Folklore 2. Animals -- Folklore

ISBN 1-84148-345-1; 1-84686-165-9 pa

LC 2004029542

"Seven familiar nursery tales are accompanied by bright, stylized, folk-art illustrations, done in paper collage and acrylic. Selections include The Cock, the Mouse and the Little Red Hen, The Gingerbread Man, The Ugly Duckling, Goldilocks, The Timid Hare (a Henny Penny story from India), The Three Little Pigs, and Stone Soup. The retellings are straightforward; most are faithful to the most commonly known versions and retain the familiar refrains. . . . The collection as a whole is delightful; the art is fresh, vibrant, and full of child appeal." SLJ

Includes bibliographical references

Blackwood, Gary L.

Legends or lies? Marshall Cavendish Benchmark 2006 72p il (Unsolved history) lib bdg $34.21

Grades: 4 5 6 7 **398.2**

1. Legends

ISBN 978-0-7614-1891-7 lib bdg; 0-7614-1891-1 lib bdg

Describes several legends that have intrigued people for centuries: the lost civilization of Atlantis, the Amazons, King Arthur, St Brendon, Pope Joan, and El Dorado

This collection "of tidbits about lingering mysteries of the past . . . [offers] more substance than most. . . . [It offers] a full-page illustration opening each chapter; reproductions, many in color; and a generously spaced format." SLJ

Includes glossary and bibliographical references

Blia Xiong

Nine-in-one, Grr! Grr! a folktale from the Hmong people of Laos. told by Blia Xiong; adapted by Cathy Spagnoli; illustrated by Nancy Hom. Children's Bk. Press 1989 30p il hardcover o.p. pa $7.95

Grades: K 1 2 **398.2**

1. Folklore -- Laos 2. Tigers -- Folklore 3. Hmong (Asian people) -- Folklore

ISBN 0-89239-048-4; 0-89239-110-3 pa

LC 89-9891

When the great god Shao promises Tiger nine cubs each year, Bird comes up with a clever trick to prevent the land from being overrun by tigers

"Simply and eloquently told, this pourquoi tale from a minority Laotian culture is boldly illustrated in a style adapted from the multi-imaged embroidered story cloths of the Hmong people. Its rhythmic text and appealing, brightly colored pictures make it a good choice for preschool story hours." Booklist

Bolt, Ranjit

The **hare** and the tortoise and other fables of La Fontaine; translated by Ranjit Bolt; illustrated by Giselle Potter. Barefoot Books 2006 64p il $19.99

Grades: 3 4 5 6 **398.2**

1. Poets 2. Fables 3. Authors 4. Children's poetry 5. Fairy tale writers

ISBN 1-905236-54-9; 978-1-905236-54-1

LC 2005-30378

"Bolt translates and recasts La Fontaine's work in rhyming, contemporary English. . . . The Fox and the Stork, The Lion and the Rat, and other familiar tales appear among these 19 selections, along with a few that are less well known. . . . Potter's double-page, naive paintings echo the humor, effectively portraying the animal and human characters. The rhymed phrasing offers an entertaining introduction to the literature of fable and pleasing read-aloud and storytelling material." SLJ

Boughn, Michael

Into the world of the dead; astonishing adventures in the underworld. Annick Press 2006 56p il lib bdg $24.95; pa $12.95

Grades: 5 6 7 8 **398.2**

1. Death -- Folklore 2. Future life -- Folklore

ISBN 1-55037-959-3 lib bdg; 1-55037-958-5 pa

"Boughn retells stories from many cultures on every continent except South America, including quite a few from Mesoamerica, Asia, Africa, and Oceania. Readers will find heroes who have traveled to and returned from the underworld as well as the gods and monsters who dwell there. Full-color and black-and-white illustrations, including reproductions, photos, and plenty of graphics of skulls, appear on every page. . . . This is a book that many young people may find appealing." SLJ

Brett, Jan

Beauty and the beast; retold and illustrated by Jan Brett. Clarion Bks. 1989 un il lib bdg $16; pa $6.95

Grades: 1 2 3 **398.2**

1. Fairy tales 2. Folklore -- France 3. Folklore

ISBN 0-89919-497-4 lib bdg; 0-395-55702-X pa

LC 88-16965

Through her great capacity to love, a kind and beautiful maid releases a handsome prince from the spell which has made him an ugly beast

"A Beauty of distinguished appearance, a delightful set of animal servants, and a suitably hideous Beast are presented in Jan Brett's distinctive, decorative style. Small details, such as tapestries mirroring the action of the tale, add to the effect of the simply written story." Horn Book Guide

Gingerbread baby. Putnam 1999 un il $16.99

Grades: K 1 2 3 **398.2**

1. Folklore 2. Toy and movable books 3. Baking -- Fiction 4. Gingerbread -- Fiction 5. Toy and movable

books -- Specimens
ISBN 0-399-23444-6

LC 98-52310

A young boy and his mother bake a gingerbread baby that escapes from their oven and leads a crowd on a chase

"Although the story remains true to the original tale, Brett has added her own touches and a surprise ending. . . . The illustrations are pure Brett and feature warm colors against a snow-white landscape." SLJ

The **mitten**; a Ukrainian folktale. adapted and illustrated by Jan Brett. anniversary ed.; Penguin Young Readers Group 2009 un il $17.99
Grades: K 1 2　　　　　　　　　　　　　　**398.2**
1. Animals -- Folklore 2. Folklore -- Ukraine
ISBN 978-0-399-25296-9; 0-399-25296-7
First published 1989 by Putnam
After Nicki accidentally drops his mitten in the forest it becomes an object of curiosity for a mole, a rabbit, a badger, a tiny brown mouse, and a big brown bear, as they all crawl into it

"Readers will enjoy the charm and humor in the portrayal of the animals as they make room for each newcomer in the mitten and sprawl in the snow after the big sneeze." Horn Book

The **three** snow bears; [by] Jan Brett. G. P. Putnam's Sons 2007 un il $16.99
Grades: K 1 2 3　　　　　　　　　　　　　**398.2**
1. Inuit -- Folklore 2. Polar bear -- Folklore
ISBN 978-0-399-24792-7

LC 2007007373

Retells the story of Goldilocks, set in an Inuit village and featuring a family of polar bears.

"Filled with the gorgeously detailed watercolor and gouache illustrations that distinguish her work, this Arctic version of the classic tale is pure Brett. . . . The plot remains true to the progression of the traditional tale and the narrative moves swiftly." SLJ

Who's that knocking on Christmas Eve. Putnam 2002 un il $16.99
Grades: K 1 2　　　　　　　　　　　　　　**398.2**
1. Folklore -- Norway 2. Christmas -- Fiction
ISBN 0-399-23873-5

LC 2001-48253

A boy from Finnmark and his ice bear help scare away some hungry trolls so that Kyri and her father can enjoy their Christmas Eve meal

This is a "vivid, well-paced retelling of an old Norwegian folktale. . . . Gorgeous endpapers depicting night-sky constellations studded with trolls, bears, and other mythical symbols complement the exquisitely detailed winter-wonderland artistry within." Booklist

Brown, Marcia
Once a mouse; a fable cut in wood. Atheneum Pubs. 1961 un il $16; pa $5.99
Grades: K 1 2 3　　　　　　　　　　　　　**398.2**
1. Fables 2. Folklore -- India
ISBN 0-684-12662-1; 0-689-71343-6 pa
Awarded the Caldecott Medal, 1962

"The illustrations are remarkably beautiful. The emotional elements of the story . . . are conveyed with just as much intensity as the purely visual ones." New Yorker

Stone soup; an old tale. told and pictured by Marcia Brown. Scribner 1947 un il $16.95; pa $6.99
Grades: K 1 2 3　　　　　　　　　　　　　**398.2**
1. Folklore -- France
ISBN 0-684-92296-7; 0-689-71103-4 pa
A Caldecott Medal honor book, 1948

"When the people in a French village heard that three soldiers were coming, they hid all their food for they knew what soldiers are. However, when the soldiers began to make soup with water and stones the pot gradually filled with all the vegetables which had been hidden away. The simple language and quiet humour of this folktale are amplified and enriched by gay and witty drawings of clever lighthearted soldiers, and the gullible 'light-witted' peasants." Cont Libr Rev

Bruchac, James
★　The **girl** who helped thunder and other Native American folktales; retold by James Bruchac and Joseph Bruchac; illustrated by Stefano Vitale. Sterling Pub. Co. 2008 96p il (Folktales of the world) $14.95
Grades: 3 4 5 6　　　　　　　　　　　　　**398.2**
1. Native Americans -- Folklore
ISBN 978-1-4027-3263-8; 1-4027-3263-5

LC 2007-16876

"The Bruchacs retell Native North American folktales in a clear yet bold voice. The anthology is arranged geographically, a logical organization that reveals the diversity of Native peoples. . . . Descriptions of each region introduce the original inhabitants of those places, as the authors provide succinct yet enriching historical and cultural context for the stories that follow. . . . Vitale's stylized oil-on-wood illustrations vividly reveal the colorful spirit of the tales, as bright blues and reds complement the earth tones found throughout." SLJ

Bruchac, Joseph
Between earth & sky; legends of Native American sacred places. written by Joseph Bruchac; illustrated by Thomas Locker. Harcourt Brace & Co. 1996 un il map hardcover o.p. pa $7
Grades: 3 4 5　　　　　　　　　　　　　　**398.2**
1. Native Americans -- Folklore
ISBN 0-15-200042-9; 0-15-202062-4 pa

LC 95-10862

"Each tale is a model of economy, gracefully distilling its message, while Locker's landscapes capture the mysticism inherent in each setting." Horn Book Guide

How Chipmunk got his stripes; a tale of bragging and teasing. as told by Joseph Bruchac & James Bruchac; pictures by Jose Aruego & Ariane Dewey. Dial Bks. for Young Readers 2001 un il hardcover o.p. pa $6.99
Grades: K 1 2 3　　　　　　　　　　　　　**398.2**
1. Bears -- Folklore 2. Chipmunks -- Folklore 3. Squirrels -- Folklore 4. Native Americans -- Folklore
ISBN 0-8037-2404-7; 0-14-250021-6 pa

LC 99-16793

"This pourquoi story is succinctly written in simple, concrete language, and repeated chants give listeners an opportunity to participate actively in the narrative's unfolding. . . . The pictures are large enough to be seen and enjoyed by a group." Bull Cent Child Books

Raccoon's last race; a traditional Abenaki story. as told by Joseph Bruchac & James Bruchac; pictures by Jose Aruego & Ariane Dewey. Dial Books for Young Readers 2004 un il $15.99

Grades: K 1 2 3   **398.2**
   1. Raccoons -- Folklore 2. Abnaki Indians -- Folklore
   ISBN 0-8037-2977-4

LC 2003-9104

Tells the story of how Raccoon, the fastest animal on earth, loses his speed because he is boastful and breaks his promises

"A solid retelling of an Abenaki legend. . . . The text reads aloud smoothly and keeps the action moving quickly. Done in pen-and-ink, gouache, and pastel, the illustrations accentuate the humor of the tale." SLJ

Thirteen moons on a turtle's back; a Native American year of moons. by Joseph Bruchac and Jonathan London; illustrated by Thomas Locker. Philomel Bks. 1992 un il $16.95; pa $5.99

Grades: K 1 2 3 4   **398.2**
   1. Children's poetry 2. Seasons -- Poetry 3. Native Americans -- Poetry 4. Native Americans -- Folklore 5. Seasons -- Juvenile literature 6. Poetry -- By individual authors
   ISBN 0-399-22141-7; 0-698-11584-8 pa

LC 91-3961

"Locker . . . has created a dramatic oil painting for each short tale. His artwork portrays seasonal changes in the land as well as the specific seasonal activities of humans and animals. The large format with minimal text will appeal to younger children, while the alternative calendar, based on changes in nature, will interest middle readers. An unusual, easy-to-use resource for librarians, teachers, and others wishing to incorporate multicultural activites throughout the year." Booklist

Turtle's race with Beaver; a traditional Seneca story. as told by Joseph Bruchac & James Bruchac; pictures by Jose Aruego & Ariane Dewey. Dial Bks. for Young Readers 2003 un il $15.99; pa $5.99

Grades: K 1 2 3   **398.2**
   1. Beavers -- Folklore 2. Turtles -- Folklore 3. Seneca Indians -- Folklore 4. Indians of North America -- Folklore -- Juvenile literature
   ISBN 0-8037-2852-2; 0-14-240466-7 pa

LC 2002-4001

When Beaver challenges Turtle to a swimming race for ownership of the pond, Turtle outsmarts Beaver, and Beaver learns to share

"Done in pen and ink, gouache, and pastel, the cheerful artwork is a wonderful match for this well-told tale." SLJ

★ The **first** strawberries; a Cherokee story. retold by Joseph Bruchac; pictures by Anna Vojtech. Dial Bks. for Young Readers 1993 un il hardcover o.p. pa $6.99

Grades: K 1 2 3   **398.2**
   1. Strawberries -- Folklore 2. Cherokee Indians --

Folklore
ISBN 0-8037-1331-2; 0-14-05409-8 pa

LC 91-31058

A quarrel between the first man and the first woman is reconciled when the Sun causes strawberries to grow out of the earth

"This retelling . . . is simply and clearly written, and as sweet as the berries the woman stops to taste. The attractive watercolors and colored-pencil illustrations show an idealized pastoral world." SLJ

★ The **great** ball game; a Muskogee story. retold by Joseph Bruchac; illustrated by Susan L. Roth. Dial Bks. for Young Readers 1994 un il $15

Grades: K 1 2 3   **398.2**
   1. Animals -- Folklore 2. Creek Indians -- Folklore
   ISBN 0-8037-1539-0

LC 93-6269

Bat, who has both wings and teeth, plays an important part in a game between the Birds and the Animals to decide which group is better

"Roth's dynamic collages combine cut papers of varied textures and hues to create a series of effective illustrations. Short and well told, this appealing pourquoi tale lends itself to reading aloud." Booklist

Bryan, Ashley
  ★ **Ashley** Bryan's African tales, uh-huh. Atheneum Bks. for Young Readers 1998 198p $22

Grades: 4 5 6   **398.2**
   1. Tales -- Africa 2. Folklore -- Africa
   ISBN 0-689-82076-3

LC 97-77743

This volume combines three previously published titles: The ox of the wonderful horns and other African folktales (1971), Beat the story-drum, pum-pum (1980), Lion and the ostrich chicks and other African folktales (1986)

This collection of African folktales is "told with Bryan's distinctive rhythmic word patterns and filled with humor, life lessons, and the antics of trickster Ananse. . . . Quality reproductions of the original woodcuts enrich this handsome volume." Horn Book Guide

★ **Beautiful** blackbird. Atheneum Bks. for Young Readers 2003 un il $16.95

Grades: K 1 2 3   **398.2**
   1. Birds -- Folklore 2. Folklore -- Zambia 3. Folklore -- Africa -- Juvenile literature
   ISBN 0-689-84731-9

LC 2002-5290

In a story of the Ila people, the colorful birds of Africa ask Blackbird, whom they think is the most beautiful of birds, to decorate them with some of his "blackening brew"

"Bryan employs boldly colored, cut-paper artwork to dramatize the action. The overlapping collage images fill the pages with energy. . . . Ready-made for participative storytelling." Booklist

Buehner, Caralyn
  Goldilocks and the three bears; [by] Caralyn Buehner; pictures by Mark Buehner. Dial Books for Young Readers 2007 un il $16.99

Grades: PreK K 1 2   **398.2**
1. Folklore 2. Bears -- Folklore
ISBN 0-8037-2939-1

LC 2005036401

In this variation on the classic folktale, a rhyming, rope-skipping, little girl rudely helps herself to the belongings of a genteel family of bears.

"This warm and pleasing retelling of the classic include a rope-jumping Goldilocks in red cowboy boots who bursts with personality. . . . The luminous oil-over-acrylic illustrations enhance the story with delightful details." SLJ

Bunting, Eve
Finn McCool and the great fish; written by Eve Bunting; illustrated by Zachary Pullen. Sleeping Bear Press 2010 un il $16.95
Grades: K 1 2 3   **398.2**
1. Fishes -- Folklore 2. Giants -- Folklore 3. Folklore -- Ireland
ISBN 1-58536-366-9; 978-1-58536-366-7

LC 2009036936

Irish giant Finn McCool is told that in order to become wise he much catch and eat the salmon that possesses knowledge, but Finn finds that he cannot bring himself to kill the miraculous fish

"Bunting makes this unfamiliar story accessible to readers. The art beautifully illustrates the green Irish countryside and makes Finn a real gentle giant." SLJ

Burleigh, Robert
Pandora; illustrated by Raul Colón. Silver Whistle/Harcourt 2002 un il $16
Grades: 3 4 5 6   **398.2**
1. Classical mythology 2. Pandora (Legendary character) 3. Mythology, Greek 4. Pandora (Greek mythology)
ISBN 0-15-202178-7

LC 2001-1282

"The text, arranged in lines like free verse, is rhythmic and clear, with short, simple sentences. . . . The romantic watercolor/colored-pencil illustrations have narrow borders and textured grounds. Blues and greens dominate the muted palette." SLJ

Burns, Batt
★ The king with horse's ears and other Irish folktales; [by] Batt Burns; illustrated by Igor Oleynikov. Sterling Pub. Co. 2009 96p il (Folktales of the world) $14.95
Grades: 4 5 6 7   **398.2**
1. Fairy tales 2. Folklore -- Ireland
ISBN 978-1-4027-3772-5; 1-4027-3772-6

LC 2007035258

"These 13 Irish tales retold by storyteller Burns follow fairies and warriors, heroes and clever thieves. . . . The stories are cleanly retold in contemporary, accessible language, and each is introduced with a short paragraph providing cultural or other information. . . . Oleynikov's paintings have a rough texture that suits the energy of the retellings and adds to the lively tone. This is a hearty collection, handsomely produced with Celtic-knot borders and gouache full-page and spot illustrations." Booklist
Includes glossary

Bushyhead, Robert H.
Yonder mountain; a Cherokee legend. as told by Robert H. Bushyhead; written by Kay Thorpe Bannon; foreword by Joseph Bruchac; illustrated by Kristina Rodanas. Marshall Cavendish 2002 un il $16.95
Grades: K 1 2 3   **398.2**
1. Folklore -- Southern States 2. Cherokee Indians -- Folklore
ISBN 0-7614-5113-7

LC 2001-32319

A Cherokee chief chooses his successor by asking three candidates to climb a mountain, thus testing their character and strength

"Beautifully illustrated with rich watercolors that fill most of the pages, this story folds its altruistic message into a vivid, entertaining tale." Booklist

Byrd, Robert
★ The hero and the minotaur; the fantastic adventures of Theseus. retold and illustrated by Robert Byrd. Dutton Children's Books 2005 un il $16.99
Grades: 3 4 5 6   **398.2**
1. Classical mythology 2. Theseus (Greek mythology) 3. Minotaur (Greek mythology)
ISBN 0-525-47391-2

LC 2004-21585

The author "interweaves the legends of Aegeus, Heracles, the Minotaur, Ariadne, and Icarus with the story of Theseus. Myths that are normally quite complicated become easy to decipher in this outstanding version, for Byrd tells the tales simply and clearly. . . . The pen-and-watercolor illustrations are painstakingly drawn and include numerous small period details that heighten the sense of history." SLJ

Caduto, Michael J.
Keepers of the night; Native American stories and nocturnal activities for children. [by] Michael J. Caduto and Joseph Bruchac; story illustrations by David Kanietakeron Fadden; chapter illustrations by Jo Levasseur and Carol Wood; foreword by Merlin D. Tuttle. Fulcrum 1994 146p il pa $15.95
Grades: Adult Professional   **398.2**
1. Nature study 2. Night -- Folklore 3. Native Americans -- Folklore
ISBN 1-55591-177-3

LC 94-2602

"The well-written chapters include discussions with illuminating scientific information." Sci Books Films
Includes glossary and bibliographical references

Campoy, F. Isabel
★ Tales our abuelitas told; a Hispanic folktale collection. [by] F. Isabel Campoy and Alma Flor Ada; illustrated by Felipe Dávalos . . . [et al.] Simon & Schuster 2006 118p il $19.95
Grades: 3 4 5 6   **398.2**
1. Folklore -- Latin America 2. Hispanic Americans -- Folklore 3. Tales -- Spain -- Juvenile literature 4. Folklore -- Spain -- Juvenile literature
ISBN 0-689-82583-5

Presents the authors' retellings of twelve traditional tales accompanied by information on origins and different versions

"All of the selections are peppered with energetic dialogue and witty detail. Children will relish their humor, especially if read aloud." SLJ

Cardenas, Teresa

Oloyou; pictures by Margarita Sada; translated by Elisa Amado. Groundwood Books 2008 un il $18.95

Grades: 2 3 4 5   398.2

1. Cats -- Folklore 2. Folklore -- Cuba 3. Bilingual books -- English-Spanish 4. Yoruba (African people) -- Folklore

ISBN 978-0-88899-795-1; 0-88899-795-7

"In this striking bilingual retelling of a Yoruba myth, Oloyou the Cat is the very first creature created by the Godchild while he is still too young to know what he is doing. More importantly, Oloyou becomes God's first friend. They are happy until Oloyou falls into Nothing, which is an oceanic kingdom presided over by Okun Aró. . . . The clarity of the writing makes this book suitable for reading aloud, while the complexity of the story will hold the interest of older readers. The oil-on-canvas illustrations are rich and bold with a mythic scope that incorporates the story's African-Caribbean roots." SLJ

Casey, Dawn

The **Barefoot** book of Earth tales; retold by Dawn Casey; illustrated by Anne Wilson. Barefoot Books 2009 95p il $19.99

Grades: 2 3 4 5 6   398.2

1. Folklore 2. Ecology -- Folklore

ISBN 978-1-84686-224-3; 1-84686-224-8

"This enchanting collection of folk tales and creation myths from different cultures encourages readers to live a more harmonious life with nature. . . . Well chosen and crafted with broad appeal, the tales are woven with subtle morals and wisdom. Each story is introduced by a brief overview about the featured locale and culture . . . and followed by a related, easy-to-replicate activity or craft. Full-page and spot illustrations and colorful decorative borders reflect the spirit and origins of each offering. Done with collaged papers with acrylic and printed backgrounds." SLJ

The **great** race; the story of the Chinese zodiac. written by Dawn Casey; illustrated by Anne Wilson. Barefoot Books 2006 un il $16.99

Grades: 1 2 3 4   398.2

1. Zodiac 2. Folklore -- China 3. Animals -- Folklore

ISBN 1-905236-77-8

LC 2005032544

Relates how the Jade Emperor chose twelve animals to represent the years in his calendar. Also discusses the Chinese calendar, zodiac, the qualities associated with each animal, and what animal rules the year in which the reader was born

"In this retelling of the ancient legend, Casey maintains the pace well. . . . The book is a visual treat, with illustrations in simple collage designs on acrylic and painted backgrounds placed in such a way as to keep the eye engaged and moving." SLJ

Cech, John

Jack and the beanstalk; retold by John Cech; illustrated by Robert Mackenzie. Sterling Pub. Co. 2008 un il $14.95

Grades: 1 2 3   398.2

1. Fairy tales 2. Giants -- Folklore 3. Folklore -- Great Britain

ISBN 978-1-4027-3064-1; 1-4027-3064-0

LC 2007001783

A boy climbs to the top of a giant beanstalk where he uses his quick wits to outsmart an ogre and make his and his mother's fortune. Includes historical notes on versions of this tale, other heroic stories, and alternate "ascension" tales.

Cech "knits fresh strands into the . . . story. This smoothly paced version, which begins with some hilarious wordplay, runs close to traditional tellings until the end, when the giant's wife joins Jack in his hasty escape. . . . MacKenzie ably ramps up the drama in the pencil-and-paint scenes." Booklist

Puss in boots; retold by John Cech; illustrated by Bernhard Oberdieck. Sterling Pub. 2010 un il (Classic fairy tale collection) $14.95

Grades: K 1 2 3   398.2

1. Fairy tales 2. Folklore -- France

ISBN 978-1-4027-4436-5; 1-4027-4436-6

LC 2008052496

A clever cat helps his poor master win fame, fortune, and the hand of a beautiful princess. Includes historical notes on versions of this tale and other fairy tales

This "offers an enjoyable retelling of the timeless story. . . . The narrative is descriptive, lively, and droll, and the colorful watercolor-and-ink illustrations, filled with period details, are intricately rendered." Booklist

Rapunzel; retold by John Cech; illustrated by Fiona Sansom. Sterling 2010 un il (Classic fairy tale collection) $14.95

Grades: K 1 2 3   398.2

1. Folklore 2. Fairy tales

ISBN 978-1-4027-6911-5; 1-4027-6911-3

A retelling of a folktale in which a beautiful girl with long golden hair is kept imprisoned in a lonely tower by a witch. Includes a note on the origins of the story.

"Cech employs clear, descriptive language that is fresh and appealing to modern readers, at times seeming to speak directly to his audience. Varying in size from inserts to double-page spreads, with the text often placed in frames, Sansom's lovely medieval paintings complement and enhance the text, depicting the action while concentrating on emotional content. . . . A spendid candidate for a crowd-pleasing read-aloud." Kirkus

The **twelve** dancing princesses; by John Cech; illustrated by Lucy Corvino. Sterling 2009 un il $14.95

Grades: K 1 2 3 4   398.2

1. Folklore 2. Fairy tales

ISBN 978-1-4027-4435-8; 1-4027-4435-8

A retelling of the traditional tale of how the king's twelve daughters wear out their shoes every night while supposedly sleeping in their locked bedroom

"In this retelling of the Grimm Brothers' tale called 'The Dancing Shoes,' several significant details have been changed. . . . Corvino has used acrylic and watercolor paints and inks, with pencil detail–particularly on faces–to create lovely illustrations in the classic fairy-tale style. This adaptation is a worthy purchase for most collections." SLJ

Chase, Richard

The **Jack** tales; told by R.M. Ward and his kindred in the Beech Mountain section of western North Carolina and by other descendants of Council Harmon (1803-1896) elsewhere in the southern mountains; with three tales from Wise County, Virginia; set down from these sources and edited by Richard Chase; with an appendix compiled by Herbert Halpert; and illustrated by Berkeley Williams, Jr. Houghton Mifflin 2003 216p il pa $7.95

Grades: 5 6 7 8 Adult Professional **398.2**
1. Folklore -- Southern States
ISBN 978-0-618-34692-9 pa; 0-618-34692-9 pa
LC 2003276676

First published 1943

A collection of folk tales from the southern Appalachians that center on a single character, the irrepressible Jack

"Humor, freshness, colorful American background, and the use of one character as a central figure in the cycle mark these 18 folk tales, told here in the dialect of the mountain country of North Carolina. A scholarly appendix by Herbert Halpert, giving sources and parallels, increases the book's value as a contribution to American folklore. Black-and-white illustrations in the spirit of the text." Booklist

Includes bibliographical references

Chen, Jiang Hong

The **magic** horse of Han Gan; [by] Chen Jiang Hong; translated by Claudia Zoe Bedrick. Enchanted Lion Books 2006 37p il $16.95

Grades: 2 3 4 **398.2**
1. Artists 2. Painters 3. Folklore -- China 4. Horses -- Folklore 5. Artists -- Folklore
ISBN 1-59270-063-2
LC 2006046393

Master artist Han Gan's painted horse comes alive to help save ancient China from attack

This is an "elegant picture book. . . . The tale is crisply and concisely told. The double-page illustrations are dominated by strong browns, blacks, and reds, and are painted directly on silk." SLJ

Chichester-Clark, Emma

★ **Goldilocks** and the three bears. Candlewick Press 2010 un il $14.99

Grades: PreK K 1 **398.2**
1. Folklore 2. Bears -- Folklore
ISBN 978-0-7636-4680-6; 0-7636-4680-6
LC 2009-14601

A retelling of the adventures of a nosy, naughty, and sassy little girl who finds the house of the three bears and helps herself to their belongings.

"This large-format edition of the traditional story offers plenty of scope for Clark's colorful illustrations. While the plot remains the same, the telling is a little more elaborate here than in most versions, with a couple of new refrains and added dialogue. . . . The controlled profusion of patterns gives the pencil-and-acrylic illustrations a busy but cheerful look. . . . Recommended for the freshness and energy of its artwork." Booklist

Clayton, Sally Pomme

Amazons! women warriors of the world. illustrated by Sophie Herxheimer. Frances Lincoln 2009 93p il $19.95

Grades: 3 4 5 6 **398.2**
1. Folklore 2. Women -- Folklore
ISBN 978-1-84507-660-3; 1-84507-660-5

"This handsome collection of folktales showcases seven empowering females, each with her own unique strengths and abilities. . . . Filled with lively language and fast-paced action, the tales introduce a pleasing range of characters and moods. . . . The illustrations employ swirling lines and vibrant color washes to reflect the setting and tone of each tale. The stories are separated by two-page interludes that provide brief facts or activities." SLJ

Includes glossary

Tales told in tents; stories from central Asia. written by Sally Pomme Clayton; illustrated by Sophie Herxheimer. Frances Lincoln 2005 64p il map $16.95; pa $8.95

Grades: 2 3 4 **398.2**
1. Folklore -- Asia
ISBN 978-1-84507-066-3; 1-84507-066-6; 978-1-84507-278-0 pa; 1-84507-278-2 pa

"In 12 traditional stories from the nomadic cultures of Central Asia, folklorist Clayton retells myth and folklore she heard in Kazakhstan, Afghanistan, and elsewhere. The lively tales include epic creation myths, rhyming riddles, trickster tales, songs, and stories of magic carpets and music. The large picture book is illustrated with richly colored line-and-watercolor paintings that evoke Central Asian traditional culture. . . . A rich resource, even for older readers, this anthology has stories that travel across the world." Booklist

Includes glossary

Climo, Shirley

The **Egyptian** Cinderella; illustrated by Ruth Heller. Crowell 1989 un il $15.95; pa $5.95

Grades: K 1 2 3 **398.2**
1. Fairy tales 2. Folklore -- Egypt
ISBN 0-690-04822-X; 0-06-443279-3 pa
LC 88-37547

In this version of Cinderella set in Egypt in the sixth century B.C., Rhodopes, a slave girl, eventually comes to be chosen by the Pharaoh to be his queen

"The beauty of the language is set off to perfection by Heller's arresting full-color illustrations." SLJ

The **Korean** Cinderella; illustrated by Ruth Heller. HarperCollins Pubs. 1993 un il $15.95; pa $6.95

Grades: K 1 2 3 **398.2**
1. Fairy tales 2. Folklore -- Korea
ISBN 0-06-020432-X; 0-06-443397-8 pa
LC 91-23268

In this version of Cinderella set in ancient Korea, Pear Blossom, a stepchild, eventually comes to be chosen by the magistrate to be his wife

"Heller's paintings are exotically lush and colorful as well as engaging. Climo includes an explanatory note about Cinderella variants (the Korean version in particular), and Heller explains the decorations, costumes, and settings she used in the illustrations. An agreeable retelling of the Cinderella story." Booklist

Monkey business; stories from around the world. illustrated by Erik Brooks. H. Holt 2005 118p il $18.95

Grades: 3 4 5 6 **398.2**

1. Folklore 2. Monkeys -- Folklore
ISBN 0-8050-6392-7

LC 2003-63956

A collection of monkey lore, fables, and stories from around the world

"This well-told and entertaining book . . . draws on pourquoi and folktales, mythology, facts, and trivia. . . . Numerous colored-pencil-and-watercolor illustrations capture the myriad cultures and creatures represented. This collection is unique, well written, and fun." SLJ

Tuko and the birds; a tale from the Philippines. illustrated by Francisco X. Mora. Holt & Co. 2008 un il $16.95

Grades: 1 2 3 **398.2**

1. Birds -- Folklore 2. Geckos -- Folklore 3. Folklore -- Philippines 4. Folklore -- Philippines -- Juvenile literature
ISBN 978-0-8050-6559-6; 0-8050-6559-8

LC 2007002826

When Tuko the gecko cries so loudly that the birds stop singing and cannot sleep, they try to trick him into moving from their home on the Philippine island of Luzon.

"Climo's retelling . . . is infused with humor. . . . Watercolor illustrations depict a village with bamboo houses and people going about their daily lives of fishing, food preparation, and play. . . . A lively choice for storytime." SLJ

Coburn, Jewell Reinhart

Domitila; a Cinderella tale from the Mexican tradition. adapted by Jewell Reinhart Coburn; illustrated by Connie McLennan. Shen's Bks. 2000 un il $16.95

Grades: 2 3 4 **398.2**

1. Fairy tales 2. Folklore -- Mexico
ISBN 1-88500-813-9

LC 99-56173

By following her mother's admonition to perform every task with care and love, a poor young Mexican girl wins the devotion of the governor's son

"The full-page oil-on-cavas illustrations are bright, sumptuous, and visually enticing. The text is bordered by proverbs rendered in both Spanish and English. Well-written and strongly illustrated." SLJ

Cohen, Caron Lee

The **mud** pony; a traditional Skidi Pawnee tale. retold by Caron Lee Cohen; illustrated by Shonto Begay. Scholastic 1988 un il hardcover o.p. pa $4.99

Grades: K 1 2 3 **398.2**

1. Horses -- Folklore 2. Pawnee Indians -- Folklore
ISBN 0-590-41526-3 pa

LC 87-23451

A poor boy becomes a powerful leader when Mother Earth turns his mud pony into a real one, but after the pony turns back to mud, he must find his own strength

"The text is powerful because it is spare and unadorned. It is extended well by the softly toned, full-color, impressionistic pictures." Helbig. This land is our land

Cousins, Lucy

★ **Yummy**; eight favorite fairy tales. Candlewick Press 2009 121p il $18.99

Grades: PreK K 1 **398.2**

1. Folklore 2. Fairy tales
ISBN 978-0-7636-4474-1; 0-7636-4474-9

"Beloved classics are successfully served by these bold, striking renditions. . . . Large, arresting gouache spreads in Cousins's signature style utilize saturated colors and thick, dark outlines against solid backgrounds. Expressive characters enhance the stories' shifting moods. Large type accentuates the dynamic texts, building each spare entry to its powerful climax." SLJ

Crews, Nina

Jack and the beanstalk. Henry Holt 2011 32p il $16.99

Grades: K 1 2 **398.2**

1. Fairy tales 2. Giants -- Folklore 3. Folklore -- Great Britain 4. Folklore -- Juvenile literature
ISBN 978-0-8050-8765-9; 0-8050-8765-6

LC 2010026951

Photo-collage illustrations and updated text provide a new look at the traditional tale of a boy who plants magic beans, climbs the beanstalk, and is captured by a giant and his wife.

"The images are quite keen, photographs and the occasional line drawing manipulated and layered to shape the story. . . . Crews' fans will be delighted; others will be drawn in by the nifty mix of folktale and photo-collage." Kirkus

Cummings, Pat

★ **Ananse** and the lizard; a West African tale. retold and illustrated by Pat Cummings. Holt & Co. 2002 un il $16.95

Grades: K 1 2 3 **398.2**

1. Anansi (Legendary character) 2. Folklore -- Ghana 3. Anansi (Legendary character) -- Legends
ISBN 0-8050-6476-1

LC 2001-1679

Ananse the spider thinks he will marry the daughter of the village chief, but instead he is outsmarted by Lizard

"Cummings' lively prose and humor are a perfect match for the story. The boxed text is accompanied by gorgeous watercolor, gouache, and pencil illustrations, rich in color and lively pattern." Booklist

Curry, Jane Louise

Hold up the sky: and other Native American tales from Texas and the Southern Plains; illustrated by James Watts. Margaret K. McElderry Bks. 2003 159p il $17.95

Grades: 4 5 6 7 **398.2**

1. Folklore -- Southern States 2. Native Americans -- Folklore
ISBN 0-689-85287-8

LC 2002-16519

Retells twenty-six tales from Native Americans whose traditional lands were in Texas and the Southern Plains, and provides a brief introduction to the history of each tribe

"Curry has carefully researched and sensitively retold tales from fourteen Native American nations. Attractive pencil drawings enhance the stories." Horn Book Guide

Includes bibliographical references

D'Aulaire, Ingri

The **terrible** troll-bird; [by] Ingri and Edgar Parin d'Aulaire. New York Review Books 2007 41p il $15.95

Grades: K 1 2 3   398.2

1. Trolls 2. Fairy tales 3. Folklore -- Norway
ISBN 978-1-59017-252-0; 1-59017-252-3

LC 2007-13020

First published 1976 by Doubleday

When four children defeat the terrible troll-bird who
has terrified their Norwegian valley for years, everyone celebrates in a merry feast.

"The d'Aulaires illustrate this rousing Scandinavian
folktale in exuberant pictures using both sketchy black-and-
white lines and mottled color." Horn Book Guide

Dabcovich, Lydia

The **polar** bear son; an Inuit tale. retold and illustrated
by Lydia Dabcovich. Clarion Bks. 1997 37p il hardcover
o.p. pa $5.95
Grades: K 1 2 3   398.2

1. Inuit -- Folklore 2. Polar bear -- Folklore 3. Inuit --
Pictorial works -- Juvenile fiction 4. Mothers and sons
-- Pictorial works -- Juvenile fiction
ISBN 0-395-72766-9; 0-395-97567-0 pa

LC 96-4780

An old woman adopts and raises a polar bear cub which
grows up and provides for her even after she has had to send
it away to save it from the jealous men of the village

"Illustrated in muted pastel colors, the pictures capture
this stark, yet beautiful, winter world." SLJ

Dayrell, Elphinstone

★ **Why** the Sun and the Moon live in the sky; an African folktale. illustrated by Blair Lent. Houghton Mifflin
1968 26p il $16; pa $6.95
Grades: K 1 2 3   398.2

1. Folklore -- Nigeria
ISBN 0-395-29609-9; 0-395-53963-3 pa

First told by the author in his book: Folk stories from
Southern Nigeria, West Africa, published 1910 in England

A Caldecott Medal honor book, 1969

"The beautifully detailed and stylized art work is based
on African sources; the artist uses cool colors for the water,
a pale blue-grey for the moon, and shades of gold and white
for the sun." Sutherland. The Best in Child Books

De las Casas, Dianne

The **gigantic** sweet potato; illustrated by Marita Gentry. Pelican Pub. Co. 2010 un il $16.99
Grades: K 1 2 3   398.2

1. Folklore -- Russia
ISBN 978-1-58980-755-6; 1-58980-755-3

LC 2010009434

Ma Farmer craves sweet potato pie but needs help to
harvest a homegrown sweet potato—in this version of the
Russian folktale, The Giant Turnip. Includes recipe and directions to make sweet potato pie.

"Colorful watercolors accompany the rhythmic text and
add a touch of foreshadowing. . . . Children will happily
join in the repetitive, cumulative text and enjoy the satisfying end. . . . This tasty selection is a solid interpretation of
the classic tale, with appealing pictures and a strong female
character." Kirkus

De Paola, Tomie

★ **Adelita**; a Mexican Cinderella story. written and illustrated by Tomie de Paola. Putnam 2002 un il hardcover
o.p. pa $6.99
Grades: K 1 2 3   398.2

1. Fairy tales 2. Folklore -- Mexico
ISBN 0-399-23866-2; 0-14-240187-0 pa

LC 2001-57873

After the death of her mother and father, Adelita is badly
mistreated by her stepmother and stepsisters until she finds
her own true love at a grand fiesta

"The prose is straightforward and crisp. . . . Making perfect use of clear, warm hues, the full-color acrylic illustrations are a feast for the eye." SLJ

The **clown** of God; an old story. told and illustrated
by Tomie de Paola. Harcourt Brace Jovanovich 1978 un
il $16; pa $7
Grades: K 1 2 3   398.2

1. Legends 2. Miracles -- Folklore 3. Christmas --
Folklore
ISBN 0-15-219175-5; 0-15-618192-4 pa

LC 78-3845

An orphan whose juggling skill led him to a career as a
traveling entertainer has grown old and clumsy and returns
as a hungry beggar to his birthplace. On Christmas Eve in
the monastery church a miracle occurs as he summons his
last strength to make his only possible offering

"Mr. de Paola has written the tale with love, tenderness,
and joy. He has executed authentic Renaissance illustrations that are magnificent in design and beauty." Child Book
Rev Serv

Jamie O'Rourke and the big potato; an Irish folktale.
retold and illustrated by Tomie dePaola. Putnam 1992 un
il hardcover o.p. pa $5.99; bd bk $5.99
Grades: K 1 2 3   398.2

1. Folklore -- Ireland 2. Folklore -- Ireland -- Juvenile
literature
ISBN 0-399-22257-X; 0-698-11603-8 pa; 0-448-
45090-9 bd bk

LC 91-10626

The laziest man in all of Ireland catches a leprechaun,
who offers a potato seed instead of a pot of gold for
his freedom

"Illustrated in dePaola's signature style, this has an inviting look. Buoyant watercolors are framed by thin orange
borders, but the potato simply can't be contained and bulges
beyond the boundaries, graphic proof of its enormous size,
an engaging read-aloud choice for Saint Patrick's Day."
Booklist

★ The **legend** of the Indian paintbrush; retold and
illustrated by Tomie dePaola. Putnam 1988 un il $16.99;
pa $7.99
Grades: K 1 2 3   398.2

1. Native Americans -- Folklore 2. Indians of North
America -- Great Plains -- Juvenile literature
ISBN 0-399-21534-4; 0-698-11360-8 pa

LC 87-20160

"The native American motifs are rendered simply and
authentically; the night sky and glorious sunset spreads are

truly beautiful with line, color, and form perfectly balanced to capture the text." Horn Book

Tomie dePaola's Favorite nursery tales. Putnam 1986 127p il $24.99
Grades: K 1 2 3   **398.2**
    1. Fables 2. Folklore
    ISBN 0-399-21319-8
LC 85-28302
"DePaola's droll, witty, and very funny illustrations capture the essence of each story from a child's point of view. . . . The beautiful layout of these pages, in which the print and pictures are perfectly at ease with one another, invites confident new readers as well as adults for reading aloud." SLJ

Tomie dePaola's front porch tales and North Country whoppers. G.P. Putnam's Sons 2007 51p il $17.99
Grades: 2 3 4 5   **398.2**
    1. Folklore -- New England 2. Folklore -- New England -- Juvenile literature
    ISBN 978-0-399-24754-5; 0-399-24754-8
LC 2007-17646
This is an "illustrated compendium of original stories, tall tales, jokes, and quips related to northern New England. . . Warm, good-humored artwork in dePaola's signature style provides an inviting setting for this flavorful collection of regional humor." Booklist

De Regniers, Beatrice Schenk
    Little sister and the month brothers; retold by Beatrice Schenk de Regniers; pictures by Margot Tomes. Marshall Cavendish Children 2009 un il $17.99
Grades: K 1 2 3   **398.2**
    1. Fairy tales 2. Slavs -- Folklore
    ISBN 978-0-7614-5546-2; 0-7614-5546-9
A reissue of the title first published 1976 by Seabury Press
A retelling of the Slavic fairy tale in which the Month Brothers' magic helps Little Sister fulfill seemingly impossible tasks which prove the undoing of her greedy stepmother and stepsister.
"Tomes's intimate, unpretentious illustrations extend the text brilliantly. A timeless treasure." Horn Book Guide

Deedy, Carmen Agra
    ★ **Martina** the beautiful cockroach; a Cuban folktale. retold by Carmen Agra Deedy; illustrated by Michael Austin. Peachtree 2007 un il $16.95
Grades: 2 3 4 5   **398.2**
    1. Folklore -- Cuba 2. Cockroaches -- Folklore
    ISBN 978-1-56145-399-3
LC 2007003108
In this humorous retelling of a Cuban folktale, a cockroach interviews her suitors in order to decide whom to marry
"Deedy's masterful retelling . . . has a rollicking voice imbued with sly tongue-in-cheek humor. The acrylic illustrations, in a hyperrealistic style . . . are rendered in a vivid tropical palette." Booklist

Demi
    King Midas; the golden touch. Margaret K. McElderry Bks. 2002 un il $19.95

Grades: 2 3 4   **398.2**
    1. Midas (Legendary character) 2. Mythology, Greek
    ISBN 0-689-83297-4
LC 99-89389
A king finds himself bitterly regretting the consequences of his wish that everything he touches would turn to gold
Demi's "unsourced but briskly amusing retelling begins with the contest when Midas's preference for Pan's shrill discord so angers the great musician Apollo that he gives the king donkey's ears. . . . The gilded special effects take center stage; still, Demi's glowing colors, decorative figures, and delicate drafting are also worthy of note. . . . This handsome book breathes new life into one of the oldest of cautionary tales." Horn Book

    ★ The **hungry** coat; a tale from Turkey. Margaret K. McElderry Books 2004 un il $19.95
Grades: K 1 2 3   **398.2**
    1. Folklore -- Turkey 2. Nasreddin Hoca (Legendary character)
    ISBN 0-689-84680-0
LC 2002-155129
After being forced to change to a fancy new coat to attend a party, Nasrettin Hoca tries to feed his dinner to the coat, reasoning that it was the coat that was the invited guest.
"Demi's retelling of this tale is compelling and includes many details that help bring both time and place into focus. Her paint-and-ink illustrations are resplendent with her trademark gold leaf and intricate borders." SLJ

DiPrimio, Pete
    The **sphinx**. Mitchell Lane Publishers 2010 48p il map (Monsters in myth) lib bdg $29.95
Grades: 4 5 6 7   **398.2**
    1. Sphinxes (Mythology)
    ISBN 978-1-58415-931-5; 1-58415-931-6
LC 2010006560
This describes the mythic Sphinx that has appeared in both Egyptian and Greek myth.
This book is "thorough and respectful of a number of ancient and modern sources and [bends] over backward to navigate often contradictory, interlinked legends. . . . A number of paintings and photos break up the otherwise text-heavy pages, and copious chapter notes and reading suggestions conclude. This is by no means entry-level stuff, but for kids handy with the basics and ready to delve deeper, [this book] will be of great use." Booklist
Includes glossary and bibliographical references

Doherty, Berlie
    Fairy tales; told by Berlie Doherty; illustrated by Jane Ray. Candlewick Press 2000 223p il $19.99
Grades: 4 5 6   **398.2**
    1. Folklore 2. Fairy tales
    ISBN 0-7636-0997-8
LC 99-89380
A collection of well-known fairy tales, such as Cinderella, Rapunzel, Aladdin and the enchanted lamp, and The fire-bird
These are "superb retellings on the earliest available sources in fresh versions sure to captivate readers anew. Ray's gold paint and folk art motifs prevail, but she also peppers the spreads with striking silhouette-collage compositions in a sumptuously designed volume." Publ Wkly

Downard, Barry

The **race** of the century; retold, written, and illustrated by Barry Downard. Simon & Schuster Books for Young Readers 2008 un il $15.99

Grades: 2 3 4   **398.2**

1. Fables 2. Rabbits -- Folklore 3. Turtles -- Folklore
ISBN 978-1-4169-2509-5; 1-4169-2509-0

LC 2006028791

Fed up with his incessant taunting, Tom Tortoise challenges Flash Harry Hare to the race of the century, which turns into a worldwide media event complete with television and newspaper coverage, photographers, and many other distractions.

"Digitally created photocollages of an animal cast, [the illustrations are] packed with silly exaggeration and humorous visual personification. . . . The sheer ludicrousness of this scenario will elicit snickering even in kids allergic to fables." Bull Cent Child Books

Eastman, Mary Huse

Index to fairy tales; including folklore, legends, and myths in collections. Scarecrow Press 1985 4v

Grades: Adult Professional   **398.2**

1. Fairy tales 2. Reference books 3. Legends -- Indexes
4. Folklore -- Indexes 5. Mythology -- Indexes

Volumes covering 1949-1972 and 1973-1977 first published by Faxon 1973 and 1979 respectively

"Although this is an essential reference book for the children's department, it is also a valuable source for the location of much folklore and fairy-tale material and should be available in adult book collections as well." Ref Sources for Small & Medium-sized Libr. 6th edition

Egielski, Richard

★ **Saint** Francis and the wolf; [by] Richard Egielski. Laura Geringer Books 2005 un il $15.99; lib bdg $16.89

Grades: 1 2 3   **398.2**

1. Saints 2. Wolves -- Folklore 3. Writers on religion
ISBN 0-06-623870-6; 0-06-623871-4 lib bdg

LC 2003-09615

"A wolf is terrorizing the Italian town of Gubbio. Knights, armies, and a threatening-looking war machine have all failed to put a stop to his terrible behavior. Only St. Francis, who can speak the wolf's language, is able to find a workable compromise for the creature and the town. The expressive cartoon art is done in Egielski's characteristic style and is full of child appeal." SLJ

Ehlert, Lois

★ **Cuckoo.** Cucu; a Mexican folktale. translated into Spanish by Gloria de Aragón Andújar. Harcourt Brace & Co. 1997 un il $16; pa $7

Grades: K 1 2 3   **398.2**

1. Mayas -- Folklore 2. Folklore -- Mexico 3. Bilingual books -- English-Spanish
ISBN 0-15-200274-X; 0-15-202428-X pa

LC 95-39560

A traditional Mayan tale which reveals how the cuckoo lost her beautiful feathers

"This tale, charmingly told in both English and Spanish, is boldly illustrated with large, brightly colored, cut-paper pictures. Inspired by folk art and crafts, the images evoke the tin work and cutout fiesta banners of Mexico." SLJ

Mole's hill; a woodland tale. Harcourt Brace & Co. 1994 un il $17; pa $7

Grades: PreK K 1 2   **398.2**

1. Moles (Animals) -- Fiction 2. Animals -- Juvenile literature 3. Seneca Indians -- Folklore -- Juvenile literature 4. Indians of North America -- Wisconsin -- Juvenile literature
ISBN 0-15-255116-6; 0-15-201890-5 pa

LC 93-31151

When Fox tells Mole she must move out of her tunnel to make way for a new path, Mole finds an ingenious way to save her home

"Ehlert's language is compact and telling. . . . The art . . . is dark-hued, appropriately nocturnal without losing spirit or contrast, and the beads stippled across the cutout cloth shapes lend interesting texture to the planes of color. . . . The story (which Ehlert says she based on a fragment of a Seneca tale, with source completely cited in the book) has charm and vigor." Bull Cent Child Books

Ehrlich, Amy

A **treasury** of princess stories; retold by Amy Ehrlich; illustrated by Gary Blythe; [paper engineering by Keith Finch] Candlewick Press 2009 un il lib bdg $19.99

Grades: 1 2 3   **398.2**

1. Folklore 2. Fairy tales 3. Pop-up books 4. Princesses -- Fiction
ISBN 978-0-7636-4478-9 lib bdg; 0-7636-4478-1 lib bdg

"Six fairy tales previously retold by Ehlrich are here compiled, repackaged, and reillustrated with pop-ups. Each begins with a sort of title page/frontispiece designed to resemble a miniature book; when the cover is opened, a beautifully rendered pop-up illustration is revealed. The stories themselves are recounted faithfully and rhythmically. Each features at least two lush illustrations as well as spot decorations." Horn Book Guide

Eilenberg, Max

★ **Beauty** and the beast; retold by Max Eilenberg; illustrated by Angela Barrett. Candlewick Press 2006 un il $17.99

Grades: 2 3 4   **398.2**

1. Fairy tales 2. Folklore -- France
ISBN 978-0-7636-3160-4; 0-7636-3160-4

LC 2006-43171

Through her great capacity to love, a kind and beautiful maid releases a handsome prince from the spell which has made him an ugly beast

"Writer and artist are both at their best in the luxury of the Beast's palace. Collectors of sumptuous fairy tale editions will not want to miss this one." Publ Wkly

Elya, Susan Middleton, 1955-

★ **Rubia** and the three osos; illustrated by Melissa Sweet. Disney/Hyperion Books 2010 un il $15.99

Grades: PreK K 1 2   **398.2**

1. Folklore 2. Stories in rhyme 3. Bears -- Folklore 4. Spanish language -- Vocabulary
ISBN 978-1-4231-1252-5; 1-4231-1252-0

LC 2009028131

Retells the story of Goldilocks and the three bears in rhyming text interspersed with Spanish words, which are defined in a glossary.

"Pencil, watercolor and collage illustrations are packed with Southwest detail and rendered in fiesta colors, adding a Latin flair, while the overtly comic depiction of the three osos and Rubia in her red cowgirl boots contributes to the lighthearted humor." Kirkus

Emberley, Ed

★ **Chicken** Little. Roaring Brook Press 2009 un il $16.95
Grades: PreK K 1 2   **398.2**
  1. Folklore 2. Animals -- Folklore
  ISBN 978-1-59643-464-6; 1-59643-464-3
                  LC 2008-49329

A retelling of the classic story of Chicken Little, who has an acorn fall on his head and runs in a panic to his friends Henny Penny, Lucky Ducky, and Loosey Goosey, to tell them the sky is falling.

"The punchy text is perfectly complemented by high-impact illustrations in collage-like planes of electric hues. The bold splashes of countless colors, contrasted against sharp fields of white, brilliantly jump out from the square pages. This is certain to become a favorite version of this story, and young readers will gleefully welcome an ending that offers no pedantic lesson." Bull Cent Child Books

★ The **red** hen; by Rebecca Emberley and Ed Emberley. Roaring Brook Press 2010 1 v. (unpaged)
Grades: PreK K 1 2   **398.2**
  1. Folklore
  ISBN 1596434929; 9781596434929
                 LC 2010284450

"When Red Hen finds a recipe for 'simply splendid cake,' she repeatedly asks the cat, the rat, and the frog for help gathering the ingredients. . . . The cat and the rat provide the familiar 'not I' but the frog croaks out a humorous 'bribbit.' . . . Set against white backgrounds, the zany characters, each with uniquely distinct eyes, pop off the pages. . . . The short, simple text allows for instant audience participation and offers a satisfying lesson on cooperation and fairness." SLJ

Endredy, James

The **journey** of Tunuri and the Blue Deer; a Huichol Indian story. illustrated by Maria Hernández de la Cruz and Casimiro de la Cruz López. Bear Cub Books 2003 32p il $15.95
Grades: 1 2 3   **398.2**
  1. Huichol Indians 2. Tales -- Mexico 3. Indians of Mexico 4. Folklore -- Mexico 5. Huichol Indians -- Folklore 6. Native Americans -- Folklore -- Mexico
  ISBN 1-59143-016-X
                 LC 2003-52298

Retells a traditional Huichol folktale in which the young Tunuri learns his place in the natural world when he meets the magical Blue Deer, and follows him on an enlightening journey.

"The colorful artwork is made from yarn that is applied to a piece of wood, an elaborate process that is a long-practiced art of the Huichol. The illustrations enhance the feel and authenticity of the story. Elaborate notes explain the sacred symbols, who the Huichol are, and how the art was created. A strong addition to folktale collections." SLJ

Ernst, Lisa Campbell

Little Red Riding Hood: a newfangled prairie tale. Simon & Schuster Bks. for Young Readers 1995 un il $16; pa $5.99
Grades: K 1 2 3   **398.2**
  1. Folklore 2. Wolves -- Folklore
  ISBN 0-689-80145-9; 0-689-82191-3 pa
                 LC 94-45723

In this "contemporary rendering of the old tale, Little Red Riding Hood wears a hooded sweatshirt and rides her bicycle, while Grandma is a robust farmer who turns the tables on the wolf. Ernst's inventive plot, enjoyable characters, and characteristic cartoon-style drawings demonstrate her mastery of the picture-book form." Horn Book Guide

Fleischman, Paul

★ **Glass** slipper, gold sandal; a worldwide Cinderella. illustrated by Julie Paschkis. Henry Holt 2007 un il $16.95
Grades: K 1 2 3 4   **398.2**
  1. Folklore 2. Fairy tales 3. Folklore -- Juvenile literature 4. Cinderella (Legendary character) -- Juvenile literature
  ISBN 978-0-8050-7953-1; 0-8050-7953-X
                 LC 2006-30615

"This inspired retelling blends many versions of Cinderella into a single, extraordinary tale. . . . As . . . Fleischman's . . . strong storytelling voice incorporates sometimes small details from different traditions, text and illustrations nimbly morph from one Cinderella story to the next, creating this brand-new version. Paschkis . . . makes use of folk art and textile patterns throughout the world in the clever background paintings behind each of her vibrant panel illustrations." Publ Wkly

Forest, Heather

The **contest** between the Sun and the Wind; an Aesop's fable. retold by Heather Forest; illustrated by Susan Gaber. August House Little Folk 2008 un il $16.95
Grades: K 1 2 3   **398.2**
  1. Fables 2. Authors 3. Folklore 4. Storytellers
  ISBN 978-0-87483-832-9; 0-87483-832-0
                 LC 2007018813

The sun and the wind test their strength by seeing which of them can cause a man to remove his coat, demonstrating the value of using gentle persuasion rather than force as a means of achieving a goal.

"Forest recasts this fable from Aesop in simple, crystalline language and occasional rhyme. . . . Gaber's wild and vivid images reflect, augment, and illuminate the story." Booklist

★ The **little** red hen; an old fable. retold by Heather Forest; illustrated by Susan Gaber. August House Little Folk 2006 un il $16.95
Grades: K 1 2 3   **398.2**
  1. Folklore 2. Animals -- Folklore 3. Chickens -- Folklore
  ISBN 0-87483-795-2
                 LC 2006040727

A rhymed retelling of the traditional tale about the industrious little red hen and her lazy friends

"Gaber's bold acrylic artwork and varied use of space . . . and the infectious, familiar refrain . . . make this an appealing storytime and readers' theater selection." SLJ

Fowles, Shelley

The **bachelor** and the bean. Farrar, Straus & Giroux 2003 un il $16

Grades: K 1 2 3   **398.2**

1. Jews -- Folklore 2. Folklore -- Morocco

ISBN 0-374-30478-5

LC 2002-23160

In this Jewish folktale from Morocco, a bachelor receives a magic pot from an imp, but it is stolen by an old woman

"Fowles' retelling . . . is lively, funny, and perfectly paced for read-alouds. But it's her watercolor-and-ink illustrations that are most distinctive. Young children will enjoy the shimmering colors and swirling patterns . . . that show the town bustle and the humor." Booklist

French, Vivian

Henny Penny; [by] Vivian French; illustrated by Sophie Windham. Bloomsbury Children's Books 2006 un il $16.95

Grades: PreK K 1 2   **398.2**

1. Folklore 2. Animals -- Folklore

ISBN 1-58234-706-9

LC 2005053688

Henny Penny and her barnyard friends are on their way to tell the king that the sky is falling when they meet a hungry fox, but Henny Penny's quick thinking saves the day

"A charmingly fleshed-out version of the traditional story. . . . Brightly colored and skillfully drawn illustrations balance perfectly with the delightful text and draw readers into their depths." SLJ

Fritz, Jean

Brendan the Navigator; a history mystery about the discovery of America. illustrated by Enrico Arno. Coward, McCann & Geoghegan 1979 31p il hardcover o.p. pa $5.99

Grades: 3 4 5   **398.2**

1. Monks 2. Saints

ISBN 0-698-20473-5; 0-698-11759-X pa

LC 78-13247

Recounts St. Brendan's life and voyage to North America long before the Vikings arrived

"Jean Fritz's narrative is beautifully cadenced, lively and wry. Her historical postscript is all right, too, and the two-color illustrations are appropriately convoluted and Celtic." N Y Times Book Rev

Galdone, Joanna

★ The **tailypo**; a ghost story. told by Joanna Galdone; illustrated by Paul Galdone. Clarion Bks. 1984 un il hardcover o.p. pa $7.95

Grades: K 1 2 3   **398.2**

1. Folklore -- United States

ISBN 0-395-30084-3 pa

LC 77-23289

First published by Seabury Press

"The energetic postures of the old man and his dogs form a strong accompaniment to the clean, vigorous storytelling, and the subtly underplayed color in the paintings not only suggests the ghostliness of the story but is pleasing in itself." Horn Book

Galdone, Paul

The **elves** and the shoemaker; retold and illustrated by Paul Galdone. Clarion Bks. 1984 un il hardcover o.p. pa $6.95

Grades: PreK K 1 2   **398.2**

1. Fairy tales 2. Folklore -- Germany

ISBN 0-89919-422-2 pa

LC 83-14979

A pair of elves help a poor shoemaker become successful, and the shoemaker and his wife reward them with elegant outfits

"The pictures in flashing hues emphasize the secret helpers' impishness; they seem to be performing the service more for a lark than in the name of sweet charity." Publ Wkly

★ The **gingerbread** boy. Clarion Bks. 1975 un il $16; pa $6.95

Grades: PreK K 1 2   **398.2**

1. Folklore 2. Fairy tales

ISBN 0-395-28799-5; 0-89919-163-0 pa

First published by Seabury Press

"A lively version of the tale of the gingerbread boy who sprang into action as soon as he was baked and gleefully eluded all would-be captors until he was finally outwitted by a fox. The artist's gingerbread boy is a strong-legged, cocky individual, who sets out on a merry race through the countryside. The action of the tale is well-paced; large, humorous illustrations with stone fences, a covered bridge, and hearty rural folk suggest a New England background, while the triumphant fox is the epitome of all slyness." Horn Book

★ **Henny** Penny; retold and illustrated by Paul Galdone. Clarion Bks. 1968 un il $16; pa $6.95

Grades: PreK K 1 2   **398.2**

1. Folklore 2. Animals -- Folklore

ISBN 0-395-28800-2; 0-89919-225-4 pa

First published by Seabury Press

A folktale also popularly known as Chicken Little. "The simple retelling has a different ending which makes the fox seem somewhat less villainous—when Henny Penny and her credulous friends follow Foxy Loxy into the cave they are never seen again and the king is never told that the sky is falling, but Foxy Loxy, his wife, and seven little foxes (appealingly portrayed in a picture as a family group) still remember the fine feast they had that day." Booklist

★ The **little** red hen; a folk tale classic. Houghton Mifflin Harcourt 2011 un il $8.99

Grades: K 1 2 3   **398.2**

1. Folklore 2. Animals -- Folklore 3. Chickens -- Folklore

ISBN 978-0-547-37018-7; 0-547-37018-0

A reissue of the edition first published 1973 by Seabury Press

The little red hen finds none of her lazy friends willing to help her plant, harvest, or grind wheat into flour, but all are eager to eat the cake she makes from it.

Galdone's retelling is "straightforward and his unassuming loose-lined pictures provide just enough embellishment." Horn Book Guide

★ The **monkey** and the crocodile; a Jataka tale from India. Clarion Bks. 1969 un il hardcover o.p. pa $6.95

Grades: PreK K 1 2   **398.2**
1. Fables 2. Jataka stories 3. Folklore -- India 4. Monkeys -- Folklore 5. Crocodiles -- Folklore
ISBN 0-89919-524-5 pa
First published by Seabury Press

The story "has the humor, plot, and movement to make it a good book for any young child, even one unused to stories: the brilliant colors, clear pictures, and brief text should make it very successful for sharing with groups of children." Horn Book

★ **Puss** in boots. Clarion Bks. 1976 un il hardcover o.p. pa $7.95
Grades: K 1 2   **398.2**
1. Fairy tales 2. Cats -- Folklore 3. Folklore -- France
ISBN 0-89919-192-4 pa
First published by Seabury Press

"Galdone follows Perrault's story line faithfully, as Puss works mischief to obtain a fortune for his master. The writing, fluid and readable, makes even this familiar tale sound fresh—no mean feat. Galdone's large, humorous caricatures—easily seen for story hour—have great gusto, and Puss is the embodiment of cleverness and knavery." SLJ

★ The **three** bears. Clarion Bks. 1972 un il $15; pa $6.95
Grades: PreK K 1 2   **398.2**
1. Folklore 2. Bears -- Folklore
ISBN 0-395-28811-8; 0-89919-401-X pa
First published by Seabury Press

In Galdone's illustrations for his retelling of the tale of Goldilocks, "his three bears are beautifully groomed, civilized creatures, living a life of rustic contentment in an astonishingly verdant forest, while his Goldilocks is a horrid, be-ringletted, overdressed child who rampages wantonly through the bears' tidy home." Times Lit Suppl

★ The **three** Billy Goats Gruff. Clarion Bks. 1973 un il $16; pa $6.95
Grades: PreK K 1 2   **398.2**
1. Goats -- Folklore 2. Folklore -- Norway
ISBN 0-395-28812-6; 0-89919-035-9 pa
First published by Seabury Press

"Galdone's illustrations are in his usual bold, clear style. The three Billy Goats Gruff are expressively drawn, and the troll looks appropriately ferocious and ugly. The large, lively, double-page spreads are sure to win a responsive audience at story hour." SLJ

★ The **three** little pigs; a folk tale classic. Houghton Mifflin Harcourt 2011 un il $8.99
Grades: K 1 2 3   **398.2**
1. Pigs -- Folklore 2. Wolves -- Folklore
ISBN 978-0-547-37020-0; 0-547-37020-2
                   LC 2011281137
A reissue of the edition published 1970 by Clarion Books
Retells the fatal episodes in the lives of two foolish pigs and how the third pig managed to avoid the same pigfalls.
Galdone's retelling is "straightforward and his unassuming loose-lined pictures provide just enough embellishment." Horn Book Guide

Gavin, Jamila
Tales from India; illustrated by Amanda Hall. Candlewick Press 2011 il
Grades: 5 6 7 8   **398.2**
1. Hindu mythology 2. Folklore -- India
ISBN 0-7636-5564-3; 978-0-7636-5564-8
                   LC 2010047651
"Gavin, . . . presents 10 classic Hindu stories, accompanied by Hall's lush and elegant gouache illustrations. . . . Readers should be drawn toward the valor, action, and dramatic transformations in these powerful tales." Publ Wkly

Gerson, Mary-Joan
Why the sky is far away; a Nigerian folktale. retold by Mary-Joan Gerson; pictures by Carla Golembe. Little, Brown 1992 un il hardcover o.p. pa $5.95
Grades: K 1 2 3   **398.2**
1. Folklore -- Nigeria
ISBN 0-316-30874-9 pa
                   LC 91-24949
A revised and newly illustrated edition of the title first published 1974 by Harcourt
The sky was once so close to the Earth that people cut parts of it to eat, but their waste and greed caused the sky to move far away
"Golembe's simple, theatrical illustrations combine monotype prints and collages in brilliant colors. . . . With its playfulness and drama, this is a fine book for story hour, especially in an ecology program." Booklist

Ginsburg, Mirra
The **Chinese** mirror; adapted from a Korean folktale by Mirra Ginsburg; illustrated by Margot Zemach. Harcourt Brace Jovanovich 1988 un il hardcover o.p. pa $6
Grades: K 1 2 3   **398.2**
1. Folklore -- Korea 2. Folklore -- Korea -- Juvenile literature
ISBN 0-15-217508-3 pa
                   LC 86-22940
"This elegantly simple little story is a seamless blend of folk-tale adaptation with illustrations that were inspired by Korean genre paintings of the eighteenth century." Horn Book

Clay boy; adapted from a Russian folk tale by Mirra Ginsburg; pictures by Jos. A. Smith. Greenwillow Bks. 1997 un il $16
Grades: K 1 2 3   **398.2**
1. Folklore -- Russia 2. Folklore -- Russia -- Juvenile literature
ISBN 0-688-14409-8; 0-688-14410-1 lib bdg
                   LC 96-33820
Wanting a son, an old man and woman make a clay boy who comes to life and begins eating everything in sight until he meets a clever goat
"The tale is adapted from a Russian folktale, and the storytelling voice is very simple and immediate. . . . In their play with scale, the illustrations express a wonderful combination of the monstrous and the cozy." Booklist

Goble, Paul
Buffalo woman; story and illustrations by Paul Goble. Bradbury Press 1984 un il hardcover o.p. pa $5.99

Grades: 2 3 4   **398.2**

1. Bison -- Folklore   2. Native Americans -- Folklore
3. Indians of North America -- Folklore -- Juvenile
literature

ISBN 0-02-737720-2; 0-689-71109-3 pa

LC 83-15704

A young hunter marries a female buffalo in the form of a
beautiful maiden, but when his people reject her he must pass
several tests before being allowed to join the buffalo nation

"Each page sparkles with the lupins and yuccas of the
Southwest and teems with native birds, butterflies, and
small animals, the richness of detail never detracting from
the overall design of the handsome illustrations. The author-
artist successfully combines a compelling version of an old
legend with his own imaginative and striking visual interpretation." Horn Book

Includes bibliographical references

The **girl** who loved wild horses; story and illustrations
by Paul Goble. Bradbury Press 1978 un il $14.95; pa
$5.99

Grades: K 1 2 3   **398.2**

1. Horses -- Folklore   2. Native Americans -- Folklore

ISBN 0-02-736570-0; 0-689-71696-6 pa

LC 77-20500

Awarded the Caldecott Medal, 1979

"Elaborate double-page spreads burst with life, revealing details of flowers and insects, animals and birds. . . .
The story is told in simple language, and the author has
included verses of a Navaho and Sioux song about horses.
Both storytelling and art express the harmony with and the
love of nature which characterize Native American culture."
Horn Book

The **legend** of the White Buffalo Woman. National
Geographic Soc. 1998 un il hardcover o.p. pa $7.95

Grades: 3 4 5   **398.2**

1. Native Americans -- Folklore   2. Teton mythology
-- Juvenile literature

ISBN 0-7922-7074-6; 0-7922-6552-1 pa

LC 97-24086

A Lakota Indian legend in which the White Buffalo
Woman presents her people with the Sacred Calf Pipe which
gives them the means to pray to the Great Spirit

"In his fluid retelling of the legend of the first peace pipe,
Goble . . . handles sweeping Lakota history succinctly and
assuredly, largely due to his compelling artwork." Publ Wkly

Includes bibliographical references

The **woman** who lived with wolves, & other stories
from the tipi; told and illustrated by Paul Goble; foreword
by Vivian Arviso Deloria. World Wisdom, Inc. 2011 un
$14.95

Grades: 3 4 5 6   **398.2**

1. Native Americans -- Folklore

ISBN 978-1-935493-20-4; 1-935493-20-5

LC 2010029180

"Goble has collected and retold 27 stories, poems, and
song lyrics from a variety of Native American tribes. . . .
Depictions of how animals and man worked in harmony
with one another permeate the stories and convey Goble's
message that humans must live with tolerance and understanding of the natural world in order for both to survive.

This collection is unique in its simplicity. The tales are accessible to young listeners as they beg to be read aloud. Most
are only a page long. The accompanying illustrations are
vintage Goble, finely detailed and painstakingly painted in
rich tones of morning sky blues, orange-hued sunsets, and
myriad chestnut, black, and amber horses." SLJ

Includes bibliographical references

Green, Roger Lancelyn

King Arthur and his Knights of the Round Table; retold
out of the old romances. with illustrations by Aubrey Beard-
sley. Knopf 1993 355p il $14.95

Grades: 5 6 7 8   **398.2**

1. Arthurian romances   2. Kings

ISBN 0-679-42311-7

LC 92-55073

A newly illustrated edition of the title first published
1953 in the United Kingdom

Relates the exploits of King Arthur and his knights from
the birth of Arthur to the destruction of Camelot

Greene, Ellin

The **little** golden lamb; retold by Ellin Greene; illustrated by Roseanne Litzinger. Clarion Bks. 2000 32p il
$15

Grades: K 1 2 3   **398.2**

1. Folklore   2. Sheep -- Folklore   3. Shepherds --
Hungary

ISBN 0-395-71526-1

LC 99-36025

A retelling of the traditional tale in which a poor, but
good-hearted lad finds his fortune with the aid of a little
golden lamb to which everyone that touches it sticks

"Greene's storytelling style is at once classic and relaxed, and the illustrations, in a soft, springtime palette, are
fittingly buoyant." Horn Book Guide

Gregorowski, Christopher

Fly, eagle, fly! an African tale. retold by Christopher
Gregorowski; pictures by Niki Daly. Margaret K. McElderry Bks. 2000 un il hardcover o.p. pa $12.99

Grades: K 1 2 3   **398.2**

1. Fables   2. Eagles -- Folklore   3. Folklore -- Africa

ISBN 0-689-82398-3; 1-4169-7599-3 pa

LC 98-45302

Original two-color illustrated edition published 1982 in
South Africa

A farmer finds an eagle and raises it to behave like a
chicken, until a friend helps the eagle learn to find its rightful
place in the sky

This "is a powerful celebration of the human spirit and
its need for independence. It is beautifully complemented
by watercolors, rich in the vibrant tones of earth and sky."
Booklist

Grifalconi, Ann

The **village** of round and square houses. Little, Brown
1986 un il lib bdg $16.95

Grades: K 1 2 3   **398.2**

1. Folklore -- Africa   2. Folklore -- Cameroon --
Juvenile literature

ISBN 0-316-32862-6

LC 85-24150

A Caldecott Medal honor book, 1987

A grandmother explains to her listeners why in their village on the side of a volcano the men live in square houses and the women in round ones

The author "illustrates her own tale, told to her by a young girl who grew up in Tos. The resting purple volcano, suddenly erupting into orange; the eerie orange sun; the villagers covered with ash; the fiery colored skies; the dense, lush jungles—all are captured beautifully by Grifalconi's art." Publ Wkly

Grimm, Jacob, 1785-1863

★ **Fairy** tales of the Brothers Grimm; edited by Noel Daniel; translated by Matthew R. Price. Taschen 2011 il $39.99

Grades: 4 5 6   398.2

1. Fairy tales 2. Folklore -- Germany

ISBN 978-3-8365-2672-2; 3-8365-2672-7

"This gorgeous treasury pairs new translations of 27 of the Grimm brothers' fairy tales with vintage illustrations dating from the 1820s to the 1950s. Brief introductions offer insight into the symbolism, themes, and contemporary relevance of each tale. Though Price and Daniel's translations feel modern . . . they honor the darkness that characterizes 'Little Red Riding Hood,' 'Snow White,' and other tales. The images show striking range. . . . The elegant presentation should entice readers to discover the cornucopia within." Publ Wkly

Grimm's fairy tales; illustrated by Arthur Rackam. Seastar Books 2001 160p il $19.95

Grades: 4 5 6   398.2

1. Fairy tales 2. Folklore -- Germany

ISBN 978-158717-092-8; 1-58717-092-2

A collection of twenty-two favorite fairy tales from the Brothers Grimm, including "Rapunzel," "The Bremen Town Musicians," "The Valiant Tailor", "The Frog Prince," "Ashenputtel," and "The Elves and the Shoemanker."

"This handsome facsimile of the 1909 edition is illustrated with twenty-one color plates and twenty-eight black-and-white drawings with an afterword by Peter Glassman." Horn Book Guide

Little Red Cap; [by] The Brothers Grimm; illustrated by Lisbeth Zwerger; translated from the German by Elizabeth D. Crawford. Minedition 2006 un il $16.99

Grades: K 1 2 3   398.2

1. Wolves -- Folklore 2. Folklore -- Germany

ISBN 0-698-40053-4

LC 2006048142

A reissue of the title first published 1983 by Morrow

This translation "gives the text a smooth pace and natural-sounding dialogue. . . . Washes in muted earth tones provide suggestions of backgrounds against which expressively drawn figures play out their familiar roles." Horn Book

Little Red Riding Hood; [by] the Brothers Grimm; illustrated by Bernadette Watts. North-South 2009 un il $16.95

Grades: K 1 2 3   398.2

1. Fairy tales 2. Wolves -- Folklore 3. Folklore -- Germany

ISBN 978-0-7358-2256-6; 0-7358-2256-5

A reissue of the edition first published 1968

A sweet little girl meets a hungry wolf in the forest while on her way to visit her grandmother.

"The well-known story is told simply and without embellishment, including some violent elements (e.g., the wolf's belly is slit open and filled with stones). The expansive illustrations use Old World folk-art elements to envelope readers in the forest landscapes." Horn Book Guide

Snow White; [by] the Brothers Grimm; illustrated by Quentin Gréban. NorthSouth Books 2009 un il $16.95

Grades: 1 2 3   398.2

1. Fairy tales 2. Folklore -- Germany

ISBN 978-0-7358-2257-3; 0-7358-2257-3

Original Belgian edition 2007

"Gréban illustrates this faithful Grimm version of the classic story with a minimum of hocus-pocus. With the notable exception of the seven dwarfs, who are dead ringers for garden gnomes, the characters are realistic-looking. Snow White is a frightened and confused young girl, the wicked queen (in disguise) becomes a stooped, old peasant woman, the jodhpurs-clad prince is appropriately regal." Horn Book Guide

The **story** of Little Red Riding Hood; [by] The Brothers Grimm; illustrated by Christopher Bing. Handprint Books 2010 un il $18.99

Grades: K 1 2 3   398.2

1. Folklore 2. Fairy tales 3. Wolves -- Folklore

ISBN 978-0-8118-6986-7; 0-8118-6986-5

LC 2009019577

"This newly illustrated fairy tale includes three versions of an old favorite. The first and primary telling is Grimm's story. The grandmother and Little Red Riding Hood are consumed by the wolf, but freed by the hunter. . . . A second, lesser-known tale shows a resourceful girl who outfoxes the wolf, and all ends happily. In Perrault's shorter, darker version, which appears on the back endpaper with its original art, the old woman and girl are eaten and not saved. . . . The new, yet traditionally styled illustrations for the first two tales are well matched to the old stories. . . . [Bing] successfully takes the story back to its traditions." SLJ

The **twelve** dancing princesses; [originally] written by the Brothers Grimm; [adapted and] illustrated by Rachel Isadora. G.P. Putnam's Sons 2007 un il $16.99

Grades: K 1 2 3   398.2

1. Folklore 2. Fairy tales 3. Folklore -- Germany -- Juvenile literature

ISBN 0-399-24744-0; 978-0-399-24744-6

LC 2007-08160

This is a retelling of the story of twelve princesses who dance secretly all night long and how their secret is eventually discovered. "Age four and up." (N Y Times Book Rev)

"Working in collages of painted, textured paper, Isadora evokes an archetypal African kingdom through sumptuous, kente cloth textiles and Serengenti-like landscapes that pop vibrantly agains primarily white backgrounds." Booklist

Haley, Gail E.

★ A **story**, a story; an African tale retold and illustrated by Gail E. Haley. Atheneum Pubs. 1970 un il $18; pa $7.99

Grades: K 1 2 3   **398.2**
1. Anansi (Legendary character) 2. Folklore -- Africa
ISBN 0-689-20511-2; 0-689-71201-4 pa
Awarded the Caldecott Medal, 1971
"The story explains the origin of that favorite African folk material, the spider tale. Here Ananse, the old spider man, wanting to buy the Sky God's stories, completes by his cleverness three seemingly impossible tasks set as the price for the golden box of stories which he takes back to earth." Sutherland. The Best in Child Books

Hamilton, Martha
The **ghost** catcher; a Bengali folktale. [by] Martha Hamilton & Mitch Weiss; illustrated by Kristen Balouch. August House Little Folk 2008 un il $16.95
Grades: PreK K 1 2   **398.2**
1. Folklore -- India 2. Ghosts -- Folklore 3. Folklore -- India -- Juvenile literature
ISBN 978-0-87483-835-0; 0-87483-835-5
LC 2007-14308
A retelling of a traditional Bengali tale in which a kind and generous Indian barber, pressed by his father then his wife to earn more money, cleverly persuades a ghost to bring him riches.
"Hamilton and Weiss relate the tale with economy and wit. . . . The illustrations' lyrical lines, colorful forms, and linen-textured backdrop create a distinctive look." Booklist

Hamilton, Virginia
★ **Bruh** Rabbit and the tar baby girl; paintings by James E. Ransome. Blue Sky Press (NY) 2003 un il $16.95
Grades: K 1 2 3   **398.2**
1. Wolves -- Folklore 2. Rabbits -- Folklore 3. African Americans -- Folklore 4. Folklore -- Juvenile literature
ISBN 0-590-47376-X
LC 2002-15529
In this retelling of the African American story, the wily Brer Rabbit outwits Brer Wolf who has set out to trap him
"Retold in Gullah, Hamilton's narrative is meticulously paced, lyrical, hilarious, and a joy to read aloud. Ransome's lush watercolors suit the story perfectly." SLJ

★ The **girl** who spun gold; illustrated by Leo & Diane Dillon. Blue Sky Press (NY) 2000 un il $16.95
Grades: K 1 2 3   **398.2**
1. Fairy tales 2. Folklore -- West Indies
ISBN 0-590-47378-6
LC 99-86365
In this West Indian retelling of "Rumpelstiltskin," Lit'mahn spins thread into gold cloth for the Quashiba, the King's new bride
"The source of this folktale is apparent in the distinctive and lilting West Indian dialect that pervades this humorous and, at times, scary telling. The lavish use of gold within the acrylic illustrations and their frames is sumptuous." SLJ

★ The **people** could fly: American Black folktales; told by Virginia Hamilton; illustrated by Leo and Diane Dillon. 2009 178p il $24.99; pa $13
Grades: 5 6 7 8   **398.2**
1. African Americans -- Folklore
ISBN 978-0-394-86925-4; 0-394-86925-7; 978-0-679-84336-8 pa; 0-679-84336-1 pa

A reissue of the title first published 1985
Coretta Scott King honor book for illustration, 1986
The author "has been successful in her efforts to write these tales in the Black English of the slave storytellers. Her scholarship is unobtrusive and intelligible. She has provided a glossary and notes concerning the origins of the tales and the different versions in other cultures. Handsomely illustrated." NY Times Book Rev
Includes bibliographical references

★ The **people** could fly: the picture book; illustrated by Leo and Diane Dillon. Knopf 2004 un il $16.95
Grades: 3 4 5 6   **398.2**
1. Slavery -- Folklore 2. African Americans -- Folklore
ISBN 0-375-82405-7
LC 2003-25579
This is a retelling of the story first published in the author's collection, The people could fly: American black folktales, published 1985
In this retelling of a folktale, a group of slaves, unable to bear their sadness and starvation any longer, calls upon the African magic that allows them to fly away
"Familiar as it is, we have never seen the story like this. Not with all these evocative images, vivid, bright and moving, leading us on a journey through territory we thought we knew." NY Times Book Rev

A **ring** of tricksters; animal tales from America, the West Indies, and Africa. illustrated by Barry Moser. Blue Sky Press (NY) 1997 111p il $19.95
Grades: 3 4 5 6   **398.2**
1. Folklore 2. Folklore -- Africa 3. Animals -- Folklore 4. Folklore -- West Indies 5. Folklore -- Africa -- Juvenile literature 6. Folklore -- West Indies -- Juvenile literature 7. African Americans -- Folklore -- Juvenile literature
ISBN 0-590-47374-3
LC 96-37543
"Hamilton's prose infuses the dialogue with depth and dimension, while Moser's spectacular, lively watercolors nearly render the impish creatures human." Publ Wkly

Han, Suzanne Crowder
The **rabbit's** tail; a story from Korea. illustrated by Richard Wehrman. Holt & Co. 1999 un il $16.95
Grades: K 1 2 3   **398.2**
1. Folklore -- Korea 2. Tigers -- Folklore 3. Rabbits -- Folklore
ISBN 0-8050-4580-5
LC 98-16627
Tiger is afraid of being eaten by a fearsome dried persimmon, but when Rabbit tries to convince him he is wrong, Rabbit loses his long tail
"The tale is vividly retold. . . . An amusing entertainment about misperceptions." SLJ

Harris, John
My **monster** notebook; [by] John Harris & Mark Todd. J. Paul Getty Museum 2011 un il $16.95
Grades: 4 5 6   **398.2**
1. Folklore 2. Monsters
ISBN 978-1-60606-050-6; 1-60606-050-3
LC 2010025302

"At its core, the volume is a descriptive list of mythological monsters, from the immortal half-woman, half-serpent Echidna to Python, the dangerous snake sent to kill baby Apollo. The notebook-style layout includes doodles, photographs, and scrap papers, making the book appear to be a relic unearthed from the ruins of a modern school locker." Horn Book Guide

Strong stuff; Herakles and his labors. fierce words by John Harris; powerful art by Gary Baseman. J. Paul Getty Museum 2005 un il map $16.95
Grades: 4 5 6 7   **398.2**
1. Classical mythology 2. Hercules (Legendary character)
ISBN 0-89236-784-9
                                    LC 2004-7904
This is a "simplified version of the 12 labors of Hercules (Herakles as the Greeks called him). . . . Each labor is allotted a spread with bright and bold illustrations featuring Herakles locked in mortal combat with the monster of the moment, accompanied by a chatty, humorous commentary." SLJ

Hartman, Bob
The **Lion** storyteller book of animal tales; animal tales old and new especially for reading aloud. illustrated by Krisztina Kállai Nagy. Lion 2011 128p il $19.99
Grades: K 1 2 3   **398.2**
1. Fables 2. Folklore 3. Animals -- Fiction
ISBN 978-0-74596-131-6; 0-74596-131-2
"Hartman vibrantly retells and updates 36 animal fables hailing from ancient Greece, Africa, Japan, India, and other world cultures. The selections include trickster, morality, and animal-origin tales . . . along with a few original stories. Nagy's bright and friendly illustrations mimic Hartman's descriptive but accessible tone. A thoughtful collection that might inspire some readers to create animal stories of their own." Publ Wkly

Mr. Aesop's story shop; illustrated by Jago Silver. Lion/Trafalgar 2011 48p il $14.99
Grades: K 1 2 3   **398.2**
1. Fables 2. Authors 3. Storytellers
ISBN 0-7459-6915-1; 978-0-7459-6915-2
"This title re-frames 10 familiar fables . . . to add new context and setting to the stories. Each entry is narrated in first person, as if Aesop himself were speaking. . . . The introduction informs young readers about what is known, and what is not, about Aesop and defines what makes a story a fable. . . . The painterly illustrations look as if they are done on textured paper and incorporate Greek architectural details. . . . A worthwhile addition to collections." Booklist

Hausman, Gerald
Horses of myth; [by] Gerald and Loretta Hausman; pictures by Robert Florczak. Dutton Children's Books 2004 100p il $12
Grades: 4 5 6 7   **398.2**
1. Folklore 2. Horses -- Folklore
ISBN 0-525-46964-8
                                    LC 2002-40809
"These five tales each feature a different type of horse, remarkable both for its individuality and the qualities representative of its breed. . . . Florczak's illustrations adapt

characteristics appropriate to the locations and time periods of each selection's origins. . . . This is an attractive volume, useful to teachers and librarians for read-alouds and of interest to horse-loving youngsters." SLJ

Hayes, Joe
Dance, Nana, dance; Cuban folktales in English and Spanish. retold by Joe Hayes; illustrated by Mauricio Trenard Sayago. Cinco Puntos Press 2008 128p il $20.95
Grades: 5 6 7 8 9   **398.2**
1. Folklore -- Cuba 2. Bilingual books -- English-Spanish
ISBN 978-1-933693-17-0; 1-933693-17-7
                                    LC 2007-38295
A collection of stories from Cuban folklore, representing the cultures of Spain, Africa, and the Caribbean.
"Each tale is accompanied by a full-page illustration that is colorful and contributes to the text. This book is a great addition to folktale and Spanish language collections. Students will enjoy these stories that could easily be incorporated into the curriculum." Libr Media Connect

Little Gold Star; a Cinderella cuento/Estrellita de oro. retold in Spanish & English by Joe Hayes; illustrated by Gloria Osuna Perez & Lucia Angela Perez. Cinco Puntos Press 2000 30p il $15.95
Grades: K 1 2 3   **398.2**
1. Fairy tales 2. Folklore -- New Mexico 3. Hispanic Americans -- Folklore 4. Bilingual books -- English-Spanish 5. Spanish language materials -- Bilingual
ISBN 0-938317-49-0
                                    LC 99-57104
In this variation of the Cinderella story, coming from the Hispanic tradition in New Mexico, Arciá and her wicked stepsisters have different encounters with a magical hawk and are left physically changed in ways that will affect their meeting with the prince
"The English text, which is made full-bodied by its many details, appears with a Spanish translation. The impressive acrylic illustrations, done in a sturdy folk-art style, are thick with color and bright with humor." Booklist

The **coyote** under the table; = El coyote debajo de la mesa: folktales told in Spanish and English. illustrations by Antonio Castro L. Cinco Puntos Press 2011 il $19.95; pa $12.95
Grades: 3 4 5 6   **398.2**
1. Folklore -- New Mexico 2. Bilingual books -- English-Spanish
ISBN 978-1-935955-21-4; 1-935955-21-7; 978-1-935955-06-1 pa; 1-935955-06-3 pa
                                    LC 2011011430
"Eight tales of tricksters and magical transformations are given a Southwestern setting by a veteran storyteller and paired to Spanish versions on facing pages. . . . Each tale opens with a realistically detailed black-and-white scene to set the comic or dramatic mood. . . . These wise and witty tales continue to repay fresh encounters." Kirkus

Henderson, Kathy
★ **Lugalbanda**; the boy who got caught up in a war. illustrated by Jane Ray. Candlewick Press 2006 72p il $16.99

Grades: 3 4 5 6 **398.2**
1. Folklore -- Iraq
ISBN 0-7636-2782-8

LC 2004-65950

An ancient Sumerian tale about the youngest and weakest of eight brothers who, caught up in an ill-advised war, uses his wits and courage and eventually becomes king.

"The adventure story and the luminous, beautifully detailed watercolors of young men and gods will easily capture today's children. The background facts about the Sumerians . . . also makes this title a valuable nonfiction resource." Booklist

Hennessy, B. G.
The **boy** who cried wolf; retold by B.G. Hennessy; illustrated by Boris Kulikov. Simon & Schuster Books for Young Readers 2006 un il $15.95
Grades: K 1 2 **398.2**
1. Folklore 2. Sheep -- Folklore 3. Wolves -- Folklore
ISBN 0-689-87433-2

LC 2004-21672

A boy tending sheep on a lonely mountainside thinks it a fine joke to cry "wolf" and watch the people come running—and then one day a wolf is really there, but no one answers his call

"The story begs to be read aloud, and the large, colorful, and amusing watercolor-and-gouache paintings are perfect for group viewing. . . . A clever take on an old favorite." SLJ

Henrichs, Wendy
I am Tama, lucky cat; a Japanese legend. illustrated by Yoshiko Jaeggi. Peachtree 2011 un il $16.95
Grades: K 1 2 3 **398.2**
1. Cats -- Folklore 2. Folklore -- Japan
ISBN 978-1-56145-589-8; 1-56145-589-X

LC 2010052072

A retelling of the traditional Japanese tale describing the origins of the beckoning cat and how it came to be a symbol of good luck.

"Evocative watercolor illustrations capture ancient Japan in this picture book retelling of the lucky-cat legend. . . . The story's tone is formal but not stilted. . . . The artist studied in Osaka and her traditional training comes through, blending formal composition with light comic touches. . . . With its compelling story and stunning art, this is a worthy addition." SLJ

Hickox, Rebecca
The **golden** sandal; a Middle Eastern Cinderella story. illustrated by Will Hillenbrand. Holiday House 1998 un il $16.95; pa $6.95
Grades: K 1 2 3 **398.2**
1. Fairy tales 2. Folklore -- Iraq
ISBN 0-8234-1331-4; 0-8234-1513-9 pa

LC 97-5071

An Iraqi version of the Cinderella story in which a kind and beautiful girl who is mistreated by her stepmother and stepsister finds a husband with the help of a magic fish

"The story is charmingly told and illustrated with paintings on vellum, giving the pictures a soft, luxurious quality." N Y Times Book Rev

Hirsh, Marilyn
The **rabbi** and the twenty-nine witches. Marshall Cavendish Children 2009 un il $17.99
Grades: K 1 2 3 **398.2**
1. Rain -- Fiction 2. Jews -- Folklore 3. Witches -- Folklore
ISBN 978-0-7614-5586-8; 0-7614-5586-8

LC 2008022985

A reissue of the title first published 1976 by Holiday House

A wise old rabbi finally rids the village of the witches that terrorize it every night that the moon is full.

Hoberman, Mary Ann
Very short fables to read together; adapted by Mary Ann Hoberman; illustrated by Michael Emberley. Little Brown & Company 2010 32p il (You read to me, I'll read to you) $16.99
Grades: K 1 2 3 **398.2**
1. Fables 2. Poetry -- By individual authors
ISBN 978-0-316-04117-1; 0-316-04117-3

"The team behind the collaborative reading series turns their attention to Aesop's fables. Two readers can recite alternating passages differentiated by color, with the closing morals to be read in unison. Emberley's pencil and watercolor spot illustrations bring fresh energy to the classic tales as well as a softening tone. . . . The jaunty rhymes and theatrical element of adopting a persona should spark enthusiasm from reluctant readers." Publ Wkly

Hodges, Margaret
★ **Dick** Whittington and his cat; retold by Margaret Hodges; illustrated by Melisande Potter. Holiday House 2006 un il $16.95
Grades: K 1 2 3 **398.2**
1. Mayors 2. Cats -- Folklore 3. Folklore -- Great Britain
ISBN 0-8234-1987-8

LC 2005-46222

Retells the legend of the poor boy in medieval England who trades his beloved cat for a fortune in gold and jewels and eventually becomes Lord Mayor of London.

"In this spare retelling of the British legend, the narrative keeps buoyant with droll dialogue. The humorous illustrations, created with colorful inks and gouache, enhance the story with expressive faces and movement that delight the eye." SLJ

Merlin and the making of the king; illustrated by Trina Schart Hyman. Holiday House 2004 un il $16.95
Grades: 3 4 5 6 **398.2**
1. Arthurian romances 2. Merlin (Legendary character) 3. Kings
ISBN 0-8234-1647-X

LC 2003-47861

"With its fairly simple vocabulary and succinct style, the lyrical narrative can be enjoyed if read independently or in a group setting. The truly distinguishing feature of this book is Hyman's detailed, colorful acrylic artwork. . . . In keeping with the feel of a medieval illuminated manuscript, each page has an attractive, elaborate border partially painted with gold ink that glows with all the richness of gold leaf." SLJ

★ **Saint** George and the dragon; a golden legend. adapted by Margaret Hodges from Edmund Spenser's Faerie Queene; illustrated by Trina Schart Hyman. Little, Brown 1984 32p il $16.95; pa $6.95
Grades: 2 3 4 5 **398.2**
1. Saints 2. Martyrs 3. Soldiers 4. Dragons -- Folklore 5. Knights and knighthood -- Folklore 6. Folklore -- England -- Juvenile literature
ISBN 0-316-36789-3; 0-316-36795-8 pa
LC 83-19980
Awarded the Caldecott Medal, 1985
Retells the segment from Spenser's The Faerie Queene, in which George, the Red Cross Knight, slays the dreadful dragon that has been terrorizing the countryside for years and brings peace and joy to the land
"Hyman's illustrations are uniquely suited to this outrageously romantic and appealing legend. . . . The paintings are richly colored, lush, detailed and dramatic. . . . This is a beautifully crafted book, a fine combination of author and illustrator." SLJ

Hogrogian, Nonny
The **contest**; adapted and illustrated by Nonny Hogrogian. Greenwillow Bks. 1976 un il lib bdg $15.89
Grades: K 1 2 3 **398.2**
1. Folklore -- Armenia
ISBN 0-688-84042-6
A Caldecott Medal honor book, 1977
"The symmetrical elements of the tale, which create arabesques of humor, are well-served by the full-color, full-page illustrations and by the pencil drawings scattered through the text. Some of the colored illustrations are bordered by oriental rug patterns, and all of the paintings and drawings are strong in their depiction of Armenian physiognomy." Horn Book

★ **One** fine day. Macmillan 1971 un il $16; pa $5.99
Grades: K 1 2 3 **398.2**
1. Foxes -- Folklore 2. Folklore -- Armenia
ISBN 0-02-744000-1; 0-02-043620-3 pa
Awarded the Caldecott Medal, 1972
When a fox drinks the milk in an old woman's jug, she chops off his tail and refuses to sew it back on unless he gives her milk back. The author-illustrator's cumulative tale, based on an Armenian folktale, tells of the many transactions the fox must go through before his tail is restored
"A charming picture book that is just right for reading aloud to small children, the scale of the pictures also appropriate for group use." Sutherland. The Best in Child Books

Hooks, William H.
Moss gown; illustrations by Donald Carrick. Clarion Bks. 1987 48p il hardcover o.p. pa $6.95
Grades: K 1 2 3 **398.2**
1. Fairy tales
ISBN 0-395-54793-8 pa
LC 86-17199
After failing to flatter her father as much as her two evil sisters, Candace is banished from his plantation and only after much time and meeting her Prince Charming, is her father able to appreciate her love
"Many children and most adults will recognize in 'Moss Gown' the Cinderella story, while the most astute may note

its resemblance to 'King Lear.' But everyone will enjoy this beautifully told North Carolina tale from the oral tradition. Carrick, a master of the dark and mysterious, has created haunting illustrations that are a wonderful complement to the story." Child Book Rev Serv

Houston, James A.
James Houston's Treasury of Inuit legends. Harcourt 2006 268p $18; pa $8.95
Grades: 5 6 7 8 **398.2**
1. Inuit -- Folklore
ISBN 978-0-15-205924-8; 978-0-15-205930-9 pa
LC 2006043577
"This collection includes four previously published stories: 'Tiktaliktak' (1965), 'The White Archer' (1967), 'Akavak' (1968), and 'Wolf Run' (1971). Noted artist Houston lived among the Inuit people for fourteen years and brought their culture to life through his books and artwork." Horn Book Guide

Huck, Charlotte S.
Princess Furball; retold by Charlotte Huck; illustrated by Anita Lobel. Greenwillow Bks. 1989 un il hardcover o.p. pa $6.99
Grades: 1 2 3 **398.2**
1. Fairy tales
ISBN 0-688-13107-7 pa
LC 88-18780
"The paintings glimmer with intense colors—Lobel's flair for both historical and humorous detail has never been more apparent, nor more luxuriously bold." SLJ

Huling, Jan
Ol' Bloo's boogie-woogie band and blues ensemble; illustrated by Henri Sorensen. Peachtree 2010 un il $16.95
Grades: 2 3 4 **398.2**
1. Animals -- Folklore 2. Folklore -- Germany 3. Musicians -- Folklore
ISBN 978-1-56145-436-5; 1-56145-436-2
Set in Louisiana, four aging animals who are no longer of any use to their masters find a new home after outwitting a gang of robbers.
"The story of the Bremen Town Musicians works just as well in the American South as it does in the Black Forest. . . . In contrast to the antic narration, Sørensen . . . contributes thoughtful, painterly landscapes of the tin-roofed buildings and dry scrub of the South, and realistic portraits of the animals. . . . Small black silhouettes adjacent to the main paintings add another layer of visual interest. Read-aloud audiences will giggle at the dialect, nonstop action, and atmospheric descriptions of Huling's . . . retelling." Publ Wkly

Husain, Shahrukh
★ The **wise** fool; fables from the Islamic world. [retold by] Shahrukh Husain; [illustrated by] Micha Archer. Barefoot Books 2011 64p il $16.99
Grades: 3 4 5 6 **398.2**
1. Folklore -- Middle East
ISBN 978-1-84686-226-7; 1-84686-226-4
LC 2010041261
A retelling of twenty-two Middle Eastern folktales about Mulla Nasreddin Hoca, a wise man remembered for his insightful and humorous stories.

"The stories are short, most no more than a page or two; the morals are unstated. They're set on full-bleed double-page spreads or opposite framed pictures in vibrant colors—blues, reds, yellow-golds and greens. Among the geometrical designs and patterns, flat perspectives and frames from which some details escape, Mulla is easily recognizable with his beard, hooked nose and turban. Readers and storytellers looking for a particular one will find this compilation easy to use, with its numbered pages and a table of contents. . . . Most of these tales will be unfamiliar to American children, making this most welcome, as well as necessary for any folklore collection." Kirkus

Hyman, Trina Schart

★ **Little** Red Riding Hood; by the Brothers Grimm retold and illustrated by Trina Schart Hyman. Holiday House 1983 un il lib bdg $16.95; pa $6.95

Grades: K 1 2 **398.2**
1. Wolves -- Folklore 2. Folklore -- Germany 3. Folklore -- Germany -- Juvenile literature
ISBN 0-8234-0470-6 lib bdg; 0-8234-0653-9 pa
LC 82-7700

This retelling "basically follows the Grimm story, although the text has been fleshed out with some extraneous details (for instance, the little girl is called Elisabeth). . . . The illustrations seem to be a labor of love; richly colored paintings of the forest teem with exquisitely detailed plant and animal life, and the interior scenes, awash with atmospheric light, are beautifully composed and executed." Horn Book

Isadora, Rachel

Hansel and Gretel; written by the Brothers Grimm; retold and illustrated by Rachel Isadora. G.P. Putnam's Sons 2009 un il $16.99

Grades: PreK K 1 2 **398.2**
1. Folklore 2. Fairy tales 3. Folklore -- Germany -- Juvenile literature
ISBN 978-0-399-25028-6; 0-399-25028-X
LC 2008018580

When they are left in the woods by their parents, two children find their way home despite an encounter with a wicked witch.

"Isadora's abbreviated retelling of the popular Grimm Brothers tale closely follows the original in both plot and detail while making the story more accessible to a younger audience. . . . She again sets her tale in Africa, piecing colorfully patterned and hand-painted papers together to create bold, busy eye-catching scenes with a strong ethnic feel." SLJ

Rapunzel; written by the Brothers Grimm; retold and illustrated by Rachel Isadora. G. P. Putnam's Sons 2008 un il $16.99

Grades: K 1 2 3 **398.2**
1. Fairy tales 2. Folklore -- Germany
ISBN 978-0-399-24772-9; 0-399-24772-6
LC 2007047104

Recasts in an African setting the familiar fairy tale in which a beautiful girl with extraordinarily long hair is imprisoned in a lonely tower by a witch.

"The story remains true to the original. . . . Colorful, vibrant oil paints and collages brighten up the story. The artwork has rich brushstrokes and is heavily patterned, and details abound." SLJ

The **fisherman** and his wife; written by the Brothers Grimm; retold and illustrated by Rachel Isadora. G. P. Putnam's Sons 2008 un il $16.99

Grades: K 1 2 3 **398.2**
1. Folklore 2. Fairy tales
ISBN 978-0-399-24771-2; 0-399-24771-8
LC 2007-18385

The fisherman's greedy wife is never satisfied with the wishes granted her by an enchanted fish.

"Isadora uses collages of paint-striated paper in tropical colors, plus occasional scraps of fabric, to give this familiar tale a generic African setting. . . . Compared to other retellings, dialogue here is minimal, suiting the story to listeners and beginning readers. . . . It's a handsome book, and a tale that sits comfortably in its new setting." Horn Book

Jacobs, Joseph

English fairy tales; with illustrations by John Batten. Knopf 1993 428p il $13.95

Grades: 4 5 6 **398.2**
1. Fairy tales 2. Folklore -- Great Britain
ISBN 0-679-42809-7
LC 93-13878

A reissue in one volume of the author's English fairy tales (1891) and More English fairy tales (1894)

A collection of more than eighty traditional stories that recount the adventures of giants, witches, princes, princesses, and animals

Jaffe, Nina

The **cow** of no color: riddle stories and justice tales from around the world; [by] Nina Jaffe and Steve Zeitlin; pictures by Whitney Sherman. Holt & Co. 1998 159p il $17

Grades: 4 5 6 7 **398.2**
1. Folklore
ISBN 0-8050-3736-5
LC 98-14167

In each of these stories, collected from around the world, a character faces a problem situation which requires that he make a decision about what is fair or just

"Sherman's black-and-white line drawings have a stark gracefulness that complements the tales' form and structure; the tales themselves are simply told with little embellishment." Bull Cent Child Books

Includes bibliographical references

The **way** meat loves salt; a Cinderella tale from the Jewish tradition. illustrated by Louise August. Holt & Co. 1998 un il music $15.95

Grades: K 1 2 3 **398.2**
1. Jews -- Folklore 2. Folklore -- Europe, Eastern
ISBN 0-8050-4384-5
LC 97-41286

The youngest daughter of a rabbi is sent away from home in disgrace, but thanks to the help of the prophet Elijah, marries the son of a renowned scholar and is reunited with her family. Includes words and music to a traditional Yiddish wedding song

"Vibrant oils of reds, yellows, and blues set off the inky black, which defines the trees and rocks, and the sashes on the women's provincial gowns. Both the writing and the art contribute to the abundant good spirit." Horn Book

James, Alison

The **star** child; translated & adapted from German by J. Alison James; illustrated by Bernadette Watts. North-South 2010 un il $16.95

Grades: PreK K 1   **398.2**

1. Fairy tales 2. Folklore -- Germany
ISBN 978-0-7358-2330-3; 0-7358-2330-8

"Poor in worldly goods but possessing 'a loving and courageous heart,' orphaned Mathilde spends a day giving away her meager possessions and reaps a splendid return. The original tale is often known as 'The Shower of Gold,' but apart from the title change and naming the girl, this sunny version faithfully recounts the story and its lesson. Watts's simply drawn and warmly colored figures encounter one another in appealing rural scenes." SLJ

James, Elizabeth

The **woman** who married a bear; retold by Elizabeth James; illustrated by Atanas. Simply Read Books 2008 un il $16.95

Grades: 2 3 4   **398.2**

1. Bears -- Folklore 2. Native Americans -- Folklore
ISBN 978-1-894965-49-1; 1-894965-49-3

"In this retelling of a West Coast First Nations' myth, a young woman tells her friends that bears are ugly, filthy, dumb animals. The Chief of the Bear People wants to punish her, but his nephew asks for her as his wife. From Mouse Woman she learns that bears can transform into humans and then into bears again. . . . Atanas's exquisite watercolor illustrations capture the natural beauty of the Pacific Coast and the distinctive culture of the First Nations people. . . . This is a welcome addition to units on Native American cultures." SLJ

Javaherbin, Mina

The **secret** message; illustrated by Bruce Whatley. Disney/Hyperion Books 2010 un il $16.99

Grades: K 1 2 3   **398.2**

1. Folklore -- Iran 2. Parrots -- Folklore
ISBN 978-1-4231-1044-6; 1-4231-1044-7

LC 2009-26231

In this retelling of a Persian folktale attributed to Jaladin Rumi , a parrot tricks a wealthy merchant into setting him free.

"This handsome picture book's intriguing title will grab children, and they won't be disappointed with the twists in both story and message. . . . Vibrant, uncluttered acrylic paintings show the large bird locked behind bars in a golden cage." Booklist

Jeffers, Susan

Hansel and Gretel; by Susan Jeffers. Rev. ed.; Dutton Children's Books 2011 il $17.99

Grades: 2 3 4   **398.2**

1. Fairy tales 2. Folklore -- Germany
ISBN 978-0-525-42221-1

LC 2011005246

A revised version of the edition published 1980 by Dial Press

When they are left in the woods by their parents, two children find their way home despite an encounter with a wicked witch.

"Those familiar with Jeffers's 1980 version (Dial) will notice that this edition includes a few changes in the illustrations and a simplified text. . . . The artwork, done once again in pen, ink, and dyes, is for the most part from the earlier edition. . . . The pictures are slightly more muted overall, but are still presented in Jeffers's very recognizable style." SLJ

Johnson, Paul Brett

★ **Fearless** Jack; adapted and illustrated by Paul Brett Johnson. Margaret K. McElderry Bks. 2001 un il hardcover o.p. pa $10.99

Grades: K 1 2 3   **398.2**

1. Folklore -- Appalachian Region 2. Folklore -- Appalachian Mountains
ISBN 0-689-83296-6; 1-416-96833-4 pa

LC 99-89184

In this Appalachian folktale, Jack wins fame and fortune after killing ten yellow jackets with one whack

"In an Appalachian twang, complete with distinct vocabulary and speech patterns, Johnson's colorful, comical, sturdy pictures are just as energetic as the story which is told." Booklist

★ **Jack** outwits the giants; adapted and illustrated by Paul Brett Johnson. Margaret K. McElderry Bks. 2002 un il hardcover o.p. pa $11.99

Grades: K 1 2 3   **398.2**

1. Giants -- Folklore 2. Folklore -- Appalachian Region
ISBN 0-689-83902-2; 1-4169-7861-5 pa

LC 2001-30811

In this Appalachian folktale, Jack outwits two giants who want fresh meat for breakfast

"Johnson interweaves several familiar motifs from many traditions while bringing an authentic mountain twang to his telling. Johnson's lively acrylics leave no doubt that these events are as comical as they are suspenseful; the equally lively dialogue makes this an especially good read-aloud." Horn Book Guide

Johnson-Davies, Denys

★ **Goha** the wise fool; retold by Denys Johnson-Davies; sewing by Hany El Saed Ahmed from drawings by Hag Hamdy Mohamed Fattouh. Books 2005 40p il $16.99

Grades: 2 3 4   **398.2**

1. Folklore -- Turkey 2. Nasreddin Hoca (Legendary character) -- Juvenile literature
ISBN 0-399-24222-8

LC 2004-15739

A collection of fourteen tales about the folk hero Nasreddin Hoca, also known as Goha, a man with a reputation for being able to answer difficult questions in a clever way.

The book is "illustrated by a team of Cairo tent makers in the form of traditional khiyamiya tapestries, with bits of bright, solid-colored fabric stitched to roughly woven, oatmeal-toned backgrounds. Many of the tales expose familiar human foibles. . . . Others amusingly illustrate wise principles." Booklist

Kajikawa, Kimiko

★ **Tsunami!** illustrated by Ed Young. Philomel Books 2009 un il $16.99

Grades: K 1 2 3   **398.2**

1. Folklore -- Japan 2. Tsunamis -- Folklore
ISBN 978-0-399-25006-4; 0-399-25006-9

LC 2008-25747

A wealthy man in a Japanese village, who everyone calls Ojiisan, which means grandfather, sets fire to his rice fields to warn the innocent people of an approaching tsunami.

"Kajikawa imbues the story with a sense of nobility. . . . Young's rough, impressionistic collages of handpainted papers, fabric, and organic material are dark and stirring." Booklist

Karlin, Barbara

James Marshall's Cinderella; illustrated by James Marshall; retold by Barbara Karlin. Dial Bks. for Young Readers 2001 un il hardcover o.p. pa $6.99

Grades: K 1 2   **398.2**

1. Folklore 2. Fairy tales
ISBN 0-8037-2730-5; 0-14-230048-9 pa

LC 2001-23097

This is a reissue of Barbara Karlin's Cinderella, published 1989 by Little, Brown

"Those seeking a condensed version of the classic fairy tale will find just what they want in Karlin's brief retelling; . . . James Marshall's witty, warts-and-all illustrations add the sparkle that brings out the best in Karlin's straightforward retelling." Horn Book

Keats, Ezra Jack

John Henry; an American legend. story and pictures by Ezra Jack Keats. Pantheon Bks. 1965 un il hardcover o.p. pa $5.99

Grades: K 1 2 3   **398.2**

1. John Henry (Legendary character) 2. Folklore -- United States 3. African Americans -- Folklore
ISBN 0-394-89052-3 pa

LC 86-27453

This is a picture book retelling of the legend of the Black American folk hero who drove spikes for the railroads

"The dynamic power with which John Henry wields his hammer is matched by the strong illustrations: brilliant oranges and reds contrast with grays and blacks that are often silhouettes; unusual backgrounds produce startling effects. A good picture-story to show to a group." Horn Book

Kellogg, Steven

Chicken Little; retold & illustrated by Steven Kellogg. Morrow 1985 un il hardcover o.p. pa $5.95

Grades: K 1 2 3   **398.2**

1. Folklore 2. Animals -- Folklore
ISBN 0-688-07045-0 pa

LC 84-25519

Chicken Little and his feathered friends, alarmed that the sky seems to be falling, are easy prey to hungry Foxy Loxy when he poses as a police officer in hopes of tricking them into his truck

"Kellogg has enlivened the text [by] giving it some modern touches (Turkey Lurkey carries golf clubs, Foxy Loxy is caught when a 'hippoliceman' tumbles out of a patrol helicopter to land him). Children have always enjoyed the repetition and cumulation of the story, as well as the silliness of the fowls who believe the sky is falling; here there's added fun." Bull Cent Child Books

★ Paul Bunyan; a tall tale. retold and illustrated by Steven Kellogg. Morrow 1984 un il lib bdg $16.89; pa $5.95

Grades: K 1 2 3   **398.2**

1. Tall tales 2. Bunyan, Paul (Legendary character)
ISBN 0-688-03850-6 lib bdg; 0-688-05800-0 pa

LC 83-26684

"Kellogg uses oversize pages for busy, detail-crowded illustrations that have vitality and humor, echoing the exaggeration and ebullience of the story." Bull Cent Child Books

Pecos Bill; a tall tale. retold and illustrated by Steven Kellogg. Morrow 1986 un il $17; pa $5.95

Grades: K 1 2 3   **398.2**

1. Tall tales 2. Pecos Bill (Legendary character)
ISBN 0-688-05871-X; 0-688-09924-6 pa

LC 86-784

Incidents from the life of Pecos Bill, from his childhood among the coyotes to his unusual wedding day

"Although there's a lot going on in these pictures, they're not cluttered; both the gradations of color and the page design smooth the lines of continuous action and tumult of humorous detail. Kellogg's portrayal of Pecos Bill as a perpetual boy will appeal to children. The retelling is a smooth adaptation for introducing young listeners to longer versions or to accompany storytelling sessions centered around tall-tale heroes." Bull Cent Child Books

★ Sally Ann Thunder Ann Whirlwind Crockett; a tall tale. retold and illustrated by Steven Kellogg. Morrow Junior Bks. 1995 un il hardcover o.p. $17

Grades: K 1 2 3   **398.2**

1. Tall tales
ISBN 0-688-14042-4; 0-688-14043-2 lib bdg; 0-688-17113-3 pa

LC 94-43782

Sally Ann is "Davy's wife and a match for any bear, alligator, or macho man in the West. As retold (and scrupulously sourced) by Kellogg, Sally Ann's early life outracing and outswimming her nine big brothers and beating all comers at the state fair . . . is but a prelude to her flight to the frontier and subsequent rescue of and marriage to Davy Crockett. . . . Kellogg's characteristically energetic paintings meet their match in this story's kinetic hyperbole; the fact that his Sally Ann and Davy look like rambunctious big kids will only add to their story-hour appeal." Bull Cent Child Books

Kim, So-Un

Korean children's favorite stories; retold by Kim So-un; illustrated by Jeong Kyoung-Sim. Tuttle 2004 95p il $16.95

Grades: 3 4 5 6   **398.2**

1. Folklore -- Korea
ISBN 0-8048-3591-8

A newly illustrated edition of The story bag, published 1955

This collection of 13 Korean folktales "includes elements shared by many cultures, such as a flood story, and others with a unique sensibility. A variety of animals appear, including tigers, both good and bad, and snakes, depicted as dragons. The delicate watercolor illustrations make the stories accessible to children." SLJ

Kimmel, Eric A.

The **adventures** of Hershel of Ostropol; retold by Eric A. Kimmel; with drawings by Trina Schart Hyman. Holiday House 1995 64p il hardcover o.p. pa $7.95

Grades: 3 4 5   **398.2**

1. Jewish legends 2. Jewish legends -- Juvenile literature

ISBN 0-8234-1210-5; 0-8234-1404-3 pa

LC 95-8907

"Hyman's wild, beautifully detailed drawings . . . capture Hershel's farcical interchange with the village creatures and characters, including the miser, the bandit, and the rabbi. With their wry idiom, these are stories for telling across generations." Booklist

Anansi and the moss-covered rock; retold by Eric A. Kimmel; illustrated by Janet Stevens. Holiday House 1988 un il lib bdg $17.95

Grades: 1 2 3 4   **398.2**

1. Anansi (Legendary character) 2. Animals -- Folklore 3. Spiders -- Folklore 4. Folklore -- West Africa

ISBN 0-8234-0689-X

LC 87-31766

Anansi the Spider uses a strange moss-covered rock in the forest to trick all the other animals, until Little Bush Deer decides he needs to learn a lesson

"The text is rhythmic, nicely building suspense to the inevitable conclusion. Stevens' complementary, colorful illustrations add detail, humor, and movement to the text." SLJ

Anansi's party time; by Eric A. Kimmel; illustrated by Janet Stevens. Holiday House 2008 un il $16.95; pa $6.95

Grades: K 1 2 3   **398.2**

1. Anansi (Legendary character) 2. Spiders -- Folklore 3. Turtles -- Folklore 4. Folklore -- West Africa

ISBN 978-0-8234-1922-7; 0-8234-1922-3; 978-0-8234-2241-8 pa; 0-8234-2241-0 pa

LC 2007002206

When Anansi the spider invites Turtle to a party just to play a trick on him, Turtle gets revenge at a party of his own

"Children will delight in hearing this tale of the spider's comeuppance. . . . Almost every page, illustrated in acrylic ink and colored pencils, has some comical element." SLJ

Even higher! Holiday House 2009 un il $16.95

Grades: K 1 2 3   **398.2**

1. Jews -- Folklore 2. Rosh ha-Shanah -- Fiction

ISBN 978-0-8234-2020-9; 0-8234-2020-5

LC 2008019710

A skeptical visitor to the village of Nemirov finds out where its rabbi really goes just before the Jewish New Year, when the villagers claim he goes to heaven to speak to God.

"Kimmel's wise, reassuring voice embellishes the story with wonderful details. . . . while keeping the narrative taut. . . . Weber's colorful, openhearted drawings immerse readers in a lost world where piety defined life and the quest for truth was the biggest adventure of all." Publ Wkly

The **fisherman** and the turtle; adapted by Eric A. Kimmel; illustrated by Martha Aviles. Marshall Cavendish Children 2008 un il $16.99

Grades: K 1 2   **398.2**

1. Folklore 2. Fairy tales 3. Aztecs -- Folklore 4. Turtles -- Folklore

ISBN 978-0-7614-5387-1; 0-7614-5387-3

A retelling of the Grimm tale about the fisherman's greedy wife, set in the land of the Aztecs

"The vivid colors of the acrylic-and-watercolor illustrations and pages bordered with motifs from Aztec art give the tale an authentic flavor." Booklist

The **flying** canoe; a Christmas story. retold by Eric A. Kimmel; illustrated by Daniel San Souci and Justin San Souci. Holiday House 2011 un il $16.95

Grades: K 1 2 3   **398.2**

1. Folklore -- Canada 2. Christmas -- Folklore 3. French Canadians -- Folklore

ISBN 0823417301; 9780823417308; 978-0-8234-1730-8; 0-8234-1730-1

LC 2011001919

On Christmas Eve, six French-Canadian trappers meet a mysterious stranger who gives them the gift of a trip to their homes in Montreal, if only they agree not to speak until they cross their own thresholds.

"This French-Canadian folktale is brought to luminous life by the San Soucis. The atmospheric artwork, done in traditional and digital media, conveys the mystery and wonder of the snowy journey. Kimmel's storytelling is rich and straightforward." SLJ

The **frog** princess; a Tlingit legend from Alaska. retold by Eric A. Kimmel; illustrated by Rosanne Litzinger. Holiday House 2006 un il $16.95

Grades: 2 3 4   **398.2**

1. Frogs -- Folklore 2. Tlingit Indians -- Folklore

ISBN 0-8234-1618-6

LC 2004049347

After rejecting all of her human suitors, the beautiful daughter of a Tlingit tribal leader declares that she would rather marry a frog from the lake

The story "is gracefully told, and [readers] will enjoy the shape-shifting magic and cultural details, which are extended in the uncluttered paintings of villagers in Tlingit costume." Booklist

★ **Gershon's** monster; a story for the Jewish New Year. retold by Eric A. Kimmel; illustrated by Jon J. Muth. Scholastic Press 2000 un il $16.95

Grades: K 1 2 3   **398.2**

1. Folklore 2. Jews -- Folklore 3. Rosh ha-Shanah -- Fiction

ISBN 0-439-10839-X

LC 99-46986

When his sins threaten the lives of his beloved twin children, a Jewish man finally repents of his wicked ways

"This presentation of a Hasidic legend has everything a reader could want: a suspenseful story, an insightful lesson and brilliantly conceived, airy pictures that accelerate the delivery of both." Publ Wkly

★ **Hershel** and the Hanukkah goblins; written by Eric A. Kimmel; illustrated by Trina Schart Hyman. Holiday House 1989 un il $16.95; pa $6.95

Grades: K 1 2 3   **398.2**
1. Jews -- Fiction 2. Fairies -- Fiction 3. Hanukkah
-- Fiction 4. Hanukkah -- Juvenile literature 5. Jews
-- Folklore -- Juvenile literature
ISBN 0-8234-0769-1; 0-8234-1131-1 pa

LC 89-1954

A Caldecott Medal honor book, 1990

This "will fit companionably with haunted castle variants. Hyman is at her best with windswept landscapes, dark
interiors, close portraiture, and imaginatively wicked creatures. Both art and history are charged with energy." Bull
Cent Child Books

Medio Pollito; a Spanish tale. adapted by Eric A. Kimmel; illustrated by Valeria DoCampo. Marshall Cavendish
2010 un il $17.99
Grades: PreK K 1 2   **398.2**
1. Folklore -- Spain 2. Chickens -- Folklore
ISBN 978-0-7614-5705-3; 0-7614-5705-4

In this version of the Spanish folktale, Medio Pollito, the
half-chick, ventures from his safe barnyard home all the way
to Madrid, aided by the friends that he helped along the way.

"Richly colored, cheerful paintings show the endearing,
plucky half chick with one leg and one wing, hopping along
the road." Booklist

The **runaway** tortilla; illustrated by Randy Cecil. Win-
slow Press (Delray Beach) 2000 un il $16.95
Grades: K 1 2 3   **398.2**
1. Folklore 2. Fairy tales 3. Hispanic Americans --
Folklore
ISBN 1-89081-718-X

LC 00-20487

In this Southwestern version of the Gingerbread Man, a
tortilla runs away from Tia Lupe and Tio Jose in Texas

"The primitive oil paintings feature a palette of sunset
colors, a rotund Tia and Tio, and a lipsticked, scowling tortilla. . . . Kimmel's saucy story joins a swarm of similar, albeit
popular, retellings of traditional tales with a Southwestern
setting." SLJ

The **spider's** gift; a Ukrainian Christmas story. retold
by Eric A. Kimmel; illustrated by Katya Krenina. Holiday
House 2010 un il $16.95
Grades: K 1 2 3   **398.2**
1. Folklore -- Ukraine 2. Spiders -- Folklore 3.
Christmas -- Folklore 4. Christmas stories -- Juvenile
literature 5. Folklore -- Ukraine -- Juvenile literature
ISBN 978-0-8234-1743-8; 0-8234-1743-3

LC 2004054162

Katrusya's family cannot afford Christmas, but they cut
a small pine tree in the forest, decorate it with buttons, and,
when baby spiders hatch in its branches, they especially enjoy the silvery webs that appear.

"Painterly illustrations work well with a charmingly retold text to introduce American children to this unusual yet
appealing holiday fable." Booklist

Kimmelman, Leslie
★ The **Little** Red Hen and the Passover matzah; illustrated by Paul Meisel. Holiday House 2010 un il $16.95
Grades: PreK K 1 2   **398.2**
1. Folklore 2. Jews -- Folklore 3. Animals -- Folklore
4. Chickens -- Folklore 5. Passover -- Folklore 6.

Folklore -- Juvenile literature
ISBN 978-0-8234-1952-4; 0-8234-1952-5

LC 2008-48488

No one will help the Little Red Hen make the Passover
matzah, but they all want to help her eat it. Includes information about Passover, a recipe for matzah, and a glossary of
Yiddish words used in the story.

"Such a clever idea! . . . By the time Kimmelman, . . . a
terrifically conversational storyteller, and Meisel, . . . a slyly
astute cartoonist, . . . are done, readers of all faiths will know
a lot more than some emotionally evocative Yiddish words."
Publ Wkly

Knutson, Barbara
Love and roast chicken; a trickster tale from the Andes.
Lerner Pub. Group 2004 un il map lib bdg $16.95
Grades: K 1 2 3   **398.2**
1. Folklore -- Peru 2. Foxes -- Folklore 3. Guinea
pigs -- Folklore 4. Native Americans -- South America
-- Folklore 5. Indians of South America -- Folklore --
Juvenile literature
ISBN 1-57505-657-7

LC 2003-18045

In this folktale from the Andes, a clever guinea pig repeatedly outsmarts the fox that wants to eat him for dinner

"Knutson's boldly outlined, vibrant woodcut-and-water-
color artwork captures the mischievous nature of the guinea
pig. . . . A thoroughly enjoyable tale that deserves a place in
most libraries." SLJ

Kopisch, August
The **helpful** elves; illustrated by Beatrice Braun-Fock.
Floris 2011 il $17.95
Grades: PreK K 1 2   **398.2**
1. Fairies -- Fiction 2. Folklore -- Germany
ISBN 978-0-86315-815-5; 0-86315-815-3

"According to legend, the city of Cologne once had tiny
helpers who would sneak into homes at night and complete
the daily chores while the townsfolk slept. . . . Until one
day the tailor's wife grew curious to see these mysterious
helpers. . . . Based on a well-known poem by Kopisch (1799-
1853) and illustrated in muted tones by Braun-Fock (1898-
1973), the charm of this tale lies in the tiny elf tabs found at
the top of each page. Together in a row, 10 elves are perched
expectantly—each made distinct with a different smile or
a long white beard-forming a miniature audience to watch
readers. . . . An enchanting . . . piece of German lore brought
to a new audience." Kirkus

Krasno, Rena
Cloud weavers; ancient Chinese legends. [by] Rena
Krasno and Yeng-Fong Chiang; illustrations from the col-
lection of Yeng-Fong Chiang. Pacific View Press 2003 96p
il $22.95
Grades: 5 6 7 8   **398.2**
1. Tales -- China 2. Folklore -- China
ISBN 1-881896-26-9

LC 2002-35911

Presents legends and tales from China, including ancient
folktales, stories that reflect Chinese traditions and virtues,
historical tales, and selections from literature

This collection "provides a showcase for some remarkable pieces of Chinese calendar art and advertising posters
from the 1920s and 1930s. . . . Prefaces provide cultural in-

sight for some stories, and the brisk retellings weave important background unobtrusively into the narrative." Booklist

Krensky, Stephen
   Anansi and the box of stories; a West African folktale. adapted by Stephen Krensky; illustrations by Jeni Reeves. Millbrook Press 2007 48p il (On my own folklore) lib bdg $25.26

Grades: 1 2 3 4   **398.2**
   1. Anansi (Legendary character) 2. Folklore -- West Africa
   ISBN 978-0-8225-6741-7
                                        LC 2006037783
Long ago in Africa, the sky god Nyame keeps all of the stories to himself, but when Anansi the spider asks their price, Nyame agrees to trade his stories if Anansi can perform four seemingly impossible tasks
   "Krensky's retelling is simple and fast-moving, ably supported by Reeve's illustrations." SLJ

   John Henry; adapted by Stephen Krensky; illustrations by Mark Oldroyd. Millbrook Press 2007 48p il (On my own folklore) lib bdg $25.26

Grades: 1 2 3 4   **398.2**
   1. John Henry (Legendary character) 2. Folklore -- United States 3. African Americans -- Folklore
   ISBN 978-1-57505-887-0 lib bdg; 1-57505-887-1 lib bdg
                                        LC 2005010187
Retells the life of the legendary African American hero who raced against a steam drill to cut through a mountain.
   This is "written in a comfortably folksy tone. . . . While the narrative has its moments of understated humor, it also involves readers. . . . Full of light and movement, Oldroyd's impressionistic pictures effectively illustrate the story." Booklist

   Paul Bunyan; adapted by Stephen Krensky; illustrated by Craig Orback. Millbrook Press 2007 42p il (On my own folklore) lib bdg $25.26

Grades: 1 2 3 4   **398.2**
   1. Tall tales 2. Bunyan, Paul (Legendary character) 3. Folklore -- United States
   ISBN 978-1-57505-888-7 lib bdg; 1-57505-888-X lib bdg
                                        LC 2005033157
Relates some of the exploits of Paul Bunyan, a lumberjack said to be taller than the trees whose pet was a blue ox named Babe.
   "With simple vocabulary and some dialogue, Krensky gives children a feeling for the characters as well as the flavor of the time and the story's setting." SLJ
   Includes bibliographical references

   Pecos Bill; adapted by Stephen Krensky; illustrations by Paul Tong. Millbrook Press 2007 44p il (On my own folklore) lib bdg $25.26

Grades: 1 2 3 4   **398.2**
   1. Tall tales 2. Pecos Bill (Legendary character) 3. Folklore -- United States
   ISBN 978-1-57505-889-4 lib bdg; 1-57505-889-8 lib bdg
                                        LC 2005033174

Relates some of the exploits of Pecos Bill, the extraordinary cowboy who was raised by coyotes, rode a mountain lion, and used a rattle snake as a rope.
   "With simple vocabulary and some dialogue, Krensky gives children a feeling for the characters as well as the flavor of the time and the story's setting." SLJ

Kurtz, Jane
   Fire on the mountain; illustrated by E. B. Lewis. Simon & Schuster Bks. for Young Readers 1994 un il hardcover o.p. pa $5.99

Grades: 1 2 3 4   **398.2**
   1. Folklore -- Ethiopia
   ISBN 0-689-81896-3 pa
                                        LC 93-11477
A clever young shepherd boy uses his wits to gain a fortune for himself and his sister from a haughty rich man
   "Lewis uses color to achieve intriguing contrast and articulates characters' faces with expression and power. Kurtz, who heard the story as a child in Ethiopia, retells it in a strong narrative voice: her language is simple and spare yet evocative." Booklist

L'Homme, Erik
   Tales of a lost kingdom; a journey into Northwest Pakistan. written by Erik L'Homme; illustrated by François Place; translated by Claudia Zoe Bedrick. Enchanted Lion Books 2007 47p il $17.95

Grades: 3 4 5 6   **398.2**
   1. Folklore -- Pakistan
   ISBN 978-1-59270-072-1; 1-59270-072-1
A collection of three authentic folktales from the ancient kingdom of Chitral at the border between Pakistan and Afghanistan. Includes a travelogue with photographs, illustrations, and a map.
   "Sardonic, bittersweet, and often tragic, these three tales reflect the hardscrabble life of this country. . . . The retellings are flavored with detail and language suitable to the oral tradition. . . . Place's elegantly simple, naive watercolor and pen-and-ink illustrations add to the attractive, hand-crafted design." SLJ

Laird, Elizabeth
   ★ **Pea** boy; and other stories from Iran. illustrated by Shirin Adl. Frances Lincoln Children's Books 2010 61p il $22.95

Grades: 3 4 5   **398.2**
   1. Folklore -- Iran
   ISBN 978-1-84507-912-3; 1-84507-912-4
Retells folktales and fables from Iran, including the story of a mouse and a cockroach who fell in love, a foolish weaver's apprentice, and a boy with the head of a chickpea.
   "Adl, who grew up in Iran, creates collages with quirky characters, a naive folk quality and a modern artistic sensibility. . . . A wonderful blend of traditional stories and original art that reflects the customs of this country." Kirkus

   A **fistful** of pearls; and other tales from Iraq. illustrated by Shelley Fowles. Frances Lincoln Children's 2008 90p il hardcover o.p. pa $7.95

Grades: 3 4 5   **398.2**
   1. Folklore -- Iraq
   ISBN 978-1-84507-811-9; 1-84507-811-X; 978-1-84507-641-2 pa; 1-84507-641-9 pa

Mythical creatures, enchanted encounters, strange serpents, and wise magicians are brought together in a compilation of Iraqi folk tales.

"This collection introduces young readers to a host of interesting characters. . . . In the introduction, Laird recalls memories of living in Iraq and provides some background for the tales. Her retellings of these folktales are flavored with humor and cultural details, as is Fowles's clever black-and-white spot art." SLJ

Langton, Jane

Saint Francis and the wolf; by Jane Langton; illustrated by Ilse Plume. Godine 2007 un il $16.95

Grades: K 1 2   **398.2**

    1. Saints 2. Folklore -- Italy 3. Wolves -- Folklore 4. Writers on religion

    ISBN 1-56792-320-8

An old and hungry wolf terrorizes the townspeople of Gubbio until Saint Francis shows the villagers how to live peacefully with the wolf.

This is written "with a smooth storyteller's pacing and an eye for kid-friendly detail. . . . Plume . . . alternates spot illustrations of flowers and plants with slightly larger scenes of Gubbio framed in Renaissance-inspired shapes. Her delicate lines and sunny watercolor palette depict the flourishing flora, fauna and stone dwellings of the Italian countryside." Publ Wkly

Lesser, Rika

★ Hansel and Gretel; illustrated by Paul O. Zelinsky; retold by Rika Lesser. Dutton Children's Bks. 1999 un il $16.99; pa $6.99

Grades: K 1 2 3   **398.2**

    1. Fairy tales 2. Folklore -- Germany

    ISBN 0-525-46152-3; 0-698-11407-8 pa

                     LC 99-10198

A reissue of the edition first published 1984 by Dodd, Mead

A Caldecott Medal honor book, 1985

A retelling of the well-known tale in which two children are left in the woods but find their way home despite an encounter with a wicked witch

"Direct and unembellished, Lesser's retelling resembles that of the earliest German edition of Grimm, published in 1812. . . . A visual feast, the illustrations frequently recall Flemish and French genre painting of the seventeenth century, while the idyllic woodland scenes reflect a later Romantic mood." Horn Book Guide

Lester, Julius

★ John Henry; pictures by Jerry Pinkney. Dial Bks. for Young Readers 1994 un il $17.99; pa $6.99

Grades: K 1 2 3   **398.2**

    1. John Henry (Legendary character) 2. Folklore -- United States 3. African Americans -- Folklore 4. Folklore -- Juvenile literature 5. John Henry (Legendary character) -- Juvenile literature

    ISBN 0-8037-1606-0; 0-14-056622-8 pa

                     LC 93-34583

A Caldecott Medal honor book, 1995

"The original legend of John Henry and how he beat the steam drill with his sledgehammer has been enhanced and enriched, in Lester's retelling, with wonderful contemporary details and poetic similes that add humor, beauty, and

strength. Pinkney's evocative illustrations—especially the landscapes, splotchy and impressionistic, yet very solid and vigorous—are little short of magnificent." Horn Book Guide

★ Uncle Remus, the complete tales; with a new introduction. as told by Julius Lester; illustrated by Jerry Pinkney. 1999 xxi, 686p il lib bdg $35

Grades: 4 5 6 7   **398.2**

    1. Animals -- Folklore 2. African Americans -- Folklore

    ISBN 0-8037-2451-9

                     LC 99-17121

Reprint in one volume of works originally published separately, 1987-1994

Lester retells stories of the trickster rabbit from African American folklore collected by Joel Chandler Harris

"This is a landmark collection. . . . Lester's retellings are sharp and flavorful and grounded in the here and now." [review of book 1] Booklist

The tales of Uncle Remus; the adventures of Brer Rabbit. as told by Julius Lester; illustrated by Jerry Pinkney. Dial Bks. 1987 151p il $19.99; pa $8.99

Grades: 4 5 6 7   **398.2**

    1. Fables 2. Animals -- Folklore 3. African Americans -- Folklore 4. African Americans -- Folklore -- Juvenile literature

    ISBN 0-8037-0271-X; 0-14-130347-6 pa

                     LC 85-20449

This adaptation of 48 Brer Rabbit stories "is the work of a writer familiar with the methodology of folkloristic and historical research but also with the techniques of flavoring fiction. . . . Pinkney's illustrations—black-and-white drawings with occasional double-page spreads in full color—are well drafted, fresh, and funny." Bull Cent Child Books

Light, Steven

Puss in boots; retold and illustrated by Steven Light. Abrams 2002 un il $14.95

Grades: K 1 2 3   **398.2**

    1. Fairy tales 2. Cats -- Folklore 3. Folklore -- France 4. Puss in Boots (Tale)

    ISBN 0-8109-4368-9

                     LC 2001-3746

A clever cat helps his poor master win fame, fortune, and the hand of a beautiful princess

"Inspired by the work of the French Rococo artist Jean-Honor Fragonard and by French decorative wallpapers, Light created patterned papers onto which he collaged the main illustrations for this story. The results are bright, busy, cheery spreads that suit his lighthearted retelling." SLJ

Livo, Norma J.

Tales to tickle your funny bone; humorous tales from around the world. [by] Norma J. Livo; foreward by Pat Mendoza. Libraries Unlimited 2007 xxvii, 206p il pa $30

Grades: Adult Professional   **398.2**

    1. Folklore 2. Wit and humor

    ISBN 978-1-59158-504-6

                     LC 2007003331

"Tall tales, noodlehead stories, urban legends, riddles, and songs fill this delightful collection of humorous tales. The selections are in shortened but lively formats for easy reading or telling. Introductory notes discuss folklore and the healing power of humor. The more than 70 stories are

arranged by genre and labeled with the country of origin. .
. . The bibliography includes books and Internet sources as
well as VHS and DVD materials. An excellent resource for
teachers, librarians, and students." SLJ

Includes bibliographical references

Long, Laurel

The **lady** & the lion; a Brothers Grimm tale. retold by
Laurel Long & Jacqueline K. Ogburn; illustrated by Laurel
Long. Dial Books 2003 un il $16.99

Grades: 2 3 4 **398.2**

1. Fairy tales 2. Folklore -- Germany

ISBN 0-8037-2651-1

With help from Sun, Moon, and North Wind, a lady
travels the world seeking to save her beloved from the evil
enchantress who turned him first into a lion, then into a dove

"The dramatic tale is smoothly told, but the illustrations,
with even more drama and lush with romance, take center
stage here. The oil paintings use flowing compositions,
swirling lines, rich colors, and a profusion of subtle patterns
to create a series of detailed scenes combining European and
Middle Eastern elements." Booklist

Louie, Ai-Ling

★ **Yeh-Shen**; a Cinderella story from China. retold
by Ai-Ling Louie; illustrated by Ed Young. Philomel Bks.
1982 un il $16.99; pa $6.99

Grades: 2 3 4 **398.2**

1. Fairy tales 2. Folklore -- China

ISBN 0-399-20900-X; 0-698-11388-8 pa

LC 80-11745

This version of the Cinderella story, in which a young
girl overcomes the wickedness of her stepsister and stepmother to become the bride of a prince, is based on ancient
Chinese manuscripts written 1000 years before the earliest
European version

"The reteller has cast the tale in well-cadenced prose,
fleshing out the spare account with elegance and grace. In
a manner reminiscent of Chinese scrolls and of decorated
folding screens, the text is chiefly set within vertical panels, while the luminescent illustrations—less narrative than
emotional—often increase their impact by overspreading
the narrow framework or appearing on pages of their own."
Horn Book

Lowery, Linda

The **tale** of La Llorona; a Mexican folktale. adapted by
Linda Lowery and Richard Keep; illustrations by Janice Lee
Porter. Millbrook Press 2008 48p il (On my own folklore)
lib bdg $25.26

Grades: 1 2 3 4 **398.2**

1. Ghost stories 2. Folklore -- Mexico

ISBN 978-0-8225-6378-5 lib bdg; 0-8225-6378-9
lib bdg

LC 2006005478

Expands on a popular Mexican folktale about a ghost
that haunts riverbanks at night, crying as she searches for
her lost children

"The illustrations are done in soft earth tones in a style
reminiscent of Mexican folk art. . . . Given the limitations
of the easy-reader format and the necessity of not terrifying young audiences too much, this is a creditable retelling."
SLJ

Includes bibliographical references

Luna, James

The **runaway** piggy; illustrated by Laura Lacamara.
Pinata Books 2010 un il

Grades: PreK K 1 2 **398.2**

1. Folklore 2. Bilingual books -- English-Spanish

ISBN 1-55885-586-6; 978-1-55885-586-1

LC 2009053971

A Mexican piggy cookie escapes from the bakery before
it can be eaten and eludes an ever-growing line of people
pursuing it. Includes recipe for piggy cookies.

"The story of The Gingerbread Man gets a lively Mexican makeover in this bilingual tale." Publ Wkly

Lunge-Larsen, Lise

★ The **hidden** folk; stories of fairies, dwarves, selkies, and other secret beings. illustrated by Beth Krommes.
Houghton Mifflin 2004 72p il $18

Grades: 3 4 5 **398.2**

1. Folklore 2. Fairy tales 3. Folklore -- Juvenile
literature

ISBN 0-618-17495-8

LC 2002-5089

Brief stories featuring such creatures as flower fairies,
elves, dwarves, and river spirits.

"The author draws on a rich tradition of legends and
myths, retelling them in an accessible manner that will captivate readers. Handsome scratchboard illustrations decorate
the pages with stylized figures and landscapes. The vivid
hues and interesting textures make an eye-catching combination." SLJ

The **troll** with no heart in his body and other tales of
trolls from Norway; retold by Lise Lunge-Larsen; woodcuts
by Betsy Bowen. Houghton Mifflin 1999 92p il hardcover
o.p. pa $7.95

Grades: 3 4 5 6 **398.2**

1. Folklore -- Norway

ISBN 0-395-91371-3; 0-618-35403-4 pa

LC 98-43244

"Lunge-Larsen presents nine Norwegian tales about the
greed and foolishness of trolls in a casual style that makes
these stories ripe for reading aloud and storytelling. Her liveliness of language and easy turn of phrase give these retellings a comforting tone despite the sometimes scary events.
Bowen's colored-ink woodblock prints, inspired by traditional Norwegian woodcarving and design, suit the monumental nature of the subject." Bull Cent Child Books

Includes bibliographical references

Lupton, Hugh

Pirican Pic and Pirican Mor; retold by Hugh Lupton;
illustrated by Yumi Heo. Barefoot Bks. (NY) 2003 un il
$16.99

Grades: K 1 2 3 **398.2**

1. Folklore -- Scotland

ISBN 1-84148-070-3

The story of two friends who go off to pick walnuts.
Their adventure begins after one friend has been busy picking the walnuts, while the other has eaten every one. Based
on a Scottish folktale

This adaptation "has a robust rhythm and language that
lends itself easily to reading or telling aloud. That energetic,
oral immediacy is enhanced by Heo's lighthearted oil paintings. Human and animal characters sporting eccentric physi-

ologies free-float among varying planes and perspectives in foreground-focused compositions infused with color and light." Bull Cent Child Books

Tales of mystery and magic; retold by Hugh Lupton; illustrated by Agnese Baruzzi. Barefoot Books 2010 63p il $19.99
Grades: 3 4 5 6　　**398.2**
 1. Folklore
 ISBN 978-1-84686-258-8; 1-84686-258-2
     LC 2008028156
"Lupton retells seven stories . . . from Chile, Greenland, India, Nigeria, North America, Russia and Scotland. The attractive page composition has spaciously placed text that rings with a storyteller's voice, while the digital collages use decorative borders to reflect ethnic characteristics. . . . Storytellers will welcome this collection, with sources provided and personal provenance to back them up, and the title will attract kids. (includes CD)." Kirkus

Lyons, Mary E.
 ★ **Roy** makes a car; based on a story collected by Zora Neale Hurston; illustrated by Terry Widener. Atheneum 2005 un il $16.95
Grades: K 1 2 3　　**398.2**
 1. Tall tales 2. Automobiles -- Folklore 3. Folklore -- United States 4. African Americans -- Folklore
 ISBN 0-689-84640-1
     LC 2004-03221
Roy Tyle, the best mechanic in the state of Florida, can clean spark plugs just by looking at them, and he takes a two dollar bet that he can make an accident-proof car.
"Perfect for reading aloud, the funny rhythmic words are well matched to Widener's exaggerated acrylic illustrations." Booklist

MacDonald, Margaret Read
 Bat's big game; retold by Margaret Read MacDonald; illustrated by Eugenia Nobati. Albert Whitman & Co. 2008 un il $16.95
Grades: K 1 2 3　　**398.2**
 1. Fables 2. Bats -- Folklore 3. Soccer -- Folkore 4. Animals -- Folklore
 ISBN 978-0-8075-0587-8; 0-8075-0587-0
"In this retelling of a traditional fable, Bat cannot decide whether he wants to be on the Animals' or the Birds' soccer team. At first he chooses the Animals, but when they start to fall behind, he switches to the Birds. When they start to lose, he tries to switch back. . . . The text is compact and has an innate rhythm characteristic of a veteran storyteller. Nobati's full-page, digitally created color illustrations are highly stylized. . . . The pictures are full of action and recreate the mood of a heated soccer game." SLJ

 Conejito; a folktale from Panama. illustrated by Geraldo Valério. August House 2006 un il $16.95
Grades: K 1 2 3　　**398.2**
 1. Folklore -- Panama 2. Rabbits -- Folklore 3. Folklore -- Juvenile literature
 ISBN 0-87483-779-0
     LC 2005-52567
In this folktale from Panama, a little rabbit and his Tia Monica outwit a fox, a tiger, and a lion, all of whom want to eat him for lunch.

"Rhyming refrains invite the participation of young listeners. . . . Valerio's splashy tropical colors and elongated, rubbery characters . . . capture the tale's bouncing energy." Booklist

Five-minute tales; more stories to read and tell when time is short. [by] Margaret Read MacDonald. August House Publishers 2007 159p $24.94; pa $14.95
Grades: Adult Professional　　**398.2**
 1. Folklore 2. Storytelling
 ISBN 978-0-87483-781-0; 0-87483-781-2; 978-0-87483-782-7 pa; 0-87483-782-0 pa
     LC 2007014511
"Quick tales in storytellers' pockets are like money in the bank. They fill in when programs are delayed, and when class periods are cut short or interrupted so that lengthier stories are no longer suitable. . . . This collection fits the bill with participation, animal, origin, riddle, romance, strange, trickster, and moral tales from around the world and for all ages. . . . Her practical guidance enables newer as well as veteran tellers to proceed confidently with these engaging stories." SLJ
Includes bibliographical references

 Go to sleep, Gecko! a Balinese folktale. retold by Margaret Read MacDonald; illustrated by Geraldo Valério. August House Little Folk 2006 un il $16.95
Grades: K 1 2　　**398.2**
 1. Geckos -- Folklore 2. Folklore -- Indonesia 3. Tales -- Indonesia -- Juvenile literature
 ISBN 978-0-87483-780-3; 0-87483-780-4
     LC 2006-40748
Retells the folktale of the gecko who complains to the village chief that the fireflies keep him awake at night but then learns that in nature all things are connected
"MacDonald's lyrical language and use of repetition help bring this folktale to life. There is just the right touch of humor in both the text and the art. The pacing is perfectly matched to the richly colored acrylic illustrations." SLJ

 How many donkeys? an Arabic counting tale. retold by Margaret Read MacDonald and Nadia Jameel Taibah; illustrations by Carol Liddiment. Albert Whitman 2009 un il $16.99
Grades: K 1 2　　**398.2**
 1. Counting 2. Arabs -- Folklore
 ISBN 978-0-8075-3424-3; 0-8075-3424-2
     LC 2008056047
When Jouha counts the ten donkeys carrying his dates to market, he repeatedly forgets to count the one he is riding on, causing him great consternation. Includes numbers written out in Arabic and in English transliteration, as well as the numerals one through ten, and a note on the origins and other versions of the story
"Bright, painterly illustrations depict the sunny desert setting; jewel-toned robes, turban, and blankets enliven the sandy palette. . . . A winning, witty, and surprisingly effective combination." Booklist

 Little Rooster's diamond button; retold by Margaret Read MacDonald; illustrated by Will Terry. Albert Whitman 2007 un il $16.95

Grades: K 1 2 3 **398.2**
1. Folklore -- Hungary 2. Roosters -- Fiction
ISBN 0807546445; 9780807546444
LC 2006-23979

In this Hungarian folktale, a rooster with a magic stomach retrieves the diamond button which was stolen from him by a greedy king

"This fine paean to cleverness and persistence is given extra zest by Terry's acrylic illustrations, which are as colorful as sparkling gems." Booklist

Surf war! a folktale from the Marshall Islands. illustrated by Geraldo Valerio. August House LittleFolk 2009 un il $16.95
Grades: K 1 2 **398.2**
1. Ecology -- Folklore 2. Folklore -- Marshall Islands
ISBN 978-0-87483-889-3; 0-87483-889-4
LC 2008042589

A bragging contest between Whale and Sandpiper turns into a battle over the beach and sea, until both parties realize that the beach and the sea, as well as sea creatures and shorebirds, are interdependent

"The illustrations dominate the pages, with the birds and their backgrounds painted with bright shades of yellow, pink, and orange, while the sea and its creatures are deeper blues, grays, and purples. This charming story provides a moral about getting along with others and caring for the environment." SLJ

Three-minute tales; stories from around the world to tell or read when time is short. August House 2004 160p $24.95; pa $17.95 **398.2**
1. Folklore 2. Short story 3. Storytelling 4. Tales
ISBN 0-87483-728-6; 0-87483-729-4 pa
LC 2004-46257

"Easy to tell, easy to teach to children and adults, and easy to remember, the 80 very short tales in this global collection are for sharing in the classroom, library, and home and around the campfire. . . . The informal, highly practical suggestions for beginners make storytelling sound easy." Booklist

Includes bibliographical references

Too many fairies; a Celtic Tale. retold by Margaret Read MacDonald; illustrated by Susan Mitchell. Marshall Cavendish Children 2010 un il $17.99
Grades: K 1 2 3 **398.2**
1. Fairies -- Folklore 2. Folklore -- Scotland
ISBN 978-0-7614-5604-9; 0-7614-5604-X
LC 2009007128

An old woman complains about all the housework she has to do, but when some fairies come to help her she finds that they are more trouble than they are worth

"This Scottish folktale is subtle but effective in its message of humility. The illustrations are folksy and warm with amusing detail. . . . A fun read-aloud." SLJ

Tunjur! Tunjur! Tunjur! a Palestinian folktale. retold by Margaret Read MacDonald; collected by Ibrahim Muhawi and Sharif Kanaana; illustrated by Alik Arzoumanian. Marshall Cavendish Children 2006 un il $16.95

Grades: K 1 2 **398.2**
1. Theft -- Fiction 2. Palestinian Arabs -- Folklore
ISBN 978-0-7614-5225-6; 0-7614-5225-7
LC 2005009719

"In this lively Palestinian tale, a woman wishes for a child to love, 'even if it is nothing more than a cooking pot.' Voila! Her wish comes true, and red Little Pot appears. . . . Reluctantly, the mother lets her pot outdoors, and its adventures include meetings with a merchant and even the royal family. Little Pot manages to roll away from each encounter with valuable stolen goods tucked inside her lid, but after her petty thefts are discovered, she receives a stinky comeuppance that is sure to please read-aloud crowds. Folklorist MacDonald's briskly paced text brims with repetitive phrases that evoke the sounds and rhythm of Little Pot's tumbling, rolling movement, and Arzoumanian's richly hued, stylized acrylics, bordered with Islamic motifs, add subtle cultural detail." Booklist

★ The **boy** from the dragon palace; a folktale from Japan. retold by Margaret Read MacDonald; illustrated by Sachiko Yoshikawa. Albert Whitman 2011 un il
Grades: K 1 2 3 **398.2**
1. Folklore -- Japan
ISBN 0-8075-7513-5; 978-0-8075-7513-0
LC 2010045965

A magical boy grants a poor flower-seller's every wish until the greedy and ungrateful man grows tired of the boy's unpleasant behavior and sends him away.

"The digitally enhanced, watercolor collage art is typically Japanese in setting, clothing and the wide-eyed . . . boy's black topknot. The text is nicely repetitive and includes satisfyingly disgusting nose-blowing effects that children will love." Kirkus

The **great** smelly, slobbery, small-tooth dog; a folktale from Great Britain. retold by Margaret Read MacDonald; illustrated by Julie Paschkis. August House Little Folk 2007 un il $16.95
Grades: PreK K 1 2 **398.2**
1. Dogs -- Folklore 2. Folklore -- Great Britain
ISBN 978-0-87483-808-4
LC 2007005504

In this British variant of a traditional tale, a great smelly, slobbery, small-tooth dog rescues a rich man from bandits and demands that the man bring his beautiful daughter to live in his castle.

"The text is perfectly paced for interactive read-alouds . . . but the active, richly colored gouache paintings, which include beautiful details, . . . will work best with small groups." Booklist

Maddern, Eric
The **cow** on the roof; illustrated by Paul Hess. Frances Lincoln 2006 un il $15.95
Grades: PreK K 1 2 **398.2**
1. Folklore
ISBN 1-84507-374-6

Shon thinks his work as a farmer is much harder than his wife's housework, so he trades places with her and both soon discover that they appreciate each other for who they are and what they do.

"Maddern recasts this familiar folktale in Wales. . . . Hess's droll, folksy watercolors are bright and humorous." SLJ

Nail soup; illustrated by Paul Hess. Frances Lincoln Children's Books 2007 un il $16.95
Grades: K 1 2 3   **398.2**
1. Folklore
ISBN 978-1-84507-479-1; 1-84507-479-3

"Maddern retells the familiar tale of a traveler who begs hospitality from a cottage dweller, promising to prepare her a delicious soup from only a nail and then hoodwinking her into providing a collection of savory ingredients. . . . The stylized views in the watercolor art favor scenes of backs and hands, but they also emphasize the playful possibilities of the text." Bull Cent Child Books

Mahy, Margaret
★ The **seven** Chinese brothers; illustrated by Jean and Mou-Sien Tseng. Scholastic 1990 un hardcover o.p. pa $5.99
Grades: 1 2 3   **398.2**
1. Fairy tales 2. Folklore -- China
ISBN 0-590-42057-7 pa

LC 88-33668

"The handsome watercolor illustrations show a sensitivity to landscape and character portrayal . . . a hint of humor, and a flair for the dramatic. Written with Mahy's accustomed storytelling skill, this book will find an eager audience as a read-aloud for elementary school children." Booklist

Malam, John
Dragons. QEB Pub. 2010 32p il map (QEB mythologies) lib bdg $28.50
Grades: 4 5 6 7   **398.2**
1. Dragons
ISBN 978-1-59566-982-7; 1-59566-982-5

LC 2008-56082

"A wealth of sidebars and captions . . . adds depth to the compelling [narrative]. Supported by vibrant color illustrations, . . . [this] fascinating and well-written [tale] will integrate well with social-science curriculums." SLJ
Includes glossary

Fairies. QEB Pub. 2010 32p il (QEB mythologies) lib bdg $28.50
Grades: 4 5 6 7   **398.2**
1. Fairies
ISBN 978-1-59566-979-7; 1-59566-979-5

LC 2008-56083

"A wealth of sidebars and captions . . . adds depth to the compelling [narrative]. Supported by vibrant color illustrations, . . . [this] fascinating and well-written [tale] will integrate well with social-science curriculums." SLJ
Includes glossary

Giants. QEB Pub. 2010 32p il (QEB mythologies) lib bdg $28.50
Grades: 4 5 6 7   **398.2**
1. Giants -- Folklore
ISBN 978-1-59566-980-3; 1-59566-980-9

LC 2009000389

"A wealth of sidebars . . . adds depth to the compelling [narrative]. Supported by vibrant color illustrations, . . .

[this] fascinating and well-written [tale] will integrate well with social-science curriculums." SLJ
Includes glossary

Monsters. QEB Pub. 2010 32p il map (QEB mythologies) $28.50
Grades: 4 5 6 7   **398.2**
1. Monsters
ISBN 978-1-59566-981-0; 1-59566-981-7

LC 2008056090

This "is filled with some of the weirdest creatures ever conceived. . . . Take the Hambaba (Iraqi myth), the hideous giant with a face of coiled intestines. Or the Flying Head (Iroquois folktale). . . . The layout, designed as if printed upon an ancient map or scroll, is great, and Follenn's artwork is a rousing example of graphic novel-style menace." Booklist

Mandell, Muriel
A **donkey** reads; adapted from a Turkish folktale by Muriel Mandell from a Turkish folktale; art by André Letria. Star Bright Books 2011 un il $16.95; pa $6.95
Grades: K 1 2 3   **398.2**
1. Donkeys -- Fiction 2. Folklore -- Turkey 3. Books and reading -- Fiction
ISBN 978-1-59572-255-3; 1-59572-255-6; 978-1-59572-256-0 pa; 1-59572-256-4 pa

LC 2010002989

In a small village in Anatolia, even the poorest villager is expected to pay tribute to a tyrranical Mongol ruler, but the wiseman, Nasreddin Hoca, finds a way to make an aged donkey seem most valuable.

"The story's clever trickery and triumph-over-wickedness elements are satisfying. The vivid illustrations have a playful reverence. . . . The last page provides some historical context for Nasreddin." Horn Book Guide

Manna, Anthony L.
The **orphan**; a Cinderella story from Greece. [by] Anthony L. Manna and Soula Mitakidou; illustrated by Giselle Potter. Schwartz & Wade 2011 un il $16.99; lib bdg $19.99
Grades: K 1 2 3   **398.2**
1. Fairy tales 2. Folklore -- Greece
ISBN 978-0-375-86691-3; 0-375-86691-4; 978-0-375-96691-0 lib bdg; 0-375-96691-9 lib bdg

LC 2010044480

In this variation on the Cinderella story set in Greece, a girl mistreated by her stepmother and stepsisters manages to captivate the prince, with help from Mother Nature and her children.

"The doll-like faces and stiff limbs of Potter's naïve-style watercolor figures suit the fairy-tale setting, and the pictures of tiny tailors and jewelers fawning before the pudgy stepsisters give the otherwise earnest story mordant humor. This Cinderella somehow seems more resourceful than her French counterpart, and her happy ending more dearly earned." Publ Wkly

Marshall, James Vance
★ **Goldilocks** and the three bears; retold and illustrated by James Marshall. Dial Bks. for Young Readers 1988 un il $15.99; pa $5.99
Grades: PreK K 1 2   **398.2**
1. Folklore 2. Bears -- Folklore 3. Folklore -- Juvenile

literature
ISBN 0-8037-0542-5; 0-14-056366-0 pa

LC 87-32983

A Caldecott Medal honor book, 1989

"Marshall's Goldilocks, the naughty little girl who disrupts a placid bear household, is no adorable blond moppet led more by curiosity than by mischievous intent. Instead, she is a sturdy, brazen, mini-hussy who stomps over the doorsill with a determined set to her mouth and a confident bounce in her step. . . . The big cartoonlike pictures depict a cozy modern setting for the respectable, suburban bears with snug rooms cluttered with books, bulbous upholstered furniture and a messy little bear's room. . . . The story contains a genuine enjoyment of Goldilock's adventures as they are reflected in Marshall's usual slapdash and rollicking illustrations." Horn Book

Hansel and Gretel; retold and illustrated by James Marshall. Dial Bks. for Young Readers 1990 un il hardcover o.p. pa $5.99

Grades: PreK K 1 2   **398.2**

1. Fairy tales 2. Folklore -- Germany
ISBN 0-14-050836-8 pa

LC 89-26011

A poor woodcutter's children, lost in the forest, come upon a house made of cookies, cakes, and candy, occupied by a wicked witch who likes to have children for dinner

"Marshall's trademark wit and slyness mark every page of this effervescent interpretation. Never has there been a more horribly magnificent witch than his—an overstuffed, cackling harridan resplendent in scarlet costume, lipstick and rouge, her hair bedecked with incongruously delicate bows." Publ Wkly

★ **Red** Riding Hood; retold and illustrated by James Marshall. Dial Bks. for Young Readers 1987 un il $15.99; pa $5.99

Grades: PreK K 1 2   **398.2**

1. Fairy tales 2. Wolves -- Folklore 3. Folklore -- Germany
ISBN 0-8037-0344-9; 0-14-054693-6 pa

LC 86-16722

This version "will have both children and their parents gripped with the drama and amused by the up-to-date dialogue. . . . The humorous, slightly sinister illustrations display Marshall's wacky style to its best advantage. Funny and wonderful for reading aloud." Horn Book

Stories from the Billabong; retold by James Vance Marshall; illustrated by Francis Firebrace. Frances Lincoln Children's Books 2009 61p il $19.95

Grades: 3 4 5 6   **398.2**

1. Aboriginal Australians -- Folklore 2. Legends -- Australia -- Juvenile literature
ISBN 978-1-84507-704-4; 1-84507-704-0

"With the help of Aboriginal storytellers who have collected the tales and myths of their people, Marshall has assembled 10 fascinating stories of the Dreamtime. . . . Each selection is beautifully told and is illustrated by a traditional artist who uses the distinctive symbols and colors of the Aboriginal people. . . . This is an engaging, colorful book that belongs in most libraries." SLJ

Martin, Rafe

The **Shark** God; story by Rafe Martin; pictures by David Shannon. Levine Bks. 2001 un il hardcover o.p. pa $5.99

Grades: K 1 2 3   **398.2**

1. Folklore -- Hawaii 2. Sharks -- Folklore
ISBN 0-590-39500-9; 0-590-39570-X pa

LC 00-40570

Because they freed a shark caught in a net, the fearsome Shark God rescues a brother and sister from the cruel king's imprisonment and helps them find a new, peaceful kingdom across the sea

"Shannon's vigorous illustrations provide a dramatic backdrop for this well-told tale." SLJ

★ The **world** before this one; a novel told in legend. with paper sculpture by Calvin Nicholls. Levine Bks. 2002 195p il hardcover o.p. pa $5.99

Grades: 4 5 6 7   **398.2**

1. Seneca Indians -- Folklore 2. Seneca mythology -- Juvenile literature 3. Tales -- New York (State) -- Juvenile literature 4. Seneca Indians -- Folklore -- Juvenile literature
ISBN 0-590-37976-3; 978-0-590-37980-9 pa; 0-590-37980-1 pa

LC 2001-23403

"Written in the style of a novel, this collection of 14 Seneca tales is presented through the retelling of one central story into which all of the others are artfully woven. . . . Martin offers sources for the tales along with an introductory note by Seneca Elder Peter Jemison. Each chapter includes a painstakingly detailed white paper sculpture of a character (often an animal) from one of the stories." SLJ

Matthews, Caitlin

Fireside stories; tales for a winter's eve. retold by Caitlin Matthews; illustrated by Helen Cann. Barefoot Books 2007 94p il $19.99

Grades: 2 3 4 5   **398.2**

1. Folklore 2. Winter -- Folklore
ISBN 978-1-846860-65-2; 1-846860-65-2

LC 2006100360

"This collection of seasonal folklore introduces readers to the Celtic and Gaelic festival of Samhain , or Summer's End; Christmas Eve in Austria; the Jewish New Year of the Trees (Tu B'Shevat); the Twelve Days of Christmas in the Czech Republic; the Twelfth Night in Russia; and Candlemas observed by the Slavey people of Canada. Each tale is accompanied by a brief introduction, setting the time and place for the story and providing necessary background information. Exquisite borders frame the text and lush watercolor illustrations enhance the narratives. Magical, mystical, humorous, and thoughtful." SLJ

Matthews, John

Trick of the tale; a collection of trickster tales. [by] John & Caitlin Matthews; illustrated by Tomislav Tomic. Candlewick Press 2008 85p il $18.99

Grades: 3 4 5 6 7 8 9 10   **398.2**

1. Folklore
ISBN 978-0-7636-3646-3; 0-7636-3646-0

LC 2007038675

An illustrated collection of tales featuring notable trickster characters such as Raven and Hare, from the folk traditions of many countries.

"Each of the 20 folktales is introduced with a detailed, full-page ink drawing that resembles a fine print, and illustrations in varying sizes appear throughout. The pictures are both energetic and eloquent, and their formal tone is echoed in generally well-shaped narrative." SLJ

McBratney, Sam

One voice, please; [retold by] Sam McBratney; illustrated by Russell Ayto. Candlewick Press 2008 167p il $15.99

Grades: 1 2 3 4   **398.2**

1. Folklore 2. Folklore -- Juvenile literature

ISBN 978-0-7636-3479-7; 0-7636-3479-4

LC 2007038294

"McBratney offers an attractive collection of 56 short, pithy traditional stories from around the world, including folktales, fables, and Biblical parables. Most are retold in two or three pages, and some are illustrated with small stylized ink drawings, which add a decorative touch and occasionally underscore a selection's humor. The tales are well chosen, and the tellings are concise, nimble, and often amusing." Booklist

McCaughrean, Geraldine

★ The **epic** of Gilgamesh; retold by Geraldine McCaughrean; illustrated by David Parkins. Eerdmans Bks. for Young Readers 2003 95p il $18

Grades: 5 6 7 8   **398.2**

1. Folklore -- Iraq

ISBN 0-8028-5262-9

LC 2003-1086

A retelling, based on seventh-century B.C. Assyrian clay tablets, of the wanderings and adventures of the god king, Gilgamesh, who ruled in ancient Mesopotamia (now Iraq) in about 2700 B.C., and of his faithful companion, Enkidu

This is "clearly a telling for our time, but one that honors its source. Parkins captures the epic's primitive power and universal emotions in rough, broadly rendered portraits." Horn Book

McClintock, Barbara

Cinderella; retold and illustrated by Barbara McClintock; from the Charles Perrault version. Scholastic Press 2005 32p il $15.99

Grades: 2 3 4   **398.2**

1. Fairy tales 2. Folklore -- France

ISBN 0-439-56145-0

LC 2003-24883

Although mistreated by her stepmother and stepsisters, Cinderella meets her prince with the help of her fairy godmother

"McClintock's faithful adaptation combines readable text and enchanting pen-and-ink and watercolor illustrations filled with minute details of architecture and dress from the era of Louis XIV." SLJ

McClure, Gillian

The **land** of the dragon king and other Korean stories. Frances Lincoln 2008 59p il $19.95

Grades: 2 3 4 5   **398.2**

1. Folklore -- Korea

ISBN 978-1-84507-805-8; 1-84507-805-5

"McClure retells and illustrates nine brief folktales in this collection, which also includes an introduction and source list. McClure's pen, ink, and watercolor drawings gracefully wrap themselves around the text, adding detail and flavor. . . . Retold in a lightly humorous vein, there's nonetheless a keen sense of justice underpinning these tales. . . . Related in straightforward yet lively prose, with just enough detail and repetition, this collection is sure to become a read-aloud favorite." SLJ

McDermott, Gerald

★ **Anansi** the spider; a tale from the Ashanti. adapted and illustrated by Gerald McDermott. Holt & Co. 1972 un il $16.95; pa $6.95

Grades: K 1 2 3   **398.2**

1. Anansi (Legendary character) 2. Folklore -- Ghana 3. Ashanti (African people) -- Folklore

ISBN 0-8050-0310-X; 0-8050-0311-8 pa

A Caldecott Medal honor book, 1973

The adaptation of this traditional tale of Ghana is based on an animated film by McDermott. It tells of Anansi, a spider, who is saved from terrible fates by his six sons and is unable to decide which of them to reward. The solution to his predicament is also an explanation for how the moon was put into the sky

This offers "brief poetic text, complemented by geometric African folk-style illustrations in pure, bold colors." SLJ

★ **Arrow** to the sun; a Pueblo Indian tale. adapted and illustrated by Gerald McDermott. Viking 1974 un il $16.99; pa $6.99

Grades: K 1 2 3   **398.2**

1. Pueblo Indians -- Folklore

ISBN 0-670-13369-8; 0-14-050211-4 pa

Awarded the Caldecott Medal, 1975

This myth tells how Boy searches for his immortal father, the Lord of the Sun, in order to substantiate his paternal heritage. Shot as an arrow to the sun, Boy passes through the four chambers of ceremony to prove himself. Accepted by his father, he returns to earth to bring the Lord of the Sun's spirit to the world of men

"The simple, brief text—which suggests similar stories in religion and folklore—is amply illustrated in full-page and doublespread pictures. . . . The strong colors and the bold angular forms powerfully accompany the text." Horn Book

★ **Coyote**: a trickster tale from the American Southwest; told and illustrated by Gerald McDermott. Harcourt Brace & Co. 1994 un il $15; pa $6

Grades: K 1 2 3   **398.2**

1. Coyote (Legendary character) 2. Native Americans -- Folklore

ISBN 0-15-220724-4; 0-15-201958-8 pa

LC 92-32979

"Coyote persuades the crows to help him fly, but he becomes so obnoxious and boastful that they abandon him in midair, so he falls back to earth. Told with playful illustrations against the glowing orange of a desert sky, the humorous Zuni tale explains how Coyote, who once had blue fur, got his dust-colored coat and black-tippped tail." Horn Book Guide

Jabuti the tortoise; a trickster tale from the Amazon. told and illustrated by Gerald McDermott. Harcourt 2001 un il hardcover o.p. pa $7

Grades: K 1 2 3   **398.2**
1. Turtles 2. Vultures 3. Turtles -- Folklore 4. Native Americans -- Folklore 5. Tales -- Amazon River Region 6. Folklore -- Amazon River Region 7. Indians of South America -- Amazon River region 8. Indians of South America -- Amazon River Region -- Folklore
ISBN 0-15-200496-3; 0-15-205374-3 pa
LC 00-11977

All the birds enjoy the song-like flute music of Jabuti, the tortoise, except Vulture who, jealous because he cannot sing, tricks Jabuti into riding his back toward a festival planned by the King of Heaven

"The story succeeds by embracing what McDermott refers to as a universal trickster theme. . . . Utilizing a radiant palette to evoke the brilliance and vitality of the region, McDermott's spreads feature his familiar geometrically drawn characters that seem to vibrate against the lush-green stylized foliage set upon hot-pink backgrounds." SLJ

★ **Monkey**; a trickster tale from India. Harcourt Children's Books 2011 un il $16.99

Grades: K 1 2 3   **398.2**
1. Folklore -- India 2. Monkeys -- Folklore 3. Crocodiles -- Folklore 4. Folklore -- India -- Juvenile literature
ISBN 978-0-15-216596-3; 0-15-216596-7
LC 2009007977

Crocodile wants to feast on Monkey's heart and Monkey must outsmart him if he is to enjoy eating mangoes all day.

"Playfully told with succinct text and illustrations, this tale will appeal to a wide audience. It is both simple and sophisticated with subtle and not-so-subtle levels of irony. The cut/torn paper illustrations are inseparable from the text." SLJ

★ **Musicians** of the sun. Simon & Schuster Bks. for Young Readers 1997 un il $17; pa $6.99

Grades: K 1 2 3   **398.2**
1. Folklore -- Mexico 2. Aztecs -- Folklore -- Juvenile literature
ISBN 0-689-80706-6; 0-689-93907-3 pa
LC 96-19891

In this retelling of an Aztec myth, Lord of the Night sends Wind to free the four musicians that the Sun is holding prisoner so they can bring joy to the world

"This work bears the hallmarks of McDermott's style: vivid colors, illustrations informed by cultural iconography and mythology, an engaging story, and complete source notes." Bull Cent Child Books

Pig-Boy; a trickster tale from Hawai'i. Harcourt Children's Books 2009 un il $16

Grades: PreK K 1 2 3   **398.2**
1. Pigs -- Folklore 2. Folklore -- Hawaii
ISBN 978-0-15-216590-1; 0-15-216590-8
LC 2006-35426

The mischievous, shape-shifting Pig-Boy gets in trouble with both the King and Pele, the goddess of fire, but always manages to slip away as his grandmother has told him to do.

"The boldly colored art is dynamic and reflects both the humor of the sprightly text and the author/illustrator's background as an animator in its visual pacing. The tale itself has just enough folkloric elements to convey action, character and setting without bogging down in detail. . . . Good rascally fun." Kirkus

Raven; a trickster tale from the Pacific Northwest. told and illustrated by Gerald McDermott. Harcourt Brace Jovanovich 1993 un il $16; pa $7

Grades: K 1 2 3   **398.2**
1. Native Americans -- Folklore
ISBN 0-15-265661-8; 0-15-202449-2 pa
LC 91-14563

A Caldecott Medal honor book, 1994

Raven, a Pacific Coast Indian trickster, sets out to find the sun

"Raven, whether he appears as a bird or child, is always marked with a distinctive design of clear-cut red, green, and blue on black, sharply contrasting with the softer hues and forms of the backgrounds and the other characters. In this way, Raven is always recognizable, even when he shifts his shape to human form. . . . Read this picture book aloud for the full effect of its simple, rhythmic text and striking artwork." Booklist

McGill, Alice
Sure as sunrise; stories of Bruh Rabbit & his walkin' talkin' friends. illustrated by Don Tate. Houghton Mifflin 2004 48p il $17

Grades: 2 3 4 5   **398.2**
1. African Americans -- Folklore
ISBN 0-618-21196-9
LC 2003-12289

"Drawing on the tales she heard from her African American family and community growing up in rural North Carolina more than 50 years ago, McGill tells five trickster stories with warmth, wit, and simple immediacy that's just right for reading aloud. . . . Based on clay models, the animal characters in human clothes are reminiscent of puppets in the big, clear oil-and-acrylic illustrations; their body language and exaggerated expressions are wonderful." Booklist

Way up and over everything; illustrated by Jude Daly. Houghton Mifflin 2008 un il $16

Grades: 2 3 4 5   **398.2**
1. Slavery -- Folklore 2. Folklore -- United States 3. African Americans -- Folklore
ISBN 978-0-618-38796-0; 0-618-38796-X
LC 2003-19384

In this retelling of a folktale, five Africans escape the horrors of slavery by flying away

"Daly's delicate and elongated figures, small in scale against the vast watercolor landscapes of the Georgia countryside, present a bird's eye view of the story and suggest the enormity of such an escape." Booklist

McGovern, Ann
Too much noise; illustrated by Simms Taback. Houghton Mifflin 1967 44p il $16; pa $6.95

Grades: K 1 2 3 **398.2**
1. Folklore
ISBN 0-395-18110-0; 0-395-62985-3 pa

"The too crowded house of a familiar old tale becomes a too noisy house in this entertaining picture-book story. Bothered by the noises in his house, an old man follows the advice of the village wise man by first acquiring and then getting rid of a cow, donkey, sheep, hen, dog, and cat. Only then can he appreciate how quiet his house is. The simplicity and straightforwardness of the folktale are evident in both the telling of the cumulative story and in the amusing colored illustrations." Booklist

Menchu, Rigoberta
The **honey** jar; [by] Rigoberta Menchu with Dante Liano; pictures by Domi; translated by David Unger. Groundwood Books/House of Anansi Press 2006 64p il $18.95
Grades: 4 5 6 **398.2**
1. Mayas -- Folklore 2. Maya mythology -- Juvenile literature
ISBN 978-0-88899-670-1; 0-88899-670-5

This is a collection of 12 Mayan folktales that the author "heard as a child. The stories range from creation stories and pourquoi tales about animals to selections that reflect a distinctive worldview, a broad awareness of nature, and a sense of humor. Using vivid colors, the naturalistic, folk-art oil paintings . . . illustrate the stories in a manner that reflects the simple spirit and directness of the tellings. An expressive collection that lends insight into the Mayan culture in which Menchu grew up." Booklist
Includes glossary

The **secret** legacy; [by] Rigoberta Menchu with Dante Liano; pictures by Domi; translated by David Unger. Groundwood Books/House of Anansi Press 2008 64p il $19.95
Grades: 4 5 6 7 8 **398.2**
1. Mayas -- Folklore 2. Folklore -- Guatemala
ISBN 978-0-88899-896-5; 0-88899-896-1

"On her first day watching over her Mayan grandfather's cornfields, young Ixkem is invited by the b'e'n , spirits in the form of small humans, to visit them underground. They feed her generously and she tells them stories that explain Mayan customs and include bits of folklore. . . . The Mexican artist Domi has provided bright paintings in a naturalistic, folk-art style. The lyrical translation preserves the storyteller's voice." SLJ

Mhlophe, Gcina
African tales; a Barefoot collection. written by Gcina Mhlophe; illustrated by Rachel Griffin. Barefoot Books 2009 95p il map
Grades: 5 6 7 8 **398.2**
1. Folklore -- Africa
ISBN 1-84686-118-7; 978-1-84686-118-5
LC 2008028042

"Each of these eight tales is preceded by information and interesting facts about the country from which it originated. A basic map of Africa helps orient readers to the location of the various countries represented. Extensive source notes are appended. . . . There are many choices that could be read aloud or told using a call-and-response format. The book design . . . is a feast for the eyes. Griffin employs a collage technique using colored beads, sewn fabric, and textured pa-

pers, and incorporates them into shapes and faces of animals and humans. . . . This compilation contains a wealth of information and will enhance folklore collections." SLJ
Includes bibliographical references

Miller, Bobbi
Davy Crockett gets hitched; retold by Bobbi Miller; illustrated by Megan Lloyd. Holiday House 2009 un il $16.95
Grades: K 1 2 3 **398.2**
1. Tall tales 2. Folklore -- United States
ISBN 978-0-8234-1837-4; 0-8234-1837-5
LC 2006050063

An accidental encounter with a thorn bush on his way to the spring dance has Davy Crockett kicking up his heels and out-dancing even the audacious Miss Sally Ann Thunder Ann Whirlwind.

"Lloyd's energetic artwork propels the narrative with effective use of light and line. . . . The text sings with rich vocabulary, making this tall tale a great choice for reading aloud." Booklist

One fine trade; retold by Bobbi Miller; illustrated by Will Hillenbrand. Holiday House 2009 un il $16.95
Grades: K 1 2 3 **398.2**
1. Weddings -- Folklore 2. Folklore -- United States 3. Peddlers and peddling -- Folklore
ISBN 978-0-8234-1836-7; 0-8234-1836-7
LC 2007-25493

Georgy Piney Woods, the best peddler who ever lived, makes several trades so his daughter can buy a wedding dress.

This is an "entertaining romp. . . . The ink and pencil scenes were scanned and digitally manipulated, with colored pencil and gouache additions to the final work. This creates a convincing depth. . . . The outlandish events and droll caricatures are supported by lively language that is full of rhythm and fun to read aloud." SLJ

Milligan, Bryce
Brigid's cloak; an ancient Irish story. written by Bryce Milligan; illustrated by Helen Cann. Eerdmans Bks. for Young Readers 2002 un il $16; pa $8
Grades: K 1 2 3 **398.2**
1. Nuns 2. Saints 3. Clothing and dress 4. Folklore -- Ireland
ISBN 0-8028-5224-6; 0-8028-5297-1 pa
LC 2001-40174

Relates a legend about the Irish slave girl who became Saint Brigid, beginning with a celestial song, a mysterious gift, and a prophecy on the night of her birth

"Borders of Celtic designs frame Cann's mixed-media pictures and add both authenticity and wonder to the tale." Booklist

Mitchell, Stephen
Genies, meanies, and magic rings; three tales from the Arabian Nights. retold by Stephen Mitchell; illustrations by Tom Pohrt. Walker & Co. 2007 181p il $16.95
Grades: 3 4 5 6 **398.2**
1. Fairy tales 2. Arabs -- Folklore 3. Arabs -- Folklore -- Juvenile literature
ISBN 978-0-8027-9639-4; 0-8027-9639-7
LC 2006-27620

A retelling of three tales from the "Arabian Nights:" "Ali Baba and the 40 thieves," "Abu Keer and Abu Seer," and "Aladdin and the magic lamp"

"The retellings are lengthy but tension builds successfully even for those familiar with the stories. Appealing pen-and-ink drawings are sprinkled thoughout." SLJ

Iron Hans; a Grimm's fairy tale. retold by Stephen Mitchell; illustrated by Matt Tavares. Candlewick Press 2007 un il $16.99

Grades: K 1 2 3   **398.2**

   1. Fairy tales 2. Folklore -- Germany

   ISBN 978-0-7636-2160-5; 0-7636-2160-9

                     LC 2006047520

With the help of Iron Hans, the wild man of the forest, a young prince makes his own way in the world and wins the hand of a princess

"Clamoring knights, galloping steeds and scenes of palace splendor crowd the pages, which rise in a vertical format as if to stress Iron Hans's nine-foot stature. . . . Complex and muscular, this is a good bet for readers who demand lots of action." Publ Wkly

Mitton, Tony

   The **storyteller's** secrets; illustrated by Peter Bailey. David Fickling Books 2010 118p il $15.99

Grades: 4 5 6   **398.2**

   1. Folklore 2. Storytelling -- Fiction

   ISBN 978-0-385-75190-2; 0-385-75190-7

"In a handsome volume profusely illustrated with a mix of silhouettes and vigorous line drawings, Mitton presents verse renditions of European tales and legends. . . . Written in ballad-style quatrains with unforced, natural sounding rhymes and cadences, the stories offer enthralling, easy-to-follow plots with clear themes. . . . Mitton links all of his selections with prose encounters between two marveling children and a mysterious old Storyteller. . . . This gathering will cast the same sort of profound spell on readers and listeners." Booklist

Moerbeek, Kees

   Aesop's fables: a pop-up book of classic tales; paper engineering by Kees Moerbeek; illustrated by Chris Beatrice & Bruce Whatley. Little Simon 2011 il $27.99

Grades: K 1 2 3 4   **398.2**

   1. Fables 2. Folklore 3. Pop-up books

   ISBN 978-1-4169-7146-7; 1-4169-7146-7

"This book makes good use of the format to showcase 10 traditional tales. Five of the fables are presented on handsomely illustrated spreads, each including a dramatic 3D sculpture that takes center stage and two smaller foldouts embellished with movable parts that contain the bulk of the text. . . . Each centerpiece pop-up does an excellent job of grabbing readers' attention and drawing them into the story. . . . Throughout, rich earthy hues, lush forest landscapes, and vivid detail make the illustrations appealing. The straightforward text aptly conveys the gist of each tale, and a brief section offers background about Aesop." SLJ

Monte, Richard

   The **dragon** of Krakow and other Polish stories. Frances Lincoln 2008 83p il hardcover o.p. pa $7.95

Grades: 3 4 5 6   **398.2**

   1. Folklore -- Poland

   ISBN 978-1-84507-812-6; 1-84507-812-8; 978-1-84507-752-5 pa; 1-84507-752-0 pa

A collection of Polish legends, myths, and lore with black-and-white illustrations.

"Monte has gathered eight beloved stories in this easy-to-read book. In the title story, a fierce dragon ravages the city until the king, with the help of a clever shoemaker, comes up with a solution. Life lessons are taught in a few of the stories. . . . The black-and-white pen-and-ink drawings are amusing and unique. A suitable addition to most fairy-tale and folklore collections." SLJ

Includes bibliographical references

The **mermaid** of Warsaw; and other tales from Poland. illustrated by Paul Hess. Frances Lincoln 2011 il pa $8.95

Grades: 4 5 6 7   **398.2**

   1. Folklore -- Poland

   ISBN 978-1-84780-164-7; 1-84780-164-1

"A gratifying and unusual collection of folktales from Poland. There are a number of good stock characters in these pages: beautiful princesses who get themselves into trouble, warty-nosed ogres, . . . buffoons who overstep themselves or commit one-too-many deadly sins. There are also talking trees, dark forests, miraculous springs and . . . monsters. . . . The tales are told . . . in an unwavering voice, with portent enough to keep an audience listening close, and Hess' artwork has the right spidery look and sinister atmosphere. . . . That the locales are ancient and real gives the whole collection added wallop." Kirkus

Montes, Marisa

   ★ **Juan** Bobo goes to work; a Puerto Rican folktale. retold by Marisa Montes; illustrated by Joe Cepeda. Harper-Collins Pubs. 2000 un il $15.95; lib bdg $15.89

Grades: K 1 2 3   **398.2**

   1. Folklore -- Puerto Rico 2. Juan Bobo (Legendary character)

   ISBN 0-688-16233-9; 0-688-16234-7 lib bdg

                     LC 99-28799

Although he tries to do exactly as his mother tells him, foolish Juan Bobo keeps getting things all wrong

"The funny, well-paced retelling smoothly incorporates Spanish words and phrases. . . . Using bold, bright Caribbean colors, Cepeda's oil paintings amplify Juan's silliness and charm. Brush strokes add texture, and background details establish the Puerto Rican setting." Booklist

Includes glossary

Morales, Yuyi

   ★ **Just** a minute; a trickster tale and counting book. Chronicle Books 2003 un il $15.95

Grades: K 1 2 3   **398.2**

   1. Counting 2. Folklore -- Mexico 3. Bilingual books -- English-Spanish

   ISBN 0-8118-3758-0

                     LC 2002-151386

In this version of a traditional tale, Senor Calavera arrives at Grandma Beetle's door, ready to take her to the next life, but after helping her count, in English and Spanish, as she makes her birthday preparations, he changes his mind

"Like the text, the rich, lively artwork draws strongly upon Mexican culture. . . . The splendid paintings and spirited storytelling—along with useful math and multicultural elements—augur a long, full life for this original folktale." Booklist

Morpurgo, Michael

★ **Beowulf**; illustrated by Michael Foreman. Candlewick Press 2006 92p il $17.99

Grades: 5 6 7 8　　　　**398.2**

1. Folklore -- Europe 2. Monsters -- Folklore

ISBN 978-0-7636-3206-9; 0-7636-3206-6

"Morpurgo retells the classic story of the courageous young warrior . . . who used his brute strength to save the neighboring Danes, then his own kinsmen, by slaying two horrible monsters, a sea serpent, and a massive dragon. . . . Many attractive full-page watercolor and pastel paintings illustrate important action-filled scenes. . . . This is a fine retelling." SLJ

Hansel and Gretel; retold by Michael Morpurgo; illustrated by Emma Chichester Clark. Candlewick Press 2008 un il $18.99

Grades: 2 3 4　　　　**398.2**

1. Fairy tales 2. Folklore -- Germany

ISBN 978-0-7636-4012-5; 0-7636-4012-3

LC 2007052335

When they are left in the woods by their parents, Hansel and Gretel find their way home despite an encounter with a wicked witch

"Leaving the basic framework of the Grimm Brothers' tale intact, Morpurgo has altered details of the plot, creating a story in which strong familial bonds allow the innocent brother and sister to overcome evil. . . . Folk-art-style paintings, in watercolor with colored-pencil outlines and facial features, range in size from small decorations and vertical strips of various widths to full-page scenes." SLJ

★ The **McElderry** book of Aesop's fables; illustrations by Emma Chichester Clark. Margaret K. McElderry Books 2005 94p il $19.95

Grades: K 1 2　　　　**398.2**

1. Fables 2. Authors 3. Storytellers

ISBN 1-4169-0290-2

LC 2004-58160

First published 2004 in the United Kingdom with title: The Orchard book of Aesop's fables

Retellings of twenty-one classic Aesop fables, including "The Hare and the Tortoise" and "Belling the Cat," in updated language.

"This large, spacious hardcover is perfectly designed for reading aloud. The text appears in big, clear type on thick paper, and Clark's gorgeous watercolors show the characters. . . . Morpurgo's adaptations of 21 short tales stay true to the tradition of humanlike animal characters and lessons that eschew heavy philosophizing in favor of warnings about ordinary folk and their foolishness." Booklist

The **Pied** Piper of Hamelin; [retold by] Michael Morpurgo; illustrated by Emma Chichester Clark. Candlewick Press 2011 il $16.99

Grades: K 1 2　　　　**398.2**

1. Folklore -- Germany

ISBN 978-0-7636-4824-4; 0-7636-4824-8

LC 2010050683

The Pied Piper pipes a village free of rats, and when the villagers refuse to pay him for the service, he pipes away their children as well.

"Chichester Clark's pencil-and-acrylic illustrations are bright and beautifully composed; the teeming rats radiate menace without being actively scary. An evocative and effective retelling of an old classic." Kirkus

★ **Sir** Gawain and the Green Knight; as told by Michael Morpurgo; illustrated by Michael Foreman. Candlewick Press 2004 114p il $18.99

Grades: 5 6 7 8　　　　**398.2**

1. Arthurian romances 2. Gawain (Legendary character) 3. Arthurian romances -- Adaptations 4. Gawain (Legendary character) -- Legends

ISBN 0-7636-2519-1

LC 2003-65527

The quest of Sir Gawain for the Green Knight teaches him a lesson in pride, humility, and honor

"Morpurgo's sprightly writing brings out all the humor as well as the horror of the original tale, and Foreman's profuse, evocative watercolor-and-pastel illustrations highlight the drama in each scene." SLJ

Mosel, Arlene

The **funny** little woman; retold by Arlene Mosel; pictures by Blair Lent. Dutton 1972 un il hardcover o.p. pa $5.99

Grades: K 1 2　　　　**398.2**

1. Folklore -- Japan

ISBN 0-14-054753-3 pa

Awarded the Caldecott Medal, 1973

While chasing a dumpling, a little lady is captured by wicked creatures from whom she escapes with the means of becoming the richest woman in Japan

"The tale unfolds in a simple tellable style. . . . Using elements of traditional Japanese art, the illustrator has made marvelously imaginative pictures. . . . All the inherent drama and humor of the story are manifest in the illustrations." Horn Book

Tikki Tikki Tembo; retold by Arlene Mosel; illustrated by Blair Lent. Holt & Co. 1968 un il $16.95; pa $6.95

Grades: K 1 2　　　　**398.2**

1. Folklore -- China 2. Personal names -- Folklore

ISBN 0-8050-0662-1; 0-312-36748-1 pa

"In this polished version of a story hour favorite, beautifully stylized wash drawings of serene Oriental landscapes are in comic contrast to amusingly visualized folk and the active disasters accruing to the possessor of a 21-syllable, irresistibly chantable name." Best Books of the Year, 1968

Mueller, Doris L.

The **best** nest; by Doris L. Mueller; illustrated by Sherry Neidigh. Sylvan Dell 2008 un il $16.95; pa $8.95

Grades: 2 3 4　　　　**398.2**

1. Birds -- Nests 2. Birds -- Folklore 3. Folklore -- Great Britain

ISBN 978-1-934359-09-9; 1-934359-09-2; 978-1-934359-25-9 pa; 1-934359-25-4 pa

LC 2007-935084

In this retelling of an old English folktale featuring birds native to the U.S., Magpie explains to the other birds how to build a nest. Some birds are impatient and fly off without listening to all the instructions, however. That is why, to this day, birds' nests come in different shapes and sizes

"The author provides support for additional activities, information about each bird, 'bird math' (problems based upon the number of broods and eggs for each species), bird care, and a 'match the nest' activity. Illustrations show each bird in mixed media with watercolor and pen and ink details." SLJ

Muller, Gerda
   Goldilocks and the three bears. Floris 2011 il $17.95
Grades: PreK K 1 2   **398.2**
   1. Bears -- Folklore
   ISBN 978-0-86315-795-0
"This delicately illustrated version of this tale, first published in France, removes some of the familiar oppositions (too hard, too soft, just right) found in earlier versions and gives the heroine a contemporary backstory (she lives in a traveling circus caravan). The charm of the book lies primarily in Muller's detailed illustrations, which are set against tan backgrounds and include an inviting fairy tale woods dotted with wildflowers and a rustic abode for the bears. . . . The story's size motif is emphasized both textually and in the art, with big, medium, and small objects appearing throughout." Publ Wkly

Muller, Robin
   The **nightwood**. Tundra Books 2010 30p il $18.95
Grades: 3 4 5   **398.2**
   1. Fairies 2. Celts -- Folklore
   ISBN 978-1-77049-209-7; 1-77049-209-7
   First published 1991 in Canada
Retells the Celtic folktale of Tamlynne, a young knight in the court of the Elfin Queen, and Elaine, who is enticed into a nearby wood and, once inside, meets and falls in love with the young knight.

"This is a wonderful, little known fairy tale, well told and captivating, and belongs in every folk literature collection." Libr Media Connect

Muth, Jon J.
   ★ **Stone** soup; retold and illustrated by Jon J. Muth. Scholastic Press 2003 un il $16.95
Grades: K 1 2 3   **398.2**
   1. Folklore
   ISBN 0-439-33909-X
                                              LC 2002-3776
"Muth's muted blue-and-gray watercolors are ideally suited to portraying the inhospitable village. . . . His respect for Chinese people and their culture makes this serving of fusion cuisine delicious and satisfying." Horn Book

Myers, Christopher
Lies and other tall tales; collected by Zora Neale Hurston; adapted and illustrated by Christopher Myers. HarperCollins Pub. 2005 un il $15.99; lib bdg $16.89
Grades: K 1 2 3   **398.2**
   1. Authors 2. Novelists 3. Dramatists 4. Tall tales 5. Memoirists 6. Folklorists 7. Short story writers 8. African Americans -- Folklore 9. African Americans -- Folklore -- Juvenile literature
   ISBN 0-06-000655-2; 0-06-000656-0 lib bdg
                                              LC 2004-22252

"Myers has adapted and illustrated some of the wild, very short, wicked stories collected by . . . Zora Neale Hurston. . . . True to the spirit of the tall-tale oral tradition, Myers' quiltlike pictures in paper and fabric collage are minimalist and exaggerated, magical and mundane. . . . Perfect for sharing with many age groups." Booklist

Myers, Tim
   The **furry**-legged teapot; retold by Tim Myers; illustrated by Robert McGuire. Marshall Cavendish Children 2007 un il $16.99
Grades: 1 2 3 4   **398.2**
   1. Folklore -- Japan
   ISBN 978-0-7614-5295-9
                                              LC 2005016935
In ancient Japan, a young tanuki, a raccoon dog that can change shapes, becomes stuck in the form of a teapot

"McGuire's acrylic spreads place the farmer's hut and monk's quarters in a lush Japanese countryside with mountains in the background. . . . Myers provides source notes for his entertaining version of the tanuki-turned-teapot story." SLJ

Naidoo, Beverley
   ★ **Aesop's** fables; [illustrated by] Piet Grobler. Frances Lincoln Children's Books 2011 48p il $18.95
Grades: 2 3 4 5   **398.2**
   1. Fables
   ISBN 978-1-84780-007-7; 1-84780-007-6
"Wearing a deliberate African patina, this refreshing collection of 16 Aesop fables takes place in the South African veld, giving these timeless moral tales a visual and verbal facelift. . . . In typical Aesop fashion, animals serve as lead characters, but Naidoo adds to the African texture by populating the tales with distinctive African animals. . . . The single-action narrative of each fable preserves the impersonal moral tone of the originals. . . . Primitive, whimsical watercolor-and-pencil illustrations preserve the African theme." Kirkus

Namm, Diane
   Greek myths; retold from the classic originals by Diane Namm; illustrated by Eric Freeberg. Sterling 2011 152p il (Classic starts) $5.95
Grades: 2 3 4 5   **398.2**
   1. Greek mythology
   ISBN 978-1-4027-7312-9; 1-4027-7312-9
                                              LC 2010039803
From Icarus's legendary flight to Orpheus's trip to the underworld, this introduces young readers to classic Greek myths.

"Namm retells 15 familiar myths in the simple, straightforward style that makes this series so accessible for emerging readers. . . . Motivations and feelings are described directly, allowing children to easily grasp the deeper meaning of the stories. The book ends with discussion questions and a note for parents and educators. . . . It will likely become a fixture in most libraries." SLJ

Nanji, Shenaaz
   Indian tales; written by Shenaaz Nanji; illustrated by Christopher Corr. Barefoot Books 2007 92p il $19.99

Grades: 3 4 5 6   398.2
1. Folklore -- India
ISBN 978-1-846860-83-6

LC 2006100357

"This anthology presents eight fluid retellings of folktales from different Indian states. . . . An introduction offers a brief overview of the country's history. . . . Each folktale is preceded by a note with facts about the state from which it originated, including explanations of festivals or terms that appear in the text. Illustrations and page borders support the texts perfectly as the folk-style paintings reflect colors of rural life." SLJ

Napoli, Donna Jo, 1948-
★ **Treasury** of Greek mythology; classic stories of gods, goddesses, heroes & monsters. National Geographic Society 2011 191p il map $24.95; lib bdg $33.90
Grades: 5 6 7 8   398.2
1. Greek mythology
ISBN 978-1-4263-0844-4; 1-4263-0844-2; 978-1-4263-0845-1 lib bdg; 1-4263-0845-0 lib bdg

LC 2011024327

"Napoli presents 25 tales introducing the major players of the Greek pantheon along with an assortment of celebrated heroes and mortals. . . . At once eloquent and elemental, these lyrically written portraits deftly detail each character's origins, realm of power, and legendary story lines. Filled with sensual imagery, the language is poetic, yet balanced by amusing asides and wry observations that add a contemporary, almost conversational accessibility. . . . Stunning stylized paintings featuring luminous colors, rich patterns, and star-infused motifs add depth and drama to the text. . . . Interesting sidebars appear throughout, providing historical, scientific, and cultural information." SLJ

Nesbit, E.
Jack and the beanstalk; [by] E. Nesbit; illustrated by Matt Tavares. Candlewick Press 2006 un il $16.99
Grades: 2 3 4   398.2
1. Fairy tales 2. Giants -- Folklore 3. Folklore -- Great Britain
ISBN 0-7636-2124-2

LC 2005050190

After climbing to the top of a huge beanstalk, a boy uses his quick wits to outsmart a giant and gain a fortune for himself and his mother

"First published in Nesbit's The Old Nursery Stories (1908), this lively retelling adds character and wit to the timeless fairy tale, and Tavares' large pencil-and-watercolor illustrations, in shades of dusky brown and green, are a fitting accompaniment to the young boy's scary encounter with the giant." Booklist

Nishizuka, Koko
The **beckoning** cat; based on a Japanese folktale. illustrated by Rosanne Litzinger. Holiday House 2009 un il $16.95
Grades: K 1 2 3   398.2
1. Cats -- Folklore 2. Folklore -- Japan 3. Folklore -- Juvenile literature
ISBN 978-0-8234-2051-3; 0-8234-2051-5

LC 2008007266

A retelling of the traditional Japanese tale describing the origins of the beckoning cat and how it came to be a symbol of good luck.

Litzinger's "full-bleed pictures—a highly tactile mix of watercolor, colored pencil, ink and gouache—combine comfortably rounded, stylized forms and a gently shaded palette to evoke a contemplative mood." Publ Wkly

Norman, Howard
Between heaven and earth; bird tales from around the world. illustrated by Leo & Diane Dillon. Harcourt 2004 78p il lib bdg $22
Grades: 4 5 6 7   398.2
1. Folklore 2. Birds -- Folklore
ISBN 0-15-201982-0

LC 2003-7874

A collection of folktales from around the world, all of which have a bird as a main character

This is "a collection of stories that are rich in cultural references from the lands of their origins. . . . The Dillons' luminous watercolor-and-pencil illustrations, detailed with patterns drawn from each tale's culture of origin, will draw readers and listeners back to the stories." Booklist

O'Malley, Kevin
The **great** race. Walker Books for Young Readers 2011 un il $16.99
Grades: K 1 2   398.2
1. Fables 2. Folklore 3. Rabbits -- Folklore 4. Turtles -- Folklore 5. Fables -- Juvenile literature
ISBN 978-0-8027-2158-7; 0-8027-2158-3

LC 2010031075

Retells the traditional tale of the tortoise and the hare as a match between the very vain Lever Lapin and Nate Turtle, who is tired of all of the publicity Lever's speed generates.

"Working in watercolor and ink, O'Malley makes fine use of the wide trim, alternating sprawling crowd shots with extreme close-ups that really distill the mano a mano dislike brewing between the opponents. A simple tale, enjoyably told." Booklist

Oberman, Sheldon
Solomon and the ant; and other Jewish folktales. retold by Sheldon Oberman; introduction and commentary by Peninnah Schram. Boyds Mills Press 2006 165p $19.95
Grades: 5 6 7 8   398.2
1. Jews -- Folklore
ISBN 1-59078-307-7

LC 2005020115

"This collection of 43 traditional Jewish stories is authoritative as well as immensely entertaining. . . . The stories, from both Ashkenazi and Sephardic traditions, are arranged more or less chronologically—from biblical days through the talmudic period to more contemporary times. There are legends, medieval fables, trickster tales, and more. . . . The stories, wonderful for storytelling and sharing, are accessible even to listeners younger than the target audience, and the notes and commentary will provide older children with context and history." Booklist
Includes bibliographical references

Ollhoff, Jim
Japanese mythology. ABDO Pub. 2011 32p il lib bdg $27.07

Grades: 5 6 7 8 **398.2**
1. Japanese mythology
ISBN 978-1-61714-723-4
LC 2010042019

'This book offers information about Japanese mythology, answering questions such as "Who is Hachiman? What is the Seven Gods of Fortune? Why are myths so important in our lives? Myths are a rich source of history. People use them to make sense of our world. Even before myths were written down, people told and retold the stories of the gods and goddesses of their homeland. Readers of Japanese Mythology will learn the history of myths, as well as their deeper meaning." (Publisher's note) "A Shinto creation story forms the backbone of [this book], which also introduces the sun goddess Amaterasu; the fabled first emperor of Japan, Jimmu; and the impish Oni." (Booklist)

"Ollhoff writes in a clear and engaging fashion, presenting complex issues in a way that will be easy for youngsters to grasp. . . . The photographs and reproductions of art tie directly to the [text]." SLJ

Olson, Arielle North
Ask the bones: scary stories from around the world; selected and retold by Arielle North Olson and Howard Schwartz; illustrated by David Linn. Viking 1999 145p il hardcover o.p. pa $5.99
Grades: 4 5 6 7 **398.2**
1. Folklore
ISBN 0-670-87581-3; 0-14-230140-X pa
LC 98-19108

A collection of scary folktales from countries around the world including China, Russia, Spain, and the United States
"David Linn's bone-chilling black-and-white illustrations . . . will stay with the reader long after the book is closed. Excellent for reading aloud, this collection will satisfy even jaded genre fans." Booklist
Includes bibliographical references

More bones; scary stories from around the world. selected and retold by Arielle North Olson and Howard Schwartz; illustrated by E.M. Gist. Viking 2008 162p il $15.99
Grades: 4 5 6 7 **398.2**
1. Folklore
ISBN 978-0-670-06339-0; 0-670-06339-8

"This tour of the world's shadowy corners is full of dark wizards, unkind witches, and other untrustworthy creatures. . . . The 22 tales, as retold by Olson and Schwartz, give a vivid glimpse into unfamiliar, unnerving territory. . . . The atmospheric illustrations, while not intricately detailed, are somewhat startling in their imagery." Booklist

Onyefulu, Ifeoma
The **girl** who married a ghost; and other tales from Nigeria. illustrated by Julia Cairns. Frances Lincoln Children's 2010 109p il $15.95
Grades: 2 3 4 5 **398.2**
1. Folklore -- Nigeria
ISBN 978-1-84780-176-0; 1-84780-176-5

A collection of nine Nigerian tales from a world where spirits rule and animals talk.
"Onyefulu retells these tales in an informal, chatty style that captures the drama. . . . The stated morals are heavy. . . . But the stories and occasional, appealing pencil drawings

move beyond the lessons, with surprising twists and turns and animal characters that steal, lie, and get their comeuppances." Booklist

Orgel, Doris
Doctor All-Knowing; a folk tale from the Brothers Grimm. retold by Doris Orgel; illustrated by Alexandra Boiger. Atheneum Books for Young Readers 2008 un il $16.99
Grades: PreK K 1 2 **398.2**
1. Folklore -- Germany
ISBN 978-1-4169-1246-0; 1-4169-1246-0

Desperate to provide enough food for himself and his daughter, a poor man sets himself up as Doctor All-Knowing and is soon called upon by a rich man to find a thief.
"Consistent in style, yet varied in size, composition, and perspective, the watercolor paintings use comic exaggeration to good effect. Vivid in both the telling and art." Booklist

Orr, Tamra
The **monsters** of Hercules. Mitchell Lane Publishers 2011 48p il map (Monsters in myth) lib bdg $29.95
Grades: 4 5 6 7 **398.2**
1. Monsters 2. Hercules (Legendary character)
ISBN 978-1-58415-927-8; 1-58415-927-8
LC 2010028764

This book about the monsters of Hercules is "thorough and respectful of a number of ancient and modern sources and [bends] over backward to navigate often contradictory, interlinked legends. . . . A number of paintings and photos break up the otherwise text-heavy pages, and copious chapter notes and reading suggestions conclude. This is by no means entry-level stuff, but for kids handy with the basics and ready to delve deeper, [this book] will be of great use." Booklist
Includes glossary and bibliographical references

The **sirens**. Mitchell Lane Publishers 2011 48p il map (Monsters in myth) lib bdg $29.95
Grades: 4 5 6 7 **398.2**
1. Sirens (Mythology)
ISBN 978-1-58415-930-8; 1-58415-930-8
LC 2010026965

This book examines the various stories that surround the myths of the Sirens.
This book is "thorough and respectful of a number of ancient and modern sources and [bends] over backward to navigate often contradictory, interlinked legends. . . . A number of paintings and photos break up the otherwise text-heavy pages, and copious chapter notes and reading suggestions conclude. This is by no means entry-level stuff, but for kids handy with the basics and ready to delve deeper, [this book] will be of great use." Booklist
Includes glossary and bibliographical references

Osborne, Mary Pope
★ **American** tall tales; wood engravings by Michael McCurdy. Knopf 1991 115p il map $22
Grades: 3 4 5 6 **398.2**
1. Tall tales 2. Folklore -- United States
ISBN 0-679-80089-1
LC 89-37235

A collection of tall tales about such American folk heroes as Sally Ann Thunder Ann Whirlwind, Pecos Bill, John Henry, and Paul Bunyan

"As tantalizing as Osborne's storytelling are McCurdy's . . . elaborate, full-color wood engravings, which in their robust stylization dramatically render the grandeur of these engrossing yarns." Publ Wkly

Includes bibliographical references

★ **Kate** and the beanstalk; written by Mary Pope Osborne; illustrated by Giselle Potter. Atheneum Bks. for Young Readers 2000 un il pa $7.99

Grades: K 1 2 3   **398.2**
1. Giants 2. Fairy tales 3. Giants -- Folklore 4. Folklore -- England 5. Folklore -- Great Britain
ISBN 0-689-82550-1; 1-4169-0818-8 pa

                LC 99-27029

In this version of the classic tale, a girl climbs to the top of a giant beanstalk, where she uses her quick wits to outsmart a giant and make her and her mother's fortune

"The text is straightforward but punctuated by some delicious dialogue. . . . Using a variety of mediums—pencil, ink, gouache, and watercolor—the illustrations are executed in Potter's signature folk-art style. They are immediate, innovative, and just the right size for story hours." Booklist

★ The **brave** little seamstress; written by Mary Pope Osborne; illustrated by Giselle Potter. Atheneum Bks. for Young Readers 2002 un il hardcover o.p. $16

Grades: K 1 2 3   **398.2**
1. Folklore 2. Fairy tales 3. Folklore -- Germany
ISBN 0-689-84486-7; 1-4169-1620-2 pa

                LC 2001-33018

A seamstress who kills seven flies with one blow outwits the king and, with the help of a kind knight, becomes a wise and kind queen

"The whimsically perky, generous text is perfectly matched to the illustrations, in Potter's signature ink-gouache-gesso-water-colors, which affix just the right amount of sauciness to the cheeky heroine." Booklist

Osborne, Will
★ **Sleeping** Bobby; [by] Will Osborne and Mary Pope Osborne; illustrated by Giselle Potter. Atheneum Books for Young Readers 2005 un il $16.95

Grades: K 1 2 3   **398.2**
1. Fairy tales 2. Folklore -- Germany
ISBN 0-689-87668-8

                LC 2004-06346

A retelling of the Grimm tale featuring a handsome prince who is put into a deep sleep by a curse until he is awakened by the kiss of a brave princess.

This "is written in a breezy, readable style, and most details of the original story have been included. . . . Potter's folk-style characters are dressed in Elizabethan garb with details such as puffed sleeves, high lace collars, and ruffs." SLJ

Otsuka, Yuzo
Suho's white horse; a Mongolian legend. retold by Yuzo Otsuka; illustrated by Suekichi Akaba; translated by Richard McNamara and Peter Howlett; instrumental by Li Bo. R.I.C. 2007 47p il $17.95

Grades: 2 3 4   **398.2**
1. Horses -- Folklore 2. Folklore -- Mongolia 3. Musical instruments -- Folkore
ISBN 1-74126-021-3

Relates how the tragic parting of a boy and his horse led to the creation of the horsehead fiddle, or morin khuur, of the Mongolian shepherds.

"First published 40 years ago in Japan . . . this big, beautiful picture book tells [a] stirring legend. . . . Children will love [Akaba's] clear watercolor paintings. . . . This includes an audio CD that features music played by a morin khuur master." Booklist

Palatini, Margie
★ **Lousy** rotten stinkin' grapes; illustrated by Barry Moser. Simon & Schuster Books for Young Readers 2009 un il $15.99

Grades: PreK K 1 2   **398.2**
1. Fables 2. Authors 3. Folklore 4. Storytellers 5. Foxes -- Folklore
ISBN 978-0-689-80246-1; 0-689-80246-3

                LC 2007015727

Retells the fable of a frustrated fox that, after many tries to reach a high bunch of grapes, decides they must be sour anyway.

"Moser's wonderful watercolor illustrations of the doubting animals executing Fox's convoluted plans are rich in humor. . . . Matched by a text that rolls off the tongue and is full of action and repetitive phrases, the book is a delight." SLJ

Park, Janie Jaehyun
The **love** of two stars; a Korean legend. retold and pictures by Janie Jaehyun Park. Groundwood Books 2005 un il $16.95

Grades: K 1 2 3   **398.2**
1. Folklore -- Korea 2. Stars -- Folklore 3. Folklore -- Juvenile literature
ISBN 0-88899-672-1

"High in the starry sky, Kyonu works as a farmer and Jingnyo as a weaver. After they fall in love, they neglect their work, leaving the people hungry and ragged, so the king allows them to meet only on the seventh day of the seventh moon month. When that day comes, however, they can't reach one another, and their tears flood the earth. Finally, the birds . . . fly up and make a bridge across the Milky Way to enable the lovers to embrace. Park's unframed double-page illustrations, painted on gessoed paper to add attractive texture, show the romantic costume drama of the Korean lovers together and apart. At the same time, the rich, dark-blue mystery of the night sky, with stars and swirling curves, will touch kids everywhere." Booklist

Partridge, Elizabeth
Kogi's mysterious journey; adapted by Elizabeth Partridge; illustrated by Aki Sogabe. Dutton Children's Bks. 2003 un il $17.99

Grades: K 1 2 3   **398.2**
1. Folklore -- Japan 2. Fishes -- Folklore 3. Artists -- Folklore
ISBN 0-525-47078-6

Kogi paints the shore of Lake Biwa, but is unable to capture the vigor and beauty that inspire him. One day, Kogi wades into the water to release a fish, and unable to resist follows in its wake, eventually becoming a fish himself, and learning what it is to be a fish in the lake

"Partridge's spare, poetic recasting of a Japanese folktale ends with the artist and his creations coming to life again as fish. Dignified and handsome, Sogabe's carefully composed cut-paper art employs muted colors to bring Kogi's inner and outer worlds to life." SLJ

Paterson, Katherine

Parzival; the quest of the Grail Knight. retold by Katherine Paterson. Lodestar Bks. 1998 127p hardcover o.p. pa $5.99

Grades: 5 6 7 8   398.2

1. Arthurian romances 2. Grail -- Folklore 3. Folklore -- England 4. Knights and knighthood -- Folklore 5. Perceval (Legendary character) -- Legends 6. Perceval (Legendary character) -- Juvenile literature

ISBN 0-525-67579-5; 0-14-130573-8 pa

LC 97-23891

A retelling of the Arthurian legend in which Parzival, unaware of his noble birth, comes of age through his quest for the Holy Grail

"Nearly 800 years old, the story has freshness, humor, grace, and depth. . . . Paterson clarifies much of the Christian doctrine that is the basis of the story, but she is never dull or pedantic." SLJ

Paye, Won-Ldy

★ **Head**, body, legs; a story from Liberia. retold by Won-Ldy Paye & Margaret H. Lippert; illustrated by Julie Paschkis. Holt & Co. 2002 un il $16.95; pa $7.95

Grades: K 1 2 3   398.2

1. Folklore -- Liberia 2. Dan (African people)

ISBN 0-8050-6570-9; 0-8050-7890-8 pa

LC 00-44856

In this tale from the Dan people of Liberia, Head, Arms, Body, and Legs learn that they do better when they work together

"This simple fable about working together is told in a straightforward text; humor is inherent in the situation. Enticing illustrations in ripe fruit colors enhance the strange, silly tale." Horn Book Guide

★ **Mrs.** Chicken and the hungry crocodile; [by] Won-Ldy Paye & Margaret H. Lippert; illustrated by Julie Paschkis. Holt & Co. 2003 un il $16.95

Grades: K 1 2 3   398.2

1. Folklore -- Liberia 2. Chickens -- Folklore 3. Crocodiles -- Folklore

ISBN 0-8050-7047-8

LC 2002-1755

When a crocodile captures Mrs. Chicken and takes her to an island to fatten her up, clever Mrs. Chicken claims that she can prove they are sisters and that, therefore, the crocodile shouldn't eat her

"Told in straightforward language this trickster tale is smart and funny. . . . The stylized gouache artwork is strong and streamlined. . . . The flat paintings recall folk art, and Crocodile's checkerboard skin reflects the patterns found in her home." SLJ

★ The **talking** vegetables; retold by Won-Ldy Paye and Margaret H. Lippert; illustrated by Julie Paschkis. Henry Holt 2006 un il $16.95

Grades: K 1 2 3   398.2

1. Anansi (Legendary character) 2. Vegetables -- Folklore 3. Folklore -- West Africa

ISBN 978-0-8050-7742-1; 0-8050-7742-1

LC 2005019757

After Spider refuses to help the villagers plant the vegetables, he is in for a surprise when he goes to pick some for himself

"From the Dan people of northeastern Liberia comes this traditional tale. . . . Paschkis's brightly colored folk-art illustrations . . . show the villagers to be an elephant, a hen, a crocodile, a leopard, a monkey, a snake, and a butterfly. . . . Read aloud, this simple but solid moralistic tale will delight youngsters and make them want to participate in the telling." SLJ

Penner, Lucille Recht

Dragons; illustrated by Peter Scott. Random House 2004 42p il (Stepping stone book) hardcover o.p. pa $3.99

Grades: 3 4 5   398.2

1. Dragons 2. Folklore

ISBN 0-307-26417-2; 0-307-46417-3 pa

LC 2003-12427

Relates myths about dragons from different countries, including where they live, what they eat, and how they look, as well as how the myths may have developed

"Carefully differentiating between reality and myth, the author intersperses bits of dragon lore . . . through the text. . . . Color illustrations showing different types of dragons add interest." Booklist

Perrault, Charles

Cinderella; or, The little glass slipper. a free translation from the French of Charles Perrault; with pictures by Marcia Brown. Scribner 1954 un il $16; pa $5.99

Grades: K 1 2 3   398.2

1. Fairy tales 2. Folklore -- France

ISBN 0-684-12676-1; 0-689-81474-7 pa

Awarded the Caldecott Medal, 1955

This is the classic story of the poor, good-natured girl who works for her selfish step-sisters until a fairy godmother transforms her into a beautiful 'princess' for just one night

"With soft, delicate colors and lines that subtly suggest, Miss Brown creates a thoroughly fairyland atmosphere, at the same time recreating the sophistication of the French Court with its golden coach, canopied bed, dazzling chandeliers, liveried footmen, curled and pompadoured ladies, and peruked (bewigged) courtiers." Libr J

Philip, Neil

Horse hooves and chicken feet: Mexican folktales; selected by Neil Philip; illustrated by Jacqueline Mair. Clarion Bks. 2003 83p il $19

Grades: 4 5 6 7   398.2

1. Folklore -- Mexico

ISBN 0-618-19463-0

LC 2002-154886

This is a "selection of 14 folktales from Mexico and people of Mexican descent from the American Southwest. The stories are simply yet effectively retold. . . . Adding considerably to the overall appeal of the book are Mair's exuberant illustrations, accomplished in the style of Mexican folk art." Booklist

Includes bibliographical references

★ The **pirate** princess and other fairy tales; by Neil Philip; illustrated by Mark Weber. Arthur A. Levine Books 2005 88p il $19.99

Grades: 4 5 6 7　　　　　　　　　　　　**398.2**

1. Fairy tales 2. Jewish legends

ISBN 0-590-10855-7

LC 2004-16949

This "volume contains seven fairy tales adapted from the stories written by seventeenth-century Hasidic rabbi Nahman ben Simha. . . . An informative four-page introduction discusses Nahman and his storytelling. The lively collection of varied tales begins with the story of a princess who turns pirate to escape unwanted suitors and rejoin the man she loves. Several of the other stories share elements of adventure, true love, promises, quests, and fortune. . . . Weber's many gouache paintings have the stylistic feeling of Chagall. . . . They capture the wit, drama, and occasional comedy of the tales." Booklist

Includes bibliographical references

Pinkney, Jerry

★ The **little** red hen. Dial Books for Young Readers 2006 un il $16.99

Grades: K 1 2 3　　　　　　　　　　　　**398.2**

1. Folklore 2. Animals -- Folklore 3. Chickens -- Folklore

ISBN 0-8037-2935-9

LC 2005-13301

A newly illustrated edition of the classic fable of the hen who is forced to do all the work of baking bread and of the animals who learn a bitter lesson from it.

This is "a lush, light-filled rendition of a folktale staple. . . . The animal's names appear in color-coded font (red for the hen, brown for the dog, etc.), making it extra-easy even for pre-readers to chime in, and the glorious, generous paintings are a real gift." SLJ

Pirotta, Saviour

Firebird; paintings by Catherine Hyde. Candlewick Press 2010 40p il $18.99

Grades: 2 3 4 5　　　　　　　　　　　　**398.2**

1. Fairy tales 2. Folklore -- Russia

ISBN 978-0-7636-5076-6; 0-7636-5076-5

LC 2010006608

With the aid of Gray Wolf, young Prince Ivan fulfills a series of tasks set for him by his father and two other kings, winning the legendary firebird, a magical horse, and the hand of Princess Helen by his efforts.

"Large and lavish, this handsome presentation builds nicely on European folktale elements. . . . Hyde's acrylic paintings are soft in focus and deep with luminous portrayals of the featured animals and dusky views of the nighttime and woodland journeys. The book's expansive layout nicely varies the use of white space and painting size. . . . A welcome choice for storytelling and reading aloud." SLJ

The **McElderry** book of Grimms' fairy tales; retold by Saviour Pirotta; illustrated by Emma Clark. Margaret K. McElderry Books 2006 126p il $19.95

Grades: 2 3 4　　　　　　　　　　　　**398.2**

1. Authors 2. Fairy tales 3. Folklorists 4. Philologists 5. Folklore -- Germany 6. Short story writers

ISBN 1-4169-1798-5

First published 2002 in the United Kingdom with title: The sleeping princess and other fairy tales from Grimm

"An appealing collection of 10 fairy tales. . . . Pirotta writes like a storyteller, with great imagery and description, and the lively stories read aloud beautifully. . . . Clark's dark, twisty branches in the forest enhance the mood of this story. The large typeface, generous use of white space, and overall design make this book one children can read themselves, and the artist's expressive illustrations contribute to the appeal." SLJ

Polacco, Patricia

★ **Luba** and the wren. Philomel Bks. 1999 un il hardcover o.p. pa $6.99

Grades: K 1 2 3　　　　　　　　　　　　**398.2**

1. Fairy tales 2. Birds -- Folklore 3. Folklore -- Russia

ISBN 0-399-23168-4; 0-698-11922-3 pa

LC 98-16353

In this variation on the story of "The Fisherman and His Wife," a young Ukrainian girl must repeatedly return to the wren she has rescued to relay her parents' increasingly greedy demands

"Polacco's signature illustrations are lush and vibrant. The regal colors of royal blue and crimson play against deep green, dappled brown, and ocher of the natural world." SLJ

Poole, Amy Lowry

★ **How** the rooster got his crown; retold and illustrated by Amy Lowry Poole. Holiday House 1999 un il $15.95

Grades: K 1 2 3　　　　　　　　　　　　**398.2**

1. Folklore -- China 2. Roosters -- Folklore

ISBN 0-8234-1389-6

LC 98-12311

In the early days of the world, when the sun refuses to come out for fear of a skillful archer's arrows, a small rooster saves the day by coaxing the sun out with his crowing

"The illustrations reflect the traditions of ancient scroll paintings; the pacing of the story is synchronized with the pictures so that the visual and verbal elements form a seamless unit." Horn Book Guide

Pringle, Laurence P.

Imagine a dragon; [by] Laurence Pringle; illustrated by Eujin Kim Neilan. Boyds Mills Press 2008 un il $16.95

Grades: 3 4 5　　　　　　　　　　　　**398.2**

1. Dragons

ISBN 978-1-56397-328-4; 1-56397-328-6

LC 2007017575

This is a history of dragons in various world cultures

"The book is interesting with lots of materials without being overwhelming. It provides a good introduction to dragon myths in world literature. The pictures, done in acrylic, are strong and powerful." Libr Media Connect

Pullman, Philip, 1946-

★ **Aladdin** and the enchanted lamp; retold by Philip Pullman; illustrated by Sophy Williams. Arthur A. Levine Books 2005 67p il $16.95

Grades: 3 4 5 **398.2**
1. Fairy tales 2. Arabs -- Folklore
ISBN 0-439-69255-5

LC 2004-8586

Recounts the tale of a poor tailor's son who becomes a wealthy prince with the help of a magic lamp he finds in an enchanted cave

"Pullman's spin on Aladdin's serendipitous adventures is satisfyingly festooned with exotic vocabulary and details. He also enlivens the telling with knowing wit. . . . Williams' numerous paintings follow Pullman's lead, with a bazaar of burnished colors and dramatic, imagination-tickling scenes." Booklist

Puttapipat, Niroot
The **musicians** of Bremen; a brothers Grimm tale. retold and illustrated by Niroot Puttapipat. Candlewick Press 2005 un il $15.99
Grades: K 1 2 3 **398.2**
1. Animals -- Folklore 2. Folklore -- Germany 3. Folklore -- Germany -- Juvenile literature
ISBN 0-7636-2758-5

LC 2005-46907

While on their way to Bremen, four aging animals who are no longer of any use to their masters find a new home after outwitting a gang of robbers

"Puttipipat makes music the strong focus of this lively version of the old Grimm folktale. . . . The dramatic ink-and-watercolor illustrations show the characters as real barnyard animals." Booklist

Quattlebaum, Mary
Sparks fly high; the legend of Dancing Point. retold by Mary Quattlebaum; pictures by Leonid Gore. Farrar, Straus & Giroux 2006 un il $16
Grades: K 1 2 3 **398.2**
1. Dance -- Folklore 2. Devil -- Folklore 3. Contests -- Folklore 4. Folklore -- Virginia 5. Folklore -- Virginia -- Juvenile literature
ISBN 978-0-374-34452-8; 0-374-34452-3

When Colonel Lightfoot and the devil hold a lengthy dance contest to see who will control a plot of land along the James River in Virginia, the result is a surprise for both participants

"Gore's textured illustrations convey the story's energy and comedy in beautifully composed scenes. . . . What really shines here, though, are the folksy words, which have all the infectious rhythm of a country dance." Booklist

Ramsden, Ashley
Seven fathers; retold by Ashley Ramsden; illustrated by Ed Young. Roaring Brook Press 2011 32p il $16.99
Grades: 2 3 4 5 **398.2**
1. Fairy tales 2. Folklore -- Norway 3. Fathers -- Folklore 4. Old age -- Folklore
ISBN 978-1-59643-544-5; 1-59643-544-5

LC 2010009674

A lone traveler, tired, hungry, and cold, finds a house and asks for a room for the night, but the old man to whom he speaks refers him to his father, and that man to his father, until he is finally rewarded for his efforts by the eldest.

"Striking collage art accompanies a fluid retelling of a lesser-known Norwegian folktale. . . . Young's minimalist yet highly expressive illustrations use a strong black line to

artfully convey the wintry setting and the stranger's encounters with the fathers." SLJ

Rascol, Sabina I.
★ The **impudent** rooster; adapted by Sabina I. Rascol; illustrated by Holly Berry. Dutton Children's Books 2004 un il $16.99
Grades: K 1 2 3 **398.2**
1. Roosters 2. Folklore -- Romania 3. Roosters -- Folklore
ISBN 0-525-47179-0

LC 2003-53141

Using his amazing swallowing ability, a rooster foils the evil plans of a greedy nobleman and brings back riches to his poor master.

"The language flows smoothly and reads aloud well. The large folk-art paintings, done in watercolors and colored pencils, depict brightly clothed characters, detailed backdrops, and a hero who grows in stature along with his deeds." SLJ

Ray, Jane
Snow White. Candlewick Press 2009 un il $19.99
Grades: 3 4 5 **398.2**
1. Fairy tales 2. Pop-up books 3. Folklore -- Germany
ISBN 978-0-7636-4473-4; 0-7636-4473-0

LC 2009007774

Retells, in six dioramas with accompanying text, the tale of the beautiful princess whose lips were red as blood, skin was white as snow, and hair was black as ebony.

"Unusual paper engineering makes this a particularly memorable version of the familiar tale. . . . Birds, squirrels, and other wildlife join viewers in looking through a die-cut screen of trees (or in interior scenes an archway) at gracefully posed, richly clad figures. The jewel-like colors, as well as Ray's almond-eyed Snow White and dusky-skinned Prince, give the tale an otherworldly air." SLJ

Robbins, Ruth
Baboushka and the three kings; illustrated by Nicolas Sidjakov; adapted from a Russian folk tale. Houghton Mifflin 1960 un il $16; pa $6.95
Grades: 1 2 3 4 **398.2**
1. Folklore -- Russia 2. Christmas -- Folklore
ISBN 0-395-27673-X; 0-395-42647-2 pa
First published by Parnassus Press
Awarded The Caldecott Medal, 1961

A retelling of the Christmas legend about the old woman who declined to accompany the three kings on their search for the Christ Child and has ever since then searched for the Child on her own. Each year as she renews her search she leaves gifts at the homes she visits, acting, in this respect, as a Russian equivalent to Santa Claus

"Mystery and dignity are in the retelling. . . . At the end of the book is the story in verse set to original music." Horn Book

Rohmer, Harriet
Uncle Nacho's hat; adapted by Harriet Rohmer; illustrations by Veg Reisberg; Spanish version, Rosalma Zubizarreta. Children's Bk. Press 1989 31p il hardcover o.p. pa $7.95
Grades: K 1 2 3 **398.2**
1. Folklore -- Nicaragua 2. Bilingual books -- English-

Spanish
ISBN 0-89239-112-X pa

LC 88-37090

"Adaptation of a Nicaraguan folktale. . . . When his niece, Ambrosia, gives Uncle Nacho a new hat, he tries unsuccessfully several times to get rid of the old, holey one. Seeing him dejected because his hat keeps coming back, Ambrosia suggests he put his mind on the new one instead. Flattened primitive paintings in brilliant, clear tropical colors and motifs enhance the fun of this comedy of errors." Helbig. This land is our land

Ross, Tony
My first nursery stories; selected and illustrated by Tony Ross. Andersen 2011 92p il $19.99
Grades: PreK K   **398.2**
   1. Folklore
   ISBN 978-1-84270-790-6; 1-84270-790-6
"Eight familiar favorites, including 'The Three Billy Goats Gruff,' 'Henny Penny,' 'Goldilocks,' and 'Jack and the Beanstalk,' appear here in a large-format edition. . . . The stories [are] nimbly told. . . . [Ross] integrates his cartoonlike drawings, full of action and bright colors, into the stories, often varying the typeface to increase the suspense. His exaggerated characters, full of motion and fun, will hold youngsters' attention." SLJ

Rounds, Glen
Ol' Paul, the mighty logger. Holiday House 1976 93p il hardcover o.p. pa $5.95
Grades: 3 4 5 6   **398.2**
   1. Bunyan, Paul (Legendary character)
   ISBN 0-8234-0713-6 pa
   First published 1936

Rumford, James
★ Beowulf; a hero's tale retold. Houghton Mifflin Company 2007 un il $17
Grades: 4 5 6 7   **398.2**
   1. Folklore -- Europe 2. Monsters -- Folklore
   ISBN 0-618-75637-X; 978-0-618-75637-7
A simplified and illustrated retelling of the exploits of the Anglo-Saxon warrior, Beowulf, and how he came to defeat the monster Grendel, Grendel's mother, and a dragon that threatened the kingdom.
"Superb on all counts—from the elegant bookmaking to the vigorous, evocative prose . . . to the pen-and-ink and watercolor illustrations that strikingly recall the work of Edmund Dulac." Horn Book

Ryan, Pam Munoz
Nacho and Lolita; illustrated by Claudia Rueda. Scholastic Press 2005 un il $16.99
Grades: 2 3 4   **398.2**
   1. Folklore -- Mexico 2. Swallows -- Folklore
   ISBN 0-439-26968-7

LC 2004-793

A very rare pitacochi bird falls in love with a swallow and plucks his colorful feathers to transform dry, barren San Juan Capistrano into a haven of flowers and flowing water, which the swallows can easily find when returning from their annual migration
"Ryan's cozy storytelling will draw listeners close, and the Colombian-born illustrator cleverly exploits the contrast between the drought-scarred backdrops and Nacho's brilliance to achieve a vibrancy that is unusual in colored-pencil illustrations." Booklist

Rylant, Cynthia
Hansel and Gretel; pictures by Jen Corace. Hyperion Books for Children 2008 un il $16.99
Grades: K 1 2   **398.2**
   1. Folklore 2. Fairy tales 3. Folklore -- Germany -- Juvenile literature
   ISBN 978-1-4231-1186-3; 1-4231-1186-9
A retelling of the well-known tale in which two children lost in the woods find their way home despite an encounter with a wicked witch who wants to eat them.
"The language is forceful and direct throughout. . . . Complementing this retelling, Corace's pen-and-ink artwork features neutral hues and sober-faced children." SLJ

Sabuda, Robert
Beauty & the beast; a pop-up book of the classic fairy tale. Little Simon 2010 un il $29.99
Grades: 1 2 3 4   **398.2**
   1. Folklore 2. Fairy tales 3. Pop-up books
   ISBN 978-1-4169-6079-9; 1-4169-6079-1
"Paper-craft-pro Sabuda extends the familiar fairy tale into a moody 3-D romance that captures, in particular, the mystery and opulence of the Beast's castle. . . . Shrewdly designed mini books package the lengthy, smoothly phrased text." Booklist

Sage, Alison
★ Rapunzel; [illustrations by] Sarah Gibb; based on the original story by the Brothers Grimm. Albert Whitman 2011 un il $16.99
Grades: 1 2 3 4   **398.2**
   1. Folklore 2. Fairy tales
   ISBN 978-0-8075-6804-0; 0-8075-6804-X
Beautiful Rapunzel is locked away in a tall, tall tower, visited only by the little creatures of the forest and the witch who has imprisoned her. Until one day a handsome prince, passing by on his horse, is transfixed by the magical sound of Rapunzel singing to her animals friends and knows he must reach her.
"Reminiscent of elaborate embroidery or tapestries, the pictures create and sustain the tale's magical atmosphere. . . . Children and adults alike will be spellbound, poring over the pages again and again, delighting each time in new details and discoveries." Kirkus

Sakade, Florence
Japanese children's favorite stories; compiled by Florence Sakade; illustrated by Yoshisuke Kurosaki. 3rd ed; Tuttle 2003 109p il $16.95
Grades: 2 3 4   **398.2**
   1. Tales -- Japan 2. Folklore -- Japan
   ISBN 0-8048-3449-0
   First published 1953
A collection of Japanese folktales.
"This enduring collection presents 20 stories to enchant and enlighten young readers. . . . Minor text revisions have little effect on the stories. . . . The text remains simple, clear, and accessible to beginning readers and storytellers alike. The 'sparkling new color illustrations' are simply Kurosaki's

original stylized scenes, repainted in bright dabs of watercolor." SLJ

San Souci, Robert

As luck would have it; from the Brothers Grimm. [by] Robert D. San Souci; illustrated by Daniel San Souci. August House/Little Folk 2008 un il $16.95

Grades: K 1 2 3 4 **398.2**

1. Folklore -- Germany

ISBN 978-0-87483-833-6; 0-87483-833-9

LC 2008000965

"Lively, comical illustrations enhance the abundant droll humor in this noodle-head tale that plays off the Grimm Brothers' 'Clever Elsie.' . . . The expressive, lucent watercolors highlighted with Prismacolor pencils portray the foolish escapades adeptly, and the anthropomorphized animal characters evocatively represent human characteristics and foibles." SLJ

★ **Cendrillon**; a Caribbean Cinderella. [by] Robert D. San Souci; illustrated by Brian Pinkney. Simon & Schuster Bks. for Young Readers 1998 un il hardcover o.p. pa $8.99

Grades: K 1 2 3 **398.2**

1. Fairy tales 2. Folklore -- Martinique

ISBN 0-689-80668-X; 0-689-84888-9 pa

LC 96-53142

A Creole variant of the familiar Cinderella tale set in Martinique and narrated by the godmother who helps Cendrillon find true love

"The narrative is full of French Creole words and phrases. . . . A fruit`a pain   (breadfruit) is transformed into the coach; six agoutis (a kind of rodent) become the horses. . . . Pinkney's art perfectly conveys the lush beauty and atmosphere of the island setting." SLJ

★ **Cut** from the same cloth; American women of myth, legend, and tall tale. collected and told by Robert D. San Souci; illustrated by Brian Pinkney; introduction by Jane Yolen. Philomel Bks. 1993 140p il hardcover o.p. pa $6.99

Grades: 4 5 6 7 **398.2**

1. Tall tales 2. Women -- Folklore 3. Folklore -- United States

ISBN 0-399-21987-0; 0-698-11811-1 pa

LC 92-5233

A collection of fifteen stories about legendary American women from Anglo-American, African American, and Native American folklore

"San Souci's language is vigorous and action verbs abound; Pinkney's black-and-white block prints match the strength of the telling. The inclusion of notes on the sources and a general bibliography make this an academic resource as well as a good collection of rolicking stories." Child Book Rev Serv

Little Gold Star; a Spanish American Cinderella tale. retold by Robert D. San Souci; illustrated by Sergio Martinez. HarperCollins Pubs. 2000 un il $15.95; lib bdg $15.89

Grades: 2 3 4 **398.2**

1. Fairy tales 2. Folklore -- Southern States 3. Hispanic Americans -- Folklore

ISBN 0-688-14780-1; 0-688-14781-X lib bdg

LC 99-50290

A Spanish American retelling of the familiar story of a kind girl who is mistreated by her jealous stepmother and stepsisters. In this version, the Virgin Mary replaces the traditional fairy godmother

"Martinez' watercolors depict homes with Spanish architectural influences in an arid, southwest desert landscape; his characters have lively, expressive faces and evocative body language. . . . This is effective fairy-tale magic transported to new terrain." Bull Cent Child Books

★ **Robin** Hood and the golden arrow; retold by Robert D. San Souci; illustrations by E.B. Lewis. Orchard Books 2010 un il $17.99

Grades: K 1 2 3 **398.2**

1. Robin Hood (Legendary character) 2. Folklore -- Great Britain

ISBN 978-0-439-62538-8; 0-439-62538-6

LC 2009015624

Retells, in easy text, of the Sheriff of Nottingham's plot to hold an archery contest in order to capture the outlaw Robin Hood, but Robin and his band of merry men arrive in disguise with a plan of their own.

"Lewis draws young readers in with the splendid cover image of Robin. . . . The watercolor pictures, reminiscent of both Pyle and N. C. Wyeth, are full of mottled greens and dappled light, with powerful figures running, shooting arrows or standing nobly. It is a feast to look upon." Kirkus

The **secret** of the stones; a folktale. retold by Robert D. San Souci; pictures by James Ransome. Phyllis Fogelman Bks. 2000 un il $16.99

Grades: K 1 2 3 **398.2**

1. African Americans 2. Folklore -- United States 3. African Americans -- Folklore

ISBN 0-8037-1640-0

LC 93-43952

When they try to find out who is doing their chores while they are working in the field, a childless couple discovers that the two stones they have brought home are actually two bewitched orphans

"Based on a tale found in both the Bantu and African-American cultures . . . the clearly told tale (which includes dialect in the dialogue) is accompanied by expressive, deep-toned illustrations." Horn Book Guide

Short & shivery; thirty chilling tales. retold by Robert D. San Souci; illustrated by Katherine Coville. Doubleday 1987 175p il hardcover o.p. pa $5.50

Grades: 4 5 6 7 **398.2**

1. Folklore 2. Ghost stories

ISBN 0-440-41804-6 pa

LC 86-29067

"A collection of spooky stories, competently adapted and retold (sometimes quite freely) from world folklore, including Japan, Africa, and Latin America, as well as Europe and the U.S. . . . The stories drawn from collections of regional American folklore are not only the freshest, but often the scariest. Sources are fully documented. . . . There are some delicious shivers here, with plenty of fodder for an active imagination, as well as excitement." SLJ

★ **Sister** tricksters; rollicking tales of clever females. retold by Robert D. San Souci; illustrated by Daniel San Souci. August House Pubs. 2006 69p il $19.95
Grades: 3 4 5 6   **398.2**
1. Animals -- Folklore 2. Folklore -- Southern States 3. Folklore -- Juvenile literature
ISBN 978-0-87483-791-9; 0-87483-791-X

LC 2006-40793

"These eight stories, featuring characters like Molly Cottontail, Miz Grasshopper, and Miz Goose, are energetically retold from Anne Virginia Culbertsons long out-of-print At the Big House (Bobbs-Merrill, 1904). . . . Delicious dialect and expressions convey a rural Southern flavor, yet the text is never hard to read or understand. . . . Stunning, richly colored, detailed, and playful paintings showing animals dressed in lavish finery introduce each lively tale." SLJ

Sootface; an Ojibwa Cinderella story. retold by Robert D. San Souci; illustrated by Daniel San Souci. Doubleday Bks. for Young Readers 1994 un il hardcover o.p. pa $6.99
Grades: 1 2 3 4   **398.2**
1. Ojibwa Indians -- Folklore
ISBN 0-440-41363-X pa

LC 93-10553

Although she is mocked and mistreated by her two older sisters, Sootface, an Ojibwa Indian maiden, wins a mighty invisible warrior for her husband with her kind and honest heart

"The San Souci version reads aloud well, and the water-color artwork illustrates the story with quiet grace." Booklist

★ **Sukey** and the mermaid; [by] Robert D. San Souci; illustrated by Brian Pinkney. Four Winds Press 1992 un il hardcover o.p. pa $5.95
Grades: 1 2 3 4   **398.2**
1. Mermaids and mermen 2. African Americans -- Folklore 3. African Americans -- Folklore -- Juvenile literature
ISBN 0-02-778141-0; 0-689-80718-X pa

LC 90-24559

Unhappy with her life at home, Sukey receives kindness and wealth from Mama Jo the mermaid

San Souci "outdoes himself here with pungent, lyrical prose that reverberates with the cadences of the South Carolina islands. . . . The supple lines of Pinkney's fluid scratchboard technique capture the grace and spirit of this magical tale and serve as the perfect foil to its darker undertones." Publ Wkly

★ The **talking** eggs; a folktale from the American South. retold by Robert D. San Souci; pictures by Jerry Pinkney. Dial Bks. for Young Readers 1989 un il $16
Grades: K 1 2 3   **398.2**
1. Folklore -- Southern States 2. Folklore -- United States -- Juvenile literature
ISBN 0-8037-0619-7

LC 88-33469

A Caldecott Medal honor book, 1990

A Southern folktale in which kind Blanche, following the instructions of an old witch, gains riches, while her greedy sister makes fun of the old woman and is duly rewarded

"Adapted from a Creole folk tale originally included in a collection of Louisiana stories by folklorist Alcee Fortier, this tale captures the flavor of the nineteenth-century South in its language and story line. . . . Jerry Pinkney's watercolors are chiefly responsible for the excellence of the book; his characters convey their moods with vivid facial expressions." Horn Book

Sanderson, Ruth
Goldilocks; retold and illustrated by Ruth Sanderson. Little, Brown Books for Young Readers 2009 un il $16.99
Grades: K 1 2 3   **398.2**
1. Folklore 2. Bears -- Folklore
ISBN 978-0-316-77885-5; 0-316-77885-0

LC 2008045298

After finding the bears' cottage in the woods and making a mess inside, Goldilocks helps the family clean up and enjoys a nice meal

"The artist warms her version of this oft-told tale with lavish accoutrements, costumes, and furniture that suggest a Scandinavian setting, which will entice viewers to explore the far corners of the pages. . . . The large, richly colored images make this an ideal classroom read-aloud, and Mama Bear's recipe for blueberry muffins offers a nice finishing touch." SLJ

Sanfield, Steve
The **adventures** of High John the Conqueror; [illustrated by John Ward] August House 1995 113p il hardcover o.p. pa $11.95
Grades: 4 5 6 7   **398.2**
1. Folklore -- United States 2. African Americans -- Folklore
ISBN 0-87483-433-3; 0-87483-774-X pa

LC 95-35825

A reissue of the title first published 1988 by Orchard Books

A collection of folk tales about High John the Conqueror, the traditional trickster hero of blacks during and immediately after the time of slavery

"Simply told in language comprehensible to very young readers, these tales are short, funny, and entertaining. . . . Fourteen full-page black-and-white pencil drawings illustrate some of the more dramatic moments in the stories." SLJ

Includes bibliographical references

Schlitz, Laura Amy
★ The **Bearskinner**; a tale of the Brothers Grimm. retold by Laura Amy Schlitz; illustrated by Max Grafe. Candlewick Press 2007 un il $16.99
Grades: 3 4 5 6   **398.2**
1. Fairy tales 2. Folklore -- Germany
ISBN 978-0-7636-2730-0; 0-7636-2730-5

LC 2007-22787

A retelling of the Grimm fairy tale in which a despondent soldier makes a pact to do the devil's bidding for seven years in return for as much money and property as he could ever want

"Schlitz narrates with clarity, grace, and sensitivity. . . . Except for the devil's coat of darkest green, Grafe's atmospheric full-page illustrations are almost monochromatic. . . . A provocative edition that should set older children thinking about the meaning of endurance and heroism." Horn Book

Schram, Peninnah

The **magic** pomegranate; by Peninnah Schram; illustrated by Melanie Hall. Millbrook Press 2008 48p il (On my own folklore) lib bdg $25.26; pa $6.95

Grades: 1 2 3 4   **398.2**

1. Fairy tales 2. Jews -- Folklore 3. Pomegranates -- Folklore

ISBN 978-0-8225-6742-4 lib bdg; 0-8225-6742-3 lib bdg; 978-0-8225-6746-2 pa; 0-8225-6746-6 pa

LC 2006036722

Three handsome and clever brothers compete to find the world's most unusual gift. Includes a note on doing good deeds, or mitzvah, and discusses the symbolism of the pomegranate in Judaism

The "tale is paired with an illustration style that nicely reflects the culture." Horn Book Guide

Includes bibliographical references

Schwartz, Alvin, 1927-1992

★ **All** of our noses are here, and other noodle tales; retold by Alvin Schwartz; pictures by Karen Ann Weinhaus. Harper & Row 1985 64p il (I can read book) lib bdg $15.89

Grades: K 1 2   **398.2**

1. Folklore 2. Wit and humor

ISBN 0-06-025288-X

LC 84-48330

This companion volume to There is a carrot in my ear, and other noodle tales, contains additional stories about members of the Brown family

"The illustrations show them looking very much like mice and always smiling and cheerful. Cousins, no doubt, to the Stupids, the family is bound to be as appealing to young readers. With a list of sources." Horn Book

★ **Ghosts!** ghostly tales from folklore. retold by Alvin Schwartz; illustrated by Victoria Chess. HarperCollins Pubs. 1991 63p il (I can read book) lib bdg $15.89; pa $3.95

Grades: K 1 2   **398.2**

1. Folklore 2. Ghost stories

ISBN 0-06-021797-9 lib bdg; 0-06-444170-9 pa

LC 90-21746

Presents seven, easy-to-read ghost stories based on traditional folk tales and legends from various countries

"All of the pen-and-watercolor illustrations are tidy and cheery and creepy. . . . Retold in a style that is simple but not choppy . . . and accompanied by a page of brief notes, all the tales will lend themselves to elaboration and innovation." Bull Cent Child Books

I saw you in the bathtub, and other folk rhymes; collected by Alvin Schwartz; pictures by Syd Hoff. Harper & Row 1989 64p il (I can read book) hardcover o.p. pa $3.99

Grades: K 1 2   **398.2**

1. Folklore

ISBN 0-06-444151-2 pa

LC 88-16111

Presents an illustrated collection of traditional folk rhymes, some composed by children

"Kids may be surprised to see their recess yells on the printed page but will relish the confirmation of significance. Hoff's full-color cartoons interpret the rhymes literally, an approach that leads to some pretty surreal results." Bull Cent Child Books

★ **In** a dark, dark room, and other scary stories; retold by Alvin Schwartz; illustrated by Dirk Zimmer. Harper & Row 1984 63p il (I can read book) $15.95; pa $3.95

Grades: K 1 2   **398.2**

1. Folklore 2. Ghost stories 3. Horror fiction

ISBN 0-06-025271-5; 0-06-444090-7 pa

LC 83-47699

This is a collection of "seven traditional tales from around the world retold in simple yet effective language. . . . The chill here springs from suspense, an eerie setting or a ghostly surprise, rather than from blood and gore. Though pared down somewhat from longer versions, the stories retain their genuine creepiness. . . . The colorfully dark illustrations are sinister without being gruesome and add a comic touch." SLJ

★ **More** scary stories to tell in the dark; collected from folklore and retold by Alvin Schwartz; illustrated by Brett Helquist. Reillustrated Harper Trophy ed Harper 2010 111 p. ill. (hardcover) $15.99

Grades: 4 5 6 7   **398.2**

1. Ghost stories 2. Horror fiction 3. Folklore -- United States

ISBN 9780060835217; 0060835214

LC 2010922248

Originally published in 1984 by Lippincott, with illustrations by Stephen Gammell.

This volume contains stories of ghosts, murders, graveyards and other horrors.

"Helquist's new illustrations for Schwartz's classic [collection] of ghost stories inhabit an altogether more benign universe than the nightmarish Stephen Gammell originals. [This edition is] handsome and accessible, ceding the stories themselves pride of place." Horn Book Guide

Includes bibliographical references (pages 105-111).

★ **Scary** stories 3; more tales to chill your bones. collected from folklore and retold by Alvin Schwartz; drawings by Stephen Gammell. HarperCollins Pubs. 1991 115p il music $15.99; lib bdg $16.89; pa $5.99

Grades: 4 5 6 7   **398.2**

1. Ghost stories 2. Horror fiction 3. Folklore -- United States

ISBN 0-06-021794-4; 0-06-021795-2 lib bdg; 0-06-440418-8 pa

LC 90-47474

Traditional and modern-day stories of ghosts, haunts, superstitions, monsters, and horrible scary things

"The book is well paced and continually captivates, surprises, and entices audiences into reading just one more page. Gammell's gauzy, cobwebby, black-and-white pen-and-ink drawings help to sustain the overall creepy mood." SLJ

Includes bibliographical references

★ **There** is a carrot in my ear, and other noodle tales; retold by Alvin Schwartz; pictures by Karen Ann Weinhaus.

Harper & Row 1982 64p il (I can read book) hardcover o.p. pa $3.95

Grades: K 1 2 **398.2**

1. Folklore 2. Wit and humor

ISBN 0-06-025234-0; 0-06-444103-2 pa

LC 80-8442

This "is a collection of six stories from sources . . . as diverse as American 'Little Moron' stories, ancient Greek tales and vaudeville pieces. Explaining in his foreword that a 'noodle is a silly person,' reteller Alvin Schwartz goes on to introduce the noodly Brown family and reveal their various foibles. . . . Most of the stories don't appear in other beginning noodle collections and will provide laughs for readers who catch the puns and absurdities the stories hinge on. The drawings by Karen Ann Weinhaus . . . show funny, pointy-proboscised folk blissfully unaware of their own goofiness." SLJ

Schwartz, Howard

Before you were born; retold by Howard Schwartz; illustrated by Kristina Swarner. Roaring Brook Press 2005 un il $16.95

Grades: K 1 2 3 **398.2**

1. Jews -- Folklore

ISBN 1-59643-028-1

LC 2003-17845

Retells a folktale in which Lailah, a guardian angel, places the indentation that everyone has on the upper lip just before a baby is born

"In spare, serene language, Schwartz reshapes a rabbinic legend. . . . Swarner's ethereal, mixed-media illustrations illuminate the spirituality of the telling." Booklist

A **coat** for the moon and other Jewish tales; selected and retold by Howard Schwartz and Barbara Rush; illustrated by Michael Iofin. Jewish Publ. Soc. 1999 81p il hardcover o.p. pa $13

Grades: 4 5 6 7 **398.2**

1. Folklore 2. Tales 3. Jews -- Folklore

ISBN 0-8276-0596-X; 0-8276-0736-9 pa

LC 98-52704

A collection of Jewish folktales from around the world, including "The Lamp on the Mountain," "The Witch Barusha," "The Sabbath Walking Stick," and "The Fisherman and the Silver Fish"

"These tales incorporate everything from the magical to the bizarre, all the while imparting specific Jewish values that have transcended time and cultural dispersion. . . . Each retelling opens with a delightfully detailed pen-and-ink illustration encircled by a key sentence or phrase from the text that gives a hint of what's to come." SLJ

A **journey** to paradise and other Jewish tales; retold by Howard Schwartz; illustrated by Giora Carmi. Pitspopany Press 2000 48p il $16.95; pa $9.95

Grades: 3 4 5 **398.2**

1. Jews -- Folklore

ISBN 0-943706-21-1; 0-943706-16-5 pa

"This collection of traditional tales from the world's far-flung Jewish community is ably selected by a well-known scholar. . . . The volume is abundantly illustrated with both spot and full-spread drawings in subdued colors." Horn Book Guide

Includes bibliographical references

Scott, Nathan Kumar

The **sacred** banana leaf; an Indonesian trickster tale. by Nathan Kumar Scott; illustrated by Radhashyam Raut. Tara 2008 un il $16.95

Grades: 2 3 4 **398.2**

1. Animals -- Folklore 2. Folklore -- Indonesia

ISBN 978-81-86211-28-1; 81-86211-28-4

"Scott's retelling has verve and humor, and the illustrations, rendered in patachitra (a traditional style of temple painting originating in eastern India) are both accessible and graceful. Saturated colors gleam from sand-toned pages, and the patterned skins of the clearly delineated animals add texture." Booklist

Seeger, Pete

★ **Abiyoyo**; based on a South African lullaby and folk story. text by Pete Seeger; illustrations by Michael Hays. Simon & Schuster Bks. for Young Readers 2001 un il $19.95; pa $6.99

Grades: K 1 2 3 **398.2**

1. Giants -- Folklore 2. Folklore -- South Africa

ISBN 0-689-84693-2; 0-689-71810-1 pa

A reissue of the title first published 1986 by Macmillan

Banished from the town for making mischief, a little boy and his father are welcomed back when they make the giant Abiyoyo disappear

"Told in the familiar Seeger style, with brief musical phrases of the one-word song incorporated in the text and printed complete at the end, and with illustrations full of light and color, this rendering of a South African tale is a pleasure. The giant is imposing but not too scary for the youngest listener leaning over the book while a parent tells the story." N Y Times Book Rev

Shannon, George

★ **More** stories to solve; fifteen folktales from around the world. told by George Shannon; illustrated by Peter Sís. Greenwillow Bks. 1991 64p il hardcover o.p. pa $4.99

Grades: 3 4 5 6 **398.2**

1. Riddles 2. Folklore

ISBN 0-688-09161-X; 0-380-73261-0 pa

"Shannon combines the folktale and the riddle in a brief collection that brings together 15 international stories." Booklist

Includes bibliographical references

Rabbit's gift; a fable from China. told by George Shannon; illustrated by Laura Dronzek. Harcourt 2007 un il $16

Grades: PreK K 1 **398.2**

1. Fables 2. Folklore -- China 3. Animals -- Folklore 4. Rabbits -- Folklore

ISBN 978-0-15-206073-2; 0-15-206073-1

LC 2006-04789

Woodland animals, each thinking of his neighbor, share a turnip left on their doorstep.

"The uncluttered illustrations, many framed in purple to compliment the purple of the turnip, perfectly capture the action of the story. The expressive faces of the animals are charming." Booklist

★ **Stories** to solve; folktales from around the world. illustrated by Peter Sís. Greenwillow Bks. 1985 55p il hardcover o.p. pa $4.99

Grades: 3 4 5 6 **398.2**

1. Riddles 2. Folklore

ISBN 0-688-04303-8; 0-380-73260-2 pa

LC 84-18656

"Each of these 14 delightful folktales is a short puzzle to be solced through cleverness, common sense or careful observations of details in the text. . . . Sis' pointillistic pen-and-ink drawings illustrate each puzzle, and sometimes clarify the solutions." SLJ

Sharpe, Leah Marinsky

★ The **goat**-faced girl; a classic Italian folktale. retold by Leah Marinsky Sharpe; illustrated by Jane Marinsky. David R. Godine 2009 un il $16.95

Grades: K 1 2 3 **398.2**

1. Fairy tales 2. Folklore -- Italy

ISBN 978-1-56792-393-3; 1-56792-393-3

LC 2009-22383

When Isabella, a beautiful but lazy young woman, agrees to marry an equally lazy prince, the sorceress who raised her gives her the head of a goat in hopes that she will learn to do things for herself.

"Rich storytelling and intricately imagined artwork make this debut a standout. . . . Marinsky's paintings, in the chalky, sun-bleached colors of the Italian renaissance, contain many small pleasures." Publ Wkly

Shelby, Anne

The **adventures** of Molly Whuppie and other Appalachian folktales; [by] Anne Shelby; illustrations by Paula McArdle. The University of North Carolina Press 2007 88p il $14.95

Grades: 4 5 6 7 **398.2**

1. Folklore -- Appalachian Mountains

ISBN 978-0-8078-3163-2

LC 2007013789

A collection of Appalachian folktales featuring Molly Whuppie and her adventures.

"Shelby has captured the language of Appalachia. . . . Her adaptations are true to the traditional folktales. . . . Young readers and listeners will make these stories their own and enjoy retelling them." SLJ

Includes bibliographical references

Shepard, Aaron

★ One-**Eye!** Two-Eyes! Three-Eyes! a very Grimm fairy tale. pictures by Gary Clement. Atheneum Books for Young Readers 2007 un il $16.95

Grades: K 1 2 3 **398.2**

1. Folklore 2. Fairy tales 3. Folklore -- Juvenile literature

ISBN 978-0-689-86740-8; 0-689-86740-9

LC 2005-00459

A retelling of the Grimm's fairy tale about a little girl who has two eyes and is horribly teased by her sisters who have one and three eyes respectively.

"The alterations to the story are consistent with the lighthearted watercolor-and-pencil illustrations. . . . Children will enjoy the humor in this reincarnation, and it will make excellent fodder for reader's theater, with a script available on the author's Web site." SLJ

★ The **princess** mouse; a tale of Finland. told by Aaron Shepard; illustrated by Leonid Gore. Atheneum Bks. for Young Readers 2003 un il hardcover o.p. pa $13.99

Grades: K 1 2 3 **398.2**

1. Fairy tales 2. Mice -- Folklore 3. Folklore -- Finland

ISBN 0-689-82912-4; 1-4169-8969-2 pa

LC 2001-55273

A retelling of a Finnish folk tale about a young man who plans to marry his mouse sweetheart

"Shepard's charmingly droll version of a Finnish folktale combines classic elements with unexpected, witty details. . . . The jewel-toned art has beautiful luminescence; the elongated, somewhat blocky look of the characters reinforces the fantasy; and the mice are downright irresistible." Booklist

The **sea** king's daughter; a Russian legend. retold by Aaron Shepard; illustrated by Gennady Spirin. Atheneum Bks. for Young Readers 1997 28p il pa $11.99

Grades: 3 4 5 6 **398.2**

1. Folklore -- Russia 2. Musicians -- Folklore

ISBN 0-689-80759-7; 0-689-84259-7 pa

LC 96-3391

A talented musician from Novgorod plays so well that the Sea King wants him to marry one of his daughters

"The telling is descriptive yet very accessible, with the art, in Spirin's majestic signature style, evoking both the mythical feel of the legend and the folk-music roots from which the story sprang." Booklist

Sherman, Pat

The **sun's** daughter; a story based on an Iroquois legend. illustrated by R. Gregory Christie. Clarion Bks. 2005 31p il $16

Grades: 2 3 4 **398.2**

1. Iroquois Indians -- Folklore

ISBN 0-618-32430-5

LC 2004-17820

"Inspired by Iroquois tales of the Corn Maiden and her sisters, this original story tells how Maize, Red Bean, and Pumpkin walked the earth spreading a bounty of food in their wake. . . . The story is charmingly told with eloquent phrasing and vocabulary. The artwork, done in a folk-art style, is energetic and exuberant, and the brush strokes are used to dramatic effect across the spreads." SLJ

Shulevitz, Uri

★ The **treasure**. Farrar, Straus & Giroux 1978 un il hardcover o.p. pa $6.95

Grades: K 1 2 3 **398.2**

1. Folklore

ISBN 0-374-37740-5; 0-374-47955-0 pa

A Caldecott Medal honor book, 1980

"Although the story is known in many cultures the retelling suggests the Hassidic tradition. . . . The eastern European influence is extended in the illustrations." Horn Book

Sierra, Judy

Can you guess my name? traditional tales around the world. selected and retold by Judy Sierra; illustrated by Stefano Vitale. Clarion Bks. 2002 110p il $20

Grades: 3 4 5 6 **398.2**

1. Folklore 2. Tales

ISBN 0-618-13328-3

LC 2002-3509

A collection of fifteen folktales from all over the world, including stories that resemble "The Three Pigs," "The Bremen Town Musicians," "Rumpelstiltskin," "The Frog Prince," and "Hansel and Gretel"

"All of the selections have dramatic dialogue and repetitive phrases and refrains, and are easy to learn. . . . Vitale's engaging folk illustrations are painted on wood. . . . This collection provides a fascinating experience with comparative literature, one that can open doors to other cultures. A must purchase for most collections." SLJ

Includes bibliographical references

★ **Nursery** tales around the world; selected and retold by Judy Sierra; illustrated by Stefano Vitale. Clarion Bks. 1996 114p il $20
Grades: K 1 2 3 4 5   **398.2**
   1. Folklore
   ISBN 0-395-67894-3
                     LC 93-2068
Presents eighteen simple stories from international folklore, grouped around six themes, such as "Runaway Cookies," "Slowpokes and Speedsters," and "Chain Tales." Includes background information and storytelling hints

"This richly illustrated compendium of folktales does double duty as a nursery story book for lap-sharing and as a sourcebook for parents and professionals. . . . Most entries feature strong rhythms and repetition that invite audience participation and develop memory. . . . Top this engaging text with Vitale's lavish oil-on-wood ethnic borders, motif vignettes, and full-page illustrations, and you have a handsome work to be valued by readers and treasured by listeners." Bull Cent Child Books

Includes bibliographical references

The **gift** of the Crocodile; a Cinderella story. illustrated by Reynold Ruffins. Simon & Schuster Bks. for Young Readers 2000 un il $17
Grades: K 1 2 3   **398.2**
   1. Fairy tales 2. Folklore -- Indonesia
   ISBN 0-689-82188-3
                    LC 98-40592
In this Indonesian version of the Cinderella story, a girl named Damura escapes her cruel stepmother and stepsister and marries a handsome prince with the help of Grandmother Crocodile

"Sierra's unadorned retelling is straightforward. . . . Ruffins's brightly colored, patterned paintings, with their angular figures and wavy landscapes, express and evoke the story's island setting." Horn Book

Silverman, Erica
Raisel's riddle; story by Erica Silverman; pictures by Susan Gaber. Farrar, Straus & Giroux 1999 un il hardcover o.p. pa $5.95
Grades: K 1 2 3   **398.2**
   1. Fairy tales 2. Jews -- Folklore
   ISBN 0-374-36168-1; 0-374-46199-6 pa
                    LC 97-29421
A Jewish version of the Cinderella story, in which a poor but educated young woman captivates her "Prince Charming" a rabbi's son, at a Purim ball

"Gaber's softly stippled spreads evoke a quiet seriousness appropriate to this thoughtful retelling." Bull Cent Child Books

Singer, Isaac Bashevis
Zlateh the goat, and other stories; pictures by Maurice Sendak; translated from the Yiddish by the author and Elizabeth Shub. Harper & Row 1966 90p il $15.95; pa $6.95
Grades: 4 5 6 7   **398.2**
   1. Jews -- Folklore
   ISBN 0-06-028477-3; 0-06-440147-2 pa
   A Newbery Award honor book, 1967
"Seven tales drawn from middle-European Jewish village life, with illustrations which extend the humor and subtlety of the situations." Hodges. Books for Elem Sch Libr

Singh, Rina
Nearly nonsense; Hoja tales from Turkey. illustrated by Farida Zaman. Tundra Books 2011 48p il $17.95
Grades: 2 3 4 5   **398.2**
   1. Folklore -- Turkey
   ISBN 978-0-88776-974-0; 0-88776-974-8
"Turkey has a particularly vibrant oral tradition, and the stories of Nasrudin Hoja—a foolish/wise man—are legion and deservedly popular. . . . When he and his son take their donkey to market, they are ridiculed whether they ride, walk, or carry the animal on their backs, proving that you can't please everyone. When Hoja wears fancy clothing, he is treated more deferentially than when he wears patched clothing, so he 'feeds' his coat to show the error of his host's behavior. Lesser-known stories are also included. . . . These retellings are unembellished, but their humor and intention are clear." SLJ

Smith, Chris
★ **One** city, two brothers; written by Chris Smith, illustrated by Aurélia Fronty. Barefoot Books 2007 un il $16.99
Grades: 2 3 4   **398.2**
   1. Brothers -- Folklore 2. Folklore -- Middle East
   ISBN 978-1-846860-42-3
To settle an inheritance dispute between two brothers, King Solomon tells a tale of how Jerusalem came to be founded.

"Based on a folktale told by both Jews and Arabs, this picture book beautifully captures the spirit of brotherhood. . . . The accomplished folk-style artwork, in shades of verdant green, heavenly blue, and harvest orange . . . adds an air of peace and hope." Booklist

Snyder, Dianne
The **boy** of the three-year nap; illustrated by Allen Say. Houghton Mifflin 1988 32p il $16.95; pa $6.95
Grades: 1 2 3   **398.2**
   1. Folklore -- Japan
   ISBN 0-395-44090-4; 0-395-66957-X pa
                    LC 87-30674
A Caldecott Medal honor book, 1989
"Japan's contribution to the trickster folktale, in which a lazy son cons a rich man, only to be outsmarted by his own, even trickier mother. Lilting prose and shimmering illustrations combine in perfect harmony." SLJ

Souhami, Jessica
King Pom and the fox; [by] Jessica Souhami. Frances Lincoln 2007 un il $16.95

Grades: K 1 2 3 **398.2**
1. Folklore
ISBN 978-1-84507-478-4; 1-84507-478-5

"In this Chinese version of 'Puss in Boots,' a young man is called King Pom because he owns a grand pomegranate tree. When a fox is caught stealing its fruit, he strikes a bargain. The fox arranges for King Pom to be rescued from the river and presented to the Emperor as a rich man, unfortunately attacked by robbers. . . . Souhami's bright, uncluttered collages are made of Ingres papers adorned with watercolor, ink, and pencil and lightly positioned on creamy backgrounds. . . . The spareness of the text matches the simplicity of the artwork." SLJ

Mrs. McCool and the giant Cuhullin; an Irish tale. Holt & Co. 2002 un il $16.95
Grades: K 1 2 3 **398.2**
1. Giants -- Folklore 2. Folklore -- Ireland
ISBN 0-8050-6852-X

LC 2001-2884

The very clever Oona saves her husband, the giant Finn McCool, by outwitting Cuhullin, who seeks to prove that he is the strongest giant in the world by beating Finn

"Painted and cut-paper illustrations in bold colors and simple shapes echo the basic drama. This is a clever, amusing version of an oft-told story." Booklist

Sausages. Frances Lincoln Children's Books 2006 un il hardcover o.p. pa $8.95
Grades: PreK K 1 2 **398.2**
1. Folklore 2. Folklore -- Juvenile literature
ISBN 978-1-84507-397-8; 1-84507-397-5; 978-1-84507-601-6 pa; 1-84507-601-X pa

"In this vibrant retelling of the Grimms' The Three Wishes, brilliantly designed paper collages capture every trace of humor in this cautionary tale. . . . A woodcutter rescues an elf from a rosebush and is granted three wishes. . . . The woodcutter asks for sausages. His wife responds with an angry reply that leaves the sausages stuck on his nose, and, of course, the last wish must be used to remove them. The story begs to be read aloud or told—the language is rich with sound effects." SLJ

The **little,** little house. Frances Lincoln 2006 32p il $15.95
Grades: K 1 2 **398.2**
1. Jews -- Folklore
ISBN 1-84507-108-5

"A delightful retelling. . . . The vibrant colors and strong contrast of the cut-paper shapes against neutral backgrounds provide great visual energy. The simple yet dramatic text makes it especially well suited to reading aloud." SLJ

The **sticky** doll trap; a trickster tale. Frances Lincoln 2011 un il $17.95
Grades: K 1 2 3 **398.2**
1. Animals -- Folklore 2. Rabbits -- Folklore 3. Folklore -- West Africa
ISBN 978-1-84780-017-6; 1-84780-017-3

Although Hare did not help the other animals find water in a drought, he manages to trick his way to more than his share, so the other creatures decide to trap him with a huge gummy doll, in a West African version of a traditional trickster tale.

"Bright collages made from Ingres papers hand-painted with watercolor inks and graphite pencil depict the savannah wildlife and horizon. The text is conversational in tone, as told from a storyteller's perspective." SLJ

Spirin, Gennady
Goldilocks and the three bears; retold and illustrated by Gennady Spirin. Marshall Cavendish Children 2009 un il $17.99
Grades: PreK K 1 2 **398.2**
1. Folklore 2. Bears -- Folklore
ISBN 978-0-7614-5596-7; 0-7614-5596-5

LC 2008026984

A simplified retelling of the adventures of a little girl walking in the woods who finds the house of the three bears and helps herself to their belongings. Includes a note on the history of the tale

"Spirin's version of this classic pairs a simple, straightforward retelling with lush Renaissance costumes and elegant page designs. The bears, rendered in watercolor and colored pencil, are solid, realistic creatures, revealing sharp teeth and claws. . . . The setting is created with richly realized essentials: solid porridge bowls, carved chairs, ornate beds, a massive stucco and wood-trimmed dwelling. . . . This . . . will be embraced for its visual clarity and sumptuous style." SLJ

★ **Little** Red Riding Hood; adapted from the Brothers Grimm by Gennady Spirin. Marshall Cavendish 2010 un il $17.99
Grades: 2 3 4 **398.2**
1. Fairy tales 2. Wolves -- Folklore 3. Folklore -- Germany
ISBN 978-0-7614-5704-6; 0-7614-5704-6

A retelling of Little Red Riding Hood's encounter with a wicked wolf while visiting her grandmother.

"This classic Grimm tale has had many interpretations over the years, but Spirin's splendid version is inspired by the lavish Dutch paintings of the 17th century. The jacket, with windmills and Renaissance cathedral spires in the background, sets the scene. . . . Grandmother, who is garbed in lace and flounces, and the hunters with their long rifles and Cavalier hats fit well into the setting. . . . Spirin places his characters up front on the page against plentiful white space, giving intensity to the unfolding drama. A simply retold and richly illustrated addition." SLJ

★ The **tale** of the Firebird; translated by Tatiana Popova. Philomel Bks. 2002 32p il $16.99
Grades: 2 3 4 **398.2**
1. Fairy tales 2. Birds -- Folklore 3. Folklore -- Russia
ISBN 0-399-23584-1

LC 2001-36660

When Prince Ivan sets out to find the Firebird for his father the tsar, he must complete a series of tasks before obtaining the Firebird and winning the hand of a beautiful princess

"The storytelling is dramatic and controlled, the language rising and falling in a cadence that encourages reading aloud. . . . Detailed and dramatic, with a golden palette that echoes crown jewels, the illustrations have an adventurous fairy-tale sweep." Bull Cent Child Books

Stampler, Ann Redisch

Shlemazel and the remarkable spoon of Pohost; illustrated by Jacqueline M. Cohen. Clarion Books 2006 39p il $16

Grades: K 1 2 3   398.2

1. Jews -- Folklore

ISBN 978-0-618-36959-1; 0-618-36959-7

LC 2005023602

A retelling of an Eastern European Jewish tale in which Shlemazel, the laziest man in town, is tricked into believing that the lucky spoon given to him by a neighbor will bring him fortune and fame, if it is used in the right way

"Employing a lively Yiddish cadence, the text is a storyteller's delight, full of humor, hyperbole, and delicious adjectives that make it a pleasure to read aloud. Jewel-toned panoramic watercolors are infused with a joyful folkloric quality well suited to the story." SLJ

★ The **rooster** prince of Breslov; illustrated by Eugene Yelchin. Clarion Books 2010 un il $16.99

Grades: K 1 2 3   398.2

1. Jews -- Folklore 2. Roosters -- Folklore

ISBN 978-0-618-98974-4; 0-618-98974-9

In this variation of a Yiddish folktale, a spoiled prince has a fit and assumes the speech and mannerisms of a rooster until he is locked in a room for seven days with a frail grizzled old man.

"Yelchin underlines the story's subtlety and humor with expressively exaggerated poses and apt caricatures rendered in minimal line and vivid gouache. . . . Stampler spells out the moral . . . [in] witty, dialogue-based storytelling." Horn Book

Steptoe, John

★ **Mufaro's** beautiful daughters; an African tale. Lothrop, Lee & Shepard Bks. 1987 un il $15.95; lib bdg $15.89

Grades: K 1 2 3   398.2

1. Fairy tales 2. Folklore -- Africa

ISBN 0-688-04045-4; 0-688-04046-2 lib bdg

LC 84-7158

A Caldecott Medal honor book, 1988; Coretta Scott King Award for illustration, 1988; Boston Globe-Horn Book Award, picture book 1987

Mufaro's two beautiful daughters, one bad-tempered, one kind and sweet, go before the king, who is choosing a wife

"The pace of the text matches the rhythm of the illustrations—both move in dramatic unity to the climax. By changing perspective the artist not only captures the lush, rich background but also the personalities of the characters with revealing studies of their faces." Horn Book

★ The **story** of Jumping Mouse; a native American legend. retold and illustrated by John Steptoe. Lothrop, Lee & Shepard Bks. 1984 un il $15.95; pa $5.95

Grades: 1 2 3   398.2

1. Mice -- Folklore 2. Native Americans -- Folklore

ISBN 0-688-01902-1; 0-688-08740-X pa

LC 82-14848

A Caldecott Medal honor book, 1985

"By keeping hope alive within himself, a mouse is successful in his quest for the far-off land. Steptoe's retelling of an unattributed tribal legend is exquisite in its use of lan-

guage and in its expansive drawings which employ dazzling subtleties of light and shadow." SLJ

Steven, Kenneth C.

Stories for a fragile planet; [written by] Kenneth Steven; [illustrated by] Jane Ray. Trafalgar Square 2011 48p il $16.99

Grades: 3 4 5 6   398.2

1. Folklore

ISBN 978-0-7459-6157-6; 0-7459-6157-6

"This appealing collection consists of 10 brief stories each with a nature theme. Settings include Ancient Greece, . . . Africa, . . . Greenland, . . . Russia, Asia, South America, and Ireland. . . . Although there are no source notes, each smoothly written story is preceded by a brief statement about its origins. The book is beautifully designed, with most of the stories illustrated with crisp, jewel-toned paintings in a primitive style." Booklist

Stevens, Janet

Coyote steals the blanket; an Ute tale. retold and illustrated by Janet Stevens. Holiday House 1993 un il lib bdg $17.95; pa $6.95

Grades: K 1 2 3   398.2

1. Fables 2. Coyote (Legendary character) 3. Ute Indians -- Folklore

ISBN 0-8234-0996-1 lib bdg; 0-8234-1129-X pa

LC 92-54415

"When Coyote swipes a blanket, thus angering the spirit of the desert, he is pursued by a rock on a rampage. This traditional trickster tale features a scraggly, scruffy yet lovable character, a narrative that will roll right off storytellers' tongues, and hilarious pictures of boastful animals trying to halt the furious boulder." SLJ

★ **Tops** and bottoms; adapted and illustrated by Janet Stevens. Harcourt Brace & Co. 1995 un il $16

Grades: K 1 2 3   398.2

1. Bears -- Folklore 2. Rabbits -- Folklore 3. African Americans -- Folklore

ISBN 0-15-292851-0

LC 93-19154

A Caldecott Medal honor book, 1996

"Bear agrees to enter into a farming partnership with Hare, but first Hare makes Bear choose which half he will receive at harvest time: tops or bottoms. Because Bear picks tops, Hare sows all root vegetables. For the second crop, Bear chooses bottoms; this time Hare grows lettuce, broccoli, and celery. Finally, the frustrated Bear demands tops and bottoms from the final season's crop. But Hare is still the winner: he grows corn [and] keeps the ears 'in the middle' for his family. . . . Steven's bold, well-composed watercolor, pencil, and gesso illustrations cover every inch of each vertically oriented double-page spread. . . . The story contains enough sly humor and reassuring predictability to captivate listeners." Horn Book

Storace, Patricia

★ **Sugar** Cane; a Caribbean Rapunzel. pictures by Raúl Colón. Jump at the Sun/Hyperion Books for Children 2007 48p il $16.99

Grades: 1 2 3 4   398.2

1. Folklore -- Caribbean region 2. Folklore -- Juvenile

literature
ISBN 0-7868-0791-1; 978-0-7868-0791-8

LC 2006-36449

"The fisherman's pregnant wife wants sugar cane, and in an attempt to satisfy her cravings he cuts some from the garden of Madame Fate, an infamous 'conjure-woman.' In return, the sorceress demands the couple's unborn child, who will be named Sugar Cane. On the girl's first birthday, the woman takes her to live in a tower without stairs. . . . One evening the lonely girl's voice attracts King, a young man renowned for his songs. Colón's colored-pencil-and-watercolor illustrations mirror the lyrical text." SLJ

Sturges, Philemon

★ The **Little** Red Hen (makes a pizza) retold by Philemon Sturges; illustrated by Amy Walrod. Dutton Children's Bks. 1999 un il $15.99
Grades: K 1 2 3   **398.2**
1. Folklore 2. Chickens -- Folklore
ISBN 0-525-45953-7

LC 99-20066

In this version of the traditional tale, the duck, the dog, and the cat refuse to help the Little Red Hen make a pizza but do get to participate when the time comes to eat it and then they wash the dishes

"There's a keen sense of the absurd here, and the hilarious cut-paper illustrations are right in tune with the zany plot." SLJ

Taback, Simms

★ **Joseph** had a little overcoat. Viking 1999 un il music $15.99
Grades: K 1 2 3   **398.2**
1. Jews 2. Coats 3. Toy and movable books 4. Jews -- Fiction 5. Folklore -- Europe, Eastern 6. Clothing and dress -- Fiction 7. Toy and movable books -- Specimens
ISBN 0-670-87855-3

LC 98-47721

A newly illustrated edition of the title first published 1977 by Random House

Awarded the Caldecott Medal, 2000

A very old overcoat is recycled numerous times into a variety of garments. Based on a Yiddish folk song, which is included

"Taback's inventive use of die-cut pages shows off his signature artwork. . . . This diverting, sequential story unravels as swiftly as the threads of Joseph's well-loved, patch-covered plaid coat." Publ Wkly

★ **Kibitzers** and fools; tales my zayda (grandfather) told me. Viking 2005 un il $16.99
Grades: K 1 2 3   **398.2**
1. Jews -- Folklore 2. Jews -- Folklore -- Juvenile literature
ISBN 0-670-05955-2

LC 2005-03859

Thirteen brief, illustrated, traditional Jewish tales, each accompanied by an appropriate saying.

"This uproarious book celebrates the shtetl scene with energetic, mixed-media pictures in bright, folk-art style. . . . Families will want to share this." Booklist

Talbott, Hudson

King Arthur and the Round Table; written and illustrated by Hudson Talbott. Books of Wonder 1995 un il $18.99
Grades: 3 4 5   **398.2**
1. Arthurian romances 2. Kings
ISBN 0-688-11340-0

LC 94-43766

"The rich watercolor tableaux . . . paint war as bloody and painful, not all glorious. The love scenes glow golden. The Round Table, huge and decorated with the signs of the zodiac, exhibits its power more than the words do. Overall, this is a rousing addition to the current pickings of Arthurian stories." SLJ

Tarnowska, Wafa'

★ **Arabian** nights; written by Wafa' Tarnowska; illustrated by Carole Hénaff. Barefoot Books 2010 125p il $24.99
Grades: 5 6 7 8   **398.2**
1. Fairy tales 2. Arabs -- Folklore
ISBN 978-1-84686-122-2; 1-84686-122-5

LC 2008028159

"With bright, lush, stylized acrylic illustrations, this collection of eight stories from A Thousand and One Nights is designed for reading aloud. . . . Throughout, the spacious paintings capture the sense of the supernatural in daily life, including magical images of people taking flight above city, trees, and desert." Booklist

Taylor, C. J.

Spirits, fairies, and merpeople; Native stories of other worlds. Tundra Books 2009 39p il $19.95
Grades: 3 4 5 6   **398.2**
1. Native Americans -- Folklore
ISBN 978-0-88776-872-9; 0-88776-872-5

"The seven brief legends in this collection hail from a range of Native cultures. Mohawk artist/storyteller Taylor includes one from her own heritage, along with one each from the Mi'kmaq, Dakota, Coos, Ojibwa, Ute, and Cree. . . . Taylor's retellings are crisp and lend themselves well to reading aloud. Each story is accompanied by a lushly hued, surrealistic painting. The powerful images featuring fearsome creatures and tiny human figures balance the taut economy of the text." SLJ

Taylor, Sean

The **great** snake; stories from the Amazon. [by] Sean Taylor; illustrated by Fernando Vilela. Frances Lincoln Children's 2008 60p il $19.95
Grades: 3 4 5 6   **398.2**
1. Folklore -- Brazil
ISBN 978-1-84507-529-3; 1-84507-529-3

A collection of nine South American folktales from sly jaguars and the slowest of sloths to spine-tingling giant serpents and white-suited strangers.

"Youngsters will be caught up in this journey, following the river from place to place, meeting kind and welcoming people who share their stories. Woodcuts stamped in black, gold, green, turquoise, and red ink on white or orange backgrounds brilliantly capture the mystery of this unfamiliar world." SLJ

Tchana, Katrin Hyman

Changing Woman and her sisters; stories of goddesses from around the world. retold by Katrin Hyman Tchana; illustrated by Trina Schart Hyman. Holiday House 2006 80p il $18.95

Grades: 5 6 7 8   **398.2**

1. Folklore 2. Gods and goddesses 3. Goddesses -- Juvenile literature

ISBN 978-0-8234-1999-9; 0-8234-1999-1

LC 2005-52504

An illustrated collection of traditional tales which feature goddesses from different cultures, including Navajo, Mayan, and Fon. Notes explain each goddess's place in her culture, the reason for the book, and how the illustrations were developed

"This large, handsome volume assembles well-chosen, well-told stories. . . . Hyman . . . contributed distinctive portrayals of the goddesses using a technique that melded photographs and found materials into full-page ink and acrylic paintings." Booklist

Includes bibliographical references

★ **Sense** Pass King; a story from Cameroon. retold by Katrin Tchana; illustrated by Trina Schart Hyman. Holiday House 2002 un il $16.95

Grades: K 1 2 3   **398.2**

1. Folklore -- Cameroon

ISBN 0-8234-1577-5

LC 00-35094

Despite a jealous king's repeated attempts to get rid of her, Ma'antah continually manages to outwit him and proves herself worthy of the name Sense Pass King

The author "gives enough details to set the scene, and her smooth pacing will keep readers on the edge of their seats. . . . Hyman's artwork suggests the African heat—layers of gold silhouettes of trees and straw-colored huts on stilts with palm-frond rooftops are artfully set off by geometrically patterned fabrics in citrus tones." Publ Wkly

★ The **serpent** slayer: and other stories of strong women; retold by Katrin Tchana; illustrated by Trina Schart Hyman. Little, Brown 2000 113p il $22.99

Grades: 4 5 6 7   **398.2**

1. Women -- Folklore

ISBN 0-316-38701-0

LC 95-35077

"Tchana offers solid retellings of the oft-anthologized ('Kate Crackernuts') and the not oft-anthologized ('Sister Lace'). . . . The thematic variety of the stories provides something for everyone. . . . Humor, suspense, romance, and horror are reflected through the medium of Hyman's powerful art." Bull Cent Child Books

Includes bibliographical references

Thomas, Joyce Carol

★ The **six** fools; collected by Zora Neale Hurston; adapted by Joyce Carol Thomas; illustrated by Ann Tanksley. HarperCollins 2006 un il $15.99; lib bdg $16.89

Grades: K 1 2 3   **398.2**

1. Authors 2. Novelists 3. Dramatists 4. Memoirists 5. Folklorists 6. Short story writers 7. Folklore -- United States 8. African Americans -- Folklore 9.

African Americans -- Folklore -- Juvenile literature

ISBN 0-06-000646-3; 0-06-000647-1 lib bdg

LC 2004-30055

A young man searches for three people more foolish than his fiancée and her parents

"This adaptation of the fool story from Hurston's Every Tongue Got to Confess . . . is light and adept. . . . The result is wonderful in voice: rich, hilarious, and satisfying. Tanksley's oil monoprints done in a folk-art style set the story in Hurston's 1920s-'30s with humor and vibrant color in a wide-ranging palette." SLJ

★ The **skull** talks back and other haunting tales; collected by Zora Neale Hurston; adapted by Joyce Carol Thomas; illustrated by Leonard Jenkins. HarperCollins 2004 56p $15.99; lib bdg $16.89

Grades: 4 5 6 7   **398.2**

1. Authors 2. Novelists 3. Dramatists 4. Short stories 5. Horror fiction 6. Memoirists 7. Folklorists 8. Horror tales 9. Horror stories 10. Short story writers 11. Children's stories, American 12. African Americans -- Folklore

ISBN 0-06-000631-5; 0-06-000634-X lib bdg

LC 2003-22215

"Thomas retells six supernatural folktales selected from Hurston's Every Tongue Got to Confess." SLJ

★ The **three** witches; collected by Zora Neale Hurston; adapted by Joyce Carol Thomas; illustrated by Faith Ringgold. HarperCollins 2006 un il $15.99; lib bdg $16.89

Grades: K 1 2 3   **398.2**

1. Authors 2. Novelists 3. Dramatists 4. Memoirists 5. Folklorists 6. Short story writers 7. Witches -- Folklore 8. Folklore -- Southern States 9. African Americans -- Folklore 10. Folklore -- Juvenile literature

ISBN 978-0-06-000649-5; 0-06-000649-8; 978-0-06-000650-1 lib bdg; 0-06-000650-1 lib bdg

LC 2005-14553

Three hungry witches set out to eat two orphaned children while their grandmother is away at the market.

"Adapting a story from Hurston's 1930s folklore collection, Every Tongue Got to Confess, Thomas makes a fast, fun, but also scary tale more accessible to young readers, while Ringgold's paintings, with thick black lines and vibrant colors, reflect both the comic exaggeration and the shivery action." Booklist

What's the hurry, Fox? and other animal stories. collected by Zora Neale Hurston; illustrated by Bryan Collier; adapted by Joyce Carol Thomas. HarperCollins Publishers 2004 un il $15.99; lib bdg $16.89

Grades: K 1 2 3   **398.2**

1. Authors 2. Novelists 3. Dramatists 4. African Americans 5. Memoirists 6. Folklorists 7. Animals -- Folklore 8. Short story writers 9. Tales -- United States 10. Folklore -- United States 11. Folklore -- Southern States 12. African Americans -- Folklore

ISBN 0-06-000643-9; 0-06-000644-7 lib bdg

LC 2003-7014

Presents a volume of pourquoi tales collected by Zora Neale Hurston from her field research in the Gulf states in the 1930s.

In her adaptations Thomas uses "simplicity, humor, wit, and a colloquial style true to the spirit of the originals. . . . Collier's double-page-spread pictures combine painting and collage to show the animal characters' sly human machinations. The stories are very short, leaving lots of space for storyteller and audience." SLJ

Tracy, Kathleen

Cerberus. Mitchell Lane Publishers 2011 48p il map (Monsters in myth) lib bdg $29.95

Grades: 4 5 6 7   **398.2**

1. Classical mythology

ISBN 978-1-58415-924-7; 1-58415-924-3

LC 2010026968

This describes myths of Cerberus, Hades three-headed watchdog who guarded the gates of the Greek Underworld.

This book is "thorough and respectful of a number of ancient and modern sources and [bends] over backward to navigate often contradictory, interlinked legends. . . . A number of paintings and photos break up the otherwise text-heavy pages, and copious chapter notes and reading suggestions conclude. This is by no means entry-level stuff, but for kids handy with the basics and ready to delve deeper, [this book] will be of great use." Booklist

Includes glossary and bibliographical references

Tseng, Grace

White tiger, blue serpent; illustrated by Jean and Mou-Sien Tseng. Lothrop, Lee & Shepard Bks. 1999 un il $16; lib bdg $16.84

Grades: 2 3 4   **398.2**

1. Fairy tales 2. Folklore -- China

ISBN 0-688-12515-8; 0-688-12516-6 lib bdg

LC 94-9757

When his mother's beautiful brocade is snatched away by a greedy goddess, a young Chinese boy faces many perils as he attempts to get it back

"Lush paintings in the manner of fifteenth-century Chinese art animate a full-bodied folktale retelling about the search for beauty." Booklist

Valeri, M. Eulalia

The **hare** and the tortoise; adaptation by Maria Eulàlia Valeri; illustrated by Max. Chronicle 2006 un il $14.95; pa $6.95

Grades: K 1 2   **398.2**

1. Fables 2. Folklore 3. Rabbits -- Folklore 4. Turtles -- Folklore 5. Bilingual books -- English-Spanish

ISBN 0-8118-5057-9; 0-8118-5058-7 pa

Recounts the traditional tale of the race between the persevering tortoise and the boastful hare in English and Spanish

"Told in a simple but richly descriptive style, the story is both entertaining and lends itself very well to reading out loud. . . . The story is aptly rendered in the English and the Spanish versions, and overall, this is handsomely executed." Booklist

Vallverdu, Josep

Aladdin and the magic lamp; from The thousand and one nights. adaptation by Josep Vallverdu; illustrated by Pep Montserrat. Chronicle Books 2006 un il $14.95; pa $6.95

Grades: K 1 2   **398.2**

1. Fairy tales 2. Arabs -- Folklore 3. Bilingual books -- English-Spanish

ISBN 0-8118-5061-7; 0-8118-5062-5 pa

Aladdin outwits an evil magician who first tries to trick him into handing over an old lamp with a genie inside and later steals Aladdin's wife and possessions.

"Told in a simple but richly descriptive style, the story is both entertaining and lends itself very well to reading out loud. . . . This is a handsomely executed English-Spanish version that will make a great addition to a child's library of favorite bedtime readings." Booklist

Van Kampen, Vlasta

It couldn't be worse! Annick Press 2003 un il lib bdg $18.95; pa $6.95

Grades: K 1 2 3   **398.2**

1. Folklore

ISBN 1-55037-783-3 lib bdg; 1-55037-782-5 pa

The farmer's family was so crowded in their one-room house that they knew that it couldn't get worse but couldn't see how to make it better. So the farmer's wife asked for advice

"Bright, cheery watercolors match the puckish charm of this folktale." Booklist

Van Laan, Nancy

Shingebiss; an Ojibwe legend. retold by Nancy Van Laan; woodcuts by Betsy Bowen. Houghton Mifflin 1997 un il $16

Grades: 2 3 4   **398.2**

1. Ducks -- Folklore 2. Ojibwa Indians -- Folklore 3. Ojibwa Indians -- Folklore -- Juvenile literature

ISBN 0-316-89627-6

LC 95-40274

Shingebiss the duck bravely challenges the Winter Maker and manages to find enough food to survive a long, harsh winter

Van Laan's "lyric text flows like a soft drum beat and, although lengthy, wastes no words. . . . The artist's rustic, spirited woodcuts appear within circular frames of thick, loose lines that give one the sense of peering through ice holes." Publ Wkly

Includes glossary and bibliographical references

The **magic** bean tree; a legend from Argentina. retold by Nancy Van Laan; paintings by Beatriz Vidal. Houghton Mifflin 1998 un il $15

Grades: K 1 2 3   **398.2**

1. Legends -- Argentina 2. Folklore -- Argentina 3. Locust trees -- Folklore 4. Quechua Indians -- Folklore 5. Native Americans -- Folklore 6. Indians of South

America -- Folklore
ISBN 0-395-82746-9

LC 96-38632

A young Quechuan boy sets out on his own to bring the rains back to his parched homeland and is rewarded by a gift of carob beans that come to be prized across Argentina

"Vidal's shimmering, folk art-style paintings are well matched to the elegant simplicity and drama of Van Laan's retelling." Booklist

Includes glossary and bibliographical references

Wada, Stephanie
  Momotaro and the island of ogres; a Japanese folktale. as told by Stephanie Wada; paintings by Kano Naganobu. George Braziller 2005 47p il $19.95
Grades: 3 4 5 6   **398.2**
  1. Folklore -- Japan 2. Folk literature, Japanese 3. Japanese fiction -- Edo period, 1600-1868
  ISBN 0-8076-1552-8
Found floating on the river inside a peach by an old couple, Momotaro grows up and fights the terrible demons who have terrorized the village for years.

"Nineteenth-century silk handscrolls, painted by master Naganobu and housed in the New York Public Library's Spencer Collection, illustrate this handsome retelling of a much-loved Japanese folktale." Booklist

Wague Diakite, Baba
  Mee-An and the magic serpent; a folktale from Mali. Groundwood Books 2007 un il $16.95
Grades: K 1 2 3 4   **398.2**
  1. Folklore -- Mali 2. Snakes -- Folklore 3. Folklore -- Mali -- Juvenile literature
  ISBN 978-0-88899-719-7; 0-88899-719-1
"Beautiful Mee-An has decided she will accept only a perfect husband, someone without a single scratch, scar, or blemish. Her magical little sister, Assa, turns herself into a fly and believes she has found such a paragon. However, he is really a serpent who plans to fatten both girls and devour them. . . . Diakité's trademark ceramic-tile illustrations are on the recto while the cleanly framed text is on the verso. A well-designed and elegantly told addition to folktale shelves." SLJ

  ★ The **hatseller** and the monkeys; a West African folktale. retold and illustrated by Baba Wagué Diakité. Scholastic Press 1999 un il $15.95
Grades: K 1 2 3   **398.2**
  1. Monkeys -- Folklore 2. Folklore -- West Africa
  ISBN 0-590-96069-5

LC 98-16250

An African version of the familiar story of a man who sets off to sell his hats, only to have them stolen by a treeful of mischievous monkeys

"Ceramic-tile paintings on each spread depict the action in fluid, bold brushwork. . . . In this retelling, Diakité's use of language is as colorful and unusual as his artwork." Publ Wkly

  The **magic** gourd. Scholastic Press 2003 32p il $16.95
Grades: 2 3 4   **398.2**
  1. Folklore -- Mali 2. Rabbits -- Folklore 3. Chameleons

-- Folklore
ISBN 0-439-43960-4

LC 2002-4731

"In a time of famine, Chameleon rewards Brother Rabbit for a kind deed with a magic gourd that fills with whatever its owner desires. King Mansa Juga steals the gourd, but clever Rabbit recovers it and teaches the greedy king a lesson. Photos of exquisitely crafted ceramic plates, bowls, and tiles bordered with traditional Mali patterns illustrate this West African tale, which is retold with both economy and flair." Horn Book Guide

Includes glossary

Waldman, Debby
  Clever Rachel; story by Debby Waldman; illustrations by Cindy Revell. Orca Book Publishers 2009 un il $19.95
Grades: K 1 2 3   **398.2**
  1. Jews -- Folklore 2. Riddles -- Fiction
  ISBN 978-1-55469-081-7; 1-55469-081-1
Retells a traditional Jewish folktale about a clever girl named Rachel who clashes with a boy named Jacob when he challenges her with his riddles, until a woman with an urgent problem shows them that they are at their best when they work together.

"The lighthearted text includes occasional Yiddish words. Energetic illustrations convey Rachel and Jacob's competitive spirits." Horn Book Guide

  A **sack** full of feathers; story by Debby Waldman; illustrations by Cindy Revell. Orca Book Publishers 2006 un il $19.95
Grades: K 1 2 3   **398.2**
  1. Jews -- Folklore 2. Gossip -- Folklore
  ISBN 1-55143-332-X
"Yankel loves to tell stories and repeat the gossip that he hears in his father's store in the shtetl. . . . Unfortunately, Yankel only hears the bits and pieces that make trouble, not how things turn out. So the rabbi decides to teach the boy a lesson by making him see that stories spread and that they can be hurtful. The fun in this retelling of a Jewish folktale is not in the lesson, but in the setting, the people, and the stories they tell. The bright acrylic folk art shows the characters gossiping, quarreling . . . and, finally, getting together." Booklist

Wang Ping
  The **dragon** emperor; a Chinese folktale. retold by Wang Ping; illustrations by Tang Ge. Millbrook Press 2008 48p il (On my own folklore) lib bdg $25.26
Grades: 1 2 3 4   **398.2**
  1. Folklore -- China 2. Dragons -- Folklore
  ISBN 978-0-8225-6740-0 lib bdg; 0-8225-6740-7 lib bdg

LC 2006036718

A jealous warrior challenges the leadership of the dragon emperor. End note discusses the dragon in Chinese folklore and culture.

The "tale is paired with an illustration style that nicely reflects the culture." Horn Book Guide

Ward, Helen
  ★ **Unwitting** wisdom; an anthology of Aesop's fables. retold & illustrated by Helen Ward. Chronicle Books 2004 un il $18.95

Grades: 3 4 5 6   **398.2**
1. Fables 2. Authors 3. Storytellers 4. Fables --
Juvenile literature
ISBN 0-8118-4450-1

LC 2003-22990

"Familiar entries from Aesop are extravagantly extended
in this stunning, oversized compendium. . . . Beautifully
rendered in pen and watercolor, the illustrations incorporate
cunning details. . . . [Ward's] language blends formal, even
florid, phrases with jocular observations and some colloquial
quips." SLJ

Wargin, Kathy-Jo
The **frog** prince; by the Brothers Grimm; as retold by
Kathy-jo Wargin; illustrated by Anne Yvonne Gilbert. Mit-
ten Press 2007 un il $18.95
Grades: K 1 2 3   **398.2**
1. Fairy tales 2. Folklore -- Germany
ISBN 978-1-58726-279-1; 1-58726-279-7

LC 2006020283

As payment for retrieving the princess's ball, the frog
exacts a promise which the princess is reluctant to fulfill

"Intricate, gloriously lush illustrations highlight this retelling of the familiar tale. Wargin has preserved much of the
tone of the original text while editing the length to make it
more palatable for younger audiences." Booklist

Washington, Donna L.
A **pride** of African tales; illustrated by James Ransome. HarperCollinsPublishers 2004 70p il $16.99; lib
bdg $17.89
Grades: 3 4 5   **398.2**
1. Folklore -- Africa 2. Folklore -- Africa -- Juvenile
literature
ISBN 0-06-024929-3; 0-06-024932-3 lib bdg

LC 94-18697

A collection of African folktales originating in the
storytelling tradition

"Ransome contributes lush, naturalistic watercolors. . .
. Storytellers looking for material will welcome this versatile offering, as will educators seeking to deepen children's
understanding of Africa's diversity and the richness of its
narrative tradition." Booklist

Includes bibliographical references

Waters, Fiona
Aesop's fables; retold by Fiona Waters; illustrated by
Fulvio Testa. Trafalgar Square 2011 il $24.99
Grades: 1 2 3 4   **398.2**
1. Fables
ISBN 978-1-84939-049-1; 1-84939-049-5

"Waters deftly adds a contemporary tone in description
and dialogue to her smooth rendering of 60 familiar and less-
well-known tales. The terse moral of each fable, concluding each one in customary style, is usually set in traditional
terms. . . . Testa's pen and watercolor drawings are fun, portraying all animals with the large eyes currently popular in
cartoon art. . . . With its many comic touches, this anthology
presents once again the humor, folly, ingenuity, and wisdom
that make Aesop so durable." SLJ

Wee, wee woman
★ The **teeny**-tiny woman; a ghost story. Clarion Bks.
1984 un il $16; pa $5.95

Grades: PreK K 1 2   **398.2**
1. Ghost stories 2. Folklore -- Great Britain
ISBN 0-89919-270-X; 0-89919-463-X pa

LC 84-4311

"Quarter-inch type will attract reticent readers, and the
comfortable, cozy country and cottage scenes defuse whatever scariness young readers might conjure up. Fences, trees,
balustrades and cupboards in murky, inky tones are designed
to suggest watchful faces and add to the atmospheric tension
of the narrative." SLJ

Willey, Margaret
★ The **3** bears and Goldilocks; illustrated by Heather
M. Solomon. Atheneum Books for Young Readers 2008
un il $16.99
Grades: PreK K 1 2 3   **398.2**
1. Folklore 2. Bears -- Folklore
ISBN 978-1-4169-2494-4; 1-4169-2494-9

LC 2007-13857

Goldilocks, ignoring her father's warning not to rush
in where she does not belong, enters a cabin in the woods,
cleans it to meet her standards, plucks from the porridge
items unappealing to her before eating a bowlful, and falls
asleep on the bed that suits her best.

"There is a rustic feel to the illustrations, rendered in
watercolor, collage, colored pencil, acrylic, and oil paint. .
. . This satisfying read-aloud offers a new twist on an old
favorite." SLJ

Clever Beatrice; an Upper Peninsula conte. illustrated
by Heather McWhorter. Atheneum Bks. for Young Readers
2001 un il $16
Grades: K 1 2 3   **398.2**
1. Tall tales 2. Giants -- Folklore 3. Folklore --
Michigan 4. Folklore -- United States
ISBN 0-689-83254-0

LC 00-42019

A small, but clever young girl outwits a rich giant and
wins all his gold

"Set in Michigan's Upper Peninsula, this is a winning
tale of brain vs. brawn. . . . Willey's telling is simple but
spirited, and her dialogue, with its slight French-Canadian
cadence, is pitch perfect. Heather Solomon's illustrations are
remarkable: watercolors augmented with collage, they have
unusual texture and depth." Horn Book

Other titles about Clever Beatrice by this author are:
Clever Beatrice and the best little pony (2004)
A Clever Beatrice Christmas (2006)

Wisnewski, Andrea
Little Red Riding Hood; retold and illustrated by An-
drea Wisnewski. David R. Godine 2006 un il $18.95
Grades: K 1 2 3   **398.2**
1. Fairy tales 2. Folklore -- Germany
ISBN 1-56792-303-8; 978-1-56792-303-2

LC 2006022122

A version of the classic story about a little girl, her
grandmother, and a not-so-clever wolf, set in nineteenth-
century rural New England

"A handsomely illustrated version of a folktale favorite.
Wisnewski's retelling is straightforward and the language
has a comfortable, folksy cadence." SLJ

Wisniewski, David

Rain player; story and pictures by David Wisniewski. Clarion Bks. 1991 un il pa $7.95; $17

Grades: 1 2 3 4 **398.2**

1. Games -- Fiction 2. Mayas -- Fiction 3. Mayas -- Legends -- Juvenile literature

ISBN 0-395-72083-4 pa; 0-395-55112-9

LC 90-44101

To bring rain to his thirsty village, Pik challenges the rain god to a game of pok-a-tok

"This original tale combines research on Mayan history and legend with a suspenseful sports story. . . . Intricate and dramatic cut-paper illustrations powerfully re-create the foliage, landscape, architecture, and clothing of the Mayan classical period. . . . An author's note provides fascinating background information on Mayan civilization and gives in-depth explanations of some of the words and phrases used in the text." Horn Book

Wormell, Christopher

Mice, morals, & monkey business; lively lessons from Aesop's Fables. Running Press 2005 un il $18.95

Grades: K 1 2 3 **398.2**

1. Fables 2. Authors 3. Storytellers

ISBN 0-7624-2404-4

"Wormell uses linocut prints to illuminate 21 of Aesop's famous life lessons. . . . The bold, black lines of the expertly rendered images and colorful accents primarily in earth tones create instantly recognizable figures. The subtle use of light and shadow adds clarity, expression, and often drama without extraneous detail." SLJ

Yolen, Jane

The Barefoot book of dance stories; [by] Jane Yolen, Heidi E. Y. Stemple; [illustrated by] Helen Cann; with story CD by Juliet Stevenson. Barefoot Books 2010 96p il $21.99

Grades: 2 3 4 5 6 **398.2**

1. Dance -- Folklore

ISBN 978-1-846862-19-9; 1-846862-19-1

LC 2008043901

"Anansi, witches, gods, goddesses, and fairies inhabit these adventurous, mysterious, and fanciful stories that capture the magical power of dance. . . . The bright watercolor and mixed-media illustrations with stylized backgrounds feature sweeping curves and patterns that swirl as if dancing across the page, as dynamic and graceful characters engage in their activities." SLJ

★ Meow; cat stories from around the world. illustrated by Hala Wittwer. HarperCollins 2005 40p il $16.99; lib bdg $17.89

Grades: K 1 2 3 **398.2**

1. Folklore 2. Cats -- Folklore 3. Cats -- Juvenile literature

ISBN 0-06-029161-3; 0-06-029162-1 lib bdg

LC 2002-06380

"A collection of 10 cat stories, plus nursery rhymes and lore drawn from sources around the world. Yolen captures the heart of each story, and the resulting text begs to be told or read aloud. . . . Wittwer's richly colored paintings fill the pages with the essence of feline charm, power, and wit. " SLJ

Mightier than the sword; world folktales for strong boys. collected and told by Jane Yolen; with illustrations by Raul Colón. Silver Whistle/Harcourt 2003 112p il $19

Grades: 4 5 6 7 **398.2**

1. Folklore

ISBN 0-15-216391-3

LC 2002-9886

A collection of folktales from around the world which demonstrate the triumph of brains over brawn

Yolen's "versions of these stories are lively, expressively written, ready for reading aloud or telling, and illustrative of her point." SLJ

Includes bibliographical references

Sister Bear; a Norse tale. adapted by Jane Yolen; illustrated by Linda Graves. Marshall Cavendish Children 2011 un il

Grades: K 1 2 3 **398.2**

1. Bears -- Folklore 2. Folklore -- Norway

ISBN 0-7614-5958-8; 978-0-7614-5958-3

LC 2010024235

Halva is traveling with her trained bear to visit the King of Denmark when they stop for the night at a cottage where, they learn, a pack of trolls is about to make its annual Christmas Eve visit, causing trouble and making a big mess. Includes author's note about the story's origins.

"There isn't a dull moment in Yolen's rousing retelling of this Norwegian folktale. . . . Grave's . . . characters have the attraction of costumed toys, and nearly every spread features a loving look at a traditional Scandinavian garment and its inticate needlework. . . . Yolen knows a good story when she sees one." Publ Wkly

Young, Ed

★ Lon Po Po; a Red-Riding Hood story from China. translated and illustrated by Ed Young. Philomel Bks. 1989 un il $16.99; pa $6.99

Grades: 1 2 3 **398.2**

1. Folklore -- China 2. Wolves -- Folklore 3. Folklore -- China -- Juvenile literature

ISBN 0-399-21619-7; 0-698-11382-9 pa

LC 88-15222

Awarded the Caldecott Medal, 1990

Three sisters staying home alone are endangered by a hungry wolf who is disguised as their grandmother

"The text possesses that matter-of-fact veracity that characterizes the best fairy tales. The watercolor and pastel pictures are remarkable: mystically beautiful in their depiction of the Chinese countryside, menacing in the exchanges with the wolf, and positively chilling in the scenes inside the house." SLJ

What about me? Philomel Bks. 2002 un il $16.99

Grades: K 1 2 3 **398.2**

1. Sufis 2. Folklore -- Middle East

ISBN 0-399-23624-4

LC 2001-45927

A young boy determinedly follows the instructions of the Grand Master in the hope of gaining knowledge, only to be surprised as how he acquires it. Based on a Sufi tale.

"Dazzling collage illustrations set the personae of the tale against muted, spatter-paint backgrounds. The figures are agile, rhythmic, graceful, and emotionally charged, interpreting the story in perfect synchronization with mood and tempo." Horn Book

★ The **sons** of the Dragon King; a Chinese legend. Atheneum Bks. for Young Readers 2004 un il $16.95
Grades: 3 4 5   **398.2**
   1. Folklore -- China
   ISBN 0-689-85184-7
                           LC 2002-154321
   The nine immortal sons of the Dragon King set out to make something of themselves, and each, with help from a watchful father, finds a role that suits his individual strengths.
   "The text is engrossing and includes an informative author's note. The illustrations, rendered in brush, ink, and cut paper, use softly smudged lines for the part of the story focused on the legend, and sharper, cleaner lines augmented by a minimal but dramatically effective use of color for the present-day segments. This elegant addition to folklore shelves should be a first purchase for most libraries." SLJ

Zelinsky, Paul O.
   Rumpelstiltskin; from the German of the Brothers Grimm. retold & illustrated by Paul O. Zelinsky. Dutton 1986 un il lib bdg $16.99; pa $6.99
Grades: K 1 2 3   **398.2**
   1. Fairy tales 2. Folklore -- Germany 3. Folklore -- Germany -- Juvenile literature
   ISBN 0-525-44265-0 lib bdg; 0-14-055864-0 pa
                         LC 86-4482
   A Caldecott Medal honor book, 1987
   A strange little man helps the miller's daughter spin straw into gold for the king on the condition that she will give him her first-born child
   "Zelinsky's painterly style and rich colors provide an evocative backdrop to this story. The medieval setting and costumes and the spools of gold thread which shine on the page like real gold are suggestive of an illuminated manuscript. . . . Zelinsky's smooth retelling and glowing pictures cast the story in a new and beautiful light." SLJ

Zemach, Margot
   The **three** little pigs; an old story. Farrar, Straus & Giroux 1989 un il hardcover o.p. pa $5.95
Grades: K 1 2   **398.2**
   1. Fables 2. Pigs -- Folklore 3. Wolves -- Folklore 4. Folklore -- Great Britain
   ISBN 0-374-37527-5; 0-374-47717-5 pa
                         LC 87-73488
   Zemach "has brought a familiar, often-told tale to life with marvelous ink-and-watercolor illustrations. Her wolf, wearing a dapper green hat and radiating slyness with every inch of his furry self, cuts a spendidly sinister figure as he attempts to wile his way to three pork chop dinners. With simple, lively sentences Zemach has related the complete story, including the apple-picking and country fair episodes." Horn Book

Ziefert, Harriet
   Little Red Riding Hood; retold by Harriet Ziefert; illustrated by Emily Bolam. Viking 2000 un il (Viking easy-to-read) hardcover o.p. pa $3.99
Grades: K 1 2   **398.2**
   1. Fairy tales 2. Wolves -- Folklore 3. Folklore --

Germany
   ISBN 0-670-88389-1; 0-14-056529-9 pa
                         LC 99-23210
   A little girl meets a hungry wolf in the forest while on her way to visit her gandmother
   This adaptation of the Grimm's fairy tale "tells the story in a brisk, straightforward style . . . [with] simple, colorful illustrations. . . . The vocabulary is appropriate for beginning readers. The lively illustrations and familiarity of the story should provide a successful reading experience." SLJ

The August House book of scary stories; spooky tales for telling out loud. edited by Liz Parkhurst. August House 2009 144p $15.95
Grades: 4 5 6 7 8   **398.2**
   1. Folklore 2. Storytelling 3. Short stories 4. Horror fiction
   ISBN 978-0-87483-915-9; 0-87483-915-7
                       LC 2009008711
   An anthology of spooky stories drawn from folklore, local history, and the storytellers' imaginations, and divided into the categories "Just Desserts and Lessons Learned," "Ghostly Guardians," "Dark Humor," "Urban Legends and Jump Tales," and "Fearless Females."
   "Each of these 20 chilling tales is meant to be told out loud and includes author notes about how to maximize the spooky effect. Middle schoolers will relish reading and sharing these tales, hoping to creep each other out." SLJ

The Blue fairy book; edited by Andrew Lang; with numerous illustrations by H. J. Ford and G. P. Jacomb Hood. Dover Publs. 1965 390p il pa $10.95
Grades: 4 5 6   **398.2**
   1. Folklore 2. Fairy tales
   ISBN 0-486-21437-0
   A reprint of the title first published 1889 by Longmans
   A collection of thirty-seven fairy tales from various countries, consisting largely of old favorites from such sources as Perrault, the Brothers Grimm, Madame D'Aulnoy, Asbjörnsen and Möe, the Arabian Nights and Swift's Gulliver's travels

English folktales; edited by Dan Keding and Amy Douglas. Libraries Unlimited 2005 231p il map (World folklore series) $35
Grades: Adult Professional   **398.2**
   1. Folklore -- Great Britain
   ISBN 1-59158-260-1
                       LC 2005016075
   "This collection of more than 50 English folktales contains a variety of stories arranged by common themes: The Fool in All His Glory, Wily Wagers and Tall Tales, Dragons and Devils, etc. The work of 22 storytellers is represented and their tellings are lively and inflected with the rhythms and speech of the regions from which their stories emanate. It is a delightful compendium for storytellers." SLJ

Grandfather tales; American-English folk tales. selected and edited by Richard Chase; illustrated by Berkeley Williams, Jr. Houghton Mifflin 1948 239p il pa $7.95
Grades: 4 5 6 7   **398.2**
   1. Folklore -- Southern States
   ISBN 0-395-06692-1; 0-618-34690-2 pa

Folklore gathered in Alabama, "North Carolina, Virginia and Kentucky. Written down only after many tellings, these [twenty-four] humorous tales are told in the vernacular of the region with added touches of local color provided by the storytellers as they meet together to keep Old-Christmas Eve. . . . Of special interest to storytellers." Booklist

Princess stories; a classic illustrated edition. compiled by Cooper Edens. Chronicle Books 2004 133p il $19.95
Grades: 2 3 4   **398.2**
1. Folklore 2. Fairy tales
ISBN 0-8118-4032-8

           LC 2003-20890

"This edition of classic princess stories showcases artists from the Golden Age of Illustration, roughly the 1880s to the 1920s. . . . Arthur Rackham, Walter Crane, Jesse Wilcox Smith, Charles Robinson, Kay Nielsen, and Edmund Dulac are among the American and European artists represented. The edition is rich in language, tone, and picture and despite the disparate nature of each artist's style, it somehow comes together as a classic whole." SLJ

Rapunzel and other magic fairy tales; selected and illustrated by Henriette Sauvant; translated by Anthea Bell. Trafalgar Square 2008 157p il $15.95
Grades: 5 6 7 8   **398.2**
1. Folklore 2. Fairy tales
ISBN 1-4052-2702-8

"Sauvant has selected 14 tales of German, English, and French origin, many of them written down by the Grimm brothers. While most of them are familiar . . . others will be unknown to most readers. . . . The illustrations, which range in size from tiny fillers to full-page and double-page pictures, appear to be painted in watercolor or acrylic on a textured surface. While some are painted in classic fairy-tale style, others are best described as surreal. . . . The sophistication of both stories and artwork makes this collection most suitable for older readers." SLJ

Tatanka and the Lakota people; a creation story. illustrated by Donald F. Montileaux. South Dakota State Historical Society Press 2006 un il $16.95
Grades: 1 2 3 4   **398.2**
1. Creation -- Folklore 2. Teton Indians -- Folklore
ISBN 0-9749195-8-6

           LC 2006016009

The transformaton of the Buffalo Nation into the Ordinary People and their salvation by Tatanka comes from this traditional creation story of the Lakota, or Sioux, Indians.

"Montileaux, an Oglala Lakota artist, illustrates the text with paintings rendered in a two-dimensional format that reflects traditional buffalo-hide paintings. The colorful, stylized images match the formal tone of the story. The English telling is clear and concise, with the corresponding Lakota text appearing alongside." SLJ

★ Trickster: Native American tales; a graphic collection. edited by Matt Dembicki. Fulcrum 2010 231p il pa $22.95
Grades: 5 6 7 8   **398.2**
1. Graphic novels 2. Folklore -- Graphic novels 3. Native Americans -- Folklore
ISBN 978-1-55591-724-1 pa; 1-55591-724-0 pa

           LC 2009-49668

"More than 40 storytellers and cartoonists have contributed to this original and provocative compendium of traditional folklore presented in authentic, colorful, and engaging sequential art. The stories are drawn from a variety of Native peoples across North America, and so the trickster character appears variously as Rabbit, a raccoon, Coyote, and in other guises; landscapes, clothing and rhythms of speech and action also vary in keeping with distinct traditions. Realistic, impressionistic, painterly, and cartoon styles of art are employed to echo and announce the tone of each tale and telling style, making this a rich visual treasure as well as cultural trove." SLJ

398.209   History, geographic treatment, biography

Aardema, Verna
   ★ Anansi does the impossible! an Ashanti tale. retold by Verna Aardema; illustrated by Lisa Desimini. Atheneum Bks. for Young Readers 1997 un il $16; pa $5.99
Grades: K 1 2 3   **398.209**
1. Anansi (Legendary character) 2. Folklore -- West Africa 3. Ashanti (African people) -- Folklore -- Juvenile literature
ISBN 0-689-81092-X; 0-689-83933-2 pa

           LC 96-20033

"Vivid, stylized collage illustrations convey the frightening force and power of the Sky God yet also reveal Anansi's own pluck and boldness. Perfect for reading or telling aloud." Booklist

Includes glossary and bibliographical references

Beneduce, Ann
   Jack and the beanstalk; retold by Ann Keay Beneduce; illustrated by Gennady Spirin. Philomel Bks. 1999 32p il $16.99
Grades: 2 3 4   **398.209**
1. Fairy tales 2. Folklore -- England 3. Folklore -- Great Britain
ISBN 0-399-23118-8

           LC 98-5722

A boy climbs to the top of a giant beanstalk, where he uses his quick wits to outsmart an ogre and make his and his mother's fortune

"Beneduce bases her version of Jack and the Beanstalk on a Victorian version, complete with a fairy guardian. . . . Spirin contributes some glorious borders for the text as well as many impressively detailed paintings, notable for their dark muted colors and mysterious, foggy look." Booklist

Bodkin, Odds
   The crane wife; retold by Odds Bodkin; illustrated by Gennady Spirin. Gulliver Bks. 1998 un il hardcover o.p. pa $7
Grades: 3 4 5   **398.209**
1. Folklore -- Japan
ISBN 0-15-201407-1; 0-15-216350-6 pa

           LC 96-35488

A retelling of the traditional Japanese tale about a poor sail maker who gains a beautiful but mysterious wife skilled at weaving magical sails

"Capturing the tale's mystery and tragedy, Spirin's watercolor-and-gouache paintings take their inspiration from Japanese art. Delicate shades of tawny gray and burnished gold predominate in the illustrations." Booklist

Casanova, Mary

The **hunter**; a Chinese folktale. retold by Mary Casanova; illustrations by Ed Young. Atheneum Bks. for Young Readers 2000 un il $16.95

Grades: K 1 2 3   **398.209**

1. Folklore -- China

ISBN 0-689-82906-X

LC 99-32166

After learning to understand the language of animals, Hai Li Bu the hunter sacrifices himself to save his village

Casanova "tells the tale in a dignified yet moving way that is complemented by the stark artwork. Arid-looking, dun-colored paper is the background for Young's masterful brush strokes." Booklist

Craft, Charlotte

★ **King** Midas and the golden touch; as told by Charlotte Craft; illustrated by K.Y. Craft. Morrow 1999 32p il $16; pa $6.99

Grades: 2 3 4   **398.209**

1. Midas (Legendary character)

ISBN 0-688-13165-4; 0-06-054063-X pa

LC 98-24035

A king finds himself bitterly regretting the consequences of his wish that everything he touches would turn to gold

"This sophisticated retelling, set in the Middle Ages, places King Midas in a sumptuous palace. . . . The elaborate oil-over-watercolor illustrations show the wondrous, tragic effects of the golden touch." Horn Book Guide

Defelice, Cynthia

Nelly May has her say; Cynthia DeFelice; pictures by Henry Cole. Margaret Ferguson Books 2013 32 p. col. ill. $16.99

Grades: K 1 2 3   **398.209**

1. Picture books for children 2. Folklore -- England

ISBN 0374398992; 9780374398996

LC 2011018484

In this children's picture book, Nelly May Nimble leaves her childhood home and 12 siblings to work for Lord Ignasius Pinkwinkle. Lord Pinkwinkle "agrees with one condition; the master of the house has special names for things, and Nelly must use those names when she speaks to him. . . . But when Lord Pinkwinkle's 'fur-faced fluffenbarker's wigger-wagger' catches fire, Nelly has to wake him and announce the fire before the house burns down. Can she remember all those silly names?" (School Library Journal)

Delacre, Lulu

Golden tales; myths, legends, and folktales from Latin America. [retold by] Lulu Delacre. Scholastic 1996 73p hardcover o.p. pa $5.99

Grades: 5 6 7 8   **398.209**

1. Folklore -- Latin America 2. Native Americans -- Folklore

ISBN 0-439-24398-X pa

LC 94-36724

This includes 12 "stories from four native cultures (Taino, Zapotec, Muisca, and Quechua), including pourquoi

tales, legends of the conquistadores, and folktales from before and after the age of Columbus. . . . [The author's] . . . retellings are done in a clear and confident voice and are accompanied by her robust, colorful oil paintings. . . . This impressively presented and referenced collection will inspire readers and tellers alike." Booklist

Includes bibliographical references

Demi

★ The **empty** pot. Holt & Co. 1990 un il $16.95; pa $6.95

Grades: K 1 2 3   **398.209**

1. Folklore -- China 2. Folklore -- China -- Juvenile literature

ISBN 0-8050-1217-6; 0-8050-4900-2 pa

LC 89-39062

"This simple story with its clear moral is illustrated with beautiful paintings. . . . A beautifully crafted book that will be enjoyed as much for the richness of its illustrations as for the simplicity of its story." SLJ

Doyle, Malachy

Tales from old Ireland; retold by Malachy Doyle; illustrated by Niamh Sharkey. Barefoot Bks. (NY) 2000 95p il $19.99; pa $16.99

Grades: 3 4 5 6   **398.209**

1. Folklore -- Ireland 2. Folklore -- Ireland -- Juvenile literature

ISBN 978-1-902283-97-5; 1-902283-97-X; 978-1-905236-32-9 pa; 1-905236-32-8 pa

A collection of seven Irish folk tales

Doyle's "retellings are simple and economical, yet contain all the lilting rhythm and musical quality for which Irish tales are famous. Sharkey's illustrations, prepared in oil and gesso on canvas, are a perfect match." SLJ

Includes bibliographical references

Fang, Linda

The **Ch'i**-lin purse; a collection of ancient Chinese stories. retold by Linda Fang; pictures by Jeanne M. Lee. Farrar, Straus & Giroux 1994 127p il hardcover o.p. pa $5.95

Grades: 5 6 7 8   **398.209**

1. Folklore -- China

ISBN 0-374-31241-9; 0-374-41189-1 pa

LC 94-9909

A collection of "Chinese stories derived from the history of the Warring States Period (770-221 B.C.E.) and from operatic versions of popular tales. Retellings are vivid, lively, and read aloud well. Many have a moral, and all are entertaining. . . . The black-and-white illustrations—one per selection—are graceful, depicting widely different epochs with amazing accuracy." SLJ

Includes glossary and bibliographical references

Garland, Sherry

Children of the dragon; selected tales from Vietnam. with illustrations by Trina Schart Hyman. Harcourt 2001 58p il $18

Grades: 3 4 5 6   **398.209**

1. Tales -- Vietnam 2. Folklore -- Vietnam

ISBN 0-15-224200-7

LC 00-8300

An illustrated collection of Vietnamese folktales with explanatory notes following each story

"This handsome volume gathers six well-told tradition-al tales not readily available elsewhere. . . . [The book is] greatly enhanced by Hyman's strong color work, romantic sensibility, and dramatic characterizations." SLJ

Gavin, Jamila

School for princes; stories from the Panchatantra. re-told by Jamila Gavin; illustrated by Bee Willey. Reprint Frances Lincoln Children's Books 2012 64 p. ill. (hard-cover) $19.99
Grades: 4 5 6   **398.209**
1. Indic mythology 2. Indian literature (English) 3. Indic literature -- Collections 4. Conduct of life -- Literary collections
ISBN 1845079906; 9781845079901
This children's book presents "a series of newly created stories in combination with five traditional tales to reveal the Panchatantra's themes. . . . Three arrogant princes change their tune in six short months as a sage uses stories to teach them the art of ruling. These fables have been introduced to people of all classes for generations to spread ideas of wisdom, kindness, friendship and unity, and self-control." (Kirkus Reviews)

Gonzalez, Lucia M.

Senor Cat's romance and other favorite stories from Latin America; retold by Lucía M. González; illustrated by Lulu Delacre. Scholastic 1997 46p il hardcover o.p. pa $5.99
Grades: 2 3 4   **398.209**
1. Folklore -- Latin America 2. Folklore -- Latin America -- Juvenile literature
ISBN 0-590-48537-7; 0-439-27863-5 pa
LC 95-34144
González tells these tales "with style and humor. The re-tellings are peppered with Spanish words, all of which are easily understood through context. Each story is followed by a short glossary and an author's note with information on the tale's origins and its variants. The vivid, sprightly paintings contain many regional details." Horn Book Guide

Heo, Yumi

The **green** frogs; a Korean folktale. retold by Yumi Heo. Houghton Mifflin 1996 un il $16; pa $6.95
Grades: K 1 2 3   **398.209**
1. Folklore -- Korea 2. Frogs -- Folklore 3. Folklore -- Korea -- Juvenile literature
ISBN 0-395-68378-5; 0-618-43228-8 pa
LC 95-19129
"Using delicate tones, flat perspectives, and somewhat abstract figures set against busy backgrounds, [Heo] cre-ates a quaint, comic effect. . . . This is a quirkier pourquoi tale than most, but it's too mischievous to be morbid." Horn Book

Jiang, Ji-li

★ The **magical** Monkey King; mischief in heaven. classic Chinese tales retold by Ji-Li Jiang; illustrated by Hui Hui Su-Kennedy. HarperCollins Pubs. 2002 122p il hard-cover o.p. pa $4.95
Grades: 3 4 5   **398.209**
1. Monkeys 2. Folklore -- China 3. Monkeys --

Folklore
ISBN 0-06-029544-9 lib bdg; 0-06-442149-X pa
LC 2001-39672
The mischievous Monkey King attempts to achieve im-mortality the easy way, gains god-like powers, and wreaks havoc in heaven
The author "provides a lively telling, and the stories move briskly. Accompanying black-and-white pictures have the look of woodcuts." Booklist

MacDonald, Margaret Read

★ **Fat** cat; a Danish folktale. retold by Margaret Read MacDonald; illustrated by Julie Paschkis. August House 2001 un il $15.95; pa $7.95
Grades: K 1 2 3   **398.209**
1. Cats 2. Mice 3. Cats -- Folklore 4. Mice -- Folklore 5. Folklore -- Denmark
ISBN 0-87483-616-6; 0-87483-765-0 pa
LC 00-68939
A greedy cat grows enormous as he eats everything in sight, including his friends and neighbors who call him fat
"The book's huge, bright illustrations are glorious. . . . The large, funny illustrations will carry well for a big-ger crowd and, combined with refrain that invites chanting along, make this a surefire hit for reading aloud." Booklist

★ **Mabela** the clever; retold by Margaret Read Mac-Donald; illustrated by Tim Coffey. Whitman, A. 2001 un il music hardcover o.p. pa $6.95
Grades: K 1 2 3   **398.209**
1. Cats -- Folklore 2. Mice -- Folklore 3. Folklore -- Africa
ISBN 0-8075-4902-9; 0-8075-4903-7 pa
LC 00-8307
An African folktale about a mouse who pays close atten-tion to her surroundings and avoids being tricked by the cat
"MacDonald's retelling of this Limba tale is engineered for storytime success. . . . Coffey's thatch-strewn paintings, rendered in acrylic on watercolor paper textured with gesso, feature lots of visibly clueless, wide-eyed mice, and his cat oozes predatory shrewdness to the very end." SLJ

McCaughrean, Geraldine

Grandma Chickenlegs; illustrated by Moira Kemp. Carolrhoda Bks. 1999 un il $15.95
Grades: K 1 2 3   **398.209**
1. Folklore -- Russia
ISBN 1-57505-415-9
LC 99-19161
In this variation of the traditional Baba Yaga story, a young girl must rely on the advice of her dead mother and her special doll when her wicked stepmother sends her to get a needle from Grandma Chickenlegs
"McCaughrean's well-paced narrative is rich in imagery and humor. . . . Kemp's colored-pencil illustrations are ren-dered with accessibly childlike simplicity, but she also uses sophisticated composition and perspectives to enhance the drama." Horn Book

Mollel, Tololwa M.

Ananse's feast; an Ashanti tale. retold by Tololwa M. Mollel; illustrated by Andrew Glass. Clarion Bks. 1997 31p il $14.95; pa $6.95

Grades: K 1 2 3 **398.209**

1. Anansi (Legendary character) 2. Folklore -- Ghana 3. Ashanti (African people) -- Folklore 4. Folklore -- Africa -- Juvenile literature

ISBN 0-395-67402-6; 0-618-19598-X pa

LC 95-17358

Unwilling to share his feast, Ananse the spider tricks Akye the turtle so that he can eat all the food himself, but Akye finds a way to get even

"Varied in composition and bright with layers of color, the oil-and-colored-pencil artwork captures the actions, reactions, and emotions of the two main characters with a great sense of playfulness and humor." Booklist

O'Connor, George

Hades. First Second 2012 76p col. ill. (Olympians)

Grades: 4 5 6 **398.209**

1. Graphic novels 2. Greek mythology 3. Persephone (Greek deity) -- Fiction 4. Mother-daughter relationship -- Fiction 5. Hades (Greek deity) -- Comic books, strips, etc. -- Juvenile literature

ISBN 9781596434349

LC 2011017563

In this book, a "tempestuous mother-daughter relationship makes up the centerpiece of [author and illustrator George] O'Connor's . . . Olympian portrait. Snatched down to the Underworld in the wake of a screaming fight with her mother Demeter, . . . raging adolescent Kore (meaning, generically 'The Maiden') initially gives her quiet, gloomy captor Hades a hard time too. After grabbing the opportunity to give herself a thorough makeover and changing her name to Persephone ('Bringer of Destruction'), though, she takes charge of her life--so surely that, when offered the opportunity to return to her remorseful mom, she lies about having eaten those pomegranate seeds so she can spend half of each year as Queen of the Dead." (Kirkus)

Includes bibliographical references.

Ollhoff, Jim

Middle Eastern Mythology; by Jim Ollhoff. ABDO Publishing Company 2011 32p il (The world of mythology) lib bdg $27.07

Grades: 5 6 7 8 **398.209**

1. Mythology -- Middle East

ISBN 1617147257; 9781617147258; 1-61714-725-7; 978-1-61714-725-8

LC 2010042977

This describes the history of myths of the Middle East, their meaning, and their gods and goddesses including Mithra, Mot, the Mesopotamian goddess Ishtar, and the Canaanite thunder god, Baal.

"Ollhoff writes in a clear and engaging fashion, presenting complex issues in a way that will be easy for youngsters to grasp. . . . The photographs and reproductions of art tie directly to the [text]." SLJ

Sierra, Judy

★ **Tasty** baby belly buttons; a Japanese folktale. illustrated by Meilo So. Knopf 1998 un il hardcover o.p. $17

Grades: K 1 2 3 **398.209**

1. Folklore -- Japan

ISBN 0-679-89369-5; 0-440-41738-4 pa

LC 98-22524

Urikohime, a girl born from a melon, battles the monstrous onis, who steal babies to eat their tasty belly buttons

"Graced with occasional delicate brushwork that seems distinctly Japanese, So's fluid, sweeping watercolors add freshness to a traditional tale of swashbuckling heroics." Booklist

Stewig, John W.

King Midas; a golden tale. told by John Warren Stewig; pictured through the mind of Omar Rayyan. Holiday House 1999 un il $15.95

Grades: 2 3 4 **398.209**

1. Midas (Legendary character)

ISBN 0-8234-1423-X

LC 98-21222

A king finds himself bitterly regretting the consequences of his wish that everything he touches would turn to gold

"Rayyan's watercolors are a phantasmagoria of irreverent details, from the statue of a fresh minotaur sticking his tongue out to a rubber duck floating in a fountain." Bull Cent Child Books

Tolman, Marije

The **island**; Ronald Tolman; Marije Tolman. Lemniscaat USA 2012 32 p. $17.95

Grades: PreK K **398.209**

1. Picture books for children 2. Islands -- Juvenile fiction 3. Polar bears -- Juvenile fiction

ISBN 1935954199; 9781935954194

In this "wordless picture book" by Marije Tolman and Ronald Tolman "you swim along with a bear on a journey through a unique archipelago. . . . With every island lies a whole new world to discover, until the bear finds the ultimate island. Has he finally come across his home, or is he merely passing through?" (Publisher's note)

Wague Diakite, Baba

The **hunterman** and the crocodile; a West African folktale. retold and illustrated by Baba Wagué Diakité. Scholastic 1997 un il $15.95

Grades: 2 3 4 **398.209**

1. Crocodiles -- Folklore 2. Folklore -- West Africa

ISBN 0-590-89828-0

LC 95-25975

"After Donso rescues a crocodile family, they turn on him and threaten to eat him. Several creatures . . . refuse his appeals for help, saying that Man has always misused them in the past. Only clever Rabbit is willing to assist him. Bold figures painted on ceramic tiles illustrate this teaching tale about 'living in harmony with nature.'" Horn Book Guide

Includes bibliographical references

Wisniewski, David

★ **Sundiata**; lion king of Mali. story and pictures by David Wisniewski. Clarion Bks. 1992 un il hardcover o.p. $5.95

Grades: 1 2 3 4 **398.209**

1. Kings 2. Legends -- Mali -- Juvenile literature

ISBN 0-395-61302-7; 0-395-76481-5 pa

LC 91-27951

The story of Sundiata, who overcame physical handicaps, social disgrace, and strong opposition to rule Mali in the thirteenth century

"Passed down through oral tradition, this historical account has the drama and depth of a folktale. The illustrations—elaborate collages inspired by the artifacts and culture of the Malinke—create a series of dramatic images. The intricacy of the paper-cuts and the richness of the colors and patterns give the artwork visual as well as narrative strength." Booklist

Stockings of buttermilk: American folktales; edited by Neil Philip; illustrated by Jacqueline Mair. Clarion Bks. 1999 124p il $20
Grades: 4 5 6 7   **398.209**
    1. Tales -- United States 2. Folklore -- United States
    ISBN 0-395-84980-2
                                             LC 98-54366
These "stories and anecdotes, rooted in Europe but harvested in America, and often from African American tellers, are nearly all surprising variants on familiar folktales. . . . Philip generally lays editorial hands on the tales lightly, if at all, learnedly discusses tale types and other matters in appended notes. . . . Jacqueline Mair's small paintings add atmosphere by mimicking folk art patchwork and embroidery patterns." Booklist
    Includes bibliographical references

398.21   Tales and lore on a specific topic

Aylesworth, Jim
    The **Gingerbread** man; retold by Jim Aylesworth; illustrated by Barbara McClintock. Scholastic 1998 un il $15.95
Grades: K 1 2 3   **398.21**
    1. Folklore 2. Fairy tales
    ISBN 0-590-97219-7
                                             LC 96-52781
A freshly baked gingerbread man escapes when he is taken out of the oven and eludes a number of pursuers until he meets a clever fox
    "This hearty retelling of the well-known tale is distinguished by cheery, lively illustrations. . . . The scenery resembles that of the eighteenth-century English artist Thomas Bewick. With even a recipe included, this is altogether an old-fashioned and enjoyable version of a favorite tale." Horn Book Guide

Cruz, Alejandro
    The **woman** who outshone the sun; the legend of Lucia Zenteno. from a poem by Alejandro Cruz Martinez; pictures by Fernando Olivera; story by Rosalma Zubizarreta, Harriet Rohmer, David Schecter. Children's Bk. Press 1991 30p hardcover o.p. pa $7.95
Grades: K 1 2 3   **398.21**
    1. Zapotec Indians -- Folklore 2. Bilingual books -- English-Spanish 3. Folklore -- Mexico -- Juvenile literature
    ISBN 0-89239-101-4; 0-89239-126-X pa
                                             LC 91-16646
Retells the Zapotec legend of Lucia Zenteno, a beautiful woman with magical powers who is exiled from a mountain village and takes its water away in punishment
    This "Hispanic folktale is skillfully told, and is solid and colorfully steeped with imagery of the earth and sky. Both

the Spanish and English read gracefully, and the poetic use of language suits the story well for telling. The illustrations have a sense of volume that is reminiscent of Orozco." SLJ

Egielski, Richard
    ★ The **gingerbread** boy. HarperCollins Pubs. 1997 un il $15.95; pa $5.95
Grades: K 1 2 3   **398.21**
    1. Folklore 2. Fairy tales 3. Folklore -- Juvenile literature
    ISBN 0-06-026030-0; 0-06-443708-6 pa
                                             LC 95-50026
    "Egielski's retelling is straightforward and retains the traditional refrain: 'Run run run as fast as you can'—it sounds just right, making a satisfying modern variation. The illustrations . . . adroitly evoke the city setting while giving a solid three-dimensionality and unique individuality to the Gingerbread Boy and his pursuers." SLJ

Gingerbread boy
    The **gingerbread** man; retold by Eric A. Kimmel; illustrated by Megan Lloyd. Holiday House 1993 un il $16.95; pa $6.95
Grades: K 1 2   **398.21**
    1. Folklore 2. Fairy tales 3. Folklore -- Juvenile literature
    ISBN 0-8234-0824-8; 0-8234-1137-0 pa
                                             LC 90-33202
A freshly baked gingerbread man escapes when he is taken out of the oven and eludes a number of animals until he meets a clever fox
    "This version softens the ending with a final page of fresh, recently baked gingerbread men. This is a story that calls for energetic art, and Lloyd provides just that in warm-toned watercolors that feature the gingerbread man zipping across the pages. A compact text and suitably large pictures make this just right for groups." Booklist

Grimm, Jacob
    Hansel and Gretel; a fairy tale. by Jacob and Wilhelm Grimm; illustrated by Dorothée Duntze; translated by Anthea Bell. North-South Bks. 2001 un il $15.95; lib bdg $15.88
Grades: 3 4 5 6   **398.21**
    1. Fairy tales 2. Folklore -- Germany
    ISBN 0-7358-1422-8; 0-7358-1423-6 lib bdg
                                             LC 2001-34537
When they are left in the woods by their parents, two children find their way home despite an encounter with a wicked witch
    "Hansel and Gretel is perhaps the most terrifying fairy tale of all, and this book doesn't cover up the universal nightmare. . . . Duntze's large, beautiful, stylized pictures show the children huddled in their home, hearing their wild monster parent shout, 'We must get rid of the children.' . . . This is not a book for the very young, but it will lead to some great discussions among older kids studying heroes and monsters." Booklist

Hong, Lily Toy
    ★ **Two** of everything; a Chinese folktale. retold and illustrated by Lily Toy Hong. Whitman, A. 1993 un il $15.95

Grades: K 1 2 3 **398.21**
1. Folklore -- China 2. Folklore -- China -- Juvenile literature
ISBN 0-8075-8157-7

LC 92-29880

A poor old Chinese farmer finds a magic brass pot that doubles or duplicates whatever is placed inside it, but his efforts to make himself wealthy lead to unexpected complications

The author "here paints with muted colors, defining rounded forms with broad outlines. Retold with verve and gentle humor, this Chinese folktale could become a read-aloud favorite." Booklist

Iron Hans
Iron John; adapted from the Brothers Grimm by Eric A. Kimmel; illustrated by Trina Schart Hyman. Holiday House 1994 un il $16.95; pa $6.95
Grades: 2 3 4 5 **398.21**
1. Fairy tales 2. Folklore -- Germany
ISBN 0-8234-1073-0; 0-8234-1248-2 pa

LC 93-7534

With help of Iron John, the wild man of the forest who is under a curse, a young prince makes his way in the world and finds his true love

"Abridged and, as the afterword explains, somewhat changed from the Grimms' tale, Kimmel's dramatic narrative flows from scene to scene with a clear sense of adventure and romance and an underlying sense of mystery. Hyman's beautifully composed illustrations . . . are notable for their rich colors and subtle interplay of light and darkness." Booklist

Jack and the bean-stalk
Jack and the beanstalk; retold and illustrated by Steven Kellogg. Morrow Junior Bks. 1991 un il $16; lib bdg $16.89; pa $6.95
Grades: K 1 2 3 **398.21**
1. Fairy tales 2. Giants -- Folklore 3. Folklore -- Great Britain 4. Folklore -- England -- Juvenile literature
ISBN 0-688-10250-6; 0-688-10251-4 lib bdg; 0-688-15281-3 pa

LC 90-45990

A boy climbs to the top of a giant beanstalk, where he uses his quick wits to outsmart a giant and make his and his mother's fortune

"Seldom has the ogre at the top of the beanstalk been depicted with such gusto! The warty, fanged, pug-nosed lout dressed in animal skins and a necklace of teeth is a wonder to behold. Steven Kellogg's humorous detail provides witty embellishment for savoring. His story line is quite faithful to the Joseph Jacobs version of the story, the sturdy text offering a strong framework for the energetic illustrations." Horn Book

Kimmel, Eric A.
Three sacks of truth; a story from France. adapted by Eric A. Kimmel; illustrated by Robert Rayevsky. Holiday House 1993 un il $15.95
Grades: 2 3 4 **398.21**
1. Fairy tales 2. Folklore -- France 3. Folklore -- France -- Juvenile literature
ISBN 0-8234-0921-X

LC 91-19265

With the aid of a perfect peach, a silver fife, and his own resources, Petit Jean outwits a dishonest king and wins the hand of a princess

"In this crisp and sprightly interpretation, storyteller Kimmel takes full advantage of the plot's sly humor, which he accentuates through many colorful, deft turns of phrase. . . . Rayevsky adds rich, predominantly earth-toned illustrations that emphasize character and expression with a slight ironic bite." Publ Wkly

Mollel, Tololwa M.
The **orphan** boy; a Maasai story. illustrated by Paul Morin. Clarion Bks. 1990 un il hardcover o.p. pa $6.95
Grades: K 1 2 3 **398.21**
1. Folklore -- Africa 2. Masai (African people) -- Folklore 3. Folklore -- Africa -- Juvenile literature
ISBN 0-89919-985-2; 0-395-72079-6 pa

LC 90-2358

"Infused with an aura of mystery, Mollel's compelling story is told skillfully and dramatically. Morin's richly textured paintings, evoking in bold colors an Africa of both parched desert and lush vegetation, are worthy companions." Publ Wkly

Rogasky, Barbara
★ The **golem**; a version. illustrated by Trina Schart Hyman. Holiday House 1996 96p il $18.95
Grades: 4 5 6 7 **398.21**
1. Rabbis 2. Jewish legends 3. Jews -- Folklore 4. Monsters -- Folklore 5. Jewish legends -- Juvenile literature 6. Jews -- Persecutions -- Juvenile literature
ISBN 0-8234-0964-3

LC 94-13040

This is "the legend of the golem—a monster created of clay—who, under the guidance of the chief rabbi of Prague, rescued the Jews from persecution by anti-Semitic Christians in the late 16th century. Rogasky's strong storytelling skills are evident. . . . Hyman's colorful, fairy tale-like illustrations bring the story to life." SLJ

Salley, Coleen
Epossumondas; written by Coleen Salley; illustrated by Janet Stevens. Harcourt 2002 un il $16
Grades: K 1 2 3 **398.21**
1. Opossums -- Folklore 2. Folklore -- Southern States
ISBN 0-15-216748-X

LC 2001-4906

A retelling of a classic tale in which a well-intentioned young possum continually takes his mother's instructions much too literally. "Ages four to seven." (Bull Cent Child Books)

"All of the elements of a good story are here. . . . Salley's text rolls off the page (and off the tongue) easily, and is accompanied by delightful watercolor and colored-pencil art." SLJ

Other titles about Epossumondas are:
Epossumondas saves the day (2006)
Epossumondas plays possum (2009)
Why Epossumondas has no hair on his tail (2004)

San Souci, Robert
The **faithful** friend; [by] Robert D. San Souci; illustrated by Brian Pinkney. Simon & Schuster Bks. for Young Readers 1995 un il $16; pa $5.99

Grades: 2 3 4   **398.21**
1. Folklore -- Martinique 2. Folklore -- Martinique --
Juvenile literature
ISBN 0-02-786131-7; 0-689-82458-0 pa

LC 93-40672

A Caldecott Medal honor book, 1996

"Pinkney's scratchboard and oil artwork switches from
bright daytime hues for most of the book to purples and
grays for scenes with the zombies and snakes, which are
very effective. . . . This excellent title contains all the elements of a well-researched folktale, and convincingly conveys the richness of the West Indian culture." SLJ

Includes bibliographical references

Vasilisa the beauty
Baba Yaga and Vasilisa the brave; as told by Marianna
Mayer; illustrated by K. Y. Craft. Morrow Junior Bks. 1994
un il $16.95
Grades: 3 4 5   **398.21**
1. Fairy tales 2. Folklore -- Russia 3. Folklore --
Russia -- Juvenile literature
ISBN 0-688-08500-8

LC 90-38514

A retelling of the old Russian fairy tale in which beautiful Vasilisa uses the help of her doll to escape from the
clutches of the witch Baba Yaga, who in turn sets in motion
the events which lead to the once ill-treated girl's marrying
the tzar

"Mayer's graceful prose conveys both the wonder and
power of the tale. Complementing the text are Craft's illustrations done in a mixture of watercolor, gouache, and oils.
The palette of red and gold set against a dark background
resembles Russian folk-art paintings on black-lacquered
wood." SLJ

Wisniewski, David
★ Golem; story and pictures by David Wisniewski.
Clarion Bks. 1996 un il $15.95; pa $6.95
Grades: 3 4 5   **398.21**
1. Jewish legends 2. Jews -- Folklore 3. Monsters --
Folklore 4. Jewish legends -- Juvenile literature
ISBN 0-395-72618-2; 0-618-89424-1 pa

LC 95-21777

Awarded the Caldecott Medal, 1997

"The fiery, crisply layered paper illustrations, portraying
with equal drama and precision the ornamental architecture
of Prague and the unearthly career of the Golem, match the
specificity and splendor of the storytelling." Publ Wkly

Wooldridge, Connie Nordhielm
Wicked Jack; adapted by Connie Nordhielm
Wooldridge; illustrated by Will Hillenbrand. Holiday House
1995 un il $16.95; pa $6.95
Grades: K 1 2 3   **398.21**
1. Folklore -- Southern States 2. Folklore -- United
States -- Juvenile literature
ISBN 0-8234-1101-X; 0-8234-1292-X pa

LC 93-13248

"The mean blacksmith defeats the devil and his young
sons with a chair that won't stop rocking, a sledgehammer
that won't stop pounding, and a fire bush that keeps on sticking. In the delectable ending, Jack, now deceased, is turned
away from the underworld by terrified demons. . . . Hillenbrand's imaginative mixed-media paintings (with smudges

of coal) have thin, robust lines, angular figures, subtle colors, and a distinctive style." Booklist

**398.22   Tales and lore of persons without
paranormal powers**

Hodges, Margaret
The kitchen knight; a tale of King Arthur. retold by
Margaret Hodges and illustrated by Trina Schart Hyman.
Holiday House 1990 un il $16.95
Grades: 3 4 5 6   **398.22**
1. Arthurian romances 2. Gareth (Legendary character)
3. Gareth (Legendary character) -- Juvenile literature
ISBN 0-8234-0787-X

LC 89-11215

A retelling of the Arthurian legend of how Sir Gareth
becomes a knight and rescues the lady imprisoned by the
fearsome Red Knight of the Red Plain

"Hyman's richly romantic illustrations are lush watercolors, framed and broken with framed insets for closeups
and framed text inside the panoramic picture. The format is
horizontal, capturing the sweep of the story. While not a tale
of King Arthur, it's a wonderful taste of Arthurian legend,
hopefully whetting young appetites for more." SLJ

Kellogg, Steven
Mike Fink; a tall tale. retold and illustrated by Steven
Kellogg. Morrow Junior Bks. 1992 un il hardcover o.p.
pa $6.95
Grades: K 1 2 3   **398.22**
1. Tall tales 2. Pioneers 3. Folklore -- United States
-- Juvenile literature
ISBN 0-688-07003-5; 0-688-13577-3 pa

LC 91-46014

Relates the extraordinary deeds of the frontiersman who
became King of the Keelboatmen on the Mississippi River

"Steven Kellogg's ebullient retelling of Mike's tall-tale
feats—illustrated with large, glowing scenes suffused with
blue and yellow and with smaller vignettes emphasizing
comic detail—follows Mike's prodigious childhood exploits, his teenage wrestling practice with Rocky Mountain
grizzlies, and his years as King of the Keelboatmen, and
closes with a final showdown with enormous steamboats
taking over the river trade." Horn Book

Yolen, Jane
Not one damsel in distress; world folktales for strong
girls. collected and told by Jane Yolen; with illustrations
by Susan Guevara. Silver Whistle Bks. 2000 116p il $17
Grades: 4 5 6 7   **398.22**
1. Women 2. Folklore 3. Fairy tales 4. Tales 5.
Women -- Folklore
ISBN 0-15-202047-0

LC 99-18509

A collection of thirteen traditional tales from various
parts of the world, each of whose main character is a fearless, strong, heroic, and resourceful woman

"This is a spirited collection with a lively pace. . . . The
stories sing and soar in Yolen's supple language, and each is
contained enough for a read-aloud." Booklist

Includes bibliographical references

Zelinsky, Paul O.

★ **Rapunzel**; retold and illustrated by Paul O. Zelinsky. Dutton Children's Bks. 1997 un il $16.99

Grades: 3 4 5   **398.22**

1. Folklore 2. Fairy tales 3. Folklore -- Germany -- Juvenile literature

ISBN 0-525-45607-4

LC 96-50260

Awarded the Caldecott Medal, 1998

A retelling of the folktale in which a beautiful girl with long golden hair is kept imprisoned in a lonely tower by a sorceress

"An elegant and sophisticated retelling that draws on early French and Italian versions of the tale. Masterful oil paintings capture the Renaissance setting and flesh out the tragic figures." SLJ

398.24   Tales and lore of plants and animals

Anansi the spider-man

Anansi and the talking melon; retold by Eric A. Kimmel; illustrated by Janet Stevens. Holiday House 1994 un il $16.95; pa $6.95

Grades: K 1 2 3   **398.24**

1. Fables 2. Anansi (Legendary character) 3. Folklore -- Africa 4. Folklore -- Africa -- Juvenile literature

ISBN 0-8234-1104-4; 0-8234-1167-2 pa

LC 93-4239

Anansi the Spider tricks Elephant and some other animals into thinking the melon in which he is hiding can talk

"The snappy narration is well suited for individual reading or group sharing. The colorful line-and-wash illustrations are filled with movement and playful energy." SLJ

★ **Anansi** goes fishing; retold by Eric A. Kimmel; illustrated by Janet Stevens. Holiday House 1992 un il $16.95; pa $6.95

Grades: K 1 2 3   **398.24**

1. Fables 2. Anansi (Legendary character) 3. Folklore -- Africa 4. Folklore -- Africa -- Juvenile literature

ISBN 0-8234-0918-X; 0-8234-1022-6 pa

LC 91-17813

Anansi the spider plans to trick Turtle into catching a fish for his dinner, but Turtle proves to be smarter and ends up with a free meal. Explains the origin of spider webs

"Children able to comprehend the wordplay will be delighted when the lazy but lovable trickster figure is outwitted by the clever turtle, and Stevens' colorful, comical illustrations are perfect for this contemporary rendition of the tale." Booklist

Country mouse and the city mouse

Town mouse, country mouse. Putnam 1994 un il $16.99; pa $6.99

Grades: K 1 2 3   **398.24**

1. Fables 2. Authors 3. Storytellers 4. Mice -- Folklore

ISBN 0-399-22622-2; 0-698-11986-X pa

LC 93-41227

A retelling of the Aesop fable. After trading houses, the country mice and the town mice discover there's no place like home

"In Brett's version, the town mice are as charming and naive as their country cousins. . . . Brett's narrative alternates the parallel mishaps of the two sets of mice with lively, smooth writing and a deft touch of humor. . . . The illustrations are rich with meticulous detail." SLJ

De Paola, Tomie

The **legend** of the poinsettia; retold and illustrated by Tomie de Paola. Putnam 1994 un il $16.99; pa $6.99

Grades: K 1 2 3   **398.24**

1. Christmas stories 2. Folklore -- Mexico 3. Flowers -- Folklore 4. Christmas -- Folklore 5. Folklore -- Mexico -- Juvenile literature

ISBN 0-399-21692-8; 0-698-11567-8 pa

LC 92-20459

When Lucida is unable to finish her gift for the Baby Jesus in time for the Christmas procession, a miracle enables her to offer the beautiful flower we now call the poinsettia

"dePaola establishes a sense of place in his use of glowing colors and architectural details as he retells another legend of miraculous transcendence." Horn Book

Hirschmann, Kris

The **werewolf**; by Kris Hirschmann. ReferencePoint Press 2012 80 p. (hardback) $27.95

Grades: 4 5 6 7 8   **398.24**

1. Werewolves

ISBN 160152238X; 9781601522382

LC 2011036347

This book on werewolves "examines these legendary creatures . . . describing their bodies, their behavior, and their monstrous transformations. It also goes snout to snout with some of history's most infamous real-life werewolves and discusses the many books and films these encounters have inspired." (Publisher's note)

"Children will get a well-rounded look at the featured subjects and how they have evolved into the creatures that still fascinate many today.—" SLJ

Includes bibliographical references and index

Johnston, Tony

The **tale** of Rabbit and Coyote; illustrated by Tomie de Paola. Putnam 1994 un il hardcover o.p. pa $5.99

Grades: K 1 2 3   **398.24**

1. Fables 2. Coyote (Legendary character) 3. Rabbit (Legendary character) 4. Zapotec Indians -- Folklore 5. Zapotec Indians -- Folklore -- Juvenile literature 6. Indians of Mexico -- Folklore -- Juvenile literature

ISBN 0-399-22258-8; 0-698-11630-5 pa

LC 92-43652

Rabbit outwits Coyote in this Zapotec tale which explains why coyotes howl at the moon

"DePaola's vivid, spicy palette of gold, red, and turquoise tones and his use of folk-art borders evoke the desert setting and complement the broad humor of Johnston's text. A glossary of the Spanish phrases that pepper the illustrations is appended." Booklist

Kellogg, Steven

★ The **three** little pigs; retold and illustrated by Steven Kellogg. Morrow Junior Bks. 1997 un il hardcover o.p. pa $6.99

Grades: K 1 2 3   **398.24**
1. Folklore 2. Pigs -- Folklore 3. Wolves -- Folklore
ISBN 0-688-08731-0; 0-688-08732-9 lib bdg; 0-06-
443779-5 pa

LC 96-34434

In this retelling of a well-known tale, Serafina Sow starts
her own waffle-selling business in order to enable her three
offspring to prepare for the future, which includes an encounter with a surly wolf

"Much of the broad humor is carried in the lively, colorful illustrations, though there's wordplay aplenty in the text
and pictures too." Booklist

Kimmel, Eric A.

Anansi and the magic stick; illustrated by Janet Stevens. Holiday House 2001 un il $16.95; pa $6.95
Grades: K 1 2 3   **398.24**
1. Anansi (Legendary character) 2. Folklore -- Africa
3. Folklore -- Africa, West
ISBN 0-8234-1443-4; 0-8234-1763-8 pa

LC 00-39608

Anansi the Spider steals Hyena's magic stick so he won't
have to do the chores, but when the stick's magic won't stop,
he gets more than he bargained for

"Kimmel tells it with cheerful energy, and Stevens' chaotic mixed-media illustrations, with lots of bright pink and
green, show Anansi's friends and neighbors . . . caught up in
the mess." Booklist

McDermott, Gerald

★ Zomo the Rabbit; a trickster tale from West Africa.
told and illustrated by Gerald McDermott. Harcourt Brace
Jovanovich 1992 un il $14.95; pa $6
Grades: K 1 2 3   **398.24**
1. Fables 2. Folklore -- Africa 3. Rabbits -- Folklore
4. Folklore -- Africa -- Juvenile literature
ISBN 0-15-299967-1; 0-15-201010-6 pa

LC 91-14558

"Like the spare text, the shapes here are boldly controlled—ideal for sharing with a group of very young children. Because of their rich patterns and sharp color contrasts,
the images in the gouache paintings, although simple, never
become simplistic." Bull Cent Child Books

Paterson, Katherine

The tale of the mandarin ducks; illustrated by Leo &
Diane Dillon. Lodestar Bks. 1989 un il hardcover o.p.
pa $6.99
Grades: 1 2 3   **398.24**
1. Fairy tales 2. Ducks -- Folklore 3. Folklore -- Japan
4. Folklore -- Japan -- Juvenile literature
ISBN 0-525-67283-4; 0-14-055739-3 pa

LC 88-30484

"A Japanese fairy tale, in picture-book format, about a
Mandarin duck caught and caged at the whim of a wealthy
Japanese lord. Separated from his mate, the bird languishes
in captivity until a compassionate servant girl sets him free.
The lord sentences the girl and her beloved to death, but they
in turn are freed and rewarded with happiness." Booklist

Puss in boots

Puss in boots; illustrated by Fred Marcellino; translated
by Malcolm Arthur. Farrar, Straus & Giroux 1990 un il
$16; pa $8.95

Grades: K 1 2 3   **398.24**
1. Fairy tales 2. Cats -- Folklore 3. Folklore -- France
4. Folklore -- France -- Juvenile literature
ISBN 0-374-36160-6; 0-374-46034-5 pa

LC 90-82136

A Caldecott Medal honor book, 1991

"Opulently designed and handsomely illustrated, this
picture book provides a fitting showcase for Perrault's artful tale of deceit and resourcefulness. Unsullied by type, the
striking front of the book features a close-up portrait of the
cat's face. Befitting a fairy tale, the artwork inside is suffused with a golden light that proclaims the story to be from
a sunnier, more dreamlike world." Booklist

Stevens, Janet

Old bag of bones; a Coyote tale. retold and illustrated
by Janet Stevens. Holiday House 1996 un il hardcover
o.p. pa $6.95
Grades: K 1 2 3   **398.24**
1. Coyote (Legendary character) 2. Shoshoni Indians
-- Folklore 3. Coyote (Legendary character) -- Juvenile
literature 4. Indians of North America -- Folklore --
Juvenile literature
ISBN 0-8234-1215-6; 0-8234-1337-3 pa

LC 95-31443

"Expressive, darkly hued illustrations complement the
lively retelling, loosely based on a Shoshoni tale, which
blends dialogue and a clipped narration for an animated, appealing story." Horn Book Guide

Taylor, Harriet Peck

Coyote places the stars; retold and illustrated by Harriet Peck Taylor. Bradbury Press 1993 un il hardcover
o.p. pa $5.99
Grades: K 1 2 3   **398.24**
1. Coyote (Legendary character) 2. Stars -- Folklore
3. Chinook Indians -- Folklore 4. Wasco Indians --
Folklore -- Juvenile literature 5. Coyote (Legendary
character) -- Juvenile literature
ISBN 0-689-81535-2 pa

LC 92-46431

"Taylor's batik-and-dye paintings are a good match for
the casual, playful rhythm of her retelling." Booklist

Trivizas, Eugene

The three little wolves and the big bad pig; illustrated
by Helen Oxenbury. Margaret K. McElderry Bks. 1993 un
il $18.99; pa $7.99
Grades: PreK K 1 2   **398.24**
1. Fables 2. Pigs -- Fiction 3. Wolves -- Fiction
ISBN 0-689-50569-8; 0-689-81528-X pa

LC 92-24829

"Trivizas laces the text with funny, clever touches. . . .
Oxenbury's watercolors capture the story's broad humor and
add a wealth of supplementary details, with exquisite renderings of the wolves' comic temerity and the pig's bellicose
stances." Publ Wkly

Ward, Helen

The hare and the tortoise; a fable from Aesop. retold
& illustrated by Helen Ward. Millbrook Press 1999 un il
$16.95; lib bdg $24.90
Grades: K 1 2 3   **398.24**
1. Fables 2. Authors 3. Folklore 4. Storytellers 5.

Rabbits -- Folklore 6. Turtles -- Folklore
ISBN 0-7613-0988-8; 0-7613-1318-4 lib bdg
LC 98-26100

Retells the events of the famous race between the boastful hare and the persevering tortoise. Includes a key to the various animals pictured in the illustrations

"A straightforward, elegant, witty retelling of an old favorite. . . . With black ink outlines meticulously delineating the creatures' fur and markings, Ward's watercolor-and-gouache paintings show each animal as both warmly cuddly and realistic." Booklist

Young, Ed
  Seven blind mice. Philomel Bks. 1992 un il $17.99; pa $7.99
Grades: K 1 2 3   **398.24**
  1. Fables 2. Mice -- Folklore 3. Folklore -- India 4. Elephants -- Folklore 5. Folklore -- India -- Juvenile literature
  ISBN 0-399-22261-8; 0-698-11895-2 pa
LC 90-35396

A Caldecott Medal honor book, 1993
  In this retelling of the "Indian folktale of the blind men and the elephant, seven blind mice approach an elephant, {and} ask what it is. . . . On Monday, Red Mouse feels the elephant's leg and proclaims 'It's a pillar.' On Tuesday, Green Mouse jumps onto the elephant's trunk and decides, 'It's a snake.' On Wednesday, Yellow Mouse checks out the tusk and says, 'It's a spear.' But on the seventh day, White Mouse scampers all over the creature and puts all the clues together. The author offers this moral, 'Knowing in part may make a fine tale, but wisdom comes from seeing the whole.' . . . Ages three to eight." (Booklist)

  "In Young's version of the familiar Indian folktale of the blind men and the elephant, seven blind mice approach an elephant, ask what it is, explore various parts of the beast, and arrive at different conclusions. . . . Many preschool and primary grade teachers will find that the book reinforces their students' learning of colors, days of the week, and ordinal numbers, while heeding the story's admonition not to lose sight of the whole in their enthusiasm for identifying the parts. Graphically, this picture book is stunning, with the cut-paper figures of the eight characters dramatically silhouetted against black backgrounds. . . . At once profound and simple, intelligent and playful." Booklist

398.25   Ghost stories

Schwartz, Alvin, 1927-1992
  ★ **Scary** stories to tell in the dark; collected from folklore by Alvin Schwartz; edited by Rachel Abrams; illustrated by Brett Helquist. Newly illustrated ed. Harper 2010 113 p. ill. (paperback) $5.99; (hardcover) $16.99
Grades: 4 5 6 7   **398.25**
  1. Ghost stories 2. Horror fiction 3. Folklore -- United States
  ISBN 9780060835200; 0060835192; 0060835206; 9780060835194

  Stories of ghosts and witches, "jump" stories, scary songs, and modern-day scary stories.

  "Helquist's new illustrations for Schwartz's classic [collection] of ghost stories inhabit an altogether more benign

universe than the nightmarish Stephen Gammell originals. [This edition is] handsome and accessible, ceding the stories themselves pride of place." Horn Book Guide

398.8   Rhymes and rhyming games

Ada, Alma Flor
  Ten little puppies; adapted from a traditional nursery rhyme in Spanish. [by] Alma Flor Ada; F. Isabel Campoy; English version by Rosalma Zubizarreta; illustrated by Ulises Wensell. Rayo 2011 un il $16.99; lib bdg $17.89
Grades: PreK   **398.8**
  1. Counting 2. Nursery rhymes 3. Dogs -- Poetry 4. Bilingual books -- English-Spanish
  ISBN 978-0-06-147043-1; 0-06-147043-0; 978-0-06-147044-8 lib bdg; 0-06-147044-9 lib bdg
LC 2010015930

Ten little puppies are lost, one by one, for different reasons, until only one little puppy remains.

  This is "one of the most popular counting rhymes in Spanish folklore. . . . Vibrant colored-pencil and watercolor illustrations are done in deep hues of green, pastels, and earth tones to create realistic images that capture the spontaneous, playful, and affectionate nature of the pups. The text can be sung or spoken in Spanish or English. The English translation skillfully utilizes rhyme to maintain the story's authenticity while accurately reflecting the original poem." SLJ

Anna Banana: 101 jump-rope rhymes; compiled by Joanna Cole; illustrated by Alan Tiegreen. Morrow Junior Bks. 1989 64p il hardcover o.p. pa $7.95
Grades: 3 4 5   **398.8**
  1. Games 2. Jump rope rhymes
  ISBN 0-688-08809-0 pa
LC 88-29108

An illustrated collection of jump rope rhymes arranged according to the type of jumping they are meant to accompany

  "Heavily inked drawings provide cartoon-style humor; sources for jump-rope rhymes and an index of first lines are appended." Booklist

Baker, Keith
  ★ **Big** fat hen; illustrated by Keith Baker. Harcourt Brace & Co. 1994 un il $15; pa $6; bd bk $6.95
Grades: PreK K 1 2   **398.8**
  1. Counting 2. Nursery rhymes 3. Chickens -- Folklore
  ISBN 0-15-200294-4; 0-15-201951-0 pa; 0-15-201331-8 bd bk
LC 93-19160

  "The text is the old rhyme, 'One, two, buckle my shoe,' and the double-page spreads show the hen and her chicks (first appearing as eggs) enacting the words. . . . Children who want to skip the counting altogether can just enjoy the singsong text and the pictures executed in acrylic paints. The big fat hen is very large and quite beautiful, with iridescent green feathers accented with purple and red; her friends are just as lovely, all colors, some with delicate patterns in their feathers." Booklist

Bodden, Valerie

Nursery rhymes. Creative Education 2010 32p il (Poetry basics) $28.50

Grades: 5 6 7 8 **398.8**

1. Nursery rhymes

ISBN 978-1-58341-778-2; 1-58341-778-8

LC 2008009157

This book describes nursery rhymes' "history, characteristics, and variations. Many examples are provided as well as ideas for how children can write their own pieces. The information is accessible, and the writing is sufficiently lively to engage readers. The well-designed pages feature a variety of art reproductions from different literary eras and some photographs." Horn Book Guide

Includes glossary and bibliographical references

Cabrera, Jane

Old Mother Hubbard. Holiday House 2001 un il hardcover o.p. bd bk $6.95

Grades: K 1 2 **398.8**

1. Dogs 2. English poetry 3. Nursery rhymes 4. Dogs -- Juvenile poetry 5. Children's poetry, English

ISBN 0-8234-1659-3; 0-8234-2132-5 bd bk

LC 00-59715

Light-hearted illustrations accompany this version of the familiar nursery rhyme about an old woman and her playful dog

"The big, close-up pictures, with thick black lines and blazing color combine slapstick and coziness. . . . The chanting rhymes and exuberant illustrations make a great read-aloud for young preschoolers." Booklist

Chapman, Jane

Sing a song of sixpence; a pocketful of nursery rhymes and tales. [by] Jane Chapman. Candlewick Press 2004 61p il $15.99

Grades: K 1 **398.8**

1. Folklore 2. Nursery rhymes 3. Children's poetry

ISBN 0-7636-2545-0

LC 2003-69565

An illustrated collection of twenty-five traditional nursery rhymes and stories, including "Jack and Jill," "Wee Willie Winkie," "Little Miss Muffet," "Three Blind Mice," "Goldilocks and the Three Bears," and "The Little Red Hen"

"With clear, bright acrylic pictures, Chapman brings an action-packed collection to preschoolers. . . . The type is large and clear, and lots of boisterous pictures decorate the big, spacious pages." Booklist

Chwast, Seymour

She sells sea shells; world class tongue twisters. Applesauce Press 2008 64p il $19.95

Grades: 3 4 5 6 **398.8**

1. Tongue twisters

ISBN 978-1-60433-009-0; 1-60433-009-0

Chwast's "visual exposé of tongue twisters teems with humor and cheek. . . . The lines and use of color are poster-like. . . . The humor can . . . be goofy or dark. . . . The punchy illustrations capture [the tongue twisters'] buoyant essence. Few will be able to resist saying them aloud." Publ Wkly

Cleary, Brian P.

Six sheep sip thick shakes; and other tricky tongue twisters. illustrations by Steve Mack. Millbrook Press 2011 31p il

Grades: 1 2 3 **398.8**

1. Tongue twisters

ISBN 1580135854 lib bdg; 9781580135856 lib bdg

LC 2010014421

This is an illustrated collection of tongue twisters. "Grades two to four." (Bull Cent Child Books)

"This high-energy collection of pleasantly rhythmic tongue twisters features a screwball cast of cartoon animals rendered in digital collages. . . . An appended guide provides tips for creating effective tongue twisters-something readers are likely to try out once they master the satisfying sounds of these silly, slippery, serpentine selections." Publ Wkly

Collins, Heather

Out came the sun; a day in nursery rhymes. Kids Can Press 2007 91p il $19.95

Grades: PreK K **398.8**

1. Nursery rhymes 2. Children's poetry

ISBN 978-1-55337-881-5; 1-55337-881-4

"Collins arranges 45 mostly familiar nursery rhymes in a sun-up to sun-down romp starring a multi-species stuffed animal family. . . . Collins's watercolors display just enough verve and domestic humor to keep her subjects from turning twee. . . . The manageable size and good-natured fun make this volume stand out." Publ Wkly

Crews, Nina

★ The **neighborhood** Mother Goose; [illustrated by] Nina Crews. Greenwillow Books 2004 63p il $15.99; lib bdg $16.89

Grades: PreK K 1 2 3 **398.8**

1. Nursery rhymes

ISBN 0-06-051573-2; 0-06-051574-0 lib bdg

LC 2003-41763

A collection of nursery rhymes, both familiar and lesser known, illustrated with photographs in a city setting.

"Nina Crews' clear, beautiful color photographs and computer manipulations bring children closeup to people like them. . . . She uses computer tools to combine photos of joyful kids in her Brooklyn neighborhood with all kinds of scenarios, realistic and wild." Booklist

A **pop**-up book of nursery rhymes. Little Simon 2009 un il (Classic collectible pop-up) $26.99

Grades: PreK K **398.8**

1. Nursery rhymes 2. Pop-up books

ISBN 978-1-4169-1825-7; 1-4169-1825-6

Matthew Reinhart adapts Mother Goose's nursery rhymes, as the characters spring to life as intricate pop-up surprises.

"Ingenious details abound—the thoughtfulness put into every movement is evident." Pub Wkly

De Paola, Tomie, 1934-

Tomie dePaola's Mother Goose. Putnam 1985 127p il $24.99

Grades: PreK K **398.8**

1. Nursery rhymes

ISBN 0-399-21258-2

LC 84-26314

This "is a large, ample, unfussy edition of every child's first staple of literature. . . . The neat, flat illustrations are darkly outlined and colored generally in the illustrator's favorite palette of clear pinks, blues, and violets and surrounded with a lot of white space. Each verse is pictured in a simple and unmistakable interpretation. . . . A perfectly basic and lovely Mother Goose, lavish yet simple, and a splendid beginning for the youngest listener." Horn Book

Dillon, Leo

Mother Goose numbers on the loose; [by] Leo & Diane Dillon. Harcourt 2007 un il $17

Grades: PreK K 1 2   **398.8**
    1. Counting 2. Nursery rhymes 3. Children's poetry 4. Counting-out rhymes
    ISBN 0-15-205676-9; 978-0-15-205676-6
                  LC 2005-37763

Presents an illustrated collection of twenty-four counting rhymes, from "Baa, baa black sheep" to "Wash the dishes, wipe the dishes"

This "is so imaginative and playful that each reading yields something new and unexpected. A cast of humans and animals parades across the stark white pages like carnival-goers, some of them sporting elaborate Renaissance masks and clothing. . . . Inventive, artistically dazzling, and full of wit." Publ Wkly

Emberley, Barbara

Drummer Hoff; adapted by Barbara Emberley; illustrated by Ed Emberley. Simon & Schuster 1987 un il $16; pa $5.95

Grades: PreK K 1 2   **398.8**
    1. Nursery rhymes
    ISBN 0-671-66248-1; 0-671-66249-X pa
                  LC 87-35755

First published 1967 by Prentice-Hall

Awarded the Caldecott Medal, 1968

"A cumulative folk rhyme is adapted in spirited style and illustrated with arresting black woodcuts accented with brilliant color. The characters who participate in the building and firing of a cannon—'Sergeant Crowder brought the powder, Corporal Farrell brought the barrel,' etc.—are hilariously rugged characters, while 'Drummer Hoff who fired it off stands by, deadpan, waiting to touch off the marvelously satisfying explosion.'" Hodges. Books for Elem Sch Libr

Fitzgerald, Joanne, 1956-

Yum! yum!! delicious nursery rhymes. [compiled and illustrated by] Joanne Fitzgerald. Fitzhenry & Whiteside 2007 un il $18.95

Grades: PreK   **398.8**
    1. Nursery rhymes 2. Food -- Poetry
    ISBN 978-1-55041-888-0; 1-55041-888-2

"A farmer's market is the setting for this charming story, set around 13 well-known nursery rhymes that deal with food. The characters are animals dressed in human clothes. Listeners will have fun hunting for the piggy who appears in every scene. . . . The small pictures, all in light pastels, are beautifully detailed. . . . Subtle humor abounds." SLJ

Galdone, Paul

Three little kittens. Clarion Bks. 1986 un il $15; pa $5.95

Grades: PreK K 1 2   **398.8**
    1. Nursery rhymes 2. Cats -- Poetry
    ISBN 0-89919-426-5; 0-89919-796-5 pa
                  LC 86-2655

Three little kittens lose, find, soil, and wash their mittens

"Galdone's characteristically exuberant pen-and-wash drawings fill these pages with feline faces, first rueful then joyful, then repentant, and finally excited about the prospects of catching 'a rat close by.' This is one of those sustained nursery rhymes that initiates youngest listeners into the concentration required for stories, and there's enough dramatic movement and color contrast in the art to hold toddlers' attention." Bull Cent Child Books

The **cat** goes fiddle-i-fee; adapted and illustrated by Paul Galdone. Clarion Bks. 1985 un il hardcover o.p. pa $6.95

Grades: K 1   **398.8**
    1. Nursery rhymes 2. Animals -- Poetry
    ISBN 0-89919-705-1 pa
                  LC 85-2686

An old English rhyme names all the animals a farm boy feeds on his daily rounds

"Galdone's line-and-watercolor illustrations have all the verve and accessible good humor associated with his work, and the varied and irresistible rhythm of the verses carries the nonsense along at a good pace, enhancing its appeal to the very young. Whether told or sung, this is a diverting selection for preschool story times." Booklist

Gustafson, Scott

Favorite nursery rhymes from Mother Goose; illustrated by Scott Gustafson. Greenwich Workshop Press 2007 96p il $19.95

Grades: PreK K 1   **398.8**
    1. Nursery rhymes 2. Children's poetry
    ISBN 978-0-86713-097-3; 0-86713-097-0

This "showcases lavish illustrations that are perfect for sharing with a group. Suffused in color and charm, the visual interpretations include many delightful details." SLJ

★ The **Helen** Oxenbury nursery collection. Alfred A. Knopf 2004 91p il $19.95; lib bdg $21.99

Grades: K 1 2 3   **398.8**
    1. Nursery rhymes 2. Poetry -- Collections
    ISBN 0-375-82992-X; 0-375-92992-4 lib bdg
                  LC 2004-58446

"The stories all feature Oxenbury's trademark winsome pencil-and-watercolor pictures. They include such favorites as 'Little Red Riding Hood,' 'Henny-Penny,' and 'The Three Little Pigs,' and are retold with drama and humor." SLJ

Hillenbrand, Will

★ **Mother** Goose picture puzzles. Marshall Cavendish Children's Books 2011 40p il $17.99

Grades: K 1 2 3   **398.8**
    1. Puzzles 2. Nursery rhymes 3. Children's poetry 4. Rebuses -- Juvenile literature
    ISBN 978-0-7614-5808-1; 0-7614-5808-5
                  LC 2010-23111

This is a "collection of nursery rhymes—jazzed up by a rebus format. . . . Playful tweaks in visually depicting both verse and action make this outing special. Each uncluttered, mixed-media spread features a rhyme . . . which appears in

large font with pictures in place of some of the words. . . .
Gently humorous touches abound. . . . This volume works as
a nifty guessing game for early readers . . . and the beloved
rhymes and detail-rich artwork should earn the project an
enthusiastic audience." Publ Wkly

Hoberman, Mary Ann

Miss Mary Mack; a hand-clapping rhyme. adapted by
Mary Ann Hoberman; illustrated by Nadine Bernard Westcott. Little, Brown 1998 un il music hardcover o.p. pa
$6.99; bd bk $6.99
Grades: PreK K 1   **398.8**
1. Songs 2. Nursery rhymes 3. Children's songs --
Texts
ISBN 0-316-93118-7; 0-316-07614-7 pa; 0-316-
36642-0 bd bk
                                            LC 96-34829
"In this expanded version of the popular hand-clapping
rhyme, the elephant (who's 'jumped so high' . . . / He reached
the sky/) . . . lands in the middle of a picnic where Mary
Mack promises him her silver buttons if he doesn't go back
to the zoo. Westcott's loose and humorous illustrations add
to the necessarily limited text. A melody line and instructions for hand-clapping are included on the front endpapers." Horn Book Guide

I saw Esau; the schoolchild's pocket book. edited by Iona
and Peter Opie; illustrated by Maurice Sendak. Candle-
wick Press 1992 160p il $19.99; pa $9.99
Grades: Adult Professional   **398.8**
1. Nursery rhymes 2. Folklore -- Great Britain 3.
English poetry -- Collections 4. Children's poetry --
Collections
ISBN 1-56402-046-0; 0-7636-1199-9 pa
                                            LC 91-71845
A revised and newly illustrated edition of the title first
published 1947 in the United Kingdom
A collection of rhymes and riddles traditionally passed
on orally from child to child
"From lamentation, pun, and insult to rebuttal, tongue-
twister, and comic complaint, these schoolyard folk rhymes
are vulgar, absurd, fierce, and utterly compelling. . . . [The
book features] Sendak's wicked, joyful illustrations. Blending the factual and the surreal, the pictures (most in color,
some in sepia or in black and white) extend the rhymes with
characters and scenarios that are gross and tender. Sendak
knows kids' ferocity and their fear." Booklist

If you love a nursery rhyme; illustrated by Susanna Lock-
heart. Barrons Educational Series 2009 un il $18.99
Grades: PreK K   **398.8**
1. Nursery rhymes
ISBN 978-0-7641-6186-5; 0-7641-6186-5
"This large-format volume features just a dozen nursery
rhymes but illustrates them with grace, style, and imaginative details. Some of the rhymes are featured on single
pages, but five appear on double-page spreads accompanied
with gatefold pages that, when opened out, move the vertical
panels in the picture's central, cut-out oval to reveal a new
scene. . . . Well designed and illustrated for active toddlers as
well as older preschoolers." Booklist

Kubler, Annie

Hop a little, jump a little! illustrated by Annie Kubler.
Child's Play 2010 un il bd bk $4.99
Grades: PreK   **398.8**
1. Nursery rhymes 2. Board books for children
ISBN 978-1-84643-341-2; 1-84643-341-X
"These board books are appealing introductions to nurs-
ery rhymes. Most pages or spreads have just one line of text,
allowing the soft, lively watercolors to take center stage."
SLJ

Lipchenko, Oleg

Humpty Dumpty and friends; nursery rhymes for the
young at heart. selected and illustrated by Oleg Lipchenko.
Tundra Books 2010 un $17.95
Grades: PreK K   **398.8**
1. Nursery rhymes
ISBN 978-1-77049-205-9; 1-77049-205-4
"Mother Goose rhymes are smartly paired and dreamily
illustrated in this beguiling collection from Lipchenko. Each
page features two poems, which often have shared elements
or themes. . . . Classics are far outnumbered by rarer rhymes
of equal charm. . . . The highly detailed and surreal nature of
Lipchenko's illustrations will keep readers poring over the
pages." Publ Wkly

Lobel, Arnold

★ The **Arnold** Lobel book of Mother Goose. Knopf
1997 176p il $21
Grades: PreK K 1 2   **398.8**
1. Nursery rhymes
ISBN 0-679-88736-9; 0-679-98736-3 lib bdg
                                            LC 97-1762
First published 1986 with title: The Random House book
of Mother Goose
This nursery rhyme collection is "a true classic, with
more than three hundred verses and Lobel's vigorous, lively,
narrative-filled illustrations." Horn Book Guide

Long, Sylvia

Sylvia Long's Mother Goose. Chronicle Bks. 1999
109p il $22.95
Grades: PreK   **398.8**
1. Nursery rhymes
ISBN 0-8118-2088-2
                                            LC 98-52311
"Human beings are replaced by animals, reptiles, and insects, all elegantly dressed, in this exuberant nursery-rhyme
collection, which includes 82 familiar and less familiar
verses." SLJ

Morris, Jackie

★ The **cat** and the fiddle; a treasury of nursery rhymes.
Francis Lincoln 2011 il $19.95
Grades: PreK K   **398.8**
1. Nursery rhymes
ISBN 978-1-84507-987-1; 1-84507-987-6
"Animals figure prominently in this collection of 40
nursery rhymes, distinguished by Morris's dreamlike watercolor illustrations. For 'Lavender's Blue' and 'Lilies Are
White' a king and queen ride a polar bear, all three crowned
with botanicals mentioned in the verse. Later, a woman in
vibrant robes knits yarn carried 'three bags full' by her enormous, shaggy black sheep. Morris places nomadic, magiste-

rial figures against pastoral backdrops, peppered with castles and cottages, creating moments of strange, bewitching beauty." Publ Wkly

Moses, Will

Will Moses Mother Goose. Philomel Bks. 2003 61p il $17.99

Grades: PreK K   398.8
   1. Nursery rhymes
   ISBN 0-399-23744-5

LC 2003-731

Folk art paintings accompany this compilation of over sixty of the best-loved Mother Goose rhymes

   "In a marvelous match of style and content Moses's . . . sprightly folk-art oil paintings make this a 'must have' Mother Goose volume. The book's tempo is set from the first page, which intersperses thumbnail vignettes with individual rhymes. . . . A turn of the page then blends the vignettes into a full-bleed panorama of busy village life." Publ Wkly

Opie, Iona Archibald

★ Here comes Mother Goose; edited by Iona Opie; illustrated by Rosemary Wells. Candlewick Press 1999 107p il $21.99

Grades: PreK K 1 2   398.8
   1. Nursery rhymes 2. Children's poetry
   ISBN 0-7636-0683-9

LC 99-14256

Presents more than sixty traditional nursery rhymes, including "Old Mother Hubbard," "I'm a Little Teapot," and "One, Two, Buckle My Shoe"

   "Wells's watercolor-and-ink pictures of somersaulting guinea pigs, mischievous rabbits, and fluffy ducklings capture the sheer joy and exuberance of the rhymes. . . . Make room on the shelves for this must-have title." SLJ

   Mother Goose's little treasures; [edited by] Iona Opie; illustrated by Rosemary Wells. Candlewick Press 2007 52p il $17.99

Grades: PreK K   398.8
   1. Nursery rhymes 2. Children's poetry
   ISBN 978-0-7636-3655-5; 0-7636-3655-X

LC 2007-24959

A collection of nursery rhymes featuring such little-known characters as the wee melodie man and Handy Spandy, Mrs. Whirly and little bonny Button-cap

   "This gem . . . shines with the charm of old-time rhymes and with Wells' beloved animal and child characters, set down in her signature style." Booklist

★ My very first Mother Goose; edited by Iona Opie; illustrated by Rosemary Wells. Candlewick Press 1996 107p il $21.99

Grades: PreK K 1 2   398.8
   1. Nursery rhymes
   ISBN 1-56402-620-5

LC 96-4904

   "The 60 plus rhymes in this collection are mostly the old-time favorites, but include some more recent ones such as 'Shoo Fly' and 'Down by the Station.' Wells illustrates the selections with her usual winsome, quirky, anthropomorphic mice, rabbits, cats, pigs, bears, etc., and even includes some people. The lavish ink-and-watercolors are filled with action and delightful details." SLJ

The Oxford dictionary of nursery rhymes; edited by Iona and Peter Opie. 2nd ed; Oxford Univ. Press 1997 xxix, 559p il $55

Grades: Adult Professional   398.8
   1. Reference books 2. Nursery rhymes -- Dictionaries
   ISBN 0-19-860088-7

LC 98-140995

First published 1951

   "The novice as well as the professional will find it an enjoyable read, as well as a learning experience." Am Ref Books Annu, 1999

Pat-a-cake; illustrated by Annie Kubler. Child's Play 2010 un il bd bk $4.99

Grades: PreK   398.8
   1. Nursery rhymes 2. Board books for children
   ISBN 978-1-84643-338-2; 1-84643-338-X

   "The rhymes stay true to the originals. One of the best aspects of the illustrations is that many different babies and toddlers are represented, including children with disabilities." SLJ

Pinkney, Jerry

Three little kittens. Dial Books for Young Readers 2010 un il

Grades: PreK K   398.8
   1. Nursery rhymes
   ISBN 0803735332; 9780803735330

LC 2009051660

Presents the classic tale of three youngsters who are careless with their mittens, but who turn out to be good little kittens after all.

   "Pinkney offers another masterful visual interpretation of a classic narrative. . . . Rendered in graphite, color pencil, and watercolor, Pinkney's sparkling-eyed young cats . . . are almost impossibly . . . cuddly and precious, exuding boundless energy and capricious emotions." Publ Wkly

★ Pocketful of posies; a treasury of nursery rhymes. [illustrated by] Salley Mavor. Houghton Mifflin Harcourt 2010 62p il $21.99

Grades: PreK K   398.8
   1. Nursery rhymes
   ISBN 978-0-618-73740-6; 0-618-73740-5

LC 2009049700

An illustrated collection of sixty-four traditional nursery rhymes.

   "Rarely have classic childhood verses been depicted with so much care and detail—and fabric. Loosely organizing the rhymes over the course of the day . . . Mavor creates a miniature world using wood felt, various stitching techniques, and found materials like acorn caps and seashells. . . . Mavor's intricate and colorful embroidered work of art makes even the best-known childhood poems feel special and new again." Publ Wkly

Polacco, Patricia

Babushka's Mother Goose. Philomel Bks. 1995 64p il hardcover o.p. pa $7.99

Grades: PreK   398.8
   1. Nursery rhymes 2. Folklore -- Russia -- Juvenile

literature

ISBN 0-399-22747-4; 0-698-11860-X pa

LC 94-32332

"The collection includes original rhymes written by Polacco as well as Ukrainian folktales and retellings from Mother Goose and Aesop that Polacco heard as a child from her own Babushka. The distinctive and humorous folk-art illustrations and delightful verses and stories make this book a joy to share with children." Horn Book Guide

Ranson, Claire

Sally go round the stars; favourite rhymes for an Irish childhood. compiled by Sarah Webb & Claire Ranson; illustrated by Steve McCarthy. O'Brien 2011 64 p.

Grades: PreK K 1 2 3   **398.8**

1. Nursery rhymes

ISBN 1847172113; 9781847172112

LC 2012418512

This book by Sarah Webb and Claire Ranson, illustrated by Steve McCarthy, is a "collection of favourite nursery rhymes known and loved throughout Ireland. It includes favourite international, British and Irish rhymes as well as special Irish favourites." The book "Includes Sally Go Round the Moon; Diddly, Diddle, Dumpling; Two Little Dicky Birds; Are Ye Right There, Michael?; Half a Pound of Tuppeny Rice; Adam and Eve and Pinch Me; and many, many more!" (Publisher's note)

Reinhart, Matthew

The **real** Mother Goose; illustrated by Blanch Fisher Wright. Scholastic 1994 128p il $9.95

Grades: PreK K 1 2   **398.8**

1. Nursery rhymes

ISBN 0-590-22517-0

First published 1916 by Rand McNally

A comprehensive collection of over three-hundred traditional nursery rhymes

Ross, Tony

Three little kittens and other favorite nursery rhymes; selected and illustrated by Tony Ross. Henry Holt and Co. 2009 90p il $16.95

Grades: PreK   **398.8**

1. Nursery rhymes 2. Children's poetry

ISBN 978-0-8050-8885-4; 0-8050-8885-7

LC 2008-925587

This is a "collection of nearly fifty classic nursery verses. . . . Illustrator Ross has sensibly taken a broad and pragmatic interpretation of the genre, so classic anonymous verse rubs shoulders with Lewis Carroll and lullabies. The presentation is invitingly simple. . . . Ross' visual style remains his usual rumply, comfortable , personable line and watercolor, his figures imbued with a gentle sense of comedy and individuality, and the illustrative vignettes are spirited and deft, sometimes approaching the masterful." Bull Cent Child Books

Schertle, Alice

★ **Pio** peep! traditional Spanish nursery rhymes. selected by Alma Flor Ada & F. Isabel Campoy; English adaptations by Alice Schertle; illustrated by Vivi Escrivá. HarperCollins Pubs. 2003 64p il $14.99; lib bdg $16.89

Grades: K 1 2 3   **398.8**

1. Nursery rhymes 2. Nursery rhymes, Spanish 3.

Nursery rhymes, Spanish American 4. Bilingual books -- English-Spanish 5. Spanish language materials -- Bilingual 6. Nursery rhymes, Spanish -- Translations into English 7. Nursery rhymes, Spanish American -- Translations into English

ISBN 0-688-16019-0; 0-688-16020-4 lib bdg

LC 2001-51641

A collection of more than two dozen nursery rhymes in Spanish, from Spain and Latin America, with English translations

"Deeply rhythmic verses, compelling rhyme schemes, and words that 'play trippingly on the tongue' characterize every verse. Schertle's excellent English adaptations are not literal translations but poetic re-creations. They retain the rhythm, meter, and general meaning of the originals. . . . Escriva's watercolor and colored-pencil illustrations use brilliant hues and detail to reconstruct a young child's world." SLJ

Seibold, J. Otto

Other goose; re-nurseried, and re-rhymed, re-mothered, and re-goosed . . . Chronicle Books 2010 69p il $19.99

Grades: 2 3 4 5   **398.8**

1. Nursery rhymes

ISBN 978-0-8118-6882-2; 0-8118-6882-6

"In the spirit of Mother Goose rhymes, many of which started as parodies, the funny rhymes and wild, vibrantly colored pictures in this picture-book collection bring the nonsense up to date with technological and cultural references kids will recognize and silliness that is universal. . . . Most if the farce and the wordplay are for sharing and reading aloud with older grade-schoolers, who will best appreciate the satire and puns as well as the busy, full-page computer graphics." Booklist

Sierra, Judy

Schoolyard rhymes; kids' own rhymes for rope skipping, hand clapping, ball bouncing, and just plain fun. illustrated by Melissa Sweet. Knopf 2005 31p il $15.95; lib bdg $17.89

Grades: K 1 2 3   **398.8**

1. Singing games 2. Jump rope rhymes 3. Children's poetry 4. Games -- Juvenile literature

ISBN 0-375-82516-9; 0-375-92516-3 lib bdg

LC 2004-4273

"Sierra has selected 50 traditional playground chants and rhymes for inclusion in this illustrated collection. . . . Sweet's comical, mixed-media art adds to the wackiness of the rhymes, with jump ropes commanding a prominent position." Booklist

Taback, Simms

★ **This** is the house that Jack built. Putnam 2002 un il $15.99; pa $6.99

Grades: K 1 2 3   **398.8**

1. Nursery rhymes 2. Children's poetry

ISBN 0-399-23488-8; 0-14-240200-1 pa

LC 00-28057

The cumulative nursery rhyme about the chain of events that started when Jack built a house

"Taback's version of the age-old cumulative rhyme is an explosion of color, energy, zaniness, and pore-over-able detail." Horn Book

Tildes, Phyllis Limbacher

Will you be mine? a nursery rhyme romance. compiled and illustrated by Phyllis Limbacher Tildes. Charlesbridge 2011 un il lib bdg $17.95; pa $7.95

Grades: PreK K 1   398.8

 1. Nursery rhymes

 ISBN 978-1-58089-244-5 lib bdg; 1-58089-244-2; 978-1-58089-245-2 pa; 1-58089-245-0 pa

          LC 2010007590

"Tildes has compiled and illustrated 18 traditional nursery rhymes that trace an 18th-century courtship to honeymoon of a farmer tabby cat and his long-lashed poodle love. The pastoral scenes of preparation for the nuptials include mice tailors, a piggy florist, and a hedgehog minister. Gouache paintings in pastel colors accompany favorites like 'Hickory, Dickory, Dock' and less-familiar poems such as 'Pretty John Watts.' . . . this picture book offers nursery rhymes in a fresh way." SLJ

Trapani, Iza

Rufus and friends: rhyme time; traditional poems extended and illustrated by Iza Trapani. Charlesbridge 2008 33p il $16.95; pa $7.95

Grades: PreK K   398.8

 1. Nursery rhymes

 ISBN 978-1-58089-206-3; 978-1-58089-207-0 pa

          LC 2007026200

In this collection of tongue-twisting nursery rhymes, the reader is asked to find hidden objects in the illustrations.

"The lively artwork was created using watercolor, ink, and colored pencils. Each actor/pooch is a different breed; they all have priceless facial expressions and vary with the situations. Children will ask for repeated readings as they search for the pictures again and again." SLJ

 Another title about Rufus is:

 Rufus and friends: school days (2010)

Rufus and friends: school days; extended and illustrated by Iza Trapani. Charlesbridge 2010 35p il lib bdg $16.96; pa $7.95

Grades: PreK K   398.8

 1. Nursery rhymes

 ISBN 978-1-58089-248-3; 1-58089-248-5; 978-1-58089-249-0 pa; 1-58089-249-3 pa

          LC 2009-4307

A collection of traditional rhymes illustrated and adapted to a school setting, with hidden objects for the reader to find in the illustrations.

"Many of the source poems will be unfamiliar, but Trapani's inventive and precise verse allows each rhyme to stand on its own. Similarly, her illustrations, in watercolor, ink and colored pencil, are bright and distinct. . . . A winner." Kirkus

★ This little piggy; lap songs, finger plays, clapping rhymes, and pantomime rhymes. edited by Jane Yolen; illustrated by Will Hillenbrand; musical arrangements by Adam Stemple. Candlewick Press 2006 80p il $19.99

Grades: PreK K 1 2   398.8

 1. Songs 2. Finger play 3. Nursery rhymes

 ISBN 0-7636-1348-7

An "anthology of approximately 60 lap rhymes, songs, clapping rhymes, and finger and foot rhymes, all presented with explanations and simple instructions for parents to play with their babies and toddlers. . . . Hillenbrand has framed the rhymes with lovely mixed-media pictures in an array of sherbet pastel colors with happy piggy families acting out the rhymes. . . . A delightful accompanying CD includes 13 songs from the text, beautifully done with vivacious accompaniment. The result is a perfect book for one-on-one sharing." SLJ

Tortillitas para mama and other nursery rhymes; Spanish and English. selected and translated by Margot C. Griego . . . [et al.]; illustrated by Barbara Cooney. Holt & Co. 1981 un il hardcover o.p. pa $5.95

Grades: PreK K 1 2   398.8

 1. Nursery rhymes 2. Folklore -- Latin America 3. Bilingual books -- English-Spanish

 ISBN 0-8050-0317-7

          LC 81-4823

A bilingual collection of 13 popular Latin American nursery rhymes

The purpose of this book "is to preserve a unique aspect of Hispanic culture which deserves to be passed down to all children. . . . The illustrations are strikingly beautiful, capturing the rich color and texture of some parts of South America. . . . [But their] homogenized view of Latin Americans can easily lead to the perpetuation of some familiar stereotypes." Interracial Books Child Bull

Winter, Jeanette

The house that Jack built. Dial Bks. for Young Readers 2000 un il hardcover o.p. pa $6.99

Grades: PreK K 1   398.8

 1. Rebuses 2. Nursery rhymes 3. Children's poetry

 ISBN 0-8037-2524-8; 0-14-230126-4 pa

          LC 99-36344

Simple rebus illustrations are used to present the familiar cumulative nursery rhyme about the antics that go on in the house built by an unsuspecting Jack

"Readers can predict who will enter the story next by watching for visual clues. The small trim size of the book and the clear, vibrant colors and simple shapes of the artwork are appealing." Horn Book Guide

398.9 Proverbs

The Night has ears; African proverbs. selected and illustrated by Ashley Bryan. Atheneum Bks. for Young Readers 1999 un il $16

Grades: K 1 2 3   398.9

 1. Proverbs 2. Proverbs, African 3. Folklore -- Africa

 ISBN 0-689-82427-0

          LC 98-48772

A collection of twenty-six proverbs, some serious and some humorous, from a variety of African tribes

"Illustrated in Bryan's distinctive multishape, multicolor style, the tempera-and-gouache art resembles stained glass. . . . A worthy supplement to cultural studies, this will also inspire students to write and illustrate their own proverbs." Booklist

400 LANGUAGE

401 Philosophy and theory

Lunge-Larsen, Lise

★ **Gifts** from the gods; written by Lise Lunge-Larsen; illustrated by Gareth Hinds. Houghton Mifflin Harcourt/ Childrens 2011 90p. $18.99

Grades: 4 5 6 7   **401**

    1. Vocabulary 2. Classical mythology

    ISBN 978-0-547-15229-5; 0-547-15229-9

                   LC 2010031635

In this book "[Lise] Lunge-Larsen and [Gareth] Hinds explain what words like echo, grace, hypnotize, and janitor have in common, tracing the origins of common words and expressions to Greek and Roman myths. Readers may know that 'arachnid' derives from the story of Arachne and that modern-day 'sirens' have mythical antecedents, but this collection . . . [also explains] the roots of 'nemesis' (the goddess of justice) or 'tantalize,' after doomed Tantalus. Lunge-Larsen provides additional context, including dictionary definitions, and quotes from children's literature. Hinds incorporates graphic novel–style elements into his . . . illustrations, including dialogue balloons and filmic perspectives." (Publishers Weekly)

"Lunge-Larsen and Hinds explain what words like echo, grace, hypnotize, and janitor have in common, tracing the origins of common words and expressions to Greek and Roman myths. . . . Lunge-Larsen provides additional context, including dictionary definitions, and quotes from children's literature. Hinds incorporates graphic novel style elements into his dynamic illustrations, including dialogue balloons and filmic perspectives. A treat for myth lovers and language lovers alike, this smart and well-executed compilation should provide readers with a deeper understanding of the ways in which language evolves and of the surprising symbolism behind certain words." Publ Wkly

411 Writing systems of standard forms of languages

Agee, Jon

★ **Z** goes home. Hyperion Bks. for Children 2003 un il $16.95

Grades: PreK K 1 2   **411**

    1. Alphabet

    ISBN 0-7868-1987-1

                   LC 2002-114205

"The letter Z abandons its allotted spot in the City Zoo sign and heads off in Agee's innovative alphabet book. Children can track the red Z's journey past an Alien, over a Bridge, into some Cake, and over Hurdles until the red-letter moment when it finally finds its way to its similarly colored friends. . . . Each letter is exemplified by a noun . . . but to make matters more interesting, the object is also shaped like the letter. . . . Bold shapes and lines create a clean, comical look." Booklist

Bayer, Jane

A **my** name is Alice; pictures by Steven Kellogg. Dial Bks. for Young Readers 1984 un il $16.99; pa $6.99

Grades: PreK K 1 2   **411**

    1. Alphabet 2. Stories in rhyme 3. Alphabet -- Juvenile literature

    ISBN 0-8037-0123-3; 0-14-054668-5 pa

                   LC 84-7059

"It is a superlative blend of visual and textual nonsense because the visual surprises keep the repetitive pattern in the text from becoming tedious. The verbal parts gradually expand in their ludicrousness, in their cataloging of zany characters and occupations." Wilson Libr Bull

Donoughue, Carol

The **story** of writing; [by] Carol Donoughue. Firefly Books 2007 48p il map $19.95

Grades: 4 5 6 7   **411**

    1. Writing -- History 2. Alphabet -- History

    ISBN 978-1-55407-306-1; 1-55407-306-5

This is an "introduction to the history of the Roman alphabet. . . . Beginning sections about early civilizations' alphabets, starting with Sumerian cuniforms, include a you-are-there narrative. . . . Later spreads cover European illuminated manuscripts and the development of printing technology. A final section [covers] Chinese characters. . . . Numerous carefully chosen color photos of artifacts . . . greatly enhance the book's appeal." Booklist

Includes bibliographical references

Ehlert, Lois

★ **Eating** the alphabet; fruits and vegetables from A to Z. Harcourt Brace Jovanovich 1989 un il $17; pa $7; bd bk $6.95

Grades: PreK K 1   **411**

    1. Fruit 2. Alphabet 3. Vegetables 4. Fruit -- Juvenile literature 5. Alphabet -- Juvenile literature 6. Vegetables -- Juvenile literature

    ISBN 0-15-224435-2; 0-15-224436-0 pa; 0-15-201036-X bd bk

                   LC 88-10906

An alphabetical tour of the world of fruits and vegetables, from apricot and artichoke to yam and zucchini

"The objects depicted, shown against a white ground, are easily identifiable for the most part, and represent the more common sounds of the letter shown. . . . Both upper- and lower-case letters are printed in large, black type. A nice added touch is the glossary which includes the pronunciation and interesting facts about the origin of each fruit and vegetable, how it grows, and its uses. An exuberant, eye-catching alphabet book." SLJ

Fleming, Denise

★ **Alphabet** under construction. Holt & Co. 2002 un il $16.95

Grades: PreK K 1 2   **411**

    1. Alphabet 2. Mice -- Fiction

    ISBN 0-8050-6848-1

                   LC 2001-5210

A mouse works his way through the alphabet as he folds the "F," measures the "M," and rolls the "R"

"Fleming has poured colored cotton fiber through hand-cut stencils to make her illustrations, which are thus bold in outline and shape and vivid with an almost incandescent coloring. Although this has the simplicity of many alphabet books, it also has momentum . . . and ingenuity in its execution." Booklist

Floca, Brian

The **racecar** alphabet. Atheneum Bks. for Young Readers 2003 un il $15.95

Grades: PreK K 1 2   **411**

1. Alphabet 2. Automobile racing -- Fiction 3. Automobiles, Racing -- Juvenile literature

ISBN 0-689-85091-3

LC 2002-2198

Automobile races highlight the letters of the alphabet

"The alphabetical text often uses alliterative phrases. . . . Although a single race appears to proceed throughout the book, the cars, drivers, tracks, and spectators change considerably from the book's opening in 1901 . . . to the conclusion in 2001. . . . Large in scale, the ink-and-watercolor artwork is bold enough to share with a story hour or classroom group, yet young racing fans will find the details absorbing. Floca's introductory note on the history of racing may interest them as well." Booklist

Hoban, Tana

★ **26** letters and 99 cents. Greenwillow Bks. 1987 un il $17.99; lib bdg $18.89; pa $6.99

Grades: PreK K 1 2   **411**

1. Coins 2. Alphabet 3. Counting 4. Alphabet -- Juvenile literature

ISBN 0-688-06361-6; 0-688-06362-4 lib bdg; 0-688-14389-X pa

LC 86-11993

This concept book "is really two books in one. 26 Letters is a delightful ABC handbook. Each page shows two letters (in both upper- and lowercase) paired with objects from airplane to zipper. Turning the book around reveals the even more creative 99 Cents. Here Hoban clearly shows youngsters how to count by pairing photos of numbers with pennies, nickels, dimes and quarters in a variety of combinations. The book counts ones from 1¢ to 30¢, by fives from 30¢ to 50¢, by tens from 50¢ to 90¢, culminating in 99¢. . . . An extremely inventive approach that will be hailed by parents, teachers and librarians." Publ Wkly

Jeffrey, Laura S.

All about Braille; reading by touch. Enslow Publishers 2004 48p il (Transportation & communication series) lib bdg $23.93

Grades: 2 3 4   **411**

1. Blind -- Books and reading 2. Braille -- Juvenile literature 3. People with visual disabilities -- Juvenile literature

ISBN 0-7660-2184-X

LC 2003-17617

This offers a brief history of braille, describes the braille alphabet and how it is used for communication for the blind.

Johnson, Stephen

★ **Alphabet** city; [by] Stephen T. Johnson. Viking 1995 un il $16.99; pa $6.99

Grades: PreK K 1 2   **411**

1. Alphabet 2. Alphabet -- Juvenile literature 3. Art appreciation -- Juvenile literature

ISBN 0-670-85631-2; 0-14-055904-3 pa

LC 95-12335

A Caldecott Medal honor book, 1995

"Only after careful scrutiny will viewers realize that these arresting images aren't photographs but compositions of pastels, watercolors, gouache and charcoal. A visual tour de force, Johnson's ingenious alphabet book transcends the genre by demanding close inspection of not just letters, but the world." Publ Wkly

Lobel, Anita

Alison's zinnia. Greenwillow Bks. 1990 un il hardcover o.p. pa $6.99

Grades: PreK K 1 2   **411**

1. Alphabet 2. Flowers -- Fiction 3. Flowers -- Juvenile literature

ISBN 0-688-08865-1; 0-688-14737-2 pa

LC 89-23700

Alison acquired an amaryllis for Beryl who bought a begonia for Crystal—and so on through the alphabet, as full-page illustrations are presented of each flower. "Preschool to grade two." (SLJ)

"More than two dozen little girls, a full alphabet of them, pick flowers for their friends: 'Alison acquired an Amaryllis for Beryl' and 'Nancy noticed a Narcissus for Olga' and so on till 'Zena zeroed in on a Zinnia for Alison.' Underneath each large handsome floral illustration is a smaller picture of the named child and her flower. Charming." N Y Times Book Rev

Macdonald, Suse

Alphabatics. Bradbury Press 1986 un il $19.95; pa $7.99

Grades: PreK K 1 2   **411**

1. Alphabet

ISBN 0-02-761520-0; 0-689-71625-7 pa

LC 85-31429

A Caldecott Medal honor book, 1987

In this book the letters of the alphabet are transformed and incorporated into twenty-six illustrations, so that the hole in "b" becomes a balloon and "y" turns into the head of a yak. "Ages two to five." (Christ Sci Monit)

MacDonald "maneuvers each letter to create a visual image as well as an object that begins with that letter." Child Book Rev Serv

Pelletier, David

The **graphic** alphabet. Orchard Bks. 1996 un il $17.95

Grades: PreK K 1 2   **411**

1. Alphabet

ISBN 0-531-36001-6

LC 96-4001

A Caldecott Medal honor book, 1997

For this "alphabet book, {Pelletier} decided that 'the illustration of the letterform had to retain the natural shape of the letter as well as represent the meaning of the word.'" (Publisher's note) "Ages four to eight." (N Y Times Book Rev)

In this alphabet book "a stylized letter Y, pink against a black background, is turned on its side and looks like a mouth open in a yawn. . . . The letter Q is repeated in squares, becoming a handsome quilt, and a three-dimensional golden H hovers over a darkened sky. Even for those who know their letters very well, some of the pictures demand a second look before the artist's view is clear. But that's the point; things can be more than or different from what they seem. An engaging book that will certainly have art-class relevance." Booklist

Robb, Don

★ **Ox,** house, stick; the history of our alphabet. illustrated by Anne Smith. Charlesbridge 2007 48p il $16.95; pa $7.95

Grades: 4 5 6 7   **411**

1. Writing -- History 2. Alphabet -- History 3. English language -- Alphabet -- Juvenile literature
ISBN 978-1-57091-609-0; 978-1-57091-610-6 pa

          LC 2005-06015

"Robb traces the history of each letter from its origin to its modern appearance in the Roman alphabet. He explains the birth of writing in pictogram form and the eventual transition to written symbols that stand for sounds. . . . Smith's whimsical paintings are a fitting companion to Robb's lighthearted text." SLJ

Van Allsburg, Chris

The **Z** was zapped; a play in twenty-six acts. performed by the Caslon Players; written and directed by Chris Van Allsburg. Houghton Mifflin 1987 un il $18.95

Grades: K 1 2 3   **411**

1. Alphabet 2. Alphabet -- Juvenile literature
ISBN 0-395-44612-0

          LC 87-14988

One by one the letters of the alphabet appear on stage, where each suffers a mishap, from "A was in an avalanche" to "Z was zapped." "Ages five to eight years." (Bull Cent Child Books)

"Children can try to guess what action has occured, thereby increasing their vocabulary and the fun, or they can turn the page and read the text, or better yet—do both. This clever romp resembles old vaudeville theater, with one curious act following the next." SLJ

Werner, Sharon

Alphabeasties and other amazing types; by Sharon Werner and Sarah Forss. Blue Apple Books 2009 un il $19.99

Grades: K 1 2 3   **411**

1. Animals 2. Alphabet
ISBN 978-1-934706-78-7; 1-934706-78-7

          LC 2009-12599

"An alphabet of animals is presented, each one cleverly composed of its initial letter in a typeface that often suits the characteristics of that creature—a spiky alligator, shaggy sheep, etc. Foldout pages allow for the impressive height of the giraffe or the length of the alligator to be revealed. . . . Young readers will enjoy the animals while older children will have a greater appreciation for the book's artistry." SLJ

413   Dictionaries of standard forms of languages

Evans, Lezlie

Can you greet the whole wide world? 12 common phrases in 12 different languages. by Lezlie Evans; illustrated by Denis Roche. Houghton Mifflin 2006 un il $16

Grades: K 1 2 3   **413**

1. Vocabulary 2. Polyglot materials
ISBN 0-618-56327-X

          LC 2005020612

Introduces young readers to common phrases such as "good morning," "thank you," and "please" in German, Hebrew, Spanish, Arabic, Russian, Hindi, Chinese, Zulu, Japanese, Italian, French, and Portuguese.

"This book is a great way to introduce the many similarities and interests of children around the world. . . . Flat, cartoon-style illustrations done in bright colors reinforce action and concepts." SLJ

Includes bibliographical references

Ogburn, Jacqueline K.

Little treasures; endearments from around the world. Houghton Mifflin 2012 il $16.99

Grades: PreK K 1 2   **413**

1. Love 2. Polyglot materials
ISBN 978-0-547-42862-8; 0-547-42862-6

"Ogburn and Raschka give families a whole new vocabulary with which to express their love, exploring terms of endearment used around the globe. Impish, doe-eyed figures rendered in broad, calligraphic brushstrokes wear with pride terms like 'ducky,' used in England, and 'kullanmuru,' which means 'nugget of gold' in Finland. Raschka forgoes painting his characters with black, brown, or white skin, instead using gleeful pinks, blues, teals, and greens. The phrases appear both in English and in their original languages . . . with phonetic pronunciations provided. . . . The message about familial love being a universal human trait is clearly and joyfully articulated; it's hard to imagine a sweeter concept." Publ Wkly

Padmanabhan, Manjula

I am different; can you find me? Charlesbridge Publishing 2011 un il $16.95; pa $7.95

Grades: K 1 2 3   **413**

1. Vocabulary 2. Picture puzzles 3. Polyglot materials 4. Language and culture
ISBN 978-1-57091-639-7; 1-57091-639-X; 978-1-57091-640-3 pa; 1-57091-640-3 pa

          LC 2010007579

First published in India

"An informational picture book presenting diverse languages to child readers, this offering . . . is a tour de force. Each page opening includes a brightly colored picture puzzle image with one item differing from the others, accompanied by the question 'Can you find me?' written in one of 16 languages from page to page and supported by phonetic pronunciation guides. Supplemental text provides information about each language, including words potentially familiar to English speakers . . . or words and phrases for readers to learn. . . . The resulting whole broadens readers' awareness of how languages evolve and adopt words from one another. . . . A substantive, engaging title." Kirkus

Park, Linda Sue

Mung-mung! a foldout book of animal sounds. illustrated by Diane Bigda. Charlesbridge 2004 un il $9.95

Grades: K 1 2   **413**

1. Vocabulary 2. Polyglot materials 3. Animals --

Juvenile literature
ISBN 1-57091-486-9

LC 2003-3765

"A multilingual guessing game for the youngest children. Each spread begins with the question, 'What kind of animal says.' and features a variety of sounds in playful handwritten typefaces. Opening a flap reveals the answer. Several languages from Europe, Asia, and the Middle East are included, as well as the sound in English to tip off youngsters. Bigda's cotton-candy-colored gouache artwork displays a lightness of line and a jazzy, freeform feel that blends well with the simple fare." SLJ

Yum! Yuck! a foldout book of people sounds from around the world. [by] Linda Sue Park, Julia Durango; illustrated by Sue Rama. Charlesbridge 2005 un il $9.95
Grades: K 1 2   **413**
1. Vocabulary 2. Polyglot materials
ISBN 1-57091-659-4

LC 2004-18955

Presenting sounds that people make to utter or cry out abruptly in various languages to express such emotion as distaste, excitement, and surprise

"This original offering is a delightful addition to the canon of multicultural picture books and a fun read-aloud guessing game." SLJ

Stojic, Manya
Hello world! greetings in 42 languages around the globe! Scholastic 2002 38p il $14.95
Grades: K 1 2   **413**
1. Vocabulary 2. Polyglot materials 3. Salutations 4. Polyglot glossaries, phrase books, etc
ISBN 0-439-36202-4

LC 2001-43615

Children from around the world say "hello" in forty-two languages, from Amharic to Zulu

"Greetings appear with a bold nearly full-page acrylic painting of a child. . . . This deceivingly simple book encourages interest in and awareness of other languages." SLJ

Weinstein, Ellen
Everywhere the cow says Moo! [by] Ellen Weinstein; illustrated by Kenneth Andersson. Boyds Mills Press 2008 un il $14.95
Grades: PreK K   **413**
1. Vocabulary 2. Polyglot materials
ISBN 978-1-59078-458-7; 1-59078-458-8

LC 2007-17566

"Via simple text and illustrations, children are told what a dog, frog, duck, rooster, and cow say in English, Spanish, French, and Japanese. . . . Each phrase has its own page featuring the animal and an iconic item (the Eiffel Tower, a bullfighter, etc.). . . . The spare and colorful cartoonlike pictures mix the look of folk art and digital precision. Bold primary colors and heavy black lines abound. A glossary includes proper and phonetic spellings." SLJ
Includes glossary

419   Sign languages

Ault, Kelly
★ **Let's** sign! every baby's guide to communicating with grownups. written by Kelly Ault; illustrated by Leo Landry. Houghton Mifflin Co. 2005 77p il $17
Grades: PreK K 1   **419**
1. Sign language
ISBN 0-618-50774-4

"After a brief and informative introduction that details the benefits of using sign language with babies, Ault presents three simple stories: Mealtime, Playtime, and Bedtime. . . . Landry's pencil-and-watercolor illustrations are child-friendly, and his depictions of the signs are both appealing and informative. . . . The signs are well chosen to reflect a child's world." SLJ

Heller, Lora
★ **Sign** language for kids; a fun & easy guide to American sign language. [by] Lora Heller. Sterling 2004 95p il $14.95
Grades: 3 4 5 6   **419**
1. Sign language 2. Sign language -- Juvenile literature
ISBN 1-4027-0672-3

LC 2003-19011

Color photos illustrate sign language for numbers, letters, colors, feelings, animals, and clothes

"Clear color photos and simple text combine to form an excellent introduction to American Sign Language (ASL)." SLJ

Lowenstein, Felicia
All about sign language; talking with your hands. Enslow Publishers 2004 48p il (Transportation & communication series) lib bdg $23.93
Grades: 2 3 4   **419**
1. Sign language 2. Sign language -- Juvenile literature 3. Sign language -- History -- Juvenile literature
ISBN 0-7660-2028-2

LC 2003-26608

This discusses "how sign language came about, the jobs where it is useful to know sign language, and people who are important to sign language. Also {includes} the manual alphabet." Publisher's note
Includes bibliographical references and index

Warner, Penny
Signing fun; American sign language vocabulary, phrases, games & activities. illustrated by Paula Gray. Gallaudet Univ. Press 2006 225p il pa $19.95
Grades: 4 5 6 7 8   **419**
1. Sign language
ISBN 1-56368-292-3

"This book is a great resource for readers who want to learn more signs, or for teachers and librarians looking for fun ways to share them with kids." SLJ

420   Specific languages

Dubosarsky, Ursula
The **word** snoop; illustrated by Tohby Riddle. Dial Books 2009 246p il $16.99

Grades: 5 6 7 8   **420**

1. English language -- History 2. English language -- History -- Juvenile literature

ISBN 978-0-8037-3406-7; 0-8037-3406-9

LC 2009-8306

First published 2008 in Australia with title: The word spy

A tour of the English language from the beginning of the alphabet in 4000 BC to modern text messaging and emoticons

"Short chapters, clear explanations, and humorous examples bring the subject to life, while word puzzles and coded messages at the end of each section invite reader participation. The attractive design adds to the appeal." Booklist

422 Etymology of standard English

Baker, Rosalie F.

In a word; 750 words and their fascinating stories and origins. by Rosalie Baker; illustrated by Tom Lopes. Cobblestone Pub. 2003 221p il $17.95

Grades: 5 6 7 8   **422**

1. English language -- Etymology

ISBN 0-8126-2710-5

LC 2003-25582

"The entries in this book discuss the meanings and derivations of 750 words and phrases. . . . While exploring word origins, Baker also touches on interesting facets of European history and Greek mythology. The jaunty illustrations are reproduced in black and shades of gray. . . . This informative book fosters an appreciation for the richness of the English language." Booklist

423 Dictionaries of standard English

★ The **American** Heritage first dictionary; rev ed; Houghton Mifflin 2009 405p il $17.95

Grades: PreK K 1 2   **423**

1. Reference books 2. English language -- Dictionaries

ISBN 978-0-547-21597-6; 0-547-21597-5

First published 2007

This dictionary includes more than 2,000 entry words, and 850 full-color photographs and drawings

Bollard, John K.

Scholastic children's thesaurus; illustrated by Mike Reed. [new and updated ed]; Scholastic Reference 2006 240p il $16.99

Grades: 4 5 6 7   **423**

1. Reference books 2. English language -- Synonyms and antonyms

ISBN 0-43979-831-0

LC 2005050010

First published 1998

An illustrated thesaurus for young readers defines more than five hundred headwords and 2,500 synonyms, providing example sentences for each synonym and including an extensive cross-referencing index.

DK Merriam-Webster children's dictionary; rev ed; Dorling Kindersley 2005 911p il map $19.99

Grades: 3 4 5 6   **423**

1. Reference books 2. English language -- Dictionaries

ISBN 0-7566-1143-1

First published 2000

Presents definitions for over 32,000 entries and includes some 3,000 illustrations interspersed throughout the text

Ferris, Jeri Chase

Noah Webster and his words; by Jeri Chase Ferris; illustrated by Vincent X. Kirsch. Houghton Mifflin Harcourt 2012 32 p. col. ill. (reinforced) $16.99

Grades: 2 3 4   **423**

1. English language -- Spelling 2. Educators -- United States -- Biography -- Juvenile literature 3. Lexicographers -- United States -- Biography -- Juvenile literature

ISBN 0547390556; 9780547390550

LC 2011013018

In this picture-book biography, author Jeri Chase Ferris tells the story of Noah Webster, who "entered Yale University and became a teacher [at age 15]. When the Revolutionary War was over, he wanted to write . . . an American spelling book that would systematize American spelling. . . . He followed his speller with a grammar text, and eventually, at age 70, published his American Dictionary of the English Language." (Kirkus Reviews)

Foster, John

Barron's junior rhyming Dictionary; illustrated by Melanie Williamson and Rupert Van Wyk. Barron's 2006 160p il pa $12.99

Grades: 3 4 5   **423**

1. Poetics 2. Reference books 3. English language -- Rhyme

ISBN 0-7641-3424-8

First published 2005 in the United Kingdom with title: Oxford junior rhyming dictionary

"Young poets will have fun perusing this book in search of the perfect rhyme. . . . Short rhymes scattered throughout are likely to encourage and inspire readers to try their hand at creating their own poems. [Illustrated with] fanciful cartoons. . . . Tips for writing limericks, nonsense nursery rhymes, and various other rhymes are included in this useful resource." SLJ

The **Kingfisher** children's illustrated dictionary & thesaurus; 2nd ed.; Kingfisher 2011 320p il $16.99

Grades: 2 3 4 5   **423**

1. Reference books 2. English language -- Dictionaries

ISBN 978-0-7534-6469-4; 0-7534-6469-1

First published 2003

"One of the challenges when designing books for children is to present information in a way that is appealing to them. The second edition of The Kingfisher Children's Illustrated Dictionary and Thesaurus meets this challenge. The design of the book makes it intuitive for students to use. . . . The illustrations and information on these pages will spark the imagination of the reader. . . . This book would be a good resource for elementary-school-age students and is recommended for both elementary-school and public libraries." Booklist

★ **Macmillan** dictionary for children; general editor, Christopher G. Morris. [rev and updated ed.]; Simon & Schuster Books for Young Readers 2007 832p il map $19.99

Grades: 2 3 4 5   **423**

1. Reference books 2. English language -- Dictionaries

ISBN 978-1-4169-3959-7; 1-4169-3959-8

LC 2007297593

First published 1975

"With 35,000 entries and more than 3,000 full-color illustrations, this attractive dictionary is a browser's delight. An introductory section explains how to find a word and includes a helpful spelling guide. . . . Eye-catching feature panels provide detailed information about words of particular interest to children. . . . An accessible and enticing addition." SLJ

The **McGraw-Hill** children's dictionary; by the Wordsmyth Collaboratory. McGraw-Hill Children's Pub. 2003 various paging il (Wordsmyth reference series) $24.95

Grades: 4 5 6 7   **423**

1. Reference books 2. English language 3. English language -- Dictionaries 4. English language -- Dictionaries, Juvenile

ISBN 1-57768-298-X

LC 2002-18796

A dictionary with word histories, synonyms, illustrations, and spelling, grammar, and usage features

"The more than 30,000 entries are easy to read, with definitions arranged in three columns. 'Word History,' 'Homophone Note,' and 'Synonyms' boxes give extra information about some words. . . . This attractive dictionary is a fine work." Booklist

The **McGraw-Hill** children's thesaurus; by the Wordsmyth Collaboratory. McGraw-Hill Children's Pub. 2003 294p (Wordsmyth reference series) $19.95

Grades: 4 5 6 7   **423**

1. Reference books 2. English language -- Synonyms and antonyms

ISBN 1-57768-296-3

LC 2002-18797

Presents an alphabetical list of more than 3000 entries, with explanations of the different meanings of each headword and its synonyms

This is "a valuable addition to the upper elementary classroom, library, or any place where children write or do homework." Am Ref Books Annu, 2003

McIllwain, John

DK Children's illustrated dictionary. Dorling Kindersley 2009 256p il $19.99

Grades: K 1 2 3   **423**

1. Reference books 2. English language -- Dictionaries

ISBN 978-0-7566-5196-1; 0-7566-5196-4

First published 1994 with title: The Dorling Kindersley children's illustrated dictionary

This dictionary offers concise definitions with numerous illustrations, and information about abbreviations, spelling, word building, facts and figures, and countries of the world

Merriam-Webster's elementary dictionary; New and expanded ed.; Merriam-Webster 2009 24a, 824p il map $17.95

Grades: 3 4 5 6   **423**

1. English language -- Dictionaries

ISBN 978-0-87779-675-6; 0-87779-675-0

LC 2008041753

First published 1986 with title: Webster's elementary dictionary

More than 36,000 entries with expanded definitions, usage examples, and nearly 1,300 quotes from classic and contemporary children's literature.

Includes bibliographical references

★ **Scholastic** children's dictionary. Scholastic Inc 2010 800p il $19.99

Grades: 3 4 5 6   **423**

1. Reference books 2. English language -- Dictionaries

ISBN 978-0-545-21858-0; 0-545-21858-6

LC 2010001521

First published 1996

Offers a dictionary that includes pronunciations, definitions, parts of speech, sample sentences, etymologies, synonyms, and cross-references

★ **Scholastic** dictionary of idioms; new & updated; Scholastic 2006 298p il pa $19.85

Grades: 4 5 6 7   **423**

1. Reference books 2. English language -- Idioms

ISBN 978-0-439-77083-5 pa; 0-439-77083-1 pa

First published 1996

This "introduction to American slang and phrase origins identifies and defines more than six hundred commonly used idioms, complementing the entries with . . . sample sentences and . . . illustrations." Publisher's note

Scholastic first dictionary; updated ed; Scholastic Reference 2006 256p il $16.99

Grades: 1 2 3   **423**

1. Reference books 2. English language -- Dictionaries

ISBN 0-439-79834-5

LC 2005049911

First published 1998

This offers definitions for approximately 1,500 words, illustrated with approximately 600 full-color photographs, and includes alternate forms for nouns, verbs, and adjectives, illustrative example sentences, and a phonetic pronunciation guide for each word

Scholastic first picture dictionary; rev ed; Scholastic Reference 2009 92p il $15.99

Grades: PreK K 1   **423**

1. Reference books 2. Picture dictionaries 3. English language -- Dictionaries

ISBN 978-0-545-13769-0; 0-545-13769-1

First published 2005

This visual dictionary "features more than 700 clearly labeled images of inanimate objects, food items and living things. A section called 'The Living Room' contains common items including a remote control, telephone and DVD player. . . . The artwork (and assorted reader-directed questions) will engage the curious." Publ Wkly

Seuss, Dr., 1904-1991

The **Cat** in the Hat beginner book dictionary; by the Cat himself and P. D. Eastman. Beginner Bks. 1964 133p il $21

Grades: K 1 2 3   **423**

1. Reference books 2. Picture dictionaries 3. English language -- Dictionaries

ISBN 0-394-81009-0; 978-0-394-91009-3

"This alphabetically arranged dictionary, illustrated with rollicking funny drawings, explains word meanings with sentences and pictures. It intends to help pre-schoolers 'recognize, remember, and really enjoy a basic vocabulary of 1,350 words.' Despite its age, this book will still appeal to young children." Peterson. Ref Books for Child. 4th edition

Terban, Marvin

Mad as a wet hen! and other funny idioms; illustrated by Giulio Maestro. Clarion Bks. 1987 64p il hardcover o.p. pa $7.95

Grades: 3 4 5   **423**

1. English language -- Idioms 2. English language -- Terms and phrases

ISBN 0-89919-479-6 pa

LC 86-17575

Illustrates and explains over 100 common English idioms, in categories including animals, body parts, and colors

"Maestro's two-color cartoonlike illustrations are amusing and informative themselves, providing visual clues that support the textual explanations. . . . Although some of the expressions included are dated, the alphabetical index enables teachers and librarians to pick and choose. This book might be particularly beneficial in schools having a large ESL program, especially for older, more advanced students." SLJ

Webster's New World children's dictionary; editor in chief, Michael Agnes. 2nd ed., rev.; Wiley Pub. 2006 928p il map $17.95

Grades: 3 4 5 6   **423**

1. Reference books 2. English language -- Dictionaries

ISBN 978-0-471-78688-7; 0-471-78688-8

LC 2005053750

First published 1991

This dictionary includes more than 33,000 entries, more than 800 notes and tips on synonyms, homonyms, prefixes, spelling, and word histories, over 750 photographs and illustrations, a thesaurus, an album of U.S. presidents, tables of weights and measures, an atlas of the world, and an album of U.S. states

"This dictionary is almost three reference books in one. . . . [It] is enjoyable to read and makes learning easy." Libr Media Connect

425   Grammar of standard English

Cleary, Brian P.

But and for, yet and nor; what is a conjunction? illustrated by Brian Gable. Millbrook Press 2010 31p il (Words are categorical) lib bdg $15.95

Grades: 2 3 4   **425**

1. English language -- Grammar

ISBN 978-0-8225-9153-5 lib bdg; 0-8225-9153-7 lib bdg

LC 2009015861

"This colorful book offers information about conjunctions and examples of how they work, all in easy-to-read rhymes. . . . The cartoon-style artwork depicts brightly colored, catlike creatures in human dress dramatizing a variety of situations. The high-energy illustrations rev up the comic intensity of the lightly humorous verse and promise to engage children in the subject." Booklist

Heller, Ruth

Fantastic! wow! and unreal! a book about interjections and conjunctions. written and illustrated by Ruth Heller. Grosset & Dunlap 1998 un il hardcover o.p. pa $7.99

Grades: K 1 2   **425**

1. English language -- Grammar 2. English language -- Conjunctions 3. English language -- Interjections

ISBN 0-448-41862-2; 0-698-11875-8 pa

LC 98-36361

Rhyming text and illustrations introduce and explain various interjections and conjunctions, including "awesome," "alas," and "yet."

Lawlor, Laurie

Muddy as a duck puddle and other American similes; illustrated by Ethan Long. Holiday House 2010 un il $16.95

Grades: 1 2 3   **425**

1. Simile 2. Simile -- Juvenile literature 3. Alphabet -- Juvenile literature 4. English language -- Juvenile literature

ISBN 978-0-8234-2229-6; 0-8234-2229-1

LC 2009-29944

"Sly and irreverent, the folk sayings collected here, one for each letter of the alphabet, stretch back over history and reflect Americans' restlessness. . . . For each letter, big, clear, brightly colored cartoons show the literal meaning in the imagery expressed in such phrases as 'crooked as a barrel of snakes,' as well as the words' sly double meanings. . . . Kids will relish the boisterous insults and ornery frontier references in both the words and the pictures." Booklist

427   Historical and geographic variations, modern nongeographic variations of English

O'Reilly, Gillian

Slangalicious; where we got that crazy lingo. text by Gillian O'Reilly; illustrations by Krista Johnson. Annick Press 2004 84p il $24.95; pa $12.95

Grades: 4 5 6 7   **427**

1. English language -- Slang 2. English language -- Etymology

ISBN 1-55037-765-5; 1-55037-764-7 pa

"This volume explores the origins and meanings of slang words by tracing the efforts of a fictional student doing an assignment. . . . After a general introduction to slang, succeeding chapters explore the colorful terminology used in the food industry, in different types of work, and in the world of sports. Also discussed are words used for money, musical terms, criminal jargon, and slang used during wartime and in different countries. . . . This is a clever way for younger students to learn about the topic. . . . Colorful, amusing illustrations appear throughout." SLJ

Includes bibliographical references

428   Standard English usage (Prescriptive linguistics)

Agee, Jon

Jon Agee's palindromania! Farrar, Straus & Giroux 2002 un il hardcover o.p. pa $6.96
Grades: 3 4 5 6   428
   1. Palindromes
   ISBN 0-374-35730-7; 0-374-40025-3 pa
                                           LC 2002-101771
This "book on word play is a creative, comedic gem." Booklist

Bacon, Pamela S.

100 + literacy lifesavers; a survival guide for librarians and teachers K-12. [by] Pamela S. Bacon and Tammy K. Bacon. Libraries Unlimited 2009 363p il pa $40
Grades: Adult Professional   428
   1. Reading 2. Teaching teams
   ISBN 978-1-59158-669-2 pa; 1-59158-669-0 pa
                                           LC 2008-45514
"This wonderful professional resource's focus is mainly school librarians and teachers, but it could be used by public librarians to generate ideas for educational programs. . . . This book is an insightful tool that provides the skills and plans for successful collaboration and evaluation of literacy efforts between teachers and librarians." Voice Youth Advocates

Includes glossary and bibliographical references

Bruno, Elsa Knight

A punctuation celebration! illustrated by Jenny Whitehead. Henry Holt and Co. 2009 un il $17.95
Grades: 1 2 3 4   428
   1. Punctuation
   ISBN 978-0-8050-7973-9; 0-8050-7973-4
                                           LC 2008018337
"Young readers will receive a better-than-average introduction to punctuation marks and their uses in this cheerfully illustrated collection of poems. Each selection presents an individual punctuation mark through rhyming verse. . . . Bruno's writing is clear and lively throughout. . . . Bright collages of children of various ethnicities engaged in diverse activities complement the text." SLJ

Budzik, Mary

Punctuation: the write stuff! [created by Basher; written by Mary Budzik] Kingfisher 2010 64p il (Basher basics) pa $7.99
Grades: 4 5 6 7   428
   1. Punctuation
   ISBN 978-0-7534-6420-5 pa; 0-7534-6420-9 pa
"This slim volume uses catchy graphic design and an informal narrative to spark interest in the subject. In a presentation reminiscent of manga and Saturday-morning cartoons, each punctuation mark is introduced as a unique character

who conveys his job through chatty dialogue. . . . The book explains the various uses of each mark and some basics of sentence structure." SLJ

Includes glossary

Cleary, Brian P.

Cool! whoa! ah! and oh! what is an interjection? illustrated by Brian Gable. Millbrook Press 2010 32p il (Words are CATegorical) lib bdg $16.98
Grades: 2 3 4   428
   1. English language -- Grammar
   ISBN 978-1-58013-594-8 lib bdg; 1-58013-594-3 lib bdg
                                           LC 2010026263
The "defines an interjection as a 'word or phrase spoken suddenly and used to show emotion,' then demonstrates its uses in a rhyming, rhythmic text. Throughout, the level of Cleary's inventive verbal humor is greatly magnified by Gable's madcap drawings of dressed animals dramatizing the sentences with cartoon-style exaggeration." Booklist

★ Hairy, scary, ordinary; what is an adjective? illustrated by Jenya Prosmitsky. Carolrhoda Bks. 2000 32p il (Words are categorical) hardcover o.p. $12.95
Grades: 2 3 4   428
   1. English language -- Grammar 2. English language -- Adjective 3. English language -- Adjective -- Juvenile literature
   ISBN 1-57505-401-9; 1-57505-419-1 pa
                                           LC 98-32132
"Descriptive words of many kinds are presented in bouncy, rhyming text. . . . The adjectives are colorfully highlighted and readers will see their function demonstrated in a wide variety of contexts. Little round cats and quirky humans, both with fat noses and wide eyes, humorously illustrate the meanings." SLJ

★ How much can a bare bear bear? what are homonyms and homophones? by Brian P. Cleary; illustrated by Brian Gable. Millbrook Press 2005 un il (Words are categorical) lib bdg $15.95
Grades: 2 3 4   428
   1. English language -- Homonyms
   ISBN 1-57505-824-3
                                           LC 2004031106
"Through rhyming wordplay, Cleary explains two parts of speech that are often difficult to understand. . . . Gable took ample advantage of the pairings to create zany cartoons that provide visual clues for readers. The grouping of each set of homophones and homonyms by color is also a helpful tool." SLJ

★ I and you and don't forget who; what is a pronoun? illustrated by Brian Gable. Carolrhoda Books 2004 un il (Words are categorical) lib bdg $14.95
Grades: 2 3 4   428
   1. English language -- Grammar 2. English language -- Pronoun
   ISBN 1-57505-596-1
                                           LC 2003-1712
Rhyming text and illustrations of comical cats present numerous examples of pronouns and their functions, from "he" and "she" to "anyone," "neither," and "which."

The "text presents the major uses of pronouns with precision, brevity, and wit. The cartoon-style ink drawings brim with irrepressible humor, while the bold use of color in the artwork adds to the high-spirited look of the pages." Booklist

Lazily, crazily, just a bit nasally; more about adverbs. by Brian P. Cleary; illustrations by Brian Gable. Millbrook Press 2008 31p il (Words are categorical) lib bdg $15.95
Grades: 2 3 4   **428**
    1. English language -- Grammar
    ISBN 978-0-8225-7848-2 lib bdg; 0-8225-7848-4
    lib bdg
                                            LC 2006033800
"A professorial feline opens this offbeat lecture with a definition of adverbs and a color-coded guide to the types found throughout the book. Readers are then drawn into another of Cleary's signature rhyming narratives, which tumbles across each page verbally and visually. . . . Knob-nosed felines done in a rainbow of colors mime numerous examples of actions that can be performed with adverbial panache." SLJ

Quirky, jerky, extra-perky; more about adjectives. by Brian P. Cleary; illustrations by Brian Gable. Millbrook Press 2007 30p il (Words are categorical) lib bdg $15.95
Grades: 2 3 4   **428**
    1. English language -- Grammar
    ISBN 978-0-8225-6709-7 lib bdg; 0-8225-6709-1
    lib bdg
                                            LC 2006010756
"Cleary offers more examples of the descriptive words in this upbeat, energetically illustrated book. Beginning with a straightforward definition of the word adjective, Cleary takes off with a series of imaginative examples presented in rhythmic, rhyming verses. . . . Colorful, comical, cartoon-style illustrations help create the madcap quality that distinguishes the series." Booklist

Stop and go, yes and no; what is an antonym? by Brian P. Cleary; illustrations by Brian Gable. Millbrook Press 2006 un il (Words are categorical) lib bdg $15.95
Grades: 2 3 4   **428**
    1. Opposites 2. English language -- Synonyms and antonyms
    ISBN 978-1-57505-860-3 lib bdg; 1-57505-860-X
    lib bdg
                                            LC 2005013991
"Cleary describes and illustrates antonyms from the obvious stop and go, yes and no, front and back, fast and slow, to the more obscure: excite and soothe, hefty and diminutive. He elaborates on reasons for celebrating opposites and also describes how to create them through the use of powerful prefixes such as un, dis, im, and non. . . . The bouncy lettering style enhances the whimsical rhymes and makes for yet another strong addition to collections of books about the English language." SLJ

Stroll and walk, babble and talk; more about synonyms. by Brian P. Cleary; illustrated by Brian Gable. Millbrook Press 2008 31p il (Words are categorical) lib bdg $15.95

Grades: 2 3 4   **428**
    1. English language -- Synonyms and antonyms
    ISBN 978-0-8225-7850-5 lib bdg; 0-8225-7850-6
    lib bdg
                                            LC 2007040360
This book "shows the fun of words with light nonsense rhymes and color cartoons of animal characters that brag and boast, lie and deceive. . . . With all the slapstick fun, the pages show and tell about shades of meaning and the importance of choosing just the right word." Booklist

The **punctuation** station; illustrations by Joanne Lew-Vriethoff. Millbrook Press 2010 37p il lib bdg $16.95
Grades: K 1 2 3   **428**
    1. Punctuation
    ISBN 978-0-8225-7852-9 lib bdg; 0-8225-7852-2
    lib bdg
                                            LC 2009015860
"Perky rhymes, animal characters, and a chaotic train-station setting provide an entertaining introduction to seven oft-used punctuation marks: periods, commas, apostrophes, quotation marks, question marks, hyphens, and exclamation points. . . . The young audience will enjoy learning the concepts as they pore over the details in the cheerful, wittily detailed cartoon art." Booklist

Edwards, Wallace
    The **cat's** pajamas. Kids Can Press 2010 un il $18.95
Grades: 3 4 5   **428**
    1. English language -- Idioms 2. English language -- Idioms -- Juvenile literature
    ISBN 978-1-55453-308-4; 1-55453-308-2
"Edwards begins this picture book with a definition of 'idiom,' and English teachers will thrill to find a book that deals with this elusive idea. . . . Edwards's illustrations show the literal meaning, which is effective in its own way. . . . A list of the real meanings is provided at the end of the book. The illustrations are handsome and detailed, which adds to the ridiculous nature of the literal interpretations. This is a useful book to introduce this figure of speech." SLJ

Fuhrken, Charles
    What every middle school teacher needs to know about reading tests (from someone who has written them) Charles Fuhrken. Stenhouse Publishers 2012 vii, 237 p.p ill. (pbk.: alk. paper) $24
Grades: Professional   **428**
    1. Achievement tests 2. Examinations -- Study guides 3. Educational tests and measurements 4. Reading (Middle school) -- Ability testing
    ISBN 1571108858; 1571109455; 9781571108852; 9781571109453
                                            LC 2011037287
This book's author, "Charles Furhrken, has spent years working with several major testing companies and contributing to the reading assessments of various testing programs." He "offers . . . strategies to help students perform well on test day." Particular focus is given to "information about reading tests, including . . . preparation materials, samples of the most frequently assessed reading standards, and . . . core-reading activities." (Publisher's note)
    Includes bibliographical references and index.

Heinrichs, Ann

Adjectives; illustrated by Dan McGeehan and David Moore. The Child's World 2011 24p il (Language rules!) lib bdg $27.07

Grades: 2 3 4   428

1. English language -- Grammar
ISBN 978-1-60253-425-4; 1-60253-425-X

LC 2010011445

This explains the ways adjectives work in reading, writing, and speaking.

This "tackles the usually humdrum mechanics of grammar using fun examples, silly sentences, and cute little monster artwork. . . . Through humor and clear and concise examples the sometimes mysterious world of grammar becomes so much easier to understand. Illustrations complement the text well, with silly characters in bright and lively colors speaking sentences using the parts of speech." Libr Media Connect

Includes glossary and bibliographical references

Adverbs; illustrated by Dan McGeehan and David Moore. The Child's World 2011 24p il (Language rules!) lib bdg $27.07

Grades: 2 3 4   428

1. English language -- Grammar
ISBN 978-1-60253-426-1; 1-60253-426-8

LC 2010011456

This explains the ways adverbs work in reading, writing, and speaking.

This "tackles the usually humdrum mechanics of grammar using fun examples, silly sentences, and cute little monster artwork. . . . Through humor and clear and concise examples the sometimes mysterious world of grammar becomes so much easier to understand. Illustrations complement the text well, with silly characters in bright and lively colors speaking sentences using the parts of speech." Libr Media Connect

Includes glossary and bibliographical references

Interjections; written by Ann Heinrichs; illustrated by Dan McGeehan and David Moore. Child's World 2010 24p il (Language rules!) lib bdg $27.07

Grades: 2 3 4   428

1. English language -- Grammar
ISBN 978-1-60253-428-5 lib bdg; 1-60253-428-4 lib bdg

LC 2010011458

This explains the ways interjections work in reading, writing, and speaking.

The book is "well organized and attractive, and [injects] humor into what might overwise be [a] fairly dry [subject]. . . . The brightly colored cartoon illustrations are amusing and clearly demonstrate . . . [the] part of speech . . . being explored. A purple-and-green monster levitates off his chair after spotting a mouse beneath it in Interjections —'Eek!.'" SLJ

Includes bibliographical references

Nouns; illustrated by Dan McGeehan and David Moore. Child's World 2011 24p il (Language rules!) lib bdg $27.07

Grades: 2 3 4   428

1. English language -- Grammar
ISBN 978-1-60253-429-2; 1-60253-429-2

LC 2010011459

This explains the ways nouns work in reading, writing, and speaking.

This "tackles the usually humdrum mechanics of grammar using fun examples, silly sentences, and cute little monster artwork. . . . Through humor and clear and concise examples the sometimes mysterious world of grammar becomes so much easier to understand. Illustrations complement the text well, with silly characters in bright and lively colors speaking sentences using the parts of speech." Libr Media Connect

Includes glossary and bibliographical references

Prefixes and suffixes; written by Ann Heinrichs; illustrated by Dan McGeehan and David Moore. Child's World 2010 24p il (Language rules!) lib bdg $27.07

Grades: 2 3 4   428

1. English language -- Grammar
ISBN 978-1-60253-430-8 lib bdg; 1-60253-430-6 lib bdg

LC 2010012343

This explains the ways prefixes and suffixes work in reading, writing, and speaking.

The book is "well organized and attractive, and [injects] humor into what might otherwise be [a] fairly dry [subject]. . . . The brightly colored cartoon illustrations are amusing and clearly demonstrate [prefixes and suffixes]." SLJ

Includes bibliographical references

Prepositions; written by Ann Heinrichs; illustrated by Dan McGeehan and David Moore. Child's World 2010 24p il (Language rules!) lib bdg $27.07

Grades: 2 3 4   428

1. English language -- Grammar
ISBN 978-1-60253-431-5 lib bdg; 1-60253-431-4 lib bdg

LC 2010011460

This explains the ways prepositions work in reading, writing, and speaking.

The book is "well organized and attractive, and [injects] humor into what might otherwise be [a] fairly dry subject. . . . The brightly colored cartoon illustrations are amusing and clearly demonstrate [prepositions]." SLJ

Includes bibliographical references

Pronouns; illustrated by Dan McGeehan and David Moore. The Child's World 2011 24p il (Language rules!) lib bdg $27.07

Grades: 2 3 4   428

1. English language -- Grammar
ISBN 978-1-60253-432-2; 1-60253-432-2

LC 2010011461

This explains the ways pronouns work in reading, writing, and speaking.

This "tackles the usually humdrum mechanics of grammar using fun examples, silly sentences, and cute little monster artwork. . . . Through humor and clear and concise examples the sometimes mysterious world of grammar becomes so much easier to understand. Illustrations complement the text well, with silly characters in bright and lively colors speaking sentences using the parts of speech." Libr Media Connect

Includes glossary and bibliographical references

Punctuation; illustrated by Dan McGeehan and David Moore. The Child's World 2011 24p il (Language rules!) lib bdg $27.07

Grades: 2 3 4   **428**

1. English language -- Grammar

ISBN 978-1-60253-433-9; 1-60253-433-0

LC 2010012344

This explains the proper use of punctuation and why it's important.

This "tackles the usually humdrum mechanics of grammar using fun examples, silly sentences, and cute little monster artwork. . . . Through humor and clear and concise examples the sometimes mysterious world of grammar becomes so much easier to understand. Illustrations complement the text well, with silly characters in bright and lively colors speaking sentences using the parts of speech." Libr Media Connect

Includes glossary and bibliographical references

Similes and metaphors; written by Ann Heinrichs; illustrated by Dan McGeehan and David Moore. Child's World 2010 24p il (Language rules!) lib bdg $27.07

Grades: 2 3 4   **428**

1. Simile 2. Metaphor

ISBN 978-1-60253-434-6 lib bdg; 1-60253-434-9 lib bdg

LC 2010012346

This explains the ways similies and metaphors work in reading, writing, and speaking.

The book is "well organized and attractive, and [injects] humor into what might otherwise be [a] fairly dry subject. . . . The brightly colored cartoon illustrations are amusing and clearly demonstrate [similies and metaphors]." SLJ

Includes bibliographical references

Synonyms and antonyms; illustrated by Dan McGeehan and David Moore. The Child's World 2011 24p il (Language rules!) lib bdg $27.07

Grades: 2 3 4   **428**

1. English language -- Synonyms and antonyms

ISBN 978-1-60253-435-3; 1-60253-435-7

LC 2010012347

This explains the ways synonyms and antonyms work in reading, writing, and speaking.

This "tackles the usually humdrum mechanics of grammar using fun examples, silly sentences, and cute little monster artwork. . . . Through humor and clear and concise examples the sometimes mysterious world of grammar becomes so much easier to understand. Illustrations complement the text well, with silly characters in bright and lively colors speaking sentences using the parts of speech." Libr Media Connect

Includes glossary and bibliographical references

Verbs; illustrated by Dan McGeehan and David Moore. The Child's World 2011 24p il (Language rules!) lib bdg $27.07

Grades: 2 3 4   **428**

1. English language -- Grammar

ISBN 978-1-60253-436-0; 1-60253-436-5

LC 2010011462

This explains the ways verbs work in reading, writing, and speaking.

This "tackles the usually humdrum mechanics of grammar using fun examples, silly sentences, and cute little monster artwork. . . . Through humor and clear and concise examples the sometimes mysterious world of grammar becomes so much easier to understand. Illustrations complement the text well, with silly characters in bright and lively colors speaking sentences using the parts of speech." Libr Media Connect

Includes glossary and bibliographical references

Heller, Ruth

Behind the mask; a book about prepositions. written and illustrated by Ruth Heller. Grosset & Dunlap 1995 un il hardcover o.p. pa $7.99

Grades: K 1 2   **428**

1. English language -- Grammar 2. English language -- Usage -- Juvenile literature 3. English language -- Grammar -- Juvenile literature

ISBN 0-448-41123-7; 0-698-11698-4 pa

LC 95-9535

Explores through rhyming text the subject of prepositions and how they're used

"Large, colorful drawings illustrate the words imaginatively." Booklist

Kites sail high: a book about verbs; written and illustrated by Ruth Heller. Grosset & Dunlap 1988 un il hardcover o.p. pa $7.99

Grades: K 1 2   **428**

1. English language -- Grammar

ISBN 0-448-10480-6; 0-698-11389-6 pa

LC 87-82718

This "book explicates and celebrates verbs of all kinds, in ebullient verses which themselves sail and soar. . . . The verses are accompanied by bold, gaily colored graphics that are especially striking for their skillful use of pattern and design." Publ Wkly

Many luscious lollipops: a book about adjectives; written and illustrated by Ruth Heller. Grosset & Dunlap 1989 un il hardcover o.p. pa $7.99

Grades: K 1 2   **428**

1. English language -- Grammar

ISBN 0-448-03151-5; 0-698-11641-0 pa

LC 88-83045

"The text begins: 'An adjective's terrific/when you want to be specific/It easily identifies/by number, color or by size/ TWELVE LARGE, BLUE, GORGEOUS butterflies.' And there they are, blue and yellow, filling a double-page spread. . . . There is great diversity and technical brilliance in the artwork, and the text has rhyme, rhythm, humor, and a very clear presentation of the concepts of different kinds of adjectives and what they do." Bull Cent Child Books

Merry-go-round; a book about nouns. written and illustrated by Ruth Heller. Grosset & Dunlap 1990 un il hardcover o.p. pa $7.99

Grades: K 1 2   **428**
1. English language -- Grammar
ISBN 0-448-40085-5; 0-698-11642-9 pa

LC 90-80645

Rhyming text and illustrations present explanations of various types of nouns and rules for their usage

"While the text will be helpful to children struggling with noun usage, the large, bountiful illustrations will appeal to everyone." Horn Book Guide

Mine, all mine; a book about pronouns. written and illustrated by Ruth Heller. Grosset & Dunlap 1997 un il hardcover o.p. pa $7.99
Grades: K 1 2   **428**
1. English language -- Grammar
ISBN 0-448-41606-9; 0-698-11797-2 pa

LC 97-10051

Introduces various types of pronouns, explains how and when to use them, and provides whimsical glimpses of what our language would be without them

"Heller has taken a part of speech and made its function perfectly and entertainingly clear. . . . The stylishly drawn, brilliantly colored, double-paged illustrations grab readers and don't let go. The exceptionally fluent, rhythmic text is printed in an unobtrusive font with pronouns highlighted in bright blue." SLJ

Up, up and away; a book about adverbs. written and illustrated by Ruth Heller. Grosset & Dunlap 1991 un il hardcover o.p. pa $7.99
Grades: K 1 2   **428**
1. English language -- Grammar 2. English language -- Usage -- Juvenile literature
ISBN 0-448-40249-1; 0-698-11663-1 pa

LC 91-70668

"Here the author explains concisely how adverbs answer precisely the questions of How? How often? When? and Where? The adverbs, in capital letters, stand out boldly and cannot be missed. . . . In the large, appealing illustrations, her penguins stand proudly, her pandas eat daintily, and her cat stares piercingly. . . . The cheerful volume . . . offers a clever introduction to kinds of words." Booklist

A **cache** of jewels and other collective nouns; written and illustrated by Ruth Heller. Grosset & Dunlap 1987 un il hardcover o.p. pa $7.99
Grades: K 1 2   **428**
1. English language -- Grammar
ISBN 0-448-19211-X; 0-698-11354-3 pa

LC 87-80254

"In light verse and brightly colored pictures, Heller provides an introduction to a specialized part of speech, the collective noun. She lists and depicts more than 25, including such familiar terms as 'batch of bread' and 'bunch of bananas,' as well as more unusual phrases. . . . The concept will stimulate the curiosity and imaginations of children with an ear for language. The illustrations, containing large, bold objects in simple yet striking compositions, ensure a visually inspiring exploration as well." Publ Wkly

Hoban, Tana
★ **Exactly** the opposite. Greenwillow Bks. 1990 un il $17.99; pa $6.99

Grades: PreK K   **428**
1. Concepts -- Juvenile literature 2. English language -- Synonyms and antonyms
ISBN 0-688-08861-9; 0-688-15473-5 pa

LC 89-27227

"Using a variety of people, animals, and objects found in outdoor settings of both the city and the country, [the author] introduces and expands on the concept of opposites in this wordless photographic book. The photographs are clear, bright, and enticing. Pairs of opposites are presented on facing pages." SLJ

Jenkins, Emily
Small, medium, large; a book about relative sizes. illustrated by Tomek Bogacki. Star Bright Books 2011 un il $19.95
Grades: PreK K 1   **428**
1. Size 2. Vocabulary
ISBN 978-1-59572-278-2; 1-59572-278-5

LC 2010050853

"Four colorful mouselike beings of varied sizes represent the concepts of small, medium, large, and extra large in bold, posterlike spreads rendered in black line and swathes of thick, textured paints. Similar characters, larger and smaller, join the original four to expand the notion of size at both ends of the scale (e.g., 'huge,' 'enormous,' 'colossal'; and 'tiny,' 'minuscule,' and 'itty-bitty' and demonstrate how many smaller sizes can stack up to equal one 'colossal' size in a splendid, culminating vertical gatefold. . . . The generous trim size, large font, simple ideas, and eye-popping shapes and colors add up to a cheerful concept book ideal for sharing with a group of young children or as a lapsit." SLJ

Leedy, Loreen
There's a frog in my throat; 440 animal sayings a little bird told me. written by Loreen Leedy & Pat Street; illustrated by Loreen Leedy. Holiday House 2003 48p il $16.95
Grades: 2 3 4 5   **428**
1. Animals -- Folklore 2. English language -- Terms and phrases
ISBN 0-8234-1774-3

LC 2002-68920

"The sayings are loosely grouped by types of animals— domestic, barnyard, winged, etc.—and each adage is accompanied by a short definition. For example, 'It's raining cats and dogs. It's raining hard.' . . . Children will pore over the pages. The collaboration of text and art makes the volume lively and humorous." SLJ

Moses, Will
Raining cats and dogs; [by] Will Moses. Philomel Books 2008 un il $17.99
Grades: 1 2 3 4 5   **428**
1. English language -- Idioms 2. Figures of speech -- Juvenile literature
ISBN 978-0-399-24233-5; 0-399-24233-3

LC 2008-10339

"In this highly appropriate pairing of folk art and sayings, Moses explains many common idioms. A colorful definition . . . a sample sentence, and one of Moses's old-fashioned Americana-style oil paintings accompany each phrase. The lesson is kept lighthearted through examples that play upon the literal meanings of each phrase, often to comedic effect." SLJ

National Geographic Society (U.S.)

Word book; learning the words in your world. National Geographic 2011 64p il (National Geographic little kids) $15.95; lib bdg $23.99

Grades: PreK   **428**

1. Vocabulary

ISBN 978-1-4263-0789-8; 1-4263-0789-6; 978-1-4263-0790-4 lib bdg; 1-4263-0790-X lib bdg

LC 2010049462

Presents hundreds of words with images representing each word, grouped together by such themes as shapes, food, games, pets, music, and seasons.

"Small, clearly labeled photos set against single-colored squares enhance the easy-to-follow design." Horn Book Guide

O'Conner, Patricia T.

Woe is I Jr; the junior grammarphobes' guide to better English in plain English. [by] Patricia O'Conner; drawings by Tom Stiglich. G.P. Putnam's Sons 2007 152p il $16.99

Grades: 4 5 6 7 8   **428**

1. English language -- Usage 2. English language -- Grammar

ISBN 978-0-399-24331-8

LC 2006020575

An adaptation of Woe is I, published 2003 for adults by Riverhead Books

The author "covers pronouns, plurals, possessives, verb usage, subject-verb agreement, capitalization, and punctuation with jargon-free explanations and entertaining examples. . . . She knows her subject, can convey her message with wit and ease, and does it all in a compact, easy-to-read format." SLJ

Reid, Alastair

Ounce, dice, trice; drawings by Ben Shahn. New York Review Books 2009 57p il $15.95

Grades: K 1 2 3   **428**

1. Vocabulary 2. Wit and humor

ISBN 978-1-59017-320-6; 1-59017-320-1

LC 2008050325

A reissue of the title first published 1958 by Atlantic-Little

"'Words have a sound and shape, in addition to their meanings. Sometimes the sound is the meaning.' This 'odd collection of words and names' includes 'light words' (lissom, sibilant), 'heavy words' (befuddled), and other fascinating categories. The author's poetic lists have been turned into picture-and-word amusement through collaboration with an illustrator whose Lear-like sketches have originality, joy, and absurdity." Horn Book Guide

Roy, Jennifer Rozines

You can write using good grammar; [by] Jennifer Rozines Roy. Enslow 2004 64p il (You can write) lib bdg $22.60

Grades: 4 5 6   **428**

1. English language -- Grammar 2. English language -- Composition and exercises

ISBN 0-7660-2084-3

LC 2002-156035

This "discusses parts of speech, punctuation, and proofreading. A list of 'Common Grammar Goofs' is appended. . . . Students will find [this book] useful." Horn Book Guide

Includes glossary and bibliographical references

Terban, Marvin

★ **Scholastic** dictionary of spelling; rev ed; Scholastic Reference 2006 272p il pa $9.99

Grades: 4 5 6   **428**

1. Spellers 2. Reference books

ISBN 978-0-439-76421-6; 0-439-76421-1

First published 1998

This spelling dictionary gives instructions for looking up a word the reader does not know how to spell, offers more than 150 memory tricks to correct commonly misspelled words, explains general spelling rules and their exceptions, and includes sections such as "The Four Longest Words in the English Language" and "The Spelling Words That Made Kids Champions." To aid pronunciation, each word is divided into syllables with the accented syllable in boldface.

Scholastic guide to grammar; [by] Marvin Terban as Professor Grammar. Scholastic Inc. 2011 255p il pa $9.99

Grades: 4 5 6 7   **428**

1. English language -- Grammar

ISBN 978-0-545-35669-5; 0-545-35669-5

This guide to English language grammar covers the parts of speech, sentences and paragraphs, spelling, capitalization, punctuation, communicating ideas through vocabulary, homonyms, homophones, homographs, figures of speech, alliteration, hyperbole, similes, personification, and idioms, and includes a thesaurus.

Truss, Lynne

Eats, shoots & leaves; why, commas really do make a difference! illustrated by Bonnie Timmons. G.P. Putnam's Sons 2006 un il $15.99

Grades: 2 3 4   **428**

1. Punctuation

ISBN 0-399-24491-3

LC 2005-28559

This version of Truss's work on punctuation is intended for children. It includes only the section on comma usage. "Primary." (Horn Book)

"Truss's picture-book version of her adult bestseller tackles the topic of commas and what can go wrong when they are misused. . . . Versions of two identically worded sentences are presented side by side, demonstrating the difference in meaning achieved when a comma is added or subtracted. Timmons's humorous watercolor cartoons bring the point home." SLJ

Twenty-odd ducks; why, every punctuation mark counts! [by] Lynne Truss; illustrated by Bonnie Timmons. G.P. Putnam's Sons 2008 un il $16.99

Grades: 2 3 4   **428**

1. Punctuation

ISBN 978-0-399-25058-3; 0-399-25058-1

LC 2007045386

This "emphasizes the importance of punctuation in general. Truss . . . makes the case that careless application can dramatically change one's meaning. To prove her point, she provides contrasting examples of the same sentence, punctuated in different ways. Timmons's charming watercolors make the change in meaning clearer." SLJ

The **girl's** like spaghetti; why, you can't manage without apostrophes! illustrated by Bonnie Timmons. G. P. Putnam's Sons 2007 un il $16.99

Grades: 2 3 4   **428**
1. Punctuation 2. Apostrophe -- Juvenile literature 3. English language -- Punctuation -- Juvenile literature
ISBN 978-0-399-24706-4; 0-399-24706-8

LC 2006-34456

This is a guide to the use of the apostrophe. "Age six and up." (N Y Times Book Rev)

"This book presents readers with two identical sentences whose meaning changes with the simple placement of the apostrophe. The plural versus the possessive is depicted through lively cartoons illustrating the sentences. Truss . . . manages to keep her lessons funny and full of kid appeal." SLJ

L is for lollygag; quirky words for a clever tongue. Chronicle Books 2008 125p $12.99

Grades: 4 5 6 7   **428**
1. Vocabulary
ISBN 978-0-8118-6021-5; 0-8118-6021-3

LC 2007021061

"Budding and accomplished wordsmiths will delight in this specialized dictionary showcasing oft-overlooked gems of the English language. . . . Each definition is related with humor, sometimes including word origination and listing equally interesting synonyms. . . . Black-and-white engravings juxtaposed with cartoons in Picassoesque profile give an old-fashioned yet offbeat air to this unusual compendium." SLJ

Includes bibliographical references

428.1

Cleary, Brian P., 1959-

Breezier, cheesier, newest, and bluest; what are comparatives and superlatives? by Brian P. Cleary; illustrations by Brian Gable. Millbrook Press 2013 31 p. col. ill. (Words are CATegorical) (reinforced) $16.95

Grades: 2 3 4   **428.1**
1. Picture books for children 2. English language -- Grammar 3. Comparison (Grammar) -- Juvenile literature 4. Grammar, comparative and general -- Adjective -- Juvenile literature
ISBN 0761353623; 9780761353621

LC 2012019105

This book is part of the Words Are CATegorical series and "presents a quick grammar lesson through a fast-paced, rhyming text and . . . cartoon-style illustrations. The introductory page defines (in prose) the terms 'comparatives' and 'superlatives.' An appended page tells (in prose) how to form comparative and superlative adjectives. And in between come the rhyming verses, briefly explaining these parts of speech and providing . . . many examples." (Booklist)

Könnecke, Ole

The **big** book of words and pictures; Ole Könnecke; translated by Monika Smith. Gecko Press 2012 22 p. $14.95

Grades: K 1   **428.1**
1. Children's literature 2. Picture books for children 3. Vocabulary -- Juvenile literature
ISBN 187757905X; 9781877579059

This children's picture book, written and illustrated by Ole Konnecke, "is a large format board book of early concept words and pictures. . . ." multiple vocabulary words and their contextual concepts are demonstrated by illustrated scenarios with animals and people, each with their own simple story to tell. (Publisher's note)

430   German and related languages

Hettinga, Donald R.

The **Brothers** Grimm; two lives, one legacy. Clarion Bks. 2001 180p il $22

Grades: 5 6 7 8   **430**
1. Authors 2. Folklorists 3. Philologists 4. Folklore -- Germany 5. Short story writers 6. Philologists -- Germany -- Biography
ISBN 0-618-05599-1

LC 00-65598

A biography of the brothers famous for collecting German folk tales

"No book for young readers presents the Grimms' intertwined lives against the larger background of early 19th-century Europe in such fascinating detail as this absorbing new biography. . . . Students will find it an excellent resource for term papers, yet it is written so clearly that it makes for enjoyable pleasure reading." SLJ

Includes bibliographical references

433   Dictionaries of standard German

Kudela, Katy R.

My first book of German words. Capstone Press 2010 32p il (A+ books: bilingual picture dictionaries) lib bdg $25.99

Grades: K 1 2 3   **433**
1. German language 2. Picture dictionaries
ISBN 978-1-4296-3296-6; 1-4296-3296-8

LC 2009005516

Simple text paired with themed photos invite the reader to learn German vocabulary and phrases.

"Ideal for children encountering multicultural friends at school and at play. . . . [This] makes simple language exchanges fun and easy. . . . The pictures are full-bleed and have the brilliant, bright look of a catalogue. . . . [This] makes for good kindergarten ready reference." Booklist

Includes bibliographical references

439   Other Germanic languages

Sussman, Joni Kibort

My first Yiddish word book; edited by Joni Kibort Sussman; pictures by Pepi Marzel. Kar-Ben Pub. 2008 32p il $17.95

Grades: K 1 2   **439**

1. Reference books 2. Yiddish language 3. Picture dictionaries

ISBN 978-0-8225-8755-2

LC 2007028347

"With this [Yiddish] picture dictionary, select vocabulary is accessible to young readers. Basic words for parts of the body, members of the family, clothing, the house, school, playground, city, grocery store, bedtime, the zoo, colors, etc., are included. All are written in block letters with English transliteration and translation. Each spread includes a large, detailed illustration with the individual items clearly identified along the bottom. The pictures are cheerful and contemporary." SLJ

443   Dictionaries of standard French

Corbeil, Jean-Claude

★ My first French English visual dictionary; [by] Jean-Claude Corbeil; Ariane Archambault. Firefly Books 2006 80p il $14.95

Grades: 3 4 5 6   **443**

1. Reference books 2. Picture dictionaries 3. French language -- Dictionaries

ISBN 978-1-55407-193-7; 1-55407-193-3

"There are 36 themes-among them 'Clothing,' 'Colors and Shapes,' 'Dinosaurs,' 'Space,' and 'Sports' selected to appeal to primary-age children. Each theme has a double-page spread of small to medium-sized individual illustrations of items allied to the theme. The other 1,300 illustrations are large and in full color and are accompanied by the English word in boldface letters with the word in the other language underneath. The typeface is large and uncluttered and easy to see. . . . Separate English and French indexes complete the book." Booklist

Kudela, Katy R.

My first book of French words; translator, Translations. com. Capstone Press 2009 32p il (A+ books: bilingual picture dictionaries) lib bdg $23.99

Grades: K 1 2 3   **443**

1. Picture dictionaries 2. French language -- Dictionaries

ISBN 978-1-4296-3295-9 lib bdg; 1-4296-3295-X lib bdg

LC 2009005510

"This simple bilingual picture dictionary is illustrated with attractive, colorful photos. Each themed spread introduces 10 words, first in English and then in French, followed by the approximate French pronunciation. . . . The 130 words cover family, body parts, clothes, toys, bedroom, bathroom, kitchen, food, farm, garden, colors, classroom, city, numbers, and useful phrases. . . . Overall, this book is appealing, useful, and easy to comprehend." SLJ

Includes bibliographical references

463   Dictionaries of standard Spanish

Corbeil, Jean-Claude

★ My first Spanish English visual dictionary; [by] Jean-Claude Corbeil; Ariane Archambault. Firefly Books 2006 80p il $14.95

Grades: 3 4 5 6   **463**

1. Reference books 2. Picture dictionaries 3. Spanish language -- Dictionaries

ISBN 978-1-55407-194-4; 1-55407-194-1

A Spanish/English visual dictionary for children: 1,600 terms annotate 1,300 realistic illustrations organized in 36 themes that children experience in their lives. Two indexes, by language, and Spanish terms include gender.

Kudela, Katy R.

My first book of Spanish words. Capstone Press 2009 32p il (A+ books: bilingual picture dictionaries) lib bdg $23.99

Grades: K 1 2 3   **463**

1. Picture dictionaries 2. Spanish language -- Dictionaries

ISBN 978-1-4296-3298-0 lib bdg; 1-4296-3298-4 lib bdg

LC 2009005518

This picture dictionary introduces common Spanish words with color photos.

Includes bibliographical references

492.4   Hebrew

Groner, Judyth Saypol

My first Hebrew word book; [by Judye Groner and Madeline Wikler]; pictures by Pepi Marzel. Kar-Ben Pub. 2005 32p il lib bdg $17.95

Grades: K 1 2   **492.4**

1. Hebrew language 2. Reference books 3. Picture dictionaries

ISBN 1-58013-126-3

LC 2004-13504

"Basic Hebrew words . . . are included. All are written in block letters with English transliteration and translation. Each spread includes a large, detailed illustration with the individual items clearly identified along the bottom. The color cartoon art is cheerful and contemporary. At the back of the book, a word list is organized alphabetically in English and includes the Hebrew words and corresponding page numbers. All in all, this is a wonderful resource." SLJ

493   Non-Semitic Afro-Asiatic languages

Giblin, James

★ The riddle of the Rosetta Stone; key to ancient Egypt. [by] James Cross Giblin. Crowell 1990 85p il hardcover o.p. pa $7.99

Grades: 5 6 7 8   **493**

1. Hieroglyphics 2. Egyptian language

ISBN 0-06-446137-8 pa

LC 89-29289

Describes how the discovery and deciphering of the Rosetta Stone unlocked the secret of Egyptian hieroglyphics

"Suspense keeps the reader glued to this fine piece of nonfiction as the mystery of hieroglyphs is slowly unraveled. . . . The author has done a masterful job of distilling information, citing the highlights, and fitting it all together in an interesting and enlightening look at a puzzling subject." Horn Book

Includes bibliographical references

495.1 Chinese

Kudela, Katy R.

My first book of Mandarin Chinese words. Capstone Press 2010 32p il (A+ books: bilingual picture dictionaries) lib bdg $25.99

Grades: K 1 2 3   **495.1**

1. Chinese language 2. Picture dictionaries

ISBN 978-1-4296-3297-3; 1-4296-3297-6

LC 2009005517

Simple text paired with themed photos invite the reader to learn Mandarin Chinese vocabulary and phrases.

"Ideal for children encountering multicultural friends at school and at play. . . . [This] makes simple language exchanges fun and easy. . . . The pictures are full-bleed and have the brilliant, bright look of a catalogue. . . . [This] makes for good kindergarten ready reference." Booklist

Includes bibliographical references

Lee, Huy Voun

1, 2, 3 go! Holt & Co. 2000 un il $17.95

Grades: K 1 2 3   **495.1**

1. Counting 2. Chinese language 3. Chinese characters

ISBN 0-8050-6205-X

LC 99-48326

An introduction to Chinese writing describing the construction, meaning, and pronunciation of simple characters used for a variety of words and the numbers one through ten

"Lee effectively displays boldly contrasted cut-paper shapes on stark white backgrounds. . . . With masterful simplicity, Lee leads readers to a preliminary appreciation of Chinese culture." Booklist

At the beach; written and illustrated by Huy Voun Lee. Holt & Co. 1994 un il hardcover o.p. pa $7.95

Grades: K 1 2 3   **495.1**

1. Chinese language 2. Writing -- Juvenile literature

ISBN 0-8050-2768-8; 0-8050-5822-2 pa

LC 93-25462

A mother amuses her young son at the beach by drawing in the sand Chinese characters, many of which resemble the objects they stand for

"The intricate, visually captivating cut-paper collages have borders with sea motifs. Useful for beginning language study and interesting due to its artistic innovation, the book includes a pronunciation guide." Horn Book Guide

Other titles in this series are:

In the leaves (2005)

In the park (1998)

In the snow (1995)

495.6 Japanese

Kudela, Katy R.

My first book of Japanese words. Capstone Press 2010 32p il (A+ books: bilingual picture dictionaries) lib bdg $25.99

Grades: K 1 2 3   **495.6**

1. Japanese language 2. Picture dictionaries

ISBN 978-1-4296-3916-3; 1-4296-3916-4

LC 2009028665

Simple text paired with themed photos invite the reader to learn Japanese vocabulary and phrases.

"Ideal for children encountering multicultural friends at school and at play. . . . [This] makes simple language exchanges fun and easy. . . . The pictures are full-bleed and have the brilliant, bright look of a catalogue. . . . [This] makes for good kindergarten ready reference." Booklist

Includes bibliographical references

500 SCIENCE

500 Natural sciences and mathematics

★ The **big** idea science book; incredible concepts that show how science works in the real world. editor, Matilda Gollon; consultant, Lisa Burke. DK Pub. 2010 304p il $29.99

Grades: 4 5 6 7   **500**

1. Science

ISBN 978-0-7566-6287-5; 0-7566-6287-7

LC 2010-281143

"Aimed at grabbing readers' general interest in science, this lively overview is split into sections on life, earth, and physical science; within each category, specific subjects are plainly labeled for easy reference. . . . Full-color photographs, drawings, and diagrams further inform, and readers can visit an interactive Web site for more exploration. For breadth of material and clarity, it's hard to beat." Publ Wkly

Bryson, Bill

A **really** short history of nearly everything. Delacorte Press 2009 169p il $19.99

Grades: 4 5 6 7   **500**

1. Science

ISBN 978-0-385-73810-1; 0-385-73810-2

A newly illustrated, abridged and adapted edition of A short history of nearly everything, published 2003 by Broadway Books for adults; this edition first published in the United Kingdom 2008

Bryson "whirls through mind-numbing notions such as the creation of the universe and the life span of an atom with good cheer and accessible, even exciting, writing. The two-page speads meander their way through the various recesses of science with a combination of explanatory prose, historical anecdotes, wry asides, and illustrations that range from helpful to comical." Booklist

Cleary, Brian P.

Mrs. Riley Bought Five Itchy Aardvarks and other painless tricks for memorizing science facts; illustrated by J.

P. Sandy. Millbrook Press 2008 48p il (Adventures in memory) lib bdg $23.93

Grades: 3 4 5 6   500

1. Memory 2. Science 3. Scientific recreations 4. Mnemonics -- Juvenile literature 5. Scientific

ISBN 978-0-8225-7819-2 lib bdg; 0-8225-7819-0 lib bdg

LC 2007-52125

"This short (48 pages), well-written, often cleverly phrased, entertaining, humorous, engaging, colorfully illustrated book should be in every school and public library. . . . [It includes] a short, informative chapter on the scientific method." Sci Books Films

Cobb, Vicki

What's the big idea? amazing science questions for the curious kid. Skyhorse 2010 197p il $19.95

Grades: 3 4 5 6   500

1. Science 2. Questions and answers 3. Matter -- Juvenile literature 4. Motion -- Juvenile literature 5. Force and energy -- Juvenile literature

ISBN 978-1-61608-013-6; 1-61608-013-2

LC 2009-46866

"The four main topics—energy, motion, matter, and life—are presented as 'big ideas' and explained through a series of two to four-page chapters that open with a kid-friendly question designed to provide insight into some of the great scientific breakthroughs. . . . Each question is introduced with an illustrated page of four students reacting (in speech bubbles) with humor and sarcasm to the question. . . . Spots of black-line cartoon-style artwork filled with color break up most pages and keep the large-point sans-serif text from overwhelming the spreads. This will be a quality addition to any collection." SLJ

Dotlich, Rebecca Kai

What is science? illustrated by Sachiko Yoshikawa. H. Holt 2006 un il $16.95

Grades: K 1 2   500

1. Science

ISBN 978-0-8050-7394-2; 0-8050-7394-9

LC 2005-20050

"Dotlich begins and ends with the line, What is science?/ So many things. In between, she enumerates some of the areas of study—astronomy, geology, paleontology, oceanography, botany, meteorology, and zoology. Each page has just a few words, in large print, superimposed on a background of boldly colored acrylic, pastel, and collage art. The rhyming text flows nicely. . . . With its large illustrations, simple text, and important concepts, this title will be enjoyed by newly independent readers, or will ignite excitement in a group. A unique look at the topic." SLJ

Goldsmith, Mike

Everything you need to know about science. Kingfisher 2009 160p il $18.99

Grades: 1 2 3 4 5   500

1. Science

ISBN 978-0-7534-6302-4; 0-7534-6302-4

"This broad, accessible encyclopedia will appeal to browsers because of the 500-plus highly realistic computer-generated illustrations, large fonts, and short paragraphs. . . . Science enthusiasts will enjoy browsing this smorgasbord of information." SLJ

Hillman, Ben

How weird is it; a freaky book all about strangeness. Scholastic 2009 47p il $15.99

Grades: 5 6 7 8   500

1. Science 2. Curiosities and wonders -- Juvenile literature

ISBN 978-0-439-91868-8; 0-439-91868-5

LC 2008-09787

Strange but facinating facts about everyday things that turn out to be extraordinary.

"Humor adds interest to the random but readable text. Large, vivid computer-manipulated photographs illustrate the information." Horn Book Guide

Hoaxed! fakes & mistakes in the world of science. by the editors of YES mag; illustrated by Howie Woo. Kids Can Press 2009 48p il lib bdg $16.95; pa $8.95

Grades: 5 6 7 8   500

1. Fraud 2. Science 3. Fraud in science -- Juvenile literature 4. Errors, Scientific -- Juvenile literature

ISBN 978-1-55453-206-3 lib bdg; 1-55453-206-X lib bdg; 978-1-55453-207-0 pa; 1-55453-207-8 pa

"Piltdown man, Richard Meinertzhagen the light-fingered bird collector, 'Stone Age' Tasaday in the Philippines, crop circles in England, cold fusion energy and UFOs in Roswell, N.M., are the fakes and mistakes described in this lively introduction to fraud in science. The breezy text opens with a clear description of the scientific process of hypothesis, experiment, publication in professional magazines and replication of results before proceeding to the many colorful fakes exposed." Kirkus

Includes index.

Murphy, Glenn

Why is snot green; and other extremely important questions (and answers) Roaring Brook Press 2009 236p il pa $9.95

Grades: 4 5 6 7   500

1. Science 2. Technology 3. Science -- Juvenile literature

ISBN 978-1-59643-500-1 pa; 1-59643-500-3 pa

"Conservation, evolution, technology, animal life, space travel, physics, and much more are discussed in this lively science book. . . . [This offers] chatty questions and answers . . . with text that is compelling, never intimidating, and sometimes deliberately outrageous. . . . Children will have fun browsing the spacious pages and sharing what they read with adults." Booklist

O'Meara, Stephen James

Are you afraid yet? the science behind scary stuff; written by Stephen James O'Meara; illustrated by Jeremy Kaposy. Kids Can Press 2009 78p il $17.95; pa $9.95

Grades: 5 6 7 8   500

1. Science 2. Supernatural

ISBN 978-1-55453-294-0; 1-55453-294-9; 978-1-55453-295-7 pa; 1-55453-295-7 pa

"This book cleverly weaves together the supernatural and the scientific in an entertaining read that answers questions about ghosts, UFOs, vampires, werewolves, and how long a decapitated head can remain conscious. Examples depicting such things in classical fiction and popular movies are seamlessly interjected between the factual explanations. Each page is filled with detailed black-and-white illustrations, emphasizing the sometimes-humorous, yet often-macabre descriptions." SLJ

Richardson, Gillian

Kaboom! explosions of all kinds. Annick Press 2009 83p il $22.95; pa $12.95

Grades: 4 5 6 7 **500**

1. Science 2. Explosions

ISBN 978-1-55451-204-1; 1-55451-204-2; 978-1-55451-203-4 pa; 1-55451-203-4 pa

"With comic-style sound-effect headings and fact boxes galore, Kaboom! highlights the supercharged of the natural and manmade worlds, from astronomy, geology, biology, herbology, and entomology to chemistry, mechanics, pyrotechnics, and art. Text is broken into asymmetrical panels for bite-size explanations. Some explosions are captured in sequence and detail with historical and high-speed photography and illustrations in comic-style panel frames. . . . Kaboom! is an engrossing attention-getter, effectively tapping the sensationalism of all types of blasts." SLJ

Schwartz, David M.

Q is for quark; a science alphabet book. written by David M. Schwartz; illustrated by Kim Doner. Tricycle Press 2001 64p il $15.95

Grades: 4 5 6 7 **500**

1. Science 2. Alphabet 3. Science -- Miscellanea -- Juvenile literature

ISBN 1-58246-021-3

LC 00-10659

Explains the meaning of scientific terms which begin with the different letters of the alphabet such as atom, black hole, and clone

"The text is filled with readable and clear explanations for some very complex concepts. . . . [Readers] will enjoy browsing through this funny and informative book." SLJ

Swanson, Diane

Nibbling on Einstein's brain; the good, the bad & the bogus in science. illustrated by Warren Clark. Annick Press 2001 104p il $24.95; pa $14.95

Grades: 5 6 7 8 **500**

1. Science -- Methodology

ISBN 1-55037-687-X; 1-55037-686-1 pa

The author "discusses topics such as the difference between correlation and cause-and-effect relationships, the importance of asking the right questions about advertisers' claims, and the links between superstition, coincidence, and probability. With a highly readable text and jaunty line illustrations, the book encourages critical thinking and skepticism when evaluating science reporting and media hype." Booklist

Watts, Claire

The **most** explosive science book in the universe; by the Brainwaves; illustrated by Lisa Swerling and Ralph Lazar; written by Claire Watts. DK Pub. 2009 60p il $19.99

Grades: 3 4 5 6 **500**

1. Science

ISBN 978-0-7566-5152-7; 0-7566-5152-2

The Brainwaves are pint-sized pals that explore the world of science including the building blocks of matter, chemistry, light, electricity and the future of science

"A sprawling, unique overview of the various scientific fields. Although students will have to hunt through the dense layout to find facts, they will likely encounter what they are searching for. . . . Appealing enough to inspire pleasure reading, the book will also serve those looking for scientific facts." SLJ

500.8 Groups of people

Thimmesh, Catherine

The **sky's** the limit; stories of discovery by women and girls. illustrated by Melissa Sweet. Houghton Mifflin 2002 73p il hardcover o.p. pa $7.95

Grades: 5 6 7 8 **500.8**

1. Science 2. Women scientists 3. Women in science 4. Science -- Miscellanea -- Juvenile literature

ISBN 0-618-07698-0; 0-618-49489-8 pa

LC 2001-39111

"The lively design and the mixed-media collage artwork is a creative delight, and the intricate ink-and-watercolor borders, inventive paintings, and childlike pictures will draw readers in. The best thing about the book, however, is Thimmesh's sparkling writing style. . . . Report writers will appreciate this, but the book will also charm browsers." Booklist

Includes bibliographical references

502 Miscellany

Murphy, Glenn

How loud can you burp? more extremely important questions (and answers!) Roaring Book Press 2009 284p il pa $10.99

Grades: 4 5 6 7 **502**

1. Science 2. Questions and answers

ISBN 978-1-59643-506-3 pa; 1-59643-506-2 pa

"'Why does pollen give you hay fever?' 'Why don't big metal ships just sink?' These are but a couple of the questions that Murphy received on the Web site he set up to solicit inquiries from kids. Written in an informal, question-and-answer format, he delivers serious scientific information in an easygoing, humorous manner, with several pages dedicated to each topic. . . . A few line drawings break up the text and sidebars highlight interesting facts or are, at times, simply funny. . . . This is an entertaining, accessible approach to science that's sure to appeal to science buffs and general browsers alike." SLJ

502.8 Auxiliary techniques and procedures; apparatus, equipment, materials

Glass, Susan

Watch out! science tools and safety. [by] Susan Glass. Heinemann Library 2007 48p il (How to be a scientist) lib bdg $21; pa $8.99

Grades: 3 4 5 6 **502.8**

1. Measurement 2. Scientific apparatus and instruments

3. Science -- Experiments
ISBN 978-1-4034-8360-7 lib bdg; 978-1-4034-8364-5 pa

LC 2006010840

Includes bibliographical references

Kramer, Stephen

Hidden worlds: looking through a scientist's microscope; photographs by Dennis Kunkel. Houghton Mifflin 2001 57p il (Scientists in the field) $16; pa $5.95

Grades: 4 5 6 7   **502.8**

1. Microscopes 2. Microscopists
ISBN 0-618-05546-0; 0-618-35405-0 pa

LC 00-58083

This book takes a "look at the work of a microscopist. Kunkel works with microscopes to explore science. . . . This book contains many of his photos, most taken with electron microscopes. . . . Several opening pages, along with the front and back endpapers, are visually dazzling. The heart of the book, though, is what readers learn about how Kunkel produces these images, and to what uses scientists put them. . . . This title offers a wealth of scientific information along with an insightful look at the world of an individual scientist." SLJ

Includes bibliographical references

Levine, Shar

★ The **ultimate** guide to your microscope; [by] Shar Levine & Leslie Johnstone. Sterling Pub. 2008 143p il pa $9.95

Grades: 5 6 7 8 9   **502.8**

1. Microscopes 2. Microscopy -- Juvenile literature
ISBN 978-1-4027-4329-0 pa; 1-4027-4329-7 pa

LC 2006-100967

"Through this fun and inviting book, readers can begin to explore the world using a microscope. Students are encouraged to learn the basics in the two first chapters and then undertake the 41 hands-on activities in the next eight chapters. Activities are presented in manageable one or two-page uniformly formatted modules." SLJ

503   Dictionaries, encyclopedias, concordances

★ **DK** first science encyclopedia; [senior editors, Currie Love, Caroline Stamps and Ben Morgan] DK Publishing 2008 127p il map $16.99

Grades: K 1 2 3 4   **503**

1. Science -- Encyclopedias
ISBN 978-0-7566-4296-9; 0-7566-4296-5

LC 2009277384

Provides a basic reference guide to life, materials, physical, earth, and space science

"On flipping to any page, readers' first impressions will be the vibrancy and beauty of the photography, but further examination reveals a wealth of interesting facts and information about the topics presented, along with real-world context for their importance." Sci Books Films

Everything you need to know; an encyclopedia for inquiring young minds. Kingfisher 2007 320p il map $24.95

Grades: PreK K 1 2 3 4   **503**

1. Reference books 2. Science -- Encyclopedias 3.

Technology -- Encyclopedias
ISBN 978-0-7534-6089-4; 0-7534-6089-0

"The encyclopedia is arranged thematically into 10 sections ('Our Earth,' 'Plants,' 'Animals,' 'Dinosaurs,' 'People and Places,' 'People Through Time,' 'My Body,' 'Science,' 'Space,' and 'Machines') with between 11 and 17 topics grouped under each. Most topics are treated in two-page spreads. . . . There is plenty of worthwhile information to answer questions and spark curiosity. . . . The volume is visually appealing, with full-color illustrations." Booklist

Jakab, Cheryl

★ The **encyclopedia** of junior science; [by] Cheryl Jakab, David Keystone. Chelsea Clubhouse 2009 10v il map set $230

Grades: 4 5 6 7   **503**

1. Reference books 2. Science -- Encyclopedias
ISBN 978-1-60413-554-1 set; 1-60413-554-9 set

LC 2008-38113

"This set introduces students to basic science concepts. Approximately 270 entries are arranged alphabetically. . . . The writing is basic, and much of the information is presented in the form of charts and bulleted lists. . . . This set would be useful for school and public libraries seeking a science encyclopedia." Booklist

The **Kingfisher** science encyclopedia; contributors, Clive Gifford . . . [et al.] updated ed; Kingfisher 2006 488p il map $24.95

Grades: 5 6 7 8   **503**

1. Reference books 2. Science -- Encyclopedias 3. Science -- Juvenile literature
ISBN 0-7534-5886-1

First published 2000

An illustrated science encyclopedia arranged in such categories as "Planet Earth," "Living Things," "Chemistry and the Elements," "Materials and Technology," "Space and Time," and "Conservation and the Environment"

"This attractive, browsable, reasonably priced encyclopedia definitely has a place beside titles offering more depth." Booklist

507   Education, research, related topics

Glass, Susan

Analyze this! understanding the scientific method. [by] Susan Glass. Heinemann Library 2007 48p il (How to be a scientist) lib bdg $21; pa $8.99

Grades: 3 4 5 6   **507**

1. Science -- Methodology
ISBN 978-1-4034-8358-4 lib bdg; 978-1-4034-8362-1 pa

LC 2006010638

Includes bibliographical references

Prove it! the scientific method in action. [by] Susan Glass. Heinemann Library 2007 48p il (How to be a scientist) hardcover o.p. lib bdg $21

Grades: 3 4 5 6   **507**
1. Science -- Experiments 2. Science -- Methodology
ISBN 978-1-4034-8359-1 lib bdg; 978-1-4034-8363-8 pa

LC 2006010639
Includes bibliographical references

Kramer, Stephen
How to think like a scientist; answering questions by the scientific method. [by] Stephen P. Kramer; illustrated by Felicia Bond. Crowell 1987 44p il $16.89
Grades: 3 4 5   **507**
1. Science -- Methodology
ISBN 978-0-690-04565-9; 0-690-04565-4

LC 85-43604
"This is a pleasant book with an open format; an amusing halftone cartoon on almost every page illustrates the child oriented experiments and supports the light tone of the book." SLJ

Science detectives; how scientists solved six real-life mysteries. by the editors of Yes Mag; illustrated by Rose Cowles. Kids Can Press 2006 48p il $15.95; pa $8.95
Grades: 4 5 6   **507**
1. Science -- Methodology
ISBN 978-1-55337-994-2; 1-55337-994-2; 978-1-55337-995-9; 1-55337-995-0 pa
This describes how scientists solved mysteries such as the spread of typhoid in 1906, the death of vultures in India in 1999, and the crash of a Swissair flight in 1998. Includes related projects.

507.8 Use of apparatus and equipment in study and teaching

Bardhan-Quallen, Sudipta
Last-minute science fair projects; when your Bunsen's not burning but the clock's really ticking. Sterling Pub. 2006 112p il $19.95
Grades: 5 6 7 8   **507.8**
1. Science projects 2. Science -- Experiments
ISBN 978-1-4027-1690-4; 1-4027-1690-7

LC 2005-34455
"The introduction goes through a stripped-down summary of things to consider in choosing a project . . . a description of what to include in the project report, and some tips on presentation. . . . The description of each project is succinct and specific, with question, hypothesis, materials, and procedures clearly outlined." Sci Books Films

Becker, Helaine
★ Science on the loose; amazing activities and science facts you'll never believe. illustrated by Claudia Dávila. Maple Tree Press 2008 64p il $22.95; pa $10.95
Grades: 3 4 5 6   **507.8**
1. Science -- Experiments
ISBN 978-1-897349-18-2; 1-897349-18-1; 978-1-897349-19-9 pa; 1-897349-19-X pa

LC 2007939081
This "is thought provoking, imaginative, and engaging, with a wonderful blend of intelligent writing, intriguing

ideas and easy-to-perform experiments. There is also plenty of humor." Sci Books Films

Bell-Rehwoldt, Sheri
Science experiments that surprise and delight; fun projects for curious kids. Capstone Press 2011 32p il (Edge books: kitchen science) lib bdg $26.65; pa $7.95
Grades: 3 4 5 6   **507.8**
1. Science -- Experiments
ISBN 978-1-4296-5428-9 lib bdg; 1-4296-5428-7 lib bdg; 978-1-4296-6253-6 pa; 1-4296-6253-0 pa

LC 2010025205
Provides step-by-step instructions for science projects using household materials and explains the science behind the experiments.
"Attractive, colorful, and full of photos, [this title] will appeal to a wide range of kids. . . . Anyone looking for a straightforward, fun, and easy science experiment will want [this title] close by." SLJ
Includes bibliographical references

Burke, Lisa
Backyard; fun experiments for budding scientists. DK Pub. 2010 23p il (I'm a scientist) $12.99
Grades: K 1 2 3   **507.8**
1. Nature 2. Science -- Experiments
ISBN 978-0-7566-6306-3; 0-7566-6306-7

LC 2010459418
"Each spread offers a science experiment with foldout flaps that demonstrate the science behind the project which introduces natural phenomena and the outside world in backyards and gardens." Publisher's note

Kitchen. DK Pub. 2010 23p il (I'm a scientist) $12.99
Grades: K 1 2 3   **507.8**
1. Science -- Experiments 2. Kitchens -- Juvenile literature 3. Science -- Experiments -- Juvenile literature
ISBN 978-0-7566-6307-0; 0-7566-6307-5
"Each spread contains a kid-friendly science experiment for very young readers which they can perform right in their own kitchen, with foldout flaps that demonstrate the science behind the project." Publisher's note

Burns, Kylie
What's going on? collecting and recording your data. Crabtree 2010 32p il (Step into science) lib bdg $26.60; pa $8.95
Grades: 4 5 6   **507.8**
1. Science -- Methodology 2. Science -- Experiments -- Juvenile literature
ISBN 978-0-7787-5155-7 lib bdg; 0-7787-5155-4 lib bdg; 978-0-7787-5170-0 pa; 0-7787-5170-8 pa
This "shows the reader how to collect and record data in a journal, as well as how to organize the data by using graphs, charts, and diagrams. . . . The colorful photographs and illustrations enhance the text. A time line showing scientific discoveries and inventions, a glossary, a list of books and websites for further information, and an index are presented at the back of the book. This . . . would be a wonderful addition to a school classroom." Sci Books Films
Includes glossary and bibliographical references

Challen, Paul C.

What just happened? reading results and making inferences. [by] Paul Challen. Crabtree 2010 32p il (Step into science) lib bdg $26.60; pa $8.95

Grades: 4 5 6 **507.8**

1. Science -- Methodology 2. Science -- Experiments -- Juvenile literature

ISBN 978-0-7787-5156-4 lib bdg; 0-7787-5156-2 lib bdg; 978-0-7787-5171-7 pa; 0-7787-5171-6 pa

This "shows the reader how to make sense of the data that have been collected and recorded during the experiment. . . . The examples of charts and graphs, along with colorful photographs and illustrations, enhance the text. A time line showing scientific discoveries and inventions, a glossary, a list of books, and websites for further information, and an index are presented at the back of the book. This . . . would be a wonderful addition to a school classroom." Sci Books Films

Includes glossary and bibliographical references

What's going to happen? making your hypothesis. [by] Paul Challen. Crabtree 2010 32p il (Step into science) lib bdg $26.60; pa $8.95

Grades: 4 5 6 **507.8**

1. Science -- Methodology

ISBN 978-0-7787-5157-1 lib bdg; 0-7787-5157-0 lib bdg; 978-0-7787-5172-4 pa; 0-7787-5172-4 pa

Learn how scientists make educated guesses called hypotheses to test their theories. . . . Readers will learn how to construct a measurable and focused hypothesis to test in an experiment.

"A time line showing important hypotheses, a glossary, a list of books and websites for further information, and an index are provided at the back of the book. This . . . would be a wonderful addition to a school classroom." Sci Books Films

Includes glossary and bibliographical references

Cobb, Vicki

Science experiments you can eat; illustrated by David Cain. rev & updated; HarperCollins Pubs. 1994 214p il hardcover o.p. pa $5.95

Grades: 5 6 7 8 **507.8**

1. Cooking 2. Science -- Experiments

ISBN 0-06-023551-9; 0-06-446002-9 pa

LC 93-13679

First published 1972

Experiments with food demonstrate various scientific principles and produce an eatable result. Includes rock candy, grape jelly, cupcakes, and popcorn

Includes glossary

See for yourself; more than 100 amazing experiments for science fairs and school projects. illustrated by Dave Klug. 2nd ed; Skyhorse Pub. 2010 192p il pa $14.95

Grades: 4 5 6 7 **507.8**

1. Science -- Experiments

ISBN 978-1-61608-083-9; 1-61608-083-3

LC 2010020800

First published 2001 by Scholastic

This is an "accessible and often intriguing collection of activities and experiments. . . . The experiments are grouped by their source of inspiration: humans, the supermarket, the toy store, drugstore, and hardware and stationery stores. . . . Cartoon-style illustrations are . . . in full color." SLJ

Squirts and spurts; science fun with water. illustrated by Steve Haefele. Millbrook Press 2000 48p il hardcover o.p. pa $7.95

Grades: 3 4 5 6 **507.8**

1. Water 2. Experiments 3. Science -- Experiments 4. Hydrodynamics -- Juvenile literature

ISBN 0-7613-1572-1 lib bdg; 0-8225-7024-6 pa

LC 00-22113

Explains the physics of water pressure, showing how it makes everyday products such as faucets, spray bottles, and water pistols work. Includes experiments

"The text succeeds in conveying sophisticated concepts through accessible language, and Steve Haefele's drawings of an exuberant, grinning narrator and her robot sidekick clearly illustrate both the broad, abstract concepts and the concrete activity steps." Booklist

We dare you! hundreds of science bets, challenges, and experiments you can do at home. [by] Vicki Cobb and Kathy Darling. Skyhorse Pub. 2007 321p il hardcover o.p. pa $14.94

Grades: 4 5 6 7 **507.8**

1. Science -- Experiments

ISBN 978-1-60239-225-0; 1-60239-225-0; 978-1-60239-775-0 pa; 1-60239-775-9 pa

LC 2007-51236

"Divided into chapters with titles such as 'The Human Wonder,' 'Fluid Feats,' 'Energy Entrapments,' and 'Mathematical Duplicity,' this volume has more than 200 experiments with clear how-to instructions. All of the projects are doable and the science behind them is explained in a kid-accessible manner. . . . Black-and-white line drawings add humor and clarify instructions. This is a great resource for teachers, parents, and budding scientists—and for any youngster who can't resist a challenge." SLJ

Includes bibliographical references

Connolly, Sean

The **book** of potentially catastrophic science; 50 experiments for daring young scientists. Workman Pub. 2010 305p il

Grades: 5 6 7 8 **507.8**

1. Science -- Experiments

ISBN 0-7611-5687-9; 978-0-7611-5687-1

LC 2010-07044

This book presents thirty-four experiments. "Each chapter starts with a brief outline of the scientific advances of the time, followed by a clarification of the science and then one or more hands-on experiments to illustrate the object or concept presented. . . . Grades five to eight." (Sci Books Films)

"This volume approaches science historically, spotlighting certain periods, processes, individuals, discoveries, and inventions. Each of the 34 chapters includes a discussion and one or two related activities, such as making a Stone Age tool, creating an earthquake in Jell-O, building a parachute for an egg drop, and extracting a banana's DNA. Safety concerns are addressed for each project, and adult help will be necessary to complete some of the experiments successfully. . . . Connolly's writing is engaging, and the historical approach works well, offering kids a quick introduction to science history and the opportunity to explore certain ideas along the way." Booklist

Gabrielson, Curt

Stomp rockets, catapults, and kaleidoscopes; 30+ amazing science projects you can build for less than $1. Chicago Review Press 2008 159p il $16.95

Grades: 3 4 5 6   **507.8**
  1. Science projects 2. Science -- Experiments
  ISBN 978-1-55652-737-1; 1-55652-737-3
                                             LC 2007-37917

"Projects include building a working model of the human hand's muscles, bones, and tendons using drinking straws, tape, and string; using a pair of two-liter bottles and a length of rubber tubing to learn how a toilet flushes; and discovering how musical instruments make sounds by fashioning a harmonica, saxophone, drum, flute, or oboe. All devices are designed to use recycled or nearly free materials and common tools." Publisher's note

Goodstein, Madeline

Ace your sports science project; great science fair ideas. [by] Madeline Goodstein, Robert Gardner, and Barbara Gardner Conklin. Enslow Publishers 2009 128p il (Ace your physics science project) lib bdg $31.93

Grades: 5 6 7 8   **507.8**
  1. Sports 2. Physics 3. Science projects 4. Science -- Experiments
  ISBN 978-0-7660-3229-3 lib bdg; 0-7660-3229-9 lib bdg
                                             LC 2008-4689

"Presents several science experiments and project ideas dealing with the physics of sports." Publisher's note
  Includes bibliographical references

Goal! science projects with soccer. Enslow Publishers 2009 104p il (Score! Sports science projects) lib bdg $31.93

Grades: 5 6 7 8   **507.8**
  1. Motion 2. Soccer 3. Force and energy 4. Science projects 5. Science -- Experiments
  ISBN 978-0-7660-3106-7 lib bdg; 0-7660-3106-3 lib bdg
                                             LC 2008-2999

"Introductions include information about the history of the sport, safety steps to follow, and the scientific method. . . . Detailed diagrams help clarify many of the directions." SLJ
  Includes glossary and bibliographical references

Hammond, Richard

Super science lab. DK Pub. 2009 96p il pa $8.99

Grades: 3 4 5   **507.8**
  1. Science -- Experiments
  ISBN 978-0-7566-5341-5 pa; 0-7566-5341-X pa

"With more than 30 scientific experiments, ranging from more traditional science-fair projects . . . this fun book has plenty of ideas to sample. Also offered are magnified images. . . . In between experiments, Hammond explores the science behind the subjects. . . . The active approach to science and scrapbook-style design, with plenty of photos, notes and asides, should win over curious kids." Publ Wkly

Harris, Elizabeth Snoke

Save the Earth science experiments; science fair projects for eco-kids. [illustrator, Orrin Lundgren] Lark Books 2008 112p il $19.95

Grades: 4 5 6   **507.8**
  1. Science projects 2. Environmental protection 3. Science -- Experiments
  ISBN 978-1-60059-322-2; 1-60059-322-4
                                             LC 2008017826

This describes science fair projects such as how to harness energy with windmills, make a biogas generator, create alternative fuels, and recycle paper

Yikes! wow! yuck! fun experiments for your first science fair. illustrated by Nora Thompson. Lark Books 2008 64p il $12.95

Grades: 3 4 5 6   **507.8**
  1. Science projects 2. Science -- Experiments
  ISBN 978-1-57990-930-7; 1-57990-930-2
                                             LC 2007-19770

"The experiments in this collection are based on everyday things in students' lives, such as Jell-O, potatoes, cereal, foggy mirrors, and exploding soda. Each one has clear, step-by-step directions and culminating questions. Ways to expand and change the projects are also included. Jokes are interspersed to add a bit of fun. . . . The illustrations offer a glimpse of what the experiment will include." SLJ
  Includes glossary

Hauser, Jill Frankel

★ **Super** science concoctions; 50 mysterious mixtures for fabulous fun. illustrations by Michael Kline. Williamson 1997 160p il pa $12.95

Grades: 3 4 5   **507.8**
  1. Scientific recreations 2. Science -- Experiments 3. Scientific recreations -- Juvenile literature
  ISBN 1-885593-02-3
                                             LC 95-47894

Over 75 science experiments with mixtures that illustrate changes in form and chemical composition
  "The sequential logic of the text make[s] this title valuable for teaching basic chemistry principles. Pen-and-ink cartoon illustrations are well placed, informative, and humorous. Safety precautions are emphasized." SLJ

Hopwood, James

Cool distance assistants; fun science projects to propel things. [by] James Hopwood. ABDO Pub. 2008 32p il (Cool science) lib bdg $25.65

Grades: 4 5 6   **507.8**
  1. Science projects 2. Science -- Experiments
  ISBN 978-1-59928-906-9 lib bdg; 1-59928-906-7 lib bdg
                                             LC 2007015625

This offers science projects about propulsion, including "Awesome Air & Water Rockets"
  The experiments "will attract boys and girls. [The] book begins with [an] upbeat introduction and three chapters about the scientific method, keeping a journal, and safety. . . . Background on the science concepts involved is presented along with a complete list of supplies. . . . The numbered instructions are easy to follow and are accompanied by small, closeup photos." SLJ

Cool dry ice devices; fun science projects with dry ice. [by] James Hopwood. ABDO Pub. 2008 32p il (Cool science) lib bdg $25.65
Grades: 4 5 6   **507.8**
1. Science projects 2. Science -- Experiments
ISBN 978-1-59928-907-6 lib bdg; 1-59928-907-5 lib bdg
LC 2007010257
This offers science projects using dry ice, including "Fast Frozen Confections"
The experiments "will attract boys and girls. [The] book begins with [an] upbeat introduction and three chapters about the scientific method, keeping a journal, and safety. . . . Background on the science concepts involved is presented along with a complete list of supplies. . . . The numbered instructions are easy to follow and are accompanied by small, closeup photos." SLJ

Hyde, Natalie
What's the plan? designing your experiment. Crabtree 2010 32p il (Step into science) lib bdg $26.60; pa $8.95
Grades: 4 5 6   **507.8**
1. Science -- Methodology 2. Science -- Experiments -- Juvenile literature 3. Science -- Methodology -- Juvenile literature
ISBN 978-0-7787-5154-0 lib bdg; 0-7787-5154-6 lib bdg; 978-0-7787-5169-4 pa; 0-7787-5169-4 pa
LC 2009-44172
This "shows readers how to gather materials and create a step-by-step procedure to test their hypotheses. . . . Colorful photographs and illustrations enhance the text. A time line showing scientific discoveries and inventions, a glossary, a list of books and websites for further information, and an index are presented at the back of the book. This . . . would be a wonderful addition to a school classroom." Sci Books Films
Includes glossary and bibliographical references

Johnson, Robin R.
What do we know now? drawing conclusions and answering the question. Crabtree 2010 32p il (Step into science) lib bdg $26.60; pa $8.95
Grades: 4 5 6   **507.8**
1. Science -- Methodology 2. Science -- Experiments -- Juvenile literature 3. Science -- Methodology -- Juvenile literature
ISBN 978-0-7787-5153-3 lib bdg; 0-7787-5153-8 lib bdg; 978-0-7787-5168-7 pa; 0-7787-5168-6 pa
LC 2009-44171
This book illustrates fun and interesting ways in which to report your results, from a science fair demonstration to a written report.
"This title . . . would be a wonderful addition to a school classroom." Sci Books Films
Includes glossary and bibliographical references

Kenda, Margaret
Science wizardry for kids; [by] Margaret Kenda [and] Phyllis S. Williams; illustrated by Deborah Gross. 2nd ed.; Barron's Educational Series 2009 242p il spiral $14.99

Grades: 3 4 5 6   **507.8**
1. Scientific recreations 2. Science -- Experiments
ISBN 978-0-7641-4177-5 spiral; 0-7641-4177-5 spiral
LC 2008049689
First published 1992
This includes over two hundred science projects including "creating an indicator out of red cabbage to test acids and bases, making an electric lemon, building a simple camera, and designing a terrarium. The directions are presented in easy-to-follow, numbered steps, and simple color drawings appear on every page." SLJ

Levine, Shar
Bathtub science; [by] Shar Levine & Leslie Johnstone; illustrations by Dave Garbot; photography by Jeff Connery. Sterling 2000 80p il hardcover o.p. pa $9.95
Grades: 3 4 5   **507.8**
1. Water 2. Science -- Experiments
ISBN 0-8069-7185-1; 1-4027-4094-8 pa
LC 2001-273784
"From a simple, familiar sink-and-float experiment to the more complicated construction of a miniature diving bell, this book covers a wide array of science experiments that can be performed in water. Clear descriptions of how to perform and understand the experiments, as well as photos of the different steps involved, make the book particularly easy to use." Horn Book Guide
Includes glossary

Sports science; [by] Shar Levine & Leslie Johnstone; illustrated by Dave Garbot; photography by Stephen Ogilvy. Sterling Pub. Co. 2006 80p il $19.95
Grades: 3 4 5   **507.8**
1. Sports 2. Science -- Experiments 3. Sports sciences -- Juvenile literature 4. Science -- Experiments -- Juvenile literature
ISBN 1-4027-1520-X
LC 2005-24367
"These 26 activities will allow children to see some real-life applications of science principles. A paragraph-length explanation of the concept being explored opens each chapter, along with mention of a specific sport or type of sport (swimming/buoyancy, various balls/aerodynamics) it relates to. . . . This book will be an appealing choice for children and for adults teaching basic science concepts to tactile and kinesthetic learners." SLJ

Lew, Kristi
Science experiments that fly and move; fun projects for curious kids. Capstone Press 2011 32p il (Edge books: kitchen science) lib bdg $26.65; pa $7.95
Grades: 3 4 5 6   **507.8**
1. Science -- Experiments
ISBN 978-1-4296-5426-5; 1-4296-5426-0; 978-1-4296-6252-9 pa; 1-4296-6252-2 pa
LC 2010025206
Provides step-by-step instructions for science projects using household materials and explains the science behind the experiments.
"Attractive, colorful, and full of photos, [this title] will appeal to a wide range of kids. . . . Anyone looking for a

straightforward, fun, and easy science experiment will want [this title] close by." SLJ

Includes glossary and bibliographical references

Margles, Samantha

Mythbusters science fair book. Scholastic 2011 128p il pa $9.99

Grades: 4 5 6 7   **507.8**

1. Science projects 2. Science -- Experiments

ISBN 978-0-545-23745-1; 0-545-23745-9

This offers "50 original ideas for science fair projects or long, boredom-riddled summer days. Much like the popular television program on which it's based, the book stays true to the scientific method. . . . Divided into chapters on chemical reactions, temperature, energy and force, and more, the two- to three-page experiments on busily designed pages feature easy step-by-step procedures." Booklist

Murphy, Pat

Exploratopia; by Pat Murphy, Ellen Macaulay, and the staff of the Exploratorium; illustrated by Jason Gorski. Little, Brown and Co. 2006 373p il $29.99

Grades: 3 4 5 6   **507.8**

1. Science -- Experiments 2. Science -- Experiments -- Juvenile literature

ISBN 978-0-316-61281-4; 0-316-61281-2

LC 2006-40942

"Practiced young experimenters ready to strike out on their own will find enticing science demonstrations on nearly every page of this inviting collection. Each of the 21 sections contains a half dozen or more entries that feature easily gathered ingredients, clear directions, and color photos or diagrams that are not only informative but often arresting as well." SLJ

Includes bibliographical references

Newcomb, Rain

Smash it! crash it! launch it! 50 mind-blowing, eye-popping science experiments. [by] Rain Newcomb & Bobby Mercer. Lark Books 2006 80p il $14.95

Grades: 4 5 6 7   **507.8**

1. Science -- Experiments 2. Physics -- Juvenile literature

ISBN 978-1-57990-795-2; 1-57990-795-4

LC 2006-05518

"Science teachers will find entertaining ways to impress their students with Newton's laws if they're willing to break a few eggs as described in this engaging book. The study of physics becomes appealing when combined with marshmallow catapults, potato popguns, and water-balloon launchers. The authors provide a brief explanation of the physical principles involved and emphasize that cleanup is required on some of the messier projects. . . . Humorous cartoon illustrations and sketchy templates supplement the descriptions of how to set up the projects. Typical household ingredients like straws, pop bottles, fruits, and lots of eggs are the materials required." SLJ

Rhatigan, Joe

Prize-winning science fair projects for curious kids; [by] Joe Rhatigan & Rain Newcomb. Lark Books 2004 112p il hardcover o.p. pa $7.95

Grades: 5 6 7 8   **507.8**

1. Science projects 2. Science -- Experiments 3.

Science projects -- Juvenile literature

ISBN 1-57990-478-5; 1-57990-750-4 pa

LC 2003-24957

"Fifty experiments in biology, the physical sciences, and chemistry are presented in an attractive and easy-to-follow format and illustrated with sharp photographs of children and of the materials needed. One of the book's strengths is the first chapter about choosing and doing a project. Ideas include checking out the validity of horoscopes, mummifying fish, testing the effectiveness of sunscreens, and testing spray-on water repellents." SLJ

Shores, Lori

How to build flipsticks. Capstone Press 2011 24p il (Hands-on science fun) lib bdg $23.99; pa $6.95

Grades: PreK K 1   **507.8**

1. Science -- Experiments

ISBN 978-1-4296-5292-6 lib bdg; 1-4296-5292-6 lib bdg; 978-1-4296-6213-0 pa; 1-4296-6213-1 pa

Simple text and full-color photos instruct readers on how to make two drawings act like a cartoon and explain the science behind the activity.

"Bright, glossy photos and irresistible ideas make these science lessons effortless fun." Booklist

How to make a bouncing egg. Capstone Press 2011 24p il (Hands-on science fun) lib bdg $23.99; pa $6.95

Grades: PreK K 1   **507.8**

1. Science -- Experiments

ISBN 978-1-4296-5291-9 lib bdg; 1-4296-5291-8 lib bdg; 978-1-4296-6214-7 pa; 1-4296-6214-X pa

Simple text and full-color photos instruct readers on how to make a bouncing egg.

"Bright, glossy photos and irresistible ideas make these science lessons effortless fun." Booklist

How to make a liquid rainbow. Capstone Press 2011 24p il (Hands-on science fun) lib bdg $23.99; pa $6.95

Grades: PreK K 1   **507.8**

1. Science -- Experiments

ISBN 978-1-4296-6216-1 lib bdg; 1-4296-6216-6 lib bdg; 978-1-4296-6216-1 pa; 1-4296-6216-6 pa

Simple text and full-color photos instruct readers on how to make a rainbow in a jar.

"Bright, glossy photos and irresistible ideas make these science lessons effortless fun." Booklist

How to make a mystery smell balloon. Capstone Press 2011 24p il (Hands-on science fun) lib bdg $23.99; pa $6.95

Grades: PreK K 1   **507.8**

1. Science -- Experiments

ISBN 978-1-4296-4494-5 lib bdg; 1-4296-4494-X lib bdg; 978-1-4296-5579-8 pa; 1-4296-5579-8 pa

LC 2010009483

Simple text and full-color photos instruct readers how to make a mystery smell balloon and explain the science behind the activity.

"Bright, glossy photos and irresistible ideas make these science lessons effortless fun." Booklist

Includes bibliographical references

Spangler, Steve

Naked eggs and flying potatoes; unforgettable experiments that make science fun. Greenleaf Book Group Press 2010 155p il (Steve Spangler science) pa $14.95

Grades: 3 4 5 6 **507.8**

1. Scientific recreations 2. Science -- Experiments
ISBN 978-1-60832-0608 pa; 1-60832-060-X pa

"Spangler uses cheap, everyday materials to invent entertaining, highly kid-appealing activities. . . . Heavily illustrated with color photos and described in funny, casual prose, the experiments will easily engage a young audience, and each is followed by a succinct explanation of the science concepts at play." Booklist

Tocci, Salvatore

More simple science fair projects, grades 3-5; illustrated by Bob Wiacek. Chelsea House Pub. 2006 48p il (Scientific American winning science fair projects) $27

Grades: 3 4 5 **507.8**

1. Science projects 2. Science -- Experiments
ISBN 0-7910-9055-8

LC 2005-57097

This "begins by describing how to exhibit information on a trifold display with the following information: background, the experimental question, materials, procedures, results, and explanations. The author then describes 18 experiments following that format. The language is clear and easy to follow. Simple drawings add a great deal to the explanations." Sci Books Films

VanCleave, Janice Pratt, 1942-

★ **Janice** VanCleave's 201 awesome, magical, bizarre & incredible experiments. Wiley 1994 118p pa $12.95

Grades: 4 5 6 7 **507.8**

1. Science -- Experiments
ISBN 0-471-31011-5

LC 93-29807

The experiments in this book "are organized by field: astronomy, biology, chemistry, earth science, and physics; the purpose, materials needed, procedure, results, and an explanation are included for each demonstration. The author writes in a clear, easy-to-understand style. . . . The book will be especially useful to teachers looking for ideas that can be adapted as hands-on activities." SLJ

Includes glossary

★ **Janice** VanCleave's 202 oozing, bubbling, dripping & bouncing experiments. Wiley 1996 120p pa $12.95

Grades: 4 5 6 7 **507.8**

1. Science -- Experiments 2. Scientific recreations -- Juvenile literature
ISBN 0-471-14025-2

LC 95-46398

Provides instructions for over 200 short experiments in astronomy, biology, chemistry, earth science, and physics

"Some activities consist merely of observation, such as 'To study parts of a feather.' Some are more complex, but all are clearly and concisely explained. Many are repeats from prior VanCleave books, but 40 are supposedly new." SLJ

Includes glossary

★ **Janice** VanCleave's 203 icy, freezing, frosty, cool & wild experiments. Wiley 1999 122p pa $12.95

Grades: 4 5 6 7 **507.8**

1. Science -- Experiments
ISBN 0-471-25223-9

LC 98-49721

This includes "experiments in astronomy, biology, chemistry, earth science, and physics. . . . Each activity includes a purpose, a list of materials, a step-by-step procedure, results, and an explanation. Experiments address such topics as the Moon's 'changing' size, how environment affects body temperature, and why ice pops are softer than ice. An excellent resource." SLJ

Janice VanCleave's big book of play and find out science projects. Wiley 2007 213p il pa $19.95

Grades: K 1 2 3 **507.8**

1. Science projects 2. Science -- Experiments
ISBN 978-0-7879-8928-6 pa; 0-7879-8928-2 pa

LC 2006-52572

This "is a compilation of 56 hands-on activities based on authentic questions asked by children. The four-part book contains activities in each of the following content areas: 'Physical Science,' 'Nature,' 'Bugs,' and 'Human Body.' . . . Adults and children will likely find it a useful tool." Sci Books Films

Includes glossary and bibliographical references

Janice VanCleave's engineering for every kid; easy activities that make learning science fun. Jossey-Bass 2007 205p il (Science for every kid series) pa $14.95

Grades: 4 5 6 7 **507.8**

1. Engineering 2. Science projects 3. Science -- Experiments 4. Engineering -- Experiments -- Juvenile literature
ISBN 978-0-471-47182-0 pa; 0-471-47182-8 pa

LC 2006-10540

Explains some of the basic physical principles of engineering, accompanied by activities that illustrate those principles

★ **Janice** VanCleave's guide to the best science fair projects; [by] Janice VanCleave. Wiley 1997 156p il pa $14.95

Grades: 4 5 6 7 **507.8**

1. Science projects 2. Science -- Experiments
ISBN 0-471-14802-4

LC 96-27512

"In the first section, VanCleave discusses scientific methodology: how to organize a project from selecting a topic through the investigatory process, the importance of keeping records, writing a final report, and the value of a nicely crafted presentation. . . . The next section—the largest by far—presents a number of double-page projects in a variety of fields. . . . A clear and informative addition." SLJ

Includes glossary and bibliographical references

Janice VanCleave's science around the year. Wiley 2000 122p il pa $12.95

Grades: 4 5 6 7 **507.8**

1. Seasons 2. Science -- Experiments
ISBN 0-471-33096-5

LC 99-53778

Presents experiments and activities in such fields as astronomy, biology, chemistry, earth science, and physics that are in some way related to one of the four seasons

Wheeler-Toppen, Jodi
Science experiments that explode and implode; fun projects for curious kids. Capstone Press 2011 32p il (Edge books: kitchen science) lib bdg $26.65; pa $7.95
Grades: 3 4 5 6   **507.8**
1. Explosions 2. Science -- Experiments
ISBN 978-1-4296-5427-2; 1-4296-5427-9; 978-1-4296-6250-5 pa; 1-4296-6250-6 pa
LC 2010027687
Provides step-by-step instructions for science projects using household materials and explains the science behind the experiments.
"Attractive, colorful, and full of photos, [this title] will appeal to a wide range of kids. . . . Anyone looking for a straightforward, fun, and easy science experiment will want [this title] close by." SLJ
Includes glossary and bibliographical references

Science experiments that fizz and bubble; fun projects for curious kids. Capstone Press 2011 32p il (Edge books: kitchen science) lib bdg $26.65; pa $7.95
Grades: 3 4 5 6   **507.8**
1. Gases 2. Bubbles 3. Science -- Experiments
ISBN 978-1-4296-5425-8 lib bdg; 1-4296-5425-2 lib bdg; 978-1-4296-6251-2 pa; 1-4296-6251-4 pa
LC 2010027684
Provides step-by-step instructions for science projects using household materials and explains the science behind the experiments.
"Attractive, colorful, and full of photos, [this title] will appeal to a wide range of kids. . . . Anyone looking for a straightforward, fun, and easy science experiment will want [this title] close by." SLJ
Includes glossary and bibliographical references

Williams, Jennifer
★ **Oobleck,** slime, & dancing spaghetti; twenty terrific at-home science experiments inspired by favorite children's books. by Jennifer Williams. Bright Sky Press 2009 192 p. ill. (paperback) $14.95
Grades: 4 5 6   **507.8**
1. Children's literature 2. Science -- Experiments -- Juvenile literature
ISBN 1933979348; 9781933979342
LC 2009000876
"Using children's literature as a springboard, this title provides a series of science experiments designed to explore concepts and ideas that spring from various stories. At the beginning of each chapter, a children's book is nicely summarized. The author then explains a related science concept, suggests discussion questions that connect the experiment to the story, and offers ideas for taking the project further. This is serious science. . . . The experiments do a really wonderful job of emphasizing the importance of observation and data collection. The writing is relatively clear. . . ." This book is great choice for home use and science units." SLJ
Includes bibliographical references.

Young, Karen Romano
Experiments to do on your family; 20 projects and experiments about sisters, brothers, parents, pets, and the rest of the gang. illustrations by David Goldin. National Geographic 2010 80p il (Science fair winners) $24.90; pa $12.95
Grades: 3 4 5 6   **507.8**
1. Psychology 2. Science -- Experiments 3. Science projects -- Juvenile literature
ISBN 978-1-4263-0692-1; 1-4263-0692-X; 978-1-4263-0691-4 pa; 1-4263-0691-1 pa
This volume provides "outlines for science fair projects in the behavioral . . . sciences. The procedures include just enough structure to help novice experimenters get started. . . . Well-placed questions encourage creativity and further thinking. [The] volume includes humorous cartoon spot illustrations and a section on preparing presentations." Horn Book Guide

Junkyard science; 20 projects and experiments about junk, garbage, waste, things we don't need anymore, and ways to recycle or reuse it--or lose it. illustrations by David Goldin. National Geographic 2010 80p il (Science fair winners) $24.90; pa $12.95
Grades: 3 4 5 6   **507.8**
1. Recycling 2. Environmental sciences 3. Science -- Experiments
ISBN 978-1-4263-0690-7; 1-4263-0690-3; 978-1-4263-0689-1 pa; 1-4263-0689-X pa
This volume provides "outlines for science fair projects in the . . . environmental . . . sciences. The procedures include just enough structure to help novice experimenters get started. . . . Well-placed questions encourage creativity and further thinking. [The] volume includes humorous cartoon spot illustrations and a section on preparing presentations." Horn Book Guide

Science activities for all students; edited by Aviva Ebner. Facts on File 2009 2v il loose-leaf $370
Grades: Adult Professional   **507.8**
1. Science projects 2. Science -- Experiments
ISBN 978-0-8160-7396-2 loose-leaf; 0-8160-7396-1 loose-leaf
LC 2008043827
Replaces Science Projects for All Students and More Science Projects for All Students, published 1998 and 2002 respectively
These "binders enable students in grades 4 through 9 with developmental or physical challenges to join their classmates in . . . hands-on [science] activities. There are 60 experiments in each binder—designed to be as inclusive as possible—in the areas of basic skills, Earth science, weather, space science, life science, and physical science. Each binder is also enhanced by approximately 250 black-and-white line illustrations." Publisher's note
Includes glossary and bibliographical references

508 Natural history

Baker, Stuart
In the Antarctic. Marshall Cavendish Benchmark 2009 32p il map (Climate change) lib bdg $19.95

Grades: 5 6 7 8 **508**

1. Greenhouse effect

ISBN 978-0-7614-4438-1 lib bdg; 0-7614-4438-6 lib bdg

LC 2009-5766

The book about climate change in the Antarctic "is perfectly organized for students. . . . Unique layout features serve as signposts and will help focus readers' attention. . . . [The book] features an outstanding chart of possible effects of global warming on the area in question, listing 'Possible Event', 'Predicted Result', and 'Impact' in short, bulleted statements." SLJ

Includes glossary

In the tropics. Marshall Cavendish Benchmark 2010 32p il map (Climate change) lib bdg $19.95

Grades: 5 6 7 8 **508**

1. Greenhouse effect

ISBN 978-0-7614-4440-4 lib bdg; 0-7614-4440-8 lib bdg

LC 2009-5768

The book about climate change in the Tropics "is perfectly organized for students. . . . Unique layout features serve as signposts and will help focus readers' attention. . . . [The book] features an outstanding chart of possible effects of global warming on the area in question, listing 'Possible Event', 'Predicted Result', and 'Impact' in short, bulleted statements." SLJ

Includes glossary

Banes, Graham L.

★ The **Kingfisher** encyclopedia of life; minutes, months, millennia--how long is a life on Earth? Kingfisher 2012 160 p. $19.99

Grades: 3 4 5 6 **508**

1. Biology 2. Longevity

ISBN 0753468913; 9780753468913

This book "focuses on 230 species . . . , categorizing them according to lifespan. The chapters start with 'Here today . . . ,' which includes bacteria that survive for less than an hour, and close with 'Time Is on My Side,' which mentions champions of longevity such as the Great Barrier Reef. . . . Spreads focusing on a life span or on species are interspersed with features highlighting biodiversity, habitats, genetics, and other influences on Earth's lifeforms." (School Library Journal)

Bardhan-Quallen, Sudipta

Nature science experiments; what's hopping in a dust bunny? illustrated by Edward Miller. Sterling 2010 64p il (Mad science) $12.95

Grades: 4 5 6 **508**

1. Nature study 2. Science -- Experiments 3. Biology -- Juvenile literature 4. Science -- Experiments -- Juvenile literature

ISBN 978-1-4027-2412-1; 1-4027-2412-8

"The first chapter of this attractive book, 'The Stuff of Life,' jumps right in by outlining the materials needed and the step-by-step process to follow to collect and isolate DNA by rinsing one's mouth with salt water. . . . Youngsters can turn to the table of contents or detailed index to choose experiments based on interest and availability of resources. . . . The chapters on bacteria and protists include color photomicrographs of the organisms, and amusing cartoon illus-

trations appear throughout. This exploration of the natural world will spark readers' interest in experimenting and questioning results." SLJ

Burnie, David

The **Kingfisher** nature encyclopedia; rev ed.; Kingfisher 2010 320p il $27.99

Grades: 4 5 6 7 **508**

1. Nature 2. Natural history 3. Reference books

ISBN 978-0-7534-6503-5; 0-7534-6503-5

First published 2004 with title: The Kingfisher illustrated nature encyclopedia

"Organized into three sections—the first on our planet's origin and the evolution of life, the second surveying the five biotic kingdoms, the third taking closer looks at 14 biomes . . .—each spread offers a topical discussion that ranges in scope from 'Seasons and Weather' or 'How Fungi Feed' to 'Protozoans' and 'Tropical Forests.' Color photos on every page add visual interest while playing supporting roles to information presented in captions and columns of lucid, not heavily technical narrative text. . . . This is a first-rate overview of its topic." SLJ

Chin, Jason

★ **Island**; a story of the Galapagos. Jason Chin. 1st ed. Roaring Brook Press 2012 40 p. (alk. paper) $16.99

Grades: 3 4 5 6 **508**

1. Birds 2. Droughts 3. Reptiles 4. Natural history -- Galapagos Islands

ISBN 1596437162; 9781596437166

LC 2011033797

The author, Jason Chin, explains "how species of reptiles and birds on the Galapagos have evolved. He begins with the birth of the islands themselves, a process in which volcanic eruptions punch successive holes in the Earth's surface as tectonic plates move over them, [and] the adaptations of the islands' animals. . . . [Chin also provides information on the] droughts [that] become more common [due to the] climate and geology." (Publishers Weekly)

Includes bibliographical references and index.

Cole, Henry

I took a walk. Greenwillow Bks. 1998 un il $16.99

Grades: PreK K 1 2 **508**

1. Nature -- Fiction 2. Animals -- Fiction 3. Nature trails -- Pictorial works -- Juvenile fiction

ISBN 0-688-15115-9

LC 97-6692

A visit to woods, pasture, and pond brings encounters with various birds, insects, and other creatures of nature. Flaps fold out to reveal the animals hidden on each two-page spread

"Executed in acrylic paint, the realistic nature scenes invite close and careful inspection." Horn Book Guide

Gates, Phil

Nature got there first; 2nd ed.; Kingfisher 2010 64p il $16.99

Grades: 3 4 5 6 **508**

1. Nature 2. Inventions 3. Technology

ISBN 978-0-7534-6410-6; 0-7534-6410-1

First published 1995

"This browsable title presents fascinating facts about inventions inspired by nature, showing the similarities between the workings of I beams and the make-up of dinosaur vertebrae; the mechanics of sailboats and the physiognomy of jellyfish; and the movements of giant squids and jet engine design. . . . The well-chosen images are both inviting and clearly illustrate the points made in the text and captions. . . . This is an informative, appealing look at the connections between natural and human design." Booklist

Includes glossary

Granström, Brita

Nature adventures; [by] Mick Manning & Brita Granstr["o]m. Frances Lincoln Children's Books 48p il $18.95

Grades: 2 3 4 5   **508**

  1. Nature study

  ISBN 978-1-84780-088-6; 1-84780-088-2

"Highly illustrated, information-packed pages entice readers to explore nature wherever they might find themselves and to take an active look at the world around them. Chapters include 'In the Town,' 'Fresh Water,' 'Woodland,' 'Field and Hedgerow,' 'Wild Country,' 'The Seashore,' and 'Through the Seasons.' Beautifully drawn artwork in pencil and watercolor provides field-guide references for budding explorers." SLJ

Includes glossary

Kalman, Bobbie

What are opposites in nature? Crabtree Pub. Co. 2010 24p il (Looking at nature) lib bdg $21.27; pa $6.95

Grades: K 1 2   **508**

  1. Nature 2. Opposites

  ISBN 978-0-7787-3326-3 lib bdg; 0-7787-3326-2 lib bdg; 978-0-7787-3346-1 pa; 0-7787-3346-7 pa

                   LC 2010016399

This book explores opposites found in nature.

"Bright, colorful photographs were selected with young readers in mind, and the type is large—perfect for reading together. . . Throughout the book are questions that challenge the reader to identify the opposites shown on the pages. . . . Parents and teachers will find . . . [this book] a great addition to a child's library." Sci Books & Films

Levinson, Nancy Smiler

★ North Pole, South Pole; illustrated by Diane Dawson Hearn. Holiday House 2002 40p il $14.95

Grades: K 1 2 3   **508**

  ISBN 0-8234-1737-9

                   LC 2001-59419

An introduction to the geography, climate, and inhabitants of the polar regions at the top and the bottom of the earth where the North Pole and the South Pole are located

"Beginning readers can find a clear and concise discussion of the differences between the poles. . . . Hearn's colorful illustrations in white, blue, and teal green depict a number of the animal inhabitants, all identified." SLJ

Lynch, Wayne

The Everglades; text and photographs by Wayne Lynch. NorthWord Books for Young Readers 2007 64p il (Our wild world: ecosystems) $16.95; pa $8.95

Grades: 4 5 6 7   **508**

  1. Natural history -- Florida 2. Natural history -- Florida

-- Everglades -- Juvenile literature

  ISBN 978-1-55971-970-4; 1-55971-970-2; 978-1-55971-971-1 pa; 1-55971-971-0 pa

                   LC 2006-101497

This "provides an up-close look at the fascinating flora and fauna of the world-famous Everglades. . . . Lynch . . . smoothly pairs engaging prose with numerous color photographs that capture the beauty of the region in both sweeping panorama and close-up detail." Booklist

McMillan, Bruce

Summer ice; life along the Antarctic peninsula. written and photo-illustrated by Bruce McMillan. Houghton Mifflin 1995 48p il map $16

Grades: 3 4 5 6   **508**

  1. Natural history -- Antarctica 2. Natural history -- Antarctica -- Juvenile literature

  ISBN 0-395-66561-2

                   LC 93-38831

"The full-color photography is brilliant in its beauty and attention to detail. However, the text is lively and knowledgeable, and could stand alone and still catch readers' interest." SLJ

Includes glossary and bibliographical references

Morrison, Gordon

★ Nature in the neighborhood; [by] Gordon Morrison. Houghton Mifflin Company 2004 32p il $16

Grades: 3 4 5 6   **508**

  1. Seasons 2. Natural history

  ISBN 0-618-35215-5

                   LC 2004-2354

"Morrison offers another quiet, layered view of a natural world that is familiar to many children. . . . His precise, pencil-and-watercolor artwork encourages viewers to look closely at common neighborhood scenes." Booklist

Potter, Jean

Nature in a nutshell for kids; over 100 activities you can do in ten minutes or less. Wiley 1995 136p il pa $12.95

Grades: 2 3 4   **508**

  1. Nature study 2. Science -- Experiments -- Juvenile literature

  ISBN 0-471-04444-X

                   LC 94-28953

"Each of the 102 experiments is easy, uses safe and mostly readily available household supplies, and is fun at the same time. Divided into seasonal sections, the activities have catchy titles, state hypotheses, list materials, lay out procedures, and finish with clear explanations. Among the noteworthy investigations are: how duck feathers react to water, how mountains are formed, what keeps a seal from freezing in icy weather, whether ants prefer sugar or aspertame, and more." SLJ

Includes glossary and bibliographical references

Rau, Dana Meachen

Day and night. Marshall Cavendish Benchmark 2010 31p il (Bookworms. Nature's cycles) lib bdg $22.79

Grades: PreK K 1   **508**
1. Day 2. Night
ISBN 978-0-7614-4094-9 lib bdg; 0-7614-4094-1
lib bdg

            LC 2008-42512
"Well composed, simple sentences tie directly to colorful, carefully chosen photos [and] . . . accurate information flows naturally. . . . A great resource for sharing one-on-one with the youngest readers." Libr Media Connect
Includes glossary

Roman, Elisabeth

World of wonders; the most mesmerizing natural phenomena on Earth. Abrams Books for Young Readers 2010 184p il $19.95
Grades: 3 4 5 6   **508**
1. Zoology 2. Earth sciences
ISBN 978-0-8109-8963-4; 0-8109-8963-8
"This refreshingly upbeat collection of random facts about Earth's creatures and natural wonders is accompanied by startlingly beautiful photographs. Each spread asks a question, such as, 'What is the most dangerous animal?' or 'What is the biggest cavern?' The answer (printed upside down beneath the question) is then followed by a short explanation or description of an unusual aspect of the animal or phenomenon. . . . This is strictly a book for browsing." SLJ

Schwartz, David M.

★ **What** in the wild? mysteries of nature concealed and revealed: ear-tickling poems. by David M. Schwartz andYael Schy; eye-tricking photos by Dwight Kuhn. Tricycle Press 2010 un il $16.99; lib bdg $19.99
Grades: K 1 2 3 4   **508**
1. Animals 2. Nature study 3. Nature poetry 4. Children's poetry 5. Natural history -- Juvenile literature
ISBN 978-1-58246-310-0; 1-58246-310-7; 978-1-58246-359-9 lib bdg; 1-58246-359-9 lib bdg
"A nifty combo of poetry (often of the concrete variety), super color photos, scientific information, and a guessing game (complete with whole-page flaps for lifting). . . . Fun as a read-alone or for one-on-one sharing, this tidy package from a talented trio will delight children (and teachers of whole curriculum, too)." SLJ
Includes bibliographical references

Wood, A. J.

Charles Darwin and the Beagle adventure; countries visited during the voyage round the world of HMS Beagle under the command of Captain Fitzroy, Royal Navy, including extracts from the works of Charles Darwin. written by A.J. Wood & Clint Twist. Candlewick Press 2009 un il map $19.99
Grades: 4 5 6 7 8   **508**
1. Evolution 2. Naturalists 3. Travel writers 4. Writers on science 5. Natural history -- Juvenile literature 6. Evolution (Biology) -- Juvenile literature
ISBN 978-0-7636-4538-0; 0-7636-4538-9

            LC 2009-921214
"This beautifully illustrated large-format book immediately appeals to both the eye and the mind. Imitating a 19th-century scrapbook to a certain extent, including various pullouts . . . the book draws the young reader in. . . . Included are copious quotes from Darwin's journals and other writings, as well as reproductions . . . of numerous 19th-century engravings, drawings, and watercolors, some from the Beagle voyage itself. . . . Integrated into the 19th-century material are modern illustrations and well-written narratives relating background information, the story of the Beagle's voyage . . . and notes on Darwin's life and work. . . . This volume provides an excellent introduction to Darwin and his accomplishments." Sci Books Films

Woodward, John

Along the shore. Brown Bear Books 2009 32p il map (Oceans alive!) lib bdg $28.50
Grades: 2 3 4 5   **508**
1. Coasts 2. Beaches 3. Seashore
ISBN 978-1-933834-61-0 lib bdg; 1-933834-61-7 lib bdg

            LC 2009-30123
This "shows and explains mudskippers, mangroves, and sea lions—all interesting life forms with which the young reader is likely to be familiar. . . . Readers also will be well exposed to a number of scientific principles . . . Excellent analogies are offered." Sci Books Films
Includes glossary and bibliographical references

508.2   Seasons

Anderson, Maxine

Explore spring! 25 great ways to learn about spring. [by Maxine Anderson; illustrated by Alexis Frederick-Frost] Nomad Press 2007 92p il pa $12.95
Grades: 2 3 4 5   **508.2**
1. Spring 2. Science -- Experiments
ISBN 978-0-9785037-4-1
Explains what spring is and why it occurs. Includes projects, activities, and experiments.
"Bold, black-and-white cartoons and occasional jokes add levity to the science. . . . The information is sound, with engaging activities to test and illuminate spring events." SLJ
Includes glossary and bibliographical references

Explore winter! 25 great ways to learn about winter. [by Maxine Anderson; illustrated by Alexis Frederick-Frost] Nomad Press 2007 92p il pa $12.95
Grades: 2 3 4 5   **508.2**
1. Winter 2. Science -- Experiments
ISBN 978-0-9785037-5-8
Explains what winter is and why it occurs. Includes projects, activities, and experiments.
"Pages of basic information are interspersed with 'Wow' facts, black-and-white cartoon illustrations, and jokes. . . . Curious readers will gain a new level of understanding about winter after reading, laughing at, and experimenting with this book." SLJ
Includes glossary and bibliographical references

Anderson, Sheila

Are you ready for fall? by Sheila M. Anderson. Lerner Publications 2010 32p il (Lightning bolt books. Seasons) lib bdg $25.26; pa $7.95

Grades: PreK K 1 2 **508.2**
1. Autumn
ISBN 978-0-7613-4586-2 lib bdg; 0-7613-4586-8 lib bdg; 978-0-7613-5672-1 pa; 0-7613-5672-X pa
LC 2009-16408

"The book explores, in simplest terms, things that we see and experience in the fall. . . . Vivid photographs accompany the text, with explanatory balloons to highlight certain points. . . . This would be an excellent book to read, chapter by chapter, to younger preschoolers and to be read by older readers and used for research up to third grade. It lends itself well to science and social studies lessons, as well as other activities." Sci Books Films

Includes glossary

Are you ready for spring? by Sheila M. Anderson. Lerner Publications 2010 32p il (Lightning bolt books. Seasons) lib bdg $25.26; pa $7.95
Grades: PreK K 1 2 **508.2**
1. Spring
ISBN 978-0-7613-4584-8 lib bdg; 0-7613-4584-1 lib bdg; 978-0-7613-5670-7 pa; 0-7613-5670-3 pa
LC 2009-16409

This "explores those attributes we most often associate with spring. The book has a lot of 'kid appeal' with its pictures and descriptions of mud puddles, rain, and flying kites. Changes in nature are subtly woven in with everyday experiences to provide a full overview of the season. The descriptions and explanations are scientifically accurate, and a diversity of ethncity and climates is shown in the colorful pictures." Sci Books Films

Includes glossary

Branley, Franklyn Mansfield
★ **Sunshine** makes the seasons; illustrated by Michael Rex. newly illustrated ed; HarperCollins Pubs. 2005 31p il (Let's-read-and-find-out science) hardcover o.p. pa $4.99
Grades: K 1 2 3 **508.2**
1. Seasons -- Juvenile literature 2. Sunshine -- Juvenile literature
ISBN 0-06-059203-6; 0-06-059205-2 pa
LC 2003-25457

First published 1974; this is a newly illustrated edition of the text revised for the 1985 edition

Describes how sunshine and the tilt of the earth's axis are responsible for the changing seasons

Includes bibliographical references

Crausaz, Anne
Seasons. Kane/Miller 2011 un il $15.99
Grades: K 1 2 **508.2**
1. Seasons 2. Seasons -- Juvenile literature
ISBN 1-61067-006-X; 978-1-61067-006-7

"Spring is when everything looks green, blooming trees smell fragrant, 'blackbirds are singing about their favorite season,' a ladybug on your hand 'might tickle,' and cherries are sweet. . . . Preschool." (Horn Book)

"With an emphasis on taste, smell, and outdoor activity, Crausaz guides readers through the seasons of the year in this understated and evocative French import. Crisp, delicate digital artwork set against mostly plain backgrounds keeps the focus on the freckled, rosy-cheeked girl." Publ Wkly

Esbaum, Jill
Everything spring. National Geographic 2010 15p il (Picture the seasons) pa $5.95
Grades: PreK K 1 **508.2**
1. Spring
ISBN 978-1-4263-0607-5; 1-4263-0607-5

"These pages burst with vibrant photographs of baby animals and closeups of buds and growth. Esbaum uses poetic prose to connect children with the joy of the season." SLJ

Hawk, Fran
Count down to Fall; illustrated by Sherry Neidigh. Sylvan Dell 2009 un il $16.95
Grades: PreK K 1 2 3 **508.2**
1. Trees 2. Autumn 3. Counting 4. Forest animals
ISBN 978-1-934359-94-5; 1-934359-94-7

"Bold, full-spread illustrations with inset details feature a variety of trees and woodland animals in this informational picture book. As the facts about trees count down, the images represent the numbers 10 to 1, while corner insets show the tree, spring and fall leaves, a seed, and occasionally the flower of the specific tree pictured, such as birch, dogwood, oak, and maple. Children will be drawn to examine the expressive images of animals and find additional ones along the detailed border featuring closeups of the tree's bark." SLJ

McKneally, Ranida
Our seasons; [by] Grace Lin and Ranida McKneally; illustrated by Grace Lin. Charlesbridge 2006 un il $15.95
Grades: K 1 2 3 **508.2**
1. Seasons
ISBN 978-1-57091-360-0; 1-57091-360-9
LC 2005-06016

"Following a brief explanation of the science behind the seasons, Lin takes readers from autumn to summer, pairing haiku verses on one page with explanations of seasonal changes on the other. . . . The gouache illustrations have plenty of child appeal and effectively tie together the poetry and the facts." SLJ

Rau, Dana Meachen
Seasons. Marshall Cavendish Benchmark 2009 31p il (Bookworms. Nature's cycles) lib bdg $22.79
Grades: PreK K 1 **508.2**
1. Seasons
ISBN 978-0-7614-4098-7 lib bdg; 0-7614-4098-4 lib bdg
LC 2008-42507

"Well composed, simple sentences tie directly to colorful, carefully chosen photos [and] . . . accurate information flows naturally. . . . A great resource for sharing one-on-one with the youngest readers." Libr Media Connect

Includes glossary

Rotner, Shelley
Every season; by Shelley Rotner & Anne Love Woodhull; photographs by Shelley Rotner. Roaring Brook Press 2007 un il $16.95
Grades: PreK K 1 **508.2**
1. Seasons
ISBN 978-1-59643-136-2; 1-59643-136-9
LC 2006-12009

With simple text and bright photographs presents a portrait of nature through the seasons of the year.

"Beautiful color photographs illustrate this picture-book. . . . What distinguishes this is the quality and selection of the photos and the lovely spare words, which repeat sounds and lines with an easy, circular rhythm that echoes the cycle of seasons and encourages child participation." Booklist

Rustad, Martha E. H.

Fall weather; cooler temperatures. illustrated by Amanda Enright. Millbrook Press 2011 24p il (Fall's here!) lib bdg $23.93

Grades: K 1 2 3   **508.2**

1. Autumn

ISBN 978-0-7613-5063-7; 0-7613-5063-2

LC 2010048309

This book about Fall weather is "outstanding for . . . its clear description of seasons and the word 'equinox.' . . . Colorful illustrations fill the spreads with active, cartoonlike boys and girls surrounded by the green, brown, and orange hues of autumn." SLJ

Schuette, Sarah L.

Let's look at fall; by Sarah L. Schuette. Capstone Press 2007 24p il (Investigate the seasons) $19.93

Grades: K 1 2   **508.2**

1. Autumn 2. Animal behavior

ISBN 978-0-7368-6705-4; 0-7368-6705-8

LC 2006020449

"The format consists of about three descriptive sentences per page in a large font, a vivid color photograph opposite, and colorful chapter titles in a larger typeface. . . . [This book is] excellent . . . for unit study and wonderful for sharing or browsing." SLJ

Includes bibliographical references

Let's look at spring; by Sarah L. Schuette. Capstone Press 2007 24p il (Investigate the seasons) $19.93

Grades: K 1 2   **508.2**

1. Spring 2. Animal behavior

ISBN 978-0-7368-6707-8; 0-7368-6707-4

LC 2006020451

"The format consists of about three descriptive sentences per page in a large font, a vivid color photograph opposite, and colorful chapter titles in a larger typeface. . . . [This book is] excellent . . . for unit study and wonderful for sharing or browsing." SLJ

Includes bibliographical references

Let's look at summer; by Sarah L. Schuette. Capstone Press 2007 24p il (Investigate the seasons) $19.93

Grades: K 1 2   **508.2**

1. Summer 2. Animal behavior

ISBN 978-0-7368-6708-5; 0-7368-6708-2

LC 2006020452

"The format consists of about three descriptive sentences per page in a large font, a vivid color photograph opposite, and colorful chapter titles in a larger typeface. . . . [This book is] excellent . . . for unit study and wonderful for sharing or browsing." SLJ

Includes bibliographical references

Let's look at winter; by Sarah L. Schuette. Capstone Press 2007 24p il (Investigate the seasons) $19.93

Grades: K 1 2   **508.2**

1. Winter 2. Animal behavior

ISBN 978-0-7368-6706-1; 0-7368-6706-6

LC 2006020508

"The format consists of about three descriptive sentences per page in a large font, a vivid color photograph opposite, and colorful chapter titles in a larger typeface. . . . [This book is] excellent . . . for unit study and wonderful for sharing or browsing." SLJ

Includes bibliographical references

Smith, Sian

Fall. Heinemann Library 2009 24p il (Seasons) lib bdg $20.71; pa $5.99

Grades: K 1   **508.2**

1. Autumn

ISBN 1-4329-2732-9 pa; 978-1-4329-2727-1 lib bdg; 1-4329-2727-2 lib bdg; 978-1-4329-2732-5 pa

LC 2008049155

This describes the clothing, weather, and human and animal activities of the Autumn.

"What distinguishes [this book] from others on the same [subject is] the vibrant, eye-catching photographs. The sentences are simple and repetitive. . . . Reading teachers will want to use this . . . for instructional purposes while early readers will feel successful mastering the text. Students will delight in the color photographs of animals and children enjoying the activities." SLJ

Spring. Heinemann Library 2009 24p il (Seasons) lib bdg $20.71; pa $5.99

Grades: K 1   **508.2**

1. Spring

ISBN 978-1-4329-2728-8 lib bdg; 1-4329-2728-0 lib bdg; 978-1-4329-2733-2 pa; 1-4329-2733-7 pa

LC 2008049156

This describes the clothing, weather, and human and animal activities of spring

"What distinguishes [this book] from others on the same [subject is] the vibrant, eye-catching photographs. The sentences are simple and repetitive. . . . Reading teachers will want to use this . . . for instructional purposes while early readers will feel successful mastering the text. Students will delight in the color photographs of animals and children enjoying the activities." SLJ

Summer. Heinemann Library 2009 24p il (Seasons) lib bdg $20.71; pa $5.99

Grades: K 1   **508.2**

1. Summer

ISBN 978-1-4329-2729-5 lib bdg; 1-4329-2729-9 lib bdg; 978-1-4329-2734-9 pa; 1-4329-2734-5 pa LC 2008049157

This describes the clothing, weather, and human and animal activities of summer

"What distinguishes [this book] from others on the same [subject is] the vibrant, eye-catching photographs. The sentences are simple and repetitive. . . . Reading teachers will want to use this . . . for instructional purposes while early readers will feel successful mastering the text. Students will delight in the color photographs of animals and children enjoying the activities." SLJ

Winter. Heinemann Library 2009 24p il (Seasons) lib bdg $20.71; pa $5.99

Grades: K 1   **508.2**
  1. Winter
  ISBN 978-1-4329-2730-1 lib bdg; 1-4329-2730-2 lib bdg; 978-1-4329-2735-6 pa; 1-4329-2735-3 pa
                                                    LC 2008049162

This describes the clothing, weather, and human and animal activities of winter

"What distinguishes [this book] from others on the same [subject is] the vibrant, eye-catching photographs. The sentences are simple and repetitive. . . . Reading teachers will want to use this . . . for instructional purposes while early readers will feel successful mastering the text. Students will delight in the color photographs of animals and children enjoying the activities." SLJ

509   History, geographic treatment, biography

Beshore, George W.
  ★ **Science** in ancient China; [by] George Beshore. Watts 1998 63p il map (Science of the past) hardcover o.p. pa $8.95

Grades: 4 5 6 7   **509**
  1. Science and civilization 2. Science -- China -- History
  ISBN 0-531-11334-5 lib bdg; 0-531-15914-0 pa
                                                    LC 97-3519

First published 1988 in the First book series

Surveys the achievements of the ancient Chinese in science, medicine, astronomy, and cosmology, and describes such innovations as rockets, wells, the compass, water wheels, and movable type

Includes glossary and bibliographical references

Cole, Joanna
  ★ The **magic** school bus and the science fair expedition; illustrated by Bruce Degen. Scholastic Press 2006 45p il $15.99

Grades: 2 3 4   **509**
  1. Scientists 2. Science -- History
  ISBN 0-590-10824-7

Ms. Frizzle takes her class on a tour through the history of science so they can get ideas for their science fair

"This has all the hallmarks of the winning series: humorous cartoon speech bubbles; instructive, funny, appealing illustrations; and clear language that explains basic concepts without condescension." Booklist

Eamer, Claire
  Before the World Was Ready; Stories of Daring Genius in Science. by Claire Eamer. Firefly Books Ltd 2013 125 p. (paperback) $14.95

Grades: 5 6 7 8   **509**
  1. Inventions 2. Scientists
  ISBN 1554515351; 9781554515356

This book looks at eight scientists and inventors. "Alfred Wegener struggled to convince geologists that the ground beneath our feet is moving. . . . Nikola Tesla's futuristic ideas about electricity were dismissed. Charles Darwin delayed publishing his controversial theory of evolution for de-

cades." Also included are Charles Babbage, Ada Lovelace, Rachel Carson, and George Cayley. (Publisher's note)

Harris, Jacqueline L.
  ★ **Science** in ancient Rome. Watts 1998 64p il map (Science of the past) hardcover o.p. pa $8.95

Grades: 4 5 6 7   **509**
  1. Science and civilization 2. Science -- Rome -- History 3. Science, Ancient -- Juvenile literature
  ISBN 0-531-20354-9; 0-531-15916-7 pa
                                                    LC 97-1901

First published 1988 in the First book series

Describes how the Romans put to use and expanded the scientific achievements of earlier civilizations

This "includes clear, easy-to-read text; simple yet effective topic headings; excellent-quality, full-color photographs and reproductions; and Internet sites." SLJ

Includes glossary and bibliographical references

Jackson, Donna M.
  ★ **Extreme** scientists; exploring nature's mysteries from perilous places. Houghton Mifflin Harcourt 2009 63p il (Scientists in the field) $18

Grades: 5 6 7 8   **509**
  1. Botanists 2. Explorers 3. Scientists 4. Spelunkers 5. Meteorologists 6. Microbiologists 7. College teachers
  ISBN 978-0-618-77706-8; 0-618-77706-7
                                                    LC 2008-36796

This volume "profiles three scientists working far out in the field. Hurricane hunter Paul Flaherty, . . . Hazel Barton, a microbiologist specializing in single-cell organisms living in extreme conditions, . . . [and] ecologist and college professor Steve Sillett, who . . . . climbs into the canopies to study redwoods. While the clearly written text includes vivid passages about the dangers these scientists face, it goes on to discuss what drives them to pursue their subjects and what they have discovered along the way. . . . The many excellent color photos portray these adventures as scientists intently focused on their work." Booklist

Includes glossary and bibliographical references

January, Brendan
  Science in colonial America. Watts 1999 64p il (Science of the past) hardcover o.p. pa $8.95

Grades: 4 5 6 7   **509**
  1. Scientists 2. Science and civilization 3. Science -- United States -- History 4. Scientists -- United States -- Biography -- Juvenile literature
  ISBN 0-531-11525-9; 0-531-15940-X pa
                                                    LC 98-10450

Describes the scientific contributions made by people in colonial America, including natural history, medicine, astronomy, and electricity

"Attractive and accessible. . . . Plentiful, accurate material." SLJ

Includes glossary and bibliographical references

McCutcheon, Marc
  ★ The **kid** who named Pluto; and the stories of other extraordinary young people in science. illustrated by Jon Cannell. Chronicle Books 2004 85p il $15.95

Grades: 4 5 6   **509**
  1. Scientists
  ISBN 0-8118-3770-X

                          LC 2003-3662

"This book profiles nine people who made significant contributions to science while still quite young. Louis Braille and Robert Goddard are among the more famous, while others, such as television pioneer Philo Farnsworth and Venetia Burney, the girl who named Pluto, are less well known. . . . The lively and lighthearted text conveys a sense of the excitement of discovery, with an appropriate amount of background information, along with the biographical facts. . . . Lively cartoon pen-and-ink illustrations, all in greens and grays, help to unify the individual chapters. " Booklist

Romanek, Trudee
  Science, medicine, and math in the early Islamic world; Trudee Romanek. Crabtree Pub. Company 2012 48 p. (reinforced library binding: alk. paper) $30.60
Grades: 4 5 6 7   **509**
  1. Science -- History 2. Medicine -- History 3. Mathematics -- History 4. Islamic civilization -- Juvenile literature 5. Science -- Islamic Empire -- History -- Juvenile literature
  ISBN 0778721701; 9780778721703; 9780778721772; 9781427195630; 9781427198402

                          LC 2012000077

This children's educational book, by Trudee Romanek, describes "the scientific contributions of the early Islamic empires to science, medicine, and mathematics. . . . This . . . book explores their public hospitals, libraries, and universities; their achievements in mathematics and astronomy, and the pursuit of alchemy; Arabic numbers; optics; music and musical instruments; poetry; and education." (Publisher's note)

Woods, Geraldine
  ★ **Science** in ancient Egypt. Watts 1998 64p il (Science of the past) hardcover o.p. pa $8.95
Grades: 4 5 6 7   **509**
  1. Science and civilization 2. Science, Ancient 3. Science -- Egypt -- History 4. Technology -- Egypt -- History
  ISBN 0-531-20341-7; 0-531-15915-9 pa

                          LC 97-649

First published 1988 in the First book series

Discusses the achievements of the ancient Egyptians in science, mathematics, astronomy, medicine, agriculture, and technology

"Well-researched and easy-to-understand. . . . Woods offers a fascinating look at the ancient Egyptians' accomplishments." SLJ

Includes glossary and bibliographical references

509.2 Scientists

Davidson, Tish
  African American scientists and inventors; by Tish Davidson. Mason Crest Publishers 2013 64 p. ill. (some col.) (Major Black contributions from Emancipation to civil rights) (library) $22.95

Grades: 4 5 6   **509.2**
  1. African American inventors 2. African American scientists
  ISBN 1422223752; 9781422223758

                          LC 2011051942

This book by Tish Davidson profiles African American scientists and inventors. "Some of them were elementary school dropouts. Others became medical doctors or college professors. Some were famous, while some toiled in obscurity. . . . Lewis Latimer devised a manufacturing process that made electric lights affordable for ordinary people. Charles Drew did pioneering work in blood storage, helping save countless lives. Garrett Woods figured out how to send messages from moving trains." (Publisher's note)

Includes bibliographical references (pages 60-61) and index.

Di Domenico, Kelly
  Women scientists who changed the world; by Kelly Di Domenico. Rosen Pub. 2012 106 p. col. ill. (library) $34.60
Grades: 5 6 7 8   **509.2**
  1. Women scientists -- Biography -- Juvenile literature
  2. Women in science -- Biography -- Juvenile literature
  ISBN 1448859999; 9781448859993

                          LC 2011032120

In this collective biography by Kelly Di Domenico, "readers meet eleven women scientists, whose research and discoveries are outstanding in their fields. . . . Readers are introduced to each scientist's life and work, including the obstacles each woman had to overcome to achieve success. Profiles include biologist Rachel Carson, orangutan researcher Birute Galdikas, and Nobel Prize-winning biochemist Ada Yonath." (Publisher's note)

Includes bibliographical references (p. 101) and index.

Miles, Liz
  Louis Pasteur; by Liz Miles. Raintree 2009 48 p. ill. (chiefly col.) (library) $32.00
Grades: 4 5 6   **509.2**
  1. Science -- History -- 19th century -- Juvenile literature
  2. Scientists -- France -- Biography -- Juvenile literature
  3. Microbiologists -- France -- Biography -- Juvenile literature
  ISBN 141093229X; 9781410932297

                          LC 2007050125

This book by Liz Miles is part of the Leveled Biographies series and looks at Louis Pasteur. "What is Pasteurization? How has Pasteur's work helped treat many diseases? The 'Leveled Biographies' series offers leveled, high-interest nonfiction in a range of text genres. Each title tells the story of one memorable life, using pictures, maps, sidebars, and engaging text to make each person's story come alive." (Publisher's note)

Includes bibliographical references (p. 46) and index.

Ottaviani, Jim
  Primates; The Fearless Science of Jane Goodall, Dian Fossey, and Biruté Galdikas. Jim Ottaviani; illustrated by Maris Wicks. First Second 2013 133 p. (hardcover) $19.99
Grades: 5 6 7 8   **509.2**
  ISBN 1596438657; 9781596438651

This nonfiction graphic novel, by Jim Ottaviani, illustrated by Maris Wicks, presents an "account of the three greatest primatologists of the last century: Jane Goodall, Dian Fossey, and Biruté Galdikas. These three ground-breaking researchers were all students of the great Louis Leakey, and each made profound contributions to primatology--and to our own understanding of ourselves." (Publisher's note)

510   Mathematics

Bodach, Vijaya

Bar graphs; by Vijaya Khisty Bodach. Capstone Press 2008 32p il (Making graphs) lib bdg $23.93; pa $7.95
Grades: K 1 2   510
  1. Graphic methods
  ISBN 978-1-4296-0040-8 lib bdg; 1-4296-0040-3 lib bdg; 978-1-4296-2870-9 pa; 1-4296-2870-7 pa
                                  LC 2007004670
This "book illustrates how to sort items and represent quantity using horizontal and vertical bars on a graph. Toy animals, fruit, pet type, and hair color are used as examples. . . . [The] title encourages readers to create their own graphs. Large, colorful photographs depict the concepts and feature ethnically diverse children. The photos and graphs complement the controlled-vocabulary [text]." SLJ
  Includes glossary and bibliographical references

Pictographs; by Vijaya Khisty Bodach. Capstone Press 2008 32p il (Making graphs) lib bdg $23.93; pa $7.95
Grades: K 1 2   510
  1. Graphic methods
  ISBN 978-1-4296-0041-5 lib bdg; 1-4296-0041-1 lib bdg; 978-1-4296-2871-6 pa; 1-4296-2871-5 pa
                                  LC 2007006948
This "introduces the idea of organizing data to 'show how many' with picture representations. Comparisons are made on a variety of topics: spotted and solid-color bunnies, how students get to school (walking, bus, and bikes), beverage preferences, and the kinds of flowers in an arrangement. . . . [The] title encourages readers to create their own graphs. Large, colorful photographs depict the concepts and feature ethnically diverse children. The photos and graphs complement the controlled-vocabulary [text]." SLJ
  Includes glossary and bibliographical references

Pie graphs; by Vijaya Khisty Bodach. Capstone Press 2007 32p il (Making graphs) lib bdg $23.93; pa $7.95
Grades: K 1 2   510
  1. Graphic methods
  ISBN 978-1-4296-0042-2 lib bdg; 1-4296-0042-X lib bdg; 978-1-4296-2872-3 pa; 1-4296-2872-3 pa
                                  LC 2007011075
"It's hard to find books that effectively explain math concerts for young children; this crystal clear entry in the Making Graphs series does just that. The book sensibly opens with an episode involving slices of strawberry pie, then points out that 'pie graphs are not just for pies.' The examples, eight in all, stay close to children's immediate concerns. . . . A big strength of this title are the pictures, primarily professional photographs of children in scenes set up to closely match the text." Booklist
  Includes bibliographical references

Tally charts; by Vijaya Khisty Bodach. Capstone Press 2008 32p il (Making graphs) lib bdg $23.93; pa $7.95
Grades: K 1 2   510
  1. Counting 2. Graphic methods
  ISBN 978-1-4296-0043-9 lib bdg; 1-4296-0043-8 lib bdg; 978-1-4296-2873-0 pa; 1-4296-2873-1 pa
                                  LC 2007010814
This "is devoted to keeping count with tally marks recorded in groups of five. This concept is illustrated with pickup sticks and then translated to pen and paper. Sports preferences, the probability of heads or tails on coin flips, and score keeping are shown. [The] title encourages readers to create their own graphs. Large, colorful photographs depict the concepts and feature ethnically diverse children. The photos and graphs complement the controlled-vocabulary [text.]" SLJ
  Includes glossary and bibliographical references

Connolly, Sean

The **book** of perfectly perilous math; 24 death-defying challenges for young mathematicians. by Sean Connolly. Workman Pub. 2012 xiii, 240 p.p ill. (alk. paper) $12.95
Grades: 4 5 6   510
  1.   Mathematical recreations 2. Word problems (Mathematics) 3. Mathematics -- Study and teaching 4. Mathematics -- Problems, exercises, etc 5. Problem solving -- Problems, exercises, etc
  ISBN 0761163743; 9780761163749
                                  LC 2012003443
This children's book by Sean Connolly "blends middle school math with fantasy. . . . These word problems are perilous, do-or-die scenarios of blood-sucking vampires . . . or [of] a rowboat of 5 shipwrecked sailors with a single barrel of freshwater. . . . They test readers on fractions, algebra, geometry, probability, expressions and equations, and more." (Publisher's note)

D'Amico, Joan

The **math** chef; over 60 math activities and recipes for kids. [by] Joan D'Amico, Karen Eich Drummond; illustrations by Tina Cash-Walsh. Wiley 1997 180p il pa $12.95
Grades: 4 5 6   510
  1. Cooking 2. Mathematics
  ISBN 0-471-13813-4
                                  LC 96-22143
Relates math and cookery by presenting math concepts and reinforcing them with recipes. Provides practice in converting from English to metric system, multiplying quantities, measuring area, estimating, and more
  "The instructional value of this book is excellent. . . . The illustrations and content are accurate and very well depicted." Sci Books Films
  Includes glossary

Flatt, Lizann

Sorting through spring; Lizann Flatt, Ashley Barron. Owlkids Books Inc. 2013 32 p. (Math in nature) $14.95
Grades: 1 2 3   510
  1. Nature -- Juvenile literature 2. Mathematics -- Juvenile literature
  ISBN 1926973593; 9781926973593
                                  LC 2012945652
"The aim of this . . . picture book is to introduce mathematical concepts such as patterning, data management,

and probability by using occurrences in nature as examples. It examines events in springtime, such as rain, bird nests, budding flowers, and baby rabbits, and asks mathematical questions about them. . . . This is the second in the 'Math in Nature' series." (Children's Literature)

Green, Dan

Math; a book you can count on! created by Basher; written by Dan Green. Kingfisher 2010 64p il $12.99; pa $7.99

Grades: 4 5 6 7   510

1. Mathematics

ISBN 978-0-7534-6620-9; 0-7534-6620-1; 978-0-7534-6419-9 pa; 0-7534-6419-5 pa

This "introduces basic mathematical terms such as zero, line, pi, quadrilaterals, ratio, bar graph, and x (representing unknown quantities). Each one, personified in the accompanying digital illustration, speaks for itself. . . . Reminiscent of Japanese cartoons, the colorful, iconic illustrations of the characters are appealing enough to disarm many mathphobic students, while those who love the subject will be in their element. . . . Appealing to a broad range of readers, this little book introduces plenty of ideas to build on while presenting familiar concepts in a fresh way." Booklist

Lee, Cora

The **great** number rumble; [a story of math in surprising places] [by] Cora Lee & Gillian O'Reilly; illustrations by Virginia Gray. Annick Press 2007 104p il $24.95; pa $14.95

Grades: 4 5 6   510

1. Mathematics

ISBN 978-1-55451-032-0; 1-55451-032-5; 978-1-55451-031-3 pa; 1-55451-031-7 pa

"When the schools in Jeremy's town ban math, there are loud cheers from the kids. . . . But Jeremy's best friend Sam, a self-proclaimed mathnik, sets out to prove that math is not only important, but fun. In the chapters that follow, Sam reveals math's presence in everyday places, including sports (types of triangles determine how a bike functions), art (artist M.C. Escher combined math patterns with imagination), even in nature (ants instinctively calculate dead reckoning—a navigation tool also used by astronauts). . . . In the end, Jeremy, his teachers, and even the Director of Education have to admit that school minus math equals all sorts of trouble." (Publisher's note) Index. "Ages nine to eleven." (Quill Quire)

"Interspersed with the story line are one-page biographies of Pythagoras, Archimedes, Hypatia of Alexandria, Sophie Germain, Charles Ludwig Dodgson, Srinivasa Ramanujan, and Andrew Wiles. Sidebars with Jeremy's thoughts on chaos theory, cash prizes for new prime numbers, laws of probability, and palindrome numbers add to the information. Full-color cartoons, diagrams, and photos appear throughout." SLJ

McKellar, Danica

Math doesn't suck; how to survive middle school math without losing your mind or breaking a nail. [by] Danica McKellar. Hudson Street Press 2007 297p il $23.95

Grades: 5 6 7 8   510

1. Mathematics

ISBN 978-1-59463-039-2; 1-59463-039-9

LC 2007017091

This "covers some of the most basic ideas of middle-grade math, including concepts relating to fractions, decimals, and ratios, making each comprehensible, interesting, and fun. Using real-world constructions, such as tangled necklaces, boyfriends, and pizza, concepts are thoroughly explained." Voice Youth Advocates

Merriam, Eve

12 ways to get to 11; written by Eve Merriam; illustrated by Bernie Karlin. Simon & Schuster Bks. for Young Readers 1993 un il hardcover o.p. pa $6.99

Grades: K 1 2 3   510

1. Counting 2. Mathematics

ISBN 0-689-80892-5 pa

LC 91-25810

Uses ordinary experiences to present twelve combinations of numbers that add up to eleven. Example: At the circus, six peanut shells and five pieces of popcorn

"Some of the double-page spreads are simpler to solve than others, which allows children to progress as they learn more about counting. The huge, vibrant cut-paper and colored-pencil pictures make the book fun, lively, and painlessly educational." Horn Book Guide

Schwartz, David M.

★ **G** is for googol; a math alphabet book. written by David M. Schwartz; illustrated by Marissa Moss. Tricycle Press 1998 57p il $15.95

Grades: 4 5 6 7   510

1. Alphabet 2. Mathematics 3. Mathematics -- Miscellanea

ISBN 1-883672-58-9

LC 98-15162

Explains the meaning of mathematical terms which begin with the different letters of the alphabet from abacus, binary, and cubit to zillion

"The text is lively and clear and will appeal to even those who think math is as dull as the kitchen floor. . . . The cartoon illustrations are colorful, amusing, and informative." SLJ

Includes glossary

Tang, Greg

Math-terpieces; the art of problem-solving. illustrated by Greg Paprocki. Scholastic Press 2003 31p il $16.95

Grades: 2 3 4   510

1. Counting 2. Set theory 3. Art appreciation

ISBN 0-439-44388-1

LC 2002-5361

A series of rhymes about artists and their works introduces counting and grouping numbers, as well as such artistic styles as cubism, pointillism, and surrealism

"Clearly written solutions to these exercises are given at the end of the book along with art definitions and brief explanations. This math-concept book is far more appealing than most." SLJ

Wyatt, Valerie

The **math** book for girls and other beings who count; written by Valerie Wyatt; illustrated by Pat Cupples. Kids Can Press 2000 64p il hardcover o.p. pa $9.95

Grades: 3 4 5 6   510

1. Mathematics

ISBN 1-55074-830-0; 1-55074-584-0 pa

This offers activities to entice "girls to stretch their math skills in measurement and probability, geometric construction and graphing, using a calculator and changing scale... . Activity directions are clear and simple, and cheerful line-and-watercolor cartoons keep the presentation breezy." Bull Cent Child Books

Includes glossary

510.92   Mathematics biography

Heiligman, Deborah

★ The **boy** who loved math; the improbable life of Paul Erdos. Deborah Heiligman; illustrated by LeUyen Pham. Roaring Brook Press 2013 48 p. (hardcover) $17.99

Grades: 1 2 3 4   510.92
1. Mathematics 2. Mathematicians -- Hungary -- Biography -- Juvenile literature
ISBN 1596433078; 9781596433076
LC 2012029744

This book is a biography of mathematician Paul Erdös. He was a child prodigy who had to be homeschooled due to his inability to sit still and follow rules. "High school was a better fit, and he made friends with students who shared his love of math. His skills became famous, but Erdös didn't know how to do laundry, cook, or even butter his own bread. He 'didn't fit into the world in a regular way.' So, he created a life that fit him instead." (School Library Journal)

"Heiligman's joyful, warm account invites young listeners and readers to imagine a much-loved boy completely charmed by numbers... The polished, disarming text offers Pham free rein for lively illustration that captures Erdos' childlike spirit." Kirkus

511   General principles of mathematics

Murphy, Stuart J.

The **sundae** scoop; illustrated by Cynthia Jabar. HarperCollins Pubs. 2003 33p il (Mathstart) hardcover o.p. pa $4.99

Grades: 1 2 3   511
1. Mathematics
ISBN 0-06-028924-4; 0-06-028925-2 lib bdg; 0-06-446250-1 pa
LC 2001-24322

This "presents the concept of combinations in a story about a group of children who host an ice-cream booth at their school picnic. With two flavors of ice cream, two sauces, and two choices of toppings, the children are surprised that eight different sundaes are available. . . . Murphy easily folds the math concepts into a lively story that will capture young readers, and Jabar reinforces the lesson with colorful , whimsical drawings of delectable ice-cream scoops." Booklist

Nagda, Ann Whitehead

★ **Tiger** math; learning to graph from a baby tiger. by Ann Whitehead Nagda and Cindy Bickel. Holt & Co. 2000 un il $17.95; pa $7.95

Grades: 2 3 4   511
1. Tigers 2. Graphic methods 3. Animals -- Infancy
ISBN 0-8050-6248-3; 0-8050-7161-X pa
LC 99-46686

Describes the growth of an orphan Siberian tiger cub, by means of words and graphs

"Easy-to-understand picture, pie or circle, bar, or line graphs, all with explanations, appear on the left; facing pages of text and clear full-color photographs are on the right." SLJ

511.3   Mathematical logic (Symbolic logic)

Berry, Minta

What comes in sets? Minta Berry. Crabtree Pub. Co. 2012 24 p. lib bdg $22.60

Grades: K 1 2   511.3
1. Set theory -- Juvenile literature 2. Set theory
ISBN 0778752682 pa; 0778752798 lib bdg; 9780778752684 pa; 9780778752790 lib bdg; 9781427196507 e-books; 9781427198099 e-books
LC 2011040391

This children's book by Minta Berry "introduces young readers to the concept of equal sets. Readers will learn to identify familiar things that come in pairs, sets of threes, fours, fives, and more." (Publisher's note) "The basic idea of sets is introduced through familiar objects: clothing, toys, kitchen items, and body parts. The activities encourage children to search through their homes for sets and make comparisons." (School Library Journal)

Murphy, Stuart J.

Dave's down-to-earth rock shop; illustrated by Cat Bowman Smith. HarperCollins Pubs. 2000 33p il (MathStart) hardcover o.p. pa $4.95

Grades: K 1 2 3   511.3
1. Set theory 2. Rocks -- Collectors and collecting
ISBN 0-06-028018-2; 0-06-028019-0 lib bdg; 0-06-446729-5 pa
LC 98-32128

As they consider sorting their rock collection by color, size, type, and hardness, Josh and Amy learn that the same objects can be organized in many different ways

"Murphy's forte is explaining complex topics in a down-to-earth manner, and that's just what he's done here. Along the way, he also includes a good deal of information about rocks, minerals, and the scientific method. Smith's full-color illustrations capture the excitement of rock hunting and include many geological and equipment details." Booklist

Seaweed soup; by Stuart Murphy; illustrated by Frank Remkiewicz. HarperCollins Pubs. 2001 31p il (MathStart) hardcover o.p. pa $4.95

Grades: K 1 2 3   511.3
1. Set theory 2. Set theory -- Juvenile literature
ISBN 0-06-028032-8; 0-06-028033-6 lib bdg; 0-06-028036-8 pa
LC 99-87634

As he asks more and more friends to join him for lunch, Turtle must make up sets of dishes to accommodate them

"A graph will help children review what they've learned, and two pages of ideas for extending the book are appended.

Remkiewicz's appealing illustrations encourage children to match sets and count items in each set." Booklst

512   Algebra

Adler, David A., 1947-

Mystery math; a first book of algebra. by David A. Adler; illustrated by Edward Miller. Holiday House 2011 1 v.

Grades: 2 3 4   **512**

1. Algebra

ISBN 0823422895; 9780823422890

LC 2010024188

Adler tackles the "topic of algebra, starting with the basics and working up from there. . . . Easy-to-understand mathematical notations guide readers through the solution to each problem, which are originally posed as word problems involving two children, Mandy and Billy, and Igor, the caretaker of a haunted house. The Halloween theme echoes the idea of algebra as the solving of mathematical mysteries, and Miller's digital artwork ups the ante with a palette strong on blacks, dark blues and lime greens." Kirkus

Anno, Masaichiro

Anno's mysterious multiplying jar; [by] Masaichiro and Mitsumasa Anno; illustrated by Mitsumasa Anno. Philomel Bks. 1983 un il $19.99; pa $7.99

Grades: 2 3 4 5   **512**

1. Factorials 2. Mathematics 3. Multiplication -- Juvenile literature

ISBN 0-399-20951-4; 0-698-11753-0 pa

LC 82-22413

Simple text and pictures introduce the mathematical concept of factorials

This book "begins with a painting of a handsome blue and white lidded jar, moves into fantasy with pictures of the water in the jar becoming a sea on which an old sailing ship is moving, transfers to an island on the sea, and goes on to describe the rooms in the houses in the kingdoms on the mountains in the countries on the island. Each time the number grows: one island, two countries, three mountains, etc. How many jars, then, were in the boxes that were in the cupboards in the rooms? . . . The explanation is in itself clear, and is expanded by other examples of factorials." Bull Cent Child Books

512.9   Foundations of algebra

Murphy, Stuart J.

Safari Park; illustrated by Steve Björkman. HarperCollins Pubs. 2002 31p il (Mathstart) hardcover o.p. pa $4.99

Grades: 2 3 4   **512.9**

1. Equations

ISBN 0-06-028914-7; 0-06-028915-5 lib bdg; 0-06-446245-5 pa

LC 00-63201

"At the new amusement park, Grandpa gives his grandkids twenty tickets each. With a little help, the kids add up the cost in tickets for rides and figure out the 'unknowns,' the number of tickets left over for snacks and games. Cartoony

watercolors keep up the carnival atmosphere, while a plot about Paul's lost tickets and the Terrible Tarantula ride adds a hint of suspense. Related activities are appended." Horn Book Guide

513   Arithmetic

Adler, David A., 1947-

Fractions, decimals, and percents; illustrated by Edward Miller. Holiday House 2010 un il $16.95

Grades: 2 3 4   **513**

1. Fractions 2. Percentage 3. Decimal fractions

ISBN 978-0-8234-2199-2; 0-8234-2199-6

LC 2008048464

"This brightly illustrated book . . . quickly presents several math concepts related to fractions, decimals, and percents. Using a county fair as a backdrop, Adler discusses how to change a number in one form to its equivalent in another; and how the value of a digit depends upon its placement in relation to a decimal point. Miller's digital artwork illustrates the ideas clearly." Booklist

Fun with Roman numerals; by David A. Adler; illustrated by Edward Miller. Holiday House 2008 un il lib bdg $16.95

Grades: 2 3 4   **513**

1. Roman numerals

ISBN 978-0-8234-2060-5 lib bdg; 0-8234-2060-4 lib bdg

LC 2007-43531

"This book provides basic information on the symbols, arrangements, and mathematical processes involving Roman numerals. Details are shared in a clear and logical manner with appropriate graphics to illustrate the concepts." Sci Books Films

Anno, Mitsumasa

Anno's magic seeds; written and illustrated by Mitsumasa Anno. Philomel Bks. 1995 un il hardcover o.p. pa $6.99

Grades: K 1 2 3   **513**

1. Mathematics 2. Mathematical recreations -- Juvenile literature

ISBN 0-399-22538-2; 0-698-11618-6 pa

LC 92-39309

The reader is asked to perform a series of mathematical operations integrated into the story of a lazy man who plants magic seeds and reaps an increasingly abundant harvest

"Anno has succeeded in combining both the moral issue of conservation of resources and arithmetical games in a charming story for young readers. A tour de force from a most original author-illustrator." Horn Book

Bang, Molly

★ **Ten,** nine, eight. Greenwillow Bks. 1983 un il $16.99; lib bdg $17.89; pa $6.99; bd bk $6.99

Grades: PreK K 1   **513**

1. Counting 2. Bedtime -- Fiction

ISBN 0-688-00906-9; 0-688-00907-7 lib bdg; 0-688-10480-0 pa; 0-688-14901-4 bd bk

LC 81-20106

A Caldecott Medal honor book, 1984

"In countdown style, the text of this counting book begins with '10 small toes all washed and warm,' and ends with '1 big girl all ready for bed.' The captions rhyme . . . and the pictures—warm, bright paintings—show a black father and child snuggling in a chair, the child yawning, and the child hugging her toy bear after some loving good night kisses." Bull Cent Child Books

Campbell, Sarah C.
★ **Growing** patterns; Fibonacci numbers in nature. photographs by Sarah C. Campbell and Richard P. Campbell. Boyds Mills Press 2010 32p il $17.95
Grades: 3 4 5   513
1. Numbers 2. Nature study 3. Fibonacci numbers -- Juvenile literature 4. Mathematics in nature -- Juvenile literature
ISBN 978-1-59078-752-6; 1-59078-752-8
LC 2009-24075
The authors "turn their attention to the Fibonacci sequence of numbers, employing photographs from nature, basic addition, and reader-directed text to explain it. . . . Besides being eye-catching, the photographs ought to prove invaluable for visual learners. . . . Kids should be left with a clear understanding of the pattern and curious about its remarkable prevalence in nature." Publ Wkly
Includes glossary

Caron, Lucille
Fraction and decimal smarts! [by] Lucille Caron, Philip M. St. Jacques. Enslow Publishers 2011 64p il lib bdg $27.93
Grades: 5 6 7 8   513
1. Fractions 2. Decimal fractions
ISBN 978-0-7660-3936-0
LC 2011008382
"This clearly written series provides definitions and examples of many concepts... examples are realistic and appropriate for the target age group." SLJ

Percent and ratio smarts! [by] Lucille Caron, Philip M. St. Jacques. Enslow Publishers 2011 64p il lib bdg $27.93
Grades: 5 6 7 8   513
1. Fractions 2. Ratios (Statistics)
ISBN 978-0-7660-3940-7
LC 2011008164

Cleary, Brian P.
The **action** of subtraction; by Brian P. Cleary; illustrated by Brian Gable. Millbrook Press 2006 30p il lib bdg $15.95
Grades: 2 3 4   513
1. Subtraction
ISBN 978-0-7613-9461-7 lib bdg; 0-7613-9461-3 lib bdg
LC 2005025881
"Subtraction is explained in rhyming text and simple, silly cartoons with excellent examples that range from angry bulldogs, hornets, and bowling pins to pieces of birthday cake, sports time-outs, and stuffed animals. . . . The illustrations are colorful and attractive." SLJ

A **fraction's** goal; parts of a whole. illustrated by Brian Gable. Millbrook Press 2011 31p il (Math is categorical) lib bdg $16.95

Grades: 2 3 4 5   513
1. Fractions
ISBN 978-0-8225-7881-9; 0-8225-7881-6
LC 2010051518
This "title presents fractions as a way to express parts of an entity (pizza) or group (jugglers). The rhyming lines of text bounce along in a genial way. . . . Brightened with eye-catching color combinations, Gable's cartoon-style illustrations express the simple mathematical ideas clearly, while his wacky critters add a good deal of humor." Booklist

Clements, Andrew
A **million** dots; illustrated by Mike Reed. Simon & Schuster Books for Young Readers 2006 un il $16.95
Grades: K 1 2 3   513
1. Million (The number)
ISBN 0-689-85824-8
LC 2004-05349
"With one million dots printed on its pages, this large-format picture book shows how big a million really is. Along the way, the text and illustrations offer plenty to look at and think about besides the rows and rows of tiny dots. On each page, Clements selects one number and connects it to a numerical fact." Booklist

Dodds, Dayle Ann
Full house; an invitation to fractions. [by] Dayle Ann Dodds; illustrated by Abby Carter. Candlewick Press 2007 un il $16.99
Grades: 1 2 3   513
1. Fractions 2. Stories in rhyme
ISBN 978-0-7636-2468-2; 0-7636-2468-3
LC 2006051847
Miss Bloom uses fractions as the six-room Strawberry Inn fills with guests and she divides her pie into sixths
"Fresh, whimsical watercolor illustrations fairly float off the pages in this title. Rhyming text invites readers to enjoy every moment at the Strawberry Inn." SLJ

Fisher, Valorie
How high can a dinosaur count? and other math mysteries. [by] Valorie Fisher. Schwartz & Wade Books 2006 un il $16.95
Grades: 1 2 3   513
1. Counting 2. Arithmetic
ISBN 0-375-83608-X
LC 2005010851
"The text for each of the 15 problems is presented on the left, using a large, clean font on a spectrum of soft pastel backgrounds. The problems are clearly explained, but lots of alliteration and some unexpected vocabulary make for interesting reading. The illustration on the right features Fisher's unique photographic technique. Richly textured patterns and hand-drawn objects are cut out and arranged, then photographed in such a way as to create whimsical tableaux with a three-dimensional feel. The characters are charming." SLJ

Fleming, Denise
★ **Count!** Holt & Co. 1992 un il $17.95; pa $7.95
Grades: PreK K 1 2   513
1. Animals 2. Counting
ISBN 0-8050-1595-7; 0-8050-4252-0 pa
LC 91-25686

The antics of lively and colorful animals present the numbers one to ten, twenty, thirty, forty, and fifty

"A fresh, upbeat concept book. Lizards, giraffes, toucans, butterflies are available for counting—if only they'll hold still long enough! Fuchsias and oranges, teals and purples, roll over the pages blending into each other in Fleming's beautiful couched paper with hand cut-stencil illustrations. Her explosions of color and motion are captivating and energizing." SLJ

Franco, Betsy

★ **Zero** is the leaves on the tree; illustrations by Shino Arihara. Tricycle Press 2009 un il $15.99

Grades: PreK K 1 2   **513**
1. Children's poetry 2. Zero (The number) 3. Seasons -- Juvenile literature
ISBN 978-1-58246-249-3; 1-58246-249-6

        LC 2008042185

Using "evocative examples from children's everyday experiences throughout the seasons, Franco explores the concept of zero. The gouache illustrations are done in soft, muted tones and have a naive charm that will have substantial child appeal." SLJ

Giganti, Paul

How many snails? a counting book. by Paul Giganti, Jr.; pictures by Donald Crews. Greenwillow Bks. 1988 un il $16.99; pa $6.99

Grades: PreK K 1 2   **513**
1. Counting
ISBN 0-688-06369-1; 0-688-13639-7 pa

        LC 87-26281

"Instead of inviting children to count static objects, Mr. Giganti poses a series of simple, direct questions designed to encourage youngsters to determine the often subtle differences between those objects. Donald Crews . . . concentrates here on decorating each page with objects that supply the necessary links to the text. Some of the pages—depicting a collection of motley dogs at the park or beautiful toy boats and trucks, cars and airplanes at a toy store—are a joy to look at." N Y Times Book Rev

Lewis, J. Patrick

Arithme-tickle; an even number of odd riddle-rhymes. illustrated by Frank Remkiewicz. Harcourt 2002 32p il $16

Grades: 2 3 4   **513**
1. Arithmetic 2. Mathematical recreations 3. Arithmetic -- Juvenile literature 4. Mathematical recreations -- Juvenile literature
ISBN 0-15-216418-9

        LC 2001-3228

"Wordplay, riddles, and math problems test readers' skill at addition, subtraction, multiplication, division, telling time, logic, and even general knowledge in this colorfully illustrated collection. Clearly meant to make math more approachable and enjoyable, this compilation includes enough genuinely complex puzzles to keep hardcore young math buffs entertained." Booklist

Long, Lynette

Marvelous multiplication; games and activities that make math easy and fun. Wiley 2000 122p il (Magical math) pa $12.95

Grades: 3 4 5 6   **513**
1. Multiplication
ISBN 0-471-36982-9

        LC 00-20473

Presents a series of activities, arranged in order of difficulty, that teach the operation of multiplication

"The cheerful ink drawings help make the [book] more inviting." Booklist

Markel, Michelle

Tyrannosaurus math; illustrations by Doug Cushman. Tricycle Press 2009 un il $15.99

Grades: 1 2 3   **513**
1. Dinosaurs 2. Arithmetic 3. Mathematics 4. Arithmetic -- Juvenile literature
ISBN 978-1-58246-282-0; 1-58246-282-8

        LC 2008042389

"From the moment he bursts out of his shell, T-Math thinks mathematically, making number sentences to express how many digits he has and the number of kids in his family. He counts footprints by twos and uses fives and tens to group and count a herd of triceratops. He checks his subtraction with addition, draws pictures to solve word problems, creates pictographs and thinks in pie graphs. And it is his estimation skills that save his sister, who gets stranded on the wrong side of a canyon after an earthquake. . . . Cushman's brightly colored acrylic illustrations nicely show readers the math involved without diminishing in any way the personalities of the dinosaurs. The ultimate melding of a topic kids love with knowledge they need." Kirkus

Mattern, Joanne

Even or odd? Rourke Pub. 2010 24p il (Little world math concepts) lib bdg $22.79; pa $7.95

Grades: PreK K   **513**
1. Number concept
ISBN 978-1-61590-292-7 lib bdg; 1-61590-292-9 lib bdg; 978-1-61590-531-7 pa; 1-61590-531-6 pa

        LC 2010009893

"Aimed at both preliterate preschoolers and emerging readers, the minimal text and images present questions and answers that introduce even and odd numbers. Magnified color photos show organized groups of everyday items . . . providing numerous opportunities for young children to practice counting by twos and identify the orphans when the groups represent odd numbers. . . . This book is a focused, one-stop resource for helping young children grasp the single, essential math concept it presents." Booklist

Includes bibliographical references

Murphy, Stuart J.

★ **Divide** and ride; illustrated by George Ulrich. HarperCollins Pubs. 1997 32p il (MathStart) hardcover o.p. pa $4.95

Grades: 1 2 3   **513**
1. Division
ISBN 0-06-026776-3; 0-06-026777-1 lib bdg; 0-06-446710-4 pa

        LC 95-26134

"Eleven friends climb aboard the Dare-Devil roller coaster and three other rides, but before each ride can begin, all of the seats must be filled. Readers follow the children as they solve each problem by dividing and then filling the empty seats with new friends. Watercolor, pen, and ink illustrations and follow-up activities accompany the story." Horn Book Guide

★ **Double** the ducks; illustrated by Valeria Petrone. HarperCollins Pubs. 2003 31p il (MathStart) hardcover o.p. lib bdg $16.89; pa $4.99
Grades: K 1   **513**
   1. Multiplication
   ISBN 0-06-028922-8; 0-06-028923-6 lib bdg; 0-06-446249-8 pa
                         LC 2001-24321
"A young cowboy cares for his five little ducks, and he scurries around to bring them three sacks of food and four bundles of hay with his two hands. When each duck brings a friend, the boy has double the ducks, so he needs to double the hay and double the food. . . . In a double-page spread at the back of the book, Murphy suggests lots of activities and games for parents to use in the kitchen and at play to make preschoolers' first steps into addition and multiplication more fun." Booklist

Earth Day-hooray! illustrated by Renee Andriani. HarperCollins Pubs. 2004 32p il (MathStart) $15.99; pa $4.99
Grades: 1 2 3   **513**
   1. Recycling 2. Place value (Mathematics)
   ISBN 0-06-000127-5; 0-06-000129-1 pa
                         LC 2002-155234
A drive to recycle cans on Earth Day teaches the children of the Maple Street School Save-the-Planet Club about place value
"Andriani's cheerful illustrations fairly teem with information about recycling and add humor and human interest to the story." SLJ
Includes bibliographical references

★ **Elevator** magic; illustrated by G. Brian Karas. HarperCollins Pubs. 1997 32p il (MathStart) hardcover o.p. pa $4.95
Grades: K 1 2   **513**
   1. Subtraction
   ISBN 0-06-026775-5; 0-06-446709-0 pa
                         LC 96-5672
"A boy meets his mother on the 10th floor of a high rise. On the way down, Mom needs to do some errands. The first stop, two floors down, is to cash a check at the Farm Bank and Trust, which is (lo and behold!) filled with horses, barns, and hay fields. Farther down is the Hard Rock Candy Store, which is not only full of candy but also the sounds and lights of a heavy metal band. Karas's zany illustrations support the main concept being taught, while picking up on the humor in the word play." SLJ

The **Grizzly** Gazette; illustrated by Steve Björkman. HarperCollins Pubs. 2003 31p il (MathStart) $15.99; lib bdg $16.89; pa $4.99
Grades: 1 2 3   **513**
   1. Percentage
   ISBN 0-06-000027-9; 0-06-000025-2 lib bdg; 0-06-000026-0 pa
                         LC 2001-24633
At Camp Grizzly the camp newspaper takes a poll each day to see who has the greatest percentage of the vote so

far in the election to chose a mascot. Includes activities for learning about percentages

Henry the fourth; illustrated by Scott Nash. HarperCollins Pubs. 1999 33p il (MathStart) $15.95; lib bdg $15.89; pa $4.95
Grades: K 1   **513**
   1. Numbers
   ISBN 0-06-027610-X; 0-06-027611-8 lib bdg; 0-06-446719-8 pa
                         LC 98-4960
A simple story about four dogs at a dog show introduces the ordinal numbers: first, second, third, and fourth
"The numerical concepts are sequential and simple enough for young children to follow. The watercolor cartoons fill the pages with action." SLJ

★ **Jack** the builder; illustrated by Michael Rex. HarperCollins Pubs. 2006 33p il (MathStart) hardcover o.p. pa $4.99
Grades: K 1   **513**
   1. Counting
   ISBN 0-06-055774-5; 0-06-055775-3 pa
"Jack stacks 2 blocks taken from a big pile. Turn the page, and a wild, colorful double-page spread shows what his simple stack becomes with the addition of a little imagination—a robot. A third block makes a hot-dog stand . . . and 2 more build 'a ferryboat out on the sea.' Eight blocks become a lookout tower, and, using 17, Jack creates a rocket ship. . . . Murphy begins and ends with simple hands-on activities for adults to help bring the math into kids' everyday life. Rex's bright illustrations will encourage even young preschoolers to point at shapes and colors as they count and add on." Booklist

Jump, kangaroo, jump! illustrated by Kevin O'Malley. HarperCollins Pubs. 1999 un il (MathStart) hardcover o.p. pa $4.95
Grades: 1 2 3   **513**
   1. Division 2. Fractions
   ISBN 0-06-027614-2; 0-06-446721-X pa
                         LC 97-45814
Kangaroo and his Australian animal friends divide themselves up into different groups for the various field day events at camp
"The simple story line presents a real-world application of fractions and division, neatly reinforced by O'Malley's expressive illustrations. Related activities are suggested." Horn Book Guide

Less than zero; illustrated by Frank Remkiewicz. HarperCollins Pubs. 2003 33p il (MathStart) $15.99; pa $4.99
Grades: K 1 2 3   **513**
   1. Arithmetic 2. Zero (The number) 3. Finance, Personal -- Juvenile literature 4. Numbers, Negative -- Juvenile literature
   ISBN 0-06-000124-0; 0-06-000126-7 pa
                         LC 2002-20732
While trying to save enough money to buy a new ice scooter, Perry the Penguin learns about managing his money and about negative numbers
Includes bibliographical references

Mall mania; illustrated by Renée Andriani. HarperCollins 2006 33p il (MathStart) $15.99; pa $4.99

Grades: K 1 2   **513**

1. Addition 2. Counting

ISBN 0-06-055776-1; 0-06-055776-X pa

"The 100th person to enter Parkside Mall will get lots of promotional gifts, and four kids from Wilson Elementary School's chess club are on hand to count up the shoppers and add the numbers together. . . . The counters use a variety of addition strategies and activities, as always, Murphy adds greatly to the math lesson by making it seem a part of daily life. Suggestions for follow-up activities, both complex and easy . . . are appended." Booklist

Includes bibliographical references

More or less; illustrated by David T. Wenzel. HarperCollinsPublishers 2005 33p il (MathStart) $15.99; pa $4.99

Grades: K 1 2 3   **513**

1. Arithmetic

ISBN 0-06-053165-7; 0-06-053167-3 pa

LC 2003-27847

"In this story, Eddie works the 'guess the age' booth at the fair. . . . The way Eddie progresses . . . leads children into the world of logical, educated guesses. . . . Youngsters who need to understand the math concept in more depth will find several activities at the conclusion of the book. . . . Sprightly watercolor artwork makes math look like fun. " Booklist

Sluggers' car wash; illustrated by Barney Saltzberg. HarperCollins Pubs. 2002 33p il (MathStart) hardcover o.p. lib bdg $17.89; pa $4.99

Grades: 1 2 3   **513**

1. Addition 2. Moneymaking projects

ISBN 0-06-028920-1; 0-06-028921-X lib bdg; 0-06-446248-X pa

LC 00-54062

When the 21st Street Sluggers, a baseball team, have a car wash to raise money, they learn to keep careful track of their dollars and cents

"Colorful illustrations both enhance the story line and elucidate the math lesson with clear tabulations for the money counting and change." SLJ

Nagda, Ann Whitehead

Cheetah math; learning about division from baby cheetahs. by Ann Whitehead Nagda in collaboration with the San Diego Zoo. Henry Holt 2007 29p il $16.95

Grades: 2 3 4   **513**

1. Cheetahs 2. Division

ISBN 978-0-8050-7645-5; 0-8050-7645-X

LC 2006030069

"Each spread includes division problems that revolve around the big cats on the left and facts about the birth and development of two baby cheetahs, Majani and Kubali, on the right. The color photography is outstanding. . . . This is a wonderful cross-curricular book and an appealing way to introduce math." SLJ

Panda math; learning about subtraction from Hua Mei and Mei Sheng. Holt & Co. 2005 29p il lib bdg $17.95

Grades: 2 3 4   **513**

1. Giant panda 2. Subtraction

ISBN 0-8050-7644-1

"This wonderful title featuring panda cubs born in the San Diego Zoo does double duty as a math book. The right side of each spread offers a captioned color photograph and text describing the growth and development of Hua Mei and Mei Sheng. The green left-hand pages provide additional details about pandas in general and these two specifically: their eating and sleeping habits, weight, and life expectancy and incorporates this information into a subtraction word problem." SLJ

Polar bear math; learning about fractions from Klondike and Snow. by Ann Whitehead Nagda and Cindy Bickel. H. Holt and Co. 2004 29p il $16.95

Grades: 2 3 4   **513**

1. Fractions 2. Polar bear

ISBN 0-8050-7301-9

LC 2003-20996

"Following the lives of two cubs that were born at the Denver Zoo and abandoned by their mother, this book provides information about polar bears and fractions. Right-hand pages tell the story of Snow and Klondike, with excellent, full-color photos showing how zoo personnel raised them from newborns until their first birthday. . . . The explanations, which combine text with pictographs, are clear and well formulated." SLJ

Rubin, Alan

How many fish? Yellow Umbrella Bks. 2003 17p il (Yellow umbrella books for early readers) $14.60

Grades: PreK K 1 2   **513**

1. Fishes 2. Counting 3. Marine animals

ISBN 0-7368-2013-2

LC 2003-924

Introduces counting by showing different numbers of fish and other creatures swimming in the sea

"Not only can beginning readers feel successful at mastering the short, repetitive sentences, but they can also excel at counting the human feet and fish under the water. Colorful illustrations enhance the text." SLJ

Schwartz, David M.

★ **How** much is a million? pictures by Steven Kellogg. Lothrop, Lee & Shepard Bks. 1985 un il $16.99; lib bdg $17.89; pa $6.99

Grades: PreK K 1 2 3   **513**

1. Counting 2. Number concept 3. Billion (The number) 4. Million (The number) 5. Trillion (The number)

ISBN 0-688-04049-7; 0-688-04050-0 lib bdg; 0-688-09933-5 pa

LC 84-5736

"Marvelosissimo the Mathematical Magician leads the reader through Steven Kellogg's scenes of fantasy to express the concepts of a million, a billion and a trillion. The text is all printed in capital letters to point out the expanding scenes portrayed in the fabulous illustrations. The idea is to make possible to children the awesome concept of large numbers. It is a delightful fantasy as a picture book, but it is even more compelling as a first reader." Okla State Dept of Educ

Slade, Suzanne

What's new at the zoo? an animal adding adventure. illustrated by Joan Waites. Sylvan Dell 2009 un il $16.95

Grades: PreK K 1 2 **513**
1. Zoos 2. Animals 3. Addition
ISBN 978-1-934359-93-8; 1-934359-93-9

"On a visit to the zoo, a young boy counts the animal babies and parents in each enclosure, the accompanying rhyme encouraging readers to do the math along with him. . . . Slade slyly sneaks in some great vocabulary, working the animal baby names into each verse. . . . Backmatter teaches two methods for adding all the numbers, a section about fact families and a matching game wherein readers can test their memories of baby names against some paragraphs of information about each animal's development. The solid math and informative backmatter make this a worthwhile addition to libraries and math programs." Kirkus

Tang, Greg
★ **Math** fables; lessons that count. illustrated by Heather Cahoon. Scholastic Press 2004 un il $16.95
Grades: K 1 2 **513**
1. Science 2. Counting 3. Conduct of life
ISBN 0-439-45399-2

LC 2002-5360
A series of rhymes about animals introduces counting and grouping numbers, as well as examples of such behaviors as cooperation, friendship, and appreciation.

"The text and perky, computer-generated cartoons show youngsters that there are many different ways of putting numbers together. . . . The enriching vocabulary is an added bonus. A fine addition to math shelves." SLJ

★ **Math** fables too; making science count. by Greg Tang; illustrated by Taia Morley. Scholastic Press 2007 un il $16.99
Grades: K 1 2 **513**
1. Science 2. Counting
ISBN 978-0-439-78351-4

LC 2006028970
"Tang offers 10 rhymes about animals that teach science concepts as well as basic arithmetic. In addition . . . each selection contains a moral. . . . The bright, bold computer-generated illustrations bring personality to the animals and create colorful displays for counting and adding." SLJ

★ The **best** of times; math strategies that multiply. illustrated by Harry Briggs. Scholastic Press 2002 un il $16.95
Grades: 2 3 4 **513**
1. Multiplication
ISBN 0-439-21044-5

LC 2002-23043
Simple rhymes offer hints on how to multiply any number by zero through ten without memorizing the multiplication tables

"Encouraging rhymes and colorful, jaunty illustrations bolster the multiplication lesson." Booklist

513.2 Arithmetic operations

Adler, David A., 1947-
Fraction fun; illustrated by Nancy Tobin. Holiday House 1996 un il $16.95; pa $6.95

Grades: 2 3 4 **513.2**
1. Fractions
ISBN 0-8234-1259-8; 0-8234-1341-1 pa

LC 96-10773
"Adler presents the concept of fractions with the tried-and-true example of dividing a pie (pizza pie, in this case), then directs readers to draw lines across paper plates and color the eight resultant wedges in various color combinations. . . . Adler doesn't shy away from correct terminology—numerators and denominators—in this primary-grade introduction. Next he launches into some hands-on experimentation. . . . Tobin supplies a jazzy, eye-popping color scheme and diagrams of exceptional clarity to illuminate the straightforward text." Bull Cent Child Books

Browne, Anthony
One gorilla; a counting book. Anthony Browne. Candlewick Press 2013 32 p. $16.99
Grades: PreK K 1 **513.2**
1. Counting 2. Picture books for children 3. Primates -- Juvenile literature
ISBN 0763663522; 9780763663520

LC 2012942388
This children's book by Anthony Browne provides children with an "array of creatures for kids to count." The book offers a "presentation of primates from gorillas to gibbons, macaques to mandrills, ring-tailed lemurs to spider monkeys . . . [and] extends the basic number concept into a look at similarities and differences -- portraying an extended family we can count ourselves part of." (Publisher's note)

Hoban, Tana
★ **Let's** count. Greenwillow Bks. 1999 un il $17.99
Grades: PreK K **513.2**
1. Counting 2. Counting -- Pictorial works -- Juvenile literature
ISBN 0-688-16008-5

LC 98-44739
Photographs and dots introduce the numbers one to one hundred

"Hoban brings us another dazzling picture book. . . . Her photos range from the simple—1 hen, 8 Dalmatian puppies—to the more sophisticated—6 twirling rings on the arms of a circus performer; 12 rolls of toilet paper unpacked and stored on a pantry shelf." Booklist

Leedy, Loreen
2 x 2; a set of spooky multiplication stories. written and illustrated by Loreen Leedy. Holiday House 1995 32p il $17.95; pa $6.95
Grades: K 1 2 3 **513.2**
1. Multiplication
ISBN 0-8234-1190-7; 0-8234-1272-5 pa

LC 94-46711
This is an "introduction to basic multiplication, with witches, cats, and monsters demonstrating the consequences of multiplying numbers from 0 to 5. The illustrations are done in muted, autumnal tones of black, blue, orange, and mustard, and arranged in a comic-strip format. . . . The concepts are clear and understandable. . . . Leedy's book presents an entertaining alternative to rote memorization." SLJ

★ **Fraction** action; written and illustrated by Loreen Leedy. Holiday House 1994 31p il $17.95; pa $6.95

Grades: K 1 2 3   **513.2**
1. Fractions
ISBN 0-8234-1109-5; 0-8234-1244-X pa
LC 93-22800

Miss Prime and her animal students explore fractions by finding many examples in the world around them

"Thickly pigmented paintings loaded with sporty animal figures add to the humorous presentation, which should make fractions not only more understandable, but also more fun for young children." Bull Cent Child Books

★ **Mission**: addition; written and illustrated by Loreen Leedy. Holiday House 1997 un il $17.95; pa $6.95
Grades: K 1 2 3   **513.2**
1. Addition
ISBN 0-8234-1307-1; 0-8234-1412-4 pa
LC 96-37149

Miss Prime and her animal students explore addition by finding many examples in the world around them

"Flat chalk-box colors predominate in the illustrations, which will please kids with their liveliness, their informality, and their cartoonlike speech balloons. . . . An attractive picture book to support the math curriculum." Booklist

★ **Subtraction** action. Holiday House 2000 32p il $17.95; pa $6.95
Grades: K 1 2 3   **513.2**
1. Subtraction
ISBN 0-8234-1454-X; 0-8234-1244-X pa
LC 99-49803

Introduces subtraction through the activities of animal students at a school fair. Includes problems for the reader to solve

This is "an action-packed volume that is perfectly suited to its audience. The softly hued cartoon animals and dialogue balloons are skillfully combined on pages divided into framed sequences." SLJ

Long, Lynette
Fabulous fractions; games and activities that make math easy and fun. Wiley 2001 122p il (Magical math) pa $12.95
Grades: 3 4 5 6   **513.2**
1. Fractions
ISBN 0-471-36981-0
LC 00-43386

This introduction to fractions includes activities using such materials as sandwiches, paper plates, cards, and dominoes

This book includes "lists of the required materials, clear and complete procedures, and a black-and-white illustration." SLJ

Marzollo, Jean
Help me learn subtraction; by Jean Marzollo; photographs by Chad Phillips. 1st American ed. Holiday House 2012 32 p. col. ill. (hardcover) $15.95; (paperback) $6.99
Grades: K 1 2   **513.2**
1. Visual literacy 2. Word problems (Mathematics) 3. Mathematics -- Study and teaching 4. Subtraction -- Juvenile literature 5. Counting-out rhymes -- Juvenile literature
ISBN 0823424014; 9780823424016; 9780823428229
LC 2011046540

Author Jean Marzollo's book "in the photograph-based Help Me Learn series . . . uses puppets, figurines, and other playful items to demonstrate [subtraction] math equations, which are presented both numerically and in words. . . . [The book utilizes] finger puppets, pipe cleaner dogs, and other objects" to help children visualize the problems. (Publishers Weekly)

Menotti, Andrea
How many jelly beans? Andrea Menotti; illustrator, Yancey Labat. Chronicle Books 2012 28 p. ill. (hardcover) $18.99
Grades: 2 3 4   **513.2**
1. Candy 2. Numbers 3. Calendars 4. Counting -- Juvenile literature 5. Jellybeans -- Juvenile literature 6. Mathematics -- Juvenile literature
ISBN 1452102066; 9781452102061
LC 2011030673

Author Andrea Menotti "takes on big numbers . . . [in this oversized book] using jelly beans as counters. When Emma and Aiden are asked how many jelly beans they want, they carry on a boasting match, resulting in escalating amounts of candy. . . . Five hundred beans cover a coffee table, and 1,000 beans are divided out over the days of a year on calendar pages." (Publishers Weekly)

Murphy, Stuart J.
Just enough carrots; illustrated by Frank Remkiewicz. HarperCollins Pubs. 1997 31p il (MathStart) $14.95; lib bdg $15.89; pa $4.95
Grades: K 1   **513.2**
1. Counting
ISBN 0-06-026778-X; 0-06-026779-8 lib bdg; 0-06-446711-2 pa
LC 96-19495

While a bunny and his mother shop in a grocery store for lunch guests, the reader may count and compare the amounts of carrots, peanuts, and worms in the grocery carts of other shoppers

"Bright, colorful illustrations, a surprise ending, and two pages of activities for adults and children extend and enhance the book's appeal." SLJ

Rose, Deborah Lee
★ **One** nighttime sea; an ocean counting rhyme. pictures by Steve Jenkins. Scholastic 2003 un il $16.95
Grades: PreK K 1 2   **513.2**
1. Night 2. Counting 3. Marine animals
ISBN 0-439-33906-5
LC 2002-8127

A counting book featuring nocturnal sea creatures, from one blue whale calf to ten turtle hatchlings, and back down to one seal pup. Includes facts about each of the twenty featured animals

"In a lapping, sealike rhythm, this enchanting counting book lulls its audience into the world beneath the waves. . . . Vivid cut-paper collages beautifully interplay with the rhymes." SLJ

Schmandt-Besserat, Denise
The **history** of counting; illustrated by Michael Hays. Morrow Junior Bks. 1999 45p il $17; lib bdg $16.93
Grades: 4 5 6 7   **513.2**
1. Counting 2. Mathematics 3. Numeration -- History

-- Juvenile literature

ISBN 0-688-14118-8; 0-688-14119-6 lib bdg

LC 96-35316

"Beginning with a look at primitive expressions of numbers, the text goes on to explain abstract counting and the methods used by the Sumerians, the Phoenicians, the Greeks, the Romans, and finally the Arabs, who brought Hindu numerals from India to Europe about 1,000 years ago. . . . Imaginatively conceived and well composed, Hays' acrylic paintings feature warm, harmonious colors and delicate plays of light and shadow against textured-linen backings. Cogently written and beautifully made." Booklist

Includes glossary

Weill, Cynthia

Count me in; a parade of numbers in English and Spanish. by Cynthia Weill; figurines by the Aguilar Sisters: Guillermina, Josefina, Irene and Concepción. Cinco Puntos Press 2012 32 p. (hardback: alk. paper) $14.95

Grades: PreK **513.2**

1. Counting 2. Mexican art 3. Picture books for children 4. Parades -- Juvenile literature 5. Numerals -- Juvenile literature

ISBN 193595539X; 9781935955399

LC 2012004538

This children's picture book helps children "practice [their] numbers in English and Spanish when [they] count the beautiful dancers, playful musicians, and happy children of Oaxaca as the Guelaguetza parade goes by! Pronounced Gal-a-get-zah, the lively celebration—full of traditional dancing and music—takes place every July deep in the heart of southern Mexico." (Publisher's note)

Winter, Jeanette

Josefina. Harcourt Brace & Co. 1996 un il $16

Grades: PreK K 1 2 **513.2**

1. Counting 2. Women artists -- Fiction

ISBN 0-15-201091-2

LC 95-34110

"In a sunny patio in Mexico, there is one rising sun in a sky where two angels keep watch over three houses. . . . Throughout her life—from her childhood through the deaths of her parents, her marriage to José, and the birth of their nine children, Josefina works the soft clay into figures to create this world. . . . Inspired by the painted clay figures decorating Josefina Aguilar's patio in Ocotlán, Mexico, Winter has crafted a picture-book vision of the folk artist's life that cleverly turns into a bilingual counting story. . . . Paired with a simple prose narrative, the artwork creates an effect that is both elegant and soothing." Booklist

513.5 Numeration systems

Geisert, Arthur

Roman numerals I to MM; Numerabilia romana uno ad duo mila: liber de difficillimo computando numerum. Houghton Mifflin 1996 xxxii $16

Grades: K 1 2 3 **513.5**

1. Counting 2. Roman numerals

ISBN 0-395-74519-5

LC 95-36247

"Geisert's detailed etchings reward extended perusal, and children will revel in the sheer abundance of pigs. A great lesson in Roman numerals." Publ Wkly

Giganti, Paul

★ Each orange had 8 slices; a counting book. by Paul Giganti, Jr.; pictures by Donald Crews. Greenwillow Bks. 1992 un il $16.99; lib bdg $17.89; pa $6.99

Grades: PreK K 1 2 **513.5**

1. Counting 2. Mathematics 3. Multiplication -- Juvenile literature

ISBN 0-688-10428-2; 0-688-10429-0 lib bdg; 0-688-13985-X pa

LC 90-24167

"This bright, well-designed book challenges young children to think analytically about what's on its pages. . . . Since the objects are organized into sets and subsets, this could be used to introduce the concept of multiplication as well as counting and addition." Booklist

Schwartz, David M.

On beyond a million; an amazing math journey. illustrated by Paul Meisel. Doubleday Bks. for Young Readers 1999 un il hardcover o.p. pa $6.99

Grades: 2 3 4 **513.5**

1. Counting 2. Decimal system

ISBN 0-385-32217-8; 0-440-41177-7 pa

LC 98-52990

"The design is busy, with sidebars and balloon comments. Each double-page spread is clearly meant to be talked about, and the discussions aren't overwhelming. . . . Awesome and yet accessible." Booklist

515 Analysis

Cleary, Brian P.

A-B-A-B-A--a book of pattern play; illustrated by Brian Gable. Millbrook Press 2010 31p il (Math is categorical) lib bdg $16.95

Grades: 2 3 4 5 **515**

1. Pattern perception 2. Patterns (Mathematics)

ISBN 978-0-8225-7880-2 lib bdg; 0-8225-7880-8 lib bdg

LC 2009-49386

"Through rhyming text and colorful illustrations, readers are given examples of simple visual and numerical patterns—from circle-square-circle-square to 1-3-5-7. . . . The buoyant narrative calls for reading aloud and the images are large enough for a modest group setting." SLJ

Murphy, Stuart J.

Beep beep, vroom vroom! illustrated by Chris Demarest. HarperCollins Pubs. 2000 33p il (MathStart) hardcover o.p. pa $4.95

Grades: K 1 **515**

1. Patterns (Mathematics) 2. Automobiles -- Juvenile literature 3. Sequences (Mathematics) -- Juvenile literature

ISBN 0-06-028016-6; 0-06-028017-4 lib bdg; 0-06-446728-7 pa

LC 98-51907

"Molly loves playing with cars, but her brother, Kevin, tells her she's too young. He lines up his 12 cars—four red, four green, four yellow—in special order on the shelf and tells her not to touch them while he's gone. . . . At the back are practical suggestions for adults and kids to find patterns on the pages and make their own patterns with pebbles, buttons, coins, and kitchen utensils. Demarest's clear, simple pastel pictures express the fun of playing with cars as the vrooming action reveals the patterns in everyday things." Booklist

Includes bibliographical references

516   Geometry

Adler, David A., 1947-
   ★ **Shape** up! illustrated by Nancy Tobin. Holiday House 1998 un il $16.95; pa $6.95
Grades: 2 3 4   **516**
   1. Shape 2. Geometry
   ISBN 0-8234-1346-2; 0-8234-1638-0 pa
                            LC 97-22236
Uses cheese slices, pretzel sticks, a slice of bread, graph paper, a pencil, and more to introduce various polygons, flat shapes with varying numbers of straight sides
"Tobin's colorful diagrams and lanky, baseball-capped tour guide make each definition and direction crystal clear, making this a useful and appealing title for extending classroom lessons or encouraging beginners to charge beyond circle-square-triangle." Bull Cent Child Books

Adler, David A., 1947-
   Perimeter, area, and volume; a monster book of dimensions. by David A. Adler; illustrated by Edward Miller. 1st ed. Holiday House 2012 32 p. col. ill. (hardcover) $16.95
Grades: 3 4 5   **516**
   1. Mathematics -- Juvenile literature 2. Measurement -- Juvenile literature 3. Dimensions 4. Weights and measures
   ISBN 0823422909; 9780823422906
                         LC 2010048653
This educational children's book by David A. Adler, illustrated by Edward Miller, provides lessons in measurement-taking within the context of a film set crewed by monsters. The book is "aligned with the Common Core State Standards for third-grade, fourth-grade, and fifth-grade mathematics in measurement and data. . . . Grab your jumbo popcorn and 3-D glasses, because you're invited to the premiere of a 3-D movie! The star-studded cast of monsters will help you calculate the perimeter of the set, the area of the movie screen, and the volume of your popcorn box." (Publisher's note)

Brocket, Jane
   Circles, stars, and squares; looking for shapes. by Jane Brocket; photographs by Jane Brocket. Millbrook Press 2013 30 p. col. ill. (library) $26.60
Grades: K 1 2   **516**
   1. Shape -- Juvenile literature 2. Plane geometry -- Juvenile literature 3. Shapes -- Juvenile literature
   ISBN 0761346112; 9780761346111
                       LC 2011050199

This children's picture book by Jane Brocket "teaches readers about two- and three-dimensional shapes. . . . The first of two loose sections looks at 'flat' shapes--circles, ovals, squares, rectangles, triangles, diamonds, and a brief mention of pentagons, hexagons and octagons--the second at 'solid' shapes--spheres, cylinders, cubes, cones, rings and eggs." (Kirkus Reviews)

Caron, Lucille
   Geometry smarts! [by] Lucille Caron, Philip M. St. Jacques. Enslow Publishers 2011 64p il lib bdg $27.93
Grades: 5 6 7 8   **516**
   1. Geometry
   ISBN 978-0-7660-3935-3
                       LC 2011008384

Ehlert, Lois
   ★ **Color** farm. Lippincott 1990 un il $17.99; lib bdg $18.89
Grades: PreK K 1   **516**
   1. Color 2. Shape
   ISBN 0-397-32440-5; 0-397-32441-3 lib bdg
                       LC 89-13561
"A delightful die-cut exploration of how shapes and colors can be layered and overlapped to create the faces of farm animals. Includes geometric pictures of a rooster, a chicken, a goose, a duck, a cat, a dog, a sheep, a pig, and a cow." Sci Child

Henkes, Kevin
   ★ **Circle** dogs; illustrated by Dan Yaccarino. Greenwillow Bks. 1998 un il $18.99; pa $6.99
Grades: PreK K 1 2   **516**
   1. Dogs -- Fiction 2. Shape -- Fiction
   ISBN 0-688-15446-8; 0-06-443757-4 pa
                       LC 97-33037
Circle dogs live in a square house with a square yard and spend a busy day eating circle snacks, digging circle holes, and sleeping
"The text is simple, almost primer-like, with lots of onomatopoetic words. . . . The lively gouache paintings in large flat areas of color have a retro look." SLJ

Hoban, Tana
   Is it larger? Is it smaller? Greenwillow Bks. 1985 un il hardcover o.p. pa $6.99
Grades: PreK K   **516**
   1. Size 2. Concepts -- Juvenile literature
   ISBN 0-688-15287-2 pa
                       LC 84-13719
"In each full-color photograph of the wordless picture book Hoban juxtaposes similar objects of differing size. In the simplest pictures only one kind of object is shown, such as three bright plastic sand cups in graduated sizes or three maple leaves. More complex compositions group several related items: measuring cups, bowls, and utensils; fish, shells, and pebbles in an aquarium. Still others contrast dissimilar objects that have common features. . . . In the photographs, Hoban demonstrates once again her mastery of the elements of composition, such as color, texture, and balance." Horn Book

   Shapes, shapes, shapes. Greenwillow Bks. 1986 un il $16.99; lib bdg $17.89; pa $6.99

Grades: PreK K **516**
1. Shape
ISBN 0-688-05832-9; 0-688-05833-7 lib bdg; 0-688-14740-2 pa

LC 85-17569

Photographs of familiar objects such as chair, barrettes, and manhole cover present a study of rounded and angular shapes

"Tana Hoban has created an excellent concept book that will encourage children to look for specific shapes in everyday urban scenes. . . . The photographs not only serve to teach shapes and colors but are works of art themselves." Appraisal

★ **So** many circles, so many squares. Greenwillow Bks. 1998 un il $16
Grades: PreK K **516**
1. Shape 2. Geometrical constructions -- Pictorial works -- Juvenile literature
ISBN 0-688-15165-5

LC 97-10110

The geometric concepts of circles and squares are shown in photographs of wheels, signs, pots, and other familiar objects

"Teachers and young children will find plenty to talk about as they look at the colorful, well-composed, and clearly defined images." Booklist

Leedy, Loreen
Seeing symmetry; written and illustrated by Loreen Leedy. Holiday House 2012 32 p. ill. (chiefly col.) (hardcover) $17.95
Grades: PreK K 1 2 **516**
1. Symmetry 2. Ratio and proportaion -- Juvenile literature
ISBN 0823423603; 9780823423606

LC 2011024038

This book presents an "introduction" to the concept of symmetry, "us[ing] a host of natural and manmade objects, as well as purely geometric designs, to illustrate horizontal, vertical, and rotational symmetry." The author asks "readers to consider whether all animals are symmetrical, to examine words for different types of symmetry in their lettering, to identify rotational symmetry in a display of buildings and furniture." (Bulletin of the Center for Children's Books)

Loughrey, Anita
Circles. QEB Pub. 2010 23p il (Shapes around me) lib bdg $24.25
Grades: PreK K 1 2 **516**
1. Shape
ISBN 978-1-59566-918-6; 1-59566-918-3

LC 2010005380

This "has a good grasp of how children best learn new math concepts. [The] book begins with a bright illustration of the shape and asks children to trace it with a finger. Subsequent pages present the shape in a variety of colorful sizes, places where it can be found, and activities. Well-thought-out, age appropriate, and attractive." Horn Book Guide

Rectangles. QEB Pub. 2010 23p il (Shapes around me) lib bdg $24.25

Grades: PreK K 1 2 **516**
1. Shape
ISBN 978-1-59566-915-5; 1-59566-915-9

LC 2010005381

This "has a good grasp of how children best learn new math concepts. [The] book begins with a bright illustration of the shape and asks children to trace it with a finger. Subsequent pages present the shape in a variety of colorful sizes, places where it can be found, and activities. Well-thought-out, age appropriate, and attractive." Horn Book Guide

Squares. QEB Pub. 2010 23p il (Shapes around me) lib bdg $24.25
Grades: PreK K 1 2 **516**
1. Shape 2. Square
ISBN 978-1-59566-917-9; 1-59566-917-5

LC 2010005382

This "has a good grasp of how children best learn new math concepts. [The] book begins with a bright illustration of the shape and asks children to trace it with a finger. Subsequent pages present the shape in a variety of colorful sizes, places where it can be found, and activities. Well-thought-out, age appropriate, and attractive." Horn Book Guide

Triangles. QEB Pub. 2010 23p il (Shapes around me) lib bdg $24.25
Grades: PreK K 1 2 **516**
1. Shape
ISBN 978-1-59566-916-2; 1-59566-916-7

LC 2010005383

This "has a good grasp of how children best learn new math concepts. [The] book begins with a bright illustration of the shape and asks children to trace it with a finger. Subsequent pages present the shape in a variety of colorful sizes, places where it can be found, and activities. Well-thought-out, age appropriate, and attractive." Horn Book Guide

Murphy, Stuart J.
★ **Bigger,** Better, BEST! illustrated by Marsha Winborn. HarperCollins Pubs. 2002 33p il (MathStart) hardcover o.p. pa $4.99
Grades: K 1 2 3 **516**
1. Size 2. Measurement 3. Area measurement
ISBN 0-06-028918-X; 0-06-028919-8 lib bdg; 0-06-446247-1 pa

LC 00-54034

"Jeff and Jenny are always fighting about who has something bigger or better, while Jill just ignores them. When the family moves to a bigger house with a separate room for each child, the two start arguing about whose room and windows are bigger. Mom then has them measure the windows with sheets of paper and the floor with newspaper. . . . [The story] carefully incorporates math without being overwhelming. The colorful and humorous illustrations add to the story." SLJ

★ **Captain** Invincible and the space shapes; illustrated by Rémy Simard. HarperCollins Pubs. 2001 33p il (MathStart) hardcover o.p. pa $4.95
Grades: K 1 2 3 **516**
1. Shape 2. Geometry 3. Geometry -- Juvenile

literature

ISBN 0-06-028022-0; 0-06-028023-9 lib bdg; 0-06-446731-7 pa

LC 00-39609

While piloting his spaceship through the skies, Captain Invincible encounters three-dimensional shapes, including cubes, cylinders, and pyramids

"An excellent tool for introducing a unit on three-dimensional shapes. . . . The bold cartoon art in deep, bright colors draws readers into this fun and exciting story. . . . The concluding reinforcement strategies and activities are very good." SLJ

★ **Hamster** champs; by Stuart J. Murphy; illustrated by Pedro Martin. HarperCollins 2005 31p il (MathStart) $15.99; pa $4.99

Grades: 1 2 3   **516**

1. Angles 2. Cats -- Fiction 3. Hamsters -- Fiction

ISBN 0-06-055772-9; 0-06-055773-7 pa

LC 2004-22471

"The humorous cartoonlike characters are fun, and plenty of good-natured banter between the hamsters and the cat helps make the concept clear." Booklist

★ **Let's** fly a kite; illustrated by Brian Floca. HarperCollins Pubs. 2000 33p il (MathStart) hardcover o.p. pa $4.95

Grades: K 1 2 3   **516**

1. Kites 2. Symmetry 3. Symmetry -- Juvenile literature 4. Ratio and proportion -- Juvenile literature

ISBN 0-06-028034-4; 0-06-028035-2 lib bdg; 0-06-446737-6 pa

LC 99-26550

Two squabbling siblings learn about symmetry when their babysitter helps them build and fly a kite

"Floca's watercolor-and-inkline cartoons enhance the story and ably depict the method used to divide everyday objects into two equal parts." SLJ

★ **Polly's** pen pal; illustrated by Remy Simard. HarperCollins 2005 30p il (MathStart) $15.99; pa $4.99

Grades: K 1 2 3   **516**

1. Measurement 2. Metric system 3. Mathematics -- Juvenile literature

ISBN 0-06-053168-1; 0-06-053170-3 pa

LC 2003-27526

"Polly has an e-mail pen pal in Montreal. As Ally uses metrics to discuss height, weight, and distances, Polly learns what they mean. No comparisons to English measurements are made but the metric measurements are likened to common objects that kids will recognize. This title features colorful . . . computer-generated cartoons." SLJ

Olson, Nathan

Cones; by Nathan Olson. Capstone Press 2008 32p il (3-D shapes) lib bdg $23.93

Grades: K 1 2   **516**

1. Cones 2. Shape 3. Geometry

ISBN 978-1-4296-0048-4 lib bdg; 1-4296-0048-9 lib bdg

LC 2006037424

This gives examples of cones such as megaphones, tops, and castle towers, and describes a simple activity.

Includes glossary and bibliographical references

Cubes; by Nathan Olson. Capstone Press 2008 32p il (3-D shapes) lib bdg $23.93

Grades: K 1 2   **516**

1. Cubes 2. Shape 3. Geometry

ISBN 978-1-4296-0049-1 lib bdg; 1-4296-0049-7 lib bdg

LC 2006037423

This gives examples of cubes, such as blocks, dice, sugar cubes, and ice cubes, and describes a simple activity.

Includes glossary and bibliographical references

Cylinders; by Nathan Olson. Capstone Press 2008 32p il (3-D shapes) lib bdg $23.93

Grades: K 1 2   **516**

1. Shape 2. Geometry 3. Cylinders

ISBN 978-1-4296-0050-7 lib bdg; 1-4296-0050-0 lib bdg

LC 2006037421

"Large color photographs show real-world examples of . . . cylinders (canned goods, birthday candles). Short descriptions flank each photo. . . . A hands-on activity will appeal to kids." Horn Book Guide

Includes glossary and bibliographical references

Pyramids; by Nathan Olson. Capstone Press 2008 32p il (3-D shapes) lib bdg $23.93

Grades: K 1 2   **516**

1. Shape 2. Geometry 3. Pyramids

ISBN 978-1-4296-0051-4 lib bdg; 1-4296-0051-9 lib bdg

LC 2006037420

"Large color photographs show real-world examples of pyramids (Hindu temple, toy tepee). . . . Short descriptions flank each photo. . . . A hands-on activity will appeal to kids." Horn Book Guide

Includes glossary and bibliographical references

Spheres; by Nathan Olson. Capstone Press 2008 32p il (3-D shapes) lib bdg $23.93

Grades: K 1 2   **516**

1. Shape 2. Geometry 3. Spheres

ISBN 978-1-4296-0052-1 lib bdg; 1-4296-0052-7 lib bdg

LC 2006037247

This offers examples of spheres such as bubbles, snowballs, oranges, and soccer balls, and describes a simple activity.

Includes glossary and bibliographical references

Rissman, Rebecca

Shapes in art. Heinemann Library 2009 24p il (Spot the shape) $14.50; pa $5.99

Grades: PreK K 1   **516**

1. Art 2. Shape

ISBN 978-1-4329-2169-9; 1-4329-2169-X; 978-1-4329-2175-0 pa; 1-4329-2175-4 pa

LC 2008043206

This describes the shapes that can be found in works of art.

This offers "vibrant photography and clarion text."
Booklist

Shapes in buildings. Heinemann Library 2009 24p il
(Spot the shape) $14.50; pa $5.99
Grades: PreK K 1   516
    1. Shape 2. Buildings
    ISBN 978-1-4329-2172-9; 1-4329-2172-X; 978-1-
    4329-2178-1 pa; 1-4329-2178-9 pa
                                          LC 2008043210
This describes the shapes that can be found in buildings.
This offers "vibrant photography and clarion text."
Booklist

Shapes in music. Heinemann Library 2009 24p il
(Spot the shape) $14.50; pa $5.99
Grades: PreK K 1   516
    1. Shape 2. Musical instruments
    ISBN 978-1-4329-2171-2; 1-4329-2171-1; 978-1-
    4329-2177-4 pa; 1-4329-2177-0 pa
                                          LC 2008043209
This describes the shapes that can be found in
musical instruments.
This offers "vibrant photography and clarion text."
Booklist

★ Shapes in sports. Heinemann Library 2009 24p il
(Spot the shape) $14.50; pa $5.99
Grades: PreK K 1   516
    1. Shape 2. Sports
    ISBN 978-1-4329-2170-5; 1-4329-2176-2; 978-1-
    4329-2176-7 pa; 1-4329-2176-2 pa
                                          LC 2008043208
This describes the shapes that can be found in sports.
This "is a near-perfect union of concept and execution.
Using . . . vibrant photography and clarion text . . . Rissman lays out a simple premise ('Shapes are all around us.')
before introducing seven shapes to come: rectangle, square,
semicircle, diamond, and so forth. . . . What is most impressive . . . are the stunning aerial photographs that turn baseball diamonds and tennis courts into dazzling intersections
of geometric patterns. This is the kind of book that will wake
readers up to the complexity of everyday items." Booklist

Shapes in the garden. Heinemann Library 2009 24p il
(Spot the shape) $14.50; pa $5.99
Grades: PreK K 1   516
    1. Shape 2. Gardens
    ISBN 978-1-4329-2168-2; 1-4329-2168-1; 978-1-
    4329-2174-3 pa; 1-4329-2174-6 pa
                                          LC 2008043205
This describes the shapes that can be found in gardens.
This offers "vibrant photography and clarion text."
Booklist

Somervill, Barbara A.
    Distance, area, and volume. Heinemann Library 2010
32p il map (Measure it!) lib bdg $29; pa $7.99
Grades: 3 4 5   516
    1. Measurement 2. Volume (Cubic content)
    ISBN 978-1-4329-3763-8 lib bdg; 1-4329-3763-4 lib
    bdg; 978-1-4329-3769-0 pa; 1-4329-3769-3 pa
                                          LC 2009-35191

"Size of text and font is suitable for this age group with
uncluttered pages designed so that text is set off with the illustrations, graphs, or drawings placed vertically. Key words
appear in bold." Libr Media Connect
Includes glossary and bibliographical references

Sullivan, Navin
    Area, distance, and volume; [by] Navin Sullivan. Mar-
shall Cavendish Benchmark 2007 44p il (Measure up!)
lib bdg $20.95
Grades: 4 5 6 7   516
    1. Geometry 2. Measurement
    ISBN 978-0-7614-2323-2 lib bdg; 0-7614-2323-0
    lib bdg
                                          LC 2006026394
An "engaging and informative [title]. . . . An excellent
blend of photographs, charts, and diagrams complements the
[text]." SLJ
Includes glossary and bibliographical references

VanCleave, Janice Pratt, 1942-
    Janice VanCleave's geometry for every kid; easy ac-
tivities that make learning geometry fun. Wiley 1994 221p
il hardcover o.p. pa $12.95
Grades: 4 5 6 7   516
    1. Geometry
    ISBN 0-471-31142-1; 0-471-31141-3 pa
                                          LC 93-43049
This "introductory text covers many topics in geometry, from lines, optical illusions, and art-related activities
to applications with protractors and the construction of basic solids. Terms are presented in a simplified fashion and
are easily understood. Graphics are clear. The hands-on activities encourage learning, creativity, and excitement." Sci
Books Films
    Includes glossary

Waxman, Laura Hamilton
    Prisms; by Laura Hamilton Waxman; illustrated by
Kathryn Mitter. Magic Wagon 2012 24 p. $27.07
Grades: 1 2 3   516
    1. Shape -- Juvenile literature 2. Prisms -- Juvenile
    literature 3. Solid geometry -- Juvenile literature 4.
    Shapes -- Juvenile literature
    ISBN 1616418753; 9781616418755
                                          LC 2012007117
This young children's book, by Laura Hamilton Waxman, illustrated by Kathryn Mitter, is part of the "Everyday
3-D Shapes" series, exploring various shapes seen in objects
of daily life. In this entry, "rhyming text and creative illustrations draw attention to prisms that are found in the world
around us." (Publisher's note)

516.2   Euclidean geometry

Green, Dan
    Algebra & geometry; anything but square. illustrated
by Simon Basher. Kingfisher 2011 il (Basher science)
$14.99; pa $8.99
Grades: 4 5 6   516.2
    1. Algebra 2. Geometry
    ISBN 978-0-7534-6627-8; 978-0-7534-6597-4 pa

519.2   Probabilities

Aboff, Marcie
   Pigs, cows, and probability. Capstone Press 2011 24p il (First facts. Data mania) lib bdg $23.99
Grades: 3 4 5 6   **519.2**
   1. Mathematics 2. Probabilities
   ISBN 978-1-4296-4529-4; 1-4296-4529-6
                                                   LC 2010000551
   "Information is presented in a few pages in a clear, concise manner. The definitions provided for words will help readers learn the [subject]. This is an excellent introduction to elementary statistics and statistical analysis." Libr Media Connect
   Includes glossary and bibliographical references

Goldstone, Bruce
   ★ **That's** a possibility! a book about what might happen. Bruce Goldstone. 1st ed. Henry Holt & Co 2013 32 p. ill. (hardcover) $16.99
Grades: 1 2 3 4   **519.2**
   1. Picture books for children
   ISBN 0805089985; 9780805089981
                                                   LC 2012036691
   This children's picture book looks at probability. "Starting with basic concepts of possibility, certainty, and impossibility ('Will an elephant hatch from this egg? That's impossible!'), [Bruce Goldstone] stages highly specific situations in photographic and digital illustrations. 'Will this butterfly land on one of the purple flowers?' he asks. 'That's probable. Can you see why?' (Spiky purple thistles dwarf and outnumber two yellow flowers, helping readers make the connection.)" (Publishers Weekly)

Leedy, Loreen
   It's probably Penny; written and illustrated by Loreen Leedy. Henry Holt 2007 un il $16.95
Grades: 1 2 3   **519.2**
   1. Probabilities
   ISBN 978-0-8050-7389-8; 0-8050-7389-2
                                                   LC 2006-02872
   "Lisa's teacher assigns the class to study probability by writing down predictions, determining results, and recording them. He demonstrates by using (and eating) jellybeans. Choosing Penny as her focal point, Lisa begins to calculate her results. . . . Leedy clearly and cleverly depicts the possibilities and choices in panels and segmented pages that feature Penny in funny poses." Booklist

Murphy, Stuart J.
   ★ **Probably** pistachio; illustrated by Marsha Winborn. HarperCollins Pubs. 2001 30p il (MathStart) hardcover o.p. pa $4.95
Grades: K 1 2 3   **519.2**
   1. Probabilities
   ISBN 0-06-028028-X; 0-06-028029-8 lib bdg; 0-06-446734-1 pa
                                                   LC 99-27695
   Readers are introduced to the concept of probability in a story about a boy who has a day in which nothing goes right
   "Winborn's watercolors playfully depict Jack's misery as things go from bad to worse. . . . A closing section has follow-up activities to extend and enrich the lesson, as well as a short list of books with related themes." Booklist

519.5   Statistical mathematics

Goldstone, Bruce
   ★ **Great** estimations. H. Holt 2006 32p il $16.95
Grades: 1 2 3 4   **519.5**
   1. Approximate computation
   ISBN 978-0-8050-7446-8; 0-8050-7446-5
                                                   LC 2005-19776
   "Laying out a mixed assemblage of toys, pipe cleaners, marbles, peanuts, and other small items, Goldstone helps viewers train themselves to estimate the size of groups of about 10 things on sight, then goes on to present similar, often fetchingly arranged, materials by hundreds and (!) thousands. He also describes 'clump counting' and 'box and count' methods. . . . This book lends itself equally well to skill building and to casual reading." Booklist

   ★ **Greater** estimations. Henry Holt and Company 2008 31p il $16.95
Grades: 1 2 3 4   **519.5**
   1. Counting 2. Approximate computation 3. Estimation theory -- Juvenile literature
   ISBN 0-8050-8315-4; 978-0-8050-8315-6
                                                   LC 2007-40894
   "Goldstone builds on the topics introduced in Great Estimations (Holt, 2006) and also discusses how to estimate length, weight, area, and volume. He does an exceptional job of breaking down the process of so that even early elementary students can comprehend it. The author also effectively introduces different methods of estimation. . . . The vivid, eye-catching photographs are the highlight of the book. . . . This lively book would be an excellent addition." SLJ

Murphy, Stuart J.
   Betcha! illustrated by S.D. Schindler. HarperCollins Pubs. 1997 33p il (MathStart) hardcover o.p. pa $4.95
Grades: 1 2 3   **519.5**
   1. Arithmetic   2. Approximate computation   3. Approximate computation -- Juvenile literature
   ISBN 0-06-026768-2; 0-06-026769-0 lib bdg; 0-06-446707-4 pa
                                                   LC 96-15486
   "On their way to a store sponsoring a contest that involves guessing the number of jellybeans in a jar, two friends encounter situations that involve numerical determinations. . . One boy counts one by one to obtain the answers, whereas the other one uses simple techniques to come up with near estimations. The easy-to-read picture-book format with only one or two sentences per page will appeal to reluctant readers. . . . The uncomplicated drawings show how the boy's brain is processing data and the skills he employs to arrive at an educated guess." SLJ

   ★ **Coyotes** all around; illustrated by Steve Björkman. HarperCollins Pubs. 2003 31p il (MathStart) $15.99; pa $4.99
Grades: 1 2 3   **519.5**
   1. Coyotes   2. Counting   3. Roadrunners   4. Approximate computation
   ISBN 0-06-051529-5; 0-06-051531-7 pa
                                                   LC 2002-151776
   A pack of coyotes tries to determine how many roadrunners and other creatures are in their vicinity, and while some

count different groups and add their totals together, Clever Coyote rounds off and estimates

"Humorous watercolor cartoons depict the action and clarify the concept. . . . Factoids about coyotes and other desert creatures appear throughout, so readers learn not only math, but also get their fair share of science sprinkled into the mix." SLJ

520 Astronomy and allied sciences

Aguilar, David A.
★ **Planets,** stars, and galaxies; a visual encyclopedia of our universe. written and illustrated by David A. Aguilar; contributing writers Christine Pulliam & Patricia Daniels. National Geographic 2007 191p il $24.95; lib bdg $38.90
Grades: 5 6 7 8 9 10 11 12   520
  1. Galaxies 2. Astronomy
  ISBN 978-1-4263-0170-4; 1-4263-0170-7; 978-1-4263-0171-1 lib bdg; 1-4263-0171-5 lib bdg
                         LC 2007061234

"This text introduces readers to the most current information available about the universe. Informatiion is presented is a clear and easy-to-understand manner. . . . The book features bright, eye-catching illustrations that Aguilar created on his computer. In addition, there are many vibrant photographs in the book that were taken by cameras here on Earth as well as by satellites and telescopes." Booklist

Includes glossary and bibliographical references

Carson, Mary Kay
★ **Beyond** the solar system; exploring galaxies, black holes, alien planets, and more: a history with 21 activities. by Mary Kay Carson. Chicago Review Press 2013 vii, 127 p.p col. ill. (paperback) $18.95
Grades: 5 6 7 8   520
  1. Creative activities 2. Astronomy -- History -- Juvenile literature
  ISBN 1613745443; 9781613745441
                         LC 2012046330

In this book, "Mary Kay Carson traces the evolution of humankind's astronomical knowledge, from the realization that we are not at the center of the universe to recent telescopic proof of planets orbiting stars outside our solar system. . . . This book contains 21 hands-on projects to further explore the subjects discussed" as well as "minibiographies of famous astronomers, a time line of major scientific discoveries . . .[and] a glossary of technical terms." (Publisher's note)

Includes bibliographical references (p. 121) and index.

Gardner, Robert
Ace your space science project; great science fair ideas. [by] Robert Gardner and Madeline Goodstein. Enslow Publishers 2009 128p il (Ace your science project) lib bdg $31.93
Grades: 5 6 7 8   520
  1. Space sciences 2. Science projects 3. Science -- Experiments
  ISBN 978-0-7660-3230-9 lib bdg; 0-7660-3230-2 lib bdg
                         LC 2008-04688

"Informative, practical, and not without dry wit, this is a good bet for replacing older books of science projects related to astronomny." Booklist

Includes bibliographical references

Garlick, Mark A.
Atlas of the universe. Simon & Schuster Books for Young Readers 2008 128p il map (Insiders) $19.99
Grades: 5 6 7 8   520
  1. Astronomy 2. Cosmology
  ISBN 978-1-4169-5558-0; 1-4169-5558-5

"Seamlessly commingling luscious, color space photographs and dramatic, sharply detailed digital imagery, this tour of the universe earns high marks for visual impact. It's not too shabby in breadth of coverage either." SLJ

Goldsmith, Mike
The **Kingfisher** space encyclopedia; Dr. Mike Goldsmith. Kingfisher 2012 159 p. (hardcover) $18.99
Grades: 4 5 6   520
  1. Astronomy -- Encyclopedias
  ISBN 0753468050; 9780753468050

In this book, "[Mike] Goldsmith skims the history of astronomy and space exploration, tours the solar system and the universe beyond, then closes with glances at dark matter and other undiscovered territory." A "spread on Global Positioning Systems" is included along with "digital images" as illustrations. (Kirkus)

Green, Dan
Astronomy; out of this world! illustrated by Simon Basher. Kingfisher 2009 128p il pa $8.95
Grades: 5 6 7 8   520
  1. Astronomy
  ISBN 978-0-7534-6290-4 pa; 0-7534-6290-7 pa

"Basher has created a portrait gallery of personified planets, comets, space probes, galaxies, several kinds of stars, and an array of other celestial bodies in a hyper-cute, pastel cartoon style. . . . Along with short bulleted lists of additional information, each figure offers a fact-based self-description. . . . Green's astro-narrative is both accurate and spiced with seldom-mentioned details." SLJ

Includes glossary

Jankowski, Connie
Space exploration. Compass Point Books 2009 40p il (Mission: science) lib bdg $26.60
Grades: 4 5 6   520
  1. Astronomy
  ISBN 978-0-7565-3958-0 lib bdg; 0-7565-3958-7 lib bdg
                         LC 2008-7722

Discusses outer space exploration and examines future possibilities such as a permanent space station, colonies in space, and journeys outside the solar system

Includes glossary

Lasky, Kathryn
★ The **librarian** who measured the earth; illustrated by Kevin Hawkes. Little, Brown 1994 48p il $16.95
Grades: 2 3 4 5   520
  1. Astronomers 2. Geographers 3. Writers on science

4. Ancient geography -- Juvenile literature
ISBN 0-316-51526-4

LC 92-42656

Describes the life and work of Eratosthenes, the Greek geographer and astronomer who accurately measured the circumference of the Earth

"Illustrating the text with warmth and humor, Hawkes' acrylic paintings capture the period details of the setting and clarify the geometric concepts used in the measurement. The often dramatic compositions vary from page to page, while the sunlit reds, oranges, and yellows glow brightly against the cooler blues and greens. . . . Entertaining as well as instructional." Booklist

Includes bibliographical references

Pinkney, Andrea Davis

★ **Dear** Benjamin Banneker; illustrated by Brian Pinkney. Harcourt Brace & Co. 1994 un il hardcover o.p. pa $7

Grades: 2 3 4   **520**

1. Astronomers 2. Mathematicians 3. Nonfiction writers 4. Clock and watch makers 5. African Americans -- Biography

ISBN 0-15-200417-3; 0-15-201892-1 pa

LC 93-31162

This offers "lucid text and striking illustrations, rendered on scratchboard and colored with oil paint." Publ Wkly

Riley, Peter D.

Space. Sea-to-Sea Publications 2011 32p il (The real scientist investigates) lib bdg $28.50

Grades: 3 4 5   **520**

1. Astronomy

ISBN 978-1-59771-284-2; 1-59771-284-1

LC 2010005375

In this book about space "solid scientific material is presented in accessible language and a visually engaging, boldly colored layout. Budding scientists are encouraged to hone their skills by recording observations, making predictions, and analyzing results. Hands-on activities are included on almost every spread. . . . The many color photos feature diverse children demonstrating the activities." SLJ

Includes glossary and bibliographical references

Sis, Peter, 1949-

★ **Starry** messenger; a book depicting the life of a famous scientist, mathematician, astronomer, philosopher, physicist, Galileo Galilei. created and illustrated by Peter Sis. Farrar, Straus & Giroux 1996 un il $18; pa $7.99

Grades: 2 3 4 5   **520**

1. Astronomers 2. Writers on science

ISBN 0-374-37191-1; 0-374-47027-8 pa

LC 95-44986

A Caldecott Medal honor book, 1997

This book traces "the astronomer's life from his birth, . . . to his childhood, . . . and finally to his years as a celebrated scientist whose experiments culminated in his construction of the first complete astronomical telescope. . . . Age six and up." (N Y Times Book Rev)

"Large, beautiful drawings reflect the ideas, events, books, maps, world view, and symbolism of the times. These intricate ink drawings, idiosyncratic in concept and beautifully tinted with delicate watercolor washes, are complemented by smaller drawings and prints that illustrate a side-

text of significant dates, time lines, quotations, comments, and explanations. . . . Those drawn to the book will find that it works on many levels, offering not just facts but intuitive visions of another world." Booklist

Space: a visual encyclopedia. DK Pub. 2010 254p il $24.99

Grades: 5 6 7 8   **520**

1. Astronomy 2. Astronautics 3. Space sciences

ISBN 978-0-7566-6277-6; 0-7566-6277-X

"Any reader wishing to gain a fair introductory understanding of astronomy in one concise book will find much satisfaction in this work. An abundance of fascinating information is contained within these pages, and the format is such that excellent and attractive related photographs and diagrams directly accompany the text. . . . The book is very well organized and very well written." Sci Books & Films

Sparrow, Giles

Cosmic! the ultimate 3-D guide to the universe. [author, Giles Sparrow; paper engineer, Richard Ferguson] DK Publishing 2008 un il $24.99

Grades: 5 6 7 8   **520**

1. Astronomy 2. Cosmology 3. Toy and movable books 4. Pop-up books

ISBN 978-0-7566-4021-7; 0-7566-4021-0

LC 2008-300768

This book "traces the history of the universe beginning with the Big Bang, discussing the structure of the solar system, planets, stars, galaxies, how the Hubble telescope functions, and the spaceships used in space exploration." Publisher's note

VanCleave, Janice Pratt, 1942-

Step-by-step science experiments in astronomy; by Janice VanCleave. Rosen Pub. 2013 80 p. col. ill. (Janice Vancleave's first-place science fair projects) (library) $33.25; (paperback) $14.15

Grades: 5 6 7 8   **520**

1. Astronomy -- Juvenile literature 2. Science -- Experiments -- Juvenile literature 3. Science projects -- Juvenile literature 4. Astronomy -- Experiments -- Juvenile literature

ISBN 1448869781; 9781448869787; 9781448884612

LC 2012000715

This book by Janice VanCleave presents 22 science experiments in astronomy for children. "Van Cleave states the basic goal of the experiments, followed by a list of necessary materials. . . . Step-by-step instructions are . . . accompanied by diagrams where needed. The results section states exactly what is expected to happen and the 'Why?' section explains in accessible terms why those specific results were achieved." (School Library Journal)

Includes bibliographical references (p. 77-78) and index

Ward, D. J.

Seven wonders of space phenomena; by D.J. Ward. Twenty-First Century Books 2011 80 p. ill. (chiefly col.) (library) $33.26

Grades: 5 6 7 8   **520**

1. Universe -- Juvenile literature 2. Astronomy -- Juvenile literature 3. Astronomy -- Miscellanea --

Juvenile literature

ISBN 0761354522; 9780761354529

LC 2010028447

This book by D.J. Ward looks at "space phenomena, such as dark matter, dark energy, and the beginning of the universe. Read what astronomers and space scientists have discovered about these amazing wonders—and what they have yet to learn." (Publisher's note)

Includes bibliographical references (p. 76-78) and index.

520.92 Astronomers

Christensen, Bonnie

I, Galileo; Bonnie Christensen. Alfred A. Knopf 2012 40 p.

Grades: 3 4 5   **520.92**

1. Inventors -- Biography 2. Physicists -- Biography 3. Astronomers -- Biography 4. Picture books for children 5. Galilei, Galileo, 1564-1642 6. Physicists -- Italy -- Biography -- Juvenile literature 7. Astronomers -- Italy -- Biography -- Juvenile literature

ISBN 0375867538; 9780307974402; 9780375867538; 9780375967535

LC 2011025100

"In this . . . picture book, blind, elderly Galileo sits . . . tells the story of his life. After speaking of his childhood and education, he recalls his scientific work, including developing an improved telescope that enabled him . . . to conclude that Copernicus' 'sun-centered theory' was correct. The church reacted . . . by placing him under house arrest and banning his books. The narrative . . . touches on many of Galileo's accomplishments." (Booklist)

522 Techniques, procedures, apparatus, equipment, materials

Cole, Michael D.

Eye on the universe; the incredible hubble space telescope. Michael D. Cole. Enslow Publishers 2013 48 p. $23.93

Grades: 4 5 6 7 8   **522**

1. Hubble Space Telescope 2. Outer space -- Exploration 3. Picture books for children 4. Astronomy -- Research -- Juvenile literature 5. Astronautics in astronomy -- Juvenile literature

ISBN 0766040771; 9780766040779

LC 2011047074

This book looks at the Hubble Space Telescope. "Orbiting high above Earth, the Hubble Telescope captures . . . wonders of space. . . . Photographs are relayed back to Earth, allowing scientists and astronomers to study parts of space that were once completely unknown. Michael D. Cole explores the . . . journey of launching this telescope into space and how it has unlocked many of the . . . mysteries in the universe." (Publisher's note)

Includes bibliographical references and index

Jefferis, David

Star spotters; telescopes and observatories. Crabtree Pub. 2009 32p il (Exploring our solar system) lib bdg $26.60; pa $8.95

Grades: 3 4 5   **522**

1. Astronomy 2. Telescopes

ISBN 978-0-7787-3725-4 lib bdg; 0-7787-3725-X lib bdg; 978-0-7787-3742-1 pa; 0-7787-3742-X pa

LC 2008-49242

"Focuses on important observatories—earthbound and orbiting—along with types of telescopes—and concludes with brief observations about binoculars and cameras. . . . [This book is] designed with easily digestible blocks of question-and-answer text sharing page space with large, sharply reproduced space photos and graphic art." SLJ

Includes glossary

Nardo, Don

Telescopes. Kidhaven Press 2005 48p il (Kidhaven science library) $23.70

Grades: 4 5 6 7   **522**

1. Telescopes

ISBN 0-7377-3060-9

This "volume explains how telescopes work and traces their history, along with the major discoveries they made possible, from Galileo's time to the present. The final chapter deals with present and planned space telescopes." Publisher's note

Includes glossary and bibliographical references

Scott, Elaine

★ Space, stars, and the beginning of time; what the Hubble telescope saw. Clarion Books 2011 66p il $17.99

Grades: 5 6 7 8   **522**

1. Astronomy 2. Hubble Space Telescope

ISBN 0-547-24189-5; 978-0-547-24189-0

LC 2010-08040

This examines "some of the data that has been collected over the two decades of the Hubble Telescope's operation. Opening chapters discuss the satellite's instrumentation and its 2009 repairs, and then the real fun begins with sections on calculating the age of the universe and its speed of expansion; the nature of dark matter, dark energy, and black holes; star formation; and planet formation, particularly outside our solar system. . . . Gasp-worthy photographs should fire up the most sluggish imaginations." Bull Cent Child Books

523 Specific celestial bodies and phenomena

Cole, Joanna

★ The magic school bus, lost in the solar system; illustrated by Bruce Degen. Scholastic 1990 un il hardcover o.p. pa $6.99

Grades: 2 3 4   **523**

1. Planets 2. Astronomy

ISBN 0590414291 pa

LC 89-10185

"The planetarium is closed for repairs, so the Magic School Bus blasts off on a real tour of the solar system. After their previous field trips, the children in Ms. Frizzle's class are all blasé about such things; as they land on the Moon, Venus, and Mars, and fly by the other planets and the Sun, they comment on what they see, generate a blizzard of one- or two-sentence reports on special topics and—even while Ms. Frizzle is temporarily left behind in the asteroid belt—crack terrible jokes." SLJ

Gardner, Robert

Far-out science projects about Earth's sun and moon; illustrations by Tom Labaff. Enslow Publishers 2007 48p il (Rockin' earth science experiments) lib bdg $23.93

Grades: 3 4 5   523

1. Science projects 2. Science -- Experiments

ISBN 978-0-7660-2736-7 lib bdg; 0-7660-2736-8 lib bdg

LC 2006-13789

A collection of science experiments such as getting direction and time from the sun, finding locations of sunrise and sunset, measuring heat from the sun, and observing the phases of the moon

This is "just right for students with limited experience looking for projects that are fairly interesting and manageable." SLJ

Includes glossary and bibliographical references

523.1   The universe, galaxies, quasars

Asimov, Isaac

The Milky Way and other galaxies; by Isaac Asimov; with revisions and updating by Richard Hantula. Gareth Stevens Pub. 2005 32p (Isaac Asimov's 21st century library of the universe) lib bdg $24.67

Grades: 4 5 6   523.1

1. Galaxies

ISBN 0-8368-3968-4

LC 2004-58313

This "examines various galactic types, structures, and superstructures, as observed by a wide array of specialized telescopes. . . . The pictures . . . are striking. . . . [An] excellent collection [enhancer]." SLJ

Includes bibliographical references

Fox, Karen C.

Older than the stars; [by] Karen C. Fox; illustrated by Nancy Davis. Charlesbridge 2010 un il lib bdg $15.95

Grades: 2 3 4 5   523.1

1. Atoms 2. Cosmology 3. Big bang theory 4. Atoms -- Juvenile literature 5. Cosmology -- Juvenile literature 6. Big bang theory

ISBN 978-1-57091-787-5 lib bdg; 1-57091-787-6 lib bdg

LC 2009-04304

"Fox and Davis tackle the challenge of creating an engaging read-aloud about the Big Bang theory with energy and style. Employing the structure of a familiar nursery rhyme, the text takes readers through the steps of the universe's expansion. . . . A text box on each spread offers a clear, concise explanation of what happened in that particular stage of the universe. . . . Perfect for the classroom, this is an intriguing introduction to a difficult-to-understand concept." SLJ

Gibbons, Gail

Galaxies, galaxies! Holiday House 2006 32p il $16.95

Grades: K 1 2 3   523.1

1. Galaxies

ISBN 978-0-8234-2002-5; 0-8234-2002-7

LC 2006-02504

"Between an opening description of the Milky Way and a closing claim that galaxy formation is still going on, the author depicts ancient astronomers at work, describes several kinds of telescopes, and profiles five distinctive galactic forms, from irregular to lenticular. Pairing brief, matter-of-fact generalizations leavened with digestible doses of specific information to painted scenes that link diverse groups of human observers to galaxies seen in blobby, broadly brushed portraits, this introduction to some of the universe's largest structures will put stars in the eyes of the most Earthbound young readers." SLJ

Goldsmith, Mike

Universe; journey into deep space. Mike Goldsmith; illustrated by Mark A. Garlick. Kingfisher 2012 48 p. (hardcover) $17.99

Grades: 4 5 6 7   523.1

1. Universe 2. Astronomy 3. Outer space

ISBN 075346876X; 9780753468760

This book, by Mike Goldsmith, illustrated by Mark A. Garlick, profiles "some of the Universe's most intriguing places, and along the way . . . [describes] the amazing history of the Cosmos. A series of . . . spreads give . . . snapshots of distant galactic locations as the reader journeys . . . from red cold Mars (3 light minutes away) to a massive Supernova (10,000 light years away) and beyond." (Publisher's note)

Jefferis, David

Galaxies; immense star islands. Crabtree Pub. 2009 32p il (Exploring our solar system) lib bdg $26.60; pa $8.95

Grades: 3 4 5   523.1

1. Galaxies

ISBN 978-0-7787-3723-0 lib bdg; 0-7787-3723-3 lib bdg; 978-0-7787-3740-7 pa; 0-7787-3740-3 pa

LC 2008-46248

This "begins with a summary look at galactic types and origins, then goes on to describe cores, halos, and other structures with special reference to the Milky Way. It closes with a smattering of advice for young sky watchers and a spread of general facts about galaxies. . . . Designed with easily digestible blocks of question-and-answer text sharing page space with large, sharply reproduced space photos and graphic art." SLJ

Includes glossary

Rau, Dana Meachen

The Milky Way and other galaxies; by Dana Meachen Rau. Compass Point Books 2005 32p il (Our solar system) $22.60

Grades: 3 4 5   523.1

1. Galaxies

ISBN 0-7565-0853-3

LC 2004-15571

The author "describes the nature of our own galaxy, then presents a gallery of other types, along with brief mentions of quasars, clusters, and superclusters. [The book is] illustrated with a mix of photos and digital art. . . . [This earns] high marks for visual appeal, and for clear, specific presentation of material." SLJ

Includes glossary and bibliographical references

Simon, Seymour

★ **Galaxies**. Morrow Junior Bks. 1988 un il hardcover o.p. pa $6.95

Grades: 3 4 5 6   **523.1**

1. Galaxies

ISBN 0-688-08002-2; 0-688-10992-6 pa

LC 87-23967

"This fine introduction to an awe-inspiring subject will surely stimulate interest in stargazing, further reading, and investigation." Horn Book

523.2   Planetary systems

Aguilar, David A.

★ **13** planets; the latest view of the solar system. National Geographic 2011 60p il $16.95; lib bdg $25.99

Grades: 5 6 7 8   **523.2**

1. Planets

ISBN 9781426307706; 1426307705; 9781426307713 lib bdg; 1426307713 lib bdg

LC 2010032510

Updated and revised edition of: 11 planets: A new view of the Solar System (2008)

Profiles each of the planets in Earth's solar system, including Pluto, Ceres, Eris, Haumea, MakeMake, the sun, the Oort cloud, comets, and more.

"Aguilar offers an amended volume reflecting the findings of the International Astronomical Union, which currently classifies eight objects in the solar system as planets and, with the addition of Haumea and Makemake, five as dwarf planets. . . . Aguilar has not only added sections on Haumea and Makemake, he has also used this opportunity to rewrite portions of the text and captions throughout the book and, in some cases, to substitute new illustrations or improve old ones for the new volume. The result is a more readable, more accurate, and more handsome edition of the previous work." Booklist

Includes bibliographical references and index.

Baines, Rebecca

Every planet has a place; a book about our solar system. by Becky Baines. National Geographic 2008 27p il (Zig zag) $14.95; lib bdg $19.90

Grades: PreK K 1   **523.2**

1. Solar system -- Juvenile literature

ISBN 978-1-4263-0313-5; 1-4263-0313-0; 978-1-4263-0314-2 lib bdg; 1-4263-0314-9 lib bdg

LC 2008-24447

Presents "factual, clearly-written information on [the solar system]. . . . Readers curiosity will be piqued by the vibrant color photographs, accommodating illustrations, large font size, and helpful captions. Special features include drawings superimposed over photographs, and a zigzag path at the end of . . . [the] book prompting readers to further explore the topic in new and fun ways." SLJ

Bredeson, Carmen

What is the solar system? Enslow Elementary 2008 32p il (I like space!) lib bdg $22.60

Grades: K 1 2 3   **523.2**

1. Planets 2. Solar system -- Juvenile literature

ISBN 978-0-7660-2944-6 lib bdg; 0-7660-2944-1 lib bdg

LC 2007-02745

This book "is beautifully illustrated, with photographs from NASA and other sources, and is well organized." Sci Books Films

Includes glossary and bibliographical references

Carson, Mary Kay

Exploring the solar system; a history with 22 activities. by Mary Kay Carson. Chicago Review Press 2008 vii, 168 p.p ill. (paperback) $17.95

Grades: 4 5 6 7   **523.2**

1. Astronomy -- Juvenile literature 2. Solar system -- Juvenile literature

ISBN 1556527152; 9781556527159

This book by Mary Kay Carson is a "mix of facts, history, and hands-on activities [about the solar system]. Beginning with a two-page table of contents with chapters arranged as planets in our solar system and an introductory time line, the author takes readers on a historical journey of what was known and/or discovered in each of eight time periods." (School Library Journal)

Goldsmith, Mike

Solar system. Kingfisher 2010 56p il (Discover science) $9.99

Grades: 1 2 3   **523.2**

1. Solar system

ISBN 978-0-7534-6447-2; 0-7534-6447-0

First published in the series Kingfisher young knowledge in 2006

"With glossy color pages, abundant visuals, and descriptive prose, this . . . title provides an accessible introduction to earth's solar system. Printed in large font, the text is well suited to newly independent readers' abilities . . . and occasionally uses familiar comparisons to aid comprehension. . . . The visual-laden pages feature a wide range of images, from stock photos to detailed renderings of planetary surfaces." Booklist

Includes glossary and bibliographical references

Greathouse, Lisa E.

Solar system. Compass Point Books 2009 40p il (Mission: science) lib bdg $26.60

Grades: 4 5 6   **523.2**

1. Solar system

ISBN 978-0-7565-4071-5 lib bdg; 0-7565-4071-2 lib bdg

LC 2008-35728

Introduces the solar system and the specific characteristics of its planets

Includes glossary

Kops, Deborah

Exploring exoplanets. Lerner Publications 2011 40p il (What's amazing about space?) lib bdg $27.93

Grades: 4 5 6   **523.2**

1. Extrasolar planets

ISBN 978-0-7613-5444-4; 0-7613-5444-1

LC 2010046109

This explains how scientists have discovered other planets in the universe similar to those in our solar system.

Includes glossary and bibliographical references

Kudlinski, Kathleen V.

Boy were we wrong about the solar system! illustrated by John Rocco. Dutton Children's Books 2008 un il $15.99

Grades: K 1 2 3   **523.2**

1. Solar system -- Juvenile literature 2. Errors, Scientific -- Juvenile literature

ISBN 978-0-525-46979-7; 0-525-46979-6

                 LC 2007-50557

This is a "debunking of such erstwhile astronomical theories as solar revolution around the Earth, concentric glass spheres dividing planetary orbits, Martian canals, and, of course, the overly elevated status of Pluto. . . . [This is illustrated with] jewel-hued, cartoonishly exaggerated paintings. . . . The concept of adults getting it dead wrong is realiably engaging." Bull Cent Child Books

Simon, Seymour

★ **Our** solar system; [by] Seymour Simon. updated ed.; Collins 2007 62p il $19.99; lib bdg $20.89

Grades: 3 4 5 6   **523.2**

1. Solar system

ISBN 978-0-06-114008-2; 0-06-114008-2; 978-0-06-114009-9 lib bdg; 0-06-114009-0 lib bdg

                 LC 2007279969

First published 1992

Describes the origins, characteristics, and future of the sun, planets, moons, asteroids, meteoroids, and comets

This "is a fine, comprehensive work on the solar system. . . . [The book includes] excellent photographs. Beautifully designed and a pleasure to use." Horn Book Guide

Tourville, Amanda Doering

Exploring the solar system. Rourke Pub. 2010 48p il (Let's explore science) $32.79; pa $9.95

Grades: 4 5 6 7   **523.2**

1. Solar system

ISBN 978-1-61590-323-8; 1-61590-323-2; 978-1-61590-562-1 pa; 1-61590-562-6 pa

                 LC 2010009910

This "moves from basic definitions . . . to more technical information, such as the formula for calculating the speed of light. Also included is up-to-date coverage of Pluto's demotion from planet to plutoid, as well as a section on dwarf planets. . . . In [this] title, well-chosen boxed examples, abundant color photos, diagrams, and an appended glossary add interest and support the engaging [text]." Booklist

Includes glossary and bibliographical references

Trammel, Howard K.

★ The **solar** system. Children's Press 2009 48p il (True book) lib bdg $26; pa $6.95

Grades: 3 4 5   **523.2**

1. Solar system

ISBN 978-0-531-16898-1 lib bdg; 0-531-16898-0 lib bdg; 978-0-531-22805-0 pa; 0-531-22805-3 pa

                 LC 2008049376

"The Solar System begins with a lineup of the usual suspects (yes, Pluto is off the hook). The way the chapters move from inner to outer planets is no surprise, but the called-out

details are cunningly illustrated and plenty fascinating. . . . . Short but solid back matter closes out [this] impressive [offering]." Booklist

Wittenstein, Vicki Oransky

Planet hunter; Goeff Marcy and the search for other earths. Boyds Mills Press 2010 48p il $17.95

Grades: 5 6 7 8   **523.2**

1. Extrasolar planets 2. Life on other planets 3. Astrophysicists 4. College teachers 5. Young adult literature -- Works 6. Biography, Individual -- Juvenile literature 7. Life on other planets -- Juvenile literature

ISBN 978-1-59078-592-8; 1-59078-592-4

"The profound thrill of searching for (and finding!) planets orbiting stars other than our own is deftly captured in this profile of Geoff Marcy, one of the great hunt's most successful practitioners. Matched to big, sharp color photos of scientists (mostly) at work and compelling speculative views of exotic suns and landscapes, Wittenstein's matter-of-fact narrative first introduces readers to Marcy and his team on the night shift . . . at the W. M. Keck Observatory atop Hawaii's Mauna Kea. . . . This handsomely packaged introduction is just the ticket for turning earthbound (for now) children into budding skywatchers." SLJ

Includes glossary and bibliographical references

523.3   Specific parts of solar system

Branley, Franklyn Mansfield

The **moon** seems to change; by Franklyn M. Branley; illustrations by Barbara and Ed Emberley. rev ed; Crowell 1987 29p il (Let's-read-and-find-out science book) hardcover o.p. pa $4.95

Grades: K 1 2 3   **523.3**

1. Moon

ISBN 0-06-445065-1 pa

                 LC 86-47747

A revised and newly illustrated edition of the title first published 1960

The author "explains the waxing and waning of the moon and compares the length of a day on earth and on the moon. Each page has colorful explanatory illustrations. . . . Branley's brief-easy-to-read text and the Emberleys' diagrams make this book a welcome addition to science collections for young children or the picture book section." SLJ

What the moon is like; by Franklyn M. Branley; illustrated by True Kelley. newly illustrated ed; HarperCollins Pubs. 2000 30p il (Let's-read-and-find-out science) hardcover o.p. lib bdg $15.89; pa $4.95

Grades: K 1 2 3   **523.3**

ISBN 0-06-027992-3; 0-06-027993-1 lib bdg; 0-06-445185-2 pa

                 LC 98-54072

A revised and newly illustrated edition of the title first published 1963 by Crowell

This book "invites readers simply to observe the moon from Earth before it delves into facts. . . . The following pages, all illustrated with clear, colorful pictures of astronauts and the lunar landscape, explore the moon's actual surface, climate, and temperature; briefly discuss lunar landings (with a map); and draw comparisons between the moon and Earth." Booklist

Carson, Mary Kay

Far-out guide to the moon. Enslow Publishers 2010 48p il (Far-out guide to the solar system) lib bdg $23.93; pa $7.95
Grades: 3 4 5   523.3
1. Moon
ISBN 978-0-7660-3189-0 lib bdg; 0-7660-3189-6 lib bdg; 978-1-59845-184-9 pa; 1-59845-184-7 pa
LC 2009006487
"Presents information about the moon, including fast facts, history, and technology used to study it." Publisher's note
Includes glossary and bibliographical references

Gibbons, Gail

The **moon** book. Holiday House 1997 un il $16.95; pa $6.95
Grades: K 1 2 3   523.3
1. Moon
ISBN 0-8234-1297-0; 0-8234-1364-0 pa
LC 96-36826
Identifies the moon as our only natural satellite, describes its movement and phases, and discusses how we have observed and explored it over the years
"Gibbons presents a great deal of information in a deceptively simple format by combining inviting illustrations with clear writing." Horn Book Guide

Landau, Elaine

The **moon**; [by] Elaine Landau. Children's Press 2007 48p il (True book) lib bdg $26
Grades: 2 3 4   523.3
1. Moon
ISBN 0-531-12562-9 lib bdg; 978-0-531-12562-5 lib bdg
LC 2007004183
This describes the phases of the moon, its composition and geography, and moon exploration.
This "matches a clearly reasoned, matter-of-fact text to plenty of small but sharply reproduced photos." SLJ
Includes glossary and bibliographical references

Simon, Seymour

★ The **moon**; rev ed.; Simon & Schuster Bks. for Young Readers 2003 un il $17.95
Grades: 4 5 6 7   523.3
1. Moon
ISBN 0-689-83563-9
LC 2001-31303
First published 1984 by Four Winds Press
A basic introduction to Earth's closest neighbor, its composition, and man's missions to it
"The digitally remastered color photographs in this update are incredible. . . . The text has undergone minimal change. . . . The facts remain true and relevant, and the writing reflects the graphics: beautiful. This is a must-have for astronomy sections." SLJ

Stewart, Melissa

Why does the moon change shape? Marshall Cavendish Benchmark 2009 32p il (Tell me why, tell me how) lib bdg $20.95
Grades: 3 4 5   523.3
1. Moon
ISBN 978-0-7614-2921-0 lib bdg; 0-7614-2921-2 lib bdg
LC 2007025247
"One or two large, well-captioned color photographs are provided per spread. [The] book concludes with an activity. [This is a] solid [introduction]." SLJ
Includes glossary and bibliographical references

Tomecek, Steve

★ **Moon**; illustrated by Liisa Chauncy Guida. National Geographic 2005 31p il (Jump into science) $16.95; lib bdg $25.90
Grades: K 1 2   523.3
1. Moon (Planet)
ISBN 0-7922-5123-7; 0-7922-8304-X lib bdg
LC 2004-8761
"Guida's artwork, in bright, saturated colors, will easily draw children into the science. . . . Tomecek's words encourage a sense of awe and wonder." Booklist

523.4   Planets, asteroids, trans-Neptunian objects of solar system

Bjorklund, Ruth

Venus. Marshall Cavendish Benchmark 2009 64p il (Space!) lib bdg o.p.; ebook $33
Grades: 4 5 6 7   523.4
1. Venus (Planet)
ISBN 978-0-7614-4251-6; 9780761445616
LC 2009014665
"Describes Venus, including its history, its composition, and its role in the solar system." Publisher's note
Includes glossary and bibliographical references

Capaccio, George

Jupiter. Marshall Cavendish Benchmark 2009 64p il (Space!) lib bdg $22.95
Grades: 4 5 6 7   523.4
1. Jupiter (Planet)
ISBN 978-0-7614-4244-8 lib bdg; 0-7614-4244-8 lib bdg; 9780761445555
LC 2008037276
"Describes Jupiter, including its history, its composition, and its role in the solar system." Publisher's note
Includes glossary and bibliographical references

Mars. Marshall Cavendish Benchmark 2010 64p il (Space!) lib bdg $22.95
Grades: 4 5 6 7   523.4
1. Mars (Planet)
ISBN 978-0-7614-4247-9 lib bdg; 0-7614-4247-2 lib bdg; 9780761445579
LC 2008037280
Describes Mars, including its history, its composition, and its role in the solar system
Includes glossary and bibliographical references

Carson, Mary Kay

Far-out guide to Jupiter. Enslow Publishers 2010 48p il (Far-out guide to the solar system) lib bdg $23.93; pa $7.95

Grades: 3 4 5   **523.4**

1. Jupiter (Planet)

ISBN 978-0-7660-3184-5 lib bdg; 0-7660-3184-5 lib bdg; 978-1-59845-186-3 pa; 1-59845-186-3 pa

LC 2008050036

"Lively writing with specific facts systematically presented and plenty of dramatic space art and photography add up to a winning formula." SLJ

Includes glossary and bibliographical references

Far-out guide to Mars. Enslow Publishers 2010 48p il (Far-out guide to the solar system) lib bdg $23.93; pa $7.95

Grades: 3 4 5   **523.4**

1. Mars (Planet)

ISBN 978-0-7660-3183-8 lib bdg; 0-7660-3183-7 lib bdg; 978-1-59845-185-6 pa; 1-59845-185-5 pa

LC 2009006485

"Presents information about Mars, including fast facts, history, and technology used to study the planet." Publisher's note

Includes glossary and bibliographical references

Far-out guide to Mercury. Enslow Publishers 2010 48p il (Far-out guide to the solar system) lib bdg $23.93; pa $7.95

Grades: 3 4 5   **523.4**

1. Mercury (Planet)

ISBN 978-0-7660-3180-7 lib bdg; 0-7660-3180-2 lib bdg; 978-1-59845-181-8 pa; 1-59845-181-2 pa

LC 2009006486

"Presents information about Mercury, including fast facts, history, and technology used to study the planet." Publisher's note

Includes glossary and bibliographical references

Far-out guide to Neptune. Enslow Publishers 2010 48p il (Far-out guide to the solar system) lib bdg $23.93; pa $7.95

Grades: 3 4 5   **523.4**

1. Neptune (Planet)

ISBN 978-0-7660-3186-9 lib bdg; 0-7660-3186-1 lib bdg; 978-1-59845-189-4 pa; 1-59845-189-8 pa

LC 2008050037

"Presents information about Neptune, including fast facts, history, and technology used to study the planet." Publisher's note

Includes glossary and bibliographical references

Far-out guide to Saturn. Enslow Publishers 2010 48p il (Far-out guide to the solar system) lib bdg $23.93; pa $7.95

Grades: 3 4 5   **523.4**

1. Saturn (Planet)

ISBN 978-0-7660-3178-4 lib bdg; 0-7660-3178-0 lib bdg; 978-1-59845-187-0 pa; 1-59845-187-1 pa

LC 2008050038

"Presents information about Saturn, including fast facts, history, and technology used to study the planet" Publisher's note

Includes glossary and bibliographical references

Far-out guide to Uranus. Enslow Publishers 2010 48p il (Far-out guide to the solar system) lib bdg $23.93; pa $7.95

Grades: 3 4 5   **523.4**

1. Uranus (Planet)

ISBN 978-0-7660-3185-2 lib bdg; 0-7660-3185-3 lib bdg; 978-1-59845-188-7 pa; 1-59845-188-X pa

LC 2008050040

"Presents information about Uranus, including fast facts, history, and technology used to study the planet." Publisher's note

Includes glossary and bibliographical references

Far-out guide to Venus. Enslow Publishers 2010 48p il (Far-out guide to the solar system) lib bdg $23.93; pa $7.95

Grades: 3 4 5   **523.4**

1. Venus (Planet)

ISBN 978-0-7660-3181-4 lib bdg; 0-7660-3181-0 lib bdg; 978-1-59845-182-5 pa; 1-59845-182-0 pa

LC 2008050041

"Presents information about Venus, including fast facts, history, and technology used to study the planet". Publisher's note

Includes glossary and bibliographical references

Far-out guide to asteroids and comets. Enslow Publishers 2010 48p il (Far-out guide to the solar system) lib bdg $23.93; pa $7.95

Grades: 3 4 5   **523.4**

1. Comets 2. Asteroids

ISBN 978-0-7660-3188-3 lib bdg; 0-7660-3188-8 lib bdg; 978-1-59845-191-7 pa; 1-59845-191-X pa

LC 2009006484

"Lively writing with specific facts systematically presented and plenty of dramatic space art and photography add up to a winning formula. . . . Carson offers a thrillingly alarmist view . . . of the (relatively) small rocks and comets that hurtle through local space to, on occasion, collide spectacularly with Earth or other planets." SLJ

Includes glossary and bibliographical references

Far-out guide to the icy dwarf planets. Enslow Publishers 2010 48p il (Far-out guide to the solar system) lib bdg $23.93; pa $7.95

Grades: 3 4 5   **523.4**

1. Planets

ISBN 978-0-7660-3187-6 lib bdg; 0-7660-3187-X lib bdg; 978-1-59845-190-0 pa; 1-59845-190-1 pa

LC 2009037810

"Lively writing with specific facts systematically presented and plenty of dramatic space art and photography add up to a winning formula." SLJ

Includes glossary and bibliographical references

Colligan, L. H.

Mercury. Marshall Cavendish Benchmark 2009 64p il (Space!) lib bdg $22.95

Grades: 4 5 6 7   523.4
   1. Mercury (Planet)
   ISBN 0-7614-4239-1 lib bdg; 9780761442394 lib
bdg; 9780761445517

LC 2008037278

"Describes Mercury, including its history, its composition, and its role in the solar system." Publisher's note

Includes glossary and bibliographical references

Hicks, Terry Allan
   Saturn. Marshall Cavendish Benchmark 2010 64p il
(Space!) lib bdg $22.95

Grades: 4 5 6 7   523.4
   1. Saturn (Planet)
   ISBN 978-0-7614-4249-3 lib bdg; 0-7614-4249-9 lib
bdg; 9780761445593

LC 2008037453

"Describes Saturn, including its history, its composition,
and its role in the solar system." Publisher's note

Includes glossary and bibliographical references

Landau, Elaine
   Beyond Pluto; [by] Elaine Landau. Children's Press
2007 48p il (True book) lib bdg $26

Grades: 2 3 4   523.4
   1. Planets
   ISBN 0-531-12565-3 lib bdg; 978-0-531-12565-6
lib bdg

LC 2007012280

This "looks past Pluto into the Kuiper Belt, the Oort
Cloud, and the search for extrasolar planets. . . . [This]
matches a clearly reasoned, matter-of-fact text to plenty of
small but sharply reproduced color photos." SLJ

Includes glossary and bibliographical references

   Jupiter; [by] Elaine Landau. Children's Press 2007
48p il (True book) lib bdg $26; pa $6.95

Grades: 2 3 4   523.4
   1. Jupiter (Planet)
   ISBN 978-0-531-12559-5 lib bdg; 0-531-12559-9 lib
bdg; 978-0-531-14789-4 pa; 0-531-14789-4 pa

LC 2007003869

First published 1991

This describes the atmosphere and geographic features
of Jupiter and the missions which have explored the planet

This "matches a clearly reasoned, matter-of-fact text to
plenty of small but sharply reproduced color photos." SLJ

Includes glossary and bibliographical references

   Mars; [by] Elaine Landau. Children's Press 2007 48p
il (True book) lib bdg $26; pa $6.95

Grades: 2 3 4   523.4
   1. Mars (Planet)
   ISBN 978-0-531-12560-1 lib bdg; 0-531-12560-2 lib
bdg; 978-0-531-14790-0 pa; 0-531-14790-8 pa

LC 2007-12260

This describes the place of Mars in the solar system, the
composition of the planet, its moons and missions to Mars

This "matches a clearly reasoned, matter-of-fact text to
plenty of small but sharply reproduced color photos." SLJ

Includes glossary and bibliographical references

   Mercury; [by] Elaine Landau. Children's Press 2007
48p il (True book) lib bdg $26; pa $6.95

Grades: 2 3 4   523.4
   1. Mercury (Planet)
   ISBN 978-0-531-12561-8 lib bdg; 0-531-12561-0 lib
bdg; 978-0-531-14791-7 pa; 0-531-14791-6 pa

LC 2007012277

This describes Mercury's place in the solar system, its
atmosphere and composition, and missions to Mercury

This "matches a clearly reasoned, matter-of-fact text to
plenty of small but sharply reproduced color photos." SLJ

Includes glossary and bibliographical references

   Neptune; [by] Elaine Landau. Children's Press 2007
48p il (True book) lib bdg $26; pa $6.95

Grades: 2 3 4   523.4
   1. Neptune (Planet)
   ISBN 978-0-531-12563-2 lib bdg; 0-531-12563-7 lib
bdg; 978-0-531-14793-1 pa; 0-531-14793-2 pa

LC 2007008257

This describes Neptune's place in the solar system, its
atmosphere and composition

This "matches a clearly reasoned, matter-of-fact text to
plenty of small but sharply reproduced color photos." SLJ

Includes glossary and bibliographical references

   Pluto; from planet to dwarf. [by] Elaine Landau. Children's Press 2007 48p il (True book) lib bdg $26; pa
$6.95

Grades: 2 3 4   523.4
   1. Pluto (Planet)
   ISBN 978-0-531-12566-3 lib bdg; 0-531-12566-1 lib
bdg; 978-0-531-14794-8 pa; 0-531-14794-0 pa

LC 2007012279

This describes Pluto's place in the solar system, its
change in status from planet to dwarf, its moons, and missions to Pluto

This "matches a clearly reasoned, matter-of-fact text to
plenty of small but sharply reproduced color photos." SLJ

Includes glossary and bibliographical references

   Saturn; [by] Elaine Landau. Children's Press 2007
48p il (True book) lib bdg $26; pa $6.95

Grades: 2 3 4   523.4
   1. Saturn (Planet)
   ISBN 978-0-531-12567-0 lib bdg; 0-531-12567-X lib
bdg; 978-0-531-14795-5 pa; 0-531-14795-9 pa

LC 2007004181

This describes Saturn's place in the solar system, its
composition, its moons and rings and missions to Saturn

This "matches a clearly reasoned, matter-of-fact text to
plenty of small but sharply reproduced color photos." SLJ

Includes glossary and bibliographical references

   Uranus; [by] Elaine Landau. Children's Press 2007
48p il (True book) lib bdg $26; pa $6.95

Grades: 2 3 4   523.4
   1. Uranus (Planet)
   ISBN 978-0-531-12569-4 lib bdg; 0-531-12569-6 lib
bdg; 978-0-531-14797-9 pa; 0-531-14797-5 pa

LC 2007012258

This describes Uranus's place in the solar system, its atmosphere, moons, and rings, and exploration

This "matches a clearly reasoned, matter-of-fact text to plenty of small but sharply reproduced color photos." SLJ

Includes glossary and bibliographical references

Venus; [by] Elaine Landau. Children's Press 2007 48p il (True book) lib bdg $26; pa $6.95

Grades: 2 3 4　　　523.4

1. Venus (Planet)

ISBN 978-0-531-12564-9 lib bdg; 0-531-12564-5 lib bdg; 978-0-531-14798-6 pa; 0-531-14798-3 pa

LC 2007004449

This describes Venus's place in the solar system, its atmosphere and composition, and missions to Venus

This "matches a clearly reasoned, matter-of-fact text to plenty of small but sharply reproduced color photos." SLJ

Includes glossary and bibliographical references

Leedy, Loreen

Messages from Mars; by Loreen Leedy and Andrew Schuerger; illustrated by Loreen Leedy. Holiday House 2006 40p il $16.95

Grades: K 1 2 3　　　523.4

1. Space flight to Mars

ISBN 978-0-8234-1954-8; 0-8234-1954-1

LC 2005-50267

"In 2106 six children, their team leader, and a 'hover-bot' (floating robot) take a voyage to Mars. . . . Along the way, they send messages back home, informally relaying information about space travel and conditions on the red planet. Cartoonlike images of the fictional characters and their spacecraft are digitally combined with photos of Mars. . . . Clever, and a good starting point for those intrigued by Mars." Booklist

Includes glossary

Miller, Ron

Seven wonders of the gas giants and their moons. Twenty-First Century Books 2011 80p il (Seven wonders) lib bdg $33.26

Grades: 5 6 7 8　　　523.4

1. Planets 2. Outer planets -- Juvenile literature

ISBN 978-0-7613-5449-9 lib bdg; 0-7613-5449-2 lib bdg; 9780761372813

LC 2010-15558

"This book describes seven phenomena about the outer planets of the solar system and their moons, including the great red spot of Jupiter and the underground sea of Europa. Index. Grades five to eight." (Sci Books Films)

This "celebrates the most unique features of Jupiter, Saturn, Uranus and Neptune, including companion moons and Saturn's mysterious rings. . . . [This] volume makes basic concepts clear in lively, energetic language that, along with the mesmerizing color photos and artists' renderings of space, will easily captivate a young audience, while up-to-date examples, including discoveries made in the last five years, will only increase the sense of immediacy and excitement." Booklist

Includes glossary and bibliographical references

Seven wonders of the rocky planets and their moons. Twenty-First Century Books 2011 80p il (Seven wonders) lib bdg $33.26

Grades: 4 5 6　　　523.4

1. Planets 2. Inner planets -- Juvenile literature

ISBN 978-0-7613-5448-2 lib bdg; 0-7613-5448-4 lib bdg; 9780761372837

LC 2010-15553

This book shows "views of features on Mercury, Venus, Earth (and its moon), and Mars. Grades five to eight." (Sci Books Films)

This "compares the fascinating diversity of Earth's land masses with those on Mars, Venus and Mercury. . . . [This] volume makes basic concepts clear in lively, energetic language that, along with the mesmerizing color photos and artists' renderings of space, will easily captivate a young audience, while up-to-date examples, including discoveries made in the last five years, will only increase the sense of immediacy and excitement." Booklist

Includes glossary and bibliographical references

Poynter, Margaret

Doomsday rocks from space. Enslow Publishers 2011 48p il (Bizarre science) lib bdg $23.93

Grades: 5 6 7 8　　　523.4

1. Comets 2. Asteroids 3. Meteorites

ISBN 978-0-7660-3673-4; 0-7660-3673-1

LC 2009053601

First published 1996 with title: Killer asteroids

"Aimed at reluctant readers, [this title is] sure to disgust and delight in equal measure. . . . [The title] will pique interest and get kids lining up at the reference desk looking for more. The text is complemented by illustrations and magnified photos of things that you would hope never to see." SLJ

Includes glossary and bibliographical references

Scott, Elaine

★ **When** is a planet not a planet? the story of Pluto. Clarion Books 2007 43p il $17

Grades: 3 4 5 6　　　523.4

1. Planets

ISBN 978-0-618-89832-9; 0-618-89832-8

"Scott takes the 2006 downgrading of Pluto from planet to dwarf planet as a teachable moment for discussing questions such as how the number of planets has changed through the centuries, what can be called a planet, and how scientists come to conclusions—and occasionally change their minds. . . . Beautifully designed, the book includes many well-captioned, color illustrations, from period portraits to NASA images to artist's conceptions." Booklist

Sherman, Josepha

Asteroids, meteors, and comets. Marshall Cavendish Benchmark 2009 64p il (Space!) lib bdg $22.95

Grades: 4 5 6 7　　　523.4

1. Comets 2. Meteors 3. Asteroids

ISBN 978-0-7614-4252-3 lib bdg; 0-7614-4252-9 lib bdg

LC 2008037281

This stands out for its "clear, accurate [presentation] of basic facts punctuated by lively turns of phrase and, sometimes, details not commonly found in the plethora of similar tours of the solar system and beyond." SLJ

Includes glossary and bibliographical references

Neptune. Marshall Cavendish Benchmark 2009 63p il (Space!) lib bdg $22.95

Grades: 4 5 6 7   **523.4**
  1. Neptune (Planet)
  ISBN 978-0-7614-4246-2 lib bdg; 0-7614-4246-4 lib bdg; 9780761445562

                   LC 2008037279
"Describes Neptune, including its history, its composition, and its role in the solar system." Publisher's note
Includes glossary and bibliographical references

Uranus. Marshall Cavendish Benchmark 2010 63p il (Space!) lib bdg $22.95
Grades: 4 5 6 7   **523.4**
  1. Astronomers 2. Uranus (Planet)
  ISBN 978-0-7614-4248-6 lib bdg; 0-7614-4248-0 lib bdg; 9780761445586

                   LC 2008037274
"Describes Uranus, including its history, its composition, and its role in the solar system." Publisher's note
Includes glossary and bibliographical references

Sparrow, Giles
  Destination Uranus, Neptune, and Pluto. PowerKids Press 2010 32p il (Destination solar system) lib bdg $23.95; pa $10
Grades: 3 4 5 6   **523.4**
  1. Uranus (Planet) 2. Neptune (Planet) 3. Pluto (Dwarf planet)
  ISBN 978-1-4358-3446-0 lib bdg; 978-1-4358-3463-7 pa

                   LC 2009-2985
Examines the outer planets, and discusses their moons, interiors, atmospheres, locations, and exploration.
  Includes glossary

Winrich, Ralph
  Pluto; a dwarf planet. by Ralph Winrich; revised and updated by Thomas K. Adamson. rev and updated; Capstone Press 2007 24p il (First facts: the solar system) lib bdg $21.26
Grades: K 1 2 3   **523.4**
  1. Pluto (Dwarf planet)
  ISBN 978-1-4296-0727-8 lib bdg; 1-4296-0727-0 lib bdg

                   LC 2006037427
First published 2005
This describes the dwarf planet Pluto, as well as other dwarf planets Ceres and Eris
"Information present in the simply phrased [narrative] is supplemented by boxes of facts . . . and sharply reproduced photos or other art." SLJ
  Includes glossary and bibliographical references

523.43   Mars

Rusch, Elizabeth
  ★ The **mighty** Mars rovers; the incredible adventures of Spirit and Opportunity. by Elizabeth Rusch. Houghton Mifflin Books for Children 2012 79 p. ill. (chiefly col.) (hardcover) $18.99; (hardcover) $18.99
Grades: 4 5 6   **523.43**
  1. Mars probes 2. Mars (Planet) -- Exploration 3.

Astronautics -- Juvenile literature
  ISBN 054747881X; 9780547478814

                   LC 2011012159
In this book, "[Elizabeth] Rusch covers not only the scientific aspects of Mars exploration but also the personalities of the people who made it happen, and profiles the rovers themselves, Spirit and Opportunity." She looks at "the behind-the-scenes efforts of launching a scientific mission." Also included are "[f]ull-color photographs," a glossary, and a list of further resources. (School Library Journal)
  Includes bibliographical references (p. 76), discography (p. 78), filmograophy (p. 78), and index.

523.45   Jupiter

Mist, Rosalind
  Jupiter and Saturn; by Rosalind Mist. QEB Pub. 2012 24 p. col. ill. (Up in space) (hardcover) $25.65
Grades: K 1 2   **523.45**
  1. Saturn (Planet) -- Juvenile literature 2. Jupiter (Planet) -- Juvenile literature
  ISBN 1609923219; 9781609923211

                   LC 2012007023
This book by Rosalind Mist, part of the Up in Space series, looks at Jupiter and Saturn. "Each planet is discussed individually, while a separate page on the solar system shows the relative size of the planets." Photographs from the Hubble Space Telescope and other space missions are included. (Booklist)

523.46   Saturn

Miller, Ron
  Saturn; Ron Miller. Twenty-First Century Books 2003 80p ill. (library) $27.93
Grades: 5 6 7 8   **523.46**
  1. Saturn (Planet)
  ISBN 9780761323600; 0761323600
Chronicles the discovery and exploration of the planet Saturn and discusses its rings and moons, its place in the solar system, and more.
  "Concepts are explained clearly, and helpful diagrams and carefully chosen illustrations assist understanding." SLJ
  Includes bibliographical references

523.49   Trans-Neptunian objects

Devorkin, David
  Pluto's secret; an icy world's tale of discovery. by Margaret Weitekamp with David DeVorkin; illustrated by Diane Kidd. Abrams Books for Young Readers 2013 40 p. (reinforced) $16.95
Grades: 2 3 4   **523.49**
  1. Picture books for children 2. Pluto (Dwarf planet) -- Juvenile literature
  ISBN 1419704230; 9781419704239

                   LC 2012033546
This children's picture book looks at Pluto. "The ninth planet from its discovery in 1930 to its demotion in 2006, Pluto has been revealing more of its 'secrets' as technology

improved, and is now considered a 'dwarf planet' in the Kuiper belt. . . . The book provides a factual history of our faraway 'dwarf,' and on its companion icy worlds, and on the discovery of Kuiper-like bands around other stars." (School Library Journal)

Includes bibliographical references.

523.6   Comets

Simon, Seymour

★ **Comets,** meteors, and asteroids. Morrow Junior Bks. 1994 un il hardcover o.p. pa $6.95

Grades: 3 4 5 6   **523.6**

1. Comets 2. Meteors 3. Asteroids

ISBN 0-688-15843-9 pa

LC 93-51251

"Simon presents basic information about comets, meteors, and asteroids in an attractive oversize book. . . . Blocks of text appear in fairly large type, usually facing a full-page illustration. . . . Simon writes in plain language, without talking down to his audience. The intriguing photographs include shots of comets and meteor showers in the sky, a meteorite in Antarctica, and an enormous impact crater in Arizona." Booklist

523.7   Sun

Branley, Franklyn Mansfield

★ The **sun,** our nearest star; by Franklyn M. Branley; illustrated by Edward Miller. HarperCollins Pubs. 2002 25p il (Let's-read-and-find-out science) hardcover o.p. pa $4.95

Grades: K 1 2   **523.7**

1. Sun

ISBN 0-06-028534-6; 0-06-028535-4 lib bdg; 0-06-445202-6 pa

LC 2001-24951

A revised and newly illustrated edition of the title first published 1961

Describes the sun and how it provides the light and energy which allow plant and animal life to exist on the earth

"This edition marks the third incarnation of an old standby. . . . The gently edited text reads better than the old one. The new design features a larger format, bolder typography, and eye-catching artwork." Booklist

Capaccio, George

The **sun**. Marshall Cavendish Benchmark 2009 64p il (Space!) lib bdg $22.95

Grades: 4 5 6 7   **523.7**

1. Sun

ISBN 978-0-7614-4242-4 lib bdg; 0-7614-4242-1 lib bdg

LC 2008037275

This stands out for its "clear, accurate [presentation] of basic facts punctuated by lively turns of phrase and, sometimes, details not commonly found in the plethora of similar tours of the solar system and beyond." SLJ

Includes glossary and bibliographical references

Carson, Mary Kay

Far-out guide to the sun. Enslow Publishers 2010 48p il (Far-out guide to the solar system) lib bdg $23.93; pa $7.95

Grades: 3 4 5   **523.7**

1. Sun

ISBN 978-0-7660-3179-1 lib bdg; 0-7660-3179-9 lib bdg; 978-1-59845-180-1 pa; 1-59845-180-4 pa

LC 2008050039

"Presents information about the sun, including fast facts, history, and technology used to study it." Publisher's note

Includes glossary and bibliographical references

Gibbons, Gail

Sun up, sun down; written and illustrated by Gail Gibbons. Harcourt Brace Jovanovich 1983 un il hardcover o.p. pa $7

Grades: K 1 2 3   **523.7**

1. Sun

ISBN 0-15-282781-1; 0-15-282782-X pa

LC 82-23420

"The illustrations clarify the text with bold, clear drawings in full color." SLJ

Landau, Elaine

The **sun**; [by] Elaine Landau. Children's Press 2007 48p il (True book) lib bdg $26; pa $6.95

Grades: 2 3 4   **523.7**

1. Sun

ISBN 978-0-531-12568-7 lib bdg; 0-531-12568-8 lib bdg; 978-0-531-14796-2 pa; 0-531-14796-7 pa

LC 2007012259

This describes the sun as a star, the sun's place in the solar system, its relationship to Earth, and how astronomers study the sun

This "matches a clearly reasoned, matter-of-fact text to plenty of small but sharply reproduced color photos." SLJ

Includes glossary and bibliographical references

Wells, Robert E.

★ **Why** do elephants need the sun? Albert Whitman & Co. 2010 un il $16.99

Grades: 2 3 4   **523.7**

1. Water 2. Photosynthesis 3. Sun

ISBN 978-0-8075-9081-2; 0-8075-9081-9

This "book, on the sun, provides an approachable introduction to the subject while laying the groundwork for understanding topics (gravity, nuclear fusion) that students will tackle in later years. Beginning with the sun itself, the presentation quickly comes down to earth in a child-friendly way, with an elephant who needs our closest star. . . . The discussion of gravity starts with the elephant, then shifts to the solar system and the sun's core. Wells also shows how people have used the sun. . . . The book's naive ink-and-watercolor illustrations are often playful in approach. Simple diagrams are often used to clarify more abstract concepts. . . . This title offers an appealing introduction to the sun, as well as a solid stepping-stone toward scientific literacy." Booklist

523.8   Stars

Abramson, Andra Serlin

Inside stars; by Andra Serlin Abramson and Mordecai-Mark Mac Low. Sterling Children's Books 2011 48p il (Inside . . .) $16.95; pa $9.95

Grades: 5 6 7 8   **523.8**
1. Stars
ISBN 978-1-4027-7709-7; 1-4027-7709-4; 978-1-4027-8162-9 pa; 1-4027-8162-8 pa
LC 2011283564

Presents an illustrated overview of stars, including information on how they affect the Earth, how scientists study them, how they are classified, how they form and die, and specific information about our star, the Sun.

"On full but not crowded-looking pages, the captions, vocabulary words and digestible blocks of text are set into and around an engagingly diverse mix of cutaway views, digital paintings and eye-widening deep-space photographs. . . . There's plenty here to stimulate both random browsers and confirmed young sky watchers." Kirkus

Includes bibliographical references

Aguilar, David A.

Super stars; the biggest, hottest, brightest, and most explosive stars in the Milky Way. National Geographic 2010 48p il $16.95; lib bdg $27.90

Grades: 4 5 6 7   **523.8**
1. Stars 2. Supergiant stars
ISBN 978-1-4263-0601-3; 1-4263-0601-6; 978-1-4263-0602-0 lib bdg; 1-4263-0602-4 lib bdg
LC 2009-37124

"Pairing dramatic space art with souped-up prose, Aguilar introduces more than a dozen types of stars and stellar phenomena. . . . Aside from the occasional alien or interstellar spacecraft set against glowing star fields, the information in both pictures and texts sticks to the facts, accurately reflecting current knowledge without ever coming close to turning into a dry recitation of data. . . . [This is an] unusually exuberant ticket to ride for young sky watchers and armchair space travelers." SLJ

Includes glossary and bibliographical references

Asimov, Isaac

The **life** and death of stars; by Isaac Asimov. rev and updated ed; Gareth Stevens Pub. 2005 32p il lib bdg $24.67

Grades: 4 5 6   **523.8**
1. Stars
ISBN 0-8368-3967-6
LC 2004-57842

This "begins with the birth of stars in dust cloud nurseries; goes on to profile the different types of stars; describes supernovas, neutron stars, and other late-stage developments; then closes with an account of our Sun's probable fate. . . . [This is an] excellent collection [enhancer]." SLJ

Includes bibliographical references

Branley, Franklyn Mansfield

The **Big** Dipper; by Franklyn M. Branley; illustrated by Molly Coxe. rev ed; HarperCollins Pubs. 1991 32p il (Let's-read-and-find-out science book) hardcover o.p. pa $4.95

Grades: K 1   **523.8**
1. Ursa Major
ISBN 0-06-445100-3 pa
LC 90-31199

A revised and newly illustrated edition of the title first published 1962

Explains basic facts about the Big Dipper, including which stars make up the constellation, how its position changes in the sky, and how it points to the North Star

Croswell, Ken

★ The **lives** of stars. Boyds Mills Press 2009 72p il $19.95

Grades: 5 6 7 8   **523.8**
1. Stars 2. Astronomy
ISBN 978-1-59078-582-9; 1-59078-582-7
LC 2008033913

"Extensive, detailed information about stars is coupled with amazing colorful photographs, many from the Hubble Space Telescope, in this stunning book. Packed with facts about the stars and their life cycle, the text often relates them to situations or objects familiar to readers." SLJ

Includes glossary

DeCristofano, Carolyn Cinami

★ A **black** hole is not a hole; Carolyn Cinami DeCristofano; Illustrated by Michael Carroll. Charlesbridge 2012 v, 74 p.p col ill. (reinforced for library use) $18.95

Grades: 4 5 6 7   **523.8**
1. Stars 2. Universe 3. Black holes (Astronomy) -- Juvenile literature
ISBN 9781570917837; 9781570917844
LC 2010022764

In this non-fiction children's book, Carolyn Cinami De-Cristofano discusses black holes. "Covering the life cycles of stars; the formation of black holes and weird optical and physical effects associated with them; more recent revelations of super-sized black holes at the centers of galaxies; and the general effects of mass on space, light, and matter, she presents a . . . picture of the strange structure and stranger physics of black holes." (Booklist)

Jackson, Ellen B.

★ The **mysterious** universe; supernovae, dark energy, and black holes. text by Ellen Jackson; photographs and illustrations by Nic Bishop. Houghton Mifflin 2008 60p il (Scientists in the field) $18

Grades: 5 6 7 8   **523.8**
1. Supernovas 2. Black holes (Astronomy)
ISBN 978-0-618-56325-8; 0-618-56325-3
LC 2007-41165

This "follows prominent astronomer Alex Filippenko and associates from the Keck Observatory in Hawaii to the Lick Observatory in California on a hunt for supernovae and related large-scale astronomical phenomena. . . . Along with depicting the scientists, the images also include massive telescopes and photos or digital simulations of galaxies, exploding stars, and other astronomical phenomena." SLJ

Includes glossary and bibliographical references

Jefferis, David

The **stars**; glowing spheres in the sky. Crabtree Pub. 2009 32p il (Exploring our solar system) lib bdg $26.60; pa $8.95

Grades: 3 4 5   **523.8**
1. Stars
ISBN 978-0-7787-3726-1 lib bdg; 0-7787-3726-8 lib
bdg; 978-0-7787-3743-8 pa; 0-7787-3743-8 pa
LC 2008-46250
"Provides an interesting, well-illustrated introduction."
Sci Books Films
Inlcudes glossary

Kim, F. S.
★ **Constellations**. Children's Press 2009 48p il (True
book) lib bdg $26; pa $6.95
Grades: 3 4 5   **523.8**
1. Constellations
ISBN 978-0-531-16895-0 lib bdg; 0-531-16895-6 lib
bdg; 978-0-531-22802-9 pa; 0-531-22802-9 pa
LC 2008050629
Though this title "dabbles in the science of planetary orbits and early stargazing gear, . . . it mostly focuses on the
rich myths surrounding the constellations, in one illustration
transforming the night sky into a draped tapestry of monsters
and gods. . . . Short but solid back matter closes out [this]
impressive [offering]." Booklist

Mack, Gail
The **stars**. Marshall Cavendish Benchmark 2009 64p
il (Space!) lib bdg $32.79
Grades: 4 5 6 7   **523.8**
1. Stars 2. Galaxies
ISBN 978-0-7614-4250-9 lib bdg; 0-7614-4250-2
lib bdg
LC 2009014655
This stands out for its "clear, accurate [presentation] of
basic facts punctuated by lively turns of phrase and, sometimes, details not commonly found in the plethora of similar
tours of the solar system and beyond." SLJ
Includes glossary and bibliographical references

Miller, Ron
Seven wonders beyond the solar system. Twenty-First
Century Books 2011 80p il (Seven wonders) lib bdg
$33.26
Grades: 5 6 7 8   **523.8**
1. Extrasolar planets
ISBN 978-0-7613-5454-3; 0-7613-5454-9
LC 2010028446
This "discusses how stars and galaxies form and how
scientists search for 'the most Earthlike planet,' as well
as the noteworthy nebulae, pulsars, and superclusters. . . .
[This] volume makes basic concepts clear in lively, energetic
language that, along with the mesmerizing color photos and
artists' renderings of space, will easily captivate a young
audience, while up-to-date examples, including discoveries
made in the last five years, will only increase the sense of
immediacy and excitement." Booklist
Includes glossary and bibliographical references

Mitton, Jacqueline
★ **Once** upon a starry night; a book of constellations.
[illustrated by] Christina Balit. National Geographic 2004
un il $16.95

Grades: K 1 2 3   **523.8**
1. Constellations 2. Classical mythology
ISBN 0-7922-6332-4
LC 2003-10993
First published 2003 in the United Kingdom
Presents facts about stars, nebulas, galaxies, and constellations and recounts the Greek myths that provided wide-
ly-known names for ten constellations, from Andromeda
to Pegasus.
"Although the stories are quite short, Mitton's vivid
word choices make the text as dynamic as Balit's striking
pictures. Partly abstract and partly representational, the artwork features bold figures of mythological characters with
silver-foil stars highlighting the points of light that make up
the constellations." Booklist

Rau, Dana Meachen
Black holes; by Dana Meachen Rau. Compass Point
Books 2005 32p il (Our solar system) $22.60
Grades: 3 4 5   **523.8**
1. Black holes (Astronomy)
ISBN 0-7565-0849-5
LC 2004-15567
"Rightly noting . . . that black holes by their very nature
can neither be seen nor directly measured, [the author] dis-
cusses what we can infer and theorize from indirect observa-
tions, then closes with a revealing 2004 discovery. . . . [This
earns] high marks for visual appeal, and for clear, specific
presentation of material." SLJ
Includes glossary and bibliographical references

Rey, H. A.
★ **Find** the constellations; 2nd ed.; Houghton Mifflin
Harcourt 2008 72p il $20; pa $9.99
Grades: 3 4 5 6   **523.8**
1. Stars 2. Constellations
ISBN 978-0-547-13140-5; 0-547-13140-2; 978-0-547-
13178-8 pa; 0-547-13178-X pa
First published 1954
"This much-needed update of Rey's classic work . . . features a cleaner typeface but retains the layout and most of the
graphics of the previous edition. . . . The primary update . .
. involves the change in Pluto's status; a great touch is the
inclusion of definitions for 'planet' and 'dwarf planet.' . . .
Statistical data . . . are updated; the planet finder now covers
the years 2007 through 2016; and there is a new list of books
for further reading. With its enduring appeal, current information, and exceptional sky charts . . . this revision should
be an essential purchase for all libraries." SLJ

Rockwell, Anne F.
Our stars; written and illustrated by Anne Rockwell.
Silver Whistle Bks. 1999 un il hardcover o.p. pa $6.99
Grades: K 1 2   **523.8**
1. Stars 2. Planets 3. Astronomy -- Juvenile literature
ISBN 0-15-201868-9; 0-15-216360-0 pa
LC 97-49518
A simple introduction to the stars, planets, and
outer space
"This book clearly explains many science facts without
'talking down' to youngsters. The storybook-style illustra-
tions, . . . invite children to look at the night sky and think
about the information presented in the text." Sci Books Films

Than, Ker
★ **Stars**. Children's Press 2009 48p il (True book)
lib bdg $26; pa $6.95
Grades: 3 4 5   **523.8**
1. Stars
ISBN 978-0-531-16899-8 lib bdg; 0-531-16899-9 lib
bdg; 978-0-531-22806-7 pa; 0-531-22806-1 pa
LC 2008051630
This introduction to stars "is simply gorgeous. The
ghostly veils of the Cat's Eye Nebula, the ominous gas pillars of the Eagle Nebula, the coral-reef depths of the Crab
Nebula—the only complaint will be that the photos aren't
bigger. The diagrams (including the cradle-to-grave 'A
Star's Life') are remarkably educational. Short but solid
back matter closes out [this] impressive [offering]." Booklist

Waxman, Laura Hamilton
Exploring black holes. Lerner Publications Company
2011 40p il (What's amazing about space?) lib bdg $27.93
Grades: 4 5 6   **523.8**
1. Black holes (Astronomy)
ISBN 978-0-7613-5442-0; 0-7613-5442-5
LC 2010035378
This book about black holes in space is "written in
simple language, [and] illustrated nicely. . . . The information presented is factually correct. . . . Every page includes
a well-chosen illustration or photograph." Sci Books Films

525   Earth (Astronomical geography)

Bailey, Jacqui
Sun up, sun down; the story of day and night. written
by Jacqui Bailey; illustrated by Matthew Lilly. Picture Window Books 2004 31p il (Science works) lib bdg $23.93
Grades: 2 3 4   **525**
1. Day 2. Night
ISBN 1-4048-0567-2
LC 2003-20119
Follows the sun from dawn to dusk to explain how light
rays travel, how shadows are formed, how the moon lights
up the night sky, and more
This "excellent science [book explains its subject] lucidly and sometimes amusingly. . . . Children will be illuminated and engaged." SLJ
Includes bibliographical references

Carson, Mary Kay
Far-out guide to Earth. Enslow Publishers 2010 48p
il (Far-out guide to the solar system) lib bdg $23.93; pa
$7.95
Grades: 3 4 5   **525**
1. Earth
ISBN 978-0-7660-3182-1 lib bdg; 0-7660-3182-9 lib
bdg; 978-1-59845-183-2 pa; 1-59845-183-9 pa
LC 2008049781
"Lively writing with specific facts systematically pre-
sented and plenty of dramatic space art and photography add
up to a winning formula." SLJ
Includes glossary and bibliographical references

Gibbons, Gail
The **reasons** for seasons. Holiday House 1995 un il
$16.95; pa $6.95
Grades: K 1 2 3   **525**
1. Seasons
ISBN 0-8234-1174-5; 0-590-90735-2 pa
LC 94-32904
"Gibbons uses simple words and clear, colorful pictures
to explain the seasons, the solstices, and the equinoxes. Be-
sides discussing the earth's tilt and orbit, she also comments
on what people and animals do in each season of the year."
Booklist

The **seasons** of Arnold's apple tree. Harcourt Brace
Jovanovich 1984 un il $17; pa $7
Grades: PreK K 1 2   **525**
1. Trees -- Fiction 2. Seasons -- Fiction 3. Apple --
Juvenile literature
ISBN 0-15-271246-1; 0-15-271245-3 pa
LC 84-4484
Arnold enjoys his apple tree through the changing year:
its springtime blossoms, the swing and tree-house it supports, its summer shade, its autumn harvest; in the winter,
the tree's branches hold strings of popcorn and berries for
the birds
"Two major concepts emerge here, the first being the
passage of the seasons, the second the valuable resource Arnold has in his apple tree. . . . Gibbons' crisp pictures ensure
that the multifaceted lesson is explicit, bright and cheery."
Booklist

Hicks, Terry Allan
Earth and the moon. Marshall Cavendish Benchmark
2009 64p il (Space!) lib bdg $22.95
Grades: 4 5 6 7   **525**
1. Earth 2. Moon
ISBN 978-0-7614-4254-7 lib bdg; 0-7614-4254-5
lib bdg
LC 2009014663
"Describes Earth and its Moon, including their history,
their composition, and their roles in the solar system." Pub-
lisher's note
Includes glossary and bibliographical references

Karas, G. Brian
★ **On** Earth; written and illustrated by G. Brian Karas.
Putnam 2005 un il $16.99
Grades: K 1 2   **525**
1. Earth
ISBN 0-399-24025-X
LC 2004-18204
"Karas covers the earth's rotation and revolution, space
and time, hemispheres, and gravity. The spare text alternates
between technical descriptions and personal experiences.
Artistic renderings of the earth and its cycles introduce dia-
grams and offer concrete images showing what happens as
day turns to night, seasons change, and the earth rotates on
its axis." Horn Book Guide

Landau, Elaine
Earth; [by] Elaine Landau. Children's Press 2007 48p
il (True book) lib bdg $26; pa $6.95

Grades: 2 3 4 **525**

1. Earth

ISBN 978-0-531-12558-8 lib bdg; 0-531-12558-0 lib bdg; 978-0-531-14788-7 pa; 0-531-14788-6 pa

LC 2007012278

Describes the planet Earth, exploring its composition, the conditions which support life, theories about how it formed, and its relationship with the moon

This "matches a clearly reasoned, matter-of-fact text to plenty of small but sharply reproduced color photos." SLJ

Includes glossary and bibliographical references

Martin, Bill

I love our Earth; [by] Bill Martin, Jr., and Michael Sampson; photographs by Dan Lipow. Charlesbridge 2006 un il $14.95

Grades: PreK K 1 2 **525**

1. Earth

ISBN 978-1-58089-106-6; 1-58089-106-3

LC 2005-06008

"Martin's simple poem celebrates the colors of varied landscapes and the glories of the seasons. Each line of text appears on half a page, under a photo of a child. The rest of each spread is devoted to a panoramic vista. The boys and girls, of varying ages, come from many racial and ethnic groups from around the globe." SLJ

Miller, Ron

Earth and the moon. 21st Cent. Bks. (Brookfield) 2003 96p il (Worlds beyond) lib bdg $25.90

Grades: 5 6 7 8 **525**

1. Earth 2. Moon

ISBN 0-7613-2358-9

LC 2001-8479

Chronicles the origin, evolution, and exploration of the Earth and the Moon, and discusses their composition, their place in our solar system, and more

This is illustrated "with a mix of NASA photos and wide-angle, computer-generated art. . . . Students with a serious interest in the physical history of the Earth and its moon will be engrossed by his account of our planet's first few billion years, the Moon's probable origin, and the rise of life." SLJ

Includes glossary and bibliographical references

Ride, Sally K.

Mission: planet Earth; our world and its climate--and how humans are changing them. [by] Sally Ride & Tam O'Shaughnessy. Roaring Brook Press 2009 80p il map (Sally Ride science) $19.95

Grades: 5 6 7 8 **525**

1. Climate -- Environmental aspects 2. Global warming -- Juvenile literature 3. Climatic changes -- Juvenile literature 4. Nature -- Effect of human beings on -- Juvenile literature

ISBN 978-1-59643-310-6; 1-59643-310-8

LC 2009-29253

"This environmental-science primer introduces a range of important concepts necessary to understand climate change and global warming. Topics include the carbon cycle, water cycle, long-range carbon emissions data, biological evidence of climate change, and much more. The authors have an extensive background in science education, and their text exhibits an excellent balance of concept thoroughness with ease of comprehension. Attractive photographs

and colorful graphics, including many charts and diagrams, are incorporated throughout." SLJ

Ross, Michael Elsohn

Earth cycles; illustrated by Gustav Moore. Millbrook Press 2001 un il (Cycles) hardcover o.p. pa $7.95

Grades: K 1 2 3 **525**

1. Geology

ISBN 0-7613-1815-1; 0-7613-1977-8 pa

LC 00-41860

"Ross discusses Earth's daily cycle of light and dark, the thirteen lunar cycles, and Earth's yearly trip around the sun. The simple text provides very basic information about periodicity and uses familiar examples to introduce new concepts. . . . Pleasing watercolors expand the text." Horn Book Guide

Simon, Seymour

★ **Earth**: our planet in space; rev ed; Simon & Schuster Bks. for Young Readers 2003 un il $17.95

Grades: 4 5 6 7 **525**

1. Earth

ISBN 0-689-83562-0

LC 2001-31304

First published 1984 by Four Winds Press

This describes the relationship between the Earth, the sun, and the moon and explains the seasons, day and night, the atmosphere, and changes in the planet's surface. Illustrated with photographs taken from space

Wells, Robert E.

What's so special about planet Earth? Albert Whitman & Co. 2009 un il $16.99

Grades: K 1 2 3 **525**

1. Earth 3. Sun

ISBN 978-0-8075-8815-4; 0-8075-8815-6

LC 2008056045

"Wells elaborates on the idea that our planet is 'a pretty good place for people to live' by, first, giving each of the other seven planets a quick flyby, then explaining how Earth's water and atmosphere create conditions suitable for life. His lively cartoon illustrations feature a pair of overall-clad young explorers (and a spaniel) boarding a jalopy-like spaceship for their spin around the solar system, then landing back on their home planet to demonstrate recycling, energy conservation, and other environmentally friendly activities." Booklist

526 Mathematical geography

Borden, Louise

Sea clocks; the story of longitude. illustrated by Erik Blegvad. Margaret K. McElderry Bks. 2003 un il $18.95

Grades: 3 4 5 6 **526**

1. Longitude 2. Navigation 3. Clocks and watches 4. Clock and watch makers

ISBN 0-689-84216-3

LC 00-45599

This "picture book introduces John Harrison, the 18th-century English carpenter turned clockmaker who spent more than 40 years perfecting a device that solved the centuries-old problem of determining longitude. . . . The writing has a measured pace that helps readers to keep the details straight and the scientific concepts are clearly explained and smoothly incorporated into the text. Blegvad's precise illustrations create a strong sense of time and place." SLJ

Galat, Joan Marie

The **discovery** of longitude; by Joan Marie Galat; illustrated by Wes Lowe. Pelican Pub. Co. 2012 32 p. (hardcover: alk. paper) $16.99

Grades: 3 4 5   526

1. Inventors 2. Longitude 3. Chronometers 4. Measuring instruments 5. Picture books for children 6. Chronometers -- History 7. Longitude -- Measurement -- History 8. Clock and watch makers -- Great Britain -- Biography

ISBN 1455616370; 9781455616374; 9781455616381

LC 2011052911

This children's book tells "the story of inventing a watch to compute longitude aboard the great sailing ships." Joan Galat explains that 300 years ago, the British government sought a way to measure longitude that was better than the current two clock system. "Enter John Harrison, carpenter and clockmaker, who toiled for over 40 years to make just such a clock." (Kirkus)

Lasky, Kathryn

★ The **man** who made time travel; pictures by Kevin Hawkes. Farrar, Straus & Giroux 2003 un il $17

Grades: 3 4 5   526

1. Longitude 2. Navigation 3. Clocks and watches 4. Mechanical engineers 5. Clock and watch makers 6. Chronometers -- History -- Juvenile literature

ISBN 0-374-34788-3

LC 2001-33266

Describes the need for sailors to be able to determine their position at sea and the efforts of John Harrison, an eighteenth century man who spent his life refining instruments to enable them to do this

"With Hawkes's luminous full-color paintings on every page, its clear science, and its compelling social commentary, this title is not to be missed." SLJ

Includes bibliographical references

526.9 Surveying

Petersen, Christine

The **surveyor**. Marshall Cavendish Benchmark 2010 48p il (Colonial people) lib bdg $29.93

Grades: 3 4 5 6   526.9

1. Surveying

ISBN 978-0-7614-4805-1; 0-7614-4805-5

This describes the life of a colonial surveyor and his importance to the community, as well as everyday life, responsibilities, and social practices during that time.

"The type font, just slightly larger than usual, makes the text very visually appealing. . . . [The] book is liberally illustrated with artwork dating from the colonial period . . . [and] information boxes offer supplemental material." Libr Media Connect

Includes glossary and bibliographical references

529 Chronology

Adamson, Thomas K.

How do you measure time? by Thomas K. and Heather Adamson. Capstone Press 2011 32p il (Measure it!) lib bdg $25.99

Grades: PreK K 1 2   529

1. Time 2. Calendars 3. Measurement

ISBN 978-1-4296-4459-4; 1-4296-4459-1

LC 2010002787

Simple text and color photographs describe the units and tools used to measure time.

"The large picture-book format and inviting color photographs make [this] clearly written [title a] welcome [addition]. . . . The [author uses] common objects, giving readers recognizable points of reference. . . . Solid." SLJ

Includes glossary and bibliographical references

Formichelli, Linda

Timekeeping; Explore the History and Science of Telling Time With 15 Projects. by Linda Formichelli, W. Eric Martin; illustrated by Sam Carbaugh. Independent Pub Group 2012 128 p. (hardcover) $21.95

Grades: 4 5 6 7 8   529

1. Time -- Juvenile literature 2. Science -- Experiments -- Juvenile literature

ISBN 1619301369; 9781619301368

This juvenile activity book, by Linda Formichelli, W. Eric Martin, with illustrations by Sam Carbaugh, is part of the "Build It Yourself" series. It teaches "the cultural history of time" through providing several activities and projects such as "making a shadow clock, tracking time like an ancient Egyptian, using a protractor to create a sundial, measuring time with water, and making a candle clock." (Publisher's note)

Gardner, Robert

It's about time! Science projects; How long does it take? Enslow Pubs. 2003 48p il (Sensational science experiments) $18.95

Grades: 3 4 5 6   529

1. Time 2. Science projects 3. Clocks and watches 4. Experiments 5. Science -- Experiments 6. Time measurements -- Experiments

ISBN 0-7660-2012-6

LC 2002-4621

This offers 18 experiments in time measurement

This is an "approachable, hands-on-book. . . . This volume is not casual reading; it deserves and requires some attention as well as adult guidance and will be rewarding to those who make the effort." Sci Books Films

Includes bibliographical references and index

Gleick, Beth

Time is when; [by] Beth Gleick; illustrated by Marthe Jocelyn. Tundra Books 2008 un il $15.95

Grades: PreK K 1   529

1. Time

ISBN 978-0-88776-870-5; 0-88776-870-9

A newly illustrated edition of the title first published 1960 by Rand McNally

"Gleick successfully answers the age-old question, 'What is time?.'. . . Breaking down time into all of its components, the author explains each one, using events that children face daily. . . . The story then builds upon each part of time as it is woven back together to make up the four seasons, explaining that a year is the time between one birthday and the next—a concept readers are sure to grasp. Jocelyn's illustrations give this account a fresh look with multicultural characters and digital clocks while still keeping an old-fashioned, nostalgic feel in the paper and fabric collages, which have bright colors and fun, busy patterns. The simple, lyrical text has a timeless quality that works well as a read-aloud and is still easy enough for beginning readers to work out on their own." SLJ

Hutchins, H. J.

A **second** is a hiccup; a child's book of time. by Hazel Hutchins; illustrated by Kady MacDonald Denton. Arthur A. Levine Books 2007 un il $16.99
Grades: PreK K 1 2   **529**
1. Time
ISBN 0-439-83106-7
LC 2006007561

"The abstract concept of time is explained in child-friendly terms. . . . Denton's charming watercolor-and-ink vignettes, showing three friends interacting with one another and with their families, celebrate their joys and accomplishments with warmth and affection. The lyrical, rhyming text answers deceptively simple childhood questions with great flair." SLJ

Jenkins, Martin

The **time** book; a brief history from lunar calendars to atomic clocks. illustrated by Richard Holland. Candlewick Press 2009 57p il map lib bdg $18.99
Grades: 4 5 6 7   **529**
1. Time 2. Calendars 3. Clocks and watches
ISBN 978-0-7636-4112-2 lib bdg; 0-7636-4112-X lib bdg
LC 2008-19706

"Conversational text, whimsical mixed-media artwork, and elegant book design combine to present an informative and entertaining romp through time." SLJ

Jenkins, Steve

★ **Just** a second. Houghton Mifflin Books for Children 2011 un il $16.99
Grades: PreK K 1 2   **529**
1. Time 2. Nature
ISBN 978-0-618-70896-3; 0-618-70896-0
LC 2011002104

This non-fiction picture book explores time and how we think about it in a different way—as a series of events in the natural world (some of them directly observable, others not) that take place in a given unit of time.

"Jenkins brings fresh perspective to the passage of time in a thought-provoking picture book that features his typically elegant cut-paper collages. . . . Back matter offers information about life spans, population growth, and Earth's history. This subtly philosophical examination of time, scale, and the mechanics of life is all but certain to leave readers reconsidering the world and their place in it." Publ Wkly

Koscielniak, Bruce

★ **About** time; a first look at time and clocks. by Bruce Koscielniak. Houghton Mifflin 2004 un il map $16

Grades: 3 4 5   **529**
1. Time 2. Calendars 3. Clocks and watches 4. Time measurements
ISBN 0-618-39668-3
LC 2003-17469

Describes the concept of time and how it has been measured throughout history, using water clocks, sundials, calendars, and atomic vibrations.

"Koscielniak gives an instructive yet entertaining march through the ages. . . . Attractive watercolor illustrations in green and tan tones enhance the text." SLJ

Maestro, Betsy

The **story** of clocks and calendars; marking a millennium. illustrated by Giulio Maestro. Lothrop, Lee & Shepard Bks. 1999 48p il hardcover o.p. pa $9.99
Grades: 3 4 5 6   **529**
1. Time 2. Calendars 3. Clocks and watches 4. Millennium -- Juvenile literature
ISBN 0-688-14548-5; 0-688-14549-3 lib bdg; 0-06-058945-0 pa
LC 98-21305

"This overview of timekeeping begins with prehistoric 'calendar sticks' and stone structures, and continues through today's ultra-precise atomic clocks. The text takes a broad multicultural approach, showing how science, history, and societal differences have influenced the calendar; the color illustrations are executed in styles that match the eras and cultures discussed in the volume." Horn Book Guide

Murphy, Stuart J.

★ **It's** about time! illustrated by John Speirs. HarperCollins Publishers 2005 33p il (MathStart) $15.99; pa $4.99
Grades: K 1 2   **529**
1. Day 2. Time 3. Night
ISBN 0-06-055768-0; 0-06-055769-9 pa
LC 2003-27524

"Each page shows an analog clock and a digital clock displaying the time, from seven o'clock one morning through the day and night to seven the next morning. The illustrations show the child's activities and, in the night, his dreams. . . . Soft pencil drawings deliniate the rounded forms of children engaged in their daily activities. The rich colors of the washes glow against the white backgrounds." Booklist

Rodeo time; by Stuart J. Murphy; illustrated by David T. Wenzel. HarperCollins 2006 33p il (MathStart) $15.99; pa $4.99
Grades: 2 3 4   **529**
1. Time 2. Rodeos
ISBN 0-06-055779-6; 0-06-055778-8 pa
LC 2005002665

"Katie and Cameron visit a rodeo with their uncle, Cactus Joe. . . . Joe gives Katie and Cameron some chores and activities, and Katie makes out a schedule to keep track of them all. Then, Katie and Cameron have to keep watch so that they don't miss any of the rodeo events. . . . The short length, light tone, and bright illustrations will help put across the concept." Booklist

Includes bibliographical references

Nagda, Ann Whitehead

Chimp math; learning about time from a baby chimpanzee. by Ann Whitehead Nagda and Cindy Bickel. Holt & Co. 2002 29p il $16.95

Grades: 2 3 4   **529**

1. Time 2. Chimpanzees

ISBN 0-8050-6674-8

LC 00-57529

"The details of the chimp's young life will fascinate readers. . . . The time lines, in particular, illuminate the narrative and can lead to classroom projects." SLJ

Older, Jules

Telling time; how to tell time on digital and analog clocks! written by Jules Older; illustrated by Megan Halsey. Charlesbridge Pub. 2000 un il $16.95; pa $6.95

Grades: K 1 2 3   **529**

1. Time 2. Clocks and watches

ISBN 0-88106-396-7; 0-88106-397-5 pa

LC 99-18764

Humorous text explains the concept of time, from seconds to hours on both analog and digital clocks, from years to millennia on the calendar

"The cartoon illustrations, showing children and many, many types of clocks are colorful, plentiful, and inviting. . . . This jovial look at time and time telling is as handy as they come." SLJ

Raum, Elizabeth

The **story** behind time. Heinemann Library 2009 32p il (True stories) lib bdg $28.21

Grades: 3 4 5   **529**

1. Time 2. Calendars 3. Clocks and watches

ISBN 978-1-4329-2343-3 lib bdg; 1-4329-2343-9 lib bdg

LC 2008037393

This offers information about time, including a history of time measurement

Includes bibliographical references

Skurzynski, Gloria

On time; from seasons to split seconds. National Geographic Soc. 2000 41p il $17.95

Grades: 4 5 6 7   **529**

1. Time 2. Time measurements

ISBN 0-7922-7503-9

LC 99-33927

Examines the ways humans have measured time throughout history and discusses the various units that are used to keep track of it

"This attractive offering is brimming with information. . . . The conversational tone helps readers get through the more difficult concepts. . . . The book is heavily illustrated with full-color drawings, photographs, and diagrams." SLJ

530 Physics

Adams, Tom

Feel the force! full of pop-up physics fun! illustrated by Thomas Flintham. Candlewick 2011 20p il (Super science)

Grades: 2 3 4   **530**

1. Physics 2. Pop-up books

ISBN 0-7636-5566-X; 978-0-7636-5566-2

"This high-energy pop-up takes a hands-on approach to physics. The text explains such concepts as force, gravity, friction, sound waves, light, and magnetism. . . . Cartoons, pop-ups, mini-books, flaps, tabs, and sidebars further elaborate on the various topics, and numerous experiments encourage further exploration and scrutiny."

Baxter, Roberta

The **particle** model of matter. Raintree 2009 48p il (Sci-hi: physical science) lib bdg $31.43; pa $8.99

Grades: 4 5 6 7   **530**

1. Atoms 2. Matter

ISBN 978-1-4109-3244-0 lib bdg; 978-1-4109-3259-4 pa

LC 2008030582

This takes a look at atoms, the building blocks of matter. It describes the different kinds of atoms, the particles that make up an atom, and the different states that matter can take

Includes bibliographical references

Bonnet, Robert L.

Home run! science projects with baseball and softball. [by] Robert L. Bonnet and Dan Keen. Enslow Publishers 2009 104p il (Score! Sports science projects) lib bdg $31.93

Grades: 5 6 7 8   **530**

1. Motion 2. Baseball 3. Force and energy 4. Science projects 5. Science -- Experiments

ISBN 978-0-7660-3365-8 lib bdg; 0-7660-3365-1 lib bdg

LC 2008-3005

"In addition to colorful, digital drawings illustrating the projects, a few photos and period prints also brighten the pages. . . . [This] will appeal to those looking for fresh science-project ideas." Booklist

Includes glossary and bibliographical references

Gaff, Jackie

Looking at solids, liquids, and gases; how does matter change? [by] Jackie Gaff. Enslow Publishers 2008 32p il (Looking at science: how things change) lib bdg $22.60

Grades: 1 2 3   **530**

1. Matter

ISBN 978-0-7660-3092-3 lib bdg; 0-7660-3092-X lib bdg

LC 2007-24514

"Fills a huge void in elementary science collections. . . . Text is arranged in succinct 'chunks,' giving important facts without overwhelming readers. . . . [This] is an essential addition." Libr Media Connect

Includes glossary and bibliographical references

Gardner, Robert

Ace your physical science project; great science fair ideas. [by] Robert Gardner, Madeline Goodstein, and Thomas R. Rybolt. Enslow Publishers 2009 128p il (Ace your physics science project) lib bdg $31.93

Grades: 5 6 7 8   **530**
1. Physics 2. Science projects 3. Science -- Experiments
ISBN 978-0-7660-3225-5 lib bdg; 0-7660-3225-6 lib bdg

LC 2008-29637

"Dozens of . . . . science activities are presented with background information, step-by-step instructions, and suggestions for extending to the science fair level. . . . Color illustrations and important safety information are included." Horn Book Guide

Includes bibliographical references

Slam dunk! science projects with basketball; [by] Robert Gardner and Dennis Shortelle. Enslow Publishers 2009 104p il (Score! sports science projects) lib bdg $31.93
Grades: 5 6 7 8   **530**
1. Physics 2. Basketball 3. Science projects 4. Science -- Experiments
ISBN 978-0-7660-3366-5 lib bdg; 0-7660-3366-X lib bdg

LC 2008-24879

"Introductions include information about the history of the sport, safety steps to follow, and the scientific method. . . . Detailed diagrams help clarify many of the directions." SLJ

Includes glossary and bibliographical references

Goodstein, Madeline
Wheels! science projects with bicycles, skateboards, and skates. Enslow Publishers 2009 104p il (Score! sports science projects) lib bdg $31.93
Grades: 5 6 7 8 9 10   **530**
1. Wheels 2. Physics 3. Science projects 4. Science -- Experiments 5. Science projects -- Juvenile literature
ISBN 978-0-7660-3107-4 lib bdg; 0-7660-3107-1 lib bdg

LC 2008-24880

"Introductions include information about the history of the sport, safety steps to follow, and the scientific method. . . . Detailed diagrams help clarify many of the directions." SLJ

Includes glossary and bibliographical references

Green, Dan
Physics; why matter matters! [by] Dan Green; Simon Basher, illustrator. Kingfisher 2008 128p il pa $8.95
Grades: 5 6 7 8   **530**
1. Physics
ISBN 978-0-7534-6214-0 pa; 0-7534-6214-1 pa

LC 2007-31805

This "introduces the elements of physics as anthropomorphic, cartoon-style characters. . . . Each of the groupings begins with an introduction and each concept is given its own spread that shows the cartoon figure and describes its 'personality.' The information is presented in a chatty and conversational tone. . . . Along with the narrative, which is written in the first person from the concept's point of view, other key facts are presented. This book would be handy as a supplement to a physics curriculum." SLJ

Includes glossary

Hartman, Eve
Light and sound; [by] Eve Hartman and Wendy Meshbesher. Raintree 2008 48p il (Sci-hi: physical science) lib bdg $22; pa $8.99

Grades: 5 6 7 8   **530**
1. Light 2. Sound
ISBN 978-1-4109-3378-2 lib bdg; 1-4109-3378-4 lib bdg; 978-1-4109-3383-6 pa; 1-4109-3383-0 pa

LC 2009-3506

A "compelling read for both browsers and science buffs. . . . Information is clearly presented and flows smoothly. . . . A treasure trove of information." SLJ

Includes glossary and bibliographical references

Lee, Cora
The **great** motion mission; a surprising story of physics in everyday life. illustrated by Steve Rolston. Annick Press 2009 114p il $24.95; pa $14.95
Grades: 4 5 6   **530**
1. Physics
ISBN 978-1-55451-185-3; 1-55451-185-2; 978-1-55451-184-6 pa; 1-55451-184-4 pa

"This book is a combination of narrative and concepts about physics. . . . Jeremy and his friends are distraught when the local summer fair is canceled in order to host a physics conference. While Jeremy helps his uncle campaign to save the fair, his new neighbor, Aubrey, sets out to prove that physics isn't only necessary, but also fun. The text is chatty and accessible to students. Topics include 'Physics and Sight,' 'Physics and Sound,' and 'Physics in Motion.' Each chapter profiles a featured physicist, from Albert Einstein to Richard Feynman. . . . Cartoon illustrations help to explain concepts such as the water cycle and wave patterns. Photographs are scattered throughout, and boxed areas highlight specific topics. This title would be especially useful for students wanting a good introduction to physics." SLJ

Includes glossary and bibliographical references

Mason, Adrienne
Change it! solids, liquids, gases and you. written by Adrienne Mason; illustrated by Claudia Davila. Kids Can Press 2006 32p il (Primary physical science) $12.95; pa $5.95
Grades: K 1 2   **530**
1. Matter 2. Science -- Experiments 3. Matter -- Properties -- Juvenile literature
ISBN 978-1-55337-837-2; 1-55337-837-7; 978-1-55337-838-9 pa; 1-55337-838-5 pa

This describes the three states of matter and includes experiments

This uses "colorful eye-catching graphics." Sci Books Films

Includes glossary

Motion, magnets and more; the big book of primary physical science. written by Adrienne Mason; illustrated by Claudia Dávila. Kids Can Press 2011 127p il $18.95
Grades: PreK K 1 2   **530**
1. Physical sciences
ISBN 978-1-55453-707-5; 1-55453-707-X

This book "is divided into four chapters that start readers off with the easy and familiar and work up to some larger science concepts, introducing and defining proper vocabulary along the way. . . . Short sentences, simple vocabulary and only a few paragraphs per page make this accessible for even the youngest of science explorers, while the 19 activities scattered throughout will deepen their understanding and hold their focus. . . . Dávila's charming digital illustrations depict rosy, round-faced multiethnic children in a variety of settings exploring the world around them." Kirkus

Ross, Michael Elsohn

Toy lab; illustrations by Tim Seeley. Carolrhoda Bks. 2003 48p il (You are the scientist) lib bdg $23.29

Grades: 3 4 5 6   530

1. Toys -- Experiments 2. Science -- Experiments 3. Physics -- Experiments -- Juvenile literature

ISBN 0-87614-456-3

LC 2001-5456

"Using the scientific method, youngsters are encouraged to experiment with toys like Slinkies, Silly Putty, Frisbees, and blocks to learn about flight, gravity, matter, pressure and waves, and objects in motion. . . . Toy Lab should pique youngsters' interest, even those who are not usually drawn to scientific experiments, and will give students some ideas for science fair projects as well." SLJ

Includes glossary

Silverstein, Alvin

Matter; by Alvin Silverstein, Virginia Silverstein, Laura Silverstein Nunn. Twenty-First Century Books 2009 112p il (Science concepts) lib bdg $31.93

Grades: 5 6 7 8   530

1. Matter

ISBN 978-0-8225-7515-3 lib bdg; 0-8225-7515-9 lib bdg

LC 2007049493

This is a "simple and straightforward [discussion] of the [subject]. The layout . . . is attractive and inviting, with full-color photographs and/or diagrams on almost every spread. In addition, the authors make good use of fact boxes. . . . [This] discusses the states of matter, the elements, chemical reactions, and more. [This title] will interest browsers and provide ample information for reports." SLJ

Includes glossary and bibliographical references

Sullivan, Navin

Weight. Marshall Cavendish Benchmark 2007 48p il (Measure up!) lib bdg $20.90

Grades: 4 5 6 7   530

1. Gravity 2. Weights and measures

ISBN 978-0-7614-2324-9 lib bdg; 0-7614-2324-9 lib bdg

"Examples using familiar objects and excellent full-color graphics help to bring concepts to life." SLJ

Includes glossary and bibliographical references

Taylor-Butler, Christine

Think like a scientist in the gym. Cherry Lake 2011 32p il (Science explorer junior) $27.07

Grades: 3 4 5   530

1. Sports 2. Physics 3. Science -- Experiments

ISBN 978-1-61080-163-8; 1-61080-163-6

"This is a kid-friendly approach to physics in particular and the scientific method in general, arranging much of the information around places and ideas kids can relate to: the gym, the track, and sports. . . . Five short chapters highlight how scientists and kids can find out how things work through experiments. . . . Photos of kids playing sports and simple but bright cartoon illustrations make this a lively read." Booklist

Weir, Jane

Matter. Compass Point Books 2009 40p il (Mission: science) lib bdg $26.60

Grades: 4 5 6   530

1. Matter

ISBN 978-0-7565-4069-2 lib bdg; 0-7565-4069-0 lib bdg

LC 2008-37624

An introduction to the scientific concept of matter, including elements, atoms, and molecules

Includes glossary

530.092 Physics--biography

Berne, Jennifer

★ On a beam of light; a story of Albert Einstein. by Jennifer Berne; illustrated by Vladimir Radunsky. Chronicle Books 2013 56 p. ill. (alk. paper) $17.99

Grades: 2 3 4 5   530.092

1. Physicists -- Biography -- Juvenile literature

ISBN 0811872351; 9780811872355

LC 2011004026

In this children's biographical story, by Jennifer Berne, illustrated by Vladimir Radunsky, "a boy rides a bicycle down a dusty road. But in his mind, he envisions himself traveling at a speed beyond imagining, on a beam of light. . . . From a boy endlessly fascinated by the wonders around him, Albert Einstein ultimately grows into a man of genius recognized the world over for profoundly illuminating our understanding of the universe." (Publisher's note)

"Radunsky's humorous, childlike drawings convey Einstein's personality as well as the important ideas in the text... provide[s] a splendid introduction to a man who never stopped questioning." Kirkus

530.1 Theories and mathematical physics

Rand, Casey

Time. Heinemann Library 2011 32p il map (Measure it!) lib bdg $29; pa $7.99

Grades: 3 4 5   530.1

1. Space and time

ISBN 978-1-4329-3766-9 lib bdg; 1-4329-3766-9 lib bdg; 978-1-4329-3772-0 pa; 1-4329-3772-3 pa

LC 2009-35210

"This book teaches the concept of time (including seasons, daylight savings, time zones)." Publisher's note

Includes glossary and bibliographical references

530.11 Relativity theory

Whiting, Jim

Space and time; Jim Whiting; photographs by Getty Images; folio illustration, Alex Ryan. 1st ed. Creative Education 2013 48 p. col. ill., col. maps (library) $35.65

Grades: 4 5 6 7   530.11

1. Physics -- Juvenile literature 2. Space and time -- Juvenile literature 3. Relativity (Physics) -- Juvenile

literature
ISBN 1608181928; 9781608181926

LC 2011040146

This book, by Jim Whiting, explores the concepts of space and time as part of the "Mysteries of the Universe" series. It appeals "to report writers and serious astronomy students. Each book carefully examines the history behind attempts to unravel explanations for the subjects, going back to Anaxagoras's work on energy in 450 B.C. all the way up to the contemporary findings of Stephen Hawking." (School Library Journal)

Includes bibliographical references (p. 46-47) and index.

530.4   States of matter

Boothroyd, Jennifer
What is a gas? by Jennifer Boothroyd. Lerner Publications Co. 2007 23p il (First step nonfiction: states of matter) lib bdg $21.27
Grades: K 1 2   **530.4**
1. Gases
ISBN 978-0-8225-6837-7 lib bdg; 0-8225-6837-3 lib bdg

LC 2006006303

"This small book introduces a single state of matter: a gas. Each page in the main section offers one or more colorful photographs and a brief line or two of large-print text. After a brief introduction to matter, the discussion moves on to the characteristics of gases and a few examples." Booklist

What is a liquid? by Jennifer Boothroyd. Lerner Publications Co. 2007 23p il (First step nonfiction: states of matter) lib bdg $21.27; pa $5.95
Grades: K 1 2   **530.4**
1. Liquids
ISBN 978-0-8225-6838-4 lib bdg; 0-8225-6838-1 lib bdg; 978-0-8225-6817-9 pa; 0-8225-6817-9 pa

LC 2006006304

This explains liquids "along with basic vocabulary. The layout is bright with many color photographs featuring children of different ethnicities. The text is spare; each spread includes, on average, three sentences." SLJ

What is a solid? by Jennifer Boothroyd. Lerner Publications Co. 2007 23p il (First step nonfiction: states of matter) lib bdg $21.27; pa $5.95
Grades: K 1 2   **530.4**
1. Solids
ISBN 978-0-8225-6836-0 lib bdg; 0-8225-6836-5 lib bdg; 978-0-8225-6816-2 pa; 0-8225-6816-0 pa

LC 2006006307

This explains solids "along with basic vocabulary. The layout is bright with many color photographs featuring children of different ethnicities. The text is spare; each spread includes, on average, three sentences." SLJ

Bradley, Kimberly Brubaker
Pop! a book about bubbles. photographs by Margaret Miller. HarperCollins Pubs. 2001 33p il (Let's-read-and-find-out science) hardcover o.p. pa $4.95

Grades: K 1   **530.4**
1. Bubbles 2. Soap bubbles
ISBN 0-06-028700-4; 0-06-028701-2 lib bdg; 0-06-445208-5 pa

LC 99-57794

Simple text explains how soap bubbles are made, why they are always round, and why they pop

"A simple, accurate text that is also fun to read. . . . Delightful color photographs of charming children making bubbles and of bubbles floating freely reinforce and extend the text. . . . This is science learning at its best." SLJ

Claybourne, Anna
The **nature** of matter; [by] Anna Claybourne. Gareth Stevens Pub. 2007 48p il (Gareth Stevens vital science: physical science) lib bdg $26.60; pa $11.95
Grades: 4 5 6 7   **530.4**
1. Matter
ISBN 978-0-8368-8088-5 lib bdg; 978-0-8368-8097-7 pa

LC 2006033732

This describes uses for matter and what happens when it changes from one form to another, the basic physical laws and properties of matter, and the various ways in which we control how matter behaves.

This is "straightforward and clear. . . . The layout is bright and colorful, with photographs and illustrations on almost every page." SLJ

Includes glossary and bibliographical references

Gardner, Robert
Melting, freezing, and boiling science projects with matter; [by] Robert Gardner. Enslow Elementary 2006 48p il (Fantastic physical science experiments) lib bdg $23.93
Grades: 4 5 6   **530.4**
1. Matter 2. Temperature 3. Science -- Experiments
ISBN 0-7660-2589-6

LC 2005033753

This offers experiments on the nature of solids, liquids, and gases and temperature.

"The ink-and-wash pictures illustrate the scientific principles as well as the equipment used in various activities. . . . Gardner's explanations are clear and his discussions lead readers to think about causes as well as what is happening to matter . . . as it changes form." Booklist

Includes glossary and bibliographical references

Hurd, Will
Changing states; solids, liquids, and gases. Heinemann Library 2009 48p il (Do it yourself) lib bdg $31.43; pa $8.99
Grades: 3 4 5 6   **530.4**
1. Gas 2. Matter 3. Solids 4. Liquids
ISBN 978-1-4329-2312-9 lib bdg; 1-4329-2312-9 lib bdg; 978-1-4329-2319-8 pa; 1-4329-2319-6 pa

LC 2008034939

The describes the fluctuating states of matter and includes experiments

This "would make an ideal supplement to science classes. A modular layout and dynamic photos keep things moving, while the experiments . . . feature lists of readily available materials, steps required to pull off the magic, and warnings as the when adult supervision is required." Booklist

Includes bibliographical references

Mason, Adrienne

Touch it! materials, matter and you. written by Adrienne Mason; illustrated by Claudia Dávila. Kids Can Press 2005 32p il (Primary physical science) $12.95; pa $5.95

Grades: K 1 2   **530.4**

1. Matter 2. Materials

ISBN 1-55337-760-5; 1-55337-761-3 pa

"Large-scale digital illustrations show children, animals, and adults commenting on and exploring the properties of matter. Some sections discuss ideas such as mass, buoyancy, or magnetism, while others suggest informal activities, for example describing different foods. Five double-page spreads present very simple science projects, beginning with a question-and-answer section followed by a short list of materials, a few steps to follow, and a brief concluding paragraph. . . . This colorful beginning science series is suitable for primary-grade students in groups and even younger children one-on-one." Booklist

Includes glossary

Oxlade, Chris

★ Changing materials; [by] Chris Oxlade. Crabtree Publishing Company 2008 32p il (Working with materials) lib bdg $26.60; pa $7.95

Grades: 2 3 4   **530.4**

1. Matter 2. Chemical reactions 3. Strength of materials

ISBN 978-0-7787-3638-7 lib bdg; 0-7787-3638-5 lib bdg; 978-0-7787-3648-6 pa; 0-7787-3648-2 pa

LC 2007027419

This describes how materials change by such processes as bending, breaking, melting, boiling, evaporating, dissolving, and burning

This "title has numerous captioned color photographs. . . . The [book offers] three simple, easy, and safe reproducible experiments. . . . Students will appreciate the pleasing design, easy-to-read font, and direct, clear writing style." Libr Media Connect

Includes glossary and bibliographical references

Cooling. Heinemann Library 2009 32p il (Changing materials) lib bdg $25.36; pa $7.99

Grades: K 1 2   **530.4**

1. Cold

ISBN 978-1-4329-3273-2 lib bdg; 1-4329-3273-X lib bdg; 978-1-4329-3278-7 pa; 1-4329-3278-0 pa

Introduces the concept of freezing points.

"A few simple activities provide opportunities to experiment. The color photographs are engaging." SLJ

Includes glossary and bibliographical references

Heating. Heinemann Library 2009 32p il (Changing materials) lib bdg $25.36; pa $7.99

Grades: K 1 2   **530.4**

1. Heat

ISBN 978-1-4329-3272-5 lib bdg; 1-4329-3272-1 lib bdg; 978-1-4329-3277-0 pa; 1-4329-3277-2 pa

Introduces the concept of boiling points.

"A few simple activities provide opportunities to experiment. The color photographs are engaging." SLJ

Includes glossary and bibliographical references

Shores, Lori

How to make bubbles. Capstone Press 2011 24p il (Hands-on science fun) lib bdg $23.99; pa $6.95

Grades: PreK K 1   **530.4**

1. Bubbles 2. Science -- Experiments

ISBN 978-1-4296-5293-3 lib bdg; 1-4296-5293-4 lib bdg; 978-1-4296-6215-4 pa; 1-4296-6215-8 pa

Simple text and full-color photos instruct readers on how to make bubbles.

"Bright, glossy photos and irresistible ideas make these science lessons effortless fun." Booklist

Spilsbury, Richard

What are solids, liquids, and gases? exploring science with hands-on activities. [by] Richard and Louise Spilsbury. Enslow Elementary 2008 32p il (In touch with basic science) lib bdg $22.60

Grades: 3 4 5   **530.4**

1. Matter 2. Science -- Experiments

ISBN 978-0-7660-3094-7 lib bdg; 0-7660-3094-6 lib bdg

LC 2007024516

This book "covers the three phases of matter described in its title. . . . Properties of each are explored. . . . The activities are all doable with simple household items, and they definitely reinforce the concepts being explored. This volume would a plus for budding scientists." Sci Books Films

Includes glossary and bibliographical references

Weakland, Mark

Bubbles float, bubbles pop. Capstone Press 2011 32p il (Science starts) lib bdg $25.99; pa $7.95

Grades: 1 2 3   **530.4**

1. Bubbles

ISBN 978-1-4296-5250-6 lib bdg; 1-4296-5250-0 lib bdg; 978-1-4296-6141-6 pa; 1-4296-6141-0 pa

LC 2010038874

Simple text and photographs explain the basic science behind bubbles.

"The text is simple and easily understood. . . . The large, up-close photographs are informative, . . . funny, . . . and intriguing." Booklist

Includes bibliographical references

Zoehfeld, Kathleen Weidner

What is the world made of? all about solids, liquids, and gases. illustrated by Paul Meisel. HarperCollins Pubs. 1998 32p il (Let's-read-and-find-out science) hardcover o.p. pa $4.95

Grades: K 1 2 3   **530.4**

1. Matter

ISBN 0-06-027143-4; 0-06-027144-2 lib bdg; 0-06-445163-1 pa

LC 97-30658

In simple text, presents the three states of matter, solid, liquid, and gas, and describes their attributes

"The explanations are clear with a simple, informal text for the new reader, and the lively line-and-water-color pictures bring in humor and common-sense." Booklist

530.8 Measurement

Adamson, Thomas K.

How do you measure length and distance? by Thomas K. and Heather Adamson. Capstone Press 2011 32p il (Measure it!) lib bdg $25.99

Grades: PreK K 1 2   **530.8**
1. Measurement
ISBN 978-1-4296-4456-3; 1-4296-4456-7
LC 2010002811

Simple text and color photographs describe the units and tools used to measure length and distance.

"The large picture-book format and inviting color photographs make [this] clearly written [title a] welcome [addition]. . . . The [author uses] common objects, giving readers recognizable points of reference. . . . Solid." SLJ

Includes glossary and bibliographical references

How do you measure liquids? by Thomas K. and Heather Adamson. Capstone Press 2011 32p il (Measure it!) lib bdg $25.99

Grades: PreK K 1 2   **530.8**
1. Liquids 2. Measurement
ISBN 978-1-4296-4457-0; 1-4296-4457-5
LC 2010002812

Simple text and color photographs describe the units and tools used to measure liquids.

"The large picture-book format and inviting color photographs make [this] clearly written [title a] welcome [addition]. . . . The [author uses] common objects, giving readers recognizable points of reference. . . . Solid." SLJ

Includes glossary and bibliographical references

How do you measure weight? by Thomas K. and Heather Adamson. Capstone Press 2011 32p il (Measure it!) lib bdg $25.99

Grades: PreK K 1 2   **530.8**
1. Weights and measures
ISBN 978-1-4296-4458-7; 1-4296-4458-3
LC 2010002784

Simple text and color photographs describe the units and tools used to measure weight.

"The large picture-book format and inviting color photographs make [this] clearly written [title a] welcome [addition]. . . . The [author uses] common objects, giving readers recognizable points of reference. . . . Solid." SLJ

Includes glossary and bibliographical references

Adler, David A., 1947-

★ How tall, how short, how faraway; illustrated by Nancy Tobin. Holiday House 1999 un il $16.95; pa $6.95

Grades: K 1 2 3   **530.8**
1. Measurement
ISBN 0-8234-1375-6; 0-8234-1632-1 pa
LC 98-18802

Introduces several measuring systems such as the Egyptian system, the inch-pound system, and the metric system

"In this wonderful hands-on concept book, easy technological measuring tools are superbly introduced and explained. . . . The informative text and colorful illustrations clearly explain the difference between customary and metric systems." Sci Child

Ball, Johnny

Why pi; how math applies to everyday life. DK Pub. 2009 93p il map $16.99

Grades: 4 5 6 7   **530.8**
1. Pi 2. Mathematics 3. Measurement
ISBN 978-0-7566-5164-0; 0-7566-5164-6

"Author Johnny Ball focuses on how people have used numbers to measure things through the ages, from the ways the ancient Egyptians measured the pyramids to how modern scientists measure time and space." Publisher's note

Cleary, Brian P.

How long or how wide? a measuring guide. illustrated by Brian Gable. Millbrook Press 2007 30p il (Math is categorical) lib bdg $15.95

Grades: K 1 2   **530.8**
1. Length measurement -- Juvenile literature
ISBN 978-0-8225-6694-6 lib bdg; 0-8225-6694-X lib bdg
LC 2006-10754

A rhyming text filled with humorous examples explains how to use and compare metric and U.S. customary units of length and introduces such tools of measurement as rulers and yardsticks.

"The book is very kid friendly, whimsical, vivid, and lively." Sci Books Films

On the scale; a weighty tale. by Brian P. Cleary; illustrated by Brian Gable. Millbrook Press 2008 31p il (Math is categorical) lib bdg $15.95

Grades: 2 3 4 5   **530.8**
1. Weights and measures
ISBN 978-0-8225-7851-2 lib bdg; 0-8225-7851-4 lib bdg
LC 2007033670

"In bubbly verse, Cleary presents a basic introduction to weights and measures. . . . Cheery, child-friendly examples are used for both English and metric measurements, progressing from smaller to larger weights in this approachable explanation of the topic. . . . Gable's watercolor cartoons depict rainbow-hued cats engaged in all manner of activities. This humorous title should prove useful in both classroom and family discussions." SLJ

Gardner, Robert

Ace your math and measuring science project; great science fair ideas. Enslow Publishers 2009 128p il (Ace your physics science project) lib bdg $31.93

Grades: 5 6 7 8   **530.8**
1. Measurement 2. Science projects 3. Weights and measures 4. Science -- Experiments
ISBN 978-0-7660-3224-8 lib bdg; 0-7660-3224-8 lib bdg
LC 2008-23926

"Dozens of . . . science activities are presented with background information, step-by-step instructions, and suggestions for extending to the science fair level. . . . Color illustrations and important safety information are included." Horn Book Guide

Includes bibliographical references

Far-out science projects with height and depth; How high is up? How low is down? Enslow Pubs. 2003 48p il (Sensational science experiments) lib bdg $18.95

Grades: 3 4 5 6 **530.8**
1. Measurement 2. Science projects 3. Experiments 4.
Science -- Experiments 5. Measurement -- Experiments
6. Altitudes -- Measurement -- Experiments
ISBN 0-7660-2016-9

LC 2002-4619

"Following a brief introduction to measurement, a review of units (metric and English standard), and a list of
safety tips, Gardner presents a series of 17 measurement activities for readers. . . . The colorful illustrations provide additional clarity for the narrative directions. . . . The activities
provide hands-on, mind-on measurement experiences with
real-world applications." Sci Books Films

Includes glossary and bibliographical references

Heavy-duty science projects with weight; how much
does it weigh? Enslow Pubs. 2003 48p il (Sensational
science experiments) lib bdg $18.95
Grades: 3 4 5 6 **530.8**
1. Gravitation 2. Measurement 3. Science projects 4.
Experiments 5. Science -- Experiments 6. Measurement
-- Experiments 7. Weight (Physics) -- Experiments
ISBN 0-7660-2013-4

LC 2002-8460

This "includes a variety of hands-on activities that use
everyday cheap materials to introduce students to many
significant physics concepts related to gravity. . . . While
challenging, the activities are accessible and interesting to
all students. . . . The language used in the volume is simple,
accurate, and scientific." Sci Books Films

Includes bibliographical references and index

Super-sized science projects with volume; how much
space does it take up? Enslow Pubs. 2003 48p il (Sensational science experiments) lib bdg $18.95
Grades: 3 4 5 6 **530.8**
1. Measurement 2. Science projects 3. Volume (Cubic
content) 4. Science -- Experiments
ISBN 0-7660-2014-2

LC 2002-153850

This "explores topics ranging from determining the volume of a quart and a liter to the amount of air in a container
of sand. Gardner's clear, informal explanations are echoed in
LaBaff's colorful illustrations." Booklist

Includes bibliographical references and index

Leedy, Loreen
★ **Measuring** Penny; written and illustrated by Loreen
Leedy. Holt & Co. 1997 un il $16.95; pa $6.95
Grades: 1 2 3 **530.8**
1. Dogs 2. Measurement
ISBN 0-8050-5360-3; 0-8050-6572-5 pa

LC 97-19108

"For a measuring project, Lisa decides to measure her
dog, Penny, and a cast of other dogs at the park. Noses, tails,
ears, paws—nothing escapes her measuring zeal. Also, time,
temperature, cost, and even value are creatively calculated
throughout a day spent caring for Penny. Leedy cleverly incorporates Lisa's notebook recordings into the illustrations,
which depict a wide range of shapes and sizes for easy visual
comparison." Horn Book Guide

Murphy, Stuart J.
★ **Room** for Ripley; illustrated by Sylvie Wickstrom.
HarperCollins Pubs. 1999 33p il (MathStart) hardcover
o.p. pa $4.95
Grades: 1 2 3 **530.8**
1. Aquariums 2. Measurement
ISBN 0-06-027621-5 lib bdg; 0-06-446724-4 pa

LC 98-26109

Uses a story about a young boy who is getting a fish
bowl ready for his new pet to introduce various units of
liquid measure

"The writing is breezy and reads like a story about a boy
who wants a pet, but the text constantly reinforces the mathematical concepts (how many cups in a pint, a quart, etc.).
The illustrations are painted in muted primary colors against
a lot of white space. . . . A fun, painless math lesson." SLJ

Parker, Victoria
How big is big? comparing plants. [by] Vic Parker.
Heinemann Library 2011 32p il (Measuring and compar-
ing) lib bdg $26; pa $7.99
Grades: 2 3 4 **530.8**
1. Plants 2. Weights and measures
ISBN 978-1-4329-3959-5 lib bdg; 1-4329-3959-9 lib
bdg; 978-1-4329-3967-0 pa; 1-4329-3967-X pa

LC 2010000932

This "contains vivid photographs, charts, and diagrams
with captions, explanations, and examples. Questions are
posed throughout . . . to entice young learners to 'stop and
think' or continue reading for more information. . . . [This]
would make an excellent addition to any classroom library."
Libr Media Connect

Includes glossary and bibliographical references

How full is full? comparing bodies of water. [by] Vic
Parker. Heinemann Library 2011 32p il map (Measuring
and comparing) lib bdg $26; pa $7.99
Grades: 2 3 4 **530.8**
1. Volume (Cubic content)
ISBN 978-1-4329-3957-1 lib bdg; 1-4329-3957-2 lib
bdg; 978-1-4329-3965-6 pa; 1-4329-3965-3 pa

LC 2010000927

This "contains vivid photographs, charts, and diagrams
with captions, explanations, and examples. Questions are
posed throughout . . . to entice young learners to 'stop and
think' or continue reading for more information. . . . [This]
would make an excellent addition to any classroom library."
Libr Media Connect

Includes glossary and bibliographical references

How heavy is heavy? comparing vehicles. [by] Vic
Parker. Heinemann Library 2011 32p il (Measuring and
comparing) lib bdg $26; pa $7.99
Grades: 2 3 4 **530.8**
1. Vehicles 2. Weights and measures
ISBN 978-1-4329-3954-0 lib bdg; 1-4329-3954-8 lib
bdg; 978-1-4329-3962-5 pa; 1-4329-3962-9 pa

LC 2010000923

This "contains vivid photographs, charts, and diagrams
with captions, explanations, and examples. Questions are
posed throughout . . . to entice young learners to 'stop and
think' or continue reading for more information. . . . [This]

would make an excellent addition to any classroom library."
Libr Media Connect

Includes glossary and bibliographical references

How long is long? comparing animals. [by] Vic Parker.
Heinemann Library 2011 32p il (Measuring and comparing) lib bdg $26; pa $7.99
Grades: 2 3 4   **530.8**
   1. Size 2. Measurement
   ISBN 978-1-4329-3958-8 lib bdg; 1-4329-3958-0 lib
   bdg; 978-1-4329-3966-3 pa; 1-4329-3966-1 pa
                 LC 2010000930
This "contains vivid photographs, charts, and diagrams
with captions, explanations, and examples. Questions are
posed throughout . . . to entice young learners to 'stop and
think' or continue reading for more information. . . . [This]
would make an excellent addition to any classroom library."
Libr Media Connect

Includes glossary and bibliographical references

Robbins, Ken
   ★ **For** good measure; the ways we say how much,
how far, how heavy, how big, how old. Roaring Brook Press
2010 un il $17.99
Grades: 3 4 5 6   **530.8**
   1. Measurement 2. Time -- Juvenile literature
   ISBN 978-1-59643-344-1; 1-59643-344-2
"By tossing in tidbits of history, word origins and meanings, Robbins takes the everyday subject of measurement
and makes it accessible, interesting and memorable. Beginning with the units for lengths and distances, readers will
not only learn about feet and inches, but also hands . . . and
cubits. . . . From distances, the author moves on to area—
measured in acres, hectares and sections—and then on to
weigh—pound, ounce, ton, stone, dram and carat. . . . Liquid
measures, dry capacity and time round out the volume. The
photographs are a good complement, clearly illustrating the
concepts without distracting from the text." Kirkus

Schwartz, David M.
   ★ **Millions** to measure; pictures by Steven Kellogg.
HarperCollins Pubs. 2003 un il $16.99; lib bdg $17.89
Grades: 2 3 4   **530.8**
   1. Measurement 2. Metric system 3. Weights and
   measures
   ISBN 0-688-12916-1; 0-06-623784-X lib bdg
                 LC 2001-39683
Marvelosissimo the Magician explains the development
of standard units of measure, and shows the simplicity of
calculating length, height, weight, and volume using the
metric system
   "Schwartz not only manages to impart a good deal of basic information . . . but also entertains the reader. He receives
ample support from illustrator Kellogg, who contributes
enough merry madness to make learning fun. Bright with
shining colors, the large, detailed pictures brim with action
and humor as well as history and math." Booklist

Somervill, Barbara A.
   Mass and weight. Heinemann Library 2011 32p il
(Measure it!) lib bdg $29; pa $7.99

Grades: 3 4 5   **530.8**
   1. Measurement 2. Weights and measures
   ISBN 978-1-4329-3765-2 lib bdg; 1-4329-3765-0 lib
   bdg; 978-1-4329-3771-3 pa; 1-4329-3771-5 pa
                 LC 2009-35208
"Size of text and font is suitable for this age group with
uncluttered pages designed so that text is set off with the illustrations, graphs, or drawings placed vertically. Key words
appear in bold." Libr Media Connect

Includes glossary and bibliographical references

Vogel, Julia
   Measuring volume; by Julia Vogel; illustrated by Luanne Marten. The Child's World 2013 24 p. col. ill. (library) $27.07
Grades: 2 3 4   **530.8**
   1. Picture books for children 2. Volume (Cubic content)
   -- Juvenile literature
   ISBN 1614732833; 9781614732839
                 LC 2012933675
In this book, part of the Simple Measurement series, Julia Vogel "addresses the topic of measuring volume with a
number of . . . examples. Pouring milk? Taking medicine?
Filling the backyard pool? Well, then you're participating
in figuring out volume." It includes a "What Equals What?"
page with equivalency charts. (Booklist)

Includes bibliographical references (p. 24) and index.

531   Classical mechanics

Bradley, Kimberly Brubaker
   Energy makes things happen; illustrated by Paul
Meisel. HarperCollins Pubs. 2003 33p il (Let's-read-and-find-out science) hardcover o.p. lib bdg $16.89; pa $4.99
Grades: K 1 2 3   **531**
   1. Force and energy 2. Energy transfer 3. Power
   resources
   ISBN 0-06-028908-2; 0-06-028909-0 lib bdg; 0-06-
   445213-1 pa
                 LC 2001-39520
This book shows how energy comes originally from the
sun and can be transferred from one thing to another
   "This worthy title uses familiar examples and a clear focus to introduce basic scientific concepts. . . . Meisel's color
illustrations of cheerful multiethnic children match the level
and tone of the text perfectly, make it more comprehensible,
and add to the book's appeal." SLJ

   Forces make things move; illustrated by Paul Meisel.
HarperCollins 2005 33p il (Let's-read-and-find-out science) $15.99; lib bdg $16.89; pa $4.99
Grades: K 1 2 3   **531**
   1. Gravity 2. Force and energy
   ISBN 0-06-028906-6; 0-06-028907-4 lib bdg; 0-06-
   445214-X pa
                 LC 2002-14763
Simple language and humorous illustrations show how
forces make things move, prevent them from starting to
move, and stop them from moving
   "Colorful line-and-watercolor-wash illustrations brighten the pages. . . . A practical starting place for understanding
forces." Booklist

Claybourne, Anna

Forms of energy. Raintree 2008 48p il (Sci-hi: physical science) lib bdg $22; pa $8.99

Grades: 5 6 7 8   **531**

1. Force and energy

ISBN 978-1-4109-3377-5 lib bdg; 1-4109-3377-6 lib bdg; 978-1-4109-3382-9 pa; 1-4109-3382-2 pa

LC 2009-3504

A "compelling read for both browsers and science buffs. . . . Information is clearly presented and flows smoothly. . . . A treasure trove of information." SLJ

Includes glossary and bibliographical references

Gut-wrenching gravity and other fatal forces; Anna Claybourne. Crabtree Publishing Company 2013 32 p. (Disgusting & dreadful science) (pbk.: alk. paper) $9.95

Grades: 4 5 6   **531**

1. Gravity -- Juvenile literature 2. Physics -- Juvenile literature 3. Force and energy -- Juvenile literature

ISBN 0778709574; 9780778709503; 9780778709572

LC 2012043529

This book by Anna Claybourne is part of the Disgusting & Dreadful Science series and focuses on gravity and other physical forces. It shares facts including that "a mouse can survive a 328-foot fall, black holes have superstrong gravity that causes 'spaghettification,' and" more. Illustrations are included. (Booklist)

Includes bibliographical references and index

Pushes and pulls. QEB Pub. 2008 24p il (Why it works) $24.25

Grades: 2 3 4 5   **531**

1. Force and energy 2. Power (Mechanics)

ISBN 978-1-59566-558-4; 1-59566-558-7

LC 2008-11713

This is "colorfully illustrated and should help young students relate better to the concepts being presented. A glossary of key words and a page of suggestions for parents and teachers to extend the learning experience round out the text." Sci Books & Films

Includes glossary and bibliographical references

Cobb, Vicki, 1938-

I fall down; illustrated by Julia Gorton. HarperCollins Publishers 2004 un il (Science play) $17.99; lib bdg $18.89

Grades: K 1 2   **531**

1. Gravity 2. Science -- Experiments

ISBN 0-688-17842-1; 0-688-17843-X lib bdg

LC 2003-1822

Simple experiments introduce the basic concept of gravity and its relationship to weight

"The digital illustrations offer clearly defined images with a distinctive, retro look. Their eye-catching pizzazz will help hold the attention of the audience. . . . Attuned to the learning style of young children, Cobb's questions and suggestions offer kids the experience of the scientific process." Booklist

Conrad, David

Gravity all around. Capstone Press 2011 24p il (Pebble plus: physical science) lib bdg $23.99

Grades: PreK K 1 2   **531**

1. Gravity

ISBN 978-1-4296-6606-0; 1-4296-6606-4

LC 2010034310

This describes the science of gravity.

This book "addresses its topic in a direct and simple manner. . . . [The] title includes a hands-on experiment with both textual and visual directions." SLJ

Includes glossary and bibliographical references

Gardner, Robert

Ace your forces and motion science project; great science fair ideas. [by] Robert Gardner and Madeline Goodstein. Enslow Publishers 2009 128p il (Ace your physics science project) lib bdg $31.93

Grades: 5 6 7 8   **531**

1. Force and energy 2. Science projects 3. Science -- Experiments

ISBN 978-0-7660-3222-4 lib bdg; 0-7660-3222-1 lib bdg

LC 2008-49778

"Presents several science experiments and project ideas about forces and motion." Publisher's note

Includes bibliographical references

Split-second science projects with speed; how fast does it go? Enslow Pubs. 2003 48p il (Sensational science experiments) lib bdg $18.95

Grades: 3 4 5 6   **531**

1. Speed 2. Science projects 3. Experiments 4. Speed -- Experiments

ISBN 0-7660-2017-7

LC 2002-4618

This serves as an "introduction to speed and velocity by providing introductory explanations and step-by-step instructions on how to set up and conduct different simple experiments. . . . Perhaps the book's strongest point is its readability. . . . The book is nicely illustrated and appealing." Sci Books Films

Includes bibliographical references and index

Gray, Susan Heinrichs

Experiments with motion; [by] Susan H. Gray. Children's Press 2011 48p il (True books: experiments) lib bdg $28; pa $6.95

Grades: 4 5 6   **531**

1. Motion 2. Science -- Experiments

ISBN 978-0-531-26346-4 lib bdg; 0-531-26346-0 lib bdg; 978-0-531-26646-5 pa; 0-531-26646-X pa

LC 2011011971

"In just four short chapters with glossy pages and plentiful color photographs, the author breaks down some fairly complicated concepts and takes readers through laws governing motion and scientific investigation. . . . Multiethnic upper elementary children demonstrate experiments using readily available everyday materials, while the text gives clear explanations." Booklist

Includes glossary and bibliographical references

Hillman, Ben

How fast is it? a zippy book all about speed. Scholastic 2008 47p il $14.99

Grades: 3 4 5   **531**
1. Speed
ISBN 978-0-439-91867-1; 0-439-91867-7
LC 2007039983
"Twenty-two full-color, full-page spreads convey the quickness (or lack) of the most ordinary things in a unique and amazing way. Examples: * How fast is a bullet-bike? * Which one is faster? A coyote or a roadrunner? * Can a sneeze be faster than a tennis serve? * How fast is the population growing? * What is the fastest-growing plant?" Publisher's note

Hopwood, James
Cool gravity activities; fun science projects about balance. [by] James Hopwood. ABDO Pub. 2008 32p il (Cool science) lib bdg $16.95
Grades: 4 5 6   **531**
1. Gravity 2. Science projects 3. Science -- Experiments
ISBN 978-1-59928-908-3 lib bdg; 1-59928-908-3 lib bdg
LC 2007010204
This offers science projects about gravity, including "The Old Cane Trick"
The projects "will attract boys and girls. [The] book begins with [an] upbeat introduction and three chapters about the scientific method, keeping a journal, and safety. . . . Background on the science concepts involved is presented along with a complete list of supplies. . . . The numbered instructions are easy to follow and are accompanied by small, closeup photos." SLJ

Macdonald, Wendy
Galileo's leaning tower experiment; a science adventure. illustrated by Paolo Rui. Charlesbridge 2009 32p il $16.95; pa $7.95
Grades: 3 4 5   **531**
1. Gravity 2. Physics 3. Astronomers 4. Writers on science
ISBN 978-1-57091-869-8; 1-57091-869-4; 978-1-57091-870-4 pa; 1-57091-870-8 pa
LC 2008010652
"In this fictionalized account of Galileo's legendary experiments on the speed of falling objects, the young professor meets a poor farm boy, Massimo, who drops bread and cheese to his uncle passing under a bridge in a boat. Stunned that the bread and cheese hit the boat at the same time, contradicting Aristotle's teachings, Galileo begins experimenting with other pairs of falling objects. . . . The story excels at teaching the concept involved and is admirably enhanced by Rui's attractive, colorful, and informative acrylics." SLJ

Mason, Adrienne
Move it! motion, forces and you. written by Adrienne Mason; illustrated by Claudia Dávila. Kids Can Press 2005 32p il (Primary physical science) $12.95; pa $5.95
Grades: K 1 2   **531**
1. Motion 2. Force and energy
ISBN 1-55337-758-3; 1-55337-759-1 pa
This explores the physics of why and how things move with simple activities such as pushing, pulling or lifting objects.
Includes glossary

O'Leary, Denyse
What are Newton's laws of motion? Crabtree Pub. Co. 2011 64p il (Shaping modern science) lib bdg $30.60; pa $10.95
Grades: 5 6 7 8   **531**
1. Motion 2. Physicists 3. Mathematicians 4. Writers on science 5. Science -- Juvenile literature
ISBN 978-0-7787-7200-2 lib bdg; 0-7787-7200-4 lib bdg; 978-0-7787-7207-1 pa; 0-7787-7207-1 pa
LC 2010-52629
This book examines how Sir Isaac Newton developed three basic laws that govern the way in which objects move. It explains how Newton expanded on the work of other scientists, including Galileo and Copernicus, to make his discovery. The book also explains how Newton's laws have influenced modern science and technology in areas such as sports and transportation.
This title is "not only written and organized well, but [it is] also gorgeous in design. Full-color photographs and illustrations are set over colorful backgrounds that add depth but not distraction. [The title] includes thought-provoking quotes from famous authors and scientists and some eyebrow-raising 'Quick Facts' throughout." SLJ
Includes glossary and bibliographical references

Phelan, Glen
Invisible force; the quest to define the laws of motion. [by] Glen Phelan. National Geographic 2006 59p il (Science quest) $17.95; lib bdg $25.90
Grades: 5 6 7 8   **531**
1. Motion 2. Gravity
ISBN 0-7922-5539-9; 0-7922-5540-2 lib bdg
LC 2005027350
This "traces the historical and scientific path to man's understanding of motion and gravity." Publisher's note
Includes glossary and bibliographical references

Riley, Peter D.
Forces; [by] Peter Riley. Sea-to-Sea Publications 2011 32p il (The real scientist investigates) lib bdg $28.50
Grades: 3 4 5   **531**
1. Force and energy 2. Science -- Methodology -- Juvenile literature
ISBN 978-1-59771-280-4 lib bdg; 1-59771-280-9 lib bdg
LC 2010-05371
In this book about forces "solid scientific material is presented in accessible language and a visually engaging, boldly colored layout. Budding scientists are encouraged to hone their skills by recording observations, making predictions, and analyzing results. Hands-on activities are included on almost every spread. . . . The many color photos feature diverse children demonstrating the activities." SLJ
Includes glossary and bibliographical references

Royston, Angela
Looking at forces and motion; how do things move? [by] Angela Royston. Enslow Publishers 2008 32p il (Looking at science: how things change) lib bdg $22.60
Grades: 1 2 3   **531**
1. Motion 2. Force and energy
ISBN 978-0-7660-3089-3 lib bdg; 0-7660-3089-X lib bdg
LC 2007-24508

"Fills a huge void in elementary science collections. . . . Text is arranged in succinct 'chunks,' giving important facts without overwhelming readers. . . . [This] is an essential addition." Libr Media Connect

Includes glossary and bibliographical references

Silverstein, Alvin

Forces and motion; [by Alvin & Virginia Silverstein & Laura Silverstein Nunn] Twenty-First Century Books 2008 112p il (Science concepts) lib bdg $31.93

Grades: 5 6 7 8   **531**

1. Motion 2. Force and energy

ISBN 978-0-8225-7514-6 lib bdg; 0-8225-7514-0 lib bdg

LC 2007-48826

"The breadth of material the authors cover in this volume is impressive. They discuss energy (kenetic and potential), forces (friction, gravity, electricity, and magnetism), simple machines (lever, wheel, pulley, ramp, and wedge), motion in fluids, and Newton's laws of motion. . . . [This offers] simple writing, many colorful pictures, and lots of examples." Sci Books Films

Includes glossary and bibliographical references

Somervill, Barbara A.

Speed and acceleration. Heinemann Library 2011 32p il (Measure it!) lib bdg $29; pa $7.99

Grades: 3 4 5   **531**

1. Speed 2. Measurement

ISBN 978-1-4329-3764-5 lib bdg; 1-4329-3764-2 lib bdg; 978-1-4329-3770-6 pa; 1-4329-3770-7 pa

LC 2009-35204

"Size of text and font is suitable for this age group with uncluttered pages designed so that text is set off with the illustrations, graphs, or drawings placed vertically. Key words appear in bold." Libr Media Connect

Includes glossary and bibliographical references

Spilsbury, Richard

What are forces and motion? exploring science with hands-on activities. [by] Richard and Louise Spilsbury. Enslow Publishers 2008 32p il (In touch with basic science) lib bdg $22.60

Grades: 3 4 5   **531**

1. Motion 2. Force and energy 3. Science -- Experiments

ISBN 978-0-7660-3095-4 lib bdg; 0-7660-3095-4 lib bdg

LC 2007024517

This book "introduces children to forces through a simple introduction to Newton's three laws, simple machines, the relationship of energy and motion through potential and kinetic energy, buoyant forces, and structural forces. . . . This volume is an excellent resource for any child who is interested in science." Sci Books Films

Includes glossary and bibliographical references

Sullivan, Navin

Speed. Marshall Cavendish Benchmark 2007 48p il (Measure up!) lib bdg $20.90

Grades: 4 5 6 7   **531**

1. Speed 2. Measurement

ISBN 978-0-7614-2325-6 lib bdg; 0-7614-2325-7 lib bdg

"Have you ever wondered how we measure different speeds? How do we know how fast an airplane travels or how much speed a shuttle needs to travel to outer space? What does speed have to do with satellites? How does the speed of light compare with the speed of sound? Speed answers these questions and explores the history of humankind's discoveries about speed." Publisher's note

Includes glossary and bibliographical references

VanCleave, Janice Pratt, 1942-

Step-by-step science experiments in energy; by Janice VanCleave. Rosen Pub. 2013 80 p. col. ill. (library) $33.25; (paperback) $14.15

Grades: 5 6 7 8   **531**

1. Energy -- Juvenile literature 2. Science -- Experiments -- Juvenile literature 3. Science projects -- Juvenile literature 4. Force and energy -- Experiments -- Juvenile literature

ISBN 144886979X; 9781448869794; 9781448884711

LC 2012006835

This book by Janice VanCleave is part of the First-Place Science Fair Projects series. The books have an introduction to the subject—here, energy, followed by 22 simple . . . experiments. Van Cleave states the basic goal of the experiments, followed by a list of necessary materials, most of which can be found around the house or easily acquired with minimal cost. Step-by-step instructions are clearly detailed and accompanied by diagrams where needed." (School Library Journal)

Includes bibliographical references and index.

Waters, Jennifer

All kinds of motion. Capstone Press 2011 24p il (Pebble plus: physical science) lib bdg $23.99

Grades: PreK K 1 2   **531**

1. Motion 2. Kinematics

ISBN 978-1-4296-6607-7; 1-4296-6607-2

LC 2010034309

This decribes the science of motion.

This book "addresses its topic in a direct and simple manner. . . . [The] title includes a hands-on experiment with both textual and visual directions." SLJ

Includes glossary and bibliographical references

Weber, Rebecca

The power of energy. Capstone Press 2011 24p il (Pebble plus: physical science) lib bdg $23.99

Grades: PreK K 1 2   **531**

1. Force and energy

ISBN 978-1-4296-6605-3; 1-4296-6605-6

LC 2010034311

This explains the science of force and energy.

This book "addresses its topic in a direct and simple manner. . . . [The] title includes a hands-on experiment with both textual and visual directions." SLJ

Include glossary and bibliographical references

532   Fluid mechanics

Cobb, Vicki

I get wet; illustrated by Julia Gorton. HarperCollins Pubs. 2002 un il $15.99; lib bdg $17.89

Grades: K 1 2   **532**
1. Water 2. Experiments 3. Water -- Experiments
ISBN 0-688-17838-3; 0-688-17839-1 lib bdg
LC 00-49882
"The simple yet well-conceived activities engage children in more than just observations—the questions and explanations are constructed to help young kids draw conclusions from their observations. Remarkably, all this is accomplished in a child-friendly, straightforward text. The illustrations are bright and energetic." Horn Book

Farndon, John
Water. Benchmark Bks. 2001 32p il (Science experiments) lib bdg $16.95
Grades: 3 4 5 6   **532**
1. Water 2. Experiments 3. Water -- Experiments 4. Science -- Experiments
ISBN 0-7614-1087-2
LC 00-60187
A collection of experiments exploring the properties of water, including ice, water, and steam, floating and sinking, heavy water, and surface tension
Includes glossary

Meiani, Antonella
Water. Lerner Publs. 2003 40p il (Experimenting with science) lib bdg $23.93
Grades: 4 5 6 7   **532**
1. Water 2. Science -- Experiments
ISBN 0-8225-0083-3
LC 2001-50773
Describes experiments with water which answer such questions as "Why are water droplets round?" and "Why do some things, like salt, dissolve in water and other things, like fish, don't?"
This offers "straightforward, well-designed experiments. . . . Numerous clear diagrams, some photos, and occasional historical sidebars extend this material, which is notable for its substance." Horn Book Guide
Includes glossary and bibliographical references

Parker, Steve, 1952-
The **science** of water; projects with experiments with water and power. [by] Steve Parker. Heinemann Library 2005 32p il (Tabletop scientist) lib bdg $29.29; pa $7.85
Grades: 4 5 6 7   **532**
1. Water 2. Science -- Experiments
ISBN 1-4034-7282-3 lib bdg; 1-4034-7289-0 pa
LC 2005007027
This "has experiments on the water cycle, water density, water as a solvent, surface tension, capillary action, buoyancy, water power, and water propulsion. . . . The colorful illustrations, organization, and ease of use of [this title makes it an] excellent [addition]." SLJ
Includes glossary

Simon, Seymour
Let's try it out in the water; by Seymour Simon and Nicole Fauteux; illustrated by Doug Cushman. Simon & Schuster Bks. for Young Readers 2000 un il $15
Grades: K 1 2   **532**
1. Floating bodies -- Experiments -- Juvenile literature
2. Buoyant ascent (Hydrodynamics) -- Experiments --

Juvenile literature
ISBN 0-689-82919-1
LC 99-20371
Presents simple activities and experiments that demonstrate buoyancy by observing why some things sink and others float in water
This does "a great job of using hands-on activities in daily life to explain basic science to young children. . . . The writers include helpful information for adults about how to teach the science as an active part of the child's ordinary experience. The exuberant, colorful pictures add to the fun." Booklist

533   Pneumatics (Gas mechanics)

Meiani, Antonella
Air. Lerner Publs. 2003 40p il (Experimenting with science) lib bdg $23.93
Grades: 4 5 6 7   **533**
1. Air 2. Science -- Experiments
ISBN 0-8225-0082-5
LC 2001-37730
Explains the properties of air through experiments which feature such topics as what air is, how much force wind has, what shape is best for flying, and how sound travels
This offers "straightforward, well-designed experiments. . . . Numerous clear diagrams, some photos, and occasional historical sidebars extend this material, which is notable for its substance." Horn Book Guide
Includes glossary and bibliographical references

Parker, Steve, 1952-
The **science** of air; projects and experiments on air and flight. [by] Steve Parker. Heinemann Library 2005 32p il (Tabletop scientist) lib bdg $29.29; pa $7.85
Grades: 4 5 6 7   **533**
1. Air 2. Science -- Experiments
ISBN 1-4034-7280-7 lib bdg; 1-4034-7287-4 pa
LC 2005006940
"The 12 experiments in [this] book have a materials list and step-by-step photo instructions. Boxed text explains the scientific ideas in each project and the processes that make it work, and offer ideas for further experimentation. The activities are followed by a history of the topic. . . . [This] title introduces air movement, air pressure, wind resistance, lift, flight, and energy from the wind. . . . The colorful illustrations, organization, and ease of use [this title makes it an] excellent [addition]." SLJ
Includes glossary

534   Specific forms of energy

Farndon, John
Sound and hearing. Benchmark Bks. 2001 32p il (Science experiments) lib bdg $16.95
Grades: 3 4 5 6   **534**
1. Sound -- Experiments 2. Hearing -- Experiments
3. Science -- Experiments 4. Senses and sensation -- Experiments
ISBN 0-7614-1091-0
LC 99-89262

A collection of experiments that explore the nature of sound and how we hear it. Activities include making a string telephone, a megaphone, and a bottle organ

Includes glossary

Gardner, Robert

Jazzy science projects with sound and music; [by] Robert Gardner. Enslow Publishers 2006 48p il (Fantastic physical science experiments) lib bdg $23.93

Grades: 4 5 6   **534**

1. Sound 2. Science -- Experiments

ISBN 0-7660-2588-8

LC 2005018729

This offers science experiments illustrating such concepts as pitch, vibration, how sound travels and how it is perceived

Includes glossary and bibliographical references

Guillain, Charlotte

Different sounds. Heinemann Library 2009 24p il (Sounds all around us) lib bdg $20.71; pa $5.99

Grades: PreK K 1   **534**

1. Sound 2. Sound waves

ISBN 978-1-4329-3202-2 lib bdg; 1-4329-3202-0 lib bdg; 978-1-4329-3208-4 pa; 1-4329-3208-X pa

LC 2008-51740

This book "introduces the basics of sound through vibrant photographs, large text, and simple sentences. . . . [A] great introduction[s] and worthy addition[s]." SLJ

Includes glossary and bibliographical references

Making sounds. Heinemann Library 2008 24p il (Sounds all around us) lib bdg $20.71; pa $5.99

Grades: PreK K 1   **534**

1. Sound

ISBN 978-1-4329-3200-8 lib bdg; 1-4329-3200-4 lib bdg; 978-1-4329-3206-0 pa; 1-4329-3206-3 pa

LC 2008-51682

This book "introduces the basics of sound through vibrant photographs, large text, and simple sentences. . . . [A] great introduction[s] and worthy addition[s]." SLJ

Includes glossary and bibliographical references

What is sound? Heinemann Library 2009 24p il (Sounds all around us) lib bdg $20.71; pa $5.99

Grades: PreK K 1   **534**

1. Sounds 2. Sound waves

ISBN 978-1-4329-3199-5 lib bdg; 1-4329-3199-7 lib bdg; 978-1-4329-3205-3 pa; 1-4329-3205-5 pa

LC 2008-51681

This describes vibrations, sound waves, and echoes.

This book "introduces the basics of sound through vibrant photographs, large text, and simple sentences. . . . [A] great introduction[s] and worthy addition[s]." SLJ

Inlcudes glossary

Hall, Pamela

Listen! Learn about sound; illustrated by Jane Yamada. Child's World 2010 24p il (Science definitions) lib bdg $22.79

Grades: PreK K 1 2   **534**

1. Sound

ISBN 978-1-60253-510-7 lib bdg; 1-60253-510-8 lib bdg

LC 2010010978

This book about sound is "attractive and succinct. . . . Large, eye-catching photos cover the recto of each spread. . . . Varying, jewel-toned accents are used in headings, highlighted glossary terms, and in a sidebar on each spread." SLJ

Includes glossary

Oxlade, Chris

Experiments with sound; explaining sound. Heinemann Library 2009 48p il (Do it yourself) $22; pa $8.99

Grades: 3 4 5 6   **534**

1. Sound 2. Science -- Experiments

ISBN 978-1-4329-2311-2; 978-1-4329-2318-1 pa

LC 2008034938

This explains the science of sound and includes such experiments as making a pan flute from straws and a homemade record player

This "would make an ideal supplement to science classes. A modular layout and dynamic photos keep things moving, while the experiments . . . feature lists of readily available materials, the steps required to pull off the magic, and warnings when adult supervision is required." Booklist

Includes bibliographical references

Riley, Peter D.

Sound; [by] Peter Riley. Sea-to-Sea Publications 2011 32p il (The real scientist investigates) lib bdg $28.50

Grades: 3 4 5   **534**

1. Sound

ISBN 978-1-59771-283-5; 1-59771-283-3

LC 2010005374

In this book about sound "solid scientific material is presented in accessible language and a visually engaging, boldly colored layout. Budding scientists are encouraged to hone their skills by recording observations, making predictions, and analyzing results. Hands-on activities are included on almost every spread. . . . The many color photos feature diverse children demonstrating the activities." SLJ

Includes glossary and bibliographical references

Spilsbury, Richard

What is sound? exploring science with hands-on activities. [by] Richard and Louise Spilsbury. Enslow Publishers 2008 32p il (In touch with basic science) lib bdg $22.60

Grades: 3 4 5   **534**

1. Sound 2. Sound waves 3. Science -- Experiments

ISBN 978-0-7660-3098-5 lib bdg; 0-7660-3098-9 lib bdg

LC 2007024520

This book "covers topics about sound, such as reflecting waves, the speed of sound, resonance, standing waves, beats, noise, and the sounds of strings. Each of seven hands-on activities for children is fully illustrated with photos of children doing the experiment. . . . This book would appeal to elementary children." Sci Books Films

Includes glossary and bibliographical references

535   Light and related radiation

Branley, Franklyn Mansfield

★ **Day** light, night light; where light comes from. by Franklyn M. Branley; illustrated by Stacey Schuett. newly il ed; HarperCollins Pubs. 1998 32p col il (Let's-read-and-find-out science) hardcover o.p. pa $4.95

Grades: K 1 2 3   **535**

1. Light
ISBN 0-06-027294-5; 0-06-027295-3 lib bdg; 0-06-445171-2 pa

LC 96-33316

First published 1975 with title: Light and darkness

Discusses the properties of light, particularly its source in heat

"This is a beautifully illustrated children's book about a basic concept in science. The pictures add to the clearly written text." Sci Books Films

Bulla, Clyde Robert

What makes a shadow? illustrated by June Otani. rev ed; HarperCollins Pubs. 1994 32p il (Let's-read-and-find-out science) lib bdg $15.89

Grades: K 1   **535**

1. Shades and shadows
ISBN 0-06-022916-0

LC 92-36350

A revised and newly illustrated edition of the title first published 1962 by Crowell

"Using short sentences and developmentally appropriate language, the author explains how shadows are formed, gives numerous examples of shadows, and describes how to make shadow pictures on the wall. Each page is illustrated with bright, colorful drawings, and the gender and cultural representation is excellent." Sci Books Films

Burnie, David

Light; written by David Burnie. DK Pub. 1999 64p il (DK eyewitness books) $15.99

Grades: 5 6 7 8   **535**

1. Light
ISBN 978-0-7894-4885-9; 0-7894-4885-8

A guide to the origins, principles, and historical study of light.

Caes, Charles J.

★ **Discovering** the speed of light; by Charles J. Caes. 1st ed. Rosen Pub. 2012 112 p. ill. (chiefly col.) (Scientist's guide to physics) (library) $34.60

Grades: 5 6 7 8   **535**

1. Light -- Speed -- Juvenile literature 2. Light -- Study and teaching -- History
ISBN 1448846994; 9781448846993

LC 2010048426

This book by Charles J. Caes is part of the "Scientist's Guide to Physics" series. It "uncovers the earliest study of the speed of light, around 550 BCE in classical Greece. From classical Greece to Galileo and later Albert Einstein, this title also details the history of the discovery of light speed measurement and theories." (VOYA)

Includes bibliographical references (p. 107-108) and index.

Claybourne, Anna

Light and dark. QEB Pub. 2008 24p il (Why it works) $24.25

Grades: 2 3 4 5   **535**

1. Light 2. Shades and shadows
ISBN 978-1-59566-556-0; 1-59566-556-0

LC 2008-11709

This is "colorfully illustrated and should help young students relate better to the concepts being presented. A glossary of key words and a page of suggestions for parents and teachers to extend the learning experience round out the text." Sci Books & Films

Includes glossary and bibliographical references

Cobb, Vicki

I see myself; illustrated by Julia Gorton. HarperCollins Pubs. 2002 un il (Science play) $15.99; lib bdg $17.89

Grades: K 1 2   **535**

1. Light 2. Optics 3. Mirrors 4. Reflection (Optics)
ISBN 0-688-17836-7; 0-688-17837-5 lib bdg

LC 00-57220

"The simple yet well-conceived activities engage children in more than just observations—the questions and explanations are constructed to help young kids draw conclusions from their observations. Remarkably, all this is accomplished in a child-friendly, straightforward text. The illustrations are bright and energetic." Horn Book

Farndon, John

Light and optics. Benchmark Bks. 2000 32p il (Science experiments) lib bdg $16.95

Grades: 3 4 5 6   **535**

1. Light 2. Optics 3. Experiments 4. Light -- Experiments 5. Optics -- Experiments
ISBN 0-7614-1090-2

LC 99-89898

A collection of experiments that explore the nature of light and how it is measured and perceived. Activities include making a shadow theater, a periscope, a microscope, a telescope, and a pinhole camera

Includes glossary

Gardner, Robert

Dazzling science projects with light and color. Enslow Elementary 2006 48p il (Fantasic physical science experiments) lib bdg $23.93

Grades: 4 5 6   **535**

1. Color 2. Light 3. Science -- Experiments 4. Light -- Juvenile literature 5. Science -- Experiments -- Juvenile literature
ISBN 0-7660-2587-X

LC 2005-09498

This "title is devoted to light and seeing, mixing colors, and more. Each of 10 chapters includes an experiment, followed by an explanation of why it works, and offers ideas for devising projects to present at a science fair. . . . Large colorful, cartoonlike drawings complement the [text]. . . . [This offers] solid information." SLJ

Includes glossary and bibliographical references

Hall, Pamela

Follow it! Learn about shadows. Child's World 2010 24p il (Science definitions) lib bdg $22.79

Grades: PreK K 1 2 **535**

1. Shades and shadows

ISBN 978-1-60253-508-4 lib bdg; 1-60253-508-6 lib bdg

LC 2010010975

"With full-page color photos and spare, interactive text, this small picture book . . . uses hands-on, everyday examples to explain basic physics. . . . Young children who love to play with shadows, making hand puppets and scary shapes, will be fascinated by the links between their playtime and science facts." Booklist

Lauw, Darlene

Light; [by Darlene Lauw & Lim Cheng Puay; series illustrator, Roy Chan Yoon Loy] Crabtree 2002 31p il (Science alive!) $25.27; pa $7.95

Grades: 3 4 5 6 **535**

1. Light 2. Optics 3. Experiments 4. Light -- Experiments 5. Optics -- Experiments

ISBN 0-7787-0560-9; 0-7787-0606-0 pa

LC 2001-42423

Presents activities that demonstrate how light works in our everyday lives. History boxes feature the scientists who made significant discoveries in the field of light

This book explains its subject matter "in a colorful and easy to understand format. . . . All experiments use easily obtainable parts and in some cases actual household items." Sci Books Films

Includes glossary

Meiani, Antonella

Light. Lerner Publs. 2003 40p il (Experimenting with science) lib bdg $23.93

Grades: 4 5 6 7 **535**

1. Light 2. Science -- Experiments

ISBN 0-8225-0084-1

LC 2001-38947

Experiments with light explain shadows and colors, and demonstrate such concepts as reflection and refraction

This offers "straightforward, well-designed experiments. . . . Numerous clear diagrams, some photos, and occasional historical sidebars extend this material, which is notable for its substance." Horn Book Guide

Includes glossary and bibliographical references

Riley, Peter D.

Light; [by] Peter Riley. Sea-to-Sea Publications 2011 32p il (The real scientist investigates ...) lib bdg $28.50

Grades: 3 4 5 **535**

1. Light 2. Science -- Experiments

ISBN 9781597712811; 1597712817

LC 2010005372

"The design of, and concepts presented . . . are exciting and appropriate for third-and-fourth grade students. Each page is filled with coloful descriptions that are appropriate for exploring light. The scientific method is outlined for each exploration, and simple techniques are offered for how to conduct exciting experiments. . . . The safety aspects of doing science experiments are covered in clear details. Any science class or children's library would be an appropriate place for this beautifully designed book." Sci Books & Films

Includes bibliographical references

Spilsbury, Louise

What is light? exploring science with hands-on activities. [by] Richard and Louise Spilsbury. Enslow Publishers 2008 32p il (In touch with basic science) lib bdg $22.60

Grades: 3 4 5 **535**

1. Light 2. Optics 3. Science -- Experiments

ISBN 978-0-7660-3097-8 lib bdg; 0-7660-3097-0 lib bdg

LC 2007024550

This book "introduces the reader to concepts such as reflection, refraction, taking pictures, using lenses, and light waves—specifically as manifested in rainbows and spectrometers. . . . What makes this volume so useful is that children are learning while they are doing the experiments. The graphics are excellent." Sci Books Films

Includes glossary and bibliographical references

535.6 Color

Barton, Chris

★ The **Day**-Glo brothers; the true story of Bob and Joe Switzer's bright ideas and brand-new colors. illustrated by Tony Persiani. Charlesbridge 2009 un il $18.95

Grades: K 1 2 3 **535.6**

1. Color 2. Paint 3. Inventors 4. Fluorescence 5. Chemical industry executives

ISBN 978-1-57091-673-1; 1-57091-673-X

LC 2008-26959

ALA ALSC Siebert Medal Honor Book (2010)

"Still in their teens in 1933, brothers Bob and Joe Switzer began experimenting with fluorescent colors and trying to create paints that would glow in the dark. . . . After years of experimentation, they succeeded in creating paints that glowed in daylight as well as ultraviolet light. . . . In stylized, digital artwork with a retro feel, Persiani illustrates early scenes of the Switzers' life in black, white, and shades of gray, then gradually introduces colors. . . . Organizing his material well and writing with a sure sense of what will interest children, Barton creates a picture book that celebrates ingenuity and invention." Booklist

Brocket, Jane

Ruby, violet, lime; looking for color. [text and photographs by Jane Brocket] Millbrook Press 2012 30p il (Jane Brocket's clever concepts) lib bdg $25.26

Grades: PreK K **535.6**

1. Color

ISBN 978-0-7613-4612-8; 0-7613-4612-0

LC 2010051757

Presents brightly colored photograph illustrations that demonstrate the three primary colors and three secondary colors, as well as brown, pink, black, white, gray, silver, and gold.

"Isolating each featured color in snapshots (often close-ups) of everyday objects, the spreads are completely filled with a grid of three to five photos that prove to readers that colors can be found anywhere and everywhere. . . . Worthy of even the most overflowing of colorful collections, this is sure to be the beginning of many a color adventure, both in school and out." Kirkus

Doran, Ella

Color; illustrations and photos by Ella Doran, David Goodman & Zoe Miller. Abrams 2006 un il $19.95

Grades: K 1 2 3   **535.6**

1. Color

ISBN 978-1-85437-697-8; 1-85437-697-7

"This riotous and bold concept book presents the basic ideas about color with simple text and clear, inviting images. . . . Arty photo collages [introduce] each of the three primary colors. . . . [The book introduces] the idea of color mixing, followed by spreads for each of the secondary colors. . . . Black and white provide an introduction to the concepts of shading and tinting. The language of color, including word associations (e.g., blue: cool, calm, sad), and different shades printed in their appropriate hues are included as are some craft activities and a few trompe l'oeils." SLJ

Farndon, John

Color. Benchmark Bks. 2000 32p il (Science experiments) lib bdg $16.95

Grades: 3 4 5 6   **535.6**

1. Color 2. Experiments 3. Color -- Experiments 4. Science -- Experiments

ISBN 0-7614-1092-9

LC 99-86994

A collection of experiments that explore the nature of color and how it is created and perceived

"Activities include creating a spectrum using a bottle of water and a piece of black cardboard, and making a color wheel. . . . The clearly illustrated, step-by-step directions for the science activities will make this a useful addition to many libraries." Booklist

Includes glossary

Hoban, Tana

★ **Colors** everywhere. Greenwillow Bks. 1995 un il $18.99; lib bdg $17.89

Grades: PreK K   **535.6**

1. Color

ISBN 0-688-12762-2; 0-688-12763-0 lib bdg

LC 93-24847

"Very young children will enjoy naming the pictured objects, while older readers will be drawn into exploring the colors' varying tones. A book children will come back to over and over." Horn Book

★ **Of** colors and things. Greenwillow Bks. 1989 un il hardcover o.p. pa $7.99

Grades: PreK K   **535.6**

1. Color

ISBN 0-688-04585-5 pa

LC 88-11101

Photographs of toys, food, and other common objects are grouped on each page according to color

"Hoban hits on a simple device to heighten a child's awareness, but what lifts this above the average concept book is the quality of its design and illustration." Booklist

Houblon, Marie

A **world** of colors; seeing colors in a new way. National Geographic 2009 43p il $16.95; lib bdg $25.90

Grades: K 1 2 3   **535.6**

1. Color

ISBN 978-1-4263-0556-6; 1-4263-0556-7; 978-1-4263-0559-7 lib bdg; 1-4263-0559-1 lib bdg

Original French edition, 2004

"This sophisticated book shows the uses of color and encourages children to find examples in their own environments. Most hues are allotted two spreads. The first one features a solid, saturated page with the color's name in a contrasting shade, facing a closeup photograph framed in black. The second includes two or three additional photos with engaging commentary or questions. . . . The images are unexpected and captivating." SLJ

Lawrence, Ellen

Color; by Ellen Lawrence; consultants: Suzy Gazlay, MA, Recipient, Presidential Award for Excellence in Science Teaching, Kimberly Brenneman, PhD, National Institute for Early Education Research, Rutgers University, New Brunswick, New Jersey. Bearport Publishing 2013 24 p. col. ill. (Science Slam: Fundamental experiments) lib bdg $23.93

Grades: K 1 2 3   **535.6**

1. Color -- Juvenile literature

ISBN 1617727385; 9781617727382

LC 2012050812

In this book by Ellen Lawrence "students will have the opportunity to conduct experiments that help them investigate what color is, as well as why things in our world are different colors. Using everyday items that kids can easily find around their homes, young students will turn into scientists as they carry out step-by-step experiments to answer intriguing questions." (Publisher's note)

Includes bibliographical references (page 24) and index

McMillan, Bruce

★ **Growing** colors. Lothrop, Lee & Shepard Bks. 1988 32p il hardcover o.p. pa $5.99

Grades: PreK K 1 2   **535.6**

1. Color 2. Fruit 3. Vegetables

ISBN 0-688-07844-3; 0-688-13112-3 pa

LC 88-2767

"A luscious-looking book that will help children identify colors. . . . This is notably a treat for kids and an example of photography as an art form in picture books." Bull Cent Child Books

536 Heat

Auch, Alison

All about temperature. Capstone Press 2011 24p il (Pebble plus: physical science) lib bdg $23.99

Grades: PreK K 1 2   **536**

1. Temperature

ISBN 978-1-4296-6608-4; 1-4296-6608-0

LC 2010034308

This explains the science of temperature.

This book "addresses its topic in a direct and simple manner. . . . [The] title includes a hands-on experiment with both textual and visual directions." SLJ

Includes glossary and bibliographical references

Gardner, Robert

Easy genius science projects with temperature and heat; great experiments and ideas. by Robert Gardner and Eric Kemer. Enslow Publishers 2009 128p il (Easy genius science projects) lib bdg $31.93

Grades: 5 6 7 8   536

1. Heat 2. Temperature 3. Science projects 4. Science -- Experiments

ISBN 978-0-7660-2939-2 lib bdg; 0-7660-2939-5 lib bdg

LC 2008-4675

"Presents several science experiments and science project ideas dealing with temperature and heat." Publisher's note

Includes glossary and bibliographical references

Really hot science projects with temperature; how hot is it? how cold is it? Enslow Pubs. 2003 48p il (Sensational science experiments) lib bdg $18.95

Grades: 3 4 5 6   536

1. Cold 2. Heat 3. Temperature 4. Science projects 5. Experiments 6. Cold -- Experiments 7. Heat -- Experiments 8. Science -- Experiments 9. Temperature -- Experiments 10. Cold -- Juvenile literature

ISBN 0-7660-2015-0

LC 2002-153849

"Includes such experiments as observing diffusion in hot and cold water and measuring the dew point. . . . Gardner's clear, informal explanations are echoed in LaBaff's colorful illustrations." Booklist

Includes bibliographical references and index

Sizzling science projects with heat and energy; [by] Robert Gardner. Enslow Elementary 2006 48p il (Fantastic physical science experiments) $23.93

Grades: 4 5 6   536

1. Heat 2. Force and energy 3. Science -- Experiments

ISBN 0-7660-2586-1

LC 2005033755

This offers science experiments concerning heat and temperature, kinetic energy, elastic potential energy, light and electric energy, insulation, and ice.

Includes glossary and bibliographical references

Rand, Casey

Temperature. Heinemann Library 2011 32p il (Measure it!) lib bdg $29; pa $7.99

Grades: 3 4 5   536

1. Measurement 2. Temperature

ISBN 978-1-4329-3767-6 lib bdg; 1-4329-3767-7 lib bdg; 978-1-4329-3773-7 pa; 1-4329-3773-1 pa

LC 2009-35275

"Size of text and font is suitable for this age group with uncluttered pages designed so that text is set off with the illustrations, graphs, or drawings placed vertically. Key words appear in bold." Libr Media Connect

Includes glossary and bibliographical references

Sullivan, Navin

Temperature; [by] Navin Sullivan. Marshall Cavendish Benchmark 2007 48p il (Measure up!) lib bdg $20.90

Grades: 4 5 6 7   536

1. Heat 2. Temperature 3. Thermometers

ISBN 978-0-7614-2322-5 lib bdg; 0-7614-2322-2 lib bdg

LC 2006011981

This is "engaging and informative. . . . The excellent blend of photographs, charts, and diagrams complements the [text]." SLJ

Includes glossary and bibliographical references

537   Electricity and electronics

Berger, Melvin

Switch on, switch off; illustrated by Carolyn Croll. Crowell 1989 32p il (Let's-read-and-find-out science book) hardcover o.p. pa $4.95

Grades: K 1 2 3   537

1. Electricity

ISBN 0-690-04786-X lib bdg; 0-06-445097-X pa

LC 88-17638

"This book presents rudimentary exploration of electricity and how electrical current flows to the light switch in a child's room. Follow the current from the generator to a power plant to the switch on the wall. Includes instructions for a simple generator. A good, first look at a topic that mystifies young scientists." Sci Child

Claybourne, Anna

Electricity. QEB Pub. 2008 24p il (Why it works) $24.25

Grades: 2 3 4 5   537

1. Electricity

ISBN 978-1-59566-559-1; 1-59566-559-5

LC 2008-11708

This is "colorfully illustrated and should help young students relate better to the concepts being presented. A glossary of key words and a page of suggestions for parents and teachers to extend the learning experience round out the text." Sci Books & Films

Includes glossary and bibliographical references

Farndon, John

Electricity. Benchmark Bks. 2001 32p il (Science experiments) lib bdg $16.95

Grades: 3 4 5 6   537

1. Electricity 2. Experiments 3. Science -- Experiments

ISBN 0-7614-1086-4

LC 00-39752

A collection of activities that explore electricity "discussing charges, circuits, conductors, and insulators. Activities include creating a Xerox effect and making an electroscope." SLJ

Includes glossary

Gardner, Robert

Easy genius science projects with electricity and magnetism; great experiments and ideas. Enslow Publishers 2009 128p il (Easy genius science projects) lib bdg $31.93

Grades: 5 6 7 8   537

1. Magnetism 2. Electricity 3. Science projects 4.

Science -- Experiments
ISBN 978-0-7660-2923-1 lib bdg; 0-7660-2923-9
lib bdg

LC 2007-38470

"Science projects and experiments about electricity and magnetism." Publisher's note

Includes glossary and bibliographical references

Energizing science projects with electricity and magnetism; [by] Robert Gardner. Enslow Elementary 2006 48p il (Fantastic physical science experiments) lib bdg $23.93

Grades: 4 5 6   **537**

1. Magnetism 2. Electricity 3. Science -- Experiments
ISBN 0-7660-2584-5

LC 2005018730

This offers science experiments concerning electric charges, magnetism and compasses, batteries, electric bulbs, and wires, and electromagnets

Includes glossary and bibliographical references

Riley, Peter D.

Electricity; [by] Peter Riley. Sea-to-Sea Publications 2011 32p il (The real scientist investigates) lib bdg $28.50

Grades: 3 4 5   **537**

1. Electricity
ISBN 978-1-59771-279-8; 1-59771-279-5

LC 2010005370

In this book about electricity "solid scientific material is presented in accessible language and a visually engaging, boldly colored layout. Budding scientists are encouraged to hone their skills by recording observations, making predictions, and analyzing results. Hands-on activities are included on almost every spread. . . . The many color photos feature diverse children demonstrating the activities." SLJ

Includes glossary and bibliographical references

Spilsbury, Richard

What is electricity and magnetism? exploring science with hands-on activities. [by] Richard and Louise Spilsbury. Enslow Elementary 2008 32p il (In touch with basic science) lib bdg $22.60

Grades: 3 4 5   **537**

1. Magnetism 2. Electricity 3. Science -- Experiments
ISBN 978-0-7660-3096-1 lib bdg; 0-7660-3096-2
lib bdg

LC 2007024518

This book "covers topics such as making and storing electricity, magnetic fields, electromagnets, and motors. Each chapter focuses on activities related to these topics. . . . There are more than enough hands-on activities to provide a child with a solid basic understanding of the relationship between magnetism and electricity." Sci Books Films

Includes glossary and bibliographical references

VanCleave, Janice Pratt, 1942-

Janice VanCleave's electricity; mind-boggling experiments you can turn into science fair projects. [by] Janice VanCleave. Wiley 1994 89p il $10.95

Grades: 4 5 6 7   **537**

1. Electricity 2. Science projects 3. Science -- Experiments
ISBN 0-471-31010-7

LC 93-40913

"The experiments move from the simple, which do not require the use of batteries, to those that require small batteries, sizes AA, AAA, C, or D. An appendix shows how to make strips of aluminum foil that can be used to form the electrical circuits that are part of some of the experiments. By encouraging students to move beyond the basic problems (with adult supervision), the author encourages them to be creative in designing science fair projects." Booklist

Includes glossary

Vogel, Julia

Plug it in! Learn about electricity; illustrated by Jane Yamada. Child's World 2010 24p il (Science definitions) lib bdg $22.79

Grades: PreK K 1 2   **537**

1. Electricity
ISBN 978-1-60253-511-4 lib bdg; 1-60253-511-6
lib bdg

LC 2010010979

This book about electricity is "attractive and succinct. . . . Large, eye-catching photos cover the recto of each spread. . . . Varying, jewel-toned accents are used in headings, highlighted glossary terms, and in a sidebar on each spread." SLJ

Includes glossary

Woodford, Chris

Experiments with electricity and magnetism. Gareth Stevens Pub. 2010 32p il (Cool science) lib bdg $28; pa $10.50

Grades: 4 5 6 7   **537**

1. Magnetism 2. Electricity 3. Science -- Experiments
ISBN 9781433934445 lib bdg; 1433934442 lib bdg; 9781433934452 pa; 1433934450 pa

LC 2009037141

"The book [is] written in an easy-to-understand, straightforward style with helpful real-life photographs... Students who need simple experiments or those who need more advanced projects will find [it] helpful." Library Media Connection

Includes bibliographical references

537.5   Electronics

Gifford, Clive

Cool tech; gadgets, games robots, and the digital world. written by Clive Gifford; consultant, Mike Goldsmith. DK Pub. 2011 143 p. col. ill. (hardcover) $19.99

Grades: 5 6 7   **537.5**

1. Technological innovations 2. Electronic apparatus and appliances 3. Games 4. Robots 5. Computers 6. Technology 7. Electronics
ISBN 0756682703; 9780756682705

LC 2011283520

This book offers "descriptions and a history of many of the prominent technological developments . . . . The topics range from coverage of notable technological breakthroughs to the individuals who made them happen. These include sections on technological products such as laptops, undersea cables, smart phones, video games, digital cameras, robots, and the Mars Rover." (SB&F: Your Guide to Science Resources for All Ages)

538 Magnetism

Branley, Franklyn Mansfield

What makes a magnet? by Franklyn M. Branley; illustrated by True Kelley. HarperCollins Pubs. 1996 31p il (Let's-read-and-find-out science) hardcover o.p. pa $4.95
Grades: K 1 2 3   **538**

1. Magnets
ISBN 0-06-026441-1; 0-06-445148-8 pa

LC 95-32181

Describes how magnets work and includes instructions for making a magnet and a compass

"Kelley's happy line drawings incorporate a humorous mouse to add safety warnings and goofy side comments. The clear diagrams and lucid explanations are both informative and engaging." Horn Book

Farndon, John

Magnetism. Benchmark Bks. 2001 32p il (Science experiments) lib bdg $16.95
Grades: 3 4 5 6   **538**

1. Magnetism 2. Experiments
ISBN 0-7614-1343-X

LC 2001-25168

A collection of activities that explore magnetism, discussing magnetic materials, magnetic poles, electricity and magnetism, Earth's magnetism, and magnetism in space
Includes glossary

Meiani, Antonella

Magnetism. Lerner Publs. 2003 40p il (Experimenting with science) lib bdg $23.93
Grades: 4 5 6 7   **538**

1. Magnetism 2. Science -- Experiments
ISBN 0-8225-0085-X

LC 2001-50464

Describes a variety of experiments that explore the world of magnets and magnetism, arranged in the categories "Magnets," "Magnetic Poles," "Magnetic Force," and "Magnetism and Electricity"

This offers "straightforward, well-designed experiments. . . . Numerous clear diagrams, some photos, and occasional historical sidebars extend this material, which is notable for its substance." Horn Book Guide
Includes glossary and bibliographical references

Vogel, Julia

Push and pull! Learn about magnets; illustrated by Jane Yamada. Child's World 2010 24p il (Science definitions) lib bdg $22.79
Grades: PreK K 1 2   **538**

1. Magnets 2. Magnetism
ISBN 978-1-60253-513-8 lib bdg; 1-60253-513-2 lib bdg

LC 2010010981

This book about magnets is "attractive and succinct. . . . Large, eye-catching photos cover the recto of each spread. . . . Varying, jewel-toned accents are used in headings, highlighted glossary terms, and in a sidebar on each spread." SLJ
Includes glossary

539 Modern physics

Claybourne, Anna

Who split the atom? Arcturus Pub. 2010 46p il (Breakthroughs in science and technology) lib bdg $32.80
Grades: 5 6 7 8   **539**

1. Atoms 2. Matter 3. Atomic structure -- Juvenile literature 4. Discoveries in science -- Juvenile literature
ISBN 978-1-84837-683-0 lib bdg; 1-84837-683-9 lib bdg

LC 2010-11015

This book explores the ways in which scientists uncovered the atom.

The book is "divided into easy to read short chapters with large, colorful photographs and graphics on every page. . . . The added inserts provide additional information to engage readers and help them connect with the scientific details." Libr Media Connect
Includes glossary and bibliographical references

539.7 Atomic and nuclear physics

Campbell, Margaret Christine

★ Discovering atoms; Margaret Christine Campbell, Natalie Goldstein. 1st ed. Rosen Pub. 2012 112 p. ill. (The scientist's guide to physics) (library) $34.60
Grades: 5 6 7 8 9   **539.7**

1. Atoms -- Juvenile literature 2. Atomic theory -- History -- Juvenile literature 3. Atomic structure -- Juvenile literature 4. Matter -- Constitution -- Juvenile literature
ISBN 1448847001; 9781448847006

LC 2010048416

This book by Margaret Christine Campbell is part of the "Scientist's Guide to Physics" series. It "presents the . . . story of the atom's discovery, which is full of bizarre theories, false starts, dead ends, and . . . intellectual insight." (Publisher's note) "Campbell includes a . . . chronological foundation upon which the discovery of elements and the creation of the periodic table build up to the discovery of the atom, atomic rays, particles, models . . . and subatomic particles." (VOYA)
Includes bibliographical references and index.

Cregan, Elizabeth R.

The atom. Compass Point Books 2009 40p il (Mission: science) lib bdg $26.60
Grades: 4 5 6   **539.7**

1. Atoms 2. Atomic theory 3. Nuclear energy
ISBN 978-0-7565-3953-5 lib bdg; 0-7565-3953-6 lib bdg

LC 2008007724

"Cregan discusses the structure of the atom, key scientists, cathode rays and electrons, radioactivity, and atom smashers. . . . The [book has an] open [layout] and large, easy-to-read type. . . . Large eye-catching and colorful photographs and illustrations appear on every page. The [book] includes a simple activity." SLJ
Includes glossary and bibliographical references

Jerome, Kate Boehm

Atomic universe; the quest to discover radioactivity. by Kate Boehm Jerome. National Geographic 2006 59p il (Science quest) $17.95; lib bdg $25.90

Grades: 5 6 7 8　　　　　　　　　**539.7**

1. Radioactivity 2. Nuclear physics

ISBN 0-7922-5543-7; 0-7922-5544-5 lib bdg

LC 2006001316

The text offers "key concepts in a pleasing and readable format that would appeal to reluctant readers." SLJ

Includes glossary and bibliographical references

Lepora, Nathan

Atoms and molecules. Marshall Cavendish Benchmark 2010 48p il (Invisible worlds) lib bdg $28.50

Grades: 4 5 6 7　　　　　　　　　**539.7**

1. Atoms 2. Molecules 3. Nanotechnology

ISBN 978-0-7614-4192-2 lib bdg; 0-7614-4192-1 lib bdg

LC 2008037237

This describes the details and characteristics of atoms and molecules that are too small for the unaided eye to see.

The narrative is "clear, well written, broken down into manageable pieces, and peppered with eye-opening facts. The numerous photographs are so phenomenal that they will inspire kids to read the text . . . so that they can wrap their minds around what they see." SLJ

Includes glossary and bibliographical references

McLean, Adam

What is atomic theory? Crabtree Pub. Co. 2011 64p il (Shaping modern science) lib bdg $30.60; pa $10.95

Grades: 5 6 7 8　　　　　　　　　**539.7**

1. Atomic theory

ISBN 978-0-7787-7197-5 lib bdg; 0-7787-7197-0 lib bdg; 978-0-7787-7204-0 pa; 0-7787-7204-7 pa

This title is "not only written and organized well, but [it is] also gorgeous in design. Full-color photographs and illustrations are set over colorful backgrounds that add depth but not distraction. [The title] includes thought-provoking quotes from famous authors and scientists and some eyebrow-raising 'Quick Facts' throughout." SLJ

Includes glossary and bibliographical references

540　Chemistry and allied sciences

Baxter, Roberta

Chemical reaction. Kidhaven Press 2005 48p il (Kidhaven science library) $27

Grades: 4 5 6 7　　　　　　　　　**540**

1. Chemistry

ISBN 0-7377-2072-7

"Baxter defines her subject and describes many different types of reactions, including acid-base reactions, oxidation, and photosynthesis. The explanations are clear and succinct. The final chapter presents some potential uses for chemical reactions, citing the development of molecular computers." SLJ

Includes glossary and bibliographical references

Coelho, Alexa

Why Is Milk White? & 200 Other Curious Chemistry Questions. Alexa Coelho and Simon Quellen Field. Independent Pub Group 2013 288 p. ill. (paperback) $14.95

Grades: 4 5 6 7 8　　　　　　　　　**540**

1. Chemistry -- Miscellanea 2. Chemistry -- Juvenile literature

ISBN 1613744528; 9781613744529

LC 2012040205

This juvenile chemistry book, by Alexa Coelho and Simon Quellen Field, is a "question-and-answer primer [that] provides straightforward, easy-to-understand explanations for inquisitive young scientists' questions. . . . From lifting latent fingerprints from a 'crime scene' using super glue (for smooth surfaces) or iodine (for paper) to hollowing out the zinc interior of a penny using muriatic acid . . . , this handy guide is [a] . . . resource for the budding chemist." (Publisher's note)

Green, Dan

Chemistry; getting a big reaction. created by Basher; written by Dan Green. Kingfisher 2010 128p il $14.99; pa $8.99

Grades: 4 5 6 7　　　　　　　　　**540**

1. Chemistry

ISBN 978-0-7534-6615-5; 0-7534-6615-5; 978-0-7534-6413-7 pa; 0-7534-6413-6 pa

This "begins with a short overview of [chemistry] and information on Antoine Lavoisier's 18th-century scientific findings. Concepts are grouped by associations: 'Basic States' (solid, liquid, etc.), 'Nuts and Bolts' (atom, ion, etc.), 'Nasty Boys' (acid, base, etc.), and more. The individual concepts are each introduced over a spread that features a computer-generated cartoon of a character representing the idea and a brief introduction to its characteristics and personality. . . . The information is presented in a chatty, first-person voice." SLJ

Juettner, Bonnie

Molecules. Kidhaven Press 2005 48p il (Kidhaven science library) $27

Grades: 4 5 6 7　　　　　　　　　**540**

1. Chemistry 2. Molecules

ISBN 0-7377-2076-X

"Juettner gives an overview of the building blocks of elements and compounds, including atoms, molecules, and the various states of matter, and describes their characteristics. The last chapter offers information on some extreme materials, such as plasma and the recently discovered Bose-Einstein condensates (BEC)." SLJ

Newmark, Ann

Chemistry; written by Ann Newmark. rev ed; DK Pub. 2005 72p il (DK eyewitness books) $15.99

Grades: 4 5 6 7　　　　　　　　　**540**

1. Chemistry

ISBN 0-7566-1385-X

First published 1993

Explores the world of chemical reactions and shows the role that chemistry plays in our world.

Van Gorp, Lynn

Elements. Compass Point Books 2009 40p il (Mission: science) lib bdg $26.60

Grades: 4 5 6 **540**

1. Chemical elements

ISBN 978-0-7565-3951-1 lib bdg; 0-7565-3951-X lib bdg

LC 2008007284

"Van Gorp provides an overview of matter and the elements and how the latter combine to form compounds; ionic and covalent bonds; the periodic table of the elements; reactions; and mixtures and solutions. The [book has an] open [layout] and large, easy-to-read type. . . . Large eye-catching and colorful photographs and illustrations appear on every page. . . . The [book] includes a simple activity." SLJ

Includes glossary and bibliographical references

540.7 Education, research, related topics

Gardner, Robert

Ace your chemistry science project; great science fair ideas. [by] Robert Gardner, Salvatore Tocci, and Kenneth G. Rainis. Enslow Publishers 2009 112p il (Ace your science project) lib bdg $31.93

Grades: 5 6 7 8 **540.7**

1. Chemistry 2. Science projects 3. Science -- Experiments

ISBN 978-0-7660-3227-9 lib bdg; 0-7660-3227-2 lib bdg

LC 2008-30800

"Presents several science projects and science project ideas about chemistry." Publisher's note

Includes bibliographical references

Ace your science project using chemistry magic and toys; great science fair ideas. Enslow Publishers 2009 128p il (Ace your science project) lib bdg $31.93

Grades: 5 6 7 8 **540.7**

1. Toys 2. Chemistry 3. Science projects 4. Science -- Experiments

ISBN 978-0-7660-3226-2 lib bdg; 0-7660-3226-4 lib bdg

LC 2008-4685

"Dozens of . . . science activities are presented with background information, step-by-step instructions, and suggestions for extending to the science fair level. . . . Color illustrations and important safety information are included." Horn Book Guide

Includes bibliographical references

Easy genius science projects with chemistry; great experiments and ideas. Enslow Publishers 2009 112p il (Easy genius science projects) lib bdg $31.93

Grades: 5 6 7 8 **540.7**

1. Chemistry 2. Science projects 3. Science -- Experiments

ISBN 978-0-7660-2925-5 lib bdg; 0-7660-2925-5 lib bdg

LC 2007-38469

This book offers science projects and experiments about chemistry divided into the following chapters: atoms, molecules, elements, and compounds; chemical reactions; oxygen and oxidation; separating and testing substances

"Illustrations are bright and useful in explaining the techniques presented. . . . An excellent resource." Sci Books Films

Includes glossary and bibliographical references

Rhatigan, Joe

Cool chemistry concoctions; 50 formulas that fizz, foam, splatter & ooze. [by] Joe Rhatigan & Veronika Gunter; illustrated by Tom LaBaff. Lark Books 2005 80p il hardcover o.p. pa $7.95

Grades: 3 4 5 6 **540.7**

1. Chemistry 2. Science -- Experiments

ISBN 1-57990-620-6; 1-57990-882-9 pa

LC 2004-13287

This describes such experiments as how to make slime, volcanoes, stalactites, water bombs, and shrunken heads (using apples and Epsom salts)

"This lively book offers an engaging introduction to science experiments. The projects . . . are simple and require household materials. . . . The zany cartoon illustrations are the perfect accompaniment to the text, which is fun and informative." SLJ

541 Chemistry

Ballard, Carol

Mixtures and solutions. Raintree 2010 48p il (Sci-hi: physical science) lib bdg $22; pa $8.99

Grades: 5 6 7 8 **541**

1. Chemistry 2. Molecules

ISBN 978-1-4109-3376-8 lib bdg; 1-4109-3376-8 lib bdg; 978-1-4109-3381-2 pa; 1-4109-3381-4 pa

LC 2009-13452

A "compelling read for both browsers and science buffs. . . . Information is clearly presented and flows smoothly. . . . A treasure trove of information." SLJ

Includes glossary and bibliographical references

Kyi, Tanya Lloyd

50 burning questions; a sizzling history of fire. illustrated by Ross Kinnaird. Annick Press 2010 104p il (50 questions series) $21.95; pa $12.95

Grades: 3 4 5 6 **541**

1. Fire

ISBN 978-1-55451-221-8; 1-55451-221-2; 978-1-55451-220-1 pa; 1-55451-220-4 pa

The author answers "questions in engagingly written vignettes that reveal how important fire has been and continues to be in nearly every aspect of human life. . . . Interspersed throughout the text are simple fire-related activities readers can perform utilizing a few common household items. . . . Kinnaird's colorful cartoon illustrations complement the text's humorous tone. . . . Accessibly written and appealingly designed." Kirkus

Includes bibliographical references

Oxlade, Chris

Mixing and separating. Heinemann Library 2009 32p il (Changing materials) lib bdg $25.36; pa $7.99

Grades: K 1 2 **541**
1. Materials
ISBN 978-1-4329-3274-9 lib bdg; 1-4329-3274-8 lib bdg; 978-1-4329-3279-4 pa; 1-4329-3279-9 pa
LC 2008-55124

"Discusses the ideas of mixtures, materials that combine to form a new marterial, and materials that cannot be combined. A few simple activities provide opportunities to experiment. The color photographs are engaging." SLJ

Includes glossary and bibliographical references

546 Inorganic chemistry

Angliss, Sarah
Gold; [by] Sarah Angliss. Benchmark Bks. 2000 32p il (The elements) lib bdg $28.50
Grades: 5 6 7 8 **546**
1. Gold
ISBN 978-0-7614-0887-1; 0-7614-0887-8
LC 98-46800

Explores the history of the precious metal gold and explains its chemistry, how it reacts, its uses, and its importance in our lives.
Includes glossary

Beatty, Richard
Boron; [by] Richard Beatty. Marshall Cavendish Benchmark 2005 32p il (The elements) lib bdg $28.50
Grades: 5 6 7 8 **546**
1. Boron
ISBN 978-0-7614-1921-1; 0-7614-1921-7
LC 2005-42159

"Included in the discussion are the uses of boron in pottery, in the nuclear industry, in living organisms, and in glassmaking. A review of the periodic table and boron's place in it, including the element's relationship to other elements, is provided." Sci Books Films
Includes glossary

Copper; [by] Richard Beatty. Benchmark Books 2001 32p il (The elements) lib bdg $28.50
Grades: 5 6 7 8 **546**
1. Copper
ISBN 978-0-7614-0945-8; 0-7614-0945-9
LC 99-54235

Explores the history of the useful metal copper and explains its chemistry, its uses, and its importance in our lives
Offers "clear, basic information, without oversimplification, in an appealing format." SLJ
Includes glossary

Manganese; [by] Richard Beatty. Benchmark Books 2005 32p il (The elements) lib bdg $28.50
Grades: 5 6 7 8 9 10 11 12 **546**
1. Manganese
ISBN 978-0-7614-1813-9; 0-7614-1813-X
LC 2004-47634
Includes glossary

Phosphorus; by Richard Beatty. Benchmark Books 2001 32p il (The elements) lib bdg $28.50

Grades: 5 6 7 8 **546**
1. Phosphorus
ISBN 978-0-7614-0946-5; 0-7614-0946-7
LC 99-88821

Explores the history of the nonmetallic element phosphorus and explains its chemistry, its reactions with other substances, its uses, and its importance in our lives
Offers "clear, basic information, without oversimplification, in an appealing format." SLJ
Includes glossary

Sulfur; [by] Richard Beatty. Benchmark Books 2000 32p il (The elements) lib bdg $28.50
Grades: 5 6 7 8 **546**
1. Sulphur
ISBN 978-0-7614-0948-9; 0-7614-0948-3
LC 99-86992

Explores the history of the element sulfur and explains its chemistry, its reactions with other substances, its uses, and its importance in our lives
Offers "clear, basic information, without oversimplification, in an appealing format." SLJ
Includes glossary

The **lanthanides**; [by] Richard Beatty. Marshall Cavendish Benchmark 2008 32p il (The elements) lib bdg $28.50
Grades: 5 6 7 8 **546**
1. Lanthanides
ISBN 978-0-7614-2687-5; 0-7614-2687-6
LC 2006-53053

Introduces the lanthanide elements, also known as the rare earth metals, discussing their physical and chemical properties, where they are found, and how they are used.
"Provides a comprehensive, yet easy-to-read overview. . . . The explanations are succinct and clear, without being oversimplified, and the layout is attractive. Diagrams and photographs complement the text on every page." SLJ
Includes glossary

Cobb, Allan B.
Cadmium; [by] Allan Cobb. Marshall Cavendish/Benchmark 2008 32p il (The elements) lib bdg $28.50
Grades: 5 6 7 8 **546**
1. Cadmium
ISBN 978-0-7614-2686-8; 0-7614-2686-8
LC 2006-51790

Introduces the element of cadmium, discussing its physical and chemical properties, where it is found, and how it is used.
"Provides a comprehensive, yet easy-to-read overview. . . . The explanations are succinct and clear, without being oversimplified, and the layout is attractive. Diagrams and photographs complement the text on every page." SLJ
Includes glossary

Cooper, Chris
Arsenic; [by] Chris Cooper. Marshall Cavendish Benchmark 2007 32p il (The elements) lib bdg $28.50
Grades: 5 6 7 8 **546**
1. Arsenic
ISBN 978-0-7614-2203-7; 0-7614-2203-X
LC 2006-43891

"Explanations are concise and clear without being over-simplified, and the arrangement is attractive. Diagrams, drawings, and photographs appear on every page and complement the text well." SLJ

Includes glossary

Dingle, Adrian

The **periodic** table; elements with style! [created by Simon Basher; written by Adrian Dingle] Kingfisher 2007 128p il pa $8.95

Grades: 4 5 6 7   546

1. Chemical elements 2. Periodic law -- Juvenile literature

ISBN 978-0-7534-6085-6 pa; 0-7534-6085-8 pa

LC 2006022515

"After a brief introduction to Mendeleev's famous table and a spread on the chart-topping loner, hydrogen, Dingle presents the elements by group. . . . Data on featured elements includes symbol, atomic number and weight, color, standard state, classification, density, boiling and melting points, . . . a diagram of the position in the periodic table, a full-page original anime-styled icon, . . . and descriptive paragraphs that rise from informative all the way to entertaining." Bull Cent Child Books

Farndon, J.

Calcium; [by] John Farndon. Benchmark Bks. 1999 32p il (The elements) lib bdg $28.50

Grades: 5 6 7 8   546

1. Calcium

ISBN 978-0-7614-0888-8; 0-7614-0888-6

LC 98-55094

Describes the origins, properties, chemical activity, and uses of the element calcium.

"Good, clear diagrams help explain the concepts . . . and full-color and black-and-white illustrations are generally interesting and informative." SLJ

Includes glossary

Hydrogen; [by] John Farndon. Benchmark Bks. 2000 32p il (The elements) lib bdg $28.50

Grades: 5 6 7 8   546

1. Hydrogen

ISBN 978-0-7614-0886-4; 0-7614-0886-X

LC 98-44692

Explores the history of the chemical element hydrogen and explains its chemistry, how it reacts, its uses, and its importance in our lives

"Good, clear diagrams help explain the concepts . . . and full-color and black-and-white illustrations are generally interesting and informative." SLJ

Includes glossary

Farndon, John

Aluminum; [by] John Farndon. Benchmark Books 2001 32p il (The elements) lib bdg $28.50

Grades: 5 6 7 8   546

1. Aluminum

ISBN 978-0-7614-0947-2; 0-7614-0947-5

Describes the discovery, versatility and other special characteristics, various uses, and affect on the human body of this most common metal in the world.

Includes glossary

Nitrogen; [by] John Farndon. Benchmark Bks. 1999 32p il (The elements) lib bdg $28.50

Grades: 5 6 7 8   546

1. Nitrogen

ISBN 978-0-7614-0877-2; 0-7614-0877-0

LC 97-37945

Discusses the origin, discovery, special characteristics, and use of nitrogen in such products as explosives and fertilizers

"The captioned, full-color drawings, photographs, and diagrams clarify the text. . . . [This] will be of interest for both general reading and report writing." SLJ

Includes glossary

Oxygen; [by] John Farndon. Benchmark Bks. 1999 32p il (The elements) lib bdg $28.50

Grades: 5 6 7 8   546

1. Oxygen

ISBN 978-0-7614-0879-6; 0-7614-0879-7

LC 97-52236

Explores the history of the chemical element oxygen and explains its chemistry, how it works in the body, and its importance in our lives.

"The captioned, full-color drawings, photographs, and diagrams clarify the text. . . . [This] will be of interest for both general reading and report writing." SLJ

Includes glossary

Gray, Leon

Iodine; [by] Leon Gray. Benchmark Books 2005 32p il (The elements) lib bdg $28.50

Grades: 5 6 7 8   546

1. Iodine

ISBN 978-0-7614-1812-2; 0-7614-1812-1

LC 2004-47644

"After discussing the structure of the iodine atom and its place on the periodic table, Gray considers its special characteristics, the history of its discovery, and its production and uses, particularly in the medical field. . . . The color illustrations include well-designed, clearly labeled diagrams and many excellent photographs. A solid choice for science collections." Booklist

Includes glossary

Tin; [by] Leon Gray. Benchmark Books 2003 32p il (The elements) lib bdg $28.50

Grades: 5 6 7 8   546

1. Tin

ISBN 978-0-7614-1551-0; 0-7614-1551-3

LC 2003-52083

Examines the characteristics, sources, and uses of the element tin, as well as tin's importance in our lives

"Numerous captioned color photos and sidebars augment the accurate and well-organized but information-dense text." Horn Book Guide

Includes glossary

Zinc; [by] Leon Gray. Marshall Cavendish Benchmark 2006 32p il (The elements) lib bdg $28.50

Grades: 5 6 7 8   546

1. Zinc

ISBN 978-0-7614-1922-8; 0-7614-1922-5

LC 2005-42163

Discusses zinc and where it can be found, how it was discovered, its special characteristics, and their importance.

"Numerous captioned photos and sidebars augment the accurate and well-organized text." Horn Book Guide

Includes glossary

Higgins, Nadia

Splash! Learn about water; illustrated by Jane Yamada. Child's World 2010 24p il (Science definitions) lib bdg $22.79

Grades: PreK K 1 2   **546**
1. Water
ISBN 978-1-60253-514-5 lib bdg; 1-60253-514-0 lib bdg

LC 2010010982

This book about water is "attractive and succinct. . . . Large, eye-catching photos cover the recto of each spread. . . . Varying, jewel-toned accents are used in headings, highlighted glossary terms, and in a sidebar on each spread." SLJ

Includes glossary

Jackson, Tom, 1972-

Fluorine; [by] Tom Jackson. Benchmark Books/ Marshall Cavendish 2004 32p il (The elements) lib bdg $28.50

Grades: 5 6 7 8   **546**
1. Flourine
ISBN 978-0-7614-1549-7; 0-7614-1549-1

LC 2003-43841

Discusses the characteristics, sources, and uses of fluorine.

"Numerous captioned color photos and sidebars augment the accurate and well-organized but information-dense text." Horn Book Guide

Includes glossary

Lithium; [by] Tom Jackson. Marshall Cavendish Benchmark 2007 32p il (The elements) lib bdg $28.50

Grades: 5 6 7 8   **546**
1. Lithium
ISBN 978-0-7614-2199-3; 0-7614-2199-8

LC 2005-55302

Explains where lithium can be found and how it was discovered, and describes its special characteristics and importance to the human body.

"Provides a comprehensive, yet easy-to-read overview in large, bold print. Explanations are concise and clear without being oversimplified, and the arrangement is attractive." SLJ

Includes glossary

Radioactive elements; by Tom Jackson. Marshall Cavendish Benchmark 2005 32p il (The elements) lib bdg $28.50

Grades: 5 6 7 8   **546**
1. Radioactivity 2. Radiochemistry -- Juvenile literature 3. Chemical elements -- Juvenile literature 4. Radioactive substances -- Juvenile literature
ISBN 978-0-7614-1923-5; 0-7614-1923-3

LC 2005-42164

Examines radioactive elements and discusses their discovery, their unique characteristics, their importance, and where they are found.

"Numerous captioned photos and sidebars augment the accurate and well-organized text." Horn Book Guide

Includes glossary

Lepora, Nathan

Chromium; [by] Nathan Lepora. Marshall Cavendish Benchmark 2005 32p il (The elements) lib bdg $28.50

Grades: 5 6 7 8   **546**
1. Chromium
ISBN 978-0-7614-1920-4; 0-7614-1920-9

LC 2005-42160

Discusses chromium and where it can be found, how it was discovered, its special characteristics, and its importance to the human body.

"Numerous captioned photos and sidebars augment the accurate and well-organized text." Horn Book Guide

Includes glossary

Molybdenum; [by] Nathan Lepora. Marshall Cavendish Benchmark 2007 32p il (The elements) lib bdg $28.50

Grades: 5 6 7 8   **546**
1. Molybdenum
ISBN 978-0-7614-2201-3; 0-7614-2201-3

LC 2005-57096

Introduces the element of molybdenum, discussing its physical and chemical properties, where it is found, and what processes or objects it is used in.

"Provides a comprehensive, yet easy-to-read overview in large, bold print. Explanations are concise and clear without being oversimplified, and the arrangement is attractive." SLJ

Includes glossary

O'Daly, Anne

Sodium; [by] Anne O'Daly. Benchmark Books 2001 32p il (The elements) lib bdg $28.50

Grades: 5 6 7 8   **546**
1. Sodium
ISBN 978-0-7614-1271-7; 0-7614-1271-9

LC 2001-25253

Discusses the characteristics, sources, and uses of sodium.

Includes glossary

Oxlade, Chris

★ **Mixing** and separating; [by] Chris Oxlade. Crabtree Pub. 2008 32p il (Working with materials) lib bdg $26.60; pa $7.95

Grades: 2 3 4   **546**
1. Matter 2. Materials
ISBN 978-0-7787-3640-0 lib bdg; 0-7787-3640-7 lib bdg; 978-0-7787-3650-9 pa; 0-7787-3650-4 pa

LC 2007027421

This defines and gives examples of mixtures and describes how materials are mixed or separated by such processes as sieving, dissolving, straining, using magnets, settling and skimming, filtering, and evaporating.

This "title has numerous captioned color photographs. . . . The [book offers] three simple, easy, safe reproducible experiments. . . . Students will appreciate the pleasing design, easy-to-read font, and direct, clear writing." Libr Media Connect

Includes glossary and bibliographical references

Sparrow, Giles

Carbon; [by] Giles Sparrow. Benchmark Bks. 1999 32p il (The elements) lib bdg $28.50

Grades: 5 6 7 8   **546**

1. Carbon

ISBN 978-0-7614-0878-9; 0-7614-0878-9

LC 97-36423

Discusses the origin, discovery, special characteristics, and uses of carbon

Includes glossary

Iron; [by] Giles Sparrow. Benchmark Bks. 1999 32p il (The elements) lib bdg $28.50

Grades: 5 6 7 8   **546**

1. Iron

ISBN 978-0-7614-0880-2; 0-7614-0880-0

LC 97-48524

Discusses the origin, discovery, special characteristics, and uses of iron.

Includes glossary

Thomas, Jens

Silicon; [by] Jens Thomas. Benchmark Books 2001 32p il (The elements) lib bdg $28.50

Grades: 5 6 7 8   **546**

1. Silicon

ISBN 978-0-7614-1274-8; 0-7614-1274-3

LC 2001-25993

Discusses the characteristics, sources, and uses of silicon.

Includes glossary

The **noble** gases; [by] Jens Thomas. Benchmark Books 2002 32p il (The elements) lib bdg $28.50

Grades: 5 6 7 8   **546**

1. Gases

ISBN 978-0-7614-1462-9; 0-7614-1462-2

LC 2002-210

Explores the history of the noble gases and explains their chemistry, their uses, and their importance in our lives.

"The well-selected photographs and diagrams are appropriate to the text." Horn Book Guide

Includes glossary

Turrell, Kerry

Tungsten; [by] Kerry Turrell. Benchmark Books 2004 32p il (The elements) lib bdg $28.50

Grades: 5 6 7 8   **546**

1. Tungsten

ISBN 978-0-7614-1548-0; 0-7614-1548-3

LC 2003-52099

Examines the characteristics, sources, and uses of the element tungsten, as well as tungsten's importance in our lives.

"Numerous captioned color photos and sidebars augment the accurate and well-organized but information-dense text." Horn Book Guide

Includes glossary

Uttley, Colin

Magnesium; [by] Colin Uttley. Benchmark Bks. 2000 32p il (The elements) lib bdg $28.50

Grades: 5 6 7 8   **546**

1. Magnesium

ISBN 978-0-7614-0889-5; 0-7614-0889-4

LC 98-53200

Explores the history of the bright-colored metal magnesium and explains its chemistry, how it reacts, its uses, and its importance in our lives.

Includes glossary

Watt, Susan

Chlorine; [by] Susan Watt. Benchmark Books 2001 32p il (The elements) lib bdg $28.50

Grades: 5 6 7 8   **546**

1. Chlorine

ISBN 978-0-7614-1272-4; 0-7614-1272-7

LC 2001-25252

Discusses the characteristics, sources, and uses of chlorine.

Includes glossary

Cobalt; [by] Susan Watt. Marshall Cavendish Benchmark 2007 32p il (The elements) lib bdg $28.50

Grades: 5 6 7 8   **546**

1. Cobalt

ISBN 978-0-7614-2200-6; 0-7614-2200-5

LC 2005-55303

Introduces the element of cobalt, discussing its physical and chemical properties, where it is found, and what processes or objects it is used in.

"Provides a comprehensive, yet easy-to-read overview in large, bold print. Explanations are concise and clear without being oversimplified, and the arrangement is attractive." SLJ

Icludes glossary

Lead; [by] Susan Watt. Benchmark Books 2001 32p il (The elements) lib bdg $28.50

Grades: 5 6 7 8   **546**

1. Lead

ISBN 978-0-7614-1273-1; 0-7614-1273-5

LC 2001-35406

Explores the history of the useful metal lead and explains its chemistry, its uses, and its importance in our lives.

Includes glossary

Mercury; [by] Susan Watt. Benchmark Books 2005 32p il (The elements) lib bdg $28.50

Grades: 5 6 7 8 9 10 11 12   **546**

1. Mercury

ISBN 978-0-7614-1814-6; 0-7614-1814-8

LC 2004-47633

This book is part "of the 28-title The Elements series. Mercury tells the history of mercury, where it is found in nature, its place in mythology, how it is mined and refined, how it forms compounds, its uses, and its position in the periodic table." Sci Books Films

Includes glossary

Silver; [by] Susan Watt. Benchmark Books 2003 32p il (The elements) lib bdg $28.50

Grades: 5 6 7 8   **546**

1. Silver

ISBN 978-0-7614-1464-3; 0-7614-1464-9

LC 2002-6080

Explores the history of silver and explains its chemistry, its uses, and its importance in our lives.

"Explanations are succinct and clear, without being oversimplified, and supplemental information is provided

in boxed sidebars. Relevant diagrams, drawings, and photographs, mainly in color, appear on every page." SLJ
Includes glossary

Zirconium; [by] Susan Watt. Marshall Cavendish Benchmark 2008 32p il (The elements) lib bdg $28.50
Grades: 5 6 7 8   **546**
1. Zirconium
ISBN 978-0-7614-2688-2; 0-7614-2688-4

              LC 2007-60885

Introduces the element of zirconium, discussing its physical and chemical properties, where it is found, and how it is used.

"Provides a comprehensive, yet easy-to-read overview. . . . The explanations are succinct and clear, without being oversimplified, and the layout is attractive." SLJ
Includes glossary

West, Krista
Bromine; [by] Krista West. Marshall Cavendish Benchmark 2008 32p il (The elements) lib bdg $28.50
Grades: 5 6 7 8   **546**
1. Bromine
ISBN 978-0-7614-2685-1; 0-7614-2685-X

              LC 2006-51812

Introduces the element of bromine and its compoinds, discussing its physical and chemical properties, where it is found, and how it is used.

"Provides a comprehensive, yet easy-to-read overview. . . . The explanations are succinct and clear, without being oversimplified, and the layout is attractive. Diagrams and photographs complement the text on every page." SLJ
Includes glossary

Woodford, Chris
Potassium; [by] Chris Woodford. Benchmark Books 2002 32p il (The elements) lib bdg $28.50
Grades: 5 6 7 8   **546**
1. Potassium
ISBN 978-0-7614-1463-6; 0-7614-1463-0

              LC 2002-18556

Describes the characteristics, sources, and uses of the element potassium

"Explanations are succinct and clear, without being oversimplified, and supplemental information is provided in boxed sidebars. Relevant diagrams, drawings, and photographs, mainly in color, appear on every page." SLJ
Includes glossary

Titanium; [by] Chris Woodford. Benchmark Books 2003 32p il (The elements) lib bdg $28.50
Grades: 5 6 7 8   **546**
1. Titanium
ISBN 978-0-7614-1461-2; 0-7614-1461-4

              LC 2001-8743

Discusses the characteristics, sources, and uses of the element titanium.

"The well-selected photographs and diagrams are appropriate to the text." Horn Book Guide
Includes glossary

Yasdua, Anita
Explore water! 25 Great Projects, Activities, Experiments. Nomad Press 2011 92 p.

Grades: 2 3 4   **546**
1. Water 2. Aqueducts 3. Water pollution 4. Water conservation 5. Water resources development
ISBN 1936313421; 9781936313426

This book for children looks at the "world of water," offering a "guide that features hands-on activities, . . . illustrations, and . . . projects about this . . . natural resource. A deluge of . . . facts and . . . information about the history and science of water teach children about topics such as the water cycle, pollution and conservation, water folklore and festivals, and the latest in water technology. With projects ranging from a rain harvester made out of plastic containers to an edible aqueduct, this . . . guide brings the world of water straight into kids' hands." (Amazon.com)

Just add water; science projects you can sink, squirt, splash & sail. Children's Press 2008 32p il (Experiment with science) lib bdg $25; pa $7.95
Grades: 5 6 7 8   **546**
1. Water chemistry -- Juvenile literature 2. Water -- Experiments -- Juvenile literature
ISBN 978-0-531-18545-2 lib bdg; 0-531-18545-1 lib bdg; 978-0-531-18762-3 pa; 0-531-18762-4 pa

              LC 2007-21682

"The book consists of nine hands-on activities that target physical science concepts inherent in water (e.g. density, buoyancy, and hardness.) . . . Students . . . will likely find the age-appropriate activities engaging and purposeful. . . . The colorful photos augment the narrative and the science is sound." Sci Books Films
Includes glossary and bibliographical references

548   Crystallography

Stangl, Jean
Crystals and crystal gardens you can grow. Watts 1990 64p il (First book) lib bdg $23
Grades: 4 5 6 7   **548**
1. Crystals 2. Science -- Experiments
ISBN 0-531-10889-9

              LC 89-38999

The author discusses the nature and structure of crystals and presents experiments in crystal formation

With "clear explanatory background on crystal formations, and easy directions for experiments, this will meet a real need in every classroom and public library collection." Bull Cent Child Books
Includes bibliographical references

549   Mineralogy

Pellant, Chris
Minerals; [by] Chris and Helen Pellant. Gareth Stevens Pub. 2009 24p il (Rock stars) lib bdg $23
Grades: 2 3 4   **549**
1. Minerals
ISBN 978-0-8368-9224-6 lib bdg; 0-8368-9224-0 lib bdg

              LC 2008016121

"Accessible and action-oriented, short but info-packed. . . . Photographs are fine, and graphics are kept extremely simple." SLJ

Includes glossary

Spilsbury, Richard

Crystals; [by] Richard and Louise Spilsbury. Heinemann Library 2011 32p il (Let's rock) $29; pa $7.99

Grades: 4 5 6   549

1. Crystals

ISBN 978-1-4329-4684-5; 1-4329-4684-6; 978-1-4329-4692-0 pa; 1-4329-4692-7 pa

LC 2010022241

"Enhanced by plenty of photos, digital paintings, and diagrams, [this examination] of [crystals treats its topic] in unusual detail. [It] describes distinguishing characteristics, creation, history, . . . and human uses in [a] central [narrative] with additional notes, suggestions for activities during walks outside, and occasional thumbnail biographies of scientists in side boxes. [The] volume ends with a simple activity." SLJ

Includes bibliographical references

Minerals; [by] Richard and Louise Spilsbury. Heinemann Library 2011 32p il (Let's rock) $29; pa $7.99

Grades: 4 5 6   549

1. Minerals

ISBN 978-1-4329-4683-8; 1-4329-4683-8; 978-1-4329-4691-3 pa; 1-4329-4691-9 pa

LC 2010022235

"Enhanced by plenty of photos, digital paintings, and diagrams, [this examination] of [minerals treats its topic] in unusual detail. [It] describes distinguishing characteristics, creation, history, . . . and human uses in [a] central [narrative] with additional notes, suggestions for activities during walks outside, and occasional thumbnail biographies of scientists in side boxes. [The] volume ends with a simple activity." SLJ

Includes bibliographical references

550   Earth sciences

Bow, James

Earth's secrets. Marshall Cavendish Benchmark 2010 48p il (Invisible worlds) lib bdg $28.50

Grades: 4 5 6 7   550

1. Earth sciences

ISBN 978-0-7614-4196-0 lib bdg; 0-7614-4196-4 lib bdg

The narrative is "clear, well written, broken down into manageable pieces, and peppered with eye-opening facts. The numerous photographs are so phenomenal that they will inspire kids to read the text . . . so that they can wrap their minds around what they see." SLJ

Includes glossary and bibliographical references

Dorion, Christiane

How the world works; a hands-on guide to our amazing planet. written by Christiane Dorion; illustrated by Beverley Young. Templar Books 2010 un il $17.99

Grades: 3 4 5   550

1. Earth sciences 2. Pop-up books

ISBN 978-0-7636-4801-5; 0-7636-4801-9

"This pop-up survey devotes pages or spreads to Earth's history and structure, the origins of life, plate tectonics, the water cycle, weather, ocean currents, the carbon cycle, greenhouse effect, plants, and food chains. In snippets of text tucked into every available nook, Dorion provides commentary ranging from basic information on seasons and other cycles to abbreviated catalogs of cloud types and kinds of boundaries between tectonic plates." SLJ

Gaff, Jackie

Looking at earth; how does it change? [by] Jackie Gaff. Enslow Publishers 2008 32p il (Looking at science: how things change) lib bdg $22.60

Grades: 1 2 3   550

ISBN 978-0-7660-3088-6 lib bdg; 0-7660-3088-1 lib bdg

LC 2007-24507

"Fills a huge void in elementary science collections. . . . Text is arranged in succinct 'chunks,' giving important facts without overwhelming readers. . . . [This] is an essential addition." Libr Media Connect

Includes glossary and bibliographical references

Gardner, Robert

Earth-shaking science projects about planet Earth; illustrations by Tom Labaff. Enslow 2007 48p il (Rockin' earth science experiments) lib bdg $23.90

Grades: 3 4 5   550

1. Geophysics 2. Science projects 3. Science -- Experiments

ISBN 978-0-7660-2733-6 lib bdg; 0-7660-2733-3 lib bdg

LC 2006-18656

This offers experiments on such topics as the roundness of Earth, the Earth's layers, the continents, plate movements, earthquakes, and volcanoes.

Includes glossary and bibliographical references

Gibbons, Gail

Planet earth/inside out. Morrow Junior Bks. 1995 un il maps hardcover o.p. pa $4.95

Grades: K 1 2 3   550

1. Geology

ISBN 0-688-09681-6 lib bdg; 0-688-15849-8 pa

LC 94-41926

Gibbons' "explanations of the earth's interior are enlivened by comparisons . . . and her plentiful pictures, with their sharp outlines and broad blocks of color, will help clarify the concepts for the youngest learners." Booklist

Gilpin, Daniel

Planet Earth; what planet are you on? created by Basher; written by Dan Gilpin. Kingfisher 2010 128p il $14.99; pa $8.99

Grades: 5 6 7 8   550

1. Earth sciences

ISBN 978-0-7534-6616-2; 0-7534-6616-3; 978-0-7534-6412-0 pa; 0-7534-6412-8 pa

LC 2010015976

Presents concepts in earth sciences using lively descriptions and cartoon illustrations personifying each concept.

"The authors blend a surprising wealth of facts into the chatty, humorous text, which is filled with analogies kids can relate to. . . . The highly approachable language, animated cast of characters, awe-inspiring facts, and conservation messages make this an appealing starting point for students seeking basic earth-science information." Booklist

Lauber, Patricia
You're aboard Spaceship Earth; illustrated by Holly Keller. HarperCollins Pubs. 1996 32p il (Let's-read-and-find-out science) hardcover o.p. pa $4.95
Grades: K 1 2 3   550
1. Earth sciences 2. Environment -- Juvenile literature
ISBN 0-06-445159-3 pa
LC 94-18704
In this book "life on our planet is compared with a manned shuttle mission that must take special care to insure the health and safety of its crew. . . . Once that concept is established, youngsters learn interesting facts about the supplies needed to survive—food, air with oxygen, and water. Lauber is adept at writing for this audience, using simple vocabulary and straightforward sentences. . . . Keller's bright and colorful drawings further explain complicated concepts such as the water cycle." SLJ

Simon, Seymour
Seymour Simon's extreme earth records; by Seymour Simon. San Francisco 2012 57 p. (hbk.: alk. paper) $17.99
Grades: 2 3 4   550
1. Earth -- Juvenile literature 2. Earth sciences -- Juvenile literature 3. Natural disasters -- Juvenile literature
ISBN 1452107858; 9781452107851
LC 2011045937
This book, by Seymour Simon, "explor[es] the most extreme parts of our amazing planet--trekking though the driest desert, climbing the snowiest mountaintops, and diving to the deepest regions of the ocean floor. Seymour Simon . . . investigates Earth's biggest, smallest, deepest, and coldest environments, animals, plants, and most severe weather." (Publisher's note)
Includes bibliographical references (p. 57) and index

Solway, Andrew
Understanding cycles and systems. Raintree 2008 48p il map (Sci-hi: Earth and space science) lib bdg $31.43; pa $8.99
Grades: 4 5 6 7   550
1. Earth sciences
ISBN 978-1-4109-3348-5 lib bdg; 1-4109-3348-2 lib bdg; 978-1-4109-3358-4 pa; 1-4109-3358-X pa
LC 2009-3531
"Multiple colorful sidebars and large and small diagrams and photographs will help students to grasp the fundamentals being discussed, and the easy but interesting science experiments will act as further reinforcements." SLJ
Includes glossary and bibliographical references

Strother, Ruth
B is for blue planet; an earth science alphabet. written by Ruth Strother and illustrated by Bob Marstall. Sleeping Bear Press 2011 40 p.
Grades: 1 2   550
1. Earth 2. Geology 3. Earth sciences 4. Picture books for children 5. English language -- Alphabet
ISBN 9781585364541
LC 2010030635
In this picture book, "[t]he . . . poetic text and . . . illustrations provide an . . . entree into . . . Earth science topics . . . while sidebars provide . . . information on each topic." (Science & Children) "Planet Earth has been home to mankind for hundreds of thousands of years and while scientists have learned a lot about it, they're still unraveling many of its mysteries. 'B is for Blue Planet: An Earth Science Alphabet' explains what we do know about our planet and what more we have to learn. [It e]xamine[s] Earth's diverse ecosystems (deserts), . . . geological wonders (karst caves), . . . weather phenomena (hurricanes), and much more." (Publisher's note)

VanCleave, Janice Pratt, 1942-
Janice VanCleave's earth science for every kid; 101 easy experiments that really work. Wiley 1991 231p il hardcover o.p. pa $12.95
Grades: 4 5 6 7   550
1. Earth sciences 2. Science -- Experiments
ISBN 0-471-53010-7 pa
LC 90-42724
Instructions for experiments, each introducing a different earth science concept
"An entertaining, educational, and nonthreatening aid to understanding earth science. The easy experiments are carefully organized." SLJ

VanCleave, Janice Pratt, 1942-
Step-by-step science experiments in earth science; by Janice VanCleave. Rosen Pub. 2013 80 p. col. ill. (library) $33.25; (paperback) $14.15
Grades: 5 6 7 8   550
1. Earth sciences -- Juvenile literature 2. Science -- Experiments -- Juvenile literature
ISBN 1448869838; 9781448869831; 9781448884674
LC 2012007944
This book by Janice VanCleave is part of the First-Place Science Fair Projects series. The books have an introduction to the subject—here, earth science, followed by 22 simple . . . experiments. Van Cleave states the basic goal of the experiments, followed by a list of necessary materials, most of which can be found around the house or easily acquired with minimal cost. Step-by-step instructions are clearly detailed and accompanied by diagrams where needed." (School Library Journal)
Includes bibliographical references (p. 78) and index.

Woodward, John
Planet Earth; written by John Woodward; consultant Kim Bryan. DK Pub. 2009 123p il (One million things) $18.99
Grades: 5 6 7 8   550
1. Earth
ISBN 978-0-7566-5235-7; 0-7566-5235-9
"The artwork is a balanced mix of stunning photography, effective illustrations, and somewhat depth-challenged Photoshop jobs. An eye-catching catchall on the natural world, this . . . is great browsing material, packed full of well-articulated information." Booklist

551 Geology, hydrology, meteorology

Blobaum, Cindy

Geology rocks! 50 hands-on activities to explore the earth. illustrations by Michael Kline. Williamson 1999 96p il pa $10.95

Grades: 4 5 6 **551**

1. Geology -- Experiments 2. Science -- Experiments
ISBN 1-885593-29-5

LC 98-53299

Presents fifty hands-on activities to introduce the science of geology and explain the formation and history of the earth

"The text is witty but conveys much factual material. The experiments can be done easily with household items and include safety precautions. . . . The book is illustrated with red-and-purple tinted cartoons and photographs." SLJ

Includes bibliographical references

Gray, Susan H.

Geology the study of rocks; Susan H. Gray. Children's Press 2012 48 p. (pbk.) $6.95

Grades: 2 3 4 5 **551**

1. Rocks 2. Geology 3. Drilling and boring (Earth and rocks)
ISBN 0531282708; 9780531246764; 9780531282700

LC 2011031091

Author Susan Heinrichs Gray presents a book on geography, the history of the earth, and the study of rocks.

Includes bibliographical references and index.

Kelly, Erica

★ Evolving planet; [by] Erica Kelly & Richard Kissel. Harry N. Abrams 2008 136p il map $19.95

Grades: 5 6 7 8 **551**

1. Evolution 2. Paleontology -- Juvenile literature 3. Natural history -- Juvenile literature
ISBN 978-0-8109-9486-7; 0-8109-9486-0

LC 2007-36342

"Based on a exhibit at Chicago's Field Museum, this big spacious volume packs in a wealth of information about evolution over four billion years. . . . There are detailed, beautiful photographs and glorious paintings on every double-page spread and the chatty text is accessible for grade-schoolers." Booklist

Includes glossary and bibliographical references

551.1 Gross structure and properties of the earth

Cole, Joanna

★ The magic school bus inside the Earth; illustrated by Bruce Degen. Scholastic 1987 40p il hardcover o.p. pa $4.95

Grades: 2 3 4 **551.1**

1. Geology
ISBN 0-590-40759-7; 0-590-40760-0 pa

LC 87-4563

In this book Ms. Frizzle teaches "geology via a field trip through the center of the earth. As her class learns about fossils, rocks, and volcanoes, so will readers, absorbing information painlessly as they vicariously travel through the caves, tunnels, and up through the cone of a volcanic island

shortly before it erupts. . . . Degen's bright, colorful artwork includes many witty details to delight observant children. Carried in cartoonlike balloons, the schoolmates' thoughts, banter, and asides add spice to the geology lesson. Bright, sassy, and savvy, the magic school bus books rate high in child appeal." Booklist

Saunders, Craig

What is the theory of plate tectonics? Crabtree Pub. Co. 2011 64p il (Shaping modern science) lib bdg $30.60; pa $10.95

Grades: 5 6 7 8 **551.1**

1. Plate tectonics 2. Geophysicists 3. Meteorologists 4. College teachers
ISBN 978-0-7787-7202-6 lib bdg; 0-7787-7202-0 lib bdg; 978-0-7787-7209-5 pa; 0-7787-7209-8 pa

LC 2010-52622

This title is "not only written and organized well, but [it is] also gorgeous in design. Full-color photographs and illustrations are set over colorful backgrounds that add depth but not distraction. [The title] includes thought-provoking quotes from famous authors and scientists and some eyebrow-raising 'Quick Facts' throughout." SLJ

Includes glossary and bibliographical references

Snedden, Robert

Earth's shifting surface. Raintree 2010 48p il (Sci-hi: Earth and space science) lib bdg $31.43; pa $8.99

Grades: 4 5 6 7 **551.1**

1. Plate tectonics
ISBN 978-1-4109-3349-2 lib bdg; 1-4109-3349-0 lib bdg; 978-1-4109-3359-1 pa; 1-4109-3359-8 pa

LC 2009-3532

"Multiple colorful sidebars and large and small diagrams and photographs will help students to grasp the fundamentals being discussed, and the easy but interesting science experiments will act as further reinforcements." SLJ

Includes glossary and bibliographical references

Storad, Conrad J.

Earth's crust. Lerner Publications Co. 2006 48p il map (Early bird Earth science) lib bdg $25.26

Grades: 3 4 5 6 **551.1**

1. Earth
ISBN 978-0-8225-5944-3 lib bdg; 0-8225-5944-7 lib bdg

LC 2005-16423

This "introduces the earth's crust. Four chapters discuss the planet's overall structure, plate tectonics, changes in the crust, and features such as mountains, faults, and volcanoes. . . . With short sentences, generously spaced lines, and large type, the text has an inviting look for young readers. The colorful illustrations include several clear diagrams and maps as well as many captioned photos. . . . A clearly written, accessible introduction." Booklist

Includes glossary

551.2   Volcanoes, earthquakes, thermal waters and gases

Benoit, Peter

The **Krakatau** eruption. Children's Press 2011 48p il (True book) lib bdg $28; pa $6.99

Grades: 3 4 5   **551.2**

1. Volcanoes

ISBN 978-0-531-20628-7 lib bdg; 978-0-531-29027-9 pa

LC 2010045930

This describes the 1883 volcanic eruption on the island of Krakatau.

"Benoit provides unbiased information that is on target for the intended audience. . . . The photographs and reproductions enhance the [text]. . . . [This book is] well-conceived." SLJ

Includes bibliographical references

Branley, Franklin Mansfield

Earthquakes; by Franklyn M. Branley; illustrated by Megan Lloyd. newly il ed.; HarperCollinsPublishers 2005 33p il (Let's-read-and-find-out science) hardcover o.p. pa $4.99

Grades: K 1 2 3   **551.2**

1. Earthquakes

ISBN 0-06-028008-5; 0-06-028009-3 lib bdg; 0-06-445188-7 pa

LC 2003-25458

A newly illustrated edition of the title first published 1990

"The most effective pictures are those that show the unseen and unseeable, such as cross-sections of mountains, volcanoes, and faults in the earth's moving crust." Booklist

Volcanoes; by Franklyn M. Branley; illustrated by Megan Lloyd. newly illustrated ed.; Collins 2008 30p il map (Let's-read-and-find-out science) $16.99; pa $5.99

Grades: 2 3 4   **551.2**

1. Volcanoes

ISBN 978-0-06-028011-6; 0-06-028011-5; 978-0-06-445189-5 pa; 0-06-445189-5 pa

LC 2006000465

A newly illustrated edition of the title first published 1985

Discusses volcanoes, what causes an eruption, and the warning signs

"The new illustrations excel at depicting ideas presented in the text and include scenes of destruction. . . . This work remains a sound, basic introduction to the topic." SLJ

Bourseiller, Philippe

Volcanoes; journey to the crater's edge. photographs by Philippe Bourseiller; adapted by Robert Burleigh; text by Helene Montardre; drawings by David Giraudon. H.N. Abrams 2003 75p il map $14.95

Grades: 4 5 6 7   **551.2**

1. Volcanoes

ISBN 0-8109-4590-8

LC 2003-971

Over thirty photographs and accompanying text reveal the facts about the world's volcanoes

"Photographer Bourseiller takes young readers to the crater's edge with truly spectacular full-color photographs. . . . The book does an excellent job of documenting the effect of volcanoes on the lives of those who live close to them, and small watercolor paintings further enliven the sense of human history." Booklist

Dwyer, Helen

Earthquakes! Marshall Cavendish Benchmark 2010 32p il map (Eyewitness disaster) lib bdg $28.50

Grades: 4 5 6   **551.2**

1. Earthquakes

ISBN 978-1-60870-001-1; 1-60870-001-1

Provides information about earthquakes through eyewitness accounts from survivors and rescue workers.

"Bold subheadings and color captions break information into readable chunks for the younger learner. Important vocabulary is in bold print. . . . An excellent addition to your science collection." Libr Media Connect

Includes glossary and bibliographical references

Fradin, Judith Bloom

★ **Earthquakes**; witness to disaster. by Judy and Dennis Fradin. National Geographic 2008 48p map (Witness to disaster) $16.95; lib bdg $26.90

Grades: 4 5 6 7   **551.2**

1. Earthquakes

ISBN 978-1-4263-0211-4; 1-4263-0211-8; 978-1-4263-0212-1 lib bdg; 1-4263-0212-6 lib bdg

LC 2007044164

"The combination of good writing and excellent graphics paired with archival and personal perspectives makes this book a valuable addition." SLJ

Includes glossary and bibliographical references

Volcano! the Icelandic eruption of 2010 and other hot, smoky, fierce, and fiery mountains. [by] Judy & Dennis Fradin. National Geographic 2010 48p il map (National Geographic kids) pa $6.95

Grades: 4 5 6 7   **551.2**

1. Volcanoes

ISBN 978-1-4263-0815-4 pa; 1-4263-0815-9 pa

"The format includes text, quotes, and facts in sidebars, as well as photographs on each page, with a colorful layout. The photographs and maps that are shown are of good quality." Sci Books & Films

Includes glossary and bibliographical references

★ **Volcanoes**; by Judy and Dennis Fradin. National Geographic 2007 48p il map (Witness to disaster) $16.95; lib bdg $26.90

Grades: 4 5 6 7   **551.2**

1. Volcanoes

ISBN 978-0-7922-5376-1; 0-7922-5376-0; 978-0-7922-5377-8 lib bdg; 0-7922-5377-9 lib bdg

LC 2006-102817

This "introduces readers to these violent eruptions, using eyewitness accounts to explain the history and science involved. They begin with a report of the 1943 birth of a volcano in Paricutín, Mexico. . . . Subsequent chapters describe other celebrated volcanoes, explain their causes and types, note the benefits of these eruptions, and clarify how they are currently predicted. . . . Numerous clear, well-chosen photographs and diagrams help to convey the great power of volcanic activity and the consequences to humans. . . . This will be useful for report writers, and a fascinating pick for browsers." Booklist

Includes bibliographical references

Hague, Bradley

Alien deep; Revealing the Mysterious Living World at the Bottom of the Ocean. by Bradley Hague. National Geographic 2012 48 p. col. ill. (hardcover: alk. paper) $17.95

Grades: 4 5 6 7 **551.2**

1. Oceanography -- Research 2. Hydrothermal vent ecology 3. Natural history -- Galapagos Islands 4. Hydrothermal vents 5. Hydrothermal vent animals

ISBN 1426310676; 9781426310676; 9781426310683

LC 2012012939

This book by Bradley Hague "depicts adventurous and thrilling elements in oceanographic fieldwork in conjunction with a National Geographic television show." (Publisher's note) "The book takes readers along on the 2011 exploration of vents in the Galapagos Reef area of the Pacific Ocean. . . . Future scientists will be hooked by the excitement of finding newly developing vents and the disappointment of finding older vents that once disappeared under layers of magma." (Booklist)

Includes bibliographical references and index.

Harrison, David Lee

★ **Volcanoes**: nature's incredible fireworks; by David L. Harrison; illustrated by Cheryl Nathan. Boyds Mills Press 2002 un il (Earthworks) $15.95

Grades: 1 2 3 **551.2**

1. Volcanoes

ISBN 1-56397-996-9

LC 2001-94536

"The surprisingly graceful text is illuminated with dynamic artwork. . . . The expressive compositions, rich in color and subtle texture, serve as literal scenes of what's happening on the earth, and there are plenty of cross sections and diagrams of what's happening beneath the earth's crust." Booklist

Includes bibliographical references

Jennings, Terry

Earthquakes and tsunamis. Smart Apple Media 2010 32p il map (Amazing planet earth) lib bdg $28.50

Grades: 4 5 6 **551.2**

1. Tsunamis 2. Earthquakes

ISBN 978-1-59920-372-0 lib bdg; 1-59920-372-3 lib bdg

LC 2008-55496

This book shows readers how the shifting plates far below the earth's surface can result in violent earthquakes and tsunamis

"Chapters are labeled as 'Case Study' or 'Science Report,' making the presentation lively. The concise explanations include just the right number of examples and clear diagrams, and have perfect color photo accompaniments." SLJ

Includes glossary

Violent volcanoes. Smart Apple Media 2010 32p il map (Amazing planet earth) lib bdg $28.50

Grades: 4 5 6 **551.2**

1. Volcanoes

ISBN 978-1-59920-374-4 lib bdg; 1-59920-374-X lib bdg

LC 2008-55499

This explains how powerful forces beneath the Earth's crust cause volcanoes to erupt

"Chapters are labeled as 'Case Study' or 'Science Report,' making the presentation lively. The concise explanations include just the right number of examples and clear diagrams, and have perfect color photo accompaniments." SLJ

Includes glossary

Levy, Matthys

Earthquakes, volcanoes, and tsunamis; projects and principles for beginning geologists. [by] Matthys Levy and Mario Salvadori. Chicago Review Press 2009 136p il pa $14.95

Grades: 5 6 7 8 **551.2**

1. Tsunamis 2. Volcanoes 3. Earthquakes

ISBN 978-1-55652-801-9 pa; 1-55652-801-9 pa

LC 2008040143

This "is an excellent introduction for young minds to the subject of earthquakes, volcanoes, and related phenomena. . . . The book is filled with projects to help young people understand the occurrence and consequences of earthquakes, volcanoes, and tsunamis." Sci Books Films

Mara, Wil

Why do earthquakes happen? Marshall Cavendish Benchmark 2011 32p il (Tell me why, tell me how) $20.95 **551.2**

1. Earthquakes

ISBN 978-0-7614-4826-6; 0-7614-4826-8

This offers information about why earthquakes happen.

This title has "clear explanations of natural phenomena, beautiful full-color illustrations, and an uncluttered design. [The] book approaches its topic in a methodical, logical fashion, using examples from a child's world." SLJ

Nault, Jennifer

Volcanoes. AV2 by Weigl Pubs. 2010 24p il map (Earth science) $27.13; pa $11.95

Grades: 3 4 5 **551.2**

1. Volcanoes

ISBN 978-1-60596-970-1; 1-60596-970-2; 978-1-60596-971-8 pa; 1-60596-971-0 pa

This book about volcanoes "intelligently mixes history, science, geography, careers, and even myths. . . . The book [is] . . . an ideal starting point for student researchers with its breakdown of different types of volcanoes, a large map of the planet's active volcanoes, an impressive time line of notable eruptions, and details of life as a volcanologist." Booklist

Person, Stephen

Devastated by a volcano! Bearport Pub. 2010 32p il map (Disaster survivors) lib bdg $25.27

Grades: 4 5 6 7 **551.2**

1. Volcanoes

ISBN 978-1-936087-50-1 lib bdg; 1-936087-50-2 lib bdg

"Captivating photos and illustrations and sidebars present interesting facts or brief anecdotes. . . . [This] should be purchased for all school and public libraries as . . . [it gives] a new perspective on the topic." Libr Media Connect

Includes glossary and bibliographical references

Reingold, Adam

Leveled by an earthquake! Bearport Pub. 2010 32p il map (Disaster survivors) lib bdg $25.27

Grades: 4 5 6 7   **551.2**

1. Earthquakes

ISBN 978-1-936087-53-2 lib bdg; 1-936087-53-7 lib bdg

LC 2009-36961

"Introduces earthquakes, describing what causes them to occur and how they are measured, along with stories of survivors who were the victims of famous earthquakes of the past." Publisher's note

Includes glossary and bibliographical references

Silverstein, Alvin

Earthquakes; the science behind seismic shocks and tsunamis. [by] Alvin Silverstein, Virginia Silverstein, and Laura Silverstein Nunn. Enslow Publishers 2010 48p il map (The science behind natural disasters) lib bdg $23.93

Grades: 4 5 6   **551.2**

1. Tsunamis 2. Earthquakes

ISBN 978-0-7660-2975-0 lib bdg; 0-7660-2975-1 lib bdg

LC 2008-38589

"Scientific explanations are accompanied by plentiful color diagrams that will help students to grasp causes and effects. . . . Photos . . . are effective, and are sometimes turned into helpful, lively diagrams by the addition of such features as wind-direction arrows." SLJ

Includes glossary and bibliographical references

Volcanoes; the science behind fiery eruptions. [by] Alvin Silverstein, Virginia Silverstein, and Laura Silverstein Nunn. Enslow Publishers 2010 48p il map (The science behind natural disasters) lib bdg $23.93

Grades: 4 5 6   **551.2**

1. Volcanoes

ISBN 978-0-7660-2972-9 lib bdg; 0-7660-2972-7 lib bdg

LC 2008-42866

"Scientific explanations are accompanied by plentiful color diagrams that will help students to grasp causes and effects. . . . Photos . . . are effective, and are sometimes turned into helpful, lively diagrams by the addition of such features as wind-direction arrows." SLJ

Includes glossary and bibliographical references

Simon, Seymour

★ Earthquakes; rev ed.; Collins 2006 30p il map pa $6.99

Grades: 3 4 5 6   **551.2**

1. Earthquakes

ISBN 978-0-06-087715-6 pa; 0-06-087715-4 pa

LC 2006279219

First published 1991 by Morrow Junior Books

Examines the phenomenon of earthquakes, describing how and where they occur, how they can be predicted, and how much damage they can inflict

Spilsbury, Louise

Shattering earthquakes; [by] Louise and Richard Spilsbury. rev and updated.; Heinemann Library 2010 32p il map (Awesome forces of nature) lib bdg $29; pa $7.99

Grades: 3 4 5 6   **551.2**

1. Earthquakes

ISBN 978-1-4329-3784-3 lib bdg; 1-4329-3784-7 lib bdg; 978-1-4329-3791-1 pa; 1-4329-3791-X pa

LC 2009037565

First published 2004

This book about earthquakes discusses "causes, characteristics, and relevant science, including progress in predicting the events. Case studies illustrate the human response. Numerous color photographs and sidebars are interwoven into the well-organized and absorbing [narrative]." SLJ

Includes glossary and bibliographical references

Violent volcanoes; [by] Louise and Richard Spilsbury. rev and updated; Heinemann Library 2010 32p il map (Awesome forces of nature) lib bdg $29; pa $7.99

Grades: 3 4 5 6   **551.2**

1. Volcanoes

ISBN 978-1-4329-3783-6 lib bdg; 1-4329-3783-9 lib bdg; 978-1-4329-3790-4 pa; 1-4329-3790-1 pa

LC 2009-37564

First published 2004

This book about volcanoes "is sure to catch the eyes of students and educators. . . . The interesting and accurate facts are presented in an easily understood vocabulary. . . . Incredible eye-catching photographs, diagrams, or maps are tastefully positioned on every page." Libr Media Connect

Includes glossary and bibliographical references

Stewart, Melissa

Inside Earthquakes. Sterling Publishing Co., Inc. 2011 48p il map (Inside . . .) $16.95; pa $9.95

Grades: 5 6 7 8   **551.2**

1. Earthquakes

ISBN 978-1-4027-5877-5; 978-1-4027-8163-6 pa

LC 2010046452

This book about earthquakes "explores its topic in an engaging way, and the many illustrations work well with adjacent text and captions. . . . The [book's] varied page layouts and attractive and the quality of photos, computer-generated images, original illustrations, and charts is . . . excellent. . . . [The book] looks at the geology of the earth's crust as well as the effects of quakes on people and cities, landforms and coastlines." Booklist

Includes bibliographical references

Inside Volcanoes. Sterling Publishing Co. 2011 48p il map (Inside) $16.95; pa $9.95

Grades: 5 6 7 8   **551.2**

1. Volcanoes

ISBN 978-1-4027-5876-8; 1-4027-5876-6; 978-1-4027-8164-3 pa; 1-4027-8164-4 pa

LC 2010046451

Examines the nature of volcanoes, how they are formed, what they look like, and how they are measured, in a text with ten foldout pages.

"With pages that fold out or flip up, well-reproduced photographs of volcanoes at rest and in action, diagrams, maps, charts, timelines and short explanations, there is much to look at and to learn. . . . Appropriately for a book that is clearly designed to stimulate interest, there are solid suggestions for both books and websites for further exploration. A good starting-place for volcano explorations." Kirkus

Stille, Darlene R.

Great shakes; the science of earthquakes. Compass Point Books 2009 43p il map (Headline science) lib bdg $27.93; pa $7.95

Grades: 5 6 7 8   **551.2**

1. Earthquakes

ISBN 978-0-7565-3947-4 lib bdg; 0-7565-3947-1 lib bdg; 978-0-7565-3368-7 pa; 0-7565-3368-6 pa

LC 2008-05739

This "is an accessible, technically accurate introduction to [earthquakes]. . . . In addition to the ludic writing, this slim volume offers . . . readers comprehensive coverage of the fundamentals of earthquakes, including the effects, plate tectonics, fault systems, seismic waves, forecasting, and safer building designs. . . . The many charts and graphs enrich the volume and clarify technical issues." Sci Books Films

Includes glossary and bibliographical references

Tagliaferro, Linda

How does a volcano become an island? Raintree 2010 32p il (How does it happen?) lib bdg $27.50; pa $7.99

Grades: 3 4 5   **551.2**

1. Islands 2. Volcanoes

ISBN 978-1-4109-3447-5 lib bdg; 1-4109-3447-0 lib bdg; 978-1-4109-3455-0 pa; 1-4109-3455-1 pa

LC 2008-52652

"Information is clearly presented using a large font, diagrams, and photographs formatted to resemble Polaroid pictures. . . . A first-rate job answering some important scientific questions." SLJ

Includes glossary and bibliographical references

Waldron, Melanie

Volcanoes; [by] Melanie Waldron. Heinemann 2007 32p il map (Mapping earthforms) hardcover o.p. lib bdg $28.21

Grades: 3 4 5   **551.2**

1. Volcanoes

ISBN 978-1-4034-9606-5 lib bdg; 1-4034-9606-4 lib bdg; 978-1-4034-9616-4 pa; 1-4034-9616-1 pa

LC 2006037722

After defining volcanoes, this describes "the actions that produce them, their effects on animals and plants, related science, . . . future possibilities, . . . and [lists] significant examples around the world. Maps, diagrams, tables, and high-quality color photographs complement the text." SLJ

Includes glossary and bibliographical references

Woods, Michael

Volcanoes; by Michael Woods and Mary B. Woods. Lerner Publications Co. 2007 64p il map (Disasters up close) lib bdg $27.93

Grades: 4 5 6   **551.2**

1. Volcanoes

ISBN 978-0-8225-4715-0 lib bdg; 0-8225-4715-5 lib bdg

LC 2005-17132

"Each page of the colorful, eye-catching book has several paragraphs of text, sidebars, and small photos, with a large photo or graphic on the facing page." Sci Books Films

Includes bibliographical references

551.3   Surface and exogenous processes and their agents

Harrison, David Lee

Glaciers; nature's icy caps. [by] David L. Harrison; illustrated by Cheryl Nathan. Boyds Mills Press 2006 un il (Earthworks) $15.95

Grades: K 1 2 3   **551.3**

1. Glaciers

ISBN 1-59078-372-7

LC 2005-24988

The author "provides a straightforward introduction to glaciers. Opening with the sinking of the Titanic, he explains how they form, move, and drop icebergs into the sea, going on to discuss where glaciers can be found and how their range shifts as Earth cycles in and out of ice ages. . . . The text reads like clear, informational prose. Nathan's digital illustrations vary in quality, but the best double-page spreads . . . are exceptionally fine." Booklist

Sepehri, Sandy

Glaciers; [by] Sandy Sepehri. Rourke Pub. 2008 32p il (Landforms) lib bdg $28.50; pa $7.95

Grades: 1 2 3 4   **551.3**

1. Glaciers

ISBN 978-1-60044-544-6 lib bdg; 1-60044-544-6 lib bdg; 978-1-60044-705-1 pa; 1-60044-705-8 pa

LC 2007012143

"The illustrations and photographs are plentiful and colorful. . . . The [volume is] well written and successfully [conveys] the basics of the topic." Sci Books Films

Includes glossary and bibliographical references

Silverman, Buffy

Exploring dangers in space; asteroids, space junk, and more. Lerner Publications 2011 40p il (What's amazing about space?) $27.93

Grades: 4 5 6   **551.3**

1. Comets 2. Meteors 3. Asteroids 4. Space debris

ISBN 978-0-7613-5446-8

LC 2010046078

This discusses meteoroids, space junk, comets and asteroids that fall to Earth, how scientists watch out for large collisions, and what they might do if Earth is in danger.

This book is "written in simple language, [and] illustrated nicely. . . . The information presented is factually correct. . . . Every page includes a well-chosen illustration or photograph." Sci Books Films

Includes bibliographical references

Simon, Seymour

★ Icebergs and glaciers. Morrow 1987 un il hardcover o.p. pa $6.99

Grades: 3 4 5 6   **551.3**

1. Glaciers 2. Icebergs

ISBN 0-688-16705-5 pa

LC 86-18142

The author "chronicles the development of glaciers and icebergs with a wonderfully clear, almost Spartan text that receives all of the support necessary from the magnificent color photographs which accompany it. . . . This book would be an excellent addition to any elementary school library or any personal juvenile collection." Appraisal

551.4 Geomorphology and hydrosphere

Brimner, Larry Dane
Caves. Children's Press 2000 47p il (True book) hardcover o.p. pa $6.95
Grades: 2 3 4   551.4
1. Caves
ISBN 0-516-21567-1; 0-516-27189-X pa
LC 99-58037
Describes the different kinds of caves, how they are formed, and the wildlife that lives within them
Includes bibliographical references

Henzel, Cynthia Kennedy
Great Barrier Reef. ABDO Pub. Co. 2011 32p il (Troubled treasures: world heritage sites) $25.65
Grades: 3 4 5   551.4
1. Coral reefs and islands
ISBN 978-1-61613-564-5; 1-61613-564-6
LC 2010021310
This "book describes in general terms [the Great Barrier Reef's] . . . creation, distinctive features, and history, as well as threats to its continued existence and both current and past restoration intitiatives. Revealing color photos taken from different heights and angles are supplemented by maps and by graphic reconstructions. . . . Henzel's distinctive approach gives this [book] unusual value for both assignment and general reading." SLJ
Includes glossary

Jennings, Terry
Massive mountains. Smart Apple Media 2010 32p il map (Amazing planet earth) lib bdg $28.50
Grades: 4 5 6   551.4
1. Mountains
ISBN 978-1-59920-370-6 lib bdg; 1-59920-370-7 lib bdg
LC 2008-55497
This book explains how mountains form and change over time
"Chapters are labeled as 'Case Study' or 'Science Report,' making the presentation lively. The concise explanations include just the right number of examples and clear diagrams, and have perfect color photo accompaniments." SLJ
Includes glossary

Sheehan, Thomas F.
Islands; [by] Thomas F. Sheehan. Rourke Pub. 2008 32p il map (Landforms) lib bdg $28.50; pa $7.95
Grades: 1 2 3 4   551.4
1. Islands
ISBN 978-1-60044-545-3 lib bdg; 1-60044-545-4 lib bdg; 978-1-60044-706-8 pa; 1-60044-706-6 pa
LC 2007012183

"The illustrations and photographs are plentiful and colorful. . . . The [volume is] well written and successfully [conveys] the basics of the topic." Sci Books Films
Includes glossary and bibliographical references

Mountains; [by] Thomas Sheehan. Rourke Pub. 2008 32p il map (Landforms) lib bdg $28.50; pa $7.95
Grades: 1 2 3 4   551.4
1. Mountains
ISBN 978-1-60044-547-7 lib bdg; 1-60044-547-0 lib bdg; 978-1-60044-708-2 pa; 1-60044-708-2 pa
LC 2007012290
"The illustrations and photographs are plentiful and colorful. . . . The [volume is] well written and successfully [conveys] the basics of the topic." Sci Books Films
Includes glossary and bibliographical references

Simon, Seymour
★ Mountains. Morrow Junior Bks. 1994 un il hardcover o.p. pa $6.99
Grades: 4 5 6 7   551.4
1. Mountains
ISBN 0-688-15477-8 pa
LC 93-11398
Introduces various mountain ranges, how they are formed and shaped, and how they affect vegetation and animals, including humans
"The striking color photographs work well with the clear text to illustrate key points and highlight the diversity among the Earth's mountain ranges." Horn Book Guide

Wilson, Hannah
Seashore; illustrated by Simon Mendez. Kingfisher 2010 18p il (Flip the flaps) $9.99
Grades: PreK K 1   551.4
1. Seashore
ISBN 978-0-7534-6445-8; 0-7534-6445-4
This "features beautiful spreads by Mendez, who paints his coastal scenes with a soft realism so accurate they are occasionally indistinguishable from photographs. Wilson, meanwhile, introduces readers to the plants and wildlife present at shorelines everywhere—not just the classic sandy beach but also salt marsh, arctic region, and mangrove swamp. Each top flap presents three questions . . . which are answered underneath. . . . Perfect for light, educational browsing." Booklist

Zoehfeld, Kathleen Weidner
How mountains are made; illustrated by James Graham Hale. HarperCollins Pubs. 1995 29p il maps (Let's-read-and-find-out science) hardcover o.p. pa $4.95
Grades: K 1 2 3   551.4
1. Geology 2. Mountains
ISBN 0-06-024510-7; 0-06-445128-3 pa
LC 93-45436
"The text and illustrations work together well in this sequential, well-organized book. Much credit goes to Hale's engaging watercolor illustrations done in cheery colors; they are simply drawn but add effective examples and diagrams." SLJ

551.46 Oceanography and submarine geology

Adamson, Thomas K.
  Tsunamis; with Walter C. Dudley, consultant. Capstone Press 2005 24p il $22.26
  Grades: 2 3 4   551.46
  1. Tsunamis
  ISBN 0-7368-5248-4

LC 2005-01640

"Adamson explains how tsunamis are caused and how they move through the ocean and grow in height as they approach the shore. He describes the damage they cause, the kinds of warning systems used to detect them, and the impact of the 2004 Indian Ocean disaster. The writing is concise but clear, and the layout features a full-page illustration facing each page of easy-to-read text. Excellent photos of the 2004 tsunami are featured, and the diagrams of the earth's plates and earthquakes are simple but informative." SLJ

Includes bibliographical references

Aronin, Miriam
  Slammed by a tsunami! Bearport Pub. 2010 32p il map (Disaster survivors) lib bdg $25.27
  Grades: 4 5 6 7   551.46
  1. Tsunamis
  ISBN 978-1-936087-48-8 lib bdg; 1-936087-48-0 lib bdg

LC 2009-34574

"Introduces tsunamis, discussing how they form and when they tend to occur, and describing the devastating effects of the 2004 tsunami in Sumatra and of some of the other well-known tsunamis of the past." Publisher's note

Includes glossary and bibliographical references

Basher, Simon
  Oceans; [making waves!] designed and created by Simon Basher; text written by Dan Green. Kingfisher 2012 128 p. ill. (paperback) $8.99; (hardcover) $14.99
  Grades: 5 6 7 8   551.46
  1. Oceanography 2. Marine ecology 3. Aquatic animals
  ISBN 0753468220; 9780753468227; 9780753468210

The book, written and illustrated by Dan Green, "shines its light into the amazing and mysterious oceans. . . . [Green] takes to the high seas with members of the Shoreline Gang and the characters in the Open-Water Crew. Readers encounter deep trenches, curious creatures, underwater mountains taller than any found on land, and the mixers and stirrers that keep the water flowing. . . . Scientific information . . . [and] a pullout wall poster of the ocean characters [helps readers understand] . . . the planet's mysterious underwater world." (reviews.clubs2.scholastic.com)

Bodden, Valerie
  To the ocean deep; by Valerie Bodden. Creative Education 2011 48 p. col. ill. (library) $34.25
  Grades: 5 6 7 8   551.46
  1. Ocean -- Juvenile literature 2. Underwater exploration -- Juvenile literature 3. Explorers -- Biography -- Juvenile literature 4. Bathyscaphe -- History -- 20th century -- Juvenile literature
  ISBN 1608180670; 9781608180677

LC 2010033416

This book by Valerie Bodden is part of the Great Expeditions series and looks at oceanic exploration expeditions. "Bodden includes brief biographies of major people involved in each expedition, interspersed with the text. There are also numerous photographs or reproductions of paintings and woodcuts from the time of the expeditions." (Library Media Connection)

Includes bibliographical references (p. 46-47) and index.

Burns, Loree Griffin
  ★ **Tracking** trash; flotsam, jetsam, and the science of ocean motion. Houghton Mifflin 2007 56p il map (Scientists in the field) $18
  Grades: 5 6 7 8   551.46
  1. Pollution 2. Ocean currents 3. Oceanographers 4. Marine debris -- Juvenile literature
  ISBN 0-618-58131-6; 978-0-618-58131-3

LC 2006-11534

This book describes "Curt Ebbesmeyer's ongoing work. . . . The oceanographer has been tracing the surface currents of the seas via the movement of plastic rubbish that has escaped from broken cargo containers. [Index.] Grades five to nine." (Bull Cent Child Books)

"The book profiles two oceanographers who devised experiments using computer-modeling programs of ocean surface current movement to predict the landfall of . . . drifting objects. . . . Spacious layout, exceptionally fine color photos, and handsome maps give this book an inviting look. . . . A unique and often fascinating book." Booklist

Includes glossary and bibliographical references

Dwyer, Helen
  Tsunamis! Marshall Cavendish Benchmark 2010 32p il map (Eyewitness disaster) lib bdg $28.50
  Grades: 4 5 6   551.46
  1. Tsunamis
  ISBN 978-1-60870-005-9; 1-60870-005-4

LC 2010001801

Provides information about tsunamis through eyewitness accounts from survivors and rescue workers.

"Bold subheadings and color captions break information into readable chunks for the younger learner. Important vocabulary is in bold print. . . . An excellent addition to your science collection." Libr Media Connect

Includes glossary and bibliographical references

Earle, Sylvia A.
  Dive! my adventures in the deep frontier. National Geographic Soc. 1999 64p il map $18.95
  Grades: 4 5 6   551.46
  1. Underwater exploration 2. Submarine diving
  ISBN 0-7922-7144-0

LC 98-11480

The author relates some of her adventures studying and exploring the world's oceans, including tracking whales, living in an underwater laboratory, and helping to design a deep water submarine

"In this extraordinary photo-essay, an eminent marine biologist and ocean explorer combines personal adventure and scientific fact with glorious color action pictures." Booklist

Includes glossary

Fradin, Judith Bloom

★ Tsunamis; witness to disaster. [by] Judy & Dennis Fradin. National Geographic 2008 48p il map (Witness to disaster) $16.95; lib bdg $20.90

Grades: 4 5 6 7 **551.46**
1. Tsunamis
ISBN 978-0-7922-5380-8; 0-7922-5380-9; 978-0-7922-5381-5 lib bdg; 0-7922-5381-7 lib bdg
LC 2008010536

This "explores the science, history, and personal experience of tsunamis and shows kids what scientists are doing to develop early warning systems so we can survive such disasters in the future." Publisher's note
Includes glossary and bibliographical references

Gibbons, Gail

Exploring the deep, dark sea. Little, Brown 1999 un il $14.95; pa $5.95

Grades: K 1 2 3 **551.46**
1. Ocean bottom 2. Marine biology 3. Underwater exploration
ISBN 0-316-30945-1; 0-316-75549-4 pa
LC 98-14443

"From the sunlight zone to the abyss, Gibbons follows the crew of a deep-diving submersible craft into the ocean depths, noting the changes in terrain and animal life at the various levels. Labels identify parts of the craft and the many animals, and explanations of the differing ecologies of the many levels are brief. Thoughtful attention to page design and narrative produce an account that is both spare and surprisingly rich." Horn Book Guide

Gray, Susan H.

Oceanography the study of oceans; Susan H. Gray. Children's Press 2012 48 p.

Grades: 2 3 4 5 **551.46**
1. Oceanography -- Juvenile literature
ISBN 0531246795; 0531282732; 9780531246795; 9780531282731
LC 2011031074

This book by Susan Heinrichs Gray is an introduction to oceanography for young readers. "Earth's oceans are almost like a foreign world, filled with millions of strange, fascinating animals and plants. Oceanographers dive into the watery depths to learn more about the incredible ocean ecosystems that make up the majority of our planet. Readers will discover how the ocean changes as it goes deeper, how deep sea animals survive in harsh environments, and more." (Google Books)
Includes bibliographical references (p. 44-45) and index

Green, Jen

The world's oceans. Smart Apple Media 2010 32p il map (Amazing planet earth) lib bdg $28.50

Grades: 4 5 6 **551.46**
1. Ocean
ISBN 978-1-59920-373-7 lib bdg; 1-59920-373-1 lib bdg
LC 2008-55500

This covers how ocean waves shape the seashore, the makeup of the ocean bed, underwater hazards, storm surges, and the effects of global warming. Interspersed with these are six "Case Study" chapters, which take an in-depth look at various oceanic events throughout history such as the creation of Iceland or the deadly tsunami that hit Indonesia in December, 2004

"Chapters are labeled as 'Case Study' or 'Science Report,' making the presentation lively. The concise explanations include just the right number of examples and clear diagrams, and have perfect color photo accompaniments." SLJ
Includes glossary

Hamilton, John

Tsunamis; [by] John Hamilton. ABDO Pub. Co. 2006 32p il map lib bdg $27.07

Grades: 2 3 4 **551.46**
1. Tsunamis
ISBN 1-59679-333-3
LC 2005040427

"Hamilton describes the 2004 Indian Ocean disaster and explains the causes and nature of tsunamis. . . . The brief but readable text adequately presents the phenomenon and the specific events. Excellent, informative color photos include several that are not common to many of the other recent books on the topic." SLJ
Includes bibliographical references

Lindop, Laurie

★ Venturing the deep sea. Twenty-First Century Books 2006 80p il map (Science on the edge) lib bdg $27.93

Grades: 5 6 7 8 **551.46**
1. Ocean bottom 2. Underwater exploration 3. Marine ecology -- Juvenile literature 4. Submarine topography -- Juvenile literature
ISBN 0-7613-2701-0
LC 2004-29729

"The science is intriguing here. . . . The photos of undersea projects, creatures, weird cave and underwater tube formations are all intriguing." Voice Youth Advocates
Includes bibliographical references

Mallory, Kenneth

Adventure beneath the sea; living in an underwater science station. [photographs by Brian Skerry] Boyds Mills Press 2010 48p il map $18.95

Grades: 4 5 6 7 **551.46**
1. Underwater exploration
ISBN 978-1-59078-607-9; 1-59078-607-6

The author "invites readers to squeeze into Aquarius, a venerable science-station habitat resting on the sea floor at a depth of 60 feet in the Florida Keys. The readable text explains the complexities of training for a weeklong stay, the aims of the scientists on the team, and what it is like to spend 24/7 in squashed companionship in a 43' × 9' cylinder as part of a crew of seven. . . . Sidebars contain interesting information. . . . Full-color photos abound." SLJ
Includes glossary and bibliographical references

★ Diving to a deep-sea volcano. Houghton Mifflin Company 2006 60p il map (Scientists in the field) $17

Grades: 5 6 7 8 **551.46**
1. Ocean bottom 2. Marine biology 3. Underwater exploration 4. Deep diving -- Juvenile literature 5. Oceanographic submersibles -- Juvenile literature
ISBN 978-0-618-33205-2; 0-618-33205-7
LC 2005-25449

This describes the exploration by marine biologist Rich Lutz and his crew of deep sea hydrothermal vents and the creatures that survive there.

"The profile of an enthusiastic scientist injects excitement into even unassuming facts." Booklist

Includes glossary and bibliographical references

Mara, Wil

How do waves form? Marshall Cavendish Benchmark 2011 32p il (Tell me why, tell me how) $20.95

Grades: 2 3 4 5   551.46

1. Tides 2. Waves

ISBN 978-0-7614-4829-7; 0-7614-4829-2

LC 2009041098

This offers information on the process of waves forming.

This title has "clear explanations of natural phenomena, beautiful full-color illustrations, and an uncluttered design. [The] book approaches its topic in a methodical, logical fashion, using examples from a child's world." SLJ

Matsen, Bradford

The incredible record-setting deep-sea dive of the bathysphere; [by] Brad Matsen. Enslow Pubs. 2003 48p il map (Incredible deep-sea adventures) lib bdg $18.95

Grades: 4 5 6 7   551.46

1. Authors 2. Inventors 3. Naturalists 4. Ocean bottom 5. Underwater exploration 6. Memoirists 7. Writers on nature 8. Writers on science 9. Hydrothermal vents -- Juvenile literature

ISBN 0-7660-2188-2

LC 2002-13822

Describes the 1934 dive of a bathysphere, or "sphere of the deep," in which two explorers, William Beebe and Otia Barton, set the world depth record and saw mysterious creatures of the deep ocean

"Attractive color photos contribute to the content." SLJ

Includes glossary and bibliographical references

Nivola, Claire A.

★ Life in the ocean; Claire A. Nivola. Frances Foster Books, Farrar Straus Giroux 2012 1 v. (unpaged) col. ill.

Grades: K 1 2 3 4   551.46

1. Biography 2. Explorers 3. Oceanography 4. Marine biologists -- United States -- Juvenile literature 5. Women marine biologists -- United States -- Juvenile literature 6. Women explorers -- United States -- Biography -- Juvenile literature

ISBN 9780374380687

LC 2011016645

This picture book presents a "biography of oceanographer Sylvia Earle, a pioneer and entrepreneur in her field who also set an example for women of the mid–20th century." It covers life on her "childhood farm," her "relocat[ion] to the Gulf Coast, and her interest [in]ocean exploration. . . . The . . . narrative highlights Earle's career and also provides a few . . . closeups from specific dives." (Publishers Weekly)

Includes bibliographical references and index

Rizzo, Johnna

Oceans; dolphins, sharks, penguins, and more!: meet 60 cool sea creatures and explore their amazing watery world. introduction by Sylvia A. Earle. National Geographic 2010 64p il $14.95; lib bdg $24.90

Grades: 4 5 6   551.46

1. Ocean 2. Marine animals

ISBN 978-1-4263-0686-0; 1-4263-0686-5; 978-1-4263-0724-9 lib bdg; 1-4263-0724-1 lib bdg

"A colorful olio of marine animals in eye-catching photos accompanies a cheerful conversational text. . . . Information boxes pop up all over the place as well, but it is the bright photos that steal the show. . . . This splashy volume is a nice introduction to a salty water-world." SLJ

Includes glossary

Schuh, Mari C.

Tsunamis. Capstone Press 2010 24p il (Earth in action) lib bdg $21.32

Grades: K 1 2   551.46

1. Tsunamis

ISBN 978-1-4296-3438-0 lib bdg; 1-4296-3438-3 lib bdg

LC 2009-2175

This book "boasts a full-page color photograph. . . . [It shows] the aftermath of a disaster . . . but there are also some diagrams showing physical mechanisms and maps highlighting commonly affected places. The left side of each spread provides a few sentences of large-print text, with short, clear explanations." SLJ

Includes glossary and bibliographical references

Simon, Seymour

★ Oceans. Morrow Junior Bks. 1990 un il $16

Grades: 3 4 5 6   551.46

1. Ocean

ISBN 0-688-09453-8

LC 89-28452

"Simon presents clear, simplified explanations of natural phenomena with well-chosen full-color photographs that go beyond decoration. He includes good black-and-white diagrams of how tides work and how waves form and transfer energy. The endpapers are maps of the world showing how and where the major currents flow." SLJ

Seymour Simon's extreme oceans; Seymour Simon. Chronicle Books 2013 60 p. col. ill. (reinforced) $17.99

Grades: 4 5 6   551.46

1. Ocean -- Juvenile literature

ISBN 1452108331; 9781452108339

LC 2012012590

In this work of children's nonfiction, author "[Seymour] Simon examines the things that are 'most,' pertaining to oceans: the tallest sea mounts, the largest waves, the highest tides in the world, the most dangerous and largest animals, the coldest and warmest waters, the biggest storms and tsunamis, and the longest journeys, as well as a closing chapter predicting scenarios if sea levels continue to rise." (School Library Journal)

Spilsbury, Louise

Sweeping tsunamis; [by] Louise and Richard Spilsbury. rev ed.; Heinemann Library 2010 32p il map (Awesome forces of nature) lib bdg $29; pa $7.99

Grades: 3 4 5 6   551.46

1. Tsunamis

ISBN 978-1-4329-3785-0 lib bdg; 1-4329-3785-5 lib bdg; 978-1-4329-3792-8 pa; 1-4329-3792-8 pa

LC 2009037567

First published 2004

This book about tsunamis "causes, characteristics, and relevant science, including progress in predicting the events. Case studies illustrate the human response. Numerous color photographs and sidebars are interwoven into the well-organized and absorbing [narrative]." SLJ

Includes glossary and bibliographical references

Stille, Darlene R.

Oceans. Children's Press 1999 47p il maps (True book) $22; pa $6.95

Grades: 2 3 4　　　　　　　　　　　　　**551.46**

1. Ocean 2. Oceanography -- Juvenile literature

ISBN 0-516-21510-8; 0-516-26768-X pa

LC 98-53857

An introduction to the ocean describing its physical characteristics, the plants and animals that live in or near it, and its importance to life on Earth

Includes bibliographical references

Tagliaferro, Linda

How does an earthquake become a tsunami? Raintree 2008 32p il map (How does it happen?) lib bdg $27.50; pa $7.99

Grades: 3 4 5　　　　　　　　　　　　　**551.46**

1. Waves 2. Tsunamis 3. Earthquakes 4. Plate tectonics

ISBN 978-1-4109-3446-8 lib bdg; 1-4109-3446-2 lib bdg; 978-1-4109-3454-3 pa; 1-4109-3454-3 pa

LC 2008-52643

"Information is clearly presented using a large font, diagrams, and photographs formatted to resemble Polaroid pictures. . . . A first-rate job answering some important scientific questions." SLJ

Includes glossary and bibliographical references

VanCleave, Janice Pratt, 1942-

Janice VanCleave's oceans for every kid; easy activities that make learning science fun. Wiley 1996 245p il map (Science for every kid series) hardcover o.p. pa $12.95

Grades: 4 5 6 7　　　　　　　　　　　　**551.46**

1. Oceanography

ISBN 0-471-12453-2 pa

LC 95-9201

Includes information on techniques and technologies of oceanography, the topology of the ocean floor, movement of the sea, properties of sea water, and life in the sea

"An engaging overview of marine sciences. Each chapter explores a topic in two to four pages, then poses questions accompanied by lucid explanations." SLJ

Includes glossary

Woodward, John

On the seabed. Brown Bear Books 2009 32p il map (Oceans alive!) lib bdg $28.50

Grades: 2 3 4 5　　　　　　　　　　　　**551.46**

1. Oceanography

ISBN 978-1-933834-64-1 lib bdg; 1-933834-64-1 lib bdg

Describes plants, animals, and different habitats that are found on the ocean's floor, and offers information on kelp forests, sunken treasure, and hydrothermal vents.

"From deep hot areas to cold places, strange, but wonderful, events and organisms are discussed. . . . Through the

various photos and the text, the reader should develop an appreciation for the diversity found on the sea floor." Sci Books Films

Includes glossary and bibliographical references

Under the waves. Brown Bear Books 2009 32p il map (Oceans alive!) lib bdg $28.50

Grades: 2 3 4 5　　　　　　　　　　　　**551.46**

1. Oceanography 2. Marine animals

ISBN 978-1-933834-62-7 lib bdg; 1-933834-62-5 lib bdg

Explores and describes both different oceans and different parts of the ocean.

"Explanations on notebook-style illustrations offer asides, a delightful extra along with appropriate maps and impressive photos. . . . Accurate details are given for such wonders as the Portuguese man-of-war, red tides, manta rays, and lion-fish." Sci Books Films

Includes glossary and bibliographical references

Voyage: Ocean: a full-speed-ahead tour of the oceans. DK Pub. 2009 128p il $24.99

Grades: 3 4 5　　　　　　　　　　　　　**551.46**

1. Ocean

ISBN 978-0-7566-4548-9; 0-7566-4548-4

"This eclectic and informative book is shaped like the porthole of a submarine. After readers open the hatch, the ocean comes alive with full-color photographs. . . . Images from the book are featured on collector's cards housed in a pocket at the end, along with stickers and a poster of ocean life. The breadth of information and special features will appeal to intrepid readers." Publ Wkly

The **deep,** deep ocean. Brown Bear Books 2009 32p il map (Oceans alive!) lib bdg $28.50

Grades: 2 3 4 5　　　　　　　　　　　　**551.46**

1. Oceanography

ISBN 978-1-933834-63-4 lib bdg; 1-933834-63-3 lib bdg

This describes "deep parts of the ocean. Colored drawings, photos, and themed factual sidebars all enhance the story, navigated by a variety of submarines. . . . Differences in temperatures from the surface to the midnight zone are elegantly explained." Sci Books Films

Includes glossary and bibliographical references

551.48　Hydrology

Chambers, Catherine

Rivers; [by] Catherine Chambers and Nicholas Lapthorn. rev and updated; Heinemann 2007 32p il map (Mapping earthforms) hardcover o.p. lib bdg $28.21

Grades: 3 4 5　　　　　　　　　　　　　**551.48**

1. Rivers

ISBN 978-1-4034-9604-1 lib bdg; 1-4034-9604-8 lib bdg; 978-1-4034-9614-0 pa; 1-4034-9614-5 pa

LC 2006037720

First published 2002

After defining rivers, this work describes "the actions that produce them, their effects on animals and plants, related science, . . . [lists] future possibilities . . . Maps, diagrams, tables, and high-quality color photographs complement the text." SLJ

Includes glossary and bibliographical references

Cole, Joanna
★ The **magic** school bus at the waterworks; illustrated by Bruce Degen. Scholastic 1986 39p il hardcover o.p. pa $4.95
Grades: 2 3 4   **551.48**
1. Water 2. Water supply
ISBN 0-590-43739-9; 0-590-40360-5 pa

LC 86-6672

The author presents "specific facts about water and a memorable image of the water cycle process. The story involves a 'strange' teacher who takes her class on a magical trip: up to the clouds—down to earth in raindrops—down a stream into a reservoir where the water is purified—finally into the underground pipes leading back to school. The illustrations both enhance the humor and provide visual presentation of the water cycle." Appraisal

Dorros, Arthur
Follow the water from brook to ocean; written and illustrated by Arthur Dorros. HarperCollins Pubs. 1991 32p il (Let's-read-and-find-out science book) $13.95; lib bdg $13.89
Grades: K 1 2 3   **551.48**
1. Water
ISBN 0-06-021598-4; 0-06-021599-2 lib bdg

LC 90-1438

Explains how water flows from brooks, to streams, to rivers, over waterfalls, through canyons and dams, to eventually reach the ocean

"An excellent presentation of introductory material about water. . . . The illustrations are simple, almost childlike, in soft colors." SLJ

Dwyer, Helen
Floods! Marshall Cavendish Benchmark 2010 32p il map (Eyewitness Disaster) lib bdg $28.50
Grades: 4 5 6   **551.48**
1. Floods
ISBN 978-1-60870-002-8; 1-60870-002-X

Provides information about floods through eyewitness accounts from survivors and rescue workers.

"Bold subheadings and color captions break information into readable chunks for the younger learner. Important vocabulary is in bold print. . . . An excellent addition to your science collection." Libr Media Connect

Includes glossary and bibliographical references

Gallant, Roy A.
Water. Benchmark Bks. 2001 48p il (Kaleidoscope) lib bdg $15.95
Grades: 3 4 5   **551.48**
1. Water
ISBN 0-7614-1040-6

LC 99-49627

Explains why water, although common, has characteristics which make it an unusual substance

"The large-print [text is] easy to read, and the explanations are clear and concise. Outstanding full-page, full-color photographs appear throughout." SLJ

Includes glossary and bibliographical references

Green, Jen
Mighty rivers. Smart Apple Media 2010 32p il map (Amazing planet earth) lib bdg $28.50
Grades: 4 5 6   **551.48**
1. Rivers
ISBN 978-1-59920-371-3 lib bdg; 1-59920-371-5 lib bdg

LC 2008-55498

Starting with a quick introduction to the water cycle, this book shows readers how rivers are formed, and how they, in turn, form waterfalls, carve out canyons, create fertile deltas, cause flooding, and have a great impact on the daily lives of people all over the world

"Chapters are labeled as 'Case Study' or 'Science Report,' making the presentation lively. The concise explanations include just the right number of examples and clear diagrams, and have perfect color photo accompaniments." SLJ

Includes glossary

Lyon, George Ella
★ **All** the water in the world. Atheneum Books for Young Readers 2011 un il $15.99
Grades: K 1 2 3   **551.48**
1. Water 2. Hydrologic cycle -- Juvenile literature
ISBN 978-1-4169-7130-6; 1-4169-7130-0

LC 2010-29530

"Lyrical text compactly describes the hydrological cycle and global contrast between plenty and dearth of the key life-giving substance. . . . The text . . . [is] lucid yet imaginative, turning scientific and geographical explanation into sonorous sound play. . . . Visuals are strong and supple: the text is creatively laid out with pattern-poem precision, and the digital art effortlessly balances crisp collage-style composite . . . and splashy, fluid splatters of pigment, providing impeccable rhythm and flow." Bull Cent Child Books

Rauzon, Mark J.
Water, water everywhere; [by] Mark J. Rauzon and Cynthia Overbeck Bix. Sierra Club Bks. for Children 1994 32p il $14.95; pa $6.95
Grades: K 1 2 3   **551.48**
1. Water
ISBN 0-87156-598-6; 0-87156-383-5 pa

LC 92-34521

Describes the forms water takes, how it has shaped Earth, and its importance to life

"Water's vital role in the life of our planet is vividly portrayed in a crisp, economical text that cultivates respect for the environment. . . . Striking, often full-page, color photographs will engage the imagination of young readers." Horn Book Guide

Sepehri, Sandy
Rivers; [by] Sandy Sepehri. Rourke Pub. 2008 32p il (Landforms) hardcover o.p. lib bdg $28.50
Grades: 1 2 3 4   **551.48**
1. Rivers
ISBN 978-1-60044-546-0 lib bdg; 1-60044-546-2 lib bdg; 978-1-60044-707-5 pa; 1-60044-707-4 pa

LC 2007012292

"The illustrations and photographs are plentiful and colorful. . . . The [volume is] well written and successfully [conveys] the basics of the topic." Sci Books Films

Includes glossary and bibliographical references

Spilsbury, Louise

Raging floods; [by] Louise and Richard Spilsbury. Heinemann Library 2010 32p il (Awesome forces of nature) lib bdg $29; pa $7.99

Grades: 3 4 5 6   551.48

1. Floods

ISBN 978-1-4329-3782-9 lib bdg; 1-4329-3782-0 lib bdg; 978-1-4329-3789-8 pa; 1-4329-3789-8 pa

LC 2009-37562

First published 2004

This book about floods "is sure to catch the eyes of students and educators. . . . The interesting and accurate facts are presented in an easily understood vocabulary. . . . Incredible eye-catching photographs, diagrams, or maps are tastefully positioned on every page." Libr Media Connect

Includes glossary and bibliographical references

Waldman, Neil

The **snowflake**; a water cycle story. [by] Neil Waldman. Millbrook Press 2003 un il $14.95

Grades: K 1 2 3   551.48

1. Snowflakes -- Juvenile literature 2. Hydrologic cycle -- Juvenile literature

ISBN 0-7613-2347-3

LC 2003-4806

Follows the journey of a water droplet through the various stages of the water cycle, from precipitation to evaporation and condensation

"The clear text is undeniably lyrical. . . . The real stunners here, though, are the dazzling, cool-toned paintings that convey the wonders of nature with delicate precision." SLJ

Wells, Robert E.

Did a dinosaur drink this water? A. Whitman 2006 un il $15.95; pa $6.95

Grades: K 1 2 3   551.48

1. Water 2. Hydrologic cycle -- Juvenile literature

ISBN 978-0-8075-8839-0; 978-0-8075-8840-6 pa

LC 2006-01039

This describes "the water cycle, explaining that the earth's water has been constantly recycled not just since dinosaur days but for billions of years. The simple text asks good questions and offers clearly worded answers, enhanced by lively, colorful ink-and-watercolor illustrations." Booklist

551.5 Meteorology

Banqueri, Eduardo

Weather. Enchanted Lion Books 2006 33p il (Field guides) $16.95

Grades: 4 5 6 7   551.5

1. Weather

ISBN 1-59270-059-4

LC 2006-42864

This "book is filled with information about all aspects of weather, from why there are seasons to predicting the weather. Complementing the scientifically accurate text is an excellent mix of drawings and photographs." Sci Books and Films

Branley, Franklyn Mansfield

Air is all around you; by Franklyn M. Branley; illustrated by John O'Brien. newly illustrated ed.; HarperCollinsPublishers 2006 36p il (Let's-read-and-find-out science) hardcover o.p. pa $4.99

Grades: K 1 2   551.5

1. Air

ISBN 0-06-059413-6; 0-06-059414-4 lib bdg; 0-06-059415-2 pa

LC 2004005043

A revised and newly illustrated edition of the title first published 1962

This "title introduces the concept of air, its presence in our world, and its importance to the environment. The text describes several interesting facts, clearly explaining ideas and incorporating experiments that are easy to reproduce at home or in the classroom. The appealing artwork supports the narrative. . . . Produced in pen and warm, earthy watercolors, the pictures are filled with amusing details." SLJ

Carson, Mary Kay

Weather projects for young scientists; experiments and science fair ideas. Chicago Review Press 2007 134p il $14.95

Grades: 4 5 6 7   551.5

1. Weather 2. Science -- Experiments 3. Science projects -- Juvenile literature

ISBN 978-1-55652-629-9; 1-55652-629-6

LC 2006-16430

This "presents difficult concepts in a very concrete, basic manner." Sci Books Films

Cosgrove, Brian

Weather; written by Brian Cosgrove. rev ed; DK Publishing 2007 72p il map (DK eyewitness books) $15.99; lib bdg $19.99

Grades: 4 5 6 7   551.5

1. Climate 2. Weather 3. Atmosphere

ISBN 978-0-7566-3006-5; 0-7566-3006-1; 978-0-7566-0737-1 lib bdg; 0-7566-0737-X lib bdg

LC 2007-281112

First published 1991 by Knopf

"Discover the world's weather—from heat waves and droughts to blizzards and floods"—Cover. Includes discussion of why the climate may change in the future.

"Accompanying the book are a poster, additional images on CD-ROM, and a useful glossary. Altogether, this book and its supplements are well crafted to motivate young learners about the importance of weather, to deepen their conceptual understanding of it, and to pique their interest in participating in its study." Sci Books Films

Includes glossary

DeLallo, Laura

Hammered by a heat wave! consultants, Daphne Thompson, Keith C. Heidorn. Bearport Pub. 2010 32p il map (Disaster survivors) lib bdg $25.27

Grades: 4 5 6 7   551.5

1. Meteorology

ISBN 978-1-936087-51-8 lib bdg; 1-936087-51-0 lib bdg

"Captivating photos and illustrations and sidebars present interesting facts or brief anecdotes. . . . [This] should be purchased for all school and public libraries as . . . [it gives] a new perspective on the topic." Libr Media Connect

Includes glossary and bibliographical references

Gardner, Robert

Ace your weather science project; great science fair ideas. [by] Robert Gardner and Salvatore Tocci. Enslow Publishers 2009 104p il (Ace your physics science project) lib bdg $31.93

Grades: 5 6 7 8   551.5

1. Weather 2. Science projects 3. Science -- Experiments

ISBN 978-0-7660-3223-1 lib bdg; 0-7660-3223-X lib bdg

LC 2008-49779

"Presents several science experiments and project ideas about weather." Publisher's note

Includes bibliographical references

Easy genius science projects with weather; great experiments and ideas. Enslow Publishers 2009 128p il (Easy genius science projects) lib bdg $31.93

Grades: 5 6 7 8   551.5

1. Weather 2. Science projects 3. Science -- Experiments

ISBN 978-0-7660-2924-8 lib bdg; 0-7660-2924-7 lib bdg

LC 2008-23972

"Science experiments and science project ideas about weather." Publisher's note

Includes glossary and bibliographical references

Stellar science projects about Earth's sky; [by] Robert Gardner; illustrations by Tom Labaff. Enslow Elementary 2007 48p il (Rockin' earth science experiments) lib bdg $23.93

Grades: 3 4 5   551.5

1. Sky 2. Science projects 3. Science -- Experiments

ISBN 978-0-7660-2732-9 lib bdg; 0-7660-2732-5 lib bdg

LC 2006-13790

This offers experiments on topics such as the weight of air, air pressure, why the sky is blue, why sunsets are red, clouds, stars, and balloons in sky and water

This is "just right for students with limited experience looking for projects that are fairly interesting and manageable." SLJ

Includes glossary and bibliographical references

Wild science projects about Earth's weather; illustrations by Tom LaBaff. Enslow 2007 48p il (Rockin' earth science experiments) lib bdg $23.93

Grades: 3 4 5   551.5

1. Weather 2. Science projects 3. Science -- Experiments

ISBN 978-0-7660-2734-3 lib bdg; 0-7660-2734-1 lib bdg

LC 2006-05897

This presents experiments on such topics as air temperature and pressure, wind direction, rainfall, and clouds.

"Each experiment is enhanced by a topical fact box and includes a supply list and step-by-step explanation." SLJ

Includes glossary and bibliographical references

Lauw, Darlene

Weather; [by Darlene Lauw and Lim Cheng Puay] Crabtree 2003 29p il (Science alive!) lib bdg $21.28; pa $7.95

Grades: 3 4 5 6   551.5

1. Weather 2. Experiments 3. Science -- Experiments 4. Meteorology -- Juvenile literature 5. Weather -- Experiments -- Juvenile literature

ISBN 0-7787-0565-X lib bdg; 0-7787-0611-7 pa

LC 2002-11641

Introduces concepts related to weather through various activities and projects

"The directions are kid friendly, and the graphics that support them are very helpful. . . . The science content is within the range of understanding of an upper elementary school student." Sci Books Films

Includes glossary

VanCleave, Janice Pratt, 1942-

Janice VanCleave's weather; mind-boggling experiments you can turn into science fair projects. [by] Janice VanCleave. Wiley 1995 89p il (Spectacular science projects series) pa $10.95

Grades: 4 5 6 7   551.5

1. Weather 2. Science projects 3. Science -- Experiments 4. Science -- Experiments -- Juvenile literature

ISBN 0-471-03231-X

LC 94-25646

"Using everyday household items, the reading audience can demonstrate to itself such phenomena as differences in climate at different points on the Earth, lightning, wind direction and intensity, clouds, rain, fronts, etc. Through excellent directions and adequate illustrations, the reader can do 20 simple experiments at little or no cost that demonstrate many aspects of the weather." Sci Books Films

Includes glossary

Vogel, Julia

Let it blow! Learn about air; illustrated by Jane Yamada. Child's World 2010 24p il (Science definitions) lib bdg $22.79

Grades: PreK K 1 2   551.5

1. Air

ISBN 978-1-60253-509-1 lib bdg; 1-60253-509-4 lib bdg

LC 2010010976

This book about air is "attractive and succinct. . . . Large, eye-catching photos cover the recto of each spread. . . . Varying, jewel-toned accents are used in headings, highlighted glossary terms, and in a sidebar on each spread." SLJ

Includes glossary

Whitt, Kelly Kizer

Solar system forecast; by Kelly Kizer Whitt; illustrated by Laurie Allen Klein. Sylvan Dell Publishing 2012 1 v. (unpaged) col. ill. (hardcover) $17.95; (paperback) $9.95; (English ebook) $9.95

Grades: 1 2 3   551.5

1. Weather forecasting 2. Pluto (Dwarf planet) 3. Planets -- Exploration 4. Solar system -- Juvenile

literature 5. Planetary meteorology -- Juvenile literature
ISBN 9781607185239; 9781607185321;
9781607185413

LC 2012007599

Author Kelly Kizer Whitt's book is narrated by "a friendly, green-skinned TV weatheralien . . . [who] begins with the Sun . . . and moves on to each planet in turn. There are additional reports for the moon Titan . . . and the dwarf planet Pluto. . . . [The story features] space-suited commuters, melted or frozen science gear and views of prominent storms, from a hurricane on Earth to Jupiter's Great Red Spot. . . . Charts, tables, diagrams, quizzes and other . . . material" provide information on "meteorological data." (Kirkus Reviews)

551.51 Composition, regions, dynamics of atmosphere

Bauer, Marion Dane

Wind; illustrated by John Wallace. Aladdin 2004 32p il (Ready-to-read) hardcover o.p. pa $3.99
Grades: K 1 2 **551.51**
1. Winds
ISBN 0-689-85442-0; 0-689-85443-9 pa

LC 2002-9656

Illustrations and simple text explain what wind is, how it is used by plants, birds, and people, and how wind can become a storm

Cobb, Vicki

I face the wind; illustrated by Julia Gorton. HarperCollins Pubs. 2003 un il (Science play) $16.99
Grades: K 1 2 **551.51**
1. Winds 2. Science -- Experiments
ISBN 0-688-17840-5; 0-688-17841-3 lib bdg

LC 2001-26480

Introduces the characteristics and actions of the wind through simple hands-on activities

"All demonstrations . . . are conducted with readily available materials. . . . Streamlined and jargon-fee though the text may be, it gets the basics across in kid-friendly terms. . . . Gorton's strong, angular graphics feature a red-headed little gal with wide-set eyes and a powerful curiosity who alternately serves as wind-tousled subject of forces real but unseen and as demonstrator for each experiment." Bull Cent Child Books

Gallant, Roy A.

Atmosphere; sea of air. Benchmark Bks. 2002 79p il (Earthworks) lib bdg $19.95
Grades: 5 6 7 8 **551.51**
1. Atmosphere 2. Meteorology
ISBN 0-7614-1366-9

LC 2001-43301

Describes the atmosphere which makes life on earth possible, explores its effects on weather and climate, and examines what causes air pollution and what can be done it

"Gallant's prose is nearly conversational in its easy delivery, but his facts are always thorough and his ideas clearly explained. . . . Crisp graphs, maps, and excellent color photos illustrate [this] fine [volume]." Booklist

Includes glossary and bibliographical references

Kaner, Etta

Who likes the wind? written by Etta Kaner; illustrated by Marie Lafrance. Kids Can Press 2006 un il (Exploring the elements) $14.95
Grades: PreK K 1 2 **551.51**
1. Winds
ISBN 1-55337-839-3

"On each double-page spread, a child expresses why he or she likes the wind ('because it pushes my boat'). The child then wonders how the event happens ('I wonder why the wind blows') and lifts a flap for a scientific explanation. The narrative sections are illustrated in child-friendly acrylics, with the explantions set off in white. Clear diagrams supplement the scientific details." Horn Book Guide

Malone, Peter

Close to the wind; the Beaufort scale. G.P. Putnam's Sons 2007 un il $16.99
Grades: 3 4 5 6 **551.51**
1. Winds 2. Admirals 3. Geographers 4. Young adult literature -- Works 5. Beaufort scale -- Juvenile literature
ISBN 0-399-24399-2; 978-0-399-24399-8

LC 2005-32672

"Captain Francis Beaufort of the Royal Navy spent the years 1805-1810 developing a graduated scale for measuring the wind. In a treatment that manages at once to be entirely informative and utterly charming, the author presents the captain's work through a rousing story. Young William Bentley . . . is a fictional midshipman on the Zephyr , a man-of-war making a voyage from Portsmouth to Naples and then to Jamaica and back. The Beaufort scale of the prevailing conditions is given on the versos, while the rectos sport exquisite watercolor-and-gouache paintings. . . . A truly lovely job of bookmaking that covers a topic rarely treated in children's literature." SLJ

Sayre, April Pulley

★ **Stars** beneath your bed; the surprising story of dust. pictures by Ann Jonas. Greenwillow Books 2005 un il $15.99; lib bdg $16.89
Grades: K 1 2 3 **551.51**
1. Dust
ISBN 0-06-057188-8; 0-06-057189-6 lib bdg

LC 2004-2108

"Dust gets a poetic treatment in a picture book that tells all about dust's what and where, and sometimes its why. Using free verse, Sayre explains how dust is made everywhere. . . . The watercolors in the well-composed two-page spreads sometimes soar . . . but there are also smaller images . . . that are equally effective." Booklist

551.55 Atmospheric disturbances and formations

Aronin, Miriam

Mangled by a hurricane! consultant, James L. Franklin. Bearport Pub. 2010 32p il map (Disaster survivors) lib bdg $25.27

Grades: 4 5 6 7 **551.55**
1. Hurricanes 2. Hurricane Katrina, 2005
ISBN 978-1-936087-49-5 lib bdg; 1-936087-49-9
lib bdg

"Captivating photos and illustrations and sidebars present interesting facts or brief anecdotes. . . . [This] should be purchased for all school and public libraries as . . . [it gives] a new perspective on the topic." Libr Media Connect

Includes glossary and bibliographical references

Bailer, Darice
Why does it thunder and lightning? Marshall Cavendish Benchmark 2011 32p il (Tell me why, tell me how) lib bdg $29.93
Grades: 2 3 4 5 **551.55**
1. Lightning 2. Thunderstorms
ISBN 978-0-7614-4825-9; 0-7614-4825-X

This offers information about thunder and lightning.

This title has "clear explanations of natural phenomena, beautiful full-color illustrations, and an uncluttered design. [The] book approaches its topic in a methodical, logical fashion, using examples from a child's world." SLJ

Branley, Franklyn Mansfield
Flash, crash, rumble, and roll; by Franklyn M. Branley; illustrated by True Kelley. newly il ed; HarperCollins Pubs. 1999 32p il (Let's-read-and-find-out science) hardcover o.p. pa $4.95
Grades: K 1 2 3 **551.55**
1. Lightning 2. Thunderstorms 3. Safety 4. Lightning -- Safety measures
ISBN 0-06-027858-7; 0-06-027859-5 lib bdg; 0-06-445179-8 pa

LC 97-43599

A revised and newly illustrated edition of the title first published 1964 by Crowell

Explains how and why a thunderstorm occurs and gives safety steps to follow when lightning is flashing

This offers "clear and informative explanations . . . [and] colorful cartoonlike pictures." Horn Book Guide

Carson, Mary Kay
★ Inside hurricanes. Sterling 2010 48p il map (Inside) $16.95; pa $9.95
Grades: 5 6 7 8 **551.55**
1. Hurricanes
ISBN 978-1-4027-5880-5; 1-4027-5880-4; 978-1-4027-7780-6 pa; 1-4027-7780-9 pa

"This trip into the eye of the storm is enveloping in more ways than one. . . . The pages fold up, or down, or left, or right, with every turn guided by an icon familiar to anyone who lives in a storm zone: a circular blue 'Hurricane Evacuation Route' road sign. This constant motion can't help but engage. . . . The design and layout is well above par, featuring excellent cutaways of storm systems, meteorological maps, thrilling photography, and a spectacular foldout Saffir-Simpson Hurricane Scale. The text is packed with info, data, and case studies broken into digestible chunks, and boxes and sidebars . . . make this . . . very appealing." Booklist

★ Inside tornadoes. Sterling 2010 48p il map (Inside) $16.95; pa $9.95

Grades: 5 6 7 8 **551.55**
1. Tornadoes
ISBN 978-1-4027-5879-9; 1-4027-5879-0; 978-1-4027-7781-3 pa; 1-4027-7781-7 pa

"This visually tempting title defines and explains the storms people call twisters, gives examples of four particularly devastating ones in this country, describes tornado watchers at work, offers hands-on activity and suggests precautions for tornado safety. . . . It includes step-by-step explanatory text, striking images and helpful graphics." Kirkus

Includes glossary and bibliographical references

Ceban, Bonnie J.
Tornadoes; disaster & survival. [by] Bonnie J. Ceban. Enslow Publishers 2005 48p il map (Deadly disasters) lib bdg $23.93
Grades: 4 5 6 7 **551.55**
1. Tornadoes
ISBN 0-7660-2383-4

LC 2004-11700

This explores the causes of tornadoes, how people survive these storms, and how they are predicted

Includes glossary and bibliographical references

Challoner, Jack
Hurricane & tornado; written by Jack Challoner. rev ed.; DK Pub. 2004 72p il map (DK eyewitness books) $15.99; lib bdg $19.99
Grades: 4 5 6 7 **551.55**
1. Storms 2. Weather 3. Natural disasters
ISBN 0-7566-0690-X; 0-7566-0689-6 lib bdg

LC 2004302408

First published 2000

Describes dangerous and destructive weather conditions around the world, such as thunderstorms, tornadoes, hurricanes, lightning, hail, and drought with photographs, historical background, and legends.

Cole, Joanna
★ The magic school bus inside a hurricane; illustrated by Bruce Degen. Scholastic 1995 un il hardcover o.p. pa $4.99
Grades: 2 3 4 **551.55**
1. Weather 2. Hurricanes 3. Meteorology
ISBN 0-590-44686-X; 0-590-44687-8 pa

LC 94-34703

"Cole presents the science in easy-to-understand terms, with Degen clarifying the concepts and adding comic relief through double-page-spread pictures that brim with details." Booklist

Demarest, Chris L.
Hurricane hunters! riders on the storm. [by] Chris L. Demarest. Margaret K. McElderry Books 2006 un il $17.95
Grades: K 1 2 3 **551.55**
1. Hurricanes 2. Weather forecasting
ISBN 978-0-689-86168-0; 0-689-86168-0

LC 2005011292

This "picture book explains the work of the large converted cargo planes that fly into hurricanes to collect weather data. . . . The pastels are particularly effective at capturing the look and feel of the powerful winds and swirling water caused by a hurricane at its height." SLJ

Includes bibliographical references

Fleisher, Paul

Lightning, hurricanes, and blizzards; the science of storms. Lerner Publications 2011 48p il (Weatherwise) lib bdg $29.27

Grades: 4 5 6 7   **551.55**

1. Blizzards 2. Lightning 3. Hurricanes

ISBN 978-0-8225-7536-8; 0-8225-7536-1

          LC 2009044918

This describes how storms form, where they strike, and what makes them so powerful.

"Chapters are well-organized and contain clear explanations. The crisp layout contains plenty of captioned photos and diagrams, as well as sidebars that feature interesting facts and suggestions for observations readers can record in their backyards." Horn Book Guide

Includes glossary and bibliographical references

Fradin, Dennis Brindell

Tornado! the story behind these twisting, turning, spinning, and spiraling storms. by Judith Bloom Fradin & Dennis Brindell Fradin. National Geographic 2011 63p il map (National Geographic kids) $16.95; lib bdg $26.90

Grades: 4 5 6 7   **551.55**

1. Tornadoes

ISBN 978-1-4263-0779-9; 1-4263-0779-9; 978-1-4263-0780-5 lib bdg; 1-4263-0780-2 lib bdg

          LC 2010042813

"Two of the four chapters describe deadly twisters in the U.S., while the others discuss the science and predictability of tornadoes. Throughout, there are first-person accounts. . . . Excellent color photos make this book a magnet for browsers, while the informative text and diagrams bring meaning to the images and provide content that students will find helpful for reports." Booklist

Includes glossary and bibliographical references

Fradin, Judith Bloom

★ Hurricanes; by Judy and Dennis Fradin. National Geographic 2007 48p il (Witness to disaster) $16.95; lib bdg $26.90

Grades: 4 5 6 7   **551.55**

1. Hurricanes

ISBN 978-1-4262-0111-0; 1-4262-0111-7; 978-1-4262-0112-7 lib bdg; 1-4262-0112-5 lib bdg

          LC 2006-103003

This describes Hurricane Katrina, the science of hurricanes, some hurricanes of the past, and the prediction of hurricanes.

This offers "dramatic first-person quotes and an array of impressive photographs." Horn Book Guide

Includes glossary and bibliographical references

Gibbons, Gail

Hurricanes! Holiday House 2009 32p il $17.95

Grades: K 1 2   **551.55**

1. Hurricanes

ISBN 978-0-8234-2233-3; 0-8234-2233-X

          LC 2009-8761

"Gibbons uses a picture-book format to detail [hurricanes'] destructive power without the information ever be-

coming too frightening. . . . Gentle watercolors are Gibbons' main weapons here, and the painted panoramas . . . are engagingly tumultuous. . . . Famous hurricanes, from Andrew to Katrina, are among the multitude of . . . topics broached in this intriguing introduction." Booklist

Tornadoes! Holiday House 2009 32p il $16.95

Grades: K 1 2 3   **551.55**

1. Tornadoes

ISBN 978-0-8234-2216-6; 0-8234-2216-X

          LC 2008035828

"Gibbons uses her trademark watercolor cartoon images and simple text to introduce readers to scientific information. . . . Gibbons's style is appealing and accessible." SLJ

Godkin, Celia

Hurricane! Fitzhenry & Whiteside 2008 un il $19.95

Grades: 2 3 4   **551.55**

1. Hurricanes

ISBN 978-1-55455-080-7; 1-55455-080-7

"An attractive, simple introduction to the effects of a hurricane on humans and on wildlife. . . . Godkin's gentle illustrations—paintings in water-soluble oil on canvas and drawings in ink and watercolor on paper—add luminous grace to this simple look at the effects of violent tropical storms. Handsome and useful." SLJ

Goin, Miriam Busch

Storms. National Geographic 2009 32p il (National Geographic kids) lib bdg $11.90; pa $3.99

Grades: K 1 2   **551.55**

1. Storms

ISBN 978-1-4263-0395-1 lib bdg; 978-1-4263-0394-4 pa

          LC 2008-51883

"Blizzards, monsoons, hurricanes: the excitement of wild, stormy weather will draw beginning readers to this dramatic title with color photos and an interactive text." Booklist

Harris, Caroline

Wild weather. Kingfisher 2005 53p il map (Kingfisher voyages) $14.95

Grades: 4 5 6 7   **551.55**

1. Storms 2. Weather

ISBN 0-7534-5931-0; 978-0-7534-5911-9

This describes weather phenomena such as monsoons, tsunamis, blizzards, tornadoes, cyclones, mirages, and El Niño.

This "book has bright and exciting pictures. . . . The organization . . . is great, and the text is easy to read." Sci Books Films

Includes glossary

Jennings, Terry

Extreme weather. Smart Apple Media 2009 32p il map (Amazing planet earth) lib bdg $28.50

Grades: 4 5 6   **551.55**

1. Storms 2. Weather

ISBN 978-1-59920-369-0 lib bdg; 1-59920-369-3 lib bdg

          LC 2009-3401

This book explains how extreme weather conditions can have devastating effects on our lives

"Chapters are labeled as 'Case Study' or 'Science Report,' making the presentation lively. The concise explanations include just the right number of examples and clear diagrams, and have perfect color photo accompaniments." SLJ

Includes glossary

Markovics, Joyce L.

Blitzed by a blizzard! by Joyce Markovics; consultant, Daphne Thompson. Bearport Pub. 2010 32p il map (Disaster survivors) lib bdg $25.27

Grades: 4 5 6 7   **551.55**

1. Blizzards

ISBN 978-1-936087-54-9 lib bdg; 1-936087-54-5 lib bdg

LC 2009-36960

"Captivating photos and illustrations and sidebars present interesting facts or brief anecdotes. . . . [This] should be purchased for all school and public libraries as . . . [it gives] a new perspective on the topic." Libr Media Connect

Includes glossary and bibliographical references

Rebman, Renee C.

How do tornadoes form? Marshall Cavendish Benchmark 2011 32p il (Tell me why, tell me how) lib bdg $29.93

Grades: 2 3 4 5   **551.55**

1. Tornadoes

ISBN 978-0-7614-4828-0; 0-7614-4828-4

LC 2009041097

This offers information on the process of tornadoes forming.

This title has "clear explanations of natural phenomena, beautiful full-color illustrations, and an uncluttered design. [The] book approaches its topic in a methodical, logical fashion, using examples from a child's world." SLJ

Royston, Angela

Hurricanes! Marshall Cavendish Benchmark 2010 32p il map (Eyewitness disaster) lib bdg $28.50

Grades: 4 5 6   **551.55**

1. Hurricanes

ISBN 978-1-60870-003-5; 1-60870-003-8

LC 2010001800

Provides information about hurricanes through eyewitness accounts from survivors and rescue workers.

"Bold subheadings and color captions break information into readable chunks for the younger learner. Important vocabulary is in bold print. . . . An excellent addition to your science collection." Libr Media Connect

Includes glossary and bibliographical references

Storms! Marshall Cavendish Benchmark 2010 32p il map (Eyewitness disaster) lib bdg $28.50

Grades: 4 5 6   **551.55**

1. Storms

ISBN 978-1-60870-004-2; 1-60870-004-6

LC 2009041697

Provides information about storms through eyewitness accounts from survivors and rescue workers.

"Bold subheadings and color captions break information into readable chunks for the younger learner. Important vocabulary is in bold print. . . . An excellent addition to your science collection." Libr Media Connect

Includes glossary and bibliographical references

Rudolph, Jessica

Erased by a tornado! Bearport Pub. 2010 32p il map (Disaster survivors) lib bdg $25.27

Grades: 4 5 6 7   **551.55**

1. Tornadoes

ISBN 978-1-936087-52-5 lib bdg; 1-936087-52-9 lib bdg

LC 2009-34363

"Captivating photos and illustrations and sidebars present interesting facts or brief anecdotes. . . . [This] should be purchased for all school and public libraries as . . . [it gives] a new perspective on the topic." Libr Media Connect

Includes glossary and bibliographical references

Schuh, Mari C.

Tornadoes. Pebble Plus 2010 24p il map (Earth in action) lib bdg $21.32

Grades: K 1 2   **551.55**

1. Tornadoes

ISBN 978-1-4296-3434-2 lib bdg; 1-4296-3434-0 lib bdg

LC 2009-2174

This book "boasts a full-page color photograph. . . . [It shows] the aftermath of a disaster . . . but there are also some diagrams showing physical mechanisms and maps highlighting commonly affected places. The left side of each spread provides a few sentences of large-print text, with short, clear explanations." SLJ

Includes glossary and bibliographical references

Shores, Lori

How to build a tornado in a bottle. Capstone Press 2011 24p il (Hands-on science fun) lib bdg $17.99; pa $6.95

Grades: PreK K 1   **551.55**

1. Tornadoes 2. Science -- Experiments

ISBN 978-1-4296-4493-8 lib bdg; 1-4296-4493-1 lib bdg; 978-1-4296-5577-4 pa; 1-4296-5577-1 pa

LC 2010013585

Simple text and full-color photos instruct readers how to build a tornado in a bottle and explain the science behind the activity.

"Bright, glossy photos and irresistible ideas make these science lessons effortless fun." Booklist

Includes bibliographical references

Silverstein, Alvin

Hurricanes; the science behind killer storms. [by] Alvin Silverstein, Virginia Silverstein, and Laura Silverstein Nunn. Enslow Publishers 2009 48p il map (The science behind natural disasters) lib bdg $23.93

Grades: 4 5 6   **551.55**

1. Hurricanes

ISBN 978-0-7660-2971-2 lib bdg; 0-7660-2971-9 lib bdg

LC 2008-26264

"Examines the science behind hurricanes, including how and where tropical storms form, the various types of tropical storms, how scientists track hurricanes, and provides hurricane safety tips." Publisher's note

Includes glossary and bibliographical references

Tornadoes; the science behind terrible twisters. [by] Alvin Silverstein, Virginia Silverstein, and Laura Silverstein

Nunn. Enslow Publishers 2009 48p il map (The science behind natural disasters) lib bdg $23.93
Grades: 4 5 6   **551.55**
  1. Tornadoes
  ISBN 978-0-7660-2976-7 lib bdg; 0-7660-2976-X lib bdg

                  LC 2008-29635

"Scientific explanations are accompanied by plentiful color diagrams that will help students to grasp causes and effects. . . . Photos . . . are effective, and are sometimes turned into helpful, lively diagrams by the addition of such features as wind-direction arrows." SLJ

Includes glossary and bibliographical references

Simon, Seymour
  ★ **Hurricanes**; updated ed; Collins 2007 31p il map $16.99; pa $6.99
Grades: 3 4 5 6   **551.55**
  1. Hurricanes
  ISBN 978-0-06-117072-0; 0-06-117072-0; 978-0-06-117071-3 pa; 0-06-117071-2 pa

                  LC 2007-280766

First published 2003
Discusses where and how hurricanes are formed, the destruction caused by legendary storms, and the precautions to take when a hurricane strikes

This is written "in a simple and precise manner. . . . The photos include computer-enhanced radar images and shots of storm damage from recent (Katrina in 2005) and historical (Glaveston in 1900) times." Sci Books Films

Includes bibliographical references

  Storms. Morrow Junior Bks. 1989 un il hardcover o.p. pa $5.95
Grades: 4 5 6 7   **551.55**
  1. Storms
  ISBN 0-688-11708-2 pa

                  LC 88-22045

This book describes the atmospheric conditions which create thunderstorms, hailstorms, lightning, tornadoes, and hurricanes and how violent weather affects the environment and people

"The half- to full-page glossy color photographs are sure to attract young readers as will the subject. Storms is an excellent way to introduce the science of meteorology to children." Sci Books Films

  ★ **Tornadoes**. Morrow Junior Bks. 1999 un il map hardcover o.p. pa $6.99
Grades: 4 5 6 7   **551.55**
  1. Tornadoes
  ISBN 0-688-14646-5; 0-06-443791-4 pa

                  LC 98-27953

Describes the location, nature, development, measurement, and destructive effects of tornadoes, as well as how to stay out of danger from them

"Incredible full-color photographs and diagrams, clearly portraying the different formations and devastating power of the windstorms, complement the text perfectly." Booklist

Spilsbury, Louise
  Howling hurricanes; [by] Louise and Richard Spilsbury. rev ed.; Heinemann Library 2010 32p il map (Awesome forces of nature) lib bdg $29; pa $7.99

Grades: 3 4 5 6   **551.55**
  1. Hurricanes
  ISBN 978-1-4329-3781-2 lib bdg; 1-4329-3781-2 lib bdg; 978-1-4329-3788-1 pa; 1-4329-3788-X pa

                  LC 2009037483

First published 2004
This book about hurricanes discusses "causes, characteristics, and relevant science, including progress in predicting the events. Case studies illustrate the human response. Numerous color photographs and sidebars are interwoven into the well-organized and absorbing [narrative]." SLJ

Includes glossary and bibliographical references

  Terrifying tornadoes; [by] Louise and Richard Spilsbury. Heinemann Library 2010 32p il map (Awesome forces of nature) lib bdg $29; pa $7.99
Grades: 3 4 5 6   **551.55**
  1. Tornadoes
  ISBN 978-1-4329-3786-7 lib bdg; 1-4329-3786-3 lib bdg; 978-1-4329-3793-5 pa; 1-4329-3793-6 pa

                  LC 2009-37459

First published 2004
This book about tornadoes "is sure to catch the eyes of students and educators. . . . The interesting and accurate facts are presented in an easily understood vocabulary. . . . Incredible eye-catching photographs, diagrams, or maps are tastefully positioned on every page." Libr Media Connect

Includes glossary and bibliographical references

Stewart, Mark
  Blizzards and winter storms. Gareth Stevens Pub. 2009 48p il map (The ultimate 10. Natural disasters) lib bdg $31
Grades: 5 6 7 8   **551.55**
  1. Storms 2. Blizzards
  ISBN 978-0-8368-9150-8 lib bdg; 0-8368-9150-3 lib bdg

                  LC 2008-28230

Blizzards and winter storms "are described, while color photos illustrate the resulting damage, conveying a significant part of the information through their captions. . . . An especially useful book." SLJ

Includes glossary and bibliographical references

Treaster, Joseph B.
  Hurricane force; in the path of America's deadliest storms. Kingfisher 2007 128p il map $16.95
Grades: 4 5 6 7 8   **551.55**
  1. Storms 2. Hurricanes
  ISBN 978-0-7534-6086-3

                  LC 2006-22517

Describes how violent storms and hurricanes are formed and notes some of history's greatest storms to hit the U.S. such as Hurricane Katrina.

This is a "gripping photo-essay. . . . There are lots of full-color photographs that bring close the high winds and surging seas of hurricanes, the shattered homes, and pictures of people rescued or lost. The extensive back matter is an integral part of the book." Booklist

Includes bibliographical references

551.56 Atmospheric electricity and optics

Kramer, Stephen

 Lightning; photographs by Warren Faidley. Carolrhoda Bks. 1992 48p il (Nature in action) hardcover o.p. pa $7.95

Grades: 4 5 6   **551.56**
 1. Lightning
 ISBN 0-87614-659-0; 0-87614-617-5 pa

LC 91-21793

"Diagrams supplement the well-written narrative in describing scientific concepts. Exceptionally fine, full-color photographs—each a work of art—perfectly illustrate the text, powerfully and spectacularly showing the majesty and might of this phenomenon." SLJ

 Includes glossary

Person, Stephen

 Struck by lightning! Bearport Pub. 2010 32p il map (Disaster survivors) lib bdg $25.27

Grades: 4 5 6 7   **551.56**
 1. Lightning
 ISBN 978-1-936087-47-1 lib bdg; 1-936087-47-2 lib bdg

"Captivating photos and illustrations and sidebars present interesting facts or brief anecdotes. . . . [This] should be purchased for all school and public libraries as . . . [it gives] a new perspective on the topic." Libr Media Connect

 Includes glossary and bibliographical references

Simon, Seymour

 Lightning. Morrow Junior Bks. 1997 un il hardcover o.p. pa $6.99

Grades: 4 5 6 7   **551.56**
 1. Lightning
 ISBN 0-688-14638-4; 0-06-088435-5 pa

LC 96-16962

Photographs and text explore the natural phenomenon of lightning

"The subject is exciting, the information is amazing, and the full-color photographs are riveting. . . . Simon's explanations are concise but thorough." Booklist

Stewart, Melissa

 ★ **Inside** lightning; illustrations by Cynthia Shaw. Sterling 2011 48p il (Inside . . .) $16.95

Grades: 5 6 7 8   **551.56**
 1. Lightning
 ISBN 978-1-4027-5878-2; 1-4027-5878-2

This book about lightning "explores its topic in an engaging way, and the many illustrations work well with adjacent text and captions. . . . The [book's] varied page layouts and attractive and the quality of photos, computer-generated images, original illustrations, and charts is . . . excellent. . . . Featuring a step-by-step, illustrated explanation of lightning formation as well as comments from people who have had close encounters with the phenomenon, Inside Lightning provides a vivid and unusually informative introduction to the subject." Booklist

 Includes bibliographical references

551.57 Hydrometeorology

Branley, Franklyn Mansfield

 Down comes the rain; by Franklyn M. Branley; illustrated by James Graham Hale. HarperCollins Pubs. 1997 31p il (Let's-read-and-find-out science) hardcover o.p. pa $4.95

Grades: K 1 2 3   **551.57**
 1. Rain 2. Clouds
 ISBN 0-06-025338-X; 0-06-445166-6 pa

LC 96-3519

A revised and newly illustrated edition of Rain & hail published 1983 by Crowell

The author explains "how water is recycled, how clouds are formed, and why rain and hail occur. A few easy science activities are included. . . . The pen-and-ink with watercolor wash paintings clearly interpret the concepts presented on each page." SLJ

 Snow is falling; by Franklyn M. Branley; illustrated by Holly Keller. HarperCollins Pubs. 2000 33p il (Let's-read-and-find-out science) hardcover o.p. pa $4.95

Grades: K 1   **551.57**
 1. Snow
 ISBN 0-06-027990-7; 0-06-027991-5 lib bdg; 0-06-445186-0 pa

LC 98-23106

A revised and newly illustrated edition of the title first published 1963 by Crowell

Describes snow's physical qualities and how quantities of it can be fun as well as dangerous

"Keller's new illustrations are a good match for the spare, informative text. A few easy activities explore snow's different properties, and a list of websites is appended." Horn Book Guide

Cassino, Mark

 ★ The **story** of snow; the science of winter's wonder. by Mark Cassino, with Jon Nelson; illustrations by Nora Aoyagi. Chronicle Books 2009 33p il $16.99

Grades: 2 3 4 5   **551.57**
 1. Snow 2. Snowflakes -- Juvenile literature
 ISBN 978-0-8118-6866-2; 0-8118-6866-4

LC 2009-04368

"Aoyagi's clean ink-and-watercolor diagrams and backgrounds allow the spectacular photographs to take center stage and provide supplemental information. Sure to get young scientists outside in the cold, particularly as it helpfully includes crystal-catching instructions." Kirkus

De Paola, Tomie

 The **cloud** book; words and pictures by Tomie de Paola. Holiday House 1975 30p il lib bdg $16.95; pa $6.95

Grades: K 1 2 3   **551.57**
 1. Clouds
 ISBN 0-8234-0259-2 lib bdg; 0-8234-0531-1 pa

The author instructs "young readers about the ten most common types of clouds, how they were named, and what they mean in terms of changing weather. Actually a very good text to use for early science instruction. Includes a scattering of traditional myths that have clouds as a basis." Adventuring with Books

Ehlert, Lois

★ **Snowballs**. Harcourt Brace & Co. 1995 un il $17;
pa $7; bd bk $6.95

Grades: PreK K 1   **551.57**

1. Snow -- Fiction 2. Snow -- Juvenile literature
ISBN 0-15-200074-7; 0-15-202095-0 pa; 0-15-
216275-5 bd bk

LC 94-47183

"Using 'good stuff' like seeds, nuts, corn kernels, and
colorful yarn kids create a wonderful snow family. Placed
on vertical page spreads, the snow characters extend the full
length of the book, a perspective that enhances the drama of
their inevitable demise when the sun comes out. Large, well-
designed illustrations effectively blend open space, colorful
paper cutouts, and real objects." Horn Book Guide

Gibbons, Gail

It's snowing! Holiday House 2011 32p il $17.95

Grades: K 1 2 3   **551.57**

1. Snow
ISBN 978-0-8234-2237-1

LC 2010029570

Introduces snow, discussing how snowflakes are formed,
what causes it to snow, where snow occurs around the world,
different types of snowstorms, and what to do during a heavy
winter storm.

"This is a crystal-clear introduction that illustrates how
snow can be dangerous, but plenty of fun, too." Booklist

Kaner, Etta

Who likes the rain? written by Etta Kaner; llustrated by
Marie Lafrance. Kids Can Press 2007 un il (Exploring the
elements) $14.95

Grades: PreK K 1 2   **551.57**

1. Rain
ISBN 978-1-55337-841-9; 1-55337-841-5

On each double-page spread, a child expresses why he or
she likes the rain ("because I can jump in puddles"). The child
then wonders how the event happens ("I wonder where puddles come from") and lifts a flap for a scientific explanation

"An attractive, straight-forward presentation of concepts
related to rain." Booklist

Who likes the snow? written by Etta Kaner; illustrated
by Marie Lafrance. Kids Can Press 2006 un il (Exploring
the elements) $14.95

Grades: PreK K 1 2   **551.57**

1. Snow
ISBN 978-1-55337-842-6; 1-55337-842-3

"This slim book is packed with fascinating information
about snow. Each spread is divided into three parts: a statement, a query, and, with the turn of a flap, a simply stated
scientific explanation. . . . Lafrance's naive acrylic paintings
have a flat appearance, as if they were carved of wood, and
clearly depict the topics being discussed." SLJ

Libbrecht, Kenneth G.

The **secret** life of a snowflake; an up-close look at the
art & science of snowflakes. [by] Kenneth Libbrecht. Voyageur Press 2010 48p il $17

Grades: 3 4 5 6   **551.57**

1. Snowflakes -- Juvenile literature
ISBN 978-0-7603-3676-2; 0-7603-3676-8

LC 2009-07892

"Extraordinary photographs of individual snowflakes
are the true highlight of this informational book. With crisp
detail and lit up with colored light, the crystals are mesmerizing in their clarity and brilliance. Libbrecht uses a first-person narration to describe the microphotography process that
he uses to create the images and then goes on to outline the
life cycle of a snowflake. . . . A solid addition to any science
collection, this book will draw in young enthusiasts, and the
beautiful photographs will engage casual browsers." SLJ

Marsico, Katie

Snowy weather days; [by] Katie Marsico. Children's
Press 2007 24p il (Scholastic news nonfiction readers)
lib bdg $19

Grades: K 1 2 3   **551.57**

1. Snow
ISBN 978-0-531-16773-1 lib bdg; 0-531-16773-9
lib bdg

LC 2006013306

Simple facts about snow.

"Young readers will take pleasure in learning simple
facts while discovering new words along the way. . . . These
full-color pictures show the featured conditions, as well as
a variety of outdoor scenes of children and adults enjoying
nature." SLJ

Includes glossary and bibliographical references

Martin, Jacqueline Briggs

★ **Snowflake** Bentley; illustrated by Mary Azarian.
Houghton Mifflin 1998 un il $16; pa $7.99

Grades: K 1 2 3   **551.57**

1. Snow 2. Farmers 3. Scientists 4. Photographers
5. Meteorologists 6. Snowflakes -- Pictorial works
-- Juvenile literature 7. Scientists -- United States --
Biography -- Pictorial works -- Juvenile literature 8.
Photographers -- United States -- Biography -- Pictorial
works -- Juvenile literature
ISBN 0-395-86162-4; 0-547-24829-6 pa

LC 97-12458

Awarded the Caldecott Medal, 1999

A biography of a self-taught scientist who photographed
thousands of individual snowflakes in order to study their
unique formations

"Azarian's woodblock illustrations, hand tinted with watercolors, blend perfectly with the text and recall the rural
Vermont of Bentley's time. . . . The story of this man's life is
written with graceful simplicity." SLJ

Rockwell, Anne F.

Clouds; by Anne Rockwell; illustrated by Frané Lessac. Collins 2008 33p il (Let's-read-and-find-out-science)
$16.99; pa $5.99

Grades: 1 2 3   **551.57**

1. Clouds
ISBN 978-0-06-029101-3; 0-06-029101-X; 978-0-06-
445220-5 pa; 0-06-445220-4 pa

"Rockwell introduces 11 different types of clouds according to their positions in the atmosphere. . . . The author
describes each type of cloud formation, explains where it is
found in the sky, and tells what kind of weather is associated
with it. Attractive folk-art-style paintings show the clouds
and children playing or working outside. The information
is solid." SLJ

Schuh, Mari C.
Avalanches. Pebble Plus 2010 24p il (Earth in action) lib bdg $21.32
Grades: K 1 2 **551.57**
1. Avalanches
ISBN 978-1-4296-3437-3 lib bdg; 1-4296-3437-5 lib bdg

LC 2009-2163
Describes avalanches, how they occur, and the damage they cause

This book "boasts a full-page color photograph. . . . [It shows] the aftermath of a disaster . . . but there are also some diagrams showing physical mechanisms and maps highlighting commonly affected places. The left side of each spread provides a few sentences of large-print text, with short, clear explanations." SLJ

Includes glossary and bibliographical references

551.6 Climatology and weather

Arnold, Caroline
El Nino; stormy weather for people and wildlife. by Caroline Arnold. Clarion Bks 1998 48 p. col. ill. (reinforced) $16.00; (paperback) $5.95
Grades: 4 5 6 7 **551.6**
1. Climate -- Juvenile literature 2. El Niño Current -- Juvenile literature 3. Climate
ISBN 0395776023; 0618551107; 9780618551101

LC 98004826
In this book, Caroline Arnold "explains how the warm current along the Peruvian coast can have a devastating impact on weather across the globe. Photographs of locations from California to Botswana to India document the effects on animals and plants and the increase in floods and hurricanes. Diagrams illustrate El Niño's formation, and a chart shows the recurring pattern in the past half century as well as the occurrence of its 'twin,' La Niña." (School Library Journal)

Includes bibliographical references (p. 45) and index.

Bailey, Gerry
Changing climate. Gareth Stevens Pub. 2011 48p il map (Planet SOS) lib bdg $31.95; pa $14.05
Grades: 4 5 6 **551.6**
1. Climate -- Environmental aspects
ISBN 978-1-4339-4962-3 lib bdg; 1-4339-4962-8 lib bdg; 978-1-4339-4963-0 pa; 1-4339-4963-6 pa

LC 2010032885
This "well-designed [book presents changing climate] . . . and how [it affects] human beings. With information about water supplies and melting ice and their impact on ecosystems, the discussion . . . of global water levels is especially enlightening. . . . The many large, colorful photos will engage readers and assist them in understanding the important concepts introduced." SLJ

Includes glossary

Baker, Stuart
In temperate zones. Marshall Cavendish Benchmark 2009 32p il map (Climate change) lib bdg $19.95

Grades: 5 6 7 8 **551.6**
1. Forest ecology 2. Greenhouse effect
ISBN 978-0-7614-4441-1 lib bdg; 0-7614-4441-6 lib bdg

LC 2009-5769
The book about climate change in the temperate zones "is perfectly organized for students. . . . Unique layout features serve as signposts and will help focus readers' attention. . . . [The book] features an outstanding chart of possible effects of global warming on the area in question, listing 'Possible Event', 'Predicted Result', and 'Impact' in short, bulleted statements." SLJ

Includes glossary

Evans, Bill
It's raining fish and spiders; by Bill Evans. Forge 2012 xiv, 223 p.p col. ill. (paperback) $18.99
Grades: 5 6 7 8 **551.6**
1. Extreme weather 2. Weather forecasting 3. Weather -- Juvenile literature 4. Severe storms -- Juvenile literature
ISBN 0765321327; 9780765321329

LC 2011278417
This book offers "information, lists, and accounts of personal experiences involving extreme weather by meteorologist and TV personality [Bill] Evans. Included are sections on tornadoes, hurricanes, and blizzards, with a good amount of information on each and . . . photos and diagrams sprinkled throughout." (Booklist)

Includes bibliographical references (p.221-222)

Gibbons, Gail
Weather words and what they mean. Holiday House 1990 un il $16.95; pa $6.95
Grades: K 1 2 3 **551.6**
1. Weather 2. Vocabulary -- Juvenile literature
ISBN 0-8234-0805-1; 0-8234-0952-X pa

LC 89-39515
The author discusses the meaning of meteorological terms such as temperature, air pressure, thunderstorm and moisture

"Gibbons' easily identifiable artistic style works well with her explanations of sometimes misunderstood weather-related terms. Drawings are appealing, attractively arranged, and closely matched to the textual information. . . . An attractive introduction for weather units in the primary grades." SLJ

Hartman, Eve
Climate change; [by] Eve Hartman and Wendy Meshbesher. Raintree 2010 48p il map (Sci-hi: Earth and space science) lib bdg $31.43; pa $8.99
Grades: 4 5 6 7 **551.6**
1. Greenhouse effect 2. Climate -- Environmental aspects
ISBN 978-1-4109-3352-2 lib bdg; 1-4109-3352-0 lib bdg; 978-1-4109-3362-1 pa; 1-4109-3362-8 pa

LC 2009-3538
Examine the causes of climate change, and how scientists gather data about global warming. Learn about the different ways people and nations are combating climate change, and how people and animals adapt to a new climate.

"Multiple colorful sidebars and large and small diagrams and photographs will help students to grasp the fundamentals being discussed, and the easy but interesting science experiments will act as further reinforcements." SLJ

Includes glossary and bibliographical references

Parker, Steve, 1952-

    Climate. QEB Pub. 2010 32p il (QEB changes in . . .) lib bdg $28.50

Grades: 3 4 5 6   **551.6**

    1. Climate

    ISBN 978-1-59566-776-2 lib bdg; 1-59566-776-8 lib bdg

                       LC 2008-56068

"The information is presented in brief paragraphs and sidebars. Suggestions for kids to help improve the planet are sprinkled throughout. . . . Students will enjoy this appealing layout and the information can spark further research on the topic[s]. . . . Either digitally or on paper, students could make fantastic presentations using a similar design." Libr Media Connect

Includes glossary

Royston, Angela

    Looking at weather and seasons; how do they change? [by] Angela Royston. Enslow Publishers 2008 32p il (Looking at science: how things change) lib bdg $22.60

Grades: 1 2 3   **551.6**

    1. Seasons 2. Weather

    ISBN 978-0-7660-3093-0 lib bdg; 0-7660-3093-8 lib bdg

                       LC 2007-24515

"Fills a huge void in elementary science collections. . . . Text is arranged in succinct 'chunks,' giving important facts without overwhelming readers. . . . [This] is an essential addition." Libr Media Connect

Includes glossary and bibliographical references

Rupp, Rebecca

    Weather; with journal illustrations by Melissa Sweet and experiment illustrations by Dug Nap. Storey Kids 2003 136p il map hardcover o.p. pa $14.95

Grades: 4 5 6 7   **551.6**

    1. Weather

    ISBN 1-58017-469-8; 1-58017-420-5 pa

                     LC 2002-152310

This includes facts about weather with instructions for 22 science projects

"A lively, upbeat presentation. Chock-full of solid information, this compendium includes lots of slightly offbeat, appealing observations. . . . Numerous, attention-grabbing visuals illustrate experiments." SLJ

Includes glossary

Simpson, Kathleen

    ★ **Extreme** weather; science tackles global warming and climate change. by Kathleen Simpson; Jonathan D.W. Kahl, consultant. National Geographic 2008 64p il map (National Geographic investigates) $17.95; lib bdg $27.90

Grades: 4 5 6 7   **551.6**

    1. Greenhouse effect 2. Weather -- Juvenile literature 3. Climate -- Environmental aspects 5. Global warming -- Juvenile literature

    ISBN 978-1-4263-0359-3; 1-4263-0359-9; 978-1-4263-0281-7 lib bdg; 1-4263-0281-9 lib bdg

This "is a well-written and engaging book. . . . Excellent descriptions of how and why these various weather patterns occur are presented. The book includes dramatic photographs and clear diagrams." Sci Books Films

Includes glossary and bibliographical references

551.609   History, geographic treatment, biography

Christie, Peter

    50 climate questions; a blizzard of blistering facts. Peter Christie; illustrated by Ross Kinnaird. Annick Press 2012 117 p. ill. (50 Questions) (paperback) $14.95; (hardcover) $22.95; (ebook) $10.99

Grades: 4 5 6 7   **551.609**

    1. Climate 2. Climate change 3. Climate -- History

    ISBN 155451374X; 9781554513741; 9781554513758; 9781554515165

This book by Peter Christie presents a "survey of the effects of climate through history and prehistory." (Kirkus Reviews) "Topics include global warming's effect on the Arctic . . . and how a cooling climate 2.5 million years ago forced early humans to diversify their diets. Christie also provides insight into weather events throughout history -- for example, how weather change contributed to civil unrest that spawned the French Revolution." (Publishers Weekly)

551.63   Weather forecasting and forecasts, reporting and reports

Breen, Mark

    ★ The **kids'** book of weather forecasting; build a weather station, read the sky & make predictions. with meteorologist Mark Breen and Kathleen Friestad; illustrations by Michael Kline. Williamson 2000 140p il maps music pa $12.95

Grades: 4 5 6 7   **551.63**

    1. Weather forecasting 2. Experiments 3. Science -- Experiments 4. Weather -- Experiments 5. Meteorology -- Experiments

    ISBN 1-88559-339-2

                     LC 99-89954

A hands-on introduction to the science of meteorology, explaining how to make equipment to measure rainfall, wind direction, and humidity, record measurements and observations in a weather log, make weather predictions, and perform other related activities

"A useful, accessible book illustrated with black-and-white diagrams and cartoons." SLJ

Includes bibliographical references

Fleisher, Paul

    Doppler radar, satellites, and computer models; the science of weather forecasting. Lerner Publications 2010 48p il map (Weatherwise) lib bdg $29.27

Grades: 4 5 6   **551.63**

    1. Weather forecasting

    ISBN 978-0-8225-7535-1; 0-8225-7535-3

                     LC 2009-44919

This describes how scientists predict the weather, the tools and instruments that help them make forecasts, and how far in advance can they make good predictions.

"Chapters are well-organized and contain clear explanations. The crisp layout contains plenty of captioned photos and diagrams, as well as sidebars that feature interesting facts and suggestions for observations readers can record in their backyards." Horn Book Guide

Includes glossary and bibliographical references

Gibbons, Gail

    Weather forecasting. Four Winds Press 1987 un il hardcover o.p. pa $5.99

Grades: K 1 2 3   **551.63**

    1. Weather forecasting

    ISBN 0-689-71683-4 pa

                LC 86-7602

"Any child can learn the basic concepts from the text at the bottom of each page, while the precocious can garner an impressive weather vocabulary by absorbing the terms labeled and defined within the artwork. Brightly illustrated with the artist's usual bold, flat colors, this book will serve as an appealing introduction to weather forecasting for young children." Booklist

552 Petrology

Aston, Dianna Hutts

    A **rock** is lively; Dianna Hutts Aston, Sylvia Long. Chronicle Books 2012 40 p. (alk. paper) $16.99

Grades: 3 4 5 6   **552**

    1. Rocks 2. Minerals

    ISBN 1452106452; 9781452106458

              LC 2011048375

This book by Dianna Hutts Aston explores "seemingly sedentary world of rocks and minerals, showing them to be anything but (when you know your geology). Boiling underground, freezing in space, colorful or drab, enormous or minuscule, health food (grits for gizzards), tools for prehistoric man and modern chimps, canvas for paleolithic art or construction material for the Taj Mahal -- rocks get around." (School Library Journal)

Davis, Barbara J.

    Minerals, rocks, and soil. Raintree 2010 48p il map (Sci-hi: Earth and space science) lib bdg $31.43; pa $8.99

Grades: 4 5 6 7   **552**

    1. Rocks 2. Minerals 3. Petrology

    ISBN 978-1-4109-3347-8 lib bdg; 1-4109-3347-4 lib bdg; 978-1-4109-3357-7 pa; 1-4109-3357-1 pa

              LC 2009-13459

"Multiple colorful sidebars and large and small diagrams and photographs will help students to grasp the fundamentals being discussed, and the easy but interesting science experiments will act as further reinforcements." SLJ

Includes glossary and bibliographical references

Faulkner, Rebecca

    Igneous rock; [by] Rebecca Faulkner. Raintree 2007 48p il (Geology rocks!) lib bdg $31.43; pa $8.99

Grades: 4 5 6   **552**

    1. Rocks

    ISBN 978-1-4109-2747-7 lib bdg; 1-4109-2747-4 lib bdg; 978-1-4109-2755-2 pa; 1-4109-2755-5 pa

              LC 2006037174

This "describes all three categories of rocks and what distinguishes them from each other, minerals, identification of igneous rocks, and their formation through volcanic activity. . . . [The book] includes quality color photographs and diagrams that do an exemplary job of expanding on the topics covered." SLJ

Includes glossary and bibliographical references

    Metamorphic rock. Raintree 2007 48p il (Geology rocks!) lib bdg $31.43; pa $8.99

Grades: 4 5 6   **552**

    1. Rocks

    ISBN 978-1-4109-2749-1 lib bdg; 1-4109-2749-0 lib bdg; 978-1-4109-2757-6 pa; 1-4109-2757-1 pa

              LC 2006037063

"This title covers the following: Squeeze and heat; Crust, mantle, and core; The world's rocks; Marvelous Metamorphism; Metamorphic rock types; Hard beauty; Metamorphic landforms." Publisher's note

Includes glossary and bibliographical references

    Sedimentary rock; [by] Rebecca Faulkner. Raintree 2007 48p il (Geology rocks!) lib bdg $31.43; pa $8.99

Grades: 4 5 6   **552**

    1. Rocks

    ISBN 978-1-4109-2748-4 lib bdg; 1-4109-2748-2 lib bdg; 978-1-4109-2756-9 pa; 1-4109-2756-3 pa

              LC 2006037173

This "covers the Earth's structure, how these rocks are formed, fossils, and the various types. [The] book includes quality color photographs and diagrams that do an exemplary job of expanding on the topics covered." SLJ

Includes glossary and bibliographical references

Gans, Roma

    Let's go rock collecting; illustrated by Holly Keller. newly il ed; HarperCollins Pubs. 1997 31p il (Let's-read-and-find-out science) hardcover o.p. pa $5.99

Grades: K 1 2   **552**

    1. Petrology -- Juvenile literature 2. Rocks -- Collectors and collecting

    ISBN 0-06-027282-1; 0-06-027283-X lib bdg; 0-06-027283-X pa

              LC 95-44999

A revised and newly illustrated edition of Rock collecting, published 1984 by Crowell

Describes the formation and characteristics of igneous, metamorphic, and sedimentary rocks and how to recognize and collect them

"The excellent diagrams, full-color photographs of specimens, and minor textual changes clarify the concepts (for example, Mohs' scale of hardness) and extend the presentation. . . . The pair of youngsters featured in Keller's brightly colored illustrations . . . convey the joys of being a rock hound." SLJ

Gardner, Robert

    Smashing science projects about Earth's rocks and minerals; [by] Robert Gardner; illustrations by Tom Labaff.

Enslow Elementary 2007 48p il (Rockin' earth science experiments) lib bdg $23.93

Grades: 3 4 5 **552**

1. Rocks 2. Minerals 3. Science projects 4. Science -- Experiments

ISBN 978-0-7660-2731-2 lib bdg; 0-7660-2731-7 lib bdg

LC 2006013788

This offers experiments about minerals and crystals, testing materials for hardness, soil, igneos, sedimentary, and metamorphic rock, and core samples.

Includes glossary and bibliographical references

Green, Dan

Rocks and minerals; a gem of a read! by Dan Green and Simon Basher; illustrated by Simon Basher. Kingfisher 2009 128p il pa $8.99

Grades: 5 6 7 8 **552**

1. Rocks 2. Minerals

ISBN 978-0-7534-6314-7 pa; 0-7534-6314-8 pa

This "presents a portrait gallery of 56 rocks and minerals (plus four kinds of fossils) composed of smiling, round-headed, usually peanut-shaped cartoon figures wearing or bearing distinctive identifiers. . . . The entries make light-hearted but unexpectedly meaty reading." Booklist

Hynes, Margaret

Rocks & fossils; foreword by Jack Horner. Kingfisher 2006 63p il (Kingfisher knowledge) $12.95

Grades: 5 6 7 8 **552**

1. Rocks 2. Fossils

ISBN 978-0-7534-5974-4; 0-7534-5974-4

LC 2005-23897

This is a "lavishly illustrated book. . . . The well-written text is pithy and comprehensible." Voice Youth Advocates

Includes glossary and bibliographical references

Rocks & minerals; illustrated by Kyle Poling. National Geographic 2010 32p il (Jump into science) $16.95; lib bdg $25.90

Grades: 1 2 3 **552**

1. Rocks 2. Minerals

ISBN 978-1-4263-0538-2; 1-4263-0538-9; 978-1-4263-0539-9 lib bdg; 1-4263-0539-7 lib bdg

LC 2010-07145

"Playful and interactive, this picture-book title . . . makes geology accessible with colorful diagrams, photos, and computer graphics. The spreads discuss how the three main types of rock are formed, as well as facts about fossils and the more than 2,500 different minerals on the planet. The visuals will capture kids." Booklist

Rocks and minerals; facts at your fingertips. DK Pub. 2012 156 p. col. ill., map (hardcover) $7.99

Grades: 5 6 7 8 **552**

1. Rocks 2. Minerals

ISBN 0756692857; 9780756692858

LC 2011277725

This book, part of the "Pocket Genius" encyclopedia series, "profiles nearly 200 types of rocks and minerals from volcanic rocks and granite to sparkling diamonds and explosive sulfur, and tells what they are made of, how they are formed and what they are used for." It "offers a . . . catalog-style presentation, which clearly lays out individual subcategories." (Publisher's note)

Smithsonian Institution

Extreme rocks & minerals! Q & A. Collins 2007 47p il $17.99; pa $6.99

Grades: 4 5 6 **552**

1. Rocks 2. Minerals

ISBN 978-0-06-089982-0; 0-06-089982-4; 978-0-06-089981-3 pa; 0-06-089981-6 pa

LC 2007001760

This describes types of rocks and minerals, how they are formed, and how people use them.

"It's hard to beat this title for a clear, accurate, and appealing survey. Illustrations are key to this subject, and the range of crisp photos is excellent." SLJ

Includes bibliographical references

Symes, R. F.

Rocks & minerals; written by R.F. Symes and the staff of the Natural History Museum, London; special photography by Colin Keates and Andreas Einsiedel. Revised ed. DK Pub. 2008 72 p. ill. (some col.) (hardcover: boxed; package) $29.99; (hardcover) $16.99

Grades: 5 6 7 8 **552**

1. Gems 2. Rocks 3. Geology -- Juvenile literature

ISBN 9780756631321 out of print; 0756637775; 9780756637774

LC 2009499083

This book is a guide to "rocks, fossils, minerals, precious metals, crystals, jewels and gemstones." Readers "see rocks that have come from outer space, stalactites as old as dinosaurs, the strange and beautiful shapes of natural crystals and priceless nuggets of gold, silver and platinum. Learn what the Earth is made of and how its rocks were formed, how early humans made the first flint tools and how diamonds and precious stones are cut, polished, and made into jewelry." (Publisher's note)

Tomecek, Steve

Everything rocks and minerals. National Geographic 2011 64p il (National Geographic kids) lib bdg $25.90; pa $12.95

Grades: 3 4 5 6 **552**

1. Rocks 2. Minerals

ISBN 978-1-4263-0801-7 lib bdg; 1-4263-0801-9 lib bdg; 978-1-4263-0768-3 pa; 1-4263-0768-3 pa

LC 2010038112

A book about rocks and minerals.

"Exploding with astounding full-color photographs and written in an appealing conversational tone, [this book is] for every kid. . . . The [text] will keep kids interested and turning pages to discover more and more facts. . . . [This] compelling, browseable, and completely engrossing [title] will delight readers." SLJ

Includes glossary and bibliographical references

Trueit, Trudi Strain

Rocks, gems, and minerals. Watts 2003 63p il (Watts library) $24; pa $8.95

Grades: 4 5 6 7 **552**

1. Rocks 2. Minerals 3. Precious stones 4. Rocks -- Juvenile literature 5. Minerals -- Juvenile literature 6.

Precious stones -- Juvenile literature
ISBN 0-531-12195-X; 0-531-16241-9 pa
LC 2001-7222
This includes "attention-grabbing photography, excellent charts and diagrams, short articles with or without photographs, and vocabulary terms that appear in bold and are explained in context." Sci Books Films
Includes glossary and bibliographical references

VanCleave, Janice Pratt, 1942-
Janice VanCleave's rocks and minerals; mind-boggling experiments you can turn into science fair projects. Wiley 1996 90p il (Spectacular science projects series) pa $10.95
Grades: 4 5 6 7 **552**
1. Rocks 2. Minerals 3. Science projects 4. Science -- Experiments
ISBN 0-471-10269-5
LC 95-10324
"VanCleave presents stunningly clear, direct, and informative projects. They are generally simple enough for self-directed students to do on their own, but a teacher's guidance would be helpful." SLJ
Includes glossary

553.2 Carbonaceous materials

Green, Robert
Coal. Cherry Lake Pub. 2010 32p il (21st century skills library. Power up!) lib bdg $27.07
Grades: 4 5 6 **553.2**
1. Coal
ISBN 978-1-60279-508-2 lib bdg; 1-60279-508-8 lib bdg
LC 2008-44184
This "provides a basic introduction to [coal]. . . . The writing is clear and succinct, and the information is accurate, timely and unbiased. The plentiful photographs are outstanding and reinforce the text. . . . Certain to appeal to young readers and their teachers." Libr Media Connect
Includes glossary and bibliographical references

Tagliaferro, Linda
How does a plant become oil? Raintree 2010 32p il (How does it happen?) lib bdg $27.50; pa $7.99
Grades: 3 4 5 **553.2**
1. Gasoline 2. Petroleum
ISBN 978-1-4109-3443-7 lib bdg; 1-4109-3443-8 lib bdg; 978-1-4109-3451-2 pa; 1-4109-3451-9 pa
LC 2008-52290
"Information is clearly presented using a large font, diagrams, and photographs formatted to resemble Polaroid pictures. . . . A first-rate job answering some important scientific questions." SLJ
Includes glossary and bibliographical references

553.4 Metals and semimetals

Raum, Elizabeth
The **story** behind gold. Heinemann Library 2009 32p il map (True stories) lib bdg $28.21

Grades: 3 4 5 **553.4**
1. Gold 2. Gold mines and mining
ISBN 978-1-4329-2340-2 lib bdg; 1-4329-2340-4 lib bdg
LC 2008037525
This offers history, ephemera, and basic facts about gold, gold mining, and the uses of gold
Includes bibliographical references

553.6 Other economic materials

Kurlansky, Mark
★ The **story** of salt; [illustrated by] S. D. Schindler. G.P. Putnam's Sons 2006 48p il map $16.99
Grades: 3 4 5 6 **553.6**
1. Salt 2. Salt -- Juvenile literature
ISBN 0-399-23998-7
LC 2005-032629
An adaptation of the author's title for adults: Salt: a world history (2002)
"The informal narrative and the exquisitely detailed, sometimes playful ink-and-watercolor illustrations dramatize the sweeping world history of salt's essential role in human life—from prehistoric times and the early voyages of discovery through the breakthrough of refrigeration and the latest drilling technology." Booklist
Includes bibliographical references

Moore, Heidi
The **story** behind salt. Heinemann Library 2009 32p il map (True stories) lib bdg $28.21
Grades: 3 4 5 **553.6**
1. Salt
ISBN 978-1-4329-2348-8 lib bdg; 1-4329-2348-X lib bdg
LC 2008037390
This describes the properties of salt and how it is used, including its history and miscellaneous facts, answering such questions as: Why is the sea salty? Why is it so easy to float in the Dead Sea? Why do people put salt on icy roads?
Includes bibliographical references

553.7 Water

Gallant, Roy A.
Water; our precious resource. Benchmark Bks. 2002 79p il map (Earthworks) lib bdg $29.93
Grades: 5 6 7 8 **553.7**
1. Water 2. Hydrology -- Juvenile literature
ISBN 0-7614-1365-0
LC 2001-43290
An in-depth look at Earth's waters and mankind's uses of water throughout history which includes ideas about planning better use of this critical resource in the future
"Gallant's prose is nearly conversational in its easy delivery, but his facts are always thorough and his ideas clearly explained. Best of all, he raises informed points that will help readers rethink their habits and realize the complexity of the issues. . . . Crisp graphs, maps, and excellent color photos illustrate [this] fine [volume]." Booklist
Includes glossary and bibliographical references

Lauw, Darlene

Water; {by Darlene Lauw and Lim Cheng Puay} Crabtree 2003 31p il (Science alive!) lib bdg $21.28; pa $7.95
Grades: 3 4 5 6 **553.7**
1. Experiments 2. Water -- Experiments 3. Science -- Experiments
ISBN 0-7787-0567-6 lib bdg; 0-7787-0613-3 pa

LC 2002-11640

Uses simple experiments to demonstrate the properties of water

"The directions are kid friendly, and the graphics that support them are very helpful. . . . The science content is within the range of understanding of an upper elementary school student." Sci Books Films

Includes glossary

Strauss, Rochelle

★ **One** well; the story of water on Earth. written by Rochelle Strauss; illustrated by Rosemary Woods. Kids Can Press 2007 32p il $17.95
Grades: 4 5 6 **553.7**
1. Water
ISBN 978-1-55337-954-6; 1-55337-954-3

"Looking at all the water on Earth . . . as 'One Well' into which all life dips to survive, Strauss presents a timely discussion of the use and abuse of a not-so-limitless resource. Liberally sprinkled with interesting facts, . . . [the book has a] readable text. . . . Woods's delicate paintings keep perfect step and provide a gentle framework for the plentiful statistical snippets." SLJ

Wick, Walter

★ A **drop** of water; a book of science and wonder. written and photographed by Walter Wick. Scholastic 1997 40p il $16.95
Grades: 4 5 6 **553.7**
1. Water 2. Science -- Experiments -- Juvenile literature
ISBN 0-590-22197-3

LC 95-30068

"This title is an elegant synthesis of science and art. . . . The close-up photographs are breathtakingly distinct; and the clarity provided by the combination of concept, text, and photography of this quality is noteworthy." Bull Cent Child Books

553.8 Gems

Moore, Heidi

The **story** behind diamonds. Heinemann Library 2009 32p il (True stories) lib bdg $28.21
Grades: 3 4 5 **553.8**
1. Diamonds
ISBN 978-1-4329-2345-7 lib bdg; 1-4329-2345-5 lib bdg

LC 2008043374

This describes the history, ephemera, basic facts, and uses of diamonds

Includes bibliographical references

560 Paleontology

Aliki

Fossils tell of long ago; rev ed; Crowell 1990 32p il (Let's-read-and-find-out science book) hardcover o.p. pa $4.95
Grades: K 1 2 3 **560**
1. Fossils
ISBN 0-06-445093-7 pa

LC 89-17247

First published 1972

"Information about how fossils are formed and discovered is presented in simple text and an appealing variety of colorful illustrations. Includes directions for creating a fossil." Sci Child

Barner, Bob

Dinosaurs roar, butterflies soar! Chronicle Books 2009 un il $16.99
Grades: K 1 2 3 **560**
1. Fossils 2. Dinosaurs 3. Butterflies
ISBN 978-0-8118-5663-8; 0-8118-5663-1

LC 2008016783

"This gently informative book describes the role butterflies played in helping dinosaurs and their environment flourish. The main text offers a simpler narrative than the supplementary and more detailed one in small type that appears below or next to it. . . . A few of the predominant theories about the dinosaurs' extinction and explanations of the continuing survival of butterflies are put forth. . . . Barner's illustrations are, as always, fantastically bright, eye-catching cut-paper collages. A useful, engaging, and illuminating book." SLJ

Bonner, Hannah

★ **When** bugs were big, plants were strange, and tetrapods stalked the earth; a cartoon prehistory of life before dinosaurs. written and illustrated by Hannah Bonner. National Geographic 2004 44p il $16.95
Grades: 3 4 5 6 **560**
1. Fossils 2. Prehistoric animals
ISBN 0-7922-6326-X

LC 2003-7818

The information is "presented with verve and humor that don't shortchange the young natural historian's quest for good explanations of the earth's distant past. . . . An exemplary curriculum support resource, but kids who dig dinosaurs will read the book purely for pleasure." Booklist

★ **When** fish got feet, sharks got teeth, and bugs began to swarm; a cartoon prehistory of life long before dinosaurs. written and illustrated by Hannah Bonner. National Geographic 2007 45p il $16.95; lib bdg $25.90
Grades: 2 3 4 5 **560**
1. Prehistoric animals 2. Paleontology -- Juvenile literature 3. Fishes, Fossil -- Juvenile literature 4. Animals, Fossil -- Juvenile literature
ISBN 978-1-4263-0078-3; 1-4263-0078-6; 978-1-4263-0079-0 lib bdg; 1-4263-0079-4 lib bdg

LC 2006-20768

"Bonner explores life on Earth during the Silurian and Devonian periods. . . . Bonner's clear, engaging writing conveys plenty of information without overwhelming readers, and her illustrations offer fascinating visual representations of unusual creatures and landscapes." SLJ

Bradley, Timothy J.
★ **Paleo** bugs; survival of the creepiest. written and illustrated by Timothy J. Bradley. Chronicle Books 2008 44p il $15.99
Grades: 4 5 6 7   560
1. Fossils 2. Insects 3. Prehistoric animals 4. Paleontology -- Juvenile literature 5. Paleoentomology -- Juvenile literature 6. Arthropoda, Fossil -- Juvenile literature
ISBN 978-0-8118-6022-2; 0-8118-6022-1
LC 2007-18174
This offers an "eye-widening gallery of extinct arthropods, from the mayfly-like heptagenia to a seven-foot-long arthropleura. . . . Bradley decks out each of his painted figures in bright hues, poses them in natural settings . . . and sets them aside a human hand or body in silhouette to suggest scale. . . . Readers will . . . pore over the pictures and come away knowing more about both these extinct animals and their modern descendants." Booklist
Includes glossary and bibliographical references

Brown, Charlotte Lewis
Beyond the dinosaurs; monsters of the air and sea. by Charlotte Lewis Brown; pictures by Phil Wilson. HarperCollinsPublishers 2007 30p il (I can read!) $15.99; lib bdg $16.89
Grades: K 1 2 3   560
1. Fossils 2. Prehistoric animals
ISBN 978-0-06-053056-3; 0-06-053056-1; 978-0-06-053057-0 lib bdg; 0-06-053057-X lib bdg
LC 2007014462
"This introduction to creatures 'just as strange and wonderful as any dinosaur' pairs a straightforward text with action-packed, life-like illustrations. . . . [It has] a spread devoted to each of 11 prehistoric animals, including the Elasmosaurus, Hainosaurus , and Archaeopteryx. Helpful pronunciation guides are included. Readers of this book will get a closeup feel for life millions of years ago." SLJ

Brown, Don
★ **Rare** treasure: Mary Anning and her remarkable discoveries. Houghton Mifflin 1999 un il hardcover o.p. pa $5.95
Grades: K 1 2 3   560
1. Fossils 2. Paleontologists 3. Ichthyosaurus -- Juvenile literature 4. Women paleontologists -- England -- Biography -- Juvenile literature
ISBN 0-395-92286-0; 0-618-31081-9 pa
LC 98-32372
Describes the life of the English girl whose discovery of an Ichthyosaurus fossil led to a lasting interest in other prehistoric animals
"Brown dwells on Mary's self-determination, focusing on her adventurous spirit . . . and lifelong quest for knowledge in her chosen field of study. . . . The understated watercolors suit the mood. Their subdued palette (ocean blues, sand browns) and simple compositions are undistracting." Bull Cent Child Books

Burton, Virginia Lee
Life story; updated ed.; Houghton Mifflin 2009 67p il $22; pa $7.99
Grades: 3 4 5   560
1. Fossils 2. Evolution 3. Natural history
ISBN 978-0-547-19508-7; 0-547-19508-7; 978-0-547-20359-1 pa; 0-547-20359-4 pa
First published 1962
"Burton's 1962 exploration of the history of life on Earth, framed as a five-act play, returns in a newly updated edition that takes current scientific information into account (Pluto, for instance, is not among the planets shown orbiting the sun). Beginning with the birth of the Sun and continuing through the Earth's creation, the emergence and evolution of animal life, up to the changing seasons of the present, it's a lyrical and informative journey." Publ Wkly

Camper, Cathy
★ **Bugs** before time; prehistoric insects and their relatives. illustrated by Steve Kirk. Simon & Schuster Bks. for Young Readers 2002 un il $16.95
Grades: 4 5 6 7   560
1. Fossils 2. Insects
ISBN 0-689-82092-5
LC 98-22872
Describes the physical characteristics, habits, and natural environment of various prehistoric insects some of which, including cockroaches, centipedes, and dragonflies, have survived into the present day
"A handsome introduction to prehistoric insects and other arthropods. . . . [Includes] up-to-date, conversational text and informative captions and date boxes. . . . Kirk's eye-catching, realistic watercolors portray a fascinating array of creatures." SLJ
Includes glossary and bibliographical references

Faulkner, Rebecca
Fossils; [by] Rebecca Faulkner. Raintree 2007 48p il map (Geology rocks!) lib bdg $31.43; pa $8.99
Grades: 4 5 6   560
1. Fossils
ISBN 978-1-4109-2752-1 lib bdg; 1-4109-2752-0 lib bdg; 978-1-4109-2760-6 pa; 1-4109-2760-1 pa
LC 2006037065
This "discusses plate tectonics, common fossils and where they are found, dinosaurs, fossil fuels, and the contributions of the study of these relics to paleontology. . . . [The] book includes quality color photographs and diagrams that do an exemplary job of expanding on the topics covered." SLJ
Includes glossary and bibliographical references

Gallant, Roy A.
Fossils. Benchmark Bks. 2000 48p il map (Kaleidoscope) lib bdg $15.95
Grades: 3 4 5   560
1. Fossils 2. Paleontology
ISBN 0-7614-1041-4
LC 99-47494
Describes what fossils are, how they are formed, and what they tell scientists about the earth's past

"The easy-to-read text offers clear explanations. . . . Well-selected, beautifully reproduced photographs and computer graphics." SLJ

Includes glossary and bibliographical references

Goldish, Meish

The **fossil** feud; Marsh and Cope's bone wars. by Meish Goldish. Bearport Pub. 2007 32p il map (Fossil hunters) lib bdg $23.96

Grades: 3 4 5 6   560

1. Fossils 2. Zoologists 3. Paleontologists

ISBN 978-1-59716-256-2 lib bdg; 1-59716-256-6 lib bdg

LC 2006011319

This "tells of the Bone Wars, a clash between two American paleontologists. In 1868, at the Haddonfield, New Jersey, marl pit, Othniel Marsh and Edward Cope established a cooperative relationship, but it deteriorated rapidly. Over the next two decades, each man established dinosaur digs in Wyoming and Colorado, spied on the other's work, and engaged in bribery, theft, and sabotage, even dynamiting fossil sites. Finally, their newspaper attacks on each other's expertise, honor, and sanity alienated the scientific community and led to the end of the Bone Wars. Goldish writes in a clear, straightforward manner, letting the story's inherent drama speak for itself. . . . The presentation is enhanced by attractive page design, which includes a paragraph or two on each page and a photo of an artifact, individuals, sites, or fossils." Booklist

Includes bibliographical references

Gray, Susan H.

Paleontology the study of prehistoric life; Susan H. Gray. Children's Press 2012 48 p.

Grades: 2 3 4 5   560

1. Paleontology -- Juvenile literature

ISBN 0329917145; 0531246809; 0531282740; 9780329917142; 9780531246801; 9780531282748

LC 2011030965

This book by Susan H. Gray provides an introduction to paleontology for young readers. It "presents general information about paleontologists . . . [and] what they learn about prehistoric animals and vegetation by studying them." (Open Library)

Includes bibliographical references (p. 44) and index

Holmes, Thom

★ **Dinosaur** scientist; careers digging up the past. Enslow Publishers 2009 128p il (Wild science careers) lib bdg $31.93

Grades: 5 6 7 8   560

1. Fossils 2. Vocational guidance

ISBN 978-0-7660-3053-4 lib bdg; 0-7660-3053-9 lib bdg

LC 2008-19634

"A great read for middle school students, the book provides vocational guidance while introducing the reader to a challenging, but very exciting, career as a paleontologist." Sci Books Films

Includes glossary and bibliographical references

Jenkins, Steve

★ **Prehistoric** actual size. Houghton Mifflin Co. 2005 un il $16

Grades: K 1 2 3   560

1. Prehistoric animals

ISBN 0-618-53578-0

LC 2004-25124

Illustrated with cut-paper artwork, "the animals pictured here include the minuscule protozoa; . . . the eight-foot-tall 'terror bird'; and the Giganotosaurus. . . . The most arresting spreads are those in which the animal is too large to picture in its entirety. . . . Information about and an illustration of the entire creature (not to scale) completes this colorful volume." Booklist

Larson, Peter L.

Bones rock! everything you need to know to be a paleontologist. [by] Peter Larson and Kristin Donnan. Invisible Cities Press 2004 204p il pa $19.95

Grades: 5 6 7 8   560

1. Fossils 2. Paleontologists -- Juvenile literature 3. Paleontology -- Vocational guidance -- Juvenile literature

ISBN 1-93122-935-X

LC 2004-413

"Illustrations include high-quality color photographs and helpful diagrams and drawings. There's fascinating information here, and Larson's enthusiasm and sound advice give plenty of encouragement to young scientists." SLJ

Includes bibliographical references

Leedy, Loreen

My teacher is a dinosaur; and other prehistoric poems, jokes, riddles, and amazing facts. written and illustrated by Loreen Leedy. Marshall Cavendish Childrens 2010 47p il $17.99

Grades: 3 4 5 6   560

1. Geology 2. Earth sciences 3. Prehistoric animals

ISBN 978-0-7614-5708-4; 0-7614-5708-9

LC 2009052901

This "introduces readers to the history of the Earth and its plants and animals. Children will have no problem following the succession of life through the pages. . . . Each spread presents one topic with a poem conveying the primary information; surrounding that poem are goofy riddles, factlets and question-limericks that expand on it. The pages are unapologetically jam-packed with information, but they never overwhelm." Kirkus

Parker, Steve, 1952-

Creatures of the sky. QEB Pub. 2011 32p il map (Wild age) lib bdg $28.50

Grades: 2 3 4   560

1. Birds 2. Fossils 3. Insects 4. Pterosaurs 5. Prehistoric animals

ISBN 978-1-59566-912-4; 1-59566-912-4

LC 2010001151

This describes prehistoric flying creatures, including insects, flying reptiles, and early birds.

"Vivid writing . . . lifts [this] otherwise ordinary [survey] a bit above average. . . . The art combines photos of fossils, distribution maps, illustrations of prehistoric monsters . . . and, on each spread, a human silhouette to indicate scale." SLJ

Land roamers. QEB Pub. 2011 32p il map (Wild age) lib bdg $28.50

Grades: 2 3 4 **560**
1. Fossils
ISBN 978-1-59566-913-1; 1-59566-913-2
LC 2010001153
This describes some prehistoric land animals.
"Vivid writing . . . lifts [this] otherwise ordinary [survey] a bit above average. . . . The art combines photos of fossils, distribution maps, illustrations of prehistoric monsters . . . and, on each spread, a human silhouette to indicate scale." SLJ
Includes glossary

Sea monsters. QEB Pub. 2011 32p il map (Wild age) lib bdg $28.50
Grades: 2 3 4 **560**
1. Fossils 2. Marine animals 3. Prehistoric animals
ISBN 978-1-59566-914-8; 1-59566-914-0
LC 2010001155
This describes prehistoric sea creatures.
"Vivid writing . . . lifts [this] otherwise ordinary [survey] a bit above average. . . . The art combines photos of fossils, distribution maps, illustrations of prehistoric monsters . . . and, on each spread, a human silhouette to indicate scale." SLJ
Includes glossary

Pellant, Chris
Fossils; [by] Chris and Helen Pellant. Gareth Stevens Pub. 2009 24p il (Rock stars) lib bdg $23
Grades: 2 3 4 **560**
1. Fossils
ISBN 978-0-8368-9223-9 lib bdg; 0-8368-9223-2 lib bdg
LC 2008016116
"Accessible and action-oriented, short but info-packed. . . . Photographs are fine, and graphics are kept extremely simple." SLJ
Includes glossary

Sabuda, Robert
Sharks and other sea monsters; [by] Robert Sabuda & Matthew Reinhart. Candlewick Press 2006 un il (Encyclopedia prehistorica) $27.99
Grades: 3 4 5 6 7 **560**
1. Prehistoric animals 2. Pop-up books 3. Extinct animals -- Juvenile literature 4. Marine animals, Fossil -- Juvenile literature
ISBN 0-7636-2229-X
LC 2005-44866
This pop-up book introduces such prehistoric creatures as giant sharks, sea scorpions, and squids.
"Gatefolds and inset minibooks expand the capacity of the book's seven spreads. . . . The sheer wonder generated by the collaborators' dimensional sleight-of-hand will more than justify purchase." Booklist

Spilsbury, Richard
Fossils; [by] Richard and Louise Spilsbury. Heinemann Library 2011 32p il (Let's rock) $29; pa $7.99
Grades: 4 5 6 **560**
1. Fossils
ISBN 978-1-4329-4682-1; 1-4329-4682-X; 978-1-4329-4690-6 pa; 1-4329-4690-0 pa
LC 2010022233

"Enhanced by plenty of photos, digital paintings, and diagrams, [this examination] of [fossils treats its topic] in unusual detail. [It] describes distinguishing characteristics, creation, history, . . . and human uses in [a] central [narrative] with additional notes, suggestions for activities during walks outside, and occasional thumbnail biographies of scientists in side boxes. [The] volume ends with a simple activity." SLJ
Includes bibliographical references

Stewart, Melissa
How does a bone become a fossil? Raintree 2010 32p il (How does it happen?) lib bdg $27.50; pa $7.99
Grades: 3 4 5 **560**
1. Fossils
ISBN 978-1-4109-3445-1 lib bdg; 1-4109-3445-4 lib bdg; 978-1-4109-3453-6 pa; 1-4109-3453-5 pa
LC 2008-52596
"Information is clearly presented using a large font, diagrams, and photographs formatted to resemble Polaroid pictures. . . . A first-rate job answering some important scientific questions." SLJ
Includes glossary and bibliographical references

Taylor, Paul D.
Fossil; written by Paul D. Taylor. rev ed; DK Pub. 2004 72p il map (DK eyewitness books) $15.99; lib bdg $19.99
Grades: 4 5 6 7 **560**
1. Fossils
ISBN 0-7566-0682-9; 0-7566-0681-0 lib bdg
First published 1990 by Knopf
This book describes different types of fossils, from algae to birds and mammals

560.9 History, geographic treatment, biography

Fern, Tracey
★ **Barnum's** bones; how Barnum Brown discovered the most famous dinosaur in the world. Tracey Fern; pictures by Boris Kulikov. Farrar Straus Giroux 2012 40 p. $17.99
Grades: 2 3 4 5 **560.9**
1. Fossils 2. Picture books for children 3. Paleontologists -- United States -- Biography -- Juvenile literature
ISBN 9780374305161
LC 2010048846
This book tells the story of "Barnum Brown," who "had a nose for fossils, trudging along behind his father as he plowed his Kansas fields, picking up ancient clams and corals. And that nose, according to [Tracey] Fern, . . . led to a lifetime of work for the American Museum of Natural History in New York. . . . A brief glimpse at Brown's early years leads to his expeditions to Patagonia and the American West, and the discovery . . . [of the] Tyrannosaurus rex." (School Library Journal)
Includes bibliographical references.

560.973

Johnson, Rebecca L.

Battle of the dinosaur bones; Othniel Charles Marsh vs. Edward Drinker Cope. by Rebecca L. Johnson. Twenty-First Century Books 2013 64 p. ill., plates, charts (Scientific rivalries and scandals) (library) $33.27

Grades: 5 6 7 8   **560.973**

1. Paleontology -- History 2. Paleontologists -- United States -- Biography -- Juvenile literature 3. Paleontology -- United States -- History -- 19th century -- Juvenile literature

ISBN 0761354883; 9780761354888

LC 2011045648

"This entry in the Scientific Rivalries and Scandals series focuses on the bitter antagonism between two pioneering nineteenth-century paleontologists. Marsh and Cope. Their contentious rivalry to discover the largest and most unusual dinosaur fossils of the American West became know as the Bone Wars and was at the forefront of American science for decades. The moral of the story is clear, revealing how rivalry can be positive and detrimental." (Booklist)

Includes bibliographical references (p. 58 - 60) and index.

567   Fossil cold-blooded vertebrates

Arnold, Caroline

Giant shark: megalodon, prehistoric super predator; illustrated by Laurie Caple. Clarion Bks. 2000 32p il $15

Grades: 3 4 5 6   **567**

1. Sharks 2. Fossils 3. Prehistoric animals 4. Carcharocles megalodon

ISBN 0-395-91419-1

LC 99-86991

Describes Megalodon, an extinct shark that was more than fifty feet long and could swallow an object the size of a small car

"This book's glowing artwork, clearly accessible text, and engrossing subject will attract readers." SLJ

O'Brien, Patrick

Megatooth! Holt & Co. 2001 un il $16.95

Grades: K 1 2 3   **567**

1. Sharks 2. Fossils 3. Prehistoric animals 4. Carcharocles megalodon

ISBN 0-8050-6214-9

LC 00-28135

"Megatooth, or Megalodon, was an ancient shark three times as large as today's great white shark. O'Brien supplies . . . several interesting facts that scientists have surmised about this fascinating creature from the huge teeth that have been found. . . . The brief text is accompanied by oversized watercolor-and-gouache illustrations." SLJ

567.9   Reptiles

Abramson, Andra Serlin

Inside dinosaurs; by Andra Serlin Abramson, Jason Brougham, and Carl Mehling; illustrated by Jason

Brougham. Sterling Innovation 2010 48p il (Inside) $16.95; pa $9.95

Grades: 5 6 7 8   **567.9**

1. Birds 2. Fossils 3. Dinosaurs

ISBN 978-1-4027-7074-6; 1-4027-7074-X; 978-1-4027-7778-3 pa; 1-4027-7778-7 pa

LC 2010010122

"This pleasantly specific overview covers not only the dinosaurs' distinctive physical characteristics (the authors include modern birds in the group), but the work of paleontologists in both field and lab, the types and typical life cycles of what are carefully dubbed 'non-avian' dinos within each 'clade,' the mass extinction of 65,000,000 years ago . . . and how new discoveries have refined theories about wings and feathers. . . . The art mixes small color photos with soft-edged paint-and-pencil reconstructions of bones, individual live portraits and prehistoric herds in natural settings. . . . [This is an] above average series entry." Kirkus

Includes glossary and bibliographical references

Arnold, Caroline

Giant sea reptiles of the dinosaur age; illustrated by Laurie Caple. Clarion Books 2007 40p il $17

Grades: 3 4 5 6   **567.9**

1. Fossils 2. Reptiles 3. Marine animals 4. Prehistoric animals 5. Paleontologists -- Juvenile literature 6. Marine reptiles

ISBN 978-0-618-50449-7; 0-618-50449-4

LC 2005-14733

Provides information about enormous reptiles who swam the seas during the dinosaur age

"Caple painstakingly re-creates the creatures Arnold introduces, but it is the undersea paintings . . . that are most effective." Booklist

Global warming and the dinosaurs; fossil discoveries at the Poles. illustrated by Laurie Caple. Clarion Books 2009 40p il map $17

Grades: 4 5 6   **567.9**

1. Fossils 2. Dinosaurs

ISBN 978-0-618-80338-5; 0-618-80338-6

LC 2008026651

"The best of Caple's watercolors . . . convincingly portray individual animals while creating beautiful effects with fine-textured surfaces and suffused light. . . . [This is a] clearly written, informative, and handsome book." Booklist

Pterosaurs; rulers of the skies in the dinosaur age. illustrated by Laurie Caple. Clarion Books 2004 40p il map $16

Grades: 3 4 5 6   **567.9**

1. Fossils 2. Pterosaurs 3. Prehistoric animals

ISBN 0-618-31354-0

LC 2003-27698

This "covers pterosaurs' ancestry, their peculiar physiology, theories about their behavior, and major fossil discoveries, frequently making abstract facts concrete through vivid comparisons. . . . Caple's neatly labeled watercolors emphasize clarity over drama, but her subjects' exotic physical oddities . . . will draw kids into the diorama-like tableaus." Booklist

Ashby, Ruth

Pteranodon; the life story of a pterosaur. by Ruth Ashby; art by Phil Wilson. Harry N. Abrams 2005 un il map $14.95

Grades: 1 2 3   567.9

1. Pterosaurs

ISBN 0-8109-5778-7

LC 2004-15612

"Ashby imagines the life of a Pteranodon from its hatching to its successful mating years later. . . . Wilson's colorful interpretations of the fossil record provide eye-catching images to enhance the narrative. Appended notes provide the reasoning behind the author's extrapolations on the pterosaur's life cycle and behaviors and the artist's bright palette. . . . this is an attractive and a rewarding look at the possibilities in a long-lost life history." SLJ

Includes bibliographical references

Bacchin, Matteo

Giant vs. giant; Argentinosaurus and Giganotosaurus. drawings and story, Matteo Bacchin; essays, Marco Signore; translated from the Italian by Marguerite Shore. Abbeville Kids 2010 61p il (Dinosaurs) $15.95

Grades: 4 5 6 7   567.9

1. Fossils 2. Dinosaurs

ISBN 978-0-7892-1013-5; 0-7892-1013-4

LC 2010-21120

This "book is split into two sections: the first contains parts . . . of a serial graphic novel about dinosaur survival, complete with dramatic narrative and grisly, to-the-death battles. The second half is a higher-level traditional nonfiction text with color photographs and diagrams, focusing on the science behind the comics. The unique format is generally engaging and effective." Horn Book Guide

T. rex and the great extinction; drawings and story, Matteo Bacchin; essays, Marco Signore; translated from the Italian by Marguerite Shore. Abbeville Kids 2010 il (Dinosaurs) $15.95

Grades: 4 5 6 7   567.9

1. Fossils 2. Dinosaurs

ISBN 9780789210142; 0789210142

LC 2010021123

This "book is split into two sections: the first contains parts . . . of a serial graphic novel about dinosaur survival, complete with dramatic narrative and grisly, to-the-death battles. The second half is a higher-level traditional nonfiction text with color photographs and diagrams, focusing on the science behind the comics. The unique format is generally engaging and effective." Horn Book Guide

Bailey, Jacqui

Monster bones; the story of a dinosaur fossil. written by Jacqui Bailey; illustrated by Matthew Lilly. Picture Window Books 2004 31p il (Science works) lib bdg $23.93

Grades: 2 3 4   567.9

1. Fossils 2. Dinosaurs

ISBN 1-4048-0565-6

LC 2003-20117

Describes how the bones of a dinosaur became fossilized, were discovered by a paleontologist, and were ultimately displayed in a museum.

This "excellent science [book explains its subject] lucidly and sometimes amusingly. . . . Children will be illuminated and engaged." SLJ

Barry, Frances

Let's look at dinosaurs. Candlewick Press 2011 un il (Flip-the flap) $12.99

Grades: PreK K 1   567.9

1. Dinosaurs 2. Pop-up books

ISBN 978-0-7636-5354-5; 0-7636-5354-3

LC 2010040127

"Gentle dinosaurs rendered in matte collage are maneuvered and concealed via flaps and simple pop-ups, while 'I wonder. . .' statements are quickly answered. . . . Barry's gently textured collages readily suggest pebbly skin and natural terrain, and even the fiercest dinosaurs have a friendliness that will please preschool-age dino-buffs." Publ Wkly

Barton, Byron

★ **Bones,** bones, dinosaur bones. Crowell 1990 un il $16.99

Grades: PreK K   567.9

1. Fossils 2. Dinosaurs 3. Fossils -- Fiction 4. Dinosaurs -- Fiction

ISBN 0-690-04825-4

LC 89-71306

"From the field search for dinosaur bones to reconstructed skeletons for museum display, paleontology as process is revealed in simple text, bold print, and flat illustrations with heavy, black outlines. Includes labeled illustrations of eight dinosaurs." Sci Child

Basher, Simon

Dinosaurs; the bare bones. written by Dan Green; illustrations by Simon Basher. Kingfisher 2012 64 p. (paperback) $7.99; (hardcover) $12.99; (prebind) $16.99

Grades: 2 3 4   567.9

1. Dinosaurs 2. Picture books for children

ISBN 0753468247; 9780753468241; 9780753468234; 9781451766288

This children's picture book by Dan Green presents a "one-stop guide to the world of dinosaurs. . . . Join the primeval party and meet terrifying Tyrannosaurus rex, huge Giganotosaurus and tiny Compsognathus. Also includes lots of information from the Triassic, Jurassic, and Cretaceous Periods, including dinosaur dinners, habitats, and fossil discoveries." (Publisher's note)

Benton, Mike

The **Kingfisher** dinosaur encyclopedia. Kingfisher 2010 159p il $19.99

Grades: 3 4 5 6   567.9

1. Fossils 2. Dinosaurs

ISBN 978-0-7534-6440-3; 0-7534-6440-3

"This thorough, fact-filled dinosaur encyclopedia contains full-color digital images of dinosaurs, in order of their appearance through geological time. . . . Profiles offer descriptions of various species' anatomy and speculations on issues like mobility, diet, and predation. Easy-to-read time lines and charts discuss the origins and extinctions of species, while abundant photographs of skeletans, dig sites, and paleontogists at work integrate relevance and texture." Publ Wkly

Bergen, David

Life-size dinosaurs. Sterling Pub. 2004 48p il $9.95

Grades: 3 4 5 6   **567.9**

1. Dinosaurs

ISBN 1-4027-1755-X

This includes life-size illustrations of such dinosaurs as Atreipus, Oviraptor, and Therizinosaurus in three 8-page-long gatefolds and four 6-page ones.

"This slim, oversize title will be eye candy indeed to dinophiles.... These vivid color illustrations are surrounded by chatty explanatory paragraphs and information boxes." SLJ

Berkowitz, Jacob

★ Jurassic poop; what dinosaurs (and others) left behind. written by Jacob Berkowitz; illustrated by Steve Mack. Kids Can Press 2006 40p il $14.95; pa $7.95

Grades: 4 5 6 7   **567.9**

1. Feces 2. Fossils 3. Dinosaurs 4. Coprolites -- Juvenile literature

ISBN 978-1-55337-860-0; 1-55337-860-1; 978-1-55337-867-9 pa; 1-55337-867-9 pa

This describes fossilized feces, or coprolites, and what we can learn from them

"Berkowitz' style is goofy and lighthearted, but there's plenty of real information. . . . The browsable format combines cartoony digital art, photographs . . . and design elements such a spiky borders and background shading." Bull Cent Child Books

Includes glossary

Bishop, Nic

★ Digging for bird-dinosaurs; an expedition to Madagascar. Houghton Mifflin 2000 48p il $16; pa $4.95

Grades: 4 5 6 7   **567.9**

1. Birds 2. Fossils 3. Dinosaurs 4. Paleontology -- Madagascar 5. Birds, Fossil -- Madagascar 6. Reptiles, Fossil -- Madagascar 7. Evolutionary paleobiology -- Madagascar

ISBN 0-395-96056-8; 0-618-1982-X pa

LC 99-36145

The story of Cathy Forster's experiences as a member of a team of paleontologists who went on an expedition to the island of Madagascar in 1998 to search for fossil birds

"Throughout the engaging, personal story, Bishop presents a great deal of information in highly readable, age-appropriate language, well matched by exceptional full-color images of scientists at work and the Malagasy landscape and people." Booklist

Includes bibliographical references

Bonner, Hannah

When dinos dawned, mammals got munched, and Pterosaurs took flight; a cartoon pre-history of life in the Triassic. Hannah Bonner. National Geographic Children's Books 2012 44 p. col. ill., col. maps (hardback) $25.90

Grades: 3 4 5 6 7   **567.9**

1. Dinosaurs 2. Triassic Period 3. Graphic novels

ISBN 9781426308628; 9781426308635

LC 2011029212

In this book Hannah Bonner "chronicles developments in the Triassic Period, during which life got a fresh lease on the planet in the wake of the massive Permian extinction. She tracks an explosion of biological diversity as the oceans were repopulated, lush forests grew and the dominant kinds of land animals went from clumsy-looking therapsids to sleek archosaurian dinosaurs and proto-crocodiles. Early mammals are already waiting in the wings." (Kirkus Reviews)

Includes bibliographical references and index

Brewster, Hugh

Dinosaurs in your backyard; illustrated by Alan Barnard. Abrams Books for Young Readers 2009 32p il $15.95

Grades: 3 4 5   **567.9**

1. Dinosaurs

ISBN 978-0-8109-7099-1; 0-8109-7099-6

LC 2008030406

First published 2008 in Canada with title: Breakout dinosaurs

"This informative book . . . transports readers back to a time when North America was defined by substantially different coastlines and divided by a broad inland seaway. Introducing some of the dinosaurs living there . . . the book uses double-page spreads that typically describe one animal in a paragraph of descriptive or dramatic text as well as a section of fast facts relating its size, weight, era, diet, and range. Large, painterly illustrations set the tone, supported by smaller maps and photos of fossils. The occasional dramatic tooth-and-claw scene is more than balanced by the weight of accessible, interesting information." Booklist

Includes bibliographical references

Brown, Charlotte Lewis

The day the dinosaurs died; written by Charlotte Lewis Brown; illustrated by Phil Wilson. HarperCollins Publishers 2006 48p il (I can read book) $15.99; lib bdg $16.89

Grades: K 1 2 3   **567.9**

1. Dinosaurs 2. Dinosaurs -- Juvenile literature 3. Extinction (Biology) -- Juvenile literature

ISBN 978-0-06-000528-3; 0-06-000528-9; 978-0-06-000529-0 lib bdg; 0-06-000529-7 lib bdg

LC 2005-15135

"Beginning with a pronunciation guide for the names of various dinosaurs, this book describes what probably happened to those reptiles 65 million years ago, when a comet or an asteroid most likely slammed into the Earth in the area of the Yucatán Peninsula. . . . Second graders will be able to read this book independently, and with its expressive, fairly naturalistic illustrations, younger children will find that it answers the question of how the dinosaurs became extinct." SLJ

Cole, Joanna

★ The magic school bus: in the time of the dinosaurs; illustrated by Bruce Degen. Scholastic 1994 un il hardcover o.p. pa $4.99

Grades: 2 3 4   **567.9**

1. Dinosaurs

ISBN 0-590-44688-6; 0-590-44639-4 pa

LC 93-5753

"An eye-catching, humorous book with bright, busy illustrations . . . packed with information." Sci Books Films

Collard, Sneed B.

★ Reign of the sea dragons; illustrated by Andrew Plant. Charlesbridge 2008 61p il $17.95; pa $8.95

Grades: 5 6 7 8 9   567.9

1. Marine animals 2. Prehistoric animals 3. Paleontology -- Juvenile literature 4. Marine reptiles, Fossil -- Juvenile literature

ISBN 978-1-58089-124-0; 978-1-58089-125-7 pa

LC 2007-26201

"An arresting dust jacket depicting a humongous pliosaur snapping huge toothy jaws at a small, long-necked plesiosaur is an attention-grabber, but it is the informative text that brings these real sea monsters to life. Collard follows his usual pattern of careful organization, with a readable text and up-to-date information. . . . Plant has provided five full-color paintings, but it is his numerous black-and-white drawings that lend sturdy anatomical and physical information. . . . Collard's discussion on extinction theories is cogent." SLJ

Includes glossary, bibliographical references, and websites

Dixon, Dougal

Amazing dinosaurs; [by] Dougal Dixon. 2nd ed.; Boyds Mills Press 2007 128p il $19.95

Grades: 3 4 5 6   567.9

1. Dinosaurs

ISBN 978-1-59078-537-9; 1-59078-537-1

LC 2006038922

First published 2000 with title: Dougal Dixon's amazing dinosaurs

This guide to dinosaurs is divided into four sections representing meat eaters, long-necked plant eaters, armored dinosaurs, and two-footed plant eaters. Each illustrated entry includes pronunciation, meaning of name, classification, size, weight, time, place, and food of a dinosaur species.

Includes glossary and bibliographical references

Plant-eating dinosaurs; by Dougal Dixon. North American ed. New Forest Press 2010 48 p. col. ill., col. maps (library) $28.50

Grades: 4 5 6 7   567.9

1. Fossils 2. Dinosaurs 3. Herbivores

ISBN 1848983336; 9781848983335

LC 2010925201

This volume "contains detailed information about dinosaurs and other prehistoric life, covering species development in chronological order. Careful links to the fossil finds that helped scientists with their explanations are found throughout. Additional text boxes cover topics from structure-function to footprints, and interpretive color illustrations and photographs further enhance the [text]." Horn Book Guide

Includes bibliographical references (p. 44-45) and index.

Prehistoric oceans. New Forest Press 2010 48p il map (Dinosaur files) lib bdg $28.50

Grades: 4 5 6 7   567.9

1. Fossils 2. Dinosaurs 3. Marine animals

ISBN 978-1-8489-8332-8; 1-8489-8332-8

This volume "contains detailed information about dinosaurs and other prehistoric life, covering species development in chronological order. Careful links to the fossil finds that helped scientists with their explanations are found throughout. Additional text boxes cover topics from structure-function to footprints, and interpretive color illus-

trations and photographs further enhance the [text]." Horn Book Guide

Includes glossary

Prehistoric skies. New Forest Press 2010 48p il map lib bdg $28.50

Grades: 4 5 6 7   567.9

1. Fossils 2. Dinosaurs 3. Prehistoric animals

ISBN 978-1-8489-8331-1; 1-8489-8331-X

Discusses the physical characteristics, behavior, diet, and fossil evidence of prehistoric animals that lived in the sky.

This volume "contains detailed information about dinosaurs and other prehistoric life, covering species development in chronological order. Careful links to the fossil finds that helped scientists with their explanations are found throughout. Additional text boxes cover topics from structure-function to footprints, and interpretive color illustrations and photographs further enhance the [text]." Horn Book Guide

Includes glossary

World of dinosaurs and other prehistoric life. Barron's 2008 112p il pa $9.99

Grades: 3 4 5   567.9

1. Fossils 2. Dinosaurs

ISBN 978-0-7641-4082-2 pa; 0-7641-4082-5 pa

This book "starts off with a color coded contents page for easy reference. Each two-page spread highlights a different creature from prehistoric life, including many lesser-known animals. . . . Wonderful illustrations capture each creature as it might have lived. Many photographs are included highlighting fossils, skeletons, and other prehistoric finds. Large font makes it more accessible to a younger reader where interest is at its highest. . . . This is a treasure trove of interesting facts without being overwhelming." Libr Media Connect

Includes glossary

Farlow, James Orville

★ **Bringing** dinosaur bones to life; how do we know what dinosaurs were really like? [by] James O. Farlow; with illustrations by James E. Whitcraft. Watts 2001 63p il lib bdg $25

Grades: 5 6 7 8   567.9

1. Fossils 2. Dinosaurs

ISBN 0-531-11403-1

LC 00-38150

"Clearly written and well organized, this book will interest children intrigued by the process of scientific thinking as well as its results." Booklist

Includes glossary and bibliographical references

Forss, Sarah

Alphasaurs and other prehistoric types; by Sharon Werner and Sarah Forss. Blue Apple Books 2012 56 p. (hardback) $22.99

Grades: 1 2 3 4   567.9

1. Alphabet 2. Picture books for children 3. Animals -- Juvenile literature 4. Dinosaurs -- Juvenile literature

ISBN 1609051939; 9781609051938

LC 2012023718

Author Sharon Werner presents a picture book for children. "Like the creatures so artfully rendered in the best-selling Alphabeasties, the dinosaurs in this stylish book are ingeniously engineered out of letters. A different typeface comprises each animal. Factual information about each dinosaur appears in multiple entries and fonts, making for an eye-catching and witty way to look at the ABC-DINO's." (Publisher's note)

French, Vivian

T. Rex; illustrated by Alison Bartlett. Candlewick Press 2004 29p il $15.99; pa $6.99; pa with audio CD $8.99
Grades: K 1 2 3   567.9
1. Dinosaurs 2. Tyrannosaurus rex -- Juvenile literature
ISBN 978-0-7636-2184-1; 0-7636-2184-6; 978-0-7636-3177-2 pa; 0-7636-3177-9 pa; 978-0-7636-3999-0 pa with audio CD; 0-7636-3999-0 pa with audio CD
LC 2003-69563
In a "dialogue with his grandfather, a boy discovers the thrill of the intellectual hunt while touring a T. Rex exhibition.... Bartlett ... working in saturated acrylics and bold shapes, travels back to the era when T. Rex was indeed king. ... The author eloquently makes the case that a willingness to seek answers, rather than merely receive them, has its own rewards." Publ Wkly

Funston, Sylvia

Dino-why? the dinosaur question and answer book. updated and rev.; Maple Tree Press 2008 64p il $22.95; pa $10.95
Grades: 4 5 6 7   567.9
1. Dinosaurs
ISBN 978-1-897349-24-3; 1-897349-24-6; 978-1-897349-25-0 pa; 1-897349-25-4 pa
LC 2007-939082
First published 1992 by Joy Street Books with title: The dinosaur question and answer book
"This book is an excellent and highly readable introduction to dinosaurs.... The questions are well conceived, and the answers ... are scientifically sound and up to date. ... The illustrations, a few of them cartoon-like, are nicely drawn and useful." Sci Books Films

Gibbons, Gail

Dinosaurs! by Gail Gibbons. Holiday House 2008 32p il $16.95
Grades: K 1 2 3   567.9
1. Dinosaurs
ISBN 978-0-8234-2143-5; 0-8234-2143-0
LC 2007034425
Simple text and illustrations introduce young readers to dinosaurs
"The combination of clear writing and lively artwork makes this an accessible choice for young dinosaur enthusiasts." Booklist

Greenwood, Marie

Amazing giant dinosaurs; [written by Marie Greenwood; illustrated by Peter Minister] DK 2012 15 p. $19.99
Grades: 2 3 4   567.9
1. Dinosaurs 2. Paleontology 3. Picture books for children 4. Toy and movable books 5. Dinosaurs -- Juvenile literature 6. Toy and movable books -- Specimens
ISBN 075669308X; 9780756693084
LC 2011279215

This book features "large foldout flaps" that create pop-up illustrations of dinosaurs. "Each dinosaur appears in a ... graphic along with a bulletin board collection of facts about its diet, habitat, behavior, and other characteristics. ... Profiles of 'Dinosaur hunters' provide insight into the paleontology profession." (Publishers Weekly)

Hartland, Jessie

★ **How** the dinosaur got to the museum. Blue Apple Books 2011 un il $17.99
Grades: 3 4 5   567.9
1. Fossils 2. Museums 3. Dinosaurs
ISBN 978-1-60905-090-0; 1-60905-090-8
LC 2011018921
"This cumulative narrative follows the journey of a set of dinosaur bones belonging to a Diplodocus longus that lived 145 million years ago to its present home in the display halls of the Smithsonian National Museum of Natural History in Washington, DC. ... It ... describes the work of many hands involved, ... starting with the dinosaur hunter who discovered the bones and the paleontologist who went to Utah to identify them and culminating with the museum director who opened the exhibit.... [The author's] verbs are interestingly varied, as are the many things these people do. The text is printed on double-page illustrations, painted in a childlike manner but detailed enough to show all the people and activities." Kirkus

Henry, Michel

Raptor; the life of a young deinonychus. illustrations by Rich Penney. Abrams Books for Young Readers 2007 un il map $15.95
Grades: 2 3 4   567.9
1. Dinosaurs 2. Deinonychus -- Juvenile literature
ISBN 978-0-8109-5775-6; 0-8109-5775-2
LC 2004-12588
This "is a beautifully illustrated book that brings a dinosaur and his environment to life. Based on informed speculation ... this book follows the life experiences of several raptors that are part of a pack that lived in the western part of North America 100 million years ago." Sci Books Films
Includes glossary and bibliographical references

Hort, Lenny

Did dinosaurs eat pizza? mysteries science hasn't solved. illustrated by John O'Brien. Henry Holt and Co. 2006 un il $15.95
Grades: K 1 2 3   567.9
1. Dinosaurs
ISBN 978-0-8050-6757-6; 0-8050-6757-4
LC 2005-12171
"The discussion opens with the idea that even though much is known about dinosaurs, there are still mysteries to solve. The pages that follow introduce a series of unanswered questions. ... Clearly written and filled with fascinating facts for dinosaur enthusiasts. ... O'Brien's detailed, often-witty ink drawings, brightened with colorful washes, interpret the facts imaginatively." Booklist

Hughes, Catherine D.

First big book of dinosaurs. National Geographic 2011 127p (National Geographic little kids) $14.95; lib bdg $21.90

Grades: PreK K 1 2 **567.9**

1. Dinosaurs

ISBN 978-1-4263-0846-8; 1-4263-0846-9; 978-1-4263-0847-5 lib ed; 1-4263-0847-7 lib bdg

LC 2011015051

"A bright, eye-catching format, naturalistic illustrations, and concise prose introduce readers to 52 dinosaur species, organized by size—small, big, giant, or gigantic. Distinguishing characteristics of each dinosaur . . . appear in a large font like a headline on each spread; informative sidebars, charts that compare each dino's size to a human, phonetic pronunciations, and lively interactive prompts . . . make this an especially engaging primer." Publ Wkly

Judge, Lita

★ **Born** to be giants; how baby dinosaurs grew to rule the world. Flash Point 2010 un il $17.99

Grades: 2 3 4 **567.9**

1. Dinosaurs 2. Dinosaurs -- Infancy -- Juvenile

ISBN 978-1-59643-443-1; 1-59643-443-0

"Expanding on the idea that the hugest dinosaurs hatched from (relatively speaking) small eggs, Judge depicts cute hatchlings with outsized heads and feet wobbling about as their gargantuan parents look on indulgently. Along with a full measure of visual appeal, she also delivers a terse but clear explanation of how scientists gain insight into dino parenting from both fossil evidence." Booklist

Includes glossary and bibliographical references

Kerley, Barbara

★ The **dinosaurs** of Waterhouse Hawkins; an illuminating history of Mr. Waterhouse Hawkins, artist and lecturer. with drawings by Brian Selznick, many of which are based on the original sketches of Mr. Hawkins. Scholastic 2001 un il

Grades: 3 4 5 **567.9**

1. Artists 2. Dinosaurs 3. Sculptors 4. Modelmakers -- Great Britain

ISBN 0-439-11494-2

LC 00058376

A Caldecott Medal honor book, 2002

This is the true story of Victorian artist Benjamin Waterhouse Hawkins, who built life-sized models of dinosaurs in the hope of educating the world about these ancient animals and what they were like. "Ages five to eight." (Bull Cent Child Books)

"Kerley suffuses her text with a sense of wonder and amazement, a tone well-matched by Selznick's lush, dramatic illustrations." Publ Wkly

Kudlinski, Kathleen V., 1950-

★ **Boy,** were we wrong about dinosaurs! illustrated by S. D. Schindler. Dutton Children's Books 2005 un il $15.99

Grades: K 1 2 3 **567.9**

1. Dinosaurs

ISBN 0-525-46978-8

LC 2003-53140

This book examines what is known about dinosaur bones, behavior, and other characteristics and how different the facts often are from what scientists, from ancient China to the recent past, believed to be true. "Ages six to ten." (Bull Cent Child Books)

"Intelligently designed and imaginatively conceived, the artwork makes the text more understandable and the whole book more beautiful. . . . Best of all, the closing paragraph acknowledges that the search is not over yet." Booklist

Includes bibliographical references

Lessem, Don

Feathered dinosaurs; by Don Lessem; illustrations by John Bindon. Lerner Publications 2005 32p il (Meet the dinosaurs) lib bdg $23.93; pa $6.95

Grades: 2 3 4 **567.9**

1. Birds 2. Dinosaurs

ISBN 0-8225-1423-0 lib bdg; 0-8225-2621-2 pa

LC 2004-19651

This covers the "links between dinosaurs and birds. . . . Lessem writes in simple language and short sentences appropriate for children transitioning out of early readers. But the brief text . . . will also read well to younger dino fans. . . . Bindon's detailed illustrations imagine the creatures in dramatic settings that will bring the drama of the ancient age alive." Booklist

Flying giants of dinosaur time. Lerner Publications Co. 2005 32p il map (Meet the dinosaurs) lib bdg $23.93; pa $6.95

Grades: 2 3 4 **567.9**

1. Pterosaurs 2. Pterodactyls

ISBN 0-8225-1424-9 lib bdg; 0-8225-2622-0 pa

LC 2004-17918

This "covers the pterosaurs and pterodactyls, extrapolating some behaviors using modern birds as models, and speculates on beak shapes and sizes in the food-gathering process. . . . The realistic, soft illustrations . . . are lively enough to please budding paleontologists. Simple, eye-catching, and informative." SLJ

Sea giants of dinosaur time. Lerner Publications Co. 2005 32p il map (Meet the dinosaurs) lib bdg $23.93; pa $6.95

Grades: 2 3 4 **567.9**

1. Dinosaurs

ISBN 0-8225-1425-7 lib bdg; 0-8225-2623-9 pa

LC 2004-17916

"A quick glimpse at eight of the larger prehistoric marine reptiles, ranging in eras from 220 million to 65 million years ago. The simple text presents a time line for these creatures, a global map of fossil finds, and some details of their physiology and distribution. The colorful double-page illustrations on blue backgrounds are accompanied by a paragraph or two of particulars." SLJ

The **fastest** dinosaurs; by Don Lessem; illustrations by John Bindon. Lerner Publications 2005 32p il (Meet the dinosaurs) lib bdg $23.93; pa $6.95

Grades: 2 3 4 **567.9**

1. Dinosaurs

ISBN 0-8225-1422-2 lib bdg; 0-8225-2620-4 pa

LC 2004-7055

This "looks at how paleontologists determine living speed when only the fossil record remains, and cites some prime examples of dinosprinters, such a Gallimimus and Troodon. The realistic, soft illustrations . . . are lively enough to please budding paleontologists. Simple, eye-catching, and informative." SLJ

The **smartest** dinosaurs; by Don Lessem; illustrations by John Bindon. Lerner Publications 2005 32p il (Meet the dinosaurs) lib bdg $23.93; pa $6.95

Grades: 2 3 4   **567.9**

1. Dinosaurs

ISBN 0-8225-1373-0 lib bdg; 0-8225-2618-2 pa

LC 2004-11152

"After a discussion of brain/body-size ratios, Lessem goes on to describe the importance of fossil finds in determining intelligence possibilities, leading to brief descriptions of seven dinosaurs that scientists feel may have been brighter than their contemporaries. . . . This is a clear look at a facet of dinosaur makeup not often touched on in other works." SLJ

The **ultimate** dinopedia; the most complete dinosaur reference ever. illustrated by Franco Tempesta; with a foreword by Rodolfo Coria. National Geographic 2010 272p il map $24.95; lib bdg $34.90

Grades: 3 4 5 6   **567.9**

1. Dinosaurs

ISBN 978-1-4263-0164-3; 1-4263-0164-2; 978-1-4263-0165-0 lib bdg; 1-4263-0165-0 lib bdg

LC 2010-07146

In the opening chapter, Lessem "presents broad basics on [dinosaur] behavior and habitats as well as a look at major discoveries in paleontology. However, it's the later chapters, which devote two pages each to specific dinosaurs, that will hook hard-core dino lovers. . . . Tempesta's full-page illustrations appear on every spread and jump off the page, and the dynamic layout . . . is immensely appealing. . . . Lessem's comprehensive overview will satisfy the interested browser as much as the ardent dinosaur enthusiast." Booklist

Includes bibliographical references

Long, John A.

★ **Dinosaurs**; [by] John Long. Simon & Schuster Books for Young Readers 2007 64p il (Insiders) lib bdg $16.99

Grades: 4 5 6 7   **567.9**

1. Dinosaurs

ISBN 978-1-4169-3857-6 lib bdg; 1-4169-3857-5 lib bdg

LC 2007-61735

"Richly hued, crisp computer-generated art and 3D model imagery serve as a stunning and sophisticated graphic counterpoint to the educational text." Publ Wkly

Includes glossary

MacLeod, Elizabeth

Monster fliers; from the time of the dinosaurs. written by Elizabeth MacLeod; illustrated by John Bindon. Kids Can Press 2010 31p il $16.95

Grades: K 1 2 3   **567.9**

1. Birds 2. Dinosaurs 3. Pterosaurs 4. Flight -- Juvenile literature 5. Dinosaurs -- Juvenile literature 6. Pterosauria -- Juvenile literature

ISBN 978-1-55453-199-8; 1-55453-199-3

"This attractive picture book [is] sure to appeal to dinophiles eager to learn more about dinosaurs' flying cousins. Nineteen pterosaurs, a few early birds, and a dromaeosaur

(a dinosaur that both walked and flew) are briefly described and illustrated in their presumed native habitats. . . . The realistic illustrations [are] painted with remarkable detail." Booklist

Macken, JoAnn Early

The **dinosaur** museum. Amicus 2010 24p il (My community) lib bdg $14.95

Grades: K 1 2   **567.9**

1. Fossils 2. Museums 3. Dinosaurs

ISBN 978-1-6075-3023-7 lib bdg; 1-6075-3023-6 lib bdg

LC 2010010554

The design offers "clear font, colorful layout, and glossy photos. . . . What's most delightful about the museum images are the juxtapositions of the fantastic (a giant dinosaur skeleton) paired with the mundane (a guy on a step-ladder using a vacuum to clean the bones. . . . A solid effort." Booklist

Manning, Phillip Lars

★ **Dinomummy**; the life, death, and discovery of Dakota, a dinosaur from Hell Creek. foreword by Tyler Lyson. Kingfisher 2007 64p il map $18.95

Grades: 4 5 6 7   **567.9**

1. Dinosaurs 2. Dinosaurs -- Juvenile literature 3. Hadrosauridae -- Juvenile literature 4. Mummified animals -- Juvenile literature

ISBN 978-0-7534-6047-4; 0-7534-6047-5

LC 2007-02878

Tells about the discovery of the fossil remains of a hadrosaur in the hills of the Hell Creek Formation in North Dakota.

"The color photographs and simple text offer a detailed account of carefully unearthing the fossil and transporting it safely to the laboratory, where many tests were performed. Dinosaurs buffs and young scientists will love this book. It is a thrilling story that is part narrative, part mystery, and part science lesson." Voice Youth Advocates

Markle, Sandra

★ **Outside** and inside dinosaurs. Atheneum Bks. for Young Readers 2000 40p il hardcover o.p. pa $7.99

Grades: 2 3 4   **567.9**

1. Fossils 2. Dinosaurs

ISBN 0-689-82300-2; 0-689-85778-0 pa

LC 99-45808

Describes the inner and outer workings of dinosaurs, discussing what has been learned about their anatomy, diet, and behavior from fossils

"Excellent, large color photos march hand in hand with Markle's readable, informative text." SLJ

Includes glossary

McGowan, Chris

Dinosaur discovery; everything you need to be a paleontologist. illustrated by Erica Lyn Schmidt. Simon & Schuster Books for Young Readers 2011 48p il $17.99

Grades: 4 5 6 7   **567.9**

1. Fossils 2. Dinosaurs

ISBN 978-1-4169-4764-6; 1-4169-4764-7; 1416947647; 9781416947646

LC 2009044604

"In-depth facts about 13 dinosaurs are interspersed with activities that teach readers about anatomy and how paleontologists understand body structure. . . . The 27 activities and experiments illustrate the concepts presented and focus on the featured dinosaurs. By following the well-written directions as well as the picture steps, budding paleontologists will explore how a tail affects balance, discover binocular vision and learn how the two parts of a bone make them both stiff and elastic. . . . Schmidt's acrylic illustrations give life to the dinosaurs, and her scientific renderings of bones could have come straight out of an anatomy textbook. . . . A thinking, active alternative for readers who fall between adult nonfiction and all the rhyming dino fare meant for the younger set." Kirkus

Most, Bernard

How big were the dinosaurs. Harcourt Brace & Co. 1994 un il $16; pa $7

Grades: PreK K 1   567.9

1. Dinosaurs

ISBN 0-15-236800-0; 0-15-200852-7 pa

LC 93-19152

Describes the size of different dinosaurs by comparing them to more familiar objects, such as a school bus, a trombone, or a bowling alley

"The colorful drawings, of children interacting with dinosaurs, will be attractive to children. The text is easy to read. This book will delight young dinosaur lovers." Sci Books Films

Munro, Roxie

Inside-outside dinosaurs. Marshall Cavendish Children 2009 un il $17.99

Grades: PreK K   567.9

1. Dinosaurs

ISBN 978-0-7614-5624-7; 0-7614-5624-4

LC 2008055322

"This large-format book offers paired double-page spreads showing each featured dinosaur twice. In the first spread, a black-and-gray skeleton in a dramatic pose stands out clearly against a white background. . . . The second spread portrays the living dinosaur within its habitat. Typically these pictures, india-ink drawings washed with colors, depict action in the background or foreground. . . . An appended section offers a bit of information about each species and identifies all the dinosaurs in the action scenes. . . . Eye-catching illustrations and minimal text make this a good choice for young dino fans." Booklist

Includes bibliographical references

Myers, Tim

If you give a T-rex a bone; illustrated by Anisa Claire Hovemann. Dawn Publications 2007 un il (A sharing nature with children book) $16.95; pa $8.95

Grades: PreK K 1 2   567.9

1. Dinosaurs 2. Dinosaurs -- Juvenile literature

ISBN 978-1-58469-097-9; 1-58469-097-6; 978-1-58469-098-6 pa; 1-58469-098-4 pa

LC 2007-08332

"The book is illustrated throughout with bright, and quite beautiful, watercolors. . . . This is a fine first introduction to prehistoric reptiles for the very young." Sci Books Films

Includes bibliographical references

Peterson, Sheryl

Pterodactyl. Creative Education 2010 48p il (Age of dinosaurs) lib bdg $34.25

Grades: 5 6 7 8   567.9

1. Dinosaurs

ISBN 978-1-58341-975-5 lib bdg; 1-58341-975-6 lib bdg

LC 2009025175

"Peterson nicely balances the known with conjecture. . . . The inviting design, on glossy pages, elegantly detours from the main text into details tantalizing . . .; informative . . .; and incredible. . . . The illustrations, from sharp diagrams to dramatic paintings to B-movie-worthy recreation scenes, add some nice flair to this solid entry." Booklist

Podesto, Martine

Dinosaurs; by Martine Podesto. Gareth Stevens 2009 102p il (My science notebook) lib bdg $31

Grades: 4 5 6   567.9

1. Dinosaurs

ISBN 978-0-8368-9213-0 lib bdg; 0-8368-9213-5 lib bdg

LC 2008-12427

"Designed to resemble a notebook with illustrated paper clips, pasting, and tape appearing on most pages, this [book] . . . offers comprehensive information. . . . supplemented by colorful drawings, diagrams, and photographs." SLJ

Includes glossary and bibliographical references

Prap, Lila

Dinosaurs?! North South Books 2010 un il $16.95

Grades: K 1 2 3   567.9

1. Birds 2. Dinosaurs 3. Evolution

ISBN 978-0-7358-2284-9; 0-7358-2284-0

"In this humorous look at evolution, Prap makes the case that all modern-day birds, including chickens, are descended from dinosaurs. The book's illustrations are fun and well-laid-out, and the witty text is chock-full of information. A group of chickens makes snarky comments about their disparate relatives . . . and side notes provide interesting details about the 'terrible lizards.' Dino lovers will clamor for this title." SLJ

Ray, Deborah Kogan

★ **Dinosaur** mountain; digging into the Jurassic Age. Frances Foster Books 2010 un il map $16.99

Grades: 3 4 5 6   567.9

1. Fossils 2. Dinosaurs 3. Paleontologists 4. Dinosaurs

ISBN 978-0-374-31789-8; 0-374-31789-5

LC 2008027877

This describes how, beginning in 1908, Earl Douglass set out to discover "a mountain in Utah that would reveal some of the grandest dinosaur skeletons anyone had ever seen. . . . Ray's expressive art . . . excels in capturing the grandeur and wonder of key moments. . . . Excited journal entries from Douglass enliven the informative text, and small sketch book-style drawings of fossils and tools add a scholarly touch." Booklist

Includes glossary and bibliographical references

Rushby, Pamela

Discovering Supercroc; by Pamela Rushby. National Geographic 2007 40p il (National Geographic science chapters) lib bdg $17.90

Grades: 3 4 5 6   **567.9**
1. Fossils 2. Crocodiles 3. Prehistoric animals
ISBN 978-1-4263-0186-5 lib bdg; 1-4263-01863-
lib bdg

LC 2007007906

"This book describes the discovery of first the jaw and then other bones belonging to SuperCroc: a forty-foot-long prehistoric crocodile. The accessible text explains how paleontologists removed the fossils and reassembled them into a skeleton, and how SuperCroc compares to today's reptiles. The many eye-catching photographs include close-ups of crocodile teeth on the striking endpapers." Horn Book Guide

Sloan, Christopher
Bizarre dinosaurs; some very strange creatures and why we think they got that way. [by] Christopher Sloan; with a foreword by James Clark and Cathy Forster. National Geographic 2008 31p il $16.95; lib bdg $25.90
Grades: 4 5 6 7   **567.9**
1. Dinosaurs 2. Dinosaurs -- Juvenile literature
ISBN 978-1-4263-0330-2; 1-4263-0330-0; 978-1-
4263-0331-9 lib bdg; 1-4263-0331-9 lib bdg
This "book should engage children of all ages who are fascinated by dinosaurs. . . . The illustrations are of uniformly high quality. . . . Each species gets two pages of text, including a full-page illustration; an inset with basic facts such as range, diet, and geological period in which it lived; a silhouette comparing their size with that of humans; and a paragraph of text." Sci Books Films

★ **How** dinosaurs took flight; the fossils, the science, what we think we know, and the mysteries yet unsolved. foreword by Dr. Xu Xing. National Geographic 2005 64p il $17.95
Grades: 5 6 7 8   **567.9**
1. Birds 2. Fossils 3. Dinosaurs 4. Birds, Fossil -- Juvenile literature 5. Birds -- Origin -- Juvenile literature
ISBN 0-7922-7298-6
This explains the evolutionary relationships between dinosaurs and birds, based on fossils and the latest research.
Includes glossary and bibliographical references

Supercroc and the origin of crocodiles; introduction by Paul Sereno. National Geographic Soc. 2002 55p il map $18.95
Grades: 5 6 7 8   **567.9**
1. Crocodiles 2. Fossil reptiles
ISBN 0-7922-6691-9

LC 2001-3976

Discusses prehistoric crocodiles, including the discovery of SuperCroc in the Sahara Desert, and the lifestyles, habitats, and conservation of modern crocodiles
"Fans of paleontology or of crocodiles will find a great deal of information clearly explained. The illustrations are up to the high National Geographic standard." Booklist
Includes glossary

Tanaka, Shelley
New dinos; The latest finds! The coolest dinosaur discoveries! written by Shelley Tanaka; illustrated by Alan Barnard. Atheneum Bks. for Young Readers 2003 48p il maps hardcover o.p. pa $9.95

Grades: 3 4 5 6   **567.9**
1. Fossils 2. Dinosaurs 3. Paleontology
ISBN 0-689-85183-9; 1-897330-55-3 pa

LC 2002-9809

Describes some of the newly discovered dinosaurs and what paleontologists have learned about these prehistoric creatures in recent years
"Vivid, dramatic illustrations are a sure draw to an already hot topic. . . . Tanaka's lively, brief text provides enough data to satisfy many readers, including true aficionados." SLJ
Includes glossary and bibliographical references

Thomson, Sarah L.
Extreme dinosaurs! Q & A; Smithsonian; [written by Sarah L. Thomson] Collins 2007 un il $16.99; pa $6.99
Grades: 3 4 5   **567.9**
1. Fossils 2. Dinosaurs
ISBN 978-0-06-089971-4; 0-06-089971-9; 978-0-06-
089967-7 pa; 0-06-089967-0 pa

LC 2006935100

"This title poses 21 questions about these perennially popular creatures and answers them with a simple text accompanied by crisp photos and/or attractive artwork. . . . [This] will surely appeal to most young dinophiles." SLJ
Includes glossary and bibliographical references

Williams, Judith
The **discovery** and mystery of a dinosaur named Jane. Enslow Publishers 2007 48p il map
Grades: 3 4 5 6   **567.9**
1. Fossils 2. Dinosaurs
ISBN 0766027090 pa; 0766027309 lib bdg;
9780766027091 pa; 9780766027305 lib bdg

LC 2006010475

This book deals with how paleontologists and researchers discovered, excavated and put on display a Tyrannosaurus skeleton found in Montana's Hell Creek formation. Glossary. Index. "Grades three to eight." (Sci Books Films)
This describes "the 2001 discovery of a fossilized dinosaur skeleton in Montana's Hell Creek Formation. . . . Williams carefully reports the entire event, from discovery through excavation and preparation to exhibition at the Burpee Museum of Natural History in Rockford, IL. Small color photos and artwork, simple diagrams, and a map help readers to visualize the complex process." SLJ
Includes bibliographical references

Woodward, John
Dinosaurs eye to eye; zoom in on the world's most incredible dinosaurs. digital sculptor Peter Minister. Dorling Kindersley 2010 96p il map $19.99
Grades: 3 4 5 6   **567.9**
1. Fossils 2. Dinosaurs
ISBN 978-0-7566-5760-4; 0-7566-5760-1
"This oversize reference book features striking digital images of dinosaurs, along with abundant information about them and the Triassic, Jurassic, and Cretaceous periods in which they thrived. . . . Action scenes . . . offer visual excitement, while diagrams, sidebars with dino-stats, and photographs of fossils emphasize the educational." Publ Wkly

Zoehfeld, Kathleen Weidner

Dinosaur parents, dinosaur young; uncovering the mystery of dinosaur families. with full-color paintings by Paul Carrick and line drawings by Bruce Shillinglaw. Clarion Bks. 2001 58p il map $17

Grades: 4 5 6 7   **567.9**

1. Fossils 2. Dinosaurs 3. Paleontology 4. Parental behavior in animals 5. Dinosaurs -- Behavior -- Juvenile literature 6. Parental behavior in animals -- Juvenile literature

ISBN 0-395-91338-1

LC 00-43101

"High-quality, color photographs of fossils of eggs and embryos and of paleontologists at work as well as line drawings and full-color paintings add to this inviting, thought-provoking book." SLJ

Includes glossary and bibliographical references

Dinosaur tracks; by Kathleen Weidner Zoehfeld; illustrated by Lucia Washburn. HarperCollinsPublishers 2007 33p il (Let's-read-and-find-out science) $15.99; lib bdg $16.89; pa $5.99

Grades: K 1 2 3   **567.9**

1. Fossils 2. Dinosaurs 3. Dinosaur tracks -- Juvenile literature

ISBN 0-06-029024-2; 978-0-06-02904-5; 0-06-029025-0 lib bdg; 978-0-06-029025-2 lib bdg; 0-06-445217-4 pa; 978-0-06-445217-5 pa

LC 2004-06242

Describes how footprints made by the dinosaurs have been preserved and what these impressions tell scientists about the animals which made them.

"The clear text is illustrated with informal, colorful spreads of kids at play on the beach where millions of years earlier dinosaurs may have 'splooshed through gloppy mud . . . [leaving] footprints behind them.'" Booklist

Where did dinosaurs come from? illustrated by Lucia Washburn. HarperCollinsPublishers 2010 40p il (Let's-read-and-find-out science book) **567.9**

1. Fossils 2. Dinosaurs

ISBN 978-0-06-029022-1; 978-0-06-445216-8 pa

LC 2009020543

Presents information about the evolution of the dinosuars, from the earliest four-limbed tetrapos of the Paleozoic age, to the meat-eating eoraptors of early Triassic, to the fully-developed dinosaurs of the Jurassic and Cretaceous periods.

"Zoehfeld is remarkably precise with language, no easy feat when writing on this topic for beginning readers, providing outstanding explanations of key evolution concepts in the finest tradition of the series. The color illustrations include anatomical details, a helpful phylognetic timeline, and imagined portrayals of dinosaurs active in verdant habitats." Horn Book

Includes glossary

DK first dinosaur encyclopedia. DK Pub. 2007 127p il $15.99

Grades: 2 3 4 5   **567.9**

1. Reference books 2. Dinosaurs -- Encyclopedias

ISBN 978-0-7566-2539-9

LC 2006016039

"Solid introductory information and strong visual appeal make this a fine choice for dinosaur fans. Crystal-clear photographs of models and artifacts fill every spread. . . . The text is clear, with enough intriguing facts to fascinate without overwhelming." SLJ

567.909

Kelsey, Elin

Canadian dinosaurs; Elin Kelsey. Reprint Maple Tree Press 2009 96 p. ill. (prebind) $28.95

Grades: 4 5 6   **567.909**

1. Fossils -- Juvenile literature 2. Dinosaurs -- Juvenile literature

ISBN 1442060409; 9781442060401

This book offers a "history of fossil hunting north of the border, including bio-material on dino-hunters past and present, followed by a compendium of carnivores and herbivores. . . . Illustrations, mainly in color, appear on every page. . . . The whole is rounded out with a list of dino locations, a time line, and a listing of institutions where these splendid fossils may be examined at leisure." (School Library Journal)

567.912   Specific dinosaurs

Dixon, Dougal

Meat-eating dinosaurs; by Dougal Dixon. North American ed. New Forest Press 2010 47 p. col. ill., col. maps (Dinosaur files) (library) $28.50

Grades: 4 5 6 7   **567.912**

1. Fossils 2. Dinosaurs 3. Carnivorous animals

ISBN 9781848983342; 1848983344

LC 2010925204

This volume "contains detailed information about dinosaurs and other prehistoric life, covering species development in chronological order. Careful links to the fossil finds that helped scientists with their explanations are found throughout. Additional text boxes cover topics from structure-function to footprints, and interpretive color illustrations and photographs further enhance the [text]." Horn Book Guide

Includes bibliographical references (p. 44-45) and index.

568   Fossil birds

Zoehfeld, Kathleen Weidner

Did dinosaurs have feathers? illustrated by Lucia Washburn. HarperCollins Publishers 2004 33p il (Let's-read-and-find-out science) $15.99; lib bdg $16.89; pa $4.99

Grades: K 1 2 3   **568**

1. Birds 2. Fossils 3. Dinosaurs 4. Archaeopteryx 5. Archaeopteryx -- Juvenile literature

ISBN 0-06-029026-9; 0-06-029027-7 lib bdg; 0-06-029027-7 pa

LC 2002-10585

Discusses the discovery and analysis of Archaeopteryx, a feathered dinosaur which may have been an ancestor of modern birds

"Using short sentences and simple words, Zoehfeld clearly explains what we know about dinosaurs with feathers. . . . Iridescent shades of blue and orange give the theropods and their settings an appealing glow." Horn Book Guide

569   Fossil mammals

Aliki

Wild and woolly mammoths; written and illustrated by Aliki. rev ed; HarperCollins Pubs. 1996 32p il hardcover o.p. pa $6.95

Grades: K 1 2 3   569

1. Mammoths 2. Mammoths -- Juvenile literature 3. Cave dwellers -- Juvenile literature

ISBN 0-06-446179-3 pa

LC 94-48217

A revised and newly illustrated edition of the title first published 1977

An easy-to-read account of the woolly mammoth, a giant land mammal which has been extinct for over 11,000 years

"With concise text and informative art, Aliki illuminates the timeless appeal of these long-gone animals—and drops a gentle warning about the possible fate of tusked decendants." Publ Wkly

Arnold, Caroline

★ **When** mammoths walked the earth; illustrated by Laurie Caple. Clarion Bks. 2002 40p il $16

Grades: 3 4 5 6   569

1. Mammoths

ISBN 0-618-09633-7

LC 2001-47192

Describes the physical characteristics, known habits, and fossil sites of mammoths, prehistoric animals closely related to the elephant

"The information is brief but thorough, with realistic watercolor illustrations depicting the giant animals and their surroundings." Booklist

Bardoe, Cheryl

Mammoths and mastodons; titans of the Ice Age. Abrams Books for Young Readers 2010 43p il map

Grades: 4 5 6 7   569

1. Fossils 2. Mammoths 3. Mastodon

ISBN 0-8109-8413-X lib bdg; 978-0-8109-8413-4 lib bdg

LC 2009-22006

The author presents a "case study in how paleontologists examine both ancient and modern clues for insights into the diets, physical development and behavior of extinct animals. Cousins to modern elephants, mammoths and mastodons once roamed large portions of the Earth, but for reasons that are not completely understood . . . vanished relatively suddenly. Focusing particularly on . . . remnants like the 55 fossilized skeletons found near one sinkhole in South Dakota and 'Lyuba,' the well preserved 'prehistoric popsicle' discovered in 2007 in Siberia, the author presents both facts and educated guesses--while leaving it clear that there is much still to be learned." (Kirkus)

"This well-designed book opens with two boys finding a strange animal dead on the arctic tundra. Their father hikes four days to a village where the news can be spread; then scientists take away the frozen baby mammoth, the first example found intact, and study it intensively. The book intersperses accounts of the scientists' research and deductions with general information about mammoths and mastodons as well as imagined scenes taking place when they walked the earth. . . . A handsome introduction." Booklist

Includes glossary and bibliographical references

Brown, Charlotte Lewis

After the dinosaurs; mammoths and fossil mammals. written by Charlotte Lewis Brown, pictures by Phil Wilson. HarperCollinsPublishers 2006 un il (I can read!) $15.99; lib bdg $16.89

Grades: K 1 2 3   569

1. Fossil mammals

ISBN 978-0-06-053053-2; 0-06-053053-7; 978-0-06-053054-9 lib bdg; 0-06-053054-5 lib bdg

LC 2005028662

"This title examines a variety of ancient mammals. It opens with a brief introduction, followed by a spread devoted to each animal. . . . The pronunciation guide is a welcome feature. The finely detailed watercolor illustrations emphasize the unusual features of each species." SLJ

Lister, Adrian

The **Ice** Age tracker's guide; illustrated by Martin Ursell. Frances Lincoln Children's Books 2010 31p il map $17.95

Grades: 4 5 6 7   569

1. Ice Age 2. Fossil mammals

ISBN 978-1-84507-718-1; 1-84507-718-0

"'Hunters' of Ice Age fauna will find the tawny pages in this 'guide' a trove of pointers for identifying a round dozen of predators and prey. What does a giant ground sloth's poop look like? Just how big is a dwarf elephant? . . . Size, shape, food, fur (if any), locations, and other tidbits are scattered about the watercolor and ink illustrations, and are reinforced by two pages of solid paragraphs of text on each creature. Lister . . . writes with authority in this lighthearted, informational work." SLJ

Manning, Mick

Woolly mammoth; [by] Mick Manning [and] Brita Granström. Frances Lincoln 2009 un il $16.95

Grades: K 1 2 3   569

1. Mammoths 2. Mammoths -- Juvenile literature

ISBN 978-1-84507-860-7; 1-84507-860-8

"Manning and Granström pair rhyming couplets, in this case describing the life of a mammoth, alongside columns of information. Simple pencil drawings fill sidebars with specific details about these huge beasts, including their habitat and natural enemies, their physical characteristics and behavior. . . . Bright watercolor-over-pencil paintings dominate the pages, which feature simple stanzas that deliver the mammoth's side of the story." SLJ

Markle, Sandra

★ **Outside** and inside woolly mammoths. Walker & Co. 2007 40p il $17.95; lib bdg $18.85

Grades: 4 5 6   569

1. Mammoths 2. Mammoths -- Juvenile literature

ISBN 978-0-8027-9589-2; 0-8027-9589-7; 978-0-8027-9590-8 lib bdg; 0-8027-9590-0 lib bdg

LC 2006027621

"Markle explains what scientists have discovered from the preserved remains of mammoths: their food, and the structure of their hair, their soft tissues, and even their DNA. Asking readers leading questions and systematically noting similarities to and differences from modern elephants, she speculates about why mammoths became extinct. . . . Except for the cover picture, the illustrations are all big, sharp color photos and digital tomography images rather than artistic recreations. A closing multimedia resource list that is accurately pitched to the level of her intended audience makes this as valuable for student use as for pleasure reading." Booklist

O'Brien, Patrick
Sabertooth. Henry Holt and Co. 2008 un il $16.95
Grades: 2 3 4 **569**
1. Dinosaurs 2. Saber-toothed tigers
ISBN 978-0-8050-7105-4; 0-8050-7105-9
LC 2007-02792
O'Brien "offers this large-format, fully illustrated volume on prehistoric cats with canine teeth so long, sharp, and curving that they are called sabertooths. After introducing several kinds of sabertooths, O'Brien focuses mainly on the Smilodon genus. . . . O'Brien writes clearly. . . . The book's main strength, though, is its excellent artwork, which portrays dramatic scenes and quiet studies of the animals with equal skill and attention to detail. A visually strong introduction." Booklist

Parker, Steve, 1952-
Ice age giants. QEB Pub. 2011 32p il (Wild age) lib bdg $28.50
Grades: 2 3 4 **569**
1. Fossils 2. Ice Age 3. Fossil mammals
ISBN 978-1-59566-911-7; 1-59566-911-6
LC 2010001152
This describes prehistoric mammals of the ice age, including giant sloths, mammoths, giant deer, giant cats, Neanderthals and modern humans.
"Vivid writing . . . lifts [this] otherwise ordinary [survey] a bit above average. . . . The art combines photos of fossils, distribution maps, illustrations of prehistoric monsters . . . and, on each spread, a human silhouette to indicate scale." SLJ
Includes glossary

Sloan, Christopher
Baby mammoth mummy; frozen in time: a prehistoric animal's journey into the 21st century. National Geographic 2011 il map $17.95; lib bdg 26.90
Grades: 4 5 6 7 **569**
1. Fossils 2. Mammoths
ISBN 978-1-4263-0865-9; 1-4263-0865-5; 978-1-4263-0866-6 lib bdg; 1-4263-0866-3 lib bdg
LC 2010044003
"From CAT scans to the use of surgical cameras, the mummy of a baby mammoth found dislodged from Siberian ice undergoes veritable CSI treatment in the Netherlands, Japan, the U.S., and in her Russian homeland as scientists scramble to discover her historic age (42,000 years), her chronological age (32 days), her diet (mother's milk), and the cause of her demise (suffocation in mud). Sloan's clear, readable text follows this journey in nicely defined stages, with explanations along the way for possibly unfamiliar processes. Plentiful photos, a pair of maps, some diagrams, and colorful artwork accompany the information." SLJ
Includes glossary and bibliographical references

Turner, Alan
★ National Geographic prehistoric mammals; illustrated by Mauricio Antón. National Geographic 2004 192p il map $29.95; lib bdg $49.90

Grades: 5 6 7 8 **569**
1. Fossil mammals 2. Mammals, Fossil
ISBN 0-7922-7134-3; 0-7922-6997-7 lib bdg
LC 2004-1189
This describes the Age of Mammals and profiles over 100 prehistoric mammals, including time lines, fact boxes, distribution maps, photos of fossils, and illustrations
"Dramatic full-color pictures . . . and captions enhance the brief, informative text." SLJ

Wheeler, Lisa
Mammoths on the move. Harcourt, Inc. 2006 un il $16
Grades: K 1 2 **569**
1. Mammoths
ISBN 0-15-204700-X
LC 2004-19112
"The text describes a group of female mammoths and their young traveling south for the winter, reaching their destination only to turn around and begin their long trek back. Wheeler uses wordplay skillfully, her verse shows originality. . . . The beautifully composed scratchboard illustrations offer strong line work, subtle use of color, and a fine sense of what migrating mammoths may have looked like." Booklist

569.9 Humans and related genera

Aronson, Marc
★ The skull in the rock; how a scientist, a boy, and Google Earth opened a new window on human origins. by Marc Aronson and Lee Berger. National Geographic 2012 64 p. (hardcover: alk. paper) $18.95
Grades: 5 6 7 8 9 10 **569.9**
1. Human origins -- Juvenile literature 2. Fossil hominids -- Juvenile literature 3. Paleoanthropology -- Juvenile literature 4. Excavations (Archeology) -- Juvenile literature 5. Paleoanthropology 6. Fossil hominids -- South Africa -- Witwatersrand Region 7. Human evolution -- South Africa -- Witwatersrand Region 8. Excavations (Archaeology) -- South Africa -- Witwatersrand Region
ISBN 1426310102; 9781426310102; 9781426310539
LC 2012012943
This book by Marc Aronson and Lee R. Berger tells the story of how "in 2008 [Berger]--with the help of his curious 9-year-old son--discovered two remarkably well preserved, two-million-year-old fossils . . . known as 'Australopithecus sediba'; a previously unknown species of ape-like creatures that may have been a direct ancestor of modern humans." (Publisher's note)
Includes bibliographical references and index.

570 Biology

★ Biology matters! Grolier 2004 10v il set $389
Grades: 5 6 7 8 9 10 **570**
1. Biology 2. Reference books
ISBN 0-7172-5979-X
LC 2003-56942
"This set presents the fundamentals of the life sciences in a clear format. . . . Volumes contain between six and eight

articles in 80 pages ... introducing its subject, presenting a brief history, and covering many aspects of its current study and applications. . . . The text is large and easy to read, and the writing is straightforward. . . . This title . . . would be a useful addition for public and school libraries." Booklist

Green, Dan

Extreme biology; from superbugs to clones... get to the edge of science. written and illustrated by Simon Basher. Kingfisher 2013 64 p. col. ill. (hardcover) $12.99

Grades: 4 5 6 7   **570**

1. Biology -- Juvenile literature
ISBN 0753470519; 9780753470510

This book written and illustrated by Simon Basher is designed to help readers "learn about the amazing research that is revolutionizing biology, from advances in medicine to genetic engineering. [Readers will] meet the world's toughest bacterium and a biologically immortal flatworm whilst learning about epigenetics, superbugs, nanomedicine and cloning. 'Extreme Biology' is a compelling guide to developments at the very forefront of science." (Publisher's note)

Kalman, Bobbie

What is symmetry in nature? Crabtree Pub. Co. 2010 24p il (Looking at nature) lib bdg $21.27; pa $6.95

Grades: K 1 2   **570**

1. Nature 2. Symmetry
ISBN 978-0-7787-3327-0 lib bdg; 0-7787-3327-0 lib bdg; 978-0-7787-3347-8 pa; 0-7787-3347-5 pa

LC 2010016400

Reveals examples of symmetry found in nature.

"Bright, colorful photographs were selected with young readers in mind, and the type is large—perfect for reading together. . . Throughout the book are questions that challenge the reader to identify the opposites shown on the pages. . . . Parents and teachers will find . . . [this book] a great addition to a child's library." Sci Books & Films

Includes glossary

Marshall Cavendish Corporation

Exploring life science. Marshall Cavendish 2000 11v set $329.95

Grades: 4 5 6   **570**

1. Reference books 2. Life sciences -- Encyclopedias
ISBN 0-7614-7135-9

LC 98-52925

Based on the high school level Encyclopedia of life sciences (1966)

"Arranged into a single alphabet, these more than 300 specific, easily digestible articles cover living things, the environment, and the life sciences themselves. Entries are enhanced by numerous crisply detailed photos, full-color drawings, and boxed closer looks at special issues or topics." SLJ

McManus, Lori

Cell systems. Heinemann Library 2011 48p il (Investigating cells) lib bdg $32

Grades: 5 6 7 8   **570**

1. Cells 2. Life (Biology)
ISBN 978-1-4329-3879-6; 1-4329-3879-7

LC 2009049974

This book looks at cell systems, including the cell, tissues, organ, and organ system hierarchy.

"The abundant graphic matter—photographs, diagrams, charts and graphs—work together with the text to create visually appealing pages. . . . [This] would be very useful in any kind of formal investigation of the topic and yet attractive enough to encourage browsing. . . . [This] . . . is exceptionally well done." Libr Media Connect

Includes glossary and bibliographical references

VanCleave, Janice Pratt, 1942-

Janice VanCleave's play and find out about nature; easy experiments for young children. Wiley 1997 122p il $29.95; pa $12.95

Grades: K 1 2   **570**

1. Nature 2. Biology 3. Science -- Experiments 4. Nature study -- Juvenile literature 5. Natural history -- Juvenile literature
ISBN 0-471-12939-9; 0-471-12940-2 pa

LC 96-2865

Provides instructions for fifty nature experiments and activities involving both plants and animals

"VanCleave's explanations are straightforward and concise. The book has a clear and uncluttered look." SLJ

Includes glossary

Step-by-step science experiments in biology; by Janice VanCleave. Rosen 2013 80 p. col. ill. (Janice Vancleave's first-place science fair projects) (library) $33.25; (paperback) $14.15

Grades: 5 6 7 8   **570**

1. Biology -- Juvenile literature 2. Science -- Experiments -- Juvenile literature
ISBN 144886982X; 9781448869824; 9781448884636

LC 2012007943

This book by Janice VanCleave presents 22 science experiments in biology for children. "Van Cleave states the basic goal of the experiments, followed by a list of necessary materials. . . . Step-by-step instructions are . . . accompanied by diagrams where needed. The results section states exactly what is expected to happen and the 'Why?' section explains in accessible terms why those specific results were achieved." (School Library Journal)

Includes bibliographical references and index.

Winston, Robert

Life as we know it; Robert Winston. 1st American ed. DK Publishing 2012 96 p. col. ill. (hardcover) $16.99

Grades: 4 5 6   **570**

1. Ecology 2. Zoology 3. Food chains (Ecology) 4. Life (Biology) -- Juvenile literature
ISBN 0756691699; 9780756691691

LC 2011277462

Author Robert Winston "begins with Earth's formation billions of years ago and continues to the present day, exploring cells, the animal kingdom, ecosystems, food chains, and creatures that tolerate extreme conditions (including bacteria that thrive in volcanic pools and coffinfish that live under high pressure on the sea floor). The book's . . . design incorporates numerous photographs, sidebars, . . . digital art, and light humor, usually in the form of speech-bubble captions for the animals." (Publishers Weekly)

570.78   Biology--student experiments

Latham, Donna

★ **Backyard** Biology; Investigate Habitats Outside Your Door With 25 Projects. by Donna Latham; illustrated by Beth Hetland. Nomad Press 2013 128 p. ill. (paperback) $15.95

Grades: 4 5 6 7   570.78

1. Biology

ISBN 1619301512; 9781619301511

This book, part of the Built It Yourself series, "incorporates 25 projects for kids to try as they explore the 'ecosystems that are outside your door.' The book's eight chapters cover biology (and microbiology), cells, and the life cycles of both plants and animals, among other topics; definitions of key terms appear throughout, as do [illustrator Beth] Hetland's cartoons and diagrams." (Publishers Weekly)

571   Internal biological processes and structures

Green, Jen

Inside animals. Marshall Cavendish Benchmark 2010 48p il (Invisible worlds) $28.50

Grades: 4 5 6 7   571

1. Cells 2. Anatomy 3. Physiology 4. Microorganisms

ISBN 978-0-7614-4195-3; 0-7614-4195-6

LC 2008037241

This describes the animal details that are too small for the unaided eye to see, and how these microscopic systems work to keep the animal alive and healthy.

The narrative is "clear, well written, broken down into manageable pieces, and peppered with eye-opening facts. The numerous photographs are so phenomenal that they will inspire kids to read the text . . . so that they can wrap their minds around what they see." SLJ

Includes glossary and bibliographical references

571.1   Animals

Singer, Marilyn

A **strange** place to call home; the world's most dangerous habitats & the animals that call them home. Marilyn Singer & Ed Young. Chronicle Books 2012 44 p. ill.

Grades: 3 4 5   571.1

1. Habitat (Ecology) 2. Exotic animals -- Juvenile literature 3. Animals -- Habitations -- Juvenile literature

ISBN 1452101205; 9781452101200

LC 2011046379

This book, describes how "[u]nder the desert's cracked and barren skin, spadefoot toads are waiting for rain. In the endless black of the deepest caves, blind fish find their way. Even in the frozen hearts of glaciers, ice worms by the billion flourish. In this . . . look at fourteen animals who defy the odds by thriving in Earth's most dangerous places, . . . poet Marilyn Singer and . . . artist Ed Young show that of all the miracles of life, it is life's persistence that astounds the most." (Publisher's note)

571.4   Biophysics

Chisholm, Sallie W., 1947-

★ **Ocean** sunlight; how tiny plants feed the seas. by Molly Bang and Penny Chisholm; illustrated by Molly Bang. Blue Sky Press 2012 48 p. (hardcover: alk. paper) $18.99

Grades: K 1 2 3 4   571.4

1. Oceanography 2. Marine biology 3. Photosynthesis 4. Sunshine -- Juvenile literature 5. Photobiology -- Juvenile literature 6. Plants -- Effect of light on -- Juvenile literature 7. Marine life -- Effect of light on -- Juvenile literature

ISBN 0545273226; 9780545273220

LC 2011024823

AAAS/Subaru SB&F Prize for Excellence in Science Books: Children's Science Picture Book (2013)

In this book, the authors "turn their attention to the ocean and its vast population of phytoplankton. . . . The . . . text follows the food chain from the tiniest of green plants (powered into life by the sun) to the biggest predators dependent on plankton-gobblers for food. The authors explain photosynthesis and the ocean layer exchange wrought by sunlight-driven currents, and even touch on the life below, where the strongest sunbeam cannot reach." (School Library Journal)

Winner, Cherie

Cryobiology. Lerner Publications Co. 2006 48p il (Cool science) lib bdg $26.60

Grades: 4 5 6   571.4

1. Cryobiology

ISBN 978-0-8225-2907-1 lib bdg; 0-8225-2907-6 lib bdg

LC 2005006158

This book "discusses how different life forms survive low temperatures, e.g., hibernating animals. . . . [The book provides] clear explanations of the science and [covers] possible benefits to humans. A variety of photos and information boxes provide an eye-catching . . . layout." Horn Book Guide

Includes glossary and bibliographical references

571.6   Cell biology

Cohen, Marina

What is cell theory? Crabtree Pub. Co. 2011 64p il (Shaping modern science) lib bdg $30.60; pa $10.95

Grades: 5 6 7 8   571.6

1. Cells

ISBN 978-0-7787-7199-9 lib bdg; 0-7787-7199-9 lib bdg; 978-0-7787-7206-4 pa; 0-7787-7206-3 pa

LC 2010052633

This title is "not only written and organized well, but [it is] also gorgeous in design. Full-color photographs and illustrations are set over colorful backgrounds that add depth but not distraction. [The title] includes thought-provoking quotes from famous authors and scientists and some eyebrow-raising 'Quick Facts' throughout." SLJ

Includes glossary and bibliographical references

Johnson, Rebecca L.

Mighty animal cells; [by] Rebecca L. Johnson; illustrations by Jack Desrocher; diagrams by Jennifer E. Fairman. Millbrook Press 2007 48p il (Microquests) lib bdg $29.27

Grades: 4 5 6 **571.6**

1. Cells

ISBN 978-0-8225-7137-7 lib bdg; 0-8225-7137-4 lib bdg

LC 2006-36394

In this introduction to animal cells, "Johnson builds one scientific concept at a time using authentic terminology and connecting new information to familiar things. . . . Full-color microscope images, drawings, and cartoons appear in a clean, uncluttered format, combining solid science with humor." Horn Book Guide

Includes glossary and bibliographical references

Lee, Kimberly Fekany

Cells. Compass Point Books 2009 40p il (Mission: science) lib bdg $26.60

Grades: 4 5 6 **571.6**

1. Cells

ISBN 978-0-7565-3954-2 lib bdg; 0-7565-3954-4 lib bdg

LC 2008007719

"Lee describes the difference between plant and animal cells, and their contents; diffusion; and cell storage, movement, and reproduction. . . . Large eye-catching and colorful photographs and illustrations appear on every page. . . . The [book] includes a simple activity." SLJ

Includes glossary and bibliographical references

571.8 Reproduction, development, growth

Mitchell, Susan K.

Animal body-part regenerators; growing new heads, tails, and legs. by Susan K. Mitchell. Enslow Publishers 2009 48p il (Amazing animal defenses) lib bdg $23.93

Grades: 4 5 6 **571.8**

1. Regeneration (Biology)

ISBN 978-0-7660-3295-8 lib bdg; 0-7660-3295-7 lib bdg

LC 2008-11453

"The closeup photos are frequent and well chosen, and accompanied by clear, simply phrased [text], which [is] more detailed than average and [takes] up most or all of the space on each page." SLJ

Includes glossary and bibliographical references

Royston, Angela

Looking at life cycles; how do plants and animals change? [by] Angela Royston. Enslow Publishers 2008 32p il (Looking at science: how things change) lib bdg $22.60

Grades: 1 2 3 **571.8**

1. Life cycles (Biology)

ISBN 978-0-7660-3091-6 lib bdg; 0-7660-3091-1 lib bdg

LC 2007-24513

"Fills a huge void in elementary science collections. . . . Text is arranged in succinct 'chunks,' giving important facts

without overwhelming readers. . . . [This] is an essential addition." Libr Media Connect

Includes glossary and bibliographical references

Silverstein, Virginia B.

★ **Growth** and development; by Alvin Silverstein, Virginia Silverstein, and Laura Silverstein Nunn. Twenty-First Century Books 2008 112p il (Science concepts) lib bdg $31.93

Grades: 4 5 6 7 **571.8**

1. Growth 2. Biology

ISBN 978-0-8225-6057-9 lib bdg; 0-8225-6057-7 lib bdg

LC 2006030299

This "considers the growth process, animals with and without skeletons, human and plant growth, and future trends as a result of medical technology. Clear organization, engaging anecdotes, and generally good photos and diagrams are strengths of the [volume]." Horn Book Guide

Includes glossary and bibliographical references

Wade, Mary Dodson

Plants grow! Enslow Elementary 2009 24p il (I like plants!) lib bdg $21.26; pa $6.95

Grades: K 1 2 **571.8**

1. Growth 2. Plants

ISBN 978-0-7660-3152-4 lib bdg; 0-7660-3152-7 lib bdg; 978-0-7660-3612-3 pa; 0-7660-3612-X pa

LC 2007039453

"The life cycle and parts of a plant are discussed in a clear, concise manner. Beautifully detailed professional photographs of plants, animals, and people complement the subject matter. [The] book includes a simple activity." SLJ

Includes glossary and bibliographical references

571.9 Diseases

Somervill, Barbara A.

Cells and disease. Heinemann Library 2011 48p il (Investigating cells) lib bdg $32

Grades: 5 6 7 8 **571.9**

1. Cells 2. Bacteria 3. Diseases

ISBN 978-1-4329-3881-9; 1-4329-3881-9

LC 2009-49981

This book describes cells and diseases.

"The abundant graphic matter—photographs, diagrams, charts and graphs—work together with the text to create visually appealing pages. . . . [This] would be very useful in any kind of formal investigation of the topic and yet attractive enough to encourage browsing. . . . [This] . . . is exceptionally well done." Libr Media Connect

Includes glossary and bibliographical references

Stewart, Melissa

Germ wars! the secrets of keeping healthy. illustrated by Janet Hamlin. Marshall Cavendish Benchmark 2010 48p il (The gross and goofy body) $29.95

Grades: 2 3 4 **571.9**

1. Bacteria 2. Immune system

ISBN 978-0-7614-4165-6; 0-7614-4165-4

LC 2008033562

This offers information on the role the immune system plays in the body science of humans and animals.

572 Biochemistry

Bang, Molly
★ **Living** sunlight; how plants bring the Earth to life. by Molly Bang & Penny Chisholm; illustrated by Molly Bang. Blue Sky Press 2009 un il $16.99
Grades: PreK K 1 2 3   **572**
1. Photosynthesis 2. Sunshine -- Juvenile literature
ISBN 978-0-545-04422-6; 0-545-04422-7
LC 2008-14238
This book "talks to young children about photosynthesis . . . in a way that tells what is actually happening on a molecular level. It also tells children why this process matters and leads them into a broad understanding of their personal connection with plant life and energy from the sun. . . . The amiable, well-informed narrator is the sun. Alight with unusual intensity, the artwork fills the pages with vibrant images. . . . Each double-page spread illustrates its lines of text with intelligence and originality." Booklist
Includes bibliographical references

Collard, Sneed B.
In the deep sea; by Sneed B. Collard III. Marshall Cavendish Benchmark 2005 43p il (Science adventures) lib bdg $29.93
Grades: 4 5 6   **572**
1. Ocean bottom 2. Bioluminescence 3. College teachers 4. Marine biologists
ISBN 0-7614-1952-7
LC 2004026489
"Describes the work of Dr. Edith Widder and other biologists in the field of bioluminescence research." Publisher's note
Includes glossary and bibliographical references

Lunis, Natalie
Glow-in-the-dark animals. Bearport Pub. 2011 24p il (Animals with super powers) lib bdg $22.61
Grades: 3 4 5   **572**
1. Bioluminescence
ISBN 978-1-61772-119-9; 1-61772-119-0
LC 2010038281
This describes animals which glow in the dark including fireflies, glowworms, fireworms, deep-sea jellyfish, anglerfish, cucujos, and dinoflagellates.
"Large color photos of animals in natural settings and clear, cogent presentations of information combine to boost this [book] well above the average for both assignments and casual browsing." SLJ
Includes glossary and bibliographical references

Sitarski, Anita
★ **Cold** light; creatures, discoveries, and inventions that glow. Boyds Mills Press 2007 48p il $16.95
Grades: 5 6 7 8   **572**
1. Light 2. Chemists 3. Physicists 4. Bioluminescence 5. Nonfiction writers 6. Writers on science 7. Luminescence -- Juvenile literature
ISBN 1-59078-468-5; 978-1-59078-468-6

"A clearly written, chatty text not only discusses the expected bioluminescent critters (think fireflies), but delves into the realms of chemiluminescence, photoluminescence, and LEDs (light-emitting diodes) as well. . . . The text lays out the historical hows and whys of cold light, its success in the natural world, and its application in medicine and domestic/industrial illumination. Clear color photos and information boxes abound." SLJ

572.8 Biochemical genetics

Johnson, Rebecca L.
Amazing DNA; [by] Rebecca L. Johnson; illustrations by Jack Desrocher; diagrams by Jennifer E. Fairman. Millbrook Press 2008 48p il (Microquests) lib bdg $29.27
Grades: 4 5 6   **572.8**
1. DNA 2. Genetics
ISBN 978-0-8225-7139-1 lib bdg; 0-8225-7139-0 lib bdg
LC 2006-102324
This describes DNA structure, cell replication and genetic transmission.
"Johnson builds one scientific concept at a time using authentic terminology and connecting new information to familiar things. . . . Full-color microscope images, drawings, and cartoons appear in a clean, uncluttered format, combining solid science with humor." Horn Book Guide
Includes glossary and bibliographical references

Rand, Casey
DNA and heredity. Heinemann Library 2011 48p il (Investigating cells) lib bdg $32
Grades: 5 6 7 8   **572.8**
1. DNA 2. Cells 3. Heredity
ISBN 978-1-4329-3880-2; 1-4329-3880-0
LC 2009049978
Learn about cells, DNA and scientists who made an impact in cell research.
"The abundant graphic matter—photographs, diagrams, charts and graphs—work together with the text to create visually appealing pages. . . . [This] would be very useful in any kind of formal investigation of the topic and yet attractive enough to encourage browsing. . . . [This] . . . is exceptionally well done." Libr Media Connect
Includes glossary and bibliographical references

573.3 Digestive system

Collard, Sneed B.
Beaks! illustrated by Robin Brickman. Charlesbridge Pub. 2002 un il hardcover o.p. pa $6.95
Grades: K 1 2 3   **573.3**
1. Birds 2. Bill (Anatomy) -- Juvenile literature
ISBN 1-57091-387-0; 1-57091-388-9 pa
LC 2001-4362
Simple text describes various bird beaks and how birds use them to eat, hunt, and gather food. Includes a quiz
"The intricate characteristics of a variety of birds' beaks are presented skillfully through words and vividly painted,

cut-and-sculpted-paper illustrations. . . . The clear text is easy to follow." SLJ

Includes bibliographical references

Deem, James M.
★ **Bodies** from the bog. Houghton Mifflin 1998 42p il hardcover o.p. pa $5.95
Grades: 4 5 6 7   **573.3**
1. Mummies 2. Archeology 3. Prehistoric peoples 4. Bog bodies -- Europe -- Juvenile literature 5. Europe -- Antiquities -- Juvenile literature 6. Prehistoric peoples -- Europe -- Juvenile literature 7. Human remains (Archaeology) -- Europe -- Juvenile literature
ISBN 0-395-85784-8; 0-618-35402-6 pa
LC 97-12010
Describes the discovery of bog bodies in northern Europe and the evidence which their remains reveal about themselves and the civilizations in which they lived

"The text is engaging and accessible, and the starkly dramatic photos are given dignity by the spacious and understated page design." Horn Book Guide

Includes bibliographical references

573.4 Endocrine and excretory systems

Goodman, Susan
★ The **truth** about poop; by Susan E. Goodman; illustrated by Elwood H. Smith. Viking 2004 40p il $15.99
Grades: 2 3 4 5   **573.4**
1. Feces 2. Animal behavior
ISBN 0-670-03674-9
LC 2003-22547
This book is "very readable, appropriately visual, and exceedingly encompassing. . . . The well-executed cartoon artwork successfully goes for the clever" Booklist

573.8 Nervous and sensory systems

Jenkins, Steve
★ **What** do you do with a tail like this? [by] Steve Jenkins & Robin Page. Houghton Mifflin 2003 un il $15
Grades: K 1 2 3   **573.8**
1. Senses and sensation 2. Questions and answers 3. Animals -- Physiology 4. Animals -- Miscellanea
ISBN 0-618-25628-8
LC 2002-11673
A Caldecott Medal honor book, 2004

"Jenkins' handsome paper-cut collages are both lovely and anatomically informative. . . . This is a striking, thoughtfully created book with intriguing facts made more memorable through dynamic art." Booklist

573.9 Miscellaneous systems and organs in animals, regional histology and physiology in animals

Souza, D. M.
Look what feet can do; by D. M. Souza. Lerner Publications Co. 2007 48p il (Look what animals can do) lib bdg $25.26

Grades: 2 3 4   **573.9**
1. Foot 2. Animals
ISBN 978-0-7613-9460-0 lib bdg; 0-7613-9460-5 lib bdg
Simple text and color photographs describe the many ways that animals use their feet

"The clean, uncluttered format, excellent color photos, and very readable type make this an attractive choice for independent reading or sharing with classroom groups." Booklist

Includes glossary and bibliographical references

Look what mouths can do; by D. M. Souza. Lerner Publications Co. 2007 48p il (Look what animals can do) lib bdg $25.26
Grades: 2 3 4   **573.9**
1. Mouth 2. Animals
ISBN 978-0-7613-9462-4 lib bdg; 0-7613-9462-1 lib bdg
LC 2005032481
This describes the many ways that animals use their mouths

This has "fun facts and sharp, clear photos. . . . Those interested in animals will be fascinated by the information provided here." SLJ

Includes bibliographical references

Look what tails can do; by D. M. Souza. Lerner Publications Co. 2007 48p il (Look what animals can do) lib bdg $25.26
Grades: 2 3 4   **573.9**
1. Tails 2. Animals
ISBN 978-0-7613-9458-7 lib bdg; 0-7613-9458-3 lib bdg
LC 2005032480
This describes the many ways in which animals use their tails

This has "fun facts and sharp, clear photos. . . . Those interested in animals will be fascinated by the information provided here." SLJ

Includes bibliographical references

574.5

Cobb, Vicki, 1938-
This place is wet; by Vicki Cobb; illustrated by Barbara Lavallee. Walker 1989 32 p. col. ill. (Imagine living here) (hardcover) $12.95; (library) $13.85; (paperback) $8.99
Grades: 1 2 3   **574.5**
1. Brazil -- Description and travel 2. Rain forests -- Juvenile literature
ISBN 9780802768803; 0802734006; 0802768814; 9780802734006
LC 89032445
This book by Vicki Cobb is part of the "Imagine Living Here geography series" which "introduc[es] the land, climate, plants, animals,and people of various places. . . . This volume transports readers to the Amazon rain forest around Manaus, Brazil. The book, in addition to the aforementioned subjects, discusses rain forest destruction, mining, pollution, and global warming." (Booklist)

575 Specific parts of and physiological systems in plants

Farndon, John

Leaves. Blackbirch Press 2006 24p il (World of plants) lib bdg $24.90

Grades: 2 3 4 5   **575**

1. Leaves

ISBN 978-1-4103-0422-3 lib bdg; 1-4103-0422-1 lib bdg

LC 2005047048

This book examines leaf shapes, the process of photosynthesis, the turning of leaves in the fall season, and unusual leaves that can trap insects

This uses "clear language and short sentences. . . . Helpful diagrams and sharp, colorful photographs supplement the [text]. . . . [This book offers] solid information in an attractive format." SLJ

Includes bibliographical references

Hicks, Terry Allan

Why do leaves change color? Marshall Cavendish Benchmark 2011 32p il (Tell me why, tell me how) lib bdg $29.93

Grades: 2 3 4 5   **575**

1. Leaves

ISBN 978-0-7614-4827-3; 0-7614-4827-6

This offers information about why leaves change color.

This title has "clear explanations of natural phenomena, beautiful full-color illustrations, and an uncluttered design. [The] book approaches its topic in a methodical, logical fashion, using examples from a child's world." SLJ

Includes glossary

575.9 Animal-like physiological processes

Lawrence, Ellen

Meat-eating plants; toothless wonders. by Ellen Lawrence. Bearport Pub. 2013 24 p. (library binding) $23.93

Grades: 1 2 3   **575.9**

1. Carnivorous plants

ISBN 1617725897; 9781617725890

LC 2012014335

This juvenile reference book, by Ellen Lawrence, "explores the world of carnivorous plants that obtain nutrients by 'eating' animals. From plants that act like sticky flypaper to trap their prey, to other plants that lure their victims into deep pitchers of liquid from which the animals will never escape, children will learn about a variety of plants that employ interesting techniques to capture food." (Publisher's note)

Includes bibliographical references and index

576.5 Genetics

Duke, Shirley Smith

You can't wear these genes. Rourke Pub. LLC 2010 48p il (Let's explore science) $32.79

Grades: 4 5 6 7   **576.5**

1. Genetics

ISBN 978-1-61590-324-5; 1-61590-324-0

LC 2010009911

This "offers a clear introduction to the complexities of genetics while inviting students to think about how their own DNA shaped who they are. In [this] title, well chosen boxed examples, abundant color photos, diagrams, and an appended glossary add interest and support the engaging [text]." Booklist

Includes glossary and bibliographical references

Gallant, Roy A.

The **treasure** of inheritance. Benchmark Bks. 2003 78p il (Story of science) lib bdg $19.95

Grades: 5 6 7 8   **576.5**

1. Genetics 2. Heredity

ISBN 0-7614-1426-6

LC 2002-10

Discusses how living things inherit traits, chronicles the history of the study of heredity, and examines current research on genetic engineering and mapping the human gene

"Readers will find accurate, readable explanations for the scientific principles here addressed. . . . Up-to-date controversies and predictions conclude the [book] . . . illustrated with well-captioned photos." Horn Book Guide

Includes glossary and bibliographical references

Simpson, Kathleen

★ **Genetics**; from DNA to designer dogs. Sarah Tishkoff, consultant. National Geographic 2008 64p il map (National Geographic investigates) $27.90

Grades: 4 5 6 7   **576.5**

1. Genetics

ISBN 978-1-4263-0361-6; 1-4263-0361-0; 978-1-4263-0327-2 lib bdg; 1-4263-0327-0 lib bdg

This discusses topics in genetics such as the identification of an Egyptian mummy by DNA testing, the genetics of pea plants studied by Gregor Mendel, cloning, the Human Genome Project, and stem cell research.

"The content is fairly exciting and should grab the attention of its target audience. . . . The photographs throughout are of high quality. . . . An engaging look at a complex topic." Booklist

Walker, Richard, 1951-

★ **Genes** & DNA; foreword by Steve Jones. Kingfisher 2003 63p il (Kingfisher knowledge) $11.95

Grades: 5 6 7 8   **576.5**

1. Genetics

ISBN 0-7534-5621-4

LC 2004-269108

This briefly discusses such topics as the role of genes in inheritance, the structure of the DNA molecule, mutations, The Human Genome Project, and genetic technology such as DNA fingerprinting, gene therapy, genetic engineering, and cloning

Includes glossary and bibliographical references

576.8 Evolution

Berkowitz, Jacob

Out of this world; the amazing search for an alien earth. Kids Can Press 2009 48p il $16.95; pa $8.95

Grades: 4 5 6 7   **576.8**

1. Life on other planets 2. Outer space -- Exploration

-- Juvenile literature
ISBN 978-1-55453-197-4; 1-55453-197-7; 978-1-55453-198-1 pa; 1-55453-198-5 pa

The author "has written a miniencyclopedic, profusely illustrated, picture book that describes, in much detail, what we all know about the universe in which we live and about the conditions that must be present on any planet in our solar system, or on an exoplanet . . . for life as we know it to exist." Sci Books Films

Bortz, Alfred B.
Astrobiology. Lerner Publications 2008 48p il map (Cool science) lib bdg $26.60
Grades: 4 5 6   **576.8**
1. Space biology 2. Life on other planets
ISBN 978-0-8225-6771-4 lib bdg; 0-8225-6771-7 lib bdg
     LC 2006033268

This describes "the search for life in the universe. Astrobiologists compare life on Earth to signs of life on other planets. They test meteorites for evidence of alien bacteria. They collect soil and atmospheric samples from other planets. They study photographs taken on space missions. And they listen for signals from alien civilizations on enormous radio dishes." Publisher's note
Includes bibliographical references

Brake, Mark
Alien Hunter's Handbook; How to Look for Extra-terrestrial Life. by Mark Brake; illustrated by Colin Jack and Geriant Ford. Kingfisher 2012 111 p. (paperback) $10.99
Grades: 4 5 6 7   **576.8**
1. Extraterrestrial beings -- Juvenile literature
ISBN 0753468859; 9780753468852

This book on extra-terrestrial life by Mark Brake "opens with an overview of the defining characteristics of life and some of Earth's remarkable creatures, such as the microscopic tardigrade, which can exist in the vacuum of space. Topics like the development of solar systems, the speed of evolution, and the formation of language also get attention, laying factual groundwork for suppositions about what alien life could look like." (Publishers Weekly)

Branley, Franklyn Mansfield
Is there life in outer space? illustrated by Edward Miller. HarperCollins Pubs. 1999 31p il (Let's-read-and-find-out science) hardcover o.p. pa $4.95
Grades: K 1 2 3   **576.8**
1. Life on other planets
ISBN 0-06-028146-4; 0-06-028145-6 lib bdg; 0-06-445192-5 pa
     LC 99-10904

A newly illustrated edition of the title first published 1984 by Crowell

Discusses some of the ideas and misconceptions about life in outer space and speculates on the existence of such life in light of recent space explorations

"Children curious about the possibility of life on distant planets will find much to think about in this speculative yet scientifically accurate text. The new illustrations, which incorporate photographs of planets, are bright and colorful." Horn Book Guide

Gamlin, Linda
Evolution; written by Linda Gamlin. rev ed.; DK Pub. 2009 72p il (DK eyewitness books) $16.99
Grades: 4 5 6 7   **576.8**
1. Evolution
ISBN 978-0-7566-5028-5; 0-7566-5028-3
First published 1993

Text about and photography of experiments, animals, plants, bones, and fossils reveal the ideas and discoveries that have changed our understanding of the natural world and how life began. Includes a CD and wall chart.

Hartman, Eve
Changing life on Earth; [by] Eve Hartman and Wendy Meshbesher. Raintree 2009 48p il (Sci-hi: life science) lib bdg $31.43; pa $8.99
Grades: 5 6 7 8   **576.8**
1. Evolution
ISBN 978-1-4109-3324-9 lib bdg; 1-4109-3324-5 lib bdg; 978-1-4109-3332-4 pa; 1-4109-3332-6 pa
     LC 2009003459

In this introduction to evolution "clear language, embedded definitions, and interesting examples illustrate abstract concepts through both text and well-chosen photographs. . . . [The book] provides a clear and useful explanation of the theory of evolution, with multiple sources of evidence and a discussion of how it helps scientists to predict the implications of changes to the environment. . . . [The] book also includes suggested activities to test ideas as well as a thorough glossary and a Webliography." SLJ
Includes glossary and bibliographical references

Jenkins, Steve
★ **Life** on earth: the story of evolution. Houghton Mifflin 2002 un il $16
Grades: 3 4 5 6   **576.8**
1. Evolution
ISBN 0-618-16476-6
     LC 2002-472

Provides an overview of the origin and evolution of life on earth and of what has been learned from the study of evolution

"Jenkins presents a superb introduction to evolution. . . . His signature cut-paper illustrations placed on white backgrounds work well. . . . Jenkins's explanations of science concepts are comprehensive and comprehensible. . . . Particularly admirable is his avoidance of any oversimplifications." Horn Book
Includes bibliographical references

Mehling, Randi
Great extinctions of the past; by Randi Mehling. Chelsea House 2007 72p il (Scientific American) lib bdg $30
Grades: 5 6 7 8   **576.8**
1. Dinosaurs 2. Prehistoric animals 3. Mass extinction of species
ISBN 978-0-7910-9049-7 lib bdg; 0-7910-9049-3 lib bdg
     LC 2006014851

Examines extinctions of prehistoric species including the dinosaurs, looks at the five largest extinctions ever, and explores the idea of a future mass extinction.

"The ideas in this book are . . . clearly explained. . . . [The book has] captioned color photos thoughout." SLJ

Includes glossary and bibliographical references

Newland, Sonya

Extinction! by Jim Pipe. Crabtree Publishing Company 2013 48 p. col. ill. (Crabtree chrome) (library) $30.60; (paperback) $9.95

Grades: 4 5 6   **576.8**

1. Extinct animals -- Juvenile literature 2. End of the world -- Juvenile literature 3. Mass extinction of species -- Juvenile literature

ISBN 0778779254; 9780778779254; 9780778779346

LC 2012032046

This book by Sonya Newland "explores both the history of extinction--dating back to the mass extinction of the Ordovician period 450 million years ago and the extinction of the dinosaurs 65 million years ago--as well as the possibility of the extinction of species in existence today. . . . In addition . . . Newland considers possible scenarios that might end life on Earth: an asteroid colliding with our planet . . . or an exploding nuclear bomb that blocks out the sun." (School Library Journal)

Includes bibliographical references and index

Pringle, Laurence P.

★ Billions of years, amazing changes; the story of evolution. Boyds Mills Press 2011 102p il $17.95

Grades: 4 5 6 7   **576.8**

1. Evolution

ISBN 978-1-59078-723-6; 1-59078-723-4

"Pringle provides an accessible introduction to complex concepts such as natural selection and genetics, paired with Jenkins's characteristically elegant collages. . . . Compelling photographs of fossils and living creatures, as well as Jenkins's paper collages, augment the substantial text. The presentation should help children gain a confident grasp on the fundamentals of evolution." Publ Wkly

Scott, Elaine

★ Mars and the search for life. Clarion Books 2008 60p il $17

Grades: 4 5 6 7   **576.8**

1. Life on other planets

ISBN 978-0-618-76695-6; 0-618-76695-2

LC 2008-07243

The author discusses "the Mars Exploration Rover (MER) and tantalizing findings that suggest that conditions on the red planet may once have been hospitable to life. . . . Illustrations are arresting and clearly captioned." Bull Cent Child Books

Includes glossary and bibliographical references

Skurzynski, Gloria

★ Are we alone? scientists search for life in space. National Geographic Society 2004 92p il $18.95

Grades: 5 6 7 8   **576.8**

1. Life on other planets

ISBN 0-7922-6567-X

LC 2003-17732

The author begins with a "history of how the idea of flying saucers and extraterrestrials became part of the American consciousness. Later chapters trace specific quests . . . for signs of life beyond earth. . . . The text remains readable

even while explaining intricate scientific concepts and complex . . . ideas. The vibrant full-color photos enhance the work impressively." Booklist

Includes glossary and bibliographical references

Solway, Andrew

Why is there life on Earth? Raintree 2012 48p il (Earth, space, and beyond) $32; pa $8.99

Grades: 5 6 7 8   **576.8**

1. Life on other planets 2. Life -- Origin

ISBN 978-1-4109-4160-2; 978-1-4109-4166-4 pa

LC 2010040160

"Delivering compact but broad summations about...life on Earth, [this] survey [is] well suited for review or reinforcement reading." SLJ

Includes glossary and bibliographical references

Turner, Pamela S.

★ Life on earth--and beyond; an astrobiologist's quest. Charlesbridge 2008 109p il map lib bdg $19.95; pa $11.95

Grades: 5 6 7 8   **576.8**

1. Space biology 2. Life on other planets 3. Astrophysicists 4. Exobiology -- Juvenile literature

ISBN 978-1-58089-133-2 lib bdg; 1-58089-133-0 lib bdg; 978-1-58089-134-9 pa; 1-58089-134-9 pa

LC 2007-01475

"Astrobiologists look outward from the Earth seeking evidence of life elsewhere in the universe. But, as this fascinating book shows, they also travel to places on Earth where extreme conditions may be similar to those on distant worlds. Turner follows astrobiologist Chris McKay as he looks for life in apparently hostile environments. . . . Illustrated with many excellent color photos and other images." Booklist

Includes bibliographical references

Walker, Robert

What is the theory of evolution? Crabtree Pub. Co. 2011 64p il (Shaping modern science) lib bdg $30.60; pa $10.95

Grades: 5 6 7 8   **576.8**

1. Evolution 2. Naturalists 3. Travel writers 4. Writers on science

ISBN 978-0-7787-7198-2 lib bdg; 0-7787-7198-9 lib bdg; 978-0-7787-7205-7 pa; 0-7787-7205-5 pa

LC 2010052628

This title is "not only written and organized well, but [it is] also gorgeous in design. Full-color photographs and illustrations are set over colorful backgrounds that add depth but not distraction. [The title] includes thought-provoking quotes from famous authors and scientists and some eyebrow-raising 'Quick Facts' throughout." SLJ

Includes glossary and bibliographical references

Weaver, Anne H.

The voyage of the beetle; a journey around the world with Charles Darwin and the search for the solution to the mystery of mysteries, as narrated by Rosie, an articulate beetle. [by] Anne H. Weaver; illustrated by George Lawrence. University of New Mexico Press 2007 80p il map $16.95

Grades: 4 5 6   **576.8**

1. Evolution 2. Naturalists 3. Travel writers 4.

Writers on science
ISBN 978-0-8263-4304-8; 0-8263-4304-X
                                    LC 2007008924

This book "is playful, creative, and beautifully conceived and executed, in terms of both the writing and the wonderful illustrations. . . . Through the eyes and narration of Darwin's fictional beetle friend Rosie, the reader is taken on the outer journey of Darwin's voyage (1831-1836) on the H.M.S. Beagle and the inner intellectual journey of Darwin's formulation of the theory of natural selection and the origin of the species." Sci Books Films
    Includes bibliographical references

Winston, Robert M. L.
    ★ **Evolution** revolution; [by] Robert Wilson. DK Pub. 2009 96p il $16.99
Grades: 5 6 7 8   **576.8**
    1. Evolution
    ISBN 978-0-7566-45243-; 0-7566-4524-7
    "The first two thirds of the book are devoted to the history of thought and research on evolution, from stories of Creation, through Darwin, to genetics. The last third looks at 'Evolution in Action.' Information on the fetuses of related species rubs shoulders with variations within species and a time line of the Earth. Visually, the book snaps with colored backgrounds, cool graphics, topflight photos, and clever word balloons coming from vintage black-and-white reproductions." SLJ

577 Ecology

Charles, Prince of Wales, 1948-
    Harmony: a vision for our future; [by] The Prince of Wales. HarperCollinsPublishers 2010 31p il $16.99
Grades: K 1 2 3   **577**
    1. Ecology 2. Environmental protection
    ISBN 978-0-06-173134-1; 0-06-173134-X
                                    LC 2010021957
Adapted for children from the adult title: Harmony: a new way of looking at our world
    "This direct appeal asks readers to consider global sustainability. Using simple text and relatable analogies, the Prince of Wales describes a planet in crisis from climate changes and shows how its inhabitants can restore harmony by observing nature's patterns and the interdependence of plants and animals. . . . This inspirational plea encourages children to think about their world and its future." Booklist
    Includes glossary

Gardner, Robert
    Ace your ecology and environmental science project; great science fair ideas. [by] Robert Gardner, Phyllis J. Perry, and Salvatore Tocci. Enslow Publishers 2009 128p il (Ace your science project) lib bdg $31.93
Grades: 5 6 7 8   **577**
    1. Ecology 2. Science projects 3. Environmental sciences 4. Science -- Experiments
    ISBN 978-0-7660-3216-3 lib bdg; 0-7660-3216-7 lib bdg
                                    LC 2008-4683
    "Dozens of . . . science activities are presented with background information, step-by-step instructions, and sug-

gestions for extending to the science fair level. . . . Color illustrations and important safety information are included." Horn Book Guide
    Includes bibliographical references

Godkin, Celia
    Wolf island. Fitzhenry & Whiteside 2007 un il $17.95; pa $9.95
Grades: K 1 2 3   **577**
    1. Ecology 2. Food chains (Ecology)
    ISBN 1-55455-007-6; 1-55455-008-4 pa
    A newly formatted edition of the title first published 1989 in Canada; first U.S. edition 1993 by Scientific American Books for Young Readers
    When a family of wolves is removed from the food chain on a small island, the impact on the island's ecology is felt by the other animals living there.
    "The food chain, especially its harsher aspects, can be difficult to explain to young children, but this gentle narrative conveys the realism without mawkish sentimentality. . . . With a large format, arresting cover, and beautiful soft-edged illustrations, this presentation offers an effective balance between a documentary and a nature story." Booklist

Gray, Susan H.
    Ecology the study of ecosystems; Susan H. Gray. Children's Press 2012 48 p. (pbk.) $6.95
Grades: 2 3 4 5   **577**
    1. Environment 2. Biodiversity 3. Environmental sciences 4. Ecology -- Juvenile literature
    ISBN 0531282694; 9780531246757; 9780531282694
                                    LC 2011030963
    Author Susan Heinrichs Gray presents a children's book on ecology and ecosystems. She provides a history of ecology and discusses how ecosystems impact human beings. Gray also looks at the research being done by ecologists on the environment today and compares different ecosystems to one another, focusing on the importance of the rain forest to our environment.
    Includes bibliographical references and index.

Housel, Debra J.
    Ecosystems. Compass Point Books 2009 40p il map (Mission: science) lib bdg $26.60
Grades: 4 5 6   **577**
    1. Ecology
    ISBN 978-0-7565-4068-5 lib bdg; 0-7565-4068-2 lib bdg
                                    LC 2008-35730
    An introduction to the ways in which plants and animals interact with each other
    Includes glossary

Latham, Donna
    Amazing biome projects you can build yourself; illustrated by Farah Rizvi. Nomad Press 2009 122p il map (Build it yourself) pa $15.95
Grades: 4 5 6 7   **577**
    1. Ecology 2. Handicraft 3. Earth sciences 4. Science -- Experiments
    ISBN 978-1-934670-40-8; 1-934670-40-5
    "Although the text addresses young 'eco explorers' directly, this book will likely be used as much by teachers, parents, and organization leaders in planning group activities.

Offering an overview of eight terrestrial biomes as well as the ocean, Latham crams a lot of information about climate, plants, animals, soil, and other characteristics onto every page. . . . Instructions for hands-on activities related to different biomes include craft projects such as pictographs and a cornhusk doll. Students can learn how to make a glacier, an erupting volcano, and a tornado in a bottle." SLJ

Includes glossary and bibliographical references

Ecology. Raintree 2009 48p il (Sci-hi: life science) lib bdg $31.43; pa $8.99

Grades: 5 6 7 8   577
1. Ecology
ISBN 978-1-4109-3328-7 lib bdg; 1-4109-3328-8 lib bdg; 978-1-4109-3336-2 pa; 1-4109-3336-9 pa
LC 2009003465

In this introduction to ecology "clear language, embedded definitions, and interesting examples illustrate abstract concepts through both text and well-chosen photographs. . . . [It] includes suggested activities to test ideas as well as a thorough glossary and a Webliography." SLJ

Includes glossary and bibliographical references

Larsen, Laurel
One night in the Everglades; Laurel Larsen; illustrated by Joyce Mihran Turley. Moonlight Pub./Taylor Trade Pub. 2012 30 p. (cloth: alk. paper) $15.95

Grades: 4 5 6   577
1. Nature study 2. Wetland ecology 3. Natural history -- Florida 4. Everglades (Fla.) -- Juvenile literature 5. Ecologists -- Florida -- Everglades -- Juvenile literature 6. Nature study -- Florida -- Everglades -- Juvenile literature 7. Natural history -- Florida -- Everglades -- Juvenile literature
ISBN 0981770045; 9780981770048; 9780981770062
LC 2012007375

This children's book, by Laurel Larsen, illustrated by Joyce Mihran Turley, "follow[s] two scientists as they spend a night in the Everglades collecting water samples, photographing wildlife, and sloshing through marshes in an attempt to understand this mysterious ecosystem. Part of a long-term effort to return the Everglades to a natural state after a century of development, the scientists try to figure out what the 'river of grass' was like prior to human settlement." (Publisher's note)

Lauber, Patricia
Who eats what? food chains and food webs. illustrated by Holly Keller. HarperCollins Pubs. 1995 32p il (Let's-read-and-find-out science) hardcover o.p. pa $4.95

Grades: K 1 2 3   577
1. Food chains (Ecology) 2. Food chains (Ecology) -- Juvenile literature
ISBN 0-06-022981-0; 0-06-022982-9 lib bdg; 0-06-445130-5 pa
LC 93-10609

"Clear, simple ink-and-watercolor drawings illustrate the clear, simple text. Informative and intriguing, this basic science book leads children to think about the complex and interdependent web of life on Earth." Booklist

Munro, Roxie
★ **Ecomazes**; 12 Earth adventures. Sterling 2010 un il $14.95

Grades: 2 3 4   577
1. Ecology 2. Maze puzzles
ISBN 978-1-4027-6393-9; 1-4027-6393-X

"These simple, themed mazes are set in full-spread renditions of biomes ranging from a tropical rain forest to a rocky, penguin-packed Antarctic beach. Munro invites viewers to trace each wandering, easy-to-follow pathway with a finger, noting distinctive landforms and keeping their eyes peeled for the tiny but precisely rendered wildlife visible on either side of the path. . . . This is truly a complete package: it's engrossing and interactive, featuring finely and accurately detailed art and covering the basics of an organizational concept that is central to our understanding of the natural world." SLJ

Rau, Dana Meachen
Food chains. Marshall Cavendish Benchmark 2009 31p il (Bookworms. Nature's cycles) lib bdg $22.79

Grades: PreK K 1   577
1. Food chains (Ecology)
ISBN 978-0-7614-4095-6 lib bdg; 0-7614-4095-X lib bdg
LC 2008-42508

"Well composed, simple sentences tie directly to colorful, carefully chosen photos [and] . . . accurate information flows naturally. . . . A great resource for sharing one-on-one with the youngest readers." Libr Media Connect

Includes glossary

Rompella, Natalie
Ecosystems; [by] Natalie Rompella. Heinemann Library 2008 48p il (Science fair projects) $30

Grades: 5 6 7 8   577
1. Ecology 2. Science projects 3. Science -- Experiments
ISBN 978-1-4034-7915-0
LC 2006039543

This "describes 10 inquiry-based science projects related to life science and ecosystems. . . . Students from mid-elementary through middle school would find little difficulty following the clearly written instructions and suggestions. . . . The illustrations consist of colorful photographs and well-labeled diagrams." Sci Books Films

Includes bibliographical references

Sayre, April Pulley
Trout are made of trees; [by] April Pulley Sayre; illustrated by Kate Endle. Charlesbridge 2008 un il lib bdg $15.95; pa $6.95

Grades: K 1 2 3   577
1. Food chains (Ecology) 2. Stream ecology -- Juvenile literature
ISBN 978-1-58089-137-0 lib bdg; 1-58089-137-3 lib bdg; 978-1-58089-138-7 pa; 1-58089-138-1 pa
LC 2007-02268

"A boy and girl, one white, one black, are exploring the stream and its inhabitants with their parents. In clear sentences, young readers follow autumn leaves as they fall from a tree into the water, are softened by algae and eaten by other creatures, which are then consumed by the trout. A more detailed explanation is included at the end of the book. Attractive collage illustrations in natural colors fill the spreads and help to explain the text. This unique introduction to how changes in nature create the food web illustrates how the whole world is interconnected." SLJ

Includes bibliographical references

Stille, Darlene R.

Nature interrupted; the science of environmental chain reactions. Compass Point Books 2009 48p il map (Headline science) lib bdg $27.93

Grades: 5 6 7 8   577

1. Ecology 2. Food chains (Ecology) 3. Environmental degradation

ISBN 978-0-7565-3949-8 lib bdg; 0-7565-3949-8 lib bdg

LC 2008007282

This "reviews the importance of subtle links in the environmental chain and the far-reaching consequences of its disruption. The possible harm to the food chain caused by the use of antibacterial soap is one case study. The flow of energy from one organism to the next in the food web and the unexpected results when this relationship is disrupted are shown in examinations of monarch butterflies, zebra mussels, and algal blooms. The color illustrations and charts . . . are clear and helpful, and the text, although information rich, is not overly difficult." SLJ

Includes glossary and bibliographical references

Suzuki, David T.

★ **You** are the Earth; know your world so you can make it better. [by] David Suzuki and Kathy Vanderlinden; art by Wallace Edwards; diagrams by Talent Pun. rev ed; Greystone Books 2010 159p il $16.95

Grades: 4 5 6 7   577

1. Ecology 2. Human ecology

ISBN 978-1-55365-476-6; 1-55365-476-5

First published 1999 with title: You are the Earth: from dinosaur breath to pizza from dirt

"After devoting a chapter to each of life's necessities—air, water, soil (earth), energy (fire), love, and a spiritual connection with the universe—the authors close with a look at three social and environmental initiatives by young people; a set of review questions (with answers); and 10 consciousness-raising activities, from science projects to storytelling. Sourced, briefly told versions of folktales from several traditions are interspersed throughout, and the plentiful illustrations include color diagrams, comics, and crisply reproduced photos. . . . [The authors'] eloquent plea to see ourselves and the Earth as interdependent will inspire readers to sit up, look around, and take a little less for granted." SLJ

Includes glossary

Toft, Kim Michelle

The **world** that we want; [by] Kim Michelle Toft. Charlesbridge 2005 un il $16.95

Grades: K 1 2 3   577

1. Habitat (Ecology)

ISBN 1-58089-114-4

LC 2004-20717

"This book offers two-page vistas that incorporate animals found in a variety of habitats, including a mangrove, a tide pool, and a reef. As viewers move from flying pelican to gliding barracuda, Toft creates ever-widening perspectives to reveal how various ecosystems relate to one another. . . . This process culminates in an impressive four-page, foldout panorama that includes all 45 animals. The minimal text cu-

mulates as well. . . . The arresting, brilliantly hued illustrations were drawn and painted on silk." SLJ

VanCleave, Janice Pratt, 1942-

Janice Vancleave's ecology for every kid; easy activities that make learning science fun. Wiley 1996 219p il maps (Science for every kid series) hardcover o.p. pa $10.95

Grades: 4 5 6 7   577

1. Ecology 2. Habitat (Ecology) 3. Science -- Experiments

ISBN 0-471-10100-1; 0-471-10086-2 pa

LC 95-6112

This book of science activities covers "25 topics, ranging from plant and animal food chains to the effect of plastics on the environment. Subjects are introduced in a 'What You Need to Know' section that gives explanation of the scientific principles, plus plenty of everyday examples. A brief preparatory exercise follows, usually in the form of an imaginative game. . . . Simple black-line drawings are crisp, uncluttered, and well placed. . . . Solid information and a generous portion of fun are combined to elevate this selection above the standard collection of experiments." SLJ

Includes glossary

Woodford, Chris

Arctic tundra and polar deserts; Revised ed. Raintree 2011 64p il map $34

Grades: 5 6 7 8 9   577

1. Tundra ecology

ISBN 978-1-4329-4172-7; 1-4329-4172-0

LC 2010012428

"...Provides detailed information suitable for middle school research projects, and browsing potential is high due to the colorful, graphic nature." Library Media Connection

Ecology; the delicate balance of life on earth. edited by Sherman Hollar. Rosen Educational Services, LLC 2012 87 p. col. ill. (library) $31.70

Grades: 5 6 7 8   577

1. Ecology -- Juvenile literature 2. Environmentalism -- Juvenile literature

ISBN 1615305076; 9781615305070

LC 2010052490

This book on ecology, edited by Sherman Hollar, "explores the formation of ecological communities and examines the biological diversity that forms the backbone of life on the planet. . . . By parsing the natural world into various ecosystems and biomes" it looks at "interaction among species and between organisms and their natural habitats". (Publisher's note)

Includes bibliographical references (p. 84) and index.

577.078   Ecology--Experiments

VanCleave, Janice Pratt, 1942-

Step-by-step science experiments in ecology; by Janice VanCleave. Rosen Pub. 2013 80 p. col. ill. (library) $33.25; (paperback) $14.15

Grades: 5 6 7 8   577.078

1. Ecology -- Juvenile literature 2. Science --

Experiments -- Juvenile literature

ISBN 1448869803; 9781448869800; 9781448884698

This book by Janice VanCleave is part of the First-Place Science Fair Projects series. The books have an introduction to the subject—here, ecology, followed by 22 simple . . . experiments. Van Cleave states the basic goal of the experiments, followed by a list of necessary materials, most of which can be found around the house or easily acquired with minimal cost. Step-by-step instructions are clearly detailed and accompanied by diagrams where needed." (School Library Journal)

Includes bibliographical references (p. 76-78) and index.

577.2   Specific factors affecting ecology

Godkin, Celia

Fire! Fitzhenry & Whiteside 2006 un il $17.95

Grades: 2 3 4   577.2

1. Forest fires 2. Forest ecology

ISBN 1-55041-889-0

"Focusing on events in one location, this handsome volume presents the cycle of forest fires in words and pictures. . . . Clear, concise writing and vivid artwork make this a fine presentation on the subject." Booklist

Peluso, Beth A.

The **charcoal** forest; how fire helps animals and plants. written and illustrated by Beth A. Peluso. Mountain Press Pub. Co. 2007 56p il pa $12

Grades: 3 4 5 6   577.2

1. Forest fires 2. Forest plants 3. Forest animals 4. Forest ecology

ISBN 978-0-87842-532-7 pa; 0-87842-532-2 pa

LC 2007003358

This "explores the new habitat created by [a forest] fire. Focusing on the Northern Rocky Mountains of the United States and Canada, the book describes twenty species of animals and plants that contribute to the reclamation and renewal of the charcoal forest." Publisher's note

Simon, Seymour

Wildfires. Morrow Junior Bks. 1996 un il hardcover o.p. pa $6.99

Grades: 4 5 6 7   577.2

1. Forest fires 2. Forest ecology

ISBN 0-688-17530-9 pa

LC 95-12653

"Exploring the place of fire in nature, Simon explains that . . . forest fires have important functions in the ecosystem. With a brilliantly clear and colorful photograph facing each page of text, the book describes the causes and the progression of the wildfires that burned areas of Yellowstone National Park in 1988, explains how the fires were beneficial in many ways. . . . Lucid writing and excellent book design." Booklist

577.3   Ecology of specific environments

Brenner, Barbara

One small place in a tree; illustrated by Tom Leonard. HarperCollins Publishers 2004 un il $15.99; lib bdg $16.89

Grades: 2 3 4   577.3

1. Forest ecology

ISBN 0-688-17180-X; 0-688-17181-8 lib bdg

LC 2002-1181

A child visitor observes as one tiny scratch in a tree develops into a home for a variety of woodland animals over many years, even after the tree has fallen.

"Brenner makes the science enjoyable and understandable, and Leonard's highly detailed, realistic illustrations provide great visual aid." Booklist

Callery, Sean

Rainforest; discover Earth's ecosystems. Kingfisher 2011 32p il map (Life cycles) $12.99

Grades: 2 3 4   577.3

1. Rain forest animals 2. Rain forest ecology 3. Food chains (Ecology)

ISBN 978-0-7534-6576-9; 0-7534-6576-0

After a brief introduction to the rain forest ecosystem "examples of three actual food chains within that ecosystem are presented . . . leaf-cutter ant, armadillo, jaguar. Well-designed double-page spreads . . . provide brief information about each creature and its place in the chain. Vivid photos and vibrantly colored pages are eye-catching. Useful food web charts summarizing content are appended." Horn Book Guide

Includes glossary

Collard, Sneed B.

Forest in the clouds; by Sneed Collard III; illustrated by Michael Rothman. Charlesbridge Pub. 2000 un il map $16.95; pa $7.95

Grades: 2 3 4   577.3

1. Cloud forests 2. Forest ecology 3. Cloud forest ecology 4. Natural history -- Costa Rica

ISBN 0-88106-985-X; 0-88106-986-8 pa

LC 98-6150

Describes some of the exotic plants and animals that live in the cloud forest of Costa Rica, and discusses some environmental threats faced by this region

"Rothman's detailed acrylic paintings, dominated by rich greens and browns, cover the better part of each spread. . . . Although valuable for reports, Collard's book will interest browsers as well." SLJ

Fleisher, Paul

Forest food webs. Lerner Publications Co. 2008 48p il (Early bird food webs) lib bdg $26.60

Grades: 2 3 4 5   577.3

1. Forest ecology 2. Food chains (Ecology)

ISBN 978-0-8225-6729-5

LC 2007-01373

"This colorful volume introduces the forest, with an emphasis on food webs. Clearly written chapters focus on topics such as plants, herbivores, carnivores, decomposers, and people's enjoyment, use, and destruction of forests in the U.S." Booklist

Includes glossary and bibliographical references

Fusco Castaldo, Nancy

Rainforests; an activity guide for ages 6-9. {by} Nancy F. Castaldo. Chicago Review Press 2003 133p il $14.95

Grades: 2 3 4 5   **577.3**

1. Rain forest ecology

ISBN 1-55652-476-5

LC 2002-152661

Provides facts and activities that explore tropical and temperate ancient forests, discusses how individuals can help preserve them, and describes well-known and unfamiliar creatures of the rain forest

"The activities are varied and interesting, ranging from science projects to crafts to recipes. . . . The book would serve as a valuable resource." SLJ

Includes bibliographical references

Gibbons, Gail

Nature's green umbrella; tropical rain forests. Morrow Junior Bks. 1994 un il maps hardcover o.p. pa $5.95

Grades: K 1 2 3   **577.3**

1. Rain forest ecology 2. Rain forests -- Juvenile literature

ISBN 0-688-12353-8; 0-688-12354-6 lib bdg; 0-688-15411-5 pa

LC 93-17569

Describes the climatic conditions of the rain forest as well as the different layers of plants and animals that comprise the ecosystem

The language is "simple, yet poetic and evocative. . . . Colorful maps pinpoint the locations of these global resources. Green vines entwine around the borders of each page and enclose the text and bright illustrations." Sci Books Films

Greenaway, Theresa

Jungle; written by Theresa Greenaway; photographed by Geoff Dann. rev ed.; DK Pub. 2004 71p il map (DK eyewitness books) $15.99

Grades: 4 5 6 7   **577.3**

1. Rain forest ecology

ISBN 0-7566-0694-2

LC 2004558978

First published 1994

Color photographs, drawings, and brief text describe the animals, plants, and ecology of tropical forests of the world

Guiberson, Brenda Z.

Rain, rain, rain forest; illustrated by Steve Jenkins. Henry Holt 2004 un il $16.95

Grades: K 1 2 3   **577.3**

1. Rain forest ecology 2. Rain forests -- Juvenile literature

ISBN 0-8050-6582-2

LC 2003-12250

"Vibrant words and sensory impressions bring the creatures' noisy cacophony and slithering, swooping motions up close, while gracefully incorporated facts convey a surprising amount of information. . . . The artist's colorful, textured images create a rich sense of atmosphere, and the precise details and lively compositions will easily draw children back to the text." Booklist

Jackson, Kay

Rain forests; by Kay Jackson. KidHaven Press 2007 48p il (Our environment) lib bdg $23.70

Grades: 5 6 7 8   **577.3**

1. Rain forests 2. Rain forest ecology

ISBN 978-0-7377-3624-3

LC 2007006892

"Jackson defines rain forests. . . . She explains why rain forests are important, . . . the causes of rain forest destruction, and current efforts to save diverse ecosystems. The writing is clear and succinct. . . . Full-color, captioned photographs and drawings appear on nearly every page." Booklist

Includes bibliographical references

Johansson, Philip

The forested Taiga; a web of life. Enslow Pubs. 2004 48p il map (World of biomes) lib bdg $18.95

Grades: 3 4 5   **577.3**

1. Forest ecology

ISBN 0-7660-2197-1

LC 2003-4436

This describes the ecology of dark evergreen forests of northern Europe, Asia and North America

This book is "extremely well written, and [it contains] ample information presented in a way that is easy to understand." Sci Books Films

Includes glossary and bibliographical references

The temperate forest; a web of life. Enslow Pubs. 2004 48p il map (World of biomes) lib bdg $18.95

Grades: 3 4 5   **577.3**

1. Ecology 2. Forest ecology

ISBN 0-7660-2198-X

LC 2003-3614

This describes the ecology of temperate forests

This book is "extremely well written, and [it contains] ample information presented in a way that is easy to understand." Sci Books Films

Includes glossary and bibliographical references

The tropical rain forest; a web of life. Enslow Pubs. 2004 48p il map (World of biomes) lib bdg $18.95

Grades: 3 4 5   **577.3**

1. Rain forest ecology

ISBN 0-7660-2199-8

LC 2003-6481

This describes the ecology of the tropical rain forests

This book is "extremely well written, and [it contains] ample information presented in a way that is easy to understand." Sci Books Films

Includes glossary and bibliographical references

Johnson, Rebecca L.

A walk in the boreal forest; with illustrations by Phyllis V. Saroff. Carolrhoda Bks. 2001 48p il map (Biomes of North America) lib bdg $23.93

Grades: 3 4 5 6   **577.3**

1. Forest ecology 2. Taigas

ISBN 1-57505-156-7

LC 00-8240

Describes the climate, seasons, plants, animals, and soil of the boreal forest, a biome or land zone, which stretches across the northern parts of North America, Europe, and Asia

"A fine overview of the plant and animal life of the boreal forest. . . . Excellent full-color photographs." SLJ

Includes glossary and bibliographical references

A **walk** in the deciduous forest; with illustrations by Phyllis V. Saroff. Carolrhoda Bks. 2001 48p il map (Biomes of North America) lib bdg $23.93

Grades: 3 4 5 6   **577.3**

1. Forest ecology 3. Forests and forestry

ISBN 1-57505-155-9

LC 00-8243

Takes readers on a walk through a forest of trees that lose their leaves in the fall, showing examples of how the animals and plants depend on each other and their environment to survive

"The simple design and clearly written, informative text will appeal to readers who enjoy nature." Horn Book Guide

Includes glossary and bibliographical references

Lasky, Kathryn

The **most** beautiful roof in the world; exploring the rainforest canopy. photographs by Christopher G. Knight. Harcourt Brace & Co. 1997 un il hardcover o.p. pa $9

Grades: 4 5 6 7   **577.3**

1. Botanists 2. Rain forest ecology

ISBN 0-15-200893-4; 0-15-200897-7 pa

LC 95-48193

Describes the work of Meg Lowman in the rainforest canopy, an area unexplored until the last ten years and home to previously unknown species of plants and animals

"Fresh in out-look and intriguing in details, this memorable book features colorful photographs that reflect the you-are-there quality of the text." Booklist

Includes glossary

Levinson, Nancy Smiler

★ **Rain** forests; illustrated by Diane Dawson Hearn. Holiday House 2008 40p il (Holiday House reader) lib bdg $15.95

Grades: K 1 2   **577.3**

1. Rain forest ecology

ISBN 978-0-8234-1899-2 lib bdg; 0-8234-1899-5 lib bdg

"Levinson offers a straightforward, simple introduction to rain forests and some of the flora and fauna found there. Most of the book deals with tropical forests and the characteristics of each of their four layers. Hearn clearly identifies the locales of her illustrations and labels the plants and animals depicted." SLJ

Levy, Janey

Discovering rain forests; [by] Janey Levy. PowerKids Press 2007 32p il map (World habitats) lib bdg $23.95

Grades: 3 4 5   **577.3**

1. Rain forests 2. Rain forest ecology

ISBN 978-1-4042-3782-7 lib bdg; 1-4042-3782-8 lib bdg

LC 2006036867

This book about rain forest ecology "includes 10 chapters with information on climate, location, plants, animals, people, conservation, and page of relevant facts and figures. Clear, colorful photographs show the landscape and the varied plants and wildlife." SLJ

Includes glossary

Lundgren, Julie K.

Forest fare; studying food webs in the forest. [by] Julie K. Lundgren. Rourke Pub. 2009 32p il map (Studying food webs) lib bdg $28.50

Grades: 3 4 5   **577.3**

1. Forest ecology 2. Food chains (Ecology)

ISBN 978-1-60472-316-8 lib bdg; 1-60472-316-5 lib bdg

LC 2008-24858

This book has "stunning photos, fascinating facts, and intriguing examples. . . . Herbivores, omnivores, and carnivores specific to . . . [the forest] ecosystem are presented. . . . 'Chew on this' insets add further interest and information. . . . [This] will appeal to readers." SLJ

Includes glossary and bibliographical references

Pfeffer, Wendy

A **log's** life; illustrations by Robin Brickman. Simon & Schuster Bks. for Young Readers 1997 un il $16

Grades: K 1 2 3   **577.3**

1. Oak 2. Forest ecology 3. Oak -- Juvenile literature 4. Forest ecology -- Juvenile literature 5. Animals -- Food -- Juvenile literature 6. Animals -- Habitations -- Juvenile literature

ISBN 0-689-80636-1

LC 95-30020

This is an "introduction to the life, death, and decay of an oak tree. The simple, informative text presents the complex cast of characters residing in or on the living tree as well as the decomposing log. . . . The verbal descriptions of this rich ecosystem are enhanced by striking illustrations of three-dimensional paper sculptures, often so realistic as to seem to be preserved natural specimens." SLJ

Pyers, Greg

The **biodiversity** of rain forests. Marshall Cavendish 2010 32p il (Biodiversity) lib bdg $28.50

Grades: 4 5 6   **577.3**

1. Rain forest ecology

ISBN 978-1-60870-073-8 lib bdg; 1-60870-073-9 lib bdg

"Page format is attractive, filled with easy-to-understand fact boxes, charts, graphs, maps and diagrams, and interesting captioned color photographs, all well-balanced within the main text." Libr Media Connect

Includes glossary

The **biodiversity** of woodlands. Marshall Cavendish 2010 32p il (Biodiversity) lib bdg $28.50

Grades: 4 5 6   **577.3**

1. Forest ecology

ISBN 978-1-60870-074-5 lib bdg; 1-60870-074-7 lib bdg

"Page format is attractive, filled with easy-to-understand fact boxes, charts, graphs, maps and diagrams, and interesting captioned color photographs, all well-balanced within the main text." Libr Media Connect

Includes glossary

Simon, Seymour

Tropical rainforests. Collins 2010 30p il $16.99; lib bdg $17.89

Grades: 3 4 5 6　　　　577.3
1. Rain forests 2. Rain forest ecology
ISBN 978-0-06-114253-6; 0-06-114253-0; 978-0-06-114254-3 lib bdg; 0-06-114254-9 lib bdg

"Simon's short overview has a familiar format: large pages of oversize text facing sharp color photos of trees, animals, and plants provide an inviting overview of the biome that is populated by the largest variety of plant and animal species on the planet, with many of them yet to be discovered. . . . Simon's careful descriptions hold a great deal of appeal for young people." SLJ

Includes glossary

Slade, Suzanne

What if there were no gray wolves? a book about the temperate forest ecosystem. illustrated by Carol Schwartz. Picture Window Books 2011 24p il map (Food chain reactions) lib bdg $25.99; pa $8.95
Grades: 2 3 4　　　　577.3
1. Wolves 2. Forest ecology
ISBN 978-1-4048-6020-9 lib bdg; 1-4048-6020-7 lib bdg; 978-1-4048-6395-8 pa; 1-4048-6395-8 pa
LC 2010009877

Discusses the temperate forest ecosystem and the role of the gray wolf in helping to maintain it, describing the wolf's place on the food chain and what would happen to the temperate forest if the gray wolf were to become extinct.

"Radiant illustrations are paired with simple, perceptive sentences to underscore the impact of the loss of [gray wolves]. . . . In a very effective convention extinct plants and animals are placed in silhouettes within many illustrations—the black void left by the loss of each species increases with each page. This . . . will engage readers on many levels." SLJ

Includes glossary and bibliographical references

Stille, Darlene R.

Tropical rain forest. Children's Press 1999 47p il (True book) lib bdg $22
Grades: 2 3 4　　　　577.3
1. Ecology 2. Rain forests 3. Rain forest ecology
ISBN 0-516-21511-6
LC 98-50753

Differentiates a tropical rain forest from all others, and describes its typical plant and animal life

"The plain style, accessible design, and beautiful photographs of landscapes and wildlife make this a good [title] for children's first research presentations." Booklist

Includes glossary and bibliographical references

Tagliaferro, Linda

Explore the tropical rain forest; by Linda Tagliaferro. Capstone Press 2007 32p il map (Explore the biomes) $16.95; pa $6.95
Grades: PreK K 1 2　　　　577.3
1. Rain forest ecology
ISBN 978-0-7368-6407-7; 0-7368-6407-5; 978-0-7368-9630-6 pa; 0-7368-9630-9 pa
LC 2006004107

This is an introduction to the tropical rain forest habitat and some of its plants and animals.

This book "uses vivid, sense-appealing language. . . . An attractive . . . format displays the captions to colorful photographs." Sci Books Films

Includes bibliographical references

Tocci, Salvatore

Life in the tropical forests. Franklin Watts 2005 63p il map (Biomes and habitats) lib bdg $25.50
Grades: 4 5 6 7　　　　577.3
1. Rain forest ecology
ISBN 0-531-12364-2
LC 2004027054

Describes the animals, plants, and people that live in rainforests and the threats to their existence

Includes glossary and bibliographical references

The **chaparral**; life on the scrubby coast. Franklin Watts 2003 63p il map (Biomes and habitats) lib bdg $25.50; pa $8.95
Grades: 4 5 6 7　　　　577.3
1. Chaparral ecology
ISBN 0-531-12303-0 lib bdg; 0-531-16671-6 pa
LC 2003-16574

A look at the plants, animals, locations, and various habitats that make up the chaparral ecosystems of the world

Vogt, Richard Carl

★ **Rain** forests. Simon & Schuster Books for Young Readers 2009 64p il (Insiders) $16.99
Grades: 4 5 6 7　　　　577.3
1. Rain forests
ISBN 978-1-4169-3866-8; 1-4169-3866-4
LC 2008061111

"The layers of a rain forest are drawn with exacting detail in every imaginable shade of green, while circular inserts zoom in on flora with accompanying stats. Running down the length of the spread are markers delineating the cutoff points for each layer—emergent, canopy, and so on. The rest of the book is similarly fine, bringing animals, reptiles, and insects into the mix. . . . Some photographs join the mostly hand-illustrated affair. . . . What will grab browsers are the 3D cover and vivid drawings on thick, oversize pages, but what will keep them reading is a cumulative sense of the rain forest as a verdant universe nearly festering with life." Booklist

Welsbacher, Anne

Protecting Earth's rain forests; by Anne Welsbacher. Lerner Publications 2009 72p il map (Saving our living Earth) lib bdg $30.60
Grades: 5 6 7 8　　　　577.3
1. Rain forests 2. Environmental protection
ISBN 978-0-8225-7562-7 lib bdg; 0-8225-7562-0 lib bdg
LC 2007-38859

"Provides a thorough, interesting discussion of multiple aspects of [rain forest protection], including historical origins, the current situation, and potential solutions. . . . Photos from around the world accompany discussions. . . . Solid choice to replace outdated books." SLJ

Includes glossary and bibliographical references

577.4 Grassland ecology

Bateman, Donna M.

Out on the prairie; Donna M. Bateman; illustrated by Susan Swan. Charlesbridge 2012 32 p. (reinforced for library use) $15.95

Grades: PreK K 1 2 **577.4**

1. Counting 2. Prairie animals 3. Picture books for children

ISBN 1580893775; 9781580893770; 9781580893787

LC 2011025782

For this counting book, "[Donna M.] Bateman Bateman has chosen representative features and creatures" of the mixed-grass prairie of Badlands National Park in South Dakota "to introduce a remarkable ecosystem. Counting from one to 10, she goes on to include pronghorns, meadowlarks, prairie dogs, grasshoppers, grouse, owls, rattlesnakes, coyotes and toads in a series of verses that also span the day from dawn to night." (Kirkus)

Collard, Sneed B.

The **prairie** builders; reconstructing America's lost grasslands. written and photographed by Sneed B. Collard III. Houghton Mifflin Co. 2005 66p il (Scientists in the field) $17; pa $8.95

Grades: 4 5 6 7 **577.4**

1. Prairies 2. Nature conservation 3. Prairie plants -- Juvenile literature 4. Prairie conservation -- Juvenile literature 5. Native plants for cultivation -- Juvenile literature

ISBN 978-0-618-39687-0; 0-618-39687-X; 978-0-547-01441-8 pa; 0-547-01441-4 pa

LC 2004-13201

This describes an effort to restore part of the native tallgrass prairie in the the 8,000-acre Neal Smith National Wildlife Refuge in Iowa

"The engaging text is accompanied by large, inviting color photographs. . . . An essential purchase for libraries in prairie regions and a worthwhile choice for others." SLJ

Includes bibliographical references

Dunphy, Madeleine

Here is the African savanna; illustrated by Tom Leonard. Hyperion Books for Children 1999 un il $14.99; lib bdg $15.99

Grades: K 1 2 3 **577.4**

1. Grassland ecology 2. Ecology -- Africa 3. Grasslands -- Africa 4. Natural history -- Africa 5. Savanna ecology -- Africa 6. Savanna ecology -- Africa -- Juvenile literature

ISBN 0-7868-0162-X; 0-7868-2134-5 lib bdg

LC 98-30007

Cumulative text describes the interdependence among the plants and animals of an African savanna

"The acrylic illustrations are rich with detail and goldtoned radiance. An endnote provides some additional information about conservation. This is an attractive, effective way to introduce ecology to young readers." Horn Book Guide

Jackson, Kay

Explore the grasslands; by Kay Jackson. Capstone Press 2007 32p il map (Explore the biomes) $16.95; pa $6.95

Grades: PreK K 1 2 **577.4**

1. Grassland ecology

ISBN 978-0-7368-6405-3; 0-7368-6405-9; 978-0-7368-9628-3 pa; 0-7368-9628-7 pa

LC 2006005641

This is a introduction to grassland ecology and some of its plants and animals

This book "uses vivid, sense-appealing language. . . . An attractive . . . format displays the captions to colorful photographs." Sci Books Films

Includes bibliographical references

Johnson, Rebecca L.

A **walk** in the prairie; with illustrations by Phyllis V. Saroff. Carolrhoda Bks. 2001 48p il map (Biomes of North America) lib bdg $23.93

Grades: 3 4 5 6 **577.4**

1. Ecology 2. Prairies 3. Prairie ecology

ISBN 1-57505-153-2

LC 00-8252

Describes the climate, soil, seasons, plants, and animals of the North American prairie and the ways in which the plants and animals depend on each other and their environment to survive

Includes glossary and bibliographical references

Levy, Janey

Discovering the tropical savanna; [by] Janey Levy. PowerKids Press 2008 32p il map (World habitats) lib bdg $23.95

Grades: 3 4 5 **577.4**

1. Grassland ecology

ISBN 978-1-4042-3783-4 lib bdg; 1-4042-3783-6 lib bdg

LC 2006103368

This book about the ecology of the tropical savanna "includes 10 chapters with information on climate, location, plants, animals, people, conservation, and page of relevant facts and figures. The [text is] concise and accessible. Clear, colorful photographs show the landscape and the varied plants and wildlife." SLJ

Includes glossary

Lion, David C.

A **home** on the prairie; by David C. Lion. Children's Press 2007 24p il (Scholastic news nonfiction readers) $20

Grades: 1 2 3 **577.4**

1. Prairie ecology

ISBN 0-516-25346-8; 978-0-516-25346-6

LC 2006002308

An introduction to prairie ecology

"Simple, easy-to-read. . . . Everything students need for reports is beautifully depicted with scenic full-color photographs of the land, the plants, and the animals that live there." SLJ

Includes bibliographical references

Lundgren, Julie K.

Grassland buffet; studying food webs in the grasslands and savannahs. [by] Julie K. Lundgren. Rourke Pub. 2009 32p il map (Studying food webs) lib bdg $28.50

Grades: 3 4 5   **577.4**
1. Grassland ecology 2. Food chains (Ecology)
ISBN 978-1-60472-318-2 lib bdg; 1-60472-318-1
lib bdg

LC 2008-24859

This book has "stunning photos, fascinating facts, and intriguing examples. . . . Herbivores, omnivores, and carnivores specific to . . . [the grassland] ecosystem are presented. . . . 'Chew on this' insets add further interest and information. . . . [This] will appeal to readers." SLJ

Includes glossary and bibliographical references

Pattison, Darcy
Prairie storms; by Darcy Pattison; illustrated by Kathleen Rietz. Sylvan Dell Pub. 2011 un il map $16.95; pa $8.95
Grades: K 1 2 3   **577.4**
1. Storms 2. Prairie animals 3. Prairie ecology
ISBN 978-1-60718-129-3; 1-60718-129-0; 978-1-60718-139-2 pa; 1-60718-139-8 pa; 978-1-60718-149-1 e-book; 1-60718-149-5 english e-book; 978-1-60718-159-0 spanish e-book; 1-60718-159-2 spanish e-book

LC 2011016339

This describes the prairie ecosystem through its ever-changing weather. Each month features a storm typical of that season and a prairie animal who must shelter, hide, escape, or endure those storms.

"Beautiful two-page framed spreads do a good job of showing an animal or bird of the plains and the weather conditions that might be currently affecting. The book gives a unique look at the differing plains habitats." Sci Books Films

Sill, Cathryn P.
Grasslands; written by Cathryn Sill; illustrated by John Sill. Peachtree Publishers 2011 un il (About habitats) $16.95
Grades: K 1 2 3   **577.4**
1. Grassland ecology
ISBN 978-1-56145-559-1; 1-56145-559-8

LC 2010026690

"With simple, informative sentences paired with beautifully detailed watercolor paintings, this title . . . will introduce young grade-schoolers to grassland ecology across the world: the climate, plants that grow there, and the wildlife that have adapted to survive in the large open spaces. . . . Great for classroom sharing." Booklist

Slade, Suzanne
What if there were no bees? a book about the grassland ecosystem. illustrated by Carol Schwartz. Picture Window Books 2010 24p il map (Food chain reactions) lib bdg $25.99; pa $8.95
Grades: 2 3 4   **577.4**
1. Bees 2. Grassland ecology 3. Fertilization of plants
ISBN 978-1-4048-6019-3 lib bdg; 1-4048-6019-3 lib bdg; 978-1-4048-6394-1 pa; 1-4048-6394-X pa

LC 2010006035

"Radiant illustrations are paired with simple, perceptive sentences to underscore the impact of the loss of [bees]. . . . In a very effective convention extinct plants and animals are placed in silhouettes within many illustrations—the black

void left by the loss of each species increases with each page. This . . . will engage readers on many levels." SLJ

Includes glossary and bibliographical references

Stille, Darlene R.
Grasslands. Children's Press 1999 47p il (True book) lib bdg $22; pa $6.95
Grades: 2 3 4   **577.4**
1. Grasslands 2. Grassland ecology
ISBN 0-516-21509-4 lib bdg; 0-516-26762-0 pa

LC 98-49728

Examines the different types of grasslands and the plant and animal life they support

Includes glossary and bibliographical references

Toupin, Laurie
Life in the temperate grasslands. Franklin Watts 2005 63p il map (Biomes and habitats) lib bdg $25.50
Grades: 4 5 6 7   **577.4**
1. Grassland ecology
ISBN 0-531-12385-5

LC 2004-13282

This describes the ecology of grasslands such as the North American prairie, the South American pampas, the African veldt and the European steppes

This is "written in an accessible and interesting, conversational style. The [author conveys] a good deal of information about topics such as adaptation, environmental threats, seasonal changes, and other essentials important to report writers and general readers." SLJ

Includes bibliographical references

Savannas; life in the tropical grasslands. [by] Laurie Peach Toupin. Franklin Watts 2005 63p il map (Biomes and habitats) lib bdg $25.50
Grades: 4 5 6 7   **577.4**
1. Grassland ecology
ISBN 0-531-12386-3

LC 2004-13281

This introduces "readers to the climate characteristics as well as plants and animals of [tropical grasslands. It is] written in an accessible and interesting, conversational style. The authors convey a good deal of information about topics such as adaptation, environmental threats, seasonal changes, and other essentials important to report writers and general readers." SLJ

Includes bibliographical references

577.5   Ecology of miscellaneous environments

Banting, Erinn
Caves; Erinn Banting. AV2 by Weigl 2012 32 p. col. ill., col. map (hardcover) $28.55; (paperback) $13.95
Grades: 4 5 6   **577.5**
1. Cave ecology
ISBN 1616906391; 1616906456; 9781616906399; 9781616906450

LC 2010050985

This book by Erinn Banting is part of the "Biomes" series. "Caves are unique ecosystems that are found on all seven continents. This book explores the plants and animals that have adapted to life in this unique environment." (Publisher's note) "Explanations of climate and physical characteristics are accompanied by appropriate diagrams and illustrations." (School Library Journal)

Bial, Raymond
★ A **handful** of dirt. Walker & Co. 2000 32p il $16.95
Grades: 3 4 5 6   577.5
1. Soils 2. Soil ecology
ISBN 0-8027-8698-7
LC 99-53632
The author "discusses how plant, animal, and mineral matter are broken down to create soil, as well as the vast amount of life forms soil supports, such as protozoa, earthworms, insects, moles, snakes, and prairie dogs. Tips on how to compost are included. The book is illustrated with crisp color photos, including several using an electron microscope." Horn Book Guide
Includes bibliographical references

Callery, Sean
Polar lands. Kingfisher 2011 il (Life cycles) $12.99
Grades: 2 3 4   577.5
1. Food chains (Ecology)
ISBN 978-0-7534-6691-9; 0-7534-6691-0
"This focuses on 11 Arctic and Antarctic animals, exploring their life cycles and the ways in which they are interconnected by a food chain. The first food chain Callery presents is hermit crab, Arctic tern, Arctic fox, polar bear. Each spread is devoted to a single animal. . . . Beautiful closeup photographs show the animals in their natural habitats eating, playing and interacting with one another. . . . A great beginning look at the lifecycles of some fascinating animals and a solid tool for learning about food chains." Kirkus

Fridell, Ron
Life in the desert. Franklin Watts 2005 63p il map (Biomes and habitats) lib bdg $25.50
Grades: 4 5 6 7   577.5
1. Deserts 2. Desert ecology
ISBN 0-531-12384-7
LC 2004027254
Presents an introduction to desert environments, in simple text with illustrations, providing information on its average temperature, climate, plant and animal life, and people
Includes glossary and bibliographical references

Hooks, Gwendolyn
Arctic appetizers; studying food webs in the arctic. [by] Gwendolyn Hooks. Rourke Pub. 2009 32p il map (Studying food webs) lib bdg $28.50
Grades: 3 4 5   577.5
1. Food chains (Ecology)
ISBN 978-1-60472-314-4 lib bdg; 1-60472-314-9 lib bdg
LC 2008-24855
This book has "stunning photos, fascinating facts, and intriguing examples. . . . Herbivores, omnivores, and carnivores specific to . . . [the arctic] ecosystem are presented. . . 'Chew on this' insets add further interest and information. . . . [This] will appeal to readers." SLJ
Includes glossary and bibliographical references

Jackson, Kay
Explore the desert; by Kay Jackson. Capstone Press 2007 32p il map (Explore the biomes) $16.95; pa $6.95
Grades: PreK K 1 2   577.5
1. Desert ecology
ISBN 978-0-7368-6404-6; 0-7368-6404-0; 978-0-7368-9627-6 pa; 0-7368-9627-9 pa
LC 2006004109
This is an introduction to desert ecology and some of its plants and animals.
This book "uses vivid, sense-appealing language. . . . An attractive . . . format displays the captions to colorful photographs." Sci Books Films
Includes bibliographical references

Johansson, Philip
The **dry** desert; a web of life. Enslow Publishers 2004 48p il (World of biomes) lib bdg $18.95
Grades: 3 4 5   577.5
1. Desert ecology 2. Deserts -- Juvenile literature
ISBN 0-7660-2200-5
LC 2003-20443
This describes the plants, animals, and ecology of deserts of the world
Includes glossary and bibliographical references

The **frozen** tundra; a web of life. Enslow Pubs. 2004 48p il map (World of biomes) lib bdg $18.95
Grades: 3 4 5   577.5
1. Tundra ecology 2. Tundras
ISBN 0-7660-2176-9
LC 2003-2271
This describes the ecology of the arctic tundra
This book is "extremely well written, and [it contains] ample information presented in a way that is easy to understand." Sci Books Films
Includes glossary and bibliographical references

Johnson, Rebecca L.
A **walk** in the tundra; with illustrations by Phyllis V. Saroff. Carolrhoda Bks. 2001 48p il map (Biomes of North America) lib bdg $23.93; pa $8.95
Grades: 3 4 5 6   577.5
1. Tundra ecology 2. Tundras
ISBN 1-57505-157-5 lib bdg; 1-57505-526-0 pa
LC 00-8245
Takes readers on a walk in the tundra, showing examples of how the animals and plants of the tundra are connected and dependent on each other and the tundra's soil and climate
"A visually pleasing title with plenty of clear, colorful photographs of the biome's flora and fauna throughout the year." SLJ
Includes glossary and bibliographical references

Levinson, Nancy Smiler
Death Valley; a day in the desert. illustrated by Diane Dawson Hearn. Holiday House 2001 29p il (Holiday House reader) $14.95
Grades: 1 2 3   577.5
1. Desert ecology 2. Ecology -- Death Valley (Calif. and Nev.) 3. Desert ecology -- Death Valley (Calif. and Nev.) 4. Natural history -- Death Valley (Calif. and

Nev.)

ISBN 0-8234-1566-X

LC 00-23305

Describes the desert habitat of Death Valley and the plants and animals that live there

"Newly independent readers will appreciate the simple text of this nonfiction easy reader. . . . The illustrations are clear and attractive." Horn Book Guide

Levy, Janey

Discovering mountains; [by] Janey Levy. PowerKids Press 2008 32p il map (World habitats) lib bdg $23.95

Grades: 3 4 5   **577.5**

1. Mountains 2. Mountain ecology
ISBN 978-1-4042-3785-8 lib bdg; 1-4042-3785-2 lib bdg

LC 2006103369

This book about mountain ecology "includes 10 chapters with information about climate, location, plants, animals, people, conservation, and a page of relevant facts and figures. The [text is] concise and accessible. Clear, colorful photographs show the landscape and the varied plants and wildlife." Booklist

Includes glossary

Discovering the Arctic tundra; [by] Janey Levy. PowerKids Press 2008 32p il map (World habitats) lib bdg $23.95

Grades: 3 4 5   **577.5**

1. Tundra ecology
ISBN 978-1-4042-3787-2 lib bdg; 1-4042-3787-9 lib bdg

LC 2006103405

This book about the ecology of the Arctic tundra "includes 10 chapters with information on climate, location, plants, animals, people, conservation, and a page of relevant facts and figures. The [text is] concise and accessible. Clear, colorful photographs show the landscape and the varied plants and wildlife." Booklist

Includes glossary

Lundgren, Julie K.

Desert dinners; studying food webs in the desert. [by] Julie K. Lundgren. Rourke Pub. 2009 32p il map (Studying food webs) lib bdg $28.50

Grades: 3 4 5   **577.5**

1. Desert ecology 2. Food chains (Ecology)
ISBN 978-1-60472-315-1 lib bdg; 1-60472-315-7 lib bdg

LC 2008-24856

This book has "stunning photos, fascinating facts, and intriguing examples. . . . Herbivores, omnivores, and carnivores specific to . . . [the desert] ecosystem are presented. . . . 'Chew on this' insets add further interest and information. . . . [This] will appeal to readers." SLJ

Includes glossary and bibliographical references

Lynch, Wayne

Sonoran Desert; text and photographs by Wayne Lynch; assisted by Aubrey Lang. NorthWord Books 2009 64p il (Our wild world ecosystems) $16.95

Grades: 5 6 7 8   **577.5**

1. Desert ecology 2. Natural history -- Sonoran Desert
ISBN 978-1-58979-389-7; 1-58979-389-7

LC 2008036635

"An in-depth look at a vibrant ecosystem. Spilling over the Mexican border into Arizona and New Mexico, the Sonoran Desert is especially rich in varied plants, animals, insects, and other critters that call it home. Lynch shares his expertise and experiences in a clearly written, conversational text, lavishly illustrated with his own crisp color photos." SLJ

Marsico, Katie

A **home** on the tundra; by Katie Marsico. Children's Press 2007 24p il (Scholastic news nonfiction readers) $20

Grades: 1 2 3   **577.5**

1. Tundra ecology
ISBN 0-516-25345-X; 978-0-516-25345-9

LC 2006002306

An introduction to tundra ecology

"Simple, easy-to-read. . . . Everything students need for reports is beautifully depicted with scenic full-color photographs of the land, the plants, and the animals that live there." SLJ

Includes bibliographical references

Moss, Miriam

This is the mountain; illustrated by Adrienne Kennaway. Frances Lincoln 2011 un il $17.95

Grades: K 1 2 3   **577.5**

1. Mountain ecology 2. Natural history -- Africa
ISBN 978-1-84507-984-0; 1-84507-984-1

"Illustrated with attractive accessible watercolors, this picture book introduces Mount Kilimanjaro, from the people and animals living on the plains around it to the mountainside and the glaciers at its peak. . . . The book has real value for children. Not only does it show life on and around Mount Kilimanjaro, it shows how the landforms and ecosystems change as one moves up the mountain." Booklist

Pascoe, Elaine

Soil; text by Elaine Pascoe; photographs by Dwight Kuhn. Blackbirch Press 2005 24p il (Nature close-up juniors) $21.20

Grades: K 1 2 3   **577.5**

1. Soil ecology
ISBN 1-4103-0311-X

LC 2004-13975

"This book introduces young readers to the wildlife lurking in the soil right under their feet and to the role of soil in plant growth. Activities include starting plants from seed and watching earthworms tunnel." Publisher's note

Includes bibliographical references

Pyers, Greg

The **biodiversity** of coasts. Marshall Cavendish 2010 32p il map (Biodiversity) lib bdg $28.50

Grades: 4 5 6   **577.5**

1. Coasts 2. Seashore ecology
ISBN 978-1-60870-069-1 lib bdg; 1-60870-069-0 lib bdg

"Page format is attractive, filled with easy-to-understand fact boxes, charts, graphs, maps and diagrams, and interesting captioned color photographs, all well-balanced within the main text." Libr Media Connect

Includes glossary

The **biodiversity** of deserts. Marshall Cavendish 2010 32p il (Biodiversity) lib bdg $28.50

Grades: 4 5 6   **577.5**

1. Desert ecology

ISBN 978-1-60870-071-4 lib bdg; 1-60870-071-2 lib bdg

"Page format is attractive, filled with easy-to-understand fact boxes, charts, graphs, maps and diagrams, and interesting captioned color photographs, all well-balanced within the main text." Libr Media Connect

Includes glossary

The **biodiversity** of polar regions. Marshall Cavendish 2010 32p il (Biodiversity) lib bdg $28.50

Grades: 4 5 6   **577.5**

ISBN 978-1-60870-072-1 lib bdg; 1-60870-072-0 lib bdg

"Page format is attractive, filled with easy-to-understand fact boxes, charts, graphs, maps and diagrams, and interesting captioned color photographs, all well-balanced within the main text." Libr Media Connect

Includes glossary

Slade, Suzanne

What if there were no lemmings? a book about the tundra ecosystem. illustrated by Carol Schwartz. Picture Window Books 2011 24p il map (Food chain reactions) lib bdg $25.99; pa $8.95

Grades: 2 3 4   **577.5**

1. Lemmings 2. Tundra ecology 3. Animals -- Arctic regions

ISBN 978-1-4048-6021-6 lib bdg; 1-4048-6021-5 lib bdg; 978-1-4048-6396-5 pa; 1-4048-6396-6 pa

LC 2010009878

Discusses the tundra ecosystem and the role of lemmings as a keystone species in helping to maintain it, describing the lemmings' place on the food chain and what would happen to the tundra if they were to become extinct.

"Radiant illustrations are paired with simple, perceptive sentences to underscore the impact of the loss of [lemmings]. . . . In a very effective convention extinct plants and animals are placed in silhouettes within many illustrations—the black void left by the loss of each species increases with each page. This . . . will engage readers on many levels." SLJ

Includes glossary and bibliographical references

Stille, Darlene R.

Deserts. Children's Press 1999 47p il (True book) hardcover o.p. pa $6.95

Grades: 2 3 4   **577.5**

1. Deserts 2. Desert ecology

ISBN 0-516-21508-6 lib bdg; 0-516-26760-4 pa

LC 98-53856

Presents a general description of deserts and describes specific desert plants, animals, people, and activities

Includes glossary and bibliographical references

Tagliaferro, Linda

Explore the tundra; by Linda Tagliaferro. Capstone Press 2007 32p il map (Explore the biomes) $16.95; pa $6.95

Grades: PreK K 1 2   **577.5**

1. Tundra ecology

ISBN 978-0-7368-6408-4; 0-7368-6408-3; 978-0-7368-9631-3 pa; 0-7368-9631-7 pa

LC 2006004108

This is an introduction to the tundra and some of its plants and animals.

This book "uses vivid, sense-appealing language. . . . An attractive . . . format displays the captions to colorful photographs." Sci Books Films

Includes bibliographical references

Wojahn, Rebecca Hogue

An **Australian** outback food chain; a who-eats-what adventure. [by] Rebecca Hogue Wojahn, Donald Wojahn. Lerner Publications 2009 64p il map (Follow that food chain) lib bdg $30.60

Grades: 3 4 5 6   **577.5**

1. Food chains (Ecology) 2. Animals -- Australia 3. Natural history -- Australia

ISBN 978-0-8225-7499-6 lib bdg; 0-8225-7499-3 lib bdg

LC 2008021117

"Numerous photos of plants and animals in their habitats appear on these pages, accompanied by an explanation of the basic elements of a food chain and definitions of terms such as predators, consumers, producers, and decomposers. What sets [this book] apart . . . is [its] 'choose your own adventure' style. . . . The authors instruct [readers] to choose one of the region's carnivores and explore its food chain, . . . [including the] dingo, saltwater crocodile, wedge-tailed eagle, [and] Gould's monitor. . . . Choices result in returning to some pages more than once and sometimes discovering a 'dead end,' a critically endangered or extinct animal. . . . The interconnections created by the choices effectively illustrate the complexity of food webs while providing information about the plants and animals that form the components. Lively, engaging writing helps sustain interest." SLJ

Includes glossary and bibliographical references

A **tundra** food chain; a who-eats-what adventure in the Arctic. [by] Rebecca Hogue Wojahn, Donald Wojahn. Lerner Publications 2009 64p il map (Follow that food chain) lib bdg $30.60

Grades: 3 4 5 6   **577.5**

1. Tundra ecology 2. Food chains (Ecology) 3. Animals -- Arctic regions

ISBN 978-0-8225-7500-9 lib bdg; 0-8225-7500-0 lib bdg

LC 2008027092

"Numerous photos of plants and animals in their habitats appear on these pages, accompanied by an explanation of the basic elements of a food chain and definitions of terms such as predators, consumers, producers, and decomposers. What sets [this book] apart . . . is [its] 'choose your own adventure' style. . . . The authors instruct [readers] to choose one of the region's carnivores and explore its food chain. Six animals (grizzly bear, snowy owl, Arctic wolf, polar bear, wolverine, and peregrine falcon) are presented. . . . Choices result in returning to some pages more than once and sometimes discovering a 'dead end,' a critically endangered or extinct animal. . . . The interconnections created by the choices effectively illustrate the complexity of food webs while providing information about the plants and animals that form the components. Lively, engaging writing helps sustain interest." SLJ

Includes glossary and bibliographical references

577.54 Desert ecology

Johnson, Rebecca L.
A **walk** in the desert; with illustrations by Phyllis V. Saroff. Carolrhoda Bks. 2001 48p il map (Biomes of North America) lib bdg $23.93; pa $8.95
Grades: 3 4 5 6   **577.54**
1. Desert plants 2. Desert animals 3. Desert ecology
ISBN 1-57505-152-4 lib bdg; 1-57505-529-5 pa
LC 00-8251

Describes the climate, soil, plants, and animals of North American deserts and the ways in which the plants and animals depend on each other and their environment to survive

"The many full-color, close-up photographs and black-and-white drawings are sure to engage readers' interest." SLJ

Includes glossary and bibliographical references

577.6 Aquatic ecology

Arnosky, Jim
The **brook** book; exploring the smallest streams. Dutton Children's Books 2008 un il $15.99
Grades: K 1 2 3   **577.6**
1. Stream plants 2. Stream animals 3. Freshwater ecology 4. Rivers -- Juvenile literature 5. Stream animals -- Juvenile literature
ISBN 978-0-525-47716-7; 0-525-47716-0

This "looks at brooks . . . and invites children to explore them. Guiding readers, Arnosky introduces the rocks at the brook's bottom, the creatures in the water, and the flowers and birds living nearby, and the animals that leave their tracks in the soft banks. [Illustrated with] luminous paintings in spring colors. . . . Attractive and useful." Booklist

Brenner, Barbara
One small place by the sea; illustrated by Tom Leonard. HarperCollins Publishers 2004 un il hardcover o.p. lib bdg $16.89
Grades: 2 3 4   **577.6**
1. Tide pool ecology
ISBN 0-688-17182-6; 0-688-17183-4 lib bdg
LC 2002-1180

For one afternoon, a child visitor observes the cycle of change within a tidepool, a small place at the edge of the sea that is home to many plants and animals

"The contents of the book are well organized, current, and accurate. The content is well illustrated, with colored pictures of the organisms, as well as many of their life habits, discussed." Sci Books Films

Fusco Castaldo, Nancy
River wild; an activity guide to North American rivers. [by] Nancy F. Castaldo. Chicago Review Press 2006 147p il pa $14.95
Grades: 4 5 6   **577.6**
1. Rivers 2. River ecology 3. Rivers -- North America -- Juvenile literature
ISBN 1-55652-585-0
LC 2005-22976

Thirty games, activites, and experiments provide an introduction to learning about how rivers are formed, the water cycle, and the animals and habitats that exist along rivers

"This book serves as a good source of information and projects." Booklist

Includes bibliographical references

Halpern, Monica
All about tide pools; by Monica Halpern. National Geographic 2007 40p il (National Geographic science chapters) $17.90
Grades: 3 4 5 6   **577.6**
1. Tide pool ecology
ISBN 978-1-4263-0184-1; 1-4263-0184-7
LC 2007007907

This is an introduction to animals and plants in tide pools and how they survive which offers suggestions for exploring this ecosystem

This "book provides a clear, engaging introduction to the topic. . . . The [book's] clear design features many well-captioned photographs . . . charts, and diagrams." Horn Book Guide

Includes glossary and bibliographical references

Hooks, Gwendolyn
Freshwater feeders; studying food webs in freshwater. Rourke Pub. 2009 32p il map (Studying food webs) lib bdg $28.50
Grades: 3 4 5   **577.6**
1. Freshwater ecology 2. Food chains (Ecology)
ISBN 978-1-60472-317-5 lib bdg; 1-60472-317-3 lib bdg
LC 2008-24857

This book has "stunning photos, fascinating facts, and intriguing examples. . . . Herbivores, omnivores, and carnivores specific to . . . [the freshwater] ecosystem are presented. . . . 'Chew on this' insets add further interest and information. . . . [This] will appeal to readers." SLJ

Includes glossary

Johansson, Philip
Lakes and rivers; a freshwater web of life. [by] Philip Johansson. Enslow Elementary 2007 48p il (Wonderful water biomes) lib bdg $23.93
Grades: 3 4 5   **577.6**
1. Lakes 2. Rivers 3. Freshwater ecology
ISBN 978-0-7660-2812-8 lib bdg; 0-7660-2812-7 lib bdg
LC 2006100470

This describes the plants, animals, and ecology of lakes and rivers.

Includes glossary and bibliographical references

Marshes and swamps; a wetland web of life. [by] Philip Johansson. Enslow Elementary 2007 48p il (Wonderful water biomes) lib bdg $23.93
Grades: 3 4 5   577.6
  1. Wetlands 2. Marsh ecology
  ISBN 978-0-7660-2814-2 lib bdg; 0-7660-2814-3 lib bdg
                                LC 2006039769
This describes the plants, animals, and ecology of marshes and swamps.
  This has "good-quality color photos. . . . Well written and engaging." SLJ
  Includes glossary and bibliographical references

The **seashore**; a saltwater web of life. Enslow Elementary 2008 48p il (Wonderful water biomes) lib bdg $23.93
Grades: 3 4 5   577.6
  1. Seashore ecology
  ISBN 978-0-7660-2811-1 lib bdg; 0-7660-2811-9 lib bdg
                                LC 2006-100600
This describes the plants, animals, and ecology of the seashore.
  This has "good-quality color photos. . . . Well written and engaging." SLJ
  Includes glossary and bibliographical references

Kudlinski, Kathleen V.
  The **seaside** switch; illustrated by Lindy Burnett. NorthWord Books for Young Readers 2007 un il $16.95
Grades: PreK K 1 2   577.6
  1. Marine biology 2. Tide pool ecology 3. Tides -- Juvenile literature 4. Tidal flats -- Juvenile literature
  ISBN 978-1-55971-964-3; 1-55971-964-8
                                LC 2006-11608
"Kudlinski's picture book uses poetic words to describe the seashore during a cycle of tides. . . . The gouache illustrations show tidal changes on a beach through the eyes of a boy, who often sketches what he sees." Booklist

Lynette, Rachel
  River food chains. Heinemann Library 2011 48p il map (Protecting food chains) lib bdg $32; pa $8.99
Grades: 4 5 6 7   577.6
  1. River ecology 2. Food chains (Ecology)
  ISBN 978-1-4329-3861-1 lib bdg; 1-4329-3861-4 lib bdg; 978-1-4329-3868-0 pa; 1-4329-3868-1 pa
                                LC 2009049552
This book explores the species found in river food chains and webs, and discusses why these food chains and webs need to be protected.
  "Featuring colorful, glossy images and accessible prose, this . . . offers a good introduction to the web of life in rivers. . . . Conservation issues are highlighted throughout, with specific suggestions for youth to get involved. . . . An informative, thought-provoking resource that conveys the fragile, interconnected web that holds ecosystems together." Booklist
  Includes glossary and bibliographical references

Marx, Trish
  ★ **Everglades** forever; restoring America's great wetland. photographs by Cindy Karp. Lee & Low Books 2004 40p il map $17.95; pa $8.95

Grades: 3 4 5 6   577.6
  1. Wetlands
  ISBN 978-1-58430-164-6; 1-58430-164-3; 978-1-60060-339-6 pa; 1-60060-339-4 pa
                                LC 2004-2934
The author offers an "introduction to the natural history and environment of the Everglades by documenting the studies of a fifth-grade class. . . . Complementing the excellent, informative text are high-quality color photographs and maps." Booklist

Morrison, Gordon
  Pond. Houghton Mifflin 2002 30p il $16
Grades: 2 3 4   577.6
  1. Ponds 2. Pond ecology 3. Pond plants 4. Pond animals
  ISBN 0-618-10271-X
                                LC 2002-3494
Observes how a glacial pond and the abundance of plants and animals that draw life from it change over the course of a year
  "Lovely, realistic watercolor paintings illustrate the text; small, detailed pencil drawings and diagrams accompany each note. . . . This lovingly crafted sketchbook has the potential to awaken in readers an awareness of the workings of nature." SLJ

Root, Phyllis
  Big belching bog; illustrations by Betsy Bowen. University of Minnesota Press 2010 un il $15.95
Grades: 2 3 4   577.6
  1. Marshes 2. Bog ecology -- Juvenile literature
  ISBN 978-0-8166-3359-3; 0-8166-3359-2
                                LC 2010018733
"Couching the adaptations of plants, insects, and animals that live in the Big Bog in Minnesota as secrets of survival, this oversize picture book becomes a real page-turner. . . . The stunning full-color woodblocks, many full spread, are beautiful enough to frame. The deep purples, browns, and teals are highlighted with stark white circles." SLJ

Sill, Cathryn P.
  Wetlands; written by Cathryn Sill; illustrated by John Sill. Peachtree 2008 un il (About habitats) $16.95
Grades: PreK K 1 2 3   577.6
  1. Wetlands
  ISBN 978-1-56145-432-7; 1-56145-432-X
                                LC 2007031280
This introduction to wetland ecology "features full-page watercolor paintings that strikingly illustrate the factual information conveyed by a sentence or two on the facing pages. . . . The artwork is stunning, filled with realistic details and a beautiful balance of colors. The format would work well as a read-aloud choice. . . . Independent readers or browsers could enjoy perusing the book themselves." SLJ

Toupin, Laurie
  Freshwater habitats; life in freshwater ecosystems. F. Watts 2005 63p il map (Biomes and habitats) lib bdg $25.50; pa $8.95
Grades: 4 5 6 7   577.6
  1. Freshwater ecology
  ISBN 0-531-12305-7 lib bdg; 0-531-16675-9 pa
                                LC 2003-16572

A look at the plants, animals, locations, and various habitats that make up the freshwater ecosystems of the world

Trumbore, Cindy

★ The **mangrove** tree; planting trees to feed families. Lee & Low Books 2011 40p il $19.95

Grades: 2 3 4   577.6

1. Mangrove ecology

ISBN 978-1-60060-459-1; 1-60060-459-5

LC 2010034501

"Roth's artwork is a treat, cut-paper and fabric collages of intense, shimmering color on a ground of paper that is electric with thick veins of fiber (photos join glossary in backmatter). . . . Hitting home hard is the project's simple practicality: no high-tech, no great infusions of capital or energy—in a word, motivating, in the best possible way." Kirkus

Wechsler, Doug

Frog heaven; ecology of a vernal pool. [by] Doug Wechsler; photographs by the author. Boyds Mills Press 2006 48p il $17.95

Grades: 3 4 5 6   577.6

1. Frogs 2. Vernal pool ecology 3. Natural history -- Delaware

ISBN 978-1-59078-253-8; 1-59078-253-4

LC 2005037562

"Wechsler offers a close-up view of a vernal pool in Delaware as it cycles through the year. . . . Wechsler's clear, color photos provide an excellent visual counterpoint to the text. This well-focused book will open readers' eyes." Booklist

Includes glossary and bibliographical references

577.68 Wetland ecology

Gibbons, Gail

Marshes & swamps. Holiday House 1998 un il $16.95; pa $6.95

Grades: K 1 2 3   577.68

1. Swamps 2. Ecology 3. Marshes 4. Wetlands

ISBN 0-8234-1347-0; 0-8234-1515-5 pa

LC 97-17995

Defines marshes and swamps, discusses how conditions in them may change, and examines the life found in and around them

"Gibbons balances a succinct, informative text with well-labeled watercolors." Horn Book Guide

577.69 Saltwater wetland and seashore ecology

Yezerski, Thomas

★ **Meadowlands**; a wetlands survival story. Thomas F. Yezerski. Farrar, Straus, Giroux 2011 40 p. il

Grades: 2 3   577.69

1. Wetland ecology 2. Meadowlands (N.J.) 3. New Jersey -- History 4. Natural history -- New Jersey

ISBN 0374349134; 9780374349134

LC 2010005503

This is an "ecological history of the Meadowlands of New Jersey, an estuary trapped in a dense industrial, commercial, and residential area. . . . Primary." (Horn Book)

This picture book explores the Meadowlands region of New Jersey, "a vast wetlands west of New York City [that] . . . was diked and drained by early European settlers and later developed and trashed. In the last 40 years, with dumping stopped and restoration begun, some wildlife has returned. . . . [Thomas F.] Yezerski surveys human uses as well as the disappearance and reappearance of other forms of life. . . . [The illustrations depict] industrial products and means of transport, . . . the varied contents of a trash mountain and . . . modern residential and commercial development. These are followed by pages showing marsh plants, worms and insects, some of the many varieties of fish that visit the waters, animals that live on the banks and birds that live there or stop by during migration." (Kirkus)

"Yezerski adroitly captures the tensions and hope in the sometimes adversarial, sometimes beneficial relationship between humans and the environment in this marvelous ecological history of the Meadowlands of New Jersey, an estuary trapped in a dense industrial, commercial, and residential area. . . . Despite humans' best efforts, the relationship is still fragile, and here captured beautifully in the expansive watercolor illustrations. . . . Each main double-page-spread illustration is bordered by tiny images with a wealth of additional taxonomical information (and sly humor) about the diverse flora and fauna (and mobsters and sports enthusiasts) of northern New Jersey." Horn Book

Includes bibliographical references

577.7 Marine ecology

Becker, Helaine

The **big** green book of the big blue sea; written by Helaine Becker; illustrated by Willow Dawson. Kids Can Press 2012 80 p. $15.95

Grades: 3 4 5   577.7

1. Science -- Experiments 2. Marine biology -- Juvenile literature 3. Marine ecology -- Juvenile literature 4. Environmental protection -- Juvenile literature

ISBN 1554537460; 9781554537464

This book, by Helaine Becker, "shows how the ocean works and why this immense ecosystem needs our protection. Experiments using everyday materials help explain scientific concepts. . . . A focus on pollution and other ecological hazards raises awareness. Young scientists will gain a hands-on understanding of how 'booms' clean oil spills and how a garbage patch roughly twice the size of Texas came to exist in the middle of the Pacific Ocean." (Publisher's note)

Callery, Sean

Ocean. Kingfisher 2011 32p il (Life cycles)

Grades: 2 3 4   577.7

1. Marine animals 2. Marine ecology 3. Food chains (Ecology)

ISBN 0-7534-6577-9; 978-0-7534-6577-6

After a brief introduction to the ocean ecosystem "examples of three actual food chains within that ecosystem are presented. . . . Well-designed double-page spreads . . . provide brief information about each creature and its place in the chain. Vivid photos and vibrantly colored pages are eye-catching. Useful food web charts summarizing content are appended." Horn Book Guide

Chin, Jason
Coral reefs. Roaring Brook Press 2011 un il $16.99
Grades: K 1 2 3   **577.7**
1. Coral reefs and islands
ISBN 978-1-5964-3563-6; 1-5964-3563-1
LC 2010045189
"Chin, who pioneered this hybrid form of straightforward nonfiction text and fanciful pictures with Redwoods (2009), offers another a statement about the power of reading for an imaginative child with this appealing introduction to a complex world. He opens and closes his narrative with accurate and clearly labeled pencil sketches of a large variety of reef-dwellers. Inside, realistic watercolor images, some in panels, some in full-bleed pages and even double-page spreads, complement the text." Kirkus

Collard, Sneed B.
On the coral reefs; by Sneed B. Collard III. Marshall Cavendish Benchmark 2005 43p il (Science adventures) lib bdg $25.64
Grades: 4 5 6   **577.7**
1. Marine ecology 2. Coral reefs and islands 3. Ecologists
ISBN 0-7614-1953-5
LC 2004030316
This describes the ecology of coral reefs and the research of marine biologist Dr. Alexandra Grutter.
Includes glossary and bibliographical references

Cousteau, Philippe
Make a splash! a kid's guide to protecting our oceans, lakes, rivers & wetlands. by Cathryn Berger Kaye; with Philippe Cousteau and EarthEcho International. Free Spirit Pub. Inc. 2013 125 p. ill. (chiefly col.) (paperback) $13.99
Grades: 3 4 5 6   **577.7**
1. Environmentalists 2. Water conservation 3. Marine ecology -- Juvenile literature 4. Environmentalism -- Juvenile literature 5. Marine pollution -- Prevention -- Juvenile literature
ISBN 1575424177; 9781575424170
LC 2012032120
This book for elementary-age readers has "colorful photos and digital drawings [that] illustrate many aspects of water on Earth, while the text provides information and tells stories of children in elementary schools around the world who have translated their own environmental concerns into action." (Booklist)

Crenson, Victoria
★ Horseshoe crabs and shorebirds; the story of a food web. illustrated by Annie Cannon. Marshall Cavendish 2003 un il lib bdg $16.95
Grades: 2 3 4   **577.7**
1. Crabs 2. Food chains (Ecology) 3. Horseshoe crabs -- Eggs 4. Ecology -- Delaware Bay (Del. and N.J.) 5. Food chains (Ecology) -- Delaware Bay (Del. and N.J.) 6. Food chains (Ecology) -- Delaware Bay (Del. and N.J.) -- Juvenile literature 7. Limulus polyphemus -- Eggs -- Delaware Bay (Del. and N.J.) -- Juvenile

literature
ISBN 0-7614-5115-3
LC 2002-156473
Presents a portrait of the Delaware Bay in the spring when a wide variety of animals, including minnows, mice, turtles, raccoons, and especially migrating shorebirds, come to feed on the billions of eggs laid by horseshoe crabs
"Crenson's text is highly descriptive and reads like an adventure story, conveying the action and excitement of nature. Cannon's watercolors fill the pages with atmosphere and motion." SLJ

Gibbons, Gail
Coral reefs. Holiday House 2007 32p il $16.95
Grades: K 1 2 3   **577.7**
1. Coral reefs and islands 2. Coral reef ecology -- Juvenile literature
ISBN 978-0-8234-2080-3; 0-8234-2080-9
LC 2006-37959
"Gibbons introduces a complex ecosystem with accessible words and inviting watercolor-washed pictures. . . . [The author explains] coral types and anatomy, how reefs form, and the symbiotic . . . relationship among reef creatures." Booklist

Hooks, Gwendolyn
Makers and takers; studying food webs in the ocean. [by] Gwendolyn Hooks. Rourke Pub. 2009 32p il map (Studying food webs) lib bdg $28.50
Grades: 3 4 5   **577.7**
1. Marine ecology 2. Food chains (Ecology)
ISBN 978-1-60472-319-9 lib bdg; 1-60472-319-X lib bdg
LC 2008-24860
This book has "stunning photos, fascinating facts, and intriguing examples. . . . Herbivores, omnivores, and carnivores specific to . . . [The ocean] ecosystem are presented. . . . 'Chew on this' insets add further interest and information. . . . [This] will appeal to readers." SLJ
Includes glossary and bibliographical references

Jackson, Kay
Explore the ocean; by Kay Jackson. Capstone Press 2007 32p il (Explore the biomes) $16.95; pa $6.95
Grades: PreK K 1 2   **577.7**
1. Marine ecology
ISBN 978-0-7368-6406-0; 0-7368-6406-7; 978-0-7368-9629-0 pa; 0-7368-9629-5 pa
LC 2006004110
This an introduction to the ocean habitat and some of its plants and animals.
This book "uses vivid, sense-appealing language. . . . An attractive . . . format displays the captions to colorful photographs." Sci Books Films
Includes bibliographical references

Johansson, Philip
The coral reef; a colorful web of life. Enslow Publishers 2007 48p il (Wonderful water biomes) lib bdg $17.95
Grades: 3 4 5   **577.7**
1. Coral reefs and islands 2. Ecology -- Juvenile

literature
ISBN 978-0-7660-2813-5 lib bdg; 0-7660-2813-5
lib bdg

LC 2006-17903

"Following a lively account of a team of divers' under-water observations, the chapters discuss types of coral reefs, their formation, and the plants and animals that inhabit them. . . . Johansson writes knowledgably and vividly, and his text, along with the well-chosen color photos, will inspire interest." Booklist

Includes glossary and bibliographical references

Parker, Steve, 1952-

Seashore; written by Steve Parker. rev ed; DK Pub. 2004 72p il (DK eyewitness books) $15.99

Grades: 4 5 6 7   577.7

1. Seashore 2. Marine plants 3. Marine animals
ISBN 0-7566-0721-3; 0-7566-0720-5 lib bdg
First published 1989 by Knopf

Brief text and photos introduce the animal inhabitants of the seashore, including fish, crustaceans, snails, and shorebirds

Pfeffer, Wendy

★ Life in a coral reef; illustrated by Steve Jenkins. Collins 2009 32p il (Let's-read-and-find-out science) $16; pa $5.99

Grades: K 1 2 3   577.7

1. Coral reefs and islands 2. Coral reef animals -- Juvenile literature 3. Coral reef ecology -- Juvenile literature
ISBN 978-0-06-029553-0; 0-06-029553-8; 978-0-06-445222-9 pa; 0-06-445222-0 pa

LC 2008000498

"Jenkins' striking paper-collage illustrations nicely complement Pfeffer's clear and engaging text in this successful explanation of what lies beneath the surface of the ocean in and around a coral reef." Booklist

Pringle, Laurence P.

Come to the ocean's edge; a nature cycle book. illustrated by Michael Chesworth. Boyds Mills Press 2003 32p il $15.95

Grades: K 1 2 3   577.7

1. Seashore ecology 2. Beaches -- Juvenile literature
ISBN 1-56397-779-6

This offers "a poetic text and beautifully composed watercolor paintings. . . . While providing a realistic view of this environment, the artwork also echoes the expressive tone of the narrative." SLJ

Pyers, Greg

The biodiversity of coral reefs. Marshall Cavendish 2010 32p il map (Biodiversity) lib bdg $28.50

Grades: 4 5 6 7   577.7

1. Coral reefs and islands
ISBN 978-1-60870-070-7 lib bdg; 1-60870-070-4 lib bdg

"Discusses the variety of living things in a coral reef's ecosystem." Publisher's note

Includes glossary

Slade, Suzanne

What if there were no sea otters? a book about the ocean ecosystem. illustrated by Carol Schwartz. Picture Window Books 2011 24p il map (Food chain reactions) lib bdg $25.99; pa $8.95

Grades: 2 3 4   577.7

1. Otters 2. Marine ecology
ISBN 978-1-4048-6018-6 lib bdg; 1-4048-6018-5 lib bdg; 978-1-4048-6397-2 pa; 1-4048-6397-4 pa

LC 2010009879

Discusses the ocean ecosystem and the role of the sea otter as a keystone species in helping to maintain it, describing the otter's place on the food chain and what would happen if the sea otter were to become extinct.

"Radiant illustrations are paired with simple, perceptive sentences to underscore the impact of the loss of [sea otters]. . . . In a very effective convention extinct plants and animals are placed in silhouettes within many illustrations—the black void left by the loss of each species increases with each page. This . . . will engage readers on many levels." SLJ

Includes glossary and bibliographical references

Taylor-Butler, Christine

A home in the coral reef; by Christine Taylor-Butler. Childrens Press 2007 24p il (Scholastic news nonfiction readers) $20

Grades: 1 2 3   577.7

1. Coral reefs and islands
ISBN 0-516-25344-1; 978-0-516-25344-2

LC 2006002305

An introduction to coral reef ecology

"Simple, easy-to-read. . . . Everything students need for reports is beautifully depicted with scenic full-color photographs of the land, the plants, and the animals that live there." SLJ

Includes bibliographical references

577.8 Synecology and population biology

Aruego, Jose

Weird friends; unlikely allies in the animal kingdom. [by] Jose Aruego and Ariane Dewey. Harcourt 2002 un il $16

Grades: K 1 2 3   577.8

1. Symbiosis
ISBN 0-15-202128-0

LC 2001-1154

"This book offers an overview of fourteen symbiotic animal relationships, such as that between rhinos and cattle egrets. . . . The brief text provides a short description of the animals, what their functions are, and how they cooperate with their allies. The brightly colored illustrations feature anthropomorphized creatures, which may attract younger naturalists." Horn Book Guide

578 Natural history of organisms and related subjects

Collard, Sneed B.

In the rain forest canopy. Marshall Cavendish Benchmark 2006 43p il (Science adventures) lib bdg $25.70

Grades: 4 5 6   **578**

1. Rain forests 2. Foresters 3. Ecologists 4. College teachers 5. Natural history -- Costa Rica 6. Rain forest ecology -- Juvenile literature 7. Forest canopy ecology -- Juvenile literature

ISBN 0-7614-1954-3

LC 2004-27940

This describes the rain forest canopy and the research of Dr. Nalini Nadkarni in Monteverde, Costa Rica

Includes glossary and bibliographical references

Kelsey, Elin

Strange new species; astonishing discoveries of life on earth. Maple Tree Press 2005 96p il $24.95; pa $16.95

Grades: 5 6 7 8   **578**

1. Biology 2. Scientists 3. Natural history 4. Discoveries in science -- Juvenile literature

ISBN 1-897066-31-7; 1-897066-32-5 pa

"This large-format book showcases new species . . . and the scientists who have discovered them. . . . The discussion ends with information on cloning, genetically modified food, and the future of life. . . . With many excellent photos, this introductory book on new species will be an intriguing addition to classroom units on classification or biology." Booklist

Strauss, Rochelle

Tree of life; the incredible biodiversity of life on Earth. Kids Can Press 2004 40p il $16.95

Grades: 5 6 7 8   **578**

1. Biological diversity 2. Biology -- Classification 3. Biology -- Juvenile literature

ISBN 1-55337-669-2

The "text first introduces the concept of a family tree for all living things, then goes on to name the five kingdoms of scientific classification. . . . The author describes the life-forms included in each species, with specific examples shown in the softly colorful illustrations accompanied by informative captions. . . . Striking, lucid, and deceptively simple." SLJ

Wildlife and plants; 3rd ed.; Marshall Cavendish 2007 20v il set $359.95

Grades: 4 5 6 7   **578**

1. Reference books 2. Plants -- Encyclopedias 3. Animals -- Encyclopedias

ISBN 978-0-7614-7693-1

First published 1994 with title: Wildlife and plants of the world

This set includes "more than 500 entries covering animals, plants, microorganisms, fungi, habitats, biomes, and overviews. . . . Entries provide a concise introduction followed by more detailed information including behavior, reproduction, characteristics, and survival tactics. . . . With its captivating information and photographs, students are sure to come to this easy-to-use set again and again." Booklist

578.4 Adaptation

Rustad, Martha E. H.

Animals in fall; preparing for winter. illustrated by Amanda Enright. Millbrook Press 2011 24p il (Fall's here!) lib bdg $23.93

Grades: K 1 2 3   **578.4**

1. Autumn 2. Winter 3. Animal behavior

ISBN 978-0-7613-5066-8; 0-7613-5066-7

LC 2010053468

This "relates the animals preparation for winter through pictures and text. . . . At the end of the book an activity that children can do to understand how extra fat can keep you warm is featured. . . . Children will enjoy the colorful, expressive illustrations." Sci Books Films

Includes glossary and bibliographical references

Silverstein, Alvin

★ **Adaptation**; by Alvin Silverstein, Virginia Silverstein, and Laura Silverstein Nunn. Twenty-First Century Books 2008 112p il (Science concepts) lib bdg $31.93

Grades: 4 5 6 7   **578.4**

1. Adaptation (Biology) 2. Evolution (Biology) -- Juvenile literature

ISBN 978-0-8225-3434-1 lib bdg; 0-8225-3434-7 lib bdg

LC 2007-02862

This "provides an accessible introduction to how living beings adapt to survive in diverse habitats. . . . The narrative gains clarity from abundant examples, colorful photos and diagrams, and fascinating sidebars." Booklist

Includes bibliographical references

578.6 Miscellaneous nontaxonomic kinds of organisms

Batten, Mary

Aliens from Earth; when animals and plants invade other ecosystems. written by Mary Batten; illustrated by Beverly Doyle. Peachtree Pubs. 2003 un il $15.95

Grades: 3 4 5 6   **578.6**

1. Plant introduction 2. Animal introduction 3. Nonindigenous pests 4. Biological invasions

ISBN 1-56145-236-X

LC 2002-13170

Explores how and why plants and animals enter ecosystems to which they are not native, as well as the consequences of these invasions for other animals, plants, and humans

"From the book title and first line of text . . . to the information-packed, full-page color illustrations, this overview of ecological missteps is nonstop intriguing." Booklist

Collard, Sneed B.

★ **Science** warriors; the battle against invasive species. written by Sneed B. Collard III. Houghton Mifflin 2008 48p il (Scientists in the field) $17

Grades: 5 6 7 8   **578.6**

1. Nonindigenous pests 2. Biological invasions 3. Scientists -- Juvenile literature

ISBN 978-0-618-75636-0; 0-618-75636-1

LC 2008-01867

"Collard focuses on four major invader species in the U.S.: the brown tree snake, . . . the red imported fire ant, . . . the melaleuca tree, . . . and the zebra mussel. . . . These are useful and thought-provoking case studies of a very large problem." Bull Cent Child Books

Includes glossary and bibliographical references

Drake, Jane

Alien invaders; species that threaten our world. [by] Jane Drake & Ann Love; illustrated by Mark Thurman. Tundra Books 2008 56p il map $19.95

Grades: 3 4 5 6   578.6

1. Nonindigenous pests 2. Biological invasions
ISBN 978-0-88776-798-2; 0-88776-798-2

"This book discusses non-native flora and fauna that endanger native species. The authors present historical cases (Irish potato blight, toad invasion in Australia), the most notorious invasive species, and threatened communities. Each double-page spread features a detailed gouache illustration, a conversational overview of problems, and some species-specific facts." Horn Book Guide

Jackson, Cari

Alien invasion; invasive species become major menaces. Gareth Stevens Pub. 2010 48p il (Current science) lib bdg $31

Grades: 4 5 6   578.6

1. Nonindigenous pests 2. Biological invasions
ISBN 978-1-4339-2057-8 lib bdg; 1-4339-2057-3 lib bdg

LC 2009002279

This "lively, well-organized [text profiles] dozens of organisms that threaten our health and well-being. Jackson succinctly describes the characteristics of more than three dozen invasive species of plants and animals. . . . One or more illustrations accompany the text on every page—a mix of sharp, color photographs and some color drawings, maps, life cycle diagrams, etc." SLJ

Includes glossary and bibliographical references

Johnson, Rebecca L.

★ Zombie makers; true stories of nature's undead. Rebecca L. Johnson. Millbrook Press 2013 48 p.

Grades: 4 5 6   578.6

1. Parasites -- Juvenile literature 2. Host-parasite relationships -- Juvenile literature
ISBN 0761386335; 9780761386339

LC 2011046181

In this book, by Rebecca L. Johnson, real biological examples of "zombies" in nature are profiled. "[D]ead people do not come back to live and start walking around, looking for trouble. But there are things that can take over the bodies and brains of innocent creatures, turning them into senseless slaves. Meet nature's zombie makers--including a fly-enslaving fungus, a suicide worm, and a cockroach-taming wasp--and their victims." (Publisher's note)

Includes bibliographical references (p. 46-47) and index

Metz, Lorijo

What can we do about invasive species? PowerKids Press 2010 24p il (Protecting our planet) lib bdg $21.25; pa $8

Grades: 2 3 4   578.6

1. Nonindigenous pests 2. Biological invasions
ISBN 978-1-4042-8084-7 lib bdg; 1-4042-8084-7 lib bdg; 978-1-4358-2487-4 pa; 1-4358-2487-3 pa

LC 2008-55828

This book provides "straightforward information . . . complemented by full-page, color photographs. . . . Links for further information . . . are housed at the publisher's Web site (which allows feedback so that readers can suggest more sites)." SLJ

Includes glossary

Owen, Ruth

Gross body invaders. Bearport Pub. 2011 24p il (Up close and gross) lib bdg $22.61

Grades: 3 4 5   578.6

1. Parasites
ISBN 978-1-61772-127-4; 1-61772-127-1

LC 2010044416

This describes small creatures which can invade the body, including head lice, eyelash mites, mosquitoes, ticks, fleas, hookworms, tapeworms, and horseflies.

"Never have the wonders of electron microscopy been more thrillingly displayed. . . . These knife-sharp, all-too-explicit photos are riveting. The [text doesn't] trail far behind in appeal either." SLJ

Includes glossary and bibliographical references

Icky house invaders. Bearport Pub. 2011 24p il (Up close and gross) lib bdg $22.61

Grades: 3 4 5   578.6

1. Microbiology 2. Household pests
ISBN 978-1-61772-124-3; 1-61772-124-7

LC 2010041241

This describes insects and other small creatures which can inhabit a home, including houseflies, fleas, dust mites, bedbugs, moths, cockroaches, woodworms, and silverfish.

"Never have the wonders of electron microscopy been more thrillingly displayed. . . . These knife-sharp, all-too-explicit photos are riveting. The [text doesn't] trail far behind in appeal either." SLJ

Includes glossary and bibliographical references

578.68   Rare and endangered species

Pobst, Sandy

★ Animals on the edge; science races to save species threatened with extinction. by Sandra Pobst; Todd K. Fuller, consultant. National Geographic 2008 64p il (National Geographic investigates) $17.95; lib bdg $27.90

Grades: 4 5 6 7   578.68

1. Endangered species 2. Wildlife conservation
ISBN 978-1-4263-0358-6; 1-4263-0358-0; 978-1-4263-0265-7 lib bdg; 1-4263-0265-7 lib bdg

This "eye-catching [title features] full-color photographs. . . . The approach is to understand the challenges to protecting endangered animals, including global warming, destruction of habitat, tagging and tracking, poaching, captive breeding, and cloning." Voice Youth Advocates

Includes glossary and bibliographical references

578.7 Organisms characteristic of specific kinds of environments

Arnosky, Jim
★ **Beachcombing**; exploring the seashore. Dutton Children's Bks. 2004 un il $15.99
Grades: K 1 2 3   578.7
  1. Seashore
ISBN 0-525-47104-9

Illustrations and text describe some of the many things that can be found on a walk along a beach, including coconuts, shark teeth, jellyfish, crabs and different kinds of shells.

"Young beachcombers will discover old and new ideas about collecting or just identifying their finds, and the book will appeal to those children who are looking for relaxing fun." SLJ

Parrotfish and sunken ships; exploring a tropical reef. by Jim Arnosky. Collins 2007 un il map $16.99; lib bdg $17.89
Grades: 2 3 4 5   578.7
  1. Coral reefs and islands 2. Natural history -- Florida
ISBN 978-0-688-17123-0; 978-0-688-17124-7 lib bdg
LC 2007010994

"With stunning watercolors and a brief, easy-to-follow text, Arnosky chronicles a boat trip he took with his wife through the coral reefs off the Florida Keys." Booklist

Cerullo, Mary M.
Life under ice; photography by Bill Curtsinger. Tilbury House 2003 37p il map $16.95
Grades: 3 4 5   578.7
  1. Marine plants 2. Marine animals 3. Natural history -- Antarctica
ISBN 0-88448-246-4
LC 2002-154451

Follows marine photographer Bill Curtsinger as he dives under the ice at Antarctica to learn about the plants and animals that thrive in this extreme habitat

"Illustrated with stunning color undersea photographs, this offers a fascinating look at the many creatures living near and beneath the waters of Antarctica. . . . The text is clear and well written, but it is the wonderful photography that distinguishes the book." Booklist

Includes glossary and bibliographical references

Conlan, Kathy
Under the ice. Kids Can Press 2002 55p il $16.95; pa $8.95
Grades: 4 5 6 7   578.7
  1. Authors 2. Marine biology 3. Marine pollution 4. Marine biologists 5. Children's authors 6. Writers on science
ISBN 1-55337-001-5; 1-55337-060-0 pa

"The first-person text creates a feeling of immediacy. . . . Well-captioned, color photos appear throughout the book. . . . Conlan . . . offers readers an engaging account of her adventurous career in scientific field research." Booklist

Ernst, Lisa Campbell
How things work in the yard. Blue Apple Books 2011 un il $14.99

Grades: K 1 2 3   578.7
  1. Urban ecology
ISBN 978-1-60905-009-2; 1-60905-009-6
LC 2010046821

"Graph paper style backgrounds emphasize the schematic approach to nature that Campbell-Ernst uses to explain how different items and creatures—such as birds, butterflies, rocks, and dirt—that can be found in a typical backyard 'work.' There's a playful aesthetic in evidence, from the bright palette and friendly cut-paper artwork to the innate humor in some of the questions themselves. . . . The various parts of the animals, plants, and objects are labeled, and brief facts about each subject dot the spreads. . . . It's an elegantly designed primer to the natural world." Publ Wkly

Guiberson, Brenda Z.
★ **Life** in the boreal forest; paintings by Gennady Spirin. Henry Holt and Co. 2009 un il $16.99
Grades: 2 3 4 5   578.7
  1. Forest ecology 2. Taiga ecology -- Juvenile literature 3. Forest animals -- Juvenile literature
ISBN 978-0-8050-7718-6; 0-8050-7718-9
LC 2008-18329

"Gorgeously intricate illustrations perfectly complement equally evocative text in this introduction to the great northern, or boreal, forest, which sprawls across the entire northern hemisphere. . . . Any child interested in animals or the outdoors will be fascinated by the array portrayed here in a series of vignettes, each of which intersperses factual information information with lively action scenes." Booklist

Kirby, Richard R.
Ocean drifters; a secret world beneath the waves. Firefly Books 2011 192p il $29.95
Grades: 5 6 7 8 9 10 11 12 Adult   578.7
  1. Marine plankton
ISBN 978-1-55407-982-7; 1-55407-982-9
LC 2011284690

"This is a very well illustrated book of some 121 full-page color photographs of microscopic marine organisms. Each illustration is accompanied by a brief description and explanation. Phytoplankton and zooplankton are featured, but also included are picoplankton, virioplankton, and bacterioplankton, with emphasis on the role played by plankton in the carbon cycle, oxygen production, and as the base of the marine food pyramid as the primary producers. Their importance in sustaining the life of the oceans, in petroleum and natural gas resources, and in climate is also discussed." Sci Books Films

Includes bibliographical references

Kummer, Patricia K.
The **Great** Barrier Reef; by Patricia K. Kummer. Marshall Cavendish Benchmark 2008 96p il map (Nature's wonders) lib bdg $24.95
Grades: 5 6 7 8   578.7
  1. Coral reefs and islands
ISBN 978-0-7614-2852-7 lib bdg; 0-7614-2852-6 lib bdg
LC 2007026661

"Provides comprehensive information on the geography, history, wildlife, peoples, and environmental issues of the Great Barrier Reef." Publisher's note

Includes glossary and bibliographical references

O'Neill, Michael Patrick

Ocean magic. Batfish 2008 45p il $19.95

Grades: 1 2 3 4   **578.7**

    1. Ocean 2. Marine animals 3. Coral reef ecology -- Juvenile literature

    ISBN 978-0-9728653-5-7; 0-9728653-5-7

                             LC 2007-904079

"O'Neill introduces readers to coral reefs, kelp forests, and the ocean bottom. Especially stunning are the photos of the Hairy Frogfish, an incredibly camouflaged member of the Anglerfish family that prowls off the coast of Florida. Nevertheless, the colorful creatures of the coral reef are the stars of this book. The author's strong support of conservation comes through loud and clear in his narrative, and photographs amplify this message by showing the amazing life-forms that could be lost." SLJ

Owen, Ruth

Creepy backyard invaders. Bearport Pub. 2011 24p il (Up close and gross) lib bdg $22.61

Grades: 3 4 5   **578.7**

    1. Insects 2. Agricultural pests

    ISBN 978-1-61772-125-0; 1-61772-125-5

                             LC 2010041212

This describes organisms which can inhabit a backyard, including earwigs, honeybees, aphids, ants, lacewings, jumping spiders, woodlice, and stinging nettles.

"Never have the wonders of electron microscopy been more thrillingly displayed. . . . These knife-sharp, all-too-explicit photos are riveting. The [text doesn't] trail far behind in appeal either." SLJ

Includes glossary and bibliographical references

Person, Stephen

The **coral** reef; a giant city under the sea. consultant, Rod Salm. Bearport Pub. 2009 32p il map (Spectacular animal towns) lib bdg $25.27

Grades: 2 3 4   **578.7**

    1. Coral reefs and islands

    ISBN 978-1-59716-869-4 lib bdg; 1-59716-869-6 lib bdg

                            LC 2009-12952

"Through excellent photographs, high-interest texts, sidebars, maps, and other material, children learn about both the animals and their habitats. The . . . . book also provides brief profiles of animals with similar habitats. . . . [This book is] much better than average 'report' titles." SLJ

Includes glossary and bibliographical references

Santoro, Lucio

Wild oceans; [by] Lucio and Meera Santoro. Little Simon 2010 un il $27.99

Grades: 2 3 4 5   **578.7**

    1. Marine biology 2. Pop-up books

    ISBN 978-1-4169-8467-2; 1-4169-8467-4

"Using the ocean as their milieu, the Santoros . . . provide solid information along with amazing visuals. Beginning with a 3-D re-creation of a tide pool, the book then moves to the open sea, where a whale rises out of the pages. An explanation of light zones underwater is illustrated by an anglerfish that lives 3,000 feet below the water's surface. Views of a coral reef and life in the frozen sea complete the treatment. Fact-filled fun." Booklist

Serafini, Frank

Looking closely across the desert. Kids Can Press 2008 un il (Looking closely) $16.95

Grades: K 1 2 3   **578.7**

    1. Deserts 2. Desert ecology -- Juvenile literature

    ISBN 978-1-55453-211-7; 1-55453-211-6

"An extreme closeup color photo of a section of a plant, animal, or other natural object set in a circle on a black background challenges readers to guess its identity. Turning the page reveals a large photo of the item in its natural setting, accompanied by two paragraphs of descriptive and informative text." SLJ

Looking closely along the shore; [by] Frank Serafini. Kids Can Press 2008 un il (Looking closely) $16.95

Grades: K 1 2 3   **578.7**

    1. Seashore

    ISBN 978-1-55453-141-7; 1-55453-141-1

This title about plants and animals of the seashore "will pique the interest of children and encourage them to seek out more information. . . . [It is] set up like a guessing game, allowing for interaction. . . . Each entry opens with a white page with large black type that asks viewers to 'Look very closely. What do you see?' The facing page is black with what seems like a hole to peep through to the next spread. . . . Readers are given a couple of possibilities to start them guessing on what image might be depicted, and, when the page is turned, an enlarged closeup is in full view, along with a few interesting facts about the plant or animal." SLJ

Looking closely around the pond. Kids Can Press 2010 un il (Looking closely) $16.95

Grades: K 1 2 3   **578.7**

    1. Ponds 2. Pond plants -- Juvenile literature 3. Pond animals -- Juvenile literature

    ISBN 978-1-55337-395-7; 1-55337-395-2

"Close-ups of a portion of a pond animal, insect, or plant on a spread invite children to guess the featured subject. . . . The animal, insect, or plant is then described in a couple of jaunty paragraphs on a page facing a full-color photograph." SLJ

Looking closely in the rain forest. Kids Can Press 2010 un il (Looking closely) $16.95

Grades: K 1 2 3   **578.7**

    1. Rain forests

    ISBN 978-1-55337-543-2; 1-55337-543-2

This "spotlights life in the tropical rain forest, including a squirrel monkey, a banana plant, a moth orchid, and a scarlet macaw. The crisp, beautiful photos and the interactive text will draw kids into both the interactive fun and scientific facts." Booklist

Looking closely inside the garden. Kids Can Press 2008 un il (Looking closely) $16.95

Grades: K 1 2 3   **578.7**

    1. Gardens 2. Plants -- Juvenile literature 3. Garden animals -- Juvenile literature

    ISBN 978-1-55453-210-0; 1-55453-210-8

"An extreme closeup color photo of a section of a plant, animal, or other natural object set in a circle on a black background challenges readers to guess its identity. Turning the page reveals a large photo of the item in its natural setting, accompanied by two paragraphs of descriptive and informative text." SLJ

Looking closely through the forest. Kids Can Press 2008 un il (Looking closely) $16.95
Grades: K 1 2 3   **578.7**
1. Forest plants 2. Forest animals 3. Forest plants -- Juvenile literature
ISBN 978-1-55453-212-4; 1-55453-212-4

This book about forest plants and animals "will pique the interest of children and encourage them to seek out more information. . . . [It is] set up like a guessing game, allowing for interaction. . . . Each entry opens with a white page with large black type that asks viewers to 'Look very closely. What do you see?' The facing page is black with what seems like a hole to peep through to the next spread. . . . Readers are given a couple of possibilities to start them guessing on what image might be depicted, and, when the page is turned, an enlarged closeup is in full view, along with a few interesting facts about the plant or animal." SLJ

Somervill, Barbara A.
Marine biologist. Cherry Lake Pub. 2009 32p il (Cool science careers) lib bdg $27.07
Grades: 3 4 5 6   **578.7**
1. Marine biology 2. Vocational guidance
ISBN 978-1-60279-504-4 lib bdg; 1-60279-504-5 lib bdg
                                        LC 2008045234
This describes the career of marine biologist, including ways to become involved in the profession, the interests and skills required, and activities for learning more
This is "highly readable. . . . Colorful photographs illustrate [the] book." SLJ
Includes glossary and bibliographical references

Stearns, Precious McKenzie
Coral reefs. Rourke Pub. 2010 24p il map (Eye to eye with endangered habitats) lib bdg $27.07; pa $7.95
Grades: 2 3 4   **578.7**
1. Coral reefs and islands
ISBN 978-1-61590-313-9 lib bdg; 1-61590-313-5 lib bdg; 978-1-61590-552-2 pa; 1-61590-552-9 pa
                                        LC 2010009856
This introduction the coral reefs "opens with dramatic facts that will grab readers. . . . This highly readable title, heavily illustrated with color photos and maps, packs in exciting geology, biology, and ecology as it makes technical information accessible." Booklist
Includes glossary and bibliographical references

Thomas, William David
Marine biologist. Gareth Stevens Pub. 2010 32p il (Cool careers: cutting edge) lib bdg $26; pa $8.95
Grades: 4 5 6   **578.7**
1. Marine biology 2. Vocational guidance
ISBN 978-1-4339-1957-2 lib bdg; 1-4339-1957-5 lib bdg; 978-1-4339-2156-8 pa; 1-4339-2156-1 pa
                                        LC 2009000239
Describes the work of a marine biologist.
This title offers "clear, solid information in a large font. . . [This] short [book is] packed with relevant, current material." SLJ
Includes glossary and bibliographical references

Wallace, Marianne D.
America's forests; guide to plants and animals. Fulcrum Pub. 2009 47p il (America's ecosystems) pa $11.95
Grades: 5 6 7 8   **578.7**
1. Forest plants 2. Forest animals 3. Forest ecology 4. Forests and forestry
ISBN 978-1-55591-595-7 pa; 1-55591-595-7 pa
                                        LC 2008041005
This "is a guide to plants and animals within the context of forest communities. Marianne Wallace . . . expertly crafts this introduction to forests. . . . The book contains abundant illustrations." Sci Books Films
Includes glossary

Wechsler, Doug
Marvels in the muck; life in the salt marshes. Boyds Mills Press 2008 48p il $17.95
Grades: 4 5 6 7   **578.7**
1. Salt marshes 2. Marsh ecology
ISBN 978-1-59078-588-1
                                        LC 2007052583
"A season-by-season look at the ecology of an oft-overlooked habitat. Wechsler's lucid text introduces the insects, birds, reptiles, crustaceans, and other critters that claim this salty expanse as home. . . . Clear color photos present species mentioned in the text." SLJ
Includes glossary and bibliographical references

Winner, Cherie
Life on the edge. Lerner Publications Co. 2006 48p il (Cool science) lib bdg $26.60
Grades: 4 5 6   **578.7**
1. Adaptation (Biology)
ISBN 978-0-8225-2499-1 lib bdg; 0-8225-2499-6 lib bdg
                                        LC 2005011071
This book "introduces creatures in extreme conditions such as thermal pools, Antarctica, and the deep sea. [The book provides] clear explanations of the science and [covers] possible benefits to humans. A variety of photos and information boxes provide an eye-catching . . . layout." Horn Book Guide
Includes glossary and bibliographical references

578.757 Soil biology

Lawrence, Ellen
Dirt; by Ellen Lawrence; consultants, Suzy Gazlay, MA, recipient of the Presidential Award for Excellence in Science Teaching and Kimberly Brenneman, PhD, National Institute for Early Education Research, Rutgers University, New Brunswick, New Jersey. Bearport Pub. Co. 2013 24 p. col. ill. (library) $23.93
Grades: K 1 2 3   **578.757**
1. Soils -- Juvenile literature 2. Soil biology -- Juvenile literature
ISBN 1617727377; 9781617727375
                                        LC 2012046349
This book on dirt by Ellen Lawrence "includes in the materials list a notebook for children to keep records of predictions, observations, and conclusions. There are seven experiments with detailed, age -- appropriate instructions

complete with pictures to support the experiments. There are also graphics that provide students with additional instructions. The author answers the questions in an appendix." (NSTA Recommends)

Includes bibliographical references and index.

579 Natural history of microorganisms, fungi, algae

Arato, Rona

Protists; algae, amoebas, plankton, and other protists. Crabtree Pub. Co. 2010 48p il (A class of their own) lib bdg $29.27; pa $9.95

Grades: 5 6 7 8   579

1. Algae 2. Protists 3. Protozoa

ISBN 978-0-7787-5377-3 lib bdg; 0-7787-5377-8 lib bdg; 978-0-7787-5391-9 pa; 0-7787-5391-3 pa

LC 2009-51386

Looks at the protist kingdom, providing information and examples of species from the major phyla, as well as information about the role of protists in the food chain and in various diseases.

"Lively section headings . . . and notes on uncommon achievements, . . . lighten the substantial load of biological terminology. Illustrated with a plethora of closeup color photos and microphotos, and closing with annotated lists of recommended Web sites, . . . [this captures] the remarkable diversity of life." SLJ

Includes glossary and bibliographical references

Bardhan-Quallen, Sudipta

Kitchen science experiments; how does your mold garden grow? illustrated by Edward Miller. Sterling 2010 64p il (Mad science) $12.95

Grades: 4 5 6   579

1. Biology 2. Microbiology 3. Science -- Experiments

ISBN 978-1-4027-2413-8; 1-4027-2413-6

LC 2010003749

"The language is as much fun as the science, including wordplay warnings . . . and the design is inviting, with colorful diagrams on each spacious, double-page spread. . . . Many students will be hooked by the fascinating revelations about the world around them." Booklist

Includes bibliographical references

Brown, Jordan

Micro mania; a really close-up look at bacteria, bedbugs & the zillions of other gross little creatures that live in, on & all around you! [by] Jordan D. Brown. Imagine! 2010 80p il $19.95

Grades: 4 5 6   579

1. Microorganisms

ISBN 978-0-9823064-2-0; 0-9823064-2-3

"This engrossing book goes into squirm-inducing detail about the bacteria, microbes, and other assorted mini-organisms that dwell in our bodies and our homes. Each spread is well laid out with plenty of white space, large text, and colorful photos of these little critters . . . and the havoc they wreak. The writing is vivid without being breathless." SLJ

Latta, Sara L.

★ The good, the bad, the slimy; the secret life of microbes. [by] Sara Latta; photographs by Dennis Kunkel. Enslow Publishers 2006 128p il lib bdg $31.93

Grades: 5 6 7 8 9   579

1. Microorganisms 2. Bacteria -- Juvenile literature 3. Microbiology -- Juvenile literature

ISBN 0-7660-1294-8

LC 2005-35405

"Explanations are simple and clear, and the layout is appealing, open, and colorful." SLJ

Includes glossary and bibliographical references

Micro monsters. Kingfisher 2010 47p il (Kingdom) $14.99; pa $8.99

Grades: 3 4 5 6   579

1. Insects 2. Microorganisms

ISBN 978-0-7534-3014-9; 0-7534-3014-2; 978-0-7534-6455-7 pa; 0-7534-6455-1 pa

This book illustrates the unseen world of microscopic monsters and shows the reader how they survive and triumph. Some pages have movable flaps to show different pictures.

"Hyper-close-up photos detail all manner of stingers, stabbers, pincers, and chompers poking out from plated exoskeletons and hairy abdomens. This . . . is a great way to sneak in some basic science learning amid the din of death and destruction." Booklist

Walker, Richard, 1951-

Microscopic life; [by] Richard Walker; foreword by Peter C. Doherty. Kingfisher 2004 63p il (Kingfisher knowledge) $12.95

Grades: 4 5 6 7   579

1. Microorganisms 2. Microbiology -- Juvenile literature

ISBN 0-7534-5778-4

LC 2004-1321

"Double-page spreads introduce viruses, bacteria, 'mini animals' (e.g., Hydra and dust mites), and other microorganisms and explain how these unseen entities affect humanity in both harmful and helpful ways. The accompanying photographic enlargements . . . are fascinating." Horn Book Guide

Weakland, Mark

Gut bugs, dust mites, and other microorganisms you can't live without. Capstone Press 2010 32p il (Fact finders. Nasty (but useful!) science) lib bdg $25.99

Grades: 3 4 5   579

1. Bacteria 2. Microorganisms

ISBN 978-1-4296-4538-6 lib bdg; 1-4296-4538-5 lib bdg

This informative guide also explains "relevant chemical processes, medical rationales, and ecological functions in reasonably specific detail. . . . A list of relevant web resources is maintained on the publisher's page." SLJ

Includes glossary and bibliographical references

Wearing, Judy

Fungi; mushrooms, toadstools, molds, yeasts, and other fungi. Crabtree 2010 48p il (A class of their own) lib bdg $29.27; pa $9.95

Grades: 5 6 7 8   **579**
1. Fungi
ISBN 978-0-7787-5375-9 lib bdg; 0-7787-5375-1 lib bdg; 978-0-7787-5389-6 pa; 0-7787-5389-1 pa

Features an examination of the four major groups of fungi: yeasts, toadstools, chytrids, and bread molds.

"Lively section headings . . . and notes on uncommon achievements, . . . lighten the substantial load of biological terminology. Illustrated with a plethora of closeup color photos and microphotos, and closing with annotated lists of recommended Web sites, . . . [thi scaptures] the remarkable diversity of life." SLJ

Includes glossary and bibliographical references

Zabludoff, Marc
The **protoctist** kingdom. Benchmark Books 2006 95p il (Family trees) lib bdg $29.92
Grades: 5 6 7 8   **579**
1. Protoctista
ISBN 0-7614-1818-0
LC 2004-21821

This examines the physical traits, adaptations, diets, habitats, and life cycles of such life forms as bacteria, amoebas, slime nets, molds, algae, coccoliths, forams, and diatoms.

"Fact-filled, yet surprisingly readable. . . . [This] title contains a wide variety of excellent-quality, full-color photographs; interesting sidebars; and diagrams." SLJ

Zamosky, Lisa
Simple organisms. Compass Point Books 2009 40p il (Mission: science) lib bdg $26.60
Grades: 4 5 6   **579**
1. Microorganisms
ISBN 978-0-7565-3955-9 lib bdg; 0-7565-3955-2 lib bdg
LC 2008-7723

An introduction to microscopic organisms, including germs

Includes glossary and bibliographical references

579.3   Prokaryotes (Bacteria)

Barker, David M.
Archaea; salt-lovers, methane-makers, thermophiles, and other archaeans. by David Barker. Crabtree Pub. 2010 48p il (A class of their own) lib bdg $29.27; pa $9.95
Grades: 5 6 7 8   **579.3**
1. Bacteria
ISBN 978-0-7787-5373-5 lib bdg; 0-7787-5373-5 lib bdg; 978-0-7787-5387-2 pa; 0-7787-5387-5 pa
LC 2009-51393

Looks at the archaea domain, providing information and examples of species from the three major phyla, as well as information about why so little is known about this diverse domain.

"Lively section headings . . . and notes on uncommon achievements, . . . lighten the substantial load of biological terminology. Illustrated with a plethora of closeup color photos and microphotos, and closing with annotated lists of recommended Web sites, . . . [this captures] the remarkable diversity of life." SLJ

Includes glossary and bibliographical references

Wearing, Judy
Bacteria; staph, strep, clostridium, and other bacteria. Crabtree 2010 48p il (A class of their own) lib bdg $29.27; pa $9.95
Grades: 5 6 7 8   **579.3**
1. Bacteria
ISBN 978-0-7787-5374-2 lib bdg; 0-7787-5374-3 lib bdg; 978-0-7787-5388-9 pa; 0-7787-5388-3 pa

Examines bacteria that are found in virtually every environment-including those that are characterized by extreme heat, cold, and depth-and, of course, bacteria that are found inside our bodies.

"Lively section headings . . . and notes on uncommon achievements, . . . lighten the substantial load of biological terminology. Illustrated with a plethora of closeup color photos and microphotos, and closing with annotated lists of recommended Web sites, . . . [this captures] the remarkable diversity of life." SLJ

Includes glossary and bibliographical references

579.6   Mushrooms

Royston, Angela
Life cycle of a mushroom; rev and updated ed.; Heinemann Library 2009 32p il (Life cycle of a) $25.36; pa $7.99
Grades: 2 3 4   **579.6**
1. Mushrooms
ISBN 978-1-4329-2530-7; 1-4329-2530-X; 978-1-4329-2547-5 pa; 1-4329-2547-4 pa
LC 2009517694

Introduces the life cycle of a mushroom, from formation of spores through underground growth of the mycelia to formation of mature mushrooms

This offers "easily accessible information in [an] attractive [package]." SLJ

Includes glossary and bibliographical references

579.8   Algae

Cerullo, Mary M.
★ **Sea** soup: phytoplankton; photography by Bill Curtsinger. Tilbury House 1999 39p il $16.95
Grades: 5 6 7 8   **579.8**
1. Phytoplankton 2. Plankton 3. Phytoplankton -- Juvenile literature
ISBN 0-88448-208-1
LC 99-39210

Discusses the microscopic organisms known as phytoplankton and the important functions they serve in replenishing earth's atmosphere, in the marine food chain, and more

"Outstanding full-color photomicroscopy dominates this slim volume on the microscopic plants at the bottom of the ocean food chain. The clearly presented information is not available in another single volume for this audience." SLJ

Includes glossary and bibliographical references

580 Natural history of plants and animals

Goodman, Emily

Plant secrets; illustrated by Phyllis Limbacher Tildes. Charlesbridge 2009 un il $16.95; pa $7.95

Grades: PreK K 1 2   **580**

1. Plants

ISBN 978-1-58089-204-9; 1-58089-204-3; 978-1-58089-205-6 pa; 1-58089-205-1 pa

LC 2008-07256

"Children will look at plants with new eyes after reading this fresh introduction. The plant cycle is introduced, beginning and ending with seeds. . . . The text will draw readers into the wonder of the topic. Bold color-coded headings introduce each of the four stages. Realistic spot illustrations, beginning with the endpapers, present the variety described in the text." SLJ

Gould, Margee

Giant plants. The Rosen Pub. Group 2011 24p il (The strangest plants on Earth) lib bdg $21.25

Grades: 3 4 5   **580**

1. Size 2. Plants

ISBN 978-1-4488-4990-1; 1-4488-4990-X

LC 2010052217

This "colorful [introduction has] bright, full-color photographs that are detailed enough to enable identification in the field. . . . [The book] includes not only the tallest and most massive plants, but also those with giant odors. One of the illustrations for the corpse flower shows kids at a greenhouse holding their noses as they observe the huge flower that smells like rotting meat. . . . Useful for reports and fun to browse, read, and learn." SLJ

Includes glossary

Levine, Shar

Plants; flowering plants, ferns, mosses, and other plants. by Shar Levine and Leslie Johnstone. Crabtree Pub. 2010 48p il (A class of their own) lib bdg $29.27; pa $9.95

Grades: 5 6 7 8   **580**

1. Plants

ISBN 978-0-7787-5376-6 lib bdg; 0-7787-5376-X lib bdg; 978-0-7787-5390-2 pa; 0-7787-5390-5 pa

LC 2009-51342

Describes the main groups of plants, including mosses, ferns, conifers, and flowering plants.

"Lively section headings . . . and notes on uncommon achievements, . . . lighten the substantial load of biological terminology. Illustrated with a plethora of closeup color photos and microphotos, and closing with annotated lists of recommended Web sites, . . . [this captures] the remarkable diversity of life." SLJ

Includes glossary and bibliographical references

Rau, Dana Meachen

Plants. Marshall Cavendish Benchmark 2009 31p il (Bookworms. Nature's cycles) lib bdg $22.79

Grades: PreK K 1   **580**

1. Plants

ISBN 978-0-7614-4097-0 lib bdg; 0-7614-4097-6 lib bdg

LC 2008-42515

"Well composed, simple sentences tie directly to colorful, carefully chosen photos [and] . . . accurate information

flows naturally. . . . A great resource for sharing one-on-one with the youngest readers." Libr Media Connect

Includes glossary

Taylor, Barbara

Inside plants. Marshall Cavendish Benchmark 2010 48p il (Invisible worlds) lib bdg $28.50

Grades: 4 5 6 7   **580**

1. Plants

ISBN 978-0-7614-4189-2 lib bdg; 0-7614-4189-1 lib bdg

LC 2008037247

This describes the plant details that are too small for the unaided eye to see, and how these microscopic systems work to keep the plant alive and healthy.

The narrative is "clear, well written, broken down into manageable pieces, and peppered with eye-opening facts. The numerous photographs are so phenomenal that they will inspire kids to read the text . . . so that they can wrap their minds around what they see." SLJ

Includes glossary and bibliographical references

Wade, Mary Dodson

Trees, weeds, and vegetables--so many kinds of plants! Enslow Elementary 2009 24p il (I like plants!) lib bdg $21.26; pa $6.95

Grades: K 1 2   **580**

1. Plants

ISBN 978-0-7660-3156-2 lib bdg; 0-7660-3156-X lib bdg; 978-0-7660-3616-1 pa; 0-7660-3616-2 pa

LC 2007039460

This does "an excellent job of introducing basic concepts about seeds and plants. Large text on colored pages explains terms and covers a lot of ground in the simplest manner imaginable. The full-color illustrations amplify the narrative." SLJ

Includes glossary and bibliographical references

580.7 Education, research, related topics

Benbow, Ann

Lively plant science projects; [by] Ann Benbow and Colin Mably; illustrations by Tom Labaff. Enslow Publishers 2009 48p il (Real life science experiments) lib bdg $23.93

Grades: 3 4 5   **580.7**

1. Botany 2. Plants 3. Science projects 4. Botany projects -- Juvenile literature 5. Science -- Experiments -- Juvenile literature

ISBN 978-0-7660-3146-3 lib bdg; 0-7660-3146-2 lib bdg

LC 2008-01745

"Color drawings, photographs, a glossary, and suggestions for further research enliven . . . [this] title . . . [and provide] solid curricular support." Booklist

Includes glossary and bibliographical references

Sprouting seed science projects; [by] Ann Benbow and Colin Mably; illustrations by Tom Labaff. Enslow Publishers 2009 48p il (Real life science experiments) lib bdg $23.93

Grades: 3 4 5 **580.7**

1. Seeds 2. Germination 3. Science projects
ISBN 978-0-7660-3147-0 lib bdg; 0-7660-3147-0
lib bdg

LC 2008-1731

"Color drawings, photographs, a glossary, and suggestions for further research enliven . . . [this] title . . . [and
provide] solid curricular support." Booklist

Includes glossary and bibliographical references

Gardner, Robert

Ace your plant science project; great science fair ideas.
[by] Robert Gardner and Phyllis J. Perry. Enslow Publishers 2009 104p il (Ace your biology science project) lib
bdg $31.93

Grades: 5 6 7 8 **580.7**

1. Plants 2. Science projects 3. Science -- Experiments
ISBN 978-0-7660-3221-7 lib bdg; 0-7660-3221-3
lib bdg

LC 2008-4687

"Presents several science experiments and project ideas
using plants." Publisher's note

Includes bibliographical references

Whitehouse, Patricia

Plants; [by] Patricia Whitehouse. Heinemann Library
2008 48p il (Science fair projects) $30

Grades: 5 6 7 8 **580.7**

1. Plants 2. Science projects 3. Science -- Experiments
ISBN 978-1-4034-7918-1

LC 2006039547

This guide to science fair projects about plants "is one
of the better 'how-to-do-a-science-fair project' books on the
market. . . . [It] guides students with initial concrete suggestions and ideas for projects, but continues to challenge students to extend their investigations. . . . The content is presented in a colorful and engaging format." Sci Books Films

Includes glossary and bibliographical references

581 Specific topics in natural history of plants

Munoz, William

Plants on the trail with Lewis and Clark; photographs
by William Muñoz. Clarion Bks. 2003 104p il map $18

Grades: 4 5 6 7 **581**

1. Plants -- United States 2. Botany -- West (U.S.) --
History -- 19th century -- Juvenile literature 3. Plant
collecting -- West (U.S.) -- History -- 19th century --
Juvenile literature
ISBN 0-618-06776-0

LC 2002-10383

Describes the journey of Lewis and Clark through the
western United States, focusing on the plants they cataloged,
their uses for food and medicine, and the plant lore of Native
American people

"Good-quality, full-color photos and reproductions
clearly extend the text. . . . The author's knowledge of and
keen interest in her subject matter is very evident in this fascinating account." SLJ

Includes bibliographical references (p. 88-90) and index

Wade, Mary Dodson

Plants live everywhere! Enslow Elementary 2009 24p
il (I like plants!) lib bdg $21.26; pa $6.95

Grades: K 1 2 **581**

1. Plants
ISBN 978-0-7660-3155-5 lib bdg; 0-7660-3155-1 lib
bdg; 978-0-7660-3615-4 pa; 0-7660-3615-4 pa

LC 2007039457

This book does "an excellent job of introducing basic
concepts about seeds and plants. Large text on colored pages
explains terms and covers a lot of ground in the simplest
manner imaginable. The full-color illustrations amplify the
narrative." SLJ

Includes glossary and bibliographical references

581.4 Adaptation

Aston, Dianna Hutts

★ A seed is sleepy; by Dianna Hutts Aston; illustrated
by Sylvia Long. Chronicle Books 2007 un il $16.95

Grades: K 1 2 3 **581.4**

1. Seeds
ISBN 978-0-8118-5520-4; 0-8118-5520-1

LC 2006-13302

"The topic is seeds, and . . . Long's masterful watercolors dominate each spread, which includes text on two levels.
Short poetic phrases in large print, aimed at younger children, give seeds accessible, anthropomorphic qualities. . . .
Paragraphs in smaller print, which tackle science concepts
and expand on the phrases, are geared to older readers."
Booklist

Farndon, John

Fruits. Blackbirch Press 2006 24p il (World of plants)
lib bdg $27.44

Grades: 2 3 4 5 **581.4**

1. Fruit
ISBN 1-4103-0424-8 lib bdg; 978-1-4103-0424-7
lib bdg

LC 2005052412

This book examines the various types of fruits, including
nuts; regions in which various fruits are grown; animals that
rely on fruit for food; and fruits in the human diet

Includes bibliographical references

Roots. Blackbirch Press 2006 24p il (World of plants)
lib bdg $27.44

Grades: 2 3 4 5 **581.4**

1. Roots (Botany)
ISBN 978-1-4103-0421-6 lib bdg; 1-4103-0421-3
lib bdg

LC 2005047045

This book examines root functions, root growth, kinds
of roots including climbing roots, and roots as food for both
humans and animals

This uses "clear language and short sentences. . . . Helpful diagrams and sharp, colorful photographs supplement the
[text]. . . . [This book offers] solid information in an attractive format." SLJ

Includes bibliographical references

Seeds. Blackbirch Press 2006 24p il (World of plants) lib bdg $27.44

Grades: 2 3 4 5   **581.4**

1. Seeds

ISBN 978-1-4103-0419-3 lib bdg; 1-4103-0419-1 lib bdg

LC 2005047047

This book examines germination, the ways seeds are spread, types and sizes of seeds, and the role of seeds in the diets of both humans and animals

This uses "clear language and short sentences. . . . Helpful diagrams and sharp, colorful photographs supplement the [text]. . . . [This book offers] solid information in an attractive format." SLJ

Includes bibliographical references

Stems. Blackbirch Press 2006 24p il (World of plants) lib bdg $27.44

Grades: 2 3 4 5   **581.4**

1. Stems (Plants)

ISBN 978-1-4103-0420-9 lib bdg; 1-4103-0420-5 lib bdg

LC 2005047049

This book examines how stems grow, the sizes of various types of stems, underground stems, and the ways people and animals use stems for food and shelter

This uses "clear language and short sentences. . . . Helpful diagrams and sharp, colorful photographs supplement the [text]. . . . [This book offers] solid information in an attractive format." SLJ

Includes bibliographical references

Galbraith, Kathryn O.

Planting the wild garden; written by Kathryn O. Galbraith; illustrated by Wendy Anderson Halperin. Peachtree 2011 32 p. il

Grades: K 1   **581.4**

1. Seeds 2. Wild plants 3. Picture books for children 4. Plants

ISBN 1561455636; 9781561455638

LC 2010026898

This picture book answers the question "how do wild plants grow and spread? In . . . prose punctuated with sound effects ('Per-chik-o-ree! Per-chiko-ree!' cries a goldfinch) . . . [Kathryn O.] Galbraith . . . explains that seeds from wild plants float in the wind, snap off plants, fall in the rain, and get carried--intentionally or unintentionally--by animals to new places where they sprout and thrive. 'A family of raccoons feasts on blackberries. . . . When they amble home again, bits of berries and seeds go with them. Next spring, new prickly canes will pop up everywhere.' [Wendy Anderson] Halperin's . . . spreads are divided into contiguous panels tinted in the lightest of watercolors, with delicate pencil shading that conveys the force of wind and rain alike." (Publishers Weekly)

"Seeds grow in wild meadows because they are carried by wind and water, birds and animals, plants and people. This title celebrates the power of these tiny wonders—so delicate, so hardy—with simple, poetic words. . . . The soft, pencil-and-watercolor images alternate expansive landscapes with small, framed details that show tiny, dramatic stories. . . . A natural choice for curriculum connections." Booklist

Goodman, Susan

Seeds, stems, and stamens; the ways plants fit into their world. by Susan E. Goodman; photographs by Michael Doolittle. Millbrook Press 2001 48p il $22.90

Grades: 2 3 4   **581.4**

1. Plants 2. Ecology 3. Adaptation (Biology) 4. Plants -- Habitat

ISBN 0-7613-1874-7

LC 00-68367

The author describes "a variety of ways plants adapt to their environment in order to survive. . . . The text is clearly and concisely written, and Doolittle's color photography is outstanding." Booklist

Gould, Margee

Prickly plants. PowerKids Press 2011 24p il (The strangest plants on Earth) lib bdg $21.25

Grades: 3 4 5   **581.4**

1. Cactus 2. Plants

ISBN 978-1-4488-4991-8; 1-4488-4991-8

LC 2010053141

This describes prickly plants including cacti, stinging nettles, the silk floss tree and the honey locust tree.

This "colorful [introduction has] bright, full-color photographs that are detailed enough to enable identification in the field. . . . Useful for reports and fun to browse, read, and learn." SLJ

Includes glossary

Heneghan, Judith

Once there was a seed; written by Judith Anderson; illustrated by Mike Gordon. Barron's 2010 32p il (Nature's miracles) pa $5.99

Grades: K 1 2   **581.4**

1. Seeds 2. Plants

ISBN 978-0-7641-4493-6 pa; 0-7641-4493-6 pa

First published 2009 in the United Kingdom

Introduces the life cycle of plants, describing how a plant is grown from a seed, sprouts roots and leaves, and eventually forms a mature plant or flower which contains new seeds.

"This proves that science for even the very youngest readers can retain the same nonfiction qualities as that for older students and still be captivating as well as educational." Libr Media Connect

Includes bibliographical references

Kim, Sue

How does a seed grow? a book with fold-out pages. photos by Tilde. Little Simon 2010 un il bd bk $7.99

Grades: PreK   **581.4**

1. Seeds 2. Board books for children 3. Plants -- Growth

ISBN 978-1-4169-9435-0; 1-4169-9435-1

"From seed to sprout to finished fruit, plants spring to life in this inventive picture book that folds out into four scenes on every spread. In a question-and-answer format, the smooth, rhyming text introduces botany basics. . . . Right-hand pages fold out to show the emerging plant in bright color photos, finally reaching an oversize scene of a child enjoying the mature fruit. . . . Both entertaining and informative." Booklist

Macken, JoAnn Early

Flip, float, fly; seeds on the move. by JoAnn Early Macken; illustrated by Pam Paparone. Holiday House 2008 un il $16.95

Grades: K 1 2 3   **581.4**

1. Seeds

ISBN 978-0-8234-2043-8; 0-8234-2043-4

LC 2006-37278

This book introduces "methods of seed distribution. Each is introduced on a double-page spread, in which a few lines of poetic text provide information succinctly. . . . Pleasing in their colors, compositions, and decorative elements, the pictures clearly show points made in the text. . . . Satisfying and well designed for both classroom sharing and individual reading." Booklist

Includes glossary and bibliographical references

Richards, Jean

A **fruit** is a suitcase for seeds; illustrated by Anca Hariton. Millbrook Press 2002 un il lib bdg $21.90

Grades: K 1 2   **581.4**

1. Fruit 2. Seeds

ISBN 0-7613-1622-1

LC 2001-32959

Provides an illustrated description of seed dispersal by which plants, most specifically fruits, travel from one place to another

"Richard's carefully worded information provides an excellent introduction to seeds, their purpose, and growth that should be easy for young children to grasp. . . . Hariton's use of bright watercolors adds sensual appeal to her illustrations." SLJ

Robbins, Ken

★ **Seeds**; text and pictures by Ken Robbins. Atheneum Books for Young Readers 2005 un il $15.95

Grades: K 1 2 3   **581.4**

1. Seeds

ISBN 0-689-85041-7

This "book focuses on seed basics: differences in shapes and sizes, and links between structure and function. . . . Seeds are show alongside the whole plants and fruits they come from. . . . The superb photographs lend themselves to scientific scrutiny: the details are sharp and clear." Horn Book

Rustad, Martha E. H.

Fall leaves; colorful and crunchy. illustrated by Amanda Enright. Millbrook Press 2011 24p il (Fall's here!) lib bdg $23.93

Grades: K 1 2 3   **581.4**

1. Autumn 2. Leaves

ISBN 978-0-7613-5062-0; 0-7613-5062-4

LC 2010053301

In this book "a young girl spies leaves changing color in the fall. She explores how different weather and amounts of sunlight allow the leaves to grow, get food and water, change color, and then fall as the seasons change. . . . In the back of the book, instructions are given for making a leaf print. . . . Children will enjoy the colorful, expressive illustrations." Sci Books Films

Includes glossary and bibliographical references

Wade, Mary Dodson

Seeds sprout! Enslow Elementary 2009 24p il (I like plants!) lib bdg $21.26; pa $6.95

Grades: K 1 2   **581.4**

1. Seeds 2. Plants

ISBN 978-0-7660-3154-8 lib bdg; 0-7660-3154-3 lib bdg; 978-0-7660-3614-7 pa; 0-7660-3614-6 pa

LC 2007039461

This book does "an excellent job of introducing basic concepts about seeds and plants. Large text on colored pages explains terms and covers a lot of ground in the simplest manner imaginable. The full-color illustrations amplify the narrative." SLJ

Includes glossary and bibliographical references

581.6   Miscellaneous nontaxonomic kinds of plants

Farrell, Courtney

Plants out of place. Rourke Pub. 2010 48p il (Let's explore science) $32.79

Grades: 4 5 6 7   **581.6**

1. Plants 2. Biological invasions 3. Food chains (Ecology)

ISBN 978-1-61590-322-1; 1-61590-322-4

LC 2010009909

This "takes a lively look at invasive plants . . . and shows both the destruction that non-native plants cause and what can be done about it. . . . In [this] title, well-chosen boxed examples, abundant color photos, diagrams, and an appended glossary add interest and support the engaging [text]." Booklist

Includes glossary and bibliographical references

Gould, Margee

Poisonous plants. PowerKids Press 2011 24p il (The strangest plants on Earth) lib bdg $21.25

Grades: 3 4 5   **581.6**

1. Poisonous plants

ISBN 978-1-4488-4989-5; 1-4488-4989-6

LC 2010050512

This "colorful [introduction has] bright, full-color photographs that are detailed enough to enable identification in the field, especially of such common poisonous plants as poison ivy, oak, and sumac. . . . Useful for reports and fun to browse, read, and learn." SLJ

Includes glossary

Souza, D. M.

Plant invaders; [by] D. M. Souza. F. Watts 2003 63p il (Watts library) lib bdg $25.50; pa $8.95

Grades: 3 4 5   **581.6**

1. Ecology 2. Plant ecology 3. Nonindigenous pests 4. Biological invasions 5. Invasive plants 6. Plant invasions

ISBN 0-531-12211-5 lib bdg; 0-531-16247-8 pa

LC 2002-8887

Discusses non-native plants, such as the kudzu vine and the tree-of-heaven, which were imported from other countries and now pose a significant threat to the ecosystems of North America

"Large, brightly colored close-up photos ranging from beautiful to bizarre are nicely placed to support the well-written [narrative.]" SLJ

Wade, Mary Dodson

People need plants! Enslow Elementary 2009 24p il (I like plants!) lib bdg $21.26; pa $6.95

Grades: K 1 2   **581.6**

1. Plants

ISBN 978-0-7660-3153-1 lib bdg; 0-7660-3153-5 lib bdg; 978-0-7660-3613-0 pa; 0-7660-3613-8 pa

LC 2007039458

"Beautifully detailed professional photographs of plants, animals, and people complement the subject matter. [The] book includes a simple activity." SLJ

Includes glossary and bibliographical references

582   Plants noted for specific vegetative characteristics and flowers

Schaefer, Lola M.

★ Pick, pull, snap! where once a flower bloomed. illustrated by Lindsay Barrett George. Greenwillow Bks. 2003 un il $15.99

Grades: K 1 2 3   **582**

1. Fruit 2. Seeds 3. Plants 4. Flowers

ISBN 0-688-17834-0

LC 2002-66818

Describes how raspberries, peanuts, corn, and other foods are produced as various plants flower, create seeds, and finally bear fruit

"On each spread, rhythmic, poetic text describes a plant's flower or husk and shows a cross section that reveals the seeds inside. A few lines of text explain a plant's growth, and then the page folds out to reveal the mature plant. . . . George's inviting, realistic color art brings youngsters up close to plants that produce familiar foods." Booklist

Includes glossary

582.13   Plants noted for their flowers

Pascoe, Elaine

Flowers; text by Elaine Pascoe; photographs by Dwight Kuhn. Blackbirch Press 2003 48p il lib bdg $23.70

Grades: 3 4 5   **582.13**

1. Flowers 2. Experiments 3. Flowers -- Experiments 4. Plants -- Juvenile literature 5. Botany projects -- Juvenile literature

ISBN 1-56711-432-6

LC 2002-151824

Describes the parts of different flowers, their role in the plants' reproduction, how to grow flowers, and how to press them. Includes activites and experiments related to flowers

This is "well organized. . . . Different-sized, sharply focused pictures complement the text on almost every page; many are remarkably detailed, extreme close-ups." SLJ

Includes bibliographical references

Souza, D. M.

Freaky flowers. Watts 2002 63p il (Watts library) lib bdg $24.50; pa $8.95

Grades: 5 6 7 8   **582.13**

1. Flowers

ISBN 0-531-11981-5 lib bdg; 0-531-16221-4 pa

LC 2001-17573

"The book begins with a short course in botany that stresses vocabulary and processes. Subsequent chapters discuss different ways plants attract pollinators through colors, odors, and habitats. The last chapter acts as a warning that many plants are endangered because their pollinators are threatened, emphasizing the balance of nature. The outstanding full-color photos feature some of the most spectacular flowers found anywhere. Small sidebars offer interesting bits of trivia about similar plants. The text is packed with biological information and pertinent vocabulary." SLJ

Includes bibliographical references

Wade, Mary Dodson

Flowers bloom! Enslow Elementary 2009 24p il (I like plants!) lib bdg $21.26; pa $6.95

Grades: K 1 2   **582.13**

1. Flowers

ISBN 978-0-7660-3157-9 lib bdg; 0-7660-3157-8 lib bdg; 978-0-7660-3617-8 pa; 0-7660-3617-0 pa

LC 2007039462

"Beautifully detailed professional photographs of plants, animals, and people complement the subject matter. [The] book includes a simple activity." SLJ

Includes glossary and bibliographical references

582.16   Trees

Bulla, Clyde Robert

A tree is a plant; illustrated by Stacey Schuett. HarperCollins Pubs. 2001 31p il (Let's-read-and-find-out science) hardcover o.p. pa $4.95

Grades: K 1 2   **582.16**

1. Trees 2. Apples

ISBN 0-06-028171-5; 0-06-028172-3 lib bdg; 0-06-445196-8 pa

LC 00-40797

A newly illustrated edition of the title first published 1960 by Crowell

The text "follows an apple plant from seed to sprout to tree, including the development of blossoms, leaves, and fruit. The functions of roots, trunk, branches, and leaves are also discussed, as well as the seasonal changes in the tree. Schuett's colorful paintings clearly illustrate topics explained in the text, while their pleasing colors, rounded forms, and small, playful animals will help keep children involved in the topic." Booklist

Ehlert, Lois

★ Red leaf, yellow leaf. Harcourt Brace Jovanovich 1991 un il $16

Grades: K 1 2 3   **582.16**

1. Trees 2. Maple -- Juvenile literature

ISBN 0-15-266197-2

LC 90-21195

"In a quiet, first-person narrative, a young child details the life cycle of a sugar maple tree. . . . The story is quite brief, and the choice of a very large typeface makes the main portion of the book accessible to beginning readers. The concluding section offers more detailed and concrete botanical information and provides hints on selecting and planting one's own tree. . . . Ehlert has combined many media to create the book's dazzling illustrations." Horn Book

Gerber, Carole
Winter trees; illustrated by Leslie Evans. Charlesbridge 2008 un il $15.95
Grades: PreK K 1 2   582.16
1. Trees 2. Winter 3. Trees in winter -- Juvenile literature 4. Trees -- Identification -- Juvenile literature
ISBN 978-1-58089-168-4; 1-58089-168-3
LC 2007-26197
"Alone in the snowy woods with his dog, a boy discovers the wonder of winter trees. . . . On every double-page spread, four lines of simple verse and bright linoleum block prints decorated with watercolor and collage capture the stark outlines and the details of what he sees, hears, and touches. . . . The blend of play, science, poetry, and art is beautiful; and notes at the back provide more facts about each tree." Booklist

Gibbons, Gail
Tell me, tree; all about trees for kids. Little, Brown 2002 un il $15.95
Grades: K 1 2 3   582.16
1. Trees
ISBN 0-316-30903-6
LC 00-64967
"The bright, watercolor illustrations show cheerful children and adults observing, planting, using, and enjoying many kinds of trees. In this simple, informative book, Gibbons provides a basic guide that is sure to please parents and teachers as well as children." Booklist

Howse, Jennifer
Trees. Weigl Publishers 2010 24p il (World of wonder: watch them grow) lib bdg $25.70; pa $9.95
Grades: 1 2   582.16
1. Trees
ISBN 978-1-60596-916-9 lib bdg; 1-60596-916-8 lib bdg; 978-1-60596-917-6 pa; 1-60596-917-6 pa
LC 2009-52098
Learn about the parts of a tree, how it matures from a tiny sprout, and how to learn its age.
The text "is simple without being simplistic; it is thoughtful and comprehensive without being overwhelming. The real appeal for teachers, students, and independent young readers, however, will be the photographs that fill the facing pages. Bold, bright, and colorful, the photographs bring you marvelously close to the subject. . . . On many different levels, this is a very appealing [book]." Libr Media Connect
Includes glossary

Lauber, Patricia
Be a friend to trees; illustrated by Holly Keller. HarperCollins Pubs. 1994 32p il (Let's-read-and-find-out science) hardcover o.p. pa $4.95
Grades: K 1 2 3   582.16
1. Trees
ISBN 0-06-021529-1 lib bdg; 0-06-445120-8 pa
LC 92-24082
"This conveys a lot of information in a simple text with clear line-and-watercolor illustrations." Booklist

Maestro, Betsy
Why do leaves change color? illustrated by Loretta Krupinski. HarperCollins Pubs. 1994 32p il (Let's-read-and-find-out science) hardcover o.p. pa $4.95
Grades: K 1 2 3   582.16
1. Autumn 2. Leaves
ISBN 0-06-022874-1 lib bdg; 0-06-445126-7 pa
LC 93-9611
Explains how leaves change their colors in autumn and then separate from the tree as the tree prepares for winter
"This is an informative concept book. . . . Krupinski's bright gouache-and-colored pencil illustrations show a boy and a girl playing in a country landscape that changes with weather and light. There are also detailed pictures of leaves in different sizes, shapes, and colors. Maestro includes simple instructions for making a leaf rubbing and for pressing leaves, as well as suggestions for places to visit where the fall foliage is special." Booklist

Pallotta, Jerry
Who will plant a tree? written by Jerry Pallotta; illustrated by Tom Leonard. Sleeping Bear Press 2010 un il $15.95
Grades: PreK K 1 2   582.16
1. Seeds 2. Trees
ISBN 978-1-58536-502-9; 1-58536-502-5
LC 2009037411
"Each spread features an animal in a different habitat that, by simply going about its everyday activities, unknowingly plants a tree. . . . The range of habitats and animals shown is impressive, from monkeys throwing figs in the jungle to Amazon River fish excreting seeds from their fruit dinners. . . . With simple, rhythmic language and engaging illustrations, this book encourages readers to see how the actions of each creature impact the Earth. An excellent accompaniment to science lessons." SLJ

Preus, Margi
Celebritrees; historic & famous trees of the world. illustrated by Rebecca Gibbon. Henry Holt & Co. 2011 un il $16.99
Grades: 2 3 4   582.16
1. Trees
ISBN 978-0-8050-7829-9; 0-8050-7829-0
"Preus introduces 14 trees famous in history or legend. Some are renowned for their age, height, girth, or other physical characteristics. For example, Methuselah, a bristlecone pine in California, is more than 4000 years old, while the Tule Tree in Mexico measures 177 feet around. Others are associated with historic events. . . . Each featured specimen receives a spread with several paragraphs of text plus Gibbon's charming colored pencil and watercolor illustrations. Readers who want to learn more about one or more of the tree varieties can find additional information at the book's end." SLJ
Includes bibliographical references

Rene, Ellen
Investigating why leaves change their color. Rosen/PowerKids 2008 24p il (Science detectives) lib bdg $15.95

Grades: 3 4 5   **582.16**
  1. Trees 2. Leaves
  ISBN 978-1-4042-4485-6 lib bdg; 1-4042-4485-9
  lib bdg

"With a chatty text, oversize font, and beautiful, full-page color photos, the open design of this . . . book . . . will invite young readers to look at the astonishing science happening around them. The page headings are appealing . . . leading into text that details the process of photosynthesis and chlorophyll's role in trapping sunlight; the botany is quite technical and will encourage kids to talk about it in the classroom and at home. . . . [This is a] fine account of one of nature's most vibrant transformations, leading kids to an elementary understanding of how the sun and sky affect each and every leaf." Booklist

583   Dicotyledons

Aaseng, Nathan
  Weird meat-eating plants. Enslow Publishers 2011
48p il (Bizarre science) lib bdg $23.93
Grades: 5 6 7 8   **583**
  1. Carnivorous plants
  ISBN 978-0-7660-3672-7; 0-7660-3672-3
                                          LC 2010016602
First published 1996 with title: Meat-eating plants
This describes meat-eating plants such as butterworts, sundews, byblis, pitcher plants, cobra lilies, venus flytraps, and bladderworts.
  "Aimed at reluctant readers, [this title is] sure to disgust and delight in equal measure. . . . [The title] will pique interest and get kids lining up at the reference desk looking for more. The text is complemented by illustrations and magnified photos of things that you would hope never to see." SLJ
  Includes glossary and bibliographical references

Bash, Barbara
  Desert giant; the world of the saguaro cactus. Sierra
Club Bks. 1989 un il hardcover o.p. pa $6.95
Grades: 3 4 5   **583**
  1. Cactus 2. Desert ecology
  ISBN 1-57805-085-5 pa
                                          LC 88-4706
"Animals find food and shelter in the towering plant of the Sonoran desert, and the local Tohono O'odom Indians have multiple uses for it. The cactus's 200-year life cycle is depicted as part of the ecosystem with colorful illustrations and clear text." Sci Child

Dickmann, Nancy
  A bean's life. Heinemann Library 2010 24p il (Watch
it grow) lib bdg $21.50; pa $5.99
Grades: PreK K 1   **583**
  1. Beans
  ISBN 978-1-4329-4142-0 lib bdg; 1-4329-4142-9 lib
  bdg; 978-1-4329-4151-2 pa; 1-4329-4151-8 pa
                                          LC 2009-49158
"Practically unique among early introductions to life cycles because death is mentioned . . . this . . . follows [a bean] . . . from . . . seed to maturity with a set of close-up color photographs, one per page, paired to large-type, one or

two-sentence captions. . . . Offers nourishing fare for young naturalists." SLJ
  Includes glossary

  An oak tree's life. Heinemann Library 2010 24p il
(Watch it grow) lib bdg $21.50; pa $5.99
Grades: PreK K 1   **583**
  1. Oak
  ISBN 978-1-4329-4143-7 lib bdg; 1-4329-4143-7 lib
  bdg; 978-1-4329-4152-9 pa; 1-4329-4152-6 pa
                                          LC 2009-49159
"Practically unique among early introductions to life cycles because death is mentioned . . . this . . . follows [an oak tree] . . . from . . . seed to maturity with a set of close-up color photographs, one per page, paired to large-type, one or two-sentence captions. . . . Offers nourishing fare for young naturalists." SLJ
  Includes glossary and bibliographical references

  A sunflower's life. Heinemann Library 2010 24p il
(Watch it grow) lib bdg $21.50; pa $5.99
Grades: PreK K 1   **583**
  1. Sunflowers
  ISBN 978-1-4329-4144-4 lib bdg; 1-4329-4144-5 lib
  bdg; 978-1-4329-4153-6 pa; 1-4329-4153-4 pa
                                          LC 2009-49161
"Practically unique among early introductions to life cycles because death is mentioned . . . this . . . follows [a sunflower] . . . from . . . seed to maturity with a set of close-up color photographs, one per page, paired to large-type, one or two-sentence captions. . . . Offers nourishing fare for young naturalists." SLJ
  Includes glossary and bibliographical references

Ganeri, Anita
  From bean to bean plant; [by] Anita Ganeri. Heine-
mann Library 2006 32p il (How living things grow) lib
bdg $25.36; pa $7.99
Grades: K 1 2 3   **583**
  1. Beans
  ISBN 1-4034-7861-9 lib bdg; 1-4034-7870-8 pa
                                          LC 2005026925
This describes the life cycle of the fava bean plant
This is "well-illustrated and informative." Sci
Books Films
  Includes glossary and bibliographical references

  From seed to apple; [by] Anita Ganeri. Heinemann
Library 2006 32p il (How living things grow) pa $7.99;
lib bdg $25.36
Grades: K 1 2 3   **583**
  1. Apples
  ISBN 1-4034-7871-6 lib bdg; 1-4034-7862-7 lib bdg
                                          LC 2005026926
This describes the life cycle of the apple from seed to blossom to fruit
  "The eye-catching color photos on each spread are bright and substantial. . . . Young readers will find [this title] interesting and [its] size manageable." SLJ
  Includes glossary and bibliographical references

  From seed to sunflower; [by] Anita Ganeri. Heinemann Library 2006 32p il (How living things grow) lib
bdg $25.36; pa $7.99

Grades: K 1 2 3 **583**

1. Sunflowers

ISBN 1-4034-7857-0 lib bdg; 1-4034-7866-X pa

LC 2005026921

This describes the life cycle of the sunflower.

This is "well-illustrated and informative." Sci Books Films

Includes glossary and bibliographical references

Gould, Margee

Meat-eating plants. PowerKids Press 2011 24p il (The strangest plants on Earth) lib bdg $21.25

Grades: 3 4 5 **583**

1. Carnivorous plants

ISBN 978-1-4488-4988-8; 1-4488-4988-8

LC 2010047870

This describes meat-eating plants including the venus flytrap, the bladderwort, the pitcher plant, and the sundew.

This "colorful [introduction has] bright, full-color photographs that are detailed enough to enable identification in the field. . . . Useful for reports and fun to browse, read, and learn." SLJ

Includes glossary

Guiberson, Brenda Z.

Cactus hotel; illustrated by Megan Lloyd. Holt & Co. 1991 un il $16.95; pa $6.95

Grades: K 1 2 3 **583**

1. Cactus 2. Desert ecology

ISBN 0-8050-1333-4; 0-8050-2960-5 pa

LC 90-41748

Describes the life cycle of the giant saguaro cactus, with an emphasis on its role as a home for other desert dwellers

"Guiberson's simple, understandable text gives an enjoyable lesson in desert ecology. Crisply attractive illustrations in color pencil and watercolor show the beauty of the desert landscape and its variety of wildlife." Booklist

Hall, Zoe

The **apple** pie tree; illustrated by Shari Halpern. Blue Sky Press (NY) 1996 un il $15.95

Grades: K 1 **583**

1. Apples 2. Cooking -- Apple -- Juvenile literature

ISBN 0-590-62382-6

LC 95-31134

"From bud to fruit, two children follow the cycle of an apple tree as it is nurtured through the seasons. . . . The story ends with a nice, warm apple pie being taken from the oven. The large pictures and text are suitable for young children. The colorful, clear-cut illustrations use a paint and paper collage technique. An end note shows how bees pollinate the tree's flowers and offers a recipe for apple pie." SLJ

Johnson, Jinny

Dandelion; illustrations by Graham Rosewarne. Smart Apple Media 2010 32p il (How does it grow?) lib bdg $28.50

Grades: 1 2 3 **583**

1. Dandelions

ISBN 978-1-59920-351-5 lib bdg; 1-59920-351-0 lib bdg

LC 2009-5693

Explains the life cycle of a dandelion

"Each stage is described on a spread that features clearly written, oversized text and a caption opposite a full-page, realistic watercolor, or, occasionally, a photograph. . . . A worthwhile purchase." SLJ

Includes glossary

Oak tree; illustrations by Graham Rosewarne. Smart Apple Media 2010 32p il (How does it grow?) lib bdg $28.50

Grades: 1 2 3 **583**

1. Oak

ISBN 978-1-59920-356-0 lib bdg; 1-59920-356-1 lib bdg

LC 2009-3399

Presents a basic overview of how an acorn grows into an oak tree and explains each stage in its development

"Each stage is described on a spread that features clearly written, oversized text and a caption opposite a full-page, realistic watercolor, or, occasionally, a photograph. . . . A worthwhile purchase." SLJ

Includes glossary and bibliographical references

Pfeffer, Wendy

From seed to pumpkin; illustrated by James Graham Hale. HarperCollins 2004 33p il (Let's-read-and-find-out science) hardcover o.p. lib bdg $16.89; pa $4.99

Grades: K 1 **583**

1. Pumpkin

ISBN 0-06-028038-7; 0-06-028039-5 lib bdg; 0-06-445190-9 pa

LC 00-54039

This explains the stages in the development of a seed into a pumpkin

Written "in simple, clear language. . . . A couple of easy recipes and experiments are appended. Appealing watercolor-and-pencil illustrations show children involved in planting and tending the pumpkins, and help make the process and the passage of time understandable to this audience." SLJ

Posada, Mia

Dandelions; stars in the grass. Carolrhoda Bks. 2000 un il lib bdg $15.95

Grades: 2 3 4 **583**

1. Dandelions

ISBN 1-57505-383-7

LC 98-53000

Rhyming text presents the dandelion, not as a weed, but as a flower of great beauty. Includes information about the flower, a recipe, and science activities

"This cheerful book is a nice combination of rhyme and information. . . . Bright and pleasing acrylic illustrations extend the text. . . . Posada includes just enough botanical detail for beginning dandelion pickers." SLJ

Includes bibliographical references

Royston, Angela

Life cycle of an oak tree; rev and updated ed.; Heinemann Library 2009 32p il (Life cycle of a) $25.36; pa $7.99

Grades: 2 3 4   **583**
  1. Oak
ISBN 978-1-4329-2531-4; 1-4329-2531-8; 978-1-4329-2548-2 pa; 1-4329-2548-2 pa

                       LC 2009517688

First published 2000

Introduces the life cycle of an oak tree, from the sprouting of an acorn through its more than 100 years of growth

This offers "easily accessible information in [an] attractive [package]." SLJ

Includes glossary and bibliographical references

585   Gymnosperms

Chin, Jason
  ★ **Redwoods**. Roaring Brook Press 2009 un il $16.95
Grades: PreK K 1 2   **585**
  1. Redwood
ISBN 978-1-59643-430-1; 1-59643-430-9

"The framing story opens with a boy finding a copy of Redwoods on a subway station bench (he's even on the cover). He delves in, and facts about the ancient trees spring to life around him. . . . Emerging from the station to find himself in the middle of a redwood forest, his adventures mirror what he's learning. . . . The straightforward narrative is given enormous energy by the inventive format and realistic watercolor illustrations. . . . Chin adeptly captures the singular and spectacular nature of redwoods in this smartly layered book." Publ Wkly

586   Seedless plants

Pascoe, Elaine
  Plants without seeds; photography by Dwight Kuhn. PowerKids Press 2003 32p il (Kid's guide to the classification of living things) $20.65
Grades: 2 3 4 5   **586**
  1. Ferns 2. Mosses
ISBN 0-8239-6315-2

                       LC 2001-7794

An introduction to the life cycles and characteristics of bryophytes, or plants without seeds, such as mosses and ferns

This "slim, well-organized . . . {introduction is} a must for schools in which plant studies are a part of the curriculum. . . . Useful for reports, with browsing appeal as well." SLJ

Includes glossary and bibliographical references

590   Animals

125 true stories of amazing animals; [inspiring tales of animal friendship & four-legged heroes, plus crazy animal antics] National Geographic||Publishers Group UK [distributor] 2012 112 p. (pbk.) $12.95
Grades: 4 5 6   **590**
  1. Animals 2. Rescue work 3. Animal behavior 4. Animals -- Anecdotes -- Juvenile literature
ISBN 142630918X; 9781426309182

                       LC 2012471745

This book is a "collection of favorite animal antics from 'National Geographic Kids' 'Amazing Animals' column [and] has a little of everything: dramatic rescues, incredible adventures, mistaken identities, strange bedfellows, odd couples, and much more." Among those featured are a "hippo that opens doors with his lips, a bison that rides in cars, an owl that goes on bike rides, and a group of elephants that play in an orchestra." (School Library Journal)

Ablow, Gail
  A **horse** in the house, and other strange but true animal stories; illustrated by Kathy Osborn. Candlewick Press 2007 un il $17.99
Grades: 2 3 4 5   **590**
  1. Animals
ISBN 978-0-7636-2838-3; 0-7636-2838-7

                       LC 2006051855

"Some of these 16 short tales would be very hard to believe, had Ablow, a journalist, not provided specific source notes for each at the end. It wouldn't be too hard to buy the moose that does laps in a Spokane swimming pool . . . —but a man successfully giving mouth-to-mouth to a distressed ornamental fish? . . . Osborn's stylized paintings capture the humor in each report. . . . Even skeptical young readers will come back for more." Booklist

Includes bibliographical references

Animals alive; the fight for survival in the wild. DK Pub. 2011 80p il map $15.99
Grades: 3 4 5 6   **590**
  1. Animals
ISBN 978-0-7566-7213-3; 0-7566-7213-9

Explains biodiversity, discusses the role animals play in ecosystems, describes the threats affecting the lives of animals, and profiles various animals, including jaguars, black rhinoceros, and bluefin tuna.

This is an "excellently crafted book. . . . The layout invites readers in through the use of different fonts and bolded words, small paragraphs, circular quotes, and fact blurbs. Each spread has stunning photos of the animals and simple illustrations. A good choice for reports, and a great read for anyone interested in endangered species." SLJ

Arnosky, Jim
  ★ **Wild** tracks! a guide to nature's footprints. [by] Jim Arnosky. Sterling Pub. Co. 2008 32p il $14.95
Grades: 1 2 3   **590**
  1. Animal tracks
ISBN 978-1-4027-3985-9; 1-4027-3985-0

                       LC 2007033972

"Tracks are separated into categories (bear, deer, cat, and so on), each presented in a two-page spread. On the left, a full-color painting displays an animal, and its tracks, in its natural habitat. On the right, information about the tracks, and how to read them, appears as pencil-sketch reproductions from Arnosky's own notebook. . . . Arnosky supplements the track identification information with fascinating related material in notebook-style entries. . . . The uniformly lovely illustrations and the compelling concept make this a book that young naturalists will enjoy year-round." Booklist

Baby animal pop! with 5 incredible, life-size foldouts. National Geographic 2011 il (National Geographic little kids) $14.95

Grades: PreK K 1 2   **590**

1. Animal babies

ISBN 978-1-4263-0765-2; 1-4263-0765-9

"This well-written book has exquisite life-size photos. Between the appealing pictures, an educational text for older children details the environment, anatomy, food, and homes of bunnies, ducklings, piglets, lambs, and ponies. The diagrams and photos give youngsters insight into the first year of the animals' lives." SLJ

Bayrock, Fiona

Bubble homes and fish farts; illustrated by Carolyn Conahan. Charlesbridge 2009 45p il $16.95; pa $7.95

Grades: 2 3 4   **590**

1. Animals 2. Bubbles

ISBN 978-1-57091-669-4; 1-57091-669-1; 978-1-57091-670-0 pa; 1-57091-670-5 pa

LC 2008-06151

"Fast Repetitive Tick (FaRT) is the term scientists use to describe the flatulencelike noise that herring make as they communicate their locations to one another other. That might be the most amusing description of the uses of bubbles in the natural world, but this entire book is enjoyable and engaging. . . . The illustrations are pale and less-detailed versions of scientifically accurate drawings overlaid with entertaining comments. . . . Creative, accessible, and fact-filled." SLJ

Berger, Gilda

101 animal records. Scholastic Inc. 2013 112 p. ill. (paperback) $8.99; (prebind) $19.65

Grades: 2 3 4 5   **590**

1. Picture books for children 2. Animals -- Juvenile literature

ISBN 0545427967; 0606315055; 9780545427968; 9780606315050

In this book, "readers will find a list of 101 animal superlatives. . . . There are such accolades as 'Loudest Insect' (the cicada) and 'Strongest Tongue' (the anteater) and 'Most Useful Insect' (the honeybee). The authors [Melvin Berger and Gilda Berger] skip an introduction, diving straight in with #1, then present a new superlative on each page accompanied by a paragraph of explanatory text." (Booklist)

Berkes, Marianne Collins

Animalogy; animal analogies. by Marianne Berkes; illustrated by Cathy Morrison. Sylvan Dell 2011 un il $16.95; pa $8.95; English ebook $9.95; Spanish ebook $9.95

Grades: PreK K 1 2 3 4   **590**

1. Animals 2. Analogy

ISBN 978-1-60718-127-9; 1-60718-127-4; 978-1-60718-137-8 pa; 1-60718-137-1 pa; 978-1-60718-147-7 English ebook; 978-1-60718-157-6 Spanish ebook

LC 2011006510

"Use this rhyming book about animals with students to explain the concept of analogies. 'Robin is to wing, as goldfish is to fin. Beaver is to build, as spider is to spin.' Body parts, size, sounds, actions, and animal classification are all included in the examples. Detailed and realistic illustrations give moose, bears, and frogs a ready-to-jump-off-the-page

appearance. . . . This book makes learning about analogies, new vocabulary, and animals easy to understand and fun." SLJ

BishopRoby, Joshua

Animal kingdom. Compass Point Books 2009 40p il (Mission: science) lib bdg $26.60

Grades: 4 5 6   **590**

1. Animals -- Classification

ISBN 978-0-7565-4057-9 lib bdg; 0-7565-4057-7 lib bdg

LC 2008-37574

An introduction to the animal kingdom, which is made up of a variety of animals that are organized into categories based on physical attributes or ancestors

Includes glossary

Cusick, Dawn

Get the scoop on animal poop; from lions to tapeworms, 251 cool facts about scat, frass, dung & more. Dawn Cusick. Imagine Pub. 2012 80 p.

Grades: 3 4 5   **590**

1. Feces 2. Wildlife 3. Excretion 4. Digestive system

ISBN 9781936140428

LC 2011025982

This book is a "guide to coprology, the study of feces. . . . Every page is packed with colorful photographs, and the text is an accumulation of snippets, a few sentences about each of the hundreds of topics." (Kirkus) "Topics covered include digestive systems of various animals, parasites, animals that eat feces, and bathroom habits. Back matter includes a guide to identify types of animal feces, a 'poo interview' with a veterinarian, activity ideas, a glossary and reading list . . . , a subject index, and an index by organism." (School Libr J)

Davies, Nicola, 1958-

Everything you need to know about animals. Kingfisher 2010 160p il $16.99

Grades: 1 2 3   **590**

1. Animals

ISBN 978-0-7534-6433-5; 0-7534-6433-0

Presents a brief overview of animal life, including types of animals and the ways their bodies are different, their means of locomotion, their food and how they find it, their senses, and how they reproduce themselves.

"As a beginner's encyclopedia of animals, this book is outstanding. The text is divided into five color-coded sections which range from the variety of animals in the world to how animals get around and get their food. . . . The text is full of colorful illustrations and the language is very readable. This is the type of book that the reader will come to again and again." Libr Media Connect

★ **Extreme** animals; the toughest creatures on Earth. illustrated by Neal Layton. Candlewick Press 2006 61p il $12.99; pa $7.99

Grades: 3 4 5 6   **590**

1. Animals 2. Adaptation (Biology) 3. Extreme environments -- Juvenile literature

ISBN 978-0-7636-3067-6; 0-7636-3067-5; 978-0-7636-4127-6 pa; 0-7636-4127-8 pa

LC 2005-43544

"There is life everywhere on Earth . . . and much of that life thrives in conditions that humans could not endure for five minutes or less. This funny and appealing little book describes who these amazing life-forms are and how they manage to survive. Simple and inviting cartoon drawings enliven the text and convey the types of extremes in an easy-to-understand manner." SLJ

Includes glossary

Faulkner, Mark

★ A **zeal** of zebras; an alphabet of collective nouns. by Woop Studios. Chronicle Books 2011 un il
Grades: PreK K   590

1. Animals 2. Alphabet
ISBN 1452104921; 9781452104928

LC 2011008011

"From the graphic designers of the Harry Potter franchise, this ABC book of collective nouns couples informative text with digitally created tableaus reminiscent of vintage posters that wryly play on the terms. . . . The thoughtful and provocative portraits will leave readers teasing out their subtleties." Publ Wkly

Gannij, Joan

Hidden hippo; written by Joan Gannij; illustrated by Clare Beaton. Barefoot Books 2008 un il $15.99
Grades: PreK K 1 2   590

1. Animals 2. Hippopotamus
ISBN 978-1-84686-170-3; 1-84686-170-5

LC 2007042677

"On safari, an unseen narrator hopes 'to see/A hippo or two,/Perhaps even three?' Clever rhyming verse details the spectacular sights along the way, such as lions, chimpanzees, and sleepy leopards. . . . This expansive tour of the African Plains is brought to life through Beaton's signature fabric appliqué collages. . . . The vibrant colors capture the hot, arid habitat. . . . Young adventurers and conservationists alike will pore over this visually stunning story." SLJ

Gibbs, Edward

★ **I** spy with my little eye. Candlewick Press 2011 un il $14.95
Grades: PreK K 1   590

1. Animals -- Color
ISBN 978-0-7636-5284-5; 0-7636-5284-9

LC 2010039167

"A classic childhood guessing game gets an elegant treatment from newcomer Gibbs in this introduction to colors and animals. . . . Defined by joyful scribbled outlines, the exuberant, friendly animal portraits dazzle." Publ Wkly

Grubman, Steve

Orangutans are ticklish; fun facts from an animal photographer. [by] Steve Grubman with Jill Davis. Schwartz & Wade Books 2010 un il $16.99
Grades: 2 3 4 5   590

1. Animals 2. Photography of animals
ISBN 978-0-375-85886-4; 0-375-85886-5

"The artfully selected facts and observations in this handsomely produced photo gallery are practically guaranteed to rivet budding naturalists, and Grubman's 13 sharply detailed studio portraits of large wild animals placed against plain, pale backgrounds put on a show that's every bit as engaging as the accompanying commentary. Grubman brings the challenges of animal photography to the fore." Booklist

Hearst, Michael

Unusual creatures; a mostly accurate account of some of the Earth's strangest animals. by Michael Hearst; illustrations by Jelmer Noordeman. Chronicle Books 2012 109 p. (alk. paper) $16.99
Grades: 3 4 5   590

1. Animals -- Juvenile literature
ISBN 1452104670; 9781452104676

LC 2011048646

In "this guide to 'unusual creatures' . . . . [Michael] Hearst introduces species like the echidna, flying snake, and narwhal, describing their physical characteristics, habitats, and behaviors, with tidbits, quizzes, and even poems. . . . Each animal appears in a matte illustration that combines naturalistic features with subtle hints of personality." (Publishers Weekly)

Hughes, Catherine D.

Little kids first big book of animals. National Geographic 2010 128p il map $14.95
Grades: K 1 2 3   590

1. Animals
ISBN 9781426307041; 1426307047; 9781426307218 lib bdg; 1426307217 lib bdg

"This book, well organized by type of habitat . . . introduces animals from all over the world. The easy-to-follow text consists of somewhat random facts about the creatures; the real stars of the show are the many vivid nature photographs." Horn Book Guide

Jenkins, Steve

★ The **Animal** Book; A Collection of the Fastest, Fiercest, Toughest, Cleverest, Shyest--and Most Surprising--animals on Earth. by Steve Jenkins. Houghton Mifflin Harcourt 2013 208 p. col. ill. (hardcover) $21.99
Grades: K 1 2 3 4 5   590

1. Picture books for children 2. Animals -- Juvenile literature
ISBN 054755799X; 9780547557991

This children's picture book by Steve Jenkins provides an "introduction to the vast animal kingdom. After a chapter of definition, information is presented in sections on animal families, senses, predators, defenses, extremes and the story of life. More facts appear in the final chapter, which serves both as index (with page numbers and thumbnails) and quick reference." (Kirkus Reviews)

★ **Biggest,** strongest, fastest. Ticknor & Fields Bks. for Young Readers 1995 un il $16; pa $5.95
Grades: K 1 2   590

1. Animals
ISBN 0-395-69701-8; 0-395-86136-5 pa

LC 94-21804

"A helpful chart at the end contains further information about each creature, such as diet and habitat. An all-round superlative effort." SLJ

Johnson, Jinny

★ **Animal** tracks & signs. National Geographic Society 2008 192p il $24.95; lib bdg $32.90
Grades: 5 6 7 8   590

1. Animals 2. Animal tracks 3. Tracking and trailing
ISBN 978-1-4263-0253-4; 1-4263-0253-3; 978-1-4263-0254-1 lib bdg; 1-4263-0254-1 lib bdg

"This attractive book describes the tracks (paw prints, bird claw prints, slimy trails) and signs (molted skin, food remains, scat, tree markings) that animals leave in their wake. . . . . A typical two-page layout includes a photo and short paragraph about the animal category, three or four colored boxes containing a photo or drawing of a specific animal (serval, bobcat), and a description of its size, geographic range, habitat, food, tracks and signs, and comments. . . . The beautiful photos vary from action . . . to informational. . . . The language is simple and readable." Voice Youth Advocates

Includes glossary and bibliographical references

Komiya, Teruyuki
Life-size zoo; from tiny rodents to gigantic elephants, an actual-size animal encyclopedia. editorial supervisor of Japanese edition, Teruyuki Komiya; photographer, Toyofumi Fukuda; Japanese translation by Makiko Oku; English language adaptation by Kristin Earhart. Seven Footer Kids 2009 43p il $17.95
Grades: PreK K 1 2   590
  1. Size 2. Zoos 3. Animals 4. Animals -- Identification -- Juvenile literature
  ISBN 978-1-934734-20-9; 1-934734-20-9
"The claim to fame for this oversize collection of animal portraits is that each animal is shown at 'actual size.' The striking photographs, taken at Japanese zoos, provide a rare opportunity to see animal faces up close. . . . Animal facts are provided in side panels that feature stick figures who engage readers. . . . The stellar photographs, playful format and informative content create a highly appealing package." Publ Wkly

More life-size zoo; lion, hippopotamus, polar bear and more: an all-new actual-size animal encyclopedia. photographer, Toshimitsu Matsuhashi; Japanese translation by Junko Miyakoshi; English language adaptation by Kristin Earhart. Seven Footer Press 2010 47p il $18.95
Grades: PreK K 1 2   590
  1. Size 2. Zoos 3. Animals
  ISBN 978-1-934734-19-3; 1-934734-19-5
This volume highlights "a second batch of zoo animals . . . in crisp, full-color photos. Some like . . . a large fruit bat, can be shown in entirety, but many others, like a fully maned African lion . . . require foldout pages for even a partial view. The eye-catching photos are the main thrust, while extra data flows along the edges of the page. . . . This is a great introduction to animals." SLJ

Levine, Shar
Animals; mammals, birds, reptiles, amphibians, fish, and other animals. by Shar Levine and Leslie Johnstone. Crabtree Pub. 2010 48p il (A class of their own) lib bdg $29.27; pa $9.95
Grades: 5 6 7 8   590
  1. Animals -- Classification 2. Animals -- Juvenile literature
  ISBN 978-0-7787-5372-8 lib bdg; 0-7787-5372-7 lib bdg; 978-0-7787-5386-5 pa; 0-7787-5386-7 pa
Looks at the animal kingdom, providing information and examples of species from the major phyla and classes, as well as case histories of newly discovered endangered species.
"Lively section headings . . . and notes on uncommon achievements, . . . lighten the substantial load of biological terminology. Illustrated with a plethora of closeup color

photos and microphotos, and closing with annotated lists of recommended Web sites, . . . [this captures] the remarkable diversity of life." SLJ

Includes glossary and bibliographical references

Lewin, Ted
  ★ **Look!** by Ted Lewin. Holiday House 2013 32 p. col. ill.
Grades: PreK K 1   590
  1. Animals -- Africa -- Juvenile literature 2. Animal ecology -- Africa -- Juvenile literature
  ISBN 9780823426072
                                          LC 2011049607
" A satisfying challenge and a fun animal adventure made thrilling by Lewin's characteristically spectacular use of light." Kirkus

McGuinness, Lisa
The **dictionary** of ordinary extraordinary animals; by Lisa McGuinness and Leslie Jonath; illustrated by Lisa Congdon. Running Press 2011 un il $18.95
Grades: K 1 2 3   590
  1. Animals -- Encyclopedias
  ISBN 978-0-7624-4063-4; 0-7624-4063-5
                                          LC 2010935841
"An alphabetically organized discussion of 150 animals, this informative guidebook combines casual descriptions of the animals with grainy illustrations reminiscent of vintage flashcards. . . . Congdon's paintings are characterized by naturalistic details and touches of surprising whimsy . . . communicating a palpable sense of wonder." Publ Wkly

McKay, Sindy
Animals under our feet; illustrated by Judith Hunt. Treasure Bay 2007 40p il (We both read) $7.99; pa $3.99
Grades: K 1 2   590
  1. Burrowing animals
  ISBN 978-1-60115-003-5; 1-60115-003-2; 978-1-60115-004-2 pa; 1-60115-004-0 pa
                                          LC 2006-932224
This "is a marvelous series for beginning readers. . . . The parent reads the left-hand page, which has complex text and new or complex words in boldface print. The child's side has supporting, but less complex, text. . . . The illustrations are well done, and the boldface type used to introduce new words to the young reader is invaluable." Sci Books Films

Myers, Jack
The **puzzle** of the platypus; and other explorations of science in action. [by] Jack Myers; illustrated by John Rice. Boyds Mills Press 2008 64p il map (Scientists probe 11 animal mysteries) $17.95
Grades: 3 4 5 6   590
  1. Animals
  ISBN 978-1-59078-556-0; 1-59078-556-8
                                          LC 2007023741
"This collection of 11 articles originally appeared in Highlights magazine during the 1990s and early 2000s. Each article tells how a scientist was able to unravel a mystery about some kind of animal. Myers's stories about dolphins, polar bears, elephants, and other animals contain many interesting scientific facts and are written in accessible and engaging prose. . . . Most of the pages have attractive watercolor illustrations." SLJ

Pittau, Francisco

★ **Out** of sight; [by] Pittau & Gervais. Chronicle Books 2010 16p il $19.99

Grades: PreK K 1   **590**

1. Animals

ISBN 9780811877121; 0811877124

LC 2010016150

"In this sophisticated guess-the-animal book, oversize pages feature large flaps offering visual clues about the animals concealed underneath. . . . The unexpected details about each animal . . . should fascinate even adults, but the core appeal is in the abstract elements that challenge readers' way of seeing." Publ Wkly

Rau, Dana Meachen

Animals. Marshall Cavendish Benchmark 2009 31p il (Bookworms. Nature's cycles) lib bdg $22.79

Grades: PreK K 1   **590**

1. Animals 2. Life cycles (Biology)

ISBN 978-0-7614-4093-2 lib bdg; 0-7614-4093-3 lib bdg

LC 2008-42513

"Well composed, simple sentences tie directly to colorful, carefully chosen photos [and] . . . accurate information flows naturally. . . . A great resource for sharing one-on-one with the youngest readers." Libr Media Connect

Includes glossary

Selsam, Millicent Ellis

Big tracks, little tracks; following animal prints. illustrated by Marlene Hill Donnelly. rev ed; HarperCollins Pubs. 1999 31p il (Let's-read-and-find-out science) hardcover o.p. pa $4.95

Grades: K 1 2 3   **590**

1. Animal tracks 2. Tracking and trailing

ISBN 0-06-028209-6; 0-06-445194-1 pa

LC 98-18315

First published with this title 1995; originally published with title How to be a nature detective

This book "teaches young readers how to track animals by finding footprints and other clues. . . . Included is a new Find Out More page with lots of hands-on activites." Publisher's note

Seuling, Barbara

Cows sweat through their noses; and other freaky facts about animal habits, characteristics, and homes. by Barbara Seuling; illustrated by Matthew Skeens. Picture Window Books 2008 40p il (Freaky facts) lib bdg $16.95

Grades: 2 3 4 5   **590**

1. Animal behavior -- Juvenile literature 2. Animals -- Habitations -- Juvenile literature

ISBN 978-1-4048-3749-2 lib bdg; 1-4048-3749-3 lib bdg

LC 2007004028

"This delightful little book contains a potpourri of facts about many members of the animal kingdom, large and small, from insects to elephants. . . . The information presented . . . is . . . fascinating." Sci Books Films

Includes glossary and bibliographical references

Silverman, Buffy

Can an old dog learn new tricks? and other questions about animals. illustrations by Colin W. Thompson. Lerner 2010 40p il (Is it a fact?) lib bdg $26.60

Grades: 4 5 6   **590**

1. Questions and answers 2. Animals -- Miscellanea

ISBN 978-0-8225-9083-5; 0-8225-9083-2

LC 2009-20587

Includes glossary and bibliographical references

Silverstein, Alvin

Dung beetles, slugs, leeches, and more; the yucky animal book. by Alvin and Virginia Silverstein, and Laura Silverstein Nunn; illustrated by Gerald Kelley. Enslow Publishers 2010 48p il (Yucky science) lib bdg $23.93

Grades: 4 5 6 7   **590**

1. Insects 2. Invertebrates 3. Animal behavior

ISBN 978-0-7660-3317-7 lib bdg; 0-7660-3317-1 lib bdg

LC 2009012281

"Written in an engaging and conversational style and full of revolting descriptions and entertaining cartoon illustrations . . . [this is] sure to turn even the strongest stomach. An introduction . . . puts 'yucky' in perspective, reminding kids that our world is diverse and that everyone has a different definition of repulsive." SLJ

Includes glossary and bibliographical references

Siwanowicz, Igor

Animals up close; zoom in on the world's most incredible creatures. DK Pub. 2009 96p il $19.99

Grades: 4 5 6   **590**

1. Animals

ISBN 978-0-7566-4513-7; 0-7566-4513-1

"An eye-catching cover will attract readers to this amazing look at some of the world's insects, fish, mammals, reptiles, amphibians, and birds. The focus is on animals small enough to fit in a child's hand. Siwanowicz showcases each creature with a spread containing a full-color, high-quality, close-up photo surrounded by multiple factual asides. . . . The book is packed with interesting material that captures the author's fascination for small creatures." SLJ

Includes glossary

Swanson, Diane

Animal aha! thrilling discoveries in wildlife science. Annick Press 2009 48p il $19.95; pa $9.95

Grades: 4 5 6   **590**

1. Animals -- Juvenile literature 2. Science -- Juvenile literature

ISBN 978-1-55451-165-5; 1-55451-165-8; 978-1-55451-164-8 pa; 1-55451-164-X pa

"An olio of 'AHA!' moments in natural science. Who knew that a Burmese python's heart enlarges to aid in digestion? Or that a parrot might comprehend human language and be able to use it creatively? Such are the tidbits in this browsable book. 'Fun Facts' and 'Fast Facts' boxes abound, and a color photo pops up on almost every page. With a lively text, this interesting pastiche will be enjoyed by kids pawing through the classroom library seeking an engaging nonfiction read." SLJ

Thomas, Keltie

Animals that changed the world. Annick Press 2010
112p il map $21.95; pa $12.95

Grades: 4 5 6 **590**

1. Animals

ISBN 978-1-55451-243-0; 1-55451-243-3; 978-1-
55451-242-3 pa; 1-55451-242-5 pa

"Thomas takes a breezy, conversational look at more
than 20 species—from microbes to codfish—that have impacted the Earth in extreme ways. . . . Animals profiled include the cat, dog, beaver, pigeon, and horse. . . . The busy
format features narrow columns of text layered on color
backgrounds alongside visually stimulating photographs,
an occasional drawing, and 'Fact Track' and 'Speak of the
Beast' sections, which explain the etymology of animal idioms." SLJ

Twist, Clint

A little book of slime; Clint Twist. Firefly Books
2012 80 p. $9.95

Grades: 3 4 5 6 7 **590**

1. Algae 2. Mucus 3. Molds (Fungi)

ISBN 1770850066; 9781770850064

Contents: What is slime? -- Slimy stuff in water -- Pond
slime -- Slime tube -- Red tide -- Lungfish -- Horrible hag-
fish -- Jellyfish -- Sea cucumber -- Sea slug -- Sea hare
-- Frogspawn -- Slimy stuff on land -- Poison arrow frog
-- Foam-nest frog -- California newt -- Water-holding frog
-- Cane toad -- Velvet worm -- Slime light -- Snail -- Banana
slug -- Slime mold beetle -- Froghopper -- Starfish stinkhorn
-- Other slimy stuff -- Saliva -- Phlegm -- Sundew plant --
Slime flux -- Decomposing vegetables -- Jelly fungus -- Lat-
tice stinkhorn -- Creeping slime -- Living snot mold.

This book "provides a[n] . . . introduction to slime in
the natural world. From pond slime and red tide to phlegm
and living snot mold, the author surveys the slick, sticky
substance produced by living organisms for protection, digestion, defense and more. In some cases the organism itself is the slime. This disparate material has been organized
into three sections: 'Slimy Stuff in Water,' 'Slimy Stuff on
Land' and 'Other Slimy Stuff.' . . . A . . . glossary defines
terms bolded in the text. There's an index but no sources or
suggestions for further research for those who want more.
"(Kirkus Reviews)

590.7 Education, research, related topics

Benbow, Ann

Awesome animal science projects; [by] Ann Benbow
and Colin Mably; illustrations by Tom Labaff. Enslow Publishers 2010 48p il (Real life science experiments) lib
bdg $23.93

Grades: 3 4 5 **590.7**

1. Animal behavior 2. Science projects

ISBN 978-0-7660-3148-7 lib bdg; 0-7660-3148-9
lib bdg

LC 2008-23932

"Color drawings, photographs, a glossary, and suggestions for further research enliven . . . [this] title . . . [and
provide] solid curricular support." Booklist

Includes glossary and bibliographical references

Gardner, Robert

Ace your animal science project; great science fair
ideas. [by] Robert Gardner . . . [et al.] Enslow Publishers
2009 128p il (Ace your biology science project) lib bdg
$31.93

Grades: 5 6 7 8 **590.7**

1. Animal behavior 2. Science projects 3. Science
-- Experiments

ISBN 978-0-7660-3220-0 lib bdg; 0-7660-3220-5
lib bdg

LC 2008-4234

"Dozens of . . . science activities are presented with
background information, step-by-step instructions, and suggestions for extending to the science fair level. . . . Color
illustrations and important safety information are included."
Horn Book Guide

Includes bibliographical references

590.72 Research

Burns, Loree Griffin

Citizen scientists; be a part of scientific discovery from
your own backyard. Loree Griffin Burns; photographs by
Ellen Harasimowicz. H. Holt 2012 80 p. col. ill., col. maps

Grades: 3 4 5 6 7 8 **590.72**

1. Suburbs 2. Animals -- Classification 3. Research
-- Citizen participation 4. Wildlife -- Geographical
distribution 5. Suburban animals -- Research -- Citizen
participation -- Juvenile literature 6. Suburban animals
-- Monitoring -- Citizen participation -- Juvenile
literature

ISBN 0805090622; 9780805090628; 9780805095173

LC 2011021673

AAAS/Subaru SB&F Prize for Excellence in Science
Books: Hands On Science Book (2013)

In this children's book, Loree Griffin Burns "brings . .
. attention to four . . . scientific projects that enlist regular
people in data collection. . . . The projects include . . . the
Monarch Watch butterfly tagging project, . . . the Audubon
Christmas Bird Count," and a "project documenting ladybug
species . . . . For each project, Burns gives detailed accounts
of the procedures employed by citizen scientists." (Horn
Book Magazine)

Includes bibliographical references and index

590.92 Animal biography

Roop, Connie

Tales of Famous Animals; Peter Roop and Connie
Roop. Scholastic 2012 112 p. (reinforced) $17.99

Grades: 4 5 6 7 8 **590.92**

1. Pets -- Juvenile literature 2. Animals -- Juvenile
literature

ISBN 0545430291; 9780545430296

This children's book, by Peter and Connie Roop, illustrated by Zachary Pullen, offers an "illustrated introduction
to some of the most fascinating and admirable animals we've
ever known! Everyone knows about President Obama's first
dog Bo, but would you believe President Adams had a pet alligator . . . ? . . . Readers will also learn about heroic animals

like Balto the sled dog and unique animals like Koko the gorilla." (Publisher's note)

591 Specific topics in natural history of animals

George, Lindsay Barrett
In the woods: who's been here? Greenwillow Bks. 1995 un il hardcover o.p. pa $7.99
Grades: PreK K 1 2 **591**
1. Forest animals
ISBN 0-688-12318-X; 0-688-16163-4 pa
LC 93-16244
A boy and girl in the autumn woods find an empty nest, a cocoon, gnawed bark, and other signs of unseen animals and their activities

"Children will be drawn to George's vivid gouache paintings, especially those depicting the animals in their natural surroundings. . . . For most childen this will be an excellent introduction to classroom nature units and the perfect prelude to a walk in the woods." Booklist

Other titles in this series are:
Around the pond: who's been here? (1996)
Around the world: who's been here? (1999)
In the garden: who's been here? (2006)
In the snow: who's been here? (1995)

Thurlby, Paul
Paul Thurlby's wildlife; Paul Thurlby. Candlewick Press 2013 32 p. $17.99
Grades: PreK K 1 **591**
1. Picture books for children 2. Animals -- Juvenile literature
ISBN 0763665630; 9780763665630
LC 2012943660
This children's picture book looks at wildlife. "A menagerie of animals is introduced," with "snippets of information [that] provide unique facts about 24 individual species; for example, 'monkeys split bananas from the bottom up—it's easier that way!' Blocky digital cartoon characters saturated in rich colors against faded backgrounds vibrantly exemplify each unique trait." (School Library Journal)

591.03 Dictionaries, encyclopedias, concordances

Spelman, Lucy
Animal encyclopedia; 2,500 animals with photos, maps, and more! National Geographic 2012 303 p. col. ill., col. maps (hardcover) $24.95; (library) $33.90
Grades: 5 6 7 **591.03**
1. Animals -- Encyclopedias
ISBN 1426310226; 9781426310225; 9781426310232
LC 2012023783
This encyclopedia about animals "is separated into vertebrate and invertebrate animals and then further subdivided by phylum. Each species gets its own page with dynamic color photos of creatures in their natural habitat, while information on variations within the species celebrates the diversity of animals across the globe." (Booklist)
Includes bibliographical references (p. 295) and index.

591.3 Genetics, evolution, age characteristics

Bleiman, Andrew
ZooBorns; zoo babies from around the world. [written by] Andrew Bleiman and [photographed by] Chris Eastland. Beach Lane Books 2010 un il $12.99
Grades: PreK K 1 **591.3**
1. Animal babies
ISBN 978-1-4424-1272-9; 1-4424-1272-0
LC 2010009590
"If a picture is worth 1,000 words, then these stunning photographs starring precious animal tykes may be priceless. The range of real-life infants featured is extraordinary in its breadth, covering such unusual zoo or aquarium residents as the crowned sifaka and the tawny frogmouth. The captivating, clear photographs pose every cub, kit and so on at its most adorable." Kirkus

Carle, Eric
★ Does a kangaroo have a mother, too? HarperCollins Pubs. 2000 un il $16.99; lib bdg $18.89; pa $6.99; bd bk $7.99
Grades: PreK K 1 **591.3**
1. Animals 2. Animals -- Infancy
ISBN 0-06-028768-3; 0-06-028767-5 lib bdg; 0-06-443642-X pa; 0-694-01456-7 bd bk
LC 99-36147
"The repetitious text is perfect for the toddler set. 'Does a lion have a mother, too? Yes! A lion has a mother. Just like me and you.' The text is repeated on every spread as the author showcases a dozen different animal mothers and their babies. . . . The vibrant artwork is classic Carle and should delight its audience." SLJ

Eamer, Claire
Super crocs & monster wings; modern animals' ancient past. [by] Claire Eamer. Annick Press 2008 93p il $19.95; pa $9.95
Grades: 4 5 6 7 **591.3**
1. Animals 2. Evolution 3. Prehistoric animals
ISBN 978-1-55451-130-3; 1-55451-130-5; 978-1-55451-129-7 pa; 1-55451-129-1 pa
"The author's conversational and often-humorous voice slides readers effortlessly through a great deal of fascinating scientific information in this title on animal evolution. After a brief but clear introduction to geologic time and Linnaean taxonomy, six chapters compare ancient and modern dragonflies, crocodilians, camelids, sloths, glyptodonts (armadillos), and beavers. . . . Jazzy fonts; crisp photos and paintings; and tilted illustrations, titles, and captions create an up-to-the-minute feel." SLJ

Jenkins, Steve
My first day; written by Steve Jenkins and Robin Page; illustrated by Steve Jenkins. Houghton Mifflin 2013 32 p. $16.99
Grades: PreK K 1 **591.3**
1. Animal babies -- Juvenile literature 2. Animal behavior -- Juvenile literature
ISBN 054773851X; 9780547738512
LC 2011048210
Authors Steve Jenkins and Robin Page present a picture book on animals. "The first day of life is different for every animal. Human newborns don't do much at all, but some

animals hit the ground running." Their book reveals "how twenty two different species, from the emperor penguin to the Siberian tiger, adapt to that traumatic first few hours of life, with or without parental help." (Publisher's note)

Kajikawa, Kimiko

Close to you; how animals bond. [by] Kimiko Kajikawa. Henry Holt 2008 un il $16.95

Grades: PreK K 1   **591.3**

1. Animal babies

ISBN 978-0-8050-8123-7; 0-8050-8123-2

LC 2007002959

"This tender title about the bonding between baby and adult animals gets some punch from additional facts appended at the end. The body of the book has a brief rhyming text, notable for its precise and engaging verbs. . . . Large, heartwarming stock photos of animal families clearly illustrate each verse. . . . The information seems carefully selected to be understandable and interesting to young children." SLJ

Kalman, Bobbie

Baby mammals; by Bobbie Kalman. Crabtree Publishing Company 2013 24 p. col. ill. (library) $22.60; (paperback) $6.95

Grades: 1 2 3 4   **591.3**

1. Mammals -- Juvenile literature 2. Animals -- Infancy -- Juvenile literature

ISBN 0778710084; 9780778710080; 9780778710134

LC 2012043723

In this book by Bobbie Kalman "close-up images of baby animals highlight the basic facts about different kinds of mammals, such as hoofed mammals, elephants, rodents, rabbits, marsupials, and primates. Children will learn about the bodies of mammals, the kinds of foods they eat, and how they are raised by their mothers after they are born. The books also show how mammals survive in different habitats." (Publisher's note)

Includes bibliographical references and index.

Patkau, Karen

Creatures yesterday and today; [by] Karen Patkau. Tundra Books 2008 un il $18.95

Grades: K 1 2 3   **591.3**

1. Animals 2. Fossils 3. Evolution 4. Prehistoric animals

ISBN 978-0-88776-833-0; 0-88776-833-4

"On the first page of this oversize book a huge diplodocus speaks. . . . Turn the page, and his descendant, a little skylark high in a tree, speaks. . . . Then there are the mollusks. . . . With large computer-created graphics in dramatic colors and a few lines of text, each double-page spread makes a similar connection for reptiles, fish, arachnids, birds, amphibians, mammals, crustaceans, and insects. . . . The amazing science will engage dinosaur fans with the wonder of evolution and the evidence of fossils." Booklist

Includes glossary

Rose, Deborah Lee

Ocean babies; illustrations by Hiroe Nakata. National Geographic 2005 un il $16.95; lib bdg $25.90

Grades: K 1 2   **591.3**

1. Animal babies 2. Marine animals 3. Infancy --

Children's literature

ISBN 0-7922-6669-2; 0-7922-8312-0 lib bdg

LC 2003-14075

Describes baby animals that live in the ocean, pointing out their many differences as well as the most important similarity.

"Nakata's cheerful watercolor paintings clearly illustrate the book's ideas while creating a beautiful undersea setting, bright with colors, teeming with varied creatures, and studded with intriguing details. Many books present information in this format, but few manage to stay as focused on the topic and sensitive to the intended audience as this one." Booklist

591.4   Physical adaptation

Aston, Dianna Hutts

★ An egg is quiet; illustrated by Sylvia Long. Chronicle Books 2006 un il $16.95

Grades: K 1 2 3   **591.4**

1. Eggs 2. Animals 3. Embryology -- Juvenile Literature

ISBN 978-0-8118-4428-4; 0-8118-4428-5

LC 2005-12090

"An exceptionally handsome book on eggs, from the delicate ova of the green lacewing to the rosy roe of the Atlantic salmon to the mammoth bulk of an ostrich egg. Aston's simple, readable text celebrates their marvelous diversity, commenting on size, shape, coloration, and where they might be found." SLJ

Baines, Rebecca

What's in that egg? a book about life cycles. by Becky Baines. National Geographic 2009 27p il $16.95; lib bdg $25.90

Grades: PreK K 1   **591.4**

1. Eggs 2. Animals 3. Embryology -- Juvenile literature

ISBN 978-1-4263-0408-8; 1-4263-0408-0; 978-1-4263-0409-5 lib bdg; 1-4263-0409-9 lib bdg

LC 2008-47895

This describes the eggs of various animals, including turtles, frogs, fish, butterflies, and swans

This title engages "children through humor, clear language, interesting facts, and abundant photos. . . . [An] excellent [introduction] for young science students." SLJ

Burnie, David

How animals work. Dorling Kindersley 2010 132p il $24.99

Grades: 5 6 7 8   **591.4**

1. Animals 2. Animal behavior

ISBN 978-0-7566-5897-7; 0-7566-5897-7

Describes the anatomy of many animal species and explains how their bodies work to help them survive. Covers such animals as birds, butterflies, elephants, crocodiles, and wolves, and includes color photos, illustrations, and diagrams.

"This beautifully photographed encyclopedia of animals is divided into categories that include movement, diet, senses, and animal families. . . . Diagrams showing internal organs and intimate closeups of eyes, skin, fur, and wings, should engage budding biologists." Publ Wkly

Cusick, Dawn

Animal eggs; an amazing clutch of mysteries & marvels! [by] Dawn Cusick & Joanne O'Sullivan. Charlesbridge 2011 48p il $14.95

Grades: K 1 2 3   **591.4**

1. Eggs

ISBN 978-0-9797455-3-9; 0-9797455-3-5

"Cusick and O'Sullivan compare the egg-laying and -hatching habits of a broad spectrum of animals. . . . Each tidily composed double-page spread offers color photographs of three or four examples of the topic under discussion, with brief descriptive paragraphs that will do double duty as quick captions for casual browsers. Although the emphasis is on protective adaptations and strategies that maximize chances for survival, the predator's point of view is not neglected. . . . [This is an] inviting offering." Bull Cent Child Books

Animal tongues. EarlyLight Books 2009 36p il $14.95

Grades: 3 4 5   **591.4**

1. Tongue 2. Animals 3. Taste -- Juvenile literature

ISBN 978-0-9797455-1-5; 0-9797455-1-9

Looks at the varied types of animal tongues and their different uses in adaption to their environment, from the sticky tongue of a chameleon, to the tongue of the lizardfish lined with teeth, to the tongue of the parrot used to make sounds.

"The facts presented are fascinating, the activities connect the reader to the text, and the photos are attention grabbing. . . . A great addition to a public or school library." Sci Books Films

Davies, Nicola, 1958-

Just the right size; why big animals are big and little animals are little. illustrated by Neal Layton. Candlewick Press 2009 61p il $14.99

Grades: 3 4 5 6   **591.4**

1. Size 2. Animals

ISBN 978-0-7636-3924-2; 0-7636-3924-9

This "book uses the 'Big Thing, Little Thing' rule (which explains how the length, surface area and cross section of an object or creature are relative to its volume and weight) . . . to explore how size affects living things. Davies's often humorous text and Layton's energetic illustrations demonstrate why humans don't have superpowers . . . and later spreads discuss the advantages and limitations of being very small or very big. . . . The spot-on comic delivery and readily comprehensible explanations make this a prime pick for readers curious about physical science in the natural world." Publ Wkly

Eamer, Claire

Lizards in the sky; animals where you least expect them. Annick 2010 97p il $21.95; pa $12.95

Grades: 3 4 5   **591.4**

1. Animals -- Habitations

ISBN 978-1-55451-265-2; 1-55451-265-4; 978-1-55451-264-5 pa; 1-55451-264-6 pa

"Eamer looks at animals living unexpected lives in unanticipated habitats. Birds and spiders underwater, snakes far out in the open ocean, fish on land, burrowing owls, and shrimp in the desert are just a few of the creatures introduced. The physiological adaptations they have made to survive are described. . . . Text boxes with factual tidbits add to the narrative. The drawings and photographs on every page

are in full color. . . . Overall, an enjoyable and fascinating title." SLJ

Fielding, Beth

Animal eyes. EarlyLight Books 2011 36p il $14.95

Grades: 1 2 3 4   **591.4**

1. Eye 2. Animals

ISBN 0979745551; 9780979745553; 978-0-9797455-5-3; 0-9797455-5-1

This book explores the morphology and behavior of animal eyes. Included are mammals, insects, birds, reptiles, amphibians, and mollusks. Glossary. Index. "Grades one to four." (Sci Books Films)

"Children who pick up this appealing book will instantly have their curiosity piqued. Each spread features a different animal and includes a full-color photo of it, close-ups of its eyes, and a few photographs of text. 'Test It Out' experiments using easily accessible materials such as colored pencils add a participatory element to the book. . . . An attractive, informative title." SLJ

★ Animal tails. EarlyLight Books 2011 36p il

Grades: 1 2 3   **591.4**

1. Tails 2. Animals

ISBN 0-9797455-8-6; 978-0-9797455-8-4

"Fielding describes how tails work for elephants, kangaroos, primates, cats, squirrels, chameleons, lizards, snakes, birds, whales, stingrays, and caterpillars. More than 13 styles of tails, such as scaly, stinging, and spraying, are paired with various functions performed by these animals. . . . The full-color photography is quite bright, clear, and eye-catching. . . . A visually appeal and interesting introduction." SLJ

Halfmann, Janet

Eggs 1 2 3; Who will the babies be? Janet Halfmann; illustrated by Betsy Thompson. 1st ed. Blue Apple Books 2012 32 p. col. ill. (hardcover) $17.99

Grades: K 1 2   **591.4**

1. Counting 2. Eggs -- Fiction 3. Picture books for children

ISBN 1609051912; 9781609051914

LC 2011038907

Author Janet Halfmann presents a picture book for children that focuses on counting skills. In the book, "words curve above and below large numbers, mimicking the subject matter: eggs and the hatchlings inside, which include newborn platypus, robins, turtles, and more . . . Gatefolds open to the right or upward, revealing the answers." (Publishers Weekly)

Hodgkins, Fran

Amazing eggs; with illustrations by Wendy Smith. Treasure Bay 2011 41p il (We both read)

Grades: K 1 2   **591.4**

1. Eggs

ISBN 1-60115-251-5; 1-60115-252-3 pa; 978-1-60115-251-0; 978-1-60115-252-7 pa

"A colorful and scientific explanation of eggs and the development of insects, reptiles, birds, and fish. The well-written, easy-to-understand text and the inviting format will encourage emerging readers to pick up the book on their own. Intended as a shared reading experience for adult and child, the dual differentiated text appears on each page, accompanied by clear, informative, full-color photos. An attractive addition that covers an important science-curriculum subject." SLJ

Hulbert, Laura

Who has these feet? illustrated by Erik Brooks. Henry Holt 2011 un il $16.99

Grades: PreK K 1 2   **591.4**

1. Foot 2. Animals

ISBN 978-0-8050-8907-3; 0-8050-8907-1

LC 2010033429

"This guess-the-animal book asks readers to identify species by looking at their feet. Hulbert describes how each animal's treads are acclimated to its particular environment: a tree frog's toes are sticky; a squirrel uses the claws on its toes to scamper along trees; and a sea turtle has flippers for swimming. A gatefold features all of the animals together. . . . Brooks's naturalistic yet affable animals will likely inspire readers to take a closer look at their own feet." Publ Wkly

Jenkins, Steve

★ Actual size. Houghton Mifflin 2004 un il $16

Grades: K 1 2 3   **591.4**

1. Size 2. Animals

ISBN 0-618-37594-5

LC 2003-17462

In "torn-and-cut paper collages, Jenkins depicts 18 animals and insects—or a part of their body—in actual size. . . . The end matter offers full pictures of the creatures and more details about their habitats and habits. Mixing deceptive simplicity with absolute clarity, this beautiful book is an enticing way to introduce children to the glorious diversity of our natural world, or to illustrate to budding scientists the importance of comparison, measurement, observation, and record keeping. A thoroughly engaging read-aloud and a must-have for any collection." SLJ

Big & little. Houghton Mifflin 1996 un il $16

Grades: K 1 2   **591.4**

1. Size 2. Shape 3. Animals

ISBN 0-395-72664-6

LC 95-41162

Jenkins "points out the differences in size between animals who are similar in other ways. The artwork combines cuttings of colored, textured papers to form animals that stand out strikingly against white backgrounds. . . . One line of text comments on the two animals' sizes, habits, or habitats. The final pages include a presentation of the comparative sizes of all the animals, [and] a paragraph of additional information about each species." Booklist

Includes bibliographical references

Kaner, Etta

Have you ever seen a hippo with sunscreen? written by Etta Kaner; illustrated by Jeff Szuc. Kids Can Press 2010 il $14.95

Grades: K 1 2 3   **591.4**

1. Animals

ISBN 978-1-55453-337-4; 1-55453-337-6

"People may wear sunscreen, sunglasses, and snowshoes, but the seven featured animals have their own physical adaptations to their environments. Large type, very brief question-and-answer text . . . and humorous illustrations make the volume accessible and entertaining for young readers." Horn Book Guide

Lunis, Natalie

Electric animals. Bearport Pub. 2011 24p il (Animals with super powers) lib bdg $22.61

Grades: 3 4 5   **591.4**

1. Platypus 2. Electric fishes

ISBN 978-1-61772-121-2; 1-61772-121-2

LC 2010034521

This describes electric animals including eels, rays, platypuses, and great white sharks.

"Large color photos of animals in natural settings and clear, cogent presentations of information combine to boost this [book] well above the average for both assignments and casual browsing." SLJ

Includes glossary and bibliographical references

Messner, Kate

★ Over and under the snow. Chronicle Books 2011 un il $16.99

Grades: PreK K 1 2   **591.4**

1. Winter 2. Animals -- Habitations

ISBN 978-0-8118-6784-9; 0-8118-6784-6

LC 2009028984

"The lyrical descriptions of the text and the gray/brown/ice-blue palette of the illustrations leave readers with a retro feel that harkens back to earlier days of children's books and bygone times when life seemed simpler. Utterly charming, and informative, to boot; readers brought up on a diet of rhymes, bright colors and adorable fluffy animals will find its simple beauty a balm." Kirkus

Miller, Debbie S.

Arctic lights, arctic nights; illustrations by Jon Van Zyle. Walker & Co. 2003 un il map $16.95; pa $7.95

Grades: 2 3 4   **591.4**

1. Animals -- Arctic regions 2. Natural history -- Alaska

ISBN 0-8027-8856-4; 0-8027-9636-2 pa

LC 2002-191047

Describes the unique light phenomena of the Alaskan Arctic and the way animals adapt to the temperature and daylight changes each month of the year

The "brief text includes not only lyrical messages about light and its partner, darkness, but also references to the reaction of wildlife to the waxing and waning. . . . Wrapped about this unfamiliar (to many of us) swirl of seasons of light are Van Zyle's superb and quietly beautiful acrylic paintings, which capture both light and dark in perfect harmony with the text." SLJ

Includes glossary

Miller, Sara Swan

★ All kinds of ears. Marshall Cavendish Benchmark 2007 48p il (All kinds of . . .) lib bdg $29.93

Grades: 3 4 5 6   **591.4**

1. Ear 2. Animals

ISBN 978-0-7614-2518-2 lib bdg; 0-7614-2518-7 lib bdg

This describes the various forms and functions of animal ears

Includes glossary and bibliographical references

★ All kinds of eyes. Marshall Cavendish Benchmark 2007 48p il (All kinds of . . .) lib bdg $29.93

Grades: 3 4 5 6   **591.4**
1. Eye 2. Animals
ISBN 978-0-7614-2519-9 lib bdg; 0-7614-2519-5
lib bdg
This describes the various forms and functions of eyes
in animals
"The excellent content and rare photographs will appeal
to children, whether for research or leisure reading." SLJ
Includes glossary and bibliographical references

★ **All** kinds of feet. Marshall Cavendish Benchmark
2007 48p il (All kinds of . . .) lib bdg $29.93
Grades: 3 4 5 6   **591.4**
1. Foot 2. Animals
ISBN 978-0-7614-2520-5 lib bdg; 0-7614-2520-9
lib bdg
This describes the various forms and functions of
animal feet
"The excellent content and rare photographs will appeal
to children, whether for research of leisure reading." SLJ
Includes glossary and bibliographical references

★ **All** kinds of mouths. Marshall Cavendish Benchmark 2007 48p il (All kinds of . . .) lib bdg $29.93
Grades: 3 4 5 6   **591.4**
1. Mouth 2. Animals
ISBN 978-0-7614-2521-2 lib bdg; 0-7614-2521-7
lib bdg
This describes the various forms and functions of
animal mouths
"The excellent content and rare photographs will appeal
to children, whether for research or leisure reading." SLJ
Includes glossary and bibliographical references

★ **All** kinds of noses. Marshall Cavendish Benchmark
2007 48p il (All kinds of . . .) lib bdg $29.93
Grades: 3 4 5 6   **591.4**
1. Nose 2. Animals
ISBN 978-0-7614-2522-9 lib bdg; 0-7614-2522-5
lib bdg
This describes the various forms and functions of
animal noses
"The excellent content and rare photographs will appeal
to children, whether for research or leisure reading." SLJ
Includes glossary and bibliographical references

★ **All** kinds of skin. Marshall Cavendish Benchmark
2007 48p il (All kinds of . . .) lib bdg $29.93
Grades: 3 4 5 6   **591.4**
1. Skin 2. Animals
ISBN 978-0-7614-2713-1 lib bdg; 0-7614-2713-9
lib bdg
This describes the shapes and functions of animal exteri-
ors found in nature, including skin, feathers, fur, and scales
Includes glossary and bibliographical references

Parker, Victoria
How small is small? comparing body parts. [by] Vic
Parker. Heinemann Library 2011 32p il (Measuring and
comparing) lib bdg $26; pa $7.99

Grades: 2 3 4   **591.4**
1. Size 2. Weights and measures
ISBN 978-1-4329-3960-1 lib bdg; 1-4329-3960-2 lib
bdg; 978-1-4329-3968-7 pa; 1-4329-3968-8 pa
        LC 2010000938
"Measure length and width and see how different parts
of the body compare." Publisher's note
Includes glossary and bibliographical references

Patkau, Karen
Creatures great and small. Tundra Books 2006 un
il $17.95
Grades: K 1 2 3   **591.4**
1. Size 2. Animals
ISBN 978-0-88776-754-8; 0-88776-754-0
"Each spread in this informational picture book shows
a large animal filling a page-and-a-half scene and a small
one from a similar classification on the right edge. . . . Sharp
lines, bold colors, and careful composition of the computer-
generated art successfully convey the rich variety of creatures and environments, accentuating similarities and differences. . . . Labeled illustrations at the back of the book
introduce concepts of scale in a clear and inviting way." SLJ
Includes glossary

Posada, Mia
Guess what is growing inside this egg. Millbrook Press
2007 un il lib bdg $15.95
Grades: K 1 2 3   **591.4**
1. Eggs 2. Animals
ISBN 978-0-8225-6192-7 lib bdg; 0-8225-6192-1
lib bdg
        LC 2006-16250
"This attractive picture book presents six animals that
hatch from eggs: penguins, alligators, ducklings, sea turtles,
spiders, and octopuses. . . . The first spread is a guessing
game, telling a little about the animal in two rhymed couplets, showing a closeup of an egg in its natural setting, and
asking 'Can you guess what is growing inside this egg?' The
next spread reveals the answer to the riddle and offers information about the featured animal's physical attributes and
behaviors. Distinctive collage-and-watercolor artwork offers eye-catching views of the animals within their habitats."
Booklist

Schaefer, Lola M.
★ **Just** one bite; 11 animals and their bites at life size!
by Lola Schaefer; illustrated by Geoff Waring. Chronicle
Books 2010 un il $17.99
Grades: K 1 2 3   **591.4**
1. Animals -- Food
ISBN 978-0-8118-6473-2; 0-8118-6473-1
"In this bold, oversized picture book, readers will see—
at actual size—how much tasty giant squid a sperm whale
can eat in one gulp . . . and how much dirt a worm can eat
at once. . . . Nine other animals and their eating habits are
illustrated. . . . The terrific, artfully composed brush, crayon
and computer-aided artwork is lavish, the perspectives dramatically up-close. The text is lively, minimal and perfect
for reading aloud." Kirkus

Schwartz, David M.
Where else in the wild? more camouflaged creatures
concealed and revealed. by David M. Schwartz and Yael

Schy; eye-tricking photographs by Dwight Kuhn. Tricycle Press 2009 un il $16.99

Grades: 2 3 4   **591.4**

1. Animals 2. Camouflage (Biology) 3. Poetry -- By individual authors

ISBN 978-1-58246-283-7; 1-58246-283-6

Presents poems and brief facts about eleven animals that rely on the ability to camouflage within nature to survive in the wilderness

"Poetry and photography work well together in this beautifully illustrated book. . . . Notable for its finesse and variety, the poetry includes rhymed verse, as well as haiku and concrete poems. A playful, informative introduction to camouflage in nature." Booklist

Where in the wild? camouflaged creatures concealed--and revealed. ear-tickling poems by David M. Schwartz and Yael Schy; eye-tricking photos by Dwight Kuhn. Tricycle Press 2007 un il $15.95

Grades: 2 3 4   **591.4**

1. Animals 2. Camouflage (Biology) 3. Poetry -- By individual authors

ISBN 978-1-58246-207-3; 1-58246-207-0

LC 2006-101406

"The well-crafted, short poems . . . offer clues to the hidden animals' identities. Beautifully photographed and designed with great attention to detail, this book will intrigue and challenge children." Booklist

Singer, Marilyn

Eggs; illustrated by Emma Stevenson. Holiday House 2008 un il $16.95

Grades: 1 2 3 4   **591.4**

1. Eggs 2. Animals

ISBN 978-0-8234-1727-8; 0-8234-1727-1

Explains the varieties, functions, and characteristics of the eggs of a multitude of creatures, including insects, birds, and reptiles

"Smoothly written, the text creates an even, almost conversational flow from page to page. . . . Stevenson contributes large and small gouache paintings in a precise yet fluid style that suits the subject well." Booklist

Includes glossary

Stewart, Melissa

Give me a hand; the secrets of hands, feet, arms, and legs. illustrated by Janet Hamlin. Marshall Cavendish Benchmark 2010 48p il (The gross and goofy body) lib bdg $20.95

Grades: 2 3 4   **591.4**

1. Foot 2. Hand 3. Human body

ISBN 978-0-7614-4158-8 lib bdg; 0-7614-4158-1 lib bdg

LC 2008033618

This offers information on the role hands, feet, arms, and legs play in the body science of humans and animals

This "offers detailed science facts in a fashion approachable enough to make a welcome supplement to school textbooks. . . . The layout is fresh, clean, and colorful, sidebars keep things conversational, and the back matter is solid." Booklist

Includes glossary and bibliographical references

Zoehfeld, Kathleen Weidner

What lives in a shell? illustrated by Helen K. Davie. HarperCollins Pubs. 1994 32p il (Let's-read-and-find-out science) hardcover o.p. pa $5.99

Grades: K 1   **591.4**

1. Shells 2. Animal defenses

ISBN 0-06-445124-0 pa

LC 93-12428

Describes such animals as snails, turtles, and crabs, which live in shells and use these coverings as protection

This book uses "interesting and accurate illustrations and just the right words. . . . The science here is good, and the explanations should cause young readers to want to learn more." Sci Books Films

591.47 Protective and locomotor adaptations, color

Collard, Sneed B.

Teeth; illustrated by Phyllis Saroff. Charlesbridge 2008 32p il lib bdg $16.95; pa $7.95

Grades: 1 2 3   **591.47**

1. Teeth 2. Animals

ISBN 978-1-58089-120-2 lib bdg; 1-58089-120-9 lib bdg; 978-1-58089-121-9 pa; 1-58089-121-7 pa

LC 2007-02266

This describes types of animal teeth, how they are used, how they grow, and the differences between teeth and horns or antlers

"Packed with exciting information, this large-size picture book combines chatty prose . . . and clear, full-color illustrations to tell amazing facts." Booklist

Wings; illustrated by Robin Brickman. Charlesbridge 2008 31p il lib bdg $16.95; pa $7.95

Grades: 1 2 3   **591.47**

1. Wings 2. Flight 3. Animals

ISBN 978-1-57091-611-3 lib bdg; 1-57091-611-X lib bdg; 978-1-57091-612-0 pa; 1-57091-612-8 pa

LC 2007-02265

This "looks at wing design and the shapes of birds, insects, and mammals, as well as at prehistoric flyers and birds that no longer fly. Human fascination with flying rounds out the discussion. Brickman's paper collages of winged animals are . . . impressive in texture and color." SLJ

Includes glossary and bibliographical references

Fielding, Beth

Animal colors; a rainbow of colors from animals around the world. EarlyLight Books 2009 32p il $14.95

Grades: K 1 2 3 4 5   **591.47**

1. Color 2. Animals 3. Animal behavior -- Juvenile literature 4. Camouflage (Biology) -- Juvenile literature 5. Protective coloration (Biology) -- Juvenile literature

ISBN 978-0-9797455-4-6; 0-9797455-4-3

"A gorgeous, in-depth look at animal colors as they occur in nature. Highly graphic and visually appealing, the book is organized first by singular colors, followed by common combinations. . . . For the youngest readers, this book can be enjoyed as simply an excellent introduction to color and to identifying the animals. For older readers, this book holds appeal as it also provides factual information, such as habitat, behavior, and diet, in bite-size doses beneath each picture. The photography is sharp and clear. . . . Simply stunning." SLJ

Halpern, Monica

Underground towns, treetops, and other animal hiding places; by Monica Halpern. National Geographic 2007 40p (National Geographic science chapters) lib bdg $17.90

Grades: 3 4 5 6   **591.47**

1. Animal defenses 2. Animals -- Habitations
ISBN 978-1-4263-0183-4 lib bdg; 1-4263-0183-9 lib bdg

           LC 2007007894

This is an introduction to hidden animal habitats, such as underground burrows, underwater, or treetops

This "book provides a clear, engaging introduction to the topic. . . . The [book's] clear design features many well-captioned photographs . . . charts, and diagrams." Horn Book Guide

Helman, Andrea

Hide and seek; nature's best vanishing acts. photographs by Gavriel Jecan. Walker Pub. Co. 2008 un il $16.95; lib bdg $17.85

Grades: 2 3 4   **591.47**

1. Animal defenses 2. Camouflage (Biology)
ISBN 978-0-8027-9690-5; 0-8027-9690-7; 978-0-8027-9691-2 lib bdg; 0-8027-9691-5 lib bdg

           LC 2007024242

"Animals' camouflage is equally effective at hiding prey from predators and predators from prey. This large-format book offers plenty of excellent photographs of animals in each category, arranged by type of habitat. . . . Throughout the book, the words seem to elaborate on the pictures." Booklist

Jenkins, Steve

★ **Living** color. Houghton Mifflin 2007 un il $17

Grades: 3 4 5 6   **591.47**

1. Animals -- Color
ISBN 978-0-618-70897-0; 0-618-70897-9

           LC 2007-12751

This "offers a pageant of the most stunning, vividly hued creatures on the planet. . . . This book opens by explaining that bright coloration goes beyond mere decoration. . . . Arranged by color, subsequent spreads feature a rainbow of animals rendered in Jenkins' celebrated cut-paper style. Each picture is accompanied by a paragraph of nicely distilled information." Booklist

★ **What** do you do when something wants to eat you? Houghton Mifflin 1997 un il $16

Grades: K 1 2 3   **591.47**

1. Animal defenses
ISBN 0-395-82514-8

           LC 96-44993

Describes how various animals, including an octopus, a bombadier beetle, a puff adder, and a gliding frog, escape danger

"Jenkins achieves remarkable anatomical detail in his boldly textured cut-paper collages; simple backgrounds keep attention tightly focused on the animals and their survival strategies." Bull Cent Child Books

Lunis, Natalie

See-through animals. Bearport Pub. 2011 24p il (Animals with super powers) lib bdg $22.61

Grades: 3 4 5   **591.47**

1. Camouflage (Biology)
ISBN 9781617721205; 1617721204

           LC 2010045408

This describes see-through animals including the clearwing butterfly, the glass frog, transparent anemone shrimp, jellyfish, the transparent sea butterfly, glass squid, transparent octopus and zebrafish and frog.

"Large color photos of animals in natural settings and clear, cogent presentations of information combine to boost this [book] well above the average for both assignments and casual browsing." SLJ

Includes bibliographical references and index.

Mitchell, Susan K.

Animal chemical combat; poisons, smells, and slime. [by] Susan K. Mitchell. Enslow Publishers 2009 48p il (Amazing animal defenses) lib bdg $23.93

Grades: 4 5 6   **591.47**

1. Animal defenses
ISBN 978-0-7660-3294-1 lib bdg; 0-7660-3294-9 lib bdg

           LC 2008-11075

"The closeup photos are frequent and well chosen, and accompanied by clear, simply phrased [text], which [is] more detailed than average and [takes] up most or all of the space on each page." SLJ

Includes glossary and bibliographical references

Animal mimics; look-alikes and copycats. [by] Susan K. Mitchell. Enslow Publishers 2009 48p il (Amazing animal defenses) lib bdg $23.93

Grades: 4 5 6   **591.47**

1. Animal defenses
ISBN 978-0-7660-3293-4 lib bdg; 0-7660-3293-0 lib bdg

           LC 2008-11449

"The closeup photos are frequent and well chosen, and accompanied by clear, simply phrased [text], which [is] more detailed than average and [takes] up most or all of the space on each page." SLJ

Includes glossary and bibliographical references

Animals with awesome armor; shells, scales, and exoskeletons. [by] Susan K. Mitchell. Enslow Publishers 2009 48p il (Amazing animal defenses) lib bdg $23.93

Grades: 4 5 6   **591.47**

1. Animal defenses
ISBN 978-0-7660-3296-5 lib bdg; 0-7660-3296-5 lib bdg

           LC 2008-11456

"The closeup photos are frequent and well chosen, and accompanied by clear, simply phrased [text], which [is] more detailed than average and [takes] up most or all of the space on each page." SLJ

Includes glossary and bibliographical references

Animals with crafty camouflage; hiding in plain sight. [by] Susan K. Mitchell. Enslow Publishers 2009 48p il (Amazing animal defenses) lib bdg $23.93

Grades: 4 5 6   **591.47**
1. Animal defenses 2. Camouflage (Biology)
ISBN 978-0-7660-3291-0 lib bdg; 0-7660-3291-4
lib bdg
LC 2008-11073
"The closeup photos are frequent and well chosen, and accompanied by clear, simply phrased [text], which [is] more detailed than average and [takes] up most or all of the space on each page." SLJ
Includes glossary and bibliographical references

Animals with wicked weapons; stingers, barbs, and quills. [by] Susan K. Mitchell. Enslow Publishers 2009 48p il (Amazing animal defenses) lib bdg $23.93
Grades: 4 5 6   **591.47**
1. Animal defenses
ISBN 978-0-7660-3292-7 lib bdg; 0-7660-3292-2
lib bdg
LC 2008-11075
"The closeup photos are frequent and well chosen, and accompanied by clear, simply phrased [text], which [is] more detailed than average and [takes] up most or all of the space on each page." SLJ
Includes glossary and bibliographical references

Morlock, Lisa
Track that scat! written by Lisa Morlock; illustrated by Carrie Anne Bradshaw. Sleeping Bear Press 2012 32 p. col. ill $15.95
Grades: K 1 2   **591.47**
1. Feces 2. Animal tracks 3. Animal behavior
ISBN 158536536X; 9781585365364
LC 2011028148
In this book, "for young Finn and her hound, . . . exploring the outdoors becomes . . . a vehicle to introduce readers to identifying commonly known animals through their tracks and, particularly, droppings. From the onset, the pair encounters -- and sometimes steps in -- a progression of animal excrement, . . . includ[ing] goose, raccoon, and bird poop." (Booklist)
"The large spreads are inviting, and the dog, a basset hound, is cute, cute, cute, and the gross factor is likely to draw kids in." SLJ

Pryor, Kimberley Jane
Amazing armor. Marshall Cavendish Benchmark 2009 32p il (Animal attack and defense) $19.95
Grades: 2 3 4   **591.47**
1. Animal defenses
ISBN 978-0-7614-4424-4; 0-7614-4424-6
LC 2009-4996
"Students will enjoy the large vivid photographs that allow for a closeup look at the animal, along with the excellent descriptions of the different survival methods. . . . Pryor does a good job of bringing the information down to a level that an elementary student would understand without losing any of the important details. . . . [This] would be a great addition to any nonfiction collection." Libr Media Connect
Includes glossary

Clever camouflage. Marshall Cavendish Benchmark 2009 32p il (Animal attack and defense) $19.95

Grades: 2 3 4   **591.47**
1. Animal defenses 2. Camouflage (Biology)
ISBN 978-0-7614-4420-6; 0-7614-4420-3
LC 2009-4997
"Students will enjoy the large vivid photographs that allow for a closeup look at the animal, along with the excellent descriptions of the different survival methods. . . . Pryor does a good job of bringing the information down to a level that an elementary student would understand without losing any of the important details. . . . [This] would be a great addition to any nonfiction collection." Libr Media Connect
Includes glossary

Mimicry and relationships. Marshall Cavendish Benchmark 2009 32p il (Animal attack and defense) $19.95
Grades: 2 3 4   **591.47**
1. Animal defenses
ISBN 978-0-7614-4421-3; 0-7614-4421-1
LC 2009-4995
"Students will enjoy the large vivid photographs that allow for a closeup look at the animal, along with the excellent descriptions of the different survival methods. . . . Pryor does a good job of bringing the information down to a level that an elementary student would understand without losing any of the important details. . . . [This] would be a great addition to any nonfiction collection." Libr Media Connect
Includes glossary

Tricky behavior. Marshall Cavendish Benchmark 2009 32p il (Animal attack and defense) $19.95
Grades: 2 3 4   **591.47**
1. Animal defenses
ISBN 978-0-7614-4425-1; 0-7614-4425-4
LC 2009-4993
"Students will enjoy the large vivid photographs that allow for a closeup look at the animal, along with the excellent descriptions of the different survival methods. . . . Pryor does a good job of bringing the information down to a level that an elementary student would understand without losing any of the important details. . . . [This] would be a great addition to any nonfiction collection." Libr Media Connect
Inlcudes glossary

Warning colors. Marshall Cavendish Benchmark 2009 32p il (Animal attack and defense) $19.95
Grades: 2 3 4   **591.47**
1. Animal defenses
ISBN 978-0-7614-4419-0; 0-7614-4419-X
LC 2009-4992
"Students will enjoy the large vivid photographs that allow for a closeup look at the animal, along with the excellent descriptions of the different survival methods. . . . Pryor does a good job of bringing the information down to a level that an elementary student would understand without losing any of the important details. . . . [This] would be a great addition to any nonfiction collection." Libr Media Connect
Includes glossary

Racanelli, Marie
Animals with armor. PowerKids Press 2010 24p il (Crazy nature) lib bdg $21.25; pa $8.25

Grades: 2 3 4 5   **591.47**

1. Animal defenses

ISBN 978-1-4358-9386-3 lib bdg; 1-4358-9386-7 lib
bdg; 978-1-4358-9864-6 pa; 1-4358-9864-8 pa

LC 2009036527

This describes the different animals that have adapted
defensive coverings, from turtles and snakes to armadillos,
snails, and bugs

This book "combines attention-grabbing information
with a well-organized format. . . . [The book has] spectacular
color photography and eye-popping facts." SLJ

Camouflaged creatures. PowerKids 2010 24p il
(Crazy nature) lib bdg $21.25; pa $8.25

Grades: 2 3 4 5   **591.47**

1. Animals 2. Camouflage (Biology)

ISBN 978-1-4358-9383-2 lib bdg; 1-4358-9383-2 lib
bdg; 978-1-4358-9858-5 pa; 1-4358-9858-3 pa

This explains how color, texture, and body shape allow animals to blend in seamlessly with their surroundings,
with examples of camouflage in lizards, moths, beetles and
other creatures

This book "combines attention-grabbing information
with a well-organized format. . . . [The book has] spectacular color photography and eye-popping facts. . . . Excellent
for reports." SLJ

Stewart, Melissa

A **rainbow** of animals. Enslow Publishers 2010 128p
il pa $10.99

Grades: 1 2 3   **591.47**

1. Animals -- Color

ISBN 978-0-7660-3706-9 pa; 0-7660-3706-1 pa

LC 2009-36706

Explains why animals come in each color of the rainbow
using examples of animals in the wild.

"In a well-thought-out format, 56 different animals from
around the globe are highlighted and grouped according to
color. From mammals to sea creatures to insects, each one
has its own spread, and brief but interesting factual details
about the color's significance are provided. . . . The large
font and vivid close-up photographs make for an eye-catching, attractive selection. Simple, effective sentences give just
enough information to inspire further investigation." SLJ

Includes bibliographical references

The **skin** you're in; the secrets of skin. illustrated by
Janet Hamlin. Marshall Cavendish Benchmark 2010 48p
il (The gross and goofy body) lib bdg $29.93

Grades: 2 3 4   **591.47**

1. Skin

ISBN 978-0-7614-4169-4; 0-7614-4169-7

LC 2008033620

This provides information on the role skin plays in the
body science of humans and animals.

This "offers detailed science facts in a fashion approachable enough to make it a welcome supplement to school textbooks. . . . The layout is fresh, clean, and colorful, sidebars
keep things conversational, and the back matter is solid."
Booklist

Includes glossary and bibliographical references

Stockdale, Susan

Stripes of all types; written and illustrated by Susan
Stockdale. Peachtree Publishers 2013 32 p. $15.95

Grades: 1 2 3   **591.47**

1. Stripes -- Juvenile literature 2. Animals -- Color --
Juvenile literature 3. Camouflage (Biology) -- Juvenile
literature

ISBN 1561456950; 9781561456956

LC 2012025541

In this children's picture book "[Susan] Stockdale pairs
. . .acrylic illustrations with . . . verse to depict 19 striped
animals. . . . The accompanying images show purple-striped
jellyfish, an eastern garter snake, ring-tailed lemurs, and an
American bittern. Elsewhere . . . a poison frog in shocking orange, yellow, and red stripes is 'propped on a log.'
Closer to home, two children cuddle with striped cats."
(Publishers Weekly)

Yaw, Valerie

Color-changing animals. Bearport Pub. 2011 24p il
(Animals with super powers) lib bdg $22.61

Grades: 3 4 5   **591.47**

1. Animal defenses 2. Animal communication 3.
Camouflage (Biology)

ISBN 978-1-61772-122-9; 1-61772-122-0

LC 2010038283

This describes color-changing animals including gray
tree frogs, snowshoe hares, cuttlefish, the mimic octopus,
the golden tortoise beetle, chameleons, seahorses, and gold-
en crab spiders.

"Large color photos of animals in natural settings and
clear, cogent presentations of information combine to boost
this [book] well above the average for both assignments and
casual browsing." SLJ

Includes glossary and bibliographical references

591.5   Behavior

Barner, Bob

Animal baths. Chronicle Books 2011 un il $15.99

Grades: PreK K 1   **591.5**

1. Baths 2. Animal behavior

ISBN 978-1-4521-0056-2; 1-4521-0056-X

LC 2011008001

"Eleven colorful two-page spreads (illustrated in cut
paper, ribbon and pastel) show a variety of animals bathing, with accompanying two-line verses. . . . Finally, there's
a little boy in a tub rub-a-dubbing and covered in bubbles.
Then, a fitting encore: A longer poem against a background
of bubbles and a child's bathtime accessories goes through
the child's whole bath routine with shoutouts to some of the
animals. . . . Barner's text is crisp and age-appropriate, but
his well-composed, clever pictures really carry the story. . . .
Well-conceived in its simplicity from beginning to end; even
pre-readers can follow along." Kirkus

Batten, Mary

Please don't wake the animals; a book about sleep.
written by Mary Batten; illustrated by Higgins Bond.
Peachtree 2008 un il $16.95

Grades: PreK K 1 2 3 **591.5**
1. Sleep 2. Animal behavior
ISBN 978-1-56145-393-1; 1-56145-393-5
LC 2007-31904

"This big bright picture book is an exciting way to talk about the biology that connects humans with many kinds of animals. 'All animals sleep,' and in all kinds of places. Predators can sleep quite safely. . . . Their prey, however, must stay alert, hardly daring to sleep at all. . . . There's also information about animals that hibernate." Booklist

Fielding, Beth
Animal baths; wild & wonderful ways animals get clean! illustrations by Susan Greenelsh. EarlyLight Books 2009 47p il $14.95
Grades: 3 4 5 **591.5**
1. Baths 2. Cleanliness 3. Animal behavior
ISBN 978-0-9797455-2-2; 0-9797455-2-7

"Written in a conversational tone, this book is divided into three parts based on how animals clean themselves. . . . Each section begins with a brief description of how and why they engage in specific activities, followed by a spread about which ones utilize this method. A full-page, softly colored drawing of the animals 'bathing' faces each page of text. This fascinating book provides some unusual details about the unique behavior of the featured creatures." SLJ

Fraser, Mary Ann
Where are the night animals? HarperCollins Pubs. 1999 29p il (Let's-read-and-find-out science) $15.95; lib bdg $15.89; pa $4.95
Grades: K 1 **591.5**
1. Night 2. Animal behavior
ISBN 0-06-027717-3; 0-06-027718-1 lib bdg; 0-06-445176-3 pa
LC 97-34683

Describes various nocturnal animals and their nighttime activities, including the opossum, brown bat, and tree frog

"The narrative approach and affable, realistic paintings make this basic science lesson accessible and engaging to the preschool audience." Horn Book Guide

Hile, Lori
Animal survival. Raintree 2011 56p il (Extreme survival) lib bdg $33.50
Grades: 4 5 6 7 **591.5**
1. Pets 2. Animals 3. Animal behavior 4. Natural disasters
ISBN 978-1-4109-3973-9; 1-4109-3973-1
LC 2010028842

This book is "fun and informative. [This] well-organized title starts with an overview [of animal survival], offers some specific examples, and includes additional facts or tips and resources. . . . [It features] dramatic archival and full-color photos on nearly every page. . . . The first chapter introduces resilient creatures that beat the odds and then follows with their journeys, animal heroes, and their work while surviving natural disasters. . . . [This is a book] that youngsters will enjoy and talk about." SLJ

Includes glossary and bibliographical references

Jenkins, Steve
★ How many ways can you catch a fly? [by] Steve Jenkins & Robin Page. Houghton Mifflin Company 2008 un il $16
Grades: PreK K 1 2 3 **591.5**
1. Animal behavior 2. Food chains (Ecology)
ISBN 978-0-618-96634-9; 0-618-96634-X
LC 2008-01864

"This picture book is about the food chain. . . . The facts about how particular animals escape danger and evade predators to stay alive are just as exciting as the facts about hunting. With clear, gorgeous, freestanding images in cut- and torn-paper collage, each double-page spread shows detailed species close up, as well as the connections between animals." Booklist

Includes bibliographical references

★ Time to eat; written and illustrated by Steve Jenkins and Robin Page. Houghton Mifflin 2011 un il $12.99
Grades: PreK K 1 2 3 **591.5**
1. Animals -- Food
ISBN 978-0-547-25032-8; 0-547-25032-0
LC 2010025127

"This small, square picture book presents an exciting introduction to what animals eat and how they collect, store, and digest their food. . . . The beautiful cut- and torn-paper collage illustrations are . . . expertly colored, detailed, and expressive . . . and the layout, featuring plenty of white space, nicely spotlights each animal in action." Booklist

Time to sleep; written and illustrated by Steve Jenkins and Robin Page. Houghton Mifflin 2011 un il $12.99
Grades: K 1 2 3 **591.5**
1. Sleep 2. Animal behavior
ISBN 978-0-547-25040-3; 0-547-25040-1
LC 2010025128

"Jenkins and Page introduce an array of creatures, showcasing how they . . . sleep. [The title concludes] with an appendix detailing further information about the featured animals. The illustrations are rendered in torn- and cut-paper collage, with each animal against a white background. . . . [The book] introduces animals from the familiar red fox to the lesser-known basilisk. Fascinating behaviors are detailed with explanations. . . . Readers will be captivated." SLJ

Knapp, Ron
Bloodsucking creatures. Enslow Publishers 2011 48p il (Bizarre science) lib bdg $23.93
Grades: 5 6 7 8 **591.5**
1. Bloodsucking animals
ISBN 978-0-7660-3671-0; 0-7660-3671-5
LC 2010009761

First published 1996 with title: Bloodsuckers

This describes bloodsucking animals such as mosquitoes, vampire bats, and fleas.

"Aimed at reluctant readers, [this title is] sure to disgust and delight in equal measure. . . . [The title] will pique interest and get kids lining up at the reference desk looking for more. The text is complemented by illustrations and magnified photos of things that you would hope never to see." SLJ

Includes glossary and bibliographical references

Lunde, Darrin

★ **After** the kill; [by] Darrin Lunde; illustrated by Catherine Stock. Charlesbridge 2011 un il lib bdg $16.95; pa $7.95

Grades: 2 3 4 5   **591.5**

1. Food chains (Ecology) 2. Animals -- Food 3. Animals -- Africa

ISBN 978-1-57091-743-1 lib bdg; 1-57091-743-4 lib bdg; 978-1-57091-744-8 pa; 1-57091-744-2 pa

LC 2010007524

This is a "blunt portrayal of animal life in the Seregeti. A lioness stalks and faltering zebra, kills it, and eats it with her family; meanwhile, white-backed vultures arrive. . . . Then come hyenas, jackals, two other types of vultures, and ultimately meat-eating beetles, until all that remains of the zebra is bones. . . . Given the inherent grisliness of the topic, the text is notably reined in and matter-of-fact, and the pictures, expansive horizontal spreads, are almost impressionistic, focusing more on the ferocity of the predators than on the details of their prey." Horn Book

Newman, Aline Alexander

Animal superstars; and more true stories of amazing animal talents. by Aline Alexander Newman. National Geographic Society 2013 111 p. col. ill. (National geographic kids. Chapters) (paperback) $5.99; (library) $14.90

Grades: 2 3 4 5   **591.5**

1. Animals 2. Animal intelligence 3. Animals -- Anecdotes 4. Animal intelligence -- Anecdotes

ISBN 1426310919; 1426310927; 9781426310911; 9781426310928

LC 2012277240

This book by Aline Alexander Newman "will feature animals who can perform amazing acts like riding motocross, foretelling the weather, and playing a guitar. These stories [may] empower them to devour the more text-heavy 'grown up' style of the book, while still keeping the story easily digestible for a hesitant reader." (Publisher's note)

Includes bibliographical references (p. 111) and index.

Pipe, Jim

Swarms; written by Jim Pipe; created and designed by David Salariya. Franklin Watts 2009 32p il (Scary creatures) lib bdg $26; pa $8.95

Grades: 3 4 5   **591.5**

1. Animal behavior

ISBN 978-0-531-21674-3 lib bdg; 0-531-21674-8 lib bdg; 978-0-531-21045-1 pa; 0-531-21045-6 pa

LC 2009010800

This describes the behavior of large groups of similar animals such as insects, birds, or fish, all moving in the same direction

This title has "two-page chapters of accessible, large-type text and bright color photos and illustrations. . . . The series distinguishes itself with 'X-Ray Vision.' When readers hold the page with this prompt up to the light, an image emerges. The X-rays mostly show the skeletal structures of the animals. Text boxes throughout add to the visual appeal. . . . [This is an] excellent [resource] for school assignments and browsing." SLJ

Includes glossary

Racanelli, Marie

Animal mimics. PowerKids Press 2010 24p il (Crazy nature) lib bdg $21.25; pa $8.25

Grades: 2 3 4 5   **591.5**

1. Animal behavior

ISBN 978-1-4358-9382-5 lib bdg; 1-4358-9382-4 lib bdg; 978-1-4358-9856-1 pa; 1-4358-9856-7 pa

Mimicry is an animal adaptation used both by prey and predators to disguise them in their habitats. The different kinds of mimicry are explored, along with specific examples of each type

This book "combines attention-grabbing information with a well-organized format. . . . [The book has] spectacular color photography and eye-popping facts. . . . Excellent for reports." SLJ

Underground animals. PowerKids 2010 24p il (Crazy nature) lib bdg $21.25; pa $8.25

Grades: 2 3 4 5   **591.5**

1. Animals

ISBN 978-1-4358-9384-9 lib bdg; 1-4358-9384-0 lib bdg; 978-1-4358-9860-8 pa; 1-4358-9860-5 pa

This describes animals that live underground from burrowers to cave-dwellers, such as earthworms, moles, ants, badgers, desert tortoises

This book "combines attention-grabbing information with a well-organized format. . . . [The book has] spectacular color photography and eye-popping facts. . . . Excellent for reports." SLJ

Ruurs, Margriet

Amazing animals; the remarkable things creatures do. illustrated by W. Allan Hancock. Tundra Books 2011 32p il $17.95

Grades: 2 3 4 5   **591.5**

1. Animal behavior

ISBN 978-0-88776-973-3; 0-88776-973-X

Detailed illustrations and short descriptions present facts about animals from around the world, including their home-building, diet, and hunting.

"Though only a few lines are devoted to each animal, the detailed paintings and surprising details should captivate readers." Publ Wkly

Settel, Joanne

Exploding ants; amazing facts about how animals adapt. Atheneum Bks. for Young Readers 1999 40p il $16.95

Grades: 4 5 6 7   **591.5**

1. Animal behavior 2. Animals -- Habits and behavior

ISBN 0-689-81739-8

LC 97-35395

Describes examples of animal behavior that may strike humans as disgusting, including the "gross" ways animals find food, shelter, and safety in the natural world

"This attractive volume presents its material as wondrous science instead of sensational effect." Booklist

Includes glossary and bibliographical references

Stewart, Melissa

Animal grossapedia; by Melissa Stewart. Scholastic 2012 107 p. (paperback) $8.99

Grades: 5 6 7   591.5

1. Biology 2. Body fluids 3. Animal behavior
ISBN 0545433487; 9780545433488

This book looks at how animals use the "gross" substances that emanate from their bodies. "Did you know Komodo dragons use their saliva to poison their prey, but mice use their saliva to heal their wounds? Could you guess that vomit is used by the sea cucumber to startle enemies and also by bees to make honey?" The book offers "an understanding of how different animals use spit, vomit, slime, poop, urine, and blood to survive." (Publisher's note)

Thimmesh, Catherine

Friends; written by Catherine Thimmesh. Houghton Mifflin 2011 un il $16.99
Grades: K 1 2 3   591.5

1. Animal behavior
ISBN 0547390106; 9780547390109; 978-0-547-
39010-9; 0-547-39010-6

LC 2010025122

This book offers a photo exploration of unlikely animal friendships.

"The photos radiate trust and warmth, and the text is soothing and reassuring." SLJ

Zelch, Patti R.

★ **Ready,** set . . . wait! what animals do before a hurricane. illustrated by Connie McLennan. Sylvan Dell 2010 un il $16.95; pa $8.95
Grades: 1 2 3 4   591.5

1. Hurricanes 2. Animal behavior
ISBN 978-1-60718-072-2; 1-60718-072-3; 978-1-
60718-083-8 pa; 1-60718-083-9 pa

"Superbly illustrated, . . . the book presents scientifically verified information on the behaviors that many animals . . . display in the days just prior to hurricanes. Prereaders will enjoy both hearing the stories and looking at the illustrations, while early readers will be able to advance through the text on their own." Sci Books Films

591.56   Behavior relating to life cycle

Bancroft, Henrietta

Animals in winter; by Henrietta Bancroft and Richard G. Van Gelder; illustrated by Helen K. Davie. rev ed; HarperCollins Pubs. 1997 32p il (Let's-read-and-find-out science) hardcover o.p. pa $4.95
Grades: K 1   591.56

1. Winter 2. Animal behavior
ISBN 0-06-027158-2; 0-06-445165-8 pa

LC 95-36246

First published 1963

Describes the many different ways animals cope with winter, including migration, hibernation, and food storage

"The words are immediate . . . and the clear, active illustrations will draw new readers to a popular subject." Booklist

Berkes, Marianne Collins

Going home; the mystery of animal migration. illustrated by Jennifer DiRubbio. Dawn 2010 un il map $16.95; pa $8.95

Grades: 2 3 4   591.56

1. Children's poetry 2. Animals -- Migration
ISBN 978-1-58469-126-6; 1-58469-126-3; 978-1-
58469-127-3 pa; 1-58469-127-1 pa

LC 2009-38568

"The illustrations enhance the text with softly colored two-page spreads. This book is perfect for a read-aloud to introduce the topic of migration. The rhyming verse flows smoothly, enhanced by the informational text." Libr Media Connect

Includes bibliographical references

Carney, Elizabeth

Great migrations; whales, wildebeests, butterflies, elephants, and other amazing animals on the move. National Geographic 2010 45p il map (National Geographic kids) $17.95; lib bdg $27
Grades: 3 4 5   591.56

1. Animals -- Migration
ISBN 9781426307003; 1426307004; 9781426307010
lib bdg; 1426307012 lib bdg

LC 2010008501

"This colorful book offers excellent photos of eight migrating animals: Mali elephants, red crabs, monarch butterflies, golden jellyfish, zebras, army ants, wildebeests, and sperm whales. . . . The writing style is often lively, tha maps are excellent, and the photos are exceptionally clear and vibrant." Booklist

Collard, Sneed B.

Animal dads; [by] Sneed B. Collard III; illustrated by Steve Jenkins. Houghton Mifflin 1997 un il $15.95; pa $5.95
Grades: K 1 2 3   591.56

1. Animal babies 2. Animal behavior
ISBN 0-395-83621-2; 0-618-03299-1 pa

LC 96-22171

"Each father and his offspring are presented on a single or double-page spread, illustrated with striking, cut-paper collage figures. The large, lifelike creatures are set against backgrounds that are true to each animal's natural habitat." SLJ

Dowson, Nick

North; the story of Arctic migration. illustrated by Patrick Benson. Candlewick Press 2011 56p il $16.99
Grades: 1 2 3   591.56

1. Animals -- Migration
ISBN 978-0-7636-5271-5; 0-7636-5271-7

LC 2010048131

"In the dark Arctic winters, few species can survive, but in short, lush summers, millions of animals return to reproduce. This combination of lyrical prose and striking illustrations conveys the mystery and magic of the far North and the cycle of darkness and rebirth that includes some astonishing migratory journeys. . . . Simple but effective, this is a beautiful introduction to a remarkable region that should encourage any child's sense of wonder." Kirkus

Fraser, Mary Ann

How animal babies stay safe. HarperCollins Pubs. 2002 33p il (Let's-read-and-find-out science) hardcover o.p. pa $4.95

Grades: K 1   **591.56**

1. Animal babies 2. Parental behavior in animals
ISBN 0-06-028803-5; 0-06-445211-5 pa

LC 00-57267

The author "describes how animal babies are cared for by their parents, including alligator babies who are carried about in their mother's mouth and young elephants who are placed in the middle of the herd for protection. Watercolor illustrations in muted colors help expand the simple text." Horn Book Guide

Jenkins, Steve

★ **Sisters** & brothers; sibling relationships in the animal world. [by] Steve Jenkins & Robin Page. Houghton Mifflin 2008 un il $16

Grades: 2 3 4   **591.56**

1. Siblings 2. Animal behavior
ISBN 978-0-618-37596-7; 0-618-37596-1

LC 2007-34305

"This riveting picture book . . . is packed with amazing facts. . . . [The subjects are] depicted in crisp, gorgeous, cut-and-torn paper collages set against lots of white space. . . . The sibling focus is a way to include a wealth of fascinating facts." Booklist

Time for a bath; written and illustrated by Steve Jenkins and Robin Page. Houghton Mifflin 2011 un il $12.99

Grades: K 1 2 3   **591.56**

1. Baths 2. Animal behavior
ISBN 978-0-547-25037-3; 0-547-25037-1

LC 2010025126

"Jenkins and Page introduce an array of creatures, showcasing how they bathe. . . . [The title concludes] with an appendix detailing further information about the featured animals. The illustrations are rendered in torn- and cut-paper collage, with each animal . . . set against a white background. . . . Readers are informed that animals bathe for different reasons: to clean themselves, to cool off, to warm up, to dissuade parasites. . . . Readers will be captivated." SLJ

Marsh, Laura

Amazing animal journeys. National Geographic 2010 48p il (Great migrations) $11.90; pa $3.99

Grades: 1 2 3   **591.56**

1. Crabs 2. Zebras 3. Walruses 4. Animals -- Migration
ISBN 978-1-4263-0742-3; 1-4263-0742-X; 978-1-4263-0741-6 pa; 1-4263-0741-1 pa

LC 2010017958

This describes the migration patterns of zebras, red crabs, and walruses.

"Dynamic full-color photographs, informative writing, and consistent organization work well together in [this volume]. . . . Along with the many photographs, the fascinating details are supported by boxes of related information, helpful definitions of new terms, and a sprinkling of entertaining jokes/riddles." SLJ

Includes glossary

Roemer, Heidi B.

Whose nest is this? by Heidi Bee Roemer; illustrated by Connie McLennan. NorthWord Books for Young Readers 2009 un il $16.95

Grades: PreK K 1 2   **591.56**

1. Birds -- Nests 2. Animals -- Habitations
ISBN 978-1-58979-386-6; 1-58979-386-2

LC 2007021870

"This picture book describes the nests of various birds, insects, mammals, fish, and reptiles. Whether it's an elf owl's cavity in a giant Saguaro, a Caribbean flamingo's mound of mud in shallow water, or a sea turtle's sandy pit, these shelters are described in brief rhymed texts. . . . The creatures are brought to life in the engaging rhymes and vivid art." SLJ

Stockdale, Susan

Carry me! animal babies on the move. written and illustrated by Susan Stockdale. Peachtree Publishers 2005 un il $15.95

Grades: K 1 2   **591.56**

1. Animal behavior
ISBN 1-56145-328-5

LC 2004-16585

"The facts of zoology are both exciting and cuddly in this science picture book with clear, bright acrylic illustrations that show how various animals carry their babies. The settings give the big picture—from the African savannah and Antarctica to South America. Then children can look closely and find animal babies tucked into pouches, clinging to bellies, propped on shoulders, perched on feet, gripped between teeth." Booklist

Includes bibliographical references

591.59   Communication

Baines, Rebecca

What did one elephant say to the other; a book about communication. by Becky Baines. National Geographic Society 2008 26p il (Zig zag) $14.95; lib bdg $19.90

Grades: PreK K 1   **591.59**

1. Elephants -- Juvenile literature 2. Animal communication -- Juvenile literature
ISBN 978-1-4263-0307-4; 1-4263-0307-6; 978-1-4263-0308-1 lib bdg; 1-4263-0308-4 lib bdg

LC 2008-07218

"Curiosity will be piqued by the vibrant color photographs, accommodating illustrations, large font size, and helpful captions. Special features include drawings superimposed over photographs, and a zigzag path at the end of . . . [the] book prompting readers to further explore the topic in new and fun ways." SLJ

Davies, Nicola, 1958-

Talk talk squawk; How and Why Animals Communicate. illustrated by Neal Layton. Walker & Company 2011 64 p.

Grades: 3 4 5   **591.59**

1. Animal communication
ISBN 0763650889 (Candlewick); 1406321184 (Walker & Co.); 9780763650889 (Candlewick); 9781406321180 (Walker & Co.)

LC 2010040794

"Davies and Layton turn to animal communication, describing how animals send and receive messages by sound, sight, smell and touch, for a variety of purposes. . . . Cartoon-like illustrations, almost doodles, done in ink and colored digitally, add humor to every page, even in the backmatter. They often include speech balloons demonstrating the animals' messages. . . . Something to crow about." Kirkus

Sayre, April Pulley

★ **Secrets** of sound; studying the calls and songs of whales, elephants, and birds. Houghton Mifflin 2002 63p il (Scientists in the field) pbk. $7.99

Grades: 4 5 6 7 **591.59**

1. Whales 2. Birdsongs 3. Elephants 4. Animal communication 5. Bioacoustics -- Juvenile literature
ISBN 9780618585465

LC 2001-51877

"The focus of this Scientists in the Field volume is scientists who study animal communication—whale songs, elephant rumbles, and nocturnal bird calls. Bioacoustics, the field encompassing their work, is a meld of biology, technology, music, and physics. . . . Christopher Clark uses underwater microphones to record whale songs. . . . Katy Payne's familiarity with the vibrations of organ music led to her discovery of the infrasound rumbles that elephants use to communicate over long distances. Bill Evans records birds at night to learn more about their migration patterns. {Glossary. Bibliography. Index.} Intermediate." (Horn Book)

"This fascinating title shows the thrill of scientific discovery up close. . . . Lots of well-edited quotes from the scientists convey their contagious enthusiasm for what they do, and sharp color photos, sound charts, and activity boxes break up the text, making it even more readable." Booklist

Includes glossary and bibliographical references

591.6 Miscellaneous nontaxonomic kinds of animals

Claybourne, Anna

100 deadliest things on the planet. Scholastic 2012 112 p. $7.99

Grades: 4 5 6 **591.6**

1. Tsunamis 2. Volcanoes 3. Animal attacks 4. Animal behavior 5. Natural disasters
ISBN 0545434378; 9780545434379

This book by Anna Claybourne looks at Earth's deadliest animals and natural disasters. "There are animals that can use an arsenal of deadly weapons--teeth, claws, stinging spines, powerful pincers, or scary suckers--to fight, hunt, or defend themselves. There are natural disasters--from towering tsunamis to massive volcanic eruptions--that can destroy whole cities in the blink of an eye." The book "includes side panels, a 'deadly factor' rating, and photos throughout." (Publisher's note)

Davies, Nicola, 1958-

What's eating you? parasites--the inside story. [by] Nicola Davies; illustrated by Neal Layton. Candlewick Press 2007 60p il $12.99

Grades: 3 4 5 6 **591.6**

1. Parasites
ISBN 978-0-7636-3460-5; 0-7636-3460-3

LC 2007-25634

"Davies uses a conversational approach to introduce readers to those weird critters that consider their host to be 'just a pantry.' . . . The subject is inherently fascinating for

kids and those who settle into read will find a good deal of information about some of the more familiar parasites. . . . The artwork adds a welcome comic veneer." Booklist

Graham, Ian

Microscopic scary creatures; written by Ian Graham; created and designed by David Salariya. Franklin Watts 2009 32p il (Scary creatures) lib bdg $26; pa $8.95

Grades: 3 4 5 **591.6**

1. Protozoa 2. Parasites 3. Microorganisms
ISBN 978-0-531-21673-6 lib bdg; 0-531-21673-X lib bdg; 978-0-531-21044-4 pa; 0-531-21044-8 pa

LC 2009-11224

This defines microscopic creatures and describes their habitats and life cycles, and their relationships to humans.

This title has "two-page chapters of accessible, large-type text and bright color photos and illustrations. . . . The series distinguishes itself with 'X-Ray Vision.' When readers hold the page with this prompt up to the light, an image emerges. The X-rays mostly show the skeletal structures of the animals. Text boxes throughout add to the visual appeal. . . . [This title is an] excellent [resource] for school assignments and browsing." SLJ

Includes glossary

Jenkins, Steve

★ **Never** smile at a monkey; and 17 other important things to remember. Houghton Mifflin Books for Children 2009 un il $16

Grades: 1 2 3 4 **591.6**

1. Dangerous animals
ISBN 978-0-618-96620-2; 0-618-96620-X

LC 2009-32964

"A visually stunning book illustrated with cut paper and torn collages. . . . This superlative illustrator has given children yet another work that educates and amazes." SLJ

Pryor, Kimberley Jane

Venom, poison, and electricity. Marshall Cavendish Benchmark 2009 32p il (Animal attack and defense) $19.95

Grades: 2 3 4 **591.6**

1. Animal defenses 2. Poisonous animals
ISBN 978-0-7614-4422-0; 0-7614-4422-X

LC 2009-4994

"Students will enjoy the large vivid photographs that allow for a close-up look at the animal, along with the excellent descriptions of the different survival methods. . . . Pryor does a good job of bringing the information down to a level that an elementary student would understand without losing any of the important details. . . . [This] would be a great addition to any nonfiction collection." Libr Media Connect

Inlcudes glossary

Racanelli, Marie

Albino animals. PowerKids Press 2010 24p il (Crazy nature) lib bdg $21.25; pa $8.25

Grades: 2 3 4 5 **591.6**

1. Albinos and albinism 2. Animals -- Color
ISBN 978-1-4358-9381-8 lib bdg; 1-4358-9381-6 lib bdg; 978-1-4358-9854-7 pa; 1-4358-9854-0 pa

This explains why different types of animals are born without skin pigmentation and about the challenges they must face in their natural environments

This book "combines attention-grabbing information with a well-organized format. . . . [The book has] spectacular color photography and eye-popping facts. . . . Excellent for reports." SLJ

Stewart, Melissa

Deadliest animals. National Geographic 2011 48p il (National Geographic readers) lib bdg $11.90; pa $3.99
Grades: K 1 2 3   **591.6**
1. Dangerous animals
ISBN 978-1-4263-0758-4 lib bdg; 1-4263-0758-6 lib ed; 978-1-4263-0757-7 pa; 1-4263-0757-8 pa
            LC 2011284182
This describes 12 dangerous species including sharks, snakes, jellyfish, bears, tigers and mosquitoes.
"Vivid nature photos show the deadly creatures in action. Silly jokes . . . and . . . sidebars maintain readers' attention." Horn Book Guide

Tourville, Amanda Doering

Animal invaders. Rourke Pub. 2010 48p il (Let's explore science) $32.79
Grades: 4 5 6 7   **591.6**
1. Animals 2. Biological invasions
ISBN 978-1-61590-319-1; 1-61590-319-4
            LC 2010009906
This describes non-native animal species.
Includes bibliographical references

591.68   Rare and endangered animals

Allgor, Marie

Endangered desert animals; by Marie Allgor; edited by Jennifer Way. PowerKids Press 2013 24 p. col. ill. (Save Earth's animals!) (library) $22.60; (paperback) $8.25
Grades: 1 2 3   **591.68**
1. Desert animals -- Juvenile literature 2. Desert ecology -- Juvenile literature 3. Endangered species -- Juvenile literature 4. Wildlife conservation -- Juvenile literature
ISBN 9781448874231; 9781448874965
            LC 2011051875
This book on endangered desert animals by Marie Allgor is part of the "Save the Earth's Animals!" series. "Before launching into the individual creatures, the title explores the region's climate and the various habitats: shrubs, cacti, and so on. The five featured animals are the slender-horned gazelle, the Egyptian vulture, Nelson's antelope squirrel, the Bactrian camel, and the desert tortoise." (Booklist)
Includes bibliographical references (p. 24) and index

Barry, Frances

Let's save the animals; a flip-the-flap book. Candlewick Press 2010 un il $12.99
Grades: PreK K   **591.68**
1. Endangered species 2. Wildlife conservation
ISBN 978-0-7636-4501-4; 0-7636-4501-X
            LC 2009-22117
"Barry's engaging entry brings young children into the conversation [about wildlife conservation] without sacrificing an ounce of kid appeal. Sporting a rounded cover, sturdy pages, and inventive die-cut flaps, this primer presents 10

endangered species in their natural habitats. . . . Barry's superb, colorful paper-collage illustrations feature close-ups of friendly looking animals." Booklist

Hirsch, Rebecca E.

Helping endangered animals; by Rebecca Hirsch. Cherry Lake Pub. 2010 32p il (Save the planet) lib bdg $27.07
Grades: 3 4 5 6   **591.68**
1. Endangered species
ISBN 978-1-60279-658-4 lib bdg; 1-60279-658-0 lib bdg
            LC 2009-38094
Examines endangered species, how human activities have contributed to shrinking numbers, and what is being done to protect animals for the future
"At the beginning of . . . [the] book, readers are given a mission and advised to be alert to the facts provided so that they can successfully answer the questions at the end. . . . Children are made to feel part of the process; suggestions for how they can become involved abound." SLJ
Includes glossary and bibliographical references

Jenkins, Martin

★ **Can** we save the tiger? Candlewick Press 2011 50p il $16.99
Grades: 1 2 3   **591.68**
1. Tigers 2. Extinct animals 3. Wildlife conservation 4. Extinction (Biology) -- Juvenile literature
ISBN 0763649090; 9780763649098; 978-0-7636-4909-8; 0-7636-4909-0
            LC 2010008899
"Magnificent artwork and a careful balance of good and bad news are the strengths of this examination of endangered species. . . . Conversational text . . . explains difficult nuances of politics and sociology with verve. White's animals—meticulously drafted and shaded with the subtlest of earth tones—could almost walk off the page. The book's large trim size allows the inclusion of many sketches of creatures in a variety of positions, while intelligent design and typography decisions make each page worth lingering over. An excellent resource." Publ Wkly

Jenkins, Steve

★ **Almost** gone; the world's rarest animals. HarperCollins Pubs. 2006 33p il (Let's-read-and-find-out science) $16.99; pa $5.99
Grades: K 1 2 3   **591.68**
1. Rare animals 2. Endangered species
ISBN 0-06-053598-9; 0-06-053600-4 pa
            LC 2004-30199
"This engaging title is informative as well as visually stunning." SLJ

Laverdunt, Damien

Small and Tall Tales of Extinct Animals; Hélène Rajcak and Damien Laverdunt; translated by Jen Craddock. Lerner Pub Group 2012 80 p. $22.95
Grades: 3 4 5   **591.68**
1. Extinct animals 2. Animals -- Encyclopedias 3. Picture books for children
ISBN 1877579068; 9781877579066
In this book, "27 animals, divided by the region they once inhabited, are featured, among them dwarf elephants,

giant ground sloths, and Haast's eagle .... Each .... creature is given a full spread with a comic strip on the left, featuring a . . . folktale, legend, or bit of history, and on the right a[n] . . . illustration of the animal, the common name, scientific name, a size chart with a comparison to a human, and a short explanation of its life and extinction." (School Library Journal)

591.7 Animal ecology, animals characteristic of specific environments

Allaire, Caroline

Let's look at the rainforest close up; written by Caroline Allaire; illustrated by Ute Fuhr and Raoul Sautai. Moonlight Pub. 2005 38 p. (First discovery close ups) $11.99
Grades: K 1 2   **591.7**
1. Picture books for children 2. Rain forests -- Juvenile literature 3. Rain forest animals -- Juvenile literature
ISBN 1851033602; 9781851033607
     LC 2012405963
This book by Caroline Allaire is part of the First Discovery Close-ups series and looks at the rainforest. It gives readers a "closer look at the 'strange half-lit world' of the rain forest, including . . . . examinations of such animals as hummingbirds, katydid grasshoppers, and heliconid caterpillars." (Booklist)

Arnosky, Jim

Watching desert wildlife. National Geographic Soc. 1998 un il hardcover o.p. pa $7.95
Grades: 3 4 5 6   **591.7**
1. Desert animals
ISBN 0-7922-7304-4; 0-7922-6737-0 pa
     LC 98-13189
Illustrations and text describe some of the animals the author encountered in the deserts of the American Southwest
"An informative and well-illustrated addition to science units on desert wildlife." Booklist

Barnhill, Kelly Regan

Monsters of the deep; deep sea adaptation. by Kelly Regan Barnhill. Capstone Press 2008 32p il (Fact finders. Extreme life) lib bdg $22.60
Grades: 2 3 4   **591.7**
1. Ocean bottom 2. Marine animals
ISBN 978-1-4296-1264-7 lib bdg; 1-4296-1264-9 lib bdg
     LC 2007-20897
This reveals "the world of deep-sea creatures. A conversational text explains how the animals have adapted to the incredible depth and darkness of the ocean's 'midnight zone.' Readers will be fascinated—or terrified—by the unusual-looking fish." Horn Book Guide
Includes glossary and bibliographical references

Bateman, Donna M.

Deep in the swamp; [by] Donna M. Bateman; illustrated by Brian Lies. Charlesbridge 2007 un il lib bdg $15.95; pa $6.95

Grades: K 1 2 3   **591.7**
1. Counting 2. Swamp animals
ISBN 978-1-57091-596-3 lib bdg; 978-1-57091-597-0 pa
     LC 2006009026
"This stunning book spotlights the flora and fauna of Florida's Okefenokee Swamp. . . . The text is a version of the familiar poem 'Over in the Meadow,' with impeccable meter. . . . Lie's meticulous and glowing acrylic illustrations feature myriad shades of green, yellow, and blue." SLJ

Bredeson, Carmen

Baby animals of lakes and ponds. Enslow Elementary 2011 24p il (Nature's baby animals) lib bdg $21.26
Grades: 1 2 3   **591.7**
1. Lakes 2. Ponds 3. Animal babies
ISBN 978-0-7660-3563-8; 0-7660-3563-8
     LC 2009037899
"The large, close-up photos . . . are irresistibly cute. The text . . . stayed focused and gives just the right amount of interesting information." Booklist
Includes glossary and bibliographical references

Baby animals of the frozen tundra. Enslow Publishers 2009 24p il map (Nature's baby animals) lib bdg $21.26
Grades: 1 2 3   **591.7**
1. Animal babies 2. Animals -- Arctic regions
ISBN 978-0-7660-3002-2 lib bdg; 0-7660-3002-4 lib bdg
     LC 2007039472
"Up-close photos and information about baby animals of the tundra biome" Publisher's note
Includes glossary and bibliographical references

Baby animals of the grasslands. Enslow Publishers 2008 23p il map (Nature's baby animals) lib bdg $21.26
Grades: 1 2 3   **591.7**
1. Grasslands 2. Animal babies
ISBN 978-0-7660-3006-0 lib bdg; 0-7660-3006-7 lib bdg
     LC 2007-29284
"Well chosen, exceedingly endearing photos highlight this [book]. . . . Accessible to new readers." SLJ
Includes glossary and bibliographical references

Baby animals of the mountains. Enslow Elementary 2011 24p il (Nature's baby animals) lib bdg $21.26
Grades: 1 2 3   **591.7**
1. Animal babies 2. Mountain animals
ISBN 978-0-7660-3562-1; 0-7660-3562-X
     LC 2009037898
"The large, closeup photos . . . are irresistibly cute. The text . . . stayed focused and gives just the right amount of interesting information." Booklist
Includes glossary and bibliographical references

Baby animals of the ocean. Enslow Publishers 2009 24p il (Nature's baby animals) lib bdg $21.26
Grades: 1 2 3   **591.7**
1. Animal babies 2. Marine animals
ISBN 978-0-7660-3003-9 lib bdg; 0-7660-3003-2 lib bdg
     LC 2007039469

"Up-close photos and information about baby animals of the ocean biome" Publisher's note

Includes glossary and bibliographical references

Baby animals of the seashore. Enslow Elementary 2011 24p il (Nature's baby animals) lib bdg $21.26

Grades: 1 2 3   591.7

1. Seashore 2. Animal babies 3. Marine animals
ISBN 978-0-7660-3565-2; 0-7660-3565-4

LC 2009037901

"The large, closeup photos . . . are irresistibly cute. The text . . . stayed focused and gives just the right amount of interesting information." Booklist

Includes glossary and bibliographical references

Baby animals of the wetlands. Enslow Elementary 2011 24p il (Nature's baby animals) lib bdg $21.26

Grades: 1 2 3   591.7

1. Wetlands 2. Animal babies
ISBN 978-0-7660-3564-5 lib bdg; 0-7660-3564-6 lib bdg

LC 2009037900

"The large, closeup photos . . . are irresistibly cute. The text . . . stayed focused and gives just the right amount of interesting information." Booklist

Includes glossary and bibliographical references

Carlson-Voiles, Polly

Someone walks by; the wonders of winter wildlife. story and illustrations by Polly Carlson-Voiles. Raven Productions 2008 un il $18.95; pa $12.95

Grades: K 1 2 3   591.7

1. Winter 2. Forest animals
ISBN 978-0-9801045-5-4; 0-9801045-5-6; 978-0-9801045-6-1 pa; 0-9801045-6-4 pa

LC 2008036871

"Set in the northern woodland in winter, this picture book shows how a variety of animals adapt to the frigid, snowy environment. . . . Poetic metaphors, internal rhymes, and repeated sounds give a lyrical tone to the prose. A typical double-page spread introduces several animals . . . in a few lines of text and two collage illustrations that combine cut papers into effective compositions enhanced with ink drawings and watercolors for details and patterns." Booklist

Cole, Joanna, 1944-

★ The **magic** school bus on the ocean floor; illustrated by Bruce Degen. Scholastic 1992 un il hardcover o.p. pa $6.99

Grades: 2 3 4   591.7

1. Ocean 2. Marine animals 3. Ocean bottom -- Juvenile literature
ISBN 0-590-41430-5; 0-590-41431-3 pa

LC 91-17695

On another special field trip on the magic school bus, Ms. Frizzle's class learns about the ocean and the different creatures that live there

"Cole's straightforward text explains the main action while energetic (but never hectic), colorful doublespread pictures supply a wealth of detail. . . . A perfect match of text and art, this is another first-class entry in a stellar series that makes science fascinating and fun." Booklist

Dawes, John

★ **Exploring** the world of aquatic life; [consultant editor, John P. Friel; authors, John Dawes and Andrew Campbell] Chelsea House Publishers 2009 6v il set $210

Grades: 5 6 7 8   591.7

1. Reference books 2. Marine animals -- Encyclopedias 3. Aquatic biology -- Juvenile literature
ISBN 978-1-60413-255-7 set; 1-60413-255-8 set

LC 2008-30416

This set "offers an introduction to the diversity of animals that inhabit oceans, rivers, and lakes. . . . Entries are arranged alphabetically. . . . [The set includes] more than 100 articles. . . . Large photographs and illustrations appear on every two-page spread. . . . With its large typeface, clear explanations, and open layout, this set will appeal to younger students and would be a useful addition to school and public libraries." Booklist

Includes bibliographical references

Grupper, Jonathan

★ **Destination:** deep sea. National Geographic Soc. 2000 31p il $16.95

Grades: 3 4 5 6   591.7

1. Marine animals
ISBN 0-7922-7693-0

LC 00-27643

Describes the physical characteristics, behavior, and habitat of various sea creatures, from familiar crabs to giant whales to tube worms

"Every stunning photograph is a celebration of ocean life." SLJ

Himmelman, John

Who's at the seashore? written and illustrated by John Himmelman. NorthWord Books 2009 un il $15.95

Grades: K 1   591.7

1. Animal behavior 2. Seashore ecology
ISBN 978-1-58979-387-3; 1-58979-387-0

LC 2008038264

"This quiet little book introduces some seaside creatures via a simple rhyming text and realistic illustrations. A ruddy turnstone uncovers a sand hopper, a watchful gull hits on the hopper, while a moon snail creates a sand collar to hold her eggs, and so on in a soft litany of beach denizens and their activities. Himmelman's larger-than-life watercolors spread across the facing pages, revealing not only the action described in the text, but also the participants in the next sequence." SLJ

Hodge, Deborah

Desert animals; written by Deborah Hodge; illustrated by Pat Stephens. Kids Can Press 2008 24p il (Who lives here?) $14.95; pa $5.95

Grades: K 1 2 3   591.7

1. Desert animals
ISBN 978-1-55453-047-2; 1-55453-047-4; 978-1-55453-048-9 pa; 1-55453-048-2 pa

This introduces animals that are built for living in the extremes of deserts, including Elf owls, sand cats, and scorpions.

Forest animals; written by Deborah Hodge; illustrated by Pat Stephens. Kids Can Press 2009 24p il (Who lives here?) $14.95; pa $5.95

Grades: K 1 2 3   591.7
1. Forest animals
ISBN 978-1-55453-070-0; 1-55453-070-9; 978-1-
55453-071-7 pa; 1-55453-071-7 pa
"This mini-guide to creatures of the northern forest features one animal per spread. A brief introduction . . . includes
facts about the animal's home, diet, young, unique features
and abilities, and/or survival techniques. The text provides
enough detail to engage readers without overwhelming
them. Uncluttered design and finely crafted realistic illustrations are strengths." Horn Book Guide

Polar animals; written by Deborah Hodge; illustrated
by Pat Stephens. Kids Can Press 2008 24p il (Who lives
here?) $14.95; pa $5.95
Grades: K 1 2 3   591.7
1. Animals -- Arctic regions
ISBN 978-1-55453-043-4; 1-55453-043-1; 978-1-
55453-044-1 pa; 1-55453-044-X pa
This book describes "the animal inhabitants of [the arctic
region]. . . . Each double-page spread highlights a specific
animal [and] . . . muted illustrations . . . effectively supplement and help explain the text." Horn Book Guide

Rain forest animals; written by Deborah Hodge; illustrated by Pat Stephens. Kids Can Press 2008 24p il (Who
lives here?) $14.95; pa $5.95
Grades: K 1 2 3   591.7
1. Rain forest animals
ISBN 978-1-55453-041-0; 1-55453-041-5; 978-1-
55453-042-7 pa; 1-55453-042-3 pa
This book describes "the animal inhabitants of [the rain
forest]. . . . Each double-page spread highlights a specific
animal [and] . . . muted illustrations . . . effectively supplement and help explain the text." Horn Book Guide

Savanna animals; written by Deborah Hodge; illustrated by Pat Stephens. Kids Can Press 2009 24p il (Who
lives here?) $14.95; pa $5.95
Grades: K 1 2 3   591.7
1. Grassland ecology 2. Animals -- Africa
ISBN 978-1-55453-072-4; 1-55453-072-5; 978-1-
55453-073-1 pa; 1-55453-073-3 pa
"This well-illustrated book introduces . . . readers to . . .
animals that live in the African savanna. . . . Basic information about the elephant, wildebeest (aka, the gnu), giraffe,
meerkat, zebra, black mamba (a snake), lion, and ostrich is
presented to two-page spreads. . . . The highlight of the book
is the excellent illustrations that complement the brief text."
Sci Books Films

Wetland animals; written by Deborah Hodge; illustrated by Pat Stephens. Kids Can Press 2008 24p il (Who
lives here?) $14.95; pa $5.95
Grades: K 1 2 3   591.7
1. Wetlands 2. Freshwater animals
ISBN 978-1-55453-045-8; 1-55453-045-8; 978-1-
55453-046-5 pa; 1-55453-046-6 pa
Introduces the animals that are built for living in or on
the water of swamps, ponds, bogs, and marshes, including
hippos, moose, capybaras, and bullfrogs.

Jenkins, Steve
★ **Down,** down, down; a journey to the bottom of the
sea. Houghton Mifflin Harcourt 2009 un il $17
Grades: 2 3 4 5   591.7
1. Ocean bottom 2. Marine animals 3. Ocean --
Juvenile literature 4. Deep-sea animals -- Juvenile
literature
ISBN 978-0-618-96636-3; 0-618-96636-6
LC 2008-36082
"Starting at the surface of the Pacific Ocean, Jenkins introduces some of the animals that inhabit descending layers
of water all the way down to the Marianas Trench. At nearly
36,000 feet, this zone has been visited only once, by human
passengers of a research vessel. Depicted in Jenkins's signature handsome collages, the denizens of each level swim
against ever-darkening backgrounds ranging from sunny
blue to deepest black. . . . The repeated message that humans
have much to explore and learn in the deeper ocean is intriguing and inviting." SLJ

★ **How** to clean a hippopotamus; a look at unusual animal partnerships. [by] Steve Jenkins & Robin Page. Houghton Mifflin Books for Children 2010 un il lib bdg $16
Grades: K 1 2 3   591.7
1. Symbiosis 2. Animal communication -- Juvenile
literature 3. Social behavior in animals -- Juvenile
literature
ISBN 978-0-547-24515-7 lib bdg; 0-547-24515-7
lib bdg
LC 2009-45452
This picture book "explores unexpected animal partnerships. . . . The spreads have an exciting, comics-inspired feel.
Each page combines panels of multiple images, rendered in
Jenkins' superbly crafted paper-collage style, with brief lines
of concise, clear text and attention-grabbing headlines. . . .
These fascinating stories from the natural world will easily
interest young people." Booklist

★ **I** see a kookaburra! discovering animal habi-
tats around the world. [by] Steve Jenkins & Robin Page.
Houghton Mifflin Co. 2005 un il map $16
Grades: K 1 2 3   591.7
1. Animals 2. Habitat (Ecology) 3. Habitat (Ecology)
-- Juvenile literature
ISBN 0-618-50764-7
LC 2004-13188
A pictorial introduction to desert, tide pool, jungle, sa-
vana, forest, and pond habitats, with examples of the animals
that live in each
"Filled with vibrant colors and palpable textures, the illustrations are breathtaking and give a real sense of the vi-
tality, diversity, and beauty of nature. A first-rate foray into
ecology that will encourage readers to explore the world
around them." SLJ
Includes bibliographical references

Johnson, Rebecca L.
★ **Journey** into the deep; discovering new ocean creatures. with a foreword by Sylvia A. Earle. Millbrook Press
2010 64p il lib bdg $31.93
Grades: 4 5 6 7   591.7
1. Ocean bottom 2. Marine animals 3. Scientific

expeditions
ISBN 978-0-7613-4148-2 lib bdg; 0-7613-4148-X
lib bdg

LC 2009049603

"This strikingly illustrated book takes its readers on a series of research voyages exploring the ocean from its shallow edges to unfathomable depths during the recently completed ten-year International Census of Marine Life. Clearly organized text and pictures combine to introduce newly discovered marine creatures of all kinds. . . . The excitement and challenge of discovery in tangible. Scientific photographs printed on blue-to-black background . . . illustrate animals mentioned in a nicely legible text. . . . Rich, revealing and rewarding." Kirkus

Includes glossary and bibliographical references

Komiya, Teruyuki
    Life-size aquarium; translated by Junko Miyakoshi. Seven Footer Press 2010 48p il $18.95
Grades: PreK K 1 2   **591.7**
    1. Marine animals
    ISBN 978-1-934734-59-9; 1-934734-59-4

This highlights "a passel of aquarium critters in crisp, full-color photos. Some, like the rockhopper penguin . . . can be shown in entirety, but many others, like . . . a long-tusked be-whiskered walrus, require foldout pages for even a partial view. The eye-catching photos are the main thrust, while extra data flows along the edges of the page." SLJ

Landstrom, Lee Ann
    Nature's yucky! 2: the desert southwest; by Lee Landstrom and Karen I. Shragg; illustrated by Rachel Rogge. Mountain Press Pub. Co. 2007 48p il pa $12
Grades: K 1 2 3   **591.7**
    1. Desert animals 2. Natural history -- Southwestern States
    ISBN 978-0-87842-529-7 pa; 0-87842-529-2 pa

LC 2006032479

This explains "the significance of adaptations of animals of the southwestern desert. . . . The illustrations are detailed and well done. . . . Each of the animals is well described." Sci Books Films

Lynette, Rachel
    Who lives in a colorful coral reef? PowerKids Press 2011 24p il map (Exploring habitats) lib bdg $21.25; pa $8.25
Grades: 2 3   **591.7**
    1. Animals 2. Coral reefs and islands
    ISBN 978-1-4488-0677-5 lib bdg; 1-4488-0677-1 lib bdg; 978-1-4488-1281-3 pa; 1-4488-1281-X pa

LC 2009-54350

Presents the various types of animals that live in a coral reef, including sea anemones, sea stars, cleaner shrimp, clown fish, and sponges.

"Sharp color photographs provide visual interest. Text is arranged in photo caption boxes or is well divided into frames spaced between the photographs in a visually pleasing array. Loads of information is packed into fairly short sentences, containing vocabulary that can be easily read by second or third graders." Libr Media Connect
    Includes glossary

Who lives in a deep, dark cave? PowerKids Press, 2011 24p il map (Exploring habitats) lib bdg $21.25; pa $8.25
Grades: 2 3   **591.7**
    1. Caves 2. Animals 3. Cave dwellers
    ISBN 978-1-4488-0676-8 lib bdg; 1-4488-0676-3 lib bdg; 978-1-4488-1277-6 pa; 1-4488-1277-1 pa
Introduces several types of animals that live in caves.

"Sharp color photographs provide visual interest. Text is arranged in photo caption boxes or is well divided into frames spaced between the photographs in a visually pleasing array. Loads of information is packed into fairly short sentences, containing vocabulary that can be easily read by second or third graders." Libr Media Connect
    Includes glossary

Who lives in a wet, wild rain forest? PowerKids Press 2011 24p il map (Exploring habitats) lib bdg $21.25; pa $8.25
Grades: 2 3   **591.7**
    1. Rain forest animals 2. Rain forest ecology
    ISBN 978-1-4488-0678-2 lib bdg; 1-4488-0678-X lib bdg; 978-1-4488-1283-7 pa; 1-4488-1283-6 pa

LC 2010000423

Introduces some of the animals of rain forests and how they live.

"Sharp color photographs provide visual interest. Text is arranged in photo caption boxes or is well divided into frames spaced between the photographs in a visually pleasing array. Loads of information is packed into fairly short sentences, containing vocabulary that can be easily read by second or third graders." Libr Media Connect
    Includes glossary

Who lives on a towering mountain? PowerKids Press 2010 24p il map (Exploring habitats) lib bdg $21.25; pa $8.25
Grades: 2 3   **591.7**
    1. Mountain animals
    ISBN 978-1-4488-0680-5 lib bdg; 1-4488-0680-1 lib bdg; 978-1-4488-1287-5 pa; 1-4488-1287-9 pa

LC 2010003466

Presents the various types of animals that live in the mountains, including snow leopards, bighorn sheep, elk, marmots, and mountain lions

"Sharp color photographs provide visual interest. Text is arranged in photo caption boxes or is well divided into frames spaced between the photographs in a visually pleasing array. Loads of information is packed into fairly short sentences, containing vocabulary that can be easily read by second or third graders." Libr Media Connect
    Includes glossary

Who lives on the icy, cold tundra. PowerKids Press 2011 24p il map (Exploring habitats) lib bdg $21.25; pa $8.25
Grades: 2 3   **591.7**
    1. Animals 2. Tundra ecology
    ISBN 978-1-4488-0675-1 lib bdg; 1-4488-0675-5 lib bdg; 978-1-4488-1279-0 pa; 1-4488-1279-8 pa

LC 2009-54351

Presents the various types of animals that live on the tundra, including polar bears, the arctic fox, the giant petrel, the emperor penguin, and musk oxen.

"Sharp color photographs provide visual interest. Text is arranged in photo caption boxes or is well divided into frames spaced between the photographs in a visually pleasing array. Loads of information is packed into fairly short sentences, containing vocabulary that can be easily read by second or third graders." Libr Media Connect

Includes glossary

Mannis, Celeste Davidson

Snapshots; the wonders of Monterey Bay. words and pictures by Celeste Davidson Mannis. Viking 2006 un il $16.99

Grades: K 1 2 3   **591.7**

1. Marine animals

ISBN 0-670-06062-3

LC 2005026407

Introduces young readers to the marine animals of Monterey Bay and the unique places that they inhabit there, offering facts and images to provide a closer look at the region's ecosystem.

"The simple text can be shared with younger children while the boxed sections provide enough detail to interest older students. With stunning photographs and text that will meet the needs of a wide range of ages, this title will be a welcome addition to most collections." SLJ

McLimans, David

Gone fishing; ocean life by the numbers. [by] David McLimans. Walker 2008 un il $16.99; lib bdg $17.89

Grades: 3 4 5   **591.7**

1. Marine animals 2. Endangered species

ISBN 978-0-8027-9770-4; 0-8027-9770-9; 978-0-8027-9564-9 lib bdg; 0-8027-9564-1 lib bdg

LC 2008014475

"Using animal-shaped numbers from 1 to 10 and back again, McLimans introduces various marine creatures and their survival status. An African penguin, sea lamprey, tiger tail sea horse, and blue-ringed octopus are among the featured species.... The black silhouetted numbers are sinuous and compelling in this unique and imaginative description of the dangers facing ocean life today." SLJ

Includes bibliographical references

Miller, Debbie S.

Survival at 120 above; by Debbie S. Miller; illustrations by Job Van Zyle. Walker & Co. 2012 40 p. col. ill. (hardback) $17.99; (reinforced) $18.89

Grades: 3 4 5   **591.7**

1. Animals 2. Climate 3. Desert animals 4. Adaptation (Biology) 5. Desert animals -- Australia -- Simpson Desert -- Juvenile literature 6. Desert ecology -- Australia -- Simpson Desert -- Juvenile literature 7. Heat adaptation -- Australia -- Simpson Desert -- Juvenile literature

ISBN 0802798136; 9780802798138; 9780802798145

LC 2011021943

Author Deborah S. Miller "records a day in the life of . . . Australia's Simpson Desert . . . as birds, mammals, reptiles, amphibians, insects and plants revel in the glory of water and relative coolness of the world's longest parallel sand dunes. . . . The book introduces young readers to many animals children have likely never seen nor heard of and helps them understand the . . . ways in which animals and other life-forms have adapted to this extreme climate. .

. . [P]ronunciation guides are incorporated within the text." (Kirkus Reviews)

Includes bibliographical references.

Survival at 40 below; illustrations by Jon Van Zyle. Walker & Co. 2010 un il $17.99; lib bdg $18.89

Grades: 2 3 4   **591.7**

1. Animals -- Arctic regions 2. Natural history -- Alaska

ISBN 978-0-8027-9815-2; 0-8027-9815-2; 978-0-8027-9816-9 lib bdg; 0-8027-9816-0 lib bdg

LC 2009013328

"Miller describes the terrain of Alaska's Gates of the Arctic National Park and explains how the seasonal changes affect a diverse array of animals . . . that live in the area year-round. . . . The text moves smoothly and quickly, offering interesting glimpses of varied hibernation patterns and the physical characteristics enabling some animals to survive winter's deep chill aboveground. . . . Van Zyle's acrylic paintings span the spreads, offering good impressionistic views of varied landscapes and fauna." SLJ

Miller, Sara Swan

Secret lives of burrowing beasts. Marshall Cavendish Benchmark 2010 48p il (Secret lives) lib bdg $29.93

Grades: 3 4 5 6   **591.7**

1. Burrowing animals

ISBN 978-0-7614-4221-9 lib bdg; 0-7614-4221-9 lib bdg

"The bright, sharp color photos . . . enhance, but take second fiddle to Miller's lively, well-knit [narrative]. . . . [This] volume closes with a generous selection of print and web resources." SLJ

Includes glossary

Secret lives of cave creatures. Marshall Cavendish Benchmark 2010 48p il (Secret lives) lib bdg $29.93

Grades: 3 4 5 6   **591.7**

1. Animals 2. Cave dwellers

ISBN 978-0-7614-4224-0 lib bdg; 0-7614-4224-3 lib bdg

"The bright, sharp color photos . . . enhance, but take second fiddle to Miller's lively, well-knit [narrative]. . . . [This] volume closes with a generous selection of print and web resources." SLJ

Includes glossary

Secret lives of deep-sea creatures. Marshall Cavendish Benchmark 2010 48p il (Secret lives) lib bdg $29.93

Grades: 3 4 5 6   **591.7**

1. Marine animals

ISBN 978-0-7614-4226-4 lib bdg; 0-7614-4226-X lib bdg

LC 2010000376

"The bright, sharp color photos . . . enhance, but take second fiddle to Miller's lively, well-knit [narrative]. . . . [This] volume closes with a generous selection of print and web resources." SLJ

Includes glossary

Secret lives of soil creatures. Marshall Cavendish Benchmark 2010 48p il (Secret lives) lib bdg $29.93

Grades: 3 4 5 6 **591.7**
1. Animals 2. Soil ecology
ISBN 978-0-7614-4229-5 lib bdg; 0-7614-4229-4
lib bdg

"The bright, sharp color photos . . . enhance, but take second fiddle to Miller's lively, well-knit [narrative]. . . . [This] volume closes with a generous selection of print and web resources." SLJ

Includes glossary

Mitton, Tony
Ocean odyssey; [illustrated by] Ant Parker. Kingfisher 2010 un il (Amazing animals) $9.99
Grades: K 1 2 3 **591.7**
1. Marine animals
ISBN 978-0-7534-3006-4; 0-7534-3006-1

"Three animal friends in human garb . . . explore the undersea world to introduce young readers to various animals in [that habitat]. The bouncy rhymed [text] and colorful cartoonlike illustrations, along with being entertaining, offer some surprisingly substantive facts about the creatures." Horn Book Guide

Rainforest romp; [by] Tony Mitton and [illustrated by] Ant Parker. Kingfisher 2009 un il (Amazing animals) $9.99 **591.7**
1. Rain forest animals
ISBN 978-0-7534-6298-0; 0-7534-6298-2

"In bouncy rhymes, Mitton describes animals that live in the rainforest. . . . Parker's vibrant cartoon illustrations show three animal friends, dressed in safari gear, exploring in the rainforest, along with the smiling creatures they encounter." Horn Book Guide

Parker, Steve, 1952-
Animal habitats. QEB Pub. 2010 32p il (QEB changes in . . .) lib bdg $28.50
Grades: 3 4 5 6 **591.7**
1. Habitat (Ecology)
ISBN 978-1-59566-773-1 lib bdg; 1-59566-773-3
lib bdg

LC 2008-56067
"Outstanding photography and informative summaries uniquely combine to make this text a must have for any elementary school library. . . . Short, succinct paragraphs and marginalia combine to appeal to readers of all ages and literary abilities. The author guides the juvenile reader through a series of environmental concerns such as the preservation of rare and endangered species, sustainability, overpopulation, biodiversity hot spots, conservation techniques, and introduced and invasive species." Sci Books Films

Includes glossary

Stewart, Melissa
Under the snow; written by Melissa Stewart; illustrated by Constance R. Bergum. Peachtree 2009 un il $16.95
Grades: K 1 2 3 **591.7**
1. Snow 2. Winter 3. Animal behavior
ISBN 978-1-56145-493-8; 1-56145-493-1

This describes how animals live under the snow in fields, forests, ponds, and wetlands

This is a "lyrical portrait. . . . Bergum's watercolor illustrations painted in panels suggest the passage of time and include close-up insets of wildlife in various habitats. . . .

Many of the facts will wow children . . . and pique interest to read more." Booklist

When rain falls; written by Melissa Stewart; illustrated by Constance R. Bergum. Peachtree 2008 un il $16.95
Grades: PreK K 1 2 **591.7**
1. Rain 2. Animal behavior 3. Animals -- Habitations -- Juvenile literature
ISBN 978-1-56145-438-9; 1-56145-438-9

LC 2007-31395
"After two children hurry inside to escape the rain, they gaze outdoors and wait for the end of the storm. Stewart elaborates on how various animals react to rain in different habitats: a forest, a field, a wetland, and a desert. The examples are clearly presented and interesting. . . . Bergum's well-rendered watercolors will facilitate group sharing." SLJ

Swinburne, Stephen R.
Ocean soup; tide pool poems. illustrated by Mary Peterson. Charlesbridge 2010 un il lib bdg $16.95
Grades: 1 2 3 **591.7**
1. Marine animals 2. Tide pool ecology 3. Animals -- Poetry
ISBN 978-1-58089-200-1 lib bdg; 1-58089-200-0
lib bdg

LC 2008026960
"This brightly illustrated, large-format book offers a collection of poems in the voices of tide-pool animals. . . . Each species is presented through first-person verse and a paragraph of information. . . . Clean, curving pencil lines with digitally added colors portray the animals in child-friendly, cartoon-style pictures." Booklist

Includes glossary and bibliographical references

Turner, Pamela S.
Prowling the seas; exploring the hidden world of ocean predators. Walker & Co. 2009 39p il map $17.99; lib bdg $18.89
Grades: 4 5 6 **591.7**
1. Ocean 2. Marine animals 3. Predatory animals
ISBN 978-0-8027-9748-3; 0-8027-9748-2; 978-0-8027-9749-0 lib bdg; 0-8027-9749-0 lib bdg

"In each chapter, a clearly delineated map makes it easy to follow the animals' routes, and many clear color photos show the animals and the scientists who study them. . . . A clearly written presentation of an unusual topic." Booklist

Webb, Sophie
Far from shore; a naturalist explores the deep ocean. written and illustrated by Sophie Webb. Houghton Mifflin Books for Children 2011 80p il $17.99
Grades: 4 5 6 7 **591.7**
1. Dolphins 2. Water birds 3. Marine animals
ISBN 978-0-618-59729-1; 0-618-59729-8

LC 2010025121
Webb "returns with another richly detailed journal of her travels as a naturalist, combining scientific information, field guide-like illustrations, and a thorough account of the day-to-day experiments of a field scientist. The setting is a four-month-long research cruise on a National Ocean and Atmospheric Administration ship to study the impact of fishing on two dolphin populations that reside in the Eastern Tropical Pacific." Horn Book

Includes glossary

591.754

Pattison, Darcy

Desert baths; by Darcy Pattison; illustrated by Kathleen Rietz. Sylvan Dell Pub. 2012 32 p. (hardcover) $17.95

Grades: K 1 2 3 4 **591.754**

1. Baths -- Fiction 2. Animal behavior -- Juvenile fiction 3. Desert animals -- Juvenile literature

ISBN 1607185253; 9781607185253; 9781607185345; 9781607185437; 9781607185529

LC 2012004377

In author Darcy Pattison's book, "all animals bathe to keep their bodies clean and healthy. Humans might use soap and water, but what do animals, especially those living in dry climates, do to keep clean?" This book explores "the desert to find out how snakes, spiders, and birds bathe. This . . . book teaches children about hygiene and how some exciting desert creatures manage to stay clean without the help of soap and water." (Publisher's note)

591.77   Marine animals

Arnosky, Jim

Shimmer & splash; the sparkling world of sea life. Jim Arnosky. Sterling Children's Books 2013 41 p. col. ill. (hardcover) $14.95

Grades: 2 3 4 5 **591.77**

1. Picture books for children 2. Marine biology -- Juvenile literature 3. Marine animals -- Juvenile literature

ISBN 1402786239; 9781402786235

LC 2012012863

In this book, author and illustrator Jim Arnosky explores life in the sea. With foldout pages and many life-size illustrations, this overview" touches "on sea life from coral reefs to sailfish, from sea jellies to fiddler crabs, all depicted in a . . . . blues and greens with splashes of yellow." The text features "personal experiences as Arnosky wades, kayaks, boats, and fishes in the 'sparkling' world of water." (School Library Journal)

Includes bibliographical references (p. 41).

Johnson, Jinny

Coral reef life; Jinny Johnson. Smart Apple Media 2012 32 p. col. ill., col. map (Watery worlds) (library) $28.50

Grades: 4 5 6 **591.77**

1. Coral reef ecology -- Juvenile literature 2. Coral reef animals -- Juvenile literature

ISBN 1599205025; 9781599205021

LC 2011012947

This book by Jinny Johnson is part of the "Watery Worlds" series. "In this book, we find out how coral reefs are formed and learn why they are so important. We look at the amazing variety of fish around the reefs and discover why the reefs themselves are in danger." (Publishers note) It "contains a map and a 'facts' page." (Library Media Connection)

Woodward, John

Ocean; an amazing window on our world. written by John Woodward; illustrations by Gary Hanna. DK Pub. 2012 59 p. col. ill. (hardcover) $10.99

Grades: 4 5 6 **591.77**

1. Picture books for children 2. Ocean -- Juvenile literature 3. Marine biology -- Juvenile literature 4. Marine animals -- Juvenile literature

ISBN 0756692377; 9780756692377

LC 2011277622

This book is part of DK Publishing's Look Closer series and allows readers to "explore different perspectives of . . . underwater scenes as they zoom in, zoom out, and go sideways, forward, and backward. . . . Specially commissioned computer-generated imagery" is included. (Publisher's note)

591.9   Animals by specific continents, countries, localities

Haas, Robert B.

African critters. National Geographic 2008 91p il $17.95; lib bdg $26.90

Grades: 3 4 5 **591.9**

1. Animals -- Africa 2. Animals -- Juvenile literature

ISBN 978-1-4263-0317-3; 1-4263-0317-3; 978-1-4263-0318-0 lib bdg; 1-4263-0318-1 lib bdg

This is a "beautiful photo-essay about African wildlife, which features pictures [Haas] took over several years in southern African game preserves. . . . Each of the chapters . . . provides fascinating details about animal behavior, and numerous boxed notes fill in more facts about numbers and anatomy. . . . This book is a must-purchase. . . . An exceptionally strong combination of action, information, and conservation." Booklist

Hooper, Meredith

Antarctic journal; the hidden worlds of Antarctica's animals. illustrated by Lucia deLeiris. National Geographic Soc. 2000 35p il maps $16.95

Grades: 3 4 5 6 **591.9**

1. Antarctica 2. Summer -- Antarctica 3. Animals -- Antarctica

ISBN 0-7922-7188-2

LC 00-35496

"Hooper describes the three-and-a-half months she and deLeiris spent at Palmer Station, Antarctica, observing marine life. . . . The realistic watercolors and black-and-white sketches work well with the detailed text." Horn Book Guide

592   Specific taxonomic groups of animals

Cerullo, Mary M.

Sea soup: zooplankton; [by] Mary M. Cerullo; photography by Bill Curtsinger. Tilbury House 2001 39p il $16.95

Grades: 5 6 7 8 **592**

1. Zooplankton 2. Plankton 3. Marine zooplankton -- Juvenile literature

ISBN 0-88448-219-7

LC 00-46721

This book "opens a pellucid window into the drifting world of mostly minute animals that, along with phytoplankton, form an aqueous 'soup' that nourishes a wide variety of sea creatures. . . . Curtsinger's often extraordinary color photos allow readers to envision the often microscopically small creatures delineated in the text. . . . This is a fascinating look at a watery zoo of creatures whose ecological importance is far beyond the measure of their size." SLJ

Includes glossary and bibliographical references

Dixon, Norma
Lowdown on earthworms. Fitzhenry & Whiteside 2005 32p il $16.95
Grades: 3 4 5   592
1. Worms 2. Earthworms -- Juvenile literature
ISBN 1-55041-114-8

"This project-oriented study combines basic facts about worm anatomy and behavior with general instructions for building, maintaining, and performing simple experiments with both a 'plastic-bottle wormery'; and a more ambitious compost bin. A mix of color photos and simple paintings offer cutaways views of worms and their burrows, representations of several types of earthworms, and pictures of finished projects." Booklist

Includes bibliographical references

Parker, Steve, 1952-
Sponges, jellyfish & other simple animals; by Steve Parker. Compass Point Books 2006 p. cm. (Animal kingdom classification)
Grades: 5 6 7 8   592
1. Sponges -- Juvenile literature. 2. Jellyfishes -- Juvenile literature. 3. Invertebrates -- Juvenile literature.
ISBN 0-7565-1614-5 (hard cover)
LC 2005029183

"Smoothly written, well-organized... With succinct text and colorful formats, [this] will appeal to students and browsers alike." SLJ

Includes bibliographical references

Pfeffer, Wendy
Wiggling worms at work; illustrated by Steve Jenkins. HarperCollins Publishers 2004 33p il (Let's-read-and-find-out science) $15.99; lib bdg $16.89; pa $4.99
Grades: K 1 2 3   592
1. Worms
ISBN 0-06-028448-X; 0-06-028449-8 lib bdg; 0-06-445199-2 pa

"This book is filled with clear explanations. . . . The concluding activities . . . are important because Jenkins's cut-paper illustrations, while lovely, include only a few anatomical details." Horn Book Guide

Trueit, Trudi Strain
Worms. Marshall Cavendish Benchmark 2009 23p il (Benchmark rebus. Creepy critters) lib bdg $22.79
Grades: PreK K 1   592
1. Worms
ISBN 978-0-7614-3966-0 lib bdg; 0-7614-3966-8 lib bdg
LC 2008-15997

"Brilliant closeup photos will help beginning readers make meaning and appeal to students who like these creatures. . . . Glossary, print and media resources for further

learning, and an about the author section conclude . . . [the] book. Reading specialists will want to be advised about [this book] . . . as will teachers. . . . This . . . is an excellent resource for beginning research projects." Publisher's note

Includes glossary and bibliographical references

593 Miscellaneous marine and seashore invertebrates

Gilpin, Daniel
Starfish, urchins & other echinoderms; by Daniel Gilpin. Compass Point Books 2006 48 p. (Animal kingdom classification)
Grades: 4 5 6   593
1. Starfishes -- Juvenile literature. 2. Sea urchins -- Juvenile literature. 3. Echinodermata -- Juvenile literature.
ISBN 0-7565-1611-0 (hard cover)
LC 2005029184

Introduces the physical characteristics, habitat, and types of echinoderms, including starfish, sea urchins, and sea cucumbers.

Includes bibliographical references

593.4 Sponges

Coldiron, Deborah
Sea sponges; by Deborah Coldiron. ABDO Pub. 2008 32p il (Underwater world) lib bdg $24.21
Grades: 2 3 4   593.4
1. Sponges
ISBN 978-1-59928-812-3 lib bdg; 1-59928-812-5 lib bdg
LC 2007-17851

"Present[s] basic information about [sea sponges]. . . . Vibrant captioned photos enhance the accessible text." Horn Book Guide

Includes glossary

593.5 Coelenterates

Gray, Susan Heinrichs
Australian spotted jellyfish; [by] Susan H. Gray. Cherry Lake Pub. 2010 32p il map (Animal invaders) $27.07
Grades: 5 6 7 8   593.5
1. Jellyfishes 2. Biological invasions
ISBN 978-1-60279-628-7; 1-60279-628-9
LC 2009024168

This offers "an introduction to the problems caused by [the Australian spotted jellyfish], a discussion of its physical characteristics and habits, a history of how it arrived in its new habitat, and an analysis of challenges encountered by those trying to limit its spread. . . . [This] stinging jelly [was] brought by cargo ships to the Gulf of Mexico and some Atlantic coastal waters." Booklist

Includes glossary and bibliographical references

King, David C.

Jellyfish; by David C. King. Marshall Cavendish Benchmark 2006 48p il map (Animals, animals) lib bdg $23.64

Grades: 3 4 5 6   **593.5**

1. Jellyfishes

ISBN 0-7614-1867-9

LC 2004-21441

Describes the physical characteristics, behavior, and habitat of jellyfish

Includes glossary and bibliographical references

Metz, Lorijo

Discovering jellyfish. PowerKids Press 2011 24p il (Along the shore) lib bdg $21.25

Grades: 3 4 5   **593.5**

1. Jellyfishes

ISBN 978-1-4488-4997-0; 1-4488-4997-7

LC 2011000159

This book about jellyfish "briefly describes the major physical and behavioral characteristics common to all [jellyfish] and one or two distinctive characteristics of about a half dozen species. . . . One or two sharp color photographs of representative species, most of which are close-ups, accompany the text on every page. . . . [This is] well organized and smoothly written in an engaging style." SLJ

Includes glossary

Spilsbury, Louise

Jellyfish. Heinemann Library 2010 24p il (A day in the life. sea animals) lib bdg $22; pa $6.49

Grades: 1 2   **593.5**

1. Jellyfishes

ISBN 978-1-4329-4000-3 lib bdg; 1-4329-4000-7 lib bdg; 978-1-4329-4007-2 pa; 1-4329-4007-4 pa

LC 2010000624

Introduces jellyfish, describing their physical characteristics, feeding habits, senses, and defense mechanisms.

This pairs "well-chosen color photos . . . with one or two sentences of simple commentary for each. . . . [Though this title] includes references to several varieties of the chosen creature, one species in particular is highlighted. . . . [Good choice] for pleasure or purpose reading." SLJ

Includes glossary and bibliographical references

Wearing, Judy

Jellyfish. Weigl Publishers 2010 24p il (World of wonder: underwater life) lib bdg $24.45; pa $8.95

Grades: K 1 2   **593.5**

1. Jellyfishes

ISBN 978-1-60596-100-2 lib bdg; 1-60596-100-0 lib bdg; 978-1-60596-101-9 pa; 1-60596-101-9 pa

LC 2009-25986

This book about jellyfish begins "with introductory information and progress[es] to more unique details of the featured creatures. Bold photographs juxtaposed on colorful background graphic will hold the attention of even the most novice readers. . . . [This book is] sure to make a splash with budding marine biologists everywhere." SLJ

Includes glossary

593.6   Anthozoa

Collard, Sneed B.

★ One night in the Coral Sea; [by] Sneed B. Collard III; illustrated by Robin Brickmann. Charlesbridge 2005 32p il $15.95; pa $6.95

Grades: 3 4 5   **593.6**

1. Corals 2. Coral reefs and islands

ISBN 1-57091-389-7; 1-57091-390-0 pa

LC 2004-3307

"On a single spring night . . . the coral in the Great Barrier Reef releases millions of eggs into the ocean. . . . Collard explains the unique spawning event and provides some background about coral and the sea creatures that share the reef. . . . Whether or not children understand the specifics of fertilization, they will be captivated by Brickman's realistic, astonishingly detailed colored-paper collages of the brilliant underwater world." Booklist

Includes glossary and bibliographical references

593.9   Echinoderms and hemichordates

Halfmann, Janet

Star of the sea; a day in the life of a starfish. illustrated by Joan Paley. H. Holt 2011 un il $16.99

Grades: K 1 2 3   **593.9**

1. Starfishes

ISBN 978-0-8050-9073-4; 0-8050-9073-8

LC 2010024952

"Simple, elegant text allows readers to follow a female ochre sea star as she comes ashore during high tide, finds and eats mussels, and is herself seized by a gull, escaping with only one ray lost. Accurate information is nicely embedded in the lyrical narration, while rich-hued watercolor collages . . . give both large-scale and close-up views." Horn Book Guide

Includes bibliographical references

Metz, Lorijo

Discovering starfish. PowerKids Press 2011 24p il (Along the shore) lib bdg $21.25

Grades: 3 4 5   **593.9**

1. Starfishes

ISBN 978-1-4488-4996-3; 1-4488-4996-9

LC 2011000152

This book about starfish "briefly describes the major physical and behavioral characteristics common to all [starfish] and one or two distinctive characteristics of about a half dozen species. . . . One or two sharp color photographs of representative species, most of which are closeups, accompany the text on every page. . . . [This is] well organized and smoothly written in an engaging style." SLJ

594   Mollusks and molluscoids

Bodden, Valerie

Slugs; Valerie Bodden. Creative Education 2013 24 p. col. ill. (library) $25.65

Grades: 1 2 3 4   **594**

1. Picture books for children 2. Slugs (Mollusks) --

Juvenile literature

ISBN 1608182339; 9781608182336

LC 2011050283

This book is part of the Creepy Creatures series by Valerie Bodden. The series uses "clear white backgrounds to showcase . . . magnified photos, while the simple, educational text is . . . arranged around the page." This entry looks at slugs, discussing "the slimy textures and spotted patterns of this mollusk, which are hermaphroditic and can produce from 20 to 100 eggs each." (Booklist)

Includes bibliographical references and index

Campbell, Sarah C.

★ **Wolfsnail**; a backyard predator. photographs by Sarah C. Campbell and Richard P. Campbell. Boyds Mills Press 2008 32p il $16.95

Grades: PreK K 1 2   **594**

1. Snails

ISBN 978-1-59078-554-6; 1-59078-554-1

LC 2007-30838

A Geisel Award honor book, 2009

"The tiny wolfsnail eats garden snails and slugs. This dramatic photo-essay . . . shows the predator stalking its prey, . . . eating it, and leaving the empty shell behind. The back matter includes a small photo of the tiny wolfsnail at its true size and lots of fascinating facts about where snails live, how they mate, and more." Booklist

Cerullo, Mary M.

Giant squid; searching for a sea monster. by Mary M. Cerullo with Clyde F.E. Roper. Capstone Press 2012 48 p. ill. (chiefly col.) (Smithsonian) (library) $26.86; (paperback) $8.95

Grades: 4 5 6   **594**

1. Giant squids -- Juvenile literature

ISBN 1429680237; 9781429675413; 9781429680233

LC 2011029181

This book "recounts some of the legends and historical clues that led to the giant squid's identification in the 19th century before focusing on Dr. Clyde Roper, a renowned specialist on cephalopods. . . . The text describes how Roper gathered facts by autopsying the carcasses of giant squids and sperm whales (its chief predator), examining other squid species, etc.; it also outlines several expeditions he led in search of a live specimen." (School Library Journal)

Coldiron, Deborah

Octopuses. ABDO Pub. 2008 32p il (Underwater world) lib bdg $24.21

Grades: 2 3 4   **594**

1. Octopuses

ISBN 978-1-59928-815-4 lib bdg; 1-59928-815-X lib bdg

LC 2007-14852

This presents "basic information about [the octopus]. . . . Vibrant captioned photos enhance the accessible text." Horn Book Guide

Includes glossary

Gilpin, Daniel

★ **Snails,** shellfish & other mollusks; by Daniel Gilpin. Compass Point Books 2006 48 p. (Animal kingdom classification)

Grades: 4 5 6   **594**

1. Snails. 2. Mollusks. 3. Shellfish.

ISBN 0-7565-1613-7 (hard cover)

LC 2005029182

"...Smoothly written, well-organized...With succinct texts and colorful formats, [this] will appeal to students and browsers alike." SLJ

Includes bibliographical references

Gray, Susan Heinrichs

Giant African snail. Cherry Lake Pub. 2009 32p il map (Animal invaders) lib bdg $27.07

Grades: 3 4 5   **594**

1. Snails 2. Biological invasions

ISBN 978-1-60279-241-8 lib bdg; 1-60279-241-0 lib bdg

LC 2008000803

Looks at the qualities of giant African snails and examines how they became an invasive species in many of the world's tropical and subtropical regions, how they cause problems in their new environments, and the ways that people have attempted to deal with them

"Clear color photographs, most of which are closeups, accompany the [text] on about every other page. . . . [This title provides] report writers with in-depth and up-to-date information on these invaders and the serious problems they cause." SLJ

Includes glossary and bibliographical references

Markle, Sandra

★ **Octopuses**. Lerner Pubs. 2007 39p il (Animal prey) lib bdg $25.26

Grades: 3 4 5   **594**

1. Octopuses

ISBN 978-0-8225-6063-0 lib bdg; 0-8225-6063-1 lib bdg

LC 2005-36350

"This title about octopuses, both predator and prey, features eye-popping color photographs of the animals on nearly every spread. Markel's lively prose brings readers right into the underwater world with sensory descriptions and details kids can relate to." Booklist

Includes bibliographical references

Metz, Lorijo

Discovering clams. PowerKids Press 2011 24p il (Along the shore) lib bdg $21.25

Grades: 3 4 5   **594**

1. Clams

ISBN 978-1-4488-4994-9; 1-4488-4994-2

LC 2011000158

This book about clams "briefly describes the major physical and behavioral characteristics common to all [clams] and one or two distinctive characteristics of about a half dozen species. . . . One or two sharp color photographs of representative species, most of which are closeups, accompany the text on every page. . . . [This is] well organized and smoothly written in an engaging style." SLJ

Miller, Sara Swan

Secret lives of seashell dwellers. Marshall Cavendish Benchmark 2010 48p il (Secret lives) lib bdg $29.93

Grades: 3 4 5 6   **594**
1. Mollusks
ISBN 978-0-7614-4228-8 lib bdg; 0-7614-4228-6
lib bdg

LC 2010000377
"The bright, sharp color photos . . . enhance, but take
second fiddle to Miller's lively, well-knit [narrative]. . . .
[This] volume closes with a generous selection of print and
web resources." SLJ
Includes glossary

Newquist, H. P.
Here there be monsters; the legendary kraken and the
giant squid. Houghton Mifflin Harcourt 2010 73p il map
$18
Grades: 4 5 6 7   **594**
1. Squids 2. Sea monsters -- Juvenile literature
ISBN 978-0-547-07678-2; 0-547-07678-9
"This intriguing book offers a chronological account of
giant squids, beginning with sailors' tales about krakens and
leading up to the groundbreaking discoveries of the past few
decades. . . . The many illustrations, in color when available,
include photos, engravings, and maps. . . . An attractive, informative book on an underrepresented topic." Booklist

Owens, L. L.
The **life** cycle of a snail. Child's World 2011 il (Life
cycles) $27.07
Grades: K 1 2 3   **594**
1. Snails
ISBN 978-1-60973-191-5; 1-60973-191-3
"The life cycle of a snail is divided as follows: egg,
hatchling, and adult. With big, clear full-page photos . . . as
well as straightforward text, readers can follow along on the
slimy journey from egg to snail. . . . This title features beautiful photos and text simple enough for very young gastropod
lovers." Booklist

Rand, Casey
Glass squid and other spectacular squid. Raintree 2011
32p il (Creatures of the deep) lib bdg $29; pa $7.99
Grades: 3 4 5 6   **594**
1. Squids
ISBN 978-1-4109-4194-7 lib bdg; 978-1-4109-4201-
2 pa

LC 2010038186
"This informative and colorful series will engage young-
er children to learn more about the sea and its creatures."
Library Media Connection
Includes glossary and bibliographical references

Redmond, Shirley-Raye
Tentacles! tales of the giant squid. illustrated by Bryn
Barnard. Random House 2003 44p il (Step into reading)
$11.99; pa $3.99
Grades: 1 2 3   **594**
1. Squids 2. Giant squids 3. Giant squids -- Juvenile
literature
ISBN 0-375-91307-6; 0-375-81307-1 pa

LC 2002-10238
Describes some of the exaggerated stories that have been
told about giant squids and also what scientists have learned
about their real physical characteristics and behavior

"An excellent choice to introduce early elementary students to nonfiction titles." Booklist

Spilsbury, Louise
Octopus. Heinemann Library 2011 24p il (A day in
the life. sea animals) lib bdg $22; pa $6.49
Grades: 1 2   **594**
1. Octopuses
ISBN 978-1-4329-4004-1 lib bdg; 1-4329-4004-X lib
bdg; 978-1-4329-4011-9 pa; 1-4329-4011-2 pa

LC 2010000922
This explores how an octopus swims, defends itself,
hunts, and sleeps.
This pairs "well-chosen color photos . . . with one or two
sentences of simple commentary for each. . . . [Though this
title] includes references to several varieties of the chosen
creature, one species in particular is highlighted. . . . [Good
choice] for pleasure or purpose reading." SLJ
Includes glossary and bibliographical references

Waxman, Laura Hamilton
Let's look at snails. Lerner Publications Company
2010 32p il (Lightning bolt books: Animal close-ups) lib
bdg $25.26
Grades: PreK K 1 2   **594**
1. Snails
ISBN 978-0-8225-7899-4 lib bdg; 0-8225-7899-9
lib bdg

LC 2007-29226
Introduces snails, describing their physical characteristics, life cycle, habitat, and predators
"Fresh photography, a creative use of graphics, and a
collagelike layout make[s] . . . [this book] eye-catching. .
. . [The] book ends with a labeled diagram of the animal, a
range map, and a further-reading list that includes print and
online resources in a single list, a nice way of validating both
types of materials." SLJ
Includes glossary

595 Arthropods

Gilpin, Daniel
Lobsters, crabs & other crustaceans; by Daniel Gilpin.
Compass Point Books 2006 48 p. (Animal kingdom clas-
sification)
Grades: 4 5 6   **595**
1. Crabs -- Juvenile literature. 2. Lobsters -- Juvenile
literature. 3. Crustacea -- Juvenile literature.
ISBN 0-7565-1612-9 (hard cover)

LC 2005029180
Introduces the physical characteristics and habitats
of crustaceans, from lobsters and shrimps to sow bugs
and barnacles.
Includes bibliographical references

595.3 Crustaceans

Metz, Lorijo
Discovering crabs. PowerKids Press 2011 24p il
(Along the shore) lib bdg $21.25

Grades: 3 4 5   **595.3**
1. Crabs
ISBN 978-1-4488-4993-2; 1-4488-4993-4
LC 2011000153

This book about crabs "briefly describes the major physical and behavioral characteristics common to all [crabs] and one or two distinctive characteristics of about a half dozen species. . . . One or two sharp color photographs of representative species, most of which are closeups, accompany the text on every page. . . . [This is] well organized and smoothly written in an engaging style." SLJ

Includes glossary

Sill, Cathryn P.
About crustaceans; a guide for children. written by Cathryn Sill; illustrated by John Sill. Peachtree Publishers 2004 un il $15.95
Grades: K 1 2   **595.3**
1. Crustaceans
ISBN 1-56145-301-3
LC 2003-16838

Describes the anatomy, behavior, and habitat of various crustaceans, including the lobster, crab, and shrimp

"Done in bright watercolors, the illustrations give a sense of these creatures' different habitats. . . . This is an excellent example of easy nonfiction, perfect for beginning readers or for sharing aloud with budding naturalists." SLJ

595.4   Chelicerates

Berger, Melvin
Spinning spiders; illustrated by S.D. Schindler. HarperCollins Pubs. 2003 33p il (Let's-read-and-find-out science) hardcover o.p. pa $4.99
Grades: K 1 2 3   **595.4**
1. Spiders
ISBN 0-06-445207-7 pa; 0-06-028696-2
LC 2001-39507

Describes the characteristics of spiders and the methods they use to trap their prey in webs

Written "in a clear, easy-to-read style. . . . Detailed, full-color illustrations, often on spreads, highlight the well-organized text." SLJ

Bishop, Nic
★ **Spiders**. Scholastic Nonfiction 2007 48p il $16.99
Grades: 1 2 3 4   **595.4**
1. Spiders
ISBN 0-439-87756-3; 978-0-439-87756-5
LC 2006-47179

"This photo-rich picture book is packed with astonishing facts about these highly successful predators. . . . General facts are here: the difference between spiders and insects; body parts; . . . how they eat; and more. Each double-page spread includes a dramatic, brilliantly colored close-up of a spider." Booklist

Bodden, Valerie
Ticks; Valerie Bodden. Creative Education 2013 24 p. col. ill. (Creepy creatures) (library) $25.65

Grades: 1 2 3 4   **595.4**
1. Ticks 2. Picture books for children
ISBN 1608182347; 9781608182343
LC 2011050287

This book is part of the Creepy Creatures series. The series uses "clear white backgrounds to showcase . . . magnified photos, while the simple, educational text is . . . arranged around the page." This book "features shots of the parasites feeding, and describes how some ticks balloon to 600 times their weight when bloated with blood." (Booklist)

Includes bibliographical references (p. 24) and index

Bredeson, Carmen
Tarantulas up close; [by] Carmen Bredeson. Enslow Elementary 2008 24p il (Zoom in on animals!) lib bdg $21.26
Grades: 1 2 3   **595.4**
1. Tarantulas
ISBN 978-0-7660-3076-3 lib bdg; 0-7660-3076-8 lib bdg
LC 2007025609

In this introduction to tarantulas, "short, large-print paragraphs describe key body parts . . . and how they function; . . . [the book outlines] hunting techniques, defense mechanisms, diet, and life cycle. Complementing the text is a large, usually full-page, sharp, color close-up of a representative species. . . . The text is well-organized and clearly written. . . . Bredeson's excellent illustrations and lucid text provide valuable insights into the nature of these hairy, and unjustly feared, spiders." SLJ

Camisa, Kathryn
Hairy tarantulas; by Kathryn Camisa. Bearport Pub. 2009 24p il (No backbone!: The world of invertebrates) lib bdg $21.28
Grades: 1 2 3   **595.4**
1. Tarantulas
ISBN 978-1-59716-704-8 lib bdg; 1-59716-704-5 lib bdg
LC 2008-12106

"Spreads include four or five simple sentences, each neatly spaced by a carriage return, facing a vivid, close-up view of the spider in action. Word balloon captions highlight details when needed and smaller photographs on the text pages provide further visual reference." SLJ

Includes glossary and bibliographical references

Ganeri, Anita
Scorpion. Heinemann Library 2011 24p il map (A day in the life: desert animals) $22; pa $6.49
Grades: K 1 2   **595.4**
1. Scorpions
ISBN 978-1-4329-4776-7; 1-4329-4776-1; 978-1-4329-4785-9 pa; 1-4329-4785-0 pa
LC 2010022827

"The engaging full-color photographs are key to [this] well-organized [book]. . . . Basic global maps show where the animal is found, and a diagram called a 'body map' labels its parts. [The text is] appropriate for the age group, and the pictures will draw in youngsters. [An] excellent [purchase] if material is needed on these animals." SLJ

Includes glossary and bibliographical references

Tarantula. Heinemann Library 2011 24p il map (A day in the life. Rain forest animals) lib bdg $22; pa $6.49
Grades: 1 2   595.4
  1. Tarantulas
  ISBN 978-1-4329-4109-3 lib bdg; 1-4329-4109-7 lib bdg; 978-1-4329-4120-8 pa; 1-4329-4120-8 pa
                                              LC 2010000970
This book follows a tarantula through its day as it sleeps, eats, and moves.

"Ganeri presents information clearly and simply in large type, two-sentence comments placed below a bright, sharply reproduced color photograph of the animal in a natural setting. . . . [This is] sufficiently specific to support assignment as well as pleasure reading." SLJ
  Includes glossary and bibliographical references

Gonzales, Doreen
  Scorpions in the dark. PowerKids Press 2010 24p il (Creatures of the night) lib bdg $21.25; pa $8.05
Grades: 2 3 4   595.4
  1. Scorpions
  ISBN 978-1-4042-8100-4 lib bdg; 1-4042-8100-2 lib bdg; 978-1-4358-3257-2 pa; 1-4358-3257-4 pa
                                              LC 2009-2076
A look at scorpions and their world in the dark.

"Basic details are complemented by eclectic trivia, . . . [and] each volume concludes with a defense of the animal . . . and why it is vital to humans. The layout is attractive, with easy-to-read text and eye-catching photography. Good for reports." SLJ
  Includes glossary

Heos, Bridget
  Stronger Than Steel; Spider Silk DNA and the Quest for Better Bulletproof Vests, Sutures, and Parachute Rope. Bridget Heos; [illustrated by] Andy Comins. Houghton Mifflin Books for Children 2013 79 p. col. ill. (hardcover) $18.99
Grades: 5 6 7 8   595.4
  1. Silk -- Juvenile literature 2. Spiders -- Juvenile literature 3. Inventions -- Juvenile literature
  ISBN 0547681267; 9780547681269
                                              LC 2012010992
This children's book, by Bridget Heos, illustrated by Andy Comis, is part of the "Scientists in the Field" series. In it "readers enter Randy Lewis' lab where they come face to face with golden orb weaver spiders, and transgenic alfalfa, silkworm silk, and goats, whose milk contains the proteins to spin spider silk--and to weave a nearly indestructible fiber." (Publisher's note)

Lasky, Kathryn
  Silk & venom; searching for a dangerous spider. photographs by Christopher G. Knight. Candlewick Press 2011 57p il map
Grades: 4 5 6 7   595.4
  1. Spiders 2. Biologists 3. Arachnologists 4. College teachers
  ISBN 0-7636-4222-3; 978-0-7636-4222-8
                                              LC 2010-41888
This book focuses on the the field work of arachnologist Greta Binford. "Binford's effort to trace the migration of Loxosceles from South American to North America . . . [led]

her to field exploration in the Dominican Republic. [Glossary. Index.] Grades four to seven." (Bull Cent Child Books)
  "Biology professor Greta Binford studies spiders in an Oregon lab and in the field in the Dominican Republic, where she searches for L. Taino, a Caribbean relative of the venomous brown recluse that might provide clues to how and when the recluse genus arrived in North America. . . . In leisurely, literary prose, Lasky presents the ancient class of arachnids before introducing the scientist and explaining her quest. . . . On most spreads, a full-bleed photograph is opposed by substantial text and one or two smaller pictures." Kirkus

Lunis, Natalie
  Deadly black widows; by Natalie Lunis. Bearport Pub. 2009 24p il (No backbone!: The world of invertebrates) lib bdg $21.28
Grades: 1 2 3   595.4
  1. Spiders
  ISBN 978-1-59716-667-6 lib bdg; 1-59716-667-7 lib bdg
                                              LC 2008-1997
A discussion of the black widow spider, the most dangerous kind of spider in the United States

"Spreads include four or five simple sentences, each neatly spaced by a carriage return, facing a vivid, close-up view of the spider in action. Word balloon captions highlight details when needed and smaller photographs on the text pages provide further visual reference." SLJ
  Includes glossary and bibliographical references

Markle, Sandra
  Black widows; deadly biters. Lerner Publications 2011 48p il (Arachnid world) lib bdg $29.27
Grades: 5 6 7 8   595.4
  1. Spiders
  ISBN 978-0-7613-5038-5; 0-7613-5038-1
This describes how black widows are similar to and different from other arachnids. Close-up photographs and diagrams reveal details about the black widow's body both inside and out. A hands-on activity compares the black widow's web to a human hair.

Markle "presents a mix of common and less-common facts . . . and her commentary accompanies a particularly strong suite of illustrations featuring large, clear, labeled outside and inside views that display body parts. Photos go beyond the standard portraits. . . . First rate." SLJ
  Includes glossary and bibliographical references

  Crab spiders; phantom hunters. Sandra Markle. Lerner Pub. Company 2012 48 p. col. ill.
Grades: 4 5 6 7   595.4
  1. Spiders 2. Zoology 3. Predatory animals
  ISBN 0761350454; 9780761350453
                                              LC 2011020443
This book is part of Sandra Markle's "Arachnid World" series. "In this book, you will learn how crab spiders are similar to and different from other arachnids. Close-up photographs and diagrams reveal extraordinary details about the crab spider's body both inside and out. A hands-on activity illustrates how a crab spider can quickly ambush a flying insect. . . . Enter the . . . world of the arachnid family with award-winning science author Sandra Markle! Too often lumped together with insects, these fascinating animals have

distinctive characteristics and habits that are all their own."
(Publisher's note)
Includes bibliographical references (p. 44-45) and index

Fishing spiders; water ninjas. Sandra Markle. Lerner
Publications Company 2012 48 p. col. ill.
Grades: 4 5 6 7   595.4
1. Spiders 2. Aquatic animals 3. Predatory animals 4.
Zoology -- Encyclopedias
ISBN 9780761350446
                                                       LC 2011020442
This book is part of Sandra Markle's "Arachnid World"
series. "In this book, you will learn how fishing spiders are
similar to and different from other arachnids. Close-up photographs and diagrams reveal extraordinary details about the
fishing spider's body both inside and out. A hands-on activity shows how the fishing spider's hairy coat helps it walk
on water.... Enter the ... world of the arachnid family with
award-winning science author Sandra Markle! Too often
lumped together with insects, these fascinating animals have
distinctive characteristics and habits that are all their own."
(Publisher's note)
Includes bibliographical references and index

Harvestmen; secret operatives. Lerner Publications
2011 48p il (Arachnid world) lib bdg $29.27
Grades: 5 6 7 8   595.4
1. Spiders
ISBN 978-0-7613-5042-2; 0-7613-5042-X
                                                       LC 2010023491
This describes how harvestmen are similar to and different from other arachnids. Close-up photographs and diagrams reveal details about the harvestmen's bodies, both
inside and out. A hands-on activity reveals how harvestmen walk on long legs using only their sense of touch to
get around.
Markle "presents a mix of common and less-common
facts . . . and her commentary accompanies a particularly
strong suite of illustrations featuring large, clear, labeled
outside and inside views that display body parts. Photos go
beyond the standard portraits. . . . First rate." SLJ
Includes glossary and bibliographical references

Jumping spiders; gold-medal stalkers. by Sandra Markle. Lerner Publications 2012 48 p. col. ill.
Grades: 4 5 6 7   595.4
1. Spiders 2. Animal behavior
ISBN 0761350470; 9780761350477
                                                       LC 2011021598
This book is part of Sandra Markle's "Arachnid World"
series. "In this book, you will learn how jumping spiders
are similar to and different from other arachnids. Close-up
photographs and diagrams reveal extraordinary details about
the jumping spider's body both inside and out. A hands-on
activity compares the reader's jumping ability with that of
a jumping spider. . . . Enter the . . . world of the arachnid
family with award-winning science author Sandra Markle!
Too often lumped together with insects, these fascinating
animals have distinctive characteristics and habits that are
all their own." (Publisher's note)
Includes bibliographical references (p. 44-45) and index

Orb weavers; hungry spinners. Lerner Publications
2011 48p il (Arachnid world) lib bdg $29.27
Grades: 5 6 7 8   595.4
1. Spiders
ISBN 978-0-7613-5039-2; 0-7613-5039-X
                                                       LC 2010023490
This describes how orb weavers are similar to and different from other arachnids. Close-up photographs and diagrams reveal details about the spider's body both inside and
out. And a hands-on activity will give you an idea of how the
orb weaver can detect prey caught in its web.
Markle "presents a mix of common and less-common
facts . . . and her commentary accompanies a particularly
strong suite of illustrations featuring large, clear, labeled
outside and inside views that display body parts. Photos go
beyond the standard portraits. . . . First rate." SLJ
Includes glossary and bibliographical references

Scorpions; armed stingers. Lerner Publications 2011
48p il (Arachnid world) lib bdg $29.27
Grades: 5 6 7 8   595.4
1. Scorpions
ISBN 978-0-7613-5037-8; 0-7613-5037-3
                                                       LC 2010004275
This describes how scorpions are similar to and different
from other arachnids. Close-up photographs and diagrams
reveal details about the scorpion's body both inside and out.
And a hands-on activity reveals how a scorpion's senses
help it find its prey.
Markle "presents a mix of common and less-common
facts . . . and her commentary accompanies a particularly
strong suite of illustrations featuring large, clear, labeled
outside and inside views that display body parts. Photos go
beyond the standard portraits. . . . First rate." SLJ
Includes glossary and bibliographical references

Sneaky, spinning, baby spiders; [by] Sandra Markle.
Walker & Company 2008 32p il $16.99; lib bdg $17.89
Grades: 3 4 5   595.4
1. Spiders 2. Animal babies
ISBN 978-0-8027-9697-4; 0-8027-9697-4; 978-0-
8027-9698-1 lib bdg; 0-8027-9698-2 lib bdg
                                                        LC 2007-49139
"Markle's intimate style beckons readers into her text
and immediately immerses them in the world of spiderlings.
. . . The full-color photographs are the work of many photographers and are filled with energy. . . . [Markle] introduces
about 14 species (of the 30,000 spiders worldwide), but she
does it in such vivid detail and with such respect and appreciation that youngsters will feel connected to these spider
moms and their babies." SLJ

Spiders; biggest! littlest! photographs by Simon Pollard. Boyds Mills Press 2004 un il $15.95
Grades: K 1 2 3   595.4
1. Size 2. Spiders
ISBN 1-59078-190-2
                                                        LC 2003-26794
This "focuses on seven spiders and explains why their
size gives them an edge over other species. . . . The book also
incorporates information about the arachnid's role as predator, its use of venom, molting, feeding methods, reproduction, etc. . . . Amazingly detailed, closeup, color photographs

appear on every spread. . . . Well organized and clearly written, this engaging work offers important insights into spider physiology not present in many other overviews." SLJ

Ticks; dangerous hitchhikers. Lerner Publications 2011 48p il (Arachnid world) lib bdg $29.27
Grades: 4 5 6 7   **595.4**
    1. Ticks
    ISBN 978-0-7613-5041-5; 0-7613-5041-1
                                                    LC 2010023484
This book about ticks offers "a clear, conversational text that will draw young people into the zoological facts with gripping, even gruesome examples that are well matched with unsparingly detailed photos. . . . The handsome design, featuring crisply magnified photos, and the approachable text from an experienced writer combine into a strong offering for both personal and classroom reading." Booklist
    Includes bibliographical references

Wolf spiders; mothers on guard. Lerner Publications 2010 48p il (Arachnid world) lib bdg $29.27
Grades: 5 6 7 8   **595.4**
    1. Spiders
    ISBN 978-0-7613-5040-8; 0-7613-5040-3
                                                    LC 2010004273
This describes how wolf spider mothers carry their young on their backs and how wolf spiders are similar to and different from other arachnids. Close-up photographs and diagrams reveal details about the spider's body both inside and out. And hands-on activities will let you experience how a wolf spider female keeps her eggs and young safe.
    Markle "presents a mix of common and less-common facts . . . and her commentary accompanies a particularly strong suite of illustrations featuring large, clear, labeled outside and inside views that display body parts. Photos go beyond the standard portraits. . . . First rate." SLJ
    Includes glossary and bibliographical references

Markle, Sandra, 1946-
Mites; master sneaks. by Sandra Markle. Lerner Publications 2012 48 p. (Arachnid world)
Grades: 4 5 6 7   **595.4**
    1. Mites 2. Animals -- Anatomy
    ISBN 9780761350460
                                                    LC 2011021462
In this book, a volume of the Arachnid World series, readers "will learn how mites are similar to and different from other arachnids. Close-up photographs, micrographs, and diagrams reveal . . . details about a mite's body both inside and out. A hands-on activity shows how quickly a few mites can multiply into hundreds." (Publisher's note) The book "discuss[es] . . . [their] physical structure, life cycle, and characteristic behaviors. . . . In 'Mites,' [author Sandra] Markle discusses a variety of these . . . creatures." (Booklist)
    Includes bibliographical references and index

Tarantulas; supersized predators. by Sandra Markle. Lerner Publications Company 2012 48 p. (Arachnid world)
Grades: 4 5 6 7   **595.4**
    1. Tarantulas
    ISBN 9780761350439
                                                    LC 2011020437
In this book, a volume of the Arachnid World series, readers "will learn how tarantulas are similar to and different

from other arachnids. Close-up photographs and diagrams reveal extraordinary details about the tarantula's body both inside and out. A hands-on activity illustrates how a tarantula grows bigger and bigger by molting." (Publisher's note) The book "discuss[es] . . . [their] physical structure, life cycle, and characteristic behaviors. . . . 'Tarantulas' looks at the lives of these large, hairy spiders and points out that they help control insect populations." (Booklist)
    Includes bibliographical references and index

Wind scorpions; killer jaws. Sandra Markle. Lerner Publications 2012 48 p. (Arachnid world) (lib. bdg.: alk. paper) $30.60
Grades: 4 5 6 7   **595.4**
    1. Scorpions 2. Animals -- Anatomy 3. Arachnids -- Juvenile literature 4. Solpugida
    ISBN 0761350489; 9780761350484
                                                    LC 2011021599
In this book, a volume of the Arachnid World series, readers "will learn how wind scorpions are similar to and very different from other arachnids. Close-up photographs and diagrams reveal extraordinary details about the wind scorpion's body both inside and out. A hands-on activity demonstrates how wind scorpions are able to pick up prey to eat it." (Publisher's note) The book "discuss[es] . . . [their] physical structure, life cycle, and characteristic behaviors. . . . 'Wind Scorpions' introduces a group of arachnids that use supersize jaws to defend themselves and to attack their prey." (Booklist)
    Includes bibliographical references and index

Montgomery, Sy
    ★ The **tarantula** scientist. Houghton Mifflin Co. 2004 80p il map (Scientists in the field) $18; pa $7.95
Grades: 4 5 6 7   **595.4**
    1. Tarantulas
    ISBN 0-618-14799-3; 0-618-91577-X pa
                                                    LC 2003-20125
Describes the research that Samuel Marshall and his students are doing on tarantulas, including the largest spider on earth, the Goliath birdeating tarantula
    "Enthusiasm for the subject and respect for both Marshall and his eight-legged subjects come through on every page of the clear, informative, and even occasionally humorous text. Bishop's full-color photos . . . are amazing." Booklist
    Includes glossary and bibliographical references

Morley, Christine
    Freaky facts about spiders; [written by Christine Morley; illustrated by Phillip Morrison] Two-Can 2007 32p il (Freaky facts) $13.95; pa $8.95
Grades: 2 3 4 5   **595.4**
    1. Spiders
    ISBN 978-1-58728-596-7; 978-1-58728-597-4 pa
                                                    LC 2006-22589
    "Competent cartoons, full-color photos, boxes, sidebars, and facts are pulled together on busy but appealing pages that deliver a shower of brief, tantalizing fact bites. In this book readers will find plenty of closeups of spiders as well as information about what they eat, how they behave, where they live, and more. The tone is casual, and the cartoons provide a light coat of comedy." Booklist

Murawski, Darlyne

Spiders and their webs; [by] Darlyne A. Murawski. National Geographic 2004 31p il $16.95

Grades: 2 3 4 5   595.4

1. Spiders 2. Spider webs -- Juvenile literature
ISBN 0-7922-6979-9

LC 2004-397

This describes nine species of spiders and how they make and use webs

"Even fainthearted arachnophobes will appreciate this gallery of spider profiles featuring full-color, telephoto views. . . . Murawski writes about her subjects with an awe and a reverence that will encourage reluctant children to move beyond spiders' creepy reputation to their fascinating features." Booklist

Includes bibliographical references

Otfinoski, Steven

Scorpions. Marshall Cavendish Benchmark 2011 il (Animals, animals) lib bdg $20.95

Grades: 3 4 5   595.4

1. Scorpions
ISBN 978-0-7614-4878-5; 0-7614-4878-0

LC 2010016035

Provides information on the anatomy, special skills, habitats, and diet of scorpions.

This offers "comprehensive text and striking, well-chosen photos. . . . [This is] packed with engaging facts and trivia, as well as an upbeat tone." Booklist

Includes glossary and bibliographical references

Simon, Seymour

★ **Spiders**; [by] Seymour Simon. updated ed.; Smithsonian 2008 31p il $16.99; pa $6.99

Grades: 3 4 5 6   595.4

1. Spiders
ISBN 978-0-06-089104-6; 0-06-089104-1; 978-0-06-089103-9 pa; 0-06-089103-3 pa
First published 2003 by HarperCollins

An introduction to the physical characteristics, behavior, and life cycle of different kinds of spiders.

"The fantastic color photos of the original edition are all here, as is Simon's crisp, informative text. . . . An attention grabber." SLJ

Stewart, Melissa

How do spiders make webs? Marshall Cavendish Benchmark 2009 32p il (Tell me why, tell me how) lib bdg $20.95

Grades: 3 4 5   595.4

1. Spiders
ISBN 978-0-7614-2920-3 lib bdg; 0-7614-2920-4 lib bdg

LC 2007025092

This "explains the differences between [spiders] and other arachnids, and how and why they spin webs. One or two large, well-captioned color photographs are provided per spread. [The] book concludes with an activity. [This is a] solid [introduction]." SLJ

Includes glossary and bibliographical references

Wadsworth, Ginger

Up, up, and away; illustrated by Patricia J. Wynne. Charlesbridge 2009 un il lib bdg $16.95

Grades: PreK K 1 2   595.4

1. Spiders
ISBN 1-58089-221-3 lib bdg; 978-1-58089-221-6 lib bdg

LC 2008040752

This traces the life cycle of a garden spider

"Simply told with well-chosen words and phrases, the story reads aloud well. . . . Wynne uses watercolor, gouache, and colored pencil to add hue and shading to the precise ink drawings that define the spiders and their surroundings." Booklist

595.6   Myriapods

Elkin, Matthew

20 fun facts about centipedes; by Matthew Elkin. Gareth Stevens Pub. 2013 32 p. col. ill. (Fun fact file: bugs!) (library) $25.25; (paperback) $10.50

Grades: 3 4 5   595.6

1. Centipedes 2. Centipedes -- Miscellanea -- Juvenile literature
ISBN 1433982307; 9781433982309; 9781433982316

LC 2012021903

This book by Matthew Elkin is part of a series " that presents a basic bulleted list of facts [with] a few sentences of information, engaging captions, and bright photographs. The basics are covered, including anatomy, eating habits, and offspring. 'Centipedes' uncovers info on the arthropods (and uncovers is the right word, as they commonly hide in cool, dark places like under rocks and, yes, in your bathroom)." (Publisher's note)

Includes bibliographical references and index.

Povey, Karen D.

Centipede; [by] Karen Povey. KidHaven Press 2004 32p il (Bugs) $22.45

Grades: 3 4 5   595.6

1. Centipedes 2. Centipedes -- Juvenile literature
ISBN 0-7377-1766-1

LC 2003-15274

Describes the physical characteristics, behavior, and habitat of centipedes.

595.7   Insects

Anderson, Margaret Jean

Bugged-out insects; [by] Margaret J. Anderson. Enslow Publishers 2011 48p il (Bizarre science) lib bdg $23.93

Grades: 4 5 6 7   595.7

1. Insects
ISBN 978-0-7660-3674-1; 0-7660-3674-X

LC 2010006474

First published 1996 with title: Bizarre insects

This describes insects such as cicadas, butterflies, praying mantises, walkingsticks, beetles, stinkbugs, botflies, mayflies, mosquitoes, bees, ants, and locusts.

"Aimed at reluctant readers, [this title is] sure to disgust and delight in equal measure. . . . [The title] will pique interest and get kids lining up at the reference desk looking for more. The text is complemented by illustrations and magnified photos of things that you would hope never to see." SLJ

Includes glossary and bibliographical references

Aronin, Miriam

★ The **ant's** nest; a huge, underground city. Bearport Pub. 2009 32p il (Spectacular animal towns) lib bdg $18.95

Grades: 2 3 4   **595.7**

1. Ants 2. Insect societies

ISBN 978-1-59716-868-7 lib bdg; 1-59716-868-8 lib bdg

LC 2009-03065

"Through excellent photographs, high-interest texts, sidebars, maps, and other material, children learn about both the animals and their habitats. The . . . book also provides brief profiles of animals with similar habitats. . . . [This book is] much better than average 'report' titles." SLJ

Includes glossary and bibliographical references

Baker, Nick

Bug zoo. DK 2010 64p il $12.99

Grades: 2 3 4   **595.7**

1. Insects 2. Collectors and collecting

ISBN 978-0-7566-6166-3; 0-7566-6166-8

LC 2010-279437

Naturalist Nick Baker shows the reader how to make miniature habitats for insects, snails and worms, some interesting aspects of their lives and how to feed the contained creatures

"This is a colorful, informative, and engaging book about keeping insects-if not as pets, then as creatures worthy of intense study. . . . Baker's enthusiasm for the subject is evident throughout. Because it provides interesting facts about insects as well as how-to tips, this title will find an audience with curious readers and would-be zookeepers alike. It may even intrigue avowed entomophobes." SLJ

Beccaloni, George

Biggest bugs life-size. Firefly Books 2010 84p il $19.95

Grades: 4 5 6 7   **595.7**

1. Insects

ISBN 978-1-55407-699-4; 1-55407-699-4

"This book presents 35 of the world's biggest, longest, and heaviest bugs. . . . Double-page spreads feature each bug's statistics, a map with its area of distribution, and straightforward text that explains its living conditions, eating habits, and life cycle. . . . The highlights, of course, are the numerous life-size and up-close full-color photographs of the bugs. . . . The visual appeal alone will entice even the most reluctant readers." Booklist

Berger, Melvin

Chirping crickets; illustrated by Megan Lloyd. HarperCollins Pubs. 1998 32p il (Let's-read-and-find-out science) lib bdg $15.89; pa $4.95

Grades: K 1 2 3   **595.7**

1. Crickets

ISBN 0-06-024962-5 lib bdg; 0-06-445180-1 pa

LC 96-51661

Describes the physical characteristics, behavior, and life cycle of crickets while giving particular emphasis to how they chirp

"Clear and detailed, the ink-and-watercolor artwork is often visually striking as well as educationally sound. . . . A well-rounded introduction." Booklist

Bishop, Nic

Butterflies; written and photographed by Nic Bishop. Scholastic Inc. 2011 31p il (Scholastic reader) pa $3.99

Grades: 1 2   **595.7**

1. Butterflies

ISBN 978-0-545-28434-9 pa; 0-545-28434-1 pa

★ **Nic** Bishop butterflies and moths. Scholastic Nonfiction 2009 48p il $17.99

Grades: 2 3 4   **595.7**

1. Butterflies

ISBN 978-0-439-87757-2; 0-439-87757-1

LC 2008-15290

"The text covers the all-important topic of metamorphosis, of course, but also discusses feeding and predation, migration, and reproduction. . . . The real draw here, though, is the art; even for Bishop, the photographs are breathtaking. . . . Kids will be drawn to this like Bishop's subject to flame." Bull Cent Child Books

Blobaum, Cindy

Insectigation! 40 hands-on activities to explore the insect world. [by] Cindy Blobaum. Chicago Review Press 2005 133p il pa $12.95

Grades: 3 4 5 6   **595.7**

1. Insects

ISBN 1-55652-568-0

"Raising mealworms, testing the visual acuity of bees, setting up a watering hole for butterflies—these are just a few of the 40 activities included in this earnest introduction to entomology. Each of eight chapters focuses on a different topic, such as physical and behavioral characteristics; metamorphosis; communication; methods to attract, collect and keep insects, etc. . . . Clear line drawings, diagrams of body parts and project materials, plus the occasional black-and-white photograph are found on almost every page. . . . The text is clearly written and well organized." SLJ

Includes bibliographical references

Bodden, Valerie

Cockroaches; Valerie Bodden. 1st ed. Creative Education 2013 24 p. col. ill. (Creepy creatures) (library) $25.65

Grades: 1 2 3 4   **595.7**

1. Cockroaches 2. Picture books for children

ISBN 1608182320; 9781608182329

LC 2011050277

This book is part of the Creepy Creatures series. The series uses "clear white backgrounds to showcase . . . magnified photos, while the simple, educational text is . . . arranged around the page." This book looks at "the 4,000 varieties of roach and [details] how they can hold their breath to crawl up drains into bathtubs." (Booklist)

Includes bibliographical references and index

Termites; Valerie Bodden. 1st ed. Creative Education 2013 24 p. col. ill. (Creepy creatures) (library) $25.65

Grades: 1 2 3 4   **595.7**

1. Picture books for children 2. Termites -- Juvenile

literature

ISBN 1608182355; 9781608182350

LC 2011050279

This children's picture book, part of the Creepy Creatures Series by Valerie Bodden, looks at termites. "Throughout most of each title, a page of large-print text, set on a plain white background, alternates with a full-page, extreme close-up photo of one or more of the featured animals. . . . Each book succinctly outlines the animals' basic structure, key body parts, distinctive characteristics of particular species, behavior, habitats, diet, natural enemies, and life cycle." (School Library Journal)

Includes bibliographical references and index

Bulion, Leslie

Hey there, stink bug! illustrated by Leslie Evans. Charlesbridge 2006 45p il lib bdg $12.95

Grades: 3 4 5 6   595.7

1. Insects 2. Insects -- Juvenile literature 3. Children's literature

ISBN 9781580893046 lib bdg; 1-58089-304-X lib bdg

LC 2005-19627

This book "describes various types of insects using different poetic forms." (Publisher's note) "Grades four to seven." (Bull Cent Child Books)

"Bulion uses gory, visceral facts to pull children into both the science and the various poetic forms. . . . Striking, watercolor-washed linoleum prints and notes about poetic forms round out this title." Booklist

Catt, Thessaly

Migrating with the monarch butterfly. PowerKids Press 2011 24p il (Animal journeys) lib bdg $21.25; pa $8.25

Grades: 2 3 4   595.7

1. Butterflies -- Migration

ISBN 978-1-4488-2546-2 lib bdg; 978-1-4488-2676-6 pa

LC 2010030647

This describes the yearly migration of the monarch butterfly, which can travel between 50 to 100 miles a day.

Cusick, Dawn

Bug butts; illustrations by Haude Levesque. Earlylight Books 2009 48p il $14.95

Grades: 3 4 5   595.7

1. Insects

ISBN 978-0-9797455-0-8; 0-9797455-0-0

This describes the diverse ways insects use their butt ends to survive and thrive.

"Provides interesting information on the posterior anatomy of insects, discussing a variety of modifications of the abdomen and anus. . . . The book is well written, informative, and very nicely illustrated." Sci Books Films

Davies, Andrew

Super-size bugs; written by Andrew Davies; photographed by Igor Siwanowicz. Sterling Publishing 2007 48p il $9.95

Grades: 3 4 5 6   595.7

1. Insects

ISBN 978-1-4027-5340-4; 1-4027-5340-3

"From the scarlet whiplike tails of a Puss Moth caterpillar to the glittering armor of the Blue Ground Beetle, from the clustered eyes of a Greenbottle Blue Tarantula to the eerily alien face of the Devil's Flower Mantis, Davies introduces a host of insects made 'supersize' by the camera lens. Paragraphs of text and detailed captions provide interesting snippets of information, but it is the superb photos that rivet the eye to these oversize pages." SLJ

Dickmann, Nancy

A bee's life. Heinemann Library 2010 24p il (Watch it grow) lib bdg $21.50; pa $5.99

Grades: PreK K 1   595.7

1. Bees

ISBN 978-1-4329-4137-6 lib bdg; 1-4329-4137-2 lib bdg; 978-1-4329-4146-8 pa; 1-4329-4146-1 pa

LC 2009-49151

"Practically unique among early introductions to life cycles because death is mentioned . . . this . . . follows [a bee] . . . from egg . . . to maturity with a set of close-up color photographs, one per page, paired to large-type, one or two-sentence captions. . . . Offers nourishing fare for young naturalists." SLJ

Includes glossary

A butterfly's life. Heinemann Library 2010 24p il (Watch it grow) lib bdg $21.50; pa $5.99

Grades: PreK K 1   595.7

1. Butterflies

ISBN 978-1-4329-4138-3 lib bdg; 1-4329-4138-0 lib bdg; 978-1-4329-4147-5 pa; 1-4329-4147-X pa

LC 2009-49152

"Practically unique among early introductions to life cycles because death is mentioned . . . this . . . follows [a butterfly] . . . from egg . . . to maturity with a set of close-up color photographs, one per page, paired to large-type, one or two-sentence captions. . . . Offers nourishing fare for young naturalists." SLJ

Dixon, Norma

Focus on flies. Fitzhenry & Whiteside 2008 32p il $18.95

Grades: 4 5 6 7   595.7

1. Flies 2. Flies -- Juvenile literature

ISBN 978-1-55005-128-5; 1-55005-128-8

This "chatty, informative title, illustrated with many clear color photos and diagrams, will hook readers with its fascinating view of a fly's 'creepy cool world.' . . . The gross details will appeal to middle-grade readers, who will then go on to learn about anatomy, metamorphosis, adaptation, diversity, classification, and flies' roles in plant pollination." Booklist

Includes bibliographical references

Dorros, Arthur

Ant cities; written and illustrated by Arthur Dorros. Crowell 1987 28p il (Let's-read-and-find-out science book) hardcover o.p. lib bdg $11.89; pa $5.99

Grades: K 1 2 3   595.7

1. Ants

ISBN 0-690-04568-9; 0-690-04570-0 lib bdg; 0-06-445079-1 pa

LC 85-48244

"Using harvester ants as a basic example, Dorros shows how the insects build tunnels with rooms for different functions and how workers, queens, and males have distinct roles in the ant hill. Along the way, she works in details of food and reproduction, ending with descriptions of other kinds of ants and suggestions for ways to observe them (including instructions for making an ant farm). The text is simple without becoming choppy, the full-color illustrations are inviting as well as informative." Bull Cent Child Books

Glaser, Linda

Dazzling dragonflies; a life cycle story. illustrated by Mia Posada. Millbrook Press 2008 un il (Linda Glaser's classic creatures) lib bdg $22.60

Grades: K 1 2 3   595.7

1. Dragonflies

ISBN 978-0-8225-6753-0 lib bdg; 0-8225-6753-9 lib bdg

LC 2007-21886

"Clearly written text and bright-hued watercolor collage illustrations introduce the life cycle of that zip-a-dipping aerialist, the dragonfly, from newly laid eggs, through months of aquatic life as a nymph, to the final metamorphosis into a glitter-winged creature. . . . [This] is basic, attractive, and easy to read." SLJ

Not a buzz to be found; insects in winter. illustrations by Jaime Zollars. Millbrook Press 2011 31p il lib bdg $25.26

Grades: K 1 2 3   595.7

1. Winter 2. Insects

ISBN 978-0-7613-5644-8; 0-7613-5644-4

LC 2011001148

"This look at how insects survive the cold may have young naturalists scouring the winter landscape to find them for themselves. From those who migrate or hibernate to ones that hide or are still eggs, Glaser has assembled a wide variety of 12 of the more common insects, including ants, ladybugs, dragonflies, honeybees, monarchs, praying mantises and black swallowtail butterflies. Short verses present readers with how each gets through the winter. . . . Gorgeous full-bleed illustrations filled with color and detail depict the insects in winter." Kirkus

Gonzales, Doreen

Crickets in the dark. PowerKids Press 2010 24p il (Creatures of the night) lib bdg $21.25; pa $8.05

Grades: 2 3 4   595.7

1. Crickets

ISBN 978-1-4042-8098-4 lib bdg; 1-4042-8098-7 lib bdg; 978-1-4358-3253-4 pa; 1-4358-3253-1 pa

LC 2009-483

A look at crickets and their world in the dark.

"Basic details are complemented by eclectic trivia, . . . [and] each volume concludes with a defense of the animal . . . and why it is vital to humans. The layout is attractive, with easy-to-read text and eye-catching photography. Good for reports." SLJ

Includes glossary

Gray, Susan Heinrichs

Emerald ash borer; by Susan H. Gray. Cherry Lake Pub. 2008 32p il map (Animal invaders) lib bdg $27.07

Grades: 3 4 5 6   595.7

1. Emerald ash borer 2. Biological invasions

ISBN 978-1-60279-112-1 lib bdg; 1-60279-112-0 lib bdg

LC 2007-34973

This describes the Emerald ash borers' "outstanding physical and behavioral characteristics at each stage in their life cycle, diet, and natural habitat, and then [explains] how they were introduced into areas outside their natural range . . . and the nature and extent of the ecological damage they have caused, and various attempts to eradicate or at least control the animals. . . . Larvae of the emerald ash borer have infested and destroyed thousands of valuable ash trees in the Midwest. . . . Clear color photographs . . . accompany the texts on about every other page. . . . [This title is] clearly written and well organized, and [has] up-to-date information." SLJ

Includes glossary

The **life** cycle of insects; [by] Susan H. Gray. Heinemann Library 2011 48p il (Life cycles) lib bdg $35; pa $8.95

Grades: 3 4 5   595.7

1. Insects

ISBN 978-1-4329-4983-9 lib bdg; 978-1-4329-4990-7 pa

LC 2010038508

This describes what an incsect is, types of insects, their life cycles, habitats, foods, defenses, and relationships to humans.

Includes glossary and bibliographical references

Hamilton, Sue L.

Swarmed by bees; [by] Sue Hamilton. ABDO Pub. Co. 2010 32p il (Close encounters of the wild kind) lib bdg $27.07

Grades: 4 5 6 7   595.7

1. Bees 2. Animal attacks

ISBN 978-1-60453-933-2 lib bdg; 1-60453-933-X lib bdg

LC 2009-45598

Readers learn of actual human-bee encounters, information about bees, survival strategies, and attack statistics.

"Students will be drawn to the realistic full-color photographs, the realistic diagrams of the creatures' bodies, the real-life stories told by victims, and the interesting, attractive formatting that includes text, diagrams, photographs, and graphics on each page. . . . [This is] exciting and attractive in a 'gross' sort of way and will appeal particularly to boys for both leisure reading and research." Libr Media Connect

Includes glossary

Hansen, Amy S.

Bugs and bugsicles; insects in the winter. [by] Amy S. Hansen; illustrations by Robert C. Kray. Boyds Mills Press 2010 32p il

Grades: 3 4 5   595.7

1. Winter 2. Insects

ISBN 1590782690; 9781590782699

"This colorful book describes what happens in winter to seven different insects: a praying mantis, a field cricket, a ladybug, a honeybee, a pavement ant, a monarch butterfly, and an Arctic woolly bear caterpillar. . . . The title concludes with an author's note and two science activities related to freezing water. A typical double-page spread includes a few paragraphs of text accompanied by large-scale illustrations." Booklist

Includes glossary and bibliographical references

Himmelman, John

Noisy bug sing-along; by John Himmelman. 1st ed. Dawn Publications 2013 32 p. (hardcover) $16.95; (paperback) $8.95

Grades: 2 3 4 **595.7**

1. Picture books for children 2. Insects -- Juvenile literature 3. Insect sounds -- Juvenile literature

ISBN 1584691913; 9781584691914; 9781584691921

LC 2012024253

This children's picture book looks at the noises made by bugs. "The opening page tells readers that bugs sing day and night, loudly and softly, and that they should sing along. . . . Each double-page spread is devoted to one insect and its sound, a sentence telling the name of the creature and what it does, followed by the sound the bug makes—in a huge display type that spreads across and fills the pages." (Kirkus)

Jango-Cohen, Judith

Bees; by Judith Jango-Cohen. Marshall Cavendish Benchmark 2006 48p il (Animals, animals) lib bdg $19.95

Grades: 3 4 5 6 **595.7**

1. Bees

ISBN 978-0-7614-2235-8 lib bdg; 0-7614-2235-8 lib bdg

LC 2005025610

"Sharp color photographs accompany the text. . . . [This is] clearly written, [and] well organized." SLJ

Includes glossary and bibliographical references

Johnson, Jinny

Butterfly; illustrations by Michael Woods. Smart Apple Media 2010 32p il (How does it grow?) lib bdg $28.50

Grades: 1 2 3 **595.7**

1. Butterflies

ISBN 978-1-59920-352-2 lib bdg; 1-59920-352-9 lib bdg

LC 2009-3397

Introduces children to the lifecycle of a butterfly

"Each stage is described on a spread that features clearly written, oversized text and a caption opposite a full-page, realistic watercolor, or, occasionally, a photograph. . . . A worthwhile purchase." SLJ

Includes glossary

Insects and creepy-crawlies; Jinny Johnson. Kingfisher 2011 32 p.

Grades: 3 4 5 **595.7**

1. Animal behavior 2. Insects -- Pictorial works 3. Insects -- Juvenile literature

ISBN 0753465922; 9780753465929

In this book, "readers get an up-close view of life in a wide variety of insect colonies through six . . . illustrated story scenes that each examine a key aspect of entomological study-from insect homes, to reproduction, life in the water, hunting and gathering, and insects that fly. Once readers absorb the key elements of the story, they explore the science through photos and fact boxes on the following page." (Publisher's note)

Simon & Schuster children's guide to insects and spiders. Simon & Schuster Bks. for Young Readers 1996 80p il $19.95

Grades: 4 5 6 7 **595.7**

1. Insects 2. Spiders

ISBN 0-689-81163-2

LC 96-27600

Provides an introduction to more than 100 insects and arachnids, giving general information about family characteristics and habits, and more specific facts about some species

"Crisp and well-designed, this is an inviting visual introduction to insects and arachnids." Booklist

Includes glossary

Knudsen, Shannon

From egg to butterfly. Lerner Publs. 2003 24p il (Start to finish) lib bdg $18.60

Grades: K 1 2 **595.7**

1. Butterflies 2. Butterflies -- Life cycles 3. Butterflies -- Life cycles -- Juvenile literature

ISBN 0-8225-0713-7

LC 2001-4652

Follows the development of a butterfly from the egg its mother lays on a plant to the fully developed insect that flies away

"Readers will be transfixed by the incredibly crisp and clear photographs accompanying the text. This up-close and intimate look at the life stages of a monarch butterfly will be an asset to any young entomologist's library." Sci Teach

Koontz, Robin Michal

What's the difference between a butterfly and a moth? by Robin Koontz; illustrated by Bandelin-Dacey. Picture Window Books 2010 24p il (What's the difference) lib bdg $25.32

Grades: K 1 2 **595.7**

1. Moths 2. Butterflies

ISBN 978-1-4048-5543-4 lib bdg; 1-4048-5543-2 lib bdg

LC 2009-6884

"Compares and contrasts the habitats, physical characteristics, location, and lifestyles of [butterflies and moths]. The picture-book format is used to great effect as it allows the two animals to be compared side by side on each spread. The bold, expressive watercolors provide the same visual impact as photographs. . . . Short sentences and highlighted fun facts make this a . . . [book] with broad appeal for both researchers and browsers." SLJ

Includes glossary

Latimer, Jonathan P.

Caterpillars; [by] Jonathan P. Latimer, Karen Stray Nolting; illustrations by Amy Bartlett Wright; foreword by Virginia Marie Peterson. Houghton Mifflin 2000 48p il (Peterson field guides for young naturalists) pbk. $5.95

Grades: 4 5 6 7 **595.7**

1. Caterpillars

ISBN 9780395979457

LC 99-38944

Describes the physical characteristics, behavior, and habitat of a variety of caterpillars, arranged by the categories "Smooth," "Bumpy," "Sluglike," "Horned," "Hairy," "Bristly," and "Spiny"

Lockwood, Sophie

Ants; by Sophie Lockwood. Child's World 2008 40p il map (World of insects) lib bdg $29.93

Grades: 4 5 6   **595.7**

1. Ants

ISBN 978-1-59296-817-6 lib bdg; 1-59296-817-1 lib bdg

LC 2006103452

This describes ants' "basic anatomy, outstanding physical and behavioral characteristics, [diet, life cycle], roles in myths and legends, and effects on humans. . . . With [its] well-organized, succinct [text] and excellent photography, [this] solid [introduction] will be [a] valuable [resource]." SLJ

Includes glossary and bibliographical references

Dragonflies; by Sophie Lockwood. Child's World 2008 40p il map (World of insects) lib bdg $29.93

Grades: 4 5 6   **595.7**

1. Dragonflies

ISBN 978-1-59296-821-3 lib bdg; 1-59296-821-X lib bdg

LC 2006103454

This describes dragonflies' "basic anatomy, outstanding physical and behavioral characteristics, [diet, life cycle], roles in myths and legends, and effects on humans. . . . With [its] well-organized, succinct [text] and excellent photography, [this] solid [introduction] will be [a] valuable [resource]." SLJ

Includes glossary and bibliographical references

Flies; by Sophie Lockwood. Child's World 2008 40p il (World of insects) lib bdg $29.93

Grades: 4 5 6   **595.7**

1. Flies

ISBN 978-1-59296-822-0 lib bdg; 1-59296-822-8 lib bdg

LC 2007000182

This describes flies' "basic anatomy, outstanding physical and behavioral characteristics, [diet, life cycle], roles in myths and legends, and effects on humans. . . . With [its] well-organized, succinct [text] and excellent photography, [this] solid [introduction] will [a] be valuable [resource]." SLJ

Includes glossary and bibliographical references

Maley, Adrienne Houk

20 fun facts about praying mantises; by Adrienne Houk Maley. 1st ed. Gareth Stevens Pub. 2013 32 p. col. ill. (library) $25.25; (paperback) $10.50

Grades: 3 4 5   **595.7**

1. Praying mantis 2. Mantodea -- Juvenile literature

ISBN 1433982404; 9781433982408; 9781433982415

LC 2012031287

This book by Adrienne Houk Maley focuses on praying mantieses and states that "female praying mantises sometimes eat the head of their mate, and then offers possible reasons for this behavior. Other entries briefly describe: key body parts, senses, defense mechanisms, hunting and/or feeding methods, diets, life cycles, etc. Captions, mounted on yellow backgrounds mimicking sticky notes, provide additional information." (Publisher's note)

Includes bibliographical references (page 31) and index.

Markle, Sandra

Hornets; incredible insect architects. by Sandra Markle. Lerner Publications Company 2008 48p il (Insect world) lib bdg $27.93

Grades: 2 3 4 5   **595.7**

1. Hornets and yellowjackets

ISBN 978-0-8225-7297-8 lib bdg; 0-8225-7297-4 lib bdg

LC 2007022290

This describes the anatomy, life cycle, and behavior of hornets

This "will please report writers, budding entomologists, and anyone who expects children's nonfiction to be as carefully documented as adult nonfiction. . . . The [book is] notable for the sharp photos placed precisely to enhance understanding. . . . The main [text is] clear and [flows] well." SLJ

Includes glossary and bibliographical references

Insects; biggest! littlest! photographs by Simon Pollard. Boyds Mills Press 2009 32p il $16.95

Grades: 2 3 4 5   **595.7**

1. Size 2. Insects 3. Insects -- Juvenile literature

ISBN 978-1-59078-512-6; 1-59078-512-6

LC 2008-33524

"This simply written introduction examines insects from the perspective of size. Employing over a dozen kinds as examples, Markle explains why those that are unusually large, small, or equipped with extraordinary body parts have an edge over predators or competing species. . . . An amazingly detailed, closeup color photograph of one or more of the insects discussed complements the text on almost every page. . . . Well organized and clearly written in an engaging style." SLJ

Includes glossary and bibliographical references

Luna moths; masters of change. by Sandra Markle. Lerner Publications Co. 2008 48p il (Insect world) lib bdg $27.93

Grades: 2 3 4 5   **595.7**

1. Moths

ISBN 978-0-8225-7302-9 lib bdg; 0-8225-7302-4 lib bdg

LC 2007025260

This describes the anatomy, life cycle, and behavior of luna moths

This "will please report writers, budding entomologists, and anyone who expects children's nonfiction to be as carefully documented as adult nonfiction. . . . The [book is] notable for the sharp photos placed precisely to enhance understanding. . . . The main [text is] clear and [flows] well." SLJ

Includes glossary and bibliographical references

★ **Praying** mantises; hungry insect heroes. Lerner Publications Company 2008 48p il (Insect world) lib bdg $27.93

Grades: 2 3 4 5   **595.7**

1. Praying mantis

ISBN 978-0-8225-7300-5 lib bdg; 0-8225-7300-8 lib bdg

LC 2007-25961

This describes the anatomy, life cycle, and behavior of praying mantises.

This "will please report writers, budding entomologists, and anyone who expects children's nonfiction to be as carefully documented as adult nonfiction. . . . The [book is] notable for the sharp photos placed precisely to enhance understanding. . . . The main [text is] clear and [flows] well." SLJ

Includes glossary and bibliographical references

Termites; hard-working insect families. by Sandra Markle. Lerner Publications Co. 2008 48p il (Insect world) lib bdg $27.93

Grades: 2 3 4 5 **595.7**

1. Termites

ISBN 978-0-8225-7301-2 lib bdg; 0-8225-7301-6 lib bdg

LC 2007025963

This describes the anatomy, life cycle, and behavior of termites

This "will please report writers, budding entomologists, and anyone who expects children's nonfiction to be as carefully documented as adult nonfiction. . . . The [book is] notable for the sharp photos placed precisely to enhance understanding. . . . The main [text is] clear and [flows] well." SLJ

Includes glossary and bibliographical references

Markovics, Joyce L.

The **honey** bee's hive; a thriving city. by Joyce Markovics; consultant, Brian V. Brown. Bearport Pub. 2009 32p il map (Spectacular animal towns) lib bdg $25.27

Grades: 2 3 4 **595.7**

1. Bees

ISBN 978-1-59716-867-0 lib bdg; 1-59716-867-X lib bdg

LC 2009-11295

Describes the activities within a honey bee hive

"Through excellent photographs, high-interest texts, sidebars, maps, and other material, children learn about both the animals and their habitats. The . . . book also provides brief profiles of animals with similar habitats. . . . [This book is] much better than average 'report' titles." SLJ

Includes glossary and bibliographical references

Marsh, Laura

Butterflies. National Geographic 2010 48p il map (Great migrations) $11.90; pa $3.99

Grades: 1 2 3 **595.7**

1. Butterflies

ISBN 978-1-4263-0740-9; 1-4263-0740-3; 978-1-4263-0739-3 pa; 1-4263-0739-X pa

This offers facts about monarch butterflies and their migration from Northern United States and Canada to the Oyamel forest of Mexico.

"Dynamic full-color photographs, informative writing, and consistent organization work well together in [this volume]. . . . Along with the many photographs, the fascinating details are supported by boxes of related information, helpful definitions of new terms, and a sprinkling of entertaining jokes/riddles." SLJ

Includes glossary

Marshall, Stephen A.

Insects A to Z. Firefly 2009 32p il lib bdg $19.95; pa $7.95

Grades: 4 5 6 **595.7**

1. Insects

ISBN 978-1-55407-555-3 lib bdg; 1-55407-555-6 lib bdg; 978-1-55407-503-4 pa; 1-55407-503-3 pa

This is an illustrated dictionary of 26 insects which includes the Latin and common names of the order, family, genus and species, as well as information on geographic distribution. Fact boxes for each entry provide information detailing each insect's scientific name, diet, average size and the location at which each was photographed.

"The photography . . . is well composed and sharply focused, with a nicely varied layout from page to page. . . . The [text is] clearly written." SLJ

Martin, Ruth

Bugs; [illustrated by Peter Scott; written by Ruth Martin; paper engineering by Andy Mansfield] Silver Dolphin Books 2009 un il (Kaleidopops) $15.95

Grades: K 1 2 3 **595.7**

1. Insects 2. Pop-up books

ISBN 978-1-59223-889-7; 1-59223-889-0

In this book about insects "iridescent insect pop-ups (which change color thanks to lenticular panels) are accompanied by brief, descriptive classifications of each species. . . . The vibrant and shiny images . . . emphasize the alien beauty of the various creepy crawlies, with less of a focus on insect anatomy." Publ Wkly

Miller, Heather

This is your life cycle; by Heather Lynn Miller; illustrated by Michael Chesworth. Clarion Books 2008 32p il $16

Grades: K 1 2 3 **595.7**

1. Dragonflies 2. Life cycles (Biology)

ISBN 978-0-618-72485-7; 0-618-72485-0

LC 2007-7245

Told in the form of a TV show, this describes the different stages of the life of Dahlia the dragonfly, including the various predators she faced, what she ate, and other facts.

"Lively, vibrant watercolor illustrations supplement the ambitious text. . . . Children will find this playful science book memorable." Libr Media Connect

Mortensen, Lori

In the trees, honeybees! illustrated by Cris Arbo. Dawn Publications 2009 un il $16.95; pa $8.95

Grades: PreK K 1 2 3 **595.7**

1. Bees

ISBN 978-1-58469-114-3; 1-58469-114-X; 978-1-58469-115-0 pa; 1-58469-115-8 pa

LC 2008038513

"Short, simple rhyming words and phrases, printed in large type on realistic illustrations, describe the amazing life cycle of the honeybee. The vibrantly colored scenes center on a beehive hidden in a tree trunk and the grass and gardens surrounding it. Brief paragraphs in a smaller font provide more information about the insect's depicted activities. . . . A wonderful choice for sharing aloud, Mortensen's finely crafted book makes a solid addition." SLJ

Mound, L. A.

Insect; written by Laurence Mound. rev ed; DK Pub. 2007 72p il (Eyewitness books) $15.99; lib bdg $19.99

Grades: 4 5 6 7   **595.7**
  1. Insects 2. Insects -- Juvenile literature
  ISBN 978-0-7566-3004-1; 0-7566-3004-5; 978-0-
  7566-0691-6 lib bdg; 0-7566-0691-8 lib bdg
                       LC 2007-281241
  First published 1990 by Knopf
  Includes glossary and bibliographical references

Munro, Roxie
  Busy builders; written and illustrated by Roxie Munro. Marshall Cavendish Children 2012 40 p. (hardcover) $17.99
Grades: 3 4 5   **595.7**
  1. Picture books for children 2. Insects -- Juvenile literature 3. Arachnids -- Juvenile literature 4. Insects -- Habitations -- Juvenile literature
  ISBN 0761461051; 9780761461050; 9780761461067
                       LC 2011017391
  This children's book, by Roxie Munro, describes "eight insects, one spider, and [offers] an inside look at the unique structures they each build. Roxie Munro's . . . art, drawn in India ink and colored ink, brings these remarkable feats of engineering into full focus. A glossary and resources to learn more are included." (Publisher's note)

Murawski, Darlyne
  Face to face with butterflies; by Darlyne A. Murawski. National Geographic 2010 31p il map (Face to face) $16.95
Grades: 3 4 5 6   **595.7**
  1. Butterflies
  ISBN 978-1-4263-0618-1; 1-4263-0618-0
  The author describes the life cycle and behavior of butterflies.
  Includes glossary and bibliographical references

  ★ **Face** to face with caterpillars; by Darlyne A. Murawski. National Geographic 2007 32p il (Face to face) $16.95; lib bdg $25.90
Grades: 3 4 5 6   **595.7**
  1. Caterpillars
  ISBN 978-1-4263-0052-3; 1-4263-0052-2; 978-1-4263-0053-0 lib bdg; 1-4263-0053-0 lib bdg
                       LC 2006-20499
  "Murawski tells how to find caterpillars and discusses their developmental stages, body parts, diet problems, and self-defense mechanisms. . . . Attractive, well written, and fascinating." SLJ
  Includes bibliographical references

Nelson, Maria
  20 fun facts about dragonflies; by Maria Nelson. 1st ed. Gareth Stevens Pub. 2013 32 p. col. ill. (Fun fact file: bugs!) (library) $25.25; (paperback) $10.50
Grades: 3 4 5   **595.7**
  1. Dragonflies 2. Dragonflies -- Juvenile literature
  ISBN 1433982358; 9781433982354; 9781433982361
                       LC 2012021207
  This book by Maria Nelson provides information on dragonflies and presents "one or two sentences per page, in large, eye-catching red print [and] offer[s] salient facts about the featured insects, usually involving an unusual physical or behavioral characteristic. Each numbered statement is followed by a short paragraph with more detail." (Publisher's note)

Nirgiotis, Nicholas
  Killer ants; illustrated by Emma Stevenson. Holiday House 2009 29p il $17.95
Grades: 2 3 4 5   **595.7**
  1. Ants 2. Predatory insects -- Juvenile literature
  ISBN 978-0-8234-2034-6; 0-8234-2034-5
                       LC 2007-46922
  This "volume presents four species of flesh-eating killer ants: army, driver, fire, and bulldog. After a dramatic opening scene and a general introduction to ants, the book spotlights each featured species in turn, devoting the most space to the army ants of the Amazon rain forest. Readers drawn by the book's title will enjoy the stories of ants attacking animals, but just as fascinating are the details of the ants' abilities, adaptations, and survival skills. . . . Stevenson . . . contributes a series of precisely drawn, useful, and sometimes dramatic gouache paintings. An informative, visually dynamic presentation." Booklist

Niver, Heather Moore
  20 fun facts about stick bugs; by Heather Moore Niver. 1st ed. Gareth Stevens Publishing 2013 32 p. col. ill. (library) $25.25; (Paperback) $10.50
Grades: 3 4 5   **595.7**
  1. Stick insects 2. Insects -- Juvenile literature
  ISBN 143398251X; 9781433982514; 9781433982521
                       LC 2012031356
  In this book by Heather Moore Niver "readers get the . . . opportunity to [see stick bugs] blending in with their natural habitat while learning many fun facts about stick bugs—including which is the longest, which resembles a lobster, and the many devious ways they avoid being caught by predators." (Publisher's note)
  Includes bibliographical references (page 31) and index.

Pringle, Laurence P.
  Cicadas! strange and wonderful. [by] Laurence Pringle; illustrated by Meryl Henderson. Boyd Mills Press 2010 32p il map $16.95
Grades: 2 3 4   **595.7**
  1. Cicadas
  ISBN 978-1-59078-673-4; 1-59078-673-4
                       LC 2010-925563
  This "provides an attractive introduction to cicadas, which typically spend 1, 13, or 17 years below ground before emerging for only a few weeks. . . . Pringle describes cicadas' physical features, behaviors, life cycle, and loss of habitat. . . . Henderson's watercolor paintings are precisely delineated, informative, and sometimes lovely as well. . . . This [is a] clearly written, informative introduction." Booklist
  Includes bibliographical references

Prischmann, Deirdre A.
  Poop-eaters; dung beetles in the food chain. by Deirdre A. Prischmann. Capstone Press 2008 32p il (Fact finders. Extreme life) lib bdg $23.93

Grades: 2 3 4   **595.7**
1. Beetles
ISBN 978-1-4296-1265-4 lib bdg; 1-4296-1265-7
lib bdg

LC 2007-20440

"The beetles' features, traits, and development are explained in breezy text, accompanied by vivid photographs and additional 'Gross!' fact boxes. . . . The volume provides an informative introduction to an underappreciated insect." Horn Book Guide

Includes glossary and bibliographical references

Rockwell, Anne F.
   Bugs are insects; by Anne Rockwell; illustrated by Steve Jenkins. HarperCollins Pubs. 2001 29p il (Let's-read-and-find-out science) hardcover o.p. lib bdg $15.89; pa $4.95
Grades: K 1 2 3   **595.7**
1. Insects
ISBN 0-06-028568-0; 0-06-028569-9 lib bdg; 0-06-445203-4 pa

LC 99-39846

Introduces common backyard insects and explains the basic characteristics of these creatures

This is a "well-written and informative book. . . . The collage illustrations are beautifully rendered with layered colored papers of a variety of textures that add both depth and details to the creatures." SLJ

   Honey in a hive; by Anne Rockwell; illustrated by S. D. Schindler. HarperCollinsPublishers 2005 33p il (Let's-read-and-find-out science) $15.99; lib bdg $16.89; pa $4.99
Grades: K 1 2 3   **595.7**
1. Bees 2. Honey
ISBN 0-06-028566-4; 0-06-028567-2 lib bdg; 0-06-445204-2 pa

LC 2003-10357

An introduction to the behavior and life cycle of honeybees, with particular emphasis on the production of honey

"Schindler's realistic artwork is both colorful and nicely matched to the text. . . . This attractive introduction to honey production will serve students well." Booklist

Rodriguez, Ana Maria
   Secret of the plant-killing ants . . . and more! Enslow Publishers 2008 48p il (Animal secrets revealed!) lib bdg $23.93
Grades: 5 6 7 8   **595.7**
1. Ants 2. Insects
ISBN 978-0-7660-2953-8 lib bdg; 0-7660-2953-0
lib bdg

LC 2007039494

"Explains why ants in the Amazon rainforest kill all but one species of plant and details other strange abilities of different types of animals." Publisher's note

Includes glossary and bibliographical references

Rotner, Shelley
   The **buzz** on bees; why are they disappearing? by Shelley Rotner and Anne Woodhull; photographs by Shelley Rotner. Holiday House 2010 un il $16.95

Grades: 2 3 4   **595.7**
1. Bees 2. Beekeeping 3. Fertilization of plants
ISBN 978-0-8234-2247-0; 0-8234-2247-X

"Excellent color photos provide an eye-catching backdrop for a simple, readable text that explains the importance of bees as pollinators and the current mystery of CCD (Colony Collapse Disorder) as hundreds of thousands of bees vanish without a trace. . . . Rotner and Woodhull offer a look at a variety of bees and other pollinators and a sample of the many products dependent on their efforts. . . . This title is eye-catching and informative." SLJ

Includes bibliographical references

Rustad, Martha E. H.
   Ants and aphids work together. Capstone Press 2011 24p il (Pebble Plus: animals working together) lib bdg $23.99; pa $6.95
Grades: K 1 2   **595.7**
1. Ants 2. Aphids 3. Symbiosis
ISBN 978-1-4296-5298-8 lib bdg; 1-4296-5298-5 lib bdg; 978-1-4296-6197-3 pa; 1-4296-6197-6 pa

LC 2010025460

Simple text and full-color photographs introduce the symbiotic relationship of ants and aphids.

In this series "the easy-to-understand examples are well selected to show of range of relationships in a variety of environments, and children will come away with some exposure to the concepts of 'parasite' and 'predator' as well." SLJ

Includes glossary and bibliographical references

Simon, Seymour
   ★ **Butterflies**. Collins 2011 30p il $17.99
Grades: 1 2 3 4   **595.7**
1. Butterflies
ISBN 978-0-06-191493-5; 0-06-191493-2

LC 2010032203

"Science writer Simon vividly explores the life cycles of butterflies and moths around the globe. . . . Simon's often breathtaking photographs offer closeup views of the insects, demonstrating color variations and their incredible transformations from pupa to adult moth or butterfly. Readers will be armed for the field with juicy vocabulary . . . and tantalizing anatomical descriptions to share." Publ Wkly

Singer, Marilyn, 1948-
   Caterpillars. EarlyLight Books 40p il $14.95
Grades: PreK K 1 2 3 4   **595.7**
1. Caterpillars
ISBN 978-0-9797455-7-7; 0-9797455-7-8

"This basic introduction to caterpillar reproduction, development, diet, survival, habitat, and anatomy is combined with powerfully clear photography that will captivate a wide audience. The book has two levels of text: simple capitalized red letters that swirl across the pages for the youngest readers to more complicated paragraphs easy enough for third or fourth graders to enjoy." SLJ

Siy, Alexandra
   Bug shots; the good, the bad, and the bugly. text and photography by Alexandra Siy; photomicrographs by Dennis Kunkel. Holiday House 2011 il $16.95

Grades: 3 4 5 6   **595.7**
  1. Insects
  ISBN 978-0-8234-2286-9; 0-8234-2286-0
                 LC 2010024063

"Insects are virtually on trial in this unusual introduction. The book begins by suggesting that readers 'Join the FBI-become a Fellow Bug Investigator' study the insects' 'mug shots,' read their 'rap sheets,' and decide if they are good or bad. After offering general information on classification, anatomy, numbers of species, etc., successive chapters focus on the 'suspects,' comprised of five large insect groups: true bugs; beetles; butterflies and moths; bees, ants, and wasps; and true flies. Each chapter describes the group's outstanding characteristics, as well as the distinctive physical and/or behavioral characteristics of representative species, their diet, harmful or beneficial effects on humans, and so on. . . . Photomicrographs of the insects or body parts illustrate the text on every page; all are brightly colored to highlight anatomical features. . . . The text is clearly written, and the photomicrographs are remarkably detailed." SLJ

★ **Mosquito** bite; [by] Alexandra Siy & Dennis Kunkel. Charlesbridge 2005 32p il $16.95; pa $6.95
Grades: 3 4 5   **595.7**
  1. Mosquitoes
  ISBN 1-57091-591-1; 1-57091-592-X pa
                 LC 2004-18959

"Black-and-white photographs of an evening game of hide-and-seek are interspersed with stunning color-enhanced microphotographs that record the life cycle of another seeker: a female Culex pipiens mosquito looking for a meal. . . . This title is fascinating for its photography and the informative text and captions." SLJ

Stewart, Melissa
  Ants. National Geographic 2010 32p il (National Geographic readers) $13.90; pa $3.99
Grades: 1 2 3   **595.7**
  1. Ants
  ISBN 978-1-4263-0609-9; 1-4263-0609-1; 978-1-4263-0608-2 pa; 1-4263-0608-3 pa
Describes different types of ants and their behavior.

  Butterfly or moth? how do you know? Enslow Publishers 2011 24p il (Which animal is which?) lib bdg $21.26; pa $6.95
Grades: 1 2 3   **595.7**
  1. Moths 2. Butterflies
  ISBN 978-0-7660-3678-9 lib bdg; 0-7660-3678-2 lib bdg; 978-1-59845-235-8 pa; 1-59845-235-5 pa
                 LC 2010003276

"This clearly written volume lays out the differences between butterflies and moths in double-page spreads that allow readers to compare the characteristics of the two animals. . . . The precisely worded, informative text is brief but does not simplify the facts. . . . Captions identify each species shown in the highly magnified, color photos." Booklist
  Includes bibliographical references

  How do bees make honey? Marshall Cavendish Benchmark 2009 32p il (Tell me why, tell me how) lib bdg $20.95

Grades: 3 4 5   **595.7**
  1. Bees 2. Honey
  ISBN 978-0-7614-2923-4 lib bdg; 0-7614-2923-9 lib bdg
                 LC 2007022935

"One or two large, well-captioned color photographs are provided per spread. [The] book concludes with an activity. [This is a] solid [introduction]." SLJ
  Includes glossary and bibliographical references

  Insect or spider? how do you know? Enslow Publishers 2011 24p il (Which animal is which?) lib bdg $21.26; pa $6.95
Grades: 1 2 3   **595.7**
  1. Insects 2. Spiders
  ISBN 978-0-7660-3681-9 lib bdg; 0-7660-3681-2 lib bdg; 978-1-59845-237-2 pa; 1-59845-237-1 pa
                 LC 2010003278

This describes the differences between insects and spiders.
This "should give budding naturalists an increased understanding of how scientists use appearance and behavior of classify sometimes-similar living things. . . . Spreads feature sharply detailed paired photographs of identified specimens seen from the same angle and at roughly equal size." SLJ
  Includes bibliographical references

Stradling, Jan
  ★ **Bugs** and spiders. Silver Dolphin Books 2009 90p il (The wonders inside) $19.95
Grades: 1 2 3 4   **595.7**
  1. Insects 2. Spiders
  ISBN 978-1-57145-907-7; 1-57145-907-3

This is a introduction to the life cycles and anatomy of a variety of insects and spiders
"The most outstanding innovation in the book consists of a series of five clear plastic overlays interspersed among the pages: these colorful overlays fit exactly over the figures on the page and bring out internal anatomic features. . . . The plethora of gorgeous drawings [is] accompanied by [an] easy-to-read, generally reliable, and highly informative text." Sci Books Films
  Includes glossary

Swanson, Diane
  Bugs up close; written by Diane Swanson; photographed by Paul Davidson. Kids Can Press 2008 40p il pa $16.95
Grades: 3 4 5 6   **595.7**
  1. Insects
  ISBN 978-1-55453-138-7 pa; 1-55453-138-1 pa

This describes "basic insect anatomy, major body parts and how they function, special adaptations of close to three dozen kinds of insects, egg-laying, metamorphosis, defense mechanisms, etc. . . . Most of the photos are so highly magnified that individual hairs, spines, and anatennae segments are clearly visible. . . . This attractive, informative overview will appeal to both browsers and budding entomologists." SLJ

Tait, Noel
  Insects & spiders. Simon & Schuster Books for Young Readers 2008 64p il map (Insiders) $16.99

Grades: 5 6 7 8   **595.7**

1. Insects 2. Spiders

ISBN 978-1-4169-3868-2; 1-4169-3868-0

LC 2008-61110

Provides an overview of insects and spiders in a book that includes detailed three-dimensional illustrations.

"Sharp, hyper-realistic, larger-than-life drawings . . . are . . . set against a plain colored background or within a natural setting. . . . [This] title succinctly describes basic anatomy; physical and behavioral characteristics common to all [insects and spiders]." SLJ

Includes glossary

Trueit, Trudi Strain

Ants; reading consultant, Nanci R. Vargus. Marshall Cavendish Benchmark 2009 23p il (Benchmark rebus. Creepy critters) lib bdg $22.79

Grades: PreK K 1   **595.7**

1. Ants

ISBN 978-0-7614-3961-5; 0-7614-3961-7

LC 2008-12152

"Brilliant close-up photos will help beginning readers make meaning and appeal to students who like these creatures. . . . Glossary, print and media resources for further learning, and an about the author section conclude . . . [the] book. Reading specialists will want to be advised about [this book] . . . as will teachers. . . . This . . . is an excellent resource for beginning research projects." Libr Media Connect

Includes glossary and bibliographical references

Beetles. Marshall Cavendish Benchmark 2010 23p il (Benchmark rebus. Creepy critters) lib bdg $22.79

Grades: PreK K 1   **595.7**

1. Beetles

ISBN 978-0-7614-3962-2; 0-7614-3962-5

LC 2008-23153

"Brilliant closeup photos will help beginning readers make meaning and appeal to students who like these creatures. . . . Glossary, print and media resources for further learning, and an about the author section conclude . . . [the] book. Reading specialists will want to be advised about [this book] . . . as will teachers. . . . This . . . is an excellent resource for beginning research projects." Libr Media Connect

Includes glossary and bibliographical references

Caterpillars. Marshall Cavendish Benchmark 2009 23p il (Benchmark rebus. Creepy critters) lib bdg $22.79

Grades: PreK K 1   **595.7**

1. Caterpillars

ISBN 978-0-7614-3963-9 lib bdg; 0-7614-3963-3 lib bdg

LC 2008-17108

"Brilliant closeup photos will help beginning readers make meaning and appeal to students who like these creatures. . . . Glossary, print and media resources for further learning, and an about the author section conclude . . . [the] book. Reading specialists will want to be advised about [this book] . . . as will teachers. . . . This . . . is an excellent resource for beginning research projects." Libr Media Connect

Includes glossary and bibliographical references

Grasshoppers. Marshall Cavendish Benchmark 2009 23p il (Benchmark rebus. Creepy critters) lib bdg $22.79

Grades: PreK K 1   **595.7**

1. Grasshoppers

ISBN 978-0-7614-3964-6 lib bdg; 0-7614-3964-1 lib bdg

LC 2008-24210

"Brilliant closeup photos will help beginning readers make meaning and appeal to students who like these creatures. . . . Glossary, print and media resources for further learning, and an about the author section conclude . . . [the] book. Reading specialists will want to be advised about [this book] . . . as will teachers. . . . This . . . is an excellent resource for beginning research projects." Publisher's note

Includes glossary and bibliographical references

VanCleave, Janice Pratt, 1942-

Janice VanCleave's insects and spiders; mind-boggling experiments you can turn into science fair projects. Wiley 1998 92p il (Spectacular science projects series) pa $10.95

Grades: 4 5 6 7   **595.7**

1. Insects 2. Spiders 3. Science projects 4. Science -- Experiments 5. Entomology projects -- Juvenile literature

ISBN 0-471-16396-1

LC 97-12595

Presents facts about insects and spiders and includes experiments, projects, and activities related to each topic

"This title is chock-full of meaningful, but not difficult, projects. . . . Clear line drawings illustrate the text on almost every page. . . . The lucid text is well organized and liberally sprinkled with safety warnings." SLJ

Includes glossary and bibliographical references

Voake, Steve

★ Insect detective; illustrated by Charlotte Voake. Candlewick Press 2010 28p il $16.99; pa $6.99

Grades: K 1 2 3   **595.7**

1. Insects

ISBN 978-0-7636-4447-5; 1-4063-1051-4; 978-0-7636-5816-8 pa

LC 2009-11152

"This charming collaboration . . . gently encourages young readers to explore their natural surroundings and observe some of the more commonly found insects in it. In spare prose, brief facts about a variety of creatures, such as leaf-miner caterpillars, ground beetles, ants, earwigs, and dragonflies, are shared, as are hints on where and how to find them. . . . Simple but elegant pen and watercolor illustrations show the creatures in their habitats." SLJ

Webster, Christine

Mosquitoes. Weigl 2010 24p il (Backyard animals) $24.45; pa $8.95

Grades: 1 2 3   **595.7**

1. Mosquitoes

ISBN 978-1-60596-086-9; 1-60596-086-1; 978-1-60596-087-6 pa; 1-60596-087-X pa

LC 2009004447

This is "packed with information and [includes] fine close-up photos." Booklist

Includes glossary

Werner, Sharon

Bugs by the numbers; facts and figures for multiple types of bugbeasties. by Sharon Werner and Sarah Forss. Blue Apple Books 2011 un il $19.99
Grades: 2 3 4   **595.7**
1. Insects 2. Counting
ISBN 978-1-60905-061-0; 1-60905-061-4
LC 2010046644

Provides readers with facts about bugs and other creepy-crawlers while introducing the concept of numbers and counting.

"Werner and Forss use 1s, 2s, and 3s, to distinguish between an ant's head, thorax, and abdomen; a mosquito consists of 75s . . . ; and a group of ladybugs are made up of numerals that correspond to the number of spots on their wings. Add in several liftable flaps and a wealth of facts about the featured species, and this duo has another winner on their hands." Publ Wkly

Wilson, J. V.

Bumblebee. Frances Lincoln 2011 il $16.95
Grades: K 1 2 3   **595.7**
1. Bees
ISBN 1847800084; 1-84780-008-4

"The pastoral life of a bumblebee queen. Her yearly cycle begins on the first day of spring, when she sleepily flies in search of food and a nest. . . . On the last day of summer, 'the old bumblebee queen flies out of her wonderful nest for the last time.' And in the autumn, all the new queens fly out to find drones to mate with before settling into another winter of sleep. Wilson's narrative is crisp and concise. . . . Kennaway's watercolors are straightforward and mostly realistic in their particulars. A valuable page about 'Helping bumblebees' and a glossary conclude the book. Informative and, in its way, lovely." Kirkus

Includes glossary

Winnick, Nick

Butterflies. Weigl Publishers 2010 24p il (World of wonder: watch them grow) lib bdg $25.70; pa $9.95
Grades: 1 2   **595.7**
1. Butterflies
ISBN 978-1-60596-928-2 lib bdg; 1-60596-928-1 lib bdg; 978-1-60596-929-9 pa; 1-60596-929-X pa
LC 2009052102

Learn about the fascinating transition these insects make from egg to caterpillar, pupa, and finally, colorful butterfly.

The text "is simple without being simplistic; it is thoughtful and comprehensive without being overwhelming. The real appeal for teachers, students, and independent young readers, however, will be the photographs that fill the facing pages. Bold, bright, and colorful, the photographs bring you marvelously close to the subject. . . . On many different levels, this is a very appealing [book]." Libr Media Connect

Includes glossary

595.76 Beetles

Gibbons, Gail

Ladybugs; by Gail Gibbons. Holiday House 2012 32 p. col. ill., col. map (hardcover) $17.95

Grades: K 1 2   **595.76**
1. Ladybugs 2. Beneficial insects 3. Picture books for children 4. Ladybugs -- Juvenile literature
ISBN 0823423689; 9780823423682
LC 2011014700

This book is about ladybugs. It features illustrations done in "watercolors, enhanced with black ink outline and detail and some crayon highlighting . . . Half of the illustrations include one or more brief notes and/or labels in addition to the oversize text. [Gail] Gibbons identifies the small beetle's body parts; shows some species of ladybugs from around the world; details the four stages of its life cycle; and discusses its usefulness to farmers and how it protects itself from predators and cold weather. Appended are some additional facts (e.g., "Ladybugs can swim") and the National Geographic websites for the U.S. and Canada." (School Library Journal)

Jenkins, Steve

The beetle book; Steve Jenkins. Houghton Mifflin Books for Children 2011 31 p. $16.99
Grades: 4 5 6 7   **595.76**
1. Beetles 2. Ecology -- Encyclopedias 3. Insects -- Encyclopedias 4. Beetles -- Juvenile literature
ISBN 9780547680842
LC 2011027129

This nonfiction natural history book presents pictures and information about an "array of beetles." Author/illustrator Steve Jenkins describes "the colors and patterns of this ubiquitous insect . . . [and] the details about the various adaptations that beetles have made over millennia in response to their environment, diet, and predators." Jenkins claims that "one out of four creatures on the planet is a beetle." (Kirkus Reviews)

Smith, Siân

Ladybugs; Sian Smith. Raintree 2013 24 p. (paperback) $8.95
Grades: PreK K   **595.76**
1. Ladybugs 2. Picture books for children 3. Ladybugs -- Juvenile literature
ISBN 1410948226; 9781410948090; 9781410948229
LC 2011041230

This children's picture book by Sian Smith "introduces readers to ladybugs. The text is presented in . . . rhyming patterns" and includes photographs. It is part of the Creepy Critters series, which "gives readers an up close and personal view of some of their favorite creepy critters." (Publisher's note)

Includes bibliographical references and index

Walker, Sally M.

Fireflies. Lerner Publs. 2001 47p il (Early bird nature books) lib bdg $22.60
Grades: K 1 2 3   **595.76**
1. Fireflies 2. Fireflies -- Juvenile literature
ISBN 0-8225-3047-3

Describes the physical characteristics, behavior and life cycle of fireflies

"The text is well organized and clearly written. . . . One or two good-quality color photographs or diagrams with informative captions appear on almost every page." SLJ

595.78 Moths and butterflies

Aston, Dianna

★ A **butterfly** is patient; by Dianna Aston; illustrated by Sylvia Long. Chronicle Books 2011 40 p. col. ill., col. maps $16.99

Grades: 1 2 **595.78**

1. Butterflies 2. Insects -- Metamorphosis 3. Picture books for children 4. Insects -- Juvenile literature
ISBN 0811864790; 9780811864794

LC 2010008548

This picture book "offers specific and accurate descriptions of metamorphosis, pollination, camouflage, migration and other butterfly features and functions, along with the differences between butterflies and moths. Imagination-stretching comparisons-'monarchs weigh only as much as a few rose petals,' the wingspan of the Arian Small Blue is 'about the length of a grain of rice'--lend wings to the body of facts, and though the author avoids direct mention of reproduction or death, a quick closing recapitulation that harks back to the opening page's hatching egg provides [a] . . . hint of life's cyclical pattern. . . . [Illustrator Sylvia] Long depicts dozens of caterpillars and butterflies, each one posed to best advantage, unobtrusively labeled." (Kirkus)

"Aston explores the development, habits, migration, and attributes of one of nature's flashier, yet familiar creations. Long's watercolors are precise but enchanting as ever. . . . A lovely mix of science and wonder." Publ Wkly

Ehlert, Lois

★ **Waiting** for wings. Harcourt 2001 un il $17

Grades: PreK K 1 2 **595.78**

1. Butterflies 2. Stories in rhyme 3. Butterfly gardens
ISBN 0-15-202608-8

LC 00-9765

Eggs clinging to leaves become caterpillars which become butterflies which lay their eggs

"A brief rhyming text and cheery tone invite readers to explore the full and half pages that form this brilliantly designed book-within-a book." Publ Wkly

Gibbons, Gail

Monarch butterfly. Holiday House 1989 un il $16.95; pa $6.95

Grades: K 1 2 3 **595.78**

1. Butterflies
ISBN 0-8234-0773-X; 0-8234-0909-0 pa

LC 89-1880

"Large-scale paintings, clearly detailed, and a simply written, sequential text describe the life cycle of the monarch butterfly and its migratory patterns. This is Gibbons at her best, providing information in a text that is cohesive and comprehensible." Bull Cent Child Books

Heiligman, Deborah

From caterpillar to butterfly; illustrated by Bari Weissman. HarperCollins Pubs. 1996 31p il (Let's-read-and-find-out science) $15.95; pa $4.95

Grades: K 1 **595.78**

1. Butterflies 2. Caterpillars 3. Butterflies -- Juvenile literature 4. Caterpillars -- Juvenile literature
ISBN 0-06-024264-7; 0-06-024268-X lib bdg; 0-06-445129-1 pa

LC 93-39055

Young children observe the metamorphosis of a caterpillar into a butterfly in a jar in their classroom

"Pen-and-ink and watercolor illustrations create a cheerful setting. . . . A small collection of butterflies commonly found in most parts of the U.S. and a list of addresses of butterfly centers are appended. An inviting book that young children can relate to and one that teachers will find valuable to support nature-study projects." SLJ

Marsh, Laura

Caterpillar to butterfly; Laura Marsh. National Geographic 2012 32 p.

Grades: K 1 2 **595.78**

1. Butterflies 2. Caterpillars 3. Insects -- Metamorphosis 4. Butterflies -- Juvenile literature 5. Caterpillars -- Juvenile literature
ISBN 1426309201; 142630921X; 9781426309205; 9781426309212

LC 2011277485

Author Laura March describes the transformation from caterpillars to butterflies, focusing on the wingspan, colors, and wing patterns of butterflies. "This level 1 Reader gives kids an up-close look at exactly how a caterpillar becomes a butterfly. . . . [The book also includes] bonus information including different types of butterflies and poisonous caterpillars." (Publisher's note)

Pasternak, Carol

How to raise monarch butterflies; a step-by-step guide for kids. Carol Pasternak. Firefly Books 2012 48 p. col. ill. (bound) $19.95

Grades: 3 4 5 6 7 **595.78**

1. Caterpillars 2. Insects -- Care 3. Monarch butterflies 4. Monarch butterfly -- Juvenile literature 5. Monarch butterfly -- Life cycles -- Juvenile literature
ISBN 1770850015; 1770850023; 9781770850019; 9781770850026

LC 2012419489

This book by Carol Pasternak presents a "detailed guide to locating and hatching. . . Monarch butterflies. . . . [R]eaders will learn about the life cycle of the Monarch and how to encourage populations in their own backyards, with tips on which plants to grow, as well as the care and feeding of their pet caterpillars. 'How to Raise Monarch Butterflies' explains what threats face Monarchs and how readers can help conserve the Monarch's feeding grounds from encroachment." (Publisher's note)

Includes bibliographical references and index.

Whalley, Paul Ernest Sutton

Butterfly & moth; written by Paul Whalley; [special photography, Colin Keates, Kim Taylor, and Dave King] Dorling Kindersley 2000 63p il (DK eyewitness books) $15.99; lib bdg $19.99

Grades: 4 5 6 7 **595.78**

1. Moths 2. Butterflies
ISBN 0-7894-5832-2; 0-7894-6556-6 lib bdg
First published 1988 by Knopf

Photographs and text explore the behavior and life cycles of butterflies and moths, examining mating rituals, camouflage, habitat, growth from pupa to larva to adult, and other aspects

595.79 Hymenoptera

Cole, Joanna

★ The **magic** school bus inside a beehive; illustrated by Bruce Degen. Scholastic 1996 47p il hardcover o.p. pa $4.99

Grades: 2 3 4   **595.79**

1. Bees 2. Honey -- Juvenile literature

ISBN 0-590-44684-3; 0-590-025721-8 pa

LC 95-38288

Ms. Frizzle "introduces her class to the insect kingdom via an excursion through a honeybee hive. Garbed in bee costumes complete with antennae, and sprayed with the proper pheromones, the students are accepted by the workers and allowed to perform such chores as foraging for nectar and pollen, building honeycombs, making honey, and feeding larvae. . . . A plethora of pseudo school reports provide additional information on the topic. Degen's colorful and amusing cartoons heighten the adventures. Clearly written and well organized." SLJ

Micucci, Charles

★ The **life** and times of the ant. Houghton Mifflin 2003 32p hardcover o.p. pa $6.95

Grades: 2 3 4   **595.79**

1. Ants 2. Ants -- Juvenile literature

ISBN 0-618-00559-5; 0-618-68949-4 pa

LC 2002-478

Describes the evolution, physical characteristics, behavior, and social nature of ants

This "offers succinct text and an impressive amount of information presented in an attractive, picture-book format." Booklist

Includes bibliographical references

★ The **life** and times of the honeybee. Ticknor & Fields Bks. for Young Readers 1995 32p il hardcover o.p. pa $6.95

Grades: 2 3 4   **595.79**

1. Bees 2. Honey

ISBN 0-395-86139-X pa

LC 93-8135

"The multitude of original watercolors bring the subject to life, provide a sense of scale and amplify the text. . . . A must acquisition for a library." Appraisal

Rissman, Rebecca

Ants; Rebecca Rissman. Raintree 2013 24 p. (lib. bdg.) $24.50

Grades: PreK K   **595.79**

1. Ants 2. Animal behavior 3. Insects -- Behavior 4. Ants -- Juvenile literature

ISBN 1410948013; 1410948145; 9781410948014; 9781410948144

LC 2011038864

This "book uses . . . rhymes and . . . images to teach readers about ants." (Publisher's note) "'Ants' begins with counting exercises that use both body segments and legs, before showing off cool photos of differently colored ants, ants marching in rows, and . . . a nest of larvae." It "concludes with a two-page exercise involving finding the titular insects within a cartoon landscape." (Booklist)

Includes bibliographical references and index.

Bees; Rebecca Rissman. Raintree 2013 24 p. (lib. bdg.) $24.50

Grades: PreK K   **595.79**

1. Bees 2. Picture books for children 3. Bees -- Juvenile literature

ISBN 1410948021; 1410948153; 9781410948021; 9781410948151

LC 2011038869

This book is part of the Creepy Critters series, which offers "readers an up close and personal view of some of their favorite creepy critters! This book introduces readers to bees. The text is presented in . . . rhyming patterns." A "cartoon-like design combined with . . . photos" is meant to be "visually appealing for young readers." (Publishers Weekly)

Includes bibliographical references and index.

596 Chordates

Bishop, Nic, 1955-

Spiders; written and photographed by Nic Bishop. Scholastic 2012 32 p. $3.99

Grades: K 1 2   **596**

1. Spiders -- Juvenile literature

ISBN 0545237572; 9780545237574

This book by Nic Bishop adapts his 2007 book of the same title for younger readers. "Designed for independent readers in first and second grades, the current book offers a completely new text that is shorter, simpler, and printed in larger type. Like its predecessor, the book discusses spiders' physical features, behaviors, and life cycles, and it provides illustrations of different species, which are clearly identified." (Booklist)

597 Cold-blooded vertebrates

Arnosky, Jim

All about sharks. Scholastic Press 2003 un il $15.95; pa $5.95

Grades: K 1 2 3   **597**

1. Sharks

ISBN 0-590-48166-5; 0-545-02600-8 pa

LC 2002-67004

Describes the physical characteristics, behavior, and survival techniques of different kinds of sharks

"Different species and families are illustrated in simple drawings, and the various parts of a shark's body are labeled and explained in a basic, easy-to-read text." SLJ

Bodden, Valerie

Sharks. Creative Education 2010 24p il (Amazing animals) lib bdg $24.25

Grades: K 1 2   **597**

1. Sharks

ISBN 978-1-58341-812-3 lib bdg; 1-58341-812-1 lib bdg

LC 2009002715

A basic exploration of the appearance, behavior, and habitat of sharks, the feared fishes of the sea. Also included is a story from folklore explaining why sharks have a bump on their heads.

This is illustrated with "dynamically colored photographs." Booklist

Includes bibliographical references

Butterworth, Christine

★ Sea horse; the shyest fish in the sea. [by] Chris Butterworth; illustrated by John Lawrence. Candlewick Press 2006 27p il $16.99; pa $6.99

Grades: K 1 2   597

1. Sea horses

ISBN 978-0-7636-2989-2; 0-7636-2989-8; 978-0-7636-4140-5 pa; 0-7636-4140-5 pa

LC 2005-50755

"Pairing a central narrative about a male Barbour's sea horse with facts in smaller type, Butterworth first pinpoints the creatures' most immediately appealing attributes . . . then goes on to discuss the males' gestational role in reproduction and survival tactics of newly independent offspring. . . . Butterworth has a flair for dynamic writing. . . . Lawrence has created vinyl engravings that masterfully capture the delicate textures of sea horses' graceful, spiny bodies and of their undersea habitats." Booklist

Catt, Thessaly

Migrating with the salmon. PowerKids Press 2011 24p il map (Animal journeys) lib bdg $21.25; pa $8.25

Grades: 2 3 4   597

1. Salmon 2. Animals -- Migration

ISBN 978-1-4488-2545-5 lib bdg; 1-4488-2545-8 lib bdg; 978-1-4488-2674-2 pa; 1-4488-2674-8 pa

LC 2010029655

Learn about the life cycle and migration patterns of the salmon.

"Keywords are bolded throughout and can be found in the glossary. The format is attractive with inset captioned photographs and page heading that seem to move across the page." Libr Media Connect

Includes glossary

Cerullo, Mary M.

The truth about great white sharks; written by Mary M. Cerullo; photographs by Jeffrey L. Rotman; illustrations by Michael Wertz. Chronicle Bks. 2000 48p il hardcover o.p. $14.95

Grades: 4 5 6 7   597

1. Sharks

ISBN 0-8118-2467-5; 0-8118-5759-X pa

LC 00-31506

This provides information "about shark anatomy, senses, eating habits, and their relationships with humans. . . . The book also contains unusual information such as how these fish are measured and photographed and why they are not able to survive in an aquarium. The attractive layout blends line drawings, full-color photographs, varied typefaces, and eye-catching graphics. Rotman's pictures are clear and informative. . . . This title will be accessible to reluctant readers and is a must for most collections." SLJ

Includes bibliographical references

Coldiron, Deborah

Eels; by Deborah Coldiron. ABDO Pub. 2008 32p il (Underwater world) lib bdg $24.21

Grades: 2 3 4   597

1. Eels

ISBN 978-1-59928-818-5 lib bdg; 1-59928-818-4 lib bdg

LC 2007-14850

"The captioned photographs are engaging. . . . 'Fast Facts' appear on some pages. . . . Provide[s] solid information for elementary school reports." Horn Book Guide

Includes glossary

Stingrays; by Deborah Coldiron. ABDO Pub. 2008 32p il (Underwater world) lib bdg $24.21

Grades: 2 3 4   597

1. Rays (Fishes)

ISBN 978-1-59928-817-8 lib bdg; 1-59928-817-6 lib bdg

LC 2007-14856

"The captioned photographs are engaging. . . . 'Fast Facts' appear on some pages. . . . Provide[s] solid information for elementary school reports." Horn Book Guide

Includes glossary

Curtis, Jennifer Keats

Seahorses; Jennifer Keats Curtis; illustrated by Chad Wallace. Henry Holt 2012 32 p.

Grades: 1 2 3   597

1. Sea horses -- Juvenile literature

ISBN 0805092390; 9780805092394

LC 2011034059

In this children's book by Jennifer Keats Curtis, illustrated by Chad Wallace, "a baby seahorse is born, turning and tumbling as he floats through ocean currents alongside his three hundred brothers and sisters. . . . [H]e changes color to fit in with the surroundings of his spectacular coral reef and sea grass surroundings; his lizard-like eyes can look in two directions at once; and when he has grown, he -- not the female -- will give birth to the next batch of whirling seahorses." (Publisher's note)

Includes bibliographical references

De la Bedoyere, Camilla

Sharks. Silver Dolphin 2009 24p il (Action files) $15.95

Grades: K 1 2 3   597

1. Sharks

ISBN 978-1-59223-933-7; 1-59223-933-1

"This lively interactive guide . . . delivers plenty of highly accessible shark-related information in tabbed chapters that cover anatomy , . . . shark life and conservation issues." Publ Wkly

Doubilet, David

★ Face to face with sharks; by David Doubilet and Jennifer Hayes. National Geographic 2009 31p il (Face to face) $16.95; lib bdg $25.90

Grades: 3 4 5 6   597

1. Sharks

ISBN 978-1-4263-0404-0; 1-4263-0404-8; 978-1-4263-0405-7 lib bdg; 1-4263-0405-6 lib bdg

LC 2008038244

The authors describe the life cycle and behavior of sharks and their own experiences with sharks in the wild

Includes glossary and bibliographical references

Ganeri, Anita

Piranha. Heinemann Library 2011 24p il map (A day in the life. Rain forest animals) lib bdg $22; pa $6.49

Grades: 1 2　　　　　　　　　　　　　　　　**597**

1. Piranhas

ISBN 978-1-4329-4108-6 lib bdg; 1-4329-4108-9 lib bdg; 978-1-4329-4119-2 pa; 1-4329-4119-4 pa

LC 2010000969

This book follows a piranha through its day as it sleeps, eats, and moves.

"Ganeri presents information clearly and simply in large type, two-sentence comments placed below a bright, sharply reproduced color photograph of the animal in a natural setting. . . . [This is] sufficiently specific to support assignment as well as pleasure reading." SLJ

Includes glossary and bibliographical references

Gibbons, Gail

Sharks. Holiday House 1992 un il $16.95; pa $6.95

Grades: K 1 2 3　　　　　　　　　　　　　　**597**

1. Sharks

ISBN 0-8234-0960-0; 0-8234-1068-4 pa

LC 91-31524

Describes shark behavior and different kinds of sharks

The author's "bold, appealing illustrations (many of them labeled and explained) are the strength of the presentation. An excellent choice for even the youngest shark fan, this will be useful for simple reports as well." Booklist

Gray, Susan Heinrichs

Walking catfish; by Susan H. Gray. Cherry Lake Pub. 2009 32p il map (Animal invaders) lib bdg $27.07

Grades: 3 4 5　　　　　　　　　　　　　　　**597**

1. Catfish 2. Biological invasions

ISBN 978-1-60279-242-5 lib bdg; 1-60279-242-9 lib bdg

LC 2008000804

"Clear color photographs, most of which are closeups, accompany the [text] on about every other page. . . . [This title provides] report writers with in-depth and up-to-date information on these invaders and the serious problems they cause." SLJ

Includes glossary and bibliographical references

Hamilton, Sue L.

Eaten by a shark; [by] Sue Hamilton. ABDO Pub. 2010 32p il (Close encounters of the wild kind) lib bdg $22.61

Grades: 4 5 6 7　　　　　　　　　　　　　　**597**

1. Sharks 2. Animal attacks

ISBN 978-1-60453-931-8 lib bdg; 1-60453-931-3 lib bdg

LC 2009-37230

In this volume, readers learn of actual human-wildlife encounters, creature information, survival strategies, and attack statistics.

"Students will be drawn to the realistic full-color photographs, the realistic diagrams of the creatures' bodies, the real-life stories told by victims, and the interesting, attractive formatting that includes text, diagrams, photographs, and graphics on each page. . . . [This is] exciting and attractive in a 'gross' sort of way and will appeal particularly to boys for both leisure reading and research." Libr Media Connect

Includes glossary

Markle, Sandra

Great white sharks; by Sandra Markle. Carolrhoda Books 2004 40p il (Animal predators) lib bdg $25.26; pa $7.95

Grades: 3 4 5 6　　　　　　　　　　　　　　**597**

1. Sharks 2. White shark -- Juvenile literature

ISBN 1-57505-731-X lib bdg; 1-57505-747-6 pa

LC 2003-23180

"The role of camouflage is aptly explained in flowing text and illustrated in clear photography. . . . The full-color photography bedazzles on almost every page." SLJ

Includes bibliographical references

Miller, Sara Swan

Seahorses, pipefishes, and their kin; Sara Swan Miller. Franklin Watts 2002 47 p. col. ill. (library) $26.50; (paperback) $6.95

Grades: 4 5 6　　　　　　　　　　　　　　　**597**

1. Picture books for children 2. Marine biology -- Juvenile literature 3. Marine animals 4. Gasterosteiformes 5. Gasterosteiformes -- Juvenile literature

ISBN 9780531121719; 0531163792; 9780531163795

LC 2001003034

This book by Sara Swan Miller is part of the Animals in Order series and looks at seahorses, pipefishes, and related animals. "These colorful series entries present a wide variety of creatures that have been sorted by scientific classification into similar groupings called orders . . . . Family names, common names, genus, species, size, and/or location are given, and paragraphs describe various behaviors (food gathering, courtship, etc.)." (School Library Journal)

Includes bibliographical references (p. 46) and index.

Musgrave, Ruth

Everything sharks; all the shark facts, photos, and fun that you can sink your teeth into. National Geographic 2011 64p il (National Geographic kids) lib bdg $25.90; pa $12.95

Grades: 3 4 5 6　　　　　　　　　　　　　　**597**

1. Sharks

ISBN 978-1-4263-0802-4 lib bdg; 1-4263-0802-7 lib bdg; 978-1-4263-0769-0 pa; 1-4263-0769-1 pa

LC 2010049108

This offers facts and photos of sharks, and scientists' tales about encounters with sharks.

"Exploding with astounding full-color photographs and written in an appealing conversational tone, [this book is] for every kid. . . . The [text] will keep kids interested and turning pages to discover more and more facts. . . . [This] compelling, browseable, and completely engrossing [title] will delight readers." SLJ

Includes glossary and bibliographical references

Pfeffer, Wendy

What's it like to be a fish? illustrated by Holly Keller. HarperCollins Pubs. 1996 32p il (Let's-read-and-find-out science) hardcover o.p. pa $4.95

Grades: K 1　　　　　　　　　　　　　　　　**597**

1. Fishes 2. Goldfish

ISBN 0-06-024429-1 lib bdg; 0-06-445151-8 pa

LC 94-6543

"By comparing goldfish to wild fish and human beings, this book describes the basic physiology of fish. The colorful illustrations are done in watercolors and pastels. . . . In a very accessible narrative that flows from point to point, the basic external anatomy of fish and such behaviors as movement, breathing, eating, and maintenance of temperature are defined in terms of caring for a goldfish in a bowl." Sci Books Films

Pringle, Laurence P.

Sharks!: strange and wonderful; by Laurence Pringle; illustrated by Meryl Henderson. Boyds Mills Press 2001 32p il $15.95

Grades: 3 4 5   597

1. Sharks

ISBN 1-56397-863-6

"Basic information about sharks—including physical characteristics, feeding habits, and their role in the chain of ocean life—is presented in clear, accessible prose. The acrylic paintings serve as a veritable catalog showcasing the variety of known sharks." Horn Book Guide

Rockwell, Anne F.

Little shark; [by] Anne Rockwell; pictures by Megan Halsey. Walker & Co. 2005 un il $15.95; lib bdg $16.85

Grades: K 1 2   597

1. Sharks 2. Sharks -- Juvenile literature

ISBN 0-8027-8955-2; 0-8027-8956-0 lib bdg

LC 2004-52611

"Rockwell invites her readers to follow a newborn shark pup as it grows, explores its ocean home on its own, and develops at last into an adult blue shark. Strung throughout the narrative . . . are interesting facts about shark physiology, behaviors, and deep-sea dangers. . . . The whole is decorated with soft watercolor-and-pencil collage illustrations that are both attractive and . . . informative." SLJ

Rodriguez, Ana Maria

Secret of the suffocating slime trap . . . and more! Enslow Publishers 2008 48p il (Animal secrets revealed!) lib bdg $23.93

Grades: 5 6 7 8   597

1. Fishes

ISBN 978-0-7660-2954-5 lib bdg; 0-7660-2954-9 lib bdg

LC 2007039493

This book offers "fascinating accounts of how scientists systematically analyzed, tested, and proved their theories or how their findings led to other, serendipitous discoveries. . . . Science experiments are thoughtfully placed to inspire exploration, and captioned, full-color photos appear throughout." SLJ

Includes glossary and bibliographical references

Rustad, Martha E. H.

Clown fish and sea anemones work together. Capstone Press 2011 24p il (Pebble Plus: animals working together) lib bdg $23.99; pa $6.95

Grades: K 1 2   597

1. Anemones 2. Clownfish 3. Symbiosis

ISBN 978-1-4296-5297-1 lib bdg; 1-4296-5297-7 lib bdg; 978-1-4296-6198-0 pa; 1-4296-6198-4 pa

LC 2010025462

Simple text and full-color photographs introduce the symbiotic relationship of clown fish and sea anemones.

In this series "the easy-to-understand examples are well selected to show of range of relationships in a variety of environments, and children will come away with some exposure to the concepts of 'parasite' and 'predator' as well." SLJ

Includes glossary and bibliographical references

Moray eels and cleaner shrimp work together. Capstone Press 2011 24p il (Pebble Plus: animals working together) lib bdg $23.99; pa $6.95

Grades: K 1 2   597

1. Eels 2. Shrimps 3. Symbiosis

ISBN 978-1-4296-5299-5 lib bdg; 1-4296-5299-3 lib bdg; 978-1-4296-6199-7 pa; 1-4296-6199-2 pa

This describes the lives of moray eels and cleaner shrimp and how they work together to survive.

In this series "the easy-to-understand examples are well selected to show of range of relationships in a variety of environments, and children will come away with some exposure to the concepts of 'parasite' and 'predator' as well." SLJ

Simon, Seymour

★ Sharks. HarperCollins Pubs. 1995 un il $16.95; pa $6.95

Grades: 2 3 4   597

1. Sharks

ISBN 0-06-023029-0; 0-06-446187-4 pa

LC 95-1593

The author "explores the fascinating undersea life of sharks, examining the truths and myths about these amazing creatures. Astounding close-up photographs enhance the informative and exciting text." Sci Child

Stewart, Melissa

Shark or dolphin? how do you know? Enslow Publishers 2011 24p il (Which animal is which?) lib bdg $21.26; pa $6.95

Grades: 1 2 3   597

1. Sharks 2. Dolphins

ISBN 978-0-7660-3680-2 lib bdg; 0-7660-3680-4 lib bdg; 978-1-59845-239-6 pa; 1-59845-239-8 pa

LC 2010003280

This describes the differences between sharks and dolphin.

This "should give budding naturalists an increased understanding of how scientists use appearance and behavior of classify sometimes-similar living things. . . . Spreads feature sharply detailed paired photographs of identified specimens seen from the same angle and at roughly equal size." SLJ

Includes bibliographical references

A place for fish; written by Melissa Stewart; illustrated by Higgins Bond. Peachtree 2011 un il map $16.95

Grades: K 1 2 3   597

1. Fishes 2. Wildlife conservation

ISBN 978-1-56145-562-1; 1-56145-562-8

"Environmental threats facing fish in various habitats around the world are introduced in a picture-book, read-aloud format. . . . Sidebars briefly describe a species affected by the threat and actions that can be taken to resolve it. Each entry repeats the same phrase, 'fish can live and grow.' The information is presented in a simple and idealistic way for young readers. The full-color illustrations on every page are very detailed, but some of the fish have humanlike eyes." SLJ

Stille, Darlene R.

The **life** cycle of fish. Heinemann Library 2011 48p il (Life cycles) lib bdg $35; pa $8.95

Grades: 3 4 5   **597**

1. Fishes

ISBN 978-1-4329-4980-8 lib bdg; 978-1-4329-4987-7 pa

LC 2010038278

This describes what a fish is, types of fishes, their life cycles, habitats, foods, defenses, and relationships to humans.

Includes glossary and bibliographical references

Stockdale, Susan

★ **Fabulous** fishes; written and illustrated by Susan Stockdale. Peachtree 2008 un il $15.95

Grades: PreK K 1 2 3   **597**

1. Fishes 2. Fishes -- Juvenile literature

ISBN 978-1-56145-429-7; 1-56145-429-X

LC 2007-29749

"With simple, rhyming text and full-page illustrations in acrylic and collage, this picture book introduces dramatic facts about more than 20 different fishes. . . . Young children will enjoy pointing out the various fish in the illustrations, while older children will switch back and forth from the pictures to the fascinating biological facts about fish behavior, habitat, and camouflage gathered in notes at the back." Booklist

Swinney, Geoff

Fish facts; illustrated by Janeen Mason. Pelican Pub. Co. 2011 48p il $17.99

Grades: 5 6 7 8   **597**

1. Fishes

ISBN 978-1-58980-908-6; 1-58980-908-4

LC 2010046220

"This comprehensive collection of facts about fish is sure to educate as well as fascinate. . . . From fish that produce light and fish that are capable of powered flight, to fish that can change sex and fish that carry their offspring in their mouths, this is chock full of both the amazing and the weird. . . . While the rather advanced vocabulary and biology that Swinney delves into mark this as a book for older readers, younger ones can certainly enjoy both the illustrations and the occasional factoid. Mason's artwork is both painstakingly detailed and realistically colored, even down to the muting effect that water has on colors. Few books come close to this one's inclusiveness." Kirkus

Turner, Pamela S.

★ **Project** Seahorse; [photographs by Scott Tuason] Houghton Mifflin Harcourt 2010 56p il (Scientists in the field) $18

Grades: 4 5 6 7   **597**

1. Sea horses 2. Fishing -- Juvenile literature 3. Young adult literature -- Works 4. Sea horses -- Juvenile literature 5. Ecology -- Philippines -- Juvenile literature

ISBN 978-0-547-20713-1; 0-547-20713-1

LC 2009-49707

"With striking images of coral-reef inhabitants, this photo-essay introduces Project Seahorse, an international effort to protect and rehabilitate the Danajon Bank, a double reef off a Philippine Island where seahorses once flourished . . . Tuason, a noted Asian marine photographer whose specialty is the Philippines, seems equally adept at photographing the

land and people and the underwater world. This is another splendid demonstration of the work of Scientists in the Field." Kirkus

Walker, Sally M.

Rays. Carolrhoda Bks. 2003 48p il (Carolrhoda nature watch book) lib bdg $23.93

Grades: 3 4 5 6   **597**

1. Rays (Fishes) 2. Endangered species 3. Rays (Fishes) -- Juvenile literature

ISBN 1-57505-172-9

LC 2001-6586

Describes the physical characteristics, behavior, life cycle, and endangered status of rays

"The crisp, well-captioned color photos highlight the many varieties of this unusual fish. Information is presented clearly." Horn Book Guide

Includes glossary

Wallace, Karen

Think of an eel; illustrated by Mike Bostock. Candlewick Press 1993 un il hardcover o.p. pa $6.99; pa with audio CD $8.99

Grades: K 1 2 3   **597**

1. Eels 2. Eels -- Juvenile literature

ISBN 1-56402-180-7; 978-0-7636-1522-2 pa; 0-7636-1522-6 pa; 978-0-7636-3994-5 pa with audio CD; 0-7636-3994-X pa with audio CD

LC 92-53131

Text and illustrations discuss the characteristics and life cycle of the eel

"Bostock's watercolor paintings illustrate the places and creatures in the text without diminishing the mystery of the eel's journey. . . . The short phrases of the prose create a rhythm almost like unrhymed verse that will please readers." Booklist

Wearing, Judy

Manta rays. Weigl Publishers 2010 24p il (World of wonder: underwater life) lib bdg $24.45; pa $8.95

Grades: K 1 2   **597**

1. Rays (Fishes)

ISBN 978-1-60596-104-0 lib bdg; 1-60596-104-3 lib bdg; 978-1-60596-105-7 pa; 1-60596-105-1 pa

LC 2009-25988

This book about mantra rays begins "with introductory information and progress[es] to more unique details of the featured creatures. Bold photographs juxtaposed on colorful background graphic will hold the attention of even the most novice readers. . . . [This book is] sure to make a splash with budding marine biologists everywhere." SLJ

Includes glossary

Seahorses. Weigl 2010 24p il (World of wonder: underwater life) lib bdg $24.45; pa $8.95

Grades: K 1 2   **597**

1. Sea horses

ISBN 978-1-60596-102-6 lib bdg; 1-60596-102-7 lib bdg; 978-1-60596-103-3 pa; 1-60596-103-5 pa

LC 2009-4986

This book about seahorses begins "with introductory information and progress[es] to more unique details of the featured creatures. Bold photographs juxtaposed on colorful background graphic will hold the attention of even the most novice readers. . . . [This book is] sure to make a splash with budding marine biologists everywhere." SLJ

Includes glossary

597.3   Selachii, Holocephali, fleshy-finned fishes

Macquitty, Miranda

Shark; written by Miranda MacQuitty. DK Pub. 2008 72 p. col. ill (hardcover) $16.99

Grades: 4 5 6 7   **597.3**

   1. Sharks -- Juvenile literature 2. Marine biology -- Juvenile literature 3. Sharks

   ISBN 0756637783; 9780756637781

                               LC 2008276031

This book is part of the DK Eyewitness Books series and focuses on sharks. The titles in this series "focus on subjects that complement students' personal interests and areas of study to make learning simple and fun." Wall charts, clip art CDs, and photographs and illustrations are included. (Publisher's note)

Mallory, Kenneth

Swimming with hammerhead sharks. Houghton Mifflin 2001 48p il (Scientists in the field) pbk. $7.99

Grades: 4 5 6 7   **597.3**

   1. Sharks 2. Hammerhead sharks 3. Hammerhead sharks -- Research -- Juvenile literature

   ISBN 9780618250790

                               LC 00-61401

"Mallory, editor-in-chief of publishing programs at the New England Aquarium, uses the context of an IMAX film production on hammerhead sharks to explain how scientists—in particular, marine biologist Pete Klimley—are studying these {animals. Index.} Intermediate." (Horn Book)

This book follows "marine biologist Pete Klimley and an IMAX film team to seamounts off Cocos Island in the Pacific Ocean to observe and film schooling hammerhead sharks. . . . A fascinating record of research and investigation, this inviting book is larded with numerous dramatic color photos." SLJ

Includes bibliographical references

Walker, Sally M.

Fossil fish found alive; discovering the coelacanth. Carolrhoda Bks. 2002 72p il map lib bdg $17.95

Grades: 5 6 7 8   **597.3**

   1. Coelacanth

   ISBN 1-57505-536-8

                               LC 2001-3815

Describes the 1938 discovery of the coelacanth, a fish previously believed to be extinct, and subsequent research about it

"Walker writes well, making this relatively unknown area of science history an exciting story of exploration and discovery. Excellent, full-color photos illustrate the text." Booklist

Includes bibliographical references

Sharks; facts at your fingertips. DK Pub. 2012 156 p. col. ill., map (hc) $7.99

Grades: 5 6 7 8   **597.3**

   1. Sharks 2. Rays (Fishes)

   ISBN 0756692865; 9780756692865

                               LC 2011277726

This book, part of the "Pocket Genius" encyclopedia series, "profiles more that 150 sharks and rays -- from the great white to the tiny dwarf lantern -- and tells what they eat, where they live and how fast they swim." It "offers a . . . catalog-style presentation, which clearly lays out individual subcategories." (Publisher's note)

597.8   Amphibians

Allen, Kathy

Deformed frogs; a cause and effect investigation. Capstone Press 2010 32p il map (Fact finders. Animals on the edge) lib bdg $25.99

Grades: 3 4 5 6   **597.8**

   1. Frogs

   ISBN 978-1-4296-4533-1 lib bdg; 1-4296-4533-4 lib bdg

                               LC 2010004412

"Excellent discussions address those who doubt the severity of the issue and those who wonder why people should care what happens to animals. The captioned photographs are timely and poignant. . . . [This] makes serious subject matter interesting and accessible." SLJ

Includes glossary and bibliographical references

Bekkering, Annalise

Frogs. Weigl 2011 24p il (World of wonder: watch them grow) lib bdg $25.70; pa $9.95

Grades: 1 2   **597.8**

   1. Frogs

   ISBN 978-1-60596-925-1 lib bdg; 1-60596-925-7 lib bdg; 978-1-60596-926-8 pa; 1-60596-926-5 pa

                               LC 2009050954

Readers will discover the world of frogs and their transition from swimming tadpoles to amphibious adults.

The text "is simple without being simplistic; it is thoughtful and comprehensive without being overwhelming. The real appeal for teachers, students, and independent young readers, however, will be the photographs that fill the facing pages. Bold, bright, and colorful, the photographs bring you marvelously close to the subject. . . . On many different levels, this is a very appealing [book]." Libr Media Connect

Includes glossary and bibliographical references

Beltz, Ellin

Frogs: inside their remarkable world. Firefly Books 2005 175p il $34.95

Grades: 5 6 7 8 9 10   **597.8**

   1. Frogs 2. Toads

   ISBN 1-55297-869-9

                               LC 2006-365517

The author "picture of the history of the frog, its anatomical makeup, its place in the natural world and the threats that are seriously reducing its numbers around the world." Publisher's note

Bishop, Nic

★ Nic Bishop frogs. Scholastic Nonfiction 2008 48p il $17.99

Grades: 2 3 4 **597.8**

1. Frogs

ISBN 978-0-439-87755-8; 0-439-87755-5

LC 2007-08699

Boston Globe-Horn Book Award honor book: Nonfiction (2008)

Bishop "presents a number of large, striking photos illustrating a clearly written discussion of the physical characteristics and habits of frogs. Dominating the book are Bishop's remarkably fine color photographs of frogs from around the world." Booklist

Includes glossary

Bluemel Oldfield, Dawn

Leaping ground frogs. Bearport 2010 24p il map (Amphibiana) lib bdg $22.61

Grades: 3 4 5 6 **597.8**

1. Frogs

ISBN 978-1-936087-35-8 lib bdg; 1-936087-35-9 lib bdg

This book about ground frogs "is informative, eye-catching, well organized, and useful for reports. . . . Large, clear color photos depict the animals in their natural habitats." SLJ

Includes glossary and bibliographical references

Bredeson, Carmen

Poison dart frogs up close; [by] Carmen Bredeson. Enslow Elementary 2008 24p il (Zoom in on animals!) lib bdg $21.26

Grades: 1 2 3 **597.8**

1. Frogs

ISBN 978-0-7660-3077-0 lib bdg; 0-7660-3077-6 lib bdg

LC 2007039467

"Short paragraphs of simply written text describe [poison dart frogs'] key body parts and how they function. . . . Behavior, diet, and care and development of the young are briefly addressed. Facing the text on each spread is a full-page, sharp, color close-up of one or more of the . . . animals in their natural habitat. . . . Bredeson's simply written and colorful [title] will provide younger readers with [a] satisfying first [introduction] to these fascinating creatures." SLJ

Includes glossary and bibliographical references

Carney, Elizabeth

Frogs! National Geographic 2009 32p il (National Geographic kids) $11.90; pa $3.99

Grades: K 1 2 **597.8**

1. Frogs

ISBN 978-1-4263-0393-7; 1-4263-0393-9; 978-1-4263-0392-0 pa; 1-4263-0392-0 pa

LC 2008014028

This "volume employs simple sentence structures to convey basic facts about frogs . . . including life cycles, habitats, and feeding information. The excellent photographs showcase a variety of species in vivid detail. Vocabulary-word text boxes and goofy jokes . . . increase accessibility." Horn Book Guide

Cowley, Joy

★ Red-eyed tree frog; story by Joy Cowley; illustrated with photographs by Nic Bishop. Scholastic Press 1999 un il $16.95

Grades: PreK K 1 2 **597.8**

1. Frogs 2. Tree frogs 3. Frogs -- Fiction 4. Rain forests -- Fiction 5. Hylidae -- Central America -- Juvenile literature

ISBN 0-590-87175-7

LC 98-15674

This frog found in the rain forest of Central America spends the night searching for food while also being careful not to become dinner for some other animal

"Stunning color photographs and a gripping interactive text." Booklist

Crump, Marty

The mystery of Darwin's frog; by Marty Crump; illustrated by Steve Jenkins and Edel Rodriquez. Boyds Mills Press 2013 40 p. ill. (reinforced) $16.95

Grades: 3 4 5 6 7 **597.8**

1. Picture books for children 2. Frogs -- Juvenile literature

ISBN 1590788648; 9781590788646

LC 2012947844

In this book, Marty Crump, a researcher who has investigated the Rhinoderma darwinii, an inch-long frog discovered by Charles Darwin in Chile in 1834, "describes the earlier investigations of this intriguing frog and records her own efforts to document how it lives in the wild. She discusses her findings and goes on to present the problems facing not only Darwin's frogs, but also frogs in general-loss of habitat, pollution, and the assault of the lethal Bd fungus." (School Library Journal)

Dickmann, Nancy

A frog's life. Heinemann Library 2010 24p il (Watch it grow) lib bdg $21.50; pa $5.99

Grades: PreK K 1 **597.8**

1. Frogs

ISBN 978-1-4329-4140-6 lib bdg; 1-4329-4140-2 lib bdg; 978-1-4329-4149-9 pa; 1-4329-4149-6 pa

LC 2009-49156

"Practically unique among early introductions to life cycles because death is mentioned . . . this . . . follows [a frog] . . . from egg . . . to maturity with a set of close-up color photographs, one per page, paired to large-type, one or two-sentence captions. . . . Offers nourishing fare for young naturalists." SLJ

Includes glossary and bibliographical references

Firestone, Mary

What's the difference between a frog and a toad? illustrated by Bandelin-Dacey. Picture Window Books 2010 24p il (What's the difference) lib bdg $25.32

Grades: K 1 2 **597.8**

1. Frogs 2. Toads

ISBN 978-1-4048-5544-1 lib bdg; 1-4048-5544-0 lib bdg

LC 2009-6885

"Compares and contrasts the habitats, physical characteristics, location, and lifestyles of [frogs and toads]. The picture-book format is used to great effect as it allows the two animals to be compared side by side on each spread.The bold, expressive watercolors provide the same visual impact as photographs. . . . Short sentences and highlighted fun facts make this . . . [a book] with broad appeal for both researchers and browsers." SLJ

Includes glossary

Ganeri, Anita

Poison dart frog. Heinemann Library 2011 24p il map (A day in the life. Rain forest animals) lib bdg $22; pa $6.49

Grades: 1 2   **597.8**

1. Frogs

ISBN 978-1-4329-4104-8 lib bdg; 1-4329-4104-6 lib bdg; 978-1-4329-4115-4 pa; 1-4329-4115-1 pa

LC 2010000959

This book follows a poison dart frog through its day as it sleeps, eats, and moves.

"Ganeri presents information clearly and simply in large type, two-sentence comments placed below a bright, sharply reproduced color photograph of the animal in a natural setting. . . . [This is] sufficiently specific to support assignment as well as pleasure reading." SLJ

Includes glossary and bibliographical references

Gibbons, Gail

Frogs. Holiday House 1993 un il $16.95; pa $6.95

Grades: K 1 2 3   **597.8**

1. Frogs 2. Frogs -- Juvenile literature

ISBN 0-8234-1052-8; 0-8234-1134-6 pa

LC 93-269

An introduction to frogs, discussing their tadpole beginnings, noises they make, their hibernation, body parts, and how they differ from toads

"Gibbons' distinctive, labeled drawings identify the features described in the text, and her subjects float, swim, jump, and dive in colorful, lifelike illustrations. . . . This attractive book will appeal to prereaders, beginning readers, and the adults who read to those groups." Booklist

Gilpin, Daniel

Tree frogs, mud puppies, & other amphibians; by Daniel Gilpin. Compass Point Books 2006 48 p. col. ill. (library) $29.99

Grades: 5 6 7 8   **597.8**

1. Picture books for children 2. Amphibians -- Juvenile literature

ISBN 0756512492; 9780756512491

LC 2005003683

This book by Daniel Gilpin is part of the Families series and looks at tree frogs, mud puppies, and other amphibians. It "discusses the large diversity of amphibians, a typical amphibian's body, ancient amphibians, and an amphibian's skin and senses. It discusses hiding and warning, movement, prey, courtship, strange breeders, and the life-cycle." (Publisher's note)

Includes bibliographical references (p. 47) and index.

Goldish, Meish

Amazing water frogs. Bearport 2010 24p il map (Amphibiana) lib bdg $22.61

Grades: 3 4 5 6   **597.8**

1. Frogs

ISBN 978-1-936087-34-1 lib bdg; 1-936087-34-0 lib bdg

This book about water frogs "is informative, eye-catching, well organized, and useful for reports. . . . Large, clear color photos depict the animals in their natural habitats." SLJ

Includes glossary and bibliographical references

Little newts. Bearport 2010 24p il map (Amphibiana) lib bdg $22.61

Grades: 3 4 5 6   **597.8**

1. Newts

ISBN 978-1-936087-38-9 lib bdg; 1-936087-38-3 lib bdg

This book about newts "is informative, eye-catching, well organized, and useful for reports. . . . Large, clear color photos depict the animals in their natural habitats." SLJ

Includes glossary and bibliographical references

Slimy salamanders. Bearport 2010 24p il map (Amphibiana) lib bdg $22.61

Grades: 3 4 5 6   **597.8**

1. Salamanders

ISBN 978-1-936087-37-2 lib bdg; 1-936087-37-5 lib bdg

This book about salamanders "is informative, eye-catching, well organized, and useful for reports. . . . Large, clear color photos depict the animals in their natural habitats." SLJ

Includes glossary and bibliographical references

Warty toads. Bearport 2010 24p il (Amphibiana) lib bdg $22.61

Grades: 3 4 5 6   **597.8**

1. Toads

ISBN 978-1-936087-36-5 lib bdg; 1-936087-36-7 lib bdg

This book about toads "is informative, eye-catching, well organized, and useful for reports. . . . Large, clear color photos depict the animals in their natural habitats." SLJ

Includes glossary and bibliographical references

Guiberson, Brenda Z.

Frog song; by Brenda Guiberson; illustrations by Gennady Spirin. Henry Holt and Company 2012 40 p. (hc) $17.99

Grades: K 1 2 3   **597.8**

1. Frogs -- Vocalization 2. Frogs -- Juvenile literature 3. Frogs -- Behavior -- Juvenile literature 4. Frogs -- Vocalization -- Juvenile literature

ISBN 0805092544; 9780805092547

LC 2011041940

This children's book, by Brenda Z. Guiberson, illustrated by Gennady Spirin, profiles exotic frogs and their sounds. "Since the time of the dinosaurs, frogs have added their birrups and bellows to the music of the earth. . . . Onomatopoeic text and . . . illustrations introduce young readers to these fascinating and important creatures, from Chile to Nepal to Australia." (Publisher's note)

Johnson, Jinny

Frog; illustrations by Graham Rosewarne. Smart Apple Media 2010 32p il (How does it grow?) lib bdg $28.50

Grades: 1 2 3   **597.8**

1. Frogs

ISBN 978-1-59920-355-3 lib bdg; 1-59920-355-3 lib bdg

LC 2008-53341

Presents an introduction to the life cycle of a frog, from its beginning as an egg, to its life as a tadpole, to its maturity as an adult frog

"Each stage is described on a spread that features clearly written, oversized text and a caption opposite a full-page, realistic watercolor, or, occasionally, a photograph. . . . A worthwhile purchase." SLJ

Includes glossary

Kolpin, Molly

Salamanders; consulting editor, Gail Saunders-Smith. Capstone Press 2010 24p il map (Pebble plus. Amphibians) lib bdg $22.65

Grades: K 1 2   **597.8**

1. Salamanders

ISBN 978-1-4296-3990-3 lib bdg; 1-4296-3990-3 lib bdg

This "is well suited to emerging readers. Dynamic, full-page color photographs complement controlled, repetitive vocabulary, printed in a large font against solid backgrounds. . . . The information and its presentation are solid." SLJ

Includes glossary and bibliographical references

Lunis, Natalie

Tricky tree frogs. Bearport 2010 24p il map (Amphibiana) lib bdg $22.61

Grades: 3 4 5 6   **597.8**

1. Frogs

ISBN 978-1-936087-33-4 lib bdg; 1-936087-33-2 lib bdg

This book about tree frogs "is informative, eye-catching, well organized, and useful for reports. . . . Large, clear color photos depict the animals in their natural habitats." SLJ

Includes glossary and bibliographical references

Markle, Sandra, 1946-

★ The **case** of the vanishing golden frogs. Milbrook Press 2011 48p il

Grades: 4 5 6   **597.8**

1. Frogs 2. Endangered species 3. Wildlife conservation

ISBN 0761351086; 9780761351085

LC 2010042642

"Notable for clarity, directness, and simplicity of writing and design alike, this volume [is] both handsome and fascinating. . . . Excellent photos, microscopic views, and maps illustrate the book." Booklist

Includes glossary and bibliographical references

★ **Hip**-pocket papa; illustrated by Alan Marks. Charlesbridge 2010 un il lib bdg $15.95

Grades: K 1 2 3   **597.8**

1. Frogs 2. Natural history -- Australia

ISBN 978-1-57091-708-0 lib bdg; 1-57091-708-6 lib bdg

LC 2008025334

"Markle writes with clarity and precision, while Marks' evocative watercolor, ink, and pencil artwork brings the frogs' world to life." Booklist

Slippery, slimy baby frogs. Walker & Co. 2006 31p il map $16.95

Grades: 3 4 5   **597.8**

1. Frogs

ISBN 978-0-8027-8062-1; 0-8027-8062-8; 978-0-8027-8063-8 lib bdg; 0-8027-8063-6 lib bdg

LC 2005-27542

"This book describes various types of frogs, from mating to adulthood. . . . The large, full-color photos provide crystal-clear closeup views of tadpoles and frogs in their natural environments, and a world map shows where the photographs were taken. While there are many other books about the life cycle of frogs, none contain the detailed information found here." SLJ

Moffett, Mark W.

Face to face with frogs. National Geographic 2008 31p il map (Face to face) $16.95; lib bdg $25.90

Grades: 3 4 5 6   **597.8**

1. Frogs

ISBN 978-1-4263-0205-3; 1-4263-0205-3; 978-1-4263-0206-0 lib bdg; 1-4263-0206-1 lib bdg

LC 2007-12445

This book has "personal accounts of [Moffett's] own explorations providing entertaining specifics to go with the arresting visuals, as casual sidebars offer information on random hoppy topics." Bull Cent Child Books

Includes glossary and bibliographical references

Pfeffer, Wendy

From tadpole to frog; illustrated by Holly Keller. HarperCollins Pubs. 1994 32p il (Let's-read-and-find-out science) $15.95; pa $4.95

Grades: K 1   **597.8**

1. Frogs 2. Frogs -- Juvenile literature

ISBN 0-06-023044-4; 0-06-445123-2 pa

LC 93-3135

"The illustrations are simple, interesting, and just right for young children. The science is accurate and presented in a way to excite young readers to get outside and look for some frogs and tadpoles." Sci Books Films

Pringle, Laurence P.

Frogs! strange and wonderful. Laurence Pringle; illustrated by Meryl Henderson. Boyds Mills Press 2012 30 p. col. ill (reinf. trade ed.) $16.95

Grades: 3 4 5 6   **597.8**

1. Frogs 2. Poisonous animals 3. Camouflage (Biology) 4. Picture books for children 5. Amphibians -- Juvenile literature

ISBN 1590783719; 9781590783719

LC 2011928834

In this book, author Laurence P. Pringle offers a "look at the similarities and differences among the many and varied species of frogs . . . The Reinwardt's flying frog glides between trees, the mantella and poison frogs come in all the colors of the rainbow and one can guess what makes the marsupial frog stand out. Camouflage, mating, development, coloring, size, locomotion, how and what they eat and how and why they make sounds are just some of the topics." (Kirkus)

Includes bibliographical references

Salas, Laura Purdie

Amphibians; water-to-land animals. illustrated by Kristin Kest. Picture Window Books 2010 24p il (Amazing science. Animal classification) lib bdg $25.32

Grades: K 1 2   **597.8**

  1. Amphibians

  ISBN 978-1-4048-5521-2 lib bdg; 1-4048-5521-1 lib bdg

           LC 2009-3290

"This is the way to introduce kids to science as well as lead them to a deeper level of understanding how the animal kingdom is divided into phylum, class, order, family, genus, and species. Excellent picture book-quality illustrations fill each page with a few well chosen words to extend visual understanding. . . . The writing is clear, age-appropriate science writing. Every school should purchase this book." Libr Media Connect

Includes glossary

Solway, Andrew

Poison frogs and other amphibians; by Andrew Solway. Heinemann Library 2006 48 p. col. ill. (Adapted for success) (library) $32.00; (paperback) $8.99

Grades: 5 6 7 8 9   **597.8**

  1. Frogs -- Juvenile literature 2. Animal defenses -- Juvenile literature 3. Amphibians -- Juvenile literature 4. Dendrobatidae -- Juvenile literature

  ISBN 140348225X; 9781403482259; 9781403482327

  out of print

           LC 2006014294

This book by Andrew Solway is part of the Adapted for Success series and looks at poison frogs. "Poison Frogs are among the most poisonous animals in the world, but how have they, and other amphibians, adapted to become so successful? The series explores how some of our favorite animals are uniquely adapted to their environment. Each book . . . covers habitat, defenses, camouflage, and the way animals find food." (Publisher's note)

Includes bibliographical references and index.

Somervill, Barbara A.

Cane toad; by Barbara A. Somervill. Cherry Lake Pub. 2008 32p il map (Animal invaders) lib bdg $26.26

Grades: 3 4 5 6   **597.8**

  1. Toads 2. Biological invasions

  ISBN 978-1-60279-115-2 lib bdg; 1-60279-115-5 lib bdg

           LC 2007-33510

This describes the cane toads' "outstanding physical and behavioral characteristics at each stage in their life cycle, diet, and natural habitat, and then [explains] how they were introduced into areas outside their natural range . . . and the nature and extent of the ecological damage they have caused, and various attempts to eradicate or at least control the animals. . . . The prolific cane toads, which are fast supplanting native amphibians in Australia, excrete a toxin powerful enough to kill the animals, and some humans unfortunate enough to ingest them. . . . Clear color photographs . . . accompany the [text] on about every other page. . . . [This title is] clearly written and well organized, and [has] up-to-date information." SLJ

Includes glossary

Stewart, Melissa

Frog or toad? how do you know? Enslow Publishers 2011 24p il (Which animal is which?) lib bdg $21.26; pa $6.95

Grades: 1 2 3   **597.8**

  1. Frogs 2. Toads

  ISBN 978-0-7660-3682-6 lib bdg; 0-7660-3682-0 lib bdg; 978-1-59845-236-5 pa; 1-59845-236-3 pa

           LC 2010003277

This describes the differences between frogs and toads. Includes bibliographical references

Salamander or lizard? how do you know? Enslow Publishers 2011 24p il (Which animal is which?) lib bdg $21.26; pa $6.95

Grades: 1 2 3   **597.8**

  1. Lizards 2. Salamanders

  ISBN 978-0-7660-3679-6 lib bdg; 0-7660-3679-0 lib bdg; 978-1-59845-238-9 pa; 1-59845-238-X pa

           LC 2010003279

This describes the differences between salamanders and lizards.

This "should give budding naturalists an increased understanding of how scientists use appearance and behavior of classify sometimes-similar living things. . . . Spreads feature sharply detailed paired photographs of identified specimens seen from the same angle and at roughly equal size." SLJ

Includes bibliographical references

A **place** for frogs; written by Melissa Stewart; illustrated by Higgins Bond. Peachtree Publishers 2010 un il map $16.95

Grades: K 1 2 3   **597.8**

  1. Frogs 2. Wildlife conservation 3. Ecology -- Juvenile literature

  ISBN 978-1-5614-5521-8; 1-5614-5521-0

           LC 2009-24515

"This wide-format book shows how people's actions have endangered frogs and what has been done to reverse those environmental threats. A typical double-page spread includes a large, detailed acrylic painting showing various frogs in their habitats. . . . Written and illustrated with young children in mind, this book is a good starting place for environmental studies." Booklist

Stille, Darlene R.

The **life** cycle of amphibians. Heinemann Library 2011 48p il (Life cycles) lib bdg $32; pa $8.99

Grades: 3 4 5   **597.8**

  1. Amphibians

  ISBN 978-1-4329-4978-5 lib bdg; 978-1-4329-4985-3 pa

           LC 2010038276

This describes how amphibians "are born or hatched, where they live, and how they grow, move, protect themselves, spend their time, and reproduce. Focusing on frogs, toads, salamanders, and caecilians, [this book] is informative."

Includes glossary and bibliographical references

Sweeney, Alyse

Toads. Capstone Press 2010 24p il map (Pebble plus. Amphibians) lib bdg $22.65

Grades: K 1 2   **597.8**
1. Toads
ISBN 978-1-4296-3991-0 lib bdg; 1-4296-3991-1
lib bdg
This "is well suited to emerging readers. Dynamic, full-page color photographs complement controlled, repetitive vocabulary, printed in a large font against solid backgrounds.... While the information and its presentation are solid." SLJ
Includes glossary and bibliographical references

Turner, Pamela S.
★ The **frog** scientist; photographs by Andy Comins. Houghton Mifflin Books for Children 2009 58p il (Scientists in the field) lib bdg $18
Grades: 5 6 7 8   **597.8**
1. Frogs 2. Biologists 3. College teachers 4. Frogs -- Juvenile literature 5. Scientists -- Juvenile literature
ISBN 978-0-618-71716-3 lib bdg; 0-618-71716-1
lib bdg
LC 2008-39770
This volume "opens with biologist Tyrone Hayes and his team collecting frogs at a pond in Wyoming. After a short chapter on Hayes' background, the discussion returns to his work: he addresses the general question of why amphibian populations world-wide are declining by studying the effects of atrizine, an agricultural pesticide, on the reproductive organs of leopard frogs from a particular pond. Well organized and clearly written.... Excellent color photos offer clear pictures of frogs and of this scientific team at work in the field and in the lab.... A vivid, realistic view of one scientist at work." Booklist
Includes glossary and bibliographical references

Whiting, Jim
Frogs in danger; by Jim Whiting. Mitchell Lane Publishers 2007 32p il (On the verge of extinction: crisis in the environment) lib bdg $25.27
Grades: 3 4 5   **597.8**
1. Frogs
ISBN 978-1-58415-585-0
LC 2007000802
This describes threats to the survival of frog species, including global warming and other environmental dangers.
"Short chapters, large font, and pronunciation guides to key words engage children doing research, but the depth of information is not compromised.... Colorful, up-close photographs are accompanied by satisfying captions." SLJ
Includes glossary and bibliographical references

Winnick, Nick
Salamanders. Weigl 2010 24p il (Backyard animals) lib bdg $24.45; pa $8.95
Grades: 1 2 3   **597.8**
1. Salamanders
ISBN 978-1-60596-084-5 lib bdg; 1-60596-084-5 lib bdg; 978-1-60596-085-2 pa; 1-60596-085-3 pa
LC 2008052060
This describes the physical characteristics, natural habitats, history, and folklore of salamanders.
This is "packed with information and [includes] fine close-up photos." Booklist
Includes glossary

597.9   Reptiles

Arnosky, Jim
★ **Slither** and crawl; eye to eye with reptiles. Sterling Pub. 2009 31p il $14.95
Grades: 2 3 4 5   **597.9**
1. Reptiles
ISBN 978-1-4027-3986-6; 1-4027-3986-9
LC 2008022493
"Arnosky's painterly eye and personal observations match handsomely in this face-to-face experience. The slim volume presents-head-on-life-size depictions of a plethora of scaly or otherwise armored critters, along with a nice selection of data included in the conversational text. Neat foldouts of a passel of snakes, an American crocodile, ... a skitter of lizards, and the heads of a variety of sea turtles add an interactive touch to the artist's outstanding acrylics." SLJ
Includes bibliographical references

Hutchinson, Mark
Reptiles. Simon & Schuster Books for Young Readers 2011 64p il (Insiders) $16.99
Grades: 4 5 6 7   **597.9**
1. Reptiles
ISBN 978-1-4424-3276-5; 1-4424-3276-4
"Arranged around the digitally rendered, sharply focused central images ... smaller inset pictures and blocks of text systematically present distinctive physical features, typical behaviors, habitats, ranges, diets, and other information about each type of reptile.... This book will wow casual browsers and budding herpetologists alike." Booklist

McCarthy, Colin
Reptile; written by Colin McCarthy; [special photography, Karl Shone ... [et al.]] Dorling Kindersley 2000 63p il (DK eyewitness books) $15.99
Grades: 4 5 6 7   **597.9**
1. Reptiles
ISBN 0-7894-5786-5
First published 1991 by Knopf
Photographs and text depict the many different kinds of reptiles, their similarities and differences, habitats, and behavior

Stille, Darlene R., 1942-
The **life** cycle of reptiles. Heinemann Library 2011 48p il map (Life cycles)
Grades: 3 4 5   **597.9**
1. Reptiles
ISBN 9781432949822 lib bdg; 9781432949891
LC 2010038507
This describes what a reptile is, types of reptiles, their life cycles, habitats, foods, and defenses.
"The book offers a good sense of the variety of reptiles in the world. The books' colorful illustrations include many fine photos from a variety of sources as well as some clearly delineated digital drawings." Booklist
Includes glossary and bibliographical references

Wilson, Hannah
Life-size reptiles; written by Hannah Wilson. Sterling 2007 48p il $9.95

Grades: 3 4 5 6   **597.9**
1. Reptiles
ISBN 1-4027-4542-7

This "covers lizards, crocodilians, and others of their cold-blooded kin. Colorful, realistic illustrations fill the pages, depicting reptiles in all their scaly/shelled splendor, many—as promised in the title—life-sized." SLJ

597.92   Turtles

Allen, Kathy
   ★ Sea turtles' race to the sea; a cause and effect investigation. Capstone Press 2011 32p il map (Animals on the edge) lib bdg $25.99
Grades: K 1 2 3   **597.92**
  1. Sea turtles 2. Endangered species
ISBN 978-1-4296-5402-9; 1-4296-5402-3
               LC 2010033003

Describes the sea turtle and its disappearing habitat.
  "The thoughtfulness with which this . . . book is arranged shows through on each page. Photos truly complement the text without overwhelming it. . . . The book merits praise for its content and its compound contribution to the environment." Sci Books Films
  Includes glossary and bibliographical references

Berger, Melvin
   Look out for turtles! illustrated by Megan Lloyd. HarperCollins Pubs. 1992 32p il (Let's-read-and-find-out science book) hardcover o.p. pa $4.95
Grades: K 1 2 3   **597.92**
  1. Turtles
ISBN 0-06-022540-8 lib bdg; 0-06-445156-9 pa
               LC 90-36894

"This simple introductory resource provides an overview of the different types of turtles and their characteristics and habits. It is a good resource for young children to use independently." Sci Child

Christopherson, Sara Cohen
   Top 50 reasons to care about marine turtles; animals in peril. Enslow Publishers 2009 103p il (Top 50 reasons to care about endangered animals) lib bdg $31.93
Grades: 4 5 6 7   **597.92**
  1. Sea turtles 2. Endangered species
ISBN 978-0-7660-3455-6 lib bdg; 0-7660-3455-0 lib bdg
               LC 2009-10555

This describes marine turtles-their life cycles, diets, young, habitats, and reasons why they are endangered animals
  "The illustrations, mostly color photographs, represent a wonderful selection of the animals and their habitats. Reluctant readers may be enticed by this . . . simply because of the great images. This . . . would make a substantial supplement to the science curriculum when studying endangered animals." Libr Media Connect
  Includes glossary and bibliographical references

Davies, Nicola, 1958-
   One tiny turtle; illustrated by Jane Chapman. Candlewick Press 2001 29p il hardcover o.p. pa with audio CD $9.99

Grades: K 1 2 3   **597.92**
  1. Turtles 2. Loggerhead turtle 3. Loggerhead turtle -- Juvenile literature
ISBN 0-7636-1549-8; 978-0-7636-4193-1 pa with audio CD
               LC 00-52326

This offers "simple, lyrical words and bright, acrylic double-page pictures. . . . Without condescension, this tells a powerful nature story for a young audience." Booklist

Gibbons, Gail
   Sea turtles. Holiday House 1995 un il $16.95; pa $6.95
Grades: K 1 2 3   **597.92**
  1. Sea turtles 2. Turtles -- Juvenile literature
ISBN 0-8234-1191-5; 0-8234-1373-X pa
               LC 94-48579

This is "a very appealing book. . . . The illustrations are lovely paintings, highlighted with black outlines and clear labels. Children should find the diagram that shows differences between sea turtles and other turtles fascinating because they are often familiar only with the latter." Sci Books Films

Guiberson, Brenda Z.
   Into the sea; illustrated by Alix Berenzy. Holt & Co. 1996 un il $16.95; pa $6.95
Grades: K 1 2 3   **597.92**
  1. Sea turtles
ISBN 0-8050-2263-5; 0-8050-6481-8 pa
               LC 95-46757

"Guiberson uses italicized sound words such as tap, tap, and scritch to draw readers into the story. Berenzy captures the essence of the text with her colored-pencil and gouache illustrations that alternate from dark to light, reflecting the various habitats." SLJ

Hall, Kirsten
   Leatherback turtle; the world's heaviest reptile. Bearport Pub. 2007 24p il map (Super sized!) lib bdg $21.28
Grades: K 1 2   **597.92**
  1. Sea turtles
ISBN 978-1-59716-393-4 lib bdg; 1-59716-393-7 lib bdg
               LC 2006033247

This describes the size, habitat, diet, and life cycle of the leatherback turtle
  This is "attractive. . . . Most spreads include two to five large-type sentences, a boxed fact, and a large colorful photograph." SLJ
  Includes glossary and bibliographical references

Lockwood, Sophie
   Sea turtles; by Sophie Lockwood. Child's World 2006 40p col. ill., col. maps (library) $29.93
Grades: 4 5 6   **597.92**
  1. Sea turtles
ISBN 1592965504; 9781592965502
               LC 2005024792

"Conservation is the dominant theme of this attractive photo-essay. . . . which has beautiful full-page color photos that bring readers close to the subject. Fast-fact boxes focus on particular species, providing spot statistics on weight, length, color, habitat, threatened or endangered status, and more." Booklist

Includes bibliographical references (p. 39) and index.

Monroe, Mary Alice

Turtle summer; a journal for my daughter. Mary Alice Monroe, Barbara J. Bergwerf. Sylvan Dell 2007 32p il $15.95

Grades: K 1 2   597.92

1. Sea turtles

ISBN 978-0-9777423-5-6; 0-9777423-5-0

LC 2006-938664

"This is a companion book to Mary Alice Monroe's novel, Swimming Lessons, the sequel to The Beach House. In the novel, the readers witness a young mother, Toy, writing a journal for her daughter, Little Lovie. This is the journal Toy is writing. Using original photographs, this scrapbook journal explains the nesting cycle of sea turtles and the natural life along the southeastern coast, including local shore birds, shells, and the sea turtle hospital." (Publisher's note) "Grades three to six." (Sci Books Films)

Rodriguez, Cindy

Sea turtles. Rourke Pub. 2010 24p il map (Eye to eye with endangered species) lib bdg $27.07

Grades: 2 3 4   597.92

1. Sea turtles

ISBN 978-1-60694-405-9 lib bdg; 1-60694-405-3 lib bdg

LC 2009-5996

Text examines the issues endangered sea turtles face and how they can be saved

"Sets out to introduce readers to [sea turtles] . . . explain the dangers they face, and detail the efforts of biologists and conservationists to save them. . . . Serviceable and informative." SLJ

Includes glossary

Spilsbury, Louise

Sea turtle. Heinemann Library 2011 24p il (A day in the life. sea animals) lib bdg $22; pa $6.49

Grades: 1 2   597.92

1. Sea turtles

ISBN 978-1-4329-4001-0 lib bdg; 1-4329-4001-5 lib bdg; 978-1-4329-4008-9 pa; 1-4329-4008-2 pa

LC 2010000626

This pairs "well-chosen color photos . . . with one or two sentences of simple commentary for each. . . . [Though this title] includes references to several varieties of the chosen creature, one species in particular is highlighted. . . . [Good choice] for pleasure or purpose reading." SLJ

Includes glossary and bibliographical references

Swinburne, Stephen R.

Turtle tide; the ways of sea turtles. illustrated by Bruce Hiscock. Boyds Mills Press 2005 un il $15.95

Grades: 2 3 4   597.92

1. Sea turtles 2. Sea turtles -- Juvenile literature

ISBN 1-59078-081-7

LC 2004-16856

"Simple, lyrical prose accompanies brilliant watercolors in this account." SLJ

Wearing, Judy

Sea turtle. Weigl 2010 24p il (World of wonder: underwater life) lib bdg $24.45; pa $8.95

Grades: K 1 2   597.92

1. Sea turtles

ISBN 978-1-60596-106-4 lib bdg; 1-60596-106-X lib bdg; 978-1-60596-107-1 pa; 1-60596-107-8 pa

LC 2009-4987

This book about sea turtles begins "with introductory information and progress[es] to more unique details of the featured creatures. Bold photographs juxtaposed on colorful background graphic will hold the attention of even the most novice readers. . . . [This book is] sure to make a splash with budding marine biologists everywhere." SLJ

Includes glossary

597.95   Lizards

Bishop, Nic

★ Lizards. Scholastic Nonfiction 2010 48p il $17.99

Grades: 2 3 4   597.95

1. Lizards

ISBN 978-0-545-20634-1; 0-545-20634-0

"Bishop introduces lizards from around the world: their habitats, egg-laying and lack of child-rearing, their specialized bodies and behaviors, their feeding and courtship. His astonishing photographs are beautifully composed and clearly reproduced. . . . The well-organized two-level text is . . . inviting." Kirkus

Includes glossary and bibliographical references

Bodden, Valerie

Komodo dragons; by Valerie Bodden. 1st ed. Creative Education 2013 24 p. col. ill. (library) $25.65

Grades: 1 2 3 4   597.95

1. Animals -- Juvenile literature 2. Komodo dragon -- Juvenile literature

ISBN 1608180875; 9781608180875

LC 2011050275

This book, part of the Amazing Animals series from author Valerie Bodden, is a "basic exploration of the appearance, behavior, and habitat of Komodo dragons, Earth's heaviest lizards. Also included is a story from folklore explaining why Indonesians respect Komodo dragons." (Publisher's note)

Includes bibliographical references and index

Collard, Sneed B. III

Sneed B. Collard III's most fun book ever about lizards; Sneed B. Collard III. Charlesbridge 2012 47 p. (reinforced for library use) $16.95

Grades: 3 4 5 6 7   597.95

1. Lizards 2. Lizards as pets 3. Wildlife photography 4. Children's literature 5. Lizards -- Miscellanea

ISBN 9781580893244; 9781580893251

LC 2011000809

This book offers an "introduction to the world of lizards [which] describes their . . . variety and life in the wild and offers cautions from a long-time reptile fan for those who want to keep lizards as pets. [Author Sneed B.] Collard . . . turns his attention . . . to modern-day lizards. After presenting an exemplar, 'Joe Lizard,' a western fence lizard, he goes on to describe other well-known species, including Komodo dragons, Gila monsters, chameleons and iguanas, as well as some with unusual talents, including 'religious lizards' that can walk on water. He covers eating and being eaten, the ways saurians keep warm and reproduce, and threats to their survival. . . . [Photographs] show lizard characteristics. . . . Captions and sidebars add further information." (Kirkus)

Cowley, Joy

★ **Chameleon** chameleon; story by Joy Cowley; illustrated with photographs by Nic Bishop. Scholastic Press 2005 un il $16.95

Grades: K 1 2   **597.95**

1. Chameleons
ISBN 0-439-66653-8

LC 2004-7291

A chameleon creeps through the rain forest avoiding danger and searching for food

This is a "stunning photo-essay. . . . Crisp, clear, full-color photos portray this reptile and its habitat. . . . An informative, thoughtfully produced science book that will be popular with a wide range of animal lovers. Excellent for browsing as well as learning." Booklist

Crump, Marty

Mysteries of the Komodo dragon; the biggest, deadliest lizard gives up its secrets. Boyd Mills Press 2010 40p il map $18.95

Grades: 3 4 5 6   **597.95**

1. Komodo dragon
ISBN 978-1-59078-757-1; 1-59078-757-9

"While Crump's lively text does not supply a stage-by-stage description of the animal's life cycle and physiology, it does give enough data to satisfy many readers and researchers. More importantly, it follows a long-term research project into the chemical makeup of 'dragon drool' and the possible practical applications of the chemicals in this deadly substance to human pharmacology. Clear, color photos depict dragons from hatchlings to adults, scientists hiding in blinds and weighing catches, and zookeepers cuddling dragons with 'gentle' dispositions. . . . A surefire selection in terms of appeal and information." SLJ

Includes glossary and bibliographical references

Gish, Melissa

Komodo dragons. Creative Education 2011 48p il (Living wild) lib bdg $23.95; pa $8.99

Grades: 5 6 7 8   **597.95**

1. Komodo dragon
ISBN 978-1-60818-080-6 lib bdg; 1-60818-080-8 lib bdg; 978-0-89812-672-3 pa; 0-89812-672-X pa

LC 2010028307

A look at Komodo dragons, including their habitats, physical characteristics such as their sawlike teeth, behaviors, relationships with humans, and threatened status in the world today.

"Stunning, full-page photographs create immediate visual interest. A brief narrative introduction sets the scene for the richer, more scientific information in the rest of the text." Booklist

Includes glossary and bibliographical references

Jango-Cohen, Judith

Let's look at iguanas. Lerner Publications Co. 2010 32p il map (Lightning bolt books: Animal close-ups) lib bdg $25.26; pa $7.95

Grades: PreK K 1 2   **597.95**

1. Iguanas
ISBN 978-0-7613-3888-8 lib bdg; 0-7613-3888-8 lib bdg; 978-0-7613-5005-7 pa; 0-7613-5005-5 pa

LC 2008-51857

Introduces desert iguanas, describing their physical characteristics, habitat, and predators.

"Fresh photography, a creative use of graphics, and a collagelike layout make[s] . . . [this book] eye-catching. . . . [The] book ends with a labeled diagram of the animal, a range map, and a further-reading list that includes print and online resources in a single list, a nice way of validating both types of materials." SLJ

Includes glossary

Lunis, Natalie

Black spiny-tailed iguana; lizard lightning! Bearport Pub. 2010 24p il map (Blink of an eye. Superfast animals!) lib bdg $22.61

Grades: 1 2 3   **597.95**

1. Iguanas 2. Lizards
ISBN 978-1-936087-91-4; 1-936087-91-X

LC 2010019671

This describes the black spiny-tailed iguana, including where it lives, what it eats, and the ways its body helps it reach its record-breaking speeds.

This "is sure to appeal to a wide variety of readers. Vibrant photos illustrate each animal from multiple perspectives, providing opportunity for readers to closely examine the animal. Information is organized by subject heading and branches into the animal's physical features and how they contribute to its speed, the animal's natural predators, and how the animal makes use of speed as a means of survival. . . This . . . will be a worthwhile addition to your nonfiction collection." Libr Media Connect

Includes glossary and bibliographical references

Somervill, Barbara A.

Monitor lizard. Cherry Lake 2010 32p il (Animal invaders) lib bdg $27.07

Grades: 5 6 7 8   **597.95**

1. Lizards 2. Biological invasions
ISBN 978-1-60279-627-0 lib bdg; 1-60279-627-0 lib bdg

This offers "an introduction to the problems caused by [the monitor lizard], a discussion of its physical characteristics and habits, a history of how it arrived in its new habitat, and an analysis of challenges encountered by those trying to limit its spread. . . . [It] describes the threat posed by these aggressive 7-foot reptiles, sold as babies by pet vendors and now loose in Florida. . . . [This] well-focused [book is] clearly written. The uncluttered page design features at least one color photo on each page." Booklist

Includes glossary and bibliographical references

Stewart, Melissa

How do chameleons change color? Marshall Cavendish Benchmark 2009 32p il (Tell me why, tell me how) lib bdg $20.95

Grades: 3 4 5   **597.95**
  1. Chameleons
  ISBN 978-0-7614-2922-7 lib bdg; 0-7614-2922-0
  lib bdg
                  LC 2007024099
  "One or two large, well-captioned color photographs are
provided per spread. [The] book concludes with an activity.
[This is a] solid [introduction]." SLJ
  Includes glossary and bibliographical references

597.96 Snakes

Bishop, Nic, 1955-
  ★ **Nic** Bishop snakes; Nic Bishop. Scholastic Nonfiction 2012 48 p. ill. (jacketed hardcover) $17.99
Grades: 3 4 5   **597.96**
  1. Snakes -- Juvenile literature
  ISBN 0545206383; 9780545206389
                  LC 2011039316
  In this juvenile zoology book, "Sibert Medal-winning
photographer Nic Bishop introduces the terrifying and beautiful world of snakes. The . . . text presents both basic information and . . . details about the appearance, habits, and
remarkable abilities of these amazing reptiles. An index and
glossary are included, along with an author's note detailing
his research and the . . . stories behind the photographs."
(Publisher's note)

Blobaum, Cindy
  Awesome snake science; 40 activities for learning
about snakes. Cindy Blobaum. 1st ed. Chicago Review
Press 2012 x, 118 p.p ill. (ebook) $11.99; (prebind)
$23.95; (paperback) $14.95
Grades: 4 5 6   **597.96**
  1. Science projects 2. Educational games 3. Science --
Experiments 4. Snakes -- Juvenile literature 5. Snakes
-- Experiments -- Juvenile literature 6. Snakes -- Study
and teaching (Elementary) -- Activity programs
  ISBN 9781613743188; 9781451775303;
9781569768075
                  LC 2011050257
  Author Cindy Blobaum's book includes "40 science
experiments, art projects, and games . . . [about snakes]
from cobras and copperheads to pythons and boas . . . Activities include making foldable fangs to learn how snakes'
teeth and jaws work together . . . [and] simulating cytotoxic
snake venom . . . Engaging, simple, and safe experiments
teach kids about the biology of snakes, such as how they
use their tongues and nostrils to detect smells, how they are
cold-blooded and sensitive to subtle changes in temperature,
and how they can detect the slightest vibrations or tremors."
(Amazon)
  Includes bibliographical references (p. 115-116)
and index.

Bodden, Valerie
  Snakes. Creative Education 2010 24p il (Amazing
animals) lib bdg $24.25

Grades: K 1 2   **597.96**
  1. Snakes
  ISBN 978-1-58341-813-0 lib bdg; 1-58341-813-X
  lib bdg
                  LC 2009002717
  A basic exploration of the appearance, behavior, and
habitat of snakes, a family of scaly reptiles. Also included is a story from folklore explaining why snakes do not
have legs.
  Includes bibliographical references

Ganeri, Anita
  Anaconda. Heinemann Library 2011 24p il map (A
day in the life. Rain forest animals) lib bdg $22; pa $6.49
Grades: 1 2   **597.96**
  1. Anacondas
  ISBN 978-1-4329-4112-3 lib bdg; 1-4329-4112-7 lib
bdg; 978-1-4329-4123-9 pa; 1-4329-4123-2 pa
                  LC 2010001135
  This book follows an anaconda through its day as it
sleeps, eats, and moves.
  "Ganeri presents information clearly and simply in large
type, two-sentence comments placed below a bright, sharply
reproduced color photograph of the animal in a natural setting. . . . [This is] sufficiently specific to support assignment
as well as pleasure reading." SLJ
  Includes glossary and bibliographical references

Gibbons, Gail
  Snakes. Holiday House 2007 32p il map $16.95
Grades: K 1 2 3   **597.96**
  1. Snakes 2. Snakes -- Juvenile literature
  ISBN 978-0-8234-2122-0; 0-8234-2122-8
                  LC 2007-24585
  "Gibbons injects a healthy dose of snake basics, delivered in her customary matter-of-fact style and illustrated
with watercolor portraits of dozens of different species, pictured mostly in natural settings." Booklist

Hamilton, Sue L.
  Bitten by a rattlesnake; [by] Sue Hamilton. ABDO
Pub. 2010 32p il (Close encounters of the wild kind) lib
bdg $27.07
Grades: 4 5 6 7   **597.96**
  1. Rattlesnakes 2. Animal attacks
  ISBN 978-1-60453-930-1 lib bdg; 1-60453-930-5
lib bdg
                  LC 2009-45423
  Readers learn of actual human-rattlesnake encounters,
information about rattlesnakes, survival strategies, and
attack statistics.
  "Students will be drawn to the realistic full-color photographs, the realistic diagrams of the creatures' bodies, the
real-life stories told by victims, and the interesting, attractive
formatting that includes text, diagrams, photographs, and
graphics on each page. . . . [This is] exciting and attractive
in a 'gross' sort of way and will appeal particularly to boys
for both leisure reading and research." Libr Media Connect
  Includes glossary

Holub, Joan
  Why do snakes hiss? and other questions about snakes,
lizards, and turtles. illustrations by Anna DiVito. Dial

Books for Young Readers 2004 46p il (Dial easy-to-read) hardcover o.p. pa $3.99

Grades: K 1 2   **597.96**

   1. Snakes 2. Reptiles 3. Questions and answers 4. Snakes -- Miscellanea -- Juvenile literature 5. Reptiles -- Miscellanea -- Juvenile literature

   ISBN 0-8037-3000-4; 0-14-240105-6 pa

                LC 2003-64948

   Questions and answers present information about the behavior and characteristics of snakes, lizards, and turtles

   "The photos and attractive ink drawings with color washes that come two to three to a page result in a colorful presentation with illustrations in different styles from many sources." Booklist

Markle, Sandra

   Rattlesnakes. Lerner Publications 2009 39p il (Animal predators) lib bdg $26.60

Grades: 4 5 6   **597.96**

   1. Rattlesnakes

   ISBN 978-1-58013-539-9 lib bdg; 1-58013-539-0 lib bdg

                LC 2008-38038

   Introduces the physical characteristics, habitat, and predatory behavior of rattlesnakes

   "Vivid close-up photographs accompany a narrative." Horn Book Guide

   Includes glossary and bibliographical references

Montgomery, Sy

   ★ The **snake** scientist; photographs by Nic Bishop. Houghton Mifflin 1999 48p il map $16; pa $5.95

Grades: 4 5 6 7   **597.96**

   1. Snakes 2. Snakes -- Research -- Juvenile literature 3. Red-sided garter snake -- Juvenile literature

   ISBN 0-395-87169-7; 0-618-11119-0 pa

                LC 98-6124

   Discusses the work of Bob Mason and his efforts to study and protect snakes, particularly red-sided garter snakes

   "The lively text communicates both the meticulous measurements required in this kind of work and the thrill of new discoveries. Large, full-color photos of the zoologist and young students at work, and lots of wriggly snakes, pull readers into the presentation." SLJ

   Includes bibliographical references

Simon, Seymour

   Giant snakes; [by] Seymour Simon. Chronicle Books 2006 un il (See more readers) lib bdg $14.95; pa $3.95

Grades: K 1 2 3   **597.96**

   1. Snakes

   ISBN 978-0-8118-5410-8 lib bdg; 0-8118-5410-8 lib bdg; 978-0-8118-5411-5 pa; 0-8118-5411-6 pa

                LC 2005-25360

   An easy-to-read illustrated introduction to large snakes.

   "The text is lively, well organized, and clear, with the many facts it presents cleverly woven into the story. The illustrations, which are beautiful, show distinctly the intricate patterns of the snakes' skin." Sci Books Films

Stewart, Melissa

   Snakes! National Geographic 2009 31p il (National Geographic kids) lib bdg $11.90; pa $3.99

Grades: K 1 2   **597.96**

   1. Snakes

   ISBN 978-1-4263-0429-3 lib bdg; 978-1-4263-0428-6 pa

                LC 2008-47001

   An introduction to the types, physical features, behavior, and pet potential of snakes.

   "The excellent photographs showcase a variety of species in vivid detail. Vocabulary-word text boxes and goofy jokes . . . increase accessibility." Horn Book Guide

597.98   Crocodilians

Bodden, Valerie

   Crocodiles. Creative Education 2010 24p il (Amazing animals) lib bdg $24.25; pa $5.99

Grades: K 1 2   **597.98**

   1. Crocodiles

   ISBN 978-1-58341-806-2 lib bdg; 1-58341-806-7 lib bdg; 978-1-926722-21-4 pa; 1-926722-21-3 pa

                LC 2009002706

   A basic exploration of the appearance, behavior, and habitat of crocodiles, a family of sharp-toothed reptiles. Also included is a story from folklore explaining why crocodiles have rough skin.

   This is illustrated with "dynamically colored photographs . . . showcasing the animal's intricately textured scales, craggy ridges, and of course, hide-rending teeth." Booklist

   Includes bibliographical references

Feigenbaum, Aaron

   American alligators; freshwater survivors. Bearport Pub. Company, Inc. 2008 32p il map (America's animal comebacks) lib bdg $25.27

Grades: 2 3 4   **597.98**

   1. Alligators

   ISBN 978-1-59716-503-7 lib bdg; 1-59716-503-4 lib bdg

                LC 2007-13160

   Explains why American alligators became an endangered species, and describes the efforts of scientists to bring them back from the brink of extinction

   "Closeup photos, maps, and an accessible text provide solid information for readers and report writers. Statistics and information about other endangered alligators are appended." Horn Book Guide

   Includes glossary and bibliographical references

Gibbons, Gail

   Alligators and crocodiles. Holiday House 2010 32p il map $17.95

Grades: K 1 2 3   **597.98**

   1. Alligators 2. Crocodiles

   ISBN 978-0-8234-2234-0; 0-8234-2234-8

   Gibbons "draws young readers into the world of alligators and crocodiles by first asking readers to distinguish between them. She describes the physical similarities and differences between the two most common species of the world's largest reptiles, as well as their habitats, habits, prey, locomotion, senses, communication, mating and nesting behavior, and status as endangered species. The author has chosen facts that will engage her readers, organized the information logically, and presented it in straightforward exposition. Pen-and-ink and watercolor illustrations show both species in their likely environment." Booklist

Gish, Melissa
Alligators. Creative Education 2010 46p il (Living wild) $23.95; pa $9.95
Grades: 5 6 7 8   597.98
 1. Alligators
 ISBN 978-1-58341-967-0; 1-58341-967-5; 978-0-89812-550-4 pa; 0-89812-550-2 pa
                                          LC 2010017372
The "book lucidly discusses conservation and the animals' often tenuous relationships with humans. The layout is uniformly simple but effective, constructed with a nice balance of main text for the report writers, smaller chunks of esoterica for browsers, and . . . killer photos." Booklist

Hamilton, Sue L.
Attacked by a crocodile; [by] Sue Hamilton. ABDO Pub. 2010 32p il (Close encounters of the wild kind) lib bdg $27.07
Grades: 4 5 6 7   597.98
 1. Crocodiles 2. Animal attacks
 ISBN 978-1-60453-929-5; 1-60453-929-1
                                          LC 2009-45514
Readers learn of actual human-crocodile encounters, information about crocodiles, survival strategies, and attack statistics.
 "Students will be drawn to the realistic full-color photographs, the realistic diagrams of the creatures' bodies, the real-life stories told by victims, and the interesting, attractive formatting that includes text, diagrams, photographs, and graphics on each page. . . . [This is] exciting and attractive in a 'gross' sort of way and will appeal particularly to boys for both leisure reading and research." Libr Media Connect
 Includes glossary

Markle, Sandra
 ★ Crocodiles; by Sandra Markle. Carolrhoda Books 2004 39p il (Animal predators) lib bdg $25.26; pa $7.95
Grades: 3 4 5 6   597.98
 1. Crocodiles
 ISBN 1-57505-726-3 lib bdg; 1-57505-742-5 pa
                                          LC 2003-15402
"The straightforward, descriptive text and superb photos give [this title] surefire appeal to middle readers." Booklist
 Includes glossary and bibliographical references

Meinking, Mary
Crocodile vs. wildebeest. Raintree 2011 32p il (Predator vs. prey) $29; pa $7.99
Grades: 1 2 3   597.98
 1. Gnus 2. Crocodiles 3. Predatory animals
 ISBN 978-1-4109-3935-7; 1-4109-3935-9; 978-1-4109-3944-9 pa; 1-4109-3944-8 pa
Explores the features of crocodiles and gnu that make them particularly suited to catch or evade.
 "The struggle between predator crocodile and its wildebeest prey is described in clear language and illustrated with engaging color photographs." Horn Book Guide

Otfinoski, Steven
 ★ Alligators; by Steven Otfinoski. Marshall Cavendish Benchmark 2009 47p il (Animals animals) lib bdg $20.95
Grades: 3 4 5 6   597.98
 1. Alligators
 ISBN 978-0-7614-2930-2 lib bdg; 0-7614-2930-1 lib bdg
                                          LC 2007-25448
"Provides comprehensive information on the anatomy, special skills, habitats, and diet of alligators." Publisher's note
 Includes glossary

Pringle, Laurence P.
Alligators and crocodiles! strange and wonderful. [by] Laurence Pringle; illustrated by Meryl Henderson. Boyds Mills Press 2009 32p il $16.95
Grades: 3 4 5   597.98
 1. Alligators 2. Crocodiles
 ISBN 978-1-59078-256-9; 1-59078-256-9
                                          LC 2008-30018
This describes alligators' and crocodiles' "habitats and nesting behavior, and explains their common anatomical features and distinguishing characteristics. . . . Henderson presents a gallery of full-body portraits of 21 crocodilian species, as well as a series of close-ups. These illustrations are drawn and colored in . . . clear, precise detail." Booklist

Riggs, Kate
Alligators; by Kate Riggs. Creative Education 2012 24 p. (Amazing animals)
Grades: K 1 2   597.98
 1. Aquatic animals 2. Alligators -- Folklore 3. Alligators -- Juvenile literature
 ISBN 1608181049; 9781608181049
                                          LC 2010049122
This book, a volume of the Amazing Animals series, offers an "exploration of the appearance, behavior, and habitat of alligators. . . . Also included is a story from folklore explaining why alligators and dogs don't get along." (Publisher's note) "This book also shows alligator hatchlings breaking free from an egg, open-jawed waiting to feed, and clinging as it rides on its mother's back. This book also addresses the question: How do you tell the difference between an alligator and a crocodile? . . . This book shares with readers how the alligator lives in the swamplands, how it hunts, raises young, and lives mostly alone." (Children's Literature)
 Includes bibliographical references (p. 24) and index

Rockwell, Anne F.
Who lives in an alligator hole? by Anne Rockwell; illustrated by Lizzy Rockwell. HarperCollins 2006 33p il (Let's-read-and-find-out science) $15.99; pa $4.99
Grades: K 1 2 3   597.98
 1. Ecology 2. Alligators
 ISBN 0-06-028530-3; 0-06-445200-X pa
Describes the habitats of these reptiles which scientists call a "keystone species" because they change the environment for their own use in a way that helps many other plants and animals.
 "Information and illustration work well together in this picture book presentation. . . . Simplified yet not anthropomorphized, the clearly delineated paintings feature alliga-

tors and other animals as the focal points of well-composed scenes." Booklist

Simon, Seymour

Crocodiles & alligators. HarperCollins Pubs. 1999 un il hardcover o.p. pa $6.99

Grades: 4 5 6 7   **597.98**

1. Alligators 2. Crocodiles

ISBN 0-06-027473-5; 0-06-443829-5 pa

LC 98-34705

Describes the physical characteristics and behavior of various members of the family of animals known as crocodilians

"The book is filled with interesting information, and the vivid, well-composed, full-color photographs and entertaining text will draw in browsers." SLJ

Stewart, Melissa

Alligator or crocodile? how do you know? Enslow Publishers 2011 24p il (Which animal is which?) lib bdg $21.26

Grades: 1 2 3   **597.98**

1. Alligators 2. Crocodiles

ISBN 978-0-7660-3677-2; 0-7660-3677-4

LC 2010003275

This explains the differences between alligators and crocodiles.

This "should give budding naturalists an increased understanding of how scientists use appearance and behavior of classify sometimes-similar living things. . . . Spreads feature sharply detailed paired photographs of identified specimens seen from the same angle and at roughly equal size." SLJ

Includes bibliographical references

598   Birds

Alderfer, Jonathan

National Geographic kids bird guide of North America; the best birding book for kids from National Geographic's bird experts. by Jonathan Alderfer. National Geographic 2013 176 p. (paperback) $15.95; (library) $23.90

Grades: 4 5 6 7 8   **598.097**

1. Birds -- North America 2. Birds -- Identification 3. Birds -- North America -- Identification -- Juvenile literature

ISBN 1426310943; 9781426310942; 9781426310959

LC 2012028615

Author "[Jonathan] Alderfer offers in-depth studies of 60 birds native to North America (plus 'mini-profiles' of another 60 specimens) in a guide for nascent birders. . . . The book is organized by region, and each bird's spread offers . . . color photographs, 'vital statistics' (including its call, diet, and habitat), maps of where it can be found, and other background." (Publishers Weekly)

Includes bibliographical references and index

Arnold, Caroline

Birds; nature's magnificent flying machines. illustrated by Patricia J. Wynne. Charlesbridge Pub. 2003 32p il $16.95; pa $6.95

Grades: 3 4 5 6   **598**

1. Birds -- Flight

ISBN 1-57091-516-4; 1-57091-572-5 pa

LC 2002-10441

An introduction to the science that explains how birds fly

"A clear, interesting book. . . . Each spread contains one or two paragraphs with a large, full-color illustration as well as smaller, captioned pictures that cover such topics as bone structure and preening. The colorful artwork consistently clarifies the concepts being discussed." SLJ

Includes glossary and bibliographical references

A bald eagle's world; written and illustrated by Caroline Arnold. Picture Window Books 2010 24p il (Caroline Arnold's animals) lib bdg $25.32

Grades: PreK K 1 2   **598**

1. Bald eagle

ISBN 978-1-4048-5741-4 lib bdg; 1-4048-5741-9 lib bdg

LC 2009033358

This narrative describes the life of a bald eagle from the time it hatches until it can fly on its own.

The story "related in the present tense, [feels] immediate and engaging. . . . The plainness of the fact boxes [contrast] with Arnold's beautiful but simple artwork, which cleanly captures the essence of [the] animal. . . . [This book's] perfectly balanced mix of facts, story, and pictures will hold young readers' attention and help then learn." Booklist

A penguin's world; written and illustrated by Caroline Arnold. Picture Window Books 2005 24p il $23.93

Grades: K 1 2 3   **598**

1. Penguins

ISBN 1-4048-1323-3

LC 2005023159

"This title follows an Adelie penguin family from scenes in which the parents build a nest and warm their eggs to final pages showcasing the four-month-old, newly independent chicks. The simple, well-paced text weaves basic concepts into the captivating narrative, and the artwork's strong colors and bold, uncluttered compositions capture the expression and movement of the birds." Booklist

Includes glossary and bibliographical references

Arnosky, Jim

★ Thunder birds; nature's flying predators. Sterling 2011 32p il $14.95

Grades: 3 4 5 6   **598**

1. Birds of prey

ISBN 978-1-4027-5661-0; 1-4027-5661-5

LC 2010019680

"Foldout pages group birds according to species and common characteristics. Lifelike owls peer at readers with deep, glassy eyes; in a section featuring birds of prey, an osprey's spectacular wing spans three panels, and journal-like passages vividly document Arnosky's observations of each bird. . . . Arnosky's enthusiasm is evident in his deftly crafted images and in the immediacy of his 'field-note' style." Publ Wkly

Bailer, Darice

Geese. Marshall Cavendish Benchmark 2010 47p il (Animals animals) lib bdg $29.93

Grades: 3 4 5 **598**
1. Geese
ISBN 978-0-7614-4840-2 lib bdg; 0-7614-4840-3
lib bdg

LC 2009019482

This offers information on the anatomy, special skills, habitats, and diet of geese.

Includes glossary and bibliographical references

Bardhan-Quallen, Sudipta

Flying eagle; illustrated by Deborah Kogan Ray. Charlesbridge 2009 un il $15.95
Grades: 1 2 3 **598**
1. Eagles
ISBN 978-1-57091-671-7; 1-57091-671-3

LC 2007-17186

"The setting is a big part of the drama in this large picture book about an eagle's search for prey in the Serengeti wildlife refuge in Tanzania. Each double-page spread includes a very short, simple rhyme with a soaring, unframed watercolor and colored-pencil picture of the bird in flight. . . . Long notes at the back about the eagle and about the Seregenti will fascinate young readers." Booklist

Barner, Bob

Penguins, penguins, everywhere! Chronicle Books 2007 un il $14.95
Grades: PreK K 1 **598**
1. Penguins
ISBN 978-0-8118-5664-5; 0-8118-5664-X

LC 2006-20960

"Colorful collages depict plump penguins performing a plethora of penguiny pastimes. . . . Barner's simply rhyming text presents a variety of the birds. . . . A final spread proffers a parade of all 17 species, including data on global location, size, and weight." SLJ

Bash, Barbara

★ **Urban** roosts: where birds nest in the city. Sierra Club Bks. 1990 un il hardcover o.p. pa $6.95
Grades: 1 2 3 4 **598**
1. Birds -- Nests
ISBN 0-316-08312-7 pa

LC 89-70187

"Excellent treatment of an unusual subject reveals that human-made places of steel, stone, and concrete are home to a variety of birds. Includes information on sparrows, finches, barn and snowy owls, swallows, swifts, nighthawks, killdeers, pigeons, wrens, crows, starlings, and falcons that have successfully adapted to city life." Sci Child

Berendt, John

My baby blue jays. Viking 2011 un il $16.99
Grades: K 1 2 3 **598**
1. Blue jays
ISBN 978-0-670-01290-9; 0-670-01290-4

LC 2010033296

The author "delivers a warm photo-essay about a pair of blue jays that make their home on his apartment balcony in New York City. While the arc of the story—nestbuilding, laying eggs, the first flight of a fledgling—is an old one, Berendt's telling is welcoming and personal, as if he were relating the story to a child in his lap while paging through a family photo album. . . . Set within scalloped borders against

a cream backdrop, the photographs provide a remarkably intimate view of the birds' lives." Publ Wkly

Bodden, Valerie

Parrots. Creative Education 2010 24p il (Amazing animals) lib bdg $24.25
Grades: K 1 2 **598**
1. Parrots
ISBN 978-1-58341-809-3 lib bdg; 1-58341-809-1
lib bdg

LC 2009002711

A basic exploration of the appearance, behavior, and habitat of parrots, a family of colorful birds. Also included is a story from folklore explaining why parrots can imitate speech.

Includes bibliographical references

Penguins. Creative Education 2010 24p il (Amazing animals) lib bdg $24.25
Grades: K 1 2 **598**
1. Penguins
ISBN 978-1-58341-810-9 lib bdg; 1-58341-810-5
lib bdg

LC 2009002712

A basic exploration of the appearance, behavior, and habitat of penguins, a family of flightless birds. Also included is a story from folklore explaining why emperor penguins are so big.

This is illustrated with "dynamically colored photographs." Booklist

Includes bibliographical references

Bouler, Olivia

★ **Olivia's** birds; saving the Gulf. Sterling Pub. 2011 32p il $14.95
Grades: 4 5 6 **598**
1. Birds 2. Nature conservation
ISBN 978-1-4027-8665-5; 1-4027-8665-4

LC 2010046002

"Eleven-year-old Bouler, who raised more than $150,000 for the Audubon Society's Gulf Coast oil spill recovery efforts through the sale of her bird paintings, pairs her artwork with casual, informative passages to create an upbeat lesson on bird identification, habitat, and nature preservation. . . . Bouler's depictions of familiar birds like the Canada goose, bald eagle, and hummingbird are carefully observed and spirited; her vivacious attitude may inspire ecologically minded readers to get involved." Publ Wkly

Burnie, David

Bird; written by David Burnie. rev ed.; DK Pub. 2008 72p il (DK eyewitness books) $15.99
Grades: 4 5 6 7 **598**
1. Birds
ISBN 978-0-7566-3768-2; 0-7566-3768-6
First published 1988 by Knopf

A photo essay on the world of birds examining such topics as body construction, feathers and flight, the adaptation of beaks and feet, feeding habits, courtship, nests and eggs, and bird watching.

Includes glossary

Cate, Annette LeBlanc

★ **Look up!** bird-watching in your own backyard. Annette LeBlanc Cate. Candlewick Press 2013 64 p. $15.99

Grades: 2 3 4 5   **598**

1. Birds

ISBN 0763645613; 9780763645618

LC 2012942416

This children's picture book puts an "emphasis on looking at the birds near home-from suburbs to inner cities." It groups "birds by colors, shapes, behaviors, feathers, calls, habitat, migration, and more" and "emphasizes the importance of observation and includes sketching instructions as a way to hone those skills on the individual aspects of a bird along with its species' characteristics." (School Library Journal)

"...Jam-packed with accurate information likely to increase any potential birder's enthusiasm and knowledge." Kirkus

Catt, Thessaly

Migrating with the Arctic tern. PowerKids Press 2011 24p il map (Animal journeys) lib bdg $21.25; pa $8.25

Grades: 2 3 4   **598**

1. Terns 2. Birds -- Migration

ISBN 978-1-4488-2542-4 lib bdg; 1-4488-2542-3 lib bdg; 978-1-4488-2668-1 pa; 1-4488-2668-3 pa

LC 2010025389

This book follows "the yearly migratory patterns of the [arctic tern] and [covers] anatomy, diet, mating, parenting, climate change as caused by people, pollution, and more. . . . [It is illustrated] with clear color photographs. . . . Go-to nonfiction for animal enthusiasts." SLJ

Includes glossary

Dunning, Joan

★ **Seabird** in the forest; the mystery of the marbled murrelet. Boyds Mills Press 2011 un il $17.95

Grades: K 1 2 3   **598**

1. Murrelets

ISBN 978-1-59078-715-1; 1-59078-715-3

"A marbled murrelet chick's early life is surprising. Most seabirds lay their eggs on the sand or high cliffs at the water's edge, but the marbled murrelet usually lays a single egg high on a branch of an old-growth tree, far from the ocean. . . . The hatched chick spends a month hunkered down on the branch, camouflaged by its own down, waiting for a parent to arrive with fish. This large-format picture book describes the life of one such chick. . . . The text runs beneath expressive illustrations, with close-ups of adult birds and their chick as well as landscapes suggesting their contrasting worlds; they support the mood of mystery and show well at a distance. Text boxes set on the illustrations add further detail. A beautiful addition." Kirkus

Evert, Laura

Birds of prey; explore the fascinating worlds of eagles, falcons, owls, vultures. by Laura Evert and Wayne Lynch; illustrations by Sherry Neidigh and John F. McGee. NorthWord 2005 191p il (Our wild world) $16.95

Grades: 3 4 5 6   **598**

1. Birds of prey

ISBN 1-55971-925-7

LC 2005000189

This "volume is divided into four sections, each addressing one of the major groups of raptors: eagles, falcons, owls, and vultures. The chapters, which have color-coded pages for quick reference, are similarly organized, making for easier reading, and deal with all aspects of the birds' life cycles and habits. Plentiful, high-quality photographs . . . and clear illustrations elucidate the narrative." SLJ

Ganeri, Anita

Macaw. Heinemann Library 2011 24p il map (A day in the life. Rain forest animals) lib bdg $22; pa $6.49

Grades: 1 2   **598**

1. Birds 2. Cage birds

ISBN 978-1-4329-4105-5 lib bdg; 1-4329-4105-4 lib bdg; 978-1-4329-4116-1 pa; 1-4329-4116-X pa

LC 2010000960

This book follows a macaw through its day as it sleeps, eats, and moves.

"Ganeri presents information clearly and simply in large type, two-sentence comments placed below a bright, sharply reproduced color photograph of the animal in a natural setting. . . . [This is] sufficiently specific to support assignment as well as pleasure reading." SLJ

Includes glossary and bibliographical references

Gibbons, Gail

Owls; [by] Gail Gibbons. Holiday House 2005 32p il $16.95; pa $6.95

Grades: K 1 2 3   **598**

1. Owls

ISBN 0-8234-1880-4; 0-8234-2014-0 pa

LC 2004-48225

A "factual look at raptors of the night, full of information tied specifically to the owls of North America. General facts on physiology, hunting tactics, digestion, habitats, and communication are offered, as is a section on mating, egg laying and incubation, and owlet development. . . . Gibbons's trademark watercolors provide lively renditions of a variety of these silent hunters. . . . This is a bright addition to owl lore for younger readers." SLJ

Gish, Melissa

★ **Eagles**. Creative Education 2010 46p il (Living wild) lib bdg $23.95; pa $9.95

Grades: 5 6 7 8   **598**

1. Eagles

ISBN 978-1-58341-968-7 lib bdg; 1-58341-968-3 lib bdg; 978-0-89812-551-1 pa; 0-89812-551-0 pa

LC 2010-17373

This "book lucidly discusses conservation and the animals' often tenuous relationship with humans. The layout is uniformly simple but effective, constructed with a nice balance of main text for the report writers, smaller chunks of esoterica for browsers, and . . . killer photos." Booklist

Hummingbirds. Creative Education 2011 46p il map (Living wild) lib bdg $23.95; pa $8.95

Grades: 5 6 7 8   **598**

1. Hummingbirds

ISBN 978-1-60818-078-3; 1-60818-078-6; 978-0-89812-670-9 pa; 0-89812-670-3 pa

LC 2010028314

A look at hummingbirds, including their habitats, physical characteristics such as their ability to hover, behaviors, relationships with humans, and admired status in the world today.

"Stunning, full-page photographs create immediate visual interest. A brief narrative introduction sets the scene for the richer, more scientific information in the rest of the text." Booklist

Includes glossary and bibliographical references

Owls. Creative Education 2011 46p il map (Living wild) lib bdg $23.95
Grades: 5 6 7 8   **598**
  1. Owls
  ISBN 978-1-60818-081-3; 1-60818-081-6
                                             LC 2010028308
  A look at owls, including their habitats, physical characteristics such as their large and observant eyes, behaviors, relationships with humans, and protected status in the world today.
  "Stunning, full-page photographs create immediate visual interest. A brief narrative introduction sets the scene for the richer, more scientific information in the rest of the text." Booklist
  Includes glossary and bibliographical references

Goldin, Augusta R.
  Ducks don't get wet; by Augusta Goldin; illustrated by Helen K. Davie. newly il ed; HarperCollins Pubs. 1999 32p il (Let's-read-and-find-out science) hardcover o.p. pa $4.95
Grades: K 1 2 3   **598**
  1. Ducks
  ISBN 0-06-027881-1; 0-06-027882-X lib bdg; 0-06-445187-9 pa
                                             LC 97-43597
  A newly illustrated edition of the title first published 1965 by Crowell
  Describes the behavior of different kinds of ducks and, in particular, discusses how all ducks use preening to keep their feathers dry
  "The text is well focused throughout. . . . Notable for its clarity, subtlety, and beauty, the artwork illustrates the text with precision and imagination." Booklist

Goldish, Meish
  California condors; saved by captive breeding. Bearport Pub. 2009 32p il map (America's animal comebacks) lib bdg $25.27
Grades: 2 3 4   **598**
  1. Condors 2. Wildlife conservation
  ISBN 978-1-59716-741-3 lib bdg; 1-59716-741-X lib bdg
                                             LC 2008-32803
  Through this true tale of wildlife survival, young readers discover the bold and creative ideas that Americans and their government have used to protect and care for the country's endangered California condors
  "Crisp photos and maps on every page work well with the text and give faces to the scientists and animals. The back matter includes a facts page, information on related species, and an up-to-date reading list." SLJ
  Includes glossary and bibliographical references

Gonzales, Doreen
  Owls in the dark. PowerKids Press 2010 24p il (Creatures of the night) lib bdg $21.25; pa $8.05
Grades: 2 3 4   **598**
  1. Owls
  ISBN 978-1-4042-8097-7 lib bdg; 1-4042-8097-9 lib bdg; 978-1-4358-3251-0 pa; 1-4358-3251-5 pa
  A look at owls and their world in the dark.
  "Basic details are complemented by eclectic trivia, ... [and the] volume concludes with a defense of the animal . . . and why it is vital to humans. The layout is attractive, with easy-to-read text and eye-catching photography. Good for reports." SLJ
  Includes glossary

Gray, Susan H.
  The **life** cycle of birds; [by] Susan H. Gray. Heinemann Library 2011 48p il (Life cycles)
Grades: 3 4 5   **598**
  1. Birds
  ISBN 9781432949792 lib bdg; 9781432949860
                                             LC 2010038277
  This describes how birds are "hatched, where they live, and how they grow, move, protect themselves, spend their time, and reproduce. . . . [This book] provides a well-organized account of avian creatures, including topics such as preening, digestion, and adaptations to different habitats." Booklist
  Includes glossary and bibliographical references

Hanel, Rachael
  Penguins. Smart Apple Media 2009 46p il (Living wild) lib bdg $32.80
Grades: 4 5 6 7   **598**
  1. Penguins
  ISBN 978-1-58341-658-7 lib bdg; 1-58341-658-7 lib bdg
                                             LC 2007008503
  "The 17 species of penguins . . . . fill [this] slim, informative [volume]. [The] overview is divided into several chapters . . . describing the shared and distinct physical characteristics of the various species, the location of their particular habitats, life cycle, social behavior, and the history of human awareness of and impact on these animals. Fine color photographs face pages of text with smaller views placed in colored sidebars or insets. The [book concludes] with current environmental threats and conservation efforts. . . . Handsome and appealing." SLJ

Harkins, Susan Sales
  Threat to the whooping crane; [by] Susan Sales Harkins and William H. Harkins. Mitchell Lane Pub. 2008 32p il map (On the verge of extinction: crisis in the environment) lib bdg $17.95
Grades: 3 4 5   **598**
  1. Cranes (Birds) 2. Endangered species 3. Whooping crane -- Juvenile literature
  ISBN 978-1-58415-685-7 lib bdg; 1-58415-685-6 lib bdg
                                             LC 2008-08037
  Describes the physical characteristics and behavior of the whooping crane, including their yearly migration patterns, and details the history of threats to the species and what steps are being made to return the crane from endangerment.

This book "provide[s] a wealth of information . . . [and is] accurate and easy for young readers to comprehend." Sci Books Films

Includes glossary and bibliographical references

Helget, Nicole Lea

Swans; by Nicole Helget. Smart Apple Media 2009 46p il (Living wild) lib bdg $32.80

Grades: 4 5 6 7   598

1. Swans

ISBN 978-1-58341-659-4 lib bdg; 1-58341-659-5 lib bdg

LC 2007015242

The "7 [species] of swans fill [this] slim, informative [volume]. [The] overview is divided into several chapters . . . describing the shared and distinct physical characteristics of the various species, the location of their particular habitats, life cycle, social behavior, and the history of human awareness of and impact on these animals. Fine color photographs face pages of text with smaller views placed in colored sidebars or insets. The [book concludes] with current environmental threats and conservation efforts. . . . Handsome and appealing." SLJ

Includes bibliographical references

Hiscock, Bruce

Ookpik; the travels of a snowy owl. Boyds Mills Press 2008 un il map $16.99

Grades: 2 3 4   598

1. Owls 2. Birds -- Migration 3. Snowy owl -- Juvenile literature

ISBN 978-1-59078-461-7; 1-59078-461-8

LC 2007-17327

A snowy owl hatches on Baffin Island and migrates over the taiga, past Ottawa, spends the winter in northern New York, and returns to his arctic home.

"An informative author's note comments on the range, size, food, courtship, nesting, growth, and survival of snowy owls. Varied in composition, well focused, and often panoramic in effect, the watercolor paintings depict the snowy owl's world as well as the bird himself. . . . The owl's journey becomes an involving story for children." Booklist

Holub, Joan

★ Why do birds sing? illustrations by Anna DiVito. Dial Books for Young Readers 2004 47p il (Dial easy-to-read) hardcover o.p. pa $3.99

Grades: K 1 2   598

1. Birds 2. Questions and answers 3. Birds -- Miscellanea -- Juvenile literature

ISBN 0-8037-2999-5; 0-14-240106-4 pa

LC 2003-64945

Questions and answers present information about the behavior and characteristics of birds

"The photos and attractive ink drawings with color washes that come two to three to a page result in a colorful presentation with illustrations in different styles from many sources." Booklist

Hoose, Phillip

★ Moonbird; a year on the wind with the great survivor B95. Phillip Hoose. Farrar Straus Giroux 2012 148 p. col. ill. (hardcover) $21.99

Grades: 5 6 7 8   598

1. Endangered species 2. Birds -- Protection 3. Wildlife conservation 4. Red knot -- Juvenile literature 5. Bird watching -- Juvenile literature 6. Red knot -- Migration -- Juvenile literature

ISBN 0374304688; 9780374304683

LC 2011035612

Robert F. Sibert Honor Book (2013)

YALSA Award for Excellence in Nonfiction for Young Adults Finalist (2013)

In this book, Phillip Hoose "explores the tragedy of extinction through a single bird species, but there is hope for survival in this story, and that hope is pinned on understanding the remarkable longevity of a single bird. . . . Hoose takes readers around the hemisphere, showing them the obstacles rufa red knots face, introducing a global team of scientists and conservationists, and offering insights about what can be done to save them before it's too late." (Kirkus Reviews)

Hudak, Heather C.

Robins; [by] Heather Hudak. Weigl Publishers Inc. 2011 24p il (World of wonder: watch them grow) lib bdg $25.70; pa $9.95

Grades: 1 2   598

1. Robins

ISBN 978-1-60596-922-0 lib bdg; 1-60596-922-2 lib bdg; 978-1-60596-923-7 pa; 1-60596-923-0 pa

LC 2010037947

Explore the life of a robin from egg to adult, as well as learn about the special ways robins communicate with each other.

The text is "well-written, providing examples that put a human face to each problem. Quotes and facts are clearly attributed, and their sources are noted in the extensive back matter. . . . Sidebars provide further information, or, more compellingly, offer stories about those touched by the topic. . . . [This] will be of great assistance to students writing reports." Libr Media Connect

Includes glossary

Jacquet, Luc

March of the penguins; [by] Luc Jacquet; including narration written by Jordan Roberts; photographs by Jérôme Maison; translated and adapted by Donnali Fifield. National Geographic 2006 160p il $30

Grades: K 1 2 3   598

1. Penguins

ISBN 0-7922-6190-9

"From summer's end in Antarctica, the book takes the reader on a journey through a year's cycle in the life of emperor penguins. . . . The quality of the photographs makes this simple story accessible to a wide audience." Sci Books Films

Johnson, Jinny

Duck; illustrations by Michael Woods. Smart Apple Media 2010 32p il (How does it grow?) lib bdg $28.50

Grades: 1 2 3   598

1. Ducks

ISBN 978-1-59920-353-9 lib bdg; 1-59920-353-7 lib bdg

LC 2008-53338

Introduces the life cycle of a duck and explains each stage in its development

"Each stage is described on a spread that features clearly written, oversized text and a caption opposite a full-page, realistic watercolor, or, occasionally, a photograph. . . . A worthwhile purchase." SLJ

Includes glossary

Johnson, Sylvia A.
Crows; by Sylvia A. Johnson. Carolrhoda Books 2005 48p il (Carolrhoda nature watch book) lib bdg $25.26
Grades: 3 4 5 6   598
1. Crows
ISBN 1-57505-628-3
LC 2004-564

This "book introduces the American crow, its broader family of corvids, and its range, habitats, cooperative breeding system, life cycle, winter migration, roosting behavior, language, and relations with people. . . . Though the clear, color photographs take up most of the space on the pages, the text offers a well-organized, informative discussion of the species." Booklist

Judge, Lita
Bird talk; what birds are saying and why. Lita Judge. Roaring Brook Press 2011 48 p.
Grades: 1 2 3 4 5   598
1. Birdsongs 2. Birds -- Behavior 3. Animal communication 4. Picture books for children
ISBN 1596436468; 9781596436466
LC 2010030353

In this picture book, "[a] simple ornithological discourse for very young readers offers several examples of feathered non-verbal communication. Over two dozen bird species--most, but not all, with North American ranges, and many fairly familiar--are shown communicating essential messages via calls, displays of plumage and other, less well-known behaviors. Birds from distant parts of the world may appear in the same opening describing behaviors that accomplish similar aims: wooing mates, camouflage, encouragement to fledglings, protection. . . . Further information about each of the species, including their habitats and ranges, appears on several pages at the back, along with a brief glossary and list of sources." (Kirkus)

Kalman, Bobbie
The life cycle of an emperor penguin; [by] Bobbie Kalman & Robin Johnson. Crabtree Pub. 2007 32p il lib bdg $25.27; pa $6.95
Grades: 2 3 4   598
1. Penguins
ISBN 978-0-7787-0630-4 lib bdg; 0-7787-0630-3 lib bdg; 978-0-7787-0704-2 pa; 0-7787-0704-0 pa
LC 2006018781

"The information is presented in a flowing narrative accompanied by color photographs and drawings that perfectly illustrate the [text]. . . . Facts are . . . outlined in a lively manner. [This work has] a wealth of factual information and would be excellent for reports." SLJ

Kelly, Irene
★ Even an ostrich needs a nest; where birds begin. Holiday House 2009 un il map $16.95

Grades: K 1 2 3   598
1. Birds -- Nests
ISBN 978-0-8234-2102-2; 0-8234-2102-3
LC 2007-51059

"This nonfiction picture book describes materials used by 40 species of birds from all parts of the world to build their unique nests and how they go about building them. . . . The diversity of materials and designs . . . make this a topic that will appeal to many. The pleasant format features text, creatively placed with the softly colored illustrations, and makes the engaging subject matter even more accessible." Booklist

It's a hummingbird's life. Holiday House 2003 un il $16.95
Grades: 2 3 4   598
1. Hummingbirds
ISBN 0-8234-1658-5
LC 00-53544

"Kelly follows the activities of the ruby-throated hummingbird throughout the seasons, relating facts and bits of trivia. . . . The tiny pen-and-ink and watercolor illustrations effectively show the features described and comparisons drawn in the narrative." SLJ

Kirby, Pamela F.
What bluebirds do. Boyds Mills Press 2009 48p il $18.95
Grades: K 1 2 3   598
1. Bluebirds 2. Birds -- Behavior
ISBN 978-1-59078-614-7; 1-59078-614-9
LC 2008-34057

"Big, full-color photos provide the drama in this personal, picture-book introduction to a common North American bird. . . . The captions include some brief commentary, and kids will feel the call for conservation as they marvel, along with Kirby, at the bird behavior she sees in her yard." Booklist

Includes glossary and bibliographical references

Landau, Elaine
Emperor penguins. Enslow Elementary 2010 31p il (Animals of the snow and ice) lib bdg $22.60
Grades: 2 3 4   598
1. Penguins
ISBN 978-0-7660-3462-4 lib bdg; 0-7660-3462-3 lib bdg
LC 2009006479

This describes emperor penguins, including habitat, eating habits, mating, babies, and conservation

"Throughout most of [this] title, a full-page, or page and a quarter, sharp, color photograph . . . alternates with a page of text. An addendum of miscellaneous facts, a short list for further reading, and some websites are appended. Landau's smoothly written, well-illustrated [title is] right on target for the intended audience." SLJ

Includes glossary and bibliographical references

Larson, Jeanette C.
Hummingbirds; facts and folklore from the Americas. written by Jeanette Larson and Adrienne Yorinks; illustrated by Adrienne Yorinks. Charlesbridge 2011 64p il $16.95; pa $8.95

Grades: 5 6 7 8 **598**
1. Hummingbirds 2. Birds -- Folklore 3. Native
Americans -- Folklore
ISBN 978-1-58089-332-9; 1-58089-332-5; 978-1-
58089-333-6 pa; 1-58089-333-3 pa
LC 2010-07578
"In a narrative that flows easily between fact and lore,
hummingbird behavior is thoroughly described and interwoven with the folktales it generated among Native American
peoples. . . . All the stories show how ancient people answered the 'how and why' questions of the behaviors they
observed, and these stories beautifully echo modern-day
scientific observations. The full-color photos of quilts and
embroidery by Yorinks invite readers to stop and savor each
one." SLJ
Includes glossary and bibliographical references

Lunis, Natalie
Peregrine falcon; dive, dive, dive! Bearport 2010 24p
il (Blink of an eye: superfast animals) lib bdg $22.61
Grades: 1 2 3 **598**
1. Falcons
ISBN 978-1-936087-93-8 lib bdg; 1-936087-93-6
lib bdg
LC 2010008023
"In terms of pure velocity, no animal can touch a diving
peregrine falcon, which this [book] . . . points out right off
the bat. Subsequent spreads cover such topics as where peregrine falcons live and their nesting habits, aerial abilities,
and, best of all, hunting techniques. . . . Dynamic, sometimes
exhilarating photos . . . accompany the straightforward text."
Booklist
Includes glossary and bibliographical references

Lynch, Wayne
Penguins! text and photographs by Wayne Lynch. Firefly Bks. (Willowdale) 1999 64p il map $19.95; pa $9.95
Grades: 4 5 6 7 **598**
1. Penguins
ISBN 1-55209-421-9; 1-55209-424-3 pa
This "is a delightful book. . . . The beautiful color photographs and the text tell a fascinating, exciting, and revealing
story." Sci Books Films

Mara, Wil
★ **Ducks**; by Wil Mara. Marshall Cavendish Bench-
mark 2009 47p il (Animals animals) $20.95
Grades: 3 4 5 6 **598**
1. Ducks
ISBN 978-0-7614-2927-2; 0-7614-2927-1
LC 2007-26004
"The material is well researched and would be an excel-
lent source for reports, and the [book has] a narrative flow
that makes [it] easy and enjoyable to read. [The] title in-
cludes expert full-color photography." SLJ
Includes glossary and bibliographical references

Markle, Sandra
Eagles. Lerner Publications Company 2009 39p il
(Animal predators) lib bdg $26.60
Grades: 4 5 6 **598**
1. Eagles
ISBN 978-1-58013-519-1; 1-58013-519-6
LC 2008038119

Introduces the physical characteristics, habitat, and predatory behavior of different types of eagles.
"Crisp photographs illustrate the hunting activities of eagles. . . . Facts are presented in a dramatic and informational
manner." Horn Book Guide
Includes glossary and bibliographical references

★ A **mother's** journey; illustrated by Alan Marks.
Charlesbridge 2005 32p il $15.95; pa $6.95
Grades: K 1 2 3 **598**
1. Penguins 2. Emperor penguin -- Juvenile literature
ISBN 1-57091-621-7; 1-57091-622-5 pa
LC 2004-18954
"A simple, lyrical text follows the fortunes of an Emper-
or penguin from laying her first egg through her epic journey to open sea seeking food and culminating in her timely
return with a belly full to regurgitate for her newly hatched
chick. The whole is perfectly accompanied by Marks's luminous blue-toned watercolors." SLJ

Marzollo, Jean
Pierre the penguin; a true story. written by Jean Marzollo; illustrated by Laura Regan. Sleeping Bear Press 2010
un il $15.95
Grades: PreK K 1 2 **598**
1. Penguins
ISBN 978-1-58536-485-5; 1-58536-485-1
LC 2009040871
Rhyming text and colorful illustrations describe the efforts of aquatic biologist Pam to help Pierre, an African penguin living at the California Academy of Sciences, when he
begins to go bald.
"Stories don't come any sweeter than this. . . . Regan's
realistic paintings work well with the text and enhance the
drama and appeal of the storytelling." SLJ

Metz, Lorijo
Discovering seagulls. PowerKids Press 2011 24p il
(Along the shore) lib bdg $21.25
Grades: 3 4 5 **598**
1. Gulls
ISBN 978-1-4488-4995-6; 1-4488-4995-0
LC 2011000154
This book about seagulls "briefly describes the major physical and behavioral characteristics common to all
[seagulls] and one or two distinctive characteristics of about
a half dozen species. . . . One or two sharp color photographs
of representative species, most of which are closeups, accompany the text on every page. . . . [This is] well organized
and smoothly written in an engaging style." SLJ
Includes glossary

Miller, Sara Swan
Woodpeckers, toucans, and their kin. Watts 2003 47p
il (Animals in order) lib bdg $25; pa $6.95
Grades: 4 5 6 **598**
1. Toucans 2. Woodpeckers 3. Honeyguides (Birds)
ISBN 0-531-12243-3 lib bdg; 0-531-16661-9 pa
LC 2002-1732
Introduces the different animals in the piciform order,
their similarities and differences, environments in which
they live, and how to observe them

This book makes "fascinating reading. . . . Photographs are glorious." Libr Media Connect

Includes glossary and bibliographical references

Momatiuk, Yva

★ **Face** to face with penguins; by Yva Momatiuk and John Eastcott. National Geographic 2009 31p il (Face to face) $16.99; lib bdg $25.90

Grades: 3 4 5 6   598

1. Penguins

ISBN 978-1-4263-0561-0; 1-4263-0561-3; 978-1-4263-0562-7 lib bdg; 1-4263-0562-1 lib bdg

LC 2009011439

The authors describe the life cycle and behavior of penguins and their own experiences with penguins in the wild.

"The exquisite photos and firsthand information provide an in-depth and personal look into the lives of these animals." SLJ

Includes glossary and bibliographical references

Munro, Roxie

Hatch! Marshall Cavendish Children's 2011 un il $17.99

Grades: 1 2 3 4   598

1. Eggs 2. Birds

ISBN 0761458824; 9780761458821; 978-0-7614-5882-1; 0-7614-5882-4

LC 2010021297

This picture book describes and helps readers learn to identify nine birds and their eggs and nests. "For each bird, we start with a two-page spread: on one side, a close-up of eggs; . . .and on the other side, a series of clues about the producers of those eggs. . . . Primary." (Horn Book)

"Munro uses a guessing game format to deliver an impressive amount of trivia about nine types of birds. 'Can you guess whose eggs these are?' is the repeated refrain that appears above clusters of eggs against a cream-colored backdrop; opposite, a silhouette of the eggs' shape contains several sentences to aid in the guessing. . . . Straightforward, but packed with information." Publ Wkly

Peterson, Roger Tory

Peterson field guide to birds of Eastern and Central North America; [by] Roger Tory Peterson, with contributions from Michael DiGiorgio [et al.] 6th ed; Houghton Mifflin Harcourt 2010 445p il map (Peterson field guide series) $19.95

Grades: 5 6 7 8 9 10 11 12 Adult   598

1. Birds -- North America 2. Birds -- Identification

ISBN 978-0-547-15246-2; 0-547-15246-9

LC 2009-37681

First published 1934 with title: A field guide to the birds

This guide to birds found east of the Rocky Mountains contains colored illustrations painted by the author, with a description of each species on the facing page. Views of young birds and seasonal variations in plumage are included.

Peterson field guide to birds of Western North America; with contributions from Michael DiGiorgio [et al.] 4th ed; Houghton Mifflin Harcourt 2010 493p il map (Peterson field guide series) pa $19.95

Grades: 5 6 7 8 9 10 11 12 Adult   598

1. Birds -- North America 2. Birds -- Western Canada

3. Birds -- Western States

ISBN 978-0-547-15270-7; 0-547-15270-1

LC 2009-39158

First published 1941 with title: A field guide to western birds

This guide illustrates over 600 species of birds on 176 color plates. In addition, over 588 range maps are included.

Piehl, Janet

Let's look at pigeons. Lerner Publications Co. 2010 32p il (Lightning bolt books: Animal close-ups) lib bdg $25.26; pa $7.95

Grades: PreK K 1 2   598

1. Pigeons

ISBN 978-0-8225-7897-0 lib bdg; 0-8225-7897-2 lib bdg; 978-1-58013-863-5 pa; 1-58013-863-2 pa

LC 2007-29224

Introduces pigeons, describing their physical characteristics, habitat, and predators

"Fresh photography, a creative use of graphics, and a collagelike layout make[s] . . . [this book] eye-catching. . . . [The] book ends with a labeled diagram of the animal, a range map, and a further-reading list that includes print and online resources in a single list, a nice way of validating both types of materials." SLJ

Includes glossary

Post, Hans

Sparrows; [by Hans Post & Kees Heij; illustrated by Irene Goede] Lemniscaat 2008 un il $16.95

Grades: PreK K 1 2   598

1. Sparrows 2. Animals -- Juvenile literature 3. English sparrow -- Juvenile literature

ISBN 978-1-59078-570-6; 1-59078-570-3

LC 2008-02563

Original Dutch edition 2006

"A year in the life of the European House Sparrow is conveyed to young readers through a friendly text and beguiling illustrations. . . . The tone of the text is both playful and informative. . . . The realistic illustrations intersperse views from the birds' prespective . . . with field guide-like pages that help illustrate bird anatomy and behavior and introduce other animals in the sparrow habitat." Horn Book

Pringle, Laurence P.

Penguins! strange and wonderful; illustrated by Meryl Henderson. Boyds Mills Press 2007 un il $16.95

Grades: 3 4 5   598

1. Penguins

ISBN 978-1-59078-090-9; 1-59078-090-6

LC 2006000521

This "highlights the diversity among the habitats, physical traits, and behaviors of the 17 amazingly adaptable species. Pringle's succinct text provides an engaging overview of penguin life. . . . Henderson's realistic paintings vary between double-page spreads of penguins in their diverse Southern Hemisphere environments and finely detailed insets that echo the text." Booklist

Includes bibliographical references

Read, Tracy C.

Exploring the world of eagles. Firefly 2010 24p il (Exploring the world of . . .) $16.95; pa $6.95

Grades: 3 4 5   **598**
  1. Eagles
  ISBN 978-1-55407-647-5; 1-55407-647-1; 978-1-
55407-656-7 pa; 1-55407-656-0 pa
This describes the American bald eagle and the golden eagle, including their anatomy and behavior and the ways they have been affected by the human environmental footprint.

This offers "an abundance of in-depth, intriguing information and [is] appropriate for research or pleasure reading. . . . Two- to four-page chapters mix smaller photos with full-page color photos, and the attractive format will help less-able readers navigate the sometimes dense, detailed paragraphs." Booklist

Rebman, Renee C.
  Vultures. Marshall Cavendish Benchmark 2011 il (Animals, animals) lib bdg $20.95
Grades: 3 4 5   **598**
  1. Vultures
  ISBN 978-0-7614-4880-8; 0-7614-4880-2
                 LC 2010016037
Provides information on the anatomy, special skills, habitats, and diet of vultures.

This offers "comprehensive text and striking, well-chosen photos. . . . [This is] packed with engaging facts and trivia, as well as an upbeat tone." Booklist
Includes glossary and bibliographical references

Savage, Stephen
  Duck. PowerKids Press 2009 32p il map (Animal neighbors) lib bdg $23.95
Grades: 3 4 5 6   **598**
  1. Ducks
  ISBN 978-1-4358-4988-4 lib bdg; 1-4358-4988-4 lib bdg
                 LC 2008-5401
This describes the life cycle, habitat, and behavior of ducks
This title features "beautiful, detailed, close-up photos of animals displayed on child-friendly page layouts. The information is well organized for reports." SLJ
Includes glossary and bibliographical references

Sayre, April Pulley
  ★ **Honk**, honk, goose! Canada geese start a family. illustrated by Huy Voun Lee. Henry Holt and Company 2009 un il $16.95
Grades: K 1 2 3   **598**
  1. Geese 2. Canada goose -- Juvenile literature
  ISBN 978-0-8050-7103-0; 0-8050-7103-2
                 LC 2008013423
"A fun read-aloud grounded by informational back matter. . . . Lee's cut-paper collage illustrations wonderfully complement the text—they're simple yet expressive." Booklist

  ★ **Vulture** view; illustrated by Steve Jenkins. Henry Holt 2007 un il $16.95
Grades: K 1 2   **598**
  1. Vultures 2. Turkey vulture -- Juvenile literature
  ISBN 978-0-8050-7557-1; 0-8050-7557-7
                 LC 2006-30766
"Sayre's poetic text begins with the sun rising. . . . The words, almost startling in their brevity, describe a group of turkey vultures as they soar in the sky, seeking food that reeks. . . . Jenkins . . . places the birds against strong, vivid colors—brilliant sky blues, hot desert reds—and gives them wide wingspans that make them seem to soar across the pages. . . . A final two-page spread . . . does a solid job of explaining how turkey vultures live." Booklist

Schulman, Janet
  ★ **Pale** Male; citizen hawk of New York City. by Janet Schulman; illustrated by Meilo So. Knopf 2008 un il $16.99; lib bdg $19.99
Grades: 3 4 5 6   **598**
  1. Hawks 2. Red-tailed hawk -- Juvenile literature
  ISBN 0-375-94558-X lib bdg; 978-0-375-84558-1; 0-375-84558-5; 978-0-375-94558-8 lib bdg
                 LC 2007-14661
This is "about the first red-tailed hawk to take up residence in New York City's Central Park since its construction in 1857. . . . The artist's evocative watercolor and colored pencil pictures perfectly capture the power and grace of the majestic raptors. . . . Readers experience New Yorkers' excitement about Pale Male and his various mates and their offspring and understand why his story has captured the interest of so many people." SLJ

Sill, Cathryn
  About hummingbirds; a guide for children. [by] Cathryn Sill; illustrated by John Sill. Peachtree Publishers 2011 un il $16.95
Grades: K 1 2 3   **598**
  1. Hummingbirds
  ISBN 1561455881; 9781561455881; 978-1-56145-588-1; 1-56145-588-1
                 LC 2010051999
"The Sills cover the [hummingbird's] diet, size, migratory habits, anatomical features, reproduction, predators, and habitats. Of special interest are their hovering skills and aerobatic displays. Each spread consists of one large-type sentence and a large watercolor depiction with just enough information for youngsters to gain an introduction to hummingbirds. The text and art combine to make this title a useful and engaging read." SLJ

"The Sills cover the [hummingbird's] diet, size, migratory habits, anatomical features, reproduction, predators, and habitats. Of special interest are their hovering skills and aerobatic displays. Each spread consists of one large-type sentence and a large watercolor depiction with just enough information for youngsters to gain an introduction to hummingbirds. The text and art combine to make this title a useful and engaging read." SLJ

Sill, Cathryn P.
  ★ **About** raptors; a guide for children. [by] Cathryn Sill; illustrated by John Sill. Peachtree 2010 un il $16.95
Grades: K 1 2   **598**
  1. Birds of prey
  ISBN 978-1-56145-536-2; 1-56145-536-9
"One short, clearly written sentence or phrase per page communicates the basics about raptors: who they are, where they live, what they eat, and how they hunt. Their similarities, such as strong feet with sharp claws, and their differences, such as locations and kinds of nests, communicate diversity in raptors throughout the world. Eighteen quality watercolors focus on the birds in their natural habitats. . . .

This book is a must-buy for all libraries interested in building a strong natural-science collection for their young patrons." SLJ

Simon, Seymour

Penguins. HarperCollins Publishers 2007 31p il (Smithsonian) $16.99; lib bdg $17.89

Grades: 2 3 4   598

1. Penguins

ISBN 978-0-06-028395-7; 0-06-028395-5; 978-0-06-028396-4 lib bdg; 0-06-028396-3 lib bdg

LC 2006-24116

This describes penguin behavior, reproduction, and feeding

This is written "in a voice perfectly attuned to the conceptual level of elementary-age readers. . . . The full-page color photographs competently capture . . . penguin appeal and are skillfully discussed in the narrative." Horn Book

Stearns, Precious McKenzie

Whooping cranes; [by] Precious McKenzie. Rourke Pub. 2010 24p il map (Eye to eye with endangered species) lib bdg $27.07

Grades: 2 3 4   598

1. Cranes (Birds)

ISBN 978-1-60694-401-1 lib bdg; 1-60694-401-0 lib bdg

LC 2009-5992

Examines the issues endangered whooping cranes face and how they can be saved

"Sets out to introduce readers to [whooping cranes] . . . explain the dangers they face, and detail the efforts of biologists and conservationists to save them. . . . Serviceable and informative." SLJ

Includes glossary

Stewart, Melissa

A place for birds; written by Melissa Stewart; illustrated by Higgins Bond. Peachtree 2009 un il $16.95

Grades: K 1 2 3   598

1. Birds

ISBN 978-1-56145-474-7; 1-56145-474-5

LC 2008036744

"This title focuses on the effects, good and bad, that human behavior has on birds, highlighting the progress that we've made toward living in harmony with our winged friends and acknowledging problems still not solved. The rhythmic main text highlights birds' needs and what people can do to see that they are met. Insets on each page then provide specific examples to drive the point home. . . . This format . . . is effective and engaging, and Bond's acrylic illustrations depict realistic scenes with a crisp vibrancy." Kirkus

Stockdale, Susan

Bring on the birds; written and illustrated by Susan Stockdale. Peachtree 2011 un il $15.95

Grades: PreK K 1 2   598

1. Birds

ISBN 1-56145-560-1; 978-1-56145-560-7

LC 2010-26893

This book celebrates the different types of birds found around the world, from dancing birds, to swimming birds, to birds with bills. Bibliography. "Ages two to six." (Publisher's note)

"This cheerful survey introduces 21 species [of birds] from varied parts of the world in spare, rhyming text and attractive acrylic paintings. . . . Picture placement follows the nice rhythm of the text with each two sets of facing framed paintings followed by a double-page view for each of the longer phrases of verse. Simple, flat stylized settings . . . showcase the lively, colorful birds. . . . Carefully crafted in charm and simplicity, the book offers many possibilities for use and enjoyment in reading aloud, browsing, and teaching." SLJ

Thomson, Ruth

The life cycle of an owl. PowerKids Press 2009 24p il lib bdg $21.23; pa $8.25

Grades: K 1 2   598

1. Owls

ISBN 978-1-4358-2833-9 lib bdg; 1-4358-2833-X lib bdg; 978-1-4358-2883-4 pa; 1-4358-2883-6 pa

LC 2008026176

This introduction to the life cycle of the owl is "arranged in a series of spreads, each of which covers a subtopic. Pages feature one to three simple sentences of large-print text and a clear, color photograph of one or more animals in various stages of growth. . . . With [its] easily accessible format, and clear [text] and photographs, [this book] will appeal to both browsers and report writers." SLJ

Underwood, Deborah

Colorful peacocks; by Deborah Underwood. Lerner Publications Co. 2007 32p il (Pull ahead books) lib bdg $22.60; pa $5.95

Grades: K 1 2 3   598

1. Peacocks

ISBN 978-0-8225-5930-6 lib bdg; 0-8225-5930-7 lib bdg; 978-0-8225-6507-9 pa; 0-8225-6507-2 pa

LC 2005017977

"This charming introduction to the peafowl family presents facts and color photographs in an easy-to-read format. Underwood covers what they eat, where they sleep, and how they care for their young. An outline drawing of a peafowl with the parts labeled and a map showing countries native to the species are included. An informative and enjoyable book." SLJ

Includes bibliographical references

Vande Griek, Susan

Loon; pictures by Karen Reczuch. Groundwood Books 2011 il $18.95

Grades: K 1 2   598

1. Loons

ISBN 978-1-55498-077-2; 1-55498-077-1

"This book follows two loon chicks from birth to maturity and has a lyrical text and lush, full-color illustrations. The acrylic-on-canvas paintings are presented from different perspectives to engage viewers—straight on, closeup, and far away." SLJ

Vogel, Carole Garbuny

The man who flies with birds; [by] Carole G. Vogel and Yossi Leshem. Kar-Ben Pub. 2009 64p il map lib bdg $18.95

Grades: 5 6 7 8   598

1. Conservationists 2. Aircraft accidents 3. Birds --

Migration

ISBN 978-0-8225-7643-3 lib bdg; 0-8225-7643-0 lib bdg

LC 2008-31198

Discusses the work of the bird expert whose lifelong study of the patterns of bird migration in Israel has led to a significant reduction in the number of collisions between aircraft and bird flocks.

"The book is heavily illustrated with good-quality color photos, maps, and diagrams, many of them captioned with incredible facts about wildlife and migration. This inspiring title on a most timely topic will appeal to those who are fascinated with wildlife, Earth science, and technology." SLJ

Includes bibliographical references

Webb, Sophie

Looking for seabirds; journal from an Alaskan voyage. Houghton Mifflin Co. 2004 48p il $16

Grades: 4 5 6 7   **598**

1. Birds 2. Diaries 3. Birds -- Alaska 4. Sea birds -- Alaska 5. Natural history -- Alaska

ISBN 0-618-21235-3

LC 2003-12420

A journal of the author's observations and adventures while working on a research vessel counting seabirds through Alaska's Aleutian Island chain

The "immediacy of the narrative . . . and the clear and colorful watercolor-and-gouache landscapes and drawings of the birds form an appealing travelogue that is as exciting as it is informative." SLJ

Webster, Christine

Ravens. Weigl Publishers 2010 24p il (Backyard animals) lib bdg $24.45; pa $8.95

Grades: 1 2 3   **598**

1. Ravens

ISBN 978-1-60596-082-1 lib bdg; 1-60596-082-9 lib bdg; 978-1-60596-083-8 pa; 1-60596-083-7 pa

LC 2009004175

This describes the physical characteristics, natural habitats, history, and folklore of ravens

This is "packed with information and [includes] fine close-up photos." Booklist

Includes glossary

Wilcox, Charlotte

Bald eagles; photographs by Jerry Boucher. Carolrhoda Bks. 2003 48p il (Carolrhoda nature watch book) lib bdg $25.26

Grades: 3 4 5 6   **598**

1. Eagles 2. Bald eagle 3. Bald eagle -- Juvenile literature

ISBN 1-57505-170-2

LC 2001-6803

Describes the physical characteristics, life cycle, and behavior of bald eagles, as well as efforts to protect them

Includes index

Willis, Nancy Carol

Red knot; a shorebird's incredible journey. Birdsong Books 2006 un il map $15.95; pa $6.95

Grades: 2 3 4   **598**

1. Sandpipers 2. Birds -- Migration 3. Red knot --

Juvenile literature

ISBN 0-9662761-4-0; 0-9662761-5-9 pa

"This title introduces an endangered sandpiper and chronologically documents her journey from Tierra del Fuego along a 20,000-mile route to the Arctic where she has her young and then makes her way back down south for the winter. . . . The smooth, simple text is complemented with well-composed, colored-pencil drawings." SLJ

Winter, Jeanette

The **tale** of Pale Male; a true story. Harcourt, Inc. 2007 un il $16

Grades: K 1 2 3   **598**

1. Hawks 2. Red-tailed hawk -- Juvenile literature

ISBN 978-0-15-205972-9; 0-15-205972-5

LC 2006-08741

"Working with acrylics on watercolor paper, Winter uses Easter-egg colors to frame her appealing cityscapes. . . . Winter blends the realistic with the fanciful throughout the story." Booklist

Wolf, Sallie

★ The **robin** makes a laughing sound; a birder's journal. designed by Micah Bornstein. Charlesbridge 2010 43p il $11.95

Grades: 5 6 7 8   **598**

1. Birds 2. Bird watching

ISBN 978-1-58089-318-3; 1-58089-318-X

LC 2008-7248

Presents observations made through every season of the year of different birds and their behavior, from robins taking a bath, to cardinals searching for food in the snow, to an owl perched on a tree at night.

"The charming, eye-catching format includes short dated nature notes written in script, some of them on glued or taped-in torn paper pieces; other paper scraps contain short typeset poems and small, labeled watercolors. . . . Pen-and-ink sketches capture a baby house sparrow, a V-formation of geese, a downy woodpecker at a suet feeder, and more. . . . This small, instructional guide may provide the inspiration for young authors with even a bit of artistic talent to begin keeping nature journals of their own." SLJ

598.3   Water birds

Gibbons, Gail

Gulls--gulls--gulls. Holiday House 1997 un il $16.95; pa $6.95

Grades: K 1 2 3   **598.3**

1. Gulls

ISBN 0-8234-1323-3; 0-8234-1664-X pa

LC 97-1266

Describes the life cycle, behavior patterns, and habitat of various species of gulls, focusing on those found in North America

"Both illustration and text provide basic, easy-to-understand facts. . . . The format is attractive with framed, simply drawn watercolor illustrations showing the birds in the foreground against bright colorful seashore or seascape backgrounds of dominant blues and greens." SLJ

Markle, Sandra, 1946-

The **long**, long journey; the godwit's amazing migration. by Sandra Markle; illustrated by Mia Posada. Millbrook Press 2013 32 p. col. ill., col. map (library) $26.60
Grades: 1 2 3   **598.3**
1. Picture books for children 2. Bar-tailed godwit -- Juvenile literature
ISBN 0761356231; 9780761356233
         LC 2012020915

This children's picture book by Sandra Markle follows the migration journey of the bar-tailed godwit chick. "Migrating 7,000 miles south from their breeding grounds, bar-tailed godwits flee the Arctic winter for the Southern-Hemisphere summer, making the longest known nonstop flight of any bird." (Kirkus Reviews)

Includes bibliographical references

McMillan, Bruce

Nights of the pufflings; written and photo-illustrated by Bruce McMillan. Houghton Mifflin 1995 32p il $16; pa $5.95
Grades: 2 3 4   **598.3**
1. Puffins
ISBN 0-395-70810-9; 0-395-85693-0 pa
         LC 94-14808

"This fascinating story, combined with gorgeous color photographs, a simple, clear text, and handsome book design, makes an appealing package. McMillan includes the pronunciation of unfamiliar Icelandic names and words within the text and follows his story with an afterwood about the North Atlantic puffins." Horn Book

Includes bibliographical references

598.4 Miscellaneous orders of water birds

McMillan, Bruce

Days of the ducklings; written and photo-illustrated by Bruce McMillan. Houghton Mifflin 2001 32p il hardcover o.p. pa $6.95
Grades: 2 3 4   **598.4**
1. Ducks 2. Eider 3. Eider -- Iceland -- Hvallátur Island -- Juvenile literature 4. Eider -- Iceland -- Hvallátur Island -- Pictorial works -- Juvenile literature
ISBN 0-618-04878-2; 0-618-86270-6 pa
         LC 00-13258

"McMillan's photographs are of extremely high quality, a wonderful blend of artistry and emotion, and his text flows well." Booklist

Includes bibliographical references

598.47 Penguins

Gibbons, Gail

Penguins! Holiday House 1998 un il maps $16.95; pa $6.95
Grades: K 1 2 3   **598.47**
1. Penguins
ISBN 0-8234-1388-8; 0-8234-1516-3 pa
         LC 98-5194

Describes the habitat, physical characteristics, and behavior of different kinds of penguins

This book has "simply written, clear text. . . . The oversized format, brightly colored illustrations, and large type font result in an eye-catching appearance that will attract young researchers and the curious minded alike." SLJ

Guiberson, Brenda Z.

★ The **emperor** lays an egg; illustrated by Joan Paley. Holt & Co. 2001 un il $16.95; pa $7.99
Grades: K 1 2 3   **598.47**
1. Penguins 2. Emperor penguin 3. Emperor penguin -- Juvenile literature 4. Parental behavior in animals -- Juvenile literature
ISBN 0-8050-6204-1; 0-8050-7636-3 pa
         LC 00-40980

"Guiberson's vivid prose fleshes out the bare bones of the penguin's life cycle. . . . Paley's collages of painted and cut papers provide exceptionally beautiful scenes of the birds." Booklist

Tatham, Betty

Penguin chick; illustrated by Helen K. Davie. HarperCollins Pubs. 2002 33p il (Let's-read-and-find-out science) $15.95; pa $4.95
Grades: K 1 2 3   **598.47**
1. Penguins 2. Emperor penguin 3. Parental behavior in animals 4. Emperor penguin -- Infancy -- Juvenile literature
ISBN 0-06-028594-X; 0-06-445206-9 pa
         LC 00-59696

This book "follows the growth of one penguin chick from egg to adulthood. The story has been told before, but the clear, simple text provides intriguing details and inherent drama that will keep young children involved straight through till the end." Booklist

598.6 Galliformes and Columbiformes

Patent, Dorothy Hinshaw

Pigeons; photographs by William Muñoz. Clarion Bks. 1997 78p il $16
Grades: 4 5 6 7   **598.6**
1. Pigeons
ISBN 0-395-69848-0
         LC 96-42072

Describes the physical characteristics, behavior, and usefulness of these birds, which have lived with people since prehistoric times

"This informative book offers a well-researched and readable text illustrated with clear, full-color photographs." Booklist

Includes glossary

598.9 Falconiformes, Caprimulgiformes, owls

Bodden, Valerie

Owls; by Valerie Bodden. 1st ed. Creative Education 2013 24 p. (Amazing animals) (paperback) $25.65
Grades: 1 2 3 4   **598.9**
1. Owls -- Juvenile literature
ISBN 1608180883; 9781608180882
         LC 2011050280

This book, by Valerie Bodden, as part of the publisher's "Amazing Animals" series, presents an introduction to various species of owls. It presents "a basic exploration of the appearance, behavior, and habitat of owls, the winged nighttime hunters. Also included is a story from folklore explaining why some owls have big eyes and ears." (Publisher's note)

Includes bibliographical references and index

Riggs, Kate

Eagles; by Kate Riggs. Creative Paperbacks 2012 24p. col. ill.

Grades: K 1 2   **598.9**

1. Eagles -- Juvenile literature

ISBN 9780898126914

LC 2012008602

"A basic exploration of the appearance, behavior, and habitat of eagles, Earth's most widespread birds of prey. Also included is a story from folklore explaining why people respect eagles." (Publisher's note)

Includes bibliographical references (p. 24) and index.

Sattler, Helen Roney

The book of North American owls; illustrated by Jean Day Zallinger. Clarion Bks. 1995 64p il maps hardcover o.p. pa $7.95

Grades: 4 5 6 7   **598.9**

1. Owls

ISBN 0-395-60524-5; 0-395-90017-4 pa

LC 91-43626

This "is a superb ornithological primer. . . . The book is lavishly illustrated." Appraisal

Includes bibliographical references

599   Mammals

Gray, Susan Heinrichs

The life cycle of mammals; [by] Susan H. Gray. Heinemann Library 2011 48p il (Life cycles) lib bdg $32; pa $8.95

Grades: 3 4 5   **599**

1. Mammals

ISBN 978-1-4329-4981-5 lib bdg; 978-1-4329-4988-4 pa

LC 2010038498

This describes what a mammal is, types of mammals, their life cycles, habitats, foods, defenses, and relationships to humans.

Includes glossary and bibliographical references

Rodriguez, Ana Maria

Secret of the singing mice . . . and more! [by] Ana Maria Rodriguez. Enslow Publishers 2008 48p il (Animal secrets revealed!) lib bdg $23.93

Grades: 5 6 7 8   **599**

1. Mammals

ISBN 978-0-7660-2956-9 lib bdg; 0-7660-2956-5 lib bdg

LC 2007-39495

This book offers "fascinating accounts of how scientists systematically analyzed, tested and proved their theories or how their findings led to other, serendipitous discoveries. . .

. Science experiments are thoughtfully placed to inspire exploration, and captioned, full-color photos appear throughout." SLJ

Includes glossary and bibliographical references

★ Exploring the world of mammals; [edited by Nancy Simmons, Richard Beatty, Amy Jane Beer] Chelsea House 2008 6v il map set $210

Grades: 5 6 7 8   **599**

1. Reference books 2. Mammals -- Encyclopedias

ISBN 978-0-7910-9651-2 set; 0-7910-9651-3 set

LC 2007028223

"This colorful and appealing set offers an introduction to the world of mammals. Most of entries are 2 to 4 pages in length. Sidebars offer extra details, and bright photographs and illustrations appear on every 2-page spread." Booklist

599.2   Marsupials and monotremes

Arnold, Caroline

A wombat's world; written and illustrated by Caroline Arnold. Picture Window Books 2008 24p il (Caroline Arnold's animals) lib bdg $26.60

Grades: PreK K 1 2   **599.2**

1. Wombats

ISBN 978-1-4048-3986-1

LC 2007032891

"This introduction to wombats combines a narrative story with boxed facts about the animals. The uncluttered cut-paper collages and simple, straightforward text show and tell events in a wombat's life over a year's time. . . . Arnold gives a mostly clear, compelling sense of the lives and characteristics of these unique animals." Booklist

Bishop, Nic

★ Nic Bishop marsupials. Scholastic 2009 48p il $17.99

Grades: 3 4 5 6   **599.2**

1. Marsupials

ISBN 978-0-439-87758-9; 0-439-87758-X

LC 2008-53379

"This broad-ranging discussion includes the Virginia opossum and related animals in the Americas before turning to the main topic, the varied marsupials of Australia. Large in scale and often exceptionally clear, the many color photos will attract animal lovers to the book. . . . This inviting title pairs some remarkable photos with a wealth of intriguing facts." Booklist

Bredeson, Carmen

Kangaroos up close; [by] Carmen Bredeson. Enslow Elementary 2008 24p il (Zoom in on animals!) lib bdg $21.26

Grades: 1 2 3   **599.2**

1. Kangaroos

ISBN 978-0-7660-3079-4 lib bdg; 0-7660-3079-2 lib bdg

"Short paragraphs of simply written text describe [kangaroos'] key body parts and how they function. . . . Behavior, diet, and care and development of the young are briefly addressed. Facing the text on each spread is a full-page, sharp, color closeup. . . . Bredeson's simply written and colorful [title] will provide younger readers with [a] satisfying first [introduction] to these fascinating creatures." SLJ

Includes glossary and bibliographical references

Doudna, Kelly

It's a baby kangaroo! ABDO Pub. Co. 2009 24p il (Baby Australian animals) $13.95

Grades: K 1 2 3   **599.2**

1. Kangaroos

ISBN 978-1-60453-576-1; 1-60453-576-8

LC 2008055075

The "book opens with a page of vital statistics: the 'baby name,' number in litter, 'weight at birth,' 'age of independence,' 'adult weight,' and 'life expectancy.' The [book] then [goes] on to describe where the animals live and their predators and conclude with a 'Fun Fact.' The photography is excellent. Sidebars on some pages include more facts or reinforce the text." SLJ

French, Jackie

★ How to scratch a wombat; where to find it . . . what to feed it . . . why it sleeps all day. illustrated by Bruce Whatley. Clarion Books 2009 85p il $16

Grades: 2 3 4 5   **599.2**

1. Wombats

ISBN 978-0-618-86864-3; 0-618-86864-X

LC 2008-02581

"Between detailed notes about wombat anatomy, behavior and habitat, French weaves in personal anecdotes from her 30-plus years of observing local wombats and caring for orphaned baby wombats. . . . French uses a friendly tone, discussing how wombats have influenced her writing career. Whatley's spot maps, diagrams and realistic b&w pencil sketches further amplify key points. A nifty blend of field notebook and memoir." Publ Wkly

Gish, Melissa

Kangaroos. Creative Education 2010 46p il (Living wild) $23.95; pa $9.95

Grades: 5 6 7 8   **599.2**

1. Kangaroos

ISBN 978-1-58341-970-0; 1-58341-970-5; 978-0-89812-553-5 pa; 0-89812-553-7 pa

LC 2010017375

"A look at kangaroos, including their habitats, physical characteristics such as the females' pouches, behaviors, relationships with humans, and valued status in the world today." Publisher's note

Heos, Bridget

What to expect when you're expecting joeys; a guide for marsupial parents (and curious kids) illustrated by Stephane Jorisch. Millbrook Press 2011 il (Expecting animal babies)

Grades: 2 3 4 5   **599.2**

1. Marsupials

ISBN 0761358595; 9780761358596

LC 2010051506

"Directed at marsupial parents of all kinds, from kangaroos and koalas to possums and bandicoots, this tongue-in-cheek guide to joey development takes it step by step, from the birth of your pinkie to where your baby goes after it leaves the pouch. Never once dropping the pretense that this is written for pouched mammals, this manages to be both

entertaining and informative. . . . [The author] uses appropriate vocabulary, making meanings clear in context and also providing a glossary. Jorisch's painted pen-and-ink sketches show lively, lightly anthropomorphized animals and add considerably to the humor." Kirkus

Includes glossary and bibliographical references

Markle, Sandra

★ Finding home; [by] Sandra Markle; illustrated by Alan Marks. Charlesbridge 2008 un il lib bdg $15.95

Grades: K 1 2 3   **599.2**

1. Koalas

ISBN 978-1-58089-122-6

LC 2007-01473

"Based on the true story of a koala that survived multiple bushfires and wandered into a residential area, this picture book, narrated in dramatic free verse, tells a gripping story of animal survival. . . . Markle's smooth, elegant poetry and Marks' expressive, realistic mixed-media images give a strong sense of the animals' terror and the mother's intense bond with her child." Booklist

Includes bibliographical references

Markovics, Joyce L.

Tasmanian devil; nighttime scavenger. by Joyce L. Markovics. Bearport Pub. 2009 32p il map (Uncommon animals) lib bdg $25.27

Grades: 1 2 3   **599.2**

1. Tasmanian devils

ISBN 978-1-59716-733-8 lib bdg; 1-59716-733-9 lib bdg

LC 2008-9307

"The explanatory text works spendidly, with large photographs that bring readers as close as they'll ever get to such beasts." Booklist

Includes glossary and bibliographical references

Montgomery, Sy

★ Quest for the tree kangaroo; an expedition to the cloud forest of New Guinea. text by Sy Montgomery; photographs by Nic Bishop. Houghton Mifflin 2006 79p il map (Scientists in the field) $18

Grades: 5 6 7 8   **599.2**

1. Zoologists 2. Tree kangaroos

ISBN 0-618-49641-6

LC 2005-34849

"The writer and photographer of this exemplary description of science field work accompanied researcher Lisa Dabek on an expedition high in New Guinea's mountains to study tree kangaroos and promote the conservation of this elusive and endangered species. . . . Montgomery . . . paces her narrative well . . . keeping the reader engaged and concerned. . . . Bishop's photographs . . . are beautifully reproduced." Publ Wkly

Racanelli, Marie

Animals with pockets. PowerKids Press 2010 24p il (Crazy nature) lib bdg $21.25; pa $8.25

Grades: 2 3 4 5   **599.2**

1. Marsupials

ISBN 978-1-4358-9385-6 lib bdg; 1-4358-9385-9 lib bdg; 978-1-4358-9862-2 pa; 1-4358-9862-1 pa

LC 2009036517

This book takes a look at different kinds of marsupials, and what makes them unique from other mammals.

This book "combines attention-grabbing information with a well-organized format. . . . [The book has] spectacular color photography and eye-popping facts. . . . Excellent for reports." SLJ

Includes glossary

Riggs, Kate

Kangaroos; by Kate Riggs. Creative Education 2012 24 p. col. ill.

Grades: K 1 2   **599.2**

1. Kangaroos 2. Animal behavior 3. Animals -- Folklore 4. Wildlife photography 5. Zoology -- Encyclopedias

ISBN 1608181081; 9781608181087

LC 2010049210

This children's book, part of Kate Riggs' "Amazing Animals" series, focuses on kangaroos. "This . . . popular series continues traveling the planet to study alligators, bats, and other fascinating animals. . . . [P]hotos are paired with . . . text to examine the featured creature's appearance, habitat, behaviors, and life cycle. . . . A basic exploration of the appearance, behavior, and habitat of kangaroos, Australia's iconic marsupials. Also included is a story from folklore explaining why kangaroos jump instead of run." (Publisher's note)

Includes bibliographical references (p. 24) and index

Sill, Cathryn P.

About marsupials; a guide for children. [by] Cathryn Sill; illustrated by John Sill. Peachtree 2006 un il $15.95

Grades: K 1 2 3   **599.2**

1. Marsupials

ISBN 1-56145-358-7

LC 2005-20582

This introduces the characteristics and behavior of 17 marsupials, such as the marsupial mole, the red kangaroo, the numbat, the spotted cuscus, the koala and tasmanian devil.

"Written with simplicity and dignity. . . . Well-suited to classroom sharing, the paintings are attractively composed and clearly delineated." Booklist

Includes glossary and bibliographical references

Webster, Christine

Opossums; [by] Christine Webster. Weigl Publishers Inc. 2008 24p il map (Backyard animals) lib bdg $24.45; pa $6.95

Grades: 2 3 4   **599.2**

1. Opossums

ISBN 978-1-59036-677-6 lib bdg; 978-1-59036-678-3 pa

LC 2006-102107

This describes the physical characteristics, behavior, and life cycle of the opossum.

"Large, full-color photos appear thoughout, and the [text is] clearly written and well organized." SLJ

Includes glossary and bibliographical references

599.3   Miscellaneous orders of placental mammals

Aronin, Miriam

The **prairie** dog's town; a perfect hideaway. Bearport Pub. 2009 32p il map (Spectacular animal towns) lib bdg $25.27

Grades: 2 3 4   **599.3**

1. Prairie dogs

ISBN 978-1-59716-870-0 lib bdg; 1-59716-870-X lib bdg

LC 2009-4064

"Introduces prairie dogs and how they live, covering the building of burrows and towns for families, different types of communication skills, and conservation efforts to protect them." Publisher's note

Includes glossary and bibliographical references

Bailer, Darice

Prairie dogs. Marshall Cavendish Benchmark 2011 il (Animals, animals) lib bdg $20.95

Grades: 3 4 5   **599.3**

1. Prairie dogs

ISBN 978-0-7614-4876-1; 0-7614-4876-4

LC 2010016033

Provides information on the anatomy, special skills, habitats, and diet of prairie dogs.

Includes glossary and bibliographical references

Cooke, Lucy

★ A **little** book of sloth; by Lucy Cooke. Margaret K. McElderry Books 2013 64 p. col. ill. (hardcover) $16.99

Grades: PreK K 1 2 3   **599.3**

1. Sloths 2. Picture books for children 3. Sloths -- Costa Rica -- Juvenile literature

ISBN 1442445572; 9781442445574

LC 2012018737

In this children's picture book, author Lucy Cooke "offers an encyclopedic look at" sloths "by way of a photo-tour of their . . . sanctuary in Costa Rica. There are sloths in pajamas (which are actually necessary because they can't control their body temperature), sloths in a 'cuddle puddle,' sloths hugging stuffed animals, [and] sloths gazing into the camera with small but trusting eyes." (Publishers Weekly)

George, Lynn

Prairie dogs; tunnel diggers. PowerKids Press 2011 24p il (Animal architects) lib bdg $21.25; pa $8.25

Grades: 1 2 3   **599.3**

1. Prairie dogs 2. Animals -- Habitations

ISBN 978-1-4488-0695-9 lib bdg; 1-4488-0695-X lib bdg; 978-1-4488-1351-3 pa; 1-4488-1351-4 pa

LC 2010008867

Includes glossary

Gibbons, Gail

Rabbits, rabbits, & more rabbits! Holiday House 2000 un il $16.95; pa $6.95

Grades: K 1 2 3   **599.3**

1. Rabbits

ISBN 0-8234-1486-8; 0-8234-1660-7 pa

LC 99-16765

Describes different kinds of rabbits, their physical characteristics, behavior, where they live, and how to care for them

"Colored washes and crayon shading enliven the clearly delineated ink drawings." Booklist

Glaser, Linda

Hello, squirrels! scampering through the seasons. by Linda Glaser; illustrated by Gay W. Holland. Millbrook Press 2006 32p il lib bdg $22.60

Grades: K 1 2   **599.3**

1. Squirrels

ISBN 978-0-7613-2887-2 lib bdg; 0-7613-2887-4 lib bdg

LC 2005003692

"The book documents a year in a squirrel's life in a first-person narration that imitates a child's voice and cadences. . . The text is filled with the kind of natural details that a child would observe. Holland's realistic colored-pencil drawings . . . are complemented by generous white space and easy-to-read print. More scientific information is provided in the answers to four questions at the end of the book." Booklist

Jango-Cohen, Judith

★ Armadillos. Benchmark Bks. 2004 47p il map (Animals, animals) lib bdg $25.64

Grades: 3 4 5 6   **599.3**

1. Armadillos

ISBN 0-7614-1617-X

LC 2003-3824

Describes the physical characteristics, behavior, and habitat of armadillos

Includes glossary and bibliographical references

Kalman, Bobbie

The life cycle of a beaver; [by] Bobbie Kalman. Crabtree 2007 32p il lib bdg $25.27; pa $6.95

Grades: 2 3 4   **599.3**

1. Beavers

ISBN 978-0-7787-0628-1 lib bdg; 0-7787-0628-1 lib bdg; 978-0-7787-0702-8 pa; 0-7787-0702-4 pa

LC 2006023330

The beaver "is described as a mammal (a term that is explained) belonging to the rodent family. Its habitat is outlined, along with information on how it builds lodges, dams, and burrows. Diet, growth, and facts about the young are included. The information is presented in a flowing narrative accompanied by color photographs and drawings that perfectly illustrate the [text]." SLJ

Markle, Sandra

Prairie dogs. Lerner Publications Company 2007 39p il map (Animal prey) lib bdg $25.26; pa $7.95

Grades: 4 5 6   **599.3**

1. Prairie dogs

ISBN 978-0-8225-6438-6 lib bdg; 0-8225-6438-6 lib bdg; 978-0-8225-6441-6 pa; 0-8225-6441-6 pa

LC 2006-598

Describes the behavior of prairie dogs in their native habitat, where they are the prey of larger animals and birds and where they must work together as a colony to create burrows and warning systems to protect themselves and their young

Includes glossary and bibliographical references

Otfinoski, Steven

Squirrels. Marshall Cavendish Benchmark 2010 47p il (Animals, animals) lib bdg $29.93

Grades: 3 4 5   **599.3**

1. Squirrels

ISBN 978-0-7614-4843-3; 0-7614-4843-8

LC 2009022628

This offers information on the anatomy, special skills, habitats, and diet of squirrels.

Includes glossary and bibliographical references

Reingold, Adam

The beaver's lodge; building with leftovers. Bearport Pub. 2009 32p il map (Spectacular animal towns) lib bdg $25.27

Grades: 2 3 4   **599.3**

1. Beavers

ISBN 978-1-59716-872-4 lib bdg; 1-59716-872-6 lib bdg

LC 2009-11723

Explores the remarkable homes built by beavers.

"Through excellent photographs, high-interest texts, sidebars, maps, and other material, children learn about both the animals and their habitats. The . . . book also provides brief profiles of animals with similar habitats. . . . [This book is] much better than average 'report' titles." SLJ

Includes glossary and bibliographical references

Stewart, Melissa

Sloths. Carolrhoda Books 2005 48p il map (Carolrhoda nature watch book) lib bdg $25.26

Grades: 3 4 5 6   **599.3**

1. Sloths

ISBN 1-57505-577-5

LC 2003-23223

In this "book, two and three-toed sloths' physical features, habitat, and environmental issues are featured. The well-composed text traces their evolution from prehistoric progenitors' to the current day. . . . With its well-captioned, full-color photos on every page and informative text, Sloths offers enough information for solid reports and general interest." SLJ

Swinburne, Stephen R.

Armadillo trail; the northward journey of the armadillo. illustrated by Bruce Hiscock. Boyds Mills Press 2009 un il $16.95

Grades: K 1 2 3   **599.3**

1. Armadillos

ISBN 978-1-59078-463-1

LC 2008028774

"In a burrow beneath a Texas field, an armadillo gives birth to four pups. As the little ones grow, they venture outside with her to hunt for food. . . . This handsome picture book offers enough detail to engage them in understanding armadillos, and a refreshing lack of sensationalism and sentimentality about events in the animals' lives." Booklist

Zuchora-Walske, Christine

Let's look at prairie dogs. Lerner Publications Co. 2010 32p il map (Lightning bolt books: Animal close-ups) lib bdg $25.26

Grades: PreK K 1 2   **599.3**
1. Prairie dogs
ISBN 978-0-7613-3891-8 lib bdg; 0-7613-3891-8
lib bdg

LC 2008-51856

Introduces prairie dogs, describing their physical characteristics, habitat, and predators

"Fresh photography, a creative use of graphics, and a collagelike layout make[s] . . . [this book] eye-catching. . . . [The] book ends with a labeled diagram of the animal, a range map, and a further-reading list that includes print and online resources in a single list, a nice way of validating both types of materials." SLJ

Includes glossary

599.35   Rodents

Bill, Tannis
★ **Pika**; life in the rocks. photographs by Jim Jacobson. Boyds Mills Press 2010 32p il $18.95
Grades: K 1 2 3   **599.35**
1. Pikas
ISBN 978-1-59078-803-5; 1-59078-803-6

"The pika is a cousin to the rabbit. . . . Using short, declarative sentences, Tannis follows the laborious life of a pika living in the Rocky Mountains. It is a daily grind of gathering leaves and branches for his hay pile, a massive thatch that can grow as large as a bathtub and that serves as a food reserve, particularly during winter months. . . . The photos capture the pika at his cutest. . . . Loaded with rich back matter on the pika and its predators, this is a cycle-of-life book that satisfies to the end." Booklist

Includes glossary and bibliographical references

Ganeri, Anita
Capybara. Heinemann Library 2011 24p il map (Day in the life. rain forest animals) lib bdg $22; pa $6.49
Grades: 1 2   **599.35**
1. Capybara
ISBN 978-1-4329-4110-9 lib bdg; 1-4329-4110-0 lib bdg; 978-1-4329-4121-5 pa; 1-4329-4121-6 pa

LC 2010001132

This book follows a capybara through its day as it sleeps, eats, and moves.

"Ganeri presents information clearly and simply in large type, two-sentence comments placed below a bright, sharply reproduced color photograph of the animal in a natural setting. . . . [This is] sufficiently specific to support assignment as well as pleasure reading." SLJ

Includes glossary and bibliographical references

Kalman, Bobbie
Baby rodents; by Bobbie Kalman. Crabtree Publishing Company 2013 24 p. col. ill. (library) $22.60; (paperback) $6.95
Grades: 1 2 3 4   **599.35**
1. Rodents 2. Animal babies -- Juvenile literature
ISBN 9780778710097; 9780778710141

LC 2012043742

This book by Bobbie Kalman presents "photographs of different kinds of rodents from cute baby chipmunks to chubby capybaras. Easy-to-understand text explains in

which habitats rodents live and how their babies are born and raised. Young readers will also learn about rodent teeth, rodent diets, how different rodents move, build their homes, and which rodents are popular pets." (Publisher's note)

Includes bibliographical references and index.

Markle, Sandra
Outside and inside rats and mice. Atheneum Bks. for Young Readers 2001 39p il hardcover o.p. pa $10.99
Grades: 2 3 4   **599.35**
1. Mice 2. Rats 3. Mice -- Anatomy -- Juvenile literature 4. Rats -- Anatomy -- Juvenile literature
ISBN 0-689-82301-0; 1-4169-7571-3 pa

LC 00-29290

Describes the external and internal physical characteristics of mice and rats and their behavior

"Markle skillfully draws readers into careful observation of outstanding close-up photographs of mice and rats. . . . The friendly text maintains its scientific rigor." Horn Book

Includes glossary

★ **Porcupines**; [by] Sandra Markle. Lerner Publications Company 2007 39p il (Animal prey) lib bdg $25.26
Grades: 3 4 5   **599.35**
1. Porcupines
ISBN 978-0-8225-6439-3 lib bdg; 0-8225-6439-4 lib bdg

LC 2006000601

This describes the physical characteristics, habits, and life cycle of porcupines

"An outstanding combination of fascinating [text] and informative, appealing photos." SLJ

Includes glossary and bibliographical references

Marrin, Albert
★ **Oh,** rats! the story of rats and people. illustrated by C.B. Mordan. Dutton Children's Books 2006 48p il $16.99
Grades: 3 4 5 6   **599.35**
1. Rats
ISBN 0-525-47762-4

LC 2004-24512

This is "lively and informative. . . . The nine short chapters are set in a handsome slim book with striking black-and-white scratchboard illustrations and muted red framing on many pages." SLJ

Includes bibliographical references

Savage, Stephen
Mouse. PowerKids Press 2009 32p il (Animal neighbors) lib bdg $23.95
Grades: 3 4 5 6   **599.35**
1. Mice
ISBN 978-1-4358-4990-7 lib bdg; 1-4358-4990-6 lib bdg

LC 2008-5414

This describes the life cycle, habitat, and behavior of mice

Rat. PowerKids Press 2009 32p il (Animal neighbors) lib bdg $23.95

Grades: 3 4 5   **599.35**
1. Rats
ISBN 978-1-4358-4991-4 lib bdg; 1-4358-4991-4
lib bdg

LC 2008-5451

This describes the life cycle, habitat, and behavior of rats
This title features "beautiful, detailed, close-up photos of animals displayed on child-friendly page layouts. The information is well organized for reports." SLJ

Sill, Cathryn P.
About rodents; [by] Cathryn Sill; illustrated by John Sill. Peachtree 2008 un il $15.95
Grades: K 1 2 3   **599.35**
1. Rodents
ISBN 978-1-56145-454-9; 1-56145-454-0

Explains what rodents are, how they live, and what they do.
"Beautifully illustrated with clear, well-composed paintings of animals, this book shows respect for its audience as well as its subject." Booklist
Includes glossary and bibliographical references

Tait, Leia
Mice. Weigl 2010 24p il (Backyard animals) lib bdg $24.45; pa $8.95
Grades: 1 2 3   **599.35**
1. Mice
ISBN 978-1-60596-080-7 lib bdg; 1-60596-080-2 lib bdg; 978-1-60596-081-4 pa; 1-60596-081-0 pa

LC 2008052059

This is "packed with information and [includes] fine close-up photos. . . . [It] does a solid job of introducing the tiny animal's habits and habitats." Booklist
Includes glossary

Webster, Christine
Porcupines. Weigl 2010 24p il (Backyard animals) lib bdg $24.45; pa $8.95
Grades: 1 2 3   **599.35**
1. Porcupines
ISBN 978-1-60596-078-4 lib bdg; 1-60596-078-0 lib bdg; 978-1-60596-079-1 pa; 1-60596-079-9 pa

LC 2009004446

This describes the physical characteristics, natural habitats, history, and folklore of porcupines.
Includes glossary

599.4   Bats

Bekkering, Annalise
Bats. Weigl 2010 24p il (Backyard animals) lib bdg $24.45; pa $8.95
Grades: 1 2 3   **599.4**
1. Bats
ISBN 978-1-60596-076-0 lib bdg; 1-60596-076-4 lib bdg; 978-1-60596-077-7 pa; 1-60596-077-2 pa

LC 2008052056

This describes the "outstanding physical and behavioral characteristics [of bats]; some historical background; natural habitats and life cycle; role in the mythology of various cultures (a short myth is recounted); and tips on how to respond to (or avoid) encounters with the creatures. . . . A large, clear color photograph of one or more of the . . . animals . . . appears on about every other page." SLJ
Includes glossary

Berman, Ruth
Let's look at bats. Lerner Publications Co. 2010 32p il (Lightning bolt books: Animal close-ups) lib bdg $25.26
Grades: PreK K 1 2   **599.4**
1. Bats
ISBN 978-0-7613-3885-7 lib bdg; 0-7613-3885-3 lib bdg

LC 2008-51858

Introduces bats, describing their physical characteristics, habitat, nocturnal behavior, and feeding habits
"Fresh photography, a creative use of graphics, and a collagelike layout make[s] . . . [this book] eye-catching. . . . [The] book ends with a labeled diagram of the animal, a range map, and a further-reading list that includes print and online resources in a single list, a nice way of validating both types of materials." SLJ
Includes glossary

Carney, Elizabeth
Bats. National Geographic 2010 31p il (National Geographic readers) pa $3.99; $11.90
Grades: 1 2 3   **599.4**
1. Bats
ISBN 978-1-4263-0710-2 pa; 1-4263-0710-1 pa; 978-1-4263-0711-9; 1-4263-0711-X

LC 2010011636

"This leveled reader offers very basic information about bats. Topics range from types of bats to bat diet to behaviors such as echolocation and hanging upside down. . . . 'Bat Myths,' such as consuming human blood, are debunked. Simple sentence structures, along with corny jokes and excellent well-captioned photos, increase accessibility." Horn Book Guide
Includes glossary

Carson, Mary Kay
★ The **bat** scientists; with photographs by Tom Uhlman. Houghton Mifflin Books for Children 2010 79p il (Scientists in the field) $18
Grades: 4 5 6 7   **599.4**
1. Bats 2. Conservation biology -- Research -- Juvenile literature
ISBN 978-0-547-19956-6; 0-547-19956-2

LC 2010006767

This describes "patient field work, rescue and conservation efforts to save bats. . . . Woven into particular researchers' stories is an enormous amount of information about bat biology and behavior. Uhlman's photographs are clearly identified in context and the backmatter supports further research." Kirkus
Includes glossary and bibliographical references

Davies, Nicola, 1958-
★ **Bat** loves the night; illustrated by Sarah Fox-Davies. Candlewick Press 2001 28p il hardcover o.p. pa $6.99
Grades: PreK K 1 2   **599.4**
1. Bats
ISBN 0-7636-1202-2; 0-7636-2438-1 pa

LC 00-66681

Bat wakes up, flies into the night, uses the echoes of her voice to navigate, hunts for her supper, and returns to her roost to feed her baby

"An enticing picture book . . . that blends story with fact. . . . Lovely, atmospheric watercolor-and-pencil illustrations show surprising detail and succeed in making an oft-maligned animal appear realistically fuzzy and appealing." Booklist

Dornfeld, Margaret

★ **Bats**; [by] Margaret Dornfeld. Benchmark Books 2004 46p il map (Animals, animals) lib bdg $25.64
Grades: 3 4 5 6　　　　　　　　　　　　　　　　599.4
1. Bats
ISBN 0-7614-1754-0
LC 2004-9342
This describes the life cycles and characteristics of bats, illustrated with color photographs.

Includes glossary and bibliographical references

Earle, Ann

Zipping, zapping, zooming bats; illustrated by Henry Cole. HarperCollins Pubs. 1995 32p il (Let's-read-and-find-out science) hardcover o.p. pa $4.95
Grades: K 1 2 3　　　　　　　　　　　　　　　599.4
1. Bats
ISBN 0-06-023480-6; 0-06-445133-X pa
LC 93-11052
"Brown bats are introduced as fliers, hunters, and contributors to good ecology in this simple discussion of the flying mammals' physical characteristics and behavior. The illustrations include realistic close-ups, informative diagrams, and scenes incorporating children. Instructions for building a bat house are included." Horn Book Guide

Gibbons, Gail

Bats. Holiday House 1999 un il $16.95; pa $6.95
Grades: K 1 2 3　　　　　　　　　　　　　　　599.4
1. Bats
ISBN 0-8234-1457-4; 0-8234-1637-2 pa
LC 99-12051
Describes different kinds of bats, their physical characteristics, habits and behavior, and efforts to protect them

"The occasional splashes of color light up brilliantly against the dark backgrounds. Well suited for classroom use, this book makes a good case for bats as an admirable part of the natural world." Booklist

Gish, Melissa

Bats. Creative Paperbacks 2010 46p il (Living wild) $23.95; pa $9.95
Grades: 5 6 7 8　　　　　　　　　　　　　　　599.4
1. Bats
ISBN 978-1-58341-966-3; 1-58341-966-7; 978-0-89812-549-8 pa; 0-89812-549-9 pa
LC 2010017371
The "book lucidly discusses conservation and the animals' often tenuous relationship with humans. The layout is uniformly simple but effective, constructed with a nice balance of main text for the report writers, smaller chunks of esoterica for browsers, and . . . killer photos." Booklist

Gonzales, Doreen

Bats in the dark. PowerKids Press 2010 24p il (Creatures of the night) lib bdg $21.25; pa $8.05
Grades: 2 3 4　　　　　　　　　　　　　　　599.4
1. Bats
ISBN 978-1-4042-8096-0 lib bdg; 1-4042-8096-0 lib bdg; 978-1-4358-3249-7 pa; 1-4358-3249-3 pa
LC 2008-53802
A look at bats and their world in the dark

"Basic details are complemented by eclectic trivia, . . . [and] each volume concludes with a defense of the animal . . . and why it is vital to humans. The layout is attractive, with easy-to-read text and eye-catching photography. Good for reports." SLJ

Includes glossary

Lunde, Darrin P.

Hello, bumblebee bat; [by] Darrin Lunde; illustrated by Patricia J. Wynne. Charlesbridge 2007 un il lib bdg $15.95
Grades: PreK K 1 2　　　　　　　　　　　　599.4
1. Bats
ISBN 978-1-57091-374-7 lib bdg; 1-57091-374-9 lib bdg
LC 2006-20952
A Geisel Award honor book, 2008

"Meet the inch-long bumblebee bat, the smallest bat species in the world. Each left-hand page poses a question to a little bat. . . . Beginning each question with the bat's memorable name heightens the pleasing sense of pattern in the text, which offers information that children can understand, but avoids overwhelming them with too many facts. Wynne . . . contributes an appealing set of pictures that complement the text." Booklist

Markovics, Joyce L.

The **bat's** cave; a dark city. by Joyce Markovics. Bearport Pub. 2009 32p il map (Spectacular animal towns) lib bdg $25.27
Grades: 2 3 4　　　　　　　　　　　　　　　599.4
1. Bats
ISBN 978-1-59716-871-7 lib bdg; 1-59716-871-8 lib bdg
LC 2009-8146
A look inside a bat's dark world, how bats hunt, sleep, and raise their young, and more

"Through excellent photographs, high-interest texts, sidebars, maps, and other material, children learn about both the animals and their habitats. The . . . book also provides brief profiles of animals with similar habitats. . . . [This book is] much better than average 'report' titles." SLJ

Includes glossary and bibliographical references

Riggs, Kate

Bats; by Kate Riggs. Creative Education 2012 24 p. col. ill.
Grades: K 1 2　　　　　　　　　　　　　　　599.4
1. Bats 2. Animals -- Food 3. Bats -- Folklore 4. Wildlife photography 5. Zoology -- Encyclopedias 6. Bats -- Juvenile literature
ISBN 1608181057; 9781608181056
LC 2010049117
This children's book is part of Kate Riggs' "Amazing Animals" series, which presents photographs and "general

facts about physiology, behaviors, eating habits, habitats, and life spans" of various animals. (Booklist) ""A basic exploration of the appearance, behavior, and habitat of bats, Earth's only flying mammals. Also included is a story from folklore explaining how bats helped shape the earth." (Publisher's note)

Includes bibliographical references (p. 24) and index

Rodriguez, Cindy

Bats. Rourke Pub. 2010 24p il map (Eye to eye with endangered species) lib bdg $27.07

Grades: 2 3 4   **599.4**
1. Bats
ISBN 978-1-60694-406-6 lib bdg; 1-60694-406-1 lib bdg

LC 2009-5997

Text examines the issues endangered bats face and how they can be saved

"Sets out to introduce readers to [bats] . . . explain the dangers they face, and detail the efforts of biologists and conservationists to save them. . . . Serviceable and informative." SLJ

Includes glossary

Stewart, Melissa

How do bats fly in the dark? Marshall Cavendish Benchmark 2009 32p il (Tell me why, tell me how) lib bdg $20.95

Grades: 3 4 5   **599.4**
1. Bats
ISBN 978-0-7614-2924-1 lib bdg; 0-7614-2924-7 lib bdg

LC 2007023821

"Provides comprehensive information on bats and the process of how they use their sensory system to find their way in the dark" Publisher's note

Includes glossary and bibliographical references

A **place** for bats; written by Melissa Stewart; illustrated by Higgins Bond. 1st ed. Peachtree Publishers 2012 32 p. col. ill. (reinforced) $16.95

Grades: K 1 2   **599.4**
1. Bats 2. Habitat (Ecology) 3. Human influence on nature
ISBN 1561456241; 9781561456246

LC 2011020468

"This book introduces 12 varieties of bats and their habitats around Canada, the United States, and Mexico, and brings to life their challenges to survive." (School Library Journal) "[Melissa] Stewart points out problems faced by bats and what specific steps people have taken . . . to help the bats, such as . . . putting up 'bat boxes' to house bats that can no longer find dead trees for shelter. The text clearly conveys the idea that people can make a difference in animal survival." (Booklist)

Includes bibliographical references.

Vogel, Julia

Bats; by Julia Vogel; illustrations by Andrew Recher. NorthWord 2007 47p il (Our wild world) $10.95; pa $7.95

Grades: 3 4 5 6   **599.4**
1. Bats
ISBN 978-1-55971-968-1; 978-1-55971-969-8 pa

LC 2006021917

The "text describes the major physical characteristics shared by all [bats], . . . behavior, distinctive characteristics of several large groups and more than two dozen species, habitats, defense mechanisms, diets, and life cycles. . . . A sharp color photograph . . . illustrates the text on most pages." Booklist

599.5   Cetaceans and sea cows

Arnosky, Jim

Jim Arnosky's All about manatees. Scholastic Nonfiction 2008 un pa $5.99

Grades: K 1 2 3   **599.5**
1. Manatees
ISBN 0-439-90361-0 pa; 978-0-439-90361-5 pa

LC 2007061717

This is an "introductory guide to manatees. . . . Artwork, captions, and paragraphs of information work together seamlessly to present the physical characteristics, behaviors, and habitats of manatees living in Florida waters, as well as the threats to their survival. Fluid paintings illustrate points in the text and depict the animals' lumbering grace." Booklist

Baker, Molly

The **secret** world of whales; illustrated by Molly Baker. Chronicle Books 2011 108p il $16.99

Grades: 4 5 6 7   **599.5**
1. Whales
ISBN 978-0-8118-7641-4; 0-8118-7641-1

LC 2010-27355

"In this small-format volume, Siebert creates a concise introduction to whales, addressing myths and stories, the history of the whaling industry, communication and intelligence, and encounters between whales and humans. With playful, anthropomorphic cartoons, striking photographs, and a discussion of the dangers facing whales—noise pollution from boats, potentially lethal sonar—readers should gain a vivid impression of their behavior in the wild, as well as an appreciation for their majesty." Publ Wkly

Catt, Thessaly

Migrating with the humpback whale. PowerKids Press 2011 24p il (Animal journeys) lib bdg $21.25; pa $8.25

Grades: 2 3 4   **599.5**
1. Whales 2. Animals -- Migration
ISBN 978-1-4488-2543-1 lib bdg; 1-4488-2543-1 lib bdg; 978-1-4488-2670-4 pa; 1-4488-2670-5 pa

LC 2010027076

This book follows "the yearly migratory patterns of the [humpback whale] and [covers] anatomy, diet, mating, parenting, climate change as caused by people, pollution, and more. . . . [It is illustrated] with clear color photographs. . . . Go-to nonfiction for animal enthusiasts." SLJ

Christopherson, Sara Cohen

Top 50 reasons to care about whales and dolphins; animals in peril. Enslow Publishers 2010 103p il (Top 50 reasons to care about endangered animals) lib bdg $31.93

Grades: 4 5 6 7   **599.5**
1. Whales 2. Dolphins 3. Endangered species
ISBN 978-0-7660-3453-2 lib bdg; 0-7660-3453-4
lib bdg

          LC 2008-48695
This describes whales and dolphins—their life cycles, diets, young, habitats, and reasons why they are endangered animals
"The illustrations, mostly color photographs, represent a wonderful selection of the animals and their habitats. Reluctant readers may be enticed by this . . . simply because of the great images. This . . . would make a substantial supplement to the science curriculum when studying endangered animals." Libr Media Connect
Includes glossary and bibliographical references

Davies, Nicola, 1958-
 Big blue whale; illustrated by Nick Maland. Candlewick Press 1997 27p il hardcover o.p. pa $6.99
Grades: K 1 2 3   **599.5**
1. Whales
ISBN 1-56402-895-X; 0-7636-1080-1 pa
          LC 96-42327
Examines the physical characteristics, habits, and habitats of the blue whale
"Davies's brief overview offers young readers exactly what they want to know about this magnificent animal, and her judicious use of comparison makes the abstract more understandable. . . . Maland's cross-hatched pen-and-ink drawings rest on blue watercolor wash backgrounds." Horn Book Guide

Esbensen, Barbara Juster
 Baby whales drink milk; illustrated by Lambert Davis. HarperCollins Pubs. 1994 32p il (Let's-read-and-find-out science) hardcover o.p. pa $4.95
Grades: K 1   **599.5**
1. Whales 2. Mammals
ISBN 0-06-445119-4 pa
          LC 92-30375
Describes the behavior of the humpback whale, with an emphasis on the fact that it is a mammal and shares the characteristics of other mammals
"Full-color paintings, mainly in watery greens and blues, show the animals in their habitat, along with a scene of a whale model in a museum and a map of migration. The book's strong point, though, is Esbensen's simple, informative text, which keeps its young audience clearly in view." Booklist

Gish, Melissa
 Killer whales. Creative Paperbacks 2010 46p il map (Living wild) $23.95; pa $9.95
Grades: 5 6 7 8   **599.5**
1. Whales
ISBN 978-1-58341-971-7; 1-58341-971-3; 978-0-89812-554-2 pa; 0-89812-554-5 pa
          LC 2010017376
"A look at killer whales, including their habitats, physical characteristics such as their unique coloration, behaviors, relationships with humans, and protected status in the world today." Publisher's note

Whales. Creative Education 2011 46p il map (Living wild) lib bdg $23.95
Grades: 5 6 7 8   **599.5**
1. Whales
ISBN 978-1-60818-084-4
          LC 2010028414
A look at whales, including their habitats, physical characteristics such as their streamlined bodies, behaviors, relationships with humans, and threatened status in the world today.
Includes glossary and bibliographical references

Goldish, Meish
 Florida manatees; warm water miracles. by Meish Goldish. Bearport Pub. 2007 32p il map (America's animal comebacks) lib bdg $18.95
Grades: 2 3 4   **599.5**
1. Manatees 2. Wildlife conservation
ISBN 978-1-59716-507-5 lib bdg; 1-59716-507-7 lib bdg
          LC 2007010311
"This accessible title discusses the environmental threats facing the Florida manatee and the efforts that saved this appealing sea creature from extinction. . . . Double-page spread feature attention-grabbing fact boxes and large, full-color photos." Booklist
Includes glossary and bibliographical references

Greenberg, Dan
 ★ **Whales**; by Dan Greenberg. Marshall Cavendish Benchmark 2009 24 p. ill. (library) $24.21
Grades: 3 4 5 6 7   **599.5**
1. Whales -- Juvenile literature 2. Marine biology -- Juvenile literature 3. Whales
ISBN 0761443460; 9780761443469
          LC 0024390
This book is part of the Benchmark Rockets: Animals series and focuses on whales. Each title "tells about and illustrates the animal world. Each animal's lives and futures are revealed in . . . dialogue with photographs and charts. The text includes what each animal eats, how it communicates, and how it lives within a community." (Library Media Connection)
"Describes the physical characteristics, habitat, behavior, diet, life cycle, and conservation status of whales." Publisher's note
Includes glossary

Greenberg, Daniel A.
 Whales; [by] Dan Greenberg, with Nina Hess. Marshall Cavendish Benchmark 2010 24p il map (Benchmark rockets. Animals) lib bdg $16.95
Grades: 3 4 5 6   **599.5**
1. Whales
ISBN 978-0-7614-4346-9; 0-7614-4346-0
          LC 2008-52110
"Describes the physical characteristics, habitat, behavior, diet, life cycle, and conservation status of whales." Publisher's note
Includes glossary

Harris, Caroline
 Whales and dolphins. Kingfisher 2010 56p il (Discover science) $9.99

Grades: 1 2 3   **599.5**
   1. Whales 2. Dolphins
   ISBN 978-0-7534-6448-9; 0-7534-6448-9

First published in the series Kingfisher young knowledge in 2005

Introduces readers to some of the largest and most acrobatic mammals in oceans and seas. Young students will discover the many types of whales and dolphins and learn about their behavior and how they survive in their watery world

"There is enough information for basic reports, but . . . [this] will also be popular with browsers. . . . [Features] large, colorful images as well as smaller, more detailed close-up." Libr Media Connect

Includes glossary and bibliographical references

Hodgkins, Fran
   ★ The **whale** scientists; solving the mystery of whale strandings. Houghton Mifflin Co. 2007 63p il map (Scientists in the field) $18
Grades: 5 6 7 8   **599.5**
   1. Whales
   ISBN 978-0-618-55673-1; 0-618-55673-7
                      LC 2006-34634

This describes the evolution of whales and their relationship to humans and offers various scientific theories about their strandings.

"Hodgkins packs her text with an impressive amount of information. . . . Well-chosen color photographs amply illustrate the well-organized discussion." SLJ

Includes glossary and bibliographical references

Landau, Elaine
   Beluga whales. Enslow Elementary 2010 31p il map (Animals of the snow and ice) lib bdg $22.60
Grades: 2 3 4   **599.5**
   1. Whales
   ISBN 978-0-7660-3459-4 lib bdg; 0-7660-3459-3 lib bdg
                      LC 2009006478

This describes beluga whales, including habitat, eating habits, mating, babies, and conservation

"Throughout most of [this] title, a full-page, or page and a quarter, sharp, color photograph . . . alternates with a page of text. An addendum of miscellaneous facts, a short list for further reading, and some websites are appended. Landau's smoothly written, well-illustrated titles are right on target for the intended audience." SLJ

Includes glossary and bibliographical references

Lourie, Peter
   ★ **Whaling** season; a year in the life of an arctic whale scientist. Houghton Mifflin Books for Children 2009 80p il map (Scientists in the field) $18
Grades: 4 5 6 7   **599.5**
   1. Inuit 2. Whales 3. Biologists 4. Bowhead whale -- Juvenile literature 5. Biology -- Fieldwork -- Juvenile literature
   ISBN 978-0-618-77709-9; 0-618-77709-1
                      LC 2009-18596

Profiles the work of John Craighead George, an Arctic whale scientist, as he studies the bowhead whale and works with the indigenous people of Alaska to better understand the history of the animal.

"Combining exemplary color photos and simple, vivid language, the chapters detail not only George's day-today methodology but also his motivation." Booklist

Includes glossary and bibliographical references

   ★ The **manatee** scientists; saving vulnerable species. Houghton Mifflin Books for Children 2011 80p il map (Scientists in the field) $18.99
Grades: 4 5 6 7   **599.5**
   1. Manatees 2. Scientists 3. Marine biology 4. Endangered species 5. Wildlife conservation
   ISBN 978-0-547-15254-7; 0-547-15254-X

This book highlights the work scientists are doing to protect the manatee, including John Reynolds, who does an aerial count of manatees from the Florida sky; Lucy Keith who spends a weekend rescuing manatees trapped in a dam in Senegal; and Fernando Rosas who takes the author on an Amazonian boat trip, looking for a young manatee he released back into the wild.

"The manatees photographed by Lourie and others add plenty of visual appeal. . . . A sturdy addition to a standard-setting nonfiction series." Booklist

Lunde, Darrin P.
   Hello, baby beluga; [by] Darrin Lunde; illustrated by Patricia J. Wynne. Charlesbridge 2011 un il $15.95; pa $6.95
Grades: PreK K 1   **599.5**
   1. Whales 2. Animal babies
   ISBN 978-1-57091-739-4; 1-57091-739-6; 978-1-57091-740-0 pa; 1-57091-740-X pa
                      LC 2010007550

"Lunde delivers facts about baby belunga whales in a simple direct-address question-and-answer format, almost as if a child is conducting a casual interview with a candid young whale. . . . Cool blues, whites, and grays dominate the illustrations, which showcase the happy calf in its arctic surroundings." Horn Book Guide

Markle, Sandra
   Killer whales; [by] Sandra Markle. Carolrhoda Books 2004 39p il (Animal predators) lib bdg $25.26; pa $7.95
Grades: 3 4 5 6   **599.5**
   1. Whales
   ISBN 1-57505-728-X lib bdg; 1-57505-743-3 pa
                      LC 2003-25944

"Dramatic, large color photos keep step with informative, readable [text]." SLJ

Includes glossary and bibliographical references

Marsh, Laura
   Whales. National Geographic 2010 48p il map (Great migrations) $11.90; pa $3.99
Grades: 1 2 3   **599.5**
   1. Whales
   ISBN 978-1-4263-0746-1; 1-4263-0746-2; 978-1-4263-0745-4 pa; 1-4263-0745-4 pa
                      LC 2010017959

This offers facts about sperm whales in an easy reader format.

"Dynamic full-color photographs, informative writing, and consistent organization work well together in [this volume]. . . . Along with the many photographs, the fascinating details are supported by boxes of related information, helpful definitions of new terms, and a sprinkling of entertaining jokes/riddles." SLJ

Includes glossary

Nicklin, Flip

★ **Face** to face with dolphins; by Flip and Linda Nicklin. National Geographic 2007 32p il (Face to face) $16.95; lib bdg $25.90

Grades: 3 4 5 6   599.5
   1. Dolphins
   ISBN 978-1-4263-0141-4; 1-4263-0141-3; 978-1-
   4263-0142-1 lib bdg; 1-4263-0142-1 lib bdg
                                              LC 2006-36273
   "The Nicklins outline the special abilities and physical features of dolphins, such as echolocation, as well as diet, reproduction, swimming habits, and threats to their existence. . . . [This] attractive, smoothly written [book], topped off with advice about self-directed research, will catch the attention of enthusiasts and motivate them toward personal investigation." SLJ

   Includes glossary and bibliographical references

   ★ **Face** to face with whales; by Flip & Linda Nicklin. National Geographic 2008 31p il map (Face to face) $16.95; lib bdg $25.95

Grades: 3 4 5 6   599.5
   1. Whales
   ISBN 978-1-4263-0244-2; 1-4263-0244-4; 978-1-
   4263-0245-9 lib bdg; 1-4263-0245-2 lib bdg
                                              LC 2007-34249
   The authors describe the life cycle and behavior of whales and their own experiences with whales in the wild.
   Includes glossary and bibliographical references

O'Connell, Jennifer

   The **eye** of the whale; a rescue story. Jennifer O'Connell. 1st hardcover ed. Tilbury House, Publishers 2012 32 p. col. ill. (hardcover) $16.95

Grades: 5 6 7 8   599.5
   1. Whales -- Juvenile literature 2. Animal rescue -- Juvenile literature 3. Humpback whale -- California -- San Francisco -- Juvenile literature 4. Wildlife rescue -- California -- San Francisco -- Juvenile literature
   ISBN 0884483355; 9780884483359
                                              LC 2012031165
   This true children's story, by Jennifer O'Connell, begins when, "near San Francisco, a distress call was radioed to shore by a local fisherman. He had discovered a humpback whale tangled in hundreds of yards of crab-trap lines. . . . A team of volunteers answered the call, and four divers risked their lives to rescue the enormous animal." (Publisher's note)

Rake, Jody Sullivan

   Blue whales up close. Capstone Press 2010 24p il (First facts. Whales and dolphins up close) lib bdg $21.32

Grades: K 1 2 3   599.5
   1. Whales
   ISBN 978-1-4296-3336-9 lib bdg; 1-4296-3336-0
   lib bdg
                                              LC 2009-6005
   This "title has colorful pages and chapter heading to capture the interest of young readers as well as short, straightforward sentence structure to keep them reading. Captivating photographs of whales in the wild are present on each

spread and feature up close images of body parts such as blow holes and baleen. . . . This . . . will be a fabulous addition to any elementary school library collection." Libr Media Connect

   Includes glossary and bibliographical references

   Humpback whales up close. Capstone Press 2010 24p il (First facts. Whales and dolphins up close) lib bdg $21.32

Grades: K 1 2   599.5
   1. Whales
   ISBN 978-1-4296-3337-6 lib bdg; 1-4296-3337-9
   lib bdg
                                              LC 2009-6004
   This "title has colorful pages and chapter heading to capture the interest of young readers as well as short, straightforward sentence structure to keep them reading. Captivating photographs of whales in the wild are present on each spread and feature up close images of body parts such as blow holes and baleen. . . . This . . . will be a fabulous addition to any elementary school library collection." Libr Media Connect

   Includes glossary and bibliographical references

   The **mystery** of whale strandings; a cause and effect investigation. Capstone Press 2010 32p il map (Fact finders. Animals on the edge) lib bdg $25.99

Grades: 3 4 5 6   599.5
   1. Whales
   ISBN 978-1-4296-4531-7 lib bdg; 1-4296-4531-8
   lib bdg
                                              LC 2010008561
   "Excellent discussions address those who doubt the severity of the issue and those who wonder why people should care what happens to animals. The captioned photographs are timely and piognant. . . . [This] makes serious subject matter interesting and accessible." SLJ
   Includes glossary and bibliographical references

Riggs, Kate

   Dolphins. Creative Education 2011 24p il (Amazing animals) $24.25; pa $5.99

Grades: K 1 2   599.5
   1. Dolphins
   ISBN 978-1-58341-989-2; 1-58341-989-6; 978-0-
   89812-562-7 pa; 0-89812-562-6 pa
                                              LC 2010019053
   "The large, beautiful photos on each spread include vivid shots of animals in action as well as close-ups of their faces. Photo captions consistently add interesting animal facts. . . . The text is laid out in a large, easy-to-read font. The text, although made up of simple sentences, conveys plenty of interesting information." Booklist

Rockwood, Leigh

   Dolphins are smart! PowerKids Press 2010 24p il (Super smart animals) lib bdg $21.25; pa $8.25

Grades: 2 3 4 5   599.5
   1. Dolphins
   ISBN 978-1-4358-9398-6 lib bdg; 1-4358-9398-0 lib
   bdg; 978-1-4358-9842-4 pa; 1-4358-9842-7 pa
   Examines the intelligence of dolphins.
   "Readers get an overview of the . . . [dolphin's] life cycle, its domestic history (where relevant), and natural habitat, and examples of how it is smart in the wild as well as

when helped by human tutelage. . . . Interesting color photographs and large, easy-to-read print will attract browsers and report writers alike." SLJ

Includes glossary

Sayre, April Pulley

Here come the humpbacks! April Pulley Sayre; illustrated by Jamie Hogan. Charlesbridge 2013 40 p. (reinforced for library use) $17.95

Grades: 2 3 4   **599.5**

1. Whales -- Juvenile literature 2. Whale watching -- Juvenile literature 3. Humpback whale -- Juvenile literature

ISBN 1580894054; 9781580894050; 9781580894067

LC 2012000785

This children's picture book by April Pulley Sayre looks at humpback whales. The male whales' singing is described. "As mother and calf move from the shallows into the open ocean, they encounter other creatures and objects, which Sayre introduces in offset text about whale-watching tours, barnacles, suckerfish, chemical pollution, and more." (Publishers Weekly)

Simon, Seymour

Dolphins. Smithsonian/Collins 2009 32p il $17.99; lib bdg $18.89

Grades: 1 2 3 4   **599.5**

1. Dolphins

ISBN 978-0-06-028393-3; 0-06-028393-9; 978-0-06-028394-0 lib bdg; 0-06-028394-7 lib bdg

LC 2008010654

"Simon presents fascinating facts about these playful mammals and describes the difference between dolphins, porpoises, and whales in terms that children can understand. Without being didactic, he discusses the physiology and habits of dolphins, as well as the greatest threat to the species—humans. Accompanied by full-page color photographs of dolphins, the text is presented with considerable white space in the margins." Booklist

Skerry, Brian

Face to face with manatees. National Geographic 2010 31p il map (Face to face) $16.95; lib bdg $25.90

Grades: 3 4 5 6   **599.5**

1. Manatees

ISBN 978-1-4263-0616-7; 1-4263-0616-4; 978-1-4263-0617-4 lib bdg; 1-4263-0617-2 lib bdg

LC 2009-40783

The author describes the life cycle and behavior of the manatee and his own experiences with manatees in the wild.

"The amazing, literally face-to-face photographs dominate the book. . . . Although written for children, this colorful, informative book will appeal to adults as well." Sci Books Films

Includes glossary and bibliographical references

Spilsbury, Louise

Dolphin. Heinemann Library 2010 24p il (A day in the life: sea animals) lib bdg $22; pa $6.49

Grades: 1 2   **599.5**

1. Dolphins

ISBN 978-1-4329-3999-1 lib bdg; 1-4329-3999-8 lib bdg; 978-1-4329-4006-5 pa; 1-4329-4006-6 pa

LC 2010000485

This pairs "well-chosen color photos . . . with one or two sentences of simple commentary for each. . . . [Though this title] includes references to several varieties of the chosen creature, one species in particular is highlighted. . . . [Good choice] for pleasure or purpose reading." SLJ

Includes glossary and bibliographical references

Stearns, Precious McKenzie

Manatees; [by] Precious McKenzie. Rourke 2010 24p il map (Eye to eye with endangered species) lib bdg $27.07

Grades: 2 3 4   **599.5**

1. Manatees

ISBN 978-1-60694-403-5 lib bdg; 1-60694-403-7 lib bdg

LC 2009-6011

This describes manatees and why they are threatened with extinction

"Sets out to introduce readers to [manatees] . . . explain the dangers they face, and detail the efforts of biologists and conservationists to save them. . . . Serviceable and informative." SLJ

Includes glossary and bibliographical references

Thomson, Sarah L.

★ Amazing whales! written by Sarah L. Thomson; photographs provided by the Wildlife Conservation Society. HarperCollins 2004 27p il (I can read book) $15.99; lib bdg $16.89

Grades: 1 2 3   **599.5**

1. Whales

ISBN 0-06-054465-1; 0-06-054466-X lib bdg

LC 2004-2473

"Thomson's superior text sustains readers' attention with interesting facts and apt comparisons. . . . Spectacular color photographs add detail and drama." SLJ

599.53   Dolphins and porpoises

Riggs, Kate

Killer whales; by Kate Riggs. Creative Education 2012 24 p. (Amazing animals)

Grades: K 1 2   **599.53**

1. Killer whales 2. Marine animals 3. Marine biology -- Juvenile literature

ISBN 9781608181094

LC 2010049129

This book offers a "look at killer whales, including their habitats, physical characteristics such as their unique coloration, behaviors, relationships with humans, and protected status." (Publisher's note) "This book shares with readers how the whale waits above water for food, how there is only one killer whale and it is found in the coldest oceans. The reader is then informed about the whale's ability to maintain its warmth thanks to blubber before attention turns toward how the whale moves and swims with the help of its strong tail and flukes." (Children's Literature)

Includes bibliographical references and index

599.6 Ungulates

Lunis, Natalie

Pronghorn; long-distance runner! Bearport Pub. 2011 24p il map (Blink of an eye. Superfast animals!) lib bdg $21.26

Grades: 1 2 3   **599.6**

  1. Pronghorn antelopes

  ISBN 978-1-936087-94-5; 1-936087-94-4

                    LC 2010011127

This decribes the pronghorn antelope, including where it lives, what it eats, and the ways its body helps it reach its record-breaking speeds.

This "is sure to appeal to a wide variety of readers. Vibrant photos illustrate each animal from multiple perspectives, providing opportunity for readers to closely examine the animal. Information is organized by subject heading and branches into the animal's physical features and how they contribute to its speed, the animal's natural predators, and how the animal makes use of speed as a means of survival. . . . This . . . will be a worthwhile addition to your nonfiction collection." Libr Media Connect

  Includes glossary and bibliographical references

599.63 Even-toed ungulates

Anderson, Jill

Giraffes; by Jill Anderson. NorthWord 2005 un il (Wild ones) $12.95; pa $8.95

Grades: K 1 2   **599.63**

  1. Giraffes

  ISBN 978-1-55971-928-5; 1-55971-928-1; 978-1-55971-929-2 pa; 1-55971-929-X pa

                    LC 2004031117

This describes the physiology, habitat, and life cycle of giraffes

"With simple, direct words and clear, closeup color photo images, this . . . does an excellent job of introducing preschoolers to basic facts about giraffe physiology and habitat, and, especially, how the animals get their food and digest it, and how they care for their young." Booklist

Bredeson, Carmen

Giraffes up close. Enslow Elementary 2008 24p il (Zoom in on animals!) lib bdg $21.26

Grades: 1 2 3   **599.63**

  1. Giraffes

  ISBN 978-0-7660-3081-7 lib bdg; 0-7660-3081-4 lib bdg

This describes the anatomy, behavior, and life cycle of the giraffe.

  Includes glossary and bibliographical references

Clarke, Penny

  ★ Hippos; written by Penny Clarke. F. Watts 2009 32p il (Scary creatures) lib bdg $26; pa $8.95

Grades: 3 4 5   **599.63**

  1. Hippopotamus

  ISBN 978-0-531-21671-2 lib bdg; 0-531-21671-3 lib bdg; 978-0-531-21042-0 pa; 0-531-21042-1 pa

                    LC 2009010798

This describes the hippo's life cycle, habitat, behavior, and relationship to humans

This title has "two-page chapters of accessible, large-type text and bright color photos and illustrations. . . . The series distinguishes itself with 'X-Ray Vision.' When readers hold the page with this prompt up to the light, an image emerges. The X-rays mostly show the skeletal structures of the animals. Text boxes throughout add to the visual appeal. . . . [This title is an] excellent [resource for school assignments and browsing." SLJ

  Includes glossary

Hatkoff, Isabella

  ★ Owen & Mzee; the true story of a remarkable friendship. told by Isabella Hatkoff, Craig Hatkoff, and Paula Kahumbu; with photographs by Peter Greste. Scholastic Press 2006 un il map $16.99

Grades: K 1 2 3   **599.63**

  1. Turtles 2. Hippopotamus 3. Indian Ocean earthquake and tsunami, 2004

  ISBN 0-439-82973-9

                    LC 2005-21341

"The text and the back matter are brimming with information about the animals, their caregivers, and the locale. This touching story of the power of a surprising friendship to mitigate the experience of loss is full of heart and hope." SLJ

  ★ Owen & Mzee: the language of friendship; told by Isabella Hatkoff, Craig Hatkoff, and Paula Kuhumbu; with photographs by Peter Greste. Scholastic Press 2007 un il $16.99

Grades: K 1 2 3   **599.63**

  1. Turtles 2. Hippopotamus

  ISBN 978-0-439-89959-8; 0-439-89959-1

                    LC 2006015612

"Owen & Mzee: The True Story of a Remarkable Friendship (Scholastic, 2006) chronicled the fascinating story of a baby hippo who was orphaned by the December 2004 tsunami and the bond he formed with Mzee, a 130-year-old Alhambra tortoise at a wildlife sanctuary in Kenya. This sequel updates readers on the status of that friendship a year and a half later, particularly with regard to the way this unusual duo has learned to communicate with one another. . . . The text is clearly written and accompanied by numerous high-quality, full-color photos of this unique pair." SLJ

  Includes bibliographical references

Jango-Cohen, Judith

Hippopotamuses; by Judith Jango-Cohen. Marshall Cavendish Benchmark 2006 47p il (Animals, animals) lib bdg $19.95

Grades: 3 4 5 6   **599.63**

  1. Hippopotamus

  ISBN 978-0-7614-2238-9 lib bdg; 0-7614-2238-2 lib bdg

                    LC 2005026015

"Describes the physical characteristics, behavior, habitat, and endangered status of hippopotamuses." Publisher's note

  Includes glossary and bibliographical references

Rumford, James

  ★ Chee-lin; a giraffe's journey. by James Rumford. Houghton Mifflin 2008 un il map $17

Grades: 1 2 3 **599.63**
1. Giraffes
ISBN 978-0-618-71720-0; 0-618-71720-X
LC 2008001863

"Linking the Chinese mythological creature, the 'cheelin', to a 1414 Chinese portrait of a giraffe, Rumford imagines how a giraffe may have journeyed to China. . . . Tweega (Swahili for 'giraffe') survives frightening voyages, cruel and tender caretakers, and cramped quarters, ending up in the emperor's spacious grounds. . . . The narrative—moving, even tender in many places—is accompanied by handsome full-page paintings, beautifully bordered with evocative motifs." Booklist

St. George, Judith
Zarafa; the giraffe who walked to the king. illustrated by Britt Spencer. Philomel Books 2009 un il $16.99
Grades: 2 3 4 **599.63**
1. Giraffes 2. Exotic animals 3. Diplomatic gifts -- Juvenile literature 4. Animals -- Transportation -- Juvenile literature
ISBN 978-0-399-25049-1; 0-399-25049-2
LC 2008-32609

This "highlights a unique historical episode, following a 19th-century giraffe, a gift from the viceroy of Egypt to Charles X, as she journeys from Africa to France. Fanciful flourishes fill Spencer's watercolor, gouache and ink art. . . . St. George's breezy, conversational text . . . moves this voyage along briskly." Publ Wkly

Tourville, Amanda Doering
A **giraffe** grows up; by Amanda Doering Tourville; illustrated by Michael Denman and William J. Huiett. Picture Window Books 2007 24p il map hardcover o.p. lib bdg $25.26
Grades: PreK K 1 2 **599.63**
1. Giraffes
ISBN 978-1-4048-3158-2 lib bdg; 1-4048-3158-4 lib bdg; 978-1-4048-3565-8 pa; 1-4048-3565-2 pa
LC 2006027307

"Each spread has an acrylic painting with a paragraph or two of text and a box of facts. . . . Easy-to-read . . . with enough information for basic reports." SLJ
Includes glossary and bibliographical references

Walden, Katherine
Warthogs. PowerKiDS Press 2009 24p il (Safari animals) lib bdg $21.25
Grades: PreK K 1 2 **599.63**
1. Warthogs
ISBN 978-1-4358-2688-5 lib bdg; 1-4358-2688-4 lib bdg
LC 2008019531

This book provides "succinctly written introductory information about [warthogs'] range, habitat, social groups, and diet. Spreads consist of one to three short, simply constructed sentences opposite crisp, color photographs, most of which represent the subject perfectly." SLJ

599.64 Bovids

Caper, William
American bison; a scary prediction. by William Caper. Bearport 2007 32p il map (America's animal comebacks) lib bdg $25.27
Grades: 2 3 4 **599.64**
1. Bison 2. Zoologists 3. Wildlife conservation 4. Zoo directors 5. Writers on nature 6. Writers on science
ISBN 978-1-59716-504-4 lib bdg; 1-59716-504-2 lib bdg
LC 2007010863

This describes how the American bison was saved from extinction by William Temple Hornaday, the American Bison Society, and the The Bronx Zoo.
This book is "well organized and [has] an easy style and an accessible vocabulary and text size . . . [and] color photographs." SLJ
Includes glossary and bibliographical references

Catt, Thessaly
Migrating with the wildebeest. PowerKids Press 2011 24p il map (Animal journeys) lib bdg $21.25; pa $8.25
Grades: 2 3 4 **599.64**
1. Gnus 2. Animals -- Migration
ISBN 978-1-4488-2544-8 lib bdg; 1-4488-2544-X lib bdg; 978-1-4488-2795-4 pa; 1-4488-2795-7 pa
LC 2010028194

Learn about the wildebeest and its migration patterns.
"Keywords are bolded throughout and can be found in the glossary. The format is attractive with inset captioned photographs and page heading that seem to move across the page." Libr Media Connect
Includes glossary

Ganeri, Anita
Arabian oryx. Heinemann Library 2011 24p il map (A day in the life: desert animals) $22; pa $6.49
Grades: K 1 2 **599.64**
1. Oryx
ISBN 978-1-4329-4769-9; 1-4329-4769-9; 978-1-4329-4778-1 pa; 1-4329-4778-8 pa
LC 2010022817

"The engaging full-color photographs are key to [this] well-organized [book]. . . . Basic global maps show where the animal is found, and a diagram called a 'body map' labels its parts. The [text is] appropriate for the age group, and the pictures will draw in youngsters. [An] excellent [purchase] if material is needed on these animals." SLJ
Includes glossary and bibliographical references

George, Jean Craighead
The **buffalo** are back; paintings by Wendell Minor. Dutton Children's Books 2010 un il $16.99
Grades: 3 4 5 **599.64**
1. Bison 2. American bison -- Juvenile literature 3. Endangered species -- Juvenile literature
ISBN 978-0-525-42215-0; 0-525-42215-3

"This handsome book discusses the history of the buffalo on the American plains. Succinctly and gracefully written, it envisions the centuries when Indians carefully managed the land, using the buffalo for food, shelter, and clothing. . . . Illustrated with beautiful landscape paintings and striking close-ups of people and animals, this book offers a very effective presentation of the buffalo's story." Booklist

Gish, Melissa

Bison. Creative Education 2011 46p il map (Living wild) $23.95

Grades: 5 6 7 8   599.64

1. Bison

ISBN 978-1-60818-077-6; 1-60818-077-8

LC 2010028305

A look at bison, including their habitats, physical characteristics such as their shaggy coats, behaviors, relationships with humans, and threatened status in the world today.

This offers "an array of interesting facts. Photography is large and beautiful—a real draw." SLJ

Includes bibliographical references

Martin, Jacqueline Briggs

★ The chiru of high Tibet; a true story. written by Jacqueline Briggs Martin; illustrated by Linda Wingerter. Houghton Mifflin Harcourt 2010 un il $17.99

Grades: 1 2 3   599.64

1. Chirus 2. Zoologists 3. Wildlife conservation 4. Nonfiction writers 5. Wildlife conservation -- Juvenile literature 6. Chiru -- China -- Tibet -- Juvenile literature

ISBN 978-0-618-58130-6; 0-618-58130-8

"The antelope-like chiru of the Chang Tang in northern Tibet were a million strong before they were hunted nearly to extinction for their marvelously soft wool. . . . Wildlife champion George Schaller . . . hoped to save the chiru by protecting the remote valley where females give birth each spring. . . . The birthing ground is now protected from poachers. Martin's account of all this is brief, dramatic, and supplemented with boxed facts, and nicely amplified in Wingerter's art." Horn Book

Includes bibliographical references

Perry, Phyllis J.

★ Buffalo. Benchmark Books 2005 48p il (Animals, animals) lib bdg $29.93

Grades: 3 4 5 6   599.64

1. Bison

ISBN 978-0-7614-1866-5 lib bdg; 0-7614-1866-0 lib bdg

LC 2004-21438

Describes the physical characteristics, behavior, and habitat of buffalo

This is "eye-catching . . . smoothly written and informative. . . . [It includes] numerous clear, closeup color photographs." SLJ

Includes glossary and bibliographical references

Walden, Katherine

Wildebeests. Rosen Pub. Group's PowerKids Press 2009 24p il (Safari animals) lib bdg $21.25; pa $8.25

Grades: PreK K 1 2   599.64

1. Gnus

ISBN 978-1-4358-2692-2 lib bdg; 1-4358-2692-2 lib bdg; 978-1-4358-3066-0 pa; 1-4358-3066-0 pa

LC 2008021587

This book provides "succinctly written introductory information about [wildebeests'] range, habitat, social groups, and diet. Spreads consist of one to three short, simply con-

structed sentences opposite crisp, color photographs, most of which represent the subject perfectly." SLJ

Includes glossary

599.65   Deer

Arnold, Caroline

A moose's world; written and illustrated by Caroline Arnold. Picture Window Books 2010 24p il (Caroline Arnold's animals) lib bdg $25.32

Grades: PreK K 1 2   599.65

1. Moose

ISBN 978-1-4048-5742-1 lib bdg; 1-4048-5742-7 lib bdg

LC 2009033360

This narrative tells the story of a moose from birth until it can live on its own.

Catt, Thessaly

Migrating with the caribou. PowerKids Press 2011 24p il map (Animal journeys) lib bdg $21.25; pa $8.25

Grades: 2 3 4   599.65

1. Caribou 2. Animals -- Migration

ISBN 978-1-4488-2541-7 lib bdg; 1-4488-2541-5 lib bdg; 978-1-4488-2666-7 pa; 1-4488-2666-7 pa

LC 2010024146

Learn about the life cycle of the caribou and its migration patterns.

"Keywords are bolded throughout and can be found in the glossary. The format is attractive with inset captioned photographs and page heading that seem to move across the page." Libr Media Connect

Inlcudes glossary

Gish, Melissa

Moose. Creative Education 2010 46p il map (Living wild) $23.95; pa $9.95

Grades: 5 6 7 8   599.65

1. Moose

ISBN 978-1-58341-973-1; 1-58341-973-X; 978-0-89812-556-6 pa; 0-89812-556-1 pa

LC 2010017378

"A look at moose, including their habitats, physical characteristics such as their imposing antlers, behaviors, relationships with humans, and secure status in the world today." Publisher's note

Heuer, Karsten

★ Being caribou; five months on foot with a caribou herd. Walker & Co. 2007 48p il map $17.95; lib bdg $18.95

Grades: 4 5 6 7   599.65

1. Caribou 2. Biologists 3. Conservationists 4. Hikers

ISBN 978-0-8027-9565-6; 0-8027-9565-X; 978-0-8027-9566-3 lib bdg; 0-8027-9566-8 lib bdg

LC 2006-27651

This is an adaptation of an adult title by the same name, published 2005 by Mountaineers Books

"The caribou calving grounds in the Arctic National Wildlife Refuge are being threatened by oil exploration. [This title] will help make kids aware of what is at stake and give them a glimpse of an extraordinary part of the world and the lengths the caribou go to traverse it. It is an important book." Quill Quire

Includes bibliographical references

Mara, Wil
★ **Deer**; by Wil Mara. Marshall Cavendish Benchmark 2009 47p il (Animals animals) $20.95
Grades: 3 4 5 6   **599.65**
  1. Deer
  ISBN 978-0-7614-2926-5; 0-7614-2926-3
        LC 2007-27328

"The material is well researched and would be an excellent source for reports, and the [book has] a narrative flow that makes [it] easy and enjoyable to read. [The] title includes expert full-color photography." SLJ

Includes glossary and bibliographical references

Riggs, Kate
Moose; by Kate Riggs. Creative Education 2012 24 p. col. ill.
Grades: K 1 2   **599.65**
  1. Moose 2. Animal behavior 3. Habitat (Ecology) 4. Animals -- Folklore 5. Zoology -- Encyclopedias
  ISBN 9781608181117
        LC 2010049131

This children's book, part of Kate Riggs' "Amazing Animals" series, focuses on moose. "This . . . popular series continues traveling the planet to study alligators, bats, and other fascinating animals. . . . [P]hotos are paired with . . . text to examine the featured creature's appearance, habitat, behaviors, and life cycle. . . . "A basic exploration of the appearance, behavior, and habitat of moose, Earth's largest deer. Also included is a story from folklore explaining how moose interact with other animals." (Publisher's note)

Includes bibliographical references (p. 24) and index

Urbigkit, Cat
★ **Path** of the pronghorn; photographs by Mark Gocke. Boyds Mills Press 2010 32p il map $17.95
Grades: 3 4 5 6   **599.65**
  1. Pronghorn antelopes
  ISBN 978-1-59078-756-4; 1-59078-756-0

"Large, eye-catching color photos accompany a quiet, informative text in this elegant book that celebrates an equally elegant North American mammal: Antilocapra americana— 'the antelope-goat of America.' Urbigkit provides enough quality information to satisfy many young researchers, and Gocke's outstanding photos record the migratory year of Wyoming's Sublette herd." SLJ

Includes bibliographical references

599.66   Odd-toed ungulates

Carson, Mary Kay
★ **Emi** and the rhino scientist; [by] Mary Kay Carson; with photographs by Tom Uhlman. Houghton Mifflin Company 2007 57p il (Scientists in the field) $18
Grades: 5 6 7 8   **599.66**
  1. Rhinoceros 2. Zoo employees 3. Animal scientists 4. Scientists -- Juvenile literature 5. Sumatran rhinoceros

-- Juvenile literature
  ISBN 978-0-618-64639-5; 0-618-64639-6
        LC 2006-34517

This describes "how Terri Roth, an expert in endangered-species reproduction at the Cincinnati Zoo, helped Emi to give birth to the first Sumatran rhino born in captivity in more than 100 years. . . . The text is full of important details, and the photographs are unfailingly crisp, bright, and full of variety." SLJ

Firestone, Mary
Top 50 reasons to care about rhinos; animals in peril. Enslow Publishers 2010 103p il (Top 50 reasons to care about endangered animals) lib bdg $31.93
Grades: 4 5 6 7   **599.66**
  1. Rhinoceros 2. Endangered species
  ISBN 978-0-7660-3457-0 lib bdg; 0-7660-3457-7 lib bdg
        LC 2008048692

This describes the different types of rhino, their life cycle, diet, young, habitat, and reasons why they are endangered animals

"The illustrations, mostly color photographs, represent a wonderful selection of the animals and their habitats. Reluctant readers may be enticed by this . . . simply because of the great images. This . . . would make a substantial supplement to the science curriculum when studying endangered animals." Libr Media Connect

Includes glossary and bibliographical references

Gish, Melissa
Rhinoceroses. Creative Education 2011 46p il map (Living wild) lib bdg $23.95
Grades: 5 6 7 8   **599.66**
  1. Rhinoceros
  ISBN 978-1-60818-083-7; 1-60818-083-2
        LC 2010028316

A look at rhinoceroses, including their habitats, physical characteristics such as their horned noses, behaviors, relationships with humans, and protected status in the world today.

Includes glossary and bibliographical references

Holmes, Mary Tavener
My travels with Clara; illustrated by Jon Cannell. J. Paul Getty Museum 2007 un il $17.95
Grades: 2 3 4   **599.66**
  1. Rhinoceros
  ISBN 978-0-89236-880-8
        LC 2006-35719

"In the mid-eighteenth century, a Dutch sea captain bought an orphaned baby rhinoceros in India, named her Clara, and toured with her around western Europe. . . . His first-person, fictionalized narrative affectionately tells of his kindness, his bond with his extraordinary companion, and the public excitement she caused. . . . Illustrations include costumed period figures and reproductions of the art Clara inspired. . . . The facts about Clara . . . are as fascintating as the art and pet story." Booklist

Momatiuk, Yva
★ **Face** to face with wild horses; by Yva Momatiuk and John Eastcott. National Geographic 2009 31p il (Face to face) $16.95; lib bdg $25.90

Grades: 3 4 5 6　　　　　　　　　　　　**599.66**
　1. Horses 2. Wild horses -- Juvenile literature
　ISBN 978-1-4263-0466-8; 1-4263-0466-8; 978-1-
　4263-0467-5 lib bdg; 1-4263-0467-6 lib bdg
　　　　　　　　　　　　　　　LC 2008-38247
　The authors describe the behavior of wild horses and
their personal encounters with them.
　Includes bibliographical references

Noble-Goodman, Katherine
　★ **Zebras**; by Katherine Noble-Goodman. Benchmark
Books 2006 48p il (Animals, animals) lib bdg $25.64
Grades: 3 4 5 6　　　　　　　　　　　　**599.66**
　1. Zebras
　ISBN 0-7614-1871-7
　Describes the physical characteristics, behavior, and
habitat of zebras
　Includes glossary and bibliographical references

Rustad, Martha E. H.
　Zebras and oxpeckers work together. Capstone Press
2011 24p il (Pebble Plus: animals working together) lib
bdg $23.99; pa $6.95
Grades: K 1 2　　　　　　　　　　　　　**599.66**
　1. Zebras 2. Symbiosis 3. Oxpeckers (Birds)
　ISBN 978-1-4296-5300-8 lib bdg; 1-4296-5300-0 lib
　bdg; 978-1-4296-6200-0 pa; 1-4296-6200-X pa
　　　　　　　　　　　　　　　LC 2010025465
　Simple text and full-color photographs introduce the
symbiotic relationship of zebras and oxpeckers.
　In this series "the easy-to-understand examples are well
selected to show of range of relationships in a variety of environments, and children will come away with some exposure to the concepts of 'parasite' and 'predator' as well." SLJ
　Includes glossary and bibliographical references

Walden, Katherine
　Rhinoceroses. PowerKids Press 2009 24p il (Safari
animals) lib bdg $21.25
Grades: PreK K 1 2　　　　　　　　　　**599.66**
　1. Rhinoceros
　ISBN 978-1-4358-2687-8 lib bdg; 1-4358-2687-6
　lib bdg
　　　　　　　　　　　　　　　LC 2008019534
　This book provides "succinctly written introductory
information about [rhinoceroses'] range, habitat, social
groups, and diet. Spreads consist of one to three short, simply constructed sentences opposite crisp, color photographs,
most of which represent the subject perfectly." SLJ
　Includes glossary and bibliographical references

599.67 Elephants

Allen, Kathy
　Elephants under pressure; a cause and effect inves-
tigation. Capstone Press 2010 32p il map (Fact finders.
Animals on the edge) lib bdg $25.99
Grades: 3 4 5 6　　　　　　　　　　　　**599.67**
　1. Elephants
　ISBN 978-1-4296-4534-8; 1-4296-4534-2
　　　　　　　　　　　　　　　LC 2010008562

"Excellent discussions address those who doubt the severity of the issue and those who wonder why people should
care what happens to animals. The captioned photographs
are timely and poignant. . . . [This] makes serious subject
matter interesting and accessible." SLJ
　Includes glossary and bibliographical references

Arnold, Katya
　★ **Elephants** can paint, too! pictures and text by Katya
Arnold. Atheneum Books for Young Readers 2005 un il
$16.95
Grades: K 1 2 3　　　　　　　　　　　　**599.67**
　1. Painting 2. Elephants 3. Art -- Juvenile literature 4.
　Asiatic elephant -- Juvenile literature
　ISBN 0-689-86985-1
　　　　　　　　　　　　　　　LC 2004-17387
　The author "tells how she trains elephants to paint and
compares the work of her human and elephant pupils. The
spare narrative is easy to understand and reads like a picture
book. . . . Arnold's amusing and colorful photographs—of
elephants and children at work—will have readers laughing
as they view them side-by-side." SLJ

Buckley, Carol
　Tarra & Bella; the elephant and dog who became best
friends. text and photography by Carol Buckley. G.P. Putnam's Sons 2009 un il $16.99
Grades: K 1 2 3 4　　　　　　　　　　　**599.67**
　1. Dogs 2. Elephants 3. Animal behavior 4. Social
　behavior in animals -- Juvenile literature
　ISBN 978-0-399-25443-7; 0-399-25443-9
　　　　　　　　　　　　　　　LC 2009-18888
　Spotlights the true-life friendship between Tarra, a retired circus elephant, and one of the Tennessee Elephant
Sanctuary's stray dogs, Bella
　"Shots of Tarra petting Bella with her trunk are among
the book's most endearing pictures, which range from snap-
shotlike to skillfully framed images; also notable are photographs that underscore the dramatic difference in the animals' sizes. . . . The animals' friendship will inspire young
readers." Publ Wkly

Cowcher, Helen
　Desert elephants. Farrar Straus Giroux 2011 un il
$16.99
Grades: K 1 2 3　　　　　　　　　　　　**599.67**
　1. Elephants 2. Desert ecology
　ISBN 978-0-374-31774-4; 0-374-31774-7
　　　　　　　　　　　　　　　LC 2010019817
　"In Mali, West Africa, the last remaining desert elephants migrate 300 miles in search of water in a circular
route just south of the Sahara Desert. In this picture book
introduction, Cowcher's beautiful watercolor-and-mixed
media illustrations chart the animals' route. . . . The present-
day interaction with people is a crucial part of the well-told
story." Booklist

Downer, Ann
　Elephant talk; the surprising science of elephant communication. Twenty-First Century Books 2011 112p il
map lib bdg $33.26

Grades: 4 5 6   **599.67**
1. Elephants 2. Animal communication
ISBN 978-0-7613-5766-7 lib bdg; 0-7613-5766-1
lib bdg

LC 2010-24880

"The complex behavior of wild elephants is introduced in a flowing narrative accompanied by full-color photographs, diagrams and maps. Downer provides an overview of elephant evolution, places the creatures in their African and Asian contexts, and describes the lives of these intelligent social animals. Her narrative then focuses on the elephants' inticate verbal and nonverbal communication techniques. . . . The illustrations and clearly labeled diagrams and maps are well placed to amplify the text. . . . Throughout this highly readable, informative title are profiles of individuals . . . who work with these animals." SLJ

Includes glossary and bibliographical references

Firestone, Mary
Top 50 reasons to care about elephants; animals in peril. Enslow Publishers 2010 103p il (Top 50 reasons to care about endangered animals) lib bdg $31.93
Grades: 4 5 6 7   **599.67**
1. Elephants 2. Endangered species
ISBN 978-0-7660-3454-9 lib bdg; 0-7660-3454-2
lib bdg

LC 2008-48690

This describes an elephant's ears, trunk and teeth, what they eat, their ancestors, the different kinds of elephants, and why they are on the endangered animals list

"The illustrations, mostly color photographs, represent a wonderful selection of the animals and their habitats. Reluctant readers may be enticed by this . . . simply because of the great images. This . . . would make a substantial supplement to the science curriculum when studying endangered animals." Libr Media Connect

Includes glossary and bibliographical references

Gibbons, Gail
Elephants of Africa. Holiday House 2008 32p il
Grades: K 1 2 3   **599.67**
1. Elephants
ISBN 0-8234-2168-6; 978-0-8234-2168-8

LC 2007051619

This book describes the habitats, physical characteristics, diet, offspring development, and behavior of the African elephant. "Grades one to four." (Sci Books Films)

"Gibbons introduces young readers to [African elephants]. Each page is filled with illustrations and a succinct but informative text that details the habitats, physical characteristics, diet, offspring development, and behavior of these dwellers of Africa's savannas and forests. . . . The text is well organized and simple to understand, enhanced by the pen-and-ink and watercolor artwork." SLJ

Jackson, Donna M.
★ The **elephant** scientist; by Caitlin O'Connell and Donna M. Jackson; photographs by Caitlin O'Connell and Timothy Rodwell. Houghton Mifflin Books for Children 2011 70p il map $17.99
Grades: 4 5 6 7   **599.67**
1. Elephants 2. Biologists 3. Ecologists
ISBN 978-0-547-05344-8; 0-547-05344-4

LC 2010014134

In this book, "O'Connell traveled to Africa in 1992 to observe wild animals; the trip turned into a job offer to study elephants at Etosha National Park; the text focuses on the scientists' work, findings, and problems encountered. The authors offer [a] . . . look at new discoveries about elephant communication and how this knowledge can be used to slow the animal's slump into extinction. Combined with . . . full-color photographs by the scientists, the elephants' world is brought to the forefront. Readers enter the researchers' camp to see their setup, fieldwork, and takedown in action. They will learn how elephant anatomy and hierarchy work together to aid in communication." (School Library Journal)

O'Connell "worked with other scientists to [identify] the vibration-sensitive cells in elephants' feet and trunks that enabled to them to 'hear' sounds transmitted through the ground. Illustrated with many well-captioned, color photos, this eye-catching book provides a sometimes fascinating look at O'Connell's work with elephants in America and in Namibia." Booklist

Joubert, Beverly
★ **Face** to face with elephants; by Beverly and Dereck Joubert. National Geographic 2008 31p il map (Face to face) $16.95; lib bdg $25.90
Grades: 3 4 5 6   **599.67**
1. Elephants
ISBN 978-1-4263-0325-8; 1-4263-0325-4; 978-1-4263-0326-5 lib bdg; 1-4263-0326-2 lib bdg

LC 2007-41229

The authors describe the life cycle and behavior of elephants and their own experiences with elephants in the wild

"The photographs are stunning, sometimes intimate, sometimes epic. . . . [This book] conveys [elephants'] magnificence and fascination." Bull Cent Child Books

Includes glossary and bibliographical references

Marsh, Laura
Elephants. National Geographic 2010 48p il map (Great migrations) $11.90; pa $3.99
Grades: 1 2 3   **599.67**
1. Elephants
ISBN 978-1-4263-0744-7; 1-4263-0744-6; 978-1-4263-0743-0 pa; 1-4263-0743-8 pa

LC 2010017961

This offers facts about elephants in an easy reader format.

"Dynamic full-color photographs, informative writing, and consistent organization work well together in [this volume]. . . . Along with the many photographs, the fascinating details are supported by boxes of related information, helpful definitions of new terms, and a sprinkling of entertaining jokes/riddles." SLJ

Includes glossary

Morgan, Jody
Elephant rescue; changing the future for endangered wildlife. Firefly Books 2004 64p il $19.95; pa $9.95
Grades: 5 6 7 8   **599.67**
1. Elephants 2. Wildlife conservation
ISBN 1-55297-595-9; 1-55297-594-0 pa

This is "well-written. . . . Stunning, full-color photographs bring [these animals] to life." SLJ

Riggs, Kate

Elephants. Creative Education 2011 24p il (Amazing animals) $24.25; pa $5.99

Grades: K 1 2   **599.67**

1. Elephants

ISBN 978-1-58341-990-8; 1-58341-990-X; 978-0-89812-563-4 pa; 0-89812-563-4 pa

LC 2010019054

"A basic exploration of the appearance, behavior, and habitat of elephants, Earth's biggest land animals. Also included is a story from folklore explaining why elephants' trunks are so long." Publisher's note

Schwabacher, Martin

Elephants; by Martin Schwabacher, with Lori Mortensen. Marshall Cavendish Benchmark 2010 24p il map (Animals) lib bdg $16.95

Grades: 3 4 5   **599.67**

1. Elephants

ISBN 978-0-7614-4343-8 lib bdg; 0-7614-4343-6 lib bdg

LC 2008-52103

"The straightforward presentation of the information and the uncluttered and attractive layout make [this] . . . good . . . for reports. Color photographs . . . are well utilized and complete a solid package." SLJ

Includes glossary and bibliographical references

599.7   Carnivores

Gonzales, Doreen

Raccoons in the dark. PowerKids Press 2010 24p il (Creatures of the night) lib bdg $21.25; pa $8.05

Grades: 2 3 4   **599.7**

1. Raccoons

ISBN 978-1-4042-8101-1 lib bdg; 1-4042-8101-0 lib bdg; 978-1-4358-3259-6 pa; 1-4358-3259-0 pa

LC 2009-2758

A look at raccoons and their world in the dark.

"Basic details are complemented by eclectic trivia, . . . [and] each volume concludes with a defense of the animal . . . and why it is vital to humans. The layout is attractive, with easy-to-read text and eye-catching photography. Good for reports." SLJ

Includes glossary

Skunks in the dark. PowerKids Press 2010 24p il (Creatures of the night) lib bdg $21.25; pa $8.05

Grades: 2 3 4   **599.7**

1. Skunks

ISBN 978-1-4042-8099-1 lib bdg; 1-4042-8099-5 lib bdg; 978-1-4358-3255-8 pa; 1-4358-3255-8 pa

LC 2009-718

A look at skunks and their world in the dark.

"Basic details are complemented by eclectic trivia, . . . [and] each volume concludes with a defense of the animal . . . and why it is vital to humans. The layout is attractive, with easy-to-read text and eye-catching photography. Good for reports." SLJ

Includes glossary

Kalman, Bobbie

Baby carnivores; by Bobbie Kalman. Crabtree Publishing Company 2013 24 p. ill. (library) $22.60; (paperback) $6.95

Grades: 1 2 3 4   **599.7**

1. Carnivorous animals 2. Food chains (Ecology) 3. Carnivorous animals -- Infancy -- Juvenile literature

ISBN 0778710106; 9780778710103; 9780778710158

LC 2012043739

This book by Bobbie Kalman presents "images of many kinds of baby carnivores that belong to a group of mammals with sharp teeth and claws. Fascinating text explains how baby carnivores are cared for by their mothers and how they learn to hunt. Young readers will learn about the food chain and where dogs, cats, bears, seals, weasels, meerkats, and other animals live." (Publisher's note)

Includes bibliographical references and index.

Leardi, Jeanette

Southern sea otters; fur-tastrophe avoided. by Jeanette Leardi. Bearport Pub. 2008 32p il map (America's animal comebacks) lib bdg $25.27

Grades: 2 3 4   **599.7**

1. Otters 2. Wildlife conservation

ISBN 978-1-59716-534-1 lib bdg; 1-59716-534-4 lib bdg

LC 2007012593

This describes efforts by scientists and environmentalists to protect southern sea otters from hunting, pollution, and other dangers

This book is "well organized and [has] an easy style and an accessible vocabulary and text size . . . [and] color photographs." SLJ

Includes glossary and bibliographical references

Lunis, Natalie

California sea lion; fast and smart. Bearport Pub. 2011 24p il map (Blink of an eye. Superfast animals!) lib bdg $22.61

Grades: 1 2 3   **599.7**

1. Seals (Animals)

ISBN 978-1-936088-08-9; 1-936088-08-8

LC 2010017683

This describes the California sea lion, where it lives, how it hunts, and the ways its body helps it reach its record-breaking speeds.

This "is sure to appeal to a wide variety of readers. Vibrant photos illustrate each animal from multiple perspectives, providing opportunity for readers to closely examine the animal. Information is organized by subject heading and branches into the animal's physical features and how they contribute to its speed, the animal's natural predators, and how the animal makes use of speed as a means of survival. . . This . . . will be a worthwhile addition to your nonfiction collection." Libr Media Connect

Includes glossary and bibliographical references

Mason, Adrienne

Skunks; written by Adrienne Mason; illustrated by Nancy Gray Ogle. Kids Can Press 2006 32p (Kids Can Press wildlife series) $10.95

Grades: 2 3 4   **599.7**

1. Skunks

ISBN 1-55337-733-8

"Focusing primarily on the four types of skunks found in North America, Mason has provided readers with an accurate, fun-to-read look at this sometimes misunderstood animal. She offers a straightforward description of the mammals habitat, appearance, predators, diet, reproduction, and human interaction. Realistically rendered watercolor illustrations appear on every spread." SLJ

Includes glossary

Otfinoski, Steven

★ **Skunks**; by Steven Otfinoski. Marshall Cavendish Benchmark 2009 47p il (Animals animals) lib bdg $20.95

Grades: 3 4 5 6　　　　　　　　　　　　**599.7**

1. Skunks

ISBN 978-0-7614-2929-6 lib bdg; 0-7614-2929-8 lib bdg

LC 2007-24117

"The material is well researched and would be an excellent source for reports, and the [book has] a narrative flow that makes [it] easy and enjoyable to read. [The] title includes expert full-color photography." SLJ

Includes glossary

Tatham, Betty

Baby sea otter; illustrated by Joan Paley. Holt & Co. 2005 un il $16.95

Grades: K 1 2　　　　　　　　　　　　　**599.7**

1. Otters

ISBN 0-8050-7504-6

LC 2004-23393

"A baby sea otter is born and cared for by her mother, who grooms her, hunts for food, feeds her, and saves her from a hungry eagle. . . . The clear, simple paragraphs of text, interspersed with the drama that the otters face daily, will keep young readers interested. Paley's lush blue and aqua-toned collages add texture and richness." SLJ

599.74　Land carnivores

Ganeri, Anita

Meerkat. Heinemann Library 2011 24p il map (A day in the life: desert animals) $22; pa $6.49

Grades: K 1 2　　　　　　　　　　　　**599.74**

1. Meerkats

ISBN 978-1-4329-4773-6; 1-4329-4773-7; 978-1-4329-4782-8 pa; 1-4329-4782-6 pa

LC 2010022821

"The engaging full-color photographs are key to [this] well-organized [book]. . . . Basic global maps show where the animal is found, and a diagram called a 'body map' labels its parts. The [text is] appropriate for the age group, and the pictures will draw in youngsters. [An] excellent [purchase] if material is needed on these animals." SLJ

Includes glossary and bibliographical references

Gibbons, Gail

Wolves. Holiday House 1994 un il $16.95; pa $6.95

Grades: K 1 2 3　　　　　　　　　　　**599.74**

1. Wolves

ISBN 0-8234-1127-3; 0-8234-1202-4 pa

LC 94-2108

"A simply written introduction that focuses on the gray, or timber, wolf. . . . Material covered includes physical characteristics, behavior within a pack, and communication by howling and body language. . . . The format is open and spacious, the print is large, and the realistic, watercolor illustrations are set against backgrounds of white and deep blues." SLJ

Goldish, Meish

Fossa; a fearsome predator. by Meish Goldish. Bearport Pub. 2009 32p il map (Uncommon animals) lib bdg $25.27

Grades: 1 2 3　　　　　　　　　　　　**599.74**

1. Fossa (Mammals)

ISBN 978-1-59716-732-1 lib bdg; 1-59716-732-0 lib bdg

LC 2008-4817

"The explanatory text works spendidly, with large photographs that bring readers as close as they'll ever get to such beasts." Booklist

Includes glossary and bibliographical references

Ryder, Joanne

Little panda; the world welcomes Hua Mei at the San Diego Zoo. Simon & Schuster 2001 un il $16.95; pa $7.99

Grades: K 1 2 3　　　　　　　　　　　**599.74**

1. Giant panda 2. Pandas -- Juvenile literature

ISBN 0-689-84310-0; 0-689-86616-X pa

"Ryder's photo-essay chronicles the life of Hua Mei, born at the World Famous San Diego Zoo in 1999. . . . Ryder's brief, almost haiku-like text is bolstered by informative paragraphs set in smaller type. The crisp, engaging photos were provided by the zoo." Booklist

Somervill, Barbara A.

Small Indian Mongoose. Cherry Lake Pub. 2010 32p il map (Animal invaders) lib bdg $27.07

Grades: 5 6 7 8　　　　　　　　　　　**599.74**

1. Mongooses 2. Biological invasions

ISBN 978-1-60279-630-0 lib bdg; 1-60279-630-0 lib bdg

LC 2009028179

This offers "an introduction to the problems caused by [the Small Indian Mongoose], a discussion of its physical characteristics and habits, a history of how it arrived in its new habitat, and an analysis of challenges encountered by those trying to limit its spread. . . . [This] considers the destructive effects of these mammals on islands (including several in Hawaii), where they were initially introduced to prey on rats. . . . [This] well-focused [book is] clearly written. The uncluttered page design features at least one color photo on each spread." Booklist

Includes glossary and bibliographical references

Walden, Katherine

Meerkats. PowerKids Press 2009 24p il (Safari animals) lib bdg $21.25

Grades: PreK K 1 2　　　　　　　　　　**599.74**

1. Meerkats

ISBN 978-1-4358-2691-5 lib bdg; 1-4358-2691-4 lib bdg

LC 2008020793

This book provides "succinctly written introductory information about [meerkats'] range, habitat, social groups, and diet. Spreads consist of one to three short, simply constructed sentences opposite crisp, color photographs, most of which represent the subject perfectly." SLJ

599.75 Cat family

Barrett, Amanda

African cats; the story behind the film. by Amanda Barrett and Keith Scholey. Disney Press 2011 205p il $35
Grades: 3 4 5 6   **599.75**
1. Lions 2. Cheetahs
ISBN 978-1-4231-3410-7; 1-4231-3410-9
"In this beautifully photographed companion book to the . . . Disneynature film, naturalists Barrett and Scholey share their experience of studying a cheetah, her six cubs, and a pride of 19 lions in the Masai Mara National Reserve. The authors gracefully chronicle the animals' social and familial dynamics, as well as their struggles for survival in a sometimes ruthless environment. Centering on the 'stars' of the film—an injured lioness with a six-month-old cub, and the mother cheetah—Barrett and Scholey lightly anthropomorphize their behaviors to construct a relatable narrative. . . . The awesome power and inscrutability of the big cats is captivating." Publ Wkly

Becker, John E.
★ **Wild** cats: past & present; illustrations by Mark Hallett. Darby Creek 2008 80p il $18.95
Grades: 5 6 7 8   **599.75**
1. Wild cats 2. Felidae -- Juvenile literature
ISBN 978-1-58196-052-5; 1-58196-052-2
"Becker provides an informative introduction to wild cats, including an account of their ancient ancestors, an overview of the family Felidae and its subdivisions, accounts of wild cats alive in the world today, and woven throughout, discussions of the endangered status of many species. . . . Clearly written and well organized, the text is enhanced by many side-bars, maps, photos, and paintings." Booklist

Bodden, Valerie
Jaguars; by Valerie Bodden. 1st ed. Creative Education 2013 24 p. col. ill. (library) $25.65
Grades: 1 2 3 4   **599.75**
1. Jaguars -- Juvenile literature
ISBN 1608180867; 9781608180868
LC 2011050284
This book, part of the Amazing Animals series, focuses on jaguars. "Jaguars, the third largest member of the cat family, are found in Mexico, Central and South America. They can spring as far as 6 meters to catch prey. Families, which include one to four cubs, live together, but by age two the cubs live alone and stalk their own territory. Like other books in the series, glossary words are explained on pages where they first are mentioned." (NSTA Recommends)
Includes bibliographical references and index.

Lions. Creative Education 2010 24p il map (Amazing animals) lib bdg $24.25

Grades: K 1 2   **599.75**
1. Lions
ISBN 978-1-58341-807-9 lib bdg; 1-58341-807-5 lib bdg
LC 2009002709
A basic exploration of the appearance, behavior, and habitat of lions, the majestic big cats of Africa and India. Also included is a story from folklore explaining why lions roar
Includes bibliographical references

Bredeson, Carmen
Lions up close; [by] Carmen Bredeson. Enslow Elementary 2008 24p il (Zoom in on animals!) $21.26
Grades: 1 2 3   **599.75**
1. Lions
ISBN 978-0-7660-3080-0; 0-7660-3080-6
LC 2007025610
This describes the anatomy, behavior, and life cycle of lions.
Includes glossary and bibliographical references

Carney, Elizabeth
Everything big cats. National Geographic 2011 64p il map (National Geographic kids) lib bdg $25.90; pa $12.95
Grades: 3 4 5 6   **599.75**
1. Wild cats
ISBN 978-1-4263-0806-2 lib bdg; 1-4263-0806-X lib bdg; 978-1-4263-0805-5 pa; 1-4263-0805-1 pa
LC 2010026963
This describes four big predators, the lion, leopard, jaguar, and tiger.
"Exploding with astounding full-color photographs and written in an appealing conversational tone, [this book is] for every kid. . . . The [text] will keep kids interested and turning pages to discover more and more facts. . . . [This] compelling, browseable, and completely engrossing [title] will delight readers." SLJ
Includes glossary and bibliographical references

Clutton-Brock, Juliet
Cat; written by Juliet Clutton-Brock. rev ed.; Dorling Kindersley 2004 72p il (DK eyewitness books) $15.99
Grades: 4 5 6 7   **599.75**
1. Cats 2. Wild cats
ISBN 0-7566-0662-4
First published 1991
Text and photographs present the anatomy, behavior, habitats, and other aspects of wild and domestic cats

Estigarribia, Diana
Cheetahs; by Diana Estigarribia. Benchmark Books 2004 46p il map (Animals, animals) lib bdg $25.64
Grades: 3 4 5 6   **599.75**
1. Cheetahs
ISBN 0-7614-1749-4
LC 2003-22600
Describes the physical characteristics, behavior, hunting methods, and habitat of cheetahs
This "beautifully crafted [book presents] information in a lively, readable manner. [It includes] excellent-quality, candid full-color photographs." SLJ
Includes glossary and bibliographical references

Firestone, Mary

Top 50 reasons to care about tigers; animals in peril. Enslow Publishers 2010 103p il (Top 50 reasons to care about endangered animals) lib bdg $31.93

Grades: 4 5 6 7 **599.75**

1. Tigers 2. Endangered species

ISBN 978-0-7660-3452-5 lib bdg; 0-7660-3452-6 lib bdg

LC 2008-48689

This describes a tiger's life, how they hunt, the purpose of its stripes, caring for young, competing with people for space, and that these animals are very close to extinction

"The illustrations, mostly color photographs, represent a wonderful selection of the animals and their habitats. Reluctant readers may be enticed by this . . . simply because of the great images. This . . . would make a substantial supplement to the science curriculum when studying endangered animals." Libr Media Connect

Includes glossary and bibliographical references

Ganeri, Anita

Jaguar. Heinemann Library 2011 24p il map (A day in the life. Rain forest animals) lib bdg $22; pa $6.49

Grades: 1 2 **599.75**

1. Jaguars

ISBN 978-1-4329-4106-2 lib bdg; 1-4329-4106-2 lib bdg; 978-1-4329-4117-8 pa; 1-4329-4117-8 pa

LC 2010000962

This book follows a day in the life of a jaguar.

"Ganeri presents information clearly and simply in large type, two-sentence comments placed below a bright, sharply reproduced color photograph of the animal in a natural setting. . . . [This is] sufficiently specific to support assignment as well as pleasure reading." SLJ

Includes glossary and bibliographical references

Gish, Melissa

Jaguars. Creative Education 2011 46p il map (Living wild) lib bdg $23.95

Grades: 5 6 7 **599.75**

1. Jaguars

ISBN 978-1-60818-079-0; 1-60818-079-4

LC 2010028315

A look at jaguars, including their habitats, physical characteristics such as their powerful jaws, behaviors, relationships with humans, and threatened status in the world today.

This offers "an array of interesting facts. Photography is large and beautiful–a real draw." SLJ

Includes glossary and bibliographical references

Leopards. Creative Education 2010 46p il (Living wild) lib bdg $34.25; pa $8.99

Grades: 5 6 7 8 **599.75**

1. Leopards

ISBN 978-1-58341-972-4 lib bdg; 1-58341-972-1 lib bdg; 978-0-89812-555-9 pa; 0-89812-555-3 pa

LC 2010017377

"A look at leopards, including their habitats, physical characteristics such as their spotted fur, behaviors, relationships with humans, and threatened status in the world today." Publisher's note

Hamilton, Sue L.

Ambushed by a cougar; [by] Sue Hamilton. ABDO Pub. Co. 2010 32p il (Close encounters of the wild kind) lib bdg $27.07

Grades: 4 5 6 7 **599.75**

1. Pumas 2. Animal attacks

ISBN 978-1-60453-928-8 lib bdg; 1-60453-928-3 lib bdg

LC 2009-45521

Readers learn of actual human-cougar encounters, information about cougars, survival strategies, and attack statistics.

"Students will be drawn to the realistic full-color photographs, the realistic diagrams of the creatures' bodies, the real-life stories told by victims, and the interesting, attractive formatting that includes text, diagrams, photographs, and graphics on each page. . . . [This is] exciting and attractive in a 'gross' sort of way and will appeal particularly to boys for both leisure reading and research." Libr Media Connect

Includes glossary

Hanel, Rachael

Tigers. Creative Education 2008 46p il map (Living wild) lib bdg $22.95

Grades: 3 4 5 **599.75**

1. Tigers

ISBN 978-1-58341-660-0 lib bdg; 1-58341-660-9 lib bdg

LC 2007-08504

This describes the behavior, life cycle, and physical characteristics of tigers and their relationships to humans.

"Children will turn first to the excellent, informatively captioned photos. . . . But this . . . also has solid, informative content to accompany the captivating visuals." Booklist

Hatkoff, Juliana

★ Leo the snow leopard; the true story of an amazing rescue. told by Juliana Hatkoff, Isabella Hatkoff, and Craig Hatkoff. Scholastic Press 2010 un il $17.99

Grades: 3 4 5 6 **599.75**

1. Snow leopard 2. Wildlife conservation

ISBN 978-0-545-22927-2; 0-545-22927-8

"This inspirational picture book conveys the importance of caring and protecting the world's wildlife. The story recounts the rescue of an orphaned snow leopard cub from Pakistan, and how the goodwill between people and nations can make a difference in the survival of endangered species. Excellent photographic detail recreates Leo's discovery by a goat herder, who in turn contacted the authorities when he got too large, and his cross-country adventure before being relocated to the Bronx Zoo in New York." SLJ

Johns, Chris

★ Face to face with cheetahs; by Chris Johns with Elizabeth Carney. National Geographic 2008 32p il map (Face to face) $16.95; lib bdg $25.90

Grades: 3 4 5 6 **599.75**

1. Cheetahs

ISBN 978-1-4263-0323-4; 1-4263-0323-8; 978-1-4263-0324-1 lib bdg; 1-4263-0324-6 lib bdg

LC 2007041220

Chris Johns describes the life cycle and behavior of cheetahs and his own experiences with cheetahs in the wild.

Includes glossary and bibliographical references

Joubert, Beverly

★ **Face** to face with leopards; by Beverly and Dereck Joubert. National Geographic 2009 31p il (Face to face) $16.95; lib bdg $25.90

Grades: 3 4 5 6   **599.75**

1. Leopards

ISBN 978-1-4263-0636-5; 1-4263-0636-9; 978-1-4263-0637-2 lib bdg; 1-4263-0637-7 lib bdg

LC 2009011441

The authors describe the life cycle and behavior of leopard and their own experiences with leopards in the wild.

"The exquisite photos and firsthand information provide an in-depth and personal look into the lives of these animals." SLJ

Includes glossary and bibliographical references

★ **Face** to face with lions; by Beverly and Dereck Joubert. National Geographic 2008 31p il (Face to face) $16.95; lib bdg $25.90

Grades: 3 4 5 6   **599.75**

1. Lions

ISBN 978-1-4263-0207-7; 1-4263-0207-X; 978-1-4263-0208-4 lib bdg; 1-4263-0208-8 lib bdg

LC 2007-11118

The authors describe the life cycle and behavior of lions and their own experiences with lions in the wild.

This is "well written and complete. . . . [It contains] many beautiful color photographs." Sci Books Films

Includes glossary and bibliographical references

Landau, Elaine

Big cats; hunters of the night. Enslow Publishers 2007 32p il (Animals after dark) $16.95

Grades: 1 2 3 4   **599.75**

1. Wild cats 2. Cats -- Juvenile literature 3. Felidae -- Juvenile literature

ISBN 978-0-7660-2770-1; 0-7660-2770-8

LC 2006-16805

This "book presents basic information on the night-hunting big cats—lions, tigers, leopards, and jaguars—in an entertaining and informative format. . . . The photographs and clear text on mostly black pages add to a rewarding reading experience." Sci Books Films

Includes bibliographical references

Lunis, Natalie

Cheetah; speed demon! Bearport Pub. 2011 24p il map (Blink of an eye. Superfast animals!) lib bdg $22.61

Grades: 1 2 3   **599.75**

1. Cheetahs

ISBN 978-1-936087-89-1; 1-936087-89-8

LC 2009-53573

This describes the cheetah, including where it lives, how it hunts, and the ways its body helps it reach its record-breaking speeds.

This "is sure to appeal to a wide variety of readers. Vibrant photos illustrate each animal from multiple perspectives, providing opportunity for readers to closely examine the animal. Information is organized by subject heading and branches into the animal's physical features and how they contribute to its speed, the animal's natural predators, and how the animal makes use of speed as a means of survival. .

. . This . . . will be a worthwhile addition to your nonfiction collection." Libr Media Connect

Includes glossary and bibliographical references

Markle, Sandra

★ **Lions**; by Sandra Markle. Carolrhoda 2004 39p il (Animal predators) lib bdg $25.26; pa $7.95

Grades: 3 4 5 6   **599.75**

1. Lions

ISBN 1-57505-727-1 lib bdg; 1-57505-744-1 pa

LC 2003-11198

"The straightforward, descriptive text and superb photos give [this title] surefire appeal to middle readers." Booklist

Includes glossary and bibliographical references

Marks, Jennifer L.

Bobcats. Capstone Press 2011 24p il map (Pebble plus. Wildcats) lib bdg $23.99

Grades: K 1 2   **599.75**

1. Bobcats

ISBN 978-1-4296-4480-8 lib bdg; 1-4296-4480-X lib bdg

LC 2010002795

"Plenty of full-page, close-up photos of . . . [bobcats] . . . in natural (or seemingly natural) settings will attract a broad audience. . . . [The book] covers geographical range (with a small map), average size, physical adaptations for the cat's habitat, typical prey, life cycle, threats, and average life span in the wild." SLJ

Includes glossary and bibliographical references

Clouded leopards. Capstone Press 2011 24p il map (Pebble plus. Wildcats) lib bdg $23.99

Grades: K 1 2   **599.75**

1. Leopards

ISBN 978-1-4296-4482-2 lib bdg; 1-4296-4482-6 lib bdg

LC 2010002797

"Plenty of full-page, close-up photos of . . . [clouded leopards] . . . in natural (or seemingly natural) settings will attract a broad audience. . . . [The book] covers geographical range (with a small map), average size, physical adaptations for the cat's habitat, typical prey, life cycle, threats, and average life span in the wild." SLJ

Includes glossary and bibliographical references

Jaguars. Capstone Press 2011 24p il map (Pebble plus. Wildcats) lib bdg $23.99

Grades: K 1 2   **599.75**

1. Jaguars

ISBN 978-1-4296-4481-5 lib bdg; 1-4296-4481-8 lib bdg

LC 2010002798

"Plenty of full-page, close-up photos of . . . [jaguars] . . . in natural (or seemingly natural) settings will attract a broad audience. . . . [The book] covers geographical range (with a small map), average size, physical adaptations for the cat's habitat, typical prey, life cycle, threats, and average life span in the wild." SLJ

Includes glossary and bibliographical references

Meinking, Mary

Polar bear vs. seal. Raintree 2011 32p il (Predator vs. prey) $29; pa $7.99

Grades: 1 2 3 **599.75**
1. Polar bear 2. Seals (Animals) 3. Predatory animals
ISBN 978-1-4109-3939-5; 978-1-4109-3948-7 pa
Explores the features of the polar bear and the seal that make them particularly suited to catch or evade the other.
"The struggle between polar bear and seal is described in clear language and illustrated with engaging color photographs." Horn Book Guide
Includes glossary and bibliographical references

Montgomery, Sy
Saving the ghost of the mountain; an expedition among snow leopards in Mongolia. text by Sy Montgomery; photographs by Nic Bishop. Houghton Mifflin Books for Children 2009 48p il map (Scientists in the field) $18
Grades: 5 6 7 8 **599.75**
1. Biologists 2. Snow leopard 3. Conservationists
ISBN 978-0-618-91645-0; 0-618-91645-8
LC 2008-36762
Author Sy Montgomery and photographer Nic Bishop accompany conservationist Tom McCarthy and his team as they travel to Mongolia's Altai Mountains to gather data about snow leopard populations in an attempt to save this endangered species
"Montgomery's enthusiasm translates well to the page and will have readers cheering for the entourage as they attempt to spot a snow leopard. This slender book abounds with information. Bishop's trademark stunning photography fills out the book with breathtaking views of the extreme environs of Central Asia and warm portraits of the charming people who live there." SLJ

Patent, Dorothy Hinshaw
Big cats; illustrations by Kendahl Jan Jubb. Walker & Co. 2005 un il map $17.95
Grades: 2 3 4 **599.75**
1. Wild cats
ISBN 0-8027-8968-4
"After mentioning the physical features and behaviors common to all or most big cats, the book looks more closely at the lion, leopard, cheetah, tiger, snow leopard, cougar, and jaguar. Patent writes with clarity, economy, and a knack for finding apt descriptions. . . . The watercolor paintings clearly represent the animals in their habitats." Booklist

Riggs, Kate
Leopards; by Kate Riggs. Creative Education 2012 24 p. col. ill.
Grades: K 1 2 **599.75**
1. Leopards 2. Animal behavior 3. Habitat (Ecology) 4. Animals -- Folklore 5. Zoology -- Encyclopedias 6. Leopard -- Juvenile literature
ISBN 1608181103; 9781608181100
LC 2010049130
This children's book, part of Kate Riggs' "Amazing Animals" series, focuses on leopards. "This . . . popular series continues traveling the planet to study alligators, bats, and other fascinating animals. . . . [P]hotos are paired with . . . text to examine the featured creature's appearance, habitat, behaviors, and life cycle. . . . "A basic exploration of the appearance, behavior, and habitat of leopards, Earth's fourth-largest cats. Also included is a story from folklore ex-

plaining why leopards and baboons don't get along." (Publisher's note)
Includes bibliographical references and index

Rodriguez, Cindy
Cougars. Rourke Pub. 2009 24p il map (Eye to eye with endangered species) lib bdg $27.07
Grades: 2 3 4 **599.75**
1. Pumas
ISBN 978-1-60694-404-2 lib bdg; 1-60694-404-5 lib bdg
LC 2009-5995
Text examines the issues endangered cougars face and how they can be saved
"Sets out to introduce readers to [cougars] . . . explain the dangers they face, and detail the efforts of biologists and conservationists to save them. . . . Serviceable and informative." SLJ
Includes glossary

Schafer, Susan
Lions; by Susan Schafer, with Susan Markowitz Meredith. Marshall Cavendish Benchmark 2010 24p il map (Animals) lib bdg $16.95
Grades: 3 4 5 **599.75**
1. Lions
ISBN 978-0-7614-4344-5 lib bdg; 0-7614-4344-4 lib bdg
LC 2008-52104
"The straightforward presentation of the information and the uncluttered and attractive layout make [this] . . . good . . . for reports. Color photographs . . . are well utilized and complete a solid package." SLJ
Includes glossary and bibliographical references

Tigers; by Susan Schafer, with Fay Robinson. Marshall Cavendish Benchmark 2010 24p il map (Animals) lib bdg $16.95
Grades: 3 4 5 **599.75**
1. Tigers
ISBN 978-0-7614-4345-2 lib bdg; 0-7614-4345-2 lib bdg
LC 2008-52109
"The straightforward presentation of the information and the uncluttered and attractive layout make [this] . . . good . . . for reports. Color photographs . . . are well utilized and complete a solid package." SLJ
Includes glossary and bibliographical references

Shores, Erika L.
Canada lynx. Capstone Press 2011 24p il map (Pebble plus. Wildcats) lib bdg $23.99
Grades: K 1 2 **599.75**
1. Lynx
ISBN 978-1-4296-4484-6 lib bdg; 1-4296-4484-2 lib bdg
LC 2010002796
"Plenty of full-page, close-up photos of . . . [the Canada Lynx] . . . in natural (or seemingly natural) settings will attract a broad audience. . . . [The book] covers geographical range (with a small map), average size, physical adaptations

for the cat's habitat, typical prey, life cycle, threats, and average life span in the wild." SLJ

Includes glossary and bibliographical references

Mountain lions. Capstone Press 2011 24p il map (Pebble plus. Wildcats) lib bdg $23.99

Grades: K 1 2   **599.75**

1. Pumas

ISBN 978-1-4296-4485-3 lib bdg; 1-4296-4485-0 lib bdg

       LC 2010002799

"Plenty of full-page, close-up photos of . . . [mountain lions] . . . in natural (or seemingly natural) settings will attract a broad audience. . . . [The book] covers geographical range (with a small map), average size, physical adaptations for the cat's habitat, typical prey, life cycle, threats, and average life span in the wild." SLJ

Includes glossary and bibliographical references

Snow leopards. Capstone Press 2011 24p il map (Pebble plus. Wildcats) lib bdg $23.99

Grades: K 1 2   **599.75**

1. Snow leopard

ISBN 978-1-4296-4483-9 lib bdg; 1-4296-4483-4 lib bdg

       LC 2010002800

"Plenty of full-page, close-up photos of . . . [snow leopards] . . . in natural (or seemingly natural) settings will attract a broad audience. . . . [The book] covers geographical range (with a small map), average size, physical adaptations for the cat's habitat, typical prey, life cycle, threats, and average life span in the wild." SLJ

Includes glossary and bibliographical references

Simon, Seymour

★ **Big** cats. HarperCollins Pubs. 1991 un il hardcover o.p. pa $6.95

Grades: 3 4 5 6   **599.75**

1. Wild cats

ISBN 0-06-021647-6; 0-06-446119-X pa

       LC 90-36374

Simon "begins with a general overview of the big cats, and then presents details on the tiger, lion, leopard, jaguar, puma, cheetah and snow leopard. . . . The author also discusses concerns about wildlife conservation." Appraisal

Squire, Ann

Cheetahs; by Ann O. Squire. Children's Press 2005 47p il (True book) lib bdg $25; pa $6.95

Grades: 2 3 4   **599.75**

1. Cheetahs

ISBN 0-516-22792-0 lib bdg; 0-516-27932-7 pa

       LC 2003-5174

"Beginning with cheetahs' best-known quality, their speed, this very readable volume goes on to discuss their prowess and limitations as hunters as well as their prey, social habits, life cycle, and use of camouflage. . . . Remarkably clear, often-dramatic color photos of cheetahs in the wild offer unusually good views of the animals." Booklist

Includes bibliographical references

599.756

Wells, Robert E.

Can we share the world with tigers? by Robert E. Wells. Albert Whitman & Company 2012 32 p. (hardcover) $16.99

Grades: 3 4 5   **599.756**

1. Ecology 2. Biodiversity conservation 3. Picture books for children 4. Bengal tiger -- India -- Juvenile literature 5. Endangered species -- India -- Juvenile literature 6. Wildlife conservation -- India -- Juvenile literature 7. Bengal tiger -- Conservation -- India -- Juvenile literature

ISBN 0807510556; 9780807510551

       LC 2011038269

In this children's picture book, "using threats to endangered Bengal tigers' survival as a springboard, [Robert E.] Wells teaches young readers about the many ways humans interfere with the natural world and its biodiversity." A tigress, her cubs, and a monkey "travel through the book together, teaching readers about habitat destruction, pollution, overharvesting, invasive species, biodiversity and extinction." (Kirkus)

599.77   Dog family

Brandenburg, Jim

★ **Face** to face with wolves; by Jim and Judy Brandenburg. National Geographic 2008 31p il map (Face to face) $16.95; lib bdg $25.90

Grades: 3 4 5 6   **599.77**

1. Wolves

ISBN 978-1-4263-0242-8; 1-4263-0242-8; 978-1-4263-0243-5 lib bdg; 1-4263-0243-6 lib bdg

       LC 2007-41217

The authors describe the life cycle and behavior of wolves and their own experiences with wolves in the wild.

This is "well written and complete. . . . [It contains] many beautiful color photographs." Sci Books Films

Includes glossary and bibliographical references

Cohn, Scotti

One wolf howls; by Scotti Cohn; illustrated by Susan Detwiler. Sylvan Dell Pub. 2009 un il $16.95; pa $8.95

Grades: PreK K 1   **599.77**

1. Months 2. Wolves 3. Counting 4. Stories in rhyme

ISBN 978-1-934359-92-1; 1-934359-92-0; 978-1-607180-37-1 pa; 1-607180-37-5 pa

The months of the year and the numbers 1 through 12 are used in rhyming text to introduce children to the behavior of wolves in natural settings

"Readers should be captivated by the animals' resilient joie de vivre as well as by their habitats' seasonal glories. The educational guide offers wolf facts, activities and details about their life cycle." Publ Wkly

Ganeri, Anita

Fennec fox. Heinemann Library 2011 24p il map (A day in the life: desert animals) lib bdg $22; pa $6.49

Grades: K 1 2   599.77
1. Foxes
ISBN 978-1-4329-4771-2 lib bdg; 1-4329-4771-0 lib
bdg; 978-1-4329-4780-4 pa; 1-4329-4780-X pa
                                          LC 2010022819
"The engaging full-color photographs are key to [this]
well-organized [book]. . . . Basic global maps show where
the animal is found, and a diagram called a 'body map' labels its parts. [The text is] appropriate for the age group, and
the pictures will draw in youngsters. [An] excellent [pur-
chase] if material is needed on these animals." SLJ
Includes glossary and bibliographical references

George, Jean Craighead
★ The **wolves** are back; paintings by Wendell Minor.
Dutton Children's Books 2008 un il lib bdg $16.99
Grades: 2 3 4 5   599.77
1. Wolves 2. Wolves -- Reintroduction -- Juvenile
literature 3. Wolves -- Yellowstone National Park --
Juvenile literature
ISBN 978-0-525-47947-5
                                          LC 2007017064
"In 1995, wolves were reintroduced to Yellowstone
Park. . . . The emphasis here is not as much on the wolves
and their habits, but on how their presence has changed
the ecosystem and returned its natural balance. . . . George
writes . . . in simple, rhythmic, informative prose. Adding to
the book's appeal are Minor's finely detailed illustrations,
featuring spectacularly rendered animals in the foreground
of the bold, western landscapes." Booklist

Goldish, Meish
Red wolves; and then there were (almost) none. Bearport Pub. 2009 32p il map (America's animal comebacks)
lib bdg $25.27
Grades: 2 3 4   599.77
1. Wolves 2. Wildlife conservation
ISBN 978-1-59716-742-0 lib bdg; 1-59716-742-8
lib bdg
                                          LC 2008-30831
Through this true tale of wildlife survival, young readers
discover the bold and creative ideas that Americans and their
government have used to protect and care for the countrys
endangered red wolves
"Crisp photos and maps on every page work well with
the text and give faces to the scientists and animals. The
back matter includes a facts page, information on related
species, and an up-to-date reading list." SLJ
Includes glossary and bibliographical references

Johnson, Jinny
Fox; illustrations by Graham Rosewarne. Smart Apple
Media 2010 32p il (How does it work?) lib bdg $28.50
Grades: 1 2 3   599.77
1. Foxes
ISBN 978-1-59920-354-6; 1-59920-354-5
                                          LC 2008-53340
Explains the life cycle of a fox.
"Each stage is described on a spread that features clearly
written, oversized text and a caption opposite a full-page,
realistic watercolor, or, occasionally, a photograph. . . . A
worthwhile purchase." SLJ
Includes glossary

Mara, Wil
★ **Coyotes**. Marshall Cavendish Benchmark 2009 48p
il (Animals animals) $20.95
Grades: 3 4 5 6   599.77
1. Coyotes
ISBN 978-0-7614-2928-9; 0-7614-2928-X
                                          LC 2007023411
"The material is well researched and would be an excellent source for reports, and the [book has] a narrative flow
that makes [it] easy and enjoyable to read. [The] title includes expert full-color photography." SLJ
Includes glossary and bibliographical references

Markle, Sandra
★ **Wolves**; by Sandra Markle. Lerner Publications
2004 40p il (Animal predators) hardcover o.p. pa $7.95
Grades: 3 4 5 6   599.77
1. Wolves
ISBN 1-57505-732-8; 1-57505-748-4 pa
                                          LC 2003-11197
"The text works well with the often striking full-color
photos that illustrate the book." Booklist
Includes glossary and bibliographical references

McAllister, Ian
The **sea** wolves; living wild in the Great Bear Rainforest. written by Ian McAllister and Nicholas Read; photographs by Ian McAllister. Orca Book Publishers 2010
121p il $19.95
Grades: 5 6 7 8   599.77
1. Wolves 2. Rain forest ecology
ISBN 978-1-55469-206-4; 1-55469-206-7
The coastal wolf, a genetically distinct strain that swims
and fishes, inhabits the Great Bear Rainforest on British Columbia's rugged west coast.
"This extensive, informative text is illustrated with remarkable photographs taken by McAllister, who has lived
in and studied the area for years. They show the lush, old-
growth forest and rocky shoreline and a variety of animals
that share this habitat, but the wolves are the stars: at rest,
at play, on the prowl and catching fish. . . . Fascinating and
useful." Kirkus

Nobleman, Marc Tyler
★ **Foxes**; by Marc Tyler Nobleman. Marshall Cavendish Benchmark 2007 47p il (Animals, animals) lib
bdg $19.95
Grades: 3 4 5 6   599.77
1. Foxes
ISBN 978-0-7614-2237-2 lib bdg; 0-7614-2237-4
lib bdg
                                          LC 2005025608
"Describes the physical characteristics, behavior, habitat, and endangered status of foxes." Publisher's note
Includes glossary and bibliographical references

Patent, Dorothy Hinshaw
When the wolves returned; restoring nature's balance
in Yellowstone. photographs by Dan Hartman and Cassie
Hartman. Walker 2008 39p il $17.95; lib bdg $18.85
Grades: 3 4 5   599.77
1. Wolves 2. Ecology -- Juvenile literature 3.
Yellowstone National Park -- Juvenile literature
ISBN 978-0-8027-9686-8; 0-8027-9686-9; 978-0-

8027-9687-5 lib bdg; 0-8027-9687-7 lib bdg
LC 2007-37141
NCTE Orbis Pictus Award honor book (2009)

When wolves were eliminated from Yellowstone National Park the natural system was out of balance. Shows the return of the wolves to the park and the natural balance being restored.

"Outstanding historical and present-day photographs of Yellowstone, its inhabitants, and its visitors capture the rugged natural beauty of the park." Horn Book

Includes bibliographical references

Person, Stephen

Arctic fox; very cool! by Stephen Person. Bearport Pub. 2009 32p il map (Uncommon animals) lib bdg $25.27

Grades: 1 2 3   **599.77**
1. Foxes
ISBN 978-1-59716-730-7 lib bdg; 1-59716-730-4 lib bdg
LC 2008-10637

"Easily readable sections detail the bitter natural habitat of the arctic fox and highlight the ways in which the animal is uniquely outfitted to survive such harsh conditions. The text works splendidly with the large, clear photographs on each page that will delight readers." Booklist

Includes glossary and bibliographical references

Read, Tracy C.

Exploring the world of coyotes. Firefly 2011 24p il (Exploring the world of) $16.95; pa $6.95

Grades: 4 5 6   **599.77**
1. Coyotes
ISBN 978-1-55407-795-3; 1-55407-795-8; 978-1-55407-796-0 pa; 1-55407-796-6 pa

This describes the physical features, habitat, diet, and behavior of coyotes.

A "well-organized [text] and good-quality pictures taken from photo archives provide the basics. [This book] reveals how North America's 'super dog' has had to adapt to survive humankind's continuous assault. . . . Insets of information in colorful circles add to the attractive configuration. [The book offers] simple language and good use of space." SLJ

Exploring the world of wolves. Firefly 2010 24p il (Exploring the world of . . .) $16.95; pa $6.95

Grades: 3 4 5   **599.77**
1. Wolves
ISBN 978-1-55407-646-8; 1-55407-646-3; 978-1-55407-655-0 pa; 1-55407-655-2 pa

This describes the anatomy and behavior of wolves.

This offers "an abundance of in-depth, intriguing information and [is] appropriate for research or pleasure reading. . . . Two- to four-page chapters mix smaller photos with full-page color photos, and the attractive format will help less-able readers navigate the sometimes dense, detailed paragraphs." Booklist

Riggs, Kate

Wolves. Creative Education 2011 24p il (Amazing animals) $24.25; pa $5.99

Grades: K 1 2   **599.77**
1. Wolves
ISBN 978-1-58341-991-5; 1-58341-991-8; 978-0-89812-564-1 pa; 0-89812-564-2 pa
LC 2010019055

"A basic exploration of the appearance, behavior, and habitat of wolves, a family of wild dogs. Also included is a story from folklore explaining why wolves are different from domestic dogs." Publisher's note

Swinburne, Stephen R.

Coyote; North America's dog. Boyds Mills Press 1999 32p il $16.95; pa $8.95

Grades: 4 5 6   **599.77**
1. Coyotes
ISBN 1-56397-765-6; 1-59078-485-5 pa

This book "packs a lot of information about North American coyotes into a small space. The author, a veteran park ranger, knows his subject well and succeeds in making it interesting to his audience. . . . The full-color photographs are clean and clear and enliven the text." Booklist

599.775   Foxes

Holland, Mary

Ferdinand Fox's first summer; by Mary Holland. Sylvan Dell Publishing 2013 32 p. ill. (reinforced) $17.95; (paperback) $9.95

Grades: K 1 2 3   **599.775**
1. Foxes -- Juvenile literature
ISBN 1607186144; 9781607186144; 9781607186267
LC 2012030121

In this children's picture book, author "[Mary] Holland presents the first part of the red fox's life cycle with the story of Ferdinand, one fox kit she photographed throughout his first summer. Short, bland paragraphs of information describe how the five fox kits grow and learn, their mother nursing and grooming them and, when they are ready, bringing back food for them to eat." (Kirkus Reviews)

599.78   Bears

Arnold, Caroline

A polar bear's world; written and illustrated by Caroline Arnold. Picture Window Books 2010 24p il (Caroline Arnold's animals) lib bdg $25.32

Grades: PreK K 1 2   **599.78**
1. Polar bear
ISBN 978-1-4048-5743-8 lib bdg; 1-4048-5743-5 lib bdg
LC 2009033366

This narrative tells the story of a polar bear from birth until it is on its own.

The story, "related in the present tense, [feels] immediate and engaging. . . . The plainness of the fact boxes contrasts with Arnold's beautiful but simple artwork, which cleanly captures the essence of [the] animal. . . . [This book's] perfectly balanced mix of facts, story, and pictures will hold young readers' attention and help them learn." Booklist

Baines, Rebecca

A **den** is a bed for a bear; a book about bears. by Becky Baines. National Geographic 2008 29p il (Zig zag) $14.95; lib bdg $19.90

Grades: PreK K 1   **599.78**

1. Bears 2. Hibernation 3. Hibernation -- Juvenile literature

ISBN 978-1-4263-0309-8; 1-4263-0309-2; 978-1-4263-0310-4 lib bdg; 1-4263-0310-6 lib bdg

LC 2008-07221

"Readers curiosity will be piqued by the vibrant color photographs, accommodating illustrations, large font size, and helpful captions. Special features include drawings superimposed over photographs, and a zigzag path at the end of . . . [the] book prompting readers to further explore the topic in new and fun ways." SLJ

Barner, Bob

Bears! bears! bears! Chronicle Books 2010 un il $14.99

Grades: PreK K 1   **599.78**

1. Bears -- Fiction

ISBN 978-0-8118-7057-3; 0-8118-7057-X

"Collages rendered in vibrant hues lead youngsters through a fanciful expedition. The colorful spreads and rhyming text will entertain children as they discover the variety of bears found around the world. . . . Two concluding spreads contain facts about bears and ursine habitats. . . . Beginning readers might like to attempt this one on their own." SLJ

Bekoff, Marc

Jasper's story; saving moon bears. by Jill Robinson & Marc Bekoff; illustrated by Gijsbert van Frankenhuyzen. Sleeping Bear Press 2013 40 p. (reinforced) $16.99

Grades: 1 2 3 4 5   **599.78**

1. Bears 2. Animal welfare 3. Wildlife rescue -- Juvenile literature 4. Asiatic black bear -- Juvenile literature

ISBN 1585367982; 9781585367986

LC 2012033687

This book by Jill Robinson was written after she encountered the practice of bear farming in China. The book "tells of one moon bear [Jasper] and how he came to symbolize the forgiveness and trust that come with love. . . . At the time of his rescue, he was both physically and emotionally battered, but through the gentle care of Robinson and her helpers, he can play and interact with other bears and humans, and seems to have forgiven the cruelties that were once inflicted upon him." (School Library Journal)

Berman, Ruth

Let's look at brown bears. Lerner Publications Co. 2010 32p il map (Lightning Bolt Books: Animal close-ups) lib bdg $25.26

Grades: PreK K 1 2   **599.78**

1. Bears

ISBN 978-0-7613-3890-1 lib bdg; 0-7613-3890-X lib bdg

LC 2008-51855

Introduces the Alaskan brown bear, describing its physical characteristics, hibernation behavior, and feeding habits

"Fresh photography, a creative use of graphics, and a collagelike layout make[s] . . . [this book] eye-catching. .

. . [The] book ends with a labeled diagram of the animal, a range map, and a further-reading list that includes print and online resources in a single list, a nice way of validating both types of materials." SLJ

Includes glossary

Bodden, Valerie

Polar bears. Creative Education 2010 24p il (Amazing animals) lib bdg $24.25

Grades: K 1 2   **599.78**

1. Polar bear

ISBN 978-1-58341-811-6 lib bdg; 1-58341-811-3 lib bdg

LC 2009002714

A basic exploration of the appearance, behavior, and habitat of polar bears, Earth's biggest land predators. Also included is a story from folklore explaining why polar bears have short tails.

This is illustrated with "dynamically colored photographs." Booklist

Includes bibliographical references

Bortolotti, Dan

Panda rescue; changing the future for endangered wildlife. Firefly 2003 64p il map lib bdg $19.95; pa $9.95

Grades: 4 5 6 7   **599.78**

1. Giant panda 2. Wildlife conservation 3. Pandas -- Juvenile literature

ISBN 1-55297-598-3 lib bdg; 1-55297-557-6 pa

This describes the panda's "natural habitat, habits, physiology, and behavior in captivity. [It also includes] a time line of conservation efforts, profiles of conservationists in the field, and forecasts of the animals' future. Throughout, the author makes clear the factors that can threaten animal populations, and discusses human attitudes toward the animals throughout history. . . . Written in accessible, lively language and nicely illustrated with exciting color photos, [this] will be useful for reports and browsing." Booklist

Davies, Nicola, 1958-

★ **Ice** bear; in the steps of the polar bear. illustrated by Gary Blythe. Candlewick Press 2005 un il $16.99

Grades: K 1 2 3   **599.78**

1. Polar bear

ISBN 0-7636-2759-3

Describes how the polar bear, also called Nanuk, thrives in the Arctic and explains the lessons that the Inuit people have learned from watching the creature.

"This inviting picture book delivers facts about polar bears and conveys respect for their adaptive success. . . . Children will be fascinated by the impressionistic oil paintings of stunning polar settings and bears at play, tenderly nursing young, and, yes, hunting seals, an activity represented by a stark image of a bear's crimson-stained muzzle that may startle the youngest readers." Booklist

De Vries, Maggie

Fraser bear; a cub's life. illustrated by Renné Benoit. Greystone Books 2010 il $16.95

Grades: 2 3 4   **599.78**

1. Bears 2. Salmon

ISBN 978-1-55365-521-3; 1-55365-521-4

"Set along British Columbia's Fraser River and arranged chronologically by months of the year, this story follows a cub from his birth through his first season of independence. With each phase of his growth, the life cycle of the chinook salmon is also explained as they migrate out to the ocean then back up the river to spawn and die, providing an abundance of rich food for Fraser and other animals. . . . A good resource for any study of the life cycle of bears or salmon." SLJ

Firestone, Mary

Top 50 reasons to care about giant pandas; animals in peril. Enslow Publishers 2010 103p il (Top 50 reasons to care about endangered animals) lib bdg $31.93
Grades: 4 5 6 7　　　　　　　　　　　　**599.78**
　　1. Giant panda　2. Endangered species
　　ISBN 978-0-7660-3451-8 lib bdg; 0-7660-3451-8
　　lib bdg
　　　　　　　　　　　　　　　LC 2008-48953
This describes the giant panda's life cycle, habitat, young, diet, living in the wild and in captivity, and why it is endangered
"The illustrations, mostly color photographs, represent a wonderful selection of the animals and their habitats. Reluctant readers may be enticed by this . . . simply because of the great images. This . . . would make a substantial supplement to the science curriculum when studying endangered animals." Libr Media Connect
Includes glossary and bibliographical references

Gish, Melissa

Pandas. Creative Education 2011 48p il (Living wild) lib bdg $23.95; pa $8.95
Grades: 5 6 7 8　　　　　　　　　　　　**599.78**
　　1. Giant panda
　　ISBN 978-1-60818-082-0 lib bdg; 1-60818-082-4 lib
　　bdg; 978-1-60818-082-0 pa; 1-60818-082-4 pa
　　　　　　　　　　　　　　　LC 2010028311
A look at pandas, including their habitats, physical characteristics such as their black-and-white fur, behaviors, relationships with humans, and threatened status in the world today.
Includes glossary and bibliographical references

Greene, Jacqueline Dembar

Grizzly bears; saving the silvertip. by Jacqueline Dembar Greene. Bearport Pub. 2008 32p il map (America's animal comebacks) lib bdg $25.27
Grades: 2 3 4　　　　　　　　　　　　**599.78**
　　1. Grizzly bear　2. Wildlife conservation
　　ISBN 978-1-59716-533-4 lib bdg; 1-59716-533-6
　　lib bdg
　　　　　　　　　　　　　　　LC 2007012606
This describes efforts by environmentals to save the silvertip grizzly bear from extinction in the American West
This book is "well organized and [has] an easy style and an accessible vocabulary and text size . . . [and] color photographs." SLJ
Includes glossary and bibliographical references

Guiberson, Brenda Z.

Ice bears; [by] Brenda Z. Guiberson; illustrated by Ilya Spirin. Henry Holt & Co. 2008 un il $16.95

Grades: 1 2 3 4　　　　　　　　　　　　**599.78**
　　1. Polar bear
　　ISBN 978-0-8050-7607-3; 0-8050-7607-7
　　　　　　　　　　　　　　　LC 2007040895
"This story of the struggle of a polar bear mother and her two cubs to survive introduces both the harsh conditions of the Arctic and the challenges of global warming for polar bears in general. Guiberson uses precise verbs and onomatopoeia to paint a picture of the daily activities of the bears while gracefully weaving in facts about their weight, diet, and climate. Spirin's detailed watercolors are surprisingly varied in depicting an essentially frozen world, using interesting perspectives." SLJ

★ Moon bear; illustrated by Ed Young. Henry Holt & Co. 2010 un il $16.99
Grades: PreK K 1 2 3　　　　　　　　　　**599.78**
　　1. Bears
　　ISBN 978-0-8050-8977-6; 0-8050-8977-2
　　　　　　　　　　　　　　　LC 2009017931
"This picture book both celebrates the endangered black moon bear in Southeast Asia and warns about the urgent threats against the species. Filled with physical details, the spare, question-and-answer text . . . is illustrated with Young's stark, large silhouette images of a beautiful, dark bear throughout the seasons." Booklist

Hamilton, Sue L.

Mauled by a bear; [by] Sue Hamilton. ABDO Pub. Co. 2010 32p il (Close encounters of the wild kind) lib bdg $27.07
Grades: 4 5 6 7　　　　　　　　　　　　**599.78**
　　1. Bears　2. Animal attacks
　　ISBN 978-1-60453-932-5 lib bdg; 1-60453-932-1
　　lib bdg
　　　　　　　　　　　　　　　LC 2009-35078
Readers learn of actual human-bear encounters, information about bears, survival strategies, and attack statistics.
"Students will be drawn to the realistic full-color photographs, the realistic diagrams of the creatures' bodies, the real-life stories told by victims, and the interesting, attractive formatting that includes text, diagrams, photographs, and graphics on each page. . . . [This is] exciting and attractive in a 'gross' sort of way and will appeal particularly to boys for both leisure reading and research." Libr Media Connect
Includes glossary

Hatkoff, Juliana

Knut; how one little polar bear captivated the world. told by Juliana, Isabella, and Craig Hatkoff, and Gerald R. Uhlich. Scholastic Press 2007 un il $16.99
Grades: 2 3 4　　　　　　　　　　　　**599.78**
　　1. Polar bear
　　ISBN 978-0-545-04716-6; 0-545-04716-1
　　　　　　　　　　　　　　　LC 2007-21379
"Knut is a German polar bear born in captivity. His story is told in simple language and accompanied by adorable, engaging close-ups of him and his primary handler, a zookeeper named Thomas Dörflein. . . . Consider this well-written, well-documented title an essential addition to every collection." SLJ

Hirsch, Rebecca E.

Top 50 reasons to care about polar bears; animals in peril. Enslow Publishers 2010 103p il (Top 50 reasons to care about endangered animals) lib bdg $31.93

Grades: 4 5 6 7   599.78

1. Polar bear 2. Endangered species

ISBN 978-0-7660-3458-7 lib bdg; 0-7660-3458-5 lib bdg

LC 2008-48693

This describes polar bears--their life cycle, diet, young, habitat, and reasons why they are endangered animals

"The illustrations, mostly color photographs, represent a wonderful selection of the animals and their habitats. Reluctant readers may be enticed by this . . . simply because of the great images. This . . . would make a substantial supplement to the science curriculum when studying endangered animals." Libr Media Connect

Includes glossary and bibliographical references

Hirschi, Ron

Our three bears; [by] Ron Hirschi; photographs by Thomas D. Mangelsen. Boyds Mills Press 2008 32p il $16.95

Grades: 2 3 4 5   599.78

1. Bears

ISBN 978-1-59078-015-2

LC 2007049380

"North America's bears—black, grizzly, and polar—are introduced in this attractive presentation made compelling by Mangelsen's full-color photographic delights. . . . Hirschi reveals the differences in each bear's hibernation patterns, habitats, diets, size, and population estimates. These short paragraphs are chock-full of information. Beginning researchers as well as young wildlife enthusiasts will find Our Three Bears well suited to their interests." SLJ

Includes bibliographical references

★ **Searching** for grizzlies; photographs by Thomas D. Mangelsen; drawings by Deborah Cooper. Boyds Mills Press 2005 un il $15.95

Grades: 3 4 5   599.78

1. Bears 2. Grizzly bear -- Juvenile literature

ISBN 1-59078-014-0

Describes the physical characteristics, behavior, and habitat primarily of grizzly bears, with some comparisons to black bears and polar bears.

"Mangelsen's fine photos and Cooper's attractive sketches accompany Hirschi's readable text bursting with the bear facts." SLJ

Kvatum, Lia

Saving Yasha; The Incredible True Story of an Adopted Moon Bear. by Lia Kvatum; photographs by Liya Pokrovskaya. National Geographic 2012 32 p. col. ill., col. maps (hardcover) $16.95; (lib. bdg.) $25.90

Grades: 1 2 3   599.78

1. Bears 2. Wildlife 3. Animal behavior

ISBN 142631051X; 9781426310515; 1426310765; 9781426310768

LC 2012288404

In this book, Lia Kvatum tells the story of "Yasha, joined later by Shum and Shiksha, [who] are nurtured by" scientists after being "orphaned by poachers . . . [in] the Siberian wild. . . . Kvatum chronicles the cubs' development as they learn to forage on their own while playing together and learning to climb trees. She also notes how important it is for human observers to remain aloof . . . to prevent the animals from becoming dependent or domesticated." (Kirkus Reviews)

Leathers, Dan

Polar bears on the Hudson Bay; by Dan Leathers. Mitchell Lane Publishers 2008 32p il map (On the verge of extinction: crisis in the environment) lib bdg $17.95

Grades: 3 4 5   599.78

1. Polar bear

ISBN 978-1-58415-586-7

LC 2007000797

This describes the life cycle of polar bears on the Hudson Bay and how they are threatened by climate change and other environmental dangers.

"Short chapters, large font, and pronunciation guides to key words engage children doing research, but the depth of information is not compromised. . . . Colorful, up-close photographs are accompanied by satisfying explanatory captions." SLJ

Includes glossary and bibliographical references

Markle, Sandra

Grizzly bears. Lerner Publications Company 2010 39p il (Animal predators) $26.60

Grades: 4 5 6   599.78

1. Grizzly bear

ISBN 978-1-58013-537-5; 1-58013-537-4

LC 2008-38120

Introduces the physical characteristics, habitat, and predatory behavior of grizzly bears.

"Vivid photographs alongside Markle's narrative, which provides factual information about grizzly bears' physical characteristics and hunting behaviors, introduce readers to these majestic and dangerous creatures." Horn Book Guide

Includes glossary and bibliographical references

★ **How** many baby pandas? Walker 2009 23p il map $15.99; lib bdg $16.89

Grades: K 1 2 3   599.78

1. Giant panda 2. Animal babies 3. Counting -- Juvenile literature

ISBN 978-0-8027-9783-4; 0-8027-9783-0; 978-0-8027-9784-1 lib bdg; 0-8027-9784-9 lib bdg

"Clear accessible text . . . and sharp photos provide an engaging, informative introduction to baby pandas, highlighting those born at China's Wolong Giant Panda Breeding Center in 2005. . . . Scientific concepts are well explained, and pages are filled with panda facts." Booklist

Includes glossary and bibliographical references

Polar bears; [by] Sandra Markle. Carolrhoda Books 2004 40p il (Animal predators) lib bdg $25.26; pa $7.95

Grades: 3 4 5 6   599.78

1. Polar bear

ISBN 1-57505-730-1 lib bdg; 1-57505-746-8 pa

LC 2003-19515

The author observes polar bears' "hunting techniques and includes information about their physical characteristics, physiology, habitats and care of young." Horn Book Guide

Includes glossary and bibliographical references

McAllister, Ian

★ **Salmon** bears; giants of the Great Bear Rainforest. [by] Ian McAllister & Nicholas Read; photographs by Ian McAllister. Orca Book Publishers 2010 89p il map pa $18.95

Grades: 5 6 7 8   **599.78**
1. Bears 2. Salmon 3. Rain forest ecology
ISBN 978-1-55469-205-7 pa; 1-55469-205-9 pa

"Read's conversational text and McAllister's excellent photos provide a perfect framework for this evocative look at the big bears of the Great Bear Rainforest of British Columbia, and an intriguing investigation of its ecological pattern of dependency. The authors present a round of seasons from one winter to the next, touching upon such topics as the effects of fish farms on wild salmon populations, what happens during a salmon run, and what the future may hold for the fish, the bears, and the Great Bear Rainforest itself... . Superbly readable, informative, and attractive." SLJ

Includes bibliographical references

Montgomery, Sy

★ **Search** for the golden moon bear; science and adventure in the Asian tropics. Houghton Mifflin 2004 80p il $17

Grades: 5 6 7 8   **599.78**
1. Bears
ISBN 0-618-35650-9

LC 2004-5236

The author reports on an expedition into Laos and Thailand in search of a rare species of bear

"The exciting narrative is complemented by an array of full-color photos. . . . This attractive and informative offering is an intelligent reportage of science as it happens." SLJ

Includes bibliographical references

Newman, Mark

Polar bears. Henry Holt & Co. 2011 un il map $16.99
Grades: K 1 2 3   **599.78**
1. Polar bear
ISBN 978-0-8050-8999-8; 0-8050-8999-3

"Irresistibly endearing polar bear photographs are the highlight of this picture book, although each spread also includes a factual statement about polar bears . . . , accompanied by smaller additional text that goes into deeper detail." Horn Book

Includes bibliographical references

Olson, Gillia M.

Polar bears' search for ice; a cause and effect investigation. Capstone Press 2010 32p il map (Fact finders. Animals on the edge) lib bdg $25.99
Grades: 3 4 5 6   **599.78**
1. Polar bear 2. Greenhouse effect
ISBN 978-1-4296-4532-4 lib bdg; 1-4296-4532-6 lib bdg

LC 2010007719

"Excellent discussions address those who doubt the severity of the issue and those who wonder why people should care what happens to animals. The captioned photographs are timely and poignant. . . . [This] makes serious subject matter interesting and accessible." SLJ

Includes glossary and bibliographical references

Rosing, Norbert

Face to face with polar bears; by Norbert Rosing with Elizabeth Carney. National Geographic 2007 32p il (Face to face) $16.95; lib bdg $25.90
Grades: 3 4 5 6   **599.78**
1. Polar bear
ISBN 978-1-4263-0139-1; 978-1-4263-0140-7 lib bdg

LC 2006032847

"Rosing tells how he and his wife tried to fend off a polar bear 'with a toothache' and a yen for their spaghetti dinner while they waited for a helicopter rescue. The book describes the animal's diet, physical features, and habitat, and the dangers of global warming. . . . [This] attractive, smoothly written [book], topped off with advice about self-directed research, will catch the attention of enthusiasts and motivate them toward personal investigation." SLJ

Includes glossary and bibliographical references

Polar bears. Firefly Books 2010 55p il map $19.95; pa $9.95
Grades: 3 4 5   **599.78**
1. Polar bear
ISBN 978-1-55407-599-7; 1-55407-599-8; 978-1-55407-623-9 pa; 1-55407-623-4 pa

LC 2010294457

Photographs and captions present the life of polar bears across the four seasons of the year. Topics covered include habitat activities, diet, anatomy, and survival.

"The high quality of the photos and their reproduction will draw many readers to this visually appealing book, which provides plenty of worthwhile information in the captions and back matter." Booklist

Ryder, Joanne

A **pair** of polar bears; twin cubs find a home at the San Diego Zoo. photos by the world-famous San Diego Zoo. Simon & Schuster Books for Young Readers 2006 un il $16.95
Grades: K 1 2   **599.78**
1. Polar bear
ISBN 0-689-85871-X

LC 2005014013

"This photo-essay introduces children to an engaging, true story from the San Diego Zoo. . . . The stars are rescued polar bear twins Tatqiq and Kalluk, who progress through the photo-rich pages from needy, quarantined cubs to fully acclimated adults with mastery over their outdoor habitat. The images, all provided by the zoo and most sharply focused and closeup, will elicit coos from readers." Booklist

Sartore, Joel

★ **Face** to face with grizzlies. National Geographic 2007 32p il (Face to face) $16.95; lib bdg $25.90
Grades: 3 4 5 6   **599.78**
1. Grizzly bear 2. Grizzly bear -- Juvenile literature
ISBN 978-1-4263-0050-9; 1-4263-0050-6; 978-1-4263-0051-6 lib bdg; 1-4263-0051-4 lib bdg

LC 2006-20500

"In accessible, exciting language, Sartore . . . describes his close encounters with bears while on assignment. . . . He matches stunning photographs of bears playing, fighting, eating, and chasing prey . . . with basic information about bears' bodies, habitats, and behavior." Booklist

Includes bibliographical references

Schreiber, Anne

Pandas. National Geographic 2010 32p il (National Geographic readers) pa $3.99

Grades: 1 2 3   **599.78**

1. Giant panda

ISBN 978-1-4263-0610-5; 1-4263-0610-5

This describes pandas and their behavior.

Schwabacher, Martin

Bears; by Martin Schwabacher with Terry Miller Shannon. Marshall Cavendish Benchmark 2010 24p il map (Animals) lib bdg $16.95

Grades: 3 4 5   **599.78**

1. Bears

ISBN 978-0-7614-3820-5 lib bdg; 0-7614-3820-3 lib bdg

"The straightforward presentation of the information and the uncluttered and attractive layout make [this] . . . good . . . for reports. Color photographs . . . are well utilized and complete a solid package." SLJ

Includes glossary and bibliographical references

Sirota, Lyn A.

Giant pandas. Capstone Press 2010 24p il map (Pebble plus. Asian animals) lib bdg $22.65

Grades: PreK K 1   **599.78**

1. Giant panda

ISBN 978-1-4296-4028-2; 1-4296-4028-6

"This . . . is an excellent resource for great pictures and information to share with students in storytimes or to support other content areas. This will be an excellent addition to nonfiction collections, especially for very young readers." Libr Media Connect

Includes bibliographical references

Swinburne, Stephen R.

★ **Black** bear; North America's bear. Boyds Mills 2003 32p il map $15.95

Grades: 3 4 5   **599.78**

1. Bears

ISBN 1-59078-023-X

An examination of black bears, their behavior and habitat.

"Stunning, full-color photos and a lively text make for an intriguing introduction to these fascinating animals." SLJ

Thomson, Sarah L.

Where do polar bears live? illustrated by Jason Chin. Collins 2010 37p il (Let's-read-and-find-out science) $16.99; pa $5.99

Grades: K 1 2 3   **599.78**

1. Polar bear

ISBN 978-0-06-157518-1; 0-06-157518-6; 978-0-06-157517-4 pa; 0-06-157517-8 pa

LC 2008056030

"This title explores a year in the life of a polar bear, focusing on facts about the animal's diet, hunting techniques, and habitat. Thomson also covers the impact of global warming on polar bears' food sources. . . . This is an affecting introduction to polar bears and their threatened existence for young children." Booklist

599.786   Polar bear

Markle, Sandra, 1946-

Waiting for ice; by Sandra Markle; illustrated by Alan Marks. Charlesbridge 2012 32 p.

Grades: 1 2 3   **599.786**

1. Polar bear -- Juvenile literature 2. Arctic region -- Juvenile literature 3. Global warming -- Juvenile literature 4. Polar bear -- Effect of global warming on

ISBN 1580892558; 9781580892551; 9781580892568

LC 2011002113

This children's book by Sandra Markle, illustrated by Alan Marks, "provides a . . . look at polar bears, the largest hunters on land, in this narrative that follows an orphaned cub barely old enough to survive on her own. Trapped on Wrangel Island in the Arctic Sea, waiting late into the fall for the annual floating pack ice to form, she and other polar bears subsist on the few animals they can find—typically only birds and walruses, as a note on global warming explains. . . . [The story offers a] look at how polar bears survive during so much of the year, when there's no ice to help them in their hunt for seals in the Arctic waters." (Kirkus)

599.79   Marine carnivores

Arnold, Caroline

A **walrus'** world; written and illustrated by Caroline Arnold. Picture Window Books 2010 24p il (Caroline Arnold's animals) lib bdg $25.32

Grades: PreK K 1 2   **599.79**

1. Walruses

ISBN 978-1-4048-5744-5 lib bdg; 1-4048-5744-3 lib bdg

LC 2009033380

This narrative tells the story of a walrus from birth until it can live on its own.

The story, "related in the present tense, [feels] immediate and engaging. . . . The plainness of the fact boxes contrasts with Arnold's beautiful but simple artwork, which cleanly captures the essence of [the] animal. . . . [This book's] perfectly balanced mix of facts, story, and pictures will hold young readers' attention and help them learn." Booklist

Harvey, Jeanne

Astro the Steller sea lion; illustrated by Shennen Bersani. Sylvan Dell Pub. 2010 un il $16.95; pa $8.95

Grades: 1 2 3   **599.79**

1. Seals (Animals) -- Fiction 2. Steller's sea lion -- Juvenile literature

ISBN 978-1-60718-076-0; 1-60718-076-6; 978-1-60718-087-6 pa; 1-60718-087-1 pa

LC 2010-921908

"Harvey tells a gentle tale of an orphaned Steller sea lion pup whose early imprinting on his human nurturers at the Marine Mammal Center in Sausalito, CA, leaves him determinedly reluctant to live in the wild on any terms. Bersani's nearly photographic illustrations keep perfect time with the simple text." SLJ

Hengel, Katherine

It's a baby Australian fur seal! ABDO 2010 24p il (Baby Australian animals) lib bdg $19.93

Grades: K 1 2 3 **599.79**
1. Animal babies 2. Seals (Animals)
ISBN 978-1-60453-574-7 lib bdg; 1-60453-574-1
lib bdg

LC 2008-55073

This book about fur seals "is a great choice. Though the focus of . . . [the] book is the animal baby, the reader will learn a great many facts. Information includes how they are born, how they are fed, age of independence, food, habitat, predators, and features that help them find food and protect themselves. . . . This . . . is a sound addition for any school library." Libr Media Connect

Includes glossary

Malam, John
Pinnipeds; written by John Malam; created and designed by David Salariya. Franklin Watts 2009 32p il (Scary creatures) lib bdg $26; pa $8.95
Grades: 3 4 5 **599.79**
1. Walruses 2. Marine mammals 3. Seals (Animals)
ISBN 978-0-531-21672-9 lib bdg; 0-531-21672-1 lib bdg; 978-0-531-21043-7 pa; 0-531-21043-X pa

LC 2009010799

This defines pinnipeds and describes their life cycles, habitats, behavior, and relationship to humans

This title has "two-page chapters of accessible, large-type text and bright color photos and illustrations. . . . The series distinguishes itself with 'X-Ray Vision.' When readers hold the page with this prompt up to the light, an image emerges. The X-rays mostly show the skeletal structures of the animals. Text boxes throughout add to the visual appeal. . . . [This title is an] excellent [resource] for school assignments and browsing." SLJ

Includes glossary

Markovics, Joyce L.
Weddell seal; fat and happy. by Joyce L. Markovics. Bearport Pub. 2009 32p il map (Uncommon animals) lib bdg $25.27
Grades: 1 2 3 **599.79**
1. Seals (Animals)
ISBN 978-1-59716-734-5 lib bdg; 1-59716-734-7 lib bdg

LC 2008-14391

"The explanatory text works spendidly, with large photographs that bring readers as close as they'll ever get to such beasts." Booklist

Includes glossary and bibliographical references

Metz, Lorijo
Discovering sea lions. PowerKids Press 2011 24p il (Along the shore) lib bdg $21.25
Grades: 3 4 5 **599.79**
1. Seals (Animals)
ISBN 978-1-4488-4992-5; 1-4488-4992-6

LC 2010047570

This book about sea lions "briefly describes the major physical and behavioral characteristics common to all [sea lions] and one or two distinctive characteristics of about a half dozen species. . . . [The book] outlines the major physical differences between [sea lions] and seals. . . . One or two sharp color photographs of representative species, most of which are closeups, accompany the text on every page. . . .

[This is] well organized and smoothly written in an engaging style." SLJ
Includes glossary

Peterson, Brenda
★ **Leopard** & Silkie; one boy's quest to save the seal pups. by Brenda Peterson; photographs by Robin Lindsey. 1st ed. Henry Holt and Co. (BYR) 2012 32 p. col. ill. (hardback) $16.99
Grades: 1 2 3 **599.79**
1. Compassion 2. Animal welfare 3. Seals (Animals)
4. Wildlife rescue -- Juvenile literature
ISBN 080509167X; 9780805091670

LC 2011029041

Author Brenda Peterson tells the story of "concerned volunteers [who] become seal sitters [in the Pacific Northwest], keeping vigil over the vulnerable baby seals that are left on the shore while their mothers hunt for food. . . . With its emphasis on human compassion, this true account teaches children to appreciate the natural world by helping in any way they can. The star of the book is six year old Miles, who organizes his own rescue mission to help the seals survive." (Publisher's note)

Includes bibliographical references.

Read, Tracy C.
Exploring the world of seals and walruses. Firefly 2011 24p il (Exploring the world of) $16.95; pa $6.95
Grades: 4 5 6 **599.79**
1. Walruses 2. Seals (Animals)
ISBN 978-1-55407-784-7; 1-55407-784-2; 978-1-55407-797-7 pa; 1-55407-797-4 pa

This describes the physical features, habitats, diets, and behavior of seals and walruses.

A "well-organized [text] and good-quality pictures taken from photo archives provide the basics. . . . [This focuses] on the different habitats and challenges faced by three pinniped subgroups: eared and earless seals and the walrus. Insets of information in colorful circles add to the attractive configuration. [The book offers] simple language and good use of space." SLJ

Rebman, Renee C.
Walruses. Marshall Cavendish Benchmark 2011 il (Animals, animals) lib bdg $20.95
Grades: 3 4 5 **599.79**
1. Walruses
ISBN 978-0-7614-4881-5; 0-7614-4881-0

LC 2010016036

This offers information on the anatomy, special skills, habitats, and diet of walruses.

This offers "comprehensive text and striking, well-chosen photos. . . . [This is] packed with engaging facts and trivia, as well as an upbeat tone." Booklist

Includes glossary and bibliographical references

Spilsbury, Louise
Seal. Heinemann Library 2011 24p il (A day in the life. sea animals) lib bdg $22; pa $6.49
Grades: 1 2 **599.79**
1. Seals (Animals)
ISBN 978-1-4329-4002-7 lib bdg; 1-4329-4002-3 lib bdg; 978-1-4329-4009-6 pa; 1-4329-4009-0 pa

LC 2010000628

This book follows a seal through its day as it sleeps, eats, and moves.

This pairs "well-chosen color photos . . . with one or two sentences of simple commentary for each. . . . [Though this title] includes references to several varieties of the chosen creature, one species in particular is highlighted. . . . [Good choice] for pleasure or purpose reading." SLJ

Includes glossary and bibliographical references

599.8 Primates

Aronin, Miriam

Aye-aye; an evil omen. by Miriam Aronin. Bearport Pub. 2009 32p il map (Uncommon animals) lib bdg $25.27

Grades: 1 2 3   599.8

1. Lemurs 2. Aye-aye (Animal)

ISBN 978-1-59716-731-4 lib bdg; 1-59716-731-2 lib bdg

LC 2008-15387

This describes the aye-aye, a lemur from Madagascar, believed, according to legend, to be an evil omen

"The explanatory text works splendidly, with large photographs that bring readers as close as they'll ever get to such beasts." Booklist

Includes glossary and bibliographical references

Barker, David

Top 50 reasons to care about great apes; animals in peril. Enslow Publishers 2010 103p il (Top 50 reasons to care about endangered animals) lib bdg $31.93

Grades: 4 5 6 7   599.8

1. Apes 2. Endangered species

ISBN 978-0-7660-3456-3 lib bdg; 0-7660-3456-9 lib bdg

LC 2008048691

This describes the great apes—their life cycle, habitats, young, and why these animals are endangered

"The illustrations, mostly color photographs, represent a wonderful selection of the animals and their habitats. Reluctant readers may be enticed by this . . . simply because of the great images." Libr Media Connect

Includes glossary and bibliographical references

Bodden, Valerie

Monkeys. Creative Education 2010 24p il (Amazing animals) lib bdg $24.25

Grades: K 1 2   599.8

1. Monkeys

ISBN 978-1-58341-808-6 lib bdg; 1-58341-808-3 lib bdg

LC 2009002710

A basic exploration of the appearance, behavior, and habitat of monkeys, a family of tree-climbing mammals. Also included is a story from folklore explaining why monkeys look like people.

Includes bibliographical references

Bow, Patricia

Chimpanzee rescue; changing the future for endangered wildlife. Firefly Books 2004 64p il (Firefly animal rescue series) $19.95; pa $9.95

Grades: 5 6 7 8   599.8

1. Chimpanzees 2. Wildlife conservation 3. Chimpanzees -- Juvenile literature 4. Endangered species -- Juvenile literature

ISBN 1-55297-909-1; 1-55297-908-3 pa

This introduces chimpanzees, how and why they are in danger, and explains what efforts are being made to protect them.

This is "well-written. . . . Stunning, full-color photographs bring [this] species to life and depict a number of individuals in the field and laboratory working to save these animals." SLJ

Bredeson, Carmen

Orangutans up close; [by] Carmen Bredeson. Enslow Elementary 2008 24p il (Zoom in on animals!) lib bdg $21.26

Grades: 1 2 3   599.8

1. Orangutan

ISBN 978-0-7660-3078-7 lib bdg; 0-7660-3078-4 lib bdg

LC 2007039466

"Short paragraphs of simply written text describe [orangutans'] key body parts and how they function. . . . Behavior, diet, and care and development of the young are briefly addressed. Facing the text on each spread is a full-page, sharp, color closeup. . . . Bredeson's simply written and colorful [title] will provide younger readers with [a] satisfying first [introduction] to these fascinating creatures." SLJ

Includes glossary and bibliographical references

Bustos, Eduardo

Going ape! Eduardo Bustos. Tundra Books of Northern New York 2012 24 p. col. ill. (hardcover) $9.95

Grades: K 1 2   599.8

1. Apes 2. Monkeys 3. Gorillas 4. Primates

ISBN 1770492828; 9781770492820

LC 2011923289

In this book, "[Eduardo] Bustos offers simple facts about a variety of primates, from the well-known gorilla to the lesser-known De Brazza's monkey." The illustrations offer "large close-ups of face of the different apes on the recto, and one or two sentences and a smaller illustration of each one on the verso." (School Library Journal)

Coxon, Michele

Termites on a stick; a chimp learns to use a tool. by Michèle Coxon. Star Bright Books 2008 un il $17.95; pa $7.95

Grades: PreK K 1 2   599.8

1. Termites 2. Chimpanzees

ISBN 978-1-59572-121-1; 1-59572-121-5; 978-1-59572-183-9 pa; 1-59572-183-5 pa

"A young chimpanzee is rewarded with a tasty treat once he figures out how to fish termites out of their nest. Simple text and realistic paintings follow Little Chimp and his mother through a day in which the youngster emulates his mother's use of a handy tool. . . . Carefully crafted, this picture-book introduction to tool-using chimps could work as a read-aloud story or as independent reading." SLJ

Ganeri, Anita

Howler monkey. Heinemann Library 2011 24p il map (A day in the life. Rain forest animals) lib bdg $22; pa $6.49

Grades: 1 2 **599.8**

1. Monkeys

ISBN 978-1-4329-4113-0 lib bdg; 1-4329-4113-5 lib bdg; 978-1-4329-4124-6 pa; 1-4329-4124-0 pa

LC 2010001137

This book follows a day in the life of a howler monkey.

"Ganeri presents information clearly and simply in large type, two-sentence comments placed below a bright, sharply reproduced color photograph of the animal in a natural setting. . . . [This is] sufficiently specific to support assignment as well as pleasure reading." SLJ

Includes glossary and bibliographical references

Lemur. Heinemann Library 2011 24p il map (A day in the life. Rain forest animals) lib bdg $22; pa $6.49

Grades: 1 2 **599.8**

1. Lemurs

ISBN 978-1-4329-4111-6 lib bdg; 1-4329-4111-9 lib bdg; 978-1-4329-4122-2 pa; 1-4329-4122-4 pa

LC 2010001134

This book follows a lemur through its day as it sleeps, eats, and moves.

"Ganeri presents information clearly and simply in large type, two-sentence comments placed below a bright, sharply reproduced color photograph of the animal in a natural setting. . . . [This is] sufficiently specific to support assignment as well as pleasure reading." SLJ

Includes glossary and bibliographical references

Orangutan. Heinemann Library 2011 24p il map (A day in the life. Rain forest animals) lib bdg $22; pa $6.49

Grades: 1 2 **599.8**

1. Orangutan

ISBN 978-1-4329-4107-9 lib bdg; 1-4329-4107-0 lib bdg; 978-1-4329-4118-5 pa; 1-4329-4118-6 pa

LC 2010000966

This book follows an orangutan through its day as it sleeps, eats, and moves.

"Ganeri presents information clearly and simply in large type, two-sentence comments placed below a bright, sharply reproduced color photograph of the animal in a natural setting. . . . [This is] sufficiently specific to support assignment as well as pleasure reading." SLJ

Includes glossary and bibliographical references

Gibbons, Gail

Gorillas. Holiday House 2010 32p il map $17.95

Grades: K 1 2 3 **599.8**

1. Gorillas

ISBN 978-0-8234-2236-4; 0-8234-2236-4

LC 2010012418

"In her familiar, winning style, Gibbons introduces wild gorillas. Through detailed watercolor illustrations, she takes readers to Africa to explore the habitat and diet of the western lowland, eastern lowland, and mountain gorillas. . . . Readers will enjoy examining the many inset diagrams and maps that accompany the informational text , and they're sure to find Gibbons's 'extras,' like the skeletal view of a gorilla's jaw, fascinating." SLJ

Gish, Melissa

Gorillas. Creative Education 2010 46p il (Living wild) $23.95; pa $9.95

Grades: 5 6 7 8 **599.8**

1. Gorillas

ISBN 978-1-58341-969-4; 1-58341-969-1; 978-0-89812-552-8 pa; 0-89812-552-9 pa

LC 2010017374

This "book lucidly discusses conservation and the animals' often tenuous relationship with humans. The layout is uniformly simple but effective, constructed with a nice balance of main text for the report writers, smaller chunks of esoterica for browsers, and . . . killer photos." Booklist

Greenberg, Daniel A.

Chimpanzees; by Dan Greenberg, with Christina Wilsdon. Marshall Cavendish Benchmark 2010 24p il map (Benchmark rockets. Animals) lib bdg $16.95

Grades: 3 4 5 **599.8**

1. Chimpanzees

ISBN 978-0-7614-4341-4; 0-7614-4341-X

LC 2008-52102

"The straightforward presentation of the information and the uncluttered and attractive layout make [this title] . . . good . . . for reports. Color photographs . . . are well utilized and complete a solid package." SLJ

Includes glossary and bibliographical references

Hatkoff, Craig

Looking for Miza; the true story of mountain gorilla family who rescued one of their own. told by Juliana Hatkoff, Isabella Hatkoff, Craig Hatkoff and Dr. Paula Kahumbu; with photographs by Peter Greste. Scholastic Press 2008 un il $16.99

Grades: 2 3 4 5 **599.8**

1. Gorillas 2. Gorilla -- Juvenile literature

ISBN 978-0-545-08540-3; 0-545-08540-3

LC 2008-09544

"In the Democratic Republic of the Congo's Virunga National Park, two rangers receive disturbing news that Miza, a baby mountain gorilla, and her mother have disappeared. When they reach Miza's family, her father, Kabirizi, has already left to look for the missing. He returns with Miza. . . . Readers will quickly respond to the vulnerable little gorilla's story, told in large color photographs as well as text." Booklist

Includes bibliographical references

Jenkins, Martin

★ Ape; illustrated by Vicky White. Candlewick Press 2007 45p il $16.99

Grades: K 1 2 3 **599.8**

1. Apes 2. Apes -- Juvenile literature

ISBN 978-0-7636-3471-1; 0-7636-3471-9

LC 2007023456

Close-up illustrations and facts about five great apes: chimps, orangutans, bonobos, gorillas, and humans.

"Working in oil and pencil, White portrays [the apes] . . . as having psychologically complex, fully realized personalities. The pictures are consistently stunning. . . . Jenkins's . . . economical, conservation-oriented text ably sets each scene . . . while occasional captions add information about the apes' habitat or behavior." Publ Wkly

Laman, Tim
★ **Face** to face with orangutans; by Tim Laman & Cheryl Knott. National Geographic 2009 31p il (Face to face) $16.95; lib bdg $25.90
Grades: 3 4 5 6   **599.8**
1. Orangutan
ISBN 978-1-4263-0464-4; 1-4263-0464-1; 978-1-4263-0465-1 lib bdg; 1-4263-0465-X lib bdg
LC 2009-00170
The authors describe orangutan behavior and their personal encounters with orangutans in Borneo.
Includes glossary and bibliographical references

Mattern, Joanne
Orangutans. Capstone Press 2010 24p il map (Pebble plus. Asian animals) lib bdg $22.65
Grades: PreK K 1   **599.8**
1. Orangutan 2. Children's literature
ISBN 978-1-4296-4030-5; 1-4296-4030-8
"This . . . is an excellent resource for great pictures and information to share with students in storytimes or to support other content areas. This will be an excellent addition to nonfiction collections, especially for young readers." Libr Media Connect
Includes bibliographical references (p. 23)

Nichols, Michael
★ **Face** to face with gorillas; by Michael Nick Nichols with Elizabeth Carney. National Geographic 2009 31p il map (Face to face) $16.95; lib bdg $25.90
Grades: 3 4 5 6   **599.8**
1. Gorillas
ISBN 978-1-4263-0406-4; 1-4263-0406-4; 978-1-4263-0407-1 lib bdg; 1-4263-0407-2 lib bdg
LC 2008023002
"Nichols has spent much of his life raising awareness about the plight of gorillas, and through brief text and accompanying photographs he shares some of his experiences as well as information about their family structure, habits, habitats, and connections to humans. . . . The attractive format will appeal to the intended audience." Booklist
Includes glossary and bibliographical references

Rockwood, Leigh
Chimpanzees are smart! PowerKids Press 2010 24p il (Super smart animals) lib bdg $21.25; pa $8.25
Grades: 2 3 4 5   **599.8**
1. Chimpanzees
ISBN 978-1-4358-9375-7 lib bdg; 1-4358-9375-1 lib bdg; 978-1-4358-9840-0 pa; 1-4358-9840-0 pa
This book examines the intelligence of chimpanzees.
"Readers get an overview of the . . . [chimpanzee's] life cycle, its domestic history (where relevant), and natural habitat, and examples of how it is smart in the wild as well as when helped by human tutelage. . . . Interesting color photographs and large, easy-to-read print will attract browsers and report writers alike." SLJ
Includes glossary

Sayre, April Pulley
Meet the howlers; illustrated by Woody Miller. Charlesbridge 2010 un il lib bdg $16.95

Grades: K 1 2   **599.8**
1. Monkeys
ISBN 978-1-57091-733-2 lib bdg; 1-57091-733-7 lib bdg
LC 2009-3953
"Sayre's . . . latest is a rhyming introduction to the howler monkeys of Central and South America. Verses appear in a jaunty typeface atop . . . Miller's full-bleed spreads; prose paragraphs in smaller type provide additional information. . . . A solid read-aloud for young animal enthusiasts." Publ Wkly

Schindel, John
Busy gorillas; [by] John Schindel, Andy Rouse. Tricycle Press 2010 un il (A busy book) bd bk $6.99
Grades: PreK   **599.8**
1. Gorillas 2. Board books for children
ISBN 978-1-58246-352-0 bd bk; 1-58246-352-2 bd bk
Simple text and color photographs describe gorillas participating in various activities.
"Intimate close-ups of winsome baby faces and blurred, movement-filled action photos combine with more standard longshots of our primate cousins. Playfully active text . . . and vivid color-block backgrounds help to keep the necessarily limited palette . . . sparkling. Another standout." Kirkus

599.813

Kalman, Bobbie
Baby primates; by Bobbie Kalman. Crabtree Publishing Company 2013 24 p. (library) $22.60; (paperback) $6.95
Grades: 1 2 3 4   **599.813**
1. Primates -- Juvenile literature 2. Habitat (Ecology) -- Juvenile literature 3. Animal babies
ISBN 0778710076; 9780778710073; 9780778710110
LC 2012043728
In this book by Bobbie Kalman "simple text and captivating photos inform young readers about [primates] and the different groups to which they belong, including monkeys, apes, humans, lemurs, and more. Children will also learn about the habitats of baby primates and why some are endangered." (Publisher's note)
Includes bibliographical references and index.

599.884 Gorillas

Eszterhas, Suzi
Gorilla. Frances Lincoln Children's Books 2012 32 p. col. ill. (hbk.) $15.99; (hbk.) $15.99
Grades: K 1 2   **599.884**
1. Gorillas 2. Wildlife photography 3. Children's literature
ISBN 1847802990; 9781847802996
This book, the first in the "Eye on the Wild series . . . follows a newborn gorilla from birth to age 6, the age of maturity, although the majority focuses on her first two years of life. From nestling in her mother's arms and napping to sucking her thumb and drinking her mother's milk . . . [Suzi]

Esterhas . . . slightly anthropomorphiz[es] the actions, feelings and intentions of her subjects . . . Backmatter offers children more facts about gorillas, along with a website for more information." (Kirkus Reviews)

Riggs, Kate

Gorillas; by Kate Riggs. Creative Education 2012 24 p. col. ill.

Grades: K 1 2   **599.884**

1. Gorillas 2. Animal behavior 3. Habitat (Ecology) 4. Animals -- Folklore 5. Zoology -- Encyclopedias 6. Gorilla -- Juvenile literature

ISBN 1608181073; 9781608181070

LC 2010049121

This children's book is part of Kate Riggs' illustrated "Amazing Animals" series, which presents "general facts about physiology, behaviors, eating habits, habitats, and life spans. . . . In 'Gorillas,' an African story answers the arguably accurate question, 'Why do gorillas do nothing but eat and sleep all day long?' Legend has it that they tried to help after a flood but goofed up so badly that they quit doing just about everything ever since." (Booklist) "A basic exploration of the appearance, behavior, and habitat of gorillas, Earth's largest apes." (Publisher's note)

"The books' easy-reading text will be a boon to both beginning and struggling readers, and the beautiful photos are inviting enough to linger over." Booklist

Includes bibliographical references (p. 24) and index

599.9   Humans

Szpirglas, Jeff

You just can't help it! your guide to the wild and wacky world of human behavior. Josh Holinaty, illustrator. Owlkids Books 2011 64p il $22.95; pa $10.95

Grades: 4 5 6 7   **599.9**

1. Human behavior 2. Human biology -- Juvenile literature

ISBN 1-926818-07-5; 1-926818-08-3 pa; 978-1-926818-07-8; 978-1-926818-08-5 pa

"How many times have you been frightened and felt the hairs on the back of your neck stand up? Or been unable to hold back a laugh? Or flinched when an object whizzed by, too close for comfort? . . . [This] book provides a cultural, historical, and sociobiological perspective on human behavior. . . . [It is an] exploration of the basic human biology that determines our reactions, social interactions, and the ways we communicate with one another." (Publisher's note) Index.

This is a "collection of curious facts and intriguing studies about human behavior. With a breezy text supported by a lively design, the author . . . presents science in a way certain to attract middle-grade and middle-school readers. Chapters on the senses, emotions, communication, and interactions with other human beings cover a variety of topics. . . . The digital art includes bits of photographs, line drawings, the use of color and shapes to help organize the print and plenty of symbols." Kirkus

Includes index

599.93   Genetics, sex and age characteristics, evolution

Goldenberg, Linda

★ Little people and a lost world; an anthropological mystery. Twenty-First Century Books 2007 112p il (Discovery!) lib bdg $31.93

Grades: 5 6 7 8   **599.93**

1. Pygmies 2. Fossil hominids 3 Excavations (Archeology) -- Indonesia 4. Excavations (Archaeology) -- Juvenile literature

ISBN 978-0-8225-5983-2 lib bdg; 0-8225-5983-8 lib bdg

LC 2005-33431

This is an account of the 2003 discovery of small fossil hominids on Flores Island, Indonesia

"This will add important insights to the study of early humans as well as, more broadly, how science and politics interact." Booklist

Includes bibliographical references

Tattersall, Ian

★ Bones, brains and DNA; the human genome and human evolution. by Ian Tattersall & Rob DeSalle; illustrated by Patricia J. Wynne. Bunker Hill Pub., Inc. 2007 47p il $16.95

Grades: 5 6 7 8   **599.93**

1. Genetics 2. Evolution 3. Human origins

ISBN 978-1-59373-056-7; 1-59373-056-X

LC 2006931578

The "text follows the trail of human evolution, basing its factual content on current data exhibited in the New Hall of Human Origins in New York City's American Museum of Natural History. Using the skills of anthropologists, archaeologists, and paleontologists, the authors track clues laid down in the fossil record, and, more importantly, in our DNA. . . . The very unsimple concepts are presented clearly, in an attractive format, with splashings of small photos, colorful artwork, diagrams, and maps to attract the eye and elucidate the text." SLJ

Thimmesh, Catherine

★ Lucy long ago; uncovering the mystery of where we came from. Houghton Mifflin Harcourt 2009 63p il $18

Grades: 4 5 6 7   **599.93**

1. Human origins 2. Fossil hominids

ISBN 978-0-547-05199-4; 0-547-05199-9

LC 2008-36761

"The 1974 discovery of the fossilized partial skeleton of a small-brained primate who apparently walked upright 3.2 million years ago in what is now Ethiopia significantly changed accepted theories about human origins. Step by step, Thimmesh presents the questions the newly discovered bones raised and how they were answered. . . . Extensive research, clear organization and writing, appropriate pacing for new ideas and intriguing graphics all contribute to this exceptionally accessible introduction to the mystery of human origins." Kirkus

600 TECHNOLOGY

600 Technology (Applied sciences)

Enz, Tammy

Repurpose it; invent new uses for old stuff. by Tammy Enz. Capstone Press 2012 32 p. col. ill. (Fact finders. Invent it) (library) $26.65

Grades: 3 4 5   600

1. Recycling 2. Art -- Juvenile literature 3. Refuse and refuse disposal -- Juvenile literature 4. Conservation of natural resources -- Juvenile literature 5. Conservation projects (Natural resources) -- Juvenile literature

ISBN 1429676361; 9781429676366

LC 2011028738

This book by Tammy Enz is part of the Invent It series "focuses on using basic engineering skills—and your own imagination—to repurpose garbage. After leading readers through the 'Six Steps of Inventing,' the book offers step-by-step numbered instructions for seven do-it-yourself projects." Examples of projects include plastic bag rain ponchos and out-of-date textbooks as hollowed-out hiding places. (Booklist)

Includes bibliographical references and index

Macaulay, David

The **new** way things work; [by] David Macaulay with Neil Ardley. Houghton Mifflin 1998 400p il $35

Grades: 4 5 6 7 8 9 10 11 12 Adult   600

1. Machinery 2. Inventions 3. Technology

ISBN 0-395-93847-3

LC 98-14224

First published 1988 with title: The way things work

Arranged in five sections this volume provides information on "the workings of hundreds of machines and devices—holograms, helicopters, airplanes, mobile phones, compact disks, hard disks, bits and bytes, cash machines. . . . Explanations [are also given] of the scientific principles behind each machine—how gears make work easier, why jumbo jets are able to fly, how computers actually compute." Publisher's note

Piddock, Charles

Future tech; from personal robots to motorized monocycles. by Charles Piddock; Dr. James Lee, consultant. National Geographic 2009 64p il (National Geographic investigates) $17.95

Grades: 5 6 7 8   600

1. Technology 2. Forecasting

ISBN 978-1-4263-0468-2; 1-4263-0468-4

"This effort takes an appreciative, uncritical look at robots, transportation, bionics, nanotechnology and future life in general. It concludes with ten specific predictions for 2025. . . . Interesting color photographs appear on almost every page and entertaining text boxes with additional related information add appeal." Kirkus

Includes glossary and bibliographical references

Solway, Andrew

Inventions and investigations. Raintree 2008 48p il (Sci-hi: physical science) lib bdg $22; pa $8.99

Grades: 5 6 7 8   600

1. Inventors 2. Inventions

ISBN 978-1-4109-3379-9 lib bdg; 1-4109-3379-2 lib bdg; 978-1-4109-3384-3 pa; 1-4109-3384-9 pa

LC 2009-3508

This explores the scientific processes used by inventors throughout history.

A "compelling read for both browsers and science buffs. . . . Information is clearly presented and flows smoothly. . . . A treasure trove of information." SLJ

Includes glossary and bibliographical references

Woodford, Chris

★ **Cool** Stuff 2.0 and how it works; written by Chris Woodford and Jon Woodcock. DK Pub. 2007 256p il $24.99

Grades: 5 6 7 8 9 10   600

1. Inventions 2. Technology

ISBN 978-0-7566-3207-6; 0-7566-3207-2

LC 2007-299442

"More than 100 entries present a wide variety of topics with high child appeal, from robot cars to high-tech toilets. . . . Full but uncluttered layouts mix photos, text boxes, diagrams, and captions to highlight key elements. . . . Readers should have an easy time understanding the basics of what each item does, how it is used, and how it works. Along with up-to-date scientific information on high-interest topics, this title has very strong browsing appeal and great booktalk potential." SLJ

Zuckerman, Amy

2030; a day in the life of tomorrow's kids. [by] Amy Zuckerman and James Daly; illustrated by John Manders. Dutton Children's Books 2009 un il $16.99

Grades: K 1 2 3   600

1. Technology 2. Forecasting 3. Technological forecasting -- Juvenile literature 4. Technological innovations -- Juvenile literature 5. Twenty-first century -- Forecasts -- Juvenile literature

ISBN 978-0-525-47860-7; 0-525-47860-4

LC 2008-14606

"A talking dog, a housecleaning robot, and a three-dimensional data orb" are among the many cool features that kids might enjoy in the future, according to this lighthearted look at 2030. The breezy narrative follows one boy through a typical day, highlighting many interesting aspects of his world. Fanciful cartoon drawings show a lively and appealing world full of new and intriguing activities that correspond neatly to modern equivalents." SLJ

608 Patents

Lee, Dora

Biomimicry; Inventions inspired by nature. written by Dora Lee; illustrated by Margot Thompson. Kids Can Press 2011 40 p. $18.95

Grades: 4 5 6   608

1. Inventions 2. Nature study 3. Human ecology 4. Technological innovations

ISBN 9781554534678

This book explores "modern innovations [that] have sprung from observation and imitation of the natural world.

In topically organized double-page spreads, [Dora] Lee describes shapes and structures, materials and designs, as well as systems for exploration, communication, rescue and delivery. . . . Three or four specific examples, each with illustrative vignettes, follow or sometimes precede the general explanation. These topics range widely and include medical marvels, new power sources, [and] biological computers and robots. . . . [The book] includes a strong ecological message: The most important natural model is the sustainable ecosystem. Through biomimicry, humans can learn to live in balance on the Earth as well." (Kirkus)

St. George, Judith
★ So you want to be an inventor? illustrated by David Small. Philomel Bks. 2002 53p il $16.99; pa $7.99
Grades: 3 4 5 6   608
1. Inventors 2. Inventions
ISBN 0-399-23593-0; 0-14-240460-8 pa
LC 2001-55447
Presents some of the characteristics of inventors by describing the inventions of people such as Alexander Graham Bell, Thomas Edison, and Eli Whitney

"St. George and Small take a skewed, funny, and informative look at the history of inventions and their inventors and what it takes to become one. . . . Small's lively, fluid caricatures make for a winning collaboration." SLJ

Includes bibliographical references

609   History, geographic treatment, biography

Barretta, Gene
Neo Leo; the ageless ideas of Leonardo da Vinci. Henry Holt & Co. 2009 un il
Grades: 2 3 4 5   609
1. Artists 2. Painters 3. Inventors 4. Scientists 5. Writers on science 6. Inventions -- History
ISBN 0805087036; 9780805087031
LC 2008038220
"This book focuses on sketches found in Leonardo's writings that reveal an understanding of inventions that would not come into being until hundreds of years after the death of this quintessential Renaissance man. Vivid watercolor illustrations depict more than a dozen, including the hang glider, contact lenses, the tank, and robots. . . . Barretta provides clear information without veering into scientific explanations." SLJ

Includes bibliographical references

Now & Ben; the modern inventions of Benjamin Franklin. by Gene Barretta. Henry Holt & Co. 2006 un il $16.95
Grades: 2 3 4 5   609
1. Authors 2. Diplomats 3. Inventors 4. Statesmen 5. Inventions 6. Scientists 7. Writers on science 8. Members of Congress
ISBN 978-0-8050-7917-3; 0-8050-7917-3
LC 2005012491
"This humorous book covers twenty-two inventions, first by showing their use in today's world . . . and a second by explaining Franklin's role in their development. . . . Read this one aloud; the busy cartoon illustrations offer plenty for listeners to contemplate." Horn Book Guide

Includes bibliographical references

Becker, Helaine
What's the big idea? inventions that changed life on Earth forever. illustrated by Steve Attoe. Maple Tree Press 2010 96p il $27.95; pa $17.95
Grades: 3 4 5 6   609
1. Inventions -- History 2. Inventions -- Juvenile literature 3. World history -- Juvenile literature
ISBN 978-1-897349-60-1; 1-897349-60-2; 978-1-897349-61-8 pa; 1-897349-61-0 pa
This book shares the big ideas behind more than thirty of the world's greatest innovations

"Identifying significant inventions in a historic timeline, this book has wonderful kid appeal. It begins with prehistory to the Middle Ages, advancing to the 1900s, finishing with not so long ago. . . . Information is displayed in short paragraphs making it easier to read than many invention books. . . . Author Helaine Becker does an excellent job of crediting diverse cultural and female contributions known or presumed." Libr Media Connect

Bender, Lionel
Invention; written by Lionel Bender. rev ed; DK Pub. 2005 72p il (DK eyewitness books) $15.99; lib bdg $19.99
Grades: 4 5 6 7   609
1. Inventions
ISBN 0-7566-1076-1; 0-7566-1075-3 lib bdg
First published 1991 by Knopf
Photographs and text explore such inventions as the wheel, gears, levers, clocks, telephones, and rocket engines.

Crowther, Robert
Robert Crowther's pop-up house of inventions; hundreds of fabulous facts about your home. Candlewick Press 2009 un il $17.99
Grades: 4 5 6 7   609
1. Inventions 2. Pop-up books
ISBN 978-0-7636-4253-2; 0-7636-4253-3
First published 2000 with title: Robert Crowther's amazing pop-up house of inventions

"As a beautifully engineered pop-up book, it is complex, highly visual, and inviting. . . . It is also durably manufactured. . . . The book is essentially an encyclopedic assortment of facts and anecdotes about the earliest forms of household appliances, furnishings, novelties, . . . games, clothing, and consumables such as soap, soda and candles. The author integrates history and science in a chatty, colorful, and humorous way that quickly draws readers into his subject." Sci Books Films

Harper, Charise Mericle
Imaginative inventions; the who, what, where, when, and why of roller skates, potato chips, marbles, and pie and more! Little, Brown 2001 32p il $14.95
Grades: K 1 2 3   609
1. Inventions -- History -- Juvenile literature
ISBN 0-316-34725-6
LC 00-62443
This "volume explains how such everyday items as gum, roller skates and potato chips came to be, describing each item in doggerel verse. With its crazy-quilt visual patterns, bouncy stanzas and fun facts, this collection of miscellany zigzags between informational and whimsical." Publ Wkly

Jedicke, Peter

Great inventions of the 20th century; by Peter Jedicke. Chelsea House 2007 72p il (Scientific American) $30

Grades: 5 6 7 8   609

1. Inventions -- History 2. Technology -- History
ISBN 978-0-7910-9048-0; 0-7910-9048-5
                                                    LC 2006014773

"The text is simple, clear, and concise. . . . [The book has] captioned color photos throughout." SLJ

Includes glossary and bibliographical references

Landau, Elaine

The history of everyday life. 21st Century Bks. 2005 56p il (Major inventions through history) $26.60

Grades: 5 6 7 8   609

1. Inventions -- History
ISBN 0-8225-3808-3

This "explores fireplaces and central heating, indoor plumbing, the washing machine, food and clothing production, and microwave ovens. . . . [It] presents information about daily living from ancient times to the present. . . . The text . . . is breezy but informative. . . . Illustrations are a mixture of period black-and-white and color photos." SLJ

Includes bibligraphical references

Lee, Richard B.

Africans thought of it! amazing innovations. [by] Bathseba Opini [and] Richard B. Lee. Annick Press 2011 48p il (We thought of it) $21.95; pa $11.95

Grades: 3 4 5 6   609

1. Inventions
ISBN 978-1-55451-277-5; 1-55451-277-8; 978-1-55451-276-8 pa; 1-55451-276-X pa

Describes the inventions created by the peoples of Africa in hunting, agriculture, architecture, metalwork, medicine, the arts, and other fields, and how they have spread through the world and continue to fit into modern African civilization.

"Vivid photographs feature authentic objects used . . . while people engaged in activities capture an enthusiastic look at the reliance on community. Colored backgrounds and borders present a busy, though uncluttered, dynamic portrayal of nuanced cultures. . . . Succinct definitions and compact descriptions provide a brief and interesting blend of the contemporary with the traditional." SLJ

Robinson, James

Inventions; foreword by James Dyson. Kingfisher 2006 63p il (Kingfisher knowledge) $12.95

Grades: 5 6 7 8   609

1. Inventions 2. Technology
ISBN 978-0-7534-5973-7; 0-7534-5973-6

"A slim, colorful overview of inventions." Kirkus
Includes glossary

Rossi, Ann

★ Bright ideas; the age of invention in America, 1870-1910. [by] Ann Rossi. National Geographic 2005 40p il (Crossroads America) $12.95

Grades: 4 5 6   609

1. Inventions -- History
ISBN 0-7922-8276-0
                                                    LC 2003-19834

This describes the history of late 19th and early 20th century inventions such as the light bulb, the telegraph, the telephone, and the automobile.

This "solid [title] for report writers may even pull in a few curious browsers because of [its] plentiful, full-color photos and reproductions. The [layout is] inviting, and the [text is] clear, informative, and readable." SLJ

Includes glossary

Ye, Ting-xing

The Chinese thought of it; amazing inventions and innovations. Annick Press 2009 48p il map (We thought of it) $19.95; pa $9.95

Grades: 5 6 7 8   609

1. Inventions -- History 2. Technology -- History
ISBN 978-1-55451-196-9; 1-55451-196-8; 978-1-55451-195-2 pa; 1-55451-195-X pa

In this survey of Chinese inventions "at least one double-page spread is devoted to each of the eleven topics: farming, working with metal, transportation and exploration, canals and bridges, weapons and warfare, paper and printing, silk, and everyday innovations. . . . The layout of the book is appealing and just right for quick reading or browsing. . . . The author's personal story about her childhood in Shanghai effectively draws the reader in." Voice Youth Advocates

Includes bibliographical references

610 Medicine and health

Auden, Scott

Medical mysteries; science researches conditions from bizarre to deadly. by Scott Auden; Elizabeth Brownell, consultant. National Geographic 2008 64p il (National Geographic investigates) $17.95; lib bdg $27.90

Grades: 4 5 6 7   610

1. Diseases 2. Medicine -- Research
ISBN 978-1-4263-0356-2; 1-4263-0356-4; 978-1-4263-0261-9 lib bdg; 1-4263-0261-4 lib bdg

This title features "full-color photographs that readers have come to expect from this publisher. . . . [It] focuses on diseases that are regarded as bizarre and are often deadly, including Creutzfeldt-Jakob, Progeria, and Morgellons. The approach is to examine the way in which these mysterious diseases were discovered and how they are being studied to find a cure. . . . [This book offers] explanations simple enough for middle school students but with enough content to make them a useful resource for high school students as well." Voice Youth Advocates

Includes glossary and bibliographical references

Bredeson, Carmen

Don't let the barber pull your teeth; could you survive medieval medicine? illustrated by Gerald Kelley. Enslow Publishers 2011 48p il (Ye yucky Middle Ages) lib bdg $23.93

Grades: 3 4 5 6   610

1. Medieval civilization 2. Medicine -- History
ISBN 978-0-7660-3693-2
                                                    LC 2010011898

This describes medieval medicine.
Includes glossary and bibliographical references

★ **Encyclopedia** of health; 4th ed.; Marshall Cavendish
2009 18v il set $514.21
Grades: 5 6 7 8 9 10   610
1. Reference books 2. Medicine -- Encyclopedias
ISBN 978-0-7614-7845-4; 0-7614-7845-0
LC 2008033014
First published 1995 with title: The Marshall Cavendish
encyclopedia of health

This reference features alphabetically arranged entries
on body function; diet and nutrition; human behavior; illness, injury and disorders; and prevention and care

"Easy-to-understand language, an attractive design, and
content that supports student research and interest lend value
to the set." Booklist

Includes bibliographical references

Goldsmith, Connie
Cutting-edge medicine. Lerner Publications Co. 2008
48p il (Cool science) lib bdg $26.60
Grades: 4 5 6   610
1. Medicine
ISBN 978-0-8225-6770-7 lib bdg; 0-8225-6770-9
lib bdg
LC 2007001946
"This book explains the many amazing ways new medical techniques are helping people live longer, healthier
lives." Publisher's note

Includes glossary and bibliographical references

Lew, Kristi
Bat spit, maggots, and other amazing medical wonders.
Capstone Press 2010 32p il (Fact finders. Nasty (but use-
ful!) science) lib bdg $25.99
Grades: 3 4 5   610
1. Medicine
ISBN 978-1-4296-4537-9 lib bdg; 1-4296-4537-7
lib bdg

This informative guide also explains "relevant chemical processes, medical rationales, and ecological functions
in reasonably specific detail. . . . A list of relevant web resources is maintained on the publisher's page." SLJ

Includes glossary and bibliographical references

Murphy, Liz
ABC doctor. Blue Apple 2007 un il $15.95
Grades: PreK K 1   610
1. Medicine 2. Medical care
ISBN 978-1-593545-93-2; 1-593545-93-2
"The basics of seeing a doctor and/or nurse are . . . explained with clever, colorful collage illustrations setting the
scene and clarifying the explanation. . . . Some medical tools
are included. Physical conditions such as fever and vomit
appear, and procedures such as a urine sample and X-ray
take readers through the alphabet. Murphy has compiled an
interesting array of terms to help children realize that medical professionals are there to help them." SLJ

Rooney, Anne
Health and medicine; the impact of science and technology. Gareth Stevens Pub. 2009 64p il (Pros and cons)
lib bdg $35

Grades: 5 6 7 8   610
1. Health 2. Medicine 3. Medical technology
ISBN 978-1-4339-1988-6 lib bdg; 1-4339-1988-5
lib bdg
LC 2008-54133
An "active layout that features color photographs, maps,
graphs or charts on every spread, this . . . [book] has much
to offer. . . . It conveniently outlines the range of views . .
. helping students to learn how to view both sides of [the]
issue[s]." SLJ

Includes glossary and bibliographical references

Sandvold, Lynnette Brent
Revolution in medicine. Marshall Cavendish Benchmark 2010 32p il (It works!) lib bdg $19.95
Grades: 3 4 5   610
1. Medical technology 2. Medicine -- History
ISBN 978-0-7614-4376-6 lib bdg; 0-7614-4376-2
lib bdg
LC 2008-54364
"This interesting, information packed [book] . . . motivates students to do their own exploring. . . . The appealing
cartoon-like photographs add humor. . . . This . . . just may
be that spark needed to create eager budding scientists." Libr
Media Connect

Includes glossary and bibliographical references

Singer, Marilyn
I'm getting a checkup; illustrated by David Milgrim.
Clarion Books 2009 32p il $16
Grades: PreK K   610
1. Medicine 2. Medical care 3. Stories in rhyme
ISBN 978-0-618-99000-9; 0-618-99000-3
LC 2007034977
"Informative and fun, this rhyming picture book will
help prepare preschoolers for a visit to the doctor's office.
The digitally rendered oil-and-pastel pictures show three
kids, each with a parent or caregiver, getting a checkup from
three different doctors. . . . Each quick rhyme is followed
by a long explanatory note. . . . The bright, cartoon-style
pictures keep the visit playful." Booklist

Woolf, Alex, 1964-
Death and disease; [by] Alex Woolf. Lucent Books
2004 48p il map (Medieval realms) $29.95
Grades: 5 6 7 8   610
1. Medieval civilization 2. Medicine -- History 3.
Public health -- History
ISBN 1-59018-533-1
LC 2003-61797
"Clear, well-organized [text] along with full-color repro-
ductions of art and artifacts and photos of period structures
immerse readers in . . . medieval life and offer sufficient in-
formation for reports." SLJ

Includes glossary and bibliographical references

610.69   Medical personnel and relationships

Marsico, Katie
The **doctor**. Marshall Cavendish Benchmark 2011 il
(Colonial people) $29.93

Grades: 3 4 5 6 **610.69**
1. Physicians 2. Medicine -- History
ISBN 978-1-60870-412-5; 1-60870-412-2
LC 2010033895
This descibes the life of a colonial doctor and his importance to the community, as well as everyday life, responsibilities, and social practices during that time.

This "lively [text] and colorful reproductions and photos will engage casual readers and researchers alike. . . . Large illustrations and thoughtful captions explain complicated scientific ideas. . . . [The] volume also includes step-by-step instructions for a related craft project. . . . [This is a] must-have." SLJ

Includes glossary and bibliographical references

610.73 Nursing and services of allied health personnel

Glasscock, Sarah
How nurses use math; math curriculum consultant: Rhea A. Stewart. Chelsea Clubhouse 2010 32p il (Math in the real world) lib bdg $28
Grades: 4 5 6 **610.73**
1. Nurses 2. Mathematics 3. Vocational guidance
ISBN 978-1-60413-607-4 lib bdg; 1-60413-607-3 lib bdg
LC 2009-20199
This describes how nurses use math in such tasks as giving eye tests, keeping records, taking the pulse, and measuring medicine and includes relevant math problems and information about how to become a nurse
Includes glossary and bibliographical references

Kenney, Karen Latchana
Nurses at work; by Karen L. Kenney; illustrated by Brian Caleb Dumm; content consultant, Judith Stepan-Norris. Magic Wagon 2010 32p il (Meet your community workers!) lib bdg $18.95
Grades: K 1 2 3 **610.73**
1. Nurses 2. Vocational guidance
ISBN 978-1-60270-651-4 lib bdg; 1-60270-651-4 lib bdg
LC 2009-2393
This book about nurses has "an uncluttered layout and consistent organization. . . . Chapter headings such as 'Problems on the Job' and 'Technology at Work,' and 'Special Skills and Training' make it easy to pinpoint specific information." SLJ
Includes glossary

610.82 Women in medicine

Harness, Cheryl
Mary Walker wears the pants; the true story of the doctor, reformer, and Civil War hero. Cheryl Harness; illustrated by Carlo Molinari. Albert Whitman & Co. 2013 32 p. (reinforced) $16.99
Grades: 2 3 4 5 **610.82**
1. Picture books for children 2. Women physicians -- Juvenile literature 3. Physicians -- United States -- Biography 4. Suffragists -- United States -- Biography

-- Juvenile literature 5. Women physicians -- United States -- Biography -- Juvenile literature
ISBN 0807549908; 9780807549902
LC 2012019531
This children's picture book focuses on the life of 19th-century "women's rights advocate, doctor, and abolitionist Mary Walker," who was "one of the first women doctors and the first woman to receive the Medal of Honor for her 'services and sufferings' during wartime." A "volunteer for the Union Army during the Civil War, her hard work and determination finally led to her appointment as an assistant surgeon in 1863, the first woman doctor in the U.S. Army." (School Library Journal)

611 Human anatomy, cytology, histology

Allen, Kathy
The human head. Capstone Press 2010 32p il (Fact finders. Anatomy class) lib bdg $23.99; pa $7.95
Grades: 3 4 5 **611**
1. Head
ISBN 978-1-4296-3338-3 lib bdg; 1-4296-3338-7 lib bdg; 978-1-4296-3882-1 pa; 1-4296-3882-6 pa
LC 2009-2793
"The vivid scientific photographs . . . and micrographs . . . are a plus. . . . On-page definitions, current further-reading lists, and a webliography maintained at the publisher's FactHound Web site all add value." SLJ
Includes glossary and bibliographical references

Delafosse, Claude
Inside the body; created by Claude Delafosse and Gallimard Jeunesse; illustrated by Pierre-Marie Valat. Reprint Moonlight Pub. 2012 36 p. col. ill. (hardcover: spiral) $12.99
Grades: K 1 2 **611**
1. Picture books for children 2. Human body -- Juvenile literature
ISBN 1851034129; 9781851034123
This children's picture book explores the human body. "This is a beginner's guide . . . with short sentences providing basic groundwork: 'You have a skeleton! This frame of bones helps you stay upright and move around.'" Some step-by-step diagrams are included that show "the process of digestion, the growth of a fetus, or the passing down of physical traits from parents and grandparents." (Booklist)

Gold, Susan Dudley
Learning about the respiratory system; Susan Dudley Gold. Enslow Publishers 2013 48 p. (library) $23.93
Grades: 5 6 7 8 **611**
1. Picture books for children 2. Respiratory system -- Juvenile literature 3. Respiratory organs -- Juvenile literature
ISBN 0766041611; 9780766041615
LC 2012011104
This book by Susan Dudley Gold is part of the Learning About the Human Body Systems series and looks at the respiratory system. She "discusses what this body system is and what organs are involved in its various processes. She discusses the potential health problems that can affect the respiratory system, such as cancer, pneumonia, and emphy-

sema, as well as ways to keep healthy and problem-free." (Publisher's note)

Includes bibliographical references and index.

Lew, Kristi
  Human organs. Capstone Press 2010 32p il (Fact finders. Anatomy class) lib bdg $23.99; pa $7.99
  Grades: 3 4 5   611
  1. Human body
  ISBN 978-1-4296-3339-0 lib bdg; 1-4296-3339-5 lib bdg; 978-1-4296-3886-9 pa; 1-4296-3886-9 pa
                                            LC 2009-2775
  "The vivid scientific photographs . . . and micrographs . . . are a plus. . . . On-page definitions, current further-reading lists, and a webliography maintained at the publisher's Fac-tHound Web site all add value." SLJ

  Includes glossary and bibliographical references

Rake, Jody Sullivan
  The **human** skeleton. Capstone Press 2010 32p il (Fact finders. Anatomy class) lib bdg $23.99; pa $7.95
  Grades: 3 4 5   611
  1. Bones 2. Skeleton
  ISBN 978-1-4296-3340-6 lib bdg; 1-4296-3340-9 lib bdg; 978-1-4296-3888-3 pa; 1-4296-3888-5 pa
                                            LC 2009-2771
  "The vivid scientific photographs . . . and micrographs . . . are a plus. . . . On-page definitions, current further-reading lists, and a webliography maintained at the publisher's Fac-tHound Web site all add value." SLJ

  Includes glossary and bibliographical references

Wheeler-Toppen, Jodi
  Human muscles. Capstone Press 2010 32p il (Fact finders. Anatomy class) lib bdg $23.99; pa $7.95
  Grades: 3 4 5   611
  1. Muscles
  ISBN 978-1-4296-3341-3 lib bdg; 1-4296-3341-7 lib bdg; 978-1-4296-3884-5 pa; 1-4296-3884-2 pa
                                            LC 2009-2766
  "The vivid scientific photographs . . . and micrographs . . . are a plus. . . . On-page definitions, current further-reading lists, and a webliography maintained at the publisher's Fac-tHound Web site all add value." SLJ

  Includes glossary and bibliographical references

612   Human physiology

Aliki
  My feet. Crowell 1990 31p il (Let's-read-and-find-out science book) hardcover o.p. pa $5.99
  Grades: PreK K 1   612
  1. Foot
  ISBN 0-690-04815-7 lib bdg; 0-06-445106-2 pa
                                            LC 89-49357
  "An extensive discussion of feet, through simple text and playful illustration, demonstrates their parts, relative sizes, what they do, and what they wear in different seasons. Includes a handicapped child whose crutches supplement feet." Sci Child

  My hands; rev ed; Crowell 1990 32p il (Let's-read-and-find-out science book) hardcover o.p. pa $5.99
  Grades: PreK K 1   612
  1. Hand
  ISBN 0-690-04880-7 lib bdg; 0-06-445096-1 pa
                                            LC 89-49158
  First published 1962
  The author "calls attention to hand structure—fingers, nails, an opposable thumb—and the special ways we use our hands to carry on everyday activities. . . . The jaunty illustrations and simple but efficient text combine for a fresh take on some very basic information." Booklist

Arnold, Caroline
  Too hot? too cold? keeping body temperature just right. Caroline Arnold; Illustrated by Annie Patterson. Charlesbridge 2013 32 p. (reinforced) $17.95; (paperback) $7.95
  Grades: 1 2 3 4 5   612
  1. Body temperature 2. Biology -- Juvenile literature 3. Body temperature -- Regulation -- Juvenile literature
  ISBN 1580892760; 9781580892766; 9781580892773
                                            LC 2012000792
  In this children's book, by Caroline Arnold and Annie Patterson, describes body heat regulation. "Have you ever wondered why you shiver when you're cold, or sweat when you're hot?" This book explores "the many different ways humans and animals adapt to heat and cold. The book includes [an] . . . explanation of cold-blooded and warm-blooded animals." (Publisher's note)

Bailey, Gerry
  Body and health; discover science through facts and fun. by Gerry Bailey & Steve Way. Gareth Stevens Pub. 2009 32p il (Simply science) lib bdg $26
  Grades: 3 4 5   612
  1. Human body 2. Human anatomy -- Juvenile literature
  ISBN 978-1-4339-0030-3 lib bdg; 1-4339-0030-0 lib bdg
                                            LC 2008-27573
  Along with facts that explore concepts across a wide range of topics, comic-strip illustrations present historical background information and foster modern-day science connections.
  "The brightly colored cover with its montage of people and cartoon characters is a real eye-catcher. This is a wonderful little book that is packed with lots of information." Sci Books Films

  Includes glossary and bibliographical references

Basher, Simon
  Human body; a book with guts! by Simon Basher and Dan Green; illustrated by Simon Basher. Kingfisher 2011 128p il $14.95; pa $8.99
  Grades: 5 6 7 8   612
  1. Human body
  ISBN 978-0-7534-6628-5; 0-7534-6628-7; 978-0-7534-6501-1 pa; 0-7534-6501-9 pa
  "Basher brings his signature informative irreverence and smiley little cartoon icons to the world of human biology. Not a comprehensive resource, but supplemental science reading doesn't come much more fun." Booklist

Bruhn, Aron

Inside the human body; illustrations by Joel Ito and Kathleen Kemly. Sterling 2010 48p il (Inside) $19.95; pa $9.95

Grades: 4 5 6   **612**

1. Human body

ISBN 978-1-4027-7091-3; 1-4027-7091-X; 978-1-4027-7779-0 pa; 1-4027-7779-5 pa

LC 2010002503

"The illustrations in [this] cool . . . [title is] enhanced by 10 large gatefolds that allow kids to dig deeper into the topics and enjoy amazing illustrations. [The] title clearly defines fact and theory, leaving puzzles for the next generation of scientists to solve. . . . [The book] touches on each of the body systems and provides a highly detailed look at a human cell." SLJ

Includes glossary and bibliographical references

Calabresi, Linda

Human body. Simon & Schuster Books for Young Readers 2008 un il (Insiders) $16.99

Grades: 4 5 6 7   **612**

1. Human body 2. Human physiology -- Juvenile literature

ISBN 978-1-4169-3861-3; 1-4169-3861-3

LC 2007-61744

This volume "offers excellent pictures of systems, organs, and even individual cells in the human body. . . . A visually dynamic introduction to the human package." Booklist

Cole, Joanna, 1944-

The magic school bus inside the human body; illustrated by Bruce Degen. Scholastic 1989 un il hardcover o.p.

Grades: 2 3 4   **612**

1. Human body 2. Physiology 3. Human anatomy 4. Metabolism -- Juvenile literature

ISBN 0-590-41426-7; 0-590-41427-5 pa

LC 8803070

"Ms. Frizzle's class leaves on a trip to the science museum, but stops for a snack along the way. Arnold is left behind when his classmates reboard the bus. Meanwhile, Ms. Frizzle has miniaturized the bus and its riders. Unwittingly, Arnold swallows it. Traveling through Arnold's insides, the class visits his digestive system, arteries, lungs, heart, brain, and muscles, finally departing through his nostrils when he sneezes. . . . Grades two to five." (Booklist)

"This is an enjoyable look at factual material painlessly packaged with the ribbons and balloons of jokes and asides meant to appeal to kids. Degen's zany, busy, full-color drawings fill the pages with action and information far beyond the text." SLJ

Fromer, Liza

My achy body. Tundra Books 2011 un il (Body works) $14.99

Grades: 2 3 4 5   **612**

1. Pain 2. Human body 3. Wounds and injuries

ISBN 978-1-77049-204-2; 1-77049-204-6

This describes bruises, scrapes, scabs, broken bones, sprains, stomach aches, earaches, and sore throats.

Includes glossary

My messy body; [by] Liza Fromer and Francine Gerstein; illustrated by Joe Weissmann. Tundra Books 2011 un il (Body works) $12.95

Grades: 2 3 4 5   **612**

1. Human body

ISBN 978-1-77049-202-8; 1-77049-202-X

This describes the purpose of the body's secretions, including tears, sweat, snot, urine, excrement, earwax, vomit, pus, and mucus.

Includes glossary

My noisy body; [by] Liza Fromer and Francine Gerstein; illustrated by Joe Weissmann. Tundra Books 2011 un il (Body works) $12.95

Grades: 2 3 4 5   **612**

1. Human body

ISBN 978-1-77049-201-1; 1-77049-201-1

This describes the meaning of sounds the body creates, including the voice, burps, hiccups, stomach growls, farts, sneezes and coughs.

The authors explain noisy body functions "with a playful attitude and with that buffet a solid body of factual information. . . . Weissmann's squiggly paintings are amusing. . . . This . . . offers a fun, frank look at sometimes taboo topics." Booklist

Gardner, Robert

Ace your human biology science project; great science fair ideas. [by] Robert Gardner and Barbara Gardner Conklin. Enslow Publishers 2009 128p il (Ace your biology science project) lib bdg $31.93

Grades: 5 6 7 8   **612**

1. Biology 2. Science projects 3. Science -- Experiments 4. Human biology -- Juvenile literature

ISBN 978-0-7660-3219-4 lib bdg; 0-7660-3219-1 lib bdg

LC 2008-30799

"Dozens of . . . science activities are presented with background information, step-by-step instructions, and suggestions for extending to the science fair level. . . . Color illustrations and important safety information are included." Horn Book Guide

Includes bibliographical references

Goddard, Jolyon

Inside the human body. Marshall Cavendish Benchmark 2010 48p il (Invisible worlds) lib bdg $28.50

Grades: 4 5 6 7   **612**

1. Human body 2. Physiology

ISBN 978-0-7614-4190-8 lib bdg; 0-7614-4190-5 lib bdg

LC 2008037254

This describes the details of the human body that are too small for the unaided eye to see, and how these microscopic systems work to keep the body alive and healthy.

The narrative is "clear, well written, broken down into manageable pieces, and peppered with eye-opening facts. The numerous photographs are so phenomenal that they will inspire kids to read the text . . . so that they can wrap their minds around what they see." SLJ

Includes glossary and bibliographical references

Green, Dan

Human body factory; the nuts and bolts of your insides. Kingfisher 2012 48 p. $16.99

Grades: 1 2 3 4   **612**

1. Biology 2. Human body 3. Picture books for children

ISBN 0753468085; 9780753468081

"This children's book describes human anatomy by comparing the body to a factory. From "the CEO sending out orders in the brain to 'waste' being sorted and delivered out of the body at the other end, the busy workers who keep everything running smoothly introduce each 'department.' All the major systems are covered, and the . . . illustrations are packed with . . . details . . . . All of this . . . artwork is backed up with . . . facts and . . . explanations of the body's essential processes." Images include "toxic signs and workers wearing biohazard suits in the large intestine, lab workers in dinghies mixing gastric juices in the stomach with a giant whisk, or park keepers on the skin keeping things clean among glades of gently swaying hairs and sweat-gland sprinklers." (Publisher's note)

Greenwood, Marie

Animals and me; [written by Marie Greenwood] DK Pub. 2010 48p il $12.99

Grades: 2 3 4 5   **612**

1. Human body 2. Physiology

ISBN 978-0-7566-6886-0; 0-7566-6886-7

Photographs and text examine different parts of the human body, explaining what they are for, and comparing them to the similar body parts of animals.

"The full-color photography is fantastic and clearly illustrates each point. Because of the wealth of information presented, this book would be enjoyed by browsers as well as students looking for report topics." SLJ

Lew, Kristi

Farts, vomit, and other functions that help your body. Capstone Press 2010 32p il (Fact finders. Nasty (but useful!) science) lib bdg $25.99

Grades: 3 4 5   **612**

1. Physiology

ISBN 978-1-4296-4539-3 lib bdg; 1-4296-4539-3 lib bdg

This informative guide also explains "relevant chemical processes, medical rationales, and ecological functions in reasonably specific detail. . . . A list of relevant web resources is maintained on the publisher's page." SLJ

Includes glossary and bibliographical references

Manning, Mick

Under your skin; your amazing body. [by] Mick Manning and Brita Granström. Albert Whitman 2007 23p il $16.95

Grades: 1 2 3   **612**

1. Human body 2. Human physiology -- Juvenile literature

ISBN 978-0-8075-8313-5; 0-8075-8313-8

LC 2007-02350

"This well-designed introduction to human body parts and their functions features eight half-page flaps that lift up to reveal simple views of internal organs. The terminology allows for different levels of comprehension . . . and the cartoon illustrations in bright colors help make the science aproachable." Horn Book Guide

Nicolson, Cynthia Pratt

Totally human; why we look and act the way we do. illustrated by Dianne Eastman. Kids Can Press 2011 40p il $16.95

Grades: 3 4 5   **612**

1. Human body 2. Psychology

ISBN 978-1-55453-569-9; 1-55453-569-7

"This playful science book introduces the biology of human evolution and behavior with an accessible, interactive text packed with information and wry, bright computer graphics on each spread. . . . The wild images . . . and the detailed text reveal astonishing answers to questions readers might never have thought to ask." Booklist

Parker, Nancy Winslow

★ **Organs!** how they work, fall apart, and can be replaced (gasp!) Greenwillow Books 2009 48p il $17.99; lib bdg $18.89

Grades: 1 2 3 4   **612**

1. Human body 2. Organs (Anatomy) -- Juvenile literature

ISBN 978-0-688-15105-8; 0-688-15105-1; 978-0-688-15106-5 lib bdg; 0-688-15106-X lib bdg

LC 2008-20718

"This is an engaging children's textbook on human anatomy and functioning. . . . Spot illustrations, charmingly rendered in colored pencil, show people with their organs in action. . . . Author Nancy Winslow Parker admirably tackles the challenge of visualizing objects that are typically masked from everyday view. . . . This fun and lighthearted book is . . . recommend[ed] for every child's library and one that will easily become a go-to reference for many years." Sci Books Films

Podesto, Martine

The **body**; by Martine Podesto. Gareth Stevens Pub. 2009 104p il (My science notebook) lib bdg $31

Grades: 4 5 6   **612**

1. Human body

ISBN 978-0-8368-9212-3 lib bdg; 0-8368-9212-7 lib bdg

LC 2008-12428

This book answers questions about the human body

"Designed to resemble a notebook with illustrated paper clips, pasting, and tape appearing on most pages, this [book] . . . offers comprehensive information. . . . supplemented by colorful drawings, diagrams, and photographs." SLJ

Includes glossary and bibliographical references

Reilly, Kathleen M.

The **human** body; 25 fantastic projects illuminate how the body works. illustrated by Shawn Braley. Nomad Press 2008 120p il $21.95; pa $15.95

Grades: 5 6 7 8   **612**

1. Human body 2. Human anatomy -- Juvenile literature 3. Science projects -- Juvenile literature

ISBN 978-1-934670-25-5; 1-934670-25-1; 978-1-934670-24-8 pa; 1-934670-24-3 pa

"The workings of the human body are expertly summarized in 11 tidy chapters, which include experiments that explain how the body works by creating models that either imitate or test its functions. . . . Many of the activities require adult supervision due to the materials required. . . . Simple drawings and cartoons enliven and illuminate the text. . . . The scientific explanations are superb." SLJ

Rockwell, Lizzy

The **busy** body book; a kid's guide to fitness. Crown 2004 un il $15.95

Grades: K 1   **612**

1. Exercise 2. Physiology

ISBN 0-375-82203-8; 0-375-92203-2 lib bdg

An introduction to the human body, how it functions, and its need for exercise.

"The text is purposely motivating, yet easy to understand and informative. The age-appropriate artwork is colorful and lively, and provides just the right amount of detail." SLJ

Rotner, Shelley

Body actions; Shelley Rotner and David A. White. Holiday House 2012 32 p. (hardcover) $16.95

Grades: 1 2 3   **612**

1. Human body 2. Nervous system 3. Digestive system 4. Musculoskeletal system 5. Picture books for children

ISBN 0823423662; 9780823423668

LC 2011007268

This children's picture book is a "brief overview of the entire human body. The nervous, skeletal, muscular, respiratory, circulatory and digestive systems; the five senses; skin, and hair are all touched on. The full-color photographs . . . feature racially diverse children, and some of the photographs include an illustration of the body system superimposed on the child." (School Library Journal)

Seuling, Barbara

Your skin weighs more than your brain; and other freaky facts about your skin, skeleton, and other body parts. by Barbara Seuling; illustrated by Matthew Skeens. Picture Window Books 2008 40p il (Freaky facts) lib bdg $23.93; pa $4.95

Grades: 2 3 4 5   **612**

1. Human body

ISBN 978-1-4048-3751-5 lib bdg; 1-4048-3751-5 lib bdg; 978-1-4048-3756-0 pa; 1-4048-3756-6 pa

LC 2007004030

A collection of amazing facts and statistics about the human body

"This quick read is a light, fun, and at times fascinating collection of various facts about the human body. . . . The book is eye-catching—a convenient and kid-friendly small size, with illustrations on every couple of pages." Sci Books Films

Includes glossary and bibliographical references

Silverstein, Alvin

Snot, poop, vomit, and more; the yucky body book. [by] Alvin Silverstein, Virginia Silverstein, and Laura Silverstein Nunn; illustrated by Gerald Kelley. Enslow Publishers 2010 48p il (Yucky science) lib bdg $23.93

Grades: 3 4 5 6   **612**

1. Human body 2. Physiology

ISBN 978-0-7660-3318-4 lib bdg; 0-7660-3318-X lib bdg

LC 2009012280

"Explores 'Yucky' things about the human body, including earwax, gas, bodily wastes, and more" Publisher's note

Includes bibliographical references

Somervill, Barbara A.

★ The **human** body. Gareth Stevens Pub. 2008 48p il (Gareth Stevens vital science: life science) lib bdg $26.60; pa $11.95

Grades: 5 6 7 8   **612**

1. Human body 2. Human physiology -- Juvenile literature

ISBN 978-0-8368-8441-8 lib bdg; 978-0-8368-8450-0 pa

LC 2007-16175

First published 2006 in the United Kingdom

This describes "human anatomy and physiology. . . . Factoids are scattered throughout the text in a fashion that captures the reader's attention and interest. . . . [The book offers] excellent graphics, namely photos and diagrams. The artwork complements and enhances the written content." Sci Books Films

Includes glossary and bibliographical references

Stewart, David Evelyn

How your body works; a good look inside your insides. written by David Stewart; illustrated by Carolyn Franklin. Children's Press 2008 32p il (Amaze) $26; pa $8.95

Grades: K 1 2   **612**

1. Human body 2. Human anatomy -- Juvenile literature 3. Human physiology -- Juvenile literature

ISBN 978-0-531-20444-3; 0-531-20444-8; 978-0-531-20455-9 pa; 0-531-20455-3 pa

This "is a bright, colorful, vivid, and easy-to-digest children's book about the basics of physiology. The book includes simple, well-illustrated chapters on the eyes, ears, intestines, cardiovascular system, liver and kidneys. . . . Organs are represented with big, colorful blocks, with very little distracting detail." Sci Books Films

Swanson, Diane

You are weird; your body's peculiar parts and funny functions. written by Diane Swanson; illustrated by Kathy Boake. Kids Can Press 2009 40p il $16.95; pa $7.95

Grades: 2 3 4 5   **612**

1. Human body

ISBN 978-1-55453-282-7; 1-55453-282-5; 978-1-55453-283-4 pa; 1-55453-283-3 pa

"This chatty, interactive humorous science book make[s] human physiology accessible and interesting, with lots of wild facts about hair, bacteria, sweat, skin, joints, muscles, and more. . . . The irreverence is right on . . . and the sound of words extend the fun without jargon." Booklist

VanCleave, Janice Pratt, 1942-

Janice VanCleave's the human body for every kid; easy activities that make learning science fun. Wiley 1995 223p hardcover o.p. pa $12.95

Grades: 4 5 6 7   **612**

1. Human body 2. Physiology 3. Human anatomy 4. Science -- Experiments 5. Physiology -- Juvenile literature

ISBN 0-471-02413-9; 0-471-02408-2 pa

LC 94-20862

"The activities described are easy to follow, are inexpensive, use readily obtainable supplies, and, most importantly, make the learning of human anatomy and physiology fun and exciting. Moreover, the material is presented in an organized, clear, and accurate manner." Sci Books Films

Walker, Richard, 1951-

    3-D human body; written by Richard Walker. DK Pub. 2011 71p il $17.99

Grades: 3 4 5 6   **612**

    1. Human body

    ISBN 978-0-7566-7216-4; 0-7566-7216-3

"Lively and informative spreads, along with augmented reality technology, introduce readers to the human body. . . . Readers can download software from the publisher's Web site, which can be used in combination with a webcam to make six spreads turn into animated AR pop-ups on a computer screen. Those who don't use the multimedia effect can still learn plenty from the book's detailed mix of photographs, digital graphics, and engaging captions that illuminate how intricate bodily components work together." Publ Wkly

    Dr. Frankenstein's human body book; the monstrous truth about how your body works. [author, Richard Walker; artist, Nick Abadzis] DK Pub. 2008 93p il $24.99

Grades: 4 5 6 7   **612**

    1. Human body 2. Human anatomy -- Juvenile literature

    ISBN 978-0-7566-4091-0; 0-7566-4091-1

"This anatomy book is as engrossing as any science fiction. Dr. Frankenstein, shown in a sepia photograph standing in a laboratory, gazing at a skull he holds in one hand, invites readers to join him as he creates a human being. . . . The story line is sustained with brief, pun-happy journal entries. . . . Gothic fonts and engraved illustrations and vignettes (in red and black and also hand-colored) blend with state-of-the-art images from MEG scans, gamma scans and other advanced technology. Clear explanations broken into easily assimilable captions and text blocks encourage the reader." Publ Wkly

    Includes glossary

    Human body; written by Richard Walker. DK Pub. 2009 72 p. ill. (chiefly col.) (DK eyewitness books) (hardcover) $16.99

Grades: 4 5 6 7   **612**

    1. Human body

    ISBN 9780756645458; 075664545X

                      LC 2009419529

In this book, text and illustrations present information on the parts of the body and how they work

    Includes glossary and bibliographical references

    Ouch! how your body makes it through a very bad day. written by Richard Walker. DK Pub. 2007 71p il $16.99

Grades: 4 5 6 7   **612**

    1. Human body

    ISBN 978-0-7566-2536-8; 0-7566-2536-X

"Tag along on a rotten day as a body copes with sneezing, getting cut, being stung by a bee, and vomiting, as well as performing more mundane actions such as urinating, tapping into its melanin supply, acting reflexively, and sweating. . . . Dramatic color graphics, both large and small, are accompanied by a multitude of informative captions. Re-

searchers who find the information on the busy pages hard to grasp can pop in the accompanying CD-ROM and catch a ride up the esophagus on a wave of vomit. . . . Eye-catching, highly pictorial, informative, and with a megadose of ick! factor." SLJ

    Includes glossary

Zoehfeld, Kathleen Weidner

    Human body. Scholastic Inc. 2010 32p il (Scholastic reader) pa $3.99

Grades: K 1   **612**

    1. Human body

    ISBN 978-0-545-23752-9 pa; 0-545-23752-1 pa

    A simple explanation of how the human body works, discussing the five senses, muscles, bones, digestion, the heart, and the brain.

"With simple chatty sentences and clearly labeled images of kids in action, this . . . title packs in fascinating facts about body parts, how they work individually and together." Booklist

    Includes glossary

612.1   Specific functions, systems, organs

Corcoran, Mary K.

    The **circulatory** story; illustrated by Jef Czekaj. Charlesbridge 2010 41p il lib bdg $17.95

Grades: 2 3 4   **612.1**

    1. Cardiovascular system 2. Blood -- Circulation

    ISBN 978-1-58089-208-7 lib bdg; 1-58089-208-6 lib bdg

                      LC 2008025332

"The author and illustrator of The Quest to Digest (2006) take young readers on an equally engaging ride through the heart, lungs, arteries, veins, capillaries, and back again. In the big, labeled cartoon illustrations a small, green Smoo-like creature rides a red blood cell down a river of plasma. . . . Corcoran's breezy commentary lays out the whole 60,000-mile system in easy-to-understand terms. . . . An irresistable invitation to go with the flow." Booklist

Gold, John Coopersmith

    Learning about the circulatory and lymphatic systems; by John C. Gold. Enslow Publishers 2013 48 p. (library) $23.93

Grades: 5 6 7 8   **612.1**

    1. Picture books for children 2. Lymphatic system -- Juvenile literature 3. Cardiovascular system -- Juvenile literature

    ISBN 0766041565; 9780766041561

                      LC 2012011099

This book by John Coopersmith Gold is part of the Learning About the Human Body Systems series and looks at the circulatory and lymphatic systems. "The circulatory system runs through the body carrying oxygen and nutrients to our cells and removes waste. It's driven by the never-resting heart, which pumps blood through more than 60,000 miles of arteries and veins. The lymphatic system regulates the amount of liquid in the body among other tasks." (Publisher's note)

    Includes bibliographical references and index.

Guillain, Charlotte

Our hearts. Heinemann Library 2010 24p il (Our bodies) lib bdg $20.71; pa $5.99

Grades: K 1 2 3   **612.1**

1. Heart

ISBN 978-1-4329-3590-0 lib bdg; 1-4329-3590-9 lib bdg; 978-1-4329-3599-3 pa; 1-4329-3599-2 pa

LC 2009-22294

This describes what the heart is, how it pumps blood through the body, and how to keep it healthy.

This explains "visually and verbally complicated medical information in a clear, understandable way. . . . Large, vivid photographs are placed alongside one or two sentences per page." Booklist

Includes bibliographical references

Kyi, Tanya Lloyd

Seeing red; the true story of blood. Annick Press 2012 121 p. (hardcover) $22.95

Grades: 4 5 6   **612.1**

1. Blood -- Juvenile literature

ISBN 1554513855; 9781554513857

This book by Tanya Lloyd Kyi, illustrated by Steve Rolston, discusses "the symbolism and reality of blood, from its role in ancient sacrifices to its uses in modern medicine and forensics. . . . Around the world, blood has always been a symbol of both life and death: blood rites, blood oaths, and blood-soaked legends. Today, we have scientific facts about blood types, transfusions, blood-borne illnesses, and crime-scene blood spatter. Yet the fluid still holds mystery." (Publisher's note)

Includes bibliographical references (p. 112-115), Internet addresses and index.

Markle, Sandra

Faulty hearts; true survival stories. Lerner Pub. 2010 48p il (Powerful medicine) lib bdg $27.93

Grades: 5 6 7 8   **612.1**

1. Heart 2. Heart diseases 3. Cardiovascular system 4. Cardiovascular system -- Juvenile literature

ISBN 978-0-8225-8699-9 lib bdg; 0-8225-8699-1 lib bdg

LC 2009-33980

This book "is extremely well done, with a number of great examples of survival stories. The examples exemplify different and important heart diseases, symptoms, and treatments. . . . That the author is a former science teacher enables her to write clearly for the intended audience. The illustrations and photographs are perfect, adding to a full understanding of the diseases described." Sci Books & Films

Includes glossary and bibliographical references

Newquist, Hp

The book of blood; from legends and leeches to vampires and veins. HP Newquist. Houghton Mifflin Books for Children 2012 160 p. ill. (chiefly col.) (hardback) $17.99

Grades: 4 5 6   **612.1**

1. Blood

ISBN 0547315848; 9780547315843

LC 2011025134

In this book, "[H.P.] Newquist . . . demystifies one of the most elemental and (literally) vital components of life as we know it. After an overview of the complex makeup of blood, Newquist dives into humankind's history with, beliefs about,

and study of blood, including missteps and misconceptions along the way . . . . Newquist goes into detail to explain how blood moves through the human body and the critical role it plays in keeping us alive." (Publishers Weekly)

Showers, Paul

Hear your heart; illustrated by Holly Keller. Harper-Collins Pubs. 2001 33p il (Let's-read-and-find-out science) hardcover o.p. pa $4.95

Grades: K 1 2 3   **612.1**

1. Heart 2. Heart -- Juvenile literature

ISBN 0-06-025410-6; 0-06-025411-4 lib bdg; 0-06-445139-9 pa

LC 99-41336

A revised and newly illustrated edition of the title first published 1968

A simple explanation of the structure of the heart and how it works

"This is an excellent introduction to the heart and how it works. . . . The open, informal design brings the physiology right into daily life. Factual, accurate, and fun." Booklist

A drop of blood; illustrated by Edward Miller. Harper-Collins Pub. 2004 32p il (Let's-read-and-find-out science) hardcover o.p. pa $4.99

Grades: K 1 2 3   **612.1**

1. Blood

ISBN 0-06-009108-8; 0-06-009109-6 lib bdg; 0-06-009110-X pa

A newly illustrated edition of the title first published 1967 and revised in 1989

A simple introduction to the composition and functions of blood

"Showers's classic introduction to this vital fluid is cleverly updated by Miller's amusing illustrations featuring a Dracula-like vampire and his Igorish friend. . . . High-quality, closeup photographs of blood cells, platelets, and fibrin under the microscope are well placed within the illustrations, and science concepts are presented with just the right amount of detail for the intended audience." SLJ

Simon, Seymour

★ The heart; our circulatory system. [by] Seymour Simon. rev ed.; Collins 2006 30p il hardcover o.p. pa $6.99

Grades: 4 5 6 7   **612.1**

1. Heart 2. Cardiovascular system

ISBN 978-0-06-087720-0; 0-06-087720-0; 978-0-06-087721-7 pa; 0-06-087721-9 pa

LC 2006-279215

First published 1996

Describes the heart, blood, and other parts of the body's circulatory system and explains how each component functions

"The text is succinct and direct, making the details understandable without losing the sense that the whole process of circulation is 'strange and wonderful.' . . . The often striking pictures include many computer-enhanced photographs as well as diagrams and highly enlarged images made possible by electron microscopes. Handsome and well-conceived in every way." Booklist [review of 1996 edition]

Tieck, Sarah

Circulatory system. ABDO Pub. 2011 32p il (Body systems) lib bdg $27.07; e-book $27.07

Grades: 2 3 4   612.1

1. Cardiovascular system

ISBN 978-1-61613-497-6 lib bdg; 1-61613-497-6 lib bdg; 978-1-61613-987-4 e-book

LC 2010019665

"Double-page spreads describe the workings of the [circulatory system] . . . with simple text on left-hand pages and large, colorful photographs or diagrams on the right. The [text touches] on common disorders (e.g., high blood pressure . . .) and healthy practices. 'Brain Food' spreads pose three questions and provide answers. Ample white space, engaging images, and 'Word of Mouth' sidebars are reader-friendly." Horn Book Guide

Includes glossary

612.2   Respiratory system

Guillain, Charlotte

Our lungs. Heinemann Library 2010 24p il (Our bodies) lib bdg $20.71; pa $5.99

Grades: K 1 2 3   612.2

1. Lungs

ISBN 978-1-4329-3594-8 lib bdg; 1-4329-3594-1 lib bdg; 978-1-4329-3603-7 pa; 1-4329-3603-4 pa

LC 2009-22298

This describes what lungs are, why we need lungs, and how to keep them healthy.

This explains "visually and verbally complicated medical information in a clear, understandable way. . . . Large, vivid photographs are placed alongside one or two sentences per page." Booklist

Includes bibliographical references

Korb, Rena

My nose; illustrated by Remy Simard; content consultant, Anthony J. Weinhaus. Magic Wagon 2010 32p il (My body) lib bdg $27.07

Grades: 1 2 3   612.2

1. Nose

ISBN 978-1-60270-808-2; 1-60270-808-8

This "volume stars a child narrator who straightforwardly describes [the nose] and how it works. A round-faced, lab-coat-wearing man appears at the bottom of every spread to provide additional details and tidbits of anatomical information. . . . Black-outlined digital-looking cartoon illustrations enliven the [text]." Horn Book Guide

Includes glossary

Simon, Seymour

Lungs; your respiratory system. [by] Seymour Simon. Smithsonian/Collins 2007 30p il hardcover o.p. $16.77; lib bdg $17.89

Grades: 3 4 5 6   612.2

1. Respiratory system 2. Lungs -- Juvenile literature 3. Respiration -- Juvenile literature

ISBN 978-0-06-054654-0; 978-0-06-054655-7 lib bdg; 0-06-054655-7 lib bdg; 0-06-054656-5 pa

LC 2006003768

"This straightforward overview of the respiratory system follows the journey of a breath through the body. Color diagrams, X-rays, and photos provide visual support. . . . The writing is concise and full of clear examples meaningful to kids." SLJ

Includes glossary and bibliographical references

Siy, Alexandra

★ Sneeze! [by] Alexandra Siy and Dennis Kunkel. Charlesbridge 2007 45p il lib bdg $16.95; pa $6.95

Grades: 4 5 6 7   612.2

1. Allergy 2. Sneezing

ISBN 978-1-57091-653-3 lib bdg; 978-1-57091-654-0 pa

LC 2005-27567

"Kunkel's big, clear, beautiful color electron micrographs on every double-page spead show everything from dust mites, mildew, and pollen to the influenza A virus." Booklist

Includes glossary and bibliographical references

Tieck, Sarah

Respiratory system. ABDO Pub. 2011 32p il (Body systems) lib bdg $27.07; e-book $27.07

Grades: 2 3 4   612.2

1. Respiratory system

ISBN 978-1-61613-501-0 lib bdg; 1-61613-501-8 lib bdg; 978-1-61613-991-1 e-book

LC 2010019652

"Double-page spreads describe the workings of the [respiratory system] . . . with simple text on lefthand pages and large, colorful photographs or diagrams on the right. The [text touches] on common disorders . . . and healthy practices. 'Brain Food' spreads pose three questions and provide answers. Ample white space, engaging images, and 'Word of Mouth' sidebars are reader-friendly." Horn Book Guide

Includes glossary

612.3   Digestive system

Corcoran, Mary K.

The quest to digest; illustrated by Jef Czekaj. Charlesbridge 2006 32p il lib bdg $16.95; pa $6.95

Grades: 2 3 4   612.3

1. Digestion 2. Gastrointestinal system -- Juvenile literature

ISBN 978-1-57091-664-9 lib bdg; 978-1-57091-665-6 pa

LC 2005-19622

"This graphically appealing, colorful, and fact-rich story describes the importance of food to the body by following an apple as it goes through the human digestion system. . . . Abundant, humorous cartoons and clever text handle explanations of belching, passing gas, and diarrhea." SLJ

Includes glossary

Donovan, Sandra, 1967-

Hawk & Drool; gross stuff in your mouth. by Sandy Donovan; illustrated by Michael Slack. Millbrook Press 2010 48p il (Gross body science) lib bdg $29.27

Grades: 4 5 6   **612.3**
1. Saliva 2. Mouth -- Diseases
ISBN 978-0-8225-8966-2 lib bdg; 0-8225-8966-4
lib bdg

LC 2008-50699

Presents disgusting facts about the human mouth, how it works to aid in digestion, the organisms that live there, and ways to keep it clean and healthy

"Solid information layered between sarcastic comments and kid-friendly terminology like fart, poop, barf, and puke will keep readers engaged. . . . Labeled, captioned (and graphic) photographs, cartoon-style illustrations, and micrographs add information." SLJ

Includes glossary and bibliographical references

Rumble & spew; gross stuff in your stomach and intestines. by Sandy Donovan; illustrated by Michael Slack. Millbrook Press 2010 48p il (Gross body science) lib bdg $29.27
Grades: 4 5 6   **612.3**
1. Intestines
ISBN 978-0-8225-8899-3 lib bdg; 0-8225-8899-4
lib bdg

LC 2008-37713

Presents disgusting facts about the human digestive system and its functions

"Solid information layered between sarcastic comments and kid-friendly terminology like fart, poop, barf, and puke will keep readers engaged. . . . Labeled, captioned (and graphic) photographs, cartoon-style illustrations, and micrographs add information." SLJ

Includes glossary and bibliographical references

Gold, Susan Dudley
Learning about the digestive and excretory systems; by Susan Dudley Gold. Enslow Publishers 2013 48 p. (library) $23.93
Grades: 5 6 7 8   **612.3**
1. Picture books for children 2. Urinary organs -- Juvenile literature 3. Digestive organs -- Juvenile literature
ISBN 0766041573; 9780766041578

LC 2012011100

This book by Susan Dudley Gold is part of the Learning About the Human Body Systems series and looks at the digestive and excretory systems. She "explains why these systems are discussed together, how they work, and ways to keep healthy." Illustrations and color photographs are included. (Publisher's note)

Includes bibliographical references and index.

Guillain, Charlotte
Our stomachs. Heinemann Library 2010 24p il (Our bodies) lib bdg $20.71; pa $5.99
Grades: K 1 2 3   **612.3**
1. Stomach 2. Digestion
ISBN 978-1-4329-3591-7 lib bdg; 1-4329-3591-7 lib bdg; 978-1-4329-3600-6 pa; 1-4329-3600-X pa

LC 2009-22295

This describes what the stomach is, what it does to food, and how to keep it healthy.

This explains "visually and verbally complicated medical information in a clear, understandable way. . . . Large,

vivid photographs are placed alongside one or two sentences per page." Booklist

Includes bibliographical references

Jakab, Cheryl
The **digestive** system; by Cheryl Jakab. Smart Apple Media 2006 32p il (Our body) lib bdg $28.50
Grades: 3 4 5   **612.3**
1. Digestion
ISBN 978-1-58340-737-0 lib bdg; 1-58340-737-5 lib bdg

LC 2005057881

This "clear, approachable book contains six chapters that [describes] the [digestive] system, how it works, diseases, treatment, and more. A final chapter promotes a healthy lifestyle and educates readers on first aid and avoiding possible problems associated with the system. Health tips appear throughout, and an activity is included. [This book is] interactive in tone and [provides] plenty of sidebar material, along with color photographs, drawings, charts, and diagrams, and a fascinating 'under the microscope' look at parts of the body." SLJ

Includes glossary

Korb, Rena
My mouth. Magic Wagon 2011 32p il (My body) lib bdg $27.07
Grades: 1 2 3   **612.3**
1. Mouth
ISBN 978-1-60270-806-8; 1-60270-806-1

This "volume stars a child narrator who straightforwardly describes [the mouth] and how it works. A round-faced, lab-coat-wearing man appears at the bottom of every spread to provide additional details and tidbits of anatomical information. . . . Black-outlined digital-looking cartoon illustrations enliven the [text]." Horn Book Guide

Includes glossary

My stomach; illustrated by Remy Simard; content consultant, Anthony J. Weinhaus. Magic Wagon 2010 32p il (My body) lib bdg $27.07
Grades: 1 2 3   **612.3**
1. Stomach
ISBN 978-1-60270-810-5; 1-60270-810-X

This "volume stars a child narrator who straightforwardly describes [the stomach] and how it works. A round-faced, lab-coat-wearing man appears at the bottom of every spread to provide additional details and tidbits of anatomical information. . . . Black-outlined digital-looking cartoon illustrations enliven the [text]." Horn Book Guide

Includes glossary

Showers, Paul
What happens to a hamburger? illustrated by Edward Miller. HarperCollins Pubs. 2001 33p il (Let's-read-and-find-out science) hardcover o.p. pa $5.99
Grades: K 1 2 3   **612.3**
1. Digestion 2. Digestive system
ISBN 0-06-027947-8; 0-06-027948-6 lib bdg; 0-06-445183-6 pa

LC 97-39007

A newly illustrated edition of the title first published 1970

Explains the processes by which a hamburger and other foods are used to make energy, strong bones, and solid muscles as they pass through the digestive system

This edition offers "attractive new illustrations, enhanced in a few places with photos that show body parts such as the epiglottis and the stomach lining. . . . Miller's digital artwork has a jaunty, retro look." Booklist

Simon, Seymour

★ **Guts**; our digestive system. [by] Seymour Simon. HarperCollins 2005 un il $16.99; lib bdg $17.89

Grades: 4 5 6 7   **612.3**

1. Digestion 2. Digestion -- Juvenile literature 3. Gastrointestinal system -- Juvenile literature

ISBN 0-06-054651-4; 0-06-054652-2 lib bdg

LC 2004-14508

"Simon's specialty of drawing in readers through large, detailed, breathtaking photos and then entertaining them with facts is again in evidence. . . . The text is enhanced with detailed colored X rays, computer-generated pictures, and microscopic photos." SLJ

Thomas, Isabel

Why do I burp? digestion and diet. Raintree 2011 32p il (Inside my body) lib bdg $29; pa $7.99

Grades: 3 4 5 6   **612.3**

1. Digestion

ISBN 978-1-4109-4014-8 lib bdg; 1-4109-4014-4 lib bdg; 978-1-4109-4025-4 pa; 1-4109-4025-X pa

LC 2010024679

"Double-page spreads begin with questions related to the . . . digestive system. The answers, in the form of short paragraphs, bulleted lists, labeled diagrams and schematics, charts, and captioned photos, pack a surprising amount of information into relatively uncluttered pages. . . . Sidebars debunk common misconceptions, give practical advice, and add quirky facts." Horn Book Guide

Includes glossary and bibliographical references

Tieck, Sarah

Digestive system. ABDO Pub. 2011 32p il (Body systems) lib bdg $27.07; e-book $27.07

Grades: 2 3 4   **612.3**

1. Digestion

ISBN 978-1-61613-498-3 lib bdg; 1-61613-498-4 lib bdg; 978-1-61758-988-1 e-book

LC 2010019663

"Double-page spreads describe the workings of the [digestive system] . . . with simple text on lefthand pages and large, colorful photographs or diagrams on the right. The [text touches] on common disorders . . . and healthy practices. 'Brain Food' spreads pose three questions and provide answers. Ample white space, engaging images, and 'Word of Mouth' sidebars are reader-friendly." Horn Book Guide

Includes glossary

612.4   Hematopoietic, lymphatic, glandular, urinary systems

Kim, Melissa

Learning about the endocrine and reproductive systems; by Melissa L. Kim. Enslow Publishers 2013 48 p. (library) $23.93

Grades: 5 6 7 8   **612.4**

1. Picture books for children 2. Endocrine glands -- Juvenile literature 3. Reproductive system -- Juvenile literature 4. Generative organs -- Juvenile literature

ISBN 0766041581; 9780766041585

LC 2012011101

This book by Melissa L. Kim is part of the Learning About the Human Body Systems series and looks at the endocrine and reproductive systems. "The endocrine system is essential to human life. It enables a person to grow, respond to change and stress, and helps turn food into energy. The reproductive system has one crucial task: that of making the next generation of people." (Publisher's note)

Includes bibliographical references and index.

612.6   Reproduction, development, maturation

Brown, Laurene Krasny

What's the big secret? talking about sex with girls and boys. [by] Laurie Krasny Brown and Marc Brown. Little, Brown 1997 31p il hardcover o.p. pa $5.95

Grades: K 1 2 3   **612.6**

1. Sex education 2. Sex (Biology) -- Juvenile literature

ISBN 0-316-10915-0; 0-316-10183-4 pa

LC 96-15521

This "picture book's subject is sex and sexuality: not simply physical differences but also gender roles, the issue of privacy, and reproduction. . . . The Browns do an outstanding and very responsible job of introducing a wide variety of terms (everything from the expected, umbilical cord, to the unexpected, masturbation, which is handled with honesty but restraint), synthesizing a great deal of information kids want to know at this age, and presenting facts in a nonthreatening but forthright context. They even manage a good deal of humor along the way. . . . The words and illustrations work extremely well together, with the busy, bright cartoon art and balloon dialogue conveying as much of the information as the text." Booklist

Butler, Dori Hillestad

★ **My** mom's having a baby! illustrated by Carol Thompson. Albert Whitman & Co. 2005 un il $15.95

Grades: 2 3 4   **612.6**

1. Pregnancy 2. Childbirth 3. Sex education

ISBN 0-8075-5344-1

LC 2004-18585

"Elizabeth describes the month-by-month development of the baby as well as the changes in Mom's body. . . . Through very direct language and clear illustrations, children will learn about a man's testicles where sperm are made and the fallopian tube where an egg is fertilized. . . . Mom answers Elizabeth's big question, 'how do Dad's sperm and your egg get together?' . . . Details are not spared when the birth is described. The playful and colorful illustrations add exuberance to the text, combining full-page paintings, cartoon panels, word balloons, and free-floating images. The joy and love felt by all of the family members is palpable. This volume is an excellent choice for those readers who are ready to ask and be told some of life's basic facts." SLJ

Cocovini, Abby

★ **What's** inside your tummy, Mommy? [by] Abby Cocovini. Henry Holt & Co. 2008 un il pa $8.95

Grades: PreK K   **612.6**
    1. Pregnancy
    ISBN 978-0-8050-8760-4 pa; 0-8050-8760-5 pa

"Cocovini has designed this oversize guide so that 'if the mommy holds the book up to her belly, you will see what the baby looks like (actual size) inside her every month!' . . . This book is warm and nonthreatening to the max, its crayoned and watercolor spot illustrations and hand-drawn timeline lending it a homey, scrapbook/journal feel. The five or so factoids on each page are shaped around easy-to-grasp, domestic concepts." Publ Wkly

Cole, Joanna

★ **How** you were born; photographs by Margaret Miller. rev & expanded ed; Morrow Junior Bks. 1993 48p il $15.95; pa $6.99

Grades: K 1 2   **612.6**
    1. Infants 2. Pregnancy 3. Childbirth 4. Embryology -- Juvenile literature
    ISBN 0-688-12059-8; 0-688-12061-X pa

LC 92-23970

A revised and newly illustrated edition of the title first published 1984

"Illustrated with photographs of culturally diverse families, Cole's text explains conception, the development of the fetus, and the birth process. A note to parents and a suggested reading list are included." J Youth Serv Libr

When you were inside Mommy; illustrated by Maxie Chambliss. HarperCollins Pubs. 2001 un il $7.99

Grades: PreK K 1   **612.6**
    1. Infants 2. Pregnancy 3. Childbirth 4. Birth
    ISBN 0-688-17043-9

LC 00-40890

This "begins with a simple explanation of a baby's development in the mother's uterus. It goes on to show the baby's birth, followed by his growth to a child of perhaps three or four years old. An appended 'Note to Parents' offers a sound approach to talking with children. . . . The simplicity and sensitivity of the writing is well matched by Chambliss' line and watercolor wash illustrations." Booklist

Fromer, Liza

My stretchy body; [by] Liza Fromer and Francine Gerstein; illustrated by Joe Weissmann. Tundra Books 2011 un il (Body works) $12.95

Grades: 2 3 4 5   **612.6**
    1. Growth
    ISBN 978-1-77049-203-5; 1-77049-203-8

This describes how we grow, including hair, skin, nails, teeth, muscles, and bones, as well as growth spurts and growing pains.
    Includes glossary

Gaff, Jackie

Looking at growing up; how do people change? [by] Jackie Gaff. Enslow Publishers 2008 32p il (Looking at science: how things change) lib bdg $22.60

Grades: 1 2 3   **612.6**
    1. Growth
    ISBN 978-0-7660-3090-9 lib bdg; 0-7660-3090-3 lib bdg

LC 2007-24509

"Fills a huge void in elementary science collections. . . . Text is arranged in succinct 'chunks,' giving important facts without overwhelming readers. . . . [This] is an essential addition." Libr Media Connect
    Includes glossary and bibliographical references

Gravelle, Karen

The **period** book; everything you don't want to ask (but need to know) by Karen Gravelle & Jennifer Gravelle; illustrations by Debbie Palen. updated ed.; Walker & Co. 2006 126p il $16.95

Grades: 4 5 6 7   **612.6**
    1. Menstruation
    ISBN 978-0-8027-8072-0; 0-8027-8072-5

LC 2008270981

First published 1996

Explains what happens at the onset of menstruation, discussing what to wear, going to the gynecologist, and how to handle various problems

"The cartoonlike illustrations and conversational tone make this updated edition a friendly, reassuring resource as well as a thorough one." Horn Book Guide

Harris, Robie H.

★ **It's** not the stork! a book about girls, boys, babies, bodies, families, and friends. illustrated by Michael Emberley. Candlewick Press 2006 59p il $16.99

Grades: K 1 2 3   **612.6**
    1. Pregnancy 2. Childbirth 3. Sex education
    ISBN 0-7636-0047-4

LC 2005-54280

"Harris opens by introducing two cartoon characters—a green-feathered bird clad in a purple shirt and blue hightop sneakers and his spike-haired friend, a bee. They wonder, 'So where DO babies come from?' Their conversational commentary, given in word balloons, is a lighthearted supplement to a more focused narrative. Told in the second person, the text is straightforward, informative, and personable. Facts are presented step-by-step, starting from the similarities and differences between boys' and girls' bodies, moving to a baby's conception, growth in the womb, and birth, ending with an exploration of different configurations of families as well as a section on 'okay' versus 'not okay' touches." SLJ

★ **It's** so amazing! a book about eggs, sperm, birth, babies, and families. illustrated by Michael Emberley. Candlewick Press 1999 81p il $21.99; pa $10.99

Grades: 2 3 4   **612.6**
    1. Pregnancy 2. Childbirth 3. Reproduction 4. Sex education 5. Human reproduction -- Juvenile literature
    ISBN 0-7636-0051-2; 0-7636-1321-5 pa

LC 98-33119

Uses bird and bee cartoon characters to present straightforward explanations of topics related to sexual development, love, reproduction, adoption, sexually transmitted diseases, and more

"While the illustrations are engaging and often hilarious, factual information is effectively presented in a clear, non-judgmental tone that will inform and assure readers." SLJ

★ **Who** has what? all about girls' bodies and boys' bodies. Candlewick Press 2011 un il $15.99
Grades: PreK K 1   612.6
    1. Human body 2. Sex education
    ISBN 978-0-7636-2931-1; 0-7636-2931-6
                        LC 2010040464

"A family outing to the beach provides the opportunity for a discussion of the similarities and differences between boys and girls. Nellie's play on the words 'everybody' and 'every body' leads Gus to wondering about body parts. Their beach visit provides an opportunity to see a variety of people and puppies, to itemize all the parts that boys and girls and dogs have in common. . . . Harris . . . matter-of-factly combines common childhood language . . . and anatomically correct terms. . . . Westcott's digital cartoonlike illustrations show different compositions of families representing a wide range of ages, races and nationalities." Kirkus

Jukes, Mavis
   ★ **Growing** up: it's a girl thing; straight talk about first bras, first periods, and your changing body. illustrations by Debbie Tilley. Knopf 1998 72p il hardcover o.p. pa $10
Grades: 4 5 6 7   612.6
    1. Girls 2. Puberty 3. Adolescence 4. Menstruation
    5. Girls -- Physiology -- Juvenile literature
    ISBN 0-679-89027-0 pa
                        LC 98-18113

This "covers body hair and shaving, perspiration and deodorant, and how to buy your first bra. The second half of the book is devoted to what to expect and how to plan for your first period. . . . The narration has an easy, comfortable voice and imparts accurate and important information." SLJ

Katz, Anne
   Girl in the know; your inside-and-out guide to growing up. written by Anne Katz; illustrated by Monika Melnychuk. Kids Can Press 2010 111p il $18.95
Grades: 4 5 6 7   612.6
    1. Puberty 2. Girls -- Health and hygiene 3. Puberty -- Juvenile literature 4. Life skills guides -- Juvenile literature 5. Girls -- Psychology -- Juvenile literature
    ISBN 978-1-55453-303-9; 1-55453-303-1

"This reassuring title is aimed at girls who want clear facts about puberty but who may not be ready to read in-depth specifics of sex and birth-control. The author . . . offers a holistic guide that covers the body changes puberty brings as well as tips about maintaining physical and emotional health. . . . The warm, straightforward, useful advice on a broad range of topics . . . will captivate both middle graders and middle-schoolers, and the frequent color drawings of stylish, diverse girls . . . reinforce the book's appeal to a wide age group." Booklist

Madaras, Lynda
   ★ **On** your mark, get set, grow! a what's happening to my body? book for younger boys. [by] Lynda Madaras; illustrations by Paul Gilligan. Newmarket Press 2008 123p il $22; pa $12

Grades: 3 4 5 6   612.6
    1. Puberty 2. Boys -- Health and hygiene
    ISBN 978-1-55704-780-9; 1-55704-780-4; 978-1-55704-781-6 pa; 1-55704-781-2 pa
                        LC 2007043095

"Madaras draws on her experience teaching sex education (called puberty classes here) to inform boys about the physical changes they will experience as they start to mature. . . . The age-appropriate presentation includes cartoon art on almost every page and a sprinkling of humor. Along with covering sex-organ growth, height, weight, and muscle gain, Madaras also discusses health and nutrition, hygiene, and 'becoming your own self.' A reassuring tone pervades the text. . . . This is an excellent resource for both children and parents." SLJ

   ★ **Ready,** set, grow! a what's happening to my body? book for younger girls. illustrations by Linda Davick. Newmarket Press 2003 127p il $22; pa $12
Grades: 3 4 5 6   612.6
    1. Puberty 2. Girls -- Health and hygiene 3. Puberty -- Juvenile literature 4. Girls -- Growth -- Juvenile literature 5. Girls -- Physiology -- Juvenile literature
    ISBN 1-55704-587-9; 1-55704-565-8 pa
                        LC 2003-9489

This "is a timely and important book. In a consistently sensitive and encouraging tone, Madaras reassures preadolescents that the changes they know are approaching or they are beginning to experience are normal, natural, and cause for celebration. Humorous sketches illustrate the emotions and stages of puberty, and keep the tone light." SLJ

   ★ The **what's** happening to my body? book for boys; [by] Lynda Madaras with Area Madaras; drawings by Simon Sullivan. 3rd rev ed.; Newmarket Press 2007 xx, 233p il $24.95; pa $12.95
Grades: 4 5 6 7   612.6
    1. Puberty 2. Adolescence 3. Sex education 4. Boys -- Health and hygiene
    ISBN 978-1-55704-769-4; 1-55704-769-3; 978-1-55704-765-6 pa; 1-55704-765-0 pa
                        LC 2007009874
First published 1984
Discusses the changes that take place in a boy's body during puberty, including information on the body's changing size and shape, the growth spurt, reproductive organs, pubic hair, beards, pimples, voice changes, wet dreams, and puberty in girls
Includes bibliographical references

   ★ The **what's** happening to my body? book for girls; [by] Lynda Madaras with Area Madaras; drawings by Simon Sullivan. 3rd rev ed.; Newmarket Press 2007 xxvi, 259p il $24.95; pa $12.95
Grades: 4 5 6 7   612.6
    1. Puberty 2. Adolescence 3. Sex education 4. Girls -- Health and hygiene
    ISBN 978-1-55704-768-7; 1-55704-768-5; 978-1-55704-764-9 pa; 1-55704-764-2 pa
                        LC 2007009862
Discusses the changes that take place in a girl's body during puberty, including information on the body's chang-

ing size and shape, pubic hair, breasts, reproductive organs, the menstrual cycle, and puberty in boys

Includes bibliographical references

Mar, Jonathan

The **body** book for boys; by Jonathan Mar and Grace Norwich. Scholastic 2010 128p il pa $8.99

Grades: 4 5 6   **612.6**

1. Boys 2. Puberty 3. Adolescence

ISBN 978-0-545-23751-2 pa; 0-545-23751-3 pa

"In this reassuring title aimed at boys just entering adolescence, the authors present frank information on such topics as hygiene, the changes brought on by puberty, exercise, and dealing with girls. The tone is kept light, and the many bright illustrations also have a fun, jokey quality." Booklist

Plaisted, Caroline

Boy talk; a survival guide to growing up. illustrated by Chris Dickason. QEB Pub. 2011 il (Growing up)

Grades: 4 5 6 7   **612.6**

1. Boys 2. Puberty

ISBN 1-60992-085-6; 978-1-60992-085-2

LC 2011009206

Discusses body changes that happen to boys during puberty, such as acne, body hair, body odor, mood swings, crushes, and more, and gives suggestions to teen boys for taking care of their hygiene and keeping good relationships.

"Using a colorful design featuring Dickason's wacky, mugging cartoon characters, this is about as appealing as a book on these topics can get, and it maintains a mildly funny, usually frank, and always healthy tone." Booklist

Girl talk; a survival guide to growing up. illustrated by Chris Dickason. QEB Pub. 2011 il (Growing up) lib bdg $23.95

Grades: 4 5 6 7   **612.6**

1. Girls 2. Puberty

ISBN 978-1-60992-084-5; 1-60992-084-8

LC 2011009125

Discusses body changes that happen to girls during puberty, such as acne, periods, cramps, body hair, mood swings, and more, and gives suggestions to teen girls for taking care of their health.

Pringle, Laurence P.

Everybody has a bellybutton; your life before you were born. by Laurence Pringle; illustrated by Clare Wood. Boyds Mills Press 1997 un il $14.95

Grades: PreK K 1 2 3   **612.6**

1. Fetus 2. Pregnancy 3. Childbirth

ISBN 1-56397-009-0

LC 95-83168

Pringle "offers a gently phrased, solidly scientific look at the growth of a baby. . . . The narrative gives specific, sensorial details that will keep even young children engaged, and the description of childbirth is matter-of-fact and undisturbing. . . . Illustrations are softly realistic pencil drawings on pink and blue backgrounds." Booklist

Includes bibliographical references

Rand, Casey

Human reproduction. Raintree 2009 48p il (Sci-hi: life science) lib bdg $31.43; pa $8.99

Grades: 5 6 7 8   **612.6**

1. Reproduction 2. Sex education

ISBN 978-1-4109-3327-0 lib bdg; 1-4109-3327-X lib bdg; 978-1-4109-3335-5 pa; 1-4109-3335-0 pa

LC 2009003464

In this introduction to human reproduction "clear language, embedded definitions, and interesting examples illustrate abstract concepts through both text and well-chosen photographs. . . . [It] includes suggested activities to test ideas as well as a thorough glossary and a Webliography." SLJ

Includes glossary and bibliographical references

Saltz, Gail

★ **Amazing** you; getting smart about your private parts. illustrated by Lynne Avril Cravath. Dutton Children's Books 2005 un il $15.99

Grades: PreK K 1   **612.6**

1. Growth 2. Reproduction 3. Sex education 4. Generative organs -- Juvenile literature

ISBN 0-525-47389-0

LC 2004-22014

"This upbeat picture book, illustrated with sunny cartoon drawings, introduces kids to basic reproductive physiology. Saltz offers simple, accessible definitions of terms, accompanied by pictures of unclothed kids and labeled diagrams of internal organs. Subsequent drawings show three stages of body development from baby to young adult, followed by an abbreviated explanation, illustrated with a heart-shaped drawing of a smiling egg and sperm, of reproduction. . . . Saltz presents the information clearly in a cheerful, positive tone." Booklist

Changing you! a guide to body changes and sexuality. [by] Gail Saltz; illustrated by Lynne Avril Cravath. Dutton Children's Books 2007 un il $16.99

Grades: 3 4 5   **612.6**

1. Puberty 2. Sex education

ISBN 978-0-525-47817-1; 0-525-47817-5

LC 2006035593

"This is an introduction to puberty and sexual intercourse in the context of a loving relationship between a man and woman. The book covers topics that kids often inquire about, such as bodily changes and how babies are born. Bright, cartoon illustrations of the human body at different stages and ages and labeled diagrams fill the pages. The clear, straightforward text uses language that young children can easily grasp while the running commentary that accompanies the art takes a lighter, more conversational approach." SLJ

Schwartz, John

Short; walking tall when you're not tall at all. Roaring Brook Press 2010 132p il $16.99

Grades: 4 5 6 7 8   **612.6**

1. Size 2. Growth 3. Body image 4. Prejudices 5. Human growth -- Juvenile literature 6. Stature, Short -- Juvenile literature

ISBN 978-1-59643-323-6; 1-59643-323-X

"In a humorous, personal voice, . . . Schwartz combines his own memories of growing up short with related discussions about physiology, statistics, popular culture, and societal prejudice, always returning to his own self-image. . . . Short kids will want every word. . . . and many readers will move on to the resource list of articles, Web sites, and scientific papers in the detailed, informal back matter." Booklist

Includes bibliographical references

Sears, William

Baby on the way; [by] William Sears, Martha Sears, and Christie Watts Kelly; illustrated by Renée Andriani. Little, Brown 2001 un il (Sears children's library) $12.95

Grades: PreK K 1 2   **612.6**

1. Infants 2. Pregnancy 3. Childbirth 4. Babies

ISBN 0-316-78767-1

LC 00-38451

This book describes how a family prepares for the arrival of a new baby and explains pregnancy and childbirth to an older sibling

"Andriani's brightly colored, cartoon-style illustrations help create the books' upbeat, yet realistic tone." Booklist

Includes bibliographical references

612.7 Musculoskeletal system, integument

Baines, Rebecca

Your skin holds you in; a book about your skin. by Becky Baines. National Geographic 2008 29p il (Zigzag) $14.95; lib bdg $19.90

Grades: PreK K 1   **612.7**

1. Skin

ISBN 978-1-4263-0311-1; 1-4263-0311-4; 978-1-4263-0312-8 lib bdg; 1-4263-0312-2 lib bdg

LC 2007-44156

"Thirteen short sentences describe skin . . . in all its glory. Additional facts appear in smaller print . . . on the same pages with the main idea sentences. Photographs of people, outlined in white and reproduced on brightly colored pages, serve as diagrams for important elements. . . . Exuberant double-page spreads encourage looking and talking." Horn Book

The **bones** you own; a book about the human body. by Becky Baines. National Geographic 2009 27p il (Zigzag) $16.95; lib bdg $25.90

Grades: PreK K 1   **612.7**

1. Bones 2. Skeleton

ISBN 978-1-4263-0410-1; 1-4263-0410-2; 978-1-4263-0411-8 lib bdg; 1-4263-0411-0 lib bdg

LC 2008-47900

This describes functions that bones perform in a human body.

This title engages "children through humor, clear language, interesting facts, and abundant photos. . . . [An] excellent [introduction] for young science students." SLJ

Barner, Bob

Dem bones; [illustrations and informational bone text by] Bob Barner. Chronicle Bks. 1996 un il $16.99

Grades: K 1 2 3   **612.7**

1. Bones 2. Skeleton

ISBN 0-8118-0827-0

LC 95-29

"A rollicking read-aloud, sing-along treat for children as they learn anatomy, rhyme, and language. . . . Scientific

facts and names combined with lyrics make this a fascinating book." Exploring Sci in the Libr

Berger, Melvin

Why I sneeze, shiver, hiccup, and yawn; illustrated by Paul Meisel. HarperCollins Pubs. 2000 un il (Let's-read-and-find-out science) hardcover o.p. pa $4.99

Grades: K 1 2 3   **612.7**

1. Reflexes 2. Nervous system

ISBN 0-06-028144-8; 0-06-445193-3 pa

LC 98-55542

A revised and newly illustrated edition of Why I cough, sneeze, shiver, hiccup & yawn, published 1983 by Crowell

An introduction to reflex acts that explains why we sneeze, shiver, hiccup, and yawn

"The writing is simple but effective, and the charming, colorful pen-and-ink and watercolors are [detailed]. . . . Attractive introductory nonfiction." SLJ

Gold, Susan Dudley

Learning about the musculoskeletal system and the skin; Susan Dudley Gold. Enslow Publishers 2013 48 p. (library) $23.93

Grades: 5 6 7 8   **612.7**

1. Picture books for children 2. Musculoskeletal system -- Juvenile literature 3. Skin -- Juvenile literature

ISBN 076604159X; 9780766041592

LC 2012011102

This book by Susan Dudley Gold is part of the Learning About the Human Body Systems series and looks at the musculoskeletal system. "Bone and muscles join forces to move us from one place to another. The musculoskeletal system controls our breathing, allows our eyes to focus, and shapes our smiles. It enables us to talk and to eat. Our strong bones support our weight. Skin wraps our body in a tough layer of tissue that keeps moisture in and germs out." (Publisher's note)

Includes bibliographical references and index.

Guillain, Charlotte

Our bones. Heinemann Library 2010 24p il (Our bodies) lib bdg $20.71; pa $5.99

Grades: K 1 2 3   **612.7**

1. Bones

ISBN 978-1-4329-3596-2 lib bdg; 1-4329-3596-8 lib bdg; 978-1-4329-3605-1 pa; 1-4329-3605-0 pa

LC 2009-22300

This describes what bones are, how they support the body, and how to keep them healthy.

This explains "visually and verbally complicated medical information in a clear, understandable way. . . . Large, vivid photographs are placed alongside one or two sentences per page." Booklist

Includes bibliographical references

Our muscles. Heinemann Library 2010 24p il (Our bodies) lib bdg $20.71; pa $5.99

Grades: K 1 2 3   **612.7**

1. Muscles

ISBN 978-1-4329-3593-1 lib bdg; 1-4329-3593-3 lib bdg; 978-1-4329-3602-0 pa; 1-4329-3602-6 pa

LC 2009-22297

This describes what muscles are, how they help us move, and how to keep them healthy.

This explains "visually and verbally complicated medical information in a clear, understandable way. . . . Large, vivid photographs are placed alongside one or two sentences per page." Booklist

Includes bibliographic references

Our skin. Heinemann Library 2010 24p il (Our bodies) lib bdg $20.71; pa $5.99

Grades: K 1 2 3   612.7

1. Skin

ISBN 978-1-4329-3597-9 lib bdg; 1-4329-3597-6 lib bdg; 978-1-4329-3606-8 pa; 1-4329-3606-9 pa

LC 2009-22301

This describes what skin is, how it protects the body, and how to keep it healthy.

This explains "visually and verbally complicated medical information in a clear, understandable way. . . . Large, vivid photographs are placed alongside one or two sentences per page." Booklist

Includes bibliographic references

Jenkins, Steve

★ **Bones**; skeletons and how they work. Scholastic Press 2010 un il $16.99

Grades: 3 4 5 6   612.7

1. Bones 2. Skeleton

ISBN 978-0-545-04651-0; 0-545-04651-3

Jenkins "begins with a single human finger bone, then shows where it fits in the hand, then attaches the arm bones and sets it aside the forelimbs of a mole, spider monkey, gray whale, turtle, and fruit bat to illustrate how they all share the same basic structure. Similar comparisons take a look at feet, legs, rib cages, necks, and heads, almost always using a consistent scale to display the relative size of elephant and stork legs or a giraffe and human neck. Jenkins provides concise chunks of text alongside his always impressive cut-paper collages. . . . The clean design of the intricate skeletons set against solid background colors is striking and provides a wonderful visual introduction to what keeps us all upright." Booklist

Kaner, Etta

And the Winner Is ... Amazing Animal Athletes. by Etta Kaner; illustrated by David Anderson. Kids Can Press 2013 32 p. ill. (hardcover) $16.95

Grades: PreK K 1 2 3   612.7

1. Animals 2. Athletics

ISBN 1554539048; 9781554539048

This book "presents the World Animal Games, with quartets of different of critters competing in a variety of Olympic-type events. A walrus and a cockatoo provide facts and color as the contestants vie for the gold in the high jump, sprinting, weight lifting, swimming, and other trials . . . . A data box for each entrant is provided, as is information on just why the winner came out on top, and how the record stands up to human athletes." (School Library Journal)

Korb, Rena

My muscles; illustrated by Remy Simard; Content Consultant; Anthony J. Weinhaus. Magic Wagon 2010 32p il (My body) lib bdg $27.07

Grades: 1 2 3   612.7

1. Muscles

ISBN 978-1-60270-807-5; 1-60270-807-X

This "volume stars a child narrator who straightforwardly describes [muscles] and how [they work]. A round-faced, lab-coat-wearing man appears at the bottom of every spread to provide additional details and tidbits of anatomical information. . . . Black-outlined digital-looking cartoon illustrations enliven the [text]." Horn Book Guide

Includes glossary

My spine; illustrated by Remy Simard; content consultant, Anthony J. Weinhaus. Magic Wagon 2010 32p il (My body) lib bdg $27.07

Grades: 1 2 3   612.7

1. Spine

ISBN 978-1-6027-0809-9; 1-60270-809-6

This "volume stars a child narrator who straightforwardly describes [the spine] and how it works. A round-faced, lab-coat-wearing man appears at the bottom of every spread to provide additional details and tidbits of anatomical information. . . . Black-outlined digital-looking cartoon illustrations enliven the [text]." Horn Book Guide

Includes glossary

Parker, Steve, 1952-

How do my muscles get strong? Raintree 2011 32p il (Inside my body) lib bdg $29; pa $7.99

Grades: 3 4 5 6   612.7

1. Muscles 2. Exercise

ISBN 978-1-4109-4017-9 lib bdg; 1-4109-4017-9 lib bdg; 978-1-4109-4028-5 pa; 1-4109-4028-4 pa

LC 2010024800

"Double-page spreads begin with questions related to the human muscular . . . . system. The answers, in the form of short paragraphs, bulleted lists, labeled diagrams and schematics, charts, and captioned photos, pack a surprising amount of information into relatively uncluttered pages. . . . Sidebars debunk common misconceptions, give practical advice, and add quirky facts." Horn Book Guide

Includes glossary and bibliographic references

The skeleton and muscles; [by] Steve Parker. Raintree 2004 48p il (Our bodies) lib bdg $29.93

Grades: 5 6 7 8   612.7

1. Skeleton 2. Musculoskeletal system 3. Muscular system

ISBN 0-7398-6622-2

LC 2003-6594

This "takes a look at bones, muscles, and joints; how they are connected and function; and how to keep them healthy. The anatomy is accurate, and the format, with plenty of pictures, diagrams, and magnified photos, is very accessible. There are also lots of lively boxed facts." Booklist

Includes bibliographic references

Simon, Seymour

Bones; our skeletal system. Morrow Junior Bks. 1998 un il hardcover o.p. pa $6.99

Grades: 4 5 6 7   612.7

1. Bones 2. Skeleton

ISBN 0-688-14645-7 lib bdg; 0-688-17721-2 pa

LC 97-44751

Describes the skeletal system and outlines the many important roles that bones play in the healthy functioning of the human body

"Simon once again proves his remarkable facility for making complicated science clear and understandable." Booklist

Muscles; our muscular system. Morrow Junior Bks. 1998 un il hardcover o.p. pa $6.99

Grades: 4 5 6 7   612.7

1. Muscles

ISBN 0-688-14642-2; 0-688-14643-0 lib bdg; 0-688-17720-4 pa

LC 97-44758

Describes the nature and work of muscles, the different kinds, and the effects of exercise and other activities on them

"The full-paged illustrations are great and include full-color photographs, MRI scans, X rays, and excellent drawings." SLJ

Stewart, Melissa

Here we grow; the secrets of hair and nails. illustrated by Janet Hamlin. Marshall Cavendish Benchmark 2010 48p il (The gross and goofy body) lib bdg $20.95

Grades: 2 3 4   612.7

1. Hair

ISBN 978-0-7614-4172-4 lib bdg; 0-7614-4172-7 lib bdg

LC 2008033563

This provides information on the role hair and nails play in the body science of humans and animals.

This "offers detailed science facts in a fashion approachable enough to make it a welcome supplement to school textbooks. . . . The layout is fresh, clean, and colorful, sidebars keep things conversational, and the back matter is solid." Booklist

Includes glossary and bibliographical references

Moving and grooving; the secrets of muscles and bones. illustrated by Janet Hamlin. Marshall Cavendish Benchmark 2010 48p il (The gross and goofy body) lib bdg $20.95

Grades: 2 3 4   612.7

1. Musculoskeletal system

ISBN 978-0-7614-4166-3 lib bdg; 0-7614-4166-2 lib bdg

LC 2008033557

This offers information on the role bones and muscles play in the body science of humans and animals

Includes glossary and bibliographical references

Tieck, Sarah

Muscular system. ABDO Pub. Co. 2011 32p il (Body systems) lib bdg $27.07; ebook $27.07

Grades: 2 3 4   612.7

1. Muscles 2. Musculoskeletal system

ISBN 978-1-61613-499-0; 1-61613-499-2 lib bdg; 978-1-61613-989-8 ebook

LC 2010019664

"Double-page spreads describe the workings of the [muscular system] . . . with simple text on left-hand pages and large, colorful photographs or diagrams on the right. The [text touches] on common disorders . . . and healthy practices. 'Brain Food' spreads pose three questions and provide

answers. Ample white space, engaging images, and 'Word of Mouth' sidebars are reader-friendly." Horn Book Guide

Includes glossary

Skeletal system. ABDO Pub. 2011 32p il (Body systems) lib bdg $27.07; e-book $27.07

Grades: 2 3 4   612.7

1. Bones 2. Skeleton

ISBN 978-1-61613-502-7 lib bdg; 1-61613-502-6 lib bdg; 978-1-61613-992-8 e-book

LC 2010019651

"Double-page spreads describe the workings of the [skeletal system] . . . with simple text on left-hand pages and large, colorful photographs or diagrams on the right. The [text touches] on common disorders . . . and healthy practices. 'Brain Food' spreads pose three questions and provide answers. Ample white space, engaging images, and 'Word of Mouth' sidebars are reader-friendly." Horn Book Guide

Includes glossary

612.8   Nervous system

Aliki

My five senses; rev ed; Crowell 1989 31p il (Let's-read-and-find-out science book) $16.95; pa $4.99

Grades: PreK K 1   612.8

1. Senses and sensation

ISBN 0-690-04792-4; 0-06-445083-X pa

LC 88-35350

First published 1962

The faculties of touch, hearing, sight, smelling and taste are introduced in relation to everyday experiences

"Each sense is used independently to observe common phenomena. Next, the author demonstrates more than one sense being used. . . . The book effectively introduced the five senses to young people." Appraisal

Boothroyd, Jennifer

What is hearing? Lerner Publications Co. 2010 32p il (Lightning Bolt Books TM-Your amazing senses) lib bdg $25.26

Grades: K 1 2   612.8

1. Sound 2. Hearing

ISBN 978-0-7613-4250-2 lib bdg; 0-7613-4250-8 lib bdg

LC 2008-51848

Describes the properties of sound and hearing, including everyday examples and information on how an ear functions

"Given [its] . . . simple sentences, colorful layout, full-page photos, and well-chosen diagrams, [this title] . . . will be useful for reports." SLJ

Includes glossary and bibliographical references

What is sight? Lerner Publications Co. 2010 32p il (Lightning Bolt Books TM-Your amazing senses) lib bdg $25.26

Grades: K 1 2   612.8

1. Vision

ISBN 978-0-7613-4248-9 lib bdg; 0-7613-4248-6 lib bdg

LC 2008-51849

Describes the importance of the sense of sight and how the human eye works, including information on color, depth perception, and protecting sight

"Given [its] . . . simple sentences, colorful layout, full-page photos, and well-chosen diagrams, [this title] . . . will be useful for reports." SLJ

Includes glossary and bibliographical references

What is smell? Lerner Publications Co. 2010 32p il (Lightning Bolt Books TM-Your amazing senses) lib bdg $25.26

Grades: K 1 2   **612.8**
1. Smell
ISBN 978-0-7613-4253-3 lib bdg; 0-7613-4253-2 lib bdg

LC 2008-51850

Provides information on the sense of smell, including why there are good and bad smells and how noses function

"Given [its] . . . simple sentences, colorful layout, full-page photos, and well-chosen diagrams, [this title] . . . will be useful for reports." SLJ

Includes glossary and bibliographical references

What is taste? Lerner Publications Co. 2010 32p il (Lightning Bolt Books TM-Your amazing senses) lib bdg $25.26

Grades: K 1 2   **612.8**
1. Taste
ISBN 978-0-7613-4251-9 lib bdg; 0-7613-4251-6 lib bdg

LC 2008-51847

Explains how human beings use their sense of taste and illustrates good and bad tastes

"Given [its] . . . simple sentences, colorful layout, full-page photos, and well-chosen diagrams, [this title] . . . will be useful for reports." SLJ

Includes glossary and bibliographical references

What is touch? Lerner Publications Co. 2010 32p il (Lightning Bolt Books TM-Your amazing senses) lib bdg $25.26

Grades: K 1 2   **612.8**
1. Touch
ISBN 978-0-7613-4252-6 lib bdg; 0-7613-4252-4 lib bdg

LC 2008-51587

The book about touch has "simple sentences, colorful layout, full-page photos, and well-chosen diagrams . . . [and] will be useful for reports." SLJ

Brocket, Jane
Spiky, slimy, smooth; what is texture? [text and photographs by Jane Brocket] Millbrook Press 2011 un il (Jane Brocket's clever concepts) lib bdg $25.26

Grades: PreK K 1 2   **612.8**
1. Touch
ISBN 978-0-7613-4614-2; 0-7613-4614-7

LC 2010028933

"Bright, attention-grabbing, and, in some cases, enlarged photographs of hard candies, duck slippers, stone walls, and other common objects give viewers the impression that they can reach out and touch them. That's exactly the point in this . . . book, which introduces texture to young children. It not only lets readers imagine what a woolly blanket or cactus plant might feel like but offers a host of adjectives, highlighted in color, to describe their textures. . . . Clever, indeed." Booklist

Cobb, Vicki
Open your eyes; discover your sense of sight. illustrations by Cynthia C. Lewis. Millbrook Press 2001 un il (Five senses) lib bdg $22.90

Grades: 2 3 4   **612.8**
1. Eye 2. Vision 3. Eye -- Juvenile literature 4. Vision -- Juvenile literature
ISBN 0-7613-1705-8

LC 2001-30394

"A discussion of the science of the eye, its parts, and how it works, and easy, child-friendly experiments on sensory perception and optical illusions result in an interesting title and an amusing look at one of our five senses. The collage illustrations are done with photographs, newspapers, and drawings. Many have humorous captions." SLJ

Your tongue can tell; discover your sense of taste. illustrations by Cynthia C. Lewis. Millbrook Press 2000 un il (Fivr senses) lib bdg $22.60; pa $7.95

Grades: 2 3 4   **612.8**
1. Taste 2. Senses and sensation
ISBN 0-7613-1473-3 lib bdg; 0-7613-1979-4 pa

LC 99-47873

Text and suggested activities explore the sense of taste, how it works, and how it can help us detect which foods are sweet, sour, salty, or spicy

Cole, Joanna
The **magic** school bus explores the senses; illustrated by Bruce Degen. Scholastic Press 1999 47p il hardcover o.p. pa $5.99

Grades: 2 3 4   **612.8**
1. Senses and sensation 2. Senses and sensation -- Juvenile literature
ISBN 0-590-44697-5; 0-590-44698-3 pa

LC 98-18662

Ms. Frizzle and her class explore the senses by traveling on the magic school bus in and out of an eye, ear, mouth, nose, and other parts of both human and animal bodies

"Along the margins are snippets of information in the form of Frizzle Facts and excerpts from kids' school reports. Degen's clever illustrations are both humorous and informative, acting as excellent visual aids for little learners." Booklist

Funston, Sylvia
It's all in your head; a guide to your brilliant brain. [by] Sylvia Funston, Jay Ingram; illustrated by Gary Clement. 2nd ed; Maple Tree Press 2005 64p il $16.95; pa $9.95

Grades: 3 4 5 6   **612.8**
1. Brain 2. Psychology
ISBN 1-897066-43-0; 1-897066-44-9 pa

First published 1994 with title: A kid's guide to the brain

This "explains how the brain controls our senses, emotions, memory, and thinking. Each chapter includes experiments, with easy-to-find items such as buttons and jelly beans, brain teasers, . . . historical information, and current theories on brain function. . . . Color photographs and whimsical illustrations make the presentation appealing." SLJ

Gardner, Robert

Ace your science project about the senses; great science fair ideas. [by] Robert Gardner . . . [et al.] Enslow Publishers 2009 112p il (Ace your biology science project) lib bdg $31.93

Grades: 5 6 7 8   612.8

1. Science projects 2. Senses and sensation 3. Science -- Experiments

ISBN 978-0-7660-3217-0 lib bdg; 0-7660-3217-5 lib bdg

LC 2008-30797

"Presents several science projects and science project ideas about the senses." Publisher's note

Includes glossary and bibliographical references

Gold, Martha V.

Learning about the nervous system; by Martha V. Gold. Enslow Publishers 2013 48 p. (library) $23.93

Grades: 5 6 7 8   612.8

1. Picture books for children 2. Nervous system -- Juvenile literature

ISBN 0766041603; 9780766041608

LC 2012011103

This book by Martha V. Gold is part of the Learning About the Human Body Systems series and looks at the nervous system. "The nervous system is made up of the brain, the spinal cord and nerves. It is responsible for telling the heart to beat, the lungs to breathe, and the muscles to move. The brain—the central command center—processes everything from understanding a teacher's instructions to enjoying a piece of chocolate cake." (Publisher's note)

Includes bibliographical references and index.

Guillain, Charlotte

How do we hear? Heinemann Library 2008 24p il (Sounds all around us) lib bdg $20.71; pa $5.99

Grades: PreK K 1   612.8

1. Sound 2. Hearing 3. Sound waves

ISBN 978-1-4329-3201-5 lib bdg; 1-4329-3201-2 lib bdg; 978-1-4329-3207-7 pa; 1-4329-3207-1 pa

LC 2008-51738

Learn about sound waves, how the human ear works, and how animals can have a special sense of hearing.

This book "introduces the basics of sound through vibrant photographs, large text, and simple sentences. . . . [A] great introduction[s] and worthy addition[s]." SLJ

Includes glossary and bibliographical references

Our brains. Heinemann Library 2010 24p il (Our bodies) lib bdg $20.71; pa $5.99

Grades: K 1 2 3   612.8

1. Brain

ISBN 978-1-4329-3592-4 lib bdg; 1-4329-3592-5 lib bdg; 978-1-4329-3601-3 pa; 1-4329-3601-8 pa

LC 2009-22296

This explains what the brain is, how it controls other body parts, and how to keep it healthy.

This explains "visually and verbally complicated medical information in a clear, understandable way. . . . Large, vivid photographs are placed alongside one or two sentences per page." Booklist

Includes bibliographical references

Hewitt, Sally

Hear this! [by] Sally Hewitt. Crabtree Pub. 2008 24p il (Let's start! science) pa $6.95

Grades: PreK K 1 2   612.8

1. Sounds 2. Hearing

ISBN 978-0-7787-4058-2 pa; 0-7787-4058-7 pa

LC 2008-5007

First published 2005 by QEB publications

This book about hearing "will provide a good starting point for younger students to learn more about their senses. . . . Most chapters are accompanied by a related activity, none are too complex for the intended audience." Libr Media Connect

Includes glossary and bibliographical references

Look here! [by] Sally Hewitt. Crabtree 2008 24p il (Let's start! science) pa $6.95

Grades: PreK K 1 2   612.8

1. Vision

ISBN 978-0-7787-4059-9 pa; 0-7787-4059-5 pa

LC 2008-5008

First published 2005 by QEB publications with title: Look out!

This book about vision "will provide a good starting point for younger students to learn more about their senses. . . . Most chapters are accompanied by a related activity, none are too complex for the intended audience." Libr Media Connect

Includes glossary and bibliographical references

Smell it! Crabtree Pub. Company 2008 24p il (Let's start! science) pa $6.95

Grades: PreK K 1 2   612.8

1. Smell

ISBN 978-0-7787-4060-5 pa; 0-7787-4060-9 pa

LC 2008-5009

First published 2005 by QEB publications with title: Smell that!

This book "will provide a good starting point for younger students to learn more about their senses. . . . Most chapters are accompanied by a related activity, none are too complex for the intended audience." Libr Media Connect

Includes glossary and bibliographical references

Tastes good! [by] Sally Hewitt. Crabtree Pub. Company 2008 24p il (Let's start! science) pa $6.95

Grades: PreK K 1 2   612.8

1. Taste

ISBN 978-0-7787-4061-2 pa; 0-7787-4061-7 pa

LC 2008-5010

First published 2005 by QEB publications

This book "will provide a good starting point for younger students to learn more about their senses. . . . Most chapters are accompanied by a related activity, none are too complex for the intended audience." Libr Media Connect

Includes glossary and bibliographical references

Touch that! [by] Sally Hewitt. Crabtree Pub. Co. 2008 24p il (Let's start! science) pa $6.95

Grades: PreK K 1 2   612.8

1. Touch

ISBN 978-0-7787-4062-9 pa; 0-7787-4062-5 pa

LC 2008-5011

First published 2005 by QEB publications

This book "will provide a good starting point for younger students to learn more about their senses.... Most chapters are accompanied by a related activity, none are too complex for the intended audience." Libr Media Connect

Includes glossary and bibliographical references

Korb, Rena

My brain; illustrated by Remy Simard; content consultant, Anthony J. Weinhaus. Magic Wagon 2011 32p il (My body) lib bdg $27.07

Grades: 1 2 3   **612.8**

1. Brain

ISBN 978-1-60270-805-1; 1-60270-805-3

This "volume stars a child narrator who straightforwardly describes [the brain] and how it works. A round-faced, lab-coat-wearing man appears at the bottom of every spread to provide additional details and tidbits of anatomical information.... Black-outlined digital-looking cartoon illustrations enliven the [text]." Horn Book Guide

Includes glossary

Larsen, C. S.

Crust and spray; gross stuff in your eyes, ears, nose, and throat. illustrated by Michael Slack. Millbrook Press 2010 48p il (Gross body science) lib bdg $29.27

Grades: 4 5 6   **612.8**

1. Ear 2. Eye 3. Nose 4. Throat

ISBN 978-0-8225-8964-8 lib bdg; 0-8225-8964-8 lib bdg

LC 2008-33777

"Solid information layered between sarcastic comments and kid-friendly terminology like fart, poop, barf, and puke will keep readers engaged.... Labeled, captioned (and graphic) photographs, cartoon-style illustrations, and micrographs add information." SLJ

Includes glossary and bibliographical references

Read, Leon

My senses. Sea-to-Sea Publications 2010 23p il (Tiger talk. All about me) lib bdg $24.25

Grades: PreK K   **612.8**

1. Senses and sensation

ISBN 978-1-59771-188-3 lib bdg; 1-59771-188-8 lib bdg

LC 2008-45010

This book about the senses "makes learning fun.... [The] book employs a simplified game of 'Where's Waldo?' by hiding a cartoon tiger on almost every page. This approach, combined with questions ... will encourage discussion and involvement." SLJ

Royston, Angela

Why do I sleep? QEB Pub. 2010 24p il (QEB my body) lib bdg $28.65

Grades: PreK K 1 2   **612.8**

1. Sleep

ISBN 978-1-59566-974-2 lib bdg; 1-59566-974-4 lib bdg

LC 2009-15226

Introduces the function and importance of sleep, and outlines good sleeping habits

"This ... is meant to be read to young children because it is written at a higher reading level than its intended audience.

The information is straightforward, well presented, and easy to understand.... [This] title is well designed, filled with color photographs, and scattered with fact boxes.... This ... will be useful in preschool and primary classrooms where health and hygiene are stressed." Libr Media Connect

Includes glossary and bibliographical references

Scott, Elaine

All about sleep from A to ZZZZ; by Elaine Scott; illustrated by John O'Brien. Viking 2008 58p il $17.99

Grades: 5 6 7 8 9 10   **612.8**

1. Sleep

ISBN 978-0-670-06188-4; 0-670-06188-3

LC 2008-6074

"This excellent overview is packed with interesting tidbits.... Scott is careful to point out which information is factual and which is theory, an important distinction.... The fanciful cartoon illustrations add to the book's appeal.... It is interesting, highly engaging, and fun to read." SLJ

Showers, Paul

Sleep is for everyone; illustrated by Wendy Watson. HarperCollins Pubs. 1997 32p il (Let's-read-and-find-out science) hardcover o.p. pa $4.99

Grades: K 1 2   **612.8**

1. Sleep

ISBN 0-06-025392-4; 0-06-025393-s lib bdg; 0-06-445141-0 pa

LC 96-49375

A newly illustrated edition of the title first published 1974 by Crowell

This volume examines "how different animals sleep, why we sleep, and what happens while we sleep and when we don't sleep enough. Colorful paper cut-out illustrations are simple and light-hearted with mottled paper as background creating a restful, gentle feeling." Horn Book Guide

Simon, Seymour

★ Eyes and ears. HarperCollins Pubs. 2003 un il hardcover o.p. pa $6.99

Grades: 4 5 6 7   **612.8**

1. Ear 2. Eye 3. Vision 4. Hearing 5. Senses and sensation

ISBN 0-688-15303-8; 978-0-06-073302-5 pa; 0-06-073302-0 pa

LC 2002-19060

Describes the anatomy of the eye and ear, how those organs function and some ways in which they may malfunction, and how the brain is also involved in our seeing and hearing

"Simon is at his very best here.... The large, exquisitely reproduced photographs from a number of sources look like fiery planets, galaxies, and monster creatures.... The anatomy and physiology are detailed and accurate, with clear diagrams." Booklist

★ The brain; our nervous system. [by] Seymour Simon. rev ed. Collins 2006 30p il $17.99; pa $6.99

Grades: 4 5 6 7   **612.8**

1. Brain 2. Nervous system

ISBN 978-0-06-087718-7; 0-06-087718-9; 978-0-06-087719-4 pa; 0-06-087719-7 pa

LC 2007-272349

First published 1997

Describes the various parts of the brain and the nervous system and how they function to enable us to think, feel, move, and remember.

Simon's "clear, concise writing style is complemented by stunning color images taken with radiological scanners, such as CAT scans, MRIs, and SEMs (scanning electron microscopes.)" SLJ [review of 1997 edition]

Includes bibliographical references

Simpson, Kathleen

The **human** brain; inside your body's control room. National Geographic 2009 64p il (National Geographic investigates) lib bdg $27.90

Grades: 5 6 7 8   **612.8**

1. Brain

ISBN 978-1-4263-0421-7 lib bdg; 1-4263-0421-8 lib bdg

"Readers will learn about . . . new brain research in this title, which includes a basic discussion of the parts of the brain, their functions, and how neurons send messages throughout the body. Information is also included about the role of the brain during sleep, dreaming, and various emotional states, as well as explanations of the various technologies available to measure brain activity. This is a well-organized, compelling introduction, sure to pique the curiosity of many children. Full-color photographs and illustrations enliven the text." SLJ

Includes bibliographical references

Stewart, Melissa

You've got nerve! the secrets of the brain and nerves. illustrated by Janet Hamlin. Marshall Cavendish Benchmark 2010 48p il (The gross and goofy body) lib bdg $20.95

Grades: 2 3 4   **612.8**

1. Nervous system

ISBN 978-0-7614-4157-1 lib bdg; 0-7614-4157-3 lib bdg

LC 2008033560

This includes information on the role the brain and nerves play in the body science of humans and animals

This "offers detailed science facts in a fashion approachable enough to make it a welcome supplement to school textbooks. . . . The layout is fresh, clean, and colorful, sidebars keep things conversational, and the back matter is solid." Booklist

Includes glossary and bibliographical references

Tieck, Sarah

Nervous system. ABDO Pub. 2011 32p il (Body systems) lib bdg $27.07; ebook $27.07

Grades: 2 3 4   **612.8**

1. Nervous system

ISBN 978-1-61613-500-3 lib bdg; 1-61613-500-X lib bdg; 978-1-61613-990-4 ebook

LC 2010019654

"Double-page spreads describe the workings of the [nervous system] . . . with simple text on left-hand pages and large, colorful photographs or diagrams on the right. The [text touches] on common disorders . . . and healthy practices. 'Brain Food' spreads pose three questions and provide answers. Ample white space, engaging images, and 'Word of Mouth' sidebars are reader-friendly." Horn Book Guide

Includes glossary

Veitch, Catherine

Sound and hearing. Heinemann Library 2009 24p il (Sounds all around us) lib bdg $20.71; pa $5.99

Grades: PreK K 1   **612.8**

1. Sound 2. Hearing 3. Sound waves

ISBN 978-1-4329-3224-4 lib bdg; 1-4329-3224-1 lib bdg; 978-1-4329-3225-1 pa; 1-4329-3225-X pa

LC 2008-51741

This book "introduces the basics of sound through vibrant photographs, large text, and simple sentences. . . . [A] great introduction[s] and worthy addition[s]." SLJ

Includes glossary

Winston, Robert M. L., 1940-

What goes on in my head? how your brain works and why you do what you do. [by] Robert Winston. DK Pub. 2010 96p il $16.99

Grades: 4 5 6 7   **612.8**

1. Brain 2. Psychology

ISBN 978-0-7566-6885-3; 0-7566-6885-9

"The author presents a great deal of scientific content and supplements it with examples, anecdotes, and current findings in the field. . . . In addition, interactive brain teasers and exercises make the science come alive. . . . The book combines vibrant colors and illustrations with explanations to keep young readers engaged." Sci Books Films

613   Personal health and safety

Ajmera, Maya

Healthy kids; Maya Ajmera, Victoria Dunning, Cynthia Pon. Charlesbridge 2012 32 p. (reinforced) $17.95

Grades: PreK K 1 2   **613**

1. Everyday life -- Juvenile literature 2. Children -- Health and hygiene -- Juvenile literature 3. Children -- Juvenile literature 4. Multiculturalism -- Juvenile literature

ISBN 1580894364; 9781580894364; 9781580894371

LC 2012000784

This book, by Maya Ajmera, Victoria Dunning, and Cynthia Pon, part of the "Global Fund of Children Book" series, offers photographs of children throughout the world doing about active and healthy daily life. Activities profiled include eating food, playing, and doing chores. Children from several countries are illustrated, including Argentina, Bhutan, Canada, Guatemala, Romania and Kenya.

Gardner, Robert

Ace your exercise and nutrition science project: great science fair ideas; [by] Robert Gardner, Barbara Gardner Conklin, and Salvatore Tocci. Enslow Publishers 2009 128p il (Ace your biology science project) lib bdg $31.93

Grades: 5 6 7 8   **613**

1. Exercise 2. Nutrition 3. Science projects 4. Science -- Experiments

ISBN 978-0-7660-3218-7 lib bdg; 0-7660-3218-3 lib bdg

LC 2008-30798

"Presents several science projects and science project ideas about exercise and nutrition." Publisher's note

Includes bibliographical references

Lehman, Robert

★ **Will** puberty last my whole life? real answers to real questions from preteens about body changes, sex, and other growing-up stuff. Julie Giesy Metzger and Robert Lehman; illustrated by Cerizo. Sasquatch Books 2011 90 p. col. ill. (pbk.) $16.95

Grades: 4 5 6 7 8   613

1. Puberty 2. Questions and answers 3. Boys -- Health and hygiene 4. Girls -- Health and hygiene 5. Puberty -- Juvenile literature 6. Teenage boys -- Physiology -- Juvenile literature 7. Teenage girls -- Physiology -- Juvenile literature 8. Interpersonal relations in adolescence -- Juvenile literature

ISBN 1570617392; 9781570617393

LC 2011038401

This book "for boys and girls between the ages of 9 and 12 has questions asked by girls in one half of the book" and "questions asked by boys are on the other side." The book contains "answers to questions pre-adolescents have about puberty, friends, feelings, sex, pimples, babies, body hair, menstruation, bras, and much more." (Amazon.com)

Miller, Edward, 1964-

★ **The monster** health book; a guide to eating healthy, being active, & feeling great for monsters & kids! [by] Edward Miller. Holiday House 2006 40p il $16.95

Grades: 2 3 4   613

1. Health 2. Nutrition

ISBN 978-0-8234-1956-2; 0-8234-1956-8

LC 2005046383

"Featuring a friendly, rotund, green monster determined to make healthy choices, this book presents basic information about food, exercise, and health. . . . Subjects include food nutrients, counting calories and understanding food labels, tips for making healthy lunches and snacks, the benefits of getting enough sleep and exercise, and ways to improve self-esteem. Miller's retro-style illustrations fill the pages with color, shapes, and humorous details, and silly jokes are tucked everywhere. . . . This lively, visually appealing book . . . belongs in children's hands." SLJ

Natterson, Cara

The **care** & keeping of you 2; the body book for older girls. Dr. Cara Natterson; illustrated by Josee Masse. American Girl 2013 96 p. (paperback) $12.99

Grades: 5 6 7 8   613

1. Puberty -- Juvenile literature 2. Life skills -- Handbooks, manuals, etc. 3. Teenage girls -- Health and hygiene -- Juvenile literature 4. Girls -- Life skills guides -- Juvenile literature

ISBN 1609580427; 9781609580421

LC 2012045813

This book, by Cara Natterson, illustrated by Josee Masse, is a body image and physiology guide written for girls going through puberty. "This . . . advice book will guide you through the next steps of growing up. . . . This book covers new questions about periods, your growing body, peer pressure, personal care, and more." (Publisher's note)

"The friendly illustrations support the overall tone and style. . . . Its neutral, matter-of-fact approach will help show readers . . . that all the changes they may be feeling are perfectly normal." SLJ

Pfeifer, Kate Gruenwald

American Medical Assocation boy's guide to becoming a teen. Jossey-Bass 2006 128p il pa $12.95

Grades: 4 5 6 7   613

1. Puberty 2. Adolescence 3. Boys -- Health and hygiene

ISBN 0-7879-8343-8

"This guide addresses puberty's changes clearly. . . . The text's approach is straightforward, accessible, and nonjudgmental, whether the topic is same-sex attraction or divorcing parents. The volume closes with an extensive resource section, including hotlines." Booklist

Includes bibliographical references

American Medical Association girl's guide to becoming a teen. Jossey-Bass 2006 128p pa $12.95

Grades: 4 5 6 7   613

1. Puberty 2. Adolescence 3. Girls -- Health and hygiene

ISBN 0-7879-8344-6

This "covers the physical and emotional changes that puberty brings, along with solid tips about grooming, diet, exercise, and other health issues, such as eating disorders. . . . The clear text communicates concepts clearly . . . and girls will find plenty of useful information." Booklist

Includes bibliographical references

Read, Leon

Keeping well. Sea-to-Sea Publications 2010 23p il (Tiger talk. All about me) lib bdg $24.25

Grades: PreK K   613

1. Health 2. Hygiene

ISBN 978-1-59771-186-9 lib bdg; 1-59771-186-1 lib bdg

LC 2008-45008

This book about keeping well "makes learning fun. . . . [The] book employs a simplified game of 'Where's Waldo?' by hiding a cartoon tiger on almost every page. This approach, combined with questions . . . will encourage discussion and involvement." SLJ

Royston, Angela

Why do I wash my hands? QEB Pub. 2010 24p il (QEB my body) lib bdg $28.65

Grades: PreK K 1 2   613

1. Hygiene

ISBN 978-1-59566-972-8 lib bdg; 1-59566-972-8 lib bdg

LC 2009-15228

Introduces the effects of germs on the skin and outlines the principles of personal hygiene.

"The information is straightforward, well presented, and easy to understand. . . . [This] title is well designed, filled with color photographs, and scattered with fact boxes." Libr Media Connect

Includes glossary and bibliographical references

Schaefer, Adam

Staying healthy; [by] A. R. Schaefer. Heinemann Library 2010 32p il (Health and fitness) lib bdg $25.36; pa $7.99

Grades: PreK K 1 **613**

1. Health 2. Hygiene 3. Exercise
ISBN 978-1-4329-2769-1 lib bdg; 1-4329-2769-8 lib
bdg; 978-1-4329-2774-5 pa; 1-4329-2774-4 pa
LC 2008-52298

Find out about the importance of a good diet, exercise,
staying clean, and what to do if you are injured or sick.

"Spare, declarative sentences coupled with bright, full-
color photos . . . [makes this book] appropriate for reading
aloud in the classroom or even during a themed story hour.
. . . While each spread introduces a new topic . . . [a] solid
[introduction] and [conclusion] make for [a] cohesive [pack-
age]." SLJ

Includes glossary and bibliographical references

Simons, Rae

At home in your body; care for the shape you're in.
Mason Crest Publishers 2010 48p il (Kids & obesity) lib
bdg $19.95; pa $7.95

Grades: 3 4 5 **613**

1. Obesity 2. Self-confidence 3. Health self-care 4.
Personal appearance
ISBN 978-1-4222-1715-3 lib bdg; 1-4222-1715-9 lib
bdg; 978-1-4222-1903-4 pa; 1-4222-1903-8 pa
LC 2010015436

Discusses healthy body types.

This book "presents the expected information about the
food pyramid, the need for physical activity, and the influence of the media on our psyches. Where the material shines
is in its holistic approach. Readers are encouraged to develop
their inner lives as much as their physical selves and to take
responsibility for their own health and eating habits. . . . This
brightly-colored, ego-boosting, responsibility-championing
. . . [book] is a winner." SLJ

Includes bibliographical references

Does television make you fat? lifestyle and obesity.
Mason Crest Publishers 2010 48p il (Kids & obesity) lib
bdg $19.95; pa $7.95

Grades: 3 4 5 **613**

1. Obesity 2. Exercise 3. Lifestyles
ISBN 978-1-4222-1712-2 lib bdg; 1-4222-1712-4 lib
bdg; 978-1-4222-1900-3 pa; 1-4222-1900-3 pa
LC 2010022849

This book about lifestyle and obesity "presents the expected information about the food pyramid, the need for
physical activity, and the influence of the media on our
psyches. Where the material shines is in its holistic approach. Readers are encouraged to develop their inner lives
as much as their physical selves and to take responsibility for
their own health and eating habits. . . . This brightly-colored,
ego-boosting, responsibility-championing . . . [book] is a
winner." SLJ

Includes bibliographical references

613.2 Dietetics

Currie, Stephen

Junk food. Cherry Lake Pub. 2009 32p il (Health at
risk) lib bdg $27.07

Grades: 4 5 6 7 8 **613.2**

1. Nutrition
ISBN 978-1-60279-284-5 lib bdg; 1-60279-284-4
lib bdg
LC 2008017498

This describes what junk food is, why it's not good for
your body, and what's being done to help us control our junk
food habit.

"Great for reports or reluctant readers." Booklist

Includes bibliographical references

Doeden, Matt

Eat right! how you can make good food choices. illustrations by Jack Desrocher. Lerner Publications 2008 64p
il (Health zone) lib bdg $30.60

Grades: 4 5 6 7 **613.2**

1. Nutrition
ISBN 978-0-8225-7552-8; 0-8225-7552-3
LC 2007043322

"This offers a highly readable, never preachy exploration into the benefits of providing quality fuel for your body.
It opens with an anecdote of a kid who snacks on soda and
chips while playing volleyball. A friend challenges him to to
eat better for a week, and he comes back with more sustained
energy and a fresh outlook. . . . The following chapters do a
great job of detailing everything from the food pyramid and
benefits of different nutrients to warnings against following
the faddish, ineffective diets." Booklist

Includes bibliographical references

Durrie, Karen

Health. Weigl 2011 il (Community helpers) $27.13

Grades: PreK K 1 2 **613.2**

1. Health 2. Nutrition
ISBN 978-1-61690-950-5; 1-61690-950-1
LC 2011024904

"A diverse group of people represents seven occupations: doctor, nurse, optometrist, fitness teacher, nutritionist,
counselor, and dentist. A large, color photo fills each double-page spread, along with a text box carrying a sentence,
such as 'I check your teeth and gums to make sure they are
healthy.' . . . All the clearly reproduced photos provide clues
that will help children guess who is speaking." Booklist

Edwards, Hazel

Talking about your weight; by Hazel Edwards and
Goldie Alexander. Gareth Stevens 2010 32p il (Healthy
living) lib bdg $26

Grades: 4 5 6 7 **613.2**

1. Obesity 2. Nutrition 3. Weight loss
ISBN 978-1-4339-3655-5; 1-4339-3655-0

"This guidebook offers a simple look at healthy lifestyle
choices involving exercise and diet. It examines people's relationships with food, body shape and genetics, eating disorders, and ways to combat obesity." Publisher's note

Furgang, Adam

Carbonated beverages; the incredibly disgusting story.
Rosen Central 2011 48p il (Incredibly disgusting food) lib
bdg $26.50; pa $11.75

Grades: 4 5 6 7   **613.2**
1. Carbonated beverages
ISBN 978-1-4488-1266-0 lib bdg; 1-4488-1266-6 lib bdg; 978-1-4488-2282-9 pa; 1-4488-2282-3 pa
LC 2010023227

This presents "straightforward information about why [carbonated beverages] are unhealthy without resorting to extreme gross-out factors. The [book contains] a breakdown of the foods' components . . . insight into how they are processed, and both short- and long-term effects of consumption. . . . Readers may or may not be disgusted, but they will definitely learn a thing or two about smart eating habits." SLJ

Includes glossary and bibliographical references

Salty and sugary snacks; the incredibly disgusting story. Rosen Central 2011 48p il (Incredibly disgusting food) lib bdg $26.50; pa $11.75
Grades: 4 5 6 7   **613.2**
1. Salt 2. Sugar 3. Nutrition 4. Snack foods
ISBN 978-1-4488-1267-7 lib bdg; 1-4488-1267-4 lib bdg; 978-1-4488-2283-6 pa; 1-4488-2283-1 pa
LC 2010025751

This book describes how salty and sugary snacks put dangerous amounts of sugar and salt into our bodies and how these unnecessary calories can have terrible effects on the body.

"Readers may or may not be disgusted, but they will definitely learn a thing or two about smart eating habits." SLJ

Includes glossary and bibliographical references

Hunt, Jamie
The **truth** about diets; what's right for you? Mason Crest Publishers 2011 48p il (Kids & obesity) lib bdg $19.95; pa $7.95
Grades: 3 4 5   **613.2**
1. Diet 2. Nutrition 3. Weight loss
ISBN 978-1-4222-1710-8 lib bdg; 1-4222-1710-8 lib bdg; 978-1-4222-1898-3 pa; 1-4222-1898-8 pa
LC 2010010014

Learn about diets and whether or not they are actually a good way to lose weight.

This "presents the expected information about the food pyramid, the need for physical activity, and the influence of the media on our psyches. Where the material shines is in its holistic approach. Readers are encouraged to develop their inner lives as much as their physical selves and to take responsibility for their own health and eating habits. . . . This brightly-colored, ego-boosting, responsibility-championing . . . [book] is a winner." SLJ

Includes bibliographical references

Johanson, Paula
Fake foods; fried, fast, and processed: the incredibly disgusting story. Rosen Central 2011 48p il (Incredibly disgusting food) lib bdg $26.50; pa $11.75
Grades: 4 5 6 7   **613.2**
1. Nutrition 2. Natural foods 3. Convenience foods
ISBN 978-1-4488-1269-1 lib bdg; 1-4488-1269-0 lib bdg; 978-1-4488-2285-0 pa; 1-4488-2285-8 pa
LC 2010020534

This presents "straightforward information about why various junk foods are unhealthy without resorting to extreme gross-out factors. The [book contains] a breakdown of the foods' components . . . insight into how they are processed, and both short- and long-term effects of consumption. . . . Readers may or may not be disgusted, but they will definitely learn a thing or two about smart eating habits." SLJ

Includes glossary and bibliographical references

King, Hazel
Carbohydrates for a healthy body; 2nd ed.; Heinemann Library 2009 48p il (Body needs) $17.99; pa $8.99
Grades: 4 5 6   **613.2**
1. Nutrition 2. Carbohydrates
ISBN 978-1-4329-2186-6; 1-4395-3782-8; 978-1-4329-2192-7 pa; 1-4329-2192-4 pa
LC 2009290513

First published 2003

Describes what carbohydrates are, what types of foods contain them, how they are digested and used to produce energy, and their role in a healthy diet.

This is "written in a clear, organized style and the full-color illustrations and photos complement the [text]." SLJ [review of 2003 edition]

Includes bibliographical references

Leedy, Loreen
The **edible** pyramid; good eating every day. written and illustrated by Loreen Leedy. rev ed.; Holiday House 2007 un il $17.95; pa $6.95
Grades: K 1 2 3   **613.2**
1. Diet 2. Nutrition
ISBN 978-0-8234-2074-2; 0-8234-2074-4; 978-0-8234-2075-9 pa; 0-8234-2075-2 pa
LC 2006036590

First published 1994

This is a "picture-book guide to healthy, delicious eating. . . . Featuring the smart cat waiter at the Edible Pyramid restaurant who recommends the menu to stylishly dressed animal customers, the bright, clear pictures show breads and grains, pasta in amazing shapes, vegetables and fruits in delicious colors, an abundance of beans, and more." Booklist

Powell, Jillian
Fats for a healthy body; 2nd ed.; Heinemann Library 2009 48p il (Body needs) lib bdg $31.43
Grades: 4 5 6   **613.2**
1. Nutrition 2. Oils and fats
ISBN 978-1-4329-2187-3 lib bdg; 1-4329-2187-8 lib bdg
LC 2009290512

First published 2003

Discusses what fats are, how they are absorbed and stored in the body, how the body uses fats, and health problems caused by fats.

Includes bibliographical references

Royston, Angela
Proteins for a healthy body; 2nd ed.; Heinemann Library 2009 48p il (Body needs) lib bdg $31.43; pa $8.99
Grades: 4 5 6   **613.2**
1. Proteins 2. Nutrition
ISBN 978-1-4329-2188-0; 1-4329-2188-6 lib bdg; 978-1-4329-2194-1 pa; 1-4329-2194-0 pa
LC 2009290511

First published 2003

"Royston looks at different kinds of proteins—antibodies, hormones, enzymes—and how vegetarians and vegans can get enough of them. . . . [This is] written in a clear, organized style and the full-color illustrations and photos complement the [text]." SLJ [review of 2003 edition]

Vitamins and minerals for a healthy body; 2nd ed.; Heinemann Library 2009 48p il (Body needs) lib bdg $31.43; pa $8.99

Grades: 4 5 6   **613.2**
1. Minerals 2. Vitamins 3. Nutrition
ISBN 978-1-4329-2189-7; 1-4329-2189-4 lib bdg; 978-1-4329-2195-8 pa; 1-4329-2195-9 pa
LC 2009293230

First published 2003

Discusses what vitamins and minerals are, how they are digested, absorbed, and used by the body, and the role of these substances in a healthy diet

Includes bibliographical references

Water and fiber for a healthy body; 2nd ed.; Heinemann Library 2009 48p il (Body needs) lib bdg $31.43; pa $8.99

Grades: 4 5 6   **613.2**
1. Water 2. Nutrition 3. Food -- Fiber content
ISBN 978-1-4329-2190-3 lib bdg; 1-4329-2190-8; 978-1-4329-2196-5 pa; 1-4329-2196-7 pa
LC 2009293229

First published 2003

Discusses what water and fiber are, what foods they can be found in, and how the body absorbs, digests, and uses these ingredients

Includes bibliographical references

Schaefer, Adam
Healthy food; [by] A. R. Schaefer. Heinemann Library 2010 32p il (Health and fitness) lib bdg $25.36; pa $7.99
Grades: PreK K 1   **613.2**
1. Diet 2. Nutrition
ISBN 978-1-4329-2768-4 lib bdg; 1-4329-2768-X lib bdg; 978-1-4329-2773-8 pa; 1-4329-2773-6 pa
LC 2008-52367

Find out what the main food groups are, and the best ways to eat these foods

"Spare, declarative sentences coupled with bright, full-color photos . . . [makes this book] appropriate for reading aloud in the classroom or even during a themed story hour. . . . While each spread introduces a new topic . . . [a] solid [introduction] and [conclusion] make for [a] cohesive [package]." SLJ

Includes glossary and bibliographical references

Simons, Rae
Bigger isn't always better; choosing your portions. Mason Crest Publishers 2011 48p il (Kids & obesity) lib bdg $19.95; pa $7.95
Grades: 3 4 5   **613.2**
1. Diet 2. Obesity 3. Nutrition 4. Eating customs
ISBN 978-1-4222-1706-1 lib bdg; 1-4222-1706-X lib bdg; 978-1-4222-1894-5 pa; 1-4222-1894-5 pa
LC 2010028159

Explores the contributions of increasingly larger portion sizes to the problem of obesity in America.

This book "presents the expected information about the food pyramid, the need for physical activity, and the influence of the media on our psyches. Where the material shines is in its holistic approach. Readers are encouraged to develop their inner lives as much as their physical selves and to take responsibility for their own health and eating habits. . . . This brightly-colored, ego-boosting, responsibility-championing . . . [book] is a winner." SLJ

Includes bibliographical references

Thompson, Helen
Cookies or carrots? you are what you eat. Mason Crest Publishers 2010 48p il (Kids & obesity) lib bdg $19.95; pa $7.95
Grades: 3 4 5   **613.2**
1. Diet 2. Nutrition
ISBN 978-1-4222-1707-8 lib bdg; 1-4222-1707-8 lib bdg; 978-1-4222-1895-2 pa; 1-4222-1895-3 pa
LC 2010025502

This book about nutrition and diet "presents the expected information about the food pyramid, the need for physical activity, and the influence of the media on our psyches. Where the material shines is in its holistic approach. Readers are encouraged to develop their inner lives as much as their physical selves and to take responsibility for their own health and eating habits. . . . This brightly-colored, ego-boosting, responsibility-championing . . . [book] is a winner." SLJ

Includes bibliographical references

Watson, Stephanie
Mystery meat; hot dogs, sausages, and lunch meats: the incredibly disgusting story. Rosen Pub. Group 2011 48p il (Incredibly disgusting food) lib bdg $26.50; pa $11.75
Grades: 4 5 6 7   **613.2**
1. Meat 2. Sausages 3. Nutrition 4. Frankfurters
ISBN 978-1-4488-1268-4 lib bdg; 1-4488-1268-2 lib bdg; 978-1-4488-2284-3 pa; 1-4488-2284-X pa
LC 2010013649

"The short but substantive chapters begin with a look at typical hot-dog ingredients and manufacturing practices, followed by discussions of how 'mystery meats,' including common, highly processed sandwich fillers, affect the body. A closing chapter about the components of a healthy diet widens the book into an opportunity for adults and kids to discuss general nutrition and includes useful tips on reading food labels. . . . Young readers will find plenty of browsing and report fodder in these pages." Booklist

Includes bibliographical references

Zahensky, Barbara A.
Diet fads. Rosen 2007 64p il (Danger zone: dieting and eating disorders) lib bdg $27.95
Grades: 4 5 6 7 8   **613.2**
1. Obesity 2. Weight loss
ISBN 978-1-4042-1999-1

"This clearly written overview emphasizes the impact of super-thin celebrity images on general self-esteem. . . . Zahensky considers the reasons people overeat and walks readers through practical steps to recognizing true hunger, making a weight-loss plan, and establishing good diet and exercise habits. She examines different types of fad and crash diets, pointing out their inherent dangers." SLJ

613.6 Personal safety and special topics of health

Catel, Patrick

Surviving stunts and other amazing feats. Raintree 2011 56p il (Extreme survival)

Grades: 4 5 6 7   **613.6**

1. Stunts

ISBN 1-4109-3969-3; 978-1-4109-3969-2

LC 2010028690

This book is "fun and informative. [This] well-organized title starts with an overview, offers some specific examples, and includes additional facts or tips and resources. Catel defines activities that encompass adventure and amazement and then leads readers through a discussion of sideshows, movies, and daring stunts (some of which include fire). . . . [It features] dramatic archival and full-color photos on nearly every page. . . . [This is a book] that youngsters will enjoy and talk about." SLJ

Includes glossary and bibliographical references

Champion, Neil

Finding food and water. Amicus 2010 32p il (Survive alive) lib bdg $28.50

Grades: 4 5 6 7   **613.6**

1. Wilderness survival

ISBN 978-1-60753-037-4 lib bdg; 1-60753-037-6 lib bdg

LC 2009030889

This offers survival tips for finding food and water in the wild, including how to know what is safe to eat or drink from land, plant, and animal sources.

This "colorful [book contains] numerous photos and illustrations that effectively break the [text] into small, readable chunks. There's lots of practical, everyday information here. . . . Brief yet gripping real-life survival stories are interspersed throughout the [book]." SLJ

Includes glossary

Finding your way. Amicus 2011 32p il (Survive alive) lib bdg $28.50

Grades: 4 5 6 7   **613.6**

1. Orienteering 2. Wilderness survival

ISBN 978-1-60753-038-1 lib bdg; 1-60753-038-4 lib bdg

LC 2009030888

"With eye-catching photographs, clear explanations, a survival skills quiz, a glossary, Web sites, and 'True Survival' stories . . . this engaging text encourages readers to figure out where they are and where they want to go." Booklist

Includes glossary

In an emergency. Amicus 2010 32p il (Survive alive) lib bdg $28.50

Grades: 4 5 6 7   **613.6**

1. Survival skills

ISBN 978-1-60753-040-4; 1-60753-040-6

LC 2010002517

This offers survival tips on what to do in emergency situations. Includes scenarios about fire, bad weather, accidents, injuries, extreme conditions, and more.'

This "colorful [book contains] numerous photos and illustrations that effectively break the [text] into small, read-

able chunks. There's lots of practical, everyday information here. . . . Brief yet gripping real-life survival stories are interspersed throughout the [book]." SLJ

Includes glossary

Making shelter. Amicus 2010 32p il (Survive alive) lib bdg $28.50

Grades: 4 5 6 7   **613.6**

1. Wilderness survival

ISBN 978-1-60753-041-1 lib bdg; 1-60753-041-4 lib bdg

LC 2010001378

This offers survival tips for building shelter in the wild, including using natural means in different regions such as the desert, forest, jungle, and cold areas. Also includes information on what to bring for aid when building shelters.

Hurley, Michael

Surviving the wilderness. Raintree 2011 56p il (Extreme survival) lib bdg $33.50

Grades: 4 5 6 7   **613.6**

1. Wilderness survival

ISBN 978-1-4109-3972-2; 1-4109-3972-3

LC 2010028839

This book is "fun and informative. [This] well-organized title starts with an overview [of wilderness survival], offers some specific examples, and includes additional facts or tips and resources. . . . [It features] dramatic archival and full-color photos on nearly every page. . . . [This is a book] that youngsters will enjoy and talk about." SLJ

Includes glossary and bibliographical references

Long, Denise

Survivor kid; a practical guide to wilderness survival. Chicago Review Press 2011 222p il $12.95

Grades: 4 5 6 7   **613.6**

1. Wilderness survival

ISBN 978-1-56976-708-5; 1-56976-708-4

LC 2011004952

"Long offers lessons on how to stay healthy and out of trouble while awaiting rescue. Her matter-of-fact, no-nonsense tone will play well with young readers, and the clear writing style is appropriate to the content. The engaging guide covers everything from building shelters to avoiding pigs and javelinas. . . . The volume invites browsing as much as studying. . . . An excellent bibliography will lead young readers to a host of fascinating websites, and 150 clipart-style line drawings complement the text." Kirkus

Includes bibliographical references

Miller, Edward, 1964-

Fireboy to the rescue! a fire safety book. Holiday House 2010 un il $16.95

Grades: K 1 2   **613.6**

1. Fire fighting 2. Fire prevention 3. Safety education

ISBN 978-0-8234-2222-7; 0-8234-2222-4

"Fireboy is a superhero intent on keeping the world's children safe from fire. After heralding all the great things fire can do . . . the cut paper-style artwork bursts into reds and yellows and oranges as all manners of things—including homes—catch aflame. . . . The snazzy presentation is entertaining in its own right. . . . Some of the especially vital details (fire alarms, extinguishers) are incorporated as photos." Booklist

Nelson, Sara Kirsten

Stay safe! how you can keep out of harm's way. by Sara Nelson; illustrated by Jack Desrocher. Lerner Publications 2008 64p il (Health zone) lib bdg $30.60

Grades: 4 5 6 7   **613.6**

1. Safety education 2. Children and strangers 3. Child sexual abuse -- Prevention

ISBN 978-0-8225-7551-1; 0-8225-7551-5

The offers safety education on such subjects as bullying in schools, inappropriate touching by family members, internet solicitations and threats in public places (such as attempted abductions).

"The format is beyond lively, with lots of color, cartoons, and an informal writing style, but it manages to present sometimes frightening material in a non-threatening and browsable way." Booklist

Includes glossary and bibliographical references

Schaefer, Adam

Staying safe. Heinemann Library 2009 32p il (Health and fitness) lib bdg $25.36; pa $7.99

Grades: PreK K 1   **613.6**

1. Safety education

ISBN 978-1-4329-2770-7 lib bdg; 1-4329-2770-1 lib bdg; 978-1-4329-2775-2 pa; 1-4329-2775-2 pa

LC 2008-52300

Find out what to do in a fire, how to stay safe in the street, and who to call in an emergency.

"Spare, declarative sentences coupled with bright, full-color photos . . . [makes this book] appropriate for reading aloud in the classroom or even during a themed story hour. . . . While each spread introduces a new topic . . . [a] solid [introduction] and [conclusion] make for [a] cohesive [package]." SLJ

Includes glossary and bibliographical references

613.7   Physical fitness

Aikman, Louise

Pilates step-by-step; [by] Louise Aikman and Matthew Harvey. Rosen Central 2011 93p il (Skills in motion) lib bdg $31.95

Grades: 5 6 7 8   **613.7**

1. Pilates method

ISBN 978-1-4488-1549-4; 1-4488-1549-5

LC 2010007510

Presents a general guide to the Pilates exercise system using a sequence of stop-action images and text instructions to illustrate some of the most common movements.

Includes bibliographical references

Atha, Antony

Fitness for young people; step-by-step. [by] Antony Atha and Simon Frost. Rosen Central 2010 93p il (Skills in motion) lib bdg $31.95

Grades: 5 6 7 8   **613.7**

1. Physical fitness

ISBN 978-1-4358-3364-7; 1-4358-3364-3

LC 2009-13245

Describes how to maintain physical fitness for youth, providing exercises that are both effective and fun.

"Colorful photographs show the entire movement of each skill presented, giving new meaning to the term 'step-by-step.' Progression borders at the bottom of the pages highlight the salient points to notice in performing each skill from beginning to end." SLJ

Includes bibliographical references

Birkemoe, Karen

★ **Strike** a pose; the Planet Girl guide to yoga. written by Karen Birkemoe; illustrated by Heather Collett. Kids Can Press 2007 96p il (Planet girl) spiral $12.95

Grades: 5 6 7 8   **613.7**

1. Yoga 2. Girls -- Health and hygiene

ISBN 978-1-55337-004-8

"This compact book offers a well-rounded overview of Hatha yoga. Using an easy conversational tone, Birkemoe relates the general practice and specific poses to reader's lives. The simple line drawings and color illustrations partner effectively with text to explain each move." SLJ

Includes glossary

Eason, Sarah

Free running; by Paul Mason and Sarah Eason. Lerner Publications 2011 il (On the radar: sports)

Grades: 5 6 7 8   **613.7**

1. Running 2. Parkour

ISBN 076137759X; 9780761377597

LC 2011000467

"Free running, also known as parkour, is a combination of speed running, gymnastics, and, in some cases, sheer fearlessness. Lovers of the sport launch over walls, clear fences in a single bound, and somersault down stairwells. This . . . captures the adrenaline-fueled energy of runners, using bold graphics, bright colors, and short interviews to showcase professionals, demonstrate moves, and trace the origins of free running." Booklist

Hunt, Jamie

Getting stronger, getting fit; the importance of exercise. Mason Crest Publishers 2011 48p il (Kids & obesity) lib bdg $19.95; pa $7.95

Grades: 3 4 5   **613.7**

1. Exercise 2. Physical fitness

ISBN 978-1-4222-1709-2 lib bdg; 1-4222-1709-4 lib bdg; 978-1-4222-1897-6 pa; 1-4222-1897-X pa

LC 2010017921

This book about nutrition and exercise "presents the expected information about the food pyramid, the need for physical activity, and the influence of the media on our psyches. Where the material shines is in its holistic approach. Readers are encouraged to develop their inner lives as much as their physical selves and to take responsibility for their own health and eating habits. . . . This brightly-colored, ego-boosting, responsibility-championing . . . [book] is a winner." SLJ

Includes bibliographical references

Jennings, Madeleine

Tai chi step-by-step; [by] Madeleine Jennings and James Drewe. Rosen Central 2011 93p il (Skills in motion) lib bdg $31.95

Grades: 5 6 7 8   **613.7**
1. Tai chi
ISBN 978-1-4488-1551-7; 1-4488-1551-7
     LC 2010008411

This book introduces both basic and higher level techniques of tai chi, with step-by-step instructions, illustrated by stop-motion sequential photography.

Includes bibliographical references

Kuskowski, Alex
   Cool relaxing; healthy & fun ways to chill out! Alex Kuskowski. ABDO Pub. Co. 2012 32 p. col. ill. (Cool health and fitness) (library) $28.50
Grades: 4 5 6   **613.7**
1. Creative activities 2. Rest -- Juvenile literature 3. Relaxation -- Juvenile literature
ISBN 1617834289; 9781617834288
     LC 2012010345

This nonfiction children's book by Alex Kuskowski presents a "hodgepodge of activities and techniques to achieve zen calm. The suggestions in this 'Cool Health and Fitness' title are all over the place--cooking, running, reading, baths, even cleaning--but that's the unspoken truth: whatever pleasantly distracts you does the trick. Eight activities are given step-by-step attention, including yoga, stretching, making a lavender pillow, and meditation." (Booklist)

Mason, Paul, 1967-
   Improving endurance. PowerKids Press 2011 32p il (Training for sports) lib bdg $25.25
Grades: 5 6 7 8   **613.7**
1. Sports 2. Exercise
ISBN 978-1-4488-3300-9; 1-4488-3300-0
     LC 2010024356

This offers "detailed tips on improving . . . endurance. All-around athletes will love this and so will kids who just want to work on getting fit." Booklist

   Improving flexibility. PowerKids Press 2011 32p il (Training for sports) lib bdg $25.25
Grades: 5 6 7 8   **613.7**
1. Sports 2. Exercise
ISBN 978-1-4488-3299-6; 1-4488-3299-3
     LC 2010024359

This offers tips on improving flexibility for sports.

"All-around athletes will love this and so will kids who just want to work on getting fit." Booklist

   Improving speed. PowerKids Press 2011 32p il (Training for sports) lib bdg $25.25
Grades: 5 6 7 8   **613.7**
1. Speed 2. Sports 3. Exercise
ISBN 978-1-4488-3302-3; 1-4488-3302-3
     LC 2010024354

This offers "detailed tips on improving speed. . . . All-around athletes will love this and so will kids who just want to work on getting fit." Booklist

   Improving strength & power. PowerKids Press 2011 32p il (Training for sports) lib bdg $25.25
Grades: 5 6 7 8   **613.7**
1. Exercise 2. Physical fitness
ISBN 978-1-4488-3301-6; 1-4488-3301-6
     LC 2010024425

This offers tips on improving strength and power for sports.

"All-around athletes will love this and so will kids who just want to work on getting fit." Booklist

Royston, Angela
   Why do I run? QEB Pub. 2010 24p il (QEB my body) lib bdg $28.65
Grades: PreK K 1 2   **613.7**
1. Running 2. Exercise 3. Physical fitness
ISBN 978-1-59566-971-1 lib bdg; 1-59566-971-X lib bdg
     LC 2009-15223

Introduces the effects of running and other exercise on the body, and outlines the principles of physical fitness and healthy, safe exercise

"The information is straightforward, well presented, and easy to understand. . . . [This] title is well designed, filled with color photographs, and scattered with fact boxes." Libr Media Connect

Includes glossary and bibliographical references

Schaefer, Adam
   Exercise; [by] A. R. Schaefer. Heinemann Library 2010 32p il (Health and fitness) lib bdg $25.36; pa $7.99
Grades: PreK K 1   **613.7**
1. Exercise
ISBN 978-1-4329-2767-7 lib bdg; 1-4329-2767-1 lib bdg; 978-1-4329-2772-1 pa; 1-4329-2772-8 pa
     LC 2008-52297

This book about exercise has "spare, declarative sentences coupled with bright, full-color photos. . . . While each spread introduces a new topic . . . [a] solid [introduction] and [conclusion] make for [a] cohesive [package]." SLJ

Includes glossary and bibliographical references

Spilling, Michael
   Yoga step-by-step; [by] Michael Spilling and Liz Lark. Rosen Central 2011 95p il (Skills in motion) lib bdg $31.95
Grades: 5 6 7 8   **613.7**
1. Yoga
ISBN 978-1-4488-1550-0; 1-4488-1550-9
     LC 2010008665

Readers are introduced to basic yoga techniques through step-by-step instructions, depicted with numerous photographs.

Includes bibliographical references

Tuminelly, Nancy
   Super simple bend & stretch; healthy & fun activities to move your body. ABDO Pub. Company 2012 32p il (Super simple exercise) lib bdg $27.07
Grades: 1 2 3   **613.7**
1. Exercise 2. Physical fitness
ISBN 978-1-61714-959-7; 1-61714-959-4
     LC 2011000963

"This volume opens with general pages on the benefits of healthy eating and physical activities as well as instructions for making a chart to track each week's efforts. Some of the book's double-page spreads explain and demonstrate several exercise ideas related to a theme. . . . Other spreads present a single activity. . . . Colorful photos show smiling children demonstrating the moves. A cheerful introduction to some basic exercises." Booklist

Includes glossary

Whitford, Rebecca

Little yoga; a toddler's first book of yoga. [by] Rebecca Whitford & Martina Selway. Holt & Co. 2005 un il $9.95

Grades: PreK K 1   **613.7**

1. Yoga
ISBN 0-8050-7879-7

"This small, square book offers a simple sequence of yoga poses designed especially for toddlers. On each cheerfully designed spread, a simple, black-outlined illustration shows a smiling toddler in a pose; on the opposite page, an animal mimics the same motion. . . . Appended material includes tips for adults to help guide children through the motions and photos of toddlers performing the poses." Booklist

613.9 Birth control, reproductive technology, sex hygiene, sexual techniques

Cole, Joanna

Asking about sex & growing up; a question-and-answer book for kids. illustrated by Bill Thomas. rev ed.; Collins 2009 89p il $15.99; pa $6.99

Grades: 4 5 6   **613.9**

1. Sex education
ISBN 978-0-06-142987-3; 0-06-142987-2; 978-0-06-142986-6 pa; 0-06-142986-4 pa

LC 2008022710

First published 1988 by Morrow Junior Books

This book "offers straightforward information about topics such as physical changes in puberty, masturbation, birth control, pregnancy, homosexuality, and STDs. . . . Libraries . . . should consider adding it as a source of basic information for curious preteens." SLJ

Harris, Robie H.

★ **It's** perfectly normal; a book about changing bodies, growing up, sex & sexual health. illustrated by Michael Emberley. 3rd ed.; Candlewick Press 2009 93p il $22.99; pa $12.99

Grades: 4 5 6 7   **613.9**

1. Puberty 2. Sex education
ISBN 978-0-7636-4483-3; 0-7636-4483-8; 978-0-7636-4484-0 pa; 0-7636-4484-6 pa

LC 2009008457

First published 1994

This provides information about sex, puberty, family relationships and reproduction, sexual decision-making and birth control, abortion laws, sexual abuse, sexual health, sexually transmitted diseases, and (new in this edition) internet safety.

"This caring, conscientious, and well-crafted book will be a fine library resource as well as a marvelous adjunct to the middle-school sex-education curriculum. . . . The bold color cartoon drawings are very candid. . . . Harris' text [is] as forthright as Emberley's art." Booklist [review of 1994 ed.]

614 Forensic medicine; incidence of injuries, wounds, disease; public preventive medicine

Spilsbury, Richard

Bones speak! solving crimes from the past. Enslow Publishers 2009 48p il (Solve that crime!) lib bdg $23.93

Grades: 5 6 7 8   **614**

1. Forensic sciences 2. Forensic anthropology
ISBN 978-0-7660-3377-1 lib bdg; 0-7660-3377-5 lib bdg

LC 2008-33309

This "title boasts in-depth information, sidebars detailing events of true crime, and activities that will increase understanding. . . . Photographs are colorful, well-captioned, and related to the text." SLJ

Includes glossary and bibliographical references

614.4 Incidence of and public measures to prevent disease

Barnard, Bryn

★ **Outbreak**; plagues that changed history. written and illustrated by Bryn Barnard. Crown Publishers 2005 47p il maps $17.95

Grades: 5 6 7 8   **614.4**

1. Diseases 2. Epidemics 3. Diseases and history -- Juvenile literature 4. Communicable diseases -- Juvenile literature
ISBN 0-375-82986-5

LC 2005-15086

This "volume explores specific plagues that have impacted society. Barnard begins with an introduction to microbes and the positive and negative effects that they can have on humans. A history of the study of microorganisms follows. The bulk of the book then focuses on specific plagues with a chapter devoted to each, including the Black Death, smallpox, yellow fever, cholera, tuberculosis, and influenza. The final chapter discusses the modern struggle against disease. . . . The evocative paintings help to clarify the text. Browsers and report writers alike will find this to be a fascinating and informative resource." SLJ

Cunningham, Kevin

Pandemics. Children's Press 2011 48p il (True book: disasters) lib bdg $28; pa $6.99

Grades: 3 4 5   **614.4**

1. Epidemics 2. Communicable diseases
ISBN 978-0-531-25423-3 lib bdg; 0-531-25423-2; 978-0-531-26628-1 pa; 0-531-26628-1 pa

LC 2011007507

This describes epidemics of smallpox, cholera, plague, influenza, and HIV/AIDS.

This is "thoughtfully designed. . . . The information . . . is right on target: concise, accurate, and thorough. . . . The photographs . . . are especially effective at putting a human face on large-scale devastation." Booklist

Includes glossary and bibliographical references

Gleason, Carrie

Feasting bedbugs, mites, and ticks. Crabtree Pub. Co. 2010 32p il (Creepy crawlies) lib bdg $26.60; pa $8.95

Grades: 4 5 6 7   **614.4**
  1. Mites 2. Ticks 3. Bedbugs
  ISBN 978-0-7787-2500-8 lib bdg; 0-7787-2500-6 lib
  bdg; 978-0-7787-2507-7 pa; 0-7787-2507-3 pa
                                                          LC 2010009552
"The informational yet easy-to-read text in double-page
spreads explains the classification, anatomy, life cycles,
and ideal feeding and living conditions for mites, ticks, and
bedbugs as well as the differences among them. . . . Children will be most interested in the long history, myths, and
lore associated with these pests as well as the eye-catching
layout, with numerous color photographs. . . . [This is an]
equally repulsive and fascinating book." Booklist
  Includes glossary and bibliographical references

Piddock, Charles
  Outbreak; science seeks safeguards for global health.
[Caryn Oryniak, consultant] National Geographic 2008
64p il (National Geographic investigates) $17.95; lib bdg
$27.90
Grades: 4 5 6 7   **614.4**
  1. Diseases 2. Epidemics 3. Medicine -- Research
  4. Public health -- Juvenile literature 5. Virus diseases
  -- Juvenile literature 6. Communicable diseases --
  Juvenile literature
  ISBN 978-1-4263-0357-9; 1-4263-0357-2; 978-1-
  4263-0263-3 lib bdg; 1-4263-0263-0 lib bdg
                                                          LC 2009-275290
This is an "introduction to the fight against infectious
diseases, including scientists who discovered various viruses and bacteria. The text outlines how we have learned
to fight nature's harmful strains and to use others to our advantage; it also provides the latest findings on bird flu and
SARS, Ebola and AIDS, and highly resistant strains of tuberculosis." Publisher's note

Platt, Richard
  Plagues, pox, and pestilence; written by Richard Platt;
illustrated by John Kelly. Kingfisher 2011 48 p. col. ill.
(hardcover) $15.99
Grades: 4 5 6   **614.4**
  1. Diseases -- Causes 2. Animals -- Diseases 3.
  Communicable diseases -- History 4. Epidemics
  -- History 5. Animals as carriers of disease 6.
  Communicable diseases -- Transmission
  ISBN 0753466872; 9780753466872
                                                          LC 2011041641
Author Richard Platt provides a "history of disease and
pestilence, told from the point of view of the bugs and pests
that cause them. The book features case histories of specific
epidemics, 'eyewitness' accounts from the rats, flies, ticks
and creepy-crawlies who spread diseases, plus plenty of
fascinating facts and figures on the biggest and worst afflic-
tions." (Publisher's note)

Walker, Richard, 1951-
  Epidemics & plagues; foreword by Denise Grady.
Kingfisher 2006 63p il (Kingfisher knowledge) hardcover
o.p. $12.95
Grades: 4 5 6 7   **614.4**
  1. Diseases 2. Epidemics
  ISBN 978-0-7534-6035-1; 0-7534-6035-1; 978-0-
  7534-6161-7 pa; 0-7534-6161-7 pa

Discusses the spread of infectious diseases and their impact on human populations, from the Black Death in medieval Europe to such modern diseases as AIDS and West Nile
virus, as well as efforts to stop the spread of these diseases.
  Includes glossary

614.5 Incidence of and public measures to
prevent specific diseases and kinds of diseases

Ballard, Carol
  AIDS and other epidemics. Gareth Stevens Pub. 2008
48p il map (What if we do nothing?) lib bdg $31
Grades: 5 6 7 8   **614.5**
  1. Epidemics 2. AIDS (Disease) 3. Communicable
  diseases
  ISBN 978-1-4339-0085-3 lib bdg; 1-4339-0085-8
  lib bdg
                                                          LC 2008029189
"Using intelligent, focused text; an open design; vivid
photos; and excellent maps, [this] book demands attention."
Booklist
  Includes bibliographical references

Murphy, Jim
  ★ An **American** plague; the true and terrifying story
of the yellow fever epidemic of 1793. Clarion Bks. 2003
165p il map $18
Grades: 5 6 7 8   **614.5**
  1. Yellow fever 2. Philadelphia (Pa.) -- History 3.
  Yellow fever -- Pennsylvania -- Philadelphia -- History
  -- 18th century 4. Yellow fever -- Pennsylvania --
  Philadelphia -- History -- 18th century -- Juvenile
  literature
  ISBN 0-395-77608-2
                                                          LC 2002-151355
A Newbery Medal honor book, 2004
"Murphy culls from a number of historical records the
story of the yellow fever epidemic that swept Philadelphia in 1793, skillfully drawing out from these sources the
fear and drama of the time and making them immediate to
modern readers. . . . Thoroughly documented, with an annotated source list, the work is both rigorous and inviting."
Horn Book

Person, Stephen
  Bubonic plague; the Black Death! Bearport Pub. 2010
32p il map (Nightmare plagues) lib bdg $25.27
Grades: 4 5 6 7   **614.5**
  1. Plague
  ISBN 978-1-936088-03-4; 1-936088-03-7
This describes what causes bubonic plague and how it
affects the body.
  "The writing is accessible and interspersed with interesting photographs and fact boxes. . . . [The book relies] on an
honest discussion of [bubonic plague and is an] . . . effective,
easily navigated [introduction]." SLJ
  Includes glossary and bibliographical references

  Malaria; super killer! Bearport Pub. 2011 32p il map
(Nightmare plagues) lib bdg $25.27

Grades: 4 5 6 7   **614.5**
1. Malaria
ISBN 978-1-936088-07-2 lib bdg; 1-936088-07-X
lib bdg

LC 2010012018

Discover what causes malaria and how it affects the body.

"The writing is accessible and interspersed with interesting photographs and fact boxes. . . . [The book relies] on an honest discussion of [malaria and is an] . . . effective, easily navigated [introduction]." SLJ

Includes glossary and bibliographical references

Reingold, Adam
Smallpox; is it over? Bearport Pub. 2010 32p il map (Nightmare plagues) lib bdg $25.27
Grades: 4 5 6 7   **614.5**
1. Smallpox
ISBN 978-1-936088-02-7; 1-936088-02-9

LC 2010009371

Discover what causes smallpox and how it affects the body.

"The writing is accessible and interspersed with interesting photographs and fact boxes. . . . [The book relies] on an honest discussion of [smallpox and is an] . . . effective, easily navigated [introduction]." SLJ

Includes glossary and bibliographical references

Rudolph, Jessica
The **flu** of 1918; millions dead worldwide! Bearport Pub. 2011 32p il map (Nightmare plagues) lib bdg $25.27
Grades: 4 5 6 7   **614.5**
1. Influenza
ISBN 978-1-936088-05-8 lib bdg; 1-936088-05-3
lib bdg

LC 2010004684

Discover what caused the Influenza epidemic of 1918 and how it affected the body.

"The writing is accessible and interspersed with interesting photographs and fact boxes. . . . [The book relies] on an honest discussion of [Influenza epidemic of 1918 and is an] . . . effective, easily navigated [introduction]." SLJ

Includes glossary and bibliographical references

615   Pharmacology and therapeutics

Hyde, Natalie
What is germ theory? Crabtree Pub. Co. 2011 64p il (Shaping modern science) lib bdg $30.60; pa $10.95
Grades: 5 6 7 8   **615**
1. Chemists 2. Germ theory of disease 3. Microbiologists 4. Writers on science
ISBN 978-0-7787-7201-9 lib bdg; 0-7787-7201-9 lib bdg; 978-0-7787-7208-8 pa; 0-7787-7208-X pa

LC 2010052631

This title is "not only written and organized well, but [it is] also gorgeous in design. Full-color photographs and illustrations are set over colorful backgrounds that add depth but not distraction. [The title] includes thought-provoking quotes from famous authors and scientists and some eyebrow-raising 'Quick Facts' throughout." SLJ

Includes glossary and bibliographical references

Petersen, Christine
The **apothecary**. Marshall Cavendish Benchmark 2010 48p il (Colonial people) lib bdg $29.93
Grades: 3 4 5 6   **615**
1. Pharmacy
ISBN 978-0-7614-4795-5; 0-7614-4795-4

LC 2009015274

This describes the life of a colonial apothecary and his importance to the community, as well as everyday life, responsibilities, and social practices during that time.

"The type font, just slightly larger than usual, makes the text very visually appealing. . . . [The] book is liberally illustrated with artwork dating from the colonial period . . . [and] information boxes offer supplemental material." Libr Media Connect

Includes glossary and bibliographical references

615.8   Specific therapies and kinds of therapies

Beccia, Carlyn
I feel better with a frog in my throat: history's strangest cures; written and illustrated by Carlyn Beccia. Houghton Mifflin Books for Children 2010 48p il $17.99
Grades: 2 3 4   **615.8**
1. Therapeutics 2. Medicine -- History 3. Medical misconceptions -- Juvenile literature
ISBN 978-0-547-22570-8; 0-547-22570-9

LC 2010-01138

This discusses some of history's "disgusting and futile medical practices. . . . [Characterized by] dry-witted artwork, conversational text, [and] engaging historical detective work, [this book] asks readers to guess which 'cures' may actually have helped a handful of ailments. . . . The author provides intriguing background information on the cures—where they arose, why they were thougth to be efficacious—and pulls more than one gem out of the nastiness." Kirkus

Bozzo, Linda
Therapy dog heroes. Enslow Publishers 2010 48p il (Amazing working dogs with American humane) lib bdg $23.93
Grades: 2 3 4   **615.8**
1. Working dogs
ISBN 978-0-7660-3200-2; 0-7660-3200-0

LC 2008048020

"The text opens with a true story of a therapy dog, and then it explains the history of the therapy dog and the training methods used to transform an ordinary dog into a canine hero." Publisher's note

Includes glossary and bibliographical references

615.9   Toxicology

Day, Jeff
Don't touch that! the book of gross, poisonous, and downright icky plants and critters. Chicago Review Press 2008 108p il pa $9.95
Grades: 3 4 5 6   **615.9**
1. Poisonous plants 2. Poisonous animals 3. Poisons

and poisoning
ISBN 978-1-55652-711-1 pa; 1-556527-11-X pa
LC 2007027466

"Packed with potentially lifesaving information, this guide is humorous without sacrificing usefulness. The author, a medical doctor, begins with some basic plants (poison ivy, poison oak, and poison sumac) that might be encountered. Drawings of the leaves are carefully labeled and accompanied by the warning not to touch any part of the plant, and not to burn it as even the smoke can irritate. Poisonous insects, spiders, amphibians, reptiles, and mammals are also included, and every entry explains why the creature's venom causes the bad reaction it does and how to treat it.... Genuinely funny, colorful drawings on every page amplify the text and make it memorable." SLJ

Jakubiak, David J.
What can we do about toxins in the environment? PowerKids Press 2011 24p il (Protecting the planet) lib bdg $21.25; pa $8.25
Grades: 2 3 4   **615.9**
1. Pollution 2. Poisons and poisoning
ISBN 978-1-4488-4987-1 lib bdg; 978-1-4488-5121-8 pa
LC 2011000151

This explains the harm that toxins do in the environment and what can be done about them.

"Every spread has a full-page, thoughtfully captioned color photograph.... School and public libraries will want [this title] to round out collections or as [an update] to replace older books." SLJ
Includes glossary

Owen, Ruth
Disgusting food invaders. Bearport Pub. 2011 24p il (Up close and gross) lib bdg $22.61
Grades: 3 4 5   **615.9**
1. Parasites 2. Food contamination
ISBN 978-1-61772-126-7; 1-61772-126-3
LC 2010044417

This describes impurities and parasites which can be found in food, including fruit flies, moths, cheese mites, mold, grubs, rat hairs and insect parts, maggots, and bacteria.

"Never have the wonders of electron microscopy been more thrillingly displayed.... These knife-sharp, all-too-explicit photos are riveting. The [text doesn't] trail far behind in appeal either." SLJ
Includes glossary and bibliographical references

616 Diseases

Calamandrei, Camilla
★ **Fever**. Marshall Cavendish Benchmark 2009 64p il (Health alert) $22.95
Grades: 4 5 6 7   **616**
1. Fever
ISBN 978-0-7614-2915-9; 0-7614-2915-8
LC 2007-26002

This "title features a handsome format, with well-chosen illustrations, a substantial amount of information, and some practical insights." Booklist
Includes glossary

Dendy, Leslie A.
★ **Guinea** pig scientists; bold self-experimenters in science and medicine. [by] Leslie Dendy and Mel Boring; with illustrations by C. B. Mordan. Henry Holt & Co. 2005 213p il $19.95
Grades: 5 6 7 8   **616**
1. Scientists 2. Medicine -- Research 3. Self-experimentation in medicine
ISBN 9780805073164; 0-8050-7316-7
LC 2004-52364

This is a collection of "stories of human 'guinea pigs' who have tested the limits of the human body for the sake of science. Starting with Sir Charles Blagden, M.D., and his heat experiments, the stories are chronologically ordered from the 1770s to 1989. Included are descriptions of experiments dealing with digestion, laughing gas, vaccinations, mosquitoes as vectors of yellow fever, radioactivity, [and] G-forces." (Sci Books Films) Index.

"The authors offer 10 ... case studies of scientists from the past several centuries who became their own test subjects.... The accounts are lively, compelling, and not always for the squeamish.... The authors cogently discuss each experiment's significance in advancing our understanding of science and medicine. Illustrated with a mix of period black-and-white photos and Mordan's nineteenth-century-style portraits ... the episodes make riveting reading." Booklist
Includes bibliographical references

Evans, Michael
The **adventures** of Medical Man; kids' illnesses and injuries explained. by Michael Evans & David Wichman; illustrated by Gareth Williams. Annick 2010 72p il $21.95; pa $12.95
Grades: 5 6 7 8   **616**
1. Diseases 2. Wounds and injuries
ISBN 978-1-55451-263-8; 1-55451-263-8; 978-1-55451-262-1 pa; 1-55451-262-X pa

"Using tangible experiences that kids can relate to, this book does a fantastic job of explaining common medical issues in an accessible way. A variety of heroic characters explain otherwise complicated and seemingly scary conditions and occurrences. Through the use of science fiction, adventure, and comics, the book covers nut allergies, concussions, broken bones, strep throat, ear infections, and asthma.... The extensive glossary is straightforward and user-friendly. The pumped-up graphic illustrations are extremely engaging and further bring these otherwise abstract concepts to life." SLJ

Murphy, Patricia J.
Illness; [by] Patricia J Murphy. Heinemann Library 2008 32p il (Tough topics) lib bdg $25.36; pa $7.99
Grades: PreK K 1 2 3   **616**
1. Diseases
ISBN 978-1-4034-9777-2 lib bdg; 978-1-4034-9782-6 pa
LC 2007005345

This "book talks about different kinds of illnesses, coping mechanisms, and varieties of medical treatments available.... Murphy gives an overview of the topic in a way that young readers can understand.... The two-page chapters include full-color photos and two paragraphs of text that are frank yet sensitive in their approach." SLJ
Includes glossary and bibliographical references

Nardo, Don

Cure quest; the science of stem cell research. by Don Nardo. Compass Point Books 2009 48p il (Headline science) lib bdg $27.93; pa $7.95

Grades: 5 6 7   **616**

1. Stem cell research

ISBN 978-0-7565-3371-7 lib bdg; 0-7565-3371-6 lib bdg; 978-0-7565-3374-8 pa; 0-7565-3374-0 pa

LC 2008-5738

Explains the science behind stem cell research.

"Color photos and graphics provide visual information; a timeline is helpful to find fast facts, and the Facthound Web site provides student with additional information." Libr Media Connect

Includes glossary and bibliographical references

Ollhoff, Jim

What are germs? ABDO Pub. Co. 2010 32p il (A history of germs) $27.07

Grades: 3 4 5 6   **616**

1. Bacteria 2. Germ theory of disease

ISBN 978-1-60453-502-0; 1-60453-502-4

"What Are Germs? includes kinds of germs and germ-fighting organizations. The short, informative chapters provide plenty of details for reports. The illustrations, many of which are color photos, enhance the information." SLJ

Includes glossary

Silverstein, Alvin

Tapeworms, foot fungus, lice, and more; the yucky disease book. by Alvin Silverstein, Virginia Silverstein, and Laura Silverstein Nunn; illustrated by Gerald Kelley. Enslow Publishers 2010 48p il (Yucky science) lib bdg $23.93

Grades: 3 4 5 6   **616**

1. Diseases 2. Medicine

ISBN 978-0-7660-3314-6 lib bdg; 0-7660-3314-7 lib bdg

LC 2009012282

"Explores 'yucky' diseases, including leprosy, plague, tapeworms, and more" Publisher's note

Includes glossary and bibliographical references

Stoyles, Pennie

The A-Z of health. Black Rabbit/Smart Apple 2010 6v il set $119.70

Grades: 5 6 7 8   **616**

1. Health 2. Reference books 3. Medicine -- Encyclopedias

ISBN 978-1-59920-654-7; 1-59920-654-4

"This reference set provides a simple, brief, and easy-to-read introduction to key aspects of physical and mental health, including various body processes and diseases as well as information on treatments and preventative measures. . . . The explanations are concise, clear, and easy to understand. In addition to the abundance of images, the large type and white space that is prevalent on every page will make this set accessible to a broad array of young readers." Booklist

616.2   Diseases of respiratory system

Chilman-Blair, Kim

Medikidz explain sleep apnea; [by] Kim Chilman-Blair and Shawn Deloache; medical content reviewed for accuracy by Paul Gringras and David Rapoport. Rosen Central 2011 40p il (Superheroes on a medical mission) lib bdg $29.25; pa $11.75

Grades: 3 4 5 6   **616.2**

1. Sleep apnea 2. Superheroes 3. Graphic novels

ISBN 978-1-4358-9459-4 lib bdg; 1-4358-9459-6 lib bdg; 978-1-4488-1841-9 pa; 1-4488-1841-9 pa

LC 2010002554

"A team of superheroes rides around on a medi-jet and whisks ill children, or their siblings, off to Mediland, a giant replica of the human body, to teach them about [sleep apnea]. . . . The comic panels are visually exciting with eye-popping colors. Inside Mediland, the science behind various conditions is expertly simplified and explained with a sometimes tongue-in-cheek repartee among the characters as well as with very basic analogies reminiscent of video games. . . . This approach makes the health issues accessible and much less scary for readers wanting to learn more for personal or academic reasons." SLJ

Includes glossary and bibliographical references

Medikidz explain swine flu; [by] Kim Chilman-Blair; medical content reviewed for accuracy by John McCauley and Calum Semple. Rosen Central 2011 40p il (Superheroes on a medical mission) lib bdg $29.25; pa $11.75

Grades: 3 4 5 6   **616.2**

1. Superheroes 2. Graphic novels 3. Swine influenza

ISBN 978-1-4358-9457-0 lib bdg; 1-4358-9457-X lib bdg; 978-1-4488-1843-3 pa; 1-4488-1843-5 pa

LC 2010003236

"A team of superheroes rides around on a medi-jet and whisks ill children, or their siblings, off to Mediland, a giant replica of the human body, to teach them about [swine flu]. . . . The comic panels are visually exciting with eye-popping colors. Inside Mediland, the science behind various conditions is expertly simplified and explained with a sometimes tongue-in-cheek repartee among the characters as well as with very basic analogies reminiscent of video games. . . . This approach makes the health issues accessible and much less scary for readers wanting to learn more for personal or academic reasons." SLJ

Includes glossary and bibliographical references

Cobb, Vicki

★ **Your** body battles a cold; written by Vicki Cobb; photomicrographs by Dennis Kunkel; illustrated by Andrew N. Harris. Millbrook Press 2009 32p il (Body battles) lib bdg $25.26

Grades: 3 4 5   **616.2**

1. Immune system 2. Cold (Disease)

ISBN 978-0-8225-6813-1; 0-8225-6813-6

LC 2008002839

Color illustrations and photomicrographs show what happens when a human body is attacked by a cold virus

"The body's immune system has never looked like this before with plasma cells using sling shots to fire antibodies into viruses, platelets riding inner tubes down a stream of blood, and viruses multiplying in a 'Germco' factory. [The] title introduces five or six defense cells, disguised as superheroes protecting the body from adversarial viruses. . . . The oversize text uses metaphors that readers will understand. . . . The micrographs will fascinate and compel young readers to read everything." SLJ

Includes glossary and bibliographical references

Glaser, Jason

Asthma. Capstone Press 2006 24p il (First facts: health matters) $21.26

Grades: K 1 2 3   **616.2**

  1. Asthma

  ISBN 978-0-7368-4287-7; 0-7368-4287-X

                               LC 2004031021

"Describes asthma and its causes, symptoms, and treatments." Publisher's note

Includes bibliographical references

Colds. Capstone Press 2006 24p il (First facts: health matters) $21.26

Grades: K 1 2 3   **616.2**

  1. Cold (Disease)

  ISBN 978-0-7368-4289-1; 0-7368-4289-6

                               LC 2004031051

"Introduces readers to the common cold, its symptoms, treatments, and prevention." Publisher's note

Includes bibliographical references

Flu. Capstone Press 2006 24p il (First facts: health matters) $21.26

Grades: K 1 2 3   **616.2**

  1. Influenza

  ISBN 978-0-7368-4290-7; 0-7368-4290-X

                               LC 2004031052

"Introduces the flu, its symptoms, treatments, and prevention." Publisher's note

Includes bibliographical references

Hoffmann, Gretchen

  ★ The **flu**. Marshall Cavendish Benchmark 2007 64p il (Health alert) lib bdg $31.36

Grades: 4 5 6 7   **616.2**

  1. Influenza

  ISBN 978-0-7614-2208-2; 0-7614-2208-0 \

                               LC 2006011980

This "title features a handsome format, with well-chosen illustrations, a substantial amount of information, and some practical insights." Booklist

Includes glossary and bibliographical references

Landau, Elaine

  ★ **Asthma**. Marshall Cavendish Benchmark 2009 32p il (Head-to-toe health) lib bdg $19.95

Grades: 2 3 4   **616.2**

  1. Asthma

  ISBN 978-0-7614-2845-9; 0-7614-2845-3

                               LC 2007-34998

"Photo illustrations are apt and age appropriate. . . . Pervading the [book] . . . is an overall sense of reassurance that even if something hurts, 'all better' is never too far away. Appealing and readable nonfiction." SLJ

Includes glossary and bibliographical references

  ★ The **common** cold. Marshall Cavendish Benchmark 2009 32p il (Head-to-toe health) lib bdg $19.95

Grades: 2 3 4   **616.2**

  1. Cold (Disease)

  ISBN 978-0-7614-2844-2; 0-7614-2844-5

                               LC 2007-35005

"Photo illustrations are apt and age appropriate. . . . Pervading the [book] . . . is an overall sense of reassurance that even if something hurts, 'all better' is never too far away. Appealing and readable nonfiction." SLJ

Includes glossary and bibliographical references

Moore-Mallinos, Jennifer

  I have asthma; illustrated by Rosa M. Cirto. Barron's 2007 35p il (What do I know about?) pa $6.99

Grades: K 1 2 3   **616.2**

  1. Asthma

  ISBN 0-7641-3785-9

After a young boy has trouble breathing during soccer practice, he is taken to his doctor who says that he has asthma, but he learns that with proper treatment and medical supervision, his asthma can be kept under control.

"The easy text, combined with soft, rounded figures in the colorful illustrations, results in a sensitively told story that offers encouragement to children suffering from this condition, complete with helpful advice." SLJ

Ollhoff, Jim

  The **flu**. ABDO Pub. Co. 2010 32p il (A history of germs) $27.07

Grades: 3 4 5 6   **616.2**

  1. Viruses 2. Influenza

  ISBN 978-1-60453-498-6; 1-60453-498-2

                               LC 2008055063

"Flu provides a concise look at the illness, pandemics, treatments, and recent strains, including H1N1. . . . The short, informative chapters provide plenty of details for reports. The illustrations, many of which are color photos, enhance the information." SLJ

Includes glossary

Robbins, Lynette

  How to deal with asthma. PowerKids Press 2010 24p il (Kids' health) lib bdg $21.25

Grades: 2 3 4   **616.2**

  1. Asthma

  ISBN 978-1-4042-8141-7 lib bdg; 1-4042-8141-X lib bdg

                               LC 2009-7653

"Hypothetical situations with fictional characters put readers in the moment and provide a solid foundation for comprehending [asthma]. . . . Robbins maintains a comforting tone, reassuring readers that it is possible to lead active lives with proper attention to diet and guidance from parents and doctors." SLJ

Includes glossary

Royston, Angela

  Asthma. Black Rabbit Books 2009 30p il (How's your health) lib bdg $27.10

Grades: 1 2 3   **616.2**

  1. Asthma

  ISBN 978-1-59920-219-8 lib bdg; 1-59920-219-0 lib bdg

                               LC 2007-35689

First published 2004 by Heinemann Library

"Encourages further learning with sidebars that help readers think concretely about the subject. . . . Altogether a pitch perfect presentation." SLJ

Includes glossary and bibliographical references

Explaining asthma. Smart Apple Media 2010 45p il (Explaining) lib bdg $34.25

Grades: 5 6 7 8   **616.2**
1. Asthma
ISBN 978-1-59920-315-7 lib bdg; 1-59920-315-4 lib bdg
LC 2008-49284

Describes what living with asthma is like, discussing symptoms, triggers, treatments, and lifestyle changes that may be necessary to prevent asthma attacks

The book provides a "basic [overview] of the health concerns related to the disease; information on diagnosis and treatment; and a discussion of the challenges or complications experienced by the affected person and their family/friends, and how to manage those problems. . . . The incorporation of quotes and personal accounts in 'Case Notes' sidebars adds to the sensitive tone found throughout [the title]." SLJ

Includes glossary

616.3   Diseases of digestive system

Allman, Toney
Obesity. Cherry Lake Pub. 2009 32p il (Health at risk) lib bdg $27.07

Grades: 4 5 6 7   **616.3**
1. Obesity
ISBN 978-1-60279-285-2 lib bdg; 1-60279-285-2 lib bdg
LC 2008017499

This describes the causes and dangers of obesity and the many efforts being made to help people control their weight.

"Great for reports or reluctant readers." Booklist
Includes bibliographical references

Bjorklund, Ruth
★ Cystic fibrosis. Marshall Cavendish Benchmark 2009 64p il (Health alert) $22.95

Grades: 4 5 6 7   **616.3**
1. Cystic fibrosis
ISBN 978-0-7614-2912-8; 0-7614-2912-3
LC 2007-46674

This "title features a handsome format, with well-chosen illustrations, a substantial amount of information, and some practical insights." Booklist

Cobb, Vicki
★ Your body battles a stomachache; written by Vicki Cobb; with photomicrographs by Dennis Kunkel; illustrations by Andrew N. Harris. Millbrook Press 2009 32p il (Body battles) lib bdg $25.26

Grades: 3 4 5   **616.3**
1. Stomach 2. Intestines 3. Immune system
ISBN 978-0-8225-7166-7 lib bdg; 0-8225-7166-8 lib bdg
LC 2008002852

Color illustrations and photomicrographs show what happens when a human digestive system is attacked by a rotavirus

"The body's immune system has never looked like this before with plasma cells using sling shots to fire antibodies into viruses, platelets riding inner tubes down a stream of blood, and viruses multiplying in a 'Germco' factory. [The] title introduces five or six defense cells, disguised as superheroes protecting the body from adversarial viruses. . . . The oversize text uses metaphors that readers will understand. . . . The micrographs will fascinate and compel young readers to read everything." SLJ

Includes glossary and bibliographical references

Glaser, Jason
Obesity. Capstone Press 2007 24p il (First facts: health matters) $21.26

Grades: K 1 2 3   **616.3**
1. Obesity
ISBN 978-0-7368-6331-5; 0-7368-6331-1
LC 2006002832

"Describes obesity, how and why it occurs, and how to treat and prevent it." Publisher's note

Includes bibliographical references

Hicks, Terry Allan
★ Obesity. Marshall Cavendish Benchmark 2009 63p il (Health alert) $22.95

Grades: 4 5 6 7   **616.3**
1. Obesity
ISBN 978-0-7614-2911-1; 0-7614-2911-5
LC 2007-31246

This "title features a handsome format, with well-chosen illustrations, a substantial amount of information, and some practical insights." Booklist

Includes glossary

Hunt, Jamie
Tired of being teased; obesity and others. Mason Crest Publishers 2010 48p il (Kids & obesity) lib bdg $19.95; pa $7.95

Grades: 3 4 5   **616.3**
1. Obesity
ISBN 978-1-4222-1711-5 lib bdg; 1-4222-1711-6 lib bdg; 978-1-4222-1899-0 pa; 1-4222-1899-6 pa
LC 2010012759

Teaches that a person is more than appearance, and discusses how to deal with being teased about one's appearance.

This book about obesity "presents the expected information about the food pyramid, the need for physical activity, and the influence of the media on our psyches. Where the material shines is in its holistic approach. Readers are encouraged to develop their inner lives as much as their physical selves and to take responsibility for their own health and eating habits. . . . This brightly-colored, ego-boosting, responsibility-championing . . . [book] is a winner." SLJ

Includes bibliographical references

Powell, Jillian
Explaining cystic fibrosis. Smart Apple Media 2010 45p il (Explaining) lib bdg $34.25

Grades: 5 6 7 8   **616.3**
  1. Cystic fibrosis
  ISBN 978-1-59920-312-6 lib bdg; 1-59920-312-X
  lib bdg

                             LC 2008-49288

Describes the illness, including its causes, how it is diagnosed, current treatments for the illness, and how those with cystic fibrosis lead everyday lives

  The book provides a "basic [overview] of the health concerns related to the disease; information on diagnosis and treatment; and a discussion of the challenges or complications experienced by the affected person and their family/friends, and how to manage those problems. . . . The incorporation of quotes and personal accounts in 'Case Notes' sidebars adds to the sensitive tone found throughout [the title]." SLJ

  Includes glossary and bibliographical references

Robbins, Lynette
  How to deal with obesity. PowerKids Press 2010 24p il (Kids' health) lib bdg $21.25

Grades: 2 3 4   **616.3**
  1. Obesity
  ISBN 978-1-4042-8143-1 lib bdg; 1-4042-8143-6
  lib bdg

                              LC 2009-8902

"Hypothetical situations with fictional characters put readers in the moment and provide a solid foundation for comprehending [obesity]. . . . Robbins maintains a comforting tone, reassuring readers that it is possible to lead active lives with proper attention to diet and guidance from parents and doctors." SLJ

  Includes glossary

Simons, Rae
  Too many Sunday dinners; family and diet. Mason Crest Publishers 2010 48p il (Kids & obesity) lib bdg $19.95; pa $7.95

Grades: 3 4 5   **616.3**
  1. Obesity 2. Heredity
  ISBN 978-1-4222-1713-9 lib bdg; 1-4222-1713-2 lib
  bdg; 978-1-4222-1901-0 pa; 1-4222-1901-1 pa

                            LC 2010019188

Discusses how obesity can be hereditary.

  This book "presents the expected information about the food pyramid, the need for physical activity, and the influence of the media on our psyches. Where the material shines is in its holistic approach. Readers are encouraged to develop their inner lives as much as their physical selves and to take responsibility for their own health and eating habits. . . . This brightly-colored, ego-boosting, responsibility-championing . . . [book] is a winner." SLJ

  Includes bibliographical references

Thompson, Helen
  Weighted down; when being overweight makes you sick. Mason Crest Publishers 2011 48p il (Kids & obesity) lib bdg $19.95; pa $7.95

Grades: 3 4 5   **616.3**
  1. Obesity
  ISBN 978-1-4222-1708-5 lib bdg; 1-4222-1708-6 lib
  bdg; 978-1-4222-1896-9 pa; 1-4222-1896-1 pa

                            LC 2010022266

Learn about the health risks associated with being overweight and how to combat excessive weight gain.

  This book "presents the expected information about the food pyramid, the need for physical activity, and the influence of the media on our psyches. Where the material shines is in its holistic approach. Readers are encouraged to develop their inner lives as much as their physical selves and to take responsibility for their own health and eating habits. . . . This brightly-colored, ego-boosting, responsibility-championing . . . [book] is a winner." SLJ

  Includes bibliographical references

616.4 Diseases of endocrine, hematopoietic, lymphatic, glandular systems; diseases of male breast

Glaser, Jason
  Juvenile diabetes. Capstone Press 2007 24p il (First facts: health matters) $21.26

Grades: K 1 2 3   **616.4**
  1. Diabetes
  ISBN 978-0-7368-6392-6; 0-7368-6392-3

                            LC 2006002820

"Describes juvenile diabetes, why it occurs, and how it is diagnosed and treated." Publisher' note

  Includes bibliographical references

Loughrey, Anita
  Explaining diabetes. Smart Apple Media 2010 45p il (Explaining) lib bdg $34.25

Grades: 5 6 7 8   **616.4**
  1. Diabetes
  ISBN 978-1-59920-314-0 lib bdg; 1-59920-314-6
  lib bdg

                            LC 2008-49290

Provides an overview of Type 1 and Type 2 diabetes, discussing causes and symptoms, recommended and required lifestyle changes, how the disease is managed, and possible complications that may occur

  The book provides a "basic [overview] of the health concerns related to the disease; information on diagnosis and treatment; and a discussion of the challenges or complications experienced by the affected person and their family/friends, and how to manage those problems. . . . The incorporation of quotes and personal accounts in 'Case Notes' sidebars adds to the sensitive tone found throughout [the title]." SLJ

  Includes glossary and bibliographical references

Pirner, Connie White
  Even little kids get diabetes; pictures by Nadine Bernard Westcott. Whitman, A. 1991 un il hardcover o.p. pa $6.95

Grades: K 1   **616.4**
  1. Diabetes
  ISBN 0-8075-2158-2; 0-8075-2159-0 pa

                            LC 90-12738

A young girl who has had diabetes since she was two years old describes her adjustments to the disease

  "Language is simple, age appropriate, and effectively gets the point across. The ink-and-watercolor drawings are lively and often upbeat. . . . Perhaps the most valuable part of the book is the 'note for parents,' which relates Pirner's personal experience over the last three years in caring for a diabetic child." SLJ

Robbins, Lynette
How to deal with diabetes. PowerKids Press 2010 24p il (Kids' health) lib bdg $21.25
Grades: 2 3 4   616.4
1. Diabetes
ISBN 978-1-4042-8144-8 lib bdg; 1-4042-8144-4 lib bdg

LC 2009-10467

"Hypothetical situations with fictional characters put readers in the moment and provide a solid foundation for comprehending [diabetes]. . . . Robbins maintains a comforting tone, reassuring readers that it is possible to lead active lives with proper attention to diet and guidance from parents and doctors." SLJ

Includes glossary

616.5   Diseases of integument

Caffey, Donna
Yikes-lice! illustrations by Patrick Girouard. Whitman, A. 1998 un il $14.95; pa $5.95
Grades: K 1 2 3   616.5
1. Lice
ISBN 0-8075-9374-5; 0-8075-9375-3 pa

LC 97-30679

Rhyming text describes what happens when a family discovers lice in the home and fights against them. Includes factual information about how lice live, spread, and can be eradicated

DerKazarian, Susan
You have head lice! by Susan DerKazarian. Children's Press 2005 31p il (Rookie read-about health) $20.50; pa $5.95
Grades: PreK K 1 2   616.5
1. Lice
ISBN 0-516-25879-6; 0-516-27920-3 pa

LC 2004-15308

This "approaches the sometimes-touchy subject of head lice in a straightforward, reassuring manner. . . . Adults wanting to explain head lice to children will find this a helpful source of basic information." Booklist

Faulk, Michelle
The case of the flesh-eating bacteria; Annie Biotica solves skin disease crimes. by Michelle Faulk. Lake Book Manufacturing, Inc. 2013 48 p. (Body system disease investigations) (library) $23.93
Grades: 5 6 7 8   616.5
1. Picture books for children 2. Skin -- Diseases -- Juvenile literature 3. Virus diseases -- Juvenile literature 4. Skin -- Infections -- Juvenile literature
ISBN 0766039455; 9780766039452

LC 2011023985

This book by Michelle Faulk "from the Body System Disease Investigations series introduces Agent Annie Biotica, a 'Disease Scene Investigator with the Major Health Crimes Unit'. This cartoon-style heroine is called in to solve

a series of skin-related medical cases . . . caused by flesh-eating bacteria, pinkeye, ringworm, chicken pox, [and] measles." (Booklist)

Includes bibliographical references (p. 47) and index

Landau, Elaine
★ Warts. Marshall Cavendish Benchmark 2010 32p il (Head-to-toe health) lib bdg $28.50
Grades: 2 3 4   616.5
1. Warts
ISBN 978-0-7614-4836-5 lib bdg; 0-7614-4836-5 lib bdg

This provides information about warts.

This "manages to pack in surprising amount information, including facts about good hygiene. The text addresses the readers directly, and the photos are real grabbers." Booklist

Includes glossary and bibliographical references

Lew, Kristi
Itch & ooze; gross stuff on your skin. illustrations by Michael Slack. Millbrook Press 2010 48p il (Gross body science) lib bdg $29.27
Grades: 4 5 6   616.5
1. Skin 2. Skin -- Diseases
ISBN 978-0-8225-8963-1 lib bdg; 0-8225-8963-X lib bdg

LC 2008-45591

Presents disgusting facts about human skin, the diseases and parasites that can cause problems with it, and how it functions to protect the body and itself.

"Solid information layered between sarcastic comments and kid-friendly terminology like fart, poop, barf, and puke will keep readers engaged. . . . Labeled, captioned (and graphic) photographs, cartoon-style illustrations, and micrographs add information." SLJ

Includes glossary and bibliographical references

Royston, Angela
Head lice. Black Rabbit Books 2009 30p il (How's your health) lib bdg $27.10
Grades: 1 2 3   616.5
1. Lice
ISBN 978-1-59920-218-1 lib bdg; 1-59920-218-2 lib bdg

First published 2001 by Heinemann Library

"Encourages further learning with sidebars that help readers think concretely about the subject. . . . Altogether a pitch perfect presentation." SLJ

Includes glossary

616.7   Diseases of musculoskeletal system

Gray, Susan Heinrichs
Living with juvenile rheumatoid arthritis. Child's World 2003 32p il (Living well) lib bdg $25.64
Grades: 4 5 6   616.7
1. Arthritis 2. Rheumatoid arthritis
ISBN 1-56766-104-1

LC 2002-2870

This title "leads off with an introduction to a young person who has [juvenile rheumatoid arthritis]. Subsequent chapters explain the physiology of the illness, what causes it, and what it's like to live with it. [The concluding section looks] at possible treatments and potential cures. [The text is] clear and simple, double spaced, and punctuated by colorful exemplary photos of kids dealing with the disease." SLJ

Includes glossary and bibliographical references

Hoffmann, Gretchen

★ **Osteoporosis**. Marshall Cavendish Benchmark 2007 64p il (Health alert) lib bdg $21.95

Grades: 4 5 6 7   **616.7**

1. Osteoporosis
ISBN 978-0-7614-2702-5; 0-7614-2702-3
LC 2007008787

This describes what it is like to have osteoporosis, what it is, its history and its diagnosis and treatment

This "title features a handsome format, with well-chosen illustrations, a substantial amount of information, and some practical insights." Booklist

Includes glossary and bibliographical references

616.8   Diseases of nervous system and mental disorders

Ali-Walsh, Rasheda

★ **I'll** hold your hand so you won't fall; a child's guide to Parkinson's disease. [by] Rasheda Ali; foreword for Muhammad Ali. Merit 2005 40p il $19.95

Grades: 2 3 4   **616.8**

1. Parkinson's disease
ISBN 1-873413-13-0

"Ali's father, Muhammad Ali, suffers from Parkinson's disease, and she answers questions children may have about the illness. . . . The text is well written and basic, without being oversimplified. . . . A short CD-ROM of the author introducing the book and its contents is included. An excellent overview written in an approachable style that will be reassuring to young readers." SLJ

Bender, Lionel

Explaining epilepsy. Smart Apple Media 2010 45p il (Explaining) lib bdg $34.25

Grades: 5 6 7 8   **616.8**

1. Epilepsy
ISBN 978-1-59920-309-6 lib bdg; 1-59920-309-X lib bdg
LC 2008-49292

Describes the nature, symptoms, and possible causes of epilepsy, gives a history of its study, and discusses its treatment

The book provides a "basic [overview] of the health concerns related to the disease; information on diagnosis and treatment; and a discussion of the challenges or complications experienced by the affected person and their family/ friends, and how to manage those problems. . . . The incorporation of quotes and personal accounts in 'Case Notes' sidebars adds to the sensitive tone found throughout [the title]." SLJ

Includes glossary and bibliographical references

Bjorklund, Ruth

★ **Cerebral** palsy. Marshall Cavendish Benchmark 2007 64p il (Health alert) lib bdg $31.36

Grades: 4 5 6 7   **616.8**

1. Cerebral palsy
ISBN 978-0-7614-2209-9; 0-7614-2209-9
LC 2006-15818

This "title features a handsome format, with well-chosen illustrations, a substantial amount of information, and some practical insights." Booklist

Includes glossary and bibliographical references

★ **Epilepsy**. Marshall Cavendish Benchmark 2007 63p il (Health alert) lib bdg $21.95

Grades: 4 5 6 7   **616.8**

1. Epilepsy
ISBN 978-0-7614-2206-8; 0-7614-2206-4
LC 2006-15816

This "title features a handsome format, with well-chosen illustrations, a substantial amount of information, and some practical insights." Booklist

Includes glossary and bibliographical references

Colligan, L. H.

★ **Sleep** disorders. Marshall Cavendish Benchmark 2009 64p il (Health alert) $22.95

Grades: 4 5 6 7   **616.8**

1. Sleep disorders
ISBN 978-0-7614-2913-5; 0-7614-2913-1

This "title features a handsome format, with well-chosen illustrations, a substantial amount of information, and some practical insights." Booklist

Includes glossary

Klosterman, Lorrie

★ **Meningitis**. Marshall Cavendish Benchmark 2007 64p il (Health alert) lib bdg $31.36

Grades: 4 5 6 7   **616.8**

1. Meningitis
ISBN 978-0-7614-2211-2; 0-7614-2211-0
LC 2006015819

This "title features a handsome format, with well-chosen illustrations, a substantial amount of information, and some practical insights." Booklist

Includes glossary and bibliographical references

Levete, Sarah

Explaining cerebral palsy. Smart Apple Media 2010 45p il (Explaining) lib bdg $34.25

Grades: 5 6 7 8   **616.8**

1. Cerebral palsy
ISBN 978-1-59920-311-9 lib bdg; 1-59920-311-1 lib bdg
LC 2008-49287

Describes the illness, including its causes, how it is diagnosed, current treatment methods, and how those with cerebral palsy live everyday lives

The book provides a "basic [overview] of the health concerns related to the disease; information on diagnosis and treatment; and a discussion of the challenges or complications experienced by the affected person and their family/ friends, and how to manage those problems. . . . The incorporation of quotes and personal accounts in 'Case Notes' sidebars adds to the sensitive tone found throughout [the title]." SLJ

Includes glossary and bibliographical references

616.85   Miscellaneous diseases of nervous system and mental disorders

Amenta, Charles A.

Russell's world; a story for kids about autism. illustrated by Monika Pollak. Magination Press 2011 un il $14.95; pa $9.95

Grades: K 1 2 3   **616.85**
1. Autism
ISBN 978-1-4338-0975-0; 1-4338-0975-3; 978-1-4338-0976-7 pa; 1-4338-0976-1 pa
                                          LC 2010048837

First published 1992 with title: Russell is extra special

"Likable young Russell puts a face on autism. Amenta's experience with his own son (now grown) shapes this heartfelt approach. This child craves routine and rituals and struggles to relate to his younger brothers. . . . Focusing on Russell's experiences, the book avoids sweeping generalizations while fairly outlining the condition's complexities. . . . Vivid mixed-media spreads include black-and-white childhood photos and display a hodgepodge of household objects and crayon scribbles. . . . Supportive without sugarcoating, this realistic account of a disorder that affects so many contains at its core a raw emotional heart." Kirkus

Andrews, Beth

Why are you so scared? a child's book about parents with PTSD. illustrated by Katherine Kirkland. Magination Press 2011 un il $14.95; pa $9.95

Grades: 1 2 3 4   **616.85**
1. Post-traumatic stress disorder
ISBN 978-1-4338-1045-9; 1-4338-1045-X; 978-1-4338-1044-2 pa; 1-4338-1044-1 pa
                                          LC 2011011082

"This straightforward, reassuring guide strives to explain some of the causes of Posttraumatic Stress Disorder . . . while not skimping on day-to-day survival tips. . . . Kirkland uses soft, hopeful illustrations that underscore the message that kids are not alone and that their parent's tired, cranky, jumpy emotions are to be expected. . . . The material is far too useful to be ignored." Booklist

Barton, Michael

It's raining cats and dogs; an autism spectrum guide to the confusing world of idioms, metaphors, and everyday expressions. Michael Barton; foreword, Delia Barton; illustrator, Michael Barton. Jessica Kingsley Publishers 2012 95 p. (alk. paper) $15.95

Grades: 3 4 5 6   **616.85**
1. Autism 2. Metaphor 3. Figures of speech 4. English language -- Idioms 5. Autistic people -- Language 6. Autism spectrum disorders -- Patients -- Language
ISBN 1849052832; 9781849052832
                                          LC 2011039514

This book offers "insight into the mind of someone with an ASD [autism spectrum disorder]. It . . . illustrates why people with ASDs have problems understanding common phrases and idioms that others accept unquestioningly as

part of everyday speech. The . . . drawings" are meant to "entertain and inspire those on the spectrum, giving them the confidence to recognise figures of speech, feel less alienated and even use idioms themselves. The drawings" are designed to "form instantly memorable references for those with ASDs to recall whenever they need to and" should "be helpful for anyone curious to understand the ASD way of thinking." (Publisher's note)

Bennett, Howard J.

Max Archer, kid detective: the case of the wet bed; illustrated by Spike Gerrell. Magination Press 2011 48p il $14.95; pa $9.95

Grades: K 1 2 3   **616.85**
1. Enuresis
ISBN 978-1-4338-0953-8; 1-4338-0953-2; 978-1-4338-0954-5 pa; 1-4338-0954-0 pa
                                          LC 2010051485

"Max is a detective who like to 'help kids with their problems'—this case takes on bedwetting. . . . Bennett strikes the right balance between story and self-help to provide a title whose tone and careful explanations both parents and kids will appreciate. . . . Even if there were not an alarming dearth of titles on this subject aimed at kids, this would stand out as a most thorough, highly readable resource." Kirkus

Brill, Marlene Targ

★ Down syndrome. Marshall Cavendish Benchmark 2007 64p il (Health alert) lib bdg $31.36

Grades: 4 5 6 7   **616.85**
1. Down syndrome 2. Down syndrome -- Juvenile literature
ISBN 978-0-7614-2207-5 lib bdg; 0-7614-2207-2 lib bdg
                                          LC 2006-15817

This "title features a handsome format, with well-chosen illustrations, a substantial amount of information, and some practical insights." Booklist

Includes glossary and bibliographical references

Capaccio, George

★ ADD and ADHD. Marshall Cavendish Benchmark 2007 64p il (Health alert) lib bdg $21.95

Grades: 4 5 6 7   **616.85**
1. Attention deficit disorder
ISBN 978-0-7614-2705-6; 0-7614-2705-8
                                          LC 2007008790

This describes what it is like to have Attention Deficit Disorder or Attention Deficit Hyperactivity Disorder, what they are, their history, and living with the disorders.

This "title features a handsome format, with well-chosen illustrations, a substantial amount of information, and some practical insights." Booklist

Includes glossary and bibliographical references

Chilman-Blair, Kim

Medikidz explain ADHD; [by] Kim Chilman-Blair and John Taddeo; medical content reviewed for accuracy by Peter D. Hill. Rosen Central 2011 40p il (Superheroes on a medical mission) lib bdg $29.25; pa $11.75

Grades: 3 4 5 6   **616.85**
1. Superheroes 2. Graphic novels 3. Attention deficit

disorder
ISBN 978-1-4358-9456-3 lib bdg; 1-4358-9456-1 lib bdg; 978-1-4488-1833-4 pa; 1-4488-1833-8 pa

LC 2010001063

"A team of superheroes rides around on a medi-jet and whisks ill children, or their siblings, off to Mediland, a giant replica of the human body, to teach them about [ADHD]. . . . The comic panels are visually exciting with eye-popping colors. Inside Mediland, the science behind various conditions is expertly simplified and explained with a sometimes tongue-in-cheek repartee among the characters as well as with very basic analogies reminiscent of video games. . . . This approach makes the health issues accessible and much less scary for readers wanting to learn more for personal or academic reasons." SLJ

Includes glossary and bibliographical references

Medikidz explain autism; [by] Kim Chilman-Blair and John Taddeo. Rosen Central 2011 40p il (Superheroes on a medical mission) lib bdg $29.25; pa $11.75
Grades: 3 4 5 6   616.85
1. Autism 2. Superheroes 3. Graphic novels
ISBN 978-1-4358-9460-0 lib bdg; 1-4358-9460-X; 978-1-4488-1835-8 pa; 1-4488-1835-4 pa

LC 2010008830

"A team of superheroes rides around on a medi-jet and whisks ill children, or their siblings, off to Mediland, a giant replica of the human body, to teach them about [autism]. . . . The comic panels are visually exciting with eye-popping colors. Inside Mediland, the science behind various conditions is expertly simplified and explained with a sometimes tongue-in-cheek repartee among the characters as well as with very basic analogies reminiscent of video games. . . . This approach makes the health issues accessible and much less scary for readers wanting to learn more for personal or academic reasons." SLJ

Includes glossary and bibliographical references

Medikidz explain depression; [by] Kim Chilman-Blair and Shawn deLoache. Rosen Central 2011 40p il (Superheroes on a medical mission) lib bdg $29.25; pa $11.75
Grades: 3 4 5 6   616.85
1. Superheroes 2. Graphic novels 3. Depression (Psychology)
ISBN 978-1-4358-9455-6 lib bdg; 1-4358-9455-3 lib bdg; 978-1-4488-1837-2 pa; 1-4488-1837-0 pa

LC 2010008833

"A team of superheroes rides around on a medi-jet and whisks ill children, or their siblings, off to Mediland, a giant replica of the human body, to teach them about [depression]. . . . The comic panels are visually exciting with eye-popping colors. Inside Mediland, the science behind various conditions is expertly simplified and explained with a sometimes tongue-in-cheek repartee among the characters as well as with very basic analogies reminiscent of video games. . . . This approach makes the health issues accessible and much less scary for readers wanting to learn more for personal or academic reasons." SLJ

Includes glossary and bibliographical references

Donovan, Sandra, 1967-
Keep your cool! what you should know about stress. illustrations by Jack Desrocher. Lerner Publications Co. 2009 64p il (Health zone) lib bdg $30.60

Grades: 4 5 6 7   616.85
1. Stress (Psychology)
ISBN 978-0-8225-7555-9; 0-8225-7555-8

LC 2007038858

This describes what causes stress and what you can do to relieve it.

"The format is beyond lively, with lots of color, cartoons, and an informal writing style, but it manages to present sometimes frightening material in a non-threatening and browsable way." Booklist

Includes glossary and bibliographical references

Levy, Joel
Phobiapedia; all the things we fear the most! Scholastic 2011 80p il pa $8.99
Grades: 4 5 6 7   616.85
1. Phobias
ISBN 978-0-545-34929-1; 0-545-34929-X

This briefly describes over 50 phobias.

"With an appealing layout, plenty of color, and enough germs, snakes, and bats to get the heart racing, this title has kid written all over it." Booklist

Quinn, Patricia O.
Attention, girls! a guide to learn all about your AD/HD. illustrated by Carl Pearce. Magination Press 2009 119p il $16.95; pa $12.95
Grades: 4 5 6 7   616.85
1. Attention deficit disorder
ISBN 978-1-4338-0447-2; 1-4338-0447-6; 978-1-4338-0448-9 pa; 1-4338-0448-4 pa

LC 2008054524

"Quinn has attention deficit hyperactivity disorder and is a medical doctor; she addresses the types of AD/HD; who can help; differences between girls and boys with AD/HD; making friends; talking with adults about the condition; relaxation techniques; and medication. Her aim is to give girls a variety of ways to manage their disorders. . . . The book is attractive and inviting with colorful cartoon illustrations, sidebars, and highlighted reminders." SLJ

Robbins, Lynette
How to deal with ADHD. PowerKids Press 2010 24p il (Kids' health) lib bdg $21.25
Grades: 2 3 4   616.85
1. Attention deficit disorder
ISBN 978-1-4042-8140-0 lib bdg; 1-4042-8140-1 lib bdg

LC 2009-6412

"Hypothetical situations with fictional characters put readers in the moment and provide a solid foundation for comprehending [ADHD]. . . . Robbins maintains a comforting tone, reassuring readers that it is possible to lead active lives with proper attention to diet and guidance from parents and doctors." SLJ

Includes glossary

How to deal with autism. PowerKids Press 2010 24p il (Kids' health) lib bdg $21.25
Grades: 2 3 4   616.85
1. Autism
ISBN 978-1-4042-8142-4 lib bdg; 1-4042-8142-8 lib bdg

LC 2009-7862

"Hypothetical situations with fictional characters put readers in the moment and provide a solid foundation for comprehending [autism]. . . . Robbins maintains a comforting tone, reassuring readers that it is possible to lead active lives with proper attention to diet and guidance from parents and doctors." SLJ

Includes glossary

Royston, Angela

Explaining down syndrome. Smart Apple Media 2010 45p il (Explaining) lib bdg $34.25

Grades: 5 6 7 8   **616.85**

1. Down syndrome

ISBN 978-1-59920-308-9 lib bdg; 1-59920-308-1 lib bdg

LC 2008-49291

This book about down syndrome provides a "basic [overview] of the health concerns related to the disease; information on diagnosis and treatment; and a discussion of the challenges or complications experienced by the affected person and their family/friends, and how to manage those problems. . . . The incorporation of quotes and personal accounts in 'Case Notes' sidebars adds to the sensitive tone found throughout [the title]." SLJ

Includes glossary

Shapiro, Ouisie

Autism and me; sibling stories. photographs by Steven Vote. Albert Whitman 2009 un il $16.99

Grades: 3 4 5 6   **616.85**

1. Autism 2. Siblings

ISBN 978-0-8075-0487-1; 0-8075-0487-4

LC 2008-31700

Children tell their stories of what it is like to live with a sibling who has autism.

"The children's emotions ring true, telling what they love about their sibling; the preaching comes from their hearts. This book would be useful in families and in classrooms to help explain both the struggles and the triumphs of living with someone who has this disorder." SLJ

Silverstein, Alvin

The **ADHD** update; understanding attention-deficit/hyperactivity disorder. [by] Alvin and Virginia Silverstein and Laura Silverstein Nunn. Enslow Publishers 2008 112p il (Disease update) lib bdg $31.93

Grades: 5 6 7 8   **616.85**

1. Attention deficit disorder 2. Attention-deficit hyperactivity disorder -- Juvenile literature

ISBN 978-0-7660-2800-5 lib bdg; 0-7660-2800-3 lib bdg

LC 2007-13853

This describes Attention-deficit hyperactivity disorder (ADHD) and its history, diagnosis and treatment, living with it, and its future

"This book is an excellent primer on AD/HD." Sci Books Films

Includes glossary and bibliographical references

The **eating** disorders update; understanding anorexia, bulimia, and binge eating. [by] Alvin and Virginia Silverstein and Laura Silverstein Nunn. Enslow Publishers 2008 128p il (Disease update) lib bdg $31.93

Grades: 5 6 7 8   **616.85**

1. Bulimia 2. Anorexia nervosa 3. Eating disorders

ISBN 978-0-7660-2802-9 lib bdg; 0-7660-2802-X lib bdg

LC 2007013985

"An introduction to the history and most up-to-date research and treatment of eating disorders." Publisher's note

Includes glossary and bibliographical references

Simons, Rae

I eat when I'm sad; food and feelings. Mason Crest Publishers 2010 48p il (Kids & obesity) lib bdg $19.95; pa $7.95

Grades: 3 4 5   **616.85**

1. Obesity 2. Weight loss 3. Eating disorders

ISBN 978-1-4222-1714-6 lib bdg; 1-4222-1714-0 lib bdg; 978-1-4222-1902-7 pa; 1-4222-1902-X pa

LC 2010007065

This book about childhood obesity makes "a compelling case by plainly stating the consequences of carrying around 'a little extra.' . . . The tone is highly sympathetic, capturing the vicious cycle of emotional eating and giving kids tools to combat weight gain." Booklist

Includes bibliographical references

Skotko, Brian

Fasten your seatbelt; a crash course on Down syndrome for brothers and sisters. [by] Brian G. Skotko and Susan P. Levine. Woodbine House 2009 191p il pa $18.95

Grades: 4 5 6 7   **616.85**

1. Siblings 2. Down syndrome

ISBN 978-1-890627-86-7 pa; 1-890627-86-0 pa

LC 2008049753

"Skotko and Levine address preteens and teenagers who have a sibling with Down syndrome, answering questions that have been generated through their work with this population. . . . With a wealth of information, numerous resources, and the reassurance that all siblings of people with disabilities sometimes go through periods of contradictory feelings, this is an excellent guide for young people who are trying to figure out how to negotiate an often-confusing relationship." SLJ

Includes bibliographical references

Snedden, Robert

Explaining autism. Smart Apple Media 2010 45p il (Explaining) lib bdg $34.25

Grades: 5 6 7 8   **616.85**

1. Autism 2. Asperger's syndrome

ISBN 978-1-59920-307-2 lib bdg; 1-59920-307-3 lib bdg

LC 2008-49285

Describes the illness, including its symptoms, how it affects physical and mental health, current treatments, and how people with autism live everyday lives

"The incorporation of quotes and personal accounts in 'Case Notes' sidebars adds to the sensitive tone found throughout [the title]." SLJ

Includes glossary and bibliographical references

Stefanski, Daniel

★ **How** to talk to an autistic kid; illustrated by Hazel Mitchell. Free Spirit 2011 43p il $12.99

Grades: 3 4 5 6 **616.85**

1. Autism

ISBN 978-1-57542-365-4; 1-57542-365-0

"Stefanski provides clear, sometimes blunt, often humorous advice for readers on how to interact with autistic classmates. An authority on this topic—he is a 14-year-old boy with autism—he begins by describing autism. . . . He describes, using a brief paragraph or two per page, some of the traits many autistic people share. . . . For each trait, he offers down-to-earth suggestions for resolving problems. . . . His insightful, matter-of-fact presentation demystifies behaviors that might confuse or disturb non-autistic classmates. Simple cartoon illustrations in black, gray and two shades of turquoise accompany the text. . . . A thought-provoking introduction to autism . . . and an essential purchase for every primary and middle-school classroom." Kirkus

Stewart, Gail

Anorexia; [by] Gail B. Stewart. Cherry Lake Pub. 2009 32p il (Health at risk) lib bdg $27.07

Grades: 4 5 6 7 **616.85**

1. Anorexia nervosa

ISBN 978-1-60279-281-4 lib bdg; 1-60279-281-X lib bdg

LC 2008017496

This explains why anorexics feel the need to keep losing weight, what can happen to them as a result of their desperate struggle to be thin, and how they can get help.

"Great for reports or reluctant readers." Booklist

Includes bibliographical references

Bulimia; [by] Gail B. Stewart. Cherry Lake Pub. 2009 32p il (Health at risk) lib bdg $27.07

Grades: 4 5 6 7 **616.85**

1. Bulimia

ISBN 978-1-60279-282-1 lib bdg; 1-60279-282-8 lib bdg

LC 2008-17497

This describes the health risks of bulimia and what can be done to help people fight this disease.

"Great for reports or reluctant readers." Booklist

Includes bibliographical references

Taylor, John F.

The **survival** guide for kids with ADD or ADHD; [by] John F. Taylor. Free Spirit Pub. 2006 119p il pa $13.95

Grades: 3 4 5 **616.85**

1. Attention deficit disorder

ISBN 978-1-57542-195-7 pa; 1-57542-195-X pa

LC 2005033737

"Packed with good advice, this guide will catch readers' eyes with its bright cover, varied fonts, and cartoon-style illustrations. The writing is clear and kid-friendly." SLJ

Van Niekerk, Clarabelle

Understanding Sam and Asperger Syndrome; [by] Clarabelle van Niekerk and Liezl Venter; illustrated by Clarabelle van Niekerk. Skeezel Press 2008 un il $17.95

Grades: PreK K 1 2 **616.85**

1. Asperger's syndrome

ISBN 978-0-9747217-1-2; 0-9747217-1-9

"A third-person past-tense narrative tells the story of Sam, a boy with Asperger Syndrome. . . . Because of the interesting story line, the positive approach, and the notion

that others can learn to help Sam instead of expecting him to change, this is an excellent introduction to the topic. The pictures are bright and lively, showing mostly happy faces. The book concludes with 10 helpful tips to remember when a friend or a classmate has Asperger's." SLJ

616.86   Substance abuse (Drug abuse)

Allman, Toney

Drugs. Cherry Lake Pub. 2009 32p il (Health at risk) lib bdg $27.07

Grades: 4 5 6 7 **616.86**

1. Drug abuse

ISBN 978-1-60279-283-8 lib bdg; 1-60279-283-6 lib bdg

LC 2008017503

This describes the dangers of drug abuse, the programs that help people get off drugs, and how to avoid drug use.

"Great for reports or reluctant readers." Booklist

Includes bibliographical references

Miller, Heather

Smoking. Cherry Lake Pub. 2009 32p il (Health at risk) lib bdg $27.07

Grades: 4 5 6 7 **616.86**

1. Smoking 2. Tobacco habit

ISBN 978-1-60279-286-9 lib bdg; 1-60279-286-0 lib bdg

LC 2008017501

This describes why smoking is dangerous, how difficult it is to stop once you start, and what efforts are underway to put the brakes on this habit.

"Great for reports or reluctant readers." Booklist

Includes bibliographical references

616.89   Mental disorders

Rashkin, Rachel

Feeling better; a kid's book about therapy. by Rachel Rashkin; illustrated by Bonnie Adamson. Magination Press 2005 48p il $14.95; pa $8.95

Grades: 4 5 6 7 **616.89**

1. Psychotherapy

ISBN 1-59147-237-7; 1-59147-238-5 pa

LC 2004022727

"Clearly written and well-organized. . . . Animated black-and-white sketches portray the girl's various emotions. This title gently encourages kids who are struggling with issues to seek help." SLJ

616.9   Other diseases

Aronin, Miriam

Tuberculosis; the white plague! Bearport Pub. 2011 32p il map (Nightmare plagues) lib bdg $25.27

Grades: 4 5 6 7 **616.9**

1. Tuberculosis

ISBN 978-1-936088-06-5; 1-936088-06-1

LC 2010010679

Discover what causes tuberculosis and how it affects the body.

"The writing is accessible and interspersed with interesting photographs and fact boxes. . . . [The book relies] on an honest discussion of [tuberculosis and is an] . . . effective, easily navigated [introduction]." SLJ

Includes glossary and bibliographical references

Berger, Melvin
   Germs make me sick! illustrated by Marylin Hafner. rev ed; HarperCollins Pubs. 1995 32p il (Let's-read-and-find-out science) hardcover o.p. pa $4.99
Grades: K 1 2 3   **616.9**
   1. Viruses 2. Bacteria 3. Diseases -- Juvenile literature
   ISBN 0-06-024250-7 lib bdg; 0-06-445154-2 pa
                                              LC 93-27059
First published 1985
Explains how bacteria and viruses affect the human body and how the body fights them
This features "Hafner's lively color cartoon illustrations. . . . [It offers a] lively combination of fact and narrative that has made this a great title for easy reading and for sharing aloud." Booklist

Blank, Alison
   Invincible microbe; tuberculosis and the never-ending search for a cure. Jim Murphy, Alison Blank. Clarion Books 2012 149 p. (hardback) $18.99
Grades: 5 6 7 8 9   **616.9**
   1. Tuberculosis 2. Lungs -- Diseases 3. Communicable diseases -- Treatment 4. Tuberculosis -- Juvenile literature 5. Microorganisms -- Juvenile literature
   ISBN 0618535748; 9780618535743
                                              LC 2011025951
This book looks at tuberculosis. It "starts with archeologists finding evidence of tuberculosis in a 500,000 year old skull and continues through to the present day. Various 'cures' such as the medieval 'king's touch' . . . , bloodletting of the 19th century, twentieth century sanatoriums and modern day drug cocktails are all discussed." Also "covered is the socioeconomic side of the disease, with a discussion of how treatment often varied depending on the race and economic status of the patient." (Children's Literature)
Includes bibliographical references

Colligan, L. H.
   ★ **Tick-**borne illnesses. Marshall Cavendish Benchmark 2009 64p il (Health alert) $22.95
Grades: 4 5 6 7   **616.9**
   1. Tick-borne diseases
   ISBN 978-0-7614-2914-2; 0-7614-2914-X
                                              LC 2007-38517
This "title features a handsome format, with well-chosen illustrations, a substantial amount of information, and some practical insights." Booklist
Includes glossary

Duke, Shirley Smith
   Infections, infestations, and disease; [by] Shirley Duke. Rourke Pub. 2010 48p il (Let's explore science) $32.79
Grades: 4 5 6 7   **616.9**
   1. Communicable diseases
   ISBN 978-1-61590-321-4; 1-61590-321-6
                                              LC 2010009908

This describes communicable diseases.
Includes bibliographical references

Glaser, Jason
   Chicken pox; consultant, James R. Hubbard. Capstone Press 2006 24p il (First facts: Health matters) $21.26
Grades: K 1 2 3   **616.9**
   1. Chickenpox
   ISBN 978-0-7368-4288-4; 0-7368-4288-8
                                              LC 2004028549
This introduction to chicken pox is "general and straightforward. Two or three simple sentences in large font appear on each page and address the causes, symptoms, appearances, and treatments." SLJ
Includes bibliographical references

   Strep throat. Capstone Press 2007 il (First facts: health matters) $21.26
Grades: K 1 2 3   **616.9**
   1. Strep throat
   ISBN 978-0-7368-6393-3; 0-7368-6393-1
                                              LC 2006002821
"Describes strep throat, how people get it, and how to treat and prevent it." Publisher's note
Includes bibliographical references

Hoffmann, Gretchen
   ★ **Chicken** pox. Marshall Cavendish Benchmark 2009 62p il (Health alert) $22.95
Grades: 4 5 6 7   **616.9**
   1. Chickenpox
   ISBN 978-0-7614-2916-6; 0-7614-2916-6
This "title features a handsome format, with well-chosen illustrations, a substantial amount of information, and some practical insights." Booklist
Includes glossary

Jarrow, Gail
   Chiggers; [by] Gail Jarrow. KidHaven Press 2004 32p il (Parasites) $22.45
Grades: 4 5 6   **616.9**
   1. Mites 2. Chiggers (Mites)
   ISBN 0-7377-1778-5
                                              LC 2003-9614
"Several short chapters briefly describe the distinctive physical and behavioral characteristics of [chiggers] and special characteristics of particular species. [The book] also [highlights] the symptoms, victims' experiences, the organisms' potential threats as disease vectors, current treatments, and prevention methods. . . . Clear, color photographs illustrate the [text]. . . . Well organized and clearly written." SLJ

Kornberg, Arthur
   Germ stories; illustrations by Adam Alaniz; photography by Roberto Kolter. University Science Books 2007 70p il $22
Grades: 2 3 4   **616.9**
   1. Bacteria 2. Microbiology
   ISBN 978-1-891389-51-1; 1-891389-51-3
                                              LC 2007-09960
"This book of poems is a visual and lyrical journey into the wonderful world of . . . germs. . . . Nobel Prize winner Arthur Kornberg gives readers a look at the structures, methods, and cycles of germs. . . . The poetry is easy and

flowing. Cartoon germs—fanged slime bacteria and wispy penicillin—are bright additions. After each poem is an electron micrograph, plus a visual comparison to help children understand just how small germs are." Libr Media Connect

Includes glossary

Landau, Elaine

★ **Chickenpox**. Marshall Cavendish Benchmark 2010 32p il (Head-to-toe health) $28.50

Grades: 2 3 4   **616.9**

1. Chickenpox

ISBN 978-0-7614-3498-6; 0-7614-3498-4

LC 2008-10782

"The book will satisfy researchers as well as those with a personal interest in the virus. . . . [This is] well-organized, informative." SLJ

Includes glossary and bibliographical references

★ **Strep** throat. Marshall Cavendish Benchmark 2010 32p il (Head-to-toe health) lib bdg $28.50

Grades: 2 3 4   **616.9**

1. Strep throat

ISBN 978-0-7614-4834-1 lib bdg; 0-7614-4834-9 lib bdg

This provides basic information about strep throat and its prevention.

This "manages to pack in a surprising amount of information, including facts about good hygiene. The text addresses the reader directly, and the photos are real grabbers." Booklist

Includes glossary and bibliographical references

Ollhoff, Jim

The **Black** Death. ABDO Pub. Co. 2010 32p il map (A history of germs) lib bdg $27.07

Grades: 3 4 5 6   **616.9**

1. Plague

ISBN 978-1-60453-497-9 lib bdg; 1-60453-497-4 lib bdg

LC 2008-55061

This book "examines the plague's origins, causes, effects, cures, and historical legacy. . . . The short, informative chapters provide plenty of details for reports. The illustrations, many of which are color photos, enhance the information." SLJ

Includes glossary

Malaria. ABDO Pub. Co. 2010 32p il (A history of germs) lib bdg $27.07

Grades: 3 4 5 6   **616.9**

1. Malaria

ISBN 978-1-60453-500-6 lib bdg; 1-60453-500-8 lib bdg

"Malaria explains why the disease is so deadly, notes types of treatments, looks at efforts to control it, and suggests the future development of a vaccine. . . . The short, informative chapters provide plenty of details for reports. The illustrations, many of which are color photos, enhance the information." SLJ

Smallpox. ABDO Pub. Co. 2010 32p il (A history of germs) lib bdg $27.07

Grades: 3 4 5 6   **616.9**

1. Smallpox 2. Physicians 3. Writers on medicine

ISBN 978-1-60453-501-3 lib bdg; 1-60453-501-6 lib bdg

"Smallpox discusses the disease's symptoms, highlights Edward Jenner's work in developing a vaccine, and touches upon the potential use of the virus as a biological weapon. . . . The short, informative chapters provide plenty of details for reports. The illustrations, many of which are color photos, enhance the information." SLJ

Includes glossary

The **germ** detectives. ABDO Pub. Co. 2010 32p il (A history of germs) lib bdg $27.07

Grades: 3 4 5 6   **616.9**

1. Bacteria 2. Chemists 3. Surgeons 4. Physicians 5. Scientists 6. Microbiology 7. Microscopists 8. Microbiologists 9. Writers on science 10. Writers on medicine 11. Nobel laureates for physiology or medicine

ISBN 978-1-60453-499-3 lib bdg; 1-60453-499-0 lib bdg

LC 2008-55062

This book "highlights the work of Antoni van Leeuwenhoek, Ignaz Semmelweis, Joseph Lister, Louis Pasteur, and Robert Koch, all of whom contributed to current knowledge about germs. . . . The short, informative chapters provide plenty of details for reports. The illustrations, many of which are color photos, enhance the information." SLJ

Includes glossary

616.97   Diseases of immune system

Ballard, Carol

Explaining food allergies. Smart Apple Media 2010 45p il (Explaining) $23.95

Grades: 5 6 7 8   **616.97**

1. Food allergy

ISBN 978-1-59920-316-4; 1-59920-316-2

LC 2008049936

This "does an excellent job of discussing complex clinical science while showing what daily life is like for kids living with food allergies, from the signs and symptoms to the tests and treatments. . . . This blend of the technical and the personal will have wide appeal." Booklist

Chilman-Blair, Kim

Medikidz explain HIV; [by] Kim Chilman-Blair and John Taddeo; medical content reviewed for accuracy by Vas Novelli and Karyn Moshal. Rosen Central 2011 40p il (Superheroes on a medical mission) lib bdg $29.25; pa $11.75

Grades: 3 4 5 6   **616.97**

1. Superheroes 2. AIDS (Disease) 3. Graphic novels

ISBN 978-1-4358-9458-7 lib bdg; 1-4358-9458-8 lib bdg; 978-1-4488-1839-6 pa; 1-4488-1839-7 pa

LC 2010001333

"A team of superheroes rides around on a medi-jet and whisks ill children, or their siblings, off to Mediland, a giant replica of the human body, to teach them about [HIV]. . . . The comic panels are visually exciting with eye-popping colors. Inside Mediland, the science behind various conditions is expertly simplified and explained with a sometimes tongue-in-cheek repartee among the characters as well as with very basic analogies reminiscent of video games. . . . This approach makes the health issues accessible and much less scary for readers wanting to learn more for personal or academic reasons." SLJ

Includes glossary and bibliographical references

Landau, Elaine

★ **Food** allergies. Marshall Cavendish Benchmark 2010 32p il (Head-to-toe health) lib bdg $28.50

Grades: 2 3 4   **616.97**

   1. Food allergy

   ISBN 978-0-7614-3500-6; 0-7614-3500-X

                        LC 2008-10785

"Color photographs appear throughout. . . . [This is] well-organized, informative." SLJ

Includes glossary and bibliographical references

Robbins, Lynette

How to deal with allergies. PowerKids Press 2010 24p il (Kids' health) lib bdg $21.25

Grades: 2 3 4   **616.97**

   1. Allergy

   ISBN 978-1-4042-8139-4 lib bdg; 1-4042-8139-8 lib bdg

                        LC 2009-2616

"Hypothetical situations with fictional characters put readers in the moment and provide a solid foundation for comprehending [allergies]. . . . Robbins maintains a comforting tone, reassuring readers that it is possible to lead active lives with proper attention to diet and guidance from parents and doctors." SLJ

Includes glossary

Royston, Angela

Allergies. Black Rabbit Books 2009 30p il (How's your health?) lib bdg $27.10

Grades: 1 2 3   **616.97**

   1. Allergy

   ISBN 978-1-59920-220-4 lib bdg; 1-59920-220-4 lib bdg

                        LC 2007-35174

First published 2004 by Heinemann Library

"Encourages further learning with sidebars that help readers think concretely about the subject. . . . Altogether a pitch perfect presentation." SLJ

Includes glossary and bibliographical references

Thomas, Pat

I think I am going to sneeze; a first look at allergies. [by] Pat Thomas; illustrated by Lesley Harker. Barron's Educational Series 2008 29p il pa $6.99

Grades: PreK K 1 2   **616.97**

   1. Allergy

   ISBN 978-0-7641-3900-0 pa; 0-7641-39002 pa

This "title covers the causes and effects of allergies and treatments and reassures youngsters that they don't have to be left out of school activities. Sidebars . . . ask questions about children's personal experiences and thoughts, which can be used as discussion starters. [The] title ends with an extensive note to parents, with practical advice for . . . helping children cope with allergies. [This is a] solid [addition] for most collections." SLJ

616.99   Tumors and miscellaneous communicable diseases

Markle, Sandra

Leukemia; true survival stories. Lerner Publications 2010 48p il (Powerful medicine) lib bdg $27.93

Grades: 5 6 7 8   **616.99**

   1. Leukemia 2. Leukemia -- Juvenile literature

   ISBN 978-0-8225-8700-2 lib bdg; 0-8225-8700-9 lib bdg

                        LC 2009-34441

This book about leukemia "will grab the attention of middle school readers. . . . The illustrations and photos are stunning with medically accurate captions. Real-life patients, whose photos are included in the text, are highlighted, with updates on their progress at the end of . . . [the] book. . . . This . . . fills the need for up-to-date books on medical topics using vocabulary that a young teenager can understand." Voice Youth Advocates

Includes glossary and bibliographical references

Silverstein, Alvin

The **breast** cancer update; [by] Alvin and Virginia Silverstein and Laura Silverstein Nunn. Enslow Publishers 2008 128p il (Disease update) lib bdg $31.93

Grades: 5 6 7 8   **616.99**

   1. Breast cancer 2. Young adult literature

   ISBN 978-0-7660-2747-3 lib bdg; 0-7660-2747-3 lib bdg

                        LC 2006-32821

This offers a history of breast cancer, a definition of it, and describes its diagnosis and treatment, prevention, and future

Includes glossary and bibliographical references

Watters, Debbie

Where's Mom's hair? a family's journey through cancer. by Debbie Watters; with Haydn and Emmett Watters; photographs by Sophie Hogan. Second Story Press 2005 31p il pa $10.95

Grades: 2 3 4   **616.99**

   1. Hair 2. Cancer

   ISBN 1-896764-94-0

"When the author underwent chemotherapy following cancer surgery, she faced the loss of her hair with courage and humor. Family and friends gathered for a 'haircutting party,' where her husband and two young sons . . . joined her in getting buzz cuts. . . . The gentle kindness conveyed in the often-humorous writing will reassure young children facing similar circumstances." SLJ

617   Surgery, regional medicine, dentistry, ophthalmology, otology, audiology

Markle, Sandra

Wounded brains; true survival stories. Lerner Publications 2011 48p il (Powerful medicine) lib bdg $27.93

Grades: 5 6 7 8   **617**

   1. Brain -- Wounds and injuries

   ISBN 978-0-8225-8704-0 lib bdg; 0-8225-8704-1 lib bdg

                        LC 2009034440

Describes several true cases of traumatic brain injury and the medical treatment that followed.

This narrative reads "like information from the Discovery Health channel, for kids: part fascinating science, part human interest story, and part 'Eew, gross!'. . . Clear, straightforward prose is supplemented by definitions and explanations of medical techniques and jargon. The numerous color photos and medical images will satisfy readers' curiosity." SLJ

Includes glossary and bibliographical references

Mullins, Matt

   Surgical technologist. Cherry Lake Pub. 2010 32p il (Cool careers: career and technical education) lib bdg $27.07

Grades: 4 5 6 7   **617**

   1. Surgery 2. Vocational guidance 3. Medical technologists

   ISBN 978-1-60279-939-4 lib bdg; 1-60279-939-3 lib bdg

                         LC 2010001437

This "provides an overview of the duties performed by these allied health professionals, requirements and training for the job, and the anticipated future of this occupation. . . . Full color, captioned photographs . . . appear on most spreads, clarifying the text. . . . This will make a useful addition to the career shelf." Booklist

Includes bibliographical references

Woog, Adam

   The **bionic** hand. Norwood House Press 2009 48p il (A great idea) lib bdg $25.27

Grades: 3 4 5 6   **617**

   1. Bionics 2. Artificial limbs

   ISBN 978-1-59953-341-4 lib bdg; 1-59953-341-3 lib bdg

                         LC 2009-15640

"Explores the development and creation of the i-LIMB which is the first commercially available bionic hand." Publisher's note

Includes glossary and bibliographical references

617.1   Injuries and wounds

Cobb, Vicki

   ★ **Your** body battles a broken bone; written by Vicki Cobb; photomicrographs by Dennis Kunkel; illustrations by Andrew N. Harris. Millbrook Press 2009 32p il (Body battles) lib bdg $25.26

Grades: 3 4 5   **617.1**

   1. Bones 2. Fractures

   ISBN 978-0-8225-7468-2; 0-8225-7468-3

                       LC 2008002837

This book provides comic illustrations and photomicrographs that describe how the body heals a broken bone

"Many of the vibrant illustrations anthropomorphize various cells and other 'battle' participants, making the science explained approachable and easy to understand. Photomicrographs further illuminate the text. These amazing pictures, taken with a scanning electron microscope, are greatly magnified and colored to highlight certain features." SLJ

Includes glossary and bibliographical references

   ★ **Your** body battles a skinned knee; written by Vicki Cobb; photomicrographs by Dennis Kunkel; illustrations by Andrew N. Harris. Millbrook Press 2009 32p il (Body battles) lib bdg $25.26

Grades: 3 4 5   **617.1**

   1. Skin 2. Immune system 3. Wounds and injuries

   ISBN 978-0-8225-6814-8; 0-8225-6814-4

                       LC 2008002826

"By combining simple yet engaging text; comic-like illustrations; and greatly magnified photomicrographs, this book describes the healing process of a bloodied knee in a fashion that is both entertaining and easy to understand." Booklist

Includes glossary and bibliographical references

Landau, Elaine

   ★ **Bites** and stings. Marshall Cavendish Benchmark 2009 32p il (Head-to-toe health) lib bdg $28.50

Grades: 2 3 4   **617.1**

   1. Bites and stings

   ISBN 978-0-7614-2850-3; 0-7614-2850-X

                       LC 2007-43022

"Photo illustrations are apt and age appropriate. . . . Pervading the [book] . . . is an overall sense of reassurance that even if something hurts, 'all better' is never too far away. Appealing and readable nonfiction." SLJ

Includes glossary and bibliographical references

   ★ **Broken** bones. Marshall Cavendish Benchmark 2009 32p il (Head-to-toe health) lib bdg $28.50

Grades: 2 3 4   **617.1**

   1. Bones 2. Fractures

   ISBN 978-0-7614-2847-3; 0-7614-2847-X

                       LC 2007-26665

"Photo illustrations are apt and age appropriate. . . . Pervading the [book] . . . is an overall sense of reassurance that even if something hurts, 'all better' is never too far away. Appealing and readable nonfiction." SLJ

Includes glossary and bibliographical references

   ★ **Bumps,** bruises, and scrapes. Marshall Cavendish Benchmark 2009 32p il (Head-to-toe health) lib bdg $28.50

Grades: 2 3 4   **617.1**

   1. Wounds and injuries

   ISBN 978-0-7614-2849-7; 0-7614-2849-6

                       LC 2007-26959

"Photo illustrations are apt and age appropriate. . . . Pervading the [book] . . . is an overall sense of reassurance that even if something hurts, 'all better' is never too far away. Appealing and readable nonfiction." SLJ

Includes glossary and bibliographical references

   ★ **Burns**. Marshall Cavendish Benchmark 2010 32p il (Head-to-toe health) lib bdg $28.50

Grades: 2 3 4   **617.1**

   1. Burns and scalds

   ISBN 978-0-7614-4832-7 lib bdg; 0-7614-4832-2 lib bdg

This provides basic information about the different types of burns a person can get.

This "manages to pack in a surprising amount of information, including facts about good hygiene. The text addresses the reader directly, and the photos are real grabbers." Booklist

Includes glossary and bibliographical references

★ **Sprains** and strains. Marshall Cavendish Benchmark 2010 32p il (Head-to-toe health) lib bdg $28.50
Grades: 2 3 4   **617.1**
  1. Wounds and injuries
  ISBN 978-0-7614-4833-4 lib bdg; 0-7614-4833-0 lib bdg

This provides basic information about the different types of sprains and strains the body can get.

This "manages to pack in a surprising amount of information, including facts about good hygiene. The text addresses the reader directly, and the photos are real grabbers." Booklist

Includes glossary and bibliographical references

Lew, Kristi
  Clot & scab; gross stuff about your scrapes, bumps, and bruises. illustrations by Michael Slack. Millbrook Press 2010 48p il (Gross body science) lib bdg $29.27
Grades: 4 5 6   **617.1**
  1. Wounds and injuries
  ISBN 978-0-8225-8965-5 lib bdg; 0-8225-8965-6 lib bdg

                    LC 2008-45626
"Solid information layered between sarcastic comments and kid-friendly terminology like fart, poop, barf, and puke will keep readers engaged. . . . Labeled, captioned (and graphic) photographs, cartoon-style illustrations, and micrographs add information." SLJ

Includes glossary and bibliographical references

Markle, Sandra
  Bad burns; true survival stories. Lerner Publications 2010 48p il (Powerful medicine) lib bdg $27.93
Grades: 5 6 7 8   **617.1**
  1. Burns and scalds
  ISBN 978-0-8225-8702-6 lib bdg; 0-8225-8702-5 lib bdg

                    LC 2009034439
Explores how advancements in medicine and technology have helped victims of severe skin burns, and includes real-life stories of burn survivors and tips on burn prevention and treatment.

This narrative reads "like information from the Discovery Health channel, for kids: part fascinating science, part human interest story, and part 'Eew, gross!'. . . Clear, straightforward prose is supplemented by definitions and explanations of medical techniques and jargon. The numerous color photos and medical images will satisfy readers' curiosity." SLJ

Includes glossary and bibliographical references

  Shattered bones; true survival stories. Lerner Publications 2010 48p il (Powerful medicine) lib bdg $27.93

Grades: 5 6 7 8   **617.1**
  1. Bones 2. Fractures
  ISBN 978-0-8225-8703-3 lib bdg; 0-8225-8703-3 lib bdg

                    LC 2009034442
Offers true stories of people who suffered broken bones, along with information on the skeleton, its structure and function, and the treatments doctors use for injuries.

This narrative reads "like information from the Discovery Health channel, for kids: part fascinating science, part human interest story, and part 'Eew, gross!'. . . Clear, straightforward prose is supplemented by definitions and explanations of medical techniques and jargon. The numerous color photos and medical images will satisfy readers' curiosity." SLJ

Includes glossary and bibliographical references

Royston, Angela
  Cuts, bruises, and breaks. Black Rabbit Books 2009 30p il (How's your health) lib bdg $27.10
Grades: 1 2 3   **617.1**
  1. Wounds and injuries
  ISBN 978-1-59920-222-8 lib bdg; 1-59920-222-0 lib bdg

"Encourages further learning with sidebars that help readers think concretely about the subject. . . . Altogether a pitch perfect presentation." SLJ

Includes glossary

617.6 Dentistry

Cobb, Vicki
  ★ **Your** body battles a cavity; written by Vicki Cobb; photomicrographs by Dennis Kunkel; illustrations by Andrew N. Harris. Millbrook Press 2009 32p il (Body battles) lib bdg $25.26
Grades: 3 4 5   **617.6**
  1. Teeth 2. Immune system
  ISBN 978-0-8225-7469-9 lib bdg; 0-8225-7469-1 lib bdg

                    LC 2008002827
With comic illustrations and photomicrographs, this shows what happens when a person gets a cavity, depicting the body's defenses as superheroes

Includes glossary and bibliographical references

Guillain, Charlotte
  Visiting the dentist. Heinmann Library 2011 24p il (Growing up) lib bdg $22; pa $6.49
Grades: PreK K 1 2   **617.6**
  1. Dentistry
  ISBN 978-1-4329-4804-7 lib bdg; 1-4329-4804-0 lib bdg; 978-1-4329-4814-6 pa; 1-4329-4814-8 pa
                    LC 2010024198
This book examines a "common, often scary [event] in children's lives and [guides] readers through [it] step-by-step. The [author discusses] the who, what, and why of [the] experience . . . By confronting . . . fears head-on, children will feel 'in the know' and be prepared to experience [this first]. The text—two sentences per page in a large font and placed on white space—is accompanied by large color photos of children, families, and adults of a variety of ethnic

backgrounds. [The] volume includes boldface vocabulary words, a picture glossary, and dos and don'ts." SLJ

Includes glossary and bibliographical references

Landau, Elaine

★ **Cavities** and toothaches. Marshall Cavendish Benchmark 2008 32p il (Head-to-toe health) lib bdg $28.50

Grades: 2 3 4   **617.6**

1. Teeth 2. Dentistry

ISBN 978-0-7614-2848-0; 0-7614-2848-8

LC 2007-19192

"Photo illustrations are apt and age appropriate.... Pervading the [book] ... is an overall sense of reassurance that even if something hurts, 'all better' is never too far away. Appealing and readable nonfiction." SLJ

Includes glossary and bibliographical references

Miller, Edward, 1964-

★ The **tooth** book; a guide to healthy teeth and gums. [by] Edward Miller. Holiday House 2008 un il $16.95

Grades: K 1 2 3   **617.6**

1. Teeth 2. Dentistry

ISBN 978-0-8234-2092-6; 0-8234-2092-2

LC 2007018302

"In this brightly illustrated picture book, Miller goes well beyond the basics of brushing, flossing, and visiting the dentist. Readers view the inside of a tooth and learn about primary and permanent teeth, decay, losing teeth, and dental first aid. Especially welcome is the emphasis on eating healthy foods and avoiding sugar.... The cleanly designed, computer-generated artwork is appealing, lively, and instructive." SLJ

Royston, Angela

Tooth decay. Black Rabbit Books 2009 30p il (How's your health) lib bdg $27.10

Grades: 1 2 3   **617.6**

1. Teeth

ISBN 978-1-59920-221-1 lib bdg; 1-59920-221-2 lib bdg

First published 2004 by Heinemann Library

"Encourages further learning with sidebars that help readers think concretely about the subject.... Altogether a pitch perfect presentation." SLJ

Includes glossary

Why do I brush my teeth? QEB Pub. 2010 24p il (QEB my body) lib bdg $28.65

Grades: PreK K 1 2   **617.6**

1. Teeth 2. Dentistry

ISBN 978-1-59566-973-5 lib bdg; 1-59566-973-6 lib bdg

LC 2009-15219

Introduces the structure and growth of the teeth, and outlines the principles of dental health and hygiene

"The information is straightforward, well presented, and easy to understand.... [This] title is well designed, filled with color photographs, and scattered with fact boxes." Libr Media Connect

Includes glossary and bibliographical references

Schuh, Mari C.

All about teeth; by Mari Schuh. Capstone Press 2008 24p il (Pebble plus. Healthy teeth) lib bdg $21.26; pa $5.95

Grades: K 1 2 3   **617.6**

1. Teeth

ISBN 978-1-4296-1238-8 lib bdg; 1-4296-1238-X lib bdg; 1-4296-1784-5 pa; 978-1-4296-1784-0 pa

LC 2007-27115

"Feature[s] bright close-up photographs ... and simple vocabulary and sentences to engage pre-readers as well as new readers." Horn Book Guide

Includes glossary and bibliographical references

Loose tooth; by Mari Schuh. Capstone Press 2008 24p il (Pebble plus. Healthy teeth) lib bdg $21.26; pa $6.95

Grades: K 1 2 3   **617.6**

1. Teeth

ISBN 978-1-4296-1243-2 lib bdg; 1-4296-1243-6 lib bdg; 978-1-4296-1789-5 pa; 1-4296-1789-6 pa

LC 2007-27208

"Feature[s] bright close-up photographs ... and simple vocabulary and sentences to engage pre-readers as well as new readers." Horn Book Guide

Includes glossary and bibliographical references

Thomas, Pat

Do I have to go to the dentist? a first look at healthy teeth. [by] Pat Thomas; illustrated by Lesley Harker. Barron's Educational Series 2008 29p il pa $6.99

Grades: PreK K 1 2   **617.6**

1. Teeth 2. Dentistry

ISBN 978-0-7641-3901-7 pa; 0-7641-3901-0 pa

This "book addresses the purpose of dental visits, what to expect, the dental exam and tooth cleaning, and cavities. ... Sidebars ... ask questions about children's personal experiences and thoughts, which can be used as discussion starters. [The] title ends with an extensive note to parents, with practical advice for lessening anxiety about going to the dentist.... [This is a] solid [addition] for most collections." SLJ

Ziefert, Harriet

ABC dentist; illustrated by Liz Murphy. Blue Apple Books 2008 un il $15.95

Grades: K 1 2 3   **617.6**

1. Alphabet 2. Dentistry

ISBN 978-1-934706-31-2; 1-934706-31-0

LC 2008005875

"From A ('appointment') to Z ('zillion times cleaner'), the bright, collage-filled pages feature facts about teeth and gums, assurances that a visit to the dentist won't hurt too much, and images of children getting care from friendly dentists and hygienists. The facts range from the basics ... to the more specialized ... while the ... illustrations ... offer a variety of views of mouths and teeth, including one nice use of an actual X-ray.... The book seeks to offer plenty of knowledge as well as comfort." Booklist

617.7　Ophthalmology

Bender, Lionel

Explaining blindness. Smart Apple Media 2010 45p il (Explaining) lib bdg $34.25

Grades: 5 6 7 8　　　　　　　　　　　　　**617.7**
1. Blind
ISBN 978-1-59920-310-2 lib bdg; 1-59920-310-3 lib bdg

LC 2008-49286

Describes blindness, including its possible causes, the different types of visual impairment, current treatments and cures, and how blind and visually impaired people live everyday lives

"The incorporation of quotes and personal accounts in 'Case Notes' sidebars adds to the sensitive tone found throughout [the title]." SLJ
Includes glossary

Glaser, Jason

Pinkeye. Capstone Press 2006 24p il (First facts: health matters) $21.26

Grades: K 1 2 3　　　　　　　　　　　　　**617.7**
1. Conjunctivitis
ISBN 978-0-7368-4292-1; 0-7368-4292-6

LC 2004031054

"Introduces pinkeye, its causes, symptoms, treatments, and prevention." Publisher's note
Includes bibliographical references

Markle, Sandra

Lost sight; true survival stories. Lerner Publications 2010 48p il (Powerful medicine) lib bdg $27.93

Grades: 5 6 7 8　　　　　　　　　　　　　**617.7**
1. Eye 2. Blind 3. Vision
ISBN 978-0-8225-8701-9 lib bdg; 0-8225-8701-7 lib bdg

LC 2009-34443

This book about vision loss "will grab the attention of middle school readers. . . . The illustrations and photos are stunning with medically accurate captions. Real-life patients, whose photos are included in the text, are highlighted, with updates on their progress at the end of . . . [the] book."
Voice Youth Advocates
Includes glossary and bibliographical references

Parker, Victoria

Having an eye test; [by] Vic Parker. Heinemann Library 2011 24p il (Growing up) lib bdg $22; pa $6.49

Grades: PreK K 1 2　　　　　　　　　　　**617.7**
1. Eye
ISBN 978-1-4329-4798-9 lib bdg; 1-4329-4798-2 lib bdg; 978-1-4329-4808-5 pa; 1-4329-4808-3 pa

LC 2010024192

This explains what to expect from an eye test.
Includes bibliographical references

617.8　Otology and audiology

Cobb, Vicki

★ **Your** body battles an earache; written by Vicki Cobb; photomicrographs by Dennis Kunkel; illustrated by Andrew N. Harris. Millbrook Press 2009 32p il (Body battles) lib bdg $25.26

Grades: 3 4 5　　　　　　　　　　　　　　**617.8**
1. Immune system 2. Ear infections
ISBN 978-0-8225-6812-4 lib bdg; 0-8225-6812-8 lib bdg

LC 2008002846

Microphotographs and comic illustrations show what happens when a person has an earache

"Many of the vibrant illustrations anthropomorphize various cells and other 'battle' participants, making the science explained approachable and easy to understand. Photomicrographs further illuminate the text." SLJ
Includes glossary and bibliographical references

Glaser, Jason

Ear infections. Capstone Press 2007 24p il (First facts: health matters) $21.26

Grades: K 1 2 3　　　　　　　　　　　　　**617.8**
1. Ear infections
ISBN 978-0-7368-6390-2; 0-7368-6390-7

LC 2006002809

"Describes ear infections, how and why they occur, and how to treat and prevent them." Publisher's note
Includes bibliographical references

Landau, Elaine

★ **Earaches**. Marshall Cavendish Benchmark 2010 32p il (Head-to-toe health) lib bdg $28.50

Grades: 2 3 4　　　　　　　　　　　　　　**617.8**
1. Ear infections
ISBN 978-0-7614-4831-0 lib bdg; 0-7614-4831-4 lib bdg

This provides basic information about earaches and their prevention.

This "manages to pack in a surprising amount of information, including facts about good hygiene. The text addresses the reader directly, and the photos are real grabbers." Booklist
Includes glossary and bibliographical references

Levete, Sarah

Explaining deafness. Smart Apple Media 2010 45p il (Explaining) lib bdg $34.25

Grades: 5 6 7 8　　　　　　　　　　　　　**617.8**
1. Deafness
ISBN 978-1-59920-313-3 lib bdg; 1-59920-313-8 lib bdg

LC 2008-49289

Discusses the history, diagnosis, and treatment of deafness, including ways to cope with living with the condition

"The incorporation of quotes and personal accounts in 'Case Notes' sidebars adds to the sensitive tone found throughout [the title]." SLJ
Includes glossary, bibliographical references and filmography

Parker, Victoria

Having a hearing test; [by] Vic Parker. Heinmann Library 2011 24p il (Growing up) lib bdg $22; pa $6.49

Grades: PreK K 1 2　　　　　　　　　　　**617.8**
1. Hearing
ISBN 978-1-4329-4799-6 lib bdg; 1-4329-4799-0 lib bdg; 978-1-4329-4809-2 pa; 1-4329-4809-1 pa

LC 2010024193

This explains how a hearing test works and possible next steps for those with hearing problems.

"The text is simple, and the pictures are big and bright." Booklist

Includes bibliographical references

617.9 Operative surgery and special fields of surgery

Jango-Cohen, Judith
  Bionics; [by] Judith Jango-Cohen. Lerner Publications Co. 2007 48p il (Cool science) lib bdg $26.60
Grades: 4 5 6 7   **617.9**
   1. Bionics 2. Artificial organs
   ISBN 978-0-8225-5937-5 lib bdg; 0-8225-5937-4 lib bdg
                     LC 2005032221
This "introduction to the field of bionics is divided into four chapters: 'Replacing Parts,' 'Fixing Malfunctions,' 'Assisting the Senses,' and 'Facing the Future.' Jango-Cohen uses a number of personal stories and references to pop culture to engage readers. . . . The explanations are clearly written and easily understood. Colorful photographs and illustrations are featured throughout the text." SLJ

Includes bibliographical references

618.92 Pediatrics

Grossberg, Blythe
  ★ **Asperger's** rules! how to make sense of school and friends. by Blythe Grossberg. Magination Press 2012 127 p. col. ill. (paperback) $9.95; (hardcover) $14.95
Grades: 5 6 7 8   **618.92**
   1. Life skills -- Juvenile literature 2. Social skills -- Juvenile literature 3. Asperger's syndrome -- Juvenile literature 4. Autism in children 5. Autistic children -- Education 6. Asperger's syndrome -- Social aspects
   ISBN 1433811286; 9781433811272; 9781433811289
                     LC 2011053483
This book by Blythe Grossberg presents a "guide for readers with Asperger's, covering feelings and emotions, teachers, asking for help, and dealing with bullies. Quizzes let readers reflect on their own approaches to situations like interacting with kids at school, and Grossberg also includes tips on how to interpret social situations. . . . Flowcharts illustrate how various conversations might progress, and other sections focus on dressing properly and eating healthful meals." (Publishers Weekly)

Reeve, Elizabeth
  The **survival** guide for kids with autism spectrum disorders (and their parents) by Elizabeth Verdick & Elizabeth Reeve; illustrated by Nick Kobyluch. Free Spirit Pub. 2012 234 p. col. ill. (pbk.) $16.99
Grades: 5 6 7 8 Adult   **618.92**
   1. Autism 2. Children with autism 3. Parents of autistic children 4. Children with autism spectrum disorders -- Juvenile literature 5. Autistic children -- Family relationships -- Juvenile literature
   ISBN 1575423855; 9781575423852; 9781575426747
                     LC 2011046520

This book "offers kids with autism spectrum disorders (ASDs) their own comprehensive resource for both understanding their condition and finding tools to cope with the challenges they face every day . . . with an emphasis on helping children gain new self-understanding and self-acceptance. Meant to be read with a parent, the book addresses questions . . . and provides strategies for communicating, making and keeping friends, and succeeding in school." (Publisher's note)

"This volume could become a treasured resource for families looking for help in successfully working through some of the problems faced by higher-functioning children with ASD." SLJ

620.1 Engineering mechanics and materials

Blaxland, Wendy
  Plates and mugs. Marshall Cavendish Benchmark 2009 32p il (How are they made?) $19.95
Grades: 3 4 5 6   **620.1**
   1. Ceramics 2. Tableware
   ISBN 978-0-7614-3809-0; 0-7614-3809-2
                     LC 2008026210
This describes how plates and mugs are made, including their history, raw materials, design, manufacture, and relationship to the environment.

Claybourne, Anna
  Materials. QEB Pub. 2008 24p il (Why it works) $24.25
Grades: 2 3 4 5   **620.1**
   1. Materials
   ISBN 978-1-59566-557-7; 1-59566-557-9
                     LC 2008-11711
This is "colorfully illustrated and should help young students relate better to the concepts being presented. A glossary of key words and a page of suggestions for parents and teachers to extend the learning experience round out the text." Sci Books & Films

Includes glossary and bibliographical references

Hillman, Ben
  How strong is it? a mighty book all about strength. [by] Ben Hillman. Scholastic Reference 2008 48p il (What's the big idea?) $14.99
Grades: 3 4 5   **620.1**
   1. Power (Mechanics)
   ISBN 978-0-439-91866-4; 0-439-91866-9
This describes the strength of such things as spiderwebs, bulldozers, wood, elephants, glue, lasers, hair, rope, and volcanoes.

"The conversational, fact-filled text and computer-manipulated illustrations add humor to this random sampling of awesome powers." Horn Book Guide

Langley, Andrew
  Glass; [by] Andrew Langley. Crabtree Pub. Co. 2009 24p il (Everyday materials) lib bdg $21.27; pa $6.95

Grades: K 1 2 3   **620.1**
1. Glass
ISBN 978-0-7787-4126-8 lib bdg; 0-7787-4126-5 lib
bdg; 978-0-7787-4134-3 pa; 0-7787-4134-6 pa
LC 2008-24157
This title "introduces [glass] in an engaging style. The
text and photos work together, progressing from a definition of the material to how it is manufactured and what it is
used for. . . . [It] concludes with a recycling section, a simple
comprehension quiz, and a topic web that offers extension
ideas. The large type, bright photos, and uncluttered layout
will allow large and small group use." SLJ
Includes glossary

Metal; [by] Andrew Langley. Crabtree Pub. Co. 2009
24p il (Everyday materials) lib bdg $21.27; pa $6.95
Grades: K 1 2 3   **620.1**
1. Metals
ISBN 978-0-7787-4127-5 lib bdg; 0-7787-4127-3 lib
bdg; 978-0-7787-4134-3 pa; 0-7787-4134-6 pa
LC 2008-24036
This title "introduces [metals] in an engaging style. The
text and photos work together, progressing from a definition of the material to how it is manufactured and what it is
used for. . . . [It] concludes with a recycling section, a simple
comprehension quiz, and a topic web that offers extension
ideas. The large type, bright photos, and uncluttered layout
will allow large and small group use." SLJ
Includes glossary

Wood; [by] Andrew Langley. Crabtree Pub. Co. 2009
24p il (Everyday materials) lib bdg $21.27; pa $6.95
Grades: K 1 2 3   **620.1**
1. Wood
ISBN 978-0-7787-4130-5 lib bdg; 0-7787-4130-3 lib
bdg; 978-0-7787-4137-4 pa; 0-7787-4137-0 pa
LC 2008-24037
This title "introduces [wood] in an engaging style. The
text and photos work together, progressing from a definition of the material to how it is manufactured and what it is
used for. . . . [It] concludes with a recycling section, a simple
comprehension quiz, and a topic web that offers extension
ideas. The large type, bright photos, and uncluttered layout
will allow large and small group use." SLJ
Includes glossary

Morris, Neil
Glass. Amicus 2010 48p il (Materials that matter) lib
bdg $28.50
Grades: 4 5 6 7   **620.1**
1. Glass
ISBN 978-1-60753-065-7 lib bdg; 1-60753-065-1
lib bdg
LC 2009029796
"The clean layout includes photographs and occasional
charts, graphs, and technical illustrations against a range of
pastel backgrounds. Inset boxes provide further detail, interesting extras, and recycling information. . . . [This book
offers] easily accessible background information for report
writers." SLJ
Includes glossary and bibliographical references

Metals. Amicus 2010 48p il (Materials that matter)
lib bdg $28.50

Grades: 4 5 6 7   **620.1**
1. Metals
ISBN 978-1-60753-066-4 lib bdg; 1-60753-066-X
lib bdg
LC 2009029797
"The clean layout includes photographs and occasional
charts, graphs, and technical illustrations against a range of
pastel backgrounds. Inset boxes provide further detail, interesting extras, and recycling information. . . . [This book
offers] easily accessible background information for report
writers." SLJ
Includes glossary and bibliographical references

Oxlade, Chris
Changing shape. Heinemann Library 2008 32p il
(Changing materials) lib bdg $25.36; pa $7.99
Grades: K 1 2   **620.1**
1. Materials
ISBN 978-1-4329-3271-8 lib bdg; 1-4329-3271-3 lib
bdg; 978-1-4329-3276-3 pa; 1-4329-3276-4 pa
LC 2008-54586
Discusses "the properties of materials and whether or not
they can bend or twist or are brittle, or are in liquid or gas
form. . . . A few simple activities provide opportunities to
experiment. The color photographs are engaging." SLJ
Includes glossary and bibliographical references

Joining materials; [by] Chris Oxlade. Crabtree Pub.
Company 2008 32p il (Working with materials) lib bdg
$26.60; pa $7.95
Grades: 2 3 4   **620.1**
1. Materials
ISBN 978-0-7787-3639-4 lib bdg; 0-7787-3639-3 lib
bdg; 978-0-7787-3649-3 pa; 0-7787-3649-0 pa
LC 2007027420
This describes how materials are joined with nuts, bolts,
and screws, glue, wood joints, welding, soldering, sewing,
tape, and velcro
This "title has numerous captioned color photographs. . .
. The [book offers] three simple, easy, and safe reproducible
experiments. . . . Students will appreciate the pleasing de-
sign, easy-to-read font, and direct, clear writing style." Libr
Media Connect
Includes glossary and bibliographical references

Shaping materials; [by] Chris Oxlade. Crabtree Pub.
Company 2008 32p il (Working with materials) lib bdg
$26.60; pa $7.95
Grades: 2 3 4   **620.1**
1. Materials
ISBN 978-0-7787-3641-7 lib bdg; 0-7787-3641-5 lib
bdg; 978-0-7787-3651-6 pa; 0-7787-3651-2 pa
LC 2007027422
This describes how materials are shaped with scissors,
molds, hammers, saws, chisels, and machine shapers, and
by folding and bending, glassblowing, and clay modeling
This "title has numerous captioned color photographs.
. . . The [book offers] three simple, easy, safe reproduc-
ible experiments. . . . Students will appreciate the pleasing
design, easy-to-read font, and direct, clear writing." Libr
Media Connect
Includes glossary and bibliographical references

Riley, Peter D.
Materials. Sea-to-Sea Publications 2011 32p il (The real scientist investigates) lib bdg $28.50
Grades: 3 4 5   620.1
1. Materials
ISBN 978-1-59771-282-8; 1-59771-282-5
LC 2010005373

In this book about materials "solid scientific material is presented in accessible language and a visually engaging, boldly colored layout. Budding scientists are encouraged to hone their skills by recording observations, making predictions, and analyzing results. Hands-on activities are included on almost every spread. . . . The many color photos feature diverse children demonstrating the activities." SLJ

Includes glossary and bibliographical references

Ward, David J.
Materials science; by D. J. Ward. Lerner Publications 2009 47p il (Cool science) lib bdg $26.60
Grades: 4 5 6   620.1
1. Materials
ISBN 978-0-8225-7588-7 lib bdg; 0-8225-7588-4
lib bdg
LC 2007042176

This describes how scientists study the microscopic parts of materials such as plastic, glass, or stainless steel, how they learn how each part makes something hard or soft, strong or weak, or good or bad at carrying heat, and how they use that knowledge to create supermaterials to help make better sports equipment, tinier computer chips, and more.

Includes glossary and bibliographical references

621   Applied physics

Spilsbury, Richard
What is energy? exploring science with hands-on activities. [by] Richard and Louise Spilsbury. Enslow Elementary 2008 32p il (In touch with basic science) lib bdg $22.60
Grades: 3 4 5   621
1. Energy resources 2. Force and energy 3. Power (Mechanics) 4. Science -- Experiments
ISBN 978-0-7660-3099-2 lib bdg; 0-7660-3099-7
lib bdg
LC 2007024521

This book includes "a discussion about what energy is and then moves on to examine heat energy, chemical energy, energy for life, electrical energy, and finally, renewable energy. Energy is such a broad topic, yet this small volume masterfully provides a good basis for understanding the concept." Sci Books Films

Includes glossary and bibliographical references

621.1   Fluid-power technologies

O'Neal, Claire
How to use waste energy to heat and light your home. Mitchell Lane Publishers 2009 47p il (Tell your parents) lib bdg $21.50

Grades: 4 5 6 7   621.1
1. Recycling 2. Waste products as fuel
ISBN 978-1-58415-765-6 lib bdg; 1-58415-765-8
lib bdg
LC 2009-4483

Explores how to reduce the amount of trash produced and stored by reusing items and recycling materials, and describes how these efforts can help protect the environment

This title "offers numerous facts and statistics, all of which are cited. . . . Chapters cover present-day issues and . . . are interspersed with full-color photographs and short 'Did You Know' trivia boxes. . . . Back matter includes detailed resource lists and 'Try This!' experiments." SLJ

Includes glossary and bibliographical references

621.3   Electrical, magnetic, optical, communications, computer engineering; electronics, lighting

Price, Sean
The story behind electricity; [by] Sean Stewart Price. Heinemann Library 2009 32p il (True stories) $28.21
Grades: 3 4 5   621.3
1. Electricity 2. Electrical engineering
ISBN 978-1-4329-2339-6; 1-4329-2339-0
LC 2008043408

This answers such questions as: How does a lightning rod work? What animals use electricity? Why did Thomas Edison have to build a power station?

Includes bibliographical references

621.31   Generation, modification, storage, transmission of electric power

Bartholomew, Alan
Electric mischief; battery-powered gadgets kids can build. written by Alan Bartholomew; illustrated by Lynn Bartholomew. Kids Can Press 2002 48p il (Kids can do it) $12.95; pa $5.95
Grades: 4 5 6   621.31
1. Electricity 2. Electric apparatus and appliances
ISBN 1-55074-923-4; 1-55074-925-0 pa

This provides instructions for building 10 electric gadgets such as a bumper car, electric dice, and a robot hand

"Projects are clearly explained and easy to follow; colorful illustrations aid understanding. Materials required . . . are readily available at hardware stores." SLJ

Benduhn, Tea
Water power; by Tea Benduhn. Weekly Reader Pub. 2009 24p il (Energy for today) lib bdg $21; pa $5.95
Grades: 2 3 4   621.31
1. Water power 2. Energy resources
ISBN 978-0-8368-9264-2 lib bdg; 0-8368-9264-X lib bdg; 978-0-8368-9363-2 pa; 0-8368-9363-8 pa
LC 2008012021

This explains how flowing water is used as an energy resource, and how it may be used in the future.

"New readers will be able to wrap their hands around the small, square size, and their minds around the clear, enlightening text. [This book has] crisp photos and strong back matter." Booklist

Includes glossary and bibliographical references

Wind power; by Tea Benduhn. Weekly Reader Pub. 2009 24p il (Energy for today) lib bdg $21; pa $5.95

Grades: 2 3 4　　　　　　　　　　　　　　**621.31**
1. Wind power 2. Energy resources
ISBN 978-0-8368-9265-9 lib bdg; 0-8368-9265-8 lib bdg; 978-0-8368-9364-9 pa; 0-8368-9364-6 pa

LC 2008012019

This explains how wind forms and the ways we may use it as an energy source in the future.

"New readers will be able to wrap their hands around the small, square size, and their minds around the clear enlightening text. [This book has] crisp photos and strong back matter." Booklist

Includes glossary and bibliographical references

Graf, Mike
How does a waterfall become electricity? Raintree 2008 32p il (How does it happen?) lib bdg $27.50; pa $7.99

Grades: 3 4 5　　　　　　　　　　　　　　**621.31**
1. Electricity 2. Water power 3. Hydrodynamics
ISBN 978-1-4109-3448-2 lib bdg; 1-4109-3448-9 lib bdg; 978-1-4109-3456-7 pa; 1-4109-3456-X pa

LC 2008-52653

The explains the cause and effect of waterfalls, and the many ways they can be used to make electricity.

"Information is clearly presented using a large font, diagrams, and photographs formatted to resemble Polaroid pictures. . . . A first-rate job answering some important scientific questions." SLJ

Includes glossary and bibliographical references

Lew, Kristi
Goodbye, gasoline; the science of fuel cells. Compass Point Books 2009 48p il (Headline science) lib bdg $27.93

Grades: 5 6 7 8　　　　　　　　　　　　**621.31**
1. Fuel cells
ISBN 978-0-7565-3521-6 lib bdg; 0-7565-3521-2 lib bdg

LC 2008011729

This "clearly examines the history and technology of hydrogen fuel cells, including the various types such as proton exchange membrane and alkaline cells. An excellent description of how the technology works gives readers an understanding of both the successes and problems relating to these promising energy sources. . . . The color illustrations and charts . . . are clear and helpful, and the text, although information rich, is not overly difficult." SLJ

O'Neal, Claire
How to use wind power to light and heat your home. Mitchell Lane Publishers 2009 47p il map (Tell your parents) lib bdg $21.50

Grades: 4 5 6 7　　　　　　　　　　　　**621.31**
1. Wind power 2. Renewable energy resources
ISBN 978-1-58415-762-5 lib bdg; 1-58415-762-3 lib bdg

LC 2009-4530

Introduces wind power, including the history of harnessing the wind for work, how modern wind power generates electricity, and how to install a turbine to a home

This book "offers numerous facts and statistics, all of which are cited. . . . Chapters cover present-day issues and . . . are interspersed with full-color photographs and short 'Did You Know' trivia boxes. . . . Back matter includes detailed resource lists and 'Try This!' experiments." SLJ

Includes glossary and bibliographical references

621.319　Transmission

Cole, Joanna
The **magic** school bus and the electric field trip; illustrated by Bruce Degen. Scholastic 1997 48p il hardcover o.p. pa $6.99

Grades: 2 3 4　　　　　　　　　　　　　**621.319**
1. Electric power 2. Electricity -- Juvenile literature 3. Electric power -- Juvenile literature
ISBN 0-590-44682-7; 0-590-44683-5 pa

LC 97-2080

Ms. Frizzle takes her class on a field trip through the town's electrical wires so they can learn how electricity is generated and how it is used

"Spiced with plenty of puns and jokes, the writing and the colorful artwork continue the series' unbeatable combination of clearly presented information and plenty of fun." Booklist

621.382　Communications engineering

Perritano, John
Revolution in communications. Marshall Cavendish Benchmark 2010 32p il (It works!) lib bdg $19.95

Grades: 3 4 5　　　　　　　　　　　　　**621.382**
1. Telecommunication
ISBN 978-0-7614-4373-5 lib bdg; 0-7614-4373-8 lib bdg

LC 2008-54347

"This interesting, information packed [book] . . . motivates students to do their own exploring. . . . The appealing cartoon-like photographs add humor. . . . This . . . just may be that spark needed to create eager budding scientists." Libr Media Connect

Includes glossary and bibliographical references

621.384　Radio and radar

Firestone, Mary
Wireless technology. Lerner Publications 2009 48p il (Cool science) lib bdg $27.93

Grades: 4 5 6　　　　　　　　　　　　　**621.384**
1. Wireless communication systems
ISBN 978-0-8225-7590-0 lib bdg; 0-8225-7590-6 lib bdg

LC 2007041102

This describes "how cutting-edge science helps people communicate better, live healthier, and have more fun!" Publisher's note

Includes glossary and bibliographical references

621.385 Telephony

Spilsbury, Richard
The **telephone**; [by] Richard and Louise Spilsbury. Heinemann Library 2011 32p il (Tales of invention) lib bdg $29; pa $7.99
Grades: 4 5 6 7   **621.385**
 1. Telephone 2. Cellular telephones
 ISBN 978-1-4329-3826-0 lib bdg; 1-4329-3826-6 lib bdg; 978-1-4329-3833-8 pa; 1-4329-3833-9 pa
                                          LC 2009049027
"Beginning with the first telegraph, the book discusses how sound travels, how speech is transmitted by wire, and how Alexander Graham Bell's first telephones worked. Then the text quickly traces later technological developments, from transatlantic cables to early cell phones to the small, light, versatile models available today. . . . The many photographs and other illustrations include excellent labeled diagrams." Booklist
 Includes bibliographical references

621.389 Security, sound recording, related systems

Gilbert, Adrian
 Top technology. Firefly 2009 32p il (Spy files) pa $6.95
Grades: 3 4 5 6   **621.389**
 1. Espionage 2. Electronic surveillance
 ISBN 978-1-55407-576-8; 1-55407-576-9
 First published 2008 in the United Kingdom
Discusses equipment and technology used by spies, including satellites, cameras, lie detectors, listening devices, and more.
 The text's "short paragraphs and great pictures are combined in a collage style that will draw readers quickly through the information. Useful for reports and browsing." SLJ
 Includes glossary

621.4 Prime movers and heat engineering

Cartlidge, Cherese
 Home windmills; by Cherese Cartlidge. Norwood House Press 2008 48p il (A great idea) lib bdg $25.27
Grades: 3 4 5 6   **621.4**
 1. Windmills
 ISBN 978-1-59953-192-2 lib bdg; 1-59953-192-5 lib bdg
                                          LC 2008-24190
 "Describes the invention and development of the home windmills." Publisher's note
 Includes glossary and bibliographical references

Woelfle, Gretchen
 The **wind** at work; an activity guide to windmills. Gretchen Woelfle. 2nd ed. Chicago Review Press 2013 vii, 145 p.p ill. (paperback) $16.95

Grades: 4 5 6   **621.4**
 1. Windmills 2. Wind power -- Juvenile literature
 ISBN 1613741006; 9781613741009
                                          LC 2012046319
 "This introduction to windmills discusses their history and function through modern times. . . . About one-third of the book is devoted to activities illustrating the properties of wind and the jobs performed by windmills. . . . The concluding chapters focus on windmills as a source of energy and suggest how to chart household energy use." (Booklist) Index. "Grades four to eight." (SLJ)
 "The historical information is excellent, and includes Persian windmills of 1000 years ago, Dutch windmills of the 17th century, and modern wind turbines. Amusing anecdotes and intriguing facts are woven into the text, keeping it lively. . . . Black-and-white historical prints, photographs, and diagrams appear throughout." SLJ
 Includes bibliographical references (pages 133-135) and index

621.43 Internal-combustion engines

Shores, Lori
 How to build a fizzy rocket. Capstone Press 2011 24p il (Hands-on science fun) lib bdg $17.99; pa $6.95
Grades: PreK K 1   **621.43**
 1. Science -- Experiments 2. Rockets (Aeronautics) -- Models
 ISBN 978-1-4296-4491-4 lib bdg; 1-4296-4491-5 lib bdg; 978-1-4296-5573-6 pa; 1-4296-5573-9 pa
                                          LC 2009051419
Simple text and full-color photos instruct readers how to build a fizzy rocket and explain the science behind the activity.
 "Bright, glossy photos and irresistible ideas make these science lessons effortless fun." Booklist
 Includes bibliographical references

621.47 Solar-energy engineering

Bang, Molly
 ★ **My** light. Blue Sky Press 2004 un il $16.95
Grades: 1 2 3   **621.47**
 1. Electricity 2. Solar energy
 ISBN 0-439-48961-X
 "Bang's strong design sense comes through in compositions that gracefully incorporate diagrams and strike a balance between graphic forms and delicate, decorative patterns. A lovely and illuminating book that presents sound science while expressing the wonder of flipping a switch and flooding a room with light." Booklist

Bearce, Stephanie
 How to harness solar power for your home. Mitchell Lane Publishers 2009 47p il map (Tell your parents) lib bdg $21.50
Grades: 4 5 6 7   **621.47**
 1. Solar energy
 ISBN 978-1-58415-761-8 lib bdg; 1-58415-761-5 lib bdg
                                          LC 2009-4529

This title about solar power "offers numerous facts and statistics, all of which are cited. . . . Chapters cover present-day issues and . . . are interspersed with full-color photographs and short 'Did You Know' trivia boxes. . . . Back matter includes detailed resource lists and 'Try This!' experiments." SLJ

Includes glossary and bibliographical references

Benduhn, Tea

Solar power; by Tea Benduhn. Weekly Reader Pub. 2008 24p il (Energy for today) lib bdg $21; pa $5.95

Grades: 2 3 4　　　　　　　　　　　　621.47

1. Solar energy

ISBN 978-0-8368-9263-5 lib bdg; 0-8368-9263-1 lib bdg; 978-0-8368-9362-5 pa; 0-8368-9362-X pa

LC 2008015515

"This title presents a surprising amount of information about solar power in brief sentences that are calibrated to newly confident readers' abilities. . . . The selection of well-chosen photos, which are crisply reproduced on each page, is particularly strong in the final chapters about solar technology. . . . The language is direct, clear, and enlightening." Booklist

Includes glossary and bibliographical references

621.48　　Nuclear engineering

Benduhn, Tea

Nuclear power; by Tea Benduhn. Weekly Reader Pub. 2009 24p il (Energy for today) lib bdg $21; pa $5.95

Grades: 2 3 4　　　　　　　　　　　　621.48

1. Nuclear energy

ISBN 978-0-8368-9262-8 lib bdg; 0-8368-9262-3 lib bdg; 978-0-8368-9361-8 pa; 0-8368-9361-1 pa

LC 2008012020

This describes how nuclear power works and how it may be used in the future.

"New readers will be able to wrap their hands around the small, square size, and their minds around the clear, enlightening text. [This book has] crisp photos and strong back matter." Booklist

Includes glossary and bibliographical references

Feigenbaum, Aaron

Emergency at Three Mile Island; by Aaron Feigenbaum. Bearport Pub. 2007 32p il map (Code red) lib bdg $23.96

Grades: 3 4 5　　　　　　　　　　　　621.48

1. Nuclear power plants

ISBN 978-1-59716-364-4 lib bdg; 1-59716-364-3 lib bdg

LC 2006031635

This "discusses the 1979 malfunction of a nuclear reactor that could have cost thousands of lives and devastated the area but, fortunately, did not. . . . The writing is clear and concise. . . . The facts are allowed to speak for themselves. The [book is] liberally laced with pertinent period photographs and numerous quotes."

Includes glossary and bibliographical references

621.5　　Pneumatic, vacuum, low-temperature technologies

Pringle, Laurence

Ice! the amazing history of the ice business. Laurence Pringle. Calkins Creek 2012 74 p. $17.95

Grades: 4 5 6 7 8　　　　　　　　　　621.5

1. Ice 2. Refrigeration 3. Food -- Preservation

ISBN 159078801X; 9781590788011

LC 2012937320

This book looks at "iceboxes, icehouses, icemen, and . . . more about the history of the harvesting, storage, and delivery of ice." Author Laurence Pringle "briefly covers early food preservation . . . before delving into the rise of the ice industry in the early 1800s, and, in particular, the harvesting of the frozen stuff at pristine Rockland Lake in New York." (School Library Journal)

Includes bibliographical references and index.

621.8　　Machine engineering

Bodden, Valerie

Levers. Creative Education 2011 23p il (Simple machines) $24.25; pa $8.99

Grades: K 1 2 3　　　　　　　　　　　621.8

1. Levers

ISBN 978-1-60818-009-7; 1-60818-009-3; 978-0-89812-580-1 pa; 0-89812-580-4 pa

"The pages are uncluttered and are typeset in a large font, making the words practically pop off the [page]. Also, the author makes the definitions that are presented simple to understand with her selection of photographs. . . . [This is] outstanding and well suited to young elementary school children." Sci Books & Films

Includes glossary

Pulleys. Creative Education 2011 23p il (Simple machines) $24.25; pa $8.99

Grades: K 1 2 3　　　　　　　　　　　621.8

1. Pulleys

ISBN 978-1-60818-010-3; 1-60818-010-7; 978-0-89812-581-8 pa; 0-89812-581-2 pa

"The pages are uncluttered and are typeset in a large font, making the words practically pop off the [page]. Also, the author makes the definitions that are presented simple to understand with her selection of photographs. . . . [This is] outstanding and well suited to young elementary school children." Sci Books & Films

Includes glossary

Screws. Creative Education 2011 23p il (Simple machines) $24.25; pa $8.99

Grades: K 1 2 3　　　　　　　　　　　621.8

1. Screws

ISBN 978-1-60818-011-0; 1-60818-011-5; 978-0-89812-582-5 pa; 0-89812-582-0 pa

"The pages are uncluttered and are typeset in a large font, making the definitions that are presented simple to understand with her selection of photographs. . . . [This is] outstanding and well suited to young elementary school children." Sci Books & Films

Includes glossary

Wheels and axles. Creative Education 2011 23p il (Simple machines) $24.25; pa $8.99

Grades: K 1 2 3   **621.8**

1. Axles 2. Wheels

ISBN 978-1-60818-013-4; 1-60818-013-1; 978-0-89812-584-9 pa; 0-89812-584-7 pa

"The pages are uncluttered and are typeset in a large font, making the words practically pop off the [page]. Also, the author makes the definitions that are presented simple to understand with her selection of photographs. . . . [This is] outstanding and well suited to young elementary school children." Sci Books & Films

Includes glossary

Caterpillar Inc.

My big book of trucks & diggers. Chronicle Books 2011 il bd bk $7.99

Grades: PreK K   **621.8**

1. Trucks 2. Construction equipment 3. Board books for children

ISBN 978-0-8118-7892-0; 0-8118-7892-9

LC 2010053590

An oversized board book featuring photos of 10 Caterpillar machines -a bulldozer, excavator, dump truck, skid steer loader, paver, motor grader, wheel loader, backhoe loader, material handler, and telehandler.

"This board book uses excellent photographs. . . . The bold colors and clear text enhance the presentation. Even though the terms are a bit challenging, the simplicity of the book and the sharp photographs will have youngsters very excited." SLJ

Coppendale, Jean

The **great** big book of mighty machines; [by] Jean Coppendale and Ian Graham. Firefly Books 2009 160p il $19.95

Grades: PreK K 1 2 3   **621.8**

1. Vehicles 2. Machinery

ISBN 978-1-55407-521-8; 1-55407-521-1

"A vehicle-lover's dream come true, this meaty volume focuses on cars, bikes, trains, tractors, rescue vehicles, construction trucks and monster trucks. Each section . . . ends with an activity page. . . . The text is easy to read and understand. Brightly colored page edges draw eyes inward to the exciting full-color photos that fill the pages." Kirkus

Includes glossary

De Medeiros, James, 1975-

Pulleys. Weigl Publishers 2009 24p il (Science matters: simple machines) lib bdg $24.45; pa $8.95

Grades: 2 3 4   **621.8**

1. Pulleys

ISBN 978-1-60596-041-8 lib bdg; 1-60596-041-1 lib bdg; 978-1-60596-042-5 pa; 1-60596-042-X pa

LC 2009-1947

Discusses what a pulley is, where it can be found, and how it is used.

"The bold, large-scale, colorful photographs . . . are sure to draw in even the most reluctant readers." SLJ

Includes glossary

De Medeiros, Michael

Screws. Weigl Publishers 2009 24p il (Science matters: simple machines) lib bdg $24.45; pa $8.95

Grades: 2 3 4   **621.8**

1. Screws

ISBN 978-1-60596-039-5 lib bdg; 1-60596-039-X lib bdg; 978-1-60596-040-1 pa; 1-60596-040-3 pa

LC 2009-1941

Discusses what a screw is, where it can be found, and how it is used.

"De Medeiros' description of the object's function is unusually elegant: Screws convert movement in a circle to movement straight ahead. . . . The back matter (including on-line suggestions, a craft, a quiz, a well-chosen glossary, and more) is strong and features what is likely the only 10-word index in existence to feature the terms nuts, bolts, and King Nebuchadnezzar." Booklist

Includes glossary

Wheels and axles. Weigl Publishers 2010 24p il (Science matters: simple machines) lib bdg $24.45; pa $8.95

Grades: 2 3 4   **621.8**

1. Axles 2. Wheels

ISBN 978-1-60596-033-3 lib bdg; 1-60596-033-0 lib bdg; 978-1-60596-034-0 pa; 1-60596-034-9 pa

LC 2009-7808

Discusses wheels and axles and how they are used in everyday life.

"The bold, large-scale photographs . . . are sure to draw in even the most reluctant readers." SLJ

Includes glossary

Gardner, Robert

Sensational science projects with simple machines; [by] Robert Gardner. Enslow Elementary 2006 48p il (Fantastic physical science experiments) $23.93

Grades: 4 5 6   **621.8**

1. Simple machines 2. Science -- Experiments

ISBN 0-7660-2585-3

LC 2005008974

"The first chapter of [this book] explains force, friction, distance, and work. The book then introduces levers, inclined planes, pulleys, etc. . . . Large colorful, cartoonlike drawings complement the [text]. . . . [This offers] solid information." SLJ

Includes glossary and bibliographical references

Hoban, Tana

Construction zone. Greenwillow Bks. 1997 un il $16.99

Grades: K 1 2   **621.8**

1. Machinery 2. Construction industry -- Juvenile literature

ISBN 0-688-12284-1

LC 96-5696

The "photos have extraordinary depth and detail." Booklist

Howse, Jennifer

Inclined planes. Weigl Publishers 2009 24p il (Science matters: simple machines) lib bdg $24.45; pa $8.95

Grades: 2 3 4   **621.8**
  1. Inclined planes
  ISBN 978-1-60596-035-7 lib bdg; 1-60596-035-7 lib bdg; 978-1-60596-036-4 pa; 1-60596-036-5 pa
                 LC 2009-25972
Discusses what an inclined plane is, where it can be found, and how it is used.
  "The bold, large-scale colorful photographs . . . are sure to draw in even the most reluctant readers." SLJ
Includes glossary

  Levers. Weigl Publishers 2009 24p il (Science matters: simple machines) lib bdg $24.45; pa $8.95
Grades: 2 3 4   **621.8**
  1. Levers
  ISBN 978-1-60596-031-9 lib bdg; 1-60596-031-4 lib bdg; 978-1-60596-032-6 pa; 1-60596-032-2 pa
                 LC 2009-1921
Discusses what a lever is, where it can be found, and how it is used.
  "The bold, large-scale, colorful photographs . . . are sure to draw in even the most reluctant readers." SLJ
Includes glossary

Kulling, Monica
  Going up! Elisha Otis's trip to the top. Monica Kulling. Tundra Books of Northern New York 2012 32 p. (hardcover) $17.95
Grades: 2 3 4   **621.8**
  1. Elevators 2. Picture books for children 3. Otis, Elisha Graves, 1811-1861
  ISBN 1770492402; 9781770492400
                 LC 2011938777
This children's book offers a biography of Elisha Otis. Fascinated by farm machines, he notes "the dangerous possibility of the hoisting platform in the factory falling if the cable breaks" and "designs a safety brake. He realizes that with this, people can also be moved up and down safely. When he gives a demonstration at the New York World's Fair, the Otis Elevator Company takes off." (Children's Literature)

Low, William
  Machines go to work. Holt & Co. 2009 un il $14.95
Grades: PreK K 1   **621.8**
  1. Machinery 2. Vehicles -- Juvenile literature
  ISBN 978-0-8050-8759-8; 0-8050-8759-1
  "The realistic digital paintings will delight youngsters; spreads alternate with three-page foldouts that show the machines at work. . . . This well-constructed picture book is a surefire hit." SLJ

Solway, Andrew
  Castle under siege! simple machines. [by] Andrew Solway. Raintree 2005 32p il lib bdg $28.21; pa $7.85
Grades: 3 4 5   **621.8**
  1. Castles 2. Simple machines
  ISBN 1-4109-1918-8 lib bdg; 1-4109-1949-8 pa
                 LC 2005014549
"The author leads readers through the construction of a castle, the workings of the drawbridge, the execution of a siege and how the inhabitants would protect the castle from attack, methods the invaders might use, and what would happen afterward to repair the damage. While readers are drawn into the action, they are also introduced to the simple

machines used during this period of time. . . . Detailed, easily interpreted diagrams are included for added understanding of concepts. Vivid and realistic photos add to the appeal. An excellent choice for research or for general interest." SLJ

Thales, Sharon
  Inclined planes to the rescue. Capstone Press 2007 24p il (Simple machines to the rescue) lib bdg $21.26
Grades: K 1 2 3   **621.8**
  1. Inclined planes 2. Simple machines
  ISBN 978-0-7368-6752-8
  This is "brightly colored, attractive . . . [and written] in language students can read and understand independently." SLJ
  Includes glossary and bibliographical references

  Levers to the rescue. Capstone Press 2007 24p il (Simple machines to the rescue) lib bdg $21.26
Grades: K 1 2 3   **621.8**
  1. Levers 2. Simple machines
  ISBN 978-0-7368-6747-4 lib bdg; 0-7368-6747-3 lib bdg
  This is "brightly colored, attractive . . . [and written] in language students can read and understand independently." SLJ
  Includes glossary and bibliographical references

  Pulleys to the rescue; by Sharon Thales. Capstone Press 2007 24p il (Simple machines to the rescue) lib bdg $21.26
Grades: K 1 2 3   **621.8**
  1. Pulleys 2. Simple machines
  ISBN 978-0-7368-6748-1 lib bdg; 0-7368-6748-1 lib bdg
                 LC 2006021503
"The presentation of the material . . . is impressive." Sci Books Films
  Includes glossary and bibliographical references

  Screws to the rescue; by Sharon Thales. Capstone Press 2007 24p il (Simple machines to the rescue) lib bdg $21.26
Grades: K 1 2 3   **621.8**
  1. Screws 2. Simple machines
  ISBN 978-0-7368-6749-8 lib bdg; 0-7368-6749-X lib bdg
                 LC 2006021502
"The presentation of the material . . . is impressive." Sci Books Films
  Includes glossary and bibliographical references

  Wedges to the rescue; by Sharon Thales. Capstone Press 2007 24p il (Simple machines to the rescue) lib bdg $21.26
Grades: K 1 2 3   **621.8**
  1. Wedges 2. Simple machines
  ISBN 978-0-7368-6750-4 lib bdg; 0-7368-6750-3 lib bdg
                 LC 2006021495
"The presentation of the material . . . is impressive." Sci Books Films
  Includes glossary and bibliographical references

Wheels and axles to the rescue. Capstone Press 2007 24p il (Simple machines to the rescue) lib bdg $21.26
Grades: K 1 2 3   **621.8**
  1. Axles 2. Wheels 3. Simple machines
  ISBN 978-0-7368-6751-1

This is "brightly colored, attractive. . . [and written] in language students can read and understand independently." SLJ

Includes glossary and bibliographical references

Tomljanovic, Tatiana
  Wedges. Weigl Publishers 2010 24p il (Science matters: simple machines) lib bdg $24.45; pa $8.95
Grades: 2 3 4   **621.8**
  1. Wedges
  ISBN 978-1-60596-037-1 lib bdg; 1-60596-037-3 lib bdg; 978-1-60596-038-8 pa; 1-60596-038-1 pa
                                                          LC 2009-1936

Discusses what a wedge is, where it can be found, and how it is used.

"The bold, large-scale, colorful, photographs . . . are sure to draw in even the most reluctant readers." SLJ

Includes glossary

Walker, Sally M.
  Put inclined planes to the test; by Sally M. Walker and Roseann Feldmann. Lerner Publications Co. 2012 40p il (How do simple machines work?) lib bdg $27.93
Grades: 3 4 5   **621.8**
  1. Inclined planes
  ISBN 978-0-7613-5324-9; 0-7613-5324-0
                                                          LC 2009032228

"Written in simple language and sentences, [this title offers a] straightforward [explanation] of how [inclined planes] work. Starting with the basics, the material gradually builds upon readers' growing understanding of the concepts presented. The experiments suggested can be performed with little assistance and with materials found in the home. Clear, distinct, color photos of children demonstrating the activities on each page help reinforce the concepts, as do the many drawings and diagrams." SLJ

Includes bibliographical references

  Put levers to the test; by Sally M. Walker and Roseann Feldmann. Lerner Publications Co. 2011 40p il (How do simple machines work?) lib bdg $27.93
Grades: 3 4 5   **621.8**
  1. Levers
  ISBN 978-0-7613-5321-8; 0-7613-5321-6
                                                          LC 2010035551

"Written in simple language and sentences, [this title offers a] straightforward [explanation] of how [levers] work. Starting with the basics, the material gradually builds upon readers' growing understanding of the concepts presented. The experiments suggested can be performed with little assistance and with materials found in the home. Clear, distinct, color photos of children demonstrating the activities on each page help reinforce the concepts, as do the many drawings and diagrams." SLJ

Includes bibliographical references

  Put pulleys to the test; [by] Sally M. Walker and Roseann Feldmann. Lerner Publications Co. 2012 40p il (Early bird physics) lib bdg $27.93

Grades: 3 4 5   **621.8**
  1. Gravity 2. Pulleys 3. Force and energy 4. Science -- Experiments
  ISBN 978-0-7613-5322-5; 0-7613-5322-4
                                                          LC 2010035395

"Written in simple language and sentences, [this] slim [title offers a] straightforward [explanation] of how [pulleys] work. Starting with the basics, the material gradually builds upon readers' growing understanding. . . The experiments suggested can be performed with little assistance and with materials found in the home. Clear, distinct, color photos of children demonstrating the activities on each page help reinforce the concepts, as do the many drawings and diagrams. Children will find [this] accessible [title] informative." SLJ

Includes bibliographical references

  Put screws to the test; by Sally M. Walker and Roseann Feldmann. Lerner Publications Company 2011 40p il (How do simple machines work?) lib bdg $27.93
Grades: 3 4 5   **621.8**
  1. Screws
  ISBN 978-0-7613-5323-2; 0-7613-5323-2
                                                          LC 2010035552

"Written in simple language and sentences, [this title offers a] straightforward [explanation] of how [screws] work. Starting with the basics, the material gradually builds upon readers' growing understanding of the concepts presented. The experiments suggested can be performed with little assistance and with materials found in the home. Clear, distinct, color photos of children demonstrating the activities on each page help reinforce the concepts, as do the many drawings and diagrams." SLJ

  Put wedges to the test; [by] Sally M. Walker and Roseann Feldmann. Lerner Publications 2012 40p il (How do simple machines work?) lib bdg $27.93
Grades: 3 4 5   **621.8**
  1. Wedges
  ISBN 978-0-7613-5325-6; 0-7613-5325-9
                                                          LC 2009032230

"Written in simple language and sentences, [this title offers a] straightforward [explanation] of how [wedges] work. Starting with the basics, the material gradually builds upon readers' growing understanding of the concepts presented. The experiments suggested can be performed with little assistance and with materials found in the home. Clear, distinct, color photos of children demonstrating the activities on each page help reinforce the concepts, as do the many drawings and diagrams." SLJ

Includes bibliographical references

  Put wheels and axles to the test; [by] Sally M. Walker and Roseann Feldmann. Lerner Publications Co. 2011 39p il (How do simple machines work?) lib bdg $27.93
Grades: 3 4 5   **621.8**
  1. Axles 2. Wheels
  ISBN 978-0-7613-5326-3; 0-7613-5326-7
                                                          LC 2010029108

"Written in simple language and sentences, [this title offers a] straightforward [explanation] of how [wheels and axles] work. Starting with the basics, the material gradually builds upon readers' growing understanding of the concepts presented. The experiments suggested can be performed with little assistance and with materials found in the home. Clear, distinct, color photos of children demonstrating the activities on each page help reinforce the concepts, as do the many drawings and diagrams." SLJ

Includes bibliographical references

Yasuda, Anita

Explore simple machines; 25 great projects, activities, experiments. illustrated by Bryan Stone. Nomad Press 2011 il (Explore your world) pa $12.95

Grades: 2 3 4   **621.8**

1. Simple machines

ISBN 978-1-936313-82-2; 1-936313-82-0

This "introduces the six simple machines in enough detail to include worm gears, all three kinds of levers, compound pulleys, and unusual examples. . . . Yasuda writes in particularly clear simple language and intersperses her explanations with historical notes, jokes . . . and 25 easy projects or demonstrations constructed from common materials." Booklist

621.9 Tools

Blaxland, Wendy

Helmets. Marshall Cavendish Benchmark 2011 32p il map (How are they made?) lib bdg $12.99

Grades: 4 5 6   **621.9**

1. Helmets 2. Plastics

ISBN 978-0-7614-4755-9 lib bdg; 0-7614-4755-5 lib bdg

LC 2009039881

"The opening spread of Helmets, which shows both a football player and an astronaut, illustrates the wide range of protective headgear, which stretches back to the leather war apparel of 3,000 BCE. Shots of gleaming orbs shuttling down assembly lines accompany text on thermoplastics, testing methods, and laws." Booklist

Includes glossary

Clements, Andrew

Workshop; illustrated by David Wisniewski. Clarion Bks. 1998 un il $16

Grades: K 1 2   **621.9**

1. Tools 2. Workshops

ISBN 0-395-85579-9

LC 97-48534

"Wisniewski's cut-paper illustrations and collage ably illustrate Clements' spare, poetic text. . . . A unique introduction to the world of wood and art for budding artisans." Bull Cent Child Books

Tomecek, Steve

Tools and machines; by Stephen M. Tomecek. Chelsea House Publishers 2010 182p il (Experimenting with everyday science) $35

Grades: 5 6 7 8   **621.9**

1. Tools 2. Machinery 3. Science -- Experiments

ISBN 978-1-60413-171-0; 1-60413-171-3

LC 2009-22332

This "offers 25 easy-to-perform activities that illuminate scientific principles. . . . [This] discusses levers, pulleys, and meters and explains how people use them in their daily lives.

. . . Following each experiment are additional comments on the science behind the experiment and link to the one that follows. Photographs, simple diagrams and illustrations, and sample data tables appear throughout, and the [layout is] clear and colorful." SLJ

Includes bibliographical references

623 Military and nautical engineering

Keenan, Sheila

★ **Castle**; how it works. David Macaulay with Sheila Keenan. Roaring Brook 2012 31 p. col. ill. (My readers) (hardcover) $15.99

Grades: 1 2 3   **623**

1. Picture books for children 2. Castles -- Juvenile literature 3. Fortification -- Juvenile literature

ISBN 1596437448; 9780395329207; 9781596437449

LC 2011962088

In this children's book, author David Macaulay provides "a tour of a medieval castle. . . . Walls keep the enemy out. Towers protect the lord and the soldiers. From the moat and portcullis to the great hall and dungeon . . . [readers can] see how a castle works as an enemy army tries to storm the walls." (Publisher's note)

Mooney, Carla

Becoming invisible; from camouflage to cloaks. Norwood House Press 2010 48p il (A great idea) lib bdg $25.27

Grades: 3 4 5 6   **623**

1. Optics 2. Camouflage (Military science)

ISBN 978-1-59953-378-0 lib bdg; 1-59953-378-2 lib bdg

LC 2010016516

This "traces the history of camouflage; looks at invisibility in stealth aircraft, films, and television today; considers current research into light and light-bending materials; and imagines future uses for invisibility technology. . . . Presenting specific, current information, [this book] will appeal to young people intrigued by inventions." Booklist

Includes glossary and bibliographical references

623.4 Ordnance

Gurstelle, William

The **art** of the catapult; build Greek ballistae, Roman onagers, English trebuchets, and more ancient artillery. Chicago Review Press 2004 172p il map $16.95

Grades: 5 6 7 8   **623.4**

1. Catapult

ISBN 1-55652-526-5

"This collection of 10 working catapult projects offers a fascinating look at world history, military strategy, and physics, related with an engaging yet lighthearted touch. . . . Instructions are clear, with full materials lists, helpful diagrams, and no skipped steps. . . . There's excellent booktalk potential here, and lively reading even for those who never get around to constructing a catapult." SLJ

Includes bibliographical references

Sheinkin, Steve

★ **Bomb**; the race to build and steal the world's most dangerous weapon. Steve Sheinkin. Roaring Brook Press 2012 266 p. ill. (hc) $19.99

Grades: 5 6 7 8 9 10 11 12 Adult   **623.4**

1. Nuclear warfare 2. Nuclear weapons 3. World War, 1914-1918 -- Chemical warfare 4. Atomic bomb -- History 5. Operation Freshman, 1942 6. Atomic bomb -- Germany -- History 7. World War, 1939-1945 -- Secret service -- Soviet Union 8. World War, 1939-1945 -- Secret service -- Great Britain 9. World War, 1939-1945 -- Commando operations -- Norway -- Vemork

ISBN 1596434872; 9781596434875

LC 2011044096

Robert F. Sibert Informational Book Medal (2013)

YALSA Award for Excellence in Nonfiction for Young Adults (2013)

John Newbery Honor Book (2013)

Author Steve Sheinkin's "story unfolds in three parts, covering American attempts to build the [atomic] bomb, how the Soviets tried to steal American designs and how the Americans tried to keep the Germans from building a bomb. It was the eve of World War II, and the fate of the world was at stake . . . all along the way spies in the United States were feeding sensitive information to the KGB." (Kirkus Reviews)

Includes bibliographical references (p. [243]-259) and index

623.7   Communications, vehicles, sanitation, related topics

Mooney, Carla

Pilotless planes. Norwood House Press 2010 48p il (A great idea) lib bdg $25.27

Grades: 3 4 5 6   **623.7**

1. Drone aircraft 2. Military aeronautics

ISBN 978-1-59953-381-0 lib bdg; 1-59953-381-2 lib bdg

LC 2010008500

This "discusses the development and use of unmanned aerial vehicles, also called UAVs or drones, such as the Predator planes currently used by the U.S. Air Force. Looking beyond military uses, the last chapter also considers future public safety, environmental, and commercial applications. . . . Presenting specific, current information, [this book] will appeal to young people intrigued by inventions." Booklist

Includes glossary and bibliographical references

623.74   Vehicles

Abramson, Andra Serlin

Fighter planes up close. Sterling 2008 48p (Up close) lib bdg $9.95

Grades: 2 3 4   **623.74**

1. Fighter planes

ISBN 978-1-4027-4796-0 lib bdg; 1-4027-4796-9 lib bdg

LC 2007008215

An introduction to fighter planes

623.82   Nautical craft

Abramson, Andra Serlin

Submarines up close. Sterling 2008 48p il (Up close) lib bdg $9.95

Grades: 2 3 4   **623.82**

1. Submarines

ISBN 978-1-4027-4797-7 lib bdg; 1-4027-4797-7 lib bdg

LC 2006102593

An introduction to submarines

Clark, Willow

Boats on the move. PowerKids Press 2010 24p il (Transportation station) lib bdg $21.25; pa $8.25

Grades: 2 3   **623.82**

1. Boats and boating -- Juvenile literature.

ISBN 978-1-4358-9336-8 lib bdg; 1-4358-9336-0 lib bdg; 978-1-4358-9760-1 pa; 1-4358-9760-9 pa

LC 2009-27410

Learn all about speedboats, military boats, boats used by the Coast Guard, and much more.

Includes glossary

Kirk, Shoshanna

T is for tugboat; navigating the seas from A to Z. [text by Shoshanna Kirk; designed by Sara Gillingham] Chronicle Books 2008 un il $15.99

Grades: 2 3 4   **623.82**

1. Ships 2. Navigation

ISBN 978-0-8118-6094-9; 0-8118-6094-9

LC 2007018333

This is an introduction to sea-related terms such as buoy, figurehead, hornpipe, and sextant

"This attractive title is an eye-pleaser filled with a mix of photographs, illustrations, and graphic images set on textured, woodgrain backgrounds. Images are both vintage and contemporary, and range from black-and-white to full-color reproductions. . . . A spread depicting an array of sailors' knots, a page illustrating Morse code, a spread labeling the parts of a ship, and the endpapers with the international code of maritime flags will be of interest to older children." SLJ

Lindeen, Mary

Ships; by Mary Lindeen. Bellwether Media 2007 24p il (Mighty machines) lib bdg $18.95

Grades: PreK K 1 2 3   **623.82**

1. Ships

ISBN 978-1-60014-060-0 lib bdg; 1-60014-060-2 lib bdg

LC 2006035262

This explains what a ship is, describes its major parts, and what it does

The glossary features "easy-to-read-and-understand definitions. . . . With [its] exciting, full-color photos on every spread [this] colorful [title] will certainly appeal to the mighty curiosity of young readers." SLJ

Includes glossary and bibliographical references

Sutherland, Jonathan

Aircraft carriers; [by] Jonathan Sutherland and Diane Canwell. Gareth Stevens Pub. 2008 32p il (Amazing ships) lib bdg $23.93

Grades: 4 5 6   **623.82**
1. Aircraft carriers
ISBN 978-0-8368-8376-3

LC 2007017049

This is an illustrated introduction to aircraft carriers from various parts of the world

"Bright colors and eye-catching photos are an enticing invitation of younger readers. . . . Vocabulary is appropriate in both text and captions. . . . Attractive, accurate, and informative." SLJ

Includes glossary and bibliographical references

Container ships and oil tankers; [by] Jonathan Sutherland and Diane Canwell. Gareth Stevens Pub. 2008 32p il (Amazing ships) lib bdg $23.93
Grades: 4 5 6   **623.82**
1. Tankers 2. Container ships
ISBN 978-0-8368-8377-0

LC 2007020479

An illustrated introduction to container ships and oil tankers from various parts of the world

"Bright colors and eye-catching photos are an enticing invitation to younger readers. . . . Vocabulary is appropriate in both text and captions. . . . Attractive, accurate, and informative." SLJ

Includes glossary and bibliographical references

Cruise ships; [by] Jonathan Sutherland and Diane Canwell. Gareth Stevens Pub. 2008 32p il (Amazing ships) lib bdg $23.93
Grades: 4 5 6   **623.82**
1. Cruise ships 2. Ocean liners
ISBN 978-0-8368-8378-7

LC 2007017050

This is an illustrated introduction to cruise ships from various parts of the world

"Bright colors and eye-catching photos are an enticing invitation to younger readers. . . . Vocabulary is appropriate in both text and captions. . . . Attractive, accurate, and informative." SLJ

Includes glossary and bibliographical references

Submarines; [by] Jonathan Sutherland and Diane Canwell. Gareth Stevens Pub. 2008 32p il (Amazing ships) lib bdg $23.93
Grades: 4 5 6   **623.82**
1. Submarines
ISBN 978-0-8368-8379-4

LC 2007017051

This is an illustrated introduction to submarines from various parts of the world

"Bright colors and eye-catching photos are an enticing invitation to younger readers. . . . Vocabulary is appropriate in both text and captions. . . . Attractive, accurate, and informative." SLJ

Includes glossary and bibliographical references

623.88   Seamanship

Mooney, Carla
Get all tied up; tying knots. Norwood House Press 2010 48p il (Creative adventure guides) lib bdg $25.27

Grades: 3 4 5 6   **623.88**
1. Knots and splices
ISBN 978-1-59953-384-1; 1-59953-384-7

LC 2010010403

"Some historical background and scientific or cultural information places the making and use of . . . knots . . . in context for young readers. [The] book has four chapters that culminate in step-by-step projects." Horn Book Guide

Includes glossary and bibliographical references

623.89   Navigation

Morrison, Taylor
The **coast** mappers. Houghton Mifflin Co. 2004 45p il map $16
Grades: 5 6 7 8   **623.89**
1. Maps 2. Surveying 3. Astronomers 4. Geographers 5. Cartographers 6. College teachers 7. Cartography -- Juvenile literature
ISBN 0-618-25408-0

LC 2003-13534

Chronicles the difficulties encountered by George Davidson and others as they attempted to create nautical charts to complete the U.S. Coast Survey of the West Coast in the mid-nineteenth century

"Cartographic methods are clearly explained through both the carefully researched text and the precise illustrations. . . . The artwork clarifies the text, depicts the breathtaking beauty of the coastline, and adds a sense of adventure." SLJ

Includes glossary and bibliographical references

Young, Karen Romano
Across the wide ocean; the why, how, and where of navigation for humans and animals at sea. Greenwillow Books 2007 78p il $18.99; lib bdg $19.89
Grades: 4 5 6 7   **623.89**
1. Ocean 2. Navigation 3. Marine animals 4. Animal navigation -- Juvenile literature
ISBN 978-0-06-009086-9; 0-06-009086-3; 978-0-06-009087-6 lib bdg; 0-06-009087-1 lib bdg

LC 2005-46146

"Readers follow such disparate entities as a loggerhead sea turtle, a nuclear submarine, and a sailboat crew seeking scientific sightings of North Atlantic right whales as Young explores the concept of navigation. . . . Larded with photos, diagrams, and maps. . . . Deceptively simple in appearance, the informative text can push some intense mental activity." SLJ

624   Civil engineering

Caney, Steven
★ **Steven** Caney's ultimate building book. Running Press 2006 596p il $29.95
Grades: 4 5 6 7 8   **624**
1. Building 2. Civil engineering
ISBN 0-7624-0409-4

"Caney examines 'building' in its broadest sense, encompassing everything from skyscrapers and bridges to bird feeders and peanut-shell 'bricks.' Opening sections investigate the history and techniques of construction, with clearly written explanations supported by black-and-white photographs and diagrams. . . . The author reinforces important concepts of design in a way that is fascinating and effective." SLJ

Fantastic feats and failures; by the editors of YES magazine. Kids Can Press 2004 52p il hardcover o.p. pa $7.95

Grades: 4 5 6 7   **624**

1. Civil engineering 2. Structural design -- Juvenile literature 3. Structural failures -- Juvenile literature

ISBN 1-55337-633-1; 1-55337-634-X pa

This "book spotlights 20 notable highs and lows in engineering. The 'feats' celebrated include the Sydney Opera House, the Brooklyn Bridge, and Canadarm (a huge, Canadian-built robotic arm used for repairs in space). Among the 'failures' are the space shuttle Challenger, the Tacoma Narrows Bridge, and the Chernobyl nuclear power plant. . . . Well organized and engagingly written. . . . Excellent photos . . . illustrate the places and events discussed, while colorful drawings visually represent concepts." Booklist

Macaulay, David

★ **Underground**. Houghton Mifflin 1976 109p il hardcover o.p. pa $9.95

Grades: 5 6 7 8 9   **624**

1. Subways 2. Building 3. Sewerage 4. Electric lines 5. Public utilities 6. Civil engineering

ISBN 0-395-24739-X; 0-395-34065-9 pa

"Introduced by a visual index—a bird's eye view of a busy, hypothetical intersection with colored indicators marking the specific locations analyzed in subsequent pages—detailed illustrations are combined with a clear, precise narrative to make the subject comprehenssible and fascinating." Horn Book

Includes glossary

Sandvold, Lynnette Brent

Revolution in construction. Marshall Cavendish Benchmark 2010 32p il (It works!) lib bdg $19.95

Grades: 3 4 5   **624**

1. Building 2. Engineering

ISBN 978-0-7614-4378-0 lib bdg; 0-7614-4378-9 lib bdg

LC 2008-54363

"This interesting, information packed [book] . . . motivates students to do their own exploring. . . . The appealing cartoon-like photographs add humor. . . . This . . . just may be that spark needed to create eager budding scientists." Libr Media Connect

Includes glossary and bibliographical references

Sullivan, George

Built to last; building America's amazing bridges, dams, tunnels, and skyscrapers. Scholastic Nonfiction 2005 128p il map $18.99

Grades: 5 6 7 8   **624**

1. Civil engineering

ISBN 0-439-51737-0

LC 2004-60996

This is a "survey of American building—from the Erie Canal to Boston's current 'Big Dig.' Chronological chapters describe the historical forces that helped drive each project

as well as the specific technological feats linked to each pioneering structure. . . . The wide selection of captivating illustrations includes archival photos and engravings, architectural drawings, and color photos. . . . Sullivan's skillful integration of social and economic history distinguishes this clear, well-designed title." Booklist

624.1   Structural engineering and underground construction

Askew, Amanda

Bulldozers. QEB Pub. 2010 24p il (Mighty machines) lib bdg $25.65; pa $5.95

Grades: PreK K 1 2   **624.1**

1. Construction equipment

ISBN 978-1-59566-925-4 lib bdg; 1-59566-925-6 lib bdg; 978-1-55407-703-8 pa; 1-55407-703-6 pa

LC 2010001217

"With huge, clear color photos of machines at work, the Mighty Machines series is an exciting way to connect books with kids' vrooming play and with what they see on the road, construction sites, and farms. . . . In Bulldozers, the parts called 'blades' and 'rippers' say it all, and the pages of full-bleed photographs show the machines building roads and even clearing a path as part of an army convoy." Booklist

Cranes. QEB Pub. 2010 24p il (Mighty machines) lib bdg $25.65; pa $5.95

Grades: PreK K 1 2   **624.1**

1. Construction equipment 2. Cranes, derricks, etc.

ISBN 978-1-59566-924-7 lib bdg; 1-59566-924-8 lib bdg; 978-1-55407-704-5 pa; 1-55407-704-4 pa

LC 2010001219

"With large, clear color photos of machines at work, the Mighty Machines series is an exciting way to connect books with kids' vrooming play and with what they see on the road, construction sites, and farms. . . . The subjects of Cranes lift containers at the docks, construct bridges, and more, and the aerial photo of a tower crane high above a cityscape is dizzying." Booklist

Includes glossary

Diggers. QEB Pub. 2010 24p il (Mighty machines) lib bdg $25.65; pa $5.95

Grades: PreK K 1 2   **624.1**

1. Construction equipment

ISBN 978-1-59566-926-1 lib bdg; 1-59566-926-4 lib bdg; 978-1-55407-705-2 pa; 1-55407-705-2 pa

LC 2010001221

"With huge, clear color photos of machines at work, the Mighty Machines series is an exciting way to connect books with kids' vrooming play, and with what they see on the road, construction sites, and farms. . . . Machines shown in Diggers are made of arms, tracks, bucket attachments, and a driver's cab and perform demolition as well as breaking up ground at a building site." Booklist

Includes glossary

Loaders. QEB Pub. 2010 24p il (Mighty machines) lib bdg $25.65; pa $5.95

Grades: PreK K 1 2   624.1

1. Construction equipment

ISBN 978-1-59566-923-0 lib bdg; 1-59566-923-X lib bdg; 978-1-55407-706-9 pa; 1-55407-706-0 pa

LC 2010001222

"With huge, clear color photos of machines at work, the Mighty Machines series is an exciting way to connect books with kids' vrooming play and with what they see on the road, construction sites, and farms. . . . Loaders covers tractors with large buckets on the front, which are used primarily at building sites but can also be found in mines and quarries, as well as being used to clear snow, repair roads, and move bales of straw on the farm." Booklist

Includes glossary

Graham, Ian

Tremendous tunnels. Amicus 2010 32p il (Super-structures) lib bdg $28.50

Grades: 5 6 7 8   624.1

1. Tunnels

ISBN 978-1-60753-134-0; 1-60753-134-8

LC 2009030865

"The vivid illustrations often help clarify points made in the text. . . . [This] colorful, informative [book offers] intriguing glimpses of notable engineering feats." Booklist

Includes glossary and bibliographical references

Hill, Lee Sullivan

Earthmovers on the move. Lerner Publications 2010 32p il (Lightning bolt books. Vroom-vroom) lib bdg $25.26

Grades: K 1 2   624.1

1. Construction equipment

ISBN 978-0-7613-3918-2; 0-7613-3918-3

LC 2009039739

This book about earthmovers has "big, high-energy color photos. . . . [The text provides] lively commentary in a mix of declarative statements and non-rhetorical questions. . . . [The] volume closes with a labeled diagram, a page of 'fun facts,' and a short list of print and web resources. . . . [This] will make a worthwhile and popular addition." SLJ

Includes glossary and bibliographical references

Mason, Adrienne

Build it! structures, systems and you. written by Adrienne Mason; illustrated by Claudia Dávila. Kids Can Press 2006 32p il (Primary physical science) $14.95; pa $5.95

Grades: K 1 2   624.1

1. Building 2. Structural engineering 3. Structural engineering -- Juvenile literature

ISBN 978-1-55337-835-8; 1-55337-835-0; 978-1-55337-836-5 pa; 1-55337-836-9 pa

This provides "a first glimpse of how structures and structural systems exist both in nature and in human-made designs. The author makes reading this book an easy and enjoyable reading experience. The book uses carefully worded descriptions, creative and vivid colors with striking graphics representations, and clear fonts." Sci Books Films

624.2 Bridges

Curlee, Lynn

★ **Brooklyn** Bridge. Atheneum Bks. for Young Readers 2001 35p il map $18

Grades: 3 4 5 6   624.2

1. Bridges 2. Bridge engineers 3. Brooklyn Bridge (New York, N.Y.) -- Juvenile literature 4. Bridges -- New York -- Design and construction -- Juvenile literature

ISBN 0-689-83183-8

LC 99-43771

"Biography, social history, and introductory engineering are . . . precisely balanced, with human-interest angles. . . . This is a grand yet practical tribute to a grand yet practical edifice." Bull Cent Child Books

Includes bibliographical references

Graham, Ian

Fabulous bridges. Amicus 2010 32p il (Superstructures) lib bdg $28.50

Grades: 5 6 7 8   624.2

1. Bridges

ISBN 978-1-60753-132-6; 1-60753-132-1

LC 2009030864

"The vivid illustrations often help clarify points made in the text. . . . [This] colorful, informative [book offers] intriguing glimpses of notable engineering feats." Booklist

Includes glossary and bibliographical references

Johmann, Carol

Bridges! amazing structures to design, build & test. [by] Carol Johmann & Elizabeth Rieth; illustrations by Michael Kline. Williamson 1999 96p il pa $12.95

Grades: 4 5 6 7   624.2

1. Bridges

ISBN 1-88559-330-9

LC 98-53272

Describes different kinds of bridges, their history, design, construction, and effects on populations, environmental dilemmas, safety, and more

"Eye-catching photographs and cartoon illustrations in blue and orange tones abound; clear organization of text and unifying page borders create an attractive graphic package. The volume includes a list of notable bridges by state and country." SLJ

625.1 Railroads

Barton, Byron

★ **Trains**. Crowell 1986 un il lib bdg $16.89

Grades: PreK K 1   625.1

1. Railroads

ISBN 0-690-04534-4

LC 85-47898

Brief text and illustrations present a variety of trains and what they do

"The concepts are simple and Barton's illustrations are just enough, and no more." Publ Wkly

Clark, Willow
Trains on the move; [by] Willow Clark. PowerKids Press 2010 24p il (Transportation station) lib bdg $21.25; pa $8.025
Grades: 2 3 **625.1**
1. Railroads
ISBN 978-1-4358-9331-3 lib bdg; 1-4358-9331-X lib bdg; 978-1-4358-9750-2 pa; 1-4358-9750-1 pa
LC 2009-21776
Learn all about the different types of trains, how they work, and how important they are
"Clark has done a fine job of including meaningful content in a limited space. . . . [This book] consists of 10 two-page chapters printed in a font of an inviting size. Full-page photos–all color except one vintage photograph–with informative captions face two-paragraph text blocks. . . . Will make readers feel they have learned something" SLJ
Includes glossary

Crowther, Robert
Trains: a pop-up railroad book. Candlewick Press 2006 un il $17.99
Grades: 2 3 4 5 **625.1**
1. Railroads 2. Pop-up books
ISBN 978-0-7636-3082-9; 0-7636-3082-9
"With pop-up effects that, appropriately enough, tend to be long, narrow, and placed in parallel tracks, this history of railroading opens with outside and inside views of a small steam locomotive and closes with a full-spread, double-tiered train station. In between, the book covers methods of propulsion, the development of passenger cars, speed and other records, tunnels, bridges, and other engineering feats. . . . Crowther simplifies technological details in his neat, brightly colored collage illustrations." SLJ

Lindeen, Mary
Trains; by Mary Lindeen. Bellwether Media 2007 24p il (Mighty machines) lib bdg $18.50
Grades: PreK K 1 2 3 **625.1**
ISBN 978-1-60014-062-4 lib bdg; 1-60014-062-9 lib bdg
LC 2006035264
This explains what a train is and discusses its major parts and what they do
The glossary features "easy-to-read-and-understand definitions. . . . With [its] exciting, full-color photos on every spread, [this] colorful [title] will certainly appeal to the mighty curiosity of young readers." SLJ
Includes glossary and bibliographical references

National Railway Museum (Great Britain)
Big book of trains; [by] National Railway Museum, York, England. DK Pub. 1998 32p il $14.99
Grades: 4 5 6 **625.1**
1. Railroads 2. Locomotives -- Juvenile literature 3. Railroads -- Trains -- Juvenile literature
ISBN 0-7894-3436-9
LC 98-18830
Describes the locomotives, cars, tunnels, stations, and functions of such trains as freight trains, channel tunnel trains, bullet trains, mountain trains, and snow trains
Includes glossary

625.26 Locomotives

Zimmermann, Karl
The Stourbridge Lion; America's First Locomotive. Karl Zimmermann; illustrated by Steven Walker. 1st ed. Boyds Mills Press 2012 32 p. ill., maps (hardcover) $16.95
Grades: 2 3 4 **625.26**
1. Steam locomotives 2. Railroads -- History 3. Transportation -- United States -- History 4. Stourbridge Lion (Steam locomotive) -- Juvenile literature 5. Steam locomotives -- United States -- History -- Juvenile literature 6. Railroads -- Pennsylvania -- Honesdale -- History -- Juvenile literature 7. Railroads -- United States -- History -- 19th century -- Juvenile literature
ISBN 1590788591; 9781590788592
LC 2011939995
Includes bibliographical references.

625.4 Local rail transit systems

McKendry, Joe
Beneath the streets of Boston; building America's first subway. written & illustrated by Joe McKendry. David R. Godine 2005 un il maps $19.95
Grades: 4 5 6 **625.4**
1. Subways 2. Subways -- Massachusetts -- Boston
ISBN 1-56792-284-8
LC 2004-16418
This book covers over twenty years of the early history of the Boston subway system
"The text is clear and well written. . . . The paintings convey the sense of story, while the drawings provide specific details. Both are equally well executed and contribute to the overall understanding of the text." SLJ

Weitzman, David L.
A subway for New York; [by] David Weitzman. Farrar, Straus and Giroux 2005 un il map $17
Grades: 4 5 6 7 **625.4**
1. Subways
ISBN 0-374-37284-5
LC 2004-56286
"Weitzman recounts the construction of [New York's] first subterranean train system, beginning above ground with descriptions of [the city's] crowded streets in 1904. . . . The text and captivating images convey the awe-inspiring scope of the project and the engineering feats that produced what remains the fastest method of navigating the city." Booklist
Includes bibliographical references

627 Hydraulic engineering

Mann, Elizabeth
Hoover Dam; with illustrations by Alan Witschonke. Mikaya Press 2001 44p il (Wonders of the world) $19.95; pa $9.95

Grades: 4 5 6 7   **627**
1. Hoover Dam (Ariz. and Nev.)
ISBN 978-1-931414-02-9; 1-931414-02-5; 978-1-
931414-13-5 pa; 1-931414-13-0 pa
LC 2001-34520
Describes the engineering, construction, and social and
historical contexts of the Hoover Dam
"A wonderfully readable, well-organized book filled
with fascinating detail." SLJ

Zuehlke, Jeffrey
The **Hoover** Dam. Lerner Publications Co. 2010 32p
il map (Lightning Bolt Books. Famous places) lib bdg
$25.26
Grades: 2 3 4   **627**
1. Hoover Dam (Ariz. and Nev.)
ISBN 978-0-8225-9408-6 lib bdg; 0-8225-9408-0
lib bdg
LC 2008-31245
Describes the Hoover Dam and includes information on
its design, construction, and environmental issues
This book uses "high-quality photos, illustrations, maps,
and diagrams. . . . Readers will enjoy learning about [the
Hoover Dam] . . . and the challenges of building and main-
taining large structures." SLJ
Includes glossary and bibliographical references

628   Sanitary engineering

Horn, Geoffrey
Environmental engineer; by Geoffrey M. Horn. Gareth Stevens Pub. 2010 32p il (Cool careers: cutting edge)
lib bdg $26; pa $8.95
Grades: 4 5 6   **628**
1. Vocational guidance 2. Sanitary engineering 3.
Environmental protection
ISBN 978-1-4339-1956-5 lib bdg; 1-4339-1956-7 lib
bdg; 978-1-4339-2155-1 pa; 1-4339-2155-3 pa
LC 2009004746
This introduction to environmental engineering careers
offers "clear, solid information in a large font. . . . [This]
short [book is] packed with relevant, current material." SLJ
Includes glossary and bibliographical references

628.1   Water supply

Cartlidge, Cherese
Water from air; water-harvesting machines. by
Cherese Cartlidge. Norwood House Press 2008 48p il (A
great idea) lib bdg $25.27
Grades: 3 4 5 6   **628.1**
1. Humidity 2. Water supply 3. Water resources
development
ISBN 978-1-59953-196-0 lib bdg; 1-59953-196-8
lib bdg
LC 2008-10780
"Describes the invention and development of water har-
vesting machines." Publisher's note
Includes glossary and bibliographical references

Person, Stephen
Saving animals from oil spills. Bearport Pub. 2011 32p
il map (Rescuing animals from disasters) lib bdg $25.27
Grades: 3 4 5 6   **628.1**
1. Oil spills 2. Animal rescue
ISBN 978-1-61772-288-2; 1-61772-288-X
LC 2011002430
"Featuring colorful, visually packed pages and readable
prose, this title . . . offers an acceessible introduction to the
impact of oil spills on a variety of creatures. . . . Throughout,
basic concepts are well conveyed, and inset text adds additional, useful commentary on each page." Booklist
Includes glossary and bibliographical references

628.9   Other branches of sanitary and municipal engineering

Abramson, Andra Serlin
Fire engines up close. Sterling 2008 48p (Up close)
lib bdg $9.95
Grades: 2 3 4   **628.9**
1. Fire engines
ISBN 978-1-4027-4798-4 lib bdg; 1-4027-4798-5
lib bdg
LC 2007008214
An introduction to fire fighters and their equipment

Allman, Toney
The **Jaws** of Life. Norwood House Press 2008 48p il
(A great idea) lib bdg $25.27
Grades: 3 4 5 6   **628.9**
1. Rescue work
ISBN 978-159953-191-5 lib bdg; 1-59953-191-7
lib bdg
LC 2008007041
"Full-color photographs and copious fun facts help make
this . . . enjoyable reading, but it's really the choice of [topic]
that is so enthralling." Booklist
Includes glossary and bibliographical references

Bingham, Caroline
Fire truck. DK Pub. 2003 29p il (Machines at work)
$8.99
Grades: K 1 2 3   **628.9**
1. Fire engines 2. Fire fighting
ISBN 0-7894-9221-0
Introduces fire engines and the work that they help fire-
fighters do in all kinds of settings
"Bingham immediately grabs the reader's attention with
brilliantly colored pictures. . . . An excellent stimulant for a
child's imagination." Sci Books Films
Includes glossary

Butler, Dori Hillestad
F is for firefighting; by Dori Hillestad Butler; illustrated
by Joan C. Waites. Pelican 2007 un il $15.95
Grades: PreK K 1   **628.9**
1. Alphabet 2. Fire fighting
ISBN 978-1-58980-420-3; 1-58980-420-1
LC 2006031113
"From 'A is for Alarm' to 'Z is for Zones,' each page
introduces a different aspect of firefighting. Crisp, colorful

illustrations depict the topics, and thick borders frame the artwork as well as the text boxes at the bottom of the pages." SLJ

Demarest, Chris L.
  Firefighters A to Z. Margaret K. McElderry Bks. 2000 un il lib bdg $16.95
  Grades: K 1   **628.9**
    1. Alphabet 2. Fire fighters 3. Fire extinction
    ISBN 0-689-83798-4
                                              LC 99-56382
  An alphabetic look at a firefighter's day
  "There's nothing babyish or cute about the robust, action-oriented pastel artwork in Firefighters A to Z. . . . Permeated with intense primary colors, the images build on one another to convey the physical nature of this dramatic but serious job. The firefighters themselves, in their bulky yellow suits and oxygen masks, appear straight out of science fiction, but the smoothly rhyming text grounds their activities in reality." Horn Book

Jango-Cohen, Judith
  Fire trucks on the move. Lerner Publications 2010 32p il (Lightning bolt books. Vroom-vroom) lib bdg $25.26
  Grades: K 1 2   **628.9**
    1. Fire engines
    ISBN 978-0-7613-6023-0 lib bdg; 0-7613-6023-9 lib bdg
                                              LC 2009039740
  This book about fire trucks has "big, high-energy color photos. . . . [The text provides] lively commentary in a mix of declarative statements and non-rhetorical questions. . . . [The] volume closes with a labeled diagram, a page of 'fun facts,' and a short list of print and web resources. . . . [This] will make a worthwhile and popular addition." SLJ
  Includes glossary and bibliographical references

Kenney, Karen Latchana
  Firefighters at work; by Karen L. Kenney; illustrated by Brian Caleb Dumm. Magic Wagon 2010 32p il (Meet your community workers!) lib bdg $18.95
  Grades: K 1 2 3   **628.9**
    1. Fire fighters 2. Vocational guidance
    ISBN 978-1-60270-648-4 lib bdg; 1-60270-648-4 lib bdg
                                              LC 2009-2384
  This book about firefighters has "an uncluttered layout and consistent organization. . . . Chapter headings such as 'Problems on the Job,' and 'Technology at Work,' and 'Special Skills and Training' make it easy to pinpoint specific information." SLJ
  Includes glossary

Landau, Elaine
  Smokejumpers; photographs by Ben Klaffke. Millbrook Press 2002 48p il lib bdg $23.90
  Grades: 3 4 5 6   **628.9**
    1. Occupations 2. Forest fires 3. Fire fighters 4. Smokejumpers 5. Wildfire fighters
    ISBN 0-7613-2324-4
                                              LC 2001-30974
  "The first half explains the physical training smokejumpers undergo and the fire-fighting theory they must learn. The second half shows what happens when a fire call comes

in. . . . The pictures and text work together beautifully. . . . This is a must-purchase for libraries in places where forest fires occur, and the true-life-adventure aspect will make it popular in other libraries as well." Booklist
  Includes glossary and bibliographical references

629   Other branches of engineering

Biggs, Brian
  Everything goes: On land. Balzer + Bray 2011 un il (Everything goes) $14.99
  Grades: PreK K 1   **629**
    1. Vehicles
    ISBN 0-06-195809-3; 978-0-06-195809-0
                                              LC 2011019349
  A young boy learns about land vehicles from bicycles to subways and trolleys as he and his father travel to the train station.
  "Biggs has a cheery cartooning style that's reminiscent of R. Crumb and ideal for populating his oversized pages with a multitude of players and detail. With running visual jokes and mini-narratives adding to the fun, Biggs gives readers lots to take in and enjoy." Publ Wkly

Ganeri, Anita
  Things that go; illustrated by Mark Bergin. Kingfisher 2010 18p il (Flip the flaps) $9.99
  Grades: PreK K 1   **629**
    1. Vehicles
    ISBN 978-0-7534-6409-0; 0-7534-6409-8
  This provides "cutaways of airplanes and trains and [shows] a fire in progress along with a spread about emergency vehicles. Some questions . . . are given suprisingly thorough answers. . . . Perfect for light, educational browsing." Booklist

Simon, Seymour
  ★ The paper airplane book; illustrated by Byron Barton. Viking 1971 48p il pa $6.99
  Grades: 3 4 5   **629**
    1. Paper crafts 2. Airplanes -- Models
    ISBN 0-14-030925-X
  Step-by-step instructions for making paper airplanes with suggestions for experimenting with them

The amazing International Space Station; by the editors of YES Mag. Kids Can Press 2003 48p il $15.95; pa $8.95
  Grades: 4 5 6   **629**
    1. Space stations 2. International Space Station -- Juvenile literature
    ISBN 1-55337-380-4; 1-55337-523-8 pa
  This describes the construction, crew, life, and work aboard the International Space Station.
  "This book packs a lot of information into clear, short chapters that are chock-full of facts, action, and cool language." SLJ

629.04   Transportation engineering

Arlon, Penelope
Emergency vehicles; by Penelope Arlon and Tory Gordon-Harris. 1st ed. Scholastic 2013 32 p. col. ill. (Scholastic discover more) (reinforced) $7.99
Grades: PreK K 1   **629.04**
1. Vehicles 2. Fire engines 3. Rescue work 4. Emergency vehicles
ISBN 0545495636; 9780545495639

LC 2012285426
This book, written by Penelope Arlon, presents a "reference book about emergency vehicles for emergent readers. 'Emergency Vehicles' is full of facts and . . . pictures of rescue vehicles. Big, annotated photos reveal . . . details of how fire trucks, ambulances, police cars, motorbikes, and helicopters really work. Alongside are explorations of more unusual vehicles . . . from superscoopers to fireboats. (Publisher's note)

Perritano, John
Revolution in transportation. Marshall Cavendish Benchmark 2010 32p il (It works!) lib bdg $19.95
Grades: 3 4 5   **629.04**
1. Transportation
ISBN 978-0-7614-4379-7 lib bdg; 0-7614-4379-7 lib bdg

LC 2008-54366
"This interesting, information packed [book] . . . motivates students to do their own exploring. . . . The appealing cartoon-like photographs add humor. . . . This . . . just may be that spark needed to create eager budding scientists." Libr Media Connect
Includes glossary and bibliographical references

629.13   Aeronautics

Adler, David A., 1947-
A **picture** book of Amelia Earhart; illustrated by Jeff Fisher. Holiday House 1998 un il $16.95; pa $6.95
Grades: 1 2 3   **629.13**
1. Air pilots 2. Missing persons 3. Women air pilots 4. Memoirists 5. Air pilots -- United States -- Biography -- Juvenile literature
ISBN 0-8234-1315-2; 0-8234-1517-1 pa

LC 96-54854
Discusses the life of the pilot who was the first woman to cross the Atlantic by herself in a plane
This offers "a straightforward, informative text full of detail. The illustrations ably reflect both the humorous and more serious moments in the narrative." Horn Book Guide
Includes bibliographical references

Bailey, Gerry
Flight. Gareth Stevens Pub. 2009 32p il (Simply science) lib bdg $26
Grades: 3 4 5   **629.13**
1. Flight 2. Aeronautics
ISBN 978-1-4339-0032-7 lib bdg; 1-4339-0032-7 lib bdg

LC 2008-27569

"In this little book, various vehicles associated with human flight are introduced . . . [and] fundamental principles underlying how these various vehicles are able to travel through the air are explained in a straightfoward and understandable manner. . . . This text will provide . . . an entertaining and informative introduction to aircraft and aerodynamic vehicles." Sci Books Films
Includes glossary and bibliographical references

Borden, Louise
Touching the sky; the flying adventures of Wilbur and Orville Wright. [by] Louise Borden & Trish Marx; illustrated by Peter Fiore. Margaret K. McElderry Bks. 2003 un il map $18.95
Grades: 3 4 5   **629.13**
1. Inventors 2. Aeronautics -- History 3. Aircraft industry executives
ISBN 0-689-84876-5

LC 2002-12041
A look at how the Wright Brothers became the first celebrities of the twentieth century through their 1909 public flying exhibitions in New York City and Germany
"Fiore's detailed watercolors dramatically and accurately record the two venues. The narrative, too, is laced with engaging facts that are successfully married to the pictures." SLJ

Brown, Don, 1949-
Ruth Law thrills a nation; story and pictures by Don Brown. Ticknor & Fields 1993 un il $16; pa $5.95
Grades: K 1 2 3   **629.13**
1. Air pilots 2. Women air pilots 3. Aeronautics -- Flights -- Juvenile literature
ISBN 0-395-66404-7; 0-395-73517-3 pa

LC 92-45701
The author discusses the flight performed by Ruth Law, who in 1916 "tried to fly from Chicago to New York City in one day. She did not succeed (she landed outside Binghamton, New York), but she broke a nonstop cross-county flying record." (Booklist) "Kindergarten to grade three." (SLJ)
"Using a simple text and effective watercolors, Brown successfully re-creates the remarkable flying feat. He sets Law in her historical context with humor and precision." Booklist

Burleigh, Robert
Flight: the journey of Charles Lindbergh; illustrated by Mike Wimmer; introduction by Jean Fritz. Philomel Bks. 1991 un il hardcover o.p. pa $6.99
Grades: 2 3 4   **629.13**
1. Generals 2. Air pilots 3. Memoirists 4. Air force officers 5. Aeronautics -- Flights
ISBN 0-399-22272-3; 0-698-11425-6 pa

LC 90-35401
Describes how Charles Lindbergh achieved the remarkable feat of flying nonstop and solo from New York to Paris in 1927
"Using Charles Lindbergh's autobiography, The Spirit of St. Louis, as the basis for his text, Burleigh vividly creates that first solo flight in words, while Wimmer fashions exhilarating pictures that are, above all else, emotional. . . . This artistic emotion . . . works terrifically with the terseness of the near-poetic text." Booklist

★ **Night** flight; Amelia Earhart crosses the Atlantic. [illustrated by] Wendell Minor. Simon & Schuster Books for Young Readers 2011 un il $16.99

Grades: K 1 2   **629.13**

1. Air pilots 2. Missing persons 3. Women air pilots 4. Memoirists 5. Aeronautics -- Flights 6. Transatlantic flights -- Juvenile literature

ISBN 1-4169-6733-8; 978-1-4169-6733-0

LC 2008-52269

This is an account of Amelia Earhart's 1932 flight across the Atlantic Ocean from Newfoundland to Ireland. Bibliography. "Grades three to six." (Bull Cent Child Books)

"A gripping narrative and dynamic art immediately pull readers into the story of Earhart's historic 1932 solo transatlantic flight. . . . Minor's . . . gouache and watercolor paintings easily convey the journey's intense drama, balancing lifelike closeups of Earhart with images of her imperiled plane. . . . Hearts will be racing. Back matter includes notes on Earhart's life." Publ Wkly

Includes bibliographical references

Carson, Mary Kay

★ The **Wright** Brothers for kids; how they invented the airplane: 21 activities exploring the science and history of flight. illustrations by Laura D'Argo. Chicago Review Press 2003 146p il pa $14.95

Grades: 4 5 6 7   **629.13**

1. Inventors 2. Aeronautics 3. Aeronautics -- History 4. Science -- Experiments 5. Aircraft industry executives

ISBN 1-55652-477-3

LC 2002-155449

This account of the Wright brothers' invention of the airplane, explains the forces of flight-lift, thrust, gravity, and drag and includes such activities as making a Chinese flying top, building a kite, bird watching, making a paper glider and a rubber-band-powered flyer

"A treasure trove of activities awaits readers of this wonderfully executed survey of the Wright brothers and their invention. The narrative flows easily and is complemented by numerous photographs that give a sense of history and this event. . . . This is a valuable resource for student reports and projects, and for classroom units." SLJ

Includes glossary and bibliographical references

Crowther, Robert

Flight: a pop-up book of aircraft. Candlewick Press 2007 un il $17.99

Grades: 2 3 4 5   **629.13**

1. Aeronautics 2. Pop-up books 3. Flight -- Juvenile literature 4. Airplanes -- Juvenile literature

ISBN 978-0-7636-3459-9; 0-7636-3459-X

This is "a history of flight, from the ancient Chinese invention of the kite to the X-43A scramjet that NASA still has under development. Along with dozens of small, simplified but clean-lined portraits of renowned aircraft, many of which 'fly' along die-cut slots, [Crowther] includes a pop-up modern air terminal, a large two-sided globe on which famous firsts are traced, and a particularly well-designed 747 cockpit with moving control levers." SLJ

Goldish, Meish

Freaky-big airplanes. Bearport Pub. 2010 24p il (World's biggest) lib bdg $22.61

Grades: 2 3 4   **629.13**

1. Airplanes

ISBN 978-1-59716-959-2 lib bdg; 1-59716-959-5 lib bdg

LC 2009-14620

Describes different types of aircraft used around the world, including information on their history, dimensions, weight, and performance

"The simply phrased narrative and captions describe what each vehicle carries, along with top speed, full weight, and other basic facts. . . . A visual glossary and a look at four other outsize flying machines . . . cap this awe-inspiring entry in the World's Biggest series." Booklist

Includes glossary and bibliographical references

Hardesty, Von

Epic flights. Kingfisher 2011 il (Epic adventure) $19.99

Grades: 5 6 7 8   **629.13**

1. Aeronautics -- History

ISBN 978-0-7534-6669-8; 0-7534-6669-4

LC 2011041637

This describes Charles Lindbergh's transatlantic flight; the Breitling Orbiter 3 which set a record for non-stop around the world flight by balloon; the Apollo 11 flight to the moon; Amy Johnson's solo flight from England to Australia in a small bi-plane; and the Voyager, which set a record by flying non-stop around the world without refueling.

"The graphics will grab readers in [this] exciting, extra-large-size [title] . . . packed with high-quality color photos on every double-page spread. Just as gripping are the narratives, captions, and technical details of exploration, adventure, and survival." Booklist

Includes glossary

Hense, Mary

How fighter pilots use math; math curriculum consultant: Rhea A. Stewart. Chelsea Clubhouse 2010 32p il (Math in the real world) lib bdg $28

Grades: 4 5 6   **629.13**

1. Air pilots 2. Aeronautics 3. Mathematics 4. Vocational guidance

ISBN 978-1-60413-605-0 lib bdg; 1-60413-605-7 lib bdg

LC 2009-20242

This describes how fighter pilots use math to judge speed, attain altitude, and maintain safety, and includes relevant math problems and information about how to become a fighter pilot

Includes glossary and bibliographical references

Hodgkins, Fran

How people learned to fly; by Fran Hodgkins; illustrated by True Kelley. HarperCollinsPublishers 2007 33p il (Let's-read-and-find-out science) $15.99; pa $5.99

Grades: K 1 2 3   **629.13**

1. Flight 2. Aeronautics

ISBN 978-0-06-029558-5; 0-06-029558-9; 978-0-06-445221-2 pa; 0-06-445221-2 pa

LC 2006000482

"This book explains the development of aircraft and the scientific principles behind them. Complex ideas, such as gravity and lift, are made accessible through concise explanations and excellent illustrations and diagrams, which are always bright, clear, and appealing." SLJ

629.133   Aircraft types

Clark, Willow
Planes on the move. PowerKids Press 2010 24p il (Transportation station) lib bdg $21.25; pa $8.25
Grades: 2 3   **629.133**
1. Airplanes 2. Aeronautics
ISBN 978-1-4358-9332-0 lib bdg; 1-4358-9332-8 lib bdg; 978-1-4358-9752-6 pa; 1-4358-9752-8 pa
Learn about all kinds of planes, including passenger planes, seaplanes, and planes used by the military.
"Clark has done a fine job of including meaningful content in a limited space. . . . [This] title consists of 10 two-page chapters printed in a font of an inviting size. Full-page photos–all color except one vintage photograph–with informative captions face two-paragraph text blocks. . . . Will make readers feel they have learned something." SLJ
Includes glossary

Graham, Ian
Aircraft; [by] Ian Graham. Black Rabbit Books 2009 32p il (How machines work) $18.95
Grades: 3 4 5   **629.133**
1. Airplanes
ISBN 978-1-59920-292-1; 1-59920-292-1
LC 2008002399
This "uses informational drawings, cutaway diagrams, and photos—including some dazzling shots of cockpit control panels. The layout is sufficiently busy to capture interest." Booklist

Hosking, Wayne
Asian kites. Tuttle 2005 63p il (Asian arts & crafts for creative kids) $12.95
Grades: 3 4 5 6   **629.133**
1. Kites 2. Handicraft
ISBN 0-8048-3545-4
"This survey offers brief anecdotes and legends along with carefully annotated construction diagrams for 15 simple kites commonly flown in Asia. . . . Closing with notes on running a kite-making workshop for children, lists of associations and sources of supplies, and a relatively extensive bibliography, this title merits, and will find, a wide audience in libraries large or small." SLJ

Keenan, Sheila
Jet plane; how it works. David Macaulay with Sheila Keenan. 1st ed. David Macaulay Studio 2012 28 p. col. ill. (My readers) (hardcover) $15.99; (paperback) $3.99
Grades: 2 3 4   **629.133**
1. Jet planes 2. Picture books for children
ISBN 1596437642; 1596437677; 9781596437647; 9781596437678
LC 2012289085
This book is part of David Macaulay's The Way Things Work series. This installment looks at the jet plane. "It weighs as much as 100 elephants, but it can fly for hours. How does a jet do that? From the engine that provides the power and wings that lift the plane off the ground to the

cockpit controls and passenger cabin, see how these modern marvels work and what makes them stay in the air." (Publisher's note)
Includes bibliographical references and index

Nahum, Andrew
Flying machine; written by Andrew Nahum, rev ed; DK Pub. 2004 72p il (DK eyewitness books) $15.99; lib bdg $19.99
Grades: 4 5 6 7   **629.133**
1. Aeronautics -- History
ISBN 0-7566-0680-2; 0-7566-0679-9 lib bdg
First published 1990 by Knopf
A photo essay tracing the history and development of aircraft from hot-air balloons to jetliners. Includes information on the principles of flight and the inner workings of various flying machines.

Oxlade, Chris
Airplanes; uncovering technology. Firefly Books 2006 52p il $16.95
Grades: 4 5 6 7   **629.133**
1. Airplanes
ISBN 1-55407-134-8
This offers "appealing visuals and plenty of well-chosen facts." SLJ

Rau, Dana Meachen
Hot air balloons. Marshall Cavendish Benchmark 2010 24p il (Surprising science) lib bdg $22.79
Grades: 2 3 4   **629.133**
1. Balloons 2. Air-cushion vehicles
ISBN 978-0-7614-4873-0; 0-7614-4873-X
"Colorfully illustrated with photographs on each page, this . . . will be well received by elementary students and educators." Libr Media Connect
Includes glossary and bibliographical references

629.2   Motor land vehicles, cycles

Cooper, Wade
On the road. Cartwheel Books 2008 30p il (Scholastic reader) pa $3.99
Grades: PreK K 1   **629.2**
1. Vehicles
ISBN 978-0-545-00720-7 pa; 0-545-00720-8 pa
"Vehicles—from lumbering tractors and cement mixers to sleek sports cars—roll across the pages of this Level One entry in the Scholastic Reader series. Each spread combines a large, crisp color photo of a vehicle, with a banner of smaller photos. The rhyming sentences are well tuned for brand-new readers." Booklist
Includes glossary

Gifford, Clive
Things that go. Kingfisher 2011 32 p. ill. $10.99
Grades: 3 4 5   **629.2**
1. Motion 2. Physics 3. Transportation 4. Science -- Encyclopedias
ISBN 0753465930; 9780753465936
This illustrated children's book "uses a series of . . . story scenes to set the stage for a[n] . . . examination of the sci-

ence behind motion. From the speed of racing, to transport on the rails, the science of heavy machinery, the physics of flight, and what keeps boats afloat. After readers absorb the elements of each story, they can explore the details through photographs and explanations on the following page. If they are interested in a particular aspect of transportation they can hop through the book following one of four icons related to their interest. Back matter offers plenty of resources for further multimedia exploration." (Publisher's note)

Mara, Wil

From locusts to...automobile anti-collision systems; by Wil Mara. Cherry Lake Pub. 2012 32 p. col. ill. (Innovations from nature) (library) $28.50; (e-book) $28.50; (paperback) $14.21

Grades: 4 5 6 7   **629.2**
     1. Biomimicry -- Juvenile literature 2. Automobiles -- Collision avoidance systems 3. Locusts
     ISBN 1610805011; 9781610805018; 9781610805889; 9781610806756
                                         LC 2012011856

"This . . . entry in the '21st Century Skills Innovation Library: Innovations from Nature' series explores how automobile manufacturers and scientists are trying to develop . . . collision avoidance systems based on the instincts of the humble locust, which has the ability to avoid oncoming objects while in a swarm. . . . [Wil] Mara describes the science of biomimicry, or 'the practice of copying nature--plants and animals--to build or improve something.'" (Booklist)

Includes bibliographical references (p. 31) and index.

Smith, Miranda

Speed machines; and other record-breaking vehicles. Kingfisher 2009 63p il (Kingfisher knowledge) $12.95

Grades: 5 6 7 8   **629.2**
     1. Speed 2. Vehicles
     ISBN 978-0-7534-6287-4; 0-7534-6287-7

"This well-organized, full-color book is packed with facts, photos, and history. It covers all aspects in history dealing with humankind's quest for speed, including land, water and air. . . . There are short blocks of main text and sidebars or blurbs to add additional information. Besides the usual suspects in books that cover this topic—cars, motorcycles, and planes—this book includes boats, gliders, hot air balloons, trains, and windsurfing among other speed machines. . . . It is an essential purchase, especially where books about racing, cars, planes, trucks, motorcycles, etc. are popular." Voice Youth Advocates

---

629.222   Gasoline-powered, oil-powered, man-powered vehicles

Bearce, Stephanie

All about electric and hybrid cars; and who's driving them. Mitchell Lane Publishers 2009 47p il (Tell your parents) lib bdg $21.50

Grades: 4 5 6 7   **629.222**
     1. Electric automobiles
     ISBN 978-1-58415-763-2 lib bdg; 1-58415-763-1 lib bdg
                                         LC 2009004528

This describes how hybrid and electric cars work and new inventions in the automotive industry, including vehicles powered by hydrogen and solar powered cars

Includes bibliographical references

Benjamin, Daniel

Prius. Marshall Cavendish Benchmark 2010 47p il (Green cars) $28.50

Grades: 3 4 5 6   **629.222**
     1. Electric automobiles
     ISBN 978-1-60870-011-0; 1-60870-011-9

"The Prius is one of the first hybrids sold in America. . . . [The] book opens with [an] . . . introduction explaining how global warming and limited oil availability are among the factors reshaping automobile design and technology. The [book provides a] clear [explanation] of how hybrid and all-electrical vehicles operate. . . . Color photos in various sizes add visual appeal." SLJ

Includes glossary and bibliographical references

Clark, Willow

Cars on the move. PowerKids Press 2010 24p il (Transportation station) lib bdg $21.25; pa $8.25

Grades: 2 3   **629.222**
     1. Automobiles
     ISBN 978-1-4358-9333-7 lib bdg; 1-4358-9333-6 lib bdg; 978-1-4358-9754-0 pa; 1-4358-9754-4 pa

Explains how cars work and shows the many different types of cars.

"Clark has done a fine job of including meaningful content in a limited space. . . . [This] title consists of 10 two-page chapters printed in a font of an inviting size. Full-page photos–all color except one vintage photograph–with informative captions face two-paragraph text blocks. . . . Will make readers feel they have learned something." SLJ

Includes glossary

Crowther, Robert

Cars; a pop-up book of automobiles. Candlewick Press 2009 un il $17.99

Grades: K 1 2 3   **629.222**
     1. Automobiles 2. Pop-up books
     ISBN 978-0-7636-4448-2; 0-7636-4448-X

"This introduction to all things automotive begins with the earliest examples that can be considered cars, finishes with a nifty foldout track scene that doubles as both stock car and Formula One, and features an intelligent array of information on luxury, everyday, and record-breaking cars in between. Most of the moving pieces are sturdily designed . . . and go a long way toward adding some pizzazz to the straightforward text." Booklist

Juettner, Bonnie

Hybrid cars; by Bonnie Juettner. Norwood House Press 2009 48p il (A great idea) lib bdg $25.27

Grades: 3 4 5 6   **629.222**
     1. Electric automobiles
     ISBN 978-1-59953-193-9 lib bdg; 1-59953-193-3 lib bdg
                                         LC 2008-22970

"Full-color photographs and copious fun facts help make this . . . enjoyable reading, but it's really the choice of [topic] that is so enthralling." Booklist

Includes glossary and bibliographical references

Lew, Kristi

Volt. Marshall Cavendish Benchmark 2010 47p il (Green cars) $28.50

Grades: 3 4 5 6   **629.222**

1. Electric automobiles

ISBN 978-1-60870-013-4; 1-60870-013-5

"The Volt is one of the first mass-produced cars to depend heavily on battery power. . . . [The] book opens with [an] . . . introduction explaining how global warming and limited oil availability are among the factors reshaping automobile design and technology. The [book provides a] clear [explanation] of how hybrid and all-electrical vehicles operate. . . . Color photos in various sizes add visual appeal." SLJ

Includes glossary and bibliographical references

Mitchell, Joyce Slayton

Crashed, smashed, and mashed; a trip to junkyard heaven. photographs by Steven Borns. Tricycle Press 2001 un il hardcover o.p. pa $7.95

Grades: 3 4 5 6   **629.222**

1. Salvage 2. Automobiles

ISBN 1-58246-034-5; 1-58246-156-2 pa

LC 00-10713

This describes an automobile junkyard where old cars are salvaged for parts and scrap metal

This book offers "excellent, clear, close-up photographs and a wealth of facts." Booklist

Includes glossary

Niver, Heather Moore

Camaros. Gareth Stevens Pub. 2011 32p il (Wild wheels) lib bdg $26.60; pa $10.50

Grades: 3 4 5 6   **629.222**

1. Automobiles

ISBN 978-1-4339-4735-3 lib bdg; 1-4339-4735-8 lib bdg; 978-1-4339-4736-0 pa; 1-4339-4736-6 pa

LC 2010032883

This book about Camaro automobiles "is sure to be . . . popular. . . . The light, somewhat breezy [text moves] quickly, presenting the history of the cars and just the right amount of information. . . . The bright, colorful illustrations are excellent. . . . A first purchase." SLJ

Includes glossary and bibliographical references

GTOs. Gareth Stevens Pub. 2011 32p il (Wild wheels) lib bdg $26.60; pa $10.50

Grades: 3 4 5 6   **629.222**

1. Automobiles

ISBN 978-1-4339-4747-6 lib bdg; 1-4339-4747-1 lib bdg; 978-1-4339-4748-3 pa; 1-4339-4748-X pa

LC 2010037589

This book about GTO automobiles "is sure to be . . . popular. . . . The light, somewhat breezy [text moves] quickly, presenting the history of the cars and just the right amount of information. . . . The bright, colorful illustrations are excellent. . . . A first purchase." SLJ

Includes glossary and bibliographical references

Portman, Michael

Chargers. Gareth Stevens Pub. 2011 32p il (Wild wheels) lib bdg $26.60; pa $10.50

Grades: 3 4 5 6   **629.222**

1. Automobiles

ISBN 978-1-4339-4739-1 lib bdg; 1-4339-4739-0 lib bdg; 978-1-4339-4740-7 pa; 1-4339-4740-4 pa

LC 2010035555

This book about Dodge Charger automobiles "is sure to be . . . popular. . . . The light, somewhat breezy [text moves] quickly, presenting the history of the cars and just the right amount of information. . . . The bright, colorful illustrations are excellent. . . . A first purchase." SLJ

Includes glossary and bibliographical references

Chevelles. Gareth Stevens Pub. 2011 32p il (Wild wheels) lib bdg $26.60; pa $10.50

Grades: 3 4 5 6   **629.222**

1. Automobiles

ISBN 978-1-4339-4743-8 lib bdg; 1-4339-4743-9 lib bdg; 978-1-4339-4744-5 pa; 1-4339-4744-7 pa

LC 2010038391

This book about Chevelle automobiles "is sure to be . . . popular. . . . The light, somewhat breezy [text moves] quickly, presenting the history of the cars and just the right amount of information. . . . The bright, colorful illustrations are excellent. . . . A first purchase." SLJ

Includes glossary and bibliographical references

Mustangs. Gareth Stevens Pub. 2011 32p il (Wild wheels) lib bdg $26.60; pa $10.50

Grades: 3 4 5 6   **629.222**

1. Automobiles

ISBN 978-1-4339-4751-3 lib bdg; 1-4339-4751-X lib bdg; 978-1-4339-4752-0 pa; 1-4339-4752-8 pa

LC 2010037587

This book about Ford Mustang automobiles "is sure to be . . . popular. . . . The light, somewhat breezy [text moves] quickly, presenting the history of the cars and just the right amount of information. . . . The bright, colorful illustrations are excellent. . . . A first purchase." SLJ

Includes glossary and bibliographical references

Torinos. Gareth Stevens Pub. 2011 32p il (Wild wheels) lib bdg $26.60; pa $10.50

Grades: 3 4 5 6   **629.222**

1. Automobiles

ISBN 978-1-4339-4755-1 lib bdg; 1-4339-4755-2 lib bdg; 978-1-4339-4756-8 pa; 1-4339-4756-0 pa

LC 2010039151

This book about Torino automobiles "is sure to be . . . popular. . . . The light, somewhat breezy [text moves] quickly, presenting the history of the cars and just the right amount of information. . . . The bright, colorful illustrations are excellent. . . . A first purchase." SLJ

Includes glossary and bibliographical references

Steggall, Susan

The life of a car. Henry Holt & Co. 2008 un il $16.95

Grades: PreK K 1 2   **629.222**

1. Automobiles

ISBN 0-8050-8747-8

"With torn-paper collages in saturated color and just three words for every spread except the last, Steggall presents the life cycle of a car from its manufacture to its destruction and recycling, when the process begins anew." SLJ

Swanson, Jennifer

★ **How** hybrid cars work; illustrated by Glen Mullaly. Child's World 2011 il (How things work) lib bdg $28.50
Grades: 4 5 6 **629.222**
1. Electric automobiles
ISBN 1-60973-217-0; 978-1-60973-217-2
LC 2011010917

"This volume is bouncy, savvy, and, above all, clear; it is hard to come away without a working knowledge of everything from the mechanics of hybrid engines to why dependence on foreign oil is bad. Hosting the series are two cartoons—a robot and a caveman—especially apt choices for a book couched in the concept of discarding old energy sources for new. . . . This is a model of how to make science appeal to young readers."
Includes bibliographical references

Warhol, Tom

Aptera. Marshall Cavendish Benchmark 2010 47p il (Green cars) $28.50
Grades: 3 4 5 6 **629.222**
1. Electric automobiles
ISBN 978-1-60870-008-0; 1-60870-008-9

"The futuristic Aptera appeared in a 'Star Trek' film. . . . [The] book opens with [an] . . . introduction explaining how global warming and limited oil availability are among the factors reshaping automobile design and technology. The [book provides a] clear [explanation] of how hybrid and all-electrical vehicles operate. . . . Color photos in various sizes add visual appeal." SLJ
Includes glossary and bibliographical references

Wheeler, Jill C.

Alternative cars; [by] Jill C. Wheeler. ABDO 2008 32p il (Eye on energy) $16.95
Grades: 3 4 5 **629.222**
1. Alternative fuel vehicles
ISBN 978-1-59928-803-1; 1-59928-803-6
LC 2007007107

This "begins with an explantion of the internal-combustion engine and its shortcomings. Wheeler then introduces readers to more efficient methods of powering automobiles, including electricity, a combination of gas and electricty, diesel fuel, hydrogen, natural gas, and ethanol. For each alternative she describes advantages, disadvantages, and the current availability of this technology. Captioned, full-color photographs . . . appear on nearly every page, complementing the clearly written text." Booklist
Includes glossary

Williams, Brian

Who invented the automobile? Arcturus Pub. 2010 46p il (Breakthroughs in science and technology) lib bdg $32.80
Grades: 5 6 7 8 **629.222**
1. Engines 2. Automobiles
ISBN 978-1-84837-681-6; 1-84837-681-2
LC 2010011019

Examines the history of the automobile.
This book is "divided into easy to read short chapters with large, colorful photographs and graphics on every page. . . . The added inserts provide additional information to engage readers and help them connect with the scientific details." Libr Media Connect

Woods, Bob

Hottest muscle cars; by Bob Woods. Enslow Publishers 2008 48p il (Wild wheels!) lib bdg $23.93; pa $7.95
Grades: 4 5 6 7 **629.222**
1. Automobiles
ISBN 978-0-7660-2872-2 lib bdg; 0-7660-2872-0 lib bdg; 978-0-7660-3611-6 pa; 0-7660-3611-1 pa
LC 2007007423

This focuses on "the beginning of America's love for muscle cars, and see why they are still loved today." Publisher's note
Includes glossary and bibliographical references

Hottest sports cars; by Bob Woods. Enslow Publishers 2008 48p il (Wild wheels!) lib bdg $23.93; pa $7.95
Grades: 4 5 6 7 **629.222**
1. Automobiles
ISBN 978-0-7660-2873-9 lib bdg; 0-7660-2873-9 lib bdg; 978-0-7660-3609-3 pa; 0-7660-3909-X pa
LC 2007007428

This focuses on "some of the world's most famous sports cars; how they began, and where they are going in the future." Publisher's note
Includes glossary and bibliographical references

Zabludoff, Marc

Ebox. Marshall Cavendish Benchmark 2010 47p il (Green cars) $28.50
Grades: 3 4 5 6 **629.222**
1. Electric automobiles
ISBN 978-1-60870-009-7; 1-60870-009-7

"The all-electric Ebox is a conversion of the gasoline-powered Toyota Scion XB. [The] book opens with [an] . . . introduction explaining how global warming and limited oil availability are among the factors reshaping automobile design and technology. The [book provides a] clear [explanation] of how hybrid and all-electrical vehicles operate. . . . Color photos in various sizes add visual appeal." SLJ
Includes glossary and bibliographical references

629.224 Trucks (Lorries)

Barton, Byron

★ **Trucks**. Crowell 1986 un il lib bdg $15.89
Grades: PreK K 1 **629.224**
1. Trucks
ISBN 0-690-04530-1
LC 85-47901

Brief text and illustrations present a variety of trucks from cement trucks to ice-cream trucks, and what they do
"A tightly focused (book) . . . featuring Barton's trademark bright, blocky graphics and spare text." Publ Wkly

Lindeen, Mary

Trucks; by Mary Lindeen. Bellwether Media 2007 24p il (Mighty machines) lib bdg $18.50
Grades: PreK K 1 2 3 **629.224**
1. Trucks
ISBN 978-1-60014-063-1 lib bdg; 1-60014-063-7 lib bdg
LC 2006035265

This explains what a truck is and describes its major parts and that they do.

The glossary features "easy-to-read-and-understand definitions. . . . With [its] exciting, full-color photos on every spread, [this] will certainly appeal to the mighty curiosity of young readers." SLJ

Includes glossary and bibliographical references

Maass, Robert

Little trucks with big jobs; [by] Robert Maass. Henry Holt & Co. 2007 un il $16.95

Grades: PreK K   **629.224**

1. Trucks

ISBN 978-0-8050-7748-3; 0-8050-7748-0

LC 2006030617

"Children are introduced to 15 little rigs and the important work they do. Simple, clear explanations accompany each full-page photograph. . . . Bright, primary colored backgrounds frame the pictures, and the text appears inside road-sign shapes. This high-interest book is sure to be popular with vehicle fans." SLJ

Mara, Wil

Trucks. National Geographic 2009 32p il (National Geographic readers) $12.99; pa $3.99

Grades: K 1 2   **629.224**

1. Trucks

ISBN 978-1-4263-0527-6; 1-4263-0527-3; 978-1-4263-0526-9 pa; 1-4263-0526-5 pa

LC 2009-21037

"Mara describes truck parts and their functions in brief, simple text for early readers. Colorful close-up photographs dominate each spread, often using arrows to point to and clarify labeled parts." Horn Book Guide

Murrell, Deborah Jane

Mega trucks. Tangerine Press 2008 32p il $6.99

Grades: PreK K 1 2   **629.224**

1. Trucks

ISBN 0-439-85056-8

First published in 2005 by Scholastic

"Discusses the parts and functions of different kinds of trucks, including tractor-trailers, loaders, and monster trucks." Publisher's note

Ransom, Candice F.

Big rigs on the move; [by] Candice Ransom. Lerner Publications 2011 32p il (Lightning Bolt Books. Vroom-vroom) lib bdg $25.26

Grades: K 1 2   **629.224**

1. Trucks

ISBN 978-0-7613-3919-9 lib bdg; 0-7613-3919-1 lib bdg

LC 2009-39738

This book about big rigs has "big, high-energy color photos. . . . [The text provides] lively commentary in a mix of declarative statements and non-rhetorical questions. . . . [The] volume closes with a labeled diagram, a page of 'fun facts,' and a short list of print and web resources. . . . [This] will make a worthwhile and popular addition." SLJ

Includes glossary and bibliographical references

Simon, Seymour

★ Seymour Simon's book of trucks. HarperCollins Pubs. 2000 un il hardcover o.p. pa $6.99

Grades: K 1 2 3   **629.224**

1. Trucks

ISBN 0-06-028473-0; 0-06-028481-1 lib bdg; 0-06-446224-2 pa

LC 99-14602

Describes various kinds of trucks and their functions, including a log truck, cement mixer truck, and sanitation truck

"The exciting photographs, many of them close-ups, will captivate youngsters. . . . The visual appeal of this book is very high and the information is clear and equally engaging." SLJ

Stille, Darlene R.

Trucks. Children's Press 1997 47p il (True book) lib bdg $22; pa $6.95

Grades: 2 3 4   **629.224**

1. Trucks

ISBN 0-516-20343-6 lib bdg; 0-516-26179-7 pa

LC 96-25727

Describes different kinds of trucks, including tractor trailers and tank trucks, pick-ups, tow trucks, fire trucks, garbage trucks, vans, and recreational vehicles

Includes bibliographical references

Zuehlke, Jeffrey

Pickup trucks on the move. Lerner Publications 2010 32p il (Lightning bolt books. Vroom-vroom) lib bdg $25.26

Grades: K 1 2   **629.224**

1. Trucks

ISBN 978-0-7613-6024-7 lib bdg; 0-7613-6024-7 lib bdg

LC 2009039747

This book about pickup trucks has "big, high-energy color photos. . . . [The text provides] lively commentary in a mix of declarative statements and non-rhetorical questions. . . . [The] volume closes with a labeled diagram, a page of 'fun facts,' and a short list of print and web resources. . . . [This] will make a worthwhile and popular addition." SLJ

Includes glossary and bibliographical references

629.225 Work vehicles

Abramson, Andra Serlin

★ Heavy equipment up close; [by] Andra Serlin Abramson. Sterling Pub. Co. 2008 47p il (Up close) $9.95

Grades: 2 3 4   **629.225**

1. Construction equipment

ISBN 978-1-4027-4799-1; 1-4027-4799-3

LC 2007019277

This is "packed with full-color photographs on pages measuring about 10 1/2 x 14 inches, many of which open out into eye-popping gatefolds. This . . . title is tailor-made for children known to gaze longingly at construction sites. Even preschoolers will enjoy the photos . . . but children who can read on their own, or sit still through each page's several pages of text, will get the most out the book's terrific mix of fun and technical vocabulary." Booklist

Lindeen, Mary

Tractors; by Mary Lindeen. Bellwether Media 2007 24p il (Mighty machines) lib bdg $18.50

Grades: PreK K 1 2 3 **629.225**

1. Tractors

ISBN 978-1-60014-061-7 lib bdg; 1-60014-061-0 lib bdg

LC 2006035263

This explains what a tractor is and discusses its major parts and what they do.

The glossary features "easy-to-read-and-understand definitions. . . . With [its] exciting, full-color photos on every spread, [this] colorful [title] will certainly appeal to the mighty curiosity of young readers." SLJ

Includes glossary and bibliographical references

629.227 Cycles

Clark, Willow

Bikes on the move. PowerKids Press 2010 24p il (Transportation station) lib bdg $21.25; pa $8.25

Grades: 2 3 **629.227**

1. Cycling 2. Bicycles

ISBN 978-1-4358-9334-4 lib bdg; 1-4358-9334-4 lib bdg; 978-1-4358-9756-4 pa; 1-4358-9756-0 pa

Learn about mountain bikes, racing bikes and lowrider bikes.

"Clark has done a fine job of including meaningful content in a limited space. . . . [This] title consists of 10 two-page chapters printed in a font of an inviting size. Full-page photos–all color except one vintage photograph–with informative captions face two-paragraph text blocks. . . . Will make readers feel they have learned something." SLJ

Includes glossary

Motorcycles on the move. PowerKids Press 2010 24p il (Transportation station) lib bdg $21.25; pa $8.25

Grades: 2 3 **629.227**

1. Motorcycles

ISBN 978-1-4358-9335-1 lib bdg; 1-4358-9335-2 lib bdg; 978-1-4358-9758-8 pa; 1-4358-9758-7 pa

Introduces the various kinds of motorcycles and their uses.

"Clark has done a fine job of including meaningful content in a limited space. . . . [This] title consists of 10 two-page chapters printed in a font of an inviting size. Full-page photos–all color except one vintage photograph–with informative captions face two-paragraph text blocks. . . . Will make readers feel they have learned something." SLJ

Includes glossary

Gibbons, Gail

Bicycle book. Holiday House 1995 un il $16.95; pa $6.95

Grades: K 1 2 3 **629.227**

1. Cycling 2. Bicycles

ISBN 0-8234-1199-0; 0-8234-1408-6 pa

LC 95-5911

"The history of bicycles, the science behind their design, descriptions of different types, their care, and safety rules are all clearly and simply presented in Gibbons's typical, inimi-

table style. Lots of color, accurate explanations, and interesting facts make this a winning choice." SLJ

Haduch, Bill

★ Go fly a bike! the ultimate book about bicycle fun, freedom & science. illustrated by Chris Murphy. Dutton Children's Books 2004 83p il $16.99

Grades: 4 5 6 7 **629.227**

1. Cycling 2. Bicycles

ISBN 0-525-47024-7

Gives the history, science, types of cycles, safety and the basics and maintenance of bicycles

"Halftone cartoonlike illustrations are scattered throughout, and a funny fact or joke appears in an inset on most pages. . . . This is a versatile, fact-packed book that can work for both research and recreational reading." Booklist

Smedman, Lisa

From boneshakers to choppers; the rip-roaring history of motorcycles. Annick Press 2007 120p il $24.95; pa $14.95

Grades: 5 6 7 8 **629.227**

1. Motorcycles

ISBN 978-1-55451-016-0; 1-55451-016-3; 978-1-55451-015-3 pa; 1-55451-015-5 pa

"Smedman defines 'motorcycles' broadly enough to include everything from Harleys to Vespas, and even bicycles, in this lively, wide-ranging history. . . . Illustrated with a generous array of action photos, historical shots, and period advertisements." Booklist

Includes bibliographical references

Woods, Bob

Hottest motorcycles; by Bob Woods. Enslow Publishers 2008 48p il (Wild wheels!) lib bdg $23.93; pa $7.95

Grades: 4 5 6 7 **629.227**

1. Motorcycles

ISBN 978-0-7660-2874-6 lib bdg; 0-7660-2874-7 lib bdg; 978-0-7660-3608-6 pa; 0-7660-3608-1 pa

LC 2007007425

This focuses on "the motorcycle's beginning, the chopper phenomenon, and motorcycle racing." Publisher's note

Includes bibliographical references

629.228 Racing cars

Rex, Michael

My race car. Holt & Co. 2000 un il lib bdg $15.95

Grades: PreK K 1 **629.228**

1 Automobile racing 2. Automobiles, Racing

ISBN 0-8050-6101-0

LC 99-31773

"'I have a race car. I drive it all the time,' says a boy sitting on the floor with his toy cars. As the pages turn, the toy world becomes reality: the boy finds himself on the track with his crew, checking his car engine, and then driving his laps. . . . Short, simple sentences create excitement . . . and Rex's bright, thick-lined cartoon drawings are appealingly energetic and clear. A great choice for young race car enthusiasts who are beginning to read on their own." Booklist

Sandler, Michael

Dynamic drag racers. Bearport Pub. 2011 24p il (Fast rides) lib bdg $22.61

Grades: 3 4 5 6 **629.228**

1. Automobiles 2. Automobile racing

ISBN 978-1-61772-138-0; 1-61772-138-7

LC 2010041872

This describes different types of vehicles used in drag races including top fuel dragsters, pro stock motorcycles, funny cars, and exhibition wheelstanders.

"Sharp, colorful photos and [a] succinct [text provides a] brief but informative [introduction] to record-setting vehicles. . . . This [book] deserves first consideration." SLJ

Includes glossary and bibliographical references

Electrifying eco-race cars. Bearport Pub. 2011 24p il (Fast rides) lib bdg $22.61

Grades: 3 4 5 6 **629.228**

1. Automobile racing 2. Electric automobiles

ISBN 978-1-61772-137-3; 1-61772-137-9

LC 2010040095

This describes earth-friendly race cars including hydrogen-fueled cars that can reach speeds of over 300 miles per hour and wind-powered speedsters that don't use a motor.

"Sharp, colorful photos and [a] succinct [text provides a] brief but informative [introduction] to record-setting vehicles. . . . This [book] deserves first consideration." SLJ

Includes glossary and bibliographical references

Hot hot rods. Bearport Pub. 2011 24p il (Fast rides) lib bdg $22.61

Grades: 3 4 5 6 **629.228**

1. Automobiles 2. Automobile racing

ISBN 978-1-61772-139-7; 1-61772-139-5

LC 2010041875

This describes hot rods including modified 1930s Ford cars, such as the "Deuce" roadster and classic Model T, VW Bugs and pumped-up pickup trucks.

"Sharp, colorful photos and [a] succinct [text provides a] brief but informative [introduction] to record-setting vehicles. . . . This [book] deserves first consideration." SLJ

Includes glossary and bibliographical references

Jet-powered speed. Bearport Pub. 2011 24p il (Fast rides) lib bdg $22.61

Grades: 3 4 5 6 **629.228**

1. Jet propulsion 2. Automobile racing

ISBN 978-1-61772-136-6; 1-61772-136-0

LC 2010037210

This describes jet-powered cars such as the Thrust2, which broke speed records using a huge jet engine that came from a British fighter plane, and the ThrustSCC which traveled faster than the speed of sound.

"Sharp, colorful photos and [a] succinct [text provides a] brief but informative [introduction] to record-setting vehicles. . . . This [book] deserves first consideration." SLJ

Includes glossary and bibliographical references

629.4 Astronautics

Aldrin, Buzz

Look to the stars. G. P. Putnam's Sons 2009 40p il $17.99

Grades: 2 3 4 **629.4**

1. Astronauts 2. Astronautics 3. Space flight 4. Air force officers 5. Nonfiction writers

ISBN 978-0-399-24721-7; 0-399-24721-1

LC 2008018575

This is "a quick overview of the past and near future of human space flight. Paired with Minor's clean-lined, realistically detailed scenes of significant aircraft, spacecraft, and high spots, [the] narrative opens with Galileo, [and] closes with the rousing suggestion that the opportunity to venture into space lies just a tantalizing few years down the road for many young readers." SLJ

Barchers, Suzanne I.

Revolution in space. Marshall Cavendish Benchmark 2010 32p il (It works!) lib bdg $19.95

Grades: 3 4 5 **629.4**

1. Astronautics

ISBN 978-0-7614-4377-3 lib bdg; 0-7614-4377-0 lib bdg

LC 2008-54365

"This interesting, information packed [book] . . . motivates students to do their own exploring. . . . [The] book starts with an invention from long ago and gradually builds on it. The scientist famous for each invention is highlighted; the brief synopsis shares his interests growing up. The ideas that ultimately inspired the invention are shown in visual 'idea clouds' sharing the process with students. Timelines show that the inventions not only took creative thought, they also took perseverance. The appealing cartoon-like photographs add humor. . . . This . . . just may be that spark needed to create eager budding scientists." Libr Media Connection

Includes glossary and bibliographical references

Benoit, Peter

The space race; by Peter Benoit. Children's Press 2012 64 p. ill. (some col.) (library) $30.00; (paperback) $8.95

Grades: 4 5 6 **629.4**

1. Astronautics -- United States 2. Space flight -- Juvenile literature 3. Astronautics -- Soviet Union -- History -- Juvenile literature 4. Astronautics -- United States -- History -- Juvenile literature 5. Space race -- History -- Juvenile literature

ISBN 0531281655; 9780531230657; 9780531281659

LC 2011031454

This book by Peter Benoit is part of the "Cornerstones of Freedom" series. It "attempts to provide an historical overview of the race between the United States and Soviet Union to explore space. . . . The book ends with a map . . . a . . . list of influential individuals, a timeline, and a glossary." (Children's Literature)

Includes bibliographical references (p. 60-61) and index.

Bortz, Alfred B.

Seven wonders of space technology; by Fred Bortz. Twenty-First Century Books 2011 80p il (Seven wonders) lib bdg $33.26; ebook $24.95

Grades: 5 6 7 8   629.4
1. Astronautics 2. Space vehicles 4. Space vehicles
-- Juvenile literature 5. Outer space -- Exploration --
Juvenile literature
ISBN 978-0-7613-5453-6 lib bdg; 0-7613-5453-0 lib
bdg; 9780761372806
LC 2010-23996

This book examines the science involved in the Great
Observatories, the International Space Station, New Horizons, Moon bases and lunar water, Mars rovers, rocketry,
and weather satellites. Glossary. Index. "Grades seven to
twelve." (Sci Books Films)

"Highlights some of astronomy's greatest technical advancements, from land observatories to spinning satellites to
moon bases. . . . [This] volume makes basic concepts clear
in lively, energetic language that, along with the mesmerizing color photos and artists' renderings of space, will easily captivate a young audience, while up-to-date examples,
including discoveries made in the last five years, will only
increase the sense of immediacy and excitement." Booklist

Includes glossary and bibliographical references

Bredeson, Carmen
John Glenn returns to orbit; life on the space shuttle.
Enslow Pubs. 2000 48p il (Countdown to space) $18.95
Grades: 4 5 6 7   629.4
1. Astronauts 2. Space flight 3. Space shuttles 4.
Senators
ISBN 0-7660-1304-9
LC 99-12490

Describes the activities aboard the space shuttle Discovery during its historic flight in 1998 when John Glenn, at age
seventy-seven, returned to space

"The accessible {text is} accompanied by plenty of well-
captioned photos and diagrams." Horn Book Guide

Includes glossary and bibliographical references

Harris, Joseph
Space exploration; impact of science and technology.
Gareth Stevens Pub. 2010 64p il map (Pros and cons) lib
bdg $35
Grades: 5 6 7 8   629.4
1. Astronautics
ISBN 978-1-4339-1989-3 lib bdg; 1-4339-1989-3
lib bdg
LC 2009-12436

"This book examines the politics of space—the space
race, weapons in space, and international cooperation, the
realities of living in space, the uses of satellites and space
probes, space age technologies that changed life on Earth,
the future of space exploration, from space tourism to space
elevators." Publisher's note

Includes glossary and bibliographical references

Jedicke, Peter
Great moments in space exploration. Chelsea House
2007 72p il (Scientific American) $30
Grades: 5 6 7 8   629.4
1. Astronautics 2. Astronautics -- History -- Juvenile
literature 4. Outer space -- Exploration -- Juvenile
literature
ISBN 978-0-7910-9046-6; 0-7910-9046-9
LC 2006-14774

This "introduction to the history of space exploration is
well illustrated with numerous photos, many from NASA.
The history is well told, with the achievements of the Soviet
Union, in particular, covered quite nicely." Sci Books Films

Includes glossary and bibliographical references

Skurzynski, Gloria
★ This is rocket science; true stories of the risk-taking
scientists who figure out ways to explore beyond Earth. National Geographic 2010 80p il $18.95; lib bdg $28.90
Grades: 5 6 7 8   629.4
1. Rocketry 2. Aeronautics 3. Aerospace engineers
ISBN 978-1-4263-0597-9; 1-4263-0597-4; 978-1-
4263-0598-6 lib bdg; 1-4263-0598-2 lib bdg
LC 2009-20386

"This concise book provides a historical, as well as contemporary, introduction to the field of aeronautical engineering with a decidedly human interest perspective. . . . This
text will be a great introduction to many of the significant
contributors to the field of rocket science." Sci Books Films

Includes glossary and bibliographical references

Stott, Carole
Space exploration; written by Carole Stott; photo-
graphed by Steve Gorton. Dorling Kindersley 2009 71p il
(DK eyewitness books) $16.99
Grades: 4 5 6 7   629.4
1. Astronautics
ISBN 978-0-7566-5828-1; 0-7566-5828-4
First published 1997 by Knopf

Describes rockets, exploratory vehicles, and other technological aspects of space exploration, satellites, space stations, and the life and work of astronauts

629.43   Unmanned space flight

Jefferis, David
Space probes; exploring beyond Earth. Crabtree Pub.
2009 32p il (Exploring our solar system) lib bdg $26.60;
pa $8.95
Grades: 3 4 5   629.43
1. Space probes
ISBN 978-0-7787-3724-7 lib bdg; 0-7787-3724-1 lib
bdg; 978-0-7787-3741-4 pa; 0-7787-3741-1 pa
LC 2008-46249

"The author explains what space probes are for, names
many that have visited each of the major planets, and then
suggests where models and mock-ups (since they can't be
observed directly) might be found. . . . [The book is] designed with easily digestible blocks of question-and-answer
text sharing page space with large, sharply reproduced space
photos and graphic art." SLJ

Includes glossary

Miller, Ron
Robot explorers. Twenty-First Century Books 2007
112p il (Space innovations) lib bdg $31.93
Grades: 4 5 6   629.43
1. Robots 2. Space probes
ISBN 978-0-8225-7152-0 lib bdg; 0-8225-7152-8
lib bdg
LC 2007002864

This describes how robots are used for space exploration
Includes bibliographical references

Siy, Alexandra

★ **Cars** on Mars; roving the red planet. Charlesbridge
2009 57p il $18.95
Grades: 5 6 7 8 **629.43**
1. Space vehicles 2. Roving vehicles (Astronautics)
-- Juvenile literature
ISBN 978-1-57091-462-1; 1-57091-462-1
LC 2008-40751
Presents an introduction to the Mars Exploration Rovers
(MERS), 'Spirit' and 'Opportunity,' with photographs of the
Mars landscape taken over a five-year period as the rovers
searched for water on the red planet
"This title will sweep readers up in an exploratory mis-
sion that has come closer than any other so far to finding sure
signs of extraterrestrial life." SLJ
Includes glossary and bibliographical references

629.44 Auxiliary spacecraft

Branley, Franklyn Mansfield

The **International** Space Station; by Franklyn M,
Branley; illustrated by True Kelley. HarperCollins Pubs.
2000 32p il (Let's-read-and-find-out science) hardcover
o.p. pa $5.95
Grades: K 1 2 3 **629.44**
1. Astronauts 2. Space stations
ISBN 0-06-028702-0; 0-06-445209-3 pa
LC 99-31897
Explains the construction and purpose of the International Space Station and the life of the astronauts on board
"The facts, including a history and background of the
station and descriptions of life in space, are presented in
a clear, easy-to-read manner. . . . Kelley's clearly labeled
drawings and configurations reinforce the concepts presented, and the watercolor illustrations add dimension to the
presentation." SLJ

Cole, Michael D.

The **Columbia** space shuttle disaster; from first liftoff
to tragic final flight. Enslow Pubs. 2003 48p il (Count-
down to space) lib bdg $18.95
Grades: 4 5 6 **629.44**
1. Space vehicle accidents
ISBN 0-7660-2295-1
LC 2003-4823
First published 1995 with title: Columbia
Details the first flight of the space shuttle Columbia, as
well as its tragic final flight
"The account offers a lot of information, helping to make
sense of a highly complicated subject. . . . The color and b&w
photographs complement the story." Libr Media Connect
Includes glossary and bibliographical references

NASA space vehicles; capsules, shuttles, and space stations. Enslow Pubs. 2000 48p il (Countdown to space)
lib bdg $18.95
Grades: 4 5 6 7 **629.44**
1. Space vehicles 2. Space vehicles -- United States

-- History -- Juvenile literature
ISBN 0-7660-1308-1
LC 99-35533
Describes American space vehicles and their uses, in-
cluding various space probes, the Mercury, Gemini, and
Apollo capsules, Skylab, the space shuttles, and the Interna-
tional Space Station
Includes glossary and bibliographical references

Holden, Henry M.

The **coolest** job in the universe; working aboard the International Space Station. Henry M. Holden. Enslow 2013
48 p. (hbk.) $23.93
Grades: 4 5 6 7 8 **629.44**
1. Space flight -- Juvenile literature 2. Space sciences
-- Juvenile literature 3. Manned space flight -- Juvenile
literature 4. Space sciences -- Research -- Juvenile
literature
ISBN 0766040747; 9780766040748
LC 2012002222
This book, by Henry M. Holden, is part of the "American Space Missions: Astronauts, Exploration, and Discovery" series. In it the daily life of astronauts working on the
International Space Station is explored. This book "focuses
on the construction of the ISS, what life is like onboard,
and the importance of the research projects conducted. . .
. Throughout, the courage, dedication, and sacrifice of the
astronauts are emphasized." (School Library Journal)
Includes bibliographical references (p. 43-45, 47)
and index

Kerrod, Robin

Space shuttles; [by] Robin Kerrod. World Almanac
Library 2005 48p il (History of space exploration) hardcover o.p. lib bdg $30
Grades: 5 6 7 8 **629.44**
1. Space shuttles
ISBN 0-8368-5709-7 lib bdg; 0-8368-5716-X pa
LC 2004-49217
Explores the successes of the shuttle program, including
the daring recovery and repair of satellites by space-walk-
ing astronauts, and examines the human and technological
costs of its tragic failures, such as the losses the Challenger
and Columbia
This "is profusely illustrated with sharply reproduced
space photos and artists' conceptions. . . . [This] makes an
important addition for any collection supporting avid young
scientists or strong science curricula." SLJ
Includes bibliographical references

Space stations; [by] Robin Kerrod. World Almanac
Library 2005 48p il (History of space exploration) hard-
cover o.p. lib bdg $30
Grades: 5 6 7 8 **629.44**
1. Space stations
ISBN 0-8368-5710-0 lib bdg; 0-8368-5717-8 pa
LC 2004-49071
Explores the history of space homes such as the Soviet's
Salyut 1, Mir, the United States's Skylab, and the Interna-
tional Space Station, a truly international venture between
several countries and scheduled for completion in 2008
This "is profusely illustrated with sharply reproduced
space photos and artists' conceptions. . . . [This] makes an

important addition for any collection supporting avid young scientists or strong science curricula." SLJ

Includes bibliographical references

Waxman, Laura Hamilton

Exploring the International Space Station. Lerner Publications 2011 40p il (What's amazing about space?) lib bdg $27.23

Grades: 4 5 6   **629.44**

1. Astronautics 2. Space stations

ISBN 978-0-7613-5443-7; 0-7613-5443-3

LC 2010035394

This describes how the International Space Station was built and how crew members live and work there.

This book is "written in simple language, [and] illustrated nicely. . . . The information presented is factually correct. . . . Every page includes a well-chosen illustration or photograph." Sci Books Films

Includes glossary and bibliographical references

629.45   Manned space flight

Bodden, Valerie

Man walks on the Moon. Creative Education 2009 48p il map (Days of change) $32.80

Grades: 5 6 7 8   **629.45**

1. Space flight to the moon

ISBN 978-1-58341-735-5; 1-58341-735-4

LC 2008009166

"With elegant design and mature prose, the Days of Change series is an ideal starting point for all manner of school projects. . . . The very first page of Man Walks on the Moon questions whether or not the feat was worth the resources, before reveling in the tech-heavy details of spaceflight and offering up some telling photos." Booklist

Includes bibliographical references

To the moon; by Valerie Bodden. Creative Education 2011 48 p. col. ill. (paperback) $12.00; (hardcover) $34.25

Grades: 5 6 7 8   **629.45**

1. Apollo project -- Juvenile literature 2. Space flight to the moon -- History -- Juvenile literature 3. Space flight to the moon -- History -- Juvenile literature

ISBN 1608180689; 9780898126662; 9781608180684

LC 2010033549

This book by Valerie Bodden on the 1969 moon landing is part of the "Great Expeditions" series. "This factual account is . . . accompanied with both black and white and color photographs. Profiles of four of the astronauts, reproductions of some of their significant journal entries, and inset boxes of supplemental information aid in understanding. Includes a table of contents, a timeline, end notes, a bibliography, and an index." (Children's Literature)

Includes bibliographical references (p. 46-47) and index.

Branley, Franklyn Mansfield

Floating in space; by Franklyn M. Branley; illustrated by True Kelley. HarperCollins Pubs. 1998 32p il (Let's-read-and-find-out science) hardcover o.p. pa $4.95

Grades: K 1 2 3   **629.45**

1. Astronauts 2. Space shuttles

ISBN 0-06-025433-5 lib bdg; 0-06-445142-9 pa

LC 97-13052

Examines life aboard a space shuttle, describing how astronauts deal with weightlessness, how they eat and exercise, some of the work they do, and more

"This is a beautifully illustrated children's book. . . . The textual information is clearly written, easy to read, and well organized." Sci Books Films

Mission to Mars; by Franklyn M. Branley; illustrated by True Kelley; foreword by Neil Armstrong. HarperCollins Pubs. 2002 33p il (Let's-read-and-find-out science) hardcover o.p. lib bdg $17.89; pa $4.99

Grades: K 1 2 3   **629.45**

1. Space flight to Mars

ISBN 0-06-029807-3; 0-06-029808-1 lib bdg; 0-06-445233-6 pa

LC 00-54036

The author invites readers to envision "themselves as members of the first Mars Mission's crew. . . . Along with a sprinkling of black-and-white and full-color photos, the illustrations mix clearly drawn schematics with scenes of crew members working busily inside the Mars Station or outside in heavy protective suits. An informative, inspirational introduction." SLJ

Bredeson, Carmen

What do astronauts do. Enslow Elementary 2008 32p il (I like space!) lib bdg $22.60

Grades: K 1 2 3   **629.45**

1. Astronautics 2. Astronauts -- Juvenile literature

ISBN 978-0-7660-2942-2 lib bdg; 0-7660-2942-5 lib bdg

LC 2007-02742

This book "is beautifully illustrated, with photographs from NASA and other sources, and is well organized." Sci Books Films

Includes bibliographical references

Brown, Don

★ **One** giant leap: the story of Neil Armstrong. Houghton Mifflin 1998 un il hardcover o.p. pa $6.95

Grades: K 1 2 3   **629.45**

1. Astronauts 2. Astronauts -- United States -- Biography -- Juvenile literature

ISBN 0-395-88401-2; 0-618-15239-3 pa

LC 97-42152

Discusses the life and accomplishments of astronaut Neil Armstrong, from his childhood in Ohio to his famous moon landing

"The sense of Armstrong as a boy growing into his childhood dream is strong in the well-constructed text, and that feeling is extended through watercolors with an airy sense of lightness that suits the emotional tone." Bull Cent Child Books

Burleigh, Robert

★ **One** giant leap; paintings by Mike Wimmer. Philomel Books 2009 un il $16.99

Grades: 1 2 3   **629.45**

1. Astronautics 2. Apollo project 3. Space flight to

the moon

ISBN 978-0-399-23883-3; 0-399-23883-2

LC 2008-15695

"Distinguished language and compelling imagery make this commemoration of the first Moon landing's 40th anniversary particularly intense. . . . The sense of immediacy is irresistible." SLJ

Chaikin, Andrew

★ **Mission** control, this is Apollo; the story of the first voyages to the moon. [by] Andrew Chaikin, with Victoria Kohl; [with paintings by] Alan Bean. Penguin Group 2009 114p il $23.99

Grades: 5 6 7 8 9   **629.45**

1. Astronautics 2. Space flight to the moon 3. Project Apollo -- Juvenile literature

ISBN 978-0-670-01156-8; 0-670-01156-8

LC 2009000833

"Based on interviews with 28 astronauts, this history of the Apollo program masterfully describes the missions and personalizes them with astronauts' own words. Chaikin starts with a brief overview of its origins and of the Mercury and Gemini missions. He then highlights the significance of each manned Apollo mission in chronological chapters, with full-page sidebars on such topics as food, TV coverage, space sickness and going to the bathroom in space. The handsome design has many photographs, diagrams of the rockets and modules and more than 30 well-reproduced paintings by Apollo 12 astronaut Bean." Kirkus

Includes bibliographical references

Cole, Michael D.

Space emergency; astronauts in danger. Enslow Pubs. 2000 48p il (Countdown to space) lib bdg $18.95

Grades: 4 5 6 7   **629.45**

1. Astronautics 2. Space vehicle accidents 3. Astronautics -- Safety measures -- Juvenile literature

ISBN 0-7660-1307-3

LC 99-26855

Describes emergencies that occurred during several space missions, including Apollo 13, Friendship 7, Gemini 8, and Mir

Includes glossary and bibliographical references

Dyer, Alan

Mission to the moon. Simon & Schuster Books for Young Readers 2009 80p il $19.99

Grades: 5 6 7 8   **629.45**

1. Space flight to the moon 2. Project Apollo -- Juvenile literature

ISBN 978-1-4169-7935-7; 1-4169-7935-2

LC 2008-61118

"Sporting a highly visual encyclopedic format, this informative book features 200 photographs documenting early research into mankind's history with the moon, early space exploration and the space race, and the Apollo missions. Detailed cross-sections of modules, space suits and other equipment offer a sound technological overview, while information on the phases, structure and surface of the moon provides added insight. . . . A DVD and poster are included." Publ Wkly

Dyson, Marianne J.

Home on the moon; living on a space frontier. National Geographic Soc. 2003 64p il $18.95

Grades: 4 5 6 7   **629.45**

ISBN 0-7922-7193-9

LC 2002-5280

Considers the moon as a frontier that has been only partially explored, looking at its history, geography, and weather, as well as what people would require to live and work there. Includes activities

"Clear writing, vivid images, interesting details, and quotes from astronauts and scientists make this a lively, fact-filled introduction." Booklist

Includes glossary and bibliographical references

Floca, Brian

★ **Moonshot**; the flight of Apollo 11. written and illustrated by Brian Floca. Atheneum Books for Young Readers 2008 un il $17.99

Grades: K 1 2 3   **629.45**

1. Astronautics 2. Space flight to the moon

ISBN 1-4169-5046-X; 978-1-4169-5046-2

LC 2007-52358

ALA ALSC Siebert Medal Honor Book (2010)

This is the story of the 1969 Apollo 11 mission to the Moon. "Grades two to five." (Bull Cent Child Books)

"Forty years after NASA's Apollo II mission first landed astronauts on the moon, this striking nonfiction picture book takes young readers along for the ride. . . . Written with quiet dignity and a minimum of fuss, the main text is beautifully illustrated with line-and-wash artwork that provides human interest, technological details, and some visually stunning scenes." Booklist

Green, Carl R.

Spacewalk; the astounding Gemini 4 mission. Carl R. Green. Enslow Publishers 2013 48 p. $23.93

Grades: 4 5 6 7 8   **629.45**

1. Gemini project 2. Outer space -- Juvenile literature 3. Space flight -- Juvenile literature

ISBN 0766040755; 9780766040755

LC 2011030869

This children's book, by Carl R. Green, "explores the astounding GEMINI 4 mission. . . . Pilot Ed White could see Hawaii, California, Texas, and Florida . . . while walking in space! . . . The first American spacewalk was a monumental achievement, and it helped push the space program toward its ultimate goal of landing men on the Moon." (Publisher's note)

Includes bibliographical references and index

Hartman, Eve

Mission to Mars; [by] Eve Hartman and Wendy Meshbesher. Raintree 2010 56p il lib bdg $33.50; pa $9.49

Grades: 5 6 7 8   **629.45**

1. Space flight to Mars

ISBN 9781-4109-3821-3 lib bdg; 1-4109-3821-2 lib bdg; 978-1-4109-3996-8 pa; 1-4109-3996-0 pa

LC 2009-53209

"Excellent black-and-white and color photos throughout are matched perfectly to the texts and well captioned. Good choices for reports and debates." SLJ

Hense, Mary

How astronauts use math; math curriculum consultant: Rhea A. Stewart. Chelsea Clubhouse 2010 32p il (Math in the real world) lib bdg $28

Grades: 4 5 6   629.45

1. Astronauts 2. Mathematics 3. Astronautics 4. Vocational guidance

ISBN 978-1-60413-610-4 lib bdg; 1-60413-610-3 lib bdg

LC 2009-23926

This describes how astronauts use math for such tasks as calculating distance, speed, and velocity, and includes relevant math problems and information about how to become an astronaut

Includes glossary and bibliographical references

Holden, Henry M.

Danger in space; surviving the Apollo 13 disaster. Henry M. Holden. Enslow Publishers 2013 48 p. $23.93

Grades: 4 5 6 7 8   629.45

1. Apollo project 2. Picture books for children 3. Apollo 13 (Spacecraft) -- Juvenile literature 4. Space vehicle accidents -- United States -- Juvenile literature

ISBN 0766040720; 9780766040724

LC 2011037734

This children's picture book tells the story of the U.S. National Aerospace and Space Administration's Apollo 13 mission. "Soaring through space at twenty-five thousand miles per hour, Apollo 13 was on course for the Moon. Suddenly, the three astronauts aboard the spacecraft heard a loud bang. A strong vibration rumbled through the crew cabin. There had been an explosion in the oxygen tank! More than two hundred thousand miles from Earth, Apollo 13 was in grave danger." (Publisher's note)

Includes bibliographical references and index

McCarthy, Meghan

Astronaut handbook. Alfred A. Knopf 2008 un il $16.99; lib bdg $19.99

Grades: K 1 2 3   629.45

1. Astronautics

ISBN 978-0-375-84459-1; 0-375-84459-7; 978-0-375-94459-8 lib bdg; 0-375-94459-1 lib bdg

LC 2007-31951

"Readers follow four aspiring astronauts from classroom to cockpit as they focus, study, practice, and ultimately take off. McCarthy applies a light, comic tone to the subject, reflected in her simple, expressive, cartoony acrylic paintings. . . . McCarthy introduces the paraphernalia of rocket travel with direct humor that understands and respects its audience." Booklist

McNulty, Faith

★ If you decide to go to the moon; illustrated by Steven Kellogg. Scholastic Press 2005 un il $16.99

Grades: K 1 2 3   629.45

1. Space flight to the moon 2. Space flight -- Juvenile literature

ISBN 0-590-48359-5

LC 2004-27755

In this "picture book, readers accompany a boy on a fascinating excursion to the moon. The lyrical text provides tips on what to pack and describes the distance to be covered. After blastoff, facts about space travel are mingled with descriptions of what the journey might be like. . . . Rich artwork complements the strong text." SLJ

McReynolds, Linda

Eight days gone; Linda McReynolds; illustrated by Ryan O'Rourke. Charlesbridge 2012 44 p. col. ill. (reinforced for library use) $16.95

Grades: 1 2 3   629.45

1. Astronauts 2. Outer space -- Exploration 3. Space flight to the moon -- Juvenile literature

ISBN 1580893643; 9781580893640

LC 2011025776

In this book, Linda McReynolds tells the story of Apollo 11. "Eighteen two-page spreads illustrate the story, and McReynolds tells it in tight four-line verses using identical rhyme schemes. . . . The rocket blasts into space, begins its orbit, and, after a uniform check, the lunar module disconnects and lands safely on the moon." McReynolds looks at astronauts Michael Collins, Neil Armstrong, and Buzz Aldrin. (Kirkus Reviews)

"The bold, punchy text and vivid illustrations combine to make this a great candidate for storytime as well as exciting solo enjoyment." SLJ

Ottaviani, Jim

T-Minus: the race to the moon; [illustrated by] Zander Cannon, Kevin Cannon. Aladdin 2009 124p il $21.99; pa $12.99

Grades: 4 5 6 7 8 9 10 11 12 Adult   629.45

1. Graphic novels 2. Apollo project -- Graphic novels 3. Gemini project -- Graphic novels 4. Space race -- Juvenile literature 5. Astronautics -- Juvenile literature 6. Space flight to the moon -- Graphic novels

ISBN 978-1-4169-8682-9; 1-4169-8682-0; 978-1-4169-4960-2 pa; 1-4169-4960-7 pa

LC 2009-920999

Ottaviani, Zander Cannon, and Kevin Cannon show what happened when the U.S. and the U.S.S.R. started the space race in the 1950s, and how it progressed to the NASA Apollo 11 mission which landed two men on the moon in July of 1969.

"Organized as a countdown, making the outcome seem inevitable, the frequent, prominent sidebars list a type of rocket, the duration of its flight, and whether the mission was a success or a failure. There are more than 30 attempts chronicled, and the shift between Soviet and U.S. successes creates an interesting balance in the narrative. . . . Ottaviani is particular with facts and eager to inspire readers with regard to the scientific process." SLJ

Platt, Richard

★ Moon landing; a pop-up celebration of Apollo 11. by Richard Platt; paper engineering by David Hawcock. Candlewick Press 2008 un il $29.99

Grades: 4 5 6 7   629.45

1. Space flight to the moon 2. Pop-up books

ISBN 978-0-7636-4046-0; 0-7636-4046-8

"This is a handsome, carefully engineered compendium. The text begins with the so-called space race between the United States and the Soviet Union in the 1950s and '60s and then offers brief descriptions of the 17 flights that made up the Apollo program. Here the emphasis is on the famous landing of the Eagle on the Moon in July 1969. The pop-ups and foldout pages on sturdy, shiny paper demonstrate the mechanical aspects of the spacecraft and offer a bold sense of both the rocketry and the trip. Small photographs and drawings surround the larger views." SLJ

Ross, Stewart

Moon: science, history, and mystery. Scholastic 2009 128p il lib bdg $18.99
Grades: 4 5 6   **629.45**
  1. Astronautics 2. Space flight to the moon
  ISBN 978-0-545-12732-5 lib bdg; 0-545-12732-7 lib bdg

"Jam-packed with information, this colorful oversize volume chronicles the race to land a person on the Moon. Alternating chapters describe Moon mythologies and superstitions, the history of astronomical study, and the efforts involved in launching a lunar expedition. . . . The photographs pop with color and action. . . . The invaluable contribution of Muslim scientists is included. . . . [The book's] multicultural history will expand any collection." SLJ
  Includes glossary

Thimmesh, Catherine

  ★ Team moon; how 400,000 people landed Apollo 11 on the moon. Houghton Mifflin Company 2006 80p il $19.95
Grades: 5 6 7 8   **629.45**
  1. Space flight to the moon
  ISBN 0-618-50757-4
                   LC 2005-10755

"Thimmesh retraces the course of the space mission that landed an actual man, on the actual Moon. It's an oft-told tale, but the author tells it from the point of view not of astronauts or general observers, but of some of the 17,000 behind-the-scenes workers at Kennedy Space Center, the 7500 Grumman employees who built the lunar module, the 500 designers and seamstresses who actually constructed the space suits, and other low-profile contributors who made the historic flight possible. . . . This dramatic account will mesmerize even readers already familiar with the event. . . . This stirring, authoritative tribute to the collective effort . . . belongs in every collection." SLJ
  Includes glossary and bibliographical references

Vogt, Gregory

  Apollo moonwalks; the amazing lunar missions. Enslow Pubs. 2000 48p il (Countdown to space) lib bdg $18.95
Grades: 4 5 6 7   **629.45**
  1. Space flight to the moon
  ISBN 0-7660-1306-5
                   LC 99-16921

Discusses the six Apollo missions that landed on the moon, describing the work performed there, what it is like to walk on the moon, and the collection of moon rocks
  Includes bibliographical references and index

  Spacewalks; the ultimate adventure in orbit. {by} Gregory L. Vogt. Enslow Pubs. 2000 48p il (Countdown to space) lib bdg $18.95
Grades: 4 5 6 7   **629.45**
  1. Space flight 2. Extravehicular activity (Space flight)
  3. Manned space flight 4. Extravehicular activity

(Manned space flight)
  ISBN 0-7660-1305-7
                   LC 99-37094

Describes the training and preparation for spacewalking, the hazards faced by astronauts, as well as the construction of spacesuits
  Includes glossary and bibliographical references

Waxman, Laura Hamilton

  Exploring space travel. Lerner Publications Company 2011 40p il (What's amazing about space?) lib bdg $27.93
Grades: 4 5 6   **629.45**
  1. Astronautics 2. Space flight
  ISBN 978-0-7613-5447-5; 0-7613-5447-6
                 LC 2010042471

This describes what it's like to be an astronaut in space.
  "Readers will come away with new knowledge, such as how scientists observe the behavior of other stars to infer the presence of exoplanets." Booklist
  Includes bibliographical references

629.46   Engineering of unmanned spacecraft

Johnson, Rebecca L.

  Satellites. Lerner Publications Co. 2006 48p il (Cool science) lib bdg $25.26
Grades: 4 5 6   **629.46**
  1. Artificial satellites
  ISBN 978-0-8225-2908-8 lib bdg; 0-8225-2908-4 lib bdg
                 LC 2004-30298

This book has "an attractive, colorful layout that will appeal to readers. Each spread includes captioned color photographs and/or illustrations; text boxes; and, often, a 'fun fact.' . . . [This] title explains what a satellite is and discusses many aspects of satellites, including how they pertain to television broadcasts, weather forecasting, and locating black holes. Numerous amazing facts are included to pique readers' interest." SLJ
  Includes bibliographical references

Kops, Deborah

  Exploring space robots. Lerner Publications 2011 40p il map (What's amazing about space?) lib bdg $27.93
Grades: 4 5 6   **629.46**
  1. Robots
  ISBN 978-0-7613-5445-1; 0-7613-5445-X
                 LC 2010044213

This explains how robots help us explore space, including a probe called New Horizons which is heading toward Pluto.
  This book is "written in simple language, [and] illustrated nicely. . . . The information presented is factually correct. . . . Every page includes a well-chosen illustration or photograph." Sci Books Films
  Includes bibliographical references

629.8 Automatic control engineering

Allman, Toney

The **Nexi** robot. Norwood House Press 2009 48p il (A great idea) lib bdg $25.27

Grades: 3 4 5 6 **629.8**

1. Robots 2. Inventors 3. Electronics engineers

ISBN 978-1-59953-342-1 lib bdg; 1-59953-342-1 lib bdg

LC 2009-14714

"The real star of this title . . . is Cynthia Breazeal, the head of the Personal Robotics Group at MIT. . . . The challenge of creating a robot with personality is understandably complex, but Allman does a fine job of making it accessible by offering up examples, and numerous photographs. . . . It's all fascinating stuff, for sure, and presented in a simple yet informative manner." Booklist

Includes glossary and bibliographical references

Chaffee, Joel

How to build a prize-winning robot. Rosen Central 2011 48p il (Robotics) lib bdg $26.50; pa $11.75

Grades: 5 6 7 8 **629.8**

1. Robots

ISBN 978-1-4488-1238-7 lib bdg; 1-4488-1238-0 lib bdg; 978-1-4488-2252-2 pa; 1-4488-2252-1 pa

LC 2010025748

"Kids who are fascinated with robots will want [this title] available." SLJ

Includes glossary and bibliographical references

Freedman, Jeri

Robots through history. Rosen Central 2011 48p il (Robotics) lib bdg $26.50; pa $11.75

Grades: 5 6 7 8 **629.8**

1. Robots

ISBN 978-1-4488-1236-3 lib bdg; 1-4488-1236-4 lib bdg; 978-1-4488-2250-8 pa; 1-4488-2250-5 pa

LC 2010024139

"Kids who are fascinated with robots will want [this title] available." SLJ

Includes glossary and bibliographical references

Graham, Ian

Robot technology. Smart Apple Media 2012 il (New technology)

Grades: 4 5 6 7 **629.8**

1. Robots

ISBN 1-599-20533-5; 978-1-599-20533-5

LC 2010044240

Describes current robotics technology, including the applications of robots in space, in the military, in industry, and around the house. Discusses the pros and cons of creating fully autonomous robots.

This "offers a fine overview for reports, and its attractive design may also entice middle-grade readers to learn more." Booklist

Payment, Simone

Robotics careers; preparing for the future. Rosen Central 2011 48p il (Robotics) lib bdg $26.50; pa $11.75

Grades: 5 6 7 8 **629.8**

1. Robots 2. Vocational guidance

ISBN 978-1-4488-1239-4 lib bdg; 1-4488-1239-9 lib bdg; 978-1-4488-2253-9 pa; 1-4488-2253-X pa

LC 2010024134

"Kids who are fascinated with robots will want [this title] available." SLJ

Includes glossary and bibliographical references

Rau, Dana Meachen

Robots. Marshall Cavendish Benchmark 2010 24p il (Surprising science) lib bdg $22.79

Grades: 2 3 4 **629.8**

1. Robots

ISBN 978-0-7614-4871-6; 0-7614-4871-3

LC 2009053764

"Colorfully illustrated with photographs on each page, this . . . will be well received by elementary students and educators." Libr Media Connect

Includes glossary and bibliographical references

Robots: from everyday to out of this world; written by the editors of Yes mag. Kids Can Press 2008 48p il $16.95; pa $8.95

Grades: 3 4 5 6 **629.8**

1. Robots

ISBN 978-1-55453-203-2; 1-55453-203-5; 978-1-55453-204-9 pa; 1-55453-204-3 pa

This "introduces robots that work (defusing bombs, assembling cars, assisting surgeons, exploring Mars) and play (riding camels, kicking soccer balls). . . . Each section is packed with fascinating information, entertaining cartoon graphics, and numerous full-color photographs. The text is hip and accessible. . . . Well-organized and engaging." Booklist

Includes glossary

Shea, Therese

The **robotics** club; teaming up to build robots. Rosen Central 2011 48p il (Robotics) lib bdg $26.50; pa $11.75

Grades: 5 6 7 8 **629.8**

1. Clubs 2. Robots

ISBN 978-1-4488-1237-0 lib bdg; 1-4488-1237-2 lib bdg; 978-1-4488-2251-5 pa; 1-4488-2251-3 pa

This title "will provide students with the information necessary to form a club and compete at making and using robots. Kids who are fascinated with robots will want [this title] available." SLJ

VanVoorst, Jennifer

Rise of the thinking machines; the science of robots. Compass Point Books 2009 48p il (Headline science) lib bdg $27.93; pa $7.95

Grades: 5 6 7 **629.8**

1. Robots

ISBN 978-0-7565-3377-9 lib bdg; 0-7565-3377-5 lib bdg; 978-0-7565-3518-6 pa; 0-7565-3518-2 pa

LC 2008-05732

"Describes various types of robots and their functions, discusses technological advancements in the field of robotics, and considers the ethical issues surrounding autonomous robots." Publisher's note

Includes glossary and bibliographical references

Woog, Adam

SCRATCHbot. Norwood House Press 2010 48p il (A great idea) lib bdg $25.27

Grades: 3 4 5 6   **629.8**

1. Robots

ISBN 978-1-59953-380-3 lib bdg; 1-59953-380-4 lib bdg

LC 2010008502

"Woog introduces a small, rolling robot with prominent whiskers, used to mimic a rodent's ability to sense its surroundings through touch. Discussions include how inventors are inspired by nature and how this appealing robot might be useful. Presenting specific, current information, [this book] will appeal to young people intrigued by inventions." Booklist

Includes glossary and bibliographical references

630   Agriculture and related technologies

Apte, Sunita

Eating green. Bearport Pub. 2009 32p il map (Going green) lib bdg $25.27

Grades: 4 5 6 7   **630**

1. Natural foods 2. Sustainable agriculture

ISBN 978-1-59716-965-3 lib bdg; 1-59716-965-X lib bdg

LC 2009-19183

"Color photographs (most full page) and a few diagrams accompany the informative text. . . . Overall, the [book] . . . is user-friendly and covers topics that are not easily found elsewhere." SLJ

Includes glossary and bibliographical references

Bailey, Gerry

Farming for the future. Gareth Stevens Pub. 2011 48p il (Planet SOS) lib bdg $31.95; pa $14.05

Grades: 4 5 6   **630**

1. Agriculture 2. Food supply

ISBN 978-1-4339-4966-1 lib bdg; 1-4339-4966-0 lib bdg; 978-1-4339-4967-8 pa; 1-4339-4967-9 pa

LC 2010032887

This well-designed book presents farming methods "and how they affect human beings. . . . [It] includes a chapter on new types of farms and foods. . . . The many large, colorful photos will engage readers and assist them in understanding the important concepts introduced." SLJ

Includes glossary

Hodge, Deborah

★ **Up** we grow! a year in the life of a small, local farm. written by Deborah Hodge; photographed by Brian Harris. Kids Can Press 2010 32p il $16.95

Grades: PreK K 1 2   **630**

1. Farm life 2. Agriculture 3. Organic farming

ISBN 978-1-55453-561-3; 1-55453-561-1

This is "a photo-essay about a year on a communal organic farm. Moving chronologically through the seasons, the spreads, illustrated with close-up photographs, follow a small collective of farmers. . . . Filled with sensory descriptions, the rhythmic text gives a strong sense of life on the farm and in the field." Booklist

Watch me grow! a down-to-earth look at growing food in the city. written by Deborah Hodge; photographed by Brian Harris. Kids Can Press 2011 32p il $16.95

Grades: PreK K 1 2   **630**

1. Gardening 2. Urban agriculture

ISBN 978-1-55453-618-4; 1-55453-618-9

This "explores ways that gardeners are growing food in community gardens, on rooftops, and in backyards. Harris contributes numerous photos of children getting in on the action—watering plants, tilling soil, and enjoying the (literal) fruits of their labor. . . . Direct and informative, this should inspire many kids to test out how green their thumbs are." Publ Wkly

Macceca, Stephanie

George Washington Carver; agriculture pioneer. by Stephanie Macceca. Compass Point Books 2010 40 p. ill. (chiefly col.) (library binding) $27.99

Grades: 4 5 6   **630**

1. African Americans 2. Agriculture -- United States 3. African American agriculturists -- Biography -- Juvenile literature 4. Agriculturists -- United States -- Biography -- Juvenile literature

ISBN 9780756543051

LC 2009034855

This book offers a biography of George Washington Carver who was "[b]orn into slavery, . . . earned a university graduate degree, and eventually became a world famous expert on plants. By experimenting with peanuts and other plants, he learned how to make many useful products from them. Carver taught students and farmers how to grow plants without damaging the soil." (Publisher's note) This book is a textbook that is intended to be used in the middle school classroom. It includes a glossary, vocabulary, and a timeline.

Includes index.

Michelson, Richard

Tuttle's Red Barn; the story of America's oldest family farm. illustrated by Mary Azarian. G.P. Putnam's Sons 2007 un il $17

Grades: K 1 2 3   **630**

1. Family farms 2. Family farms -- Juvenile literature

ISBN 978-0-399-24354-7; 0-399-24354-2

LC 2007-07514

Michelson and Azarian "salute 12 generations of Tuttles from Dover, N.H., operators of the longest continuously running family farm in the country. . . . Each chapter focuses on the male Tuttle who inherits the farm, and that Tuttle, glimpsed in his youth, observes some history. . . . In Azarian's tableau-like woodcuts, styles change while character endures. Her hand-crafted aesthetic enhances the story's warmth and humanity." Publ Wkly

Parker, Steve, 1952-

Food and farming. QEB Pub. 2010 32p il (QEB changes in . . .) lib bdg $28.50

Grades: 3 4 5 6   **630**

1. Farms 2. Agriculture 3. Food supply

ISBN 978-1-59566-775-5 lib bdg; 1-59566-775-X lib bdg

LC 2008-56069

"The information is presented in brief paragraphs and sidebars. Suggestions for kids to help improve the planet are sprinkled throughout. . . . Students will enjoy this appealing layout and the information can spark further research on the topic. . . . Either digitally or on paper, students could make fantastic presentations using a similar design." Libr Media Connect

Includes glossary

Rosen, Michael J.

★ **Our** farm; four seasons with five kids on one family's farm. written and photographed by Michael J. Rosen. Darby Creek Pub. 2008 144p il $18.95

Grades: 4 5 6 7 8   630

1. Family life 2. Farm life -- United States 3. Farms -- Juvenile literature 4. Farm life -- Juvenile literature

ISBN 978-1-58196-067-9; 1-58196-067-0

A journal of one year on the Bennett farm in central Ohio. Shows how one family, with the help of relatives and friends, creates a life and livelihood on a 150-acre farm.

"This engaging book is an unsentimental, appreciative look into the world of one farm family." SLJ

Vogel, Julia

Local farms and sustainable foods. Cherry Lake 2010 32p il (Save the planet) lib bdg $27.07

Grades: 3 4 5 6   630

1. Farms 2. Sustainable agriculture

ISBN 978-1-60279-660-7 lib bdg; 1-60279-660-2 lib bdg

LC 2009-38096

Teaches young readers about locally grown fruits and vegetables

"At the beginning of . . . [the] book, readers are given a mission and advised to be alert to the facts provided so that they can successfully answer the questions at the end. . . . Children are made to feel part of the process; suggestions for how they can become involved abound." SLJ

Includes glossary and bibliographical references

Watterson, Carol

The **edible** alphabet; 26 reasons to love the farm. illustrated by Michela Sorrentino. Tricycle Press 2011 un il $16.99; lib bdg $19.99

Grades: K 1 2 3   630

1. Farms 2. Alphabet 3. Farm produce 4. Domestic animals

ISBN 1-58246-421-9; 1-58246-422-7 lib bdg; 978-1-58246-421-3; 978-1-58246-422-0 lib bdg

LC 2010030478

"This informative alphabet book focuses on the importance of agricultural and animal farms. For each letter, Watterson uses bouncy alliteration to introduce her subjects. . . . Sorrentino matches Watterson's friendly prose with lively mixed-media collages that include polka-dotted fowl and cars fashioned from zucchini, while interactive prompts and intriguing facts give readers a lot to munch on." Publ Wkly

630.9   Agriculture and related technologies-- Historical, geographic treatment

Richardson, Gillian

10 plants that shook the world; Gillian Richardson; illustrated by Kim Rosen. Annick Press 2013 132 p. (hardcover) $24.95

Grades: 4 5 6 7 8   630.9

1. Plants 2. Agriculture -- History

ISBN 1554514452; 9781554514458

This book, by Gillian Richardson, illustrated by Kim Rosen, profiles ten plants with significant histories. It describes how "countries went to war to control trade centers for pepper . . . , a grass called papyrus became the first effective tool for sharing knowledge through writing . . . , Europeans in the 1600s cut down rainforests to grow sugar, contributing to soil erosion . . . [and] dependence on the potato caused one of the greatest tragedies in history." (Publisher's note)

"With bold, lively caricatures from Rosen throughout, it's an intriguing and well-designed study of the ways plants have helped start wars, cure diseases, and advance technology." Pub Wkly

631.3   Tools, machinery, apparatus, equipment

Peterson, Cris

★ **Fantastic** farm machines; photographs by David R. Lundquist. Boyd Mills Press 2006 un il $17.95

Grades: K 1 2 3   631.3

1. Agricultural machinery

ISBN 1-59078-271-2

LC 2005-33561

"Peterson gives readers an accurate firsthand view of modern, often computerized equipment used on today's farms. Her easy-to-understand text describes both the machines and their functions. . . . The short, informative paragraphs are surrounded by excellent color photographs that extend the text." SLJ

631.4   Soil science

Bourgeois, Paulette

The **dirt** on dirt; by Paulette Bourgeois with Kathy Vanderlinden; illustrated by Martha Newbigging. Kids Can Press 2008 48p il $15.95; pa $7.95

Grades: 3 4 5 6   631.4

1. Soils 2. Soil ecology 3. Soils -- Juvenile literature

ISBN 978-1-55453-101-1; 1-55453-101-2; 978-1-55453-1028 pa; 1-55453-102-0 pa

"From dirty toes, fossils, earthworms, and animal burrows to buried treasure, cities, and dog bones, this engaging introduction to soil touches on a wide variety of topics clearly and concisely. 'Fun with Dirt' experiments and activities demonstrate concepts and stimulate imagination. Illustrated with well-captioned photographs and cartoon-style sketches." Booklist

Gardner, Robert

Super science projects about Earth's soil and water; [by] Robert Gardner; illustrations by Tom Labaff. Enslow

Elementary 2007 48p il (Rockin' earth science experiments) $17.95

Grades: 3 4 5   **631.4**

1. Soils 2. Water 3. Science projects 4. Science -- Experiments

ISBN 978-0-7660-2735-0; 0-7660-2735-X

LC 2006006680

This is a "selection of earth-science projects, all focused on soil and water concepts, such as evaporation, the water cycle, and the components of soil. Each experiment is clearly explained in step-by-step instructions, illustrated with Labaff's clean-lined diagrams and formatted on uncluttered pages." Booklist

Includes glossary and bibliographical references

Hall, Pamela

Dig in! Learn about dirt; illustrated by Jane Yamada. Child's World, Inc. 2010 24p il (Science definitions) lib bdg $22.79

Grades: PreK K 1 2   **631.4**

1. Soils

ISBN 978-1-60253-507-7 lib bdg; 1-60253-507-8 lib bdg

LC 2010010974

This book about soil is "attractive and succinct. . . . Large, eye-catching photos cover the recto of each spread. . . . Varying, jewel-toned accents are used in headings, highlighted glossary terms, and in a sidebar on each spread." SLJ

Includes glossary

Spilsbury, Richard

Soil; [by] Richard and Louise Spilsbury. Heinemann Library 2011 32p il (Let's rock) $29; pa $7.99

Grades: 4 5 6   **631.4**

1. Soils

ISBN 978-1-4329-4685-2; 1-4329-4685-4; 978-1-4329-4693-7 pa; 1-4329-4693-5 pa

LC 2010022242

"Enhanced by plenty of photos, digital paintings, and diagrams, [this examination] of [soil treats its topic] in unusual detail. [It] describes distinguishing characteristics, creation, history, . . . and human uses in [a] central [narrative] with additional notes, suggestions for activities during walks outside, and occasional thumbnail biographies of scientists in side boxes. [The] volume ends with a simple activity." SLJ

Includes bibliographical references

631.5   Cultivation and harvesting

Juettner, Bonnie

The **seed** vault. Norwood House Press 2009 48p il (A great idea) lib bdg $25.27

Grades: 3 4 5 6   **631.5**

1. Seeds 2. Endangered species 3. Biological diversity 4. Plants -- Collection and preservation

ISBN 978-1-59953-343-8 lib bdg; 1-59953-343-X lib bdg

LC 2009-16567

"With a mix of scientific terminology and accessible sentence structure, the [book] effectively [describes] how the [idea] took shape and were put into practice by the scientists

involved. . . . Color photographs are included on every page and provide a visual complement to the [text]." SLJ

Includes glossary and bibliographical references

Rustad, Martha E. H.

Fall harvests; bringing in food. illustrated by Amanda Enright. Millbrook Press 2011 24p il (Fall's here!) lib bdg $23.95

Grades: K 1 2 3   **631.5**

1. Autumn 2. Agriculture

ISBN 978-0-7613-5067-5; 0-7613-5067-5

LC 2010053467

"This offers . . . information about planting or reaping, and directions for making a cornhusk doll. . . . Colorful illustrations fill the spreads with active, cartoonlike boys and girls surrounded by the green, brown, and orange hues of autumn." SLJ

631.8   Fertilizers, soil conditioners, growth regulators

Barker, David

Compost it. Cherry Lake Pub. 2010 32p il (Save the planet) lib bdg $27.95

Grades: 3 4 5 6   **631.8**

1. Compost

ISBN 978-1-60279-656-0 lib bdg; 1-60279-656-4 lib bdg

LC 2009038092

"Written as dispatches from an imaginary journalist, the pages follow several individuals who explain different types of composting: a soil ecologist, . . . a home owner, . . . an apartment dweller, . . . and, finally, the manager of large-scale, urban operation. The creative, uncrowded format features text printed in an old-fashioned typewriter font on a notebook-paper background, numerous color photos, and facts boxes. . . . This upbeat, lucid overview of compost and its benefits is a strong choice." Booklist

Glaser, Linda

Garbage helps our garden grow; a compost story. story by Linda Glaser; photography by Shelley Rotner. Millbrook 2010 32p il lib bdg $25.26

Grades: K 1 2 3   **631.8**

1. Compost

ISBN 978-0-7613-4911-2 lib bdg; 0-7613-4911-1 lib bdg

"Clear, vivid photos give this simple introduction to composting a realistic look that makes the process look downright doable. . . . Most of Rotner's excellent photos feature one or two children as they scrape their dinner plates into a bucket indoors, add kitchen and yard waste to the compost bin outside, observe the leaves and food rotting over time, add the compost to their vegetable garden, put new plants into the ground, and watch them grow." Booklist

632   Plant injuries, diseases, pests

Mooney, Carla

Sunscreen for plants. Norwood House Press 2009 48p il (A great idea) lib bdg $25.27

Grades: 3 4 5 6   **632**
1. Plants
ISBN 978-1-59953-344-5 lib bdg; 1-59953-344-8
lib bdg

LC 2009-15641

"With a mix of scientific terminology and accessible sentence structure, the [book] effectively [describes] how the [idea] took shape and were put into practice by the scientists involved. . . . Color photographs are included on every page and provide a visual complement to the [text]." SLJ

Includes glossary and bibliographical references

633.1 Cereals

Aliki

Corn is maize; the gift of the Indians. written and illustrated by Aliki. Crowell 1976 33p il (Let's-read-and-find-out science book) hardcover o.p. pa $5.99
Grades: K 1 2 3   **633.1**
1. Corn
ISBN 0-690-00975-5 lib bdg; 0-06-445026-0 pa
In this book, the author provides a history of corn, or maize, and "also the life cycle of the plant itself, its growth and reproductive patterns, and its many uses. Excellent illustrations by the author help convey both cultural aspects and technological uses of corn." Sci Child

Gibbons, Gail

Corn; by Gail Gibbons. Holiday House 2008 32p il $16.95
Grades: K 1 2 3   **633.1**
1. Corn
ISBN 978-0-8234-2169-5; 0-8234-2169-4

LC 2007051632

"The colorful watercolors are sure to attract even the most reluctant readers. . . . A simple, yet informative and engaging look at an important food source." SLJ

Landau, Elaine

Corn. Children's Press 1999 47p il (True book) lib bdg $22; pa $6.95
Grades: 2 3 4   **633.1**
1. Corn 2. Corn -- Juvenile literature
ISBN 0-516-21026-2 lib bdg; 0-516-26759-0 pa

LC 98-47332

Examines the history, cultivation, and uses of corn
"Landau does her usual fine job of explaining a topic so that it is understandable to kids." Booklist

Includes glossary and bibliographical references

Wheat. Children's Press 1999 47p il (True book) lib bdg $22; pa $6.95
Grades: 2 3 4   **633.1**
1. Wheat 2. Wheat -- Juvenile literature
ISBN 0-516-21029-7 lib bdg; 0-516-26792-2 pa

LC 98-47333

Examines the history, cultivation, and uses of wheat
Includes glossary and bibliographical references

Micucci, Charles

The **life** and times of corn; written and illustrated by Charles Micucci. Houghton Mifflin Books for Children 2009 32p il $16
Grades: 2 3 4   **633.1**
1. Corn
ISBN 978-0-618-50751-1; 0-618-50751-5

LC 2008040466

This focuses on the science, uses and history of corn
This is an "entertaining and informative mix of bite-size scientific information and historical facts and mouth-watering watercolors." Booklist

Includes bibliographical references

Reynolds, Jan

★ **Cycle** of rice, cycle of life; a story of sustainable farming. Lee & Low Books 2009 un il map $19.95
Grades: 3 4 5   **633.1**
1. Rice 2. Sustainable agriculture 3. Sustainable agriculture -- Juvenile literature 5. Rice -- Bali (Indonesia) -- Juvenile literature
ISBN 978-1-60060-254-2; 1-60060-254-1

LC 2008-30518

This is "filled with beautiful color images. . . . [It is written] in precise, accessible language. . . . Reynolds offers young readers a broad, deep understanding of the concept, even as she provides a fascinating introduction to a specific culture." Booklist

Includes glossary

Sobol, Richard

The **life** of rice; from seedling to supper. Candlewick Press 2010 36p il map (Traveling photographer) $17.99
Grades: 3 4 5 6   **633.1**
1. Rice
ISBN 978-0-7636-3252-6; 0-7636-3252-X

LC 2009-15138

"Turning his lens to the rice fields of Thailand, Sobol begins this affectionate account with a description of the Royal Plowing Ceremony that kicks off the planting season and continues through cultivation and into the harvest. Brief explanations of the growing stages of rice are accompanied by beautiful color photographs of the fields in their various phases. . . . Sobol offers an interesting look at a country and its people, and their relationship to the land. The writing is accessible and lively, providing a unique, specific look at one of the world's most important staples." SLJ

633.3 Legumes, forage crops other than grasses and legumes

Bial, Raymond

The **super** soybean. Albert Whitman & Co. 2007 40p il $16.95
Grades: 4 5 6   **633.3**
1. Soybean 2. Soybean -- Juvenile literature 3. Soybean products -- Juvenile literature
ISBN 978-0-8075-7549-9; 0-8075-7549-6

LC 2007-14165

"Pairing a densely informational text with color photos, mostly of soybeans being grown and harvested, [the author] traces their cultivation's historical background, catalogs many of the uses to which they are put, and . . . trumpets enthusiastic appreciation for their twin roles as a major U.S. export and a renewable natural resource." Booklist

633.5   Fiber crops

Moore, Heidi

The **story** behind cotton. Heinemann Library 2009 32p il (True stories) $28.21

Grades: 3 4 5   **633.5**

1. Cotton

ISBN 978-1-4329-2341-9; 1-4329-2341-2

LC 2008043334

This offers history, ephemera, and basic facts about cotton and its production and uses.

Includes bibliographical references

633.8   Other crops grown for industrial processing

Smith, Danna

Balloon trees; by Danna Smith; illustrated by Laurie Allen Klein. Sylvan Dell Publishing 2013 32 p. (English hardcover) $17.95

Grades: PreK K 1 2   **633.8**

1. Rubber -- Juvenile literature   2. Rubber plants -- Juvenile literature

ISBN 1607186128; 9781607186120; 9781607186243

LC 2012030119

In this children's book, by Danna Smith, illustrated by Laurie Allen Klein, "rhyming couplets and effective illustrations describe the general process by which latex is extracted from trees, converted into a colorful mix, shaped into forms, treated and sent to stores to be sold as balloons. Each double-page spread shows a separate step, watched over by what looks like a warbler with an observant eye." (Kirkus)

634   Orchards, fruits, forestry

Dickmann, Nancy

An **apple's** life. Heinemann Library 2010 24p il (Watch it grow) lib bdg $21.50; pa $5.99

Grades: PreK K 1   **634**

1. Apples

ISBN 978-1-4329-4141-3 lib bdg; 1-4329-4141-0 lib bdg; 978-1-4329-4150-5 pa; 1-4329-4150-X pa

LC 2009-49157

This title shows the reader how an apple begins life, grows, and reproduces.

"Practically unique among early introductions to life cycles because death is mentioned . . . this . . . follows [an apple] . . . from . . . seed to maturity with a set of close-up color photographs, one per page, paired to large-type, one or two-sentence captions. . . . Offers nourishing fare for young naturalists." SLJ

Includes glossary

Esbaum, Jill

Apples for everyone. National Geographic 2009 16p il (Picture the seasons) pa $5.95

Grades: K 1 2   **634**

1. Apples

ISBN 978-1-4263-0523-8 pa; 1-4263-0523-0 pa

LC 2009-12719

Discusses how apples develop from blossoms to fruit, how they are harvested, how people use them, the history of apples in the United States, and different varieties of them

This does "a fabulous job of conjuring up the sights, smells, and sensations of a brisk autumn. Using minimal text with National Geographic's typically fine photographs, Esbaum brings out familiar, comforting details of the outdoors. . . . The writing flows with sensory details." Booklist

Farmer, Jacqueline

Apples; illustrated by Phyllis Limbacher Tildes. Charlesbridge 2007 un il map lib bdg $16.95; pa $6.95

Grades: 1 2 3 4   **634**

1. Apples

ISBN 978-1-57091-694-6 lib bdg; 1-57091-694-2 lib bdg; 978-1-57091-695-3 pa; 1-57091-695-0 pa

LC 2006-20942

"Farmer provides a wealth of information here. The process of grafting is clearly explained, as are the differences between apple juice and cider, the nutritional value of the popular fruit, and the apple in history and legend. A handy chart detailing the various kinds of apples and their appropriate uses is included, as is a page of facts and records and a recipe for apple pie. Watercolor illustrations feature a multicultural cast of smiling children. The pictures accurately reflect the text and are attractive." SLJ

Gibbons, Gail

Apples. Holiday House 2000 un il $17.95; pa $6.95

Grades: K 1 2 3   **634**

1. Apples   2. Apples -- Juvenile literature

ISBN 0-8234-1497-3; 0-8234-1669-0 pa

LC 99-54246

Explains how apples were brought to America, how they grow, their traditional uses and cultural significance, and some of the varieties grown

"With its cheerful, bright illustrations and clear, simple presentation, this title will be the perfect pick for the perennial fall apple-book requests." SLJ

The **berry** book. Holiday House 2002 un il $16.95

Grades: K 1 2 3   **634**

1. Berries   2. Cooking

ISBN 0-8234-1697-6

LC 2001-40602

Describes different types of berries and how they grow. Includes recipes with berry ingredients

This is a "brief, informative account. . . . Cheerful illustrations with clear labels enliven the accessible text." Horn Book Guide

Kellogg, Steven

★ **Johnny** Appleseed; a tall tale retold and illustrated by Steven Kellogg. Morrow Junior Bks. 1988 un il $16.95; lib bdg $16.89

Grades: K 1 2 3   **634**

1. Frontier and pioneer life   2. Pioneers   3. Fruit growers   4. Frontier and pioneer life -- Juvenile literature

ISBN 0-688-06417-5; 0-688-06418-3 lib bdg

LC 87-27317

"Oversize pages have given Kellogg a fine opportunity for pictures that are on a large scale, colorful and animated if often busy with details. His version of Chapman's life is more substantial than the subtitle (A TallTale) would indicate, since the text makes clear the difference between what Chapman really did and what myths grew up about his work, his life, his personality, and his achievements. There's some exaggeration, but on the whole the biography is factual and written with clarity." Bull Cent Child Books

Landau, Elaine

Apples. Children's Press 1999 47p il (True book) hardcover o.p. lib bdg $25

Grades: 2 3 4   **634**
1. Apples
ISBN 0-516-21024-6 lib bdg; 0-516-26571-7 pa
LC 98-47327

Surveys the history, cultivation, and uses of apples and describes the different kinds

This "will fill a need for young report writers." Booklist

Includes glossary and bibliographical references

Bananas. Children's Press 1999 47p il (True book) lib bdg $22; pa $6.95

Grades: 2 3 4   **634**
1. Banana
ISBN 0-516-21025-4 lib bdg; 0-516-26574-1 pa
LC 98-47328

Examines the history, cultivation, and uses of bananas

Includes glossary and bibliographical references

Maestro, Betsy

How do apples grow? illustrated by Giulio Maestro. HarperCollins Pubs. 1992 32p il (Let's-read-and-find-out science book) hardcover o.p. pa $5.99

Grades: K 1 2 3   **634**
1. Apples
ISBN 0-06-020056-1 lib bdg; 0-06-445117-8 pa
LC 91-9468

Describes the life cycle of an apple from its initial appearance as a spring bud to that point in time when it becomes a fully ripe fruit

"Clear, complete. . . . Inquisitive children will find simple yet scientifically accurate answers to their questions about apple trees and their fruit. Large illustrations and limited text facilitate group-reading. The endearing, soft-toned drawings are clearly labelled, providing an excellent teaching tool or reference point for the science teacher." Sci Child

Malam, John

Grow your own smoothie. Heinemann Library 2011 32p il (Grow it yourself!) lib bdg $26; pa $7.99

Grades: K 1 2   **634**
1. Cooking 2. Strawberries 3. Vegetable gardening
ISBN 978-1-4329-5111-5 lib bdg; 978-1-4329-5118-4 pa
LC 2010049836

This describes how to grow strawberries and how to make a strawberry smoothie.

Includes glossary and bibliographical references

Moses, Will

Johnny Appleseed; the story of a legend. Philomel Bks. 2001 un il $16.99

Grades: 3 4 5 6   **634**
1. Frontier and pioneer life 2. Pioneers 3. Fruit growers 4. Frontier and pioneer life -- Middle West -- Juvenile literature 5. Apple growers -- United States -- Biography -- Juvenile literature
ISBN 0-399-23153-6
LC 00-44600

This is a "picture-book biography of John Chapman, aka Johnny Appleseed. . . . Starting in 1774, the year of Chapman's birth, Moses briefly covers Chapman's early childhood, and then quickly moves on to his young adult years, when he leaves home for the frontier. The bulk of the book documents Chapman's rich adult life and celebrates his odd ways. . . . The paintings . . . are filled with rich detail and are unforgettable." Booklist

Includes bibliographical references

Rustad, Martha E. H.

Fall apples; crisp and juicy. illustrated by Amanda Enright. Millbrook Press 2011 24p il (Fall's here!) lib bdg $23.93

Grades: K 1 2 3   **634**
1. Apples 2. Cooking
ISBN 978-0-7613-5064-4; 0-7613-5064-0
LC 2010051510

"In this book, the reader discovers how fall apples grow and the many things that you can make with them. . . . Colorful illustrations enhance the lively text." Sci Books Films

Includes glossary and bibliographical references

Smucker, Anna Egan

Golden delicious; a Cinderella apple story. by Anna Egan Smucker; illustrated by Kathleen Kemly. Albert Whitman & Company 2008 un il $16.99

Grades: 1 2 3   **634**
1. Apples
ISBN 978-0-8075-2987-4; 0-8075-2987-7
LC 2007052792

This is "the story of the discovery and successful marketing of the Golden Delicious apple. The narrative is simple and direct, with an occasional flair. . . . Kemly's soft pastel illustrations provide interesting historical details, including dress and transportation, and help to move the story along. An author's note gives more background, along with details about the grafting process." SLJ

Ziefert, Harriet

One red apple; paintings by Karla Gudeon. Blue Apple Books 2009 un il $16.99 **634**
1. Apples
ISBN 978-1-934706-67-1; 1-934706-67-1
LC 2009012663

This follows the life cycle of an apple: from fruit growing on the tree to market, to picnic, to seed, to sapling and tree, and finally to a new apple.

"With lyrical text and folk-style artwork, this handsome picture book celebrates the pleasures of a favorite food while accentuating nature's cycles and Earth's bounty." SLJ

634.11

Codell, Raji Esme

Seed by seed; the legend and legacy of Johnny "Appleseed" Chapman. by Esme Raji Codell; illustrations by Lynne Rae Perkins. Greenwillow Books 2012 32 p. (trade ed.) $16.99

Grades: K 1 2 3 **634.11**

1. Legendary characters 2. Picture books for children 3. Frontier and pioneer life -- Middle West -- Juvenile literature 4. Apple growers -- United States -- Biography -- Juvenile literature

ISBN 0061455156; 9780061455155; 9780061455162

LC 2011033653

In this children's picture book, the author looks at American folk hero John Chapman, also known as Johnny Appleseed, and answers the question "Why should we remember him today, more than two hundred years later, and call him a hero?" by presenting the "five tenets Chapman lived by: 'Use what you have. Share what you have. Respect nature. Try to make peace where there is war. You can reach your destination by taking small steps.'" (Publishers Weekly)

634.9 Forestry

Jakubiak, David J.

What can we do about deforestation? PowerKids Press 2011 24p il (Protecting our planet) lib bdg $21.25; pa $8.25

Grades: 2 3 4 **634.9**

1. Deforestation

ISBN 978-1-4488-4986-4 lib bdg; 1-4488-4986-1 lib bdg; 978-1-4488-5119-5 pa; 1-4488-5119-X pa

LC 2011000160

This explains the importance of forests and trees in our environment, the reasons for deforestation and the damage caused by the destruction of trees.

"Every spread has a full-page, thoughtfully captioned color photograph. . . . School and public libraries will want [this title] to round out collections or as [an update] to replace older books." SLJ

Includes glossary

Morris, Neil

Wood. Amicus 2011 48p il map (Materials that matter) lib bdg $28.50

Grades: 4 5 6 7 **634.9**

1. Wood

ISBN 978-1-60753-070-1 lib bdg; 1-60753-070-8 lib bdg

LC 2010001621

"The clean layout includes photographs and occasional charts, graphs, and technical illustrations against a range of pastel backgrounds. Inset boxes provide further detail, interesting extras, and recycling information. . . . [This book offers] easily accessible background information for report writers." SLJ

Includes glossary and bibliographical references

Morrison, Taylor

Wildfire. Houghton Mifflin Co. 2006 48p il $17

Grades: 4 5 6 **634.9**

1. Wildfires 2. Forest fires 3. Wildfires -- Juvenile literature 5. Forest fires -- Juvenile literature

ISBN 978-0-618-50900-3; 0-618-50900-3

LC 2005-30483

This is an "overview of the people involved in fighting wildfires and the techniques and equipment they use. Detailed paintings aid in explaining how firefighters work and in describing the natural conditions that lead to initial fires and more dangerous developments. . . . The pages are packed with visual and textual information." SLJ

Includes glossary and bibliographical references

Silverstein, Alvin

★ Wildfires; the science behind raging infernos. [by] Alvin and Virginia Silverstein and Laura Silverstein Nunn. Enslow Publishers 2010 48p il map (The science behind natural disasters) lib bdg $23.93

Grades: 4 5 6 **634.9**

1. Wildfires

ISBN 978-0-7660-2973-6 lib bdg; 0-7660-2973-5 lib bdg

LC 2008-48025

"Scientific explanations are accompanied by plentiful color diagrams that will help students to grasp causes and effects. . . . Photos . . . are effective, and are sometimes turned into helpful, lively diagrams by the addition of such features as wind-direction arrows." SLJ

Includes glossary and bibliographical references

Trammel, Howard K.

Wildfires; by Howard K. Trammel. Children's Press 2009 48 p. col. ill. (library) $29

Grades: 4 5 6 **634.9**

1. Wildfires -- Juvenile literature 2. Natural disasters -- Juvenile literature

ISBN 0531168875; 9780531168875

LC 2008014796

This book by Howard K. Trammel is part of the True Books: Earth Science series and looks at wildfires. The series answers questions such as "what makes the earth quake, rivers flood, and volcanoes blow their tops? How do natural forces become natural disasters?" (Publisher's note)

635 Garden crops (Horticulture)

Berkes, Marianne

What's in the garden? by Marianne Berkes; illustrated by Cris Arbo. 1st ed. Dawn Publications 2013 32 p. ill. (hardcover) $16.95; (paperback) $8.95

Grades: K 1 2 **635**

1. Gardens -- Poetry 2. Picture books for children 3. Gardening -- Juvenile literature 4. Kitchen gardens -- Juvenile literature 5. Vegetable gardening -- Juvenile literature 6. Cooking (Vegetables) -- Juvenile literature

ISBN 1584691891; 9781584691891; 9781584691907

LC 2012024245

This children's gardening book from Marianne Berkes combines "rhyming verses with recipes celebrating the garden's bounty. . . . From the popular ants on a log to the more daring French onion soup, breakfast-y carrot muffins to a dessert of blueberry pie, young chefs are likely to get a wide introduction to both the products of the garden and the culinary arts." (Kirkus Reviews)

Cohen, Whitney

The **book** of gardening projects for kids; 101 ways to get kids outside, dirty, and having fun. Whitney Cohen and John Fisher. 1st ed. Timber Press 2012 264 p. col. ill. $29.95

Grades: Adult   **635**

1. Gardening 2. Gardens -- Guidebooks 3. Gardens -- Activity Projects 4. Gardening for children

ISBN 1604693738; 9781604692457

LC 2011036778

In this book, "Whitney Cohen and John Fisher draw on years of experience in the Life Lab Garden Classroom and gardening with their own children to teach parents how to integrate the garden into their family life, no matter its scope or scale. The book features . . . gardening advice, including how to design a play-friendly garden, ideas for fun-filled theme gardens, and how to cook and preserve the garden's bounty. 101 . . . garden activities are also featured." (Publisher's note)

Creasy, Rosalind

Blue potatoes, orange tomatoes; illustrations by Ruth Heller. Sierra Club Bks. for Children 1994 40p il hardcover o.p. pa $6.95

Grades: 3 4 5   **635**

1. Vegetables 2. Vegetable gardening 3. Vegetables -- Juvenile literature 4. Cooking -- Vegetables -- Juvenile literature

ISBN 0-87156-576-5; 0-87156-919-1 pa

LC 92-38800

Describes how to plant and grow a variety of colorful vegetables, including red corn, yellow watermelons, and multicolored radishes, and includes recipes

"With interesting and authentic information about gardening accompanied by brilliant, life-like illustrations, this book will not only promote the delight in growing plants but enhance the wonder in the natural world right in your own backyard." Appraisal

Ehlert, Lois, 1934-

★ **Growing** vegetable soup; written and illustrated by Lois Ehlert. Harcourt Brace Jovanovich 1987 un il $17; pa $7; bd bk $6.95

Grades: PreK K 1 2   **635**

1. Vegetable gardening -- Juvenile literature

ISBN 0-15-232575-1; 0-15-232580-8 pa; 0-15-205055-8 bd bk

LC 86-22812

"Brightly-colored large illustrations and a boldly-worded text show how to plant and grow vegetables for Dad's soup. Shocking pinks, reds and greens give the illustrations an almost three-dimensional quality and will be good for large audiences of preschoolers." Child Book Rev Serv

Esbaum, Jill

Seed, sprout, pumpkin, pie. National Geographic 2009 16p il (Picture the seasons) pa $5.95

Grades: K 1 2   **635**

1. Pumpkin

ISBN 978-1-4263-0582-5 pa; 1-4263-0582-6 pa

LC 2009-12735

Discusses how pumpkins grow, the different varieties of pumpkins, and the many ways people use them

"Using minimal text with National Geographic's typically fine photographs, Esbaum brings out familiar, comforting details of the outdoors. . . . Perfect for Halloween, [this] is a veritable festival of orange featuring . . . panoramas of pumpkin fields and market stands, . . . the rarely appreciated pumpkin flower, pumpkins so big people make boats out of them, and . . . jack-'o-lanterns. . . . Fun, cozy, evocative stuff." Booklist

Fridell, Ron

Life cycle of a pumpkin; [by] Ron Fridell and Patricia Walsh. rev ed; Heinemann Library 2009 32p il (Life cycle of a) $25.36; pa $7.99

Grades: 2 3 4   **635**

1. Pumpkin

ISBN 978-1-4329-2527-7; 1-4329-2527-X; 978-1-4329-2544-4 pa; 1-4329-2544-X pa

LC 00011234

First published 2002

"From seed to seedling, vine, and finally full-grown fruit, the life cycle of the pumpkin is clearly and colorfully described. Bright and engaging full-color photographs amplify the text on each page." SLJ

Includes bibliographical references

Gaarder-Juntti, Oona

What in the world is a green garden? ABDO Pub. Co. 2011 24p il (Going green) lib bdg $24.21

Grades: 1 2 3 4   **635**

1. Sustainable agriculture

ISBN 978-1-61613-188-3; 1-61613-188-8

LC 2010004322

"The lively layout design, featuring colorful headings, short paragraphs, and attractive photographs, has a scrapbook-like quality. . . . [The title explains] how all our choices require energy and resources, and encourage readers to make changes in their lifestyles. . . . [This] . . . will inspire and empower readers to make a difference." SLJ

Includes glossary and bibliographical references

Gibbons, Gail

The **pumpkin** book. Holiday House 1999 un il $16.95; pa $6.95

Grades: K 1 2 3   **635**

1. Pumpkin

ISBN 0-8234-1465-5; 0-8234-1636-4 pa

LC 98-45267

Describes how pumpkins come in different shapes and sizes, how they grow, and their traditional uses and cultural significance. Includes instructions for carving a pumpkin and drying the seeds

"Bold, clear watercolor illustrations and a concise text work together. . . , Gibbons succeeds once again at covering a topic in a useful way at just the right level for beginning readers." SLJ

The **vegetables** we eat; by Gail Gibbons. Holiday House 2007 32p il $16.95

Grades: K 1 2 3   **635**

1. Vegetables

ISBN 0-8234-2001-9; 978-0-8234-2001-8

LC 2005052654

"A clear, informative introduction to eight groups of vegetables, categorized by the part of the plant that is eaten. For each group, Gibbons includes an illustration of one representative veggie as it grows in a garden. The rest of the page includes illustrations of related plants. . . . The author offers basic suggestions for starting a garden and shows how produce goes from large farms to processing plants and grocery stores. . . . Familiar paneled illustrations and accessible text combine to present a simple, effective approach to the topic." SLJ

Grow it, cook it. DK Pub. 2008 80p il $15.99
Grades: 3 4 5 6   **635**
    1. Cooking 2. Vegetable gardening
    ISBN 978-0-7566-3367-7; 0-7566-3367-2

This "title combines instructions for growing edible plants with recipes based on the harvest. . . . The lush photos of ripening vegetables . . . will spark children's curiosity and inspire them to learn more. . . . Most children will need help . . . as they prepare the delicious, often sophisticated culinary treats. . . . An attractive introduction to both gardening and healthy meals." Booklist

Hirsch, Rebecca E.
Growing your own garden; by Rebecca Hirsch. Cherry Lake Pub. 2010 32p il (Save the planet) lib bdg $27.07
Grades: 3 4 5 6   **635**
    1. Vegetable gardening
    ISBN 978-1-60279-657-7 lib bdg; 1-60279-657-2 lib bdg
               LC 2009-38093

"At the beginning of . . . [the] book, readers are given a mission and advised to be alert to the facts provided so that they can successfully answer the questions at the end. . . . Children are made to feel part of the process; suggestions for how they can become involved abound." SLJ

Includes glossary and bibliographical references

Malam, John
Grow your own sandwich. Heinemann Library 2011 32p il (Grow it yourself!) lib bdg $26; pa $7.99
Grades: K 1 2   **635**
    1. Cooking 2. Tomatoes 3. Vegetable gardening
    ISBN 978-1-4329-5108-5 lib bdg; 978-1-4329-5115-3 pa
               LC 2010049833

This describes how to grow tomatoes and how to make a cheese and tomato sandwich.

Includes glossary and bibliographical references

Grow your own soup. Heinemann Library 2011 32p il (Grow it yourself!) lib bdg $26; pa $7.99
Grades: 2 3 4   **635**
    1. Cooking 2. Pumpkin 3. Vegetable gardening
    ISBN 978-1-4329-5106-1 lib bdg; 978-1-4329-5113-9 pa
               LC 2010049830

This describes how pumpkins grow, how to plant and raise your own, and how to make pumpkin soup.

Includes glossary and bibliographical references

Morris, Karyn
★ The **Kids** Can Press jumbo book of gardening; written by Karyn Morris; illustrated by Jane Kurisu. Kids Can Press 2000 240p il pa $14.95
Grades: 4 5 6 7   **635**
    1. Gardening
    ISBN 1-55074-690-1

"Sections cover general information; fruit, vegetable, and flower gardens; noninvasive native plants; gardens that attract wildlife; and group projects. Projects range from a few annuals in a container and thickets designed with native wildlife in mind to community gardens. Directions are clear, with plenty of diagrams and illustrations." Booklist

Ready set grow! quick and easy gardening projects. DK Pub. 2010 79p il $12.99
Grades: 3 4 5   **635**
    1. Gardening
    ISBN 978-0-7566-5887-8; 0-7566-5887-X

"Sunny and energetic spreads feature more than 30 garden project ideas, aimed at getting kids outdoors and in the dirt. Photographs and illustrations teach the basics about plant cultivation. . . . Recycling is a recurring theme, . . . many of the garden-related projects tend toward the whimsical, . . . and there's a strong emphasis on growing edible plants. . . . The fun, easy, and green concepts should have readers eagerly awaiting spring." Publ Wkly

Robbins, Ken
Pumpkins. Roaring Brook Press 2006 un il $14.95
Grades: K 1 2   **635**
    1. Pumpkin
    ISBN 978-1-59643-184-3; 1-59643-184-9
               LC 2005-33023

"With color photos that equal any painting for artistry of composition and sensitivity, Robbins has created a book that is certain to become an autumn favorite." SLJ

Rockwell, Anne F.
One bean; pictures by Megan Halsey. Walker & Co. 1998 un il hardcover o.p. pa $6.95
Grades: K 1 2   **635**
    1. Beans 2. Beans -- Development 3. Lima bean -- Juvenile literature
    ISBN 0-8027-8648-0; 0-8027-7572-1 pa
               LC 97-36249

"An easy-to-read text combines with lively illustrations to create the story of what happens to one small bean when it interacts with some soil, just a little water, a lot of sunlight, and a young child's tender care." Sci Child

Rustad, Martha E. H.
Fall pumpkins; orange and plump. illustrated by Amanda Enright. Millbrook Press 2011 24p il (Fall's here) lib bdg $23.93
Grades: K 1 2 3   **635**
    1. Pumpkin
    ISBN 978-0-7613-5065-1; 0-7613-5065-9
               LC 2010048310

The author "takes the young reader on a journey to learn how pumpkins are planted, tended, and grown. . . . The book also shows the reader how to use fully grown pumpkins: carving them for Halloween, making roasted pumpkins seeds, and us the pumpkin meat to make pumpkin pie. . . . The illustrations are very colorful." Sci Books Films

Includes glossary and bibliographical references

Sayre, April Pulley

Touch a butterfly; wildlife gardening with kids. April Pulley Sayre. 1st ed. Roost Books 2013 xiv, 207 p.p (paperback) $19.95

Grades: Adult Professional   **635**

1. Wildlife attracting 2. Gardening -- Juvenile literature 3. Garden animals 4. Gardening to attract wildlife

ISBN 1590309170; 9781590309179

LC 2012021579

This book, by April Pulley Sayre, offers instructions on how to "turn your garden into a hummingbird hotspot, a haven for butterflies, and a thriving ecosystem that will delight and inspire the young and young-at-heart. . . . Begin to see your yard from an animal's perspective; discover plants that attract colorful birds and bugs; embrace sensory experiences that native plants and creatures bring; and understand how your yard fits into the surrounding landscape." (Publisher's note)

635.9   Flowers and ornamental plants

Bearce, Stephanie

A kid's guide to container gardening. Mitchell Lane Publishers 2009 48p il (Gardening for kids) lib bdg $29.95

Grades: 3 4 5 6   **635.9**

1. Container gardening

ISBN 978-1-58415-814-1 lib bdg; 1-58415-814-X lib bdg

LC 2009001314

This is a guide to growing plants in tubs, buckets, and other containers

This book is "filled with information, which is divided into neat chapters written in a chatty, enthusiastic voice. . . . [The book features] large type, embedded with bolded vocabulary words, . . . as well as sharp color photos on every page." Booklist

Includes bibliographical references

A kid's guide to making a terrarium. Mitchell Lane Publishers 2009 48p il (Gardening for kids) lib bdg $29.95

Grades: 3 4 5 6   **635.9**

1. Terrariums

ISBN 978-1-58415-813-4 lib bdg; 1-58415-813-1 lib bdg

LC 2009001319

This book is "filled with information, which is divided into neat chapters written in a chatty, enthusiastic voice. . . . [The book features] large type, embedded with bolded vocabulary words, . . . as well as sharp color photos on every page." Booklist

Includes bibliographical references

636   Animal husbandry

Gunter, Veronika Alice

Pet science; 50 purr-fectly woof-worthy activities for you & your pets. by Veronika Alice Gunter and Rain Newcomb; illustrated by Tom LaBaff. Lark Books 2006 80p il $14.95

Grades: 3 4 5 6   **636**

1. Pets 2. Science -- Experiments 3. Pets -- Juvenile literature

ISBN 1-57990-786-5

LC 2005-4860

This "book of 50 activities encourages budding ethnologists to investigate, explore, and record their pet's behavior. . . . Delightful four-color illustrations fill the pages. . . . This engaging book is a delightful way to bring science to young children." Sci Books Films

Includes glossary

Jones, Charlotte Foltz

The king who barked; real animals who ruled. illustrated by Yayo. Holiday House 2009 40p il $16.95

Grades: 3 4 5   **636**

1. Famous animals -- Juvenile literature 2. Human-animal relationships -- Juvenile literature

ISBN 978-0-8234-1925-8; 0-8234-1925-8

LC 2008-25669

"The brief accounts in this whimsical collection of animal anecdotes introduce symbolic leaders such as goat mayors, dog-kings, and a rhinoceros who won a seat on the São Paulo city council in a write-in campaign. The stories, which are arranged by continent of origin, hail from legends and oral histories, though some are more recent and better documented. Yayo's acrylic-on-canvas paintings capture the topsy-turvy spirit of the tales and add playful details." SLJ

Includes bibliographical references

Keenan, Sheila

★ Animals in the house; a history of pets and people. Scholastic Nonfiction 2007 112p il $17.99

Grades: 4 5 6   **636**

1. Pets

ISBN 978-0-439-69286-1; 0-439-69286-5

"Keenan provides an overview of pets andtheir people. Beginning with statistics about pet ownership, the text goes on to describe how animals and humans came together . . . and discusses how this relationship has changed and deepened. . . . Eye-catchingly designed, the format uses Photoshop to best advantage, providing interesting graphics, popping borders, and plenty of pictures featuring adorable animals." Booklist

Includes bibliographical references

Love, Ann

Talking tails; the incredible connection between people and their pets. [by] Ann Love & Jane Drake; illustrated by Bill Slavin. Tundra Books 2010 80p il $22.95

Grades: 3 4 5 6   **636**

1. Pets 2. Human-animal relationships -- Juvenile literature

ISBN 978-0-88776-884-2; 0-88776-884-9

"Focusing mainly on dogs and cats but with some attention to fish, reptiles, rodents, and birds, Love and Drake celebrate the affection that connects people with their pets.

Along with providing a historical overview of animal domestication, . . . the authors profile some famous real pets. . . . They run through major cat and dog breeds; discuss characteristic instincts, personalities, behavior, and body language; and explain how to plan for, choose, . . . and care for an animal. . . . Slavin skillfully captures the bountiful warmth here. . . . This will draw animal lovers like a magnet." Booklist

Martin, Claudia

Farming. Marshall Cavendish Benchmark 2010 64p il (Working animals) $28.50

Grades: 4 5 6 7   636

1. Agriculture 2. Domestic animals

ISBN 978-1-60870-162-9; 1-60870-162-X

LC 2010006895

"Attractively designed and packed with information. . . . The composition of each page is attractively set up with well-selected and reproduced stock and historical photos." SLJ

Montgomery, Sy

Temple Grandin; how the girl who loved cows embraced autism and changed the world. by Sy Montgomery. Houghton Mifflin Harcourt 2012 147 p. col. ill. $17.99

Grades: 4 5 6 7 8   636

1. Autism 2. Cattle 3. Biography 4. Women scientists -- Biography 5. Animal welfare -- United States -- Juvenile literature 6. Livestock -- Housing -- United States -- Juvenile literature 7. Livestock -- Handling -- United States -- Juvenile literature 8. Autistic people -- United States -- Biography -- Juvenile literature 9. Animal scientists -- United States -- Biography -- Juvenile literature 10. Animal specialists -- United States -- Biography -- Juvenile literature 11. Women animal specialists -- United States -- Biography -- Juvenile literature

ISBN 0547443153; 9780547443157

LC 2011039911

AAAS/Subaru SB&F Prize for Excellence in Science Books: Middle Grade Science Book (2013)

This book by Sy Montgomery presents a biography of autistic animal scientist Temple Grandin. Sy Montgomery argues that "though one never outgrows autism, it doesn't condemn those who have it to unproductive lives, and an appendix, 'Temple's Advice for Kids on the Spectrum,' provides first-hand wisdom. Photos and diagrams depict Grandin's work as well as documenting her early life and career." (Kirkus Reviews)

Includes bibliographical references and index.

Steele, Christy

Cattle ranching in the American West; by Christy Steele. World Almanac Library 2005 48p il map (America's westward expansion) lib bdg $30; pa $11.95

Grades: 5 6 7 8   636

1. Cattle 2. Ranch life

ISBN 0-8368-5787-9 lib bdg; 0-8368-5794-1 pa

LC 2004-56769

This volume describing Western cattle ranching is "richly illustrated with historical photographs, illustrations, maps, and quotes from primary sources presented in sidebars." SLJ

Includes bibliographical references

Tafuri, Nancy

★ **Spots,** feathers, and curly tails. Greenwillow Bks. 1988 un il $16.95

Grades: PreK K 1 2   636

1. Domestic animals 2. Domestic animals -- Miscellanea -- Juvenile literature

ISBN 0-688-07536-3; 0-688-07537-1 lib bdg

LC 87-15638

Questions and answers highlight some outstanding characteristics of farm animals, such as a chicken's feathers and a horse's mane

"In the watercolor illustrations with black pen outline, Nancy Tafuri manages in the simplest style to give energy and personality to the animals through the angle of a head or the set of a snout. The story will provide a successful experience for both child and adult reader and is an ideal book for the beginning reader to entertain a younger sibling in a game they'll both enjoy." Horn Book

Turner, Pamela S.

★ **Hachiko**; written by Pamela S. Turner; illustrated by Yan Nascimbene. Houghton Mifflin 2004 un il $15

Grades: K 1 2 3   636

1. Dogs -- Fiction

ISBN 0-618-14094-8

LC 2002-155546

This "picture book pays tribute to one of the world's lesser-known animal heroes: Hachiko, a dog who kept vigil for nearly 10 years at a Tokyo train station, waiting for his deceased master to return from work. Turner unfolds this poignant true story in the natural, unaffected voice of Kentaro, a fictional little boy, who wonders at the dog's unswerving devotion. Unobtrusive details evoke a sense of place . . . as does Nascimbene's spare line-and-watercolor artwork, reminiscent of Japanese woodblock prints. . . . This will resonate with any child who has loved a dog and been loved in return." Booklist

636.08   Specific topics in animal husbandry

Curtis, Jennifer Keats

Sanctuaries; by Jennifer Keats Curtis; with Karine Aigner [and nine others] Sylvan Dell Publishing 2013 32 p. (Animal helpers) (English hardcover) $17.95

Grades: K 1 2   636.08

1. Animal rescue -- Juvenile literature 2. Animal sanctuaries -- Juvenile literature 3. Wildlife refuges -- Juvenile literature

ISBN 160718611X; 9781607186113; 9781607186236

LC 2012039949

In this book, "using examples from six animal-rescue organizations . . . [Jennifer Keats] Curtis describes what wild-animal sanctuaries do. Short informational paragraphs are set on . . . photographs of animals being cared for. The account begins with a series of portraits of shelter animals: several tigers, a binturong, a declawed Canadian lynx, a pair of blind bobcats and a bear. The author goes on to describe animal medical and dental treatments, training and enrichment." (Kirkus Reviews)

Doner, Kim

On a road in Africa; [by] Kim Doner; afterword by Chryssee Perry Martin. Tricycle Press 2008 un il $15.95

Grades: PreK K 1 2 **636.08**

1. Stories in rhyme 2. Wildlife conservation 3. Animals -- Africa

ISBN 978-1-58246-230-1; 1-58246-230-5

LC 2007-18199

"This is a lovely picture book to share as a rhyming story, animal book, or cultural introduction." Libr Media Connect

Kehret, Peg

Animals welcome; a life of reading, writing, and rescue. Peg Kehret. W.W. Norton & Co. Inc. 2012 272 p. (hardback) $16.99

Grades: 4 5 6 7 **636.08**

1. Wildlife 2. Autobiography 3. Animal behavior 4. Animal rescue -- United States -- Anecdotes -- Juvenile literature 5. Animal welfare -- United States -- Anecdotes -- Juvenile literature 6. Animal shelters -- United States -- Anecdotes -- Juvenile literature

ISBN 0525423990; 9780525423997

LC 2011035440

Author Peg Kehret shares "her life on a small wildlife sanctuary, . . . the tragedy of her husband's sudden death, and the pain of losing Pete, the shelter cat who co-authored three of her books." In addition to stories of animal rescue and facts about birds and animals, the book is "a personal glimpse into the life of an author who loves animals, and the philosophy by which she lives." (Publisher's note)

Larson, Kirby

Two Bobbies; a true story of Hurricane Katrina, friendship, and survival. [by] Kirby Larson and Mary Nethery; illustrations by Jean Cassels. Walker & Co. 2008 un il $16.99

Grades: K 1 2 3 **636.08**

1. Cats 2. Dogs 3. Hurricane Katrina, 2005

ISBN 978-0-8027-9754-4; 0-8027-9754-7

"Abandoned during the [Hurricane] Katrina evacuations, pets Bobbi [the dog] and Bob Cat wander dangerous, debris-strewn streets seeking food and water. Eventually taken to a rescue shelter, the Bobbies show distress when separated but remain calm when together. Workers then discover that Bob Cat is blind and that Bobbi seems to serve as his seeing-eye dog. . . . The descriptive, sometimes folksy prose and realistically rendered gouache illustrations accessibly convey the Bobbies' experiences and mutual devotion. . . . This moving story about the importance of friendship and home highlights the plight of the hurricane's lost and left-behind animals, as well as the value of animal shelters." Booklist

636.088 Animals for specific purposes

Grayson, Robert

Transportation. Marshall Cavendish Benchmark 2010 64p il (Working animals) $28.50

Grades: 4 5 6 7 **636.088**

1. Pack animals (Transportation)

ISBN 978-1-60870-167-4; 1-60870-167-0

LC 2010006899

"Describes animals that people all over the world use to transport people and goods, such as elephants, horses, yaks, water buffalo, and dogs." Publisher's note

Includes glossary and bibliographical references

Halls, Kelly Milner

Saving the Baghdad Zoo; a true story of hope and heroes. by Kelly Milner Halls, with William Sumner. Greenwillow Books 2010 64p il map $17.99

Grades: 4 5 6 7 **636.088**

1. Zoos 2. Wildlife conservation 3. Army officers 4. Iraq War, 2003- -- Juvenile literature

ISBN 978-0-06-177202-3; 0-06-177202-X

LC 2008-52820

"This eye-opening tale of compassion and cooperation chronicles the mission of an international team of military personnel, zoo staffers, veterinarians, and relief workers to rescue neglected animals in Baghdad. . . . Sobering and uplifting photographs—many taken by Sumner—underscore both the direness of the situation and the spirit of hope that drove the project." Publ Wkly

Includes bibliographical references

Kent, Deborah

★ Animal helpers for the disabled. Watts 2003 63p il (Watts library) hardcover o.p. $25.50

Grades: 4 5 6 7 **636.088**

1. Dogs 2. Guide dogs 3. Working animals 4. Animals and the handicapped 5. Animals -- Training 6. Animals -- Therapeutic use 7. Animals as aids for people with disabilities -- Juvenile literature

ISBN 0-531-12017-1; 0-531-16663-5 pa

LC 2002-8885

Explores the history of guide dogs, service animals, and assistance dogs, and discusses the process of training them to help people who have physical disabilities

This is an "informative, often inspirational and thought-provoking [book]." Booklist

Includes bibliographical references

Laidlaw, Rob

Wild animals in captivity; [by] Rob Laidlaw. Fitzhenry & Whiteside 2008 48p il $19.95

Grades: 5 6 7 8 **636.088**

1. Zoos 2. Animal welfare

ISBN 978-1-55455-025-8; 1-55455-025-4

"A passionate, well-written, and well-researched argument against the practices of most zoos around the world. . . . Describes the damage done when animals are unnaturally confined and moved to inhospitable climates, and compares the wild and captive lives of polar bears, orcas, elephants, and great apes—the four species most harmed by captivity. . . . The issues raised in this important and powerful book will resonate with young and old." SLJ

Markle, Sandra

Animal heroes; true rescue stories. by Sandra Markle. Millbrook Press 2009 64p il lib bdg $29.27

Grades: 4 5 6 7 **636.088**

1. Pets 2. Animals 3. Rescue work

ISBN 978-0-8225-7884-0 lib bdg; 0-8225-7884-0 lib bdg

LC 2007-50435

"Nine stories, based on interviews with the grateful survivors, describe how brave animals rescued people in catastrophic circumstances. Each edgy retelling reveals details that only the participants could know, including sounds, smells, sights, and the knowledge that at any moment they could die, deepening the tension. Mixed in are Markle's broad and perfectly attuned insights about animal behavior." SLJ

Includes glossary and bibliographical references

636.089   Veterinary medicine

Jackson, Donna M.

ER vets; life in an animal emergency room. Houghton Mifflin 2005 88p il $17

Grades: 5 6 7 8   636.089

1. Veterinary medicine 2. Veterinarians -- Juvenile literature 3. Veterinary emergencies -- Juvenile literature

ISBN 0-618-43663-4

"With plentiful, excellent-quality photographs, this highly visual book offers a behind-the-scenes look at an emergency animal hospital in Colorado. . . . A section on grief counseling for families with critically ill pets and a spread on how to put together a pet first-aid kit are included. Well-researched and well-written, ER Vets is an engaging book on a hot topic." SLJ

636.1   Horses

Bailer, Darice

Donkeys. Marshall Cavendish Benchmark 2011 il (Animals, animals) lib bdg $20.95

Grades: 3 4 5   636.1

1. Donkeys

ISBN 978-0-7614-4875-4; 0-7614-4875-6

LC 2010033889

Provides information on the anatomy, special skills, habitats, and diet of donkeys.

This offers "comprehensive text and striking, well-chosen photos. . . . [This is] packed with engaging facts and trivia, as well as an upbeat tone." Booklist

Includes glossary and bibliographical references

Barnes, Julia

Horses at work; [by] Julia Barnes. North American ed.; Gareth Stevens 2006 32p il (Animals at work) lib bdg $23.93

Grades: 3 4 5   636.1

1. Horses 2. Working animals

ISBN 0-8368-6225-2

LC 2005054066

This describes horses' uses throughout history, their relationship with humans, habitat, diet, and appearance.

This is "well-written, well-organized, . . . visually appealing and fun to read." SLJ

Includes bibliographical references

Bowers, Nathan

4-H guide to training horses. Voyageur Press 2009 176p il $18.99

Grades: 5 6 7 8   636.1

1. Horses -- Training

ISBN 978-0-7603-3627-4; 0-7603-3627-X

LC 2009015299

This provides "sound and comprehensive information. [The book] covers basic training techniques and riding skills such as mounting, saddling, reining, stopping and starting, and posture among other topics. The training techniques offer insight into equine behavior based on their history as prey animals. The authors also emphasize that horse owners' success will be determined by how much effort they are willing to expend on their relationship with their animals. The many color photographs clearly depict the methods and activities that are taking place, and the accompanying images further clarify what is happening and its significance." SLJ

Includes glossary

Bozzo, Linda

My first horse; [by] Linda Bozzo. Enslow Elementary 2007 32p il (My first pet library from the American Humane Association) lib bdg $22.60

Grades: 1 2 3   636.1

1. Horses

ISBN 978-0-7660-2753-4 lib bdg; 0-7660-2753-8 lib bdg

LC 2006014969

This offers brief basic advice on selecting a horse and caring for it.

Includes glossary and bibliographical references

Crosby, Jeff

Harness horses, bucking broncos & pit ponies; a history of horse breeds. written and illustrated by Jeff Crosby and Shelley Ann Jackson. Tundra Books 2011 69p il map $21.99

Grades: 4 5 6 7   636.1

1. Horses

ISBN 978-0-88776-986-3; 0-88776-986-1

"After a brief introduction, the animals are grouped by the roles they have played in relation to people: 'Rapid Transit,' 'Military Advantage,' 'Horsepower,' 'Equine Entertainment,' and 'Feral Horses.' The concise and interesting information on each of the 43 breeds is accompanied by an illustration of the type as well as one of the horse in action and often includes a small map showing its origins. The excellent painterly pictures clearly capture the unique life of each horse." SLJ

Includes bibliographical references

Draper, Judith

My first horse and pony book; [by] Judith Draper. Kingfisher 2005 47p il $9.95

Grades: K 1 2 3   636.1

1. Horses 2. Horsemanship

ISBN 0-7534-5878-0

This "guide covers the basics about horses and ponies, including physical characteristics, care and feeding, grooming, and stabling. After discussing proper clothing and tacking up, the author takes a look at English and Western riding. . . . The photos are excellent—bright and clear—and precisely illustrate what the text is describing." SLJ

★ My first horse and pony care book; [by] Judith Draper. Kingfisher 2006 48p il $9.95

Grades: K 1 2 3   **636.1**
1. Horses 2. Horsemanship
ISBN 978-0-7534-5989-8; 0-7534-5989-2
                                        LC 2006005962
"Draper focuses on pony breeds commonly used in the
United Kingdom and on English-style riding and tack. The
information about feeding, grooming, and riding is detailed,
accurate, and accessible. . . . The photographs are beautiful
and in sharp focus. . . . This book is a must-have for young
horse lovers." SLJ
Includes glossary

Gibbons, Gail
Horses! Holiday House 2003 un il $17.95; pa $6.95
Grades: K 1 2 3   **636.1**
1. Horsemanship 2. Horses -- Juvenile literature
ISBN 0-8234-1703-4; 0-8234-1875-8 pa
                                        LC 2003-41683
Presents information on horses, including their physical
characteristics, behavior, and how to ride a horse
"Attractive, full-color labeled illustrations fill every
page, with many expanding on a particular point in the main
text. . . . The book's accessible format will attract browsers
as well as legions of young would-be equestrians." Booklist

Hamilton, Libby
Horse: the essential guide for young equestrians; writer,
Libby Hamilton; illustrators: Sophie Allsopp . . . [et al.]
Candlewick Press 2008 24p il $15.99
Grades: 2 3 4 5   **636.1**
1. Horses
ISBN 978-0-7636-3547-3; 0-7636-3547-2
"This clever and pleasing guide contains a wealth of
information on horses, including history, breeds, care and
grooming, equipment, riding, and shows. Facts and tips are
presented in an imaginative and lively format. The excellent,
realistic illustrations are colorful and accurate and even occasionally humorous." SLJ

Holub, Joan
★ Why do horses neigh? illustrations by Anna DiVito.
Dial Bks. for Young Readers 2003 46p il (Dial easy-to-
read) hardcover o.p. pa $3.99
Grades: K 1 2   **636.1**
1. Horses 2. Questions and answers 3. Human-animal
relationships 4. Horses -- Miscellanea -- Juvenile
literature
ISBN 0-8037-2770-4 lib bdg; 0-14-230119-1 pa
                                        LC 2001-47476
Questions and answers present information about the
behavior and characteristics of horses and their interactions
with humans
The book has "a bright, appealing format that combines
jaunty original art and well-chosen photos." Booklist

Jeffrey, Laura S.
★ Horses; how to choose and care for a horse. Enslow Publishers 2004 48p il (American Humane pet care
library) lib bdg $23.93
Grades: 3 4 5   **636.1**
1. Pets 2. Horses 3. Horsemanship -- Juvenile literature
ISBN 0-7660-2519-5
                                        LC 2003-22970

Provides information on owning a horse, including how
to choose among different breeds and how to groom, house,
feed, and keep a horse healthy
This offers "children solid information . . . at a level they
can understand. Many endearing photos . . . make [this book]
fun to look at." Booklist
Includes glossary and bibliographical references

Lewin, Ted
★ Stable. Roaring Brook Press/Flash Point 2010 un
il $17.99
Grades: K 1 2 3   **636.1**
1. Horses
ISBN 978-1-59643-467-7; 1-59643-467-8
                                        LC 2009-44431
"Lewin conveys the spirit of a Brooklyn institution
through sumptuously detailed, luminous watercolors. Kens-
ington Stables, a relic from the days when horses provided
necessary transportation, shelters 37 animals, large and
small. . . . The straightforward, present-tense prose conveys
the central point that horses are important to the community,
and they should be preserved." Kirkus

Lomberg, Michelle
Horse. Weigl Publishers 2009 32p il (My pet) lib bdg
$26; pa $9.95
Grades: 3 4 5   **636.1**
1. Pets 2. Horses
ISBN 978-1-60596-092-0 lib bdg; 1-60596-092-6 lib
bdg; 978-1-60596-093-7 pa; 1-60596-093-4 pa
                                        LC 2009-25974
Information about how to house, feed, and care
for horses.
"With clear, formal writing, and extensive coverage . . .
[this title is] useful for reports. . . . Numerous color photographs, charts . . . and question-and-answer boxes supplement the [text]." SLJ
Includes glossary

Lunis, Natalie
Miniature horses. Bearport 2010 24p il (Peculiar
pets) lib bdg $22.61
Grades: 3 4 5   **636.1**
1. Horses
ISBN 978-1-59716-861-8 lib bdg; 1-59716-861-0
lib bdg
                                        LC 2009-10379
Introduces the miniature horse, describing its physical
characteristics, history, and behavior, and discussing the care
and diet that it needs
"The language . . . is lively . . . [and] the illustrations are
vivid, with photos offering some amusing shots. . . . This
[book] . . . will hold readers' attention, but also challenge
them to consider the responsibilities required of owners of
unusual creatures." SLJ
Includes glossary and bibliographical references

MacLeod, Elizabeth
Why do horses have manes? Kids Can Press 2009
64p $14.95
Grades: 3 4 5 6   **636.1**
1. Horses
ISBN 978-1-55453-312-1; 1-55453-312-0

In a question and answer format "this slim volume covers standard information . . . and branches out to the more esoteric. . . . Freestanding text sections with a light and engaging tone combined with glossy photo vignettes of horses vamping for the camera make the book highly browsable." Horn Book Guide

Mack, Gail

Horses. Marshall Cavendish Benchmark 2010 48p il (Great pets) lib bdg $29.93

Grades: 2 3 4　　　　　　　　　　　　**636.1**
　1. Horses
　ISBN 978-0-7614-4147-2 lib bdg; 0-7614-4147-6 lib bdg
　　　　　　　　　　　　　LC 2008037262

"Describes the characteristics and behavior of pet horses, also discussing their physical appearance and place in history." Publisher's note

Includes glossary and bibliographical references

Niven, Felicia Lowenstein

Learning to care for a horse. Enslow Publishers 2010 48p il (Beginning pet care with American Humane) lib bdg $23.93

Grades: 2 3 4　　　　　　　　　　　　**636.1**
　1. Horses
　ISBN 978-0-7660-3196-8; 0-7660-3196-9
　　　　　　　　　　　　　LC 2008048961

"Readers will learn how to choose a horse and care for a horse, from what kind of horse is best for them and how long they live." Publisher's note

Includes glossary and bibliographical references

Peterson, Cris

Horsepower; the wonder of draft horses. photographs by Alvis Upitis. Boyds Mills Press 1997 un il $16.95; pa $9.95

Grades: K 1 2 3　　　　　　　　　　　**636.1**
　1. Horses 2. Working animals -- Juvenile literature
　ISBN 1-56397-626-9; 1-56397-943-8 pa
　　　　　　　　　　　　　LC 96-84679

"Crisp, full-color photographs accompany the short, smoothly written text." SLJ

Ransford, Sandy

Horse & pony breeds; written by Sandy Ransford; photographed by Bob Langrish. Kingfisher (NY) 2003 64p il (Kingfisher riding club) $14.95; pa $8.99

Grades: 4 5 6 7　　　　　　　　　　　**636.1**
　1. Horses
　ISBN 0-7534-5575-7; 0-7534-6075-0 pa
　　　　　　　　　　　　　LC 2003-272944

An "overview of an international array of horse and pony breeds including many that may be unfamiliar to American children. The book covers the majority of breeds in half-page treatments that feature at least a paragraph of commentary and a captioned side body, and a full-color photograph that points out conformation differences particular to each breed. . . . An attractive, informative book that is sure to please both readers and browsers." SLJ

Includes glossary

Horse & pony care; written by Sandy Ransford; photographed by Bob Langrish. Kingfisher (NY) 2002 64p il (Kingfisher riding club) hardcover o.p. pa $8.95

Grades: 4 5 6 7　　　　　　　　　　　**636.1**
　1. Horses
　ISBN 0-7534-5439-4; 0-7534-5744-X pa

This offers instructions on such topics as washing and clipping a pony, exercise routines and caring for pastureland, and includes information about types of feed and how much feed a pony needs

"Children who have a horse or want one will find a good deal of information in this attractive, photo-rich book. There are clear instructions. . . . The full-color photos are well composed, fully captioned, and quite thorough." Booklist

★ The **Kingfisher** illustrated horse & pony encyclopedia; written by Sandy Ransford; photographed by Bob Langrish. Kingfisher 2004 224p il $24.95

Grades: 4 5 6 7　　　　　　　　　　　**636.1**
　1. Horses 2. Horsemanship
　ISBN 0-7534-5781-4
　　　　　　　　　　　　　LC 2003-27293

"The first part of the book covers the life cycle, domestication, and types of horses and ponies. . . . The second part deals with how to care for these animals and discusses horsemanship from taking riding lessons to training and driving a horse. . . . Filled with appealing photos of young people interacting with their four-legged friends, this title is an extremely useful addition to any collection." SLJ

Rockwood, Leigh

Horses are smart! PowerKids Press 2010 24p il (Super smart animals) lib bdg $21.25; pa $8.25

Grades: 2 3 4 5　　　　　　　　　　　**636.1**
　1. Horses
　ISBN 978-1-4358-9399-3 lib bdg; 1-4358-9399-9 lib bdg; 978-1-4358-9838-7 pa; 1-4358-9838-9 pa
　Examines the intelligence of horses.

"Bright, colorful, captioned photographs complement the text. Rockwood does an excellent job of simplifying the information without making it choppy or boring." Libr Media Connect

Includes glossary

Simon, Seymour

★ **Horses**. HarperCollins Pubs. 2006 un il $15.99; lib bdg $16.89

Grades: 2 3 4　　　　　　　　　　　　**636.1**
　1. Horses
　ISBN 0-06-028944-9; 0-06-028945-7 lib bdg
　　　　　　　　　　　　　LC 2004-30392

"Simon provides the basic facts, which include the importance of horses to humans throughout history, their evolution, physical traits, interactions among themselves, and the various breeds. The information is clear and accurate. The striking color photos will capture readers attention." SLJ

Wilsdon, Christina

For horse-crazy girls only; everything you want to know about horses. illustrated by Alecia Underhill. Feiwel and Friends 2010 150p il $14.99

Grades: 4 5 6 7   **636.1**
1. Horses
ISBN 978-0-312-60323-6; 0-312-60323-1
LC 2010015677

"Filled with quizzes, trivia, top 10 lists, and information about equine behavior, history, sports, and more, this guide-book aims straight at the hearts of horse-loving tweens. . . . The book runs the gamut from how to pick a horse's name to horses in popular culture, the evolution of the species, and horse-related events nationwide. The many sidebars, tidbits, and anecdotes encourage casual browsing-horse lovers will be in heaven." Publ Wkly

636.2   Cattle and related animals

Barnes, Julia
Camels and llamas at work; [by] Julia Barnes. Gareth Stevens 2006 32p il map (Animals at work) lib bdg $23.93
Grades: 3 4 5   **636.2**
1. Camels 2. Llamas 3. Working animals
ISBN 0-8368-6222-8
LC 2005054065

This is "well-written, well-organized, . . . visually appealing and fun to read." SLJ
Includes bibliographical references

Boynton, Sandra
Amazing cows; udder absurdity for children. Workman Pub. 2010 89p il $15.99; pa $10.95
Grades: K 1 2   **636.2**
1. Cattle
ISBN 978-0-7611-6371-8; 0-7611-6371-9; 978-0-7611-6214-8 pa; 0-7611-6214-3 pa
LC 2010034583

Jokes, humorous stories and poems, a comic book and other misinformation about cows.

"Not since the heyday of Gary Larson has so much ado-ration been shown to bovines. With her trademark irrever-ence, Boynton offers an impassioned and hyperbolic ode to cows, replete with jokes, a spread devoted to cow fashion, a cow 'myth' that takes place in ancient Athens . . . , limericks, and puns aplenty. . . . It's pure fun." Publ Wkly

Diemer, Lauren
Cows. Weigl Publishers 2010 24p il (World of wonder: watch them grow) lib bdg $25.70; pa $9.95
Grades: 1 2   **636.2**
1. Cattle
ISBN 978-1-60596-919-0 lib bdg; 1-60596-919-2 lib bdg; 978-1-60596-920-6 pa; 1-60596-920-6 pa
LC 2009052101

Learn about how cows are born and grow up, as well as their role in the world.

The text "is simple without being simplistic; it is thought-ful and comprehensive without being overwhelming. The real appeal for teachers, students, and independent young readers, however, will be the photographs that fill the facing pages. Bold, bright, and colorful, the photographs bring you marvelously close to the subject. . . . On many different levels, this is a very appealing [book]." Libr Media Connect
Includes glossary

Freedman, Russell
★ In the days of the vaqueros; America's first true cowboys. Clarion Bks. 2001 70p il $18; pa $9.99
Grades: 4 5 6 7   **636.2**
1. Cowhands 2. Ranch life 3. Mexican Americans 4. Southwest, New -- History -- Juvenile literature 5. Ranch life -- Southwest, New -- History -- Juvenile literature 6. Southwest, New -- Social life and customs -- Juvenile literature 7. Frontier and pioneer life -- Southwest, New -- Juvenile literature 8. Mexican American cowboys -- Southwest, New -- History -- Juvenile literature
ISBN 0-395-96788-0; 978-0-395-96788-1; 978-0-547-13365-2 pa; 0-547-13365-0 pa
LC 2001-17357

The author "tells the story with depth, clarity, and a vigor that conveys the thrilling excitement of the work and the macho swagger of the culture. . . . The book's design is beautiful, with spacious type on thick paper, and the daz-zling illustrations—prints, paintings, and photos on almost every page." Booklist
Includes glossary and bibliographical references

Peterson, Cris
Clarabelle; making milk and so much more. [by] Cris Peterson; photographs by David R. Lundquist. Boyds Mills Press 2007 un il $16.95
Grades: 1 2 3   **636.2**
1. Cattle 2. Dairying
ISBN 1-59078-310-7; 978-1-59078-310-8

This focuses on "a dairy farm in northern Wisconsin, in-troduced through the daily life of a single cow, Clarabelle. In describing the basics of cow physiology and care and the dairy's operations, Peterson illuminates facts with compari-sons that will grab kids' attention. . . . Lundquist's sharp, close-up photographs . . . . will easily draw curious kids back into the science." Booklist
Includes glossary

Pinkney, Andrea Davis
★ Bill Pickett, rodeo-ridin' cowboy; written by Andrea D. Pinkney; illustrated by Brian Pinkney. Harcourt Brace & Co. 1996 un il hardcover o.p. pa $7
Grades: K 1 2 3   **636.2**
1. Rodeos 2. Cowhands 3. Cowboys 4. African Americans -- Biography
ISBN 0-15-200100-X; 0-15-202103-5 pa
LC 95-35920

Describes the life and accomplishments of the son of a former slave whose unusual bulldogging style made him a rodeo star

"The story is told with verve, relish, and just enough of a cowboy twang, with Pinkney giving an excellent overview of the history of rodeos and black cowboys in a closing note. Husband Brian Pinkney's pictures, in his typical scratch-board technique, are well suited to the story, their lines and colors swirling with movement and excitement on the deep black surface." Booklist
Includes bibliographical references

636.3   Sheep and goats

Minden, Cecilia
  Sheep. Cherry Lake Pub. 2010 24p il (21st century junior library: farm animals) lib bdg $22.80
Grades: 1 2 3   **636.3**
  1. Sheep
  ISBN 978-1-60279-544-0 lib bdg; 1-60279-544-4 lib bdg

                                  LC 2009-3318
This is an introduction to sheep as farm animals
This manages "to parlay [its] low page count into surprisingly deep and wide-ranging discussions on the various aspects of [the sheep's] existence. . . . It's the text that is so impressive, with its use of simple, explanatory language to introduce unusually advanced vocabulary. . . . [The] animal is not only shown in its natural (and often adorable) state but also as meat on a plate. Info boxes called 'Think!' expand the discussion even further." Booklist
Includes glossary and bibliographical references

Urbigkit, Cat
  The shepherd's trail; [by] Cat Urbigkit. Boyds Mills Press 2008 32p il $16.95
Grades: 2 3 4   **636.3**
  1. Sheep 2. Shepherds
  ISBN 978-1-59078-509-6

                                LC 2007017475
This "discusses the migration of domestic sheep in the western U.S. . . . Clear color photos offer close-ups of individual animals and long-range views of the flocks and the often striking landscapes. Topics discussed in the text include the roles of sheepherders, camptenders, herding dogs, guardian dogs, and sheepshearers, as well as details of the sheep's lives through the cycle of a year." Booklist

  A young shepherd. Boyd Mills Press 2006 un il $15.95
Grades: K 1 2 3   **636.3**
  1. Sheep 2. Shepherds 3. Shepherds -- Juvenile literature
  ISBN 1-59078-364-6
  "This photo-essay features a 12-year-old 4-H member (Urbigkit's son) who tends his own flock of sheep. Urbigkit . . . communicates Cass' commitment to his task in compelling photos that showcase the gamboling baby animals. . . . The close-up look at a fascinating, animal-focused activity will appeal even to readers who rarely rub shoulders with livestock." Booklist

636.4   Swine

Gibbons, Gail
  Pigs. Holiday House 1999 un il $16.95; pa $6.95
Grades: K 1 2 3   **636.4**
  1. Pigs
  ISBN 0-8234-1441-8; 0-8234-1554-6 pa

                                  LC 98-28807
Examines the basic characteristics, common breeds, intelligence, behavior, life cycle, and uses of pigs

"Bright with spring greens and yellows, this attractive book introduces pigs through simple sentences and many colorful pictures." Booklist

King-Smith, Dick
  ★ All pigs are beautiful; illustrated by Anita Jeram. Candlewick Press 1993 un il (Read and wonder) hardcover o.p. pa $6.99; pa with audio CD $9.99
Grades: K 1 2 3   **636.4**
  1. Pigs
  ISBN 978-0-7636-1433-1 pa; 0-7636-1433-5 pa; 978-0-7636-4195-5 pa with audio CD; 0-7636-4195-2 pa with audio CD

                                  LC 92-53136
The author "interlards fond reminiscences of porkers he has known with interesting facts about them that are sure to keep children absorbed. His tone is affectionate, amusing, and informative. Jeram's pen-and-ink and watercolor illustrations, done in soft, earthy colors, are a warm match for the text." SLJ

Minden, Cecilia
  Pigs. Cherry Lake Pub. 2010 24p il (21st century junior library: farm animals) lib bdg $22.80
Grades: 1 2 3   **636.4**
  1. Pigs
  ISBN 978-1-60279-542-6 lib bdg; 1-60279-542-8 lib bdg

                                  LC 2009-3676
This is an introduction to pigs as farm animals
This manages "to parlay [its] low page count into surprisingly deep and wide-ranging discussions on the various aspects of [the pig's] existence. . . . It's the text that is so impressive, with its use of simple, explanatory language to introduce unusually advanced vocabulary. . . . [The] animal is not only shown in its natural (and often adorable) state but also as meat on a plate. Info boxes called 'Think!' expand the discussion even further ([The book] encourages readers to ask why some of their friends may not eat pork)." Booklist
Includes glossary and bibliographical references

Rockwood, Leigh
  Pigs are smart! PowerKids Press 2010 24p il (Super smart animals) lib bdg $21.25; pa $8.25
Grades: 2 3 4 5   **636.4**
  1. Pigs
  ISBN 978-1-4358-9373-3 lib bdg; 1-4358-9373-5 lib bdg; 978-1-4358-9834-9 pa; 1-4358-9834-6 pa
  Examines the intelligence of pigs
  "Readers get an overview of the . . . [pig's] life cycle, its domestic history (where relevant), and natural habitat, and examples of how it is smart in the wild as well as when helped by human tutelage. . . . Interesting color photographs and large, easy-to-read print will attract browsers and report writers alike." SLJ
  Includes glossary

636.5 Chickens and other kinds of domestic birds

Dickmann, Nancy

A **chicken's** life. Heinemann Library 2011 24p il (Watch it grow) lib bdg $21.50; pa $5.99

Grades: PreK K 1   **636.5**

1. Chickens

ISBN 978-1-4329-4139-0 lib bdg; 1-4329-4139-9 lib bdg; 978-1-4329-4148-2 pa; 1-4329-4148-8 pa

LC 2009-49153

"Practically unique among early introductions to life cycles because death is mentioned . . . this . . . follows [a chicken] . . . from egg . . . to maturity with a set of close-up color photographs, one per page, paired to large-type, one or two-sentence captions. . . . Offers nourishing fare for young naturalists." SLJ

Includes glossary and bibliographical references

Gibbons, Gail

Chicks & chickens. Holiday House 2003 un il $17.95; pa $6.95

Grades: K 1 2 3   **636.5**

1. Chickens

ISBN 0-8234-1700-X; 0-8234-1939-8 pa

LC 2002-27472

An introduction to the physical characteristics, behavior, and life cycle of chickens, as well as a discussion of how chickens are raised on farms

The author "offers lots of solid information as well as bits of trivia that will be of interest to this audience. Cartoon illustrations are large, colorful, and plentiful." SLJ

Heppermann, Christine

City chickens; by Christine Heppermann. Houghton Mifflin Books for Children 2012 47 p. ill. (chiefly col.) (hardcover) $16.99; (ebook) $16.99

Grades: 4 5   **636.5**

1. Animal housing 2. Animal behavior 3. Birds -- Protection 4. Chickens 5. Animal welfare 6. Animal shelters 7. Chickens -- Minnesota -- Anecdotes -- Juvenile literature 8. Animal welfare -- Minnesota -- Anecdotes -- Juvenile literature 9. Animal shelters -- Minnesota -- Anecdotes -- Juvenile literature

ISBN 0547518307; 9780547518305; 9780547518336

LC 2011009754

In author Christine Hepperman's book, she provides stories of adopted chickens. "Just outside of downtown Minneapolis, follow the sounds of crowing and clucking and you will find Mary Britton Clouse's Chicken Run Rescue. Over the years, Mary and her husband have given hundreds of homeless birds a safe place to rest until they can be adopted by caring families." (Publisher's note)

Includes bibliographical references.

Kindschi, Tara

4-H guide to raising chickens. Voyageur Press 2010 176p il pa $18.99

Grades: 5 6 7 8   **636.5**

1. Chickens

ISBN 978-0-7603-3628-1 pa; 0-7603-3628-8 pa

LC 2009015300

"This title has everything one ever wanted to know about chickens but didn't know enough to ask. Eight chapters di-

vide the text into broad topics such as getting started, choosing a breed, housing equipment, and exhibiting chickens. . . . Line drawings and charts give additional information, and the excellent color photography is profuse." SLJ

Includes glossary and bibliographical references

Minden, Cecilia

Ducks. Cherry Lake Pub. 2010 24p il (21st century junior library: farm animals) lib bdg $22.80

Grades: 1 2 3   **636.5**

1. Ducks

ISBN 978-1-60279-546-4 lib bdg; 1-60279-546-0 lib bdg

LC 2009-5033

This is an introduction to ducks as farm animals

This manages "to parlay [its] low page count into surprisingly deep and wide-ranging discussions on the various aspects of [the duck's] existence. . . . It's the text that is so impressive, with its use of simple, explanatory language to introduce unusually advanced vocabulary. In [this book] readers learn such terminology as clutch, dabbling, and gland. . . . [The] animal is not only shown in its natural (and often adorable) state but also as meat on a plate. Info boxes called 'Think!' expand the discussion even further." Booklist

Includes glossary and bibliographical references

Sklansky, Amy E.

Where do chicks come from? illustrated by Pam Paparone. HarperCollins Publishers 2005 un il (Let's-read-and-find-out science) hardcover o.p. pa $4.99

Grades: K 1 2   **636.5**

1. Eggs 2. Chickens 3. Chickens -- Life cycles -- Juvenile literature

ISBN 0-06-028892-2; 0-06-028893-0 lib bdg; 0-06-445212-3 pa

LC 2003-7711

Describes what happens day-by-day for the three weeks from the time a hen lays an egg until the baby chick hatches

This offers "clear and accurate text. . . . The illustrations are soft and friendly, but retain enough realism for children to understand the subject matter. . . . This is an enjoyable and informative introduction to scientific information." SLJ

Wearing, Judy

Chickens. Weigl 2011 24p il (World of wonder: watch them grow) lib bdg $25.70; pa $9.95

Grades: 1 2   **636.5**

1. Eggs 2. Chickens

ISBN 978-1-60596-913-8 lib bdg; 1-60596-913-3 lib bdg; 978-1-60596-914-5 pa; 1-60596-914-1 pa

LC 2009050943

Learn about the transition these birds make from egg to chick, and finally, to full-grown chicken.

The text is "well-written, providing examples that put a human face to each problem. Quotes and facts are clearly attributed, and their sources are noted in the extensive back matter. . . . Sidebars provide further information, or, more compellingly, offer stories about those touched by the topic. . . . [This] will be of great assistance to students writing reports." Libr Media Connect

Includes glossary and bibliographical references

636.6 Birds other than poultry

Altman, Linda Jacobs

Parrots. Benchmark Bks. 1999 32p il (Perfect pets)
lib bdg $28.50

Grades: 3 4 5 6   **636.6**

1. Pets 2. Parrots 3. Parrots -- Juvenile literature
ISBN 0-7614-1102-X

LC 99-49672

Provides information about the history, physical characteristics, choosing, and care of all kinds of parrots

"The writing is clear and informative. . . . Colorful,
nicely detailed, framed photographs and reproductions of
the animals are interspersed throughout." SLJ

Includes glossary and bibliographical references

Bozzo, Linda

My first bird; [by] Linda Bozzo. Enslow Elementary
2007 32p il (My first pet library from the American Humane Association) lib bdg $22.60

Grades: 1 2 3   **636.6**

1. Cage birds
ISBN 978-0-7660-2749-7 lib bdg; 0-7660-2749-X
lib bdg

LC 2006008405

"The material is brief, providing a general overview. .
. . [Illustrated with] attractive, heartwarming color photographs." SLJ

Includes glossary and bibliographical references

Haney, Johannah

Parrots. Marshall Cavendish Benchmark 2008 48p il
(Great pets) lib bdg $29.93

Grades: 2 3 4   **636.6**

1. Parrots
ISBN 978-0-7614-2998-2 lib bdg; 0-7614-2998-0
lib bdg

LC 2008-24335

"Describes the characteristics and behavior of pet parrots, also discussing their physical appearance and place in
history." Publisher's note

Includes glossary and bibliographical references

Small birds. Marshall Cavendish Benchmark 2010
46p il (Great pets) lib bdg $29.93

Grades: 2 3 4   **636.6**

1. Cage birds
ISBN 978-0-7614-4150-2 lib bdg; 0-7614-4150-6
lib bdg

LC 2008037258

"Describes the characteristics and behavior of small pet
birds, also discussing their physical appearance and place in
history." Publisher's note

Includes glossary and bibliographical references

Jeffrey, Laura S.

Birds; how to choose and care for a bird. Enslow Publishers 2004 48p il (American humane pet care library)
lib bdg $23.93

Grades: 3 4 5   **636.6**

1. Pets 2. Birds 3. Birds as pets 4. Cage birds --
Juvenile literature
ISBN 0-7660-2515-2

LC 2003-22966

Provides information on keeping birds as pets, including
how to choose and care for a bird

Includes bibliographical references and index

Mead, Wendy

Top 10 birds for kids; [by] Wendy Mead. Enslow Publishers 2008 48p il (Top pets for kids with American Humane) lib bdg $23.93

Grades: 2 3 4 5   **636.6**

1. Pets 2. Cage birds
ISBN 978-0-7660-3072-5 lib bdg; 0-7660-3072-5
lib bdg

LC 2007-38479

"Includes beautiful full-color photos showing the animals at their best. Judicious use of text boxes, crisp fonts,
and white space will make it easy for readers to follow the
flow of information." SLJ

Includes glossary and bibliographical references

Niven, Felicia Lowenstein

Learning to care for a bird. Enslow Publishers 2010
48p il (Beginning pet care with American Humane) lib
bdg $23.93

Grades: 2 3 4   **636.6**

1. Cage birds
ISBN 978-0-7660-3192-0; 0-7660-3192-6

LC 2008048964

"Readers will learn how to choose, train, and care for a
bird." Publisher's note

Includes glossary and bibliographical references

Rockwood, Leigh

Parrots are smart! PowerKids Press 2010 24p il (Super smart animals) lib bdg $21.25; pa $8.25

Grades: 2 3 4 5   **636.6**

1. Parrots
ISBN 978-1-4358-9376-4 lib bdg; 1-4358-9376-X lib
bdg; 978-1-4358-9844-8 pa; 1-4358-9844-3 pa
Examines the intelligence of parrots.

"Bright, colorful, captioned photographs complement
the text. Rockwood does an excellent job of simplifying the
information without making the text choppy or boring." Libr
Media Connect

Includes glossary and bibliographical references

Spinner, Stephanie

Alex the parrot; no ordinary bird. by Stephanie Spinner; illustrations by Meilo So. Alfred A. Knopf 2012 41
p. $17.99

Grades: 1 2 3 4   **636.6**

1. Birds 2. Parrots 3. Animal intelligence 4. African
gray parrot -- Juvenile literature
ISBN 0375868461; 9780375868467; 9780375968464

LC 2011014381

In this picture-book biography, author Stephanie Spinner tells the story of how "Irene Pepperberg's African gray
parrot learned to speak and understand English so well [that]
he changed both public and scientific beliefs about animal
communication and cognition. Named Alex, for Avian
Learning Experiment, the parrot was randomly acquired
from a pet shop for graduate student Pepperberg's research."
(Kirkus Reviews)

636.7 Dogs

Altman, Linda Jacobs
Big dogs. Benchmark Bks. 2001 32p il (Perfect pets)
lib bdg $15.95
Grades: 3 4 5 6   636.7
1. Dogs 2. Pets
ISBN 0-7614-1101-1
                                        LC 99-49674
Provides information about the history, physical char-
acteristics, choice, training and care of various breeds of
large dogs
Includes glossary and bibliographical references

American Kennel Club
★ The **Complete** dog book for kids; official publication of the American Kennel Club. Howell Book House
1996 274p il maps hardcover o.p. pa $22.95
Grades: 4 5 6 7   636.7
1. Dogs
ISBN 0-87605-458-0; 0-87605-460-2 pa
                                        LC 96-29228
This "begins with a general section that advises readers
on buying a dog, responsibilities, rewards, and how to match
a dog with one's situation. . . . More than 100 dogs are profiled, with information on history, appearance, health, and
'fun facts.' Crisp color photographs accompany each article.
. . . A final section gives good advice about nutrition and
health issues." Booklist

Baines, Becky
Everything dogs; All the canine facts, photos, and fun
that you can get your paws on! by Becky Baines; with Dr.
Gary Weitzman. National Geographic 2012 64 p. col. ill.
(paperback) $12.95; (library) $21.90
Grades: 3 4 5   636.7
1. Picture books for children 2. Dogs -- Juvenile
literature
ISBN 1426310242; 1426310250; 9781426310249;
9781426310256
                                        LC 2012289035
This book by Becky Baines looks at dogs. "Baines starts
with the basics ('What is a dog?') and moves on to discuss
small and large breeds, answer doggie-related questions
('Why do dogs roll in smelly stuff?'), and imagine your pet's
daily schedule. . . . This also presents a chart for decoding
canine moods and looks at the dog family, which includes
coyotes, dingoes, and jackals, among others." (Booklist)
Includes bibliographical references (page 62) and index.

Barnes, Julia
Pet dogs; [by] Julia Barnes. Gareth Stevens Pub. 2007
un il (Pet pals) lib bdg $23.93
Grades: 2 3 4 5   636.7
1. Dogs
ISBN 0-8368-6777-7
                                        LC 2006042378
This places dogs "within the context of [their] wild roots
and [their] relationship to humans. . . . Barnes explains what
makes the animal an ideal pet, recommends how to be a
good caregiver, and reveals how the creature communicates
(as well as how to answer). The [book mixes] practical advice with trivia in a way that children will find informative

and easy to navigate. Crisp, full-color photos enhance the
[text]." SLJ
Includes glossary and bibliographical references

Bial, Raymond
Rescuing Rover; saving America's dogs. Houghton
Mifflin 2011 80p il
Grades: 4 5 6 7   636.7
1. Dogs 2. Animal welfare
ISBN 0-547-34125-3; 978-0-547-34125-5
                                        LC 2010025123
"This accessible, amply illustrated title offers and in-
formative introduction to canine-rescue endeavors. After
recounting his own moving story of adopting a rescue dog,
Bial provides a history of human-dog relationships. . . . Bial
also explores rescue organizations, such as the ASPCA. . . .
Bial frankly discusses the abuse many dogs experience . . . as
well as euthanasia. . . . Historical and contemporary photos;
extensive book lists . . .; websites; and detailed index complete this well-presented resource." Booklist
Includes bibliographical references

Bidner, Jenni
Is my dog a wolf? how your pet compares to its wild
cousin. Lark Books 2006 64p il $9.95
Grades: 3 4 5 6   636.7
1. Dogs 2. Wolves 3. Wolves -- Juvenile literature
ISBN 978-1-57990-732-7; 1-57990-732-6
                                        LC 2005-34865
"This book identifies instinctual behaviors in wolves,
such as pack living, licking and biting at one another, and
howling, and describes how they are manifested in the common house dog, even though the species changed thousands
of years ago. . . . Clear color photographs beautifully illustrate the text. This informative, entertaining title is suitable
for reports and for general reading." SLJ

Biniok, Janice
The **miniature** schnauzer. Eldorado Ink 2010 112p il
(Our best friends) lib bdg $34.95
Grades: 4 5 6 7   636.7
1. Dogs
ISBN 978-1-932904-61-1 lib bdg; 1-932904-61-1
lib bdg
"The Our Best Friends series continues to be an ideal
resource for those kids (or even adults) looking for a cradle-
to-grave primer on responsible pet ownership. . . . These
[books] offer far more than the customary cursory enticements and warnings usually aimed at first-time animal
caregivers, with in-depth information on health issues and
extensive explanations of the various types of species. . .
. This is required (if sobering) reading for the serious pet
owner." Booklist
Includes bibliographical references

The **rottweiler**. Eldorado Ink 2010 112p il (Our best
friends) lib bdg $34.95
Grades: 4 5 6 7   636.7
1. Dogs
ISBN 978-1-932904-64-2 lib bdg; 1-932904-64-6
lib bdg
"The Our Best Friends series continues to be an ideal
resource for those kids (or even adults) looking for a cradle-
to-grave primer on responsible pet ownership. . . . These

[books] offer far more than the customary cursory enticements and warnings usually aimed at first-time animal
caregivers, with in-depth information on health issues and
extensive explanations of the various types of species. . .
. This is required (if sobering) reading for the serious pet
owner." Booklist

Includes bibliographical references

Bozzo, Linda

Fire dog heroes. Enslow Publishers 2010 48p il
(Amazing working dogs with American Humane) lib bdg
$23.93

Grades: 2 3 4　　　　　　　　　　　　　**636.7**

1. Arson 2. Working dogs 3. Fire fighting

ISBN 978-0-7660-3202-6; 0-7660-3202-7

LC 2008048019

"The text opens with a true story of an arson dog, and
then it explains the history of the arson K-9 team and the
training methods used to transform an ordinary dog into a
canine hero." Publisher's note

Includes glossary and bibliographical references

My first dog; [by] Linda Bozzo. Enslow Elementary
2007 32p il (My first pet library from the American Humane Association) lib bdg $22.60

Grades: 1 2 3　　　　　　　　　　　　　**636.7**

1. Dogs

ISBN 978-0-7660-2754-1 lib bdg; 0-7660-2754-6
lib bdg

LC 2006008404

"The material is brief, providing a general overview. .
. . [Illustrated with] attractive, heartwarming color photographs." SLJ

Includes glossary and bibliographical references

Search and rescue dog heroes. Enslow Publishers 2010
48p il (Amazing working dogs with American Humane) lib
bdg $23.93

Grades: 2 3 4　　　　　　　　　　　　　**636.7**

1. Rescue dogs

ISBN 978-0-7660-3201-9; 0-7660-3201-9

LC 2008048018

"The text opens with a true story of a search and rescue
(SAR) dog, and then it explains the history of the SAR K-9
team and the training methods used to transform an ordinary
dog into a canine hero." Publisher's note

Includes glossary and bibliographical references

Calmenson, Stephanie

May I pet your dog? the how-to guide for kids meeting dogs (and dogs meeting kids) by Stephanie Calmenson;
illustrated by Jan Ormerod. Clarion Books 2007 32p il
$9.95

Grades: PreK K 1 2　　　　　　　　　　　**636.7**

1. Dogs 2. Dogs -- Juvenile literature

ISBN 978-0-618-51034-4; 0-618-51034-6

LC 2005-34955

Harry the dog explains how to safely meet him and
his friends.

"Straightforward guidelines and a positive, encouraging
tone make this book appealing and practical. Young dog lovers will delight in the variety of breeds shown in the bright,
clear illustrations." SLJ

Rosie; a visiting dog's story. photographs by Justin Sutcliffe. Clarion Bks. 1994 47p il hardcover o.p. pa $6.95

Grades: K 1 2 3　　　　　　　　　　　　　**636.7**

1. Dogs 2. Pet therapy -- Juvenile literature 3. Dogs
-- Training -- Juvenile literature

ISBN 0-395-65477-7; 0-395-92722-6 pa

LC 93-21243

"Rosie is the true story of an endearing Tibetan terrier
who works as a therapy dog with Delta Society's Pet Partners Program of New York City. Rosie's tenderness and enthusiasm come through in Sutcliffe's fantastic photos that
chronicle Rosie's training and first visit to a children's hospital and a nursing home." Child Book Rev Serv

Carnesi, Monica

Little dog lost; a true story of a brave dog named Baltic.
Nancy Paulsen Books 2012 il $15.99

Grades: PreK K　　　　　　　　　　　　　**636.7**

1. Dogs 2. Animal rescue

ISBN 978-0-399-25666-0; 0-399-25666-0

On a cold winter day, a curious dog wandered onto a
frozen river, and before he knew it he was traveling fast on a
sheet of ice. Many people tried to help, but the dog could not
be reached. Finally, after two nights and seventy-five miles,
the little dog was saved by a ship out in the Baltic Sea.

"The story is told simply and charmingly. The author's
use of the present tense gives the narrative immediacy, and
with very brief sentences, some dialogue and questions
posed to readers, Carnesi imbues the tale with a strong sense
of drama that will captivate young listeners." Kirkus

Coren, Stanley

Why do dogs have wet noses? Kids Can Press 2006
63p il $14.95; pa $9.95

Grades: 3 4 5 6　　　　　　　　　　　　　**636.7**

1. Dogs 2. Dogs -- Juvenile literature

ISBN 1-55337-657-9; 1-55337-658-7 pa

"This interesting, entertaining book has chapters on
'How Humans and Dogs Became Friends,' 'How Dogs See
the World,' 'How Dogs Talk,' and 'How Dogs Think.' The
question-and-answer format is interspersed with facts and
stories in sidebars. . . . . Beautiful full-color photos show
many breeds." SLJ

Crosby, Jeff

Little lions, bull baiters & hunting hounds; a history
of dog breeds. written and illustrated by Jeff Crosby and
Shelley Ann Jackson. Tundra Books 2008 72p il $19.95

Grades: 2 3 4 5　　　　　　　　　　　　　**636.7**

1. Dogs

ISBN 978-0-88776-815-6; 0-88776-815-6

LC 2007927387

"Featuring more than breeds that are categorized as
hunting, herding, working, or companion dogs, this attractive volume includes interesting and sometimes unusual
facts about canines. . . . The painterly illustrations are often
action-packed. . . . There is also a brief history of the origin
of dogs and a succinct look at mixed breeds. . . . This is a
great browsing book." SLJ

Includes bibliographical references

Dennis, Brian

★ **Nubs**; the true story of a mutt, a Marine & a miracle. by Brian Dennis, Kirby Larson, and Mary Nethery. Little, Brown Books for Young Readers 2009 un il $17.99

Grades: K 1 2 3 **636.7**

1. Dogs 2. Iraq War, 2003-2011 -- Personal narratives

ISBN 978-0-316-05318-1; 0-316-05318-X

LC 2009003808

This is a "hugely inspirational true account. . . . The gritty, low-res shots of the two companions against the bleak Iraqi horizon are married with text so gracefully that many of the compositions could be book jackets." Booklist

Gaines, Ann

Top 10 dogs for kids; [by] Ann Graham Gaines. Enslow Publishers 2008 48p il (Top pets for kids with American Humane) lib bdg $23.93

Grades: 2 3 4 5 **636.7**

1. Dogs

ISBN 978-0-7660-3070-1 lib bdg; 0-7660-3070-9 lib bdg

LC 2007-24510

"Includes beautiful full-color photos showing the animals at their best. Judicious use of text boxes, crisp fonts, and white space will make it easy for readers to follow the flow of information." SLJ

Includes glossary and bibliographical references

George, Jean Craighead

★ **How** to talk to your dog; illustrated by Sue Truesdell. HarperCollins Pubs. 2000 26p il $9.95

Grades: 2 3 4 **636.7**

1. Dogs 2. Pets 3. Human-animal communication 4. Dogs -- Behavior -- Juvenile literature

ISBN 0-06-027092-6

LC 98-41515

Describes how dogs communicate with people through their behavior and sounds and explains how to talk back to them using sounds, behavior, and body language

"The mixed photography (of George, representing the humans) and illustration (an endearingly scruffy yellow mutt is the main canine representative) is . . . effective. . . . This will be an accessible and perhaps paradigm-shifting introduction for young readers." Bull Cent Child Books

Gewirtz, Elaine Waldorf

Fetch this book. Eldorado Ink 2010 112p il (Our best friends) lib bdg $34.95

Grades: 4 5 6 7 **636.7**

1. Dogs -- Training

ISBN 978-1-932904-60-4 lib bdg; 1-932904-60-3 lib bdg

This "is a dog-training manual, with pet-care advice only in reference to training. [This] well-written [book provides] examples to support [its] points and solid online and text resources and feature [a] clean, uncluttered [layout]. . . . There is plenty of practical information that motivated readers can glean from [this title]." SLJ

Includes bibliographical references

The **bulldog**. Eldorado Ink 2010 112p il (Our best friends) lib bdg $34.95

Grades: 4 5 6 7 **636.7**

1. Dogs

ISBN 978-1-932904-58-1 lib bdg; 1-932904-58-1 lib bdg

"The Our Best Friends series continues to be an ideal resource for those kids (or even adults) looking for a cradle-to-grave primer on responsible pet ownership. These [books] offer far more than the customary cursory enticements and warnings usually aimed at first-time animal caregivers, with in-depth information on health issues and extensive explanations of the various types of species. . . . This is required (if sobering) reading for the serious pet owner." Booklist

Includes bibliographical references

Gibbons, Gail

Dogs. Holiday House 1996 32p il $16.95; pa $6.95

Grades: K 1 2 3 **636.7**

1. Dogs

ISBN 0-8234-1226-1; 0-8234-1335-7 pa

LC 95-24966

An introduction to dogs including their history, types of breeds, senses, and ways of communication

"There is something for all dog enthusiasts here. A good choice for both reports and pleasure reading." SLJ

Goldish, Meish

Ground zero dogs; by Meish Goldish. Bearport Pub. 2013 32 p. col. ill. (library binding) $25.27

Grades: 2 3 4 **636.7**

1. Search dogs 2. Picture books for children 3. September 11 terrorist attacks, 2001 4. Rescue dogs -- Juvenile literature 5. September 11 Terrorist Attacks, 2001 -- Juvenile literature

ISBN 1617725765; 9781617725760

LC 2012003341

This children's picture book is part of the Dog Heroes series. The book introduces "readers to a select few of the roughly 300 search-and-rescue dogs that used their agile feet and powerful senses of smell . . . to locate both survivors and bodies among the World Trade Center rubble. . . . Salty helped his blind owner escape alive from the seventy-first floor, and Trakr uncovered a woman who had been buried for 24 hours." (Booklist)

Includes bibliographical references and index

Goodman, Susan E.

It's a dog's life; how man's best friend sees, hears, and smells the world. written by Susan E. Goodman; illustrated by David Slonim. 1st ed. Roaring Brook Press 2012 32 p. col. ill.

Grades: 2 3 4 **636.7**

1. Dogs -- Juvenile literature 2. Dogs -- Juvenile humor 3. Dogs -- Behavior -- Juvenile literature 4. Dogs -- Evolution -- Juvenile literature

ISBN 9781596434486

LC 2011022965

This book by Susan E. Goodman and illustrated by David Slonim focuses on dog breeds and dog behavior. "Have you ever wondered what your dog sees when he looks at a sunset? Or what she smells when she has her nose to the ground? And what IS your pooch trying to say when he looks at you with those big puppy eyes? . . . [Goodman] answers those questions and a whole lot more." (Publisher's note)

Includes bibliographical references.

Gorrell, Gena K.

Working like a dog; the story of working dogs through history. Tundra 2003 156p il pa $16.95

Grades: 4 5 6 7   **636.7**

1. Working dogs

ISBN 0-88776-589-0

"Gorrell begins by tracing the evolution of 'household canids' from the wild into the civilized world. Other chapters delve into the many ways in which these animals have been viewed throughout history, what makes particular breeds right for certain jobs, dogs at war, famous pooches, etc. . . . The well-captioned, black-and-white photographs and reproductions add greatly to a narrative that's packed with intriguing details." SLJ

Includes bibliographical references

Grogan, John

Marley; a dog like no other. Collins 2007 196p il $16.99; lib bdg $17.89

Grades: 4 5 6   **636.7**

1. Dogs 2. Journalists 3. Memoirists 4. Labrador retriever -- Juvenile literature

ISBN 978-0-06-124033-1; 978-0-06-124034-8 lib bdg

LC 2007-08600

"Grogan's anecdotal adaptation of his bestselling memoir, Marley & Me: Life and Love with the World's Worst Dog speaks to a middle-grade audience. . . . The narrative maintains all the energy, humor and poignancy of the adult book. . . . Grogan leaves young readers with fond memories of this exasperating yet thoroughly endearing creature." Publ Wkly

Hart, Joyce

Big dogs; by Joyce Hart. Marshall Cavendish Benchmark 2008 48p il (Great pets) lib bdg $29.93

Grades: 2 3 4   **636.7**

1. Dogs

ISBN 978-0-7614-2707-0 lib bdg; 0-7614-2707-4 lib bdg

LC 2007013042

This is an "enthusiastic, warm [introduction]. . . . [It is] clearly written and [is] the most thorough, honest [introduction] to owning [big dogs] for this audience." SLJ

Includes glossary and bibliographical references

Small dogs. Marshall Cavendish Benchmark 2008 48p il (Great pets) lib bdg $29.93

Grades: 2 3 4   **636.7**

1. Dogs

ISBN 978-0-7614-2995-1 lib bdg; 0-7614-2995-6 lib bdg

LC 2007-36784

"Describes the characteristics and behavior of small dogs, also discussing their physical appearance and place in history." Publisher's note

Includes glossary and bibliographical references

Hoffman, Mary Ann

Guard dogs. Gareth Stevens Pub. 2011 24p il (Working dogs) lib bdg $22.60; pa $8.15

Grades: 2 3 4   **636.7**

1. Working dogs

ISBN 978-1-4339-4647-9 lib bdg; 1-4339-4647-5 lib bdg; 978-1-4339-4648-6 pa; 1-4339-4648-3 pa

LC 2010035241

This describes guard "dogs and the training they receive. The short chapters, complemented by numerous color photographs, provide examples of particular breeds that do [this] job and show how their characteristics are suited for the tasks. The charts provided are especially helpful, covering commands and more specific tasks. There is enough information to make the [text] feel fresh. . . . A solid choice for readers looking for more than cute pictures." SLJ

Herding dogs. Gareth Stevens Pub. 2011 24p il (Working dogs) lib bdg $22.60; pa $8.15

Grades: 2 3 4   **636.7**

1. Dogs

ISBN 978-1-4339-4655-4 lib bdg; 1-4339-4655-6 lib bdg; 978-1-4339-4656-1 pa; 1-4339-4656-4 pa

LC 2010035243

This describes herding "dogs and the training they receive. The short chapters, complemented by numerous color photographs, provide examples of particular breeds that do [this] job and show how their characteristics are suited for the tasks. The charts provided are especially helpful, covering commands and more specific tasks. There is enough information to make the [text] feel fresh. . . . A solid choice for readers looking for more than cute pictures." SLJ

Holub, Joan

★ **Why** do dogs bark? Dial Bks. for Young Readers 2001 48p il (Dial easy-to-read) $13.99

Grades: K 1 2   **636.7**

1. Dogs

ISBN 0-8037-2504-3

LC 00-23984

Questions and answers present information about the origins, behavior, and characteristics of dogs and their interaction with humans

This book combines "appealing color photos and sprightly cartoons with an informative, easy-to-read text." Booklist

Houston, Dick

Bulu, African wonder dog. Random House 2010 323p il $15.99; lib bdg $18.99

Grades: 5 6 7 8   **636.7**

1. Dogs 2. Wildlife conservation

ISBN 978-0-375-84723-3; 0-375-84723-5; 978-0-375-94720-9 lib bdg; 0-375-94720-5 lib bdg

LC 2009015804

"In the Nyanja language, bulu means 'wild dog,' and that's what Steve and Anna Tolan named the beloved little Jack Russell mix they adopted. Disregarding warnings about the dangers of raising a dog in the bush, the Tolans moved from England to rural Zambia to fulfill their lifelong dream of setting up an animal rescue and conservation center. . . . Bulu's energy, high spirits, and loyalty to his masters make the book read like a praise song to dogs. Houston's account is an animal-lover's delight, complete with the action-adventure of surviving the bush, fighting poachers, and spreading a message of conservation." Booklist

Huneck, Stephen

Even bad dogs go to heaven; more from the dog chapel. Abrams 2010 un il $19.95

Grades: 2 3 4   **636.7**

1. Dogs 2. Bereavement

ISBN 978-0-8109-9629-8; 0-8109-9629-4

"After recovering from a near-fatal illness, Huneck established a chapel dedicated to the relationship between dogs and their owners on his property in Vermont. . . . The introduction is lengthy . . . but touching. It is illustrated with color photographs of the small chapel. . . . Following the introduction, the artist presents about 30 short sayings about dogs, one per spread, in large informal print and illustrates each one with his characteristic style. The sayings are clever and celebrate the richness that pets bring to life. They also offer comfort for those who might have lost a beloved canine friend. The illustrations are simple and solid, but brightly colored and have a gentle humor of their own." SLJ

Jackson, Emma

A home for Dixie; the true story of a rescued puppy. by Emma Jackson, with full-color photographs by Bob Carey. Collins 2008 un il $16.99; lib bdg $17.89

Grades: 1 2 3 4   **636.7**

1. Dogs

ISBN 978-0-06-144962-8; 0-06-144962-8; 978-0-06-144963-5 lib bdg; 0-06-144963-6 lib bdg

LC 2008-006049

"In this photo-essay, the author, a high school student, chronicles her quest for a puppy, her family's decision to adopt one, and their trip to Aunt Mary's Doghouse—a non-profit rescue agency—to find the right animal. . . . The book's strengths are the large, full-color, often full-page photos of the appealing pup and her new owner. The Web sites recommended for potential pet owners are regularly updated." SLJ

Jeffrey, Laura S.

Dogs; how to choose and care for a dog. Enslow Publishers 2004 48p il (American humane pet care library) lib bdg $23.93

Grades: 3 4 5   **636.7**

1. Dogs 2. Pets

ISBN 0-7660-2520-9

LC 2003-22971

Explains who to consult, where to go to pick the right dog, and how to keep them happy and healthy

Includes glossary and bibliographical references

Jenkins, Steve

★ Dogs and cats; written and illustrated by Steve Jenkins. Houghton Mifflin Co. 2007 un il $16

Grades: 1 2 3 4   **636.7**

1. Cats 2. Dogs 3. Cats -- Juvenile literature 4. Dogs -- Juvenile literature

ISBN 978-0-618-50767-2; 0-618-50767-1

LC 2006-24654

"The lively narrative provides a copious amount of information, examining each species in human history, describing evolution and domestication, highlighting physical characteristics and behaviors, and finishing up with amazing facts about each animal. The layout is excellent, with images dominating the text. Jenkins's cut and torn-paper collages are stunning." SLJ

Johnson, Jinny

Dogs and puppies; [by] Jinny Johnson. Smart Apple Media 2008 32p il (Get to know your pet) $27.10

Grades: 3 4 5 6   **636.7**

1. Dogs

ISBN 978-1-59920-089-7; 1-59920-089-9

LC 2007-52598

"Spreads include in-depth care instruction, and 'Q & A' sidebars that answer common behavioral questions. . . . The layout is clear, with full color photos and illustrations breaking up the text." SLJ

Includes glossary

Katz, Jon

★ Meet the dogs of Bedlam Farm; a true story. Henry Holt and Company 2011 un il $16.99

Grades: K 1 2 3   **636.7**

1. Farm life 2. Working dogs

ISBN 978-0-8050-9219-6; 0-8050-9219-6

LC 2010011698

"Border collies Rose and Izzy; Frieda, a rottweiler/German shepherd mix; and black Lab Lenore are four dogs living on Bedlam Farm in Upstate New York. Katz lives on the farm and has written about it for older audiences. . . . The large, full-color photographs are totally engaging and capture the animals' distinct personalities. . . . The writing is crisp and clear, and the stories (each dog gets its own turn) are sweet and filled with gentle humor." SLJ

Kehret, Peg

Shelter dogs; amazing stories of adopted strays. Whitman, A. 1999 un il $14.95

Grades: 3 4 5   **636.7**

1. Dogs 2. Animal shelters 3. Dog adoption 4. Dogs -- United States -- Anecdotes -- Juvenile literature 5. Dog adoption -- United States -- Anecdotes -- Juvenile literature 6. Animal shelters -- United States -- Anecdotes -- Juvenile literature

ISBN 0-8075-7334-5

LC 98-34760

Tells the stories of eight stray dogs that were adopted from animal shelters and went on to become service dogs, actors, and heroes

"The writing is clear and straightforward, letting the drama and pathos of the dogs' triumphs, and the owners' dedication, carry the stories." SLJ

Laidlaw, Rob

No shelter here; Making the world a kinder place for dogs. Rob Laidlaw. Pajama Press 2012 63 p.

Grades: 3 4 5 6 7 8   **636.7**

1. Dogs 2. Animal rights 3. Animal welfare

ISBN 0986949558; 9780986949555

This book provides an "informative and visually varied introduction to problems affecting dogs worldwide. In a short, colorful volume with sidebars and photographs on nearly every page, professional dog advocate [Rob] Laidlaw . . . presents facts about how dogs live, provides an overview of the cruelty dogs face at the hands of humans and offers profiles of young activists who are working to better dogs' lives. . . . A list of animal welfare websites points interested readers toward further information." (Kirkus)

Includes bibliographical references and index.

Lunis, Natalie

Greyhound; canine blur! Bearport Pub. 2011 24p il map (Blink of an eye. Superfast animals!) lib bdg $22.61
Grades: 1 2 3   **636.7**

1. Dogs 2. Animal locomotion

ISBN 978-1-936087-90-7; 1-936087-90-1

LC 2010010576

This describes the greyhound dog, including where it was first bred, why it was so helpful to hunters, and the ways its body helps it reach its record-breaking speeds.

This "is sure to appeal to a wide variety of readers. Vibrant photos illustrate each animal from multiple perspectives, providing opportunity for readers to closely examine the animal. Information is organized by subject heading and branches into the animal's physical features and how they contribute to its speed, the animal's natural predators, and how the animal makes use of speed as a means of survival. . . This . . . will be a worthwhile addition to your nonfiction collection." Libr Media Connect

Includes glossary and bibliographical references

McCarthy, Meghan

The **incredible** life of Balto. Alfred A. Knopf 2011 un il $16.99; lib bdg $19.99
Grades: K 1 2   **636.7**

1. Sled dogs 2. Diphtheria 3. Balto (Dog) -- Juvenile literature

ISBN 978-0-375-84460-7; 0-375-84460-0; 978-0-375-94460-4 lib bdg; 0-375-94460-5 lib bdg

LC 2009-52707

"After making an arduous journey to deliver medicine to combat diphtheria in Nome, Alaska, in 1925, Balto and his owner at first enjoy fame. But after a statue and a starring movie role, Balto's fortunes change when he's sold to a vaudeville act. . . . Straightforward narration keeps this picture-book biography moving toward its happy conclusion. . . . It's an accessible introduction to the story of Balto, and a reminder of the fickle nature of fame." Publ Wkly

Mehus-Roe, Kristin

Dogs for kids! everything you need to know about dogs. by Kristin Mehus-Roe. BowTie Press 2007 384p il pa $14.95
Grades: 4 5 6 7   **636.7**

1. Dogs

ISBN 978-1-931993-83-8 pa; 1-931993-83-1 pa

LC 2006035434

"If you are looking for a book about canines that is entertaining as well as immensely informative, this is it. In a lively, conversational tone, Mehus-Roe offers a vast amount of material, from the history of dogs to vacationing with a pet, and provides practical and upbeat explanations, ideas, offbeat tidbits, and pertinent details." SLJ

Includes bibliographical references

Morn, September B.

The **pug.** Eldorado Ink 2010 112p il (Our best friends) lib bdg $34.95
Grades: 4 5 6 7   **636.7**

1. Dogs

ISBN 978-1-932904-63-5 lib bdg; 1-932904-63-8 lib bdg

"The Our Best Friends series continues to be an ideal resource for those kids (or even adults) looking for a cradle-to-grave primer on responsible pet ownership. . . . These [books] offer far more than the customary cursory enticements and warnings usually aimed at first-time animal caregivers, with in-depth information on health issues and extensive explanations of the various types of species. . . . This is required (if sobering) reading for the serious pet owner." Booklist

Includes bibliographical references

Niven, Felicia Lowenstein

Learning to care for a dog. Enslow Publishers 2010 48p il (Beginning pet care with American Humane) lib bdg $23.93
Grades: 2 3 4   **636.7**

1. Dogs

ISBN 978-0-7660-3190-6; 0-7660-3190-X

LC 2008048962

"Readers will learn how to choose, train, and care for a dog." Publisher's note

Includes glossary and bibliographical references

Patent, Dorothy Hinshaw

★ **Saving** Audie; a pit bull puppy gets a second chance. photographs by William Muñoz. Walker & Company 2011 un il $16.99; lib bdg $17.89
Grades: 2 3 4   **636.7**

1. Dogs 2. Animal welfare 3. Football players 4. Dog rescue -- Juvenile literature 5. Animal welfare -- Juvenile literature 6. Pit bull terriers -- Juvenile literature

ISBN 978-0-8027-2272-0; 0-8027-2272-5; 978-0-8027-2273-7 lib bdg; 0-8027-2273-3 lib bdg

LC 2010-36547

When Michael Vick's dog fighting ring was discovered, more than forty dogs were rescued. But their struggle was far from over. Most animal advocates believed the former fighting dogs were too damaged to save, but Audie and his kennel mates would prove them wrong when public outcry and the publicity surrounding Michael Vick's punishment won them a chance at a happy life.

"Munoz's photographs range from moody . . . to adorable. . . . Patent wrings emotion from her understated text and remains nonjudgmental about Vick's reemergence." Booklist

Prap, Lila

Doggy whys. North-South Books 2011 un il $16.95
Grades: 2 3 4   **636.7**

1. Dogs

ISBN 0-7358-4014-8; 978-0-7358-4014-0

"Although this book could have coasted by entirely on the strength of the funky, ruff-n-tuff cartoon pooches that are the centerpiece of each spread, Prap goes one better and provides insightful information on why dogs are so, well, darn doggy. . . . A few of her inquiries will enlighten even veteran fact hounds." Booklist

Rajczak, Kristen

Pulling dogs. Gareth Stevens Pub. 2011 24p il (Working dogs) lib bdg $22.60; pa $8.15

Grades: 2 3 4   **636.7**

1. Working dogs 2. Sled dog racing
ISBN 978-1-4339-4663-9 lib bdg; 1-4339-4663-7 lib
bdg; 978-1-4339-4664-6 pa; 1-4339-4664-5 pa

LC 2010037168

This describes pulling "dogs and the training they receive. The short chapters, complemented by numerous color
photographs, provide examples of particular breeds that do
[this] job and show how their characteristics are suited for
the tasks. The charts provided are especially helpful, covering commands and more specific tasks. There is enough
information to make the [text] feel fresh. . . . A solid choice
for readers looking for more than cute pictures." SLJ

Rescue dogs. Gareth Stevens Pub. 2011 24p il (Working dogs) lib bdg $22.60; pa $7

Grades: 2 3 4   **636.7**

1. Rescue dogs
ISBN 978-1-4339-4667-7 lib bdg; 1-4339-4667-X lib
bdg; 978-1-4339-4668-4 pa; 1-4339-4668-8 pa

LC 2010037169

This describes rescue "dogs and the training they receive. The short chapters, complemented by numerous color
photographs, provide examples of particular breeds that do
[this] job and show how their characteristics are suited for
the tasks. The charts provided are especially helpful, covering commands and more specific tasks. There is enough
information to make the [text] feel fresh. . . . A solid choice
for readers looking for more than cute pictures." SLJ

Rockwood, Leigh

Dogs are smart! PowerKids Press 2010 24p il (Super
smart animals) lib bdg $21.25; pa $8.25

Grades: 2 3 4 5   **636.7**

1. Dogs
ISBN 978-1-4358-9374-0 lib bdg; 1-4358-9374-3 lib
bdg; 978-1-4358-9836-3 pa; 1-4358-9836-2 pa
Examines the intelligence of dogs.

"Bright, colorful, captioned photographs complement
the text. Rockwood does an excellent job of simplifying the
information without making the text choppy or boring." Libr
Media Connect

Includes glossary

Rogers, Tammie

4-H guide to dog training and dog tricks. Voyageur Press
2009 176p il pa $18.99

Grades: 5 6 7 8 9 10   **636.7**

1. Dogs -- Training
ISBN 978-0-7603-3629-8; 0-7603-3629-6

LC 2009-17040

"This is not simply a how-to-train book; it is also a guide
to cultivating a respectful relationship with your dog. The
excellent information is comprehensive, and it is presented
in a clear and detailed style. The author covers different
training methods, discussing the tools needed from food to
collar selection. Using this manual, dog owners can move
through the basics (sit, down, etc.) to obedience competition
and fun tricks and activities." SLJ

Includes bibliographical references

Rutherford, Clarice

★ A **dog** is a dog; and that's why he's so special. by
Clarice Rutherford. Alpine 2012 xi, 98 p.p col. ill. (paperback: alk. paper) $14.95

Grades: 4 5 6   **636.7**

1. Pets 2. Wolves 3. Animal behavior 4. Dogs --
Behavior -- Juvenile literature 5. Dogs -- Training --
Juvenile literature
ISBN 1577791037; 9781577791034

LC 2009003029

"The author, Clarice Rutherford, brings her many years
of experience with dogs into this book, and explains dogs,
how to manage, train, as well as understand them . . . The
reader will learn the basic history of dogs and their relationship to the wolf. How the dog's brain develops and the
importance of early socialization and basic training is explained, as well as how the genetics and instincts of the wolf
play an important role in the behavior of the dog." (Barnes
& Noble)

Includes bibliographical references and index.

Schweitzer, Karen

The **beagle**. Eldorado Ink 2010 112p il (Our best
friends) lib bdg $34.95

Grades: 4 5 6 7   **636.7**

1. Dogs
ISBN 978-1-932904-57-4 lib bdg; 1-932904-57-3
lib bdg

"The Our Best Friends series continues to be an ideal
resource for those kids (or even adults) looking for a cradle-
to-grave primer on responsible pet ownership. . . . These
[books] offer far more than the customary cursory enticements and warnings usually aimed at first-time animal
caregivers, with in-depth information on health issues and
extensive explanations of the various types of species. . .
. This is required (if sobering) reading for the serious pet
owner." Booklist

Includes bibliographical references

The **dachshund**. Eldorado Ink 2010 112p il (Our best
friends) lib bdg $34.95

Grades: 4 5 6 7   **636.7**

1. Dogs
ISBN 978-1-932904-59-8 lib bdg; 1-932904-59-X
lib bdg

"The Our Best Friends series continues to be an ideal
resource for those kids (or even adults) looking for a cradle-
to-grave primer on responsible pet ownership. . . . These
[books] offer far more than the customary cursory enticements and warnings usually aimed at first-time animal
caregivers, with in-depth information on health issues and
extensive explanations of the various types of species. . .
. This is required (if sobering) reading for the serious pet
owner." Booklist

Includes bibliographical references

Simon, Seymour

★ **Dogs**. HarperCollinsPublishers 2004 un il $17.99;
lib bdg $18.89; pa $6.99

Grades: 1 2 3 4   **636.7**

1. Dogs 2. Dogs -- Juvenile literature
ISBN 0-06-028942-2; 0-06-028943-0 lib bdg; 978-0-
06-446255-6 pa; 0-06-446255-2 pa

LC 2003-12484

Provides a basic introduction to the physical characteristics and behavior of dogs

"The striking color photos, including many close-ups, create a feeling of intimacy. . . . Simon succeeds in addressing his topic in clear, easily understood vocabulary without writing down to children." SLJ

Singer, Marilyn

A **dog's** gotta do what a dog's gotta do; dogs at work. Holt & Co. 2000 86p il $16

Grades: 3 4 5 6   **636.7**

1. Working dogs 2. Dogs -- Juvenile literature 3. Working animals -- Juvenile literature

ISBN 0-8050-6074-X

Describes how dogs use their physical abilities, intelligence, and training by humans to perform a variety of jobs, including working in the movies, catching burglars, delivering messages, and cheering up children in hospitals

"Dog lovers will appreciate this readable, informative look at canines and the work they do." Booklist

Stamper, Judith Bauer

Eco dogs. Bearport Pub. 2011 32p il (Dog heroes) lib bdg $25.27

Grades: 3 4 5   **636.7**

1. Working dogs 2. Endangered species

ISBN 978-1-61772-152-6; 1-61772-152-2

           LC 2010041191

"Eco Dogs help scientists by sniffing out scat, which is analyzed for signs of pollutants or changes in the food chain that might have harmful effects on the environment and on indigenous species. [This book is] engaging not just because the content is so compelling, but also because the [author has] highlighted specific dogs currently working in [this field]. The use of real names and full-color photographs on every page, many contributed by the individuals who work with these dogs, makes reading [this book] a personal experience. . . . [An] excellent [introduction] to [this new [development] in service-dog training." SLJ

Includes glossary and bibliographical references

Urbigkit, Cat

Brave dogs, gentle dogs; how they guard sheep. Boyds Mills Press 2005 32p il $15.95; pa $8.95

Grades: K 1 2 3   **636.7**

1. Sheep dogs

ISBN 1-59078-317-4; 978-1-59078-674-1 pa

           LC 2004-16855

A "photo-essay on guardian dogs. Accompanied by clear, full-color photos, the simple, informative text describes the raising of these sheepdogs and their natural proclivity for guarding 'their' flocks." SLJ

The **guardian** team; on the job with Rena and Roo. Boyds Mills Press 2011 32p il

Grades: K 1 2 3   **636.7**

1. Sheep 2. Donkeys 3. Ranch life 4. Working dogs

ISBN 1590787706; 9781590787700

"Orphaned wild burro Roo and litter-runt puppy Rena become livestock guardians and, eventually, friends on the author's ranch. They are initially paired to protect lamb orphans from predators. Youthful, mutual wariness eventually unfolds into friendship between the two. . . . Heartwarming

photos and clear, accessible text combine to make this story a winner." SLJ

Includes bibliographical references

Whitehead, Sarah

How to speak dog. Scholastic Reference 2008 96p il pa $6.99

Grades: 4 5 6 7 8   **636.7**

1. Dogs

ISBN 978-0-545-02078-7 pa; 0-545-02078-6 pa

Explains how to read a dog's body language and vocalizations and presents step-by-step instructions for training, housebreaking, teaching tricks, and playing several types of games.

This is "well-organized and interesting. . . . Whitehead discusses, and clearly shows in good-quality, full-color photographs, various canine emotions." SLJ

636.73   Working and herding dogs

Katz, Jon

Lenore finds a friend; a true story from Bedlam Farm. Story and photographs by Jon Katz. Henry Holt and Company 2012 32 p. (hc) $15.99

Grades: K 1 2 3   **636.73**

1. Friendship 2. Animal behavior 3. Picture books for children 4. Farm life -- Juvenile fiction 5. Animals -- Anecdotes 6. Animal communication -- Juvenile literature 7. Emotions in animals -- Anecdotes -- Juvenile literature 8. Social behavior in animals -- Anecdotes -- Juvenile literature 9. Working dogs -- New York (State) -- Anecdotes -- Juvenile literature 10. Farm life -- New York (State) -- West Hebron -- Anecdotes -- Juvenile literature

ISBN 080509220X; 9780805092202

           LC 2011029040

This children's picture book is based on the story of the friendship between puppy Lenore and ram Brutus at Bedlam Farm. Lenore "was lonely because the other animals . . . were not friendly towards her. Rose, the other dog at the farm, was too busy herding the sheep" to play. Lenore starts making friends with Brutus by giving him daily kisses. "Despite Rose's attempts to keep Lenore away from Brutus, Lenore does not give up and the friendship . . . grows." (Children's Literature)

Kimmel, Elizabeth Cody

Balto and the great race; illustrated by Nora Koerber. Random House 1999 99p il map (Stepping stone book) hardcover o.p. pa $3.99

Grades: 3 4 5   **636.73**

1. Diphtheria 2. Sled dog racing 3. Dogs -- Juvenile literature 4. Alaska -- History -- Juvenile literature

ISBN 0-679-99198-0 lib bdg; 0-679-89198-6 pa

           LC 98-35753

Recounts how the sled dog Balto saved Nome, Alaska, in 1925 from a diphtheria epidemic by delivering medicine through a raging snowstorm

"Kimmel's writing deftly combines geography, sled racing, and historical background with the gripping adventure of Balto's race to save lives. In many ways, the book reads like fast-paced fiction. Koerber's serviceable black-and-white illustrations appear throughout and reflect the action. Sure to appeal to beginning chapter-book readers." SLJ

636.8 Cats

Barnes, Julia

Pet cats; [by] Julia Barnes. Gareth Stevens Pub. 2007 32p il (Pet pals) lib bdg $23.93

Grades: 2 3 4 5 **636.8**

1. Cats

ISBN 0-8368-6776-9

LC 2006042377

"In spreads filled with color photographs, Barnes presents a short explanation of the feline family tree, as well as the history of cat-human relationships, before delving into cat breeds, characteristics, and behavior. Final sections offer ideas for new cat owners." Booklist

Includes glossary and bibliographical references

Bidner, Jenni

Is my cat a tiger? how your cat compares to its wild cousins. Lark Books 2006 64p il $9.95

Grades: 3 4 5 6 **636.8**

1. Cats 2. Wild cats

ISBN 1-57990-815-2

LC 2006023356

"This book shows how domestic cats compare with their wild cousins. Specifically, it addresses what domestic behavior reveals about wild roots. . . . The color photographs are fantastic. . . . This is a fascinating volume." SLJ

Biniok, Janice

Mixed breed cats. Eldorado Ink 2010 112p il (Our best friends) lib bdg $34.95

Grades: 4 5 6 7 **636.8**

1. Cats

ISBN 978-1-932904-62-8 lib bdg; 1-932904-62-X lib bdg

This "is a cradle-to-grave overview of a cat's life. . . . [This] well-written [book provides] examples to support [its] points and solid online and text resources and feature [a] clean, uncluttered [layout]. . . . There is plenty of practical information that motivated readers can glean from [this title]. [It] debunks some presumptions about domesticated felines, commenting that the 'finicky eater' tag is unwarranted, and that cats are easier to train than people think." SLJ

Includes bibliographical references

Bozzo, Linda

My first cat; [by] Linda Bozzo. Enslow Elementary 2007 32p il (My first pet library from the American Humane Association) lib bdg $22.60

Grades: 1 2 3 **636.8**

1. Cats

ISBN 978-0-7660-2750-3 lib bdg; 0-7660-2750-3 lib bdg

LC 2006008403

This offers brief basic advice on selecting a cat and caring for it.

Includes glossary and bibliographical references

George, Jean Craighead

How to talk to your cat; illustrated by Paul Meisel. HarperCollins Pubs. 2000 28p il $9.95

Grades: 2 3 4 **636.8**

1. Cats 2. Pets 3. Human-animal communication 4. Cats -- Behavior -- Juvenile literature

ISBN 0-06-027968-0

LC 98-41517

Describes how cats communicate with people through their behavior and sounds and explains how to talk back to them using sounds, behavior, and body language

"The writing style is breezy, conversational, and amusing, and is helped along by the many color illustrations. The photographs of the author are cleverly combined with humorous cartoon drawings of cats that display a great deal of intelligence and comedic personality. . . . A useful and readable addition to any pet collection." SLJ

Gibbons, Gail

Cats. Holiday House 1996 un il hardcover o.p. $16.95

Grades: K 1 2 3 **636.8**

1. Cats

ISBN 0-8234-1253-9; 0-8234-1410-8 pa

LC 96-3953

Presents information about the physical characteristics, senses, and behavior of cats, as well as how to care for these animals and some general facts about them

"This easy-to-read picture book will appeal to lovers of the popular pet. Brightly colored illustrations identify different breeds, while the informative . . . text describes physical and behavioral traits of kittens and cats." Horn Book Guide

Hart, Joyce

Cats; by Joyce Hart. Marshall Cavendish Benchmark 2008 48p il (Great pets) lib bdg $29.93

Grades: 2 3 4 **636.8**

1. Cats

ISBN 978-0-7614-2710-0 lib bdg; 0-7614-2710-4 lib bdg

LC 2007016462

This is an "enthusiastic, warm [introduction]. . . . [It is] clearly written and [is] the most thorough, honest [introduction] to owning [pet cats] for this audience." SLJ

Holub, Joan

Why do cats meow? illustrations by Anna DiVito. Dial Books for Young Readers 2001 46p il (Dial easy-to-read) hardcover o.p. pa $3.99

Grades: K 1 2 **636.8**

1. Cats

ISBN 0-8037-2503-5; 0-14-056788-7 pa

LC 00-23985

Questions and answers present information about the history, behavior, and characteristics of cats and their interaction with humans

"Packed with interesting information and illustrated with an abundance of cartoon artwork and color photographs." Horn Book Guide

Jeffrey, Laura S.

Cats; how to choose and care for a cat. Enslow Publishers 2004 48p il (American humane pet care library) lib bdg $23.93

Grades: 3 4 5　　　　　　　　　　　　　　636.8
1. Cats　2. Pets
ISBN 0-7660-2516-0

LC 2003-22967

Provides information on cats as pets, including how to choose among different breeds, find a cat to buy or adopt, and how to feed and keep a cat healthy

This offers "children solid information about pet selection and care at a level they can understand." SLJ

Includes glossary and bibliographical references

Johnson, Jinny

Cats and kittens; [by] Jinny Johnson. Black Rabbit Books 2009 32p il (Get to know your pet) $27.10
Grades: 3 4 5 6　　　　　　　　　　　636.8
1. Cats
ISBN 978-1-59920-088-0; 1-59920-088-0

LC 2007-43435

"Spreads include in-depth care instruction, and 'Q & A' sidebars that answer common behavioral questions. . . . The layout is clear, with full color photos and illustrations breaking up the text." SLJ

Includes glossary

MacLeod, Elizabeth

Why do cats have whiskers? Kids Can Press 2008 64p il $14.95
Grades: 3 4 5 6　　　　　　　　　　　636.8
1. Cats
ISBN 978-1-55453-196-7; 1-55453-196-9

"With its lively text and copious photographs, this title offers readers an accessible introduction to the world of felines. . . . MacLeod's interesting facts and anecdotes are sure to keep young cat owners engaged." Horn Book Guide

Malam, John

Grow your own cat toy. Heinemann Library 2011 32p il (Grow it yourself!) lib bdg $26; pa $7.99
Grades: 2 3 4　　　　　　　　　　　　636.8
1. Gardening 2. Handicraft 3. Catnip
ISBN 978-1-4329-5110-8 lib bdg; 1-4329-5110-6;
978-1-4329-5117-7 pa; 1-4329-5117-3 pa

LC 2010049835

This describes the catnip plant and why cats like it, how to grow it, and how to make a catnip toy.

This book "turns the idea [of growing a catnip toy] into a fun and fascinating project. . . . A big part of the book's appeal is the crisp color photographs. . . . Simple sentences in an easily read typeface . . . are just right for the elementary-school age group. . . . A well-done package in every way." Booklist

Includes glossary and bibliographical references

Myron, Vicki

Dewey the library cat; a true story. [by] Vicki Myron with Bret Witter. Little, Brown 2010 214p $16.99
Grades: 4 5 6 7 8　　　　　　　　　　636.8
1. Cats 2. Libraries
ISBN 978-0-316-06871-0; 0-316-06871-3

Adapted from: Dewey: the small town library cat who touched the world, published 2008 by Grand Central Publisher for adults

"From the opening chapter, when librarian Vicki Myron finds a fragile, freezing kitten in the book return, children will be hooked on her heartwarming story about Dewey Readmore Books. . . . Anecdotes such as Dewey's fascination with rubber bands, his bizarre behavior during a bat invasion, and his finicky eating habits are ideal booktalk material. So are descriptions of Dewey's tender, intuitive interactions with people of all ages and backgrounds." Booklist

Niven, Felicia Lowenstein

Learning to care for a cat. Enslow Publishers 2010 48p il (Beginning pet care with American Humane) lib bdg $23.93
Grades: 2 3 4　　　　　　　　　　　　636.8
1. Cats
ISBN 978-0-7660-3191-3; 0-7660-3191-8

LC 2008048963

"Readers will learn how to choose, train, and care for a cat." Publisher's note

Includes glossary and bibliographical references

Rau, Dana Meachen

Top 10 cats for kids; [by] Dana Meachen Rau. Enslow Publishers 2008 48p il (Top pets for kids with American Humane) lib bdg $23.93
Grades: 2 3 4 5　　　　　　　　　　　636.8
1. Cats
ISBN 978-0-7660-3071-8 lib bdg; 0-7660-3071-7 lib bdg

LC 2007-24440

"Includes beautiful full-color photos showing the animals at their best. Judicious use of text boxes, crisp fonts, and white space will make it easy for readers to follow the flow of information." SLJ

Includes glossary and bibliographical references

Rebman, Renee C.

Cats. Marshall Cavendish Benchmark 2009 47p il (Animals, animals) lib bdg $20.95
Grades: 3 4 5　　　　　　　　　　　　636.8
1. Cats
ISBN 978-0-7614-3975-2

LC 2008020918

Provides comprehensive information on the anatomy, special skills, habitats, and diet of cats.

Includes glossary and bibliographical references

Simon, Seymour

★ Cats. HarperCollins Pub. 2004 un il lib bdg $16.89; pa $6.99
Grades: 1 2 3 4　　　　　　　　　　　636.8
1. Cats 2. Cats -- Juvenile literature
ISBN 0-06-028940-6; 0-06-028941-4 lib bdg; 0-06-446254-4 pa

LC 2003-8337

Discusses the history, physical characteristics, behavior, and various breeds of cats, and provides basic information on caring for one as a pet.

"The striking color photos, including many closeups, create a feeling of intimacy. . . . Simon succeeds in addressing his topic in clear, easily understood vocabulary without writing down to children." SLJ

Tildes, Phyllis Limbacher

Calico's cousins; cats from around the world. Charlesbridge Pub. 1999 un il lib bdg $15.95; pa $6.95

Grades: K 1 2 3   **636.8**
1. Cats
ISBN 0-88106-648-6 lib bdg; 0-88106-649-4 pa
LC 98-4011

"Calico, a domestic longhair cat, introduces various breeds by describing both their origin and common traits. Each double-page spread features realistic illustrations of several cats in an environment appropriate to their origin, and a map at the end provides geographical reference." Horn Book Guide

Whitehead, Sarah
How to speak cat. Scholastic 2009 96p il pa $6.99
Grades: 4 5 6 7 8   **636.8**
1. Cats
ISBN 978-0-545-02079-4 pa; 0-545-02079-4 pa

"This pet-care book focuses on developing a relationship with a pet. The author states that the communication process is a two-way street, and she describes how readers can translate a cat's body language and vocalizations. . . . the bright color photographs of children with their cats on every page will appeal greatly to readers. This is a fun book that offers a good understanding of its audience and subject." SLJ

636.9   Other mammals

Barnes, Julia
Elephants at work; [by] Julia Barnes. Gareth Stevens 2006 32p il map (Animals at work) lib bdg $23.93
Grades: 3 4 5   **636.9**
1. Elephants 2. Working animals
ISBN 0-8368-6224-4
LC 2005054067

This describes uses of elephants throughout history, their relationship with humans, habitat, diet, and appearance

This is "well-written, well-organized, ... visually appealing and fun to read." SLJ

Includes bibliographical references

Pet guinea pigs; [by] Julia Barnes. Gareth Stevens Pub. 2007 32p il (Pet pals) lib bdg $23.93
Grades: 2 3 4 5   **636.9**
1. Guinea pigs
ISBN 0-8368-6779-3
LC 2006042373

This places guinea pigs "within the context of [their] wild roots and [their] relationship to humans. From there, Barnes explains what makes the animal an ideal pet, recommends how to be a good caregiver, and reveals how the creature communicates (as well as how to answer). The [book mixes] practical advice with trivia in a way that children will find informative and easy to navigate. Crisp, full-color photos enhance the [text]." SLJ

Includes glossary and bibliographical references

Pet rabbits; [by] Julia Barnes. Gareth Stevens Pub. 2007 32p il (Pet pals) lib bdg $32.92
Grades: 2 3 4 5   **636.9**
1. Rabbits
ISBN 0-8368-6781-5
LC 2006042374

This places rabbits "within the context of [their] wild roots and [their] relationship to humans. From there, Barnes explains what makes the animal an ideal pet, recommends how to be a good caregiver, and reveals how the creature communicates (as well as how to answer). The [book mixes] practical advice with trivia in a way that children will find informative and easy to navigate. Crisp, full-color photos enhance the [text]." SLJ

Includes glossary and bibliographical references

Bjorklund, Ruth
Rabbits; by Ruth Bjorklund. Marshall Cavendish Benchmark 2008 48p il (Great pets) lib bdg $28.50
Grades: 2 3 4   **636.9**
1. Rabbits
ISBN 978-0-7614-2708-7 lib bdg; 0-7614-2708-2 lib bdg
LC 2007013044

The offers an introduction to rabbits as pets and how to choose and care for them

This is an "enthusiastic, warm [introduction]. . . . [This is] clearly written and [is] the most thorough, honest [introduction] to owning a pet [rabbit] for this audience." SLJ

Includes glossary and bibliographical references

Bozzo, Linda
My first guinea pig and other small pets; [by] Linda Bozzo. Enslow Elementary 2007 32p il (My first pet library from the American Humane Association) lib bdg $22.60
Grades: 1 2 3   **636.9**
1. Mice 2. Pets 3. Rats 4. Ferrets 5. Gerbils 6. Rabbits 7. Hamsters 8. Guinea pigs
ISBN 978-0-7660-2752-7 lib bdg; 0-7660-2752-X lib bdg
LC 2006014970

This offers advice on selecting and caring for small pets including guinea pigs, hamsters, gerbils, rabbits, ferrets, rats, and mice.

Includes glossary and bibliographical references

Ellis, Carol
Hamsters and gerbils. Marshall Cavendish Benchmark 2009 46p il (Great pets) $20.95
Grades: 2 3 4   **636.9**
1. Gerbils 2. Hamsters
ISBN 978-0-7614-2999-9; 0-7614-2999-9
LC 2008-24336

"Describes the characteristics and behavior of pet hamsters and gerbils, also discussing their physical appearance and place in history." Publisher's note

Includes glossary and bibliographical references

Foran, Jill
Guinea pig. Weigl 2010 32p il (My pet) lib bdg $26; pa $9.95
Grades: 3 4 5   **636.9**
1. Pets 2. Guinea pigs
ISBN 978-1-60596-090-6 lib bdg; 1-60596-090-X lib bdg; 978-1-60596-091-3 pa; 1-60596-091-8 pa
LC 2009-5128

Information about how to house, feed, and care for guinea pigs.

"With clear, formal writing, and extensive coverage . . . [this title is] useful for reports. . . . Numerous color photographs, charts . . . and question-and-answer boxes supplement the [text]." SLJ

Includes glossary

Gaines, Ann

Top 10 small mammals for kids; [by] Ann Graham Gaines. Enslow Publishers 2008 48p il (Top pets for kids with American Humane) lib bdg $23.93

Grades: 2 3 4 5   636.9

1. Pets 2. Mammals

ISBN 978-0-7660-3075-6 lib bdg; 0-7660-3075-X lib bdg

LC 2007-38480

"Includes beautiful full-color photos showing the animals at their best. Judicious use of text boxes, crisp fonts, and white space will make it easy for readers to follow the flow of information." SLJ

Includes glossary and bibliographical references

Ganeri, Anita

★ Rabbits. Heinemann 2009 32p il (A pet's life) $17.75

Grades: 3 4 5   636.9

1. Rabbits

ISBN 978-1-4329-3394-4; 1-4329-3394-9

"Pretty much everything a child needs to know about taking care of rabbits in this title. . . . The book is organized in a logical way that will keep kids focused. . . . [The book uses] a good-size typeface and clear, adorable photos. . . . Fact-filled, fun to look at, and a pleasure to read." Booklist

Hamilton, Lynn

Ferret. Weigl 2010 32p il (My pet) lib bdg $26; pa $9.95

Grades: 3 4 5   636.9

1. Pets 2. Ferrets

ISBN 978-1-60596-096-8 lib bdg; 1-60596-096-9 lib bdg; 978-1-60596-097-5 pa; 1-60596-097-7 pa

LC 2009-4985

Information about how to house, feed, and care for ferrets.

"With clear, formal writing, and extensive coverage . . . [this title is] useful for reports. . . . Numerous color photographs, charts . . . and question-and-answer boxes supplement the [text]." SLJ

Includes glossary

Haney, Johannah

Ferrets. Marshall Cavendish Benchmark 2010 46p il (Great pets) lib bdg $29.93

Grades: 2 3 4   636.9

1. Pets 2. Ferrets

ISBN 978-0-7614-4153-3 lib bdg; 0-7614-4153-0 lib bdg

LC 2009020561

"Describes the characteristics and behavior of pet ferrets, also discussing their physical appearance and place in history." Publisher's note

Includes glossary and bibliographical references

Holub, Joan

★ Why do rabbits hop? and other questions about rabbits, guinea pigs, hamsters, and gerbils. illustrations by Anna DiVito. Dial Bks. for Young Readers 2002 46p il (Dial easy-to-read) hardcover o.p. pa $3.99

Grades: K 1 2   636.9

1. Pets 2. Gerbils 3. Rabbits 4. Hamsters 5. Guinea pigs 6. Questions and answers 7. Rabbits as pets 8. Rabbits -- Miscellanea -- Juvenile literature 9. Gerbils as pets -- Miscellanea -- Juvenile literature 10. Hamsters as pets -- Miscellanea -- Juvenile literature 11. Guinea pigs as pets -- Miscellanea -- Juvenile literature

ISBN 0-8037-2771-2 lib bdg; 0-14-230120-5 pa

LC 2001-47477

Questions and answers present information about the behavior and characteristics of rabbits, guinea pigs, hamsters, and gerbils and their interaction with humans

"The text is both interesting and informative. . . . [The book has] a bright, appealing format that combines jaunty original art and well-chosen photos." Booklist

Jeffrey, Laura S.

Hamsters, gerbils, guinea pigs, rabbits, ferrets, mice, and rats; how to choose and care for a small mammal. Enslow Publishers 2004 48p il (American humane pet care library) lib bdg $23.93

Grades: 3 4 5   636.9

1. Mice 2. Pets 3. Rats 4. Ferrets 5. Mammals 6. Rabbits 7. Hamsters 8. Guinea pigs 9. Pets -- Juvenile literature 10. Mammals -- Juvenile literature

ISBN 0-7660-2518-7

LC 2003-22969

Explains the different personalities of several small mammals, where to go to pick the right one, and how to keep them happy and healthy

Includes glossary and bibliographical references

Johnson, Jinny

Guinea pigs; [by] Jinny Johnson. Black Rabbit Books 2009 32p il (Get to know your pet) $27.10

Grades: 3 4 5 6   636.9

1. Guinea pigs

ISBN 978-1-59920-211-2; 1-59920-211-5

LC 2007-43437

"Spreads include in-depth care instruction, and 'Q & A' sidebars that answer common behavioral questions. . . . The layout is clear, with full color photos and illustrations breaking up the text." SLJ

Includes glossary

Hamsters and gerbils; [by] Jinny Johnson. Black Rabbit Books 2009 32p il (Get to know your pet) $27.10

Grades: 3 4 5 6   636.9

1. Gerbils 2. Hamsters

ISBN 978-1-59920-092-7; 1-59920-092-9

LC 2007-52813

"Spreads include in-depth care instruction, and 'Q & A' sidebars that answer common behavioral questions. . . . The layout is clear, with full color photos and illustrations breaking up the text." SLJ

Includes glossary

Rabbits; [by] Jinny Johnson. Black Rabbit Books 2009 32p il (Get to know your pet) $27.10

Grades: 3 4 5 6   **636.9**
1. Rabbits
ISBN 978-1-59920-090-3; 1-59920-090-2
LC 2007-43436
"Spreads include in-depth care instruction, and 'Q & A' sidebars that answer common behavioral questions. . . . The layout is clear, with full color photos and illustrations breaking up the text." SLJ
Includes glossary

Rats and mice; [by] Jinny Johnson. Black Rabbit Books 2009 32p il (Get to know your pet) $27.10
Grades: 3 4 5 6   **636.9**
1. Mice 2. Rats
ISBN 978-1-59920-091-0; 1-59920-091-0
LC 2007-52815
"Spreads include in-depth care instruction, and 'Q & A' sidebars that answer common behavioral questions. . . . The layout is clear, with full color photos and illustrations breaking up the text." SLJ
Includes glossary

Lewin, Ted
★ **Balarama**; a royal elephant. [by] Ted and Betsy Lewin. Lee & Low Books 2009 un il $19.95
Grades: 3 4 5 6   **636.9**
1. Elephants 2. Festivals -- Juvenile literature 3. Asiatic elephant -- Juvenile literature
ISBN 978-1-60060-265-8; 1-60060-265-7
LC 2009-1499
"Ted Lewin's brilliant, realistic watercolors capture the sun-drenched pageantry of Mysore as well as the dusty, filtered light of the forest, while Betsy Lewin's lively cartoons aptly depict the action and personalities involved. The story has pathos and tension." SLJ

Lunis, Natalie
Furry ferrets. Bearport 2010 24p il (Peculiar pets) lib bdg $22.61
Grades: 3 4 5   **636.9**
1. Pets 2. Ferrets
ISBN 978-1-59716-860-1 lib bdg; 1-59716-860-2 lib bdg
LC 2009-10378
Introduces the furry ferret, describing its physical characteristics, habitat, and behavior, and discussing the care and diet that it needs if it is kept as a pet
"The language . . . is lively . . . [and] the illustrations are vivid, with photos offering some amusing shots. . . . This [book] . . . will hold readers' attention, but also challenge them to consider the responsibilities required of owners of unusual creatures." SLJ
Includes glossary and bibliographical references

McNicholas, June
Rats. Heinemann Lib. 2003 48p il (Keeping unusual pets) $24.22
Grades: 4 5 6 7   **636.9**
1. Rats
ISBN 1-4034-0283-3
LC 2002-3164
Describes how to select a pet rat, what to feed it, and when to take it to the vet, as well as how to keep a pet scrapbook

"A valuable, accessible resource." Booklist
Includes bibliographical references

Newcomb, Rain
Is my hamster wild? the secret lives of hamsters, gerbils & guinea pigs. by Rain Newcomb & Rose McLarney. Lark Books 2008 64p il $9.95
Grades: 2 3 4   **636.9**
1. Gerbils 2. Hamsters 3. Guinea pigs
ISBN 978-1-60059-242-3; 1-60059-242-2
LC 2007-44312
"Crisp photo album-style pictures with humorous captions reinforce the deft main text." Horn Book Guide

Niven, Felicia Lowenstein
Learning to care for small mammals. Enslow Publishers 2010 48p il (Beginning pet care with American Humane) lib bdg $23.93
Grades: 2 3 4   **636.9**
1. Ferrets 2. Rabbits 3. Rodents
ISBN 978-0-7660-3195-1; 0-7660-3195-0
This describes how to care for small mammals such as rabbits, guinea pigs, gerbils, hamsters, rats, mice, or ferrets.
"The pictures are colorful and engaging, with a no-fuss layout. The text is easy to follow, pitched at just the right level for the audience." SLJ
Includes glossary and bibliographical references

Petrylak, Ashley
Guinea pigs. Marshall Cavendish Benchmark 2009 44p il (Great pets) lib bdg $29.93
Grades: 2 3 4   **636.9**
1. Guinea pigs
ISBN 978-0-7614-4148-9 lib bdg; 0-7614-4148-4 lib bdg
LC 2008037238
"Describes the characteristics and behavior of pet guinea pigs, also discussing their physical appearance and place in history." Publisher's note
Includes glossary and bibliographical references

Richardson, Adele
Caring for your hamster; by Adele Richardson. Capstone Press 2007 24p il (Positively pets) $21.26
Grades: K 1 2 3   **636.9**
1. Hamsters
ISBN 978-0-7368-6387-2; 0-7368-6387-7
LC 2005035852
This is a "concise, competent [introduction] to the responsibility and fun of being a pet owner. . . . Attractive and well suited for young readers in both tone and content. The clear color photographs display the animals in all their glory." SLJ
Includes bibliographical references

Sobol, Richard
An elephant in the backyard; text and photographs by Richard Sobol. Dutton Children's Books 2004 un il $17.99
Grades: K 1 2 3   **636.9**
1. Elephants 2. Asiatic elephant -- Juvenile literature
ISBN 0-525-47288-6
LC 2003-52492

Describes how special elephants are in the village of Tha Kleng in Thailand and looks at the life of one particular young elephant named Wan Pen.

This is an "engaging photo-essay. Large, colorful photographs enhance the text. . . . The text is packed with interesting tidbits about these large mammals." SLJ

636.935

Boruchowitz, David E.

Sugar gliders; David E. Boruchowitz; [editor, Thomas Mazorlig] T.F.H. 2012 111 p. (Animal planet. Pet care library) (pbk.: alk. paper) $10.95

Grades: 4 5 6 7   **636.935**

1. Sugar gliders as pets -- Juvenile literature 2. Sugar glider 3. Sugar gliders as pets

ISBN 0793837111; 9780793837113

LC 2011049947

This book on sugar gliders by David E. Boruchowitz is part of the "Animal Planet Pet Care Library" series. "According to Boruchowitz, they make excellent house pets due to their affinity for cuddling in tiny places. . . . Every aspect of ownership is covered, from basic dietary requirements to grooming and socialization." (Booklist)

Includes bibliographical references and index

637   Processing dairy and related products

Aliki

Milk from cow to carton; rev ed; HarperCollins Pubs. 1992 31p il (Let's-read-and-find-out science book) hardcover o.p. pa $5.95

Grades: K 1 2 3   **637**

1. Milk 2. Cattle 3. Dairying

ISBN 0-06-445111-9 pa

LC 91-23807

First published 1974 by Crowell with title: Green grass and white milk

Briefly describes how a cow produces milk, how the milk is processed in a dairy, and how various other dairy products are made from milk

This features "full-color artwork. . . . An excellent primary-level introduction to dairy science." Booklist

Gibbons, Gail

The **milk** makers. Macmillan 1985 un il hardcover o.p. pa $5.99

Grades: K 1 2 3   **637**

1. Milk 2. Cattle 3. Dairying 4. Dairy cattle -- Juvenile literature

ISBN 0-02-736640-5; 0-689-71116-6 pa

LC 84-20081

Explains how cows produce milk and how it is processed before being delivered to stores

"Starting with dairy cows grazing at pasture, nothing is overlooked in the procedure, from the role of the calf to winter feed and shelter, the function of four stomachs, milking, milk handling, and the operation of a dairy. Diagrams of the cow stomachs as well as the machines used at farm and dairy leave no question unanswered, although city children will be unfamiliar with what it means to breed a cow. Finally, there

is a pictorial list of the many other dairy products found in most homes." Sci Books Films

Malam, John

Journey of a glass of milk; John Malam. Heinemann Library 2013 32 p. (hb) $26.65

Grades: 1 2 3   **637**

1. Milk supply 2. Picture books for children 3. Milk -- Juvenile literature 4. Milk trade -- Juvenile literature 5. Dairy processing -- Juvenile literature

ISBN 1432966030; 9781432966034; 9781432966102

LC 2011050559

This book is part of the "Journey of a . . . " series that "looks at how common products end up in our homes, starting with the raw materials and ending with the finished goods. This title looks at the journey of a glass of milk; examining how cows are milked, how the milk is treated, how it is packaged, transported and distributed to stores, and how it is sold and eventually drunk!" (Publisher's note)

Includes bibliographical references and index

Peterson, Cris

Extra cheese, please! mozzarella's journey from cow to pizza. photographs by Alvis Upitis. Boyds Mills Press 1994 un il $16.95; pa $9.95

Grades: K 1 2 3   **637**

1. Cheese 2. Dairying 3. Cheese -- Juvenile literature 4. Dairying -- Juvenile literature

ISBN 1-56397-177-1; 1-59078-246-1 pa

LC 93-70876

"Nicely balanced pages contain brief blocks of clearly written text and many full-color photographs." SLJ

Includes glossary and bibliographical references

638   Insect culture

Burns, L. G.

★ The **hive** detectives; chronicle of a honey bee catastrophe. with photographs by Ellen Harasimowicz. Houghton Mifflin Books for Children 2010 66p il (Scientists in the field) $18

Grades: 5 6 7 8 9 10   **638**

1. Beekeeping 2. Honeybee -- Juvenile literature 3. Bee culture -- Juvenile literature

ISBN 978-0-547-15231-8; 0-547-15231-0

LC 2009-45249

"Not long after beekeepers encountered a devastating new problem in their hives in 2006, a team of bee scientists began working to discover the causes of colony collapse disorder (CCD), now attributed to a combination of factors possibly including pesticides, nutrition, mites and viruses. . . . Mock notebook pages break up the narrative with biographies of the individual scientists, information about who and what can be found inside the hive and the features of bee bodies. An appendix adds varied fascinating facts about bees—again using the format of an illustrated research journal. Harasimowicz's clear, beautifully reproduced photographs support and extend the text." Kirkus

Includes glossary and bibliographical references

Fujiwara, Yumiko

Honey; a gift from nature. written by Yumiko Fujiwara; illustrated by Hideko Ise. Kane/Miller 2006 un il (Nature: a child's eye view) pa $7.95

Grades: PreK K 1   **638**

1. Bees 2. Honey 3. Honey -- Juvenile literature 4. Honeybee -- Juvenile literature

ISBN 1-929132-94-8 pa; 978-1-929132-94-2 pa

LC 2005-930528

Original Japanese edition 1997

A young Japanese girl spends the day with her beekeeping father in the mountains where he keeps his hives. Explains how bees gather nectar, how it is turned into honey, and how the honey is collected.

Harkins, Susan Sales

Design your own butterfly garden; by Susan Sales Harkins and William H. Harkins. Mitchell Lane Publishers 2008 48p il (Gardening for kids) lib bdg $29.95

Grades: 3 4 5 6   **638**

1. Butterfly gardens

ISBN 978-1-58415-638-3 lib bdg; 1-58415-638-4 lib bdg

LC 2008-2245

Introduces the principles of butterfly gardening, discussing how to plan the garden, what flowers to plant there, and how to maintain it in all seasons

"All the tasks delineated are well within the scope of children's abilities, and the items needed to complete them are not hard to find. . . . [The book has] excellent full-color photography and include[s] charts and diagrams to assist in the completion of the projects." SLJ

Includes bibliographical references

Malam, John

Grow your own butterfly farm. Heinemann Library 2011 32p il (Grow it yourself!) lib bdg $26; pa $7.99

Grades: K 1 2   **638**

1. Gardening 2. Butterflies

ISBN 978-1-4329-5109-2 lib bdg; 978-1-4329-5116-0 pa

LC 2010049834

This describes how to grow a flower garden which attracts butterflies.

Includes glossary and bibliographical references

639   Hunting, fishing, conservation, related technologies

Lomberg, Michelle

Spider. Weigl Publishers 2009 32p il (My pets) lib bdg $26; pa $9.95

Grades: 3 4 5   **639**

1. Pets 2. Spiders

ISBN 978-1-60596-094-4 lib bdg; 1-60596-094-2 lib bdg; 978-1-60596-095-1 pa; 1-60596-095-0 pa

LC 2009-25979

Information about how to house, feed, and care for spiders.

"With clear, formal writing, and extensive coverage . . . [this title is] useful for reports. . . . Numerous color photo-

graphs, charts . . . and question-and-answer boxes supplement the [text]." SLJ

Includes glossary

Richardson, Adele

Caring for your hermit crab; by Adele Richardson. Capstone Press 2007 24p il (Positively pets) $21.26

Grades: K 1 2 3   **639**

1. Pets 2. Crabs

ISBN 978-0-7368-6388-9; 0-7368-6388-5

LC 2006006390

This is a "concise, competent [introduction] to the responsibility and fun of being a pet owner. . . . Attractive and well suited for young readers in both tone and content. The clear color photographs display the animals in all their glory." SLJ

Includes bibliographical references

639.2   Commercial fishing, whaling, sealing

Foster, Mark

★ Whale port; a history of Tuckanucket. written by Mark Foster; illustrated by Gerald Foster. Houghton Mifflin Company 2007 64p il $18

Grades: 4 5 6 7   **639.2**

1. Whaling 2. Whaling -- New England -- Juvenile literature 3. City and town life -- New England -- History -- Juvenile literature

ISBN 978-0-618-54722-7; 0-618-54722-3

LC 2006018772

This describes the history of whaling in New England through the fictional village of Tuckanucket and Zachariah Taber, his family and neighbors.

The village is "depicted in precisely detailed ink and crayon pictures. . . . The Fosters . . . have elegantly synthesized a tremendous amount of information into a beguiling format." Horn Book

Kurlansky, Mark

★ The cod's tale; illustrated by S.D. Schindler. Putnam 2002 43p il map $16.99

Grades: 3 4 5 6   **639.2**

1. Fishes 2. Codfish 3. Commercial fishing 4. Atlantic cod 5. Fisheries -- History 6. Cod fisheries -- History 7. Atlantic cod -- Juvenile literature 8. Cod fisheries -- History -- Juvenile literature

ISBN 0-399-23476-4

LC 00-68412

"Schindler's line-and-watercolor scenes are rendered with the delicate hatching of fine engraving and suffused with gentle humor. . . . This is a classic example of an unlikely subject made not only likely but fascinating and informative through authorial and illustrative craftsmanship." Bull Cent Child Books

Includes bibliographical references

McKissack, Patricia C.

★ Black hands, white sails; the story of African-American whalers. [by] Patricia C. McKissack & Fredrick L. McKissack. Scholastic Press 1999 xxiv, 152p il $17.95

Grades: 5 6 7 8   **639.2**
1. Whaling 2. Abolitionists 3. African Americans
ISBN 0-590-48313-7

LC 99-11439

A Coretta Scott King honor book for text, 2000

A history of African-American whalers between 1730 and 1880, describing their contributions to the whaling industry and their role in the abolitionist movement

"A well-researched and detailed book." SLJ

Includes bibliographical references

McMillan, Bruce

Salmon summer; written and photo-illustrated by Bruce McMillan. Houghton Mifflin 1998 32p il $17

Grades: 2 3 4   **639.2**
1. Salmon 2. Fishing 3. Kodiak Island (Alaska) -- Social life and customs -- Pictorial works -- Juvenile literature
ISBN 0-395-84544-0

LC 97-29679

A photo essay describing a young native Alaskan boy fishing for salmon on Kodiak Island as his ancestors have done for generations

"McMillan documents the goings on with his trademark crystal-clear color photographs and an engaging text." Booklist

Includes glossary and bibliographical references

Sandler, Martin W.

★ **Trapped** in ice! an amazing true whaling adventure. Scholastic Nonfiction 2006 168p il $16.99

Grades: 5 6 7 8   **639.2**
1. Whaling 2. Whaling -- Arctic regions -- Juvenile literature
ISBN 0-439-74363-X

LC 2005-42644

"In 1871, people aboard 32 whaling ships discovered just how dangerous Arctic waters could be after they ignored warnings of an early winter. As conditions worsened, the ships were trapped by ice, forcing the 1,219 people to abandon the vessels or die. Sandler's account of this true story is both informative and absorbing. . . . Well-chosen illustrations and side notes on such topics as life aboard ship and women at sea extend readers' understanding." Booklist

Includes glossary and bibliographical references

Somervill, Barbara A.

Commercial fisher. Cherry Lake Pub. 2011 32p il (Cool careers) lib bdg $27.07

Grades: 4 5 6 7   **639.2**
1. Commercial fishing 2. Vocational guidance
ISBN 978-1-60279-986-8; 1-60279-986-5

LC 2010029123

This book begins "with a personal story of a teen and then [segues] into the occupation [of commercial fisher]. . . . [It covers] the necessary training and skills for the job (and options for obtaining them), a typical day, salary expectations, and well-known professionals in the field. The [text is] accessible and clearly written. . . . The [volume has] a generous number of clear color photographs that depict people at work." SLJ

Includes glossary and bibliographical references

639.3 Culture of cold-blooded vertebrates

Bjorklund, Ruth

Lizards. Marshall Cavendish Benchmark 2009 48p il (Great pets) $20.95

Grades: 2 3 4   **639.3**
1. Lizards
ISBN 978-0-7614-2997-5; 0-7614-2997-2

LC 2008-17560

"Describes the characteristics and behavior of pet lizards, also discussing their physical appearance and place in history." Publisher's note

Includes glossary and bibliographical references

Cone, Molly

★ **Come** back, salmon; how a group of dedicated kids adopted Pigeon Creek and brought it back to life. photographs by Sidnee Wheelwright. Sierra Club Bks. for Children 1992 48p il $16.95; pa $7.95

Grades: 3 4 5 6   **639.3**
1. Salmon 2. Wildlife conservation
ISBN 0-87156-572-2; 0-87156-489-0 pa

LC 91-29023

Describes the efforts of the Jackson Elementary School in Everett, Washington, to clean up a nearby stream, stock it with salmon, and preserve it as an unpolluted place where the salmon could return to spawn

"The photographs are superb. . . . Personal and inspiring, the text alternates between descriptions of the project, background information about pollution and renewal, and dialogue of the students recorded; additional scientific information is displayed in panels set off from the main text." Horn Book

Includes glossary

Craats, Rennay

Gecko. Weigl Publishers 2009 32p il (My pet) lib bdg $26; pa $9.95

Grades: 3 4 5   **639.3**
1. Pets 2. Geckos
ISBN 978-1-60596-098-2 lib bdg; 1-60596-098-5 lib bdg; 978-1-60596-099-9 pa; 1-60596-099-3 pa

LC 2009-25985

Information about how to house, feed, and care for geckos.

"With clear, formal writing, and extensive coverage . . . [this title is] useful for reports. . . . Numerous colorful photographs, charts . . . and question-and-answer boxes supplement the [text]." SLJ

Includes glossary

Gaines, Ann

Top 10 reptiles and amphibians for kids; [by] Ann Graham Gaines. Enslow Publishers 2008 48p il (Top pets for kids with American Humane) lib bdg $23.93

Grades: 2 3 4 5   **639.3**
1. Pets 2. Reptiles 3. Amphibians
ISBN 978-0-7660-3074-9 lib bdg; 0-7660-3074-1 lib bdg

LC 2007047884

"Includes beautiful full-color photos showing the animals at their best. Judicious use of text boxes, crisp fonts, and white space will make it easy for readers to follow the flow of information." SLJ

Includes glossary and bibliographical references

Hamilton, Lynn
Turtle. Weigl Publishers 2009 32p il (My pet) lib bdg $26; pa $9.95
Grades: 3 4 5   639.3
1. Pets 2. Turtles
ISBN 978-1-60596-088-3 lib bdg; 1-60596-088-8 lib bdg; 978-1-60596-089-0 pa; 1-60596-089-6 pa
LC 2009-25973
Information about how to house, feed, and care for turtles.

"With clear, formal writing, and extensive coverage . . . [this title is] useful for reports. . . . Numerous color photographs, charts . . . and question-and-answer boxes supplement the [text]." SLJ

Includes glossary

Haney, Johannah
Frogs. Marshall Cavendish Benchmark 2009 48p il (Great pets) lib bdg $29.93
Grades: 2 3 4   639.3
1. Pets 2. Frogs
ISBN 978-0-7614-4151-9 lib bdg; 0-7614-4151-4 lib bdg
LC 2008037242
"Describes the characteristics and behavior of pet frogs, also discussing their physical appearance and place in history." Publisher's note

Includes glossary and bibliographical references

Turtles; [by] Johannah Haney. Marshall Cavendish Benchmark 2008 48p il (Great pets) lib bdg $28.50
Grades: 2 3 4   639.3
1. Pets 2. Turtles
ISBN 978-0-7614-2709-4 lib bdg; 0-7614-2709-0 lib bdg
LC 2006038157
The offers an introduction to turtles as pets and how to choose and care for them

This is an "enthusiastic, warm [introduction]. . . . [It is] clearly written and [is] the most thorough, honest [introduction] to owning a pet [turtle] for this audience." SLJ

Includes glossary and bibliographical references

Hart, Joyce
Snakes. Marshall Cavendish Benchmark 2008 48p il (Great pets) $20.95
Grades: 2 3 4   639.3
1. Pets 2. Snakes
ISBN 978-0-7614-2996-8; 0-7614-2996-4
LC 2008-24333
"Describes the characteristics and behavior of pet snakes, also discussing their physical appearance and place in history." Publisher's note

Includes glossary and bibliographical references

Hernandez-Divers, Sonia
Geckos. Heinemann Lib. 2003 48p il (Keeping unusual pets) lib bdg $24.22

Grades: 3 4 5 6   639.3
1. Pets 2. Geckos
ISBN 1-4034-0282-5
LC 2002-3163
This offers information about geckos and advice about keeping them as pets

"Lively and informative, with photos scattered across and around the pages . . . [this offers] a wealth of valuable advice." SLJ

Includes glossary and bibliographical references

Lunis, Natalie
Green iguanas. Bearport Pub. 2010 24p il map (Peculiar pets) lib bdg $25.26
Grades: 3 4 5   639.3
1. Pets 2. Iguanas
ISBN 978-1-59716-863-2 lib bdg; 1-59716-863-7 lib bdg
LC 2009-17545
Introduces the green iguana, describing its physical characteristics, habitat, and behavior, and discussing the care and diet that it needs if it is kept as a pet

"The language . . . is lively . . . [and] the illustrations are vivid, with photos offering some amusing shots. . . . This [book] . . . will hold readers' attention, but also challenge them to consider the responsibilities required of owners of unusual creatures." SLJ

Includes glossary and bibliographical references

Niven, Felicia Lowenstein
Learning to care for reptiles and amphibians. Enslow Publishers 2010 48p il (Beginning pet care with American Humane) lib bdg $23.93
Grades: 2 3 4   639.3
1. Reptiles 2. Amphibians
ISBN 978-0-7660-3194-4; 0-7660-3194-2
This describes how to care for pet reptiles and amphibians such as frogs, geckos, snakes, salamanders, newts, and turtles.

Includes glossary and bibliographical references

Schafer, Susan
Lizards. Benchmark Bks. 2001 32p il (Perfect pets) lib bdg $15.95
Grades: 3 4 5 6   639.3
1. Pets 2. Lizards 3. Lizards as pets 4. Lizards as pets -- Juvenile literature
ISBN 0-7614-1103-8
LC 99-58088
Describes various kinds of lizards while focusing on those which could best serve as pets by indicating the food they need and the care they require

Includes glossary and bibliographical references

639.34   Fish culture in aquariums

Aliki
★ My visit to the aquarium. HarperCollins Pubs. 1993 un il $15.95; pa $6.95
Grades: K 1 2 3   639.34
1. Marine animals 2. Marine aquariums 3. Freshwater

animals 4. Aquariums -- Juvenile literature
ISBN 0-06-021458-9; 0-06-446186-6 pa

LC 92-18678

During his visit to an aquarium, a boy finds out about the characteristics and environments of many different marine and freshwater creatures

"Fish facts, selected for their child-appeal and delivered in a brisk, conversational tone, are neatly organized by marine environment. . . . The dominant blues and greens of Aliki's watercolors are not only cool and inviting; they also provide visual continuity amid the riot of brightly colored fish." Booklist

Bozzo, Linda

My first fish; [by] Linda Bozzo. Enslow Publishers 2007 32p il (My first pet library from the American Humane Association) lib bdg $22.60

Grades: 1 2 3   **639.34**

1. Fishes 2. Aquariums
ISBN 978-0-7660-2751-0 lib bdg; 0-7660-2751-1 lib bdg

LC 2006010500

"This book explores how to choose the right fish and how to care for your new pet." Publisher's note

Includes glossary and bibliographical references

Buckmaster, Marjorie L.

Freshwater fishes; [by] Marjorie L. Buckmaster. Marshall Cavendish Benchmark 2007 48p il (Great pets) $19.95

Grades: 2 3 4   **639.34**

1. Fishes 2. Aquariums
ISBN 978-0-7614-2712-4

LC 2007017809

The offers an introduction to freshwater fish as pets and how to choose and care for them.

This is an "enthusiastic, warm [introduction]. . . . [It is] clearly written and [is] the most thorough, honest [introduction] to owning [pet fish] for this audience." SLJ

Jeffrey, Laura S.

Fish; how to choose and care for a fish. Enslow Publishers 2004 48p il (American humane pet care library) lib bdg $23.93

Grades: 3 4 5   **639.34**

1. Pets 2. Fishes 3. Aquariums 4. Aquarium fishes 5. Aquarium fishes -- Juvenile literature
ISBN 0-7660-2517-9

LC 2003-22968

Explains how to set up a personalized aquarium, pick the right fish, and how to keep them happy and healthy

Includes glossary and bibliographical references

Niven, Felicia Lowenstein

Learning to care for fish. Enslow Publishers 2010 48p il (Beginning pet care with American Humane) lib bdg $23.93

Grades: 2 3 4   **639.34**

1. Fishes 2. Aquariums
ISBN 978-0-7660-3193-7; 0-7660-3193-4

This describes how to care for pet fish.

"The pictures are colorful and engaging, with a no-fuss layout. The text is easy to follow, pitched at just the right level for the audience." SLJ

Includes glossary and bibliographical references

Rau, Dana Meachen

Top 10 fish for kids; [by] Dana Meachen Rau. Enslow Publishers 2008 48p il (Top pets for kids with American Humane) lib bdg $23.93

Grades: 2 3 4 5   **639.34**

1. Fishes 2. Aquariums
ISBN 978-0-7660-3073-2 lib bdg; 0-7660-3073-3 lib bdg

LC 2007-32319

"Includes beautiful full-color photos showing the animals at their best. Judicious use of text boxes, crisp fonts, and white space will make it easy for readers to follow the flow of information." SLJ

Includes glossary and bibliographical references

Richardson, Adele

Caring for your fish; by Adele Richardson. Capstone Press 2007 24p il (Positively pets) $21.26

Grades: K 1 2 3   **639.34**

1. Fishes 2. Aquariums
ISBN 978-0-7368-6386-5; 0-7368-6386-9

LC 2005035854

This is a "concise, competent [introduction] to the responsibility and fun of being a pet owner. . . . Attractive and well suited for young readers in both tone and content. The clear color photographs display the animals in all their glory." SLJ

Includes bibliographical references

639.9   Conservation of biological resources

Buckley, Carol

Just for elephants. Tilbury House 2006 un il $16.95

Grades: 3 4 5 6   **639.9**

1. Elephants 2. Wildlife conservation 3. Elephants -- Juvenile literature
ISBN 978-0-88448-283-3; 0-88448-283-9

LC 2006-22283

"This is a beautifully written, compelling story of a conscientious drive to care for these animals in a humane way." SLJ

Curtis, Jennifer Keats

Animal helpers; wildlife rehabilitators. Jennifer Keats Curtis. Sylvan Dell Pub. 2012 32 p. (hardcover) $17.95

Grades: K 1 2   **639.9**

1. Animals 2. Veterinarians 3. Wildlife rehabilitation
ISBN 1607186713; 9781607186717; 9781607186724; 9781607186731; 9781607186748

LC 2012937373

This "photographic journal takes readers 'behind the scenes' at four different wildlife rehabilitation centers" that help "wild animals when they are injured, become ill, or are orphaned." It shows "backyard animals as they are nursed back to health and released back to the wild when possible." (Publisher's note)

Fleming, Denise, 1950-

★ **Where** once there was a wood. Holt & Co. 1996 un il $16.95; pa $6.95

Grades: K 1 2   **639.9**

1. Habitat (Ecology) 2. Wildlife conservation

ISBN 0-8050-3761-6; 0-8050-6482-6 pa

LC 95-18906

"Lush, textured collage artwork features a stunning combination and arrangement of colors with brilliant hues juxtaposed against muted earth tones. . . . The gentle, poetic narration is never overpowered by the pictures." SLJ

Includes bibliographical references

George, Jean Craighead

A **tarantula** in my purse; and 172 other wild pets. written and illustrated by Jean Craighead George. Harper-Collins Pubs. 1996 134p il hardcover o.p. pa $5.99

Grades: 4 5 6   **639.9**

1. Pets 2. Artists 3. Authors 4. Naturalists 5. Illustrators 6. Women authors 7. Authors, American 8. Children's authors 9. Wildlife conservation -- Personal narratives -- Juvenile literature

ISBN 0-06-023626-4; 0-06-446201-3 pa

LC 95-54151

"Told in a casual and thoroughly engaging manner, the stories will enchant all animal lovers and even those who aren't." SLJ

Hatkoff, Juliana

Winter's tail; how one little dolphin learned to swim again. told by Juliana Hatkoff, Isabella Hatkoff, and Craig Hatkoff. Scholastic Press 2009 un il $16.99

Grades: 3 4 5 6   **639.9**

1. Dolphins 2. Artificial limbs

ISBN 978-0-545-12335-8; 0-545-12335-6

"A compassionate look at the true odyssey of an orphaned Atlantic bottlenose dolphin. Rescued from a crab trap, with severe injuries, 'Winter' was brought to the Clearwater (FL) Marine Aquarium and, despite the heroic efforts of the staff, lost her tail. . . . Winter caught the attention of a prosthetic engineer, and the Hatkoffs' clear text follows the efforts of a mixed team from the aquarium and Hanger Prosthetics & Orthotics to design a workable 'tail' to keep her healthy. Full-color photos reveal the cooperative efforts of the human team and Winter in this journey toward a more normal life." SLJ

Lasky, Kathryn

★ **Interrupted** journey; illustrated by Christopher Knight. Candlewick Press 2001 un il hardcover o.p. pa $6.99

Grades: 3 4 5 6   **639.9**

1. Sea turtles 2. Rare animals 3. Wildlife conservation 4. Wildlife rescue 5. Lepidochelys kempii

ISBN 0-7636-0635-9; 0-7636-2883-2 pa

LC 99-57126

Describes efforts to protect sea turtles, particularly Kemp's ridley turtles, and help them reproduce and replenish their once-dwindling numbers

"There's a sense of wonder in the simple words and the huge, thrilling color pictures in this photo-essay." Booklist

Montgomery, Sy

★ **Kakapo** rescue; saving the world's strangest parrot. text by Sy Montgomery; photographs by Nic Bishop. Houghton Mifflin 2010 73p il map (Scientists in the field) $18

Grades: 4 5 6 7   **639.9**

1. Parrots 2. Endangered species 3. Wildlife conservation 4. Kakapo -- Juvenile literature

ISBN 978-0-618-49417-0; 0-618-49417-0

LC 2009-45250

Awarded the Robert F. Sibert Medal, 2011

Montgomery and Bishop head "to a remote island off the southern tip of New Zealand, where they join a local government-sponsored research team that is working to save the Kakapo parrot from extinction. . . . Montgomery's delight in her subject is contagious, and throughout her enthusiastic text, she nimbly blends scientific and historical facts with immediate, sensory descriptions of fieldwork. Young readers will be fascinated. . . . Bishop's photos of the creatures and their habitat are stunning." Booklist

Stetson, Emily

Kids' easy-to-create wildlife habitats; [by] Emily Stetson. Williamson Books 2004 128p il map (Quick starts for kids!) pa $12.95

Grades: 2 3 4   **639.9**

1. Habitat (Ecology) 2. Wildlife conservation

ISBN 0-8249-8665-2

LC 2004-40871

This "book shows children how to observe and support wildlife around their homes, schools, and communities. Packed with useful information. . . . With sound advice and many helpful illustrations, precisely drawn in blue and gray ink, this offers children small ways to support wildlife close to home." Booklist

640   Home and family management

Ernst, Lisa Campbell, 1957-

How things work in the house; Lisa Campbell Ernst. 1st ed. Blue Apple Books 2012 1 v. (unpaged) col. ill. (hardcover) $16.99

Grades: 1 2 3   **640**

1. Kitchen utensils 2. Questions and answers 3. Household equipment and supplies 4. Home economics -- Equipment and supplies -- Juvenile literature

ISBN 1609051890; 9781609051891

LC 2011038908

In her book, author Lisa Campbell Ernst "explains what can be done with things in our houses" and how things work. "The varied uses of . . . bananas . . . and spoons" are discussed. "Similarly, popcorn, sandwiches, scissors, glue, piggy banks and kazoos are featured." The book offers a "glimpse at how things work in our houses . . . [and] everyday worlds." (Kirkus Reviews)

Gaarder-Juntti, Oona

What in the world is a green home? ABDO Pub. Co. 2010 24p il (Going green) lib bdg $24.21

Grades: 1 2 3 4   **640**
1. Housing -- Environmental aspects
ISBN 978-1-61613-189-0 lib bdg; 1-61613-189-6
lib bdg

LC 2010004340

"The lively layout design, featuring colorful headings, short paragraphs, and attractive photographs, has a scrapbook-like quality.... [The title explains] how all our choices require energy and resources, and encourage readers to make changes in their lifestyles.... [This] ... will inspire and empower readers to make a difference." SLJ

Includes glossary and bibliographical references

641.3   Food

Burleigh, Robert
Chocolate; riches from the rainforest. Abrams 2002
un il $16.95
Grades: 3 4 5 6   **641.3**
1. Chocolate 2. Chocolate -- History 3. Chocolate processing 4. Chocolate industry -- History
ISBN 0-8109-5734-5

LC 2001-3744

Traces the history of chocolate from a drink of the Olmec and Maya and later in Europe to its popularity around the world today

"Chocolate's fascinating story pairs with mouth watering photos in this handsome, picture-book-size overview." Booklist

Includes glossary and bibliographical references

Butterworth, Chris
How Did That Get in My Lunchbox? the story of food. [by] Chris Butterworth; illustrated by Lucia Gaggiotti. Candlewick 2013 25 p. il $5.99
Grades: K 1 2 3   **641.3**
1. Food 2. Nutrition 3. Food/Juvenile literature
ISBN 0763665037; 9780763665036

LC 2010003034

"Taking stock of the contents of a typical school lunchbox, Butterworth and Gaggiotti serve up [an] ... overview of seven familiar ingredients' journeys, from the bread holding a sandwich together to the chocolate chips in a cookie.... [The book follows food] from the farm (or grove or orchard) through the production process (at the mill, the bakery, the dairy, etc.) to the delivery of the final product. [Index.] Primary." (Horn Book)

"With reader-directed prose and cheerfully retro artwork, Butterworth and Gaggiotti use a balanced meal—sandwich, fruit, veggies, juice box, and cookie—to explain how foodstuffs make it from farms, dairies, and factories into kids' lunches." Publ Wkly

Chapman, Garry
Coffee; by Garry Chapman and Gary Hodges. Black Rabbit 2010 32p il (World commodities) lib bdg $28.50
Grades: 5 6 7 8   **641.3**
1. Coffee
ISBN 978-1-59920-584-7 lib bdg; 1-59920-584-X
lib bdg
"The first part of the book discusses how coffee beans are grown, treated, prepared, and enjoyed around the world.

... The second section offers an opportunity to use the commodity of coffee to understand such economics concepts as supply and demand or futures trading.... Finally, the book spins through a look at fair trade practices; political, environmental, and social issues surrounding coffee trade; and the sustainability and outlook of the global coffee industry. In all, the book gleans a pretty impressive and diverse array of accessible information from such a small bean." Booklist

Includes glossary

Cleary, Brian P.
Apples, cherries, red raspberries; what is in the fruits group? illustrations by Martin Goneau; consultant, Jennifer K. Nelson. Millbrook Press 2010 31p il (Food is CATegorical) lib bdg $25.26
Grades: K 1 2 3   **641.3**
1. Fruit 2. Nutrition
ISBN 978-1-58013-589-4 lib bdg; 1-58013-589-7
lib bdg

LC 2009049582

"With highly readable bits and pieces about which yummy foods have which nutrients and vitamins [this book is] .. . just right for sharing with young kids, introducing the value of healthy foods and exercise through silly rhymes, puns, zany color cartoons of cats in wild action. The scenarios .. . range from cat characters picking apples in an orchard to a big cat that triumphs in a boxing ring after eating 'cool' bananas." Booklist

Green beans, potatoes, and even tomatoes; what is in the vegetable group? by Brian P. Cleary; illustrations by Martin Goneau; consultant, Jennifer K. Nelson. Millbrook Press 2010 31p il (Food is CATegorical) lib bdg $25.26
Grades: K 1 2 3   **641.3**
1. Nutrition 2. Vegetables
ISBN 978-1-58013-588-7 lib bdg; 1-58013-588-9
lib bdg

LC 2009-49592

"With highly readable bits and pieces about which yummy foods have which nutrients and vitamins [this book is] .. . just right for sharing with young kids, introducing the value of healthy foods and exericse through silly rhymes, puns, and zany color cartoons of cats in wild action.... Sweet potatoes, carrots, and more are portrayed as both wholesome and tasty." Booklist

D'Amico, Joan
The science chef; 100 fun food experiments and recipes for kids. [by] Joan D'Amico, Karen Eich Drummond; illustrations by Tina Cash-Walsh. Wiley 1995 180p il $12.95
Grades: 4 5 6   **641.3**
1. Food 2. Cooking 3. Science -- Experiments 4. Food -- Juvenile literature 5. Cooking -- Juvenile literature 6. Science -- Experiments -- Juvenile literature
ISBN 0-471-31045-X

LC 94-9045

This includes facts about food, recipes, and experiments with food

"Attractively illustrated with black-and-white line drawings, easy and interesting to read, and filled with tidbits of information." SLJ

Includes glossary

De Paola, Tomie
The **popcorn** book. Holiday House 1978 un il lib
bdg $16.95; pa $6.95
Grades: K 1 2 3   **641.3**
  1. Popcorn
  ISBN 0-8234-0314-9 lib bdg; 0-8234-0533-8 pa
                                          LC 77-21456
The author-artist's "amusing soft-color pictures—each
bordered with a lavender frame—show action in the past or
the present while a few lines of text or balloon speeches describe what is happening." Horn Book

Eamer, Claire
The **world** in your lunch box; the wacky history and
weird science of everyday foods. Claire Eamer; artwork by
Sa Boothroyd. Annick Press 2012 121 p.
Grades: 4 5 6   **641.3**
  1. Nutrition 2. Food -- History 3. Food -- Composition
  4. Food -- Juvenile literature
  ISBN 1554513936; 9781554513932
This book by Claire Eamer presents an "exploration of
food history and food science . . . '[E]verything's interesting if you take the time to learn about it,' says the cooking
teacher, who challenges his students to keep a record of their
lunches and research their backgrounds. . . . . The lunches
described are usually well-balanced. From each, the author
has chosen a selection of ingredients, providing examples
of their use in history and offering . . . science connections.
Most topics are covered in a single page [along with] cartoon-styled drawings . . . [and] jokes . . . Ten favorite food
facts conclude the narrative, but there are also suggestions
for further reading, an extensive bibliography and even an
index". (Kirkus)
  Includes bibliographical references and index.

Gaarder-Juntti, Oona
  What in the world is green food? ABDO Pub. Co. 2010
24p il (Going green) lib bdg $24.21
Grades: 1 2 3 4   **641.3**
  1. Food -- Environmental aspects
  ISBN 978-1-61613-192-0 lib bdg; 1-61613-192-6
  lib bdg
                                          LC 2010004321
  "The lively layout design, featuring colorful headings,
short paragraphs, and attractive photographs, has a scrapbook-like quality. . . . [The title explains] how all our choices
require energy and resources, and encourage readers to make
changes in their lifestyles. . . . [This] . . . will inspire and
empower readers to make a difference." SLJ
  Includes glossary and bibliographical references

Hewitt, Sally
  Your food. Crabtree Pub. Co. 2009 32p il (Green
team) $26.60; pa $8.95
Grades: 3 4 5 6   **641.3**
  1. Food
  ISBN 978-0-7787-4099-5; 0-7787-4099-4; 978-0-
  7787-4106-0 pa; 0-7787-4106-0 pa
                                          LC 2008023291
  "The color graphics and layouts are highly appealing and
will definitely be attractive to young readers. . . . This . . . is
an excellent resource for school libraries, science teachers,
and community sponsors." Libr Media Connect
  Includes glossary

Jango-Cohen, Judith
  The **history** of food; [by] Judith Jango-Cohen. Twenty-First Century Books 2006 56p il (Major inventions
through history) lib bdg $26.60
Grades: 5 6 7 8   **641.3**
  1. Food -- History
  ISBN 0-8225-2484-8
                                          LC 2004-23022
  This history of food "discusses canning, pasteurization,
refrigeration, supermarkets, and genetically modified foods.
. . . The text . . . is breezy but informative; unfamiliar terms
are defined. Illustrations are a mixture of period black-and-
white and color photos." SLJ
  Includes bibliographical references

Landau, Elaine
  Popcorn; illustrated by Brian Lies. Charlesbridge Pub.
2003 32p il hardcover o.p. pa $7.95
Grades: 2 3 4   **641.3**
  1. Popcorn
  ISBN 1-57091-442-7 lib bdg; 1-57091-443-5 pa
                                          LC 2002-2271
  Provides a history of one of America's favorite snack
foods, presenting its origins, nutritional information
and recipes
  "Lies' brightly colored acrylic illustrations enhance the
humor of the text. . . . This will be useful for classroom
projects and report writers as well as entertaining reading."
Booklist
  Includes bibliographical references

Llewellyn, Claire
  Cooking with fruits and vegetables; by Claire Llewellyn
with recipes by Clare O'Shea. Rosen Central 2011 48p il
(Cooking healthy) lib bdg $27.95
Grades: 5 6 7 8   **641.3**
  1. Fruit 2. Cooking 3. Vegetables
  ISBN 978-1-4488-4844-7; 1-4488-4844-X
                                          LC 2010039333
  This book pairs "facts about [fruits and vegetables], including where it is eaten, with eye-catching photos. . . . Each
course (section) has an overview of the vegetable group . .
. followed by recipes from all over the world. They vary in
difficulty. . . . The cooking directions are clear and straightforward. . . . [The book is] profusely illustrated with full-col-
or photos. Students who are learning to cook will appreciate
[this] excellently organized [read]." SLJ
  Includes bibliographical references

Malam, John
  Grow your own snack. Heinemann Library 2011 32p
il (Grow it yourself!) lib bdg $26; pa $7.99
Grades: 2 3 4   **641.3**
  1. Beans 2. Cooking 3. Vegetable gardening
  ISBN 978-1-4329-5107-8 lib bdg; 978-1-4329-5114-
  6 pa
                                          LC 2010049849
  This describes how to grow broad beans, and how to fry
them for a snack.
  Includes glossary and bibliographical references

Menzel, Peter

★ **What** the world eats; photographed by Peter Menzel; written by Faith D'Aluisio. Tricycle Press 2008 160p il map $22.99

Grades: 4 5 6 7 8   **641.3**

1. Diet 2. Eating customs 3. Food -- Pictorial works 4. Food habits -- Juvenile literature

ISBN 978-1-58246-246-2; 1-58246-246-1

LC 2007-41439

An adaptation of Hungry Planet, published 2005 by Ten Speed Press for adults

"Stunning color photographs of mealtimes and daily activities illustrate the warm, informative, anecdotal narratives. . . . This is a fascinating, sobering, and instructive look at daily life around the world." Booklist

Includes bibliographical references

Micucci, Charles

★ The **life** and times of the peanut. Houghton Mifflin 1997 31p il music hardcover o.p. pa $6.95

Grades: 2 3 4   **641.3**

1. Peanuts 2. Peanuts -- Juvenile literature

ISBN 0-395-72289-6; 0-618-03314-9 pa

LC 96-1290

"The author presents information on how peanuts grow, how they are farmed, where they are produced . . . and how they are used worldwide. What sets this book apart is Micucci's amusing and creative techniques for bringing statistics to life. . . . The artwork is attractive . . . with great attention to line, movement, and color, all carefully placed on the pages." Booklist

Miller, Jeanne

Food science. Lerner Publications 2009 48p il (Cool science) lib bdg $27.93

Grades: 4 5 6   **641.3**

1. Food

ISBN 978-0-8225-7589-4 lib bdg; 0-8225-7589-2 lib bdg

This describes how food scientists "explore how cooking changes food, create dishes that surprise the senses, and help farmers grow food in healthier ways." Publisher's note

Includes glossary and bibliographical references

Peterson, Cris

★ **Seed** soil sun; earth's recipe for food. photographs by David R. Lundquist. Boyd Mills Press 2010 un il $17.95

Grades: PreK K 1 2   **641.3**

1. Food 2. Seeds 3. Plants

ISBN 978-1-59078-713-7; 1-59078-713-7

The children's book discusses "[p]hotosynthesis . . . [and how] plants take our planet's basic resources (sunlight, water, and air) and generate food and oxygen. . . . Peterson's . . . text is [accompanied by David Lundquist's] . . . photography [that] illustrates her account, which features maize as an example. Lundquist shows . . . worms that till the soil as well as corn plants ranging from seedlings, through knee-highs, to full-grown harvestable stalks." (Science)

"Peterson explains how most food comes from seeds, which—thanks to nutrients from soil and energy from the sun—grow into fruits and vegetables. Lundquist's color photographs . . . may have kids considering an attempt at growing their own food." Publ Wkly

Includes bibliographical references

Price, Sean

The **story** behind chocolate; [by] Sean Stewart Price. Heinemann Library 2009 32p il map lib bdg $28.21

Grades: 3 4 5   **641.3**

1. Chocolate

ISBN 978-1-4329-2347-1 lib bdg; 1-4329-2347-1 lib bdg

LC 2008037524

"Price explains how chocolate was discovered and became popular, its ingredients, the chocolate-making process, and how companies like Hershey and Cadbury became successful. . . . The well-organized [text is] informative and clearly written, and the numerous color photographs and drawings are eye-catching and complement the [narrative] well." SLJ

Includes bibliographical references

Reilly, Kathleen M.

Food; 25 amazing projects investigate the history and science of what we eat. illustrated by Farah Rizvi. Nomad Press 2010 124p il (Build it yourself) pa $15.95

Grades: 4 5 6   **641.3**

1. Food

ISBN 978-1-934670-59-0; 1-934670-59-6

"This broad overview of food touches on its history and future, production and packaging, social and cultural practices, and health and safety concerns. . . . The information presented and questions posed on food packaging, megafarming, locally grown vs. commercially grown foods, free-range grazing, and healthy food choices make this a particularly up-to-date survey. . . . Every chapter concludes with two to three hands-on activities that range from cooking to science and art projects. . . . This soup-to-nuts look at the business and consumption of food will make a good addition to most collections." SLJ

Includes glossary and bibliographical references

Robbins, Ken

★ **Food** for thought; the stories behind the things we eat. Roaring Brook Press 2009 45p il $17.95

Grades: 2 3 4   **641.3**

1. Food

ISBN 978-1-59643-343-4; 1-59643-343-4

LC 2007-44062

"Robbins focuses on a mouthwatering array of produce: apples, oranges, potatoes, tomatoes, grapes, bananas, mushrooms, and pomegranates. Each spacious spread combines Robbins' vibrantly hued photographs with engaging text filled with information about each food, including its nutritional content, history, current methods of cultivation, and appearance in figures of speech ('couch potato'), as well as mythology and folklore. . . . The enticing images will draw young readers into the captivating assortment of facts." Booklist

Sayre, April Pulley

★ **Go**, go, grapes! April Pulley Sayre. 1st ed. Simon & Schuster 2012 1v. (unpaged) col. ill. (hardcover) $16.99

Grades: K 1 2   **641.3**

1. Fruit 2. Children's poetry 3. Picture books for

children 4. Grapes -- Juvenile literature
ISBN 1442433906; 9781442433908

LC 2011011602

In this book, April Pulley Sayre presents photographs of "the standard apple, orange, banana, grapes and berries, [and] she entices readers with such exotics as tamarillo, kiwano, guava, rambutan, currant, durian and . . . dragon fruit. . . . Sayre shows off the colors and textures. . . . Several fruits are cut to show off their insides, such as the seeds of the kiwi and pomegranate and the intriguing cross sections of a lychee and mangosteen." (Kirkus Reviews)

★ Rah, rah, radishes! a vegetable chant. Beach Lane Books 2011 un il $14.99
Grades: PreK K   641.3
1. Vegetables 2. Food -- Poetry
ISBN 978-1-4424-2141-7; 1-4424-2141-X
LC 2010034360

Photographs of vegetables and rhyming text celebrate vegetables in all their colorful and tasty variety.

"Each page calls out a cheer-worthy vegetable in two short lines of text, accompanied by a large, colorful photograph. . . . With its upbeat, easy-to-digest text and large, clear images, this book will become a go-to choice in spring-themed preschool storytimes and early elementary health or environmental units." SLJ

Sylver, Adrienne
Hot diggity dog; the history of the hot dog. illustrated by Elwood H. Smith. Dutton Children's Books 2010 un il $16.99
Grades: K 1 2 3   641.3
1. Frankfurters
ISBN 978-0-525-47897-3; 0-525-47897-3

"How did hot dogs become so popular? asks Sylver in this popular history of the wiener. . . . Accompanied by Smith's handsomely goofy, retro artwork, the narrative offers sidebars with factual tidbits galore." Kirkus

Thornhill, Jan
Who wants pizza? the kids' guide to the history, science & culture of food. Maple Tree Press 2010 64p il $22.95; pa $10.95
Grades: 4 5 6   641.3
1. Food 2. Agriculture
ISBN 978-1-897349-96-0; 1-897349-96-3; 978-1-897349-97-7 pa; 1-897349-97-1 pa

This discusses "where food comes from and if there's enough to go around. Amid color photographs and sidebars, Thornhill writes concisely about hunter-gatherers, agriculture, processed foods, globalization, and poverty, among numerous other topics, providing a straightforward and balanced overview of the modern food industry, and the choices readers have when it comes to their own meals." Publ Wkly

641.5 Cooking

Arroyo, Sheri L.
How chefs use math; math curriculum consultant, Rhea A. Stewart. Chelsea Clubhouse 2010 32p il (Math in the real world) lib bdg $28

Grades: 4 5 6   641.5
1. Cooks 2. Cooking 3. Mathematics 4. Vocational guidance
ISBN 978-1-60413-608-1 lib bdg; 1-60413-608-1 lib bdg
LC 2009-14180

This describes how chefs use math for such tasks as measuring ingredients, watching temperatures, buying food, setting menu prices, and managing restaurant and catering businesses, and includes relevant math problems and information about how to become a chef

Includes glossary and bibliographical references

Batmanglij, Najmieh
Happy Nowruz; cooking with children to celebrate the Persian New Year. [by] Najmieh Batmanglij. Mage Publishers 2008 119p il $40
Grades: 4 5 6 7 8   641.5
1. New Year 2. Eating customs 3. Middle Eastern cooking 4. Iran -- Social life and customs
ISBN 1-933823-16-X; 978-1-933823-16-4
LC 2007-036047

"Combining a cookbook format with straightforward, informational text, this amply illustrated title offers a detailed introduction to the history and customs surrounding Nowruz, the Persian New Year. . . . The covered spiral binding allows pages to remain open while cooking, and the uncluttered, attractive format, featuring color photos of kids in the kitchen and whimsical illustrations, will attract interested browsers." Booklist

Beery, Barbara
Barbara Beery's pink princess party cookbook; photography by Zac Williams. Simon & Schuster Books for Young Readers 2011 55p il spiral $15.99
Grades: 2 3 4 5   641.5
1. Cooking 2. Parties 3. Entertaining
ISBN 978-1-4424-1231-6; 1-4424-1231-3
LC 2010017691

"Beery offers ideas for six themed celebrations, such as a mermaid princess party, a garden fairy princess party, and a spa princess party. They all include delicate but easy-to-follow recipes for punch, cookies, cakes, sushi, and decorations, as well as themed crafts such as body lotion and floral headbands. These are well-planned ideas, with plenty of full-color photographs to support the text." SLJ

Behnke, Alison
Cooking the Central American way; [by] Alison M. Behnke, in consultation with Griselda Aracely Chacon and Kristina Anderson. Lerner Publications Co. 2005 72p il (Easy menu ethnic cookbooks) lib bdg $25.26
Grades: 5 6 7 8   641.5
1. Central American cooking
ISBN 978-0-8225-1236-3; 0-8225-1236-X
LC 2004-11870

An introduction to the cooking of Central America. Includes glossary

Cooking the Mediterranean way; culturally authentic foods, including low-fat and vegetarian recipes. Alison M. Behnke, in consultation with Anna and Lazaros Christoforides. Lerner Publications 2005 72p il map (Easy menu ethnic cookbooks) lib bdg $25.26

Grades: 5 6 7 8   **641.5**
   1. Mediterranean cooking
   ISBN 0-8225-1237-8; 978-0-8225-1237-0
                        LC 2004-11054
   An introduction to Mediterranean cooking and food habits, featuring traditional recipes and including information on the history, geography, customs, and people of this region of the world.
   Includes glossary

Cooking the Middle Eastern way; culturally authentic foods including low-fat and vegetarian recipes. Alison Behnke in consultation with Vartkes Ehramjian. Lerner Publications Co. 2005 72p il map (Easy menu ethnic cookbooks) lib bdg $25.26
Grades: 5 6 7 8   **641.5**
   1. Middle Eastern cooking
   ISBN 978-0-8225-1238-7; 0-8225-1238-6
                        LC 2004-19658
"This volume begins with an introduction to the history and varied cultures of the Middle East, followed by lists of cooking tips, utensils, terminology, and regional ingredients as well as a discussion of healthy, low-fat choices. . . . This is a well-designed, attractive source of recipes for Middle Eastern fare." Booklist
   Includes glossary

Berman, Karen
Easy-peasy recipes; snacks and treats to make and eat. Karen Berman; [edited by] Kirsten Hall. Running Press Kids 2012 40 p. $14.95
Grades: 1 2 3   **641.5**
   1. Cooking 2. Cookbooks 3. Children -- Nutrition
   ISBN 0762444436; 9780762444434
                       LC 2011937816
   This cookbook by Karen Berman is "geared toward independent child chefs. The 13 snack and treat recipes . . . [include] a taco-salad pirate face, a breakfast buffet shaped like a train with individual cars and a berry-and-yogurt-snow-capped mountain. To assemble these creations, young chefs are directed to use a pair of (washed) safety scissors instead of knives. . . . 'Do It Another Way' sections accompanying each recipe give readers ideas for substituting ingredients or trying new ones." (Kirkus Reviews)

Blaxland, Wendy
   American food. Smart Apple Media 2012 32p il map (I can cook!) lib bdg $28.50
Grades: 3 4 5 6   **641.5**
   1. Cooking
   ISBN 978-1-59920-667-7; 1-59920-667-6
                       LC 2011005443
   Describes historical, cultural, and geographical factors that have influenced the cuisine of the United States. Includes recipes to create American food.
   This includes "recipes with kid appeal. . . . Captioned, full-color photographs provide step-by-step directions. . . . [An] ideal [supplement] to culture and country studies." SLJ
   Includes glossary

   Chinese food. Smart Apple Media 2012 32p il map (I can cook!) lib bdg $28.50

Grades: 3 4 5 6   **641.5**
   1. Chinese cooking
   ISBN 978-1-59920-671-4; 1-59920-671-4
                       LC 2011005448
   Describes historical, cultural, and geographical factors that have influenced the cuisine of China. Includes recipes to create Chinese food.
   This includes "recipes with kid appeal. . . . Captioned, full-color photographs provide step-by-step directions. . . . [An] ideal [supplement] to culture and country studies." SLJ
   Includes glossary

   French food. Smart Apple Media 2012 32p il map (I can cook!) lib bdg $28.50
Grades: 3 4 5 6   **641.5**
   1. French cooking
   ISBN 978-1-59920-669-1; 1-59920-669-2
                       LC 2011005445
   Describes historical, cultural, and geographical factors that have influenced the cuisine of France. Includes recipes to create French food.
   This includes "recipes with kid appeal. . . . Captioned, full-color photographs provide step-by-step directions. . . . [An] ideal [supplement] to culture and country studies." SLJ
   Includes glossary

   Italian food. Smart Apple Media 2012 32p il map (I can cook!) lib bdg $28.50
Grades: 3 4 5 6   **641.5**
   1. Italian cooking
   ISBN 978-1-59920-670-7; 1-59920-670-6
                       LC 2011005446
   Describes historical, cultural, and geographical factors that have influenced the cuisine of Italy. Includes recipes to create Italian food.
   Includes glossary

   Mexican food. Smart Apple Media 2012 32p il map (I can cook!) lib bdg $28.50
Grades: 3 4 5 6   **641.5**
   1. Mexican cooking
   ISBN 978-1-59920-668-4; 1-59920-668-4
                       LC 2011005444
   Describes historical, cultural, and geographical factors that have influenced the cuisine of Mexico. Includes recipes to create Mexican food.
   This includes "recipes with kid appeal. . . . Captioned, full-color photographs provide step-by-step directions. . . . [An] ideal [supplement] to culture and country studies." SLJ
   Includes glossary

   Middle Eastern food. Smart Apple Media 2012 32p il map (I can cook!) lib bdg $28.50
Grades: 3 4 5 6   **641.5**
   1. Middle Eastern cooking
   ISBN 978-1-59920-672-1
                       LC 2011005450
   Describes historical, cultural, and geographical factors that have influenced the cuisine of the Middle East. Includes recipes to create Middle-Eastern food.

This includes "recipes with kid appeal. . . . Captioned, full-color photographs provide step-by-step directions. . . . [An] ideal [supplement] to culture and country studies." SLJ

Includes glossary

Bloomfield, Jill

Jewish holidays cookbook; by Jill Colella Bloomfield; Janet Ozur Bass, consultant; photography by Angela Coppola. DK Pub. 2008 128p il spiral bdg $19.99

Grades: 4 5 6 7   **641.5**

1. Jewish cooking 2. Jewish holidays

ISBN 978-0-7566-4089-7 spiral bdg; 0-7566-4089-X spiral bdg

"More than 40 recipes are included for celebrations from Shabbat to Lag B'Omer. Several introductions explain cooking tools, kitchen safety, and the general principles of keeping kosher, and brief background information is given for each holiday. Simple step-by-step instructions make the recipes easy. . . . Beautiful color photographs, both full page and spot, whet the appetite." SLJ

Bowers, Sharon

Ghoulish goodies. Storey Pub. 2009 153p il pa $14.95

Grades: 3 4 5 6   **641.5**

1. Desserts 2. Halloween 3. Holiday cooking

ISBN 978-1-60342-146-1 pa; 1-60342-146-7 pa

LC 2009007802

This offers recipes for Halloween-themed desserts such as Monster Eyeballs, Chocolate Spider Clusters, Buried Alive Cupcakes, and Screaming Red Punch

"Perfect for Halloween and beyond, this conveniently organized, well-illustrated cookbook is sure to be a crowd-pleaser. . . . Most recipes are complemented by a full-color photograph of the finished product. . . . Hauntingly appetizing." SLJ

Cornell, Kari A.

Cooking the Indonesian way; [by] Kari A. Cornell and Merry Anwar. Lerner Publications Company 2004 72p il (Easy menu ethnic cookbooks) lib bdg $25.26

Grades: 5 6 7 8   **641.5**

1. Indonesian cooking

ISBN 978-0-8225-4127-1; 0-8225-4127-0

LC 2003-11205

Introduces the land, people, and regional cooking of Indonesia and includes recipes for such dishes as pork sate, corn fritters, and chicken in coconut cream sauce.

Includes glossary

Cooking the southern African way; by Kari Cornell in consultaiton with Peter Thomas. Lerner Publications Co. 2005 72p il map (Easy menu ethnic cookbooks) lib bdg $25.26

Grades: 5 6 7 8   **641.5**

1. South African cooking

ISBN 978-0-8225-1239-4; 0-8225-1239-4

LC 2004-11869

Introduces the history, land, and food of South Africa and includes recipes.

Includes glossary

D'Amico, Joan

★ The coming to America cookbook; delicious recipes and fascinating stories from America's many cultures. [by] Joan D'Amico, Karen Eich Drummond. Wiley 2005 180p il pa $14.95

Grades: 5 6 7 8   **641.5**

1. Cooking

ISBN 0-471-48335-4

LC 2004-14947

The authors "provide information about American immigrants from 18 nations as well as recipes representing each group. . . . Accompanied by line drawings of ethnic families choosing, preparing, and eating food, . . . chapters discuss each country's climate, history, major waves of emigration, and traditional foods. Typically, three recipes follow. . . . Teachers and students looking for recipes from American immigrant cultures will make good use of this handy resource." Booklist

Dodge, Abigail Johnson

★ Around the world cookbook. DK Publishing 2008 124p il map spiral bdg $19.99

Grades: 3 4 5 6   **641.5**

1. Cooking

ISBN 978-0-7566-3744-6 spiral bdg; 0-7566-3744-9 spiral bdg

"This book presents more than 50 step-by-step recipes for ethnic cuisine. Dodge opens with instructions for basic cooking skills, an illustrated list of kitchen tools, a glossary of terms used in the recipes, and tips for working with different types of ingredients. . . . Possibly tricky steps are clarified with photographs and captions." SLJ

Ejaz, Khadija

Recipe and craft guide to India. Mitchell Lane Publishers 2010 63p il map (World crafts and recipes) lib bdg $33.95

Grades: 4 5 6 7 8   **641.5**

1. Handicraft 2. Indic cooking

ISBN 978-1-58415-938-4 lib bdg; 1-58415-938-3 lib bdg

LC 2010008950

Provides recipes for several popular Indian dishes and includes instructions on creating colorful and traditional Indian crafts.

This provides "plenty of ideas for adding tasty treats and impressive visual aids to cultural reports or presentations." SLJ

Includes glossary and bibliographical references

Gerasole, Isabella

The Spatulatta cookbook; by Isabella and Olivia Gerasole; photographs by John Zich. Scholastic 2007 128p il spiral bdg $16.99

Grades: 3 4 5 6   **641.5**

1. Cooking

ISBN 978-0-439-02250-7 spiral bdg; 0-439-02250-9 spiral bdg

"This lively, colorful companion book to the Gerasole sisters' Web site . . . contains an enticing array of dishes both sweet and savory, easy and complicated. . . . Beautifully reproduced color photos show the completed dishes and smaller photos show some of the steps. . . . This book strikes a great balance between fun and practical." SLJ

Includes glossary

Gold, Rozanne

Kids cook 1-2-3; recipes for young chefs using only 3 ingredients. illustrated by Sara Pinto. Bloomsbury Children's Books 2006 144p il $17.95

Grades: 3 4 5 6   641.5

1. Cooking

ISBN 978-1-58234-735-6; 1-58234-735-2

LC 2006-00623

"This very basic cookbook offers 125 recipes for breakfast, lunch, dinner, healthy snacks, side dishes, and desserts. The recipes are clearly presented, and are broken into easy-to-follow steps." SLJ

Gregory, Josh

Chef. Cherry Lake Pub. 2011 32p il (Cool careers) lib bdg $27.07

Grades: 4 5 6 7   641.5

1. Cooks 2. Cooking 3. Vocational guidance

ISBN 978-1-60279-985-1; 1-60279-985-7

LC 2010029085

This book begins "with a personal story of a teen and then [segues] into the occupation [of chef]. . . . [It covers] the necessary training and skills for the job (and options for obtaining them), a typical day, salary expectations, and well-known professionals in the field. The [text is] accessible and clearly written. . . . The [volume has] a generous number of clear color photographs that depict people at work." SLJ

Includes glossary and bibliographical references

Hargittai, Magdolna

Cooking the Hungarian way; by Magdolna Hargittai. rev and expanded; Lerner Publications Co 2003 72p il map (Easy menu ethnic cookbooks) lib bdg $25.26

Grades: 5 6 7 8   641.5

1. Hungarian cooking

ISBN 978-0-8225-4132-5; 0-8225-4132-7

LC 2001-6612

First published 1986

An overview of Hungarian cookery, including information about the country's geography, history, holidays, and festivals. Features simple recipes, menu planning, and information about low-fat cooking and vegetarian options

Includes glossary and bibliographical references

Hopkinson, Deborah

★ Fannie in the kitchen; the whole story from soup to nuts of how Fannie Farmer invented recipes with precise measurements. pictures by Nancy Carpenter. Atheneum Bks. for Young Readers 2001 un il hardcover o.p. pa $7.99

Grades: K 1 2 3   641.5

1. Cooking 2. Cookbook writers 3. School administrators

ISBN 0-689-81965-X; 0-689-86987-5 pa

LC 97-46712

Fannie Farmer is a mother's helper in the Shaw house, where the daughter gives her the idea of writing down precise instructions for measuring and cooking, which eventually became one of the first modern cookbooks

"A clever introduction to the renowned nineteenth century cook. . . . The collage artwork is exceptional—elegant as well as whimsical. Carpenter brings together original pen-and-ink artwork and engravings, all washed in watercolor, to create a houseful of expressive characters and abundant, often witty details." Booklist

Hughes, Helga

Cooking the Austrian way; [by] Helga Hughes. rev and expanded ed; Lerner Publications 2004 72p il map (Easy menu ethnic cookbooks) lib bdg $25.26

Grades: 5 6 7 8   641.5

1. Austrian cooking

ISBN 978-0-8225-4102-8; 0-8225-4102-5

LC 2002-152146

First published 1990

An introduction to the cooking of Austria including such traditional recipes as Wiener schnitzel, potato noodles, and Sacher cake. Also includes information on the geography, customs, and people of this European country

"Updated to include low-fat and vegetarian options. . . . Color photos and definitions of cooking terms and unusual ingredients will aid novice cooks." Horn Book Guide

Includes glossary

Ichord, Loretta Frances

Skillet bread, sourdough, and vinegar pie; cooking in pioneer days. illustrated by Jan Davey Ellis. Millbrook Press 2003 64p il map hardcover o.p. pa $8.95

Grades: 3 4 5   641.5

1. Cooking 2. Frontier and pioneer life -- West (U.S.) 3. Frontier and pioneer life -- United States -- Juvenile literature

ISBN 0-7613-1864-X lib bdg; 0-7613-9521-0 pa

LC 2002-8157

Presents a look at what was eaten in the American West by pioneers on the trail, cowboys on cattle drives, and gold miners in California camps, with available ingredients, cooking methods, and equipment. Includes recipes and appendix of classroom cooking directions

"This unique title effectively combines recipes with history, a must for any collection needing information on the old West." Libr Media Connect

Includes bibliographical references

Karmel, Annabel

My favorite recipes. DK Pub. 2011 96p il $14.99

Grades: 3 4 5 6   641.5

1. Cooking

ISBN 978-0-7566-7195-2; 0-7566-7195-7

"These recipes . . . look good enough to eat. Each one includes a full-page, full-color picture of the dish, as well as step-by-step instructions, with smaller pictures. . . . All recipes need adult assistance, and some require more than basic cooking skills. The recipes are organized in four sections: light bites, main meals, fruity treats, and cakes and cookies. They include children's favorites like spaghetti and chicken dippers . . . as well as more exotic dishes like paella and lamb tagine. Where this cookbook really shines is in the creative and fun plating. Karmel often creates faces or animals out of a dish. . . . A bright and colorful cookbook that is sure to appeal to children." SLJ

Katsoris, Nick

Loukoumi's celebrity cookbook; featuring favorite childhood recipes by over 50 celebrities. Nick Katsoris. Dream Day Press/NK Publications/Loukoumi Books 2011 87 p. (hardcover) $19.95

Grades: 4 5 6   **641.5**

    1. Cookbooks 2. Children's literature

    ISBN 0984161015; 9780984161010

    Gourmand World Cookbook Award (2012) -"Best Charity Cookbook in the United States"

This cookbook "opens with a story about a lamb, Loukoumi, and her friends, a dog, a monkey, and a cat, that are hungry. The cast of . . . animals joins Aunt Cat Cora, who gives tips about making a cake. The recipe follows, with the table of contents finally appearing on page 22, divided into sections: 'Weekend Breakfasts,' 'Lunchtime Favorites,' 'After School Snacks,' 'Family Meals,' and 'Delicious Desserts.'" (School Library Journal)

Katzen, Mollie

    ★ **Honest** pretzels; and 64 other amazing recipes for cooks ages 8 & up. Tricycle Press 1999 177p il hardcover o.p. pa $17.99

Grades: 4 5 6   **641.5**

    1. Vegetarian cooking 2. Pretzels -- Juvenile literature

    ISBN 1-88367-288-0; 978-1-58246-305-6 pa; 1-58246-305-0 pa

                        LC 99-20184

Provides step-by-step instructions for a variety of vegetarian recipes, arranged in such categories as "Breakfast Specials," "Soups, Sandwiches & Salads for Lunch or Supper," and "Desserts and a Few Baked Things"

"Small, colorful drawings illustrate most of the cooking instructions and brighten many of the other pages as well." Booklist

    ★ **Salad** people and more real recipes; a new cookbook for preschoolers and up. Tricycle Press 2005 93p il $17.95

Grades: K 1 2 3   **641.5**

    1. Cooking

    ISBN 1-58246-141-4

"Katzen offers a range of vegetarian, kid-friendly recipes in an artistic, innovative format. Each recipe receives two spreads. The first contains detailed, step-by-step instructions for adults; the second, directed to children, illustrates stages of preparation in a series of clear, boxed drawings. Katzen's whimsical color pictures of dancing produce and animals decorate the pages. . . . These detailed, practical, and inspired ideas may extend far beyond the kitchen, helping adults approach parenting in new ways and helping kids develop a lifelong interest and confidence in healthy food." Booklist

LaPenta, Marilyn

    Way cool drinks. Bearport Pub. 2011 24p il (Yummy tummy recipes) lib bdg $22.61

Grades: 3 4 5 6   **641.5**

    1. Cooking 2. Beverages

    ISBN 978-1-61772-163-2; 1-61772-163-8

                        LC 2011017444

This offers recipes for fruit drinks such as mango tango, fruit fusion, and blueberry bash smoothie.

"All 14 recipes are easy to follow with little more than four or five listed steps, clearly defined serving sizes, and minimal prep time. A healthy tip and oather facts are included with each recipe." Booklist

    Includes glossary and bibliographical references

LaRoche, Amelia

    Recipe and craft guide to France. Mitchell Lane Publishers 2010 63p il map (World crafts and recipes) lib bdg $33.95

Grades: 4 5 6 7 8   **641.5**

    1. Handicraft 2. French cooking

    ISBN 978-1-58415-936-0 lib bdg; 1-58415-936-7 lib bdg

                        LC 2010008949

Provides recipes for several popular French dishes and includes instructions on creating crafts using household items.

This provides "plenty of ideas for adding tasty treats and impressive visual aids to cultural reports or presentations." SLJ

    Includes glossary and bibliographical references

Lagasse, Emeril

    ★ **Emeril's** there's a chef in my world! recipes that take you places. illustrated by Charles Yuen; photographs of Emeril Lagasse and children by Quentin Bacon. HarperCollins Publishers 2006 210p il $22.99

Grades: 5 6 7 8   **641.5**

    1. Cooking

    ISBN 978-0-06-073926-3; 0-06-073926-6

                        LC 2005-15133

"The famous chef introduces dishes from around the world, dividing the recipes into familiar food categories—sweets, snacks, sandwiches, entrees, etc. . . . The recipes, from latkes to egg-drop soup, are good choices for openminded eaters. . . . Many children will enjoy the mix of maps, flags, cartoon drawings, and color photos . . . and the cultural facts woven into each recipe." Booklist

Larson, Jennifer S.

    Delicious vegetarian main dishes; by Jennifer S. Larson; photographs by Brie Cohen. Millbrook Press 2013 32 p. col. ill. (library) $26.60

Grades: 1 2 3 4   **641.5**

    1. Cooking 2. Vegetarian cooking 3. Vegetarian cooking -- Juvenile literature 4. Entrées (Cooking) -- Juvenile literature

    ISBN 0761366350; 9780761366355

                        LC 2012020923

This book by Jennifer S. Larson presents "easy-to-follow recipes such as baked potato pile up, lemony couscous, crispy tofu sticks, and tasty tortilla towers. [Also included are] simple drawings of important steps as well as photographs of the finished dishes. This book also provides key information, such as an equipment list, a technique list, safety tips, notes on special ingredients, and more." (Publisher's note)

    Includes bibliographical references (page 32) and index.

Lee, Frances

    Fun with Chinese cooking. PowerKids Press 2009 32p il (Let's get cooking!) lib bdg $18.95; pa $11.75

Grades: 4 5 6 7 **641.5**
1. Chinese cooking
ISBN 978-1-4358-3453-8 lib bdg; 1-4358-3453-4 lib
bdg; 978-1-4358-3475-0 pa; 1-4358-3475-5 pa
LC 2009010337

This includes recipes for such Chinese dishes as spring
rolls and braised mushrooms, and highlights the history and
dishes that surround the Chinese New Year.

"The photography is exceptional, with children engaged
in the cooking process. . . . Children, and the adults who
assist them, will spend hours together mastering the techniques." SLJ

Locricchio, Matthew
★ The **2nd** international cookbook for kids; photo-
graphs by Jack McConnell. Marshall Cavendish 2008 176p
il $18.99
Grades: 5 6 7 8 **641.5**
1. Cooking
ISBN 978-0-7614-5513-4
LC 2008003178

The recipes are "presented in a challenging yet teen-
friendly step-by-step sequence. The book is best for patient
chefs with kitchen experience and adventurous appetites.
Informative sidebars provide facts about the recipes and cultures." Horn Book Guide

★ The **international** cookbook for kids; by Matthew
Locricchio; photographs by Jack McConnell. Reprint Mar-
shall Cavendish 2012 175p il $12.99
Grades: 5 6 7 8 **641.5**
1. Cooking 2. Cookery, International -- Juvenile
literature
ISBN 9780761463139
LC 2004-5894

This includes "60 classic recipes from Italy, France,
China, and Mexico, ... chef's tips discussing ingredients,
nutrition, and technique, safety section discussing basic
kitchen precautions, cooking terms and definitions." Publisher's note

Mattern, Joanne
Recipe and craft guide to China. Mitchell Lane Publishers 2010 63p il map (World crafts and recipes) lib
bdg $33.95
Grades: 4 5 6 7 8 **641.5**
1. Handicraft 2. Chinese cooking
ISBN 978-1-58415-937-7 lib bdg; 1-58415-937-5
lib bdg
LC 2010009242

Provides recipes for several popular Chinese dishes and includes instructions on creating crafts using
household items.

This provides "plenty of ideas for adding tasty treats and
impressive visual aids to cultural reports or presentations."
SLJ

Includes glossary and bibliographical references

McCallum, Ann
Eat your math homework; recipes for hungry minds.
illustrated by Leeza Hernandez. Charlesbridge 2011 46p
il $16.95; pa $7.95

Grades: 2 3 4 **641.5**
1. Cooking 2. Mathematics
ISBN 978-1-57091-779-0; 1-57091-779-5; 978-1-
57091-780-6 pa; 1-57091-780-9 pa
LC 2010033631

"McCallum combines math with cooking in this attractive book. After a brief introduction and a few basic cooking
tips, she explains the Fibonacci sequence and shows how to
demonstrate it using chunks of fruit on skewers. Fractions
are expressed through fried flour tortillas cut into fractional
portions; tessellations with two-tone brownies; tangrams
with flat cookies; variables and pi with pizza and probability with trail mix. In six-page chapters, the recipe sounds
good, the math is clearly explained, and there's a playfulness
of presentation that makes each activity look inviting. The
mixed-media illustrations feature dressed rabbits, whose
zany attitudes broaden their appeal. . . . Witty and smart."
Booklist

Mendez, Sean
One world kids cookbook; easy, healthy and affordable
family meals. foreword by Ferran Adrià. Interlink 2011
96p il $20
Grades: 4 5 6 **641.5**
1. Cooking
ISBN 978-1-56656-866-1; 1-56656-866-8

"International recipes for families interested in cooking
a variety of world cuisines together. This colorful, amply illustrated cookbook emphasizes the educational, nutritional
and social benefits of cooking with children, offering 19
recipes from as many nations. The book devotes four pages
to each recipe and country, along with enriching notes on
food and cultural facts. The country's flag is depicted with a
map locating the country, followed by a double-page spread
documenting how to create each recipe. . . . This cookbook
offers complex, authentic international flavors without over-
complicating the process, and the result is something you'd
really enjoy having for dinner. A deliciously engaging fusion
of cookbook and cultural lesson." Kirkus

Mofford, Juliet Haines
Recipe and craft guide to Japan. Mitchell Lane Publishers 2010 63p il map (World crafts and recipes) lib
bdg $33.95
Grades: 4 5 6 7 8 **641.5**
1. Handicraft 2. Japanese cooking
ISBN 978-1-58415-933-9 lib bdg; 1-58415-933-2
lib bdg
LC 2010008951

Provides recipes for several popular Japanese dishes and
includes instructions on creating traditional Japanese crafts
using household items.

This provides "plenty of ideas for adding tasty treats and
impressive visual aids to cultural reports or presentations."
SLJ

Includes glossary and bibliographical references

Recipe and craft guide to the Caribbean. Mitchell Lane
Publishers 2010 64p il map (World crafts and recipes) lib
bdg $33.95

Grades: 4 5 6 7 8 **641.5**
1. Handicraft 2. Caribbean cooking
ISBN 978-1-58415-935-3 lib bdg; 1-58415-935-9
lib bdg
LC 2010009240

Provides recipes for several popular Caribbean dishes and includes instructions on creating traditional Caribbean crafts using household items.

This provides "plenty of ideas for adding tasty treats and impressive visual aids to cultural reports or presentations." SLJ

Includes glossary and bibliographical references

Reusser, Kayleen
Recipe and craft guide to Indonesia. Mitchell Lane Publishers 2010 64p il map (World crafts and recipes) lib bdg $33.95
Grades: 4 5 6 7 8 **641.5**
1. Handicraft 2. Indonesian cooking
ISBN 978-1-58415-934-6 lib bdg; 1-58415-934-0
lib bdg
LC 2010009243

Provides recipes for several popular Indonesian dishes and includes instructions on creating crafts using household items.

This provides "plenty of ideas for adding tasty treats and impressive visual aids to cultural reports or presentations." SLJ

Includes glossary and bibliographical references

Sheen, Barbara
Foods of Chile. KidHaven Press 2011 64p il map (A taste of culture) $28.75
Grades: 4 5 6 **641.5**
1. Chilean cooking
ISBN 978-0-7377-5421-6; 0-7377-5421-4
LC 2010035995

"Demonstrating that a nation's cuisine springs from its geography, history, and traditions, [this volume explores Chile's background], the availability of fresh ingredients, and recipes that followed. . . . Culturally specific foods are described alongside some accompanying recipes and photos of people enjoying the dishes." Horn Book Guide

Includes glossary and bibliographical references

Foods of Cuba. KidHaven Press 2011 64p il map (A taste of culture) $28.75
Grades: 4 5 6 **641.5**
1. Cuban cooking
ISBN 978-0-7377-5113-0; 0-7377-5113-4
LC 2010030795

"Demonstrating that a nation's cuisine springs from its geography, history, and traditions, [this volume explores Cuba's background], the availability of fresh ingredients, and recipes that followed. . . . Culturally specific foods are described alongside some accompanying recipes and photos of people enjoying the dishes." Horn Book Guide

Includes glossary and bibliographical references

Foods of Egypt. KidHaven Press 2010 64p il map (A taste of culture) $28.75

Grades: 4 5 6 **641.5**
1. Egyptian cooking
ISBN 978-0-7377-4843-7; 0-7377-4843-5
LC 2009038461

"Sheen explores how different native dishes and types of local celebrations emerge from [Egypt's] culture and surroundings. [An] introductory [map] with a [key] to areas of food production illuminate the country's cuisine by identifying geographical landforms and climate. Traditions and tastes are described in accessible detail; key recipes are included and unfamiliar foods are pictured." Horn Book Guide

Includes glossary and bibliographical references

Foods of Ireland. KidHaven Press 2011 64p il map (A taste of culture) $28.75
Grades: 4 5 6 **641.5**
1. Irish cooking
ISBN 978-0-7377-5114-7; 0-7377-5114-2
LC 2010018791

"Sheen explores how different native dishes and types of local celebrations emerge from [Ireland's] culture and surroundings. [An] introductory [map] with a [key] to areas of food production illuminate the country's cuisine by identifying geographical landforms and climate. Traditions and tastes are described in accessible detail; key recipes are included and unfamiliar foods are pictured." Horn Book Guide

Includes glossary and bibliographical references

Foods of Kenya. KidHaven Press 2010 64p il map (A taste of culture) $28.75
Grades: 4 5 6 **641.5**
1. African cooking 2. Kenyan cooking
ISBN 978-0-7377-4813-0; 0-7377-4813-3
LC 2009048378

"Sheen explores how different native dishes and types of local celebrations emerge from [Kenya's] culture and surroundings. [An] introductory [map] with a [key] to areas of food production illuminate the country's cuisine by identifying geographical landforms and climate. Traditions and tastes are described in accessible detail; key recipes are included and unfamiliar foods are pictured." Horn Book Guide

Includes glossary and bibliographical references

Foods of Korea. KidHaven Press 2011 64p il map (A taste of culture) $26.75
Grades: 4 5 6 **641.5**
1. Korean cooking
ISBN 978-0-7377-5115-4; 0-7377-5115-0
LC 2010018789

"Demonstrating that a nation's cuisine springs from its geography, history, and traditions, [this volume explores Korea's background], the availability of fresh ingredients, and recipes that followed. . . . Culturally specific foods are described alongside some accompanying recipes and photos of people enjoying the dishes." Horn Book Guide

Includes glossary and bibliographical references

Foods of Peru. KidHaven Press 2011 64p il map (A taste of culture) $28.75
Grades: 4 5 6 **641.5**
1. Peruvian cooking
ISBN 978-0-7377-5346-2; 0-7377-5346-3
LC 2010032959

"Demonstrating that a nation's cuisine springs from its geography, history, and traditions, [this volume explores Peru's background], the availability of fresh ingredients, and recipes that followed. . . . Culturally specific foods are described alongside some accompanying recipes and photos of people enjoying the dishes." Horn Book Guide

Includes glossary and bibliographical references

Tuminelly, Nancy

Cool creepy food art; easy recipes that make food fun to eat! ABDO Pub. Company 2011 32p il (Cool food art) lib bdg $25.65

Grades: 3 4 5   **641.5**

1. Food 2. Cooking

ISBN 978-1-61613-363-4; 1-61613-363-5

LC 2010003286

This offers recipes for such dishes as severed finger pizza; floating head cider, to die for dip, eyeball spaghetti, gross-out pita, garbage goop, bloody hand punch, and snot stick pretzels.

"Photographs provide clear step-by-step instructions as well as images of the finished products." Horn Book Guide

Includes glossary

Cool fruit & veggie food art; easy recipes that make food fun to eat! ABDO Pub. Company 2010 32p il (Cool food art) lib bdg $25.65

Grades: 3 4 5   **641.5**

1. Food 2. Fruit 3. Cooking -- Vegetables

ISBN 978-1-61613-364-1; 1-61613-364-3

LC 2010003285

Provides step-by-step instructions for creating fruit and vegetable food art, such as a funny face salad, an apple flutterfly, and a flying cucumber; and includes tips on techniques.

"Photographs provide clear step-by-step instructions as well as images of the finished products." Horn Book Guide

Includes glossary

Cool snack food art; easy recipes that make food fun to eat! ABDO Pub. Company 2010 32p il (Cool food art) lib bdg $25.65

Grades: 3 4 5   **641.5**

1. Food 2. Snack foods

ISBN 978-1-61613-367-2; 1-61613-367-8

LC 2010003573

Provides step-by-step instructions for creating snack food art, such as chili snake dogs, a peanut butter and candy pizza, and a sweet treat flowerpot; and includes tips on techniques.

Includes glossary

Walker, Barbara Muhs

The **Little** House cookbook; frontier foods from Laura Ingalls Wilder's classic stories. by Barbara M. Walker; illustrated by Garth Williams. Harper & Row 1979 240p il $16.95; pa $9.95

Grades: 5 6 7 8   **641.5**

1. Authors 2. Cooking 3. Novelists 4. Frontier and pioneer life 5. Western writers 6. Children's authors 7. Young adult authors

ISBN 0-06-026418-7; 0-06-446090-8 pa

LC 76-58733

Recipes based on the pioneer food written about in the "Little House" books of Laura Ingalls Wilder, along with quotes from the books and descriptions of the food and cooking of pioneer times

"Illustrated by Williams's familiar warm drawings, the adaptations of menus from pioneer days include paragraphs describing the Wilder and Ingalls families working together, preparing holiday meals, individual foods, special treats and staple fare." Publ Wkly

Includes bibliographical references

Webb, Lois Sinaiko

Holidays of the world cookbook for students; [by] Lois Sinaiko Webb and Lindsay Grace Roten. updated and rev.; Greenwood 2011 442p il map $95; pa $32.95

Grades: 5 6 7 8 9 10   **641.5**

1. Cooking 2. Holidays

ISBN 978-0-313-38393-9; 0-313-38393-6; 978-0-313-39790-5 pa; 0-313-39790-2 pa; 978-0-313-38394-6 ebook

LC 2011-8458

First published 1995 by Oryx Press

"The recipes appear with each country entry, and the countries are arranged in alphabetical order within each region: Africa, Asia and the South Pacific, the Caribbean, Europe, Latin America, the Middle East, and North America." Publisher's note

Yolen, Jane

Fairy tale feasts; a literary cookbook for young readers and eaters. [by] Jane Yolen and Heidi E. Y. Stemple; illustrated by Philippe Beha. Crocodile Books 2006 197p il $24.95

Grades: 2 3 4 5   **641.5**

1. Cooking 2. Folklore

ISBN 1-56656-543-6

This "folds fairy tales into a cookbook of kid-friendly recipes. The stories, with the exception of one original story by Yolen, represent mostly European folktales, and Yolen retells them with her usual verve and ease. . . . Each story is paired with at least one recipe that connects with the story's themes or references. . . . Stemple's recipes require adult supervision, but the resulting dishes, as well as Beha's spare, whimsical spot illustrations, will capture children's fancy." Booklist

Jewish fairy tale feasts; stories retold by Jane Yolen; recipes by Heidi E.Y. Stemple; illustrations by Sima Elizabeth Shefrin. 1st American ed. Crocodile Books, an imprint of Interlink Pub. Group, Inc. 2012 200 p. (hardcover) $25

Grades: 2 3 4 5   **641.5**

1. Fairy tales 2. Jewish cooking 3. Cooking -- Juvenile literature 4. Jewish cooking -- Juvenile literature

ISBN 1566569095; 9781566569095

LC 2012016174

This children's book, by Jane Yolen, Heidi E. Y. Stemple, illustrated by Sima Elizabeth Shefrin, offers Jewish cooking recipes and fairy tales to accompany them. "Here you'll find Yolen's . . . retellings of Jewish tales from around the world paired with Stemple's recipes-for everything from challah to matzo brei to pomegranate couscous, tzimmes chicken, and rugelah, in creative versions of classic dishes that any family will delight in cooking together." (Publisher's note)

Includes bibliographical references and index

641.509 History, geographic treatment, biography

Hartland, Jessie

Bon appetit! the delicious life of Julia Child. Jessie Hartland. Schwartz & Wade Books 2012 48 p. (hbk.) $17.99

Grades: 2 3 4 5   **641.509**

1. Women cooks 2. Women -- Biography 3. Picture books for children 4. Women cooks -- United States -- Biography 5. Women cooks -- United States -- Biography -- Juvenile literature

ISBN 0375869441; 0375969446; 9780375869440; 9780375969447

LC 2011018658

This juvenile biography, by Jessie Hartland, follows "Julia Child--chef, author, and television personality--from her childhood in Pasadena, California, to her life as a spy in WWII, . . . to the publication of 'Mastering the Art of French Cooking,' to the funny moments of being a chef on TV. This is a comprehensive and enchanting picture book biography, told in many panels and jam-packed with lively, humorous, and child-friendly details." (Publisher's note)

Includes bibliographical references.

641.594

Bucholz, Dinah

The **unofficial** Narnia cookbook; from Turkish delight to gooseberry fool--over 150 recipes inspired by the Chronicles of Narnia. Dinah Bucholz. Sourcebooks Jabberwocky 2012 233 p. $19.99

Grades: 4 5 6   **641.594**

1. Cookbooks 2. Narnia (Imaginary place)

ISBN 1402266413; 9781402266416

In this cookbook by Dinah Bucholz "each recipe is clearly tied to particular incidents and chapters in the books of Narnia. . . . While striving to stick to the actual meals in the stories (Eel Stew! Boar's Head!), [Bucholz] creates or re-creates Beautiful Breakfasts; Snacks, Teas, and Meals on the Run; Lunch and Dinner Menus; and Fabulous Feasts in four chapters." (Kirkus)

641.6 Cooking specific materials

Llewellyn, Claire

Cooking with meat and fish; [by] Claire Llewellyn, Clare O'Shea. Rosen Central 2011 48p il map (Cooking healthy) lib bdg $27.95

Grades: 5 6 7 8   **641.6**

1. Meat 2. Cooking 3. Seafood

ISBN 978-1-4488-4845-4; 1-4488-4845-8

LC 2010039337

A description of each type of meat and fish, how to cook them in a healthy manner, and recipe examples of each.

This book pairs "facts about [meat and fish], including where it is eaten, with eye-catching photos. . . . Each course (section) has an overview of the . . . [meat] followed by recipes from all over the world. They vary in difficulty. . . . The cooking directions are clear and straightforward. . . . [The book is] profusely illustrated with full-color photos.

Students who are learning to cook will appreciate [this] excellently organized [read]." SLJ

Includes glossary and bibliographical references

MacLeod, Elizabeth

Chock full of chocolate; written by Elizabeth MacLeod; illustrated by June Bradford. Kids Can Press 2005 40p il (Kids can do it) hardcover o.p. pa $6.95

Grades: 4 5 6   **641.6**

1. Cooking 2. Chocolate

ISBN 1-55337-762-1; 1-55337-763-X pa

This includes recipes for chocolate cookies, cakes, and other desserts.

641.8 Cooking specific kinds of dishes and preparing beverages

DeVore, Janna

Ballerina cookbook; photographs by Zac Williams. Gibbs Smith 2011 70p il $14.99

Grades: 2 3 4 5 6   **641.8**

1. Ballet 2. Parties 3. Desserts

ISBN 978-1-4236-0793-9; 1-4236-0793-7

LC 2010030688

"An elegant and beautifully arranged cookbook of desserts and drinks. The recipes are organized into four sections: 'Ballerina Basics,' 'The Nutcracker,' 'Sleeping Beauty,' and 'Swan Lake.' The recipes have 'ballerina' names that for the most part describe the dish. . . . The overall layout is appealing with the recipe on one page and a luscious, full-page picture on the other. . . . The recipes are perfect for a party or a tasty treat any day of the week." SLJ

Dunnington, Rose

Sweet eats; mmmore than just desserts. [by] Rose Dunnington. Lark Books 2008 112p $9.95

Grades: 3 4 5 6   **641.8**

1. Baking 2. Desserts

ISBN 978-1-60059-236-2; 1-60059-236-8

LC 2007037094

This "offers mouthwatering recipes, explains how to cook safely and efficiently, and introduces basic skills. In a breezy first-person style, the author covers such useful aspects as how to organize a work space, safety tips, the tools needed, and how and why to do things. The 35 recipes include a pie crust and various frostings/toppings and are accompanied by plenty of full-color visual aids along the way." SLJ

Includes glossary

Gibbons, Gail

Ice cream; the full scoop. by Gail Gibbons. Holiday House 2006 un il $16.95

Grades: K 1 2 3   **641.8**

1. Ice cream, ices, etc.

ISBN 978-0-8234-2000-1; 0-8234-2000-0

LC 2005052575

"Gibbons explains how this favorite food developed from flavored ice to the creamy dessert we know today, describes the invention and workings of the ice-cream maker, follows the journey from cow to factory to grocery-store shelves, and mentions the innovative creation of the cone. . .

. The narrative is simple and direct and the cartoon illustrations are colorful and cheerful." SLJ

Goodman, Susan

All in just one cookie; by Susan E. Goodman; illustrated by Timothy Bush. Greenwillow Books 2006 un il $16.99; lib bdg $17.89

Grades: 2 3 4   **641.8**

1. Baking 2. Cookies

ISBN 978-0-06-009092-0; 0-06-009092-8; 978-0-06-009093-7 lib bdg; 0-06-009093-6 lib bdg

LC 2005040308

"As Grandma gathers the ingredients for her chocolate-chip cookies, her cat collects facts about the process of making butter, vanilla, baking soda, and other cookie components. . . . Cartoonlike illustrations show where each ingredient comes from, along with side comments from the cat and dog." Horn Book Guide

Love, Ann

Sweet! the delicious story of candy. [by] Ann Love & Jane Drake; illustrated by Claudia Dávila. Tundra Books 2007 64p il map $19.95

Grades: 4 5 6 7   **641.8**

1. Candy

ISBN 978-0-88776-752-4

"This history of things sweet and sugary is a yummy feast. The prose is chatty and inviting. Color cartoon illustrations show multiethnic people in the process of making or enjoying everything from honey to ice cream to cotton candy (called candy floss here) to jelly beans and chocolate." SLJ

MacLeod, Elizabeth

Bake and make amazing cakes; written by Elizabeth MacLeod; illustrated by June Bradford. Kids Can Press 2001 40p il (Kids can do it) hardcover o.p. pa $5.95

Grades: 4 5 6   **641.8**

1. Cake

ISBN 1-55074-849-1; 1-55074-848-3 pa

In this book "there are four cake recipes; three icing recipes; and 19 different creations, including cakes in the shape of a mouse, a house, a butterfly, and a bus. . . . The directions are clear and the format is clean." SLJ

Bake and make amazing cookies; written by Elizabeth MacLeod; illustrated by June Bradford. Kids Can Press 2004 40p il (Kids can do it) hardcover o.p. pa $6.95

Grades: 4 5 6   **641.8**

1. Cookies

ISBN 1-55337-631-5; 1-55337-632-3 pa

This offers "32 recipes under four headings 'Holidays,' 'For Special People,' 'Seasons,' and 'Just for Fun.' This book is sure to please bakers. The step-by-step instructions . . . are easy to follow, and the ingredients/tools listed are readily available or easily obtainable. . . . Each recipe is accompanied by precise, softly colored illustrations." SLJ

Morris, Ann

Bread, bread, bread; photographs by Ken Heyman. Lothrop, Lee & Shepard Bks. 1989 un il hardcover o.p. pa $5.95

Grades: PreK K 1   **641.8**

1. Bread

ISBN 0-688-06335-7; 0-688-12275-2 pa

LC 88-26677

This photo essay shows different kinds of bread around the world from baguettes to challah

"Each picture offers a strong ethnic identity or a thought-provoking human interaction, with captions of only a few words in large print. An unusual index . . . gives background information about the pictures, citing the countries of origin and a few facts about each type of bread." SLJ

Paulsen, Gary

The tortilla factory; paintings by Ruth Wright Paulsen. Harcourt Brace & Co. 1995 un il hardcover o.p. pa $7

Grades: K 1 2 3   **641.8**

1. Tortillas

ISBN 0-15-292876-6; 0-15-201698-8 pa

LC 93-48590

"Paulsen traces the journey of the corn, from harvest and grinding, to the tortilla factory, where people turn the corn flour into tortillas that, filled with beans, 'give strength to the brown hands that work the black earth to plant yellow seeds.' . . . Replete with the lush greens of healthy plants, the rich browns of adobe buildings and fertile soil, and the vibrant gold of ears of corn, the highly satisfying illustrations reinforce the reverential mood established by the spare poetic narrative." Horn Book

Raum, Elizabeth

The story behind bread. Heinemann Library 2009 32p il (True stories) lib bdg $28.21

Grades: 3 4 5   **641.8**

1. Bread

ISBN 978-1-4329-2346-4 lib bdg; 1-4329-2346-3 lib bdg

LC 2008037394

The story behind "bread covers the history of the staple and its importance, the harvesting of grains, and the equipment used to bring it 'From Fields to Tables.' Readers will learn, for example, that bagels were originally created in the shape of a stirrup to honor the King of Poland. . . . The well-organized [text is] informative and clearly written, and the numerous color photographs and drawings are eye-catching and complement the [narrative] well." SLJ

Includes bibliographical references

Smart, Denise

The children's baking book; recipes & styling by Denise Smart; photography by Howard Shooter. DK 2009 128p il $17.99

Grades: 3 4 5   **641.8**

1. Baking

ISBN 0-7566-5788-1; 978-0-7566-5788-8

Instructions for making bread, pastry, muffins, cakes and cookies. Includes more than 50 easy-to-follow recipes.

"This accessible baking book features more than 50 sweet and savory recipes . . . with full-color photographs that show both preparations and tasty end results. Divided into sections on cookies and baked goods, dough, cakes, and pastry, the recipes are further labeled with levels of difficulty. . . . The sweet-toothed should find the mouthwatering pictures and straightforward instructions hard to resist." Publ Wkly

Tuminelly, Nancy

Cool cake & cupcake food art; easy recipes that make food fun to eat! ABDO Pub. Company 2011 32p il (Cool food art) lib bdg $25.65

Grades: 3 4 5   **641.8**
1. Cake 2. Food 3. Baking
ISBN 978-1-61613-362-7; 1-61613-362-7
LC 2010003287

Provides step-by-step instructions for creating cake and cupcake food art, such as a flower garden cake, a portly panda, and a hole in one cupcake; and includes tips on techniques.

"Photographs provide clear step-by-step instructions as well as images of the finished products." Horn Book Guide
Includes glossary

Cool sandwich food art; easy recipes that make food fun to eat! ABDO Pub. Company 2011 32p il (Cool food art) lib bdg $25.65

Grades: 3 4 5   **641.8**
1. Food 2. Sandwiches
ISBN 978-1-61613-366-5; 1-61613-366-X
LC 2010003475

Provides step-by-step instructions for creating sandwich food art, such as a peanut butter and jelly flower, a happy hippo hoagie, and a caterpillar wrap; and includes tips on techniques.

Includes glossary

642   Meals and table service

Duncan, Karen

The **good** fun! book; 12 months of parties that celebrate service. by Karen Duncan & Kate Hannigan Issa; illustrated by Anthony Alex LeTourneau. Blue Marlin Publications 2010 un il $15.95

Grades: 3 4 5 6   **642**
1. Cooking 2. Parties 3. Handicraft 4. Social action
ISBN 978-0-9792918-5-2; 0-9792918-5-2
LC 2010025848

"For each month of the year, Duncan and Issa suggest a party with a service theme. For example, they suggest making Valentines for children at a local hospital in February, cleaning up a park for Earth Day in April, or making jacko-lanterns for a nursing home in October. The ideas are realistic, age appropriate, and thoughtful. The authors have done a good job mixing fun with function. . . . Each plan contains two ideas, a treat recipe, a craft, and information about a national charity related to the theme. The book is illustrated with child-friendly color cartoons featuring youngsters doing good deeds." SLJ

Includes bibliographical references

646   Sewing, clothing, management of personal and family life

Neitzel, Shirley

The **jacket** I wear in the snow; pictures by Nancy Winslow Parker. Greenwillow Bks. 1989 un il $16.99; pa $6.99

Grades: PreK K 1 2   **646**
1. Stories in rhyme 2. Snow -- Fiction 3. Clothing and dress -- Fiction 4. Clothing and dress -- Juvenile literature
ISBN 0-688-08028-6; 0-688-04587-1 pa
LC 88-18767

A young girl names all the clothes that she must wear to play in the snow

"Written in cheerful, cumulative verse that recalls the well-known favorite nursery rhyme 'The House That Jack Built,' the text, with its easy-going rhythm, will be simple for children to recite from memory. . . . The artist's drawings are executed in . . . watercolor, pencil, and pen; they combine with the large typeface and a generous amount of white space to create a tremendously appealing book." Horn Book

646.2   Sewing and related operations

Plumley, Amie Petronis

Sewing school; 21 sewing projects kids will love to make. [by] Amie Petronis Plumley & Andria Lisle; photography by Justin Fox Burks. Storey Pub. 2010 143p il $16.95

Grades: 3 4 5 6   **646.2**
1. Sewing
ISBN 978-1-60342-578-0; 1-60342-578-0
LC 2010022154

"This large-format book offers appealing projects illustrated with color photos of step-by-step directions as well as kids engaged in sewing and showing off work. The opening 12 lessons begin with topics such as threading a needle, knotting the thread, and making a basic running stitch. After covering basic knowledge and skills, the presentation moves on to instructions for fun easy projects." Booklist

Sadler, Judy Ann

Simply sewing; written by Judy Ann Sadler; illustrated by Jane Kurisu. Kids Can Press 2004 48p il (Kids can do it) hardcover o.p. pa $6.95

Grades: 4 5 6   **646.2**
1. Sewing
ISBN 1-55337-659-5; 1-55337-660-9 pa

This "book opens with a section on sewing supplies. . . . Subsequent chapters discuss fabric and the basics of hand and machine stitching. . . . Each of the 12 projects is accompanied by a color photo, step-by-step color illustrations, and a list of supplies needed. . . . This attractive book has a wide assortment of ideas to spark interest." SLJ

646.4   Clothing and accessories construction

D'Cruz, Anna-Marie

Make your own masks. PowerKids Press 2009 24p il (Do it yourself projects!) lib bdg $23.95; pa $9.40

Grades: 2 3 4   **646.4**
1. Handicraft 2. Masks (Facial)
ISBN 978-1-4358-2853-7 lib bdg; 1-4358-2853-4 lib bdg; 978-1-4358-2923-7 pa; 1-4358-2923-9 pa
LC 2008033677

This offers "step-by-step instructions and full-color photos to illustrate the crafts. Projects have a broad cultural representation and are not gender specific. Materials are easily obtained. [The projects include] an Aztec skull, a Bwa sun mask, a Greek Medusa, and a Viking mask." SLJ

Includes glossary and bibliographical references

Make your own purses and bags. PowerKids Press 2009 24p il (Do it yourself projects!) lib bdg $23.95; pa $9.40

Grades: 2 3 4　　　　　　　　　　　　　　　**646.4**
　　1. Bags 2. Handicraft
　　ISBN 978-1-4358-2856-8 lib bdg; 1-4358-2856-9 lib bdg; 978-1-4358-2929-9 pa; 1-4358-2929-8 pa
　　　　　　　　　　　　　　　　LC 2008033671

This offers "step-by-step instructions and full-color photos to illustrate the crafts. Projects have a broad cultural representation and are not gender specific. Materials are easily obtained. . . . A Didgeridoo pencil case and an MP3-player case are among the projects [included]." SLJ

Includes glossary and bibliographical references

Petersen, Christine
　　The **tailor**. Marshall Cavendish Benchmark 2011 il (Colonial people) $29.93

Grades: 3 4 5 6　　　　　　　　　　　　　**646.4**
　　1. Tailoring
　　ISBN 978-1-60870-417-0; 1-60870-417-3
　　　　　　　　　　　　　　　　LC 2010016864

This describes the life of a colonial tailor and his importance to the community, as well as everyday life, responsibilities, and social practices during that time.

This "lively [text] and colorful reproductions and photos will engage casual readers and researchers alike. . . . Large illustrations and thoughtful captions explain complicated scientific ideas. . . . [The] volume also includes step-by-step instructions for a related craft project. . . , [This is a] must-have." SLJ

Includes glossary and bibliographical references

Schwarz, Renee
　　Making masks; written and illustrated by Renée Schwarz. Kids Can Press 2002 40p il (Kids can do it) $12.95; pa $5.95

Grades: 4 5 6　　　　　　　　　　　　　　**646.4**
　　1. Handicraft 2. Masks (Facial) 3. Masks (Facial) -- Juvenile literature
　　ISBN 1-55074-929-3; 1-55074-931-5 pa

This offers instructions for creating a variety of masks using such materials as cardboard, felt, paper, and pipe cleaners

This includes "appealing projects and easy-to-follow directions. . . . Schwarz does a good job constructing and illustrating a variety of masks." SLJ

Torres, Laura
　　Rock your wardrobe. QEB Pub. 2010 32p il (Rock your . . .) lib bdg $28.50

Grades: 4 5 6　　　　　　　　　　　　　　**646.4**
　　1. Fashion 2. Handicraft 3. Clothing and dress
　　ISBN 978-1-59566-937-7; 1-59566-937-X
　　　　　　　　　　　　　　　　LC 2010010671

This book "gives kids easy step-by-step ways to . . . fashion clothes with simple, easily found scraps and a little glue and paint. Colorful photographs show youngsters crafting appealing T-shirts . . . etc., some of which are created from

recycled found items. All are projects they can complete by themselves." Horn Book Guide

646.7　Management of personal and family life

Buchholz, Rachel
　　How to survive anything; shark attack, quicksand, embarrassing parents, pop quizzes, and other perilous situations. illustrations by Chris Philpot. National Geographic 2011 176p il (National geographic kids) pa $12.95

Grades: 5 6 7 8　　　　　　　　　　　　　**646.7**
　　1. Life skills 2. Survival skills
　　ISBN 978-1-4263-0774-4; 1-4263-0774-8
　　　　　　　　　　　　　　　　LC 2010028045

"Buchholz doles out hilarious and handy advice for suffering though both natural and manmade catastrophes. Part survival guide and part self-help book, it provides honest, tongue-in-cheek answers to questions teens may be reluctant to ask out loud, in addition to imparting disaster preparedness strategies. It's a clever, winning combination. Superb full-color digital illustrations and photographs and a lively, conversational tone will catch and keep readers' attention, and the list-heavy layout is fun to read and easy to understand." SLJ

Chancellor, Deborah
　　Happy and healthy. QEB Pub. 2011 32p il (For girls!) lib bdg $18.95

Grades: 2 3 4 5　　　　　　　　　　　　　**646.7**
　　1. Life skills 2. Personal grooming 3. Girls -- Health and hygiene
　　ISBN 978-1-60992-104-0; 1-60992-104-6
　　　　　　　　　　　　　　　　LC 2011006913

This guide for girls gives advice on how to keep healthy, including exercise and keeping fit, creative cooking, skin and hair care, healthy foods, and sports.

"Each lively, readable spread is packed with color photos, computer graphics, and lots of boxes filled with facts, lists, and practical suggestions." Booklist

Heinrichs, Ann
　　The **barber**. Marshall Cavendish Benchmark 2010 48p il (Colonial people) lib bdg $29.93

Grades: 3 4 5 6　　　　　　　　　　　　　**646.7**
　　1. Barbers and barbershops
　　ISBN 978-0-7614-4800-6; 0-7614-4800-4
　　　　　　　　　　　　　　　　LC 2009018626

"The type font, just slightly larger than usual, makes the text very visually appealing. . . . [The] book is liberally illustrated with artwork dating from the colonial period . . . [and] information boxes offer supplemental material." Libr Media Connect

Includes glossary and bibliographical references

646.700

Buchanan, Andrea J.
　　The **daring** book for girls; Andrea Buchanan, Miriam Peskowitz; illustrated by Alexis Seabrook. 1st ed. Collins 2007 viii, 279 p.p ill. (some col.), col. map (hardcover) $26.95

Grades: 4 5 6 7 8 9   **646.700**

1. Girls 2. Amusements 3. Recreation 4. Curiosities and wonders 5. Girls in literature 6. Girls -- Conduct of life 7. Girls -- Life skills guides

ISBN 0061472573; 9780061472572

LC 2007031986

This book is "filled with interesting activities to try and important facts [girls] may not know, but are sure to keep them busy for hours. The authors cover everything from making a lemon-powered clock to the history of writing and cursive, from how to paddle a canoe to the Periodic Table of the Elements." (School Library Journal)

Includes bibliographical references (p. 274-276).

647.9 Specific kinds of public households and institutions

Mara, Wil

The **innkeeper**. Marshall Cavendish Benchmark 2010 48p il (Colonial people) lib bdg $29.93

Grades: 3 4 5 6   **647.9**

1. Hotels and motels

ISBN 978-0-7614-4796-2; 0-7614-4796-2

LC 2009011873

This describes the life of a colonial innkeeper and his importance to the community, as well as everyday life, responsibilities, and social practices during that time.

"The type font, just slightly larger than usual, makes the text very visually appealing. . . . [The] book is liberally illustrated with artwork dating from the colonial period . . . [and] information boxes offer supplemental material." Libr Media Connect

Includes glossary and bibliographical references

648 Housekeeping

Barber, Nicola

Moving to a new house. PowerKids Press 2009 24p il (The big day!) lib bdg $21.25; pa $8.25

Grades: PreK K 1   **648**

1. Moving

ISBN 978-1-4358-2841-4 lib bdg; 978-1-4358-2897-1 pa

LC 2008026222

"Children in kindergarten will enjoy [this book] as [a read-aloud] . . . while those at the end of first grade will be able to read [it] independently. The writing is straightforward and reassuring, and the content provides a realistic view of what youngsters might experience in [a new home]. . . . [The book] mentions the possibility of feeling strange in the new environment, but also discusses how quickly the child will adjust and make new friends." SLJ

Includes bibliographical references

Parker, Victoria

Moving; [by] Vic Parker. Heinemann Library 2011 24p il (Growing up) lib bdg $22; pa $6.49

Grades: PreK K 1 2   **648**

1. Moving

ISBN 978-1-4329-4800-9 lib bdg; 1-4329-4800-8 lib bdg; 978-1-4329-4810-8 pa; 1-4329-4810-5 pa

LC 2010024194

This explains what to expect from a move across the street or across the country.

Includes bibliographical references

649 Child rearing; home care of people with disabilities and illnesses

Buckley, Annie

Be a better babysitter; by Annie Buckley. Child's World 2007 32p il (Girls rock!) lib bdg $24.21

Grades: 5 6 7 8   **649**

1. Babysitting

ISBN 1-59296-740-X

LC 2006001639

This "describes what babysitting entails, examines pros and cons, discusses safety issues, offers tips for doing a good job, and suggests saving as much as half of any money earned. . . . [This] realistic [title is] well written and [provides] excellent information." SLJ

Includes bibliographical references

Chasse, Jill D.

The **babysitter's** survival guide; fun games, cool crafts, and how to be the best babysitter in town. illustrated by Jessica Secheret. Sterling Pub. Co. 2010 107p il $12.95

Grades: 5 6 7 8   **649**

1. Babysitting

ISBN 978-1-4027-4654-3; 1-4027-4654-7

LC 2009-2538

"This useful, up-to-date handbook offers plenty of practical advice with a wise emphasis on safety, which makes it a good choice for new sitters as well as those with experience. Chassé starts with information on starting a business, including references, advertising, and interviewing. Child development is a main focus; suggested activities and tips on interaction with children at different developmental stages will be appreciated by sitters and parents alike. . . . Occasional two-color cartoons feature diverse children and sitters." SLJ

Includes bibliographical references

Danzig, Dianne

Babies don't eat pizza; the big kids' book about baby brothers and baby sisters. by Dianne Danzig; illustrated by Debbie Tilley. Dutton Children's Books 2009 un il $16.99

Grades: PreK K   **649**

1. Infants 2. Siblings

ISBN 978-0-525-47441-8; 0-525-47441-2

"Focusing on day-to-day living with an infant, the text adopts an unfussy tone that subtly flatters readers as being sensible and mature (relatively speaking). . . . Tilley's ink and watercolor cartoons are sunny and empathic . . . and include plenty of visual jokes to encourage anxious kids—and their parents—to bond. Headings on most spreads make this volume eminently browsable—and therefore a handy family resource." Publ Wkly

Sears, William

★ **What** baby needs; [by] William Sears, Martha Sears and Christie Watts Kelly; illustrated by Renée Andriani. Little, Brown 2001 un il (Sears children's library) $12.95
Grades: K 1 2   **649**

1. Infants 2. Siblings
ISBN 0-316-78828-7

LC 00-37529

This "is a warm look at how life in the family changes to accommodate the needs of a newborn, and the care an infant requires. . . . The lighthearted, full-color cartoons bring some welcome new images to baby books: breastfeeding, babywearing (including both a dad and a mom with an infant in a baby sling), and the newborn snoozing near the parents' bed." SLJ

Includes bibliographical references

Wells, Rosemary

My shining star; raising a child who is ready to learn. [by] Rosemary Wells. Scholastic Press 2006 un il $8.99
Grades: PreK K   **649**

1. Parenting
ISBN 0-439-84701-X

LC 2005010481

"Young children will enjoy the adorable bunny characters and the small size that is just right for their little hands. But this gem of a picture book is directed to adults—and it belongs in the big hands of every teacher and parent. On each colorful spread, Wells expands on 10 principles to help any child succeed. The direct, simple advice is illustrated with Wells' favorite rabbits demonstrating the recommendations." Booklist

650.1 Personal success in business

Orr, Tamra

A **kid's** guide to earning money; by Tamra Orr. Mitchell Lane Publishers 2008 47p il (Money matters: a kid's guide to money) lib bdg $29.95
Grades: 4 5 6   **650.1**

1. Personal finance 2. Money-making projects for children
ISBN 978-1-58415-643-7 lib bdg; 1-58415-643-0 lib bdg

LC 2008-2253

"This chatty, interactive guide offers practical suggestions for finding jobs, from babysitting and dogwalking to delivering newspapers. . . . Also included is useful advice on setting price points, how to cut costs, and what the labor laws allow for kids under 18, as well as a frank view of the negatives associated with the working world. . . . Stress is laid on the importance of getting parental permission before setting out on the trail to riches." Booklist

Includes glossary and bibliographical references

652 Processes of written communication

Bell-Rehwoldt, Sheri

Speaking secret codes. Capstone Press 2010 32p il (Edge books: making and breaking codes) lib bdg $26.65

Grades: 4 5 6 7   **652**

1. Ciphers 2. Cryptography
ISBN 978-1-4296-4569-0 lib bdg; 1-4296-4569-5 lib bdg

LC 2010004163

"Spoken codes in history, including the Underground Railroad and POWs during the Vietnam War, are introduced by using various examples of word substitutions. Educators will appreciate the concise information provided by codes that have shaped world history. . . . Historical photographs, highlighted vocabulary words and definitions, and do-it-yourself suggestions will keep readers interested." SLJ

Includes glossary and bibliographical references

Blackwood, Gary L.

Mysterious messages; a history of codes and ciphers. [by] Gary Blackwood; designed and illustrated by Jason Henry. Dutton Children's Books 2009 170p il $16.99
Grades: 5 6 7 8   **652**

1. Ciphers 2. Cryptography
ISBN 978-0-525-47960-4; 0-525-47960-0

LC 2008-48970

"This well-written history of cryptography begins with a pottery-glaze formula encrypted in cuneiform on a clay tablet (1500 BCE) and traces the uses of secret messages in statecraft, espionage, warfare, crime, literature, and business up to the present. Along the way, Blackwood . . . discusses the historical development of coding and encryption and tells many good stories of messages ciphered and deciphered. . . . The many sidebars and illustrations, including photos, reproductions of artworks and artifacts, and the pictures demonstrating the codes themselves, contribute to the book's approachable look." Booklist

Gilbert, Adrian

Codes and ciphers. Firefly 2009 32p il (Spy files) pa $6.95
Grades: 3 4 5 6   **652**

1. Ciphers 2. Espionage 3. Cryptography
ISBN 978-1-55407-573-7 pa; 1-55407-573-4 pa
First published 2008 in the United Kingdom

Discusses the difference between codes and ciphers, common codes and ciphers that have been used during wars, and how to create simple ciphers

This "gives an excellent overview of the historical and practical use of codes and ciphers in spy work. . . . The [text's] short paragraphs and great pictures are combined in a collage style that will draw readers quickly through the information." SLJ

Includes glossary

Gregory, Jillian

Breaking secret codes. Capstone Press 2010 32p il (Edge books: making and breaking codes) lib bdg $26.65
Grades: 4 5 6 7   **652**

1. Ciphers 2. Cryptography
ISBN 978-1-4296-4568-3 lib bdg; 1-4296-4568-7 lib bdg

LC 2010004162

"Educators will appreciate the concise information provided by codes that have shaped world history. Sample cryptographs are scattered throughout the pages, along with other noteworthy facts. Historical photographs, highlighted vocabulary words and definitions, and do-it-yourself suggestions will keep readers interested." SLJ

Includes glossary and bibliographical references

Making secret codes. Capstone Press 2010 32p il (Edge books: making and breaking codes) lib bdg $26.65
Grades: 4 5 6 7   **652**
  1. Ciphers 2. Cryptography
  ISBN 978-1-4296-4567-6 lib bdg; 1-4296-4567-9 lib bdg
                LC 2010004161

"Educators will appreciate the concise information provided by codes that have shaped world history. Sample cryptographs are scattered throughout the pages, along with other noteworthy facts. Historical photographs, highlighted vocabulary words and definitions, and do-it-yourself suggestions will keep readers interested." SLJ

Includes glossary and bibliographical references

Mitchell, Susan K.
  Spy codes and ciphers. Enslow Publishers 2011 48p il (The secret world of spies) lib bdg $23.93
Grades: 4 5 6   **652**
  1. Spies 2. Ciphers 3. Espionage 4. Cryptography
  ISBN 978-0-7660-3709-0
                LC 2010006176

Discusses different methods of secret communications used by spies, such as Morse code, the Enigma machine, the Najavo language, and digital steganography, and includes career information.

Includes glossary and bibliographical references

658   General management

Bochner, Arthur Berg
  The **new** totally awesome business book for kids (and their parents) with twenty super businesses you can start right now! [by] Arthur Bochner & Rose Bochner; foreword by Andriane G. Berg. rev and updated 3rd ed.; Newmarket Press 2007 188p il pa $9.95
Grades: 4 5 6 7   **658**
  1. Small business 2. Money-making projects for children
  ISBN 978-1-55704-757-1 pa; 1-55704-757-X pa
                LC 2007002637

First published 1995 with title: The totally awesome business book for kids

A comprehensive look at the basic financial and management aspects of moneymaking businesses for children

"This book can certainly be thought provoking for young people with an entrepreneurial spirit. . . . The illustrations are lively and engaging, and the text non-threatening." Voice Youth Advocates

Includes bibliographical references

Mooney, Carla
  Starting a business; have fun and make money. Norwood House Press 2010 48p il (Creative adventure guides) lib bdg $25.27
Grades: 3 4 5 6   **658**
  1. Business enterprises 2. Money-making projects for children
  ISBN 978-1-59953-386-5; 1-59953-386-3

This book "outlines a small business plan for kids, with examples of successful young entrepreneurs." Horn Book Guide

Includes glossary and bibliographical references

662   Technology of explosives, fuels, related products

Benduhn, Tea
  Ethanol and other new fuels; by Tea Benduhn. Weekly Reader Pub. 2009 24p il (Energy for today) lib bdg $21; pa $5.95
Grades: 2 3 4   **662**
  1. Energy resources 2. Alcohol as fuel
  ISBN 978-0-8368-9260-4 lib bdg; 0-8368-9260-7 lib bdg; 978-0-8368-9359-5 pa; 0-8368-9359-X pa
                LC 2008014483

This describes how ethanol and other new fuels work and how they can be used in the future.

"New readers will be able to wrap their hands around the small, square size, and their minds around the clear, enlightening text. [This book has] crisp photos and strong back matter." Booklist

Includes glossary and bibliographical references

Cobb, Vicki
  Fireworks; photographs by Michael Gold. Millbrook Press 2005 48p il (Where's the science here?) lib bdg $23.93
Grades: 3 4 5   **662**
  1. Fireworks
  ISBN 0-7613-2771-1
                LC 2004-29823

"From pictures of different types of display formations to those of chemicals being loaded into mortar tubes, readers will find interesting illustrations that support the text in Fireworks. They will learn about the science of pyrotechnics and be exposed to words like chemical reaction, combustion, and lift charges. Sections offer a historical overview of the evolution of the study of fire, the mechanics of building fireworks . . . how explosions are timed, and how pyrotechnicians avoid nasty surprises." SLJ

Rau, Dana Meachen
  Fireworks. Marshall Cavendish Benchmark 2010 24p il (Surprising science) $22.79
Grades: 2 3 4   **662**
  1. Fireworks
  ISBN 978-0-7614-4868-6; 0-7614-4868-3
                LC 2009053723

This book "opens with the experience of watching fireworks, traces their history from China to Europe to colonial America, and discusses the rocketry and chemistry that make them possible. Although the discussions are relatively short, they provide good, basic knowledge as well as some intriguing details. . . . Rau provides information about the dangers of fireworks as well. . . . The book's paper quality and page layouts are quite good, maximizing the effectiveness of the clear, colorful photos and well-chosen period art-works that illustrate the text." Booklist

Includes glossary and bibliographical references

664   Food technology

Cobb, Vicki

Junk food; photographs by Michael Gold. Millbrook 2005 48p il (Where's the science here?) lib bdg $23.93
Grades: 3 4 5   **664**
1. Food industry 2. Food -- Composition
ISBN 0-7613-2773-8

The author "focuses on food chemistry, not nutrition, in examinations of six seductive snack foods (popcorn, corn chips, chocolate, candy, potato chips, and soda). Well-digested explanations and low-tech projects reinforce Cobb's reputation for snappy hands-on science writing for children. . . . Gold's photos stand well above those in most nonfiction science series and directly support Cobb's intentions." Booklist

Gardner, Robert

Ace your food science project; great science fair ideas. [by] Robert Gardner, Salvatore Tocci, and Thomas R. Rybolt. Enslow Publishers 2009 128p il (Ace your science project) lib bdg $31.93
Grades: 5 6 7 8   **664**
1. Food 2. Science projects 3. Science -- Experiments
ISBN 978-0-7660-3228-6 lib bdg; 0-7660-3228-0
lib bdg
            LC 2008-49780

"Presents several science experiments and project ideas using food." Publisher's note

Includes bibliographical references

McCarthy, Meghan

★ **Pop!** the accidental invention of bubble gum. Simon & Schuster Books for Young Readers 2010 un il $15.99
Grades: 1 2 3   **664**
1. Inventors 2. Bubble gum 3. Accountants 4. Food industry executives
ISBN 978-1-4169-7970-8; 1-4169-7970-0
            LC 2008-49272

Traces the 1928 invention of bubble gum by a hardworking accountant at a candy company, describing how in his spare time he experimented with different recipes and ingredients to eventually create the product known today as Double Bubble.

"Kids who enjoy blowing gum bubbles may never have considered how the treat came to be, but here, in easy language and with amusing illustrations, McCarthy changes that. . . . The acrylic paintings portray humor throughout, in part by peopling the book with googly-eyed characters who are often chewing a wad of gum." Booklist

Petersen, Christine

The **miller.** Marshall Cavendish Benchmark 2011 il (Colonial people) $29.93
Grades: 3 4 5 6   **664**
1. Flour mills
ISBN 978-1-60870-416-3; 1-60870-416-5
            LC 2010033890

This describes the life of a colonial miller and his importance to the community, as well as everyday life, responsibilities, and social practices during that time.

This "lively [text] and colorful reproductions and photos will engage casual readers and researchers alike. . . . Large illustrations and thoughtful captions explain complicated scientific ideas. . . . [The] volume also includes step-by-step instructions for a related craft project. . . . [This is a] must-have." SLJ

Includes glossary and bibliographical references

Ridley, Sarah

A **chocolate** bar; [by] Sarah Ridley. Gareth Stevens Pub. 2006 32p il (How it's made) lib bdg $23.93
Grades: 3 4 5   **664**
1. Chocolate
ISBN 0-8368-6293-7
            LC 2005054075

First published 2005 in the United Kingdom

This presents "the origins of a chocolate bar, from a Ghana cocoa farm to a factory. The facts are clear and well organized; each spread shows a logical progression in the process, and sharp color photos and maps will help cement the concepts in readers' minds." Booklist

Rotner, Shelley

Where does food come from? by Shelley Rotner and Gary Goss; photographs by Shelley Rotner. Millbrook Press 2006 32p il lib bdg $22.60
Grades: K 1 2   **664**
1. Food 2. Food industry
ISBN 0-7613-2935-8
            LC 2005000874

Explains where various foods originate from, how food is grown, and brought to supermarkets and other stores, in simple text with illustrations.

"Large print, a well-spaced text, varied typeface, simple explanations, and appealing color photos of children on every page make this book a pleasant reading experience. . . . This is a book that teachers, librarians, and parents will find useful, informative, and fun to share." SLJ

665   Technology of industrial oils, fats, waxes, gases

Walker, Niki

Hydrogen; running on water. [by] Niki Walker. Crabtree Pub. 2007 32p il (Energy revolution) lib bdg $25.20; pa $8.95
Grades: 5 6 7 8   **665**
1. Hydrogen as fuel
ISBN 978-0-7787-2915-0 lib bdg; 0-7787-2915-X lib bdg; 978-0-7787-2929-7 pa; 0-7787-2929-X pa
            LC 2006014369

This describes various sources of hydrogen power, including natural gas, gasified coal, fuel from water, and biomass gas, and how it is stored and distributed, and offers energy conservation tips.

Includes glossary

665.5 Petroleum

Benduhn, Tea

Oil, gas, and coal; by Tea Benduhn. Weekly Reader Pub. 2009 24p il (Energy for today) lib bdg $21; pa $5.95

Grades: 2 3 4   **665.5**

1. Coal 2. Gasoline 3. Natural gas 4. Energy resources
ISBN 978-0-8368-9261-1 lib bdg; 0-8368-9261-5 lib bdg; 978-0-8368-9360-1 pa; 0-8368-9360-3 pa

LC 2008015517

This describes what fossil fuels are, how they work as energy sources, and their future.

"New readers will be able to wrap their hands around the small, square size, and their minds around the clear, enlightening text. [This book has] crisp photos and strong back matter." Booklist

Includes glossary and bibliographical references

Rockwell, Anne F.

What's so bad about gasoline? fossil fuels and what they do. by Anne Rockwell; illustrated by Paul Meisel. Collins 2009 33p il (Let's-read-and-find-out science) $16.99; pa $5.99

Grades: 1 2 3   **665.5**

1. Gasoline 2. Air pollution 3. Energy resources 4. Energy conservation 5. Greenhouse effect 6. Fossil fuels -- Juvenile literature
ISBN 978-0-06-157528-0; 0-06-157528-3; 978-0-06-157527-3 pa; 0-06-157527-5 pa

LC 2007-52947

"Rockwell presents the basic facts about how gasoline is produced, how it was first discovered, and its uses. She then discusses how gasoline and other fossil fuels . . . have contributed to polluting the environment. Suggestions are offered on how to cut back our gas consumption, and alternatives such as solar power, wind power, nuclear energy, and alternative fuels are addressed. . . . Detailed pen-and-ink and watercolor drawings in shades of blue and brown appear throughout, and text balloons help provide humor to various scenarios." SLJ

666 Ceramic and allied technologies

Blaxland, Wendy

Bottles and jars. Marshall Cavendish Benchmark 2011 32p il map (How are they made?) lib bdg $28.50

Grades: 3 4 5 6   **666**

1. Plastics 2. Glassware 3. Glass -- History
ISBN 978-0-7614-4752-8 lib bdg; 0-7614-4752-0 lib bdg

LC 2009040080

This discusses how bottles and jars are made, including their history, raw materials, design, manufacture, packaging and distribution, marketing and advertising, and their relationship to the environment.

Includes glossary

Koscielniak, Bruce

Looking at glass through the ages; by Bruce Koscielniak. Houghton Mifflin Co. 2006 un $16

Grades: 3 4 5 6   **666**

1. Glass -- History
ISBN 0-618-50750-7

LC 2005003916

"A handsome book on the history of glassmaking. Starting with faience, developed in Egypt around 2500 B.C., the author's precisely worded, carefully detailed text and watercolor artwork explain the steps for producing various types of glass and glassware. . . . Much information is compacted into the smoothly written narrative. Captioned illustrations are well matched with the text and extend the information value of the book." SLJ

Petersen, Christine

The glassblower. Marshall Cavendish Benchmark 2011 il (Colonial people) $29.93

Grades: 3 4 5 6   **666**

1. Glassblowing
ISBN 978-1-60870-413-2; 1-60870-413-0

LC 2010033901

This describes the life of a colonial glassblower and his importance to the community, as well as everyday life, responsibilities, and social practices during that time.

This "lively [text] and colorful reproductions and photos will engage casual readers and researchers alike. . . . Large illustrations and thoughtful captions explain complicated scientific ideas. . . . [The] volume also includes step-by-step instructions for a related craft project. . . . [This is a] must-have." SLJ

Includes glossary and bibliographical references

Stewart, Melissa

How does sand become glass? Raintree 2010 32p il (How does it happen?) lib bdg $27.50; pa $7.99

Grades: 3 4 5   **666**

1. Sand 2. Glass 3. Erosion
ISBN 978-1-4109-3449-9 lib bdg; 1-4109-3449-7 lib bdg; 978-1-4109-3457-4 pa; 1-4109-3457-8 pa

LC 2008-52654

"Information is clearly presented using a large font, diagrams, and photographs formatted to resemble Polaroid pictures. . . . A first-rate job answering some important scientific questions." SLJ

Includes glossary and bibliographical references

668 Technology of other organic products

Rhatigan, Joe

Soapmaking; 50 fun & fabulous soaps to melt & pour. Lark Books 2003 112p il (Kids' crafts) $19.95

Grades: 3 4 5 6   **668**

1. Soap 2. Handicraft
ISBN 1-57990-416-5

LC 2003-883

This describes soapmaking projects beginning with choosing a soap base and selecting molds, adding fragrance, color, or other extras. Projects include eyeball soaps, making soap popsicles, smiley faces, a soapasaurus, alphabet soap, a soap bracelet and a clear bar with an embedded photo.

"This book has a wonderful, 'squeaky-clean' appearance and a perfect combination of text, color photography, design, and child models." SLJ

Wagner, Lisa

Cool melt & pour soap; [by] Lisa Wagner. ABDO Pub. 2005 32p il (Cool crafts) lib bdg $22.78

Grades: 4 5 6   **668**

1. Soap 2. Handicraft

ISBN 1-59197-741-X

LC 2004-46291

This guide to soap crafting "discusses premade bases, coloring and fragrance, layered soaps, treasure-packed soaps, relief soaps, and packaging ideas." SLJ

668.4   Plastics

Langley, Andrew

Plastic; [by] Andrew Langley. Crabtree Pub. Co. 2009 24p il (Everyday materials) lib bdg $21.27; pa $6.95

Grades: K 1 2 3   **668.4**

1. Plastics

ISBN 978-0-7787-4129-9 lib bdg; 0-7787-4129-X lib bdg; 978-0-7787-4136-7 pa; 0-7787-4136-2 pa

LC 2008-25324

This title "introduces [plastics] in an engaging style. The text and photos work together, progressing from a definition of the material to how it is manufactured and what it is used for. . . . [It] concludes with a recycling section, a simple comprehension quiz, and a topic web that offers extension ideas. The large type, bright photos, and uncluttered layout will allow large and small group use." SLJ

Includes glossary

Morris, Neil

Plastics. Amicus 2010 48p il (Materials that matter) lib bdg $28.50

Grades: 4 5 6 7   **668.4**

1. Plastics

ISBN 978-1-60753-068-8 lib bdg; 1-60753-068-6 lib bdg

LC 2009051435

"The clean layout includes photographs and occasional charts, graphs, and technical illustrations against a range of pastel backgrounds. Inset boxes provide further detail, interesting extras, and recycling information. . . . [This book offers] easily accessible background information for report writers." SLJ

Includes glossary and bibliographical references

670   Manufacturing

Slavin, Bill

Transformed; how everyday things are made. written by Bill Slavin with Jim Slavin; illustrated by Bill Slavin. Kids Can Press 2005 160p il $24.95

Grades: 4 5 6 7   **670**

1. Manufactures

ISBN 1-55337-179-8

This describes the manufacture of such items "as baseballs, plastic dinosaurs, toothpaste, cereal, paper, and bricks. Each two-page spread covers the making of one of the 69 items in numbered paragraphs. The pictures are the best

part—clear watercolor and ink images, made all the more engaging by folks in overalls directing the action." Booklist

Includes glossary and bibliographical references

671   Manufacture of products from specific materials

Blaxland, Wendy

Cans. Marshall Cavendish Benchmark 2011 32p il map (How are they made?) lib bdg $28.50

Grades: 3 4 5 6   **671**

1. Cans

ISBN 978-0-7614-4753-5 lib bdg; 0-7614-4753-9 lib bdg

LC 2009039876

This discusses how cans are made, including their history, raw materials, design, manufacture, packaging and distribution, marketing and advertising, production, and their relationship to the environment.

674   Lumber processing, wood products, cork

Blaxland, Wendy

Pencils. Marshall Cavendish Benchmark 2009 32p il (How are they made?) $19.95

Grades: 3 4 5 6   **674**

1. Pencils

ISBN 978-0-7614-3807-6; 0-7614-3807-6

LC 2008026215

This describes how pencils are made, including raw materials, design, manufacture, and relationship to the environment.

675   Leather and fur processing

Petersen, Christine

The tanner. Marshall Cavendish Benchmark 2011 il (Colonial people) $29.93

Grades: 3 4 5 6   **675**

1. Leather industry

ISBN 978-1-60870-418-7; 1-60870-418-1

LC 2010033896

This describes the life of a colonial tanner and his importance to the community, as well as everyday life, responsibilities, and social practices during that time.

This "lively [text] and colorful reproductions and photos will engage casual readers and researchers alike. . . . Large illustrations and thoughtful captions explain complicated scientific ideas. . . . [The] volume also includes step-by-step instructions for a related craft project. . . . [This is a] must-have." SLJ

Includes glossary and bibliographical references

676 Pulp and paper technology

Langley, Andrew

Paper products; [by] Andrew Langley. Crabtree Pub. Co. 2009 24p il (Everyday materials) lib bdg $21.27; pa $6.95

Grades: K 1 2 3 **676**

1. Paper 2. Papermaking

ISBN 978-0-7787-4128-2 lib bdg; 0-7787-4128-1 lib bdg; 978-0-7787-4135-0 pa; 0-7787-4135-4 pa

LC 2008-24011

This title "introduces [paper products] in an engaging style. The text and photos work together, progressing from a definition of the material to how it is manufactured and what it is used for. . . . [It] concludes with a recycling section, a simple comprehension quiz, and a topic web that offers extension ideas. The large type, bright photos, and uncluttered layout will allow large and small group use." SLJ

Includes glossary

Morris, Neil

Paper. Amicus 2010 48p il (Materials that matter) lib bdg $28.50

Grades: 4 5 6 7 **676**

1. Paper

ISBN 978-1-60753-067-1 lib bdg; 1-60753-067-8 lib bdg

LC 2009051436

"The clean layout includes photographs and occasional charts, graphs, and technical illustrations against a range of pastel backgrounds. Inset boxes provide further detail, interesting extras, and recycling information. . . . [This book offers] easily accessible background information for report writers." SLJ

Includes glossary and bibliographical references

677 Textiles

Langley, Andrew

Wool; [by] Andrew Langley. Crabtree Pub. Co. 2009 24p il (Everyday materials) lib bdg $21.27; pa $6.95

Grades: K 1 2 3 **677**

1. Wool

ISBN 978-0-7787-4131-2 lib bdg; 0-7787-4131-1 lib bdg; 978-0-7787-4138-1 pa; 0-7787-4138-9 pa

LC 2008-25323

This title "introduces [wool] in an engaging style. The text and photos work together, progressing from a definition of the material to how it is manufactured and what it is used for. . . . [It] concludes with a recycling section, a simple comprehension quiz, and a topic web that offers extension ideas. The large type, bright photos, and uncluttered layout will allow large and small group use." SLJ

Includes glossary

Morris, Neil

Textiles. Amicus 2010 48p il (Materials that matter) lib bdg $28.50

Grades: 4 5 6 7 **677**

1. Fabrics

ISBN 978-1-60753-069-5 lib bdg; 1-60753-069-4 lib bdg

LC 2009051434

"The clean layout includes photographs and occasional charts, graphs, and technical illustrations against a range of pastel backgrounds. Inset boxes provide further detail, interesting extras, and recycling information. . . . [This book offers] easily accessible background information for report writers." SLJ

Includes glossary and bibliographical references

Sobol, Richard

★ The story of silk; from worm spit to woven scarves. Richard Sobol. Candlewick Press 2012 36 p. col. ill., col. maps (reinforced) $17.99

Grades: 2 3 4 5 **677**

1. Thailand 2. Silkworms 3. Silk -- Juvenile literature

ISBN 0763641650; 9780763641658

LC 2012942294

This children's educational book answers the question "What does worm spit have to do with the world's most luxurious fabric? . . . Join author and photographer Richard Sobol as he picks up his camera once more and travels to a small village in Thailand for an in-depth exploration of the story of silk and the labor-intensive process of making it." (Publisher's note)

678 Elastomers and elastomer products

Allman, Toney

Recycled tires; by Toney Allman. Norwood House Press 2008 48p il (A great idea) lib bdg $25.27

Grades: 3 4 5 6 **678**

1. Tires 2. Recycling

ISBN 978-1-59953-197-7 lib bdg; 1-59953-197-6 lib bdg

LC 2008-15736

"'Describes the invention and development of recycled rubber tires." Publisher's note

Includes glossary and bibliographical references

680 Manufacture of products for specific uses

Tunis, Edwin

★ Colonial craftsmen and the beginnings of American industry; written and illustrated by Edwin Tunis. Johns Hopkins Univ. Press 1999 159p pa $18.95

Grades: 4 5 6 7 **680**

1. Handicraft 2. Decorative arts 3. Handicraft -- United States -- History 4. Industries -- United States -- History

ISBN 0-8018-6228-0

LC 99-20398

The author describes the working methods and products, houses and shops, town and country trades, individual and group enterprises by which the early Americans forged the economy of the New World. He discusses such trades as papermaking, glassmaking, shipbuilding, printing, and metalworking

"An oversize book that is impressively handsome and that should be tremendously useful; well-organized and superbly illustrated, the text is comprehensive, lucid, and detailed. . . . An extensive index is appended." Chicago. Children's Book Center

681   Precision instruments and other devices

Rau, Dana Meachen

Become an explorer; make and use a compass. Norwood House Press 2010 48p il (Creative adventure guides) lib bdg $25.27

Grades: 3 4 5 6   **681**

1. Compass

ISBN 978-1-59953-383-4; 1-59953-383-9

LC 2010010359

"Some historical background and scientific or cultural information places the making and use of . . . compasses in context for young readers. [The] book has four chapters that culminate in step-by-step projects." Horn Book Guide

Includes glossary and bibliographical references

682   Small forge work (Blacksmithing)

Petersen, Christine

The blacksmith. Marshall Cavendish Benchmark 2010 48p il (Colonial people) lib bdg $29.93

Grades: 3 4 5 6   **682**

1. Blacksmithing

ISBN 978-0-7614-4799-3; 0-7614-4799-7

This describes the life of a colonial blacksmith and his importance to the community, as well as everyday life, responsibilities, and social practices during that time.

"The type font, just slightly larger than usual, makes the text very visually appealing. . . . [The] book is liberally illustrated with artwork dating from the colonial period . . . [and] information boxes offer supplemental material." Libr Media Connect

Includes glossary and bibliographical references

683   Hardware and household appliances

Blaxland, Wendy

Knives and forks. Marshall Cavendish Benchmark 2009 32p il (How are they made?) $19.95

Grades: 3 4 5 6   **683**

1. Cutlery 2. Tableware

ISBN 978-0-7614-3805-2; 0-7614-3805-X

LC 2008026214

This describes how knives and forks are made, including their history, raw materials, design, manufacture, and relationship to the environment.

684   Furnishings and home workshops

Robertson, J. Craig

The kids' building workshop; 15 woodworking projects for kids and parents to build together. [by] J. Craig and

Barbara Robertson, with their daughters Camille and Allegra. Storey Kids 2004 136p il $22.96; pa $12.95

Grades: 3 4 5 6   **684**

1. Woodwork

ISBN 1-58017-572-4; 1-58017-488-4 pa

LC 2004-1521

"The first section, 'Setting Up Shop: Getting to Know Your Tools,' includes a basic introduction to hammering, sawing, drilling, block planing, and measuring. Next, 'Down to Business: Building Your Own Projects' puts these tools and techniques to work in simple, yet cleverly designed, kid-friendly projects that increase in complexity. . . . Clear instructions, black-and-white photos, and cutting diagrams are included for each one. . . . Practical and enjoyable introduction to the subject." SLJ

685   Leather and fur goods, and related products

Blaxland, Wendy

Sneakers. Marshall Cavendish Benchmark 2009 32p il (How are they made?) $19.95

Grades: 4 5 6   **685**

1. Sneakers

ISBN 978-0-7614-3810-6; 0-7614-3810-6

LC 2008026211

This is an "introduction to athletic shoes and the global trade involved in their manufacture and marketing. . . . A typical page offers a paragraph or more of informative text as well as a color photo and, perhaps, a small sidebar." Booklist

Cobb, Vicki

Sneakers; photographs by Michael Gold. Millbrook Press 2006 48p il (Where's the science here?) lib bdg $23.93

Grades: 3 4 5   **685**

1. Sneakers

ISBN 0-7613-2772-X

LC 2004-29816

"From photographs of the inside of a sneaker factory to X-rays of the foot to a picture of how rubber is extracted from a rubber tree, readers will find a new angle to spark their interest in Sneakers. They will learn about how sneakers are designed and made, and even how to test their fit. [An] attractive [choice] that [relates] science to [a topic] that fascinate kids." SLJ

D'Cruz, Anna-Marie

Make your own slippers and shoes. PowerKids Press 2009 24p il (Do it yourself projects!) lib bdg $23.95; pa $9.40

Grades: 2 3 4   **685**

1. Shoes 2. Handicraft

ISBN 978-1-4358-2852-0 lib bdg; 1-4358-2852-6 lib bdg; 978-1-4358-2921-3 pa; 1-4358-2921-2 pa

LC 2008033669

Learn how to make different types of shoes from around the world using easy-to-find materials.

Includes glossary and bibliographical references

Heinrichs, Ann
The **shoemaker**. Marshall Cavendish Benchmark 2010
48p il (Colonial people) lib bdg $29.93
Grades: 3 4 5 6   **685**
1. Shoemakers
ISBN 978-0-7614-4798-6; 0-7614-4798-9
LC 2009007938

This describes the life of a colonial shoemaker and his
importance to the community, as well as everyday life, responsibilities, and social practices during that time

"The type font, just slightly larger than usual, makes the
text very visually appealing. . . . [The] book is liberally illustrated with artwork dating from the colonial period . . .
[and] information boxes offer supplemental material." Libr
Media Connect

Includes glossary and bibliographical references

686   Printing and related activities

D'Cruz, Anna-Marie
Make your own books. PowerKids Press 2009 24p il
(Do it yourself projects!) lib bdg $23.95; pa $9.40
Grades: 2 3 4   **686**
1. Books 2. Handicraft 3. Bookbinding
ISBN 978-1-4358-2855-1 lib bdg; 1-4358-2855-0 lib
bdg; 978-1-4358-2927-5 pa; 1-4358-2927-1 pa
LC 2008033659

Projects for creating many different kinds of books from
easy-to-find materials

Includes glossary and bibliographical references

Petersen, Christine
The **printer**. Marshall Cavendish Benchmark 2010
48p il (Colonial people) lib bdg $29.93
Grades: 3 4 5 6   **686**
1. Printing -- History
ISBN 978-0-7614-4802-0; 0-7614-4802-0
LC 2009044588

This describes the life of a colonial printer and his importance to the community, as well as everyday life, responsibilities, and social practices during that time.

"The type font, just slightly larger than usual, makes the
text very visually appealing. . . . [The] book is liberally illustrated with artwork dating from the colonial period . . .
[and] information boxes offer supplemental material." Libr
Media Connect

Includes glossary and bibliographical references

686.2   Printing

Adler, David A., 1947-
A **picture** book of Louis Braille; illustrated by John
& Alexandra Wallner. Holiday House 1997 un il $16.95;
pa $6.95
Grades: 1 2 3   **686.2**
1. Blind 2. Inventors 3. Teachers of the blind 4. Blind
-- Books and reading
ISBN 0-8234-1291-1; 0-8234-1413-2 pa
LC 96-38453

Presents the life of the nineteenth-century Frenchman,
accidentally blinded as a child, who originated the raised dot

system of reading and writing used by the blind throughout
the world

"The text is simple yet informative. . . . Adler sprinkles
in interesting facts about early 19th-century France that help
readers better grasp Braille's world. . . . Softly colored illustrations in line and watercolor add visual clues for younger
children." SLJ

Koscielniak, Bruce
Johann Gutenberg and the amazing printing press.
Houghton Mifflin Co. 2003 un il $16
Grades: 2 3 4   **686.2**
1. Inventors 2. Printers 3. Printing -- History
ISBN 0-618-26351-9
LC 2002-151176

A history of the modern printing industry, including how
paper and ink are made, looking particularly at the printing press invented by Gutenberg around 1450 but also at
its precursors

"The pleasing line drawings and the subtle hues of Bos-
cielniak's watercolors give the illustrations an informal look
that makes their informative content all the more accessible." Booklist

687   Clothing and accessories

Kent, Peter
Peter Kent's big book of armor; from armadillos to
armored cars. Kingfisher 2010 64p il $16.99
Grades: 1 2 3 4   **687**
1. Armor
ISBN 978-0-7534-6423-6; 0-7534-6423-3

Describes the history of armor and protective clothing,
from prehistoric protection and the armors of ancient Egypt
and Assyria to medieval and modern armor, armored transport, and fortified buildings.

"With its broad definition of armor and the plentiful
color illustrations, this informative volume will appeal to a
large audience for pleasure reading, as well as providing a
solid volume for research purposes." Libr Media Connect

Includes glossary

688.7   Recreational equipment

Blaxland, Wendy
Basketballs. Marshall Cavendish Benchmark 2011
32p il map (How are they made?) lib bdg $28.50
Grades: 3 4 5 6   **688.7**
1. Basketball 2. Sporting goods
ISBN 978-0-7614-4751-1 lib bdg; 0-7614-4751-2
lib bdg
LC 2009039874

This book "starts out with the raw materials used to
make [basketballs]. . . . Next, [a] time [line] handily [sums]
up basketball from 1891 to 1992, when composite rubber
balls were developed. . . . Design and stages of production
are then explained. . . . Nicely designed and well executed."
SLJ

Includes glossary

Fridell, Ron

   Sports technology. Lerner Publications 2009 48p il (Cool science) lib bdg $27.93

Grades: 4 5 6   **688.7**

   1. Sports 2. Technology

   ISBN 978-0-8225-7587-0 lib bdg; 0-8225-7587-6 lib bdg

                              LC 2007050905

This describes "how science helps athletes stay safer, perform better, and have more fun." Publisher's notes

Includes glossary and bibliographical references

Hirschmann, Kris

   LEGO toys. Norwood House Press 2008 48p il (A great idea) lib bdg $25.27

Grades: 3 4 5 6   **688.7**

   1. Toys

   ISBN 978-1-59953-194-6 lib bdg; 1-59953-194-1 lib bdg

                              LC 2008010712

Describes the invention and development of LEGO toys

"Full-color photographs and copious fun facts help make this . . . enjoyable reading, but it's really the choice of [topic] that is so enthralling." Booklist

Includes glossary and bibliographical references

Oxlade, Chris

   Gadgets and games; Chris Oxlade. Capstone Heinemann Library 2013 56 p. col. ill. (Design and engineering for STEM) (library) $33.50; (paperback) $9.49

Grades: 5 6 7   **688.7**

   1. Electronics 2. Industrial design 3. Product life cycle -- Juvenile literature 4. Toys -- Design and construction -- Juvenile literature 5. Household appliances -- Design and construction -- Juvenile literature 6. Electronic apparatus and appliances -- Design and construction -- Juvenile literature

   ISBN 1432970364; 9781432970314; 9781432970369

                              LC 2012013468

This book, part of the Design and Engineering for STEM series, looks at electronic devices and mobile games. It looks at the life cycle of these items, or "the stages from their design, manufacture, and sale to their use, maintenance, and disposal." Topics include "prototyping, the sourcing of components, the production process, the decisions made by designers and engineers, and recycling." (Publisher's note)

Includes bibliographical references (p. 54) and index.

Ross, Stewart

   Sports technology. Smart Apple Media 2011 il (New technology)

Grades: 4 5 6 7   **688.7**

   1. Sports

   ISBN 1-599-20534-3; 978-1-599-20534-2

                              LC 2010044241

Describes the technological advances in the sports industry, including the technology used to create better equipment, sports wear, judging tools, and playing surfaces.

This "offers a fine overview for reports, and its attractive design may also entice middle-grade readers to learn more." Booklist

Wulffson, Don L.

   Toys! amazing stories behind some great inventions. [by] Don Wulffson; with illustrations by Laurie Keller. Holt & Co. 2000 137p il $16.95

Grades: 4 5 6 7   **688.7**

   1. Toys 2. Inventions

   ISBN 0-8050-6196-7

                              LC 99-58440

Describes the creation of a variety of toys and games, from seesaws to Silly Putty and toy soldiers to Trivial Pursuit

"Each of the 25 chapters is illustrated with small, humorous drawings and discusses a particular toy or game's origin and development. The book ends with a bibliography and a list of Web sites. Good, readable fare for browsing or light research." Booklist

Includes bibliographical references

690   Construction of buildings

Barton, Byron

   Building a house. Greenwillow Books 1981 un il lib bdg $17.89; pa $6.99

Grades: PreK K 1   **690**

   1. Houses 2. Building 3. House construction

   ISBN 978-0-688-84291-8 lib bdg; 0-688-84291-7 lib bdg; 978-0-688-09356-3 pa; 0-688-09356-6 pa

"In the simplest possible book on building a house, a step-by-step, one-line description is given of the major factors in construction. Such workers as bricklayers, carpenters, plumbers, electricians, and painters do their own jobs until the small, bright red-and-green house is completed and a family moves in. Flat drawings in brilliant primary colors enable the very young to visualize the methods of housebuilding." Horn Book

   ★ **Machines** at work. Crowell 1987 un il $17.99; bd bk $7.99

Grades: PreK K 1   **690**

   1. Building 2. Building -- Juvenile literature 3. Machinery -- Juvenile literature

   ISBN 0-694-00190-2; 0-694-01107-X bd bk

                              LC 86-24221

"The short, punchy narrative reinforces the dynamics of the illustrations. . . . This should be a popular read-aloud for preschoolers and satisfying read-alone for beginners." Publ Wkly

Byers, Ann

   Jobs as green builders and planners. Rosen Pub. 2010 80p il (Green careers) lib bdg $30.60

Grades: 5 6 7 8   **690**

   1. Building 2. Vocational guidance 3. Environmental science

   ISBN 978-1-4358-3566-5 lib bdg; 1-4358-3566-2 lib bdg

                              LC 2009015517

This "well-conceived [introduction focuses] on various jobs in [building and construction planning], the education and experience required, and expected earnings. The [book is] well organized, making it easy to gain an overview of the major aspects of the work. . . . [This book] will make [a] good [addition] to career collections. Photographs from the field and website and contact information for professional organizations add value." SLJ

Includes glossary and bibliographical references

Gibbons, Gail

How a house is built. Holiday House 1990 un il $16.95; pa $6.95

Grades: K 1 2 3   690

1. Houses 2. Building 3. House construction -- Juvenile literature

ISBN 0-8234-0841-8; 0-8234-1232-6 pa

LC 90-55107

This book describes how the surveyor, heavy machinery operators, carpenter crew, plumbers, and other workers build a house

"With her customary bright illustrations, Gibbons gives a fine introduction to the construction of a wood-frame house. . . . Construction machines and materials as well as parts of the house are identified, and each stage of construction logically follows the others. Workers are drawn in both sexes and several skin tones." Booklist

Hudson, Cheryl Willis

★ Construction zone; photographs by Richard Sobol; text by Cheryl Willis Hudson. Candlewick Press 2006 un il $15.99

Grades: 2 3 4   690

1. Building

ISBN 0-7636-2684-8

"Large photographs of the construction of the MIT Stata Center in Cambridge, MA, are the core of this book. The simple text explains the process from the design by Frank O. Gehry to the completed building. Construction-zone activity, equipment, and jargon are pictured and explained. . . . Words in bold . . . are defined and explained at the bottom of the page on which they appear. . . . Children will be fascinated by both the picture story and the informative text." SLJ

Macaulay, David

★ Unbuilding. Houghton Mifflin 1980 78p il $18; pa $9.95

Grades: 4 5 6 7 8 9   690

1. Building 2. Skyscrapers

ISBN 0-395-29457-6; 0-395-45425-5 pa

LC 80-15491

This fictional account of the dismantling and removal of the Empire State Building describes the structure of a skyscraper and explains how such an edifice would be demolished

"Save for the fact that one particularly stunning double-page spread is marred by tight binding, the book is a joy: accurate, informative, handsome, and eminently readable." Bull Cent Child Books

Newhouse, Maxwell

The house that Max built. Tundra Books 2008 un il $18.95

Grades: K 1 2 3   690

1. House construction 2. Building -- Juvenile literature 3. Dwellings -- Juvenile literature

ISBN 978-0-88776-774-6; 0-88776-774-5

"When Max decides to build a house beside the lake, 'he needs a lot of help.' This simple introduction takes readers through the major steps of the construction, from the archi-

tect's drawings to the completed house. In one or two sentences per page, the present-tense narrative neatly applies the personal viewpoint of the homeowner to each construction phase. . . . Warmly rendered folk-art-style oil paintings show the house coming together over time. . . . [This has] strong visual appeal and just enough detail." SLJ

Ritchie, Scot

Look at that building! a first book of structures. written and illustrated by Scot Ritchie. Kids Can Press 2011 32 p. col. ill. (hardcover) $16.95

Grades: PreK K 1 2 3 4   690

1. Houses 2. Buildings 3. Picture books for children 4. Building

ISBN 1554536960; 9781554536962

This book introduces young readers to basic construction concepts through the eyes of five friends keen on building a doghouse for their pet pooch, Max. To find out more about the task, Yulee, Martin, Nick, Sally and Pedro head to the library, where they learn about foundations, beams, frames and other building fundamentals.

"Winsome cartoon art shows a mutlicultural group of friends taking steps to tackle their project. . . . Budding architects and anyone researching the process will appreciate this colorful overview." Booklist

Schwarz, Renee

Birdfeeders. Kids Can Press 2005 40p il (Kids can do it) $12.95; pa $6.95

Grades: 4 5 6   690

1. Bird feeders 2. Birds -- Juvenile literature

ISBN 1-55337-699-4; 1-55337-700-1 pa

This offers instructions for constructing nine types of bird feeders composed of recycled or common household materials such as flowerpots, juice cans, Frisbees and ketchup bottles.

Birdhouses. Kids Can Press 2005 40p il (Kids can do it) $12.95; pa $6.95

Grades: 4 5 6   690

1. Woodwork 2. Birdhouses

ISBN 1-55337-549-1; 1-55337-550-5 pa

This "shows and tells how to build nine birdhouses using inexpensive materials such as wood, plastic drainage pipes, flower pots, and even an old boot. . . . Small, clear pictures illustrate the step-by-step directions." Booklist

Somervill, Barbara A.

Green general contractor. Cherry Lake Pub. 2011 32p il (Cool careers) lib bdg $27.07

Grades: 4 5 6 7   690

1. Building 2. Vocational guidance 3. Sustainable architecture

ISBN 978-1-60279-987-5; 1-60279-987-3

LC 2010029535

This book begins "with a personal story of a teen and then [segues] into the occupation [of general contractor]. . . . [It covers] the necessary training and skills for the job (and options for obtaining them), a typical day, salary expectations, and well-known professionals in the field. The [text is] accessible and clearly written. . . . The [volume has] a generous number of clear color photographs that depict people at work." SLJ

Includes glossary and bibliographical references

694 Wood construction

Walker, Lester

Carpentry for children; preface by David Macaulay. Overlook Press 1982 208p il hardcover o.p. pa $14.95

Grades: 4 5 6 7   694

1. Carpentry 2. Handicraft
ISBN 0-87951-990-8 pa

LC 82-3469

A step-by-step guide to carrying out such carpentry projects as a birdhouse, candle chandelier, doll cradle, puppet theater, and coaster car

696 Utilities

Gregory, Josh

Plumber. Cherry Lake Pub. 2011 32p il (Cool careers) lib bdg $27.07

Grades: 4 5 6 7   696

1. Plumbing 2. Vocational guidance
ISBN 978-1-60279-984-4; 1-60279-984-9

LC 2010029538

This book begins "with a personal story of a teen and then [segues] into the occupation [of plumber]. . . . [It covers] the necessary training and skills for the job (and options for obtaining them), a typical day, salary expectations, and wellknown professionals in the field. The [text is] accessible and clearly written. . . . The [volume has] a generous number of clear color photographs that depict people at work." SLJ

Includes glossary and bibliographical references

Raum, Elizabeth

★ The story behind toilets. Heinemann Library 2009 32p il (True stories) $19.75

Grades: 2 3 4   696

1. Toilets
ISBN 978-1-4329-2350-1; 1-4329-2350-1

LC 2008037392

"Virtually everything related to toilets is covered, from the bodily functions that require such facilities all the way to the technology of the toilets of tomorrow. . . . 'A Short History of Toilets' is the most surprising chapter, with its running time line of toilet innovations. . . . Raum has the arcana down. . . . But there's real educational value here, too, notably in the discussion of sewage plants, the debate over pay toilets, the international scope of health problems related to poor sanitation, and the twisty time line that ends the book." Booklist

Includes bibliographical references

700 ARTS

700 The arts

Ajmera, Maya

★ To be an artist; [by] Maya Ajmera & John D. Ivanko; foreword by Jacques d'Amboise. Charlesbridge 2004 un il $15.95

Grades: K 1 2 3   700

1. Arts 2. Creative ability 3. Arts -- Juvenile literature
ISBN 1-57091-503-2

LC 2003-8154

This includes "photographs of youngsters from many different countries engaged in a variety of art forms, including dancing, singing, writing, and painting. The bold text introduces each discipline and is supported with more extensive descriptions of the individual endeavors and the nature of artistic expression in general. . . . This vibrant book pulsates with the energy and sense of accomplishment that accompanies participation in the arts." SLJ

Johnson, Dolores

★ The Harlem Renaissance; by Dolores Johnson with Virginia Schomp. Marshall Cavendish Benchmark 2008 80p il (Drama of African-American history) lib bdg $23.95

Grades: 5 6 7 8   700

1. Harlem Renaissance 2. African American arts
ISBN 978-0-7614-2641-7

LC 2007034691

This is an account of the flowering of African American art, literature, music, and political commentary of the 1920s and 1930s centered in the Harlem section of New York City.

Includes glossary and bibliographical references

McArthur, Meher

An ABC of what art can be; pictures by Esther Pearl Watson. J. Paul Getty Museum 2010 un il $17.95

Grades: 2 3 4 5   700

1. Art 2. Alphabet
ISBN 978-0-89236-999-7; 0-89236-999-X

LC 2009-15387

"This lighthearted artist's alphabet finds inspiration from many forms. . . . Each page is unique in the color and style choices enriching the text and is unified by the collage style used throughout. . . . Watson's fun-loving illustrations are a good match for McArthur's rhyming text. An enjoyable alphabet for young artists." SLJ

Speaking of art; colorful quotes by famous painters. edited by Bob Raczka. Millbrook Press 2010 31 p. col. ill.

Grades: 3 4 5   700

1. Art 2. Artists -- Quotations 3. Art -- Quotations, maxims, etc
ISBN 9780761350545

LC 2009023484

This book presents information about eighteen famous artists and answers questions such as "When did Vincent Van Gogh feel most alive? Why did Juan Gris always pet a dog with his left hand? . . . Art lover [and author] Bob Raczka pairs . . . quotes by famous painters with . . . examples of their best work. The result is a . . . gallery of observations about the joys and the mysteries of art. From Edgar Degas' The Rehearsal (1878-79) to Georgia O'Keeffe's Evening Star, No. III (1917) to Romare Bearden's Family (1986), you'll discover the works - and the wisdom - of eighteen artistic masters." (Publisher's note)

Includes bibliographical references

700.23

Apodaca, Blanca

Behind the canvas; an artist's life. by Blanka Apodaca and Michael Serwich. Teacher Created Materials 2012 48 p. (paperback) $8.96; (prebind) $18.99

Grades: 4 5 6   **700.23**

1. Artists -- Juvenile literature   2. Art -- Technique -- Juvenile literature

ISBN 1433348268; 145177074X; 9781433348266; 9781451770742

This book is part of the TIME for Kids Nonfiction Readers series and looks at the lives of artists. "Most of the books tie the subject to related professions, sharing ways in which students could help solve the dilemmas. . . . Colorful photographs with extensive captioning, 'Dig Deeper' sections that provide added detail and ask probing questions, diagrams, and informative maps all help guide students." (Library Media Connection)

700.917

Flatt, Lizann

Arts and culture in the early Islamic world; Lizann Flatt. Crabtree Pub. Company 2012 48 p. col. ill., col. map (reinforced library binding: alk. paper) $30.60

Grades: 5 6 7   **700.917**

1. Islamic art   2. Islamic civilization

ISBN 0778721671; 9780778721673; 9780778721741; 9781427195609; 9781427198372

LC 2012000074

This book by Lizann Flatt is part of the "Life in the Early Islamic World" series. It "introduces the important roles that many of the arts, but especially calligraphy, architecture, and the decorative arts, have had in Islamic culture, in which art is meant to be 'useful as well as beautiful.'" (Booklist) "The main texts are supplemented with blue boxes of information, subsections, and many high-quality reproductions, maps, and paintings." (School Library Journal)

701   Philosophy and theory of fine and decorative arts

Benduhn, Tea

What is color? Crabtree Pub. Co. 2009 24p il (Get art smart) lib bdg $15.95; pa $6.95

Grades: K 1 2 3   **701**

1. Color in art

ISBN 978-0-7787-5123-6 lib bdg; 0-7787-5123-6 lib bdg; 978-0-7787-5137-3 pa; 0-7787-5137-6 pa

LC 2009-22914

Isolates the artistic element of color, discusses what thoughts and feelings can be conveyed by different colors, and examines how they contribute to a work of art through various examples

This book has a "first-person plural tone that uses accessible, well-thought-out phrases. Concrete visual examples are in the form of frequent and excellent reproductions of fine art in a variety of mediums. . . . [A] respectable and respectful resource[s]." SLJ

Includes glossary and bibliographical references

What is shape? Crabtree Pub. 2009 24p il (Get art smart) lib bdg $15.95; pa $6.95

Grades: K 1 2 3   **701**

1. Shape

ISBN 978-0-7787-5139-7 lib bdg; 0-7787-5139-2 lib bdg; 978-0-7787-5125-0 pa; 0-7787-5125-2 pa

This describes how shapes of all kinds, including geometric shapes and the organic shapes found in nature, can be used in art.

This book has a "first-person plural tone that uses accessible, well-thought-out phrases. Concrete visual examples are in the form of frequent and excellent reproductions of fine art in a variety of mediums. . . . [A] respectable and respectful resource[s]." SLJ

Includes glossary and bibliographical references

Ehlert, Lois

★ **Color** zoo. Lippincott 1989 un il $17.99; lib bdg $17.89; bd bk $7.99

Grades: PreK K 1   **701**

1. Color   2. Shape

ISBN 0-397-32259-3; 0-397-32260-7 lib bdg; 0-694-01067-7 bd bk

LC 87-17065

A Caldecott Medal honor book, 1990

"Not only an effective method for teaching basic concepts, the book is also a means for sharpening visual perception, which encourages children to see these shapes in other contexts." Horn Book

Fitzgerald, Stephanie

What is texture? Crabtree Pub. Co. 2009 24p il (Get art smart) lib bdg $15.95; pa $6.95 **701**

1. Handicraft   2. Art -- Technique

ISBN 978-0-7787-5127-4 lib bdg; 0-7787-5127-9 lib bdg; 978-0-7787-5141-0 pa; 0-7787-5141-4 pa

LC 2009-22917

Introduces different kinds of texture and how they are used in art, and includes information on making a rubbing

This book has a "first-person plural tone that uses accessible, well-thought-out phrases. Concrete visual examples are in the form of frequent and excellent reproductions of fine art in a variety of mediums. . . . [A] respectable and respectful resource[s]." SLJ

Includes glossary and bibliographical references

Gonyea, Mark

★ **A book** about color. Henry Holt & Co. 2010 un il $19.99

Grades: 1 2 3 4 5   **701**

1. Color in art

ISBN 978-0-8050-9055-0; 0-8050-9055-X

"Topics presented include primary and secondary colors, warm and cool colors, saturation, and the addition of black and white. In the digital illustrations, simple forms in solid colors stand out sharply against white or other solid backgrounds. . . . This attractive volume offers plenty to observe, ponder, and discuss." Booklist

Hensley, Laura

Art for all; what is public art? Raintree 2010 32p il
(Culture in action) $29

Grades: 5 6 7 8   **701**

1. Art

ISBN 978-1-4109-3923-4; 1-4109-3923-5

LC 2009051126

This "briefly surveys public art, from murals and graffiti
to obelisks and religious statues. . . . A world map shows the
locations of 16 public artworks mentioned in the text. . . .
The quality of the illustrations is fine. . . . Given the book's
broad scope and few pages, it accomplishes a good deal.
Three activities, a time line, a glossary, and a brief bibliography round out this attractive presentation." Booklist

Includes glossary and bibliographical references

Kutschbach, Doris

The art treasure hunt; I spy with my little eye. Doris
Kutschbach. Prestel 2012 48 p. $14.95

Grades: 3 4 5   **701**

1. Art 2. Painters 3. Picture books for children

ISBN 3791370979; 9783791370972

LC 2011942236

In this book, readers "are . . . challenged to find details
'hidden' in some of the world's greatest paintings. On each
double-page spread, a large reproduction of a masterpiece
such as Kandinsky's 'Heavenly Blue,' Seurat's 'A Sunday
Afternoon on the Island of La Grande Jatte,' Rousseau's
'The Dream' or Breugel's 'Children's Games' is paired with
a list of items to search for: a dog, an umbrella, or a ball, for
instance." (Publisher's note)

Meredith, Susan

What is form? by Susan Markowitz Meredith. Crabtree Pub. Co. 2009 24p il (Get art smart) lib bdg $15.95;
pa $6.95

Grades: K 1 2 3   **701**

1. Composition (Art)

ISBN 978-0-7787-5124-3 lib bdg; 0-7787-5124-4 lib
bdg; 978-0-7787-5138-0 pa; 0-7787-5138-4 pa

Introduces the concept of form, demonstrates how it is
used in art, and includes information on reliefs, sculpture,
and identifying forms in everyday life

This book has a "first-person plural tone that uses accessible, well-thought-out phrases. Concrete visual examples
are in the form of frequent and excellent reproductions of
fine art in a variety of mediums. . . . [A] respectable and
respectful resource[s]." SLJ

Includes glossary and bibliographical references

What is line? by Susan Markowitz Meredith. Crabtree
Pub. Co. 2009 24p il (Get art smart) lib bdg $15.95; pa
$6.95

Grades: K 1 2 3   **701**

1. Line (Art)

ISBN 978-0-7787-5122-9 lib bdg; 0-7787-5122-8 lib
bdg; 978-0-7787-5136-6 pa; 0-7787-5136-8 pa

LC 2009-22912

Identifies lines in art and demonstrates how differently
shaped lines are used to create texture, movement, patterns,
and emotion.

This book has a "first-person plural tone that uses accessible, well-thought-out phrases. Concrete visual examples
are in the form of frequent and excellent reproductions of

fine art in a variety of mediums. . . . [A] respectable and
respectful resource[s]." SLJ

Includes glossary and bibliographical references

What is space? by Susan Markowitz Meredith. Crabtree Pub. Co. 2009 24p il (Get art smart) lib bdg $15.95;
pa $6.95

Grades: K 1 2 3   **701**

1. Space and time in art

ISBN 978-0-7787-5126-7 lib bdg; 0-7787-5126-0 lib
bdg; 978-0-7787-5140-3 pa; 0-7787-5140-6 pa

Introduces the concept of space; how differences in
space are used in art; and includes information on distance,
form, and overlap.

This book has a "first-person plural tone that uses accessible, well-thought-out phrases. Concrete visual examples
are in the form of frequent and excellent reproductions of
fine art in a variety of mediums. . . . [A] respectable and
respectful resource[s]." SLJ

Includes glossary and bibliographical references

Museum of Modern Art (New York, N.Y.)

Make art mistakes; an inspired sketchbook for everyone. Chronicle Books 2010 un il $16.99

Grades: 3 4 5 6   **701**

1. Art

ISBN 978-0-8118-7076-4; 0-8118-7076-6

"This lively sketchbook contains decorative graphic
spreads and prompts that ask readers to integrate their
own words and drawings. Quotations from artists such as
O'Keeffe and Picasso invite deeper reflection on making art
while loosely introducing themes on line, color, pattern, and
texture. Most of the exercises emphasize free expression . . .
while others introduce concepts like perspective. Young artists are likely to enjoy the balance between instruction and
independent exploration." Publ Wkly

Renshaw, Amanda

★ The art book for children; [texts by Amanda Renshaw and Gilda Williams Ruggi] Phaidon Press 2005 79p
il $19.95

Grades: 2 3 4 5   **701**

1. Art appreciation 2. Art -- Juvenile literature 3. Art
-- History -- Juvenile literature 5. Art appreciation --
Juvenile literature

ISBN 978-0-7148-4530-2

Invites the reader to take a closer look at art work while
pointing out tiny details hidden in famous works of art, providing information about a work or an artist, or explaining
the techniques used to create the pieces

This is "an excellent, accessible introduction to art that
speaks directly to children without condescension." Booklist

★ The art book for children: book two; text by Amanda Renshaw. Phaidon Press 2007 79p il $19.95

Grades: 2 3 4 5   **701**

1. Art appreciation

ISBN 978-0-7148-4706-1

"Each double-page spread features a top-quality reproduction of an artwork, accompanied by simple text that will
engage both young children and mature, independent readers. . . . The brief words . . . encourage viewers to imagine
themselves in the scenes, to find objects in the compositions,
or to reflect on the moods and activities depicted and in their

own lives. This interactive approach creates a wonderful introduction to the history of Western art." Booklist

Tomecek, Steve

Art & architecture; by Stephen M. Tomecek. Chelsea House Publishers 2010 174p il (Experimenting with everyday science) $35

Grades: 4 5 6 7   **701**

1. Architecture 2. Art and science 3. Science -- Experiments 4. Art -- Study and teaching

ISBN 978-1-60413-168-0; 1-60413-168-3

LC 2009030195

"This fun and informative book features 25 simple experiments using common household items and foods such as blueberries, colored cellophane, food coloring, Magic Markers, miniature marshmallows, and wooden toothpicks to demonstrate principles and inspire creative thought about the intersection of science with the visual and mechanical arts. The six chapters include activities that illuminate certain scientific aspects of each respective subject. . . . Accessible for independent reading by children with a scientific bent or curiosity about how the world works, these experiments would also be useful for scout projects or science clubs." SLJ

Includes bibliographical references

702.8   Auxiliary techniques and procedures; apparatus, equipment, materials

Hanson, Anders

Cool collage; the art of creativity for kids! [by] Anders Hanson. ABDO Pub. Co. 2009 32p il (Cool art) lib bdg $24.21

Grades: 2 3 4   **702.8**

1. Collage

ISBN 978-1-60453-146-6 lib bdg; 1-60453-146-0 lib bdg

LC 2008-8641

This book about collage making is "well organized, with clearly written sections . . . and several clever projects and exercises. . . . [It] should have substantial child appeal." SLJ

Includes glossary

Luxbacher, Irene

1   2 3 I can collage! [by] Irene Luxbacher. Kids Can Press 2009 23p il (Starting art) $14.95; pa $6.95

Grades: 2 3 4   **702.8**

1. Collage

ISBN 978-1-55453-313-8; 1-55453-313-9; 978-1-55453-314-5 pa; 1-55453-314-7 pa

Collage activities with step-by-step instructions will help kids create a whale, a crab, a sea turtle and more.

★ The **jumbo** book of art; written and illustrated by Irene Luxbacher. Kids Can Press 2003 208p il pa $14.95

Grades: 4 5 6 7   **702.8**

1. Color 2. Drawing 3. Painting 4. Sculpture 5. Art -- Study and teaching

ISBN 1-55074-762-2

"Each of the four chapters is devoted to instructing readers in the basics of one technique—drawing, creating with color, sculpture, and mixed-media projects, respectively—

and then inspires those readers to let loose and have fun making something beautiful. . . . The book features clear layouts, well-written definitions of terms, full-color illustrations, and more than 90 projects. . . . This practical, lively, and smart package is a must-have for every art and elementary school classroom, and a welcome addition to most library collections." SLJ

Includes glossary

Vry, Silke

13 art illusions children should know; Silke Vry. Prestel Pub. Random House 2012 48 p. (hardcover) $14.95

Grades: 4 5 6   **702.8**

1. Optical illusions 2. Art -- Juvenile literature

ISBN 379137110X; 9783791371108

LC 2012939037

This book by Silke Vry is part of the "Children Should Know" series. "This collection features artworks that incorporate a variety of methods for tricking our eyes: including trompe l'oeil, clever uses of color and perspective, Surrealism, and Photo-Realism. Arranged thematically, each work is presented in a two-page spread. . . . [T]exts explain the methods the artists employed to shape their illusions." (Publisher's note)

704   Special topics in fine and decorative arts

Barber, Nicola

★ Islamic empires; [by] Nicola Barber. Raintree 2005 48p il map (History in art) $31.43

Grades: 4 5 6 7   **704**

1. Islam 2. Islamic art

ISBN 1-4109-0522-5

LC 2004-7527

This is an introduction to the art, culture, and history of Islamic empires.

This book has "a depth of content that is unusual in art-history books for this age group. . . . [It] is amply illustrated with full-color photographs and reproductions. . . . Well-written, informative." SLJ

Includes bibliographical references

Coyne, Jennifer Tarr

Come look with me: discovering women artists for children; [by] Jennifer Tarr Coyne. Lickle 2005 32p il $15.95

Grades: 3 4 5   **704**

1. Women artists 2. Art appreciation

ISBN 1-890674-08-7

Introduces twelve women artists, including Faith Ringgold, Mary Cassatt, Frida Kahlo, and Grandma Moses, each with a short biography, a full-page color plate, a description of the image, and a set of discussion questions.

"This offering encourages children to learn biographical facts about artists and to look closely at the images and think about artistic decisions. . . . Each spread features a beautifully reproduced image." Booklist

January, Brendan

★ Native American art & culture; [by] Brendan January. Raintree 2005 56p il map (World art & culture) lib bdg $23; pa $9.99

Grades: 5 6 7 8   **704**

1. Native Americans 2. Native American art

ISBN 978-1-4109-1108-7 lib bdg; 1-4109-1108-X lib bdg; 978-1-4109-2118-5 pa; 1-4109-2118-2 pa

LC 2004-8072

"January investigates the many art forms of the Native American tribes. . . . Chapters are dedicated to pottery, textiles, carving, and painting as well as body art, architecture, ceremonies, songs, and dances. . . . Numerous color photographs of both ancient and modern artwork are included on each spread, and they are exceptional. . . . This fresh look at Native American culture through its artwork will be a welcome alternative for reports and classroom discussion, and the popularity of the subject matter and appealing design will attract readers outside the classroom environment." SLJ

Includes bibliographical references

Raczka, Bob

Before they were famous; how seven artists got their start. Millbrook Press 2010 32p il (Art adventures) $25.26

Grades: 4 5 6 7   **704**

1. Artists 2. Creative ability

ISBN 978-0-7613-6077-3; 0-7613-6077-8

LC 2009049596

"Short biographies written in conversational, jargon-free text introduce seven great artists, as young beginners and then as creators of famous works. From Dürer and Michelangelo to Picasso and Dali, the featured artists are presented chronologically on uncluttered, open spreads that include beautiful full-page reproductions. . . . Great preparation for a gallery visit, this will appeal to older readers, too, for its exciting, never-condescending talk about the pictures and the artists who created them." Booklist

Rolling, James Haywood

Come look with me: discovering African American art for children; [by] James Haywood Rolling, Jr. Lickle 2005 32p il $15.95

Grades: 3 4 5   **704**

1. Art appreciation 2. African American art

ISBN 1-890674-07-9

This volume presents 12 works of African American art "reproduced in full color and accompanied by descriptive information; the facing page contains several questions designed to engage young viewers and an adult in conversation as well as a few paragraphs of background. . . . Artists . . . include . . . Palmer Hayden and Clementine Hunter . . . Henry Ossawa Tanner, Romare Bearden, and Jacob Lawrence." SLJ

704.9 Iconography

Bingham, Jane

Society & class; [by] Jane Bingham. Raintree 2006 56p il map (Through artists' eyes) lib bdg $32.86

Grades: 4 5 6 7   **704.9**

1. Society in art 2. Art appreciation 3. Social classes in art

ISBN 1-4109-2237-5

LC 2005025028

This "succinctly looks at how artists have depicted the lives of farmers, hunters, rulers, slaves, soldiers, and mer-

chants throughout history. Social change such as the French and American Revolutions inspired artists, while the rise of Communism and Fascism had a chilling effect on art. . . . The full-color reproductions are well chosen and of good quality. The information is brief, but it provides a well-thought-out overview of these artistic interpretations." SLJ

Includes bibliographical references

Luxbacher, Irene

★ The **jumbo** book of outdoor art; written and illustrated by Irene Luxbacher. Kids Can Press 2006 144p il pa $16.95

Grades: 3 4 5 6   **704.9**

1. Art 2. Nature craft

ISBN 978-1-55337-680-4 pa; 1-55337-680-3 pa

"Four major sections (Digging Deep, Going Green, It's All Elemental, and Fertile Ground) each contain more than a dozen activities and/or experiments. Good-quality illustrations and photos bring these ideas to life. . . . Children will polish their creative skills with a wide variety of artistic experiences, such as a secret garden, silly sprouts, terrific topiaries, beautiful batik, super spider's web, weathervanes, great flowing fountain, sparkling ice chandeliers, and more." SLJ

Raczka, Bob

Action figures; paintings of fun, daring, and adventure. Millbrook Press 2010 31p il lib bdg $25.26

Grades: 1 2 3 4   **704.9**

1. Art appreciation

ISBN 978-0-7613-4140-6 lib bdg; 0-7613-4140-4 lib bdg

LC 2008053976

"Eighteen paintings, and not a bowl of fruit in sight. Whether it is the knockout punch of George Bellows's Dempsey and Firpo or the fiery blasts of Diego Rivera's The Conquest of Mexico, this art is not about sitting still. Raczka threads selections together using few words. . . . The book includes works in various styles, dating from 1450 to 1962. Rounded out with some fun facts about the selections, this enjoyable collection presents an array of action-packed art fit for independent perusal or group discussion." SLJ

The **art** of freedom; how artists see America. by Bob Raczka. Millbrook Press 2008 32p il lib bdg $25.26

Grades: 1 2 3   **704.9**

1. American art 2. Art appreciation 3. United States in art

ISBN 978-0-8225-7508-5

LC 2007023831

"The 18 beautifully reproduced works of art in this collection cut a swath across the country—including farms and cities, baseball and jazz, hard work and sacrifice, native peoples and immigrants. . . . Concise notes about each picture at the back of the book will help children and those reading to them find out more about the artists and their work." Booklist

709 Art History, geographic treatment, biography

Ayres, Charlie

Lives of the great artists. Thames & Hudson 2008 96p il $19.95

Grades: 5 6 7 8   **709**

1. Artists 2. Art -- History

ISBN 978-0-500-23853-0; 0-500-23853-7

LC 2008-91000

Presents illustrated and age-appropriate imaginary tours of the studios of famous artists from Leonardo da Vinci and Michelangelo to Monet and van Gogh, in an anecdotal reference that is complemented by reproductions of famous works and introductory portraits

This is "brightly written and augmented with activities, Web resources, and fun facts. . . . The works of art chosen to represent each artist are heavy on the drama and detail, resulting in high kid appeal and interesting captions. . . . The layout is clean and clear." SLJ

Children's book of art; an introduction to the world's most amazing paintings and sculptures. DK Pub. 2009 139p il $24.99

Grades: 4 5 6 7   **709**

1. Art appreciation 2. Art -- History

ISBN 978-0-7566-5511-2; 0-7566-5511-0

"From prehistoric to modern times, this expertly designed survey delivers a wealth of information. Much more than a mere time line, the focus shifts from artist to movement to medium with fluidity. Gallery pages examine how particular subjects are depicted in art from a variety of cultures and time periods. Hundreds of color reproductions are sure to hold readers' interest. . . . The vast amount of information presented is neither overwhelming nor superficial." SLJ

Cocca-Leffler, Maryann

Edgar Degas: paintings that dance; written and illustrated by Maryann Cocca-Leffler. Grosset & Dunlap 2001 un il (Smart about art) hardcover o.p. pa $5.99

Grades: 2 3 4   **709**

1. Artists 2. Painters 3. Artists, French 4. Painters -- France -- Biography -- Juvenile literature

ISBN 0-448-42520-3; 0-448-42520-3 pa

LC 2001-23149

Written in the format of a school report by a fictitious student named Kristin Cole, this recounts events in the life of the French artist Degas and offers insight into his work

Illustrated with "charming childlike drawings and reproductions of the artist's paintings in scrapbook-style layouts. . . . [This] is a successful blend of fact and humor that makes sophisticated concepts completely accessible and even entertaining." Booklist

Finger, Brad

13 American artists children should know. Prestel 2010 46p il $14.95

Grades: 4 5 6   **709**

1. American art 2. Art appreciation 3. Artists -- United States

ISBN 978-3-7913-7036-1; 3-7913-7036-7

"Beginning with Winslow Homer and ending with Andy Warhol and Jasper Johns, this picture-book overview introduces 13 well-known American artists. On each double-page spread, short biographies combine with richly reproduced images of the artists' famous works. . . . Finger . . . writes with clarity and enthusiasm." Booklist

Includes glossary

Guery, Anne

Alphab'art; by Anne Guery, Olivier Dussutour. Frances Lincoln 2009 un il $19.95

Grades: 3 4 5 6   **709**

1. Alphabet 2. Art appreciation

ISBN 978-1-84780-013-8; 1-84780-013-0

One letter of the alphabet is concealed in each of these 26 paintings by some of the masters of Western art, including Picasso, Dalí, Van Gogh, Matisse, Giotto, Chagall, Mondrian, Hopper, Kandinsky, Klee, Magritte, and Bosch.

"Readers are challenged by representational and abstract paintings spanning seven centuries, as the text encourages close inspection of the art. . . . This [is a] rich, well-thought-out book." SLJ

Johnson, Stephen

A is for art; an abstract alphabet. [by] Stephen T. Johnson. Simon & Schuster Books for Young Readers 2008 un il $16.99

Grades: K 1 2 3   **709**

1. Alphabet 2. Abstract art 3. Art, Abstract -- Juvenile literature 4. English language -- Alphabet -- Juvenile literature

ISBN 978-0-689-86301-1; 0-689-86301-2

LC 2007-30224

"This exciting alphabetic compendium began with a dictionary. Following years of study and work as a realistic painter, Johnson found himself wanting to explore abstract art. He started by collecting words for each letter of the alphabet. Then, he created a piece based on their meanings. . . . The works vary from paintings and collages to sculptures to installations, and an index reveals the locations of the hidden letters as well as dimensions and materials for the pieces. Children will enjoy seeing everyday objects like candy used in his creations, and will no doubt be inspired to come up with some abstract art of their own." SLJ

Lane, Kimberly

Come look with me: Asian art. Charlesbridge 2008 32p il $15.95

Grades: 3 4 5   **709**

1. Asian art 2. Art appreciation

ISBN 978-1-890674-19-9; 1-890674-19-2

LC 2007037926

"The book is intended to introduce children to fine art in various Asian countries in an accessible manner, and it succeeds. . . . Lane presents a dozen full-color reproductions, done in various mediums and representing different time periods, along with background information and discussion starters." SLJ

Come look with me: Latin American art; [by] Kimberly Lane. Charlesbridge 2007 32p il $15.95

Grades: 3 4 5   **709**

1. Art appreciation 2. Latin American art

ISBN 978-1-890674-20-5

LC 2006034237

This book provides an introduction to Latin American art, pairing reproductions of works of art with questions about the artists lives and work.

"The paintings are reproduced in full color on high-quality paper. The writing is lively and interesting, yet the discussions of artistic ideas and theories are concise and easy to understand." SLJ

Raczka, Bob

  ★ **Name** that style; all about isms in art. by Bob Raczka. Millbrook Press 2008 32p il (Art adventures) lib bdg $25.26; pa $9.95

Grades: 5 6 7 8   **709**

  1. Art -- History

  ISBN 978-0-8225-7586-3 lib bdg; 0-8225-7586-8 lib bdg; 978-1-58013-824-6 pa; 1-58013-824-1 pa

                      LC 2008000312

"Beginning with naturalism and ending with photorealism, with many stops along the way, this compact overview documents the shifts, both in terms of technique as well as subject matter, that differentiate each style from its predecessors. Each 'ism' gets a two-page spread, with a beautifully reproduced example. . . . This is . . . indispensible for any middle-grade classrooms introducing art history." Booklist

  Where in the world? around the globe in 13 works of art. [by] Bob Raczka. Millbrook Press 2007 31p il map lib bdg $25.26; pa $9.95

Grades: 4 5 6 7 8   **709**

  1. Art appreciation

  ISBN 978-0-8225-6371-6 lib bdg; 0-8225-6371-1 lib bdg; 978-0-8225-6372-3 pa; 0-8225-6372-X pa

                      LC 2006014895

"On this armchair tour around the world, Raczka introduces different artists and works of art. All evoke a strong sense of place. . . . Each reproduction is accompanied by a lively text describing the locale and time period, biographical information about the artist, and other interesting tidbits." SLJ

Schumann, Bettina

  13 women artists children should know; [by] Bettina Schumann; [translated from German by Jane Michael] Prestel 2009 46p il $14.95

Grades: 5 6 7 8   **709**

  1. Women artists 2. Art appreciation

  ISBN 978-3-7913-4333-4; 3-7913-4333-5

This is profiles women artists such as Sofonisba Anguissola, Maria Sybilla Merian, Mary Cassatt, Georgia O'Keeffe, Frida Kahlo, Louise Bourgeois, and Cindy Sherma

This "large-format, brightly colored [survey proves a] solid, even inspiring [introduction] to the art world. . . . Leading questions encourage budding artists to use the featured subjects and artworks as inspiration." Horn Book Guide

  Includes glossary

Shoemaker, Marla K.

  Art museum opposites; [by] Katy Friedland, Marla K. Shoemaker. Temple University Press 2010 un il $16.95

Grades: PreK K 1 2 3   **709**

  1. Opposites 2. Art appreciation

  ISBN 978-1-4399-0523-4; 1-4399-0523-1

                      LC 2010020731

This is a "collection of fine art in a child-friendly format. Each spread pairs full-color reproductions that suggest opposites. For example, Chagall's A Wheatfield on a Summer's Afternoon is juxtaposed with Miró's Dog Barking at the Moon to suggest 'day' and 'night.' Friedland and Shoemaker have chosen a wide variety of art from ancient to modern times. . . . The layouts are attractively designed. . . . Each paired entry includes a short paragraph that discusses the two pieces exhibited. The authors ask questions and suggest activities. . . . The thoughtfully written text adds interest to the illustrations." SLJ

Wenzel, Angela

  13 artists children should know; [translation by Jane Michael] Prestel 2010 46p il $14.95

Grades: 4 5 6   **709**

  1. Artists 2. Art appreciation 3. Art -- History

  ISBN 978-3-7913-4173-6; 3-7913-4173-1

This profiles 13 artists such as Leondardo da Vinci, Vincent Van Gogh, Vermeer, and Henri Matisse

This "large-format, brightly colored [survey provides a] solid, even inspiring [introduction] to the art world. . . . Leading questions encourage budding artists to use the featured subjects and artworks as inspiration." Horn Book Guide

  Includes glossary

709.04   20th century, 1900-1999

Finger, Brad

  13 modern artists children should know. Prestel 2010 il $14.95

Grades: 4 5 6   **709.04**

  1. Artists 2. Art appreciation 3. Modern art

  ISBN 978-3-7913-7015-6; 3-7913-7015-4

This "large-format, brightly colored [survey provides a] well-oranized [introduction] to the [modern] art world. . . . [It provides] short bios and reproductions of one or more works that illustrate the artist's accomplishments. Leading questions encourage budding artists to use the featured subjects and artworks as inspiration." Horn Book Guide

  Includes glossary

Raimondo, Joyce

  ★ **Express** yourself! activities and adventures in expressionism. Watson-Guptill Publications 2005 48p il (Art explorers) $12.95

Grades: 2 3 4 5   **709.04**

  1. Art appreciation 2. Expressionism (Art)

  ISBN 0-8230-2506-3

An introduction to Expressionism which includes guidance for related activities as well as brief biographies of six artists: Edvard Munch, Vincent van Gogh, Ernst Ludwig Kirchner, Visily Kandinsky, Willem de Kooning, and Jackson Pollock

"The layout is particularly attractive, with crisp, full-color photos and drawings set against brightly colored borders; the text and captions are easy to read. . . . This book will be welcomed by teachers, parents, and would-be artists." Booklist

★ **Imagine** that! activities and adventures in surrealism. Watson-Guptill Publications 2004 48p il (Art explorers) $13.95

Grades: 2 3 4 5   **709.04**
   1. Surrealism 2. Art appreciation
   ISBN 0-8230-2502-0

LC 2003-19487

An introduction to Surrealism which includes guidance for related activities as well as brief biographies of six artists: Salvador Dali, Rene Magritte, Max Ernst, Joan Mir, Merit Oppenheim, and Frida Kahlo

"One of the strengths of this book is the inclusion of artwork produced by children. . . . It offers a wealth of intriguing and easy-to-do activities." SLJ

Make it pop! activities and adventures in Pop art. [by] Joyce Raimondo. Watson-Guptill Publications 2006 48p il (Art explorers) $12.95

Grades: 2 3 4 5   **709.04**
   1. Pop art 2. Art appreciation
   ISBN 0-8230-2507-1; 978-0-8230-2507-7

LC 2006012957

"Raimondo introduces six prominent Pop artists—Roy Lichtenstein, Andy Warhol, Robert Rauschenberg, Jasper Johns, Claes Oldenburg, and George Segal. First she describes each man's creative technique, and then she invites readers to observe one of their well-known works by asking questions. . . . Most of the required materials can be found around the house or are readily available at a craft store, and written instructions for each project are easy to follow." SLJ

What's the big idea? activities and adventures in abstract art. Watson-Guptill 2008 48p il (Art explorers) $13.95

Grades: 2 3 4 5   **709.04**
   1. Abstract art 2. Art appreciation
   ISBN 978-0-8230-9998-6; 0-8230-9998-9

"Using the works of famous abstract artists, Raimondo invites readers to discover this genre. Her tone is lively and inquisitive. . . . The activities encourage the investigation of shapes, colors, and patterns, as well as personal creativity. Instructions are clear and thorough. . . . The color photos are reproductions are well chosen and the vivid layout will draw readers to the featured works and projects." SLJ

Spilsbury, Richard
   Pop art. Heinemann Library 2009 48p il (Art on the wall) lib bdg $23

Grades: 5 6 7 8 9 10   **709.04**
   1. Pop art
   ISBN 978-1-4329-1368-7 lib bdg; 1-4329-1368-9 lib bdg

LC 2008020358

This describes how Pop art began, some of the movement's artists, and the influence of Pop art

This title succeeds "in presenting a bird's-eye view of [Pop art] without oversimplification. Information on individual artists is included in the broader context of the movement. Visually exciting, with plenty of color, [the layout is] hip and should appeal to the target audience." SLJ

Includes glossary and bibliographical references

709.2   Biography

Bernier-Grand, Carmen T.
   Pablo Picasso; I the king, yo el rey. by Carmen T. Bernier-Grand; illustrated by David Diaz. 1st ed. Marshall Cavendish 2012 64 p. ill. (hardcover) $19.99

Grades: 5 6 7   **709.2**
   1. Art -- History
   ISBN 0761461779; 9780761461777

LC 2011032177

This biography of painter Pablo Picasso is written "in free-verse style. . . . The artist's strong will and drive are demonstrated in his decision to wander Madrid with sketchbook in lieu of attending art school; by his insistent attempts to develop his own style (e.g., his Blue Period; his fascination with masklike faces; his creation of Cubism); by his move to Paris; and his insatiable desire for women." (School Library Journal)

Krull, Kathleen
   ★ Lives of the artists; masterpieces, messes (and what the neighbors thought) written by Kathleen Krull; illustrated by Kathryn Hewitt. Harcourt Brace & Co. 1995 96p il $21

Grades: 4 5 6 7   **709.2**
   1. Artists 2. Artists -- Biography -- Juvenile literature
   ISBN 0-15-200103-4

LC 94-35357

"Krull's brief biographies provide basic facts as well as intriguing details. The subjects chosen range from the famous (Michelangelo Buonarroti) to the infamous (Andy Warhol) to the less well known. Hewitt's caricaturelike illustrations reflect and extend the lively text." Horn Book Guide

Includes glossary and bibliographical references

Stanley, Diane
   ★ Leonardo da Vinci. Morrow Junior Bks. 1996 un il $16.95; lib bdg $15.93; pa $6.95

Grades: 4 5 6 7   **709.2**
   1. Artists 2. Painters 3. Scientists 4. Artists, Italian 5. Writers on science
   ISBN 0-688-10437-1; 0-688-10438-X lib bdg; 0-688-16155-3 pa

LC 95-35227

"Stanley begins with a brief introduction to the Italian Renaissance and then looks at the life of the artist. The text pages feature a series of sketches from Leonardo's notebooks. These vivid drawings, chosen to reflect ideas and events in the story, juxtapose well with the large illustrations created with colored pencil, gouache, and watercolors on the facing pages. . . . The craftsmanship that makes this biography so solid in concept, appealing in design, and accessible in presentation extends to the scholarship behind it, as glimpsed in the appended postscript and bibliographies." Booklist

Winter, Jonah
   Just behave, Pablo Picasso! by Jonah Winter; pictures by Kevin Hawkes. Arthur A. Levine Books, an imprint of Scholastic 2012 48 p.

Grades: 1 2 3 4   **709.2**
   1. Conformity 2. Child artists 3. Creative ability
   ISBN 9780545132916; 9780545132923

LC 2011026234

This book offers aspiring children artists encouragement through the story of artist Pablo "Picasso [who] did not always behave. He refused to conform to popular taste or replicate his own successes. . . . In covering his early years (his experimentation with style, perspective, and color were not always appreciated), the author delivers a . . . message to today's young artists: don't be discouraged if your creative efforts are criticized." (School Library Journal)

709.3   Specific continents, countries, localities

Campbell-Hinshaw, Kelly
   Ancient Mexico; [by] Kelly Campbell-Hinshaw. Chronicle Books 2007 32p il (Art across the ages) hardcover o.p. pa $4.95
Grades: 2 3 4   **709.3**
   1. Mexican art
   ISBN 0-8118-5670-4; 0-8118-5671-2 pa
"A brief text and striking photos introduce the art of ancient Mexico in this distinctive early reader, which features artifacts such as stone and clay sculptures, a jade mask, a wall painting, and a shield decorated with feathers and inlaid gold. . . . This offers a visually impressive introduction to the arts of Mexico's earliest cultures." Booklist

Langley, Andrew
   ★ **Ancient** Greece. Raintree 2005 48p il (History in art) lib bdg $31.43; pa $8.99
Grades: 4 5 6 7   **709.3**
   1. Greek art
   ISBN 978-1-4109-0517-8 lib bdg; 1-4109-0517-9 lib bdg; 978-1-4109-2035-5 pa; 1-4109-2035-6 pa
                         LC 2004-7523
The author shows "how art provides primary-source information about everyday and family life, beliefs and religion, and philosophy and mythology in . . . ancient [Greece]. . . . The [book follows] a well-organized format that makes the history accessible for reports, but the [author takes the book] beyond a reports-only status. Captions for the two or three illustrations per spread are clear." SLJ
   Includes glossary and bibliographical references

711   Area planning (Civic art)

Macaulay, David
   ★ **City**: a story of Roman planning and construction. Houghton Mifflin 1974 112p il $18; pa $10.99
Grades: 4 5 6 7 8 9 10   **711**
   1. Civil engineering 2. Roman architecture 3. City planning -- Rome
   ISBN 0-395-19492-X; 0-395-34922-2 pa LC 74-4280
"By following the inception, construction, and development of an imaginary Roman city, the account traces the evolution of Verbonia from the selection of its site under religious auspices in 26 B.C. to its completion in 100 A.D." Horn Book
   Includes glossary

   Rome antics. Houghton Mifflin 1997 79p il $18

Grades: 4 5 6 7   **711**
   1. Rome (Italy) -- Description -- Juvenile literature
   ISBN 0-395-82279-3
                         LC 97-20941
"Modern Rome is seen through the skewed perspective of a homing pigeon's erratic flight through the city streets as she delivers a message to an artist in a garret. . . . Macaulay adds sly touches of humor to the pen-and-ink sketches. . . . The book includes a map of the city 'As the pigeon flies' with each structure numbered, and an addendum shows the 22 featured buildings with a paragraph or two of interesting facts about each one." SLJ

712   Landscape architecture (Landscape design)

Gourley, Robbin
   ★ **First** garden; the White House garden and how it grew. written and illustrated by Robbin Gourley; foreword by Alice Waters. Clarion Books 2011 36p il $16.99
Grades: 1 2 3 4   **712**
   1. Vegetable gardening 2. Obama, Michelle 3. White House Gardens (Washington, D.C.)
   ISBN 978-0-547-48224-8; 0-547-48224-8
                      LC 2010024643
The White House kitchen garden, part of Michelle Obama's campaign to encourage healthful eating, was established in 2009. This book tells the story of Mrs. Obama's garden, as well as the story of the White House grounds, the other gardens that came before, the White House children who have played there, and the teamwork that led to the garden now flourishing on the South Lawn.
"In the many watercolor illustrations, splashes of color show up brilliantly against the bright, white pages. Although Gourley includes plenty of factoids for kids intrigued by past and present residents of the White House, she also makes gardening look enjoyable and rewarding. . . . Gourley's clear, focused writing and lively illustrations will keep children engaged." Booklist
   Includes bibliographical references

720   Architecture

Barker, Geoff P.
   Incredible skyscrapers. Amicus 2011 32p il (Superstructures) lib bdg $28.50
Grades: 5 6 7 8   **720**
   1. Skyscrapers
   ISBN 978-1-6075-3133-3; 1-6075-3133-X
                      LC 2009044044
"The vivid illustrations often help clarify points made in the text. . . . [This] colorful, informative [book offers] intriguing glimpses of notable engineering feats." Booklist
   Includes bibliographical references

Curlee, Lynn
   ★ **Skyscraper**. Atheneum Books for Young Readers 2007 40p il $17.99
Grades: 3 4 5 6   **720**
   1. Skyscrapers
   ISBN 0-689-84489-1

"Dramatic paintings and lucid prose highlight this excellent history of skyscrapers." SLJ

Farrell, Courtney

Build it green. Rourke Pub. LLC 2010 48p il (Let's explore science) lib bdg $32.79

Grades: 4 5 6 7   **720**

1. Sustainable architecture

ISBN 978-1-61590-320-7 lib bdg; 1-61590-320-8 lib bdg

LC 2010009907

This "introduces concepts of eco-friendly architecture with specific examples, from abode houses to Earthships, while it talks about the large impact that small home energy-saving adjustments, such as water-conserving toilets, can make. . . . In [this] title, well-chosen boxed examples, abundant color photos, diagrams, and an appended glossary add interest and support the engaging [text]." Booklist

Includes glossary and bibliographical references

Hale, Christy

★ **Dreaming** up; a celebration of building. Christy Hale. Lee & Low Books, Inc. 2012 40 p. (hardcover) $18.95

Grades: K 1 2 3   **720**

1. Creative ability 2. Building -- Juvenile literature 3. Imagination -- Juvenile fiction 4. Children's art 5. Architecture -- Juvenile literature

ISBN 1600606512; 9781600606519

LC 2012007376

Boston Globe-Horn Book Honor: Nonfiction (2013).

Author Christy Hale presents a story about architecture and play. "Children building--Concrete poetry--Pair them with notable structures from around the world and see children's constructions taken to the level of architectural treasures. Here is a unique celebration of children's playtime explorations and the surprising ways childhood experiences find expression in the dreams and works of innovative architects. Come be inspired to play--dream--build--discover!" (Publisher's note)

Hosack, Karen

Buildings; [by] Karen Hosack. Raintree 2009 32p il map (What is art?) lib bdg $27.50

Grades: 5 6 7 8   **720**

1. Buildings 2. Architecture

ISBN 978-1-4109-3165-8 lib bdg; 1-4109-3165-X lib bdg

LC 2008-9700

This "features public spaces and private residences created from a variety of materials. Every page includes a paragraph about the structure with glossary terms in bold type. . . . [Title is] consistent in quality of design and content." SLJ

Includes glossary and bibliographical references

Laroche, Giles

What's inside; fascinating structures around the world. Houghton Mifflin Books for Children 2009 un il $17

Grades: 4 5 6 7   **720**

1. Architecture 2. Historic buildings -- Juvenile literature

ISBN 978-0-618-86247-4; 0-618-86247-1

LC 2008-33832

"This beautiful book presents interior and exterior views of 14 extraordinary structures, from King Tut's tomb and the Temple of Kukulcan to the Sydney Opera House and the Georgia Aquarium. . . . The text is good, the organization is clever, but it's the art here that is truly masterful. The illustrations are made from layers and layers of cut and painted paper." SLJ

Macaulay, David

★ **Building** big. Houghton Mifflin 2000 192p il $30; pa $12.95

Grades: 5 6 7 8 9 10   **720**

1. Dams 2. Bridges 3. Tunnels 4. Engineering 5. Skyscrapers 6. Architecture

ISBN 0-395-96331-1; 0-618-46527-8 pa

LC 00-28116

"Macaulay combines his detailed yet vaguely whimsical illustrations with simple, straightforward prose that breaks down complex architectural and engineering accomplishments into easily digestible tidbits that don't insult the intelligence of the reader of any age." N Y Times Book Rev

Includes glossary

Oxlade, Chris

Skyscrapers; uncovering technology. Firefly Books 2006 52p il $16.95

Grades: 4 5 6 7   **720**

1. Skyscrapers

ISBN 1-55407-136-4

"This tour of big buildings flits around the world and through history with a kaleidoscopic mix of small, finely detailed artrists' renditions and five-sentence-or-less text munchies. . . . It also features four mylar overlays that offer an inside look at a few towering structures. . . . Blending eye-catching visuals with specific facts and comparisons, this quick survey will please both browsers and assignment-driven readers." Booklist

Parker, Victoria

How tall is tall? comparing structures. [by] Vic Parker. Heinemann Library 2011 32p il (Measuring and comparing) lib bdg $26; pa $7.99

Grades: 2 3 4   **720**

1. Skyscrapers 2. Weights and measures

ISBN 978-1-4329-3955-7 lib bdg; 1-4329-3955-6 lib bdg; 978-1-4329-3963-2 pa; 1-4329-3963-7 pa

LC 2010000924

This "contains vivid photographs, charts, and diagrams with captions, explanations, and examples. Questions are posed throughout . . . to entice young learners to 'stop and think' or continue reading for more information. . . . [This] would make an excellent addition to any classroom library." Libr Media Connect

Includes glossary and bibliographical references

Paxmann, Christine

From mud huts to skyscrapers; architecture for children. by Christine Paxmann; illustrated by Anne Ibelings. Prestel Pub. Random House 2012 64 p. ill. (hardcover) $19.95

Grades: 4 5 6   **720**

1. Picture books for children 2. Architecture -- Juvenile

literature
ISBN 3791371134; 9783791371139

LC 2012939038

This book "takes readers on a journey through time, exploring well-known structures such as the pyramids, Hagia Sophia, Versailles, and the Guggenheim Museum. Each spread is dedicated to a single building; in addition to a detailed illustration of the structure, it also includes information about the architect, the architectural style, and/or definitions of particular details." (School Library Journal)

Price, Sean

The **story** behind skyscrapers; [by] Sean Stewart Price. Heinemann Library 2009 32p il (True stories) $28.21
Grades: 3 4 5   **720**

1. Skyscrapers
ISBN 978-1-4329-2349-5; 1-4329-2349-8

LC 2008043411

This offers a history of skyscrapers along with miscellaneous facts about them.
Includes bibliographical references

Roeder, Annette

13 buildings children should know; [translator, Jane Michael] Prestel 2009 46p il $14.95
Grades: 5 6 7 8   **720**

1. Architecture
ISBN 978-3-7913-4171-2; 3-7913-4171-5

"The famous buildings featured in this pictorial collection include Notre Dame cathedral in Paris, Neuschwanstein Castle in Germany, New York City's Guggenheim Museum and the Beijing National Stadium (built for the 2008 Olympics), each pictured in color photographs, cross-sections and/or ground plans, with time lines tracing the buildings' developments and changes over time. . . . A sound introduction to some impressive structures." Publ Wkly

Spilsbury, Louise

Can buildings speak? [by] Louise and Richard Spilsbury. Cherrytree Books 2009 24p il (Start-up art and design) lib bdg $24.25
Grades: 2 3 4   **720**

1. Buildings 2. Architecture
ISBN 978-1-84234-523-8 lib bdg; 1-84234-523-0 lib bdg

LC 2007-46389

This title has "readers examining all sorts of structures, from their local school to Antonio Gaudí's Casa Batlló in Barcelona, Spain. . . . Includes a wide range of possible activities to extend the information provided, often suggesting further research on the Internet. . . . [This book is] well designed, with a large, bold font; clear and ample photography; and interesting layout." SLJ

Stern, Steven L.

Building greenscrapers; consultant, Frank Robbins. Bearport Pub. 2009 32p il (Going green) lib bdg $25.27
Grades: 4 5 6 7   **720**

1. Skyscrapers 2. Sustainable architecture
ISBN 978-1-59716-962-2 lib bdg; 1-59716-962-5 lib bdg

LC 2009-12494

"Color photographs (most full page) and a few diagrams accompany the informative text. . . . Overall, the [book] . .

. is user-friendly and covers topics that are not easily found elsewhere." SLJ
Includes glossary and bibliographical references

720.47   Architecture and the environment

Kaner, Etta

Earth-friendly buildings, bridges, and more; the eco-journal of Corry Lapont. written by Etta Kaner; illustrated by Stephen MacEachern. Kids Can Press 2012 64 p. ill. $18.95
Grades: 3 4 5   **720.47**

1. Urban ecology 2. English Channel Tunnel 3. Sustainable architecture
ISBN 1554535700; 9781554535705

Author Etta Kaner addresses topics including "site selection, planning, designing, the integration of green engineering solutions (like using rainwater for cooling) and nifty details on the how-tos of constructing eco-friendly structures. Across a series of two-page spreads, [protagonist] Corry explores not only new buildings (domes and skyscrapers) but also such diverse projects as the Vizcaya Bridge (Spain), the English Channel Tunnel and the locks of Ottawa's Rideau Canal, as well as dams, dikes and levees." (Kirkus Reviews)

"Though sustainable architecture is becoming more and more a part of school curriculum and family discussions, there are surprisingly few books available on the topic. This handsome, information-rich, yet brief illustrated "eco-journal" fills a gap--and more." Kirkus

720.9   History, geographic treatment, biography

Zaunders, Bo

★ **Gargoyles,** girders, & glass houses; magnificent master builders. illustrated by Roxie Munro. Dutton Children's Books 2004 48p il $17.99
Grades: 3 4 5 6   **720.9**

1. Architects 2. Architecture -- History 3. Architecture -- Juvenile literature
ISBN 0-525-47284-3

LC 2003-28192

The author and illustrator "tell the stories of Brunelleschi's dome of Santa Maria del Fiore, the mosques of Mimar Koca Sinan, the sculpture and architecture of Brazil's Lisboa, the Roeblings' Brooklyn Bridge, Eiffel's tower in Paris, the buildings of Barcelona's Gaudi, and Van Alen's Chrysler Building in New York City. Zaunders' narrative approach to nonfiction adds an appealing dimension to these artistic and engineering feats. Munro's often-beautiful ink drawings with color washes capture the special qualities of each construction." Booklist
Includes bibliographical references

721   Architectural materials

Knight, Margy Burns

Talking walls; illustrated by Anne Sibley O'Brien. Tilbury House 1992 un il map hardcover o.p. pa $8.95

Grades: 3 4 5   **721**
1. Walls 2. World history
ISBN 0-88448-102-6; 0-88448-154-9 pa

LC 91-67867

An illustrated description of walls around the world and their significance

"A praiseworthy celebration of similarities and differences among the world's peoples. . . . Young readers will recognize such landmarks as the Great Wall of China, the cave walls of Lascaux, the Wailing Wall and the Vietnam Memorial. More surprising selections feature the work of Australian aborigines, Indian Hindus, Islamic Egyptians, Native Americans and Africans. The narrative is respectful and egalitarian, with the clear intent of valuing no one people over another. O'Brien's . . . well-designed and affecting pastels cover each spread." Publ Wkly

725 Specific types of structures

Graham, Ian
    Amazing stadiums. Amicus 2010 32p il (Superstructures) lib bdg $28.50
Grades: 5 6 7 8   **725**
1. Stadiums
ISBN 978-1-6075-3131-9; 1-6075-3131-3

LC 2009044043

"The vivid illustrations often help clarify points made in the text. . . . [This] colorful, informative [book offers] intriguing glimpses of notable engineering feats." Booklist
   Includes glossary and bibliographical references

Low, William
    Old Penn Station; [by] William Low. Henry Holt and Co. 2007 un il $16.95
Grades: 3 4 5 6   **725**
1. Railroad stations 2. Historic buildings 3. Pennsylvania Station (New York, N.Y.)
ISBN 978-0-8050-7925-8; 0-8050-7925-4

LC 2006015359

"Low contributes both words and pictures in this ode to New York City's Pennsylvania Station. Introductory pages describe why and how the glorious train station was erected. Later spreads focus on how the building was utilized before it fell into disuse and was finally demolished to make way for the smaller, subterranean station used today. . . . The artwork . . . is magnificent. Full-spread, oil-and-digital, mixed-media paintings depicting people moving through the beautiful structure will draw children into Low's underlying message: 'Buildings are not just concrete and steel. They are the heart and soul of all great cities.'" Booklist
   Includes bibliographical references

Nardo, Don
    Roman amphitheaters. Watts 2002 63p il (Watts library) lib bdg $25.50; pa $8.95
Grades: 5 6 7 8   **725**
1. Roman architecture 2. Architecture, Roman -- Juvenile literature 3. Amphitheaters -- Rome -- Juvenile literature
ISBN 0-531-12036-8 lib bdg; 0-531-16224-9 pa

LC 2001-17769

The author discusses the Colosseum in Rome as an example of how amphitheaters were constructed and "provides a brief cultural context; a history of the development of the building type; and a history of the . . . [Colosseum] including how it was built, what it was used for, and what happened after the society that created it lost prominence. . . . The writing is informative and engaging and not oversimplified. The illustrations are mainly clear, high-quality, full-color photographs." SLJ
   Includes glossary and bibliographical references

726 Buildings for religious and related purposes

Curlee, Lynn
   ★ **Parthenon**. Atheneum Books for Young Readers 2004 un il $17.95
Grades: 3 4 5 6   **726**
1. Athens (Greece) -- Buildings, structures, etc -- Juvenile literature 2. Parthenon (Athens, Greece)
ISBN 0-689-84490-5

LC 2003-2615

A detailed history of the Parthenon exploring its construction and restoration.
   This is a "splendid introduction to Greece's most renowned monument. . . . [The author's] examination of the architectural details is particularly accurate and absorbing. . . . The limpid, forthright prose matches artwork of similar clarity and elegant simplicity. The acrylic paintings balance areas of flat color with finely controlled line." SLJ

Henzel, Cynthia Kennedy
    Taj Mahal. ABDO Pub. Co. 2011 32p il map (Troubled treasures: world heritage sites) $25.65
Grades: 3 4 5   **726**
1. Taj Mahal (Agra, India)
ISBN 978-1-61613-568-3; 1-61613-568-9

LC 2010021306

This "book describes in general terms [the Taj Mahal's] construction, . . . distinctive features, and history, as well as threats to its continued existence and both current and past restoration intitiatives. Revealing color photos taken from different heights and angles are supplemented by maps and by graphic reconstructions. . . . Henzel's distinctive approach gives this [book] unusual value for both assignment and general reading." SLJ
   Includes glossary

Hyman, Teresa L.
    Pyramids; [by] Teresa Hyman. KidHaven Press 2004 48p il (Wonders of the world) lib bdg $23.70
Grades: 3 4 5 6   **726**
1. Pyramids
ISBN 0-7377-2055-7

LC 2004-12063

This "introduces structures in ancient Egypt, Africa, Cambodia, and Mexico and is full of large, colorful photos and illustrations. . . . Attractive, readable." SLJ
   Includes bibliographical references

Macaulay, David
   ★ **Mosque**. Houghton Mifflin 2003 96p il $18

Grades: 4 5 6 7 8 9 10   **726**
1. Mosques -- Juvenile literature 2. Mosques -- Design
and construction
ISBN 0-618-24034-9

LC 2003-177

"Once again Macaulay uses clear words and exemplary
drawings to explore a majestic structure's design and construction. . . . In his respectful, straightforward explanation
of the mosque's design, Macaulay offers an unusual, inspiring perspective into Islamic society." Booklist

Includes glossary

★ **Pyramid**. Houghton Mifflin 1975 80p il $20; pa
$9.95
Grades: 4 5 6 7 8 9 10   **726**
1. Pyramids
ISBN 0-395-21407-6; 0-395-32121-2 pa

LC 75-9964

The construction of a pyramid in 25th century B.C.
Egypt is described. "Information about selection of the site,
drawing of the plans, calculating compass directions, clearing and leveling the ground, and quarrying and hauling the
tremendous blocks of granite and limestone is conveyed as
much by pictures as by text." Horn Book

Includes glossary

Mann, Elizabeth
The **Parthenon**; illustrations by Yuan Lee. Mikaya
Press 2006 47p il (Wonders of the world) $22.95
Grades: 4 5 6 7   **726**
1. Athens (Greece) -- History 2. Parthenon (Athens,
Greece)
ISBN 1-931414-15-7

This "volume introduces the history of ancient Athens
culminating in the building of the Parthenon. . . . [The text
is] well-researched and clearly written. . . . The color illustrations include an excellent map of Greece, photos of artifacts and sculptures, and many clearly deliniated, large-scale
paintings." Booklist

726.6   Cathedrals

Macaulay, David
★ **Building** the book Cathedral. Houghton Mifflin
1999 112p il $29.95
Grades: 4 5 6 7 8 9   **726.6**
1. Cathedrals 2. Gothic architecture 3. Architecture,
Gothic
ISBN 0-395-92147-3

LC 99-17975

"On its twenty-fifth anniversary, the author recounts the
origins of his first book and suggests revisions he'd make
in light of what he's learned. . . . Most of the original Cathedral: the story of it's construction is reproduced in this
oversized celebratory volume, along with lots of preliminary
sketches, new commentary, and revised, or newly deployed,
art. . . . Touches of informal humor further enliven a book
that's already mesmerizing for both its original content and
its insights into this author-illustrator's incisive, ebulliently
creative mind." Horn Book

728.8   Large and elaborate private dwellings

Humphrey, Paul
Building a castle; by Paul Humphrey. Arcturus Pub.
2012 32 p. col. ill. (library) $28.50
Grades: 4 5 6   **728.8**
1. Castles -- Design and construction -- Juvenile
literature 2. Castles -- Europe -- Design and construction
-- Juvenile literature
ISBN 1848585594; 9781848585591

LC 2011051450

This book by Paul Humphrey "takes readers on a journey from the very beginnings of castles as fortresses to the
lavish tourist destinations of today." The text, along with
"contextual photographs, staged reenactments, and detailed
diagrams offers . . . [an] overview of how an architectural
structure reveals the culture, class system, and daily life of
the Middle Ages. Castles from the Czech Republic, Scotland, England, Turkey, and Holland are highlighted." (Children's Literature)

Scarre, Christopher
The **Palace** of Minos at Knossos; [by] Chris Scarre and
Rebecca Stefoff. Oxford University Press 2003 47p il map
(Digging for the past) $21.95
Grades: 4 5 6 7   **728.8**
1. Archaeologists 2. Excavations (Archeology)
-- Greece 3. Excavations (Archaeology) -- Greece --
Knossos (Extinct city) -- Juvenile literature
ISBN 0-19-514272-1

LC 2003-3712

Discusses the ancient Minoan civilization of Knossos,
Crete, as manifested by the excavations of that city by the
archaeologist Sir Arthur Evans.

"Many excellent photos and diagrams, mainly in color;
time lines . . . and explanations of archaeological stratig-
raphy and of the mysterious Linear B writing are included.
The book is concise, clear, entertaining, and factual." SLJ

Includes bibliographical references

729   Design and decoration of structures and accessories

Hill, Isabel (Isabel T.)
Urban animals. Star Bright Books 2009 un il $17.95;
pa $7.95
Grades: K 1 2 3   **729**
1. Animals in art 2. Architectural decoration and
ornament
ISBN 978-1-59572-209-6; 1-59572-209-2; 978-1-
59572-210-2 pa; 1-59572-210-6 pa

LC 2009028378

"Vivid photographs invite children to look closely at a
variety of city buildings to find a column adorned with a
dog's face, a bronze frieze featuring flying geese, etc. On
each double-page spread, lefthand pages show wide views
while right-hand pages zoom in on the highlighted animal.
The child-friendly topic and approach and the small trim
size make this a winning introduction to architecture." Horn
Book Guide

Macaulay, David

★ **Built** to last. Houghton Mifflin Harcourt 2010 272p il $24.99

Grades: 4 5 6 7 8 9 10   **729**

1. Castles 2. Cathedrals 3. Architecture 4. Young adult literature 5. Castles -- Juvenile literature 6. Mosques -- Juvenile literature 7. Cathedrals -- Juvenile literature 8. Mosques -- Design and construction 9. Architecture, Medieval -- Juvenile literature

ISBN 978-0-547-34240-5; 0-547-34240-3

"Significantly updating the Caldecott Honor-winning Castle (1977) and Cathedral (1973) with new text and full-color illustrations, this hefty volume combines them with a very lightly revised Mosque (2003) for a three-in-one architectural spree. No mere colorization of the black-and-white originals of the first two books, . . . the all-new, often breathtaking images have been drawn by hand and then digitally colored to harmonize, beautifully with the look of Mosque. . . . Take a moment to mourn the originals, then celebrate this entirely worthy revision." Kirkus

730   Sculpture and related arts

Raczka, Bob

★ **3-D ABC**; a sculptural alphabet. by Bob Raczka. Millbrook Press 2007 32p il lib bdg $23.93

Grades: K 1 2 3   **730**

1. Alphabet 2. Sculpture

ISBN 978-0-7613-9456-3 lib bdg; 0-7613-9456-7 lib bdg

LC 2005013472

"This alphabetically arranged primer on 20th-century sculpture includes Marcel Duchamp's Bicycle Wheel, Constantin Brancusi's The Kiss (paired with Robert Indiana's Love), and Claes Oldenburg's Spoonbridge and Cherry. The selections are international in scope, and the media range from scrap metal and found objects to wood and fluorescent lights." SLJ

730.9   History, geographic treatment, biography of sculpture and related arts together, of sculpture alone

Niepold, Mil

Oooh! Picasso; [by] Mil Niepold & Jeanyves Verdu. Tricycle Press 2009 un il (The Oooh! artist) $14.95

Grades: 2 3 4   **730.9**

1. Artists 2. Painters 3. Sculpture 4. Art appreciation

ISBN 978-1-58246-265-3; 1-58246-265-8

LC 2008010646

"Niepold and Verdu introduce five of Picasso's sculptures. For each one, a close-up detail of the artwork is shown first, along with the question, 'What is this?' Two more spreads present zoomed-in images with possible answers, followed by a third spread showing the entire sculpture along with a statement like, 'oooh! i am a guitar.' . . . Bold text floating on bright solid-color pages complements the pictures. A photo of the artist is appended along with reproductions of the artworks and identifying information. . . . This book will ignite readers' imaginations and is both an

effective gateway to art appreciation for young children and a fun exercise for elementary students." SLJ

730.92   Biography

Fritz, Jean

Leonardo's horse; illustrated by Hudson Talbott. Putnam 2001 un il $16.99

Grades: 4 5 6 7   **730.92**

1. Artists 2. Bronzes 3. Painters 4. Air pilots 5. Scientists 6. Art collectors 7. Airline employees 8. Writers on science 9. Patrons of the arts 10. Horses in art -- Juvenile literature 11. Bronzes, American -- 20th century -- Juvenile literature 12. Cavallo di Leonardo (Milan, Italy) -- Juvenile literature

ISBN 0-399-23576-0

LC 00-41550

"Combining biography, history, and art, Fritz's absorbing text is both a lively introduction to Leonardo and a tribute to Dent." Booklist

731   Sculpture

Kenney, Karen Latchana

Super simple masks; fun and easy-to-make crafts for kids. ABDO Pub. Company 2010 32p il (Super simple crafts) lib bdg $17.95

Grades: K 1 2 3 4   **731**

1. Handicraft 2. Masks (Sculpture)

ISBN 978-1-60453-627-0 lib bdg; 1-60453-627-6 lib bdg

LC 2009-357

"Colorful photos; clean layout in a bright, primary palette; and large, abundant step-by-step instructional photos give [this book] great appeal. The . . . crafts . . . are functional and attractive. . . . Readily obtainable household materials and easy-to-follow instructions mean that children can do these crafts independently." SLJ

Includes glossary

Wenzel, Angela

13 sculptures children should know. Prestel 2010 il $14.95

Grades: 4 5 6   **731**

1. Sculpture 2. Art appreciation

ISBN 978-3-7913-7010-1; 3-7913-7010-3

This "large-format, brightly colored [survey provides a] well-oranized [introduction] to the . . . world [of sculpture]. [It] highlights a variety of works from antiquity to modern times. . . . Leading questions encourage budding artists to use the featured subjects and artworks as inspiration." Horn Book Guide

Includes glossary

731.4   Techniques and procedures

Hanson, Anders

Cool sculpture; the art of creativity for kids. [by] Anders Hanson. ABDO Pub. Co. 2009 32p il (Cool art) lib bdg $24.21

Grades: 2 3 4   731.4
1. Sculpture -- Technique
ISBN 978-1-60453-144-2 lib bdg; 1-60453-144-4
lib bdg

LC 2008-22324

This book about sculpture is "well organized, with
clearly written sections . . . and several clever projects and
exercises. . . . [It] should have substantial child appeal." SLJ
Includes glossary

Luxbacher, Irene
1 2 3 I can build! Kids Can Press 2009 23p il (Starting
art) $14.95; pa $6.95
Grades: 2 3 4   731.4
1. Sculpture -- Technique
ISBN 978-1-55453-315-2; 978-1-55453-316-9 pa

"Illustrated step-by-step projects show kids how to build
small structures out of household materials, encouraging
both hands-on creativity and imaginative play. Clear photos of brightly colored materials appear on spacious layouts
against white backgrounds. Each project looks sharp and appealing, with sketched cartoon characters adding liveliness
and humor." SLJ

1 2 3 I can sculpt! Kids Can Press 2007 23p il (Starting art) $12.95
Grades: 2 3 4   731.4
1. Sculpture -- Technique
ISBN 978-1-55453-038-0; 1-55453-038-5

This "introduces the various types of simple materials
and techniques that can be used to create animal sculptures.
This book is . . . project-oriented, although such concepts
as three-dimensionality, texture, and balance are mentioned.
Children can make an egg-carton crocodile, an aluminum-
foil-and-clay snake, a clay-and-pipe-cleaner giraffe, a paper-
bag dinosaur, and more. . . . [The book has] lively pages with
color photos and easy-to-follow directions." SLJ

Spilsbury, Louise
What is sculpture? [by] Louise and Richard Spilsbury.
Cherrytree Books 2009 24p il (Start-up art and design)
lib bdg $24.25
Grades: 2 3 4   731.4
1. Sculpture
ISBN 978-1-84234-525-2 lib bdg; 1-84234-525-7
lib bdg

LC 2007-46393

"Includes a wide range of possible activities to extend
the information provided, often suggesting further research
on the Internet. . . . [This book is] well designed, with a
large, bold font; clear and ample photography; and interesting layout." SLJ

736   Other plastic arts

Alexander, Chris
Difficult origami; by Chris Alexander. Capstone Press
2009 32p il (Snap books) lib bdg $25.26

Grades: 3 4 5 6   736
1. Origami
ISBN 978-1-4296-2022-2 lib bdg; 1-4296-2022-6
lib bdg

LC 2007-52196

This book includes "clearly illustrated diagrams and attractive photos of the completed projects using different colors and textures of paper." SLJ
Includes glossary and bibliographical references

Sort-of-difficult origami; by Chris Alexander. Capstone
Press 2009 32p il (Snap books) lib bdg $25.26
Grades: 3 4 5 6   736
1. Origami
ISBN 978-1-4296-2023-9 lib bdg; 1-4296-2023-4
lib bdg

LC 2007-52208

This book includes "clearly illustrated diagrams and attractive photos of the completed projects using different colors and textures of paper." SLJ
Includes glossary and bibliographical references

Boursin, Didier
Folding for fun; origami for ages 4 and up. Firefly
Books 2007 63p il $19.95
Grades: K 1 2 3 4 5   736
1. Origami
ISBN 978-1-55407-253-8; 1-55407-253-0

This offers instructions for 16 origami projects including
balls, boats, twirlers, boxes, hats, and airplanes.

"The pages combine a dynamic array of images, including ink illustrations of the folding steps and color photos
of young people playing with their finished work. . . . This
how-to will appeal to a wide range of children . . . as well as
the adults and teens who work with them." Booklist

Origami for everyone; beginner-intemediate-advanced.
Firefly 2011 il pa $29.95; pa $19.95
Grades: 3 4 5 6   736
1. Origami
ISBN 978-1-55407-958-2; 1554079586; 978-1-55407-
792-2 pa; 1-55407-792-3 pa

"Though most (possibly all) of the photographs and step
diagrams for these 68 paper-folding projects are recycled
from Boursin's earlier collections, he has both revised the
instructions and commentary and grouped the models according to estimated difficulty. After an extensive opening
tutorial of folds and bases adorned with savvy general folding tips, he offers a randomly ordered assortment of aircraft,
animals, stars, ornaments, and spinners. . . . The author's
lighthearted, fanciful outlook gives this extensive sampler a
bright and inviting tone." SLJ

Harbo, Christopher L.
Easy animal origami. Capstone Press 2011 24p (First
facts: easy origami) lib bdg $23.99
Grades: 1 2 3   736
1. Origami 2. Animals in art
ISBN 978-1-4296-5384-8; 1-4296-5384-1

LC 2010024791

Provides instructions and photo-illustrated diagrams for
making a variety of easy animal origami models.

"There is one project per brightly colored spread, with
the boxed pictures of the steps large enough to see the fold-

ing process. . . . Further appeal comes from the fact that many of the origami figures do not have to remain stationary. Some can be manipulated and played with after completion. . . . There may only be seven projects in [the] book, but they are more than enough to hold the interest of young ones smitten by the idea of folding paper into shapes." SLJ

Includes bibliographical references

Easy holiday origami. Capstone Press 2011 24p il (First facts: easy origami) lib bdg $23.99
Grades: 1 2 3   **736**
1. Origami 2. Holiday decorations
ISBN 978-1-4296-5387-9; 1-4296-5387-6
LC 2010024785
Provides instructions and photo-illustrated diagrams for making a variety of easy holiday origami models.

"There is one project per brightly colored spread, with the boxed pictures of the steps large enough to see the folding process. . . . Further appeal comes from the fact that many of the origami figures do not have to remain stationary. Some can be manipulated and played with after completion. . . . There may only be seven projects in [the] book, but they are more than enough to hold the interest of young ones smitten by the idea of folding paper into shapes." SLJ

Includes bibliographical references

Easy ocean origami. Capstone Press 2011 24p il (First facts: easy origami) lib bdg $23.99
Grades: 1 2 3   **736**
1. Origami
ISBN 978-1-4296-5385-5; 1-4296-5385-X
LC 2010024786
Provides instructions and photo-illustrated diagrams for making a variety of easy water-related origami models.

"There is one project per brightly colored spread, with the boxed pictures of the steps large enough to see the folding process. . . . Further appeal comes from the fact that many of the origami figures do not have to remain stationary. Some can be manipulated and played with after completion. . . . There may only be seven projects in [the] book, but they are more than enough to hold the interest of young ones smitten by the idea of folding paper into shapes." SLJ

Includes bibliographical references

Easy origami toys. Capstone Press 2011 24p il (First facts: easy origami) lib bdg $23.99
Grades: 1 2 3   **736**
1. Toys 2. Origami
ISBN 978-1-4296-5386-2; 1-4296-5386-8
LC 2010024788
Provides instructions and photo-illustrated diagrams for making a variety of easy origami toys.

"There is one project per brightly colored spread, with the boxed pictures of the steps large enough to see the folding process. . . . Further appeal comes from the fact that many of the origami figures do not have to remain stationary. Some can be manipulated and played with after completion. . . . There may only be seven projects in [the] book, but they are more than enough to hold the interest of young ones smitten by the idea of folding paper into shapes." SLJ

Includes bibliographical references

Henry, Sally
Paper folding; [by] Sally Henry. PowerKids Press 2009 32p il (Make your own crafts) lib bdg $25.25
Grades: 3 4 5 6   **736**
1. Origami 2. Paper crafts
ISBN 978-1-4358-2507-9 lib bdg; 1-4358-2507-1 lib bdg
LC 2008-4524
"After describing different kinds of paper, Henry explains the difference between a fold, a crease, and a burnished fold, and then lists all the other supplies besides paper (glue, rubber cement) that should be on hand. The rest of the book devotes two-page spreads to each project. . . . The ideas are fantastic. . . . This will keep plenty of hands and minds busy." Booklist

Includes glossary

Jackson, Paul
Origami toys; that tumble fly and spin. Gibbs Smith 2010 127p il $19.99 **736**
1. Toys 2. Origami
ISBN 1-4236-0524-1; 978-1-4236-0524-9
"In this handsomely packaged volume, Jackson offers 29 elegantly simple toys that he has either invented or modified. The models . . . include percussive 'instruments,' a wriggling fish, dogs, . . . a spinning star, two gliders, and even a catapult. . . . The particularly clear step diagrams use standard origami notation, and the directions that accompany them are just as easy to follow. . . . [This is an] above-average offering." SLJ

Krier, Ann Kristen
Totally cool origami animals. Sterling Pub. 2007 96p il $19.95
Grades: 4 5 6   **736**
1. Origami
ISBN 978-1-4027-2448-0; 1-4027-2448-9
LC 2006029593
"Each of these twenty-eight origami animal projects is accompanied by clear step-by-step instructions and photos. Projects are conveniently labeled 'beginner,' 'intermediate,' or 'advanced.' . . . The projects . . . are typically well explained. Paper-folders of all abilities should be able to tackle these projects with success." Horn Book Guide

Meinking, Mary
Easy origami; by Mary Meinking. Capstone Press 2009 32p il (Snap books) lib bdg $25.26
Grades: 3 4 5 6   **736**
1. Origami
ISBN 978-1-4296-2020-8 lib bdg; 1-4296-2020-X lib bdg
LC 2008-1677
This book includes "clearly illustrated diagrams and attractive photos of the completed projects using different colors and textures of paper." SLJ

Includes glossary and bibliographical references

Not-quite-so-easy origami; by Mary Meinking. Capstone Press 2009 32p il (Snap books) lib bdg $25.26

Grades: 3 4 5 6   **736**
1. Origami
ISBN 978-1-4296-2021-5 lib bdg; 1-4296-2021-8
lib bdg

LC 2008-1679

This book includes "clearly illustrated diagrams and attractive photos of the completed projects using different colors and textures of paper." SLJ
Includes glossary and bibliographical references

Nguyen, Duy
Monster origami. Sterling Pub. 2007 96p il pa $9.95
Grades: 5 6 7 8   **736**
1. Origami 2. Monsters
ISBN 978-1-4027-4014-5 pa; 1-4027-4014-X pa

LC 2007003244

This "volume offers step-by-step instructions for using paper to create 'creatures of horror from books and movies.' . . . Nguyen begins with an overview of basic folds, each demonstrated in clear illustrations. . . . Nguyen shows, in easy-to-follow diagrams, how to use the folds in intricate combinations to create an array of familiar, frightening characters, ranging from Count Dracula to Godzilla's foe, King Ghidora. A final spread shows color photographs of the finished projects." Booklist

Origami birds. Sterling Pub. 2006 96p il $19.95
Grades: 5 6 7 8   **736**
1. Origami 2. Birds in art
ISBN 978-1-4027-1932-5; 1-4027-1932-9

LC 2005037669

This offers instructions for creating origami representations of 19 species of birds including cardinals, cockatoos, falcons, flying ducks, parakeets, and penguins
"The instructions are direct and thorough. . . . Spare line drawings show each step of construction, and color photos spotlight the finished project against a background photo of the bird's natural habitat." Booklist

Zombigami; paper folding for the living dead. Sterling 2011 il pa $9.95
Grades: 5 6 7 8   **736**
1. Origami 2. Zombies
ISBN 978-1-4027-8646-4; 1-4027-8646-8
"Featuring both a detachable photo gallery of folded ghouls placed in atmospheric settings and a package of origami paper in suitably ominous colors and patterns, this collection of 13 undead figures may not survive intact for long but offers experienced paper folders hours of creepy fun. Nguyen opens with a tutorial of creases and folding symbology then . . . goes on to show how each figure is folded with plenty of carefully drawn and clearly labeled step diagrams. Nonetheless, most of these models are challenging projects." SLJ

Owen, Ruth
Valentine's Day origami; by Ruth Owen. PowerKids Press 2013 32 p. col. ill. (library) $26.50; (paperback) $11.75
Grades: 4 5 6   **736**
1. Origami -- Juvenile literature 2. Valentine's Day -- Juvenile literature 3. Valentine decorations -- Juvenile

literature
ISBN 1448878659; 9781448878659; 9781448879243

LC 2012009647

"This . . . title in the Holiday Origami series encourages young people to create an original I-love-you offering. . . . After a brief history of the origin and traditions of Valentine's Day, the origami instructions start off simply, with pictures and directions on exactly how and when to fold and crease. First, there are two spreads with 9 steps that show how to make an origami heart. Later, 13 steps over four pages show how to make a red rose. Nine steps make a heart box." (Booklist)

737.4   Coins

Reid, Margarette S.
Lots and lots of coins; illustrations by True Kelley. Dutton Children's Books 2010 un il $16.99
Grades: K 1 2 3   **737.4**
1. Coins
ISBN 978-0-525-47879-9; 0-525-47879-5

LC 2009053286

"In this cheerful book, a boy tells about an interest he shares with his dad: coin collecting. . . . Throughout the book, text shares the pages with brightly colored, mixed-media artwork, captions, and speech or thought balloons. Photos of common coins appear in boxes along with a little information, and the backs of the state quarters appear on one double-page spread. . . . With an upbeat tone and plenty of interesting facts, this is a fine introduction to coin collecting for young children." Booklist
Includes bibliographical references

738   Ceramic arts

Andrews-Goebel, Nancy
★ The **pot** that Juan built; pictures by David Diaz. Lee & Low Bks. 2002 un il $16.95
Grades: K 1 2 3   **738**
1. Artists 2. Pottery 3. Ceramists 4. Pottery -- Technique -- Juvenile literature
ISBN 1-58430-038-8

LC 2001-38139

A cumulative rhyme summarizes the life's work of renowned Mexican potter, Juan Quezada. Additional information describes the process he uses to make his pots after the style of the Casas Grandes people.
"This unusual book is set up to allow for differing levels of reading expertise. . . . One page contains a catchy cumulative rhyme modeled on 'This Is the House That Jack Built,' which outlines the process of making a pot. The facing page offers a clearly written prose presentation. . . . Diaz's arresting illustrations, rendered in Adobe Photoshop, use yellows, oranges, and reds in a layered effect that seems to glow with an inward light." SLJ

Spilsbury, Louise
Mother nature, designer; [by] Louise and Richard Spilsbury. Cherrytree Books 2008 24p il (Start-up art and design) lib bdg $24.25

Grades: 2 3 4 **738**
1. Nature craft
ISBN 978-1-84234-526-9 lib bdg; 1-84234-526-5
lib bdg

LC 2007-46390

First published 2007 in the United Kingdom

"Examines the patterns and colors that exist naturally in habitats and animal life, tells how they have inspired great artists such as Henri Rousseau. . . . Includes a wide range of possible activities to extend the information provided, often suggesting further research on the Internet. . . . [This book is] well designed, with a large, bold font; clear and ample photography; and interesting layout." SLJ

738.092 Biography

Cheng, Andrea
Etched in clay; the life of Dave, enslaved potter and poet. Andrea Cheng; with woodcuts by the author. Lee & Low Books 2012 144 p. (hardcover: alk. paper) $17.95
Grades: 4 5 6 **738.092**
1. Slaves 2. Potters 3. African American poets 4. African American potters 5. Slaves -- South Carolina
ISBN 160060451X; 9781600604515; 9781600608933

LC 2012027280

In this children's biography in verse, Caldecott Honor-winner Andrea Cheng looks at the "life of the enslaved potter Dave," who wrote poetry. "Records indicate Dave, who was born in the United States in 1801, was most likely purchased at a slave auction at age 17 by Harvey Drake, who, with his uncles, held the Pottersville Stoneware Manufactory in South Carolina. Dave took to the wheel within weeks and went on to become one of the most accomplished potters in the region." (Kirkus Reviews)

738.1 Techniques, procedures, apparatus, equipment, materials

Cuxart, Bernadette
Modeling clay animals; easy-to-follow projects in simple steps. Barron's 2010 95p il pa $9.99
Grades: 1 2 3 4 **738.1**
1. Clay 2. Handicraft 3. Animals in art
ISBN 978-0-7641-4579-7 pa; 0-7641-4579-7 pa

"In this well-put-together resource, Cuxart shows readers how to make more than 50 different figures using clay and other materials. The book begins with basic tips and instructions and then devotes a page or two to each of the projects. . . . For each one there are illustrated step-by-step instructions and a photo of the final product. The instructions are primarily visual and are accompanied by a sentence or two of text. They are very clear, and even fairly young children should be able to follow the directions without much adult intervention. Some of the final products are more stylized than others, but all are appealing." SLJ

Kenney, Karen Latchana
Super simple clay projects; fun and easy-to-make crafts for kids. ABDO Pub. Company 2010 32p il (Super simple crafts) lib bdg $17.95

Grades: K 1 2 3 4 **738.1**
1. Clay 2. Pottery 3. Handicraft
ISBN 978-1-60453-623-2 lib bdg; 1-60453-623-3
lib bdg

LC 2009-351

"Colorful photos; clean layout in a bright, primary palette; and large, abundant step-by-step instructional photos give [this book] great appeal. The . . . crafts . . . are functional and attractive. . . . [The book] shows kids how to make a pencil holder out of an empty can, for example. . . . Readily obtainable household materials and easy-to-follow instructions mean that children can do these crafts independently." SLJ

Includes glossary

Llimos, Anna
Easy clay crafts in 5 steps. Enslow Elementary 2008 31p il (Easy crafts in 5 steps) lib bdg $22.60
Grades: 2 3 4 **738.1**
1. Clay 2. Ceramics
ISBN 978-0-7660-3085-5 lib bdg; 0-7660-3085-7
lib bdg
Original Spanish edition 2005

The offers instructions for 14 clay craft projects, among them a pear-shaped box, a flower vase, and a paperweight

The text is "easy to read, and the results are quirky and pleasing; steps are illustrated with bright photographs." Horn Book Guide

Includes bibliographical references

738.5 Mosaics

Harris, Nathaniel
Mosaics. PowerKids Press 2009 30p il (Stories in art) lib bdg $25.25
Grades: 4 5 6 7 **738.5**
1. Mosaics
ISBN 978-1-4042-4438-2; 1-4042-4438-7

LC 2007052714

"After introducing the ancient roots of mosaic art in many cultures, this colorfully illustrated book discusses the methods used in making mosaics. Each of the next six double-page spreads presents a single, narrative mosaic. . . . Four mosaic craft ideas follow, with detailed instructions and photos of key construction steps as well as finished products. . . . [Illustrated with] fine color photos. . . . This book nicely combines art appreciation with hands-on learning." Booklist

739.2 Work in precious metals

Mara, Wil
The **silversmith**. Marshall Cavendish Benchmark 2010 48p il (Colonial people) lib bdg $29.93
Grades: 3 4 5 6 **739.2**
1. Silverwork
ISBN 978-0-7614-4804-4; 0-7614-4804-7

LC 2009035563

This describes the life of a colonial silversmith and his importance to the community, as well as everyday life, responsibilities, and social practices during that time.

"The type font, just slightly larger than usual, makes the text very visually appealing. . . . [The] book is liberally illustrated with artwork dating from the colonial period . . . [and] information boxes offer supplemental material." Libr Media Connect

Includes glossary and bibliographical references

739.27 Jewelry

Kenney, Karen Latchana

Super simple jewelry; fun and easy-to-make crafts for kids. ABDO Pub. Co. 2010 32p il (Super simple crafts) lib bdg $17.95

Grades: K 1 2 3 4   **739.27**

  1. Jewelry 2. Handicraft

ISBN 978-1-6045-3625-6 lib bdg; 1-6045-3625-X lib bdg

       LC 2009000354

"From bright jewelry pendants made from metal washers to necklaces made from scrap-paper beads, the likable projects featured in this slim title create bright baubles from easy-to-find, inexpensive materials. Each spread combines sharp photos both during construction and then in their finished state, and the book's design makes following along easy." Booklist

741.2 Techniques, procedures, apparatus, equipment, materials

Emberley, Ed

Ed Emberley's big green drawing book. Little, Brown 1979 91p il hardcover o.p. pa $10.99

Grades: 2 3 4 5   **741.2**

  1. Drawing

ISBN 0-316-23596-2 pa

       LC 79-16247

The author "combines basic shapes (circles, triangles, lines, squiggles) to create a variety of cartoon people and animals. The crisp green-and-black illustrations on a white background are large and well spaced. . . . As in his other drawing books, Emberley's wordless step-by-step method is easy to follow; even very young children can successfully reproduce the simple but appealing figures." SLJ

Ed Emberley's big red drawing book. Little, Brown 1987 un il hardcover o.p. pa $10.99

Grades: 2 3 4 5   **741.2**

  1. Drawing

ISBN 0-316-23435-4 pa

       LC 87-3091

The author explains "how to create objects and figures by building up a series of simple lines and squiggles into a more complicated and complete whole. The color red suggests most of the subjects, among them a U.S. flag, a fire engine, and assorted red-and-green Christmas items." Booklist

Ed Emberley's drawing book: make a world. Little, Brown 1972 un il hardcover o.p. pa $6.99

Grades: 2 3 4 5   **741.2**

  1. Drawing

ISBN 0-316-78972-0 pa

"The final three pages, which supply suggestions for making comic strips, posters, mobiles and games, help make the volume particularly appealing. For all developing artists and even plain scribblers." Horn Book

★ Ed Emberley's fingerprint drawing book. Little, Brown 2000 un il hardcover o.p. pa $7.99

Grades: 2 3 4 5   **741.2**

  1. Drawing

ISBN 0-316-23215-7; 0-316-78969-0 pa

       LC 00-31026

"A step-by-step approach to drawing for beginners and those who are artistically challenged. Each figure introduced can be made with a basic fingerprint or more, and then lines and dots are placed beneath the form to take budding artists to a complete picture. It is so easy to do that even very young children can enjoy a simple art adventure." SLJ

Ed Emberley's great thumbprint drawing book. Little, Brown 1977 37p il lib bdg $15.95; pa $6.95

Grades: 2 3 4 5   **741.2**

  1. Drawing

ISBN 0-316-23613-6 lib bdg; 0-316-23668-3 pa

       LC 76-57346

"There is little text; most of the book consists of illustrations, step-by-step, of making pictures out of thumbprints. A few Emberley embellishments and a page that suggests other ways of making prints (carrot or potato) are included." Bull Cent Child Books

Hanson, Anders

Cool drawing; the art of creativity for kids! [by] Anders Hanson. ABDO Pub. Co. 2009 32p il (Cool art) lib bdg $24.21

Grades: 2 3 4   **741.2**

  1. Drawing

ISBN 978-1-60453-142-8 lib bdg; 1-60453-142-8 lib bdg

       LC 2008-8642

This book about drawing is "well organized, with clearly written sections . . . and several clever projects and exercises. . . . [It] should have substantial child appeal." SLJ

Includes glossary and bibliographical references

Luxbacher, Irene

1 2 3 I can draw! Kids Can Press 2008 23p il (Starting art) $14.95; pa $5.95

Grades: 2 3 4   **741.2**

  1. Drawing

ISBN 978-1-55453-039-7; 1-55453-039-3; 978-1-55453-152-3 pa; 1-55453-152-7 pa

"A creative, eye-catching illustrated cover will attract kids to this book, and the large print; softly colored, childlike drawings; and simple sentences are sure to keep them interested in pursuing art on their own. A 'self-portrait' shows how position, figure, clothing, facial expressions, and hair are combined to create a lively piece of artwork. Materials needed are clearly labeled and accompanied by sharp color photos or neat sketches. In three easy steps, children can see how to use lines and shapes to draw faces, features, expressions, a figure drawing, or an astronaut. . . . This title is sure to please beginning artists." SLJ

Temple, Kathryn

★ **Drawing**; the only drawing book you'll ever need to be the artist you've always wanted to be. [by] Kathryn Temple. Lark Books 2005 112p il (Art for kids) $17.95

Grades: 5 6 7 8   **741.2**

1. Drawing

ISBN 1-57990-587-0

LC 2004-17909

This "introduction to essential drawing techniques builds from the starting points of lines and simple shapes. . . . Eight concise chapters explore seeing with artist's eyes, line drawing, light and shadow, proportion and scale, perspective, drawing faces, drawing bodies, and using imagination. The succinct text reads smoothly and is written in a clear, understandable style. Sample sketches and crisp, color photographs extend the text." SLJ

741.5   Cartoons, graphic novels, caricatures, comics

Abadzis, Nick

★ **Laika**. First Second Books 2007 205p il

Grades: 5 6 7 8 9 10 11 12 Adult   **741.5**

1. Graphic novels 2. Space flight -- Graphic novels 3. Soviet Union -- History -- 1953-1991 -- Graphic novels

ISBN 1-59643-101-6; 978-1-59643-101-0

LC 2006-51907

This graphic novel tells the story of Laika, the dog sent into space aboard Sputnik II. Bibliography. "Grades six to ten." (Bull Cent Child Books)

"Although the tightly packed and vividly inked panels of Abadzis's art tell an impressively complex tale . . . Laika's palpable spirit is what readers will remember." Publ Wkly

Aguirre, Jorge

★ **Giants** beware! written by Jorge Aguirre; illustrated by Rafael Rosado. First Second 2012 202 p.

Grades: 3 4 5   **741.5**

1. Humorous graphic novels 2. Adventure graphic novels 3. Giants -- Graphic novels 4. Fairy tales -- Graphic novels 5. Fairy tales 6. Graphic novels

ISBN 1596435828; 9781596435827

LC 2011030471

In this children's graphic novel, "spunky Claudette is set on becoming a monster slayer like her father. . . . When she hears the story of a giant on the loose, she is determined to leave her home--accompanied by her cowardly brother, Gaston, and best friend Marie--in order to set things right. . . . When Claudette discovers that not all stories are as they seem, she and her friends must fool the adults who have come to bring them home to protect an innocent monster." (Publishers Weekly)

Ames, Lee J.

Draw 50 animal 'toons; [by] Lee J. Ames and Bob Singer. Doubleday 2000 un il (Draw 50) hardcover o.p. pa $8.95

Grades: 4 5 6 7   **741.5**

1. Animals in art 2. Cartooning -- Technique

ISBN 978-0-385-49142-6; 0-385-49142-5; 978-0-767-90544-2 pa; 0-767-90544-X pa

LC 00020750

"Step-by-step method shows how to draw cartoon animals, including dogs, mice, and a skateboarding crocodile." Publisher's note

Arni, Samhita

★ **Sita's** Ramayana; Moyna Chitrakar, illustrator. Groundwood Books 2011 il $24.95

Grades: 5 6 7 8   **741.5**

1. Graphic novels 2. Hindu mythology -- Graphic novels

ISBN 978-1-55498-145-8; 1-55498-145-X

"The Ramayana is the story of the exiled prince Rama and his beautiful wife, Sita. When she is kidnapped by a love-struck demon king, her husband's efforts to rescue her result in a war that eventually involves not only demons and mortals, but also gods, monsters, and even animals. . . . Here, a Patua scroll painter has adapted it as a fast-paced, brilliantly bold graphic novel. All of the suspense, treachery, sorcery, and pathos of this epic is depicted in homemade natural dyes layered onto paper in energetic lines, rhythmic patterns, and fields of hot, bright colors. . . . This book would be a must-purchase based on the strength of its dramatic story and arresting art, enhanced by superior design and high-quality production. Brilliant and fresh." SLJ

Artell, Mike

Funny cartooning for kids. Sterling Pub. 2007 128p il $17.95

Grades: 3 4 5 6   **741.5**

1. Drawing 2. Cartooning -- Technique

ISBN 978-1-4027-2260-8

"This volume approaches the basics of traditional cartooning with what is funny—what creates humor. Pointing out the difference between 'regular' illustrations and cartoons, the author divides the book into chapters that give readers instruction in six areas—exaggeration; simplification; animals and objects doing 'people' things; people in different poses; unusual body types and gestures; and monsters, weird creatures, and aliens. . . . Black-and-white pen-and-ink drawings throughout are designed to encourage readers to add and create their own individual changes to cartoon figures." SLJ

Baltazar, Art

Billy Batson and the magic of Shazam!: Mr. Mind over matter; Art Baltazar & Franco, writers; Byron Vaughns, artist & covers; David Tanguay, colors; Steve Wands, Travis Lanham, letterers. DC Comics 2011 un il pa $12.99

Grades: 3 4 5   **741.5**

1. Graphic novels 2. Superhero graphic novels 3. Captain Marvel (Fictional character)

ISBN 978-1-4012-2993-1; 1-4012-2993-X

Eleven-year-old Billy Batson has been given an amazing gift: The magic word Shazam!, which transforms him into Captain Marvel and gives him incredible superpowers. In this volume, Billy and his superpowered sister, Mary Marvel, fight side by side (and, occasionally, with each other) in amazing adventures featuring the world's greatest villains.

"Baltazar has hit upon exactly the right note with stories that will appeal solidly to young readers. . . . He also bothers to write up to young readers rather than down, with resonant themes, strong emotional stakes, battles won through wit as well as strength, and a complex narrative that works on many levels." Booklist

Tiny Titans: welcome to the treehouse. DC Comics 2009 144p il $12.99

Grades: K 1 2 3   **741.5**

1. Graphic novels 2. Humorous graphic novels 3. Superhero graphic novels

ISBN 978-1-4012-2078-5

Here are the Teen Titans as never seen before: as little kids. They all attend Sidekick City Elementary School, where their principal and teachers are supervillains, and they get into playground showdowns with the Fearsome Five. Baltazar and Franco, who have created such characters as Patrick the Wolf Boy, present a series of short stories, most one or two pages long, featuring little kid versions of Robin, Starfire, Wonder Girl, Cassie, Speedy, Kid Flash, Cyborg, Beast Boy, Raven, and more. While these stories are written for the young readers, the humor may also appeal to teens and adults.

Other titles in this series are:

Tiny Titans: adventures in awesomeness (2009)
Tiny Titans: Sidekickin' it (2010)
Tiny Titans go camping (2010)
Tiny Titans and the science fair (2010)

Bannister (Person)

The **shadow** door; art by Bannister; story by Nykko; [colors by Jaffre; translation by Carol Klio Burrell] Graphic Universe 2009 46p il (The Elsewhere chronicles) lib bdg $27.93; pa $6.95

Grades: 4 5 6 7   **741.5**

1. Graphic novels 2. Horror graphic novels

ISBN 978-0-7613-4459-9 lib bdg; 0-7613-4459-4 lib bdg; 978-0-7613-3963-2 pa; 0-7613-3963-9 pa

LC 2008-39442

Four friends discover a movie projector that opens a passageway into a world threatened by creatures of shadow, where their only weapon is light

"This is an undeniably attractive offering, as the artwork, with deep darks and effervescent lights splayed across large, glossy pages, is strikingly rendered. . . . [This] should have no problem gaining an appreciative readership." Booklist

Other titles in this series are:

Shadow spies (2009)
Master of shadows (2009)

Barba, Corey

Yam: bite-size chunks. Top Shelf Productions 2008 88p il pa $10

Grades: PreK K 1 2 3   **741.5**

1. Graphic novels 2. Stories without words 3. Humorous graphic novels 4. Friendship -- Graphic novels

ISBN 978-1-60309-014-8 pa; 1-60309-014-2 pa

Yam is a little boy who wears a hooded suit and has a magical backpack. On the island of La Leche de la Luna, Yam meets a sentient cupcake, cheers up a crying raincloud with a lollipop, plays with his friends Gato and Mary, and has a four-legged pet TV that sleeps in bed with him. Along with short stories that originally appeared as mini comics and in Nickelodeon Magazine, the book includes an original story in which Yam develops a crush on a beautiful toy seller

in town. He spends so much time daydreaming about her that he neglects all his friends.

"The wordless panels are quite effective with the tenderly drawn art powerfully conveying nuanced moments." SLJ

Barks, Carl

Walt Disney's Donald Duck: lost in the Andes. Fantagraphics 2011 $24.99

Grades: 2 3 4 5 6   **741.5**

1. Cartoons and caricatures

ISBN 978-1-60699-474-0; 1-60699-474-3

"One of comics revered masters gets a fresh new reprinting worthy of his work and accessible to kids. . . . Barks toiled for Disney in anonymity throughout the 1940s and '50s while creating such great characters as Scrooge McDuck and Gyro Gearloose. This volume finds him at a creative peak. . . . In the title story Donald and his three nephews travel deep into a magical Andes region to find the source of the square eggs scientists covet. . . . The best stories, however, set up Donald and his nephews as foes, a simple motivation comically escalating until the only result is total disaster. . . . Despite the dark undertones, the comic expressions and dialogue is still laugh-out-loud funny." Publ Wkly

Bendis, Brian Michael

Takio, vol. 1. Marvel Icon 2011 un il $9.95

Grades: 5 6 7 8   **741.5**

1. Graphic novels 2. Superhero graphic novels 3. Sisters -- Graphic novels

ISBN 978-0-7851-5326-9; 0-7851-5326-8

"This entertaining graphic novel features a crunchy and kinetic art style, quick pacing, realistic dialogue, and enough action to appeal to most middle-school readers." Booklist

Bliss, Harry

★ **Luke** on the loose; a Toon Book. TOON Books 2009 32p il map $12.95

Grades: PreK K 1 2   **741.5**

1. Graphic novels 2. Humorous graphic novels

ISBN 978-1-935179-00-9; 1-935179-00-4

LC 2008-35699

A young boy's fascination with pigeons soon erupts into a full-blown chase around Central Park, across the Brooklyn Bridge, through a fancy restaurant, and into the sky

"The cartoon panels are so successful at engaging readers that young children do not have to be able to read the text to enjoy the story. Each drawing is filled with humorous details." SLJ

Bouchard, Hervé

Harvey; how I became invisible. [by] Hervé Bouchard and Janice Nadeau; translated by Helen Mixter. Groundwood Books/House of Anansi Press 2010 un il $19.95

Grades: 5 6 7 8   **741.5**

1. Graphic novels 2. Death -- Fiction 3. Fathers -- Fiction 4. Bereavement -- Fiction 5. Family life -- Fiction 6. Graphic novels -- Juvenile literature

ISBN 978-1-55498-075-8; 1-55498-075-5

Original French edition 2009

"This open-ended book is deserving of discussion, difficult though it may be." Booklist

Bullock, Mike

Lions, tigers, and bears, vol. 1: Fear and pride; [by] Mike Bullock and Jack Lawrence. Image Comics 2006 128p il pa $12.99

Grades: 2 3 4 5 6   **741.5**

1. Graphic novels 2. Adventure graphic novels

ISBN 1-58240-657-X

When Joey Price has to move away from his grandmother, she gives him a new set of stuffed animals that she says will guard him from nightmares. And one night, he discovers that the stuffed animals are real, and unfortunately, so are the Beasties, the nightmares in his closet

Caldwell, Ben

Fantasy! cartooning; [by] Ben Caldwell. Sterling Pub. Co. 2005 95p il pa $9.95

Grades: 5 6 7 8   **741.5**

1. Drawing 2. Fantasy in art 3. Cartoons and comics 4. Cartooning -- Technique

ISBN 1-4027-1612-5

LC 2005041676

Caldwell's "drawing style is . . . a blend of modern Disney (Hercules, Mulan), Don Bluth (Dragon's Lair), and the Cartoon Network (Powderpuff Girls, Samurai Jack, Star Wars: Clone Wars). . . . Caldwell shows original thinking, and his technique is exciting, modern, and unique." SLJ

Cammuso, Frank

Knights of the lunch table: the dodgeball chronicles. Graphix 2008 141p pa $9.99

Grades: 3 4 5 6   **741.5**

1. Graphic novels 2. Humorous graphic novels 3. School stories -- Graphic novels

ISBN 978-0-439-90322-6 pa; 0-439-90322-X pa

Artie King's family has moved and now he has to start at a new school, Camelot Middle School. Dodgeball is the big game at Camelot, and the Horde is a champion team; the Horde members are also the worst bullies in the school. . . . Artie immediately gets into trouble with Joe, the leader of the Horde. . . . However, he manages to open the broken old locker . . . [which] provides mysterious, useful stuff, such as a lunch. Joe challenges Artie to a dodgeball game; Artie has new friends Percy and Wayne who'll help him, and then he meets Gwen. And science teacher Mr. Merlyn is also on his side.

"Arthurian legend gets an update for young readers in this outstanding graphic novel. . . . The funny, fast-paced tale of young Arthur's quest to defeat the bullies stands well on its own. The appealing illustrations are full of color, action, and life." SLJ

Other titles in this series are:

Knights of the lunch table: the dragon players (2009)

Knights of the lunch table: the battling bands (2011)

★ Otto's orange day; a Toon Book. by Frank Cammuso & Jay Lynch. TOON Books 2008 40p il $12.95

Grades: K 1 2   **741.5**

1. Graphic novels 2. Cats -- Graphic novels 3. Color -- Graphic novels 4. Magic -- Graphic novels

ISBN 978-0-9799238-2-1; 0-9799238-2-4

LC 2007040759

"This is a text-book example of how to use page composition, expanding panel size, color, and stylized figures to make sequential art fresh, energetic, and lively." Booklist

Casty

Walt Disney's Mickey Mouse and the world to come. Boom Kids! 2010 un il pa $9.99

Grades: 3 4 5 6   **741.5**

1. Graphic novels 2. Science fiction graphic novels 3. Mickey Mouse (Cartoon character)

ISBN 978-1-60886-562-8; 1-60886-562-2

Mickey Mouse and his friend from the future Eega Beeva take an amazing journey into the future.

"Disney fans, both children and adults, will enjoy [this] graphic [novel]." SLJ

Cavallaro, Michael

L. Frank Baum's The Wizard of Oz; the graphic novel. Puffin Books 2005 176p pa $9.99

Grades: 3 4 5 6 7 8   **741.5**

1. Authors 2. Dramatists 3. Journalists 4. Graphic novels 5. Fantasy graphic novels 6. Children's authors

ISBN 0-14-240471-3

LC 2006-273599

This graphic novel adaptation remains true to the story by Baum: Dorothy and her dog Toto are whisked to Oz, where they meet the Tin Woodsman, the Cowardly Lion, and the Scarecrow and they all journey to find the Wizard to grant their desires.

"The black-and-white illustrations are action packed, and the characters, with their Bazooka Joe eyes, combine classic comic touches with the popular manga style. Reluctant readers will gravitate toward the cartoon cover." SLJ

Chantler, Scott

Tower of treasure. Kids Can Press 2010 112p il (Three thieves) $17.99; pa $8.95

Grades: 3 4 5 6   **741.5**

1. Graphic novels 2. Adventure graphic novels 3. Circus -- Fiction 4. Thieves -- Fiction 5. Acrobats and acrobatics -- Fiction

ISBN 978-1-55453-414-2; 1-55453-414-3; 978-1-55453-415-9 pa; 1-55453-415-1 pa

"Young gymnast Dessa, searching for her kidnapped twin brother, joins two fellow circus performers in an attempted heist, a prison escape and a merry chase through and out of the fortress of Kingsbridge. . . . Artfully using exchanged glances and wordless panels to add both humor and emotional depth, Chantler introduces a likable trio of thieves in a medieval-ish setting. . . . The banter among the three is sharp and witty and balances the visual pacing effortlessly. Fast paced, cleanly illustrated, great fun." Kirkus

Another title in this series is:

The sign of the black rock (2011)

Colfer, Eoin

★ Artemis Fowl: the graphic novel; adapted by Eoin Colfer and Andrew Donkin; art by Giovanni Rigano; color by Paolo Lammana. Hyperion Books for Children 2007 un il $18.99; pa $9.99

Grades: 4 5 6 7 8 9   **741.5**

1. Graphic novels 2. Fantasy graphic novels 3. Adventure graphic novels

ISBN 978-0-7868-4881-2; 0-7868-4881-2; 978-0-7868-4882-9 pa; 0-7868-4882-0 pa

Twelve-year-old genius and criminal mastermind Artemis Fowl runs his missing father's crime empire and gets his hands on a book that will give him access to the underground

fairy world. This graphic novel adaptation gives the book a
European look and color palette

"Excellent use of color and shading gives the panels a
tremendous sense of light with enchanting effect. Characters are expressively brought to life with fun, exaggerated
style." SLJ

Collar, Orpheus

★ The **Red** Pyramid. Hyperion 2012 192 p. (Kane
chronicles) (hardback) $21.99

Grades: 4 5 6 7   741.5

1. Occult fiction -- Juvenile fiction 2. Fantasy fiction
-- Juvenile fiction 3. Siblings -- Fiction 4. Secret
societies -- Fiction 5. Gods and goddesses -- Fiction 6.
Voyages and travels -- Fiction

ISBN 1423150686; 9781423150688

This is the first installment of the Kane chronicles.
"Since their mother's death, Carter and Sadie have become
near strangers. While Sadie has lived with her grandparents
in London, her brother has traveled the world with their
father, the brilliant Egyptologist, Dr. Julius Kane. . . . [Dr.
Kane] unleashes the Egyptian god Set, who banished him
to oblivion and forces the children to flee for their lives."
(Publisher's note)

"The first-person narrative shifts between Carter and
Sadie, giving the novel an intriguing dual perspective made
more complex by their biracial heritage and the tension between the siblings. . . . This fantasy adventure delivers . .
. young protagonists with previously unsuspected magical
powers, a riveting story marked by headlong adventure, a
complex background rooted in ancient mythology, and wry,
witty twenty-first-century narration." Booklist

Collicutt, Paul

City in peril! Templar Books/Candlewick Press 2009
un il (Robot City) pa $8.99

Grades: 3 4 5   741.5

1. Graphic novels 2. Mystery graphic novels 3. Science
fiction graphic novels 4. Robots -- Graphic novels

ISBN 978-0-7636-4120-7 pa; 0-7636-4120-0 pa

LC 2009-931660

In Robot City, a metropolis of 15 million humans and
1 million robots, Curtis, the Colossal CoastGuard Robot
works as part of a team of robots and humans to keep the
Robot City Bay safe. In the middle of the night, the Red Star
oil rig sends out a desperate distress call when something
attacks it in the middle of a storm. Curtis, who looks like a
light house on huge, long legs, helps to save the crew on the
oil rig, but there's something out there in the ocean, and it
means to attack Robot City. He has suffered damage in one
of his legs, but Curtis knows he has to stop the menace. This
science fiction adventure is full of action and derring-do with
colorful retro-style comic book illustrations. Young readers,
as well as adults, will appreciate the twist in the story.

"Curtis is a walking, talking lighthouseheaded robot who
protects the coast of Robot City with his trusty human crew,
Ali and Steve. When an oil rig out at sea catches fire, Curtis
rushes to the rescue and then investigates the fishy mystery
of the causes of this near disaster. . . . The illustrations . . . are
full of retro-comicbook-style action and classic movieserial
banter." Kirkus

Conway, Gerry

Crawling with zombies; Gerry Conway, writer; Paulo
Henrique, artist; based on the series by Franklin W. Dixon.
Papercutz 2010 un il (The Hardy Boys: the new case files)
$10.99; pa $6.99

Grades: 4 5 6 7   741.5

1. Graphic novels 2. Mystery graphic novels 3.
Zombies -- Graphic novels

ISBN 978-1-59707-219-9; 1-59707-219-2; 978-1-
59707-220-5 pa; 1-59707-220-6 pa

"This mix of the Hardy Boys with zombies is . . . a fast-
paced story that should entice reluctant readers. Frank and
Joe race motorcycles, communicate with ATAC (American
Teens Against Crime), and try to solve the mystery of why
teenagers who've been participating in flash mob stunts
called 'zombie crawls' (because they dress and act like zombies) have started losing control of themselves in a decidedly zombielike way. The book is a simple page-turner. . . .
Henrique's artwork is colorful, shiny, and bright, a pleasing
mix of traditional American cartoon and Japanese manga
styles." SLJ

Coudray, Philippe

★ **Benjamin** Bear in "Bright ideas!" a Toon book. by
Philippe Coudray. Toon Books 2013 32 p. $12.95

Grades: PreK K 1   741.5

1. Animals -- Graphic novels 2. Picture books for
children 3. Graphic novels 4. Bears -- Fiction 5.
Humorous stories

ISBN 1935179225; 9781935179221

LC 2012022895

This children's picture book is part of the Benjamin Bear
series, where the bear and his animal friends appear in minimalist fables drawn . . . from French cartoonist [Philippe]
Coudray's original series. . . . In 'Can I Get a Ride?' [Ben-
jamin] picks up one woodland hitchhiker after another until,
in the last panel, tables turn and they have to carry him. In
'See-Saw,' he 'helps' a fox carry a log (and demonstrates a
principle of physics) not by lifting the long end, but by hopping onto the short end." (Kirkus)

Benjamin Bear in Fuzzy thinking; a Toon book. Toon
Books 2011 32p il $12.99

Grades: PreK K 1 2   741.5

1. Graphic novels 2. Humorous graphic novels 3.
Bears -- Graphic novels

ISBN 978-1-935179-12-2; 1-935179-12-8

LC 2011000801

Although he is a very serious bear, Benjamin Bear has a
funny way of doing things, like drying dishes on a rabbit's
back or sharing his sweater without taking it off.

"Coudray's droll vignettes in a muted palette will be the
perfect enticement for those with a visual sense of humor
who are just starting to read." Kirkus

Craddock, Erik

BC mambo. Random House Children's Books 2009
95p il (Stone rabbit) lib bdg $11.99; pa $5.99

Grades: 2 3 4 5   741.5

1. Graphic novels 2. Rabbits -- Graphic novels

ISBN 978-0-375-93922-6 lib bdg; 0-375-93922-9 lib
bdg; 978-0-375-84360-0 pa; 0-375-84360-4 pa

LC 2008-00681

After Stone Rabbit is transported back to prehistoric times, his bottle of barbecue sauce becomes the key ingredient in a power-hungry Neanderthal's plan to dominate the world

Craddock "brings a brightly colored, zany cartoon quality to the story and art, with the hero rabbit falling into one peril after another. The proposed fast-food empire is just the kind of plot that young readers can follow; reading this book is just as fun as watching Saturday morning cartoons." Booklist

Other titles in this series are:
Pirate palooza (2009)
Deep-space disco (2009)
Superhero stampede (2009)

Crane, Jordan
The **clouds** above. Fantagraphics 2005 216p il $18.95
Grades: 3 4 5 6 7 8   741.5
1. Graphic novels 2. Fantasy graphic novels
ISBN 1-560976-27-6
Simon and his cat Jack embark on an adventure among the clouds one day when Simon skips school and finds a rickety stairway leading skyward. They find a friendly cloud, flee thunderstorms and trick a flock of belligerent birds, only to find themselves back at school.

"Everything's exciting . . . and the dialogue is witty and bubbly. . . . The book is a joy to look at—Crane's loose, gliding lines burst with character, and his compositional gifts make every panel worth contemplating on its own." Publ Wkly

Dahl, Michael
Alien snow; illustrated by Roberta Pares. Stone Arch Books 2011 un il (Good vs evil) lib bdg $22.65
Grades: 4 5 6 7   741.5
1. Graphic novels 2. Good and evil -- Fiction 3. Extraterrestrial beings -- Fiction
ISBN 978-1-4342-2090-5; 1-4342-2090-7
LC 2010004111
"When young Noah Urbain walks into an antique shop, he unknowinly walks into a trap. . . . In this story, told from two perspectives ('evil' and 'good'), the storekeeper traps Noah in a snow globe. . . . The ultralow word count . . . and suspenseful action of this title . . . will help lure in reluctant readers." Booklist

Davis, Eleanor
★ **Stinky**; a Toon Book. RAW Junior 2008 40p il $12.95
Grades: K 1 2 3   741.5
1. Graphic novels 2. Humorous graphic novels 3. Monsters -- Graphic novels 4. Friendship -- Graphic novels
ISBN 978-0-9799238-4-5; 0-9799238-4-0
LC 2007-94387
A Geisel Award honor book, 2009
Stinky the monster is sort of a young Shrek—a little grumpy, he loves pickles and likes his swamp nicely yucky and mucky, with no kids. Kids are gross, they like to take baths. When a new boy dares to build a treehouse in the middle of his swamp, Stinky takes action with all kinds of crazy plans to scare the boy away. However, every plan backfires, so what's a monster to do?

"The charming cartoon artwork, full of humorous details, complements the text, and the muted color scheme makes Stinky endearing rather than scary. The simple vocabulary and repetition of words make the text accessible for emergent readers." SLJ

★ The **secret** science alliance and the copycat crook. Bloomsbury 2009 153p il $18.99; pa $10.99
Grades: 3 4 5 6 7 8   741.5
1. Graphic novels 2. School stories 3. Humorous graphic novels 4. Adventure graphic novels 5. Inventors -- Fiction 6. Graphic novels -- Juvenile literature
ISBN 978-1-59990-142-8; 1-59990-142-0; 978-1-59990-396-5 pa; 1-59990-396-2 pa
LC 2008-45399
Eleven-year-old Julian Calendar thought changing schools would mean leaving his "nerdy" persona behind, but instead he forms an alliance with fellow inventors Greta and Ben and works with them to prevent an adult from using one of their gadgets for nefarious purposes

"With its frenetically eye-catching, full-color panels chock-full of humorous and informative detail, Davis's first (of many, one hopes) graphic adventure of the SSA pumps new life into the kids' secret society formula." Kirkus

Dawson, Willow
Lila & Ecco's do-it-yourself comics club. Kids Can Press 2010 112p il $16.95
Grades: 4 5 6 7   741.5
1. Graphic novels 2. Cartoons and caricatures
ISBN 978-1-55453-438-8; 1-55453-438-0
Twelve-year-olds Lila and Ecco are obsessed with comics. Every summer, they dress up as their favorite characters to attend the local comic book convention. This year, after they stumble into a workshop of comics creators, Lila and Ecco come to an exciting realization they can make their very own comic books!.

"Is it a story of two friends creating a comic, or a step-by-step guide to making comics? Why, it's both, actually. And what's most surprising is not that the guide is so comprehensive and easy to follow but that the framing story not only couches the lessons in comfortable language but is also diverting in its own right. . . . Dawson's savvy, sassy black-and-white art gives the static idea of instructions some pep, and the information is quite complete." Booklist

De Campi, Alex
Kat & Mouse: Teacher torture; [by] Alex de Campi; art by Frederica Manfredi. Tokyopop 2006 96p il pa $5.99
Grades: 4 5 6 7 8 9   741.5
1. Graphic novels 2. Mystery fiction 3. Mystery graphic novels
ISBN 1-59816-548-8
Middle schooler Kat starts at a posh school where her father has been hired as the new science teacher, but all is not well. Accidents happen in the science lab, and an anonymous student threatens worse unless Kat's dad passes all the rich, popular students. Kat decides to investigate, aided by her one new friend, Mouse, the rebellious computer nerd and would-be CSI investigator.

Deas, Mike
Dalen & Gole; scandal in Port Angus. Orca Book Publishers 2011 123p il pa $9.95

Grades: 4 5 6 7   **741.5**
1. Graphic novels 2. Science fiction graphic novels 3. Extraterrestrial beings -- Graphic novels
ISBN 978-1-55469-800-4; 1-55469-800-6

Dalen and Gole, refugees on Earth from the distant planet of Budap, must solve the mystery of diminishing fish stocks and save their home planet from an evil plot.

Deas "provides solid graphics, pacing, dialogue, and humor. . . . A fun mystery-adventure that's just right for young space cases." Booklist

Delporte, Yvan

The **purple** smurfs; by Yvan Delporte and Peyo. Papercutz 2010 55p $10.99; pa $5.99
Grades: 1 2 3 4   **741.5**
1. Graphic novels
ISBN 978-1-59707-207-6; 1-59707-207-9; 978-1-59707-206-9 pa; 1-59707-206-0 pa

Deutsch, Barry

★ **Hereville**: how Mirka got her sword; colors by Jake Richmond. Amulet Books 2010 137p il $15.95
Grades: 4 5 6 7   **741.5**
1. Graphic novels 2. Fantasy graphic novels 3. Jews -- Graphic novels 4. Dragons -- Graphic novels 5. Graphic novels -- Juvenile literature
ISBN 978-0-8109-8422-6; 0-8109-8422-9
                             LC 2010-924236

Mirka and her family live in an Orthodox Jewish village called Hereville. All she really wants to do is fight dragons, but what she has to fight is a troublesome pig that talks. Then Mirka meets the witch who lives nearby, and then confronts a troll, and soon she finds she has much more adventure than she knows how to handle.

"Deutsch creates authentic characters spiced with just enough fantasy to surprise. . . . Details of Orthodox daily life are well blended into the art and given just the right touches of explanation to keep readers on track." Booklist

Duffy, Chris

★ **Nursery** rhyme comics; 50 timeless rhymes by 50 celebrated cartoonists. First Second 2011 il $18.99
Grades: K 1 2 3 4 5   **741.5**
1. Graphic novels 2. Nursery rhymes
ISBN 978-1-59643-600-8; 1-59643-600-X

"No fewer than 50 cartoonists and comic-book artists provide distinctive visual riffs on as many nursery rhymes in this memorable showcase. . . . Visually far more complicated than the usual toddler-friendly nursery fare, this is best saved for older children. . . . As much as the visual styles may vary, the high levels of wit and invention never falter." Kirkus

Eliopoulos, Chris

Okie Dokie Donuts; open for business! Top Shelf 2011 il $9.95
Grades: 1 2 3   **741.5**
1. Graphic novels 2. Baking -- Fiction 3. Robots -- Fiction
ISBN 978-1-603090-68-1; 1-603090-68-1

"Big Mama, proprietor of Okie Dokie Donuts, is so beloved and her donuts so coveted that she is regaled in rhyming song by her customers every morning. . . . Mr. Mayweather [is] a kitchen-appliance salesman. His new ware, Mr. Baker, is a doughnut-making robot that will streamline

the workload and multiply the profits. . . . Young readers may well see what's coming . . . especially when Mr. Baker's ingredient slot is accidentally loaded with garbage, but that won't detract one iota from the fun. . . . Eliopoulos creates a confection of zaniness, from the breathless slapstick and the wild, blocky art right down to the childlike lettering that fills the speech balloons." Booklist

Espinosa, Rod

The **courageous** princess. Dark Horse Comics 2007 240p il pa $9.95
Grades: 3 4 5 6 7 8 9   **741.5**
1. Graphic novels 2. Fantasy graphic novels 3. Princesses -- Graphic novels
ISBN 978-1-59307-719-8

Plain Princess Mabelrose doesn't get along with the other, prettier princesses, but her intelligence helps her when a dragon kidnaps her. Instead of waiting for rescue, Mabelrose escapes, taking a friendly hedgehog and a few useful-looking items (a pouch, a length of rope) that she doesn't know are magic.

Farshtey, Greg

Bionicle #1: rise of the Toa Nuva. Papercutz 2008 un il $12.95; pa $7.95
Grades: 3 4 5 6   **741.5**
1. Graphic novels 2. Adventure graphic novels 3. Science fiction graphic novels
ISBN 978-1-59707-110-9; 978-1-59707-109-3 pa

Six mighty heroes the Toa arrive on a tropical island to find a land under siege. The Great Spirit Mata Nui has been cast into an unending sleep by the evil Makuta. Now Makuta is attacking the island's Matoran villagers with vicious Rahi beasts. The Toa must combine their skills and elemental and mask powers to defeat Makuta and restore peace to the island.

"The art is vivid and attention grabbing, and the story line, which weaves in Polynesian mythology, is exciting and action-packed." SLJ

Flight explorer; edited by Kazu Kibuiski. Villard 2008 112p il pa $10
Grades: 4 5 6 7   **741.5**
1. Graphic novels 2. Fantasy graphic novels 3. Humorous graphic novels 4. Adventure graphic novels 5. Science fiction graphic novels
ISBN 978-0-345-50313-8 pa; 0-345-50313-9 pa

This anthology includes stories that Kibuishi kept from Flight Volume 4 because they had all-ages appeal, as well as stories submitted especially for this volume. Kibuishi's own Copper and his talking dog cross a deep canyon by leaping onto mushrooms, only to discover the vegetation is intelligent. Kean Soo's Jellaby and his human friends frolic in the snow. Missile Mouse by Jake Parker defends a village on another planet, only to discover his coming was prophesied (this story includes two uses of the word "crap"). The other stories will appeal to younger readers, while some of the humor will also appeal to older readers. Other than the one bad word in "Missile Mouse" (noted above), there shouldn't be any other content that would keep this book out of most elementary and middle schools.

"Every story has a layout that promotes an acute sense of pacing and showcases the crisp, defined, full-color art." SLJ

Ford, Christopher

Stickman Odyssey; an epic doodle. Philomel Books 2011 200p il $12.99

Grades: 5 6 7 8   **741.5**

1. Graphic novels 2. Humorous graphic novels 3. Adventure graphic novels 4. Greek mythology -- Graphic novels

ISBN 978-0-399-25426-0; 0-399-25426-9

LC 2010-36900

In this humorous take on the Odyssey, Zozimos, banished from his country by his evil stepmother, has many adventures as he prepares to return home to reclaim the throne that is rightfully his.

"The black-and-white illustrations are occasionally simple to the point of hilarity. . . . There is subtlety and depth here, however, and the contrast between the intentionally plain characters and their seemingly larger-than-life (but ultimately universal) quests . . . makes the final product both the promised Greek epic tale and an examination of the ways in which modern humans are isolated and lost. . . . Ford balances allegory and madcap quest so perfectly that the book inspires reflection even while it is clearly a quick-reading, ridiculous, often gross adventure." Bull Cent Child Books

Friesen, Ray

Cupcakes of doom! Don't Eat Any Bugs Productions 2008 98p il pa $12.95

Grades: 3 4 5 6 7 8   **741.5**

1. Graphic novels 2. Humorous graphic novels 3. Adventure graphic novels 4. Pirates -- Graphic novels

ISBN 978-0-9802314-1-0 pa; 0-9802314-1-8 pa

The Pirate band led by Captain Scurvybeard must do battle with the Vikings to decide the fate of the kingdom called Pellmellia. With a decidedly shifty fellow named Flambe testing them to see if they deserve to be pirates, Yoho Joseph, Peglegless Pete (he's just a kid), Lester the parrot, Pete's sister Jamie, and the rest of the crew must find the long lost recipe for the Cupcakes of Doom, or the Deliciously-Evil Viking Pie will take over as the people's favorite baked good. The book is full of silly humor, wacky characters (including identical twin sea serpents and a Viking penguin), and a lot of action without violence or bad language. The book is suitable for younger readers, but adults will enjoy the silliness and catch more of the jokes

Piranha pancakes. Don't Eat Any Bugs Productions 2011 93p il (A lookit! book) pa $9.95

Grades: 3 4 5   **741.5**

1. Graphic novels

ISBN 978-0-9802314-3-4; 0-9802314-3-4

This is a "wild conglomeration of humor that has just about nothing to do with piranha pancakes. Returning characters Melville and Tbyrd feature in a number of stories, . . . though to call them stories would not be quite accurate. They, like the characters themselves, are actually just opportunities to fire a continuous fusillade of visual puns, screwball shenanigans, and metatextual references to the fact that everything going on exists within a comic. . . . Friesen matches his wildfire wit with charming, animation-style art that, in addition to distinctly defining the characters in a way that the text doesn't have time to, offers a great deal of visual variation." Booklist

Fuji, Machiko

The big adventures of Majoko, volume 1; illustrated by Tomomi Mizuna. UDON Entertainment 2009 200p il (Manga for kids) pa $7.99

Grades: 3 4 5 6 7 8   **741.5**

1. Manga 2. Graphic novels 3. Fantasy graphic novels 4. Witches -- Graphic novels

ISBN 978-1-89737-681-2 pa; 1-89737-681-2 pa

"Young witch Majoko sends her diary to the human world to find an adventuring partner and through it finds shy, quiet Nana. Together the two girls have a rollicking series of escapades. . . . Characters are simply drawn, but the backgrounds are nicely detailed and the plot elements are clearly thought out and easy to follow. . . . The content is very appropriate for the intended audience." Booklist

Gagne, Michel

The saga of Rex. Image 2010 200p il $17.99

Grades: 4 5 6   **741.5**

1. Graphic novels 2. Foxes -- Graphic novels 3. Science fiction -- Graphic novels

ISBN 978-1-60706-322-3; 1-60706-322-0

The adorable little fox named Rex is plucked from his home world by a mysterious spaceship and transported to the arcane world of Edernia, where he meets Aven, an enigmatic biomorph with a flying saucer.

"While children may enjoy this graphic novel for its gorgeous art—especially the cute characters—its story line will more likely be appreciated by older readers. The almost wordless story isn't meant to be read on a literal level but instead on more a mystical and dreamlike level. . . . Gagné . . . offers a sensitive and intriguing graphic novel for people who like a little enigma in what they read." Publ Wkly

Giarrano, Vince

★ Comics crash course; [by] Vincent Giarrano. Impact Books 2004 127p il pa $19.99

Grades: 5 6 7 8   **741.5**

1. Drawing 2. Cartoons and comics 3. Cartoons and caricatures

ISBN 1-58180-533-0

LC 2004-43969

This is a guide to creating comic book stories and characters.

This offers "plenty of great art advice, striking imagery, and just enough edginess to satisfy most aspiring comic-book artists. . . . An excellent introduction to comic drawing, composition, and graphic storytelling." SLJ

Giarrusso, Chris

G-Man, volume 1: learning to fly. Image Comics 2010 un il pa $9.99

Grades: 3 4 5 6   **741.5**

1. Graphic novels 2. Humorous graphic novels 3. Superhero graphic novels

ISBN 978-1-60706-270-7 pa; 1-60706-270-4 pa

Mikey G. is G-Man, the newest superhero on the block, in a town full of superheroes (he made his cape from the family's magic blanket). His friends Billy Demon, Tan Man, Sparky, and the Suntrooper are all ready to help, but G-Man also has to deal with his older brother Great Man (aka Dave) and their superhero dad, Mr. G.

This "hits all the right notes, from its friendly cartoon figures to the occasionally hilarious one-liners." Booklist

Gownley, Jimmy

Amelia rules!: the whole world's crazy! ibooks 2003 176p $24.95; pa $14.95

Grades: 3 4 5 6   **741.5**

1. Graphic novels 2. Humorous graphic novels 3. Friendship -- Graphic novels 4. Family life -- Graphic novels

ISBN 0-9712169-3-2; 0-9712169-2-4 pa

"Amelia . . . is getting used to life with her newly divorced mom and her hip, young aunt Tanner; settling in at a strange new school; and finding a group of friends. Amelia is no sweet innocent, nor are her three G.A.S.P (Gathering of Awesome Superpals) buddies: Reggie, superhero in the making; Rhonda, Amelia's tough bete noire with a fourth-grade 'thing' for Reggie; and quiet, mysterious Pajamaman. Jealousy, meanness, sadness, and confusion, as well as surprising generosity, and love crisscross the pages in energetic, freewheeling, full-color cartoon art that unwraps a kid's-eye view of life honestly, poignantly, and with a hefty dollop of melodrama." Booklist

Other titles in this series are:

Amelia rules!: What makes you happy? (2004)

Amelia rules! Superheroes (2005)

Amelia rules! a very ninja Christmas (2009)

Amelia rules! When the past is a present (2010)

Amelia rules! The tweenage guide to not being unpopular (2010)

Amelia rules! True things (adults don't want kids to know (2010)

Amelia rules! Amelia and the other side of yuletide (2011)

Amelia rules! Amelia vs. the sneeze barf (2011)

Amelia rules! The meaning of life and other stuff (2011)

Grant, Alan

Robert Louis Stevenson's Strange case of Dr. Jekyll and Mr. Hyde; adapted by Alan Grant; illustrated by Cam Kennedy; colored and lettered by Jamie Grant. Tundra Books 2008 40p il pa $11.95

Grades: 6 7 8 9 10   **741.5**

1. Poets 2. Authors 3. Novelists 4. Graphic novels 5. Horror graphic novels 6. Essayists 7. Travel writers 8. Short story writers

ISBN 978-0-88776-882-8 pa; 0-88776-882-2 pa

"Stevenson's classic tale takes on a new format in a vivid graphic novel. This mysterious story of the struggle between good and evil is one that has been popular since its publication and continues to hold its appeal. Much about this adaptation honors the original version of the story—the language of the period remains true, and the drawings of 1880s London and the furnishings and fashion within it are realistic as well." Voice Youth Advocates

★ Graphic novels and comic books; edited by Kat Kan. The H.W. Wilson Co. 2010 195p il (Reference shelf) pa $35

Grades: Adult Professional   **741.5**

1. Graphic novels 2. Comic books, strips, etc. 3. Graphic novels -- History and criticism 4. Comic books, strips, etc. -- History and criticism

ISBN 978-0-8242-1100-4; 0-8242-1100-6

LC 2010-34209

"This collection of articles from scholarly journals, newspapers, and blogs gives a well-rounded overview of graphic novels, as well as a strong argument for their place in schools and libraries. The first section chronicles the growing mainstream acceptance of graphic novels in the United States. . . . Susequent sections look at these books as complex works of literature, as education and literacy aids, and as significant additions to library collections, with advice for librarians on how to purchase, catalog, file, and promote them. In the final section, readers hear from writers and artists . . . who clearly convey the joy they get from this medium. This is both an entertaining and highly practical read." SLJ

Includes bibliographical references

Gravel, Elise

A day in the office of Doctor Bugspit. Blue Apple 2011 il (Balloon toons) $10.99

Grades: K 1 2 3   **741.5**

1. Graphic novels 2. Physicians -- Fiction 3. Extraterrestrial beings -- Fiction

ISBN 978-1-60905-092-4; 1-60905-092-4

"Looking like a cross between a slug and a sock puppet in Gravel's crudely drawn, garishly colored cartoons, alien Doctor Bugspit plies his trade. He blithely dispenses jars of 'Fix-It-Up Syrup' (made from sock juice, dead flies, moldy meat, pickle juice and ear wax) and other nostrums to extraterrestrial patients complaining of maladies ranging from split brains . . . to an all-body outbreak of toes. . . . Presented in a loose assortment of graphic panels, page-sized or smaller, this . . . will exert a strong draw on budding graphic-novel fans as well as children fascinated by yucky stuff." Kirkus

Guibert, Emmanuel

Sardine in outer space; [by] Emmanuel Guibert; illustrated by Joann Sfar; translated by Sasha Watson; colorist, Walter Pezzali. First Second 2006 128p il pa $12.95

Grades: 3 4 5 6   **741.5**

1. Graphic novels 2. Humorous graphic novels 3. Science fiction graphic novels

ISBN 978-1-59643-126-3 pa; 1-59643-126-1 pa

LC 2005-21790

In this volume of twelve interconnected stories, little space pirate Sardine cruises in the spaceship Huckleberry with Uncle Yellow Shoulder and Little Louie. They do battle with Supermuscleman, who runs a tough space orphanage where children are taught "good behavior"

"Sfar's off-kilter, slightly uglified art, reminiscent of a toned-down Beavis and Butthead, gives the simple fun an unusual punch." Booklist

Other titles in this series are:

Sardine in outer space 2 (2006)

Sardine in outer space 3 (2007)

Sardine in outer space 4 (2007)

Sardine in outer space 5 (2008)

Sardine in outer space 6 (2009)

Hale, Dean

★ Rapunzel's revenge; [by] Shannon and Dean Hale; illustrated by Nathan Hale. Bloomsbury 2008 144p il map $18.99; pa $14.99

Grades: 5 6 7 8   **741.5**

1. Graphic novels 2. Fantasy graphic novels 3. Humorous graphic novels 4. Fairy tales -- Graphic

novels

ISBN 1-59990-070-X; 1-59990-288-5 pa; 978-1-59990-070-4; 978-1-59990-288-3 pa

LC 2007-37670

In this graphic novel, Rapunzel escapes "from the enchanted tree where Mother Gothel imprisoned her. Rapunzel sets off alone through the ghost towns and Badlands of Gothel's Reach. She is determined to find Gothel's Villa and teach Mother Gothel a long-overdue lesson for her years of treachery and lies, and help her real mother get out of the mine camps where Mother Gothel has kept her enslaved." (Publisher's note) "Grades four to seven." (Bull Cent Child Books)

"The dialogue is witty, the story is an enticing departure from the original, and the illustrations are magically fun and expressive." SLJ

Another title about these characters is:

Calamity Jack (2009)

Hale, Shannon

Calamity Jack; [by] Shannon Hale, Dean Hale, and Nathan Hale. Bloomsbury 2010 144p il $19.99; pa $14.99

Grades: 5 6 7 8   741.5

1. Graphic novels 2. Fairy tales -- Graphic novels

ISBN 978-1-59990-076-6; 1-59900-076-9; 978-1-59990-373-6 pa; 1-59990-373-3 pa

LC 2008-41332

In this graphic novel interpretation of "Jack and the beanstalk," Jack is a born schemer who climbs a magical beanstalk in the hope of exacting justice from a mean giant and gaining a fortune for his widowed mother, aided by some friends.

"The urban setting suits this retelling of the familiar beanstalk tale; Nathan Hale's art gives it a steampunk twist, and the addition of fairy-tale creatures like giants and pixies is natural and convincing." Booklist

Hart, Christopher

Drawing the new adventure cartoons; cool spies, evil guys and action heroes. Sixth & Spring Books 2008 126p il pa $19.95

Grades: 4 5 6 7   741.5

1. Drawing 2. Cartoons and caricatures

ISBN 978-1-933027-60-9 pa; 1-933027-60-6 pa

"This fun guide works best for those with some previous figure-drawing experience. . . . Sections on 'Drawing the Head,' 'Drawing the Teen Action Body,' and 'Using Body Language to Convey Emotion' offer detailed and, for the most part, step-by-step instructions. Subsequent sections . . . provide examples of unique and zany aspects of adventure-style characters. . . . Throughout the book, Hart also includes useful tip boxes, often demonstrating how not to draw a character. These suggestions are invaluable, providing insight into creating kinetic and expressive cartoons." SLJ

Kids draw Manga Shoujo; [by] Christopher Hart. Watson Guptill Publications 2005 54p il (Kids draw) pa $10.95

Grades: 1 2 3 4   741.5

1. Drawing 2. Cartoons and comics 3. Cartoons and caricatures

ISBN 0-8230-2622-1

LC 2004-19367

"Each page takes a character, then shows a step-by-step rendering starting with simple shapes and adding more detailed lines until the final figure is realized. Manga Shoujo is full of clean, bold colors and lines. . . . Hart's books are designed for young, casual fans who will appreciate the simplicity of the drawing style and will use these titles as an easy introduction to this art." SLJ

You can draw cartoon animals; a simple step-by-step drawing guide. Walter Foster 2009 120p il (Just for kids!) pa $12.99

Grades: 2 3 4 5 6   741.5

1. Drawing 2. Cartoons and caricatures

ISBN 978-1-60058-611-8 pa; 1-60058-611-2 pa

"Hart begins by giving some general guidelines for drawing head and body shapes, and line thickness. Then he demonstrates, step by step, how to draw a variety of animals, both wild and domesticated. He includes an informative paragraph at the beginning of each set of instructions and side notes for some of the steps. . . . The projects are simple but yield a pleasing result reminiscent of animated characters the target age group might see on TV. Colored boarders at the top and bottom of each page unify the book and add visual appeal. Sure to be a favorite." SLJ

The **cartoonist's** big book of drawing animals; [by] Christopher Hart. Watson-Guptill Publications 2008 224p il pa $21.95

Grades: 3 4 5 6   741.5

1. Drawing 2. Animals in art 3. Cartoons and caricatures

ISBN 978-0-8230-1421-7 pa; 0-8230-1421-5 pa

LC 2007-29102

"The simple text that accompanies each drawing explains the artist's choices and focuses readers' attention on important details in each drawing. Children will love this thorough and easy-to-use how-to guide." SLJ

Hastings, Jon

Terrabella Smoot and the unsung monsters. SLG Publishing 2005 48p il $10.95

Grades: K 1 2 3   741.5

1. Graphic novels 2. Fantasy graphic novels 3. Monsters -- Fiction 4. Monsters -- Graphic novels

ISBN 1-59362-017-9

When she becomes separated from her family on the way to the Monster of the Year celebration, young monster Terrabella meets up with a loose-lipped dip and other creatures as she makes her way to Lord Thonk's castle. There, she discovers that Lord Thonk, the Monster of the Year, has imprisoned all the monster servants who actually performed the monstrous deeds, and she finds a way to bring justice to the celebration

Hatke, Ben

★ **Zita** the spacegirl. Book One First Second 2011 182p Book One il pa $10.99; $17.99

Grades: 3 4 5 6   741.5

1. Graphic novels 2. Science fiction graphic novels 3. Graphic novels -- Juvenile literature

ISBN 1-59643-446-5 pa; 1-59643-695-6; 978-1-59643-446-2 pa; 978-1-59643-695-4

When her best friend is abducted by an alien doomsday cult, Zita leaps to the rescue and finds herself a stranger on a strange planet.

Hatke "doles out an increasingly loony and charming array of aliens, robots, and unclassifiable blobs and hairy things for Zita . . . to encounter. It's fun, plenty funny, and more than a little random. Kids will love it." Booklist

Hayes, Geoffrey

★ **Benny** and Penny in just pretend; a Toon Book. [by] Geoffrey Hayes. RAW Junior 2008 32p il $12.95

Grades: PreK K 1 **741.5**

1. Graphic novels 2. Mice -- Graphic novels 3. Siblings -- Graphic novels

ISBN 978-0-9799238-0-7; 0-9799238-0-8

"The sweet, delicately colored illustrations have an old-fashioned feel that gives the familiar sibling story a timeless quality. . . . The text uses a limited vocabulary with sufficient repetition to help with word recognition. . . . A charmer that will invite repeated readings." Booklist

Other titles about Benny and Penny are:

Benny and Penny in the big no-no! (2009)

Benny and Penny in the toy breaker (2010)

★ **Patrick** in A teddy bear's picnic and other stories; a Toon book. Toon Books 2011 32p il $12.95

Grades: PreK K 1 2 **741.5**

1. Graphic novels 2. Bullies -- Fiction 3. Teddy bears -- Fiction 4. Mother-child relationship -- Fiction

ISBN 978-1-935179-09-2; 1-935179-09-8

LC 2010-40209

The adventures of Patrick the little teddy bear as he goes on a picnic with his mother, tries to avoid his nap, goes to the bakery to buy cookies, and contends with the bullying Big Bear.

"The bears have an endearing physicality . . . and Hayes displays a keen awareness of the volatility of a child's moods. . . . The rich vocabulary talks to kids on their own level but will also gently push their reading abilities." Booklist

Helfand, Lewis

Conquering Everest; the lives of Edmund Hillary and Tenzing Norgay. illustrated by Amit Tayal. Kalyani Navyug Media 2011 91p il (Campfire Graphic Novels Series) pa $12.99

Grades: 5 6 7 8 **741.5**

1. Mountaineering 2. Mountaineers 3. Nonfiction writers

ISBN 978-93-80741-24-6; 93-80741-24-3

LC 2011321480

"The exploits of two young men mad for climbing mountains are retold in graphic panels. . . . Tayal captures their likeness in flurries of small but visually varied cartoon scenes, often placing figures in front of reworked photos of forbidding ice fields and peaks. Helfand fills the dialogue-heavy narrative with specific biographical details amd exciting accounts of some of the great triumphs and tragedies of Himalayan mountaineering. . . . A vivid double character portrait, enhanced by equally sharp glimpses of climbing techniques, strategies and hazards." Kirkus

Hergé, 1907-1983

The **adventures** of Tintin, vol. 1; Tintin in America, Cigars of the Pharaoh, The Blue Lotus. Little, Brown 1994 192p il $18.99

Grades: 4 5 6 7 8 9 **741.5**

1. Graphic novels 2. Adventure graphic novels 3. Tintin (Fictional character) -- Graphic novels

ISBN 0-316-35940-8

Tintin, the heroic boy reporter from France, travels to America where he outwits gangsters in Chicago of the 1930s and adventures in the Wild West; sails the Mediterranean Sea with faithful dog Snowy and finds himself in a mystery involving a movie tycoon, drugs, and cigars in an ancient Egyptian tomb; then he travels to India to finally solve the mystery. This Little, Brown edition reprints some of the early Tintin adventures published in the 1930s in a 3-in-1 volume. This is the first in a series that reprints most of the Tintin stories by Herge. Librarians and teachers should note that the books retain some stereotypical depictions of people of other cultures and remember that these were acceptable and expected at the time of original publication.

The **secret** of the unicorn; Hergé; [translated by Leslie Lonsdale-Cooper and Michael Turner]. Joy Street Books 1991 62 p. col. ill. (pb) $10.99

Grades: 3 4 5 **741.5**

1. Cartoons and comics 2. Adventure graphic novels 3. Tintin (Fictional character) 4. Buried treasure -- Graphic novels 5. Buried treasure -- Fiction 6. Adventure and adventurers -- Fiction

ISBN 0316358320; 0316359025

LC 92153472

In this graphic novel, "[t]he . . . plot revolves around young reporter Tintin, his dog Snowy, and his friend Captain Haddock, who discover a riddle left by Haddock's ancestor, the 17th century Sir Francis Haddock, which could lead them to the hidden treasure of the pirate Red Rackham. In order to unravel the riddle, Tintin and Haddock must obtain three identical models of Sir Francis' ship, the 'Unicorn,' but discover that criminals are also after these model ships, and are willing to kill in order to obtain them." (Wikipedia)

Herrod, Mike

Doggie dreams. Blue Apple Books 2011 il (Balloon toons) $10.99

Grades: K 1 2 3 **741.5**

1. Graphic novels 2. Dogs -- Fiction 3. Dreams -- Fiction

ISBN 978-1-60905-065-8; 1-60905-065-7

LC 2010046646

Simple text and illustrations in comic book style reveal a dog's dreams, which feature abundant food, singing, and an opportunity to demonstrate courage.

"Unfussy illustrations of the ambitious pup in repose enhance the story's humor." Horn Book Guide

Hoena, B. A.

Jack and the beanstalk: the graphic novel; retold by Blake A. Hoena; illustrated by Ricardo Tercio. Stone Arch Books 2009 33p il $21.26

Grades: 2 3 4 5 **741.5**

1. Graphic novels 2. Fairy tales -- Graphic novels

ISBN 978-1-4342-0766-1

LC 2008-6722

When Jack sells the family cow for a handful of beans, his mother is not pleased. However, they are magic beans, and when Jack plants them, a giant beanstalk grows. Curious about where the beanstalk has gone, Jack climbs it, and finds a giant's home up there. As he brings back such things as a chicken that lays golden eggs, his mother exclaims that he is finding his father's old treasures. But sooner or later, the giant will catch Jack. This graphic novel adaptation includes information about the history of the tale, along with a short glossary and reading questions.

Holm, Jennifer L.

★ **Babymouse**: queen of the world. Random House Books for Young Readers 2005 91p il lib bdg $12.99; pa $5.95

Grades: 3 4 5 6   741.5

1. Graphic novels 2. Humorous graphic novels 3. Babymouse (Fictional character) 4. Mice -- Fiction 5. Mice -- Graphic novels 6. Friendship -- Graphic novels
ISBN 0-375-93229-1 lib bdg; 0-375-83229-7 pa
LC 2004-51166

"In this energetic comic . . . Babymouse, a wise-cracking rodent stand-in for your average, adventure-seeking nine-year-old, strives to capture popular Felicia's goodwill, finally achieving her end at the expense of Wilson Weasel, truest of friends. But, wouldn't you know it, Felicia's world has little to offer a smart, fun-loving mouse, after all." Booklist

Other titles in this series are:
Babymouse: beach babe (2006)
Babymouse: burns rubber (2010)
Babymouse: cupcake tycoon (2010)
Babymouse: dragonslayer (2009)
Babymouse: heartbreaker (2006)
Babymouse: mad scientist (2011)
Babymouse: monster mash (2008)
Babymouse: our hero (2005)
Babymouse: puppy love (2007)
Babymouse: rock star (2006)
Babymouse: the musical (2009)
Babymouse: skater girl (2007)
Camp Babymouse (2007)
A very Babymouse Christmas (2011)

★ **Squish**, Super Amoeba; by Jennifer L. Holm & Matthew Holm. Random House 2011 90p il (Squish) lib bdg $12.99; pa $6.99

Grades: 3 4 5   741.5

1. Graphic novels 2. School stories 3. Amebas -- Fiction 4. Bullies -- Fiction 5. Superheroes -- Fiction
ISBN 978-0-375-93783-5 lib bdg; 0-375-93783-8 lib bdg; 978-0-375-84389-1 pa; 0-375-84389-2 pa
LC 2010-08004

"The hilarious misadventures of a hapless young every-lad who happens to be an amoeba. . . . If ever a new series deserved to go viral, this one does." Kirkus

"Another title in this series is:
Brave new pond (2011)

Horowitz, Anthony

Stormbreaker: the graphic novel; [by] Anthony Horowitz; adapted Antony Johnston; illustrated by Kanako Damerum & Yusuru Takasaki. Philomel Books 2006 un il (Alex Rider) pa $14.99

Grades: 5 6 7 8   741.5

1. Graphic novels 2. Spies -- Graphic novels
ISBN 0-399-24633-9

In this graphic novel version on Horowitz's novel, fourteen-year-old Alex Rider is coerced into continuing his uncle's dangerous work for Britain's intelligence agency, MI6.

"If it's possible, this is even more rapidly paced than the novel. Alex remains an appealing hero here, and the idea of a heroic teen up against insidious adults continues to be an extremely powerful draw for readers." Booklist

Ita, Sam

★ The **Odyssey**; a pop-up book. Sterling 2011 il $26.95

Grades: 4 5 6 7   741.5

1. Graphic novels 2. Adventure graphic novels 3. Pop-up books
ISBN 978-1-4027-5867-6; 1-4027-5867-7

"A highlight-reel version of Odysseus' journey home, framed as a graphic novel and plastered with fantastically dramatic pop-ups and other special effects. Opening with Penelope working on a tapestry that transforms into an entirely different scene with the drop of a step-flap, the tale plunges on into the many escapes of Odysseus and his crew. . . . Ita . . . tells the tale in balloons of colloquial dialogue. . . . Even newbies will be riveted by this nonstop, high-energy retelling. Homer himself would be agog." Kirkus

Kibuishi, Kazu

★ **Amulet**, book one: The Stonekeeper. Graphix 2008 185p $21.99; pa $9.99

Grades: 3 4 5 6 7 8   741.5

1. Graphic novels 2. Fantasy graphic novels 3. Mystery graphic novels 4. Adventure graphic novels
ISBN 978-0-439-84680-6; 0-439-84680-3; 978-0-439-84681-3 pa; 0-439-84681-1 pa

After a family tragedy, Emily, Navin, and their mother move to an ancestral home to start a new life. When their mother is kidnapped by a tentacled creature, Em and Navin have to figure out how to set things straight and save their mother's life.

"Filled with excitement, monsters, robots, and mysteries, this fantasy adventure will appeal to many readers." SLJ

Other titles in this series are:
Amulet: The Stonekeeper's curse (2009)
Amulet: The Cloud Searchers (2010)
Amulet: The Last Council (2011)

Copper. Graphix/Scholastic 2010 94p il $21.99; pa $12.99

Grades: 5 6 7 8   741.5

1. Graphic novels 2. Adventure graphic novels 3. Science fiction graphic novels 4. Dogs -- Graphic novels
ISBN 978-0-545-09892-2; 0-545-09892-0; 978-0-545-09893-9 pa; 0-545-09893-9 pa

A collection of graphic novel adventures about a boy named Copper and his dog, Fred, including "navigating a dangerous forest of giant mushrooms, [and] surviving a crash landing in a homemade airplane—that run from lyrical to the downright apocalyptic. Illustrated in a deceptively simple style, its solemn tenor and deep strangeness . . . will likely inspire heavy investment from those who prefer a somewhat off-kilter read." Booklist

Kim, Susan

★ City of spies; [by] Susan Kim [and] Laurence Klavan; illustrated by Pascal Dizin. First Second 2010 172p il pa $17

Grades: 4 5 6 7   **741.5**

1. Graphic novels 2. Adventure graphic novels 3. Spies -- Graphic novels

ISBN 1-59643-262-4 pa; 978-1-59643-262-8 pa

This graphic novel, set in New York City during World War II, tells the story of Kim and Klavan, who are hunting for Nazi spies. Grades seven to ten. (Bull Cent Child Books)

"With her mother gone and a father who has better things to do than be bothered raising a daughter, Evelyn is sent to live with her unconventional Aunt Lia in the bohemian art world of 1942 New York City. . . . Evelyn spends much of her time in the company of imaginary superheroes, fouling up the plans of Nazi spies. Before long she finds an unlikely friend in the building superintendent's son, Tony. Together, they . . . stumble upon an actual Nazi plot. With stupefying precision, Dizin's art channels Hergé's Tintin in tone, palette, and with the remarkable expressiveness of the clean, flexible figures. . . . With villains and danger that just border on the genuinely scary, the tale is filled not only with a thrilling sense of excitement but also with a child's longing for a grown-up to believe in." Booklist

Kochalka, James

Dragon Puncher. Top Shelf 2010 36p il $9.95

Grades: PreK K 1 2   **741.5**

1. Graphic novels 2. Cats -- Graphic novels 3. Dragons -- Graphic novels

ISBN 978-1-60309-057-5; 1-60309-057-6

This is the story of The Dragon Puncher, a cute but ruthless kitty in an armored battle suit who is dedicated to defeating dangerous dragons, and his would-be sidekick Spoony-E (a fuzzy little fellow armed with a wooden spoon) .

This is illustrated using Kochalka's "signature child-like figures collaged onto photographed backgrounds with the faces of himself, his son, and his cat. . . . Through Kochalka's guerilla, one-man-and-a-pen style of creation, it magically captures the exact sense of zaniness often discovered in . . . playtime. . . . Remarkably, it does this without losing coherence; and with huge panels and spare dialogue that will amuse kids and adults, it's also the rare graphic novel that makes an excellent read-aloud." Booklist

Johnny Boo: the best little ghost in the world! Top Shelf Productions 2008 40p pa $9.95

Grades: K 1 2 3   **741.5**

1. Graphic novels 2. Humorous graphic novels 3. Ghosts -- Graphic novels 4. Friendship -- Graphic novels

ISBN 978-1-60309-013-1

"Johnny Boo may be the best little ghost in the world, with the best little ghost pet, Squiggle, but that doesn't mean he's ready to face down scary Ice Cream Monster. When the monster turns out not to be scary after all, Johnny and Squiggle take it on as a new, if unpredictable, friend. Kochalka's simple line drawings and bright crayon colors stand out in this sweet, silly graphic novel. . . . The dialogue is fairly simple but never simplistic, and the text is printed clearly enough to make the book accessible to children just beginning to pick up chapter books." Booklist

Other titles in this series are:

Johnny Boo: Twinkle power (2009)

Johnny Boo and the happy apples (2009)

Johnny Boo and The mean little boy (2010)

Kovac, Tommy

Wonderland; written by Tommy Kovac; illustrated by Sonny Liew. Disney Press 2008 159p il $19.99

Grades: 4 5 6 7 8   **741.5**

1. Graphic novels 2. Fantasy graphic novels

ISBN 978-1-4231-0451-3; 1-4231-0451-X

First published as single-issue comics by SLG Publishing

"Ever wonder what happened in Wonderland after Alice left? Follow the quirky tale of Mary Ann, the meticulous and dutiful housekeeper for the White Rabbit, as she continues the tale. Her boss is now wanted for treason by the Queen of Hearts for allowing the Alice Monster to enter the kingdom--off with his head! On the run and fearing for their lives, Mary Ann and White Rabbit encounter the meddlesome Cheshire Cat, the ever-contentious troublemaker, sending the White Rabbit straight into the clutches of the queen and poor Mary Ann tumbling into the Treacle Well. . . . This is a terrific look at a great classic. The energetic, action-packed illustrations complement the story in Disney-cartoon style, making for a great read for all ages" SLJ

Krosoczka, Jarrett J.

Lunch Lady and the League of Librarians. Alfred A. Knopf 2009 un il lib bdg $11.99; pa $5.99

Grades: 3 4 5 6 7 8   **741.5**

1. Graphic novels 2. Humorous graphic novels 3. Games -- Graphic novels 4. Librarians -- Graphic novels 5. School stories -- Graphic novels 6. School children -- Food -- Graphic novels

ISBN 978-0-375-94684-4 lib bdg; 0-375-94684-5 lib bdg; 978-0-375-84684-7 pa; 0-375-84684-0 pa

LC 2008043117

The school lunch lady, a secret crime fighter, sets out to stop a group of librarians bent on destroying a shipment of video games, while a group of students known as the Breakfast Bunch provides back-up

"The black-and-white pen-and-ink illustrations have splashes of yellow in nearly every panel. The clean layout, featuring lots of open space, is well suited for the intended audience. . . . With its appealing mix of action and humor, this clever, entertaining addition to the series should have wide appeal." SLJ

Other titles about the Lunch Lady are:

Lunch lady and the cyborg substitute (2009)

Lunch Lady and the author visit vendetta (2009)

Lunch Lady and the summer camp shakedown (2010)

Lunch Lady and the bake sale bandit (2010)

Lunch Lady and the field trip fiasco (2011)

Larson, Hope

Chiggers; [by] Hope Larson; lettered by Jason Azzopardi. Atheneum Books for Young Readers 2008 170p il $17.99; pa $9.99

Grades: 5 6 7 8 9   **741.5**

1. Graphic novels 2. Camps -- Fiction 3. Friendship -- Graphic novels

ISBN 978-1-4169-3584-1; 978-1-4169-3587-2 pa

LC 2008-09557

When Abby returns to the same summer camp she always goes to, she is dismayed to find that her old friends have changed, and the only person who wants to be her friend is the strange new girl, Shasta.

"Chiggers provides a ticket to summer fun. Larson delicately handles both the usual middle-school angst and the additional pressures that come with being somewhat different. . . . The content is perfect for upper elementary and middle school students." SLJ

Le Gall, Frank

Freedom! Frank Le Gall; illustrated by Flore Balthazar; coloring by Robin Doo. Graphic Universe 2012 40 p. col. ill.

Grades: 2 3 4   **741.5**
1. Cats -- Graphic novels 2. Mice -- Graphic novels 3. Freedom -- Juvenile fiction 4. Animal babies -- Juvenile fiction 5. Graphic novels 6. Cats -- Fiction 7. Mice -- Fiction 8. Animals -- Infancy -- Fiction
ISBN 0761378847; 9780761378846
LC 2011021726

This illustrated children's book features "Miss Annie [who] is a kitten, and she does all of the expected kitten activities—playing with pens and yarn, napping on armchairs, and begging for food. But she does the unexpected, too, like befriending a mouse she knows she's supposed to hunt. On her first adventure outside of the house, she meets two older cats, Zeno and Miss Rostropovna, who guide her through the big, new world. Annie has a wide range of expressions, from her perked ears to the tip of her pert tail." (Publishers Weekly)

"A charming balance of cartoon and natural kitty-ness in full-color, eight-panel pages, this cat's-eye view of life will induce purrs in feline fans everywhere." Kirkus

Rooftop cat; by Frank Le Gall; illustrated by Flore Balthazar; coloring by Robin Doo. 1st American ed. Lerner/Graphic Universe 2012 40 p. col. ill. (paperback) $6.95; (lib. bdg.: alk. paper) $29.27

Grades: 2 3 4   **741.5**
1. Graphic novels 2. Cats -- Fiction 3. Children's literature 4. Mice -- Fiction 5. Animals -- Infancy -- Fiction
ISBN 0761385479; 9780761385479; 9780761378853
LC 2011025646

The author, Frank Le Gall, presents another entry in his Miss Annie book series. "Miss Annie is just a kitten, but she loves having adventures on the rooftops outside her home. When a gang of dangerous alley cats invade her street, Miss Annie will have to prove her bravery and determination . . . and her loyalty to her very best friend, a mouse." (Publisher's note)

Lemke, Donald

Zinc Alloy: Super Zero; illustrated by Douglas Holgate. Stone Arch Books 2009 33p il $21.26

Grades: 2 3 4 5 6 7   **741.5**
1. Graphic novels 2. Humorous graphic novels 3. Superhero graphic novels 4. Robots -- Graphic novels 5. Bullies -- Graphic novels
ISBN 978-1-4342-0762-3
LC 2008-6712

Zack Allen loves to read comics, especially Robo Hero; unfortunately, he's the kind of kid that bullies like to pick on, and they have done so. Then Zack builds his own robot suit; he was just going to get the bullies to stop, but when he hears about a runaway train, he uses the suit to become a new superhero Zinc Alloy! He's going to have to work on controlling things a lot better, though how will he explain broken doors to his mom? The book includes a short history of comic books and the glossary includes definitions for "noogies" and "wet willies."

Lepp, Royden

David: Shepard's song, vol. 1. Cross Culture Entertainment/Alias Enterprises 2005 72p il pa $8.99

Grades: 3 4 5 6 7 8 9   **741.5**
1. Bible stories 2. Graphic novels 3. Kings 4. Biblical characters 5. Bible stories -- Graphic novels
ISBN 1-933428-82-1

Anointed by the prophet Samuel as a young boy and mocked by his family, young David is hunted even by King Saul himself. While hiding in a cave, David looks back on the day that Samuel found him tending the sheep and anointed him to become the next King of Israel. This retelling can be exciting for any young reader.

Littlefield, Holly

The **rooftop** adventure of Minnie and Tessa, factory fire survivors; by Holly Littlefield; adaptation by Amanda Doering Tourville; illustrated by Ted Hammond and Richard Carbajal. Graphic Universe 2011 31p il (History's kid heroes) $26.60

Grades: 3 4 5 6   **741.5**
1. Graphic novels 2. Catholics -- Fiction 3. Immigrants -- Fiction 4. Jews -- United States -- Fiction
ISBN 978-0-7613-6179-4; 0-7613-6179-0
LC 2010028952

Adapted from the 1996 novel, Fire at the Triangle factory, by Holly Littlefield

Two immigrant friends, Jewish Minnie and Catholic Tessa, work long hours at New York City's Triangle Shirtwaist Factory, and when a fire breaks out on March 25, 1911, trapping dozens of workers inside, they help one another to escape the flames. Includes facts about the factory, the fire, and its aftermath.

"Presented in graphic novel form, the dark intensity of the illustrations engages the reader." Jewish Book World

Includes bibliographical references

Liu, Na

★ **Little** White Duck; a childhood in China. by Andrés Vera Martínez and Na Liu; illustrated by Andrés Vera Martínez. Graphic Universe 2012 96 p. col. ill. (lib. bdg.: alk. paper) $29.27; (pbk.) $9.95

Grades: 4 5 6   **741.5**
1. China -- History -- 1976- 2. Biographical graphic novels 3. Graphic novels 4. China -- History -- 1976-2002 -- Comic books, strips, etc
ISBN 0761365877; 9780761365877; 9780761381150; 0761381155

LC 2011005347

This graphic novel provides a "glimpse into Chinese girlhood during the 1970s and '80s." It begins with the 3-year-old narrator trying to understand the death of Chairman Mao. "From there, her life unfolds in short sketches. . . . She explains about the four pests that plague China . . . and her stomach-turning school assignment to catch rats and deliver the severed tails to her teacher . . . [as well as] the origins of Chinese New Year, her favorite holiday." (Kirkus Reviews)

"This picturesque treasure introduces Chinese culture through a personal perspective that is both delightful and thought-provoking." SLJ

Long, Ethan

Rick & Rack and the great outdoors. Blue Apple 2010 un il (Balloon toons) $10.99

Grades: 1 2 3 **741.5**

1. Graphic novels 2. Deer -- Fiction 3. Nature -- Fiction 4. Raccoons -- Fiction 5. Friendship -- Fiction

ISBN 978-1-60905-034-4; 1-60905-034-7

LC 2010-32388

Rick the raccoon and Rack the deer spend a day fishing, tracking wild animals, and canoeing on a lake.

"This graphic novel takes beginning readers through three very short and humorous stories. . . . This . . . puts the comics medium to good use: tracking the visual elements of the story will help emerging readers decode the text with ease." Booklist

Luciani, Brigitte

A hubbub; illustrated by Eve Tharlet. Graphic Universe 2010 32p il (Mr. Badger and Mrs. Fox) pa $6.95; lib bdg $25.26

Grades: 1 2 3 **741.5**

1. Graphic novels 2. Badgers -- Fiction 3. Toleration -- Fiction 4. Cats -- Graphic novels 5. Foxes -- Graphic novels 6. Stepfamilies -- Fiction 7. Siblings -- Graphic novels

ISBN 0-7613-5626-6 lib bdg; 978-0-7613-5632-5 pa; 0-7613-5632-0 pa; 978-0-7613-5626-4 lib bdg

LC 2010005714

Ginger the fox learns that, even though life with just her mother was very different, being part of a family can be a good thing, such as when some unwanted cats try to take over the children's clubhouse.

"Tharlet's delicately detailed panels never look crowded despite plenty of speech balloons. Above-average fare for younger graphic-fiction fans." Kirkus

The meeting; illustrated by Eve Tharlet. Graphic Universe 2010 32p il (Mr. Badger and Mrs. Fox) lib bdg $25.26; pa $6.95

Grades: 1 2 3 **741.5**

1. Graphic novels 2. Foxes -- Graphic novels 3. Badgers -- Graphic novels 4. Siblings -- Graphic novels

ISBN 978-0-7613-5625-7 lib bdg; 0-7613-5625-8 lib bdg; 978-0-7613-5631-8 pa; 0-7613-5631-2 pa

LC 2009032617

Having lost their home, a fox and her daughter move in with a badger and his three children, but when the youngsters throw a big party hoping to prove that they are incompatible, their plan backfires.

"Rendered as a beginning graphic novel, the story and characters are presented with plenty of heart and soul: expressive anthropomorphic faces and postures and rich dialogue require and reward engagement. Watercolor panels vary in size on folio pages, and balloons contain an easy-to-read font." Booklist

Another title in this series is:

A hubbub (2010)

Lynch, Jay

Mo and Jo: fighting together forever; a toon book. by [illustrator] Dean Haspiel & [writer] Jay Lynch. RAW Junior 2008 40p il $12.95

Grades: K 1 2 3 **741.5**

1. Graphic novels 2. Humorous graphic novels 3. Superhero graphic novels 4. Siblings -- Graphic novels

ISBN 978-0-9799238-5-2

Mona and Joey are battling twins, and everything they do turns into a fight. They both love the same superhero, the Mighty Mojo. One day he comes to their house and says he needs to retire and gives them his costume, which has all his powers

"The text is peppered with puns and some clever idiom work, reinforced by repetition as well as what's happening in the clean panels and art." Booklist

Macdonald, Fiona

Journey to the Center of the Earth; by Jules Verne; Fiona Macdonald, adapter; illustrated by Penko Gelev. Barron's Educational Series, Inc. 2007 48p il (Graphic classics) $15.99; pa $8.99

Grades: 3 4 5 6 7 8 **741.5**

1. Authors 2. Novelists 3. Graphic novels 4. Adventure graphic novels 5. Children's authors 6. Science fiction writers

ISBN 978-0-7641-5982-4; 978-0-7641-3495-1 pa

In Hamburg, Germany in 1863, eccentric Professor Otto Lidenbrock acquires a book by the sixteenth-century alchemist, Arne Saknussemm; the book includes a parchment page written in coded runes, and Lidenbrock's nephew Axel helps him decode it. To Axel's horror, the message tells of a way to get to the Center of the Earth, and Lidenbrock drags him along on the adventure.

The "story progresses in short two-page episodes, helped along by a few sentences of narration under each frame. Detailed illustrations in muted colors work with . . . the dim underground setting. . . . Dramatic, action-filled scenes and highly expressive faces catch readers eyes and pull them into the [story]." SLJ

Kidnapped; by Robert Louis Stevenson; Fiona Macdonald, adapter; illustrated by Penko Gelev. Barron's Educational Series, Inc. 2007 48p il (Graphic classics) $15.99; pa $8.99

Grades: 3 4 5 6 7 8 **741.5**

1. Poets 2. Authors 3. Novelists 4. Graphic novels 5. Adventure graphic novels 6. Essayists 7. Travel writers 8. Short story writers

ISBN 978-0-7641-5980-0; 978-0-7641-3494-4 pa

Orphaned David Balfour goes to his uncle, who first tries to kill him and then tricks him into going onboard a ship that leaves Scotland with David aboard. David befriends a passenger, Alan Breck, then learns he's a Jacobite in exile. They survive a shipwreck, witness a murder, and become fugitives on the run back in Scotland.

The "story progresses in short two-page episodes, helped along by a few sentences of narration under each frame. Detailed illustrations in muted colors work with the stormy, furtive story. . . . Dramatic, action-filled scenes and highly expressive faces catch readers eyes and pull them into the [story]." SLJ

Macherot, R.

Sibyl-Anne vs. Ratticus; translated from the French by Kim Thompson. Fantagraphics 2011 64p il $16.99

Grades: 5 6 7 8   741.5

1. Graphic novels 2. Mice -- Graphic novels
ISBN 978-1-60699-452-8; 1-60699-452-2

"This collection of comics, originally published in Spirou magazine in 1966 and 1967, contains several stories in which the mouse Sibyl-Anne and her friends fight back the greedy villain Ratticus. This is the first time that American audiences will be able to appreciate this story arc from the golden age of Franco-Belgian comics. . . . [The stories] are lighthearted and sometimes surreal adventures that use an artistic style reminiscent of classic comics such as Blondie or Pogo. The colors are bright and the creatures are adorable. . . . An enjoyable read for kids, teens, and even adults." SLJ

Mack, Jeff

Hippo and Rabbit in three short tales. Scholastic/Cartwheel Books 2011 32p il (Scholastic reader) pa $3.99

Grades: K 1 2   741.5

1. Graphic novels 2. Humorous graphic novels 3. Rabbits -- Fiction 4. Friendship -- Fiction 5. Hippopotamus -- Fiction
ISBN 978-0-545-27445-6; 0-545-27445-1

LC 2010-13567

Friends Hippo and Rabbit are very different in size, but they have fun together as they eat breakfast (Rabbit eats vegetables, Hippo has a cheeseburger), play on the swing (Rabbit has to try very hard to push Hippo), and then comfort each other during a thunderstorm at night.

"With a low word count and simple sentences [this is] suitable for newly independent readers. . . . The book can be used as a supplemental reader in the classroom, but the stories are fun enough for recreational reading at home. " Booklist

Another title about Hippo and Rabbit is:
Hippo and Rabbit in 3 more tales: Brave like me (2011)

Manning, Matthew K.

Ali Baba and the forty thieves; retold by Matthew K. Manning; illustrated by Ricardo Osnaya. Stone Arch Books 2010 63p il lib bdg $26.65; pa $6.95

Grades: 4 5 6   741.5

1. Graphic novels 2. Folklore -- Graphic novels
ISBN 978-1-4342-1988-6 lib bdg; 1-4342-1988-7 lib bdg; 978-1-4342-2776-8 pa; 1-4342-2776-6 pa

LC 2010020144

"Ali Baba is a poor man who stumbles upon a hidden cave where a band of thieves hides its loot, opening the cave with the phrase open sesame and closing it with close sesame. When he brings some of the treasure home, his greedy brother, Kasim, finds out and forces Ali Baba to tell him everything; but the thieves discover Kasim in their cave and kill him. When they hunt after Ali Baba, it takes the courage and cunning of the servant girl Marjana to save Ali Baba and his family. Osnaya's stylish art and Manning's story combine to make a dynamic comic book." Booklist

Martin, Ann M.

The **Baby**-sitter's Club: Kristy's great idea; a graphic novel. [text by Ann M. Martin; art] by Raina Telgemeier. Scholastic Graphix 2006 192p il $16.99; pa $8.99

Grades: 3 4 5 6   741.5

1. Graphic novels 2. Friendship -- Graphic novels 3. Babysitting -- Graphic novels
ISBN 0-439-80241-5; 0-439-73933-0 pa

LC 2005-37749

Follows the adventures of Kristy and the other members of the Baby-sitters Club as they deal with crank calls, uncontrollable two-year-olds, wild pets, and parents who do not always tell the truth. A graphic novel based on the 1988 book by the same name.

"Comics artist Telgemeier's clean-lined, black-and-white art with stark black details nicely differentiates the four personable seventh-graders who parlay their babysitting experience into a business." Booklist

Other titles about the Baby-sitters Club are:
The truth about Stacey (2006)
Mary Anne saves the day (2007)
Claudia and Mean Janine (2008)

McCann, Jim

★ **Return** of the Dapper Men; written by Jim McCann; art by Janet Lee; lettered by Dave Lanphear; edited by Stephen Christy. Archaia Comics 2010 un il $24.95

Grades: 4 5 6 7 8   741.5

1. Graphic novels 2. Science fiction graphic novels 3. Robots -- Graphic novels
ISBN 978-1-932386-90-5; 1-932386-90-4

"In the dreamy land of Anorev, children, all under age 11, live underground among intricate gear-work mechanisms, while elegant robots live in abandoned houses aboveground. . . . All are perpetually stuck in the same day, and time has, essentially, ceased to mean anything—until 314 Dapper Men rain from the sky and set in motion the impetus for change. . . . Where this book truly stands out is how well the story works in concert with Lee's stunning artwork, which employs an art nouveau sheen. . . . A true dazzler that speaks on multiple levels for both child and adult readers and one that gets richer with each read." Booklist

McCranie, Stephen

★ **Mal** and Chad; the biggest, bestest time ever. Philomel Books 2011 218p il pa $9.99

Grades: 2 3 4 5   741.5

1. Graphic novels 2. Adventure graphic novels 3. Dogs -- Graphic novels 4. Schools -- Graphic novels 5. Time travel -- Graphic novels
ISBN 978-0-399-25221-1; 0-399-25221-5

LC 2010036904

Fourth-grade genius Mal and his talking dog Chad shrink themselves to microscopic size and travel through time, but girls and the school bully present bigger challenges.

"McCranie captures both the big-eyed, round-headed cartoon adorableness of his characters and the realistic (though age-appropriate) menace of the dinosaurs with equal aplomb. . . . An unusually satisfying read." Booklist

McGuiness, Dan

Pilot & Huxley: the first adventure. Graphix 2011 62p il pa $7.99

Grades: 3 4 5   741.5

1. Graphic novels 2. Adventure graphic novels
ISBN 978-0-545-26504-1 pa; 0-545-26504-5 pa

"After a late video-game rental puts them on the wrong side of some aliens who want to destroy Earth, innocent boys Pilot and Huxley are transported into an alternate dimension where Huxley's name is the ultimate swear word and boats sail on bees instead of water. . . . Our heroes will see a city inside a dragon's nose and a burger made of live rat before the exciting conclusion. It's delightfully surreal and filled with imaginative dialogue. . . . McGuinness's illustrations are colorful and kinetic, fitting the tale's many humorous twists. " Publ Wkly

Another title in this series is:

Pilot & Huxley: the next adventure (2011)

Pilot & Huxley: the next adventure. Graphix 2011 60p il pa $7.99

Grades: 3 4 5   **741.5**

1. Graphic novels 2. Adventure graphic novels

ISBN 978-0-545-26845-5; 0-545-26845-1

Pilot and Huxley just want to get home, but an unexpected glitch hurtles them into the holiday lands instead. Now they're stuck in a bizarre world where ghouls and zombies in Halloween Land are friendly, and Santa and his elves in Christmas Land are evil.

"The book is full of inspired nonsense." Kirkus

McLeod, Bob

★ **SuperHero** ABC. HarperCollins Pubs. 2006 40p il $15.99; lib bdg $16.89; pa $7.99

Grades: PreK K 1 2   **741.5**

1. Alphabet 2. Graphic novels 3. Superheroes -- Fiction 4. Superheroes (Fictional characters) -- Fiction

ISBN 0-06-074514-2; 0-06-074515-0 lib bdg; 0-06-074516-9 pa

LC 2004-22180

Humorous SuperHeroes such as Goo Girl and The Volcano represent the letters of the alphabet from A to Z.

"There's strong appeal here for the youngest comic-book fans, with many doses of humor along the way. Each figure has special powers, of course, which readers learn about through alliterative captions and action-packed illustrations." SLJ

Medley, Linda

★ **Castle** waiting. Fantagraphics 2006 456p il $29.95

Grades: 5 6 7 8 9 10 11 12   **741.5**

1. Fairy tales 2. Graphic novels 3. Fantasy graphic novels

ISBN 1-56097-747-7

All of Medley's previously self-published comics are collected here in one volume for the first time. The titular castle was the home of Sleeping Beauty, whose story is retold from the viewpoint of the flibbertigibbet ladies in waiting. After the flighty princess awakens with the kiss of a handsome but not too bright prince, the castle becomes a sanctuary for various misfits. Readers will find references to many fairy tales, folk tales, and nursery rhymes in Medley's book, and her clean, clear black-and-white art reflects the works of classic illustrators such as Arthur Rackham.

Meister, Cari

Clues in the attic; illustrated by Rémy Simard. Stone Arch Books 2010 25p il (My 1st graphic novel) $21.32; pa $3.95

Grades: K 1 2   **741.5**

1. Graphic novels 2. Mystery graphic novels 3.

Siblings -- Graphic novels

ISBN 978-1-4342-1889-6; 1-4342-1889-9; 978-1-4342-2283-1 pa; 1-4342-2283-7 pa

"Siblings Ben and Sofia investigate strange noises that they hear coming from above them. . . . [This title provides an] effective early-reader [equivalent] to comics and graphic novels. [Its] traditional beginning-reader trim size as well as bold and brightly colored illustrations are appealing to novice readers, while the inclusion of a 'How to Read a Graphic Novel' section, a glossary, discussion questions, and writing prompts will appeal to parents and teachers. The texts include simple sentences that closely match the art, while panels are limited to a maximum of four per page. Good fun for early graphic-novel readers." SLJ

Morse, Scott

★ **Magic** Pickle; with color by Jose Garibaldi. Scholastic/Graphix 2008 un il pa $9.99

Grades: 2 3 4 5   **741.5**

1. Graphic novels 2. Humorous graphic novels 3. Superhero graphic novels

ISBN 978-0-439-87995-8 pa; 0-439-87995-7 pa

"Starting with an irresistibly goofy premise, Morse layers on sly humor, astute references, and blazing action, turning in a charming, slam-bang story." Booklist

Other titles in this series are:

Magic Pickle and the Planet of the Grapes (2008)

Magic Pickle vs. the Egg Poacher (2008)

Magic Pickle and the Garden of Evil (2009)

Magic Pickle and the Creature from the Black Legume (2009)

Mortensen, Lori

The **missing** monster card; illustrated by Rémy Simard. Stone Arch Books 2010 25p il (My 1st graphic novel) $21.32; pa $3.95

Grades: K 1 2   **741.5**

1. Graphic novels 2. Mystery graphic novels

ISBN 978-1-4342-1888-9; 1-4342-1888-0; 978-1-4342-2284-8 pa; 1-4342-2284-5 pa

"Ethan has just found a rare Monster Card in the pack he bought, and he wants to show it to his friend Zack, but when he goes to Zack's house the next day, the card isn't in his jacket pocket. The two friends search for the card to solve the mystery. . . . The book provides a short tutorial on how to navigate the panels and uses sound effects, dialogue balloons, and brief narrative text to tell the story. . . . A brief glossary, discussion questions, and writing prompts provide teachers with easy lesson plans for classroom use. The bright colors and cartoony illustrations add to the appeal for beginning readers." Booklist

Mouly, Francoise

Big fat Little Lit; [edited by] Art Spiegelman and Francoise Mouly. Puffin 2006 144p il pa $14.99

Grades: 2 3 4 5 6 7 8   **741.5**

1. Graphic novels 2. Folklore -- Graphic novels

ISBN 0-14-240706-2

This volume collects all three previously published Little Lit books: Little Lit: Once Upon a Time, Little Lit: Strange Stories for Strange Kids, and Little Lit: It Was a Dark and Silly Night. Many comics creators and children's book writers and illustrators contributed stories, including Ian Falconer, Daniel Clowes, Maurice Sendak, David Sedaris, Chris Ware, Jules Feiffer, Barbara McClintock, Crockett Johnson, J. Otto Siebold, Neil Gaiman, Art Spiegelman, and Lemony Snicket.

★ The **TOON** treasury of classic children's comics; selected and edited by Art Spiegelman and Françoise Mouly; introduction by Jon Scieszka. Abrams ComicArts 2009 350p il $40

Grades: 3 4 5 6 **741.5**
1. Comic books, strips, etc.
ISBN 978-0-8109-5730-5; 0-8109-5730-2
LC 2009009830

"These stories are terrifically funny, joltingly exuberant, bafflingly bizarre, and best of all, compiled into one hearty, hefty, handsome volume." Booklist

Naujokaitis, Pranas T.
The **totally** awesome epic quest of the brave boy knight. Blue Apple Books 2011 40p il (Balloon toons) $10.99

Grades: K 1 2 3 **741.5**
1. Graphic novels 2. Monsters -- Fiction 3. Buried treasure -- Fiction 4. Knights and knighthood -- Fiction
ISBN 978-1-60905-099-3; 1-60905-099-1
LC 2011019009

A young boy and his furry friend, Butterscotch, as brave knights, battle a green monster that is destroying a princess's kingdom, seek a hidden treasure, and patrol the kingdom.

"The tales are loopily involving, allowing both the boy and the girl to play big parts, with humor that comes in broad strokes that Naujokaitis vividly paints on the faces of the actors." Kirkus

Nobleman, Marc Tyler
★ **Boys** of Steel; The Creators of Superman. Random House Childrens Books 2013 40 p. (library) $19.99; (paperback) $7.99

Grades: 4 5 6 7 **741.5**
1. Superman (Fictional character) 2. Superhero comic books, strips, etc.
ISBN 9780375938023; 0449810631; 9780449810637

This book by Marc Tyler Nobleman and illustrated by Ross MacDonald "tells how writer Jerry Siegel and artist Joe Shuster, two misfit teens in Depression-era Cleveland who were more like Clark Kent than his alter ego, created this superhero [Superman] and published his adventures in comic-book format." (Publishers Weekly)

Nytra, David
The **secret** of the stone frog; a Toon graphic novel. by David Nytra. Toon Books 2012 80 p. $14.95

Grades: 2 3 4 5 **741.5**
1. Fantasy graphic novels 2. Siblings -- Juvenile fiction 3. Fantasy 4. Graphic novels 5. Brothers and sisters -- Fiction
ISBN 1935179187; 9781935179184
LC 2011050431

In this children's book by David Nytra, "Leah and her younger brother, Alan, awake to find their beds relocated to the middle of a lush forest. They soon come across a stone frog that guides them toward their home. . . . Their long, strange trip is full of bees, fanciful lions, and a subway ride . . . After they make a narrow escape when an entire town . . . comes alive, the story ends with our hero and heroine back in their beds as a new day begins." (School Library Journal)

O'Brien, Anne Sibley
★ The **legend** of Hong Kil Dong, the Robin Hood of Korea. Charlesbridge 2006 un il $14.95

Grades: 3 4 5 6 7 **741.5**
1. Graphic novels 2. Hong Kil Dong (Legendary character) 3. Folklore -- Korea -- Juvenile literature
ISBN 978-1-58089-302-2; 1-58089-302-3
LC 2005-56941

Hong Kil Dong is the son of a powerful government minister and one of his servants; this means the father will not recognize his son as his own. The boy grows up with great intelligence and wit, and leaves home to find his fortune. He learns martial arts and magic, and when he encounters thieves who rob only because corrupt government officials have ruined them, he turns the thieves into an army to right the wrongs. This story is based on a seventeenth century Korean legend.

Includes bibliographical references

O'Connor, George
Athena; grey-eyed goddess. First Second 2010 76p il (Olympians) $16.99; pa $9.99

Grades: 5 6 7 8 **741.5**
1. Graphic novels 2. Classical mythology 3. Athena (Greek deity)
ISBN 978-1-59643-649-7; 1-59643-649-2; 978-1-59643-432-5 pa; 1-59643-432-5 pa

"O'Connor's drawings, full of energetic diagonals and expressive faces, are nicely balanced by spare settings and minimalistic backgrounds. A sophisticated color palette, full of midtones and subtle contrasts, and panel layouts that vary from page to page further distinguish the art. The author's affection for his subject is evident in a chatty note. Profiles of major characters, notes, and discussion questions appear in addition to the usual back matter. An exceptional graphic novel." SLJ

Includes bibliographical references

Hera: the goddess and her glory. First Second 2011 76p il (Olympians) pa $9.99

Grades: 5 6 7 8 **741.5**
1. Graphic novels 2. Hera (Greek deity) 3. Classical mythology
ISBN 978-1-59643-433-2; 1-59643-433-3

"O'Connor picks a few telling episodes from the goddess' legacy for a more nuanced tale of Zeus' long-suffering, acid-tongued queen. Central to this reclamation project are the 10 labors she indirectly visits upon Heracles. . . . With dedication to the source material, even at its thorniest, and fantastic artwork, O'Connors top-notch Olympians series continues to drive home the point that not only were these gods and goddesses the world's first superheroes but their labyrinthine web of weak-willed failings, spiteful jealousies, and titanic retaliations made for the world's foremost, must-see soap opera." Booklist

Poseidon; earth shaker. by George O'Connor. 1st ed. Roaring Brook Press 2012 80 p. (Olympians) (paperback) $9.99; (hardcover) $16.99

Grades: 4 5 6 **741.5**
1. Greek mythology -- Graphic novels 2. Poseidon (Greek deity) -- Graphic novels 3. Mythology, Greek

-- Juvenile literature
ISBN 1596437383; 1596438282; 9781596437388;
9781596438286

LC 2011052219

This graphic novel, by George O'Connor, is part of the "Olympians" series, featuring the mythology of the Greco-Roman gods. "The fifth installment of the Olympians series of graphic novels . . . turns the spotlight on that most mysterious and misunderstood of the Greek gods. . . . Thrill to such famous myths as Theseus and the Minotaur, Odysseus and Polyphemos, and the founding of Athens—and learn how the tempestuous Poseidon became the King of the Seas." (Publisher's note)

Includes bibliographical references and index

★ **Zeus**; king of the gods. Roaring Brook Press 2010 76p il (Olympians) $16.99; pa $9.99

Grades: 5 6 7 8   **741.5**

1. Graphic novels 2. Zeus (Greek deity) 3. Classical mythology 4. Graphic novels -- Juvenile literature 5. Zeus (Greek deity) -- Juvenile literature
ISBN 978-1-59643-431-8; 1-59643-625-5; 978-1-59643-432-5 pa; 1-59643-431-7 pa

Retells in graphic novel format stories from Greek mythology about the exploits of the young Zeus and how he rallied an army and overthrew his father, Kronos, to become king of the gods

"It's [the] balance between respect for myth and adherence to comic-book form that works so wonderfully well here." Bull Cent Child Books

O'Donnell, Liam

Power play; illustrated by Mike Deas. Orca Book Publishers 2011 64p il (Graphic guide adventure) pa $9.95

Grades: 3 4 5 6 7 8 9   **741.5**

1. Graphic novels 2. Mystery graphic novels
ISBN 978-1-55469-069-5; 1-55469-069-2

Siblings Devin and Nadia team up with their friend Marcus, Marcus' stepbrother Bounce, and Bounce's best friend Pema when they all attend the World Leaders Summit, where Marcus' father, Dr. Ashmore is scheduled to speak. The friends find themselves mixed up in a fight between some of the most powerful people in the world and those who want more equitable rights to clean water and other environmental concerns.

An enjoyable story with educational value, this strong mystery is presented along with information about world politics, power, and the benefits of political protest for social good." Booklist

O'Malley, Kevin

Desk stories. Albert Whitman 2011 32p il

Grades: 1 2 3   **741.5**

1. Graphic novels 2. Schools -- Graphic novels
ISBN 0-8075-1562-0; 978-0-8075-1562-4

LC 2010050423

Six separate stories tell, in words and cartoons, the surprising history and activities of the ordinary school desk.

"Presented in a graphic-novel format, six fanciful, silly stories incorporate situations that any child who has endured a tedious class will appreciate. . . . This lighthearted offering will likely produce cheers rather than jeers and makes a great choice for reluctant readers." Booklist

Parker, Jake

Missile Mouse: the star crusher. Graphix 2010 172p (Missile Mouse) $21.99; pa $10.99

Grades: 3 4 5 6   **741.5**

1. Graphic novels 2. Adventure graphic novels 3. Science fiction graphic novels 4. Mice -- Graphic novels
ISBN 978-0-545-11714-2; 0-545-11714-3; 978-0-545-11715-9 pa; 0-545-11715-1 pa

"When his mission to recover an ancient star compass goes wrong, intrepid Galactic Security Agent Missile Mouse finds himself saddled with a partner. . . . The two are to retrieve a missing scientist who holds the key to a horrible weapon, the Star Crusher, in his hereditary memory. . . . [This is] a gem in story and art. Bright, action-filled, at times wordless panels keep the pages turning. Intelligent space opera and a realistically rounded hero will have young fans of the future demanding the next volume." Kirkus

Another title about Missile Mouse is:
Missle Mouse: rescue on Tankium 3 (2011)

Pearson, Luke

Hilda and the Midnight Giant; Luke Pearson. Consortium Book Sales & Dist 2012 chiefly col. ill.

Grades: 4 5 6 7 8   **741.5**

1. Occult fiction 2. Girls -- Fiction 3. Forests and forestry -- Fiction
ISBN 1907704256; 9781907704253

In this book, the "protagonist finds her world turned upside down as she faces the prospect of leaving her snow-capped birthplace for the hum of the megalopolis, where her mother (an architect) has been offered a prestigious job. During Hilda's daily one-and-a-half hour trek to school she looks for ways to stall her mother's decision. She conspires with the beings of the mystical Blue Forest to delay the inevitable. Will they help or hinder her? More importantly, who is this mysterious Midnight Giant? This is the first part of the Hildafolk series, a series that follows Hilda on her many adventures and travels through the magical fjords and enchanted mountains of her birthplace as she unravels the mysteries of the supernatural world that surrounds her." (Amazon.com)

Petersen, David

★ **Mouse** Guard: Fall 1152. Archaia Studios Press 2007 un il $24.95

Grades: 5 6 7 8   **741.5**

1. Graphic novels 2. Fantasy graphic novels 3. Mice -- Graphic novels
ISBN 978-1-932386-57-8; 1-932386-57-2

In a medieval world populated by animals, mice have their own civilization but live in constant peril from predators. They live in hidden towns protected by the Guard, who also escort travelers between towns. Three young members of the Guard, Lieam, Saxon, and Kenzie, go in search of a missing grain merchant. They find him dead in the belly of a snake who tried to eat them; but they also find evidence that the dead merchant is a traitor. Now they need to find out to whom he was betraying the Guard and why. While this story features animals and is suitable for most readers who can handle some fighting action, there's nothing cute or Disney-esque in the art. Characters die, this is a serious story, but readers who have read Bone or the Harry Potter series can handle the action in this book. This is the first in a series.

Another title is this series is:

Mouse Guard: Winter 1152 (2009)

Petrucha, Stefan

Mickey Mouse: 300 Mickeys; writers, Stefan Petrucha . . . [et al.]; artists, Cèsar Ferioli Pelaez . . . [et al.] Boom! Kids 2011 un il pa $9.99
Grades: 3 4 5   **741.5**
   1. Graphic novels 2. Mickey Mouse (Cartoon character)
   ISBN 978-1-60886-627-4; 1-60886-627-0

A collection of four Mickey Mouse stories, including tales about a cloning experiment gone wrong that leads to countless copies of Mickey Mouse and an attack by an army of robot presidents during Mickey and Minnie's vacation to Mount Rushmore.

"This book combines classic comics stories with original comics from Italy and the U.S. featuring Mickey Mouse and a few of his friends. . . . The colorful art . . . is right on model with the Disney characters. Anyone who has enjoyed Mickey Mouse cartoons will have fun with these adventures, full of action and humor that is just right for younger readers." Booklist

Phelan, Matt

   ★ **Around** the world. Candlewick Press 2011 240p il $24.99
Grades: 4 5 6 7   **741.5**
   1. Graphic novels 2. Voyages and travels
   ISBN 978-0-7636-3619-7; 0-7636-3619-3
                                                           LC 2010043153

"Phelan presents three true stories of around-the-world adventures inspired by Jules Verne's Around the World in Eighty Days that, even though they were undertaken in the late 1800s, would be hardly less arduous today. Thomas Stevens, Joshua Slocum, and Nellie Bly saw the world from the seat of a bicycle, aboard a 36-foot sloop, and via trains and ships, respectively. The small, specific pleasures of Phelan's work . . . are showcased in panels laid out in horizontal bands, reinforcing the linear, ever-onward nature of each narrative. The use of limited color palettes enhances the artist's characteristic delicate, expressive pen-and-ink drawings without overpowering them, allowing each traveler's character to be the dominant story element. . . . Design elements such as borders and frames lend a jaunty festivity to a graphic novel that will appeal to aficionados of the form and any reader in search of engrossing true journeys." SLJ

   ★ The **storm** in the barn. Candlewick Press 2009 201p il $24.99; pa $14.99
Grades: 4 5 6 7 8 9   **741.5**
   1. Graphic novels 2. Adventure graphic novels 3. Kansas -- Graphic novels 4. Monsters -- Graphic novels 5. Dust storms -- Graphic novels
   ISBN 978-0-7636-3618-0; 0-7636-3618-5; 978-0-7636-5290-6 pa; 0-7636-5290-3 pa

In Kansas of 1937, the land has been in the grip of the Dust Bowl for four years, and eleven-year-old Jack Carter has seen his family worn down by it. But the day Jack outruns a dust storm all the way home from town, he glimpses something odd in the abandoned Talbot barn, and he tries to find the courage to go into the barn and confront what is there.

"Children can read this as a work of historical fiction, a piece of folklore, a scary story, a graphic novel, or all four. Written with simple, direct language, it's an almost wordless

book: the illustrations' shadowy grays and blurry lines eloquently depict the haze of the dust. A complex but accessible and fascinating book." SLJ

Pien, Lark

   Long Tail Kitty. Blue Apple Books 2009 51p il $14.95
Grades: 1 2 3 4   **741.5**
   1. Graphic novels 2. Humorous graphic novels 3. Cats -- Graphic novels 4. Friendship -- Graphic novels
   ISBN 978-1-934706-44-2

Long Tail Kitty comes to children's books from Pien's webcomic. Pien colored Gene Yang's American Born Chinese. Here, she uses watercolor washes over precise ink to depict the everyday adventures of Long Tail Kitty.

"The volume's appeal lies in the tidy, thoughtfully shaded panels and the cast's playful banter and witty barbs." Horn Book

Pilkey, Dav

   The **adventures** of Ook and Gluk; Kung-fu cavemen from the future. by George Beard and Harold Hutchins. Blue Sky Press 2010 175p il $9.99
Grades: 3 4 5   **741.5**
   1. Graphic novels 2. Kung fu -- Graphic novels 3. Time travel -- Graphic novels
   ISBN 978-0-545-17530-2; 0-545-17530-5
                                                           LC 2010-904867

Friends Ook and Gluk are always getting into trouble with their village chief until they pass through a portal into a future run by the chief's descendant, where they learn kung fu so they can return to the past and free their people.

Powell, Martin

   The **seven** voyages of Sinbad; retold by Martin Powell; illustrated by Ferran [Daniel Perez] Stone Arch Books 2010 63p il lib bdg $26.65; pa $6.95
Grades: 4 5 6   **741.5**
   1. Graphic novels 2. Folklore -- Graphic novels
   ISBN 978-1-4342-1987-9 lib bdg; 1-4342-1987-9 lib bdg; 978-1-4342-2775-1 pa; 1-4342-2775-8 pa
                                                           LC 2010020159

Sinbad the sailor "recounts his miraculous travels to a beggar before giving him the riches to set out on his own adventures. . . . The artwork is as comics-inspired as it gets—all dramatic poses and forced perspective. [This] may succeed in introducing . . . Sinbad to new readers." SLJ

   The **tall** tale of Paul Bunyan: the graphic novel; retold by Martin Powell; illustrated by Aaron Blecha. Stone Arch Books 2010 35p il (Tall tale) $22.65
Grades: 1 2 3 4   **741.5**
   1. Tall tales 2. Graphic novels 3. Bunyan, Paul (Legendary character) 4. Folklore -- Graphic novels
   ISBN 978-1-4342-1897-1; 1-4342-1897-X

The legendary woodsman Paul Bunyan was the biggest man who ever lived. One day, Paul finds a big blue ox frozen in the snow. He nurses the behemoth back to health, and names his new companion Babe.

"The book is complemented by excellent design work that mixes advertising tropes with frontier photographic elements to help reinforce the legendary quality of the myth." SLJ

Pyle, Kevin C.

Take what you can carry; Kevin C. Pyle. Henry Holt and Co. 2012 176 p. chiefly ill. (some col.) (hc) $12.99

Grades: 4 5 6 **741.5**

1. Teenagers -- Graphic novels 2. Shoplifting -- Graphic novels 3. Japanese Americans -- Evacuation and relocation, 1942-1945 -- Graphic novels

ISBN 0805082867; 9780805082869

LC 2011924430

In this graphic novel, in "1977 suburban Chicago, Kyle runs wild with his friends and learns to shoplift from the local convenience store. In 1941 Berkeley, the Himitsu family is forced to leave their home for a Japanese-American internment camp, and their teenage son must decide how to deal with his new life. But though these boys are growing up in wildly different places and times, their lives intersect in more ways than one, as they discover compassion, learn loyalty, and find renewal." (Publisher's note)

Rafter, Dan

Atlas; illustrated by Adam Ellis . . . [et al.] Bluewater Comics 2010 un il pa $9.99

Grades: 5 6 7 8 **741.5**

1. Graphic novels 2. Superhero graphic novels

ISBN 978-1-61623-931-2; 1-61623-931-X

"Atlas is a typical square-jawed superhero; in fact, he's pretty angular and blocky all over. His other primary characteristics are that he's always hungry and that he's kind of a dim bulb. As the story begins, his long-suffering partner, Wonder Boy, has to drag him away from yet another Chicago-style hot dog to fight some villains who are threatening the city. . . . The artwork is well suited to this witty story. The images are eye-catching and filled with life and humor." SLJ

Ransom, Candice F.

The lifesaving adventure of Sam Deal, shipwreck rescuer; adaptation by Amanda Doering Tourville; illustrated by Zachary Trover. Graphic Universe 2011 31p il (History's kid heroes) lib bdg $26.60; pa $8.95

Grades: 2 3 4 **741.5**

1. Graphic novels 2. Horses -- Graphic novels 3. Shipwrecks -- Graphic novels 4. African Americans -- Graphic novels

ISBN 978-0-7613-6177-0 lib bdg; 0-7613-6177-4 lib bdg; 978-0-7613-6196-1 pa; 0-7613-6196-0 pa

LC 2009051719

In 1896, ten-year-old Sam Deal and Ginger, the wild horse he has tamed, assist an all-Black lifesaving crew as they attempt to rescue survivors of a shipwreck off North Carolina's Outer Banks.

This book provides an "exciting [glimpse] into the past, with just the right amount of tension and intensity to capture readers' attention. . . . [It] will serve as [a] good [introduction] to graphic novels and historical fiction for early readers. Added bonuses are the brief yet informative [introduction] and [afterword] providing more facts about the [setting]." SLJ

Includes bibliographical references

Reinhart, Matthew

DC super heroes: The ultimate pop-up book. Little, Brown 2010 un il $29.99

Grades: PreK K 1 2 **741.5**

1. Pop-up books 2. Superheroes -- Fiction

ISBN 978-0-316-01998-9; 0-316-01998-4

"The illustrations in this detailed and decidedly heroic pop-up compendium of superheroes and supervillains feel ripped from the pages of classic DC comics. Favorites like Superman, Batman, and Wonder Woman get their own majestic spreads . . . while mini-booklets highlight their allies, nemeses, and histories. Each spread is dramatic and dynamic. . . . Expertly crafted and superfun." Publ Wkly

Renier, Aaron

Spiral-bound. Top Shelf Productions 2005 144p il pa $14.95

Grades: 4 5 6 7 8 9 **741.5**

1. Graphic novels 2. Mystery graphic novels

ISBN 1-891830-50-3

"Turnip the elephant is using the summer to find his artistic voice through sculpture, his friend Stucky the dog is building a submarine, and Ana the rabbit is working on the town's underground newspaper. Their stories all wind around the town's deep, dark secret about the monster that lives in the pond. . . . The characters seem like real children, wholesome without being too sweet, and Renier's art is light and fun, a sort of Babar meets underground comix." Booklist

★ The Unsinkable Walker Bean; written and illustrated by Aaron Renier; colored by Alec Longstreth. First Second 2010 191p il pa $13.99

Grades: 5 6 7 8 **741.5**

1. Graphic novels 2. Adventure graphic novels 3. Graphic novels -- Juvenile literature

ISBN 978-1-59643-453-0 pa; 1-59643-453-8 pa

The story "centers around a cursed skull stolen from the lair of two deep-sea crustacean witches. Like all who look upon the skull, Walker's beloved grandpa falls deathly ill when he finds it, and the boy sets out to return the skull from whence it came. . . . The generous page size lets [the] reader dive into Renier's quavery and painstakingly detailed cartooning, and he really shows off his stuff with a bounty of full-splash dazzlers. . . . Exciting, deep, funny, and scary, with tremendous villains and valor galore." Booklist

Reynolds, Aaron

Joey Fly, private eye in Creepy crawly crime; illustrations by Neil Numberman. Henry Holt & Co. 2009 96p il (Joey Fly, private eye) $16.95; pa $9.95

Grades: 3 4 5 6 **741.5**

1. Graphic novels 2. Mystery graphic novels

ISBN 978-0-8050-8242-5; 0-8050-8242-5; 978-0-8050-8786-4 pa; 0-8050-8786-9 pa

LC 2007-40041

"In a city inhabited by insects, Joey fly is a private eye combating crime for a fee. . . . Young readers will be amused by this noir-type story filled with classic detective dialogue and swarms of insect humor." Booklist

Another title about Joey Fly is:

Joey Fly, private eye in big hairy drama (2010)

Robbins, Trina

The Maltese mummy; illustrated by Tyler Page. Graphic Universe 2011 59p il (Chicagoland Detective Agency) $29.27; pa $9.99

Grades: 4 5 6 7   **741.5**

1. Graphic novels 2. Mystery graphic novels
ISBN 978-0-7613-4615-9; 0-7613-4615-5; 978-0-
7613-5636-3 pa; 0-7613-5636-3 pa

A friend has vanished, a mummy's amulet is missing, and there's a weirdo out there looking for human brains and hearts. The Chicagoland Detective Agency—run by Megan, Raf, and his talking dog Bradley—have more than enough cases on their hands (and paws). But where to start?

"The Goth look is actually cheerful and supports the juvenile humor quite well. . . . Those who want plots that are more Scooby Doo than Nancy Drew will enjoy this silly romp of a mystery." SLJ

The **big** flush; by Trina Robbins; illustrated by Tyler Page. Graphic Universe 2012 59 p. $6.95

Grades: 3 4 5   **741.5**

1. Ghost stories 2. School stories 3. Mystery fiction 4. Graphic novels 5. Dogs -- Fiction 6. Ghosts -- Fiction 7. Schools -- Fiction 8. Spirit possession -- Fiction 9. Japanese Americans -- Fiction
ISBN 0822591618; 9780761381655; 9780822591610
                     LC 2011044490

In this mystery, a "ghost is haunting the girls' bathroom at Pine Lake Academy, but that isn't the interesting part of the story. The interesting thing is that she's singing 'Alexander's Ragtime Band.' Anyone who drinks the water ends up possessed, and even a manly young detective like Raf Hernandez finds himself saying, 'How I love the Turkey Trot! But Auntie says the Turkey Trot and the Grizzly Bear are vulgar and will corrupt today's youth.'" (Kirkus)

The **drained** brains caper; [by] Trina Robbins and Tyler Page. Lerner Publishing Group/Graphic Universe 2010 64p il (Chicagoland Detective Agency) lib bdg $27.97; pa $6.95

Grades: 4 5 6 7   **741.5**

1. Graphic novels 2. Mystery graphic novels 3. Humorous graphic novels 4. Brainwashing -- Fiction 5. Schools -- Graphic novels 6. Japanese Americans -- Graphic novels
ISBN 978-0-7613-4601-2 lib bdg; 0-7613-4601-5 lib bdg; 978-0-7613-5635-6 pa; 0-7613-5635-5 pa
                     LC 2009-32620

Required to attend summer school after moving to Chicagoland, thirteen-year-old manga-love Megan Yamamura needs help from twelve-year-old computer genius Raf Hernandez to escape the maniacal principal's mind control experiment.

This tells "an entertaining story. . . . Page's black-and-white cartooning has a loose manga slant, with peppy goofiness popping out from stippled screen tones." Booklist

Another title in this series is:
The Maltese mummy (2011)

Roberts, Scott

Patty-cake and friends: color collection. SLG Publishing 2006 104p il pa $12.95

Grades: 4 5 6 7 8 9 10 11 12   **741.5**

1. Graphic novels 2. Humorous graphic novels 3. Friendship -- Graphic novels 4. Family life -- Graphic novels
ISBN 1-59362-030-6

Patty-Cake (real name Patricia Bakerman), her family and her neighborhood friends star in a series of true-to-life everyday adventures and misadventures, including getting even with her older sister at the pool, helping her best friend Irving get even with his pesky older brother, going on her first train ride with her dad, and more. Roberts' exaggerated cartoon style is reminiscent of old Tex Avery cartoons, as characters fully express their emotions particularly anger and surprise. Some use of frank language may keep this book in public library collections.

Roche, Art

★ **Cartooning**; the only cartooning book you'll ever need to be the artist you've always wanted to be. Lark Books 2005 111p il (Art for kids) $17.95

Grades: 3 4 5 6   **741.5**

1. Drawing 2. Cartoons and comics 3. Cartooning -- Technique
ISBN 1-57990-623-0

"This how-to guide is a step above the average cartooning instruction book. The glossy, full-color pages are visually attractive. . . . Roche's engaging writing style is informative and fun. . . . His loose, spacious cartooning style is perfect for beginners or kids who might be intimidated by more detail-oriented techniques." SLJ

Roman, Dave

Astronaut Academy: Zero gravity. First Second Books 2011 185p il $16.99; pa $9.99

Grades: 4 5 6 7 8 9 10   **741.5**

1. Graphic novels 2. Humorous graphic novels 3. Science fiction graphic novels 4. School life -- Graphic novels
ISBN 978-1-59643-756-2; 1-59643-756-2; 978-1-59643-20-6 pa; 1-59643-620-4 pa
                     LC 2010-941434

Hakata Soy has been the leader of a futuristic superhero team, but he has given that up and just wants to be a normal student at Astronaut Academy, a school on a space station, where students take such courses as anti-gravity gymnastics and fire-throwing. Other students include Doug Hiro, who always wears his space helmet, rich girl Maribelle Mellonbelly, Miyumi San (Maribelle's rival), and egotistical Billy Lee. Hakata Soy has some trouble adjusting to school life, and things get much worse when the villainous Gotcha Birds steal a robotic twin to Hakata Soy and reprogram it to kill him. The comics originally appeared as web comics, then as mini comics that Roman took to various comic cons; this is the first trade book collection of the stories. Middle grade students, boys and girls, will enjoy this book, which is full of humor and action with little actual violence.

"Students like the introspective Hakata Soy, the space-gymnastics-obsessed Doug Hiro, and the snooty rich girl Mirabelle Mellonbelly meet up at Astronaut Academy, a middle school where the zany mixes with the postmodern. . . . Silliness is high on the agenda, aided by minimal, cartoonish art that plays on manga tropes but also manages to build character into the simple lines of a face. . . . This is one for readers looking for more involved and complex comedy than a cursory glance at the images might lead one to expect." Booklist

Roop, Peter

The **stormy** adventure of Abbie Burgess, lighthouse keeper; by Peter Roop and Connie Roop; adapted by Amanda Doering Tourville; illustrated by Zachary Trover. Graphic Universe 2011 31p il (History's kid heroes) lib bdg $26.60; pa $8.95

Grades: 3 4 5 6   741.5

1. Graphic novels 2. Lighthouse keepers 3. Lighthouses -- Graphic novels

ISBN 978-0-7613-6172-5 lib bdg; 0-7613-6172-3 lib bdg; 978-0-7613-6191-6 pa; 0-7613-6191-X pa

LC 2010006748

Based on Peter & Connie Roop's Keep the lights burning, Abbie, published 1985 by Carolrhoda Books

In Maine in 1856 seventeen-year-old Abbie Burgess lives with her family on a tiny island where her father is the lighthouse keeper. A storm hits when her father is away and Abbie must keep the lights burning until he returns.

This book provides an "exciting [glimpse] into the past, with just the right amount of tension and intensity to capture readers' attention. . . . [It] will serve as [a] good [introduction] to graphic novels and historical fiction for early readers. Added bonuses are the brief yet informative [introduction] and [afterword] providing more facts about the [setting]." SLJ

Includes bibliographical references

Rosenstiehl, Agnes

★ **Silly** Lilly and the four seasons. Toon Books 2008 36p il $12.95

Grades: PreK K 1   741.5

1. Graphic novels 2. Humorous graphic novels 3. Seasons -- Graphic novels

ISBN 978-0-9799238-1-4; 0-9799238-1-6

"Rosenstiehl follows Lilly . . . as she undertakes simple, familiar activities through the seasons. . . . Lilly is bold and engaging. . . . The text is very brief, . . . the colors are warm and bright, and the panels are large enough to draw in children new to books and reading." Booklist

Another title about Silly Lilly is:

Silly Lilly in what will I be today? (2011)

Rosenstiehl, Agnès

Silly Lilly in what will I be today? RAW Junior 2010 32p il $12.95

Grades: PreK K 1   741.5

1. Graphic novels 2. Week -- Fiction 3. Occupations -- Fiction

ISBN 978-1-935179-08-5; 1-935179-08-X

LC 2010005308

No job is too tough for Silly Lilly: first she's a cook who paints, then an acrobat who tumbles, then a vampire.

"This concept book meets comic is an excellent addition for beginning readers. . . . Almost all of the text appears in word bubbles written in very basic vocabulary level in simple sentences. The India ink and watercolor cartoon illustrations are clear, with white backgrounds to keep the scenes uncluttered. . . . A fine example of a book that knows its audience." SLJ

Rosinsky, Natalie M.

Graphic content! the culture of comic books. Compass Point Books 2010 64p il (Pop culture revolutions) lib bdg $31.99

Grades: 5 6 7 8 9 10   741.5

1. Comic books, strips, etc. -- History and criticism

ISBN 978-0-7565-4241-2 lib bdg; 0-7565-4241-3 lib bdg

Traces the origins of comic books and discusses the emergence of superheroes, censorship issues, their depiction of increased social diversity, and their impact on society

"This slim and splashily designed book . . . does an admirable job of keeping things succinct yet thorough. . . . [The author] maintains a nice international scope throughout. . . . This is a super resource to have on hand to give a broader context of the medium and its fascinating history." Booklist

Write your own graphic novel. Compass Point Books 2009 64p il (Write your own) lib bdg $33.26

Grades: 5 6 7 8 9 10 11 12   741.5

1. Graphic novels -- Authorship

ISBN 978-0-7565-3856-9 lib bdg; 0-7565-3856-4 lib bdg

LC 2008-6506

This book offers tips, advice, end encouragement to readers who might want to try their hand at writing their own comics and graphic novels. Rosinsky uses many examples from Stone Arch and Capstone Press books along with many others, and the "case study" side bars provide glimpses into the work of such graphic novelists as Marjane Satrapi, Art Spiegelman, and Craig Thompson. The back matter includes a list of suggested graphic novels that are suitable for teen readers

"Students wishing to explore the graphic-novel format will benefit from clear explanations of how to portray heroes and villains, use dramatic dialogue, and create a story map. Excerpts from several popular graphic novels are included." SLJ

Runton, Andy

Owly: The way home and The bittersweet summer; [by] Andy Runton. Top Shelf 2004 160p il pa $10

Grades: K 1 2 3 4 5 6 7 8 9 10 11 12   741.5

1. Graphic novels 2. Owls -- Graphic novels 3. Friendship -- Graphic novels

ISBN 1-891830-62-7

LC 2005298860

Rotund little Owly befriends Wormy despite their differences, and together they help a couple of hummingbirds and learn that friendship doesn't end with separation.

"The whimsical black-and-white art is done with great facility for expressing emotion, and Runton's reliance on icons and pictures in lieu of the usual dialogue makes the story perfect for give-and-take between children and their parents." Booklist

Other titles in this series are:

Owly vol. 2: Just a little blue (2005)

Owly vol. 3: Flying lessons (2005)

Russell, P. Craig

★ **Coraline**; based on the novel by Neil Gaiman; adapted and illustrated by P. Craig Russell; colorist, Lovern Kindzierski; letterer, Todd Klein. HarperCollins 2008 186p il $18.99; lib bdg $19.89

Grades: 4 5 6 7   741.5

1. Graphic novels 2. Horror graphic novels

ISBN 978-0-06-082543-0; 978-0-06-082544-7 lib bdg

LC 2007-930658

"An adaptation of Gaiman's 2002 novel Coraline, . . . a tale of childhood nightmares. As in the original story, Coraline wanders around her new house and discovers a door leading into a mirror place, where she finds her button-eyed 'other mother,' who is determined to secure Coraline's love one way or another. This version is a virtuoso adaptation. . . . A master of fantastical landscapes, Russell sharpens the realism of his imagery, perserving the humanity of the characters and heightening the horror." Booklist

Salati, Giorgio

Race for the Ultrapods; writers, Giorgio Salati & Alessandro Ferrari; artists, Roberta Migheli & Antonello Dalena. Boom Kids! 2010 un il (Disney's Hero Squad: Ultraheroes) pa $9.99

Grades: 4 5 6 7   741.5
1. Graphic novels 2. Superhero graphic novels
ISBN 978-1-60886-560-4; 1-60886-560-6

It's the year 2734 and the only one standing in the way of earth's utter destruction . . . Mickey Mouse?! In this volume, the battle for the Ultrapods is reaching it's boiling point as The Duck Avenger and the Ultraheroes clash with the villainous Emil Eagle and his Sinister Seven.

"Disney fans, both children and adults, will enjoy [this] graphic [novel]." SLJ

Santat, Dan

Sidekicks. Arthur A. Levine Books 2011 215p il $24.99; pa $12.99

Grades: K 1 2   741.5
1. Graphic novels 2. Superhero graphic novels 3. Pets -- Graphic novels 4. Graphic novels -- Juvenile literature
ISBN 978-0-439-29811-7; 0-439-29811-3; 978-0-439-29819-3 pa; 0-439-29819-9 pa

LC 2010034704

When Captain Amazing feels he is getting too old to be a reliable superhero, he tries to hire a new sidekick, but his pets have different ideas.

"Despite the presence of its charming animal characters, Santat produces much more of a dramatic adventure than a hilarious romp. . . . Realistic relationship dynamics come out. . . . Well-crafted art balances the lighthearted and the rough-and-tumble art works equally well for the character moments and the epic battle at the end." Booklist

Sava, Scott Christian

★ **Hyperactive**; by Scott Christian Sava; artist, Joseph Bergin. IDW Publishing/Worthwhile Children's Books 2009 108p il pa $12.99

Grades: 3 4 5 6 7 8   741.5
1. Graphic novels 2. Humorous graphic novels 3. Adventure graphic novels 4. Superhero graphic novels
ISBN 978-1-60010-313-1; 1-60010-313-8

"Joey Johnson learns he can move at super speed and puts his power to good use doing household chores. But when word gets out, a shady executive sees the opportunity to make big bucks off of Joey's super DNA. . . . With its surprise ending, which suggests more to come, a readership of young boys will ensure that this one flies off the shelf at the speed of light." Booklist

Sfar, Joann

Little Vampire; stories and drawings by Joann Sfar; colors by Walter; translated by Alexis Siegel and Edward Gauvin. First Second 2008 92p il pa $13.95

Grades: 3 4 5 6   741.5
1. Graphic novels 2. Vampires -- Graphic novels 3. School stories -- Graphic novels
ISBN 1-59643-233-0 pa; 978-1-59643-233-8 pa

LC 2007-38498

First published in France

An unusual friendship forms between a vampire and a human, when Little Vampire leaves notes on homework Michael has left at school. "Grades four to seven." (Bull Cent Child Books)

"Joann Sfar's art is surreal, with vivid colors, busy panels and fabulous monsters." KLIATT

★ The **little** prince; adapted from the book by Antoine de Saint-Exupéry; translated by Sarah Ardizzone; colour by Brigitte Findakly. Houghton Mifflin Harcourt 2010 110p il $19.99

Grades: 5 6 7 8 9   741.5
1. Authors 2. Novelists 3. Air pilots 4. Graphic novels 5. Fantasy graphic novels 6. Essayists 7. Children's authors 8. Air pilots -- Graphic novels 9. Extraterrestrial beings -- Graphic novels
ISBN 978-0-547-33802-6; 0-547-33802-3

"On the surface, this is a straight graphic-novel retelling of the narrator pilot getting stranded in the desert, where he meets a curious little boy who claims to be from a wee planet very far away. . . . The ultimately tricky task is to honor the source but not sound like an adaptation (otherwise, why not just read the original?) and Sfar nails it on both counts. . . . Everything is handled with both reverence and ingenuity." Booklist

Shiga, Jason

★ **Meanwhile**. Abrams/Amulet 2010 un il $15.95

Grades: 4 5 6 7 8 9   741.5
1. Graphic novels 2. Science fiction graphic novels
ISBN 978-0-8109-8423-3; 0-8109-8423-7

LC 2009-39844

"In this graphic novel mind boggler . . . readers play the role of little Jimmy and on the first page make the seemingly innocuous decision of ordering a vanilla or chocolate ice-cream cone. Tubes connect panels in all directions and veer off into tabs to other pages, creating a head-spinningly tangled web of story. . . . The crux is that Jimmy stumbles into the lab of an affable mad scientist and is allowed to tinker with three inventions: a mind reader, a time machine, and the Killitron, which obliterates all life on earth aside from the user's. . . . It's maddening and challenging, all right, but that's precisely what makes it so crazy fun." Booklist

Shioya, Hitoshi

Dinosaur hour!, vol. 1; story and art by Hitoshi Shioya; [translation, Katherine Schilling] Viz Media/Vizkids 2009 192p il $7.99

Grades: 3 4 5 6   741.5
1. Manga 2. Graphic novels 3. Humorous graphic novels 4. Dinosaurs -- Graphic novels
ISBN 978-1-4215-2648-5

Shioya takes dinosaurs from the various prehistoric periods and puts them into slapstick situations. In short comics stories, herbivores such as Protoceratops and carnivores such as Tyrannosaurus Rex interact, often with the herbivores getting eaten. In one story, a couple of Protoceratops decide to check out the story that Tyrannosaurus Rex can't see well, but it doesn't stop the carnivore from chomping on both of them. In other stories, smaller carnivores try to tackle a stegosaurus, who uses its tail to sweep them away. Dinosaurs make bets with each other, play pranks, deal with ghosts and bullies. The almost inevitable getting eaten part isn't portrayed graphically (beyond a T. Rex holding a couple of Protoceratops in its mouth), so younger readers who like dinosaurs and enjoy silly humor can enjoy this manga.

Sias, Ryan

    Zoe and Robot: let's pretend. Blue Apple 2011 un il (Balloon Toons) $10.99

    Grades: K 1 2 3   **741.5**

    1. Graphic novels 2. Humorous graphic novels 3. Robots -- Graphic novels 4. Imagination -- Graphic novels

    ISBN 978-1-60905-063-4; 1-60905-063-0

                           LC 2010046829

    A young girl named Zoe wants Robot to play pretend with her, but she has to teach Robot how to pretend, because "Robots do not know how to pretend." From imagining a pile of pillows is a mountain to feeling the wind from a whirring fan, Zoe tries to help Robot. Finally, she draws mountains on a pair of goggles that she puts on Robot.

    "The colorful art and simple panel designs make it easy to follow the story. . . . Beginning readers can easily catch the visual cues that help them interpret the simple dialogue, and they will enjoy the humor. . . . This is a fun, easy-to-read graphic novel for beginning readers." Booklist

Siegel, Siena Cherson

    ★ **To** dance; a ballerina's graphic novel. [by] Siena Cherson Siegel; [illustrated by] Mark Siegel. Simon & Schuster 2006 un il pa $9.99

    Grades: 4 5 6 7   **741.5**

    1. Ballet 2. Authors 3. Novelists 4. Ballet dancers 5. Graphic novels 6. Autobiographical graphic novels 7. Comic book writers 8. Puerto Ricans -- Biography

    ISBN 1-4169-2687-9 pa

    In this memoir of her youth in dance from ages six to eighteen, Siegel tells what it was like to be totally involved in dance, in ballet—all the joys and the physical pain. She worked as a young dancer with George Ballanchine. Her absolute desire to be a dancer took her from her native Puerto Rico to New York City to study. Her simple but heartfelt narration is ably illustrated by her husband Mark Siegel.

The **sign** of the black rock; written and illustrated by Scott Chantler. Kids Can Press 2011 il (Three thieves)

    Grades: 3 4 5 6   **741.5**

    1. Graphic novels 2. Adventure graphic novels

    Three goodhearted fugitives stop at a roadside inn during a ferocious thunderstorm. Narrow escapes ensue as Grig, the scheming and selfish innkeeper, endeavors to capture the trio and secure a reward from the Queen. Tensions mount further as the Queen's Dragons arrive at the tavern, hot on the trail of the fugitives and immediately suspicious of the smarmy Grig.

    "Chantler not only shows an ability to pack plenty of clearly defined action into his graphic panels, but also devel-

ops unusually nuanced characters through glances, gestures, subtleties of facial expression and the occasional quick flashback. . . . Readers should start with the first volume to get the characters' back stories, but here's an animated, breathlessly paced adventure that's just hitting its stride." Kirkus

Slavin, Bill

    Big city Otto: elephants never forget. Kids Can Press 2011 il

    Grades: 3 4 5 6   **741.5**

    1. Graphic novels 2. Adventure graphic novels 3. Elephants -- Fiction

    ISBN 1-55453-476-3; 1-55453-477-1 pa; 978-1-55453-476-0; 978-1-55453-477-7 pa

    "Simpleton pachyderm Otto enlists his friend, a clever green parrot named Crackers, to help him find Otto's very best friend, Georgie, a chimpanzee who was stolen from their African jungle home by 'the man with the wooden nose.' The duo must make their way out of the jungle and soon find themselves across the pond in America, in the big city. When the pair falls in with a gang of crooked gators who take advantage of Otto's unfortunate peanut allergy (to help them steal gator-ade, of course), Otto and Crackers need to learn who is trustworthy—and who is out to take advantage of their naivete. Slavin's lush, full-color illustrations have a yesteryear feel with a dash of European influence." Kirkus

Smith, Jeff

    Bone: crown of horns; by Jeff Smith; with color by Steve Hamaker. Scholastic Graphix 2009 212p il pa $9.99; $19.99

    Grades: 4 5 6 7 8   **741.5**

    1. Graphic novels 2. Fantasy graphic novels 3. Adventure graphic novels

    ISBN 978-0-439-70632-2 pa; 0-439-70632-7 pa; 978-0-439-70631-5; 0-439-70631-9

    "The quality and consistency of both artwork and story makes this series and its climatic conclusion, one of the best graphic novel series for readers of all ages." Voice Youth Advocates

    ★ **Little** Mouse gets ready. TOON Books 2009 32p il $12.95

    Grades: PreK K 1   **741.5**

    1. Graphic novels 2. Humorous graphic novels 3. Mice -- Graphic novels 4. Clothing and dress -- Graphic novels

    ISBN 978-1-935179-01-6; 1-935179-01-2

                           LC 2008-55403

    ALA ALSC Geisel Award Honor Book (2010)

    "Little Mouse is eager to go to the barn with his mother. He slowly and methodically gets dressed, which is quite an accomplishment for the little guy, only to be reminded, in classic noodlehead fashion, that mice don't wear clothes. . . . The cartoon illustrations are large and uncomplicated without being babyish, and the punch line is preceded with places for knowing giggles." SLJ

Snider, Jesse

    Toy Story; some assembly required. [by] Jesse Snider and Jake Black; illustrated by Tanya Roberts . . . [et al.] Boom Kids 2010 un il pa $9.99

Grades: 3 4 5 6 **741.5**

   1. Graphic novels 2. Toys -- Graphic novels

   ISBN 978-1-60886-570-3; 1-60886-570-3

"The toys are afraid that Andy will be bringing home some new (and possibly better) toys from the dinosaur museum so they decide to tag along on the trip. . . . The characters are true to the animated adventures, which will make loyal fans happy. The colors are vibrant and help to convey the mood of each illustration." SLJ

Sonishi, Kenji

   Leave it to PET!: the misadventures of a recycled super robot, vol. 1; story & art by Kenji Sonishi; translation, Katherine Schilling; touch-up art & lettering, John Hunt; editor, Traci N. Todd. Viz Media/VizKids 2009 192p il $7.99

Grades: 3 4 5 6 **741.5**

   1. Manga 2. Graphic novels 3. Humorous graphic novels 4. Recycling -- Graphic novels

   ISBN 978-1-4215-2649-2

PET (polyethylene terephthalate, a type of recyclable plastic) was a simple plastic bottle until nine-year-old Noboru recycled him. Now PET is a super robot programmed to "repay" Noboru for recycling him by helping him. Unfortunately for Noboru, PET's help usually ends up causing even more trouble; being a super robot doesn't mean PET has a clue about what he is doing. The book includes lots of short stories that follow the formula of Noboru getting into a bit of a fix, calling for PET, then getting into more trouble as PET does the wrong thing. Some of the stories do include some information about recycling plastics and aluminum, which is done somewhat differently in Japan than in the U.S.

Soo, Kean

   Jellaby: monster in the city. Hyperion Books 2009 172p il pa $9.99

Grades: 4 5 6 7 8 9 **741.5**

   1. Graphic novels 2. Fantasy graphic novels 3. Monsters -- Graphic novels 4. Friendship -- Graphic novels

   ISBN 978-1-4231-0565-7 pa; 1-4231-0565-6 pa

Beginning right where the first book ended, Portia, Jason, and Jellaby continue on their way to Toronto, walking after Portia panicked and they got off the train. They're searching for a way home for Jellaby, and they think a door somewhere in Exhibition Place, where the Canadian National Exhibition is taking place, holds a clue. Portia feels torn between wanting to help her friend yet not wanting to say goodbye forever, and her ambivalence causes a rift between her and Jason. When she doesn't want to trust a masked magician who seems to know too much about them and Jellaby, Portia leaves Jason. They all end up in the Automotive Building, where the masked man leads Jason and Jellaby down below the building, while Portia seems to find her long lost father. But is he really her father, and just what is waiting for Jason and Jellaby under the Automotive Building? Soo again uses a mostly purple color palette.

Spires, Ashley

   ★ **Binky** the space cat. Kids Can Press 2009 64p il $16.95; pa $7.95

Grades: 2 3 4 5 **741.5**

   1. Graphic novels 2. Humorous graphic novels 3. Cats -- Graphic novels 4. Space flight -- Graphic novels

   ISBN 978-1-55453-309-1; 1-55453-309-0; 978-1-55453-419-7 pa; 1-55453-419-4 pa

Binky the cat lives with two humans (an unnamed mother and son) in what he thinks of as a space station. He's determined to become a space cat and venture into outer space with his stuffed mousie Ted, and to that end he gets his space cat kit through the mail, complete with instructions to build a space ship.

"Spires's mix of sly, dry and slapstick humor in her first graphic novel is perfect. . . . Details in the muted watercolor illustrations, like mousie Ted covering his nose as Binky releases 'space gas,' will keep readers of all ages giggling, whether they're cat lovers or not." Kirkus

   Other titles about Binky are:

   Binky to the rescue (2010)

   Binky under pressure (2011)

Stanley, John

   Little Lulu, vol. 1: My dinner with Lulu; [by] John Stanley and Irving Tripp. Dark Horse Comics 2005 200p il pa $9.95

Grades: 4 5 6 7 8 9 10 11 12 Adult **741.5**

   1. Graphic novels 2. Humorous graphic novels 3. Friendship -- Graphic novels

   ISBN 1-59307-318-6

Lulu Moppet plays with best friend Tubby, except when he hangs out with the other neighborhood boys and tries to keep girls out of their clubhouse; she deals with terrible toddler Alvin by weaving extravagant tales featuring herself; and other everyday adventures. This is the first volume of a series that will eventually reprint every Little Lulu comic for new young readers.

   Other titles in this series are:

   Little Lulu vol. 2: Sunday afternoon

   Little Lulu vol. 3: Lulu in the doghouse

   Little Lulu vol. 4: Lulu goes shopping

   Little Lulu vol. 5: Lulu takes a trip

   Little Lulu vol. 6: Letters to Santa

   Little Lulu vol. 7: Lulu's umbrella

   Little Lulu vol. 8: Late for school

   Little Lulu vol. 9: Lucky Lulu

   Little Lulu vol. 10: All dressed up

   Little Lulu vol. 11: April fools

   Little Lulu vol. 12: Leave it to Lulu

   Little Lulu vol. 13: Too much fun

Steig, Jeanne

   ★ **Cats,** dogs, men, women, ninnies, & clowns; the lost art of William Steig. with illustrations by William Steig. Abrams 2011 il $40

Grades: Adult Professional **741.5**

   1. Artists 2. Authors 3. Cartoonists 4. Illustrators 5. American wit and humor 6. Authors, American 7. Children's authors

   ISBN 978-0-8109-9577-2; 0-8109-9577-8

                      LC 2010041853

"A treasure trove of hundreds of previously unpublished illustrations by children's book icon Steig, this compendium is organized thematically (people, dogs, 'odd ducks,' etc.); the late Steig's wife, Jeanne, introduces each section with delightful, insightful anecdotes." Publ Wkly

Steinberg, David

★ **Sound** off! by D. J. Steinberg; illustrated by Brian Smith. Grosset & Dunlap 2008 un il (Adventures of Daniel Boom AKA Loud Boy) pa $5.99

Grades: 3 4 5   **741.5**

1. Graphic novels 2. Superhero graphic novels
ISBN 978-0-448-44698-1

LC 2007019009

"Bursting with action, color, and intriguing characters . . . this works in every way. Smith's visual wit, which puts a retro gloss on cartoon art of the 1950s, is on display without sidetracking the story, and pacing and plotting are superb." Booklist

Steinke, Aron Nels

The **Super** Duper Dog Park. Blue Apple Books 2011 il (Balloon toons) $10.99

Grades: K 1 2 3   **741.5**

1. Graphic novels 2. Dogs -- Fiction 3. Amusement parks -- Fiction
ISBN 978-1-60905-093-1; 1-60905-093-2

LC 2011019077

Dog lovers and their canine friends make their way to the Super Duper Dog Park on Dog Island, where dogs ride bicycles, make music, and enjoy a perfect day.

"Steinke's text is geared to be easy reading, but it is not without cleverness: snatches of rhyme or onomatopoeic devices that give a good taste of sound. . . . The artwork follows the text's accessible engagement. . . . Both colorful and high spirited, this title will give new readers a good run for their money." Kirkus

Stephens, Jay

Heroes! draw your own superheroes, gadget geeks & other do-gooders. [by] Jay Stephens. Lark Books 2007 64p il $12.95; pa $5.95

Grades: 4 5 6 7   **741.5**

1. Drawing 2. Superheroes 3. Cartoons and caricatures
ISBN 978-1-57990-934-5; 1-57990-934-5; 978-1-60059-179-2 pa; 1-60059-179-5 pa

LC 2006101661

"Stephens shows just how to draw [superheroes]. . . . Stephens does a good job organizing his material, beginning with a bit of history, then moving quickly to hero heads, . . . and on to masks, disguises, physical features, power effects, and action moves. The brightly colored illustrations offer plenty of how-to info and lots of great heroes, male and female, to use as models." Booklist

Monsters! draw your own mutants, freaks & creeps. [by] Jay Stephens. Lark Books 2007 64p il $12.95; pa $5.95

Grades: 4 5 6 7   **741.5**

1. Drawing 2. Monsters in art 3. Cartoons and caricatures
ISBN 978-1-57990-935-2; 1-57990-935-3; 978-1-60059-178-5 pa; 1-60059-178-7 pa

LC 2006036104

This offers instruction in drawing such cartoon monsters as Dockula, the aquatic nibbler; Skeeterman, the campground creep; and Spook Ook, the attic thumper

Robots! draw your own androids, cyborgs & fighting bots. [by] Jay Stephens. Lark Books 2007 64p il $12.95

Grades: 4 5 6 7   **741.5**

1. Drawing 2. Robots in art 3. Cartoons and caricatures
ISBN 978-1-57990-937-6; 1-57990-937-X

LC 2007027637

"With simple detailed instructions, an inviting text, and entertaining cartoon scenarios, . . . Stephens explains, step by step, how to draw a variety of robots." Booklist

Storrie, Paul D.

★ **Beowulf**; monster slayer: a British legend. story by Paul D. Storrie; pencils and inks by Ron Randall. Lerner Publishing Group/Graphic Universe 2008 48p il (Graphic myths and legends) lib bdg $26.60

Grades: 4 5 6 7   **741.5**

1. Graphic novels 2. Monsters -- Graphic novels
ISBN 978-0-8225-6757-8 lib bdg; 0-8225-6757-1 lib bdg

LC 2006-39094

An adaptation of the epic poem in which the hero Beowulf slays the monster Grendel

This "reads like ancient poetry. . . . The action and character design are strong and clear, with solid, comfortable storytelling that is strongly helped by capable color artwork." SLJ

Sturm, James

★ **Adventures** in cartooning; how to turn your doodles into comics. [by] James Sturm, Andrew Arnold, Alexis Frederick-Frost. First Second 2009 109p il pa $12.95

Grades: 2 3 4 5   **741.5**

1. Drawing 2. Graphic novels 3. Graphic novels -- Authorship 4. Comic books, strips, etc. -- Authorship 5. Cartooning -- Technique -- Juvenile literature
ISBN 978-1-59643-369-4 pa; 1-59643-369-8 pa

"In fairy-tale fashion, the Magic Cartooning Elf helps a young princess with writer's block produce her first comic. A story-within-a-story emerges. . . . Simple cartooning basics offered after the story are quite appealing; even the most reluctant artist may be inspired to pick up a pencil and give it a shot. Entertaining and surprisingly edifying." Kirkus

Telgemeier, Raina

Drama; Raina Telgemeier; with color by Gurihiru. 1st ed. Graphix 2012 233 p. chiefly ill.

Grades: 3 4 5 6 7   **741.5**

1. Graphic novels 2. School stories 3. Middle schools -- Fiction 4. Schools -- Fiction 5. Theater -- Fiction 6. Interpersonal relations -- Fiction
ISBN 0545326982; 0545326990; 9780545326988; 9780545326995

LC 2011040748

Stonewall Honor Book (2013)

Author Raina Telgemeier's book focuses on a middle school drama production. "Callie loves theater . . . [S]he's the set designer for the stage crew, and this year she's determined to create a set worthy of Broadway on a middle-school budget. But how can she, when she doesn't know much about carpentry, ticket sales are down, and the crew members are having trouble working together?" (Publisher's note)

Includes bibliographical references

★ **Smile**. Scholastic/Graphix 2010 213p il $21.99; pa $10.99

Grades: 5 6 7 8 **741.5**
1. Graphic novels 2. Autobiographical graphic novels 3. Dentistry -- Graphic novels 4. Friendship -- Graphic novels 5. Graphic novels -- Juvenile literature 6. Personal appearance -- Graphic novels
ISBN 978-0-545-13205-3; 0-545-13205-3; 978-0-545-13206-0 pa; 0-545-13206-1 pa

LC 2008-51782

Boston Globe-Horn Book Award honor book: Nonfiction (2010)

Sixth grader Raina just wants to be normal, but when she falls down going home from a Girl Scout meeting, she severely injures her two front teeth, and this starts her down a long road with braces, surgery, retainers, embarrassing headgear—all sure to make her stand out from her middle school classmates for all the wrong reasons. There's also a major earthquake, then boy confusion, friends who turn out not to be good friends, sibling jealousy, all the stuff that makes life interesting, if not fun. Telgemeier wrote and drew the autobiographical Smile as a webcomic; this volume collects the story in color.

"The dental case that Telgemeier documents in this graphic memoir was extreme: a random accident led to front tooth loss when she was 12, and over the next several years, she suffered through surgery, implants, headgear, false teeth, and a rearrangement of her remaining incisors. . . . Both adults and kids . . . are vividly and rapidly portrayed. . . . Telgemeier's storytelling and full-color cartoony images form a story that will cheer and inspire any middle-schooler dealing with orthodontia." Booklist

Thielbar, Melinda
The **ancient** formula; a mystery with fractions. illustrated by Tintin Pantoja. Graphic Universe 2010 46p il (Manga math mysteries) lib bdg $29.27
Grades: 1 2 3 4 **741.5**
1. Graphic novels 2. Mystery graphic novels 3. Kung fu -- Graphic novels 4. Schools -- Graphic novels 5. Mathematics -- Graphic novels
ISBN 978-0-7613-4907-5 lib bdg; 0-7613-4907-3 lib bdg

LC 2010001431

The students of Sifu Faiza's Kung Fu School use their knowledge of fractions as they try to discover what happened to Leung Jan's long-lost healing formula.

"The book is a great read and provides the reader with mathematical instruction, practice solving problems, and entertainment all at once. . . . The images and colors are exciting and vibrant." Sci Books Films

Thompson, Jill
Magic Trixie; written and illustrated by Jill Thompson; lettered by Jason Arthur. Harper Trophy 2008 93p il pa $7.99
Grades: 3 4 5 **741.5**
1. Graphic novels 2. Fantasy graphic novels 3. Humorous graphic novels 4. Magic -- Graphic novels
ISBN 978-0-06-117045-4 pa

LC 2007-24298

Magic Trixie is feeling a bit put out; everything in her house seems to revolve around her baby sister, and she doesn't get to do anything fun. If that wasn't bad enough, Show & Tell time is coming up at Monstersorri School, and

all her classmates have seen all her tricks too many times. She'll have to come up with a new one that's really special.

"Bright colors and a whimsical style make everything friendly rather than scary. Underneath the supernatural trappings lies a classical story of sibling envy to which every big sister and big brother can relate." Booklist
Other titles in this series are:
Magic Trixie sleeps over (2008)
Magic Trixie and the dragon (2009)

★ **Scary** Godmother; written and illustrated by Jill Thompson. Dark Horse 2010 207p il $24.99
Grades: 3 4 5 **741.5**
1. Graphic novels 2. Supernatural graphic novels 3. Halloween -- Graphic novels
ISBN 978-1-59582-589-6; 1-59582-589-4

It's Halloween night and it's up to Scary Godmother to show one little girl just how much fun spooky can be! Meet Hannah Marie, who, with the help of Scary Godmother, stands up to her mean-spirited cousin Jimmy and her fear of monsters on her first Halloween adventure with the big kids. Later, Hannah joins forces with Orson, the vampire boy, to unravel a mystery near and dear to their hearts.

This is a "collection compiling all four of Thompson's original Scary Godmother stories plus extra goodies. Told in often-rhyming prose and word balloons on vibrant pages that balance a visually lavish picture book aesthetic with sequential-art page composition, the stories burst with complex color tones and creepy cartoon figures." Booklist

Torres, J.
Into the woods; J. Torres; illustrated by Faith Erin Hicks. Kids Can Press 2012 100 p. col. ill. (hardcover) $17.95
Grades: 1 2 3 4 5 **741.5**
1. Magic -- Graphic novels 2. Sasquatch -- Graphic novels 3. Totems and totemism -- Graphic novels
ISBN 1554537118; 9781554537112

In this graphic fantasy novel, "city boy Rufus is staying at his grandmother's house on the edge of a forest for a few days without his parents," and he "decides to explore the woods. He meets a girl named Penny. . . . When looking for her in the woods, Rufus finds a glowing necklace in a tree. After reading the word on the back, he turns into Bigfoot! . . . There's danger in the forest as well as magic, and when Penny disappears, Rufus . . . use[s] the totem to effect a rescue." (Kirkus Reviews)

Townsend, Michael
Kit Feeny: on the move. Alfred A. Knopf 2009 un il lib bdg $12.99; pa $5.99
Grades: 3 4 5 **741.5**
1. Graphic novels 2. Moving -- Fiction 3. Bullies -- Fiction 4. Friendship -- Fiction
ISBN 978-0-375-95614-0 lib bdg; 0-375-95614-X lib bdg; 978-0-375-85614-3 pa; 0-375-85614-5 pa

LC 2008-37443

When plucky Kit Feeny moves to a new town, he immediately makes an enemy of the sadistic school bully and must struggle to find friends who share his interests.

"Kit, a mischievous, silly, ambiguous anthropomorphic animal, . . . is an easy hero to cheer for in this graphic novel, which reluctant readers will find hard to put down." Booklist
Another title about Kit Feeny is:

Kit Feeny: the ugly necklace (2009)

Kit Feeny: the ugly necklace. Alfred A. Knopf 2009 un lib bdg $12.99; pa $5.99
Grades: 3 4 5 **741.5**
1. Graphic novels 2. Bears -- Fiction 3. Gifts -- Fiction 4. Family life -- Fiction
ISBN 978-0-375-95615-7 lib bdg; 0-375-95615-8 lib bdg; 978-0-375-85615-0 pa; 0-375-85615-3 pa
LC 2008040155

Kit Feeny, a young bear, enters into a competition with his sisters to see who can give their mother the best birthday present

Trondheim, Lewis
Monster Christmas; [Joe Johnson, translation; Lea Hernandez, lettering] Papercutz 2011 32p il (Monster) $9.99
Grades: K 1 2 3 **741.5**
1. Graphic novels 2. Monsters -- Graphic novels 3. Christmas -- Graphic novels 4. Family life -- Graphic novels
ISBN 978-1-59707-288-5; 1-59707-288-5
Orginal French edition, 1999

"A brother, Petey, and a sister, Jean, go on a Christmas vacation to the snowy mountains with their Mom and Dad and pet monster, Kriss. On the way they encounter another monster chasing Santa Claus and have to rely on their creativity, quick thinking, and a monster of their own to save Santa and themselves. Both Trondheim's art and the English-language translation create a story that could come from the mind of a child, despite its bizarre creatures and sudden surprises. Yet it's also the work of a talented artist channeling that childish wonder into a finely crafted tale for young audiences." Publ Wkly

Tiny Tyrant; by Lewis Trondheim; translated from the French by Alexis Siegel; illustrated by Fabrice Parme. First Second Books 2007 124p il $12.95
Grades: 4 5 6 7 8 9 10 11 12 Adult **741.5**
1. Graphic novels 2. Humorous graphic novels
ISBN 978-1-59643-094-5
LC 2006021479

"Tiny child-king Ethelbert is spoiled and difficult, expecting to have his every whim fulfilled-or else. . . . In the end, though, he becomes a hero. The dynamic cartoons are filled with details and riddled with humor; most pages have between six and eight small pictures. . . . This title will have wide appeal. It's young and accessible enough for elementary-grade kids, but teens will also be charmed by the rascally king." SLJ

Varon, Sara
Bake sale. First Second 2011 157p il $19.99; pa $16.99
Grades: 3 4 5 6 **741.5**
1. Graphic novels 2. Cupcakes -- Graphic novels 3. Bakers and bakeriesGraphic novels
ISBN 978-1-59643-740-1; 1-59643-740-5; 978-1-59643-419-6 pa; 1-59643-419-8 pa
LC 2010051587

"The book has a mellow, easygoing feel, using soft colors and showing many yummy foods. As an added bonus, recipes for how to make the various scrumptious meals read-

ers watch Cupcake prepare are provided. . . . Varon's art is simple and cozy, making this sweet tale a confection of its own." Publ Wkly

Venable, Colleen A. F.
Hamster and cheese; illustrated by Stephanie Yue. Graphic Universe 45p il (Guinea Pig, pet shop private eye) lib bdg $27.93; pa $6.95
Grades: 2 3 4 **741.5**
1. Mystery graphic novels 2. Animals -- Graphic novels 3. Hamsters -- Graphic novels 4. Guinea pigs -- Graphic novels
ISBN 978-0-7613-4598-5 lib bdg; 0-7613-4598-1 lib bdg; 978-0-7613-5479-6 pa; 0-7613-5479-4 pa

"Who is stealing Mr. Venezi's sandwiches? The befuddled pet-shop owner misidentifies the store's animals, leading the hamsters to think they're koalas. . . . Hamisher the koala-hamster thinks Sasspants the guinea pig is a private investigator because the second G on her cage's sign has fallen off, so he asks her to investigate. . . . Young readers will appreciate the zaniness of the pet shop and the fun mystery, and Yue's colorful art uses a straightforward panel design that's easy to follow." Booklist

Other titles in this series are:
And then there were gnomes (2010)
The ferret's a foot (2011)
Fish you were here (2011)

Venditti, Robert
★ The **lightning** thief: the graphic novel; by Rick Riordan; adapted by Robert Venditti; art by Attila Futaki; color by Jose Villarrubia; layouts by Orpheus Collar; lettering by Chris Dickey. Disney/Hyperion Books 2010 un il (Percy Jackson and the Olympians) $19.99; pa $9.99
Grades: 5 6 7 8 **741.5**
1. Graphic novels 2. Greek mythology -- Graphic novels
ISBN 978-1-4231-1696-7; 1-4231-1696-8; 978-1-4231-1710-0 pa; 1-4231-1710-7 pa
LC 2010035512

After learning that he is the son of a mortal woman and Poseidon, god of the sea, twelve-year-old Percy is sent to a summer camp for demigods like himself, and joins his new friends on a quest to prevent a war between the gods.

This graphic novel adaptation of Rick Riordan's novel "succeeds in spectacular fashion. . . . The book retains the excellent pacing of the original and gives a face to Riordan's vision of the mythological made modern. Futaki's artwork is exemplary but what leaves such a lasting impression is Villarrubia's coloring, which reveals both subtlety and spectacle when needed." Publ Wkly

Vernon, Ursula
Dragonbreath: curse of the were-wiener. Dial Books for Young Readers 2010 208p il $12.99
Grades: 3 4 5 6 7 **741.5**
1. School stories 2. Dragons -- Fiction 3. Iguanas -- Fiction 4. Frankfurters -- Fiction
ISBN 978-0-8037-3469-2; 0-8037-3469-7
LC 2009049358

When Danny Dragonbreath's best friend Wendell the iguana is bitten by one of the hot dogs from his school lunch, he begins to turn into a were-wiener.

"The book is just spooky enough for young readers who don't want to get too scared, and it features the return of the monster potato salad." Booklist

Walker, Landry Q.

The **Incredibles**: secrets & lies; writer, Landry Walker; artist, Marcio Takara. Boom Kids! 2010 un il pa $9.99
Grades: 3 4 5 6 **741.5**
1. Graphic novels 2. Superhero graphic novels
ISBN 978-1-60886-583-3; 1-60886-583-5

Mrs. Incredible must save the day when the Eiffel Tower explodes; and Mr. Incredible, Dash, and Violet track down a mysterious thief.

"The illustrations are true to the popular movies. . . . This fast-paced story with well-known characters will engage readers." SLJ

Walt Disney's Uncle Scrooge; around the world in 80 bucks. Boom Kids! 2010 un il pa $9.99
Grades: 3 4 5 6 **741.5**
1. Graphic novels
ISBN 978-1-60886-566-6; 1-60886-566-5

Follows Uncle Scrooge and Donald's adventures, after his rival John D. Rockerduck challenges Scrooge to travel around the world on a budget.

"Disney fans, both children and adults, will enjoy [this] graphic [novel]." SLJ

Watson, Andi

★ **Glister** and the haunted teapot. Image Comics 2007 un il pa $5.99
Grades: 4 5 6 **741.5**
1. Graphic novels 2. Ghosts -- Graphic novels
ISBN 978-1-58240-853-8 pa; 1-58240-853-X pa

"Strange things happen around Glister Butterworth, and that is why she does not bat an eye when a haunted teapot arrives at her door. It is haunted by the ghost of Phillip Bulwark-Stratton, whose long-winded literary works have fallen out of favor. . . . British author/artist Watson, creator of the fan-favorite Skeleton Key aims at a younger but still sophisticated audience with his new bi-monthly series. . . . Each issue will be digest-sized and include a self-contained story. Fans of the series will want to read every issue." Voice Youth Advocates

Weigel, Jeff

★ **Thunder** from the sea; adventure on board the HMS Defender. G. P. Putnam's Sons 2010 46p il $17.99
Grades: 3 4 5 6 **741.5**
1. Graphic novels 2. Adventure graphic novels 3. Naval art and science -- Graphic novels
ISBN 978-0-399-25089-7
LC 2009-32801

In 1805, during the Napoleonic Wars, twelve-year-old Jack Hoyton becomes a member of the crew of HMS Defender, a midsize ship in the British Royal Navy. The Defender patrols along a portion of the French coast to block French ships, but a major gun emplacement in Dumont hampers the ship's efforts. When some of the crew land to fill their barrels with fresh water, French gunmen fire upon them, killing an officer and wounding a crewman. The Captain assigns Jack to be part of the crew that will land and take the guns; when the men arrive, they find that there

is no small village, but a major shipbuilding facility, and they're captured.

"Weigel's old-fashioned comics art shows lots of authentic details of eighteenth-century shipboard life, and there is some battle violence. . . . This picture-book-size graphic novel should find a ready audience of young adventure-loving readers." Booklist

Includes bibliographical references

Wetterer, Margaret K.

The **snowshoeing** adventure of Milton Daub, blizzard trekker; by Margaret K. Wetterer and Charles M. Wetterer; adaptation by Emma Carlson Berne; illustrated by Zachary Trover. Graphic Universe 2011 31p il (History's kid heroes) lib bdg $26.60; pa $8.95
Grades: 2 3 4 **741.5**
1. Graphic novels 2. Adventure graphic novels 3. Snowshoers 4. Blizzards -- Graphic novels
ISBN 978-0-7613-6175-6 lib bdg; 0-7613-6175-8 lib bdg; 978-0-7613-6194-7 pa; 0-7613-6194-4 pa
LC 2009051717

An 1888 blizzard has paralyzed much of the Northeast United States, but twelve-year-old Milton Daub puts on a pair of homemade snowshoes and braves the storm to bring food and medicine to many of his neighbors in the Bronx, New York.

This book provides an "exciting [glimpse] into the past, with just the right amount of tension and intensity to capture readers' attention. . . . [It] will serve as [a] good [introduction] to graphic novels and historical fiction for early readers. Added bonuses are the brief yet informative [introduction] and [afterword] providing more facts about the [setting]." SLJ

Includes bibliographical references

White, Mike

Amity Blamity, book one. SLG 2011 un il pa $10.95
Grades: 4 5 6 **741.5**
1. Graphic novels 2. Farm life -- Graphic novels
ISBN 978-1-59362-209-1; 1-59362-209-0

"Four-year-old Gretchen doesn't speak. Thankfully, she's got her potbellied pig, Chester, who's not only something of a motormouth but an ambitious one at that. He's the founder of Pig Corp. . . . Their main threat is Gretchen's lazy ex-jailbird uncle, Downey. . . . The resulting humor is enjoyable funny-paper fare. . . . Quirky talking-animal fare with just enough edge to tickle." Booklist

Wight, Eric

★ **Frankie** Pickle and the closet of doom; written and illustrated by Eric Wight. Simon & Schuster Books for Young Readers 2009 79p il $9.99
Grades: 2 3 4 5 **741.5**
1. Graphic novels 2. Humorous graphic novels 3. Cleanliness -- Fiction 4. Family life -- Fiction 5. Imagination -- Fiction 6. Family life -- Graphic novels 7. Orderliness -- Graphic novels
ISBN 978-1-4169-6484-1; 1-4169-6484-3
LC 2008-30865

Fourth-grader Frankie Piccolini has a vivid imagination when it comes to cleaning his disastrously messy room, but eventually even he decides that it is just too dirty.

"Wight's hilarious twists of language are matched with a wicked sense of fun in the illustrations and frequent sequential-paneled episodes of pretend play." Kirkus

Other titles about Frankie Pickle are:

Frankie Pickle and the Pine Run 3000 (2010)

Frankie Pickle and the mathematical menace (2011)

Zornow, Jeff

The **legend** of Sleepy Hollow; adapted and illustrated by Jeff Zornow; based upon the works of Washington Irving. Magic Wagon 2007 un il (Graphic horror) $18.95

Grades: 5 6 7 8 9 10 11 12　　　　　**741.5**

ISBN 978-1-60270-060-4; 1-60270-060-5

LC 2007-9615

This "is an entertaining and faithful, if much adapted version of Irving's classic story. Zornow's illustrations are the highlight of the work, successfully bringing the characters of the story to life." Booklist

741.6　Graphic design, illustration, commercial art

★ **Artist** to artist; 23 major illustrators talk to children about their art. Philomel Books 2007 105p il $30

Grades: 4 5 6 7　　　　　**741.6**

1. Illustrators 2. Illustration of books 3. Picture books for children

ISBN 978-0-399-24600-5

"This anthology celebrates and elucidates contemporary picture-book art. . . . Ashley Bryan, Quentin Blake, Leo Lionni, Alice Provensen, and Gennady Spirin are among the contributors, whose comments are formatted as signed letters illustrated with childhood photographs. . . . Each artist includes glorious self-portraits and a gatefold page that reveals a marvelous array of sketches, color mixes, and studio scenes. All readers will find something that piques curiosity or provides insight." Booklist

Carle, Eric

The **art** of Eric Carle. Philomel Bks. 1996 125p il $35; pa $19.99

Grades: Adult Professional　　　　　**741.6**

1. Illustration of books 2. Picture books for children

ISBN 0-399-22937-X; 0-399-24002-0 pa

LC 95-24940

This is "both a textual and visual anthology: in addition to Carle's autobiographical chapter and the text of his 1990 speech at the Library of Congress, chapters include accolades from Ann Beneduce (Carle's U.S. editor) and from Dr. Viktor Christen (Carle's German editor). A photoessay on the artist's collage technique rubs shoulders with a forty-page gallery of his illustrations over the last quarter of a century, which precedes a look at some of his quick sketches and an illustrated bibliography of his oeuvre. The book's inviting layout may appeal to artistic youngsters as well as grown Carle fans, and the information about his working process, particularly the technical details, is absorbing." Bull Cent Child Books

Ellabbad, Mohieddine

The **illustrator's** notebook; [translated from the Arabic by Sarah Quinn] Groundwood Books/House of Anansi Press 2006 30p il $16.95

Grades: 5 6 7 8　　　　　**741.6**

1. Artists 2. Illustrators 3. Illustration of books 4. Illustration of books -- Juvenile literature

ISBN 0-88899-700-0

"Part children's book, part autobiography, part design treatise, this hard-to-categorize Egyptian import is full of wonders from start to finish. Ellabbad uses excerpts from his notebooks to discuss ways of seeing art from an artist's perspective and as someone from an Arabic culture. Printed like the Egyptian edition—read right to left—the pages are magnificently and surprisingly illustrated, juxtaposing Arabic script (English translations appear in the margins), watercolor paintings, pasted-in photos and pictures from comic books, and all manner of characters from Eastern and Western cultures." SLJ

Evans, Dilys

★ **Show** & tell; exploring the fine art of children's book illustration. [by] Dilys Evans. Chronicle Books 2008 143p il $24.99

Grades: Adult Professional　　　　　**741.6**

1. Illustrators 2. Illustration of books

ISBN 978-0-8118-4971-5; 0-8118-4971-6

LC 2006027981

This "book focuses on twelve illustrators, ranging from classic stars such as Hilary Knight and Trina Schart Hyman to new talents such as Bryan Collier and David Shannon; each . . . chapter talks about the artist's process and life and explores in depth the artistic achievements in particular books, with page reproductions included for close viewing and exploration. The style is chatty yet informed, and the careful scrutiny of the illustrations will be conceptually enlightening to many readers seeking to develop their skill in assessing art." Bull Cent Child Books

Kushner, Tony

The **art** of Maurice Sendak; 1980 to present. text by Tony Kushner. Abrams 2003 223p il $60

Grades: Adult Professional　　　　　**741.6**

1. Artists 2. Authors 3. Illustrators 4. Set designers 5. Children's authors

ISBN 0-8109-4448-0

LC 2003-9293

This "collection presents 350 illustrations, many of which are drawings for set and costume design work, . . . others of which are posters for plays and for events such as the New York is Book Country fair. . . . Sendak's precise, intensely shaded yet welcoming shapes and figures have lost none of their luster. They would ordinarily be enough in themselves in a survey like this, but Kushner's lovely, funny, partisan text . . . lifts the book to another level." Publ Wkly

Includes bibliographical references

Maguire, Gregory

Making mischief; a Maurice Sendak appreciation. William Morrow 2009 200p il $27.50

Grades: Adult Professional　　　　　**741.6**

1. Artists 2. Authors 3. Illustrators 4. Set designers

5. Children's authors
ISBN 978-0-06-168916-1; 0-06-168916-5
LC 2009017357

"Maguire constructs a thoughtful and accessible overview of Sendak's works and artistic process, making for a tender homage to the famed artist that only a true fan could produce. . . . He presents a series of five essays, expounding upon the various influences seen in Sendak's work. . . as well as an analysis of motifs and techniques. Maguire often allows the art to speak for itself, displaying a generous selection of Sendak's illustrations, both famed and lesser known." Bull Cent Child Books

Nahson, Claudia J.
The **snowy** day and the art of Ezra Jack Keats; Claudia J. Nahson; with an essay by Maurice Berger. Jewish Museum, under the auspices of the Jewish Theological Seminary of America 2011 104p il $27.50
Grades: Adult Professional
741.6
1. Artists 2. Authors 3. Illustrators 4. Authors, American 5. Children's authors
ISBN 978-0-300-17022-1; 0-300-17022-X
LC 2011007880

"Keats's Caldecott-winning story about a boy's wintertime exploration of his neighborhood turns 50 in 2012; this fascinating examination of Keats and his oeuvre, complete with 80 full-color reproductions, coincides with the first major U.S. exhibition devoted to his work. . . . Nahson, curator at the Jewish Museum, writes that The Snowy Day reflected Keats's interest in 'rendering visible what has hitherto been invisible to his audience, be that an inner-city child, a message graffitied on a wall, or a dilapidated building.' Her essay joins one from historian/art critic Maurice Berger that makes abundantly clear the book's societal importance." Publ Wkly

Includes bibliographical references

Neuburger, Emily K.
★ A **Caldecott** celebration; seven artists and their paths to the Caldecott medal. rev ed.; Walker & Co. 2008 55p il $19.95; lib bdg $20.85
Grades: Adult Professional
741.6
1. Illustrators 2. Caldecott Medal 3. Illustration of books
ISBN 978-0-8027-9703-2; 0-8027-9703-2; 978-0-8027-9704-9 lib bdg; 0-8027-9704-0 lib bdg
LC 2007-23132

First published 1998
Profiles seven Caldecott award winning books and their authors, including Robert McCloskey's "Make Way for Ducklings," Marcia Brown's "Cinderella," Maurice Sendak's "Where the Wild Things Are," William Steig's "Sylvester and the Magic Pebble," Chris Van Allsburg's "Jumanji," David Wiesner's "Tuesday," and Mordicai Gerstein's "The Man Who Walked Between the Towers"

"The value of this volume is that Marcus makes these exceptional author/illustrators, and the processes by which they created their award-winning picture books, accessible to children and to adults who value children's literature." SLJ

Reading Is Fundamental, Inc.
The **art** of reading; forty illustrators celebrate RIF's 40th anniversary. with a foreword by Leonard S. Marcus. Dutton Bks. 2005 96p il lib bdg $19.99
Grades: Adult Professional
741.6
1. Illustrators 2. Illustration of books
ISBN 0-525-47484-6

"Forty well-known, well-loved children's book illustrators share memories of a book . . . seminal to their development as readers and artists, and offer accompanying pieces of art—reimagined from those books. . . . This is a lovingly conceived, cohesive, and distinctively designed treasure. . . . Leonard S. Marcus's insightful and affecting foreword sets just the right anticipatory tone for readers who will be treated to spectacular pictures and often-moving personal statements." SLJ

Say, Allen
★ **Drawing** from memory; Allen Say. 1st ed. Scholastic Press 2011 63 p. il map $17.99
Grades: 3 4 5 6
741.6
1. Artists 2. Authors 3. Illustrators 4. Autobiography -- Graphic novels 5. Children's authors 6. Japanese Americans -- Biography
ISBN 9780545176866; 0545176867
LC 2011016324

Sibert Honor Book, 2012
This book "opens with a . . . watercolor map of Japan on the left, framed in a rectangle, while on the right is a . . watercolor of Yokohama's seashore and fishing village, with two black-and-white photographs pasted on: Say as a child, and the stone beach wall. The early arc takes readers from [Allen] Say's 1937 birth, through family moves to escape 1941 bombings and then Say's nigh-emancipation at age 12, when his mother supported him in his own Tokyo apartment. The one-room apartment 'was for me to study in, but studying was far from my mind this was going to be my art studio!' The art table's drawer handle resembles a smile. . . . [A]pprenticing with famous cartoonist Noro Shinpei, Say works dedicatedly on comic panels, still-lifes and life drawing. Nothing—not political unrest, not U.S. occupation, not paternal disapproval—derails his singular goal of becoming a cartoonist." (Kirkus)

"Say's account is complex, poignant, and unfailingly honest. Say's fans—and those who also feel the pull of the artist's life—will be captivated." Publ Wkly

Stevens, Janet
From pictures to words; a book about making a book. written and illustrated by Janet Stevens. Holiday House 1995 un il $16.95
Grades: K 1 2 3
741.6
1. Authorship 2. Picture books for children 3. Authorship -- Juvenile literature 4. Creative writing -- Juvenile literature 5. Picture books for children -- Juvenile literature
ISBN 0-8234-1154-0
LC 94-18976

"The straightforward text carefully presents information while maintaining the narrative flow. Dialogue balloons and funny asides from the characters keep the presentation lively." SLJ

Tan, Shaun

★ The **bird** king; an artist's notebook. Shaun Tan. Arthur A. Levine Books 2013 128 p. (hardcover: alk. paper) $19.99

Grades: 3 4 5 6 7   **741.6**
   1. Artists' notebooks
   ISBN 0545465133; 9780545465137
                                                LC 2012016625

This book by author and illustrator Shaun Tan "is a collection of sketches, random jottings, preliminary designs for book, film and theatre projects, sketchbook pages and drawings from life. Each of these represent some aspect of a working process, whereby stories generally evolve from visual research and free-wheeling doodles. They are also 'unfinished' pieces created in a single sitting, not originally intended for publication." (Publisher's note)

Under the spell of the moon; art for children from the world's great illustrators. [edited by Patricia Aldana; texts translated by Stan Dragland] Groundwood Books 2004 80p il $25

   Grades: Adult Professional   **741.6**
   1. Illustrators 2. Illustration of books 3. Illustrated children's books -- Juvenile literature
   ISBN 0888995598

This volume includes the work of thirty-three illustrators of books for children. The illustrators "each have a double page including both their illustration and a short piece of text (written either by them or another author), or a traditional verse or saying. . . . Original texts in a language other than English are included, followed by a translation by Canadian poet and editor Stan Dragland. . . . Age four and up." (Quill Quire)

This "collection features the artwork of children's book illustrators who, together, represent more than 25 countries. Each double-page spread includes a different artist's image accompanied by a poem, nursery rhyme, song, or bit of non-sense that appears in both English and the illustrator's native language. . . . Katherine Paterson offers a stirring introduction that discusses IBBY (The International Board on Books for Young People)." Booklist

741.9   Collections of drawings

Pericoli, Matteo

See the city; the journey of Manhattan unfurled. [by] Matteo Pericoli. Alfred A. Knopf 2004 un il $15.95

Grades: 4 5 6 7   **741.9**
   1. Drawing 2. Drawing -- Technique 3. Manhattan (New York, N.Y.) -- In art
   ISBN 0-375-82469-3
                                                LC 2003-25881

"This depiction of Manhattan began as two continuous scrolls, one of the East Side, one of the West Side, each 37 feet long, which were published in 2001 (Random). The drawings in pen and ink depict the city skyline from the perspective of a boat tour taken around the island by Pericoli. . . . A personal narrative accompanies the drawings, affording insight into the creative processes of writing and illustrating. This is a fascinating work." SLJ

Volavkova, Hana

★ --I never saw another butterfly-- children's drawings and poems from Terezin concentration camp, 1942-1944. edited by Hana Volavková; foreword by Chaim Potok; afterword by Vaclav Havel. expanded 2nd ed; Schocken Bks. 1993 xxii, 106p il hardcover o.p. pa $17.50

Grades: 4 5 6 7   **741.9**
   1. Child artists 2. Children's writings 3. Holocaust, 1933-1945
   ISBN 0-8052-1015-6 pa
                                                LC 92-50477

Original Czech edition, 1959; first American edition published 1964 by McGraw-Hill

"Of the 15,000 children who passed through Terezin before going to Auschwitz, only 100 lived. This book is a collection of poems and drawings by some of them. . . . This touching book adds another facet to library collections on the Holocaust." SLJ

743   Drawing and drawings by subject

Ames, Lee J.

Draw 50 aliens, UFO's galaxy ghouls, milky way marauders, and other extra terrestrial creatures; [by] Lee J. Ames with Ric Estrada. Doubleday 1998 un il (Draw 50) hardcover o.p. pa $8.95

Grades: 4 5 6 7   **743**
   1. Drawing
   ISBN 978-0-385-49144-0; 0-385-49144-1; 978-0-385-49145-7 pa; 0-385-49145-X pa
                                                LC 98-20077

A step-by-step guide to drawing outer space creatures

Draw 50 animals. Doubleday 1974 un il (Draw 50) hardcover o.p. pa $8.95

Grades: 4 5 6 7   **743**
   1. Drawing 2. Animal painting and illustration
   ISBN 978-0-385-07712-5; 0-385-07712-2; 978-0-385-19519-5 pa; 0-385-19519-2 pa
                                                LC 73-13083

This book provides step-by-step instructions for drawing animals ranging from penguins and seals to elephants and monkeys

Draw 50 athletes. Doubleday 1985 un il (Draw 50) hardcover o.p. pa $8.95

Grades: 4 5 6 7   **743**
   1. Drawing 2. Athletes in art
   ISBN 978-0-385-19055-8; 0-385-19055-7; 978-0-385-24638-5 pa; 0-385-24638-2 pa
                                                LC 83-45569

This book "consists of single-page spreads, each devoted to one athlete. Each figure is drawn in a series of six or more steps, starting with a basic shape and ending with a stylish, somewhat detailed india ink drawing." Booklist

Draw 50 baby animals; the step-by-step way to draw kittens, lambs, chicks, and other adorable offspring. Broadway Books 2003 un il (Draw 50) hardcover o.p. pa $8.95

Grades: 4 5 6 7 **743**
1. Drawing 2. Animals in art 3. Drawing -- Technique
ISBN 978-0-767-91283-9; 0-767-91283-7; 978-0-767-91284-6 pa; 0-767-91284-5 pa

LC 2002-33247

Step-by-step instructions for drawing fifty baby animals.

Draw 50 beasties and yugglies and turnover uglies and things that go bump in the night. Doubleday 1988 il (Draw 50) hardcover o.p. pa $8.95
Grades: 4 5 6 7 **743**
1. Drawing 2. Monsters in art 3. Drawing -- Juvenile literature
ISBN 978-0-385-24625-5; 0-385-24625-0; 978-0-385-26767-0 pa; 0-385-26767-3 pa

LC 88-16143

Provides step-by-step instructions for drawing monsters, goons, and gruesome beasts

Ames "encourages readers to take plenty of time and suggests very lightly sketching out the step-by-step drawings so that mistakes may be rectified. This one, with its popular subject of imaginative monsters and other nightmare inhabitants, will be a sure-fire circulator." SLJ

Draw 50 birds; [by] Lee J. Ames with Tony D'Adamo. Doubleday 1996 un il (Draw 50) hardcover o.p. pa $8.95
Grades: 4 5 6 7 **743**
1. Drawing 2. Birds in art
ISBN 978-0-385-47006-3; 0-385-47006-1; 978-0-385-47163-3 pa; 0-385-47163-7 pa

LC 96-27621

Draw 50 boats, ships, trucks & trains. Doubleday 1976 un il (Draw 50) hardcover o.p. pa $8.95
Grades: 4 5 6 7 **743**
1. Drawing 2. Vehicles in art
ISBN 978-0-385-08903-6; 0-385-08903-1; 978-0-385-23630-0 pa; 0-385-23630-1 pa

LC 75-19011

Step-by-step instructions for drawing fifty different ships, boats, trucks, and trains

Draw 50 buildings and other structures. Doubleday 1980 un il (Draw 50) hardcover o.p. pa $8.95
Grades: 4 5 6 7 **743**
1. Drawing 2. Buildings in art
ISBN 978-0-385-14401-8; 0-385-14401-6; 978-0-385-41777-8 pa; 0-385-41777-2 pa

LC 79-7483

This is similar in format to the author's other books. Step by step procedures enable the reader to draw houses from the U.S. and Ireland, bridges and even a torii (a Japanese gateway)

Draw 50 cats. Doubleday 1986 un il (Draw 50) hardcover o.p. pa $8.95
Grades: 4 5 6 7 **743**
1. Drawing 2. Cats in art 3. Animal painting and illustration
ISBN 978-0-385-23484-9; 0-385-23484-8; 978-0-385-24640-8 pa; 0-385-24640-4 pa

LC 86-8964

Step-by-step instructions on how to draw a variety of cats, including domestic breeds, wild cats, cuddly kittens, and celebrity cats

Draw 50 dinosaurs and other prehistoric animals; with a foreword by George Zappler. Doubleday 1977 un il (Draw 50) hardcover o.p. pa $8.95
Grades: 4 5 6 7 **743**
1. Drawing 2. Dinosaurs in art 3. Animal painting and illustration
ISBN 978-0-385-11134-8; 0-385-11134-7; 978-0-385-19520-1 pa; 0-385-19520-6 pa

LC 76-7285

Step-by-step instructions for drawing a variety of dinosaurs and other prehistoric animals

Draw 50 dogs. Doubleday 1981 un il (Draw 50) hardcover o.p. pa $8.95
Grades: 4 5 6 7 **743**
1. Drawing 2. Dogs in art 3. Animal painting and illustration
ISBN 978-0-385-15686-8; 0-385-15686-3; 978-0-385-23431-3 pa; 0-385-23431-7 pa

LC 79-6853

"Ames' six-step drawings guide youngsters along toward fashioning their own canine figures. Each species starts out with an ultrasimple shape; ovals, circles, or rectangular extensions suggest developing proportions that lead to the completed sketch." Booklist

Draw 50 endangered animals; [by] Lee J. Ames with Warren Budd. Doubleday 1992 un il (Draw 50) hardcover o.p. pa $8.95
Grades: 4 5 6 7 **743**
1. Drawing 2. Animals in art 3. Animal painting and illustration
ISBN 978-0-385-41191-2; 0-385-41191-X; 978-0-385-46985-2 pa; 0-385-46985-3 pa

LC 92-23092

Step-by-step instructions on how to draw a variety of threatened species from all over the world

Draw 50 famous faces. Doubleday 1978 un il (Draw 50) hardcover o.p. pa $8.95
Grades: 4 5 6 7 **743**
1. Drawing 2. Portraits
ISBN 978-0-385-13217-6; 0-385-13217-4; 978-0-385-23432-0 pa; 0-385-23432-5 pa

LC 77-15878

Step-by-step instructions for drawing historical figures, statesmen, sports, stars, and entertainers

Draw 50 flowers, trees, and other plants. Doubleday 1994 un il (Draw 50) hardcover o.p. pa $8.95
Grades: 4 5 6 7 **743**
1. Drawing 2. Plants in art 3. Flowers in art 4. Botanical illustration
ISBN 978-0-385-47004-9; 0-385-47004-5; 978-0-385-47150-3 pa; 0-385-47150-5 pa

LC 94-7192

Draw 50 holiday decorations; [by] Lee J. Ames with Ray Burns. Doubleday 1987 un il (Draw 50) hardcover o.p. pa $8.95
Grades: 4 5 6 7   743
  1. Drawing 2. Holiday decorations
  ISBN 978-0-385-19057-2; 0-385-19057-3; 978-0-385-26770-0 pa; 0-385-26770-3 pa

LC 87-15581

Step-by-step instructions for drawing a variety of holiday subjects such as Baby New Year, Cupid and his arrow, July 4th rockets, turkey, pumpkin, Easter basket, Santa Claus, and a menorah

Draw 50 horses. Doubleday 1984 un il (Draw 50) hardcover o.p. pa $8.95
Grades: 4 5 6 7   743
  1. Horses in art 2. Animal painting and illustration 3. Drawing -- Technique
  ISBN 978-0-385-17640-8; 0-385-17640-6; 978-0-385-17642-2 pa; 0-385-17642-2 pa

LC 81-43646

Step-by-step instructions for drawing different breeds of horses in a variety of poses

Draw 50 monsters, creeps, superheroes, demons, dragons, nerds, dirts, ghouls, giants, vampires, zombies, and other curiosa. Doubleday 1983 un il (Draw 50) hardcover o.p. pa $8.95
Grades: 4 5 6 7   743
  1. Drawing 2. Monsters in art
  ISBN 978-0-385-17637-8; 0-385-17637-6; 978-0-385-17639-2 pa; 0-385-17639-2 pa

LC 80-3006

A "demonstration of how to draw a lengthy lineup of cartoon superheroes and assorted creeps, villains, monsters, and miscellaneous odd creatures. Each page features step-by-step directions, beginning with a simple basic shape that becomes ever more elaborate until the final version sits triumphantly at the bottom right corner of each page." Booklist

Draw 50 people; [by] Lee J. Ames with Creig Flessel. Doubleday 1993 un il (Draw 50) hardcover o.p. pa $8.95
Grades: 4 5 6 7   743
  1. Portraits 2. Drawing -- Technique
  ISBN 978-0-385-41193-6; 0-385-41193-6; 978-0-385-41194-3 pa; 0-385-41194-4 pa

LC 93-20631

Draw 50 people of the Bible; [by] Lee J. Ames and Andre Le Blanc. Doubleday 1995 un il (Draw 50) hardcover o.p. pa $8.95
Grades: 4 5 6 7   743
  1. Drawing
  ISBN 978-0-385-47005-6; 0-385-47005-3; 978-0-385-47162-6 pa; 0-385-47162-9 pa

LC 95-24361

[Draw 50 series] Doubleday 1974 21v
Grades: 4 5 6 7   743
  1. Drawing
Each volume presents step-by-step instructions for drawing a variety of animals, people, or objects

Bergin, Mark
  How to draw pets. PowerKids Press 2011 32p il (How to draw) lib bdg $25.25; pa $11.75
Grades: 4 5 6 7   743
  1. Animals in art 2. Drawing -- Technique
  ISBN 978-1-4488-4511-8 lib bdg; 978-1-4488-4517-0 pa

LC 2010049184

"The cover features sketches of a cat, dog, and rabbit, allowing children to see both structure as well as finished product. Inside, the book starts by showing pictures of animals drawn with different materials such as pencils, ink, charcoals, and pastels, and explains what each medium accomplishes. Next comes an introduction to perspective and looks at different parts of animals. The familiar circle method then gets kids drawing pets from head to tails. . . . The amount of information throughout is just right: thorough but not overwhelming." Booklist
  Includes glossary

Court, Rob
  How to draw cars and trucks; [by] Rob Court. Child's World 2005 32p il (Scribbles Institute) lib bdg $21.36
Grades: 4 5 6   743
  1. Trucks 2. Drawing 3. Automobiles
  ISBN 1-59296-148-7

LC 2004-3729

This volume does "more than deconstruct objects into basic shapes then reconstruct them to show budding artists how to draw. [It] also [provides] information about select information of what's being drawn . . . which makes artists look harder at details and helps them better understand what they are creating. . . . [The author] introduces a few drawing fundamentals—perspective, shading, and composition—and supplies tips on choosing drawing pencils and using color to enliven a picture. . . . There's a lot more than just drawing practice here." Booklist

Emberley, Ed
  Ed Emberley's drawing book of faces. Little, Brown 1975 32p il hardcover o.p. pa $6.95
Grades: 2 3 4 5   743
  1. Drawing 2. Face in art
  ISBN 0-316-23655-1 pa
Provides step-by-step instructions for drawing a wide variety of faces reflecting various emotions and professions

Farrell, Russell
  All about drawing horses & pets. Walter Foster 2010 80p (All about drawing) $34.25; pa $9.95
Grades: K 1 2 3   743
  1. Horses in art 2. Animals in art 3. Drawing -- Technique
  ISBN 978-1-936309-06-1; 1-936309-06-8; 978-1-600585-80-7 pa; 1-600585-80-9 pa

LC 2010004211

First published 2008 in paperback
"Starting with simple geometric shapes, readers are led step-by-step through stages to draw [horses and pets]; close observation is presented as key to drawing lifelike forms. Photos or illustrations of the real creatures are included with 'Fun Facts' about them for readers' reference." Horn Book Guide

All about drawing sea creatures & animals; illustrated by Russell Farrell and Diana Fisher. Walter Foster 2010 80p il (All about drawing) $34.25; pa $9.95
Grades: K 1 2 3   **743**
1. Marine animals in art 2. Drawing -- Technique
ISBN 978-1-936309-08-5; 1-936309-08-4; 978-1-600585-81-4 pa; 1-600585-81-7 pa
First published 2008 in paperback
"Starting with simple geometric shapes, readers are led step-by-step through stages to draw [sea creatures and animals]; close observation is presented as key to drawing lifelike forms. Photos or illustrations of the real creatures are included with 'Fun Facts' about them for readers' reference." Horn Book Guide

Fisher, Diana
All about drawing dinosaurs & reptiles. Walter Foster 2011 80p (All about drawing) $34.25
Grades: K 1 2 3   **743**
1. Reptiles in art 2. Dinosaurs in art 3. Drawing -- Technique
ISBN 978-1-936309-07-8; 1-936309-07-6
LC 2010004210
"Starting with simple geometric shapes, readers are led step-by-step through stages to draw [dinosaurs and reptiles]; close observation is presented as key to drawing lifelike forms. Photos or illustrations of the real creatures are included with 'Fun Facts' about them for readers' reference." Horn Book Guide

Kesselring, Susan
5 steps to drawing faces; illustrated by Dana Regan. Child's World 2011 il lib bdg $25.64
Grades: 3 4 5 6   **743**
1. Face in art 2. Drawing -- Technique
ISBN 978-1-60973-197-7; 1-60973-197-2
"This colorful guide to drawing faces opens with an introductory section that provides drawing tips and a list of tools to get started, and offers supportive advice. . . . Different spreads are devoted to drawing the specific features of eyes, nose, and mouth. The book then goes on to explain how to create various facial expressions. . . . The inviting format and simple step-by-step instructions make this a good place for budding artists to begin." Booklist
Includes glossary and bibliographical references

Lipsey, Jennifer
I love to draw horses! [by] Jennifer Lipsey. Lark Books 2008 48p il (My very favorite art book) $9.95
Grades: 3 4 5 6   **743**
1. Drawing 2. Horses in art
ISBN 978-1-60059-152-5; 1-60059-152-3
LC 2007-49048
"This drawing guide presents basics (starting with circles) for beginning artists. Readers will discover a wealth of information as they sketch a variety of equine subjects in action. . . . The accessible instructions are presented with finished, illustrated demonstrations in colored pen to create an easy-to-use and attractive how-to for young artists." SLJ

Masiello, Ralph
Ralph Masiello's Halloween drawing book; Ralph Masiello. Charlesbridge 2012 48 p. (softcover) $7.95

Grades: 2 3 4   **743**
1. Halloween -- Juvenile literature 2. Drawing -- Technique -- Juvenile literature 3. Halloween in art -- Juvenile literature
ISBN 1570915415; 9781570915413; 9781570915420
LC 2011036736
In this book, author and illustrator Ralph Masiello "brings a haunting twist to his popular drawing series. Step-by-step diagrams show young artists how to draw ghosts, witches, jack-o'-lanterns, skeletons, a haunted house, and more. Just follow the simple steps to create creepy critters and eerie objects. Bonus challenge steps show you how to add frightfullyfun details to your drawings." (Publisher's note)

Ralph Masiello's robot drawing book. Charlesbridge 2011 un lib bdg $16.95; pa $7.95
Grades: 2 3 4 5   **743**
1. Robots in art 2. Drawing -- Technique
ISBN 978-1-57091-535-2 lib bdg; 1-57091-535-0 lib bdg; 978-1-57091-536-9 pa; 1-57091-536-9 pa
LC 2010033634
"Masiello begins with a discussion of how to use circles, squares, and other basic forms to draw robot parts like switches, plugs, and antennae. He includes a brief discussion of drawing and coloring tools and shows young artists how to draw eight different robots. . . . The instructions are simple enough for primary-grade students to have success without adult assistance. Masiello's creations are humorous, old-fashioned, and two dimensional." SLJ

Peffer, Jessica
DragonArt; how to draw fantastic dragons and fantasy creatures. Impact Books 2005 127p il pa $19.99
Grades: 5 6 7 8   **743**
1. Dragons 2. Drawing 3. Mythical animals
ISBN 1-58180-657-4
LC 2005013013
This is a guide to drawing dragons and other mythical beasts such as griffins, guardian gargoyles, and deadly basilisks.
"This book has great writing and superb illustrations and manages to do everything right from the front cover to the index." SLJ

Roza, Greg
Drawing Dracula. Windmill Books 2011 24p il (Drawing movie monsters step-by-step) lib bdg $25.65; pa $12.85
Grades: 3 4 5 6   **743**
1. Monsters in art 2. Drawing -- Technique 3. Motion pictures -- History and criticism
ISBN 978-1-61533-015-7 lib bdg; 1-61533-015-1 lib bdg; 978-1-61533-021-8 pa; 1-61533-021-6 pa
LC 2010004901
A "surefire [hit] with movie fans and aspiring artists, [this volume traces] the cinematic history of [Dracula] and gives step-by-step instructions on how to bring [him] to life on paper. The instructions and accompanying illustrations explaining how to draw the [monster start] with basic shapes such as circles and rectangles and gradually adding more details. . . . Each pose comes from a notable cinematic depiction of the monster . . . and includes a brief description of the movie with entertaining trivia about its cultural significance,

special effects, or popularity over time. The drawing poses are logically organized in chronological order. . . . With text printed in a large, clear font and simply structured sentences, [this book provides] an accessible introduction to film history, and young artists will undoubtedly enjoy trying their hand at depicting [the monster] in a variety of poses." SLJ

Includes glossary and bibliographical references

Drawing Frankenstein. Windmill Books 2011 24p il (Drawing movie monsters step-by-step) lib bdg $25.65; pa $12.85

Grades: 3 4 5 6   **743**

1. Monsters in art 2. Drawing -- Technique 3. Motion pictures -- History and criticism

ISBN 978-1-61533-014-0 lib bdg; 1-61533-014-3 lib bdg; 978-1-61533-019-5 pa; 1-61533-019-4 pa

LC 2010004900

A "surefire [hit] with movie fans and aspiring artists, [this volume traces] the cinematic history of [Frankenstein] and gives step-by-step instructions on how to bring [him] to life on paper. The instructions and accompanying illustrations explaining how to draw the [monster start] with basic shapes such as circles and rectangles and gradually adding more details. . . . Each pose comes from a notable cinematic depiction of the monster . . . and includes a brief description of the movie with entertaining trivia about its cultural significance, special effects, or popularity over time. The drawing poses are logically organized in chronological order. . . . With text printed in a large, clear font and simply structured sentences, [this book provides] an accessible introduction to film history, and young artists will undoubtedly enjoy trying their hand at depicting [the monster] in a variety of poses." SLJ

Includes glossary and bibliographical references

Drawing Godzilla. Windmill Books 2010 24p il (Drawing movie monsters step-by-step) lib bdg $25.65; pa $12.85

Grades: 3 4 5 6   **743**

1. Monsters in art 2. Drawing -- Technique 3. Motion pictures -- History and criticism

ISBN 978-1-61533-013-3 lib bdg; 1-61533-013-5 lib bdg; 978-1-61533-017-1 pa; 1-61533-017-8 pa

LC 2010004899

A "surefire [hit] with movie fans and aspiring artists, [this volume traces] the cinematic history of [Godzilla] and gives step-by-step instructions on how to bring [him] to life on paper. The instructions and accompanying illustrations explaining how to draw the [monster start] with basic shapes such as circles and rectangles and gradually adding more details. . . . Each pose comes from a notable cinematic depiction of the monster . . . and includes a brief description of the movie with entertaining trivia about its cultural significance, special effects, or popularity over time. The drawing poses are logically organized in chronological order. . . . With text printed in a large, clear font and simply structured sentences, [this book provides] an accessible introduction to film history, and young artists will undoubtedly enjoy trying their hand at depicting [the monster] in a variety of poses." SLJ

Includes glossary and bibliographical references

Drawing King Kong. Windmill Books 2011 24p il (Drawing movie monsters step-by-step) lib bdg $25.65; pa $12.85

Grades: 3 4 5 6   **743**

1. Monsters in art 2. Drawing -- Technique 3. Motion pictures -- History and criticism

ISBN 978-1-61533-016-4 lib bdg; 1-61533-016-X lib bdg; 978-1-61533-023-2 pa; 1-61533-023-2 pa

LC 2010006166

A "surefire [hit] with movie fans and aspiring artists, [this volume traces] the cinematic history of [King Kong] and gives step-by-step instructions on how to bring [him] to life on paper. The instructions and accompanying illustrations explaining how to draw the [monster start] with basic shapes such as circles and rectangles and gradually adding more details. . . . Each pose comes from a notable cinematic depiction of the monster . . . and includes a brief description of the movie with entertaining trivia about its cultural significance, special effects, or popularity over time. The drawing poses are logically organized in chronological order. . . . With text printed in a large, clear font and simply structured sentences, [this book provides] an accessible introduction to film history, and young artists will undoubtedly enjoy trying their hand at depicting [the monster] in a variety of poses." SLJ

Includes glossary and bibliographical references

743.6   Drawing animals

Kellogg, Steven

★ The **mysterious** tadpole; new illustrations and text by Steven Kellogg. 25th anniversary ed; Dial Bks. for Young Readers 2002 un il $16.99; pa $6.99

Grades: PreK K 1 2   **743.6**

1. Birds in art 2. Pets -- Fiction 3. Colored pencil drawing -- Technique

ISBN 0-8037-2788-7; 0-14-240140-4 pa

LC 2001-53776

First published 1977

"Louis receives a birthday present from his uncle in Scotland: Alphonse, an amiable tadpole that outgrows his bowl, the bathtub, and even the apartment. . . . The new illustrations are bigger, bolder, brighter, and brimming with lively details." Booklist

745   Decorative arts

Dhom, Christel

The **Advent** Craft and Activity Book; Stories, Crafts, Recipes and Poems for the Christmas Season. Christel Dhom. Floris Books 2012 144 p. $19.95

Grades: 4 5 6   **745**

1. Advent 2. Baking 3. Children's stories 4. Handicraft for children

ISBN 0863159125; 9780863159121

This book is a "compendium of old-fashioned craft projects, recipes and stories was written by a Waldorf kindergarten teacher in Germany and translated for English-speaking countries. . . . Recipes for holiday cookies and candies are included, with measurements given in both grams and ounces. Craft projects include traditional advent wreaths, beeswax candles and Nativity figures made from unspun sheep's wool." (Kirkus)

Hart, Avery

★ **Ancient** Greece! 40 hands-on activities to experience this wondrous age. [by] Avery Hart & Paul Mantell; illustrations by Michael Kline. Williamson 1999 104p il pa $12.95

Grades: 4 5 6 7   **745**

1. Handicraft 2. Activity programs in education -- Juvenile literature

ISBN 1-885593-25-2

LC 98-35762

Introduces the places, people, historical events, myths, culture, and philosophy of ancient Greece. Includes forty hands-on activities, such as making an early Greek theater, building an Ionic temple, and pressing olives for oil

This is "a clever title that encourages learning and creativity." SLJ

Includes bibliographical references

Major, John S.

Caravan to America; living arts of the Silk Road. [by] John S. Major and Betty J. Belanus. Cricket Bks. 2002 130p il map hardcover o.p. pa $15.95

Grades: 4 5 6 7   **745**

1. Arts 2. Cookbook writers 3. Cooking teachers

ISBN 0-8126-2666-4; 0-8126-2677-X pa

LC 2002-5477

Profiles eight artists and artisans now living in America who are originally from the "Silk Road," an ancient network of caravan trails through which trade goods, ideas, and arts pass between Asia and the Mediterranean

"Full of colorful and informative archival and contemporary photographs and drawings. . . . Each person's story is told in an interesting manner, and information about their specialty and its history is woven throughout the text. . . . Not only is the work informative, but it is handsome as well." SLJ

Includes glossary and bibliographical references

Tejubehan (Singer)

★ **Drawing** from the City; Teju Behan. Pgw 2012 28 p. $35.95

Grades: 3 4 5 6 7 8   **745**

1. India 2. Artists 3. Poverty

ISBN 9380340176; 9789380340173

This "autobiographical art book recounts self-taught artist Teju Behan's journey from an impoverished childhood in rural India, through her family's efforts to improve their lot in a tent city in Mumbai, and into her adulthood, when she lived as a singer and artist with her husband. . . . Hand-screen-printed illustrations comprised of intricate linework and patterns of dots underscore elements of the text." (Kirkus)

745.2   Industrial art and design

Arato, Rona

Design it! the ordinary things we use every day and the not-so-ordinary ways they came to be. illustrations by Claudia Newell. Tundra Books 2010 71p il pa $20.95

Grades: 4 5 6 7   **745.2**

1. Industrial design 2. Inventors -- Juvenile literature 3. Inventions -- Juvenile literature

ISBN 978-0-88776-846-0 pa; 0-88776-846-6 pa

"This book opens with an explanation of what industrial designers do and with whom they work to make better products. Brief chapters then cover such topics as home, communications, lighting, and toy design and include a good-design checklist that takes function, usability, ergonomics, aesthetics, and greenness into consideration. The language is chatty and inviting, and the pages are full of cartoon illustrations and text superimposed on colorful geometric backgrounds. Sidebars offer a wealth of further information." SLJ

Welsbacher, Anne

Earth-friendly design; by Anne Welsbacher. Lerner Publications Company 2009 72p il (Saving our living Earth) lib bdg $30.60

Grades: 5 6 7 8   **745.2**

1. Industrial design 2. Environmental protection

ISBN 978-0-8225-7564-1 lib bdg; 0-8225-7564-7 lib bdg

LC 2007-35925

"Provides a thorough, interesting discussion of multiple aspects of [Earth-friendly design], including historical origins, the current situation, and potential solutions. . . . Photos from around the world accompany discussions. . . . [This is a] solid choice to replace outdated books." SLJ

Includes glossary and bibliographical references

745.4   Pure and applied design and decoration

Gonyea, Mark

★ **Another** book about design; complicated doesn't make it bad. Henry Holt & Co. 2007 un il $19.95

Grades: 3 4 5   **745.4**

1. Design

ISBN 978-0-8050-7576-2; 0-8050-7576-3

LC 2006-43705

The author demonstrates "how ideas such as foreground and background, repetition and size of shapes, and positive and negative space can affect a final composition. The definitions of terms are as minimal and clear as the visuals. . . . [This] will leave kids eager to play with the concepts in their own pictures." Booklist

★ A **book** about design; complicated doesn't make it good. Henry Holt & Co. 2005 un il $18.95

Grades: 3 4 5   **745.4**

1. Design

ISBN 0-8050-7575-5

LC 2004-08982

"This stylish, square volume delivers a cheerful manifesto on graphic design. . . . Chatty, brief chapters present principles of composition, line, color, and contrast, as well as techniques for drawing attention to 'what's important' on a page. . . . The text, set against pure white backdrops, is easy to read, and the artwork's elemental shapes and bright colors illustrate the theories in ways that children will readily grasp." Booklist

745.5   Handicrafts

Alter, Anna

What can you do with an old red shoe? a green activity book about re-use. [by] Anna Alter. Henry Holt & Co. 2009 32p il $16.95

Grades: 1 2 3   **745.5**

1. Salvage 2. Recycling 3. Handicraft
ISBN 978-0-8050-8290-6; 0-8050-8290-5

LC 2008018341

"Recycling becomes lots of fun in this sprightly activity book. Alter offers 13 projects, and . . . . the finished products are usually items kids will want to use. . . . The instructions are clear and simple . . . and what really makes this a standout is Alter's adorable artwork featuring a coterie of animals at work and play. Short poems introduce each project." Booklist

Balchin, Judy

Crafty activities; over 50 fun and easy things to make. by Judy Balchin . . . [et al.] Search 2007 un il pa $19.95

Grades: 4 5 6 7   **745.5**

1. Handicraft
ISBN 978-1-84448-250-4 pa; 1-84448-250-2 pa

"The book is divided into six chapters—mosaics, printing, lettering, papier-mâché, handmade cards, and origami—with projects ranging from simple leaf prints to an elaborate necklace made from dried pasta. . . . The photos of smiling kids showing off their creations, the attractive, spacious page design, and, above all the ingenious projects will attract kids—as well as teachers." Booklist

Bell-Rehwoldt, Sheri

The **kids'** guide to building cool stuff; by Sheri Bell-Rehwoldt. Capstone Press 2009 32p il (Kids' guides) lib bdg $23.99

Grades: 4 5 6 7   **745.5**

1. Amusements 2. Handicraft 3. Science -- Experiments
ISBN 978-1-4296-2276-9 lib bdg; 1-4296-2276-8 lib bdg

LC 2008-29687

This provides instructions for building such items as a kite, a balloon rocket, a paper boat, a milk carton bird feeder, and a plastic plate hovercraft

Includes glossary and bibliographical references

Bull, Jane

★ **Make** it! by Jane Bull. DK Pub. 2008 62p il $14.99

Grades: 1 2 3 4   **745.5**

1. Recycling 2. Handicraft
ISBN 978-0-7566-3837-5; 0-7566-3837-2

LC 2008006636

"From its unique cardboard cutout 'picture-frame' cover to its 3 'Rs' to recycling, this craft book lives up to its motto: 'Don't trash it-treasure it!' As good for its ideas in suggesting alternate materials as for its instructions, it will be sheer joy for young crafters. . . . The projects are easy and clever, and all of the pages are profusely illustrated with large, colorful photos of a boy and girl working on the crafts." SLJ

Check, Laura

Create your own candles; 30 easy-to-make designs. illustrations by Norma Jean Martin-Jourdenais. Williamson Books 2004 62p il (Quick starts for kids!) pa $8.95

Grades: 5 6 7 8   **745.5**

1. Candles 2. Candlemaking -- Juvenile literature
ISBN 1-88559-352-X

LC 2004-40870

"Check begins this useful resource with 'Ten Hot Safety Tips.' . . . Next, she lists and describes basic equipment. . . . The projects range from simple beeswax candles to molded candles, hand-dipped candles, and gel candles." SLJ

Dall, Mary Doerfler

Little Hands create! art & activities for kids ages 3 to 6. [by] Mary Dall; illustrations by Sarah Rakitin. Williamson Books 2004 118p il (Williamson Little Hands book) pa $9.95

Grades: K 1 2   **745.5**

1. Handicraft
ISBN 1-88559-365-1

LC 2004-40872

"Although Dall's text is addressed to the little ones who will be making these projects . . . it's really for adult helpers, who can read the instructions aloud as they shepherd their charges through a wealth of crafts activities—from twisted-paper jewelry to pictures and sculptures. Most of the projects depend on readily available materials. . . . The directions are clear. . . . Dall extends the fun with some bright, silly poems and occasional suggestions of simple games to play or picture books that dovetail nicely with the craft. . . . Great for teachers, daycare providers, or anyone looking for rainy-day activities for the very young." Booklist

Durkin, Kath

Paint it! by Kath Durkin. QEB Pub. 2012 32 p. col. ill. (hardcover) $28.50

Grades: 3 4 5   **745.5**

1. Picture books for children 2. Art -- Technique -- Juvenile literature 3. Handicraft -- Juvenile literature 4. Painting -- Technique -- Juvenile literature
ISBN 1609922751; 9781609922757

LC 2012012110

This book by Kath Durkin is part of the Art Smart series and "provides detailed . . . directions for 12 different painting projects appropriate for kids of varying artistic abilities. The projects encompass a wide range of painting techniques, including watercolors, acrylics, and graffito." (Booklist)

Fox, Tom

★ **Snowball** launchers, giant-pumpkin growers, and other cool contraptions; [by] Tom Fox. Sterling Pub. 2006 127p il pa $9.95

Grades: 4 5 6 7   **745.5**

1. Handicraft
ISBN 978-0-8069-5515-5 pa; 0-8069-5515-5 pa

LC 2005032781

"The 20 projects in this collection range from a simple 'Heartbeat Monitor' to a fairly complex 'Moth-Bot,' a wheeled vehicle that moves toward light with the flick of a switch. Most have strong kid appeal. . . . Instructions are written in an engaging, conversational tone, with background information about concepts such as gravity and electricity woven into the text." SLJ

Garner, Lynne

★ **African** crafts; fun things to make and do from West Africa. Chicago Review Press 2008 48p il $12.95

Grades: 4 5 6 **745.5**

1. Handicraft 2. African art

ISBN 978-1-55652-748-7; 1-55652-748-9

First published 2004 in the United Kingdom

Presents an overview of West African culture and provides step-by-step instructions for using simple household materials to make such traditional items as a mask, a coiled pot, block-printed and woven cloths, and a drum.

"Despite the generic title, the focus is on one country, Ghana, and that is the strength of this hands-on crafts book, illustrated with clear step-by-step instructions and lots of color photos. . . . Written in chatty style, the spaciously laid out chapters cover adinkra block printing, pot coiling, mask making, music makers, and kente strip weaving. . . . An excellent source for school and home." Booklist

Haab, Sherri

★ **Dangles** and bangles; 25 funky accessories to make and wear. by Sherri Haab and Michelle Haab; with illustrations by Barbara Pollak. Watson-Guptill Publications 2005 96p il pa $9.95

Grades: 5 6 7 8 **745.5**

1. Jewelry 2. Handicraft

ISBN 0-8230-0064-8

This describes "jewelry hardware, . . . tools, glues and adhesives, and . . . craft supplies, as well as ideas about where to purchase these materials. A spread on basic techniques explains how to work with cord and elastic, glue, rings/pins, etc. The projects . . . range from necklaces to key chains to hair accessories. . . . The mix of colorful photographs, full-page paintings of stylishly dressed youngsters, and varied typefaces makes for an attractive layout. Packed full of wonderful ideas, this irresistible title will be popular with young crafters as well as with adults who plan craft programs." SLJ

Hankin, Rosie

Crafty kids; fun projects for you and your toddler. Barron's 2006 64p il pa $8.99

Grades: PreK K **745.5**

1. Handicraft

ISBN 0-7641-3542-2

"Designed for parents to use with young children, the 28 projects in this collection are both fun and simple to put together. . . . Most of the projects are constructed from paper plates and colored or painted papers that have been cut into simple, often geometric shapes and then adorned with cotton balls, stickers, or marker designs." Booklist

Hendry, Linda

Cat crafts; written and illustrated by Linda Hendry. Kids Can Press 2002 40p il (Kids can do it) $12.95; pa $5.95

Grades: 4 5 6 **745.5**

1. Cats 2. Handicraft

ISBN 1-55074-964-1; 1-55074-921-8 pa

This includes instructions for 17 craft projects including a spider cat toy, a scratch pad, a catnip fish, and decorated placemats, earrings, and bookends

"Nicely designed, double-page spreads show the project step-by-step, each one clearly and succinctly described and illustrated with a color drawing." Booklist

Dog crafts; written and illustrated by Linda Hendry. Kids Can Press 2002 40p il (Kids can do it) $12.95; pa $5.95

Grades: 4 5 6 **745.5**

1. Dogs 2. Handicraft

ISBN 1-55074-960-9; 1-55074-962-5 pa

This includes instructions for 17 craft projects including decorated jars, picture frames, placemats, jewelry, and bookends

"Nicely designed, double-page spreads show the project step-by-step, each one clearly and succinctly described and illustrated with a color drawing." Booklist

Horse crafts; written and illustrated by Linda Hendry. Kids Can Press 2006 40p il (Kids can do it) $12.95; pa $6.95

Grades: 4 5 6 **745.5**

1. Horses 2. Handicraft

ISBN 1-55337-646-3; 1-55337-647-1 pa

This includes instructions for craft projects including drawing a horse, making a silhouette, a pencil top, a lampshade, a pin, a browband cover, a mirror, a plaque, a clipboard, a pillow, a keepsake box, a blue jean bag, bookends, a CD box, and a sock horse.

Henry, Sandi

Making amazing art; 40 activities using the 7 elements of art design. by Sandi Henry; illustrated by Sarah Rakitin Cole. Williamsonbooks 2007 128p il (Kids can) $16.99; pa $12.99

Grades: 2 3 4 5 **745.5**

1. Art 2. Design 3. Handicraft

ISBN 978-0-8249-6794-9; 0-8249-6794-1; 978-0-8249-6795-6 pa; 0-8249-6795-X pa

LC 2006101173

"Each chapter in this well-organized, heavily illustrated book features one element—line, texture, color, etc.—with five or six projects that cleverly support it. . . . Icons display three challenge levels; step-by-step instructions help to ensure success." SLJ

Jocelyn, Marthe

Sneaky art; crafty surprises to hide in plain sight. Marthe Jocelyn. Candlewick Press 2013 64 p. $12.99

Grades: 3 4 5 **745.5**

1. Handicraft for children

ISBN 0763656488; 9780763656485

LC 2012942615

This children's craft book, by Marthe Jocelyn, is a "how-to manual for creating removable and shareable art projects from easily found materials. The sneaky part is in the installation! Each work of art is custom-created for display in public places. . . . This utterly unique guide--part craft book, part art-philosophy--offers a stylish and sweet . . . spirit of fun meant to put a smile on the faces of strangers and loved ones alike." (Publisher's note)

Kenney, Karen Latchana

Super simple art to wear; fun and easy-to-make crafts
for kids. ABDO Pub. Company 2010 31p il (Super simple
crafts) lib bdg $17.95

Grades: K 1 2 3 4   **745.5**
1. Handicraft
ISBN 978-1-60453-622-5 lib bdg; 1-60453-622-5
lib bdg

               LC 2009-349

"Colorful photos; clean layout in a bright, primary palette; and large, abundant step-by-step instructional photos
give [this book] great appeal. The . . . crafts . . . are functional and attractive. [The book] demonstrates [for instatnce]
how to paint shoelaces. . . . Readily obtainable household
materials and easy-to-follow instructions mean that children
can do these crafts independently." SLJ
Includes glossary

Llimos, Anna

Easy cardboard crafts in 5 steps. Enslow Elementary
2008 31p il (Easy crafts in 5 steps) lib bdg $22.60

Grades: 2 3 4   **745.5**
1. Handicraft
ISBN 978-0-7660-3083-1 lib bdg; 0-7660-3083-0
lib bdg

Original Spanish edition 2005

This "has instructions for 14 projects, among them a
folder, drum, and hang-glider. . . . A materials list is provided
for each item, with general supplies and recyclables sufficient for most crafts. The simple directions are adequately
spaced on the page and accompanied by step-by-step color
photos." SLJ
Includes bibliographical references

Easy cloth crafts in 5 steps. Enslow Elementary 2008
31p il (Easy crafts in 5 steps) lib bdg $22.60

Grades: 2 3 4   **745.5**
1. Handicraft
ISBN 978-0-7660-3084-8 lib bdg; 0-7660-3084-9
lib bdg

Original Spanish edition 2005

This "has instructions for 14 projects, among them . . .
a tray, turtle, and clown. . . . A materials list is provided for
each item, with general supplies and recyclables sufficient
for most crafts. The simple directions are adequately spaced
on the page and accompanied by step-by-step color photos."
SLJ
Includes bibliographical references

Easy earth-friendly crafts in 5 steps. Enslow Elementary 2008 31p il (Easy crafts in 5 steps) lib bdg $22.60

Grades: 2 3 4   **745.5**
1. Recycling 2. Handicraft
ISBN 978-0-7660-3086-2 lib bdg; 0-7660-3086-5
lib bdg

Original Spanish edition 2005

This offers instructions for 14 crafts using recycled materials such as bottle caps, egg cartons, and bottles, among
them a coin purse, a spinning top, and a doll

The text is "easy to read, and the results are quirky and
pleasing; steps are illustrated with bright photographs."
Horn Book Guide
Includes bibliographical references

Haunted house adventure crafts. Enslow Elementary
2010 32p il (Fun adventure crafts) lib bdg $22.60; pa
$6.95

Grades: 1 2 3   **745.5**
1. Halloween 2. Handicraft
ISBN 978-0-7660-3730-4 lib bdg; 0-7660-3730-4 lib
bdg; 978-0-7660-3731-1 pa; 0-7660-3731-2 pa

             LC 2009041462

Original Spanish edition 2008

"In simple language and bright pictures, 11 crafts are
laid out, including the magnum opus: a cardboard haunted
house. . . . Small illustrated versions of the final products
cavort across the pages, and story ideas conclude." Booklist
Includes bibliographical references

Milord, Susan

★ **Mexico!** 40 activities to experience Mexico past &
present. illustrations by Michael Kline. Williamson 1998
96p il maps pa $10.95

Grades: 3 4 5   **745.5**
1. Handicraft 2. Activity programs in education --
Juvenile literature
ISBN 1-88559-322-8

             LC 98-34153

"Milord provides an amazing amount of information
about Mexico, ranging from ancient history through the
Spanish conquest to contemporary life. Activities include
such standards as making an Ojo de Dios and a piñata, but
there are also directions for creating marzipan skulls for the
Day of the Dead celebration, as well as recipes for salsa,
tortillas, and hot chocolate. . . . This is an excellent starting
point for students investigating this culture." SLJ
Includes bibliographical references

Monaghan, Kimberly

Organic crafts; 75 earth-friendly art activities. [by]
Kimberly Monaghan. Chicago Review Press 2007 140p
pa $14.95

Grades: 2 3 4 5   **745.5**
1. Handicraft 2. Nature craft
ISBN 978-1-55652-640-4 pa; 1-55652-640-7 pa

             LC 2006031659

"These activities, crafts, and games are arranged by
type of material used, such as rocks, pebbles, and shells;
soil, clay, and sand, etc. There's a wide range of interesting projects, including clay beads, a glittering sand castle,
potpourri, a sea sparkler, a wind sock, a gourd birdhouse,
broken-china mosaics, homemade paper, rock sculpture, and
garden chimes. Children will also learn how to make natural
glue cornstarch paint, and salt clay." SLJ
Includes bibliographical references

My art book; amazing art projects inspired by masterpieces.
DK Pub. 2011 80p il $15.99

Grades: 3 4 5 6   **745.5**
1. Art 2. Handicraft
ISBN 978-0-7566-7582-0; 0-7566-7582-0

"Representing a variety of cultures and styles, this book
highlights 14 famous artworks and offers a craft project related to each one. The arrangement is roughly chronological, beginning with the cave paintings of Lascaux, France,
and ending with the Pop Art of Andy Warhol. Each work is
reproduced in a high-quality color photograph and described
in a few paragraphs of succinct but interesting text. The

projects are varied and appealing, and no two use the same medium or technique. . . . A great resource for teaching art history though hands-on activities." SLJ

Oldham, Todd
★ **Kid** made modern. AMMO 2009 184p il $22.95
Grades: 3 4 5 6   **745.5**
1. Design 2. Handicraft 3. Art appreciation -- Juvenile literature
ISBN 978-1-934429-36-5; 1-934429-36-8
LC 2009-934393
"This activity book from renowned designer Oldham uses the work of Mid-Century modern visual artists—including Isamu Noguchi, Alexander Calder, and Charles and Ray Eames—as springboards for 52 hands-on creative projects. Brief tutorials introduce skills and techniques, paired with full-color photos of kids and the various processes. . . . There's much here to capture the eye of ambitious, crafty readers." Publ Wkly

Owen, Cheryl
Gifts for kids to make. Hamlyn 2006 128p il pa $14.95
Grades: K 1 2 3 4 5   **745.5**
1. Gifts 2. Handicraft
ISBN 0-600-61502-2
"This useful volume is divided into six categories—bric-a-brac, stationery, scented gifts, floral garden gifts, accessories, and edible treats—with 7 to 10 projects in each. Examples are magnets, bookmarks, gift wrap, birdfeeder, glasses case, and cookies. . . . The items are appealing to children and age appropriate. Both the written and visual instructions are clear and easy to follow." SLJ

Press, Judy
The **little** hands big fun craft book; illustrated by Loretta Trezzo Braren. 2nd ed.; Williamson 2008 142p il pa $12.99
Grades: PreK K 1   **745.5**
1. Handicraft
ISBN 978-0-8249-6827-4 pa; 0-8249-6827-1 pa
First published 1996
This craft book for young children includes 70 projects

Robinson, Fay
★ **Hispanic**-American crafts kids can do! [by] Fay Robinson. Enslow Elementary 2006 32p il (Multicultural crafts kids can do!) $22.60
Grades: 3 4 5   **745.5**
1. Handicraft
ISBN 0-7660-2459-8
LC 2005033800
This offers instructions for creating 10 crafts from Mexico, Panama, and Central and South America including piñatas, maracas, molas, Mayan weavings, and Mexican pottery.
"The title gets it right. These are crafts kids can do, and, more important, will want to do. . . . Kids get to see each project in colorful, step-by-step photographs." Booklist
Includes bibliographical references

Ross, Kathy
Bedroom makeover crafts; illustrated by Nicole in den Bosch. Millbrook Press 2008 47p il (Girl crafts) lib bdg $26.60; pa $7.95

Grades: 3 4 5   **745.5**
1. Handicraft
ISBN 978-0-8225-7593-1 lib bdg; 0-8225-7593-0 lib bdg; 978-1-58013-823-9 pa; 1-58013-823-3 pa
LC 2007001894
"This title contains step-by-step directions for an array of room accessories that includes everything from earring dolls and doorknob covers to small tables and trash baskets. Materials are readily obtained and directions are clear and easy to follow." SLJ

Crafts for kids who are learning about dinosaurs; illustrated by Jan Barger. Millbrook Press 2008 48p il lib bdg $26.60
Grades: 2 3 4   **745.5**
1. Dinosaurs 2. Handicraft
ISBN 978-0-8225-6809-4 lib bdg; 0-8225-6809-8 lib bdg
LC 2006100645
"These 22 projects include a necklace, a bathtub toy, puppets, a pencil topper, a tape dispenser, and more. Brief facts about dinosaurs are matched with each craft. Each project has a list of materials needed and illustrations for the 3 to 15 steps. . . . A welcome addition for young dinosaur fans." SLJ

Earth-friendly crafts; clever ways to reuse everyday items. [by] Kathy Ross; illustrated by Celine Malepart. Millbrook Press 2009 48p il lib bdg $26.60
Grades: 3 4 5 6   **745.5**
1. Recycling 2. Handicraft
ISBN 978-0-8225-9099-6 lib bdg; 0-8225-9099-9 lib bdg
LC 2008025481
"This clear, colorful title offers a selection of environmentally focused projects that encourage kids to reduce, reuse, and recycle. Both practical and eye-catching, the projects, from pencil cups to decorative pins, rely on everyday discarded items that many kids will find around their homes. . . . [The crafts] are presented in line drawings that demonstrate the construction step by step along with color photos of the finished product." Booklist

Sadler, Judy Ann
The **new** jumbo book of easy crafts; written by Judy Ann Sadler; illustrated by Caroline Price. Kids Can Press 2009 176p il pa $18.95
Grades: PreK K 1 2   **745.5**
1. Handicraft
ISBN 978-1-55453-239-1 pa; 1-55453-239-6 pa
First published 2001 with title: The Kids Can Press jumbo book of easy crafts
This includes instructions for over 150 crafts divided into four themed sections: Imagine and Create, Wear and Use, Make and Play and Decorate and Celebrate

Silver, Patricia
Face painting; written by Patricia Silver (Patty the clown); illustrated by Louise Phillips. Kids Can Press 2000 40p il (Kids can do it) pa $5.95
Grades: 4 5 6   **745.5**
1. Face painting
ISBN 1-55074-845-9; 1-55074-689-8 pa

The author "includes step-by-step instructions for 16 of the most commonly requested faces, rules for safety, and the all-important cleanup tips. Clear, full-color photographs and drawings of children in the makeup accompany the instructions. These simple illustrations are charming and helpful." SLJ

Sirrine, Carol

Cool crafts with old jeans; green projects for resourceful kids. Capstone Press 2010 32p il (Snap books. Green crafts) lib bdg $26.65

Grades: 3 4 5 6　　　　　　　　　　745.5

1. Recycling 2. Handicraft 3. Jeans (Clothing)
ISBN 978-1-4296-4006-0 lib bdg; 1-4296-4006-5 lib bdg

"Steps are easy to follow and well documented, and the projects encourage experimentation and creativity. Materials are generally easy to find. . . . This . . . is original, well-presented, and bound to inspire classroom and individual projects." SLJ

Includes glossary and bibliographical references

Cool crafts with old t-shirts; green projects for resourceful kids. Capstone Press 2010 32p il (Snap Books. Green crafts) lib bg $26.65

Grades: 3 4 5 6　　　　　　　　　　745.5

1. Salvage 2. Handicraft
ISBN 1-4296-4009-X lib bdg; 978-1-4296-4009-1 lib bdg

"Steps are easy to follow and well documented, and the projects encourage experimentation and creativity. Materials are generally easy to find. . . . This . . . is original, well-presented, and bound to inspire classroom and individual projects." SLJ

Includes glossary and bibliographical references

Cool crafts with old wrappers, cans and bottles; green projects for resourceful kids. Capstone Press 2010 32p il (Snap books. Green crafts) lib bdg $26.65

Grades: 3 4 5 6　　　　　　　　　　745.5

1. Salvage 2. Handicraft
ISBN 978-1-4296-4008-4 lib bdg; 1-4296-4008-1 lib bdg

"Steps are easy to follow and well documented, and the projects encourage experimentation and creativity. Materials are generally easy to find. . . . This . . . is original, well-presented, and bound to inspire classroom and individual projects." SLJ

Includes glossary and bibliographical references

Torres, Laura

Rock your school stuff. QEB Pub. 2010 32p il (Rock your . . .) lib bdg $28.50

Grades: 4 5 6　　　　　　　　　　745.5

1. Handicraft 2. Schools -- Equipment and supplies
ISBN 978-1-59566-936-0; 1-59566-936-1

LC 2010010670

This book "gives kids easy step-by-step ways to . . . personalize school supplies. . . . Colorful photographs show youngsters crafting [such items as beaded pens, recycled paperclip bookmarks, backpack zipper pulls] . . . some of which are created from recycled found items. All are projects they can complete by themselves." Horn Book Guide

Warwick, Ellen

Everywear; written by Ellen Warwick; illustrated by Bernice Lum. Kids Can Press 2008 80p il (Planet girl) $14.95

Grades: 5 6 7 8　　　　　　　　　　745.5

1. Handicraft 2. Dress accessories 3. Jewelry making -- Juvenile literature 4. Dress accessories -- Juvenile literature
ISBN 978-1-55337-799-3; 1-55337-799-0

"After several opening pages that introduce supplies, . . . very basic stitching skills, and terminology, girls turn to the . . . issue of hair: woven-ribbon bands, jazzed-up chopsticks; fabric-flower-bedecked combs; reversible ponytail wraps. Next come body adornments . . . followed by stuff to stow it in, of clutched, dangled, and toted varieties. Each project features a list of supplies, . . . clearly numbered steps with cartoon-styled illustrations . . . and full-color photograph of the finished item. . . . [This has] genuine sleepover appeal." Bull Cent Child Books

Wolf, Laurie Goldrich

Recyclo-gami; 40 crafts to make your friends green with envy! Running Press Teens 2010 112p il $14.95

Grades: 4 5 6 7　　　　　　　　　　745.5

1. Recycling 2. Handicraft
ISBN 978-0-7624-4052-8; 0-7624-4052-X

"Wolf's fun, resourceful projects offer straightforward ways to reuse common materials to make accessories, jewelry, household decorations, games, and gifts. Leftover tissue or wrapping paper can be used to create decoupage plates; old crayons are melted and baked into molds to make multicolored crayons; and unused CDs and DVDs are transformed into funky, freeform bowls when melted in the oven. . . . The ease of most of the activities should inspire readers to see the recycling bin as a potential treasure trove." Publ Wkly

745.54　Papers

Garza, Carmen Lomas

★ Making magic windows; creating papel picado/cut-paper art with Carmen Lomas Garza. Children's Bk. Press 1999 61p il pa $9.95

Grades: 3 4 5 6　　　　　　　　　　745.54

1. Handicraft 2. Paper crafts 3. Paper work 4. Paper work -- Juvenile literature
ISBN 0-89239-159-6

LC 98-38518

Provides instructions for making paper banners and more intricate cut-outs. Includes diagrams for creating specific images

"Based on workshops conducted by the artist, the step-by-step instructions and illustrations have been fine-tuned and are clear and easy to follow. . . . Multiculturally authentic and a guaranteed kid-crowd pleaser, this workbook is enthusiastically recommended for all craft collections." Booklist

Latno, Mark

The paper boomerang book; build them, throw them, and get them to return every time. Chicago Review Press 2010 245p il pa $12.95

Grades: 5 6 7 8 **745.54**
1. Boomerangs 2. Paper crafts
ISBN 978-1-56976-282-0 pa; 1-56976-282-1 pa
LC 2010007251

"In a unique . . . guide Latno . . . [explains] how to make, fine-tune, and decorate a type of paper boomerang that can be constructed with commonly available materials and thrown with (relative) safety indoors. The instructions and simply drawn diagrams are embedded in a history of boomerangs and throwing sticks, a challenging technical discussion of the physics of boomerangs and gyroscopes, and very detailed descriptions of the characteristics of railroad board (Latno's preferred paper) and alternatives, plus art-and-craft materials that can be used to dress up finished models." SLJ

Includes glossary and bibliographical references

Llimos, Anna
Easy paper crafts in 5 steps. Enslow Elementary 2008 31p il (Easy crafts in 5 steps) lib bdg $22.60
Grades: 2 3 4 **745.54**
1. Paper crafts
ISBN 978-0-7660-3087-9 lib bdg; 0-7660-3087-3 lib bdg
Original Spanish edition 2005

This offers instructions for 14 paper craft projects, among them a basket, a butterfly, and pop-up card

The text is "easy to read, and the results are quirky and pleasing; steps are illustrated with bright photographs." Horn Book Guide

Includes bibliographical references

Torres, Laura
Rock your party. QEB Pub. 2010 32p il (Rock your . . .) lib bdg $28.50
Grades: 4 5 6 **745.54**
1. Parties 2. Handicraft 3. Paper crafts
ISBN 978-1-59566-935-3; 1-59566-935-3
LC 2010010668

This book "gives kids easy step-by-step ways to make decorations for their . . . parties. . . . Colorful photographs show youngsters crafting appealing . . . party hats, etc. some of which are created from recycled found items. All are projects they can complete by themselves." Horn Book Guide

Walsh, Danny
The **cardboard** box book; 25 things to make and do with empty boxes. by Danny, Jake, and Niall Walsh; [photographs by Martin Norris; illustrations by Josh Halloran] Watson-Guptill 2006 112p il pa $12.95
Grades: 3 4 5 **745.54**
1. Boxes 2. Handicraft
ISBN 0-8230-0610-7
LC 2005935223

"An eye-catching cover showcases a few of these projects designed for indoor or outdoor play, and the book's lively design and layout, featuring bold colors and various fonts, will draw in young crafters. Opening chapters discuss where to find boxes of different sizes, what a basic tool kit consists of, how to use paint and glitter, when adult help is needed, and the time involved in constructing the creations." SLJ

745.58   Beads, found and other objects

Boonyadhistarn, Thiranut
Beading; bracelets, barrettes, and beyond. by Thiranut Boonyadhistarn. Capstone Press 2007 32p il (Snap books) $25.26
Grades: 4 5 6 7 **745.58**
1. Beadwork
ISBN 978-0-7368-6472-5; 0-7368-6472-5
LC 2006004102

This describes how to create such bead crafts as safety-pin bracelets and bag charms.

"Girls will appreciate these ideas for recreating fashion trends and for achieving the artistic effects that they want. . . . Page layouts are lively and attractive. The projects use easily obtainable materials, and the directions are simple and well numbered." SLJ

Includes bibliographical references

Llimos, Anna
Easy bead crafts in 5 steps. Enslow Elementary 2008 31p il (Easy crafts in 5 steps) lib bdg $22.60
Grades: 2 3 4 **745.58**
1. Beadwork
ISBN 978-0-7660-3757-1 lib bdg; 0-7660-3757-6 lib bdg
Original Spanish edition 2005

This offers instructions for 14 bead craft projects, among them a bracelet and ring, a bookmark, and a belt

The text is "easy to read, and the results are quirky and pleasing; steps are illustrated with bright photographs." Horn Book Guide

Includes bibliographical references

Ross, Kathy
Beautiful beads; illustrated by Nicole in den Bosch. Millbrook Press 2009 48p il lib bdg $26.60
Grades: 2 3 4 5 **745.58**
1. Beadwork
ISBN 978-0-8225-9214-3 lib bdg; 0-8225-9214-2 lib bdg
LC 2008044441

"A diverse collection of 21 fun and unique projects. Young readers will learn how to make different types of beads (fabric, textured, thread, ribbon, sparkle stem), two games, a felt-bead bracelet, a cluster pin, a seed-bead flower magnet, whimsical items (beaded dog, spaghetti doll, and others), a bookmark, a tissue box, and more. The colors are vivid, and the illustrations perfectly complement the text." SLJ

Scheunemann, Pam
★ **Cool** beaded jewelry; [by] Pam Scheunemann. ABDO Pub. 2005 32p il (Cool crafts) $22.78
Grades: 4 5 6 **745.58**
1. Jewelry 2. Beadwork
ISBN 1-59197-739-8
LC 2004-46292

This "has an extensive section on bead history, sizes, shapes, types, and metal findings (clasps, etc.). Projects include a memory wire bracelet, a beaded necklace and bracelet, daisy chain necklace, and beaded rings." SLJ

Sirrine, Carol

Cool crafts with old CDs; green projects for resourceful kids. Capstone Press 2010 32p il (Snap books. Green crafts) lib bdg $26.65

Grades: 3 4 5 6   **745.58**

1. Salvage 2. Compact discs 3. Plastics craft

ISBN 978-1-4296-4007-7 lib bdg; 1-4296-4006-5 lib bdg

"Steps are easy to follow and well documented, and the projects encourage experimentation and creativity. Materials are generally easy to find. . . . This . . . is original, well-presented, and bound to inspire classroom and individual projects." SLJ

Includes glossary and bibliographical references

745.59 Making specific objects

Hufford, Deborah

★ Greeting card making; send your personal message. by Deborah Hufford. Capstone Press 2006 32p il (Snap books crafts) lib bdg $25.26

Grades: 3 4 5   **745.59**

1. Handicraft 2. Greeting cards

ISBN 0-7368-4385-X

LC 2005006899

"A pop-up birthday cake, a dried flower-petal design, and a lacey valentine are among the homemade card ideas featured in this simple, easy-to-follow title. . . . Introductory pages cover basic paper folds and materials; later spreads present mostly clear, step-by-step instructions." Booklist

Includes glossary and bibliographical references

Kenney, Karen Latchana

Super simple magnets; fun and easy-to-make crafts for kids. ABDO Pub. Co. 2010 32p il (Super simple crafts) lib bdg $17.95

Grades: K 1 2 3 4   **745.59**

1. Magnets 2. Handicraft

ISBN 978-1-60453-626-3 lib bdg; 1-60453-626-8 lib bdg

LC 2009-355

"Colorful photos; clean layout in a bright, primary palette; and large, abundant step-by-step instructional photos give [this book] great appeal. The . . . crafts . . . are functional and attractive. . . . Readily obtainable household materials and easy-to-follow instructions mean that children can do these crafts independently." SLJ

Includes glossary

745.592 Toys, models, miniatures, related objects

Castleforte, Brian

Papertoy monsters; 50 cool papertoys you can make yourself! Workman Pub. Co. 2010 233p il pa $16.95

Grades: 4 5 6 7   **745.592**

1. Paper crafts 2. Monsters in art

ISBN 978-0-7611-5882-0 pa; 0-7611-5882-0 pa

"Twenty-five 'papertoy' artists contribute 50 original monster designs made of colorful cardstock that can be punched out and glued together to form three dimensional

cartoon characters, each with its own quirky backstory. The menagerie includes the tentacled OctoPup, who devours small boats; Yucky Chuck, a serrated-toothed 'mutant lunchbox monster'; and Lester Rottenbottom, a teacher-turned-mad-scientist. The designers' enthusiasm for their subjects should inspire readers to invent their own monsters on the blank templates provided." Publ Wkly

Harbo, Christopher L.

Paper airplanes: Captain, level 4. Capstone Press 2010 32p il (Edge books. Paper airplanes) lib bdg $26.65

Grades: 3 4 5 6   **745.592**

1. Paper crafts 2. Airplanes -- Models

ISBN 978-1-4296-4744-1 lib bdg; 1-4296-4744-2 lib bdg

LC 2010001003

This "includes a list of basic materials and an overview of folding instructions and techniques. . . . Along with hints on how to hold the plane for take-off to maximize strengths are suggestions on conducting friendly competitions with the finished products. Sure to keep readers busy for hours." SLJ

Includes bibliographical references

Paper airplanes: Copilot, level 2. Capstone Press 2010 32p il (Edge books. Paper airplanes) lib bdg $26.65

Grades: 3 4 5 6   **745.592**

1. Paper crafts 2. Airplanes -- Models

ISBN 978-1-4296-4742-7 lib bdg; 1-4296-4742-6 lib bdg

LC 2010001004

This "includes a list of basic materials and an overview of folding instructions and techniques. . . . Along with hints on how to hold the plane for takeoff to maximize strengths are suggestions on conducting friendly competitions with the finished products. Sure to keep readers busy for hours." SLJ

Includes bibliographical references

Paper airplanes: Flight school, level 1. Capstone Press 2010 32p il (Edge books. Paper airplanes) lib bdg $26.65

Grades: 3 4 5 6   **745.592**

1. Paper crafts 2. Airplanes -- Models

ISBN 978-1-4296-4741-0 lib bdg; 1-4296-4741-8 lib bdg

LC 2010001005

This "includes a list of basic materials and an overview of folding instructions and techniques. . . . Along with hints on how to hold the plane for takeoff to maximize strengths are suggestions on conducting friendly competitions with the finished products. Sure to keep readers busy for hours." SLJ

Includes bibliographical references

Paper airplanes: Pilot, level 3. Capstone Press 2010 32p il (Edge books. Paper airplanes) lib bdg $26.65

Grades: 3 4 5 6   **745.592**

1. Paper crafts 2. Airplanes -- Models

ISBN 978-1-4296-4743-4 lib bdg; 1-4296-4743-4 lib bdg

LC 2010001006

This "includes a list of basic materials and an overview of folding instructions and techniques. . . . Along with hints on how to hold the plane for takeoff to maximize strengths are suggestions on conducting friendly competitions with the finished products. Sure to keep readers busy for hours." SLJ

Includes bibliographical references

The **kids'** guide to paper airplanes. Capstone Press 2009 32p il (Kids' guides) $23.93
Grades: 4 5 6 7 **745.592**
1. Paper crafts 2. Airplanes -- Models
ISBN 978-1-4296-2274-5; 1-4296-2274-1
LC 2008029688

"Using colorful, vivid, and clear step-by-step illustrations, Harbo demonstrates how to construct everything from the classic Dart to the circular Space Ring to the 18-step Silent Huntress." Booklist
Includes glossary and bibliographical references

Mercer, Bobby
The **flying** machine book; build and launch 35 rockets, gliders, helicopters, boomerangs, and more. Bobby Mercer. Chicago Review Press 2012 ix, 197 p.p ill. (pbk.) $14.95
Grades: 4 5 6 **745.592**
1. Flight 2. Aeronautics 3. Airplanes -- Models 4. Models and modelmaking 5. Paper airplanes 6. Flying-machines -- Models
ISBN 9781613740866
LC 2011041174

This book provides "step-by-step instructions for 35 aerodynamic projects . . . Physics teacher [Bobby] Mercer . . . here provides . . . directions for building a variety of flying machines including rockets, gliders, helicopters, boomerangs and assorted launchers. An opening chapter called Flight School introduces the Bernoulli principle and four forces: lift, thrust, drag and weight. . . . Each subsequent chapter begins with more flight school, repeating the relevant principles and applying them to the different forms of flying machines described. Many of the constructions use similar techniques and most are not difficult. The models are made of common materials: card stock and old folders, drinking straws, rubber bands and duct tape." (Kirkus Reviews)

Rigsby, Mike
★ **Amazing** rubber band cars; easy-to-build wind-up racers, models, and toys. [by] Mike Rigsby. Chicago Review Press 2007 121p il lib bdg $12.95
Grades: 4 5 6 7 **745.592**
1. Toys 2. Handicraft 3. Automobiles -- Models
ISBN 978-1-55652-736-4 lib bdg; 1-55652-736-5 lib bdg
LC 2007013969

This offers instructions for making toy and model cars "using mostly cardboard, glue, pencils, rubber bands, and a few other easily obtainable materials. . . . Readers will learn about corrugated and flat cardboard, and how to use glue and work with templates. Excellent instructions are accompanied by black-and-white photos every step of the way. . . . These projects are fun to construct, and inquisitive minds will be fascinated by the moving cars." SLJ

Schwarz, Renee
Wind chimes and whirligigs. Kids Can Press 2007 40p il (Kids can do it) $12.95; pa $6.95

Grades: 4 5 6 **745.592**
1. Handicraft 2. Whirligigs 3. Wind chimes
ISBN 978-1-55337-868-6; 1-55337-868-7; 978-1-55337-870-9 pa; 1-55337-870-9 pa

"A colorfully designed and artfully arranged photographic cover is the perfect introduction to the 12 unique and creative projects within. An overall neat appearance and precise, vibrant illustrations or sharp photos add to the attractive layout. . . . The techniques, using plastic, nylon fishing line, tape, glue, and screwdrivers, are carefully explained." SLJ

Thomson, Ruth
Toys and models; photography by Neil Thomson. Sea-to-Sea Publications 2010 32p il (World of design) lib bdg $28.50
Grades: 4 5 6 7 **745.592**
1. Toys 2. Handicraft 3. Models and modelmaking
ISBN 978-1-59771-209-5 lib bdg; 1-59771-209-4 lib bdg
LC 2008-43868

This "volume presents examples of crafts made around the world, then offers six simple items inspired by these goods that children can make (mostly using recycled materials). The directions allow for easy replication, while information about the crafts provides a window into world cultures. . . . The colorful close-up photographs provide . . . interesting details." Horn Book Guide
Includes glossary and bibliographical references

745.593 Useful objects

Maurer, Tracy
Scrapbook starters; [by] Tracy Nelson Maurer. Rourke Pub. LLC 2009 32p il (Creative crafts for kids) lib bdg $29.95
Grades: 3 4 5 6 **745.593**
1. Scrapbooks
ISBN 978-1-6069-4343-4 lib bdg; 1-6069-4343-X lib bdg
LC 2009003900

"This attractive title . . . guides young readers through the basics of starting, designing, and maintaining a scrapbook. . . . Boxed tips, supply lists, and full-color photos of scrapbooking kids in action, along with completed projects, add visual interest. . . . A solid resource on a popular subject." Booklist

Mooney, Carla
Light your way; make a candle. Norwood House Press 2010 48p il (Creative adventure guides) lib bdg $25.27
Grades: 3 4 5 6 **745.593**
1. Candles
ISBN 978-1-59953-387-2; 1-59953-387-1
LC 2010010399

"Some historical background and scientific or cultural information places the making and use of candles . . . in context for young readers. [The] book has four chapters that culminate in step-by-step projects." Horn Book Guide
Includes glossary and bibliographical references

Price, Pamela S.

★ **Cool** scrapbooks; [by] Pam Price. ABDO Pub.
2005 32p il (Cool crafts) lib bdg $25.65

Grades: 4 5 6   **745.593**

1. Scrapbooks
ISBN 1-59197-744-4

LC 2004-46290

This guide to scrapbooks "addresses the use of photos,
embellishments, adding words, computer possibilities, and
more. . . . [This book lists] required materials, [has] small
color photos, and [includes] clearly explained, numbered
steps." SLJ

Ransom, Candice F.

Scrapbooking just for you! how to make fun, personal,
save-them-forever keepsakes. [by] Candice Ransom. Sterling Pub. 2010 120p il $14.95

Grades: 4 5 6 7   **745.593**

1. Scrapbooks
ISBN 978-1-4027-4096-1; 1-4027-4096-4

LC 2008038982

"Ransom's well-organized introduction showcases her
enthusiasm for scrapbooking and also includes material for
more experienced crafters. . . . High-quality color photos
that are a good match with the directions make the pages
pop, and directions are clear." SLJ

745.594 Decorative objects

Ancona, George

★ The **pinata** maker: El pinatero. Harcourt Brace &
Co. 1994 un il hardcover o.p. pa $9

Grades: K 1 2 3   **745.594**

1. Paper crafts 2. Bilingual books -- English-Spanish
ISBN 0-15-261875-9; 0-15-200060-7 pa

LC 93-2389

Describes how Don Ricardo, a craftsman from Ejutla de
Crespo in southern Mexico, makes piñatas for all the village
birthday parties and other fiestas

"Ancona tells his story in both English and Spanish, with
both languages on every page. His clear, bright, full-color
photographs complement the detailed text, giving the reader
much additional information." Horn Book

Bledsoe, Karen E.

Chinese New Year crafts; [by] Karen E. Bledsoe. Enslow Publishers 2005 32p il (Fun holiday crafts kids can
do) lib bdg $22.60

Grades: 2 3 4   **745.594**

1. Handicraft 2. Chinese New Year
ISBN 0-7660-2347-8

LC 2004-9622

This includes directions for ten craft projects related to
Chinese New Year including a dragon-streamer puppet, a
ribbon lantern, and Chinese zodiac pictures

This is "aesthetically pleasing with . . . bright colorful
pages, clear concise instructions on the left side and photographs of various stages of the final product on the right. . .
. Use of everyday items such as paper cups, cupcake liners,
and construction paper makes these activities practical for
both students and teachers." SLJ

Includes bibliographical references

Di Salle, Rachel

Junk drawer jewelry; written by Rachel Di Salle and
Ellen Warwick; illustrated by Jane Kurisu. Kids Can Press
2006 40p il (Kids can do it) hardcover o.p. pa $6.95

Grades: 4 5 6   **745.594**

1. Jewelry 2. Handicraft
ISBN 978-1-55337-965-2; 978-1-55337-966-9 pa

This introduces the "world of jewelry crafting. . . . Projects of varying difficulty include bracelets, necklaces, rings,
wristbands, chokers, and earrings. Each project is accompanied by a color photo, a You Will Need list, and step-by-step
instructions. This book will be a popular addition to libraries." SLJ

Fritsch, P.

Pennsylvania Dutch Halloween scherenschnitte; written and illustrated by Peter V. Fritsch. Pelican 2011 78p
il $19.95

Grades: 3 4 5 6   **745.594**

1. Paper crafts 2. Pennsylvania Dutch folk art 3.
Halloween -- Poetry
ISBN 978-1-58980-956-7; 1-58980-956-4

LC 2011012276

"In the tradition of Pennsylvania Dutch folk art, Fritsch
arranges scherenschnitte (scissor-cut) silhouettes against
flaming orange backgrounds. Short poems, which appear
both in the Pennsylvania Dutch dialect and in English, mine
folklore with rascally and sometimes frightening results,
and are set against often symmetrical scenes of angular cats,
ghosts, witches, and other devilish creatures. An elegant
treat harkens back to early American celebrations of Halloween." Publ Wkly

Gnojewski, Carol

Cinco de Mayo crafts; [by] Carol Gnojewski. Enslow
Publishers 2004 32p il (Fun holiday crafts kids can do)
lib bdg $22.66

Grades: 2 3 4   **745.594**

1. Handicraft 2. Cinco de Mayo
ISBN 0-7660-2344-3

LC 2004-9624

This includes instructions for ten craft projects related
the Cinco de Mayo including a peace votive, sombrero, and
paper poncho

This is "aesthetically pleasing with . . . bright colorful
pages, clear concise instructions on the left side and photographs of various stages of the final product on the right. . .
. Use of everyday items such as paper cups, cupcake liners,
and construction paper makes these activities practical for
both students and teachers." SLJ

Includes bibliographical references

Levine, Shar

Extreme balloon tying; more than 40 over-the-top projects. [by] Shar Levine & Michael Ouchi. Sterling Pub. Co.
2006 91p il pa $9.95

Grades: 3 4 5 6   **745.594**

1. Balloons 2. Handicraft
ISBN 978-1-4027-2465-7 pa; 1-4027-2465-9 pa

LC 2006007319

This explains "how to make balloon figures. . . . The
book offers complete, step-by-step directions for a variety
of appealing projects, illustrated with exceptionally precise
drawings and color photos." Booklist

McGee, Randel

Paper crafts for Chinese New Year; [by] Randel McGee. Enslow Elementary 2008 48p il (Paper craft fun for holidays) lib bdg $23.93

Grades: 2 3 4   **745.594**

1. Paper crafts 2. Chinese New Year

ISBN 978-0-7660-2950-7 lib bdg; 0-7660-2950-6 lib bdg

LC 2007014026

This explains the significance of Chinese New Year and offers instructions for making paper crafts including a dancing dragon puppet, a lion dancer mask, a lai see or red gift envelope, shadow puppets, a tangram, a chinese lantern, firecracker decorations, and Chinese symbols and banners.

"The crafts contain materials lists and color photos of the steps and of the finished product. The directions are easy to follow, and enlargeable patterns are provided." SLJ

Includes bibliographical references

Paper crafts for Christmas; [by] Randel McGee. Enslow Elementary 2009 48p il (Paper craft fun for holidays) lib bdg $23.93

Grades: 2 3 4   **745.594**

1. Christmas 2. Paper crafts

ISBN 978-0-7660-2952-1 lib bdg; 0-7660-2952-2 lib bdg

Provides a brief introduction to the history of Christmas, and Christmas-themed paper craft ideas

"Filled with cultural facts . . . [this book offers] much more than just basic craft ideas. . . . Kids will . . . enjoy piecing together these appealing projects. . . . A pop-up card that sends Santa down the chimney is particularly inventive." Booklist

Paper crafts for Day of the Dead; [by] Randel McGee. Enslow Elementary 2008 48p il (Paper craft fun for holidays) lib bdg $23.93

Grades: 2 3 4   **745.594**

1. Paper crafts 2. All Souls' Day

ISBN 978-0-7660-2951-4 lib bdg; 0-7660-2951-4 lib bdg

LC 2007013987

This explains the significance of the Mexican Day of the Dead, and offers instructions for paper crafts including paper marigolds, a skeleton candy basket, happy skeleton figures, skeleton pets, paper clothes for skeletons, a skull mask, papel cortado window banners, and Aztec animal decorations.

"The crafts contain materials lists and color photos of the steps and of the finished product. The directions are easy to follow, and enlargeable patterns are provided." SLJ

Includes bibliographical references

Paper crafts for Halloween; [by] Randel McGee. Enslow Elementary 2009 48p il (Paper craft fun for holidays) lib bdg $23.93

Grades: 2 3 4   **745.594**

1. Halloween 2. Paper crafts

ISBN 978-0-7660-2947-7 lib bdg; 0-7660-2947-6 lib bdg

LC 2007014048

"Filled with cultural facts, [this book offers] . . . much more than just basic craft ideas. . . . Kids will . . . enjoy piecing together these appealing projects." Booklist

Includes bibliographical references

Paper crafts for Kwanzaa; [by] Randel McGee. Enslow Elementary 2008 48p il (Paper craft fun for holidays) lib bdg $23.93

Grades: 2 3 4   **745.594**

1. Kwanzaa 2. Paper crafts

ISBN 978-0-7660-2949-1 lib bdg; 0-7660-2949-2 lib bdg

LC 2007014039

This explains the significance of Kwanzaa and offers instructions for paper crafts including a kinara pop-up card, a mkeka mat, a muhindi or ear of corn, standing Kwanzaa figures, a standing fruit tree, cut-outs of the Nguzo Saba or Seven Guiding Principles, a lion, and an African-style hat.

"The crafts are attractive and easy to make with adult help, and they use common supplies." SLJ

Includes bibliographical references

Paper crafts for Valentine's Day. Enslow Publishers 2008 48p il (Paper craft fun for holidays) lib bdg $23.93

Grades: 2 3 4   **745.594**

1. Paper crafts 2. Valentine's Day

ISBN 978-0-7660-2948-4 lib bdg; 0-7660-2948-4 lib bdg

LC 2007014041

Explains the significance of Valentine's Day and offers instructions for making paper crafts including a Cupid figure, a heart sculpture, a lacy heart card, a pop-up heart card, a valentine heart crown, heart flowers, a stick puppet, and a Danish woven heart basket.

"These eight crafts are simple to complete, with easy-to-follow instructions. A color photo of the finished piece is included." SLJ

Includes bibliographical references

Rau, Dana Meachen

Get connected; make a friendship bracelet. Norwood House Press 2010 48p il (Creative adventure guides) lib bdg $25.27

Grades: 3 4 5 6   **745.594**

1. Beadwork 2. Bracelets

ISBN 978-1-59953-385-8; 1-59953-385-5

LC 2010010404

"Some historical background and scientific or cultural information places the making and use of . . . jewelry . . . in context for young readers. [The] book has four chapters that culminate in step-by-step projects." Horn Book Guide

Includes glossary and bibliographical references

Trusty, Brad

The **kids'** guide to balloon twisting; by Brad and Cindy Trusty. Capstone Press 2011 32p il (Kids' guides) lib bdg $26.65

Grades: 4 5 6 7   **745.594**

1. Balloons 2. Handicraft

ISBN 978-1-4296-5444-9; 1-4296-5444-9

LC 2010036470

Gives kids step-by-step instructions about how to twist balloon animals and other shapes.

"Rare is the kid not dazzled by the squeaking, twisting balloon maestros out there, and this brightly illustrated, step-by-step guide makes it easy—well, easy-ish." Booklist

Includes bibliographical references

Jazzy jewelry. Kingfisher 2007 48p il (Ecocrafts) pa $7.95

Grades: 3 4 5 6 **745.594**

1. Jewelry 2. Recycling 3. Handicraft

ISBN 978-0-7534-5969-0 pa; 0-7534-5969-8 pa

This offers instructions for making jewelry out of recycled materials such as buttons, bottle caps, beads, safety pins, fabric scraps, chop sticks, key rings, and plastic bags.

745.6 Calligraphy, heraldic design, illumination

Hanson, Anders

Cool calligraphy; the art of creativity for kids. [by] Anders Hanson. ABDO Pub. Co. 2009 32p il (Cool art) lib bdg $24.21

Grades: 2 3 4 **745.6**

1. Calligraphy

ISBN 978-1-60453-145-9 lib bdg; 1-60453-145-2 lib bdg

LC 2008-19885

This book about calligraphy is "well organized, with clearly written sections . . . and several clever projects and exercises. . . . [It] should have substantial child appeal." SLJ

Includes glossary

Winters, Eleanor

★ 1 2 3 calligraphy! letters and projects for beginners and beyond. Sterling Pub. Co. 2006 128p il $14.95

Grades: 4 5 6 7 **745.6**

1. Calligraphy

ISBN 1-4027-1839-X; 978-1-4027-1839-7

LC 2005022071

"Twenty well-written, easy-to-follow explanatory chapters are filled with plenty of practical exercises. Chapters are grouped into three parts with the first reviewing calligraphy basics, vocabulary, and types of writing instruments. The second part teaches italic, swing gothic, and modern gothic alphabets. Finally, creative projects such as stationery, envelopes, signs, and 'calligrams' are described." SLJ

745.7 Decorative coloring

Wagner, Lisa

★ Cool painted stuff; [by] Lisa Wagner. ABDO Pub. 2005 32p il (Cool crafts) $22.78

Grades: 4 5 6 **745.7**

1. Painting 2. Handicraft

ISBN 1-59197-742-8

LC 2004-53117

This guide to painted crafts "includes four projects (in six or seven steps): a flowered mini-tote, checkered frame, treasure box, and fancy flowerpot. [This book lists] required materials, [has] small color photos, and [includes] clearly explained, numbered steps." SLJ

746 Textile arts

Torres, Laura

Rock your room. QEB Pub. 2010 32p il (Rock your . . .) $28.50

Grades: 4 5 6 **746**

1. Handicraft 2. Interior design

ISBN 978-1-59566-938-4; 1-59566-938-8

This book "gives kids easy step-by-step ways to make decorations for their rooms . . . . Colorful photographs show youngsters crafting appealing . . . wall decorations, . . . etc., some of which are created from recycled found items. All are projects they can complete by themselves." Horn Book Guide

Warwick, Ellen

Injeanuity; written by Ellen Warwick; illustrated by Bernice Lum. Kids Can Press 2006 80p il (Planet girl) spiral bdg $12.95

Grades: 5 6 7 8 **746**

1. Sewing 2. Handicraft 3. Denim -- Juvenile literature 4. Textile crafts -- Juvenile literature 5. Jeans (Clothing) -- Juvenile literature

ISBN 978-1-55337-681-1 spiral bdg; 1-55337-681-1 spiral bdg

"Warwick combines a love of denim with some simple crafts that will have readers thinking and feeling like fashion designers. . . . [The book] includes 17 projects from re-wearable jeans to purses and wallets to bolsters and footstools to halters and skirts and more. All include clear, easy-to-follow instructions and informative illustrations." SLJ

746.1 Products and processes

Roessel, Monty

Songs from the loom; a Navajo girl learns to weave. text and photographs by Monty Roessel. Lerner Publs. 1995 48p il (We are still here) lib bdg $21.27; pa $6.95

Grades: 3 4 5 6 **746.1**

1. Weaving 2. Navajo Indians 3. Fabrics -- Juvenile literature 4. Weaving -- Juvenile literature 5. Navajo Indians -- Juvenile literature

ISBN 0-8225-2657-3 lib bdg; 0-8225-9712-8 pa

LC 94-48765

"Ten-year-old Jaclyn's grandmother teaches her the art of traditional Navajo rug-weaving. Jaclyn learns the songs and stories that invest the weaving with meaning, as well as the use of the proper tools and techniques. The color photographs of contemporary Navajo life are clear and engrossing, enhancing the solid text." Horn Book Guide

Includes glossary and bibliographical references

746.4 Needlework and handwork

Sadler, Judy Ann

★ The jumbo book of needlecrafts; written by Judy Ann Sadler . . . [et al.]; illustrated by Esperaça Melo . . . [et al.] Kids Can Press 2005 208p il $16.95

Grades: 4 5 6 **746.4**

1. Needlework

ISBN 1-55337-793-1

A compilation with a new introduction of 5 books previously published: Knitting by Judy Ann Sadler (2002); Crocheting by Gwen Blakely Kinsler (2003); Simply sewing by Judy Ann Sadler (2004); Embroidery by Judy Ann Sadler (2004); Quilting by Biz Storms (2001)

This is a "how-to guide to the basics of knitting, crocheting, embroidery, quilting, and sewing. . . . The volume begins with helpful suggestions on gathering supplies, measuring, selecting fabric, and stitching. The rest of the book presents detailed, step-by-step directions on basic techniques for projects that range from very simple to intricate. . . . Color drawings and photographs are appealing as well as instructive. . . . An excellent addition to needlework collections." SLJ

746.41 Weaving, braiding, matting unaltered vegetable fibers

Swett, Sarah
Kids weaving; [by] Sarah Swett; photographs by Chris Hartlove; illustrations by Lena Corwin. Stewart, Tabori & Chang 2005 128p il $19.95
Grades: 4 5 6 7   **746.41**
1. Weaving
ISBN 1-58479-467-4
     LC 2005000650
"Swett introduces this craft with a simple weaving of a checkerboard note card—a task requiring two pieces of paper and a pair of scissors. After mastering the technique with several different small projects, she explains how to weave a hideout out of sticks and vines in the yard. She demonstrates techniques on a cardboard loom and progresses to skills for weaving on a pipe loom. These projects show the whimsical and the practical, the useful and the decorative aspects of the art. Hartlove's excellent-quality, full-color photos depict children enjoying the craft in many different settings. . . . In addition, the helpful step-by-step drawings clearly depict the processes and techniques." SLJ

Includes bibliographical references

746.42 Nonloom weaving and related techniques

Sadler, Judy Ann
Hemp jewelry; written by Judy Ann Sadler; illustrated by June Bradford. Kids Can Press 2005 40p il (Kids can do it) hardcover o.p. pa $6.96
Grades: 4 5 6   **746.42**
1. Jewelry 2. Macrame 3. Beadwork 4. Macramé 5. Handicraft -- Juvenile literature 6. Jewelry making -- Juvenile literature
ISBN 1-55337-774-5; 1-55337-775-3 pa
This "provides instructions for making jewelry from strands of hemp that are woven in various patterns while incorporating beads, clasps, and other findings. . . . Attractive and easy to follow. . . . Detailed, step-by-step instructions, . . . are clearly illustrated with large-scale, colorful ink-and-wash drawings." Booklist

★ Knotting; make your own basketball nets, guitar straps, sports bags and more! written by Judy Ann Sadler;

illustrated by Céleste Gagnon. Kids Can Press 2006 40p il (Kids can do it) $12.95; pa $6.99
Grades: 4 5 6   **746.42**
1. Handicraft 2. Knots and splices
ISBN 1-55337-541-6; 1-55337-834-2 pa
This describes how use rope to make various types of knots, lanyards, guitar straps, ladders, hanging holders, swings, dog leashes, and basketball nets.

746.43 Knitting, crocheting, tatting

Blanchette, Peg
12 easy knitting projects. Williamson Books 2006 63p il (Quick starts for kids!) pa $8.95
Grades: 3 4 5 6   **746.43**
1. Knitting
ISBN 0-8249-6785-2
     LC 2005029247
"With its wide margins, color illustrations on every page, and well-spaced text, this book will appeal to beginners and accomplished knitters. It discusses the four basic yarn weights, lists materials, and offers step-by-step instructions for basic stitches, making fringe, and more. An icon indicates the complexity of each project." SLJ

Bradberry, Sarah
★ Kids knit! simple steps to nifty projects. [by] Sarah Bradberry. Sterling Pub. Co. 2004 96p il hardcover o.p. pa $9.95
Grades: 5 6 7 8   **746.43**
1. Knitting
ISBN 0-8069-7733-7; 978-1-4027-4057-2 pa; 1-4027-4057-3 pa
     LC 2004-19375
Presents basic knitting techniques and instructions for making a backpack, pillow, doll, and other simple projects
This "book works equally well for beginners and experienced knitters. . . . Besides the requisite information on knitting and purling, there are invaluable tips about finishing garments, fixing mistakes, and adding embellishments. The projects have been chosen with an eye toward simplicity, yet they have real appeal." Booklist

Davis, Jane
★ Crochet; fantastic jewelry, hats, purses, pillows & more. Lark Books 2005 112p il (Kids' crafts) $19.95; pa $9.95
Grades: 5 6 7 8   **746.43**
1. Crocheting
ISBN 978-1-57990-477-7; 1-57990-477-7; 978-1-60059-138-9 pa; 1-60059-138-8 pa
     LC 2004-13288
This describes basic crochet techniques and includes instructions for 50 projects
"The book is a pleasure to look at. . . . Photographs are large and crisp. . . . Davis clearly knows what kids like. . . . Both visual and text explanations are very clear. . . . This is a must for your craft shelves." Booklist

Guy, Lucinda
Kids learn to crochet; [by] Lucinda Guy & François Hall. Trafalgar Square Books 2008 96p il pa $15.95

Grades: 2 3 4   **746.43**
1. Crocheting
ISBN 978-1-57076-395-3 pa; 1-57076-395-X pa
LC 2008900190
"Softly hued, whimsical color illustrations are superimposed on sharp, vivid color photos in this eye-catching introduction. In step-by-step fashion, children will learn how (with adult guidance) to crochet a pen or pencil topper, cute critters, flowers, a bag, and more. Adorable mice guide children throughout with their 'Pip Says' and 'Peg Says' tips." SLJ

Kids learn to knit; [by] Lucinda Guy & Francois Hall. Trafalgar Square Pub. 2007 96p il pa $14.95
Grades: 2 3 4   **746.43**
1. Knitting
ISBN 1-56076-335-6
"After introducing the basics of knitting, the tools, and the materials, the handbook starts at the beginning (the slip knot, broken down into four steps); casting on (three steps); the knit stitch (five steps); and binding off (four steps). Each simply explained step is illustrated with at least one clear, larger-than-life illustration. Knitters . . . can proceed to sections on the purl stitch and the stockinette stitch, followed by six projects. . . . With breezy ink-and-watercolor cartoons of frolicking animals as well as bright photos, this book infuses instructions and advice with a welcome dose of fun." Booklist

Junor, Betty
Fun & funky knits; over 20 simple knit stitch projects. by Betty Junor. 1st North American ed. Barron's Educational Series, Inc. 2012 80 p. col. ill. (paperback) $7.99
Grades: 4 5 6   **746.43**
1. Knitting 2. Sewing -- Technique 3. Needlework -- Patterns 4. Knitting -- Patterns
ISBN 1438001746; 9781438001746
LC 2012932175
Author Betty Junor presents a book on knitting projects, "starting with very basic instructions and recommending the use of brilliantly colored yarns." Junor discusses slipknots, casting off, and finishing and gives directions for making headbands, belts, drawstring bags, and purses. She also shows readers how to make knitted flowers and how to incorporate pompoms into projects. (Publisher's note)

Sadler, Judy Ann
Quick knits; written by Judy Ann Sadler; illustrated by Esperança Melo. Kids Can Press 2006 40p il (Kids can do it) hardcover o.p. pa $6.95
Grades: 4 5 6   **746.43**
1. Knitting
ISBN 978-1-55337-963-8; 1-55337-963-2; 978-1-55337-964-5 pa; 1-55337-964-0 pa
This provides instructions for basic knitting stitches and simple projects including scarves, hats, cuffs, a wallet, a pillow, foot mats, slippers, and a sweater
"This attractively designed title features clear, colorful illustrations and an easy-to-follow text." SLJ

746.44   Embroidery

Sadler, Judy Ann
Embroidery; written by Judy Ann Sadler; illustrated by June Bradford. Kids Can Press 2004 40p il (Kids can do it) $12.95; pa $6.95
Grades: 4 5 6   **746.44**
1. Embroidery
ISBN 1-55337-616-1; 1-55337-617-X pa
"With an attractively designed cover featuring photos of sample projects, this book is sure to encourage interest in needlework." SLJ

746.46   Patchwork and quilting

Rau, Dana Meachen
Quilting for fun! Compass Point Books 2009 48p il (For fun) lib bdg $25.26
Grades: 3 4 5   **746.46**
1. Quilting
ISBN 978-0-7565-3860-6 lib bdg; 0-7565-3860-2 lib bdg
LC 2008008274
This covers the basics of quilting, a brief history, and instructions for five quilting projects
"Varied typefaces and colors, large print, good spacing, and lively and creative arrangement make [this book] attractive, and color photos and other illustrations throughout are easy to follow. . . . Materials are easily obtainable from craft stores, and some are readily available at home." SLJ
Includes glossary and bibliographical references

Storms, Biz
Quilting; written by Biz Storms; illustrated by June Bradford. Kids Can Press 2001 40p il (Kids can do it) $12.95; pa $5.95
Grades: 4 5 6   **746.46**
1. Quilting
ISBN 1-55074-967-6; 1-55074-805-X pa
"Quilting uses step-by-step instructions keyed to excellent color illustrations to present basics. Ten kid-pleasing projects of increasing difficulty follow—from an appliquéd tee shirt to a full-size quilt—each as appealingly and clearly presented as the last." Booklist

746.9   Other textile products

Bertoletti, John C.
How fashion designers use math; math curriculum consultant: Rhea A. Stewart. Chelsea Clubhouse 2010 32p il (Math in the real world) lib bdg $28
Grades: 4 5 6   **746.9**
1. Mathematics 2. Fashion design 3. Fashion -- Vocational guidance
ISBN 978-1-60413-606-7 lib bdg; 1-60413-606-5 lib bdg
LC 2009-22683
This describes how designers use math to measure, create, and produce their fashions, and includes problems to solve and information about how to become a fashion designer

"Color photos of designers in action combine with diagrams that further clarify the easily digestible text." Booklist

Includes glossary and bibliographical references

Blaxland, Wendy

Sweaters. Marshall Cavendish Benchmark 2011 32p il map (How are they made?) lib bdg $12.99

Grades: 4 5 6 **746.9**

1. Wool 2. Knitting 3. Sweaters

ISBN 978-0-7614-4756-6 lib bdg; 0-7614-4756-3 lib bdg

LC 2009039882

This describes how sweaters are made, including their history, parts, design, wool and synthetic fibers, raw materials, manufacture, packaging and distribution, marketing and advertising, and their affects on the environment

Includes glossary

747 Interior decoration

Weaver, Janice

★ It's your room; a decorating guide for real kids. [by] Janice Weaver and Frieda Wishinsky; illustrated by Claudia Dávila. Tundra Books 2006 63p il pa $14.95

Grades: 5 6 7 8 **747**

1. Interior design

ISBN 0-88776-711-7

"Budding interior designers and readers who want to personalize their rooms will appreciate this title. It is filled with step-by-step guidelines for creating a budget, selecting paint colors and fabrics, organizing closets and desks, laying everything out, and adding finishing touches. The illustrations will be a hit with first-time decorators just starting to develop their own color sense." SLJ

748.5 Stained, painted, leaded, mosaic glass

Kenney, Karen Latchana

Super simple glass jar art; fun and easy-to-make crafts for kids. ABDO Pub. Co. 2010 32p il (Super simple crafts) lib bdg $17.95

Grades: K 1 2 3 4 **748.5**

1. Glass 2. Handicraft

ISBN 978-1-60453-624-9 lib bdg; 1-60453-624-1 lib bdg

LC 2009-352

"Colorful photos; clean layout in a bright, primary palette; and large, abundant step-by-step instructional photos give [this book] great appeal. The . . . crafts . . . are functional and attractive. . . . Readily obtainable household materials and easy-to-follow instructions mean that children can do these crafts independently." SLJ

Includes glossary

750 Painting and paintings

Cressy, Judith

★ Can you find it? Abrams 2002 40p il $15.95

Grades: 2 3 4 5 **750**

1. Painting 2. Art appreciation 3. Painting --

Appreciation -- Juvenile literature

ISBN 0-8109-3279-2

LC 2002-18358

"Nineteen paintings from New York City's Metropolitan Museum of Art were chosen for careful scrutiny in this book. Next to each striking, full-color reproduction is a list of items to search for: e.g., '2 cats, 6 lotus blossoms, 3 eye amulets,' etc., for a painting from ancient Egypt. The works of art are from around the globe and range from illuminated manuscripts to 20th-century canvases. Designed to encourage discovery, the tiny, sometimes indistinct details will keep children engrossed for hours." SLJ

Other titles in this series are:

Can you find it, too? by Judith Cressey (2004)

Can you find it inside? by by Jessica Schulte (2005)

Can you find it outside? by Jessice Schulte (2005)

Can you find it? America by Linda Falken (2010)

D'Harcourt, Claire

★ Masterpieces up close; by Claire d'Harcourt. Chronicle Books 2006 63p il $22.95

Grades: 4 5 6 7 **750**

1. Painting 2. Art appreciation 3. Painting -- Appreciation -- Juvenile literature 4. Painting -- Themes, motives -- Juvenile literature

ISBN 0-8118-5403-5

LC 2004-16341

"From Giotto to Warhol, d'Harcourt selects some of the most famous icons of Western art for a closer look. . . . The format of this oversize volume [consists of] boldly colored spreads featuring a central, large image surrounded by smaller details from it. Interesting tidbits and questions accompany each small picture, inviting viewers to wonder, think, and question what they see. . . . The last pages include lift-the-flap copies of the paintings and biographical sketches of the artists. A visually striking volume for browsers and art education." SLJ

Micklethwait, Lucy

Children; a first art book. Frances Lincoln Children's 2006 un il $14.95

Grades: K 1 2 3 **750**

1. Painting 2. Children in art 3. Art appreciation

ISBN 1-84507-116-6

"This title uses works by 18 different artists to illustrate its theme. Children are shown in nine activities, from Reading and writing to Sleeping. . . . The artwork represents several cultures and ethnic groups, as well as styles and time periods. Text is minimal—just enough to encourage conversation about the reproductions. An excellent first exposure to fine art, and great preparation for museum visits." SLJ

In the picture; get looking! get thinking! Frances Lincoln 2010 un il $17.95

Grades: K 1 2 3 4 **750**

1. Painting 2. Art appreciation

ISBN 978-1-84507-636-8; 1-84507-636-2

Micklethwait "combines familiar techniques that fold a hunt-and-find game into a survey of such diverse artworks as Marc Chagall's dreamy 1911 painting I and the Village and an amazingly intricate 1590s battle scene from the Mughal Empire text The Akbarnama. Intriguing close-ups pulled from each artwork appear across from a crisp reproduction of the full image. . . . Additional activities . . . are included on each spread and an extensive, appended section." Booklist

Raczka, Bob

★ **Artful** reading; [by] Bob Raczka. Millbrook Press 2007 32p il lib bdg $25.26

Grades: 1 2 3 4   **750**

1. Painting 2. Reading in art 3. Art appreciation
ISBN 978-0-8225-6754-7

                                       LC 2006035083

"Through 23 works of art, Raczka shows the timeless appeal of reading. . . . Simple sentences serve as captions to these masterpieces. . . . Each work is clearly labelled, and endnotes provide information about the artists and their paintings, among them Edgar Degas and Dante Gabriel Rossetti." SLJ

★ **More** than meets the eye; seeing art with all five senses. by Bob Raczka. Millbrook Press 2003 32p il hardcover o.p. pa $9.95

Grades: K 1 2 3   **750**

1. Painting 2. Art appreciation 3. Art appreciation -- Juvenile literature 4. Painting -- Appreciation -- Juvenile literature
ISBN 0-7613-2797-5 lib bdg; 0-7613-1994-8 pa

                                       LC 2003-343

Provides images of paintings and new, sensory ways to experience them, such as tasting the milk in Vermeer's "The Milkmaid," hearing the music in Tanner's "The Banjo Lesson," or feeling the fur in da Vinci's "Lady with an Ermine."

"Raczka's short, rhyming text gives structure to the book, but the color reproductions of well-chosen, vivid paintings steal the show. This art book rests on a simple concept, beautifully executed." Booklist

★ **Unlikely** pairs; fun with famous works of art. [by] Bob Raczka. Millbrook Press 2006 31p il lib bdg $23.93; pa $9.95

Grades: 4 5 6 7   **750**

1. Painting 2. Art appreciation
ISBN 0-7613-2936-6 lib bdg; 0-7613-2378-3 pa

                                       LC 2003-14078

Invites the reader to discover fourteen funny stories produced by pairing twenty-eight paintings from different eras and styles

"Raczka deserves an A+ for cleverness. . . . Rodin's The Thinker is juxtaposed with Klee's modernistic painting of a chessboard so that the statue looks as if it is contemplating the next move. Siméon-Chardin's picture of a boy blowing soap bubbles seems to be creating Kandinsky's Several Circles. Each selection takes up a page and is reproduced in crisp color. . . . This book is an amusing way to introduce children to famous works of art." SLJ

Schulte, Jessica

Can you find it inside? H.N. Abrams 2005 un il $10.95

Grades: 2 3 4 5   **750**

1. Painting 2. Art appreciation
ISBN 0-8109-5794-9

                                       LC 2005000990

"Two-line rhymes present clues to help young readers find details in paintings from the collections of the Metro-politan Museum of Art. Each painting, or portion of it, is matched with three couplets." SLJ

Wenzel, Angela

13 paintings children should know. Prestel 2009 il $14.95

Grades: 5 6 7 8   **750**

1. Painting 2. Art appreciation
ISBN 978-3-7913-4323-5; 3-7913-4323-8

This "large-format, brightly colored [survey provides a] solid, even inspiring [introduction] to the art world. . . . Leading questions encourage budding artists to use the featured subjects and artworks as inspiration." Horn Book Guide

Includes glossary

750.1   Philosophy and theory

Richardson, Joy

Looking at pictures; an introduction to art for young people. with illustrations by Charlotte Voake. rev ed.; Abrams Books for Young Readers 2009 80p il $21.95

Grades: 4 5 6 7   **750.1**

1. Painting 2. Art appreciation
ISBN 978-0-8109-8288-8; 0-8109-8288-9

                                       LC 2008055684

First published 1997

This "exploration of thirteenth- to twentieth-century European paintings examines the subject matter and techniques used and also delves into how the pieces were restored. Other topics covered are pigments, the use of light and perspective, the depiction of special events and daily life, and painting people and nature. Occasional well-placed illustrations supplement the numerous color reproductions." Horn Book Guide

Includes bibliographical references

Wolfe, Gillian

Look! Drawing the line in art. Frances Lincoln 2008 44p il $17.95

Grades: 3 4 5   **750.1**

1. Art appreciation
ISBN 978-1-84507-824-9; 1-84507-824-1

"Each spread introduces a different technique, such as 'strong lines' and 'leafy lines' and shows a work of fine art demonstrating it, reproduced with clarity and in full color. Occasionally, the text defines artistic techniques, such as perspective and shading. Each spread has kid-friendly ideas for making one's own creations. . . . There is a wide range of dates for the art featured, beginning in the 1600s and ending in 2003. The text describes how each piece was created and includes some anecdotal stories about the artist and the work. . . . This is an accessible introduction to art history." SLJ

Look! Seeing the light in art. Frances Lincoln 2007 45p il $16.95

Grades: 3 4 5   **750.1**

1. Art appreciation
ISBN 978-1-84507-467-8; 1-84507-467-X

"Wolfe invites readers to examine how artists have tried to convey qualities of light in works that represent night, day, rainstorms, sunlight, heat, cold, and use light to create the texture and shape of objects. Each spread includes a suggestion for an art activity . . . as well as a page of accessible text, in large print, that presents questions and observations designed to draw viewers back into the well-reproduced artworks. With a few exceptions, the artists represented are well-known, male, European masters, such as Caravaggio and Renoir." Booklist

751.4   Techniques and procedures

Hanson, Anders

Cool painting; the art of creativity for kids. [by] Anders Hanson. ABDO Pub. Co. 2009 32p il (Cool art) lib bdg $24.21

Grades: 2 3 4   751.4

   1. Painting -- Technique

   ISBN 978-1-60453-143-5 lib bdg; 1-60453-143-6 lib bdg

                         LC 2008-22243

This book about painting is "well organized, with clearly written sections . . . and several clever projects and exercises. . . . [It] should have substantial child appeal." SLJ

   Includes glossary

Lipsey, Jennifer

   ★ I love to finger paint! [by] Jennifer Lipsey. Lark Books 2006 48p il (My very favorite art book) $9.95

Grades: K 1 2 3   751.4

   1. Finger painting

   ISBN 1-57990-771-7

                       LC 2005034821

"Lipsey describes a variety of painting techniques that can be used to create intriguing designs—finger and handprinting, patterning, scraping and scratching, texturing, even painting with feet and palms. Pictures in a rainbow of brilliant colors accompany the instructions, supplying children with examples to copy and inspiration to extend what they have learned to make more pictures. Excellent for teachers, and, with oversight from adults, for kids themselves." Booklist

   ★ I love to paint! Lark Books 2005 48p il (My very favorite art book) $9.95

Grades: K 1 2 3   751.4

   1. Painting 2. Painting -- Technique

   ISBN 1-57990-630-3

This offers instruction in such techniques as finger painting, watercolors, scratch art, sponge painting, using straws to blow paint around the pages, and stenciling

   "Here's a book that is as attractive as it is useful. . . . This is exceptionally well organized." Booklist

Luxbacher, Irene

   1 2 3 I can paint! Kids Can Press 2007 23p il (Starting art) $14.95; pa $5.95

Grades: 2 3 4   751.4

   1. Painting -- Technique

   ISBN 978-1-55453-037-3; 978-1-55453-150-9 pa; 1-55453-150-0 pa; 1-55453-037-7

This "introduces aspiring artists to some materials and techniques that can be successfully used to create pictures with paint. Luxbacher discusses primary and secondary col-

ors; backgrounds; color tones; cool warm, and complementary colors; perspective and line; and several brush strokes. The brief text offers clear definitions of terms and easy-to-follow instructions for projects. . . . The artwork . . . will be easy for children to replicate." Booklist

Peot, Margaret

   ★ Inkblot; drip, splat, and squish your way to creativity. Boyds Mills Press 2011 56p il $19.95

Grades: 4 5 6 7   751.4

   1. Ink painting 2. Art -- Technique -- Juvenile literature 3. Painting -- Technique -- Juvenile literature

   ISBN 1-59078-720-X; 978-1-59078-720-5

                       LC 22010-929541

This describes how to make inkblots and use them in art and as inspiration for writing and other forms of creativity.

   "Peot's own entrancing inkblots . . . plus a few guest blots, illustrate every step, showing how the pure blot becomes a final artwork. . . . Readers get clear directions and lively encouragement." Kirkus

   Includes bibliographical references

751.7   Specific forms

Bingham, Jane

   Graffiti. Raintree 2009 32p il (Culture in action) $28.21; pa $7.99

Grades: 5 6 7 8   751.7

   1. Graffiti 2. Mural painting and decoration

   ISBN 978-1-4109-3401-7; 1-4109-3401-2; 978-1-4109-3418-5 pa; 1-4109-3418-7 pa

                       LC 2008054323

"According to the time line in the . . . book, graffiti can be traced back to 60,000 BCE and paintings on cave walls. A note on the contents page states that it is illegal to draw on other people's property without permission. The different types of graffiti described are interesting, and some of the artwork is beautiful. A section on problems talks about ugly tags (short nicknames), the expense of cleanup, and how some cities have legal graffiti walls. . . . Well organized and with bright, colorful photography, [this] introductory [title gives] readers good basic knowledge." SLJ

   Includes glossary and bibliographical references

Harris, Nathaniel

   Wall paintings. PowerKids Press 2009 30p il (Stories in art) lib bdg $25.25

Grades: 4 5 6 7   751.7

   1. Mural painting and decoration

   ISBN 978-1-4042-4440-5 lib bdg; 1-4042-4440-9 lib bdg

                       LC 2007-52739

"This title explains the concept of wall paintings and how they were executed by using well-known examples. . . . Pages are well-designed with a paragraph about the painting and a section which gives some background information. . . . This is a useful addition to the art shelves." Libr Media Connect

   Includes glossary and bibliographical references

757 Human figures

Raczka, Bob

★ **Here's** looking at me; how artists see themselves. [by] Bob Raczka. Millbrook Press 2006 32p il lib bdg $23.93

Grades: 3 4 5 6   **757**

1. Artists 2. Self-portraits 3. Artists -- Juvenile literature

ISBN 978-0-7613-3404-0 lib bdg; 0-7613-3404-1 lib bdg

LC 2005006144

This is a "top-notch introduction to self-portraiture." SLJ

Thomson, Ruth

Portraits. Chelsea Clubhouse 2004 32p il (First look at art) $14.95

Grades: 2 3 4 5   **757**

1. Portraits 2. Art appreciation

ISBN 0-7910-7948-1

LC 2003-14428

First published 2003 in the United Kingdom

This describes various types of portraits including profiles and silhouettes, self-portraits, depictions of royalty, multiple faces, heroic portraits, and collage portraits, and includes related art activities.

"Teachers will find easy-to-understand art lessons and projects and students will find inspiration in [this] well-organized, attractive [title]." SLJ

Includes glossary

759 History, geographic treatment, biography

Kelley, True

Claude Monet: sunshine and waterlilies; written and illustrated by True Kelley. Grosset & Dunlap 2001 un il (Smart about art) $14.89; pa $7.50

Grades: 2 3 4   **759**

1. Artists 2. Painters 3. Artists, French 4. Painters -- France -- Biography -- Juvenile literature

ISBN 0-448-42613-7; 0-448-42522-X pa

LC 2001-23147

Written in the format of a school report by a fictitious student named Kristin Cole, this recounts the events in the life of the French artist and offers insight into his work

Illustrated with "charming childlike drawings and reproductions of the artist's paintings in scrapbook-style layouts. . . . [This] is a successful blend of fact and humor that makes sophisticated concepts completely accessible and even entertaining." Booklist

Markel, Michelle

The **fantastic** jungles of Henri Rousseau; by Michelle Markel; illustrated by Amanda Hall. Eerdmans Books for Young Readers 2012 34 p. (alk. paper) $17.00

Grades: PreK K 1 2 3   **759**

1. Outsider art 2. Painters -- France -- Biography 3. Painters -- France -- Biography -- Juvenile literature

ISBN 0802853641; 9780802853646

LC 2011035838

This children's picture book chronicles the life and work of "France's most celebrated naïve painter -- Henri Rous-

seau. . . . When was in his 40s, Rousseau . . . began to recreate himself as an artist. Though he had no formal training and few financial resources, he persevered. . . . Rousseau was ridiculed repeatedly by critics and artists, yet he continued to create his exotic, seemingly unsophisticated paintings." (Kirkus Reviews)

Monet, Claude

Monet's impressions; words and pictures. Chronicle Books 2009 un il $15.99

Grades: K 1 2 3   **759**

1. Art appreciation 2. Impressionism (Art)

ISBN 978-0-8118-7056-6; 0-8118-7056-1

LC 2009004287

"This simple, stunning title pairs details from the artist's paintings with short quotations from his letters and from articles in which he was quoted. At the back of the book, each painting is reproduced in full, with captions (medium, size, location) and a source for each quote. High-quality printing ensures that each brushstroke is in clear focus, and that colors are true." SLJ

Niepold, Mil

Oooh! Matisse; [by] Mil Niepold and Jeanyves Verdu. Tricycle Press 2007 un il $14.95

Grades: 2 3 4   **759**

1. Artists 2. Painters

ISBN 978-1-58246-227-1; 1-58246-227-5

LC 2006102319

"'What is this?' reads the text on the opening page of this vivid visual conundrum, which opens with four elongated, purplish-blue tear shapes set on a goldenrod background. The answer . . . is: 'Yellow, I am the sun and blue, I am the fingers that shield my eyes.' Four other color-and-shape constructs are presented in a similar manner. . . . The format seems simple, but this is really a sophisticated eye-opener." Booklist

Serres, Alain

★ **And** Picasso painted Guernica; written and designed by Alain Serres; translated by Rosalind Price. Allen & Unwin Children's 2010 51p il $24.99

Grades: 5 6 7 8   **759**

1. Artists 2. Painters 3. War in art

ISBN 978-1-74175-994-5; 1-74175-994-3

Original French edition, 2007

"Serres explains the mechanics of cubism . . . , tells the story of the horrifying German bombing of the civilians of Guernica and Picasso's reaction to it . . . , and finishes by tracing the rest of Picasso's career as he paints 'all the beauty of the world and its monstrous face as well.' The oversize pages are packed with period photographs and color reproductions of Picasso's sketches and paintings, each captioned in detail, with a double gatefold of Guernica at the center. . . . A passionate and intelligent tribute to the transformative power of art." Publ Wkly

759.05   Painting -- 1800-1899

Raimondo, Joyce

★ **Picture** this! activities and adventures in impressionism. Watson-Guptill 2004 48p il (Art explorers) $12.95

Grades: 3 4 5   **759.05**

1. Art appreciation 2. Impressionism (Art) 3. Art appreciation -- Juvenile literature 4. Impressionism (Art) -- Juvenile literature 5. Impressionism (Art) -- Technique -- Juvenile literature

ISBN 0-8230-2503-9

LC 2004-7356

"With step-by-step activities, full-color reproductions, and examples of children's imitative art, this slim volume provides a creative and simple introduction to the Impressionists. . . . Brief biographies of the painters are appended. A highly useful and entertaining book." SLJ

Sabbeth, Carol

★ **Monet** and the impressionists for kids; their lives and ideas, 21 activities. Chicago Review Press 2002 140p il pa $17.95

Grades: 5 6 7 8   **759.05**

1. Art appreciation 2. Impressionism (Art) 3. Impressionism (Art) -- Juvenile literature 4. Art, French -- 19th century -- Juvenile literature 5. Impressionist artists -- France -- Biography -- Juvenile literature

ISBN 1-55652-397-1

LC 2001-47191

Discusses the nineteenth-century French art movement known as Impressionism, focusing on the works of Monet, Renoir, Degas, Cassatt, Cezanne, Gauguin, and Seurat

"A beautifully designed introduction to Impressionism. . . . Sabbeth also includes 21 appealing extension activities such as recipes, crafts, games, and writing suggestions. Quality color reproductions on glossy pages, and varied, attractive layouts add to the book." SLJ

Includes glossary and bibliographical references

Van Gogh and the Post-Impressionists for kids; their lives and ideas, 21 activities. Chicago Review Press 2011 160p il

Grades: 4 5 6 7   **759.05**

1. Artists 2. Painters 3. Art appreciation 4. Postimpressionism (Art)

ISBN 1-56976-275-9; 978-1-56976-275-2

LC 2010053908

"The bulk of this wonderfully thorough study of Post-Impressionist artists focuses on van Gogh, with smaller sections devoted to Paul Gauguin, Henri de Toulouse-Lautrec, Paul Signac, and Emile Bernard. The highly engaging text follows the artists' lives with crisp writing and vivid detail, delving into their family backgrounds and relationships, and doesn't sugarcoat dark and gritty incidents such as van Gogh's self-inflicted ear amputation. Information is well organized. . . . Full-color reproductions of paintings discussed in the text add visual interest, and educational sidebars expound on topics mentioned in the main narrative. . . . With its creative, hands-on ideas for teaching art technique and history, this book is an excellent resource for students and teachers." SLJ

Includes glossary and bibliographical references

Sellier, Marie

Renoir's colors. Getty 2010 il bd bk $16.95

Grades: PreK K 1 2   **759.05**

1. Artists 2. Painters 3. Color in art 4. French painting 5. Board books for children

ISBN 978-1-60606-003-2 bd bk; 1-60606-003-1 bd bk

"Lift-the-flap windows spotlight pure colors in details of the artist's work. Turn the page to see the entire work, with a few simple lines of text guiding the eye to other shades of the highlighted color or adding an anecdote about the piece or model. Well-chosen paintings of familiar subjects . . . keep this small collection of fine art accessible to even the youngest child. This fine-art concept book is simply designed and superbly printed." SLJ

759.06   Painting -- 1900-1999

Barsony, Piotr

The **stories** of the Mona Lisa; an imaginary museum tale about the history of modern art. Piotr Barsony; translated from the French by Joanna Oseman. Skyhorse Publishing 2012 55 p. (hardcover: alk. paper) $19.95

Grades: 5 6 7 8   **759.06**

1. Art -- History 2. Mona Lisa (Painting) 3. Art movements -- Juvenile literature 4. Painting, Modern -- Juvenile literature

ISBN 1620872285; 9781620872284

LC 2012015603

"As [this book by Pietr Barsony] begins, a little girl asks: 'Dad, will you tell me a story?' The story her painter father tells is a history of art with the Mona Lisa as its central character. . . . He takes daughter and readers both on a journey of discovery through an imaginary museum. . . . Each painting is of only the Mona Lisa. . . . They are his own responses to and interpretations of Leonardo's masterpiece as filtered through the vision of other artists and movements." (Kirkus Reviews)

Raczka, Bob

No one saw; ordinary things through the eyes of an artist. Millbrook Press 2002 32p il lib bdg $23.90; pa $9.95

Grades: K 1 2 3   **759.06**

1. Modern painting 2. Art appreciation 3. Painting, Modern -- 19th century 4. Painting, Modern -- 20th century

ISBN 0-7613-2370-8 lib bdg; 0-7613-1648-3 pa

LC 2001-30006

"Reproductions of sixteen famous paintings, set against complementary backgrounds, reflect their creators' unique viewpoints, while a gentle rhyming text comments on the masterpieces ('No one saw mothers like Mary Cassatt. / No one saw Sunday like Georges Seurat'). The selections serve the impressionist through modern works well and conclude that 'nobody sees the world like you.'" Horn Book Guide

759.13 United States

Bryant, Jen

★ A **splash** of red; the life and art of Horace Pippin. by Jen Bryant; illustrated by Melissa Sweet. Alfred A. Knopf 2013 40 p. (hard cover) $17.99

Grades: K 1 2   **759.13**

1. Painters -- Biography 2. Veterans -- Biography 3. African American painters -- Biography -- Juvenile literature 4. Painters -- United States -- Biography -- Juvenile literature

ISBN 0375867120; 9780375867125; 9780375967122

LC 2012003209

This children's picture book by Jen Bryant presents a "portrait of African-American artist Horace Pippin (1888-1946). . . . From Pippin's young childhood . . . to his Army service in World War I, to the well-deserved fame that arrived only late in his life, he 'couldn't stop drawing.' When a military injury threatens Pippin's painting ability, he tries wood burning--'[u]sing his good arm to move the hurt one'-- and works his way back to painting." (Kirkus Reviews)

Close, Chuck, 1940-

Chuck Close; face book. by Chuck Close. Abrams Books for Young Readers 2012 64 p.

Grades: 3 4 5 6 7   **759.13**

1. Face in art 2. Vision disorders 3. Artists -- Interviews 4. Artists -- United States -- Biography 5. Artists -- United States -- Biography -- Juvenile literature

ISBN 9781419701634

LC 2011034557

In this book, "[Chuck] Close discloses struggles with childhood ill health and severe dyslexia. He tells how . . . he adjusted for his prosopagnosia (face blindness). . . . He also discloses the many 'hows' of his . . . technique: how he uses gridded photos to build his faces and how he works from his wheelchair and wields his brush with less-abled hands. . . . At the book's . . . center is the . . . opportunity to 'mix 'n' match' various eyes, noses and mouths among 14 of the artist's . . . self-portraits." (Kirkus)

Duggleby, John

★ **Story** painter: the life of Jacob Lawrence. Chronicle Bks. 1998 55p il $16.95

Grades: 4 5 6 7   **759.13**

1. Artists 2. Painters 3. Illustrators 4. African American artists 5. African American painters -- Biography 6. African Americans in art -- Juvenile literature

ISBN 0-8118-2082-3

LC 98-4513

A biography of the African American artist who grew up in the midst of the Harlem Renaissance and became one of the most renowned painters of the life of his people

"Lawrence's expressionistic, stark paintings, in excellent full-page color reproduction . . . nicely complement Duggleby's measured account of a materially poor but culturally rich childhood and Lawrence's subsequent struggles and successes." Publ Wkly

Includes bibliographical references

Falken, Linda C.

Can you find it? America; by Linda Falken. Abrams Books for Young Readers 2010 34p il $16.95

Grades: 2 3 4 5   **759.13**

1. Art appreciation 2. American painting

ISBN 978-0-8109-8890-3; 0-8109-8890-9

This "invites sharp-eyed viewers to pick out tiny details in 20 American paintings, textiles, and prints from the Met's collections. The selections include work from anonymous folk artists to the more recent likes of Faith Ringgold and Red Grooms. The pictures are all reproduced with knife-edged clarity. . . . Not only good preparation for a museum visit but also excellent practice for developing good general observation skills." Booklist

Gherman, Beverly

Norman Rockwell; storyteller with a brush. Atheneum Bks. for Young Readers 2000 57p il $19.95

Grades: 4 5 6 7   **759.13**

1. Artists 2. Painters 3. Illustrators 4. Artists -- United States 5. Painters -- United States -- Biography -- Juvenile literature

ISBN 0-689-82001-1

LC 98-36546

Describes the life and work of the popular American artist who depicted both traditional and contemporary subjects, including children, family scenes, astronauts, and the poor

"The format of the biography is appealing and attractive. The pages are replete with color reproductions of Rockwell's paintings as well as photographs of the man and his family. The text is well researched and authentic; the writing style is free-flowing and the words capture the naturalness of Rockwell's paintings." SLJ

Includes bibliographical references

Honoring our ancestors; stories and pictures by fourteen artists. edited by Harriet Rohmer. Children's Bk. Press 1999 31p il $15.95

Grades: 3 4 5 6   **759.13**

1. Artists 2. Minorities in art 3. Artists -- United States 4. Minorities in art -- Juvenile literature 5. Minority artists -- United States -- Psychology -- Juvenile literature

ISBN 0-89239-158-8

LC 98-38686

Fourteen artists and picture book illustrators present paintings with descriptions of ancestors or other sources of inspiration that have inspired them

This is "rewarding in its breadth and vivacity. The portraits are thematically rich yet accessible; generally, the texts are cheerful and resist sentimentality." Horn Book Guide

Lawrence, Jacob

The **great** migration; an American story. paintings by Jacob Lawrence; with a poem in appreciation by Walter Dean Myers. HarperCollins Pubs. 1993 un il hardcover o.p. pa $8.99

Grades: 4 5 6 7   **759.13**

1. African Americans in art

ISBN 0-06-023037-1; 0-06-443428-1 pa

LC 93-16788

"Lawrence is a storyteller with words as well as pictures: his captions and his own 1992 introduction to this book are the best commentary on his work." Booklist

Lincoln's Gettysburg address; a pictorial interpretation painted by James Daugherty. James Daugherty. Albert Whitman & Co. 2013 48 p.

Grades: 1 2 3 4   **759.13**

1. Gettysburg (Pa.) 2. Lincoln, Abraham, 1809-1865

ISBN 9780807545508

LC 2012013288

This children's book, illustrated by Caldecott Honoree and Newbery Medalist James Daugherty, presents the text of U.S. President Abraham Lincoln's Gettysburg Address. "The Gettysburg Address is one of the most influential speeches in our history, written by Abraham Lincoln at a crucial period in his presidency and in United States history." (Publisher's note)

759.2   European painting

Wenzel, Angela

  13 art mysteries children should know. Prestel 2011 45p il $14.95

Grades: 4 5 6   **759.2**

1. Art 2. Artists 3. Painting

ISBN 978-3-7913-7044-6; 379-1-37044-8

Presents information about thirteen mysteries from the art world, including questions about the Mona Lisa, van Gogh, and the street artist Banksy.

"Excellent-quality reproductions appear throughout. This is definitely a different approach for introducing young people to various aspects of art history. . . . The illustrations are well chosen to support these succinct inquiries into some perplexing puzzlements from the world of art." SLJ

759.4   French painting

Parker, Marjorie Blain

  ★ **Colorful** dreamer; the story of artist Henri Matisse. Marjorie Blain Parker; illustrated by Holly Berry. Dial Books For Young Readers 2012 32 p. (hardcover) $16.99

Grades: 3 4 5   **759.4**

1. Painters 2. Picture books for children 3. Artists -- France -- Biography -- Juvenile literature

ISBN 0803737580; 9780803737587

LC 2011035446

This "picture-book biography covers [Henri] Matisse's entire life but focuses on his career aspirations and achievements." The text includes "details such as young Henri's dream of becoming a magician and his skill with a peashooter. . . . Black-and-white drawings represent the artist's dull youth and colorful paintings are introduced when his career takes off." (School Library Journal)

" Berry's illustrations are the star of the show... The style of the artwork evokes Matisse more and more as the story progresses, ending, as his career did, with paper cut-out collage... A must for art teachers, and a nice addition to history and biography collections." Kirkus

759.9   Other geographic areas

Gogh, Vincent van

  ★ **Vincent's** colors; words and pictures by Vincent van Gogh. Chronicle Books 2005 un il $14.95

Grades: K 1 2 3   **759.9**

1. Color in art 2. Artists, Dutch

ISBN 0-8118-5099-4

"This text is pulled directly from the letters Van Gogh wrote about his paintings to his brother, Theo. Each line of the rhyming stanzas is accompanied by a rich, full-color reproduction of one of the artist's key works. . . . Van Gogh's poetic descriptions will hold the attention of young readers; even preschoolers will enjoy the simple text and vibrant pictures. The brilliant colors and brush strokes are reproduced faithfully." SLJ

Raczka, Bob

  The **Vermeer** interviews; conversations with seven works of art. as imagined by Bob Raczka. Millbrook Press 2009 32p il (Art adventures) lib bdg $25.27

Grades: 3 4 5 6   **759.9**

1. Artists 2. Painters 3. Artists, Dutch 4. Art appreciation

ISBN 978-0-8225-9402-4 lib bdg; 0-8225-9402-1 lib bdg

LC 2008024969

"Raczka makes Johannes Vermeer's masterpieces accessible by employing an interview format. Clearly stating that these 'conversations' are 'as imagined' by the author, 'Bob' asks the subjects of seven paintings a series of questions about themselves and their surroundings, allowing them to give details about the art techniques, historical context, and cultural elements." SLJ

Includes bibliographical references

Winter, Jonah

  ★ **Frida**; illustrated by Ana Juan. Levine Bks. 2002 un il $16.95; pa $5.99

Grades: K 1 2 3   **759.9**

1. Artists 2. Painters 3. Women artists 4. Artists, Mexican 5. Painters -- Mexico -- Biography -- Juvenile literature

ISBN 0-590-20320-7; 0-590-20321-5 pa

LC 00-51421

This "illustrated short biography argues that the seeds of iconic painter Frida Kahlo's genius were planted during her childhood. . . . Winter consistently manages to convey much with a few well-chosen words, and the illustrations are appropriately awash with traditional Mexican folk art motifs and characters. Especially pleasing are Juan's surreal, Kahlo like touches." Horn Book

759.9494   Swiss painting

Vry, Silke

  Paul Klee for children; Silke Vry; [translation, Jane Michael] Prestel 2011 95 p. $14.95

Grades: 4 5 6   **759.9494**

1. Art -- Technique -- Juvenile literature 2. Art

appreciation -- Juvenile literature
ISBN 3791370774; 9783791370774

LC 2011937220

This book, by SIlke Vry, is about the art work of Paul Klee. "Paul Klee's playful paintings are a natural introduction for children to the world of creativity and art. . . . The German artist was fascinated by children's drawings, and incorporated their energy and simplicity into his own work. This . . . introduction to Klee's paintings focuses on the artist's love of color and symbols, his lighthearted technique, and his belief that music and painting were inextricably linked." (Publisher's note)

759.972 Mexican painting

Rubin, Susan Goldman

★ Diego Rivera; an artist for the people. by Susan Goldman Rubin. Abrams Books for Young Readers 2013 56 p. (reinforced) $21.95

Grades: 5 6 7 8   **759.972**

1. Mural painting and decoration -- Juvenile literature
2. Painters -- Mexico -- Biography -- Juvenile literature
ISBN 0810984113; 9780810984110

LC 2012010022

This book, by Susan Goldman Rubin, "offers young readers . . . insight into the life and artwork of the famous Mexican painter and muralist [Diego Rivera]. The book follows Rivera's career, looking at his influences and tracing the evolution of his style. His work often called attention to the culture and struggles of the Mexican working class. . . . The book contains a list of museums where you can see Rivera's art, a historical note, a glossary, and a bibliography." (Publisher's note)

Includes bibliographical references and index

760.2 Miscellany

Hanson, Anders

Cool printmaking; the art of creativity for kids. [by] Anders Hanson. ABDO Pub. Co. 2009 32p il (Cool art) lib bdg $24.21

Grades: 2 3 4   **760.2**

1. Prints 2. Printing
ISBN 978-1-60453-147-3 lib bdg; 1-60453-147-9 lib bdg

LC 2008-22323

This book about printmaking is "well organized, with clearly written sections . . . and several clever projects and exercises. . . . [It] should have substantial child appeal." SLJ

Includes glossary

Luxbacher, Irene

1 2 3 I can make prints! Kids Can Press 2008 24p il (Starting art) $14.95; pa $5.95

Grades: 2 3 4   **760.2**

1. Prints 2. Printing
ISBN 978-1-55453-040-3; 1-55453-040-7; 978-1-55453-153-0 pa; 1-55453-153-5 pa

"This book presents brightly colored, framed examples and ink cartoons to invite young readers to make prints. Simple stamp prints fill the pages, as well as relief, intaglio, and block prints, with examples of patterns and symmetry. . . . A child-friendly format introduces the prints: each art project entails only three easy-to-follow steps, and embellishments add creativity and instruction. . . . Luxbacher presents bold, eye-catching examples in an easy-to-understand, entertaining manner." SLJ

761 Printmaking

Boonyadhistarn, Thiranut

Stamping art; imprint your designs. by Thiranut Boonyadhistarn. Capstone Press 2007 31p il $25.26

Grades: 4 5 6 7   **761**

1. Handicraft 2. Rubber stamp printing
ISBN 978-0-7368-6477-0; 0-7368-6477-6

LC 2006004077

This "describes how to make stamps from common household objects, create 'embossed' cards, make a 'stained glass' lampshade, and more." SLJ

Includes bibliographical references

Price, Pamela S.

★ Cool rubber stamp art; [by] Pam Price. ABDO Pub. Co. 2005 32p il (Cool crafts) lib bdg $22.78

Grades: 4 5 6   **761**

1. Handicraft 2. Rubber stamp printing
ISBN 1-59197-743-6

LC 2004-53123

This describes five rubber stamp art projects: "a terracotta flowerpot, spring greeting card, wrapping paper, canvas beach bag, and homemade stamps (sponge, string, leaf). . . . [This book lists] required materials, [has] small color photos, and [includes] clearly explained, numbered steps. . . . [It will] will appeal to children." SLJ

Ross, Kathy

One-of-a-kind stamps and crafts; illustrated by Nicole in den Bosch. Millbrook Press 2010 48p il (Girl crafts) lib bdg $25.26; pa $7.95

Grades: 3 4 5 6   **761**

1. Handicraft 2. Rubber stamp printing
ISBN 978-0-8225-9216-7 lib bdg; 0-8225-9216-9 lib bdg; 978-1-58013-885-7 pa; 1-58013-885-3 pa

LC 2009020626

"This book describes how to create 20 stamps as well as an ink-pad storage shelf and a stamp storage box. . . . Decorative top borders add to the overall neat, well-spaced pages. The projects include readily available supplies, step-by-step instructions, and clear color illustrations. . . . An enhancement to craft collections." SLJ

769.92 Biography

Ray, Deborah Kogan

Hokusai; the man who painted a mountain. Foster Bks. 2001 un il $18

Grades: 3 4 5 6   **769.92**

1. Artists 2. Artists, Japanese 3. Printmakers -- Japan -- Biography -- Juvenile literature
ISBN 0-374-33263-0

LC 00-50395

"The text and evocative artwork provide details and scenes of everyday Japanese life in the 19th century. The illustrations include accomplished soft watercolor and colored-pencil paintings, labeled Chinese characters, drawings from the artist's sketchbooks, and a reproduction of Hokusai's 'The Great Wave off Kanagawa.'" SLJ

Includes bibliographical references

770 Photography, computer art, cinematography, videography

Finger, Brad

13 photos children should know. Prestel 2011 45p il lib bdg $14.95
Grades: 4 5 6   770
  1. Modern history 2. Documentary photography
  ISBN 978-3-7913-7047-7; 3-7913-7047-2
Examines the history behind thirteen popular photographs, including the moon landing, the fall of the Berlin Wall, and the wedding of Prince Charles and Princess Diana.

Friedman, Debra

★ **Picture** this; fun photography and crafts. Kids Can Press 2003 40p il (Kids can do it) hardcover o.p. pa $5.95
Grades: 4 5 6   770
  1. Handicraft 2. Photography
  ISBN 1-55337-046-5; 1-55337-047-3 pa
"Clearly written instructions and ideas, illustrated with color diagrams and photographs . . . explores such concepts as light and shadow, action, and point of view. The crafts include framing and matting as well as suggestions for arranging pictures in a scrapbook." SLJ

Includes glossary

Partridge, Elizabeth

Restless spirit: the life and work of Dorothea Lange. Viking 1998 122p il hardcover o.p. pa $12.99
Grades: 6 7 8 9   770
  1. Photographers 2. Women photographers 3. Women photographers -- United States -- Biography -- Juvenile literature
  ISBN 0-670-87888-X; 0-14-230024-1 pa
                                LC 98-9807
A biography of Dorothea Lange, whose photographs of migrant workers, Japanese American internees, and rural poverty helped bring about important social reforms
"Generously placed throughout this accessibly written biography are the photographic images that make Lange a pre-eminent artist of the century. The book is elegantly designed and the photographic reproductions are excellent." Bull Cent Child Books

Includes bibliographical references

775 Digital photography

Johnson, Daniel

4-H guide to digital photography. Voyageur Press 2009 176p $18.99

Grades: 5 6 7 8   775
  1. Digital photography
  ISBN 978-0-7603-3652-6; 0-7603-3652-0
                            LC 2009014679
This guide to digital photography offers "sound and comprehensive information. . . . [It] features numerous excellent photos that support the text. It explores types of digital cameras, how to take good photos, the complexities of lighting, managing images . . . and the importance of just enjoying this activity. Types of photography such as landscape and macro are explained. The author does an excellent job of discussing the importance of both technological details and artistic creativity." SLJ

Includes glossary

Rabbat, Suzy

Using digital images. Cherry Lake Pub. 2010 32p il (Super smart information strategies) lib bdg $27.07
Grades: 3 4 5 6   775
  1. Digital photography
  ISBN 978-1-60279-954-7 lib bdg; 1-60279-954-7 lib bdg
                            LC 2010018941
"The information on deciding between file formats and resolutions in Using Digital Images will be tremendously helpful, and some beginner techniques on taking and editing effective photos are a nice bonus." Booklist

Includes bibliographical references

778.5 Cinematography and videography

Green, Julie

Shooting video to make learning fun. Cherry Lake Pub. 2010 32p il (Super smart information strategies) lib bdg $27.07
Grades: 3 4 5 6   778.5
  1. Digital video recording 2. Motion pictures -- Production and direction
  ISBN 978-1-60279-955-4 lib bdg; 1-60279-955-5 lib bdg
                            LC 2010002022
"This books helps students learn how to harness the power of video to inform and entertain. Includes background information and practical hands on activities." Publisher's note

Includes bibliographical references

779 Photographic images

Delannoy, Isabelle

★ **Our** living Earth; a story of people, ecology, and preservation. by Isabelle Delannoy; photographs by Yann Arthus-Bertrand. Harry N. Abrams 2008 157p il $24.95
Grades: 5 6 7 8   779
  1. Human geography 2. Aerial photography
  ISBN 978-0-8109-7132-5; 0-8109-7132-1
                            LC 2008010324
"Wrapped around Arthus-Bertrand's magnificent aerial photographs from around the world, Delannoy's text is organized thematically, covering fresh water, biodiversity, oceans, land, cities, people, food, and climate. . . . Read-

ers will find surprising information and images to ponder. Almost every page supports the overarching theme that social justice and environmental protection are inextricably related. . . . This volume raises awareness, and the striking images, astonishing statistics, and brief explanations will stimulate readers to investigate further and possibly to take action." SLJ

Haas, Robert B.

★ **I** dreamed of flying like a bird; my adventures photographing wild animals from a helicopter. National Geographic 2010 64p il $17.95; lib bdg $27.90

Grades: 2 3 4　　　　　　　　　　　　　　779

1. Aerial photography 2. Photography of animals 3. Animals -- Africa 4. Animals -- Africa -- Juvenile literature

ISBN 978-1-4263-0693-8; 1-4263-0693-8; 978-1-4263-0694-5 lib bdg; 1-4263-0694-6 lib bdg

LC 2009-52955

"Haas, a veteran wildlife photographer, proffers another set of photos from several of his albums for adults. Here he accompanies the pictures . . . with anecdotal commentary on the hazards and pleasures of viewing nature from an aerial perspective. . . . This . . . [provides] young viewers with an unusual perspective on the natural world." Booklist

Includes glossary and bibliographical references

Hoban, Tana

Shadows and reflections. Greenwillow Bks. 1990 un il $16.99

Grades: PreK K　　　　　　　　　　　　　779

1. Shades and shadows 2. Shades and shadows -- Juvenile literature

ISBN 978-0-688-07089-2; 0-688-07089-2

LC 89-30461

Photographs without text feature shadows and reflections of various objects, animals, and people

"This imaginative, wordless book of color photographs is a visual treat, offering witty and subtle sets of images for enriching the eyes of children and adults." SLJ

780　Music

Aliki

★ **Ah,** music! written and illustrated by Aliki. HarperCollins Pubs. 2003 47p il $17.99; pa $6.99

Grades: K 1 2 3　　　　　　　　　　　　780

1. Music 2. Music -- History and criticism 3. Music -- History and criticism -- Juvenile literature

ISBN 0-06-028719-5; 0-06-446236-6 pa

LC 2001-26476

This introduction to music defines such terms as rhythm, melody, pitch, and volume, gives a brief description of written music, instruments of the orchestra, vocal parts, harmony, dynamics, and tempo, cultural diversity in dance and music, and gives a brief outline of musical history

"Terms are explained in an easy, child-friendly manner. . . . Aliki's love of her subject shines through. This enjoyable title is best shared one-on-one and its format makes it ideal for browsing." SLJ

Anderson, M. T.

★ **Handel,** who knew what he liked; illustrated by Kevin Hawkes. Candlewick Press 2001 un il hardcover o.p. pa $6.99

Grades: 4 5 6　　　　　　　　　　　　　780

1. Composers 2. Composers -- Biography -- Juvenile literature

ISBN 0-7636-1046-1; 0-7636-2562-0 pa

LC 00-57210

In this biography Handel, who would later compose some of the world's most beautiful music, is shown as a stubborn little boy with a mind of his own

The author "infuses the composer's story with warmth and color, humor and humanity. . . . Relating pithy stories with plain words and short sentences, Anderson never forgets his audience in his enthusiasm for his subject." Booklist

Lach, William

★ **Can** you hear it? Abrams Books for Young Readers 2007 39p il $18.95

Grades: 2 3 4 5　　　　　　　　　　　　780

1. Art and music

ISBN 978-0-8109-5721-3

"This visual and aural feast invites parents, educators, and young listeners to 'listen and look' at 13 examples of pictorial music and visual masterpieces. The introduction prepares readers with an explanation of the connections between composers' notes and art images. A woodblock print by Utagawa Hiroshige, the pointillism of Seurat, and landscapes by Jacob van Ruisdael and Thomas Cole are among those included in the presentation. The paired examples invite listeners to identify solo instruments or orchestral themes that characterize an image found in the visual art." SLJ

Nathan, Amy

Meet the musicians; from prodigy (or not) to pro. Henry Holt and Co. 2006 168p il $17.95

Grades: 5 6 7 8　　　　　　　　　　　　780

1. Music 2. Musicians

ISBN 978-0-8050-7743-8; 0-8050-7743-X

LC 2005026508

The author "interviewed 13 of the New York Philharmonic's members, representing 11 different instruments, and spun their articulate comments into brief, readable profiles, supplemented by various sidebars—among them, an invaluable feature outlining pros and cons of individual instruments. . . . The practical advice mixed with inspirational words strikes just the right note for children at many different stages in their musical education." Booklist

Includes bibliographical references

780.89　Ethnic and national groups

Igus, Toyomi

★ **I** see the rhythm; paintings by Michele Wood; text by Toyomi Igus. Children's Bk. Press 1998 32p il $18.95; pa $7.95

Grades: 4 5 6 7　　　　　　　　　　　　780.89

1. African American music 2. African Americans -- Music -- History and criticism 3. African Americans

-- Music -- History and criticism -- Juvenile literature
ISBN 0892391510; 0892392129; 0-89239-151-0;
0-89239-212-9 pa

LC 97-29310

Coretta Scott King Award for illustration

Text and illustrations combine to give an "overview of African American music. . . . {A} time line sets the social context, and brief paragraphs describe the various types of music, from African origins and slave songs through ragtime; the blues; big band, bebop, and cool jazz; gospel; rhythm and blues; and the contemporary sounds of rock, hip-hop, and rap." (Booklist) "Grades four to eight." (Bull Cent Child Books)

"The text, made up of free verse and music lyrics, incorporates different font sizes, shapes, and colors to underline the mood of each genre. . . . The colors of each full-page scenario underline the mood. . . . This book celebrates music with art and words and successfully blends all three." SLJ

780.9 History, geographic treatment, biography

Children's book of music; an introduction to the world's most amazing music and its creators. DK Publishing 2010 142p il $24.99
Grades: 3 4 5 6   **780.9**
1. Music -- History and criticism
ISBN 978-0-7566-6734-4; 0-7566-6734-8

LC 2010564872

"Concise summaries and eye-catching photography are combined in this chronological look at music 'from the first hum' to digital recording and reactable electronic instruments. The book explores the nature of music, its origins, and varied sounds. The organization creates a useful resource for research as well as for casual browsing. . . . While the information is succinct, there is enough depth for basic information and unusual facts. . . . Thirty-five musical highlights are included on the CD . . . each tagged by an icon and explanation within the book, provide teaching and listening aids. A solid resource for any library." SLJ

Includes glossary

Solway, Andrew

Africa; [by] Andrew Solway. Heinemann Library 2008 48p il (World of music) lib bdg $22
Grades: 5 6 7 8   **780.9**
1. African music
ISBN 978-1-4034-9891-5 lib bdg; 1-4034-9891-1 lib bdg

LC 2006100578

This introduction to African music discusses "instruments, dance, and vocal styles. The photographs presented are wonderfully colorful in quality and narrative. Topics covered include history, famous players, current styles, pop-culture, politics, world-wide connections." Libr Media Connect

Includes glossary and bibliographical references

Latin America and the Caribbean; [by] Andrew Solway. Heinemann Library 2008 48p il (World of music) lib bdg $22

Grades: 5 6 7 8   **780.9**
1. Music -- Latin America 2. Music -- Caribbean region
ISBN 978-1-4034-9889-2 lib bdg; 1-4034-9889-X lib bdg

LC 2006100579

This introduction to music of Latin America and the Caribbean discusses "instruments, dance, and vocal styles. The photographs presented are wonderfully colorful in quality and narrative. Topics covered include history, famous players, current styles, pop-culture, politics, and world-wide connections." Libr Media Connect

Includes glossary and bibliographical references

Underwood, Deborah

Australia, Hawaii, and the Pacific; [by] Deborah Underwood. Heinemann Library 2008 48p il (World of music) lib bdg $22
Grades: 5 6 7 8   **780.9**
1. Music -- Hawaii 2. Music -- Oceania 3. Music -- Australia
ISBN 978-1-4034-9894-6 lib bdg; 1-4034-9894-6 lib bdg

LC 2006100576

This introduction to the music of Australia, Hawaii, and the Pacific discusses "instruments, dance, and vocal styles. The photographs presented are wonderfully colorful in quality and narrative. Topics covered include history, famous players, current styles, pop-culture, politics, and world-wide connections." Libr Media Connect

Includes glossary and bibliographical references

780.92 Biography

Krull, Kathleen

★ **Lives** of the musicians; good times, bad times (and what the neighbors thought) written by Kathleen Krull; illustrated by Kathryn Hewitt. Harcourt Brace Jovanovich 1993 96p il $21; pa $12
Grades: 4 5 6 7   **780.92**
1. Authors 2. Singers 3. Pianists 4. Composers 5. Dramatists 6. Violinists 7. Librettists 8. Folk musicians 9. Jazz musicians 10. Conductors (Music) 11. Memoirists 12. Songwriters 13. Music teachers 14. Classical musicians 15. Theatrical directors 16. Composers -- Biography -- Juvenile literature
ISBN 0-15-248010-2; 0-15-216436-7 pa

LC 91-33497

"Twenty (including both Gilbert and Sullivan) composers, from Vivaldi to Gershwin, are here profiled in a series of irreverent, anecdotal vignettes, each stylishly illustrated with an elegant caricature." Bull Cent Child Books

Includes glossary and bibliographical references

780.94 Music of Europe

Allen, Patrick

Europe; [by] Patrick Allen. Heinemann Library 2008 48p il (World of music) lib bdg $22

Grades: 5 6 7 8   **780.94**
1. Music -- Europe
ISBN 978-1-4034-9890-8 lib bdg; 1-4034-9890-3
lib bdg

LC 2006100580

This introduction to European music discusses "instruments, dance, and vocal styles. The photographs presented are wonderfully colorful in quality and narrative. Topics covered include history, famous players, current styles, pop-culture, politics, and world-wide connections." Libr Media Connect

Includes glossary and bibliographical references

781.2   Elements of music

Tomecek, Steve
Music; [by] Stephen M. Tomecek. Chelsea House 2010 165p il (Experimenting with everyday science) $35
Grades: 5 6 7 8   **781.2**
1. Musical instruments 2. Science -- Experiments 3. Music -- Acoustics and physics
ISBN 978-1-60413-169-7; 1-60413-169-1

LC 2009-22333

This "offers 25 easy-to-perform activities that illuminate scientific principles. . . . Topics . . . include the history of music, various instruments, and how scientific principles explain the creation of sounds. . . . Following each experiment are additional comments on the science behind the experiment and link to the one that follows. Photographs, simple diagrams and illustrations, and sample data tables appear throughout, and the [layout is] clear and colorful." SLJ

Includes bibliographical references

781.49   Recording of music

Miles, Liz
Making a recording. Raintree 2009 32p il (Culture in action) $28.21; pa $7.99
Grades: 5 6 7 8   **781.49**
1. Sound recordings 2. Music industry -- Vocational guidance
ISBN 978-1-4109-3392-8; 1-4109-3392-X; 978-1-4109-3409-3 pa; 1-4109-3409-8 pa

LC 2009000416

This "is a must-read for any aspiring musician. A brief history is followed by a discussion of modern techniques, and technical terms are explained in simple language. Fun activities include designing a label. . . . Well organized and with bright, colorful photography, [this] introductory [title gives] readers good basic knowledge." SLJ

Includes glossary and bibliographical references

781.5   Kinds of music

Stringer, Lauren
When Stravinsky met Nijinsky; two artists, their ballet, and one extraordinary riot. Lauren Stringer. Houghton Mifflin Harcourt 2013 32 p. $16.99
Grades: K 1 2   **781.5**
1. Picture books for children 2. Rite of spring

(Choreographic work)
ISBN 0547907257; 9780547907253

LC 2012025330

In this children's picture book looks at the dramatic reaction to "The Rite of Spring," a collaboration between Igor Stravinsky and Vaslav Nijinsky. It "introduces the two men and how they worked alone, while noting that they both dreamed of something different. Their collaboration brought the world 'The Rite of Spring' . . . which opened to a riot in Paris during its premier[e]." (Booklist)

781.62   Folk music

Handyside, Chris
★ Folk. Heinemann Library 2006 48p il (A history of American music) lib bdg $31.43
Grades: 5 6 7 8   **781.62**
1. Folk music
ISBN 1-4034-8150-4

This history of folk music is an "excellent, clear [introduction]. . . . [It] starts with the post-Civil War era, when folklorists gathered slave songs. It describes the music's commercial success beginning with early recordings of the Carter family and Jimmie Rodgers in the 1920s and continuing with Leadbelly, Woody Guthrie, Pete Seeger, and the many musicians who became popular during the folk revival of the late 50s and early 60s. . . . It concludes with sections on folk rock, punk rock, and the future of folk music." SLJ

Includes bibliographical references

Orozco, Jose-Luis
★ De colores and other Latin-American folk songs for children; selected, arranged, and translated by José-Luis Orozco; illustrated by Eliza Kleven. Dutton Children's Bks. 1994 56p il hardcover o.p. pa $7.99
Grades: K 1 2 3   **781.62**
1. Folk songs 2. Children's songs 3. Folklore -- Latin America 4. Bilingual books -- English-Spanish 5. Latin American folk songs -- Juvenile literature
ISBN 0-525-45260-5; 0-14-056548-5 pa

"Each of the 27 songs is presented with background notes; lyrics in both Spanish and English; simple arrangements for the voice, piano, and guitar; and suggestions for group sing-alongs and musical games. . . . The book is a delight for the eyes as well as the ear. . . . Kleven provides bountiful illustrations—the endpapers are sunshine bright with a crisp quilt of yellow flowers, and playful borders that ripple with colorful patterns and miniature pictures line the edge of every page." Booklist

781.642   Country music

Bertholf, Bret
★ Long gone lonesome history of country music; by Bret Bertholf. Little, Brown 2007 un il $18.99
Grades: 4 5 6   **781.642**
1. Country music
ISBN 978-0-316-52393-6; 0-316-52393-3

LC 2005016036

"This tongue-in-cheek overview features a folksy narrative of how and why country music developed in the barns and back roads of rural America. The text . . . covers instruments, early recordings, yodeling, . . . the Great Depression, gospel, movie cowboys, a 'paper-doll' spoof of singers' costumes, hillbilly jazz, World War II, . . . and much more. While poking fun at itself . . . the book offers a vast amount of historical fact amid a multitude of caricatures of country stars. . . . The ever-changing backgrounds and fonts with colored-pencil and crayon illustrations carry an amazing variation of detail." SLJ

781.643 Blues

Handyside, Chris

★ **Blues**; [by] Christopher Handyside. Heinemann Library 2006 48p il (A history of American music) lib bdg $31.43

Grades: 5 6 7 8   781.643

1. Blues music

ISBN 1-4034-8148-2

LC 2005019280

"This book charts the development of this uniquely American Music form from the 1600s through to the present. It also shows how social, economic, and regional factors have all helped to shape the blues over time and, in turn, how this music has gone on to influence other genres." Publisher's note

Includes glossary and bibliographical references

781.644 Soul

Aretha, David

Awesome African-American rock and soul musicians; David Aretha. Enslow Publishers, Inc. 2012 112 p. ill. (African-American Collective Biographies) (library) $31.93

Grades: 5 6 7   781.644

1. Rock musicians 2. Soul musicians 3. African American musicians 4. African American rock musicians -- Biography -- Juvenile literature 5. Soul musicians -- United States -- Biography -- Juvenile literature

ISBN 1598451405; 9781598451405

LC 2011019956

"From the African-American Collective Biographies series, this volume introduces nine significant figures in rock and soul music: Chuck Berry, Ray Charles, Little Richard, James Brown, Aretha Franklin, Jimi Hendrix, Diana Ross, Stevie Wonder, and Prince. After a general introduction to rock and soul music, each chapter looks at the individual performer's life, career, musical style, achievements, and contributions to the field." (Booklist)

Includes bibliographical references (p. 108-109) and index.

Handyside, Chris

★ **Soul** and R&B; [by] Christopher Handyside. Heinemann Library 2006 48p il (A history of American music) lib bdg $31.43

Grades: 5 6 7 8   781.644

1. Soul music 2. Rhythm and blues music

ISBN 1-4034-8153-9

LC 2005019324

"This book charts the development of this uniquely American music form from the 1800s through to the present. It also shows how social, economic, and regional factors have all helped to shape soul and R&B over time and, in turn, how this music has gone on to influence other genres." Publisher's note

Includes glossary and bibliographical references

781.65 Jazz

Dillon, Leo

★ **Jazz** on a Saturday night; [by] Leo & Diane Dillon. Blue Sky Press 2007 un il $16.99

Grades: PreK K 1 2   781.65

1. Jazz music 2. Jazz musicians 3. Children's poetry 4. Jazz musicians -- Juvenile literature

ISBN 0-590-47893-1; 978-0-590-47893-1

LC 2006-34009

This takes readers on "an imaginary Saturday night concert featuring seven . . . [jazz] greats, from Thelonius Monk to John Coltrane. Rhythmic text acts as an introduction to the legendary musicians. . . . The sophisticated illustrations . . . recall Harlem Renaissance paintings. . . . Brief biographies of the seven featured artists serve as endnotes, while a bonus CD briefly explores jazz instruments and features an original song that shares the book's title." Publ Wkly

Handyside, Chris

★ **Jazz**; [by] Christopher Handyside. Heinemann Library 2006 48p il (A history of American music) lib bdg $31.43

Grades: 5 6 7 8   781.65

1. Jazz music

ISBN 1-4034-8149-0

LC 2005019305

"This book charts the development of this uniquely American Music form from the 1600s through to the present. It also shows how social, economic, and regional factors have all helped to shape Jazz over time and, in turn, how this music has gone on to influence other genres." Publisher's note

Includes glossary and bibliographical references

Marsalis, Wynton

★ **Jazz** A-B-Z; [by] Wynton Marsalis and Paul Rogers; with biographical sketches by Phil Schaap. Candlewick Press 2005 un il $24.99

Grades: 5 6 7 8 9 10   781.65

1. Jazz music 2. Jazz musicians 3. Alphabet -- Juvenile literature

ISBN 978-0-7636-3434-6

LC 2005-48448

This is an illustrated alphabetically arranged introduction to jazz musicians.

This is a "witty, stunningly designed alphabet catalog. . . . The biographical sketches and notes on poetic forms by Phil Schaap are concise and genuinely informative. . . . Rogers's pastiche full-page portraits, his use of expressive typography and the smaller vignettes he sprinkles throughout are bound to heighten any reader's appreciation of both the musicians and the music.... [Marsalis offers] clever ... poems, wordplays, odes and limericks." N Y Times Book Rev

Pinkney, Andrea Davis

★ **Duke** Ellington; the piano prince and his orchestra. illustrated by Brian Pinkney. Hyperion Bks. for Children 1998 un il $15.95; pa $5.99

Grades: 2 3 4   **781.65**

1. Composers 2. Jazz musicians 3. Band leaders 4. African Americans -- Biography

ISBN 0-7868-0178-6; 0-7868-1420-9 pa

LC 96-46031

A Caldecott Medal honor book, 1999; Coretta Scott King honor book for illustration, 1999

A brief recounting of the career of this jazz musician and composer who, along with his orchestra, created music that was beyond category

This is "written in a folksy, colloquial style.... The warmly colored, exquisitely designed scratchboard illustrations have a grand time evoking the sounds of Ellington's music." Horn Book Guide

Includes bibliographical references

781.66   Rock (Rock 'n' roll)

George-Warren, Holly

Shake, rattle, & roll; the founders of rock & roll. words by Holly George-Warren; pictures by Laura Levine. Houghton Mifflin 2001 un il hardcover o.p. pa $5.95

Grades: 3 4 5 6   **781.66**

1. Musicians 2. Rock music 3. Rock musicians -- Biography -- Juvenile literature

ISBN 0-618-05540-1; 0-618-43229-9 pa

LC 00-33480

"A wonderfully entertaining browsing book that will also fill a gap in most music collections." SLJ

Guillain, Charlotte

Punk; music, fashion, attitude! Raintree 2011 32p il (Culture in action) lib bdg $29

Grades: 5 6 7 8   **781.66**

1. Punk rock music

ISBN 978-1-4109-3916-6; 1-4109-3916-2

LC 2009052585

"Guillain delves into the history of punk and follows its influence on modern art, fashion, and politics.... [This volume is] quick, interesting, up-to-date ... with plenty of supportive, captioned, full-color photographs. [It] also [provides] related project suggestions." SLJ

Includes glossary and bibliographical references

Handyside, Chris

★ **Rock.** Heinemann Library 2006 48p il (A history of American music) lib bdg $31.43

Grades: 5 6 7 8   **781.66**

1. Rock music

ISBN 1-4034-8150-4

This history of rock music is an "excellent, clear [introduction].... [It] opens with the mid-1950s advent of rock n roll and continues with surf music, girl groups, the British

invasion, psychedelic rock, heavy metal, punk, and grunge. Featured musicians range from Elvis Presley to Kurt Cobain." SLJ

Includes bibliographical references

Stamaty, Mark Alan

★ **Shake,** rattle & turn that noise down! how Elvis shook up music, me, and mom. Alfred A. Knopf 2010 un il $17.99; lib bdg $20.99

Grades: 2 3 4   **781.66**

1. Actors 2. Singers 3. Rock music 4. Cartoonists 5. Rock musicians

ISBN 978-0-375-84685-4; 0-375-84685-9; 978-0-375-94685-1 lib bdg; 0-375-94685-3 lib bdg

LC 2008-02231

"Dividing each page into multiple panels with sizable chunks of text allows Stamaty to cram a lot of information into the picture-book format.... [The book] makes a convincing case that that old, dead singer really was cool." Booklist

782.1   Opera

Siberell, Anne

★ **Bravo!** brava! a night at the opera; behind the scenes with composers, cast, and crew. introduction by Frederica von Stade. Oxford Univ. Press 2001 64p il $19.95

Grades: 4 5 6 7   **782.1**

1. Opera 2. Questions and answers

ISBN 0-19-513966-6

LC 2001-21206

This "book introduces all features of the opera, including stars, stagehands, set designers, conductors, and supernumeraries.... Cartoon artwork illustrates the text, and a world map highlighting the settings of well-known operas is also included, as are curtain diagrams, plot summaries of favorite operas, and sample costumes." Horn Book Guide

Includes glossary and bibliographical references

782.25   Small-scale vocal forms

Igus, Toyomi

★ **I** see the rhythm of gospel; paintings by Michele Wood; text by Toyomi Igus. Zonderkidz 2010 40p il $16.99

Grades: 4 5 6 7   **782.25**

1. Gospel music 2. African American music 3. Gospel music -- Juvenile literature 4. African Americans -- History -- Juvenile literature

ISBN 978-0-310-71819-2; 0-310-71819-8

LC 2010-08987

"Gospel music—its origins and its effects on the souls and stories of African Americans—gets a strong, loving treatment here.... Igus [provides] the stirring text and Wood the inventive folk art.... Adding to the book's usefulness is a terrific CD with five songs spanning the history of gospel music." Booklist

Nelson, Kadir

★ **He's** got the whole world in his hands. Dial Books for Young Readers 2005 un il $16.99

Grades: K 1 2 **782.25**
1. Spirituals (Songs)
ISBN 0-8037-2850-6

LC 2004-23075

An illustrated version of the well-known spiritual song
"Nelson uses pencils, oils, and watercolors to create a
series of striking, beautifully composed pictures. . . . Nelson
envisions the song in a highly personal and involving manner while embodying its strength and spirit." Booklist

All night, all day; a child's first book of African-American
spirituals. selected and illustrated by Ashley Bryan; musical arrangements by David Manning Thomas. Atheneum Pubs. 1991 48p il music hardcover o.p. pa $6.99
Grades: K 1 2 3 4 **782.25**
1. Spirituals (Songs) 2. Spirituals (Songs) -- Juvenile
literature
ISBN 0-689-31662-3; 0-689-86786-7 pa

LC 90-753145

"An exuberance of warm color and great variety in pattern and design distinguish the illustrations. . . . Excellent
piano accompaniments and guitar chords further enrich the
beautiful, wholly gratifying book." Horn Book

★ Let it shine; three favorite spirituals. [illustrated by]
Ashley Bryan. Atheneum Books for Young Readers
2007 un il $16.99
Grades: K 1 2 3 **782.25**
1. Spirituals (Songs) 2. Spirituals (Songs) -- Juvenile
literature
ISBN 0-689-84732-7

"The inspiring words of three well-known spirituals,
'This Little Light of Mine,' 'Oh, When the Saints Go Marching In,' and 'He's Got the Whole World in His Hands,' are
matched with powerful construction-paper collage illustrations. Each double-page spread of this oversize picture book
is an explosion of shapes and bright colors." Booklist

★ This little light of mine; illustrated by E. B. Lewis. Simon & Schuster Books for Young Readers 2005 32p
il $16.95
Grades: K 1 2 3 **782.25**
1. Spirituals (Songs) 2. Spirituals (Songs) -- Juvenile
ISBN 0-689-83179-X

"A visual interpretation of an African-American spiritual. It is morning when the book opens, and readers are
greeted by a smiling boy. Throughout the day, he spreads
his own special brand of joy wherever he goes. . . . Lewis's
watercolor illustrations across double pages effectively convey emotions of happiness and the giving and sharing of
oneself." SLJ

782.28   Carols

Spirin, Gennady
We three kings; illustrated by Gennady Spirin. Ath-
eneum Books for Young Readers 2007 un il $16.99
Grades: K 1 2 3 **782.28**
1. Carols
ISBN 978-0-689-82114-1; 0-689-82114-X

"This handsome picture book illustrates the verses and
repeated choruses of the Christmas carol 'We Three Kings.'

. . . Created with watercolors and colored pencils, the formally composed and richly detailed illustrations create a distinctive world, with landscapes reminiscent of Renaissance
paintings." Booklist

782.4   Secular forms

Ho, Minfong
★ **Hush!** a Thai lullaby. pictures by Holly Meade.
Orchard Bks. 1996 un il hardcover o.p. pa $6.99
Grades: PreK K 1 2 **782.4**
1. Lullabies
ISBN 0-531-07166-9 pa

LC 95-23251

A Caldecott Medal honor book, 1997

"A mother goes to each animal, from lizard to water buffalo to elephant, trying to quiet noises that might wake her
child. When the animals are silenced and the mother finally
falls asleep, the baby lies awake, with wide eyes and a smile.
Ho's rhythmic text is fine for reading aloud. . . . The setting,
apparently a remote Thai village, is gently evoked in cut paper and ink pictures that are bold enough to be used with
groups. . . . The comforting earth tones suit the quiet nature
of the story." Booklist

782.42   Songs

Bates, Ivan
★ **Five** little ducks; illustrated by Ivan Bates. Scholas-
tic 2006 un il $12.99
Grades: K 1 2 **782.42**
1. Songs 2. Counting 3. Ducks -- Songs
ISBN 0-439-74693-0

LC 2005000112

One by one, five little ducks wander away from their
mother until her lonely quack brings them all waddling back

"Bates's muted watercolors bring a lively energy . . . to
this beloved song. The artist's sweet and nostalgic adaptation is unique for its gentle and warm tone." SLJ

Baum, Maxie
I have a little dreidel; illustrated by Julie Paschkis.
Scholastic Press 2006 un il $9.99
Grades: K 1 2 **782.42**
1. Songs 2. Children's songs 3. Children's poetry 4.
Hanukkah stories 5. Hanukkah -- Songs
ISBN 0-439-64997-8; 978-0-439-64997-1

LC 2005-31318

An illustrated retelling of the classic Hannukah song,
with directions for playing the dreidel game and a recipe for
making latkes.

"A favorite Hanukkah song is given new life in this
charmingly illustrated variation. . . . Distinctive, folk-art-
style illustrations feature a mix of patterns and vibrant solids, thick lines and simple shapes, while the bottom third of
each spread frames the text in a bold blue-and-white woodcutlike design." SLJ

Berkes, Marianne Collins

Over in Australia; amazing animals Down Under. by Marianne Berkes; illustrated by Jill Dubin. Dawn Publications 2011 un il $16.95; pa $8.95

Grades: PreK K   **782.42**

   1. Songs 2. Counting 3. Animals -- Songs 4. Animals -- Australia

ISBN 978-1-58469-135-8; 1-58469-135-2; 978-1-58469-136-5 pa; 1-58469-136-0 pa

                         LC 2010031038

"Berkes incorporates some of Australia's unique animals in her latest variant of the familiar song, 'Over in the Meadow.' . . . Dubin's charming paper collages deftly use a variety of patterns plus a bonus 'hidden' animal noted on one of the informative pages after the song text. That section also includes more facts about all the mentioned animals, offers suggestions for class activities, explains Dubin's illustration process, and provides the score for those unfamiliar with the tune." SLJ

Boynton, Sandra

Blue Moo; 17 jukebox hits from way back never; deluxe illustrated songbook. lyrics and drawings by Sandra Boynton; music by Sandra Boynton & Michael Ford. Workman Pub. Co. 2007 64p il $16.95

Grades: K 1 2 3   **782.42**

   1. Songs

ISBN 978-0-7611-4775-6; 0-7611-4775-6

A book and audio CD of songs in the style of 1950s pop music.

"Grandparents, parents, and children alike can enjoy this collection. . . . Boynton has combined a roster of celebrity singers, good humor, and lots of creativity for a gift of music and fun for every member of the family." SLJ

Dog train; deluxe illustrated lyrics book of the unpredictable rock-and-roll journey. music by Sandra Boynton & Michael Ford; lyrics and drawings by Sandra Boynton. Workman Pub. 2005 64p il $17.95

Grades: K 1 2 3   **782.42**

   1. Songs 2. Rock music

ISBN 0-7611-3966-4

                         LC 2005051801

"This collection of songs erupts with energy, humor, and a strong dose of rock n roll. . . . The book has a spread for each song—a colorful, cheerful illustration and excerpts of lyrics—followed by complete lyrics and musical scores at the end. An About the Artists section includes a photo and biographical sketch of each artist who performs on the accompanying CD." SLJ

Philadelphia chickens; a too-illogical zoological musical revue: deluxe illustrated lyrics book of the original cast recording of the unforgettable (though completely imaginary) stage spectacular. music by Sandra Boynton & Michael Ford; lyrics and drawings by Sandra Boynton. Workman Pub. 2002 64p il $16.95

Grades: K 1 2 3   **782.42**

   1. Songs 2. Musicals

ISBN 0-7611-2636-8

                         LC 2002-27049

This is "a book-and-CD package billed as an 'imaginary musical revue.' The first 32 pages contain lyrics and illustrations, the second half of the book includes musical notation

and additional lyrics for each song. An all-star cast, including Meryl Streep, Laura Linney, Eric Stoltz and the Bacon Brothers, headlines the musical recording, which features a variety of original show tunes." Publ Wkly

Sandra Boynton's One shoe blues; starring B.B. King. Workman 2009 59p il $10.95

Grades: PreK K 1 2 3   **782.42**

   1. Songs 2. Singers 3. Guitarists 4. Blues musicians 5. Puppets and puppet plays -- Fiction 6. Lost and found possessions -- Fiction

ISBN 978-0-7611-5138-8; 0-7611-5138-9

                         LC 2009035847

"Boynton transforms a song from her 2007 book-and-CD title Blue Moo: 17 Jukebox Hits from Way Back Never into a stand-alone book-plus-DVD, starring blues legend B.B. King. Boynton weaves the lyrics of her original song into an extended tale about some colorful sock puppets who watch King perform the song in a cozy country house. . . . Still photographs from Boynton's music video and other complementary shots illustrate the story. . . . In addition to King's humorous and engaging performance (complete with sock puppet accompaniment), the DVD contains other kid-pleasing tidbits." Publ Wkly

Cabrera, Jane

Old MacDonald had a farm; [by] Jane Cabrera. Holiday House 2008 un il $16.95

Grades: PreK K   **782.42**

   1. Farm life -- Songs 2. Folk songs -- United States

ISBN 978-0-8234-2141-1

                         LC 2007034036

First published 2007 in the United Kingdom

"A gray-haired, rosy-cheeked Old MacDonald starts off by introducing his young-looking wife, with 'a kiss kiss here, and a kiss kiss there. . . .' Then it's off to the fields, barn, and pond to meet his dog, sheep, horse, hens, goat, ducks, cow, and pig. . . . Cabrera's bright, splotchy illustrations follow the text, with full spreads devoted to each verse. Young children can read along easily enough and can probably add their own verses to the mix." SLJ

The wheels on the bus. Holiday House 2011 un il $16.95

Grades: PreK K   **782.42**

   1. Songs 2. Animals -- Songs

ISBN 978-0-8234-2350-7; 0-8234-2350-6

                         LC 2011000120

In this version of the classic song, animal passengers roar, flap, and chatter while riding a bus.

"Readers will enjoy the journey Cabrera illustrates with her easily recognizable style—bright hues outlined in black, with a finger-paint–like texture." Kirkus

Collins, Judy

When you wish upon a star; performed by Judy Collins; paintings by Eric Puybaret; music by Ned Washington; lyrics by Leigh Harline. Charlesbridge 2011 il $17.95

Grades: PreK K 1 2   **782.42**

   1. Songs 2. Wishes -- Songs

ISBN 978-1-936140-35-0; 1-936140-35-7

                         LC 2011004945

"A short introductory verse and the song's lyrics accompany the illustrations, glossy spreads that feature an international group of children—an Eskimo, an Asian child in a bamboo hat, a boy in a turban, and half a dozen others. All of them spot a brilliant star, smiling in the sky; soon after, a woman in a blue cape and fairy wings materializes and leads the children to a country with jaunty toy buildings and candy-cane trees. . . . There, the children's wishes are fulfilled. . . . Puybaret's polished drafting gives the spreads a compelling combination of splendor and restraint." Publ Wkly

Coots, John Frederick

Santa Claus is comin' to town; written by J. Fred Coots & Haven Gillespie; illustrated by Steven Kellogg. Harper-Collins 2004 un il hardcover o.p. pa $6.99

Grades: K 1 2 3   **782.42**
   1. Songs 2. Santa Claus 3. Christmas music 4. Christmas -- Songs 5. Santa Claus -- Songs 6. Children's songs -- United States -- Texts
   ISBN 0-688-14938-3; 0-06-443865-1 pa
                  LC 2003-1821

This "manages to get the rhythm of the music right onto the page. . . . The pictures are packed, and the design is witty." Horn Book

Crews, Nina

★ The **neighborhood** sing-along. Greenwillow Books 2011 63p il $17.99

Grades: K 1 2 3   **782.42**
   1. Songs 2. Children's songs
   ISBN 978-0-06-185063-9; 0-06-185063-2; 978-0-06-185064-6 lib bdg; 0-06-185064-0 lib bdg
                  LC 2010010340

A collection of songs, both familiar and lesser known, illustrated with photographs in a city setting.

"A valuable collective cultural inheritance resides in these songs, and though there are other, more comprehensive volumes available (some including the music), this bright, attractive package is a good introduction." SLJ

DiPucchio, Kelly S.

Sipping spiders through a straw; campfire songs for monsters. lyrics by Kelly DiPucchio; pictures by Gris Grimly. Scholastic Press 2008 un il $15.99

Grades: 2 3 4   **782.42**
   1. Songs 2. Monsters
   ISBN 978-0-439-58401-2; 0-439-58401-9

"This book of eighteen clever song parodies captures exactly the type of thing kids might come up with on their own. Grisly watercolor and mixed-media illustrations awash in appropriately putrid shades of brown and gray will definitely appeal to its target readers: those with a ghoulish sense of humor who are not easily grossed out by disgusting monsters or bodily fluids." Horn Book Guide

Dylan, Bob

Man gave names to all the animals; illustrated by Jim Arnosky. Sterling 2010 un il $17.95

Grades: K 1 2 3   **782.42**
   1. Songs 2. Animals -- Songs
   ISBN 978-1-4027-6858-3; 1-4027-6858-3

"Through vivid paintings of a primeval planet teeming with wildlife, Arnosky translates Dylan's 1979 song about the naming of Earth's animals into a gorgeous picture book. Full lyrics and a CD of the original song are included. In Dylan's narrative, Man takes note of the characteristics of

various animals, including a bear, cow, bull, pig, and sheep, and determines a name for each creature. . . . A list of 170 species appears in the back of the book, with hints on locating each creature on Arnosky's website." SLJ

Engels, Christiane

Knick knack paddy whack; illustrated by Christiane Engel; sung by SteveSongs. Barefoot Books 2008 un il $16.99

Grades: PreK K   **782.42**
   1. Counting 2. Folk songs
   ISBN 978-1-84686-144-4; 1-84686-144-6
                  LC 2007-25046

An illustrated version of the traditional counting song that tells of the ten things 'this old man' played before he came rolling home.

"This bright, lively, new interpretation of the classic children's song incorporates numbers, musical-instrument families, and a multiethnic group of adorable children who march along with the 'old man' of the song. . . . With its inventive use of numbers, music, and collage illustrations, it's a worthy addition." SLJ

Fatus, Sophie

Here we go round the mulberry bush; [by] Sophie Fatus and Fred Penner. Barefoot Books 2007 un il $16.99

Grades: PreK K 1 2   **782.42**
   1. Songs
   ISBN 978-1-84686-035-5; 1-84686-035-0
                  LC 2006025656

Presents ten verses of the popular song, with illustrations of children from different cultures as they get ready for school.

"The double-page spreads, rendered in bold acrylics, are separated into fours to show the kids side by side. This artfully underscores cultural diversity while uniting the children through their similar routines. Music and a CD of the song are included." Horn Book Guide

Harburg, E. Y.

Over the rainbow; performed by Judy Collins; music by Harold Arlen; lyrics by E.Y. Harburg; paintings by Eric Puybaret. Imagine Pub. 2010 un il $17.95

Grades: K 1 2 3   **782.42**
   1. Songs
   ISBN 978-1-936140-00-8; 1-936140-00-4

Illustrates the well-known song with paintings of a young girl's search for happiness.

"A musical classic inspires the creation of new images of sweeping horizons and fanciful creatures. The book includes a CD by singer Judy Collins. Her crystal-clear voice floats seamlessly through the lyrics. . . . Two additional songs interpreted by Collins make this brief CD a treasure—'I See the Moon' . . . and 'White Coral Bells.' Readers are treated to deep jewel tones as Puybaret carefully pulls them from one image to another with a succession of dreamlike scenes. . . . The art is unique, delicate, and detailed." SLJ

Henderson, Kathy

Hush, baby, hush! lullabies from around the world. illustrated by Pam Smy. Frances Lincoln Children's Books 2011 43p il $17.95

Grades: PreK K 1　　　　　　　　　**782.42**
1. Lullabies
ISBN 978-1-84507-967-3; 1-84507-967-1

"This collection includes 29 lullabies from countries including Japan, Nigeria, Malawi and Greenland. . . . Music for about half the lullabies is provided. Most songs are printed in their original languages, but lullabies in languages such as Arabic and Korean are transliterated instead of being rendered in original scripts. Animated oil-and-colored-pencil paintings show adults and children in fully-realized landscapes, city streets, marketplaces and bedrooms. . . . This attractive presentation is appropriate as a baby gift, for daycare and preschool collections and public libraries." Kirkus

Hillenbrand, Will
★ **Down** by the station. Harcourt Brace & Co. 1999 un il music $17; pa $6.99
Grades: K 1 2　　　　　　　　　**782.42**
1. Songs 2. Animals -- Songs 3. Railroads -- Songs 4. Children's songs -- Texts 5. Zoo animals -- Songs and music 6. Animals -- Infancy -- Songs and music
ISBN 0-15-201804-2; 0-15-216790-0 pa
LC 98-41770

In this version of a familiar song, baby animals ride to the children's zoo on the zoo train

"This twist on an old favorite combines sunny illustrations, playful humor, and appealing animals." SLJ

Hinojosa, Tish
Cada nino/Every child; a bilingual songbook for kids. illustrated by Lucia Angela Perez. Cinco Puntos Press 2002 56p il music hardcover o.p. pa $9.95
Grades: K 1 2 3　　　　　　　　**782.42**
1. Songs 2. Bilingual books -- English-Spanish
ISBN 0-9383-1760-1; 0-9383-1779-2 pa

"Hinojosa has gathered 11 traditional, original, and adapted songs to celebrate both Hispanic culture and universal experiences and feelings. A brief author's note in English and Spanish prefaces the music, with chords and melody, and verses in both languages. . . . Lovely, bright, folk-art illustrations, brimming with pattern play and whimsical details, create magical worlds of familiar objects and experiences as they incorporate cultural elements. . . . A CD is available for separate purchase." Booklist

Hoberman, Mary Ann
Mary had a little lamb; adapted by Mary Ann Hoberman; illustrated by Nadine Bernard Westcott. Little, Brown 2003 un il (Sing-along stories) $15.95
Grades: K 1 2　　　　　　　　　**782.42**
1. Sheep 2. Songs 3. Sheep -- Songs 4. Children's songs -- Texts
ISBN 0-316-60687-1
LC 2002-72478

This expanded version of the traditional rhyme shows what happens after the lamb gets to school. Includes music on the last page

"This playful extension of the original nursery rhyme adds to the nonsense with simple words and clear, slapstick watercolor-and-ink illustrations." Booklist

The **eensy**-weensy spider; adapted by Mary Ann Hoberman; illustrated by Nadine Bernard Westcott. Little, Brown 2000 un il hardcover o.p. pa $6.99

Grades: K 1 2 3　　　　　　　　**782.42**
1. Songs 2. Finger play 3. Spiders -- Songs
ISBN 0-316-36330-8; 0-316-73412-8 pa
LC 99-25701

An expanded version of the familiar children's finger-play rhyme describing what the little spider does after being washed out of the water-spout

"Whimsical, watercolor cartoons capture the lighthearted tone of the verse. . . . This sprightly adaptation lends itself to singing aloud and is sure to be a hit." SLJ

Isadora, Rachel
★ **12** days of Christmas; [illustrated by] Rachel Isadora. G.P. Putnam's Sons 2010 un il map $16.99
Grades: PreK K 1 2　　　　　　　**782.42**
1. Riddles 2. Folk songs 3. Christmas -- Songs 4. Carols -- Juvenile literature 5. Rebuses -- Juvenile literature
ISBN 978-0-399-25073-6; 0-399-25073-5
LC 2009052862

Sets the traditional Christmas carol in Africa, using a combination of text and rebuses. Includes author's note about some of the African traditions depicted.

This is "illustrated with . . . visually arresting collages that incorporate African fabrics. . . . In this interpretation, the maids milk goats and the lords are masked dancers from Mali. . . . This change of setting gives the old song new zest." Kirkus

Jackson, Jill
Let there be peace on earth; and let it begin with me. by Jill Jackson & Sy Miller; [illustrated by David Diaz] Tricycle Press 2009 un il $18.99
Grades: PreK K 1 2　　　　　　　**782.42**
1. Songs 2. Peace -- Songs
ISBN 978-1-58246-285-1; 1-58246-285-2
LC 2008043122

Illustrates the award-winning song about each person's responsibility to help bring about world peace. Includes a history of the song and biographical notes on the husband and wife songwriting team.

"Diaz's luminous artwork brings [the song] to life for picture-book audiences. . . . The CD contains 12 peace-themed, secular songs. The arrangements are airy and fun for children." SLJ

Johnson, James Weldon
★ **Lift** every voice and sing; by James Weldon Johnson; illustrated by Bryan Collier. Amistad 2007 un il $16.99; lib bdg $17.89
Grades: K 1 2 3　　　　　　　　**782.42**
1. Songs 2. African American music
ISBN 978-0-06-054147-7; 978-0-06-145897-2 lib bdg
LC 2007008602

An illustrated version of the song that has come to be considered the African American national anthem

"Collier's stirring textured collage-and-watercolor illustrations . . . express his Christian faith and his profound sense of connection with his people's historic struggle." Booklist

Katz, Alan
Mosquitoes are ruining my summer! and other silly dilly camp songs. illustrated by David Catrow. Margaret K. McElderry Books 2011 un il $16.99

Grades: 3 4 5 **782.42**
1. Songs 2. Camps -- Songs
ISBN 978-1-4169-5568-9; 1-4169-5568-2
LC 2009021167
Familiar tunes are given new words relating to summer camp, including "Whose Idea Was This Dumb Hike" sung to the tune of "Twinkle Twinkle Little Star."

"Few elements of the camp-going experience are exempt from the tongue-in-cheek riffing, and the lively cartoon-style illustrations extend the hyperbolic humor through caricature and perspective." Booklist

On top of the potty and other get-up-and-go songs; [by] Alan Katz; [illustrations] David Catrow. Margaret K. McElderry Books 2008 un il $16.99
Grades: PreK **782.42**
1. Songs 2. Toilet training -- Songs
ISBN 978-0-689-86215-1; 0-689-86215-6
LC 2007-9004
Well-known songs with new lyrics encourage toddlers to trade in their diapers for the potty chair, including 'If You Gotta Go Do Poopy,' sung to the tune of 'If You're Happy and You Know It.'

"Great for toilet training, this picture book provides adults with a different way to sing and talk about that crucial time when toddlers move from diapers to underwear, potty chair, and toilet. . . . Lots of youngsters and their caregivers will have fun with this." Booklist

Smelly locker; silly dilly school songs. illustrated by David Catrow. Margaret K. McElderry Books 2008 un il $16.99
Grades: K 1 2 3 **782.42**
1. Songs 2. Children's songs 3. Schools -- Songs 4. Schools -- Juvenile literature
ISBN 978-1-4169-0695-7; 1-4169-0695-9
LC 2006-36814
Well-known songs, including "Oh Susannah" and "Take Me Out to the Ballgame," are presented with new words and titles, such as "Heavy Backpack!" and "I Don't Want to Do Homework!"

This is "an irreverent, entertaining commentary in song about school life. . . . With exaggerated features and hilarious body language, Catrow's expressive cartoon characters capture the bizarre and ridiculous elements of the text." SLJ

Katz, Karen
The **babies** on the bus. Henry Holt 2011 32p il $14.99
Grades: PreK K **782.42**
1. Songs
ISBN 978-0-8050-9011-6; 0-8050-9011-8
LC 2010039229
"'The Wheels on the Bus' gets a facelift with new illustrations and a few new verses focused on babies. Each of the 13 verses is complete on a spread. Bright colors and simple patterns are eye-catching for all, but will have special appeal for babies and toddlers. Katz's familiar round-faced youngsters of different ethnicities will delight readers." SLJ

Langstaff, John M.
Frog went a-courtin' retold by John Langstaff; with pictures by Feodor Rojankovsky. Harcourt Brace Jovanovich 1955 un il music $16; pa $7

Grades: K 1 2 3 **782.42**
1. Folk songs 2. Mice -- Songs 3. Frogs -- Songs
ISBN 0-15-230214-X; 0-15-633900-5 pa
Awarded the Caldecott Medal, 1956
"Retelling of a merry old Scottish ballad with many-colored illustrations about the marriage between Mr. Frog and Miss Mouse. A composite American version set to Appalachian mountain music." Chicago Public Libr

Oh, a-hunting we will go; [by] John Langstaff; pictures by Nancy Winslow Parker. Atheneum Pubs. 1974 un il music hardcover o.p. pa $6.99
Grades: K 1 2 **782.42**
1. Folk songs 2. Animals -- Songs
ISBN 0-689-71503-X pa
The nonsense verses of this folk song trace the hunt for such animals as an armadillo, a fox, and a snake, and describe the imagined treatment of each animal once it is caught

"The 12 stanzas are complemented by Parker's droll crayon illustrations (the fox caught in the box is watching TV), and a score for guitar and piano is appended. An amusing addition to 'song' picture books." SLJ

★ **Over** in the meadow; with pictures by Feodor Rojankovsky. Harcourt Brace & Co. 1957 un il music hardcover o.p. pa $7
Grades: K 1 2 **782.42**
1. Counting 2. Folk songs 3. Animals -- Songs
ISBN 0-15-258854-X; 0-15-670500-1 pa
"This old counting rhyme tells of ten meadow families whose mothers advise them to dig, run, sing, play, hum, build, swim, wink, spin and hop. The illustrations, half in full color, show the combination of realism and imagination which little children like best. The tune, arranged simply, is on the last page, and children will have fun acting the whole thing out." Horn Book

Leodhas, Sorche Nic
Always room for one more; illustrated by Nonny Hogrogian. Holt & Co. 1965 un il music $14.95; pa $5.95
Grades: K 1 2 3 **782.42**
1. Folk songs
ISBN 0-8050-0331-2; 0-8050-0330-4 pa
Awarded the Caldecott Medal, 1966
"A picture book based on an old Scottish folk song about hospitable Lachie MacLachlan, who invited in so many guests that his little house finally burst. Rhymed text . . . a glossary of Scottish words, and music for the tune are combined into an effective whole." Hodges. Books for Elem Sch Libr

Lightfoot, Gordon
★ **Canadian** railroad trilogy; art by Ian Wallace. Groundwood Books/House of Anansi Press 2010 un il
Grades: 2 3 4 5 **782.42**
1. Children's songs 2. Railroads -- Songs 3. Railroads -- History 4. Railroads -- History -- Juvenile literature
ISBN 0888999534; 9780888999535
This is an illustrated version of Gordon Lightfoot's song written in Canadia's centennial year, 1967, to commemorate the building of the Canadian Pacific Railroad. "Age four and up." (Quill Quire)

"Wallace's . . . sprawling, dreamlike paintings pay homage to the Canadian landscape; they accompany the lyrics of Lightfoot's 1967 song. . . . Mountains, forests, coastline, and plains roll past as on a railway journey—miles of lonely wilderness the Canadian Pacific Railway was built to span. . . . Wallace doesn't avoid showing the realities of the railway workers lives. . . . It's a huge and unusual project, and Wallace has executed it with admirable care." Publ Wkly

Long, Laurel
★ The **twelve** days of Christmas; illustrated by Laurel Long. Dial Books for Young Readers 2011 il $16.99
Grades: PreK K   **782.42**
1. Songs 2. Folk songs 3. Christmas -- Songs
ISBN 978-0-8037-3357-2; 0-8037-3357-7
LC 2008015774
An illustrated version of the traditional song.
"Long's lyrical and lush oil paintings, reminiscent of Russian icon art, combined with a tricky interactive element, make this version of the traditional carol special." SLJ

Lyon, George Ella
Which side are you on? the story of a song. artwork by Christopher Cardinale. Cinco Puntos Press 2011 un il $17.95
Grades: 3 4 5   **782.42**
1. Miners 2. Labor unions 3. Coal mines and mining -- Songs
ISBN 978-1-933693-96-5; 1-933693-96-7
LC 2010037398
This tells the story of a song which was written in 1931 by Florence Reece in a rain of bullets. Florence's husband Sam was a coal miner in Kentucky. Miners went on strike until they could get better pay, safer working conditions, and health care. The company hired thugs to attack the organizers like Sam Reece. George Ella Lyon tells this story through the eyes of one of Florence's daughters.
"Ribbons of song lyrics weave across scenes of the miners' tools of their trade and the guns of hired company toughs. A thorough author's note follows the text, ending with the song's musical notation and one version of the words on the back cover. The use of music as a protest element makes an interesting addendum to resources on union history or the time period." SLJ

Mallett, David
★ **Inch** by inch; the garden song. pictures by Ora Eitan. HarperCollins Pubs. 1995 un il music hardcover o.p. pa $5.95
Grades: K 1 2   **782.42**
1. Songs 2. Children's songs 3. Gardens -- Songs 4. Gardening -- Juvenile literature 5. Folk songs -- Juvenile literature
ISBN 0-06-443481-8 pa
LC 93-38352
"In this picture-book version of the song first published in 1975 . . . a young child plants seeds . . . weeds and tends them, and finally, gleans a bountiful harvest. . . . Employing a variety of media including cut paper, Eitan uses color and space to create a striking effect." SLJ

Martin, Steve
Late for school; illustrated by C. F. Payne. Grand Central 2010 un il $17.95

Grades: PreK K 1 2   **782.42**
1. Songs 2. Schools -- Songs
ISBN 978-0-446-55702-3; 0-446-55702-1
An illustrated song about the difficulties of getting to school on time, with an audio CD of the author singing the song with banjo accompaniment.
"In Payne's . . . hands, Martin's goofy verse achieves its comic impact on a cinematic scale. . . . Kids will relish Martin's subversive madness." Publ Wkly

Norworth, Jack
Take me out to the ball game; performed by Carly Simon; written by Jack Norworth; illustrated by Amiko Hirao. Imagine 2011 un il $17.95
Grades: PreK K 1 2   **782.42**
1. Songs 2. Baseball -- Songs
ISBN 978-1-936140-26-8; 1-936140-26-8
LC 2010035438
Text and illustrations present the well-known song about baseball games, with the ball players depicted as animals.
"It's a visual tour de force, with double-page spreads of large, action-packe, brilliantly colored scenes in startingly off-center perspective. A Carly Simon CD accompanies the book, and youngsters will have a wonderful time reading and singing along." Kirkus

Orozco, Jose-Luis
★ **Diez** deditos. Ten little fingers & other play rhymes and action songs from Latin America; selected, arranged, and translated by José-Luis Orozco; illustrated by Elisa Kleven. Dutton Children's Bks. 1997 56p il music $19.99; pa $7.99
Grades: K 1 2 3   **782.42**
1. Songs 2. Finger play 3. Folklore -- Latin America 4. Bilingual books -- English-Spanish
ISBN 0-525-45736-4; 0-14-230087-9 pa
"This collection of fingerplays and action songs in Spanish and English comes with clear instructions for physical movements and simple musical notation. A brief sentence or paragraph introduces each entry. . . . Orozco's selections, some traditional, some written by himself, include versifications on such child-appealing subjects as dancing, singing, animals, weather, and food. . . . Kleven's collage illustrations practically pop off the pages with flashy colors and rich details that make each bustling composition a viewer's delight." Bull Cent Child Books

★ **Fiestas**: a year of Latin American songs of celebration; selected, arranged, and translated by José-Luis Orozco; illustrated by Elisa Kleven. Dutton Children's Bks. 2002 48p il music $17.99
Grades: K 1 2 3   **782.42**
1. Songs 2. Festivals 3. Bilingual books -- English-Spanish
ISBN 0-525-45937-5
"Orozco presents 22 songs that center around holidays. . . . Arranged by month, each song is presented with a paragraph of background, the music for the melody (with guitar chords), and the lyrics in both Spanish and English. . . . Kleven's bright borders and busy illustrations . . . make this not only an exemplary songbook, but also a stunning visual experience." SLJ

Paxton, Tom

The **marvelous** toy; words and music by Tom Paxton; illustrated by Steve Cox. Imagine Publishing 2009 un il $17.95

Grades: PreK K 1 2   **782.42**

1. Songs 2. Toys -- Songs

ISBN 978-0-9822939-2-8; 0-9822939-2-5

In this picture book adaptation of Paxton's song, a "boy receives [a] toy from his father, they enjoy it together, and the boy passes it on to his own son with similar enthusiasm. . . . Although the spindly, alien-looking toy is never completely visible, the rainbow-colored protrusions that are shown emit airbrushed beams, while sparks zoom and zip behind it, illuminating the night and leaving a trail of magic in its wake. . . . Four Paxton songs are enclosed on a CD." Publ Wkly

Pinkney, Brian

★ **Hush**, little baby; adapted and illustrated by Brian Pinkney. Greenwillow Books 2006 un il $15.99; lib bdg $17.89

Grades: K 1 2   **782.42**

1. Lullabies 2. Children's songs 3. Folk songs -- United States

ISBN 978-0-06-055993-9; 0-06-055993-4; 978-0-06-055994-6 lib bdg; 0-06-055994-2 lib bdg

LC 2005-08216

"Pinkney sets his version of the traditional Appalachian folksong in an African American household of the early 1900s. . . . Ink-on-clayboard scenes show a distraught toddler girl comforted by a playful father and older brother, who sing, dance, and, of course, offer a series of whimsical gifts. . . . An appended musical arrangement gives the tune a jazzy beat to match the wheeling, undulating figures in the story." Booklist

Raffi

Baby Beluga; illustrated by Ashley Wolff. Crown 1990 un il music (Raffi songs to read) hardcover o.p. pa $5.99; bd bk $6.99

Grades: K 1 2   **782.42**

1. Songs 2. Children's songs 3. Whales -- Songs

ISBN 0-517-58362-3 pa; 0-517-70977-5 bd bk

LC 89-49367

Presents the illustrated text to the song about the little white whale who swims wild and free

"Wolff's striking double-page spreads show the young whale among its fellow Arctic Sea inhabitants. Diversifying her views, the illustrator eyes Baby Beluga and mother swimming together underwater; takes an aerial angle, looking down on the whales from a puffin's perspective; and observes the icy yet welcoming formations where seals, polar bears, and an Eskimo find shelter. . . . An inviting approach to reading encouragement." Booklist

Down by the bay; illustrated by Nadine Bernard Westcott. Crown 1987 un il music (Raffi songs to read) hardcover o.p. pa $5.99; bd bk $6.99

Grades: K 1 2   **782.42**

1. Songs 2. Children's songs

ISBN 0-517-56645-1 pa; 0-517-80058-6 bd bk

LC 87-750291

This illustrated version of one of Raffi's songs depicts a variety of unusual sights to be seen "down by the bay"

The "cheerful nonsense verses are illustrated with equal cheer. Westcott's scraggly lines and bright, clear colors humorously portray the busy children, jolly animals, and frantic mothers that populate the song." SLJ

Five little ducks; illustrated by Jose Aruego and Ariane Dewey. Crown 1989 un il (Raffi songs to read) hardcover o.p. pa $5.99; bd bk $6.99

Grades: K 1 2   **782.42**

1. Songs 2. Ducks -- Songs

ISBN 0-517-58360-7; 0-517-56945-0 pa; 0-517-80057-8 bd bk

LC 88-3752

When her five little ducks disappear one by one, Mother Duck sets out to find them

Raven, Margot

Happy birthday to you! the mystery behind the most famous song in the world. by Margot Theis Raven; paintings by Chris K. Soentpiet. Sleeping Bear Press 2008 un il $17.95

Grades: 1 2 3 4   **782.42**

1. Songs 2. Pianists 3. Educators 4. Songwriters

ISBN 978-1-58536-169-4; 1-58536-169-0

LC 2007037438

"A lovely succession of watercolor paintings depicts the latter half of the 19th century in Louisville and illuminates the thoughtful expressions and joyful faces of the Hill family. . . . [This is] an eye-opener for history and trivia lovers in all libraries." SLJ

Ray, Jane

★ The **twelve** days of Christmas. Candlewick Press 2011 un il $16.99

Grades: PreK K 1   **782.42**

1. Songs 2. Folk songs 3. Christmas -- Songs

ISBN 978-0-7636-5735-2; 0-7636-5735-2

LC 2010052222

On each of the twelve days of Christmas, more and more gifts arrive from the recipient's true love.

"Ray's intricate illustrations offer a wealth of details to explore up close. The images are slightly busy for sharing with a large group, but irresistible for a smaller group or one-on-one. A very nice version indeed." SLJ

Reid, Rob

Children's jukebox; the select subject guide to children's musical recordings. 2nd ed; American Library Association 2007 284p pa $55

Grades: Adult Professional   **782.42**

1. Reference books 2. Children's libraries 3. Songs -- Indexes 4. Subject headings -- Children's recordings

ISBN 0-8389-0940-X pa; 978-0-8389-0940-9 pa

LC 2006103175

First published 1995

This is an index to 548 recordings for children with 147 subject headings, plus subcategories

Includes discography

Roslonek, Steve

The **shape** song swingalong; written and sung by SteveSongs; illustrated by David Sim. Barefoot 2011 il $16.99; pa $9.99

Grades: PreK K 1 2   **782.42**
1. Shape 2. Songs
ISBN 978-1-84686-671-5; 1-84686-671-5; 978-1-
84686-679-1 pa; 1-84686-679-0 pa

"Children in primary colored, mixed-media spreads create the very scenes that they inhabit, using large crayons
to draw various shapes that form everything from a city of
brick skyscrapers to a sunny beach where Sim's naïf figures
ride a purple waterslide. A jazzy song by the children's musical group SteveSongs describes the children's drawings
and the shapes that they use to create specific images. . .
. The shape-focused chorus, bouncy verses, and whimsical
storytelling should have kids singing along with the included
CD recording, which also features a video animation of the
story." Publ Wkly

Roth, Susan L.
★ **Hanukkah,** oh Hanukkah; [by] Susan L. Roth. Dial
Books for Young Readers 2004 un il $10.99; pa $5.99
Grades: K 1 2   **782.42**
1. Songs 2. Hanukkah 3. Hanukkah -- Songs 4.
Children's songs -- Texts
ISBN 0-8037-2843-3; 0-14-240701-1 pa
LC 2003-13165
A family of mice celebrates the eight days of Hannukah
with friends in this illustrated version of the holiday song
"Cloth and paper collages done in many different pat-
terns and textures add interest to the cozy tableaux. . . . The
lovely colors and the appealing tune make this a good holi-
day choice." SLJ

Rueda, Claudia
Let's play in the forest while the wolf is not around; by
Claudia Rueda. Scholastic Press 2006 un il $16.99
Grades: PreK K 1   **782.42**
1. Folk songs 2. Singing games 3. Wolves -- Songs 4.
Animals -- Songs
ISBN 0-439-82323-4
LC 2005030531
In this adaptation of the traditional French and Latin
American song, animals play in the forest while a scary wolf
slowly dresses and becomes hungrier and hungrier
"On flat backgrounds, the angular, minimally detailed
but colorful digital images, enhanced with a few light pencil
strokes, show the animals at play in the forest, always chanting the same line. . . . This is a great song for toddlers to act
out as they are getting dressed." Booklist

Sedaka, Neil
Waking up is hard to do; illustrated by Daniel Miyares.
Imagine 2010 un il $17.95
Grades: PreK K 1 2 3   **782.42**
1. Songs
ISBN 978-1-936140-13-8; 1-936140-13-6
LC 2010001402
"Sedaka has rewritten the lyrics of his 1962 and 1975
chart-topping tune to create this child-pleasing book. The
alarm clock is ringing, birds are singing, breakfast is warming, and school is calling. The repeated chorus, 'Wakin' up is
hard to do,' will allow children to chime in. . . . The charming art has fun details and an adorable cast of animal characters. . . . A CD includes the title track as well as two new
songs: 'Lightnin' Jim' and 'Sing.'" SLJ

Seeger, Ruth Crawford
★ **American** folk songs for children in home, school,
and nursery school; a book for children, parents, and
teachers. by Ruth Crawford Seeger; illustrated by Barbara
Cooney. Oak Publications 2002 190p il pa $24.95
Grades: PreK K 1 2 3 4 Adult Professional   **782.42**
1. Songs 2. Folk music -- United States
ISBN 978-0-8256-0346-4 pa; 0-8256-0346-3 pa
First published 1948 by Doubleday
"This is a unique collection. It will probably be the au-
thoritative source for American folk songs for children for
many, many years." Saturday Review of Books

Seskin, Steve
Sing my song; a kid's guide to songwriting. starring
Steve Seskin and a chorus of creative kids; illustrated by Eve
Aldridge . . . [et al.] Tricycle Press 2008 32p il $18.99
Grades: 1 2 3 4 5   **782.42**
1. Songwriters and songwriting
ISBN 978-1-58246-266-0; 1-58246-266-6
LC 2007046966
"Seskin has tapped a mother lode of musical enthusiasm
in this book by showing young readers the 'how to' necessary to create songs and set them to music. Following 12
excellent examples and step-by-step instructions, readers
discover how to put together the parts of a song. Musical
terms are defined, song forms are suggested, and a CD of
tunes provides sample accompaniment as Seskin backs up
his relaxed vocals on guitar and with choruses from various
schools." SLJ

Spirin, Gennady
★ **The twelve** days of Christmas; illustrated by Gen-
nady Spirin. Marshall Cavendish 2009 un il $16.99
Grades: K 1 2 3   **782.42**
1. Songs 2. Folk songs 3. Christmas -- Songs 4.
Christmas -- Juvenile literature
ISBN 978-0-7614-5551-6; 0-7614-5551-5
LC 2008-06476
On each of the twelve days of Christmas, unusual and
fanciful gifts arrive to celebrate the season.
"This holiday favorite is brought to life through Spirin's
gorgeous illustrations. . . . The elaborately detailed and exquisitely executed artwork, rendered in watercolor and colored pencil, has a Renaissance feel. Roman numerals are
placed on the tree or the base of the tree planter to indicate
which day is being celebrated. As the oval inset fills with
calling birds, golden rings, swans-a-swimming, etc., readers
will enjoy trying to count all the gifts. A must-have." SLJ

Staines, Bill
★ **All** God's critters; song by Bill Staines; pictures by
Kadir Nelson. Simon & Schuster Books for Young Readers
2009 un il $16.99
Grades: PreK K 1   **782.42**
1. Songs 2. Animals -- Songs
ISBN 978-0-689-86959-4; 0-689-86959-2
LC 2008-23624
Celebrates how all the animals in the world make their
own music in their own way, some singing low, some
singing higher.
The song "is brought to rollicking life by Nelson's art-
work. . . . Each delightful spread [is] full-to-bursting with .

.. critters' energy. . . . The oversize type of the lyrics nearly shouts off the page." Booklist

Stotts, Stuart
★ **We** shall overcome; a song that changed the world. by Stuart Stotts; foreword by Pete Seeger; with illustrations by Terrance Cummings. Clarion Books 2009 72p il $18
Grades: 5 6 7 8   **782.42**
1. African Americans -- Civil rights -- Songs
ISBN 978-0-547-18210-0; 0-547-18210-4
LC 2009022578
"This smart, effective telling has few missteps. From the informative black-and-white photographs to the solid back matter to the CD sung by Pete Seeger, it is a complete package." Booklist

They Might Be Giants (Musical group)
Kids go! [by] They Might Be Giants; illustrations by Pascal Campion. Simon & Schuster 2009 un il $19.99
Grades: K 1 2 3   **782.42**
1. Songs
ISBN 978-0-7432-7275-9; 0-7432-7275-7
LC 2009019668
An illustrated version of the song 'Go, Kid, Go,' exhorting the reader to get up and move around
"With just a hint of retro style about them, Campion's thick and loose black ink lines provide a sense of fluidity in riotous scenes that use a limited but appealing palette of green, gray, and peach, splashed over lots of white space. Befitting the action words in the text, the font size bounces from small to large, adding to the energetic tone. . . . An accompanying DVD features an animated video of the song." Publ Wkly

Vetter, Jennifer Riggs
Down by the station; illustrations by Frank Remkiewicz. Tricycle Press 2009 un il $15.99
Grades: PreK K   **782.42**
1. Songs 2. Vehicles
ISBN 978-1-58246-243-1; 1-58246-243-7
LC 2008011308
This illustrated version of the traditional song expands and describes more vehicles, different locations, and their unique sounds, from puffer-billies to racecars and rockets
"Remkiewicz uses candy-bright colors and a hint of goofy elasticity in his slightly busy watercolor art. With enough repetition to tempt early readers to try the text on their own, the book will also attract the lap-sit crowd." SLJ

Voake, Charlotte
★ **Tweedle** dee dee; [by] Charlotte Voake. Candlewick Press 2008 un il $16.99
Grades: PreK K 1 2   **782.42**
1. Folk songs -- United States
ISBN 978-0-7636-3797-2; 0-7636-3797-1
LC 2007040414
Illustrations of a forest in spring and simple text provide a variation on the traditional folk song, "The green leaves grew around"
The pages are "washed with pale green and covered with squiggly line drawings and watercolors. . . . The minimal text invites a read-aloud—and even before arriving at the musical score on the final spread, readers are likely to find themselves singing." Publ Wkly

Yolen, Jane
★ **Apple** for the teacher; thirty songs for singing while you work. collected and introduced by Jane Yolen; music arranged by Adam Stemple; art edited by Eileen Michaelis Smiles. Harry N. Abrams 2005 117p il $24.95
Grades: 4 5 6 7   **782.42**
1. Songs 2. Work -- Songs
ISBN 0-8109-4825-7
LC 2004-24404
"Yolen has brought together a collection of 30 work songs . . . which represent a wide variety of occupations. . . . She introduces each job, explaining unusual vocabulary and references in the songs. . . . The artwork . . . is elegant. Ranging from sculpture to paintings to needlework, each selection of Americana has been carefully matched to the occupation, beautifully reproduced on high-quality paper, and meticulously identified." Booklist

Zelinsky, Paul O.
★ **Knick**-knack paddywhack! a moving parts book. adapted from the counting song and illustrated by Paul O. Zelinsky; paper engineering by Andrew Baron. Dutton 2002 un il $18.99
Grades: K 1 2 3   **782.42**
1. Songs 2. Counting
ISBN 0-525-46908-7
A young boy sets out on a walk—pull the tabs and tiny old men from One to Ten act out the familiar refrain of the traditional counting song on and all around him.
"This glorious title is a paper-engineering and bookmaking marvel as well as a freewheeling romp." SLJ

★ **The** 12 days of Christmas; a pop-up celebration by Robert Sabuda. anniversary edition; Little Simon 2006 un il $26.95
Grades: K 1 2 3   **782.42**
1. Folk songs 2. Pop-up books 3. Christmas -- Songs
ISBN 978-1-4169-2792-1; 1-4169-2792-1
A reissue of the edition first published 1996
This pop-up version of the popular Christmas folk song about gift-giving features "a partridge popping, snow scattering, and lords a-leaping off the page. . . . For this . . . anniversary edition . . . paper engineer Robert Sabuda encloses . . . extra pages with a pop-up Christmas tree with real lights aglow, and a . . . pop-up ornament of two turtledoves." Publisher's note

De colores; illustrated by David Diaz. Marshall Cavendish 2008 un il $16.99
Grades: K 1 2 3   **782.42**
1. Songs 2. Bilingual books -- English-Spanish
ISBN 978-0-7614-5431-1; 0-7614-5431-4
LC 2007022133
"This popular folk song, which is also the anthem of the United Farm Workers of America, celebrates the arrival of spring and the connectedness of humankind. Diaz's joyful pictures bring the words to life. Rendered in acrylic, colored pencil, and pencil, the vibrant, fanciful artwork features flying and floating people as well as giant-sized roosters, chickens, and birds. . . . Presented in Spanish and English, each line is illustrated on an expansive spread. Piano music and historical information about the song are included." SLJ

Deck the halls; [illustrations by] Norman Rockwell. Atheneum Books for Young Readers 2008 un il $16.99
    Grades: PreK K 1 2   **782.42**
    1. Songs 2. Christmas -- Songs
    ISBN 978-1-4169-1771-7; 1-4169-1771-3
                                          LC 2007037461
"The traditional Christmas carol is illustrated with
Rockwell's heartwarming visions of holiday cheer. The art
come[s] from a variety of sources—magazine covers, advertisements, holiday cards—and matches the lyrics surprisingly well. . . . Handsomely nostalgic." SLJ

The Farmer in the dell; illustrated by Alexandra Wallner.
Holiday House 1998 un il music $15.95
    Grades: K 1   **782.42**
    1. Folk songs -- United States
    ISBN 0-8234-1382-9
                                          LC 97-44206
An illustrated version of the traditional game song accompanied by music
"Wallner's primitive folk art sparkles with life, action,
and energy. The colored pen-and-ink illustrations are packed
with details." SLJ

Favorite folk songs; The Peter Yarrow songbook. [com-
piled by Peter Yarrow]; illustrated by Terry Widener.
Sterling Pub. 2008 48p il (Peter Yarrow songbook
series) $16.95
    Grades: PreK K 1 2   **782.42**
    1. Folk songs
    ISBN 978-1-4027-5961-1; 1-4027-5961-4
                                          LC 2008022435
An illustrated compilation of folk songs with an audio CD of the songs performed by Peter Yarrow and his
daughter Bethany.
"Widener's acrylic paintings are expansive and gorgeous, but the [CD is] the real treasure here." SLJ

The Fox went out on a chilly night; an old song. illustrated
by Peter Spier. Doubleday 1961 un il music hardcover
o.p. pa $6.95
    Grades: K 1 2 3   **782.42**
    1. Foxes -- Songs 2. Folk songs -- United States
    ISBN 0-385-07990-7; 0-440-40829-6 pa
Set in New England, this old song tells about the trip the
fox father made to town to get some of the farmer's plump
geese for his family's dinner, and how he manages to evade
the farmer who tries to shoot him
"A true picture book in the Caldecott-Brooke tradition.
Fine drawings, lovely colors, and pictures so full of amusing
details that young viewers will make fresh discoveries every
time they . . . scrutinize these beautiful, action-filled pages."
Horn Book

★ I hear America singing! folk songs for American families. collected and arranged by Kathleen Krull; illustrated by Allen Garns; introductory note by Arlo Guthrie.
Knopf 2003 145p il $24.95
    Grades: 3 4 5 6   **782.42**
    1. Folk songs -- United States
    ISBN 0-375-82527-4
First published 1992 without CD with title: Gonna sing
my head off!

"Work songs, love songs, ballads and blues, lullabies,
spirituals, protest songs, and sheer nonsense make up this
entertaining collection of 62 traditional and contemporary
favorites. For each song, Krull provides the simplest piano
and guitar arrangements in a clear double-page spread design that includes the words to all the verses. . . . The exuberant illustrations, mostly in bright pastels, manage to be both
familiar and dramatic. . . . Informal notes at the head of each
song give something about history, origin, performance, and
possibilities for variation." Booklist

In the hollow of your hand; slave lullabies. collected by Alice McGill; pictures by Michael Cummings. Houghton
Mifflin 2000 un il music $18
    Grades: 5 6 7 8   **782.42**
    1. Sleep 2. Slavery 3. Lullabies 4. African Americans
    5. Mother and child 6. Slavery -- Poetry 7. Sleep
    -- Juvenile poetry 8. African Americans -- Poetry
    9. Mother and child -- Juvenile poetry 10. African
    Americans -- Juvenile poetry 11. American poetry --
    African American authors 12. Slavery in literature --
    Juvenile literature 13. Lullabies, American -- African
    American authors 14. Children's poetry, American
    -- African American authors 15. African Americans
    -- Intellectual life -- Juvenile literature 16. Slaves --
    United States -- Intellectual life -- Juvenile literature
    17. Lullabies, American -- African American authors --
    History and criticism -- Juvenile literature 18. Children's
    poetry, American -- African American authors -- History
    and criticism -- Juvenile literature
    ISBN 0-395-85755-4
                                          LC 97-20269
A collection of lullabies orally transmitted by African-
American slaves revealing their hardships and sorrows as
well as soothing notes of well-being and belief in a better
time to come
"This moving collection of 13 folk lullabies is a powerful way to communicate what family life was like under
slavery. . . . Opposite each song is a handsome full-page quilt
collage contributed by Michael Cummings. . . . There's full
musical notation at the back, and a CD of the songs, sung by
McGill, is included. The people's words are achingly beautiful, and the combination with history and personal experience makes this an enduring collection." Booklist

Let's sing together; The Peter Yarrow songbook. [selected
by Peter Yarrow]; illustrated by Terry Widener. Sterling Pub. 2009 48p il (Peter Yarrow songbook series)
$16.95
    Grades: PreK K 1 2   **782.42**
    1. Folk songs
    ISBN 978-1-4027-5963-5; 1-4027-5963-0
"The lyrics of 12 folk songs, rooted in several cultural
traditions, are illustrated in Widener's simple yet resonant
folk art style, which creatively mingles conventional, earth-
toned scenarios . . . with images featuring vividly hued,
fanciful flourishes. . . . The author provides guitar chords,
historical notes and personal anecdotes for each song. On the
included CD, Yarrow sings each song, accompanied by his
talented daughter Bethany Yarrow and a quartet of children.
An energetic and uplifting package." Publ Wkly

★ National anthems of the world; edited by Michael Ja-
mieson Bristow. 11th ed.; Weidenfeld & Nicolson
2006 629p $90

Grades: 5 6 7 8 9 10 11 12 Adult   **782.42**

1. National songs

ISBN 0-304-36826-1

First published 1943 in the United Kingdom with title:
National anthems of the United Nations and France

This volume contains national anthems of about 198 nations, including melody and accompaniment. Words are presented in the native language with transliteration provided
where necessary. English translations follow. Brief historical
notes on the adoption of each anthem are included

"An essential reference resource for all libraries." Libr J

Sleepytime songs; The Peter Yarrow songbook. [compiled
by] Peter Yarrow; illustrated by Terry Widener. Sterling Pub. 2008 48p il (Peter Yarrow songbook series)
$16.95

Grades: PreK K 1 2   **782.42**

1. Lullabies 2. Folk songs -- United States

ISBN 978-1-4027-5962-8; 1-4027-5962-2

LC 2008022530

"Yarrow, best known as the Peter of Peter, Paul, and
Mary, here offers a wonderful compilation of bedtime songs,
complete with CD. Beginning with a warm introduction
from Yarrow about singing to children, the book continues
with two-page spreads containing the lyrics of the songs, set
against Widener's imaginative art." Booklist

Weave little stars into my sleep; Native American lullabies.
edited by Neil Philip; photographs by Edward S. Curtis.
Clarion Bks. 2001 un il $16

Grades: 2 3 4   **782.42**

1. Lullabies 2. Native American literature 3. Lullabies,
American -- Indian authors

ISBN 0-618-08856-3

LC 00-60324

Published in the United Kingdom with title: Where did
you fall from?

This is a "book of 15 lullabies, selected, adapted, and,
in some cases, reworked from original Native American
material. Striking, carefully chosen photographs, originally
published in the early 1900s, portray the spirit of the words."
Booklist

Includes bibliographical references

★ The twelve days of Christmas; illustrated by Ilse Plume.
David R. Godine 2005 un il $17.95

Grades: K 1 2 3   **782.42**

1. Songs 2. Folk songs 3. Christmas -- Songs

ISBN 978-1-56792-300-1; 1-56792-300-3

LC 2005013368

A reissue of the edition first published 1990 by Harper
& Row

"Plume has drawn on her studies of old manuscripts,
books of hours, miniatures, and bestiaries, plus her knowledge of Italy to produce a rich tribute to the Italian Renaissance. Paintings, as if executed on old vellum or parchment,
depict a young woman in fancy dress and her true love resplendent in garden and household settings enjoying each
day's gifts. The text, variously framed, is surrounded by
flower embellishments, birds, vines, and other natural bits.

. . . Words and music with piano accompaniment and guitar
chords in the key of F are included." SLJ

782.421   Rock (Rock 'n' roll) songs

Behnke, Alison Marie

Death of a dreamer; the assassination of John Lennon.
Alison Marie Behnke. Twenty-First Century Books 2012
96 p.

Grades: 5 6 7 8   **782.421**

1. Assassination 2. Rock musicians -- Political activity
3. Rock musicians -- England -- Biography 4. Rock
musicians 5. Murder -- New York (State) -- New York
-- Juvenile literature 6. Rock musicians -- England --
Biography -- Juvenile literature 7. Murderers -- New
York (State) -- Biography -- Juvenile literature

ISBN 0822590360; 9780822590361

LC 2010005550

In this young adult book, "[t]win narratives converge in
New York City on December 8, 1980, when John Lennon
was murdered by Mark David Chapman. [Alison Marie]
Behnke calls the murder an assassination, and by the general
definition of the word--'to murder (a usually prominent person) by sudden or secret attack, often for political reasons'-
-the murder of John Lennon might qualify. Lennon was political by the end of his life, writing 'Give Peace a Chance,'
which became the anthem of the peace movement, but he
was hardly a revolutionary, as Behnke terms him. Chapman was not especially political, and he didn't really seem
to know why he attacked Lennon; it was certainly not from
any well-thought-out political motives, as the author herself
describes." (Kirkus)

Includes bibliographical references (p. 92), discography
(p. 93), filmography (p. 93), and index

Brewer, Paul

The **Beatles** were fab (and they were funny) by Kathleen Krull and Paul Brewer; illustrated by Stacy Innerst.
Harcourt Children's Books 2013 40 p. col. ill. (reinforced)
$16.99

Grades: 2 3 4   **782.421**

1. Wit and humor 2. Rock musicians -- England --
Biography 3. Rock musicians -- England -- Juvenile
humor

ISBN 054750991X; 9780547509914

LC 2012025483

This book, by Kathleen Krull, Paul Brewer, and illustrated by Stacy Innerst, explores when "the Beatles burst onto
the music scene in the early 1960s, . . . their off-the-charts
talent and offbeat humor made them the most famous band
on both sides of the Atlantic. . . . [This] text and expressive,
quirky paintings chronicle the phenomenal rise of Beatlema-
nia, showing how the Fab Four's sense of humor helped the
lads weather everything that was thrown their way." (Publisher's note)

Carle, Eric

★ **Today** is Monday; pictures by Eric Carle. Philomel
Bks. 1993 un il music hardcover o.p. pa $6.99

Grades: K 1 2 3   **782.421**

1. Songs 2. Children's songs 3. Food -- Songs 4.
Animals -- Songs 5. Food -- Songs -- Juvenile literature

6. Week -- Songs -- Juvenile literature
ISBN 0-399-21966-8; 0-698-11563-5 pa

LC 91-45866

Each day of the week brings a new food, until on Sunday all the world's children can come and eat it up

This song "gets new life in a picture book bursting with food, animals, and lots of energy. Beginning with the grinning cat on the cover . . . a zooful of animals act out the lyrics: snakes get tangled in spaghetti, elephants use their trunks to slurp 'Zoooop,' and pelicans catch fish on Friday. With text at a minimum, Carle's always innovative artwork steps center stage in an oversize format that allows gloriously colored collages to spread over two pages." Booklist

Christensen, Bonnie

★ **Woody** Guthrie, poet of the people. Knopf 2001 un il hardcover o.p. pa $7.99

Grades: 3 4 5 6   **782.421**

1. Singers 2. Folk musicians 3. Memoirists 4. Songwriters 5. Folk singers -- United States -- Biography -- Juvenile literature
ISBN 0-553-11203-1; 0375811133; 0375911138 lib bdg

LC 00-65504

This book tells "the life story of American songwriter Woody Guthrie. . . . Grades three to six." (Bull Cent Child Books)

"Christensen makes a fine union of a spirited, vibrant text and hand-colored woodcuts that are sinewy and emotionally compelling." Booklist

Hort, Lenny

★ The **seals** on the bus; illustrated by G. Brian Karas. Holt & Co. 2000 un il $17.95

Grades: K 1 2   **782.421**

1. Buses 2. Songs 3. Animal sounds 4. Animals -- Songs 5. Children's songs -- Texts
ISBN 0-8050-5952-0

LC 99-33612

Different animals—including seals, tigers, geese, rabbits, monkeys, and more—make their own sounds as they ride all around the town on a bus

"Karas' artwork combines cut paper, gouache, acrylic, and pencil to create a series of pleasingly varied scenes of cheerful chaos. A good story hour choice." Booklist

Katz, Alan

Take me out of the bathtub and other silly dilly songs; illustrated by David Catrow. Margaret K. McElderry Bks. 2001 un il $15

Grades: K 1 2 3   **782.421**

1. Songs 2. Humorous songs 3. Humorous songs -- Texts 4. Children's songs -- United States -- Texts
ISBN 0-689-82903-5

LC 99-89390

Well-known songs, including "Oh Susannah" and "Row Row Row Your Boat," are presented with new words and titles, such as "I'm So Carsick" and "Go Go Go to Bed"

"Catrow's animated double-spread pictures are at least as silly as the song lyrics, offering action-filled scenes bursting with odd-looking creatures." Booklist

Schroeder, Alan, 1961-

Baby Flo; Florence Mills lights up the stage. by Alan Schroeder; illustrated by Cornelius Van Wright & Ying-Hwa Hu. Lee & Low Books 2012 40 p. (hardcover: alk. paper) $18.95

Grades: 1 2 3   **782.421**

1. Biography 2. African American singers -- Biography -- Juvenile literature
ISBN 1600604102; 9781600604102

LC 2011036553

This book, by Alan Schroeder, tells the story of "[Baby Florence] Mills [who] was singing and dancing just about as soon as she could talk and walk. . . . Baby Flo went on to become an international superstar during the Harlem Renaissance . . . but first she had to overcome a case of stage fright and discover that winning wasn't everything. Here is the spirited story of that spunky young girl learning to chase her dreams with confidence." (Publisher's note)

Taback, Simms

★ **There** was an old lady who swallowed a fly. Viking 1997 un il $16.99

Grades: K 1 2 3   **782.421**

1. Folk songs 2. Animals -- Songs 3. English folk songs -- Juvenile literature
ISBN 0-670-86939-2

A Caldecott Medal honor book, 1998

Simms Taback's illustrated version of the folk song in which an old lady swallows a variety of progressively larger animals

"Each page is full of details and humorous asides. . . . A die-cut hole allows readers to see inside [the old lady's] belly, first the critters already devoured and, with the turn of the page, the new animal that will join the crowd in her ever-expanding stomach. . . . The text is handwritten on vivid strips of paper that are loosely placed on the patterned page, thus creating a lively interplay between the meaning of the words and their visual power." SLJ

Watson, Renée

★ **Harlem's** little blackbird; Renee Watson; illustrated by Christian Robinson. 1st ed. Random House Children's Books 2012 1 v. (unpaged) (trade) $17.99

Grades: 2 3 4   **782.421**

1. African American singers 2. Picture books for children 3. Singers -- New York (State) -- New York -- Biography -- Juvenile literature 4. African American singers -- New York (State) -- New York -- Biography -- Juvenile literature
ISBN 0375869735; 9780375869730; 9780375969737; 9780375985379

LC 2011043314

Author Renée Watson tells the story of "Florence Mills, [who] knew that she was blessed with a gift--a sweet, bird-like singing voice that everyone loved. But she also knew firsthand the profound ache of racism. When she moved to New York City, the stages got bigger, the lights grew brighter, and offers that could make her an international star were hers for the taking. Instead, Florence chose shows that helped promote other black performers. And she sang songs that heralded the call for civil rights." (reneewatson.net)

Hush, little baby; a folk song. with pictures by Marla Frazee. Harcourt Brace & Co. 1999 un il hardcover o.p. pa $7

Grades: K 1 2 **782.421**

1. Lullabies 2. Folk songs 3. Folk songs -- United States 4. Folk songs, English -- Texts
ISBN 0-15-201429-2; 0-15-204761-1 pa

LC 98-9608

In an old lullaby a baby is promised an assortment of presents from its adoring parent

"True to the song's Appalachian roots, Frazee sets the traditional lullaby in the hills of West Virginia, with big, detailed pictures that add character and exaggerated sibling rivalry to the nonsense story. . . . The music is on the last page, and Frazee's clear narrative pictures in acrylics and pencil capture the rhythm of the words, the historic particulars of the place, the nighttime farce, and the universal family scenarios of jealousy and love." Booklist

783   Music for single voices

Fishkin, Rebecca Love

Singing; a practical guide to pursuing the art. Compass Point Books 2010 48p il (Performing arts) lib bdg $28.65

Grades: 5 6 7 8 **783**

1. Singing 2. Vocational guidance
ISBN 978-0-7565-4362-4 lib bdg; 0-7565-4362-2 lib bdg

LC 2010012607

This guide on a singing career includes tips on education, technique, and more.

"Meant for students contemplating a career in the field . . . [this book goes] beyond basic introductions and into more detail about what it takes to make it as a professional. . . . [The author maintains] . . . a frank, realistic tone, stressing the importance of hard work and dedication. Great [resource] . . . for those wanting to make their passions more than just a hobby." SLJ

Includes glossary and bibliographical references

Landau, Elaine

Is singing for you? Lerner Publications 2011 40p il (Ready to make music) lib bdg $27.93

Grades: 4 5 6 7 **783**

1. Singing
ISBN 978-0-7613-5427-7 lib bdg; 0-7613-5427-1 lib bdg

LC 2009052350

Helps readers explore the art of singing. This book covers the basics, including tips for getting started and info on vocal technique.

"Landau covers all the bases so that prospective musicians have the information they need. . . . Kids thinking about taking up an instrument will find . . . [this book] helpful in their decision-making process." SLJ

Includes glossary and bibliographical references

784.19   Instruments

D'Cruz, Anna-Marie

Make your own musical instruments. PowerKids Press 2009 24p il (Do it yourself projects!) lib bdg $23.95; pa $9.40

Grades: 2 3 4 **784.19**

1. Handicraft 2. Musical instruments
ISBN 978-1-4358-2854-4 lib bdg; 1-4358-2854-2 lib bdg; 978-1-4358-2925-1 pa; 1-4358-2925-5 pa

LC 2008033667

This offers "step-by-step instructions and full-color photos to illustrate the crafts. Projects have a broad cultural representation and are not gender specific. Materials are easily obtained. . . . [Projects include] castanets, bongo drums, and a jazz washboard." SLJ

Includes glossary and bibliographical references

Helsby, Genevieve

★ **Those** amazing musical instruments; [by] Genevieve Helsby; with Marin Alsop as your guide. Sourcebooks Jabberwocky 2007 176p il $19.95

Grades: 4 5 6 7 8 9 **784.19**

1. Musical instruments
ISBN 978-1-4022-0825-6; 1-4022-0825-1

LC 2007013821

This is "a guide to instruments commonly found in an orchestra. . . . Utilizing large print; ample, colorful illustrations; and an open format, the book is logically organized into chapters about each of the musical instrument families, including keyboards, the voice, and modern electronic instruments. Throughout, readers are prompted to listen to the accompanying CD-ROM, which features more than 100 musical samples. Information is clearly presented, and the author's enthusiasm for her subject is contagious." SLJ

VanHecke, Susan

★ **Raggin',** jazzin', rockin' a history of American musical instrument makers. Boyds Mills Press 2011 136p il $17.95

Grades: 5 6 7 8 9 **784.19**

1. Musical instruments 2. Manufacturing executives 3. Musical instrument makers
ISBN 1-59078-574-6; 978-1-59078-574-4

LC 2010-04877

This is a history of American musical instrument making, including the stories of the Zildjian family's cymbals, Steinway's pianos, Charles Gerard Conn's brass instruments, C. F. Martin's guitars, William F. Ludwig's drums, Hammond keyboards, Fender electric guitars, and Moog synthesizers.

"Musicians and music lovers look no further. [This] is a book for everyone. . . . This is an interesting book." Voice Youth Advocates

Includes bibliographical references

Wiseman, Ann Sayre

Making music; [by] Ann Sayre Wiseman and John Langstaff; illustrations by Ann Sayre Wiseman. Storey Bks. 2003 96p il hardcover o.p. pa $9.95

Grades: 3 4 5 6 **784.19**

1. Handicraft 2. Musical instruments 3. Musical instruments -- Construction
ISBN 1-58017-513-9; 1-58017-512-0 pa

LC 2003-54218

First published 1979 by Scribner with title: Making musical things

Includes instructions for making a variety of simple musical instruments from ordinary household items

Includes glossary and bibliographical references

784.2 Full orchestra (Symphony orchestra)

Ganeri, Anita

★ The **young** person's guide to the orchestra; Benjamin Britten's composition on CD narrated by Ben Kingsley. book written by Anita Ganeri. Harcourt Brace & Co. 1996 56p il $25

Grades: 4 5 6 7   **784.2**

1. Orchestra 2. Music appreciation 3. Musical instruments

ISBN 0-15-201304-0

LC 95-41478

"Accompanying this book on orchestral music is a CD featuring Britten's A Young Person's Guide to the Orchestra . . . as well as Dukas' The Sorcerer's Apprentice. The book begins with an overview of the orchestra and then centers around groups of instruments, explaining a bit of their history and their sound's distinctive quality. . . . The book also introduces eight famous composers, world music, Benjamin Britten, and the background of The YoungPerson's Guide to the Orchestra. . . . Handsome and useful." Booklist

Includes glossary

Koscielniak, Bruce

★ The **story** of the incredible orchestra; an introduction to musical instruments and the symphony orchestra. Houghton Mifflin 2000 un il $16; pa $6.95

Grades: 2 3 4   **784.2**

1. Orchestra 2. Musical instruments

ISBN 0-395-96052-5; 0-618-31112-2 pa

LC 98-43933

Describes the orchestra, the families of instruments of which it is made, and the individual instruments in each family

"The illustrations are dense with gentle color and filled with scenes of musicians at play and pictures of instruments, with banner labels adding more information. . . . A lot of information about who invented what and how it's played is packed into these engaging pages." Booklist

784.4 Light orchestra

Brown, Monica

Tito Puente, Mambo King; Tito Puente, Rey del Mambo. by Monica Brown; illustrated by Rafael Lopez; translated by Adriana Dominguez. HarperCollins 2013 32 p. col. ill. (hardcover) $17.99

Grades: 2 3 4   **784.4**

1. Puente, Tito, 1923-2000 -- Juvenile literature 2. Salsa musicians -- United States -- Biography -- Juvenile literature

ISBN 0061227838; 9780061227837

LC 2012025493

This children's picture-book biography of Tito Puente presents a "bilingual tribute to the salsa drummer and band leader extraordinaire. [Monica] Brown's narrative . . . takes her preschool and primary audience from Tito's toddlerhood . . . through childhood loves: drum lessons, dancing and stickball on the streets of Harlem. Bouncing through the musician's adulthood, Brown highlights early gigs, a Navy stint . . . and regular shows at the Palladium in New York City." (Kirkus Reviews)

786 Specific instruments and their music

Ganeri, Anita

Pianos and Keyboards. Smart Apple Media 2011 il (How the world makes music)

Grades: 4 5 6   **786**

1. Keyboard instruments

ISBN 1-599-20479-7; 978-1-599-20479-6

LC 2010052912

Describes various keyboard instruments from around the world, such as the familiar piano and organ, along with other keyboard instruments such as the accordian, harpsichord, and the hurdy-gurdy.

"The text reads smoothly, the layout is attractive. . . . This will be useful for collections serving schools, especially those assigning instrument reports." Booklist

Includes glossary and bibliographical references

786.2 Keyboard instruments

Reich, Susanna

★ **Clara** Schumann; piano virtuoso. Clarion Bks. 1999 118p il $18; pa $9.95

Grades: 5 6 7 8   **786.2**

1. Pianists 2. Women composers 3. Pianists -- Germany -- Biography -- Juvenile literature

ISBN 0-395-89119-1; 0-618-55160-3 pa

LC 98-24510

Describes the life of the German pianist and composer who made her professional debut at age nine and who devoted her life to music and to her family

"This thoroughly researched book draws on primary sources, both Clara's own diaries and her voluminous correspondence with her husband. . . . Reich's lucid, quietly passionate biography is liberally illustrated with photographs and reproductions." Horn Book Guide

786.8 Percussion instruments

Ganeri, Anita

Drums and percussion instruments. Smart Apple Media 2011 il (How the world makes music) lib bdg $28.50

Grades: 4 5 6   **786.8**

1. Percussion instruments

ISBN 978-1-599-20478-9

LC 2010043356

Describes various percussion instruments from around the world, including current drum kits, orchestral instruments such as the xylophone, and more traditional drums from Africa and Asia.

Includes glossary and bibliographical references

786.9   Drums and devices used for percussive effects

Greenwood, Mark

Drummer boy of John John; by Mark Greenwood; illustrations by Frané Lessac. Lee & Low 2012 40 p. (hardcover: alk. paper) $18.95

Grades: PreK K 1 2 3   **786.9**

1. Music 2. Biography 3. Musical instruments 4. Steel drum (Musical instrument) -- Juvenile literature 5. Musicians -- Trinidad and Tobago -- Biography -- Juvenile literature

ISBN 1600606520; 9781600606526

LC 2011045370

In author Mark Greenwood's book, "Carnival is coming, and the villagers of John John, Trinidad, are getting ready to jump up and celebrate with music, dancing, and a parade. Best of all, the Roti King has promised free rotis--tasty fried pancakes filled with chicken, herbs, and spices--for the best band in the parade. . . . With ingenuity and the help of his friends, Winston takes on the Carnival bands, drumming his way to victory--and to the Roti King's prized treat." (Publisher's note)

Landau, Elaine

Are the drums for you? Lerner Publications 2011 40p il (Ready to make music) lib bdg $27.93

Grades: 4 5 6 7   **786.9**

1. Drums 2. Percussion instruments

ISBN 978-0-7613-5426-0 lib bdg; 0-7613-5426-3 lib bdg

LC 2009-48971

Hear what professional drummers like about their instrument, and learn what skills a good drummer needs.

"Landau covers all the bases so that prospective musicians have the information they need. . . . Kids thinking about taking up an instrument will find . . . [this book] helpful in their decision-making process." SLJ

Includes glossary and bibliographical references

787   Stringed instruments (Chordophones)

Ganeri, Anita

Stringed instruments. Smart Apple Media 2011 il (How the world makes music) lib bdg $28.50

Grades: 4 5 6   **787**

1. Stringed instruments

ISBN 978-1-599-20480-2

LC 2010042418

Describes various stringed instruments from around the world including familiar instruments such as the guitar and violin, along with other traditional instruments such as the Japanese Koto and Indian lutes.

787.2   Violins

Landau, Elaine

Is the violin for you? Lerner Publications 2011 40p il (Ready to make music) lib bdg $27.93

Grades: 4 5 6 7   **787.2**

1. Violins

ISBN 978-0-7613-5423-9 lib bdg; 0-7613-5423-9 lib bdg

LC 2009045609

Hear what professional violinists like about their instrument, and learn what skills a good violinist needs.

"Landau covers all the bases so that prospective musicians have the information they need. . . . Kids thinking about taking up an instrument will find . . . [this book] helpful in their decision-making process." SLJ

Includes glossary and bibliographical references

787.87   Guitars

Blaxland, Wendy

Guitars. Marshall Cavendish Benchmark 2011 32p il map (How are they made?) lib bdg $12.99

Grades: 4 5 6   **787.87**

1. Guitars

ISBN 978-0-7614-4754-2 lib bdg; 0-7614-4754-7 lib bdg

LC 2009039880

This describes how guitars are made including their history, parts, materials, design, manufacture, packaging and distribution, marketing and advertising, and affect on the environment

"There is a bounty of color photos, including fascinating contructiion shots as well as pics of axe-wielding notables Les Paul, Bruce Springsteen, and Prince." Booklist

Includes glossary

Landau, Elaine

Is the guitar for you? Lerner Publications 2011 40p il (Ready to make music) lib bdg $27.93

Grades: 4 5 6 7   **787.87**

1. Guitars

ISBN 978-0-7613-5424-6 lib bdg; 0-7613-5424-7 lib bdg

LC 2009-48750

Hear what professional guitarists like about their instrument, and learn what skills a good guitarist needs.

"Landau covers all the bases so that prospective musicians have the information they need. . . . Kids thinking about taking up an instrument will find . . . [this book] helpful in their decision-making process." SLJ

Includes glossary and bibliographical references

788   Wind instruments (Aerophones)

Ganeri, Anita

Brass instruments. Smart Apple Media 2011 il (How the world makes music) lib bdg 28.50

Grades: 4 5 6   **788**

1. Wind instruments

ISBN 978-1-599-20477-2

LC 2010053889

Describes various brass instruments from around the world, such as the familiar trumpet and trombone, along with historical instruments such as the Alphorn, serpent, and traditional instruments still played today, including the didgeridoo and the dung-chen.

Includes glossary and bibliographical references

Wind instruments. Smart Apple Media 2011 il (How the world makes music) lib bdg $28.50
Grades: 4 5 6 **788**
1. Wind instruments
ISBN 978-1-599-20482-6

LC 2010042423

Describes various wind instruments from around the world, such as the familiar clarinet, saxophone, and flute, along with other traditional instruments such as the Chinese flute, nose flute, and pan pipes.

Landau, Elaine
Is the flute for you? Lerner Publications 2011 40p il (Ready to make music) lib bdg $27.93
Grades: 4 5 6 7 **788**
1. Flutes
ISBN 978-0-7613-5420-8 lib bdg; 0-7613-5420-4 lib bdg

LC 2009048970

Hear what professional flutists like about their instrument, and learn what skills a good flutist needs.

"Landau covers all the bases so that prospective musicians have the information they need. . . . Kids thinking about taking up an instrument will find . . . [this book] helpful in their decision-making process." SLJ

Includes glossary and bibliographical references

Is the trumpet for you? Lerner Publications 2011 40p il (Ready to make music) lib bdg $27.93
Grades: 4 5 6 7 **788**
1. Trumpet
ISBN 978-0-7613-5422-2 lib bdg; 0-7613-5422-0 lib bdg

LC 2009048280

Hear what professional trumpeters like about their instrument, and learn what skills a good trumpeter needs.

"Landau covers all the bases so that prospective musicians have the information they need. . . . Kids thinking about taking up an instrument will find . . . [this book] helpful in their decision-making process." SLJ

Includes glossary and bibliographical references

788.7 Saxophones

Golio, Gary
Spirit seeker; John Coltrane's musical journey. by Gary Golio; paintings by Rudy Gutierrez. Clarion Books 2012 48 p. (hardcover) $17.99
Grades: 3 4 5 6 7 **788.7**
1. Music and religion 2. Creation (Literary, artistic, etc.) -- Juvenile literature 3. Saxophonists -- United States -- Biography -- Juvenile literature 4. Jazz musicians -- United States -- Biography -- Juvenile literature
ISBN 0547239947; 9780547239941

LC 2011045948

Includes bibliographical references and discography.

This book, by Gary Golio, illustrated by Rudy Gutierrez, explores the musical career of Jazz saxophonist John Col-

trane. "Growing up, John was a seeker. He wondered about spirit, and the meaning of life. And whether music could be a key to unlocking those mysteries. . . . This is the story of a shy, curious boy from a deeply religious family who grew up to find solace and inspiration in his own unique approach to both spirituality and music." (Publisher's note)

788.9 Brass instruments (Lip-reed instruments)

Lynette, Rachel
Miles Davis; legendary jazz musician. by Rachel Lynette. KidHaven Press 2010 48 p. ill. (some col.) (hardcover) $29.95
Grades: 5 6 7 8 **788.9**
1. Jazz music 2. Jazz musicians -- United States -- Biography -- Juvenile literature
ISBN 0737750340; 9780737750348

LC 2009045056

This biography of Miles Davis by Rachel Lynette is part of the Innovators series. Lynette "pinpoints the many works in which Davis pushed musical boundaries." She "refrains from mentioning the album Bitches Brew by name, instead offering . . . 'Davis and his band made an album that sold more than . . . any other jazz record ever.'" (Booklist)

Includes bibliographical references and index.

790 Recreational and performing arts

Glenn, Joshua
Unbored; the essential field guide to serious fun. [compiled by] Joshua Glenn & Elizabeth Foy Larsen; design by Tony Leone. Bloomsbury USA 2012 352 p. (hardback) $25
Grades: 5 6 7 **790**
1. Amusements -- Juvenile literature 2. Games -- Juvenile literature 3. Handicraft -- Juvenile literature 4. Recreation -- Juvenile literature
ISBN 1608196410; 9781608196418

LC 2012012368

This activity book by Elizabeth Foy Larsen and Joshua Glen, illustrated by Heather Kasunick and Mister Reusch, "provides kids with information to round out their world view and inspire them to learn more. From how-tos on using the library or writing your representative to a graphic history of video games, the book isn't shy about teaching. Yet the bulk of the 350-page mega-resource presents hands-on activities." (Publisher's note)

790.06 Organizations and management of recreation

Rosen, Michael J.
Let's build a playground; Michael J. Rosen. Candlewick Press 2013 32 p. (reinforced) $15.99
Grades: 2 3 4 5 **790.06**
1. Playgrounds 2. Community development
ISBN 0763655325; 9780763655327

LC 2012943649

This book, by Michael J. Rosen, illustrated by Ellen Kelson and Jennifer Cecil, is part of the "Kaboom! Books" series. It describes how "two hundred kids and grown-ups in an Indianapolis community got together to build the playground in this book--one of over two thousand that Ka-BOOM! has helped create." (Publisher's note)

790.1   General kinds of recreational activities

Ball, Jacqueline A.
Traveling green. Bearport Pub. 2009 32p il (Going green) lib bdg $25.27
Grades: 4 5 6 7   **790.1**
    1. Travel -- Environmental aspects
    ISBN 978-1-59716-964-6 lib bdg; 1-59716-964-1 lib bdg
                             LC 2009-19836
"Color photographs (most full page) and a few diagrams accompany the informative text[s]. . . . Overall, the [book] . . . is user-friendly and covers topics that are not easily found elsewhere." SLJ
Includes glossary and bibliographical references

Bell-Rehwoldt, Sheri
    The **kids'** guide to classic games. Capstone Press 2009 32p il (Kids' guides) lib bdg $23.99
Grades: 4 5 6 7   **790.1**
    1. Games
    ISBN 978-1-4296-2273-8 lib bdg; 1-4296-2273-3 lib bdg
                             LC 2008-29686
This provides instructions and rules for indoor and outdoor games such as ping-pong soccer, ringer, paper football, spiderweb, tug-of-war, and pipeline
Includes glossary and bibliographical references

Conner, Bobbi
    Unplugged play; no batteries, no plugs, pure fun. illustrations by Amy Patacchiola. Workman Pub. 2007 xxv, 401p il $27.95; pa $16.95
Grades: Adult Professional   **790.1**
    1. Play 2. Games
    ISBN 978-0-7611-4114-3; 978-0-7611-4390-1 pa
                            LC 2007-23999
"Conner has compiled more than 710 games and activities sorted by age level. Good old-fashioned play and fun are the motto here with simple props from around the house or just an imagination. The book is separated into three major parts: 'Toddler Play,' 'Preschool Play,' and 'Grade School Play.' Each has a section on solo play, ideas for parent and child, playing with others, and birthday-party activities. Each chapter and section is loaded with ideas and suggestions for simple crafts. There is such a wealth of information in this book." SLJ

Danks, Fiona
    Run wild! outdoor games and adventures. [by] Fiona Danks and [photography by] Jo Schofield. Frances Lincoln 2011 159p il pa $24.95
Grades: 5 6 7 8   **790.1**
    1. Games 2. Parties 3. Handicraft 4. Nature study 5. Outdoor life 6. Storytelling
    ISBN 978-0-7112-3172-6; 0-7112-3172-9

"This large-format book introduces a cornucopia of ideas for outdoor activities, along with mesmerizing color photos of children and teens creatively enjoying themselves in fields, woods, backyards, and at rivers and beaches. . . . From skimming stones to making leaf masks to whittling walking sticks to following treasure trails, here's an enticing array of ideas for outdoor fun and wilderness discovery." Booklist

Davies, Huw
    The **games** book; written by Huw Davies; illustrated by Lisa Jackson. Scholastic 2009 118p il pa $9.99
Grades: 1 2 3 4 5 6   **790.1**
    1. Games
    ISBN 978-0-545-13403-3 pa; 0-545-13403-X pa
                            LC 2009004292
"This small book takes a look at the games in simpler times. There are no electronics, batteries, cell phones, or videos involved. They mostly require physical and/or mental action along with the use of an imagination and some sweat, and maybe a little dirt. There are old favorites such as Red Rover and Simon Says as well as Rummy, Hangman, and I Spy. The clear instructions are easy for early readers to follow." SLJ

Drake, Jane
    The **kids** winter handbook; [by] Jane Drake & Ann Love; illustrated by Heather Collins. Kids Can Press 2001 127p il $18.95; pa $12.95
Grades: 4 5 6 7   **790.1**
    1. Handicraft 2. Recreation 3. Nature craft
    ISBN 1-55337-033-3; 1-55074-969-2 pa
This offers ideas for winter activities such as sewing, observing the night sky, identifying animal tracks, storytelling, cooking, crafts, and games
"Most of the projects are inexpensive to make, and supplies are easy to obtain, making these interesting alternatives to holiday boredom or too much TV. Many of the activities, especially those that are science related, are also suitable for the classroom." SLJ

Ferrer, J. J.
    The **art** of stone skipping and other fun old-time games; stoopball, jacks, string games, coin flipping, line baseball, jump rope, and more. by J.J. Ferrer; illustrated by Todd Dakins. Charlesbridge Pub., Inc. 2012 192 p. (paperback) $14.95
Grades: K 1 2 3 4 5 6 7 8 9 10 11 12 Adult   **790.1**
    1. Games
    ISBN 1936140748; 9781936140749
                            LC 2012015052
This book, by J. J. Ferrer, offers a "collection of timeless games that guarantees kids a good time- by themselves, with a group of friends, or with family. Includes ball games . . . , card games . . . , sack races, and old favorites such as Duck, Duck, Goose and Red Rover. There is also a chapter for car games. Simple instructions explain the rules, how many people can play, the object of the game, and what you need." (Publisher's note)
Includes bibliographical references and index.

Gillman, Claire

The **kids'** summer fun book; great games, activities, and adventures for the entire family. [by] Claire Gillman & Sam Martin. Barron's 2011 128p il pa $12.99

Grades: 3 4 5 6   **790.1**

1. Games 2. Sports 3. Summer 4. Cooking 5. Handicraft 6. Recreation

ISBN 978-0-7641-4581-0; 0-7641-4581-9

This offers ideas for summer activities such as beach parties, sand castle building, hiking and camping trips, kite flying, snorkeling, croquet, fishing, games, water sports, handicrafts, and cooking.

The **kids'** winter fun book; homespun adventures for family fun. [by] Claire Gillman & Sam Martin. Barron's 2011 128p il pa $12.99

Grades: 3 4 5 6   **790.1**

1. Sports 2. Winter 3. Cooking 4. Amusements 5. Handicraft 6. Recreation 7. Indoor games

ISBN 978-0-7641-4726-5; 0-7641-4726-9

This book "offers a variety of activities, games, crafts, and opportunities for family bonding throughout the winter. Indoor projects include knitting scarves, making a snow globe, and creating an obstacle course. Among the outdoor activities are hiking, winter photography, ice skating, and making a sled; more than a dozen recipes for items like caramel apples and winter stew are also included." Publ Wkly

Goldstone, Bruce

100 ways to celebrate 100 days. Henry Holt and Company 2010 un il $16.99

Grades: K 1 2 3   **790.1**

1. Amusements 2. Recreation

ISBN 978-0-8050-8997-4; 0-8050-8997-7

"Bright color photographs that pop from white backgrounds invite youngsters to celebrate the first 100 days of school by doing things: 'Recycle 100 cans'; 'Walk 100 steps in any direction.' 'Make a snake with 100 beads'; and even mop. Highlighting the ideas shown on each spread is a number line in 100 hues, which are also backgrounds for saying hello in 100 languages. . . . A more clever collection of 100 ideas is hard to imagine. A must-have for schools." SLJ

Hines-Stephens, Sarah

Show off; how to do absolutely everything one step at a time. [by] Sarah Hines Stephens and Bethany Mann. Candlewick Press 2009 224p il $18.99

Grades: 5 6 7 8   **790.1**

1. Amusements 2. Handicraft 3. Recreation

ISBN 978-0-7636-4599-1; 0-7636-4599-0

LC 2009015847

"This lively illustrated activity book delivers concise instructions for a variety of indoor and outdoor activities. Projects include crafts, pranks and magic tricks; ideas for nature exploration; and other purely entertaining feats. . . . The instructions are heavy on graphics and light on detail, making for an eye-catching but potentially frustrating experience. But readers should enjoy the irreverence and variety." Publ Wkly

Regan, Lisa

Games on the move! QEB Pub. 2011 32p il (Games handbook) lib bdg $27.10

Grades: 3 4 5   **790.1**

1. Games

ISBN 978-1-59566-933-9; 1-59566-933-7

LC 2010018098

First published 2010 in the United Kingdom

These travel games "will keep kids occupied and engaged. . . . The games are formatted by degree of difficulty with easier activities at the beginning; almost all of them take up a single page and can be learned by following the three-step directions. Surrounding these explanations are bright illustrations, suggestions for altering the game if there is a solo player or to make it more challenging, and an occasional fact related to the activity." SLJ

Outdoor games! QEB Pub. 2011 32p il (Games handbook) lib bdg $27.10

Grades: 3 4 5   **790.1**

1. Games

ISBN 978-1-59566-934-6; 1-59566-934-5

LC 2010014187

First published 2010 in the United Kingdom

These games "will keep kids occupied and engaged. . . . The games are formatted by degree of difficulty with easier activities at the beginning; almost all of them take up a single page and can be learned by following the three-step directions. Surrounding these explanations are bright illustrations, suggestions for altering the game if there is a solo player or to make it more challenging, and an occasional fact related to the activity." SLJ

Party games. QEB Pub. 2011 32p il (Games handbook) lib bdg $27.10

Grades: 3 4 5   **790.1**

1. Games 2. Parties

ISBN 978-1-59566-932-2; 1-59566-932-9

LC 2010014188

First published 2010 in the United Kingdom

These party games "will keep kids occupied and engaged. . . . The games are formatted by degree of difficulty with easier activities at the beginning; almost all of them take up a single page and can be learned by following the three-step directions. Surrounding these explanations are bright illustrations, suggestions for altering the game if there is a solo player or to make it more challenging, and an occasional fact related to the activity." SLJ

Rowell, Victoria

Tag, toss & run; 40 classic lawn games. Paul Tukey & Victoria Rowell. Storey Pub. 2012 207 p. (pbk.: alk. paper) $14.95

Grades: Adult Professional   **790.1**

1. Games 2. Outdoor recreation 3. Games -- Juvenile literature 4. Outdoor games -- Juvenile literature

ISBN 1603425608; 9781603425605

LC 2011049410

This book on "family lawn games" presents a "guide to 40 time-tested favorites -- from classics like capture the flag, croquet, badminton, and bocce to the lesser-known Cherokee marbles, cornhole, and Kubb. The authors offer a quick overview of the basic structure of each game, as well as strategies for playing and tips for creating fun variations." (Publisher's note)

Includes bibliographical references and index.

791   Public performances

Gerstein, Mordicai, 1935-
★ The **man** who walked between the towers. Roaring Brook Press 2003 un il $17.95; lib bdg $24.90
Grades: PreK K 1 2 3   **791**
   1. Tightrope walking 2. Aerialists
   ISBN 0-7613-1791-0; 0-7613-2868-8 lib bdg
                                    LC 2003-9040
Awarded the Caldecott Medal, 2004
A lyrical evocation of Philippe Petit's 1974 tightrope walk between the World Trade Center towers
"The pacing of the narrative is as masterful as the placement and quality of the oil-and-ink paintings. . . . Gerstein captures his subject's incredible determination, profound skill, and sheer joy." SLJ

Lusted, Marcia Amidon
   Entertainment. ABDO Pub. Company 2011 112p il (Inside the industry) $23.95
Grades: 5 6 7 8   **791**
   1. Performing arts -- Vocational guidance
   ISBN 978-1-61714-799-9; 1-61714-799-0
                                    LC 2010041255
This "well-designed [book describes] a variety of careers in [entertainment]. Because [it helps] readers assess if these positions are suitable for their personality types and backgrounds, the [title is a] good [choice] for career exploration and self-discovery. [It is] also useful for research and reports. . . . Sidebars and full-color photos appear throughout." SLJ
   Includes bibliographical references

791.06   Organizations and management

Rau, Dana Meachen
   Roller coasters. Marshall Cavendish Benchmark 2010 24p il (Surprising science) lib bdg $22.79
Grades: 2 3 4   **791.06**
   1. Roller coasters
   ISBN 978-0-7614-4872-3; 0-7614-4872-1
                                    LC 2009053722
"Colorfully illustrated with photographs on each page, this . . . will be well received by elementary students and educators." Libr Media Connect
   Includes glossary and bibliographical references

791.3   Circuses

Helfer, Ralph
   The **world's** greatest elephant; illustrated by Ted Lewin. Philomel Books 2006 un il $16.99
Grades: 1 2 3   **791.3**
   1. Circus 2. Elephants
   ISBN 0-399-24190-6
                                    LC 2005-06490
The true story of the lives and travels of the circus elephant Modoc who travelled widely and experienced dangerous adventures with his owner and trainer Bram Gunterstein.
   "The large picture-book format is the typical choice for Lewin's fine watercolors, boldly portraying the dramatic

episodes of the elephants life and the story of friendship, separation, and reunion. This bold and heartwarming adventure tale should have wide appeal." SLJ

791.43   Motion pictures

Bliss, John
   Art that moves; animation around the world. Raintree 2011 32p il (Culture in action) lib bdg $29
Grades: 5 6 7 8   **791.43**
   1. Animated films
   ISBN 978-1-4109-3922-7; 1-4109-3922-7
                                    LC 2009051125
This "is a good choice for children interested in animated movies. Bliss looks at techniques from the early beginnings to modern times and mentions recent film releases such as Cars (2006) and Where the Wild Things Are (2010). . . . [This volume is] quick, interesting, up-to-date . . . with plenty of supportive, captioned, full-color photographs. [It] also [provides] related project suggestions." SLJ
   Includes bibliographical references

Brown, Don
   Mack made movies. Roaring Brook Press 2003 un il $16.95; lib bdg $23.90
Grades: 2 3 4   **791.43**
   1. Actors 2. Motion picture producers and directors 3. Motion picture directors 4. Motion picture producers
   ISBN 0-7613-1538-1; 0-7613-2504-2 lib bdg
                                    LC 2002-6357
A simple biography of the director whose silent films immortalized such slapstick clowns as the Keystone Kops, Charlie Chaplin, Fatty Arbuckle, Mabel Normand, and Ben Turpin
   This offers a "concise, brilliantly understated text. . . . Especially fine in conveying facial expression, Brown's spare, fluid sketches, softly washed in sepia and butterscotch tones, cunningly capture the look of the times." Booklist

Cech, John
   Imagination and innovation; the story of Weston Woods. with a foreword by Maurice Sendak. Scholastic Press 2009 175p il $29.99
Grades: Adult Professional   **791.43**
   1. Animated films 2. Children's literature 3. Motion picture producers and directors 4. Motion picture executives
   ISBN 978-0-545-08922-7; 0-545-08922-0
                                    LC 2009014207
"This is a fascinating look at Weston Woods and its creator, Morton Schindel. Rich with full-color archival photographs, detailed production notes, animation cels, and first-person accounts, the book gives readers a personal, behind-the-scenes look at the man and the studio that has animated most of the great works of children's literature from the mid-20th century to the present." SLJ

Cohn, Jessica
   Animator. Gareth Stevens Pub. 2010 32p il (Cool careers: cutting edge) lib bdg $26; pa $8.95

Grades: 4 5 6　　　　　　　　　　791.43
　1. Vocational guidance 2. Animation (Cinematography)
ISBN 978-1-4339-1953-4 lib bdg; 1-4339-1953-2 lib
bdg; 978-1-4339-2152-0 pa; 1-4339-2152-9 pa
　　　　　　　　　　　　LC 2009002006

Describes the work of an animator.

This title offers "clear, solid information in a large font. .
. . [This] short [book is] packed with relevant, current material." SLJ

Includes glossary and bibliographical references

Higgins, Nadia

　Jennifer Lawrence; The hunger games' girl on fire.
by Nadia Higgins. Lerner Publications Company 2013 32
p. col. ill. (Pop culture bios: action movie stars) (library)
$26.60

Grades: 4 5 6　　　　　　　　　　791.43
　1. Hunger games (Motion picture) 2. Actors -- United
　States -- Biography -- Juvenile literature
　ISBN 1467707430; 9781467707435
　　　　　　　　　　　　LC 2012031010

This book is part of the Pop Culture Bios: Action Movie
Stars series. It "features 22-year-old Jennifer Lawrence, best
known to young people as the actress who played Katniss in
'The Hunger Games.' [Nadia] Higgins describes how Lawrence grew up in Kentucky and then, at age 14, left school
and took up acting in New York. After a few television and
movie roles, she received a Best Actress Oscar nomination
for 'Winter's Bone.'" (Booklist)

Includes bibliographical references and index

Kinney, Jeff

　The **wimpy** kid movie diary; how Greg Heffley went
Hollywood. Amulet Books 2010 199p il $14.95
Grades: 4 5 6 7　　　　　　　　　791.43
　1. Motion pictures -- Production and direction
　ISBN 978-0-8109-9616-8; 0-8109-9616-2
　　　　　　　　　　　　LC 2010001859

"Diary of a Wimpy Kid was made into a movie in 2010.
The process is here chronicled, through text, photos, and illustrations. Many details are included, from the way the actors were chosen to how the moldy cheese was filmed. The
process is explained clearly and will be interesting to new
and seasoned Kid fans and future filmmakers alike." Horn
Book Guide

McDonald, Megan

　Judy Moody goes to Hollywood; behind the scenes
with Judy Moody and friends. by Megan McDonald with
Richard Haynes; set photography by Suzanne Tenner. Can-
dlewick Press 2011 144p il map $14.99
Grades: 2 3 4　　　　　　　　　　791.43
　1. Motion pictures -- Production and direction
　ISBN 978-0-7636-5551-8; 0-7636-5551-1
　　　　　　　　　　　　LC 2011283432

"This behind the scenes look to the 2011 movie Judy
Moody and the NOT Bummer Summer is filled with facts
about the characters and the actors who play them. It also
gives a surprisingly detailed yet accessible view of movie-
making, explaining key elements of everything from set design to lighting." Horn Book Guide

O'Brien, Lisa

　Lights, camera, action! making movies and TV from
the inside out. [by] Lisa O'Brien; illustrated by Stephen
MacEachern. 2nd ed.; Maple Tree Press 2007 64p il
$21.95; pa $12.95
Grades: 4 5 6 7　　　　　　　　　791.43
　1. Acting 2. Motion pictures -- Production and direction
　ISBN 978-1-897066-88-1; 1-897066-88-0; 978-1-
　897066-89-8 pa; 1-897066-89-9 pa
First published 1998 by Firefly Books

This book "follows Johnny, a young aspiring actor, as he
auditions for and gets a part in a new movie called The Mists
of Time. Author Lisa O'Brien examines the development
and production of movies from early concept through final
production. Along the way, readers get a guided tour of the
world of acting, from finding an agent, through to 'acting' an
audition, to handling the media." Publisher's note

Reynolds, David West

　Star wars: incredible cross sections; illustrated by
Hans Jenssen & Richard Chasemore. DK Pub. 1998 32p
il $19.95
Grades: 4 5 6 7　　　　　　　　　791.43
　1. Star Wars films
　ISBN 0-7894-3480-6
　　　　　　　　　　　　LC 98-22878

This book "includes diagrams for the Millennium Falcon,
T-65 X-wing, Blockade Runner, Tie Fighters, Sandcrawler,
and BLT-A4 Y-wing, among others. An elaborate four-page
fold-out analyzes the Death Star in minute detail. . . . AT-AT
Walkers, AT-STs, snowspeeders, and speeder bikes are also
included. Diagrams are surrounded by inserts of fascinating
trivia, history, and technical notes." Voice Youth Advocates

791.44　Radio

McCarthy, Meghan

　★ **Aliens** are coming! the true account of the 1938 War
of the worlds radio broadcast. Knopf 2006 un il $16.95;
lib bdg $18.99
Grades: 1 2 3　　　　　　　　　　791.44
　1. War of the worlds (Radio program)
　ISBN 0-375-83518-0; 0-375-93518-5 lib bdg
　　　　　　　　　　　　LC 2005-08941

"In an average American living room of 1938, folks
gather around the radio for a night's entertainment, when
there's a new bulletin: 'Aliens are coming!' Orson Welles'
infamous Halloween trick, his October 30 broadcast of H.
G. Wells' War of the Worlds, is greatly excerpted and put
together with quirky, imaginative artwork that reinforces the
fantasy. . . . Using a 1930's art style, and a palette comprising mostly muted grays and reds, McCarthy evokes an era
gone by. . . . This is packed with age-appropriate thrills and
scares." Booklist

791.5　Puppetry and toy theaters

D'Cruz, Anna-Marie

　Make your own puppets. PowerKids Press 2009 24p
il (Do it yourself projects!) lib bdg $23.95; pa $9.40

Grades: 2 3 4 **791.5**
   1. Handicraft 2. Puppets and puppet plays
   ISBN 978-1-4358-2851-3 lib bdg; 1-4358-2851-8 lib
bdg; 978-1-4358-2919-0 pa; 1-4358-2919-0 pa
LC 2008033661

This offers "step-by-step instructions and full-color
photos to illustrate the crafts. Projects have a broad cultural
representation and are not gender specific. Materials are easily obtained. . . . [Projects include] a Venus flytrap and a
Chinese dragon." SLJ
   Includes glossary and bibliographical references

Exner, Carol R.
   Practical puppetry A-Z; a guide for librarians and
teachers. [by] Carol R. Exner. McFarland 2005 267p il
pa $39.95
Grades: Adult Professional **791.5**
   1. Puppets and puppet plays
   ISBN 0-7864-1516-9
LC 2005010590

"Exner presents the art of puppetry as a creative and engaging way to snag the interests of both adults and children.
Presented in alphabetical order, approximately 135 entries
cover everything from starting a puppetry business to puppetry history to creating numerous kinds of puppets: glove,
sponge, life-size, even marionettes. . . . This is an excellent
resource for school or public libraries." Booklist
   Includes bibliographical references

Kennedy, John E.
   ★ **Puppet** planet. North Light Books 2006 79p il
$16.99
Grades: 4 5 6 7 **791.5**
   1. Puppets and puppet plays
   ISBN 978-1-58180-794-3; 1-58180-794-5
LC 2005033711

This book offers twelve "puppet projects, each using a
variety of techniques, [and] features 'action panels' so readers can see how each puppet comes to life. [It also] Includes
staging ideas to play up each project's uniqueness." Publisher's note

Minkel, Walter
   ★ **How** to do The three bears with two hands; per-
forming with puppets. American Lib. Assn. 2000 154p
il pa $28
Grades: Adult Professional **791.5**
   1. Children's libraries 2. Puppets and puppet plays
   ISBN 0-8389-0756-3
LC 99-28228

This guide to performing puppet plays in libraries offers advice on such topics as voice control and manipulation
technique, script writing and adaptation, puppets, stages,
scenery and props, and includes five puppet show scripts
and stage-building plans
   Includes bibliographical references

791.8 Animal performances

Collard III, Sneed B.
   The **world** famous Miles City Bucking Horse Sale.
Bucking Horse Books 2010 64p il $18

Grades: 5 6 7 8 **791.8**
   1. Horses 2. Rodeos
   ISBN 0984446001; 9780984446001; 978-0-9844460-
0-1; 0-9844460-0-1

"Collard takes readers inside the Miles City [Montana]
Bucking Horse Sale, a four-day event that draws visitors
from across the country. Started in 1951 as a sale of wild
horses, it's evolved into a jamboree of music, rodeo, food,
contests, and a parade. . . . Plenty of action-filled color photographs break up the narrative. . . . Handsomely designed, .
. . this is a fascinating look at a fresh topic."

"Collard takes readers inside the Miles City [Montana]
Bucking Horse Sale, a four-day event that draws visitors
from across the country. Started in 1951 as a sale of wild
horses, it's evolved into a jamboree of music, rodeo, food,
contests, and a parade. . . . Plenty of action-filled color photographs break up the narrative. . . . Handsomely designed, .
. . this is a fascinating look at a fresh topic." Booklist
   Includes glossary

Grayson, Robert
   Performers. Marshall Cavendish Benchmark 2010
64p il (Working animals) lib bdg $28.50
Grades: 4 5 6 7 **791.8**
   1. Animals in entertainment
   ISBN 978-1-60870-165-0 lib bdg; 1-60870-165-4
lib bdg
LC 2010006893

"Describes the role of animals in movies, sporting
events, and various competitions." Publisher's note
   Includes glossary and bibliographical references

Laidlaw, Rob
   On parade; the hidden world of animals in entertainment. Fitzhenry & Whiteside 2010 55p il $19.95
Grades: 4 5 6 **791.8**
   1. Zoos 2. Circus 3. Animal welfare 4. Animals in
entertainment
   ISBN 978-1-55455-143-9; 1-55455-143-9

This book examines animals at the zoo and circus, animals working in movies and television, violence in the world
of performing animals and offers ways to improve conditions and prevent animal abuse.
   The author's "clearly argued text; crisp, captioned color
photos; and appended list of organizations make this an important source for animal advocates." Booklist

Munro, Roxie
   Rodeo; by Roxie Munro. Bright Sky Press 2007 un
il $15.95
Grades: PreK K 1 2 **791.8**
   1. Rodeos
   ISBN 978-1-933979-03-8
LC 2007015245

"Clear, concise text and clever lift-the-flap illustrations
capture the action and excitement of a rodeo." SLJ

Schubert, Leda
   ★ **Ballet** of the elephants; illustrated by Robert Andrew Parker. Roaring Brook Press 2006 un il $17.95
Grades: K 1 2 3 **791.8**
   1. Ballet 2. Circus 3. Dancers 4. Composers 5.
Elephants 6. Choreographers 7. Circus executives
8. Elephants -- Juvenile literature 9. Circus polka

(Choreographic work: Balanchine) -- Juvenile literature
ISBN 1-59643-075-3

LC 2005-02670

The story of how "Circus polka" a dance of 50 elephants and 50 ballerinas, conceived by John Ringling North, choreographed by George Balanchine to music written by Igor Stravinsky, was created

"Schubert's book tells an astonishing true story. . . . The words are simple and lyrical . . . and the beautiful, freely sketched double-page ink-and-watercolor art celebrates the excitement of the animals' dance." Booklist

792   Stage presentations

Chrisp, Peter
Welcome to the Globe; the story of Shakespeare's theater. written by Peter Chrisp. Dorling Kindersley 2000 48p il (Dorling Kindersley readers) $12.95; pa $3.95
Grades: 1 2 3   **792**
1. Poets 2. Authors 3. Dramatists 4. Theaters -- England -- London -- Juvenile literature 5. Theater -- England -- London -- History -- 17th century -- Juvenile literature
ISBN 0-7894-6641-4; 0-7894-6640-6 pa

LC 00-21931

Various characters, including a waterman, an actor, a gallant, and an apple seller, from Shakespeare's London describe the Globe Theatre from their own perspective

"Illustrations and photographs are excellent, showing details of the building and the people." SLJ
Includes glossary

Jacobs, Paul DuBois
★ **Putting** on a play; drama activities for kids. [by] Paul DuBois Jacobs and Jennifer Swender; illustrated by Debra Spina Dixon. Gibbs Smith 2005 64p il pa $9.95
Grades: 2 3 4   **792**
1. Theater -- Production and direction
ISBN 1-58685-767-3

LC 2005011249

"This little book is a powerhouse of information. . . . An excellent beginning resource for any child or group of children interested in theater." SLJ

Kenney, Karen Latchana
Cool costumes; how to stage your very own show. ABDO Pub. Company 2010 32p il (Cool performances) lib bdg $17.95
Grades: 4 5 6   **792**
1. Costume 2. Theater
ISBN 978-1-60453-714-7 lib bdg; 1-60453-714-0 lib bdg

LC 2009-1751

Includes step-by-step instructions on how to create royalty robes, animal ears, baseball T-Shirts and more

"Simple language, colorful page design, and detailed step-by-step photos invite children to gather some easily available houselhold items, apply paint and some imagination, and put on a play—or just play." SLJ
Includes glossary and webliography

Cool makeup; how to stage your very own show. ABDO Pub. Company 2010 32p il (Cool performances) lib bdg $17.95
Grades: 4 5 6   **792**
1. Theatrical makeup
ISBN 978-1-60453-715-4 lib bdg; 1-60453-715-9 lib bdg

LC 2009-1752

Offers instructions and step-by-step pictures to reveal how theatrical makeup can create the illusion of facial hair, bruises and wounds, animals, skeletons, or old age.

"Simple language, colorful page design, and detailed step-by-step photos invite children to gather some easily available household items, apply paint and some imagination, and put on a play—or just play." SLJ
Includes glossary and webliography

Cool productions; how to stage your very own show. ABDO Pub. Co. 2010 32p il (Cool performances) lib bdg $17.95
Grades: 4 5 6   **792**
1. Theater -- Production and direction
ISBN 978-1-60453-716-1 lib bdg; 1-60453-716-7 lib bdg

LC 2009-405

Includes step-by-step instructions on how to make flyers, tickets, programs and more

"Simple language, colorful page design, and detailed step-by-step photos invite children to gather some easily available household items, apply paint and some imagination, and put on a play—or just play." SLJ
Includes glossary

Cool scripts & acting; how to stage your very own show. ABDO Pub. Company 2010 32p il (Cool performances) lib bdg $17.95
Grades: 4 5 6   **792**
1. Acting 2. Drama -- Technique 3. Theater -- Production and direction
ISBN 978-1-60453-717-8 lib bdg; 1-60453-717-5 lib bdg

LC 2009-406

Includes step-by-step instructions on how to write a script, use stage directions, play acting games and more

"Simple language, colorful page design, and detailed step-by-step photos invite children to gather some easily available household items, apply paint and some imagination, and put on a play—or just play." SLJ
Includes glossary

Cool sets & props; how to stage your very own show. ABDO Pub. Company 2010 32p il (Cool performances) lib bdg $17.95
Grades: 4 5 6   **792**
1. Theaters -- Stage setting and scenery
ISBN 978-1-60453-718-5 lib bdg; 1-60453-718-3 lib bdg

LC 2009-408

"This volume focuses on the primarily cardboard and paper objects that motivated youngsters can turn into backdrops, set pieces, and props. Photo examples set the bar high (though many are achievable), and the text breaks down the creation process into bite-size chunks. It's fairly challenging stuff, but the information is metered out so efficiently that patience, not artistic ability, will be the key to success." Booklist

Includes glossary and webliography

Cool special effects; how to stage your very own show. ABDO Pub. Company 2010 32p il (Cool performances) lib bdg $17.95

Grades: 4 5 6   792

1. Stage lighting 2. Theaters -- Stage setting and scenery

ISBN 978-1-60453-719-2 lib bdg; 1-60453-719-1 lib bdg

LC 2009-1753

Offers instructions on creating special effects for a theatrical production, including information on different light effects, keeping a prompt book, and recording your own sound effects

"Simple language, colorful page design, and detailed step-by-step photos invite children to gather some easily available household items, apply paint and some imagination, and put on a play—or just play." SLJ

Includes glossary and webliography

McLean, Dirk

Curtain up! a book for young performers. illustrated by France Brassard. Tundra Books 2010 un il $17.95

Grades: K 1 2 3   792

1. Theater -- Fiction

ISBN 978-0-88776-899-6; 0-88776-899-7

"This brief, straightforward depiction of a young girl's theatrical experiences provides a realistic and accurate glimpse into the art. Amaya's dream is to be on the stage, and her mother has been helping her with her memorization and articulation. She auditions for a musical and is chosen to play the lead in a professional play. . . . The realistic illustrations are done in a pastel palette and bring the personalities of the characters to life." SLJ

Schumacher, Thomas L.

How does the show go on? an introduction to the theater. by Thomas Schumacher with Jeff Kurtti. 2nd ed; Disney 2008 128p il $22.95

Grades: 4 5 6 7   792

1. Theater

ISBN 978-1-4231-2031-5; 1-4231-2031-0

"Filled with lavish color photos of Disney theater productions, this eye-catching volume has clever chapter titles, beginning with 'Overture,' which tells about 'styles of theaters' and 'kinds of shows.' In 'Act One' and 'Act Two,' aspects of the front and back of the house are discussed, including the marquee, the box office, props, special effects, and so on. Interspersed throughout the facts and photos are 'Stage Notes,' where bits of trivia are doled out." SLJ

Skog, Jason

Acting; a practical guide to pursuing the art. Compass Point Books 2010 48p il (Performing arts) lib bdg $28.65

Grades: 5 6 7 8   792

1. Acting 2. Vocational guidance

ISBN 978-0-7565-4364-8 lib bdg; 0-7565-4364-9 lib bdg

LC 2010012604

A guide for those interested in a career in acting, and includes tips on education, technique, and more.

"Meant for students contemplating a career in the field . . . [this book goes] beyond basic introductions and into more detail about what it takes to make it as a professional. . . . [The author maintains] . . . a frank, realistic tone, stressing the importance of hard work and dedication. Great [resource] . . . for those wanting to make their passions more than just a hobby." SLJ

Includes glossary and bibliographical references

Underwood, Deborah

Staging a play. Raintree 2009 32p il (Culture in action) $28.21; pa $7.99

Grades: 5 6 7 8   792

1. Theater -- Production and direction

ISBN 978-1-4109-3396-6; 1-4109-3396-2; 978-1-4109-3413-0 pa; 1-4109-3413-6 pa

LC 2009000417

This "discusses the various professionals involved in a production, such as actors, costume designers, prop masters, and stage handlers. Well organized and with bright, colorful photography, [this] introductory [title gives] readers good basic knowledge." SLJ

Includes glossary and bibliographical references

792.09   History, geographic treatment, biography

Aliki

★ **William** Shakespeare & the Globe; written & illustrated by Aliki. HarperCollins Pubs. 1999 48p il hardcover o.p. pa $6.99

Grades: 4 5 6 7 8 9   792.09

1. Poets 2. Authors 3. Dramatists 4. Theaters -- England -- London -- Reconstruction -- Juvenile literature 5. Theater -- England -- London -- History -- 16th century -- Juvenile literature

ISBN 0-06-027820-X; 0-06-443722-1 pa

LC 98-7903

"A logically organized and engaging text, plenty of detailed illustrations with informative captions, and a clean design provide a fine introduction to both bard and theater." Horn Book Guide

792.309

Schubert, Leda

★ **Monsieur** Marceau; Leda Schubert; illustrated by Gérard DuBois. Roaring Brook Press 2012 p. cm.

Grades: 2 3 4   792.309

1. Marceau, Marcel, 1923-2007 2. Mimes -- France -- Juvenile literature

ISBN 9781596435292

LC 2011033798

This book by Leda Schubert, illustrated by Gérard DuBois, provides a "picture book biography [of] . . . Marcel Marceau, the world's most famous mime. . . . [Marceau] enthralled audiences around the world for more than fifty years. When he waved his hand or lifted his eyebrow he was able to speak volumes without ever saying a word. But few know the story of the man behind those gestures" (Publisher's note)

Includes bibliographical references and index

792.6 Musical plays

Amendola, Dana

A **day** at the New Amsterdam Theatre; photos by Gino Domenico; written by Dana Amendola. Disney Editions 2004 125p il $24.95

Grades: 4 5 6 7   **792.6**

1. Theater

ISBN 0-7868-5438-3

"This title covers a day in the life of Disney's The Lion King, the long-running Broadway musical. . . . A clock in a corner of each spread guides readers through the day as box-office personnel, makeup designers, dancers, actors, cleaning staff, and others do their jobs. Each spread includes several full-color photos that are often gritty, sometimes glamorous. . . . This unique volume provides an honest, realistic, eye-opening look at the behind-the-scenes work that goes into the running of a Broadway show." SLJ

792.602

Michael, Ted

So you wanna be a superstar? the ultimate audition guide. by Ted Michael; with contributions by Nic Cory & Mara Jill Herman; introduction by Lea Salonga; edited by Lisa Cheng. RP Kids 2012 151 p. (paperback: consumable) $10.95; (paperback) $10.95; (ebook) $10.95

Grades: 4 5 6 7 8   **792.602**

1. Auditions 2. Voice culture

ISBN 0762446102; 9780762446100; 9780762447015 pdf

LC 2012932845

This book by Ted Michael presents a guide for " hopeful musical theater, show choir, a cappella, and glee club singers" with advice designed to help readers "train [their] vocal cords, pick the right audition material, and become comfortable with the spotlight. Interactive quizzes . . . and words of advice from industry professionals" are also included. (Publisher's note)

792.7 Variety shows and theatrical dancing

Dillon, Leo

★ **Rap** a tap tap; here's Bojangles--think of that! [by] Leo & Diane Dillon. Blue Sky Press (NY) 2002 un il $15.95

Grades: PreK K 1 2 3   **792.7**

1. Actors 2. Tap dancing 3. Stories in rhyme 4. African Americans 5. Tap dancers

ISBN 0-590-47883-4

LC 2001-43896

In illustrations and rhyme describes the dancing of Bill "Bojangles" Robinson, one of the most famous tap dancers of all time

"The spreads feature a bouncy text and eye-catching art. . . . The paintings have the effect of collage and employ

strong city shapes, with bridges, buildings, and park benches pressed against feather-white backgrounds." Booklist

792.8 Ballet and modern dance

Augustyn, Frank

★ **Footnotes**; dancing the world's best-loved ballets. [by] Frank Augustyn and Shelley Tanaka. Millbrook Press 2001 94p il $17.95

Grades: 5 6 7 8   **792.8**

1. Ballet

ISBN 0-7613-1646-9

LC 00-50075

"Footnotes uses seven classical ballets as a jumping-off point to talk about the evolution of this unique art form, partnering, dancer as actor, training, costumes, choreography, and some of the world's most well-known performers." SLJ

Collins, Pat Lowery

I am a dancer; by Pat Lowery Collins; illustrated by Mark Graham. Millbrook Press 2008 un il lib bdg $22.60

Grades: PreK K 1 2 3   **792.8**

1. Dance

ISBN 978-0-8225-6369-3 lib bdg; 0-8225-6369-X lib bdg

LC 2007021885

"This book shows girls and boys in various movements that can be defined as dance steps. . . . Graham's beautiful oil paintings are filled with solidly built children on the move, while some of the backgrounds are almost ethereal. Even the brushstrokes convey action. This book is a lovely merging of art and poetry and gives a delightful sense of joyful motion." SLJ

Friedman, Lise

Becoming a ballerina; a nutcracker story. by Lise Friedman; photographs by Mary Dowdle. Penguin Group 2012 44 p. (hardcover) $18.99

Grades: 4 5 6   **792.8**

1. Ballet 2. Athletes 3. Picture books for children 4. Ballerinas -- Juvenile literature 5. Ballet dancing -- Juvenile literature

ISBN 0670013927; 9780670013920

LC 2012000867

This book follows "13-year-old Fiona, a real-life fledgling ballerina, on her journey from hopeful auditionee to starring performer as Clara in the Boston Ballet's production of 'The Nutcracker.' . . . Fiona talks about her aches and pains ('Sometimes hurt so much that I want to cry'), her sacrifices ('I miss going to birthday parties and the movies, being in school talent shows, sleepovers--normal stuff'), [and] the fierce competition." (Publishers Weekly)

Gladstone, Valerie

A **young** dancer; the life of an Ailey student. photographs by Jose Ivey. Henry Holt and Co. 2009 un il $18.95

Grades: 1 2 3 4   **792.8**

1. Ballet 2. Dancers 3. Students 4. African American dancers 5. Ballet dancers -- Juvenile literature

ISBN 978-0-8050-8233-3; 0-8050-8233-6

LC 2008-18343

"This book about a 13-year-old African American dancer ... combines strong color photos and lively first-person text. Iman Bright is a student at New York City's Ailey School, founded by the late Alvin Ailey.... A wide range of readers will find inspiration in Iman's dedication and in her joyful approach to her discipline." Booklist

Goodman, Joan E.
Ballet bunnies; written and illustrated by Joan Elizabeth Goodman. Marshall Cavendish 2008 un il $14.99
Grades: K 1 2 **792.8**
1. Ballet
ISBN 978-0-7614-5392-5; 0-7614-5392-X
LC 2007-11907
This ballet primer demonstrates basic technique in ballet, from warm-ups to the barre to the hop, skip, twirl, and wiggle fun of centerwork.
"The simply drawn acrylic illustrations show the boys and girls demonstrating positions, and the easy-to-understand text gives further guidance.... This is a gentle introduction." SLJ
Includes glossary

Greenberg, Jan
★ **Ballet** for Martha; making Appalachian Spring. [by] Jan Greenberg and Sandra Jordan; illustrated by Brian Floca. Flash Point 2010 48p il $17.99
Grades: 2 3 4 **792.8**
1. Ballet 2. Artists 3. Dancers 4. Composers 5. Sculptors 6. American music 7. Choreographers 8. Dance teachers 9. Industrial designers
ISBN 978-1-59643-338-0; 1-59643-338-8
Robert F. Sibert Medal honor book, 2011
Tells the story behind the creation of "Appalachian Spring," describing Aaron Copland's composition and Martha Graham's intense choreography.
"Matching the mood of Graham's moves, the writing is pared down but full of possibilities. Floca's ink-and-watercolor artwork nimbly shifts from the prosaic . . . to the visionary . . . to the several-spread finale of the ballet itself. The book as a whole beautifully captures the process of artistic creation." Booklist

Isadora, Rachel
★ **Lili** at ballet. Putnam 1993 un il hardcover o.p. pa $6.99
Grades: PreK K 1 2 **792.8**
1. Ballet -- Fiction 2. Ballet -- Juvenile literature
ISBN 0-399-22423-8; 0-698-11408-6 pa
LC 92-8429
Lili dreams of becoming a ballerina and goes to her ballet lessons four afternoons a week
"Isadora uses pastel shades of purple, pink, green, and blue with bold splashes of black. This is a prettily illustrated book that captures the magic and hard work involved in ballet." SLJ
Other titles about Lili are:
Lili backstage (1997)
Lili on stage (1995)

Kupesic, Rajka
The **white** ballets. Tundra Books 2011 40p il $19.95

Grades: 4 5 6 7 **792.8**
1. Ballet -- Stories, plots, etc.
ISBN 978-0-88776-923-8; 0-88776-923-3
This retells the stories of Swan Lake, Giselle, and La Bayadère and includes information and comments on the three ballets.
"The tales are well told, and the author, a former ballerina, provides information on the history of the ballet. Each painting in gold leaf and oil represents a scene from one of the ballets. The richly colored illustrations are very stylized with graceful figures dressed in flowing, romantic costumes, and Kupesic elaborates on the details, symbols, and characters in her artwork.... For ballet enthusiasts this is a unique look at these classics." SLJ

Marsico, Katie
Choreographer. Cherry Lake Pub. 2011 il (Cool arts careers) lib bdg $18.95
Grades: 4 5 6 7 **792.8**
1. Dance 2. Choreographers 3. Vocational guidance
ISBN 978-1-61080-136-2; 1-61080-136-9
LC 2011001170
"Illustrated with color photos of the famous, the young, and the fabulously festooned, this is a sturdy presentation of facts and case studies that will bring the process of professional choreography home to those students considering such a competitive and demanding career." Booklist
Includes bibliographical references

Mellow, Mary Kate
Ballet for beginners; featuring the School of American Ballet. by Mary Kate Mellow and Stephanie Troeller. Imagine! 2010 80p il $14.95
Grades: 3 4 5 6 **792.8**
1. Ballet
ISBN 978-1-936140-01-5; 1-936140-01-2
"The education of a dancer's body and mind is a long and complicated process, and this book tells that story with a lighthearted grace and brio." SLJ

Nelson, Marilyn
Beautiful ballerina; photographs by Susan Kuklin. Scholastic Press 2009 un il $17.99
Grades: PreK K 1 2 **792.8**
1. Ballet 2. African American dancers
ISBN 978-0-545-08920-3; 0-545-08920-4
LC 2009009135
"The description 'poetry in motion' may be taken quite literally in this paean to the young dancers who train at the Dance Theatre of Harlem. The heartfelt poem's playful words could make a lively read-aloud dance-along, and young balletomanes will be intrigued by the girls in the photographs. The phrase 'Beautiful ballerina, you are the dance' is repeated throughout and invites audience participation." SLJ

Relota, Agatha
Carla and Leo's world of dance; illustrations by Thierry Perez. Thames & Hudson 2011 il $19.95
Grades: 3 4 5 6 **792.8**
1. Dance
ISBN 978-0-500-51560-0; 0-500-51560-3
"Ten-year-old Carla and her friend, Leo, sign up for ballroom-dance classes. As they learn the Viennese waltz,

foxtrot, swing, merengue, mambo, cha-cha, rumba, salsa, and tango, their teacher offers information on the history and culture of these dances. The format has a comic-book, poster-art style with the print highlighted in rectangular colored shapes. The bold, linear illustrations of the dancers fill the pages as Carla and Leo demonstrate the steps with grace and zest. . . . This is not a how-to manual but a celebration and introduction to the diverse dances. The enthusiasm of these two characters is infectious, and the slick artwork captures the elegance and drama of these movements and makes them look like lots of fun." SLJ

Solway, Andrew

Modern dance; [by] Andrew Solway. Heinemann Library 2009 48p il (Dance) lib bdg $31.43

Grades: 4 5 6 7 8   **792.8**

1. Modern dance

ISBN 978-1-4329-1376-2 lib bdg; 1-4329-1376-X lib bdg

LC 2008-14295

This book "is enhanced by eye-catching photography that shows costumes, famous dancers, technique and people dancing. . . . [Those] thinking about dance as a career will find this . . . helpful. . . . [This] is a definite must have." Libr Media Connect

Includes glossary and bibliographical references

Thompson, Lauren

★ Ballerina dreams; a true story. by Lauren Thompson; photographs by James Estrin. Feiwel & Friends 2007 un il $16.95

Grades: PreK K 1 2   **792.8**

1. Ballet 2. Cerebral palsy

ISBN 978-0-312-37029-6; 0-312-37029-6

LC 2006036338

"Five adorable little girls are given the opportunity to learn to dance like ballerinas and eventually perform on stage. This is no small accomplishment since the girls have cerebral palsy and other muscle disorders and several wear leg braces. . . . This is an inspiring portrayal of determination and love that will foster empathy among young readers. The colorful photographs of this dancing community working toward a common goal accurately and sensitively capture the struggles and joyful enthusiasm of all of the participants." SLJ

Troupe, Thomas Kingsley

If I were a ballerina; illustrated by Heather Heyworth. Picture Window Books 2010 24p il (Dream big) lib bdg $25.32; pa $7.95

Grades: K 1 2 3   **792.8**

1. Ballet

ISBN 978-1-4048-5532-8 lib bdg; 1-4048-5532-7 lib bdg; 978-1-4048-5706-3 pa; 1-4048-5706-0 pa

LC 2009-3295

This "begins with a small girl who imagines herself as a star onstage, dancing to beautiful music played by a glorious orchestra. Then the story tracks back to imagined ballet classes, where she envisions the pointed shoes she would wear and the barre exercises she would do with the other dancers before practicing at home. The simple, first-person narrative and clear, digitally enhanced color drawings partner well together, and even young preschoolers will enjoy

the fun blend of the fantasy . . . and facts, including ballet's five basic positions." Booklist

Includes glossary

Vaughan, Carolyn

Invitation to ballet; by Carolyn Vaughan; works of art by Edgar Degas; illustrated by Rachel Isadora. Abrams Books for Young Readers 2012 31 p. col. ill. $16.95

Grades: 2 3 4   **792.8**

1. Dance in art 2. Ballet dancers 3. Artists -- Biography 4. Ballet -- Juvenile literature 5. Ballet in art -- Juvenile literature

ISBN 1419702602; 9781419702600

LC 2011019046

The author Carolyn Vaughan presents provides a book "with a brief history of ballet and a biography of . . . French impressionist Edgar Degas. . . . [Vaughan explains] what happens in ballet class [to young children]. . . . [Illustrations show] modern-day girls and boys practicing ballet positions, [dances,] and steps . . . [and] works of art by . . . Degas." (Publisher's note)

Veitch, Catherine

Dancing. Heinemann Library 2009 24p il (Sports and my body) lib bdg $21.36; pa $6.49

Grades: 1 2   **792.8**

1. Dance

ISBN 978-1-4329-3501-6 lib bdg; 1-4329-3501-1 lib bdg; 978-1-4329-3502-3 pa; 1-4329-3502-X pa

LC 2009-8962

Readers learn what dancing is, how it can help them stay healthy, and how they can dance safely.

This book relates "activity to health . . . [and] explains that in order to stay healthy, children should get plenty of rest, eat healthy food, and drink plenty of water." SLJ

Includes glossary

792.9 Stage productions

Cox, Carole

Shakespeare kids; performing his plays, speaking his words. Libraries Unlimited 2010 xx, 126p il pa $30

Grades: Adult Professional   **792.9**

1. Poets 2. Authors 3. Dramatists 4. Theater -- Production and direction

ISBN 978-1-59158-838-2 pa; 1-59158-838-3 pa

LC 2009041731

This is a "a practical guide for performing Shakespeare's plays, albeit in condensed form, without changing his poetic dialogue. . . . Cox gears her work to teachers of students in grades 3-8, librarians, or adults leading recreational programs, providing precise, detailed instructions on all facets of youth-oriented Shakespearean play production. . . . The text is clear and concise . . . Black-and-white photos capture specific moments that illustrate the performers' enthusiasm." SLJ

Includes bibliographical references

793　Indoor games and amusements

Gunter, Veronika Alice

★ The **ultimate** indoor games book; the 200 best boredom busters ever! [by] Veronika Alice Gunter. Lark Books 2005 128p il hardcover o.p. pa $7.95

Grades: 3 4 5 6　　　　　　　　　　　　　793

1. Indoor games

ISBN 1-57990-625-7; 1-60059-198-1 pa

LC 2005006054

"This compilation of brain games, ball games, pen-and-paper games, etc., provides a good supply of ideas that will appeal to most any player in a variety of circumstances. The activities are suitable for individuals or two or more players. Most of the suggestions require little or no equipment." SLJ

King, Bart

Bart's king-sized book of fun. Gibbs Smith 2010 304p pa $19.99

Grades: 4 5 6　　　　　　　　　　　　　793

1. Amusements

ISBN 978-1-4236-0641-3; 1-4236-0641-8

LC 2010011438

"This is a lively and entertaining collection of tricks, jokes, facts, recipes, games, pranks, wordplay, and all-around fun. Inventions include airbag pants, a disco ball made from old CDs, and a remote-control pumpkin. Creative costume ideas include a piñata, an alien, chewed gum, a shooting star, and more. . . . An activity book extraordinaire for cool kids everywhere." SLJ

Includes bibliographical references

Regan, Lisa

Indoor games! QEB Pub. 2011 32p il (Games handbook) lib bdg $27.10

Grades: 3 4 5　　　　　　　　　　　　　793

1. Indoor games

ISBN 978-1-59566-931-5; 1-59566-931-0

LC 2010014139

First published 2010 in the United Kingdom

These indoor games "will keep kids occupied and engaged. . . . The games are formatted by degree of difficulty with easier activities at the beginning; almost all of them take up a single page and can be learned by following the three-step directions. Surrounding these explanations are bright illustrations, suggestions for altering the game if there is a solo player or to make it more challenging, and an occasional fact related to the activity." SLJ

793.2　Parties and entertainments

Guillain, Charlotte

My first sleepover. Heinemann Library 2011 24p il (Growing up) lib bdg $22; pa $6.49

Grades: PreK K 1 2　　　　　　　　　　　793.2

1. Sleepovers

ISBN 978-1-4329-4802-3 lib bdg; 1-4329-4802-4 lib bdg; 978-1-4329-4812-2 pa; 1-4329-4812-1 pa

LC 2010024196

This book examines a "common, often scary [event] in children's lives and [guides] readers through [it] step-by-step. The [author discusses] the who, what, and why of [the] experience . . . By confronting . . . fears head-on, children will feel 'in the know' and be prepared to experience [this first]. The text—two sentences per page in a large font and placed on white space—is accompanied by large color photos of children, families, and adults of a variety of ethnic backgrounds. [The] volume includes boldface vocabulary words, a picture glossary, and dos and don'ts." SLJ

Includes glossary and bibliographical references

Kenney, Karen Latchana

Cool family parties; perfect party planning for kids. Abdo Pub. 2011 il (Cool parties) lib bdg $27.07

Grades: 3 4 5 6　　　　　　　　　　　793.2

1. Parties

ISBN 978-1-61714-973-3; 1-61714-973-X

LC 2011003503

This book about family parties "has a lot of child appeal. The vivid photos and well-organized and readable content provide great springboards for party ideas. . . . Step-by-step crafts, sample menus, and easy-to-replicate games and activities add to the fun." SLJ

Cool holiday parties; perfect party planning for kids. Abdo Pub. Co. 2011 il (Cool parties) lib bdg $27.07

Grades: 3 4 5 6　　　　　　　　　　　793.2

1. Parties　2. Holidays

ISBN 978-1-61714-974-0; 1-61714-974-8

LC 2011003504

This book about holiday parties "has a lot of child appeal. The vivid photos and well-organized and readable content provide great springboards for party ideas. . . . Step-by-step crafts, sample menus, and easy-to-replicate games and activities add to the fun." SLJ

Cool international parties; perfect party planning for kids. ABDO Pub. Co. 2011 il (Cool parties) lib bdg $27.07

Grades: 3 4 5 6　　　　　　　　　　　793.2

1. Parties

ISBN 978-1-61714-975-7

LC 2011003498

This book about international parties "has a lot of child appeal. The vivid photos and well-organized and readable content provide great springboards for party ideas. . . . Step-by-step crafts, sample menus, and easy-to-replicate games and activities add to the fun." SLJ

Includes glossary and bibliographical references

Cool slumber parties; perfect party planning for kids. ABDO Pub. Co. 2011 il (Cool parties) lib bdg $27.07

Grades: 3 4 5 6　　　　　　　　　　　793.2

1. Parties　2. Sleepovers

ISBN 978-1-61714-976-4; 1-61714-976-4

LC 2011004213

This book about slumber parties "has a lot of child appeal. The vivid photos and well-organized and readable content provide great springboards for party ideas. . . . Step-by-step crafts, sample menus, and easy-to-replicate games and activities add to the fun." SLJ

Cool sports parties; perfect party planning for kids. Abdo Pub. Co. 2012 il (Cool parties) lib bdg $27.07

Grades: 3 4 5 6   **793.2**
1. Sports 2. Parties
ISBN 978-1-61714-977-1; 1-61714-977-2

LC 2011004214

This book about sports parties "has a lot of child appeal.
The vivid photos and well-organized and readable content
provide great springboards for party ideas. . . . Step-by-step
crafts, sample menus, and easy-to-replicate games and activities add to the fun." SLJ

Cool theme parties; perfect party planning for kids.
ABDO Pub. Co. 2011 il (Cool parties) lib bdg $27.07
Grades: 3 4 5 6   **793.2**
1. Parties
ISBN 978-1-61714-978-8; 1-61714-978-0

LC 2011004215

This book about theme parties "has a lot of child appeal.
The vivid photos and well-organized and readable content
provide great springboards for party ideas. . . . Step-by-step
crafts, sample menus, and easy-to-replicate games and activities add to the fun." SLJ

McGillian, Jamie Kyle
Sleepover party! games and giggles for a fun night.
[by] Jamie Kyle McGillian. Sterling Pub. 2007 95p il
$14.95
Grades: 3 4 5 6   **793.2**
1. Parties
ISBN 978-1-4027-2978-2; 1-4027-2978-2

LC 2006029509

"An attractive, girl-friendly compendium of party-plan-
ning ideas. All of the basics are covered, such as house rules,
what to make/buy, 'Top 10 Things to Get Straight before the
Party,' invitations, menus, music, and more. . . . Dozens of
indoor and outdoor games . . . and craft ideas are briefly described. The chapter on food includes snacks, dinners, desserts, breakfasts, and goodie-bag ideas." SLJ

Ross, Kathy
The **best** birthday parties ever! a kid's do-it-yourself
guide. art by Sharon Lane Holm. Millbrook Press 1999
78p il lib bdg $24.90; pa $9.95
Grades: 2 3 4   **793.2**
1. Games 2. Parties 3. Birthdays 4. Handicraft 5.
Birthdays -- Juvenile literature 6. Children's parties --
Juvenile literature
ISBN 0-7613-1410-5 lib bdg; 0-7613-0989-6 pa

LC 98-27503

Provides instructions for the invitations, games, crafts,
table decorations, and cakes for a dozen birthday parties
based on such themes as outer space, puppets, and dinosaurs

"The book is appealing. The illustrations are colorful and
plentiful." SLJ

793.3 Social, folk, national dancing

Ancona, George
★ **Capoeira**; game! dance! martial art! [by] George
Ancona. Lee & Low Books 2007 un il $18.95

Grades: 3 4 5 6   **793.3**
1. Capoeira (Dance)
ISBN 978-1-58430-268-1

LC 2006028866

This offers "uncomplicated words and engaging, step-
by-step photographs of young capoeristas in action. . . . Ancona's . . . enthusiasm and awe for his subject is contagious."
Booklist
Includes glossary and bibliographical references

★ **Ole!** Flamenco. Lee & Low 2010 un il map $19.95
Grades: 5 6 7 8   **793.3**
1. Flamenco 2. Flamenco -- Juvenile literature
ISBN 978-1-60060-361-7; 1-60060-361-0

LC 2010-22272

Ancona tells "the story of flamenco, an art form that's
more than dancing and has been around for hundreds of
years. He begins with a short introduction that chronicles his
visit to Spain. . . . He then returns readers to Santa Fe, New
Mexico, where a group of young people are learning flamenco. A helpful map traces the art form's roots, while the text
explains both the history of the Gypsies and flamenco. Full-
color photographs capture the excitement and dazzle. . . .
All aspects of flamenco are explored, including movements,
facial expressions, and sound effects." Booklist
Includes glossary and bibliographical references

Fishkin, Rebecca Love
Dance; a practical guide to pursuing the art. content adviser, Hannah Seidel and Chris Ferris and dancers; reading
adviser, Alexa L. Sandmann. Compass Point Books 2011
48p il (Performing arts) lib bdg $28.65
Grades: 5 6 7 8   **793.3**
1. Dance 2. Vocational guidance
ISBN 978-0-7565-4363-1 lib bdg; 0-7565-4363-0
lib bdg

LC 2010012605

This guide about a career in dance includes tips on education, technique, and more.

"Meant for students contemplating a career in the field .
. . [this book goes] beyond basic introductions and into more
detail about what it takes to make it as a professional. . .
. [The author maintains] . . . a frank, realistic tone, stressing the importance of hard work and dedication. Great [re-
source] . . . for those wanting to make their passions more
than just a hobby." SLJ
Includes glossary and bibliographical references

Garofoli, Wendy
Hip-hop dancing. Capstone Press 2011 4v il lib bdg
ea $30.65
Grades: 4 5 6   **793.3**
1. Dance 2. Hip-hop
ISBN 978-1-4296-5484-5 v1; 1-4296-5484-5 v1;
978-1-4296-5485-2 v2; 1-4296-5485-6 v2; 978-1-
4296-5486-9 v3; 1-4296-5486-9 v3; 978-1-4296-
5487-6 v4; 1-4296-5487-2 v4

LC 2010030394

Provides instructions for joining or starting a hip-hop
dance crew, and includes information about real-life crews.

"These volumes cover the basic moves as well as more
detailed movements often seen on television programs. . . .
Everything about the set is jazzy and current. Sentences are
short and direct, with a small-sized font detailing step-by-

step instructions and fact boxes extending the information." Booklist

Includes bibliographical references

Haney, Johannah

  Capoeira. Marshall Cavendish Benchmark 2011 il (Martial arts in action) $29.93

Grades: 4 5 6 7   **793.3**

  1. Capoeira (Dance)

  ISBN 978-0-7614-4932-4; 978-1-6087-0362-3 e-book

                           LC 2010013829

This describes the history, equipment, and technique of capoeira.

This treats "martial arts with the dignity that serious enthusiasts bring to the sport. . . . Illustrations include not only photos of modern gear and from films but also historical images." Booklist

Keeler, Patricia A.

  ★ **Drumbeat** in our feet. Lee & Low 2006 un il $16.95

Grades: 3 4 5   **793.3**

  1. Dance -- Africa

  ISBN 1-58430-264-X

This "book opens with a concise overview of the origins of African dance traditions that highlights the diversity of African peoples, cultures, and landscapes. Other two-page chapters cover how dances are passed on to children, different types of dances, image dances (those that mimic animal movements), costumes and body painting, honoring spirits and ancestors, musical instruments, drums, call-and-response songs, masked dancers, and performance. Keeler's watercolor-and-pencil illustrations impart a sense of vibrancy, movement, and joy. . . . A fresh, uplifting, and captivating offering." SLJ

793.7   Games not characterized by action

Macaulay, David

  ★ **Black** and white. Houghton Mifflin 1990 un il hardcover o.p. pa $7.99

Grades: 1 2 3   **793.7**

  1. Cattle -- Fiction 2. Railroads -- Fiction 3. Literary recreations -- Juvenile literature

  ISBN 0-395-52151-3; 0-618-63687-0 pa

                           LC 89-28888

Awarded the Caldecott Medal, 1990

Four brief "stories" about parents, trains, and cows, or is it really all one story? The author recommends careful inspection of words and pictures to both minimize and enhance confusion

"The magic of Black and White comes not from each story, . . . but from the mysterious interactions between them that creates a fifth story. . . . Eventually, the stories begin to merge into a surrealistic tale spanning several levels of reality. . . . Black and White challenges the reader to use text and pictures in unexpected ways." Publ Wkly

  Shortcut. Houghton Mifflin 1995 un il $15.95; pa $7.95

Grades: 1 2 3   **793.7**

  1. Literary recreations -- Juvenile literature

  ISBN 0-395-52436-9; 0-618-00607-9 pa

                           LC 95-2542

"This picture book concerns six humans whose paths cross and recross in the eight chapters of brief text and distinctive artwork. Albert and his horse, June, take their wagon of melons to market, sell them, and go home. . . . Patty's pet pig, Pearl, wanders onto an abandoned railroad line. . . . Professor Tweet is studying birds when suddenly his hot air balloon breaks free and heads toward a nearby cathedral spire. . . . Seemingly inconsequential details in one story become the moving forces in another." Booklist

Scieszka, Jon

  ★ **Math** curse; illustrated by Lane Smith. Viking 1995 un il $16.99

Grades: 2 3 4 5   **793.7**

  1. Mathematics -- Fiction 2. Mathematical recreations -- Juvenile literature

  ISBN 0-670-86194-4

                           LC 95-12341

When the teacher tells her class that they can think of almost everything as a math problem, one student acquires a math anxiety which becomes a real curse

"Bold in design and often bizarre in expression, Smith's paintings clearly express the child's feelings of bemusement, frustration, and panic as well as her eventual joy when she overcomes the math curse. . . . A child-centered, witty picture book." Booklist

793.73   Puzzles and puzzle games

Agee, Jon

  Smart feller fart smeller & other Spoonerisms. Hyperion Books 2006 un il $14.95

Grades: 3 4 5 6   **793.73**

  1. Spoonerisms 2. Riddles, Juvenile

  ISBN 0-7868-3692-X

                           LC 2005-929187

"Using full-page black-and-white cartoons that play with the mixed-up words, Agee captures the fun of spoonerisms. The farce of the verbal puns is extended by pictures that caricature everyone. . . . A brief introduction explains what a spoonerism is, and the last page summarizes 'what they said' with 'what they meant to say.'" Booklist

Chedru, Delphine

  Spot it again! find more hidden creatures. translated from French by Scott Auerbach. Abrams Books for Young Readers 2011 un il $14.95

Grades: PreK K 1   **793.73**

  1. Picture puzzles

  ISBN 978-0-8109-9736-3; 0-8109-9736-3

                           LC 2010020924

Original French edition 2009

This "conceals 16 more small creatures within its modish patterns. The simple and lively text prompts readers to poke among the flaps, die cuts, and vibrant lines and shapes to find snails, hungry earthworms, crying crocodiles, and more. . . . Beautifully designed from its large size to its rounded corners and heavy stock, this interactive adventure concludes with a search for sleepwalking sheep on a night-time spread. Children will enjoy this striking volume." SLJ

Spot it! find the hidden creatures. Abrams Books for Young Readers 2009 un il $14.95
Grades: PreK K 1   **793.73**
   1. Picture puzzles
   ISBN 978-0-8109-0632-7; 0-8109-0632-5
           LC 2008032549
"This rounded-corner volume employs op-art designs to hide 15 creatures, and a farm girl, for viewers to find. The searches vary in difficulty. . . . The bright patterns vary from packed geometrics to a gathering of flowers, mushrooms, or trees. . . . Great for one-on-one lap sharing." SLJ

Cole, Joanna
   Why did the chicken cross the road? and other riddles, old and new; compiled by Joanna Cole and Stephanie Calmenson; illustrated by Alan Tiegreen. Morrow Junior Bks. 1994 64p il hardcover o.p. pa $7.95
Grades: 3 4 5   **793.73**
   1. Riddles
   ISBN 0-688-12204-3
           LC 94-2582
The authors "begin with a brief explanation about the origin of riddles and proceed with a collection of over two hundred, classic and new. Though many of the riddles appear in other collections, the book, illustrated with black-and-white line drawings, will be useful for its short bibliography and subject index." Horn Book Guide

Hall, Katy
   ★ **Creepy** riddles; [by] Katy Hall and Lisa Eisenberg; pictures by S.D. Schindler. Dial Bks. for Young Readers 1998 48p il (Dial easy-to-read) hardcover o.p. pa $3.99
Grades: K 1 2   **793.73**
   1. Riddles 2. Riddles, Juvenile 3. Supernatural -- Wit and humor 4. Supernatural -- Juvenile humor
   ISBN 0-8037-1684-2; 0-14-130988-1 pa
           LC 94-37524
"A collection of riddles about vampires, ghosts, ghouls, and assorted monsters. . . . The illustrations are a scream. Schindler uses a find-nibbed pen to include lots of subtle details before adding vivid watercolor washes. . . . A superior choice for most joke or beginning-to-read collections." SLJ

   ★ **Dino** riddles; by Katy Hall and Lisa Eisenberg; pictures by Nicole Rubel. Dial Bks. for Young Readers 2002 40p il (Dial easy-to-read) hardcover o.p. pa $3.99
Grades: K 1 2   **793.73**
   1. Jokes 2. Riddles 3. Dinosaurs -- Wit and humor
   ISBN 0-8037-2239-7; 0-14-250179-4 pa
           LC 97-49947
A collection of riddles relating to dinosaurs, such as "What do you get if you cross a dinosaur with a rabbit? Tricerahops!" and "What did dinosaur campers cook over the fire? Dino-s'mores!"
   "Rubel's informal ink-and-marker illustrations are suitably silly. . . . This will be just right for joke-book junkies, beginning readers, and teachers looking to breathe new life into staid dinosaur units." Bull Cent Child Books

   Ribbit riddles; by Katy Hall and Lisa Eisenberg; pictures by Robert Bender. Dial Bks. for Young Readers 2001 40p il (Dial easy-to-read) hardcover o.p. pa $3.99
Grades: K 1 2   **793.73**
   1. Frogs 2. Jokes 3. Riddles 4. Riddles, Juvenile 5. Frogs -- Juvenile humor
   ISBN 0-8037-2525-6; 0-14-240056-4 pa
           LC 99-89174
A collection of riddles and jokes about frogs. Example: What do little frogs like to eat on a hot summer day? Hopsicles!
   "The distinctive art, cell-vinyl on layers of acetate, has a shimmery, almost fuzzy look that catches the eye—and the jokes." Booklist

   ★ **Simms** Taback's great big book of spacey, snakey, buggy riddles; riddles by Katy Hall and Lisa Eisenberg; [illustrated by Simms Taback] Viking 2008 un il $17.99
Grades: K 1 2 3   **793.73**
   1. Riddles
   ISBN 978-0-670-01121-6; 0-670-01121-5
   "Taback brings his vibrant trademark exuberance to this picture-book riddle collection, which fairly hums with fun. Rainbow-bright colors pop off black backgrounds, making the riddles bigger than life. As the title suggests, space, snakes, and bugs dominate the subject matter." Booklist

   Snakey riddles; by Katy Hall and Lisa Eisenberg; pictures by Simms Taback. Dial Bks. for Young Readers 1990 48p il (Dial easy-to-read) hardcover o.p. pa $3.99
Grades: K 1 2   **793.73**
   1. Riddles 2. Riddles -- Juvenile literature 3. Snakes -- Humor -- Juvenile literature
   ISBN 0-14-037141-9 pa
           LC 88-23687
An illustrated collection of riddles about snakes
   "Riddle lovers will groan with delight at some of these riddles. . . . The best thing about the book is the cleverly drawn, lively cartoon illustrations. Long, colorful snakes form borders framing the text and picture for each riddle." SLJ

   Turkey riddles; by Katy Hall and Lisa Eisenberg; pictures by Kristin Sorra. Dial Bks. for Young Readers 2002 40p il (Dial easy-to-read) hardcover o.p. pa $3.99
Grades: K 1 2   **793.73**
   1. Jokes 2. Riddles 3. Turkeys 4. Riddles, Juvenile 5. Turkeys -- Juvenile humor
   ISBN 0-8037-2530-2; 0-14-240369-5 pa
           LC 2001-47475
A collection of nearly three dozen riddles featuring turkeys, such as "What happened when Tom Turkey stepped up to the plate? He hit a fowl ball"
   "The art, with cross-hatched details, is bright and appealing. . . . Great for a good time alone, with friends, or even in a classroom." Booklist

Kalz, Jill
   An **A-MAZE-ing** amusement park adventure; illustrated by Mattia Cerato. Picture Window Books 2010 32p il (A-MAZE-ing adventures) lib bdg $25.99

Grades: K 1 2 3   **793.73**
  1. Maps 2. Maze puzzles 3. Amusement parks
ISBN 978-1-4048-6023-0 lib bdg; 1-4048-6023-1
lib bdg

                      LC 2010009865

"Fantastically illustrated, the adventures take the form of overhead maps, which allow Cerato to give in to her every twisty, turny impulse. . . . The first maze is a view of an entire amusement park, while subsequent mazes zero in on individual areas. . . . It's impressively orchestrated and enjoyable. . . . Navigating maps is an important real-world skill and is rarely—let's face it, never—this much fun." Booklist

Kidslabel (Firm)
  Spot 7 School; by KIDSLABEL. Chronicle Books 2006 un il (Seek & find) $12.95
Grades: K 1 2 3 4   **793.73**
  1. Puzzles
ISBN 978-0-8118-5324-8; 0-8118-5324-1

                      LC 2005026114

Original Japanese edition 2003
"This book has colorful, busy photos of objects and lists of items associated with school for readers to locate. . . . It also offers viewers some additional tasks: the two pages of each spread are identical except for seven differences, and each left-hand page contains a riddle, the answer to which is found on the page. . . . The clear images depict imaginative groupings. . . . It offers entertainment and an opportunity to hone observational skills rolled into one." SLJ
  Other titles in this series are:
  Spot 7 Christmas (2006)
  Spot 7 Animals (2007)
  Spot 7 Spooky (2007)
  Spot 7 Toys (2008)

Lankford, Mary D.
  Mazes around the world; by Mary D. Lankford; illustrated by Karen Dugan. Collins 2008 26p il $16.99; lib bdg $17.89
Grades: 3 4 5   **793.73**
  1. Maze puzzles
ISBN 978-0-688-16519-2; 0-688-16519-2; 978-0-688-16520-8 lib bdg; 0-688-16520-6 lib bdg

                      LC 2007008580

"Lankford traces the history of mazes from the ancient Egyptian Labyrinth . . . to today's mazes in North America's corn fields. . . . Each left-hand page offers an engaging account of a particular maze or type of maze, depicted on the facing page in a charming painting by Dugan. . . . Drawing from many cultures and historical periods, this well-researched, accessible book explores a topic with inherent child appeal." Booklist
  Includes bibliographical references

Maestro, Giulio
  Riddle roundup; a wild bunch to beef up your word power. Clarion Bks. 1989 64p il hardcover o.p. pa $7.95
Grades: 2 3 4   **793.73**
  1. Riddles 2. Word games
ISBN 0-89919-537-7 pa

                      LC 86-33403

A collection of sixty-one riddles based on different kinds of word play such as puns, homonyms, and homographs

Maestro, Marco
  What do you hear when cows sing? and other silly riddles. by Marco and Giulio Maestro; pictures by Giulio Maestro. HarperCollins Pubs. 1996 48p il (I can read book) hardcover o.p. pa $3.95
Grades: K 1 2   **793.73**
  1. Riddles
ISBN 0-06-444227-6 pa

                      LC 94-18686

"The subjects of the riddles will be familiar to most readers—trains, bugs, mice, fish, boats. . . . Most of the selections involve plays on words, but some are relatively straightforward. . . . Children will love the silly pictures, laugh at the riddles, enjoy sharing them with others, and expand their vocabularies all at the same time." SLJ

Marzollo, Jean
  I spy a Christmas tree; riddles by Jean Marzollo; photographs by Walter Wick. Scholastic 2010 un il $9.99
Grades: PreK K 1 2   **793.73**
  1. Christmas 2. Picture puzzles
ISBN 978-0-545-22092-7; 0-545-22092-0
Rhyming verses ask readers to find hidden objects in the photographs of Christmas tree ornaments and toys.

  I spy an egg in a nest; riddles by Jean Marzollo; photographs by Walter Wick. Scholastic 2011 un il (Scholastic reader) pa $3.99
Grades: PreK K 1 2   **793.73**
  1. Picture puzzles
ISBN 978-0-545-22093-4 pa; 0-545-22093-9 pa

                      LC 2009051611

This visual game book consists of a series of rhymed riddles listing objects that children must locate in the accompanying photographs of subjects relating to spring.
  "Sharpening children's visual discrimination and concentration, this colorful book offers a fun approach to reading skills." Booklist

  I spy school days; a book of picture riddles. photographs by Walter Wick; riddles by Jean Marzollo. Scholastic 1995 33p il $18.95
Grades: K 1 2 3 4   **793.73**
  1. Puzzles 2. Puzzles -- Juvenile literature
ISBN 0-590-48135-5

                      LC 94-43629

"This riddle book in verse follows the . . . format of large, oversized pages chock-full of objects and realia. This time, the double-page spreads are devoted to unifying activities or themes associated with school, chalkboard, a puppet show, art or science classrooms, a playground, etc. The full-color photographs are sharp, bright, and busy." SLJ

Munro, Roxie
  Amazement park; by Roxie Munro. Chronicle Books 2005 37p il $16.95
Grades: K 1 2 3   **793.73**
  1. Maze puzzles
ISBN 0-8118-4581-8

                      LC 2004-8482

This book includes "12 . . . mazes to navigate. . . . All mazes lead from one page to the next and then back again to the first one. . . . The mazes do get tricky and sometimes completely confusing, but an answer key is included for those who get stuck. The cartoon art is eye-catching and colorful." SLJ

Another book of maze puzzles by this author is:
Mazescapes (2001)

Mazeways: A to Z; by Roxie Munro. Sterling Pub. Co., Inc. 2007 un il $12.95
Grades: K 1 2 3   **793.73**
1. Alphabet 2. Maze puzzles
ISBN 978-1-4027-3774-9; 1-4027-3774--2

LC 2007001586

"Each letter is featured on a spread or a page with directions for traveling through the maze and finding different objects along the way. . . . Back pages provide solutions. This engaging title works as an interactive alphabet book, an introduction to mapping skills, or to sharpen visual discrimination skills." SLJ

Nickle, John
Alphabet explosion! search and count from alien to zebra. [by] John Nickle. Schwartz & Wade Books 2006 un il $16.95
Grades: K 1 2 3   **793.73**
1. Puzzles 2. Alphabet
ISBN 0-375-83598-9

LC 2005024372

"Each wordless page features animals and objects whose names begin with a featured letter. A number indicates how many items are buried within the picture. . . . Nickle's finely rendered scenes are imaginative, humorous, and sophisticated, and he incorporates a free-flowing range of artistic styles that adds energy to the pages.." Booklist

Rosenthal, Amy Krouse
Wumbers; it's a word cr8ed with a number! wri10 by Amy Krouse Rosenthal; illustr8ed by Tom Lichtenheld. Chronicle Books 2012 40 p. col. ill. (alk. paper) $16.99
Grades: K 1 2 3   **793.73**
1. Word games 2. Word games -- Juvenile literature
ISBN 1452110220; 9781452110226

LC 2011041591

This children's picture book by Amy Krouse Rosenthal "combines words and numbers ('wumbers') that challenge readers to use their number recognition and phonological skills. . . . From a boy and girl enjoying their '10ts' to the smiling child who is 'el8ed' because he lost his first '2th,' [Tom] Lichenheld's ink and pastel coloring-book-style drawings supply visual clues to decoding the text." (School Library Journal)

Schnur, Steven
Autumn; an alphabet acrostic. illustrated by Leslie Evans. Clarion Bks. 1997 un il $16
Grades: K 1 2 3   **793.73**
1. Autumn 2. Alphabet 3. Acrostics 4. Autumn -- Juvenile literature
ISBN 0-395-77043-2

LC 96-50219

"A fall riddle is presented for each letter of the alphabet. The answer is spelled out in the first letter of each line. The riddles are spare with striking images. . . . Evans's stunning hand-colored linoleum block prints are clear, bright, and provide sharp clues for the riddles. . . . This delightful alphabet book with a new twist will provide inspiration and challenges for a wide audience." SLJ

Summer; an alphabet acrostic. illustrated by Leslie Evans. Clarion Books 2001 un il $16
Grades: K 1 2 3   **793.73**
1. Summer 2. Alphabet 3. Acrostics
ISBN 0-618-02372-0

LC 00-31674

"This concept book features a short poem in which the first letter of each line spells out the word it represents. 'Daisy' becomes 'Dragonflies dart/And hover,/Inspecting white flowers with/Sunlike/Yellow centers.' The sheer inventiveness of each poem is impressive. . . . Neatly framed linoleum-block illustrations feature rich colors and bold lines that capture the brightness of the days." SLJ

Sirett, Dawn
Hide and seek first words; [written by Dawn Sirett; photography by Dave King]. DK Publishing 2010 48p il $12.99
Grades: PreK   **793.73**
1. Vocabulary 2. Picture puzzles
ISBN 978-0-7566-6300-1; 0-7566-6300-8

LC 2010280415

"This seek-and-find, with its colorful collection of photographic puzzles, will capture the attention of young children and draw them into the book. Working with an adult to locate the brightly colored objects hidden throughout loosely themed spreads . . . preschoolers will also be helping build reading readiness and verbal skills through short rhyming text and object labeling." Horn Book Guide

Steig, William
★ **C D B**. Simon & Schuster Bks. for Young Readers 2000 47p il $16; pa $4.99
Grades: 2 3 4 5   **793.73**
1. Games 2. Word games 3. Word games -- Juvenile literature
ISBN 0-689-83160-9; 0-671-66689-4 pa

LC 99-32720

First published 1968 by Windmill Bks.
Letters and numbers are used to create the sounds of words and simple sentences 4 u 2 figure out with the aid of illustrations
Readers "will delight in puzzling out the letter-and-number messages, aided by the simple, thickly outlined drawings and an answer key." Booklist

C D C? Farrar, Straus & Giroux 2003 57p il $16
Grades: 2 3 4 5   **793.73**
1. Word games
ISBN 0-374-31233-8

LC 2002-111704

A color illustrated edition of the title first published 1984
Letters, numbers, and symbols are used to create the sounds of words and simple sentences which U R expected to figure out with the aid of illustrations. Includes an answer key
"Flawlessly executed, purely pleasurable, the book is definitely 'D-Q-R' for doldrums at any season." Horn Book

Steiner, Joan

Look-alikes; photography by Thomas Lindley. Little, Brown 1998 un il $13.95

Grades: K 1 2 3 4   **793.73**

1. Puzzles 2. Picture puzzles

ISBN 0-316-81255-2

LC 97-32795

"Bursting with creativity, this work of visual genius will set imaginations soaring." Publ Wkly

Look-alikes Christmas; [by] Joan Steiner; photography by Ogden Gigli. Little, Brown 2003 un il lib bdg $14.95

Grades: K 1 2 3 4   **793.73**

1. Puzzles 2. Christmas 3. Picture puzzles -- Juvenile literature

ISBN 0-316-81187-4

LC 2003-47406

Simple verses challenge readers to identify the everyday objects used to construct nine three-dimensional Christmas scenes, including a cathedral, Nutcracker ballet, and Santa's workshop.

"In both presentation and delivery, this is clever, ingenious, and fun both for readers and nonreaders." SLJ

Look-alikes around the world; concept, constructions & text by Joan Steiner; design by Stephen Blauweiss; photography by Ogden Gigli. Little, Brown and Company 2007 un il $15.99

Grades: K 1 2 3 4   **793.73**

1. Puzzles

ISBN 978-0-316-81172-9; 0-316-81172-6

LC 2007012332

"Using everyday objects . . . artist Joan Steiner has created three-dimensional scenes of more than 40 famous landmarks and familiar vacation locales. . . . Complete with photographs of the actual sites, . . . facts, and more than 500 look-alikes to search for, this [is in the format of a] postcard album." Publisher's note

Other titles in this series are:

Look-alikes (1998)

Look-alikes Jr (1999)

Look-alikes Christmas (2003)

Look-alikes, jr. photography by Thomas Lindley. Little, Brown 1999 un il $13.95

Grades: K 1 2 3   **793.73**

1. Puzzles

ISBN 0-316-81307-9

LC 99-11683

Simple verses challenge readers to identify the everyday objects used to construct eleven three-dimensional scenes, including a house, kitchen, bedroom, school bus, train, farm, and rocket

"The design is both witty and cunning, offering lots of just-hard-enough opportunities for looking and finding." Horn Book

Wick, Walter

★ Can you see what I see? picture puzzles to search and solve. Scholastic 2002 35p il $13.95

Grades: PreK K 1 2   **793.73**

1. Puzzles 2. Picture puzzles

ISBN 0-439-16391-9

LC 2001-49032

Presents twelve brain-teasing hidden picture puzzles to solve

"With its range of activities and perspective-shifting challenges, this is sure to appeal to a wide age group of children, who won't be satisfied until they've solved the last puzzle." Booklist

Other titles in this series are:

Can you see what I see?: Cool collections (2004)

Can you see what I see?: Dream machine (2003)

Can you see what I see?: On a scary scary night (2008)

Can you see what I see?: Once upon a time (2006)

Can you see what I see?: Seymour and the juice box boat (2004)

Can you see what I see: Seymour makes new friends (2006)

Can you see what I see?: The night before Christmas (2005)

Can you see what I see?: Treasure ship (2010)

★ I spy; a book of picture riddles. photographs by Walter Wick; riddles by Jean Marzollo; design by Carol Devine Carson. Scholastic 1992 33p il $13.95

Grades: K 1 2 3 4   **793.73**

1. Puzzles 2. Puzzles -- Juvenile literature

ISBN 0-590-45087-5

LC 91-28268

This visual game book consists of "a series of rhymed riddles listing objects that children must locate in the accompanying photographs. Each double-page spread features crisp, full-color shots featuring an abundance of familiar items. The objects range from large and easy-to-spot to tiny and partially hidden. . . . An appealing book for children and adults to share and enjoy together." SLJ

Other titles in this series are:

I spy a Christmas tree (2010)

I spy Christmas (1992)

I spy extreme challenger! (2000)

I spy fantasy (1994)

I spy fun house (1993)

I spy gold challenger! (1998)

I spy mystery (1993)

I spy school days (1995)

I spy spooky night (1996)

I spy super challenger! (1997)

I spy treasure hunt (1999)

I spy ultimate challenger! (2003)

I spy year-round challenger! (2003)

793.74   Mathematical games and recreations

Ball, Johnny

Go figure! DK Pub. 2005 96p il map $15.99

Grades: 4 5 6 7   **793.74**

1. Mathematics 2. Mathematical recreations

ISBN 0-7566-1374-4

A collection of math activities that include brainteasers, magic tricks, and mind-reading games

"A dynamic book. . . . Blocks of color, diagrams, and photo collages contribute to the exciting layout. . . . A fun romp for number and puzzle lovers." SLJ

Polonsky, Lydia

  Math for the very young; a handbook of activities for
parents and teachers. [by] Lydia Plonsky . . . [et al.]; illustrated by Marcia Miller. Wiley 1995 210p il hardcover
o.p. pa $14.95

Grades: Adult Professional   **793.74**

  1. Mathematical recreations

  ISBN 0-471-01671-3; 0-471-01647-0 pa

                              LC 94-20861

"This guide suggests ways to introduce math to children
through everyday activities. Sections include making a record book about the child and the family as well as activities
for each month of the year, geometric crafts, math games,
counting rhymes and stories, and ways to use math in the
home and on the road." Booklist

  Includes bibliographical references

Tang, Greg

  Math appeal; mind-stretching math riddles. illustrated
by Harry Briggs. Scholastic Press 2003 un il $16.95

Grades: 2 3 4   **793.74**

  1. Mathematical recreations

  ISBN 0-439-21046-1

                            LC 2002-5354

Rhyming anecdotes present opportunities for simple
math activities and hints for solving

  "Bright, whimsical illustrations and clever rhymes introduce challenging exercises. . . . In a note, Tang states that
his goal is 'to encourage clever, creative thinking,' and the
questions posed do that." SLJ

  ★ **Math** potatoes; mind-stretching brain food. illustrated by Harry Briggs. Scholastic Press 2005 un il $16.95

Grades: 2 3 4   **793.74**

  1. Mathematical recreations

  ISBN 0-439-44390-3

                            LC 2004-16638

"This picture book uses all kinds of visual tricks to demonstrate how to make arithmetic faster and easier. On each
double-page spread, a rhyming verse has fun with a variety
of subjects. Most rhymes are about foods . . . and the bright,
computer-generated pictures are as playful as the words. .
. . The games are complex, the visuals are tricky, and although the rhyme seems straightforward . . . readers must
think carefully about adding, subtracting, and multiplying."
Booklist

  The **grapes** of math; mind-stretching math riddles. illustrated by Harry Briggs. Scholastic Press 2001 un il
$16.95

Grades: 2 3 4   **793.74**

  1. Mathematical recreations   2. Word problems
(Mathematics)

  ISBN 0-439-21033-X

                            LC 00-30062

Illustrated riddles introduce strategies for solving a variety of math problems in using visual clues

  "This clever collection of puzzles could spark the interest of even the mathematically challenged. . . . The simple,
staccato rhymes and crisp lines of the artwork keep attention focused, while those who find themselves stumped
can consult the 'Answers' section at the back of the book."
Publ Wkly

793.8   Magic and related activities

Barnhart, Norm

  Amazing magic tricks: a beginner level; by Norm
Barnhart. Capstone Press 2009 32p il (Magic Tricks) lib
bdg $23.93

Grades: 4 5 6   **793.8**

  1. Magic tricks

  ISBN 978-1-4296-1942-4 lib bdg; 1-4296-1942-2
lib bdg

                            LC 2008-2572

"Numbered steps, clearly illustrated by crisp photographs, guide students through the preparation and performance of such classic magician's fare as 'The Magical
Sailor's Knot.'. . . The books' design, with the text neatly
packaged in boxes, will attract reluctant readers." SLJ

  Includes glossary and bibliographical references

  Amazing magic tricks: apprentice level; by Norm
Barnhart. Capstone Press 2009 32p il (Magic Tricks) lib
bdg $23.93

Grades: 4 5 6   **793.8**

  1. Magic tricks

  ISBN 978-1-4296-1943-1 lib bdg; 1-4296-1943-0
lib bdg

                            LC 2008-2573

"Numbered steps, clearly illustrated by crisp photographs, guide students through the preparation and performance of such classic magician's fare as 'The Magical
Sailor's Knot.'. . . The books' design, with the text neatly
packaged in boxes, will attract reluctant readers." SLJ

  Includes glossary and bibliographical references

  Amazing magic tricks: expert level; by Norm Barnhart.
Capstone Press 2009 32p il (Magic Tricks) lib bdg $23.93

Grades: 4 5 6   **793.8**

  1. Magic tricks

  ISBN 978-1-4296-1945-5 lib bdg; 1-4296-1945-7
lib bdg

                            LC 2008-2574

"Numbered steps, clearly illustrated by crisp photographs, guide students through the preparation and performance of such classic magician's fare as 'The Magical
Sailor's Knot.'. . . The books' design, with the text neatly
packaged in boxes, will attract reluctant readers." SLJ

  Includes glossary and bibliographical references

  Amazing magic tricks: master level; by Norm Barnhart. Capstone Press 2009 32p il (Magic Tricks) lib bdg
$23.93

Grades: 4 5 6   **793.8**

  1. Magic tricks

  ISBN 978-1-4296-1944-8 lib bdg; 1-4296-1944-9
lib bdg

                            LC 2008-2575

"Numbered steps, clearly illustrated by crisp photographs, guide students through the preparation and performance of such classic magician's fare as 'The Magical
Sailor's Knot.'. . . The books' design, with the text neatly
packaged in boxes, will attract reluctant readers." SLJ

  Includes glossary and bibliographical references

Becker, Helaine

Magic up your sleeve; amazing illusions, tricks, and science facts you'll never believe. illustrated by Claudia Dávila. Maple Tree Press 2010 64p il $22.95; pa $10.95

Grades: 3 4 5 6   **793.8**

1. Science 2. Magic tricks

ISBN 978-1-897349-75-5; 1-897349-75-0; 978-1-897349-76-2 pa; 1-8973497-6-9 pa

"Thirty tricks are presented covering optical illusions, mind reading, 'math magic,' chemistry, and physics. All directions are clear and easy to follow. . . . The digital cartoon illustrations are nicely executed and add flashes of humor to the scenarios. . . . A welcome addition that should vanish off library shelves." SLJ

Colgan, Lynda

Mathemagic! number tricks. written by Lynda Colgan; illustrated by Jane Kurisu. Kids Can Press 2011 40p il $16.95

Grades: 3 4 5   **793.8**

1. Magic tricks 2. Mathematical recreations

ISBN 978-1-55453-425-8; 1-55453-425-9

"Colgan introduces 10 magic tricks that are accomplished using mathematical principles. The directions are clear and easy to follow, and each trick is followed by an explanation of how it actually works, as well as suggestions for performing it effectively for an audience. Interesting historical tidbits occasionally appear in sidebars. The simple cartoon illustrations add interest and clarify how the tricks are accomplished." SLJ

Includes glossary

Jennings, Madeleine

Magic step-by-step; [by] Madeleine Jennings and Colin Francome. Rosen Central 2010 89p il (Skills in motion) lib bdg $31.95

Grades: 5 6 7 8   **793.8**

1. Magic tricks

ISBN 978-1-4358-3363-0; 1-4358-3363-5

LC 2009-13221

Presents step-by-step instructions on performing magic tricks, including card tricks, rope tricks, and sleight of hand.

"Colorful photographs show the entire movement of each skill presented, giving new meaning to the term 'step-by-step.' Progression borders at the bottom of the pages highlight the salient points to notice in performing each skill from beginning to end." SLJ

Includes bibliographical references

Tremaine, Jon

Magic with numbers. QEB Pub. 2010 32p il (Magic handbook) lib bdg $28.50

Grades: 4 5 6   **793.8**

1. Numbers 2. Magic tricks 3. Mathematical recreations

ISBN 978-1-59566-945-2; 1-59566-945-0

LC 2010014138

Provides step-by-step instructions for fifteen magic tricks using numbers, including profiles of famous magicians.

This "is uncommonly good. . . . [The book] uses sharp, comprehensible illustrations set up on old-fashioned marbled backdrops. . . . Best of all, the friendly, crystal-clear

[text] makes this one of the most coherent [books] in the genre." Booklist

Magical illusions. QEB Pub. 2010 32p il (Magic handbook) lib bdg $28.50

Grades: 4 5 6   **793.8**

1. Magic tricks

ISBN 978-1-59566-944-5; 1-59566-944-2

LC 2010008525

This volume explains how to perform magic tricks that involve creating illusions.

This "is uncommonly good. . . . [The book] uses sharp, comprehensible illustrations set up on old-fashioned marbled backdrops. . . . Best of all, the friendly, crystal-clear [text] makes this one of the most coherent [books] in the genre." Booklist

Paper tricks. QEB Pub. 2010 32p il (Magic handbook) lib bdg $28.50

Grades: 4 5 6   **793.8**

1. Magic tricks 2. Paper crafts

ISBN 978-1-59566-852-3; 1-59566-852-7

LC 2010017910

This offers instructions for magic tricks using paper.

This "is uncommonly good. . . . [The book] uses sharp, comprehensible illustrations set up on old-fashioned marbled backdrops. . . . Best of all, the friendly, crystal-clear [text] makes this one of the most coherent [books] in the genre." Booklist

Pocket tricks. QEB Pub. 2010 32p il (Magic handbook) lib bdg $28.50; pa $13.50

Grades: 4 5 6   **793.8**

1. Magic tricks

ISBN 978-1-59566-853-0 lib bdg; 1-59566-853-5 lib bdg; 978-1-84835-443-2 pa; 1-84835-443-6 pa

LC 2010008526

This volume explains how to perform simple magic tricks using items that are commonly in a person's pocket.

This "is uncommonly good. . . . [The book] uses sharp, comprehensible illustrations set up on old-fashioned marbled backdrops. . . . Best of all, the friendly, crystal-clear [text] makes this one of the most coherent [books] in the genre." Booklist

Includes bibliographical references

Wyler, Rose

Magic secrets; by Rose Wyler and Gerald Ames; pictures by Arthur Dorros. rev ed.; Harper & Row 1990 63p il (I can read book) hardcover o.p. pa $3.99

Grades: K 1 2   **793.8**

1. Magic tricks 2. Magic -- Juvenile literature

ISBN 0-06-444153-9 pa

LC 89-35841

A revised and newly illustrated edition of the title first published 1967

Easy magic tricks for the aspiring young magician

"Most of the magic tricks presented here are easily understood and appear to be simple to learn and to execute with ample practice." SLJ

793.8092   Magicians (Performers)

Jarrow, Gail

★ The **amazing** Harry Kellar; great American magician. Gail G. Jarrow. Calkins Creek 2012 96 p. col. ill. $17.95

Grades: 3 4 5 6 7 8   **793.8092**

   1. Magicians 2. Optical illusions

   ISBN 1590788656; 9781590788653

                       LC 2011940465

This book is a biography of Harry Keller (later Kellar), "the first dean of the Society of American Magicians, a man [magician Harry] Houdini regarded as a mentor. . . . Few secrets of the illusions are revealed here, but [Gail] Jarrow makes it clear that it was Kellar's art that made them seem like real magic." The book also includes "[d]ozens of . . . Kellar posters" and a "timeline, bibliography, [and] annotated sources." (Kirkus)

794.1   Chess

Basman, Michael

   Chess for kids; written by Michael Basman. Dorling Kindersley 2001 45p il $12.99; pa $6.99

Grades: 4 5 6 7   **794.1**

   1. Chess 2. Chess for children -- Juvenile literature

   ISBN 0-7894-6540-X; 0-7566-1807-X pa

                       LC 00-59018

This guide to chess explains the rudiments of the game, techniques and winning strategies

"A solid introduction for novices and good for skilled players wanting to develop their strategies and find out about chess clubs and tournaments." Booklist

King, Daniel

   ★ **Chess;** from first moves to checkmate. New ed.; Kingfisher 2010 64p il pa $8.99

Grades: 5 6 7 8 9 10 11 12   **794.1**

   1. Chess

   ISBN 978-0-7534-1930-4

   First published 2000

Introduces the rules and strategies of chess, as well as its history and some of the great players and matches.

794.8   Electronic games

Egan, Jill

   How video game designers use math; math curriculum consultant: Rhea A. Stewart. Chelsea Clubhouse 2010 32p il (Math in the real world) lib bdg $28

Grades: 4 5 6   **794.8**

   1. Mathematics 2. Video games 3. Computer games 4. Computer animation 5. Vocational guidance

   ISBN 978-1-60413-603-6 lib bdg; 1-60413-603-0 lib bdg

                       LC 2009-24173

This describes how video game designers use math to create and produce their games and includes relevant math problems and information about how to become a video game designer

Includes glossary and bibliographical references

Jozefowicz, Chris

   Video game developer. Gareth Stevens Pub. 2010 32p il (Cool careers: cutting edge) lib bdg $26; pa $8.95

Grades: 4 5 6   **794.8**

   1. Video games 2. Computer games 3. Vocational guidance

   ISBN 978-1-4339-1958-9 lib bdg; 1-4339-1958-3 lib bdg; 978-1-4339-2157-5 pa; 1-4339-2157-X pa

                       LC 2008053549

This introduction to video game developer careers offers "clear, solid information in a large font. . . . [This] short [book is] packed with relevant, current material." SLJ

Includes glossary and bibliographical references

Oxlade, Chris

   Gaming technology. Smart Apple Media 2011 il (New technology) lib bdg $34.25

Grades: 4 5 6 7   **794.8**

   1. Video games 2. Computer games

   ISBN 9781599205311

                       LC 2010044239

Describes the technology used for creating and playing video games. Includes information on how different platforms work and the direction video game technology may be going.

This "offers a fine overview for reports, and its attractive design may also entice middle-grade readers to learn more." Booklist

Includes glossary and bibliographical references

796   Athletic and outdoor sports and games

Berman, Len

   The **greatest** moments in sports. Sourcebooks 2009 136p il $16.99

Grades: 5 6 7 8   **796**

   1. Sports

   ISBN 978-1-4022-2099-9; 1-4022-2099-5

                       LC 2009023686

"Forty years as a sportscaster gives Berman plenty of experience to choose the 25 greatest sports moments. His writing is lively, humorous, and informative—just right to sustain kids' (or adults') interest. Quality photos throughout are another plus. . . . An audio CD that includes many of the moments as they were broadcast live is part of the package." SLJ

Includes bibliographical references

   The **greatest** moments in sports; upsets and underdogs. Len Berman. Sourcebooks Jabberwocky 2012 iv, 124 p.p ill. (hardcover) $19.99

Grades: 5 6 7 8   **796**

   1. Sports upsets -- History

   ISBN 140227226X; 9781402272264

In this sports book, "[Len] Berman offers his take on 25 of the most unexpected victories. . . . Youngsters learn about Billy Mills's surprise win of Olympic Gold for the 10,000 meter run in 1964, and Mexico's Little League World Series win of 1957. Text boxes . . . [present] biographical information and quick glimpses into the records of the 'champions' versus the 'underdogs.' The accompanying CD offers additional insight from Berman on 10 of the upsets." (School Library Journal)

Blumenthal, Karen

Let me play; the story of Title IX, the law that changed the future of girls in America. Atheneum Books for Young Readers 2005 152p il $19.95

Grades: 6 7 8 9 10   **796**

1. Women athletes 2. Sex discrimination

ISBN 0-689-85957-0

LC 2004-1450

Title IX legislation assured "that 'no one could be closed out of any educational program or activity receiving federal money simply because of sex.' After explaining the genesis of the legislation, . . . Blumenthal discusses how evolving guidelines and interpretations brought girls' school athletic programs into its purview. [Bibliography. Index.] Grades nine to twelve." (Bull Cent Child Books)

"The author looks at American women's evolving rights by focusing on the history and future of Title IX, which bans sex discrimination in U.S. education. . . . The images are . . . gripping, and relevant political cartoons and fact boxes add further interest. Few books cover the last few decades of American women's history with such clarity and detail." Booklist

Includes bibliographical references

Hile, Lori

Surviving extreme sports. Raintree 2011 56p il (Extreme survival) lib bdg $33.50

Grades: 4 5 6 7   **796**

1. Extreme sports 2. Wilderness survival

ISBN 978-1-4109-3968-5; 1-4109-3968-5

LC 2010028689

This book is "fun and informative. [This] well-organized title starts with an overview [of extreme sports], offers some specific examples, and includes additional facts or tips and resources. . . . [It features] dramatic archival and full-color photos on nearly every page. . . . [This is a book] that youngsters will enjoy and talk about." SLJ

Includes glossary and bibliographical references

Howell, Brian

Sports. ABDO Pub. Co. 2011 112p il (Inside the industry) lib bdg $23.95

Grades: 5 6 7 8   **796**

1. Sports -- Vocational guidance

ISBN 978-1-61714-804-0; 1-61714-804-0

LC 2010042558

This " well-designed [book describes] a variety of careers in [sports]. Because [it helps] readers assess if these positions are suitable for their personality types and backgrounds, the [title is a] good [choice] for career exploration and self-discovery. [It is] also useful for research and reports. . . . Sidebars and full-color photos appear throughout." SLJ

Includes bibliographical references

Kelley, K. C.

Weird races. Child's World 2011 24p il (Weird sports) lib bdg $25.64

Grades: 3 4 5 6   **796**

1. Racing

ISBN 978-1-60954-376-1; 1-60954-376-1

LC 2010042898

This describes sports such as lawnmower racing, bed racing, wife carrying, street luge, cheese rolling, and toilet racing.

"Both the writing and the visual style are exuberant-without relying too much on exclamation points." Booklist

Weird sports moments. Child's World 2011 24p il (Weird sports) lib bdg $25.64

Grades: 3 4 5 6   **796**

1. Sports 2. Curiosities and wonders

ISBN 978-1-60954-377-8; 1-60954-377-7

LC 2010042899

This describes weird moments in sports such as the outfield bonfire, football vs. the band, celebrating too early, and run the other way.

"Both the writing and the visual style are exuberant-without relying too much on exclamation points." Booklist

Krull, Kathleen

★ Lives of the athletes; thrills, spills (and what the neighbors thought) written by Kathleen Krull; illustrated by Kathryn Hewitt. Harcourt Brace & Co. 1997 96p il $21

Grades: 4 5 6 7   **796**

1. Actors 2. Athletes 3. Baseball players 4. Football players 5. Golfers 6. Surfers 7. Hurdlers 8. Swimmers 9. Decathletes 10. Ice skaters 11. High jumpers 12. Mountaineers 13. Pentathletes 14. Army officers 15. Hockey players 16. Soccer players 17. Tennis players 18. Martial artists 19. Javelin throwers 20. Olympic athletes 21. Basketball players 22. Nonfiction writers 23. Runners (Athletes) 24. Volleyball players 25. Athletes -- Biography -- Juvenile literature

ISBN 0-15-200806-3

LC 95-50702

"Krull profiles twenty legendary athletes of the twentieth century who broke new ground in their sports and often broke through racial or gender barriers as well. . . . The brief biographies are enhanced by unusual details of personality and Hewitt's lively caricatures of the subjects." Horn Book

Includes bibliographical references

Ralston, Birgitta

Snow play; how to make forts & slides & winter campfires plus the coolest Loch Ness monster and 23 other brrrilliant [i.e. brilliant] project in the snow. Artisan 2010 111p il $14.95

Grades: 4 5 6 7 8 9 10 11 12 Adult   **796**

1. Snow 2. Outdoor recreation

ISBN 978-1-57965-405-4; 1-57965-405-3

"Opening with explanations of different types of snow and the various tools needed to work with it, this how-to book describes more than two dozen projects, most of which will require adult help and supervision. . . . Ratings of difficulty, the number of people and tools needed, the type of snow required, and the time frame are included with each project. Short snow-related facts appear throughout. . . . A brief listing of worldwide snow festivals, snow hotels and igloos, and an ice museum completes the package. While kids can certainly use this book to inspire ideas for winter fun, adults will find it equally useful, especially for generating ideas for family projects." SLJ

Rand, Casey

Graphing sports. Heinemann Library 2009 32p il (Real world data) $28.21; pa $7.99

Grades: 5 6 7 8   796

  1. Graphic methods 2. Sports -- Statistics
ISBN 978-1-4329-2621-2; 1-4329-2621-7; 978-1-4329-2630-4 pa; 1-4329-2630-6 pa

LC 2009001189

This explains sports related concepts through charts and graphs.

"The writing is spot-on for the audience. Most importantly, the statistics used are well chosen and instantly understandable, and the text clearly explains how each type of graph can be used to best display different types of data." SLJ

Includes glossary and bibliographical references

Rose, Julianna

Go out and play! favorite outdoor games from Kaboom! 1st ed. Candlewick Press 2011 vii, 96 p.p col. ill. (paperback) $11.99

Grades: 3 4 5   796

  1. Games 2. Recreation
ISBN 0763655309; 9780763655303

LC 2011046634

This resource book is a "collection of 69 group games . . . to encourage children to engage in outdoor play. . . . Organized according to game type, the book focuses on versions of tag, hide-and-seek, ball games, team games, sidewalk games, circle games and races. . . . Sections at the beginning and end tell adults how to best be partners in children's play and how to create safe play spaces that will get kids outdoors." (Kirkus Reviews)

"This lively offering describes and outlines simple games that center on physical activity, including multiple versions of tag, hide-and-seek, ball games, race games, and 'no-rules games.' Each game is introduced in basic language, with a brief sidebar highlighting the number of players, recommended ages, space required, and suggested materials. Enlivened with cartoon spot art and photographs of children at play, the book should give readers plenty of activity options come spring." Publ Wkly

Includes bibliographical references.

Strother, Scott

★ The adventurous book of outdoor games; classic fun for daring boys and girls. [by] Scott Strother. Sourcebooks 2008 293p il pa $14.99

Grades: 4 5 6 7 Adult Professional   796

  1. Games
ISBN 978-1-4022-1443-1 pa; 1-4022-1443-X pa

This book "outlines more than 100 games, each at different activity levels set by the amount of physical exertion required. . . . Each game discusses the number of players, ages, time allotted, and type of playing field, followed by a brief description of equipment, startup, object of the game, and how to play. . . . The easy-to-read, easy-to-follow format will provide hours of imaginative play for all of those who are willing to try. An excellent resource for parents, teachers, and activity directors and even for children themselves." SLJ

Watson, S. B.

Weird animal sports. Child's World 2011 24p il (Weird sports) lib bdg $25.64

Grades: 3 4 5 6   796

  1. Sports 2. Animals 3. Curiosities and wonders
ISBN 978-1-60954-3754; 1-60954-375-0

LC 2010042897

This describes sports such as turkey bowling, frog jumping, race car hamsters, camel racing, and elephant soccer.

"Both the writing and the visual style are exuberant—without relying too much on exclamation points." Booklist

Weird sports of the world. Child's World 2011 24p il (Weird sports) lib bdg $25.64

Grades: 3 4 5 6   796

  1. Sports 2. Curiosities and wonders
ISBN 978-1-60954-378-5; 1-60954-378-5

LC 2010042901

This describes sports such as parkour, tough guy, unicycle hockey, mountain boarding, chess boxing, and waterfall kayaking.

"Both the writing and the visual style are exuberant-without relying too much on exclamation points." Booklist

Weird throwing and kicking sports. Child's World 2011 24p il (Weird sports) lib bdg $25.64

Grades: 3 4 5 6   796

  1. Sports 2. Curiosities and wonders
ISBN 978-1-6095-4379-2; 1-6095-4379-3

LC 2010044026

This describes sports such as fish flinging, toe wrestling, stone tossing, stick kicking, and blanket riding.

"Both the writing and the visual style are exuberant-without relying too much on exclamation points." Booklist

Includes bibliographical references

Woods, Mark

Xtreme! Extreme sports facts and stats; [by] Mark Woods and Ruth Owen. Gareth Stevens Pub. 2011 32p il (Top score math) lib bdg $26.60

Grades: 4 5 6   796

  1. Extreme sports
ISBN 978-1-4339-5020-9; 1-4339-5020-9

LC 2010029612

This book, "chock-full of numbers, presents 'facts and stats' associated with [extreme sports]. Figures include sports records, players' heights, jersey numbers, and surfing speeds. . . . [The book succeeds] at entertaining and instructing fans through engaging text and quiz challenges." Horn Book Guide

796.1 Miscellaneous games

Birmingham, Maria

Weird zone; sports. Maria Birmingham. Owlkids Books Inc. 2013 128 p. (Weird zone) $22.95

Grades: 4 5 6 7   796.1

  1. Sports -- Juvenile literature
ISBN 1926973607; 9781926973609

LC 2012948714

This book on unusual sports by Maria Birmingham is part of the "Weird Zone" book series. It includes such sports as "rolling down a hill in a plastic ball (aka 'zorbing') . . . professional-grade pillow fighting . . . lawn-mower racing . . . [and] extreme ironing. . . . Each sport gets a two-page spread." (Kirkus Reviews)

★ The **Eentsy**, weentsy spider: fingerplays and action rhymes; compiled by Joanna Cole and Stephanie Calmenson; illustrated by Alan Tiegreen. Morrow Junior Bks. 1991 64p il music hardcover o.p. pa $8.99

Grades: K 1 2 3   **796.1**

1. Songs 2. Finger play
ISBN 0-688-10805-9 pa

LC 90-44594

"Tiegreen uses a few simple lines to create a cast of multicultural characters whose enthusiasm is infectious. . . . An attractive, upbeat addition to the finger-play collection." Booklist

Includes bibliographical references

★ **Miss** Mary Mack and other children's street rhymes; compiled by Joanna Cole and Stephanie Calmenson; illustrated by Alan Tiegreen. Morrow Junior Bks. 1990 64p hardcover o.p. pa $7.95

Grades: K 1 2 3   **796.1**

1. Games 2. Nursery rhymes
ISBN 0-688-09749-9 pa

LC 89-37266

This is a collection of over 100 traditional childhood hand-clapping and street rhymes

"Tiegreen's lighthearted pen-and-ink illustrations are sure to tickle the fancy of young readers. . . . A book that's sure to produce smiles in any story hour or program." SLJ

796.2 Activities and games requiring equipment

Bell-Rehwoldt, Sheri
The **kids'** guide to jumping rope. Capstone Press 2011 32p il (Kids' guides) lib bdg $26.65

Grades: 4 5 6 7   **796.2**

1. Rope skipping
ISBN 978-1-4296-5443-2; 1-4296-5443-0

LC 2010035018

Describes the sport of jumping rope, including how-to information on jumps and tricks.

This includes "plentiful photos of giddy girls (and a few guys) madly skipping rope. . . . This makes jumping rope look like the best time in the world." Booklist

Includes bibliographical references

796.22 Skateboarding

Fitzpatrick, Jim
Skateboarding. Cherry Lake Pub. 2009 32p il (Innovation in sports) lib bdg $27.07

Grades: 4 5 6 7   **796.22**

1. Skateboarding
ISBN 978-1-60279-259-3 lib bdg; 1-60279-259-3 lib bdg

LC 2008007548

This describes skateboarding history, equipment, safety, and health benefits

This "stands out by emphasizing monumental shifts and advances in the events themselves. . . . Concise and occasionally revelatory." Booklist

Includes glossary and bibliographical references

Spencer, Russ
Skateboarding; by Russ Spencer. Child's World 2005 32p il (Kids' guides) lib bdg $24.21

Grades: 4 5 6   **796.22**

1. Skateboarding
ISBN 1-59296-210-6

LC 2003-27370

This "opens with an explanation of the sport and gives reasons why people enjoy it. The four chapters that follow cover background and development, equipment, technique, and stars and competitions. The excellent color photos are clear and exciting." SLJ

Includes bibliographical references

Stock, Charlotte
Skateboarding step-by-step; [by] Charlotte Stock and Ben Powell. Rosen Central 2010 91p il (Skills in motion) lib bdg $31.95

Grades: 5 6 7 8   **796.22**

1. Skateboarding
ISBN 978-1-4358-3365-4; 1-4358-3365-1

LC 2009-11414

Presents instructions on skateboarding from learning to skateboard to executing jumps, flips, and tricks.

"Colorful photographs show the entire movement of each skill presented, giving new meaning to the term 'step-by-step.' Progression borders at the bottom of the pages highlight the salient points to notice in performing each skill from beginning to end." SLJ

Includes bibliographical references

796.3 Ball games

Rosen, Michael J.
Balls!: round 2; illustrations by John Margeson. Darby Creek Pub. 2008 80p il $18.95

Grades: 3 4 5 6   **796.3**

1. Sports 2. Sporting goods 3. Ball games -- Juvenile literature 4. Balls (Sporting goods) -- Juvenile literature
ISBN 978-1-58196-066-2; 1-58196-066-2

"Rosen offers a lighthearted look at a variety of balls, covering their production and history, and how they're used in sports. . . . The author highlights balls used in baseball, softball, bowling, bocce, croquet, shot put, billiards, and lacrosse. Each sport receives a brief introduction . . . complemented by color photographs, cartoons, and graphics. There's an emphasis on fun science, with simple puzzles and experiments. . . . Rosen serves up a feast of whimsical trivia and wordplay, and he rounds out this collection with sections on marbles and extreme goofballs." SLJ

Includes bibliographical references

796.323 Basketball

Bekkering, Annalise

NCAA Basketball. Weigl Publishers 2010 32p il map (Sporting championships) lib bdg $26; pa $9.95

Grades: 3 4 5   796.323

1. Basketball

ISBN 978-1-60596-634-2 lib bdg; 1-60596-634-7 lib bdg; 978-1-60596-635-9 pa; 1-60596-635-5 pa

LC 2009-8366

This sets the NCAA Basketball championship "within the context of the sport and explains what you need to know when watching the big [event]." Booklist

Includes glossary and bibliographical references

Burns, Brian

Basketball step-by-step; [by] Brian Burns and Mark Dunning. Rosen Central 2010 95p il (Skills in motion) lib bdg $31.95

Grades: 5 6 7 8   796.323

1. Basketball

ISBN 978-1-4358-3360-9; 1-4358-3360-0

LC 2009-14417

An introduction to the skills needed to play basketball uses a sequence of stop-action images and text instructions to illustrate such offensive and defensive moves as inside pivot and shoot, blocking out, and overhead pass.

"Colorful photographs show the entire movement of each skill presented, giving new meaning to the term 'step-by-step.' Progression borders at the bottom of the pages highlight the salient points to notice in performing each skill from beginning to end." SLJ

Includes bibliographical references

Doeden, Matt

The greatest basketball records; by Matt Doeden. Capstone Press 2009 32p il (Sports records) lib bdg $17.95

Grades: 4 5 6 7 8   796.323

1. Basketball

ISBN 978-1-4296-2006-2 lib bdg; 1-4296-2006-4 lib bdg

LC 2008-2033

This "has enough historical insight and trivia to remain appealing over time.... Brief, lively sentences sum up individual feats and set them in context.... [This] should appeal to a wide audience." SLJ

Includes glossary and bibliographical references

Gibbons, Gail

My basketball book. HarperCollins Pubs. 2000 un il $6.99

Grades: K 1 2   796.323

1. Basketball

ISBN 0-688-17140-0

LC 99-87902

Introduces the basics of the game of basketball, describing the players, court, techniques, and rules of play

Includes glossary

Gifford, Clive

Basketball; [by] Clive Gifford. PowerKids Press 2009 32p il (Personal best) lib bdg $25.25

Grades: 4 5 6 7 8   796.323

1. Basketball

ISBN 978-1-4042-4444-3 lib bdg; 1-4042-4444-1 lib bdg

LC 2007-42989

This guide to basketball "offers well-organized and easy-to-follow instructions, focusing on rules, clothing, specific skills, and competitions.... Informative, readable." SLJ

Includes bibliographical references

Labrecque, Ellen

Basketball; by Ellen Labrecque. Cherry Lake Pub. 2009 32p il (Innovation in sports) lib bdg $27.07

Grades: 4 5 6 7   796.323

1. Basketball

ISBN 978-1-60279-256-2 lib bdg; 1-60279-256-9 lib bdg

LC 2008002044

This describes basketball history, rules, equipment, training, and great players

This "stands out by emphasizing monumental shifts and advances in the events themselves.... Concise and occasionally revelatory." Booklist

Includes glossary and bibliographical references

Macy, Sue

Basketball belles; how two teams and one scrappy player put women's hoops on the map. illustrated by Matt Collins. Holiday House 2010 un il $16.95

Grades: 1 2 3 4   796.323

1. Women athletes 2. Basketball players 3. Basketball -- Biography 4. Women basketball players -- Juvenile literature

ISBN 0-8234-2163-5; 978-0-8234-2163-3

LC 2009-42498

This book is told from the perspective of Agnes Morley, who played on Stanford University's women's basketball team. It is a play-by-play account of an 1896 game played between Morley's team and the University of California at Berkeley team. "Ages six to nine." (Bull Cent Child Books)

"In this rousing picture book, Macy and Collins take readers to the (very) early days of women's basketball through the eyes of Agnes Morley, who offers a play-by-play account of an 1896 game between Stanford and Berkeley—the first ever between two women's basketball teams. ... Whether Agnes is wrangling with a calf on her family's ranch or diving for a loose ball, her determination shines through in Collins's dynamic, painterly digital spreads." Publ Wkly

McClellan, Ray

Basketball. Bellwether Media 2010 24p il (Blastoff! readers. My first sports) $19.95

Grades: K 1 2 3   796.323

1. Basketball

ISBN 978-1-60014-279-6; 1-60014-279-6

LC 2009-8186

Simple text and full color photographs introduce beginning readers to the sport of basketball.

Includes glossary and bibliographical references

Robinson, Tom

Basketball. Norwood House Press 2010 64p il (Girls play to win) lib bdg $26.60

Grades: 4 5 6 7 **796.323**
1. Basketball
ISBN 978-1-59953-388-9; 1-59953-388-X
LC 2010009814

Covers the history, rules, fundamentals and significant personalities of the sport of women's basketball. Topics include: techniques, strategies, competitive events, and equipment.

"With an easy design and format, the [text is] highly accessible to even the most reluctant readers and [provides] great exposure and insight into the world of female professional sports." Horn Book Guide

Includes glossary and bibliographical references

Slade, Suzanne
Basketball; how it works. Capstone Press 2010 48p il (Science of sports) lib bdg $29.32; pa $7.95
Grades: 4 5 6 7 **796.323**
1. Basketball
ISBN 978-1-4296-4021-3 lib bdg; 1-4296-4021-9 lib bdg; 978-1-4296-4873-8 pa; 1-4296-4873-2 pa

The book's "photograph-heavy design works to engage its audience, while the easy-to-read [text explains] the science." Horn Book Guide

Includes glossary

Stewart, Mark
Swish; the quest for basketball's perfect shot. by Mark Stewart and Mike Kennedy. Millbrook Press 2009 64p il lib bdg $25.26
Grades: 5 6 7 8 **796.323**
1. Basketball
ISBN 978-0-8225-8752-1 lib bdg; 0-8225-8752-1 lib bdg
LC 2008-24958

"The wide pages offer plenty of room for well-spaced text, sidebars, and illustrations. Each page has at least one picture, with mostly color photos, and the many action shots make the book more exciting. With information on women's and men's basketball at both collegiate and professional levels, this is a nice addition to sports collections." Booklist

Includes bibliographical references

Thomas, Keltie
★ **How** basketball works. Maple Tree Press 2005 64p il hardcover o.p. $16.95
Grades: 5 6 7 8 **796.323**
1. Basketball
ISBN 1-89706-618-X; 1-89706-619-8 pa

This guide to basketball offers information about the game's origins, history, and equipment as well as positions, training, skills, stats, & rules of the game. It also offers tips and fascinating factoids.

"The writing style is razzle-dazzle energetic. . . . . The layout features numerous sidebars and brightly colored photos and digital drawings. Even longtime fans will learn something from this engaging, enthusiastic book." Booklist

Thornley, Stew
Kevin Garnett; champion basketball star. by Stew Thornley. Enslow Publishers 2013 48 p. col. ill. (library) $23.93
Grades: 4 5 6 7 **796.323**
1. Picture books for children 2. Basketball players --

United States -- Biography -- Juvenile literature
ISBN 0766040283; 9780766040281
LC 2011031517

This book by Stew Thornley is a children's picture book biography of professional basketball player Kevin Garnett. In his "career, Garnett has won MVP trophies and other individual awards, but his NBA championship ring is most important to him. The team has always come first for KG." (Publisher's note)

Includes bibliographical references (p. 47) and index.

Kobe Bryant; champion basketball star. by Stew Thornley. Enslow Publishers 2013 48 p. col. ill. (library) $23.93
Grades: 4 5 6 7 **796.323**
1. Picture books for children 2. Bryant, Kobe, 1978- -- Juvenile literature 3. Basketball players -- United States -- Biography -- Juvenile literature
ISBN 0766040291; 9780766040298
LC 2011038174

This picture book by Stew Thornley is a biography of professional basketball player Kobe Bryant. "He can swish shots from long range or drive to the basket for a vicious dunk. Bryant once scored 81 points in a single game! He can also dish it to his teammates and play lockdown defense. . . . The Los Angeles Lakers superstar has won five NBA titles since coming out of high school, and he has earned many individual awards." (Publisher's note)

Tim Duncan; champion basketball star. by Stew Thornley. Enslow Publishers 2013 48 p. col. ill. (library) $23.93
Grades: 4 5 6 7 **796.323**
1. Basketball players -- United States -- Biography
ISBN 0766040305; 9780766040304
LC 2011050440

This book by Stew Thornley is part of the Sports Star Champions series and looks at basketball player Tim Duncan. The texts "focus on the athletes' professional careers, with very little information about their personal lives. . . . Each book ends with career statistics, the player's address, and a brief list for further reading." (School Library Journal)

Includes bibliographical references (p. 47) and index.

Woods, Mark
Slam dunk! basketball facts and stats. [by] Mark Woods and Ruth Owen. Gareth Stevens Pub. 2011 32p il (Top score math) lib bdg $26.60
Grades: 4 5 6 **796.323**
1. Basketball
ISBN 978-1-4339-5017-9; 1-4339-5017-0
LC 2010029685

This book, "chock-full of numbers, presents 'facts and stats' associated with [basketball]. Figures include sports records, players' heights, jersey numbers, and surfing speeds. . . . [The book succeeds] at entertaining and instructing fans through engaging text and quiz challenges." Horn Book Guide

Yancey, Diane
Basketball. Lucent Books 2011 112p il (Science behind sports) lib bdg $33.45

Grades: 5 6 7 8   **796.323**
1. Basketball
ISBN 978-1-4205-0293-0; 1-4205-0293-X
LC 2010035239

This "explores the scientific principles such as momentum, gravity, friction, and aerodynamics, plus many more, behind [basketball]. . . . [The author discusses the sport's] origins, history, and changes, . . . the biomechanics and physiology of playing, related health and medical concerns, and the causes and treatment of sports-related injuries. Additional information tells how exercise, diet and nutrition, warming up, and training relate to peak performance and enjoyment of the sport. . . . [The book] has features on possible side effects of anabolic steroid use; how MRIs work; and how various improvements to the courts, basketballs, shoes, and uniforms have affected the game. The action photography . . . is fantastic. . . . [A must-have] for sports fans, athletes, science students, and even anyone considering a career in sports-related medicine, coaching, or other connected fields." SLJ

Includes glossary and bibliographical references

796.325   Volleyball

Crossingham, John
Spike it volleyball; [by] John Crossingham. Crabtree Pub. Co. 2008 32p il (Sports starters) lib bdg $18.95; pa $6.95
Grades: 2 3 4   **796.325**
1. Volleyball
ISBN 978-0-7787-3143-6 lib bdg; 0-7787-3143-X lib bdg; 978-0-7787-3175-7 pa; 0-7787-3175-8 pa
LC 2008004853

This "offers a sturdy overview of volleyball, from rules and scoring to basic moves. The accessible text lays out clear explanations of terms and concepts. . . . The eye-catching design combines large color photos of athletes in action with smaller inset pictures." Booklist

McDougall, Chros
Volleyball. Norwood House Press 2010 64p il (Girls play to win) lib bdg $26.60
Grades: 4 5 6 7   **796.325**
1. Volleyball
ISBN 978-1-59953-392-6; 1-59953-392-8
LC 2010009810

Covers the history, rules, fundamentals and significant personalities of the sport of women's volleyball. Topics include: techniques, strategies, competitive events, and equipment.

"With an easy design and format, the [text is] highly accessible to even the most reluctant readers and [provides] great exposure and insight into the world of female professional sports." Horn Book Guide

Includes glossary and bibliographical references

796.332   American football

Buckley, James
The Child's World encyclopedia of the NFL; by James Buckley, Jr. . . . [et al.] Child's World 2007 4v il

Grades: 3 4 5 6 7   **796.332**
1. Reference books 2. Football -- Encyclopedias
ISBN 978-1-59296-922-7 v1; 978-1-59296-923-4 v2; 978-1-59296-924-1 v3; 978-1-59296-925-8 v4
LC 2007005662

This encyclopedia of the National Football League is "full of color photos; significant names, terms, and events; and plenty of popular football figures. The authors are all experienced sportswriters and editors." Booklist

Ultimate guide to football; by James Buckley, Jr. Franklin Watts 2010 160p il $30; pa $7.99
Grades: 4 5 6 7   **796.332**
1. Football
ISBN 978-0-531-20752-9; 0-531-20752-8; 978-0-531-21023-9 pa; 0-531-21023-5 pa
LC 2009011003

This guide to football covers "historical highlights and delectable ephemera . . . with spreads covering each NFL team interspersed among chatty tales. . . . The highlighter-green color scheme matches the loud, vibrant layout and heightens the contrasting black-and-white player photos, while sporadic cartoons add some pep to the presentation." Booklist

Includes bibliographical references

Diemer, Lauren
Rose Bowl. Weigl Publishers 2010 32p il map (Sporting championships) lib bdg $26; pa $9.95
Grades: 3 4 5   **796.332**
1. Football
ISBN 978-1-60596-638-0 lib bdg; 1-60596-638-X lib bdg; 978-1-60596-639-7 pa; 1-60596-639-8 pa
LC 2009-8362

This sets the Rose Bowl "within the context of the sport and explains what you need to know when watching the [event]." Booklist

Includes glossary and bibliographical references

Doeden, Matt
Play football like a pro; key skills and tips. Capstone Press 2011 32p il (Play like the pros) lib bdg $25.32; pa $6.95
Grades: 3 4 5   **796.332**
1. Football
ISBN 978-1-4296-4825-7 lib bdg; 1-4296-4825-2 lib bdg; 978-1-4296-5646-7 pa; 1-4296-5646-8 pa
LC 2010007243

"Provides instructional tips on how to improve one's football skills, including quotes and advice from professional coaches and athletes." Publisher's note

Includes glossary and bibliographical references

Dougherty, Terri
The **greatest** football records; by Terri Dougherty. Capstone Press 2009 32p il (Sports records) lib bdg $17.95
Grades: 4 5 6 7 8   **796.332**
1. Football
ISBN 978-1-4296-2007-9 lib bdg; 1-4296-2007-2 lib bdg
LC 2008-2035

This "has enough historical insight and trivia to remain appealing over time. . . . Brief, lively sentences sum up individual feats and set them in context. . . . [This] should appeal to a wide audience." SLJ

Includes glossary and bibliographical references

Gibbons, Gail

My football book. HarperCollins Pubs. 2000 un il $6.99

Grades: K 1 2   **796.332**

1. Football 2. Football -- Juvenile literature
ISBN 0-688-17139-7

LC 99-87202

Introduces the basics of the game of football, describing the players, field, and how the game is played

"What shines through [in this book] is Gibbons's dedication to presenting the game as fun. . . . The illustrations, especially those of the players, clearly reflect the action." SLJ

Includes glossary

Gifford, Clive

Football. Marshall Cavendish Benchmark 2009 30p il (Tell me about sports) $19.95

Grades: 3 4 5   **796.332**

1. Football
ISBN 978-0-7614-4456-5; 0-7614-4456-4

LC 2009-4828

"An introduction to football, including techniques, rules, and the training regimen of professional athletes in the sport." Publisher's note

Includes glossary and bibliographical references

Gigliotti, Jim

Defensive backs. Gareth Stevens Pub. 2010 48p il (Game day. Football) lib bdg $31

Grades: 3 4 5   **796.332**

1. Football
ISBN 978-1-4339-1964-0 lib bdg; 1-4339-1964-8 lib bdg

LC 2009-6801

"The attractive page design showcases a mix of colorful photographs along with some vintage black-and-white shots, all within an attractive green border that shows yardage marks on a field. . . . This [book] . . . will generate discussion and sharing of opinions about favorite players and record book statistics." SLJ

Includes glossary and bibliographical references

Football. Cherry Lake Pub. 2009 32p il (Innovation in sports) lib bdg $27.07

Grades: 4 5 6 7   **796.332**

1. Football
ISBN 978-1-60279-257-9 lib bdg; 1-60279-257-7 lib bdg

LC 2008002305

This describes football history, rules, equipment, training and strategy, and innovators

This "stands out by emphasizing monumental shifts and advances in the events themselves. . . . Concise and occasionally revelatory." Booklist

Includes glossary and bibliographical references

Linebackers. Gareth Stevens Pub. 2010 48p il (Game day. Football) lib bdg $31

Grades: 3 4 5   **796.332**

1. Football
ISBN 978-1-4339-1959-6 lib bdg; 1-4339-1959-1 lib bdg

LC 2009-6802

"The attractive page design showcases a mix of colorful photographs along with some vintage black-and-white shots, all within an attractive green border that shows yardage marks on a field. . . . This [book] . . . will generate discussion and sharing of opinions about favorite players and record book statistics." SLJ

Includes glossary and bibliographical references

Linemen. Gareth Stevens Pub. 2010 48p il (Game day. Football) lib bdg $31

Grades: 3 4 5   **796.332**

1. Football
ISBN 978-1-4339-1960-2 lib bdg; 1-4339-1960-5 lib bdg

LC 2009-2272

"The attractive page design showcases a mix of colorful photographs along with some vintage black-and-white shots, all within an attractive green border that shows yardage marks on a field. . . . This [book] . . . will generate discussion and sharing of opinions about favorite players and record book statistics." SLJ

Includes glossary and bibliographical references

Receivers. Gareth Stevens Pub. 2010 48p il (Game day. Football) lib bdg $31

Grades: 3 4 5   **796.332**

1. Football
ISBN 978-1-4339-1962-6 lib bdg; 1-4339-1962-1 lib bdg

LC 2008-55595

"The attractive page design showcases a mix of colorful photographs along with some vintage black-and-white shots, all within an attractive green border that shows yardage marks on a field. . . . This [book] . . . will generate discussion and sharing of opinions about favorite players and record book statistics." SLJ

Includes glossary and bibliographical references

Kelley, K. C.

Quarterbacks. Gareth Stevens Pub. 2010 48p il (Game day. Football) lib bdg $31

Grades: 3 4 5   **796.332**

1. Football
ISBN 978-1-4339-1961-9 lib bdg; 1-4339-1961-3 lib bdg

LC 2008-55596

"The attractive page design showcases a mix of colorful photographs along with some vintage black-and-white shots, all within an attractive green border that shows yardage marks on a field. . . . This [book] . . . will generate discussion and sharing of opinions about favorite players and record book statistics." SLJ

Includes glossary and bibliographical references

Running backs. Gareth Stevens Pub. 2010 48p il (Game day. Football) lib bdg $31

Grades: 3 4 5   **796.332**
   1. Football
   ISBN 978-1-4339-1963-3 lib bdg; 1-4339-1963-X
lib bdg

LC 2009-2277

"The attractive page design showcases a mix of colorful photographs along with some vintage black-and-white shots, all within an attractive green border that shows yardage marks on a field. . . . This [book] . . . will generate discussion and sharing of opinions about favorite players and record book statistics." SLJ

Includes glossary and bibliographical references

Marsico, Katie
   Football; by Katie Marsico and Cecilia Minden. Cherry Lake Pub. 2009 32p il (Real world math: Sports) lib bdg $27.07
Grades: 4 5 6   **796.332**
   1. Football 2. Arithmetic
   ISBN 978-1-60279-247-0 lib bdg; 1-60279-247-X
lib bdg

LC 2008-1165

This book "starts with a short story on the history of [football], fundamental rules, and a math challenge in every chapter. . . . [This book] will pique your imagination." Sci Books Films

Includes glossary and bibliographical references

McClellan, Ray
   Football. Bellwether Media 2010 24p il (Blastoff! readers. My first sports) $19.95
Grades: K 1 2 3   **796.332**
   1. Football
   ISBN 978-1-60014-194-2; 1-60014-194-3

LC 2009-8187

"Simple text and full color photographs introduce beginning readers to the sport of football." Publisher's note

Includes glossary and bibliographical references

Rappoport, Ken
   Peyton Manning; champion football star. by Ken Rappoport. Enslow Publishers 2013 48 p. col. ill. (library) $23.93
Grades: 4 5 6 7   **796.332**
   1. Quarterbacks (Football) 2. Football players -- United States -- Biography -- Juvenile literature 3. Quarterbacks (Football) -- United States -- Biography -- Juvenile literature
   ISBN 0766040275; 9780766040274

LC 2011052759

This book is part of the Sports Star Champion series and looks at quarterback Peyton Manning. The "texts focus on the athletes' professional careers, with very little information about their personal lives. Occasional sidebars add additional interest, and each book ends with career statistics, the player's address, and a brief list for further reading." (School Library Journal)

Includes bibliographical references (p. 47) and index.

Stewart, Mark
   Touchdown; the power and precision of football's perfect play. by Mark Stewart and Mike Kennedy. Millbrook Press 2009 64p il lib bdg $27.93

Grades: 5 6 7 8   **796.332**
   1. Football
   ISBN 978-0-8225-8751-4 lib bdg; 0-8225-8751-3
lib bdg

LC 2008044295

"This attractive book opens with an intriguing history of American football. . . . Next, 10 double-page spreads feature 'Ten Unforgettable Touchdowns' in both professional and collegiate games from 1913 to 2006. After a chapter on 'touchdown makers,' spotlighting outstanding players . . . comes a short section on notable touchdown bloopers and another on trick plays and the element of surprise. . . . Photos, period prints, and reproductions of trading cards illustrate the text while adding color to the pages. . . . This nicely designed book provides plenty of on-the-field drama as well as pertinent information in a smoothly written overview of the touchdown." Booklist

Thomas, Keltie
   How football works; illustrated by Stephen MacEachern. Owlkids 2010 64p il (How sports work) $22.95; pa $12.95
Grades: 3 4 5   **796.332**
   1. Football
   ISBN 978-1-897349-87-8; 1-897349-87-4; 978-1-897349-88-5 pa; 1-897349-88-2 pa

"A wide range of football facts are packed into every double-page spread of this picture-book overview of the sport. The covered topics include the history of the game, the changing turf of the NFL, equipment, and some of the most memorable clashes and players. Each short chapter is laid out with boxes containing a few paragraphs of information, along with color photos and illustrations. Young readers are bound to enjoy this browser-friendly approach, which presents an array of facts that can be absorbed quickly." Booklist

796.334   Soccer (Association football)

Bazemore, Suzanne
   Soccer: how it works. Capstone Press 2010 48p il (Science of sports) lib bdg $29.32; pa $7.95
Grades: 4 5 6 7   **796.334**
   1. Soccer
   ISBN 978-1-4296-4025-1 lib bdg; 1-4296-4025-1 lib bdg; 978-1-4296-4876-9 pa; 1-4296-4876-7 pa

"Describes the science behind the sport of soccer, including kicking, ball control, and goalkeeping." Publisher's note

Includes glossary

Forest, Christopher
   Play soccer like a pro; key skills and tips. Capstone Press 2011 32p il (Play like the pros) lib bdg $25.32; pa $6.95
Grades: 3 4 5   **796.334**
   1. Soccer
   ISBN 978-1-4296-4827-1 lib bdg; 1-4296-4827-9 lib bdg; 978-1-4296-5647-4 pa; 1-4296-5647-6 pa

LC 2010007244

"Provides instructional tips on how to improve one's soccer skills, including quotes and advice from professional coaches and athletes." Publisher's note

Includes glossary and bibliographical references

Gibbons, Gail

My soccer book. HarperCollins Pubs. 2000 un il $6.99

Grades: K 1 2   **796.334**

   1. Soccer 2. Soccer -- Juvenile literature

   ISBN 0-688-17138-9

                            LC 99-34514

Briefly describes the equipment, terminology, rules, positions, and plays of one of the world's most popular games

This "small, snappily designed book [is] attractive, accessible. . . . Diverse groups of children, drawn in Gibbons' typically bright colors and cheery style, demonstrate sports equipment and game plays." Booklist

Includes glossary

Gifford, Clive

The **Kingfisher** soccer encyclopedia. Kingfisher 2010 144p il $19.99

Grades: 5 6 7 8   **796.334**

   1. Reference books 2. Soccer -- Encyclopedias

   ISBN 978-0-7534-6397-0; 0-7534-6397-0

   First published 2006

"Gifford does an excellent job of covering most aspects of the game from its history of a hundred-plus years to its current rules and tactics, teams, competitions, and famous players. Each section is clearly identified and provides additional information about the game. . . . Students involved in the sport or interested in specific teams or players will appreciate this book." Voice Youth Advocates

Includes glossary and bibliographical references

My first soccer book; Clive Gifford. Kingfisher 2012 48 p. col. ill. (hardcover) $12.99

Grades: 2 3 4   **796.334**

   1. Soccer 2. Soccer -- Training

   ISBN 0753467836; 9780753467831

                        LC 2012036444

In this children's picture book about soccer, "[Clive] Gifford discusses the field, positions, gear, and basic rules, then moves on to warm-ups and stretching. The book's main section offers double-page spreads on topics such as ball control, passing, shooting, goalkeeping, tackling, and paying attention to the referee." (Booklist)

Soccer; Clive Gifford. 1st ed. PowerKids Press 2009 32 p. col. ill. (Personal best) (library) $26.50

Grades: 4 5 6 7 8   **796.334**

   1. Soccer

   ISBN 9781404244412; 1404244417

                        LC 2007042997

This guide to soccer "offers well-organized and easy-to-follow instructions, focusing on rules, clothing, specific skills, and competitions. . . . Informative, readable." SLJ

Soccer skills; Clive Gifford. Kingfisher 2005 48 p. col. ill. (paperback) $6.99

Grades: 4 5 6   **796.334**

   1. Soccer -- Training 2. Soccer -- Training -- Juvenile literature.

   ISBN 0753459329; 9780753459324

                        LC 2005006232

This book presents an "overview of tactics and moves for beginning soccer players by a well-known expert in the field. After an initial chapter on referees and rules, [Clive]

Gifford goes on to ball control, various passing techniques, and shooting and tacking skills. Four pages are devoted to goaltending. The text consists of brief paragraphs of information placed around the illustrations rather than a flowing narrative." (School Library Journal)

Includes bibliographical references (p. 47) and index.

Guillain, Charlotte

Soccer. Heinemann Library 2009 24p il (Sports and my body) lib bdg $21.36; pa $6.49

Grades: 1 2   **796.334**

   1. Soccer

   ISBN 978-1-4329-3456-9 lib bdg; 1-4329-3456-2 lib bdg; 978-1-4329-3461-3 pa; 1-4329-3461-9 pa

                        LC 2009-7082

Learn what soccer is, how it can help them stay healthy, and how they can play soccer safely.

This book relates "activity to health . . . [and] explains that in order to stay healthy, children should get plenty of rest, eat healthy food, and drink plenty of water." SLJ

Includes glossary

Hornby, Hugh

Soccer; written by Hugh Hornby; photographed by Andy Crawford. DK Pub. 2008 70p il (DK eyewitness books) $15.99

Grades: 4 5 6 7   **796.334**

   1. Soccer

   ISBN 978-0-7566-3779-8; 0-7566-3779-1

                        LC 2008276290

   First published 2000

Examines all aspects of the game of soccer: its history, rules, techniques, tactics, equipment, playing fields, competitive play, and more.

Hyde, Natalie

Soccer science. Crabtree Pub. Co. 2009 32p il (Sports science) lib bdg $26.60; pa $8.95

Grades: 3 4 5 6   **796.334**

   1. Soccer

   ISBN 978-0-7787-4537-2 lib bdg; 0-7787-4537-6 lib bdg; 978-0-7787-4554-9 pa; 0-7787-4554-6 pa

                        LC 2008-46276

This book approachs soccer "from a scientific angle, describing some of the physics behind [the] pursuit and how athletes can use this knowledge to improve performance. . . . Fascinating facts . . . [such as] information about the soccer robots in the RoboCup, are presented in a captivating, lively manner. . . . The layout features colorful text boxes interspersed among photographs." SLJ

Includes glossary

Jennings, Madeleine

Soccer step-by-step; [by] Madeleine Jennings and Ian Howe. Rosen Central 2010 95p il (Skills in motion) lib bdg $31.95

Grades: 5 6 7 8   **796.334**

   1. Soccer

   ISBN 978-1-4358-3362-3; 1-4358-3362-7

                        LC 2009-12538

Presents instructions on the basic movements of soccer, including passing, shooting, and goalkeeping.

"Colorful photographs show the entire movement of each skill presented, giving new meaning to the term 'step-by-step.' Progression borders at the bottom of the pages highlight the salient points to notice in performing each skill from beginning to end." SLJ

Includes bibliographical references

Kassouf, Jeff

Soccer. Norwood House Press 2011 64p il (Girls play to win) lib bdg $26.60

Grades: 4 5 6 7   **796.334**

1. Soccer

ISBN 978-1-59953-464-0; 1-59953-464-9

LC 2011011037

Covers the history, rules, fundamentals, and significant personalities of the sport of women's soccer. Topics include: techniques, strategies, competitive events, and equipment.

Includes glossary and bibliographical references

Kelley, K. C.

Soccer. Cherry Lake Pub. 2008 32p il (Innovation in sports) lib bdg $27.07

Grades: 4 5 6 7   **796.334**

1. Soccer

ISBN 978-1-60279-261-6 lib bdg; 1-60279-261-5 lib bdg

LC 2008006749

This describes soccer history, rules, styles of play, equipment, and innovators

This "stands out by emphasizing monumental shifts and advances in the events themselves. . . . Concise and occasionally revelatory." Booklist

Includes glossary and bibliographical references

Stewart, Mark

★ Goal!: the fire and fury of soccer's greatest moment; [by] Mark Stewart and Mike Kennedy. Millbrook Press 2010 64p il lib bdg $27.93

Grades: 5 6 7 8   **796.334**

1. Soccer

ISBN 978-0-8225-8754-5 lib bdg; 0-8225-8754-8 lib bdg

LC 2009014098

"This well-written book explores the nuances of scoring in the world's most popular sport. A quick history of the game lays the groundwork with details that may be new to even hard-core fans. The second chapter jumps right into the good stuff with descriptions of 10 of the most famous goals. . . . Also included is a rundown of the best male and female scorers from the early twentieth century to the present and weird anomalies and amusing anecdotes from soccer lore." Booklist

Wendorff, Anne

Soccer. Bellwether Media 2010 24p il (Blastoff! readers. My first sports) $19.95

Grades: K 1 2 3   **796.334**

1. Soccer

ISBN 978-1-60014-329-8; 1-60014-329-6

LC 2009-8183

"Simple text and full color photographs introduce beginning readers to the sport of soccer." Publisher's note

Includes glossary and bibliographical references

Woods, Mark

Goal! soccer facts and stats. [by] Mark Woods and Ruth Owen. Gareth Stevens Pub. 2011 32p il (Top score math) lib bdg $26.60

Grades: 4 5 6   **796.334**

1. Soccer

ISBN 978-1-4339-5015-5; 1-4339-501505

LC 2010029686

This book, "chock-full of numbers, presents 'facts and stats' associated with [soccer]. Figures include sports records, players' heights, jersey numbers, and surfing speeds. . . . [The book succeeds] at entertaining and instructing fans through engaging text and quiz challenges." Horn Book Guide

Includes glossary

796.34   Racket games

Smolka, Bo

Lacrosse. Norwood House Press 2011 64p il (Girls play to win) lib bdg $26.60

Grades: 4 5 6 7   **796.34**

1. Lacrosse

ISBN 978-1-59953-463-3; 1-59953-463-0

LC 2011011050

Covers the history, rules, fundamentals, and significant personalities of the sport of women's lacrosse. Topics include: techniques, strategies, competitive events, and equipment.

Includes glossary and bibliographical references

796.342   Tennis (Lawn tennis)

Bow, Patricia

Tennis science. Crabtree Pub. Co. 2009 32p il (Sports science) lib bdg $26.60; pa $8.95

Grades: 3 4 5 6   **796.342**

1. Tennis

ISBN 978-0-7787-4539-6 lib bdg; 0-7787-4539-2 lib bdg; 978-0-7787-4556-3 pa; 0-7787-4556-2 pa

LC 2008-48874

This book approachs tennis "from a scientific angle, describing some of the physics behind [the] pursuit and how athletes can use this knowledge to improve performance. . . . Fascinating facts . . . are presented in a captivating, lively manner. . . . The layout features colorful text boxes interspersed among photographs." SLJ

Includes glossary and bibliographical references

Gifford, Clive

Tennis; [by] Clive Gifford. Sea-to-Sea Publications 2009 30p il (Know your sport) lib bdg $27.10

Grades: 5 6 7 8   **796.342**

1. Tennis

ISBN 978-1-59771-153-1 lib bdg; 1-59771-153-5 lib bdg

LC 2008-7322

"Describes the equipment, courts, training, moves, and competitions of tennis. Includes step-by-step descriptions of moves." Publisher's note

Includes glossary

Marsico, Katie

Tennis; [by] Katie Marsico and Cecilia Minden. Cherry Lake Pub. 2009 32p il (Real world math: Sports) lib bdg $27.07

Grades: 4 5 6   **796.342**

1. Tennis 2. Arithmetic

ISBN 978-1-60279-248-7 lib bdg; 1-60279-248-8 lib bdg

LC 2008-1179

This book "starts with a short story on the history of [tennis], fundamental rules, and a math challenge in every chapter. . . . [This book] will pique your imagination." Sci Books Films

Includes glossary and bibliographical references

Wendorff, Anne

Tennis. Bellwether Media 2010 24p il (Blastoff! readers. My first sports) $19.95

Grades: K 1 2 3   **796.342**

1. Tennis

ISBN 978-1-60014-328-1; 1-60014-328-8

LC 2009-8188

"Simple text and full color photographs introduce beginning readers to the sport of tennis." Publisher's note

Includes glossary and bibliographical references

Woods, Mark

Ace! tennis facts and stats. [by] Mark Woods and Ruth Owen. Gareth Stevens Pub. 2011 32p il (Top score math) lib bdg $26.60

Grades: 4 5 6   **796.342**

1. Tennis

ISBN 978-1-4339-4986-9; 1-4339-4986-9

LC 2010025704

This book, "chock-full of numbers, presents 'facts and stats' associated with [tennis]. Figures include sports records, players' heights, jersey numbers, and surfing speeds. . . . [The book succeeds] at entertaining and instructing fans through engaging text and quiz challenges." Horn Book Guide

796.352 Golf

Freedman, Russell

Babe Didrikson Zaharias; the making of a champion. Clarion Bks. 1999 192p il $18

Grades: 5 6 7 8 9 10   **796.352**

1. Women athletes 2. Golfers 3. Hurdlers 4. High jumpers 5. Javelin throwers 6. Olympic athletes 7. Athletes -- United States -- Biography -- Juvenile literature 8. Women athletes -- United States -- Biography -- Juvenile literature

ISBN 0-395-63367-2

LC 98-50208

A biography of Babe Didrikson, who broke records in golf, track and field, and other sports, at a time when there were few opportunities for female athletes

"Freedman's measured yet lively style captures the spirit of the great athlete. . . . Plenty of black-and-white photos capture Babe's spirit and dashing good looks; the documentation . . . is impeccable." Horn Book

Includes bibliographical references

Gifford, Clive

Golf: from tee to green; the essential guide for young golfers. Sea-to-Sea Publications 2010 64p il (Know your sport) $16.99

Grades: 5 6 7 8   **796.352**

1. Golf

ISBN 978-1-59771-217-0; 1-59771-217-5

LC 2008045861

Presents an instructional guide to the sport of golf, with information on different aspects of play and the equipment used.

"This book will be welcomed by young golf enthusiasts, whether they're beginners or experienced players. . . . A useful and attractive guide." Horn Book Guide

Includes bibliographical references

Kelley, K. C.

Golf. Cherry Lake Pub. 2009 32p il (Innovation in sports) lib bdg $27.07

Grades: 4 5 6 7   **796.352**

1. Golf

ISBN 978-1-60279-262-3 lib bdg; 1-60279-262-3 lib bdg

LC 2008002045

This describes golf history, rules, balls, and club technology, and innovators

This "stands out by emphasizing monumental shifts and advances in the events themselves. . . . Concise and occasionally revelatory." Booklist

Includes bibliographical references

Michelson, Richard

Twice as good; the story of William Powell and clearview, the only golf course designed, built and owned by an African-American. written by Richard Michelson; illustrated by Eric Velasquez. Sleeping Bear Press 2011 32 p. col. ill. $16.95

Grades: 2 3 4   **796.352**

1. African American businesspeople 2. Golfers -- United States -- Biography 3. Discrimination in sports 4. Golf course architects -- United States -- Biography 5. Golf courses -- United States -- Design and construction -- History -- Juvenile literature

ISBN 1585364665; 9781585364664

LC 2011029114

This children's picture book tells the story of "Willie Powell . . . [who] dreamed of becoming a professional golfer, but his accomplishments went far beyond playing the game of golf. Willie was often denied the opportunity to play golf because he was African American. Determined, he decided to build his own course, and welcome people of all color to play golf." (Publisher's note)

"An inspirational story, suitable for Black History Month and for children interested in the game of golf." LJ

Webster, Christine

Masters Golf Tournament. Weigl Publishers 2009 32p il map (Sporting championships) lib bdg $26; pa $9.95

Grades: 3 4 5   **796.352**

1. Golf

ISBN 978-1-60596-640-3 lib bdg; 1-60596-640-1 lib bdg; 978-1-60596-641-0 pa; 1-60596-641-X pa

LC 2009-12346

This sets the Masters Golf Tournament "within the context of the sport and explains what you need to know when watching the big [event]." Booklist

Includes glossary and bibliographical references

796.357 Baseball

Adler, David A., 1947-
Lou Gehrig; the luckiest man. illustrated by Terry Widener. Harcourt Brace & Co. 1997 un il $17; pa $7
Grades: 2 3 4   **796.357**
1. Baseball players 2. Baseball -- Biography
ISBN 0-15-200523-4; 0-15-202483-3 pa
LC 95-7997
Traces the life of the Yankees' star ballplayer, focusing on his character and his struggle with the terminal disease amyotrophic lateral sclerosis

"Adler's restrained tone makes his description of Gehrig's stoic and uncomplaining struggle all the more moving. The illustrations, meticulously detailed . . . also pack an emotional wallop." Horn Book Guide

A **picture** book of Jackie Robinson; illustrated by Robert Casilla. Holiday House 1994 un il $17.95; pa $6.95
Grades: 1 2 3   **796.357**
1. Baseball players 2. African American athletes 3. Army officers 4. Baseball -- Biography
ISBN 0-8234-1122-2; 0-8234-1304-7 pa
LC 93-27224
"A brief look at the life of baseball great Jackie Robinson. The subject's childhood, sporting accomplishments, and later endeavors are touched upon, as are the bigotry and prejudice he faced as the first African American to play in the major leagues. . . . Casilla's full-and double-page watercolors provide attractive backgrounds for the text. A sound introduction to a significant figure." SLJ

Bertoletti, John C.
How baseball managers use math; math curriculum consultant: Rhea A. Stewart. Chelsea Clubhouse 2010 32p il (Math in the real world) lib bdg $28
Grades: 4 5 6   **796.357**
1. Baseball 2. Mathematics 3. Vocational guidance
ISBN 978-1-60413-604-3 lib bdg; 1-60413-604-9 lib bdg
LC 2009-16265
"The layout for [this] slim [title] is bright and colorful with a photograph and a 'You Do the Math' problem to solve and large, easy-to-read text on every spread. An answer key is included in the back matter, along with a page detailing the career choices and the educational requirements. . . . [It] includes such topics as how managers rely on player statistics to make decisions and why the pitch count is important to monitor. [This title] would be useful to supplement lessons on mathematics. [It] will also appeal to students wanting to learn more about math as it relates to specific careers." SLJ

Includes glossary and bibliographical references

Bildner, Phil
★ The **unforgettable** season; the story of Joe DiMaggio, Ted Williams and the record-setting summer of '41. il-

lustrated by S. D. Schindler. G. P. Putnam's Sons 2011 un il $16.99
Grades: 1 2 3   **796.357**
1. Baseball 2. Baseball players 3. Baseball managers 4. Baseball -- History -- Juvenile literature
ISBN 978-0-399-25501-4; 0-399-25501-X
LC 2010007382
"In a narrative that's conversational yet informative, Bildner dives into the baseball season of 1941, alternately focusing on Yankee slugger DiMaggio, who had a 56-game hitting streak, and Red Sox star Williams, who ended the season with a batting average of .406. Bildner builds suspense with taut descriptions of critical on-field moments . . . while Schindler's paintings capture the ballpark energy." Publ Wkly

Bow, James
Baseball science. Crabtree Pub. 2009 32p il (Sports science) lib bdg $26.60; pa $8.95
Grades: 3 4 5 6   **796.357**
1. Baseball
ISBN 978-0-7787-4534-1 lib bdg; 0-7787-4534-1 lib bdg; 978-0-7787-4551-8 pa; 0-7787-4551-1 pa
LC 2008-46274
This describes baseball skills and techniques from a scientific point of view.

Includes glossary and bibliographical references

Buckley, James
Ultimate guide to baseball. Shoreline Pub. 2010 160p il $30; pa $7.99
Grades: 4 5 6 7   **796.357**
1. Baseball
ISBN 978-0-531-20750-5; 0-531-20750-1; 978-0-531-21021-5 pa; 0-531-21021-9 pa
LC 2009043684
"This is a wide-ranging, brisk overview of the game. Sections briefly skim baseball history, hitting, pitching, defense and baserunning, and the World Series. Each major league team is introduced in a thumbnail sketch. . . . Other topics include baseball slang and nicknames, the 11 ways to get on base, and the author's choices for the best defensive players of all time. . . . Buckley writes with a lightly humorous touch that should appeal to fans and browsers." SLJ

Includes bibliographical references

Child's World (Firm)
The **Child's** World encyclopedia of baseball; by James Buckley, Jr. . . . [et al.] Child's World 2009 5v il set $247.75
Grades: 4 5 6 7 8   **796.357**
1. Baseball -- Encyclopedias
ISBN 978-1-60253-175-8 set; 1-60253-175-7 set
LC 2008039461
In this baseball encyclopedia, the authors "definitely convey an enthusiasm for their subject." Booklist

Coleman, Janet Wyman
Baseball for everyone; stories from the great game. by Janet Wyman Coleman with Elizabeth V. Warren. Abrams 2003 48p il $16.95

Grades: 4 5 6 **796.357**
1. Baseball
ISBN 0-8109-4580-0

LC 2002-155971

An illustrated history of baseball, covering the origins of the game, some of its best-known players, and significant changes in rules and practices throughout the nineteenth and twentieth centuries

"Drawing on The Perfect Game, Warren's adult book and exhibit of the same name at New York's American Folk Art Museum, . . . this elegant volume may well be irresistible to fans of America's favorite pastime. . . . [This offers] lively, informative text . . . enticingly packaged with a plethora of photographs, memorabilia and often astonishing folk art." Publ Wkly

Cook, Sally
Hey batta batta swing! the wild old days of baseball. [by] Sally Cook & James Charlton; illustrated by Ross MacDonald. Margaret K. McElderry Books 2007 48p il $17.99
Grades: 3 4 5 6 **796.357**
1. Baseball 2. Baseball -- History -- Juvenile literature
ISBN 978-1-4169-1207-1; 1-4169-1207-X

LC 2006-08132

"The authors present a lively, puckish history of baseball's earliest years, relating what young readers actually want to know. . . . Boldface words in the text identify jargon, most of which is still used today, and definitions stud the page borders. The jaunty tone is flawlessly matched by MacDonald's illustrations, with their wriggling lines and Katzenjammer Kids colors." Booklist

Curlee, Lynn
★ Ballpark; the story of America's baseball fields. Atheneum Books for Young Readers 2005 41p il $17.95
Grades: 3 4 5 6 **796.357**
1. Baseball 2. Stadiums 3. Baseball fields -- History -- Juvenile literature
ISBN 0-689-86742-5

LC 2003-23144

This is a "succinct and thoughtful overview. . . . Stylized, full-page acrylic paintings add to the nostalgic tone of the book." SLJ

Dreier, David
Baseball; how it works. Capstone Press 2010 48p il (Science of sports) lib bdg $29.32; pa $7.95
Grades: 4 5 6 7 **796.357**
1. Baseball
ISBN 978-1-4296-4020-6 lib bdg; 1-4296-4020-0 lib bdg; 978-1-4296-4872-1 pa; 1-4296-4872-4 pa
"The well-designed layout, featuring glossy color visuals, is stimulating, and the concepts are further reinforced in brief definitions that appear at the bottom of many pages and in an appended glossary. . . . The clever approach will help draw interest and build understanding." Booklist
Includes glossary

Frager, Ray
Baltimore Orioles. ABDO Pub. Co. 2011 48p il (Inside MLB) $31.35

Grades: 4 5 6 **796.357**
1. Baseball
ISBN 978-1-61714-036-5; 1-61714-036-8

LC 2010036557

"Written by [a] professional [sportswriter], peppered with well-chosen quotations and illustrated with photos on every page turn, this [book about the Baltimore Orioles] will interest die-hard baseball fans and is likely to engage reluctant readers." Horn Book Guide
Includes glossary and bibliographical references

Freedman, Lew
Boston Red Sox. ABDO Pub. Co. 2011 48p il (Inside MLB) $31.35
Grades: 4 5 6 **796.357**
1. Baseball
ISBN 9781617140372; 1617140376

LC 2010036554

"Written by [a] professional [sportswriter], peppered with well-chosen quotations and illustrated with photos on every page turn, this [book about the Boston Red Sox] will interest diehard baseball fans and is likely to engage reluctant readers." Horn Book Guide
Includes glossary and bibliographical references

Gibbons, Gail
My baseball book. HarperCollins Pubs. 2000 un il $6.99
Grades: K 1 2 **796.357**
1. Baseball 2. Baseball -- Juvenile literature
ISBN 0-688-17137-0

LC 99-32945

An introduction to baseball, describing the equipment, playing field, rules, players, and process of the game
"The information is well augmented by clearly labeled, colorful drawings." SLJ
Includes glossary

Gitlin, Marty
Softball. Norwood House Press 2011 64p il (Girls play to win) lib bdg $26.60
Grades: 4 5 6 7 **796.357**
1. Softball
ISBN 978-1-59953-465-7; 1-59953-465-7

LC 2011011051

Covers the history, rules, fundamentals, and significant personalities of the sport of women's softball. Topics include: techniques, strategies, competitive events, and equipment.
Includes glossary and bibliographical references

Glaser, Jason
Batter. Gareth Stevens 2011 48p il (Play ball: baseball) lib bdg $31.95; pa $14.05; ebook $31.95
Grades: K 1 2 3 **796.357**
1. Baseball
ISBN 978-1-4339-4619-6 lib bdg; 1-4339-4619-X lib bdg; 978-1-4339-4620-2 pa; 1-4339-4620-2 pa; 978-1-4339-4622-6 ebook

LC 2010039132

"A well-conceived, up-to-date look at the particular skills needed to play [batter] in baseball. [This] volume discusses the [batter's] evolution through baseball history, describes the player's responsibilities during games, and highlights famous players. Clearly written and amply illustrated with photos of recent and current stars, [this book offers] solid information for young baseballers and casual fans alike." Horn Book Guide

Includes glossary and bibliographical references

Catcher. Gareth Stevens Pub. 2011 48p il (Play ball: baseball) lib bdg $31.95

Grades: K 1 2 3   **796.357**
1. Baseball
ISBN 9781433944840 pa; 9781433944833 lib bdg
LC 2010035720

"A well-conceived, up-to-date look at the particular skills needed to play [catcher] in baseball. [This] volume discusses the [catcher's] evolution through baseball history, describes the player's responsibilities during games, and highlights famous players. Clearly written and amply illustrated with photos of recent and current stars, [this book offers] solid information for young baseballers and casual fans alike." Horn Book Guide

Infielders. Gareth Stevens 2011 48p il (Play ball: baseball) lib bdg $31.95; pa $14.05; e-book $31.95

Grades: K 1 2 3   **796.357**
1. Baseball
ISBN 978-1-4339-4487-1 lib bdg; 1-4339-4487-1 lib bdg; 978-1-4339-4488-8 pa; 1-4339-4488-X pa; 987-1-4339-4490-1 e-book
LC 2010026667

"A well-conceived, up-to-date look at the particular skills needed to play [infield] in baseball. [This] volume discusses the [infielder's] evolution through baseball history, describes the player's responsibilities during games, and highlights famous players. Clearly written and amply illustrated with photos of recent and current stars, [this book offers] solid information for young baseballers and casual fans alike." Horn Book Guide

Outfielders. Gareth Stevens 2011 48p il (Play ball: baseball) lib bdg $31.95; pa $14.05; e-book $31.95

Grades: K 1 2 3   **796.357**
1. Baseball
ISBN 978-1-4339-4491-8 lib bdg; 1-4339-4491-8 lib bdg; 978-1-4339-4492-5 pa; 1-4339-4492-5 pa; 978-1-4339-4494-9 e-book
LC 2010030690

"A well-conceived, up-to-date look at the particular skills needed to play [outfield] in baseball. [This] volume discusses the [outfielder's] evolution through baseball history, describes the player's responsibilities during games, and highlights famous players. Clearly written and amply illustrated with photos of recent and current stars, [this book offers] solid information for young baseballers and casual fans alike." Horn Book Guide

Includes glossary and bibliographical references

Pitcher. Gareth Stevens 2011 48p il (Play ball: baseball) lib bdg $31.95; pa $14.05; ebook $31.95

Grades: K 1 2 3   **796.357**
1. Baseball
ISBN 978-1-4339-4495-6 lib bdg; 1-4339-4495-2 lib bdg; 978-1-4339-4496-3 pa; 1-4339-4496-3 pa; 978-1-4339-4498-7 ebook
LC 2010039136

"A well-conceived, up-to-date look at the particular skills needed to play [pitcher] in baseball. [This] volume discusses the [pitcher's] evolution through baseball history, describes the player's responsibilities during games, and highlights famous players. Clearly written and amply illustrated with photos of recent and current stars, [this book offers] solid information for young baseballers and casual fans alike." Horn Book Guide

Includes glossary and bibliographical references

Golenbock, Peter
★ **Hank** Aaron; brave in every way. illustrated by Paul Lee. Harcourt 2001 un il $16

Grades: 1 2 3   **796.357**
1. Baseball players 2. African American athletes 3. Baseball -- Biography 4. Baseball players -- United States -- Biography -- Juvenile literature
ISBN 0-15-202093-4
LC 00-8855

A biography of the Hall of Fame baseball player who broke Babe Ruth's career home run record

"This richly illustrated biography . . . deftly tells the athlete's story. . . . Lee's strong, full-page acrylic illustrations in rich tones and textures work well and give the story depth and intensity." SLJ

Teammates; written by Peter Golenbock; designed and illustrated by Paul Bacon. Harcourt Brace Jovanovich 1990 un il $16; pa $7

Grades: 1 2 3 4   **796.357**
1. Baseball players 2. African American athletes 3. Army officers 4. Baseball -- Biography 5. Baseball -- History -- Juvenile literature
ISBN 0-15-200603-6; 0-15-284286-1 pa
LC 89-38166

Describes the racial prejudice experienced by Jackie Robinson when he joined the Brooklyn Dodgers and became the first black player in Major League baseball and depicts the acceptance and support he received from his white teammate Pee Wee Reese

"Golenbock's bold and lucid style distills this difficult issue, and brings a dramatic tale vividly to life. Bacon's spare, nostalgic watercolors, in addition to providing fond glimpses of baseball lore, present a haunting portrait of one man's isolation. Historic photographs of the major characters add interest and a touch of stark reality to an unusual story, beautifully rendered." Publ Wkly

Hetrick, Hans
Play baseball like a pro; key skills and tips. Capstone Press 2011 32p il (Play like the pros) lib bdg $25.32; pa $6.95

Grades: 3 4 5   **796.357**
1. Baseball
ISBN 978-1-4296-4824-0 lib bdg; 1-4296-4824-4 lib bdg; 978-1-4296-5644-3 pa; 1-4296-5644-1 pa
LC 2010007241

"Provides instructional tips on how to improve one's baseball skills, including quotes and advice from professional coaches and athletes." Publisher's note

Includes glossary and bibliographical references

Jennings, Madeleine

Baseball step-by-step; [by] Madeleine Jennings, Alan Smith, and Alan Bloomfield. Rosen Central 2009 95p il (Skills in motion) lib bdg $31.95

Grades: 5 6 7 8   **796.357**

1. Baseball

ISBN 978-1-4358-3361-6; 1-4358-3361-9

         LC 2009-13246

An introduction to the skills needed to play baseball uses a sequence of stop-action images and text instructions to illustrate the moves needed to pitch, catch, field, hit, and run bases.

"Colorful photographs show the entire movement of each skill presented, giving new meaning to the term 'step-by-step.' Progression borders at the bottom of the pages highlight the salient points to notice in performing each skill from beginning to end." SLJ

Includes bibliographical references

Kelly, David A.

Miracle mud: Lena Blackburne and the secret mud that changed baseball. by David A. Kelly; illustrated by Oliver Dominguez. Milbrook Press 2013 32 p. (lib. bdg.: alk paper) &16.95

Grades: 3 4 5   **796.357**

1. Baseball -- History 2. Picture books for children 3. Sports -- United States -- Marketing -- Juvenile literature 4. Inventors -- United States -- Biography -- Juvenilve literature 5. Baseball players -- United States -- Biography -- Juvenile literature 6. Baseball -- United States -- Equipment and supplies -- Juvenile literature

ISBN 0761380922; 9780761380924

         LC 2012020917

This children's picture book is a biography of baseball player Lena Blackburne. "Blackburne was never an outstanding player, but he will go down in history for developing a solution to the wet, soggy baseballs that could be difficult to throw during a game. One day after fishing, he stepped in some soft, gooey mud and an idea was born. Because the mud took the shine off any new white baseball, he began to sell it." (School Library Journal)

Kisseloff, Jeff

Who is baseball's greatest pitcher? Cricket Bks. 2003 181p il $15.95

Grades: 5 6 7 8   **796.357**

1. Baseball

ISBN 0-8126-2685-0

         LC 2003-1245

Asks the reader to compare the statistics for thirty-three of baseball's greatest starting pitchers and decide who is the best

"Accomplishments and anecdotes are related in an informative and entertaining manner. . . . Anyone who enjoys baseball will be delighted with this information-packed, informal book." SLJ

Includes bibliographical references

Lipsyte, Robert

★ Heroes of baseball; the men who made it America's favorite game. [by] Robert Lipsyte. Atheneum Books for Young Readers 2006 92p il $19.95

Grades: 4 5 6 7   **796.357**

1. Baseball -- Biography 2. Baseball players -- Juvenile literature

ISBN 0-689-86741-7; 978-0-689-86741-5

         LC 2005010841

"Using as a focus some of baseball's greats—Big Al Spalding, Babe Ruth, Mickey Mantle, Jackie Robinson, Curt Flood . . . —Lipsyte offers a strong history of the game and its place in American culture. . . . Although much of this material, including the pictures, might be familiar to young readers already absorbed in the game, it is nicely laid out and colorfully formatted. Lipsyte has a clear, vivid style." Booklist

Includes glossary and bibliographical references

McClellan, Ray

Baseball. Bellwether media 2010 24p il (Blastoff! readers. My first sports) $19.95

Grades: K 1 2 3   **796.357**

1. Baseball

ISBN 978-1-60014-277-2; 1-60014-277-X

         LC 2009-8157

"Simple text and full color photographs introduce beginning readers to the sport of baseball." Publisher's note

Includes glossary and bibliographical references

Moss, Marissa

Barbed wire baseball; by Marissa Moss; illustrated by Yuko Shimizu. Abrams Books for Young Readers 2013 48 p. (reinforced) $18.95

Grades: 3 4 5   **796.357**

1. Baseball -- History 2. Japanese Americans -- Evacuation and relocation, 1942-1945 -- Juvenile literature 3. World War, 1939-1945 -- Juvenile literature 4. Baseball -- United States -- History -- 20th century -- Juvenile literature

ISBN 1419705210; 9781419705212

         LC 2012010021

This children's book, by Marissa Moss, illustrated by Yuko Shimizu, profiles a 1940s Japanese American baseball player. "Kenichi 'Zeni' Zenimura dreams of playing professional baseball, . . . [and] he grows up to be a successful player, playing with Babe Ruth and Lou Gehrig! When the Japanese attack Pearl Harbor in 1941, Zeni and his family are sent to one of ten internment camps. . . . Zeni brings the game of baseball to the camp, along with a sense of hope." (Publisher's note)

Nelson, Kadir

★ We are the ship; the story of Negro League baseball. words and paintings by Kadir Nelson; forward by Hank Aaron. Jump at the Sun 2008 88p il $18.99

Grades: 2 3 4   **796.357**

1. Baseball 2. Negro leagues 3. African American athletes 4. Negro leagues -- History -- Juvenile literature 5. African American baseball players -- Juvenile literature 6. Baseball -- United States -- History -- Juvenile literature

ISBN 978-0-7868-0832-8; 0-7868-0832-2

Awarded the Sibert Medal, 2009

The author "delivers a history of the Negro Leagues in a sumptuous volume that no baseball fan should be without. Using a folksy vernacular, a fictional player gives an insider account of segregated baseball. . . . As illuminating as the text is, Nelson's muscular paintings serve as the true draw. His larger-than-life players have oversized hands, elongated bodies and near-impossible athleticism." Publ Wkly

Nevius, Carol

    Baseball hour; illustrated by Bill Thomson. Marshall Cavendish 2008 un il $16.99

Grades: 1 2 3   **796.357**

    1. Baseball

    ISBN 978-0-7614-5380-2; 0-7614-5380-6

                               LC 2007014254

This "picture book follows a multicultural group of boys and girls through their team's baseball practice. . . . The rhyming, rhythmic text works well enough, but . . . the photorealistic artwork, which a note describes as 'rendered in mixed media,' steal the show. Technically impressive, the black, white, and sepia illustrations capture form, details, action, and gesture well." Booklist

Rappaport, Doreen

    Dirt on their skirts; the story of the young women who won the world championship. [by] Doreen Rappaport, Lyndall Callan; pictures by E.B. Lewis. Dial Bks. for Young Readers 1999 un il $16.99

Grades: K 1 2 3   **796.357**

    1. Baseball -- Fiction

    ISBN 0-8037-2042-4

                                LC 98-47080

Margaret experiences the excitement of watching the 1946 championship game of the All-American Girls Professional Baseball League as it goes into extra innings.

"With its economy of language and telling period details, this book provides an exciting slice of sports history and an appealing bit of Americana. . . . Lewis's finely wrought watercolor paintings deftly capture the crowd and the action on the field." SLJ

Rappoport, Ken

    Alex Rodriguez; champion baseball star. by Ken Rappoport. Enslow Publishers 2013 48 p. col. ill. (Sports star champions) (library) $23.93

Grades: 4 5 6 7   **796.357**

    1. Baseball players -- Biography 2. Baseball players -- United States -- Biography -- Juvenile literature

    ISBN 0766040267; 9780766040267

                              LC 2011043754

"Of the forty-three glossy story pages in the book, fifteen describe . . . [baseball player Alex Rodriguez's] career from 2004 forward. A Career Statistics Chart follows his performance through 2011. Color photos include A-Rod's early baseball career through 2011. Many of his impressive stats are discussed, including being the only major league player to hit thirty home runs and drive in one hundred runs in thirteen consecutive seasons." (Children's Literature)

    Derek Jeter; champion baseball star. by Ken Rappoport. Enslow Publishers 2013 48 p. col. ill. (Sports star champions) (library) $23.93

Grades: 4 5 6 7   **796.357**

    1. Baseball players -- Biography 2. Baseball players

-- United States -- Biography -- Juvenile literature

    ISBN 0766040259; 9780766040250

                              LC 2011033514

This book by Ken Rappoport, part of the Sports Star Champions series, presents a biography of "New York Yankees shortstop" Derek Jeter, who "has led the Yankees to five World Series titles and has won several individual awards." (Publisher's note) The "book ends with career statistics, the player's address, and a brief list for further reading." (School Library Journal)

Robinson, Sharon, 1950-

    Jackie Robinson; American hero. by Sharon Robinson. Scholastic, Inc. 2013 48 p. $16.99

Grades: 4 5 6   **796.357**

    1. Picture books for children 2. African American baseball players -- Biography -- Juvenile literature 3. Baseball players -- United States -- Biography -- Juvenile literature

    ISBN 054556915X; 9780545569156

                              LC 2012046058

This book by Jackie Robinson's daughter Sharon Robinson is a biography of "the famous African American baseball player" that looks at "the significance of how a young black ballplayer broke the racial barrier and helped desegregate Major League Baseball. . . . The author gives a brief overview from childhood, to marriage, to death while showcasing myriad black-and-white family photos." (School Library Journal)

Skead, Robert

    Something to prove; the great Satchel Paige vs. rookie Joe DiMaggio. by Robert Skead; illustrated by Floyd Cooper. Carolrhoda Books 2013 32 p. ill. (library) $16.95

Grades: 2 3 4 5   **796.357**

    1. Baseball -- Juvenile literature 2. Baseball players -- United States -- Social conditions -- Juvenile literature 3. Discrimination in baseball -- United States -- History -- Juvenile literature

    ISBN 0761366199; 9780761366195

                              LC 2012019709

This children's book, by Robert Skead, tells how "in 1936, the New York Yankees wanted to test a hot prospect named Joe DiMaggio to see if he was ready for the big leagues. They knew just the ballplayer to call: Satchel Paige, the best pitcher anywhere, black or white. For the game, Paige joined a group of amateur African American players, and they faced off against a team of white major leaguers plus young DiMaggio." (Publisher's note)

Smith, Charles R., 1969-

    Diamond life; baseball sights, sounds, and swings. Orchard Bks. 2004 28p il $15.95

Grades: 2 3 4   **796.357**

    1. Baseball

    ISBN 0-439-43180-8

"Smith captures the colorful language and vivid images of the game. . . . The energetic, playful language begs to be read aloud. Combined with bright colors, bold print in a variety of fonts, and exceptional photography, this book is a winner." SLJ

Stars in the shadows; the Negro league all-star game of 1934. Charles R. Smith Jr.; illustrated by Frank Morrison. Atheneum 2012 106 p. ill. (hardcover) $14.99

Grades: 2 3 4   **796.357**

1. Negro leagues 2. African American athletes 3. Radio broadcasting of sports 4. Baseball -- History

ISBN 0689866380; 9780689866388

LC 2011017469

In this chapter book, "[Charles R.] Smith uses a fictional radio sports announcer to introduce the players on both Negro League East-West Classic teams. . . . The story takes place during a time when baseball was segregated and fans voted for their favorite players to make the All-Star roster. Within a basic organization plan of nine innings, or chapters, the author writes in a poetic narrative style." (School Library Journal)

"Some of the best-ever baseball players face off in 1934 at the second annual Negro League All-Star game in Chicago. . . . Cool Papa Bell, Josh Gibson, Willie Wells, Satchel Paige and Oscar Charleston are legendary names despite the segregation that kept them from competing in one integrated league for their entire careers. The concept behind this slim volume is excellent—a story in poems told in nine innings, each inning properly divided into the top of the inning and bottom. Graphite illustrations lend an old-timey feel to the text, and various advertisements, fan comments and even a performance by the Jubilee Singers complete the event." Kirkus

Includes bibliographical references.

Stewart, Mark

Long ball; the legend and lore of the home run. [by] Mark Stewart and Mike Kennedy. Millbrook Press 2006 64p il lib bdg $22.60

Grades: 4 5 6 7   **796.357**

1. Baseball

ISBN 978-0-7613-2779-0 lib bdg; 0-7613-2779-7 lib bdg

LC 2005015041

"The highly readable text is extended by excellent graphics, photographs, and reproductions of baseball cards and magazine covers." Booklist

Includes bibliographical references

Stout, Glenn

Baseball heroes. Houghton Mifflin Harcourt 2011 121p il (Good sports) pa $5.99

Grades: 3 4 5 6   **796.357**

1. Baseball players 2. Army officers 3. Baseball -- Biography

ISBN 978-0-547-41708-0 pa; 0-547-41708-X pa

LC 2010006760

"This strong title . . . focuses on the careers of four trailblazing ballplayers: Hank Aaron, Jackie Robinson, Fernando Valenzuela, and Ila Borders. . . . Stout writes with conviction and does not sugar-coat the hateful, sometimes racially motivated comments these players endured. . . . Stout's action-packed, suspenseful descriptions of milestone games will easily draw young people's interest." Booklist

Tavares, Matt

Becoming Babe Ruth; Matt Tavares. Candlewick Pr 2013 40 p. $16.99

Grades: K 1 2 3   **796.357**

1. Baseball players -- Biography

ISBN 0763656461; 9780763656461

LC 2012942357

Author Matt Tavares presents a biography of George Herman Ruth, more commonly known as Babe Ruth. At "Saint Mary's Industrial School for Boys," George is "expected to study hard and follow a lot of rules. But there is one good thing about Saint Mary's: almost every day, George gets to play baseball. Here, under the watchful eye of Brother Matthias, George evolves as a player and as a man." (Publisher's note)

Teitelbaum, Michael

Baseball; by Michael Teitelbaum. Cherry Lake Pub. 2009 32p il (Innovation in sports) lib bdg $18.95

Grades: 5 6 7 8   **796.357**

1. Baseball

ISBN 978-1-60279-255-5 lib bdg; 1-60279-255-0 lib bdg

LC 2008-2310

This title "traces the many leaps forward in the history of baseball. [It] chronicles innovations that changed the game. . . . Nice-sized color photographs and sidebars . . . accompany the concise and easy-to-follow text." Booklist

Includes glossary and bibliographical references

Thorn, John

First pitch; how baseball began. Beach Ball Books 2011 40p il pa $14.99

Grades: 4 5 6 7   **796.357**

1. Baseball -- History

ISBN 978-1-936310-04-3; 1-936310-04-X

"Packed with vintage images and photographs, this history of baseball takes readers from the origins of the sport to the present day. . . . Thorn . . . writes clearly and eloquently. . . . Fans who think they know baseball may discover they have much to learn." Publ Wkly

Tocher, Timothy

Odd ball; hilarious, unusual, and bizarre baseball moments. illustrated by Stacy Curtis. Marshall Cavendish 2011 64p il $15.99

Grades: 3 4 5   **796.357**

1. Baseball

ISBN 978-0-7614-5813-5; 0-7614-5813-1

LC 2010013847

"Tocher and Curtis serve up an enjoyable, offbeat collection of trivia. . . . Tocher's deftly limned accounts are broadly humorous and supplemented by Curtis's giggle-inducing cartoons. . . . Ranging from baseball's early days to the present, this collection offers an appealing selection of entertaining baseball facts." SLJ

Vernick, Audrey

★ **Brothers** at bat; the true story of an amazing all-brother baseball team. by Audrey Vernick; Illustrated by Steven Salerno. Clarion Books 2012 39 p.

Grades: 3 4 5   **796.357**

1. Brothers 2. Baseball -- History 3. Picture books for children 4. Baseball players -- Biography 5. Baseball teams -- New Jersey -- History 6. Baseball teams -- United States -- History 7. Brothers -- New Jersey -- Biography -- Juvenile literature 8. Brothers -- United

States -- Biography -- Juvenile literature
ISBN 9780547385570

LC 2011025645

This biographical picture book depicts "a time when local baseball was part of the American landscape, one family fielded its own team. The Acerra family numbered 16 children, 12 of whom were brothers who all loved to play baseball. The boys played in high school and later formed their own semi-pro team. They played wherever they could get a good game and were known as highly skilled players and crowd pleasers. They shared a special closeness and loyalty. . . . That loyalty extended to a love of country as six of them fought in World War II. . . . After the war they continued to play in local leagues, with younger brothers taking over when big brothers aged out. In 1997 they were recognized by the Baseball Hall of Fame as the all-time longest playing all-brother team." (Kirkus)

Weatherford, Carole Boston

★ A **Negro** league scrapbook; foreword by Buck O'Neil. Boyds Mills Press 2005 48p il $19.95

Grades: 4 5 6 7   **796.357**
1. Baseball 2. Negro leagues 3. African American athletes
ISBN 1-59078-091-4

LC 2004-19324

"Weatherford's text covers . . . a summation of the history of the Negro Leagues and sections on the pitchers, hitters, utility men, various teams, and so forth. Each topic is briefly covered on a spread of text with black-and-white photos and full-color realia designed to look like a scrapbook. Topics are introduced with a few lines of verse. . . . The book is especially successful in conveying the significance of the Negro Leagues to the black community, and in detailing the realities of segregation. . . . This title succeeds as a thoughtful introduction." SLJ

Winter, Jonah

★ **You** never heard of Willie Mays?! by Jonah Winter; illustrations by Terry Widener. Schwartz & Wade Books 2013 40 p. (trade) $17.99

Grades: K 1 2 3   **796.357**
1. Baseball -- History 2. Baseball players -- United States -- Biography -- Juvenile literature
ISBN 0375868445; 9780375868443; 9780375968440

LC 2011047347

This children's book, by Jonah Winter, profiles the baseball star Willy Mays. "Many believe him to be the best baseball player that ever lived. . . . In . . . [this] picture book biography, young readers can follow Mays's unparalleled career from growing up in Birmingham, Alabama, to playing awe-inspiring ball in the Negro Leagues and then the Majors, where he was center fielder for the New York (later San Francisco) Giants." (Publisher's note)

Wise, Bill

Silent star; the story of deaf major leaguer William Hoy. by Bill Wise; illustrated by Adam Gustavson. Lee & Low Books 2012 40 p. col. ill. (hardcover: alk. paper) $18.95; (ebook) $18.95

Grades: 3 4 5   **796.357**
1. Deaf athletes -- Biography 2. Baseball players -- Biography 3. Deaf athletes -- United States -- Biography

4. Baseball players -- United States -- Biography
ISBN 1600604110; 9781600604119; 9781600609763

LC 2011036827

This "picture-book biography of William Ellsworth Hoy (1862-1961), one of the first deaf players in major league baseball . . . follows Hoy from his childhood . . . through his chance discovery by in amateur league coach and his ascent into the minor leagues and beyond. [Bill] Wise outlines the hardships and prejudices Hoy encountered at every turn . . . but Hoy's determination cuts through all the doubt he faced, and some of the records he set stand to this day." (Publishers Weekly)

Wong, Stephen

Baseball treasures; by Stephen Wong; photographs by Susan Einstein. Collins 2007 58p il $16.99; lib bdg $17.89

Grades: 5 6 7 8   **796.357**
1. Baseball -- History 2. Baseball -- Collectibles
ISBN 978-0-06-114464-6; 0-06-114464-9; 978-0-06-114473-8 lib bdg; 0-06-114473-8 lib bdg

LC 2006036069

This describes collectibles connected with the history of baseball, including balls, gloves and bats, jerseys, baseball cards, World Series memorabilia, and trophies.

This is "a well-designed, well-illustrated book for kids. . . . The text manages to impart the essential information without becoming bogged down in too much detail." Booklist

796.4   Weight lifting, track and field, gymnastics

Bobrick, Benson

A **passion** for victory: the story of the Olympics in ancient and early modern times; the story of the Olympics in ancient and early modern times. Benson Bobrick. Alfred A. Knopf 2012 xvi, 143 p.p ill. (hardback) $19.99

Grades: 4 5 6 7   **796.4**
1. Olympic games 2. Sports tournaments
ISBN 9780375868696; 9780375968693

LC 2011016036

The book offers an "account of the Olympic Games and their place in history. . . . [Athletes] Milo of Croton, Jim Thorpe, Johnny Weissmuller and Jesse Owens are given their due here. The photo-essay format conveys their stories . . . as well as the glory, shenanigans and pettiness of the Olympics throughout history. Almost every full-page spread includes at least one photograph, and the text . . . addresses the cultural context of the games." (Kirkus Reviews)

Includes bibliographical references.

Schwartz, Heather E.

Gymnastics. Lucent Books 2011 96p il (Science behind sports) lib bdg $33.45

Grades: 5 6 7 8   **796.4**
1. Gymnastics
ISBN 978-1-4205-0277-0; 1-4205-0277-8

LC 2010033544

This "explores the scientific principles such as momentum, gravity, friction, and aerodynamics, plus many more, behind [gymnastics]. . . . [The author discusses the sport's] origins, history, and changes, . . . the biomechanics and physiology of playing, related health and medical concerns, and the causes and treatment of sports-related injuries. Additional information tells how exercise, diet and nutrition, warming up, and training relate to peak performance and enjoyment of the sport.... One of the most interesting chapters ... is 'The Psychology of Gymnastics,' which discusses fears, force of will, honing the competitive edge, and the pressure to succeed.... [This volume is] jam-packed full of information. [A must-have] for sports fans, athletes, science students, and even anyone considering a career in sports-related medicine, coaching, or other connected fields." SLJ

Includes glossary and bibliographical references

796.42   Track and field

Adler, David A., 1947-
A **picture** book of Jesse Owens; [by] David Adler; illustrated by Robert Casilla. Holiday House 1992 un il lib bdg $16.95; pa $6.95
Grades: 1 2 3   **796.42**
1. Track athletics 2. African American athletes 3. Olympic athletes 4. Runners (Athletes)
ISBN 0-8234-0966-X lib bdg; 0-8234-1066-8 pa
LC 91-44735
A simple biography of the noted black track star who competed in the 1936 Berlin Olympics

"The portrait presented, although brief, is accurate and touches on the major events of the track-and-field champion's life.... Casilla contributes full-page watercolor paintings that nicely complement and expand the writing." SLJ

Gifford, Clive
Track and field; [by] Clive Gifford. PowerKids Press 2009 32p il (Personal best) lib bdg $25.25
Grades: 4 5 6 7 8   **796.42**
1. Track athletics
ISBN 978-1-4042-4442-9 lib bdg; 1-4042-4442-5 lib bdg
LC 2007-42984
This guide to track and field "offers well-organized and easy-to-follow instructions, focusing on rules, clothing, specific skills, and competitions.... Informative, readable." SLJ

Includes bibliographical references

Track athletics; [by] Clive Gifford. Sea-to-Sea Publications 2009 30p il (Know your sport) lib bdg $27.10
Grades: 5 6 7 8   **796.42**
1. Track athletics
ISBN 978-1-59771-154-8 lib bdg; 1-59771-154-3 lib bdg
LC 2008-7323
"Describes the equipment, training, moves, and running events of track competitions. Includes step-by-step descriptions of moves." Publisher's note
Includes glossary

Lang, Heather
Queen of the track; Alice Coach, olympic high-jump champion. Heather Lang; illustrated by Floyd Cooper. 1st ed. Boyds Mills Press 2012 40 p. col. ill. (reinforced trade ed.) $16.95

Grades: 3 4 5   **796.42**
1. Olympic games 2. Black athletes 3. Olympic athletes
ISBN 1590788508; 9781590788509
LC 2011939994
Author Heather Lang tells the story of "the 1948 Olympics in London, [where] members of the U.S. Women's Track and Field team went down to defeat one by one. Any hope of winning rested on Alice Coachman. Thousands of spectators stayed late for the high-jump event and witnessed history as she became the first African American woman to win an Olympic gold medal. In time for the 2012 Olympic Games in London, this book follows Coachman on her journey from rural Georgia, where she overcame adversity both as a woman and as a black athlete, to her triumph in Wembly Stadium." (Publisher's note)
Includes bibliographical references.

Malaspina, Ann
Touch the sky; Alice Coachman, Olympic high jumper. by Ann Malaspina; illustrated by Eric Velasquez. Albert Whitman 2012 32 p.
Grades: 2 3 4   **796.42**
1. Picture books for children 2. Women athletes -- Juvenile literature 3. Track athletics -- Juvenile literature 4. African American athletes -- Juvenile literature 5. Jumping -- United States -- Juvenile literature 6. Track and field athletes -- United States -- Juvenile literature 7. African American women athletes -- United States -- Juvenile literature
ISBN 080758035X; 9780807580356
LC 2011008564
This children's picture book by Ann Malaspina tells the story of the African American Olympic high jumper Alice Coachman. "In Alice's Georgia hometown, there was no track where an African-American girl could practice, so she made her own crossbar with sticks and rags.... Her dream to compete at the Olympics came true in 1948. This is a ... free-verse story of the first African-American woman to win an Olympic gold medal. Photos ... are also included." (Publisher's note)
Includes bibliographical references.

Marsico, Katie
Running; [by] Katie Marsico and Cecilia Minden. Cherry Lake Pub. 2009 32p il (Real world math: Sports) lib bdg $27.07
Grades: 4 5 6   **796.42**
1. Running 2. Arithmetic 3. Track athletics
ISBN 978-1-60279-249-4 lib bdg; 1-60279-249-6 lib bdg
LC 2008-1167
This book "starts with a short story on the history of [running], fundamental rules, and a math challenge in every chapter.... [This book] will pique your imagination." Sci Books Films
Includes glossary and bibliographical references

McDougall, Chros
Track & field. Norwood House Press 2011 64p il (Girls play to win) lib bdg $26.60

Grades: 4 5 6 7   **796.42**
  1. Track athletics
  ISBN 978-1-59953-467-1; 1-59953-467-3
                                  LC 2011011053
  Covers the history, rules, fundamentals, and significant personalities of the sport of women's track and field. Topics include: techniques, strategies, competitive events, and equipment.
  Includes glossary and bibliographical references

Wiseman, Blaine
  Boston Marathon. Weigl Publishing 2011 32p il (Sporting championships) lib bdg $26; pa $10.95
Grades: 3 4 5   **796.42**
  1. Boston Marathon 2. Marathon running
  ISBN 978-1-61690-124-0 lib bdg; 1-61690-124-1 lib bdg; 978-1-61690-125-7 pa; 1-61690-125-X pa
  This sets the Boston Marathon "within the context of the sport and explains what you need to know when watching the [event]." Booklist
  Includes bibliographical references

796.44 Gymnastics

Veitch, Catherine
  Gymnastics. Heinemann Library 2009 24p il (Sports and my body) lib bdg $21.36; pa $6.49
Grades: 1 2   **796.44**
  1. Gymnastics
  ISBN 978-1-4329-3454-5 lib bdg; 1-4329-3454-6 lib bdg; 978-1-4329-3459-0 pa; 1-4329-3459-7 pa
                                  LC 2009-7084
  Readers learn what gymnastics is, how it can help them stay healthy, and how they can do gymnastics safely.
  This book relates "activity to health . . . [and] explains that in order to stay healthy, children should get plenty of rest, eat healthy food, and drink plenty of water." SLJ
  Includes glossary

Wendorff, Anne
  Gymnastics. Bellwether Media 2010 24p il (Blastoff! readers. My first sports) $19.95
Grades: K 1 2 3   **796.44**
  1. Gymnastics
  ISBN 9781600143274; 160014327X
                                  LC 2009-8181
  Simple text and full color photographs introduce beginning readers to the sport of gymnastics.
  Includes glossary and bibliographical references

796.440 Biography

Burford, Michelle
  Grace, gold and glory; my leap of faith: the Gabrielle Douglas story. by Gabrielle Douglas; with Michelle Burford. Zondervan 2012 222 p. ill. (hardcover) $24.99
Grades: 4 5 6 7 8   **796.440**
  1. Gymnastics 2. Olympic athletes 3. Women gymnasts -- United States -- Biography 4. Women

Olympic athletes -- United States -- Biography
  ISBN 0310740614; 9780310740612
                                  LC 2012042389
  This book is a "first-person account of 2012 Olympic gold medalist [Gabrielle] Douglas's life from birth to the Olympics written in collaboration with [Michelle] Burford. . . . Douglas mentions the lows—her family lived in their van for months when she was an infant—and bullying, but never dwells on them. . . . Supported by her mother and siblings, and by her strong faith in God, she sees herself as capable of achieving greatness 'because God has equipped me with all I need to succeed.'" (Publishers Weekly)

Washburn, Kim
  Heart of a champion; the Dominique Dawes story. Kim Washburn. Zonderkidz 2012 123 p. ill. (softcover) $6.99
Grades: 4 5 6   **796.440**
  1. Olympic games 2. Blacks -- Biography 3. African American women 4. African American athletes 5. Christian biography 6. Gymnasts -- United States -- Biography -- Juvenile literature
  ISBN 0310722683; 9780310722687
                                  LC 2012008588
  Author Kim Washburn tells the story of gymnast Dominique Dawes, who "competed in three Olympic games and was one of two women to be the first African American to medal in gymnastics. She was also a member of the celebrated Magnificent Seven, the team that won the gold medal in Atlanta in 1996 over the dominant Russian and Romanian squads. . . . Washburn offers up many of Dawes' less illustrious moments, . . . including disappointing performances at World Championships, a brief stint on Broadway, and her search for a lasting and fulfilling career." (Booklist)

796.48 Olympic games

Butterfield, Moira
  Events. Sea-to-Sea Publications 2011 il (The Olympics) lib bdg $19.95
Grades: 4 5 6 7   **796.48**
  1. Olympic games
  ISBN 978-1-5977-1321-4; 1-5977-1321-X
                                  LC 2011006465
  This describes events of the Olympics.
  Includes glossary and bibliographical references

  History. Sea-to-Sea Publications 2011 il (The Olympics) lib bdg $28.50
Grades: 4 5 6 7   **796.48**
  1. Olympic games
  ISBN 978-1-5977-1319-1; 1-5977-1319-8
                                  LC 2011006470
  This is a history of the Olympics.
  Includes glossary and bibliographical references

  Scandals. Sea-to-Sea Publications 2011 il (The Olympics) lib bdg $28.50
Grades: 4 5 6 7   **796.48**
  1. Olympic games 2. Sports -- Corrupt practices
  ISBN 978-1-5977-1320-7; 1-5977-1320-1
                                  LC 2011006473

"The book is divided into chapters that cover such topics as bribes, doping, and political problems. Along with famous events, such as the tragedy at the Munich Olympics, in which Israeli athletes were murdered, and the Marion Jones running scandal, in which she was stripped of her medals, there are other shocking and suprising moments. . . . This . . . volume, full of historical and contemporary photos, gives readers a lot to think about." Booklist

Macy, Sue
★ **Swifter,** higher, stronger; a photographic history of the Summer Olympics. by Sue Macy; foreword by Bob Costas. updated for the 2008 Summer Olympics; National Geographic 2008 96p il $18.95; lib bdg $27.90
Grades: 4 5 6 7   **796.48**
  1. Olympic games
  ISBN 978-1-4263-0290-9; 1-4263-0290-8; 978-1-4263-0302-9 lib bdg; 1-4263-0302-5 lib bdg
  First published 2004
A detailed look at the history of the Olympic Games, from their origins in Ancient Greece, through their rebirth in nineteenth century France, to the present, highlighting the contributions of individuals to the Games' success and popularity.
  "While other books on the topic go into more depth on specific sports, athletes, or historical events, none are as enthusiastically broad or as enjoyable to read as this one. And, it's superbly illustrated with colorful, well-chosen, and enticing photographs." SLJ [review of 2004 ed.]
  Includes bibliographical references

796.5   Outdoor life

George, Jean Craighead
★ **Pocket** guide to the outdoors; [by] Jean Craighead George; with Twig C. George . . . [et al.] Dutton Children's Books 2009 138p il pa $9.99
Grades: 5 6 7 8   **796.5**
  1. Camping 2. Outdoor life 3. Wilderness survival 4. Outdoor life -- Juvenile literature 5. Outdoor recreation -- Juvenile literature
  ISBN 978-0-525-42163-4 pa; 0-525-42163-7 pa
  "This survival guide is the book to read before a wilderness adventure. In short, clearly written chapters, it provides practical tips about ways to enjoy nature and includes information about building shelters, starting fires, making a fishing line and cleaning a fish, outdoor cooking, identifying animal tracks and edible and poisonous plants, and the basics of orienteering. Safety is always considered. Drawings and clearly labeled sketches help with identification." SLJ
  Includes bibliographical references

Schofield, Jo
  Make it wild; 101 things to make and do outdoors. [by] Jo Schofield and Fiona Danks. Frances Lincoln 2010 159p il pa $24.95
Grades: 4 5 6 7 8   **796.5**
  1. Nature craft 2. Outdoor life
  ISBN 978-0-7112-2885-6; 0-7112-2885-X
  "Using the raw materials nature has to offer, the authors offer clear, concise instructions on how to create ephemeral art, outdoor toys, jewelry, sculptures, and dozens of other

things using materials like clay, ice, leaves, sand, and wood. The instructions offer good guidance but also encourage children to use their own creativity and imagination to craft the final product. The projects range in level of difficulty and, depending on the age of the child, can be done individually or in collaboration with siblings, peers, or parents. The authors include safety instructions and recommendations for further resources on outdoor creative exercises. The activities will teach problem solving and commonsense, useful skills; instill a deeper appreciation of nature; and encourage creativity and ingenuity. An excellent choice for any library collection." Booklist

796.52   Walking and exploring by kind of terrain

Athans, Sandra K.
  Tales from the top of the world; climbing Mount Everest with Pete Athans. by Sandra K. Athans. Millbrook Press 2013 64 p. ill. (lib. bdg.: alk. paper) $31.93
Grades: 4 5 6   **796.52**
  1. Mountaineering 2. Mount Everest (China and Nepal) 3. Mountaineers -- Biography 4. Mountaineering -- Everest, Mount (China and Nepal)
  ISBN 0761365060; 9780761365068
                                                          LC 2011045834
In this book by Sandra K. Athans and Pete Athans, "readers are invited to accompany Pete Athans (who has climbed Everest some 14 times and stood on top of the world on 7 different occasions) on the arduous journey from below base camp to the summit. The matter-of-fact text is broken by tales of Athans's personal adventures . . . and all are decorated with a plethora of color photos." (School Library Journal)
  Includes bibliographical references (p. 61) and index

Bodden, Valerie
  To the top of Mount Everest; by Valerie Bodden. 1st ed. Creative Education 2012 48 p. ill. (some col.) (paperback) $12.00; (library) $34.25
Grades: 5 6 7 8   **796.52**
  1. Exploration -- Juvenile literature 2. Mount Everest (China and Nepal) -- Juvenile literature 3. Mountaineering -- Everest, Mount (China and Nepal) -- History 4. Mountaineers -- Everest, Mount (China and Nepal) -- Biography -- Juvenile literature
  ISBN 1608180700; 9780898126686; 9781608180707
                                                          LC 2010033553
  This book by Valerie Bodden is part of the Great Expeditions series and looks at expeditions to the top of Mount Everest. "Bodden includes brief biographies of major people involved in each expedition, interspersed with the text. There are also numerous photographs or reproductions of paintings and woodcuts from the time of the expeditions." (Library Media Connection)
  Includes bibliographical references and index.

Cleare, John
  Epic climbs. Kingfisher 2011 64p il (Epic adventure) $19.95
Grades: 5 6 7 8   **796.52**
  1. Mountaineering
  ISBN 978-0-7534-6573-8; 0-7534-6573-6

"Cleare gives the history of five of the most famous and dangerous mountains to climb: Eiger, K2, Everest, McKinley, and Matterhorn. Each section has a short, easy-to-read summary that gives the history of climbers who have conquered these peaks. Full-color photos include the view from the top and historical and contemporary climbing equipment." SLJ

Jenkins, Steve

★ The **top** of the world; climbing Mount Everest. Houghton Mifflin 1999 un il $16; pa $6.95

Grades: 2 3 4   **796.52**

1. Mountaineering 2. Mount Everest (China and Nepal) 3. Everest, Mount (China and Nepal) 4. Mountaineering -- Everest, Mount (China and Nepal) -- Juvenile literature

ISBN 0-395-94218-7; 0-618-19676-5 pa

LC 98-42748

"Jenkins' papercut illustrations are extraordinary—feathery light to catch the effect of fog radiating off the mountains, mottled and striated to replicate rocky plateaus, pebbled to look like ice flowers. . . . A very attractive book, with plenty of substance for curious children." Booklist

Includes bibliographical references

Skreslet, Laurie

To the top of Everest; [by] Laurie Skreslet with Elizabeth MacLeod. Kids Can Press 2001 56p il hardcover o.p. pa $9.95

Grades: 4 5 6 7   **796.52**

1. Mountaineering

ISBN 1-55074-721-5; 1-55074-814-9 pa

This is an account of Skreslet's "1982 trek up Everest when he became one of the first Canadians to make it to the top. Skreslet takes readers through every exciting, excruciating element of the climb. Beautiful color photographs abound." Booklist

Includes glossary

796.54 Camping

Champion, Neil

Fire and cooking. Amicus 2010 32p il (Survive alive) lib bdg $19.95

Grades: 4 5 6 7   **796.54**

1. Fires 2. Camping 3. Wilderness survival

ISBN 978-1-60753-039-8 lib bdg; 1-60753-039-2 lib bdg

LC 2010001626

This offers survival tips for building a fire and cooking in the wild, including information on different kinds of fires. Also discusses how to know what to cook and utensils to use.

This "colorful [book contains] numerous photos and illustrations that effectively break the [text] into small, readable chucks. There's lots of practical, everyday information here. . . . Brief yet gripping real-life survival stories are interspersed throughout the [book]." SLJ

796.6 Cycling and related activities

Bow, James

Cycling science. Crabtree Pub. Co. 2009 32p il (Sports science) lib bdg $26.60; pa $8.95

Grades: 4 5 6   **796.6**

1. Cycling

ISBN 978-0-7787-4535-8 lib bdg; 0-77874535-X lib bdg; 978-0-7787-4552-5 pa; 0-7787-4552-X pa

LC 2008-46275

This book approachs cycling "from a scientific angle, describing some of the physics behind [the] pursuit and how athletes can use this knowledge to improve performance. . . . Fascinating facts . . . are presented in a captivating, lively manner. . . . The layout features colorful text boxes interspersed among photographs." SLJ

Includes glossary and bibliographical references

Guillain, Charlotte

Cycling. Heinemann Library 2009 24p il (Sports and my body) lib bdg $21.36; pa $6.49

Grades: 1 2   **796.6**

1. Cycling

ISBN 978-1-4329-3457-6 lib bdg; 1-4329-3457-0 lib bdg; 978-1-4329-3462-0 pa; 1-4329-3462-7 pa

LC 2009-7085

Readers learn what cycling is, how it can help them stay healthy, and how they can cycle safely.

This book relates "activity to health . . . [and] explains that in order to stay healthy, children should get plenty of rest, eat healthy food, and drink plenty of water." SLJ

Includes glossary

Macy, Sue

★ Wheels of change; how women rode the bicycle to freedom (with a few flat tires along the way) National Geographic 2011 96p il map $18.95; lib bdg $27.90

Grades: 4 5 6 7 8   **796.6**

1. Cycling 2. Bicycles 3. Gender role 4. Women athletes 5. Sex role 6. Feminism -- Juvenile literature 7. Women -- United States -- History 8. Cycling for women -- Juvenile literature

ISBN 978-1-4263-0761-4; 1-4263-0761-6; 978-1-4263-0762-1 lib bdg; 1-4263-0762-4 lib bdg

LC 2010-27141

This is an "engaging look at the emancipating impact that bikes had on late-nineteenth-century U.S. women. The eye-catching chapters, filled with archival images . . . zero in on the profound ways that bicycles subverted traditional notions of femininity. . . . Macy seamlessly weaves together research, direct quotes . . . and historical overviews that put the facts into context, while sidebars expand on related topics. . . . A strong, high-interest choice for both classroom and personal reading." Booklist

Robinson, Laura

★ Cyclist bikelist; a book for every rider. illustrated by Ramón K. Pérez. Tundra Books 2010 55p il pa $17.95

Grades: 4 5 6 7   **796.6**

1. Cycling 2. Bicycles

ISBN 978-0-88776-784-5; 0-88776-784-2

The author "covers a broad range of topics, from choosing and caring for a bike to differences in tires, how gear ratios work, and even proper dress and nutrition. She also provides a quick overview of the bicycle's history and inspiring sketches of several renowned racers. . . . Supplemented by photos of different types of bikes, Pérez's bright, cartoon-style pictures add both humor and . . . sharply drawn details. A first-rate guide." Booklist

Schoenherr, Alicia

Mountain biking; by Alicia and Rusty Schoenherr. Child's World 2005 32p il (Kids' guides) lib bdg $24.21
Grades: 4 5 6   **796.6**
    1. Mountain biking
    ISBN 1-59296-209-2

LC 2003-27371

This "opens with an explanation of the sport and gives reasons why people enjoy it. The four chapters that follow cover background and development, equipment, technique, and stars and competitions. The excellent color photos are clear and exciting." SLJ

Includes bibliographical references

796.7   Driving motor vehicles

Nelson, Kristin L.

Monster trucks on the move. Lerner Publications 2011 32p il (Lightning bolt books. Vroom-vroom) lib bdg $25.26
Grades: K 1 2   **796.7**
    1. Trucks
    ISBN 978-0-7613-6022-3 lib bdg; 0-7613-6022-0 lib bdg

LC 2009038530

This book about monster trucks has "big, high-energy color photos. . . . [The text provides] lively commentary in a mix of declarative statements and non-rhetorical questions. . . . [The] volume closes with a labeled diagram, a page of 'fun facts,' and a short list of print and web resources. . . . [This] will make a worthwhile and popular addition." SLJ

Includes glossary and bibliographical references

796.72   Automobile racing

Arroyo, Sheri L.

How race car drivers use math; math curriculum consultant: Rhea A. Stewart. Chelsea Clubhouse 2010 32p il (Math in the real world) lib bdg $28
Grades: 4 5 6   **796.72**
    1. Mathematics 2. Automobile racing 3. Vocational guidance
    ISBN 978-1-60413-609-8 lib bdg; 1-60413-609-X lib bdg

LC 2009-21476

"The layout for [this slim [title] is bright and colorful with a photograph and a 'You Do the Math' problem to solve and large, easy-to-read text on every spread. An answer key is included in the back matter, along with a page detailing the career choices and the educational requirements. . . . In [this title], readers learn about qualifying times, track designs, and tracking fuel. . . . [This title] would be useful to supplement lessons on mathematics. [It] will also appeal to students wanting to learn more about math as it relates to specific careers." SLJ

Includes glossary and bibliographical references

Eagen, Rachel

NASCAR; written by Rachel Eagen. Crabtree Pub. Co. 2007 32p il (Automania!) lib bdg $25.20; pa $8.95
Grades: 4 5 6   **796.72**
    1. Automobile racing
    ISBN 978-0-7787-3007-1 lib bdg; 0-7787-3007-7 lib bdg; 978-0-7787-3029-3 pa; 0-7787-3029-8 pa

LC 2006012406

"Eagen has done an excellent job explaining the National Association of Stock Car Automobile Racing—the history, the modification of the cars, the drivers, and the competitions—while conveying a sense of the magnitude of the sport's current fan base. Her lucid, interesting text gets a lift from plenty of high-energy photos." Booklist

Egan, Erin

★ **Hottest** race cars; by Erin Egan. Enslow Publishers 2007 48p il (Wild wheels!) $17.95
Grades: 4 5 6   **796.72**
    1. Automobile racing
    ISBN 978-0-7660-2871-5; 0-7660-2871-2

LC 2007007427

"Along with presenting a bit of racing's history, Egan unravels confusion about the three kinds of open-wheel competitions (Formula One, Indy, and Champ). Then she takes a quick but revealing look at major car components. . . . Information on driver's gear, race strategy, and more, along with a sprinkling of anecdotes . . . fill the rest of the pages, which are loaded with color photos." Booklist

Includes glossary and bibliographical references

Howse, Jennifer

NASCAR Sprint Cup. Weigl Publishers 2009 32p il map (Sporting championships) lib bdg $26; pa $9.95
Grades: 3 4 5   **796.72**
    1. Automobile racing
    ISBN 978-1-60596-636-6 lib bdg; 1-60596-636-3 lib bdg; 978-1-60596-637-3 pa; 1-60596-637-1 pa

LC 2009-12344

This sets the NASCAR Sprint Cup "within the context of the sport and explains what you need to know when watching the big [event]." Booklist

Includes glossary and bibliographical references

Kelley, K. C.

Hottest NASCAR machines; by K. C. Kelley. Enslow Publishers 2008 48p il (Wild wheels!) lib bdg $23.93
Grades: 4 5 6 7   **796.72**
    1. Automobile racing
    ISBN 978-0-7660-2869-2 lib bdg; 0-7660-2869-0 lib bdg

LC 2007007426

"Experience the thrill of a NASCAR race, and learn about the cars, personalities, and races associated with this sport." Publisher's note

Includes glossary and bibliographical references

Piehl, Janet

Formula one race cars on the move. Lerner Publications 2010 32p il (Lightning bolt books. Vroom-vroom) lib bdg $25.26

Grades: K 1 2   **796.72**

1. Automobile racing

ISBN 978-0-7613-3920-5 lib bdg; 0-7613-3920-5 lib bdg

LC 2009039745

This book about race cars has "big, high-energy color photos. . . . [The text provides] lively commentary in a mix of declarative statements and non-rhetorical questions. . . . [The] volume closes with a labeled diagram, a page of 'fun facts,' and a short list of print and web resources. . . . [This] will make a worthwhile and popular addition." SLJ

Includes glossary and bibliographical references

Pimm, Nancy Roe

The **Daytona** 500; the thrill and thunder of the great American race. Milbrook Press 2011 64p il (Spectacular sports) lib bdg $29.27

Grades: 5 6 7 8   **796.72**

1. Automobile racing

ISBN 978-0-7613-6677-5; 0-7613-6677-6

LC 2010027263

"Pimm, who worked in the pit box during her husband Ed Pimm's NASCAR racing days, offers an informative introduction to the Daytona 500. Beginning in 1903 . . . this traces the event's history and discusses the cars, drivers, strategies, and memorable moments. Colorful photos illustrate the clear text, while the many sidebars spotlight related facts." Booklist

Includes bibliographical references

796.8   Combat sports

Bjorklund, Ruth

Aikido. Marshall Cavendish Benchmark 2011 il (Martial arts in action) $29.93

Grades: 4 5 6 7   **796.8**

1. Aikido

ISBN 978-0-7614-4931-7; 978-1-6087-0361-6 e-book

LC 2010013820

This describes the history, equipment, and technique of aikido.

This treats "martial arts with the dignity that serious enthusiasts bring to the sport. . . . Illustrations include not only photos of modern gear and from films but also historical images." Booklist

Ditchfield, Christin

Wrestling. Children's Press 2000 47p il (True book) hardcover o.p. lib bdg $25

Grades: 2 3 4   **796.8**

1. Wrestling

ISBN 0-516-21611-2 lib bdg; 0-516-27033-8 pa

LC 99-28191

Describes the history, rules, and styles of wrestling

Includes bibliographical references

Ellis, Carol

Judo and jujitsu. Marshall Cavendish Benchmark 2011 il (Martial arts in action) $29.93

Grades: 4 5 6 7   **796.8**

1. Judo 2. Jiu-jitsu

ISBN 978-0-7614-4933-1; 978-1-6087-0363-0 e-book

LC 2010013821

This describes the history, equipment, and technique of judo and jujitsu.

This treats "martial arts with the dignity that serious enthusiasts bring to the sport. . . . Illustrations include not only photos of modern gear and from films but also historical images." Booklist

Kendo. Marshall Cavendish Benchmark 2010 47p il (Martial arts in action) $29.93

Grades: 4 5 6 7   **796.8**

1. Kendo

ISBN 978-0-7614-4935-5; 0-7614-4935-3

LC 2010013827

This book about kendo offers "an introduction, a brief history, and expectations for students who begin taking classes. . . . [This title is] outstanding, using an approachable voice without fictionalizing and presenting the history of [kendo] in a way that makes it feel relevant." SLJ

Includes glossary and bibliographical references

Wrestling. Marshall Cavendish Benchmark 2010 47p il (Martial arts in action) $29.93

Grades: 4 5 6 7   **796.8**

1. Wrestling

ISBN 978-0-7614-4941-6; 0-7614-4941-8

LC 2010013819

This book about wrestling offers "an introduction, a brief history, and expectations for students who begin taking classes. . . . [This title is] outstanding, using an approachable voice without fictionalizing and presenting the history of [wrestling] in a way that makes it feel relevant." SLJ

Includes glossary and bibliographical references

Gifford, Clive

Martial arts. Marshall Cavendish Benchmark 2009 30p il (Tell me about sports) $19.95

Grades: 3 4 5   **796.8**

1. Martial arts

ISBN 978-0-7614-4457-2; 0-7614-4457-2

LC 2008-55993

"An introduction to martial arts, including techniques, rules, and the training regimen of professional athletes in the sport." Publisher's note

Includes glossary and bibliographical references

Haney-Withrow, Anna

Tae kwon do. Marshall Cavendish Benchmark 2011 il (Martial arts in action) $29.93

Grades: 4 5 6 7   **796.8**

1. Tae kwon do

ISBN 978-0-7614-4940-9; 978-1-6087-0368-5 e-book

LC 2010013828

This describes the history, equipment, and technique of tae kwon do.

This treats "martial arts with the dignity that serious enthusiasts bring to the sport. . . . Illustrations include not only photos of modern gear and from films but also historical images." Booklist

Hicks, Terry Allan

Karate. Marshall Cavendish Benchmark 2010 47p il (Martial arts in action) $29.93

Grades: 4 5 6 **796.8**

1. Karate

ISBN 978-0-7614-4934-8; 0-7614-4934-5

LC 2010013818

This books looks at karate including its history, fighting techniques, training methods, and the values of respect and discipline.

This treats "martial arts with the dignity that serious enthusiasts bring to the sport. . . . Illustrations include not only photos of modern gear and from films but also historical images." Booklist

Includes glossary

Lewin, Ted

★ At Gleason's gym. Roaring Brook Press 2007 un il $17.95

Grades: 2 3 4 5 **796.8**

1. Boxing 2. Gymnasiums -- Juvenile literature

ISBN 978-1-59643-231-4; 1-59643-231-4

LC 2006-32176

"Gleason's gym in Brooklyn is where 'the world works out.' . . . Nine-year-old Sugar Boy Younan, National Silver Gloves Champion, 110-pound division, goes there to shadow box and spar with partners. This glorious tribute to Gleason's . . . packs a punch of its own, with a text that is both moving and informative and with vibrant artwork so realistic that readers can practically smell the sweat." Booklist

Mack, Gail

Kickboxing. Marshall Cavendish Benchmark 2011 il lib bdg $29.93

Grades: 4 5 6 7 **796.8**

1. Kickboxing

ISBN 978-0-7614-4936-2; 978-1-6087-0366-1 e-book

LC 2010014798

This describes the history, equipment, and technique of kickboxing.

This treats "martial arts with the dignity that serious enthusiasts bring to the sport. . . . Illustrations include not only photos of modern gear and from films but also historical images." Booklist

Mason, Paul, 1967-

Boxing. Sea-to-Sea Publications 2011 32p il (Combat sports) lib bdg $28.50

Grades: 4 5 6 **796.8**

1. Boxing

ISBN 978-1-59771-273-6; 1-59771-273-6

"...[Provides] an inviting look for students who are learning about techniques and for examining records and statistics... Use to refresh an older collection." SLJ

Includes glossary and bibliographical references

Watkins, Richard Ross

Gladiator; by Richard Watkins. Houghton Mifflin 1997 80p il map hardcover o.p. pa $8.95

Grades: 4 5 6 7 **796.8**

1. Gladiators 2. Gladiators -- Juvenile literature

ISBN 0-395-82656-X; 0-618-07032-X pa

LC 96-21107

Describes the history of gladiators, including types of armor, use of animals, amphitheaters, and how the practice fit into Roman society for almost 700 years

"In a balanced treatment of a potentially sensational topic, Watkins provides colorfully written, detailed accounts of the fights as well as pithy discussions of what gladiators meant to the Romans and what they tell us about Roman society. . . . The solid gray-and-white drawings illustrate the text effectively." Booklist

Includes glossary and bibliographical references

Wiseman, Blaine

Ultimate fighting. Weigl Publishers 2011 il (Sporting championships) lib bdg $26; pa 10.95

Grades: 3 4 5 **796.8**

1. Martial arts

ISBN 978-1-61690-130-1 lib bdg; 1-61690-130-6 lib bdg; 978-1-61690-131-8 pa; 1-61690-131-4 pa

LC 2010038886

This sets the ultimate fighting championship "within the context of the sport and explains what you need to know when watching the [event]." Booklist

Wouk, Henry

Kung fu. Marshall Cavendish Benchmark 2010 47p il (Martial arts in action) $29.93

Grades: 4 5 6 **796.8**

1. Kung fu

ISBN 978-0-7614-4937-9; 0-7614-4937-X

LC 2010013842

Centuries ago a small band of warrior monks living in the remote forests of ancient China created a mysterious and unique style of fighting that used no weapons. It is known today as kung fu. This is the story of how that once secret martial art has become one of the most famous in the world

This treats "martial arts with the dignity that serious enthusiasts bring to the sport. . . . Illustrations include not only photos of modern gear and from films but also historical images." Booklist

Includes glossary

796.812 Wrestling

Jones, Patrick

The main event; the moves and muscle of pro wrestling. Patrick Jones. Millbrook Press 2013 64 p. (lib. bdg.; alk. paper) $31.93

Grades: 4 5 6 **796.812**

1. Wrestling 2. Wrestling -- History

ISBN 0761386351; 9780761386353

LC 2011046180

This book is a "history of wrestling as 'sports entertainment'—read that as meaning staged—from [Patrick] Jones. This is . . . the art of making the blows and throws look like the real thing while the outcome has been predetermined." He tracks "the evolution of the various professional circuits and the shenanigans of the promoter Vince McMahon" and tells stories of wrestlers like "Gorgeous George, Strangler

Lewis, Andre the Giant, Hulk Hogan, The Undertaker, [and] The Rock." (Kirkus)

796.815   Oriental martial arts forms

Mason, Paul, 1967-
Judo; [by] Paul Mason. Sea-to-Sea Publications 2009
30 p. col. ill. (Know your sport) (library) $27.10
Grades: 5 6 7 8   **796.815**
   1. Judo
   ISBN 978-1-59771-151-7; 1-59771-151-9
                 LC 2008007318
"Describes the equipment, training, moves, and competitions of judo. Includes step-by-step descriptions of moves." Publisher's note
   Includes index.

796.9   Ice and snow sports

Woods, Bob
Snowboarding; by Bob Woods. Child's World 2005
32p il (Kids' guides) lib bdg $24.21
Grades: 4 5 6   **796.9**
   1. Snowboarding
   ISBN 1-59296-211-4
                 LC 2003-27365
This "opens with an explanation of the sport and gives reasons why people enjoy it. The four chapters that follow cover background and development, equipment, technique, and stars and competitions. The excellent color photos are clear and exciting." SLJ
   Includes bibliographical references

796.91   Ice skating

Marsico, Katie
Speed skating; [by] Katie Marsico and Cecilia Minden. Cherry Lake Pub. 2009 32p il (Real world math: Sports) lib bdg $27.07
Grades: 4 5 6   **796.91**
   1. Arithmetic 2. Ice skating
   ISBN 978-1-60279-250-0 lib bdg; 1-60279-250-X lib bdg
                 LC 2008-806
This book "starts with a short story on the history of [speed skating], fundamental rules, and a math challenge in every chapter. . . . [This book] will pique your imagination." Sci Books Films

McDougall, Chros
Figure skating. Norwood House Press 2010 64p il (Girls play to win) lib bdg $26.60
Grades: 4 5 6 7   **796.91**
   1. Ice skating
   ISBN 978-1-59953-389-6; 1-59953-389-8
                 LC 2010009809
"This begins with a look back at the origin of [figure skating] and the traces the young women who played a role in skating from the olden days to today. The first of six chapters describes skating basics . . . and then the progression

of stars begins. . . . Color photos, sidebars, and boxed explanations break up the text. . . . A nicely compact history." Booklist
   Includes glossary and bibliographical references

Thomas, Keltie
How figure skating works; illustrated by Stephen MacEachern. OwlKids 2009 64p il $22.95; pa $10.95
Grades: 3 4 5 6   **796.91**
   1. Ice skating
   ISBN 978-1-897349-58-8; 1-897349-58-0; 978-1-897349-59-5 pa; 1-897349-59-9 pa
"This lively overview features clear, well-written explanations of the technical elements of figure skating and anecdotes from skating history. The readable text is supplemented with eye-catching photos, cartoon illustrations, and simple diagrams and charts." SLJ
   Includes glossary

796.93   Skiing and snowboarding

Kenney, Karen Latchana
Skiing & snowboarding. Norwood House Press 2010
64p il (Girls play to win) lib bdg $26.60
Grades: 4 5 6 7   **796.93**
   1. Skiing 2. Snowboarding
   ISBN 978-1-59953-391-9; 1-59953-391-X
                 LC 2010009808
Covers the history, rules, fundamentals and significant personalities of the sports of women's skiing and snowboarding. Topics include: techniques, strategies, competitive events, and equipment.
   "With an easy design and format, the [text is] highly accessible to even the most reluctant readers and [provides] great exposure and insight into the world of female professional sports." Horn Book Guide
   Includes glossary and bibliographical references

Schwartz, Heather E.
Snowboarding. Lucent Books 2011 il (Science behind sports) $33.45
Grades: 5 6 7 8   **796.93**
   1. Snowboarding
   ISBN 978-1-4205-0322-7; 1-4205-0322-7
                 LC 2010033274
This "explores the scientific principles such as momentum, gravity, friction, and aerodynamics, plus many more, behind [snowbarding]. . . . [The author discusses the sport's] origins, history, and changes, . . . the biomechanics and physiology of playing, related health and medical concerns, and the causes and treatment of sports-related injuries. Additional information tells how exercise, diet and nutrition, warming up, and training relate to peak performance and enjoyment of the sport. . . . The action photography . . . is fantastic. . . . [This volume is] jam-packed full of information. [A must-have] for sports fans, athletes, science students, and even anyone considering a career in sports-related medicine, coaching, or other connected fields." SLJ
   Includes glossary and bibliographical references

796.94   Snowmobiling

Woods, Bob

Snowmobile racers. Enslow Publishers 2010 48p il (Kid racers) lib bdg $23.93

Grades: 5 6 7 8   **796.94**

1. Snowmobiles

ISBN 978-0-7660-3487-7 lib bdg; 0-7660-3487-9 lib bdg

LC 2009020784

This describes snowmobiles and races for kids, discussing which snowmobiles qualify, how they are built and raced, who the best drivers are, what to look for in a snowmobile, safety, good sportsmanship, and how racing activities can be a good part of family life.

"The easily digestible text gets more visual weight on the page, but there are plenty of captioned color photos depicting different sorts of races as well as recreational snowmobiling." Booklist

Includes glossary and bibliographical references

796.96   Ice games

Wiseman, Blaine

Stanley Cup. Weigl Publishers 2011 32p il map (Sporting championships) lib bdg $26; pa $10.95

Grades: 3 4 5   **796.96**

1. Hockey

ISBN 978-1-61690-127-1 lib bdg; 1-61690-127-6 lib bdg; 978-1-61690-128-8 pa; 1-61690-128-4 pa

LC 2010006164

This sets the Stanley Cup "within the context of the sport and explains what you need to know when watching the [event]." Booklist

796.962   Ice hockey

Adams, Carly

Queens of the ice; they were fast, they were fierce, they were teenage girls. Lorimer 2011 131p il (Record books) $16.95; pa $9.95

Grades: 5 6 7 8   **796.962**

1. Hockey 2. Women athletes

ISBN 978-1-55277-721-3; 1-55277-721-9; 978-1-55277-720-6 pa; 1-55277-720-0 pa

"Filled with exciting action, this . . . title . . . showcases the history of the Preston Rivulettes, a Canadian hockey team of teenage girls who played together for 10 seasons, from 1931 until 1940, without losing a game and at a time when many believed that girls could not play the sport and needed chaperones. . . . Adams deepens the story with the historical background of the Great Depression and the team's struggle to find money. Occasional achival photos and boxed inserts add to the clear, readable account." Booklist

Johnstone, Robb

Hockey; rev ed.; Weigl Publishers 2009 24p il (In the zone) $24.45; pa $8.95

Grades: 4 5 6 7   **796.962**

1. Hockey

ISBN 978-1-6059-6130-9; 1-6059-6130-2; 978-1-6059-6131-6 pa; 1-6059-6131-0 pa

LC 2009005607

First published 2001

"Colorful, informative. . . . For those just showing an interest in the bone-crushing sport, [this is] an excellent place to get their bearings. Using short, mostly two-page chapters, Johnstone explains the genesis of the sport, the gear needed, the rules, the positions, and the leagues, before concluding with biographies of eight legendary NHL players." Booklist

McClellan, Ray

Hockey. Bellwether Media 2010 24p il (Blastoff! readers. My first sports) $19.95

Grades: K 1 2 3   **796.962**

1. Hockey

ISBN 978-1-60014-330-4; 1-60014-330-X

LC 2009-8180

"Simple text and full color photographs introduce beginning readers to the sport of hockey." Publisher's note

Includes bibliographical references

McKinley, Michael

Ice time; the story of hockey. Tundra Books 2006 80p il $18.95

Grades: 5 6 7 8   **796.962**

1. Hockey 2. Hockey -- Canada -- Juvenile literature

ISBN 978-0-88776-762-3; 0-88776-762-1

"This straightforward history of hockey emphasizes the professional game and Canadian players. . . . Hockey enthusiasts will find this a welcome arrival." Booklist

McMahon, Dave

Hockey. Norwood House Press 2010 64p il (Girls play to win) lib bdg $26.60

Grades: 4 5 6 7   **796.962**

1. Hockey

ISBN 978-1-59953-390-2; 1-59953-390-1

LC 2010009811

Covers the history, rules, fundamentals and significant personalities of the sport of women's hockey. Topics include: techniques, strategies, competitive events, and equipment.

"With an easy design and format, the [text is] highly accessible to even the most reluctant readers and [provides] great exposure and insight into the world of female professional sports." Horn Book Guide

Includes glossary and bibliographical references

Sharp, Anne Wallace

Ice hockey. Lucent Books 2011 112p il map (Science behind sports) lib bdg $33.45

Grades: 5 6 7 8   **796.962**

1. Hockey

ISBN 978-1-4205-0281-7; 1-4205-0281-6

LC 2010025670

This book about ice hockey highlights "performance; chapter headings include topics such as 'Training and Nutrition,' 'High-Tech Equipment,' and 'Injuries and Treatments.' Physics, biology, and psychology concepts related to the [sport] are . . . wrapped into technical discussions of moves and techniques. Many photographs of pros and novices in action add interest." Horn Book Guide

Includes glossary and bibliographical references

Stewart, Mark

Score! the action and artistry of hockey's magnificent moment. Millbrook Press 2010 64p il $29.27

Grades: 5 6 7 8   **796.962**
1. Hockey
ISBN 978-0-8225-8753-8; 0-8225-8753-X

"Stewart and Kennedy take readers on a chatty, photo-studded tour of the art of scoring in the rink. This intermediate-level hockey book definitely isn't for beginners. . . . What savvy readers will get, however, is a bounty of information on the game's defining goals, goal scorers, and goal-scoring techniques. . . . This makes a worthy addition to any sports shelf." Booklist

796.98   Winter Olympic games

Macy, Sue

★ **Freeze** frame; a photographic history of the Winter Olympics. National Geographic 2006 96p il map $18.95

Grades: 5 6 7 8 9 10   **796.98**
1. Olympic games 2. Winter sports
ISBN 0-7922-7887-9; 978-0-7922-7887-0

Highlights in the history of the Winter Olympics from their inception in 1924 to today, including profiles of the Olympic athletes and information on the lesser-known winter sports. Also includes an Olympic almanac with information about each Olympiad.

This book "has spectacular photographs and clear, captivating prose." SLJ

Includes bibliographical references

797   Aquatic and air sports

Kelley, K. C.

Weird water sports. Child's World 2011 24p il (Weird sports) lib bdg $25.64

Grades: 3 4 5 6   **797**
1. Water sports
ISBN 978-1-60954-380-8; 1-60954-380-8
LC 2010044028

This describes sports such as noodling, bog bike racing, concrete canoeing, underwater hockey, and river surfing.

"Both the writing and the visual style are exuberant-without relying too much on exclamation points." Booklist

797.1   Aquatic sports

Bass, Scott

Kayaking; by Scott Bass. Child's World 2005 32p il (Kids' guides) lib bdg $24.21

Grades: 4 5 6   **797.1**
1. Kayaks and kayaking
ISBN 1-59296-208-4
LC 2003-27372

This "opens with an explanation of the sport and gives reasons why people enjoy it. The four chapters that follow

cover background and development, equipment, technique, and stars and competitions. The excellent color photos are clear and exciting." SLJ

Includes bibliographical references

Storey, Rita

Sailing. Sea-to-Sea Publications 2011 30p il (Know your sport) lib bdg $28.50

Grades: 4 5 6   **797.1**
1. Sailing
ISBN 978-1-59771-286-6
LC 2010003439

This "volume provides an introduction to the equipment, techniques, and safety measures for [sailing]. . . . Instructive photographs help illustrate such concepts as [tacking a sailboat], . . . while engaging stock images capture the excitement on the water. The [volume concludes] with racing information, profiling top racers, rules, and tactics." Horn Book Guide

Includes glossary

Thorpe, Yvonne

Canoeing and kayaking. Sea-to-Sea Publications 2011 30p il (Know your sport) $28.50

Grades: 4 5 6   **797.1**
1. Canoes and canoeing 2. Kayaks and kayaking
ISBN 9781597712859
LC 2010003438

This "volume provides an introduction to the equipment, techniques, and safety measures for [canoeing and kayaking]. . . . Instructive photographs help illustrate such concepts as . . . paddling a kayak, while engaging stock images capture the excitement on the water. The [volume concludes] with racing information, profiling top racers, rules, and tactics." Horn Book Guide

Includes glossary

Wurdinger, Scott D.

Kayaking; by Scott Wurdinger and Leslie Rapparlie. Creative Education 2006 48p il (Adventure sports) $21.95

Grades: 5 6 7 8   **797.1**
1. Kayaks and kayaking
ISBN 978-1-58341-397-5
LC 2005051057

"Strong, full-page color photographs illustrate this overview of kayaking. . . . Tracing the use of kayaks back thousands of years, the authors touch on the history of the boats before moving on to contemporary usage for sports and recreation. . . . The exciting views . . . will instantly draw browsers and serious readers alike." Booklist

Includes bibliographical references

797.2   Swimming and diving

Arroyo, Sheri L.

How deep sea divers use math; math curriculum consultant: Rhea A. Stewart. Chelsea Clubhouse 2010 32p il (Math in the real world) lib bdg $28

Grades: 4 5 6   **797.2**

  1. Mathematics 2. Scuba diving 3. Vocational guidance
  ISBN 978-1-60413-611-1 lib bdg; 1-60413-611-1
  lib bdg

                         LC 2009-18413

"The layout for [this] slim [title] is bright and colorful with a photograph and a 'You Do the Math' problem to solve and large, easy-to-read text on every spread. An answer key is included in the back matter, along with a page detailing the career choices and the educational requirements. . . . [It] discusses how divers use math to determine how much air they will need in their tanks and use grids to map underwater shipwrecks. The mathematical topics covered include measurement, estimation, data analysis, and problem solving. . . . [This title] would be useful to supplement lessons on mathematics. [It] will also appeal to students wanting to learn more about math as it relates to specific careers." SLJ

  Includes glossary and bibliographical references

Boudreau, Helene

  Swimming science. Crabtree Pub. Co. 2009 32p il (Sports science) lib bdg $26.60; pa $8.95

Grades: 3 4 5 6   **797.2**

  1. Swimming
  ISBN 978-0-7787-4538-9 lib bdg; 0-7787-4538-4 lib bdg; 978-0-7787-4555-6 pa; 0-7787-4555-4 pa

                         LC 2008-48870

This book approachs swimming "from a scientific angle, describing some of the physics behind [the] pursuit and how athletes can use this knowledge to improve performance. . . . Fascinating facts . . . [such as] a discussion of the swimmer who covered 3,270 miles down the Amazon River . . . are presented in a captivating, lively manner. . . . The layout features colorful text boxes interspersed among photographs." SLJ

  Includes glossary and bibliographical references

Gifford, Clive

  Swimming; [by] Clive Gifford. PowerKids Press 2009 32p il (Personal best) lib bdg $25.25

Grades: 4 5 6 7 8   **797.2**

  1. Swimming
  ISBN 978-1-4042-4443-6 lib bdg; 1-4042-4443-3 lib bdg

                         LC 2007-43003

This guide to swimming "offers well-organized and easy-to-follow instructions, focusing on rules, clothing, specific skills, and competitions. . . . Informative, readable." SLJ

Guillain, Charlotte

  Swimming. Heinemann Library 2009 24p il (Sports and my body) lib bdg $21.36; pa $6.49

Grades: 1 2   **797.2**

  1. Swimming
  ISBN 978-1-4329-3455-2 lib bdg; 1-4329-3455-4 lib bdg; 978-1-4329-3460-6 pa; 1-4329-3460-0 pa

                         LC 2009-7083

Learn what swimming is, how it can help them stay healthy, and how they can swim safely.

  This book relates "activity to health . . . [and] explains that in order to stay healthy, children should get plenty of rest, eat healthy food, and drink plenty of water." SLJ

  Includes glossary and bibliographical references

Hoblin, Paul

  Swimming & diving. Norwood House Press 2011 64p il (Girls play to win) lib bdg $26.60

Grades: 4 5 6 7   **797.2**

  1. Diving 2. Swimming
  ISBN 978-1-59953-466-4; 1-59953-466-5

                         LC 2011011038

Covers the history, rules, fundamentals, and significant personalities of the sport of women's swimming and diving. Topics include: techniques, strategies, competitive events, and equipment.

  Includes glossary and bibliographical references

Lourie, Peter

  First dive to shark dive. Boyds Mills Press 2006 48p il $17.95 **797.2**

  1. Scuba diving 2. Scuba diving -- Juvenile literature
  ISBN 1-59078-068-X

                         LC 2005-24987

"In this photo-essay, a father and his 12-year-old daughter, Suzanna, fly to Andros, in the Bahamas, so Suzanna can learn to scuba dive. During an intense seven days, she becomes certified and makes four dives. The narrative . . . . also covers information about the island . . . the ocean and its inhabitants . . . and the old Andros traditions. . . . Stunning color photographs . . . reveal why Suzanna wanted to be certified to dive." Booklist

Minden, Cecilia

  Swimming; [by] Cecilia Minden and Katie Marsico. Cherry Lake Pub. 2009 32p il (Real world math: Sports) lib bdg $27.07

Grades: 4 5 6   **797.2**

  1. Swimming 2. Arithmetic
  ISBN 978-1-60279-246-3 lib bdg; 1-60279-246-1 lib bdg

                         LC 2008-1198

This book "starts with a short story on the history of [swimming], fundamental rules, and a math challenge in every chapter. . . . [This book] will pique your imagination." Sci Books Films

  Includes glossary and bibliographical references

Timblin, Stephen

  Swimming. Cherry Lake Pub. 2009 32p il (Innovation in sports) lib bdg $27.07

Grades: 4 5 6 7   **797.2**

  1. Swimming
  ISBN 978-1-60279-258-6 lib bdg; 1-60279-258-5 lib bdg

                         LC 2008002046

This describes swimming history, rules, equipment, training, and swimming stars

  This "stands out by emphasizing monumental shifts and advances in the events themselves. . . . Concise and occasionally revelatory." Booklist

  Includes glossary and bibliographical references

Wendorff, Anne

  Swimming. Bellwether Media 2010 24p il (Blastoff! readers. My first sports) $19.95

Grades: K 1 2 3   **797.2**

1. Swimming

ISBN 978-1-60014-326-7; 1-60014-326-1

     LC 2009-8182

Simple text and full color photographs introduce beginning readers to the sport of swimming.

Includes glossary and bibliographical references

798.4   Horse racing

Joyce, Gare

     Northern Dancer; king of the racetrack. Gare Joyce. Fitzhenry & Whiteside 2011 72 p.

Grades: 4 5 6   **798.4**

1. Northern Dancer (Race horse) -- Juvenile literature

ISBN 1554551633; 9781554551637

This book by Gare Joyce focuses on the racing horse Northern Dancer. "As a colt, he was unimpressive. . . . Eventually, the colt that nobody wanted took the racing world by storm. Northern Dancer won the Kentucky Derby, and went on to win the Preakness Stakes of Baltimore, and nearly won the Belmont of New York. On retirement, Northern Dancer became the greatest horse stud in history, worth over $40 million by 1981." (Publisher's note)

McCarthy, Meghan

     ★ **Seabiscuit**; the wonder horse. Simon & Schuster Books for Young Readers 2008 un il $15.99

Grades: K 1 2 3   **798.4**

1. Horse racing 2. Seabiscuit (Race horse) 3. Race horses -- Juvenile literature

ISBN 978-1-4169-3360-1; 1-4169-3360-3

     LC 2008-06729

"The book covers Seabiscuit's transformation from scruffy loser to—well, scruffy winner, his loyal team of owner, trainer, and jockey, and his appeal to the economically pinched crowds; the saga here culminates in Seabiscuit's famous match with War Admiral. . . . The account is simplified for the youngest audiences, and they'll get the high points of the story . . . without getting lost in detail. . . . The cartooning is genuinely comic at times; the acrylic paintings are subtly toned, though, with gray touches muting the colors slightly." Bull Cent Child Books

Scanlan, Lawrence

     The **big** red horse; the story of Secretariat and the loyal groom who loved him. with photos by Raymond Woolfe. Harper Trophy 2011 166p il pa $7.99

Grades: 4 5 6 7   **798.4**

1. Horse racing 2. Stablehands

ISBN 978-0-06-202669-9; 0-06-202669-0

"This biography of the legendary racehorse provides many intimate details about his daily life and incredible prowess. . . . His good looks and tremendous athletic ability enabled him to win the Triple Crown at a record-breaking pace and the hearts of the American people. Scanlan focuses on the special relationship between Secretariat and his groom, Eddie Sweat. . . . Black-and-white photos are scattered throughout. . . . This solid book will have special appeal for horse lovers." SLJ

Tate, Nikki

     Behind the scenes: the racehorse. Fitzhenry & Whiteside 2008 72p il $22.95; pa $18.95

Grades: 5 6 7 8   **798.4**

1. Horse racing 2. Horse racing -- Juvenile literature 4. Racetracks (Horse racing) -- Juvenile literature

ISBN 978-1-55455-018-0; 1-55455-018-1; 978-1-55455-032-6 pa; 1-55455-032-7 pa

"A short history of horse racing opens this attractive and informative book. Tate discusses the breeding, training, and care of the horses but devotes plenty of space to the people who are involved in the sport. . . . The many color photos . . . are quite clear and well matched to the text." Booklist

Wiseman, Blaine

     Kentucky Derby. Weigl Publishers 2010 32p il (Sporting championships) lib bdg $26; pa $10.95

Grades: 3 4 5   **798.4**

1. Horse racing 2. Kentucky Derby

ISBN 978-1-61690-121-9 lib bdg; 1-61690-121-7 lib bdg; 978-1-61690-122-6 pa; 1-61690-122-5 pa

This sets the Kentucky Derby "within the context of the sport and explains what you need to know when watching the [event]." Booklist

Includes bibliographical references

798.8   Dog racing

Blake, Robert J.

     ★ **Togo**. Philomel Bks. 2002 un il $16.99

Grades: K 1 2 3   **798.8**

1. Dogs 2. Dogs -- Fiction 3. Sled dogs -- Juvenile literature 4. Iditarod Trail Sled Dog Race, Alaska -- Juvenile literature

ISBN 0-399-23381-4

     LC 2001-45926

In 1925, Togo, a Siberian husky who loves being a sled dog, leads a team that rushes to bring diphtheria antitoxin from Anchorage to Nome, Alaska

The author "paints a vivid word-picture of bitter, deadly conditions and the grueling effort required to surmount them, reinforcing it with dramatic art." Booklist

Miller, Debbie S.

     The **great** serum race; blazing the Iditarod Trail. illustrations by Jon van Zyle. Walker & Co. 2002 un il map hardcover o.p. pa $8.95

Grades: 3 4 5   **798.8**

1. Dogs 2. Iditarod Trail Sled Dog Race, Alaska 3. Mushers -- Alaska -- Juvenile literature 4. Sled dogs -- Alaska -- Juvenile literature 5. Diphtheria antitoxin -- Juvenile literature 6. Diphtheria -- Alaska -- Nome -- Juvenile literature 7. Iditarod National Historic Trail (Alaska) -- History -- Juvenile literature

ISBN 0-8027-8811-4; 0-8027-8812-2 lib bdg; 0-8027-7723-2 pa

     LC 2001-56777

The story of the heroic role played by sled dogs, including the Siberian husky Togo, in the delivery of antitoxin serum to those stricken with diphtheria in 1925 Nome. Includes historical notes about the event as well as about the Iditarod Sled Dog Race which commemorates it

"Zyle, official artist of the Iditarod and a musher himself, has created vivid, full-spread paintings to bring the story to life. . . . This is an excellent account told with lots of detail and drama." SLJ

Includes bibliographical references

799.1 Fishing

Lindeen, Carol

Freshwater fishing; by Carol K. Lindeen. Capstone Press 2011 32p il (Blazers. Wild outdoors) lib bdg $25.32
Grades: 2 3 4   **799.1**
  1. Fishing
  ISBN 978-1-4296-4810-3 lib bdg; 1-4296-4810-4 lib bdg
                    LC 2010001015

This "will fill a gap in many rural communities. . . . Blocks of text or 'Wild Facts' are scattered among the pages providing humorous or memorable trivia. . . . Close-up photography fills the pages and shows safe hunting attire." SLJ

Includes glossary and bibliographical references

799.2 Hunting

Adamson, Thomas K.

Bowhunting. Capstone Press 2011 32p il (Blazers. Wild outdoors) lib bdg $25.32
Grades: 2 3 4   **799.2**
  1. Hunting 2. Bow and arrow
  ISBN 978-1-4296-4808-0 lib bdg; 1-4296-4808-2 lib bdg
                    LC 2009053410

This "will fill a gap in many rural communities. . . . Blocks of text or 'Wild Facts' are scattered among the pages providing humorous or memorable trivia. . . . Close-up photography fills the pages and shows safe hunting attire." SLJ

Includes glossary and bibliographical references

Deer hunting. Capstone Press 2011 32p il (Blazers. Wild outdoors) lib bdg $25.32
Grades: 2 3 4   **799.2**
  1. Deer hunting
  ISBN 978-1-4296-4807-3 lib bdg; 1-4296-4807-4 lib bdg
                    LC 2009053412

Describes how to hunt deer, including the skills and patience required for the hunt, the proper guns and ammunition needed, and the safety skills every hunter should follow.

This "will fill a gap in many rural communities. . . . Blocks of text or 'Wild Facts' are scattered among the pages providing humorous or memorable trivia. . . . Close-up photography fills the pages and shows safe hunting attire." SLJ

Includes glossary and bibliographical references

Duck hunting. Capstone Press 2011 32p il (Blazers. Wild outdoors) lib bdg $25.32
Grades: 2 3 4   **799.2**
  1. Ducks 2. Hunting
  ISBN 978-1-4296-4809-7 lib bdg; 1-4296-4809-0 lib bdg
                    LC 2010001097

This "will fill a gap in many rural communities. . . . Blocks of text or 'Wild Facts' are scattered among the pages providing humorous or memorable trivia. . . . Close-up photography fills the pages and shows safe hunting attire." SLJ

Includes glossary and bibliographical references

Peterson, Judy Monroe

Big game hunting. Rosen Central 2011 64p il map (Hunting: pursuing wild game!)) lib bdg $29.25; pa $12.95
Grades: 5 6 7 8   **799.2**
  1. Hunting
  ISBN 978-1-4488-1240-0 lib bdg; 1-4488-1240-2 lib bdg; 978-1-4488-2270-6 pa; 1-4488-2270-X pa
                    LC 2010006859

In this introduction to big game hunting "Peterson displays an impressive grasp of the pastime by throwing in almost everything: types of guns and bows, safety laws, licenses, land access, animal behavior, clothing, methods of hunting, and preparing harvested meat. . . . [The book] is jam-packed with info. . . . A green-heavy design, bright photoss of hunters . . . and prey, and above average back matter close out this solid entry." Booklist

Includes bibliographical references

Wolny, Philip

Waterfowl. Rosen Central 2011 64p il (Hunting: pursuing wild game!) lib bdg $29.25; pa $12.95
Grades: 4 5 6 7   **799.2**
  1. Hunting 2. Water birds
  ISBN 978-1-4488-1243-1 lib bdg; 1-4488-1243-7 lib bdg; 978-1-4488-2273-7 pa; 1-4488-2273-4 pa
                    LC 2010017396

This guide to waterfowl hunting covers what to wear and pack, shooting strategies, the construction of duck blinds, gun safety, hunting permits and licenses, and other laws relating to hunting limits, seasons, and private and public property.

Includes bibliographical references

800 LITERATURE, RHETORIC & CRITICISM

808 Rhetoric and collections of literary texts from more than two literatures

Children's writer's & illustrator's market; edited by Alice Pope. Writer's Digest Books il
Grades: Adult Professional   **808**
  1. Publishers and publishing 2. Authorship -- Handbooks, manuals, etc.
  Annual. First published 1998

This reference includes listings of children's book publishers, magazines, agents, art reps, contests, clubs, conferences, awards, and grants with contact information, along with articles and interviews on a variety of subjects relating to children's writing, illustrating, and publishing

Includes bibliographical references

Christelow, Eileen

★ **What** do authors do? Clarion Bks. 1995 32p il hardcover o.p. pa $5.95

Grades: 1 2 3   **808**

1. Authors 2. Authorship 3. Illustrators 4. Publishers and publishing 5. Authors -- Juvenile literature 6. Authorship -- Juvenile literature 7. Illustrators -- Juvenile literature 8. Publishers and publishing -- Juvenile literature

ISBN 0-395-71124-X; 0-395-86621-9 pa

LC 94-19725

"Christelow packs a great deal of humor as well as information into her attractive pages. Best of all, she infuses the whole with a sense of the zest and love that writers feel for their work." Booklist

Cleary, Brian P.

Skin like milk, hair of silk; what are similes and metaphors? illustrated by Brian Gable. Millbrook Press 2009 il (Words are categorical) lib bdg $15.95

Grades: 2 3 4   **808**

1. Simile 2. Metaphor

ISBN 978-0-8225-9151-1; 0-8225-9151-0

LC 2008049643

"Cleary provides brief definitions of similes and metaphors, offers roughly 15 examples of each one, and explains how they are used. Large pen-and-ink illustrations feature cartoon cats rendered in bold, vibrant colors. The style is fun and inviting." SLJ

Cornwall, Phyllis

Put it all together. Cherry Lake Pub. 2010 32p il (Super smart information strategies) lib bdg $27.97

Grades: 3 4 5 6   **808**

1. Report writing

ISBN 978-1-60279-643-0 lib bdg; 1-60279-643-2 lib bdg

LC 2009027806

"The appealing layout includes manageable paragraphs, a variety of engaging illustrations, and examples that clearly guide readers through each topic. In [this book], strategies include gathering resources, organizing information, and ways of presenting discoveries." SLJ

Includes glossary and bibliographical references

Fletcher, Ralph

★ **How** to write your life story; [by] Ralph Fletcher. Collins 2007 102p $15.99; pa $5.99

Grades: 5 6 7 8   **808**

1. Authorship 2. Autobiography -- Authorship

ISBN 978-0-06-050770-1; 978-0-06-050769-5 pa

LC 2007010990

A guide to help write an autobiography

"Fletcher gives readers and educators many practical and supportive tips. . . . Interspersed within the text are interviews with Jack Gantos, Kathi Appelt, and Jerry Spinelli, along with passages from the author's own memoir." SLJ

Fox, Kathleen

Plagiarism! Plagiarism! 25 fun games and activities to teach documenting and sourcing skills to students. Upstart Books 2011 56p il pa $14.95

Grades: Adult Professional   **808**

1. Authorship 2. Plagiarism

ISBN 978-1-60213-050-0; 1-60213-050-7

"This handy book is aimed at teaching a tricky concept to primary and elementary grade children. The author pro-

vides a discussion of sources, rewording, when to use quotation marks, etc. Each activity is written in the style of a lesson plan." SLJ

Greenwood, Cathleen

So, you wanna be a writer? how to write, get published, and maybe even make it big! Vicki Hambleton, Cathleen Greenwood. Aladdin/Beyond Words 2012 186 p. ill. (So, you wanna be ..) (pbk.) $9.99

Grades: 4 5 6   **808**

1. Vocational guidance 2. Authorship -- Handbooks, manuals, etc. 3. Authorship -- Marketing -- Juvenile literature 4. Authorship -- Vocational guidance -- Juvenile literature

ISBN 9781582700434 2001 edition.; 1582700435 2001 edition; 9781582703534 2012 edition; 1582703590 2012 edition; 9781582703596 2012 edition; 9781442452916 2012 edition

LC 2011046252

This book presents a "[s]oup-to-nuts overview on all aspects of developing a writing career, from picking a genre to publicizing a finished work." It includes "myriad interviews, not only of established professionals such as Wendelin Van Draanen and Todd Strasser, but of young writers who may not be as familiar. Additionally, the authors sample some of these young wordsmiths' work . . . It includes quizzes, writing exercises to loosen up the brain and a handy section on further resources as well as a . . . short glossary of terms that all professional writers should know." (Kirkus Reviews)

Leedy, Loreen

★ **Look** at my book; how kids can write & illustrate terrific books. written and illustrated by Loreen Leedy. Holiday House 2004 32p il $16.95

Grades: K 1 2 3   **808**

1. Authorship 2. Handicraft 3. Bookbinding 4. Illustration of books 5. Book design 6. Authorship -- Juvenile literature 7. Book design -- Juvenile literature 8. Illustration of books -- Juvenile literature

ISBN 0-8234-1590-2

LC 2003-41713

Provides ideas and simple directions for writing, illustrating, designing, and binding books.

"Following the writing process fairly closely . . . [the author] takes readers through a step-by-step formula that almost guarantees a successful product. . . . Lively, colorful illustrations expand and interpret the text." SLJ

Mack, James

Journals and blogging; [by] Jim Mack. Raintree 2009 32p il (Culture in action) $28.21; pa $7.99

Grades: 5 6 7 8   **808**

1. Diaries 2. Weblogs

ISBN 978-1-4109-3406-2; 1-4109-3406-3; 978-1-4109-3423-9 pa; 1-4109-3423-3 pa

LC 2009000490

This "encourages readers to write as a way to express their feelings. It describes different types of journals and blogs. A page on Internet safety and the danger of downloading material encourages adult supervision. . . . Well organized and with bright, colorful photography, [this] introductory [title gives] readers good basic knowledge." SLJ

Includes glossary and bibliographical references

Miles, Liz

Writing a screenplay. Raintree 2009 32p il (Culture in action) $28.21; pa $7.99

Grades: 5 6 7 8 **808**

1. Drama -- Technique

ISBN 978-1-4109-3407-9; 1-4109-3407-1; 978-1-4109-3424-6 pa; 1-4109-3424-1 pa

This covers writing for "film and television. Plot, location, characters, dialogue, and mood are a few of the components discussed. . . . Well organized and with bright, colorful photography, [this] introductory [title gives] readers good basic knowledge." SLJ

Includes glossary and bibliographical references

Morrison, Lillian

It rained all day that night; autographs, rhymes & inscriptions. compiled by Lillian Morrison; illustrated by Christy Hale. August House 2003 80p il $16.95; pa $9.95

Grades: 3 4 5 6 **808**

1. Poetry 2. Autograph verse 3. Autograph albums 4. Children's poetry, American 5. American poetry -- Collections

ISBN 0-87483-735-9; 0-87483-726-X pa

LC 2003-51987

An illustrated compilation of short poems and other inscriptions from autograph albums, arranged by such themes as friendship, school, and nonsense.

"Morrison has created a stunning collection of autograph verses. . . . Hale's ink-and-watercolor paintings dance across each page, extending the sentiment . . . implicit in each verse." SLJ

Rau, Dana Meachen

Ace your creative writing project. Enslow Elementary 2009 48p il (Ace it! information literacy) lib bdg $23.93

Grades: 3 4 5 **808**

1. Creative writing

ISBN 978-0-7660-3395-5 lib bdg; 0-7660-3395-3 lib bdg

LC 2008024888

This describes where writers get their ideas, your story's characters and setting, writing, revising, and presenting your writing

Includes bibliographical references

Ace your writing assignment. Enslow Elementary 2009 48p il (Ace it! information literacy) lib bdg $23.93

Grades: 3 4 5 **808**

1. English language -- Composition and exercises

ISBN 978-0-7660-3394-8 lib bdg; 0-7660-3394-5 lib bdg

LC 2008024887

This describes how to make writing better and more interesting

Includes bibliographical references

Rosinsky, Natalie M.

Write your own biography; by Natalie M. Rosinsky. Compass Point Books 2008 64p il (Write your own) lib bdg $31.93

Grades: 5 6 7 8 **808**

1. Biography -- Authorship

ISBN 978-0-7565-3366-3 lib bdg; 0-7565-3366-X lib bdg

LC 2007011471

"Rosinsky adroitly leads readers through the challenging process of researching and writing a biography. Chapters include helpful suggestions, excerpts from published works, and writing exercises. Full-color photos, charts, and graphics break up the text." SLJ

Includes glossary and bibliographical references

Sendak, Maurice, 1928-2012

★ My brother's book; Maurice Sendak; [edited by] Michael di Capua. HarperCollins 2013 32 p. (hardcover bdg.) $18.95

Grades: 4 5 6 7 8 **808**

1. Poetry 2. Poetry -- Collections

ISBN 0062234897; 9780062234896

LC 2012942549

In this book, "with influences from Shakespeare and William Blake, [Maurice] Sendak pays homage to his late brother, Jack, whom he credited for his passion for writing and drawing. Pairing Sendak's . . . poetry with his . . . artwork, . . . Sendak's tribute to his brother is an expression of both grief and love. . . . Pulitzer Prize--winning literary critic and Shakespearean scholar Stephen Greenblatt contributes a[n] . . . introduction." (Publisher's note)

Tadjo, Veronique

★ Talking drums; a selection of poems from Africa south of the Sahara. edited and illustrated by Véronique Tadjo. Bloomsbury Children's Books 2003 96p il map $15.95

Grades: 5 6 7 8 **808**

1. African poetry 2. African poetry (English) 3. African poetry -- Collections 4. African poetry -- Translations into English

ISBN 1-58234-813-8

LC 2003-52173

A collection of traditional and twentieth-century poems from sub-Saharan Africa, written in or translated into English, that expresses the spirit and history of this region

"The contemporary and the traditional are both well represented in this lively anthology. . . . Illustrated with small, black-and-white folk-art drawings, the collection ranges widely, including poems of love, sorrow, and pride. . . . This [is a] fine resource for social studies and literature classes, which will also be great for reading aloud." Booklist

Includes glossary

Writing and publishing; the librarian's handbook. edited by Carol Smallwood. American Library Association 2010 189p (ALA guides for the busy librarian) pa $65

Grades: Adult Professional **808**

1. Authorship 2. Library science

ISBN 978-0-8389-0996-6; 0-8389-0996-5

LC 2009-25047

"This important writer's guide is readable from cover to cover or by bits and pieces and is a helpful and handy read for every librarian." Libr Media Connect

Includes bibliographical references

808.06   Rhetoric of specific kinds of writing

Fletcher, Ralph

Guy-write; what every guy writer needs to know. by Ralph Fletcher. 1st ed. Christy Ottaviano Books/Henry Holt and Co. 2012 166 p. ill. (hardcover) $15.99

Grades: 4 5 6   **808.06**

1. Writing 2. Boys -- Books and reading 3. Authors -- Juvenile literature 4. Authorship -- Juvenile literature 5. Illustrators -- Juvenile literature

ISBN 0805094040; 9780805094046

LC 2011033487

Author Ralph "Fletcher offers a new writing guide with advice aimed squarely at boys. . . . He lets guy writers know it's OK to write what they love: humor, grossness, battles, fantasy and horror. And he counsels guy writers on how to talk with their teachers about writing what they love to satisfy assignments. Along the way Fletcher peppers the text with general writing tips and suggestions for ways to make all types of writing stronger and more enjoyable." (Kirkus Reviews)

808.1   Rhetoric in specific literary forms

Prelutsky, Jack

★ Pizza, pigs, and poetry; how to write a poem. Greenwillow Books 2008 191p il $16.99; pa $5.99

Grades: 4 5 6   **808.1**

1. Poets 2. Authors 3. Poetics 4. Singers 5. Translators 6. Children's authors 7. Poetry -- By individual authors 8. Poetry -- Authorship -- Juvenile literature

ISBN 978-0-06-143449-5; 0-06-143449-3; 978-0-06-143448-8 pa; 0-06-143448-5 pa

LC 2007-36738

"Along with easy-to-follow tips for creating verse, haiku, and concrete poetry, the reigning Children's Poet Laureate offers insights into his own thought processes, . . . glimpses of his childhood, and personal anecdotes. . . . Prelutsky tucks in more than a dozen examples of his own work, plus 10 two-and-part-of-a-third line 'poem starts.'" Booklist

Wolf, Allan

Immersed in verse; an informative, slightly irreverent & totally tremendous guide to living the poet's life. [by] Allan Wolf; illustrated by Tuesday Mourning. Lark Books 2006 112p il $14.95

Grades: 5 6 7 8   **808.1**

1. Poetics

ISBN 1-57990-628-1

LC 2005024825

Contains advice, ideas, writing activities, and encouragement from a working poet for aspiring poets. Includes poems by a variety of poets from the unknown to the famous, including Langston Hughes, E.E. Cummings, Eve Merriam, and more

"This how-to guide—chock-full of examples—is sure to inspire and nurture young poets. The information is intensive without being overwhelming, wise without being didactic. Wolf's love of language is evident throughout." SLJ

Includes glossary and bibliographical references

808.3   Rhetoric of fiction

Bullard, Lisa

You can write a story! a story-writing recipe for kids. by Lisa Bullard; illustrated by Deborah Haley Melmon. Two-Can 2007 47p il $16.95

Grades: 2 3 4   **808.3**

1. Authorship 2. Creative writing 3. Fiction -- Technique

ISBN 978-1-58728-587-5; 1-58728-587-8

LC 2006016771

"Bullard takes a clever approach to teaching children the basic steps in story composition by treating the process as a cooking exercise. She begins with the basic ingredients of character, setting, and action, and then takes readers through the various ways they can add flavorings to their stories, including spicy settings, tempting titles, and the all-important taste test (revising). . . . The clear, engaging text speaks directly to a child. . . . Melmon's cartoon illustrations are bright, amusing, and strategically placed to add interest." Booklist

Includes bibliographical references

Hershenhorn, Esther

S is for story; a writer's alphabet. written by Esther Hershenhorn; illustrated by Zachary Pullen. Sleeping Bear Press 2009 un il $17.95; lib bdg $7.95

Grades: 3 4 5 6   **808.3**

1. Alphabet 2. Authorship 3. Fiction -- Technique

ISBN 978-1-58536-439-8; 1-58536-439-8; 978-1-58536-511-1 lib bdg; 1-58536-511-4 lib bdg

LC 2009005433

"This engaging, instructive introduction to writing stands out. The concepts paired with each letter cover elements of story (plot, characters); technique (revision, journaling); and basic practices for fostering creativity (observe). Short poems; clear, enthusiastic explanations; tips; and quotes from well-known children's authors appear on each page." Booklist

Levine, Gail Carson

★ Writing magic; creating stories that fly. Collins 2006 167p $16.99; pa $5.99

Grades: 5 6 7 8   **808.3**

1. Authorship 2. Creative writing 3. Fiction -- Technique 4. Fiction -- Authorship -- Juvenile literature

ISBN 978-0-06-051961-2; 0-06-051969-4; 978-0-06-051960-5 pa; 0-06-051960-6 pa

LC 2006-00481

"Levine, best known for Ella Enchanted (1997), offers middle-graders ideas about making their own writing take flight. . . . Among the topics she covers are shaping character, beginnings and endings, revising, and finding ideas. . . . Each chapter concludes with writing exercises. . . . A terrific item to have on hand for writing groups or for individual young writers who want to improve." Booklist

Litwin, Laura Baskes

Write horror fiction in 5 simple steps; Laura Baskes Litwin. Enslow Publishers 2013 48 p. $23.93

Grades: 4 5 6   **808.3**

1. Horror fiction -- Authorship -- Juvenile literature 2. Horror tales -- Technique -- Juvenile literature 3. Horror

tales -- Authorship -- Juvenile literature
ISBN 076603836X; 9780766038363

LC 2010038776

This book by Laura Baskes Litwin, part of the Creative Writing in 5 Simple Steps series, "shows aspiring writers how to write a terrifying tale of horror. . . . A good horror story is like a good ride at an amusement park. Feeling scared without having to face real danger is exhilarating. The story builds with tantalizing ideas. The reader inches out on the coaster track, knowing the precarious drop is seconds away." (Publisher's note)

Includes bibliographical references, filmography and index

Mazer, Anne

★ **Spilling** ink; a young writer's handbook. by Anne Mazer and Ellen Potter; illustrated by Matt Phelan. Flash Point 2010 275p il $17.99; pa $9.99

Grades: 5 6 7 8   **808.3**

1. Authorship 2. Creative writing 3. Fiction -- Technique 4. Authorship -- Juvenile literature 5. Fiction -- Authorship -- Juvenile literature
ISBN 978-1-59643-514-8; 1-59643-514-3; 978-1-59643-628-2 pa; 1-59643-628-X pa

"Two fine writers put their heads together and come up with an equally fine guide to their craft for beginners. . . . Mazer speaks to beginnings . . . while Potter tackles endings; and both have diverting things to say about everything that happens in between, whether it's the narrative voice or (eek) writer's block. [They are] always agreeable, practical, and commonsensical in their approach. . . . Their text is enlivened with sidebar features, personal anecdotes, and suggestions to readers for exercising their new skills. . . . Such devices, along with the authors' unfailing good humor, will go a long way to convincing their audience that writing can actually be fun! A notion that is nicely underscored by Phelan's engaging and always appealing illustrations." Booklist

808.5   Rhetoric of speech

Bullard, Lisa

Ace your oral or multimedia presentation. Enslow Elementary 2009 48p il (Ace it! information literacy) lib bdg $23.93

Grades: 3 4 5   **808.5**

1. Multimedia 2. Public speaking
ISBN 978-0-7660-3391-7 lib bdg; 0-7660-3391-0 lib bdg

LC 2008024885

"Learn how to research, write, practice, and present an oral or multimedia presentation with confidence" Publisher's note

Includes bibliographical references

808.8   Collections of literary texts from more than two literatures

The **big** book for toddlers; edited by Alice Wong & Lena Tabori. Welcome Books 2009 219p il $24.95

Grades: PreK K   **808.8**

1. Games 2. Handicraft 3. Fairy tales 4. Nursery

rhymes
ISBN 978-1-59962-071-8; 1-59962-071-5

"Full-bleed vintage illustrations by Jessie Willcox Smith, Maxfield Parrish, Margaret Evans Price and others grace the pages of this cheerful . . . hardcover book, divided into five sections: arts and crafts activities, condensed fairy tales, songs, games and nursery rhymes. The projects are simple and have buoyant instructions, . . . songs such as 'Old MacDonald' and 'Ants Go Marching' include musical notation; and familiar stories and rhymes appear as well. The lively assemblage will appeal to toddlers, and the heirloom images should captivate them as well as nostalgic adults." Publ Wkly

Classic horse stories; compiled by Christina Rossetti Darling and Blue Lantern Studio. Chronicle Books 2010 144p $19.99

Grades: 4 5 6   **808.8**

1. Horses 2. Literature -- Collections
ISBN 978-0-8118-6569-2; 0-8118-6569-X

LC 2010008550

"This compilation of stories, poems, and artwork celebrates the relationship between horses and their devotees. Darling pulls from a wide range of familiar, beloved material: excerpts from Steinbeck's The Red Pony, Farley's The Black Stallion, and Lewis's The Horse and His Boy join poetry from Shakespeare, Farjeon, and Stevenson. Varied paintings and illustrations from throughout the 20th century underscore the point that the book offers something for all tastes." Publ Wkly

De Paola, Tomie

Joy to the world; Christmas stories and songs. G.P. Putnam's Sons 2010 111p il lib bdg $24.99

Grades: K 1 2 3   **808.8**

1. Carols 2. Christmas 3. Literature -- Collections
ISBN 978-0-399-25536-6; 0-399-25536-2

LC 2010284499

"This handsome omnibus includes three of dePaola's adaptations of traditional Christmas legends—The Night of Las Posadas, The Story of the Three Wise Kings, and The Legend of the Poinsettia—in addition to five selections from Tomie dePaola's Book of Christmas Carols. The distinctions of tone and style reveal a versitility with which this illustrator is not always credited." Horn Book Guide

Everything I need to know I learned from a children's book. Roaring Brook 2009 233p $29.99

Grades: Adult Professional   **808.8**

1. Children's literature -- History and criticism
ISBN 978-1-59643-395-3; 1-59643-395-7

"Over 100 noteworthy figures, from Ursula K. Le Guin to Jay Leno, convey lessons learned from specific children's books in this affirming collaboration, which is divided into six thematic sections and features full-color images. For each selection, a contributor provides a brief essay about how the book influenced him or her, accompanied by an excerpt. . . . A moving patchwork message about the transformative powers of reading." Publ Wkly

Griffiths, Andy

Killer koalas from outer space; and lots of other very bad stuff that will make your brain explode! illustrations by Terry Denton. Feiwel and Friends 2011 172p il $12.99

Grades: 3 4 5 6　　　　　　　　　　**808.8**
1. Literature -- Collections
ISBN 978-0-312-36789-3; 0-312-36789-9

Portions of this book were originally published in Australia as "The Bad Book" and "The Very Bad Book"

"Sometimes bad can be very, very good indeed. Griffiths proves this time and again in this hilarious collection of rude, lewd and crude poems, jokes and cautionary tales. Deliciously revolting characters in stories . . . are sure to leave young, potty-humor-loving readers in stitches. Denton's edgy, stick-figure illustrations only add to the fun, upping the gross-out ante and giving the collection a frenetic energy that makes the book nearly impossible to put down. . . . The genius of this subversive little tome lies in its perfect combination of zany subject matter that will appeal to a broad spectrum of readers and a format that make it easily accessible to beginning and struggling readers." Kirkus

Julie Andrews' collection of poems, songs, and lullabies; edited by Julie Andrews and Emma Walton Hamilton; paintings by James McMullan. Little, Brown Books for Young Readers 2009 192p il $24.99
Grades: K 1 2 3　　　　　　　　　**808.8**
1. Songs 2. Lullabies 3. Poetry -- Collections
ISBN 978-0-316-04049-5; 0-316-04049-5

LC 2009-5121

"Julie Andrews and her daughter's selection of material for children contains works by figures as diverse as Emily Dickinson, Langston Hughes, Rodgers and Hammerstein, A.A. Milne and Shel Silverstein, as well as offerings by Andrews and Hamilton. McMullan's paintings express the sometimes silly, sometimes melancholic temperaments of the pieces, which together form a tapestry of human emotions and experiences, grand and small. The broad potpourri of voices, given a modern yet comforting flair by the artwork, is bound to become a favorite. An audio CD with poems read by Andrews and Hamilton is included." Publ Wkly

The **Norton** anthology of children's literature; the traditions in English. Jack Zipes, general editor . . . [et al.] W.W. Norton 2005 xxxviii, 2471p il pa $65
Grades: Adult Professional　　　　　**808.8**
1. Literature -- Collections 2. Children's literature, English 3. Children's literature, American 4. Children's literature -- History and criticism
ISBN 0-393-97538-X

LC 2004-54172

A collection of fairy tales, picture books, nursery rhymes, fantasy, alphabets, chapbooks, and comics published in English since 1659, representing 170 authors and illustrators, and including more than ninety complete works and excerpts from others

"The delights are abundant. . . . A mile wide and very deep, this is an invaluable resource for professionals, but fun for casual perusing, too." Publ Wkly

Includes bibliographical references

Spinelli, Eileen
Today I will; a year of quotes, notes, and promises to myself. [by] Eileen & Jerry Spinelli; illustrated by Julia Rothman. Alfred A. Knopf 2009 un il $15.99; lib bdg $18.99
Grades: 5 6 7 8　　　　　　　　　　**808.8**
1. Quotations 2. Conduct of life 3. American literature

-- Collections
ISBN 978-0-375-84057-9; 0-375-84057-5; 978-0-375-96230-1 lib bdg; 0-375-96230-1 lib bdg

LC 2008047869

"The Spinellis turn their skills to inspiring readers with quotes and promises for every day of the year. There is a single-page entry for each day, and each one begins with a quote from children's literature. . . . Each quote is followed by an explanatory note. Each note is then summarized into a short promise on which readers can reflect. . . . The book covers a vast array of topics and themes, from serious to silly, and is inspiring and helpful." SLJ

808.81　　Collections in specific forms

All the wild wonders; poems of our Earth. edited by Wendy Cooling; illustrated by Piet Grobler. Frances Lincoln 2010 42p $19.95
Grades: 2 3 4 5　　　　　　　　　　**808.81**
1. Nature poetry 2. Poetry -- Collections
ISBN 978-1-84780-073-2; 1-84780-073-4

"The selections from more than 30 poets in this anthology celebrate the beauty of the wild and warn of the danger that threatens the environment. . . . With a multiracial cast, Grobler's moving, pencil-and-watercolor illustrations extend the global, environmental connections. . . . Great for sharing, this will grab conservationists with both the warnings and the hope." Booklist

A **children's** treasury of poems; illustrations by Linda Bleck. Sterling 2008 un il $12.95
Grades: PreK K 1 2　　　　　　　　**808.81**
1. Poetry -- Collections
ISBN 978-1-4027-4498-3; 1-4027-4498-6

"This collection of 19 humorous poems includes Robert Louis Stevenson's 'Bed in Summer,' Vachel Lindsay's 'The Little Turtle,' Edward Lear's 'The Owl and the Pussycat,' and Gelett Burgess's 'The Purple Cow,' among other familiar verses. Playful, cartoonlike illustrations with cutout characters and details superimposed on sturdy pages give the book texture and help create a novel effect. Different ethnicities are represented in the illustrations, although most are of fanciful animals and fairies. Young children should find the childlike format appealing." SLJ

Driscoll, Michael
★ A **child's** introduction to poetry; listen while you learn about the magic words that have moved mountains, won battles and made us laugh and cry. illustrated by Meredith Hamilton. Black Dog & Leventhal 2003 90p il $19.95
Grades: 4 5 6 7　　　　　　　　　　**808.81**
1. Poetry -- Collections 2. Poetry -- History and criticism
ISBN 1-57912-282-5

"The first section discusses the different forms the genre takes: nursery rhyme, narrative verse, ballad, free verse, pastoral, etc. Driscoll offers a clear explanation of each type and defines any difficult, associated vocabulary. Commentary on each example and a note on where to find the recording on the accompanying CD is provided for each selection. The second section covers individual poets from Homer to Maya Angelou and offers at least one example or excerpt from each writer's work. The brief introductions to the forms and poets are lively and often amusing. Readers will find the varied layouts and warm cartoon watercolors inviting." SLJ

Includes glossary and bibliographical references

Eric Carle's animals, animals. Philomel Bks. 1989 87p $21.99; pa $7.99

Grades: 2 3 4 5 **808.81**

1. Animals -- Poetry 2. Poetry -- Collections 3. Children's poetry -- Collections 4. Animals -- Poetry -- Juvenile literature

ISBN 0-399-21744-4; 0-698-11855-3 pa

LC 88-31646

"Illustrations take center stage in Eric Carle's Animals Animals . . . compiled by Laura Whipple. The well-chosen poems are from a variety of sources—the Bible, Shakespeare, Japanese Haiku, Pawnee Indian, weather sayings and contemporary poets like Judith Viorst, Ogden Nash, and Jack Prelutsky. On many pages the poem may be only two or three lines but the pictures are full-page spreads in Mr. Carle's familiar vividly colored, collage style." Kobrin Letter

Eric Carle's dragons dragons and other creatures that never were. Philomel Bks. 1991 69p il $21.99; pa $12.99

Grades: 2 3 4 5 **808.81**

1. Poetry -- Collections 2. Mythical animals -- Poetry 3. Children's poetry -- Collections 4. Mythical animals -- Poetry -- Juvenile literature

ISBN 0-399-22105-0; 0-399-22837-3 pa

LC 91-11986

An illustrated collection of poems about dragons and other fantastic creatures by a variety of authors

"The collection offers a sumptuous viewing of Carle's rich blend of tissue-paper and paint collages and a grand introduction to the imaginary beasts. Laura Whipple concludes this adroit compilation with a brief commentary on the fabulous animals as 'a magical part of our human heritage.'" Horn Book

Includes glossary

A **family** of poems; my favorite poetry for children. [selected by] Caroline Kennedy; paintings by Jon J. Muth. Hyperion Books for Children 2005 143p il $19.95

Grades: 3 4 5 6 **808.81**

1. Poetry -- Collections

ISBN 0-7868-5111-2

An anthology of over 100 poems divided into categories such as "About Me," "Animals," "Adventure" and "Bedtime," including works by such poets as A.A. Milne, Robert Louis Stevenson, Jack Prelutsky, Edward Lear, Robert Frost, William Wordsworth, T.S. Eliot, Carl Sandberg, William Shakespeare.

"From the cover photograph of Kennedy as a toddler reading to her teddy to the red linen-textured endpapers; from her thoughtful introduction and words of encouragement to children at the beginning of each section of carefully chosen poems to Muth's beautifully executed watercolors, this volume is a treasure." SLJ

★ A **foot** in the mouth; poems to speak, sing, and shout. [edited by Paul B. Janeczko; illustrated by Chris Raschka] Candlewick Press 2009 64p il $17.99

Grades: 4 5 6 7 **808.81**

1. Children's poetry 2. Poetry -- Collections

ISBN 978-0-7636-0663-3; 0-7636-0663-4

LC 2008-935581

"The poems in Janeczko and Raschka's collection . . . are not complacent, although plenty are funny and some are familiar. . . . Punchy collages flutter across airy white pages in loose visual arrangements; torn scraps of origami paper layer with fluid lines in tart color. Janeczko introduces the collection with the idea that 'Poetry is sound,' a pleasure to vocalize and memorize. . . . Readers will be emboldened to join in the 'song.'" Publ Wkly

Julie Andrews' treasury for all seasons; poems and songs to celebrate the year. selected by Julie Andrews & Emma Walton Hamilton; paintings by Marjorie Priceman. Little, Brown and Company 2012 192 p. $19.99

Grades: K 1 2 3 **808.81**

1. Songbooks 2. Children's poetry 3. Seasons -- Poetry

ISBN 0316040517; 9780316040518

LC 2011053202

This book is a "compilation of poems and songs (including some of [Julie] Andrews and [Emma Walton] Hamilton's own) from more than 75 writers, organized by month. Summer sees . . . poems about discovery and outdoor activity, with works by Billy Collins, Joy Harjo, and E.B. White; fall poems include nature, back-to-school, and Thanksgiving themes, with pieces by Emily Dickinson, Sandra Cisneros, and others. Caldecott Honor artist [Marjorie] Priceman" illustrates. (Publishers Weekly)

Leave your sleep; selected by Natalie Merchant; pictures by Barbara McClintock. Frances Foster Books 2012 48 p. (hardcover) $24.99

Grades: K 1 2 3 **808.81**

1. Songbooks 2. Children's poetry 3. Poetry -- Collections

ISBN 0374343683; 9780374343682

LC 2011047064

This book is a children's poetry collection. "For her 2010 hit album with the same title, [Natalie] Merchant composed music for 30 19th- and 20th-century British and American poems, some written for children and some written about childhood. For this volume, she's selected 19 of those poems (18 from the CD set and one other), describing them as 'representing the long conversation I had with my daughter during the first six years of her life.'" (Kirkus Reviews)

My village; rhymes from around the world. collected by by Danielle Wright; illustrated by Mique Moriuchi; introduction by Michael Rosen. Frances Lincoln Children's 2010 53p il $19.95

Grades: PreK K 1 2 **808.81**

1. Nursery rhymes 2. Poetry -- Collections

ISBN 978-1-84780-086-2; 1-84780-086-6

"A sunny cover invites readers into this collection of nursery rhymes from around the world. Selections from 22 countries presented in both English and the original language are included as well as the original script/alphabet when appropriate. . . . The rhymes are well chosen and range from funny and bouncy to quiet and thoughtful. The brightly colored collage illustrations complement them well." SLJ

★ **National** Geographic book of animal poetry; 200 poems that squeak, soar, and roar. [edited by] J. Patrick Lewis. National Geographic 2012 183 p.
Grades: 2 3 4 5   **808.81**
1. Animals -- Poetry -- Collections 2. Animals -- Poetry
ISBN 1426310099; 9781426310096; 9781426310546
LC 2012010404

This collection of poetry about animals, edited by J. Patrick Lewis, features "lighthearted poems from the likes of Basho and Ben Franklin, Leadbelly, Jack Prelutsky and Joyce Sidman . . . [and] animal photographs. Lewis adds advice for budding animal poets to the . . . bibliography and multiple indexes at the end." (Kirkus)

Includes bibliographical references and index

The **Oxford** book of story poems; [compiled by] Michael Harrison and Christopher Stuart-Clark. Oxford University Press 2006 175p il pa $18.95
Grades: 5 6 7 8   **808.81**
1. Poetry -- Collections
ISBN 978-0-19-276344-0 pa; 0-19-276344-X pa
LC 2007282711
First published 1990

This anthology contains "narrative verse by British and American poets, from traditional ballads such as 'Sir Patrick Spens' to contemporary poems such as Judith Nicholls' 'Storytime.' . . . The poets include Carroll, Keats, de la Mare, Kennedy, Lear, Lindsay, Longfellow, Noyes, Poe, Southey, and Tolkien. . . . A handy collection of story poems for reading aloud or alone." Booklist [review of 1990 edition]

★ **Poetry** speaks: who I am; poems of discovery, inspiration, independence, and everything else. Sourcebooks Jabberwocky 2010 136p $19.99
Grades: 5 6 7 8 9 10   **808.81**
1. Poetry -- Collections
ISBN 978-1-4022-1074-7; 1-4022-1074-4

This collection "aims at middle-grade readers with more than 100 strikingly diverse poems by writers including Poe, Frost, Nikki Giovanni, and Sandra Cisneros. The works are slotted together in mindful thematic order, beside occasional spot art. . . . Pairing a contemporary poem like Toi Derricotte's 'Fears of the Eighth Grade' alongside Keats's 'When I Have Fears That I May Cease to Be,' results in a refreshing lack of literary hierarchy that enables disparate works to build and reflect upon one another. An accompanying CD features recordings of 44 of the poems. . . . A sound and rewarding introduction to the joys of poetry." Publ Wkly

Rhymes round the world; [compiled by] Kay Chorao. Dutton Children's Books 2009 40p il $17.99
Grades: PreK K 1   **808.81**
1. Poetry -- Collections
ISBN 978-0-525-47875-1; 0-525-47875-2
LC 2008013887

"These 40 poems and songs offer children a taste of many different cultures. Most are anonymous or traditional nursery rhymes; a few are by English or American poets. The tone is light and joyous. Sweet illustrations of babies and toddlers engaged in playful activities depict the universality of children everywhere." SLJ

★ **River** of words; young poets and artists on the nature of things. edited by Pamela Michael; introduced by Robert Hass. Milkweed Editions 2008 298p il hardcover o.p. pa $18
Grades: 4 5 6 7 8 9   **808.81**
1. Nature poetry 2. Children's art 3. Children's writings 4. Teenagers' writings 5. Poetry -- Collections
ISBN 978-1-57131-685-1; 1-57131-685-X; 978-1-57131-680-6 pa; 1-57131-680-9 pa

"In 1995 Michael and Hass . . . cofounded the River of Words project, designed to connect students' art and poetry education to the natural world immediately around them. . . . The poems and pictures in this handsomely designed volume have been culled from yearly contests. . . . The works are startling, many of them dislocating and highly complex." Publ Wkly

Sail away with me; old and new poems. selected and written by Jane Collins-Philippe; illustrated by Laura Beingessner. Tundra Books 2010 un il $15.95
Grades: K 1 2 3   **808.81**
1. Sea poetry 2. Children's poetry 3. Poetry -- Collections
ISBN 978-0-88776-842-2; 0-88776-842-3

"Starting off with 'My Bonnie Lies Over the Ocean' and other folk-song favorites, this picture-book poetry collection celebrates the sea and sailing traditions. . . . The lively watercolor illustrations extend the images i the words. . . . Ranging in theme from adventure to nonsense, these poems will be fun for reading aloud." Booklist

Starry night, sleep tight; a bedtime book of lullabies. illustrated by Gail Yerrill. Tiger Tales 2009 un il $12.95
Grades: PreK   **808.81**
1. Lullabies 2. Poetry -- Collections
ISBN 978-1-58925-844-0; 1-58925-844-4

"This collection of familiar lullabies and poems is enhanced by soft, dreamlike artwork and attractively designed, quiltlike borders. The classic verses and songs are coupled with soft and lovable illustrations of animals and sprinkled with a touch of glitter to make bedtime seem magical." SLJ

The **tree** that time built; a celebration of nature, science, and imagination. selected by Mary Ann Hoberman and Linda Winston; [illustrations by Barbara Fortin] Sourcebooks Jabberwocky 2009 209p il $19.99
Grades: 5 6 7 8   **808.81**
1. Nature poetry 2. Science -- Poetry 3. Poetry -- Collections
ISBN 978-1-4022-2517-8; 1-4022-2517-2
LC 2009032608

An anthology of more than 100 poems celebrating the wonders of the natural world and encouraging environmental awareness. Includes an audio CD that comprises readings of 44 of the poems, many performed by the poets themselves.

"Classic works by Walt Whitman, Emily Dickinson, Christina Rossetti, and the like, and selections from contemporary poets are included. . . . This handsome collection is especially appropriate for classroom use and instruction. . . . From the playful to the profound, the poems invite reflection and inspire further investigation." SLJ

Includes glossary and bibliographical references

War and the pity of war; edited by Neil Philip; illustrated by Michael McCurdy. Clarion Bks. 1998 96p il $20

Grades: 5 6 7 8 9 10 **808.81**

1. War poetry 2. Children's poetry 3. War -- Poetry 4. Poetry -- Collections 5. War -- Juvenile poetry

ISBN 0-395-84982-9

LC 97-32897

"The selections, covering conflicts from ancient Persia to modern-day Bosnia, are by a wide variety of poets, from the well known (Tennyson, Whitman, Sandburg, Auden), to the obscure (Anakreon from ancient Greece and 11th-century Chinese poet Bunno). . . . The stark and simple scratchboard drawings are reminiscent of the Ernie Pyle illustrations from World War II and are as memorable as the best propaganda." SLJ

★ Winter poems; selected by Barbara Rogasky; illustrated by Trina Schart Hyman. Scholastic 1994 40p il $15.95; pa $5.99

Grades: 3 4 5 6 **808.81**

1. Winter -- Poetry 2. Poetry -- Collections 3. Children's poetry -- Collections 4. Seasons -- Poetry -- Juvenile literature 5. English poetry -- Collections -- Juvenile literature 6. American poetry -- Collections -- Juvenile literature

ISBN 0-590-42872-1; 0-590-42873-X pa

LC 91-24419

"Rogasky has selected a wide range of poems—25 in all—dating from 10th-century Japan to the contemporary U.S. The best of the ages is represented, with familiar favorites from Shakespeare, Thomas Hardy, Robert Frost, Emily Dickinson, Carl Sandburg, etc. . . . Hyman's illustrations perfectly capture the spirit of that season, with acrylics in deep, chilling shades. . . . A beautiful presentation of outstanding quality." SLJ

808.88 Collections of miscellaneous writings

Alcorn, Stephen

A gift of days; the greatest words to live by. Atheneum Books for Young Readers 2009 115p il $21.99

Grades: 5 6 7 8 **808.88**

1. Quotations 2. Celebrities

ISBN 978-1-4169-6776-7; 1-4169-6776-1

LC 2007-48766

"Beautifully designed and imaginatively conceptualized, this volume presents 366 days and 366 quotations from famous people, tagged to the days they were born. Alcorn lays this out on each double-page spread with a stunning polychrome-relief block-print bordered with pattern on one leaf and, facing, a week of birthdays and quotes. These images are often brilliantly inventive. . . . Librarians, educators and historically minded kids will take much pleasure from looking up birthdays to see the associated wisdom from women and men across the ages." Kirkus

809 History, description, critical appraisal of more than two literatures

Carpenter, Humphrey

The Oxford companion to children's literature; [by] Humphrey Carpenter and Mari Prichard. Oxford Univ. Press 1984 586p il hardcover o.p. pa $70

Grades: Adult Professional **809**

1. Reference books 2. Children's literature -- Dictionaries

ISBN 0-19-211582-0; 0-19-860228-6 pa

LC 83-15130

"One volume work with brief critiques of authors, illustrators, books, characters, and radio and television programs. Largely British in coverage of materials but does include most Newbery winners as well as well-known American, Australian and Canadian authors. Contemporary and historical subjects related to children's literature are examined." N Y Public Libr. Ref Books for Child Collect. 2d edition

Krull, Kathleen

★ Lives of the writers; comedies, tragedies (and what the neighbors thought) written by Kathleen Krull; illustrated by Kathryn Hewitt. 1st ed. Harcourt Brace & Co. 1994 96 p. col. ill. (reinforced) $21

Grades: 4 5 6 7 **809**

1. Poets 2. Authors 3. Humorists 4. Novelists 5. Dramatists 6. Historians 7. Journalists 8. Young adult literature/Works 9. Authors/Biography/Juvenile literature

ISBN 0152480099; 9780152480097

LC 93032436

This volume presents biographical sketches of writers. Arranged "in chronological order by date of birth, the selection of writers begins with Murasaki Shikibu, the first-century Japanese author of 'The Tale of Genji' . . . and concludes with Isaac Bashevis Singer, the Jewish American storyteller who died in 1991." (Horn Book Magazine)

This offers "views of twenty writers . . . from various countries and historical periods. Included are William Shakespeare, Edgar Allan Poe, Mark Twain, Zora Neale Hurston, Isaac Bashevis Singer, and many others." Publisher's note

Includes bibliographical references (p. 96) and index.

Sutton, Roger

A family of readers; the book lover's guide to children's and young adult literature. [by] Roger Sutton and Martha V. Parravano; foreword by Gregory Maguire. Candlewick Press 2010 350p il $22; pa $14.99

Grades: Adult Professional **809**

1. Children -- Books and reading 2. Teenagers -- Books and reading 3. Children's literature -- History and criticism

ISBN 978-0-7636-3280-9; 0-7636-3280-5; 978-0-7636-5755-0 pa; 0-7636-5755-7 pa

"This collection of essays from editors, reviewers, and authors emanates enthusiasm for books and reading. . . . Each section begins with an overview, followed by a selection of essays. The first chapter addresses the very smallest book lovers, and the last tackles the needs of young adults. Each chapter is followed by an annotated list of books. A complete bibliography and biographical sketches of the contributors are included in the end. . . . It should be required reading for every youth services librarian." Voice Youth Advocates

The Oxford encyclopedia of children's literature; Jack Zipes, editor in chief. Oxford University Press 2006 4v il set $495

    Grades: Adult Professional   **809**

    1. Reference books 2. Children's literature 3. Authors -- Biography 4. Children's literature -- Encyclopedias 6. Children's literature -- History and criticism

    ISBN 978-0-19-514656-1; 0-19-514656-5

                      LC 2005-34390

    "The 3200 signed articles in this set include brief discussions of the work of major writers, important trends, genres, characters, organizations, and noteworthy publications and people in the field. All of the alphabetical articles are clearly written and most include cross-references. . . . There is no comparable single work that brings together all aspects of the topic, making this a valuable resource." SLJ

    Includes bibliographical references

809.1   Literature in specific forms other than miscellaneous writings

Bodden, Valerie

    Concrete poetry. Creative Education 2010 32p il (Poetry basics) $28.50

    Grades: 5 6 7 8   **809.1**

    1. Poetry -- History and criticism

    ISBN 978-1-58341-775-1; 1-58341-775-3

                      LC 2008009156

    This book describes concrete poetry's "history, characteristics, and variations. Many examples are provided as well as ideas for how children can write their own pieces. The information is accessible, and the writing is sufficiently lively to engage readers. The well-designed pages feature a variety of art reproductions from different literary eras and some photographs." Horn Book Guide

    Includes glossary and bibliographical references

    Haiku. Creative Education 2010 32p il (Poetry basics) $19.95

    Grades: 5 6 7 8   **809.1**

    1. Haiku

    ISBN 978-1-58341-776-8; 1-58341-776-1

                      LC 2008-9158

    Presents history and examples of the Japanese form of poetry called haiku.

    "The information is accessible, and the writing is sufficiently lively to engage readers. The well-designed pages feature a variety of art reproductions from different literary eras and some photographs." Horn Book Guide

    Includes glossary and bibliographical references

    Limericks. Creative Education 2010 32p il (Poetry basics) $19.95

    Grades: 5 6 7 8   **809.1**

    1. Limericks

    ISBN 978-1-58341-777-5; 1-58341-777-X

                      LC 2008-9159

    This describes limericks' "history, characteristics, and variations. Many examples are provided as well as ideas for

how children can write their own pieces. The information is accessible, and the writing is sufficiently lively to engage readers. The well-designed pages feature a variety of art reproductions from different literary eras and some photographs." Horn Book Guide

    Includes glossary and bibliographical references

810   Literatures of specific languages and language families

Dude! stories and stuff for boys. edited by Sandy Asher and David Harrison. Dutton Childrens Books 2006 258p il $17.99

    Grades: 4 5 6 7   **810**

    1. Boys 2. American literature -- Collections

    ISBN 0-525-47684-9

                      LC 2005025060

    "These 18 original stories, plays, and poems by prize-winning writers range from entertaining to challenging and offer an array of characters and experiences. In Bill C. Davis' intimate, thought-provoking 'Family Meeting,' a boy whose stepbrother committed suicide discovers the value of life. Jamie Adoff's 'Twelve' is a rap poem about experiencing violence but still retaining hope. Jose Cruz Gonzalez's play Watermelon Kisses is an amusing, credible portrayal of brotherly love and squabbles. The selections, which include many well-written gems, will resonate with and also amuse middle-grade boys." Booklist

Here there be dragons; illustrated by David Wilgus. Harcourt Brace & Co. 1993 149p il hardcover o.p. pa $10

    Grades: 5 6 7 8   **810**

    1. Dragons -- Fiction 2. American literature -- Collections

    ISBN 0-15-201705-4 pa

                      LC 92-23194

    "Yolen has compiled a collection of her poetry and prose about dragons of all sizes, shapes and dispositions. She introduces each piece with a brief description including the circumstances surrounding its writing. . . . The poetry, like the prose, varies in length but will enthrall readers. David Wilgus' pen and ink drawings further enhance the book." Book Rep

★ **Wachale!** poetry and prose on growing up Latino in America; edited by Ilan Stavans. Cricket Publs. 2001 146p $16.95

    Grades: 5 6 7 8   **810**

    1. Latinos (U.S.) 2. Hispanic Americans 3. Bilingual books -- English-Spanish 4. American literature -- Hispanic American authors -- Collections

    ISBN 0-8126-4750-5

                      LC 2001-47189

    A bilingual collection of poems, stories, and other writings which celebrates diversity among Latinos.

    "This collection would make a fine classroom text, great for reading aloud and for stimulating students from everywhere to write about their roots and celebrate their shifting places across borders." Booklist

    Includes glossary and bibliographical references

Wilkin, Binnie Tate

African and African American images in Newbery Award winning titles; progress in portrayals. Scarecrow Press 2009 195p pa $40

Grades: Adult Professional   **810**

1. Newbery Medal 2. African Americans in literature 3. Children's literature -- History and criticism

ISBN 978-0-8108-6959-2 pa; 0-8108-6959-4 pa

LC 2009017726

"The author has exhaustively examined all books that have won the Newbery Medal and been cited as honor books since the award's creation in 1922. Her purpose is to evaluate the representation of Africans and African Americans, and to describe how these groups are portrayed in each title's historical context. . . . Books with the most positive images are awarded three pluses, while books with marginal African-American characters are indicated with an 'M.' . . . An essential volume for scholars, teachers, and librarians." SLJ

Includes bibliographical references

811   American poetry

Ada, Alma Flor

★ **Gathering** the sun; an alphabet in Spanish and English. English translation by Rosa Zubizarreta; illustrated by Simón Silva. Lothrop, Lee & Shepard Bks. 1997 un il $16.95; pa $6.99

Grades: 2 3 4   **811**

1. Alphabet 2. Children's poetry 3. Mexican Americans -- Poetry 4. Alphabet -- Juvenile literature 5. Poetry -- By individual authors 6. Bilingual books -- English-Spanish 7. Mexican Americans -- Juvenile literature 8. Agricultural laborers -- Juvenile literature

ISBN 0-688-13903-5; 0-688-17067-7 pa

"Using the Spanish alphabet as a template, Ada has written 27 poems that celebrate both the bounty of the harvest and the Mexican heritage of the farmworkers and their families. The poems, presented in both Spanish and English, are short and simple bursts of flavor. . . . Silva's sun-drenched gouache paintings are robust, with images sculpted in paint." Booklist

Adoff, Arnold

★ **Roots** and blues; a celebration. paintings by R. Gregory Christie. Clarion Books 2011 88p il

Grades: 4 5 6   **811**

1. Children's poetry 2. Blues music -- Poetry 3. African Americans -- Poetry 4. Poetry -- By individual authors 5. Blues (Music) -- History and criticism -- Juvenile literature

ISBN 0547235542; 9780547235547

LC 2009-26625

Adoff tells the story of the blues in this collection of sixty poems and prose pieces. "Grades eight to twelve." (Bull Cent Child Books)

"In this visceral collaboration, Adoff and Christie honor the enduring legacy of blues music. Vibrant, haunting acrylic paintings portray crowded slave ships, chain gang labor, and the crackling energy of juke joints. . . . Several poems titled 'Listening' capture the sounds of the decades in which they're set . . . and mimic the rhythms and repetitions of the blues. . . . This is a challenging, openhearted collection with

images and poems that bleed into one another, but also stand powerfully alone." Publ Wkly

Agee, Jon

★ **Orangutan** tongs; poems to tangle your tongue. Hyperion Books for Children 2009 47p il $16.99

Grades: 2 3 4 5   **811**

1. Humorous poetry 2. Tongue twisters 3. Children's poetry 4. Poetry -- By individual authors

ISBN 978-1-4231-0315-8; 1-4231-0315-7

LC 2008-13941

"This collection is loaded with tricky tongue-twisting rhymes that will challenge readers. . . . In addition to being just plain funny, Agee is a wordsmith and accomplished illustrator, factors that have produced another must-have winner from a comic master." SLJ

Ahlberg, Allan

Everybody was a baby once, and other poems; illustrator Bruce Ingman. Candlewick Press 2010 63p il $15.99

Grades: PreK K 1   **811**

1. Children's poetry 2. Infants -- Poetry 3. Poetry -- By individual authors

ISBN 978-0-7636-4682-0; 0-7636-4682-2

"From the creators of The Pencil, these 19 poems cover whimsical territory and feature kids, angels, sausages, and monsters, rendered in kinetic, childlike sketches. A few poems strike nostalgic, melancholy notes . . . but most are upbeat, with gently jazzy rhythms. . . . The Lilliputian cast and memorable verse could make this a dog-eared favorite." Publ Wkly

Alarcon, Francisco X.

Iguanas in the snow and other winter poems; poems, Francisco X. Alarcón; illustrations, Maya Christina Gonzalez. Children's Bk. Press 2001 31p il hardcover o.p. pa $7.95

Grades: 2 3 4   **811**

1. Winter -- Poetry 2. Winter -- Juvenile poetry 3. Poetry -- By individual authors 4. Bilingual books -- English-Spanish 5. California, Northern -- Juvenile poetry

ISBN 0-89239-168-5; 0-89239-202-9 pa

LC 00-65667

"Brief, zippy verses express delight in such simple things as a family frolic in the snow and the wonder of giant redwoods. . . . The selections are short of line and long on meter, with a rhythmic roll that begs reading aloud. . . . Gonzalez's illustrations are bright and busy, catching the playful cadence of the words." SLJ

Angelou, Maya

Amazing peace; a Christmas poem. by Maya Angelou; paintings by Steve Johnson and Lou Fancher. Schwartz & Wade Books 2008 un il $17.99; lib bdg $20.99

Grades: 3 4 5   **811**

1. Christmas -- Poetry 2. Poetry -- By individual authors

ISBN 978-0-375-84150-7; 0-375-84150-4; 978-0-375-94327-0 lib bdg; 0-375-94327-7 lib bdg

"This poem was largely inspired by the terrible natural disasters occurring throughout the world when Angelou was invited to read at the 2005 White House tree-lighting ceremony. Thus, the opening lines rumble and roil almost menacingly to illustrate the climate of doubt and anxiety into which the spirit of Christmas arrives. Hope enters as a whisper and grows until it is 'louder than the explosion of bombs.' . . . Johnson and Fancher's paintings, rendered in oil, acrylic, and fabric on canvas, elegantly depict a calm, snow-blanketed village where children play, families shop, and artisans ply their crafts. . . . This is a comforting book that gets to the heart of what Christmas should mean. As an added treat, Angelou reads the poem on the accompanying CD." SLJ

★ **Maya** Angelou; edited by Edwin Graves Wilson; illustrated by Jerome Lagarrigue. Sterling Pub. 2007 48 p. col. ill. (Poetry for young people) (hardcover) $14.95
Grades: 4 5 6 7   **811**
  1. Poets, American 2. African Americans -- Poetry 3. Poetry -- By individual authors
  ISBN 9781402720239; 1402720238
                       LC 2006013803
"Wilson's introduction . . . addresses how Angelou's life has informed her imagination. . . . Twenty-five poems show her concern with the African-American experience. . . . Dignity, pride, and resiliancy are at this collection's core. . . . Footnotes offer definitions of colloquialisms and difficult words. Lagarrigue's painterly artwork uses golds, greens, and violets to capture the luminescent quality of the poems. . . . This [is a] distinguished work." SLJ

Archer, Peggy
  From dawn to dreams; poems for busy babies. illustrated by Hanako Wakiyama. Candlewick Press 2007 un il $15.99
Grades: PreK   **811**
  1. Infants -- Poetry 2. Poetry -- By individual authors
  ISBN 978-0-7636-2467-5; 0-7636-2467-5
                       LC 2006051832
"15 poems cover the gamut of activities in which babies and toddlers participate: a first step, clomping around in adult shoes, exploring faces in a mirror, introducing oneself to the family cat, and so on. . . . The oil-on-paper illustrations are in a style reminiscent of art in the 1950s. On various pages, the text is surrounded by a zigzag frame that adds to the old-fashioned feel." SLJ

  Name that dog! puppy poems from A to Z. illustrations by Stephanie Buscema. Dial Books for Young Readers 2010 un il $16.99
Grades: PreK K 1 2 3   **811**
  1. Dogs -- Poetry 2. Poetry -- By individual authors
  ISBN 978-0-8037-3322-0; 0-8037-3322-4
                       LC 2009009286
"This picture book poetry collection presents a rogue's gallery of pooches in selections designed to help an unidentified dog owner name his or her new pet. . . . The poems, representing a variety of styles, read smoothly and are complemented by Buscema's energetic, stylized illustrations." Booklist

Argueta, Jorge
  Talking with Mother Earth; poems. illustrated by Lucia Angela Perez. Groundwood Books 2006 un il $15.95
Grades: 3 4 5 6   **811**
  1. Nature poetry 2. Racism -- Poetry 3. Pipil Indians -- Poetry 4. Poetry -- By individual authors 5. Bilingual

books -- English-Spanish
  ISBN 0-88899-626-8
  This presents poems which explore a Pipil Nahua Indian boy's connection to Mother Earth and how it heals the wounds of racism.
  "This literary offering stands out for its beauty and depth of expression. . . . Pérez's illustrations are colorful, detailed, and appealing, incorporating many indigenous icons." SLJ

Aronica-Buck, Barbara
  Over the moon; the Broadway lullaby project. Easton Studio Press 2012 46 p.
Grades: 3 4 5   **811**
  1. Lullabies
  ISBN 1935212702; 9781935212706
  This book compiled by Kate Dawson and Jodi Glucksman presents a "collection of original lullabies and illustrations featuring music by some of Broadway's biggest stars and brightest composers with illustrations by acclaimed Children's artists and Broadway set designers. . . . each offering a . . . visual interpretation of a song from the CD bound in the book." (Publisher's note)

Bagert, Brod
  School fever; by Brod Bagert; pictures by Robert Neubecker. Dial Books for Young Readers 2008 un il $16.99
Grades: 1 2 3   **811**
  1. Schools -- Poetry 2. Poetry -- By individual authors
  ISBN 978-0-8037-3201-8; 0-8037-3201-5
                       LC 2007-9324
  This is a book of "poems, most of which follow a basic rhyming pattern, [and] touch on a number subjects and school situations near and dear to children. . . . The fun illustrations, completed with ink and a computer, really capture the essence of the poems." Libr Media Connect

Bates, Katharine Lee
  ★ **America** the beautiful; illustrated by Chris Gall. Little, Brown 2004 un il $16.95
Grades: K 1 2 3   **811**
  1. Songs -- United States 2. Children's poetry, American 3. United States -- Juvenile poetry
  ISBN 0-316-73743-7
                       LC 2003-54552
  Four verses of the nineteenth-century poem later set to music, illustrated by the author's great-great-grandnephew
  "Children will be stirred by Gall's pictures. Using hand engraving on clay-covered board and enhancing elements such as color with a computer, he offers a series of pictures resembling woodcuts in form and WPA paintings in style." Booklist

Behn, Harry
  Halloween; illustrated by Greg Couch. North-South Bks. 2003 un il $15.95; lib bdg $16.50
Grades: 1 2 3   **811**
  1. Halloween 2. American poetry 3. Halloween -- Poetry 4. Children's poetry, American 5. Halloween -- Juvenile poetry 6. Poetry -- By individual authors 7. Supernatural -- Juvenile poetry
  ISBN 0-7358-1609-3; 0-7358-1766-9 lib bdg
                       LC 2002-43238
  "A skeleton, a witch, and a devil go out to trick-or-treat, but are frightened by every sound they hear and everything

they see. Larger-than-life, vivid illustrations bring this simple rhyming verse to life on each haunting spread." SLJ

Bernier-Grand, Carmen T.

Cesar; si, se puede! yes, we can! illustrated by David Diaz. Marshall Cavendish 2004 48p il $16.95

Grades: 3 4 5 6 **811**

1. Children's poetry 2. Agricultural laborers 3. Labor leaders 4. Mexican Americans -- Poetry 5. Poetry -- By individual authors
ISBN 0-7614-5172-2

LC 2003-26866

"The lyrical language describes events and paints evocative pictures to which children will relate. Diaz's stylized, computer-drawn, folk-art illustrations capture the subject's private and public life." SLJ

Inlcudes glossary and bibliographical references

Berry, James

Carnival of the animals; poems inspired by Saint-Saens' music. by James Berry . . . [et al.]; edited by Judith Chernaik; illustrated by Satoshi Kitamura. Candlewick Press 2006 un il $16.99

Grades: K 1 2 3 4 **811**

1. Children's poetry 2. Music -- Poetry 3. Animals -- Poetry 4. American poetry -- Collections
ISBN 0-7636-2960-X

LC 2005-48445

"Chernaik commissioned 13 poets to respond to the musical animal portraits in Saint-Saens' kid-friendly Carnival of the Animals . . . Their concise, vibrant word painting will forge an instant connection with children. . . . The poems . . . can be appreciated with or without the accompanying 55-minute CD of music and readings. . . . Having said that, separating this from its inspirational basis would miss the point; children will find it fascinating to see how their own impressions of the original works match the poets'—not to mention illustrator Kitamura's, whose engaging watercolors shift fluidly among the poems' many moods while lending the whole a welcome cohesion." Booklist

Blackaby, Susan

★ **Nest**, nook & cranny; poems by Susan Blackaby; illustrated by Jamie Hogan. Charlesbridge 2010 48p il $15.95

Grades: 3 4 5 6 **811**

1. Habitat (Ecology) 2. Animals -- Poetry 3. Poetry -- By individual authors
ISBN 978-1-58089-350-3; 1-58089-350-3

LC 2009004302

"This lively poetry collection pairs verse about animals with black-and-white drawings of creatures in their natural habitats. . . . The various settings, accompanied by notes on nature, will grab young conservationists. . . . Teachers will welcome the extensive final notes on animal habitats and poetic forms for science and creative-writing classes." Booklist

Blackall, Sophie

★ **Spinster** Goose; twisted rhymes for naughty children. [by] Lisa Wheeler & Sophie Blackall. Atheneum Books for Young Readers 2011 41p il $16.99

Grades: 3 4 5 **811**

1. Parodies 2. Nursery rhymes 3. Children's poetry 4.

Poetry -- By individual authors
ISBN 978-1-4169-2541-5; 1-4169-2541-4

"This collection of Mother Goose parodies . . . is as elegant as it is, like Mary, 'quite contrary.' The no-nonsense Spinster Goose oversees a reform school. . . . Blackall's pallid vignettes balance chilly poise and mordant humor. . . . Wheeler adds some intellectual depth to the original nursery rhymes while grossifying them. . . . Though some may shrink from its clever ghastliness, kids with twisted senses of humor will feel right at home." Publ Wkly

Brooks, Gwendolyn

★ **Bronzeville** boys and girls; illustrated by Faith Ringgold. newly illustrated ed.; Amistad/HarperCollins Publishers 2007 41p il $16.99; lib bdg $18.89

Grades: K 1 2 3 **811**

1. Children's poetry 2. African Americans -- Poetry 3. Poetry -- By individual authors
ISBN 978-0-06-029505-9; 0-06-029505-8; 978-0-06-029506-6 lib bdg; 0-06-029506-6 lib bdg

LC 2006-01947

A newly illustrated edition of the title first published 1956

"Brooks's deceptively simple poems for children combined with Ringgold's vibrant illustrations help to rejuvenate this collection first published in 1956. . . . Each poem is tightly constructed, rhythmic and distinctive. . . . Ringgold's bold illustrations, outlined with her signature thick black lines, are among some of her best and most narrative works since Tar Beach." Publ Wkly

Brown, Calef

★ **Flamingoes** on the roof; poems and paintings by Calef Brown. Houghton Mifflin 2006 un il $16

Grades: 3 4 5 6 **811**

1. Humorous poetry 2. Children's poetry 3. Poetry -- By individual authors
ISBN 0-618-56298-2

LC 2004-25125

"These 29 nonsense poems, written in a variety of rhymed meters, are deliciously loaded with alliterative and assonant sounds and filled with delightful doggerel. . . . Full-page, flat acrylic illustrations, most painted in harmonious jewel tones, face single-toned pages of text in a variety of colors." SLJ

★ **Hallowilloween**; nefarious silliness. Houghton Mifflin Books for Children 2010 un il $16.99

Grades: 2 3 4 5 **811**

1. Humorous poetry 2. Children's poetry 3. Monsters -- Poetry 4. Poetry -- By individual authors
ISBN 978-0-547-21540-2; 0-547-21540-1

"Brown's playful collection of poems and paintings is likely to inspire as many giggles as it does shivers. Readers meet a werewolf named Jack, Duncan the shrunken head, and an unhappy mummy. . . . Brown's acrylic illustrations add to the creepy silliness: an artful mix of naive and stylized, whimsical details and vibrant color. Young readers will relish the wordplay and find themselves torn to choose a favorite among this wacky menagerie." SLJ

Soup for breakfast; poems and pictures. Houghton Mifflin Co. 2008 un il $16

Grades: K 1 2 3 **811**

1. Humorous poetry 2. Children's poetry 3. Poetry

-- By individual authors
ISBN 978-0-618-91641-2; 0-618-91641-5

LC 2007047734

Brown's "fun-filled poems feature an unpredictable range of topics and imagery.... He offsets each poem with one of his flat, idiosyncratic paintings; with their oddball beasts and improbable color combinations, his pictures are somewhere between surreal and folk art." Publ Wkly

Brown, Margaret Wise

Nibble nibble; [by] Margaret Wise Brown; paintings by Wendell Minor. HarperCollins 2007 un il $16.99; lib bdg $17.89

Grades: PreK K 1   **811**

1. Rabbits -- Poetry 2. Poetry -- By individual authors
ISBN 978-0-06-059208-0; 0-06-059208-7; 978-0-06-059209-7 lib bdg; 0-06-059209-5 lib bdg

LC 2006029869

A collection of poetry about rabbits

"Large, almost tactile paintings of birds, butterflies, and bunnies combine well with the flow of Brown's charming poems, originally published in 1959.... Onomatopoeic and motion words are reflected in the pictures with their ground-level perspective. These five beautifully and newly illustrated poems will enchant another generation of children." SLJ

Bryan, Ashley

Sing to the sun; poems and pictures by Ashley Bryan. HarperCollins Pubs. 1992 un il pa $6.95

Grades: 2 3 4 5   **811**

ISBN 0-06-443437-0

LC 91-38359

A collection of poems and paintings celebrating the ups and downs of life

"With an energetic beat that's hard to resist, Bryan drums out poetry with a Caribbean sway. These short poems that sing the praises of everyday joys are further charged by the riotous primary colors Bryan splashes around." Booklist

Bulion, Leslie

At the sea floor cafe; odd ocean critter poems. written by Leslie Bulion; illustrated by Leslie Evans. Peachtree Publishers 2011 45p il $14.95

Grades: 5 6 7 8   **811**

1. Marine animals -- Poetry 2. Poetry -- By individual authors
ISBN 978-1-56145-565-2; 1-56145-565-2

LC 2010026691

"Using complex poetry forms and cleverly constructed lines, Bulion plays tribute to sea creatures.... Evans's spare, well-placed hand-colored linoleum block prints hold their own without overwhelming the text." Horn Book Guide

Burleigh, Robert

★ Home run; the story of Babe Ruth. illustrated by Mike Wimmer. Harcourt Brace & Co. 1998 un il hardcover o.p. pa $7

Grades: K 1 2 3   **811**

1. Baseball 2. Baseball players 3. Baseball -- Fiction
ISBN 0-15-200970-1; 0-15-204599-6 pa

LC 95-10038

A poetic account of the legendary Babe Ruth as he prepares to make a home run

"With a flowing minimal text, Burleigh brings the Babe to life through the moment of one at bat.... Wimmer's sprawling, photorealistic oil paintings depict the larger-than-life figure and his surroundings with folksy Norman Rockwell-like charm." SLJ

★ Hoops; illustrated by Stephen T. Johnson. Harcourt Brace & Co. 1997 un il hardcover o.p. pa $6

Grades: 6 7 8 9   **811**

1. Children's poetry 2. Basketball -- Poetry 3. Poetry -- By individual authors 4. Basketball -- Juvenile literature
ISBN 0-15-201450-0; 0-15-216380-8 pa

LC 96-18440

Illustrations and poetic text describe the movement and feel of the game of basketball

"Burleigh's staccato text is well matched by Johnson's dynamic pastels. Muted colors and a strong sense of motion as bodies leap and lift, pounce and poke, aptly complement the words." SLJ

Child, Lydia Maria Francis

Over the river and through the wood; the New England boy's song about Thanksgiving day. [by] L. Maria Child; illustrated by Matt Tavares. Candlewick Press 2011 un il $16.99

Grades: 2 3 4   **811**

1. Thanksgiving Day -- Poetry 2. Poetry -- By individual authors
ISBN 978-0-7636-2790-4; 0-7636-2790-9

LC 2010038878

"A charming and dynamic rendition of the song about Thanksgiving Day, originally published in 1844. All 12 original verses are included, each old-fashioned scene appropriately matching the text. Tavares's watercolor, ink, and pencil illustrations are crisp and bright, expertly capturing the wind-whipped outdoor scenes of the sleigh moving from page to page and ultimately to grandfather's house for a feast." SLJ

Ciardi, John

★ You read to me, I'll read to you; drawings by Edward Gorey. Lippincott 1962 64p il hardcover o.p. pa $7.95

Grades: 1 2 3 4   **811**

1. Humorous poetry 2. Poetry -- By individual authors
ISBN 0-06-446060-6 pa

Thirty-five "imaginative and humorous poems for an adult and a child to read aloud together. Written in a basic first-grade vocabulary, the poems to be read by the child alternate with poems to be read by the adult." Booklist

Clayton, Dallas

Make magic! do good! Dallas Clayton. Candlewick Press 2012 112 p. $17.99

Grades: 3 4 5   **811**

1. Children's poetry 2. Friendship -- Poetry
ISBN 0763657468; 9780763657468

LC 2012942305

This is a poetry collection for children by Dallas Clayton. "Recurring themes in the nearly 50 poems include seizing the day, making friends of enemies, being kind, and blazing one's own trail. 'You won't be fast forever/ so the clever thing to do/ is to stop and help the others keep up/ because

someday/ they'll be you,' writes Clayton in 'Running!'"
(Publishers Weekly)

Clements, Andrew

Dogku; [by] Andrew Clements; illustrations by Tim
Bowers. Simon & Schuster Books for Young Readers 2007
un il $16.99
Grades: 1 2 3 4 **811**
1. Haiku 2. Dogs -- Poetry 3. Poetry -- By individual
authors
ISBN 978-0-689-85823-9; 0-689-85823-X
LC 2006003691

"A stray dog's first day in a family's home is more or less
a test of whether he'll get to stay. . . . [The author] tells the
entire tale in haiku, a remarkably effective vehicle for delivering such a sweet and simple story. . . . While each haiku is
typically spare, Bowers's vibrant illustrations are busy and
bright, filling the pages with the same unbounded energy as
the lovable pooch." SLJ

Coombs, Kate

Water sings blue; ocean poems. by Kate Coombs; illustrated by Meilo So. Chronicle Books 2012 36 p.
Grades: PreK K 1 2 3 **811**
1. Sea poetry 2. Ocean -- Poetry 3. Children's poetry
4. Poetry -- Collections 5. Picture books for children
ISBN 9780811872843
LC 2010030163

This picture book presents "twenty-three poems and . . .
watercolor paintings [that] pay tribute to the wonders of the
ocean world. . . . [Kate Coombs] invites young readers into
her celebration with an opening 'Song of the Boat' and ends
with the message of the 'Tideline'. . . . [In another poem]
Gulper Eel's 'astronomical maw' is compared to a black
hole." (Kirkus Reviews)

Corcoran, Jill

Dare to dream--change the world; edited by Jill Corcoran; illustrated by J. Beth Jepson. 1st ed. Kane Miller 2012
38 p. col. ill. (hardcover) $15.99
Grades: 3 4 5 **811.6**
1. Poetry -- Collections 2. Heroes and heroines --
Poetry
ISBN 1610670655; 9781610670654
This book presents "an illustrated collection of poems
celebrating those who have, as the title indicates, 'changed
the world.'" A "biographical poem, brief text and topical poem . . . illuminate each person's achievements. . . .
Subjects range from the contemporary (Temple Grandin,
Steven Spielberg) to the historical (Jonas Salk), and from
the well-known to the obscure (Father Greg Boyle)."
(Kirkus Reviews)

Cox, Kenyon

Mixed beasts; or, A miscellany of rare and fantastic
creatures; compiled by Professor Julius Duckworth O'Hare,
Esq. illustrations by Wallace Edwards; verses by Kenyon
Cox. Kids Can Press 2005 un il $17.95
Grades: 3 4 5 **811**
1. Nonsense verses 2. Children's poetry 3. Animals
-- Poetry 4. Poetry -- By individual authors
ISBN 1-55337-796-6
"These original nonsense poems about a miscellany of
odd beasts comprised of a mixture of two species, such as

a Rhinocerostrich, a Bumblebeaver, a Kangarooster, and a
Camelelephant, are clever and funny. Full-page, detailed
illustrations of exotic flora and fauna as well as preposterous creatures are rendered in watercolor, colored pencil, and
gouache. The humor of the selections is carried out in the
art." SLJ

Crawley, Dave

Reading, rhyming, and 'rithmetic; poems by Dave
Crawley; illustrations by Liz Callen. Wordsong 2010 31p
il $17.95
Grades: 3 4 5 **811**
1. Schools -- Poetry 2. Poetry -- By individual authors
ISBN 978-1-59078-565-2; 1-59078-565-7
LC 2009019917
This anthology focuses on school-themed poems.
"The verses flow easily and the rhymes are engaging and
well done. Each one lends itself to being read aloud. Kids
will love this collection. The illustrations are pleasant, hu-
morous, and just enough to complement the verses." Libr
Media Connect

Dakos, Kalli

A funeral in the bathroom; and other school bathroom
poems. illustrated by Mark Beech. Albert Whitman & Co.
2011 47p il
Grades: 3 4 5 **811**
1. Schools -- Poetry 2. Bathrooms -- Poetry 3. Poetry
-- By individual authors
ISBN 0-8075-2675-4; 978-0-8075-2675-0
LC 2010045591
"Dakos's humorous, bittersweet poems and Beech's
mischievous illustrations center on the school bathroom as a
place of refuge, camaraderie, and, of course, necessity. . . . A
heartfelt collage of relatable moments." Publ Wkly

Dant, Traci

Some kind of love; a family reunion in poems. illustrated by Eric Velasquez. Marshall Cavendish Children 2010
un il $17.99
Grades: K 1 2 3 **811**
1. Children's poetry 2. Family reunions -- Poetry 3.
African Americans -- Poetry 4. Poetry -- By individual
authors
ISBN 978-0-7614-5559-2; 0-7614-5559-0
LC 2008-20878
"'Must be some kind of love.' That is the refrain that
starts off each moving poem in this picture book about an
annual African American family reunion, told in free verse
from the viewpoint of a nine-year-old boy. Handsome oil
paintings show the 'giant sleepover,' with group pictures of
multiple generations, as well as closeups of cousins sharing
bikes, eating fried chicken, and sleeping four boys to a bed."
Booklist

Dawes, Kwame Senu Neville

★ I saw your face; [drawings by] Tom Feelings; text
by Kwame Dawes; afterword by Jerry Pinkney. Dial Books
2004 un il $16.99
Grades: 3 4 5 **811**
1. Face in art 2. Children's poetry 3. Blacks --
Poetry 4. Blacks -- Juvenile literature 5. Poetry -- By

individual authors
ISBN 0-8037-1894-2

LC 2004-00241

A poem and portraits of children illustrate the shared beauty and heritage of people of African descent living throughout the world.

"Accompanied by Dawes's celebratory verses, page after page of evocative drawings are set in Africa, the Caribbean, England, and the American South." Horn Book Guide

Dotlich, Rebecca Kai
★ **Over** in the pink house. Wordsong/Boyds Mills Press 2004 30p il $15.95
Grades: K 1 2 3 **811**
1. Jump rope rhymes 2. Poetry -- By individual authors
ISBN 1-59078-027-2

"These 32 original rhymes are infused with fresh, colorful imagery and toe-tapping rhythm. Appropriate for reading or chanting aloud while jumping rope, each one has a lighthearted, whimsical quality. The vibrantly colored illustrations are equally playful." SLJ

Durango, Julia
★ **Under** the mambo moon; illustrated by Fabricio Vanden Broeck. Charlesbridge Pub. 2011 un il lib bdg $12.95
Grades: 3 4 5 **811**
1. Music -- Poetry 2. Latin Americans -- Poetry 3. Poetry -- By individual authors
ISBN 157091723X; 9781570917233; 1-57091-723-X; 978-1-57091-723-3

LC 2008007255

"In understated verse, a girl named Marisol explores the role that music plays in her Latino community, introducing the people who visit her father's music store. . . . Grainy grayscale scenes inside the store alternate with kinetic acrylic and colored-pencil tableaus, placed opposite the visitors' monologues. . . . A vivid mingling of poetry, narrative, and art."

"In understated verse, a girl named Marisol explores the role that music plays in her Latino community, introducing the people who visit her father's music store. . . . Grainy grayscale scenes inside the store alternate with kinetic acrylic and colored-pencil tableaus, placed opposite the visitors' monologues. . . . A vivid mingling of poetry, narrative, and art." Publ Wkly

Eliot, T. S. (Thomas Stearns), 1888-1965
★ **Old** Possum's book of practical cats; illustrated by Axel Scheffler. Harcourt Children's Books 2009 64p il $16
Grades: 3 4 5 6 **811**
1. Children's poetry 2. Cats -- Poetry 3. Poetry -- By individual authors
ISBN 978-0-547-24827-1; 0-547-24827-X

"Scheffler brings his considerable illustrative talents to this new edition of Eliot's much-loved collection of cat whimsy, first published in 1939. Scheffler's cartoon felines, with their expressive eyes, are a deliciously animated cast. . . . These cats by turns baffle and delight the humans around them." SLJ

Elliott, David
In the sea; David Elliott; illustrated by Holly Meade. 1st U.S. ed. Candlewick Press 2012 32 p. col. ill.
Grades: 1 2 3 **811**
1. Children's poetry 2. American poetry -- Collections 3. Marine animals -- Juvenile poetry 4. Marine animals -- Poetry 5. Poetry -- By individual authors
ISBN 9780763644987; 0763644986

LC 2010047666

This book of poems for children by David Elliot and illustrated by Holly Meade presents an "exploration of life in the sea. From the tiny sea horse 'dainty as a wish,' to the clown fish, which is 'not an enemy / of anemone,' to the blue whale who sings 'of shipwrecked sailors down below,' 20 creatures are celebrated with rhymes that accentuate their quirks and charm." (Booklist)

★ **In** the wild; illustrated by Holly Meade. Candlewick Press 2010 un il
Grades: 1 2 3 **811**
1. Children's poetry 2. Animals -- Poetry 3. Animals -- Juvenile literature 4. Poetry -- By individual authors
ISBN 0-7636-4497-8; 978-0-7636-4497-0

LC 2009008244

A woodcut-illustrated collection of poems that celebrates wild animals. "Preschool, primary." (Horn Book)

"A lion standing alone on a grassy plain leads off the assortment of 14 mammals introduced in short, reflective poems and bold, energetic woodblock scenes. . . . Mead's woodblock prints . . . have just a hint of humor and capture the powerful wild nature of the creatures. . . . The poems are read-aloud gems." SLJ

Esbensen, Barbara Juster
★ **Swing** around the sun; poems. art by Cheng-Khee Chee . . . [et al.] Carolrhoda Bks. 2003 un il lib bdg $16.95
Grades: 2 3 4 **811**
1. Seasons 2. American poetry 3. Seasons -- Poetry 4. Seasons -- Juvenile poetry 5. Children's poetry, American 6. Poetry -- By individual authors
ISBN 0-87614-143-2

LC 2002-7980

A newly illustrated edition of the title first published 1965 by Lerner

A collection of poems that celebrates the seasons, with illustrations for each season by a different Minnesota artist

"A rich, vibrant reading and viewing experience. . . . The poetry's impact is heightened by masterful new illustrations from four distinguished artists. . . . Cheng-Khee Chee's textured watercolors sprout and bloom across the pages of 'Spring.' Janice Lee Porter's 'Summer' oil pastels hum with energetic color and sinuous shapes. Mary GrandPré ushers in fall with a warmer palette of pastels. . . . Finally, Stephen Gammell's snowscapes, spattered in icy grays and blue capture winter's wild spirit." SLJ

Farrar, Sid
The **year** comes round; haiku through the seasons. Sid Farrar; illustrated by Ilse Plume. Albert Whitman & Co. 2012 32 p. $16.99
Grades: K 1 2 3 **811**
1. Haiku 2. Nature poetry 3. Children's poetry 4. Seasons -- Poetry 5. Haiku, American 6. Months --

Juvenile poetry 7. Nature -- Juvenile poetry
ISBN 0807581291; 9780807581292

LC 2011015478

This book, by Sid Farrar, illustrated by Ilse Plume, offers "[t]welve nature-themed haiku accompanied by lush illustrations [that] take the reader from January to December." Describing natural elements such as fireflies and frost on windowpanes, this collection seeks "to introduce children to the traditional Japanese poetry form." (Publisher's note)

Fehler, Gene
   Change-up; baseball poems. illustrated by Donald Wu. Clarion Books 2009 48p il $16
Grades: 2 3 4 5   **811**
   1. Children's poetry 2. Baseball -- Poetry 3. Baseball -- Juvenile literature 4. Poetry -- By individual authors
   ISBN 978-0-618-71962-4; 0-618-71962-8
                                                       LC 2008-21950
"Thirty-six brief poems follow a baseball player's year. . . . Fehler's verses offer simple images and the delights of the game's terse play-by-play. . . . Wu's comically exaggerated illustrations are done in acrylic and colored pencils. With its charming wordplay and humor, this book should win an audience." SLJ

Field, Eugene
   Wynken, Blynken, and Nod; written by Eugene Field; illustrated by Giselle Potter. Schwartz & Wade Books 2008 un il $16.99; lib bdg $19.99
Grades: PreK K 1 2   **811**
   1. Children's poetry 2. Sleep -- Poetry 3. Poetry -- By individual authors
   ISBN 978-0-375-84196-5; 0-375-84196-2; 978-0-375-94596-0 lib bdg; 0-375-94596-2 lib bdg
                                                       LC 2007-09568
"Field's soothing lullaby of a poem (1889) is handsomely visualized via the classic device of translating the contents of a child's own room into the stuff of dreams. Potter's appealing dreamlike art features a moon-faced child and the three eponymous figures who are as like him . . . as peas in a pod. . . . An idyllic and imaginative new look at an old favorite." Horn Book

Fisher, Aileen Lucia
   Do rabbits have Christmas? poems. by Aileen Fisher; illustrated by Sarah Fox-Davies. Henry Holt 2007 un il $16.95
Grades: PreK K 1 2   **811**
   1. Nature poetry 2. Winter -- Poetry 3. Christmas -- Poetry 4. Poetry -- By individual authors
   ISBN 978-0-8050-7491-8; 0-8050-7491-0
                                                       LC 2006030504
"This well-chosen verse collection features 15 short poems culled from eight of Fisher's books. . . . Clean and precise, the poems create indeliable but often delicate images. Fox-Davies' endearing paintings reflect the childlike tone and quiet appreciation of nature inherent in the verse." Booklist

Fitch, Sheree
   ★ **Night** Sky Wheel Ride; Sheree Fitch; illustrated by Yayo. Tradewind 2012 32 p. $16.95

Grades: PreK K 1 2   **811**
   1. Fairs -- Poetry 2. Stories in rhyme
   ISBN 189658067X; 9781896580678

This illustrated narrative children's poem, by Sheree Fitch and illustrated by the artist Yayo, "take[s] . . . a spectacular ride through the imagination. We fly past illustrations displaying a [kaleidoscope] of colors. Magical, fun fair creatures appear and disappear in a jungle of cotton-candy trees." (Publisher's note)

Fleischman, Paul
   ★ **Big** talk; poems for four voices. illustrated by Beppe Giacobbe. Candlewick Press 2000 44p il $17.99; pa $7.99
Grades: 4 5 6 7   **811**
   1. Children's poetry, American 2. Poetry -- By individual authors
   ISBN 0-7636-0636-7; 0-7636-3805-6 pa
                                                       LC 99-46882
A collection of poems to be read aloud by four people, with color-coded text to indicate which lines are read by which readers
"Each poem is more demanding, and more rewarding, than the last. Giacobbe highlights the humor in strips of vignettes that run along the bottom of the page. This is 'toe-tapping, tongue-flapping fun.'" Horn Book Guide

   ★ **I** am phoenix: poems for two voices; illustrated by Ken Nutt. Harper & Row 1985 51p il hardcover o.p. pa $5.99
Grades: 4 5 6 7   **811**
   1. Children's poetry 2. Birds -- Poetry 3. Poetry -- By individual authors
   ISBN 0-06-446092-4 pa
                                                       LC 85-42615
A collection of poems about birds to be read aloud by two voices
"Devotés of the almost lost art of choral reading should be among the first to appreciate this collection. . . . Printed in script form, the selections . . . have a cadenced pace and dignified flow; their combination of imaginative imagery and realistic detail is echoed by the combination of stylized fantasy and representational drawings in the black and white pictures, all soft line and strong nuance." Bull Cent Child Books

   ★ **Joyful** noise: poems for two voices; illustrated by Eric Beddows. Harper & Row 1988 44p il $15.99; lib bdg $16.89; pa $5.99
Grades: 4 5 6 7   **811**
   1. Insects -- Poetry 2. Poetry -- By individual authors
   ISBN 0-06-021852-5; 0-06-021853-3 lib bdg; 0-06-446093-2 pa
                                                       LC 87-45280
Awarded the Newbery Medal, 1989
"There are fourteen poems in the handsomely designed volume, with stylish endpapers and wonderfully interpretive black-and-white illustrations. Each selection is a gem, polished perfection." Horn Book

Fletcher, Ralph
   A **writing** kind of day; poems for young poets. illustrations by April Ward. Wordsong/Boyds Mills Press 2005 32p il $17.95; pa $9.95

Grades: 3 4 5   **811**
ISBN 1-59078-276-3; 1-59078-353-0 pa
"A young writer's daily experiences and concerns are folded into poems to which many readers can relate. . . . Varied in mood and tone, the offerings entertain as they celebrate words and language. . . . Ward's black-and-white illustrations use a variety of mediums, including pencil, photography, computer-generated images, and ink. " SLJ

Florian, Douglas

★ **Autumnblings**; poems and paintings by Douglas Florian. Greenwillow Bks. 2003 48p il $15.99; lib bdg $16.89
Grades: 2 3 4 5   **811**
1. Autumn 2. American poetry 3. Autumn -- Poetry 4. Autumn -- Juvenile poetry 5. Children's poetry, American 6. Poetry -- By individual authors
ISBN 0-06-009278-5; 0-06-009279-3 lib bdg
               LC 2002-29780
A collection of poems that portray the essence of the season between summer and winter
"Short verse lines make the entries particularly suitable for reading aloud or reciting. . . . The illustrations, luminous watercolors touched with colored pencils, often move beyond the decorative to witty visual commentary or elegant, streamlined scenes." Bull Cent Child Books

★ **Bing** bang boing; poems and drawings by Douglas Florian. Harcourt Brace & Co. 1994 144p il hardcover o.p. pa $8
Grades: 2 3 4 5   **811**
1. Nonsense verses 2. Children's poetry 3. Poetry -- By individual authors 4. Nonsense verses -- Juvenile literature
ISBN 0-15-233770-9; 0-15-205860-9 pa
               LC 94-3894
An illustrated collection of more than 150 nonsense verses
"The author's spare, pen-and-ink drawings, like the poems themselves, deftly explore the comic potential in each combination of words. With a few clean lines, he creates an original, funny vision." SLJ

★ **Comets,** stars, the Moon, and Mars; space poems and paintings. Harcourt 2007 45p il $16
Grades: 2 3 4 5   **811**
1. Children's poetry 2. Astronomy -- Poetry 3. Poetry -- By individual authors
ISBN 978-0-15-205372-7; 0-15-205372-7
               LC 2006-08274
This "book looks at astronomy through the magnifying, clarifying lens of poetry. Each double-page spread features a short, accessible poem about a subject such as the sun, each of its planets, a comet, a constellation, or the universe, set with an impressive painting." Booklist

★ **Dinothesaurus**; prehistoric poems and paintings. by Douglas Florian. Atheneum 2009 43p il $17.99
Grades: 2 3 4 5   **811**
1. Children's poetry 2. Dinosaurs -- Poetry 3. Poetry -- By individual authors 4. Dinosaurs -- Juvenile literature
ISBN 978-1-4169-7978-4; 1-4169-7978-6
"Florian's freeflowing, witty collection of poems and collages about dinosaurs is a giganotosaurus delight. . . . The poems marry facts with a poet's eye for detail. . . . The heart

of the book is in its humor, the spontaneity of both illustrations and poems, and Florian's slightly askew view of the Mesozoic creatures." Publ Wkly
Includes glossary and bibliographical references

★ **Handsprings**; poems & paintings by Douglas Florian. Greenwillow Books 2006 48p il $15.99; lib bdg $16.89
Grades: 2 3 4 5   **811**
1. Children's poetry 2. Spring -- Poetry 3. Poetry -- By individual authors
ISBN 0-06-009280-7; 0-06-009281-5 lib bdg
               LC 2005-04567
A collection of short poems about spring
This includes "twenty-nine exuberant poems coupled with whimsical paintings distinguished for their warm colors, spare imagery, and a peculiar, sweet grace." Horn Book

★ **Laugh**-eteria; poems and drawings by Douglas Florian. Harcourt Brace & Co. 1999 157p $17; pa $8
Grades: 2 3 4 5   **811**
1. American poetry 2. Humorous poetry 3. Humorous poetry, American 4. Children's poetry, American 5. Poetry -- By individual authors
ISBN 0-15-202084-5; 0-15-206148-7 pa
               LC 98-20047
A collection of more than 100 humorous poems on such topics as ogres, pizza, fear, school, dragons, trees, and hair
"Florian's pithy poems echo playground chants (and sometimes, better yet, jeers) in their rhythmic recitability . . . and his focus on orality and absurdity makes them thematically irresistible. The line drawings have a sophisticated quirkiness." Bull Cent Child Books

★ **Omnibeasts**; animal poems and paintings by Douglas Florian. Harcourt 2004 95p il $18
Grades: 2 3 4 5   **811**
1. Animals -- Poetry 2. Poetry -- By individual authors
ISBN 0-15-205038-8
               LC 2003-18823
A compilation of animal poems selected from the author's previously published collections
This "is a treasure chest of wit and charm. The author weaves information into each poem, combining fun and fact. Combined with Florian's signature watercolors . . . each short offering occupies its own spread. This book has enormous appeal for readers of many ages." SLJ

★ **Poetrees**. Beach Lane Books 2010 45p il $16.99
Grades: 3 4 5 6   **811**
1. Children's poetry 2. Trees -- Poetry 3. Trees -- Juvenile literature 4. Poetry -- By individual authors
ISBN 978-1-4169-8672-0; 1-4169-8672-3
               LC 2009-03025
"Florian focuses on trees (seeds, bark, leaves, roots, and tree rings) and introduces readers to 13 species from around the world. An oversize, double-page illustration accompanies each poem. . . . The selections are accessible and concise, with child-friendly wordplay and artful design. . . . The primitive illustrations—crafted on 'primed paper bags' using mixed media including gouache watercolor paints, col-

ored pencils, rubber stamps, oil pastels, and collage—range in nuance from whimsy to mystery and reverence." SLJ

★ **Summersaults**; poems & paintings by Douglas Florian. Greenwillow Bks. 2002 48p il $16.99; lib bdg $17.89

Grades: 2 3 4 5   811
 1. American poetry 2. Summer -- Poetry 3. Children's poetry, American 4. Poetry -- By individual authors
 ISBN 0-06-029267-9; 0-06-029268-7 lib bdg
                                              LC 2001-23619
"Florian ably captures the freedom and exuberance of the season in bright, new greens, sun-baked browns, and images of leaping, grinning figures. The gleeful puns, wordplay, and creative grammar will charm youngsters." Booklist

★ **Winter** eyes; poems & paintings by Douglas Florian. Greenwillow Bks. 1999 48p il $16

Grades: 2 3 4 5   811
 1. Winter -- Poetry 2. Winter -- Juvenile poetry 3. Children's poetry, American 4. Poetry -- By individual authors
 ISBN 0-688-16458-7
                                              LC 98-19483
A collection of poems about winter, including "Sled," "Icicles," and "Ice Fishing"
"The short rhyming lines are clear and will be easy to read aloud, and the softly toned watercolor-and-colored-pencil pictures show snowy winter scenes, some realistic, some playful." Booklist

★ **Zoo's** who; poems and paintings by Douglas Florian. Harcourt 2005 47p il $17

Grades: K 1 2 3   811
 1. Children's poetry 2. Animals -- Poetry 3. Poetry -- By individual authors
 ISBN 0-15-204639-9
                                              LC 2004-4576
A collection of short poems about animals
"There's plenty of humor throughout. . . . The artwork . . . always has unexpected bits. . . . The more astute the reader, the better the time he or she will have with this." Booklist

Florian, Douglas, 1950-
 ★ **UnBEElievables**; honeybee poems and paintings. Douglas Florian. Beach Lane Books 2012 32 p. col. ill. (hardcover) $16.99

Grades: 1 2 3 4 5   811
 1. Beehives 2. Children's poetry 3. Bees -- Juvenile poetry 4. Children's poetry, American 5. Honeybee -- Juvenile poetry 6. Bees -- Ecology -- Juvenile poetry
 ISBN 1442426527; 9781442426528
                                              LC 2011005613
This children's picture book presents a collection of poetry about bees. "The 14 poems introduce the roles of the queen, drones and workers and touch on such matters as anatomy, development from egg to bee, and even Colony Collapse Disorder." (Kirkus Reviews)
"Florian bestows yet another pleasing mix of punny poems and colorful collages that blend whimsy and fact... Spreads like "Swarm" epitomize Florian's skill at combining pithy rhymes, well-chosen facts and playfully tongue-in-cheek pictures." Kirkus
 Includes bibliographical references

Forbes, Robert L.
 Beast Friends Forever; by Robert L. Forbes; illustrated by Ronald Searle. Penguin Group USA 2013 80 p. (hardcover) $19.95

Grades: 4 5 6 7   811
 1. Animal courtship 2. Animals -- Poetry 3. Animals -- Juvenile literature
 ISBN 1590208080; 9781590208083
In this book of children's poetry by Robert Forbes, "animal courtship is infused with quirky human characteristics and some sneaky social commentary. Readers meet Lancelot the Ocelot, doing time for 'his romance turned to tragedy, ending in a crime.' And Babette the Skunk, having studied with 'Parisian perfumers,' has fashioned a new scent, 'packaged in black and called "In-d-scent,"/It's sure to enflame any white-striped gent.'" (School Library Journal)

Forler, Nan
 Winterberries and apple blossoms; reflections and flavors of a Mennonite year. paintings by Peter Etril Snyder. Tundra Books 2011 39p il $22.95

Grades: 4 5 6 7   811
 1. Cooking 2. Months -- Poetry 3. Mennonites -- Poetry 4. Poetry -- By individual authors
 ISBN 978-1-77049-254-7; 1-77049-254-2
With a poem for every month of the year, young Naomi introduces us to her family and hosts a journey through the seasonal rhythms of her rural Mennonite community. Includes a recipe for each month of the year.
This includes "12 evocative poems. . . . Snyder . . . contributes smudgy, sunlit acrylic scenes that convey a close-knit family that works, plays, and prays together. Along with Forler's graceful verse, and recipes for every season, it all adds up to a warm portrait of a community seldom found in the spotlight." Publ Wkly

Frampton, David
 ★ **Mr.** Ferlinghetti's poem. Eerdmans Books for Young Readers 2006 un $18

Grades: K 1 2 3   811
 1. Summer -- Poetry 2. Fire fighters -- Poetry 3. Poetry -- By individual authors
 ISBN 0-8028-5290-4
                                              LC 2005024287
"Frampton's exuberant pictures match well with an equally vivacious poem. . . . Frampton's signature woodcuts are wonderful, balancing cool and warm colors, and also managing to look both blocky and fluid at the same time." SLJ

Franco, Betsy
 ★ **Bees,** snails, and peacock tails shapes--naturally; [by] Betsy Franco; illustrated by Steve Jenkins. Margaret K. McElderry Books 2008 un il $16.99

Grades: PreK K 1 2   811
 1. Nature poetry 2. Shape -- Poetry 3. Poetry -- By individual authors
 ISBN 978-1-4169-0386-4; 1-4169-0386-0
                                              LC 2006-12094
"The pair behind Birdsongs tackles another science topic—geometry in the animal world. Whether addressing hexagonal beehive cells or a snail's spiral shell, brisk rhymes draw attention to nature's math. . . . Striking color combinations make the illustrations pop. This inviting book is bound

to spark more careful observation of the shapes and colors in the reader's natural world." Publ Wkly

Messing around on the monkey bars; illustrated by Jessie Hartland. Candlewick Press 2009 45p il $17.99
Grades: 3 4 5   **811**
1. Children's poetry 2. Schools -- Poetry 3. Schools -- Juvenile literature 4. Poetry -- By individual authors
ISBN 978-0-7636-3174-1; 0-7636-3174-4
"A cheeky romp through elementary schoolchildren's academic and social lives. Though readers could tackle the poems alone, differences in typeface cue the possibility for two readers to share the poems aloud. . . . Hartland's energetic gouache illustrations adopt a naive style that matches the playful spirit of the text while serving as a splendid complement to its evocation of children's voices." Kirkus

A **curious** collection of cats; concrete poems. illustrations by Michael Wertz. Tricycle Press 2009 un il $16.99
Grades: PreK K 1 2 3   **811**
1. Children's poetry 2. Cats -- Poetry 3. Cats -- Juvenile literature 4. Poetry -- By individual authors
ISBN 978-1-58246-248-6; 1-58246-248-8
LC 2008-11359
"Thirty-two unusual, concrete poems, one per page with a single exception, are matched by Wertz's monoprints. The words move in several directions and sometimes inhabit multiple objects. The poems are so embedded within the illustrations that it is hard to imagine them without the artwork. . . . Cat lovers will recognize their felines stretching, purring, and napping." SLJ

Frost, Robert, 1874-1963
Birches; illustrated by Ed Young. Holt & Co. 1988 un il hardcover o.p. pa $8.95
Grades: 3 4 5   **811**
1. Trees -- Poetry 2. Poetry -- By individual authors
ISBN 0-8050-7230-6 pa
LC 86-4787
An illustrated version of the well-known poem written in 1916, about birch trees and the pleasures of climbing them
"The freedom called for in the sweep and depth of Frost's words should not be hemmed in by rigidly defined illustrations, and Young allows this license, giving the viewer ample opportunity to absorb and be absorbed by the imagery. The text is set two to three lines to a page, with the poem repeated in its entirety at the end." Booklist

★ **Robert** Frost; edited by Gary D. Schmidt; illustrated by Henri Sorensen. Sterling 1994 48p il (Poetry for young people) $14.95; pa $6.95
Grades: 4 5 6 7   **811**
1. Children's poetry 2. Poetry -- By individual authors
ISBN 0-8069-0633-2; 1-4027-5475-2 pa
LC 94-11161
This volume "contains a three-page overview of the poet's life, 29 poems selected and arranged around the seasons of the year, brief and apt commentaries on each, and a useful index of titles and subject matter. The realistic watercolor illustrations capture the delicate beauty of a New England spring and the glory of fall while still suggesting the around-the-corner chill of winter, a disquiet echoing throughout much of Frost's poetry." SLJ

George, Kristine O'Connell
Book! illustrated by Maggie Smith. Clarion Bks. 2001 31p il $9.95; bd bk $5.95
Grades: PreK K   **811**
1. American poetry 2. Stories in rhyme 3. Books and reading 4. Books -- Juvenile poetry 5. Children's poetry, American 6. Books and reading -- Fiction
ISBN 0-395-98287-1; 0-547-15409-7 bd bk
LC 00-65600
"When the toddler narrator opens a present and discovers a volume entitled Bunnies, he and the book immediately become inseparable." Publ Wkly

★ **Emma** Dilemma: big sister poems. Clarion Books 2011 47p il $16.99
Grades: K 1 2 3   **811**
1. Children's poetry 2. Sisters -- Poetry 3. Poetry -- By individual authors
ISBN 0618428429; 9780618428427; 978-0-618-42842-7; 0-618-42842-9
LC 2008-50647
"A likable fourth-grader shares her frustrations about her preschool-age sister, Emma, in candid narrative poems. . . . There are tender moments, genuinely conveyed in Carpenter's expressive pen-and-ink illustrations. . . . The vignettes form such a vivid portrait of Emma and Jessica that readers may feel as if they personally know them." Publ Wkly

★ **Little** dog poems; illustrated by June Otani. Clarion Bks. 1999 40p il $12
Grades: K 1 2   **811**
1. American poetry 2. Dogs -- Poetry 3. Dogs -- Juvenile poetry 4. Children's poetry, American 5. Poetry -- By individual authors
ISBN 0-395-82266-1
LC 97-46678
"The language is simple and concrete enough for the youngest listeners. Otani's pen and watercolor illustrations make a fine complement to the verse." Horn Book Guide

★ **Old** Elm speaks; tree poems. illustrated by Kate Kiesler. Clarion Bks. 1998 48p il $15; pa $5.95
Grades: 2 3 4   **811**
1. American poetry 2. Trees -- Poetry 3. Trees -- Juvenile poetry 4. Children's poetry, American 5. Poetry -- By individual authors
ISBN 0-395-87611-7; 0-618-75242-0 pa
LC 97-49333
A collection of short, simple poems which present images relating to trees in various circumstances and throughout the seasons
"George conveys a deep understanding of nature, here particularly of trees, in a way that is readily accessible to children. Kiesler's warm oil paintings beautifully complement the poems." Booklist

Toasting marshmallows; camping poems. illustrated by Kate Kiesler. Clarion Bks. 2001 48p il $15
Grades: 3 4 5   **811**
1. Camping 2. American poetry 3. Camping -- Poetry 4. Camping -- Juvenile poetry 5. Children's poetry,

American 6. Poetry -- By individual authors
ISBN 0-618-04597-X

LC 00-56984

"All of the selections convey a child-focused sense of wonder. . . . The poems are varied and inventive, replete with marvelous images and universal truths. . . . Each one is accompanied by a well-executed and evocative acrylic painting." SLJ

★ The **great** frog race and other poems; pictures by Kate Kiesler; with an introduction by Myra Cohn Livingston. Clarion Bks. 1997 40p il $15; pa $5.95
Grades: 3 4 5 **811**
1. Children's poetry 2. Poetry -- By individual authors
ISBN 0-395-77607-4; 0-618-60478-2 pa

LC 95-51090

A collection of poems about frogs and dragonflies, wind and rain, a visit to the tree farm, the garden hose, and other aspects of country life

"George's astute imagery pairs beautifully with Kiesler's rich, warm-toned oil paintings to impart a strong sense of the pleasures of rural landscape." Booklist

Gerstein, Mordicai, 1935-
Dear hot dog; poems about everyday stuff. Abrams 2011 un il
Grades: PreK K 1 2 **811**
1. Poetry -- By individual authors
ISBN 0810997320; 9780810997325

This collection of poems follows three friends from the time they wake up and brush their teeth to when they snuggle up for bed with their favorite stuffed animal.

This is "lyrical yet accessible. . . . Gerstein infuses humanity into a toothbrush, shoes, a bowl, a kite, leaves and an ice-cream cone. His acrylic illustrations are in harmony with his verses; sharp black lines and rich colors that spread outside their outlines, giving a dreamy yet vivid effect." Kirkus

Gibson, Amy
Around the world on eighty legs; illustrated by Daniel Salmieri. Scholastic Press 2010 un il $18.99
Grades: K 1 2 **811**
1. Children's poetry 2. Animals -- Poetry 3. Animals -- Juvenile literature 4. Poetry -- By individual authors
ISBN 978-0-439-58755-6; 0-439-58755-7

LC 2009007160

"Gibson's collection of poems cleverly presents creatures from all across the globe in witty, rhythmic, and well-crafted verse. Instructional and entertaining, the poems nicely balance information with humor and wordplay. . . . Emphasizing humor over naturalism, Salmieri's . . . illustrations match the playfulness of Gibson's verse point for point." Publ Wkly

Giovanni, Nikki
★ **Spin** a soft black song: poems for children; illustrated by George Martins. rev ed; Hill & Wang 1985 57p il hardcover o.p. pa $4.95
Grades: 3 4 5 6 **811**
1. African Americans -- Poetry 2. Poetry -- By individual authors
ISBN 0-374-46469-3 pa

LC 84-19287

First published 1971

A poetry collection which recounts the feelings of black children about their neighborhoods, American society, and themselves

"A beautifully illustrated book of poems about black children for children of all ages. . . . Simple in theme but a very moving collection nonetheless." Read Ladders for Hum Relat. 5th edition

★ The **sun** is so quiet; poems. illustrations by Ashley Bryan. Holt & Co. 1996 31p il $14.95
Grades: K 1 2 3 **811**
1. Nature poetry 2. Children's poetry 3. Poetry -- By individual authors
ISBN 0-8050-4119-2

LC 95-39357

A collection of poems primarily about nature and the seasons but also concerned with chocolate and scary movies

"Of the 13 poems presented here, 12 appeared in books published between 1973 and 1993. The new poem, entitled 'Connie,' represents the best of Giovanni: a series of quick-silver images that capture a mood to perfection. Painted in Bryan's signature style, the illustrations fill the pages with sunny colors and bold patterns." Booklist

Gottfried, Maya
★ **Our** farm; by the animals of Farm Sanctuary. [by] Maya Gottfried [and] Robert Rahway Zakanitch. Alfred A. Knopf 2010 un il $17.99; lib bdg $20.99
Grades: PreK K 1 2 3 **811**
1. Children's poetry 2. Animals -- Poetry 3. Farm life -- Poetry 4. Animals -- Juvenile literature 5. Poetry -- By individual authors
ISBN 978-0-375-86118-5; 0-375-86118-1; 978-0-375-96118-2 lib bdg; 0-375-96118-6 lib bdg

LC 2009-14885

"This homage to the shelter for neglected and abused farm animals where Gottfried served as a volunteer is a book of poems and accompanying paintings that will raise awareness both of the Sanctuary and the sad reasons for which such a place exists. But it has more to recommend it. The poems are 'narrated' by some of the shelter's inhabitants. . . . There's a disarming innocence throughout, and the best of the selections are enchanting. Zakanitch's illustrations are superb. Each one is a collectible work of art, exhibiting a masterful technique, tenderness, subtlety, and humor." SLJ

Graham, Joan Bransfield
★ **Flicker** flash; poems by Joan Bransfield Graham; illustrated by Nancy Davis. Houghton Mifflin 1999 un il $15; pa $6.95
Grades: K 1 2 3 **811**
1. American poetry 2. Light -- Poetry 3. Light -- Juvenile poetry 4. Children's poetry, American 5. Poetry -- By individual authors
ISBN 0-395-90501-X; 0-618-31102-5 pa

LC 98-12956

A collection of poems celebrating light in its various forms, from candles and lamps to lightning and fireflies

"A vivid fusion of ingenious concrete poetry and boldly colored graphics." SLJ

Grandits, John
★ **Blue** lipstick; concrete poems. Clarion Books 2007 un il $15; pa $5.95

Grades: 5 6 7 8 9 10   **811**
1. Children's poetry 2. Poetry -- By individual authors
3. Teenagers -- Juvenile literature
ISBN 978-0-618-56860-4; 0-618-56860-3; 978-0-618-
85132-4 pa; 0-618-85132-1 pa
LC 2006-23332

"This selection introduces readers to Jessie, who impulsively purchases blue lipstick, but later, regretfully decides
to give it 'the kiss-off.' Jessie is big sister to Robert, who
was featured in Grandits's Technically, It's Not My Fault
(Clarion, 2004). As he did in that terrific collection, the author uses artful arrangements of text on the page, along with
54 different typefaces, to bring his images and ideas to life.
. . . This irreverent, witty collection should resonate with a
wide audience." SLJ

★ **Technically,** it's not my fault; concrete poems. by
John Grandits. Clarion Books 2004 un il $15; pa $5.95
Grades: 5 6 7 8   **811**
1. Children's poetry 2. Poetry -- By individual authors
ISBN 0-618-42833-X; 0-618-50361-7 pa
LC 2004-231

A collection of concrete poems on such topics as roller
coasters, linguini, basketball, and sisters

"Grandits combines technical brilliance and goofy good
humor to provide an accessible, fun-filled collection of poems, dramatically brought to life through a brilliant book
design." SLJ

Grant, Shauntay
Up home; artwork by Susan Tooke; story by Shauntay
Grant. Nimbus Publishing 2009 un il $19.95
Grades: K 1 2 3   **811**
1. Poets 2. Authors 3. Journalists 4. Children's poetry
5. Children's authors 6. African Americans -- Poetry
ISBN 978-1-55109-660-5; 1-55109-660-9

This illustrated poem evokes the author's memories of
growing up in the Canadian town of Preston, Nova Scotia.

"Deceptively simple, the poetic narrative vividly conveys an array of remembered images, sights, sounds, and
emotions, all of which are brought to life in Tooke's realistic
acrylic images." SLJ

Gray, Rita
One big rain; poems for rainy days. compiled by Rita
Gray; illustrated by Ryan O'Rourke. Charlesbridge 2010
30 p. $9.95
Grades: 2 3 4   **811**
1. Children's poetry 2. Rain -- Poetry 3. Children's
poetry 4. Seasons -- Juvenile poetry 5. American
poetry -- Collections 6. Children's poetry, American 7.
Haiku -- Translations into English 8. Rain and rainfall
-- Juvenile poetry
ISBN 1570917167; 9781570917165; 978-1-57091-
716-5; 1-57091-716-7
LC 2009026748

"With five short poems for each season of the year, this
unassuming anthology offers a sampling of poems about
rain. . . . Gray's collection of poems, nicely balanced in tone,
style, and origin, includes eight Japanese haiku in translation and short works by a number of American poets, some
renowned and others little known. Understated in color and
somewhat stylized in form, the oil-on-paper illustrations

capture the seasons of the year as well as the moods of the
verse."

"With five short poems for each season of the year, this
unassuming anthology offers a sampling of poems about
rain. . . . Gray's collection of poems, nicely balanced in tone,
style, and origin, includes eight Japanese haiku in translation and short works by a number of American poets, some
renowned and others little known. Understated in color and
somewhat stylized in form, the oil-on-paper illustrations
capture the seasons of the year as well as the moods of the
verse." Booklist

Includes bibliographical references and index

Greenfield, Eloise
Brothers & sisters; family poems. illustrated by Jan
Spivey Gilchrist. Amistad 2009 32p il $17.99; lib bdg
$18.89
Grades: K 1 2 3   **811**
1. Children's poetry 2. Siblings -- Poetry 3. African
Americans -- Poetry 4. Poetry -- By individual authors
5. Brothers and sisters -- Juvenile literature
ISBN 978-0-06-056284-7; 0-06-056284-6; 978-0-06-
056285-4 lib bdg; 0-06-056285-4 lib bdg
LC 2008020209

"Greenfield's poetic observations and commentaries
succinctly capture siblings at various ages and stages. . . .
With only a few lines, the author grasps the love and admiration, the frustration and hurt, the fun and aggravation that
they can engender. . . . The illustrator is equally as skillful in
depicting the wide range of emotions and ages in the faces
of the individual African Americans peopling the paintings.
The realistic watercolors fit around and beside the poems,
using the white space to highlight the art and give balance
to the pages." SLJ

★ The **Great** Migration; journey to the North. Harp-
erCollins Children's Books 2010 un il $16.99
Grades: K 1 2 3   **811**
1. Children's poetry 2. African Americans -- Poetry 3.
Poetry -- By individual authors
ISBN 978-0-06-125921-0; 0-06-125921-7
LC 2008-43821

"Collaborators Greenfield and Gilchrist . . . shape an
evocative portrait of African-Americans who moved North
during the Great Migration between 1915 and 1930 to escape Ku Klux Klan fueled racism and to secure better lives.
. . . Chronicling the journey by train, lilting poetry and
pictures capture a sense of both apprehension and hope. .
. . Making intriguing use of photographs of people, news
headlines, maps, and painted elements, each of Gilchrist's
collages has a distinctive look and lighting, ranging from
conventional portraits of the travelers to more abstract images." Publ Wkly

★ **Honey,** I love, and other love poems; pictures by Di-
ane and Leo Dillon. Crowell 1978 un il $14.95; pa $5.95
Grades: 2 3 4   **811**
1. Love poetry 2. African Americans -- Poetry 3.
Poetry -- By individual authors
ISBN 0-690-01334-5; 0-06-443097-9 pa
LC 77-2845

"These 16 poems explore facets of warm, loving relationships with family, friends and schoolmates as experienced by a young Black girl. Central to the theme of the

book is the idea that the child loves herself and is very confident in expressing that love." Interracial Books Child Bull

When the horses ride by; children in the times of war. poems by Eloise Greenfield; illustrations by Jan Spivey Gilchrist. Lee & Low Books 2006 un il $17.95

Grades: 2 3 4   **811**
1. War poetry 2. Poetry -- By individual authors
ISBN 978-1-58430-249-0; 1-58430-249-6
LC 2005015393

Collection of poems about children around the world, focusing on the children's perceptions of war and how the turmoil of war affects their lives.

"Combining 17 rhythmic poems with dramatic illustrations, this title addresses a complex topic. Greenfield's deceptively simple verses express universal truths about both conflict and childhood." SLJ

Grimes, Nikki

At Jerusalem's gate; poems of Easter. with woodcuts by David Frampton. Eerdmans Books for Young Readers 2005 un il $20

Grades: 5 6 7 8   **811**
1. Children's poetry 2. American poetry 3. Easter -- Poetry 4. Easter -- Juvenile Poetry 5. Children's poetry, American 6. Poetry -- By individual authors
ISBN 0-8028-5183-5
LC 2003-1089

"Twenty-two poems trace the events celebrated by Christians as Easter Week, from Jesus' entry into Jerusalem through his appearance to disciples after the Resurrection. . . . Grades five to eight." (Bull Cent Child Books)

"Each poem is preceded by a brief synopsis of the event, often accompanied by the author's own musings and queries, which prompt readers to think and ask questions of their own. . . . Bold, handsome woodcuts reinforce the powerful drama depicted in poetry. An outstanding effort." SLJ

★ **Meet** Danitra Brown; illustrated by Floyd Cooper. Lothrop, Lee & Shepard Bks. 1994 un il hardcover o.p. pa $6.99

Grades: 2 3 4   **811**
1. Children's poetry 2. Friendship -- Poetry 3. African Americans -- Poetry 4. Poetry -- By individual authors
ISBN 0-688-15471-9 pa
LC 92-43707

"A collection of 13 original poems that stand individually and also blend together to tell a story of feelings and friendship between two African-American girls. . . . Cooper's distinguished illustrations in warm dusty tones convey the feeling of closeness. The poignant text and lovely pictures are an excellent collaboration." SLJ

Other titles about Danitra Brown are:
Danitra Brown, class clown (2005)
Danitra Brown leaves town (2002)

Thanks a million; poems by Nikki Grimes; pictures by Cozbi A. Cabrera. Greenwillow Books 2006 31p il $15.99; lib bdg $16.89

Grades: K 1 2 3   **811**
1. Children's poetry 2. Poetry -- By individual authors
ISBN 0-688-17292-X; 0-688-17293-8 lib bdg
LC 2004-54158

"Sixteen thoughtful poems about being thankful for everyday things. Grimes uses a variety of forms that include haiku, a riddle, and a rebus in selections that speak directly to the experiences of young children. . . . Cabreras acrylic illustrations are distinctive, folksy, and effective." SLJ

★ **What** is goodbye? illustrations by Raúl Colón. Hyperion Books for Children 2004 un il $15.99

Grades: 4 5 6 7   **811**
1. Death -- Poetry 2. Family life -- Poetry 3. Poetry -- By individual authors
ISBN 0-7868-0778-4
LC 2002-72987

Alternating poems by a brother and sister convey their feelings about the death of their older brother and the impact it had on their family.

"Grimes handles these two voices fluently and lucidly, shaping her characters through her form. Colón's paintings in muted colors combine imagism with realism to create an emotional dreamscape on nearly every page." SLJ

★ **When** Gorilla goes walking; by Nikki Grimes; illustrated by Shane Evans. Orchard Books 2007 un il $16.99

Grades: PreK K 1 2   **811**
1. Cats -- Poetry 2. African Americans -- Poetry 3. Poetry -- By individual authors
ISBN 978-0-439-31770-2
LC 2006017194

"In interlinked poems, Cecilia, a young African American girl, introduces her 'cool cat'—a fierce, tailless, gray shorthair named Gorilla. . . . In spare, expressive lines and bold colors, Evans' dynamic paintings capture the messy intimacy of the cat and human bond." Booklist

★ **A pocketful** of poems; illustrated by Javaka Steptoe. Clarion Bks. 2001 30p il $15

Grades: K 1 2 3   **811**
1. Haiku 2. American poetry 3. City and town life 4. Haiku, American 5. Nature -- Juvenile poetry 6. Children's poetry, American 7. City and town life -- Poetry 8. Poetry -- By individual authors 9. City and town life -- Juvenile poetry
ISBN 0-395-93868-6
LC 00-24232

"Tiana has round glasses, a wide mouth, and long braids; she opens her hands full of letters and her pocket full of words. Each page has two facing poems, both in Tiana's voice: one is short and bracing, the other is a haiku in the standard five-seven-five syllable configuration. . . . The first poem in a pair is set in standard type; the haiku usually floats or sways or sashays amidst the illustrations. . . , Steptoe is a fabulously inventive collagist. He does amazing things not only with cut and torn paper and string but also with drinking straws, aluminum plates, and stray beads." Booklist

Gutman, Dan

★ **Casey** back at bat; paintings by Steve Johnson and Lou Fancher. HarperCollins 2007 un il $16.99; lib bdg $17.89

Grades: K 1 2 3 4   **811**
1. Children's poetry 2. Baseball -- Poetry 3. Poetry

-- By individual authors

ISBN 978-0-06-056025-6; 0-06-056025-8; 978-0-06-056026-3 lib bdg; 0-06-056026-6 lib bdg

LC 2006029468

"Gutman revisits and updates Thayer's classic baseball poem. This time around . . . Casey hits a fly ball that soars out of the park and keeps on going. It crosses the Atlantic Ocean and has an unfortunate encounter with a tower in Pisa before continuing on to the Sphinx in Egypt. . . . It passes dinosaurs . . . and astronauts before heading back to Earth. The ride is uproarious from start to finish, and Gutman's broadly humorous verse hits all the right notes. . . . Johnson and Fancher's paintings have a playfully nostalgic look, with a mix of textured papers and newsprint splashed across the surfaces of uniforms." SLJ

Hale, Sarah Josepha

Mary had a little lamb; by Sarah Josepha Hale; illustrated by Laura Beith. Marshall Cavendish 2011 il $12.99
Grades: PreK K 1 2   811

1. Nursery rhymes 2. Sheep -- Poetry 3. Poetry -- By individual authors

ISBN 978-0-7614-5824-1; 0-7614-5824-7

LC 2010012807

"Though Mary Had a Little Lamb was published in 1830, it seems anything but old-fashioned in this jaunty picture book. . . . The characters clothing and the many touches of fantasy and humor lift the poem out of its historical period and into some timeless, lighthearted landscape of the imagination. All six verses appear, from the very familiar to the nearly forgotten, and each illustrated with one or more double-page pictures that magnify the hilarity. . . . Even the potentially unctuous-sounding ending verse is lightened by the joyous spirit and amusing details in the accompanying illustrations, digital collages combining fabric elements with acrylic and gouache painting. A child-pleasing version of the well-known poem." Booklist

Harley, Avis

★ **African** acrostics; a word in edgeways. poems by Avis Harley; photographs by Deborah Noyes. Candlewick Press 2009 un il $17.99; pa $6.99
Grades: 4 5 6 7   811

1. Acrostics 2. Children's poetry 3. Animals -- Africa 4. Animals -- Poetry 5. Animals -- Juvenile literature 6. Poetry -- By individual authors

ISBN 978-0-7636-3621-0; 0-7636-3621-5; 978-0-7636-5818-2 pa

LC 2008017916

This volume depicts "such wild animals as giraffes, zebras, and lions, in poems written to contain acrostics, in which beginning or ending letters from the poetry lines can be used to spell other words." (Publisher's note) "Grades four to six." (Bull Cent Child Books)

"Harley has written 18 poems, each one featuring a different animal. All are written as acrostics, with most of them based on the first letter of each line, but several with more unusual patterns. . . . Much of Harley's poetry consists of carefully crafted descriptive word imagery that is right on target. . . . Most of the full-page, full-color photos of the animals are perfect companions to the facing selections." SLJ

★ **Sea** stars; saltwater poems. [by] Avis Harley; photographs by Margaret Butschler. Wordsong 2006 35p il $16.95
Grades: 3 4 5   811

1. Marine animals -- Poetry 2. Poetry -- By individual authors

ISBN 978-1-59078-429-7; 1-59078-429-4

LC 2006000931

"Butschler's beautiful color photographs came first, and her visual images of creatures on the seashore and in the aquarium inspired Harley's brief, concrete poems—from haiku and tanka to rhyming couplets and nursery rhyme parody. The wordplay will grab readers . . . and so will the exquisite images in both words and pictures." Booklist

The **monarch's** progress; poems with wings. written and illustrated by Avis Harley. Wordsong 2008 32p il $16.95
Grades: 3 4 5   811

1. Butterflies -- Poetry 2. Poetry -- By individual authors

ISBN 978-1-59078-558-4

"This collection of 18 illustrated poems celebrates butterflies in general and monarchs in particular. Cleverly written with obvious attention to craft, the poetry varies in form from rhymed couplets to acrostic verse to haiku and explores topics such as the physical differences between the larval and adult stages, the way monarch wings look when magnified, and the usefulness of having taste sensors in one's feet. Accompanying each poem is a color-pencil drawing, often featuring precise lines and intense hues." Booklist

Harrison, David L.

Vacation; we're going to the ocean. poems by David Harrison; illustrations by Rob Shepperson. Wordsong 2009 62p il $16.95
Grades: 2 3 4   811

1. Ocean -- Poetry 2. Vacations -- Poetry 3. Family life -- Poetry 4. Poetry -- By individual authors

ISBN 978-1-59078-568-3; 1-59078-568-1

LC 2008017718

"These delightful poems center on a family's trip to the ocean and are told from the perspective of young Sam. . . . This book, with its expressive art that expands on the humor in each poem, should have wide appeal." SLJ

Hauth, Katherine B.

What's for dinner? quirky, squirmy poems from the animal world. illustrated by David Clark. Charlesbridge 2011 48p il lib bdg $16.95; pa $7.95
Grades: 3 4 5   811

1. Children's poetry 2. Animals -- Poetry 3. Poetry -- By individual authors 4. Animals -- Food -- Juvenile literature

ISBN 978-1-57091-471-3 lib bdg; 1-5709-1471-0 lib bdg; 978-1-57091-472-0 pa; 1-57091-472-9 pa

LC 2010-07588

"Hauth's funny, eloquent poems celebrate the often-grisly realities of the food chain, depicted in Clark's scraggly ink and watercolor illustrations. A mole gags on a banana slug, a rat 'gets a hug' from a boa constrictor, and a flattened toad becomes a roadkill restaurant. . . . Appended notes provide

additional animal facts. A satisfying mix of tutelage and repartee." Publ Wkly

Havill, Juanita

I heard it from Alice Zucchini; poems about the garden. by Juanita Havill; illustrated by Christine Davenier.
Chronicle Books 2006 29p il $15.95

Grades: K 1 2 3 4   **811**

1. Gardens -- Poetry 2. Gardening -- Poetry 3. Poetry
-- By individual authors

ISBN 978-0-8118-3962-4; 0-8118-3962-1

LC 2004013365

"Havill's collection of verse captures the science and
backyard magic of growing things. . . . Davenier extends
the fanciful imagery in scenes of lively, gossiping plants and
animals, rendered in her signature watercolor-washed ink
sketches." Booklist

Heidbreder, Robert

Noisy poems for a busy day. Kids Can Press 2012 40
p. col. ill. (hardcover) $16.95

Grades: K 1 2   **811**

1. Day 2. Children 3. Poetry -- Collections

ISBN 1554537061; 9781554537068

This children's picture book by Robert Heibreder presents "a collection of (mostly) five-line poems that recreate the sounds and actions of a preschooler's day. . . . The
collection is structured in the shape of a day, and Lori Joy
Smith's child-like illustrations introduce us to five children
whose lives involve toast and jam, goofing around, playing
tag, kissing dogs, turning somersaults, going down the slide,
and watching clouds." (Quill and Quire)

Herrera, Juan Felipe

★ Laughing out loud, I fly; poems in English and
Spanish. drawings by Karen Barbour. HarperCollins Pubs.
1998 un il $15.99

Grades: 6 7 8 9   **811**

1. Mexican Americans -- Poetry 2. Poetry -- By
individual authors 3. Bilingual books -- English-
Spanish 4. Mexican Americans -- Juvenile poetry

ISBN 0-06-027604-5

LC 96-45476

A collection of poems in Spanish and English about
childhood, place, and identity

"Barbour's black-and-white drawings accompany each
poem, delicately underlining its images but allowing the
strong sensuality of the words to seep into readers' minds."
SLJ

Hines, Anna Grossnickle

★ Peaceful pieces; poems and quilts about peace.
Henry Holt 2011 32p il

Grades: PreK K 1 2   **811**

1. Peace -- Poetry 2. Poetry -- By individual authors

ISBN 0805089969; 9780805089967

LC 2010011697

"Hines pairs poems with images of her handmade quilts
to reflect on the theme of peace. Several works focus on individual relationships: when two sisters fight, their mother
makes them face each other at close range, which diffuses
their anger into laughter. . . . Poems like 'Soldier Daddy' are
socially resonant. . . . Often Hines needs just a few words to
convey oceans of meaning. . . . The beauty and painstaking

detail evident in each quilt brings the book's vision a stitch
closer." Publ Wkly

Pieces; a year in poems & quilts. Greenwillow Bks.
2001 un il $15.95; lib bdg $15.89

Grades: K 1 2 3   **811**

1. Nature 2. Quilts 3. Seasons 4. Nature poetry
5. American poetry 6. Nature -- Juvenile poetry 7.
Seasons -- Juvenile poetry 8. Children's poetry,
American 9. Poetry -- By individual authors 10. Quilts
-- Pictorial works -- Juvenile literature

ISBN 0-688-16963-5; 0-688-16964-3 lib bdg

LC 99-86463

Poems about the four seasons, as reflected in the natural
world, are accompanied by photographs of quilts made by
the author

"An appendix explains Hines's meticulous quilting process. . . . Hines takes her quilter's stash of fabric swatches
and her wordsmith's metaphors for memories of the seasons,
and pieces together a unified, artistic whole. An outstanding
book for aspiring quilters or anyone at all." Publ Wkly

Includes bibliographical references

★ Winter lights; a season in poems & quilts. Greenwillow Bks. 2005 un il $16.99; lib bdg $17.89

Grades: K 1 2 3   **811**

1. Quilts 2. Winter -- Poetry 3. Holidays -- Poetry 4.
Poetry -- By individual authors

ISBN 0-06-000817-2; 0-06-000818-0 lib bdg

"Winter is the time of lights, and Hines celebrates the
season in thoughtful poems and pictures of gorgeous quilts
full of bright, beautiful colors. Christmas is only one of the
light-producing celebrations that Hines illuminates. The
feast of Santa Lucia, Hanukkah, Kwanzaa, and the Chinese
New Year are spectacularly introduced with short bursts of
poetry and quilts that capture the spirit of the day." Booklist

Hoberman, Mary Ann

Forget-me-nots; poems to learn by heart. selected by
Mary Ann Hoberman; illustrated by Michael Emberley. Megan Tingley Books 2012 143 p.

Grades: PreK K   **811**

1. Children's poetry 2. Poetry -- Memorizing 3. Poetry
-- Collections 4. Children's poetry, American

ISBN 031612947X; 9780316129473

LC 2011025119

This poetry collection is a "compendium of verse . . .
chosen with children in mind. The Children's Poet Laureate
from 2008 to 2010, [Mary Ann] Hoberman chose 123 poems
that are memorable in both senses of the word. They're 'easy
to remember' (though she concedes that the longer ones will
take more time) and 'worth remembering.' In an appended
section, she discusses an approach to learning poems by
heart, making the process a game with a specific prize."
(Booklist)

★ You read to me, I'll read to you; very short stories
to read together. illustrated by Michael Emberley. Little,
Brown 2001 un il $15.95

Grades: K 1 2 3   **811**

1. American poetry 2. Books and reading 3. Children's
poetry, American 4. Poetry -- By individual authors

ISBN 0-316-36350-2

LC 00-35230

"These rhyming short stories are written in three columns: a left and right-hand column for each of the two readers meant to alternate in the reading of most of the text, and a middle italicized column indicating that the two readers should read those lines together. . . . Each short story covers a two-page spread and features . . . two characters, one for each reader; story subjects range from animals to friendship. . . . Grades two to three." (Bull Cent Child Books)

"Hoberman offers 13 rhymed variations on the theme of getting together to read. The short poems are designed to be read aloud by two voices, with occasional parts to share. . . . The energy never flags, neither in Hoberman's trademark bouncy rhythms nor in Emberley's exuberant illustrations, which picture a wonderful array of children and animals tumbling across the pages." Booklist

★ **You** read to me, I'll read to you: very short scary tales to read together; illustrated by Michael Emberley. Little, Brown 2007 32p il $16.99

Grades: K 1 2 3   **811**

1. Monsters -- Poetry 2. Poetry -- By individual authors
ISBN 978-0-316-01733-6

"The fourth uproarious poetry picture book in Hoberman and Emberley's popular You Read to Me, I'll Read to You series continues the pattern of simple, rhyming, illustrated stories for two voices. . . . The clear words with gorgeously gruesome, comic-style pictures tell of wild action and monster characters as lurid as they come." Booklist

Hoce, Charley

Beyond Old MacDonald; funny poems from down on the farm. illustrated by Eugenie Fernandes. Wordsong/Boyds Mills Press 2005 31p il $16.95

Grades: K 1 2 3   **811**

1. Farm life -- Poetry 2. Poetry -- By individual authors
ISBN 1-59078-312-3

"Hoce employs wordplay in many of these 30 selections. . . . The humor is age appropriate and poems about 'ants in my plants' and a hoarse horse will appeal to children who are beginning to enjoy playing with language. . . . This book is fun, but it's also excellent for classroom use; a 'Wordplay Guide' that indicates language skills, such as identifying homophones, personification, and idioms, is appended." SLJ

Holbrook, Sara

Zombies! evacuate the school! illustrations by Karen Sandstrom. Wongsong 2010 56p il $16.95

Grades: 2 3 4 5   **811**

1. Schools -- Poetry 2. Poetry -- By individual authors
ISBN 978-1-59078-820-2; 1-59078-820-6

"With a breezy and comedic touch, Holbrook shines a light on school experiences, from academic pursuits to classroom rivalries to gym-class exploits. Humor reigns, and readers will identify with themes and emotions. . . . Many of the poems utilize an inner voice and encourage self-reflection. They are brief and accessible. . . . Sandstrom's pen-and-ink illustrations provide additional humor." SLJ

Hopkins, Lee Bennett, 1938-

★ **City** I love; by Lee Bennett Hopkins; illustrated by Marcellus Hall. Abrams Books for Young Readers 2009 un il $16.95

Grades: K 1 2 3 4   **811**

1. City and town life -- Poetry 2. Poetry -- By individual

authors
ISBN 978-0-8109-8327-4; 0-8109-8327-3

LC 2008008226

"A backpack-toting, humble hound with wanderlust and a winged companion tour several of the world's cities. Hopkins's 18 poems observe skyscrapers, hot-dog vendors, subways, taxis, bridges, bright lights, and the diversity of people and pigeons. . . . These polished poems are equally matched by Hall's graphic-style cartoons, which offer many added layers of narrative delight as well as beautiful colors and an eye-catching sense of design." SLJ

I am the book; poems selected by Lee Bennett Hopkins; illustrated by Yayo. Holiday House 2010 un il $16.95

Grades: K 1 2   **811**

1. Books and reading -- Poetry 2. American poetry -- Collections
ISBN 0823421198; 9780823421190

LC 2009014743

"This collection of poems by contemporary writers celebrates the joys of reading. . . . In Yayo's acrylic spreads, an open book becomes a whale's tail, a treasure box, and a drifting raft, emphasizing the transformative potential of words." Publ Wly

Hughes, Langston

★ **Langston** Hughes; edited by Arnold Rampersad & David Roessel; illustrations by Benny Andrews. Sterling Pub. 2006 48p il (Poetry for young people) $14.95

Grades: 5 6 7 8   **811**

1. African Americans -- Poetry 2. Poetry -- By individual authors
ISBN 1-4027-1845-4; 978-1-4027-1845-8

LC 2005025369

A brief profile of African American poet Langston Hughes accompanies some of his better known poems for children.

"This charming collection of 26 poems is vibrantly illustrated with depictions of African Americans in varied settings. . . . This will be a welcome introduction to Hughes's poetry for elementary students, and it includes sufficient detail to make it useful and enjoyable for older students." SLJ

★ **My** people; photographs by Charles R. Smith Jr. Atheneum Books for Young Readers 2009 un il $17.99

Grades: K 1 2 3   **811**

1. African Americans -- Poetry 2. Poetry -- By individual authors
ISBN 978-1-4169-3540-7; 1-4169-3540-1

LC 2008025604

ALA EMIERT Coretta Scott King Illustrator Award (2010)

"Introducing the poem two or three words at a time, Smith pairs each phrase with a portrait of one or more African Americans; printed in sepia, the faces of his subjects materialize on black pages. . . . Smith's faces emerge into the light, displaying the best that humanity has to offer—intelligence, wisdom, curiosity, love and joy." Publ Wkly

★ The **Negro** speaks of rivers; [by] Langston Hughes; with illustrations by E. B. Lewis. Disney Jump at the Sun Books 2009 un il $16.99

Grades: K 1 2 3   **811**

1. Rivers -- Poetry 2. African Americans -- Poetry 3.

Poetry -- By individual authors

ISBN 978-0-7868-1867-9; 0-7868-1867-0

ALA EMIERT Coretta Scott King Illustrator Award Honor Book (2010)

Children will "easily connect with these luminous, soul-stirring pictures that honor both African American heritage and the whole human family. Transcendent images for a transcendent poem." Booklist

★ The **dream** keeper and other poems; including seven additional poems. [by] Langston Hughes; illustrated by Brian Pinkney. 75th anniversary ed.; Alfred A. Knopf 2007 83p il $16.99

Grades: 4 5 6 7   811

1. African Americans -- Poetry 2. Poetry -- By individual authors

ISBN 978-0-679-84421-1

First published 1932; this is a reissue of the 1994 edition

A collection of sixty-six poems, selected by the author for young readers, including lyrical poems, songs, and blues, many exploring the black experience

"Black-and-white scratchboard illustrations in Pinkney's signature style express the emotion and beat of the poetry. . . . The poems are . . . colloquial and direct yet mysterious and complex." Booklist

Hughes, Langston, 1902-1967

★ **I,** too, am America; Langston Hughes; illustrated by Bryan Collier. Simon & Schuster Books for Young Readers 2012 40 p.

Grades: K 1 2 3   811

1. Railroads -- Fiction 2. Picture books for children 3. African Americans -- Poetry 4. United States -- History -- Poetry

ISBN 1442420081; 9781442420083

LC 2011002879

Coretta Scott King Illustrator Book Award (2013)

In this picture book, a "celebration of Pullman porters is the focus of this . . . edition of Langston Hughes' classic poem. . . . [It] begin[s] with . . . a speeding train before moving on to large portraits of African American porters serving white passengers aboard a luxury train. . . . [T]he porters gather left-behind items--newspapers, blues and jazz albums--and toss them from the train. . . . [T]he words and music fall into the hands of African Americans across the country." (Booklist)

Iyengar, Malathi Michelle

Tan to tamarind; poems about the color brown. poems by Malathi Michelle Iyengar; illustrations by Jamel Akib. Children's Book Press 2009 30p il $16.95

Grades: K 1 2 3   811

1. Color -- Poetry 2. Poetry -- By individual authors

ISBN 978-0-89239-227-8; 0-89239-227-4

LC 2008022225

"Illustrated with pastel pictures in warm autumn colors, both dark and light, the simple poems celebrate the diversity and the connections in nature, culture, place, and language among blacks, Latinos, Indians, Native Americans, and many mixed-race kids. All the names for brown—from tan to honey, beige, and ocher—show the wonder of the senses." Booklist

Janeczko, Paul B.

★ **Wing** nuts; screwy haiku. by Paul B. Janeczko and J. Patrick Lewis; illustrated by Tricia Tusa. Little, Brown 2006 un il $15.99

Grades: 2 3 4   811

1. Children's poetry 2. Poetry -- By individual authors

ISBN 0-316-60731-2

LC 2005-07970

"This book introduces senryu, a Japanese verse form that can involve the evasive, the punny, the parodic, and the slapstick. . . . The highly spirited verses feature witty word-play and puns. . . . This book fulfills its purpose to revive and invigorate the language, and does so with humor. In her ink-and-watercolor cartoons, Tusa uses a soft palette, strong lines, and abundant white space to define the comical characters." SLJ

Johnson, Dinah

Hair dance! words by Dinah Johnson; photographs by Kelly Johnson. Henry Holt 2007 un il $16.95

Grades: K 1 2   811

1. Hair -- Poetry 2. Girls -- Poetry 3. African Americans -- Poetry 4. Poetry -- By individual authors 5. Hairstyles -- Juvenile literature

ISBN 978-0-8050-6523-7; 0-8050-6523-7

LC 2006-30616

"This vibrant offering pairs colorful photographs of African-American girls with upbeat verses. The youngsters are shown alone and together, and their moods and expressions vary from shy and pensive to bold and exuberant. They wear their hair loose and natural, and in barrettes, beads, Afro puffs, or braids that 'fly high into the sky.' . . . Most of the verses are short and rhythmic and read aloud like a jump-rope rhyme." SLJ

Includes bibliographical references

Katz, Alan

Oops! poems by Alan Katz; drawings by Edward Koren. Margaret K. McElderry Books 2008 132p il $17.99

Grades: 3 4 5 6   811

1. Humorous poetry 2. Children's poetry 3. Poetry -- By individual authors

ISBN 978-1-4169-0204-1; 1-4169-0204-X

LC 2005-32439

"This collection of more than 100 short, funny, rhyming poems never lags. It includes occasional (rather funny) potty humor. . . . Puns and other groaners abound and are sure to delight young readers, especially boys. . . . Koren's pen-and-ink cartoons resemble the art in Shel Silverstein's collections. The illustrations match the tone of the book and sometimes add extra interpretations of the poems. This is a great choice for reluctant poetry readers and aspiring class clowns." SLJ

Poems I wrote when no one was looking; drawings by Edward Koren. Margaret K. McElderry Books 2011 153p il $17.99

Grades: 3 4 5   811

1. Humorous poetry 2. Poetry -- By individual authors

ISBN 978-1-4169-3518-6; 1-4169-3518-5

LC 2007052523

"Accompanied by Koren's impish, characteristically furry caricatures, Katz's comedic poems take aim at familiar experiences like family squabbling and avoiding homework, while offering child-centric observations about the world. . . . Kids will revel in the gently wicked jokes . . . and mild gross-out gags . . . that run throughout the collection." Publ Wkly

Kennedy, X. J.

City kids; street and skyscraper rhymes. illustrated by Philippe Béha. Tradewind Books 2010 104p il $17.95
Grades: 3 4 5　　　　811
　　1. Children's poetry 2. City and town life -- Poetry 3. Poetry -- By individual authors
　　ISBN 978-1-896580-44-9; 1-896580-44-0
"The urban world is examined from every angle in this lively collection of verse about city life. Most can apply to cities generally, though there are specific poems about Toronto, San Francisco, London, and others. . . . Béha's illustrations have a naïf, crayon-scrawled exuberance, and most match the upbeat tone of Kennedy's verse." Publ Wkly

Kinerk, Robert

Oh, how Sylvester can pester! and other poems more or less about manners. pictures by Drazen Kozjan. Simon & Schuster Books for Young Readers 2011 28p il $16.99
Grades: K 1 2 3　　　　811
　　1. Children's poetry 2. Etiquette for children and teenagers 3. Etiquette -- Poetry 4. Poetry -- By individual authors
　　ISBN 1-4169-3362-X; 978-1-4169-3362-5
　　　　　　　　　　LC 2010000771
In these illustrated poems "Kinerk pokes fun at what can happen when good manners are neglected." (Publisher's note) "Primary." (Horn Book)
"The rhymes in this picture book about manners have fun with names and with nonsense. . . . The clear, bright digital pictures extend the farce." Booklist

Lang, Diane

Vulture verses; love poems for the unloved. written by Diane Lang; illustrated by Lauren Gallegos. Prospect Park Media 2012 32 p.
Grades: 2 3 4　　　　811
　　1. Didactic poetry 2. Animals -- Poetry 3. Children's poetry 4. Animals -- Juvenile poetry 5. Children's poetry, American
　　ISBN 0983459452; 9780983459453
　　　　　　　　　　LC 2012002823

Larios, Julie Hofstrand

★ **Imaginary** menagerie; a book of curious creatures. poems by Julie Larios; [illustrated by] Julie Paschkis. Harcourt 2008 32p il $16
Grades: K 1 2 3　　　　811
　　1. Children's poetry 2. Mythical animals -- Poetry 3. Poetry -- By individual authors 4. Animals, Mythical -- Juvenile literature
　　ISBN 978-0-15-206325-2
　　　　　　　　　　LC 2006-37442
This is a collection of poems about "mythical creatures. . . . Working in a range of styles, Larios creates accessible, atmospheric poems full of sounds and rhythms that are best read aloud. . . . Paschkis' beautifully patterned pictures use motifs such as Nordic designs scrawled across the trolls'

bridge to correspond to each creature's country of origin." Booklist

★ **Yellow** elephant; a bright bestiary. poems by Julie Larios; paintings by Julie Paschkis. Harcourt 2006 31p il $16
Grades: K 1 2 3　　　　811
　　1. Children's poetry 2. Color -- Poetry 3. Animals -- Poetry 4. Poetry -- By individual authors
　　ISBN 0-15-205422-7
　　　　　　　　　　LC 2004-25163
"The animals featured in these well-crafted poems flash with color and emotion. Each spread features a picture of a brightly hued animal, and Larios' rhythms and sounds skillfully reinforce the memorable, evocative images. . . . Together with Paschkis' vibrant, patterned, gouache paintings, the poems beautifully show how color and sound create mood and imagery." Booklist

Lawrence, Jacob

★ **Harriet** and the Promised Land. Simon & Schuster Bks. for Young Readers 1993 un il $18; pa $6.99
Grades: 2 3 4 5　　　　811
　　1. Abolitionists 2. Children's poetry 3. Underground railroad -- Poetry 4. Poetry -- By individual authors
　　ISBN 0-671-86673-7; 0-689-80965-4 pa
　　　　　　　　　　LC 92-33740
A newly illustrated edition of the title first published 1968 by Windmill Books
"The strength of this volume is in the forceful, stylized paintings by the famous black artist, which capture the degradation of slavery." Brooklyn. Art Books for Child

Lesynski, Loris

Crazy about soccer. Annick Press 2012 47 p. $22.95
Grades: 3 4 5　　　　811
　　1. Soccer -- Poetry 2. Children's poetry 3. Picture books for children
　　ISBN 1554514223; 9781554514229
This poetry collection "celebrates the sport of soccer. . . . From the commiseration offered to players who must persevere through squalls in 'Rain Game' to . . . 'Turf Burn,' which . . . describes the perils of artificial grass, [Loris] Lesynski's verse explores the gamut of soccer experiences. The format varies, with verses that range from brief . . . , such as the sole line comprising 'The Concussion Discussion,' to the lengthier 'How to Be a Referee,' which pays homage to . . . game officials." (Kirkus)

Levy, Debbie

Maybe I'll sleep in the bathtub tonight; and other funny bedtime poems. illustrated by Stephanie Buscema. Sterling Pub. 2010 24p il $14.95
Grades: PreK K 1 2　　　　811
　　1. Humorous poetry 2. Bedtime -- Poetry 3. Poetry -- By individual authors
　　ISBN 978-1-4027-4944-5; 1-4027-4944-9
　　　　　　　　　　LC 2008-48826
"These cozy rhymes for sharing at bedtime have a lot of fun with wordplay, from the literal interpretations of sleepover, showing kids on a roof, and sleep tight (I unkinked myself and vowed: / Tonight I will sleep loose!), to a familiar nursery lullaby. . . . Young children with their caregivers will giggle at the humorous scenes, illustrated with

colorful gouache pictures, which could make a good prelude to the usual soothing lullabies." Booklist

★ The **year** of goodbyes; a true story of friendship, family and farewells. Disney-Hyperion Books 2010 136p il $16.99

Grades: 5 6 7 8   **811**

1. Jews -- Poetry 2. Holocaust, 1933-1945 -- Poetry 3. Poetry -- By individual authors

ISBN 978-1-4231-2901-1; 1-4231-2901-6

LC 2009-18671

"Artfully weaving together her mother's poesiealbum (autograph/poetry album), diary, and her own verse, Levy crafts a poignant portrait of her Jewish mother's life in 1938 Nazi Germany that crackles with adolescent vitality." Publ Wkly

Lewis, J. Patrick

★ **Birds** on a wire; a Renga 'round town. [by] J. Patrick Lewis & Paul B. Janeczko; illustrations by Gary Lippincott. Wordsong 2008 un il $17.95

Grades: 2 3 4   **811**

1. Renga 2. Children's poetry 3. Poetry -- By individual authors

ISBN 978-1-59078-383-2; 1-59078-383-2

LC 2006-11582

"In the Japanese verse form called renga, a cousin to the haiku, two or more poets take turns, each playing off the previous verse so that the narrative is propelled in constantly new and surprising directions. Lewis and Janeczko, both accomplished youth poets, prove just how compelling this form can be.... Mirroring the verse form, each of Lippincott's two-page spreads offers visual clues as to what the next will hold as well as echoes of the previous one.... This lovely picture book is an impeccable synthesis of text and image, each simultaneously playing off the other in ways insightful and visceral." Booklist

★ **Blackbeard,** the pirate king; several yarns detailing the legends, myths, and real-life adventures of history's most notorious seaman. told in verse by J. Patrick Lewis. National Geographic Society 2006 un il map $16.95; lib bdg $25.90

Grades: 3 4 5   **811**

1. Pirates 2. Children's poetry 3. Pirates -- Poetry 4. Poetry -- By individual authors

ISBN 0-7922-5585-2; 0-7922-5586-0 lib bdg

LC 2005-29514

"Lewis crafts sophisticated verse around the few facts and many fictions told of Edward Teach, otherwise known as Blackbeard, the seventeenth century pirate king. In antique type, the poems are either set against parchment-style backgrounds or against one of the book's diverse images, which include paintings by N. C. Wyeth, and Caspar David Friedrich, as well as archival prints and striking modern paintings. Despite the broad range of art styles, the story flows cohesively throughout, vividly evoking the buccaneer's adventures in swashbuckling lines that read aloud well." Booklist

Countdown to summer; a poems for every day of the school year. illustrations by Ethan Long. Little, Brown and Co. 2009 un il $15.99

Grades: 4 5 6   **811**

1. Schools -- Poetry 2. Poetry -- By individual authors

ISBN 978-0-316-02089-3; 0-316-02089-3

LC 2008016772

"180 poems are here gathered to be enjoyed on a vitamin-like one-a-day basis. . . . Some verses are long, some short, some thought-provoking, some laugh-provoking. Long's penciled spot art provides an agreeable visual accompaniment." Kirkus

★ **Doodle** dandies; poems that take shape. J. Patrick Lewis, words; Lisa Desimini, images; with design and typography by Ann Bobco and Lisa Desimini. Atheneum Bks. for Young Readers 1998 un il hardcover o.p. pa $7.99

Grades: 1 2 3 4   **811**

1. American poetry 2. Visual poetry 3. Visual poetry, American 4. Children's poetry, American 5. Poetry -- By individual authors

ISBN 0-689-81075-X; 0-689-84889-7 pa

LC 9601920

This is a collection of poems each of which appears on the page in the shape of its subject so that the poem looks like whatever it's about. "Grades three to six." (SLJ)

"Every page of this book is well designed, creating words and images that work together in harmony. . . . Doodle Dandies captures the joy that wordplay can bring." SLJ

Edgar Allan Poe's apple pie; math puzzlers in classic poems. written by J. Patrick Lewis; illustrated by Michael H. Slack. Harcourt 2012 37 p.

Grades: 4 5 6   **811**

1. Children's poetry 2. Mathematics -- Poetry 3. Mathematical recreations 4. Word problems (Mathematics) 5. Poetry -- Parodies, imitations, etc. 6. Children's poetry, American 7. English poetry -- Adaptations 8. American poetry -- Adaptations 9. Mathematics -- Juvenile poetry 10. Mathematical recreations -- Juvenile literature

ISBN 9780547513386

LC 2011025735

The author J. Patrick Lewis "combines math and language arts with this collection of humorous poetry parodies that present readers with math word problems to solve. Fourteen famous poets and some of their more prominent works are the basis for Lewis' parodies, which . . . retain the structure, rhyme and rhythm of the originals." The book presents challenges based on works by poets including Walt Whitman, Emily Dickinson, and Shel Silverstein on mathematics concepts such as fractions, decimals, and perimeter. (Kirkus)

If you were a chocolate mustache; J. Patrick Lewis. WordSong 2012 159 p. $18.95

Grades: 3 4 5   **811**

1. Children's poetry 2. Dragons -- Poetry 3. Turtles -- Poetry

ISBN 159078927X; 9781590789278

LC 2012939794

For this book, "in offbeat poems that include haikus, limericks, riddles, and wordplay of every kind, current children's poet laureate [J. Patrick] Lewis offers quirky contemplations, silly vignettes, and improbable events." Here, "a dragon serves as a clothes dryer, Bigfoot laments that he can't find stylish shoes in his size, and an old turtle complains to the sky that there is 'nothing new under the sun,' only to have his claim challenged by a snowflake." (Publishers Weekly)

★ **Monumental** verses. National Geographic 2005 31p il $16.95; lib bdg $25.90

Grades: 5 6 7 8   **811**
1. Monuments -- Poetry 2. Poetry -- By individual authors

ISBN 0-7922-7135-1; 0-7922-7139-4 lib bdg

"Lewis offers 14 poems celebrating monumental structures. From the remnants of civilizations at Stonehenge, Easter Island, and Machu Picchu to the more modern achievements of the Taj Mahal, the Eiffel Tower, and the Statue of Liberty, the subjects are varied and the accompanying photos are striking." Booklist

★ **Once** upon a tomb; gravely humorous verses. illustrated by Simon Bartram. Candlewick 2006 un il $16.99

Grades: 3 4 5   **811**
1. Death -- Poetry 2. Poetry -- By individual authors

ISBN 0-7636-1837-3

"Proving himself to be anything but a grave man, Lewis offers 22 irreverent epitaphs and other mortuary verses, each of which is paired with a large, polished portrait or burial scene created in richly hued acrylics.... This rare look at the lighter side of death should elicit plenty of surprised giggles from young audiences." Booklist

Please bury me in the library; illustrated by Kyle M. Stone. Harcourt 2005 32p il $16

Grades: 3 4 5   **811**
1. Children's poetry 2. Books and reading -- Poetry 3. Poetry -- By individual authors 4. Libraries -- Juvenile literature

ISBN 0-15-216387-5

LC 2003-26983

A "collection of 16 poems celebrating books, reading, language, and libraries.... The brief selections encompass various forms, from an eight-word acrostic to haiku to rhyming quatrains and couplets.... The poems are accompanied by richly dark artwork. The thickly applied acrylic paint and mixed-media illustrations ... [have] a comically grotesque air, and add comprehension to the verses." SLJ

★ **Self** -portrait with seven fingers; the life of Marc Chagall in verse. [by] J. Patrick Lewis &Jane Yolen. Creative Editions 2011 38p il $18.99

Grades: 5 6 7 8   **811**
1. Artists 2. Painters 3. Jews -- Poetry 4. Artists -- Poetry 5. Jews -- Biography

ISBN 978-1-56846-211-0; 1-56846-211-5

LC 2009034767

"Lewis and Yolen pair 14 poems about Marc Chagall (1887–1985) with reproductions of more than a dozen of his paintings (as well as vintage photographs) in this moving account of the artist's Jewish upbringing in what is now Belarus, ... his ascent in the art world, and his loves and losses, including arrest by the Nazis while living in Paris.... The duo's emphatic and empathetic verse is put into context by informative biographical sidebars that appear beneath each

poem. A study in resilience, dedication, and wide-ranging talent." Publ Wkly

Includes bibliographical references

Skywriting; poems to fly. illustrated by Laszlo Kubinyi. Creative Editions 2010 32p il $25.65

Grades: 3 4 5 6   **811**
1. Flight -- Poetry 2. Poetry -- By individual authors

ISBN 978-1-56846-203-5; 1-56846-203-4

LC 2008014229

"Tracing the history of flight, this collection of poems celebrates the daring dreams of humans, from Icarus's doomed journey ... to modern space shuttles.... Kubinyi's precise linework and sense of movement are well-matched to the mechanical subject matter and capture the spirit of flight across the ages." Publ Wkly

Spot the plot; a riddle book of book riddles. illustrated by Lynn Munsinger. Chronicle Books 2009 un il $15.99

Grades: K 1 2 3   **811**
1. Riddles 2. Riddles, Juvenile 3. Books and reading -- Poetry 4. Poetry -- By individual authors 5. Children's stories -- Stories, plots, etc.

ISBN 978-0-8118-4668-4; 0-8118-4668-7

LC 2008-03206

"Short poetic riddles are presented on spreads, each providing the clues in both text and illustrations of the plot of a well-known children's story. Two young detectives and their dog are looking at such activities as farm animals typing letters in a field (Click, Clack, Moo), a train running along snowy railway tracks (The Polar Express), or a pumpkin coach careening along as it's drawn by a bunch of rats (Cinderella).... This book is perfect for an interactive read-aloud." SLJ

Under the kissletoe; Christmastime poems. [by] J. Patrick Lewis; illustrations by Rob Shepperson. Wordsong 2007 32p il $16.95

Grades: 2 3 4   **811**
1. Christmas -- Poetry 2. Poetry -- By individual authors

ISBN 978-1-59078-438-9; 1-59078-438-3

LC 2006038984

"In Lewis's collection of poems ... affable wit and infectious cadence bring fresh energy to traditional yuletide images.... Shepperson's brightly shaded, borderline cartoon-y illustrations balance humor with warmth." Horn Book

★ **When** thunder comes; poems for civil rights leaders. by J. Patrick Lewis, 2011-2013 Children's Poet Laureate; illustrated by R. Gregory Christie. Chronicle Books 2012 44 p. (alk. paper) $16.99

Grades: 4 5 6   **811**
1. Children's poetry 2. Civil rights -- Juvenile literature 3. Children's poetry, American

ISBN 1452101191; 9781452101194

LC 2011045938

In this collection, "Children's Poet Laureate J. Patrick Lewis gives ... voice to seventeen heroes of civil rights... . Illustrated by five ... artists, this ... collection of poems invites the reader to hear in each verse the thunder that lies in every voice, no matter how small." Civil rights figures profiled include "Coretta Scott King, Harvey Milk, Mohandas Gandhi, Nelson Mandela, Sylvia Mendez, Aung San Suu

Kyi, . . . Andrew Goodman, and Michael Schwerner." (Publisher's note)

The **World's** Greatest; poems. [written by] J. Patrick Lewis; [illustrated by Keith Graves] Chronicle Books 2008 33p il $16.99

Grades: K 1 2 3 **811**

1. Children's poetry 2. World records -- Poetry 3. Poetry -- By individual authors

ISBN 978-0-8118-5130-5; 0-8118-5130-3

LC 2007-14717

"This sprightly, clever collection centers on facts found in various editions of the 'Guinness Book of Records.' . . . The droll, distinct illustrations created using acrylic paint and colored pencils capture perfectly the humor and vigor of the text. This attractive book is saturated with color and will charm children who understand its adroit wordplay." SLJ

★ The **brothers'** war; Civil War voices in verse. including photographs by Civil War photographers. National Geographic 2007 31p il $17.95; lib bdg $20.90

Grades: 5 6 7 8 9 10 **811**

1. Children's poetry 2. Poetry -- By individual authors

ISBN 978-1-4263-0036-3; 978-1-4263-0037-0 lib bdg

LC 2006-103275

"This heartrending collection of original poems paired with photographs by Civil War photographers makes real what statistics about war cannot—that the casualties of any war have human faces. Lewis . . . writes poignantly and lyrically. . . . An elegant design of gold, silver and black handsomely frames the text and photographs." Publ Wkly

★ The **house**; illustrated by Roberto Innocenti. Creative Editions 2009 un il $19.95

Grades: 4 5 6 7 **811**

1. Houses -- Poetry 2. Poetry -- By individual authors

ISBN 978-1-56846-201-1; 1-56846-201-8

"The walls in a stone farmhouse literally talk in this first-person narrative that deals with the ravages of time and their effects on the structure and its inhabitants. After a brief history, the house (constructed in 1656, 'a plague year') fast forwards to the dawn of the 20th century, when children discover its ruins. The quatrains, one to a spread, alternate between an AABB and ABBA rhyme scheme, thus avoiding singsong predictability. . . . Children will pore over Innocenti's marvelously detailed spreads, composed in an oversize, vertical format and set in an Italian hill town. . . . In the subset of books dealing intelligently with the effects of time on a single location, this is a provocative choice." SLJ

The **underwear** salesman; and other jobs for better or verse. [by] J. Patrick Lewis; illustrated by Serge Bloch. Atheneum Books for Young Readers 2009 un il $16.99

Grades: 3 4 5 **811**

1. Work -- Poetry 2. Occupations -- Poetry 3. Poetry -- By individual authors

ISBN 978-0-689-85325-8; 0-689-85325-4

LC 2008025884

"Puns are everywhere in this playful, rhyming survey of jobs, and the collage illustrations extend the verbal fun with wry, literal images." Booklist

Lobel, Arnold

Odd owls & stout pigs; a book of nonsense. color by Adrianne Lobel. Harper 2009 31p il $15.99; lib bdg $16.89

Grades: PreK K 1 2 **811**

1. Humorous poetry 2. Owls -- Poetry 3. Pigs -- Poetry 4. Poetry -- By individual authors

ISBN 978-0-06-180054-2; 0-06-180054-6; 978-0-06-180055-9 lib bdg; 0-06-180055-4 lib bdg

LC 2009001406

Presents a linked collection of brief rhymes featuring owls and pigs

"This collection of nonsense rhymes and poems explodes with fun and frivolity. . . . The verses cover a wide variety of topics, and the words create sound patterns that will engage listeners. . . . Original illustrations were scanned and enhanced with oil pastels and colored pencils. They play buoyantly off Mr. Lobel's clever text and provide a breezy feel." SLJ

★ The **frogs** and toads all sang; color by Adrianne Lobel. HarperCollinsPublishers 2009 29p il $16.99; lib bdg $17.89

Grades: PreK K 1 2 **811**

1. Frogs -- Poetry 2. Toads -- Poetry 3. Poetry -- By individual authors

ISBN 978-0-06-180022-1; 978-0-06-180023-8 lib bdg

LC 2008051768

A collection of poems featuring frogs, toads, and polliwogs

"Originally created by the late Lobel as a handmade book for a fellow author, these poems and pencil sketches (skillfully given washes of color by his daughter, Adrianne) are the progenitors of Lobel's classic Frog and Toad series. But even kids who haven't spent much time with those amphibious friends will find plenty to enjoy. . . . The drawings of genteelly domesticated amphibians large and small bring to mind the spontaneity, intimacy and exuberance of the sketchpad." Publ Wkly

Longfellow, Henry Wadsworth

Hiawatha; pictures by Susan Jeffers. Dial Bks. for Young Readers 1983 un il hardcover o.p. pa $6.99 **811**

1. Native Americans -- Poetry 2. Native Americans -- Folklore 3. Poetry -- By individual authors

ISBN 0-14-055882-9 pa

LC 83-7225

Verses excerpted from the poem first published 1855 with title: Song of Hiawatha

"Jeffers has captured the essence of this brief section from the classic poem. . . . The pale tints of the pictures are in complete harmony with nature and with the text and show in detail how Hiawatha might have seen his world. A fine first exposure to the poem for children and a beautiful artistic experience." SLJ

Low, Alice

The **fastest** game on two feet and other poems about how sports began; illustrated by John O'Brien. Holiday House 2009 40p il $17.95

Grades: 3 4 5 6 **811**

1. Sports -- Poetry 2. Poetry -- By individual authors

ISBN 978-0-8234-1905-0; 0-8234-1905-3

LC 2007013441

"These 19 poems, each for a different sport, score a goal. Under the title, a short paragraph establishes a context for the origin of the sport. . . . The poems are tightly phrased and put a spin on the historical information of how the sport has evolved. O'Brien's signature style of dappled watercolors-over-ink comically underscores the theme that sports are fun." Kirkus

Lujan, Jorge

Doggy slippers; poems by Jorge Luján (with the contribution of Latin American children); translated by Elisa Amado; pictures by Isol. Groundwood Books/House of Anansi Press 2010 un il $18.95

Grades: PreK K 1   **811**
1. Pets -- Poetry 2. Poetry -- By individual authors
ISBN 978-0-88899-983-2; 0-88899-983-6

"Using suggestions from kids in Mexico and Argentina, Luján crafts this refreshing collection of 12 free-verse poems about children's pets. . . . Abstract, whimsical illustrations in a retro palette of brown, gold, olive and aqua rely on squiggly pencil outlines to economically define details and highlight sublime and ridiculous aspects from each poem. . . . Poetic pet snapshots packaged with panache and translated with aplomb." Kirkus

MacLachlan, Patricia

I didn't do it; [by] Patricia MacLachlan and Emily MacLachlan Charest; illustrated by Katy Schneider. Katherine Tegan Books 2010 un il $16.99

Grades: PreK K 1 2   **811**
1. Children's poetry 2. Dogs -- Poetry 3. Poetry -- By individual authors
ISBN 978-0-06-135833-3; 0-06-135833-9

LC 2009-27541

This is a "charming volume of verses showing the thoughts of puppies of many breeds. . . . The verses are short, and the authors seem to understand canines and their likes, dislikes and self discipline (or lack thereof). Humor abounds, as do the activities, and illustrated in lively, textured oil paintings that make breeds clearly recognizable." Kirkus

★ **Once** I ate a pie; by Patricia MacLachlan and Emily MacLachlan Charest; illustrated by Katy Schneider. Joanna Cotler Books 2006 un il $15.99; lib bdg $16.89; pa $6.99

Grades: K 1 2 3   **811**
1. Children's poetry 2. Dogs -- Poetry 3. Poetry -- By individual authors
ISBN 978-0-06-073531-9; 0-06-073531-7; 978-0-06-073532-6 lib bdg; 0-06-073532-5 lib bdg; 978-0-06-073533-3 pa; 0-06-073533-3 pa

LC 2004-22225

"Free-verse poems about 14 individual dogs sprawl across oversize spreads accompanied by large oil illustrations. The poems and paintings together delightfully capture each distinct personality in few words and with broad strokes of the brush." SLJ

Maddox, Marjorie

Rules of the game; baseball poems. illustrated by John Sandford. Wordsong 2009 32p il $16.95

Grades: 5 6 7 8   **811**
1. Children's poetry 2. Baseball -- Poetry 3. Poetry

-- By individual authors
ISBN 978-1-59078-603-1; 1-59078-603-3

LC 2008-19018

"Sports fans will find themselves nodding in recognition of Maddox's sophisticated grasp of the game's intricacies, while language mavens will appreciate her joyous wordplay and dead-on command of poetic devices. . . . Sandford's charcoal pencil drawings, backed by sepia-toned pages . . . impart a classy timelessness to the book that's a nice match to its subject." Booklist

Mitton, Tony

Gnash, gnaw, dinosaur! prehistoric poems with lift-the-flap surprises! written by Tony Mitton; illustrated by Lynne Chapman. Kingfisher 2009 un il $12.99

Grades: PreK K 1 2 3   **811**
1. Dinosaurs -- Poetry 2. Poetry -- By individual authors
ISBN 978-0-7534-6226-3; 0-7534-6226-5

"Mitton's rhyming verses impart a fair amount of information about their dinosaur subjects, reflecting their behavior, food and eating habits and habitats. . . . Chapman's illustrations reflect the text's subtle fact-underneath-fun manner. . . . With great vocabulary, verses that scan well and a large trim size, this fits well into dinosaur-themed storytimes." Kirkus

Rumble, roar, dinosaur! more prehistoric poems with lift-the-flap surprises! written by Tony Mitton; illustrated by Lynne Chapman. Kingfisher 2010 un il $12.95

Grades: PreK K 1 2 3   **811**
1. Dinosaurs -- Poetry 2. Poetry -- By individual authors
ISBN 978-0-7534-1932-8; 0-7534-1932-7

LC 2010007498

"With its expressive cartoon dinosaurs, this lift-the-flap poetry book . . . emphasizes fun over science. The rhymes have plenty of bounce." Publ Wkly

Moore, Clement Clarke

★ The **night** before Christmas; [illustrated by] Charles Santore. Applesauce 2011 il $18.95

Grades: PreK K 1   **811**
1. Christmas -- Poetry 2. Santa Claus -- Poetry 3. Poetry -- By individual authors
ISBN 978-1-60433-237-7; 1-60433-237-9

Santore "brings to life Moore's 'A Visit from St. Nicholas' in characteristically elegant and detail-rich paintings. His is a very traditional vision, as he brings readers inside a stately colonial home, tastefully appointed with wreaths, garlands, and stockings. . . . It's a gorgeous interpretation of a beloved holiday classic." Publ Wkly

★ The **night** before Christmas; illustrated by Richard Jesse Watson. HarperCollins Pubs. 2006 un il hardcover o.p. pa $6.99

Grades: K 1 2 3   **811**
1. Christmas -- Poetry 2. Santa Claus -- Poetry 3. Poetry -- By individual authors
ISBN 0-06-075741-8; 0-06-075742-6 lib bdg; 978-0-06-075744-1 pa; 0-06-075744-2 pa

"Watson presents a modern, hip, and playful version of the classic poem with Santa cruising in a rocket-ship-style sleigh into an ordinary American '50s town, dressed like a biplane aviator. Multicultural elves, including one with dreadlocks and carrying a boom box and another in an Asian jacket carrying an origami paper crane, decorate the text side of each spread. Watson's imaginative style, dynamic composition, and use of perspective are stunning and exciting." SLJ

'Twas the night before Christmas; illustrated by Christopher Wormell. Running Press Kids 2010 un il $16.95
Grades: PreK K 1 **811**
   1. Christmas -- Poetry 2. Santa Claus -- Poetry 3. Poetry -- By individual authors
   ISBN 978-0-7624-2717-8; 0-7624-2717-5
The well-known poem about an important Christmas visitor.
"With their strong black lines and deep colors, Wormell's signature block prints are a fittingly iconic pairing for Moore's holiday classic. . . . This is an enchanting and elegant adaptation." Publ Wkly

Moore, Lilian
   ★ **Beware,** take care; fun and spooky poems. by Lilian Moore; illustrated by Howard Fine. Henry Holt and Co. 2006 un il $16.95
Grades: PreK K 1 2 **811**
   1. Fear -- Poetry 2. Monsters -- Poetry 3. Supernatural -- Poetry 4. Poetry -- By individual authors
   ISBN 978-0-8050-6917-4; 0-8050-6917-8
                      LC 2005020257
Poems first published in the author's Spooky Rhymes and Riddles (1973) and See My Lovely Poison Ivy (1975)
"The ghosts, monsters, and dragons are amusing and not the least bit scary in this congenial picture-book gathering of short verses. . . . Illustrated with humor and warmth, these poems are simple enough for independent readers and silly enough to evoke chuckles and giggles during read-aloud sharing." SLJ

Mural on Second Avenue, and other city poems; illustrated by Roma Karas. Candlewick Press 2005 un il $16.99
Grades: K 1 2 3 **811**
   1. City and town life -- Poetry 2. Poetry -- By individual authors
   ISBN 0-7636-1987-6
                      LC 2002-73702
"These 17 poems, all but one of which were chosen from Moore's previous collections, celebrate life in the city. . . . The poems appear on pages covered in bright oil paintings. . . . These poems speak loudly to children." SLJ

Mora, Pat
   ★ **Yum!** mmmm! que rico! Americas' sproutings: haiku. illustrated by Rafael López. Lee & Low 2007 un il map lib bdg $16.95
Grades: 1 2 3 4 **811**
   1. Fruit 2. Haiku 3. Vegetables 4. Children's poetry 5. Food -- Poetry 6. Haiku -- Juvenile literature 7. Poetry -- By individual authors
   ISBN 978-1-58430-271-1 lib bdg; 1-58430-271-2 lib bdg
                      LC 2006-38199
"This inventive stew of food haiku celebrates indigenous foods of the Americas. Each of the 13 poems appears on a gloriously colorful double-page spread, accompanied by a sidebar that presents information about the origin of the food. . . . The acrylic-on-wood-panel illustrations burst with vivid colors and stylized Mexican flair." Booklist
   Includes bibliographical references

Mordhorst, Heidi
   Pumpkin butterfly; poems from the other side of nature. illustrations by Jenny Reynish. Wordsong 2009 32p il $16.95
Grades: 3 4 5 6 **811**
   1. Nature poetry 2. Poetry -- By individual authors
   ISBN 978-1-59078-620-8; 1-59078-620-3
                      LC 2009019918
"A collection of 23 nature poems cycles through the seasons, emphasizing the play between the outward and the hidden realms. The vocabulary and imagery stretch the maturing apprehension of young readers. . . . The use of contrasts . . . vividly convey an observant look at what is often overlooked. . . . Reynish's decorative illustrations reflect a thoughtful and purposeful artistic hand." Kirkus

Myers, Christopher
   ★ **We** are America; a tribute from the heart. Walter Dean Myers, Christopher Myers. HarperCollins Children's Books 2011 1 v. (unpaged) $16.99; lib bdg $17.89
Grades: 3 4 5 6 **811**
   1. Children's poetry, American
   ISBN 978-0-06-052308-4; 0-06-052308-5; 978-0-06-052309-1 lib bdg; 0-06-052309-3 lib bdg; 0060523085; 0060523093; 9780060523084; 9780060523091
                      LC 2007011852
Walter Dean and Christopher Myers pay "homage to the entire United States in a soul-searching, free-verse poem examining the people, ideals, and promise of America. . . . Christopher Myers's evocative paintings often juxtapose different eras. . . . Closing notes explicate quotations that lace the pages and identify figures shown in the artwork. . . . Few will be unmoved by this stirring and provocative collaboration." Publ Wkly

Myers, Walter Dean, 1937-
   ★ **Blues** journey; illustrated by Christopher Myers. Holiday House 2003 un il $18.95; pa $8.95
Grades: 4 5 6 **811**
   1. Blues music -- Poetry 2. African Americans -- Poetry 3. Poetry -- By individual authors
   ISBN 978-0-8234-1613-4; 0-8234-1613-5; 978-0-8234-2079-7 pa; 0-8234-2079-5 pa
                      LC 2001-16645
"In this picture book for older readers, Myers offers blues-inspired verse that touches on the black-and-blue moments of individual lives. . . . Much of Myers' poetry here is terrific, by turn, sweet, sharp, ironic, but it's the memorable collage artwork, executed in the bluest of blue ink and brown paper, that will draw readers first." Booklist

   ★ **Harlem**; a poem. pictures by Christopher Myers. Scholastic 1997 un il $16.95
Grades: 5 6 7 8 9 10 **811**
   1. African Americans -- Poetry 2. Poetry -- By individual authors
   ISBN 0-590-54340-7
                      LC 96-8108

A Caldecott Medal honor book, 1998

A poem celebrating the people, sights, and sounds of Harlem

"Myers's paean to Harlem sings, dances, and swaggers across the pages, conveying the myriad sounds on the streets. . . . Christopher Myers's collages add an edge to his father's words, vividly bringing to life the sights and scenes of Lenox Avenue." Horn Book Guide

★ **Jazz**; illustrated by Christopher Myers. Holiday House 2006 un il $18.95; pa $8.95

Grades: 4 5 6 7   811

1. Children's poetry 2. Jazz music -- Poetry 3. Jazz -- Juvenile literature 4. Poetry -- By individual authors
ISBN 978-0-8234-1545-8; 0-8234-1545-7; 978-0-8234-2134-2 pa; 0-8234-2173-2 pa

LC 2005-52639

Illustrations and poetry celebrate the roots of jazz music

"Walter Dean Myers infuses his lines . . . with so much savvy syncopation that readers can't help but be swept up in the rhythms. . . . Christopher Myers lays black-inked acetate over brilliant, saturated acrylics. The resulting chiaroscuro conjures the deep shadows and lurid reflections of low-lit after-dark jazz clubs." Publ Wkly

Nash, Ogden

★ **Lineup** for yesterday; illustrated by C. F. Payne. Creative Editions 2011 55p il $19.99

Grades: 3 4 5 6   811

1. Alphabet 2. Baseball -- Poetry 3. Poetry -- By individual authors
ISBN 978-1-56846-212-7; 1-56846-212-3

LC 2010040121

"Baseball legends of yesteryear come alive more or less alphabetically in Nash's pithy verses. Twenty-four players of the first half of the 20th century are profiled in playful, humorous short poems with an ABCB rhyme scheme. . . . The verses are accompanied by statistical information and delightful, large-scale, closeup depictions of the players in action, rendered by Payne in layers of colored pencil, acrylics, water colors and a variety of other media. . . . Following each group of three or four verses, and headed by a diminutive version of the appropriate illustration, Nash's daughter Linell Nash Smith provides more detailed information about each player. She also contributes a charming introduction." Kirkus

Nelson, Marilyn

★ **Sweethearts** of rhythm; the story of the greatest all-girl swing band in the world. written by Marilyn Nelson; illustrated by Jerry Pinkney. Dial Books 2009 un il $21.99

Grades: 4 5 6 7   811

1. Women musicians 2. Jazz music -- Poetry 3. Jazz -- Juvenile literature 4. Poetry -- By individual authors
ISBN 978-0-8037-3187-5; 0-8037-3187-6

LC 2008-46255

"On all fronts, a resonant performance." Publ Wkly

Nesbitt, Kenn

My hippo has the hiccups; and other poems I totally made up. illustrated by Ethan Long. Sourcebooks Jabberwocky 2009 155p il $17.99

Grades: 2 3 4   811

1. Poetry -- By individual authors
ISBN 978-1-4022-1809-5; 1-4022-1809-5

LC 2008-48478

"This is a zany and at times challenging volume of more than 100 poems, 39 of which are read by the author on an accompanying CD. Nesbitt's consistent rhythms and unforced rhymes make these poems readable . . . [and] Long's spare line illustrations add humorous touches. This will be a popular addition to most collections." SLJ

Nye, Naomi Shihab

Come with me; poems for a journey. images by Dan Yaccarino. Greenwillow Bks. 2000 32p il $15.95; lib bdg $15.89

Grades: 3 4 5 6   811

1. Poetry -- By individual authors
ISBN 0-688-15946-X; 0-688-15947-8 lib bdg

LC 99-34164

"Sixteen poems depict different aspects of going places: subjects include imaginary voyages, the pace of travel, arrival in new places, the trajectory of words, and personal journeys of growth. . . . Nye uses sophisticated metaphor and oblique evocations of emotion in simple and concrete phraseology, making the poems conceptually challenging yet literarily accessible. The visuals are bold and dramatic, making excellent use of collage and mixed media." Bull Cent Child Books

O'Neill, Mary Le Duc

Hailstones and halibut bones; adventures in color. newly illustrated by John Wallner. Doubleday 1989 un il $15.95; pa $9.95

Grades: K 1 2 3   811

1. Children's poetry 2. Color -- Poetry 3. Color -- Juvenile literature 4. Poetry -- By individual authors
ISBN 978-0-385-24484-8; 0-385-24484-3; 978-0-385-41078-6 pa; 0-385-41078-6 pa

LC 88-484

A newly illustrated edition of the title first published 1961

Twelve poems reflect the author's feelings about various colors

"Wallner has created montages of each poem's images and colored them with various hues of the featured color. The results do complement the moods of the poems." SLJ

Ode, Eric

When you're a pirate dog and other pirate poems; Eric Ode, Jim Harris. Pelican Pub. 2012 40 p.

Grades: 1 2 3   811

1. Humorous poetry 2. Children's poetry 3. Pirates -- Poetry 4. Pirates -- Juvenile poetry 5. Children's poetry, American
ISBN 1455614939; 9781455614936; 9781455614943

LC 2011036785

This children's poetry collection by Eric Ode, illustrated by Jim Harris, is centered on pirates. "Pirates find their literary voices in this rollicking romp on the salty seas. Hilarity ensues as they go about their tasks narrated in poetry and song. The jolly illustrations bring their adventures, above and below decks, to life. See all their silly exploits in this swashbuckling adventure!" (Publisher's note)

Paolilli, Paul

Silver seeds; a book of nature poems. by Paul Pao-lilli and Dan Brewer; paintings by Steve Johnson and Lou Fancher. Viking 2001 un il $15.99; pa $6.99

Grades: K 1 2 3   **811**

1. Nature 2. Nature poetry 3. American poetry 4. Children's poetry, American 5. Poetry -- By individual authors
ISBN 0-670-88941-5; 0-14-250010-0 pa

LC 00-9469

"Paolilli and Brewer have selected 15 . . . words on which to build nature poems. The first letter of the first word in each line of a poem is part of another word that is the title (or subject) of the poem." Booklist

Park, Linda Sue

★ **Tap** dancing on the roof; sijo (poems) illustrated by Istvan Banyai. Clarion Books 2007 un il $16

Grades: 4 5 6   **811**

1. Sijo 2. Children's poetry 3. Poetry -- By individual authors
ISBN 978-0-618-23483-7; 0-618-23483-7

LC 2006-24901

Park's "sijo skip lightly from breakfast . . . to bedtime . . . with excursions to the backyard, the classroom, and the beach. . . . The sijo's contours are clean and spare, quali-ties echoed in the blue-gray, black and white architecture and crisp shadows of Banyai's . . . digital illustrations." Publ Wkly

Patz, Nancy

★ **Who** was the woman who wore the hat? written and illustrated by Nancy Patz. Dutton 2003 un il $14.99

Grades: 3 4 5   **811**

1. Jews -- Poetry 2. Poetry -- By individual authors
ISBN 0-525-46999-0

LC 2003-545123

"When author Patz saw an unlabeled woman's hat in a glass case in the Jewish Historical Museum in Amsterdam, she wondered whose it could be. . . . She drew the hat in her sketchbook and eventually created this quiet tribute to the woman—any Jewish woman—who might have been forced to leave her home in Amsterdam for a cruel fate in the Nazi extermination camps. Patz combines an accessible prose poem . . . with collages that blend historical photographs with her own sketches. A chronology of the Holocaust com-pletes the book." Booklist

Peters, Lisa Westberg

★ **Earthshake**; poems from the ground up. pictures by Cathie Felstead. Greenwillow Bks. 2003 32p il $16.99; lib bdg $17.89

Grades: 3 4 5   **811**

1. Geology -- Poetry 2. Poetry -- By individual authors
ISBN 0-06-029265-2; 0-06-029266-0 lib bdg

LC 2002-32177

Presents twenty-two poems about geology. End notes provide information about the earth's surface and interior, types of rocks, and how volcanoes, glaciers, and erosion modify the landscape

"Exuberant, silly, and serious by turns, the selections engage imagination with often-humorous wordplay. The simple yet clever collages, many of which incorporate clip-art elements, deepen the intellectual and emotional content, yet keep a light tone." SLJ

Volcano wakes up! illustrated by Steve Jenkins. Henry Holt and Company 2010 un il $16.99

Grades: 2 3 4   **811**

1. Volcanoes -- Poetry 2. Poetry -- By individual authors
ISBN 0805082875; 9780805082876; 978-0-8050-8287-6; 0-8050-8287-5

LC 2008-38225

"Personified features of a Hawaiian landscape speak in verse during a day in the life of a waking volcano, rendered in Jenkins's atmospheric trademark cut-paper collages. . . . A humorous, imaginative, and artful concept." "Personified features of a Hawaiian landscape speak in verse during a day in the life of a waking volcano, rendered in Jenkins's atmospheric trademark cut-paper collages. . . . A humorous, imaginative, and artful concept." Publ Wkly

Podwal, Mark H.

★ **Jerusalem** sky; stars, crosses, and crescents. Dou-bleday Book for Young Readers 2005 un $15.95; lib bdg $17.99

Grades: 3 4 5   **811**

1. Religious poetry 2. Poetry -- By individual authors
ISBN 0-385-74689-X; 0-385-90927-6 lib bdg

A series of illustrated poems about the city of Jerusalem and its importance to Jews, Christians, and Muslims

"With beautiful poems and vivid, impressionistic art-work, Podwal captures the hope and tears the city evokes among followers of the three monotheistic religions of the world." Booklist

Prelutsky, Jack

★ **Awful** Ogre running wild; by Jack Prelutsky; illus-trations by Paul O. Zelinsky. Greenwillow Books 2008 40p il $17.99; lib bdg $18.89

Grades: 2 3 4 5   **811**

1. Monsters -- Poetry 2. Poetry -- By individual authors
ISBN 978-0-06-623866-1; 0-06-623866-8; 978-0-06-623867-8 lib bdg; 0-06-623867-6 lib bdg

LC 2007027683

In a series of poems, Awful Ogre has a picnic with a lovely ogress, visits Grandma, exercises, paints a picture, enters a cook-off, attends a concert, causes a commotion, swims, goes through other activities

"Prelutsky shows his sure sense of rhythm and rhyme as well as his child-pleasing sense of humor in this series of 17 clearly written poems. Most appear on double-page spreads, accompanied by large ink-and-watercolor illustrations that reflect the tone of the verse." Booklist

★ **Awful** Ogre's awful day; poems by Jack Prelutsky; pictures by Paul O. Zelinsky. Greenwillow Bks. 2001 39p il $15.95; pa $6.99

Grades: 2 3 4 5   **811**

1. Monsters -- Poetry 2. Poetry -- By individual authors
ISBN 0-688-07778-1; 0-06-077459-2 pa

LC 99-54323

In a series of poems, Awful Ogre rises, grooms himself, dances, pens a letter, and goes through other activities as the day passes

"Awful Ogre proves an ideal agent for Prelutsky's oversize humor. . . . Zelinsky presents Awful Ogre as a grotesque but goofy innocent, sillier than he is sinister. . . . A virtuoso performance by two master funny-bone-ticklers." Publ Wkly

Be glad your nose is on your face and other poems; some of the best of Jack Prelutsky. illustrated by Brandon Dorman. Greenwillow Books 2008 194p il $22.99
Grades: PreK K 1 2 3   **811**
   1. Poetry -- By individual authors
   ISBN 978-0-06-157653-9; 0-06-157653-0
                       LC 2008013371
"This fat, sunny volume brings together 112 of Prelutsky's poems. Most are old favorites from the past four decades, but 15 of them have never been published before. Kicking off with a letter from the poet, the book contains five sections, each concluding with a page of activities such as word games and drawing prompts. Digital illustrations with lavish details and colors stand out nicely from the ample white space. . . . A CD features the author reading 30 of the poems to a . . . musical accompaniment." SLJ

★ **Behold** the bold umbrellaphant; and other poems. illustrations by Carin Berger. Greenwillow Books 2006 31p il $16.99; lib bdg $17.89
Grades: 3 4 5 6   **811**
   1. Humorous poetry 2. Children's poetry 3. Poetry -- By individual authors
   ISBN 978-0-06-054317-4; 0-06-054317-5; 978-0-06-054318-1 lib bdg; 0-06-054318-3 lib bdg
                       LC 2005-22185
Each poem in this collection "is about a creature that is part animal and part inanimate object. For instance, the Alarmadillos have alarm clocks for bodies, and the Ballpoint Penguins can write with their beaks. The poems are full of fun and wit, with wordplay and meter that never miss a beat. The whimsical illustrations use cut-print media, old-fashioned print images, and a variety of paper textures to create a rich visual treat well suited to the poetry." SLJ

★ **Good** sports; illustrated by Chris Raschka. Alfred A. Knopf 2007 un il $16.99; lib bdg $19.99
Grades: 2 3 4 5   **811**
   1. Children's poetry 2. Sports -- Poetry 3. Sports -- Juvenile literature 4. Poetry -- By individual authors
   ISBN 978-0-375-83700-5; 978-0-375-93700-2 lib bdg
                       LC 2006-05092
"This picture book uses poetry to express the physical sensations and wide-ranging emotions of participating in sports. Prelutsky's smoothly rhyming quatrains, ideal for recitation, cover team sports . . . as well as several individual ones and celebrate disciplined efforts as exuberantly as non-competitive play. . . . Raschka's watercolors extend the high-energy verses without overwhelming them." Booklist
   Includes bibliographical references

★ The **Headless** Horseman rides tonight; more poems to trouble your sleep. illustrated by Arnold Lobel. Greenwillow Bks. 1980 38p il hardcover o.p. pa $6.99
Grades: 2 3 4 5   **811**
   1. Monsters -- Poetry 2. Poetry -- By individual authors
   ISBN 0-688-11705-8 pa
                       LC 80-10372

The author's "rhymes are as lethal, lithe, and literate as ever and Lobel wrings every atmospheric ounce out of them." SLJ

If not for the cat; haiku by Jack Prelutsky; paintings by Ted Rand. Greenwillow Books 2004 40p il $16.99; lib bdg $17.89
Grades: 1 2 3 4   **811**
   1. Haiku 2. Children's poetry 3. Animals -- Poetry 4. Poetry -- By individual authors
   ISBN 0-06-059677-5; 0-06-059678-3 lib bdg
                       LC 2003-17064
"Each of the 17 haiku in this collection explores the essence of an animal, the words forming a sort of riddle answered in Rand's accompanying double-page illustration. . . . Prelutsky shows his command of word choice through a minimalist form that is perfectly matched by Rand's control of his mixed-media artwork to create a wonderful celebration of the art of haiku." SLJ

In Aunt Giraffe's green garden; pictures by Petra Mathers. Greenwillow Books 2007 63p il $16.99; lib bdg $17.89
Grades: K 1 2 3   **811**
   1. Children's poetry 2. Animals -- Poetry 3. Poetry -- By individual authors
   ISBN 978-0-06-623868-5; 0-06-623868-4; 978-0-06-623869-2 lib bdg; 0-06-623869-2 lib bdg
                       LC 2005035928
This is a "picture-book poetry collection of gleeful nonsense verse and captivating illustrations. . . . The bouncing, rhyming couplets are best read aloud. . . . Mathers' watercolor artwork greatly enhances each selection." Booklist

★ **It's** Christmas! by Jack Prelutsky; pictures by Marylin Hafner. HarperCollins Publishers 2008 46p il (I can read!) $16.99
Grades: K 1 2 3   **811**
   1. Christmas -- Poetry 2. Poetry -- By individual authors
   ISBN 978-0-06-053706-7; 0-06-053706-X
                       LC 2007040112
A newly illustrated edition of the title first published 1981 by Greenwillow Books
This collection of Christmas poems covers such topics as Christmas trees, mistletoe, Santa Claus, a Christmas play, and gifts.
"Hafner's line-and-watercolor pictures illustrate the bouncing, rhyming words in clear, playful holiday scenes." Booklist

★ **It's** Thanksgiving! by Jack Prelutsky; pictures by Marylin Hafner. HarperCollins 2007 44p il (I can read!) $15.99; lib bdg $16.89
Grades: 1 2 3   **811**
   1. Thanksgiving Day -- Poetry 2. Poetry -- By individual authors
   ISBN 978-0-06-053710-4; 978-0-06-053709-8 lib bdg
                       LC 2007014465
First published 1982 by Greenwillow Books
A collection of twelve Thanksgiving Day poems

★ **It's** Valentine's Day; pictures by Yossi Abolafia. Greenwillow Bks. 1983 47p il (Greenwillow read-alone books) hardcover o.p. pa $5.95

Grades: 1 2 3 **811**

1. Valentine's Day -- Poetry 2. Poetry -- By individual authors

ISBN 0-688-14652-X pa

LC 83-1449

"The 14 poems here range from the genuine joy of 'It's Valentine's Day' . . . to the giddy goofiness of 'I love you more than applesauce' or 'Jelly Jill loves Weasel Will'. . . . The rhymes are generally simple but clever and the line drawings in red and blue, with their expressive faces and explanatory vignettes, add tremendously to the enjoyment of the poetry." SLJ

★ **It's** snowing! it's snowing! winter poems. illustrated by Yossi Abolafia. HarperCollins Pubs. 2006 48p il (I can read book) $15.99; lib bdg $16.89

Grades: 1 2 3 **811**

1. Winter -- Poetry 2. Poetry -- By individual authors

ISBN 0-06-053715-9; 0-06-053716-7 lib bdg

A newly illustrated edition of the title first published 1984 by Greenwillow Bks.

A collection of short poems about winter

"The sounds of the rhyming words are as much fun as the snow action in these 16 poems . . . accompanied by exuberant line-and-watercolor illustrations that capture all the play in the cold." Booklist

★ **Monday's** troll; poems by Jack Prelutsky; pictures by Peter Sis. Greenwillow Bks. 1996 39p il hardcover o.p. $16

Grades: 2 3 4 5 **811**

1. Children's poetry 2. Supernatural -- Poetry 3. Poetry -- By individual authors

ISBN 0-688-09644-1; 0-688-14373-3 lib bdg; 0-688-17529-5 pa

LC 95-7085

A collection of seventeen poems about such unsavory characters as witches, ogres, wizards, trolls, giants, a yeti, and seven grubby goblins

This "collection overflows with energy, tongue-in-cheek wit, rich vocabulary, and rollicking rhyme and meter. The oil and gouache paintings on gesso backgrounds are equally playful, as each gold-bordered, double-page spread adds more layers of meaning to the words." SLJ

★ **My** dog may be a genius; poems. [drawings by James Stevenson] Greenwillow Books 2008 159p il $18.99; lib bdg $19.89

Grades: 2 3 4 5 **811**

1. Children's poetry 2. Children's poetry, American. 3. Poetry -- By individual authors

ISBN 978-0-06-623862-3; 978-0-06-623863-0 lib bdg

LC 2007-19462

"Prelutsky has created yet another volume of short poems with guaranteed child appeal. Again he has assembled a zany cast of imaginary creatures and machines. . . . Prelutsky plays with language and does not shy away from challenging vocabulary. . . . Stevenson's simple signature drawings

capture the spirit of each poem with just the right amount of illustration." SLJ

★ **Nightmares**: poems to trouble your sleep; illustrated by Arnold Lobel. Greenwillow Bks. 1976 38p il lib bdg $17.89

Grades: 2 3 4 5 **811**

1. Monsters -- Poetry 2. Poetry -- By individual authors

ISBN 0-688-84053-1

LC 76-4820

This "collection of poems is calculated to evoke icy apprehension, and the poems about wizards, bogeymen, ghouls, ogres (well, one poem apiece to each or to others of their ilk) are exaggerated just enough to bring simultaneous grins and shudders. Prelutsky uses words with relish and his rhyme and rhythm are, as usual, deft. Lobel's illustrations are equally adroit, macabre yet elegant." Bull Cent Child Books

★ **Ride** a purple pelican; pictures by Garth Williams. Greenwillow Bks. 1986 64p il $17.95; pa $7.95

Grades: K 1 2 3 **811**

1. Nursery rhymes 2. Nonsense verses 3. Poetry -- By individual authors 4. Nonsense verses -- Juvenile literature

ISBN 0-688-04031-4; 0-688-15625-8 pa

LC 84-6024

A collection of short nonsense verses and nursery rhymes

"Prelutsky has caught the rhythm and spirit of nursery rhymes in 29 short poems about drum-beating bunnies, bullfrogs on parade, Chicago winds, giant sequoias and other wondrous things. Many of these easy-to-remember poems are filled with delicious sounding American and Canadian place names. Garth Williams' full-color, full-page illustrations are good complements to the poems. Highly recommended." Child Book Rev Serv

Scranimals; poems by Jack Prelutsky; pictures by Peter Sis. Greenwillow Bks. 2002 40p il $16.99; lib bdg $18.89

Grades: 2 3 4 5 **811**

1. Nonsense verses 2. Nonsense verses, American 3. Children's poetry, American 4. Poetry -- By individual authors

ISBN 0-688-17819-7; 0-688-17820-0 lib bdg

LC 2001-23620

"The verse sparkles with wit and mad invention. . . . Sis' art picks up on the strange and otherworldly aspects of the poems, evincing a surreal and haunting edge to its intricately lined visions." Bull Cent Child Books

★ **Something** big has been here; drawings by James Stevenson. Greenwillow Bks. 1990 160p il $17.95

Grades: 3 4 5 **811**

1. Humorous poetry 2. Children's poetry 3. Poetry -- By individual authors 4. Humorous poetry -- Juvenile literature

ISBN 0-688-06434-5

LC 89-34773

An illustrated collection of humorous poems on a variety of topics

"Puns and verbal surprises abound. Clever use of alliteration and abundant variety in the sound and texture of words add to the pleasure.. ... Stevenson's small cartoons of snaggle-toothed animals and deadpan children extend and expand the mad humor of the poems, supporting but never overwhelming their good-natured fun. A fine prescription against the blues at any time of year." Horn Book

★ **Tyrannosaurus** was a beast; illustrated by Arnold Lobel. Greenwillow Bks. 1988 31p il hardcover o.p. pa $6.99
Grades: 2 3 4 5   **811**
   1. Dinosaurs -- Poetry 2. Poetry -- By individual authors
   ISBN 0-688-06443-4 lib bdg; 0-688-11569-1 pa
                                          LC 87-25131
A collection of humorous poems about dinosaurs
   "Fourteen dinosaurs meet their match in this outstanding author/illustrator team. While Prelutsky's short, pithy, often witty verses sum up their essential characters, Lobel's line and watercolor portraits bring the beasts to life, enormous yet endearingly vulnerable." Booklist

★ **What** a day it was at school! poems by Jack Prelutsky; pictures by Doug Cushman. Greenwillow Books 2006 39p il $15.99; lib bdg $16.89
Grades: K 1 2 3   **811**
   1. Children's poetry 2. Schools -- Poetry 3. Poetry -- By individual authors
   ISBN 978-0-06-082336-8; 0-06-082336-4; 978-0-06-082335-1 lib bdg; 0-06-082335-6 lib bdg
                                          LC 2005-48968
   "Cushman has interpreted Prelutsky's school-aged protagonist as a cat. The feline's journal contains 17 poems about everyday joys and predicaments. . . . Lively and fun, with perfect meter and an abundance of interesting word choices, these poems beg to be read aloud. And they will be. Cushman has created an appealing school environment with a variety of colorful cartoon animal characters that are happily compatible with Prelutsky's silly and energetic verse." SLJ

★ The **carnival** of the animals; music by Camille Saint-Saëns; new verses by Jack Prelutsky; illustrated by Mary GrandPré; with a fully orchestrated CD of the Camille Saint-Saëns music. Alfred A. Knopf 2010 un $19.99; lib bdg $22.99
Grades: 2 3 4 5   **811**
   1. Animals -- Poetry 2. Poetry -- By individual authors
   ISBN 978-0-375-86458-2; 0-375-86458-X; 978-0-375-96458-9 lib bdg; 0-375-96458-4 lib bdg
                                          LC 2009008734
   This is an illustrated collection of verses inspired by Camille Saint-Saens' musical suite The carnival of the animals.
   "This delightful collection of new poems . . . serves as both helpful libretto and stand-alone treasure. The poems correlate to the animal-themed movements and neatly capture each creature's essence. . . , GrandPré's . . . vibrant acrylic and paper collage scenes exude the same imaginative insight. . . . An accompanying CD contains music performed by the Württemberg Chamber Orchestra and poems read by Prelutsky." Publ Wkly

★ The **dragons** are singing tonight; pictures by Peter Sis. Greenwillow Bks. 1993 39p il $16; pa $6.95

Grades: 2 3 4 5   **811**
   1. Children's poetry 2. Dragons -- Poetry 3. Poetry -- By individual authors 4. Dragons -- Poetry -- Juvenile literature
   ISBN 0-688-09645-X; 0-688-12511-5 lib bdg; 0-688-16162-6 pa
                                          LC 92-29013
   "Dragons are verbally and visually portrayed in this collection with wonder, whimsy, and a touch of wistfulness. . . . The oil and gouache paintings on a gesso background have marvelous details and unexpected bursts of humor." SLJ

★ The **frogs** wore red suspenders; rhymes by Jack Prelutsky; pictures by Petra Mathers. Greenwillow Bks. 2002 63p il $16.95; lib bdg $16.89; pa $6.99
Grades: K 1 2 3   **811**
   1. Nursery rhymes 2. American poetry 3. Nonsense verses 4. Children's poetry, American 5. Poetry -- By individual authors
   ISBN 0-688-16719-5; 0-688-16720-9 lib bdg; 0-06-073776-X pa
                                          LC 00-68128
   A collection of 28 "lighthearted poems, many of which invoke place names in the United States. . . . The mild humor lies not in the action but in Prelutsky's deft use of language, particularly effective shared aloud. The result is enjoyable, but it is Petra Mathers's illustrations that make the book memorable. Demurely naive, her cheerful, delicately delineated human and animal characters focus on their activities with becoming modesty and grace." Horn Book

★ The **new** kid on the block: poems; drawings by James Stevenson. Greenwillow Bks. 1984 159p il $17.95; lib bdg $17.93
Grades: 3 4 5 6   **811**
   1. Humorous poetry 2. Children's poetry 3. Poetry -- By individual authors 4. Humorous poetry -- Juvenile literature
   ISBN 0-688-02271-5; 0-688-02272-3 lib bdg
                                          LC 83-20621
   "The author's rollicking, silly poems bounce and romp with fun; Stevenson's cartoon-like sketches capture the hilarity with equal skill. A book everyone will enjoy dipping into." Child Book Rev Serv

★ A **pizza** the size of the sun; poems by Jack Prelutsky; drawings by James Stevenson. Greenwillow Bks. 1996 159p il $18; lib bdg $17.93
Grades: 3 4 5 6   **811**
   1. Humorous poetry 2. Children's poetry 3. Poetry -- By individual authors 4. Humorous poetry -- Juvenile literature
   ISBN 0-688-13235-9; 0-688-13236-7 lib bdg
                                          LC 95-35930
   This collection of humorous poems is "filled with zany people, improbable creatures, and rhythm and rhyme galore, all combining to celebrate the unusual, the mundane, and the slightly gruesome. . . . Each page is brimming with Stevenson's complementary, droll watercolors, reproduced here in black and white." SLJ

The **swamps** of Sleethe; poems from beyond the solar system. illustrated by Jimmy Pickering. Alfred A. Knopf 2009 un il $16.99; lib bdg $19.99

Grades: 3 4 5 6 **811**

1. Children's poetry 2. Extrasolar planets -- Poetry 3. Poetry -- By individual authors 4. Extraterrestrial beings -- Poetry

ISBN 978-0-375-84674-8; 0-375-84674-3; 978-0-375-94674-5 lib bdg; 0-375-94674-8 lib bdg

LC 2008006530

"Nineteen poems with jaunty rhythms lure readers to some very menacing planets. Almost all tell of the horrors to be found in worlds beyond our solar system.... Dark colors with sharp contrasts help define these worlds in mixed-media illustrations. Some of the unusual planet names are anagrams to solve with answers in the back of the book. Science-fiction and poetry lovers should unite over this slim and entertaining volume." SLJ

Prelutsky, Jack, 1940-

★ **I've** lost my hippopotamus; Jack Prelutsky; illustrations by Jackie Urbanovic. 1st ed. Greenwillow Books 2012 143 p. ill. (trade bdg.) $18.99; (lib. bdg.) $19.89

Grades: K 1 2 3 4 5 **811**

1. Humorous poetry 2. Animals -- Poetry 3. Children's poetry 4. Humorous poetry, American 5. Children's poetry, American

ISBN 0062014579; 9780062014573; 9780062014580

LC 2011002636

This children's book by Jack Prelutsky, illustrated by Jackie Urbanovic, offers "more than 100 . . . poems that poke holes in the serious facade of the adult world. A snake performs arithmetic, a boy is puzzled by the rainstorm in his bedroom, . . . and a thirsty centipede drinks too much water." (Publishers Weekly)

★ **Stardines** swim high across the sky and other poems; by Jack Prelutsky; illustrations by Carin Berger. Greenwillow Books 2012 40 p.

Grades: K 1 2 3 **811**

1. Children's poetry 2. Imaginary creatures -- Poetry 3. Children's poetry, American 4. Imaginary creatures -- Juvenile poetry

ISBN 9780062014641; 9780062014658

LC 2011025993

This children's poetry collection, by Jack Prelutsky, illustrated by Carin Berger, presents lyric descriptions of two dozen imaginary "creatures of animal and inanimate origin. . . . Procrastinating pandas, self-adhering geese and cacophonous magpies are a few of the carefully selected creatures on display . . . ," embellished by multi-media dioramas by Berger. (Kirkus Reviews)

Raczka, Bob

★ **Guyku**; a year of haiku for boys. illustrated by Peter H. Reynolds. Houghton 2010 un il

Grades: 1 2 3 **811**

1. Haiku 2. Children's poetry 3. Boys -- Poetry 4. Seasons -- Poetry 5. Haiku -- Juvenile literature 6. Poetry -- By individual authors

ISBN 0547240031; 9780547240039

Claudia Lewis Award for Poetry, 2011

This is a collection of seventeen-syllable poems about a boy's life. "Primary." (Horn Book)

"The poems in this picture-book collection capture natural moments that boys, and many girls, have while playing outdoors. Each season is addressed, and moments like riding bikes in the spring with baseball cards attached to the wheels to mimic the sound of a motorcycle almost define spring. . . . The artwork and the text dovetail beautifully and help set the inquisitive and playful intent of the poems. . . . This wonderful collection will resonate with all children. . . . The pen, ink, and watercolor illustrations mirror the simplicity of each entry and capture the expressions of the boys and their adventures honestly." SLJ

★ **Lemonade,** and other poems squeezed from a single word; illustrations by Nancy Doniger. Roaring Brook Press 2011 43p il

Grades: 2 3 4 5 **811**

1. Children's poetry 2. Poetry -- By individual authors

ISBN 1596435410; 9781596435414

LC 2010-24807

"Each poem is displayed in two formats, first a patterned visual that . . . aligns the letters in each word under the relevant titular letter, . . . and then a simple one-word-per-line arrangement. . . . Grades three to seven." (Bull Cent Child Books)

"Raczka offers an accessible, playful poetry collection. . . . Doniger's spare illustrations add quirky appeal without distracting from the inventive formations of type." Booklist

Rex, Adam

★ **Frankenstein** makes a sandwich. Harcourt 2006 40p il $16

Grades: 2 3 4 5 **811**

1. Children's poetry 2. Monsters -- Poetry 3. Poetry -- By individual authors

ISBN 0-15-205766-8

LC 2005-13678

A collection of humorous poems about monsters such as Frankenstein, The Creature from the Black Lagoon, Count Dracula, The Invisible Man, Godzilla, and The Phantom of the Opera

"Told with smooth, unstrained rhymes, each selection captures its subject's voice. Rex uses an impressive variety of techniques and media in the artwork while paying homage to famed illustrators. . . . The book is fresh, creative, and funny, with just enough gory detail to cause a few gasps." SLJ

★ **Frankenstein** takes the cake. Harcourt 2008 39p il lib bdg $16

Grades: 2 3 4 5 **811**

1. Children's poetry 2. Monsters -- Poetry 3. Poetry -- By individual authors

ISBN 978-0-15-206235-4 lib bdg; 0-15-206235-1 lib bdg

LC 2007-44634

Frankenstein wants to marry his undead bride in peace, but his best man, Dracula, is freaking out about the garlic bread, and the Headless Horseman wishes everyone would stop drooling over his pumpkin head.

"With maniacal glee, Rex . . . delivers spot-on rhymes about B-movie monsters, loosely organized around the nuptials of Frankenstein and his bride. . . . Rex's eclectic imagery and freewheeling verse will have readers going back for seconds." Publ Wkly

Rockwell, Thomas

Emily Stew; with some side dishes. illustrated by David McPhail. Roaring Brook Press 2010 43p il $16.99

Grades: 2 3 4 5   **811**

1. Children's poetry 2. Poetry -- By individual authors

ISBN 978-1-59643-336-6; 1-59643-336-1

This is "a wildly inventive poetic portrait of a riveting character who's made up—rather literally—of a stew of contradictions. Moody and prone to the most erratic behavior, Emily is depicted in these playful rhymed vignettes as an eccentric yet eminently recognizable and likable young creature.... McPhail's pen-and-ink spot art helps capture the defiant Emily as she asserts her individuality in scenes ranging from dancing with a fish to being eaten by a tiger." Kirkus

Rosen, Michael J.

★ The **Hound** dog's haiku; and other poems for dog lovers. [illustrated by] Mary Azarian. Candlewick Press 2011 56p il

Grades: 2 3 4   **811**

1. Haiku 2. Dogs -- Poetry 3. Poetry -- By individual authors

ISBN 0-7636-4499-4; 978-0-7636-4499-4

"These delightful selections will engage haiku composers and dog lovers. . . . Twenty canines are represented, with each dog given a fully illustrated spread; the breed's name is in large letters and the haiku on the opposing page is in a smaller font. Endnotes take the form of visual avatars culled from the illustrations, with a short paragraph about the breed. Fetch this title full of wordplay, creative romps, and pet prompts for a fun read." SLJ

★ The **cuckoo's** haiku; and other birding poems. illustrated by Stan Fellows. Candlewick Press 2009 un il $17.99

Grades: 2 3 4   **811**

1. Haiku 2. Children's poetry 3. Birds -- Poetry 4. Birds -- Juvenile literature 5. Poetry -- By individual authors

ISBN 978-0-7636-3049-2; 0-7636-3049-7

LC 2008-21417

"A rare gift for young and old alike, this exquisite book about birds combines delicate verses and stunning watercolors that celebrate the natural world. Designed as if it were a birder's notebook, the book provides an intriguing haiku for each bird, dazzling paintings of the species in their habitats, as well as notes about their behaviors and traits." Publ Wkly

Ruddell, Deborah

★ A **whiff** of pine, a hint of skunk; a forest of poems. illustrated by Joan Rankin. Margaret K. McElderry Books 2009 un il $16.99

Grades: 3 4 5   **811**

1. Nature poetry 2. Forest animals -- Poetry 3. Poetry -- By individual authors

ISBN 978-1-4169-4211-5; 1-4169-4211-4

LC 2007-38023

"Twenty-three evocative poems about forest animals, beautifully illustrated. Literary variety serves this collection well, with many different lengths, rhyme schemes and moods. The common elements in Ruddell's verse are economy and an observer's respect for her subjects. . . . Similarly, Rankin's watercolors show respect via their accuracy and

detail, while still capturing the various flavors of the poems." Kirkus

Salas, Laura Purdie

Bookspeak! poems about books. written by Laura Purdie Salas; illustrated by Josée Bisaillon. Clarion Books 2011 un il $16.99

Grades: PreK K 1 2   **811**

1. Books and reading -- Poetry 2. Poetry -- By individual authors

ISBN 978-0-547-22300-1; 0-547-22300-5

LC 2010043173

"This collection of poems makes its message clear: books are where it's at. Sala's polished verse demonstrates a deep love for all aspects of books. . . . Bisaillon's mixed media illustrations are dizzyingly inventive, their bright colors, sampling of typography, and whimsical details underscoring the idea of the potential that awaits between the covers." Publ Wkly

San Jose, Christine

Every second something happens; poems for the mind and senses. selected by Christine San José and Bill Johnson; illustrations by Melanie Hall. Wordsong 2009 48p il $17.95

Grades: PreK K 1 2   **811**

1. American poetry -- Collections

ISBN 978-1-59078-622-2; 1-59078-622-X

LC 2008024115

"Fun for reading aloud, the very short verses in this collection are easy, rhythmic, and immediate. Some are written by young kids and some by children's poets, and there are even a few lines from Shakespeare. . . . Hall's clear colorful illustrations never overwhelm the words as they show kids in action." Booklist

Sandburg, Carl

★ **Carl** Sandburg; edited by Frances Schoonmaker Bolin; illustrated by Steve Arcella. Sterling 1995 48p il (Poetry for young people) $14.95; pa $6.95

Grades: 4 5 6 7   **811**

1. Poetry -- By individual authors

ISBN 0-8069-0818-1; 1-4027-5471-X pa

LC 94-30777

"The 33 poems in Sandburg vary in length and theme, but most are the staples of anthologies, e.g., 'Fog,' 'Arithmetic,' and 'We Must Be Polite.' The surrealistic illustrations, which appear to be rendered in pastels, are appealing; the soft edges and warm tones work well with Sandburg's imagery." SLJ

Rainbows are made: poems; selected by Lee Bennett Hopkins; wood engravings by Fritz Eichenberg. Harcourt Brace Jovanovich 1982 81p il hardcover o.p. pa $13

Grades: 5 6 7 8   **811**

1. Poetry -- By individual authors

ISBN 0-15-265481-X pa

LC 82-47934

This book "offers some 70 short poems by Carl Sandburg and groups them by theme: the seasons, the sea, the imaginative mind, etc. Each theme explores different aspects of poetic creativity as envisioned by Sandburg and illustrated by Fritz Eichenberg's wood engravings. Eichenberg has truly captured the power and vigorousness of Sandburg's verse." SLJ

Scanlon, Liz Garton
★ **All** the world; illustrated by Marla Frazee. Beach Lane Books 2009 un il $17.99
Grades: PreK K 1 **811**
  1. Children's poetry 2. Beaches -- Poetry 3. Family life -- Poetry 4. Poetry -- By individual authors
  ISBN 978-1-4169-8580-8; 1-4169-8580-8
                  LC 2008-51057
ALA ALSC Caldecott Medal Honor Book (2010)
"Charming illustrations and lyrical rhyming couplets speak volumes in celebration of the world and humankind, combining to create a lovely book that will be appreciated by a wide audience. The pictures, made with black Prismacolor pencil and watercolors, primarily follow a multicultural family from a summer morning on the beach through a busy day and night." SLJ

Schertle, Alice
★ **Button** up! [illustrations by] Petra Mathers. Harcourt 2009 33p il $16
Grades: PreK K 1 2 **811**
  1. Children's poetry 2. Animals -- Poetry 3. Clothing and dress -- Poetry 4. Poetry -- By individual authors
  ISBN 978-0-15-205050-4; 0-15-205050-7
                  LC 2007-42839
An illustrated collection of poetry features animals wearing an array of shoes, jackets, hats, and other fun attire to demonstrate their unique personalities.
"Mathers' charming watercolors show a variety of decked out animals in vignettes and double-page spreads that add to the humor. . . . The whimsical illustrations pair perfectly with the wittiness of the text, and the whole is a clever and original poetic treat." Booklist

Scieszka, Jon
Truckery rhymes; written by Jon Scieszka; characters and environments developed by the Design Garage David Shannon, Loren Long, David Gordon. Simon & Schuster Books for Young Readers 2009 57p il $17.99
Grades: PreK K 1 2 3 **811**
  1. Nursery rhymes 2. Trucks -- Poetry 3. Poetry -- By individual authors
  ISBN 978-1-4169-4135-4; 1-4169-4135-5
                  LC 2007037439
"This collection of lively truck-themed 'Mother Goose' rhymes is filled with humor. . . . The digital illustrations are colorful, energetic, and playful: the vehicles have personality plus. . . . This effervescent picture book will zoom off your shelves." SLJ

Service, Robert W.
★ The **cremation** of Sam McGee; by Robert W. Service; paintings by Ted Harrison; introduction by Pierre Berton. 20th anniversary ed.; Kids Can Press 2006 un il $17.95
Grades: 4 5 6 7 **811**
  1. Poetry -- By individual authors
  ISBN 978-1-55453-092-2; 1-55453-092-X
  Text first published 1907. This is a reissue of the edition first published 1986 in Canada and 1987 in the United States by Greenwillow Bks.

This poem "has gripped readers and listeners for decades. . . . [The illustrator] obviously appreciates the humor inherent in the text. . . . As Pierre Berton observes in his introduction, [Harrison's] 'style is unique: part Oriental, part native American, part Ted Harrison.'" Horn Book

Shange, Ntozake
★ **Freedom's** a-callin' me; poems by Ntozake Shange; paintings by Rod Brown. Amisatd/Collins 2012 il $16.99
Grades: 4 5 6 7 **811**
  1. Slavery -- Poetry 2. African Americans -- Poetry 3. Underground railroad -- Poetry
  ISBN 978-0-06-133741-3; 0-06-133741-2
                  LC 2010050515
The author and illustrator present "a series of poems and paintings that express the hope and frustration of enslaved people trying to navigate the Underground Railroad. Using dialect to convey a Southern cadence, Shange's poems communicate powerful emotions. . . . These poems are a cry from the heart. . . . The expressive, impressionistic paintings capture attention with their bold strokes and vivid coloring." SLJ

★ **We** troubled the waters; poems by Ntozake Shange; paintings by Rod Brown. Amistad/Collins 2009 un il $16.99; lib bdg $17.89
Grades: 4 5 6 7 8 9 10 **811**
  1. Poetry -- By individual authors 2. African Americans -- Civil rights -- Poetry
  ISBN 978-0-06-133735-2; 0-06-133735-8; 978-0-06-133737-6 lib bdg; 0-06-133737-4 lib bdg
                  LC 2008025360
"Each spread pairs a poem with blurred, expressive acrylic paintings, and the pages feature both well-known civil rights leaders and ordinary people who endured oppression. . . . The messages are haunting. . . . The colloquial lines, indelible images, and comparisons between then and now will keep readers talking." Booklist

Shannon, George
Busy in the garden; poems by George Shannon; pictures by Sam Williams. Greenwillow Books 2006 36p il $15.99; lib bdg $16.89
Grades: K 1 2 **811**
  1. Children's poetry 2. Gardening -- Poetry 3. Poetry -- By individual authors 4. Gardening -- Juvenile literature
  ISBN 0-06-000464-9; 0-06-000465-7 lib bdg
                  LC 2003-56863
A collection of short poems and riddles about planting seeds, watching garden vegetables dance, and growing jack-o-lanterns.
"The best selections are immediately accessible and bounce with humor and an irresistible beat. Williams' lively watercolor-and-pencil illustrations of children and animals digging in the rows shine with the colors of spring." Booklist

Chicken scratches; Grade A poultry poetry and rooster rhymes. by George Shannon & Lynn Brunelle; illustrated by Scott Menchin. Chronicle Books 2010 un il $14.99
Grades: K 1 2 3 **811**
  1. Chickens -- Poetry
  ISBN 978-0-8118-6648-4; 0-8118-6648-3

"This attractive volume features 16 wacky rhyming verses. The somewhat irreverent poems include odes to imagined daily lives of opera-singing and sumo-wrestling chickens to complex egg laying and eating. . . . Rendered in pen and colored digitally, the simple yet expressive cartoon illustrations really bring out the fun of the poetry." SLJ

Shapiro, Karen Jo

I must go down to the beach again; [by] Karen Jo Shapiro; illustrated by Judy Love. Charlesbridge 2007 48p il lib bdg $14.95; pa $5.95

Grades: 4 5 6 7   811

1. Parodies 2. Humorous poetry 3. Poetry -- By individual authors

ISBN 978-158089-143-1 lib bdg; 1-58089-143-8 lib bdg; 978-158089-144-8 pa; 1-58089-144-6 pa

LC 2006009029

"Shapiro offers parodies of 23 classic British and American poems. . . . It is clear in reading her selections that the author knows the sources through and through and that she is quite a good poet in her own right. . . . Love's black-and-white pen-and-ink drawings underscore the humor in each selection." SLJ

Shields, Carol Diggory

★ **Almost** late to school and more school poems; illustrated by Paul Meisel. Dutton Children's Bks. 2003 40p il $15.99; pa $6.99

Grades: 2 3 4   811

1. Humorous poetry 2. Schools -- Poetry 3. Poetry -- By individual authors

ISBN 0-525-45743-7; 0-14-240328-8 pa

"The 22 energetic selections reflect the typical day-to-day activities and problems including being late for school, the first day, having to go to the bathroom, fund-raising, and other events. Shields utilizes a variety of forms including a concrete poem, poems for two voices, and a jump-rope rhyme. Meisel's vibrant cartoon illustrations are lively and fun and capture the poems' humor and insight." SLJ

★ **English,** fresh squeezed! 40 thirst-for-knowledge-quenching poems. by Carol Diggory Shields; illustrations by Tony Ross. Handprint Books 2004 80p il $14.95

Grades: 4 5 6 7   811

1. English language -- Poetry 2. Poetry -- By individual authors

ISBN 1-59354-053-1

LC 2004-53905

"Shields presents humorous poems both celebrating and bemoaning parts of speech, grammatical rules, and other annoyances of English class. Her rhyming verse is generally snappy and pointed. . . . Ross's spot illustrations in black and white with a blue tone add visual amusement without overwhelming." SLJ

Someone used my toothbrush! and other bathroom poems. illustrated by Paul Meisel. Dutton Children's Books 2010 32p il $16.99

Grades: PreK K 1 2 3   811

1. Bathrooms -- Poetry 2. Poetry -- By individual authors

ISBN 978-0-525-47937-6; 0-525-47937-6

Comic, kid-centric poems about the bathroom.

"This collection of 21 short poems is right on target with its rhymed glimpses into the cheerful chaos of family life. . . . The colorful cartoons add just the right tone. They are light and funny, featuring a multicultural cast of characters. There's a lot to like in this clever and appealing collection." SLJ

Shore, Diane ZuHone

★ **This** is the dream; by Diane Z. Shore and Jessica Alexander; illustrated by James Ransome. HarperCollinsPublishers 2006 un il $15.99; lib bdg $16.89

Grades: 2 3 4   811

1. Children's poetry 2. Poetry -- By individual authors 3. African Americans -- Civil rights -- Poetry

ISBN 0-06-055519-X; 0-06-055520-3 lib bdg

LC 2003-26554

"A chronicle of the Civil Rights movement presented through lyrical verses and distinguished illustrations. Ransome juxtaposes collaged archival photographs and newspaper clippings with his paintings. . . . Each succinct and evocative verse is accompanied by a double-page image." SLJ

This is the game; by Diane Z. Shore; illustrated by Owen Smith. HarperCollinsPublishers 2011 32p il $16.99

Grades: K 1 2 3   811

1. Baseball -- Poetry 2. Poetry -- By individual authors

ISBN 978-0-06-055522-1; 0-06-055522-X

LC 2008047700

"In this picture-book celebration of baseball, aspects of the game are described in verse and illustrated with, bold double-page spreads." Booklist

Sidman, Joyce

Butterfly eyes and other secrets of the meadow; written by Joyce Sidman; illustrated by Beth Krommes. Houghton Mifflin Co. 2006 un il $16

Grades: 3 4 5 6   811

1. Children's poetry 2. Animals -- Poetry 3. Meadows -- Poetry 4. Poetry -- By individual authors

ISBN 0-618-56313-X

LC 2005-03921

"Eight pairs of 'poetry riddles' present such related elements as the spittlebug . . . and the xylem sap it sucks from its host plant. A spread giving answers to the riddle and adding specific details . . . follows each pair of poems. . . . Kromme's scratchboard illustrations are splendid. . . . An elegantly conceived, beautifully integrated volume." Horn Book

★ **Dark** Emperor and other poems of the night; written by Joyce Sidman; illustrated by Rick Allen. Houghton Mifflin Harcount 2010 29p il $16.99

Grades: 3 4 5 6   811

1. Children's poetry 2. Night -- Poetry 3. Forest animals -- Poetry 4. Night -- Juvenile literature 5. Poetry -- By individual authors

ISBN 978-0-547-15228-8; 0-547-15228-0

A Newbery Medal honor book, 2011

"This picture book combines lyrical poetry and compelling art with science concepts. . . . Poems about the woods at night reveal exciting biology facts that are explained in long notes on each double-page spread. . . . In an opening note, Allen explains his elaborate, linoleum-block printmaking technique, and each atmospheric image shows the creatures and the dense, dark forest with astonishing clarity." Booklist

★ **Eureka!** poems about inventors. illustrated by K. Bennett Chavez. Millbrook Press 2002 48p il lib bdg $24.90
Grades: 4 5 6   811
1. Inventors 2. American poetry 3. Inventors -- Poetry 4. Children's poetry, American 5. Inventors -- Juvenile poetry 6. Poetry -- By individual authors
ISBN 0-7613-1665-5
     LC 00-56620
"Chavez's full-color, surrealistic illustrations add depth, character, and feeling to the selections. . . . The entire book reads beautifully." SLJ

★ **Meow** ruff; a story in concrete poetry. written by Joyce Sidman; illustrated by Michelle Berg. Houghton Mifflin 2006 un il $16
Grades: 1 2 3   811
1. Cats -- Poetry 2. Dogs -- Poetry 3. Rain -- Poetry 4. Poetry -- By individual authors
ISBN 0-618-44894-2
"Sidman develops a simple tale about a cat and dog trapped in a rainstorm, coding much of the substance right into the physical landscape. . . . Berg, who created the pictures digitally and is also the book's graphic designer, intelligently showcases the concept of words as building blocks in a stylized landscape of flat colors, two-dimensional forms, and wildly mutating typefaces." Booklist

★ **Song** of the water boatman; & other pond poems. written by Joyce Sidman; illustrated by Beckie Prange. Houghton Mifflin 2005 un il $16
Grades: 3 4 5   811
1. Ponds -- Poetry 2. Poetry -- By individual authors
ISBN 0-618-13547-2
A Caldecott Medal honor book, 2006
A collection of poems that provide a look at some of the animals, insects, and plants that are found in ponds, with accompanying information about each.
"In this strikingly illustrated collection, science facts combine with vivid poems about pond life through the seasons. . . . Throughout, plants and animals come alive in the bold woodcut prints." Booklist

★ **Swirl** by swirl; spirals in nature. Houghton Mifflin Harcourt 2011 40p il $16.99
Grades: PreK K 1 2   811
1. Nature poetry 2. Shape -- Poetry 3. Poetry -- By individual authors
ISBN 978-0-547-31583-6; 0-547-31583-X
     LC 2010040724
"Krommes's scratchboard illustrations suffuse every spread with color, shape, and movement, vividly depicting spirals in nature. . . . Sidman's very simple text provides the perfect backdrop: powerful, poetic, good for reading aloud and reading again. . . . This book is elegantly constructed, and as poetry, picture book, or nonfiction, a success in every way." Horn Book

This is just to say; poems of apology and forgiveness. by Joyce Sidman; illustrated by Pamela Zagarenski. Houghton Mifflin Co. 2007 47p il $16
Grades: 4 5 6   811
1. Children's poetry, American. 2. Apologizing -- Juvenile poetry. 3. Poetry -- By individual authors
ISBN 978-0-618-61680-0; 0-618-61680-2
     LC 2006009820
"Mrs. Merz assigns her sixth-grade students to write poems of apology, and what emerges is a surprising array of emotions, poetic forms, and subjects. . . . Sidman's ear is keen, capturing many voices. Her skill as a poet accessible to young people is unmatched. Zagarenski's delicately outlined collage drawings and paintings are created on mixed backgrounds—notebook paper, paper bags, newspaper, graph paper, school supplies." SLJ

★ **Ubiquitous**; celebrating nature's survivors. poetry by Joyce Sidman; illustrated by Beckie Prange. Houghton Mifflin 2010 un il $17
Grades: 2 3 4 5   811
1. Children's poetry 2. Animals -- Poetry 3. Poetry -- By individual authors
ISBN 978-0-618-71719-4; 0-618-71719-6
Sidman and Prange "offer another winning blend of poetry, science, and art in this picture-book collection that celebrates the earth's most resilient and long-lived species. . . . Each dynamic spread features a poem, a prose paragraph, and a captivating illustration that work together to reinforce both the science concepts and the awe they inspire. Prange's watercolor-tinted linocut illustrations beautifully expand both the information and imagery in the words." Booklist

Siebert, Diane
★ **Tour** America; a journey through poems and art. by Diane Siebert; illustrated by Stephen T. Johnson. Chronicle Books 2006 un il map $17.95
Grades: 3 4 5 6   811
1. Poetry -- By individual authors
ISBN 978-0-8118-5056-8; 0-8118-5056-0
     LC 2005027125
"This stunning tour of America highlights 26 of the poet's favorite sights . . . Siebert's striking word choices and images reflect the essence of each subject. . . . A double-page map at the beginning of the book alerts readers to the exciting destinations they will experience, and a smaller map and inset box of additional information for each sight increase the educational value. Johnson masterfully varies his medium and art style to reflect the mood of each locale. There are quiet watercolors . . . and dynamic collages . . . as well as pastels, oils, acrylics, and photos." SLJ

Sierra, Judy
★ **Monster** Goose; illustrated by Jack E. Davis. Harcourt 2001 un il $17; pa $7
Grades: 2 3 4 5   811
1. Monsters 2. Nursery rhymes 3. American poetry 4. Monsters -- Poetry 5. Children's poetry, American 6. Monsters -- Juvenile poetry 7. Nursery rhymes -- Adaptations 8. Poetry -- By individual authors
ISBN 0-15-202034-9; 0-15-205417-0 pa
     LC 00-8808
A collection of parodies of Mother Goose rhymes featuring monsters

"Davis, working in acrylics and colored pencil, crowds his illustrations with monsters, vermin and gross gags. . . . This volume strikes a nice balance between goofy and ghastly." Publ Wkly

Silverstein, Shel

★ **Don't** bump the glump and other fantasies; [by] Shel Silverstein. HarperCollins Publishers 2008 un il $17.99; lib bdg $18.89

Grades: 3 4 5 6   **811**

  1. Humorous poetry 2. Poetry -- By individual authors

  ISBN 978-0-06-149338-6; 978-0-06-149619-6 lib bdg

             LC 2007036737

First published 1964 by Simon & Schuster with title: Uncle Shelby's zoo: don't bump the glump!

"This collection of 45 poems tours readers past imaginary creatures. . . . There's no question that the intensity of Silverstein's watercolor palette adds to the fun." Publ Wkly

★ **Every** thing on it; poems and drawings by Shel Silverstein. Harper 2011 194p il $19.99; lib bdg $20.89

Grades: 3 4 5 6   **811**

  1. Humorous poetry 2. Nonsense verses 3. Poetry -- By individual authors

  ISBN 978-0-06-199816-4; 0-06-199816-8; 978-0-06-199817-1 lib bdg; 0-06-199817-6 lib bdg

The second original book to be published since Silverstein's passing in 1999, this poetry collection includes more than one hundred and thirty never-before-seen poems and drawings completed by the cherished American artist and selected by his family from his archives.

"Silverstein's inspired word play and impish sense of humor are in abundant evidence. His signature line drawings accompany many of the poems and complete the jokes of some. . . . Adults who grew up with Uncle Shelby will find themselves wiping their eyes by the time they get to the end of this collection; children new to the master will find themselves hooked." Kirkus

★ **Falling** up; poems and drawings by Shel Silverstein. HarperCollins Pubs. 1996 171p il $17.99; lib bdg $18.89

Grades: 3 4 5 6   **811**

  1. Humorous poetry 2. Nonsense verses 3. Children's poetry 4. Poetry -- By individual authors 5. Humorous poetry -- Juvenile literature

  ISBN 0-06-024802-5; 0-06-024803-3 lib bdg

             LC 96-75736

This "collection includes more than 150 poems. . . . As always, Silverstein has a direct line to what kids like, and he gives them poems celebrating the gross, the scary, the absurd, and the comical. The drawings are much more than decoration. They often extend a poem's meaning and, in many cases, add some great comedy." Booklist

★ **Runny** Babbit; a billy sook. HarperCollins Pub. 2005 89p il $17.99; lib bdg $18.89

Grades: 3 4 5 6   **811**

  1. Humorous poetry 2. Poetry -- By individual authors

  ISBN 0-06-025653-2; 0-06-028404-8 lib bdg

In this book "readers are introduced to Runny Babbit and his friends . . . and are encouraged to plunge headlong into this phonemic flipflop world of funny poems. . . . Complete with signature comical bold line drawings that provide visual clues, the poems require concentration to translate the

silly phrases. . . . Children will love these clever poems and without prompting will probably create their own." SLJ

★ **Where** the sidewalk ends; the poems & drawings of Shel Silverstein. 30th anniversary special ed; HarperCollins 2004 183p il $17.99; lib bdg $18.89

Grades: 3 4 5 6 7 8 9 10   **811**

  1. Humorous poetry 2. Nonsense verses 3. Poetry -- By individual authors

  ISBN 0-06-057234-5; 0-06-058653-2 lib bdg

             LC 2004-269335

First published 1974

"There are skillful, sometimes grotesque line drawings with each of the 127 poems, which run in length from a few lines to a couple of pages. The poems are tender, funny, sentimental, philosophical, and ridiculous in turn, and they're for all ages." Sat Rev

★ **A light** in the attic; Special edition; Harper 2009 185p il $18.99

Grades: 3 4 5 6   **811**

  1. Humorous poetry 2. Nonsense verses 3. Poetry -- By individual authors

  ISBN 978-0-06-190585-8; 0-06-190585-2

First published 1981

This collection of more than one hundred poems "will delight lovers of Silverstein's raucous, rollicking verse and his often tender, whimsical, philosophical advice. . . . The poems are tuned in to kids' most hidden feelings, dark wishes and enjoyment of the silly. . . . The witty line drawings are a full half of the treat of this wholly satisfying anthology by the modern successor to Edward Lear and Hilaire Belloc." SLJ [review of 1981 edition]

Singer, Marilyn

★ **Central** heating; poems about fire and warmth. illustrated by Meilo So. Alfred A. Knopf 2005 41p il $15.95; lib bdg $17.99

Grades: 4 5 6 7   **811**

  1. Fire -- Poetry 2. Heat -- Poetry 3. Poetry -- By individual authors

  ISBN 0-375-82912-1; 0-375-92912-6 lib bdg

             LC 2004-4274

"The complicated nature of fire is explored in Singer's energetic short poems and So's deceptively simple single-color illustrations. . . . This title . . . belongs on library shelves everywhere." SLJ

First food fight this fall and other school poems; by Marilyn Singer; illustrated by Sachiko Yoshikawa. Sterling 2008 42p il $14.95

Grades: K 1 2 3 4   **811**

  1. Schools -- Poetry 2. Poetry -- By individual authors

  ISBN 978-1-4027-4145-6; 1-4027-4145-6

             LC 2007043386

"Twenty-nine poems, in the voices of a dozen children who ride the school bus together, depict various activities that take place in and out of the classroom. Bright, cartoon illustrations in acrylics, pastels, and collage capture the youngsters' boundless energy. . . . These poems resonate with mischievous good cheer." SLJ

★ **Mirror** mirror; illustrated by Josée Masse. Dutton Children's Books 2010 un il $16.99

Grades: 3 4 5 6   **811**
1. Children's poetry 2. Fairy tales -- Poetry 3. Poetry -- By individual authors
ISBN 978-0-525-47901-7; 0-525-47901-5; 0525479015; 9780525479017

LC 2009017917

A collection of short poems which, when reversed, provide new perspectives on the fairy tale characters they feature.

"This appealing collection . . . is a marvel to read. . . . The vibrant artwork is painterly yet unfussy and offers hints to the characters who are narrating the poems. An endnote shows children how to create a 'reverse' poem. This is a remarkably clever and versatile book." SLJ

A **full** moon is rising; poems. pictures by Julia Cairns. Lee & Low Books 2011 48p il $19.95
Grades: 1 2 3 4   **811**
1. Poetry -- By individual authors
ISBN 978-1-60060-364-8; 1-60060-364-5

LC 2010034693

"Singer's sparkling verses celebrate the majesty of the moon as experienced in settings around the world, each distinctly conveyed in Cairns's perceptive watercolors. . . . The lunar celebration even extends beyond Earth, with a scientist in the International Space Station contemplating both Earth's moon and the Martian moon, Phobos. The breadth of perspectives creates a stirring portrait of a familiar but no less marvelous sight." Publ Wkly

★ A **stick** is an excellent thing; poems celebrating outdoor play. illustrated by LeUyen Pham. Clarion Books 2012 il $16.99
Grades: PreK K 1 2   **811**
1. Imagination -- Poetry 2. Outdoor recreation -- Poetry 3. Poetry -- By individual authors
ISBN 978-0-547-12493-3; 0-547-12493-7

LC 2011009848

"Singer presents the full spectrum of outdoor activities in rhymed poems consummately animated by Pham's vibrant drawings. . . . While many of the snappy lyrics show off the pleasures of moving . . . a real strength of the collection is its engagement of the imagination. . . . Pham's evocative artwork heightens the imagination's importance in play, with her digitally colored pencil-and-ink renderings so finely textured that they radiate a warmth as arresting as Ezra Jack Keats'. A thrilling integration of verse and image." Kirkus

Singer, Marilyn, 1948-
★ **Follow** follow; a book of reverso poems. by Marilyn Singer; illustrated by Josée Masse. Dial Books for Young Readers 2013 32 p. (hardcover: acid-free paper) $16.99
Grades: 1 2 3 4   **811**
1. Children's poetry 2. Fairy tales -- Poetry 3. Children's poetry, American 4. Characters and characteristics in literature -- Juvenile poetry
ISBN 0803737696; 9780803737693

LC 2012014359

This children's book, by Marilyn Singer, illustrated by Josee Masse, offers several fairy tales in the form of "reversos--a poetic form in which the poem is presented forward and then backward. . . . Read these . . . poems from top to bottom and they mean one thing. Then reverse the lines and

read from bottom to top and they mean something else--it is almost like magic!" (Publisher's note)

The **superheroes'** employment agency; by Marilyn Singer; illustrated by Noah Z. Jones. Clarion Books 2012 39 p. col. ill. (hardcover) $16.99
Grades: 1 2 3   **811**
1. Magic -- Fiction 2. Superheroes -- Fiction 3. Supernatural -- Fiction 4. Superheroes -- Juvenile poetry
ISBN 0547435592; 9780547435596

LC 2011025722

Author Marilyn Singer's book features "underemployed B-list superheroes. . . . Got rats and mice? Call on the . . . Verminator! Supernatural foes will flee from the garlic foam wielded by Muffy the Vampire Sprayer. . . . Along with having distinct individual powers and abilities, several of these eager job seekers combine to offer enhanced services. Armored Sir Knightly and The Masked Man, both aging veterans, can team up to entertain at children's parties, for instance." (Kirkus Reviews)

Sklansky, Amy E.
Out of this world; poems and facts about space. by Amy E. Sklansky; illustrated by Stacey Schuett. Alfred A. Knopf 2012 40 p.
Grades: 3 4 5   **811**
1. Outer space -- Poetry 2. Outer space -- Juvenile literature 3. Space sciences -- Juvenile literature
ISBN 0375857915; 0375864598; 0375964592; 0375987339; 9780375857911; 9780375864599; 9780375964596; 9780375987335

LC 2011032506

This children's book combines astronomy and other space science facts, space-themed poetry by Amy Sklansky, and illustrations and supplemental educational diagrams by Stacey Schuett. "The mysteries of the universe and the science of space exploration are perennially popular subjects, . . . Amy Sklansky has written . . . poems about planets and stars and rockets and moon landings and satellites. Each poem is supported by additional facts and explanations in the margins." Schuett's illustrations depict various subjects such as the Earth's atmospheric layers, star systems and other planets. (Publisher's note)

Smith, Hope Anita
★ **Mother** poems; words and pictures by Hope Anita Smith. Henry Holt and Co. 2009 72p il $16.95
Grades: 4 5 6 7   **811**
1. Death -- Poetry 2. Mothers -- Poetry 3. Bereavement -- Poetry 4. African Americans -- Poetry 5. Poetry -- By individual authors
ISBN 978-0-8050-8231-9; 0-8050-8231-X

LC 2008-18342

"Smith writes about an African American child's grief at the sudden death of her mother. . . . Like the poetry, Smith's simple, torn-paper collages in a folk-art style show the close embraces and vignettes without overwhelming the words." Booklist

Snyder, Betsy
I haiku you; Betsy Snyder. Random House Childrens Books 2012 32 p. (trade) $9.99

Grades: PreK K 1   **811**
1. Haiku 2. American poetry 3. Children's poetry 4. Haiku, American 5. Children's poetry, American
ISBN 0375867503; 9780375867507; 9780375967504; 9780375981265

LC 2012008884

Author Betsy Snyder presents a "collection of haiku [that] captures special moments of friendship and appreciation from a child's point of view. Love is explored in its broadest sense as a cast of winsome, ethnically diverse children are featured in everyday activities such as making snow angels, riding a bicycle and sharing a purple Popsicle." (Kirkus Reviews)

Soto, Gary
Canto familiar; [illustrated by Annika Nelson] Harcourt Brace & Co. 1995 79p il $18; pa $5.95
Grades: 4 5 6   **811**
1. Children's poetry 2. Mexican Americans -- Poetry 3. Poetry -- By individual authors
ISBN 978-0-15-200067-7; 0-15-200067-4; 978-0-15-205885-2 pa; 0-15-205885-0 pa

LC 94-24218

"This collection of simple free verse captures common childhood moments at home, at school, and in the street. Many of the experiences are Mexican American . . . and occasional Spanish words are part of the easy, colloquial, short lines. . . . The occasional full-page, richly colored woodcuts by Annika Nelson capture the child's imaginative take on ordinary things." Booklist

★ **Neighborhood** odes; illustrated by David Diaz. Harcourt Brace Jovanovich 1992 68p il hardcover o.p. pa $5.95
Grades: 4 5 6   **811**
1. Children's poetry 2. Hispanic Americans -- Poetry 3. Poetry -- By individual authors
ISBN 0-15-256879-4; 0-15-205364-6 pa

LC 91-20710

"Twenty-one poems, all odes, celebrate life in a Hispanic neighborhood. Other than the small details of daily life— peoples' names or the foods they eat—these poems could be about any neighborhood. With humor, sensitivity, and insight, Soto explores the lives of children. . . . David Diaz's contemporary black-and-white illustrations, which often resemble cut paper, effortlessly capture the varied moods— happiness, fear, longing, shame, and greed—of this remarkable collection. With a glossary of thirty Spanish words and phrases." Horn Book

Stevenson, James
★ **Corn-fed**; poems by James Stevenson; with illustrations by the author. Greenwillow Bks. 2002 48p il hardcover o.p. lib bdg $15.89
Grades: 2 3 4 5   **811**
1. Poetry -- By individual authors
ISBN 0-06-000597-1; 0-06-000598-X lib bdg

LC 2001-33261

A collection of short poems with such titles as "Coney Island movie," "Why bicycles are locked up," and "Aquarium"

"These musings are shot through with Stevenson's wry scrutiny of and appreciation for, the world around him. . . ."

Spare but appealing, these poetic ponderings render the ordinary fresh." Horn Book Guide

★ **Popcorn**; poems by James Stevenson; with illustrations by the author. Greenwillow Bks. 1998 64p il $16
Grades: 2 3 4 5   **811**
1. Poetry -- By individual authors
ISBN 0-688-15261-9

LC 97-6320

A collection of short poems with such titles as "Popcorn," "Driftwood," and "My new bird book"

"With a physical immediacy and a casual voice, Stevenson's poems capture quiet, intensely moving moments of daily life in a small seaside town, and his exquisite, understated watercolors extend the concrete particulars of the words." Booklist

Sturges, Philemon
Down to the sea in ships; illustrated by Giles Laroche. Putnam's 2005 un il $16.99
Grades: 3 4 5   **811**
1. Boats and boating -- Poetry 2. Poetry -- By individual authors
ISBN 0-399-23464-0

LC 2002-67957

Poems describe a variety of watercraft, from birch bark canoes to cruise ships, and reveal their impact on the world.

"A seamless collection of finely honed but telling histories of important ships in fully realized poems. . . . Laroche's boats, made of cut paper and paint, appear to lift from the waves and float in their pictorial waters. This author and illustrator work wonders together." SLJ

Swaim, Jessica
Scarum fair; poems by Jessica Swaim; illustrations by Carol Ashley. Wordsong 2010 31p il $17.95
Grades: 3 4 5   **811**
1. Monsters -- Poetry 2. Poetry -- By individual authors
ISBN 978-1-59078-590-4; 1-59078-590-4

LC 2008040336

"Clever writing pulls children into a creepy carnival of 29 humorous poems. . . . Dark background colors add a sense of foreboding as the cartoon children meet the ghouls illustrated in acrylics, graphite, and pen and ink." SLJ

Thayer, Ernest Lawrence
★ **Casey** at the bat; a ballad of the republic sung in the year 1888. [by] Ernest L. Thayer; illlustrated by C.F. Payne. Simon & Schuster Bks. for Young Readers 2003 un il lib bdg $16.95
Grades: K 1 2 3   **811**
1. Baseball 2. American poetry 3. Baseball -- Poetry 4. Baseball -- Juvenile poetry 5. Children's poetry, American 6. Poetry -- By individual authors 7. Baseball players -- Juvenile poetry
ISBN 0-689-85494-3

LC 2002-3472

Poem first published 1888

A narrative poem about the celebrated baseball player who strikes out at the crucial moment of the game

"Payne's caricatures, rendered in a mix of acrylics, watercolor ink, oils, and colored pencils, are a marvel of texture and personality." SLJ

Ernest L. Thayer's Casey at the bat; a ballad of the Republic sung in the year 1888. reported by Ernest L. Thayer; illustrated by Christopher Bing. Handprint Books 2000 un il $17.95

Grades: 3 4 5 6 **811**
1. Baseball -- Poetry 2. Baseball players -- Poetry 3. Poetry -- By individual authors
ISBN 1-929766-00-9
LC 00-37010

A Caldecott Medal honor book, 2001

"Thayer's classic poem of the 19th-century baseball legend has been revived for a new generation in this creatively designed package. . . . Bing has orchestrated every detail to great effect. Each double spread, rendered in ink and brush on scratchboard, is a scene from the poem. The multitude of lines adds energy; the multiple perspectives create interest." SLJ

Thomas, Joyce Carol
★ **Brown** honey in broomwheat tea; poems by Joyce Carol Thomas; illustrated by Floyd Cooper. HarperCollins Pubs. 1993 un il $16.95; pa $6.99

Grades: K 1 2 3 **811**
1. Children's poetry 2. African Americans -- Poetry 3. Poetry -- By individual authors
ISBN 0-06-021087-7; 0-06-443439-7 pa
LC 91-46043

"A dozen poems rooted in home, family, and the African American experience combine with a series of warm and evocative watercolors in this highly readable and attractive picture book." Booklist

★ The **blacker** the berry; poems. illustrated by Floyd Cooper. HarperCollins 2008 un il $16.99; lib bdg $17.89

Grades: PreK K 1 2 **811**
1. Children's poetry 2. African Americans -- Poetry 3. Poetry -- By individual authors 4. African Americans -- Juvenile literature
ISBN 978-0-06-025375-2; 0-06-025375-4; 978-0-06-025376-9 lib bdg; 0-06-025376-2 lib bdg
Coretta Scott King Award for illustration, 2009
Coretta Scott King honor book for text, 2009

"Black comes in all shades from dark to light, and each is rich and beautiful in this collection of simple, joyful poems and glowing portraits that show African American diversity and connections." Booklist

Thomas, Patricia
Nature's paintbox; a seasonal gallery of art and verse. [by] Patricia Thomas; illustrated by Craig Orback. Millbrook Press, Inc. 2007 un il lib bdg $16.95

Grades: 2 3 4 **811**
1. Seasons -- Poetry 2. Poetry -- By individual authors
ISBN 978-0-8225-6807-0
LC 2006035079

"The verse connects each season with the artist's medium, beginning with pen and ink for winter, then cycling through pastel chalk for springs, watercolor for summer, and oils for fall. . . . This picture book is both intriguing to look at and excellent for reading aloud." Booklist

Updike, John
★ A **child's** calendar; illustrations by Trina Schart Hyman. Holiday House 1999 un il $16.95

Grades: K 1 2 3 **811**
1. American poetry 2. Months -- Poetry 3. Months -- Juvenile poetry 4. Children's poetry, American 5. Poetry -- By individual authors
ISBN 0-8234-1445-0
LC 98-46166

A newly illustrated edition of the title first published 1965 by Knopf

A Caldecott Medal honor book, 2000

"Hyman's colorful illustrations portray a multiracial family living in rural New Hampshire. . . . Each evocative illustration has its own story to tell, celebrating the small moments in children's lives with clarity and sensitivity, with empathy and joy." Booklist

Van Wassenhove, Sue
The **seldom**-ever-shady glades; poems and quilts by Sue Van Wassenhove. Wordsong 2008 32p il $17.95

Grades: 3 4 5 6 **811**
1. Nature poetry 2. Birds -- Poetry 3. Poetry -- By individual authors
ISBN 978-1-59078-352-8
LC 2007018099

"Through exuberant poems and quilted illustrations . . . Van Wassenhove offers an unusual tour of the delicate Everglades habitat. . . . Van Wassenhove's creative application of quilting techniques to depict the rippled surfaces and shifting hues of a wetland environment will draw fascinated gazes." Booklist

Vardell, Sylvia M.
Poetry people; a practical guide to children's poets. Libraries Unlimited 2007 170p $50

Grades: Adult Professional **811**
1. Poets 2. Poetry 3. Reference books 4. Children's poetry 5. Poetry -- Study and teaching 6. Poetry -- By individual authors
ISBN 978-1-59158-443-8; 1-59158-443-4
LC 2007003329

This is "a comprehensive survey of 62 contemporary children's poets. Each of the one- to two-page entries begins with a brief biography and includes Web sites, bibliographies, suggestions for use and reading of specific poems, plus connections to other children's literature. . . . This book will be welcomed by all adults interested in connecting children with poetry." SLJ

Includes bibliographical references

Viorst, Judith
If I were in charge of the world and other worries; poems for children and their parents. illustrated by Lynne Cherry. Atheneum Pubs. 1981 56p il lib bdg $16.95; pa $4.95

Grades: 3 4 5 6 **811**
1. Humorous poetry 2. Poetry -- By individual authors
ISBN 0-689-30863-9 lib bdg; 0-689-70770-3 pa
LC 81-2342

"Forty-one lively, funny poems written from a wry, self-deprecating point of view. Some poems verge on adult feelings—such as a broken heart or a lyrical appreciation of spring—but most of them deal with children's worries, to which the author seems to be specially attuned." Horn Book

Walker, Alice

There is a flower at the tip of my nose smelling me; by Alice Walker; illustrated by Stefano Vitale. HarperCollinsPublishers 2006 un il $16.99; lib bdg $17.89

Grades: 2 3 4   **811**

1. Senses and sensation -- Poetry 2. Poetry -- By individual authors

ISBN 978-0-06-057080-4; 0-06-057080-6; 978-0-06-057081-1 lib bdg; 0-06-057081-4 lib bdg

LC 2005014517

"Walker celebrates the beauty of the world and our connection to it through a series of short verses that praise the senses. . . . Vitale's vibrant, jewel-toned illustrations embolden the folk-art simplicity of each verse." SLJ

Why war is never a good idea; illustrations by Stefano Vitale. HarperCollins Publishers 2007 un il $16.99; lib bdg $17.89

Grades: 3 4 5   **811**

1. War poetry 2. Children's poetry 3. Poetry -- By individual authors

ISBN 978-0-06-075385-6; 0-06-075385-4; 978-0-06-075386-3 lib bdg; 0-06-075386-2 lib bdg

LC 2006036255

Simple, rhythmic text explores the wanton destructiveness of War, which has grown old but not wise, as it demolishes nice people and beautiful things with no consideration for the consequences

"A thought-provoking, eloquent poem and brilliant art combine to bring the abstract concept of war to a personal, immediate level." SLJ

Weatherford, Carole Boston

★ Birmingham, 1963. Wordsong 2007 39p il $17.95

Grades: 3 4 5 6   **811**

1. Children's poetry 2. Bombings -- Poetry 3. Poetry -- By individual authors 4. African Americans -- Civil rights -- Poetry 5. Hate crimes -- Birmingham (Ala.) -- Juvenile literature 6. Bombings -- Alabama -- Birmingham -- Juvenile literature

ISBN 978-1-59078-440-2; 1-59078-440-5

LC 2006038105

"In free verse, a fictional 10-year-old tells of actual events leading up to the Ku Klux Klan bombing of the Sixteenth Street Baptist Church on September 15, 1963, and of the four young girls who died in the explosion. On each double-page spread, a few lines of spare poetry . . . are placed opposite a stirring, unframed archival photograph. . . . The quiet yet arresting book design will inspire readers." Booklist

Remember the bridge; poems of a people. designed by Semador Megged. Philomel Bks. 2002 53p il $17.99

Grades: 5 6 7 8   **811**

1. African Americans -- Poetry 2. Children's poetry, American 3. Poetry -- By individual authors 4. African Americans -- Juvenile poetry

ISBN 0-399-23726-7

LC 2001-36161

"The author evokes imagined and actual individual experiences of the people . . . in the historical black-and-white photos, drawings, and etchings. . . . This celebratory, visually striking book will be appreciated in most collections." SLJ

Weinstock, Robert

Food hates you too; and other poems. Hyperion Books for Children 2009 26p il $15.99

Grades: 2 3 4 5   **811**

1. Children's poetry 2. Food -- Poetry 3. Poetry -- By individual authors

ISBN 978-1-4231-1391-1; 1-4231-1391-8

"This hilarious collection of poems about food stretches the imagination and vocabulary. . . . Varying in length and form, . . . the poetry is fresh, funny, and challenging. . . . Full-color and sometimes delightfully bizarre mixed-media illustrations offer clever asides . . . goofy perspectives, . . . and amusing visual scenarios." SLJ

Whitehead, Jenny

Holiday stew; by Jenny Whitehead. Henry Holt & Co. 2007 64p il $17.95

Grades: 2 3 4   **811**

1. Holidays -- Poetry 2. Poetry -- By individual authors

ISBN 978-0-8050-7715-5; 0-8050-7715-4

LC 2006011144

This poetry collection is "a celebration of a year's worth of holidays. . . . The collection is organized by season, and each of the 78 original poems is accompanied by a richly detailed ink illustration. Neither the rhyme nor the meter is forced, and the poems remain rooted in child-based experiences." SLJ

Wilbur, Richard

The disappearing alphabet; illustrated by David Diaz. Harcourt Brace & Co. 1998 un il hardcover o.p. pa $7

Grades: 3 4 5   **811**

1. Alphabet 2. American poetry 3. Alphabet -- Poetry 4. Children's poetry, American 5. Poetry -- By individual authors 6. English language -- Alphabet -- Juvenile poetry

ISBN 0-15-201470-5; 0-15-216362-X pa

LC 97-24617

A collection of twenty-six short poems pondering what the world would be like if any letters of the alphabet should disappear

"The poems presented here were first printed in The Atlantic Monthly magazine. A series of rhyming couplets of varying lengths, they range from the innocently whimsical to the cleverly sophisticated. Diaz uses computer-generated illustrations to add just the right touches to the verses; the images are lush and playful at the same time." SLJ

Willard, Nancy

★ A visit to William Blake's inn; poems for innocent and experienced travelers. illustrated by Alice and Martin Provensen. Harcourt Brace Jovanovich 1981 44p il $16; pa $7

Grades: 2 3 4 5   **811**

1. Nonsense verses 2. Poetry -- By individual authors

ISBN 0-15-293822-2; 0-15-293823-0 pa

LC 80-27403

Awarded the Newbery Medal, 1982; A Caldecott Medal honor book, 1982

"Nancy Willard's fantasy is pure pleasure, and her joy is expressed in the juxtaposition of sense and nonsense. . . . Done chiefly in glowing tawny colors, the pictures are highly decorative, and the whole book, printed on buff paper speckled to simulate an antique look, presents an elegant appearance." Horn Book

Williams, Vera B.

Amber was brave, Essie was smart; the story of Amber and Essie told here in poems and pictures by Vera B. Williams. Greenwillow Bks. 2001 un il $15.95; lib bdg $15.89; pa $7.99

Grades: 3 4 5   **811**

1. Sisters 2. American poetry 3. Sisters -- Poetry 4. Sisters -- Juvenile poetry 5. Children's poetry, American 6. Poetry -- By individual authors

ISBN 0-06-029460-4; 0-06-029461-2 lib bdg; 0-06-057182-9 pa

LC 00-48438

Two sisters help each other deal with life while their mother is working and their father has been sent to jail

"An engaging, affecting view of the bonds between sisters, this balances reality with hope and love as it shows how small moments tell a big story." Booklist

Wilson, Karma

What's the weather inside? poems by Karma Wilson; drawings by Barry Blitt. Margaret McElderry Books 2009 170p il $17.99

Grades: 2 3 4   **811**

1. Humorous poetry 2. Children's poetry 3. Poetry -- By individual authors

ISBN 978-1-4169-0092-4; 1-4169-0092-6

LC 2006-23623

"This collection of more than 100 poems features comical wordplay . . . as well as lots of fun riffs on Mother Goose rhymes and fairy tales. Many are about family, friends, and school. . . . Blitt's line drawings are a great match for the verses. They are funny, dynamic, and full of personality." SLJ

Wong, Janet S.

Knock on wood; poems about superstitions. written by Janet S. Wong; illustrated by Julie Paschkis. Margaret K. McElderry Bks. 2003 33p il $17.95

Grades: 3 4 5   **811**

1. Superstition 2. American poetry 3. Superstition -- Poetry 4. Children's poetry, American 5. Poetry -- By individual authors

ISBN 0-689-85512-5

LC 2002-8319

A collection of seventeen original poems about superstitions, including walking under a ladder, breaking a mirror, and knocking on wood. Includes notes about the superstitions

"Some selections are haunting, and some humorous. . . . Paschkis creates an exquisite backdrop for the verses. Presented on a panoramic spread, each poem and facing watercolor scene have matching frames, anchoring them as reflections of one another. . . . There is much to ponder in both words and pictures." SLJ

Twist; yoga poems. written by Janet S. Wong; illustrated by Julie Paschkis. Margaret K. McElderry Books 2007 39p il $17.99

Grades: 2 3 4 5   **811**

1. Children's poetry 2. Yoga -- Poetry 3. Poetry -- By

individual authors

ISBN 0-689-87394-8; 978-0-689-87394-2

LC 2005-15888

"This collection of 16 poems touches on the uplifting and emotional aspects of yoga, putting words to the spirit of the poses and evoking the energy and feelings of the practice. . . . Paschkis's watercolor paintings frame both the poem and a child performing the pose with colorful fauna, flora, and people that suggest India as well as that particular exercise." SLJ

Worth, Valerie

★ All the small poems and fourteen more; pictures by Natalie Babbitt. Farrar, Straus & Giroux 1994 194p il hardcover o.p. pa $6.95

Grades: 2 3 4 5   **811**

1. Children's poetry 2. Poetry -- By individual authors

ISBN 0-374-40345-7 pa

LC 94-8810

"As the title implies, all the original collaborations between this poet and artist are collected in this volume, which includes ninety-nine poems and an additional fourteen new ones. The earlier works have been widely praised, for good reason, and the new verses are every bit as worthy as their predecessors." Horn Book

★ Animal poems; pictures by Steve Jenkins. Farrar, Straus & Giroux 2007 un il $17

Grades: 4 5 6   **811**

1. Children's poetry 2. Animals -- Poetry 3. Poetry -- By individual authors

ISBN 0-374-38057-0; 978-0-374-38057-1

LC 2005-56812

A collection of twenty-three illustrated poems about animals

"This pairing of . . . Worth's exquisite poems with Jenkins's . . . extraordinary, cut-paper illustrations make this a volume to treasure. . . . Each poem in this handsome volume is a gem—full of crisp language, vivid images and thoughtful ideas." Publ Wkly

Peacock and other poems; pictures by Natalie Babbitt. Farrar, Straus & Giroux 2002 40p il $15

Grades: 2 3 4 5   **811**

1. American poetry 2. Children's poetry, American 3. Poetry -- By individual authors

ISBN 0-374-35766-8

LC 2001-23828

A collection of short blank verse about common sights and objects such as "umbrella," "pencil," "crayons"

"The illustrations, minimalist in form but not in impact, match the incisive delicacy of the poems, twenty-six in all— and each is a delight." Horn Book

Pug and other animal poems; Valerie Worth; pictures by Steve Jenkins. Margaret Ferguson Books, Farrar Straus Giroux 2012 40 p. $16.99

Grades: 2 3 4 5   **811**

1. Animals -- Poetry 2. Children's poetry

ISBN 0374350248; 9780374350246

LC 2010034300

This juvenile poetry collection, by Valerie Worth, illustrated by Steve Jenkins, "examines a wide range of animal behavior, from the fleetingness of a fly sipping spilled milk to the constant steely presence of a powerful bull; the greedy meal of a street rat to a cat's quiet gift of a dead mouse on the doorstep." (Publisher's note)

Yolen, Jane

★ **Birds** of a feather; poems by Jane Yolen; photographs by Jason Stemple; foreword by Donald Kroodsma. Wordsong 2011 32p il $17.95

Grades: 3 4 5   **811**

1. Birds -- Poetry 2. Poetry -- By individual authors

ISBN 978-1-59078-830-1; 1-59078-830-3

"Striking photographs of birds that might be seen in the eastern United States illustrate this . . . collection of 14 poems in varied forms. . . . Semple's splendid photographs show birds in the wild. . . . The colors are true, and the details sharp; careful focus and composition make the birds the center of attention. . . . Short sidebars add interesting, informative details about each species." Kirkus

Bug off! creepy, crawly poems. by Jane Yolen; photographs by Jason Stemple. 1st ed. Wordsong 2012 30 p. col. ill. (reinforced) $16.95

Grades: 3 4 5   **811.54**

1. Children's poetry 2. Insects -- Poetry 3. Spiders -- Poetry

ISBN 1590788621; 9781590788622

LC 2011939947

Author Jane Yolen presents a book of poetry for children. In the collection, "[f]ly, praying mantis, butterfly, ants, honey bee, lovebug, daddy longlegs, spider, dragonfly, tick, ladybug and grasshopper each take a spread, the photo opposite a page of text that includes the poem and a paragraph of facts. Most of Yolen's poems rhyme, and an author's note encourages readers to create their own poems." (Kirkus)

The **Emily** sonnets; the life of Emily Dickinson. by Jane Yolen; illustrations by Gary Kelley. 1st ed. Creative Editions 2012 40 p. col. ill. (reinforced) $19.99

Grades: 5 6 7   **811**

1. Dickinson, Emily, 1830-1886 -- Poetry

ISBN 1568462158; 9781568462158

LC 2011040841

This book by Jane Yolen presents 15 sonnets about poet Emily Dickinson. "The selections are constructed in various voices. . . . In the first five pieces, Emily speaks of the family's brick house, her close relationship with her sister Vinnie, her schooling, her variance with her family's religious beliefs, and the companionship of her dog. . . . The other speakers . . . tell of her always dressing in white, her life as a recluse, and her work." (School Library Journal)

An **egret's** day; poems by Jane Yolen; photographs by Jason Stemple. Wordsong 2009 30p il $17.95

Grades: 3 4 5   **811**

1. Herons -- Poetry

ISBN 978-1-59078-650-5; 1-59078-650-5

LC 2008051688

"Poetry and short informative paragraphs combine to celebrate both the elegance and the natural history of the American egret. Haiku, free verse, rhyming couplets and even a limerick are just some of the forms Yolen masterfully uses to engage readers on both aesthetic and scientific levels. Gorgeous photography completes this carefully designed literary science piece with scenes of the egret's daily life." Kirkus

A **mirror** to nature; poems about reflection. [by] Jane Yolen; photographs by Jason Stemple. Wordsong 2009 31p il $17.95

Grades: 3 4 5   **811**

1. Nature poetry 2. Poetry -- By individual authors

ISBN 978-1-59078-624-6

LC 2008031760

"Water acts as a mirror in this picture book that combines short poems with full-page color photographs of animals in the wild. . . . The poetic forms are well matched to the mood in the pictures. . . . Drawn by the rich play in words and pictures, kids will see reflections, strange and beautiful, in the the natural world." Booklist

Young, Ed

★ **Beyond** the great mountains; a visual poem about China. Chronicle Books 2005 32p il $17.95

Grades: 4 5 6 7   **811**

1. Poetry -- By individual authors

ISBN 0-8118-4343-2

"The book is comprised of 14 lines, each of which is accompanied by its own double-page illustration, done in cut-and torn-paper collage. Young also provides the ancient characters for the images he presents. . . . Designed to be read vertically, each page is flipped up to reveal the accompanying illustration. In this way, the entire book becomes a piece of art, a visual treat of sublime colors and textures that joins with text and characters to describe the vastness and beauty of China." SLJ

Zimmer, Tracie Vaughn

Cousins of clouds; elephant poems. illustrated by Megan Halsey and Sean Addy. Clarion Books 2011 31p il $16.99

Grades: 3 4 5   **811**

1. Children's poetry 2. Elephants -- Poetry 3. Poetry -- By individual authors   ISBN 978-0-618-90349-8; 0-618-90349-6

This collection of poems and factoids celebrates the "wonders of elephants," from glorious winged creatures of myth to the realities of their precarious modern existence. With a wide-ranging stock of lore and fact, Vaughn limns the complex relationship between humans and the largest land animals. In "Inspiration," she observes that their image is etched in the "imagination/of all mankind,/a behemoth of hope." Poems like "Ivory" and "Grace," however, remind readers that elephants have been hunted and used for hard labor and public performance. . . . "Fortress" graphically depicts the protective instincts of female elephants, while "Elephant Blues" places cartoon drawings and verses atop colored sheets of music." (School Library Journal)

"Against fanciful collage backdrops portraying pachyderms in an array of styles and arrangements, Zimmer pairs prose and mostly free-verse tributes to elephants and those who care for them. . . . She writes with passion and sympathy. . . . Along with giving each spread a different look and palette, the illustrators inject dashes of visual wit. . . . Both informative and heartfelt." Kirkus

★ **Steady** hands; poems about work. by Tracie Vaughn Zimmer; illustrated by Megan Halsey and Sean Addy. Clarion Books 2009 48p il $16

Grades: 4 5 6　　　　　　　　　　　　　　**811**

1. Work -- Poetry 2. Occupations -- Poetry 3. Poetry -- By individual authors

ISBN 978-0-618-90351-1; 0-618-90351-8

LC 2007038848

"Inventive, complicated collages and well-crafted poems focus on the activities of working people in this eye-catching book. With an observant eye, Zimmer . . . captures different individuals performing work with 'steady hands.'. . . . Halsey and Addy's . . . hip collages combine individual cut-outs of people along with drawings, photos, textured backgrounds and designs." Publ Wkly

811.008　American poetry -- Collections

The **20th** century children's poetry treasury; selected by Jack Prelutsky; illustrated by Meilo So. Knopf 1999 87p il $19.95

Grades: 3 4 5 6　　　　　　　　　　　　**811.008**

1. English poetry 2. American poetry 3. Children's poetry, English 4. Children's poetry, American 5. American poetry -- Collections 6. English poetry -- 20th century 7. American poetry -- 20th century

ISBN 0-679-89314-8; 0-679-99314-2 lib bdg

LC 99-23988

A collection of more than 200 poems by such modern poets as Nikki Grimes, John Ciardi, Karla Kuskin, Ted Hughes, e.e. cummings, Eve Merriam, Deborah Chandra, Arnold Adoff, and more than 100 others

"While all of these selections have been published elsewhere, the format and illustrations in this collection give them new life. . . . So's watercolor illustrations are, by turn, impressionistic, childlike, silly, and serious, as called for by the tone of the poems featured. . . . . A splendid collection." SLJ

African American poetry; edited by Arnold Rampersad and Marcellus Blount; illustrated by Karen Barbour. Sterling Pub Co Inc. 2013 48 p. ill. (hardcover) $14.95

Grades: 3 4 5 6 7　　　　　　　　　　**811.008**

1. American poetry -- Asian American authors

ISBN 1402716893; 9781402716898

This book of poetry by African American authors"introduces 27 poets from the days of Phillis Wheatley to well-established poets writing in the 21st century. A four-page introduction outlines historical periods and influences. Presented chronologically, the entries begin with a paragraph describing the poet's life and work. Paul Laurence Dunbar, Countee Cullen, Langston Hughes, Lucille Clifton, Maya Angelou, and others are joined by George Moses Horton . . .and others." (School Library Journal)

Amazing faces; edited by Lee Bennett Hopkins; illustrated by Chris Soentpiet. Lee & Low 2010 un il $18.95

Grades: 2 3 4 5　　　　　　　　　　　**811.008**

1. Children's poetry 2. American poetry -- Collections 3. Emotions -- Juvenile literature

ISBN 978-1-60060-334-1; 1-60060-334-3

"Illustrated with large, handsome watercolor portraits, the 16 poems in this anthology celebrate the rich diversity of American kids—what makes each one special and the connections between them. . . . A great collection for sharing at home and in the classroom." Booklist

★ **America** at war; poems. selected by Lee Bennett Hopkins; illlustrated by Stephen Alcorn. Margaret K. McElderry Books 2008 84p il $21.99

Grades: 5 6 7 8　　　　　　　　　　　**811.008**

1. War poetry 2. Children's poetry 3. War poetry, American 4. American poetry -- Collections

ISBN 978-1-4169-1832-5; 1-4169-1832-9

LC 2006-08723

"This handsome anthology, expressing Americans' varied experience during wartime, is a fine selection of poems accessible to children. . . . The poems will touch readers with their sharp poignancy and undeniable power. Throughout the well-designed book, the expressive watercolor artwork enhances the poetry." Booklist

The **arrow** finds its mark; a book of found poems. edited by Georgia Heard; illustrated by Antoine Guilloppé. Roaring Brook Press 2012 38 p.

Grades: 3 4 5　　　　　　　　　　　　**811.008**

1. American poetry 2. Children's poetry 3. Poetry -- Collections

ISBN 1596436654; 9781596436657

LC 2011017180

This poetry collection, edited by Georgia Heard with illustrations by Antoine Guillope, features material from "Twitter feeds, school notes, advertisements, street signs. . . .poetry in . . . unlikely places [by] thirty contemporary poets. Imagine picking up a scrap of paper off the floor or reading a sign at a gas station or looking at graffiti on the subway and finding poetry in these words. The literary equivalent of a collage, found poems take existing text, reorder and refashion it, and present it as a poem." (Publisher's note)

★ **Ashley** Bryan's ABC of African-American poetry. Atheneum Bks. for Young Readers 1997 un il hardcover o.p. pa $7.99

Grades: K 1 2 3　　　　　　　　　　　**811.008**

1. Alphabet 2. African Americans -- Poetry 3. Alphabet -- Juvenile literature 4. Children's poetry -- Collections 5. American poetry -- African American authors -- Collections 6. American poetry -- African American authors -- Juvenile literature

ISBN 0-689-81209-4; 0-689-84045-4 pa

LC 96-25148

Each letter of the alphabet is represented by a line from a poem by a different African American poet, describing an aspect of the black experience

This book is illustrated "by Bryan's vivid tempera and gouache paintings. . . . The selections . . . display a loving acquaintance with poets from James Weldon Johnson to Rita Dove. While there is a full range of emotions, joy and pride predominate." SLJ

★ The **Beauty** of the beast; poems from the animal kingdom. selected by Jack Prelutsky; illustrated by Meilo So; opening poems for each section especially written

for this anthology by Jack Prelutsky. Knopf 1997 101p
il $19.95

Grades: 4 5 6   **811.008**

1. Animals -- Poetry 2. Poetry -- Collections 3.
Children's poetry -- Collections 4. Animals -- Poetry
-- Juvenile literature

ISBN 0-679-87058-X

LC 96-14423

"Prelutsky has selected a remarkable array of poems full
of movement and sound. . . . Each page has several poems
and bright watercolors that writhe with texture." SLJ

Includes bibliographical references

★ **Behind** the museum door; poems to celebrate the wonders of museums. selected by Lee Bennett Hopkins;
illustrated by Stacey Dressen-McQueen. Abrams Books
for Young Readers 2007 un il $16.95

Grades: 3 4 5   **811.008**

1. Art -- Poetry 2. Museums -- Poetry 3. American
poetry -- Collections

ISBN 978-0-8109-1204-5; 0-8109-1204-X

LC 2006013576

"This collection of poems touches on the sights and
sensations a group of children experience on a field trip. .
. . Selections are by such poets as Lilian Moore, Jane Yolen, Alice Schertle, and Myra Cohn Livingston. . . . Each
of Dressen-McQueen's folk-art-style 'exhibits,' carefully
crafted in acrylic paint, oil pastel, and colored pencil, successfully captures and reinforces the mood of its accompanying poem." SLJ

★ The **Bill** Martin Jr. Big book of poetry; edited by Bill
Martin Jr., with Michael Sampson; foreword by Eric
Carle; afterword Steven Kellogg. Simon & Schuster
Books for Young Readers 2008 175p $21

Grades: PreK K 1 2 3   **811.008**

1. Children's poetry 2. American poetry -- Collections

ISBN 978-1-4169-3971-9; 1-4169-3971-7

"The almost 200 selections in this big handsome anthology . . . have a singing beat. . . . The collection brings together poems from Robert Frost, Christina Rossetti, Langston Hughes, Nikki Grimes, Aliki, Jack Prelutsky, and many
other well-known poets. Accompanying the poems are pictures from many of the best picture-book illustrators whose
work . . . extends the words' lyrical rhythms and playfulness." Booklist

★ **Cool** salsa; bilingual poems on growing up Latino in
the United States. edited by Lori M. Carlson; introduction by Oscar Hijuelos. Holt & Co. 1994 xx, 123p il
hardcover o.p. pa $6.99

Grades: 5 6 7 8 9 10   **811.008**

1. Bilingual books -- English-Spanish 2. American
poetry -- Hispanic American authors -- Collections

ISBN 0-8050-3135-9; 978-0-449-70436-3 pa; 0-449-
70436-X pa

LC 93-45798

"This collection presents poems by 29 Mexican-American, Cuban-American, Puerto Rican, and other Central and
South American poets, including Sandra Cisneros, Luis J.
Rodriguez, Pat Mora, Gary Soto, Ana Castillo, Oscar Hijuelos, Ed J. Vega, Judith Ortiz-Cofer, and other Latino writers
both contemporary and historical. Brief biographical notes

on the authors are provided. All the poems deal with experiences of teenagers." Book Rep

★ A **dazzling** display of dogs; concrete poems by Betsy
Franco; illustrations by Michael Wertz. Tricycle Press
2011 un il $16.99; lib bdg $19.99

Grades: PreK K 1 2 3   **811.008**

1. Children's poetry 2. Dogs -- Poetry 3. Dogs --
Juvenile literature 4. Poetry -- By individual authors

ISBN 978-1-58246-343-8; 1-58246-343-3; 978-
1-58246-387-2 lib bdg; 1-58246-387-5 lib bdg;
1582463433; 1582463875 lib bdg; 9781582463438;
9781582463872 lib bdg

LC 2010018014

"In an exuberant collection of concrete dog pems . . . the
whimsy of Franco's poems is matched by the modern-meets-
retro collages into which they are integrated. . . . Franco and
Wertz persuasively convey canine behavior, from devoted
companion to inner wolf, as well as the trials and treasured
moments familiar to many owners. Dog lovers won't want
to miss this clever, jubilant gem." Publ Wkly

Dizzy dinosaurs; silly dino poems. edited by Lee Bennett
Hopkins; illustrated by Barry Gott. Harper 2011 44p il
(I can read!) $16.99; pa $3.99

Grades: K 1 2 3   **811.008**

1. Children's poetry 2. Dinosaurs -- Poetry 3. American
poetry -- Collections 4. Dinosaurs -- Juvenile literature
5. Humorous poetry -- Juvenile literature

ISBN 978-0-06-135839-5; 0-06-135839-8; 978-0-06-
135841-8 pa; 0-06-135841-X pa

"Nineteen dinosaur poems plus a pronunciation guide
to dinosaur names make up this easy reader collection. . .
. The poets do surprisingly well at writing poems using the
short words and easy vocabulary of an I Can Read book. . .
. Gott's paintings exaggeate the dinosaurs comically, giving
the prehistoric critters a variety of bright colors and showing
their disparate sizes by including other animals. . . . Even
non-dino-fans will enjoy the humor of these dinosaurs set
amidst ordinary modern life." Horn Book

★ The **entrance** place of wonders; poems of the Harlem
Renaissance. selected by Daphne Muse; illustrated by
Charlotte Riley-Webb. Abrams 2006 un il $15.95

Grades: 3 4 5   **811.008**

1. Children's poetry 2. Harlem Renaissance 3.
American poetry -- African American authors --
Collections

ISBN 0-8109-5997-6

"Twenty poems written during the Harlem Renaissance
are perfectly paired with exuberant oil paintings. Familiar
poets such as Countee Cullen, Langston Hughes, James
Weldon Johnson, and Claude McKay are joined by less immediately recognized names such as Effie Lee Newsome,
Dorothy Vena Johnson, and Gladys May Caseley-Hayford.
Their collective work, firmly grounded in this exciting explosion of African-American culture, affirms the joy of life
and of personal growth and discovery." SLJ

An **eyeball** in my garden; and other spine-tingling poems.
selected and edited by Jennifer Cole Judd and Laura

Wynkoop; with illustrations by Johan Olander. Marshall Cavendish Childrens 2010 64p il $15.99

Grades: 3 4 5 6 **811.008**

1. Monsters -- Poetry 2. Supernatural -- Poetry 3. American poetry -- Collections

ISBN 978-0-7614-5655-1; 0-7614-5655-4

LC 2010008081

"This compilation of new poems covers scary as well as silly Halloween territory. For every truly chilling ghost train, there's a witch's shopping list or a monster that turns out to be the speaker's own reflection. Easily flowing meter in most of the pieces makes for smooth read-alouds. Black-and-white ink illustratiions are appropriately spooky." Horn Book Guide

Falling down the page; [compiled] by Georgia Heard. Roaring Brook Press 2009 47p il $16.95

Grades: 3 4 5 6 **811.008**

1. Children's poetry 2. Lists -- Juvenile literature 3. American poetry -- Collections

ISBN 978-1-59643-220-8; 1-59643-220-9

LC 2007-38870

"Thirty-two 'list' poems are presented in a dynamic design and trim size. . . . The accessible yet thought-provoking selections are from mostly well-known poets such as Marilyn Singer, Lee Bennett Hopkins and Rebecca Kai Dotlich, and include a couple from Heard. . . . The poems will spark imagination." Kirkus

★ **For** laughing out loud; poems to tickle your funnybone. selected by Jack Prelutsky; illustrated by Marjorie Priceman. Knopf 1991 84p il $17

Grades: 3 4 5 6 **811.008**

1. Humorous poetry 2. American poetry -- Collections 3. Children's poetry -- Collections 4. Humorous poetry -- Juvenile literature 5. Nonsense verses -- Juvenile literature

ISBN 0-394-82144-0

LC 90-33010

A collection of humorous poems by writers including Ellen Raskin, Karla Kuskin, Ogden Nash, and Arnold Lobel

"These nonsense verses by a wide variety of poets combine the domestic and the gross, deadpan and slapstick, with a lilting rhythm and satisfying rhyme. . . . The design is ebullient, often with several poems appearing on a double-page spread surrounded by wildly energetic wash-and-line illustrations." Booklist

Give me wings; poems selected by Lee Bennett Hopkins; illustrated by Ponder Goembel. Holiday House 2010 31p il $16.95

Grades: PreK K 1 2 **811.008**

1. Flight -- Poetry 2. American poetry -- Collections

ISBN 978-0-8234-2023-0; 0-8234-2023-X

LC 2009014744

"In this series of poems about wings and flight, with offerings from Langston Hughes, W.H. Auden, April Halprin Wayland, and others, readers can embark on a journey through the skies. . . . Paired with Goembel's depictions of often-winged children borne aloft, sometimes tentatively, sometimes with confidence and exuberance, the poems create a contemplative tribute to flight." Publ Wkly

Got geography! poems. selected by Lee Bennett Hopkins; pictures by Philip Stanton. Greenwillow Books 2006 32p il $15.99; lib bdg $16.89

Grades: 3 4 5 **811.008**

1. Geography -- Poetry 2. American poetry -- Collections

ISBN 0-06-055601-3; 0-06-055602-1 lib bdg

LC 2004-59662

"Sixteen selections from a variety of poets explore the curiosity piqued by maps, globes, the land we live on, and places far away. The gentle, often-moving verses cover a wide spectrum of ways to explore the Earth from mapping the world to examining its surface to finding one's place within it. . . . The bright acrylic-and-watercolor illustrations bring energy to the pages and set the mood for each poem." SLJ

Hamsters, shells, and spelling bees; school poems. edited by Lee Bennett Hopkins; pictures by Sachiko Yoshikawa. HarperCollins 2008 46p il (I can read!) $16.99; lib bdg $17.89

Grades: PreK K 1 2 **811.008**

1. Schools -- Poetry 2. American poetry -- Collections

ISBN 978-0-06-074112-9; 0-06-074112-0; 978-0-06-074113-6 lib bdg; 0-06-074113-9 lib bdg

LC 2007020881

"Contributed by well-known poets for young people (Jane Yolen, J. Patrick Lewis, Alice Schertle, among others), the poems in this bright compilation . . . describe a wide range of school experiences. . . . The selections range in style from haikus to free verse, although many poems follow a bouncy, rhyming structure. All are written in accessible words targeted straight to emerging readers. . . . [Illustrated with] jellybean-bright cartoon-style illustrations." Booklist

★ **Hanukkah** lights; holiday poetry. selected by Lee Bennett Hopkins; pictures by Melanie Hall. HarperCollins 2004 28p il (I can read book) $15.99; lib bdg $16.89

Grades: K 1 2 3 **811.008**

1. Hanukkah 2. American poetry 3. Hanukkah -- Poetry 4. Judaism -- Juvenile poetry 5. Children's poetry, American 6. Hanukkah -- Juvenile poetry 7. American poetry -- Collections

ISBN 0-06-008051-5; 0-06-008052-3 lib bdg

LC 2003-18901

A collection of poems that celebrate the activities and experiences of Hanukkah

"The poems are simple, evocative, and rhythmic without lapsing into a singsong cadence. Hall's expressive artwork creates an appealing contemporary tone with vivid pastels and a smattering of collage." SLJ

★ **Heart** to heart; new poems inspired by twentieth-century American art. edited by Jan Greenberg. Abrams 2001 80p il map $19.95

Grades: 5 6 7 8 9 10 **811.008**

1. American art 2. Art, American 3. Art -- 20th century 4. Art, Modern -- 20th century 5. American poetry -- Collections

ISBN 0-8109-4386-7

LC 99-462335

Michael L. Printz Award honor book, 2002

A compilation of poems by Americans writing about American art in the twentieth century, including such writers as Nancy Willard, Jane Yolen, and X. J. Kennedy.

"From a tight diamante and pantoum to lyrical free verse, the range of poetic styles will speak to a wide age group. . . . Concluding with biographical notes on each poet and artist, this rich resource is an obvious choice for teachers, and the exciting interplay between art and the written word will encourage many readers to return again and again to the book." Booklist

★ **Here's** a little poem; a very first book of poetry. collected by Jane Yolen and Andrew Fusek Peters; illustrated by Polly Dunbar. Candlewick Press 2007 104p il $21.99

Grades: PreK　　　　　　　　　　　**811.008**
1. Children's poetry 2. American poetry -- Collections
ISBN 978-0-7636-3141-3; 0-7636-3141-8
　　　　　　　　　　　　　　　　LC 2006-40621

"This big, spacious anthology of more than 60 poems is a wonderful first book to read with babies and toddlers over and over again. . . . The clear, active, mixed-media illustrations show very young children outdoors and in; morning to bedtime; loving, teary, absurd, furious." Booklist

★ **Hip** hop speaks to children; a celebration of poetry with a beat. editor, Nikki Giovanni; advisory editors, Tony Medina, Willie Perdomo, Michele Scott; series editor, Dominique Raccah; illustrators, Kristen Balouch, Michele Noiset, Jeremy Tugeau, Alicia Vergel de Dios, and Damian Ward. Sourcebooks Jabberwocky 2008 72p il $19.99

Grades: 3 4 5 6　　　　　　　　　　**811.008**
1. American poetry -- Collections 2. American poetry -- African American authors -- Collections
ISBN 978-1-4022-1048-8; 1-4022-1048-5
　　　　　　　　　　　　　　　　LC 2008004627

"Editor Giovanni states, 'Poetry with a beat. That's hip hop in a flash,' and she goes on to link hip-hop to grand opera and present a capsule history of African American vernacular music. This features a wide-ranging selection of 51 entries, plus a CD with new or previously released recorded versions of 29, some with music. The poets range from Langston Hughes and W.E.B. DuBois to Kanye West, Mos Def, and Queen Latifah. . . . Although created by five illustrators, the art shares both vibrant colors and a dancing free-spirited look that matches the general tone of the poetry." Booklist

★ **I** am the darker brother; an anthology of modern poems by African Americans. edited and with an afterword by Arnold Adoff; drawings by Benny Andrews; introduction by Rudine Sims Bishop; foreword by Nikki Giovanni. rev ed; Simon & Schuster Bks. for Young Readers 1997 208p il hardcover o.p. pa $5.99

Grades: 6 7 8 9 10　　　　　　　　　**811.008**
1. Children's poetry -- Collections 3. American poetry -- African American authors -- Collections 4. American poetry -- African American authors -- Juvenile literature
ISBN 0-689-81241-8; 0-689-80869-0 pa
　　　　　　　　　　　　　　　　LC 97-144181

First published 1968

This anthology presents "the African-American experience through poetry that speaks for itself. . . . Because of the

historical context of many of the poems, the book will be much in demand during Black History Month, but it should be used and treasured as part of the larger canon of literature to be enjoyed by all Americans at all times of the year. An indispensable addition to library collections." SLJ

★ **I**, too, sing America; three centuries of African American poetry. [selected and annotated by] Catherine Clinton; illustrated by Stephen Alcorn. Houghton Mifflin 1998 128p il $21

Grades: 6 7 8 9　　　　　　　　　　**811.008**
1. African Americans -- Poetry 2. American poetry -- Afro-American authors 3. American poetry -- African American authors -- Collections
ISBN 0-395-89599-5
　　　　　　　　　　　　　　　　LC 97-46137

"For each poet, Clinton provides a biography and a brief, insightful commentary on the poem(s) she has chosen, including a discussion of political as well as literary connections. Alcorn's dramatic, full-page, full-color illustrations opposite each poem evoke the quiltlike patterns and rhythmic figures of folk art." Booklist

★ **In** daddy's arms I am tall; African Americans celebrating fathers. illustrated by Javaka Steptoe. Lee & Low Bks. 1997 un il $15.95; pa $6.95

Grades: K 1 2 3　　　　　　　　　　**811.008**
1. Children's poetry 2. Fathers -- Poetry 3. African Americans -- Poetry 4. American poetry -- Collections 5. Fathers -- Juvenile literature
ISBN 1-880000-31-8; 1-58430-016-7 pa
　　　　　　　　　　　　　　　　LC 97-7311

Coretta Scott King Award for illustration

A collection of poems celebrating African-American fathers by Angela Johnson, E. Ethelbert Miller, Carole Boston Weatherford, and others

"Certain poems . . . elevate this collection above the mundane, but it is the illustrations that set this volume apart. Steptoe uses a variety of materials and techniques and art forms to enhance the language of the poems, including torn paper, collages, realia, paintings, and drawings." Horn Book

Incredible inventions; poems selected by Lee Bennett Hopkins; illustrations by Julia Sarcone-Roach. Greenwillow Books 2009 27p il $17.99; lib bdg $18.89

Grades: 1 2 3 4　　　　　　　　　　**811.008**
1. Inventions -- Poetry 2. American poetry -- Collections
ISBN 978-0-06-087245-8; 0-06-087245-4; 978-0-06-087246-5 lib bdg; 0-06-087246-2 lib bdg
　　　　　　　　　　　　　　　　LC 2008003830

"Ingenious inventions are the focus of this lively picture-book poetry collection. Contributed by both well-known and emerging poets, the selections represent a wide range of styles. . . . The subjects, drawn from a young person's everyday world, add to the poems' accessiblity. . . . The mixed-media artwork's well-designed compositions add energy without overwhelming the words." Booklist

★ **A kick** in the head; selected by Paul B. Janeczko; illustrated by Chris Raschka. Candlewick Press 2005 61p il $17.99; pa $9.99

Grades: 4 5 6 7　　　　　　　　　　**811.008**
1. Children's poetry 2. Poetry -- Collections 3.

American poetry -- Collections
ISBN 978-0-7636-0662-6; 0-7636-0662-6; 978-0-7636-4132-0 pa; 0-7636-4132-4 pa

LC 2004-48508

"Raschka's high-spirited, spare torn-paper-and-paint collages ingeniously broaden the poems' wide-ranging emotional tones. . . . Clear, very brief explanations of poetic forms . . . accompany each entry; a fine introduction and appended notes offer further information. . . . This is the introduction that will ignite enthusiasm." Booklist

Knock at a star; a child's introduction to poetry. [compiled by] X. J. Kennedy and Dorothy M. Kennedy; illustrated by Karen Lee Baker. rev ed; Little, Brown 1999 180p il hardcover o.p. pa $12.99
Grades: 3 4 5 6   **811.008**
1. Children's poetry, English 2. Children's poetry, American 3. English poetry -- Collections 4. American poetry -- Collections
ISBN 0-316-48436-9; 0-316-48800-3 pa

LC 98-21572

A revised and newly illustrated edition of the title first published 1982

An anthology of mostly very short poems by standard, contemporary, and anonymous poets, intended to stimulate interest in reading and writing poetry

"Karen Lee Baker's small, shaded-pencil drawings capture the many moods of the verse." Booklist

★ **Lives**: poems about famous Americans; selected by Lee Bennett Hopkins; illustrated by Leslie Staub. HarperCollins Pubs. 1999 31p il $15.99
Grades: 4 5 6 7   **811.008**
1. American poetry -- Collections
ISBN 0-06-027767-X; 0-06-027768-8 lib bdg

LC 98-29851

A collection of poetic portraits of sixteen famous Americans from Paul Revere to Neil Armstrong, by such authors as Jane Yolen, Nikki Grimes, and X. J. Kennedy

"Hopkins's eloquent introduction praises the power of poetry. Concluding 'Notes on the Lives' give readers useful biographical information. Full-page portraits feature Staub's distinctive, flat, primitive style, and their backgrounds have details particular to the subject. . . . A winning combination of poems and illustrations." SLJ

★ **Marvelous** math; a book of poems. selected by Lee Bennett Hopkins; illustrated by Karen Barbour. Simon & Schuster Bks. for Young Readers 1997 31p il hardcover o.p. pa $6.99
Grades: 3 4 5   **811.008**
1. Mathematics -- Poetry 2. American poetry -- Collections
ISBN 0-689-80658-2; 0-689-84442-5 pa

LC 96-21597

Presents such poems as "Math Makes Me Feel Safe," "Fractions," "Pythagoras," and "Time Passes," by such writers as Janet S. Wong, Lee Bennett Hopkins, and Ilo Orleans

"Rhymed and open verse styles are represented, as are a variety of tones. . . . Barbour's lively illustrations dance and play around the poems. Her boldly outlined watercolor figures, often wearing ill-fitting hats, fill the pages with childlike whimsy." SLJ

More pocket poems; selected by Bobbi Katz; illustrated by Deborah Zemke. Dutton Children's Books 2009 28p il $17.99
Grades: K 1 2 3   **811.008**
1. American poetry -- Collections
ISBN 978-0-525-42076-7; 0-525-42076-2

LC 2008013883

"This brightly illustrated anthology presents 44 short poems for children. . . . [It has a] thematic arrangement by season, cycling from spring to winter. . . . Writers represented include Eve Merriam, Emily Dickinson, Alan Benjamin, Langston Hughes, Arnold Lobel, Myra Cohn Livingston, Betsy Franco, Aileen Fisher, Jack Prelutsky, and John Ciardi. Lively, upbeat paintings illustrate each verse." Booklist

★ **My** America; a poetry atlas of the United States. selected by Lee Bennett Hopkins; illustrated by Stephen Alcorn. Simon & Schuster Bks. for Young Readers 2000 83p il $21.95
Grades: 4 5 6 7   **811.008**
1. Children's poetry, American 2. American poetry -- Collections 3. United States -- Juvenile poetry
ISBN 0-689-81247-7

LC 98-47402

A collection of poems evocative of seven geographical regions of the United States, including the Northeast, Southeast, Great Lakes, Plains, Mountain, Southwest, and Pacific Coast States.

"Some poems are purposive, but the best . . . capture places and people in all their diversity. Stephen Alcorn's handsome, multi-textured pictures . . . avoid literal interpretation and capture the sweep of the land and the rhythm of the words." Booklist

The **Oxford** book of children's verse in America; edited by Donald Hall. Oxford University Press 1985 xxxviii, 319p $39.95; pa $19.95
Grades: 5 6 7 8 9 10 11 12 Adult   **811.008**
1. American poetry -- Collections 2. Children's poetry -- Collections 3. American poetry -- Collections -- Juvenile literature
ISBN 0-19-503539-9; 0-19-506761-4 pa

LC 84-20755

"A fine and carefully winnowed collection of American poetry is gathered in a book that will interest students of children's literature and young people who simply enjoy browsing." Horn Book

★ The **Place** my words are looking for; what poets say about and through their work. selected by Paul B. Janeczko. Bradbury Press 1990 150p il $17.95
Grades: 4 5 6 7   **811.008**
1. Poetics 2. American poetry -- Collections 3. Children's poetry -- Collections 4. American poets -- Juvenile literature
ISBN 0-02-747671-5

LC 89-39331

"More than forty contemporary poets are included: Eve Merriam, X. J. Kennedy, Felice Holman, Gary Soto, Mark Vinz, Karla Kuskin, and John Updike, among others. Their contributions vary widely in theme and mood and style, though the preponderance of the pieces are written in modern idiom and unrhymed meter. The accompanying comments frequently are as insightful and eloquent as the poems themselves." Horn Book

Poetry speaks to children; editor, Elise Paschen; illustrators, Judy Love, Wendy Rasmussen, Paula Zinngrabe Wendland. Sourcebooks 2005 104p il $19.95

Grades: 3 4 5 6　　　　　　　　　**811.008**
1. American poetry -- Collections
ISBN 1-4022-0329-2; 978-1-4022-0329-9

"A fine, basic collection. Approximately half of the 97 selections are read or performed on the accompanying CD. The book provides a mix of adult writers (Rita Dove, Seamus Heaney, and Billy Collins, among others) and those whose work is specifically for children, such as X. J. Kennedy and Mary Ann Hoberman. Topics include childhood, animals, nonsense poems, and humor. . . . The three illustrators have captured the different tones of the selections." SLJ

★ A **Poke** in the I; [selected by] Paul Janeczko; illustrated by Chris Raschka. Candlewick Press 2001 35p il hardcover o.p. pa $7.99

Grades: 4 5 6 7 8 9 10　　　　　　　**811.008**
1. American poetry 2. Concrete poetry, American 3. Children's poetry, American 4. American poetry -- Collections
ISBN 0-7636-0661-8; 0-7636-2376-8 pa

LC 00-33675

"Thirty concrete poems of all shapes and sizes are carefully laid on large white spreads, extended by Raschka's quirky watercolor and paper-collage illustrations. . . . Beautiful and playful, this title should find use in storytimes, in the classroom, and just for pleasure anywhere." SLJ

★ The **Random** House book of poetry for children; selected and introduced by Jack Prelutsky; illustrated by Arnold Lobel. Random House 1983 248p il $19.95; lib bdg $21.99

Grades: 3 4 5 6　　　　　　　　　**811.008**
1. English poetry -- Collections 2. American poetry -- Collections 3. Children's poetry -- Collections
ISBN 0-394-85010-6; 0-394-95010-0 lib bdg

LC 83-2990

In this anthology emphasis "is placed on humor and light verse; but serious and thoughtful poems are also included. . . . Approximately two thirds of the selections were written within the past forty years—the splendid contributions of such writers as John Ciardi, Aileen Fisher, Dennis Lee, Myra Cohn Livingston, David McCord, Eve Merriam, and Lilian Moore. [There are] . . . samplings of earlier poets from Shakespeare and Blake to Emily Dickinson and Walter de la Mare." Horn Book

★ **Read** a rhyme, write a rhyme; poems selected by Jack Prelutsky; illustrated by Meilo So. Alfred A. Knopf 2005 23p il $16.95

Grades: 2 3 4　　　　　　　　　**811.008**
1. Poetics 2. Children's poetry 3. American poetry -- Collections
ISBN 0-375-82286-0

LC 2004-26501

"Prelutsky designed this collection to jumpstart children's creative juices. Three short poems were chosen for each theme: dogs, food, birthdays, bugs, cows, friends, snow, turtles, rain, and self. He also includes a poemstart:

an unfinished verse, along with advice and lists of rhyming words, so that readers can complete the poem on their own. The compiler displays a fine sense for lighthearted, kid-friendly poetry. . . . So's watercolor-and-ink illustrations add playfully jumbled perspectives." SLJ

★ **Read**-aloud rhymes for the very young; selected by Jack Prelutsky; illustrated by Marc Brown; with an introduction by Jim Trelease. Knopf 1986 98p il $19.95; lib bdg $21.99

Grades: K 1 2　　　　　　　　　**811.008**
1. Nursery rhymes 2. English poetry -- Collections 3. American poetry -- Collections 4. Children's poetry -- Collections
ISBN 0-394-87218-5; 0-394-97218-X lib bdg

LC 86-7147

"Prelutsky has selected and combined joyous, sensitive poems . . . by such traditional poets as Dorothy Aldis and A. A. Milne, as well as by more contemporary poets such as Karla Kuskin, Dennis Lee, and Prelutsky himself. All are lively, rhythmic poems that young children will enjoy. . . . Brown's bright pastel illustrations effectively use framing, action, and cheerful creatures to echo the light tone of the book. The poems are arranged with others of the same topic and include popular concerns of small children such as animals, bath time, dragons, and play. Teachers and librarians will appreciate poems about seasons, months, holidays, and special events that can be easily incorporated into story hours and classroom life." SLJ

★ **Sharing** the seasons; a book of poems. selected by Lee Bennett Hopkins; illustrated by David Diaz. Margaret K. McElderry Books 2010 83p il $21.99

Grades: 3 4 5　　　　　　　　　**811.008**
1. Seasons -- Poetry 2. American poetry -- Collections
ISBN 978-1-4169-0210-2; 1-4169-0210-4

LC 2009-19297

"This dynamic collection features 48 poems—12 for each of the seasons—mingling previously published poems by Carl Sandburg, Karla Kuskin, and others, with new works by several poets, including Hopkins. The diverse, accessible selections create a mosaic that stirs the senses. Diaz's ethereal silhouettes of animals and people, which resemble layered, cut-paper shadows, are ornately inlaid with nature motifs." Publ Wkly

Sky magic; poems. selected by Lee Bennett Hopkins; illustrated by Mariusz Stawarski. Dutton Children's Books 2009 31p il $17.99

Grades: 1 2 3　　　　　　　　　**811.008**
1. Children's poetry 2. Stars -- Poetry 3. American poetry -- Collections
ISBN 978-0-525-47862-1; 0-525-47862-0

LC 2008034222

"Hopkins has gathered 14 poems about the sun, moon, and stars. Some are by well-known authors, like Carl Sandburg and Tennessee Williams, while others are less familiar. Almost all of the selections are short, wistful, free verse, and well crafted. The dreamlike tone is reflected in Stawarski's quasi-surrealistic illustrations." SLJ

★ **Soul** looks back in wonder; [illustrated by] Tom Feelings. Dial Bks. 1993 un il hardcover o.p. pa $7.99
Grades: 4 5 6 7 **811.008**
1. African Americans -- Poetry 2. Children's poetry -- Collections 4. American poetry -- Collections -- Juvenile literature 5. American poetry -- African American authors -- Collections 6. American poetry -- African American authors -- Juvenile literature
ISBN 0-8037-1001-1; 0-14-056501-9 pa
LC 93-824
Coretta Scott King Award for illustration
Artwork and poems by such writers as Maya Angelou, Langston Hughes, and Askia Toure portray the creativity, strength, and beauty of their African American heritage
"This thoughtful collection of poetry is unique. . . . Feelings selected sketches done while he was in West Africa, South America, and at home in America. The original drawings were enhanced with colored pencils, colored papers, stencil cut-outs, and other techniques to give a collage effect. Marbled textures bring vibrancy to the work." Horn Book

★ **Switching** on the moon; a very first book of bedtime poems. collected by Jane Yolen and Andrew Fusek Peters; illustrated by G. Brian Karas. Candlewick Press 2010 95p il $21.99
Grades: PreK K **811.008**
1. Lullabies 2. Children's poetry 3. Night -- Poetry 4. Sleep -- Poetry 5. Bedtime -- Poetry 6. American poetry -- Collections
ISBN 0763642495; 9780763642495; 978-0-7636-4249-5; 0-7636-4249-5
LC 2008025442
This is an anthology of sixty poems for bedtime reading by authors from Britain, Canada and the United States. Subjects include "the moon, dreams, lullabies, stars, bathtime, bedtime, the dark, night sounds, toothbrushes. [Indexes.] Preschool." (Horn Book)
"Yolen and Peters's 60-poem anthology reveals the many faces of nighttime through the words of these collaborators as well as poets that include Tennyson, Plath, Lee Bennett Hopkins, and Mary Ann Hoberman. . . . With Kara's mixed-media illustrations creating a chalky, dreamlike atmosphere, this book is made for bedtime." Publ Wkly

There's no place like school; classroom poems. selected by Jack Prelutsky; illustrations by Jane Manning. Greenwillow Books 2010 32p il $16.99; lib bdg $17.89
Grades: K 1 2 3 **811.008**
1. Schools -- Poetry 2. American poetry -- Collections
ISBN 978-0-06-082338-2; 0-06-082338-0; 978-0-06-082339-9 lib bdg; 0-06-082339-9 lib bdg
LC 2009020373
This is a "picture-book collection of poems that range from the classroom to the cafeteria to the playground. Contributed by well-known poets, including Carol Diggory Shields and Lee Bennett Hopkins, the mostly rhyming, lighthearted selections hit familiar targets. . . . The energetic, fruit-juice-hued watercolor scenes hum with cheerful energy and subversive humor and, like the poems, capture the chaotic intensity and fun of a typical school day." Booklist

★ **Words** with wings; a treasury of African-American poetry and art. selected by Belinda Rochelle. HarperCollins Pubs. 2001 un il lib bdg $18.99
Grades: 4 5 6 7 **811.008**
1. American poetry 2. African Americans in art 3. Afro-Americans 4. Afro-Americans in art 5. African Americans -- Poetry 6. Afro-Americans -- Juvenile poetry 7. Afro-Americans in art -- Juvenile literature 8. Children's poetry, American -- Afro-American authors 9. American poetry -- African American authors -- Collections
ISBN 0-688-16415-3
LC 00-26864
Pairs twenty works of art by African-American artists such as Horace Pippin and Jacob Lawrence with twenty poems by African-American poets such as Langston Hughes, Countee Cullen, and Lucille Clifton
"Most of the combinations are stunning. . . . Short biographical paragraphs on each poet and artist round out this moving presentation." SLJ

812 American drama in English

Black, Ann N.
Readers theatre for middle school boys; investigating the strange and mysterious. illustrated by Cody Rust. Teachers Idea Press 2008 190p il (Readers theatre) pa $30
Grades: Adult Professional **812**
1. Readers' theater 2. Drama -- Collections 3. Children's reading -- Projects 4. Plays for library presentation
ISBN 978-1-59158-535-0 pa; 1-59158-535-X pa
LC 2007034923
"This book provides solid offerings of Readers Theater scripts for educators working with middle school boys. Selections include adaptations of such creepy classics as 'The Legend of Sleepy Hollow,' 'The Masque of the Red Death,' . . . and 'The Monkey's Paw.' The scripts have a new, fresh feel, and contain plenty of elements to capture and maintain adolescent males' attention." Libr Media Connect
Includes bibliographical references

Bruchac, Joseph
Pushing up the sky: seven Native American plays for children; illustrated by Teresa Flavin. Dial Bks. for Young Readers 2000 94p il hardcover o.p. $21.99
Grades: 3 4 5 **812**
1. Native American drama 2. Plays 3. Drama -- Collections 4. Children's plays, American 5. Indians of North America -- Drama 6. Indians of North America -- Juvenile drama
ISBN 0-8037-2168-4; 0-8037-2535-3 pa
LC 98-20483
Uses drama to tell seven different stories from Native American traditions including the Abenaki, Ojibway, Cherokee, Cheyenne, Snohomish, Tlingit, and Zuni
"The short, simple scripts are accessible to young, inexperienced actors. . . . Suggestions are given for easy-to-make costumes, props, and scenery. A variety of pen-and-ink drawings illustrate the plays, as well as one lively gouache illustration per selection." SLJ
Includes bibliographical references

Dabrowski, Kristen

My first monologue book; 100 monologues for young children. by Kristen Dabrowski. Smith and Kraus 2006 112p (Young actors series) pa $11.95

Grades: 2 3 4 5 6   **812**

1. Acting 2. Monologues

ISBN 1-57525-533-2 pa; 978-1-57525-533-0 pa

LC 2006938162

"Dabrowski offers short, accessible selections on common topics such as games, families, food, friends, school, and wishes. The true-to-life experiences and emotions are delivered in a child's voice and run the gamut from funny to serious." SLJ

My second monologue book; famous and historical people: 101 monologues for young children. Smith and Kraus 2008 115p il (My first acting series) pa $11.95

Grades: 2 3 4 5 6   **812**

1. Acting 2. Monologues

ISBN 978-1-57525-601-6 pa; 1-57525-601-0 pa

LC 2008927862

Presents over a hundred monologues focusing on ordinary and famous people designed for use by children who are just starting with acting

"The monologues and activities will fire the imaginations of young students." SLJ

My third monologue book; places near and far: 102 monologues for young children. Smith and Kraus Publishers 2008 116p il (My first acting series) pa $11.95

Grades: 2 3 4 5 6   **812**

1. Acting 2. Monologues

ISBN 978-1-57525-602-3

LC 2008927864

This collection of monologues is "divided into four parts: places you know (the woods, grandma's house), places in the United States (Laredo, TX; Flagstaff, AZ), foreign countries (Italy, Morocco), and imaginary and far-out places (Hogwarts, an alien world). . . . Concluding activities range from figuring out where the character is, to circling or underlining grammar clues, to completing a travel journal. [This is a] good [addition] as [it suggests] well-rounded activities for students to practice reading, writing, speaking, and both critical and imaginative thinking." SLJ

Fredericks, Anthony D.

African legends, myths, and folktales for readers theatre; illustrated by Bongaman. Teachers Ideas Press 2008 xxiii, 166p il map (Readers theatre) pa $25

Grades: Adult Professional   **812**

1. Folk literature 2. Readers' theater 3. Tales -- Africa 4. Folklore -- Africa 5. Drama -- Collections 6. Children's reading -- Projects 7. Plays for library presentation 8. School libraries -- Services to blacks

ISBN 978-1-59158-633-3 pa; 1-59158-633-X pa

LC 2007-44594

Author Tony Fredericks and illustrator, Bongaman, present readers theatre scripts based on traditional African folklore. Includes background information for teachers on each African country, as well as instruction and presentation suggestions, and additional resources for studies of African folklore

"For the most part, the stories . . . are short, lively, and often humorous. . . . A valuable volume." SLJ

Includes bibliographical references

Levine, Karen

★ Hana's suitcase on stage; original story by Karen Levine; play by Emil Sher. Second Story 2007 171p il (Holocaust remembrance book for young readers) pa $18.95

Grades: 5 6 7 8   **812**

1. Children's plays 2. Holocaust victims 3. Holocaust, 1933-1945 -- Drama

ISBN 978-1-89718-705-0 pa; 1-89718-705-X pa

"Set in the Tokyo Holocaust Center, the two-act play opens with the woman and two of her student helpers questioning and searching for answers to the suitcase's history. . . . Act II blends characters of Ishioka and her students with Hana and her family, each group individually recounting their stories in alternating voices. As with the original book, this title succeeds in recreating a striking representation of one child's tragic and beautiful life in a terrifying world of hate and prejudice. This volume will serve as one of the most effective teaching models for Holocaust curriculums available. Photographs and facsimiles of Nazi documents are included." SLJ

Shepard, Aaron

Stories on stage; children's plays for reader's theater (or readers theatre), with 15 Play scripts from 15 authors. 2nd ed; Shepard 2005 160p pa $15

Grades: Adult Professional   **812**

1. Readers' theater 2. Drama -- Collections

ISBN 0-938497-22-7

First published 1993 in H. W. Wilson Co.

A collection of twenty-two plays adapted from folk tales, short stories, myths, and novels and intended for use in reader's theater programs

"With its mix of humor, fantasy, and multicultural tales . . . this book gives teachers both a fun and useful tool for bringing reading and literature to their students." SLJ

813   American fiction in English

Ada, Alma Flor

Under the royal palms; a childhood in Cuba. Atheneum Bks. for Young Readers 1998 85p il $15

Grades: 4 5 6 7   **813**

1. Authors 2. Educators 3. Dramatists 4. Women authors 5. Authors, American 6. Children's authors 7. Cuba -- Social life and customs 8. Cuba -- Intellectual life -- Juvenile literature 9. Cuba -- Social life and customs -- Juvenile literature 10. Authors, Cuban -- 20th century -- Biography -- Juvenile literature 11. Authors, American -- 20th century -- Biography -- Juvenile literature

ISBN 0-689-80631-0

LC 97-48887

The author recalls her life and impressions growing up in Cuba

"The attention paid to small daily things as well as the occasional awareness of historical events will encourage readers to look for their own family stories." Booklist

Barracca, Debra

★ The **adventures** of Taxi Dog; by Debra and Sal Barracca; pictures by Mark Buehner. Dial Bks. for Young Readers 1990 30p il $16.99; pa $5.99

Grades: PreK K 1 2   **813**

1. Stories in rhyme 2. Dogs -- Fiction 3. Taxicabs -- Fiction

ISBN 0-8037-0671-5; 0-14-056665-1 pa

LC 89-1056

"In snappy, rhymed lines, Maxi recalls his days as a stray and his adoption by taxi-driving Jim. Applying oil paint over acrylics, Buehner creates color with lush character. The hues' intense depth, coupled with the artist's finesse with perspective, will draw readers into the action." Booklist

Other titles about Maxi, the Taxi Dog are:

Maxi, the hero (1991)

Maxi, the star (1993)

A Taxi Dog Christmas (1994)

Borden, Louise

The **little** ships; the heroic rescue at Dunkirk in World War II. illustrated by Michael Foreman. Margaret K. McElderry Bks. 1997 un il hardcover o.p. pa $6.99

Grades: K 1 2 3   **813**

1. World War, 1939-1945 -- Fiction 2. Dunkerque (France), Battle of, 1940 -- Fiction 3. Dunkerque (France), Battle of, 1940 -- Juvenile literature

ISBN 0-689-80827-5; 0-689-85396-3 pa

LC 95-52557

A young English girl and her father take their sturdy fishing boat and join the scores of other civilian vessels crossing the English Channel in a daring attempt to rescue Allied and British troops trapped by Nazi soldiers at Dunkirk

"Borden's descriptive style is potent, and Foreman's watercolors perfectly express the dulled and watery scenes of devastation, the exhausted and hopeful soldiers awaiting rescue." Horn Book Guide

Bunting, Eve

★ **Flower** garden; written by Eve Bunting; illustrated by Kathryn Hewitt. Harcourt Brace & Co. 1994 un il $16; pa $7; bd bk $10.95

Grades: K 1 2 3   **813**

1. Stories in rhyme 2. Flowers -- Fiction 3. Birthdays -- Fiction

ISBN 0-15-228776-0; 0-15-202372-0 pa; 0-15-206516-4 bd bk

LC 92-25766

"The simple rhymed verse, which skips along in pace with the child's anticipation, is smoothly integrated with the vibrant, lifelike paintings." Booklist

Ehlert, Lois

★ **Feathers** for lunch. Harcourt Brace Jovanovich 1990 un il $17; pa $7

Grades: PreK K 1 2   **813**

1. Stories in rhyme 2. Cats -- Fiction 3. Birds -- Fiction 4. Birds -- Juvenile literature

ISBN 0-15-230550-5; 0-15-200986-8 pa

LC 89-29459

"Ehlert has attempted many things in these pages—for instance, the birds are all drawn life-size—and has succeeded in all of them; her lavish use of bold color against generous amounts of white space is graphically appealing,

and the large type, nearly one-half-inch tall, invites attempts by those just beginning to read. An engaging, entertaining, and recognizably realistic story." Horn Book

★ **Nuts** to you! Harcourt Brace Jovanovich 1993 un il $17; pa $7

Grades: PreK K 1 2   **813**

1. Stories in rhyme 2. Squirrels -- Fiction

ISBN 0-15-257647-9; 0-15-205064-7 pa

LC 92-19441

"A frisky squirrel digs up bulbs and steals birdseed from a nearby feeder; in his boldest act, he enters the young narrator's apartment through a tear in the window screen. The quick-thinking child entices the mischievous squirrel back outside with some peanuts. . . . The story, told in brisk rhyme, is a fast-paced romp, and the large, dramatically styled collages will dazzle even the largest audiences. . . . The four concluding pages offer basic information about squirrels." Horn Book

Fleischman, Sid

★ The **abracadabra** kid; a writer's life. Greenwillow Bks. 1996 198p il hardcover o.p. $16.99

Grades: 5 6 7 8   **813**

1. Authors 2. Magicians 3. Magazine editors 4. Authors, American 5. Children's authors 6. Young adult authors

ISBN 0-688-14859-X; 0-688-15855-2 pa

LC 95-47382

This autobiography, "turns real life into a story complete with cliffhangers. And it's a classic boy's story, from card tricks and traveling magic shows to World War II naval experiences and screen-writing gigs for John Wayne movies. En route, we learn how Fleischman learned the craft of writing." Bull Cent Child Books

Includes bibliographical references

Fleming, Denise

★ **Barnyard** banter. Holt & Co. 1994 un il $17.95; pa $7.95; bd bk $7.95

Grades: PreK K 1 2   **813**

1. Stories in rhyme 2. Animals -- Fiction

ISBN 0-8050-1957-X; 0-8050-5581-9 pa; 0-8050-6594-6 bd bk

LC 93-11032

All the farm animals are where they should be, clucking and mucking, mewing and cooing, except for the missing goose

"Strong rhythm and rhyme, plus fun onomatopoetic animal sounds, demand reading aloud. But even more delightful than the engaging text are Fleming's spectacular illustrations. . . . They create realistically textured, bold, bright settings for the whimsical critters to romp through." SLJ

★ **In** the small, small pond. Holt & Co. 1993 un il $17.95; pa $7.95

Grades: PreK K 1   **813**

1. Stories in rhyme 2. Pond ecology -- Fiction

ISBN 0-8050-2264-3; 0-8050-5983-0 pa

LC 92-25770

A Caldecott Medal honor book, 1994

Illustrations and rhyming text describe the activities of animals living in and near a small pond as spring progresses to autumn

"The brilliant, primitive illustrations were made by pouring colored cotton pulp through hand-cut stencils. Against the eye-catching colors, the four-word rhymes in bold black print dance, each double-page spread picturing and describing a different creature. Text, pictures, layout, and design are all beautifully done." SLJ

★ **In** the tall, tall grass. Holt & Co. 1991 un il $17.95; pa $7.99

Grades: PreK K 1   **813**

1. Stories in rhyme 2. Animals -- Fiction

ISBN 0-8050-1635-X; 0-8050-3941-4 pa

LC 90-26444

Rhymed text (crunch, munch, caterpillars lunch) presents a toddler's view of creatures found in the grass from lunchtime till nightfall, such as bees, ants, and moles

"Boldly colored in grassy greens, sunny yellows, and evening blues, the impressionistic illustrations make this a real treat for eyes as well as ears." Booklist

Fradin, Dennis Brindell

Zora! the life of Zora Neal Hurston. Judith Bloom Fradin and Dennis Brindell Fradin. Clarion Books 2012 xi, 180 p.p. ill. $17.99

Grades: 5 6 7 8   **813**

1. African American authors -- Biography 2. African American women -- Biography -- Juvenile literature 3. African American authors -- Biography -- Juvenile literature 4. Folklorists -- United States -- Biography -- Juvenile literature 5. Authors, American -- 20th century -- Biography -- Juvenile literature

ISBN 0547006950; 9780547006956

LC 2011025949

This book by Dennis Brindell Fradin and Judith Bloom Fradin presents a "biography of . . . African-American author . . . [Zora Neale] Hurston. . . . Beginning with a . . . scene of the 59-year-old Hurston, already a well-known author, working as a white family's domestic helper because she needed a paycheck, the Fradins . . . establish the complexities of Zora's inner and external worlds, before offering highlights of her life in chronological order." (Publishers Weekly)

Includes bibliographical references and index.

Fritz, Jean

Harriet Beecher Stowe and the Beecher preachers. Putnam 1994 144p il $15.99; pa $5.99

Grades: 5 6 7 8   **813**

1. Authors 2. Novelists 3. Abolitionists 4. Women authors 5. Authors, American 6. Children's authors 7. Nonfiction writers 8. Short story writers

ISBN 0-399-22666-4; 0-698-11660-7 pa

LC 93-6408

This is a biography of the abolitionist author of "Uncle Tom's Cabin" with an emphasis on the influence of her preacher father and her family on her life and work.

"Written with vivacity and insight, this readable and engrossing biography is an important contribution to women's history as well as to the history of American letters." Horn Book

Includes bibliographical references

Geisert, Arthur

★ **Pigs** from 1 to 10. Houghton Mifflin 1992 32p il hardcover o.p. pa $6.95

Grades: 1 2 3 4   **813**

1. Counting 2. Pigs -- Fiction 3. Puzzles -- Juvenile literature

ISBN 0-395-58519-8; 0-618-21611-1 pa

LC 92-5097

Ten pigs go on an adventurous quest. The reader is asked to find all ten of them, and the numerals from zero to nine, in each picture

"Geisert's inventiveness knows no bounds, and his illustrations both inspire the imagination and convey a homey charm. The final page, a triumphant aggregation of pigs and numbers, is especially endearing." Publ Wkly

Guarino, Deborah

Is your mama a llama? illustrated by Steven Kellogg. Scholastic 1989 un il hardcover o.p. pa $6.99; bd bk $6.99

Grades: PreK K   **813**

1. Stories in rhyme 2. Llamas -- Fiction 3. Animals -- Fiction 4. Riddles -- Juvenile literature

ISBN 0-590-41387-2 lib bdg; 0-439-59842-7 pa; 0-590-25938-5 bd bk

LC 87-32315

A young llama asks his friends if their mamas are llamas and finds out, in rhyme, that their mothers are other types of animals

"The lines are clean as well as exuberant, the colors well-blended as well as bright, and the compositions uncluttered as well as appealing. An ingenious page design invites choral participation, and the ending will encourage a cozy hiatus for bed/nap time." Bull Cent Child Books

Hamanaka, Sheila

All the colors of the earth. Morrow Junior Bks. 1994 un il $17.99; pa $6.99

Grades: 1 2 3 4   **813**

1. Stories in rhyme

ISBN 0-688-11131-9; 0-688-17062-5 pa

LC 93-27118

Reveals in verse that despite outward differences children everywhere are essentially the same and all are lovable

"A poetic picture book and an exemplary work of art. . . . Hamanaka's oil paintings are all double-page spreads filled with the colors of earth, sky, and water, and the texture of the artist's canvas shines through. The text is arranged in undulant waves across each painting." SLJ

Hamilton, Virginia

★ **Virginia** Hamilton: speeches, essays, and conversations; edited by Arnold Adoff & Kacy Cook. Blue Sky Press 2010 368p $29.99

Grades: 8 9 10 11 12 Adult Professional   **813**

1. Authorship 2. Children's literature -- History and criticism

ISBN 978-0-439-27193-6; 0-439-27193-2

LC 2009031676

"A groundbreaking writer of children's fiction, folktales, biography, and picture books, Hamilton won every major award, and much of this book is made up of her acceptance speeches, including those for the Newbery, Hans Christian Andersen, and Coretta Scott King awards, as well as her Arbuthnot and Zena Sutherland lectures. Aimed at a general audience, the book employs a tone both scholarly and informal, as Hamilton talks about her career as a woman and a black writer in America and about the form and content of her work in general and with particular titles. . . . Many speeches include introductions by children's literature scholars and editors, who add perspective on Hamilton's lasting influence, while family members fill in biographical details. A must for YAs who love her books, this will also appeal to librarians, teachers, and children's literature students." Booklist

Includes bibliographical references

Juster, Norton

The **annotated** Phantom tollbooth; by Norton Juster; illustrations by Jules Feiffer; introduction and notes by Leonard Marcus. Alfred A. Knopf 2011 284p il $29.99; lib bdg $32.22

Grades: Adult Professional   **813**

1. Authors 2. Architects 3. Children's authors
ISBN 978-0-375-85715-7; 0-375-85715-X; 978-0-375-95715-4 lib bdg; 0-375-95715-4 lib bdg

LC 2011013174

"Still ferrying dazzled readers to Dictionopolis and beyond 50 years after his first appearance, young Milo is accompanied this time through by encyclopedic commentary from our generation's leading (and most readable) expert on the history of children's literature and publishing. . . . Leonard opens with typically lucid and well-organized pictures of both Juster's and Feiffer's formative years and later careers, interwoven with accounts of the book's conception, publication and critical response. In notes running alongside the ensuing facsimile, he puts on an intellectual show. . . . he delivers notes on topics as diverse as the etymological origins of "BALDERDASH!" and mimetic architecture to textual parallels with the Wizard of Oz and echoes of Winsor McKay and George Grosz in the art. Family photos, scrawled notes and images of handwritten and typescript manuscript pages further gloss a work that never ages nor fails to astonish." Kirkus

Kehret, Peg

Five pages a day; a writer's journey. Whitman, A. 2002 185p lib bdg $15.99

Grades: 4 5 6 7   **813**

1. Authors 2. Women authors 3. Authors, American 4. Children's authors 5. Children's stories -- Authorship -- Juvenile literature 6. Authors, American -- 20th century -- Biography -- Juvenile literature
ISBN 0-8075-8650-1

LC 2002-16768

A biography of the author of numerous books for young people, describing her childhood bout with polio, how she became a writer, family relationships, and the importance of writing in her life

"With the same eye for well-chosen details that characterizes her other writing, [Kehret] mines her experiences for anecdotes young readers will appreciate." Booklist

Lester, Helen

Author; a true story. Houghton Mifflin 1997 32p il $11

Grades: K 1 2 3   **813**

1. Authors 2. Authorship 3. Women authors 4. Children's authors 5. Elementary school teachers
ISBN 0-395-82744-2

LC 96-9645

An "autobiographical look at the evolution of a writer describes Lester's experiences—including her earliest three-year-old scribbles and the acceptance of her first manuscript (on the seventh try). Illustrated with Lester's own rather childlike illustrations, this lighthearted but realistic (and helpful) guide for the writer has lots of fresh tips for young authors-in-the-making." Horn Book Guide

Lowry, Lois

Looking back; a book of memories. Houghton Mifflin 1998 181p il $17

Grades: 5 6 7 8   **813**

1. Authors 2. Novelists 3. Women authors 4. Authors, American 5. Young adult authors 6. Authors, American -- 20th century -- Biography -- Juvenile literature
ISBN 0-395-89543-X

LC 98-11376

Using family photographs and quotes from her books, the author provides glimpses into her life

"A compelling and inspirational portrait of the author emerges from these vivid snapshots of life's joyful, sad and surprising moments." Publ Wkly

Martin, Bill

Polar bear, polar bear, what do you hear? by Bill Martin, Jr.; pictures by Eric Carle. Holt & Co. 1991 un il $16.95; bd bk $7.95

Grades: PreK K   **813**

1. Stories in rhyme 2. Animals -- Fiction 3. Animal communication -- Juvenile literature
ISBN 0-8050-1759-3; 0-8050-5388-3 bd bk

LC 91-13322

Zoo animals from polar bear to walrus make their distinctive sounds for each other, while children imitate the sounds for the zookeeper

"Carle's characteristically inventive, jewel-toned artwork forms a seamless succession of images that fairly leap off the pages." Publ Wkly

★ The **maestro** plays; by Bill Martin, Jr.; pictures by Vladimir Radunsky. Holt & Co. 1994 un il $15.95

Grades: K 1 2 3   **813**

1. Stories in rhyme 2. Musicians -- Fiction
ISBN 0-8050-1746-1

LC 94-1916

"At center stage is a clown-like creature, 'The Maestro,' who plays a progression of instruments. And how does he play? In an intriguing variety of ways, including some that are easy enough to understand ('flowingly, glowingly, knowingly, showingly, goingly') and some that will require youngsters to use their imaginations ('nippingly, drippingly, zippingly, clippingly, pippingly.'" Publ Wkly

McPhail, David M.

★ **Pigs** aplenty, pigs galore! [by] David McPhail. Dutton Children's Bks. 1993 un il hardcover o.p. pa $6.99

Grades: PreK K 1 2   **813**

1. Stories in rhyme 2. Pigs -- Fiction
ISBN 0-525-45079-3; 0-14-055313-4 pa

LC 92-27986

"The rhyme is bouncy enough, but it's the pictures that will have parents and kids howling. Using deep watercolors set against a black background, McPhail presents a magnificent group of porkers, whose capacity for costumes and capers is truly wondrous." Booklist

Other titles about the pigs are:

Pigs ahoy! (1995)

Those can-do pigs (1996)

Miller, William

Zora Hurston and the chinaberry tree; illustrated by Cornelius Van Wright and Ying-hwa Hu. Lee & Low Bks. 1994 un il $15.95; pa $6.95

Grades: K 1 2 3   **813**

1. Authors 2. Novelists 3. Dramatists 4. Women authors 5. African American authors 6. Memoirists 7. Folklorists 8. Short story writers

ISBN 1-880000-14-8; 1-880000-33-4 pa

LC 94-1291

"Conveying the changing expressions on the face of the young Hurston as easily as they show the grandeur of the sky at nightfall, the versatile artists neatly capture the emotions in this lucidly told story." Publ Wkly

Paulsen, Gary

★ **How** Angel Peterson got his name; and other outrageous tales about extreme sports. Wendy Lamb Bks. 2003 111p hardcover o.p. pa $5.99

Grades: 5 6 7 8   **813**

1. Authors 2. Sled dog racers 3. Authors, American 4. Children's authors 5. Short story writers 6. Young adult authors 7. Authors, American -- 20th century -- Biography -- Juvenile literature

ISBN 0-385-72949-9; 0-385-90090-2 lib bdg; 978-0-440-22935-3 pa; 0-440-22935-9 pa

LC 2002-7668

Author Gary Paulsen relates tales from his youth in a small town in northwestern Minnesota in the late 1940s and early 1950s, such as skiing behind a souped-up car and imitating daredevil Evel Knievel

"Writing with humor and sensitivity, Paulsen shows boys moving into adolescence believing they can do anything. . . . None of them dies (amazingly), and even if Paulsen exaggerates the teensiest bit, his tales are side-splittingly funny and more than a little frightening." Booklist

★ **My** life in dog years; with drawings by Ruth Wright Paulsen. Delacorte Press 1998 137p il $15.95; pa $6.50

Grades: 4 5 6 7   **813**

1. Dogs 2. Authors 3. Sled dog racers 4. Authors, American 5. Children's authors 6. Short story writers 7. Young adult authors 8. Dogs -- United States -- Anecdotes -- Juvenile literature 9. Dog owners -- United States -- Biography -- Juvenile literature 10. Authors, American -- 20th century -- Biography -- Juvenile literature

ISBN 0-385-32570-3; 0-440-41471-7 pa

LC 97-40254

The author describes some of the dogs that have had special places in his life, including his first dog, Snowball, in the Philippines; Dirk, who protected him from bullies; and Cookie, who saved his life

"Paulsen differentiates his canine friends beautifully, as only a keen observer and lover of dogs can. At the same time, he presents an intimate glimpse of himself, a lonely child of alcoholic parents, who drew strength and solace from his

four-legged companions and a love of the great outdoors. Poignant but never saccharine, honest, and open." Booklist

Peet, Bill

★ **Bill** Peet: an autobiography. Houghton Mifflin 1989 190p il hardcover o.p. pa $15

Grades: 4 5 6 7   **813**

1. Artists 2. Authors 3. Illustrators 4. Authors, American 5. Children's authors

ISBN 0-395-50932-7; 0-395-68982-1 pa

LC 88-37067

A Caldecott Medal honor book, 1990

"Every page of this oversized book is illustrated with Peet's unmistakable black-and-white drawings of himself and the people, places, and events described in the text. Familiar characters from his books and movies appear often." SLJ

Pilkey, Dav

The **Hallo**-wiener. Blue Sky Press (NY) 1995 un il $16.95; pa $5.99

Grades: PreK K 1 2   **813**

1. Dogs -- Fiction 2. Halloween stories 3. Halloween -- Fiction

ISBN 0-590-41703-7; 0-439-07946-2 pa

LC 94-40949

All the other dogs make fun of Oscar the dachshund until one Halloween when, dressed as a hot dog, Oscar bravely rescues the others

"Pilkey's bold, colorful illustrations add life to his simple tale of courage and friendship." Horn Book Guide

Rosen, Michael J.

Elijah's angel; a story for Chanukah and Christmas. illustrated by Aminah Brenda Lynn Robinson. Harcourt Brace Jovanovich 1992 un il hardcover o.p. pa $6

Grades: 2 3 4   **813**

1. Clergy 2. Artists 3. Sculptors 4. Barbers 5. Woodworkers 6. Jews -- Fiction 7. Hanukkah stories 8. Christmas stories 9. Artists -- Fiction 10. Hanukkah -- Fiction 11. Christmas -- Fiction

ISBN 0-15-201556-2; 0-15-225394-7 pa

LC 91-37552

At Christmas-Hanukkah time, Elijah Pierce, a black Christian woodcarver gives a carved angel to Michael, a young Jewish friend, who struggles with accepting the Christmas gift until he realizes that friendship means the same thing in any religion

"Perhaps because it's based on reality, Michael and Elijah's relationship rings sweetly true. The naive-style paintings, done in house paint on scrap rags, boldly simulate woodcuts, and though the artwork is not pretty, it, too, has the feel of reality." Booklist

Scieszka, Jon

★ The **Frog** Prince continued; story by Jon Scieszka; paintings by Steve Johnson. Viking 1991 un il $15.99; pa $6.99

Grades: 2 3 4 5   **813**

1. Fairy tales 2. Frogs -- Fiction

ISBN 0-670-83421-1; 0-14-054285-X pa

LC 90-26537

After the frog turns into a prince, he and the Princess do not live happily ever after and the Prince decides to look for a witch to help him turn back into a frog

"The dialogue is witty; the plot, as logical as it is offbeat. Steve Johnson's paintings, executed in a rich and somber palette, are like stage settings; his depiction of the various characters is inspired." Horn Book

Small, David
  George Washington's cows. Farrar, Straus and Giroux 1994 un il hardcover o.p. pa $6.95
Grades: PreK K 1 2   **813**
  1. Generals 2. Presidents 3. Stories in rhyme 4. Animals -- Fiction
  ISBN 0-374-32535-9; 0-374-42534-5 pa
               LC 93-39989
Humorous rhymes about George Washington's farm where the cows wear dresses, the pigs wear wigs, and the sheep are scholars

"Small's watercolors immeasurably extend his zany poem and make maximum use of the double-page spreads. Cleverly designed and well-executed scenes are filled with silly details that children will love." Booklist

Soto, Gary
  Too many tamales; illustrated by Ed Martinez. Putnam 1992 un il $16.99; pa $7.99
Grades: PreK K 1 2   **813**
  1. Christmas stories 2. Christmas -- Fiction 3. Mexican Americans -- Fiction
  ISBN 0-399-22146-8; 0-698-11412-4 pa
               LC 91-19229
Maria tries on her mother's wedding ring while helping make tamales for a Christmas family get together, but panic ensues when hours later, she realizes the ring is missing

This is "a very funny story, full of delicious surprise. The handsome, realistic oil paintings, in rich shades of brown, red, and purple, are filled with light, evoking the togetherness of an extended family." Booklist

Spinelli, Jerry
  ★ Knots in my yo-yo string; the autobiography of a kid. Knopf 1998 148p il hardcover o.p. pa $10.95
Grades: 4 5 6 7   **813**
  1. Authors 2. Magazine editors 3. Authors, American 4. Children's authors
  ISBN 0-679-98791-6; 0-679-88791-1 pa
               LC 97-30827
This Italian-American Newbery Medalist presents a humorous account of his childhood and youth in Norristown, Pennsylvania

"There is an 'everyboy' universality to Spinelli's experiences, but his keen powers of observation and recall turn the story into a richly rewarding personal history." Horn Book Guide

Stewart, Sarah
  The library; pictures by David Small. Farrar, Straus & Giroux 1995 un il $16.50; pa $6.95
Grades: K 1 2 3   **813**
  1. Stories in rhyme 2. Picture books 3. Librarianship -- Poetry 4. Books and reading -- Fiction
  ISBN 0-374-34388-8; 0-374-44394-7 pa
               LC 94-30320

Elizabeth Brown loves to read more than anything else, but when her collection of books grows and grows, she must make a change in her life

"Framed watercolors give the book an old-fashioned, scrapbooklike appearance. . . . Small black-ink line drawings decorate the verses below and often add an additional touch of humor. This is a funny, heartwarming story about a quirky woman with a not-so-peculiar obsession." SLJ

Thurber, James
  ★ Many moons; illustrated by Marc Simont. Harcourt Brace Jovanovich 1990 un il $17
Grades: 1 2 3 4   **813**
  1. Fairy tales 2. Princesses -- Fiction
  ISBN 0-15-251872-X
               LC 89-36465
A newly illustrated edition of the title first published 1943

Though many try, only the court jester is able to fulfill Princess Lenore's wish for the moon.

"Simont proves a noble successor to Louis Slobodkin, and his buoyant watercolors, full of poignancy and subtle merriment, more than do justice to Thurber's beloved tale. . . . Even staunch traditionalists will find it hard to resist this new version." Publ Wkly

817 American humor and satire in English

Brewer, Paul
  You must be joking! lots of cool jokes. compiled and illustrated by Paul Brewer; foreword by Kathleen Krull. Cricket Books 2003 107p il $16.95
Grades: 3 4 5 6   **817**
  1. Jokes 2. Riddles 3. Wit and humor 4. Wit and humor, Juvenile
  ISBN 0-8126-2661-3
               LC 2002-13926
A collection of over two hundred jokes and riddles, grouped by subject, plus tips on writing, learning, and telling jokes.

"The cartoon sketches scattered throughout the text add to the humor. A gem among joke books." SLJ

  You must be joking, two! even cooler jokes, plus 11 1/2 tips for laughing yourself into your own stand-up comedy routine. written and illustrated by Paul Brewer. Cricket Books 2007 92p il $16.95
Grades: 3 4 5 6   **817**
  1. Jokes 2. Riddles 3. Wit and humor
  ISBN 978-0-8126-2752-7; 0-8126-2752-0
               LC 2007014450
Includes riddles, jokes, and knock-knocks about monsters, aliens, cyberspace, school, pirates, animals, birds, and bugs

"An introduction plus the 11 ½ Tips will inspire readers to look at everyday events with an eye for humor and offer some suggestions on keeping children's attention, jokes to avoid, stage fright, and more. Black-and-white drawings introduce each chapter and spot art is sprinkled throughout the book. Most collections should make room for this one." SLJ

Freymann, Saxton

Knock, knock! [by] Saxton Freymann . . . [et al.] Dial Books for Young Readers 2007 un il $16.99

Grades: K 1 2   817

1. Jokes 2. Knock-knock jokes 3. American wit and humor -- Juvenile literature

ISBN 978-0-8037-3152-3; 0-8037-3152-3

LC 2006-39463

"14 children's book artists . . . illustrate a different groan-inducing knock-knock joke in signature style. Saxton Freymann uses photos of lettuce ('Lettuce who?' 'Lettuce in!') made to look like pigs. Tomie de Paola creates two love-struck gorillas to illustrate 'Gorilla who?' 'Gorilla my dreams, I love you!' and so on. . . . The artwork is . . . just great and varied enough to keep children turning the pages." Booklist

Rosenthal, Amy Krouse

The **wonder** book; drawings by Paul Schmid. Harper 2010 79p il $17.99

Grades: 2 3 4   817

1. Wit and humor 2. Wit and humor, Juvenile 3. Word games -- Juvenile literature

ISBN 978-0-06-142974-3; 0-06-142974-0

LC 2008-939052

"Here is a joyous, totally original potpourri of stories, poems, lists, palindromes, visual jokes, and random observations about the universal delights and conundrums of childhood. Set squarely in the world of the 21st-century child . . . these varied musings nonetheless speak to everyone's inner child, young or old. . . . Simple, evocative, and childlike black-and-white line drawings, in concert with judicious and varied use of white space, perfectly capture the happy/sad/serious/silly moods of the selections." SLJ

818   American miscellaneous writings in English

Brown, Don

★ **American** boy: the adventures of Mark Twain; written and illustrated by Don Brown. Houghton Mifflin 2003 un il $16

Grades: 2 3 4   818

1. Authors 2. Humorists 3. Novelists 4. Essayists 5. Satirists 6. Memoirists 7. Travel writers 8. Authors, American 9. Short story writers

ISBN 0-618-17997-6

LC 2002-151177

Provides a brief biography of the noted American writer who was born Samuel Clemens

"The boyhood of writer Samuel Clemens is irresistible, with much of his youth inspiring scenes in his works that have become folklore in their own right. Brown does a spirited job of telling some of those stories. . . . Brown's strengths as an artist, making evocative vistas and suggesting architecture and flora, are in evidence here." Booklist

Includes bibliographical references

Cooper, Floyd

★ **Coming** home; from the life of Langston Hughes. Philomel Bks. 1994 un il lib bdg $16.95; pa $6.99

Grades: K 1 2 3   818

1. Poets 2. Authors 3. Novelists 4. Dramatists 5. African American authors 6. Poets, American 7. Short story writers 8. Young adult authors

ISBN 0-399-22682-6 lib bdg; 0-698-11612-7 pa

LC 93-36332

This "biography highlights pivotal events in Hughes's life, emphasizing his loneliness as a child and his development as a poet. . . . Cooper's hazy illustrations in gold, brown, and sepia tones reveal keen observations of people and neighborhood. The text and art combine to create a fine tribute and introduction to the writer's life." Horn Book

Includes bibliographical references

Lewis, J. Patrick

Last laughs; animal epitaphs. J. Patrick Lewis and Jane Yolen; illustrated by Jeffrey Stewart Timmins. Charlesbridge 2012 48 p. ill. (reinforced for library use) $16.95

Grades: 3 4 5 6   818

1. Obituaries 2. Death in literature 3. Animals in literature 4. Animals -- Juvenile humor 5. Animals -- Juvenile poetry

ISBN 1580892604; 9781580892605

LC 2011025702

Author J. Patrick Lewis provides "30 tombstone remembrances [for a variety of animals]. . . . Sometimes they are gruesome, as with the newt, 'so small, / so fine, / so squashed / beneath / the crossing / sign.' There are the macabre and the simply passing: 'In his pond, / he peacefully soaked, / then, ever so quietly / croaked.' [Other animals include] . . . the eel . . . [and] the piranha." (Kirkus Reviews)

McCurdy, Michael

Walden then & now; an alphabetical tour of Henry Thoreau's pond. Charlesbridge 2010 un il lib bdg $16.95

Grades: 4 5 6 7   818

1. Authors 2. Alphabet 3. Naturalists 4. Essayists 5. Pacifists 6. Writers on nature 7. Nonfiction writers 8. Natural history -- Massachusetts

ISBN 978-1-58089-253-7 lib bdg; 1-58089-253-1 lib bdg

LC 2009-26645

"Elegiac woodcarvings evoke the setting of Henry Thoreau's Walden Pond as the text weaves past and present in this lengthy alphabet poem. On each spread, consecutive letters face one another, making a couplet of the lines. A dark, but not somber, woodcarving illustrates each letter, and an explanatory paragraph expands upon the information in the verse. . . . The book ends with entries from Thoreau's diary and McCurdy's inspiration and starting point for this book. Purchase as an introduction to Thoreau and for poetry shelves." SLJ

Paulsen, Gary

★ **Caught** by the sea; my life on boats. Delacorte Press 2001 103p maps $15.95; pa $5.50

Grades: 5 6 7 8   818

1. Authors 2. Ocean travel 3. Boats and boating 4. Sled dog racers 5. Authors, American 6. Children's authors 7. Short story writers 8. Young adult authors 9. Ocean travel -- Juvenile literature 10. Boats and boating -- Juvenile literature 11. Authors, American -- 20th century -- Biography -- Juvenile literature

ISBN 0-385-32645-9; 0-440-40716-8 pa

LC 2001-17336

"Paulsen traces his life at sea, from buying his first sail-boat to getting lost in the Pacific to encountering sharks. . . . His sometimes comic, sometimes near-fatal sea-going errors make for absorbing, captivating reading." Booklist

Sandburg, Carl

The **Sandburg** treasury; prose and poetry for young people. introduction by Paula Sandburg; illustrated by Paul Bacon. Harcourt Brace Jovanovich 1970 480p il hardcover o.p. pa $24

Grades: 5 6 7 8   818

1. American literature

ISBN 0-15-202678-9 pa

This volume brings together all of Sandburg's books for young people; his whimsical stories, two books of poetry, a version of his biography of Abraham Lincoln, and portions of his autobiography specially edited for children

818.602

Griffiths, Andy

What Body Part Is That? A Wacky Guide to the Funniest, Weirdest, and Most Disgustingest Parts of Your Body. by Andy Griffiths; illustrated by Terry Denton. 1st U.S. ed. Feiwel & Friends 2012 ix, 180 p.p ill. (hardcover) $12.99

Grades: 3 4 5   818.602

1. Human anatomy -- Juvenile literature 2. Wit and humor, Juvenile 3. Human body -- Juvenile humor 4. Human anatomy -- Juvenile humor

ISBN 0312367902; 9780312367909

LC 2012288587

"This humorous book is about every body part and then some -- from your head to your toes and everything in-between that you can and can't see." (Library Media Connection) Author "[Andy] Griffiths' anatomical tour in general steers clear of anything that would be marked as correct on a test. From 'Ears can be big or small, depending on their size' to 'Capillaries are the larval form of butterflies,' he offers . . . inanities about 68 mostly real body features." (Kirkus Reviews)

820   English and Old English (Anglo-Saxon) literatures

Krull, Kathleen

★ A **pot** o' gold; a treasury of Irish stories, poetry, folklore, and (of course) blarney. selected and adapted by Kathleen Krull; illustrated by David McPhail. Hyperion Books For Children 2004 181p il map hardcover o.p. pa $9.99

Grades: 3 4 5 6   820

1. Irish literature 2. Folklore -- Ireland 3. Ireland -- Literary collections

ISBN 0-7868-0625-7; 1-4231-1752-2 pa

LC 2001-39058

A collection of stories, folklore, poetry, and songs from Ireland, including works by authors such as James Joyce and Oscar Wilde as well as classic myths, stories and poems about Finn McCool, fairies, leprechauns and saints Patrick and Bridget

"Children will love the limericks and the folk riddles. McPhail's signature full-color illustrations enliven the pages and add tremendous appeal for younger readers. The stunning cover and spine shimmer with the gold promised in the title and honor the intricate designs found in the Book of Kells. This is an eclectic grouping and an excellent introduction to the country's culture." SLJ

Includes bibliographical references

821   English poetry

Brown, Calef

His shoes were far too tight; poems. by Edward Lear; selected and introduced by Daniel Pinkwater and illustrated by Calef Brown. Chronicle Books 2010 un il $16.99

Grades: K 1 2 3   821

1. Nonsense verses 2. Poetry -- By individual authors

ISBN 978-0-8118-6792-4; 0-8118-6792-7; 0811867927; 9780811867924

LC 2010008549

"Pinkwater and Brown honor a fellow champion of absurdity, Edward Lear, in this frisky collection. Even before readers get to the poems, a cartoon self-portrait of Lear in the introduction . . . hints at the revelry that's to follow. Brown's elegantly quirky collages convey the gentle lunacy of the Owl and the Pussycat . . . and lesser-known characters. . . . These seasoned collaborators provide an assuring nudge for readers to embrace Lear's sumptuously silly verse." Publ Wkly

Carroll, Lewis, 1832-1898

★ **Jabberwocky**; the classic poem from Lewis Carroll's Through the looking glass, and what Alice found there. reimagined and illustrated by Chistopher Myers. 1st ed. Jump at the Sun/Hyperion Books for Children 2007 1 v. (unpaged) col. ill. $15.99

Grades: 4 5 6 7   821

1. Nonsense verses 2. Children's poetry 3. Poetry -- By individual authors

ISBN 978-1-4231-0372-1; 1-4231-0372-6

LC 2007018337

This reinterpretation of Lewis Carroll's poem about the Jabberwock uses a basketball court as setting. "Ages five to nine." (N Y Times Book Rev)

"Myers cleverly translates Carroll's nonsense poem into a contemporary tale through sports imagery. . . . The spectacular paintings have silhouetted figures on vibrant backgrounds. . . . The jaunty text is in capital letters in an extra-large black font, with some words highlighted in color." SLJ

Cohen, Barbara

★ **Canterbury** tales; [by] Geoffrey Chaucer; selected, translated, and adapted by Barbara Cohen; illustrated by Trina Schart Hyman. Lothrop, Lee & Shepard Bks. 1988 87p il $24.99

Grades: 4 5 6 7   821

1. Poets 2. Authors 3. Middle Ages 4. Poetry -- By individual authors

ISBN 0-688-06201-6

LC 86-21045

"Cohen's evident love and respect for Chaucer's writing keep her close to the text. Her writing retains the flavor of the times and the spirit of Chaucer's words while her prose retelling, enriched by Hyman's lively full-color paintings, enhances the book's appeal to young people. . . . An excellent introduction to The Canterbury Tales for young readers." Booklist

Dahl, Roald

★ **Vile** verses. Viking 2005 191p il $25

Grades: 4 5 6   **821**

1. Humorous poetry 2. Poetry -- By individual authors
ISBN 0-670-06042-9

A collection of Roald Dahl's poems, many previously published in his novels, such as Charlie and the Chocolate Factory and James and the , Giant Peach,and illustrated by various artists such as Tony Ross, Lane Smith, Quentin Blake, and Chris Riddle

"This vivacious addition to poetry collections will amuse a broad audience." SLJ

Howitt, Mary Botham

The **spider** and the fly; based on the poem by Mary Howitt; with illustrations by Tony DiTerlizzi. Simon & Schuster Bks. for Young Readers 2002 un il $16.95

Grades: K 1 2 3   **821**

1. Flies -- Poetry 2. Spiders -- Poetry 3. Poetry -- By individual authors
ISBN 0-689-85289-4

LC 2002-5760

An illustrated version of the well-known poem about a wily spider who preys on the vanity and innocence of a little fly

"Rendered in black-and-white gouache and pencil, then reproduced in silver-and-black duotone, the paintings have a spooky quality perfectly suited to retelling this melancholy tale. Ms. Fly, with her whimsical flower umbrella and Roaring '20s attire, captures the flavor of an old-time Hollywood heroine." SLJ

Hughes, Ted, 1930-1998

Collected poems for children; pictures by Raymond Briggs. Farrar, Straus and Giroux 2007 259p il $18

Grades: 3 4 5 6   **821**

1. Children's poetry 2. Poetry. 3. Children's poetry, English. 4. Poetry -- By individual authors
ISBN 978-0-374-31429-3; 0-374-31429-2

LC 2006-37437

First published 2005 in the United Kingdom

This is a "collection of 250 poems by the late English poet laureate Ted Hughes. . . . Children will love the sounds of the rhythmic lines, and Briggs' scattering of small black-and-white drawings perfectly captures the tiny details in the words." Booklist

Includes bibliographical references

Kipling, Rudyard, 1865-1936

If; a father's advice to his son. [by] Rudyard Kipling; photographs by Charles R. Smith. Atheneum Books for Young Readers 2007 un il $14.99

Grades: 4 5 6   **821**

1. Poetry -- By individual authors
ISBN 978-0-689-87799-5; 0-689-87799-4

LC 2006005312

"Kipling's powerful poem comes to life for a contemporary audience in atmospheric photographs that use the

metaphor of sports. A lovely shot of a boy heading a soccer ball accompanies the opening couplet: 'If you can keep your head/when all about you/are losing theirs/and blaming it on you.' The mood and actions in most of the illustrations clearly invoke the verse." SLJ

Lear, Edward, 1812-1888

The **complete** verse and other nonsense; compiled and edited with an introduction and notes by Vivien Noakes. Penguin Bks. 2002 566p il pa $18

Grades: 4 5 6 7 8 9 10 11 12 Adult   **821**

1. Nonsense verses 2. Nonsense verses, English 3. Nonsense literature, English 4. Poetry -- By individual authors
ISBN 0-14-200227-5

LC 2002-28998

This volume "presents all of Lear's verse and other nonsense writings, including stories, letters, and illustrated alphabets, as well as previously unpublished material, line drawings, and . . . [an] introduction by scholar Vivien Noakes." Publisher's note

Includes bibliographical references

★ **Edward** Lear; edited by Edward Mendelson; illustrated by Laura Huliska-Beith. Sterling 2002 48p il (Poetry for young people) $14.95; pa $6.95

Grades: 4 5 6 7   **821**

1. Limericks 2. Nonsense verses 3. Poetry -- By individual authors
ISBN 0-8069-3077-2; 1-4027-7294-7 pa

LC 2001-20112

"In an analytical introduction, Mendelson looks at Lear's serious and silly sides before selecting 15 limericks and 18 longer poems, all of which feature odd creatures adapting to, or reveling in, their differences. Sporting conical noses or other physical peculiarities, Huliska-Beit's smiling, rubber-limbed figures dance through vertiginously tilted, brightly colored minimalist settings. . . . Thought- and laugh-provoking." Booklist

★ **Edward** Lear's The duck & the kangaroo; illustrated by Jane Wattenberg. Greenwillow Books 2009 un il $17.99

Grades: PreK K 1 2   **821**

1. Nonsense verses 2. Ducks -- Poetry 3. Kangaroos -- Poetry 4. Poetry -- By individual authors
ISBN 0-06-136683-8; 978-0-06-136683-3

LC 2008024126

"Duck, envious of Kangaroo's hop . . . asks to ride upon the larger animal's back. Upon reflection, Kangaroo expresses his concern that Duck's wet and cold feet will give him rheumetism. Duck solves the problem by wearing beautifully knitted socks. . . . Wattenberg's quirky photo collages . . . are perfectly suited for Lear's nonsensical text." Booklist

★ The **owl** and the pussycat; by Edward Lear; illustrated by Anne Mortimer. Katherine Tegen Books 2006 un il $15.99; lib bdg $16.89

Grades: K 1 2 3   **821**

1. Nonsense verses 2. Cats -- Poetry 3. Owls -- Poetry 4. Poetry -- By individual authors
ISBN 0-06-027228-7; 0-06-027229-5 lib bdg

LC 2003015476

After a courtship voyage of a year and a day, Owl and Pussy finally buy a ring from Piggy and are blissfully married

"Lear's poem is beautifully illustrated with a mixture of elaborate, stylized borders and sumptuous portrayals of natural elements like verdant plant and tree leaves and colorful tropical flowers." SLJ

The **owl** and the pussycat and other nonsense; Edward Lear; illustrated by Robert Ingpen. Palazzo 2012 48 p. col. ill.

Grades: 2 3 4   **821**

1. Nonsense verses 2. Animals -- Poetry 3. Children's poetry 4. English poetry 5. Animals -- Juvenile poetry 6. Children's poetry, English

ISBN 9780957148307

LC 2011287935

This children's collection, by Edward Lear, illustrated by Robert Ingpen, honors the 200th birthday anniversary of the poet and "features seven of his poems, including 'The Owl and the Pussycat,' 'The Jumblies,' and 'The Dong with a Luminous Nose.' . . . For readers who want to immerse themselves in the writer's world, there is some biographical information as well as some reproductions of his paintings and a letter." (School Library Review)

Milne, A. A.

★ **Now** we are six; with decorations by Ernest H. Shepard. Dutton 1961 104p il $22.99; pa $4.99

Grades: K 1 2 3   **821**

1. Poetry -- By individual authors

ISBN 0-525-44960-4; 0-14-0361234-3 pa

First published 1927. Reprinted September 1961 in this completely new format designed by Warren Chappell. Verso of title page

"The boy or girl who has liked 'When were were very young' and 'Winnie-the-Pooh' will enjoy reading about Alexander Beetle who was mistaken for a match, the knight whose armor didn't squeak, and the old sailor who had so many things which he wanted to do. There are other entertaining poems, also, and many pictures as delightful as the verses." Pittsburgh

★ **When** we were very young; with decorations by Ernest H. Shepard. Dutton 1961 102p il $11.99; pa $6.99

Grades: K 1 2 3   **821**

1. Poetry -- By individual authors

ISBN 0-525-44445-9; 0-14-036123-5 pa

First published 1924. Reprinted September 1961 in this completely new format designed by Warren Chappell. Verso of title page

"Mr. Milne's gay jingles have found a worthy accompaniment in the charming illustrations of Mr. Shepard." Saturday Rev

Stevenson, Robert Louis

★ **A child's** garden of verses; by Robert Louis Stevenson; illustrated by Tasha Tudor. rev format ed; Simon & Schuster Books for Young Readers 1999 67p il $19.99

Grades: K 1 2 3   **821**

1. Scottish poetry 2. Poetry -- By individual authors

ISBN 0-689-82382-7

LC 98-19561

"Verses known and loved by one generation after another. Among the simpler ones for preschool children are: Rain; At the Seaside; and Singing." Right Book for the Right Child

Williams, Marcia

★ **Chaucer's** Canterbury Tales; retold and illustrated by Marcia Williams. Candlewick Press 2007 45p il $16.99

Grades: 4 5 6 7   **821**

1. Poets 2. Authors 3. Middle Ages 4. Poetry -- By individual authors

ISBN 978-0-7636-3197-0; 0-7636-3197-3

A retelling in comic strip form of Geoffrey Chaucer's famous work in which a group of pilgrims in fourteenth-century England tell each other stories as they travel on a pilgrimage to the cathedral at Canterbury

"Chaucer's pilgrims come to life in the energetic retelling of nine tales. . . . The watercolor-and-ink cartoon-art displayed in a comic-book format is a perfect match for the raucous and sometimes-raw humor." SLJ

822.3   Drama of Elizabethan period, 1558-1625

Coville, Bruce

William Shakespeare's A midsummer night's dream. Dial Bks. 1996 un $17.95; pa $7.99

Grades: 5 6 7 8 9   **822.3**

1. Poets 2. Authors 3. Audiobooks 4. Dramatists

ISBN 0-8037-1784-9; 0-14-250168-9 pa

LC 94-12600

A simplified prose retelling of Shakespeare's play about the strange events that take place in a forest inhabited by fairies who magically transform the romantic fate of two young couples.

"Coville introduces the story and also conveys something of the poetry and drama. Nolan's framed graphite and watercolor paintings express the dreaminess and absurdity of the play, and the pictures have a theatrical flair." Booklist

William Shakespeare's Macbeth; retold by Bruce Coville; pictures by Gary Kelley. Dial Bks. 1997 un il $18

Grades: 5 6 7 8 9   **822.3**

1. Poets 2. Authors 3. Dramatists

ISBN 0-8037-1899-3

LC 97-7582

A simplified prose retelling of Shakespeare's play about a man who kills his king after hearing the prophesies of three witches

"Kelley's framed pastel illustrations of the hideous hags will hold kids from the start, and Coville's dramatic narrative will keep them reading. . . . Words and pictures are true to the dark, brooding spirit of the play." Booklist

William Shakespeare's Romeo and Juliet; retold by Bruce Coville; pictures by Dennis Nolan. Dial Bks. 1999 un il $16.99

Grades: 5 6 7 8 9   **822.3**

1. Poets 2. Authors 3. Dramatists 4. Verona (Italy) -- Juvenile fiction 5. Romeo (Fictitious character) -- Juvenile fiction 6. Juliet (Fictitious character) -- Juvenile fiction

ISBN 0-8037-2462-4

LC 98-36178

A simplified prose retelling of Shakespeare's play about two young people who defy their warring families' prejudices and dare to fall in love

"Coville's treatment is generally faithful to the original and is nicely enhanced by Dennis Nolan's lushly romantic illustrations. . . . This is an accessible and enticing introduction to one of Shakespeare's most popular works." Booklist

William Shakespeare's Twelfth night; retold by Bruce Coville; illustrated by Tim Raglin. Dial Bks. 2003 un il $16.99

Grades: 5 6 7 8 9   **822.3**
1. Poets 2. Authors 3. Dramatists 4. Brothers and sisters -- Juvenile fiction 5. Survival after airplane accidents, shipwrecks, etc -- Juvenile fiction
ISBN 0-8037-2318-0

LC 2001-28252

This "provides a short, prose version of Shakespeare's Twelfth Night. . . . Though simplified, the story is intact and bits of the original language are preserved. Large-scale ink drawings, warmed with tints of color and shaded with crosshatching, clearly depict the action." Booklist

Nettleton, Pamela Hill
William Shakespeare; playwright and poet. by Pamela Hill Nettleton. Compass Point Books 2005 112p il map (Signature lives) lib bdg $30.60

Grades: 5 6 7 8   **822.3**
1. Poets 2. Authors 3. Dramatists
ISBN 0-7565-0816-9

LC 2004-23081

Profiles the life and work of William Shakespeare

"This biography is one of the best available for younger students. Nettleton supplements what little is actually known about the bard's life with detailed and accurate information about everyday life in England during the period, the theater, and publishing practices of the time. The text is enhanced by full-color illustrations and black-and-white reproductions." SLJ

Includes bibliographical references

Packer, Tina
★ **Tales** from Shakespeare; retold by Tina Packer; illustrated by Gail de Marcken . . . [et al.] Scholastic Press 2004 192p il $24.95

Grades: 5 6 7 8   **822.3**
1. Poets 2. Authors 3. Dramatists
ISBN 0-439-32107-7

LC 2003-42710

Tina Packer retells ten of Shakespeare's plays. The stories are illustrated by various artists: Macbeth by Barry Moser, The Tempest by Mark Teague, Othello by Kadir Nelson, Twelfth Night by Chesley McLaren, Romeo and Juliet by David Shannon, Much Ado About Nothing by Mary Grand-Pre, King Lear by Leo and Diane Dillon, As You Like It by Barbara McClintock, A Midsummer Night's Dream by Gail De Marcken, and Hamlet by P.J. Lynch

This is "a treasure trove of well-told tales. In these adaptations, Packer captures the essence of the playwright's words and ideas, placing them in concise and clearly told stories. . . . Each illustrator sets the appropriate tone for and conveys the mood of the tale, and the breadth of artistic interpretations gives the book appeal to a wide audience." SLJ

Raum, Elizabeth
Twenty-first-century Shakespeare. Raintree 2011 32p il (Culture in action) lib bdg $29

Grades: 5 6 7 8   **822.3**
1. Poets 2. Authors 3. Dramatists 4. Dramatists, English 5. Authors, English
ISBN 978-1-4109-3920-3; 1-4109-3920-0

LC 2009050693

This "discusses modern adaptations of the Bard's classic works; teachers may find this a useful resource to help students see how Shakespeare remains a part of today's culture. [This volume is] quick, interesting, up-to-date . . . with plenty of supportive, captioned, full-color photographs. [It] also [provides] related project suggestions." SLJ

Includes glossary and bibliographical references

Stanley, Diane
★ **Bard** of Avon: the story of William Shakespeare; by Diane Stanley and Peter Vennema; illustrated by Diane Stanley. Morrow Junior Bks. 1992 un il hardcover o.p. pa $6.99

Grades: 4 5 6 7   **822.3**
1. Poets 2. Authors 3. Dramatists
ISBN 0-688-09108-3; 0-688-09109-1 lib bdg; 0-688-16294-0 pa

LC 90-46564

A brief biography of the world's most famous playwright, using only historically correct information

"A remarkably rounded picture of Shakespeare's life and the period in which he lived is presented . . . together with a thoughtful attempt to relate circumstances in his personal life to the content of his plays. . . . The text is splendidly supported by the illustrations, which are stylized, yet recognizable, and present a clear view of life in the late sixteenth century. A discerning, knowledgeable biography, rising far above the ordinary." Horn Book

Includes bibliographical references

Weiner, Miriam
Shakespeare's Seasons; created by Miriam Weiner; illustrations by Shannon Whitt; edited by Miriam Weiner & Shannon Whitt. Downtown Bookworks 2012 1 v. (unpaged) col. ill. (hardcover) $16.99

Grades: K 1 2 3   **822.3**
1. Seasons
ISBN 1935703579; 9781935703570

In this book by author Miriam Weiner, "tiny snippets of Shakespeare form the text for an illustrated almanac. . . . Readers see children on the beach flying kites and building sandcastles, watched by a woman with a book. The beachscape is visually anchored by the head of a woman with long hair, hinting that this may be a memory. . . . The longest quote is eight lines but most are four or less. . . . [Weiner incorporates] The Winter's Tale, The Tempest . . . [and] As You Like It." (Kirkus Reviews)

823   English fiction

Bannerman, Helen
★ The **story** of Little Babaji; illustrated by Fred Marcellino. HarperCollins Pubs. 1996 un il $16.99; pa $7.95

Grades: PreK K 1 2 **823**
1. Fables 2. Tigers -- Fiction
ISBN 0-06-205064-8; 0-06-008093-0 pa

In this edition of the Story of Little Black Sambo, originally published 1899, the characters have been given Indian names

Babaji gives his new clothing to tigers who threaten to eat him, but they chase one another around a tree until they turn to butter

"Marcellino has set the story of Little Black Sambo in India. . . . Except for a change of names . . . Bannerman's text is essentially unaltered, retaining the narrative rhythm that has always paced a tightly patterned plot. Marcellino's watercolor paintings project a toy-like quality that emphasizes humor over suspense." Bull Cent Child Books

Colbert, David
The **magical** worlds of Harry Potter; David Colbert. Updated and complete ed. Berkley Books 2008 xi, 209 p.p ill. (paperback) $14.00
Grades: 5 6 7 8 **823**
1. Authors 2. Novelists 3. Fantasy writers 4. Children's authors 5. Young adult authors 6. Fantasy fiction -- History and criticism 7. Rowling, J.K. 1965 -- characters
ISBN 0425223183; 9780425223185
LC 2008274096

First published 2001 in the United Kingdom; first United States edition 2002

Explores the sources and meanings of aspects of the literary world of Harry Potter within myths, legends, and history.

"Long after the enthusiasm for Harry and friends has abated, this small volume will serve as a resource to answer questions that may result from reading other stories in the genre." SLJ [review of 2002 edition]

Includes bibliographical references (p. 317-318) and index.

Mahy, Margaret
17 kings and 42 elephants; pictures by Patricia MacCarthy. Dial Bks. for Young Readers 1987 26p il $16.99
Grades: K 1 2 3 **823**
1. Stories in rhyme 2. Animals -- Fiction
ISBN 0-8037-0458-5
LC 87-5311

A newly illustrated edition of the title first published 1972 in the United Kingdom

Seventeen kings and forty-two elephants romp with a variety of jungle animals during their mysterious journey through a wild, wet night

"This book takes you on a jungle journey you will never forget. . . . The text is lyrical, humorous, and full of nonsense and fantasy. Children and adults will be charmed by the melodic use of language and the beautiful batik illustrations." Child Book Rev Serv

Wells-Cole, Catherine
Charles Dickens; England's most captivating storyteller. written by Catherine Wells-Cole; including extracts from the works of Charles Dickens. 1st U.S. ed. Candlewick/Templar Books 2011 28 p. ill., maps (some col.) (Historical notebook) (hardcover) $19.99

Grades: 7 8 9 10 11 12 **823**
1. Authors 2. Novelists 3. Authors, English
ISBN 0763655678; 9780763655679
LC 2011013677

This book by Catherine Wells-Cole "provides a . . . glimpse into the life" of author Charles Dickens. "Like a scrapbook, the book includes excerpts from Dickens' personal letters, illustrations from his original books, family photos, and other images from the Victorian age. . . . Double-page spreads focus on Dickens' childhood, family life, and fame. Other spreads focus on topics that influenced his writing, including schools, prisons, and workhouses." (Library Media Connection)

"In this scrapbook homage to Dickens, each page teems with images and reproductions, from letters to book excerpts to maps, all pertaining to a different area of Dickens's life and work. The topics range widely, skimming the surface of both the esteemed author's life and the subjects that interested him most. . . . The gorgeous, high-quality reproductions make a strong visual impact, and while the flaps, folds, and envelopes make readers work to uncover information, most will be quickly drawn into the hunt for more treasured tidbits about Dickens and his time." SLJ

828 English miscellaneous writings

Thomas, Dylan
★ A **child's** Christmas in Wales; illustrated by Chris Raschka. Candlewick Press 2004 un il $17.99
Grades: 2 3 4 5 6 7 8 9 **828**
1. Christmas -- Wales 2. Poets, Welsh -- 20th century -- Biography
ISBN 0-7636-2161-7
LC 2003-65274

The Welsh poet Dylan Thomas recalls the celebration of Christmas with his family and the feelings it evoked in him as a child.

"Applied to torn paper, the ink and watercolors spread through the fibers, freely forming soft outlines and shadows. The result is an intriguing contemporary take on a story that is by now part of the rather staid canon of Christmas classics." N Y Times Book Rev

831 German poetry

Rasmussen, Halfdan
★ A **little** bitty man and other poems for the very young; Halfdan Rasmussen; translated by Marilyn Nelson and Pamela Espeland; illustrated by Kevin Hawkes. Candlewick Press 2011 29 p.
Grades: PreK K 1 **831**
1. Children's poetry, Danish -- Translations into English
ISBN 9780763623791
LC 2009007515

"A charming collection of poems finds an American audience in a splendid translation. . . . Rasmussen (1915-2002) was a beloved Danish poet, known both for his human-rights writings as well as nonsense verse for children. A sweet compendium of the latter is translated here . . . and animated by Hawkes' dynamic, colorful acrylic-and-pencil renderings, effectively capturing the playfulness of Rasmussen's verse in both sound and image." Kirkus

841 French poetry

Cendrars, Blaise
★ **Shadow**; translated and illustrated by Marcia Brown from the French of Blaise Cendrars. Scribner 1982 un il $17; pa $6.99
Grades: 1 2 3   **841**
1. French poetry 2. Children's poetry 3. Shades and shadows -- Poetry 4. Poetry -- By individual authors
ISBN 0-684-17226-7; 0-689-71875-6 pa
LC 81-9424
Original text first published in France
Awarded the Caldecott Medal, 1983
"Inspired by the exotic atmosphere and the dramatic possibilities of the text, Brown has choreographed a sequence of almost theatrical illustrations, placing human and animal figures—and their shadows—against brilliant, contrasting, always changing settings. Resplendent—yet controlled—in color, texture, and form, the work is an impressive, sophisticated example of the art of the picture book." Horn Book

861 Spanish poetry

Argueta, Jorge
★ **A movie** in my pillow; story by Jorge Argueta; illustrations by Elizabeth Gómez. Children's Bk. Press 2001 31p il $15.95
Grades: 3 4 5 6   **861**
1. Immigrants -- Poetry 2. Hispanic Americans -- Poetry 3. Children's poetry, Salvadoran 4. Poetry -- By individual authors 5. Bilingual books -- English-Spanish 6. Children's poetry, Salvadoran -- Translations into English
ISBN 0-89239-165-0
LC 00-55582
"Gómez's rich and bright paintings fill every spread with . . . joy and literal humor. . . . An excellent addition to any poetry collection." SLJ

Lujan, Jorge
Colors! Colores! by Jorge Luján; illustrated by Piet Grobler; translated by John Oliver Simon and Rebecca Parfitt. Groundwood Books 2008 36p il $17.95
Grades: K 1 2   **861**
1. Children's poetry 2. Color -- Poetry 3. Color -- Juvenile literature 4. Poetry -- By individual authors 5. Bilingual books -- English-Spanish
ISBN 978-0-88899-863-7; 0-88899-863-5
This is "a fully illustrated collection of 11 brief, free-verse poems linked by a common theme: colors. Each poem appears in English and then in Spanish on a double-page spread surrounded by white space and accompanied by an eye-catching watercolor painting. . . . Gobler . . . interprets the verse through watercolor paintings that are as spare and fanciful as the writing." Booklist

Messengers of rain and other poems from Latin America; edited by Claudia M. Lee; illustrated by Rafael Yock-teng; translations by Andrew C. Leone . . . [et al.] Douglas & McIntyre 2002 80p il $18.95
Grades: 3 4 5 6   **861**
1. Spanish poetry -- Collections 2. Spanish American poetry -- Translations into English 3. Children's poetry, Spanish American -- Translations into English
ISBN 0-88899-470-2
"The 64 poems from 19 countries include 20th-century classics and more recent selections, and represent women, indigenous writers, and widely published names such as Octavio Paz and Rafael Pombo. . . . Yockteng's fanciful watercolors head each section with a full-page spread, and spots brighten the pages between, here and there, without distracting from the poems." SLJ

883 Classical Greek epic poetry and fiction

Landmann, Bimba
★ **The fate** of Achilles. Getty 2011 il $19.95
Grades: 4 5 6 7   **883**
1. Poets 2. Authors
ISBN 978-1-60606-085-8; 1-60606-085-6
"Landmann (The Incredible Voyage of Ulysses) continues her retelling of Homer's epics with this haunting version of the Iliad. Ghostly, Giacometti-style figures accompany the story of Achilles's life, from his baptism in the river Styx . . . to his departure for Troy, . . . the death of his dearest friend, . . . and his reconciliation with the father of the enemy he has slain. . . . Readers with the patience to sit through saga-length narratives will be fascinated by her prose, which moves easily through the sprawling epic without feeling ponderous or hurried. These kinds of retellings are few and far between, and hers are magic." Publ Wkly

★ **The incredible** voyage of Ulysses; text and illustrations by Bimba Landmann. Getty Publications 2010 un il $19.95
Grades: 4 5 6 7   **883**
1. Poets 2. Authors
ISBN 978-1-60606-012-4; 1-60606-012-0
"With narrative restraint and illustrative power, Landmann's . . . retelling of Homer's Odyssey follows Ulysses as he battles frightening creatures and endures the treachery of the gods while sailing home to Ithaca. . . . The paintings, worked with swift, bold strokes, combine the solemn stiffness of Greek statuary with the prophetic sweep of William Blake's imaginings." Publ Wkly

891 East Indo-European and Celtic literatures

Laird, Elizabeth
Shahnameh; the Persian book of kings. Retold by Elizabeth Laird; illustrated by Shirin Adl. Frances Lincoln Children's Books 2012 129 p.
Grades: 2 3 4 5   **891**
1. Epic poetry 2. Persian legends -- Juvenile literature 3. Persian mythology -- Juvenile literature
ISBN 1847802532; 9781847802538
This children's book, by Elizabeth Laird, illustrated by Shirin Adl, is a "collection of stories and myths from ancient Persia, written into an epic poem by . . . Firdousi in the 10th

century. . . . The tales describe the beginning of the world, and include amazing birds who bring up orphaned Kings, . . . a feisty princess who goes to war incognito, and above all the great hero Rostam, who tragically kills his own son Sohrab, not knowing his identity." (Publisher's note)

895.6 Japanese literature

Kobayashi, Issa

★ **Today** and today; by Kobayashi Issa; pictures by G. Brian Karas. Scholastic Press 2007 un il $16.99

Grades: K 1 2 3   895.6

1. Haiku 2. Children's poetry

ISBN 0-4395-9078-7

LC 2003-26684

"Karas uses the haiku of the eighteenth-century Japanese poet Issa to limn a gentle, understated tale of one family over a year. . . . The translations . . . are simply and clearly crafted. . . . Kara's art, using rice paper, paint, and pencil, is precise, enticing, and evocative." Booklist

897 Literatures of North American native languages

★ **Dancing** teepees: poems of American Indian youth; selected by Virginia Driving Hawk Sneve, with art by Stephen Gammell. Holiday House 1989 32p il $17.95; pa $8.95

Grades: 4 5 6   897

1. Native Americans -- Poetry

ISBN 0-8234-0724-1; 0-8234-0879-5 pa

LC 88-11075

An illustrated collection of poems from the oral tradition of Native Americans

This is an "eclectic collection, drawn from a variety of tribal traditions. Printed on heavy paper, the book is illustrated with a catalogue of marvelously rendered designs and motifs, ranging from those of the Northwest Coast to the intricate beadwork patterns of the Great Lakes and the zig-zag geometric borders of Southwestern pottery." N Y Times Book Rev

900 HISTORY

904 Collected accounts of events

Blackwood, Gary L.

Enigmatic events. Marshall Cavendish Benchmark 2005 72p il (Unsolved history) lib bdg $29.93

Grades: 4 5 6 7   904

1. Disasters 2. Curiosities and wonders 3. History -- Miscellanea

ISBN 0-7614-1889-X

LC 2004-23755

Explores several events that have baffled scientists and historians for years, such as the demise of the dinosaurs, the "lost colony" of Roanoke, the sinking of the Main, and the Hindenberg disaster

This collection of "tidbits about lingering mysteries of the past . . . [offers] more substance than most. . . . [This offers] a full-page illustration opening each chapter; reproductions, many in color; and a generously spaced format." SLJ

Includes glossary and bibliographical references

Guiberson, Brenda Z.

★ **Disasters**; natural and man-made catastrophes through the centuries. Henry Holt and Company 2010 228p il $18.99

Grades: 5 6 7 8 9   904

1. Disasters 2. Natural disasters

ISBN 978-0-8050-8170-1; 0-8050-8170-4

LC 2009018908

"The subtitle provides an accurate outline of the contents of this lively treatment of disasters from smallpox to Hurricane Katrina. In each chapter, Guiberson outlines the sources of the disaster, the results, and means of obviating the problems that caused these tragedies. For example, the chapter on the Great Chicago Fire begins with the construction of the city over unstable marshland. . . . This kind of exhaustive background serves to create an understanding of the contributory issues and demonstrates possible preventive steps. Guiberson's compellingly written exegesis is equally good in the other nine chapters. Well-placed, black-and-white reproductions and photos extend the text. A perfect example of solid historical research coupled with engaging writing." SLJ

Includes bibliographical references

909 World history

Adams, Simon

★ The **Kingfisher** atlas of world history; a pictorial guide to the world's people and events, 10,000 BCE-present. Kingfisher 2010 181p il map $24.99

Grades: 4 5 6 7   909

1. World history 2. Historical geography

ISBN 978-0-7534-6388-8; 0-7534-6388-1

"This colorful and fact-packed book is not only informative but well organized. Sections cover 'The Ancient World,' 'The Medieval World,' 'Exploration and Empire,' and 'The Modern World,' and each section contains 15 or 16 thematic maps presented in chronological order. . . . It is very useful and entertaining as well as data-filled." Booklist

910 Geography and travel

Goodman, Joan E.

A **long** and uncertain journey: the 27,000 mile voyage of Vasco da Gama; by Joan Elizabeth Goodman; illustrated by Tom McNeely. Mikaya Press 2001 47p il map (Great explorers book) $22.95

Grades: 4 5 6 7   910

1. Explorers 2. Explorers -- Portugal -- Biography -- Juvenile literature 3. Discoveries in geography -- Portuguese -- Juvenile literature

ISBN 0-9650493-7-X

LC 00-63795

"McNeely's full-page illustrations, which vibrate with life and action, lighten the format, and quotations from the diary of an anonymous sailor on the voyage add fascinating detail and vivid description. . . . A good resource for reports, but the book is also intelligently written and exciting." Booklist

Jenkins, Steve

★ **Hottest,** coldest, highest, deepest. Houghton Mifflin 1998 un il $16

Grades: K 1 2   910

1. Geography 2. Geography -- Miscellanea 3. Geography -- Juvenile literature
ISBN 0-395-89999-0

LC 97-53080

Describes some of the remarkable places on earth, including the hottest, coldest, windiest, snowiest, highest, and deepest

This book "uses striking colorful paper collage illustrations. . . . This eye-catching introduction to geography will find a lot of use in libraries and classrooms." SLJ

Includes bibliographical references

Rockwell, Anne F.

★ **Our** earth; written and illustrated by Anne Rockwell. Harcourt Brace & Co. 1998 un il hardcover o.p. pa $6

Grades: K 1 2   910

1. Geography
ISBN 0-15-201679-1; 0-15-202383-6 pa

LC 97-1247

A simple introduction to geography which explains such things as how the earth was shaped, how islands are born from volcanoes, and how gushing springs affect rivers

"The watercolor-and-gouache illustrations are very accessible. The pictures should provoke questions; parents and teachers can use the answers to provide kids with more information." Booklist

Rumford, James

Traveling man: the journey of Ibn Battuta, 1325-1354; written, illustrated, and illuminated by James Rumford. Houghton Mifflin 2001 un il map hardcover o.p. pa $7.99

Grades: 3 4 5 6   910

1. Travelers 2. Voyages and travels 3. Travel writers 4. Asia -- Description 5. Voyages and travels -- Juvenile literature 6. Asia -- Description and travel -- Juvenile literature 7. Africa -- Description and travel -- Juvenile literature
ISBN 0-618-08366-9; 0-618-43233-7 pa

LC 00-57257

"Rumford's presentation is lavish and undeniably impressive. Ibn Battuta's route snakes across the spreads to create an extended map, with text boxes serving as stopping points along the way. Lush watercolor scenes, awash in gold highlights, are frequently borded by equally lush calligraphy quotes, rendered in Arabic, Persian, or Chinese." Bull Cent Child Books

Includes glossary

Wojtanik, Andrew, 1989-

The **National** Geographic Bee ultimate fact book; countries A to Z. Andrew Wojtanik. National Geographic 2012 384 p. maps (pbk.) $21.90; (reinforced library binding) $21.90

Grades: 5 6 7 8 9 10   910

1. Atlases 2. Nations 3. Geography 4. Geography -- Encyclopedias
ISBN 1426309473; 1426309635; 9781426309472; 9781426309632

LC 2011282873

This book "provides statistical information for the world's 195 countries at a glance. The book starts off with a world map and full-page continental maps. Individual entries for countries are listed alphabetically. . . . A glossary explains terms that may be unfamiliar to students . . . . Each country entry includes a map with longitude and latitude and basic facts: continent, size, population, and capital." (Voice of Youth Advocates)

Includes bibliographical references (p. 382)

910.2 Miscellany

Ching, Jacqueline

Jobs in green travel and tourism. Rosen Pub. 2010 80p il (Green careers) lib bdg $30.60

Grades: 5 6 7 8   910.2

1. Tourist trade 2. Vocational guidance 3. Environmental movement 4. Environmental protection 5. Travel -- Environmental aspects
ISBN 978-1-4358-3571-9 lib bdg; 1-4358-3571-9 lib bdg

LC 2009016587

This "well-conceived [introduction focuses] on various jobs in [travel and tourism], the education and experience required, and expected earnings. The [book is] well organized, making it easy to gain an overview of the major aspects of the work. . . . [This book] will make [a] good [addition] to career collections. Photographs from the field and website and contact information for professional organizations add value." SLJ

Includes glossary and bibliographical references

910.3 Dictionaries, encyclopedias, concordances, gazetteers

Gifford, Clive

The **Kingfisher** geography encyclopedia; 2nd ed., rev. and updated ed.; Kingfisher 2011 487p il map $34.99

Grades: 4 5 6 7   910.3

1. Reference books 2. Geography -- Encyclopedias
ISBN 978-0-7534-6575-2; 0-7534-6575-2

Statistics, text, and color maps reveal the physical geography, peoples, politics, governments, languages, religions, and currencies of each nation of the world.

"The geographical descriptions are well written and include striking photos. The text is large and easy to read. . . . It is a great book to keep around the library for students to browse and dream about their next journey." Voice Youth Advocates

★ Junior worldmark encyclopedia of the nations; Timothy L. Gall, Susan Bevan Gall, and Derek M. Gleason, editors. 6th ed; Gale, Cengage Learning 2012 3200 p. 10v col. ill. (set: alk. paper) $677

Grades: 5 6 7 8 **910.3**

1. Geography -- Encyclopedias 2. World history -- Encyclopedias 3. Political science -- Encyclopedias

ISBN 1414463138; 9781414463131; 9781414463148; 9781414463155; 9781414463162; 9781414463179; 9781414463186; 9781414463193; 9781414463209; 9781414463216; 9781414463223; 9781414463230; 9781414490861

LC 2011050016

First published 1996

This book series, edited by Timothy L. Gall, Susan Bevan Gall, and Derek M. Gleason, is a juvenile national encyclopedia. "Each volume . . . starts with a table of contents for the specific volume and a guide to country articles. Each country profile, organized alphabetically, begins with . . . capital, flag, anthem, monetary unit, weights and measures. . . Thirty-five color-coded subheadings and their corresponding numbers, as well as geographical profiles, complete each section." (Booklist)

"This new edition contains 196 countries of the world and the Palestinian Territories. Color maps... photos, and charts enhance the overall attractiveness of this updated set... This well-written encyclopedia would be a valuable resource for elementary, middle-school, and public libraries." Booklist

Includes bibliographical references and index

910.4 Accounts of travel and facilities for travelers

Aronson, Marc

★ The **world** made new; why the Age of Exploration happened & how it changed the world. [by] Marc Aronson & John W. Glenn. National Geographic 2007 64p il map $17.95; lib bdg $27.90

Grades: 4 5 6 7 **910.4**

1. Explorers 2. Exploration

ISBN 978-0-7922-6454-5; 978-0-7922-6978-6 lib bdg

LC 2006022091

"This highly pictorial, readable overview provides significant depth of coverage. . . . The illustrations, most in full color, make ample and appropriate use of period prints as well as contemporary illustrations and photographs. The result is a visual feast that fleshes out the . . . remarkably evenhanded narrative." SLJ

Includes glossary and bibliographical references

Benoit, Peter

The **Titanic** disaster. Children's Press 2011 il (True book: disasters) lib bdg $26; pa $6.95

Grades: 3 4 5 **910.4**

1. Shipwrecks

ISBN 978-0-531-20627-0 lib bdg; 0-531-20627-0 lib lib; 978-0-531-29026-2 pa; 0-531-29026-3 pa

LC 2010045932

This describes the sinking of the Titanic in 1912.

"Benoit provides unbiased information that is on target for the intended audience. . . . The photographs and repro-

ductions enhance the [text]. . . . [This book is] well-conceived." SLJ

Includes bibliographical references

Bristow, David

★ **Sky** sailors; true stories of the balloon era. [by] David L. Bristow. Farrar Straus Giroux 2010 134p il $18.99

Grades: 4 5 6 7 **910.4**

1. Balloons

ISBN 978-0-374-37014-5; 0-374-37014-1

LC 2009037285

"This lively look at escapades of daring men—and a surprising number of women—who risked their lives flying in balloons will appeal to adventure, history and science buffs—and perhaps steampunk fans as well. Each of the nine chapters, which are chronologically arranged, focuses on an exciting story, starting with the first confirmed human balloon flight in 1783 . . . and ending with Dolly Shepherd, a young British woman in the early 1900s who parachuted out of balloons, hanging onto a trapeze. . . . Useful captions accompany many full-color illustrations of artwork and photographs." Kirkus

Includes bibliographical references

Brown, Don

★ **All** stations! distress! April 15, 1912, the day the Titanic sank. Roaring Brook Press 2008 un il (Actual times) $17.95

Grades: 2 3 4 **910.4**

1. Shipwrecks 2. Shipwrecks -- North Atlantic Ocean -- Juvenile literature

ISBN 978-1-59643-222-2; 1-59643-222-5

LC 2008-08934

"Don Brown recounts the complicated, compact last moments of the [Titanic's] only voyage. . . . The tale ends with something of the later lives of the survivors. . . . The glory of All Stations! Distress! is in Brown's moody watercolors done with a brush dipped in stardust and frozen mist." Horn Book

Cerullo, Mary M.

★ **Shipwrecks**; exploring sunken cities beneath the sea. [by] Mary M. Cerullo. Dutton Children's Books 2009 64p il $18.99

Grades: 5 6 7 8 **910.4**

1. Shipwrecks 2. Underwater archaeology -- Juvenile literature 3. Underwater exploration -- Juvenile literature

ISBN 978-0-525-47968-0; 0-525-47968-6

LC 2008-48967

This focuses "on two wrecks: the Henrietta Marie, sunk in 1700 near the Florida Keys, and the Portland, sunk in 1898 off the coast of Massachusetts. The book makes the convincing case that these wrecks are important not only for historical reasons but also for the underwater ecosystems their structures now host. . . . This delivers both education and shivers." Booklist

Clifford, Barry

Real pirates; the untold story of the Whydah from slave ship to pirate ship. by Barry Clifford and Kenneth J. Kinkor with Sharon Simpson; photography by Kenneth Garrett. National Geographic 2008 175p il map $16.95

Grades: 4 5 6 7   **910.4**

1. Pirates 2. Archeology 3. Shipwrecks 4. Slave trade
ISBN 978-1-4263-0279-4; 1-4263-0279-7

LC 2008299778

"Clifford, an underwater archaeological explorer, used research and the artifacts recovered from the Whydah to tell the story of its life as a slave galley and pirate ship. In the process, he dispels many myths about buccaneers. . . . Photographs of artifacts . . . and the recovery crew at work combine with large visually appealing paintings of dramatic battle, storm, and courtroom scenes. . . . The book is a fascinating blend of history, ocean-diving recovery, and archaeology, and demonstrates archaeology in action and the role artifacts play in informing us about the past." SLJ

Includes bibliographical references

Denenberg, Barry

★ **Titanic** sinks! Viking 2011 72p il

Grades: 5 6 7 8   **910.4**

1. Shipwrecks
ISBN 0670012432; 9780670012435

LC 2011012040

This is a "gripping recounting of the Titanic's doomed maiden voyage, chronicled in the tabloid-style pages of a fictional magazine. . . . Melding fact and fiction, the book compiles dramatic headlines, articles that range from news bulletins about the building of the ship to a chatty tour of its lavish interior, and an array of stunning period photographs." Publ Wkly

Gibbons, Gail

★ **Sunken** treasure. Crowell 1988 32p il hardcover o.p. pa $6.95

Grades: K 1 2 3   **910.4**

1. Shipwrecks 2. Buried treasure
ISBN 0-690-04736-3 lib bdg; 0-06-446097-5 pa

LC 87-30114

"Gibbons concentrates on the ancient Spanish galleon, the Atocha, which sank off the coast of Florida in 1662, describing under labeled headings the sinking, the search, the find, recording, salvage, restoration and preservation, cataloguing, and eventual distribution of the treasure. . . . A handsomely designed book, well organized, and easily accessible to younger readers." Horn Book

Hagglund, Betty

Epic treks. Kingfisher 2011 64p il (Epic adventure) $19.99

Grades: 5 6 7 8   **910.4**

1. Explorers 2. Voyages and travels
ISBN 978-0-7534-6668-1; 0-7534-6668-6

LC 2011041638

"The graphics will grab readers in [this] exciting, extra-large-size [title] . . . packed with high-quality color photos on every double-page spread. Just as gripping are the narratives, captions, and technical details of exploration, adventure, and survival. . . . Epic Treks covers Lewis and Clark, Livingston and Stanley, Burk and Wells, and Amundsen and Scott, each journey an exciting adventure filled with details about what they endured and what they found, as well as their failures and shortcomings." Booklist

Includes glossary

Hopkinson, Deborah

★ **Titanic**; voices from the disaster. by Deborah Hopkinson. Scholastic Press 2012 289 p.

Grades: 5 6 7 8   **910.4**

1. Titanic (Steamship) 2. Shipwrecks -- Juvenile literature
ISBN 0545116740; 9780545116749

LC 2011006695

YALSA Award for Excellence in Nonfiction for Young Adults Finalist (2013)

Robert F. Sibert Honor Book (2013)

In this book about the sinking of the Titanic, author Deborah "Hopkinson begins with a description of the ship . . . and introduces some of the passengers who embarked on its maiden voyage. The narrative shifts . . . to the disaster itself with a litany of things gone wrong. . . . [M]emoirs . . . are interlaced throughout the text, as survivors testified . . . on the relative chaos or calm, heroism or cowardice, of passengers and crew." (Bulletin of the Center for Children's Books)

Includes bibliographical references

Jenkins, Martin

Titanic; [illustrated by] Brian Sanders. Candlewick Press 2008 31p il map $29.99

Grades: 4 5 6   **910.4**

1. Shipwrecks
ISBN 978-0-7636-3795-8; 0-7636-3795-5

LC 2007-36029

This follows the Titanic's history from the shipyard to its tragic end.

"A series of vignettes and drawings depict the last moments of the tragedy and are helpful to those interested in details. Archival photographs, drawings, sidebars, and inserts extend and clarify the text." Horn Book Guide

Kentley, Eric

Story of the Titanic; illustrated by Steve Noon; written by Eric Kentley. DK Pub. 2001 32p il $17.95

Grades: 4 5 6 7   **910.4**

1. Shipwrecks
ISBN 0-7894-7943-5

LC 2001-28432

"This book, with its oversize format, brief, informative text, and large illustrations, will be a first choice for many children." Booklist

Includes glossary

Marschall, Ken

★ **Inside** the Titanic; illustrated by Ken Marschall; text by Hugh Brewster. Little, Brown 1997 32p il $19.95

Grades: 4 5 6 7   **910.4**

1. Shipwrecks
ISBN 0-316-55716-1

LC 97-382

"Color cutaway paintings of the Titanic in this oversize book allow readers to view every deck as they follow two 12-year-old boys exploring the vessel, and to see how the liner struck the iceberg and sank." Booklist

Includes glossary and bibliographical references

McPherson, Stephanie Sammartino

★ **Iceberg** right ahead! the tragedy of the Titanic. Twenty-First Century Books 2011 112p il

Grades: 4 5 6 7 8 **910.4**
1. Shipwrecks
ISBN 9780761367567

LC 2011002352

"With innumerable books, movies, documentaries, novels, and biographies all telling versions of the Titanic story, it would seem that there is little more to learn, yet by providing more details and some of the most up-to-date research, McPherson's compelling, thoughtful narrative proves otherwise. . . . The layout includes plenty of period photographs, diagrams, artwork, and sidebars with interesting tangential tidbits, making for a thorough resource. . . . A comprehensive, well-written, thoroughly researched title." SLJ

Includes bibliographical references

Mundy, Robyn
Epic voyages. Kingfisher 2011 64p il (Epic adventure) $19.99
Grades: 5 6 7 8 **910.4**
1. Explorers
ISBN 978-0-7534-6574-5; 0-7534-6574-4

"The graphics will grab readers in [this] exciting, extra-large-size [title] . . . packed with high-quality color photos on every double-page spread. Just as gripping are the narratives, captions, and technical details of exploration, adventure, and survival. . . . [This] book covers Magellan, Cook, Shackleton, Heyedahl and also Chichester, who, in 1966, sailed alone around the world." Booklist

Riggs, Kate
Pirates. Creative Education 2010 24p il (Great warriors) $24.25; pa $8.99
Grades: K 1 2 **910.4**
1. Pirates
ISBN 978-1-60818-002-8; 1-60818-002-6; 978-0-89812-573-3 pa; 0-89812-573-1 pa

LC 2010019611

A introduction to the roving warriors known as pirates, including their history, lifestyle, weapons, and how they remain a part of today's culture by their continued existence.

This title makes pirates "accessible to students just beginning to read on their own. The text and design of the [book is] spare, and vocabulary words are introduced unobtrusively. . . . The concepts are simple, but introduced without oversimplification that might lead to misunderstandings. [This is an] excellent [introduction] and fun to read aloud." SLJ

Includes glossary and bibliographical references

Ross, Stewart
★ **Into** the unknown; how great explorers found their way by land, sea, and air. Candlewick Press 2011 un il map $19.99
Grades: 4 5 6 7 **910.4**
1. Explorers 2. Explorers -- Juvenile literature 3. Discoveries in geography -- Juvenile literature
ISBN 978-0-7636-4948-7; 0-7636-4948-1

LC 2010038720

"Biesty's trademark amusing, informatively detailed illustrations are a highlight of this entertaining examination of several voyages of exploration. . . . Chapters cover an impressive range of exploration. In addition to the usual suspects, they include a 340 B.C.E. Greek voyage to the Arctic Circle; Chinese Admiral Zheng He to India; [and] David

Livingston and Mary Kingsley into the African interior. . . . Each chapter includes a fold-out section of illustrations with a map of the journey and a cross-section of the method of transportation. . . . An altogether agreeable package for armchair explorers." Kirkus

910.92 Geographers, travelers, explorers regardless of country of origin

Fritz, Jean
Around the world in a hundred years; from Henry the Navigator to Magellan. illustrated by Anthony Bacon Venti. Putnam 1994 128p il map hardcover o.p. pa $8.99
Grades: 4 5 6 7 **910.92**
1. Princes 2. Explorers 3. Colonial administrators 4. Exploration -- Juvenile literature
ISBN 0-399-22527-7; 0-698-11638-0 pa

LC 92-27042

"Fritz examines the voyages of ten explorers, acknowledging that their contributions, though deserving of recognition, were dearly bought. Opening and closing chapters summarize the fourteenth-century world view and indicate later expansion of geographic understanding. As always, Fritz tempers scholarship with humor in this brief volume—illustrated with drawings in pencil—which reads like an adventure story." Horn Book Guide

Includes bibliographical references

911 Historical geography

Chrisp, Peter
Atlas of ancient worlds; author, Peter Chrisp; consultant, Philip Parker. DK Pub. 2009 96p il map $21.99
Grades: 4 5 6 7 8 **911**
1. Reference books 2. Historical atlases 3. Ancient civilization
ISBN 978-0-7566-4512-0; 0-7566-4512-3

This atlas consists "of maps and illustrations accompanied by extensive captions outlining the cultures of many civilizations. Each section begins with a map of a continent and a table of contents detailing which peoples will be discussed in it. Each civilization is covered in a chapter spread that includes a small map of the extent of each empire and many photos, pictures, and captioned drawings. . . . The accompanying clip art CD contains images of many of the artifacts as well as of the maps found in the book. . . . This atlas offers a wonderful introduction to [ancient civilizations] as well as solid geography basics." SLJ

Includes glossary

Leacock, Elspeth
★ **Places** in time; a new atlas of American history. [by] Elspeth Leacock and Susan Buckley; illustrations by Randy Jones. Houghton Mifflin 2001 48p il $15; pa $6.95
Grades: 4 5 6 7 **911**
1. Reference books 2. Children's atlases 3. United States -- Historical geography -- Juvenile literature 4. United States -- History -- Miscellanea -- Juvenile literature
ISBN 0-395-97958-7; 0-618-3113-0 pa

LC 00-59741

This book presents "20 sites in American history at the moment of their historical significance, beginning in 1200 (Cahokia) and ending in 1953. Places and times include New Plymouth—1627, Charlestown—1739, Saratoga—1777, Philadelphia—1787, Abilene—1871, and Chicago—1893. The detailed cutaway views of homes, forts, and mills are impressive enough to keep readers looking again and again. These fascinating slices of life stir the imagination and lead to questions and further research." SLJ

Includes bibliographical references

Todras, Ellen H.

Explorers, trappers, and pioneers; by Ellen H. Todras. Kingfisher 2012 32 p. ill. (paperback) $9.99

Grades: 4 5 6 **911**
1. America -- Exploration -- Juvenile literature 2. Frontier and pioneer life -- United States -- Juvenile literature
ISBN 0753465159; 9780753465158

This book by Ellen H. Todras is part of the "All About America" series. It "begins with the Vikings landing in Newfoundland 1,000 years ago and concludes with the Oklahoma Land Rush in 1889." It "offers 13 highly illustrated double-page spreads that present topics using a few paragraphs of information, related text boxes, and several color illustrations and five or more captioned illustrations." (Booklist)

912 Graphic representations of surface of earth and of extraterrestrial worlds

★ **Beginner's** United States atlas; a it's your country, be a part of it! National Geographic 2009 128p il map $18.95

Grades: 1 2 3 4 **912**
1. Atlases 2. Reference books
ISBN 978-1-4263-0512-2; 1-4263-0512-5

Provides information about the United States, including state flags, birds, flowers, and capitals, as well as key points about the water, people, and physical features of each state

Boyer, Crispin

National Geographic kids ultimate U.S. road trip atlas; maps, games, activities, and more for hours of backseat fun. by Crispin Boyer. 1st ed. National Geographic 2012 128 p. col. ill., col. maps (pbk.: alk. paper) $5.99; (lib. bdg.: alk. paper) $14.90

Grades: 4 5 6 **912**
1. Atlases 2. Road maps 3. United States -- Historical geography -- Maps 4. Recreation areas -- United States -- Maps 5. Outdoor recreation -- United States -- Maps
ISBN 1426309333; 1426309341; 9781426309335; 9781426309342

LC 2011034647

This book, by author Crispin Boyer, "includes . . . road maps of each state and Washington, D.C., and a map of the United States. State symbols, cool things to do, boredom busters, fun facts, wacky roadside attractions, and games accompany the maps. . . . In the back matter [there is] a comprehensive index . . . for kids to look up names and places." (Publisher's note)

Includes bibliographical references and index.

Crane, Nicholas

Barefoot Books world atlas. Barefoot Books 2011 56p

Grades: 3 4 5 **912**
1. Maps 2. Atlases 3. Geography
ISBN 1-84686-333-3; 978-1-84686-333-2

"This fresh and informative atlas offers engaging, fact-filled overviews of Earth's oceans and continents. Mini-books, flaps, and sidebars address topics ranging from 'People and Places' to 'Transport.' Dean's maps are crowded with warmly illustrated people, animals, places, and objects that represent particular areas of the world. . . . With its emphasis on sustainability, interconnectedness, and diversity, the book offers young armchair travelers and globe-trotters much to discover. Includes a removable world map. An app is also available." Publ Wkly

Leedy, Loreen

★ **Mapping** Penny's world. Holt & Co. 2000 un il map $17; pa $7.95

Grades: 1 2 3 **912**
1. Dogs 2. Maps 3. Boston terrier 4. Dogs -- Fiction 5. Maps -- Fiction
ISBN 0-8050-6178-9; 0-8050-7262-4 pa

LC 99-48327

After learning about maps in school, Lisa maps all the favorite places of her dog Penny

"The concepts are clear, and the digital-painting and photo-collage illustrations are uncluttered and ably clarify the text." SLJ

★ **National** Geographic atlas of the world; 9th ed.; National Geographic Society 2010 153p il $175

Grades: 5 6 7 8 9 10 **912**
1. Atlases 2. Reference books
ISBN 978-1-4262-0634-4

First published 1963

"The National Geographic Society presents more than 80 large-format color maps grouped by continent portraying the world with detailed, digitally painted terrain modeling. Each continent is introduced by satellite, political, and physical maps. Political maps for regions and specific countries follow." Libr J

★ **National** Geographic Kids beginner's world atlas; 3rd ed.; National Geographic 2011 il map $27.90

Grades: K 1 2 3 **912**
1. Atlases 2. Reference books
ISBN 978-1-4263-0839-0; 1-4263-0839-6

First published 1999 with title: National Geographic beginner's world atlas

This is an "eye-catching atlas for the child who is ready to learn about the world beyond his or her own community. Enticing panoramic photographs introduce each continent, and easy-to-decipher maps make this oversize volume one that will fascinate inquisitive young children given to browsing." Booklist

★ **National** Geographic United States atlas for young explorers; 3rd ed.; National Geographic 2008 175p il map $24.95

Grades: 4 5 6 7 **912**
1. Atlases 2. Reference books
ISBN 978-1-4263-0255-8; 1-4263-0255-X

First published 1999

This atlas offers maps of each of the states in the United States, divided into five geographical regions, plus U.S. territories. Each state map indicates physical features such as mountains and rivers, national forests, cities, major interstate roads, and industries, and is accompanied by color photos and facts about the state. An introductory section describes how to use the companion web site for more information, maps of the United States biomes, climates, natural hazards, political states, population, ethnic diversity, and energy use.

★ **National** Geographic world atlas for young explorers; 3rd ed.; National Geographic 2007 191p il map $24.95

Grades: 3 4 5 6   912
1. Atlases 2. Reference books
ISBN 978-1-4263-0088-2
First published 1998

This atlas includes photographs taken from space, political and physical maps, flags and statistics, and links to additional images and information on a companion website.

Student atlas; Dorling Kindersley, Inc. 6th ed. DK Pub. 2013 176 p. ill. (hardcover) $14.99

Grades: 5 6 7 8   912
1. Atlases 2. Geography -- Juvenile literature
ISBN 0756663199; 9780756663193

This book from DK Publishing is part of the Student Atlas series. It is a "single-volume guide to the nations of the world. [It's] fully revised and updated, and packed with clear, detailed maps highlighting landscape, industry, land use, population, climate and environmental issues." (Publisher's note)

Parker, Victoria

How far is far? comparing geographical distances. [by] Vic Parker. Heinemann Library 2011 32p il (Measuring and comparing) lib bdg $26; pa $7.99

Grades: 2 3 4   912
1. Maps 2. Measurement
ISBN 978-1-4329-3956-4 lib bdg; 1-4329-3956-4 lib bdg; 978-1-4329-3964-9 pa; 1-4329-3964-5 pa
LC 2010000926

This "contains vivid photographs, charts, and diagrams with captions, explanations, and examples. Questions are posed throughout . . . to entice young learners to 'stop and think' or continue reading for more information. . . . [This] would make an excellent addition to any classroom library." Libr Media Connect

Includes glossary and bibliographical references

916 Geography of and travel in Africa

Bodden, Valerie

To the heart of Africa; by Valerie Bodden. Creative Education 2011 48 p. col. ill. (library) $34.25

Grades: 5 6 7 8   916
1. Africa -- Exploration -- Juvenile literature 2. Exploration and discovery --Juvenile literature 3. Explorers -- Scotland -- Biography -- Juvenile literature 4. Explorers -- Africa, Southern -- Biography -- Juvenile literature 5. Missionaries, Medical -- Africa, Southern

-- Biography -- Juvenile literature
ISBN 1608180662; 9781608180660
LC 2010033414

This book by Valerie Bodden is part of the Great Expeditions series and looks at expeditions into Africa. "Bodden includes brief biographies of major people involved in each expedition, interspersed with the text. There are also numerous photographs or reproductions of paintings and woodcuts from the time of the expeditions." (Library Media Connection)

Includes bibliographical references (p. 46-47) and index.

917 Geography of and travel in North America

Butts, Edward

Shipwrecks, monsters, and mysteries of the Great Lakes; [by] Ed Butts. Tundra Books 2010 80p il pa $14.95

Grades: 4 5 6 7   917
1. Shipwrecks 2. Sea monsters -- Juvenile literature 3. Shipwrecks -- Great Lakes -- Juvenile literature
ISBN 978-1-77049-206-6 pa; 1-77049-206-2 pa

"In 1679, a French ship called the Griffon left Green Bay on Lake Michigan, bound for Niagara with a cargo of furs. Neither the Griffon nor the five-man crew was ever seen again. . . . Its disappearance was probably the result of the first shipwreck on a Great Lake. Since then, more than six thousand vessels, large and small, have met tragic ends. . . . Shoals and reefs, uncharted rocks, and sandbars could snare a ship or rip open a hull. Unpredictable winds could capsize a vessel at any moment. . . . The wreckage of ships and the bones of the people who sail them litter the bottoms of the five lakes: Ontario, Erie, Huron, Michigan, and Superior. Ed Butts has gathered stories and lake lore in this [volume]." (Publisher's note) "Ages nine to twelve." (Quill Quire)

Clark, Diane C.

★ A **kid's** guide to Washington, D.C. [written by Diane C. Clark; illustrations and maps by Richard E. Brown] rev and updated ed.; Harcourt, Inc. 2008 154p il map pa $14

Grades: 3 4 5 6   917
1. Puzzles 2. Children -- Travel 3. Washington (D.C.)
ISBN 978-0-15-206125-8 pa; 0-15-206125-8 pa
LC 2007-015509

First published 1989

"Brimming with useful information in both text and sidebars, this sturdy, large-format guidebook covers a broad array of topics, everything from a brief history of Washington, D.C., to practical advice on how to get around the city. . . . The extensive appendix now lists 128 places to see and gives their locations in the city and online. Shades of blue and red add color to the pages, which usually include graphic elements such as photos and line drawings. An attractive, practical guide for young visitors to Washington." Booklist

Koehler-Pentacoff, Elizabeth

Jackson and Bud's bumpy ride; America's first cross-country automobile trip. by Elizabeth Koehler-Pentacoff; illustrated by Wes Hargis. Millbrook Press 2009 un il

Grades: 1 2 3   **917**
   1. Physicians   2. Automobile travel
   ISBN 0822578859; 9780822578857

                      LC 2008012752
   An account of the first cross-country automobile trip in
the United States made in 1903 by Dr. Horatio Jackson, mechanic Sewall J. Crocker, and bulldog Bud
   "Short sentences and readable prose capture much of the
triumph and challenge of the 63-day trip. . . . The animated,
cartoon illustrations are lighthearted and detailed, and add
much to the narrative." SLJ
   Includes bibliographical references

Patent, Dorothy Hinshaw
   Animals on the trail with Lewis and Clark; photographs
by William Muñoz. Clarion Bks. 2002 118p il map $18
Grades: 4 5 6 7   **917**
   1. Animals -- United States   2. West (U.S.) -- Description
and travel -- Juvenile literature
   ISBN 0-395-91415-9

                      LC 2001-42200
   Retraces the Lewis and Clark journey and blends their
observations of previously unknown animals with modern
information about those same animals
   "The spacious page layouts, beautiful illustrations, and
well-written text help ensure that this historically significant
story will be read and enjoyed." Booklist
   Includes bibliographical references

Rubbino, Salvatore
   ★ A **walk** in New York. Candlewick Press 2009 37p
il map $16.99
Grades: 2 3 4   **917**
   1. New York (N.Y.) -- Description and travel
   ISBN 978-0-7636-3855-9; 0-7636-3855-2

                      LC 2008-20787
   This follows a wide-eyed boy and his dad on their walk
around Manhattan, from Grand Central Terminal to the top
of the Empire State Building, from Greenwich Village to the
Statute of Liberty. Includes lots of facts and trivia and a gatefold of the Empire State Building.
   "The book's large trim size and the illustrator's perspective provide an entertaining and palpable sense of scale as
the small boy marvels at skyscrapers and landmarks. . . .
Neophytes and jaded residents alike will embrace this vibrant and enticing slice of the Big Apple." Pub Wkly

Schanzer, Rosalyn
   ★ **How** we crossed the West; the adventures of Lewis
& Clark. National Geographic Soc. 1997 un il hardcover
o.p. pa $7.95
Grades: 3 4 5   **917**
   1. Explorers   2. Territorial governors
   ISBN 0-7922-3738-2; 0-7922-6726-5   pa

                      LC 96-6585
   "Pithy and sometimes humorous, the text tells of con-
tacts with Native Americans, encounters with wildlife . . . .
and the hardships of the trail. Warm in color and accessible
in style, the acrylic paintings have a folk-art inspiration."
Booklist

917.3   Geography of and travel in United States

Bodden, Valerie
   Through the American West; by Valerie Bodden. Creative Education 2011 48 p. col. ill. (library) $34.25
Grades: 5 6 7 8   **917.3**
   1. Lewis and Clark Expedition (1804-1806) -- Juvenile
literature
   ISBN 1608180654; 9781608180653

                      LC 2010033413
   This book by Valerie Bodden is part of the "Great Expeditions" series. It describes an expedition "led by William
Clark and Meriwether Lewis to explore the wilderness to
the west and look for an all water route to the Pacific Ocean.
They were aided by Sacagawea, a Shoshone Indian. The
adventures and hardships of the arduous three-year journey
include both the achievements and the disappointments encountered along the way". (Children's Literature)
   Includes bibliographical references (p. 46-47) and index.

National Geographic kids national parks guide U.S.A. the
   most amazing sights, scenes, and cool activities from
   coast to coast. National Geographic. National Geographic Society 2012 160 p.
   Grades: 4 5 6   **917.3**
   1. National parks and reserves -- United States --
   Guidebooks
   ISBN 9781426309311; 9781426309328

                      LC 2011034235
   This children's guidebook of America's National Parks,
by Sarah Wassner Flynn, features "tips on exploration, information about animals, sidebars, checklists, fun facts, maps,
cool things to do, and much more. Conservation information, a 'find out more' section, glossary, and index add ample
back matter to round out this book." (Publisher's note)
   Includes bibliographical references and index **917.804**

919   Geography of and travel in Australasia, Pacific Ocean islands, Atlantic Ocean islands, Arctic islands, Antarctica and on extraterrestrial worlds

Martin, Jacqueline Briggs
   ★ **The lamp,** the ice, and the boat called Fish; based
on a true story. pictures by Beth Krommes. Houghton Mifflin 2001 un il $15
Grades: 3 4 5 6   **919**
   1. Inuit
   ISBN 0-618-00341-X

                      LC 99-35303
   "The quiet, intriguing language, with a poet's attention
to sound, will lull young ones into the story's drama, as
will Beth Krommes' captivating scratchboard illustrations."
Booklist

O'Brien, Patrick
   ★ **You** are the first kid on Mars. G.P. Putnam's Sons
2009 un il $16.99
Grades: K 1 2 3   **919**
   1. Life on other planets
   ISBN 978-0-399-24634-0; 0-399-24634-7

                      LC 2008-29486

"This intriguing vision of space exploration should set imaginations soaring." Publ Wkly

919.89 Antarctica--geography

Bodden, Valerie

To the South Pole; by Valerie Bodden. Creative Education 2011 48 p. col. ill. (library) $34.25

Grades: 5 6 7 8   **919.89**

1. South Pole -- Exploration -- Juvenile literature 2. Amundsen, Roald, 1872-1928 -- Juvenile literature 3. Explorers -- Norway -- Biography -- Juvenile literature
ISBN 1608180697; 9781608180691

LC 2010033552

This book by Valerie Bodden, part of the "Great Expeditions" series, presents "a history of Roald Amundsen's . . . 1911 trip to the South Pole, detailing the challenges encountered, the individuals involved, the discoveries made, and how the expedition left its mark upon the world." (Publisher's note) . Major historical milestones and details about the search for the southernmost tip of the world are related in" addition to "profiles of four of the major explorers". (Children's Literature)

Includes bibliographical references (p. 46-47) and index.

Dowdeswell, Evelyn

Scott of the Antarctic; Evelyn Dowdeswell, Julian Dowdeswell, and Angela Seddon. Heinemann Library 2013 32 p. (hb) $26.65

Grades: 2 3 4   **919.89**

1. Explorers 2. South Pole
ISBN 1432968904; 9781432968908; 9781432968915

LC 2011037936

This book "[e]xamines Antarctica and [explorer] Robert Scott's epic expedition to the South Pole." (WorldCat) To "commemorate the 100th anniversary of Scott[']s Antarctic trek, and his tragic death before returning home, this book charts the epic race to the South Pole." (Google Books)

Includes bibliographical references and index

92   Individual biography

Aaron, Hank, 1934-

★ Tavares, Matt. **Henry** Aaron's dream. Candlewick Press 2010 un il $16.99; pa $6.99

Grades: 3 4 5   92

1. Baseball players 2. African American athletes 3. Baseball -- Biography 4. African American baseball players -- Juvenile literature
ISBN 978-0-7636-3224-3; 0-7636-3224-4; 978-07636-6129-8 pa

LC 2008037417

"Well-written text and brilliantly composed art highlight the poignancy and triumph in Aaron's story. This rousing tribute should resonate with a wide audience." SLJ

Ada, Alma Flor, 1938-

Parker-Rock, Michelle. **Alma** Flor Ada; an author kids love. Enslow Publishers 2008 48p bibl il por (Authors kids love) lib bdg $23.93

Grades: 3 4 5   92

1. Authors 2. Educators 3. Dramatists 4. Women authors 5. Cuban Americans 6. Authors, American 7. Children's authors
ISBN 978-0-7660-2760-2 lib bdg; 0-7660-2760-0 lib bdg

LC 2008004641

"The frequent use of direct quotes makes the [text] particularly enjoyable. . . . Kids will be fascinated with Ada's childhood home in Cuba. . . . Well written, interesting, and useful for reports." SLJ

Includes bibliographical references

Adams, Abigail, 1744-1818

Adler, David A. A **picture** book of John and Abigail Adams; by David A. Adler and Michael S. Adler; illustrated by Ronald Himler. Holiday House 2010 un il $17.95

Grades: 1 2 3   92

1. Spouses of presidents 5. Presidents -- United States
ISBN 978-0-8234-2007-0; 0-8234-2007-8

LC 2006050069

"This excellent picture-book biography introduces the childhoods, courtship, and family life of John and Abigail Adams as well as their years in public service. . . . Himler's graceful and well-composed drawings are brightened with luminous washes." Booklist

Includes bibliographical references

Adams, John, 1735-1826

Adler, David A. A **picture** book of John and Abigail Adams; by David A. Adler and Michael S. Adler; illustrated by Ronald Himler. Holiday House 2010 un il $17.95

Grades: 1 2 3   92

1. Presidents 2. Vice-presidents 3. Parents of presidents 4. Spouses of presidents
ISBN 978-0-8234-2007-0; 0-8234-2007-8

LC 2006050069

"This excellent picture-book biography introduces the childhoods, courtship, and family life of John and Abigail Adams as well as their years in public service. . . . Himler's graceful and well-composed drawings are brightened with luminous washes." Booklist

Includes bibliographical references

Adams, Samuel, 1722-1803

★ Fritz, Jean. **Why** don't you get a horse, Sam Adams? illustrated by Trina Schart Hyman. 1974 47p il $15.99; pa $5.99

Grades: 2 3 4   92

1. Statesmen 2. Members of Congress 3. Writers on politics
ISBN 0-399-23401-2; 0-698-11416-7 pa

"A piece of history far more entertaining and readable than most fiction. . . . The author has humanized a figure of the Revolution: Adams emerges a marvelously funny and believable man. The illustrations play upon his foibles; they are, in fact, even more outrageously mocking than the text. A tour de force, for both author and illustrator." Horn Book

Albers, Josef, 1888-1976

★ Wing, Natasha. An **eye** for color: the story of Josef Albers; illustrated by Julia Breckenreid. Holt & Co. 2009 un il $16.99

Grades: 3 4 5 6   92
1. Artists 2. Painters 3. Color in art 4. Artists, German
5. Printmakers 6. Art teachers
ISBN 978-0-8050-8072-8; 0-8050-8072-4

LC 2008038214

"This creative biography explores how Albers, perhaps best known for his paintings of squares in different color combinations, 'saw art in the simplest things.' . . . After visiting Mexico—Albers is shown climbing an abstract templelike structure of colorful rectangles—he reflects on the effects of combining different colors. . . . An accessible and lively introduction to this artist and to color theory." Publ Wkly

Includes glossary and bibliographical references

Alcott, Louisa May, 1832-1888

McDonough, Yona Zeldis. **Louisa**; the life of Louisa May Alcott. illustrated by Bethanne Andersen. Henry Holt and Co. 2009 un il $17.99
Grades: 2 3 4   92
1. Authors 2. Novelists 3. Women authors 4. Authors, American 5. Young adult authors
ISBN 978-0-8050-8192-3; 0-8050-8192-5

LC 2008-38222

"McDonough clearly lays out the essentials of Alcott's life story. Often striking and occasionally memorable, Andersen's gouache-and-pastel illustrations use strong shapes and rich colors to create iconic images." Booklist

Includes bibliographical references

Aldrin, Buzz

★ Aldrin, Buzz, 1930- **Reaching** for the moon; paintings by Wendell Minor. HarperCollins Children's Books 2005 un il $16.99; lib bdg $17.89; pa $6.99
Grades: 2 3 4   92
1. Astronauts 2. Air force officers 3. Nonfiction writers
ISBN 0-06-055445-2; 0-06-055446-0 lib bdg; 0-06-055447-7 pa

LC 2004-6247

Aldrin "discusses his childhood interest in flight, his military training and academic preparation for a career as an astronaut, and . . . his pride and excitement in both his Gemini 12 extravehicular activity and his moon walk. . . . Ages five to nine." (Bull Cent Child Books)

"In this picture book, Aldrin, the second man to step foot on the moon, relates the life events that led him to the space program and his assignment on Apollo 11. . . . Minor's colorful and precisely rendered illustrations help this effort really take off, especially in the images of Aldrin's space journeys." Booklist

Alexander, the Great, 356-323 B.C.

Adams, Simon. **Alexander**; the boy soldier who conquered the world. National Geographic 2005 64p il map (World history biographies) $17.95; lib bdg $27.90
Grades: 4 5 6 7   92
1. Ancient civilization 2. Kings
ISBN 0-7922-3660-2; 0-7922-3661-0 lib bdg

This describes the life and times of Alexander the Great. This is a "handsomely designed [book]. . . . illustrated with maps and many color photographs of art and sculpture that give substance to [the era]. . . . Adams does not down-

play Alexander's brutality or all-consuming ambition and includes examples of both." SLJ

Includes bibliographical references

Demi. **Alexander** the Great; written and illustrated by Demi. Marshall Cavendish 2010 59p il $19.99
Grades: 4 5 6 7   92
1. Kings and rulers 2. Kings
ISBN 978-0-7614-5700-8; 0-7614-5700-3

"Demi's meticulous, expansive story highlights the achievements of Alexander the Great, who conquered much of the known world (to the Greeks) in only 12 years. . . . Illustrated with Demi's customary skill, ... Alexander's conflicts and victories will delight young history lovers with their daring." Publ Wkly

Ali, Muhammad, 1942-

★ Bolden, Tonya. The **champ!** the story of Muhammad Ali. illustrated by R. Gregory Christie. Alfred A. Knopf 2004 un il $17.95; lib bdg $19.99; pa $6.99
Grades: 2 3 4 5   92
1. African American athletes 2. Boxers (Persons) 3. Boxing -- Biography
ISBN 0-375-82401-4; 0-375-92401-9 lib bdg; 0-440-41782-1 pa

LC 2004-10082

A biography of the African American boxer

"In simple, clear, and lively text, Bolden introduces both Ali the fighter and Ali the activist. . . . The words interact well with Christie's sturdy acrylic paintings." Booklist

Myers, Walter Dean, 1937- **Muhammad** Ali; the people's champion. illustrated by Alix Delinois. Collins Amistad 2010 un il $16.99; lib bdg $17.89
Grades: 1 2 3   92
1. African American athletes 2. Boxers (Persons) 3. Boxing -- Biography
ISBN 978-0-06-029131-0; 0-06-029131-1; 978-0-06-029132-7 lib bdg; 0-06-029132-X lib bdg

LC 2009-05326

"The curious mix of bravado and humility constituting the life of Muhammad Ali receives a sensitive exploration in this vibrantly illustrated biography. . . . Delinois is with Myers every step, using wild splotches of paint and scribbles of chalk not only to capture the velocity of a punch but also fill in contexual blanks. . . . Unexpectedly far reaching, this is a Muhammed Ali for the thinking child." Booklist

★ Smith, Charles R., 1969- **Twelve** rounds to glory: the story of Muhammad Ali; illustrated by Bryan Collier. Candlewick Press 2007 80p il $19.99
Grades: 5 6 7 8   92
1. African American athletes 2. Boxers (Persons) 3. Boxing -- Biography
ISBN 978-0-7636-1692-2; 0-7636-1692-3

LC 2007-25998

"Rap-style cadences perfectly capture the drama that has always surrounded the boxer's life. . . . Collier's compelling watercolor collages with their brown overtones beautifully portray Ali's determination and strength." SLJ

Winter, Jonah. **Muhammad** Ali; champion of the world. written by Jonah Winter; illustrated by François

Roca. Schwartz & Wade Books 2007 un il $16.99; lib bdg $19.99

Grades: 2 3 4 5 **92**

1. African American athletes 2. Boxers (Persons) 3. Boxing -- Biography

ISBN 978-0-375-83622-0; 0-375-83622-5; 978-0-375-93787-3 lib bdg; 0-375-93787-0 lib bdg

LC 2006-101855

"Winter and Roca offer a rousing tribute to Ali's spirit, determination, and strength of will in this picture-book biography. . . . Winter's highly charged prose is well matched by Roca's eye-catching oil paintings, which vividly capture Ali's proud, defiant character and detail the racism he encountered and the hero worship he inspired." SLJ

Ali, Rubina

Ali, Rubina. **Slumgirl** dreaming; Rubina's journey to the stars. [by] Rubina Ali in collaboration with Anne Berthod and Divya Dugar. Delacorte Press 2009 187p il pa $9.99

Grades: 5 6 7 8 **92**

1. Actors 2. Children

ISBN 978-0-385-73908-5 pa; 0-385-73908-7 pa

LC 2009029305

The young actress describes her life growing up in the slums of Mumbai, her experiences on the set of the film "Slumdog Millionaire," and how her life has changed as a result of her role in the film

"The writing here has a journalistic feel. It is not poetic or especially nuanced. But in a sea of cookie-cutter biography series, this book stands out. It has heart, and is aimed at an age group that will identify with Ali in essential ways." SLJ

Alonso, Alicia

★ Bernier-Grand, Carmen T. **Alicia** Alonso; prima ballerina. illustrated by Raúl Colón. Marshall Cavendish Children's 2011 64p il $19.99

Grades: 4 5 6 7 **92**

1. Cubans 2. Ballet dancers 3. Choreographers 4. Dance directors

ISBN 978-0-7614-5562-2; 0-7614-5562-0

LC 2010018269

"An informative, beautifully illustrated introduction to the world-renowned dancer. Alonso's focused life and illustrious career are made even more remarkable by the fact that she lost her peripheral vision at age 19 and had to learn to visualize both the stage set and the dance itself in order to execute spins and lifts, and to choreograph ballets. Each one is presented as a titled one-page piece in abbreviated poetic prose; many face full-page textured paintings rendered in Colón's distinctive mix of watercolor, colored, and lithograph pencils." SLJ

Includes bibliographical references

Alvarez, Luis W., 1911-1988

Venezia, Mike. **Luis** Alvarez; wild idea man. written and illustrated by Mike Venezia. Children's Press 2010 32p il (Getting to know the world's greatest inventors & scientists) lib bdg $28; pa $6.95

Grades: 2 3 4 **92**

1. Physicists 2. Nobel laureates for physics

ISBN 978-0-531-23703-8 lib bdg; 0-531-23703-6 lib bdg; 978-0-531-20777-2 pa; 0-531-20777-3 pa

LC 2009-356

"Employing oversized font, judicious use of white space, and appealing illustrations . . . readers learn about physicist Luis Alvarez and his numerous contributions to early 20th-century science. . . . Student researchers will appreciate the glossary and index, since there are no chapter headings or subheadings. This title, . . . serves equally well for research assignments, biography units, or as engaging leisure reading for aspiring scientists." Libr Media Connect

Includes glossary

Andersen, Hans Christian, 1805-1875

★ Varmer, Hjordis. **Hans** Christian Andersen; his fairy tale life. illustrated by Lilian Brogger; translated by Tiina Nunnally. Groundwood Books 2005 111p il $19.95

Grades: 5 6 7 8 **92**

1. Authors 2. Novelists 3. Dramatists 4. Authors, Danish 5. Children's authors 6. Short story writers

ISBN 0-88899-690-X

"Most of this book describes Andersen's childhood and belated schooling, showing his poverty and the grief he experienced over the death of his beloved father, as well as several horrifying events such as being forced by a teacher to witness the beheading of three young people. . . . The biography is divided into 11 chapters, set up as if they were stories. . . . The writing flows smoothly, with many details provided to help students picture the places and events. Brøgger's haunting, mixed-media illustrations add to the somber and at times surreal feeling of the text." SLJ

Anderson, Marian, 1897-1993

★ Freedman, Russell. The **voice** that challenged a nation; Marian Anderson and the struggle for equal rights. Clarion Books 2004 114p il $18

Grades: 5 6 7 8 **92**

1. African American women 2. African American singers 3. Opera singers 4. African Americans -- Civil rights 5. African American women -- Biography

ISBN 0-618-15976-2

LC 2003-19558

A Newbery Medal honor book, 2005

In the mid-1930s, Marian Anderson was a famed vocalist who had been applauded by European royalty and welcomed at the White House. But, because of her race, she was denied the right to sing at Constitution Hall in Washington, D.C. This is the story of her resulting involvement in the civil rights movement of the time.

"In his signature prose, plain yet eloquent, Freedman tells Anderson's triumphant story, with numerous black-and-white photos and prints that convey her personal struggle, professional artistry, and landmark civil rights role." Booklist

Includes bibliographical references

★ Hopkinson, Deborah. **Sweet** land of liberty; written by Deborah Hopkinson; illustrated by Leonard Jenkins. Peachtree 2007 un il $16.95

Grades: K 1 2 3 4 **92**

1. Lawyers 2. Opera singers 3. Secretaries of the interior 4. African Americans -- Biography 5. African

Americans -- Civil rights
ISBN 1-56145-395-1; 978-1-56145-395-5

LC 2006024331

"Jenkins' powerful, bright, mixed-media collages show and tell the connections, past, present, and future." SLJ

★ Ryan, Pam Munoz. **When** Marian sang: the true recital of Marian Anderson, the voice of a century; libretto by Pam Muñoz Ryan; staging by Brian Selznick. Scholastic Press 2002 un il $16.95
Grades: 2 3 4   92
1. African American women 2. African American singers 3. Opera singers 4. African American women -- Biography
ISBN 0-439-26967-9

LC 2001-49508

An introduction to the life of Marian Anderson, extraordinary singer and civil rights activist, who was the first African American to perform at the Metropolitan Opera, whose life and career encouraged social change

"This book masterfully distills the events in the life of an extraordinary musician. . . . Working with a sepia-toned palette, Selznick's paintings shimmer with emotion." Publ Wkly

Anderson, Tillie
★ Stauffacher, Sue. **Tillie** the terrible Swede; how one woman, a sewing needle, and a bicycle changed history. Alfred A. Knopf 2011 un il $17.99; lib bdg $20.99
Grades: K 1 2   92
1. Cycling 2. Women athletes
ISBN 978-0-375-84442-3; 0-375-84442-2; 978-0-375-94442-0 lib bdg; 0-375-94442-7 lib bdg

LC 2010-07083

"Reaching back more than a century, Stauffacher and McMenemy resurrect the story of pioneering woman cyclist Tillie Anderson. . . . Racing in a self-created aerodynamic outfit . . . Anderson both scandalized and thrilled 1890s America as she shattered records for speed and endurance, leaving competitors and conventional wisdom in the dust. . . . Stauffacher's . . . writing is as sprightly and heartfelt as ever, and to her credit, she connects Tillie's accomplishments to the building women's rights movement. An excellent afterword, tucked on the inside back cover, provides fascinating historical context for Anderson's story." Publ Wkly

Anderson, Walter Inglis, 1903-1965
★ Bass, Hester. The **secret** world of Walter Anderson; illustrated by E.B. Lewis. Candlewick Press 2009 un il $17.99
Grades: 2 3 4 5   92
1. Artists 2. Artists -- United States
ISBN 978-0-7636-3583-1; 0-7636-3583-9

LC 2008029674

"This sensitive portrait of Anderson—'the most famous American artist you've never heard of'—paints him as a solitary man who kept a private room hidden from his wife and children and often took his rowboat to the Mississippi Gulf Coast's isolated Horn Island to glean inspiration. Subdued watercolors evoke the artist's love of the natural world. . . . A powerful tribute to the lengths artists will go for their passions." Publ Wkly

Andrews, Roy Chapman, 1884-1960
★ Bausum, Ann. **Dragon** bones and dinosaur eggs: a photobiography of Roy Chapman Andrews. National Geographic Soc. 2000 64p il map $17.95
Grades: 5 6 7 8   92
1. Fossils 2. Dinosaurs 3. Explorers 4. Zoologists 5. Naturalists 6. Travel writers 7. Writers on nature 8. Writers on science 9. Museum administrators
ISBN 0-7922-7123-8

LC 99-38363

A biography of the great explorer-adventurer, who discovered huge finds of dinosaur bones in Mongolia, pioneered modern paleontology field research, and became the director of the American Museum of Natural History

"Bausum's account reads smoothly, and a layout dense with captioned sepia photographs and quotes from Andrews provides plenty of oases for readers as they follow him through the desert." Bull Cent Child Books

Includes bibliographical references

Appleseed, Johnny, 1774-1845
Worth, Richard. **Johnny** Appleseed; select good seeds and plant them in good ground. Enslow Publishers 2010 128p il map (Americans: the spirit of a nation) $23.95
Grades: 4 5 6 7   92
1. Apples 2. Frontier and pioneer life 3. Pioneers 4. Fruit growers
ISBN 978-0-7660-3352-8; 0-7660-3352-X

LC 2008048701

"This nicely illustrated and sourced [biography] . . . includes full-page sidebars." Booklist

Includes glossary and bibliographical references

Yolen, Jane. **Johnny** Appleseed; the legend and the truth. by Jane Yolen; illustrated by Jim Burke. HarperCollinsPublishers 2008 un il $16.99; lib bdg $17.89
Grades: K 1 2 3   92
1. Apples 2. Frontier and pioneer life 3. Pioneers 4. Fruit growers
ISBN 978-0-06-059135-9; 0-06-059135-8; 978-0-06-059136-6 lib bdg; 0-06-059136-6 lib bdg

LC 2005017789

"In this comely, homespun picture-book biography, Yolen assembles the fact and fiction surrounding America's favorite orchardist into a tale both substantive and lyrical. . . . Burke's striking paintings conform to a natural, yarn-dyed palette of apple reds, forest greens, meadow golds, and midnight blues." Booklist

Archimedes, ca. 287-212 B.C.
Hightower, Paul. The **greatest** mathematician; Archimedes and his eureka! moment. Enslow Publishers 2010 128p il (Great minds of ancient science and math) lib bdg $31.93
Grades: 5 6 7 8   92
1. Mathematicians 2. Writers on science
ISBN 978-0-7660-3408-2 lib bdg; 0-7660-3408-9 lib bdg

LC 2008051818

This biography is a "solid [choice], as . . . [it provides] a good overview of the cultural and political landscape of the times, as well as pictures." SLJ

Includes glossary and bibliographical references

Armstrong, John Barclay, 1850-1913

Alter, Judy. **John** Barclay Armstrong; Texas Ranger. by Judy Alter. Bright Sky Press 2007 59p il $14.95

Grades: 4 5 6 7   **92**

1. Sheriffs 2. Texas Rangers

ISBN 978-1-931721-86-8

"Born in 1850 and raised in Tennessee, Armstrong went west to seek his fortune. At 25, he joined the Texas Rangers and soon came to embody the legendary qualities of these remarkable lawmen. He is an interesting character, and the author aptly tells his tale. The archival black-and-white photos add authenticity and help bring the man to life." SLJ

Armstrong, Louis, 1900-1971

★ Kimmel, Eric A. A **horn** for Louis; by Eric A. Kimmel; illustrated by James Bernardin. Random House 2005 86p il $11.95; lib bdg $13.99; pa $3.99

Grades: 2 3 4   **92**

1. Singers 2. Jazz musicians 3. African American musicians 4. Band leaders 5. Trumpet players

ISBN 0-375-83252-1; 0-375-93252-6 lib bdg; 978-0-375-84005-0 pa

LC 2005004151

"Adapted from an unpublished memoir, this beginning chapter book is an account of [Louis] Armstrong's youthful acquisition of his first true horn. . . . Kimmel's skilled narrative accentuates the diversity of the boys surroundings and the early influence of local music upon his innate gift. Bernardins dynamic black-and-white artwork captures the vivacious subject well and includes many period and cultural details." SLJ

Weinstein, Muriel Harris. **Play,** Louis, play! the true story of a boy and his horn. illustrated by Frank Morrison. Bloomsbury Books for Young Readers 2010 99p il $15.99

Grades: 3 4 5   **92**

1. Singers 2. Jazz musicians 3. African American musicians 4. Band leaders 5. Trumpet players

ISBN 978-1-59990-375-0; 1-59990-375-X

LC 2010025974

"With a bouncy, freewheeling tone that would make her subject proud, Weinstein tells the story of Louis Armstrong's childhood from the point of view of his first cornet, . . . Morrison's sketchy black-and-white spot art livens up an already ebullient chapter-book biography of a true artistic pioneer." Booklist

Arn Chorn-Pond

Lord, Michelle. A **song** for Cambodia; by Michelle Lord; illustrated by Shino Arihara. Lee & Low 2008 un il $16.95

Grades: 3 4 5   **92**

1. Musicians 2. Flutists 3. Human rights activists

ISBN 978-1-60060-139-2; 1-60060-139-1

LC 2007026248

A biography of Arn Chorn-Pond who, as a young boy in 1970s Cambodia, survived the Khmer Rouge killing fields because of his skill on the khim, a traditional instrument, and later went on to help heal others and revive Cambodian music and culture.

"Filled with drama and tragedy, this picture-book biography skillfully telescopes Arn's tumultuous boyhood. Realistic gouache illustrations depict the terrors of war but refrain from showing graphic violence. Amazing and inspiring." Booklist

Ashe, Arthur, 1943-1993

Hubbard, Crystal. **Game,** set, match, champion Arthur Ashe; illustrated by Kevin Belford. Lee & Low Books 2010 un il $19.95

Grades: 3 4 5 6   **92**

1. African American athletes 2. Tennis players 3. Nonfiction writers 4. Tennis -- Biography

ISBN 978-1-60060-366-2; 1-60060-366-1

LC 2010013304

"Tennis legend Ashe's life, on and off the court, is the focus of this stirring picture-book biography . . . which combines a detailed narrative with powerful acrylic paintings." Booklist

Astaire, Adele, 1896-1981

Orgill, Roxane. **Footwork;** the story of Fred and Adele Astaire. illustrated by Stephane Jorisch. Candlewick Press 2007 un il $17.99

Grades: 2 3 4 5   **92**

1. Actors 2. Dancers 3. Singers

ISBN 978-0-7636-2121-6; 0-7636-2121-8

LC 2006-40068

The biography of Fred and Adele Astaire, from their humble beginnings to Broadway stars.

Orgill's text "brims with well-chosen biographical and period details, and . . . Jorisch's whisper-weight, line-and-watercolor drawings convey the fizz of the footwork and the gritty backdrop of steam trains and stage doors." Booklist

Includes bibliographical references

Astaire, Fred

Orgill, Roxane. **Footwork;** the story of Fred and Adele Astaire. illustrated by Stephane Jorisch. Candlewick Press 2007 un il $17.99

Grades: 2 3 4 5   **92**

1. Actors 2. Dancers 3. Singers

ISBN 978-0-7636-2121-6; 0-7636-2121-8

LC 2006-40068

The biography of Fred and Adele Astaire, from their humble beginnings to Broadway stars.

Orgill's text "brims with well-chosen biographical and period details, and . . . Jorisch's whisper-weight, line-and-watercolor drawings convey the fizz of the footwork and the gritty backdrop of steam trains and stage doors." Booklist

Includes bibliographical references

Audubon, John James, 1785-1851

★ Davies, Jacqueline. The **boy** who drew birds: a story of John James Audubon; illustrated by Melissa Sweet. Houghton Mifflin Co. 2004 un il map $15

Grades: 2 3 4   **92**

1. Birds 2. Artists 3. Painters 4. Naturalists 5. Ornithologists 6. Writers on science 7. Artists -- United States

ISBN 0-618-24343-7

LC 2004-971

This describes how John James Audubon studied and painted birds

"Sweet's mixed-media collage artwork includes sensitive pencil sketches and ink drawings washed with watercolors and gouache, as well as elements such as photos of bird nests and bones. . . . This handsome book makes a beguiling introduction to the painter." Booklist

Includes bibliographical references

Aung San Suu Kyi

Rose, Simon. **Aung** San Suu Kyi. 2011 il por (Remarkable people) $27.13; pa $12.95

Grades: 4 5 6 7   92

1. Political prisoners 2. Women political activists 3. Dissenters 4. Political leaders 5. Nonfiction writers 6. Human rights activists 7. Nobel laureates for peace
ISBN 978-1-61690-833-1; 1-61690-833-5; 978-1-61690-834-8 pa; 1-61690-834-3 pa

LC 2011011584

This looks at Aung San Suu Kyi's "life, accomplishments, and challenges while including a page of quotes, an annotated list of contemporaries and influences, starter suggestions for writing a paper, and a time line and glossary. [The book] looks into the Nobel Peace Prize– winning Myanmar activist, whose struggle for democracy has landed her under house arrest multiple times." Booklist

Baker, Alia Muhammad

★ Winter, Jeanette. The **librarian** of Basra; a true story from Iraq. Harcourt, Inc. 2004 32p il $16

Grades: PreK K 1 2 3   92

1. Books 2. Libraries 3. Librarians 4. Iraq War, 2003
ISBN 0-15-205445-6

LC 2004-12969

The story of Alia Muhammad Baker, a librarian in Basra, Iraq, who managed to rescue seventy percent of the library's collection before the library burned in the Iraq War in 2003

"Winter's bright, folk-art style does much to mute the horrific realties of war. . . . The librarian's quiet bravery serves as a point of entry into a freighted topic." Booklist

Baker, Josephine, 1906-1975

★ Winter, Jonah. **Jazz** age Josephine; illustrated by Marjorie Priceman. Atheneum 2012 il $16.99

Grades: K 1 2 3   92

1. Actors 2. Dancers 3. Singers 4. Jazz music 5. African American singers 6. African American women -- Biography
ISBN 978-1-4169-6123-9; 1-4169-6123-2

"Even though the ranks of picture-book biographies of significant artists (many of whom kids have likely never heard of) have swollen considerably in recent years, this one about the singer, dancer, and all-around entertainer Josephine Baker still manages to dazzle. . . . The biographical details . . . are covered in broad strokes, with more attention given to recreating the style and swagger of her onstage performances. . . . Winter's syncopated language dances nearly as much as the energized, loose-limbed figures in Priceman's kinetic artwork to convey the spirit, as much as the life, of the subject." Booklist

Banneker, Benjamin, 1731-1806

Maupin, Melissa. **Benjamin** Banneker. Child's World 2010 39p il map (Journey to freedom) lib bdg $20.92

Grades: 3 4 5 6   92

1. Astronomers 2. Mathematicians 3. Nonfiction writers 4. Clock and watch makers 5. African

Americans -- Biography
ISBN 978-1-60253-117-8 lib bdg; 1-60253-117-X lib bdg

LC 2009003639

A biography of the African American scientist and mathematician

"Maupin has created an accessible account of Banneker's like and accomplishments. Short, uncomplicated text is interspersed with sepia-tone primary source photographs and documents." Booklist

Includes bibliographical references

Barnum, P. T. (Phineas Taylor), 1810-1891

★ Fleming, Candace. The **great** and only Barnum; the tremendous, stupendous life of showman P.T. Barnum. illustrated by Ray Fenwick. Schwartz & Wade Books 2009 151p il $18.99; lib bdg $21.99

Grades: 5 6 7 8   92

1. Circus 2. Circus executives
ISBN 978-0-375-84197-2; 0-375-84197-0; 978-0-375-94597-7 lib bdg; 0-375-94597-0 lib bdg

LC 2008-45847

"In this sweeping yet cohesive biography, Fleming so finely tunes Barnum's legendary ballyhoo that you can practically hear the hucksterism and smell the sawdust. . . . The material is inherently juicy, but credit Fleming's vivacious prose, bountiful period illustrations, and copious source notes for fashioning a full picture on one of the forebearers of modern celebrity." Booklist

Includes bibliographical references

Barrie, J. M. (James Matthew), 1860-1937

★ Yolen, Jane. **Lost** boy; the story of the man who created Peter Pan. illustrated by Steve Adams. Dutton Children's Books 2010 un il $17.99

Grades: 2 3 4   92

1. Authors 2. Novelists 3. Dramatists 4. Authors, Scottish 5. Essayists 6. Satirists
ISBN 978-0-525-47886-7; 0-525-47886-8

LC 2009-24697

"This handsome picture-book biography presents the life of James Barrie, the creator of Peter Pan. . . . Adams' paintings provide evocative views of Barrie and his world. Yolen smoothly relates intriguing incidents from Barrie's childhood and adult life without making comments or drawing conclusions." Booklist

Includes bibliographical references

Barton, Clara, 1821-1912

Krensky, Stephen. **Clara** Barton. DK Pub. 2011 128p il (DK biography) $14.99; pa $5.99

Grades: 5 6 7 8   92

1. Nurses 2. Red Cross officials 3. Social welfare leaders
ISBN 978-0-7566-7279-9; 0-7566-7279-1; 978-0-7566-7278-2 pa; 0-7566-7278-3 pa

Describes the life and accomplishments of Clara Barton, a teacher who organized efforts to bring nursing care to wounded soldiers during the Civil War and who went on to become the founder of the American Red Cross.

"Barton is placed in historical context, and key concepts, such as the causes of the Civil War, the struggle for women's suffrage, and the importance of the Geneva Convention, are explained. Compact in form, the text is complemented by full-color and archival photographs and reproductions on every spread. . . . An excellent resource for reports that will also appeal to fans of biography." SLJ

Includes bibliographical references

Somervill, Barbara A. **Clara** Barton; founder of the American Red Cross. Compass Point Books 2007 112p bibl il por lib bdg $23.95

Grades: 5 6 7 8   92

1. Nurses 2. Red Cross officials 3. Social welfare leaders

ISBN 978-0-7565-1888-2 lib bdg; 0-7565-1888-1 lib bdg

LC 2006027071

"With an open design, clear type, and period prints and photos on every double-page spread, this highly readable biography . . . does a great job of setting Barton's personal story within the history of her time." Booklist

Includes bibliographical references

Wade, Mary Dodson. **Amazing** civil war nurse Clara Barton. Enslow Publishers 2009 24p il (Amazing Americans) lib bdg $21.26

Grades: 1 2 3   92

1. Nurses 2. Red Cross officials 3. Social welfare leaders

ISBN 978-0-7660-3281-1 lib bdg; 0-7660-3281-7 lib bdg

LC 2008-24889

"Colorful photos are found throughout, with a timeline, dictionary, websites concerning the topic, as well as an index making . . . [this] book a wonderful introduction to nonfiction features." Libr Media Connect

Includes glossary

Bates, Peg Leg, 1907-1998

★ Barasch, Lynne. **Knockin'** on wood; starring Peg Leg Bates. by Lynne Barasch. Lee & Low Books 2004 un il $16.95

Grades: 2 3 4   92

1. Dancers 2. Handicapped 3. Tap dancing 4. African American dancers 5. Hotel executives 6. Tap dancers -- United States -- Biography -- Juvenile literature 7. Dancers with disabilities -- United States -- Biography -- Juvenile literature

ISBN 1-58430-170-8

LC 2003-22905

A picture book biography of Clayton "Peg Leg" Bates, an African American who lost his leg in a factory accident at the age of twelve and went on to become a world-famous tap dancer

"Sprightly ink-and-watercolor art ably depicts both the poverty of Bates' early life and the colorful world of entertainment. . . . Barasch subtly sets the story against American racism." Booklist

Baum, L. Frank, 1856-1919

Krull, Kathleen. The **road** to Oz; twists, turns, bumps, and triumphs in the life of L. Frank Baum. illustrated by Kevin Hawkes. Alfred A. Knopf 2008 un il $17.99; lib bdg $20.99

Grades: 2 3 4 5   92

1. Authors 2. Dramatists 3. Journalists 4. Authors,

American 5. Children's authors

ISBN 978-0-375-83216-1; 0-375-83216-5; 978-0-375-93216-8 lib bdg; 0-375-93216-X lib bdg

LC 2007-41526

This picture-book biography of the author of The Wonderful Wizard of Oz "displays Krull's usual stylistic strengths: a conversational tone, well-integrated facts, vivid anecdotes, and sly asides. . . . Hawkes' ink-and-acrylic illustrations . . . support the sense of Baum as a multifaceted, fascinating individual." Booklist

Beebe, William, 1877-1962

Sheldon, David. **Into** the deep; the life of naturalist and explorer William Beebe. Charlesbridge 2009 un il lib bdg $16.95

Grades: 2 3 4   92

1. Authors 2. Explorers 3. Zoologists 4. Naturalists 5. Memoirists 6. Writers on nature

ISBN 978-1-58089-341-1 lib bdg; 1-58089-341-4 lib bdg

LC 2008-25341

"This colorful introduction to Beebe's life for younger readers opens with his parents' encouragement of his interests in the natural world and his early work as a curator and collector of birds before he developed the idea of observing animals in their native habitat and began to focus on undersea life. . . . Sheldon's lush double-page paintings, in acrylic, gouache and India ink, show young Will surrounded by animals, alive and stuffed, and the older man at work in a variety of settings. . . . A fine offering for would-be explorers." Kirkus

Includes bibliographical references

Beethoven, Ludwig van, 1770-1827

Bauer, Helen. **Beethoven** for kids; his life and music with 21 activities. Chicago Review Press 2011 129p il

Grades: 4 5 6 7   92

1. Composers

ISBN 1-56976-711-4; 978-1-56976-711-5

LC 2011018131

"This introduction to the towering classical composer sets the story of his life and work in the context of the revolutionary events of early-19th-century Europe. . . . The author's own extensive musical experience contributes to the breadth of this title. Sidebars and historical prints add further information about musical forms and instruments, historical events and people mentioned. . . . This will be particularly useful for parents and classroom teachers hoping to make the study of great music more interesting." Kirkus

Includes bibliographical references

Martin, Russell. The **mysteries** of Beethoven's hair; [by Russell Martin and Lydia Nibley] Charlesbridge 2009 120p il lib bdg $15.95

Grades: 5 6 7 8   92

1. Composers

ISBN 978-1-57091-714-1 lib bdg; 1-57091-714-0 lib bdg

LC 2008-07257

"Based on Martin's adult book Beethoven's Hair: An Extraordinary Historical Odyssey and Scientific Mystery Solved (Broadway, 2000), this reworking for a young audience presents an intriguing interdisciplinary story. Martin and Nibley trace the labyrinthine journey of a lock of

Beethoven's hair encased in a glass and wooden locket from the 18th century to the present. . . . This is a most unusual, thoroughly researched detective story written in a clearly accessible and lively tone. Black-and-white photos and reproductions appear throughout. . . . It is . . . an incredibly readable and absorbing selection that demonstrates the multidimensional nature of true scholarship." SLJ

Viegas, Jennifer. **Beethoven's** world; [by] Jennifer Viegas. Rosen Pub. Group 2008 64p il (Music throughout history) lib bdg $29.25

Grades: 5 6 7 8   **92**

1. Composers

ISBN 1-4042-0724-4 lib bdg; 978-1-4042-0724-0 lib bdg

LC 2005028917

This "book begins with an introduction briefly addressing social issues of the day, historical background, or other significant information. . . . Successive chapters discuss the [man's] early [life], family background, social status, personality characteristics, musical training and education, obstacles or challenges, and influences. A chapter . . . focuses on the musician's well-known compositions, describing through lively and colorful language some of the musical elements employed . . . The format and layout are appealing and uncluttered." SLJ

Includes glossary and bibliographical references

Bell, Alexander Graham, 1847-1922

Carson, Mary Kay. **Alexander** Graham Bell; giving voice to the world. [by] Mary Kay Carson. Sterling 2007 124p il (Sterling biographies) lib bdg $12.95; pa $5.95

Grades: 6 7 8 9   **92**

1. Inventors   2. Teachers of the deaf   3. Telecommunications executives

ISBN 978-1-4027-4951-3 lib bdg; 1-4027-4951-1 lib bdg; 1-4027-3230-9 pa; 978-1-4027-3230-0 pa

LC 2007003502

"Carson introduces Bell's life, giving readers an excellent picture of why this man became so famous. . . . [The book provides] clear, concise information in an easy-to-follow format with captioned photographs and illustrations on most pages." SLJ

Includes glossary and bibliographical references

Garmon, Anita. **Alexander** Graham Bell invents; by Anita Garmon. National Geographic 2007 40p il (National Geographic history chapters) lib bdg $17.90

Grades: 2 3 4   **92**

1. Inventors   2. Teachers of the deaf   3. Telecommunications executives

ISBN 978-1-4263-0189-6

LC 2007007828

This biography of the inventor is "nicely illustrated with photos, paintings, engravings, and facsimiles. [It is] just right for emerging chapter-book readers. . . . Useful for reports . . . and interesting pleasure reading." SLJ

Includes glossary and bibliographical references

Bernstein, Leonard, 1918-1990

★ Rubin, Susan Goldman. **Music** was IT: young Leonard Bernstein. Charlesbridge 2011 178p il lib bdg $19.95

Grades: 5 6 7 8   **92**

1. Composers   2. Conductors (Music)   3. Jews --

Biography

ISBN 1-58089-344-9 lib bdg; 978-1-58089-344-2 lib bdg; 978-1-60734-276-2 e-book

LC 2010-07584

This is a biography of composer and conductor Leonard Bernstein. Bibliography. Index. "Grades five to nine." (Bull Cent Child Books)

"An impeccably researched and told biography of Leonard Bernstein's musical apprenticeship, from toddlerhood to his conducting debut with the New York Philharmonic at age 25. . . . Drawn from interviews, family memoirs and other print resources, quotations are well-integrated and assiduously attributed. Photos, concert programs, early doodles and letters, excerpts from musical scores and other primary documentation enhance the text. Excellent bookmaking— from type to trim size—complements a remarkable celebration of a uniquely American musical genius." Kirkus

Bhutto, Benazir

Naden, Corinne J. **Benazir** Bhutto. Marshall Cavendish Benchmark 2010 96p il (Leading women) $39.93

Grades: 5 6 7 8   **92**

1. Prime ministers   2. Women politicians   3. Political leaders

ISBN 978-0-7614-4952-2; 0-7614-4952-3

In this biography "readers learn about Bhutto's student years at Radcliffe College and her rise to prime minister of Pakistan, the first woman to lead a Muslim state. . . . The [woman's life is] revealed within the political and historical context of [her] times and [includes] quotes from autobiographical material. . . . Color and black-and-white photos are included. . . . The compact size, chronological organization, and accessible writing [style makes this biography a] good [resource] for reports." SLJ

Includes bibliographical references

Bieber, Justin, 1994-

Bieber, Justin. **Justin** Bieber: first step 2 forever; my story. HarperCollins Children's Books 2010 236p il $21.99

Grades: 4 5 6 7   **92**

1. Singers   2. Pop musicians

ISBN 978-0-06-203974-3; 0-06-203974-1

"Bieber, the platinum-selling singer/songwriter . . . debuts with an account of his 16-year-old life that's cheeky yet entirely in line with his safe and wholesome image. . . . The book covers his upbringing in Ontario, his early introduction to music, YouTube stardom, his love of pranks, and the stratospheric success he now enjoys—all interspersed with lyrics, tweets, and numerous full-bleed photographs of Bieber." Publ Wkly

Yasuda, Anita. **Justin** Bieber. 2011 24p il (Remarkable people) lib bdg $27.13; pa $12.95

Grades: 4 5 6 7   **92**

1. Singers   2. Pop musicians

ISBN 978-1-61690-667-2 lib bdg; 1-61690-667-7 lib bdg; 978-1-61690-672-6 pa; 1-61690-672-3 pa

LC 2010051002

This looks at Justin Bieber's "life, accomplishments, and challenges while including a page of quotes, an annotated list of contemporaries and influences, starter suggestions for writing a paper, and a time line and glossary. . . . [This book] tracks the music sensation from 12-year-old YouTube phenom to the kind of celebrity who's earned such numbing fun facts as 'Justin has a dog named Sam.'" Booklist

Black Elk, 1863-1950

★ Nelson, S. D. **Black** Elk's vision; a Lakota story. Abrams Books for Young Readers 2010 47p il $19.95
Grades: 5 6 7 8   92
1. Shamans 2. Oglala Indians 3. Indian leaders
ISBN 978-0-8109-8399-1; 0-8109-8399-0
LC 2009-9392
"This handsomely designed, large-format book tells the story of Black Elk (1863-1950), a Lakota man who saw many changes come to his people. . . . Often quoting from Black Elk Speaks (1932), Nelson makes vivid the painful ways life changed for the Lakotain in the 1800s. . . . Colorful, imaginative artwork, created using pencils and acrylic paints, is interspersed with nineteenth-century photos, underscoring that this dramatic account reflects the experiences of a man who witnessed history." Booklist

Bly, Nellie, 1864-1922

★ Macy, Sue. **Bylines**: a photobiography of Nellie Bly; foreword by Linda Ellerbee. National Geographic 2009 64p il map $19.95; lib bdg $28.90
Grades: 5 6 7 8   92
1. Authors 2. Journalists 3. Women journalists 4. Nonfiction writers
ISBN 978-1-4263-0513-9; 1-4263-0513-3; 978-1-4263-0514-6 lib bdg; 1-4263-0514-1 lib bdg
LC 2008-52329
"This is a biography of the American reporter. Grades five to nine." (Bull Cent Child Books)
"This detailed biography of the trailblazing 19th-century journalist incorporates photographs of Bly and her subjects. The extensive text explores the details of a life spent seeking justice. . . . A thorough introduction to the life of a fascinating figure." Publ Wkly

Blériot, Louis, 1872-1936

★ Provensen, Alice. The **glorious** flight: across the Channel with Louis Bleriot, July 25, 1909; [by] Alice and Martin Provensen. Viking 1983 39p il $17.99; pa $6.99
Grades: 1 2 3 4   92
1. Air pilots 2. Aeronautical engineers 3. Airplanes -- Design and construction
ISBN 978-0-670-34259-4; 0-670-34259-9; 978-0-14-050729-4; 0-14-050729-9 pa
LC 82-7034
Awarded the Caldecott Medal, 1984
"A pleasing text recounts Bleriot's adventures with gentle humor and admiration for his earnest, if accident-prone, determination. Best of all, the pictures shine with the illustrator's delight in the wondrous flying machines themselves." Horn Book

Boone, Daniel, 1734-1820

Spradlin, Michael P. **Daniel** Boone's great escape; [by] Michael P. Spradlin; illustrated by Ard Hoyt. Walker & Co. 2008 un il $16.95; lib bdg $17.85
Grades: K 1 2 3   92
1. Escapes 2. Explorers 3. Shawnee Indians 4.

Frontier and pioneer life 5. Scouts 6. Pioneers
ISBN 978-0-8027-9581-6; 0-8027-9581-1; 978-0-8027-9582-3 lib bdg; 0-8027-9582-X lib bdg
LC 2007-50382
"Spradlin . . . and Hoyt . . . deliver a thrilling adventure about famed 18th-century frontiersman Daniel Boone. The storytelling is immediate and swift. . . . Gripping prose relates Boone's experiences as the Shawnee hold him captive from February to June in 1778, until he makes a daring escape to warn fellow settlers of an impending attack. Hoyt's skillful blend of closeups and eye-level perspectives pulls readers right into the action. Maintaining the tight-as-a drum tension, the watercolor-and-ink scenes show the escapee hightailing it through thick forests." Publ Wkly

Brady, Tom

Wilner, Barry. **Tom** Brady; a football star who cares. Enslow Publishers, Inc. 2011 48p il (Sport stars who care) lib bdg $23.93; pa $7.95
Grades: 3 4 5   92
1. Football players 2. Football -- Biography
ISBN 978-0-7660-3773-1 lib bdg; 0-7660-3773-8 lib bdg; 978-1-59845-233-4 pa; 1-59845-233-9 pa
LC 2010041784
A biography of the quarterback for the New England Patriots who also works for charities.
This is "especially good for book reports." Booklist
Includes glossary and bibliographical references

Braille, Louis, 1809-1852

★ Freedman, Russell. **Out** of darkness: the story of Louis Braille; illustrated by Kate Kiesler. Clarion Bks. 1997 81p il $16.95; pa $7.95
Grades: 4 5 6 7   92
1. Blind 2. Inventors 3. Teachers of the blind 4. Blind -- Books and reading
ISBN 0-395-77516-7; 0-395-96888-7 pa
LC 95-52353
"Without melodrama, Freedman tells the momentous story in quiet chapters in his best plain style, making the facts immediate and personal. . . . A diagram explains how the Braille alphabet works, and Kate Kessler's full-page shaded pencil illustrations are part of the understated poignant drama." Booklist

Branson, Richard

Goldsworthy, Steve. **Richard** Branson. 2011 il (Remarkable people) $27.13; pa $12.95
Grades: 4 5 6 7   92
1. Businessmen 2. Financiers 3. Retail executives 4. Airline executives 5. Telecommunications executives
ISBN 978-1-61690-671-9; 978-1-61690-676-4 pa
LC 2010051145
A biography of British financier Richard Branson.

Breckinridge, Mary, 1881-1965

★ Wells, Rosemary. **Mary** on horseback; three mountain stories. pictures by Peter McCarty. Dial Bks. for Young Readers 1998 53p il $16.99; pa $4.99
Grades: 4 5 6 7   92
1. Nurses 2. Midwives 3. Medical care -- Kentucky -- History -- Juvenile literature
ISBN 0-670-88923-7; 0-14-130815-X pa
LC 97-43409

Tells the stories of three families who were helped by the work of Mary Breckinridge, the first nurse to go into the Appalachian Mountains and give medical care to the isolated inhabitants. Includes an afterword with facts about Breckinridge and the Frontier Nursing Service she founded

"These beautifully written stories will remain with the reader long after the book is closed." Booklist

Breitbart, Siegmund, 1883-1925

Rubinstein, Robert E. **Zishe** the strongman; by Robert Rubinstein; illustrations by Woody Miller. Kar-Ben Pub. 2010 un il lib bdg $17.95; pa $7.95

Grades: K 1 2 3   92

1. Strong men 2. Bodybuilders 3. Jews -- Poland 4. Circus performers 5. Jews -- Biography

ISBN 978-0-7613-3958-8 lib bdg; 0-7613-3958-2 lib bdg; 978-0-7613-3960-1 pa; 0-7613-3960-4 pa

LC 2009001875

"This picture book in warm sepia tones tells of a Polish Jew who emigrated to the U.S. in the early twentieth century and became a famous circus strongman. . . . This title makes a lively addition to other stories of Yiddish immigration." Booklist

Bridges, Ruby

★ Bridges, Ruby. **Through** my eyes: the autobiography of Ruby Bridges; articles and interviews compiled and edited by Margo Lundell. Scholastic Press 1999 63p il $16.95

Grades: 4 5 6   92

1. Travel agents 2. Civil rights activists 3. African Americans -- Civil rights

ISBN 0-590-18923-9

LC 98-49242

Ruby Bridges recounts the story of her involvement, as a six-year-old, in the integration of her school in New Orleans in 1960

"Profusely illustrated with sepia photos—including many gritty journalistic reproductions—this memoir brings some of the raw emotions of a tumultuous period into sharp focus. . . . A powerful personal narrative that every collection will want to own." SLJ

Donaldson, Madeline. **Ruby** Bridges. Lerner Publications 2009 48p il (History maker bios) $27.93

Grades: 3 4 5   92

1. School integration 2. Travel agents 3. Civil rights activists 4. African Americans -- Civil rights

ISBN 978-0-7613-4220-5; 0-7613-4220-6

LC 2008046526

"Donaldson recounts the story of this young African American girl who, in 1960 at the age of six, integrated New Orleans' William Franz Elementary School. . . . Donaldson's book is illustrated will fill-color drawings and carefully chosen period photos. . . . The book . . . makes a good introduction for report writers too young for Bridges' own memoir, Through My Eyes (1999)." Booklist

Includes bibliographical references

Bridgman, Laura Dewey, 1829-1889

Alexander, Sally Hobart. **She** touched the world: Laura Bridgman, deaf-blind pioneer; by Sally Hobart Alexander and Robert Alexander. Clarion Books 2008 100p il $18

Grades: 5 6 7 8   92

1. Deaf 2. Blind 3. Students 4. Physicians 5. Philanthropists 6. Humanitarians 7. Teachers of the blind

ISBN 978-0-618-85299-4; 0-618-85299-9

"At the age of three, in 1832, Laura Bridgman contracted scarlet fever and lost her sight, her hearing, her sense of smell, and much of her sense of taste. Her family sent her to Dr. Samuel [Gridley] Howe at the New England Institute for the Education of the Blind, and by the age of 10, Laura was world-famous for her accomplishments. . . . Alexander . . . presents a well-written and thoroughly researched biography of this remarkable woman, with numerous black-and-white photos." Booklist

Includes bibliographical references

Brown, John, 1800-1859

★ Hendrix, John. **John** Brown; his fight for freedom. written and illustrated by John Hendrix. Abrams Books for Young Readers 2009 39p il $18.95

Grades: 4 5 6 7   92

1. Abolitionists 2. Slavery -- United States 3. Slavery -- History -- Juvenile literature

ISBN 978-0-8109-3798-7; 0-8109-3798-0

LC 2008-45969

The author "traces how John Brown went from conducting slaves along the Underground Railroad to espousing violent insurrection as a means to end slavery. . . . Reinforcing Brown as a larger-than-life folk hero, the pictures are exhilarating. . . . By embracing Brown's complexity, especially in the well-argued afterword, Hendrix sows acres of fertile ground for discussion." Booklist

Bruchac, Joseph, 1942-

Parker-Rock, Michelle. **Joseph** Bruchac; an author kids love. Enslow Publishers, Inc. 2009 48p il (Authors kids love) lib bdg $23.93

Grades: 3 4 5   92

1. Poets 2. Authors 3. Storytellers 4. College teachers 5. Magazine editors 6. Authors, American 7. Children's authors 8. Nonfiction writers

ISBN 978-0-7660-3160-9 lib bdg; 0-7660-3160-8 lib bdg

LC 2008-33051

"Clearly written, [this] outstanding [biography provides] many interesting details about the [subject's] personal [life] and [includes] photos that enhance the [text]." SLJ

Includes glossary and bibliographical references

Bryan, Ashley, 1923-

★ Bryan, Ashley. **Ashley** Bryan; words to my life's song. with photographs by Bill McGuinness. Atheneum Books for Young Readers 2009 58p il $18.99

Grades: 3 4 5 6   92

1. Artists 2. Authors 3. Illustrators 4. African American artists 5. African American authors 6. College teachers 7. Authors, American 8. Children's authors

ISBN 978-1-4169-0541-7; 1-4169-0541-3

LC 2008-14369

"In rich collages of words and pictures, this highly visual autobiography introduces artist Ashley Bryan's life and his vision of the world around him. . . . Photos of Bryan's world and reproductions of his often bright-hued and inherently vibrant artworks appear on every page. . . . They infuse the entire presentation with energy, color, and joy. . . . Beautifully designed, the book creates an original, stimulating, and inspiring portrait of the artist . . . as well as a celebration of his vision." Booklist

Buchanan, James, 1791-1868

Burgan, Michael. **James** Buchanan. Marshall Cavendish Benchmark 2011 112p il (Presidents and their times) lib bdg $23.95

Grades: 5 6 7 8   92

1. Presidents 2. Senators 3. Members of Congress 4. Secretaries of state

ISBN 978-0-7614-4810-5; 0-7614-4810-1

LC 2009025933

This offers information on President James Buchanan and places him within his historical and cultural context. Also explored are the formative events of his times and how he responded.

"The abundant sidebars provide a good deal of background information that will be helpful to students. . . . Attractive . . . as well as useful." Booklist

Includes glossary and bibliographical references

Burningham, John, 1936-

Burningham, John. **John** Burningham; preface by Maurice Sendak; commentary by Brian Alderson. Candlewick Press 2009 223p il $70

Grades: Adult Professional   92

1. Artists 2. Authors 3. Illustrators 4. Authors, English 5. Children's authors

ISBN 978-0-7636-4434-5; 0-7636-4434-X

"The British author and illustrator has garnered an international reputation for combining imaginative, offbeat illustrations with highly funny, original stories for children. In this oversize, lavishly illustrated volume, Burningham relates his life story from his nonconformist schooling and his early meanderings around the world to his various artistic ventures, picture books being only one of his endeavors. . . . Students of children's literature will be intrigued by Maurice Sendak's short preface and by the six-page opening commentary by children's literature scholar Brian Alderson. A fascinating and insightful treat for Burningham aficionados." SLJ

Caesar, Julius, 100-44 B.C.

Galford, Ellen. **Julius** Caesar; the boy who conquered an empire. [by] Ellen Galford. National Geographic 2007 64p il map (World history biographies) $17.95; lib bdg $27.90

Grades: 5 6 7 8   92

1. Statesmen 2. Historians 3. Emperors -- Rome

ISBN 978-1-4263-0064-6; 978-1-4263-0065-3 lib bdg

LC 2006020777

A biography of the Roman emperor

This "visually appealing [title is] packed with excellent photographs and reproductions, interesting sidebars, and [has] a time line running along the bottom of every page. . . . [This book is] useful, well-written." SLJ

Includes glossary and bibliographical references

Calder, Alexander, 1898-1976

★ Stone, Tanya Lee. **Sandy's** circus; a story about Alexander Calder. illustrated by Boris Kulikov. Viking 2008 un il $16.99

Grades: 1 2 3   92

1. Artists 2. Sculptors 3. Circus in art 4. Artists -- United States 5. Sculpture -- History -- Juvenile literature

ISBN 978-0-670-06268-3; 0-670-06268-5

LC 2008-08380

"This beautifully illustrated picture-book biography . . . [offers a] spare, direct story that focuses on Calder's youth and what are, perhaps, his most kid-accessible artworks: his wire sculptures of circus performers. . . . Kulikov's elegant, fanciful, multimedia collages extend the story." Booklist

Includes bibliographical references

Campanella, Roy, 1921-1993

Adler, David A. **Campy**; the Roy Campanella story. by David A. Adler; illustrated by Gordon C. James. Viking Penguin 2007 un il $15.99

Grades: 2 3 4   92

1. Baseball players 2. African American athletes 3. Baseball -- Biography

ISBN 0-670-06041-0

LC 2005023314

"Roy Campanella . . . was the second African American signed by Branch Rickey to play for the Brooklyn Dodgers. . . . Adler . . . capably reprises Campy's on-field triumphs . . . and off-field tragedy (he was paralyzed in a car accident in 1958), while James delivers evocative illustrations in the soft-focus, pastel-heavy style that has become standard for baseball." nostalgia. Booklist

Includes bibliographical references

Cannon, Annie Jump, 1863-1941

Gerber, Carole. **Annie** Jump Cannon, astronomer; illustrated by Christina Wald. Pelican Pub. 2011 un il $16.99

Grades: 2 3 4 5   92

1. Deaf 2. Astronomers 3. Women astronomers 4. Curators

ISBN 9781589809116; 1589809114

LC 2011012147

"This inspiring picture-book biography of a trailblazer in the field presents insight into the challenges of women interested in science during the late 19th and early 20th centuries. Cannon was born in 1863 and as a young girl her mother nurtured her interest in the night sky. . . . When her father learned that Wellesley College was the only women's college offering physics classes, he enrolled her. She graduated with a degree in physics and had a successful career in astronomy. . . . The realistic illustrations capture the time period and complement the text. They're scientifically accurate. . . . A solid resource." SLJ

Carson, Rachel, 1907-1964

★ Ehrlich, Amy. **Rachel**; the story of Rachel Carson. illustrated by Wendell Minor. Silver Whistle/Harcourt 2003 un il $16

Grades: 2 3 4   92

1. Authors 2. Conservationists 3. Women scientists 4. College teachers 5. Marine biologists 6. Writers on nature 7. Writers on science

ISBN 0-15-216227-5

LC 00-13115

This "anecdotal biography of nature writer and environmentalist Carson focuses on incidents that influenced

Carson's thinking and career aspirations. . . . Minor's . . . impressively realistic watercolor and gouache paintings lend a pleasing cohesiveness to the volume." Publ Wkly

Scherer, Glenn. **Who** on earth is Rachel Carson? mother of the environmental movement. [by] Glenn Scherer and Marty Fletcher. Enslow Publishers 2009 112p il (Scientists saving the earth) lib bdg $31.93
Grades: 5 6 7 8   92
  1. Authors 2. Biologists 3. Conservationists 4. Women scientists 5. Environmentalists 6. College teachers 7. Marine biologists 8. Writers on nature 9. Writers on science
  ISBN 978-1-59845-116-0 lib bdg; 1-59845-116-2 lib bdg
                                                LC 2008028498
"The writing is clear and informative. . . . Color photographs are relevant and of good quality." SLJ
Includes bibliographical references

Carver, George Washington, 1864?-1943
  ★ Bolden, Tonya. **George** Washington Carver. Abrams Books for Young Readers 2008 41p il $18.95
Grades: 3 4 5 6   92
  1. Botanists 2. Scientists 3. African Americans -- Biography 4. Biography, Individual -- Juvenile literature
  ISBN 978-0-8109-9366-2; 0-8109-9366-X
                                                LC 2007-28069
NCTE Orbis Pictus Award honor book (2009)
This is a biography of "the slave-born black scientist. . . . Offering sourced quotations throughout, Bolden covers subtleties that simpler treatments tend to bypass. . . . Photos and reproductions, many of Carver's own paintings, are exceptional, and their arrangement in the style of an old-fashioned album lends the book a suitable gravitas. . . . [The book is] absorbing." Booklist
Includes bibliographical references

Harness, Cheryl. The **groundbreaking**, chance-taking life of George Washington Carver and science & invention in America; by Cheryl Harness. National Geographic 2008 143p il map (Cherly Harness histories) $16.95; lib bdg $25.90
Grades: 4 5 6 7   92
  1. Botanists 2. Scientists 3. African Americans -- Biography
  ISBN 978-1-4263-0196-4; 1-4263-0196-0; 978-1-4263-0197-1 lib bdg; 1-4263-0197-9 lib bdg
                                                LC 2007029316
"Harness presents Carver as a man who, regardless of constant hardship and racial prejudice, persevered to become a beloved teacher and devoted scientist. . . . The author raises challenging questions throughout. . . . The lively prose style conveys his sense of passion and adventure about the man and his intellectual pursuits, and the simple black-and-white drawings add a further sense of drama." SLJ
Includes bibliographical references

Cassatt, Mary, 1844-1926
  Harris, Lois V. **Mary** Cassatt; impressionist painter. [by] Lois V. Harris. Pelican 2007 32p il $15.95

Grades: 2 3 4   92
  1. Artists 2. Painters 3. Women artists
  ISBN 978-1-58980-452-4
                                                LC 2007011755
"With large, crisply reproduced, color artwork on nearly every page, this picture-book biography of American Impressionist Mary Cassatt will appeal to a broad age-range of readers." Booklist

Catherine, Duchess of Cambridge, 1982-
  Doeden, Matt. **Prince** William & Kate; a royal romance. Lerner Publications 2011 48p il lib bdg $26.60
Grades: 5 6 7 8   92
  1. Princes 2. Princesses
  ISBN 978-0-7613-8029-0; 0-7613-8029-9
                                                LC 2011003413
"This short and sweet volume accents what down-to-earth and normal newlyweds Prince William and Kate Middleton are really like. After a brief recap of the couple's engagement interview, the book goes on to profile the pair individually and then as a duo. . . . This is an upbeat, readable narrative about a handsome, appealing couple. The color photographs are well chosen." Booklist
Includes glossary and bibliographical references

Champlain, Samuel de, 1567-1635
  MacLeod, Elizabeth. **Samuel** de Champlain; written by Elizabeth MacLeod; illustrated by John Mantha. Kids Can Press 2008 32p il (Kids Can Read) $14.95; pa $3.95
Grades: 1 2 3   92
  1. Explorers
  ISBN 978-1-55453-049-6; 1-55453-049-0; 978-1-55453-050-2 pa; 1-55453-050-4 pa
  A biography of the French explorer of Canada
This is a "fresh, short [biography] for newly independent readers. . . . The writing is clear if sedate, and the type is large. Abundant pen-and-ink illustrations are finely rendered and enhance [the] text." SLJ

Champollion, Jean François, 1790-1832
  Rumford, James. **Seeker** of knowledge; the man who deciphered Egyptian hieroglyphs. Houghton Mifflin 2000 un il $15; pa $6.95
Grades: 3 4 5   92
  1. Hieroglyphics 2. Archaeologists 3. Egyptologists -- France -- Biography -- Juvenile literature
  ISBN 0-395-97934-X; 0-618-33345-2 pa
                                                LC 99-37254
A biography of the French scholar whose decipherment of the Egyptian hieroglyphic language made the study of ancient Egypt possible
"Despite the book's traditional picture-book appearance, with a short text and nicely rendered watercolor art, the topic requires and gets sturdy treatment. . . . Those intrigued by hieroglyphs . . . will find this a useful introduction." Booklist

Chanel, Coco, 1883-1971
  ★ Matthews, Elizabeth. **Different** like Coco. Candlewick Press 2007 un il $16.99
Grades: 2 3 4   92
  1. Fashion designers 2. Perfumers 3. Cosmetics industry executives 4. Fashion -- Juvenile literature
  ISBN 978-0-7636-2548-1; 0-7636-2548-5
                                                LC 2006-40622

"A celebration of the life of a major fashion designer and independent spirit. . . . The story is accompanied, appropriately, by elegant pen-and-ink and watercolor cartoons that capture her struggles as a young woman, as well as her innate sense of style." SLJ

Chaplin, Charlie, 1889-1977

★ Fleischman, Sid. **Sir** Charlie; Chaplin, the funniest man in the world. Greenwillow Books 2010 268p il $19.99; lib bdg $20.89

Grades: 5 6 7 8 9   **92**

1. Actors 2. Comedians 3. Motion pictures 4. Motion picture directors 5. Motion picture producers

ISBN 0-06-189640-3; 0-06-189641-1 lib bdg; 978-0-06-189640-8; 978-0-06-189641-5 lib bdg

LC 2009019689

This is a biography of the actor and director who starred in such films as City Lights (1931), Modern Times (1940), The Great Dictator (1947) and Limelight (1952). Chronology. Bibliography. Index. Grades six to ten. (Bull Cent Child Books)

"This lively and engaging account of a poor Cockney boy who became the world's greatest silent-movie comedian is a must for biography collections. . . . Brief, easily digestible chapters, an extensive time line, and plenty of photos make the book's well-researched content accessible and appealing." SLJ

Chapman, Oscar L., 1896-1978

★ Hopkinson, Deborah. **Sweet** land of liberty; written by Deborah Hopkinson; illustrated by Leonard Jenkins. Peachtree 2007 un il $16.95

Grades: K 1 2 3 4   **92**

1. Lawyers 2. Opera singers 3. Secretaries of the interior 4. African Americans -- Biography 5. African Americans -- Civil rights

ISBN 1-56145-395-1; 978-1-56145-395-5

LC 2006024331

"Jenkins' powerful, bright, mixed-media collages show and tell the connections, past, present, and future." SLJ

Chavez, Cesar, 1927-1993

Adler, David A. A **picture** book of Cesar Chavez; by David A. Adler and Michael S. Adler; illustrated by Marie Olofsdotter. Holiday House 2010 un il $17.95

Grades: 1 2 3 4   **92**

1. Migrant labor 2. Agricultural laborers 3. Labor leaders 4. Mexican Americans -- Biography

ISBN 978-0-8234-2202-9; 0-8234-2202-X

LC 2009039319

"The selfless struggles of labor leader Chávez are given a tempered and lucid treatment in this educational overview. . . . Olofsdotter keeps her illustrations gentle and ennobling. The characters are drawn in the intentionally stiff style that fits with the depth-challenged folk art backgrounds, most of which are dominated by the color of sand. . . . An elegant introduction to a man who inspired thousands." Booklist

Includes bibliographical references

★ Krull, Kathleen. **Harvesting** hope; the story of Cesar Chavez. illustrated by Yuyi Morales. Harcourt 2003 un il $17

Grades: 2 3 4   **92**

1. Migrant labor 2. Agricultural laborers 3. Labor leaders 4. Mexican Americans -- Biography

ISBN 0-15-201437-3

LC 2002-5096

A biography of Cesar Chavez, from age ten when he and his family lived happily on their Arizona ranch, to age thirty-eight when he led a peaceful protest against California migrant workers' miserable working conditions

"The brief text creates a remarkably complex view of Chavez—his experiences and feelings. Krull's empathetic words are well paired with artist Yuyi Morales's mixed-media acrylic paintings, which are suffused with a variety of emotions. . . . The pictures glow with intense shades of gold, green, pink, and orange." Horn Book

Chisholm, Shirley, 1924-2005

Raatma, Lucia. **Shirley** Chisholm. Marshall Cavendish Benchmark 2010 96p il (Leading women) $39.93

Grades: 4 5 6 7   **92**

1. Women politicians 2. Members of Congress 3. Presidential candidates 4. African American women -- Biography

ISBN 978-0-7614-4953-9; 0-7614-4953-1

"The arresting portrait on the cover will guide readers right into this well-written [biography of] . . . the first African American woman to enter Congress. . . . Raatma vividly explains what was happening in the country at the time and uses those events effectively as a backdrop. The many photos, both black and white and color, are good choices for the well-designed book." Booklist

Includes bibliographical references

Clemens, Susy, 1872-1894

★ Kerley, Barbara. The **extraordinary** Mark Twain (according to Susy) illustrated by Edwin Fotheringam. Scholastic Press 2010 un il $17.99

Grades: 2 3 4 5   **92**

1. Authors 2. Biography 3. Humorists 4. Novelists 5. Authorship 6. Essayists 7. Satirists 8. Memoirists 9. Travel writers 10. Authors, American 11. Short story writers

ISBN 978-0-545-12508-6; 0-545-12508-1

LC 2009-04752

"Wanting to present a portrait of her papa beyond that of just humorist and author, Mark Twain's 13-year-old daughter Susy spent a year chronicling her observations and reflections. . . . Kerley contextualizes the teenager's admiring musings with vivid familial backdrops. . . . Minibooklets titled 'Journal' appear in the fold of many spreads, containing excerpts from Susy's notebook. . . . Adding dynamic flair to the limited palettes of each digitally created scene are curlicues representing words, which emanate wildly from pen tips, pages, and mouths. Author notes about Susy and her father, a time line of Twain's life, and tips for writing an 'extraordinary biography' complete this accessible and inventive vision of a American legend." Publ Wkly

Clemente, Roberto, 1934-1972

★ Perdomo, Willie. **Clemente!** illustrated by Bryan Collier. Henry Holt & Co. 2010 un il $16.99

Grades: 1 2 3   **92**

1. Baseball players 2. Baseball -- Biography

ISBN 978-0-8050-8224-1; 0-8050-8224-7

"Perdomo's witty, passionate account of the beloved Puerto Rican baseball pioneer takes an unusual approach.

The child narrator, whose father is president of the Roberto Clemente fan club, was named in honor of the great player, and little Clemente can tell you just about everything there is to know about the man. . . . Collier's kinetic artwork uses collage to explosive effect. . . . More than just a biography, this book warmly illustrates the parent-child bond that is one of the finer by-products of sports fandom." Booklist

★ Winter, Jonah. **Roberto** Clemente; pride of the Pittsburgh Pirates. illustrated by Raul Colón. Atheneum Books for Young Readers 2005 un il $16.95
Grades: 2 3 4   92
1. Baseball players 2. Baseball -- Biography 3. Puerto Ricans -- Biography
ISBN 0-689-85643-1
LC 2003-25546
This is a biography of the baseball player. Ages five to eight. (Bull Cent Child Books)
"Winter tells the . . . story of how Clemente's passionate love of the game and unrivaled work ethic took him from poverty in Puerto Rico . . . to World Series triumph with the Pittsburgh Pirates and, later . . . to near-mythic status as a role model for young Latino ballplayers. Soaked in pastoral greens and browns, Colon's evocatively grainy, soft-focus illustrations, rendered with a mix of watercolors, colored pencils, and litho pencils, capture perfectly the worlds in which Clemente was most at home. . . . Baseball history brought vividly to life for a younger audience." Booklist

Cleopatra, Queen of Egypt, d. 30 B.C.
Blackaby, Susan. **Cleopatra**; Egypt's last and greatest queen. Sterling Pub. 2009 124p il (Sterling biographies) $12.95; pa $5.95
Grades: 5 6 7 8   92
1. Queens
ISBN 978-1-4027-6540-7; 1-4027-6540-1; 978-1-4027-5710-5 pa; 1-4027-5710-7 pa
LC 2008030146
"Villainess or goddess, a great queen or a selfish and overly ambitious woman—readers get to decide. They will be drawn into this biography by a description of a legendary magnificent banquet given by Mark Antony for Cleopatra. The lively narrative maintains interest from her birth in 69 BCE to her death in 31 BCE. . . . Sidebars, color photographs, and reproductions appear throughout. . . . This book leaves readers fascinated and eager to learn more about her time in history." SLJ
Includes glossary and bibliographical references

Shecter, Vicky Alvear. **Cleopatra** rules! the amazing life of the original teen queen. Boyds Mills Press 2010 128p il map $17.95
Grades: 5 6 7 8   92
1. Queens
ISBN 1590787188; 9781590787182
LC 2009-26737
This is a biography of "Cleopatra VII, the last pharaoh of Egypt." (Publisher's note) "Grades six to ten." (Bull Cent Child Books)
"This attractive book presents Cleopatra's story through an unusual text, informative sidebars, and excellent color illustrations. . . . Calling attention to the writing as much as its story, the text includes puns, informal language, and

contemporary metaphors. . . . Shecter's solid research is evident." Booklist
Includes glossary and bibliographical references

Cleveland, Grover, 1837-1908
Otfinoski, Steven. **Grover** Cleveland. Marshall Cavendish Benchmark 2011 112p il (Presidents and their times) lib bdg $23.95
Grades: 5 6 7 8   92
1. Mayors 2. Governors 3. Presidents 4. District attorneys
ISBN 978-0-7614-4811-2; 0-7614-4811-X
LC 2009029689
This offers information on President Grover Cleveland and places him within his historical and cultural context. Also explored are the formative events of his times and how he responded.
"The abundant sidebars provide a good deal of background information that will be helpful to students. . . . Attractive . . . as well as useful." Booklist
Includes glossary and bibliographical references

Clinton, Hillary Rodham, 1947-
Blashfield, Jean F. **Hillary** Clinton. Marshall Cavendish Benchmark 2010 112p il (Leading women) $39.93
Grades: 4 5 6 7   92
1. Lawyers 2. Women politicians 3. Senators 4. Secretaries of state 5. Spouses of presidents 6. Presidential candidates
ISBN 978-0-7614-4954-6; 0-7614-4954-X
A biography of the Secretary of State and former Senator, presidential candidate, and First Lady.
Includes bibliographical references

Cogswell, Alice
★ McCully, Emily Arnold. **My** heart glow: Alice Cogswell, Thomas Gallaudet and the birth of American sign language. Hyperion Books for Children 2008 un il $15.99
Grades: 2 3 4   92
1. Deaf 2. Sign language 3. Teachers of the deaf 4. Deafness -- Juvenile literature 5. Sign language -- Juvenile literature
ISBN 978-1-4231-0028-7; 1-4231-0028-X
This is the story of Thomas Gallaudet and his deaf neighbor, Alice Cogswell, and how Gallaudet established a school for the deaf in the United States and developed American Sign Language.
"Emily Arnold McCully's watercolor illustrations are beautifully rendered. . . . Not only does this book accurately present the engrossing story of Alice and Gallaudet, it is also an excellent resource for teaching diversity and encouraging empathy for others." Libr Media Connect

Coleman, Bessie, 1896?-1926
★ Grimes, Nikki. **Talkin'** about Bessie: the story of aviator Elizabeth Coleman; illustrated by E. B. Lewis. Orchard Bks. 2002 un il $16.95
Grades: 3 4 5   92
1. Air pilots 2. Women air pilots 3. African American pilots
ISBN 0-439-35243-6
Coretta Scott King Award for illustration, 2003
"Following a brief introduction to Coleman's life, the story, couched in a fictional framework, opens in the parlor

of a house in Chicago, where friends and relatives gather to mourn Bessie's death. Each spread features one person speaking about Bessie. . . . Lewis' paintings, subdued in tone and color, reflect the spirit of the verse through telling details and sensitive, impressionistic portrayals." Booklist

Includes bibliographical references

Colt, Samuel, 1814-1862

Wyckoff, Edwin Brit. The **man** behind the gun: Samuel Colt and his revolver. Enslow Publishers 2010 32p il (Genius at work! Great inventor biographies) lib bdg $22.60

Grades: 4 5 6   92

    1. Inventors 2. Firearms industry 3. Gunsmiths 4. Manufacturing executives

    ISBN 978-0-7660-3446-4 lib bdg; 0-7660-3446-1 lib bdg

                              LC 2009-28129

"Readers will learn about Samuel Colt, the revolver, and mass production." Publisher's note

Includes glossary and bibliographical references

Coltrane, John, 1926-1967

Weatherford, Carole Boston. **Before** John was a jazz giant: a song of John Coltrane; [illustrated by] Sean Qualls. Henry Holt & Co. 2008 un il $16.95

Grades: K 1 2 3   92

    1. Jazz musicians 2. African American musicians 3. Saxophonists

    ISBN 978-0-8050-7994-4; 0-8050-7994-7

                              LC 2007-07196

Coretta Scott King honor book for illustration, 2009

"The beat of lyrical words and the beauty of the beautiful illustrations express how, as a child, jazz-musician Coltrane heard music in the world around him. Vibrant with color and movement, double-page spreads in acrylic, collage, and pencil extend the images about the magical sounds of everyday things." Booklist

Columbus, Christopher

Fritz, Jean. **Where** do you think you're going, Christopher Columbus? pictures by Margot Tomes. Putnam 1980 80p il maps $15.99; pa $5.99

Grades: 2 3 4   92

    1. Explorers

    ISBN 0-399-20723-6; 0-698-11580-5 pa

                              LC 80-11377

Discusses the voyages of Christopher Columbus who was determined to beat everyone in the race to the Indies

"Reducing a life as well-documented as Columbus's to 80 pages must result in some simplifications of fact or context, but in this case they are not readily apparent. Mrs. Fritz's breezy narrative gives us a highly individual Columbus. . . . Margot Tomes's three-color illustrations are attractive, amusing and informative." N Y Times Book Rev

Cone, Claribel, 1864-1929

★ Fillion, Susan. **Miss** Etta and Dr. Claribel; Bringing Matisse to America. David R. Godine 2011 83p il $18.95

Grades: 4 5 6 7   92

    1. Artists 2. Painters 3. Physicians 4. Art collectors

    ISBN 978-1-56792-434-3; 1-56792-434-4

                              LC 2010048937

"An affectionate, lively examination of the reciprocal relationship between a great artist and two great art lovers.

Etta and Claribel Cone, unmarried sisters from a wealthy Baltimore family . . . [were] discerning collectors of modern art, particularly that of Henri Matisse. . . . Their account is lavishly illustrated in full color by reproductions from the Cone Collection at the Baltimore Museum of Art and Matisse-inflected paintings by the author, who drew extensively on the Cone archive that is also housed at the museum. . . . This appealing work stands as both a portrait of two unconventional women and a celebration of the possibilties of arts patronage." Kirkus

Cone, Etta, 1870-1949

★ Fillion, Susan. **Miss** Etta and Dr. Claribel; Bringing Matisse to America. David R. Godine 2011 83p il $18.95

Grades: 4 5 6 7   92

    1. Artists 2. Painters 3. Physicians 4. Art collectors

    ISBN 978-1-56792-434-3; 1-56792-434-4

                              LC 2010048937

"An affectionate, lively examination of the reciprocal relationship between a great artist and two great art lovers. Etta and Claribel Cone, unmarried sisters from a wealthy Baltimore family . . . [were] discerning collectors of modern art, particularly that of Henri Matisse. . . . Their account is lavishly illustrated in full color by reproductions from the Cone Collection at the Baltimore Museum of Art and Matisse-inflected paintings by the author, who drew extensively on the Cone archive that is also housed at the museum. . . . This appealing work stands as both a portrait of two unconventional women and a celebration of the possibilties of arts patronage." Kirkus

Copernicus, Nicolaus, 1473-1543

Andronik, Catherine M. **Copernicus;** founder of modern astronomy. rev ed; Enslow Publishers 2009 128p bibl il (Great minds of science) lib bdg $31.93

Grades: 5 6 7 8   92

    1. Astronomers

    ISBN 978-0-7660-3013-8 lib bdg; 0-7660-3013-X lib bdg

                              LC 2008-23940

First published 2002

"A highly readable book that presents a good balance between the biographical information needed to understand Copernicus as a man and the scientific explanations necessary to understand his work. . . . Good-quality, black-and-white reproductions, illustrations, and photographs add interest to the clearly written text." SLJ [review of 2002 edition]

Includes glossary and bibliographical references

Corwin, Jeff

Corwin, Jeff. **Jeff** Corwin: a wild life; the authorized biography. Penguin Group 2009 100p il pa $6.99

Grades: 4 5 6 7   92

    1. Biologists 2. Naturalists 3. Conservationists 4. Television personalities

    ISBN 978-0-14-241403-3 pa; 0-14-241403-4 pa

                              LC 2009008092

"The host of Animal Planet . . . and other popular TV programs blends his exciting adventure in the wild with his passionate call for conservation. . . . An insert of beautifully reproduced color photos from his global travels show him with a giraffe in Kenya, a moose in Alaska, and more. . . .

The adventures are thrilling, and the messages are urgent."
Booklist

Cosgrove, Miranda, 1993-

Yasuda, Anita. **Miranda** Cosgrove. Weigl 2011 24p
il (Remarkable people) $27.13; pa $12.95

Grades: 4 5 6 7   92

1. Actors 2. Singers

ISBN 978-1-6169-0668-9; 1-6169-0668-5; 978-1-
6169-0673-3 pa; 1-6169-0673-1 pa

LC 2010051144

A biography of actress and singer Miranda Cosgrove

Coup, W. C., 1857-1895

Covert, Ralph. **Sawdust** and spangles: the amazing life
of W.C. Coup; [by] Ralph Covert, G. Riley Mills; illustrated
by Giselle Potter. Abrams Books for Young Readers 2007
un il $16.95

Grades: K 1 2 3   92

1. Circus 2. Circus executives

ISBN 978-0-8109-9351-8; 0-8109-9351-1

LC 2006031981

"As a boy, William Cameron Coup left home to run
away with the circus. . . . He eventually became one of the
industry's most successful and inventive entrepeneurs. This
picture book biography relates Coup's story in an accessible
. . . way. Potter's illustrations are beautifully rendered, interpreting Coup's life and world with quirky energy and imaginative color." Horn Book Guide

Cousteau, Jacques Yves, 1910-1997

Berne, Jennifer. **Manfish**: a story of Jacques Cousteau;
illustrated by Eric Puybaret. Chronicle Books 2008 un il
$16.99

Grades: K 1 2 3   92

1. Ocean 2. Authors 3. Scientists 4. Skin diving
5. Divers 6. Naval officers 7. Oceanographers 8.
Nonfiction writers 9. Underwater exploration --
Juvenile literature

ISBN 0-8118-6063-9; 978-0-8118-6063-5

LC 2007-30513

This is a biography of the underwater explorer and marine naturalist. "Ages six to nine." (Bull Cent Child Books)

"Writing in simple poetic language, both lyrical and
concise . . . Berne offers a luminous picture-book biography
of about Jacques Cousteau. . . . Puybaret's smooth-looking
acrylic paintings extend the words' elegant simplicity and
beautifully convey the sense of infinite, underwater space."
Booklist

★ Yaccarino, Dan. The **fantastic** undersea life of
Jacques Cousteau. Knopf 2009 un il $16.99; lib bdg
$19.99

Grades: K 1 2 3   92

1. Ocean 2. Authors 3. Scientists 4. Skin diving
5. Divers 6. Naval officers 7. Oceanographers 8.
Nonfiction writers

ISBN 978-0-375-85573-3; 978-0-375-95573-0 lib bdg

LC 2008-04581

"Yaccarino deftly provides information about important
events in Cousteau's life while conveying the excitement
and wonder that the ocean explorer experienced. . . . Effective layout and page design plus colorful gouache illustrations result in a striking visual presentation." SLJ

Coville, Bruce

Parker-Rock, Michelle. **Bruce** Coville; by Michelle
Parker-Rock. Enslow Publishers 2008 48p bibl il por (Authors kids love) lib bdg $23.93

Grades: 3 4 5   92

1. Authors 2. Authors, American 3. Children's authors

ISBN 978-0-7660-2755-8 lib bdg; 0-7660-2755-4
lib bdg

LC 2006015873

A biography of the popular children's author, Bruce Coville, based on a interview.

The text is "interesting and conversational throughout. .
. . [A] colorful [cover], family photos, and a font size that's
not too intimidating all contribute to the [book's] appeal. . . .
Suitable for reports or for pleasure reading." SLJ

Includes glossary and bibliographical references

Crandall, Prudence, 1803-1890

★ Jurmain, Suzanne. The **forbidden** schoolhouse;
the true and dramatic story of Prudence Crandall and her
students. Houghton Mifflin 2005 150p il $18

Grades: 5 6 7 8   92

1. Teachers 2. Educators 3. Abolitionists 4. African
Americans -- Education

ISBN 0-618-47302-5

This is the story of Prudence Crandall, who, in 1831,
opened a school for African American girls in Canterbury,
Connecticut.

"A compelling, highly readable book. . . . Writing with
a sense of drama that propels readers forward . . . Jurmain
makes painfully clear what Crandall and her students faced.
. . . Including a number of sepia-toned and color photographs
as well as historical engravings, the book's look will draw in
readers." Booklist

Includes bibliographical references

Crazy Horse, Sioux Chief, ca. 1842-1877

Brimner, Larry Dane. **Chief** Crazy Horse; following
a vision. Marshall Cavendish Benchmark 2009 41p il
(American heroes) lib bdg $20.95

Grades: 2 3 4   92

1. Indian chiefs

ISBN 978-0-7614-3061-2

LC 2008002868

A biography of Crazy Horse, warrior chief of the Oglala
tribe of the Sioux nation

This "concise and well-written [title covers] key biographical facts without overwhelming young readers, and
[includes] captioned illustrations and reproductions, most
of which are in color. Text is large, and the layout is age-
appropriate and attractive, with wide margins." SLJ

Includes glossary and bibliographical references

Crews, Donald

Crews, Donald. **Bigmama's**. Greenwillow Bks. 1991
un il $16; lib bdg $15.93; pa $5.95

Grades: K 1 2 3   92

1. Artists 2. Authors 3. Country life 4. Illustrators
5. Photographers 6. Authors, American 7. Children's
authors 8. African Americans -- Biography 9. Family
life -- Juvenile literature 10. Country life -- Juvenile

literature

ISBN 0-688-09950-5; 0-688-09951-3 lib bdg; 0-688-15842-0 pa

LC 90-33142

Visiting Bigmama's house in the country, young Donald Crews finds his relatives full of news and the old place and its surroundings just the same as the year before

"This is an evocative celebration of the joy and wonder of childhood; would that every child had such a summer. The last page is a hauntingly lovely remembrance. The illustrations are perfect and make this a truly beautiful book." Child Book Rev Serv

Crum, George, fl. 1853

Taylor, Gaylia. **George** Crum and the Saratoga chip; illustrated by Frank Morrison. Lee & Low Books 2006 32p il $16.95

Grades: 2 3 4   92

1. Cooks 2. Cooking 3. Racially mixed people

ISBN 978-1-58430-255-1; 1-58430-255-0

LC 2005015313

"Part Native American, part African American, George Crum coped with prejudice as a boy in New York State during the 1830s. As a young man, he became an excellent cook and was hired as a chef at a renowned restaurant in Saratoga Springs. . . . Once . . . Crum retrieved [a] dish of French fries, whittled them into very thin slices, and cooked them in hot oil, creating the forerunner of the potato chip. . . . This picture-book biography describes dramatic moments that reveal Crum's creativity, artistic temperament, and relentless pursuit of perfection. Buoyant acrylic illustrations accentuate the absurdity of situations, depicting the jaunty chef, all angles and energy." Booklist

Includes bibliographical references

Curie, Marie, 1867-1934

Cregan, Elizabeth R. **Marie** Curie; pioneering physicist. Compass Point Books 2009 40p il map (Mission: Science) lib bdg $26.60

Grades: 4 5 6   92

1. Chemists 2. Physicists 3. Women scientists 4. Nobel laureates for physics

ISBN 978-0-7565-3960-3

This biography of the discoverer of radium "does a good job of connecting the scientist's work to our lives today. . . . [The] book has a variety of graphics including diagrams, photos, and reproductions of paintings and sketches. [This volume is] a definite plus for a school library or the juvenile collection in a public library." Libr Media Connect

★ Krull, Kathleen. **Marie** Curie; [illustrations by] Boris Kulikov. Viking 2007 128p il (Giants of science) $15.99

Grades: 5 6 7 8   92

1. Chemists 2. Physicists 3. Women scientists 4. Nobel laureates for physics

ISBN 978-0-670-05894-5; 0-670-05894-7

LC 2007-24251

"The compelling and conversational narrative (ably assisted by Kulikov's black-and-white drawings) portrays a brilliant . . . woman with plenty of idiosyncrasies, and the story of her discovery of radium . . . is as engaging as any of her personal dramas and challenges." Horn Book

McClafferty, Carla Killough. **Something** out of nothing; Marie Curie and radium. Farrar, Straus & Giroux 2006 134p il $18

Grades: 5 6 7 8 9 10   92

1. Chemists 2. Physicists 3. Women scientists 4. Nobel laureates for physics

ISBN 0-374-38036-8; 0374380368

LC 2004056414

This is a biography of the Polish chemist. Bibliography. Index. "Grades five to eight." (Bull Cent Child Books)

This "biography examines Curie's life and work as a groundbreaking scientist and as an independent woman. . . . The groundbreaking science is as thrilling as the personal story. . . . The spacious design makes the text easy to read, and occasional photos . . . bring the story closer." Booklist

Curtis, Christopher Paul

Parker-Rock, Michelle. **Christopher** Paul Curtis; an author kids love. Enslow Publishers 2009 48p il (Authors kids love) lib bdg $23.93

Grades: 1 2 3   92

1. Authors 2. African American authors 3. Authors, American 4. Children's authors 5. Government employees

ISBN 978-0-7660-3161-6 lib bdg; 0-7660-3161-6 lib bdg

LC 2009022379

A biography of the author of the Newbery honor book The Watsons Go to Birmingham—1963 and the Newbery winner Bud, not Buddy

Includes glossary and bibliographical references

Custer, George Armstrong, 1839-1876

Anderson, Paul Christopher. **George** Armstrong Custer; the Indian Wars and the Battle of the Little Bighorn. [by] Paul Christopher Anderson. PowerPlus Books 2004 112p il (Library of American lives and times) lib bdg $31.95

Grades: 4 5 6 7   92

1. Generals 2. Little Bighorn, Battle of the, 1876 3. Army officers 4. Native Americans -- Wars

ISBN 0-8239-6631-3

LC 2002-153404

A biography of the Civil War general who died at the Battle of the Little Bighorn

This "is not an apologia but a carefully measured analysis. . . . Stunning reproductions and photos provide a clear sense of the times and settings." SLJ

Includes bibliographical references

Cézanne, Paul, 1839-1906

Burleigh, Robert. **Paul** Cezanne; a painter's journey. H.N. Abrams 2006 31p il $17.95

Grades: 4 5 6 7   92

1. Artists 2. Painters 3. Artists, French

ISBN 0-8109-5784-1

LC 2005011779

"Burleigh offers brief insights into Cézanne's personal life, such as his relationship with his father, who did not support his sons interest in art. However, the emphasis is on interpreting some individual paintings and understanding the artist's various styles, including the impact of the Impressionists and his evolution to a freer and simpler manner of expression in his later years. . . . The high-quality reproductions demonstrate Burleigh's points. . . . A solid, lively introduction." SLJ

Dahl, Roald

Dahl, Roald. **More** about Boy; Roald Dahl's tales from childhood. Farrar, Straus, and Giroux 2009 229p il $16.99
Grades: 5 6 7 8   **92**
1. Authors 2. Authors, English 3. Children's authors 4. Short story writers   ISBN 978-0-374-35055-0; 0-374-35055-8

LC 2009016118

First published 2008 in the United Kingdom
"Containing the entire text and artwork from Dahl's 1984 autobiography Boy, this reworked and expanded version also incorporates previously unpublished materials from the Roald Dahl Museum and Story Centre in England, as well as excerpts that have appeared in earlier books. . . . Dahl's revealing writing, open and full of wicked humor, is certain to endear the beloved writer . . . to a new generation." Publ Wkly

Dahl, Roald. The **missing** golden ticket and other splendiferous secrets; illustrated by Quentin Blake. Puffin Books 2010 115p il pa $4.99
Grades: 3 4 5 6   **92**
1. Authors 2. Authors, English 3. Children's authors 4. Short story writers
ISBN 978-0-14-241742-3 pa; 0-14-241742-4 pa

LC 2010021712

"Containing excerpts from earlier tributes to Dahl's work and wit, this is an eclectic and funny collection of tidbits by and about the late author. The kernel of the book is 'Spotty Powder,' a characteristically droll chapter from an early draft of Charlie and the Chocolate Factory. . . . Highly entertaining, it's a sparkling window into Dahl's vivid personality and oeuvre." Publ Wkly

Dalai Lama XIV, 1935-

Kimmel, Elizabeth Cody. **Boy** on the lion throne; the childhood of the 14th Dalai Lama. with a foreword by His Holiness the Dalai Lama. Roaring Brook Press 2009 146p il map $18.95
Grades: 4 5 6 7   **92**
1. Buddhism 2. Buddhist leaders 3. Political leaders 4. Nobel laureates for peace
ISBN 978-1-59643-394-6; 1-59643-394-9

Follows the childhood of Lhamo Thondup, who was identified at the age of two as the fourteenth reincarnation of the Dalai Lama, describing the humble life he was born into and how his life changed after he was recognized

"Kimmel is reverent without being adulatory, and her explanation of the Dalai Lama's relationship with Maoist China is presented in simple, clear language. This is a strange and fascinating story told in an engaging style, and young readers will find lots to keep them turning the pages." Bull Cent Child Books

Includes bibliographical references

Darwin, Charles, 1809-1882

Ashby, Ruth. **Young** Charles Darwin and the voyage of the Beagle; written by Ruth Ashby. Peachtree 2009 116p il map $12.95
Grades: 4 5 6   **92**
1. Evolution 2. Naturalists 3. Travel writers 4. Writers

on science 5. Natural history -- Juvenile literature
ISBN 978-1-56145-478-5; 1-56145-478-8

LC 2008-36747

"Beginning with the letter inviting him to sail aboard the Beagle, this traditional biography relates Darwin's life with an emphasis on the trip that led him to forge his theory about natural selection. Ashby makes good use of Darwin's own writing, sprinkling quotes throughout the text, which allow his adventures and opinions to come to life. . . . This biography will work well for book reports . . . providing accurate and readable information about the scientist and his journey." Booklist

Includes bibliographical references

★ Krull, Kathleen. **Charles** Darwin; illustrated by Boris Kulikov. Viking 2010 144p il (Giants of science) $15.99
Grades: 5 6 7 8   **92**
1. Evolution 2. Naturalists 3. Travel writers 4. Writers on science
ISBN 978-0-670-06335-2; 0-670-06335-5

LC 2010-07315

"Krull once again offers an illuminating, humanizing portrait of a famous scientist. . . . Krull . . . writes in easily paced, lively, conversational prose, knitting together interesting facts, anecdotes, and historical overviews into a fascinating whole. She offers clear definitions of not only Darwin's theories but also how his discoveries built on previous scientists' work. . . . Kulikov's whimsical ink drawings and well-culled list of resources round out this strong entry in the series." Booklist

Lasky, Kathryn. **One** beetle too many: the extraordinary adventures of Charles Darwin. Candlewick Press 2009 un il $17.99; pa $6.99
Grades: 3 4 5 6   **92**
1. Evolution 2. Naturalists 3. Travel writers 4. Writers on science 5. Evolution (Biology) -- Juvenile literature
ISBN 0-7636-1436-X; 978-0-7636-1436-2; 978-0-7636-5821-2 pa

LC 2002-71254

Describes the life and work of the renowned nineteenth-century biologist who transformed conventional Western thought with his theory of natural evolution.

"Distilling tough concepts into light, conversational prose, Lasky . . . gives middle-graders a just-right introduction to Charles Darwin. . . . Trueman . . . up-ends perspective with multilayed mixed-media illustrations; mostly paint, these also incorporate bits of flowers and weeds as well as string, paper, and fabric. . . . Highly accessible." Publ Wkly

Markle, Sandra. **Animals** Charles Darwin saw; an around-the-world adventure. illustrated by Zina Saunders. Chronicle Books 2009 45p il $16.99
Grades: 2 3 4 5   **92**
1. Animals 2. Evolution 3. Naturalists 4. Travel writers 5. Writers on science 6. Natural history -- Juvenile literature
ISBN 978-0-8118-5049-0; 0-8118-5049-8

LC 2007-53058

Looks at the animals that Charles Darwin saw throughout his life, from his early explorations in local woods and fields to his travels on the HMS Beagle, and how they influenced his later thought.

"Sandra Markle tells Darwin's story in clear prose spiced with interesting vignettes, . . . and Zina Saunders brings the scenes alive with colorful woodcut illustrations." N Y Times Book Rev

McGinty, Alice B. **Darwin**; illustrated by Mary Azarian. Houghton Mifflin Books for Children 2009 un il $18
Grades: 1 2 3 4   **92**
1. Evolution 2. Naturalists 3. Travel writers 4. Writers on science 5. Natural history -- Juvenile literature
ISBN 978-0-618-99531-8; 0-618-99531-5
LC 2008-33930
"After tracing Charles Darwin's youth and education, this fully illustrated biography focuses on his five-year voyage about the HMS Beagle. . . . Azarian . . . illustrates the book using handsome woodcut prints painted with watercolors. . . . The interplay of the clearly written third-person text with Darwin's own words and occasional quotes from his contemporaries creates a multifaceted view that leads to a broader understanding." Booklist

★ Schanzer, Rosalyn. **What** Darwin saw; the journey that changed the world. National Geographic 2009 47p il map $17.95; lib bdg $26.90
Grades: 3 4 5 6   **92**
1. Evolution 2. Naturalists 3. Travel writers 4. Writers on science 5. Natural history -- Juvenile literature
ISBN 978-1-4263-0396-8; 1-4263-0396-3; 978-1-4263-0397-5 lib bdg; 1-4263-0397-1 lib bdg
LC 2008-39809
"Schanzer uses Darwin's own words, taken from his journals, books, and letters, in the speech balloons of her graphic depiction of the voyage of the Beagle. This is not a full biography, but begins with Darwin's acceptance of the offer to sail on the expedition and ends with the presentation of his theory of evolution in 1860. Bright, watercolor cartoons accurately portray landscapes and specimens while also creating a vivid sense of adventure." SLJ
Includes bibliographical references

Sis, Peter. The **tree** of life: a book depicting the life of Charles Darwin, naturalist, geologist & thinker. Frances Foster Bks./Farrar, Straus & Giroux 2003 un il map $18
Grades: 4 5 6 7   **92**
1. Naturalists 2. Travel writers 3. Writers on science
ISBN 0-374-45628-3
LC 2002-40706
Presents the life of the famous nineteenth-century naturalist using text from Darwin's writings and detailed drawings by Sis
"Muted tones of blue, green, and tan, and finely hatched drawings in the manner of old prints lend a period look to the pages. Beautifully conceived and executed, the presentation is a humorous and informative tour de force that will absorb and challenge readers." SLJ

Dave, ca. 1800-ca. 1870
★ Hill, Laban Carrick. **Dave**, the potter; artist, poet, slave. illustrated by Bryan Collier. Little, Brown Books for Young Readers 2010 un il $16.99
Grades: K 1 2 3 4   **92**
1. Slaves 2. Artists 3. American pottery 4. African

American artists 5. African American authors 6. Ceramists 7. Poets, American 8. Slavery -- United States
ISBN 0-316-10731-X; 978-0-316-10731-0
LC 2010-06382
A Caldecott Medal honor book, 2011
This is a biography of the artist known as Dave, who "spent most of his life in a rural South Carolina district famed for its stoneware. . . . [Dave's] creations included mammoth storage pots. . . . Sometimes he signed his name and put the date. Other times he wrote verse [on the pot], usually a short rhyme. . . . Ages three to six." (N Y Times Book Rev)
"The life of an astonishingly prolific and skilled potter who lived and died a slave in 19th-century South Carolina is related in simple, powerful sentences that outline the making of a pot. The movements of Dave's hands are described using familiar, solid verbs: pulling, pinching, squeezing, pounding. . . . The pithy lines themselves recall the short poems that Dave inscribed on his pots. Collier's earth-toned watercolor and collage art extends the story, showing the landscape, materials, and architecture of a South Carolina farm. . . . A lengthy author's note fleshes out what is known of the man's life story and reproduces several of his two-line poems." SLJ

David-Neel, Alexandra, 1868-1969
★ Brown, Don. **Far** beyond the garden gate: Alexandra David-Neel's journey to Lhasa. Houghton Mifflin 2002 un il $16
Grades: 3 4 5   **92**
1. Authors 2. Buddhism 3. Explorers 4. Travelers 5. Travel writers 6. Religious scholars 7. Asian studies specialists
ISBN 0-618-08364-2
LC 2002-222
Describes the life and travels of Alexandra David-Neel, who became a scholar of Buddhism and Tibet in the early twentieth century and trekked thousands of miles to reach Llasa, the Tibetan capital.
This "tells a fascinating tale. . . . David-Neel's vivid quotes are interspersed throughout the story. . . . The beiges, grays, and whites of Brown's palette capture the feeling of the unfamiliar world into which the woman and her companion ventured." SLJ
Includes bibliographical references

De Paola, Tomie, 1934-
★ De Paola, Tomie. **26** Fairmount Avenue; written and illustrated by Tomie dePaola. Putnam 1999 56p il $14.99; pa $6.99
Grades: 2 3 4   **92**
1. Artists 2. Authors 3. Painters 4. Illustrators 5. Authors, American 6. Children's authors
ISBN 0-399-23246-X; 0-698-11864-2 pa
LC 98-12918
A Newbery Medal honor book, 2000
Children's author-illustrator Tomie De Paola describes his experiences at home and in school when he was a boy. "Age four and up." (Commonweal)
"A disarmingly unselfconscious reminiscence. . . . The immediacy of detail resists nostalgia, and dePaola is wise to what recent graduates of his picture books will find interest-

ing. Neat sketches and silhouettes will draw browsers in to this satisfying easy chapter book." Horn Book Guide

De Paola, Tomie. **Christmas** remembered; [by] Tomie dePaola. G. P. Putnam's Sons 2006 86p il $19.99; pa $9.99

Grades: 5 6 7 8   **92**
1. Artists 2. Authors 3. Painters 4. Christmas 5. Illustrators 6. Authors, American 7. Children's authors
ISBN 0-399-24622-3; 0-14-241481-6 pa
LC 2005032658

The children's author and artist shares his love of Christmas in 15 memories, which span six decades

"Brightening the pages are illustrations in varied styles and media, from an intriguing portrait of dePaola's Italian grandmother to decorative paper collages to iconic paintings of great stillness and beauty.... Written with dialogue and humor as well as reflection." Booklist

De Paola, Tomie. **For** the duration; a 26 Fairmount Avenue book; the war years. written and illustrated by Tomie dePaola. Putnam's Sons 2009 99p il $15.99

Grades: 2 3 4   **92**
1. Artists 2. Authors 3. Painters 4. Illustrators 5. World War, 1939-1945 6. Authors, American 7. Children's authors
ISBN 978-0-399-25209-9; 0-399-25209-6

From gas rationing to air-raid drills, as long as the war lasts, life is going to be different for Tomie. And sometimes different is hard. Fortunately, Tomie still has school, his family, and the things he's good at to carry him through.

"DePaola's style and word choices are just right for his audience, and the point of view is consistently that of a second grader. Full-page and spot art black-and-white pencil drawings and silhouette art by the author illustrate this must-read title for fans of the series." SLJ

De Paola, Tomie. **I'm** still scared; a 26 Fairmount Avenue book, book 6. written and illustrated by Tomie dePaola. G. P. Putnam's Sons 2006 83p il $13.99; pa $5.99

Grades: 2 3 4   **92**
1. Artists 2. Authors 3. Painters 4. Illustrators 5. Authors, American 6. Children's authors 7. World War, 1939-1945 -- United States
ISBN 0-399-24502-2; 0-14-240826-3 pa
LC 2005-13500

"DePaola picks up his autobiographical series right where his last title, Things Will Never Be the Same (2003), left off: December, 7, 1941. Now in second grade, little Tomie describes the reactions to the Pearl Harbor bombings, first at home, then at church, and finally at school.... Once again, the warm, childlike narration captures both the specifics of the time and universal experiences that will connect with most children. The shaded, black-and-white sketches on each page extend the story's small, revealing moments." Booklist

De Paola, Tomie. **On** my way; a 26 Fairmount Avenue book. written and illustrated by Tomie dePaola. Putnam 2001 73p il $13.99; pa $6.99

Grades: 2 3 4   **92**
1. Artists 2. Authors 3. Painters 4. Illustrators 5. Authors, American 6. Children's authors 7. Authors,

American -- 20th century -- Biography -- Juvenile literature
ISBN 0-399-23583-3; 0-698-11948-7 pa
LC 00-38229

"This is the third installment of De Paola's memoirs of childhood. It "culminates with the artist entering first grade and finally . . . getting to learn to read. . . . The memoir begins in the previous spring, with the crisis of baby sister Maureen's pneumonia.. . . There are happier times as well.. . . Primary." (Horn Book)

"The saga of dePaola's early life related in 26 Fairmount Avenue . . ., and Here We All Are . . . continues with this reminiscence of kindergarten and first grade. dePaola describes his baby sister Maureen's recovery from pneumonia, a family trip to the 1939 World's Fair, and his theatrical debut as the blushing bride in a "Tiny Tot Bridal Party".... The humor is clear and the selection of incidents indicates the author has a comfortable familiarity with the concerns of his audience." Bull Cent Child Books

De Paola, Tomie. **Why?** a 26 Fairmount Avenue book. written and illustrated by Tomie dePaola. G. P. Putnam's Sons 2007 85p il $14.99

Grades: 2 3 4   **92**
1. Artists 2. Authors 3. Painters 4. Illustrators 5. Authors, American 6. Children's authors
ISBN 978-0-399-24692-0
LC 2006011911

"This seventh installment in dePaola's autobiography covers New Year's Day through April 20, 1942. . . . Tomie overhears talk of rationing and hoarding, peeks out from behind blackout curtains, and notes that, due to the war, Fleer bubblegum will no longer be available. As ever, the author fills the story with authentically childlike details. . . . The black-and-white full-page and spot pictures convey emotions effectively." SLJ

Desmond, Viola Irene
Warner, Jody. **Viola** Desmond won't be budged! pictures by Richard Rudnicki. Groundwood Books/House of Anansi Press 2010 un il $18.95

Grades: K 1 2 3   **92**
1. Hairstylists 2. Race discrimination 3. Blacks -- Canada 4. Civil rights activists
ISBN 978-0-88899-779-1; 0-88899-779-5

"Using a cadenced style that echoes the oral tradition of African-Canadians, Warner recounts the story simply, allowing children to see raw discrimination for what it was. Rudnicki uses bold acrylics in vivid colors to tell the story. He captures the style, dress and look of the period." Kirkus

Devi, Dulari
Devi, Dulari. **Following** my paint brush; text by Gita Wolf. Tara Books 2011 un il $17.50

Grades: 3 4 5 6   **92**
1. Artists 2. Painters 3. Women artists 4. Artists, Indian
ISBN 978-93-80340-11-1; 93-80340-11-7

This is the story of Dulari Devi, a domestic helper who went on to become an artist in the Mithila style of folk painting from Bihar, eastern India.

"Set against plain white backgrounds, Devi's artwork . . . vibrates with bold reds, yellows, and greens. The focus of Devi's artwork is her immediate environment—religious imagery, trees, pottery, fish, and children at play—her delicate linework adding complexity and texture to the mural-like tableaus." Publ Wkly

Dickens, Charles, 1812-1870

Manning, Mick. **Charles** Dickens; scenes from an extraordinary life. [illustrated by] Brita Granström. Frances Lincoln 2011 un il $18.95

Grades: 2 3 4 5   92

1. Authors 2. Novelists 3. Authors, English
ISBN 978-1-84780-187-6; 1-84780-187-0

"Dickens narrates his own life story in this biography. . . . Loosely rendered pencil-and-watercolor scenes with speech-bubble interjections from characters take center stage, while small illustrated sidebars provide additional context. . . . A bonus: tidy comic strip panels provide quick summaries of several Dickens novels, which may whet readers' appetite to further explore his writing." Publ Wkly

Rosen, Michael, 1946- **Dickens**; his work and his world. illustrated by Robert Ingpen. Candlewick Press 2005 95p il $19.99

Grades: 5 6 7 8   92

1. Authors 2. Novelists 3. Authors, English
ISBN 0-7636-2752-6

LC 2004-61847

"The art adds to the richness of a volume designed and written with care." Booklist

Drew, Charles Richard, 1904-1950

Venezia, Mike. **Charles** Drew; doctor who got the world pumped up to donate blood. written and illustrated by Mike Venezia. Children's Press 2009 32p il (Getting to know the world's greatest inventors & scientists) $28

Grades: 2 3 4   92

1. Blood 2. Surgeons 3. Inventors 4. Physicians 5. College teachers 6. African Americans -- Biography
ISBN 978-0-531-23725-0; 0-531-23725-7

LC 2008-27648

Charles Drew "is the individual credited with discovering how to extract plasma from whole blood and store it for long periods. . . . The book . . . is written in simple terms for children and focuses on the barriers [Drew] faced as an African-American in a pre-civil-rights-era United States. . . . There are interesting pictures of Drew's life, as well as other pictures of blood plasma being used to save the lives of soldiers on the battlefield. . . . [This] is a biography that is outside of the ordinary." Sci Books Films

Du Bois, W. E. B. (William Edward Burghardt), 1868-1963

Whiting, Jim. **W.E.B.** Du Bois; civil rights activist, author, historian. Mason Crest Publishers 2010 64p il (Transcending race in America: biographies of biracial achievers) $22.95; pa $9.95

Grades: 5 6 7 8   92

1. Authors 2. Novelists 3. Historians 4. Editors 5. Essayists 6. Sociologists 7. Nonfiction writers 8. Civil rights activists 9. African Americans -- Biography 10. African Americans -- Civil rights
ISBN 978-1-4222-1618-7; 1-4222-1618-7; 978-1-4222-1632-3 pa; 1-4222-1632-2 pa

LC 2009022049

"The author openly discusses Du Bois' political and ideological struggles, which concluded with his move to Ghana and admittance into the Communist Party. . . . The book . . . provides solid information about Du Bois." Booklist

Includes glossary and bibliographical references

Dylan, Bob, 1941-

Burckhardt, Marc. **When** Bob met Woody; the story of the young Bob Dylan. illustrated by Marc Burckhardt. Little, Brown 2011 40p il $17.99

Grades: 3 4 5   92

1. Rock musicians
ISBN 978-0-316-11299-4; 0-316-11299-2

LC 2010-43030

This picture book biography follows Bob Zimmerman as he renames himself after his favorite poet, Dylan Thomas, and leaves his mining town to pursue his love of music in New York City. There, he meets his folk music hero and future mentor, Woody Guthrie.

"Golio excels at portraying Zimmerman's angst as he flounders for meaning and even invents for himself a more colorful backstory. Burckhardt's acrylics have the fractured look of damaged paintings, and . . . [convey] gravity and emotion. Back matter, including quotation sources, is superb. A stirring introduction to two musical legends." Booklist

Includes bibliographical references

Délano, Poli, 1936-

Delano, Poli. **When** I was a boy Neruda called me Policarpo; illustrated by Manuel Monroy. Groundwood Books/House of Anansi Press 2006 84p il $15.95

Grades: 5 6 7 8   92

1. Poets 2. Authors 3. Diplomats 4. Novelists 5. Poets, Chilean 6. Memoirists 7. Short story writers 8. Nobel laureates for peace 9. Nobel laureates for literature
ISBN 0-88899-726-4

In this book, the author "offers seven vignettes, interspersed with six of Neruda's . . . poems and biographical information, to give middle-grade readers a sense of what it was like to grow up in the constant presence of a kindly, though spoiled and eccentric, celebrity. . . . Grades four to six." (MultiCult Rev)

"Based on the author's childhood remembrances of when he and his diplomat parents lived with Tío Pablo [Neruda] in Mexico, these seven chapters reveal both the genius and the eccentricities of the Nobel Prize-winning Chilean poet. . . . The chapters are short, well written, and filled with interesting details that will open up a new and exotic world. . . . Monroy's pen-and-sepia-toned drawings are . . . at times humorous, at times dramatic, but always enticing." SLJ

Earhart, Amelia, 1898-1937

★ Fleming, Candace. **Amelia** lost: the life and disappearance of Amelia Earhart. Schwartz & Wade Books 2011 118p il map

Grades: 4 5 6 7   92

1. Air pilots 2. Missing persons 3. Women air pilots 4. Memoirists
ISBN 0-375-84198-9; 0-375-94598-9 lib bdg; 978-0-375-84198-9; 978-0-375-94598-4 lib bdg

LC 2010-05279

Fleming "offers a fresh look at this famous aviatrix. Employing dual narratives—straightforward biographical chapters alternating with a chilling recounting of Earhart's final flight and the search that followed—Fleming seeks to uncover the 'history of the hype,' pointing out numerous examples in which Earhart took an active role in mythologizing her own life. . . . Frequent sidebars, well-chosen maps, archival documents, and photos further clarify textual references without disturbing the overall narrative flow." Booklist

Tanaka, Shelley. **Amelia** Earhart; the legend of the lost aviator. by Shelley Tanaka; illustrated by David Craig. Abrams Books for Young Readers 2008 48p il map $18.95
Grades: 3 4 5 6   **92**
1. Air pilots 2. Missing persons 3. Women air pilots 4. Memoirists
ISBN 978-0-8109-7095-3; 0-8109-7095-3
      LC 2007-39749
NCTE Orbis Pictus Award (2009)
This is an account of the life of aviator Amelia Earhart from her childhood up to the time she disappeared on a flight in 1937.
"This title is notable . . . for its smooth, powerful storytelling, ample gallery of well-chosen photographs, and nicely placed sidebar information on such topics as flight delays, navigation, and around-the-world flight records." Bull Cent Child Books
Includes bibliographical references

Earle, Sylvia A., 1935-
Reichard, Susan E. **Who** on earth is Sylvia Earle? undersea explorer of the ocean. Enslow Publishers 2009 112p il (Scientists saving the earth) lib bdg $31.93
Grades: 5 6 7 8   **92**
1. Botanists 2. Marine biology 3. Women scientists 4. Underwater exploration 5. Divers 6. Marine biologists
ISBN 978-1-59845-118-4 lib bdg; 1-59845-118-9 lib bdg
      LC 2008032014
"The writing is clear and informative. . . . Color photographs are relevant and of good quality." SLJ
Includes glossary and bibliographical references

Earnhardt, Dale, Jr.
Rappoport, Ken. **Dale** Earnhardt, Jr. a car racer who cares. Enslow Publishers, Inc. 2011 48p il (Sports stars who care) lib bdg $23.93; pa $7.95
Grades: 3 4 5   **92**
1. Automobile racing 2. Automobile racing drivers
ISBN 978-0-7660-3777-9 lib bdg; 0-7660-3777-0 lib bdg; 978-1-59845-228-0 pa; 1-59845-228-2 pa
      LC 2010014947
This is a biography of race car driver Dale Earnhardt Jr. and founder of the Dale Jr. Foundation.
This is "especially good for book reports." Booklist
Includes glossary and bibliographical references

Eastman, George, 1854-1932
Kulling, Monica. **It's** a snap! George Eastman's first photograph. illustrated by Bill Slavin. Tundra Books 2009 un il (Great idea) $17.95
Grades: 2 3 4   **92**
1. Inventors 2. Philanthropists 3. Photography -- History 4. Manufacturing executives 5. Kodak camera

-- Juvenile literature 6. Photographic industry -- History -- Juvenile literature
ISBN 978-0-88776-881-1; 0-88776-881-4
"This picture-book biography begins in 1877, in Rochester, NY, with Eastman buying his first camera. . . . The picture-taking process took too long and the bored townspeople headed home before he could develop the wet plate. Eastman was determined to make photography easier and more affordable for everyone. During the next eight years, he invented the dry plate, the first roll of film, and the Kodak camera, and started the Eastman Kodak Company. The book will entertain and inform readers. . . . Slavin's pen-and-ink and watercolor illustrations . . . complement the text." SLJ

Ederle, Gertrude, 1905-2003
Adler, David A. **America's** champion swimmer: Gertrude Ederle; written by David A. Adler; illustrated by Terry Widener. Harcourt 2000 un il $16; pa $7
Grades: 2 3 4   **92**
1. Swimming 2. Women athletes 3. Swimmers 4. Olympic athletes
ISBN 0-15-201969-3; 0-15-205251-8 pa
      LC 98-54954
Describes the life and accomplishments of Gertrude Ederle, the first woman to swim the English Channel and a figure in the early women's rights movement
This book "illustrated with richly colored acrylic paintings . . . captures the highlights of Ederle's life in evocative images and telling details that will appeal to children." N Y Times Book Rev

Edison, Thomas A. (Thomas Alva), 1847-1931
★ Brown, Don. A **wizard** from the start: the incredible boyhood & amazing inventions of Thomas Edison. Houghton Mifflin Books for Children 2010 un il $16
Grades: 2 3 4   **92**
1. Inventors 2. Inventions -- Juvenile literature
ISBN 978-0-547-19487-5; 0-547-19487-0
"Focusing on the great inventor's youth, roughly from age eight to mid-20s, this anecdotal picture-book biography is both engaging and accessible. . . . Youngsters will find much to relate to. . . . Brown's signature sketches combine digital imagery and watercolors and reflect the period costume and key moments in Edison's early life." SLJ

★ Carlson, Laurie M. **Thomas** Edison for kids; his life and ideas: 21 activities. [by] Laurie Carlson. Chicago Review Press 2006 147p il $14.95
Grades: 5 6 7 8   **92**
1. Inventors 2. Science -- Experiments
ISBN 1-55652-584-2
      LC 2005025659
"Part biography, part science activity book, this resource will appeal to casual researchers and novice inventors. It contains a wealth of full-page primary source archival photographs, sidebars, and short biographical profiles of Edison's contemporaries, in addition to short and straightforward experiments." Voice Youth Advocates
Includes bibliographical references

Kesselring, Susan. **Thomas** Edison. Child's World 2010 24p il (Basic biographies) lib bdg $22.79

Grades: PreK K 1   **92**
1. Inventors
ISBN 978-1-60253-345-5; 1-60253-345-8
LC 2009029374
This biography of Thomas Edison "pairs intelligent, brief text with abundant photos. Simple but never basic." Booklist

Venezia, Mike. **Thomas** Edison; inventor with a lot of bright ideas. written and illustrated by Mike Venezia. Children's Press 2008 32p il (Getting to know the world's greatest inventors & scientists) lib bdg $28; pa $6.95
Grades: 2 3 4   **92**
1. Inventors
ISBN 0-531-14978-1 lib bdg; 978-0-531-14978-2 lib bdg; 0-531-22209-8 pa; 978-0-531-22209-6 pa
LC 2008002306
In this biography of inventor Thomas Edison "the humor and silly scenarios depicted in the cartoon drawings will draw readers back into the smooth, straightforward language." Booklist

Edmonds, S. Emma E. (Sarah Emma Evelyn), 1841-1898
Hendrix, John. **Nurse,** soldier, spy: the story of Sarah Edmonds, a Civil War hero; [illustrated by] John Hendrix. Abrams Books for Young Readers 2011 47p il $18.95
Grades: 2 3 4   **92**
1. Spies 2. Nurses 3. Women soldiers 4. Soldiers -- United States
ISBN 978-0-8109-9735-6; 0-8109-9735-5
LC 2010-23171
A story of a nineteen-year-old woman who disguised herself as a man to avoid an unwanted marriage and who distinguished herself as a male nurse during the Civil War, and later as a spy for the Union Army.
"In ink-and-wash illustrations Hendrix . . . displays his knack for visual narrative. . . . This large-format picture book illustrates Edmonds' courage and determination while conveying a good deal of information in a highly readable way." Booklist

Jones, Carrie. **Sarah** Emma Edmonds was a great pretender; the true story of a Civil War spy. illustrations by Mark Oldroyd. Carolrhoda Books 2011 un il $17.95
Grades: 2 3 4   **92**
1. Spies 2. Nurses 3. Women soldiers 4. Soldiers -- United States
ISBN 978-0-7613-5399-7; 0-7613-5399-2
This is "an entertaining and powerful Civil War era story about living by one's own rules. Realizing she would never satisfy her father's desire for a son, teenage Sarah Emma Edmonds fled from Canada to America where she assumed the identity of Frank Thompson. Edwards then joined the Union Army, first as a male nurse, then as a spy, passing herself off as a slave and, later, as an Irish peddler. . . . In Oldroyd's full-bleed spreads, characterized by strong cross-hatching and angular shapes, Edmonds's eyes twinkle with her secret knowledge, while Jones delivers her story with the assuredness of a natural storyteller." Publ Wkly

Einstein, Albert, 1879-1955
★ Brown, Don. **Odd** boy out: young Albert Einstein. Houghton Mifflin 2004 un il $16

Grades: 2 3 4   **92**
1. Physicists 2. Nobel laureates for physics
ISBN 0-618-49298-4
LC 2003-17701
An introduction to the work and early life of the twentieth-century physicist whose theory of relativity revolutionized scientific thinking.
"Brown's pen-and-ink and watercolor illustrations [are] rendered in a palette of dusky mauve and earthy brown. . . . Through eloquent narrative and illustration, Brown offers a thoughtful introduction to an enigmatic man." SLJ

★ Delano, Marfe Ferguson. **Genius**; a photobiography of Albert Einstein. National Geographic 2005 64p il $17.95; lib bdg $27.90; pa $7.95
Grades: 5 6 7 8   **92**
1. Physicists 2. Nobel laureates for physics
ISBN 0-7922-9544-7; 0-7922-9545-5 lib bdg; 1-4263-0294-0 pa
LC 2004-15001
A biography of the German American physicist.
This "combines a solid text with a particularly attractive format. . . . Delano offers just enough information about Einstein's theories to give a sense of his work. . . . Oversize and filled with well-selected photographs, the book is very handsome." Booklist

Kesselring, Susan. **Albert** Einstein. Child's World 2010 24p il (Basic biographies) lib bdg $22.79
Grades: PreK K 1   **92**
1. Physicists 2. Nobel laureates for physics
ISBN 978-1-60253-338-7; 1-60253-338-5
LC 2009029363
This "pairs intelligent, brief text with abundant photos. Simple but never basic." Booklist

★ Krull, Kathleen. **Albert** Einstein; illustrated by Boris Kulikov. Viking 2009 141p il (Giants of science) $15.99
Grades: 5 6 7 8   **92**
1. Physicists 2. Nobel laureates for physics 3. Physics -- Juvenile literature 4. Science -- History -- Juvenile literature
ISBN 978-0-670-06332-1; 0-670-06332-0
LC 2009-16037
"Krull delivers a splendidly humane biography of that gold standard of brilliance, Albert Einstein. . . . Drawing extensively on Einstein's writings, she presents a fully rounded portrait of a man whose genius combined with a bad temper and arrogance, to the detriment of his own professional advancement, not to mention his relationships with women and his children. Using concrete examples, the author brings such mind-bending notions as his General Theory of Relativity within the grasp of child readers." Kirkus

Meltzer, Milton. **Albert** Einstein. Holiday House 2008 32p il $16.95
Grades: 3 4 5   **92**
1. Physicists 2. Scientists 3. Nobel laureates for physics
ISBN 978-0-8234-1966-1; 0-8234-1966-5
LC 2006-43676

"Meltzer offers a sound, cogent introduction to Einstein in this attractive volume, which discusses the scientist's work and its significance within a lively account of his life. . . . Well-chosen black-and-white photos and a few documents illustrate the narrative that takes both its subject and its audience seriously." Booklist

Includes bibliographical references

Eisenhower, Dwight D. (Dwight David), 1890-1969

Mara, Wil. **Dwight** Eisenhower. Marshall Cavendish Benchmark 2011 112p il (Presidents and their times) lib bdg $34.21

Grades: 5 6 7 8   92

1. Generals 2. Presidents 3. College presidents
ISBN 978-0-7614-4812-9; 0-7614-4812-8

LC 2009033042

"The size makes it ideal for that one-hundred page biography assignment; the readability makes the titles accessible to reluctant readers in high school; the succinct, well-presented information makes the volumes fitting for initial research at both the middle and high school level." Voice Youth Advocates

Includes glossary and bibliographical references

Eleanor, of Aquitaine, Queen, consort of Henry II, King of England, 1122?-1204

Kramer, Ann. **Eleanor** of Aquitaine; the queen who rode off to battle. National Geographic 2006 64p il map (World history biographies) $17.95; lib bdg $27.90

Grades: 5 6 7 8   92

1. Queens
ISBN 0-7922-5895-9; 0-7922-5896-7 lib bdg

An illustrated biography of the medieval queen who traveled to the Crusades with her first husband King Louis VII of France and later married King Henry II of England.

Includes glossary and bibliographical references

Elizabeth I, Queen of England, 1533-1603

★ Adams, Simon. **Elizabeth** I; the outcast who became England's queen. [by] Simon Adams. National Geographic 2005 64p il map (World history biographies) $17.95; lib bdg $27.90

Grades: 4 5 6 7   92

1. Queens
ISBN 0-7922-3649-1; 0-7922-3654-8 lib bdg

LC 2005001359

An illustrated introduction to the life and times of the 16th century queen of England

"Accomplishments and hardships are clearly explained with supporting quotes and facts. . . . Beautifully illustrated and visually appealing." SLJ

Includes glossary and bibliographical references

Stanley, Diane. **Good** Queen Bess: the story of Elizabeth I of England; by Diane Stanley and Peter Vennema; illustrated by Diane Stanley. HarperCollins Pubs. 2001 un il $16.99

Grades: 4 5 6 7   92

1. Queens
ISBN 0-688-17961-4

LC 00-47267

A reissue of the title first published 1990 by Four Winds Press

Follows the life of the strong-willed queen who ruled England in the time of Shakespeare and the defeat of the Spanish Armada

"The handsome illustrations . . . are worthy of their subject. Although the format suggests a picture-book audience, this biography needs to be introduced to older readers who have the background to appreciate and understand this woman who dominated and named an age." SLJ

Includes bibliographical references

Ellington, Duke, 1899-1974

Stein, Stephanie. **Duke** Ellington; his life in jazz with 21 activities. [by] Stephanie Stein Crease. Chicago Review Press 2009 148p il (For kids) pa $16.95

Grades: 5 6 7 8   92

1. Composers 2. Jazz musicians 3. Band leaders
ISBN 978-1-55652-724-1; 1-55652-724-1

LC 2008-23742

"This large-format book combines an illustrated biography of Duke Ellington with activities designed to offer insights into Ellington s era and his music. An informative account in an attractive...format." Booklist

Includes bibliographical references, discography, and filmography

Farnsworth, Philo T., 1906-1971

★ Krull, Kathleen. The **boy** who invented TV: the story of Philo Farnsworth; illustrated by Greg Couch. Alfred A. Knopf 2009 un il $16.99; lib bdg $19.99

Grades: 3 4 5   92

1. Inventors 2. Television 3. Broadcasting engineers
ISBN 978-0-375-84561-1; 0-375-84561-5; 978-0-375-94561-8 lib bdg; 0-375-94561-X lib bdg

LC 2008-35500

"This entertaining book explores the life of inventor Philo Farnsworth, who discovered how to transmit images electronically, leading to the first television. . . . Krull's substantial, captivating text is balanced by Couch's warm, mixed-media illustrations." Publ Wkly

Includes bibliographical references

Farris, Christine

★ Farris, Christine. **March** on! the day my brother Martin changed the world. [by] Christine King Farris; illustrated by London Ladd. Scholastic Press 2008 un il $17.99

Grades: 2 3 4   92

1. Clergy 2. Civil rights demonstrations 3. College teachers 4. Nonfiction writers 5. Civil rights activists 6. Nobel laureates for peace 7. African Americans -- Civil rights
ISBN 978-0-545-03537-8; 0-545-03537-6

LC 2007038620

"Describing the 1963 March on Washington, Farris, the older sister of Martin Luther King Jr., maintains the deft touch that made My Brother Martin so moving. . . . Farris . . . effectively uses plain language and well-chosen facts to explain her brother's extraordinary achievements. . . . Ladd . . . demonstrates a rare talent for portraiture. . . . His King looks human—in other words, capable of inspiring the reader." Publ Wkly

Ferris, George Washington Gale, 1859-1896

Sneed, Dani. **Ferris** wheel!: George Ferris and his amazing invention; by Dani Sneed. Enslow 2008 32p il (Genius at work!: great inventor biographies) lib bdg $22.60

Grades: 4 5 6   92

1. Inventors 2. Ferris wheels 3. Civil engineers

ISBN 978-0-7660-2834-0 lib bdg; 0-7660-2834-8 lib bdg

LC 2007010605

"Color and black-and-white photos and color graphics add to the information on most pages. [This book is] easy to read and full of enough facts to make a solid basis for research." SLJ

Includes glossary and bibliographical references

Fibonacci, Leonardo, ca. 1170-ca. 1240

★ D'Agnese, Joseph. **Blockhead**; the life of Fibonacci. illustrated by John O'Brien. Henry Holt and Company 2010 40p il $16.99

Grades: 2 3 4 5   92

1. Numbers 2. Mathematicians 3. Fibonacci numbers -- Juvenile literature

ISBN 0-8050-6305-6; 978-0-8050-6305-9

LC 2009005264

This is a biography of Leonardo Fibonacci, the twelfth-century mathematician who discovered the numerical sequence named for him. "Intermediate." (Horn Book)

"D'Agnese's introduction to medieval Europe's greatest mathematician offers both a coherent biographical account—spun, with some invented details, from very sketchy historical records—and the clearest explanation to date for younger readers of the numerical sequence that is found throughout nature and still bears his name. O'Brien's illustrations place the prosperously dressed, woolly headed savant in his native Pisa and other settings." Booklist

Fillmore, Millard, 1800-1874

Gottfried, Ted. **Millard** Fillmore; by Ted Gottfried. Marshall Cavendish Benchmark 2007 96p il (Presidents and their times) lib bdg $22.95

Grades: 5 6 7 8   92

1. Presidents 2. Vice-presidents 3. Members of Congress

ISBN 978-0-7614-2431-4

LC 2006019707

"Primary-source materials and quotes, helpful insets, and carefully selected . . . reproductions bring history to life and help make [this] clearly written [biography] highly readable." SLJ

Includes glossary and bibliographical references

Fitzgerald, Ella

★ Orgill, Roxane. **Skit**-scat raggedy cat: Ella Fitzgerald; written by Roxane Orgill; illustrated by Sean Qualls. Candlewick Press 2010 un il $17.99

Grades: 2 3 4   92

1. Singers 2. African American singers 3. Pop musicians 4. African American women -- Biography

ISBN 978-0-7636-1733-2; 0-7636-1733-4

LC 2009-47407

This is "a stylish portrayal of Ella Fitzgerald. . . . There's no question that Orgill and Qualls know what makes [jazz] so catchy: it's slinky, rhythmic, and joyful and on full display in both the lively text and swinging artwork." Booklist

★ Pinkney, Andrea Davis. **Ella** Fitzgerald; the tale of a vocal virtuosa. by Andrea Davis Pinkney with Scat Cat Monroe; illustrated by Brian Pinkney. Hyperion 2002 un il $16.99

Grades: 2 3 4   92

1. Singers 2. African American women 3. African American singers 4. Pop musicians 5. African American women -- Biography

ISBN 0-7868-0568-4; 0-7868-2493-X lib bdg

"Scat Cat Monroe, a jazzy feline in a zoot suit, tells Fitzgerald's life story. . . . The general details of an extraordinary life—when, what, where, and how—are related in rhythmic, vivid language that matches the verve of the hand-colored scratchboard illustrations." Bull Cent Child Books

Fitzgerald, Larry, 1983-

Sandler, Michael. **Larry** Fitzgerald. Bearport Pub. 2010 24p il map (Football heroes making a difference) lib bdg $22.61

Grades: 2 3 4   92

1. Football players 2. Football -- Biography

ISBN 978-1-936087-58-7; 1-936087-58-8

LC 2009028305

A look at the life and career of the famous football player. Includes glossary and bibliographical references

Ford, Henry, 1863-1947

★ Mitchell, Don. **Driven**; a photobiography of Henry Ford. foreword by Lee Iacocca. National Geographic 2010 64p il map $18.95; lib bdg $27.90

Grades: 5 6 7 8   92

1. Businessmen 2. Philanthropists 3. Automobile industry 4. Automobile executives 5. Automobiles -- Juvenile literature

ISBN 978-1-4263-0155-1; 1-4263-0155-3; 978-1-4263-0156-8 lib bdg; 1-4263-0156-1 lib bdg

LC 2009-07136

"Mitchell introduces readers to the founder of the auto company. . . . Thoughts, feelings, and quotes abound, and they are well sourced. . . . The writing is clear, and the organization is chronological. . . . Driven combines fine photography and an inviting text to depict Ford's life and his impact on the world." SLJ

Includes bibliographical references

Forten, James, 1766-1842

Figley, Marty Rhodes. **Prisoner** for liberty; by Marty Rhodes Figley; illustrations by Craig Orback. Millbrook Press 2008 48p il (On my own history) lib bdg $25.26

Grades: 2 3 4   92

1. Abolitionists 2. Philanthropists 3. Sailmakers 4. African Americans -- Biography

ISBN 978-0-8225-7280-0 lib bdg; 0-8225-7280-X lib bdg

LC 2006028582

"In dramatic words and vivid paintings, this [book] . . . celebrates the heroism of an African American teen in the Revolutionary War. Born free, 15-year-old James Forten joined the crew of the Royal Louis as a sailor. When the British captured the ship, he refused the chance to escape to help a sickly white friend. . . . This inspiring, personal story will help draw early readers into U.S. history." Booklist

Includes bibliographical references

Fossey, Dian

Kushner, Jill Menkes. **Who** on earth is Dian Fossey? defender of the mountain gorillas. Enslow Publishers 2009 112p il (Scientists saving the earth) lib bdg $31.93

Grades: 5 6 7 8   92

1. Authors 2. Gorillas 3. Women scientists 4. Murder victims 5. Primatologists 6. Writers on science

ISBN 1-59845-117-0 lib bdg; 978-1-59845-117-7 lib bdg

LC 2008029376

"The book is filled with factual information, yet is written in a manner that makes both Fossey and her gorillas come to life for the reader." Sci Books Films

Includes glossary and bibliographical references

Foucault, Jean Bernard Léon, 1819-1868

Mortensen, Lori. **Come** see the Earth turn: the story of Leon Foucault; illustrations by Raúl Allén. Tricycle Press 2010 un il $17.99

Grades: 3 4 5   92

1. Physicists 2. Scientists

ISBN 978-1-58246-284-4; 1-58246-284-4

A biography of the scientist who proved that the Earth spins on its axis.

"Mortensen's prose infuses this small scientific drama with remarkable tension, while Allén's dramatically lit paintings, often organized into elegant panels, have a cinematic quality and amplify the action even further." Publ Wkly

Frank, Anne, 1929-1945

★ Metselaar, Menno. **Anne** Frank: her life in words and pictures; from the archives of The Anne Frank House. [by] Menno Metselaar and Ruud van der Rol; translated by Arnold J. Pomerans. Roaring Brook Press 2009 215p il map pa $12.99

Grades: 5 6 7 8   92

1. Children 2. Diarists 3. Holocaust victims 4. Jews -- Netherlands 5. Holocaust, 1933-1945 6. World War, 1939-1945 -- Jews

ISBN 978-1-59643-546-9; 1-59643-546-1; 978-1-59643-547-6 pa; 1-59643-547-X pa

First published 2004 in the Netherlands with title: The story of Anne Frank

Boston Globe-Horn Book Award honor book: Nonfiction (2010)

"Beginning with a single photograph of the cover of Anne Frank's diary and the quote, 'One of my nicest presents,' this small, beautifully formatted book is accessible, compelling, and richly pictorial. . . . The book immediately immerses readers in the girl's life via a series of family photographs, many previously unpublished. Divided chronologically, the accompanying text is enhanced by diary entries, resulting in a historically succinct yet descriptive presentation. . . . Even for those collections where Anne Frank is well represented, this is a moving and valuable book." SLJ

Franklin, Benjamin, 1706-1790

★ Byrd, Robert. **Electric** Ben; the amazing life and times of Benjamin Franklin. Penguin Group 2012 40 p. (hardcover) $17.99

Grades: 3 4 5   92

1. Biography 2. Inventions -- History 3. United States -- History 4. Printers -- United States -- Biography -- Juvenile literature 5. Inventors -- United States -- Biography -- Juvenile literature 6. Statesmen -- United States -- Biography -- Juvenile literature 7. Scientists -- United States -- Biography -- Juvenile literature

ISBN 0803737491; 9780803737495

LC 2011050493

Boston Globe-Horn Book Award: Nonfiction (2013). Robert F. Sibert Honor Book (2013)

This book by Robert Byrd presents a biography of Benjamin Franklin. "A true Renaissance man, Benjamin Franklin was the first American celebrity. In pictures and text, master artist Robert Byrd documents Franklin's numerous and diverse accomplishments, from framing the Constitution to creating bifocals." The book contains "facts, quotes, and captions, while the . . . illustrations make a . . . tribute to the brilliant American." (Publisher's note)

Fleming, Candace. **Ben** Franklin's almanac; being a true account of the good gentleman's life. Atheneum Bks. for Young Readers 2003 120p il $19.95

Grades: 5 6 7 8   92

1. Authors 2. Diplomats 3. Inventors 4. Statesmen 5. Scientists 6. Writers on science 7. Members of Congress 8. Statesmen -- United States

ISBN 0-689-83549-3

LC 2002-6136

Brings together eighteenth century etchings, artifacts, and quotations to create the effect of a scrapbook of the life of Benjamin Franklin

"An authoritative work of depth, humor, and interest, presenting Franklin in all his complexity, ranging from the heroic to the vulgar, the saintly to the callous." SLJ

Freedman, Russell. **Becoming** Ben Franklin; how a candle-maker's son helped light the flame of liberty. 1st ed. Holiday House 2013 86 p. col. ill. (hardcover) $24.95

Grades: 5 6 7 8   92

1. Franklin, Benjamin, 1706-1790 -- Juvenile literature 2. Founding Fathers of the United States -- Juvenile literature 3. Printers -- United States -- Biography -- Juvenile literature 4. Inventors -- United States -- Biography -- Juvenile literature 5. Statesmen -- United States -- Biography -- Juvenile literature 6. Scientists -- United States -- Biography -- Juvenile literature

ISBN 0823423743; 9780823423743

LC 2012002971

This book is a biography of Ben Franklin. Russell Freedman "chose episodes that reflect how the young man, disgruntled with being his brother's apprentice, made a life for himself . . . . By describing the obstacles Franklin overcame in establishing his print shop in Philadelphia, Freedman delineates a . . . path between his subject's early ambition and his ease with people to his success in business and then to his later roles as a diplomat, revolutionary, and public servant." (School Library Journal)

Includes bibliographical references (p. 78-82) and index.

★ Fritz, Jean. **What's** the big idea, Ben Franklin? illustrated by Margot Tomes. Putnam Pub. Group 1976 46p il $15.99; pa $5.99

Grades: 2 3 4   **92**
 1. Authors 2. Diplomats 3. Inventors 4. Statesmen
 5. Scientists 6. Writers on science 7. Members of
Congress
 ISBN 0-399-23487-X; 0-698-11372-1 pa
The text "focuses on Franklin's multifaceted career but
also gives personal details and quotes some of his pithy
sayings. Enough background information about colonial
affairs is given to enable readers to understand the importance of Franklin's contributions to the public good but not
so much that it obtrudes on his life story. Although the text
is not punctuated by references or footnotes, a page of notes
(with numbers for pages referred to) is appended." Bull Cent
Child Books

 ★ Harness, Cheryl. The **remarkable** Benjamin Franklin; written & illustrated by Cheryl Harness. National Geographic Society 2005 47p il $17.95
Grades: 2 3 4   **92**
 1. Authors 2. Diplomats 3. Inventors 4. Statesmen
 5. Scientists 6. Writers on science 7. Members of
Congress
 ISBN 0-7922-7882-8
                                              LC 2004-20504
"Beginning with Franklin's birth, Harness explores the
activities that filled his days from his quest to open his own
print shop to his role in the American Revolution to his personal intrigues and inventions. Her conversational writing
style and vivid illustrations will appeal to readers just becoming acquainted with this important figure." SLJ
Includes bibliographical references

 Miller, Brandon Marie. **Benjamin** Franklin, American
genius; his life and ideas, with 21 activities. Chicago Review Press 2009 125p il pa $16.95
Grades: 4 5 6 7   **92**
 1. Authors 2. Diplomats 3. Inventors 4. Statesmen
 5. Scientists 6. Writers on science 7. Members of
Congress
 ISBN 978-1-55652-757-9 pa; 1-55652-757-8 pa
                                              LC 2009012456
"Miller does an excellent job of presenting a synopsis
of Franklin's life in a highly readable manner. . . . Imbedded
in each chapter are asides that further elaborate on Franklin's life and times and activities that coordinate with the
text or the historical facts presented. The directions are easy
to follow and enhance the overall presentation, especially
in terms of classroom connections. Illustrations accompany
each project and reproductions of primary documents, renderings, and paintings provide added value." SLJ
Includes glossary and bibliographical references

 Rushby, Pamela. **Ben** Franklin; printer, author, inventor, politician. by Pamela Rushby. National Geographic
2007 40p il (National Geographic history chapters) lib
bdg $17.90
Grades: 2 3 4   **92**
 1. Authors 2. Diplomats 3. Inventors 4. Statesmen
 5. Scientists 6. Writers on science 7. Members of
Congress 8. Statesmen -- United States
 ISBN 978-1-4263-0191-9
                                              LC 2007007896

This biography of Benjamin Franklin is "nicely illustrated with . . . paintings, engravings, and facsimiles. . . . [It is]
just right for emerging chapter-book readers. . . . Useful . . .
for reports . . . and interesting pleasure reading." SLJ
Includes glossary and bibliographical references

 ★ Schroeder, Alan. **Ben** Franklin; his wit and wisdom
from A to Z. illustrated by John O'Brien. Holiday House
2011 un il $16.95
Grades: 2 3 4   **92**
 1. Authors 2. Diplomats 3. Inventors 4. Statesmen
 5. Scientists 6. Writers on science 7. Members of
Congress 8. Statesmen -- United States
 ISBN 978-0-8234-1950-0; 0-8234-1950-9
                                              LC 2010024062
"Alphabetically arranged, but far more than just an alphabet book, this guide to the life of Ben Franklin covers
his upbringing, his prominence in early America, his many
inventions, and his beliefs and writings. Given the breadth
of Franklin's accomplishments, it shouldn't be surprising
that each letter gets more than one word. . . . O'Brien's ink
and watercolor images contribute ample humor, and Schroeder creates a well-rounded, fascinating portrait of an iconic
American." Publ Wkly

Fritz, Jean
 ★ Fritz, Jean. **Homesick**: my own story; illustrated
with drawings by Margot Tomes and photographs. Putnam
1982 163p il $16.99; pa $5.99
Grades: 5 6 7 8   **92**
 1. Authors 2. Women authors 3. Children's authors
 ISBN 0-399-20933-6; 0-698-11782-4 pa
                                              LC 82-7646
 A Newbery Medal honor book, 1983
"The descriptions of places and the times are vivid in a
book that brings to the reader, with sharp clarity and candor,
the yearnings and fears and ambivalent loyalties of a young
girl." Bull Cent Child Books

Fulton, Robert, 1765-1815
 Herweck, Don. **Robert** Fulton; engineer of the steamboat. Compass Point Books 2009 40p il (Mission: Science) lib bdg $26.60
Grades: 4 5 6 7   **92**
 1. Engineers 2. Inventors 3. Steamboats
 ISBN 978-0-7565-3961-0 lib bdg; 0-7565-3961-7
lib bdg
                                              LC 2008007728
Covers the life and accomplishments of American inventor and mechanic, Robert Fulton, who is best known for
building the first successful steamboat

Galilei, Galileo, 1564-1642
 ★ Panchyk, Richard. **Galileo** for kids; his life and
ideas: 25 activities. foreword by Buzz Aldrin. Chicago Review Press 2005 166p il map pa $16.95
Grades: 5 6 7 8   **92**
 1. Astronomers 2. Writers on science
 ISBN 1-55652-566-4
                                              LC 2004-22936
 A biography of the Renaissance scientist and his times
with related activities
"Clear . . . writing places Galileo squarely within the
historical context of the turbulent Italian Renaissance. . . .

Panchyk's title is a good choice for those interested in integrating history and science curriculums." SLJ

Includes bibliographical references

★ Steele, Philip. **Galileo**; the genius who faced the Inquisition. National Geographic 2005 64p il (World history biographies) $17.95; lib bdg $27.90

Grades: 4 5 6 7　　　　　　　　　　　　　　　　92

1. Astronomers 2. Writers on science

ISBN 0-7922-3656-4; 0-7922-3657-2 lib bdg

LC 2005-01357

An illustrated introduction to the 16th century astronomer and his times

"Accompliments and hardships are clearly explained with supporting quotes and facts. . . . Beautifully illustrated and visually appealing." SLJ

Gallaudet, T. H. (Thomas Hopkins), 1787-1851

★ McCully, Emily Arnold. **My** heart glow: Alice Cogswell, Thomas Gallaudet and the birth of American sign language. Hyperion Books for Children 2008 un il $15.99

Grades: 2 3 4　　　　　　　　　　　　　　　　92

1. Deaf 2. Sign language 3. Teachers of the deaf 4. Deafness -- Juvenile literature 5. Sign language -- Juvenile literature

ISBN 978-1-4231-0028-7; 1-4231-0028-X

This is the story of Thomas Gallaudet and his deaf neighbor, Alice Cogswell, and how Gallaudet established a school for the deaf in the United States and developed American Sign Language.

"Emily Arnold McCully's watercolor illustrations are beautifully rendered. . . . Not only does this book accurately present the engrossing story of Alice and Gallaudet, it is also an excellent resource for teaching diversity and encouraging empathy for others." Libr Media Connect

Wyckoff, Edwin Brit. **Sign** language man: Thomas H. Gallaudet and his incredible work. Enslow Elementary 2010 32p il (Genius at work! Great inventor biographies) lib bdg $22.60

Grades: 4 5 6　　　　　　　　　　　　　　　　92

1. Sign language 2. Deaf -- Education 3. Teachers of the deaf 4. Deaf -- Means of communication

ISBN 978-0-7660-3447-1 lib bdg; 0-7660-3447-X lib bdg

LC 2010005359

"Read about Thomas H. Gallaudet, who helped develop and teach American Sign Language." Publisher's note

Includes glossary and bibliographical references

Gama, Vasco da, 1469-1524

★ Calvert, Patricia. **Vasco** da Gama; so strong a spirit. [by] Patricia Calvert. Benchmark Books 2005 96p il map (Great explorations) lib bdg $29.93

Grades: 5 6 7 8　　　　　　　　　　　　　　　92

1. Explorers 2. Explorers -- Portugal -- Biography -- Juvenile literature 3. Discoveries in geography -- Portuguese -- Juvenile literature

ISBN 0-7614-1611-0

LC 2003-22946

Recounts the voyages undertaken by fifteenth-century Portuguese explorer Vasco da Gama to strengthen his nation's power by establishing a sea trade route to India.

Includes bibliographical references

Gandhi, Mahatma, 1869-1948

★ Wilkinson, Philip. **Gandhi**; the young protester who founded a nation. National Geographic 2005 64p il (World history biographies) $17.95; lib bdg $27.90

Grades: 4 5 6 7　　　　　　　　　　　　　　　92

1. Authors 2. Journalists 3. Passive resistance 4. Essayists 5. Pacifists 6. Memoirists 7. Political leaders 8. Writers on politics

ISBN 0-7922-3647-5; 0-7922-3648-3 lib bdg

"Double-page spreads describe phases in Gandhi's life, from childhood to his tragic death, detailed in Wilkinson's straightforward, succinct language and in anecdotes, which will capture young people's attention and also humanize the great leader." Booklist

Includes glossary and bibliographical references

Garnett, Kevin, 1976-

Wilner, Barry. **Kevin** Garnett; a basketball star who cares. Enslow 2011 48p il (Sports stars who care) $23.93

Grades: 3 4 5　　　　　　　　　　　　　　　　92

1. Basketball players 2. Basketball -- Biography

ISBN 978-0-7660-3772-4; 0-7660-3772-X

This is a biography of the forward for the Boston Celtics who, through his 4XL Foundation, helps teens prepare for careers in business and who donated more than $1 million to help rebuild areas devastated by Hurricane Katrina.

This is "especially good for book reports." Booklist

Gaudí, Antoni, 1852-1926

★ Rodriguez, Rachel. **Building** on nature; the life of Antoni Gaudi. illustrated by Julie Paschkis. Henry Holt & Co. 2009 un il $16.99

Grades: 1 2 3　　　　　　　　　　　　　　　　92

1. Architects 2. Architecture -- Juvenile literature

ISBN 978-0-8050-8745-1; 0-8050-8745-1

LC 2008-38213

This is a biography of "the Catalonian architect Antoni Gaudi. The immediacy of the present-tense narrative is simple, direct, and at times piercingly poetic. . . . Paschkis doesn't try to reproduce the delicate exoticism of Gaudi's buildings in a line-for-line manner but rather soaks up the wondrous strange oozing from his designs and renders their dreamlike qualities in pointed details and large-scale impressions." Booklist

Gee, Maggie

★ Moss, Marissa. **Sky** high: the true story of Maggie Gee; illustrated by Carl Angel. Tricycle Press 2009 un il $16.99

Grades: 3 4 5　　　　　　　　　　　　　　　　92

1. Authors 2. Novelists 3. Air pilots 4. Women air pilots 5. World War, 1939-1945 -- Aerial operations

ISBN 978-1-58246-280-6; 1-58246-280-1

LC 2008042387

This is a biography of the Asian American World War II air pilot, Maggie Gee

"Based on interviews with Gee, this has a lovely, personal feel to it. And while some of the faces in the acrylic and colored-pencil illustrations are a bit stiff, the scenes themselves exude a panoramic joy." Booklist

Gehry, Frank

Bodden, Valerie. **Frank** Gehry. Creative Education 2009 48p il (Xtraordinary artists) lib bdg $32.80

Grades: 4 5 6 7   92
  1. Architects
  ISBN 978-1-58341-662-4 lib bdg; 1-58341-662-5
  lib bdg
                                        LC 2007004201
This is a biography of architect Frank Gehry
  This offers an "interesting [layout]; big, high-quality
reproductions and photographs on heavy paper; insightful
quotes from diverse sources; and . . . an excerpt from an
essay about [Gehry] at the end of the book. Readers get a
strong sense of [the] artist's personality along with an excellent survey of his work." SLJ
  Includes bibliographical references

Genghis Khan, 1162-1227
  ★ Demi. **Genghis** Khan. Marshall Cavendish Chil-
dren 2009 un il $19.99
Grades: 4 5 6 7   92
  1. Mongols 2. Kings and rulers 3. Kings
  ISBN 978-0-7614-5547-9; 0-7614-5547-7
                                        LC 2008006001
A reissue of Chingis Khan, published 1991 by Henry
Holt & Co.
  A biography of the Mongol leader and military-strategist
who, at the height of his power, was supreme master of the
largest empire ever created in the lifetime of one man.
  "Demi has managed to portray a fierce conqueror as a
sympathetic character who follows a strict code that places
loyalty, obedience, and discipline above all else. . . . The
artist achieves a clever grandeur with the liberal use of iridescent gold and detailed scenes that spill out of their gilded
borders and nearly off the pages. . . . This handsome biography is a feast for the eyes from cover to cover." Booklist

George III, King of Great Britain, 1738-1820
  ★ Fritz, Jean. **Can't** you make them behave, King
George? pictures by Tomie de Paola. Putnam 1977 45p il
$16.99; pa $6.99
Grades: 2 3 4   92
  1. Kings
  ISBN 0-399-23304-0; 0-698-11402-7 pa
                                        LC 75-33722
  "As a boy, George is seen to have had struggles in de-
portment; as King George III, he is mystified that the colonists refuse to be taught. Bits of history, a sense of George's
personality, and the loneliness of being king are all conveyed
with good humor. The artist's drawings evoke more chuckles." LC. Child Books, 1977

Gibson, Althea, 1927-2003
  Deans, Karen. **Playing** to win: the story of Althea Gib-
son; by Karen Deans; illustrated by Elbrite Brown. Holiday
House 2007 un il $16.95
Grades: 1 2 3 4   92
  1. Women athletes 2. African American athletes 3.
Tennis players 4. Tennis -- Biography
  ISBN 0-8234-1926-6
                                        LC 2004052275
  "Not only was Gibson a record-breaking tennis player,
but she also played an important role in breaking down racial
barriers. . . . The multimedia illustrations are well matched
to the power and fluidity of the text, particularly in capturing
the champion in action. . . . This well-written and attractive

biography will be a popular addition to most collections."
SLJ
  Includes bibliographical references

  ★ Stauffacher, Sue. **Nothing** but trouble; the story of
Althea Gibson. illustrated by Greg Couch. Alfred A. Knopf
2007 un il $16.99; lib bdg $19.99
Grades: 2 3 4 5   92
  1. Women athletes 2. African American athletes 3.
Tennis players 4. Tennis -- Biography 5. Tennis --
Juvenile literature
  ISBN 978-0-375-83408-0; 978-0-375-93408-7 lib bdg
                                        LC 2006-12605
A biography of the first African American tennis player
to win at Wimbleton and Forest Hills in 1957 and 1958
  "Couch's kinetic illustrations done in acrylic with digital
imaging wonderfully enhance the text. Althea stands out in
a blur of color against somber sepia, blue, and olive-drab
backgrounds. The prose is rhythmic and has the cadence of
the street, and it's a treat to read aloud." SLJ

Giff, Patricia Reilly
  Giff, Patricia Reilly. **Don't** tell the girls; a family memoir. by Patricia Reilly Giff. Holiday House 2005 131p il
$16.95
Grades: 4 5 6 7   92
  1. Authors 2. Teachers 3. Women authors 4. Authors,
American 5. Children's authors
  ISBN 0-8234-1813-8
                                        LC 2004-47452
  "Giff reflects on her childhood and her family, going
back through several generations. Spotlighting her two
grandmothers, she lovingly relates remembered conversations and incidents involving the one she knew well before
turning to the other grandmother, whom she never met. . . .
This little book has much to offer thoughtful children. . . .
With . . . sharply reproduced family photos and documents,
this handsome book's small format reflects its intimate, conversational style." Booklist

Glenn, John, 1921-
  Mitchell, Don. **Liftoff**; a photobiography of John
Glenn. National Geographic Society 2006 64p il $17.95;
lib bdg $27.90
Grades: 5 6 7 8   92
  1. Astronauts 2. Senators 3. Statesmen -- United States
  ISBN 0-7922-5899-1; 0-7922-5900-9 lib bdg
                                        LC 2005-30916
This is a biography of the American astronaut, pilot, and
U.S. Senator from Ohio.
  This is "well-written and well-illustrated." Sci
Books Films
  Includes bibliographical references

Gogh, Vincent van, 1853-1890
  Bodden, Valerie. **Vincent** van Gogh. Creative Education 2009 48p il (Xtraordinary artists) lib bdg $32.80
Grades: 4 5 6 7   92
  1. Artists 2. Painters 3. Artists, Dutch
  ISBN 978-1-58341-663-1 lib bdg; 1-58341-663-3
lib bdg
                                        LC 2007002118
  This biography of the artist offers an "interesting [lay-
out]; big, high-quality reproductions and photographs on

heavy paper; insightful quotes from diverse sources; and meaty selections of the artist's own writing . . . at the end of the book. Readers get a strong sense of [the] artist's personality along with an excellent survey of his work." SLJ

Includes bibliographical references

Goodall, Jane, 1934-

★ McDonnell, Patrick. **Me** . . . Jane. Little, Brown 2011 $15.99

Grades: PreK K 1 2   92

1. Chimpanzees 2. Women scientists 3. Primatologists 4. Writers on nature 5. Nonfiction writers

ISBN 978-0-316-04546-9; 0-316-04546-2; 0316045462; 9780316045469

LC 2010019756

This book is "inspirational. . . . McDonnell's homey, earth-toned pen and watercolor pictures give way to that most famous of all Goodall photographs, where the young scientist and an even younger chimp reach across their worlds to touch hands. The simple and intimate paintings are accented with casually arrayed stamped motifs and some of Goodall's childhood drawings." Horn Book

★ Winter, Jeanette. The **watcher**: Jane Goodall's life with the chimps. Schwartz & Wade Books 2011 un il $17.99; lib bdg $20.99

Grades: PreK K 1 2   92

1. Chimpanzees 2. Women scientists 3. Primatologists 4. Writers on nature 5. Nonfiction writers

ISBN 978-0-375-86774-3; 0-375-86774-0; 978-0-375-96774-0 lib bdg; 0-375-96774-5 lib bdg

LC 2010005280

"This tranquil picture-book biography establishes from the beginning that Jane Goodall has always had the right temperment for the work that made her famous. . . . The theme of persistence, particularly in relation to observing animals, shapes the spare, inviting text, which takes Goodall from backyard observations to scientific study of chimpanzees in Tanzania. In Winter's signature stylized paintings, the jungle is rendered in cool blues and greens." Horn Book

Greenberg, Hank, 1911-1986

Sommer, Shelley. **Hammerin'** Hank Greenberg; baseball pioneer. Calkins Creek 2011 135p il $17.95

Grades: 5 6 7 8   92

1. Baseball players 2. Jews -- Biography 3. Baseball -- Biography

ISBN 1-59078-452-9; 978-1-59078-452-5

"Greenberg grew up in an Orthodox Jewish family in New York and went on to be a Hall-of-Fame first baseman and left fielder, playing most of his career with the Detroit Tigers in the 1930s and 1940s. . . . Sommer presents a fast-moving, straightforward biography. . . . Numerous black-and-white photos enhance the text. . . . An excellent choice for kids who enjoy delving into baseball history." Booklist

Greene, Nathanael, 1742-1786

Mierka, Gregg A. **Nathanael** Greene; the general who saved the Revolution. [by] Gregg A. Mierka. OTTN Pub. 2007 88p il map (Forgotten heroes of the American Revolution) $23.95; pa $12.95

Grades: 5 6 7 8   92

1. Generals 2. Society of Friends

ISBN 978-1-59556-012-4; 1-59556-012-2; 978-1-59556-017-9 pa; 1-59556-017-3 pa

LC 2006021044

"This lively profile combines an engrossing account of the Revolutionary War with healthy measures of images and passages drawn from primary—and sometimes previously unpublished—sources." Booklist

Includes bibliographical references

Gross, Elly Berkovits, 1929-

Gross, Elly Berkovits. **Elly**; my true story of the Holocaust. [by] Elly Berkovits Gross. Scholastic Press 2009 125p il $14.99

Grades: 4 5 6 7   92

1. Poets 2. Authors 3. Holocaust survivors 4. Memoirists 5. Jews -- Romania 6. Holocaust, 1933-1945 -- Personal narratives

ISBN 978-0-545-07494-0; 0-545-07494-0

Relates how the author was torn from her happy home and sent to Birkenau by the Nazis, describing how she worked long hours and fought for survival before being set free at the end of the war and beginning a new life in America.

"As a powerful reminder of man's capacity for inhumanity, this memoir is essential reading." Booklist

Guthrie, Woody, 1912-1967

Burckhardt, Marc. **When** Bob met Woody; the story of the young Bob Dylan. illustrated by Marc Burckhardt. Little, Brown 2011 40p il $17.99

Grades: 3 4 5   92

1. Rock musicians

ISBN 978-0-316-11299-4; 0-316-11299-2

LC 2010-43030

This picture book biography follows Bob Zimmerman as he renames himself after his favorite poet, Dylan Thomas, and leaves his mining town to pursue his love of music in New York City. There, he meets his folk music hero and future mentor, Woody Guthrie.

"Golio excels at portraying Zimmerman's angst as he flounders for meaning and even invents for himself a more colorful backstory. Burckhardt's acrylics have the fractured look of damaged paintings, and . . . [convey] gravity and emotion. Back matter, including quotation sources, is superb. A stirring introduction to two musical legends." Booklist

Includes bibliographical references

Guyton, Tyree

Shapiro, J. H. **Magic** trash; a story of Tyree Guyton and his art. [by] J.H. Shapiro; illustrated by Vanessa Newton. Charlesbridge 2011 32p il

Grades: K 1 3 4   92

1. Artists

ISBN 1580893856 lib bdg; 9781580893855 1

LC 2010023524

"Multicolored, multilayered, multimedia illustrations trace the life of Tyree Guyton and his visionary artwork, which used reclaimed trash to turn a derelict Detroit street into community-activist art. . . . Readers whiz through Tyree's story, propelled by his energy and zinging, trippy triplets that cap each significant event in his life. . . . An inspiring, exciting introduction to avant-garde art and social commentary, this biography convinces young readers that art can exist, thrive and effect change outside in the real world." Kirkus

Gág, Wanda, 1893-1946

Ray, Deborah Kogan. **Wanda** Gag; the girl who lived to draw. [by] Deborah Kogan Ray. Viking Childrens Books 2008 un il $16.99

Grades: 2 3 4   **92**

1. Artists 2. Authors 3. Illustrators 4. Women authors 5. Authors, American 6. Children's authors

ISBN 978-0-670-06292-8; 0-670-06292-8

LC 2008-13132

"This charming biography of the creator of Millions of Cats . . . shows how Gág's family and childhood inspired her lifelong pursuit of art. . . . Each page of text is introduced with a quote from the subject's diaries and letters, and faces a white-framed illustration reflecting the Old World charm of her childhood, which comes to life with Ray's evocative paintings." SLJ

Hale, Bruce, 1957-

Parker-Rock, Michelle. **Bruce** Hale; an author kids love. Enslow Publishers 2008 48p bibl il por (Authors kids love) lib bdg $23.93

Grades: 3 4 5   **92**

1. Artists 2. Authors 3. Illustrators 4. Storytellers 5. Authors, American 6. Children's authors 7. Children's literature -- Authors and illustrators

ISBN 978-0-7660-2758-9 lib bdg; 0-7660-2758-9 lib bdg

LC 2007029319

A biography of the author of the Chet Gecko mystery series for children, based on an interview

"The frequent use of direct quotes makes the [text] particularly enjoyable. . . . Kids will be fascinated with . . . Hale's hat collection and love of surfing. . . . Well written, interesting, and useful for reports." SLJ

Halvorsen, Gail

★ Tunnell, Michael. **Candy** bomber; the story of the Berlin airlift's chocolate pilot. Charlesbridge 2010 110p il

Grades: 4 5 6 7   **92**

1. Air pilots 2. Air force officers

ISBN 1-58089-336-8; 1-58089-337-6 pa; 978-1-58089-336-7; 978-1-58089-337-4 pa

This book takes place "[i]n 1948, after World War II, [in] Berlin, . . . [where Michael] Tunnell tells us that pilot Gail Halvorsen spent a night in the city, noticing kids behind a fence watching the planes land. He offered sticks of Doublemint gum to two of the kids, who passed them around so their pals could get a whiff. . . . Soon people all over began sending candy-and-handkerchief parachutes to Halvorsen and other pilots to drop over Berlin." (School Library Journal)

"Curious about the city into which he ferried goods during the Berlin Airlift in 1948, pilot Gail Halvorsen stayed over to visit, met some children, and offered to drop candy and gum when he next flew over. This simple idea grew into a massive project with reverberations today. Tunnell tell this appealing story . . . clearly and chronologically, weaving just enough background for twenty-first century readers and

illustrating almost every page with black-and-white photographs, many from Halvorsen's own collection." Booklist

Includes bibliographical references

Hamilton, Alexander, 1757-1804

★ Fritz, Jean. **Alexander** Hamilton; the outsider. illustrations by Ian Schoenherr. G.P. Putnam's Sons 2011 144p il

Grades: 5 6 7 8   **92**

1. Statesmen 2. Statesmen -- United States 3. Secretaries of the treasury

ISBN 039925546X; 9780399255465

LC 2010006008

Fritz "provides a brisk, well-written account introducing Founding Father Alexander Hamilton as an outsider to America. . . . Fast moving and engaging, this straightforward biography acknowledges Hamilton's flaws while portraying him as an intelligent, energetic man who rose to the challenge of his times. . . . In addition to the black-and-white reproductions of period paintings and prints that illustrate the text, Schoenherr's striking, engraving-like images of Hamilton as scholar, soldier, aide-decamp, statesman, and duelist introduce each section." Booklist

Includes bibliographical references

Hancock, John, 1737-1793

Adler, David A. A **picture** book of John Hancock; by David A. Adler and Michael S. Adler; illustrated by Ronald Himler. Holiday House 2007 un il $16.95

Grades: 1 2 3   **92**

1. Governors 2. Statesmen 3. Colonial leaders 4. Members of Congress

ISBN 978-0-8234-2005-6; 0-8234-2005-1

LC 2005052649

"This biography begins with what is probably Hancock's most famous act, the signing of the Declaration of Independence. It then takes readers back to the beginning of his life to tell how he became such an important and influential part of America's Revolutionary War. . . . Himler's watercolors in muted tones offer visual guides to historical events. This title . . . is a solid addition to biography collections." SLJ

Includes bibliographical references

★ Fritz, Jean. **Will** you sign here, John Hancock? pictures by Trina Schart Hyman. Putnam Pub. Group 1976 47p il hardcover o.p. pa $5.99

Grades: 2 3 4   **92**

1. Governors 2. Statesmen 3. Colonial leaders 4. Members of Congress

ISBN 0-399-23306-7; 0-698-11440-X pa

"An affectionate look at a flamboyant, egocentric, but kindly, patriot, the book is a most enjoyable view of history. . . . The delightful illustrations exactly suit the times and the extraordinary character of John Hancock." Horn Book

Harvey, William, 1578-1657

Yount, Lisa. **William** Harvey; discoverer of how blood circulates. [by] Lisa Yount. rev ed.; Enslow Publishers 2008 128p il map (Great minds of science) lib bdg $31.93

Grades: 5 6 7 8   **92**

1. Biologists 2. Physicians 3. Physiologists 4. Writers on science 5. Writers on medicine 6. Blood

-- Circulation

ISBN 978-0-7660-3010-7 lib bdg; 0-7660-3010-5 lib bdg

LC 2007020301

First published 1994

"A biography of the seventeenth-century English physician William Harvey and includes related activities for readers." Publisher's note

Includes glossary and bibliographical references

Hatshepsut, Queen of Egypt

★ Galford, Ellen. **Hatshepsut**; the princess who became king. National Geographic 2005 64p il map (World history biographies) $17.95; lib bdg $27.90

Grades: 4 5 6 7   92

1. Queens 2. Kings and rulers

ISBN 0-7922-3645-9; 0-7922-3646-7 lib bdg

This "presents the life of Queen Hatshepsut, who ruled Egypt as pharaoh during the New Kingdom, around 3500 years ago. Illustrated with clear, color photos of artifacts and sites as well as colorful maps, the text discusses aspects of Egyptian life such as education and religion in Hatshepsut's life. . . . With a clearly written text and many handsome photos, this provides an accessible introduction to Hatshepsut and her times." Booklist

Hawking, Stephen W., 1942-

Venezia, Mike. **Stephen** Hawking; cosmologist who gets a big bang out of the universe. written and illustrated by Mike Venezia. Children's Press 2009 32p il (Getting to know the world's greatest inventors & scientists) $28

Grades: 2 3 4   92

1. Cosmology 2. Physicists 3. Handicapped 4. Black holes (Astronomy) 5. College teachers 6. Writers on science

ISBN 978-0-531-23728-1; 0-531-23728-1

LC 2008-27650

"This exemplary . . . biography will inform and motivate young readers. It introduces Stephen Hawking as a physicist and cosmologist. . . . [The author] introduces a few of Hawking's cosmological ideas in clear, but simple, ways that communicate the nature of the ideas and how scientific understanding is developed by a community of scientists. There are colorful telescopic photographs, entertaining cartoons, and numerous photographs of Hawking's professional and personal life." Sci Books Films

Henry, John William, 1847-ca. 1875

★ Nelson, Scott Reynolds. **Ain't** nothing but a man; my quest to find the real John Henry. [by] Scott Reynolds Nelson with Marc Aronson. National Geographic 2008 64p il $18.95; lib bdg $27.90

Grades: 4 5 6 7 8   92

1. John Henry (Legendary character) 2. Railroad workers 3. Railroads -- History 4. African Americans -- Biography 5. Biography, Individual -- Juvenile literature 6. John Henry (Legendary character) -- Juvenile literature

ISBN 978-1-4263-0000-4; 1-4263-0000-X; 978-1-4263-0001-1 lib bdg; 1-4263-0001-8 lib bdg

LC 2007-12446

This describes the author's research to find the real man who inspired the songs and legends about the African American steel-driving hero.

"The layout is attractive, with a sepia and beige background for the text and sepia-toned photographs. . . . This is an excellent example of how much detective work is needed for original research." SLJ

Includes bibliographical references

Henry, Patrick, 1736-1799

★ Fritz, Jean. **Where** was Patrick Henry on the 29th of May? illustrated by Margot Tomes. Putnam Pub. Group 1975 47p il $16.99; pa $6.99

Grades: 2 3 4   92

1. Statesmen 2. Colonial leaders

ISBN 0-399-23305-9; 0-698-11439-6 pa

"The color pictures are artful evocations of the [18th] century in America and the text presents Patrick Henry as a human being—not a sterilized historic 'figure.'" Publ Wkly

Henson, Jim

Krull, Kathleen. **Jim** Henson; the guy who played with puppets. paintings by Steve Johnson and Lou Fancher. Random House 2011 35p il $16.99; lib bdg $19.99

Grades: K 1 2 3   92

1. Television programs 2. Puppets and puppet plays 3. Puppeteers

ISBN 978-0-375-85721-8; 0-375-85721-4; 978-0-375-95721-5 lib bdg; 0-375-95721-9 lib bdg

LC 2010043837

"Krull, Johnson, and Fancher offer an inspiring and timely portrait of the late Henson. The book covers Henson's upbringing, experimentation with and study of puppetry, and the creation and success of his beloved Muppets on TV and on the big screen. . . . Johnson and Fancher's paintings exude a warm, nostalgic glow as they show the early roots of Henson's creativity and behind-the-scenes images of him at work." Publ Wkly

Includes bibliographical references

Henson, Matthew Alexander, 1866-1955

Hopkinson, Deborah. **Keep** on! the story of Matthew Henson, co-discoverer of the North Pole. written by Deborah Hopkinson; illustrated by Stephen Alcorn. Peachtree Publishers 2009 un il $17.95

Grades: 2 3 4   92

1. Explorers 2. African Americans -- Biography

ISBN 978-1-56145-473-0; 1-56145-473-7

LC 2008031118

"Written in articulate and straightforward prose, and accompanied by quotes from Henson, Keep On! tells the story of an inspiring and courageous figure and is enhanced by Alcorn's dramatic, sweeping scenes." SLJ

★ Johnson, Dolores. **Onward**; a photobiography of African-American polar explorer Matthew Henson. National Geographic 2006 64p il $17.95

Grades: 5 6 7 8   92

1. Explorers 2. African Americans -- Biography

ISBN 0-7922-7914-X

LC 2005-05837

"The quest to be the first to reach the North Pole is an exciting adventure story, and Henson got there first, as part of the ninth expedition led by Robert Peary in 1909. But Henson was African American, labeled as Peary's 'Negro manservant,' and he did not get full recognition until 2001. This . . . . focuses on the physical details of the dangerous

Arctic journeys . . . the repeated failures and the teamwork, as well as Henson's skills, stamina, and essential role in forging relationships with the Inuit. . . . The book design is beautiful: thick paper, spacious type, and stirring photos that capture the icy storms as well as the people involved in the history." Booklist

Hepburn, Audrey, 1929-1993

Cardillo, Margaret. **Just** being Audrey; illustrated By Julia Denos. Balzer + Bray 2011 un il
Grades: 1 2 3   92
  1. Actors
  ISBN 006185283X; 9780061852831
                             LC 2010003982
"Growing up in WW II–era Europe, Audrey wanted only to be a dancer, but the other girls made fun of her physical hurdles. . . . She was spotted by entertainment heavyweights . . . and quickly catapulted to fame. Denos' soft pastel illustrations cut just the right Audrey outline . . . and fans will especially enjoy picking out the movie roles depicted in a two-page spread of costumes. Her later humanitarian deeds are given their due, but it is Audrey's simple kindness that is emphasized throughout." Booklist
Includes bibliographical references

Herrera, Juan Felipe, 1948-

Herrera, Juan Felipe. The **upside** down boy; story by Juan Felipe Herrera; illustrations by Elizabeth Gómez. Children's Bk. Press 2000 31p il $15.95
Grades: K 1 2 3   92
  1. Poets 2. Authors 3. Children's authors 4. Young adult authors 5. Mexican Americans -- Biography 6. Bilingual books -- English-Spanish 7. Mexican American poets -- Biography -- Juvenile literature 8. Poets, American -- 20th century -- Biography -- Juvenile literature
  ISBN 0-89239-162-6
                                 LC 99-49113
The author recalls the year when his farm worker parents settled down in the city so that he could go to school for the first time
"Herrera's poetic prose sings with a unique voice in both languages, and Gómez's illustrations are colorful and ethereal." Horn book guide

Heschel, Abraham Joshua, 1907-1972

★ Michelson, Richard. **As** good as anybody: Martin Luther King Jr. and Abraham Joshua Heschel's amazing march toward freedom; by Richard Michelson; illustrated by Raul Colón. Knopf 2008 un il $16.99; lib bdg $19.99
Grades: 2 3 4   92
  1. Clergy 2. Rabbis 3. Theologians 4. Jews -- Biography 5. Nonfiction writers 6. Civil rights activists 7. Nobel laureates for peace 8. African Americans -- Biography 9. African Americans -- Civil rights
  ISBN 978-0-375-83335-9; 0-375-83335-8; 978-0-375-93335-6 lib bdg; 0-375-93335-2 lib bdg
This is the story of how Abraham Joshua Heschel, a Polish rabbi who escaped the Holocaust, and Martin Luther King worked together for African American civil rights.
"Michelson writes in poetic language. . . . Also admirable is Michelson's ability to convey complex historical concepts . . . in clear, potent terms that will speak directly to readers. . . . In both palette and style, Colón's colored-pencil

and watercolor art . . . suggests the past, but his themes carry into today's headlines." Booklist

Hillary, Edmund Sir

Coburn, Broughton. **Triumph** on Everest: a photobiography of Sir Edmund Hillary. National Geographic Soc. 2000 64p il map $17.95; pa $7.95
Grades: 4 5 6 7   92
  1. Mountaineering 2. Mountaineers 3. Nonfiction writers
  ISBN 0-7922-7114-9; 0-7922-7932-8 pa
                                LC 00-27009
A biography of Edmund Hillary, whose love of snow, mountains, and the outdoor life culminated in his conquering the highest peak in the world
"Threaded with quotes from Hillary's own writings, and full of fine, blue-toned photographs, the engrossing text presents the life of a reticent but world-renowned mountaineer, adventurer, and philanthropist." SLJ
Includes bibliographical references

Hodgman, Ann

Hodgman, Ann. **How** to die of embarrassment every day. Henry Holt and Co. 2011 208p il $16.99
Grades: 5 6 7 8   92
  1. Authors 2. Women authors 3. Cookbook writers 4. Authors, American 5. Children's authors
  ISBN 978-0-8050-8705-5; 0-8050-8705-2
                                LC 2010-49004
Hodgman offers a "chatty personal narrative . . . focusing on her childhood years and her tendency to land herself into humiliating situations. . . . The generous supply of spot art and relevant images from Hodgman's childhood adds to the browsibility. . . . There's . . . plenty of humor . . . but more importantly there's a tacit message about the survivability of embarrassment and the fact that we all, even seemingly perfect and polished adults, spend our lives goofing up." Bull Cent Child Books

Hodgman, Ann. The **house** of a million pets; with illustrations by Eugene Yelchin. Henry Holt & Co. 2007 263p il $16.95
Grades: 3 4 5 6   92
  1. Pets 2. Authors 3. Cookbook writers 4. Children's authors 5. Pets -- Juvenile literature
  ISBN 978-0-8050-7974-6; 0-8050-7974-2
                                LC 2006-36447
This is a "witty and personable narrative. . . . Yelchin's inky animal vignettes are inviting, with a cheerful impudence in their scrawled lines that perfectly matches the text." Bull Cent Child Books

Honda, Sōichirō, 1906-1991

Weston, Mark. **Honda**; the boy who dreamed of cars. illustrated by Katie Yamasaki. Lee & Low Books 2008 un il $17.95
Grades: 3 4 5   92
  1. Executives 2. Businesspeople 3. Automobile industry 4. Automobile executives 5. Automobiles -- Juvenile literature
  ISBN 978-1-60060-246-7; 1-60060-246-0
                               LC 2007049040
"Weston's writing is clear and accessible. . . . The book reads like a story, with fictionalization of Honda's thoughts

and dialogue. . . . Yamasaki's acrylic illustrations dominate each page. At first glance they seem representational, but on closer inspection readers will find little men climbing on the engine parts, . . . [and] miniature cars going around a globe and down Honda's arm. . . . Yamasaki's creative composition makes the pictures interesting and dynamic." SLJ

Hopper, Edward, 1882-1967

★ Rubin, Susan Goldman. **Edward** Hopper; painter of light and shadow. Abrams Books for Young Readers 2007 47p il $18.95

Grades: 5 6 7 8   92

1. Artists 2. Painters 3. Artists -- United States
ISBN 978-0-8109-9347-1; 0-8109-9347-3

LC 2006-31978

"On every page of this beautifully designed biography, readers will find a reproduction of Hopper's work, matched to clear, eloquent commentary. . . . Readers . . . will come back to read about the man and look at his art again and again." Booklist

Includes bibliographical references

Houdini, Harry, 1874-1926

Biskup, Agnieszka. **Houdini**; the life of the great escape artist. illustrated by Pat Kinsella. Capstone Press 2011 32p il (Graphic library: American graphic) lib bdg $29.32; pa $7.95

Grades: 4 5 6 7   92

1. Magicians 2. Biographical graphic novels 3. Nonfiction writers
ISBN 978-1-4296-5474-6 lib bdg; 1-4296-5474-0 lib bdg; 978-1-4296-6268-0 pa; 1-4296-6268-9 pa

LC 2010024848

In graphic novel format, explores the life of Harry Houdini and describes some of his most daring escapes.

"The illustrations are eye-catching and the narration is presented simply, yet compellingly. . . . Fact-filled, entertaining, and accessible." SLJ

Includes bibliographical references

Carlson, Laurie M. **Harry** Houdini for kids; his life and adventures with 21 magic tricks and illusions. Chicago Review Press 2009 136p il pa $16.95

Grades: 4 5 6 7   92

1. Magicians 2. Magic tricks 3. Nonfiction writers
ISBN 978-1-55652-782-1 pa; 1-55652-782-9 pa

LC 2008021404

"Reluctant readers (as well as budding troublemakers) will flock to this biography/handbook hybrid about one of the most famous magicians who ever lived. Even for those familiar with Houdini's fascinating story, Carlson's snappy writing gives it new life. . . . Nearly every page is enlivened with period photographs, boxed sections containing biographies and definitions, and, most important, 21 magic tricks that will have readers breaking out their deck of cards and practicing their sleight of hand." Booklist

★ Fleischman, Sid. **Escape!** the story of the great Houdini. Greenwillow Books 2006 210p il $18.99; lib bdg $19.89

Grades: 5 6 7 8   92

1. Magicians 2. Nonfiction writers
ISBN 978-0-06-085094-4; 0-06-085094-9; 978-0-06-085095-1 lib bdg; 0-06-0850957-1 lib bdg

LC 2005052631

"Fleischman looks at Houdini's life through his own eyes, as a fellow magician. . . . Fleischman's tone is lively and he develops a relationship with readers by revealing just enough truth behind Houdini's razzle-dazzle to keep the legend alive. . . . Engaging and fascinating." SLJ

Includes bibliographical references

Krull, Kathleen. **Houdini**; the world's greatest mystery man and escape king. in a production written by Kathleen Krull; and illustrated by Eric Velasquez. Walker & Co. 2005 un il hardcover o.p. pa $6.95

Grades: 2 3 4   92

1. Magicians 2. Nonfiction writers
ISBN 0-8027-8953-6; 0-8027-8954-4 lib bdg; 0-8027-9646-X pa

LC 2004-49493

"Framed descriptions of some of Houdini's most famous stunts are interspersed within the overview of his life. The author's crisp narrative style and careful choice of detail are evident here. . . . Velasquez's impressive framed, posed oil paintings portray the magician's intensity and sense of showmanship." SLJ

Includes bibliographical references

★ Weaver, Janice. **Harry** Houdini; the legend of the world's greatest escape artist. illustrations, Chris Lane. Abrams 2011 48p il $18.95

Grades: 4 5 6   92

1. Magicians 2. Nonfiction writers
ISBN 978-1-4197-0014-9; 1-4197-0014-6

The life of Harry Houdini and his less famous partner, his brother Dash, includes details of his well-known career as a magician, as well as his interest in exposing fake mediums and other frauds. Sidebars highlight topics related to the early 20th century, such as child labor, the dime museums, and early aviation, an interest of Houdini's.

Weaver's "well-researched biography of Harry Houdini paints a complex picture of the escape artist. . . . Each spread is visually inviting, mixing b&w photographs and colorful playbills, sometimes alongside moody full-page paintings from Lane, . . . which contribute to an overall air of mystery. A well-rounded addition to the children's bookshelf." Publ Wkly

Houston, Samuel, 1793-1863

★ Fritz, Jean. **Make** way for Sam Houston; illustrations by Elise Primavera. Putnam 1986 109p il map hardcover o.p. pa $5.99

Grades: 4 5 6   92

1. Governors 2. Statesmen 3. Senators 4. Army officers
ISBN 0-399-21303-1; 0-698-11646-1 pa

LC 85-25601

"Artfully weaving the threads of fact, Fritz creates a biography that is both interesting and informative. Developing Houston as a human character that readers can identify with as well as admire, and drawing him against the scene of

America's own political turmoil, Fritz gives us a book to be read and to be felt." Voice Youth Advocates

Includes bibliographical references

Howe, Samuel Gridley, 1801-1876

Alexander, Sally Hobart. **She** touched the world: Laura Bridgman, deaf-blind pioneer; by Sally Hobart Alexander and Robert Alexander. Clarion Books 2008 100p il $18

Grades: 5 6 7 8   92

1. Deaf 2. Blind 3. Students 4. Physicians 5. Philanthropists 6. Humanitarians 7. Teachers of the blind

ISBN 978-0-618-85299-4; 0-618-85299-9

"At the age of three, in 1832, Laura Bridgman contracted scarlet fever and lost her sight, her hearing, her sense of smell, and much of her sense of taste. Her family sent her to Dr. Samuel [Gridley] Howe at the New England Institute for the Education of the Blind, and by the age of 10, Laura was world-famous for her accomplishments. . . . Alexander . . . presents a well-written and thoroughly researched biography of this remarkable woman, with numerous black-and-white photos." Booklist

Includes bibliographical references

Hudson, Henry, d. 1611

★ Weaver, Janice. **Hudson**; written by Janice Weaver; illustrated by David Craig. Tundra Books 2010 47p il map $22.95

Grades: 3 4 5 6   92

1. Explorers

ISBN 978-0-88776-814-9; 0-88776-814-8

This is a biography of the explorer. "The grandson of a trader, Hudson sailed under both British and Dutch flags, looking for a northern route to China. Although none of his voyages led to the discovery of a northwest passage, he did explore what is now Hudson's Bay and what is now New York City." (Publisher's note) Index. "Ages eight to twelve." (Quill Quire)

"This dramatic picture-book biography about Henry Hudson, who discovered neither the new land nor the passage to Asia he sought, makes the explorer's lack of success a gripping read. . . . Weaver is clear about what is fact and what is supposition, and the tumultuous early-seventeenth-century history is meticulously documented. . . . Craig's glowing period portraits, landscapes, and watercolors of the ship in dangerous seas intensify the drama, and archival prints and maps add interest." Booklist

Includes bibliographical references

Hunter, Clementine, 1886?-1988

★ Whitehead, Kathy. **Art** from her heart: folk artist Clementine Hunter; [illustrated by] Shane Evans. G.P. Putnam's Sons 2008 un il $16.99

Grades: 4 5 6 7   92

1. Artists 2. Folk art 3. Painters 4. Women artists 5. African American artists 6. Centenarians

ISBN 978-0-399-24219-9; 0-399-24219-8

LC 2006-34458

"Whitehead's lyrical text speaks of Hunter's perseverance and talent as well as of the simplicity, love of nature, and caring of friends and family that informed her work. Evans bolsters Whitehead's words with bold mixed-media illustrations that portray Hunter in hard times and in good." SLJ

Hutchinson, Anne Marbury, 1591-1643

Atkins, Jeannine. **Anne** Hutchinson's way; [by] Jeannine Atkins; pictures by Michael Dooling. Farrar, Straus and Giroux 2007 un il $17

Grades: 2 3 4   92

1. Colonists 2. Dissenters 3. Religious leaders

ISBN 0-374-30365-7

"Anne Hutchinson arrives with her family in Massachusetts colony in 1634 and begins preaching scripture from her home after finding herself in disagreement with the minister's beliefs. . . . Atkins is able to take the issue of religious freedom and make it personal by telling the story through the eyes of Hutchinson's young daughter, Susanna. . . . A sense of sturdiness is everywhere here: in the story . . . and in Dooling's impressive artwork, plain in color but rugged in its portrayal of the demands of colony life. Illustrated in a photo-realistic style that makes the long-ago events seem close." Booklist

Hypatia, ca. 370-415

★ Love, D. Anne. **Of** numbers and stars; the story of Hypatia. by D. Anne Love; illustrated by Pam Paparone. Holiday House 2006 un il $16.95

Grades: 2 3 4   92

1. Philosophers 2. Mathematicians 3. Women mathematicians

ISBN 0-8234-1621-6

LC 2003064725

"In fourth-century C.E. Egypt, women had few opportunities. How Hypatia, daughter of mathematician Theon, became one of the greatest philosophers of her day makes fascinating reading. . . . Attractive paintings add life to a clear and captivating text that offers a unique contribution to units about Egypt, philosophers, or women in history." SLJ

Includes bibliographical references

Irving, Washington, 1783-1859

★ Harness, Cheryl. The **literary** adventures of Washington Irving; American storyteller. by Cheryl Harness. National Geographic Society 2008 43p il $17.95; lib bdg $27.90

Grades: 2 3 4 5   92

1. Authors 2. Historians 3. Essayists 4. Biographers 5. Authors, American 6. Children's authors

ISBN 978-1-4263-0438-5; 1-4263-0438-2; 978-1-4263-0439-2 lib bdg; 1-4263-0439-0 lib bdg

LC 2008024975

A biography of the American author of The adventures of Rip Van Winkle and The Legend of Sleepy Hollow.

"Pairing insightful text with paintings organized into comic-book-style frames, Harness captures with exuberance everything that made Irving's life so exciting." Booklist

Includes bibliographical references

Jalāl al-Dīn Rūmī, Maulana, 1207-1273

★ Demi. **Rumi**; whirling dervish. written and illustrated by Demi. Marshall Cavendish Children 2009 31p il $19.99

Grades: 4 5 6 7   92

1. Poets 2. Persian poetry

ISBN 978-0-7614-5527-1; 0-7614-5527-2

LC 2008012920

"Demi presents this picture-book introduction to the thirteenth-century mystical poet. . . . Demi condenses her famous subject's life into a brief but substantive text. . . . She adds frequent excerpts from Rumi's poems and writings. . . . In an introductory note, Demi cites Turkish miniatures as her inspiration for the small-scale, elaborately patterned pictures, rendered in Turkish and Chinese inks with gold overlay. . . . The gilded, celebratory pictures create shimmering beauty from the smallest details." Booklist

James, LeBron

Gatto, Kimberly. **Lebron** James; a basketball star who cares. [by] Kimberly A. Gatto. Enslow Publishers, Inc. 2011 48p il (Sport stars who care) lib bdg $23.93; pa $7.95

Grades: 3 4 5   92
1. Basketball players 2. Basketball -- Biography
ISBN 978-0-7660-3776-2 lib bdg; 0-7660-3776-2 lib bdg; 978-1-59845-231-0 pa; 1-59845-231-2 pa
LC 2010014921
A biography of basketball star Lebron James, who helps those in need through several charities, from the Boys and Girls Clubs of America to his own LeBron James Family Foundation.

This is "especially good for book reports." Booklist
Includes glossary and bibliographical references

Yasuda, Anita. **Lebron** James. 2011 24p il (Remarkable people) $27.13; pa $12.95

Grades: 4 5 6 7   92
1. Basketball players 2. Basketball -- Biography
ISBN 978-1-6169-0669-6; 1-6169-0669-3; 978-1-6169-0674-0 pa; 1-6169-0674-X pa
LC 2010051003
This looks at Lebron James' "life, accomplishments, and challenges while including a page of quotes, an annotated list of contemporaries and influences, starter suggestions for writing a paper, and a time line and glossary. . . . [This book] follows basketball's 'King James' from his early life with a single teen mother to his splashy entry into the NBA at age 19." Booklist

Jay-Z

Richard Spilsbury. **Jay-Z**. Heinemann Library 2013 48 p. (Titans of business) (pbk.) $8.99

Grades: 4 5 6 7   92
1. Businessmen 2. Rap musicians 3. Success in business
ISBN 1432964305; 1432964372; 9781432964306; 9781432964375
LC 2011050758
This book, part of the Titans of Business series, looks at rapper and entrepreneur Jay-Z. "Starting with Jay-Z's early life as Shawn Corey Carter in a poor Brooklyn neighborhood, the biography recounts how he overcame his difficult adolescence as a drug dealer with his desire to be a musician." (Booklist)
Includes bibliographical references and index

Jefferson, Thomas, 1743-1826

Miller, Brandon Marie. **Thomas** Jefferson for kids; his life and times, with 21 activities. Chicago Review Press 2011 ix, 132p il $16.95

Grades: 4 5 6 7   92
1. Architects 2. Presidents 3. Vice-presidents 4.

Essayists 5. Presidents -- United States
ISBN 978-1-56976-348-3; 1-56976-348-8
LC 2011019318
"Miller offers a thorough and methodical overview of Jefferson's life and political career. . . . The presentation is expecially forthright about Jefferson's ownership of slaves and his fathering of children with Sally Hemmings. . . . The volume offers the chance to delve into Jefferson's life and be inspired by the range of his interests." Kirkus
Includes bibliographical references

Jemison, Mae C.

Jemison, Mae C. **Find** where the wind goes; moments from my life. [by] Mae Jemison. Scholastic Press 2001 196p il hardcover o.p. $16.95

Grades: 5 6 7 8   92
1. Astronauts 2. Physicians 3. African American women 4. African American women -- Biography 5. African American women astronauts -- Biography -- Juvenile literature
ISBN 0-439-13195-2; 0-439-13196-0 pa
LC 00-41008
"Mae Jemsion, doctor, scientist, astronaut, and professor, here tells of the formative incidents of her life. . . . The author discusses her youth—her days in the South, her family's move to Chicago's South Side, school experiences, and growing up—as well as her later life and her place in the space program. . . . Grades five to eight." (Bull Cent Child Books)

"Dr. Jemison, the first woman of color to travel in space, shares her life story in this autobiographical selection." Book Rep

Joan, of Arc, Saint, 1412-1431

Demi, 1942- **Joan** of Arc. Marshall Cavendish Children 2011 un il $19.99

Grades: 3 4 5   92
1. Saints 2. Christian saints
ISBN 978-0-7614-5953-8; 0-7614-5953-7
LC 2011001123
"Joan of Arc's story told in the ravishing line and color of Demi's art. . . . The text unequivocally treats the 15th-century Joan as a saint, casting the craven King Charles VII as the villain he was. Joan's life is recounted with a strong emphasis on prayer and the will of God, from her beginnings as a devout peasant girl who heeded angelic and saintly voices through her victories and defeats to her imprisonment, trial and martyrdom at the stake. . . . A young female hero par excellence." Kirkus

Jobs, Steven, 1955-2011

Goldsworthy, Steve. **Steve** Jobs. Weigl 2011 24p il (Remarkable people) $27.13; pa $12.95 92
1. Entrepreneurs 2. Businesspeople 3. Computer industry 4. Computer scientists 5. Computer industry executives 6. Electronics industry executives
ISBN 978-1-6169-0670-2; 1-6169-0670-7; 978-1-6169-0675-7 pa; 1-6169-0675-8 pa
LC 2010050999
This looks at Steve Jobs' "life, accomplishments, and challenges while including a page of quotes, an annotated list of contemporaries and influences, starter suggestions for writing a paper, and a time line and glossary. . . . [This book] kicks off as current as possible with a picture of the bearded

Apple CEO displaying an iPad, before getting into the ups (he became a multimillionaire in just two years) and downs (his struggle with cancer)." Booklist

Venezia, Mike. **Steve** Jobs & Steve Wozniak; geek heroes who put the personal in computers. written and illustrated by Mike Venezia. Children's Press 2010 32p il (Getting to know the world's greatest inventors & scientists) lib bdg $28

Grades: 2 3 4   92

1. Entrepreneurs 2. Businesspeople 3. Computer industry 4. Computer scientists 5. Electronics engineers 6. Computer industry executives 7. Electronics industry executives

ISBN 978-0-531-23730-4 lib bdg; 0-531-23730-3 lib bdg

Venezia "describes the extraordinary childhoods of Jobs and Wozniak.... Imperceptibly, Venezia brings a broad history of computers into the picture by demonstrating simultaneously how Jobs and Wozniak were influenced by early computer pioneers and how they then made their mark on the world.... Venezia's thoughtful writing style and carefully chosen photos and graphics allows children to use their imagination and see part of themselves in the two 'heroes' of the title." Sci Books Films

Johnson, Jack, 1878-1946

★ Smith, Charles R., 1969- **Black** Jack: the ballad of Jack Johnson; [by] Charles R. Smith Jr.; illustrated by Shane W. Evans. Roaring Brook Press 2010 un il $16.99

Grades: K 1 2 3   92

1. African American athletes 2. Boxers (Persons) 3. Boxing -- Biography 4. Boxing -- Juvenile literature

ISBN 978-1-59643-473-8; 1-59643-473-2

A picture book biography in verse of boxer Jack Jackson, the first African American heavyweight champion of the world

"The elegant simplicity and rat-a-tat rhythms land some stunners. . . . [The book is] enhanced by Evans' lithe and swaggering artwork, which lends a tremendous visual charisma, grace, and grandeur to the man." Booklist

Includes bibliographical references

Johnson, Lyndon B. (Lyndon Baines), 1908-1973

Gold, Susan Dudley. **Lyndon** B. Johnson. Marshall Cavendish Benchmark 2009 112p il (Presidents and their times) lib bdg $34.21

Grades: 5 6 7 8   92

1. Presidents 2. Vice-presidents 3. Senators 4. Members of Congress 5. Presidents -- United States

ISBN 978-0-7614-2837-4 lib bdg; 0-7614-2837-2 lib bdg

LC 2007038518

A biography of the thirty-sixth president of the United States discusses his personal life, education, and political career and covers the formative events of his time

Includes glossary and bibliographical references

Johnson, Mamie, 1935-

★ Green, Michelle Y. A **strong** right arm: the story of Mamie Peanut Johnson; introduction by Mamie Johnson. Dial Bks. for Young Readers 2002 111p il $15.99; pa $5.99

Grades: 4 5 6 7   92

1. Women 2. Women athletes 3. Baseball players 4. African Americans 5. African American athletes 6. Johnson, Mamie 7. Collectibles dealers 8. Baseball -- Biography 9. African American baseball players -- Biography -- Juvenile literature 10. Baseball players -- United States -- Biography -- Juvenile literature 11. Women baseball players -- United States -- Biography -- Juvenile literature

ISBN 0-8037-2661-9; 0-14-240072-6 pa

LC 2001-28616

"Johnson was a pitcher with the Negro Leagues' Indianapolis Clowns from 1953 to 1955. In the introduction, Johnson speaks directly and movingly to the reader about her meeting with author Green, who then lets the famous ballplayer tell her own story in a lively first-person narrative. Johnson's ebullient personality and determination fairly leap off the page." Booklist

Includes bibliographical references

Jones, John Paul, 1747-1792

Cooper, Michael L. **Hero** of the high seas; John Paul Jones and the American Revolution. National Geographic 2006 128p il map $21.95; lib bdg $32.90

Grades: 5 6 7 8   92

1. Admirals 2. Naval officers

ISBN 0-7922-5547-X; 0-7922-5548-8 lib bdg

LC 2005-36256

"Cooper charts his subject's life from a scandal-ridden Scottish captain on a trading ship to a man of self-invention who came to the American colonies to start a new life and became a naval hero. Jones is presented as a loyal captain, an arrogant leader, a determined sailor, and a flagrant social climber. The narrative style will appeal to reluctant readers, for it reads like a chronicle of thrilling naval adventures. . . . The text is clear and understandable." SLJ

Includes bibliographical references

Jordan-Fenton, Christy

Jordan-Fenton, Christy. **Fatty** legs; a true story. [by] Christy Jordan-Fenton and Margaret Pokiak-Fenton; artwork by Liz Amini-Holmes. Annick Press 2010 104p il $21.95; pa $12.95

Grades: 3 4 5 6   92

1. Inuit 2. Authors 3. Artisans 4. Children's authors 5. Native Americans -- Canada 6. Inuit -- Canada -- Juvenile literature

ISBN 978-1-55451-247-8; 1-55451-247-6; 978-1-55451-246-1 pa; 1-55451-246-8 pa

This book chronicles the unbreakable spirit of an Inuit girl while attending an Arctic residential school.

"Dark, expressive original paintings are dotted throughout the story and complement the serious tone of the narrative. . . . An excellent addition to any biography collection, the book is fascinating and unique, and yet universal in its message." SLJ

Jordan-Fenton, Christy. A **stranger** at home; a true story. [by] Christy Jordan-Fenton and Margaret Pokiak-Fenton; artwork by Liz Amini-Holmes. Annick Press 2011 124p il $21.95; pa $12.95

Grades: 3 4 5 6   92

1. Inuit 2. Authors 3. Artisans 4. Children's authors

5. Native Americans -- Canada
ISBN 978-1-55451-362-8; 1-55451-362-6; 978-1-55451-361-1 pa; 1-55451-361-8 pa

"After two years in Catholic residential school, 10-year-old Olemaun returns to Tuktoyaktuk on Canada's Arctic coast, a stranger to her friends and family, unaccustomed to the food and clothing and unable to speak or understand her native language. Margaret Pokiak's story continues after the events of Fatty Legs (2010), which described her boarding-school experience. In this stand-alone sequel, she describes a year of reintegration into her Inuvialuit world. . . . Olemaun's spirit and determination shine through this moving memoir." Kirkus

Jordan, Michael, 1963-
Cooper, Floyd. **Jump!** from the life of Michael Jordan. Philomel Books 2004 un il $15.99
Grades: K 1 2 3   92
1. Basketball 2. Baseball players 3. African American athletes 4. Olympic athletes 5. Basketball players
ISBN 0-399-24230-9
LC 2003-25071
This is a "childhood profile of basketball legend Michael Jordan. Each double-page spread features powerful portraits of Jordan. . . . Children who view Jordan as a deity on the court will take comfort in Cooper's stories, written in casual, colloquial language." Booklist
Includes bibliographical references

Joseph, Nez Percé Chief, 1840-1904
Biskup, Agnieszka. **Thunder** rolling down the mountain; the story of Chief Joseph and the Nez Perce. illustrated by Rusty Zimmerman. Capstone Press 2011 32p il (Graphic library: American graphic) lib bdg $29.32; pa $7.95
Grades: 4 5 6 7   92
1. Biographical graphic novels 2. Indian chiefs 3. Nez Percé Indians
ISBN 978-1-4296-5472-2 lib bdg; 1-4296-5472-4 lib bdg; 978-1-4296-6270-3 pa; 1-4296-6270-0 pa
LC 2010027914
In graphic novel format, explores the battles and hardships faced by Chief Joseph and the Nez Perce when they were forced to leave their homelands.
"The illustrations are eye-catching and the narration is presented simply, yet compellingly. . . . Fact-filled, entertaining, and accessible." SLJ
Includes bibliographical references

Englar, Mary. **Chief** Joseph, 1840-1904. Blue Earth Books 2004 32p (American Indian biographies) lib bdg $23.93
Grades: 3 4 5   92
1. Nez Perce Indians 2. Indian chiefs 3. Native Americans -- Biography
ISBN 0-7368-2444-8
LC 2003-11071
A biography of the peace chief who ended the Nez Percé War by surrendering to United States soldiers in 1877, believing that he would be permitted lead his people back to their ancestral lands in Idaho. Includes a recipe for berry fritters and directions for "the stick game."
This "very accessible [title is] well illustrated with maps, photographs, and paintings, and [it offers] an introduction to

American Indian history as well as specific information for reports." Booklist

Jumper, Betty Mae, 1923-2011
★ Annino, Jan Godown. **She** sang promise: the story of Betty Mae Jumper, Seminole tribal leader; illustrated by Lisa Desimini; afterword by Moses Jumper, Jr. National Geographic 2010 33p il map lib bdg $26.90
Grades: 1 2 3   92
1. Nurses 2. Seminole Indians 3. Storytellers 4. Indian leaders
ISBN 978-1-4263-0592-4 lib bdg; 1-4263-0592-3 lib bdg
LC 2009-16066
"Elected in 1967 as one of the first women tribal leaders in modern times, Seminole Betty Mae Tiger Jumper overcame oppression and prejudice, starting in her childhood. This picture-book biography tells her story in a dramatic present-tense narrative that blends details of her life with the historical struggle of her people. . . . The large collage paintings in bright colors blend old and new traditions, the natural world, and Seminole artwork." Booklist
Includes glossary and bibliographical references

Kahanamoku, Duke, 1890-1968
Crowe, Ellie. **Surfer** of the century; the life of Duke Kahanamoku. illustrations by Richard Waldrep. Lee & Low Books 2007 un il map $18.95
Grades: 3 4 5 6   92
1. Actors 2. Surfing 3. Swimming 4. Surfers 5. Swimmers 6. Olympic athletes
ISBN 978-1-58430-276-6
LC 2006036562
"The text is concise and readable, ably supported by Waldrep's full-page color art on every spread. These vibrant, action-filled illustrations . . . add much to the book's overall appeal. Well researched and fact-filled." SLJ

Kahlo, Frida, 1907-1954
★ Frith, Margaret. **Frida** Kahlo; the artist who painted herself. written by Margaret Frith; illustrated by Tomie DePaola. Grosset & Dunlap 2003 un il (Smart about art) hardcover o.p. pa $5.99
Grades: 2 3 4   92
1. Artists 2. Painters 3. Women artists 4. Artists, Mexican
ISBN 0-448-43239-0; 0-448-42677-3 pa
LC 2003-5221
Biography of Mexican artist Frida Kahlo, written as a child's school report
"Kahlo's story is clear, concise, and accessible. All of the basic facts are here, along with many personal details that enliven the narrative. . . . The well-written prose is beautifully complemented both by photos of Kahlo and of some of her best-known paintings and by dePaola's splendid trademark illustrations, all set against vividly colored backgrounds." SLJ

Kearton, Cherry
Bond, Rebecca. **In** the belly of an ox: the unexpected photographic adventures of Richard and Cherry Kearton; written and illustrated by Rebecca Bond. Houghton Mifflin Books for Children 2009 un il $16

Grades: K 1 2 3   92
1. Naturalists 2. Photographers 3. Photography of birds 4. Birds -- Nests 5. Wildlife photography -- Juvenile literature
ISBN 978-0-547-07675-1; 0-547-07675-4
"In the late 19th century, these nature-loving brothers spent their youth navigating the British countryside. . . . When they were older, the boys devised a method to photograph wild birds in their nests. . . . Bond's graceful watercolors depict the brothers as they piece together their disguises and gain recognition for their innovative approach to photography. The brothers' dedication and ingenuity are especially resonant, and their elaborate costumes will amuse but also inspire." Publ Wkly

Kearton, Richard, 1862-1928
Bond, Rebecca. **In** the belly of an ox: the unexpected photographic adventures of Richard and Cherry Kearton; written and illustrated by Rebecca Bond. Houghton Mifflin Books for Children 2009 un il $16
Grades: K 1 2 3   92
1. Naturalists 2. Photographers 3. Photography of birds 4. Birds -- Nests 5. Wildlife photography -- Juvenile literature
ISBN 978-0-547-07675-1; 0-547-07675-4
"In the late 19th century, these nature-loving brothers spent their youth navigating the British countryside. . . . When they were older, the boys devised a method to photograph wild birds in their nests. . . . Bond's graceful watercolors depict the brothers as they piece together their disguises and gain recognition for their innovative approach to photography. The brothers' dedication and ingenuity are especially resonant, and their elaborate costumes will amuse but also inspire." Publ Wkly

Keaton, Buster, 1895-1966
★ Brighton, Catherine. **Keep** your eye on the kid; the early years of Buster Keaton. Roaring Brook Press 2008 un il $16.95
Grades: 3 4 5   92
1. Actors 2. Motion picture producers and directors 3. Motion picture directors 4. Silent films -- Juvenile literature 5. Biography, Individual -- Juvenile literature
ISBN 978-1-59643-158-4; 1-59643-158-X
LC 2007-16534
This is a first-person account of the early years of Buster Keaton, who started performing as a child with his parents in vaudeville and "grew up to become a famous movie producer and performer. . . . Brighton's cartoon drawings shaded in umber and gray tones have a graphic look quite appropriate to the comic subject. The account ends with a brief look at the elaborate stage falls typical of Keaton's movie humor, and a full-page author's note gives added information on his career." SLJ
Includes bibliographical references.

Keckley, Elizabeth, ca. 1818-1907
★ Jones, Lynda. **Mrs.** Lincoln's dressmaker: the unlikely friendship of Elizabeth Keckley and Mary Todd Lincoln; by Lynda D. Jones. National Geographic 2009 80p il $18.95; lib bdg $27.90
Grades: 5 6 7 8   92
1. Memoirists 2. Dressmakers 3. Spouses of presidents 4. Slavery -- United States 5. African American women

-- Biography
ISBN 978-1-4263-0377-7; 1-4263-0377-7; 978-1-4263-0378-4 lib bdg; 1-4263-0378-5 lib bdg
LC 2008-29314
"Readers may be familiar with the ups and downs of Lincoln's life, but details of Keckley's story . . . will give them new insights into the life of a slave, in this case, one who was educated and had a profession." Booklist
Includes bibliographical references

Kehret, Peg, 1936-
Kehret, Peg. **Small** steps; the year I got polio. Anniversary ed; Albert Whitman 2006 205p il $15.95; pa $6.99
Grades: 4 5 6   92
1. Authors 2. Poliomyelitis 3. Women authors 4. Authors, American 5. Children's authors
ISBN 978-0-8075-7459-1; 0-8075-7459-7; 978-0-8075-7458-4 pa; 0-8075-7458-9 pa
LC 2006005136
First published 1996
Kehret "writes in an approachable, familiar way, and readers will be hooked from the first page on." SLJ
Includes bibliographical references

Keller, Helen, 1880-1968
Amoroso, Cynthia. **Helen** Keller; by Cynthia Amoroso and Robert B. Noyed. Child's World 2010 24p il (Basic biographies) lib bdg $22.79
Grades: PreK K 1   92
1. Deaf 2. Blind 3. Authors 4. Memoirists 5. Humanitarians 6. Teachers of the deaf 7. Inspirational writers 8. Teachers of the blind 9. Social welfare leaders
ISBN 978-1-60253-341-7; 1-60253-341-5
LC 2009029369
This biography of Helen Keller "pairs intelligent, brief text with abundant photos. Simple but never basic." Booklist
Includes bibliographical references

Delano, Marfe Ferguson. **Helen's** eyes; a photobiography of Annie Sullivan, Helen Keller's teacher. [foreword by Keller Johnson Thompson] National Geographic 2008 63p il map $17.95; lib bdg $27.90
Grades: 4 5 6 7   92
1. Deaf 2. Blind 3. Authors 4. Teachers 5. Memoirists 6. Humanitarians 7. Teachers of the deaf 8. Inspirational writers 9. Teachers of the blind 10. Social welfare leaders
ISBN 978-1-4263-02-9-1; 1-4263-0209-6; 978-1-4263-0210-7 lib bdg; 1-4263-0210-X lib bdg
"There are many biographies of Helen Keller and Annie Sullivan, but this one is very nicely done. . . . The book is honest in its portrayals, especially of Sullivan. . . . What makes this oversize book so appealing is the clean design, with large typeface. The many fascinating photographs are sometimes placed over historical documents." Booklist
Includes bibliographical references

Lawlor, Laurie. **Helen** Keller: rebellious spirit. Holiday House 2001 168p il $22.95
Grades: 5 6 7 8   92
1. Deaf 2. Blind 3. Authors 4. Memoirists 5. Humanitarians 6. Inspirational writers 7. Social

welfare leaders

ISBN 0-8234-1588-0

LC 00-36950

A "biography of the most famous deaf and blind person in history. Drawing on social and scientific studies of deafness and blindness as well as on American history texts, Lawlor puts Keller's experiences in context. . . . At the same time, readers get a strong feel for Keller's personality and for the personalities of Annie Sullivan, Alexander Graham Bell, and other major figures in her life. Aided by numerous well-chosen photographs and excerpts from Keller's writings." Horn Book

Includes bibliographical references

Sullivan, George. **Helen** Keller; her life in pictures. foreword by Keller Johnson Thompson. Scholastic Nonfiction 2007 80p il $17.99

Grades: 4 5 6 7   92

1. Deaf 2. Blind 3. Authors 4. Memoirists 5. Humanitarians 6. Inspirational writers 7. Social welfare leaders

ISBN 0-439-91815-4; 978-0-439-91815-2

LC 2006-51401

"Accompanied by brief, simply phrased commentary from Sullivan, this suite of photos portrays Keller from early childhood into her 80s. . . . This profile will serve equally well as an introduction, or as supplementary reading for confirmed admirers." Booklist

Includes bibliographical references

Kellerman, Annette, 1888-1975

Corey, Shana. **Mermaid** Queen; the spectacular true story of Annette Kellerman, who swam her way to fame, fortune, & swimsuit history! illustrated by Edwin Fotheringham. Scholastic Press 2008 un il $17.99

Grades: K 1 2 3   92

1. Actors 2. Swimming 3. Women athletes 4. Swimmers

ISBN 978-0-439-69835-1; 0-439-69835-9

LC 2007-52664

"Fotheringham's glorious artwork is filled with period details and dress, high-dives and stunts, and priceless expressions on the faces of amazed audiences. . . . This well-written and brightly illustrated account is a perfect pearl." SLJ

Kennedy, John F. (John Fitzgerald), 1917-1963

★ Heiligman, Deborah. **High** hopes; a photobiography of John F. Kennedy. National Geographic 2003 63p il map $17.95

Grades: 4 5 6 7   92

1. Presidents 2. Senators 3. Members of Congress 4. Presidents -- United States 5. Presidents -- United States -- Biography -- Juvenile literature 6. Presidents -- United States -- Pictorial works -- Juvenile literature

ISBN 0-7922-6141-0

LC 2003-7819

Photographs and text trace the life of President John F. Kennedy.

The text "successfully captures the spirit that makes Kennedy an enduring figure in our history. . . . This well-

designed book features large, well-chosen, black-and-white photographs." SLJ

Includes bibliographical references

Rappaport, Doreen. **Jack's** path of courage; the life of John F. Kennedy. written by Doreen Rappaport; illustrated by Matt Tavares. Hyperion Books for Children 2010 un il $17.99

Grades: 2 3 4 5   92

1. Presidents 2. Senators 3. Members of Congress 4. Presidents -- United States

ISBN 978-1-4231-2272-2; 1-4231-2272-0

"In her signature succinct style, Rappaport fuses facts about Kennedy's personal and public lives with quotations from his writings and speeches. . . . Tavares's light and shadow-infused paintings balance lifelike portrayals of Kennedy with renderings of dramatic events. . . . An evenhanded, graphically stirring biography." Publ Wkly

Includes bibliographical references

King, Coretta Scott, 1927-2006

★ Shange, Ntozake. **Coretta** Scott; poetry by Ntozake Shange; paintings by Kadir Nelson. Amistad/Katherine Tegen Books 2009 un il lib bdg $18.89; $17.99

Grades: K 1 2 3   92

1. Clergy 2. Singers 3. Nonfiction writers 4. Civil rights activists 5. Nobel laureates for peace 6. African Americans -- Civil rights 7. African American women -- Biography ISBN 978-0-06-125365-2 lib bdg; 0-06-125365-0 lib bdg; 978-0-06-125364-5; 0-06-125364-2

LC 2008-10486

Nelson's "jacket portrait of Coretta Scott, monumental and tender at the same time, sets the tone for this intimate picture biography. The artist's full-bleed paintings, powerfully molded and saturated with color, depict crucial moments in Scott's life. . . . Shange's . . . rhythmic lines and format syntax roll like waves . . . carrying readers on a soul-stirring ride." Publ Wkly

King, Martin Luther, Jr., 1929-1968

★ Farris, Christine. **March** on! the day my brother Martin changed the world. [by] Christine King Farris; illustrated by London Ladd. Scholastic Press 2008 un il $17.99

Grades: 2 3 4   92

1. Clergy 2. Civil rights demonstrations 3. College teachers 4. Nonfiction writers 5. Civil rights activists 6. Nobel laureates for peace 7. African Americans -- Civil rights

ISBN 978-0-545-03537-8; 0-545-03537-6

LC 2007038620

"Describing the 1963 March on Washington, Farris, the older sister of Martin Luther King Jr., maintains the deft touch that made My Brother Martin so moving. . . . Farris . . . effectively uses plain language and well-chosen facts to explain her brother's extraordinary achievements. . . . Ladd . . . demonstrates a rare talent for portraiture. . . . His King looks human—in other words, capable of inspiring the reader." Publ Wkly

★ Farris, Christine. **My** brother Martin; a sister remembers growing up with the Rev. Dr. Martin Luther King Jr. by Christine King Farris; illustrated by Chris Soentpiet.

Simon & Schuster Bks. for Young Readers 2003 35p il $17.95

Grades: K 1 2 3   **92**
1. Clergy 2. College teachers 3. Nonfiction writers 4. Civil rights activists 5. Nobel laureates for peace 6. African Americans -- Biography 7. African Americans -- Civil rights

ISBN 0-689-84387-9

LC 2001-44681

Looks at the early life of Martin Luther King, Jr., as seen through the eyes of his older sister.

"The warmth of the text is exquisitely echoed in Soentpiet's realistic, light-filled watercolor portraits. . . . This outstanding book belongs in every collection." SLJ

★ Michelson, Richard. **As** good as anybody: Martin Luther King Jr. and Abraham Joshua Heschel's amazing march toward freedom; by Richard Michelson; illustrated by Raul Colón. Knopf 2008 un il $16.99; lib bdg $19.99

Grades: 2 3 4   **92**
1. Clergy 2. Rabbis 3. Theologians 4. Jews -- Biography 5. Nonfiction writers 6. Civil rights activists 7. Nobel laureates for peace 8. African Americans -- Biography 9. African Americans -- Civil rights

ISBN 978-0-375-83335-9; 0-375-83335-8; 978-0-375-93335-6 lib bdg; 0-375-93335-2 lib bdg

This is the story of how Abraham Joshua Heschel, a Polish rabbi who escaped the Holocaust, and Martin Luther King worked together for African American civil rights.

"Michelson writes in poetic language. . . . Also admirable is Michelson's ability to convey complex historical concepts . . . in clear, potent terms that will speak directly to readers. . . . In both palette and style, Colón's colored-pencil and watercolor art . . . suggests the past, but his themes carry into today's headlines." Booklist

★ Myers, Walter Dean, 1937- **I've** seen the promised land; the life of Dr. Martin Luther King, Jr. illustrated by Leonard Jenkins. HarperCollins Publishers 2004 un il $15.99; lib bdg $16.89

Grades: K 1 2 3   **92**
1. Clergy 2. Nonfiction writers 3. Civil rights activists 4. Nobel laureates for peace 5. African Americans -- Biography 6. African Americans -- Civil rights 7. African Americans -- Biography -- Juvenile literature 8. Baptists -- United States -- Clergy -- Biography -- Juvenile literature 9. Civil rights workers -- United States -- Biography -- Juvenile literature 10. African Americans -- Civil rights -- History -- 20th century -- Juvenile literature

ISBN 0-06-027703-3; 0-06-027704-1 lib bdg

LC 2003-4098

Pictures and easy-to-read text introduce the life of civil rights leader Dr. Martin Luther King, Jr.

"This eloquent picture book presents a brief overview of King's life and accomplishments. . . . Jenkins's stunning collage artwork dramatically reflects the events described in the narrative." SLJ

★ Rappaport, Doreen. **Martin's** big words: the life of Dr. Martin Luther King, Jr. illustrated by Bryan Collier. Hyperion Bks. for Children 2001 un il $15.99; pa $6.99

Grades: K 1 2 3   **92**
1. Clergy 2. Nonfiction writers 3. Civil rights activists 4. Nobel laureates for peace 5. African Americans -- Biography 6. African Americans -- Civil rights

ISBN 0-7868-0714-8; 1-4231-0635-0 pa

LC 00-40957

A Caldecott Medal honor book, 2002; A Coretta Scott King honor book for illustration, 2002

"Rappaport's spare narrative captures the essentials of the man, the movement he led, and his policy of nonviolence. . . . Collier's collage art is glorious. Combining cut-paper, photographs, and watercolor he expresses his own Christian faith and King's power 'to make many different things one.'" Booklist

★ Shange, Ntozake. **Coretta** Scott; poetry by Ntozake Shange; paintings by Kadir Nelson. Amistad/Katherine Tegen Books 2009 un il lib bdg $18.89; $17.99

Grades: K 1 2 3   **92**
1. Clergy 2. Singers 3. Nonfiction writers 4. Civil rights activists 5. Nobel laureates for peace 6. African Americans -- Civil rights 7. African American women -- Biography

ISBN 978-0-06-125365-2 lib bdg; 0-06-125365-0 lib bdg; 978-0-06-125364-5; 0-06-125364-2

LC 2008-10486

Nelson's "jacket portrait of Coretta Scott, monumental and tender at the same time, sets the tone for this intimate picture biography. The artist's full-bleed paintings, powerfully molded and saturated with color, depict crucial moments in Scott's life. . . . Shange's . . . rhythmic lines and format syntax roll like waves . . . carrying readers on a soul-stirring ride." Publ Wkly

Watkins, Angela Farris. **My** Uncle Martin's big heart; illustrated by Eric Velasquez. Abrams 2010 un il $18.95

Grades: PreK K 1 2   **92**
1. Clergy 2. Nonfiction writers 3. Civil rights activists 4. Nobel laureates for peace 5. African Americans -- Civil rights

ISBN 978-0-8109-8975-7; 0-8109-8975-1

"In this warm, handsome picture book, Watkins celebrates her loving relationship as a small preschooler with 'Uncle M. L.' . . . The girl speaks about taking pride in her uncle's political role as a civil rights leader and national hero. Even more, though, she focuses on personal moments. . . . Velasquez is at his best here. . . . He shows the affection that the child and her uncle share." Booklist

Knight, Margaret, 1838-1914

McCully, Emily Arnold. **Marvelous** Mattie; how Margaret E. Knight became an inventor. Farrar, Straus & Giroux 2006 un il $16

Grades: K 1 2 3   **92**
1. Inventors 2. Women inventors

ISBN 0-374-34810-3

LC 2004-56415

Margaret (or Mattie) "Knight's design for a safer loom saved textile workers from injuries and death. . . . She fought in court and won the right to patent her most famous invention, a machine that would make paper bags. Mattie's story is told in a style that is not only easy to understand, but that is also a good read-aloud. The watercolor-and-ink illustrations capture the spirited inventor and support the text in style and design." SLJ

Knox, Henry, 1750-1806

★ Silvey, Anita. **Henry** Knox; bookseller, soldier, patriot. pictures by Wendell Minor. Clarion Books 2010 40p il $17.99

Grades: 2 3 4 5　　　　　　　　　　　　　　　　92

1. Generals

ISBN 978-0-618-27485-7; 0-618-27485-5

LC 2009045353

"When the first shots were fired at Lexington and Concord, Henry Knox was a portly young bookseller who avidly read books on military science and discussed them with the British officers who frequented his Boston shop. He would soon put his theoretical knowledge to practical use, for he was placed in charge of the Continental Army's artillery. . . . The first half of this fully illustrated book deftly portrays Knox as a likable, optimistic youth, while the second half shows him as a determined 25-year-old officer leading the expedition that freed Boston in 1776. . . . Painted on wooden panels, Minor's acrylic art creates a vivid sense of the period in varied scenes crafted with a fine grasp of composition, texture, and color." Booklist

Kobayashi, Issa, 1763-1827

★ Gollub, Matthew. **Cool** melons--turn to frogs!: the life and poems of Issa; story and Haiku translations by Matthew Gollub; illustrations by Kazuko G. Stone; calligraphy by Keiko Smith. Lee & Low Bks. 1998 un il $16.95; pa $9.95

Grades: 3 4 5 6　　　　　　　　　　　　　　　　92

1. Haiku 2. Poets 3. Authors 4. Japanese poetry

ISBN 1-880000-71-7; 1-58430-241-0 pa

LC 98-13087

A biography and introduction to the work of the Japanese haiku poet whose love for nature finds expression in the more than thirty poems included in this book

This contains the life of the poet "told in simple language; lots of his exquisite and accessible haiku; limpid watercolor and colored pencil illustrations reminiscent of Japanese prints and drawings; and beautiful Japanese calligraphy." Booklist

Korczak, Janusz, 1878-1942

Bogacki, Tomek. The **champion** of children; the story of Janusz Korczak. Farrar Straus Giroux 2009 un il $17.99

Grades: 1 2 3 4　　　　　　　　　　　　　　　　92

1. Authors 2. Pediatricians 3. Jews -- Poland 4. Holocaust victims 5. Children's authors 6. Holocaust, 1933-1945

ISBN 978-0-374-34136-7; 0-374-34136-2

LC 2008-16188

This is a "picture-book biography of the Holocaust-era children's advocate and doctor. Early Polish childhood life and interests quickly move into the doctor's student days and expand to his renowned, democratically run orphanage. . . . He steadfastly stayed with his children during the Nazi invasion and deportation and ultimately perished with them at Treblinka. . . . Though this is a story that ends in dark despair, the author succeeds in creating a positive, upbeat atmosphere with his palette of muted reds, blues and greens." Kirkus

Kouanchao, Malichansouk, 1971-

Youme. **Mali** under the night sky; a Lao story of home. written and illustrated by Youme. Cinco Puntos Press 2010 un il $17.95

Grades: K 1 2　　　　　　　　　　　　　　　　92

1. Artists 2. Women artists

ISBN 978-1-933693-68-2; 1-933693-68-1

Relates the true story of Laotian American artist Malichansouk Kouanchao, who enjoyed her early childhood playing in the wilderness until civil war forced her family to leave for another country, allowing her to bring only her memories of her homeland.

This story "is told in a simple, straightforward manner, from a child's point of view. . . . The focus remains tightly on Mali's experiences and feelings, keeping it accessible to young readers. . . . The watercolor illustrations, while naive in style, convey a real sense of place." SLJ

Koufax, Sandy, 1935-

★ Winter, Jonah. **You** never heard of Sandy Koufax!? illustrations by Andre Carrilho. Schwartz & Wade Books 2009 un il $17.99; lib bdg $20.99 92

1. Baseball players 2. Jews -- Biography 3. Baseball -- Biography 4. Baseball -- History -- Juvenile literature

ISBN 978-0-375-83738-8; 0-375-83738-8; 978-0-375-93738-5 lib bdg; 0-375-93738-2 lib bdg

LC 2007-41860

The author relates "the story of arguably the greatest left-handed pitcher in baseball history as if he were an unnamed teammate along for the ride. . . . Winter makes a point to emphasize that at the time, . . . Koufax was one of very few Jewish players, and he encountered his share of prejudice. . . . Carrilho's digitally enhanced graphite artwork, which resembles highly expressionistic cartoons, emphasizes movement, . . . with touches of deep gold and swift strokes of red against Dodger blue." Booklist

Includes glossary

Kublai Khan, 1216-1294

★ Krull, Kathleen. **Kubla** Khan; the emperor of everything. illustrated by Robert Byrd. Viking Children's Books 2010 un il $17.99

Grades: 2 3 4　　　　　　　　　　　　　　　　92

1. Mongols 2. Kings

ISBN 978-0-670-01114-8; 0-670-01114-2

LC 2010007322

"Krull assembles a convincingly grand impression of Kubla Khan and his vast accomplishments. . . . The grandiosity of his reign is well depicted in Bryd's Eastern-style artwork, which provides a subtle buttress to the narrative arc. . . . A solid choice for reports that is also scintillating enough for pleasure reading." Booklist

Includes bibliographical references

La Salle, Robert Cavelier, sieur de, 1643-1687

Goodman, Joan E. **Despite** all obstacles: La Salle and the conquest of the Mississippi; by Joan Elizabeth Goodman; illustrated by Tom McNeely. Mikaya Press 2001 47p il map (Great explorers book) $19.95

Grades: 4 5 6 7　　　　　　　　　　　　　　　　92

1. Explorers 2. Explorers -- France -- Biography -- Juvenile literature 3. Canada -- History -- To 1763 (New France) -- Juvenile literature 4. Explorers -- Mississippi River -- Biography -- Juvenile literature 5. Mississippi

River Valley -- History -- To 1803 -- Juvenile literature
ISBN 1-931414-01-7

LC 2001-31732

A biography of the man who explored the St. Lawrence, Ohio, Illinois, and Mississippi rivers, and who claimed America's heartland for King Louis XIV and France

"Vivid color illustrations and Goodman's exciting writing style will attract both researchers and pleasure readers." Voice Youth Advocates

Law, Westley Wallace, 1923-2002

Haskins, James. **Delivering** justice; W.W. Law and the fight for civil rights. [by] Jim Haskins; illustrated by Benny Andrews. Candlewick Press 2005 un il $16.99

Grades: 2 3 4   92

1. Postal employees 2. Civil rights activists 3. African Americans -- Civil rights

ISBN 0-7636-2592-2

LC 2005-47114

A biography of Westley (W. W.) Law, a mail carrier who played a leading role in the civil rights movement

"With handsome, full-page illustrations in oil and collage, this picture-book biography tells the stirring story of a quiet hero." Booklist

Lawrence, Jacob, 1917-2000

Collard, Sneed B. **Jacob** Lawrence; a painter's story. Marshall Cavendish Benchmark 2009 41p bibl il por (American heroes) lib bdg $20.95

Grades: 2 3 4   92

1. Artists 2. Painters 3. Illustrators 4. African American artists 5. Artists -- United States

ISBN 978-0-7614-4058-1 lib bdg; 0-7614-4058-5 lib bdg

LC 2008034819

This introduces "young readers to one of the preeminent twentieth-century African American artists. Collard recounts a few important touchstones of Lawrence's life . . . but mostly frames the narrative around his works. . . . The narrative is concise, but not to the point of simplicity. . . . Reproductions of paintings and period photos alternate each page of the text." Booklist

Includes glossary and bibliographical references

Lazarus, Emma, 1849-1887

★ Silverman, Erica. **Liberty's** voice: the story of Emma Lazarus; illustrated by Stacey Schuett. Dutton Children's Books 2011 un il $17.99

Grades: 2 3 4 5   92

1. Poets 2. Authors 3. Novelists 4. Women poets 5. Philanthropists 6. Poets, American 7. Social reformers 8. Jews -- Biography

ISBN 0-525-47859-0; 978-0-525-47859-1

LC 2010-13186

This is a biography of the American poet whose lines are inscribed on the Statue of Liberty. "Grades three to five." (Bull Cent Child Books)

"A well-known poet in her day, Emma Lazarus was initially hesitant to pen the poem that would make her famous, 'The New Colossus,' which is engraved on the base of the Statue of Liberty. . . . But her dedication to the plight of immigrant Russian Jews . . . ultimately inspired her message to the 'huddled masses yearning to breathe free.' In a straightforward and smooth narrative style, Silverman . . .

tells the story of Lazarus' life and work. The accompanying ink-and-watercolor illustrations serve the historical setting, characters, and plot well." Booklist

Includes bibliographical references

Ledger, Heath, 1979-2008

Watson, Stephanie. **Heath** Ledger; talented actor. ABDO Pub. Company 2010 112p il (Lives cut short) lib bdg $32.79

Grades: 5 6 7 8   92

1. Actors

ISBN 978-1-60453-789-5 lib bdg; 1-60453-789-2 lib bdg

LC 2009034353

This discusses Heath Ledger's "early life, providing details that give insight into later success and troubles and maintaining a laudatory tone that focuses on the individual's artistic achievements and hard work to achieve fame. Details [such as] explaining that Jack Nicholson warned Heath Ledger about the Joker role . . . are bound to resonate with readers. Numerous photos and sidebars appear throughout. [A] worthwhile [resource] for reports as well as popular reading." SLJ

Includes bibliographical references

Lee, Bruce, 1940-1973

Mochizuki, Ken. **Be** water, my friend; the early years of Bruce Lee. illustrated by Dom Lee. Lee & Low Books 2006 un il $16.95

Grades: K 1 2 3   92

1. Actors 2. Martial arts 3. Martial artists

ISBN 1-58430-265-0

"This distinctive-looking book offers a smoothly written text and many handsome, textured acrylic paintings done in tones of brown and cream." Booklist

Lee, Sammy, 1920-

★ Yoo, Paula. **Sixteen** years in sixteen seconds; the Sammy Lee story. illustrations by Dom Lee. Lee & Low Books 2005 un il $16.95

Grades: 2 3 4   92

1. Diving 2. Physicians 3. Korean Americans 4. Divers 5. Olympic athletes

ISBN 1-58430-247-X

LC 2004-20962

"Yoo introduces Sammy Lee, the son of Korean immigrants who overcame formidable odds to become an Olympic diving champion as well as a doctor. . . . Washed in nostalgic sepia tones, Dom Lee's acrylic-and-wax textured illustrations are reminiscent of his fine work in Ken Mochizuki's watershed Baseball Saved Us (1993) and like Yoo's understated words, the uncluttered images leave a deep impression." Booklist

Lennon, John, 1940-1980

Anderson, Jennifer Joline. **John** Lennon; legendary musician & Beatle. ABDO 2010 112p il (Lives cut short) lib bdg $32.79

Grades: 5 6 7 8   92

1. Singers 2. Rock musicians 3. Songwriters

ISBN 978-1-60453-790-1 lib bdg; 1-60453-790-6 lib bdg

LC 2009034354

This discusses the John Lennon's "early life, providing details that give insight into later success and troubles and maintaining a laudatory tone that focuses on the individual's artistic achievements and hard work to achieve fame. Details [such as] explaining that . . . John Lennon had no musical training . . . are bound to resonate with readers. Numerous photos and sidebars appear throughout. [A] worthwhile [resource] for reports as well as popular reading." SLJ

Includes glossary and bibliographical references

Rappaport, Doreen. **John's** secret dreams; the life of John Lennon. written by Doreen Rappaport; illustrated by Bryan Collier. Hyperion Books for Children 2004 un il $16.99

Grades: 4 5 6 7   **92**
  1. Singers 2. Rock musicians 3. Songwriters
  ISBN 0-7868-0817-9

LC 2003-57116

"Using a combination of simple prose, song lyrics, and illustration, this heartfelt picture-book biography traces Lennon's life from his childhood to his death. Striking in both its simplicity and complexity, it captures this enigmatic singer, artist, songwriter, and folk hero in a way that will move and fascinate those too young to remember the man but are surrounded by his music and myth." SLJ

Leonardo, da Vinci, 1452-1519
Anderson, Maxine. **Amazing** Leonardo da Vinci inventions you can build yourself. Nomad Press 2006 122p il map (Learn some hands-on history) pa $14.95

Grades: 5 6 7 8   **92**
  1. Artists 2. Painters 3. Handicraft 4. Inventions 5. Scientists 6. Renaissance 7. Artists, Italian 8. Writers on science
  ISBN 0-9749344-2-9

"Anderson has combined biography with doable activities that mirror ideas found in Leonardo's notebooks. Using common household objects (duct tape, foil, cereal boxes, paper-towel tubes, etc.), readers can make a parachute, hydrometer, invisible ink, walk-on-water shoes, etc. Anderson introduces each project with an explanation of why Leonardo came up with the idea and whether he created just the sketch or the sketch and the object. Detailed steps and illustrations provide clarity." SLJ

★ Krull, Kathleen. **Leonardo** da Vinci; illustrated by Boris Kulikov. Viking 2005 128p il (Giants of science) $15.99

Grades: 5 6 7 8   **92**
  1. Artists 2. Painters 3. Scientists 4. Renaissance 5. Artists, Italian 6. Writers on science
  ISBN 0-670-05920-X

This is a "biography of Leonardo da Vinci that highlights his scientific approach to understanding the physical world. The first half of the book describes Leonardo's apprenticeship and his work as an artist in Milan. The second half relates events in his later life, emphasizing his observation and investigation of the human body and nature. . . . Six excellent ink drawings illustrate this attractive volume. A very readable, vivid portrait set against the backdrop of remarkable times." Booklist

Includes bibliographical references

Phillips, John. **Leonardo** da Vinci; the genius who defined the Renaissance. National Geographic 2006 64p bibl il (World history biographies) $17.95; lib bdg $27.90; pa $6.95

Grades: 5 6 7 8   **92**
  1. Artists 2. Painters 3. Scientists 4. Renaissance 5. Artists, Italian 6. Writers on science
  ISBN 978-0-7922-5385-3; 0-7922-5385-X; 978-0-7922-5386-0 lib bdg; 0-7922-5386-8 lib bdg; 978-1-4263-0248-0 pa; 1-4263-0249-7 pa

Examines the life of Renaissance genius Leonardo da Vinci, discussing his inquiries and accomplishments in art and various fields of science

Includes bibliographical references

Lewis, Ida, 1842-1911
Moss, Marissa. The **bravest** woman in America; illustrations by Andrea U'Ren. Tricycle Press 2011 un il $16.99

Grades: K 1 2 3   **92**
  1. Lighthouses 2. Lighthouse keepers
  ISBN 1-58246-369-7; 978-1-58246-369-8

LC 2010008917

This picture book tells the story of Ida Lewis. "In 1857, when she was fifteen, the family moved to the lighthouse at Lime Rock (which guards Rhode Island's Newport Harbor), where Mr. Lewis was lighthouse keeper. Soon after, illness disabled him; Ida took over his duties and, at sixteen, . . . rescued four boys whose boat had capsized. . . . It was the first of many rescues during a lifelong career for which she received a Congressional Lifesaving Medal. . . . Preschool, primary." (Horn Book)

"Moss's . . . short, stirring biography of 19th-century lighthouse keeper Ida Lewis centers on Lewis's first rescue, at age 16, off the coast of Rhode Island. . . . U'Ren's . . . bold, mixed-media illustrations capture the power and many moods of the sea, from calm ultramarine to the foam-topped dark slate and deep green of stormy waters. Heavy brushstrokes and black outlines . . . suggest the deliberate strength with which Ida carried out her vocation." Publ Wkly

Lewis, John, 1940-
★ Haskins, James. **John** Lewis in the lead; a story of the civil rights movement. [by] Jim Haskins and Kathleen Benson; illustrations by Benny Andrews. Lee & Low 2006 un il $17.95

Grades: 3 4 5   **92**
  1. Members of Congress 2. Civil rights activists 3. African Americans -- Civil rights
  ISBN 1-58430-250-X

LC 2005-35472

"Born in a sharecropper family in the segregated South in 1940, John Lewis grew up to lead many protests for civil rights, and he has served in Congress for the last 20 years. In this handsome picture book for older readers, the authors blend information on Lewis' political contributions with the history of the civil rights struggle. . . . Andrews' dramatic, folk-art-style, color-saturated illustrations combine handsome individual portraits of Lewis with overviews of the horrific street violence by mobs, police, and troopers." Booklist

Lewis, Maud, 1903-1970

Bogart, Jo Ellen. **Capturing** joy: the story of Maud Lewis; illustrated by Mark Lang. Tundra Books 2011 un il pa $8.95

Grades: 3 4 5 6   **92**

1. Artists 2. Painters 3. Handicapped 4. Women artists 5. Artists, Canadian 6. Folk artists

ISBN 978-1-77049-262-2; 1-77049-262-3

First published 2002

"More than an account of a fascinating life, Bogart's introduction to this Canadian painter is a lesson in self-determination. It is the story of a young woman who, despite multiple birth defects and the crippling effects of rheumatoid arthritis, painstakingly created Christmas cards and paintings showing scenes and people lovingly recollected from her own experience. Living in a tiny house with no electricity or indoor plumbing, Lewis painted on scraps of wood and cardboard, using remnants of paint from fishing boats that her husband found on his fish-peddling route. Her style is primitive folk art, often brightly hued. . . . Each spread has a full-page reproduction of a Lewis painting, and each text page includes a realistic, black-and-white pencil drawing by Lang. . . . A lovely and inspiring book." SLJ

Li Cunxin

Li Cunxin. **Dancing** to freedom; the true story of Mao's last dancer. illustrated by Anne Spudvilas. Walker & Co. 2008 un il $16.95; lib bdg $17.85

Grades: K 1 2 3   **92**

1. Ballet 2. Ballet dancers 3. Securities brokers

ISBN 978-0-8027-9777-3; 0-8027-9777-6; 978-0-8027-9778-0 lib bdg; 0-8027-9778-4 lib bdg

LC 2007-37150

"A poignant memoir of a boy caught in the difficulties of life in Maoist China, this is the author's own story of how he was given a chance to break the bonds of his bleak life and become an international star. . . . [Li] was offered the chance to dance with the Houston Ballet, and his greatest dream was realized when his parents were finally able to come to the U.S. to see him perform. This fascinating, heartfelt story is perfectly matched by Spudvilas's masterful paintings." SLJ

Lichtenstein, Roy, 1923-1997

★ Rubin, Susan Goldman. **Whaam!**: the art & life of Roy Lichtenstein. Abrams 2008 47p il $18.95

Grades: 4 5 6 7   **92**

1. Artists 2. Pop art 3. Painters 4. Sculptors 5. Printmakers 6. Artists -- United States

ISBN 978-0-8109-9492-8; 0-8109-9492-5

LC 2007-42048

"Rubin presents an overview of a modern master with clear writing and an abundance of his eye-popping works, all framed on pages that mirror the artist's signature use of primary colors and Benday dots." Booklist

Lincoln family

★ Rabin, Staton. **Mr.** Lincoln's boys; being the mostly true adventures of Abraham Lincoln's trouble-making sons, Tad and Willie. by Staton Rabin; illustrated by Bagram Ibatoulline. Penguin Group 2008 un il $16.99

Grades: 1 2 3   **92**

1. Lawyers 2. Presidents 3. Pioneers 4. State legislators 5. Members of Congress 6. Children of presidents 7. Presidents -- United States

ISBN 978-0-670-06169-3; 0-670-06169-7

LC 2008-1774

"Tad and Willie, the mischievous sons of President Abraham Lincoln, scampered around the White House surprising and irritating almost everyone. Their pranks, however, delighted their father, who was faced with the grim realities of the Civil War. . . . Fictionalized dialogue throughout is believable. A large part of the appeal of this book can be credited to Ibatoulline's masterful illustrations. Evocative and detailed, they fill the pages with visual information and emotion. Readers will be intrigued by the antics of these famous children." SLJ

Includes bibliographical references

Lincoln, Abraham, 1809-1865

Aylesworth, Jim. **Our** Abe Lincoln; an old tune with new lyrics. adapted by Jim Aylesworth; illustrated by Barbara McClintock. Scholastic Press 2009 un il $16.99

Grades: PreK K 1 2   **92**

1. Songs 2. Lawyers 3. Presidents 4. Children's songs 5. State legislators 6. Members of Congress 7. Presidents -- United States

ISBN 978-0-439-92548-8; 0-439-92548-7

LC 2007-31060

"With a fresh approach to Lincoln that is both delightful and accurate, Aylesworth sets history to the tune of 'The Old Gray Mare' and the derivative song 'Our Abe Lincoln Came Out of the Wilderness,' which was popular during the 16th president's campaign. . . . McClintock captures the exuberance with charming visuals that outline significant aspects of the leader's life and lore. Scenes rendered in watercolor and pen and ink feature a multicultural cast." SLJ

★ Brewer, Paul. **Lincoln** tells a joke; how laughter saved the President (and the country) [by] Kathleen Krull & Paul Brewer; illustrated by Stacy Innerst. Harcourt 2010 un il $16

Grades: 2 3 4   **92**

1. Lawyers 2. Presidents 3. Wit and humor 4. State legislators 5. Members of Congress

ISBN 0-15-206639-X; 978-0-15-206639-0

LC 2009-24197

This biography of the American president focuses on his use of wit and humor, and his love of language. "Ages seven to ten." (Bull Cent Child Books)

"Moving through the sixteenth president's many challenges, from family deaths to lost elections to fighting slavery, the text emphasizes how Lincoln coped with a joke on his tongue and a smile on his lips. . . . Innerst's acrylic artwork feels homey and humorous." Booklist

Burleigh, Robert. **Abraham** Lincoln comes home; [by] Robert Burleigh; paintings by Wendell Minor. Henry Holt and Co. 2008 un il $16.95

Grades: 2 3 4   **92**

1. Lawyers 2. Presidents 3. State legislators 4. Members of Congress 5. Presidents -- United States

ISBN 978-0-8050-7529-8; 0-8050-7529-1

LC 2007040030

"Following Lincoln's death, his body was taken back to Illinois for burial. Burleigh focuses on one boy's perceptions as he and his father travel through the night by horse-drawn carriage to see the funeral train pass. . . . Minor's gouache watercolors capture the prairie as well as multiple perspectives of the train, while Burleigh's prose is almost poetic." SLJ

Denenberg, Barry. **Lincoln** shot! a president's life remembered. chief writer, Barry Denenberg; artist, Christopher Bing. Feiwel and Friends 2008 40p il $24.95
Grades: 5 6 7 8   92
1. Lawyers 2. Presidents 3. State legislators 4. Members of Congress 5. Presidents -- United States
ISBN 978-0-312-37013-8; 0-312-37013-X
LC 2007-48851
"The concept is that this is a commemorative edition of 'The National News' published one year after Lincoln's death . . . Also included is an engaging, readable yet detailed account of Lincoln's life. . . . [This book] is an example of how high-quality bookmaking can turn a history lesson into an authentic experience." Booklist

★ Freedman, Russell. **Abraham** Lincoln and Frederick Douglass; the story behind an American friendship. by Russell Freedman. Houghton Mifflin Harcourt 2012 119 p.
Grades: 4 5 6 7 8   92
1. Friendship 2. Abolitionists -- United States 3. United States -- History -- 1861-1865, Civil War -- Biography 4. Friendship -- United States -- Juvenile literature 5. Presidents -- United States -- Biography -- Juvenile literature 6. African American abolitionists -- Biography -- Juvenile literature
ISBN 9780547385624
LC 2011025953
This book tells the story of Abraham Lincoln, "the 16th president, . . . [along] with his friend and ally, abolitionist Frederick Douglass. The story opens with Douglass anxiously waiting to meet Lincoln for the first time to air grievances about the treatment of African-American soldiers during the Civil War. . . . Subsequent chapters detail the leaders' often parallel biographies. Both were self-made and shared a passion for reading, rising from poverty to prominence." (Publishers Weekly)
Includes bibliographical references (p. [108]-109) and index

★ Freedman, Russell. **Lincoln**: a photobiography. Clarion Bks. 1987 149p il $18; pa $7.95
Grades: 5 6 7 8 9 10   92
1. Lawyers 2. Presidents 3. State legislators 4. Members of Congress 5. Presidents -- United States
ISBN 0-89919-380-3; 0-395-51848-2 pa
LC 86-33379
Awarded the Newbery Medal, 1988
This is "a balanced work, elegantly designed and enhanced by dozens of period photographs and drawings, some familiar, some refreshingly unfamiliar." Publ Wkly
Includes bibliographical references

Giblin, James. **Good** brother, bad brother; the story of Edwin Booth and John Wilkes Booth. Clarion Books 2005 244p il $22
Grades: 5 6 7 8   92
1. Actors 2. Lawyers 3. Brothers 4. Presidents 5.

Murderers 6. State legislators 7. Members of Congress
ISBN 0-618-09642-6
LC 2004-21260
This is a dual biography of John Wilkes Booth, who assassinated Abraham Lincoln, and his brother, Edwin, an actor. Bibliography. Index. "Middle school, high school." (Horn Book)
Giblin "frames the intertwined tale of two brothers with accounts of their families, friends, the Civil War, and nineteenth-century theater. . . . Alcoholism and depression afflicted the family, but Giblin is brilliant at showing that darkness was only one part of a life. . . . Giblin's book will engross readers until the very last footnote." Booklist
Includes bibliographical references

Gilpin, Caroline Crosson. **Abraham** Lincoln. National Geographic 2013 31 p. (paperback) $3.99; (library) $13.90
Grades: 1 2 3   92
1. Slaves -- Emancipation -- Juvenile literature 2. Presidents -- United States -- Biography -- Juvenile literature
ISBN 1426310854; 9781426310850; 9781426310867
LC 2012031885
In this book, "readers will learn about the . . . life and legacy of our 16th President of the United States, Abraham Lincoln and his historic decision to abolish slavery. Readers will also learn why this decision impacted the United States, as well as the extent of Lincoln's impact as a fearless leader of the Civil War." (Publisher's note)

Harness, Cheryl. **Abe** Lincoln goes to Washington, 1837-1865; written and illustrated by Cheryl Harness. National Geographic Soc. 1997 un il maps $18
Grades: 2 3 4   92
1. Lawyers 2. Presidents 3. State legislators 4. Members of Congress 5. Presidents -- United States
ISBN 0-7922-3736-6
LC 96-9587
Portrays Lincoln's life as a lawyer in Springfield, a devoted husband and father, and president during the Civil War years
"The text gallops through years of history, with sudden stops for surprisingly vivid little scenes. . . . Filled with color and action, Harness' paintings and maps dominate the pages and provide a wealth of historical detail as well as a humanizing view of the Lincolns." Booklist
Includes bibliographical references

Herbert, Janis. **Abraham** Lincoln for kids; his life and times with 21 activities. [by] Janis Herbert. Chicago Review Press 2007 149p il pa $14.95
Grades: 4 5 6 7   92
1. Lawyers 2. Presidents 3. State legislators 4. Members of Congress 5. Presidents -- United States
ISBN 978-1-55652-656-5 pa; 1-55652-656-3 pa
LC 2007009052
"This attractive biographical guide offers a good mixture of information, anecdotes, and activities, balancing facts about Lincoln's personal and family life with the record of

his accomplishments as president and a broader view of his times." Booklist

Includes glossary and bibliographical references

Kalman, Maira. **Looking** at Lincoln. Nancy Paulsen Books 2012 1 v.

Grades: K 1 2 3 4 5   **92**

1. Picture books for children 2. Presidents -- United States -- Biography 3. Presidents -- United States -- Biography -- Juvenile literature

ISBN 9780399240393

LC 2011046953

'This children's book offers an account of former U.S. President "Abraham Lincoln [who] is one of the first giants of history children are introduced to.... Lincoln's legacy is everywhere - there he is on your penny and five-dollar bill. And we are still the United States because Lincoln helped hold them together. But who was he, really? The little girl in this book wants to find out. Among the many other things, she discovers our sixteenth president was a man who believed in freedom for all, had a dog named Fido, loved Mozart, apples, and his wife's vanilla cake, and kept his notes in his hat. From his boyhood in a log cabin to his famous presidency and untimely death, Kalman shares Lincoln's ... life with young readers." (Publisher's note)

Includes bibliographical references

★ Rabin, Staton. **Mr.** Lincoln's boys; being the mostly true adventures of Abraham Lincoln's trouble-making sons, Tad and Willie. by Staton Rabin; illustrated by Bagram Ibatoulline. Penguin Group 2008 un il $16.99

Grades: 1 2 3   **92**

1. Lawyers 2. Presidents 3. Pioneers 4. State legislators 5. Members of Congress 6. Children of presidents

ISBN 978-0-670-06169-3; 0-670-06169-7

LC 2008-1774

"Tad and Willie, the mischievous sons of President Abraham Lincoln, scampered around the White House surprising and irritating almost everyone. Their pranks, however, delighted their father, who was faced with the grim realities of the Civil War.... Fictionalized dialogue throughout is believable. A large part of the appeal of this book can be credited to Ibatoulline's masterful illustrations. Evocative and detailed, they fill the pages with visual information and emotion. Readers will be intrigued by the antics of these famous children." SLJ

Includes bibliographical references

★ Rappaport, Doreen. **Abe's** honest words; the life of Abraham Lincoln. [illustrated by] Kadir Nelson. Hyperion Books for Children 2008 44p il $16.99

Grades: 2 3 4   **92**

1. Lawyers 2. Presidents 3. State legislators 4. Members of Congress 5. Presidents -- United States

ISBN 1-4231-0408-0; 978-1-4231-0408-7

LC 2006-43608

"This collaboration between Rappaport and Nelson provides a sweeping arc of Lincoln's life.... Rappaport writes in the very free verse and on each page echoes her narrative with prescient samplings of Lincoln's words. In generously sized artwork ... Nelson makes the familiar face ... exciting again.... The exceptional art, along with Rappaport's and

Lincoln's words, makes this a fine celebration of a man who needs little introduction." Booklist

Includes bibliographical references

Sheinkin, Steve. **Lincoln's** Grave Robbers. Scholastic 2013 224 p. $16.99

Grades: 5 6 7 8   **92**

1. Grave robbing 2. Counterfeits and counterfeiting

ISBN 0545405726; 9780545405720

This book is an "account of the attempted heist of Abraham Lincoln's body in 1876." Steve Sheinkin first "delv[es] into the history of counterfeiting.... James Kennally, leader of one of the largest counterfeiting rings in the Midwest, masterminded the plot to steal the late president's body from the Lincoln Monument," intending "to ransom the purloined corpse" and extort "the government for a tidy sum of money and the freedom of his jailed, top-notch engraver." (Publishers Weekly)

St. George, Judith. **Stand** tall, Abe Lincoln; [by] Judith St. George; illustrated by Matt Faulkner. Philomel Books 2007 un il $16.99

Grades: 2 3 4   **92**

1. Lawyers 2. Presidents 3. State legislators 4. Members of Congress

ISBN 978-0-399-24174-1

LC 2006024877

"This account of Lincoln's childhood is written in fast-paced short sentences. St. George ... uses a folksy, conversational style.... Faulkner's humorous illustrations are a perfect match for the text.... The expressive images are done in a caricature style, with slightly exaggerated hands, feet, and heads." SLJ

Includes bibliographical references

Thomson, Sarah L. **What** Lincoln said; by Sarah L. Thomson; art by James Ransome. Collins 2009 un il $17.99; lib bdg $18.89

Grades: K 1 2 3   **92**

1. Lawyers 2. Presidents 3. State legislators 4. Members of Congress

ISBN 978-0-06-084819-4; 0-06-084819-7; 978-0-06-084820-0 lib bdg; 0-06-084820-0 lib bdg

LC 2008020095

"By using Lincoln's own words, Thomson builds a portrait that relates his statements to significant events in his life.... Short descriptions of the circumstances and a related quote are set on bold, colorful spreads. Ransome delivers a larger-than-life portrait of this homely president with acrylic, almost cartoonlike paintings.... An engaging overview, this is a worthy introduction to this famous president." SLJ

Lincoln, Mary Todd, 1818-1882

★ Jones, Lynda. **Mrs.** Lincoln's dressmaker: the unlikely friendship of Elizabeth Keckley and Mary Todd Lincoln; by Lynda D. Jones. National Geographic 2009 80p il $18.95; lib bdg $27.90

Grades: 5 6 7 8   **92**

1. Memoirists 2. Dressmakers 3. Spouses of presidents 4. Slavery -- United States 5. African American women

-- Biography
ISBN 978-1-4263-0377-7; 1-4263-0377-7; 978-1-
4263-0378-4 lib bdg; 1-4263-0378-5 lib bdg

LC 2008-29314

"Readers may be familiar with the ups and downs of Lin-coln's life, but details of Keckley's story . . . will give them new insights into the life of a slave, in this case, one who was educated and had a profession." Booklist

Includes bibliographical references

Linné, Carl von, 1707-1778

Anderson, Margaret Jean. **Carl** Linnaeus; father of classification. [by] Margaret J. Anderson. rev ed; Enslow Publishers 2009 128p il (Great minds of science) lib bdg $31.93

Grades: 5 6 7 8 9   92
1. Botanists 2. Naturalists 3. Writers on science
ISBN 978-0-7660-3009-1 lib bdg; 0-7660-3009-1
lib bdg

LC 2008-23941

First published 1997

"Budding scientists will surely draw inspiration from this biography of Linnaeus. . . . Anderson creates a dra-matic narrative fully capable of keeping readers enthralled." Kirkus

Includes glossary and bibliographical references

Lockwood, Belva Ann, 1830-1917

Bardhan-Quallen, Sudipta. **Ballots** for Belva; the true story of a woman's race for the presidency. by Sudipta Bard-han-Quallen; illustrated by Courtney A. Martin. Abrams Books for Young Readers 2008 un il $16.95

Grades: 2 3 4 5   92
1. Lawyers 2. Feminism 3. Suffragists 4. Women lawyers 5. Women politicians 6. Lecturers 7. Presidential candidates
ISBN 978-0-8109-7110-3; 0-8109-7110-0

LC 2007049842

"This picture-book biography introduces [Belva Ann Lockwood], the woman who ran for president more than a century ago. . . . She obtained a law degree, fought for equal rights, and ultimately became the first woman to re-ceive certified votes during her 1884 presidential campaign. . . . Quotes from Lockwood and others enliven the text. . . . Handsome illustrations clearly set the time and place, and Lockwood's fortitude comes through in her posture and fa-cial expressions." SLJ

Lomax, John Avery, 1867-1948

Hopkinson, Deborah. **Home** on the range; John A. Lo-max and his cowboy songs. illustrated by S. D. Schindler. G. P. Putnam's Sons 2009 un il $16.99

Grades: 2 3 4   92
1. Ethnomusicologists 2. Folklorists 3. Musicologists 4. Folk songs -- United States 5. Songs -- Juvenile literature
ISBN 978-0-399-23996-0; 0-399-23996-0

LC 2008-16802

This traces the early career of John A Lomax, the collec-tor and recorder of American folk songs.

This a "colorful narrative. . . . Glimpses of his thoughts and emotions . . . as well as dialogue help personalize the story. . . . Schindler's . . . realistic illustrations, painted with a light touch in muted hues, ably capture the expressions of

skeptical cowboys . . . . or the eagerness with which Lomax goes about his work." Publ Wkly

Longworth, Alice Roosevelt, 1884-1980

★ Kerley, Barbara. **What** to do about Alice? how Al-ice Roosevelt broke the rules, charmed the world, and drove her father Teddy crazy! illustrated by Edwin Fotheringham. Scholastic Press 2008 un il $16.99

Grades: K 1 2 3   92
1. Presidents -- United States -- Family
ISBN 978-0-439-92231-9; 0-439-92231-3

LC 2006-38372

Boston Globe-Horn Book Award honor book: Nonfic-tion (2008)

"The daughter of Theodore Roosevelt, ... Alice had a joie de vivre that she called 'eating up the world.' . . . Ker-ley's text has the same rambunctious spirit as its subject. . . . The large format gives Fotheringhame . . . plenty of room for spectacular art, which includes use of digital media." Booklist

Lorenz, Konrad

Greenstein, Elaine. The **goose** man; the story of Kon-rad Lorenz. Clarion Books 2009 32p il $16

Grades: K 1 2 3   92
1. Geese 2. Scientists 3. Ethologists 4. Writers on nature 5. Writers on science 6. Animal behavior -- Juvenile literature 7. Nobel laureates for physiology or medicine
ISBN 978-0-547-08459-6; 0-547-08459-5

LC 2008-44618

"From childhood, Konrad Lorenz was fascinated by ducks and geese, growing up to become a prizewinning sci-entist who offered new insights into animal behavior. This picture-book biography . . . summarizes his life's work with geese. . . . The pastel illustrations, in gouache, ink and col-ored pencil, use a technique that includes scratchboard ef-fects and is childlike in style. . . . These pictures tell the story as clearly as the simple text, whose language and frequent repetition make this scientific biography easily accessible to beginning readers." Kirkus

Includes bibliographical references

Louis, Joe, 1914-1981

Adler, David A. **Joe** Louis; America's fighter. written by David A. Adler; illustrated by Terry Widener. Harcourt 2005 un il $16

Grades: 2 3 4   92
1. Soldiers 2. African American athletes 3. Boxers (Persons) 4. Boxing -- Biography
ISBN 0-15-216480-4

LC 2003-12817

The life story of Joe Louis, heavyweight champion box-er, with the complete history of his career in the ring.

"This creative team's collaboration packs a powerful punch. . . . The action-packed acrylics capture the setting and emotions—Widener's signature muscular figures are particularly apt here." SLJ

Includes bibliographical references

★ De la Pena, Matt. A **nation's** hope; the story of boxing legend Joe Louis. illustrated by Kadir Nelson. Dial Books for Young Readers 2011 un il $17.99

Grades: 1 2 3   **92**
  1. Soldiers 2. African American athletes 3. Boxers
(Persons) 4. Boxing -- Biography 5. Boxing -- Juvenile
literature
ISBN 978-0-8037-3167-7; 0-8037-3167-1
                                                   LC 2010-13477
"Nelson's . . . photographically realistic, luminescent oil
paintings bring to life this lyrical tribute to boxing legend
Joe Louis. Focusing on Louis's 1938 rematch against German Max Schmeling . . . de la Peña . . . in his first picture
book, shows how the event unified a racially divided country
for one evening. . . . Spare, evocative verse melds with the
eloquent illustrations to create palpable energy around the
fight and Louis's struggle to the top. . . . A dramatic introduction to a pugilist who symbolized many things for an entire
country." Publ Wkly

Lyons, Maritcha Rémond, 1848-1929
  ★ Bolden, Tonya. **Maritcha**; a nineteenth-century
American girl. Abrams 2005 47p il $17.95
Grades: 4 5 6 7 8 9 10   **92**
  1. Teachers 2. African American women 3. Civic
leaders 4. African American women -- Biography 5.
African Americans -- New York (N.Y.)
ISBN 0-8109-5045-6
                                                   LC 2004-05849
"The high quality of writing and the excellent documen-
tation make this a first choice for all collections." SLJ

Maathai, Wangari, 1940-2001
  ★ Johnson, Jen Cullerton. **Seeds** of change; planting a
path to peace. illustrated by Sonia Lynn Sadler. Lee & Low
2010 un il $18.95
Grades: 2 3 4   **92**
  1. Biologists 2. Conservationists 3. Environmentalists
4. Nobel laureates for peace
ISBN 978-1-60060-367-9; 1-60060-367-X
Coretta Scott King/John Steptoe New Talent Award (Illustrator), 2011
  This picture biography "draws on Wangari Maathai's
autobiographical writing to present an overview of the activist's life from childhood to the present. . . . Richer than other
treatments of Maathai for children and more grounded in her
work's implicit feminism, this details her education in Nai-
robi and the United States, her imprisonment for activism
and her scientific and environmental work, resulting in the
planting of 30,000,000 trees and economic empowerment
for Kenyan women. Sadler's beautiful scratchboard illustrations incise white contoured line into saturated landscapes of
lush green leaf patterns, brilliant-hued textiles and undulating, stylized hills. . . . Vibrant and accomplished." Kirkus

  ★ Napoli, Donna Jo. **Mama** Miti: Wangari Maathai
and the trees of Kenya; illustrated by Kadir Nelson. Simon
& Schuster Books for Young Readers 2010 un il $16.99
Grades: K 1 2 3   **92**
  1. Biologists 2. Conservationists 3. Environmentalists
4. Nobel laureates for peace 5. Forest ecology --
Juvenile literature
ISBN 978-1-4169-3505-6; 1-4169-3505-3
                                                   LC 2008-23604
"Napoli adopts a folkloric narrative technique to showcase the life work of Wangari Maathai, whose seminal role
in Kenya's reforestation earned her the Nobel Peace Prize in

2004. When, one after the other, women journey to Maathai
to seek counsel about scarce food, disappearing firewood
and ailing animals, she tells them, 'Plant a tree.'. . . Nelson's
pictures, a jaw-dropping union of African textiles collaged
with oil paintings, brilliantly capture the villagers' clothing and the greening landscape. The richly modulated oils
portray the dignified, intent gazes of Maathai and other Ke-
nyans. . . . This is, in a word, stunning." Kirkus
  Includes bibliographical references

  Nivola, Claire A. **Planting** the trees of Kenya; the story
of Wangari Maathai. Farrar, Straus & Giroux 2008 un il
$16.95
Grades: 2 3 4   **92**
  1. Biologists 2. Conservationists 3. Environmentalists
4. Nobel laureates for peace
ISBN 978-0-374-39918-4; 0-374-39918-2
                                                   LC 2006038249
"Kenyan activist Wangari Maathai was awarded the Nobel Peace Prize in 2004 for her environmental and human
rights achievements. Founder of the Green Belt Movement,
she has encouraged people to repair their economy, land, and
health with simple, environmentally friendly acts, such as
planting more trees. This beautiful picture-book biography
echoes the potent simplicity of Maathai's message with direct, spare prose and bright, delicate watercolors." Booklist

  Winter, Jeanette. **Wangari's** trees of peace; a true story
from Africa. Harcourt 2008 un il $17
Grades: K 1 2 3   **92**
  1. Biologists 2. Conservationists 3. Environmentalists
4. Nobel laureates for peace
ISBN 978-0-15-206545-4; 0-15-206545-8
                                                   LC 2007-34810
"Wangari Maathai, the 2004 Nobel Peace Prize winner
whose Green Belt Movement has planted 30 million trees
in Kenya, is the subject of Winter's . . . eloquent picture biography. . . . The tightly focused text moves quickly without
sacrificing impact. . . . Winter's images appear in framed,
same-size squares on each page, creating a flat, frieze-like
effect." Publ Wkly

Madison, Dolley, 1768-1849
  Adler, David A. A **picture** book of Dolley and James
Madison; by David A. Adler and Michael S. Adler; illustrat-
ed by Ronald Himler. Holiday House 2009 un il $17.95
Grades: 1 2 3   **92**
  1. Presidents 2. Members of Congress 3. Secretaries
of state 4. Spouses of presidents 5. Presidents -- United
States
ISBN 978-0-8234-2009-4; 0-8234-2009-4
                                                   LC 2007041178
"Adler's picture-book biography focuses mainly on the
War of 1812, but also mentions Madison's contributions
to the Constitution and the creation of the three branches
of government. Although this is a biography of the couple,
there is more specific information on James Madison than
on Dolley. Still, readers do learn some interesting facts about
her. . . . Adler's writing is clear yet not oversimplified, and is
without fictionalization." SLJ
  Includes bibliographical references

★ Brown, Don. **Dolley** Madison saves George Washington; written and illustrated by Don Brown. Houghton Mifflin Co. 2007 un il $16

Grades: 1 2 3   92

   1. Artists 2. Generals 3. Painters 4. Presidents 5. War of 1812 6. Spouses of presidents

   ISBN 978-0-618-41199-3; 0-618-41199-2

                LC 2006-09813

   "While First Lady, [Dolley Madison] redecorated the President's Mansion, ensuring that Gilbert Stuart's portrait of George Washington was prominently displayed. However, it was during the War of 1812 that she earned the gratitude of her nation when, despite the fact that the 100 soldiers assigned to protect the mansion ran off, she bravely remained behind to make sure that the painting as well as important government documents were saved from otherwise certain destruction by British forces. Pen and ink and watercolors effectively depict the simplicity and roughness of Colonial life and convey with humor the spirit of the time and characters." SLJ

Madison, James, 1751-1836

Adler, David A. A **picture** book of Dolley and James Madison; by David A. Adler and Michael S. Adler; illustrated by Ronald Himler. Holiday House 2009 un il $17.95

Grades: 1 2 3   92

   1. Presidents 2. Members of Congress 3. Secretaries of state 4. Spouses of presidents

   ISBN 978-0-8234-2009-4; 0-8234-2009-4

                LC 2007041178

   "Adler's picture-book biography focuses mainly on the War of 1812, but also mentions Madison's contributions to the Constitution and the creation of the three branches of government. Although this is a biography of the couple, there is more specific information on James Madison than on Dolley. Still, readers do learn some interesting facts about her. . . . Adler's writing is clear yet not oversimplified, and is without fictionalization." SLJ

   Includes bibliographical references

Elish, Dan. **James** Madison; [by] Dan Elish. Marshall Cavendish Benchmark 2007 96p il (Presidents and their times) lib bdg $22.95

Grades: 5 6 7 8   92

   1. Presidents 2. Members of Congress 3. Secretaries of state

   ISBN 978-0-7614-2432-1

                LC 2006036856

A biography of the fourth president of the United States.

   "Primary-source materials and quotes, helpful insets, and carefully selected . . . reproductions bring history to life and help make [this] clearly written [biography] highly readable." SLJ

   Includes glossary and bibliographical references

Maiman, Theodore Harold, 1927-2007

Wyckoff, Edwin Brit. **Laser** man; Theodore H. Maiman and his brilliant invention. [by] Edwin Brit Wyckoff. Enslow Elementary 2008 32p il (Genius at work!: great inventor biographies) lib bdg $20.60

Grades: 4 5 6   92

   1. Lasers 2. Engineers 3. Physicists

   ISBN 978-0-7660-2848-7 lib bdg; 0-7660-2848-8 lib bdg

                LC 2006034680

A biography of Theodore H. Maiman, the engineer who invented the laser

   Includes glossary and bibliographical references

Malcolm X, 1925-1965

Gunderson, Jessica. **X**: the biography of Malcolm X; illustrated by Seitu Hayden. Graphic Library 2011 32p il (Graphic library: American graphic) lib bdg $29.32; pa $7.95

Grades: 4 5 6 7   92

   1. Black Muslims 2. Biographical graphic novels 3. Black Muslim leaders 4. Civil rights activists 5. African Americans -- Biography

   ISBN 978-1-4296-5471-5 lib bdg; 1-4296-5471-6 lib bdg; 978-1-4296-6267-3 pa; 1-4296-6267-0 pa

                LC 2010037029

In graphic novel format, explores the life and death of Malcolm X.

   "The illustrations are eye-catching and the narration is presented simply, yet compellingly. . . . Fact-filled, entertaining, and accessible." SLJ

   Includes glossary and bibliographical references

★ Myers, Walter Dean, 1937- **Malcolm** X; a fire burning brightly. illustrated by Leonard Jenkins. HarperCollins Pubs. 2000 un il $15.95

Grades: 3 4 5 6   92

   1. Black Muslim leaders 2. Civil rights activists 3. African Americans -- Biography 4. Black Muslims -- Biography -- Juvenile literature

   ISBN 0-06-027707-6

                LC 99-21527

   "Myers's spare and eloquent narrative makes the complexities of Malcolm X's story accessible without compromising its integrity. The book has appeal for reluctant teen readers as well as younger readers. The sophisticated paintings blend realism with abstraction to heighten the underlying emotional drama of scenes." Horn Book Guide

Mandela, Nelson

★ Kramer, Ann. **Mandela**; the rebel who led his nation to freedom. National Geographic 2005 63p il (World history biographies) $17.95; lib bdg $27.90

Grades: 4 5 6 7   92

   1. Presidents 2. Political prisoners 3. Political leaders 4. Human rights activists 5. Nobel laureates for peace

   ISBN 0-7922-3658-0; 0-7922-3659-9 lib bdg

   "This biography introduces readers not only to Mandela, but also to the political turmoil that affected South Africa for over a century. It begins with his birth, and covers his school years, his political ventures, imprisonment, release, presidency, Nobel Peace Prize, and retirement. Full-color photographs appear throughout and a time line runs along the bottom of each spread. . . . the book is well worth purchasing." SLJ

   Includes glossary and bibliographical references

★ Mandela, Nelson. **Nelson** Mandela: long walk to freedom; abridged by Chris van Wyk; illustrated by Paddy Bouma. Roaring Book Press 2009 un il $16

Grades: 2 3 4 5　　　　　　　　　　　　　　　**92**

1. Presidents 2. Political prisoners 3. Political leaders 4. Human rights activists 5. Nobel laureates for peace

ISBN 978-1-59643-566-7; 1-59643-566-6

"Abridged from Mandela's 1994 autobiography, this picture book distills the basic facts of his childhood, his education, and the influences that led him to become one of the world's most renowned political activists. In a simple, yet effective manner, he describes the growing system of apartheid, and the unjust treatment of blacks in South Africa is made clear without horrifying details. . . . The writing is clear, providing chronological detail for even young students new to the concept and history of apartheid. Full-page, color paintings accompany the text on every spread and depict crucial moments from the narrative in a way that both complements and enhances the story." SLJ

Mankiller, Wilma

Sonneborn, Liz. **Wilma** Mankiller. Marshall Cavendish Benchmark 2010 112p il (Leading women) $39.93

Grades: 5 6 7 8　　　　　　　　　　　　　　　**92**

1. Cherokee Indians 2. Indian chiefs

ISBN 978-0-7614-4959-1; 0-7614-4959-0

LC 2009029399

"The story of Mankiller's lifelong work for the Cherokee Nation and her role as its first female principal chief will absorb readers. The [woman's life is] revealed within the political and historical context of [her] times and [includes] quotes from autobiographical material. . . . Color and black-and-white photos are included. . . . The compact size, chronological organization, and accessible writing [style makes this biography a] good [resource] for reports." SLJ

Manley, Effa, 1900-1981

★ Vernick, Audrey. **She** loved baseball: the Effa Manley story; written by Audrey Vernick; illustrated by Don Tate. Collins 2010 un il

Grades: 1 2 3　　　　　　　　　　　　　　　**92**

1. African American athletes 2. Baseball executives 3. Baseball -- Biography 4. African American women -- Biography

ISBN 0061349208; 9780061349201

This is a picture book biography of Effa Manley, the African American baseball team owner and first and only woman ever inducted into the Baseball Hall of Fame.

"Tate's energetic illustrations harmonize well with Vernick's fresh and engaging text. History favors the individuals in the spotlight: here's an entertaining portrait of a woman who made significant strides behind the scenes." Publ Wkly

Manning, Peyton, 1976-

Wilner, Barry. **Peyton** Manning; a football star who cares. Enslow Publishers, Inc. 2011 48p il (Sport stars who care) lib bdg $23.93; pa $7.95

Grades: 3 4 5　　　　　　　　　　　　　　　**92**

1. Football players 2. Football -- Biography

ISBN 978-0-7660-3774-8 lib bdg; 0-7660-3774-6 lib bdg; 978-1-59845-232-7 pa; 1059845-232-0 pa

LC 2010014946

"The text traces Manning's athletic prowess from his playing days in elementary and high school, his successful

college career, and, of course, his outstanding professional play, with Manning winning MVP four times. . . . A large typeface, a striking design, and plenty of color photographs will entice readers, even reluctant ones. Stats, a glossary, and suggested resources for learning more complete this attractive package." Booklist

Includes glossary and bibliographical references

Marceau, Marcel, 1923-2007

Spielman, Gloria. **Marcel** Marceau; master of mime. illustrated by Manon Gauthier. Kar-Ben Pub. 2011 un il lib bdg $17.95

Grades: 3 4 5　　　　　　　　　　　　　　　**92**

1. Mime 2. Actors 3. Mimes 4. Jews -- Biography 5. World War, 1939-1945 -- France

ISBN 978-0-7613-3961-8; 0-7613-3961-2

LC 2010027787

"Readers are introduced to the world-famous reviver of the lost art of mime in this attractive and accessible picture-book biography. Melding Marceau's childhood and evolution as an artist with world events, Spielman reveals how the young son of a kosher butcher in Strasbourg, France, pursued his dream, despite the Nazi invasion in 1939. . . . Gauthier's childlike mixed-media illustrations feature myriad rosy-cheeked characters and capture both the whimsy of Marceau's performances and the more somber conditions of war-torn France." SLJ

Marley, Bob

★ Medina, Tony. **I** and I; Bob Marley. illustrated by Jesse Joshua Watson. Lee & Low Books 2009 un il $19.95

Grades: 4 5 6　　　　　　　　　　　　　　　**92**

1. Singers 2. Reggae musicians

ISBN 978-1-60060-257-3; 1-60060-257-6

LC 2008-33485

"In the words and rhythms of Jamaican patois, Medina's lyrical, direct lines make the most sense when read in tandem with the extensive appended notes. . . . Like the words, Watson's beautifully expressive acrylic paintings evoke a strong sense of Marley's remarkable life and his Caribbean homeland." Booklist

Includes bibliographical references

Martini, Helen, 1912-

Lyon, George Ella. **Mother** to tigers; illustrations by Peter Catalanotto. Atheneum Bks. for Young Readers 2003 un il $16.95

Grades: K 1 2 3　　　　　　　　　　　　　　　**92**

1. Zoos 2. Zoo directors 3. Zoo keepers -- United States -- Juvenile literature

ISBN 0-689-84221-X

LC 00-45375

"Lyon's succinct, yet elegant, prose emphasizes Martini's dedication to the animals in her care. . . . Catalanotto's watercolor, charcoal, and torn-paper art is particularly effective here." Booklist

Matisse, Henri

Anholt, Laurence. **Matisse**; the king of color. Barron's 2007 un il $14.99

Grades: 2 3 4 5　　　　　　　　　　　　　　　**92**

1. Artists 2. Painters 3. Artists, French

ISBN 0-7641-6047-8

"Anholt tells the story behind Matisse's final masterpiece—Chapelle du Rosaire. During a serious illness, the artist becomes friends with his nurse, Monique, and he draws and paints several pictures of her. When his health improves, she leaves the man who has been like a grandfather to her and joins a strict religious order. Years later, the two friends are reunited when Matisse moves into a villa close to the nunnery. As a final gift for Monique, now Sister Jacques-Marie, he designs a simple chapel for the nuns. . . . The bright and cheerful illustrations draw heavily on Matisse's drawings, paintings, and collages. Facts about the artist's life and style are also skillfully woven into the story and illustrations." SLJ

★ Fillion, Susan. **Miss** Etta and Dr. Claribel; Bringing Matisse to America. David R. Godine 2011 83p il $18.95
Grades: 4 5 6 7   92
1. Artists 2. Painters 3. Physicians 4. Art collectors 5. Art -- Collectors and collecting
ISBN 978-1-56792-434-3; 1-56792-434-4
LC 2010048937
"An affectionate, lively examination of the reciprocal relationship between a great artist and two great art lovers. Etta and Claribel Cone, unmarried sisters from a wealthy Baltimore family . . . [were] discerning collectors of modern art, particularly that of Henri Matisse. . . . Their account is lavishly illustrated in full color by reproductions from the Cone Collection at the Baltimore Museum of Art and Matisse-inflected paintings by the author, who drew extensively on the Cone archive that is also housed at the museum. . . . This appealing work stands as both a portrait of two unconventional women and a celebration of the possibilties of arts patronage." Kirkus

Welton, Jude. **Henri** Matisse. Watts 2002 46p il (Artists in their time) $22; pa $6.95
Grades: 5 6 7 8   92
1. Artists 2. Painters 3. Artists, French 4. Artists -- France -- Biography -- Juvenile literature
ISBN 0-531-12228-X; 0-531-16621-X pa
LC 2002-69106
Discusses the life and career of this French artist, describing and giving examples of his work
This offers a "clear and lively [text]. . . . Captioned, full-color and black-and-white photographs and art reproductions are liberally scattered throughout." SLJ

Matzeliger, Jan, 1852-1889
Mitchell, Barbara. **Shoes** for everyone: a story about Jan Matzeliger; illustrations by Hetty Mitchell. Carolrhoda Bks. 1986 63p il (Carolrhoda creative minds book) hardcover o.p. pa $8.95
Grades: 3 4 5   92
1. Inventors 2. Shoe industry 3. African American inventors 4. Clothing industry executives
ISBN 0-87614-290-0; 0-87614-473-3 pa
LC 86-4157
A biography of the half-Dutch half-black Surinamese man who, despite the hardships and prejudice he found in his new Massachusetts home, invented a shoe-lasting machine that revolutionized the shoe industry in the late nineteenth century
This is "a compelling story of human endeavor. A clear text blessedly allows the extraordinary individual in focus,

Jan Matzeliger, . . . to emerge without undue exclamatory adulation." Bull Cent Child Books

McCloskey, Robert, 1914-2003
McCloskey, Jane. **Robert** McCloskey; a private life in words and pictures. Seapoint Books 2011 il $24.95
Grades: Adult Professional   92
1. Artists 2. Authors 3. Illustrators 4. Authors, American 5. Children's authors
ISBN 978-0-9786899-6-4; 0-9786899-6-8
In this "biography of the great author/illustrator, his younger daughter reconstructs his life, her recollections nicely complemented by scores of beautifully reproduced illustrations from her father's books as well as photos and never-before-published sketches and paintings. The text is artless in the best sense, not a formal biography but a sequence of significant circumstances and events as Jane observed them." Horn Book

McCoy, Elijah, 1844-1929
Kulling, Monica. **All** aboard!: Elijah McCoy's steam engine; illustrated by Bill Slavin. Tundra Books 2010 un il (Great idea) $17.95
Grades: K 1 2 3   92
1. Inventors 2. Railroads 3. African American inventors
ISBN 978-0-88776-945-0; 0-88776-945-4
A picture book biography of the African American inventor of the oil cup, patented in 1872, which continuously greased the engines of steam locomotives.
This is "an engaging biography. . . . Expressive watercolors . . . capture the time period, allowing readers to imagine what life was like in this era, and add energy and touches of humor." SLJ

Meir, Golda, 1898-1978
Blashfield, Jean F. **Golda** Meir. Marshall Cavendish Benchmark 2010 112p il (Leading women) $39.93
Grades: 5 6 7 8   92
1. Diplomats 2. Prime ministers 3. Women politicians 4. Cabinet members 5. Jews -- Biography
ISBN 978-0-7614-4960-7; 0-7614-4960-4
"Meir survived pogroms in Russia as a child and became prime minister of Israel. . . . The [woman's life is] revealed within the political and historical context of [her] times and [includes] quotes from autobiographical material. . . . Color and black-and-white photos are included. . . . The compact size, chronological organization, and accessible writing [style makes this biography a] good [resource] for reports." SLJ
Includes bibliographical references

Menchú, Rigoberta
Menchu, Rigoberta. The **girl** from Chimel; [by] Rigoberta Menchú with Dante Liano; pictures by Domi; translated by David Unger. House of Anansi Press 2005 54p il $16.95
Grades: 4 5 6 7   92
1. Mayas 2. Memoirists 3. Indian leaders 4. Human rights activists 5. Nobel laureates for peace
ISBN 0-88899-666-7
This is "Menchú's account of her childhood in the small village of Chimel, Guatamala. . . . Short sketches provide glimpses of Menchú's early years; lyrical language and re-

peated phrases such as 'when I was a girl in Chimel' link the text to oral storytelling. . . . Each chapter sports a vivid oil painting by Domi, featuring thick strokes of bright oranges, purples, greens, and reds and a naive approach that lends a folk-art feel, effectively capturing the action and emotion of the stories." Bull Cent Child Books

Mendel, Gregor, 1822-1884
Bardoe, Cheryl. **Gregor** Mendel; the friar who grew peas. illustrated by Jos. A. Smith. Abrams Books for Young Readers 2006 un il $18.95

Grades: 2 3 4   92
1. Genetics 2. Scientists 3. Geneticists 4. Genetics -- History -- Juvenile literature
ISBN 0-8109-5475-3

LC 2005-22957

A picture book biography of the scientist who became known as the father of genetics

"This slim, oversize volume is as much a treat for the eye as it is for the curious mind. Smith's crisp, realistic paintings, often flooded with the bright green of pea plants, accompany Bardoe's readable text." SLJ

Includes bibliographical references

Van Gorp, Lynn. **Gregor** Mendel; genetics pioneer. science contributor, Sally Ride Science. Compass Point Books 2008 40p il (Mission: Science) lib bdg $26.60

Grades: 4 5 6   92
1. Genetics 2. Scientists 3. Geneticists
ISBN 978-0-7565-3963-4 lib bdg; 0-7565-3963-3 lib bdg

LC 2008-07725

A biography of scientist Gregor Mendel, with an introduction to the principles of genetics

This "will entice students to become excited about an assignment or just satisfy their own curiosity. . . . The text . . . does a good job of connecting the scientist's work to our lives today. . . . [The] book has a variety of graphics including diagrams, [and] photos." Libr Media Connect

Merian, Maria Sibylla, 1647-1717
★ Engle, Margarita. **Summer** birds: the butterflies of Maria Merian; pictures by Julie Paschkis. Henry Holt & Co. 2010 un il $16.99

Grades: K 1 2 3   92
1. Artists 2. Painters 3. Zoologists 4. Butterflies 5. Naturalists 6. Caterpillars 7. Illustrators 8. Women artists 9. Women scientists 10. Caterpillars -- Juvenile literature 11. Butterflies -- Metamorphosis -- Juvenile literature
ISBN 978-0-8050-8937-0; 0-8050-8937-3

LC 2009-05267

"Born in Frankfurt in 1647, Maria Sibylla Merian disagreed with the conventional wisdom . . . that 'summer birds,' or butterflies, were 'beasts of the devil' that sprang alive from the mud . . . . Engle writes in the voice of Maria as a young teen, who carefully watches the slow transformation of caterpillars to winged adults, painting everything that she sees. . . . In expertly pared-down language, the poetic lines deftly fold in basic science concepts about life cycles, along with biographical details that are further developed in an appended historical note. Paschkis' brilliantly colored and patterned paintings are an exuberant counterpoint to the minimal words." Booklist

Michelangelo Buonarroti, 1475-1564
★ Stanley, Diane. **Michelangelo**. HarperCollins Pubs. 2000 un il $18.99; pa $6.99

Grades: 4 5 6 7   92
1. Artists 2. Painters 3. Sculptors 4. Architects 5. Renaissance 6. Artists, Italian
ISBN 0-688-15085-3; 0-06-052113-9 pa

A biography of the Renaissance sculptor, painter, architect, and poet, well known for his work on the Sistine Chapel in Rome's St. Peter's Cathedral

This is "as readable as it is useful. . . . Integrating Michelangelo's art with Stanley's watercolor, gouache, and colored-pencil figures and settings has the desired effect: readers will be dazzled with the master's ability, while at the same time pulled into his daily life and struggles." SLJ

Includes bibliographical references

Miller, Norma, 1919-
Miller, Norma. **Stompin'** at the Savoy; the story of Norma Miller. collected and edited by Alan Govenar; illustrated by Martin French. Candlewick Press 2006 54p il $15.99

Grades: 3 4 5 6   92
1. Dancers 2. African American women 3. African American dancers 4. African American women -- Biography
ISBN 0-7636-2244-3

LC 2004-57916

This is an autobiography of the African American jazz dancer of the Harlem Renaissance

This "sizzles with spirit and swings with vitality. . . . Miller tells her story with humor and candor. . . . Stylized black-and-white illustrations, produced digitally and in mixed media, nearly swing right off the pages." SLJ

Mohapatra, Jyotirmayee, 1978-
Woog, Adam. **Jyotirmayee** Mohapatra; by Adam Woog. KidHaven Press 2006 48p il $24.95

Grades: 4 5 6 7   92
1. Social action 2. Feminists 3. Women -- India 4. Children's rights advocates
ISBN 0-7377-3611-9

LC 2006009121

"Mohapatra grew up in a rural village in India and became a leader in the fight for the rights of girls and women. . . . The power of one individual to inspire others to action is clearly expressed in this well-written profile. Full-color photos and a map enhance the presentation." SLJ

Includes bibliographical references

Monet, Claude, 1840-1926
Maltbie, P. I. **Claude** Monet; the painter who stopped the trains. illustrated by Jos. A. Smith. Abrams Books for Young Readers 2010 32p il $18.95

Grades: K 1 2 3   92
1. Artists 2. Painters 3. Artists, French 4. Railroads in art
ISBN 978-0-8109-8961-0; 0-8109-8961-1

LC 2009039459

"Inspired by his son's love of trains, Monet decided to show art critics that impressionism could be more than just seascapes. For three months in 1877, he painted on the platform of the Saint-Lazare train station in Paris. . . . Smith expertly illuminates the changing landscape of an evolving world, as Maltbie's thoughtful story of inspiration and imagination highlights a less remembered portion of Monet's work." Publ Wkly

Includes bibliographical references

Monroe, James, 1758-1831

Naden, Corinne J. **James** Monroe; [by] Corinne J. Naden and Rose Blue. Marshall Cavendish Benchmark 2009 96p il map (Presidents and their times) lib bdg $34.21

Grades: 5 6 7 8   92
    1. Presidents 2. Secretaries of state
    ISBN 978-0-7614-2838-1 lib bdg; 0-7614-2838-0 lib bdg

                              LC 2007-29480
"Provides comprehensive information on President James Monroe and places him within his historical and cultural context. Also explored are the formative events of his times and how he responded." Publisher's note

Includes glossary and bibliographical references

Montezuma, Carlos, 1866?-1923

Capaldi, Gina. A **boy** named Beckoning: the true story of Dr. Carlos Montezuma, Native American hero; adapted and illustrated by Gina Capaldi. Carolrhoda Books 2008 32p il lib bdg $16.95

Grades: 2 3 4   92
    1. Physicians 2. Physicists 3. Indian leaders 4. Native Americans -- Biography
    ISBN 978-0-8225-7644-0

                             LC 2007021745
"Capaldi uses Montezuma's own words to tell this gripping story of a Yavapai boy who was captured by the Pima in 1871 and grew up to become a prominent doctor and Native American spokesperson. Solidly researched, the well-written text follows Wassaja (later renamed Carlos Montezuma) as he was sold into slavery and purchased by a kind Italian photographer. . . . The illustrations are stunning, with multiple perspectives and rich gold and brown tones." SLJ

Includes bibliographical references

Moran, Thomas, 1837-1926

Judge, Lita. **Yellowstone** Moran; painting the American West. Viking 2009 un il $16.99

Grades: K 1 2 3   92
    1. Artists 2. Painters 3. Engravers 4. West (U.S.) in art 5. Artists -- United States
    ISBN 978-0-670-01132-2; 0-670-01132-0

                             LC 2008049879
"In 1871, American artist Thomas Moran journeyed with a team of geologists through the Rocky Mountains to 'the land called the Yellowstone,' observing and sketching the landscape around him. Judge's watercolor illustrations capture the movement and pristine energy of the wilderness along with the team's arduous journey over rocks, ravines and woods." Publ Wkly

Includes bibliographical references

Morgan, Julia

★ Mannis, Celeste Davidson. **Julia** Morgan built a castle; by Celeste Mannis; illustrated by Miles Hyman. Viking 2006 un il $17.99

Grades: 1 2 3 4   92
    1. Architects 2. Women architects
    ISBN 0-670-05964-1

                             LC 2004-17401
A picture book biography of "a groundbreaking female architect. Luminescent illustrations, created using soft pastels and pencils in a golden-peach palette, appear to glow with the light of California and France, both seminal locations in Morgan's life. . . . Filled with rich vocabulary, the narrative employs scrumptious architectural terms such as Baroque, flying buttresses, and teakwood cornice." SLJ

Morris, Esther Hobart, 1814-1902

White, Linda. **I** could do that! Esther Morris gets women the vote. [by] Linda Arms White; pictures by Nancy Carpenter. 1st ed; Farrar, Straus and Giroux 2005 32p il

Grades: 2 3 4   92
    1. Suffragists 2. Women -- Suffrage 3. Justices of the peace
    ISBN 0-374-33527-3

                             LC 2003-51417
In 1869, a woman whose "can-do" attitude had shaped her life was instrumental in making Wyoming the first state to allow women to vote, then became the first woman to hold public office in the United States.

"White's carefully shaped text is amplified by Carpenter's folksy oils, which combine prim, period details and witty exaggerations." Booklist

Includes bibliographical references

Mozart, Maria Anna, 1751-1829

★ Fancher, Lou. **For** the love of music; the remarkable story of Maria Anna Mozart. paintings by Steve Johnson and Lou Fancher. Tricycle Press 2011 un il $16.99; lib bdg $19.99

Grades: 1 2 3   92
    1. Composers 2. Musicians 3. Music -- Juvenile literature
    ISBN 978-1-58246-326-1; 1-58246-326-3; 978-1-58246-391-9 lib bdg; 1-58246-391-3 lib bdg
"In an intimate tribute to musical prodigy Maria Anna Mozart (sister of Wolfgang Amadeus), Rusch organizes biographical passages into sonata movements, with musical terms used to mark events in Maria's life. . . . Rusch's rich prose and Johnson and Fancher's lavishly detailed collages—melding paint, paper, fabrics, and weathered musical notation—seamlessly blend to form a moving portrait of an unsung musician." Publ Wkly

Includes bibliographical references

Mozart, Wolfgang Amadeus, 1756-1791

★ Fancher, Lou. **For** the love of music; the remarkable story of Maria Anna Mozart. paintings by Steve Johnson and Lou Fancher. Tricycle Press 2011 un il $16.99; lib bdg $19.99

Grades: 1 2 3   92
    1. Composers 2. Musicians 3. Music -- Juvenile literature
    ISBN 978-1-58246-326-1; 1-58246-326-3; 978-1-58246-391-9 lib bdg; 1-58246-391-3 lib bdg
"In an intimate tribute to musical prodigy Maria Anna Mozart (sister of Wolfgang Amadeus), Rusch organizes biographical passages into sonata movements, with musical terms used to mark events in Maria's life. . . . Rusch's

rich prose and Johnson and Fancher's lavishly detailed collages—melding paint, paper, fabrics, and weathered musical notation—seamlessly blend to form a moving portrait of an unsung musician." Publ Wkly

Includes bibliographical references

Riggs, Kate. **Wolfgang** Amadeus Mozart. Creative Education 2009 48p il (Xtraordinary artists) lib bdg $32.80
Grades: 4 5 6 7   **92**
  1. Composers
  ISBN 978-1-58341-664-8 lib bdg; 1-58341-664-1 lib bdg
        LC 2007008963
This biography of the composer offers an "interesting [layout]; big, high-quality reproductions and photographs on heavy paper; insightful quotes from diverse sources; and meaty selections of the artist's own writing . . . at the end of the book. Readers get a strong sense of [Mozart's] personality along with an excellent survey of his work." SLJ

Includes bibliographical references

Stanley, Diane. **Mozart,** the wonder child; a puppet play in three acts. Collins 2009 un il $17.99; lib bdg $18.89
Grades: 3 4 5   **92**
  1. Composers 2. Puppets and puppet plays
  ISBN 978-0-06-072674-4; 0-06-072674-1; 978-0-06-072676-8 lib bdg; 0-06-072676-8 lib bdg
        LC 2008-10487
"Stanley takes a look at one of the Western world's most celebrated prodigies, wee Wolfgang Mozart. . . . [Stanley] manages a neat overview of her subject's life in surprisingly few pages. . . . The illustrations treat the proceedings as a marionette show performed by the famous Salzberg Marionettes." Bull Cent Child Books

Includes bibliographical references

Weeks, Marcus. **Mozart**; the boy who changed the world with his music. [by] Marcus Weeks. National Geographic 2007 64p il map (World history biographies) $17.95; lib bdg $27.90
Grades: 5 6 7 8   **92**
  1. Composers
  ISBN 978-1-4263-0002-8; 1-4263-0002-6; 978-1-4263-0003-5 lib bdg; 1-4263-0003-4 lib bdg
        LC 2006020783
An introduction to the life and music of the composer and musician Mozart.
This "visually appealing [title is] packed with excellent photographs and reproductions, interesting sidebars, and have a time line running along the bottom of every page. . . . [The book is] useful, well-written." SLJ

Includes bibliographical references

Muir, John, 1838-1914
Lasky, Kathryn. **John** Muir; America's first environmentalist. illustrated by Stan Fellows. Candlewick Press 2006 41p il $16.99
Grades: 3 4 5   **92**
  1. Authors 2. Naturalists 3. Writers on nature
  ISBN 0-7636-1957-4
A biography of John Muir, naturalist and founder of the Sierra Club, whose travels, speeches and writings led direct-

ly to the creation of the Yosemite National Park in 1890 and other national parks that followed.
"Lasky's clear prose quotes liberally from diary entries Muir recorded. . . . True to Muir's vision, Fellows' spacious double-page watercolors show the beauty of the wide landscapes in storm and sunshine as well as the tiny details in a single meadow." Booklist

Includes bibliographical references

Wadsworth, Ginger. **Camping** with the president; illustrated by Karen Dugan. Calkins Creek 2009 32p il $16.95
Grades: 3 4 5   **92**
  1. Authors 2. Governors 3. Presidents 4. Naturalists 5. Vice-presidents 6. Environmental movement 7. National parks and reserves 8. Writers on nature 9. Nobel laureates for peace
  ISBN 978-1-59078-497-6; 1-59078-497-9
        LC 2008024155
"Inspired by conservationist John Muir's nature essays, President Theodore Roosevelt traveled west, visiting national parks and learing more about their resources. Wadsworth's well written, lively account highlights the pair's 1903 exploration of the Yosemite wilderness, as well as America's early conservation movement, in an accessible and engaging picture book for older readers. Dugan's abundant, intricately rendered watercolors portray the stunning vistas and wildlife and are set against white backgrounds." Booklist

Includes bibliographical references

Naismith, James, 1861-1939
Wyckoff, Edwin Brit. The **man** who invented basketball: James Naismith and his amazing game. Enslow Publishers 2007 32p bibl il por (Genius at work!: great inventor biographies) lib bdg $22.60
Grades: 4 5 6   **92**
  1. Physicians 2. Game inventors 3. College teachers 4. Basketball coaches 5. Basketball -- History 6. Physical education teachers
  ISBN 978-0-7660-2846-3 lib bdg; 0-7660-2846-1 lib bdg
        LC 2006018655
This "introduces the man behind one of today's most high-profile sports. . . . Young hoops devotees will enjoy the details of a favorite sport's infancy. . . . Crisp photos, illustrations, and a sidebar featuring Naismith's original 13 rules break up the accessible text." Booklist

Includes glossary and bibliographical references

Nakahama, Manjiro, 1827-1898
★ Blumberg, Rhoda. **Shipwrecked!**: the true adventures of a Japanese boy. HarperCollins Pubs. 2000 80p il map hardcover o.p. pa $7.99
Grades: 5 6 7 8   **92**
  1. Survival after airplane accidents, shipwrecks, etc. 2. Interpreters 3. Japanese -- United States 4. Shipwreck victims -- Japan
  ISBN 0-688-17484-1; 0-688-17485-X pa
        LC 99-86664
In 1841, rescued by an American whaler after a terrible shipwreck leaves him and his four companions castaways on a remote island, fourteen-year-old Manjiro learns new laws and customs as he becomes the first Japanese person to set foot in the United States

"Exemplary in both her research and writing, Blumberg hooks readers with anecdotes that astonish without sensationalizing, and she uses language that's elegant and challenging, yet always clear. Particularly notable is the well-chosen reproductions of original artwork." Booklist

Includes bibliographical references

Napoleon I, Emperor of the French, 1769-1821

Burleigh, Robert. **Napoleon**; the story of the little corporal. Abrams Books for Young Readers 2007 43p il map $18.95

Grades: 4 5 6 7   92

1. Emperors

ISBN 978-0-8109-1378-3; 0-8109-1378-X

LC 2006-23610

"Burleigh's straightforward style and clear focus make accessible this account of the rapid rise and fall of the skilled military leader and emperor of France. The period artwork, accompanied by helpful captions, enhances the cleanly designed presentation." Horn Book Guide

Neruda, Pablo, 1904-1973

★ Brown, Monica. **Pablo** Neruda; poet of the people. illustrations by Julie Paschkis. Henry Holt and Co. 2011 un il

Grades: PreK   92

1. Poets 2. Authors 3. Diplomats 4. Novelists 5. Poets, Chilean 6. Nobel laureates for peace 7. Nobel laureates for literature

ISBN 080509198X; 9780805091984

LC 2010025320

This is a picture-book introduction to the Chilean poet. "Primary, intermediate." (Horn Book)

"This gentle tribute to Chilean poet Neruda explores his formative experiences, from searching for 'beetles and birds' eggs' in the forest to discovering his love for books. . . . Brown and Paschkis paint a compelling portrait of a man who saw the world as a joyful, complex, and beautiful poem waiting to be unveiled." Publ Wkly

Includes bibliographical references

Delano, Poli. **When** I was a boy Neruda called me Policarpo; illustrated by Manuel Monroy. Groundwood Books/House of Anansi Press 2006 84p il $15.95

Grades: 5 6 7 8   92

1. Poets 2. Authors 3. Diplomats 4. Novelists 5. Poets, Chilean 6. Memoirists 7. Short story writers 8. Nobel laureates for peace 9. Nobel laureates for literature

ISBN 0-88899-726-4

In this book, the author "offers seven vignettes, interspersed with six of Neruda's . . . poems and biographical information, to give middle-grade readers a sense of what it was like to grow up in the constant presence of a kindly, though spoiled and eccentric, celebrity. . . . Grades four to six." (MultiCult Rev)

"Based on the author's childhood remembrances of when he and his diplomat parents lived with Tío Pablo [Neruda] in Mexico, these seven chapters reveal both the genius and the eccentricities of the Nobel Prize-winning Chilean poet. . . . The chapters are short, well written, and filled with interesting details that will open up a new and exotic world. . . . Monroy's pen-and-sepia-toned drawings are . . . at times humorous, at times dramatic, but always enticing." SLJ

Newton, Isaac Sir, 1642-1727

Hollihan, Kerrie Logan. **Isaac** Newton and physics for kids; his life and ideas with 21 activities. Chicago Review Press 2009 131p il map pa $16.95

Grades: 4 5 6 7   92

1. Physicists 2. Scientists 3. Mathematicians 4. Writers on science

ISBN 978-1-55652-778-4 pa; 1-55652-778-0 pa

LC 2008048635

"Hollihan introduces readers to the scientific brilliance, as well as the social isolation, of this giant figure, blending a readable narrative with an attractive format that incorporates maps, diagrams, historical photographs, and physics activities." Booklist

Includes bibliographical references

★ Krull, Kathleen. **Isaac** Newton; illustrated by Boris Kulikov. Viking 2006 126p il (Giants of science) $15.99

Grades: 5 6 7 8   92

1. Physicists 2. Scientists 3. Mathematicians 4. Writers on science

ISBN 0-670-05921-8

LC 2005017741

This "profiles Sir Isaac Newton, the secretive, obsessive, and brilliant English scientist who invented calculus, built the first reflecting telescope, developed the modern scientific method, and discerned many of our laws of physics and optics. . . . The lively, conversational style will appeal to readers. . . . Kulikov's humorous pen-and-ink drawings complement the lighthearted text of this fascinating introduction." Booklist

Steele, Philip. **Isaac** Newton; the scientist who changed everything. [by] Philip Steele. National Geographic Society 2007 64p il map (World history biographies) $17.95; lib bdg $27.90

Grades: 4 5 6 7   92

1. Physicists 2. Scientists 3. Mathematicians 4. Writers on science

ISBN 978-1-4263-0114-8; 978-1-4263-0115-5 lib bdg

LC 2006020772

"The cradle-to-grave text includes vivid descriptions of Newton's youth. . . . The dynamic format is a draw; numerous mostly archival images . . . and a time-line border add interest and cultural context on each spacious page." Booklist

Includes bibliographical references

Nezahualcóyotl, King of Texcoco, 1402-1472

★ Serrano, Francisco. The **poet** king of Tezcoco; a great leader of Ancient Mexico. illustrated by Pablo Serrano; biography translated and adapted by Trudy Balch; poetry translated by Jo Anne Engelbert. Groundwood Books/House of Anansi Press 2007 35p il $18.95

Grades: 4 5 6 7   92

1. Aztecs 2. Kings

ISBN 978-0-88899-787-6; 0-88899-787-6

"In the fifteenth century, the land where Mexico City now sprawls was a vast, green kingdom called Tezcoco. This . . . introduces one of Tezcoco's greatest rulers, a Toltec royal named Nezahualcoyotl. . . . The folk-art inspired illustrations echo the area's artistic traditions with beautiful patterning and symbolic imagery and flat , simplified characters reminiscent of hieroglyphics. Groundbreaking in its coverage of exciting history, this book offers details that are rarely presented to young people." Booklist

Nightingale, Florence, 1820-1910

Gorrell, Gena K. **Heart** and soul: the story of Florence Nightingale. Tundra Bks. 2000 146p il map hardcover o.p. pa $11.95

Grades: 5 6 7 8   92

1. Nurses 2. Nonfiction writers
ISBN 0-88776-494-0; 0-88776-703-6 pa

A biography of the 19th century English woman known as the founder of modern nursing

"This highly readable and well-researched biography does an excellent job of integrating the social and medical conditions of Nightingale's time. . . . Enlivening the narrative are black-and-white reproductions of drawings . . . and period photographs." SLJ

Includes bibliographical references

Nixon, Richard M. (Richard Milhous), 1913-1994

★ Aronson, Billy. **Richard** M. Nixon; [by] Billy Aronson. Marshall Cavendish Benchmark 2007 96p il (Presidents and their times) lib bdg $22.95

Grades: 5 6 7 8   92

1. Presidents 2. Vice-presidents 3. Senators 4. Nonfiction writers 5. Members of Congress
ISBN 978-0-7614-2428-4

LC 2006013839

Aronson "is able to paint a picture so full that readers will come away feeling that they know the man and understand at least some of the forces that shaped him. . . . The narrative moves chronologically, marching through the war years, Nixon's tenure in Congress and as vice-president, his presidential loss to JFK, his successful efforts to remake himself as a politician, and his years as president. . . . The typeface is clear, the photographs are well chosen." Booklist

Includes glossary and bibliographical references

Noguchi, Isamu, 1904-1988

Hale, Christy. The **East**-West house; Noguchi's childhood in Japan. Lee & Low Books 2009 un il $17.95

Grades: 3 4 5 6   92

1. Artists 2. Sculptors 3. Japanese Americans 4. Industrial designers
ISBN 978-1-60060-363-1; 1-60060-363-7

LC 2008053728

"The mixed-media collage illustrations reflect the blend of East and West. . . . Thoroughly documented and heavily reliant on primary sources. . . . An original and thought-provoking addition to biography or art collections." SLJ

Nuñez Cabeza de Vaca, Alvar, 16th cent.

Lourie, Peter. **On** the Texas trail of Cabeza de Vaca; 1st ed.; Boyds Mills Press 2008 48p il map $17.95

Grades: 4 5 6 7   92

1. Explorers 2. Historians 3. Travel writers 4. Government officials 5. Colonial administrators
ISBN 978-1-59078-492-1; 1-59078-492-8

LC 2007049180

"In 1527, Governor Pánfilo de Narváez sailed westward from Spain to explore the land that stretched between present-day Florida and Mexico, colonizing and conquering. With him, as his treasurer and sheriff, was Cabeza de Vaca. . . . He [returned] with a wealth of information, codified in

La Relación , his account of his experience. Then, 475 years later, Lourie set out to follow Cabeza de Vaca's trail through Texas. . . . This well-researched, beautifully composed book is the result. Using primary sources and period reproductions as well as the author's experiences and contemporary pictures, it highlights historical information within the context of current circumstances. Beautifully placed photos, reproductions, maps, and sidebars enhance the fluid text." SLJ

Includes bibliographical references

O'Keeffe, Georgia, 1887-1986

Bryant, Jennifer. **Georgia's** bones; [illustrated by] Bethanne Anderson. Eerdmans Books for Young Readers 2005 32p il $16

Grades: K 1 2 3   92

1. Artists 2. Painters 3. Women artists
ISBN 0-8028-5217-3

LC 2004-6800

Artist Georgia O'Keeffe was interested in the shapes she saw around her, from her childhood on a Wisconsin farm to her adult life in New York City and New Mexico

"Bryant writes in spare, lyrical verse, honoring her subject's idiosyncratic impressions and precise observation of the natural world. . . . Cow skulls, southwestern landscapes, and oversize flowers are present and accounted for, but the swooping brushstrokes and earthy textures are unmistakably Andersen's own." Booklist

Rodriguez, Rachel. **Through** Georgia's eyes; illustrated by Julie Paschkis. Henry Holt and Co. 2006 un il $16.95

Grades: K 1 2 3   92

1. Artists 2. Painters 3. Women artists 4. Artists -- United States
ISBN 978-0-8050-7740-7; 0-8050-7740-5

LC 2005012479

"Rodríguez gently tells this inspirational artist's story . . . with quiet simplicity. . . . Using short, strong sentences and phrases, the author emphasizes the artist's creative force. Paschkis extends the words with the visual simplicity of colorful, cut-paper collages." SLJ

Winter, Jeanette. **My** name is Georgia; a portrait. Harcourt Brace & Co. 1998 un il $16; pa $7

Grades: K 1 2 3   92

1. Artists 2. Painters 3. Women artists 4. Artists -- United States
ISBN 0-15-201649-X; 0-15-204597-X pa

LC 97-7087

This book on Georgia O'Keeffe "follows the artist's journey from home to school in Chicago, to New York, to Texas, and back to New York, . . . and finally to New Mexico. . . . Ages nine to twelve." (Horn Book)

"Winter mirrors the artist's stark imagery and strong personality in spare, poetic text and folk art—inspired illustrations." Publ Wkly

Includes bibliographical references

Oakley, Annie, 1860-1926

Wills, Charles A. **Annie** Oakley: a photographic story of a life; [by] Chuck Wills. DK Pub. 2007 128p il (DK biography) $14.99

Grades: 4 5 6 7   **92**
1. Entertainers 2. Marksmen
ISBN 978-0-7566-2986-1

A biography of the sharp-shooter in Buffalo Bill's Wild West Show, from her humble Quaker heritage, her childhood filled with poverty and abuse, to her rise to international fame.

"This highly readable book has a rich layout of photographs and illustrations on every spread." SLJ

Obama, Barack, 1961-

Abramson, Jill. **Obama**; the historic journey. Young reader's ed.; Callaway 2009 94p il map $24.95
Grades: 5 6 7 8   **92**
1. Lawyers 2. Presidents 3. Racially mixed people 4. Senators 5. State legislators 6. Nobel laureates for peace
ISBN 978-0-670-01208-4; 0-670-01208-4

LC 2009-5051

"This scaled down, teen-friendly version of The New York Times's adult biography is geared for middle school students. Containing many of the same photos, it provides a brief overview of the President's life, information that has been revealed over the election year and during his administration. . . . Its allure is in the many photographs with captions, sidebars, speech quotes, and charts. The book is nicely organized. The writing is direct and simple, explaining things such as convention delegates. . . . The book should entice young readers to explore his life further." Voice Youth Advocates

Feinstein, Stephen. **Barack** Obama. Enslow Publishers 2008 24p il map por (African-American heroes) lib bdg $21.26
Grades: K 1 2 3   **92**
1. Lawyers 2. Presidents 3. Racially mixed people 4. Senators 5. State legislators 6. Nobel laureates for peace
ISBN 978-0-7660-2893-7 lib bdg; 0-7660-2893-3 lib bdg

LC 2007036363

This is a "slim introduction to the [president] that begins with his childhood in Hawaii and Indonesia. Feinstein's upbeat text, divided into very short chapters, focuses on details that will capture kids' interest." Booklist

Includes bibliographical references

Grimes, Nikki. **Barack** Obama; son of promise, child of hope. illustrated by Bryan Collier. Simon & Schuster Books for Young Readers 2008 un il $16.99
Grades: 1 2 3 4   **92**
1. Lawyers 2. Presidents 3. Racially mixed people 4. Senators 5. State legislators 6. Nobel laureates for peace
ISBN 978-1-4169-7144-3; 1-4169-7144-0

LC 2008-06245

Who Obama "is and where he comes from is conveyed in beautifully poetic language [and] . . . the illustrator's impressive interpretation of the author's text takes the story to a more meaningful visual level for younger readers." Libr Media Connect

Includes bibliographical references

Kesselring, Susan. **Barack** Obama. Child's World 2010 24p il (Basic biographies) lib bdg $22.79
Grades: K 1 2   **92**
1. Lawyers 2. Presidents 3. Racially mixed people 4. Senators 5. State legislators 6. Nobel laureates for peace
ISBN 978-1-60253-339-4; 1-60253-339-3

LC 2009029365

This "provides a clear description of the man's life before and during his presidency and outlines some of his duties, without delving into politics. The books' clear and relevant black-and-white and color photographs sport captions that aid understanding of the subject matter." SLJ

Includes bibliographical references

Weatherford, Carole Boston. **Obama**; only in America. illustrated by Robert Barrett. Marshall Cavendish Children 2010 un il $17.99
Grades: 2 3 4 5   **92**
1. Lawyers 2. Presidents 3. Racially mixed people 4. Senators 5. State legislators 6. Nobel laureates for peace
ISBN 978-0-7614-5641-4; 0-7614-5641-4

LC 2009006338

"Weatherford puts an amazing amount of information about Barack Obama into a rhythmic text that is also wonderfully concise. Most of the major moments of Obama's life are here, both personal and professional. . . . The book makes Obama seem both larger than life yet also someone beset with struggles with which readers can identify. . . . Barrett's illustrations, oils on canvas, add a soft focus to the events." Booklist

Obama, Michelle

Brophy, David. **Michelle** Obama; meet the First Lady. by David Bergen Brophy. HarperCollins 2009 114p il $16.99; pa $6.99
Grades: 5 6 7 8   **92**
1. Lawyers 2. Spouses of presidents 3. Hospital administrators 4. African American women -- Biography
ISBN 978-0-06-177991-6; 0-06-177991-1; 978-0-06-177990-9 pa; 0-06-177990-3 pa

A brief biography of Michelle Obama, wife of President Barack Obama

"The author . . . mixes personal data with information about the political process that brought the Obamas to the White House. . . . This biography is a must-have for all school libraries." Voice Youth Advocates

Includes glossary

Colbert, David. **Michelle** Obama; an American story. Houghton Mifflin Harcourt 2009 151p il $16
Grades: 5 6 7 8   **92**
1. Lawyers 2. Spouses of presidents 3. Hospital administrators 4. African American women -- Biography
ISBN 978-0-547-24941-4; 0-547-24941-1

This biography delves into "the subject of The First Lady's family roots. . . . It offers a strong sense of who Obama was as a child, her solid upbringing, and her adult choices, all bolstered with numerous quotes from Obama and those who know her best. . . . Two sections of color photos and appended source notes for direct quotes complete this timely, highly readable biography." Booklist

Hopkinson, Deborah. **Michelle**; illustrated by A.G. Ford. Katherine Tegen Books 2009 un il $17.99; lib bdg $18.89

Grades: K 1 2 3   **92**

1. Lawyers 2. Presidents 3. Senators 4. State legislators 5. Spouses of presidents 6. Hospital administrators 7. Nobel laureates for peace 8. African American women -- Biography

ISBN 978-0-06-182739-6; 0-06-182739-8; 978-0-06-182743-3 lib bdg; 0-06-182743-6 lib bdg

LC 2009014551

This biography of the First Lady "touches on Michelle's childhood years in a loving working-class family, her academic accomplishments, courtship, marriage, careers and role as devoted mother and active supporter of her husband's presidential campaign. The straightforward, accessible text at times assumes dramatic overtones. . . . Ford's paintings offer likenesses of Michelle and her family, often capturing facial expressions and nuances of posture and gesture with uncanny realism. This warm, respectful portrait succeeds in presenting its subject as both inspirational and relatable." Publ Wkly

Kesselring, Susan. **Michelle** Obama. Child's World 2010 24p il (Basic biographies) lib bdg $22.79

Grades: PreK K 1   **92**

1. Lawyers 2. Spouses of presidents 3. Hospital administrators 4. African American women -- Biography

ISBN 978-1-60253-343-1; 1-60253-343-1

LC 2009029597

This biography of the First Lady "pairs intelligent, brief text with abundant photos. Simple but never basic." Booklist

Includes bibliographical references

Odetta, 1930-2008

Alcorn, Stephen. **Odetta**, the queen of folk; poem by Samantha Thornhill; conceived and illustrated by Stephen Alcorn. Scholastic Press 2010 un il

Grades: K 1 2 3   **92**

1. Singers 2. Folk music 3. Folk musicians 4. African American women -- Biography

ISBN 0-439-92818-4; 978-0-439-92818-2

LC 2009-5104

"Thornhill's poem pays powerful tribute to the folk-singing legend, beginning with early experiences that shaped her music . . . and her first exposure to segregation when her family moved to Los Angeles. . . . Filled with stars, candles, lightning bolts, music notes, and angels, Alcorn's rousing compositions borrow from folk art traditions, religious imagery, graphic design, and 1960s album cover art, creating a rich tapestry that trumpets the power of this singular figure." Publ Wkly

Paganini, Nicolò, 1782-1840

Frisch, Aaron. **Dark** fiddler: the life and legend of Nicolo Paganini; [by] Aaron Frisch; illustrated by Gary Kelley. Creative Editions 2008 un il lib bdg $17.95

Grades: 3 4 5 6   **92**

1. Composers 2. Violinists

ISBN 978-1-56846-200-4 lib bdg; 1-56846-200-X lib bdg

"Readers may not be familiar with the name Paganini, but after one look at the dramatic cover, with the spectral violinist staring back, a slight smile on his lips, they will want to find out more. . . . The folksy tone of the narrative will draw kids close as the story of Paganini's life unfolds. All this is set against breathtaking, chalklike art." Booklist

Paige, Satchel, 1906-1982

★ Adler, David A. **Satchel** Paige; don't look back. written by David A. Adler; illustrated by Terry Widener. Harcourt 2006 un il $16

Grades: K 1 2 3   **92**

1. Baseball players 2. African American athletes 3. Baseball -- Biography

ISBN 978-0-15-205585-1; 0-15-205585-1

LC 2005026354

A brief illustrated biography of the baseball player who, after a long career in the Negro Leagues, joined the Cleveland Indians and became the first African American to pitch in the World Series.

"Widener's acrylic paintings elongate and exaggerate the figures, using a rubbery perspective and old-fashioned hues to great effect." Booklist

Includes bibliographical references

Palmer, Joseph, 1791-1875

Hyatt, Patricia Rusch. The **quite** contrary man; a true American tale. illustrated by Kathryn Brown. Abrams Books for Young Readers 2010 un il $16.95

Grades: K 1 2 3   **92**

1. Beards 2. Social reformers

ISBN 978-0-8109-4065-9; 0-8109-4065-5

LC 2009052211

In nineteenth century New England, Joseph Palmer flouts the law against wearing a beard and is accused by his fellow citizens of being unpatriotic and sinful, stubbornly refusing to shave even when he is sent to jail.

"Although these are serious themes, this picture book offers a positive story with a happy ending, and much of the tone is due to Brown's pleasant and well-designed illustrations in pen and ink and watercolor, which set the scenes helpfully and support the folksy language." Booklist

Park, Linda Sue, 1960-

Parker-Rock, Michelle. **Linda** Sue Park; an author kids love. Enslow Publishers 2009 48p il (Authors kids love) lib bdg $23.93

Grades: 3 4 5   **92**

1. Authors 2. Authors, American 3. Children's authors

ISBN 978-0-7660-3158-6 lib bdg; 0-7660-3158-6 lib bdg

LC 2008-44549

"Clearly written, [this] outstanding [biography provides] many interesting details about the [subject's] personal [life] and [includes] photos that enhance the [text]." SLJ

Includes glossary and bibliographical references

Parkhurst, Charley, 1812-1879

Kay, Verla. **Rough**, tough Charley; by Verla Kay; illustrated by Adam Gustavson. Tricycle Press 2007 un il $15.95

Grades: K 1 2 3   **92**

1. Male impersonators 2. Coach drivers 3. Women -- West (U.S.) 4. Frontier and pioneer life -- California

ISBN 978-1-58246-184-7; 1-58246-184-8

LC 2006026611

"Many folks thought they knew the real Charley Parkhurst (1812-1879): a scrappy orphan . . . who became one of the bravest, fastest, saltiest and most respected stagecoach drivers in Gold Country. . . . But everybody had Charley wrong, for . . . Charley had successfully disguised the fact that he was actually a woman. . . . Gustavson's . . . lush, realistic oil illustrations are a lavish counterpoint to Kay's spare verse, [and] are suffused with the romance and roughness of a bygone era." Publ Wkly

Parks, Rosa, 1913-2005

Amoroso, Cynthia. **Rosa** Parks; by Cynthia Amoroso and Robert B. Noyed. Child's World 2010 24p il (Basic biographies) lib bdg $22.79

Grades: PreK K 1   92

1. Civil rights activists 2. African Americans -- Civil rights 3. African American women -- Biography

ISBN 978-1-60253-344-8; 1-60253-344-X

LC 2009029372

This biography of Rosa Parks "pairs intelligent, brief text with adundant photos. Simple but never basic." Booklist

Includes bibliographical references

★ Giovanni, Nikki, 1943- **Rosa**; illustrated by Bryan Collier. Henry Holt 2005 32p il $16.95

Grades: 3 4 5   92

1. African American women 2. Civil rights activists 3. African Americans -- Civil rights 4. African American women -- Biography

ISBN 0-8050-7106-7

A Caldecott Medal honor book, 2006

This book tells the story of Rosa Parks's "refusal to yield her seat to a white bus rider and that act's direct connection with the Montgomery bus boycott. . . . Ages six to nine." (Bull Cent Child Books)

"Paired very effectively with Giovanni's passionate, direct words, Collier's large watercolor-and-collage illustrations depict Parks as an inspiring force that radiates golden light, and also as part of a dynamic activist community." Booklist

Pasteur, Louis, 1822-1895

Zamosky, Lisa. **Louis** Pasteur; founder of microbiology. Compass Point Books 2009 40p il map (Mission: Science) lib bdg $26.60

Grades: 4 5 6   92

1. Chemists 2. Scientists 3. Microbiologists 4. Writers on science

ISBN 978-0-7565-3962-7

LC 2008007726

This biography of the father of microbiology "does a good job of connecting the scientist's work to our lives today. . . . [The] book has a variety of graphics including diagrams, photos, and reproductions of paintings and sketches. [This volume is] a definite plus for a school library or the juvenile collection in a public library." Libr Media Connect

Includes glossary and bibliographical references

Patch, Sam, 1807-1829

Cummins, Julie. **Sam** Patch; daredevil jumper. [illustrated by Michael Allen Austin] Holiday House 2009 un il $16.95

Grades: PreK K 1 2   92

1. Stunt performers 2. Factory workers 3. Adventure

and adventurers -- Juvenile literature

ISBN 978-0-8234-1741-4; 0-8234-1741-7

LC 2007-34624

This "chronicles the short life of early-19th-century stuntman Sam Patch. . . . The conversational style briskly moves the tale from Sam's childhood jumping exploits to the showstopping stunts of his brief but world-famous career. . . . Austin's . . . sepia-infused acrylics set a tone alternating between whimsical and haunting. The dynamic illustrations make exaggerated use of light and perspective." Publ Wkly

Patrick, Saint, 373?-463?

De Paola, Tomie. **Patrick**: patron saint of Ireland. Holiday House 1992 un il lib bdg $16.95; pa $6.95

Grades: K 1 2 3   92

1. Saints 2. Christian saints 3. Missionaries

ISBN 0-8234-0924-4 lib bdg; 0-8234-1077-3 pa

LC 91-19417

Relates the life and legends of Patrick, the patron saint of Ireland

"The combination of book design, text, and illustration is suitably reverent but never saccharine; the whole is a well-executed treatment of an appealing subject." Horn Book

Paul, Les, 1915-2009

Wyckoff, Edwin Brit. **Electric** guitar man: the genius of Les Paul; [by] Edwin Brit Wyckoff. Enslow Elementary 2008 32p il (Genius at work!: great inventor biographies) lib bdg $22.60

Grades: 4 5 6   92

1. Inventors 2. Guitarists

ISBN 978-0-7660-2847-0 lib bdg; 0-7660-2847-X lib bdg

LC 2006034681

"Without the electronic guitar invented by Les Paul, music would never have been the same. In this biography of Paul's life and career, Edwin Brit Wyckoff shares how the rambunctious boy from Waukesha, Wisconsin, was propelled to stardom by his unrivaled playing ability and technological prowess." Publisher's note

Includes glossary and bibliographical references

Pavlov, Ivan Petrovich, 1849-1936

Saunders, Barbara R. **Ivan** Pavlov; exploring the mysteries of behavior. Enslow Publishers 2006 112p il por (Great minds of science) lib bdg $31.93

Grades: 5 6 7 8   92

1. Scientists 2. Behaviorism 3. Physiologists 4. Writers on medicine 5. Nobel laureates for physiology or medicine

ISBN 0-7660-2506-3

LC 2005031648

This is a biography of Russian scientist Ivan Pavlov, best known for his experiments with dogs, which were key to the development of behaviorism, and who won the 1904 Nobel Prize for his research on digestion

"The accessible [text has] an inviting, open format and [offers] many anecdotes. . . . Good-quality photos and illustrations complement the [narrative]." SLJ

Includes glossary and bibliographical references

Peary, Marie Ahnighito, 1893-1978

Kirkpatrick, Katherine A. **Snow** baby; the Arctic childhood of Admiral Robert E. Peary's daring daughter. [by]

Katherine Kirkpatrick. Holiday House 2007 50p il map $16.95

Grades: 5 6 7 8   92

1. Admirals 2. Explorers 3. Children of prominent persons

ISBN 978-0-8234-1973-9; 0-8234-1973-8

LC 2006-02016

"Born north of the Arctic Circle in 1893, Marie Ahn-ighito Peary published her own version of her youth in 1934 (The Snowbaby's Own Story), on which this book is based. Kirkpatrick's engaging text captures the girl's adventurous spirit and the opportunities that her father's life as an explorer presented, as well as her love of the North and her Inuit friends." SLJ

Peary, Robert Edwin, 1856-1920

Kirkpatrick, Katherine A. **Snow** baby; the Arctic child-hood of Admiral Robert E. Peary's daring daughter. [by] Katherine Kirkpatrick. Holiday House 2007 50p il map $16.95

Grades: 5 6 7 8   92

1. Admirals 2. Explorers 3. Children of prominent persons

ISBN 978-0-8234-1973-9; 0-8234-1973-8

LC 2006-02016

"Born north of the Arctic Circle in 1893, Marie Ahn-ighito Peary published her own version of her youth in 1934 (The Snowbaby's Own Story), on which this book is based. Kirkpatrick's engaging text captures the girl's adventurous spirit and the opportunities that her father's life as an explorer presented, as well as her love of the North and her Inuit friends." SLJ

Pelé, 1940-

★ Cline-Ransome, Lesa. **Young** Pele; soccer's first star. illustrated by James E. Ransome. Schwartz & Wade Bks. 2007 un il

Grades: K 1 2 3   92

1. Soccer players 2. Soccer -- Biography 3. Soccer -- Juvenile literature

ISBN 0-375-83599-7; 0-375-93599-1 lib bdg; 978-0-375-83599-5; 978-0-375-93599-2 lib bdg

This is a biography of the soccer player and author of My Life and the Beautiful Game (1977). "Primary." (Horn Book)

"With handsome oil paintings and a stirring story, this picture-book biography will first grab children with its action. Just as exciting, though, is the account of Brazilian-born Pelé's personal struggle—his amazing rise from poverty to international soccer stardom." Booklist

Pele. **For** the love of soccer! illustrated by Frank Morrison. Disney-Hyperion Books 2010 un il $16.99

Grades: K 1 2 3   92

1. Soccer 2. Athletes 3. Soccer players

ISBN 978-1-4231-1538-0; 1-4231-1538-4

LC 2009-15890

"In a spare narrative enlivened by typography of various sizes and colors, soccer legend Pele underscores his lifelong passion for soccer. . . . Following two time lines simultaneously, Morrison's . . . energetic, fluid paintings spotlight Pele's soccer moves beside those of a young player today. . . . Though the narrative links the two players throughout,

a warmhearted ending ties their stories together visually, as Pele signs a ball for the boy." Publ Wkly

Penrose, Antony

Penrose, Antony. The **boy** who bit Picasso. Abrams Books for Young Readers 2011 47p il $16.95

Grades: 3 4 5   92

1. Artists 2. Painters 3. Artists, French 4. Archivists 5. Children of prominent persons

ISBN 978-0-8109-9728-8; 0-8109-9728-2

LC 2010009444

Presents a story of Tony, the son of photographer Lee Miller and painter-writer Sir Roland Penrose, who shares his childhood memories of his special friend—a world-famous artist by the name of Pablo Picasso.

"Numerous b&w photographs appear, along with original drawings by contemporary children. Reproductions of Picasso's works demonstrate the influence Penrose's family had on Picasso's art. . . . It's a fascinating and highly personal vision of the artist." Publ Wkly

Perón, Eva, 1919-1952

Favor, Lesli J. **Eva** Peron. Marshall Cavendish Benchmark 2010 112p il (Leading women) $39.93

Grades: 5 6 7 8   92

1. Women politicians 2. Spouses of presidents

ISBN 978-0-7614-4962-1; 0-7614-4962-0

A biography of the influential and admired First Lady of Argentina.

Includes bibliographical references

Peterson, Adrian

Sandler, Michael. **Adrian** Peterson. Bearport Pub. 2010 24p il map (Football heroes making a difference) lib bdg $22.61

Grades: 2 3 4   92

1. Football players 2. Football -- Biography

ISBN 978-1-936087-59-4 lib bdg; 1-936087-59-6 lib bdg

LC 2009033352

Looks at the life and accomplishments of the star running back of the Minnesota Vikings.

Includes glossary and bibliographical references

Peterson, Roger Tory, 1908-1996

Thomas, Peggy. **For** the birds: the life of Roger Tory Peterson; illustrated by Laura Jacques. Calkins Creek 2011 il $16.95

Grades: 2 3 4 5   92

1. Birds 2. Artists 3. Naturalists 4. Illustrators 5. Ornithologists 6. Writers on nature

ISBN 978-1-59078-764-9; 1-59078-764-1

"Intrigued from childhood by the wildlife around him, Roger Tory Peterson grew up to publish, in 1934, the first pocket-sized bird guide. . . . Using language and imagery relevant to her topic, Thomas . . . provides a lively chronological narrative. . . . Jacques' hyper-realistic mixed-media paintings have sharp edges and blended shadows, giving the appearance of acylics and collage digitally combined. . . . An excellent addition to the 'sense of wonder' shelf." Kirkus

Phelps, Michael, 1985-

Torsiello, David P. **Michael** Phelps; swimming for Olympic gold. Enslow Publishers 2009 48p il (Hot celebrity biographies) lib bdg $23.93

Grades: 2 3 4   92

1. Athletes 2. Swimming 3. Swimmers 4. Olympic athletes

ISBN 978-0-7660-3591-1 lib bdg; 0-7660-3591-3 lib bdg

LC 2008-48700

"Quality design, including an interesting color palette, distinguishes [this profile] . . . [which] is illustrated with large, recent color photos. The tone is light but not breathless; the writing is solid." SLJ

Includes glossary

Picasso, Pablo, 1881-1973

Jacobson, Rick. **Picasso**; soul on fire. [by] Rick Jacobson; illustrated by Laura Fernandez & Rick Jacobson. Tundra Books 2004 un il $15.95; pa $8.95

Grades: 3 4 5   92

1. Artists 2. Painters 3. Artists, French

ISBN 978-0-88776-599-5; 0-88776-599-8; 978-1-77049-263-9 pa; 1-77049-263-1 pa

This is an introduction the life of the artist, exploring his influences, selected works, and his creative processes.

"Written in simple, clear language. . . . The softly radiant oil paintings are mostly full page and enhance the enjoyment of the book. . . . This eloquent tribute will serve as an introduction to Picasso and to an artist's inspirations." SLJ

Penrose, Antony. The **boy** who bit Picasso. Abrams Books for Young Readers 2011 47p il $16.95

Grades: 3 4 5   92

1. Artists 2. Painters 3. Artists, French 4. Archivists 5. Children of prominent persons

ISBN 978-0-8109-9728-8; 0-8109-9728-2

LC 2010009444

Presents a story of Tony, the son of photographer Lee Miller and painter-writer Sir Roland Penrose, who shares his childhood memories of his special friend—a world-famous artist by the name of Pablo Picasso.

"Numerous b&w photographs appear, along with original drawings by contemporary children. Reproductions of Picasso's works demonstrate the influence Penrose's family had on Picasso's art. . . . It's a fascinating and highly personal vision of the artist." Publ Wkly

Pike, Lip, 1845-1893

Michelson, Richard. **Lipman** Pike; America's first home run king. written by Richard Michelson; illustrated by Zachary Pullen. Sleeping Bear Press 2011 un il $16.95

Grades: 2 3 4   92

1. Baseball players 2. Jews -- Biography 3. Baseball -- Biography

ISBN 978-1-58536-465-7; 1-58536-465-7

LC 2010032367

This is a picture book biography of Lipman Pike, the son of Jewish immigrants from Holland, who became, in the 1850s, one of America's first professional baseball players.

"Michelson effortlessly hurtles the story through Lip's career . . . and baseball fans will be fascinated by the details. . . . Pullen's unmistakable, big-headed caricatures make this

an ideal companion to Jonah Winter's You Never Heard of Sandy Koufax?! (2009)." Booklist

Pinchot, Gifford, 1865-1946

Hines, Gary. **Midnight** forests; a story of Gifford Pinchot and our national forests. illustrated by Robert Casilla. Boyds Mills Press 2005 un il $16.95

Grades: 3 4 5   92

1. Governors 2. Conservationists 3. Forests and forestry 4. Foresters

ISBN 1-56397-148-8

LC 2003-26876

"This picture-book biography introduces Gifford Pinchot, a wealthy young American who studied forestry in France and returned home to put his knowledge to good use in his own country. Appointed Secretary of Agriculture in 1898, he later joined forces with Theodore Roosevelt to turn 16 million acres into national forests. . . . Mirroring the quiet prose, the dignified pencil-and-watercolor illustrations depict Pinchot at work and in quiet contemplation." Booklist

Includes bibliographical references

Pippin, Horace, 1888-1946

Venezia, Mike. **Horace** Pippin; written and illustrated by Mike Venezia. Children's Press 2008 32p il (Getting to know the world's greatest artists) lib bdg $28

Grades: 3 4 5   92

1. Artists 2. Painters 3. African American artists

ISBN 978-0-531-18527-8 lib bdg; 0-531-18527-3 lib bdg

LC 2007016127

A biography of the African American artist best known for his paintings of life in America during slavery and the years of segregation.

"Though the [text is] simply written, [this title contains] a wealth of information. . . . [The book has] many reproductions of the [artist's] works as well as those of the masters who influenced [him]. To help illustrate his points, Venezia has incorporated his own cartoon-style illustrations." SLJ

Planck, Max, 1858-1947

Weir, Jane. **Max** Planck; revolutionary physicist. Compass Point Books 2009 40p il (Mission: science) lib bdg $26.60

Grades: 4 5 6   92

1. Physicists 2. Nobel laureates for physics

ISBN 978-0-7565-4073-9 lib bdg; 0-7565-4073-9 lib bdg

LC 2008-37622

Biography of the physicist Max Planck

Includes glossary and bibliographical references

Pocahontas, d. 1617

Brimner, Larry Dane. **Pocahontas**; bridging two worlds. Marshall Cavendish Benchmark 2009 41p il (American heroes) lib bdg $20.95

Grades: 2 3 4   92

1. Princesses 2. Powhatan Indians 3. Indian leaders

ISBN 978-0-7614-3065-0

This traces the life of Pocahontas from her birth in about 1595 to her death and considers the impact her life had on American history

This "concise and well-written [title covers] key biographical facts without overwhelming young readers, and [includes] captioned illustrations and reproductions, most of which are in color. Text is large, and the layout is age-appropriate and attractive, with wide margins." SLJ

Krull, Kathleen. **Pocahontas**; princess of the New World. [by] Kathleen Krull; pictures by David Diaz. Walker 2007 un il $16.95; lib bdg $17.85

Grades: K 1 2 3   **92**

    1. Princesses 2. Powhatan Indians 3. Indian leaders
    ISBN 978-0-8027-9554-0; 0-8027-9554-4; 978-0-8027-9555-7 lib bdg; 0-8027-9555-2 lib bdg

                  LC 2006025723

This focuses on "the mischievous girl Matoaka, affectionately nicknamed Pocahontas. Primary sources provide the basic facts. . . . Diaz's cut-paper collage illustrations literally glow with vibrancy. He uses a palette of tropical colors—lemon yellow, lime green, ocean blue, and orange." SLJ

Pokiak-Fenton, Margaret

    Jordan-Fenton, Christy. **When** I was eight; illustrated by Gabrielle Grimard. Annick Press 2013 32 p. (reinforced) $21.95

Grades: 1 2 3 4   **92**

    1. Inuit -- Biography 2. Girls -- Education
    ISBN 1554514916; 9781554514915

In this children's book, by Christy Jordan-Fenton and Margaret Pokiak-Fenton, "Olemaun is eight and knows a lot of things. But she does not know how to read. She must travel to the outsiders' school to learn. . . . The nuns at the school take her Inuit name and call her Margaret. . . . Margaret's tenacious character draws the attention of a black-cloaked nun who tries to break her spirit at every turn. But she is more determined than ever to read." (Publisher's note)

Pollock, Jackson, 1912-1956

    ★ Greenberg, Jan. **Action** Jackson; [by] Jan Greenberg and Sandra Jordan; illustrated by Robert Andrew Parker. Roaring Brook Press 2002 32p il hardcover o.p. pa $6.95

Grades: 3 4 5 6   **92**

    1. Artists 2. Painters 3. Artists -- United States
    ISBN 0-7613-1682-5; 0-7613-2770-3 lib bdg; 0-312-36751-1 pa

                  LC 2002-6211

Imagines Jackson Pollock at work during the creation of one of his paint-swirled and splattered canvases

"Using spare, lyrical words, the authors layer the exciting story with deep observations about what art is and how it is made. . . . Parker's scribbly pen-and-watercolor illustrations get the mood just right; the loose lines have an improvised, energetic quality that echoes Pollock's painting." Booklist

    Includes bibliographical references

Polo, Marco, 1254-1323?

    Demi. **Marco** Polo; written and illustrated by Demi. Marshall Cavendish 2008 un il map $19.99

Grades: 4 5 6 7   **92**

    1. Explorers 2. Travelers 3. Voyages and travels 4. Travel writers
    ISBN 978-0-7614-5433-5; 0-7614-5433-0

"This elegant, scholarly picture-book biography brings the explorer's fantastic journey to life. . . . Demi weaves her subject's own accounts into a seamless tale of wonder. . . . The delicately rendered illustrations, painted with Chinese inks and gold overlays . . . capture the exotic beauty of 13th-century China." SLJ

Markle, Sandra. **Animals** Marco Polo saw; an adventure on the Silk Road. illustrated by Daniela Jaglenka Terrazzini. Chronicle Books 2009 45p il $16.99

Grades: 3 4 5 6   **92**

    1. Explorers 2. Travelers 3. Voyages and travels 4. Travel writers 5. Animals -- Asia
    ISBN 978-0-8118-5051-3; 0-8118-5051-X

                  LC 2007053057

"This intriguing book discusses generally agreed-upon details of Marco Polo's explorations in Mongolia and the Far East, and speculates about the moths, jackals, van cats, zebu, oxen, Persian lions, snow cats, and camels he may have met along the way. . . . The text is enhanced by color, mixed-media illustrations that occupy one page or the top half of each spread. . . . A useful introduction to 13th-century history." SLJ

McCarty, Nick. **Marco** Polo; the boy who traveled the medieval world. National Geographic 2006 64p il map (World history biographies) $17.95; lib bdg $27.90

Grades: 5 6 7 8   **92**

    1. Explorers 2. Travelers 3. Voyages and travels 4. Travel writers
    ISBN 0-7922-5893-2; 0-7922-5894-0 lib bdg

A biography of the Italian explorer who became famous for his travels in Asia

    Includes glossary and bibliographical references

Twist, Clint. **Marco** Polo; history's great adventurer. Candlewick Press 2011 un il (Historical notebooks) $19.99

Grades: 5 6 7 8   **92**

    1. Explorers 2. Travelers 3. Voyages and travels 4. Travel writers
    ISBN 978-0-7636-5286-9; 0-7636-5286-5

                  LC 2010040131

First published 2010 in the United Kingdom with title: Marco Polo; geographer of distant lands

"In this sumptuous scrapbook, excerpts from Marco Polo's own account of his travels are paired with beautiful maps, drawings, and illustrations. . . . This volume is well suited to browsing, and many readers will want to spend time poring over the many details." SLJ

Powell, John Wesley, 1834-1902

    ★ Ray, Deborah Kogan. **Down** the Colorado; John Wesley Powell, the one-armed explorer. Frances Foster Books/Farrar, Straus & Giroux 2007 un il $17

Grades: 3 4 5   **92**

    1. Explorers 2. Geologists
    ISBN 0-374-31838-7; 978-0-374-31838-3

                  LC 2006-43994

"This picture-book biography traces the life of explorer John Wesley Powell, whose landmark journey in 1869 down the Colorado River made him a national hero. Each double-page spread combines text on one side describing an episode from Powell's life with a stunning, full-page illustration on the opposite side. . . . An exciting adventure story and an instructive account of the exploration of the West." Booklist

Presley, Elvis, 1935-1977

Collins, Terry. **Elvis**; a graphic novel. illustrated by Michele Melcher. Capstone Press 2011 32p il (Graphic library: American graphic) lib bdg $29.32; pa $7.95

Grades: 4 5 6 7   92

1. Actors 2. Singers 3. Rock musicians 4. Biographical graphic novels

ISBN 978-1-4296-5476-0 lib bdg; 1-4296-5476-7 lib bdg; 978-1-4296-6266-6 pa; 1-4296-6266-2 pa

LC 2010024847

In graphic novel format, explores the life of Elvis Presley and describes his return to stardom through his '68 Comeback Special.

"The illustrations are eye-catching and the narration is presented simply, yet compellingly. . . . Fact-filled, entertaining, and accessible." SLJ

Includes glossary and bibliographical references

Quimby, Harriet, 1875-1912

Moss, Marissa. **Brave** Harriet; the first woman to fly the English Channel. illustrated by C.F. Payne. Silver Whistle Bks. 2001 un il $16

Grades: K 1 2 3   92

1. Air pilots 2. Women air pilots 3. Aeronautics -- Flights

ISBN 0-15-202380-1

LC 99-50463

Harriet Quimby, the first American woman to have received a pilot's license, describes her April 1912 solo flight across the English Channel, the first such flight by any woman

"Moss writes effectively in first person, putting readers in touch with Quimby's dreams and determination through direct, vivid language. The mixed media artwork combines paints and pastels in a series of beautiful scenes." Booklist

Whitaker, Suzanne. The **daring** Miss Quimby; by Suzanne George Whitaker; illustrated by Catherine Stock. Holiday House 2009 un il $16.95

Grades: 1 2 3   92

1. Air pilots 2. Women air pilots

ISBN 978-0-8234-1996-8; 0-8234-1996-7

LC 2008022569

A biography of Harriet Quimby, who, in 1911 "became the first American woman to earn a pilot's license. . . . Whitaker's spare, engaging narrative and Stock's lively watercolors bring this little-known female adventurer to life." Booklist

Reagan, Ronald, 1911-2004

Burgan, Michael. **Ronald** Reagan; a photographic story of a life. DK Pub. 2011 128p il (DK biography) $14.99; pa $5.99

Grades: 5 6 7 8   92

1. Actors 2. Governors 3. Presidents

ISBN 978-0-7566-7075-7; 0-7566-7075-6; 978-0-7566-7074-0 pa; 0-7566-7074-8 pa

"Burgan's survey covers the basic facts in a positive but not propagandistic introduction. . . . Featuring small but clear photos or boxed commentary on every page and capped with a substantial . . . multimedia resource list, this compact volume . . . gives readers a broad picture of his achievements and a sense of his compelling personal style." Booklist

Includes bibliographical references

Marsico, Katie. **Ronald** Reagan. Marshall Cavendish Benchmark 2011 112p il (Presidents and their times) lib bdg $23.95

Grades: 5 6 7 8   92

1. Actors 2. Governors 3. Presidents

ISBN 978-0-7614-4814-3; 0-7614-4814-4

LC 2009044590

This offers information on President Ronald Reagan and places him within his historical and cultural context. Also explored are the formative events of his times and how he responded.

"The abundant sidebars provide a good deal of background information that will be helpful to students. . . . Attractive . . . as well as useful." Booklist

Includes glossary and bibliographical references

Ream, Vinnie, 1847-1914

★ Fitzgerald, Dawn. **Vinnie** and Abraham; [by] Dawn Fitzgerald; illustrated by Catherine Stock. Charlesbridge 2007 un il lib bdg $15.95

Grades: 2 3 4   92

1. Artists 2. Sculptors 3. Women artists

ISBN 978-1-57091-658-8 lib bdg; 1-57091-658-6 lib bdg

LC 2006009033

"This picture-book biography presents Vinnie Ream as a young woman who transcended the conventions of her time through determination and a remarkable talent for sculpture. . . . After Lincoln's assassination, Congress commissioned her to sculpt a marble statue of the late president, which is still on display in the Capital rotunda. Fitzgerald's clearly written narrative portrays Vinnie as a hardworking, resolute person who succeeded through her own gifts and the help of others who believed in her. Stock's watercolor paintings light up the pages." Booklist

Reeves, Bass, 1838-1910

★ Nelson, Vaunda Micheaux. **Bad** news for outlaws; the remarkable life of Bass Reeves, deputy U.S. Marshal. illustrations by R. Gregory Christie. Carolrhoda Books 2009 un il lib bdg $17.95

Grades: 3 4 5   92

1. Law enforcement 2. Frontier and pioneer life 3. Sheriffs 4. African Americans -- Biography

ISBN 978-0-8225-6764-6 lib bdg; 0-8225-6764-4 lib bdg

LC 2008001188

ALA EMIERT Coretta Scott King Author Award (2010)

This is a biography of Bass Reeves, a former slave who was recruited as a deputy United States Marshal in the area that was to become Oklahoma. Chronology. Grades three to six. (Bull Cent Child Books)

"Kids will have no trouble loping into this picture-book biography. Born a slave, Reeves became one of the most feared and respected Deputy U.S. Marshals to tame the West. . . . The text, especially, gets into the tall-tale spirit of things. . . . An exciting subject captured with narrative panache and visual swagger." Booklist

Reinhardt, Django, 1910-1953

★ Christensen, Bonnie. **Django**. Roaring Brook Press 2009 un il $17.99

Grades: 1 2 3 4   92

1. Guitarists 2. Jazz musicians

ISBN 978-1-59643-422-6; 1-59643-422-8

ALA Schneider Family Book Award (2010)

"Richly expressive paint and ink illustrations portray the hard-earned successes of Django Reinhardt, whose childhood was spent traveling with his impoverished gypsy family, where music was a constant and illuminating presence. . . . Christensen's soft, rhythmic prose echoes her evocative images as Django explores the music scene of 1920s Paris, before suffering serious burns on his hands and leg when his wagon catches fire. Despite his injuries, Reinhardt teaches himself to play again. . . . A sensuous tribute to an illustrious musician." Publ Wkly

Reiss, Johanna

★ Reiss, Johanna. The **upstairs** room. Crowell 1972 273p hardcover o.p. pa $5.99

Grades: 5 6 7 8 9 10   92

1. Authors 2. Holocaust survivors 3. Children's authors 4. Jews -- Netherlands 5. World War, 1939-1945 -- Jews 6. Holocaust, 1933-1945 -- Personal narratives

ISBN 0-690-85127-8; 0-06-440370-X pa

A Newbery Medal honor book, 1973

"In a vital, moving account the author recalls her experiences as a Jewish child hiding from the Germans occupying her native Holland during World War II. . . . Ten-year-old Annie and her twenty-year-old sister Sini, . . . are taken in by a Dutch farmer, his wife, and mother who hide the girls in an upstairs room of the farm house. Written from the perspective of a child the story affords a child's-eye-view of the war." Booklist

Renoir, Auguste, 1841-1919

Somervill, Barbara A. **Pierre**-Auguste Renoir; [by] Barbara Somervill. Mitchell Lane 2007 48p il (Art profiles for kids) lib bdg $29.95

Grades: 5 6 7 8   92

1. Artists 2. Painters 3. Artists, French

ISBN 978-1-58415-566-9 lib bdg; 1-58415-566-3 lib bdg

LC 2007000661

Profiles the famous French artist best known for his portraits and his paintings such as "The Luncheon of the Boating Party" that depict people enjoying themselves

"The glossy pages allow for good reproductions of paintings as well as a few photos. . . . Back matter includes a glossary, chronology, chapter notes for quotes, lists of books and Internet sites, and a Timeline in History . . . offers a concise, readable account of the artist's life." Booklist

Includes glossary and bibliographical references

Revere, Paul, 1735-1818

★ Fritz, Jean. **And** then what happened, Paul Revere? pictures by Margot Tomes. Coward, McCann & Geoghegan 1973 45p il $16.99; pa $5.99

Grades: 2 3 4   92

1. Artisans 2. Metalworkers 3. Revolutionaries

ISBN 0-399-23337-7; 0-698-11351-9 pa

This "description of Paul Revere's ride to Lexington is funny, fast-paced, and historically accurate; it is given added interest by the establishment of Revere's character: busy, bustling, versatile, and patriotic, a man who loved people and excitement. The account of his ride is preceded by a description of his life and the political situation in Boston, and it concludes with Revere's adventures after reaching Lexington." Bull Cent Child Books

Giblin, James. The **many** rides of Paul Revere; by James Cross Giblin. Scholastic Press 2007 85p il map $17.99

Grades: 4 5 6 7   92

1. Artisans 2. Metalworkers 3. Revolutionaries

ISBN 978-0-439-57290-3; 0-439-57290-8

LC 2006-38369

"This well-organized biography presents a lucid account of Revere's childhood, his limited education, his training in his father's workshop, his brief military career, and his adult life as a silversmith, family man, and Revolutionary War leader. . . . Giblin presents salient facts and intriguing details to create a well-rounded and credible image of the man. Among the many illustrations are period portraits, narrative paintings, engravings, drawings, and maps as well as photos of significant sites and artifacts." Booklist

Includes bibliographical references

Mortensen, Lori. **Paul** Revere's ride; illustrated by Craig Orback. Picture Window Books 2010 32p il map (Our American story) lib bdg $23.99

Grades: 2 3 4   92

1. Artisans 2. Metalworkers 3. Revolutionaries 4. Statesmen -- United States

ISBN 978-1-4048-5537-3; 1-4048-5537-8

LC 2009-6893

Highlights the life and accomplishments of Paul Revere, including the events leading up to his famous ride to warn of the British attack on Concord.

This book is "illustrated with well-executed, full-page, color illustrations, maps, and photos. . . . [It has] accurate, clearly written information that students can use for either leisure reading or reports." SLJ

Includes glossary and bibliographical references

Rey, H. A. (Hans Augusto), 1898-1977

★ Borden, Louise. The **journey** that saved Curious George; the true wartime escape of Margret and H. A. Rey. illustrated by Allan Drummond. Houghton Mifflin 2005 72p il $17

Grades: 3 4 5 6   92

1. Artists 2. Authors 3. Illustrators 4. Jewish refugees 5. Authors, American 6. Children's authors

ISBN 0-618-33924-8

LC 2004-01015

This "book tells the story of Margret and H. A. Rey. Part 1 concerns their childhoods in Germany, their lives together in Rio de Janeiro and Paris in the 1920s and 1930s, and the growing menace after war broke out in 1939. As German-born Jews, they were suspect in many quarters. Part 2 recalls the Reys' flight from Paris and the couple's escape to Lisbon, Rio, and finally New York. They were carrying several illustrated manuscripts, including The Adventures of FiFi, later retitled Curious George. Photos, reproductions of documents, and artwork appear throughout the book, as do Drummond's spirited ink-and-watercolor illustrations,

brimming with action and details. The text . . . reads well."
Booklist

Rey, Margret

★ Borden, Louise. The **journey** that saved Curious George; the true wartime escape of Margret and H. A. Rey. illustrated by Allan Drummond. Houghton Mifflin 2005 72p il $17

Grades: 3 4 5 6   92

1. Artists 2. Authors 3. Illustrators 4. Jewish refugees
ISBN 0-618-33924-8

LC 2004-01015

This "book tells the story of Margret and H. A. Rey. Part 1 concerns their childhoods in Germany, their lives together in Rio de Janeiro and Paris in the 1920s and 1930s, and the growing menace after war broke out in 1939. As German-born Jews, they were suspect in many quarters. Part 2 re-calls the Reys' flight from Paris and the couple's escape to Lisbon, Rio, and finally New York. They were carrying several illustrated manuscripts, including The Adventures of FiFi, later retitled Curious George. Photos, reproductions of documents, and artwork appear throughout the book, as do Drummond's spirited ink-and-watercolor illustrations, brimming with action and details. The text . . . reads well."
Booklist

Ringgold, Faith

Venezia, Mike. **Faith** Ringgold; written and illustrated by Mike Venezia. Children's Press 2008 32p il (Getting to know the world's greatest artists) lib bdg $28

Grades: 3 4 5   92

1. Artists 2. Authors 3. Illustrators 4. Women artists
5. African American artists 6. Children's authors
ISBN 978-0-531-18526-1 lib bdg; 0-531-18526-5 lib bdg

LC 2007016125

This examines the work and life of Faith Ringgold, an African American artist who works in a variety of mediums including textiles, paintings, and prints, and is best known for her story quilts.

"Though the [text is] simply written, [this title contains] a wealth of information. . . . [The book has] many reproduc-tions of the [artist's] works as well as those of the masters who influenced [her]. To help illustrate his points, Venezia has incorporated his own cartoon-style illustrations." SLJ

Rivera, Diego, 1886-1957

★ Tonatiuh, Duncan. **Diego** Rivera; his world and ours. Abrams Books for Young Readers 2011 32p il $15.95

Grades: K 1 2 3   92

1. Artists 2. Painters 3. Artists, Mexican
ISBN 978-0-8109-9731-8; 0-8109-9731-2

LC 2010032618

"Tonatiuh relates key moments in the famous muralist's life and ponders what would capture his interest if he were alive today. The stylized brown figures are shown in pro-file with open mouths, exaggerated features, and heads that seem hinged to the bodies. . . . In scenes both thoughtful and humorous, Tonatiuh contrasts interpretations of Rivera's work with renderings of imagined work today. . . . An in-spired approach that combines child appeal, cultural anthro-pology, and art history." SLJ

Robeson, Paul, 1898-1976

Greenfield, Eloise. **Paul** Robeson; illustrated by George Ford. Lee & Low Books 2009 un il $18.95; pa $9.95

Grades: 2 3 4 5   92

1. Actors 2. Singers 3. Football players 4. Political activists 5. Civil rights activists 6. African Americans -- Biography
ISBN 978-1-60060-256-6; 1-60060-256-8; 978-1-60060-262-7 pa; 1-60060-262-2 pa

LC 2008030420

First published 1975 by HarperCollins

"Vibrant, monochromatic acrylic illustrations . . . use shading and depth to convey tremendous emotion. Powerful movements and vivid expressions enhance the narrative. . . . This book offers a fully developed portrayal of the man." SLJ

Robinson, Jackie, 1919-1972

Amoroso, Cynthia. **Jackie** Robinson; by Cynthia Amo-roso and Robert B. Noyed. Child's World 2010 24p il (Basic biographies) lib bdg $22.79

Grades: PreK K 1   92

1. Baseball players 2. African American athletes 3. Army officers 4. Baseball -- Biography
ISBN 978-1-60253-342-4; 1-60253-342-3

LC 2009029371

This biography of Jackie Robinson "pairs intelligent, brief text with abundant photos. Simple but never basic." Booklist

Includes bibliographical references

★ Burleigh, Robert. **Stealing** home; written by Robert Burleigh; illustrated by Mike Wimmer. Simon & Schuster Books for Young Readers 2007 un il $16.99

Grades: 1 2 3 4   92

1. Baseball players 2. African American athletes 3. Army officers 4. Baseball -- Biography
ISBN 978-0-689-86276-2; 0-689-86276-8

LC 2006-01048

"Burleigh employs two narrative voices, one a spare, lyrical moment-by-moment replay of [Jackie] Robinson's bold steal home from third base in the first game of the 1955 World Series against the New York Yankees. . . . Historical sidebars on each spread supplement this dramatic, immedi-ate account, providing anecdotes about the era, Robinson's struggles . . . plus highlights of his baseball career . . . and personal life. Wimmer's textured, animated oil paintings de-pict the game action at close range and with lifelike clarity." Publ Wkly

O'Sullivan, Robyn. **Jackie** Robinson plays ball; by Robyn O'Sullivan. National Geographic 2007 40p il (Na-tional Geographic history chapters) lib bdg $17.90

Grades: 2 3 4   92

1. Baseball players 2. African American athletes 3. Army officers 4. Baseball -- Biography
ISBN 978-1-4263-0190-2

LC 2007007893

This biography of Jackie Robinson is "nicely illustrated with photos. . . . [It is] just right for emerging chapter-book readers. . . . Useful . . . for reports . . . and interesting pleasure reading." SLJ

Includes glossary and bibliographical references

Robinson, Sharon. **Promises** to keep: how Jackie Robinson changed America. Scholastic 2004 64p il $16.95
Grades: 4 5 6 7   92
  1. Baseball players 2. African American athletes 3. Army officers 4. Baseball -- Biography
  ISBN 0-439-42592-1
LC 2003-42709
"Robinson's daughter, Sharon, describes her father's youth, his rise to become major-league baseball's first African American player, and his involvement in the civil rights movement. . . . Her private view of her father's accomplishments, placed within the context of American sports and social history, makes for absorbing reading. An excellent selection of family and team photographs and other materials . . . illustrate this fine tribute." Booklist

Robinson, Sharon. **Testing** the ice: a true story about Jackie Robinson; illustrated by Kadir Nelson. Scholastic Press 2009 un il $16.99
Grades: 1 2 3 4   92
  1. Baseball players 2. African American athletes 3. Army officers 4. Baseball -- Biography
  ISBN 978-0-545-05251-1; 0-545-05251-3
LC 2008-38838
As a testament to his courage, Jackie Robinson's daughter shares memories of him, from his baseball career to the day he tests the ice for her, her brothers, and their friends.
"Robinson neatly sums up the significance of her father's achievements while depicting him as a loving family man. Nelson's large paintings, done in pencil, watercolor, and oils, dramatically convey Robinson's public persona, the intensely competitive athlete, and contrasts that with the relaxed, yet commanding father Sharon and her brothers knew." SLJ

Romo, Tony, 1980-
Sandler, Michael. **Tony** Romo. Bearport Pub. 2010 24p il (Football heroes making a difference) lib bdg $22.61
Grades: 2 3 4   92
  1. Football players 2. Football -- Biography
  ISBN 978-1-936087-60-0 lib bdg; 1-936087-60-X lib bdg
LC 2009031216
A look at the life and career of the football star.
Includes bibliographical references

Roosevelt, Eleanor, 1884-1962
Fleming, Candace. **Our** Eleanor; a scrapbook look at Eleanor Roosevelt's remarkable life. Atheneum Books for Young Readers 2005 176p il $19.95
Grades: 5 6 7 8   92
  1. Diplomats 2. Columnists 3. Humanitarians 4. Social activists 5. Spouses of presidents 6. United Nations officials
  ISBN 0-689-86544-9
LC 2004-22825
Told in scrapbook style, this biography looks behind the politics to present First Lady Eleanor Roosevelt in her many roles: wife and mother, United Nations delegate, popular columnist, civil rights crusader, and champion of the underprivileged.
"Each of the seven chapters leads readers through the subject's busy life with short sections of text filled with well-documented first-person accounts and direct quotes. .

. . Not a spread goes by without incredible archival photographs or reproductions, newspaper and magazine clippings, handwritten letters, and diary entries. . . . They all provide relevant and fascinating insight." SLJ

★ Rappaport, Doreen. **Eleanor,** quiet no more; written by Doreen Rappaport; illustrated by Gary Kelley. Hyperion 2009 un il $16.99
Grades: 2 3 4 5   92
  1. Diplomats 2. Columnists 3. Humanitarians 4. Social activists 5. Spouses of presidents 6. United Nations officials
  ISBN 978-0-7868-5141-6; 0-7868-5141-4
"The narrative moves swiftly through the important moments in [Eleanor] Roosevelt's life . . . but along with accomplishments, Rappaport does something more subtle—she shows the way Eleanor grew into herself. Crisp sentences focus the narrative and are bolstered by the quotes that end each page. . . . The accompanying art is composed of rich, beautifully crafted paintings that also catch Roosevelt's growing sense of purpose." Booklist

Roosevelt, Franklin D. (Franklin Delano), 1882-1945
Krull, Kathleen. A **boy** named FDR; how Franklin D. Roosevelt grew up to change America. illustrated by Steve Johnson & Lou Fancher. Alfred A. Knopf 2010 un il $17.99; lib bdg $20.99
Grades: 3 4 5   92
  1. Governors 2. Presidents 3. Handicapped 4. Philatelists 5. Presidents -- United States
  ISBN 978-0-375-85716-4; 0-375-85716-8; 978-0-375-95716-1 lib bdg; 0-375-95716-2 lib bdg
LC 2009-22089
Focuses on Franklin D. Roosevelt's childhood years and summarizes his achievements as president.
"Full-page, painterly artwork evokes the times and the determination of FDR, and Krull has a knack for ferreting out interesting anecdotes that humanize the facts. Informative backmatter provides a dated list of his life and famous words and sources. Well done." Kirkus

Panchyk, Richard. **Franklin** Delano Roosevelt for kids; his life and times with 21 activities. [by] Richard Panchyk. Chicago Review Press 2007 147p il pa $14.95
Grades: 4 5 6 7   92
  1. Governors 2. Presidents 3. Handicapped 4. Philatelists
  ISBN 978-1-55652-657-2 pa; 1-55652-657-1 pa
LC 2007003484
"There are many interesting photos . . . and they are all sufficiently captioned. . . . Information about the Roosevelts [is] presented in a lively, engaging manner." SLJ
Includes bibliographical references

St. George, Judith. **Make** your mark, Franklin Roosevelt; [by] Judith St. George; illustrated by Britt Spencer. Philomel Books 2007 un il $16.99
Grades: 2 3 4   92
  1. Governors 2. Presidents 3. Handicapped 4. Philatelists
  ISBN 978-0-399-24175-8; 0-399-24175-2
LC 2006008921
"This illustrated biography . . . explores . . . the influences that shaped Roosevelt's life with stories that will delight

young readers. . . . Throughout, Spencer's spirited water-color, gouache, and ink illustrations bring to life the culture and background of this American icon." SLJ

Includes bibliographical references

Roosevelt, Theodore, 1858-1919

★ Brown, Don. **Teedie**; the story of young Teddy Roosevelt. Houghton Mifflin Books for Children 2009 un il $16

Grades: 2 3 4   92
1. Governors 2. Presidents 3. Vice-presidents 4. Nobel laureates for peace
ISBN 978-0-618-17999-2; 0-618-17999-2
                                           LC 2008033879

"Teedie led a privileged life in one of New York City's wealthiest households, but was a sickly child. His asthma didn't stop him from being curious or from reading widely. . . . Teedie became Teddy when he entered Harvard University in 1876. After graduation, Roosevelt sought his own way. . . . He traveled, became an outdoorsman, a politician, and ultimately the youngest president of the United States. Line and wash illustrations add movement and a playful tone to the serious text, which generously incorporates quotes from Roosevelt." SLJ

Includes bibliographical references

Elish, Dan. **Theodore** Roosevelt; by Dan Elish. Marshall Cavendish Benchmark 2008 96p il (Presidents and their times) lib bdg $22.95

Grades: 5 6 7 8   92
1. Governors 2. Presidents 3. Vice-presidents 4. Nobel laureates for peace
ISBN 978-0-7614-2429-1
                                           LC 2006012987

A biography of the president
"Primary-source materials and quotes, helpful insets, and carefully selected photographs and/or reproductions bring history to life and help make [this] clearly written [biography] highly readable." SLJ

Includes glossary and bibliographical references

Fritz, Jean. **Bully** for you, Teddy Roosevelt! illustrations by Mike Wimmer. Putnam 1991 127p il hardcover o.p. pa $5.99

Grades: 5 6 7 8   92
1. Governors 2. Presidents 3. Vice-presidents 4. Nobel laureates for peace
ISBN 0-399-21769-X; 0-698-11609-7 pa
                                           LC 90-8142

Follows the life of the twenty-sixth president, discussing his conservation work, hunting expeditions, family life, and political career

"Jean Fritz gives a rounded picture of her subject and deftly blends the story of a person and a picture of an era." Bull Cent Child Books

Includes bibliographical references

Harness, Cheryl. The **remarkable**, rough-riding life of Theodore Roosevelt and the rise of empire America; painstakingly written and illustrated by Cheryl Harness. National Geographic 2007 144p il map $16.95; lib bdg $25.90

Grades: 4 5 6 7   92
1. Governors 2. Presidents 3. Vice-presidents 4.

Nobel laureates for peace 5. Presidents -- United States
ISBN 978-1-4263-0008-0; 1-4263-0008-5; 978-1-4263-0009-7 lib bdg; 1-4263-0009-3 lib bdg
                                           LC 2006029039

"Animated writing and intricate black-and-white illustrations drive this biography of the ever-enthusiastic twenty-sixth president of the United States. An extensive running timeline at the bottom of the pages emphasizes the dramatic changes that occurred during Roosevelt's life. The book is jam-packed with information." Horn Book Guide

Includes bibliographical references

Hollihan, Kerrie Logan. **Theodore** Roosevelt for kids; his life and times + 21 activities. Chicago Review Press 2010 133p il pa $16.95

Grades: 5 6 7 8   92
1. Governors 2. Handicraft 3. Presidents 4. Vice-presidents 5. Nobel laureates for peace
ISBN 978-1-55652-955-9 pa; 1-55652-955-4 pa

"What stands out in this volume is the writing, which presents history as an engaging and informative story. . . . The projects are interesting and accessible. . . . Both useful and entertaining, this is a worthy addition to most collections." SLJ

Keating, Frank. **Theodore**; illustrated by Mike Wimmer. Simon & Schuster Books for Young Readers 2006 un il $16.95

Grades: K 1 2 3   92
1. Governors 2. Presidents 3. Vice-presidents 4. Nobel laureates for peace
ISBN 0-689-86532-5
                                           LC 2003-17046

A picture book biography of the 26th president of the United States
"This handsome, well-researched biography is as dignified as its subject. Using a spare, readable style, the author captures Roosevelt's spirit and determination." SLJ

★ Kerley, Barbara. **What** to do about Alice? how Alice Roosevelt broke the rules, charmed the world, and drove her father Teddy crazy! illustrated by Edwin Fotheringham. Scholastic Press 2008 un il $16.99

Grades: K 1 2 3   92
1. Presidents -- United States -- Family
ISBN 978-0-439-92231-9; 0-439-92231-3
                                           LC 2006-38372

Boston Globe-Horn Book Award honor book: Nonfiction (2008)

"The daughter of Theodore Roosevelt, . . . Alice had a joie de vivre that she called 'eating up the world.' . . . Kerley's text has the same rambunctious spirit as its subject. . . . The large format gives Fotheringhame . . . plenty of room for spectacular art, which includes use of digital media." Booklist

St. George, Judith. **You're** on your way, Teddy Roosevelt! illustrated by Matt Faulkner. Philomel Books 2004 un il $16.99

Grades: 2 3 4   92
1. Governors 2. Presidents 3. Vice-presidents 4.

Nobel laureates for peace

ISBN 0-399-23888-3

LC 2003-21534

"St. George's skill in presenting information with a light touch keeps the pace lively, while Faulkner's gouache illustrations . . . further animate the narrative." Horn Book Guide

Includes bibliographical references

Wade, Mary Dodson. **Amazing** president Theodore Roosevelt. Enslow Publishers 2009 24p il (Amazing Americans) lib bdg $21.26

Grades: 1 2 3   92

1. Governors 2. Presidents 3. Vice-presidents 4. Nobel laureates for peace

ISBN 978-0-7660-3284-2 lib bdg; 0-7660-3284-1 lib bdg

LC 2008-24892

"Colorful photos are found throughout, with a timeline, dictionary, websites concerning the topic, as well as an index making . . . [this] book a wonderful introduction to nonfiction features." Libr Media Connect

Includes glossary

Wadsworth, Ginger. **Camping** with the president; illustrated by Karen Dugan. Calkins Creek 2009 32p il $16.95

Grades: 3 4 5   92

1. Authors 2. Governors 3. Presidents 4. Naturalists 5. Vice-presidents 6. Environmental movement 7. National parks and reserves 8. Writers on nature 9. Nobel laureates for peace

ISBN 978-1-59078-497-6; 1-59078-497-9

LC 2008024155

"Inspired by conservationist John Muir's nature essays, President Theodore Roosevelt traveled west, visiting national parks and learing more about their resources. Wadsworth's well written, lively account highlights the pair's 1903 exploration of the Yosemite wilderness, as well as America's early conservation movement, in an accessible and engaging picture book for older readers. Dugan's abundant, intricately rendered watercolors portray the stunning vistas and wildlife and are set against white backgrounds." Booklist

Includes bibliographical references

Ross, Betsy, 1752-1836

White, Becky. **Betsy** Ross; illustrated by Megan Lloyd. Holiday House 2011 il $16.95

Grades: K 1 2   92

1. Generals 2. Presidents 3. Dressmakers 4. Needleworkers 5. Flags -- United States

ISBN 978-0-8234-1908-1; 0-8234-1908-8

LC 2009054296

"Fourteen spreads with four to six rhythmic words on each one tell the story of the first American flag. . . . The large, simple text, paired with the irresistible appliqué art, makes this a perfect introduction to the Stars and Stripes. Using cotton fabric, embroidery thread, dye, paint, and linoleum-block prints, Lloyd captures the period, hard work, and ingenuity of this favorite colonial figure." SLJ

Rothschild, Lionel Walter Rothschild, Baron, 1868-1937

Judge, Lita. **Strange** creatures; the story of Walter Rothschild and his museum. Hyperion 2011 un il $17.99

Grades: 1 2 3   92

1. Zoology 2. Zoologists 3. Members of Parliament

ISBN 1-4231-1389-6; 978-1-4231-1389-8

This is a biography of the British zoologist and banker. Rothschild "used his own income to finance [zoological] expeditions and ultimately built a museum to house his collection on the family's grounds. . . . Ages five to eight." (Bull Cent Child Books)

"Walter Rothschild, the shy eldest son of Lord Nathan Rothschild, never took an interest in the family banking business, instead developing an all-consuming veneration for the wild; at age seven, he began collecting living animals like kangaroos and kiwi birds for his 'museum.' Judge's expressive watercolors convey Rothschild's inquisitiveness and his parents' angst over such mishaps as a giant lizard escape. . . . Children should get a kick out of this 19th-century misfit who relentlessly pursued his unconventional passion." Publ Wkly

Rowling, J. K., 1965-

Peterson-Hilleque, Victoria. **J.K.** Rowling, extraordinary author. ABDO Pub. Company 2010 112p il (Essential lives) $32.79

Grades: 5 6 7 8   92

1. Authors 2. Novelists 3. Women authors 4. Fantasy writers 5. Authors, English 6. Children's authors 7. Young adult authors

ISBN 978-1-61613-517-1; 1-61613-517-4

LC 2010000503

This biography of author J. K. Rowling "toggles between the subject's personal and professional life. . . . [The book] offers sidebar . . . definitions of particular characters or events in the 'Harry Potter' series. The writing is accessible, the format is open, and full-color photos appear throughout." SLJ

Includes glossary and bibliographical references

Rudolph, Wilma, 1940-1994

★ Krull, Kathleen. **Wilma** unlimited: how Wilma Rudolph became the world's fastest woman; illustrated by David Diaz. Harcourt Brace & Co. 1996 un il $17; pa $7

Grades: 2 3 4   92

1. Women athletes 2. African American athletes 3. Olympic athletes 4. Runners (Athletes) 5. Track athletics -- Biography

ISBN 0-15-201267-2; 0-15-202098-5 pa

LC 95-32105

A biography of the African-American woman who overcame crippling polio as a child to become the first woman to win three gold medals in track in a single Olympics

"Brightly colored paintings contrast with sepia-toned photographic backgrounds, creating juxtapositions that extend both the text and the pictures in the foreground. Krull's understated conversational style is perfectly suited to Rudolph's remarkable and inspiring story." Horn Book Guide

Wade, Mary Dodson. **Amazing** Olympic athlete Wilma Rudolph. Enslow Publishers 2009 24p il (Amazing Americans) lib bdg $21.26

Grades: 1 2 3   92

1. Women athletes 2. Track athletics 3. African American athletes 4. Olympic athletes 5. Runners

(Athletes)
ISBN 978-0-7660-3282-8 lib bdg; 0-7660-3282-5
lib bdg

LC 2008-24890

"The book features a design that is clear and inviting with a full-page photo on every double-page spread." Booklist

Includes glossary and bibliographical references

Rustin, Bayard, 1910-1987

★ Brimner, Larry Dane. **We** are one: the story of Bayard Rustin. Calkins Creek 2007 48p il $17.95

Grades: 5 6 7 8   92

1. Civil rights activists 2. African Americans -- Biography 3. African Americans -- Civil rights
ISBN 1-59078-498-7

"Brimner sets Rustin's personal story against the history of segregation in his time and focuses on his leadership role . . . in the struggle for civil rights. On each page, the clearly written, informal text is accompanied by eloquently captioned archival photos." Booklist

Includes bibliographical references

Ruth, Babe, 1895-1948

Yomtov, Nelson. The **Bambino**: the story of Babe Ruth's legendary 1927 season; illustrated by Tim Foley. Capstone Press 2011 32p il (Graphic library: American graphic) lib bdg $29.32; pa $7.95

Grades: 4 5 6 7   92

1. Baseball players 2. Biographical graphic novels 3. Baseball -- Biography
ISBN 978-1-4296-5473-9 lib bdg; 1-4296-5473-2 lib bdg; 978-1-4296-6265-9 pa; 1-4296-6265-4 pa

LC 2010024764

In graphic novel format, follows Babe Ruth through the 1927 season and describes his attempt to break his own home run record.

"The illustrations are eye-catching and the narration is presented simply, yet compellingly. . . . Fact-filled, entertaining, and accessible." SLJ

Includes glossary and bibliographical references

Sís, Peter, 1949-

★ Sís, Peter, 1949- The **wall**; growing up behind the Iron Curtain. Farrar, Straus and Giroux 2007 un il $18

Grades: 4 5 6 7 8 9 10   92

1. Artists 2. Authors 3. Cold war 4. Animators 5. Illustrators 6. Set designers 7. Children's authors
ISBN 978-0-374-34701-7; 0-374-34701-8

LC 2006-49149

Boston Globe-Horn Book Award: Nonfiction (2008)

"The author pairs his remarkable artistry with journal entries, historical context and period photography to create a powerful account of his childhood in Cold War-era Prague." Publ Wkly

Saint-Georges, Joseph Boulogne, chevalier de, 1745-1799

Brewster, Hugh. The **other** Mozart; the life of the famous Chevalier de Saint George. [by] Hugh Brewster; illustrated by Eric Velasquez. Abrams Books for Young Readers 2007 48p il $18.95

Grades: 4 5 6 7   92

1. Nobility 2. Composers 3. Violinists 4. Racially

mixed people
ISBN 978-0-8109-5720-6; 0-8109-5720-5

LC 2006-07488

"Born to a white plantation owner and a black slave in eighteenth-century Guadeloupe, Joseph Bologne grew up to become the Chevalier de Saint-George, one of France's most accomplished composers. In this picture-book biography for middle-graders, Brewster introduces his subject's fascinating life. . . . Archival images and Velasquez's arresting full-page portraits will captivate many young readers." Booklist

★ Cline-Ransome, Lesa. **Before** there was Mozart: the story of Joseph Boulogne, Chevalier de Saint-George; illustrated by James Ransome. Schwartz & Wade Books 2011 un il $17.99; lib bdg $20.99

Grades: 1 2 3 4   92

1. Nobility 2. Composers 3. Violinists 4. Racially mixed people
ISBN 978-0-375-83600-8; 0-375-83600-4; 978-0-375-93621-0 lib bdg; 0-375-93621-1 lib bdg

LC 2008-48825

"Born in Guadeloupe, Joseph Boulogne was the son of a black slave and a white plantation owner of French nobility. When Joseph's family moved to France, he enrolled in school and, despite facing racial prejudice, devoted himself to mastering the violin. . . . Joseph composed six operas (as well as other pieces of music), stood before audiences on the same stages as Mozart, and performed before Louis XVI and Marie Antoinette. Ransome's mixed-media paintings join tropical motifs with the sumptuous colors and prints of affluent Paris society, and his faces glow with vitality. Readers will likely marvel at why such a compelling figure has not received more attention." Publ Wkly

Santos-Dumont, Alberto, 1873-1932

Griffith, Victoria. The **fabulous** flying machines of Alberto Santos-Dumont; illustrated by Eva Montanari. Abrams Books for Young Readers 2011 il $16.95

Grades: 1 2 3 4   92

1. Airships 2. Engineers 3. Inventors 4. Air pilots 5. Aeronautics -- History
ISBN 978-1-4197-0011-8; 1-4197-0011-1

LC 2010048781

"Dumont is credited as being the first one to get an airplane off the ground under its own power, in 1906. In this fictionalized account, readers learn of the man's idiosyncratic and highly inventive nature. Although he was born in Brazil, he later made Paris his home where he became a larger-than-life personality, partly because of his reputation for—and the spectacle of—his chosen mode of transportation to run everyday errands: a dirigible. His quest to move through the air at a faster pace and for greater distances led to his invention of a biplane. . . . Montanari captures the look, dress, and formality of the era in her splendid, impressionistic pastel, chalk, and oil paintings. The endnotes add details and facts about the life of this charismatic, adventurous man and mark his place in aviation history." SLJ

Includes bibliographical references

Sarg, Tony, 1882-1942

★ Sweet, Melissa. **Balloons** over Broadway; the true story of the puppeteer of Macy's Parade. Houghton Mifflin Books for Children 2011 40p il $16.99

Grades: K 1 2   92
1. Artists 2. Parades 3. Illustrators 4. Thanksgiving
Day 5. Puppets and puppet plays 6. Puppeteers
ISBN 978-0-547-19945-0; 0-547-19945-7
LC 2010044181
Flora Stieglitz Straus Award (2012); Golden Kite Award:
Picture Book Illustration (2011); Lupine Award (Maine):
Picture Book (2011); Robert F. Sibert Informational Book
Medal (2012)

"Tony Sarg . . . the man who invented the giant balloons of the Macy's Thanksgiving Day Parade, has found a
worthy biographer in . . . Sweet. . . . With lighthearted watercolors, fanciful scrapbooking, and collaged typography,
Sweet shows how Sarg, a self-taught immigrant, combined
an indomitable curiosity with an engineer's know-how and a
forever-young imagination. The story walks readers through
each stage of Sarg's development as a master of puppetry—
his childhood fascination with mechanics and marionettes,
his first big break as a developer of window displays for Macy's, and his early earthbound parade creations (essentially
air-filled rubber bags that were steered down the street). . .
. Sweet captures it all in what is truly a story for all ages."
Publ Wkly

Sasaki, Sadako, 1943-1955
Coerr, Eleanor. **Sadako**; illustrated by Ed Young. Put-
nam 1993 un il $17.95; pa $6.99
Grades: 1 2 3 4   92
1. Children 2. Leukemia 3. Leukemia patients 4.
Atomic bomb -- Physiological effect 5. Hiroshima
(Japan) -- Bombardment, 1945 -- Juvenile literature
ISBN 0-399-21771-1; 0-698-11588-0 pa
LC 92-41483
"This is the same story as the author's Sadako and the
Thousand Paper Cranes, told through an entirely new text.
In this abbreviated version, the beautiful, limpid prose and
crisp dialogue further telescope Sadako's fight with leuke-
mia. . . . Young's pastels vividly capture all the moods of the
narrative, place, and characters. . . . A masterful collabora-
tion." SLJ

★ Coerr, Eleanor. **Sadako** and the thousand paper
cranes; paintings by Ronald Himler. Putnam 1977 64p il
$16.99; pa $5.99
Grades: 3 4 5 6   92
1. Children 2. Leukemia 3. Leukemia patients 4.
Atomic bomb -- Physiological effect
ISBN 0-399-20520-9; 0-698-11802-2 pa
LC 76-9872
"A story about a young girl of Hiroshima who died from
leukemia ten years after the dropping of the atom bomb. Her
dreams of being an outstanding runner are dimmed when
she learns she has the fatal disease. But her spunk and bravery, symbolized in her efforts to have faith in the story of
the golden crane, are beautifully portrayed by the author."
Babbling Bookworm

Savage, Augusta Christine, 1892-1962
Schroeder, Alan. **In** her hands; the story of sculptor
Augusta Savage. illustrated by JaeMe Bereal. Lee & Low
Books 2009 un il $19.95
Grades: 3 4 5 6   92
1. Artists 2. Sculptors 3. Women artists 4. Harlem

Renaissance 5. African American artists
ISBN 978-1-60060-332-7; 1-60060-332-7
LC 2009003859
"Young readers will . . . find this a solid introduction to
the art world and a daring but lesser-known African American artist. Bereal's . . . expansive, richly hued one and two-
page spreads fit nicely with the text and deftly capture the
emotions of the story." Booklist

Schaller, George B.
Turner, Pamela S. A **life** in the wild; George Schaller's
struggle to save the last great beasts. Farrar, Straus and Giroux 2008 103p il map $21.95
Grades: 5 6 7 8   92
1. Zoologists 2. Wildlife conservation 3. Nonfiction
writers 4. Animal behavior -- Juvenile literature
ISBN 978-0-374-34578-5; 0-374-34578-3
LC 2007-42844
"The author interviewed Schaller and had access to his
photos, which allowed her to capture beautifully the spirit
of Schaller's work. The book is organized chronologically,
and each chapter covers a geographic area and the principal
animals that Schaller studied there. . . . Animal lovers and
conservation-minded students will enjoy this excellent introduction to Schaller and his ideals." Voice Youth Advocates
Includes bibliographical references

Schliemann, Heinrich, 1822-1890
★ Schlitz, Laura Amy. The **hero** Schliemann; the
dreamer who dug for Troy. illustrated by Robert Byrd. Can-
dlewick Press 2006 72p il $12.23
Grades: 4 5 6   92
1. Archeologists 2. Excavations (Archeology) 3.
Archaeologists 4. Excavations (Archaeology) -- Turkey
-- Troy (Extinct city) -- Juvenile literature
ISBN 0-7636-2283-4
LC 2005046916
This is a biography of the archaeologist who rediscov-
ered ancient Troy. "Intermediate." (Horn Book)
"In this slim biography, Schlitz introduces Heinrich
Schliemann, a nineteenth-century 'storyteller, archaeologist,
and crook,' who led a search for the lost cities of Homer's
epic poems." Booklist
Includes bibliographical references

Schulz, Charles M.
Amoroso, Cynthia. **Charles** Schulz; by Cynthia Amo-
roso and Robert B. Noyed. Child's World 2010 24p il
(Basic biographies) lib bdg $22.79
Grades: PreK K 1   92
1. Cartoonists
ISBN 978-1-60253-340-0; 1-60253-340-7
LC 2009029366
A biography of the cartoonist who created Charlie
Brown in the strip "Peanuts."
This "pairs intelligent, brief text with abundant photos.
Simple but never basic." Booklist
Includes bibliographical references

★ Gherman, Beverly. **Sparky**: the life and art of
Charles Schulz. Chronicle Books 2010 125p il $16.99
Grades: 5 6 7 8   92
1. Cartoonists
ISBN 978-0-8118-6790-0; 0-8118-6790-0

A look at the life and influences of Charles Schulz, creator of the beloved comic strip Peanuts.

"Gherman's clear and direct prose is just right for portraying the life of the famous cartoonist for young readers. The splashy, bright design, with multicolored pages and several of Schulz's cartoons included, makes this a cheery read that may well introduce the Peanuts comic strip to a new generation, who likely know Charlie Brown mostly through the holiday TV specials. An informative yet lighthearted look at the life of an American icon." Kirkus

Scidmore, Eliza Ruhamah, 1856-1928

Zimmerman, Andrea. **Eliza's** cherry trees; Japan's gift to America. illustrated by Ju Hong Chen. Pelican Pub. Co. 2011 un il $16.99

Grades: 3 4 5 6   92
1. Photographers 2. Cherry trees 3. Travel writers
ISBN 1-58980-954-8; 978-1-58980-954-3

LC 2010046163

"This is an inspiring, heartwarming story of determination and spirit. The writing flows well, and the lush illustrations are reminiscent of Impressionist paintings." SLJ

Scieszka, Jon, 1954-

Scieszka, Jon. **Knucklehead**; tall tales and mostly true stories of growing up Scieszka. Viking 2008 106p il $16.99; pa $12.99

Grades: 4 5 6 7   92
1. Authors 2. Authors, American 3. Children's authors
ISBN 978-0-670-01106-3; 0-670-01106-1; 978-0-670-01138-4 pa; 0-670-01138-X pa

LC 2008-16870

"Scieszka . . . has written an autobiography about boys, for boys and anyone else interested in baseball, fire and peeing on stuff. . . . The text is divided into two- to three-page nonsequential chapters and peppered with scrapbook snapshots and comic-book-ad reproductions. . . . By themselves, the chapters entertain with abrupt, vulgar fun. Taken together, they offer a look at the makings of one very funny author." Booklist

Scott, Wendell, 1921-1990

Weatherford, Carole Boston. **Racing** against the odds; the story of Wendell Scott, stock car racing's African-American champion. illustrated by Eric A. Velasquez. Marshall Cavendish Children 2009 un il $17.99

Grades: 3 4 5   92
1. Automobile racing 2. African American athletes 3. Automobile racing drivers
ISBN 978-0-76145-465-6; 0-76145-465-9

LC 2008010711

"In this stirring biography of Scott, the only black race car driver to win a NASCAR race, Velasquez's expressive pastels showcase the driver's determination and resourcefulness. . . . With as much attention paid to Scott's life off the track as on, readers won't need to be racing fans to be drawn in." Publ Wkly

Selkirk, Alexander, 1676-1721

★ Kraske, Robert. **Marooned**; the strange but true adventures of Alexander Selkirk, the real Robinson Crusoe. illustrated by Robert Andrew Parker. Clarion Books 2005 120p il map $15

Grades: 5 6 7 8   92
1. Sailors 2. Survival after airplane accidents, shipwrecks, etc.
ISBN 0-618-56843-3

LC 2004-28769

"In 1704, English sailing master Alexander Selkirk was marooned on Juan Fernandez, an isolated Pacific island. . . . In 1709, two English ships rescued him, hired him as a second mate, and later captured a Spanish treasure ship. . . . Kraske offers a well-focused look at life in several quite different settings during the early eighteenth century as well as an absorbing telling of Selkirk's story." Booklist

Includes glossary and bibliographical references

Sendler, Irena, 1910-2008

★ Rubin, Susan Goldman. **Irena** Sendler and the children of the Warsaw Ghetto; illustrated by Bill Farnsworth. Holiday House 2011 40p il $18.95

Grades: 3 4 5 6   92
1. Jews -- Poland 2. Holocaust, 1933-1945 3. World War, 1939-1945 -- Poland 4. World War, 1939-1945 -- Jews -- Rescue
ISBN 978-0-8234-2251-7; 0-8234-2251-8

LC 2010-23667

"Irena Sendler stands out on the list of righteous Gentiles for her incredibly daring methods of hiding and transporting nearly 400 babies and children out of Nazi-occupied Poland. . . . Rubin's documentary-style narrative is smoothly interspersed with dialogue taken from interviews conducted with many of the now-adult survivors. . . . Farnsworth's moody oil renditions authentically capture the tension, fear, despair and darkness of the period." Kirkus

Vaughan, Marcia. **Irena's** jars of secrets; illustrated by Ron Mazellan. Lee & Low Books 2011 il $18.95

Grades: 3 4 5   92
1. Humanitarians 2. Jews -- Poland 3. Holocaust, 1933-1945 4. World War, 1939-1945 -- Children 5. World War, 1939-1945 -- Jews -- Rescue
ISBN 978-1-60060-439-3; 1-60060-439-0

LC 2011016386

"Vaughan tells the true story without embellishment, employing stark, unadorned syntax that never wavers into pathos, sentiment or myth. It is a definition of quiet heroism. Mazellan's very dark, deeply shadowed oil paintings capture the unabated terror and sorrow. Children should read this work with an adult who is armed with some knowledge of the material. Powerful." Kirkus

Sequoyah, 1770?-1843

★ Rumford, James. **Sequoyah**; the Cherokee man who gave his people writing. Houghton Mifflin 2004 un il $16

Grades: 1 2 3 4   92
1. Cherokee Indians 2. Artisans 3. Metalworkers 4. Indian leaders
ISBN 0-618-36947-3

LC 2004-00980

"Rumford presents the seminal events in Sequoyah's life, culminating in his invention of the Cherokee syllabary. The author writes with a concise eloquence that echoes the oral tradition and makes this one of those rare gems of read-aloud nonfiction. . . . Done in ink, watercolor, pastel, and pencil, the illustrations were adhered to a rough piece of wood, and its textures were highlighted through the use of chalk and colored pencil. . . . The parallel text in Cherokee . . . makes this beautiful book readily accessible to Cherokee children in their own language." SLJ

Wade, Mary Dodson. **Amazing** Cherokee writer Sequoyah. Enslow Publishers 2009 24p il (Amazing Americans) lib bdg $21.26

Grades: 1 2 3   **92**

    1. Cherokee Indians 2. Artisans 3. Metalworkers 4. Indian leaders

    ISBN 978-0-7660-3285-9 lib bdg; 0-7660-3285-X lib bdg

                                      LC 2008-24893

"Colorful photos are found throughout, with a timeline, dictionary, websites concerning the topic, as well as an index making . . . [this] book a wonderful introduction to nonfiction features." Libr Media Connect

    Includes glossary

Seuss, Dr., 1904-1991

Cohen, Charles D. The **Seuss,** the whole Seuss, and nothing but the Seuss; a visual biography of Theodor Seuss Geisel. Random House 2004 390p il $35; lib bdg $36.99

Grades: Adult Professional   **92**

    1. Artists 2. Authors 3. Humorists 4. Illustrators 5. Authors, American 6. Children's authors 7. Children's literature -- Authorship 8. Artists -- United States -- Biography 9. Illustration of books -- United States 10. Authors, American -- 20th century -- Biography

    ISBN 0-375-82248-8; 0-375-92248-2 lib bdg

                                        LC 2003-20526

This is a "profile of the creator of Horton, the Grinch, and the Cat in the Hat. . . . Crisp full-color illustrations on every page of the coffee-table volume will pull readers into Cohen's accessible recap of Theodore Geisel's career, which is enhanced with just enough personal information to bring everything together. . . . [The volume includes] clear reproductions of posters, book illustrations, newspaper cartoons, and book pages, with intriguing background information." Booklist

★ Krull, Kathleen. The **boy** on Fairfield Street; how Ted Geisel grew up to become Dr. Seuss; paintings by Steve Johnson and Lou Fancher; with decorative illustrations by Dr. Seuss. Random House 2004 43p il $16.95; lib bdg $18.99

Grades: K 1 2 3   **92**

    1. Artists 2. Authors 3. Humorists 4. Illustrators 5. Authors, American 6. Children's authors

    ISBN 0-375-82298-4; 0-375-92298-9 lib bdg

                                        LC 2003-1754

Introduces the life of renowned children's author and illustrator Ted Geisel, popularly known as Dr. Seuss, focusing on his childhood and youth in Springfield, Massachusetts

"Johnson and Fancher's lovely, full-page illustrations are supplemented by samples of Dr. Seuss's artwork. . . . Krull's work is a terrific look at the boyhood of one of the most beloved author/illustrators of the 20th century." SLJ

Sewall, May Wright, 1844-1920

Boomhower, Ray E. **Fighting** for equality; a life of May Wright Sewall. [by] Ray E. Boomhower. Indiana Historical Society Press 2007 160p il $17.95

Grades: 4 5 6   **92**

    1. Feminism 2. Educators 3. Reformers 4. Suffragists

    5. Lecturers 6. Pacifists

    ISBN 978-0-87195-253-0; 0-87195-253-X

                                        LC 2007008517

"This accessible volume tells of the life and work of suffragist and educator [May] Wright Sewall. . . . Archival black-and-white photos enhance the text." Horn Book Guide

    Includes bibliographical references

Shakur, Tupac

Harris, Ashley Rae. **Tupac** Shakur; multi-platinum rapper. ABDO Pub. Co. 2010 112p il (Lives cut short) lib bdg $32.79

Grades: 5 6 7 8   **92**

    1. Poets 2. Actors 3. Hip-hop 4. Rap music 5. African American musicians 6. Rap musicians

    ISBN 978-1-60453-791-8; 1-60453-791-4

This discusses Tupac Shakur's early life, "providing details that give insight into later success and troubles and maintaining a laudatory tone that focuses on the individual's artistic achievements and hard work to achieve fame. Details [such as] explaining . . . that Tupac Shakur was a standout student in high school are bound to resonate with readers. Numerous photos and sidebars appear throughout. [A] worthwhile [resource] for reports as well as popular reading." SLJ

Shuster, Joe, 1914-1992

★ Nobleman, Marc Tyler. **Boys** of steel; the creators of Superman. illustrated by Ross MacDonald. Knopf 2008 un il $16.99; lib bdg $19.99

Grades: 1 2 3   **92**

    1. Artists 2. Cartoonists 3. Illustrators 4. Superman (Fictional character) 5. Comic book writers

    ISBN 978-0-375-83802-6; 0-375-83802-3; 978-0-375-93802-3 lib bdg; 0-375-93802-8 lib bdg

                                        LC 2007041606

"This book brings the young men behind the Man of Steel to a picture-book audience. Along with the compressed account of the partnership between nerdy high-school outcasts Joe Shuster and Jerry Siegel, Nobleman includes insights about superheroes' cultural significance and the chord struck by Superman. . . . It's hard to imagine a better sidekick for the text than MacDonald's illustrations, which capture the look of 1930s comics with their sepia-toned, stylized imagery." Booklist

Siegel, Jerry, 1914-1996

★ Nobleman, Marc Tyler. **Boys** of steel; the creators of Superman. illustrated by Ross MacDonald. Knopf 2008 un il $16.99; lib bdg $19.99

Grades: 1 2 3   **92**

    1. Artists 2. Cartoonists 3. Illustrators 4. Superman (Fictional character) 5. Comic book writers

    ISBN 978-0-375-83802-6; 0-375-83802-3; 978-0-375-93802-3 lib bdg; 0-375-93802-8 lib bdg

                                        LC 2007041606

"This book brings the young men behind the Man of Steel to a picture-book audience. Along with the compressed account of the partnership between nerdy high-school outcasts Joe Shuster and Jerry Siegel, Nobleman includes insights about superheroes' cultural significance and the chord struck by Superman. . . . It's hard to imagine a better sidekick for the text than MacDonald's illustrations, which capture the look of 1930s comics with their sepia-toned, stylized imagery." Booklist

Sikorsky, Igor

Wyckoff, Edwin Brit. **Helicopter** man: Igor Sikorsky and his amazing invention. Enslow 2010 32p il (Genius at work! Great inventor biographies) lib bdg $22.60
Grades: 4 5 6   92
1. Helicopters 2. Aeronautical engineers 3. Aeronautics -- History 4. Aircraft industry executives
ISBN 978-0-7660-3445-7; 0-7660-3445-3
LC 2009-15881
This is the story of Igor Sikorsky's life, and how he built the first successful helicopter.
Includes glossary and bibliographical references

Sitting Bull, Dakota Chief, 1831-1890

Bruchac, Joseph. A **boy** called Slow: the true story of Sitting Bull; illustrated by Rocco Baviera. Philomel Bks. 1994 un il $16.99; pa $6.99
Grades: 1 2 3   92
1. Dakota Indians 2. Indian chiefs
ISBN 0-399-22692-3; 0-698-11616-X pa
LC 93-21233
The author "recounts the early years of the young Lakota boy who grows from an unprepossessing child named 'Slow,' to a youth whose careful and deliberate actions bring honor to the name, to a young warrior whose courage in defeating the Crow earns him his father's vision name Tatan'ka Iyota'ke—Sitting Bull." Bull Cent Child Books

Turner, Ann Warren. **Sitting** Bull remembers; paintings by Wendell Minor. HarperCollinsPublishers 2007 un il $16.99; lib bdg $17.89
Grades: 3 4 5 6   92
1. Dakota Indians 2. Little Bighorn, Battle of the, 1876 3. Indian chiefs
ISBN 978-0-06-051399-3; 0-06-051399-3; 978-0-06-051400-6 lib bdg; 0-06-051400-0 lib bdg
LC 2006-29870
"In this first-person, fictionalized account, Sitting Bull is living in captivity near the end of his life and remembering his past. . . . Turner's writing is lyrical, almost poetic. The story is poignant and sympathetic to the plight of the Native peoples who were driven from their land and forced to live on tiny reservations. . . . The well-crafted art adds drama and depth to the story." SLJ

Smalls, Robert, 1839-1915

Halfmann, Janet. **Seven** miles to freedom; the Robert Smalls story. by Janet Halfmann; illustrated by Duane Smith. Lee & Low Books 2008 un il $17.95
Grades: 3 4 5   92
1. Slaves 2. State legislators 3. Members of Congress 4. Slavery -- United States 5. African Americans -- Biography 6. African Americans -- Civil rights
ISBN 978-1-60060-232-0; 1-60060-232-0
LC 2007029274
This "will grab readers with exciting action. . . . Spacious, impressionistic oil paintings accompany [the] text." Booklist

Smith, Elinor, 1911-2010

★ Brown, Tami Lewis. **Soar**, Elinor! pictures by François Roca. Farrar Straus Giroux 2010 un il $16.99

Grades: 2 3 4 5   92
1. Air pilots 2. Women air pilots
ISBN 978-0-374-37115-9; 0-374-37115-6
LC 2008-30405
"Elinor Smith began talking flying lessons in 1921 when she was only 10 years old. At 16, she was the youngest person in the U.S., man or woman, to earn a pilot's license. The climax of this picture-book biography is when Smith achieved acclaim as the first person to fly a plane under . . . four of New York City's bridges. . . . Brown's narration is fluent, engaging, and full of dialogue. . . . [The book features] realistic oil illustrations. . . . Roca uses minimal background detail and skillfully arranges scenes to focus attention on the emotions and faces of the characters while still maintaining historical and geographical accuracy." SLJ
Includes bibliographical references

Smith, Louise, 1916-2006

★ Rosenstock, Barbara. **Fearless**; the story of racing legend Louise Smith. [by] Barb Rosenstock; illustrated by Scott Dawson. Dutton Children's Books 2010 un il $16.99
Grades: K 1 2   92
1. Automobile racing 2. Automobile drivers 3. Automobile racing drivers
ISBN 978-0-525-42173-3; 0-525-42173-4
LC 2009-53252
"Dawson's gorgeous, light-infused acrylics convey Louise's self-assured nature, while race scenes capture the rush of adrenaline in a blur of glinting metal. Rosenstock's upbeat prose finishes on a high note, with aging Louise flying down a country road. . . . This debut for both author and illustrator is a winner." Publ Wkly

Sneve, Virginia Driving Hawk

Sneve, Virginia Driving Hawk. The **Christmas** coat; memories of my Sioux childhood. illustrated by Ellen Beier. Holiday House 2011 un il $16.95
Grades: K 1 2 3   92
1. Authors 2. Christmas 3. Novelists 4. Dakota Indians 5. Clothing and dress 6. Christmas stories 7. Children's authors 8. Young adult authors 9. Native Americans -- Biography
ISBN 978-0-8234-2134-3; 0-8234-2134-1
LC 2010029562
Virginia's coat is too small and hardly protects her from the frigid South Dakota winter. As Christmas approaches, all the children on the Sioux reservation look forward to receiving boxes full of clothing sent by congregations in the East. Virginia spots a beautiful gray fur coat but holds back tears as it is claimed by one of her classmates. Later, Virginia can't believe what Mama brings home. Based on an event from the author's childhood.
"Virginia's personality shines through in this poignant story that entertains and informs without recourse to sterotypes." Kirkus

Snyder, Grace, 1882-1982

Warren, Andrea. **Pioneer** girl; a true story of growing up on the prairie. with a new afterword by the author. University of Nebraska Press 2009 104p il map pa $14.95
Grades: 5 6 7 8   92
1. Frontier and pioneer life 2. Quiltmakers 3.

Centenarians
ISBN 978-0-8032-2526-8 pa; 0-8032-2526-1 pa

LC 2009-20883

First published 1998 by Morrow Junior Books

Biography of Nebraska homesteader, Grace McCance Snyder

"This new edition offers an afterword that includes information about black homesteaders, Native Americans, and the specific tasks of women, especially quilting. . . . Although it is written for younger readers than a teen audience, readability and intense subject matter should make the book popular with those readers." Voice Youth Advocates

Includes bibliographical references

Sockalexis, Louis, 1871-1913

Wise, Bill. **Louis** Sockalexis; Native American baseball pioneer. by Bill Wise; illustrated by Bill Farnsworth. Lee & Low Books 2007 un il $16.95

Grades: 2 3 4 5   92

1. Baseball players 2. Baseball -- Biography 3. Native Americans -- Biography
ISBN 978-1-58430-269-8

LC 2006017730

"This picture book offers a rousing introduction to the life of the first Native American to play major league baseball. . . . Wise and Farnsworth collaborate to great effect in rendering this story both informative and poignant. The color-drenched paintings do an excellent job of bringing this period to life and capturing the intense emotion of the ballpark drama." SLJ

Includes bibliographical references

Soto, Gary

Abrams, Dennis. **Gary** Soto; foreword by Kyle Zimmer. Chelsea House Pubs. 2008 120p bibl il por (Who wrote that?) $30

Grades: 5 6 7 8   92

1. Poets 2. Authors 3. Novelists 4. Mexican American authors 5. Essayists 6. College teachers 7. Authors, American 8. Children's authors 9. Young adult authors 10. Mexican Americans -- Biography
ISBN 978-0-7910-9529-4; 0-7910-9529-0

LC 2007045509

A biography of the popular Mexican American author for children and young adults.

Includes bibliographical references

Sotomayor, Sonia, 1954-

Gitlin, Marty. **Sonia** Sotomayor; Supreme Court justice. by Martin Gitlin. ABDO Pub. Co. 2011 112p il (Essential lives) $32.79

Grades: 5 6 7 8   92

1. Judges 2. Women judges 3. District attorneys 4. Supreme Court justices 5. Hispanic Americans -- Biography
ISBN 978-1-61613-518-8; 1-61613-518-2

LC 2010000499

This biography of Supreme Court Justice Sonia Sotomayor "toggles between the subject's personal and professional life; [it] offers sidebar explanations of legal issues. . . . The writing is accessible, the format is open, and full-color photos appear throughout." SLJ

Includes glossary and bibliographical references

McElroy, Lisa Tucker. **Sonia** Sotomayor; first Hispanic U.S. Supreme Court justice. Lerner Publications 2010 48p il lib bdg $26.60

Grades: 5 6 7 8   92

1. Judges 2. Women judges 3. District attorneys 4. Supreme Court justices 5. Hispanic Americans -- Biography
ISBN 978-0-7613-5861-9 lib bdg; 0-7613-5861-7 lib bdg

LC 2009037703

"Well organized and straightforward, this biography is appealing with its bright photographs and bold, easy-to-read font. Starting with Sotomayor's childhood in the Bronx, the author covers the justice's life and career up to her nomination to the Supreme Court. . . . An informative, interesting, and, most of all, inspiring read." SLJ

Includes bibliographical references

Winter, Jonah. **Sonia** Sotomayor; a judge grows in the Bronx. illustrated by Edel Rodríguez. Atheneum Books for Young Readers 2009 un il $16.99

Grades: K 1 2 3   92

1. Judges 2. Women judges 3. District attorneys 4. Supreme Court justices 5. Hispanic Americans -- Biography 6. Bilingual books -- English-Spanish
ISBN 978-1-4424-0303-1; 1-4424-0303-9

LC 2009031659

A biography of the Bronx-born Latina Supreme Court justice.

"This timely, accessible picture-book biography, which features both English and Spanish text on every page, brings Sotomayer's exciting rags-to-riches story to young readers. . . . Winter lets the small details convey the drama, which is amplified in the mixed-media illustrations in warm shades of red and brown." Booklist

Squires, Emily Swain, 19th cent.

Hailstone, Ruth. The **white** ox; the journey of Emily Swain Squires. [illustrations by] Dan Burr; [written by] Ruth Hailstone. Calkins Creek 2009 un il $18.95

Grades: 2 3 4   92

1. Mormons 2. Immigrants 3. Frontier and pioneer life 4. Pioneers
ISBN 978-1-59078-555-3; 1-59078-555-X

LC 2008024154

Hailstone's "narrative describes the real-life journey of ten-year-old Emily Swain Squires (her great-great grandmother), who traveled ahead of her family from England to Salt Lake City around 1863. During the hardest part of the journey, walking across the plains, she befriended a weary white ox, which gave her enough strength to complete the long trek. Burr uses a digital version of oil painting in Photoshop, applied to a traditional surface, to create 15 stunning and dramatic spreads that appear historically accurate in every detail. Children will be swept up by the lovely art and the tale of Emily's remarkable journey." Kirkus

Standish, Myles, 1584?-1656

Harness, Cheryl. The **adventurous** life of Myles Standish; and the amazing-but-true survival story of Plymouth Colony. painstakingly written and illustrated by Cheryl Harness. National Geographic 2006 144p il map (Cheryl Harness history) $16.95; lib bdg $25.90

Grades: 4 5 6 7 **92**
1. Pilgrims (New England colonists) 2. Colonists 3. Pilgrim fathers 4. Colonial leaders
ISBN 978-0-7922-5918-3; 0-7922-5918-1; 978-0-7922-5919-0 lib bdg; 0-7922-5919-X lib bdg

"Harness chronicles the history of the Plymouth Pilgrims from their troubles in England to their first years in North America, with the focus on Standish. Separating documented history from speculation, the narrative explains religious movements, introduces key figures, and gives a balanced account of Pilgrim-Indian relationships. . . . The tone is casual. . . . A reader-friendly approach to history." Booklist
Includes bibliographical references

Stanton, Elizabeth Cady, 1815-1902

★ Stone, Tanya Lee. **Elizabeth** leads the way: Elizabeth Cady Stanton and the right to vote; illustrations by Rebecca Gibbon. Henry Holt & Co. 2008 un il $16.95
Grades: 1 2 3 **92**
1. Feminism 2. Suffragists 3. Women -- Suffrage
ISBN 978-0-8050-7903-6; 0-8050-7903-3
LC 2007002833

This is "a short, incisive biography covering some of the high points of Stanton's life, beginning with her shocking realization about how unfairly the law treated women, which translated into Stanton's work for women's suffrage. . . . The child-pleasing artwork features characters a bit reminiscent of clothespin dolls, but the cameos of action, matched by full-page pictures, make the history accessible." Booklist

Stein, Gertrude, 1874-1946

Winter, Jonah. **Gertrude** is Gertrude is Gertrude is Gertrude; written by Jonah Winter; illustrated by Calef Brown. Atheneum Books for Young Readers 2009 un il $16.99
Grades: K 1 2 3 **92**
1. Poets 2. Authors 3. Novelists 4. Women authors 5. Essayists 6. Memoirists 7. Literary critics 8. Authors, American 9. Private secretaries
ISBN 978-1-4169-4088-3; 1-4169-4088-X
LC 2007-01447

Winter "crafts a Steinesque 'word portrait' of the modernist author. Stein wears a serene smile in Brown's . . . patchy acrylic images, and by her side is an enigmatic Alice B. Toklas. . . . Winter's nonlinear prose echoes The Autobiography of Alice B. Toklas, and his fugues suit a poet fond of repetition (and babble). Brown's idiosyncratic visuals and complementary palette . . . befit this impresario of experimental artists and writers on the Rive Gauche." Publ Wkly

Stowe, Harriet Beecher, 1811-1896

Adler, David A. A **picture** book of Harriet Beecher Stowe; illustrated by Colin Bootman. Holiday House 2003 un il $17.95; pa $6.95
Grades: K 1 2 3 **92**
1. Authors 2. Novelists 3. Abolitionists 4. Women authors 5. Authors, American
ISBN 0-8234-1646-1; 0-8234-1878-2 pa
LC 2002-27626

Details the life and achievements of abolitionist Harriet Beecher Stowe whose book, Uncle Tom's Cabin, is said to have started the Civil War

"This biography offers easily accessible information supported by realistic, evocative oil paintings." SLJ
Includes bibliographical references

Su, Shih, 1036 or 7-1101

Demi. **Su** Dongpo; Chinese genius. Lee & Low Books 2006 un il map $24
Grades: 3 4 5 6 **92**
1. Poets 2. Authors 3. Authors, Chinese 4. Calligraphers
ISBN 978-1-58430-256-8; 1-58430-256-9
LC 2005030437

"Beautifully designed and produced, the book features delicately limned, brilliantly colored paintings of scenes from Su Dongpo's life, outlined in scarlet and bordered with thin bands of gold. A visually striking introduction to the man sometimes referred to as Su Shi or Su Tung-po." Booklist

Sullivan, Anne, 1866-1936

Amoroso, Cynthia. **Helen** Keller; by Cynthia Amoroso and Robert B. Noyed. Child's World 2010 24p il (Basic biographies) lib bdg $22.79
Grades: PreK K 1 **92**
1. Deaf 2. Blind 3. Authors 4. Memoirists 5. Humanitarians 6. Teachers of the deaf 7. Inspirational writers 8. Teachers of the blind 9. Social welfare leaders
ISBN 978-1-60253-341-7; 1-60253-341-5
LC 2009029369

This biography of Helen Keller "pairs intelligent, brief text with abundant photos. Simple but never basic." Booklist
Includes bibliographical references

Delano, Marfe Ferguson. **Helen's** eyes; a photobiography of Annie Sullivan, Helen Keller's teacher. [foreword by Keller Johnson Thompson] National Geographic 2008 63p il map $17.95; lib bdg $27.90
Grades: 4 5 6 7 **92**
1. Deaf 2. Blind 3. Authors 4. Teachers 5. Memoirists 6. Humanitarians 7. Teachers of the deaf 8. Inspirational writers 9. Teachers of the blind 10. Social welfare leaders
ISBN 978-1-4263-02-9-1; 1-4263-0209-6; 978-1-4263-0210-7 lib bdg; 1-4263-0210-X lib bdg

"There are many biographies of Helen Keller and Annie Sullivan, but this one is very nicely done. . . . The book is honest in its portrayals, especially of Sullivan. . . . What makes this oversize book so appealing is the clean design, with large typeface. The many fascinating photographs are sometimes placed over historical documents." Booklist
Includes bibliographical references

Suzuki, Hiromi

★ Barasch, Lynne. **Hiromi's** hands. Lee & Low Books 2007 un il $17.95
Grades: K 1 2 3 **92**
1. Cooks 2. Cooking 3. Gender role 4. Japanese Americans 5. Sex role 6. Japanese Americans -- Juvenile literature
ISBN 978-1-58430-275-9
LC 2006017283

This picture book biography tells the story of sushi chef Hiromi Suzuki. "Primary." (Horn Book)

"Ink-and-watercolor scenes are rendered in salmon and grays; each childhood is captured in black-and-white snapshots. . . . An inspiring story." SLJ

Tallchief, Maria

Tallchief, Maria. **Tallchief**; America's prima ballerina. by Maria Tallchief with Rosemary Wells; illustrations by Gary Kelley. Viking 1999 un il $15.99

Grades: 3 4 5   **92**
1. Ballet 2. Ballet dancers 3. Native American women 4. Dance teachers
ISBN 0-670-88756-0
LC 98-35783

Ballerina Maria Tallchief describes her childhood on an Osage reservation, the development of her love of dance, and her rise to success in that field

"Through eloquent words, readers are immediately drawn into the first-person narrative. . . . As beautiful as the text is, so too are Kelley's pictures. The large illustrations, several covering double-page spreads, are rendered in soft pastels." SLJ

Tatum, Art, 1910-1956

★ Parker, Robert Andrew. **Piano** starts here: the young Art Tatum. Schwartz & Wade Books 2008 un il $16.99; lib bdg $19.99

Grades: K 1 2 3   **92**
1. Pianists 2. Jazz musicians 3. African American musicians
ISBN 978-0-375-83965-8; 0-375-83965-8; 978-0-375-93965-5 lib bdg; 0-375-93965-5 lib bdg
LC 2006-102105

This is a "a biography of famed jazz pianist Art Tatum. . . . A subtle sophistication shines through Parker's easygoing yet dynamic watercolors. . . . Parker's unhurried account could inspire visions of jazz greatness among young musicians." Publ Wkly

Includes bibliographical references

Taylor, Annie Edson, 1838-1921

★ Van Allsburg, Chris, 1949- **Queen** of the Falls. Houghton Mifflin Harcourt 2011 un il $18.99

Grades: 3 4 5   **92**
1. Teachers 2. Stunt performers
ISBN 0-547-31581-3; 978-0-547-31581-2
LC 2010006780

This picture book tells the story of how "a retired sixty-two-year-old charm school instructor named Annie Edson Taylor, seeking fame and fortune, decided to . . . go over Niagara Falls in a wooden barrel." (Publisher's note) "Primary, intermediate." (Horn Book)

"Any kid who has beheld Niagara Falls—or even taken a good look at pictures of it—will be suitably gobsmacked by the true story of charm-school teacher Annie Edson Taylor, who, at age 62, decided on a whim to fund her golden years by being the first person over the falls. . . . On October 24, 1901, [a] reinforced and padded 160-pound [barrel] was dropped into the water in front of thousands of nervous spectators. Van Allsburg's trademark framed illustrations have the unnerving stillness of old-timey photos." Booklist

Taylor, Major, 1878-1932

Brill, Marlene Targ. **Marshall** Major Taylor; world champion bicyclist, 1899-1901. by Marlene Targ Brill. Twenty-First Century Books 2008 112p il (Trailblazer biography) lib bdg $31.93

Grades: 5 6 7 8   **92**
1. Bicycle racing 2. African American athletes 3.

Cyclists
ISBN 978-0-8225-6610-6 lib bdg; 0-8225-6610-9 lib bdg
LC 2006003883

"Marshall Taylor, an African American bicyclist who, despite facing prejudice in racing and in life, achieved world renown at the turn of the last century. . . . Brill's accessible, personable prose vividly relates Taylor's experiences." Booklist

Includes bibliographical references

Tenzing Norgay, 1914-1986

Burleigh, Robert. **Tiger** of the snows; Tenzing Norgay; the boy whose dream was Everest. [by] Robert Burleigh and [illustrated by] Ed Young. Simon & Schuster 2006 un il $16.95

Grades: 3 4 5 6   **92**
1. Mountaineering 2. Mountaineers
ISBN 0-689-83042-4
LC 2005-00469

Presents the true story of Nepalese Sherpa Tenzing Norgay who, realizing his own dreams, helped Sir Edmund Hillary reach the summit of Mount Everest.

"Young's hauntingly beautiful illustrations capture the mystery and grandeur of these dangerously high peaks with somber-hued pastels, predominantly blues and purples, set against black backgrounds. . . . A stunning and lyrical ode to a contemplative man and his amazing achievement." SLJ

Thurman, Howard, 1900-1981

Jackson Issa, Kai. **Howard** Thurman's great hope; by Kai Jackson Issa; illustrated by Arthur L. Dawson. Lee & Low Books 2008 un il $16.95

Grades: 2 3 4 5   **92**
1. Clergy 2. Theologians 3. College teachers 4. Inspirational writers
ISBN 978-1-60060-249-8; 1-60060-249-5
LC 2007050093

"Reds, blues, and yellows pop against brown wood desks or whitewashed walls in vivid, realistic oil paintings. The author drew from Thurman's memoir and papers to create this accessible, engaging biography." SLJ

Tillage, Leon, 1936-

★ Tillage, Leon. **Leon's** story; [by] Leon Walter Tillage; collage art by Susan L. Roth. Farrar, Straus & Giroux 1997 107p il hardcover o.p. pa $6.95

Grades: 4 5 6 7 8 9 10   **92**
1. African Americans -- Biography
ISBN 0-374-34379-9; 0-374-44330-0 pa
LC 96-43544

The son of a North Carolina sharecropper recalls the hard times faced by his family and other African Americans in the first half of the twentieth century and the changes that the civil rights movement helped bring about

The author's "voice is direct, the words are simple. There is no rhetoric, no commentary, no bitterness. . . . This quiet drama will move readers of all ages . . . and may encourage them to record their own family stories." Booklist

Tingle, Tim

★ Tingle, Tim. **Saltypie**; a Choctaw journey from darkness into light., with illustrations by Karen Clarkson. Cinco Puntos Press 2010 40p il

Grades: 2 3 4 5   92
1. Blind 2. Grandmothers 3. Choctaw Indians 4. Storytellers
ISBN 1933693673; 9781933693675
"Tingle tells his family's story from their origins in Oklahoma Choctaw country to their life in Texas. The account spans generations and weaves in ghosts from the past to the present day. . . . The author was six that he learned that his grandmother was blind. Tingle was a junior in college when he got word that Mawmaw was having surgery. As the family gathered at the hospital, they told stories about their past, and he heard about her days as an orphan at an Indian boarding school and the discrimination she encountered living in Texas. . . . The large, full-spread illustrations are vibrant and vital in moving the story along. A lovely piece of family history." SLJ

Toulouse-Lautrec, Henri de, 1864-1901
Burleigh, Robert. **Toulouse**-Lautrec; the Moulin Rouge and the City of Light. Abrams 2005 32p il $17.95
Grades: 3 4 5   92
1. Artists 2. Painters 3. Lithographers 4. Artists, French
ISBN 0-8109-5867-8
This "volume introduces the life and art of Toulouse-Lautrec. . . . Burleigh relates the facts in a way that is comprehensible to children, without talking down to them. . . . The book's format allows for many illustrations, including period photos and paintings of Paris by artists such as Pissarro and Renoir, which are cleverly mingled with reproductions of Toulouse-Lautrec's arresting drawings, paintings, and lithographs, many in color. . . . A beautifully designed book that provides a lively, accessible introduction to the artist's life and work." Booklist

Toussaint Louverture, 1743?-1803
★ Rockwell, Anne F. **Open** the door to liberty!: a biography of Toussaint L'Ouverture; illustrated by R. Gregory Christie. Houghton Mifflin Books for Children 2009 64p il $18
Grades: 5 6 7 8   92
1. Generals 2. Revolutionaries 3. Blacks -- Biography 4. Slavery -- West Indies
ISBN 978-0-618-60570-5; 0-618-60570-3
LC 2007-25746
"In this eye-opening biography, Rockwell makes a strong case that Toussaint L'Ouverture is one of the most overlooked heroes of the eighteenth century. A freed slave of the French colony of St. Domingue (what we now know as Haiti), L'Ouverture was 48 when he was so inspired by his people's uprising against the French that he joined them and, through his oratory and strategical skills, became their leader. In 1793, he led history's first triumphant slave rebellion, but the resulting freedom would not last long. . . . Evocative paintings in primary colors help tell the story." Booklist
Includes bibliographical references

Truth, Sojourner, d. 1883
Clinton, Catherine. **When** Harriet met Sojourner; illustrated by Shane W. Evans. Katherine Tegen Books 2008 un il $16.99; lib bdg $17.89
Grades: K 1 2 3   92
1. Abolitionists 2. Memoirists 3. Slavery -- United

States 4. African American women -- Biography
ISBN 978-0-06-050425-0; 0-06-050425-0; 978-0-06-050426-7 lib bdg; 0-06-050426-9 lib bdg
LC 2006-19099
"Clinton imagines what might have been said during a meeting between Harriet Tubman and Sojourner Truth, who both found themselves in Boston one day in October 1864. Their meeting is the climax of this picture book, which tells the stories of the two heroes in clear, simple words on alternating double-page spreads. Evans' dramatic collage-style illustrations evoke the quilts the women worked on, piecing together their history." Booklist

★ Pinkney, Andrea Davis. **Sojourner** Truth's stepstomp stride; [by] Andrea Davis Pinkney & Brian Pinkney. Disney Jump at the Sun Books 2009 un il $16.99
Grades: K 1 2 3   92
1. Feminism 2. Abolitionists 3. Memoirists 4. African American women -- Biography 5. Slavery -- History -- Juvenile literature
ISBN 978-0-7868-0767-3; 0-7868-0767-9
The Pinkneys "collaborate on an upbeat yet nuanced picture biography of Sojourner Truth, whose slave name was Isabella. . . . Andrea Davis Pinkney's narrative adopts a confidential, admiring tone, tracing Truth's years of enslaved toil, her subsequent escape, deep religious faith and narration of her life story to abolitionist Olive Gilbert. . . . Brian Pinkney's watercolors, in washes of ochre and slate blue contoured in inky black, utilize a dry-brush technique well suited for depicting Truth's hardscrabble youth and unyielding commitment to justice." Kirkus

Rockwell, Anne F. **Only** passing through: the story of Sojourner Truth; by Anne Rockwell; illustrated by Gregory Christie. Knopf 2000 un il $16.95; lib bdg $18.99
Grades: 3 4 5   92
1. Feminism 2. Abolitionists 3. African American women 4. Memoirists 5. African American women -- Biography
ISBN 0-679-89186-2; 0-679-99186-7 lib bdg
LC 00-35736
Rockwell's narrative "is both conversational and immediately riveting. . . . The semi-abstract paintings are inspirational rather than representational, their authority residing in the presence Christie imparts to this heroine." Bull Cent Child Books

Tubman, Harriet, 1820?-1913
Clinton, Catherine. **When** Harriet met Sojourner; illustrated by Shane W. Evans. Katherine Tegen Books 2008 un il $16.99; lib bdg $17.89
Grades: K 1 2 3   92
1. Abolitionists 2. Memoirists 3. Slavery -- United States 4. African American women -- Biography
ISBN 978-0-06-050425-0; 0-06-050425-0; 978-0-06-050426-7 lib bdg; 0-06-050426-9 lib bdg
LC 2006-19099
"Clinton imagines what might have been said during a meeting between Harriet Tubman and Sojourner Truth, who both found themselves in Boston one day in October 1864. Their meeting is the climax of this picture book, which tells the stories of the two heroes in clear, simple words on alternating double-page spreads. Evans' dramatic collage-style

illustrations evoke the quilts the women worked on, piecing together their history." Booklist

Turner, Glennette Tilley. An **apple** for Harriet Tubman; [by] Glennette Tilley Turner; illustrated by Susan Keeter. Albert Whitman & Co. 2006 un il $15.95
Grades: 2 3 4   92
   1. Apples 2. Abolitionists 3. African American women 4. Slavery -- United States 5. African American women -- Biography
   ISBN 978-0-8075-0395-9; 0-8075-0395-9
                LC 2005037360
"At age seven, Tubman's job was to care for the baby of an unkind white woman, who whipped her. Later, the overseer of an orchard lashes her for eating an apple.... Ketter's unframed, thickly painted pictures depict the slave child's cruel working conditions and her brave escape and rescue, culminating as Tubman buys a house and plants apple trees, which produce fruit for everyone to share. The story, with its concrete details, works as both fact and metaphor, bringing the transformation full circle—from the scars of suffering to the fruit of freedom." Booklist
Includes bibliographical references

★ Weatherford, Carole Boston. **Moses**; when Harriet Tubman led her people to freedom. illustrated by Kadir Nelson. Hyperion 2006 un il $15.99
Grades: 2 3 4   92
   1. Abolitionists 2. Underground railroad 3. African American women -- Biography
   ISBN 0-7868-5175-9
A Caldecott Medal honor book, 2007
Describes Tubman's spiritual journey as she hears the voice of God guiding her north to freedom on that very first trip to escape the brutal practice of forced servitude.
"This is a "handsome, poetic account.... Shifting perspectives and subtle details ... underscore the narrative's spirituality.... Tubman's beautifully furrowed face is expressive and entrancing." SLJ

Tutankhamen, King of Egypt
Demi. **Tutankhamun**; written and illustrated by Demi. Marshall Cavendish Children 2009 un il map $19.99
Grades: 4 5 6 7   92
   1. Kings and rulers 2. Kings
   ISBN 978-0-7614-5558-5; 0-7614-5558-2
                LC 2008029313
"The unmistakable designs and opulent glitter of ancient Egyptian art gleam on every page of Demi's picture-book introduction to Tutankhamun. Beginning with King Tut's great-grandfather, Demi presents the broad historical context surrounding the young monarch's reign.... Demi's language, organized into brief but pithy paragraphs, is clear. ... It's the beautiful illustrations that will attract and hold a young audience most, and as usual, Demi incorporates artistic motifs and materials appropriate to her subject." Booklist

Twain, Mark, 1835-1910
★ Burleigh, Robert. The **adventures** of Mark Twain by Huckleberry Finn; with considerable help from Robert Burleigh and [illustrated by] Barry Blitt. Atheneum Books for Young Readers 2011 un il
Grades: 2 3 4   92
   1. Authors 2. Humorists 3. Novelists 4. Essayists 5.

Satirists 6. Memoirists 7. Travel writers 8. Authors, American
   ISBN 0689830416; 9780689830419
                LC 2010006512
This is a biography of Mark Twain told from the perspective of one of his characters. "Grades two to five." (Bull Cent Child Books)
"The neat switcheroo in this picture-book biography has the story of Mark Twain's life told by one of his most endearing characters, Huck Finn.... Although Huck's narration is almost overwhelmingly folksy, his undeniably cheery tone is infectious.... Blitt ... provides jaunty, cartoony pen-and-watercolor artwork, with exaggerated, tall-tale figures and period charm aplenty." Booklist

★ Fleischman, Sid. The **trouble** begins at 8; a life of Mark Twain in the wild, wild West. Greenwillow Books 2008 224p il $18.99; lib bdg $19.89
Grades: 5 6 7 8   92
   1. Authors 2. Humorists 3. Novelists 4. Essayists 5. Satirists 6. Memoirists 7. Travel writers 8. Authors, American 9. Short story writers 10. Biography, Individual -- Juvenile literature
   ISBN 0-06-134431-1; 0-06-134432-X lib bdg; 978-0-06-134431-2; 978-0-06-134432-9 lib bdg
                LC 2007-37891
This biography of Mark Twain focuses on his travels. Grades five to nine. (Bull Cent Child Books)
"Fleischman writes a charming biography of Samuel Clemens before he became Mark Twain, the great American novelist.... Written with a sense of humor and wit that honors Twain, this book is sprinkled with famous Twain quotes, excerpts of his writing, and pictures of Twain and other primary documents from the era Clemens spent both on the Mississippi River and in the West." Voice Youth Advocates
Includes bibliographical references

★ Kerley, Barbara. The **extraordinary** Mark Twain (according to Susy) illustrated by Edwin Fotheringam. Scholastic Press 2010 un il $17.99
Grades: 2 3 4 5   92
   1. Authors 2. Biography 3. Humorists 4. Novelists 5. Authorship 6. Essayists 7. Satirists 8. Memoirists 9. Travel writers 10. Authors, American 11. Short story writers
   ISBN 978-0-545-12508-6; 0-545-12508-1
                LC 2009-04752
"Wanting to present a portrait of her papa beyond that of just humorist and author, Mark Twain's 13-year-old daughter Susy spent a year chronicling her observations and reflections.... Kerley contextualizes the teenager's admiring musings with vivid familial backdrops.... Minibooklets titled 'Journal' appear in the fold of many spreads, containing excerpts from Susy's notebook.... Adding dynamic flair to the limited palettes of each digitally created scene are curlicues representing words, which emanate wildly from pen tips, pages, and mouths. Author notes about Susy and her father, a time line of Twain's life, and tips for writing an 'extraordinary biography' complete this accessible and inventive vision of a American legend." Publ Wkly

Velázquez, Diego, 1599-1660

Venezia, Mike. **Diego** Velazquez; written and illustrated by Mike Venezia. Children's Press 2004 32p il (Getting to know the world's greatest artists) lib bdg $26; pa $6.95

Grades: K 1 2 3   92

1. Artists 2. Painters 3. Artists, Spanish 4. Painters -- Spain -- Biography -- Juvenile literature

ISBN 0-516-22580-4 lib bdg; 0-516-26980-1 pa

LC 2003-4590

Describes the life and career of the seventeenth-century Spanish artist famous for his portraits of royalty.

"The unusually abundant full-color reproductions more than justify this series' longevity, as do Venezia's lighthearted cartoons, which foster welcome associations between 'art appreciation' and 'fun.'" Booklist

Vivaldi, Antonio, 1678-1741

Shefelman, Janice Jordan. **I**, Vivaldi; written by Janice Shefelman; illustrated by Tom Shefelman. William B. Eerdmans Pub. Co. 2007 un il $18

Grades: 3 4 5   92

1. Composers 2. Violinists

ISBN 978-0-8028-5318-9; 0-8028-5318-8

LC 2006-20120

This is a picture book "biography of composer Antonio Vivaldi. . . . The first-person narration offers an accessible and personable view of Vivaldi's intense passion for music. . . . Stunning ink-and-watercolor scenes evoke the ornate, shadowy church interiors and gilded ornamentation of 17th century Venice." Publ Wkly

Wagner, Honus, 1874-1955

★ Yolen, Jane. **All** star! Honus Wagner and the most famous baseball card ever. illustrated by Jim Burke. Philomel Books 2010 un il $17.99

Grades: 2 3 4   92

1. Baseball cards 2. Baseball players 3. Baseball coaches 4. Baseball managers 5. Baseball -- Biography

ISBN 978-0-399-24661-6; 0-399-24661-4

LC 2009-15066

Biography of Honus Wagner and an explanation of why his baseball card is worth almost $3 million.

"The treatment of Wagner's hardscrabble early years . . . is particularly masterful. . . . An eloquently understated tribute to that archetypal American combination of stoicism, decency, drive, and sheer talent." Publ Wkly

Wagué Diakité, Baba

Wague Diakite, Baba. A **gift** from childhood; memories of an African boyhood. Groundwood Books 2010 134p il $18.95

Grades: 5 6 7 8   92

1. Artists 2. Authors 3. Illustrators 4. Children's authors

ISBN 978-0-88899-931-3; 0-88899-931-3

"Diakite's . . . illustrated memoir focuses on his childhood in a small Malian village. . . . Interspersed with Diakite's recounting of his youth . . . are stories about his grandfather's brokering peaceful relations with the French, a blacksmith who stymies Death, and others. . . . Diakite's precise language and vibrant illustrations, created on earthenware tiles, form an engrossing story of community life. Studded with Malian proverbs, metaphors, and morals . . .

it's a memoir alive with far more voices than just that of the author." Publ Wkly

Waldman, Neil, 1947-

Waldman, Neil. **Out** of the shadows; an artist's journey. Boyds Mills Press 2006 144p il $21.95

Grades: 5 6 7 8   92

1. Artists 2. Authors 3. Illustrators 4. Jews -- Biography 5. Children's authors

ISBN 1-59078-411-1

Neil Waldman reveals how his passion for art emerged in the kitchen of his family's apartment, where he discovered the work of Vincent Van Gogh and the ability to use illustration as a means to escape the sadness that plagued his home.

"Young artists, as well as readers who wonder about the person behind the pictures they have seen, will appreciate every element of this book: well-constructed story, visual richness, and uncompromising honesty." Booklist

Walker, C. J., Madame, 1867-1919

Lasky, Kathryn. **Vision** of beauty; the story of Sarah Breedlove Walker; illustrated by Nneka Bennett. Candlewick Press 2000 un il $14.99

Grades: 3 4 5   92

1. Philanthropists 2. African American women 3. African American businesspeople 4. Cosmeticians 5. Cosmetics industry executives 6. African American women executives

ISBN 9780763664282

LC 99-19594

This is a biography of the African American entrepreneur who founded a cosmetics company and became a millionaire. "Grades three to five." (Bull Cent Child Books)

"Lasky's engaging account moves smoothly through events in Walker's life. . . . The illustrations . . . are attractive and rich in historical detail." Booklist

Walking Coyote

Bruchac, Joseph, 1942- **Buffalo** song; by Joseph Bruchac; illustrated by Bill Farnsworth. Lee & Low Books 2008 un il $17.95

Grades: 1 2 3   92

1. Bison 2. Kalispel Indians 3. Wildlife conservation 4. Animal rescue workers 5. Native Americans -- Biography

ISBN 978-1-58430-280-3; 1-58430-280-1

LC 2007024912

This biography is "partly fictionalized. . . . Bruchac's long, eloquent afterword fills in the facts. . . . [It is illustrated with] Farnsworth's beautiful, full-bleed oil paintings." Booklist

Walton, Sam

Blumenthal, Karen. **Mr.** Sam; how Sam Walton built Wal-Mart and became America's richest man. Penguin Group 2011 183p il $17.99

Grades: 5 6 7 8   92

1. Businessmen 2. Discount stores 3. Retail executives

ISBN 978-0-670-01177-3; 0-670-01177-0

LC 2010049520

"This spectacular success story tracks Walton's rise from lower-middle-class origins to, by the mid-1980s, the top of the 'America's Richest' list. . . . Written in a fluid, journalistic style and enhanced by photos, boxed-out 'Sam stories,' charts tracking changes in Americans' spending habits, and a lavish source list, this account of the man who created what is today the world's largest company makes compelling reading." Booklist

Warhol, Andy, 1928?-1987

★ Christensen, Bonnie. **Fabulous!** a portrait of Andy Warhol. Henry Holt and Co. 2011 un il $16.99
Grades: 3 4 5 6   92
1. Artists -- United States 2. Pop art -- Juvenile literature
ISBN 978-0-8050-8753-6; 0-8050-8753-2
LC 2010027840

"Spanning Warhol's rise to fame, this thoughtful account begins and ends with brief, fictionalized scenes that take place in 1966, illuminating the pop artist's popularity and success in contrast to the challenges he overcame to achieve recognition. The bulk of the narrative is fact-based, tracing major milestones in Warhol's personal and professional life through well-organized chronological flashbacks. . . . The differences between fine and commercial art, and Warhol's success in melding the two styles, are addressed in a way that is easy to understand even for someone with no background in art history. Christensen skillfully conveys emotion and mood through vivid, bold collage illustrations." SLJ
Includes bibliographical references

★ Rubin, Susan Goldman. **Andy** Warhol; pop art painter. H.N. Abrams 2006 48p il $18.95
Grades: 4 5 6 7   92
1. Artists 2. Pop art 3. Artists -- United States 4. Motion picture directors
ISBN 0-8109-5477-X
LC 2005-13238

"Andy Warhol was a colorful figure who revolutionized how the world looks at art. Rubin's coherent and interesting narrative is filled with quotes by the artist and people who knew him. . . . Excellent-quality black-and-white and full-color photographs of Warhol and his family and reproductions of his paintings and those of others who influenced him appear throughout." SLJ

Washington, Booker T., 1856-1915

Brimner, Larry Dane. **Booker** T. Washington; getting into the schoolhouse. Marshall Cavendish Benchmark 2009 41p il (American heroes) lib bdg $20.95
Grades: 2 3 4   92
1. Slaves 2. Authors 3. Educators 4. African American educators 5. Memoirists 6. Nonfiction writers 7. Civil rights activists 8. African Americans -- Biography
ISBN 978-0-7614-3063-6
LC 2008002870

A biography of Booker T. Washington, who rose from slavery to become a great African-American leader and educator

This "concise and well-written [title covers] key biographical facts without overwhelming young readers, and [includes] captioned illustrations and reproductions, most of which are in color. Text is large, and the layout is age-appropriate and attractive, with wide margins." SLJ
Includes glossary and bibliographical references

Washington, George, 1732-1799

Adler, David A. **George** Washington; an illustrated biography. by David A. Adler. Holiday House 2004 274p il map $24.95
Grades: 5 6 7 8   92
1. Generals 2. Presidents 3. Presidents -- United States
ISBN 0-8234-1838-3
LC 2003-67606

This "look at America's premier founding father literally spans his lifetime and attempts to focus . . . on how Washington's early character formation impacted his decisions as a military officer and later as president. . . . The illustrations are largely engravings from the late 19th century. . . . The writing style is accessible without ever falling prey to oversimplification." SLJ

Allen, Kathy. **President** George Washington; illustrated by Len Ebert. Picture Window Books 2010 32p il (Our American story) lib bdg $23.99
Grades: 2 3 4   92
1. Generals 2. Presidents
ISBN 978-1-4048-5539-7; 1-4048-5539-4
LC 2009-6894

Highlights the life and accomplishments of the Commander in Chief of the Continental Army and first president of the United States.

This title is "illustrated with well-executed, full-page, color illustrations, maps, and photos. . . . [It has] accurate, clearly written information that students can use for either leisure reading or reports." SLJ
Includes glossary and bibliographical references

Dolan, Edward F. **George** Washington; [by] Edward F. Dolan. Marshall Cavendish Benchmark 2008 96p il (Presidents and their times) lib bdg $32.79
Grades: 5 6 7 8   92
1. Generals 2. Presidents
ISBN 978-0-7614-2427-7 lib bdg; 0-7614-2427-X lib bdg
LC 2006037802

This biography of the first president of the United States "is illustrated with color photos and contains boxed descriptions of key historical events, artwork, and political concepts experienced during the time period. . . . This . . . will be of great use both for biographical research and for enriching the curriculum." Libr Media Connect
Includes glossary and bibliographical references

Malaspina, Ann. **Phillis** sings out freedom; the story of George Washington and Phillis Wheatley. illustrated by Susan Keeter. Albert Whitman 2010 un il $16.99
Grades: 2 3 4   92
1. Poets 2. Slaves 3. Authors 4. Generals 5. Presidents 6. Women poets 7. African American authors 8. Poets, American 9. African American women -- Biography
ISBN 978-0-8075-6545-2; 0-8075-6545-8

"Camped in Cambridge in the fall of 1775, General Washington despairs that his soldiers won't ever be able to defeat the British. In Providence, freed slave Phillis Wheatley pens a poem of encouragement to Washington. Malaspina intertwines information about Wheatley's early life with wartime events. . . . Keeter's rich oil paintings are full of period details that help to clarify both the war scenes and Wheatley's life." Booklist

Miller, Brandon Marie. **George** Washington for kids; his life and times with 21 activities. [by] Brandon Marie Miller. Chicago Review Press 2007 130p il pa $14.95
Grades: 4 5 6 7   92
1. Generals 2. Presidents
ISBN 1-55652-655-5 pa; 978-1-55652-655-8 pa
This book covers Washington's life and includes 21 hands-on projects based on his experiences and the times in which he lived.
This is "accessible and absorbing . . . clearly written and informative. . . . Primary quotes are interposed throughout, and illustrations, photographs, and visual aids are plentiful and well placed." SLJ

Mooney, Carla. **George** Washington; 25 great projects you can build yourself. illustrated by Samuel Carbaugh. Nomad 2011 121p il (Build it yourself) $21.95; pa $15.95
Grades: 4 5 6 7   92
1. Generals 2. Handicraft 3. Presidents
ISBN 978-1-934670-64-4; 1-934670-64-2; 978-1-934670-63-7 pa pa; 1-934670-63-4 pa
"The life of George Washington lends itself remarkably well to a variety of kid-friendly crafts that don't require old-fashioned materials or 18th-century skills. . . . The projects separate biographical chapters that are thorough and clear. . . . Sidebars with vocabulary words, quotes, interesting facts about the man and his time, and 'What if?' questions regarding pivotal moments in Washington's life add to the text. These sidebars, as well as amusing cartoon illustrations, make the subject light and approachable." SLJ
Includes glossary and bibliographical references

★ Rockwell, Anne F. **Big** George: how a shy boy became President Washington; [by] Anne Rockwell; illustrated by Matt Phelan. Harcourt 2009 un il $17
Grades: K 1 2 3   92
1. Generals 2. Presidents
ISBN 0-15-216583-5; 978-0-15-216583-3
LC 2002-4984
Portrays George Washington as a shy boy who wasn't afraid of anything except talking to people, but who grew up to lead an army against the British and serve as president of the new nation
This "adulatory biography offers plenty for contemporary kids to connect with. . . . But it's Phelan's . . . extraordinary artwork that cements the bond with readers. As his pencil-and-gouache scenes review Washington's life up to the presidency, his scenes bristle with immediacy, dramatic tension and emotional insight." Publ Wkly

White, Becky. **Betsy** Ross; illustrated by Megan Lloyd. Holiday House 2011 il $16.95
Grades: K 1 2   92
1. Generals 2. Presidents 3. Dressmakers 4. Needleworkers 5. Flags -- United States
ISBN 978-0-8234-1908-1; 0-8234-1908-8
LC 2009054296
"Fourteen spreads with four to six rhythmic words on each one tell the story of the first American flag. . . . The large, simple text, paired with the irresistible appliqué art,

makes this a perfect introduction to the Stars and Stripes. Using cotton fabric, embroidery thread, dye, paint, and linoleum-block prints, Lloyd captures the period, hard work, and ingenuity of this favorite colonial figure." SLJ

Weber, EdNah New Rider
Weber, EdNah New Rider. **Rattlesnake** Mesa; stories from a native American childhood. by EdNah New Rider Weber; photographs by Richela Renkun. Lee & Low Books 2004 132p il $18.95
Grades: 4 5 6 7   92
1. Native Americans 2. Artisans 3. Memoirists 4. Storytellers 5. Native Americans -- Biography
ISBN 1-58430-231-3
LC 2004-2385
"Weber describes her experiences with warmth and affection in this unusually compelling memoir. Striking black-and-white photos . . . add to the book's appeal." Horn Book Guide

Wells-Barnett, Ida B., 1862-1931
Dray, Philip. **Yours** for justice, Ida B. Wells; the daring life of crusading journalist. written by Philip Dray; illustrated by Stephen Alcorn. Peachtree Publishers 2008 un il $18.95
Grades: 2 3 4   92
1. Authors 2. Journalists 3. Essayists 4. Nonfiction writers 5. Newspaper executives 6. Civil rights activists 7. African Americans -- Civil rights 8. African American women -- Biography
ISBN 978-1-56145-417-4; 1-56145-417-6
LC 2007-4016
"Dray introduces this civil rights crusader and journalist who campaigned tirelessly to end the practice of lynching. . . . Alcorn's ink-and-watercolor illustrations have a fluid quality, conveying both action within the story and movement from one scene to the next. . . . This makes a good choice for middle-grade readers." Booklist
Includes bibliographical references

★ Myers, Walter Dean, 1937- **Ida** B. Wells; let the truth be told. illustrated by Bonnie Christensen. HarperCollinsPublishers 2008 37p il $16.99; lib bdg $17.89
Grades: 2 3 4 5   92
1. Authors 2. Journalists 3. Essayists 4. Nonfiction writers 5. Newspaper executives 6. Civil rights activists 7. African Americans -- Civil rights 8. African American women -- Biography
ISBN 978-0-06-027705-5; 0-06-027705-X; 978-0-06-027706-2 lib bdg; 0-06-027706-8 lib bdg
LC 2007-40107
"Myers deals with Wells-Barnett's career—from child of slaves, to teacher, to writer and organizer in the causes of anti-lynching and women's suffrage—in a style accessible to younger elementary audiences. . . . Each spread features a limited amount of text, and sourced quotations from Well-Barnett are frequently appended in red. Christensen's shaggy line and watercolor illustrations soften the rougher edges of the drama without straying into cartoonishness." Bull Cent Child Books

West, Benjamin, 1738-1820

Brenner, Barbara. The **boy** who loved to draw: Benjamin West; illustrated by Olivier Dunrea. Houghton Mifflin 1999 un il $15; pa $6.99

Grades: K 1 2 3   **92**

1. Artists 2. Painters 3. Artists -- United States
ISBN 0-395-85080-0; 0-618-31089-4 pa

LC 97-5183

Recounts the life story of the Pennsylvania artist who began drawing as a boy and eventually became well known on both sides of the Atlantic

"Naive in style and reminiscent of some colonial art, the illustrations present clear visual expressions of the activities and emotions related in the story. . . . A fascinating look at art in colonial times, and a likable portrait of the artist as a young boy." Booklist

Wheatley, Phillis, 1753-1784

Clinton, Catherine. **Phillis's** big test; written by Catherine Clinton; illustrated by Sean Qualls. Houghton Mifflin 2008 un il $16

Grades: 1 2 3 4   **92**

1. Poets 2. Slaves 3. Authors 4. Women poets 5. African American authors 6. Poets, American 7. Slavery -- United States
ISBN 978-0-618-73739-0; 0-618-73739-1

LC 2007-13241

"This picture-book biography deals with a transformative moment in the life of Phillis Wheatley, the first African American to publish a book of poetry. In 1772, 18 members of the intelligentsia from the Massachusetts Bay Colony . . . gathered to question the 17-year-old slave to ascertain the authorship of the poems she claimed were her own. . . . Qualls's uncluttered acrylic and collage compositions employ strong diagonal lines, swirling ribbons of thought, and a combination of opaque images and outlined, transparent figures over washes of color to create visual interest. . . . A formal tone, an occasional quaint turn of phrase, and a typeface with an irregular impression create the flavor of a time past. Clinton and Qualls offer an elegant introduction to an important individual." SLJ

Lasky, Kathryn. A **voice** of her own: the story of Phillis Wheatley, slave poet; illustrated by Paul Lee. Candlewick Press 2003 un il $17.99; pa $7.99

Grades: 3 4 5   **92**

1. Poets 2. Slaves 3. Authors 4. Women poets 5. African American authors 6. Poets, American 7. Slavery -- United States
ISBN 0-7636-0252-3; 0-7636-2878-6 pa

LC 2001-47139

A biography of an African girl brought to New England as a slave in 1761 who became famous on both sides of the Atlantic as the first Black poet in America

Written "in evocative language that's rich with historical detail. . . . This will serve as a good introduction to Wheatley's life and times for young children, who will appreciate Lee's full-page, historically accurate acrylics." Booklist

Malaspina, Ann. **Phillis** sings out freedom; the story of George Washington and Phillis Wheatley. illustrated by Susan Keeter. Albert Whitman 2010 un il $16.99

Grades: 2 3 4   **92**

1. Poets 2. Slaves 3. Authors 4. Generals 5. Presidents

6. Women poets 7. African American authors 8. Poets, American 9. Presidents -- United States 10. African American women -- Biography
ISBN 978-0-8075-6545-2; 0-8075-6545-8

"Camped in Cambridge in the fall of 1775, General Washington despairs that his soldiers won't ever be able to defeat the British. In Providence, freed slave Phillis Wheatley pens a poem of encouragement to Washington. Malaspina intertwines information about Wheatley's early life with wartime events. . . . Keeter's rich oil paintings are full of period details that help to clarify both the war scenes and Wheatley's life." Booklist

Whitfield, Simon, 1975-

Whitfield, Simon. **Simon** says gold: Simon Whitfield's pursuit of athletic excellence; by Simon Whitfield with Cleve Dheensaw. Orca Publishers 2009 118p il pa $14

Grades: 5 6 7 8   **92**

1. Athletes 2. Track athletics 3. Triathletes
ISBN 978-1-55469-141-8 pa; 1-55469-141-9 pa

"In 2000, Whitfield won a gold medal in the inaugural triathlon race held in the Sydney Summer Olympics. . . . He tells his story with candor, and he sheds light on the dark side of early success and the pressures athletes face. Sidebars offer more information on the sport of triathlon, and scrapbook-style color photographs enliven the tale." SLJ

Whitman, Narcissa Prentiss, 1808-1847

Harness, Cheryl. The **tragic** tale of Narcissa Whitman and a faithful history of the Oregon Trail; written and illustrated by Cheryl Harness. National Geographic Society 2006 144p il map (Cheryl Harness history) $16.95; lib bdg $25.90

Grades: 4 5 6 7   **92**

1. Frontier and pioneer life 2. Overland journeys to the Pacific 3. Pioneers 4. Missionaries
ISBN 0-7922-5920-3; 0-7922-7890-9 lib bdg

LC 2005-30930

This "introduces a nineteenth-century pioneer and missionary. . . . [She and her husband Marcus Whitman] journeyed along the Oregon Trail to the Waiilatpu Mission, where they ministered to the Cayuse. . . . Harness' chatty, conversational style makes the pair accessible to modern readers, and frequent quotes from Narcissa's diaries and letters and a time line help to frame the story in light of world and national events. Harness' black-line illustrations . . . help to break up the text for younger readers." Booklist

Includes bibliographical references

Whitman, Walt, 1819-1892

★ Kerley, Barbara. **Walt** Whitman; words for America. illustrated by Brian Selznick. Scholastic Press 2004 un il $16.95

Grades: 4 5 6 7   **92**

1. Poets 2. Authors 3. Essayists 4. Poets, American
ISBN 0-439-35791-8

LC 2003-20085

A biography of the American poet whose compassion led him to nurse soldiers during the Civil War, to give voice to the nation's grief at Lincoln's assassination, and to capture the true American spirit in verse

"Delightfully old-fashioned in design, [the book's] oversized pages are replete with graceful illustrations and snippets of poetry. The brilliantly inventive paintings add vibrant testimonial to the nuanced text." SLJ

Wiesenthal, Simon

★ Rubin, Susan Goldman. The **Anne** Frank Case: Simon Wiesenthal's search for the truth; illustrated by Bill Farnsworth. Holiday House 2009 40p il $18.95

Grades: 4 5 6 7   92

1. Authors 2. Children 3. Architects 4. Holocaust survivors 5. Diarists 6. Essayists 7. Memoirists 8. Nazi hunters 9. Jewish leaders 10. Holocaust victims 11. Jews -- Biography 12. Holocaust, 1933-1945
ISBN 978-0-8234-2109-1; 0-8234-2109-0

LC 2007-28396

"In 1958, Holocaust deniers disrupted a theater performance of The Diary of Anne Frank. In response, the well-known Nazi hunter Simon Wiesenthal vowed to prove Anne's story true. . . . This 'hook' is the framing story for a picture-book biography chronicling Wiesenthal's experiences during World War II and illustrating the development of his unusual career." SLJ

Includes glossary and bibliographical references

Wilder, Laura Ingalls, 1867-1957

Anderson, William T. **Pioneer** girl: the story of Laura Ingalls Wilder; by William Anderson; illustrated by Dan Andreasen. HarperCollins Pubs. 1998 un il hardcover o.p. pa $6.99

Grades: 2 3 4   92

1. Authors 2. Novelists 3. Women authors 4. Frontier and pioneer life 5. Western writers 6. Authors, American 7. Children's authors 8. Young adult authors
ISBN 0-06-027243-0; 0-06-027244-9 lib bdg; 0-06-446234-X pa

LC 96-31203

Recounts the life story of the author of the "Little House" books, from her childhood in Wisconsin to her old age at Rocky Ridge Farm

"Laura Ingalls Wilder's many fans will delight in this inviting biographical overview in a picture-book format, graced by Andreasen's dreamy landscapes, glowing prairie skies and warm character portraits." Publ Wkly

Berne, Emma Carlson. **Laura** Ingalls Wilder; by Emma Carlson Berne. ABDO Pub. 2008 112p il map $22.95

Grades: 4 5 6 7   92

1. Authors 2. Novelists 3. Women authors 4. Frontier and pioneer life 5. Western writers 6. Authors, American 7. Children's authors 8. Young adult authors
ISBN 978-1-59928-843-7; 1-59928-843-5

LC 2007012513

"Beginning in 1929 with the events that led up to the publication of Little House in the Big Woods, this readable biography further amplifies Wilder's life and correlates it with her books. . . . This volume is packed with relevant material, a time line, archival photographs, quotes from primary sources, and an official Web site." SLJ

Includes glossary and bibliographical references

Wilder, Laura Ingalls. A **Little** House traveler; writings from Laura Ingalls Wilder's journeys across America. by Laura Ingalls Wilder. HarperCollins 2006 344p il $16.99; pa $7.99

Grades: 5 6 7 8   92

1. Authors 2. Novelists 3. Women authors 4. Western writers 5. Authors, American 6. Children's authors 7. Young adult authors
ISBN 978-0-06-072491-7; 0-06-072491-9; 978-0-06-072492-4 pa; 0-06-072492-7 pa

LC 2005014975

"This volume combines three Wilder travel diaries: On the Way Home, recounting the 1894 trip from South Dakota to Missouri, with husband Almanzo and daughter Rose; West from Home, featuring letters written by Laura to Almanzo during her 1915 solo visit to Rose in San Francisco; and The Road Back, highlighting Laura's previously unpublished record of a 1931 trip with Almanzo to De Smet, South Dakota, and the Black Hills. . . . This offers an amazing look at a beloved author, as well as a fascinating account of travel before interstate highways and air-conditioning." Booklist

Wilder, Laura Ingalls. **West** from home; letters of Laura Ingalls Wilder to Almanzo Wilder, San Francisco, 1915. edited by Roger Lea MacBride; historical setting by Margot Patterson Doss. Harper & Row 1974 124p il hardcover o.p. pa $5.99

Grades: 6 7 8 9   92

1. Authors 2. Novelists 3. Women authors 4. Western writers 5. Authors, American 6. Children's authors 7. Young adult authors
ISBN 0-06-024110-1; 0-06-440081-6 pa

LC 73-14342

This collection is "edited from letters sent to her beloved husband while Laura spent two months in late 1915 visiting their daughter and immersing herself in the sights of bustling San Francisco and the exciting Panama-Pacific Exposition. Wilder readers of all ages will lose themselves in this trip— the adults with nostalgia and wholesome pleasure, the youth with wonder and awe over the sights vividly described in her inimitable combination of homespun literary and journalistic styles." Child Book Rev Serv

William, Prince, Duke of Cambridge, 1982-

Doeden, Matt. **Prince** William & Kate; a royal romance. Lerner Publications 2011 48p il lib bdg $26.60

Grades: 5 6 7 8   92

1. Princes 2. Princesses
ISBN 978-0-7613-8029-0; 0-7613-8029-9

LC 2011003413

"This short and sweet volume accents what down-to-earth and normal newlyweds Prince William and Kate Middleton are really like. After a brief recap of the couple's engagement interview, the book goes on to profile the pair individually and then as a duo. . . . This is an upbeat, readable narrative about a handsome, appealing couple. The color photographs are well chosen." Booklist

Includes glossary and bibliographical references

Williams, Daniel Hale, 1856-1931

Venezia, Mike. **Daniel** Hale Williams; surgeon who opened hearts and minds. written and illustrated by Mike Venezia. Children's Press 2010 32p il (Getting to know the world's greatest inventors & scientists) lib bdg $28

Grades: 2 3 4   92

1. Surgeons 2. Physicians 3. Writers on medicine 4.

African Americans -- Biography
ISBN 978-0-531-23729-8 lib bdg; 0-531-23729-X
lib bdg
Venezia "describes the life of Daniel Hale Williams, a
pioneering physician working during the late 19th and early
20th centuries who achieved fame as one of the first open-
heart surgeons. The book tells an inspiring story. . . . The
colorful cartoons and historical photographs . . . complement
the text well." Sci Books Films

Williams, J. W., 1929-
Barbour, Karen. **Mr.** Williams. Henry Holt and Co.
2005 29p il $16.95
Grades: K 1 2 3   92
1. Farmers 2. Country life 3. African Americans
ISBN 0-8050-6773-6
LC 2004-22182
"Recounting stories told by J. W. Williams, a friend of
her mother's, Barbour captures the essence of a black Louisiana farmer's life in the early 20th century. . . . The words
are succinct but evocative of a larger picture. . . . The ink-
and-gouache illustrations, punctuated with well-placed bits
of fabric collage, are perfect." SLJ

Williams, Lindsey, 1987-
Houle, Michelle E. **Lindsey** Williams; gardening for
impoverished families. [by] Michelle Houle. KidHaven
Press 2008 48p il (Young heroes) lib bdg $27.45
Grades: 4 5 6 7   92
1. Gardening 2. Food relief 3. Social action 4.
Gardeners 5. Humanitarians
ISBN 978-0-7377-3867-4 lib bdg; 0-7377-3867-7
lib bdg
LC 2007022923
This "introduces 20-year-old Lindsey Williams, who has
won numerous awards, including the International Eco-Hero
Award, for her groundbreaking work with agriculture and
hunger issues. . . . Williams has developed growing techniques that produce more food using fewer natural resources. . . . The straightforward text, with many quotes from Williams, will draw children into the science and environmental
issues." Booklist
Includes glossary and bibliographical references

Williams, Roger, 1604?-1683
Avi. **Finding** Providence: the story of Roger Williams;
story by Avi; illustrations by James Watling. HarperCollins
Pubs. 1997 46p il (I can read chapter book) hardcover
o.p. pa $3.99
Grades: 2 3 4   92
1. Clergy 2. Colonial leaders 3. Writers on religion
ISBN 0-06-025179-4; 0-06-444216-0 pa
LC 95-46360
After being forced to leave the Massachusetts Bay Col-
ony, Roger Williams travels south and, with the help of the
Narragansett Indians, founds Providence, Rhode Island
"Plentiful dialogue speeds the action along, and even
the philosophical issues are cogently presented for young
readers in the form of Williams' interrogation at the trial.
Watling's watercolors have a roughhewn quality appropiate
to the early colonies, and his grave figures are charged with
tension." Bull Cent Child Books

Williams, Ted, 1918-2002
Bowen, Fred. **No** easy way; the story of Ted Williams
and the last .400 season. illustrations by Charles S. Pyle.
Dutton Children's Books 2010 un il lib bdg $16.99
Grades: 1 2 3   92
1. Baseball players 2. Baseball managers 3. Baseball
-- Biography
ISBN 978-0-525-47877-5 lib bdg; 0-525-47877-9
lib bdg
LC 2009-17920
This recounts the 1941 baseball season in which Ted
Williams hit .406 for the Boston Red Sox.
"Unlike many decades-old baseball stories, this one
hasn't lost its appeal over the years, and Bowen makes the
most of it in terms kids will understand. Pyle's illustrations,
combined with vintage photographs, capture the drama of
Williams at bat." Booklist

Williams, William Carlos, 1883-1963
★ Bryant, Jennifer. A **river** of words: the story of Wil-
liam Carlos Williams; written by Jen Bryant; illustrated by
Melissa Sweet. Eerdmans Books for Young Readers 2008
un il $17
Grades: 1 2 3 4   92
1. Poets 2. Authors 3. Physicians 4. Essayists 5.
Poets, American 6. Short story writers
ISBN 978-0-8028-5302-8; 0-8028-5302-1
LC 2007-49347
A Caldecott Medal honor book, 2009
This picture book biography of William Carlos Williams
traces childhood events that lead him to become a doctor
and a poet.
Bryant's "simple, spare language matches her subject
well. Sweet's mixed-media collages will draw varying age
groups. . . . [This is an] inspiring title." Booklist

Wilson, Woodrow, 1856-1924
Marsico, Katie. **Woodrow** Wilson. Marshall Caven-
dish Benchmark 2011 112p il (Presidents and their times)
$23.95
Grades: 5 6 7 8   92
1. Governors 2. Presidents 3. College presidents 4.
Nobel laureates for peace
ISBN 978-0-7614-4815-0; 0-7614-4815-2
LC 2009041116
This offers information on President Woodrow Wilson
and places him within his historical and cultural context.
Also explored are the formative events of his times and how
he responded.
"The abundant sidebars provide a good deal of back-
ground information that will be helpful to students. . . . At-
tractive . . . as well as useful." Booklist
Includes glossary and bibliographical references

Winfrey, Oprah
Weatherford, Carole Boston. **Oprah**; the little speaker.
illustrated by London Ladd. Marshall Cavendish Children
2010 un il $17.99
Grades: K 1 2 3   92
1. Entertainers 2. Philanthropists 3. Television
personalities 4. Talk show hosts 5. Television
producers 6. African American women -- Biography
ISBN 978-0-7614-5632-2; 0-7614-5632-5
LC 2009006339

This picture book biography of Oprah Winfrey "focuses solely on her childhood. An author's note at the beginning sets the stage for the true rags-to-riches story about a poor girl on a Mississippi pig farm who became an entertainer, entrepreneur, and philanthropist. . . . The narrative portrays a bright, spunky child . . . while the soft-edged, acrylic illustrations paint a determined, sober-faced girl." Booklist

Wong, Anna May, 1905-1961

Yoo, Paula. **Shining** star: the Anna May Wong story; by Paula Yoo; illustrated by Lin Wang. Lee & Low Books 2009 un il $17.95

Grades: 2 3 4 5   92

1. Actors 2. Chinese Americans -- Biography
ISBN 978-1-60060-259-7; 1-60060-259-2

LC 2008042673

"Lin Wang's . . . elegant paintings in muted hues capture the actress's emotions in her expressive eyes framed by dark bangs. . . . The conversational narrative uses many descriptive vignettes. . . . A fascinating account of the life of a determined actress." Publ Wkly

Woodhull, Victoria C., 1838-1927

Krull, Kathleen. A **woman** for president; the story of Victoria Woodhull. illustrations by Jane Dyer. Walker & Co 2004 un il $16.95; lib bdg $17.85

Grades: 3 4 5   92

1. Feminism 2. Suffragists 3. Women in politics 4. Feminists 5. Presidential candidates
ISBN 0-8027-8908-0; 0-8027-8909-9 lib bdg

LC 2004-49483

"Woodhull is a fascinating figure, and Krull's lively and astute writing does her justice. . . . The watercolors, cast with a golden glow, are handsome." Booklist

Includes bibliographical references

Wozniak, Stephen, 1950-

Venezia, Mike. **Steve** Jobs & Steve Wozniak; geek heroes who put the personal in computers. written and illustrated by Mike Venezia. Children's Press 2010 32p il (Getting to know the world's greatest inventors & scientists) lib bdg $28

Grades: 2 3 4   92

1. Entrepreneurs 2. Businesspeople 3. Computer industry 4. Computer scientists 5. Electronics engineers 6. Computer industry executives 7. Electronics industry executives
ISBN 978-0-531-23730-4 lib bdg; 0-531-23730-3 lib bdg

Venezia "describes the extraordinary childhoods of Jobs and Wozniak. . . . Imperceptibly, Venezia brings a broad history of computers into the picture by demonstrating simultaneously how Jobs and Wozniak were influenced by early computer pioneers and how they then made their mark on the world. . . . Venezia's thoughtful writing style and carefully chosen photos and graphics allows children to use their imagination and see part of themselves in the two 'heroes' of the title." Sci Books Films

Wright, David, 1982-

Rappoport, Ken. **David** Wright; a baseball star who cares. Enslow 2011 il (Sports stars who care) $23.93

Grades: 3 4 5   92

1. Baseball players 2. Baseball -- Biography
ISBN 978-0-7660-3775-5; 0-7660-3775-4

A biography of the all-star third baseman for the New York Mets who has worked with charities and who established the David Wright Foundation.

This is "especially good for book reports." Booklist

Wright, Orville, 1871-1948

Collins, Mary. **Airborne**: a photobiography of Wilbur and Orville Wright. National Geographic Soc. 2003 63p il maps $18.95

Grades: 4 5 6 7   92

1. Inventors 2. Aeronautics -- History 3. Aircraft industry executives
ISBN 0-7922-6957-8

LC 2002-5279

Examines the lives of the Wright brothers and discusses their experiments and triumphs in the field of flight

"The well-chosen photos give readers a feel for Kitty Hawk—windy, sandy, solitary. This is an exceptionally well-informed picture of the Wright brothers and what their 100-year-old achievement really meant." SLJ

★ Freedman, Russell. The **Wright** brothers: how they invented the airplane; with original photographs by Wilbur and Orville Wright. Holiday House 1991 129p il hardcover o.p. pa $14.95

Grades: 5 6 7 8 9 10   92

1. Inventors 2. Aeronautics -- History 3. Aircraft industry executives
ISBN 0-8234-0875-2; 0-8234-1082-X pa

LC 90-48440

A Newbery Medal honor book, 1992

In this "combination of photography and text, Freedman reveals the frustrating, exciting, and ultimately successful journey of these two brothers from their bicycle shop in Dayton, Ohio, to their Kitty Hawk flights and beyond. . . . An essential purchase for younger YAs." Voice Youth Advocates

Includes bibliographical references

O'Sullivan, Robyn. The **Wright** brothers fly; by Robyn O'Sullivan. National Geographic 2007 40p il (National Geographic history chapters) lib bdg $17.90

Grades: 2 3 4   92

1. Inventors 2. Aeronautics -- History 3. Aircraft industry executives
ISBN 978-1-4263-0188-9

LC 2007007895

This history of the Wright brothers is "nicely illustrated with photos. . . . [It is] just right for emerging chapter-book readers. . . . Useful . . . for reports . . . and interesting pleasure reading." SLJ

Includes glossary and bibliographical references

Venezia, Mike. The **Wright** brothers; inventors whose ideas really took flight. written and illustrated by Mike Venezia. Children's Press 2010 32p il (Getting to know the world's greatest inventors & scientists) lib bdg $28

Grades: 2 3 4   92

1. Inventors 2. Aeronautics 3. Aircraft industry

executives
ISBN 978-0-531-23732-8 lib bdg; 0-531-23732-X
lib bdg

LC 2009030222

This "explores the development of the Wright brothers
by way of their early childhood environment and interests,
which ultimately contributed to their successful attainment
of the first powered aircraft. . . . Young readers will gain
insights into the brothers' inventive and entrepreneurial lives
from a humanistic perspective, as well as developing a sense
of the qualities that are associated with contributors to advancements in technology." Sci Books Films

Wright, Patience Lovell, 1725-1786

★ Shea, Pegi Deitz. **Patience** Wright; America's first
sculptor, and revolutionary spy. [by] Pegi Deitz Shea; illustrated by Bethanne Andersen. Henry Holt 2007 un il
$17.95

Grades: 4 5 6   92
1. Spies 2. Artists 3. Sculptors 4. Women artists
ISBN 978-0-8050-6770-5; 0-8050-6770-1

LC 2005021696

A biography of Patience Wright, born in 1725, who became a sculptor and a spy for the American colonies

"Shea writes with a dynamic simplicity that brings
Wright to life. At the same time, she seamlessly incorporates
information about the war and events leading up to it into
her text." Booklist

Wright, Richard, 1908-1960

★ Miller, William. **Richard** Wright and the library
card; illustrated by Gregory Christie. Lee & Low Bks.
1997 un il hardcover o.p. pa $6.95

Grades: K 1 2 3   92
1. Authors 2. Novelists 3. Dramatists 4. Essayists 5.
Nonfiction writers 6. Short story writers 7. Libraries
-- Fiction 8. African Americans -- Fiction 9. Books and
reading -- Fiction 10. Discrimination in education --
United States -- Juvenile literature 11. Afro-American
authors -- 20th century -- Biography -- Juvenile literature
ISBN 1-880000-57-1; 1-880000-88-1 pa

LC 97-6847

Based on a scene from Wright's autobiography, Black
boy, in which the seventeen-year-old African-American borrows a white man's library card and devours every book as
a ticket to freedom

"Christie's powerful impressionistic paintings in acrylic
and colored pencil show the harsh racism in the Jim Crow
South. . . . Words and pictures express the young man's
loneliness and confinement and, then, the power he found
in books." Booklist

Wright, Wilbur, 1867-1912

Collins, Mary. **Airborne**: a photobiography of Wilbur
and Orville Wright. National Geographic Soc. 2003 63p
il maps $18.95

Grades: 4 5 6 7   92
1. Inventors 2. Aeronautics -- History 3. Aircraft
industry executives
ISBN 0-7922-6957-8

LC 2002-5279

Examines the lives of the Wright brothers and discusses
their experiments and triumphs in the field of flight

"The well-chosen photos give readers a feel for Kitty
Hawk—windy, sandy, solitary. This is an exceptionally
well-informed picture of the Wright brothers and what their
100-year-old achievement really meant." SLJ

★ Freedman, Russell. The **Wright** brothers: how they
invented the airplane; with original photographs by Wilbur
and Orville Wright. Holiday House 1991 129p il hardcover o.p. pa $14.95

Grades: 5 6 7 8 9 10   92
1. Inventors 2. Aeronautics -- History 3. Aircraft
industry executives
ISBN 0-8234-0875-2; 0-8234-1082-X pa

LC 90-48440

A Newbery Medal honor book, 1992

In this "combination of photography and text, Freedman
reveals the frustrating, exciting, and ultimately successful
journey of these two brothers from their bicycle shop in
Dayton, Ohio, to their Kitty Hawk flights and beyond. . . . An
essential purchase for younger YAs." Voice Youth Advocates

Includes bibliographical references

O'Sullivan, Robyn. The **Wright** brothers fly; by
Robyn O'Sullivan. National Geographic 2007 40p il (National Geographic history chapters) lib bdg $17.90

Grades: 2 3 4   92
1. Inventors 2. Aeronautics -- History 3. Aircraft
industry executives
ISBN 978-1-4263-0188-9

LC 2007007895

This history of the Wright brothers is "nicely illustrated
with photos. . . . [It is] just right for emerging chapter-book
readers. . . . Useful . . . for reports . . . and interesting pleasure
reading." SLJ

Includes glossary and bibliographical references

Venezia, Mike. The **Wright** brothers; inventors whose
ideas really took flight. written and illustrated by Mike
Venezia. Children's Press 2010 32p il (Getting to know
the world's greatest inventors & scientists) lib bdg $28

Grades: 2 3 4   92
1. Inventors 2. Aeronautics 3. Aircraft industry
executives
ISBN 978-0-531-23732-8 lib bdg; 0-531-23732-X
lib bdg

LC 2009030222

This "explores the development of the Wright brothers
by way of their early childhood environment and interests,
which ultimately contributed to their successful attainment
of the first powered aircraft. . . . Young readers will gain
insights into the brothers' inventive and entrepreneurial lives
from a humanistic perspective, as well as developing a sense
of the qualities that are associated with contributors to advancements in technology." Sci Books Films

Yaccarino, Dan

★ Yaccarino, Dan. **All** the way to America; the story
of a big Italian family and a little shovel. Alfred A. Knopf
2011 un il $16.99; lib bdg $19.99

Grades: K 1 2 3   92
1. Artists 2. Authors 3. Genealogy 4. Illustrators 5.
Italian Americans 6. Authors, American 7. Children's

authors

ISBN 0-375-86642-6; 0-375-96642-0 lib bdg; 978-0-375-86642-5; 978-0-375-96642-2 lib bdg

LC 2010017549

"In this picture book, Yaccarino shares his family history. Starting with his great-grandfather Michele Iaccarino's immigration to America, he gives a simplified rundown of each generation's career and family life. Advice passed from parent to child creates a narrative connection among generations. . . . The text is clear and simple . . . [and] readers' interest will be held fast by the bright illustrations. In his typical retro style, Yaccarino creates a world of friendly, rounded people set against stylized background scenery. . . . The story will make an excellent family-history discussion starter." SLJ

York, ca. 1775-ca. 1815

★ Pringle, Laurence P. **American** slave, American hero; York of the Lewis and Clark Expedition. [by] Laurence Pringle; illustrations by Cornelius Van Wright and Ying-Hwa Hu. Calkins Creek Books 2005 40p il $17.95
Grades: 3 4 5   92

1. Slaves 2. Explorers 3. Slavery -- United States

ISBN 978-1-59078-282-8; 1-59078-282-8

LC 2005037352

"With a detailed text and handsome watercolor paintings, this illustrated biography celebrates the heroic role of Clark's personal slave on the famous expedition out west in 1804, with the horror of slavery in the background." Booklist

Includes bibliographical references

Young, Ed

★ Young, Ed. The **house** Baba built; an artist's childhood in China. Little, Brown and Co. 2011 48p il $17.99
Grades: 2 3 4 5   92

1. Artists 2. Authors 3. Illustrators 4. Authors, American 5. Children's authors

ISBN 978-0-316-07628-9; 0-316-07628-7

LC 2011005396

"In this picture book memoir by the Caldecott Medalist, which opens in 1931 (the year he was born), the stock market has crashed, and China is in turmoil. Young's father, Baba, persuades a landowner in Shanghai to let him construct a huge brick house on his land; Baba promises to return the house after 20 years, long enough to keep his family safe until WWII ends. Young's creation, shaped with help from author Libby Koponen, is as complex and labyrinthine as Baba's house, with foldout pages that open to reveal drawings, photos, maps, and memories. Tender portraits of his siblings, torn-paper collages showing tiny figures at play, and old photos of stylish adults intermingle, as if they'd been found forgotten in a drawer." Publ Wkly

Zaharias, Babe Didrikson, 1911-1956

Van Natta, Don, 1964- **Wonder** girl; the magnificent sporting life of Babe Didrikson Zaharias. Little, Brown and Co. 2011 403p il $27.99
Grades: 5 6 7 8   92

1. Women athletes 2. Golfers 3. Hurdlers 4. High jumpers 5. Javelin throwers 6. Olympic athletes

ISBN 978-0-316-05699-1; 0-316-05699-5

LC 2010041794

Describes the life and times of LPGA founder Babe Didrikson, the Texas woman who achieved All-American status in basketball, won gold medals in track and field in the 1932 Olympics, and became the first woman to play against men in a PGA tournament.

This is an "engaging biography. . . . Van Natta marvelously narrates the forgotten life of the 'greatest all-around athlete of all time,' a story that every American sport fan should relish." Publ Wkly

Includes bibliographical references

Zhu, Xiao-Mei

LeBlanc, Andre. The **red** piano; [illustrated by] Barroux; translated by Justine French. Wilkins Farago 2010 40p il $16.99
Grades: 2 3 4 5   92

1. Pianists 2. Music teachers

ISBN 978-0-9806070-1-7; 0-9806070-1-9

"The experiences of Chinese-born French pianist Khu Xiao-Mei inspire this poignant, picture-book biography set during the Cultural Revolution. Separated from her family and forbidden to pursue classical music studies, a young girl in exile clandestinely collects Bach preludes and practices the piano in a hut on the outskirts of her rural village. When she and her accomplice, an elderly villager who hides the piano, are discovered, they are tortured and ridiculed, and the piano is destroyed. An ambiguous ending sends the girl from the camp into a murky sunset with her secreted music notebooks in tow. Leblanc's clipped, elegant phrases tell a woeful, abstracted story that is well-matched with Barroux's arresting paintings in inky brown and shocking red. . . . The dramatic imagery offers an accessible, vivid picture of life during the time of Chairman Mao." Booklist

Zitkala-Sa, 1876-1938

★ Pearce, Q. L. **Red** Bird sings; the story of Zitkala-Sa; by Gina Capaldi & Q.L. Pearce; illustrated by Gina Capaldi. Carolrhoda Books 2011 32p il lib bdg $17.95
Grades: 3 4 5 6   92

1. Authors 2. Women authors 3. Women musicians 4. Yankton Indians 5. Political activists 6. Essayists 7. Indian leaders 8. Authors, American 9. Short story writers 10. Native Americans -- Biography

ISBN 978-0-7613-5257-0; 0-7613-5257-0

LC 2011003014

This children's biography describes the life of "Gertrude Simmons Bonnin of the Yankton Sioux, later known as Zitkala-Sa [who] bridged the nineteenth and twentieth centuries, and the white and Indian cultures . . . readers follow her school days, her later career as a political advocate for Indian rights, and her struggle to reconcile her determination for personal advancement with feelings of guilt for abandoning her family." The book includes "[f]irst-person narration adapted from Zitkala-Sa's own writings and supplemented with 'additional primary and secondary sources'". (Bulletin of the Center for Children's Books)

"Capaldi and Pearce document the life of Gertrude Simmons, an author, musician, and activist best known by her pen name, Zitkala-Sa (Red Bird). Drawing from semiautobiographical stories that Zitkala-Sa wrote for the Atlantic Monthly in the early 1900s, Capaldi and Pearce eloquently describe her experience at a Quaker boarding school, where she laments the loss of her culture, but also develops passions for violin and women's suffrage. . . . Capaldi's understated illustrations integrate solid colors and doll-like characterizations with reproductions of period materials, while appended information on Sitkala-Sa rounds out this fascinating portrait." Publ Wkly

Includes bibliographical references

Zuckerberg, Mark

Woog, Adam. **Mark** Zuckerberg, Facebook creator. KidHaven Press 2009 48p il map (Innovators) $28.25

Grades: 4 5 6 7   **92**

1. Businesspeople 2. Internet executives

ISBN 978-0-7377-4566-5; 0-7377-4566-5

LC 2009013458

"This brisk, readable [biography the creator of Facebook] . . . presents an appealing picture of the shy, lonely future billionaire . . . This is fascinating and relevant stuff." Booklist

Includes bibliographical references

920   Biography, genealogy, insignia

Adler, David A.

Heroes for civil rights; by David A. Adler; illustrated by Bill Farnsworth. Holiday House 2007 32p il $16.95

Grades: 3 4 5   **920**

1. African Americans -- Biography 2. African Americans -- Civil rights

ISBN 978-0-8234-2008-7

LC 2006038185

"Adler presents biographical sketches of several individuals and the defining actions or events in their lives as they relate to the roles they played during the Civil Rights Movement. . . . The format is attractive, with the easy-to-read text facing a full-page illustration. Farnsworth's oil paintings complement the simple presentations by featuring a large portrait of each individual, with one or more smaller pictures of a significant moment superimposed on it." SLJ

Includes bibliographical references

Bausum, Ann

★ **Our** country's first ladies; [by] Ann Bausum; with a foreword by First Lady Laura Bush. National Geographic 2007 127p il $19.95; lib bdg $28.90

Grades: 5 6 7 8   **920**

1. Presidents' spouses -- United States

ISBN 978-1-4263-0006-6; 978-1-4263-0007-3 lib bdg

LC 2006021284

"A well-researched, thoughtfully written, attractive account. Fact boxes provide basic information such as birth and death dates, marriage dates, and children's names; a 'Did You Know' section shares interesting personal tidbits. Periodic time lines help to place the women's lives within the broader events of history. There is enough information here for simple reports. Interesting facts and anecdotes will hold readers' attention. . . . An excellent layout and clear, colorful photographs and reproductions will further entice readers." SLJ

Includes bibliographical references

Beccia, Carlyn

The **raucous** royals; test your royal wits: crack codes, solve mysteries, and deduce which royal rumors are true. Houghton Mifflin 2008 64p il $17

Grades: 4 5 6 7   **920**

1. Nobility 2. Historiography 3. Kings and rulers 4. Biography, Collective -- Juvenile literature 5. Kings and rulers -- Biography -- Juvenile literature

ISBN 978-0-618-89130-6; 0-618-89130-7

LC 2008-298419

"Thirteen beliefs about rulers receive an acerbic and irreverent interrogation in this blend of royal-watching and skeptical investigation. The royal rumors, arranged chronologically, start with the real story behind Prince Dracula and Richard III's murderous ways, stopping en route at Napoleon's short stature and Marie Antoinette's 'let them eat cake' utterance, and finish up with Catherine the Great's death and King George's madness. . . . The energy and gleefully gossipy nature makes this a fine companion for Krull's Lives of . . . series, while its verve particularly recommends it as an entrée into historiography and critical thinking." Bull Cent Child Books

Includes bibliographical references

Bolden, Tonya

Portraits of African-American heroes; paintings by Ansel Pitcairn. Dutton Children's Books 2003 88p il $18.99; pa $11.99

Grades: 4 5 6 7   **920**

1. African Americans -- Biography

ISBN 0-525-47043-3; 0-14-240473-X pa

LC 2002-75911

"Each profile lists expected biographical information, but offers even more by way of keen insights into a subject's personality based on interviews and information drawn from personal memoirs. . . . Pitcairn's beautifully rendered sepia-toned portraits make each subject jump from the page, beckoning children to come ever closer and learn." Booklist

Bragg, Georgia

★ **How** they croaked; the awful ends of the awfully famous. Walker & Co. 2011 178p il $17.99; lib bdg $18.89

Grades: 5 6 7 8   **920**

1. Death 2. Biography 3. Celebrities -- Death -- Juvenile literature

ISBN 978-0-8027-9817-6; 0-8027-9817-9; 978-0-8027-9818-3 lib bdg; 0-8027-9818-7 lib bdg

LC 2010-08659

"Bragg chronicles with ghoulish glee the chronic or fatal maladies that afflicted 19 historical figures. Nonsqueamish readers will by entranced by her riveting descriptions. . . . The author tucks quick notes on at least marginally relevant topics, such as leeching, scurvy, presidential assassins, and mummy eyes . . . between the chapters. . . . O'Malley's cartoon portraits and spot art add just the right notes of humor to keep the contents from becoming too gross." Booklist

Cook, Michelle

★ **Our** children can soar; a celebration of Rosa, Barack, and the pioneers of change. illustrations by Cozbi A. Cabrera . . . [et al.]; foreword by Marian Wright Edelman. Bloomsbury 2009 un il $16.99; lib bdg $17.89

Grades: K 1 2   **920**

1. African Americans -- History 2. African Americans

-- Biography
ISBN 978-1-59990-418-4; 1-59990-418-7; 978-1-
59990-419-1 lib bdg; 1-59990-419-5 lib bdg
LC 2009-1730

"The spreads understandably represent an array of artistic styles and media, yet they form a cohesive and affecting collective portrait. . . . Additional images from Leo and Diane Dillon, James Ransome, E.B. Lewis, Eric Velasquez and others, corroborate Children's Defense Fund founder Marian Wright Edelman's assertion, in the book's foreword, that African-American history is 'the story of hope.'" Publ Wkly

Cotter, Charis

Born to write; the remarkable lives of six famous authors. Annick Press 2009 167p il $24.95; pa $14.95
Grades: 5 6 7 8   920
1. Authors
ISBN 978-1-55451-192-1; 1-55451-192-5; 978-1-
55451-191-4 pa; 1-55451-191-7 pa

A collective biography of authors Lucy Maud Montgomery, Christopher Paul Curtis, C. S. Lewis, E.B. White, Madeleine L'Engle, and Philip Pullman

"Younger readers will find the presentation of the book appealing, with many colorful photographs and illustrations; however, more mature readers will gain the most enjoyment as they discover the backgrounds and inspirations of some of their favorite writers. . . . An excellent resource for reports and pleasure reading." SLJ

Kids who rule; the remarkable lives of five child monarchs. Annick Press 2007 120p il map $24.95; pa $14.95
Grades: 5 6 7 8   920
1. Queens 2. Emperors 3. Kings and rulers 4.
Buddhist leaders 5. Political leaders 6. Nobel laureates for peace 7. Queens -- Biography -- Juvenile literature 8. Children -- Biography -- Juvenile literature 9. Kings and rulers -- Biography -- Juvenile literature
ISBN 978-1-55451-062-7; 1-55451-062-7; 978-1-
55451-061-0 pa; 1-55451-061-9 pa

This "book discusses five people who became monarchs as children: Tutankhamen of Egypt, Mary Queen of Scots, Queen Christina of Sweden, China's Emperor Puyi, and the fourteenth Dalai Lama. . . . The illustrations, many in color, include portrait paintings, engravings, and maps as well as photos of people, places, and artifacts. . . . This appealing collective biography presents five unusual children whose stories are well worth reading." Booklist

Cummins, Julie

★ **Women** daredevils; thrills, chills, and frills. illustrated by Cheryl Harness. Dutton Children's Books 2008
48p il $17.99
Grades: 3 4 5 6   920
1. Stunt performers 2. Women -- Biography 3.
Daredevils -- Juvenile literature
ISBN 978-0-525-47948-2; 0-525-47948-1
LC 2007-18102

"Cummins introduces 10 women stunt performers, active from 1880 to 1929. . . . Each story includes broad historical context with facts about women's status and societal expectations. . . . Cummins' lively text provides a sense of each individual by including quotes and physical descriptions. . . . Harness' richly colored, detailed illustrations . . . are expressive, realistic, and filled with action." Booklist

Drucker, Malka

Portraits of Jewish American heroes; by Malka Drucker; illustrated by Elizabeth Rosen. Dutton Children's Books 2008 96p il $22.99
Grades: 4 5 6   920
1. Jews -- United States -- Biography
ISBN 978-0-525-47771-6; 0-525-47771-3
LC 2007-028481

"From Albert Einstein and Bella Abzug to Ruth Bader Ginsburg, Hank Greenberg, and Steven Spielberg, this invitingly illustrated collective biography celebrates 20 Jewish American heroes in all their diversity. . . . The nicely designed volume includes full-page portraits of the subjects in various media. . . . Drucker's eloquent, chatty style opens up big issues about Judaism as a source of idealism and for a just, compassionate society." Booklist

Includes bibliographical references

Fortey, Jacqueline

Great scientists; written by Jacqueline Fortey. DK Pub. 2007 72p il map (DK eyewitness books) $15.99
Grades: 5 6 7 8   920
1. Scientists 2. Science -- Juvenile literature
ISBN 978-0-7566-2974-8; 0-7566-2974-8
LC 2007-298205

This introduces readers to the great scientists and their discoveries from ancient history to modern times.

"An accompanying CD provides clip art taken from the book; this art can prove invaluable to both teachers and students. . . . A very fine book for elementary and middle school students and those who teach them." Sci Books and Films

Fradin, Dennis B.

The **founders**; the 39 stories behind the U.S. Constitution. [by] Dennis Brindell Fradin; illustrated by Michael McCurdy. Walker & Co. 2005 162p il map $22.95; lib bdg $23.95
Grades: 4 5 6 7   920
1. Statesmen -- United States
ISBN 0-8027-8972-2; 0-8027-8973-0 lib bdg

"The makers of the U.S. Constitution are profiled in two or three pages each, in sections introduced by a brief note about their home states. McCurdy's black-and-white scratchboard illustrations are properly stately and engaging. Readers will find great nuggets of fact." Booklist

Includes bibliographical references

★ **Funny** business; conversations with writers of comedy. compiled and edited by Leonard S. Marcus. Candlewick Press 2009 214p il $21.99
Grades: 5 6 7 8 9 10   920
1. Authors 2. Authorship 3. Wit and humor 4.
Children's literature 5. Wit and humor, Juvenile 6.
Authorship -- Juvenile literature 8. Authors, American
-- Biography -- Juvenile literature
ISBN 978-0-7636-3254-0; 0-7636-3254-6

This book comprises interviews with writers of humorous books for young people: Judy Blume, Beverly Cleary, Sharon Creech, Christopher Paul Curtis, Anne Fine, Daniel Handler, Carl Hiaasen, Norton Juster, Dick King-Smith, Hilary McKay, Daniel Pinkwater, Louis Sachar, and Jon Scieszka. Index. "Intermediate, middle school." (Horn Book)

"In 12 entertaining interviews . . . Marcus's compilation explores the childhoods, writing processes and senses of humor of well-known writers for children, including Judy Blume, Beverly Cleary, Daniel Handler, Norton Juster and Jon Scieszka. Marcus's evident knowledge of his subjects' writing makes for some intriguing questions and answers. . . . Photographs, manuscript pages and even e-mail chains between the writers and their editors add fascinating tidbits." Publ Wkly

George-Warren, Holly

Honky-tonk heroes & hillbilly angels; the pioneers of country & western music. words by Holly George-Warren; pictures by Laura Levine. Houghton Mifflin 2006 32p il $16

Grades: 3 4 5 6   920

1. Musicians 2. Country music 3. Country musicians -- Juvenile literature

ISBN 0-618-19100-3

LC 2003-5364

Profiles important and influential performers of country and western music, including the Carter Family, Roy Acuff, Gene Autry, Bill Monroe, Patsy Cline, and Loretta Lynn.

"Concise but thorough. . . . Colorful, stylized, folk art of the performers and/or their instruments is included." SLJ

Gifford, Clive

10 inventors who changed the world; written by Clive Gifford; illustrated by David Cousens. Kingfisher 2009 63p il $14.99

Grades: 4 5 6 7   920

1. Inventors 2. Inventions

ISBN 978-0-7534-6259-1; 0-7534-6259-1

"The innovative efforts of nine men and one woman are presented here. Some of the names will be familiar (Galileo, Franklin, Edison, Curie) while others will prove less so (Isambard Kindgom Brunel, Glenn Curtiss, Sergei Korolev). Starting in ancient times with Archimedes, the chronology ends in modern times with Korolev, a Soviet-era rocket designer. Each section offers a succinct yet thorough biography of the inventors. Striking graphic-novel-style art is a visual aid to draw readers into each setting and era." SLJ

10 kings & queens who changed the world; written by Clive Gifford; illustrated by David Cousens. Kingfisher 2009 63p il map $14.99

Grades: 4 5 6 7   920

1. Kings and rulers

ISBN 978-0-7534-6252-2; 0-7534-6252-4

"Cousens' bright graphic novel-style artwork is the grabber here; he uses theatrical angles to portray each historical figure as a chiseled or beautiful adventurer. . . . The writing is clear, packed with information, and presented in agile paragraphs that twist around the scenes of war, plotting, and murder." Booklist

Haven, Kendall F.

Reluctant heroes; true five-minute-read adventure stories for boys. Libraries Unlimited 2008 169p pa $30

Grades: Adult Professional   920

1. Storytelling 2. Heroes and heroines 3. Children's reading -- Psychological aspects

ISBN 978-1-59158-749-1 pa; 1-59158-749-2 pa

LC 2008014017

"These 25 true stories are divided into three sections: 'Stories from History,' 'Stories from the Modern World,'

and 'Stories from the Natural World.' Each one offers a short history or explanation to place events in context and concludes with suggestions for further reading. . . . Appropriate as partnered works to nonfiction topics, these brief entries create useful classroom writing prompts or simply entertaining read-alouds. Quick-moving action and dialogue place readers squarely in the midst of dangerous, momentous events." SLJ

Includes bibliographical references

Hodgkins, Fran

Champions of the ocean; illustrations by Cris Arbo. Dawn Publications 2009 144p il (Earth heroes) pa $11.95

Grades: 5 6 7 8   920

1. Scientists 2. Oceanography 3. Environmentalists 4. Oceanographers

ISBN 978-1-58469-119-8 pa; 1-58469-119-0 pa

LC 2009-17926

This is a collective biography of oceanographers William Beebe, Archie Carr, Jacques-Yves Cousteau, Margaret Wentworth Owings, Eugenie Clark, Roger Payne, Sylvia Earle, and Tierney Thys.

This is illustrated with "black-and-white photographs and illustrations. [The book] provides young readers with fascinating facts and insights. . . . This volume is an excellent introduction to the biography genre, as well as a terrific research book." Sci Books Films

Includes bibliographical references

Housel, Debra J.

Ecologists; from Woodward to Miranda. Compass Point Books 2009 40p il (Mission: science) lib bdg $26.60

Grades: 4 5 6   920

1. Ecology 2. Environmentalists

ISBN 978-0-7565-4076-0 lib bdg; 0-7565-4076-3 lib bdg

LC 2008-35733

Profiles ecologists John Woodward, Aldo Leopold, Rachel Carson, Ruth Patrick, Eugene Odum, Lan Lubchenco, and Neo Martinez

Includes glossary and bibliographical references

Jankowski, Connie

Astronomers; from Copernicus to Crisp. Compass Point Books 2009 40p il (Mission: science) lib bdg $26.60

Grades: 4 5 6   920

1. Astronomers

ISBN 978-0-7565-3965-8 lib bdg; 0-7565-3965-X lib bdg

LC 2008-8325

Explores the lives and discoveries of noted astronomers from the fifteenth to the twenty-first century.

Includes glossary and bibliographical references

Kiernan, Denise

★ Signing our lives away; the fame and misfortune of the men who signed the Declaration of Independence. by Denise Kiernan & Joseph D'Agnese. Quirk 2009 255p $19.95

Grades: 5 6 7 8   920

1. Statesmen -- United States

ISBN 978-1-59474-330-6; 1-59474-330-4

"Kiernan and D'Agnese present readers with astonishing individual portraits of all the signers [of the Declaration of Independence] in an attempt both to dispel some of the mythology surrounding the document as well as to establish a place in the historical discourse for those men not named Jefferson, Hancock, Franklin, or Adams. The marvelously arranged work lends itself to either straightforward reading or skipping around. . . . An entertaining and effective narrative of about three to five pages per individual is presented." SLJ

Includes bibliographical references

Kimmel, Elizabeth Cody

Ladies first; 40 daring American women who were second to none. [by] Elizabeth Cody Kimmel; foreword by Stacy Allison. National Geographic 2006 192p il $18.95

Grades: 5 6 7 8   **920**

1. Women -- Biography

ISBN 0-7922-5393-0

LC 2005005113

This offers "introductions to forty of America's most brilliant and courageous women. Each essay is three pages in length and includes a fourth full-page portrait of the woman being introduced. . . . The women chosen achieved greatness in a wide range of endeavors, from athletics to the arts to politics. . . . Students will find these excellent essays useful as an introduction to the women portrayed and as a good jumping off point for further research." Voice Youth Advocates

Includes bibliographical references

Krull, Kathleen

★ **Lives** of extraordinary women; rulers, rebels (and what the neighbors thought) written by Kathleen Krull; illustrated by Kathryn Hewitt. Harcourt 2000 95p il $21

Grades: 4 5 6 7   **920**

1. Queens 2. Saints 3. Diplomats 4. Empresses 5. Explorers 6. Travelers 7. Suffragists 8. Abolitionists 9. Prime ministers 10. Women in politics 11. Regents 12. Feminists 13. Pacifists 14. Columnists 15. Dissenters 16. Memoirists 17. Humanitarians 18. Indian chiefs 19. Archaeologists 20. Indian leaders 21. Cabinet members 22. Social activists 23. Political leaders 24. Nonfiction writers 25. Women -- Biography 26. Members of Congress 27. Spouses of presidents 28. Human rights activists 29. United Nations officials 30. Nobel laureates for peace 31. Women in politics -- Biography -- Juvenile literature 32. Women heads of state -- Biography -- Juvenile literature

ISBN 0-15-200807-1

LC 99-6840

"Each entry offers a tightly written biography, often filled with delicious anecdote. . . . Each biographical essay is accompanied by one of Hewitt's full-page, full-color caricatures. Both artful and witty, the illustrations provide perfect accompaniments to the often breezy and accessible text." N Y Times Book Rev

Includes bibliographical references

★ **Lives** of the presidents; fame, shame (and what the neighbors thought) written by Kathleen Krull; illustrated by Kathryn Hewitt. updated ed.; Harcourt Children's Books 2011 104p il $21

Grades: 4 5 6 7   **920**

1. Presidents -- United States

ISBN 978-0-547-49809-6; 0-547-49809-8

First published 1998

"This new edition is sure to be even more popular than the original title (Harcourt, 1998) as it includes Presidents George W. Bush and Barack Obama, who are given the same cheeky-but-respectful treatment as their predecessors. . . . [Krull] provides further information on ex-Presidential activity since 1998, such as Jimmy Carter's Nobel Prize, Ronald Reagan's passing, and the Clintons' post-White House work. All other entries and art are virtually unaltered. Guaranteed to inject some levity into the ubiquitous presidential biography assignment, the 2011 Lives of the Presidents is a must-have for elementary schools and public libraries." SLJ

Includes bibliographical references

The **brothers** Kennedy; John, Robert, Edward. illustrated by Amy June Bates. Simon & Schuster Books for Young Readers 2010 40p il $16.99

Grades: 2 3 4   **920**

1. Brothers 2. Statesmen 3. Presidents 4. Senators 5. Attorneys general 6. Political leaders 7. Members of Congress 8. Siblings of presidents 9. Presidential candidates

ISBN 978-1-4169-9158-8; 1-4169-9158-1

"Focusing on John, Robert, and Edward, the book describes the Kennedys' early family life and highlights a pivotal event for each featured sibling. . . . The stylized artwork [is] rendered in pencil, watercolor, and gouache. . . . The likenesses are strong, and the images set a historic tone." Booklist

Includes bibliographical references

Malnor, Bruce

Champions of the wilderness; by Bruce and Carol L. Malnor; illustrated by Anisa Claire Hovemann. Dawn Publications 2009 143p il (Earth heroes) pa $11.95

Grades: 5 6 7 8   **920**

1. Environmentalists 2. Biography, Collective -- Juvenile literature

ISBN 978-1-58469-116-7 pa; 1-58469-116-6 pa

LC 2008-53670

"This is a short gem of a book that includes short biographies of eight 'heroes' who have championed the preservation and/or conservation of wilderness areas around the world over the past two centuries. Henry David Thoreau, John Muir, Teddy Roosevelt, Aldo Leopold, Richard St. Barbe Baker, Mardy Murie, David Suzuki, and Wangari Maathai are the heroes in question. The storytelling is fluent and engaging." Sci Books Films

Includes bibliographical references

Malnor, Carol

Champions of wild animals; by Carol L. and Bruce Malnor; illustrations by Anisa Claire Hovemann. Dawn Publications 2010 144p il (Earth heroes) pa $11.95

Grades: 5 6 7 8   **920**

1. Naturalists 2. Endangered species 3. Wildlife conservation 4. Naturalists -- Juvenile literature 5. Endangered species -- Juvenile literature 6. Wildlife conservationists -- Juvenile literature

ISBN 978-1-58469-123-5 pa; 1-58469-123-9 pa

LC 2010-16030

This describes "the youth and careers of eight of the world's greatest environmentalists who championed the protection of wildlife, including William Hornaday (saved the bison from extinction), Ding Darling (A Duck's Best Friend), Rachel Carson (author of Silent Spring), Roger Tory Peterson (Inventor of the Modern Field Guide), R.D. Lawrence (Storyteller for Wolves), E.O. Wilson (Lord of the Ants), Jane Goodall (Champion for Chimps), and Ian and Saba Douglas-Hamilton (Saving the Elephants)." Publisher's note

Includes bibliographical references

Nathan, Amy

Meet the dancers; from ballet, Broadway, and beyond. Henry Holt 2008 231p il $18.95

Grades: 5 6 7 8   920

1. Dance 2. Dancers 3. Ballet dancers -- Juvenile literature

ISBN 978-0-8050-8071-1; 0-8050-8071-6

LC 2007-27589

"This collective biography reveals the paths that 16 diverse dancers followed to become professionals and to join prestigious companies. . . . The tone of the text is conversational. . . . The pictures dramatically capture how talented these performers are. Anyone, whether considering a career in dance or not, will be inspired and educated by these up-close-and-personal accounts." SLJ

Pinkney, Andrea Davis

★ Let it shine; stories of Black women freedom fighters. illustrated by Stephen Alcorn. Harcourt 2000 107p il $20

Grades: 4 5 6 7   920

1. Slaves 2. Authors 3. Midwives 4. Educators 5. Journalists 6. Abolitionists 7. Philanthropists 8. Essayists 9. Memoirists 10. Political leaders 11. Nonfiction writers 12. Members of Congress 13. Newspaper executives 14. Presidential advisers 15. Civil rights activists 16. Organization officials 17. Political party leaders 18. Presidential candidates 19. African Americans -- Civil rights 20. African American women -- Biography 21. African Americans -- Civil rights -- History 22. African American women civil rights workers -- Biography

ISBN 0-15-201005-X

LC 99-42806

This "collective biography tells of 10 extraordinary black women. From Sojourner Truth to Shirley Chisholm, this is also a view of African American history through individual lives. . . . Stephen Alcorn's allegorical oil portraits are dramatic and beautiful. . . . The immediacy of the text and the spacious design of the large volume make this a natural for reading aloud." Booklist

Includes bibliographical references

Rappaport, Doreen

★ We are the many; a picture book of American Indians. illustrated by Cornelius Van Wright and Ying-Hwa Hu. HarperCollins Pubs. 2002 28p il hardcover o.p. lib bdg $17.89

Grades: 2 3 4   920

1. Native Americans -- Biography

ISBN 0-688-16559-1; 0-06-001139-4 lib bdg

LC 2001-39820

"One incident from each person's life is re-created, giving a quick, snapshot-style view of the individual's contribution to the world. . . . The text is large, and sentences are ac-

cessible to emerging readers. . . . There is some fictionalizing . . . but it is limited and does not detract from the overall worth of the title." SLJ

Rivera, Raquel

Arctic adventures; tales from the lives of Inuit artists. pictures by Jirina Marton. Groundwood Books/House of Anansi Press 2007 47p il $18.95

Grades: 3 4 5 6   920

1. Artists 2. Sculptors 3. Artists, Inuit 4. Printmakers 5. Inuit -- Art 6. Inuit artists -- Juvenile literature 7. Inuit -- Canada -- Juvenile literature

ISBN 978-0-88899-714-2; 0-88899-714-0

"This dynamic picture book draws on memoir, legend, art, and history to tell true dramatized events in the lives of four modern Inuit artists. . . . Beautiful illustrations in colored pencil and mixed media show the individual people and creatures in the Arctic landscape. . . . After each story, there is a brief, straightforward biography of the artist, a photo, and a reproduction of his or her work." Booklist

Includes glossary and bibliographical references

Roop, Peter

Tales of famous heroes; by Peter and Connie Roop; illustrated by Rebecca Zomchek. Scholastic 2010 106p il $17.99

Grades: 3 4 5 6   920

1. Heroes and heroines

ISBN 978-0-545-23750-5; 0-545-23750-5

"The lives of inspirational figures are presented in such an engaging manner that readers will not be able to stop after reading just one. The 17 profiles highlight important events from the individual's childhood, demonstrating how each was set on course for greatness. Current famous people, such as Sonia Sotomayor, Barack Obama, and Nelson Mandela, are included, as well as historical figures like Winston Churchill and Sojourner Truth. . . . The book is illustrated with caricature-type portraits superimposed on archival photographs. Each biography is made up of easy-to-read paragraphs designed for beginners or less capable older readers. An engaging collective biography." SLJ

Rosenberg, Aaron

The Civil War; one event, six people. Scholastic 2011 160p il map (Profiles) $14.99

Grades: 5 6 7 8   920

1. Nurses 2. Slaves 3. Authors 4. Lawyers 5. Generals 6. Presidents 7. Abolitionists 8. Photographers 9. Memoirists 10. Police officials 11. State legislators 12. College presidents 13. Members of Congress 14. Red Cross officials 15. Social welfare leaders

ISBN 978-0-545-28926-9; 0-545-28926-2

"This collective biography . . . introduces Abraham Lincoln, Frederick Douglass, Clara Barton, George McClellan, Robert E. Lee, and Matthew Brady. Single paragraph summaries of each subject's historical relevance are followed by resumes of their lives that focus on how each affected and was affected by the Civil War and that point out connections between them all. . . . Archival photographs are instuctive." Booklist

Includes bibliographical references

Stout, Glenn

Yes she can! women's sports pioneers. Houghton Mifflin Harcourt 2011 117p il (Good sports) pa $5.99

Grades: 4 5 6 7　　　　　　　　　　　　　　**920**

1. Women athletes

ISBN 978-0-547-41725-7; 0-547-41725-X

"In chapters devoted to swimmer Trudy Ederle, runners Louise Stokes and Tidye Pickett, jockey Julie Krone, and Indy car driver Danica Patrick, Stout covers each woman's hard work, setbacks, and triumphs without minimizing the challenges and disappointments along the way. . . . Accessible and inspirational." Publ Wkly

Thimmesh, Catherine

★ **Girls** think of everything; illustrated by Melissa Sweet. Houghton Mifflin 2000 57p $16; pa $6.95

Grades: 5 6 7 8　　　　　　　　　　　　　　**920**

1. Women 2. Admirals 3. Chemists 4. Students 5. Inventors 6. Inventions 7. Physicists 8. Women inventors 9. Computer scientists 10. Home economists 11. Clothing industry executives 12. Office supply industry executives 13. Inventions -- United States -- History -- Juvenile literature 14. Women inventors -- United States -- Biography -- Juvenile literature

ISBN 0-395-93744-2; 0-618-19563-7 pa

LC 99-36270

"Ten women and two girls are given a few pages each. Included are Mary Anderson, who invented the windshield wiper (after she was told it wouldn't work); Ruth Wakefield, who, by throwing chunks of chocolate in her cookie batter, gave Toll House cookies to the world; and young Becky Schroeder, who invented Glo-paper because she wanted to write in the dark. The text is written in a fresh, breezy manner, but it is the artwork that is really outstanding." Booklist

Waldman, Neil

A **land** of big dreamers; voices of courage in America. selected and illustrated by Neil Waldman. Millbrook Press 2010 32p il lib bdg $16.95

Grades: 3 4 5　　　　　　　　　　　　　　**920**

1. Courage 2. American national characteristics

ISBN 978-0-8225-6810-0; 0-8225-6810-1

LC 2010001185

"Thirteen prominent American men and women are briefly profiled in this collection. Chronologically ranging from Thomas Jefferson to Barack Obama, each entry features an inspiring quote from its subject and a concise explanation of his or her context in history. Opposite each page of text is a watercolor painting by the author depicting an image or montage of the notable individual and illustrating the work they achieved or how they lived. Each one evokes the emotions the book is meant to inspire: courage, strength and determination." Kirkus

Winter, Jonah

Peaceful heroes; illustrated by Sean Addy. Arthur A. Levine Books 2009 56p il $17.99

Grades: 4 5 6 7　　　　　　　　　　　　　　**920**

1. Peace 2. Heroes and heroines

ISBN 978-0-439-62307-0; 0-439-62307-3

LC 2008-48311

"Starting off with Jesus, Gandhi, King, and Sojourner Truth, this collective biography goes on to profile many less well-known peace activists across the world. . . . The de-

tailed portraits never deny the horrifying realities that the peace-seeking leaders are fighting against. With the chatty interactive text, there are handsome full-page pictures of each activist, rendered in oil, acrylic, and collage in shades of red and brown." Booklist

Wild women of the Wild West; illustrated by Susan Guevara. Holiday House 2011 il $16.95

Grades: 2 3 4　　　　　　　　　　　　　　**920**

1. Women -- Biography 2. Frontier and pioneer life -- West (U.S.)

ISBN 978-0-8234-1601-1; 0-8234-1601-1

LC 2010030911

"This book introduces 16 figures who made their mark between the California Gold Rush and the end of the 19th century. . . . Each page-long biographical sketch is written in a delightful colloquial style that gives the text verve and sparkle. Each biography is accompanied by a full-page, watercolor and ink portrait of the subject. All are based on historical photos and show the women as strong and powerful." SLJ

Includes bibliographical references

Yolen, Jane

Sea queens; women pirates around the world. illustrated by Christine Joy Pratt. Charlesbridge 2008 103p il $18.95

Grades: 4 5 6 7　　　　　　　　　　　　　　**920**

1. Women pirates 2. Women -- Biography

ISBN 978-1-58089-131-8; 1-58089-131-4

LC 2007026983

This offers "12 portraits of sword-swinging, seafaring women throughout history, from Artemisia, in 500 B.C.E. Persia, to Madame Ching, an early nineteenth-century Chinese woman and named here as 'the most successful pirate in the world.' . . . The scratchboard illustrations work well as portraits. . . . The book is filled with fascinating, dramatically told stories and sidebars." Booklist

Includes bibliographical references

920.003　Dictionaries, encyclopedias, concordances of biography as a discipline

Rockman, Connie C.

Tenth book of junior authors and illustrators; edited by Connie C. Rockman. Wilson, H.W. 2008 803p autog il por (Junior authors & illustrators series) hardcover o.p. $120

Grades: Adult Professional　　　　　　　**920.003**

1. Reference books 2. Children's literature 3. Young adult literature 4. Authors -- Dictionaries 5. Illustrators -- Dictionaries 6. Children's literature -- Bio-bibliography 7. Children's literature -- History and criticism 8. Young adult literature -- History and criticism 9. Children's literature -- Authors and illustrators

ISBN 978-0-8242-1066-3; 0-8242-1066-2

LC 2008043312

This volume covers some 200 authors and illustrators of books for children and young adults including David Almond, Blue Balliett, Terry Pratchett, and Laura Vaccaro Seeger. For 17 authors and artists whose careers include significant new works and honors since their profile in earlier editions of the series, newly written entries are featured

"Standard resource for libraries serving young readers and students studying children's and young adult literature." Booklist

Includes bibliographical references

Something about the author; facts and pictures about authors and illustrators of books for young people. Gale Res. il

Grades: Adult Professional **920.003**
1. Reference books 2. Authors -- Dictionaries 3. Illustrators -- Dictionaries 4. Children's literature -- Bio-bibliography

First published 1971. Frequency varies

"This important series gives comprehensive coverage of the individuals who write and illustrate books for children. Each new volume adds about 100 profiles. Entries include career and personal data, a bibliography of the author's works, information on works in progress and references to further information." Safford. Guide to Ref Materials for Sch Libr Media Cent. 5th edition

Something about the author: autobiography series. Gale Res. il

Grades: Adult Professional **920.003**
1. Reference books 2. Authors -- Dictionaries 3. Illustrators -- Dictionaries 4. Children's literature -- Bio-bibliography

First published 1986

An "ongoing series in which juvenile authors discuss their lives, careers, and published works. Each volume contains essays by 20 established writers or illustrators (e.g., Evaline Ness, Nonny Hogrogian, Betsy Byars, Jean Fritz) who represent all types of literature, preschool to young adult. . . . Some articles focus on biographical information, while others emphasize the writing career. Most, however, address young readers and provide family background, discuss the writing experience, and cite some factors that influenced it. Illustrations include portraits of the authors as children and more recent action pictures and portraits. There are cumulative indexes by authors, important published works, and geographical locations mentioned in the essays." Safford. Guide to Ref Books for Sch Libr Media Cent. 5th edition

920.02   General collections of biography

Donovan, Sandy
   Lethal leaders and military madmen; by Sandy Donovan. Lerner Publications Company 2013 32 p. col. ill. (library) $26.60

Grades: 5 6 7 8 **920.02**
1. Picture books for children 2. Kings and rulers -- Juvenile literature 3. Dictators -- Juvenile literature 4. Military government -- Juvenile literature

ISBN 1467706094; 9781467706094

LC 2012018444

This book by Sandy Donovan is part of the Shockzone Villains series and looks at political and military leaders. "Some of history's most ruthless leaders are headed your way. Some of these rulers schemed their way to the top.

Others just conquered everything around them." (Publisher's note)

920.72   Women

Biography for beginners: women who made a difference. Favorable Impressions 2011 $49

Grades: 3 4 5 6 **920.72**
1. Reference books 2. Women -- Biography

ISBN 978-1-931360-43-2

LC 2011017258

This is a "collection of 60 biographies of women who made an impact in their fields. . . . Each 6- to 10-page article is accompanied by well-chosen illustrations of the women. . . . The articles . . . are written at the appropriate level for elementary-school to middle-grade students and divided into sections that use bold type for the first few words to catch the reader's eye. The use of quotes from the subjects and others enhances the biographies and makes them more personal. . . . The biographies . . . serve as solid resources for young readers." Booklist

Includes glossary and bibliographical references

Branzei, Sylvia
   Adventurers; Sylvia Branzei; illustrated by Melissa Sweet. Running Press 2011 96 p. ill., maps (ebook) $10.95; (paperback) $10.95

Grades: 3 4 5 6 7 **920.72**
1. Women 2. Adventure and adventurers 3. Women -- Biography -- Juvenile literature 4. Women adventurers -- Biography -- Juvenile literature 5. Adventure and adventurers -- Biography -- Juvenile literature

ISBN 9780762443857; 0762436964; 9780762436965

LC 2009923889

This book "provides 6- to 8-page biographical sketches of 12 women who are 'the stuff of legends.' Each one is identified with a character trait, e.g. balloonist Sophie Blanchard is 'Intrepid' and Margaret Bourke-White is 'Relentless,' although most of the adjectives could apply to every subject, as [Sylvia] Branzei makes plain." Among those included are Amelia Earhart, Nellie Bly, Susan Butcher, and Kit Deslauriers. (School Library Journal)

   Cowgirls; illustrated by Sylvia Branzei; by Melissa Sweet. Running Press Kids 2011 96 p. ill. (some col.), map (paperback) $10.95

Grades: 3 4 5 6 7 **920.72**
1. Picture books for children 2. Cowgirls -- Juvenile literature 3. Ranch life -- West (U.S.) -- Juvenile literature 4. Cowgirls -- West (U.S.) -- History -- Juvenile literature 5. Cowgirls -- West (U.S.) -- Biography -- Juvenile literature

ISBN 0762436956; 9780762436958

LC 2009923890

This book "profiles 12 sketches of working cowgirls and rodeo riders from the 19th century through the present day. The term 'cowgirl' also covers other Western types: stagecoach driver Mary Fields is here, along with outlaw Sally Skull and 'Little Sure-Shot' Annie Oakley. 'Lady cowboy poet' Georgie Sicking will probably be new to most readers; one of her poems is included." (School Library Journal)

Includes bibliographical references (p. 92-96)

León, Vicki

  ★ **Outrageous** women of the Middle Ages; by Vicki Leon. Wiley 1998 ix, 118 p.p ill., maps hardcover o.p. (paperback) $14.95; (prebind) $23.95

Grades: 4 5 6 7 8   **920.72**

  1. Middle Ages 2. Women -- History 3. Women -- Biography

  ISBN 9780471170044; 9781435280090

           LC 97030307

In this book, Vicki Leon looks at women of the Middle Ages. She "tells of a Viking killed by a severed head, a queen who knew the meaning of congregating frogs, and much more. The stories and sidebars provide a detailed picture of the times. . . . The women profiled lived in the 6th through 14th centuries in Europe, Asia, and Africa. Their spheres included everything from astronomy to warfare. They were nomads and empresses." (School Library Journal)

  Includes bibliographical references (p. 115-117).

McCann, Michelle Roehm

  Girls who rocked the world; heroines from Sacagawea to Natalie Portman. Michelle Roehm McCann and Amelie Welden. Simon & Schuster 2012 p. cm. (hardcover: alk. paper) $18.99

Grades: 5 6 7 8   **920.72**

  1. Feminism 2. Women -- History 3. Women -- Biography 4. Girls -- Biography -- Juvenile literature

  ISBN 9781582703022; 9781582703619

           LC 2011050502

  Author Michelle Roehm McCann presents "examples of strong, independent female role models, all of whom first impacted the world as teenagers or younger." The book "spans a variety of achievements, interests, and backgrounds, from Harriet Tubman and Coco Chanel to S.E. Hinton and Maya Lin--each with her own incredible story of how she created life-changing opportunities for herself and the world." (Publisher's note)

  Includes bibliographical references and index.

929   Genealogy, names, insignia

Ollhoff, Jim

  Beginning genealogy; expert tips to help you trace your own ancestors. ABDO Pub. Co. 2011 32p il (Your family tree) $18.95

Grades: 4 5 6 7   **929**

  1. Research 2. Genealogy

  ISBN 978-1-61613-460-0; 1-61613-460-7

           LC 2009050812

This is "great . . . for kids interested in genealogy. . . . [It does] a wonderful job of presenting the fundamentals of genealogical research in a clear and exciting manner. . . . Understanding and properly using primary documents is stressed throughout. . . . [An] attractive, spacious [layout]; full-color, sharp images; clearly labeled diagrams; and scattered maps add information and appeal." SLJ

  Includes glossary

  Collecting primary records. ABDO Pub. Co. 2011 32p il (Your family tree) $18.95

Grades: 4 5 6 7   **929**

  1. Research 2. Genealogy

  ISBN 978-1-61613-461-7; 1-61613-461-5

           LC 2009050811

  This describes how to collect primary records for geneological research.

  This is "great . . . for kids interested in genealogy. . . . [It does] a wonderful job of presenting the fundamentals of genealogical research in a clear and exciting manner. . . . Understanding and properly using primary documents is stressed throughout. . . . [An] attractive, spacious [layout]; full-color, sharp images; clearly labeled diagrams; and scattered maps add information and appeal." SLJ

  Includes glossary

  DNA; window to the past: how science can help untangle your family roots. ABDO Pub. Co. 2011 32p il map (Your family tree) $18.95

Grades: 4 5 6 7   **929**

  1. Genetics 2. Genealogy

  ISBN 978-1-61613-462-4; 1-61613-462-3

           LC 2009050808

  This explains how DNA is used in geneology.

  This is "great . . . for kids interested in genealogy. . . . [It does] a wonderful job of presenting the fundamentals of genealogical research in a clear and exciting manner. . . . Understanding and properly using primary documents is stressed throughout. . . . [An] attractive, spacious [layout]; full-color, sharp images; clearly labeled diagrams; and scattered maps add information and appeal." SLJ

  Includes glossary

  Filling the family tree. ABDO Pub. Co. 2011 32p il (Your family tree) lib bdg $18.95

Grades: 4 5 6 7   **929**

  1. Research 2. Genealogy

  ISBN 978-1-61613-464-8; 1-61613-464-X

           LC 2009050806

  This is "great . . . for kids interested in genealogy. . . . [It does] a wonderful job of presenting the fundamentals of genealogical research in a clear and exciting manner. . . . Understanding and properly using primary documents is stressed throughout. . . . [An] attractive, spacious [layout]; full-color, sharp images; clearly labeled diagrams; and scattered maps add information and appeal." SLJ

  Using your research; how to check your facts and use your information. ABDO Pub. Co. 2011 32p il (Your family tree) lib bdg $18.95

Grades: 4 5 6 7   **929**

  1. Research 2. Genealogy

  ISBN 978-1-61613-465-5; 1-61613-465-8

           LC 2009050805

  Presents a brief guide on how to check facts and use other information in genealogical research.

  This is "great . . . for kids interested in genealogy. . . . [It does] a wonderful job of presenting the fundamentals of genealogical research in a clear and exciting manner. . . . Understanding and properly using primary documents is stressed throughout. . . . [An] attractive, spacious [layout]; full-color, sharp images; clearly labeled diagrams; and scattered maps add information and appeal." SLJ

  Includes glossary

Waddell, Dan

Who do you think you are? be a family tree detective. Candlewick Press 2011 24p il $19.99

Grades: 2 3 4 5   **929**

1. Genealogy

ISBN 978-0-7636-5547-1; 0-7636-5547-3

    LC 2010050054

"This guide to genealogy . . . takes readers through the steps of tracing their origins, starting with a who's who of possible extended family members and an explanation of genes. Waddell provides oral history interview tips, Internet search guidelines, and suggestions such as consulting censuses for clues about deceased relatives. Flaps and other interactive features hold additional information. . . . Those with an interest in the topic should discover useful insights, ideas, and tips for conducting research." Publ Wkly

929.9 Forms of insignia and identification

Allen, Kathy

The first American flag; illustrated by Siri Weber Feeney. Picture Window Books 2010 32p il map (Our American story) lib bdg $23.99

Grades: 2 3 4   **929.9**

1. Flags -- United States

ISBN 978-1-4048-5541-0 lib bdg; 1-4048-5541-6 lib bdg

    LC 2009-6892

An introduction to the American flag and its symbolism discusses the features and history of early American flags

This title is "illustrated with well-executed, full-page, color illustrations, maps, and photos. . . . [It has] clearly written information that students can use for either leisure reading or reports." SLJ

Includes glossary and bibliographical references

Bateman, Teresa

★ Red, white, blue, and Uncle who? the stories behind some of America's patriotic symbols. illustrated by John O'Brien. Holiday House 2001 64p il $16.95; pa $6.95

Grades: 4 5 6 7   **929.9**

1. National emblems 2. National monuments

ISBN 0-8234-1285-7; 0-8234-1784-0 pa

    LC 00-57258

This "volume presents 17 'patriotic symbols,' an umbrella term that encompasses everything from the flag to Uncle Sam, from Mount Rushmore to the Korean War Memorial. Bateman finds plenty of interesting information to share about each symbol or site, and browsers will be entertained by the many stories of origination, construction, and history." Booklist

Includes bibliographical references

Jackson, Donna M.

The name game; a look behind the labels. illustrated by Ted Stearn. Viking 2009 64p il $16.99

Grades: 4 5 6 7 8   **929.9**

1. Names

ISBN 978-0-670-01197-1; 0-670-01197-5

    LC 2008-37705

"All kinds of entertaining and random facts are found in this quirky book. Tips for naming pets and companies

are given, in a chapter each, along with hints for remembering people's names, explanations of conventions in other countries, and the system of choosing hurricane monikers. Sports, people, and geographic locations all have different sections. Black-and-white cartoons add a bit of humor. Students will navigate this book with ease." SLJ

930 History of specific continents, countries, localities; extraterrestrial worlds

Adams, Simon

The Kingfisher atlas of the ancient world; illustrated by Katherine Baxter. Kingfisher 2006 44p il $15.95

Grades: 4 5 6 7   **930**

1. Reference books 2. Ancient civilization 3. Historical geography

ISBN 978-0-7534-5914-0; 0-7534-5914-0

"Featuring seventeen . . . hand-illustrated maps and . . . with . . . information about ancient civilizations and peoples, this is [a] . . . pictorial guide to what the world was like between 10,000 B.C. and A.D. 1000. Each . . . map shows the major sites from a particular civilization or group of civilizations. . . . Feature spreads use photographs of cultural and architectural artifacts, as well as additional information, to focus in greater depth on the key cultures of Egypt, Greece, and Rome." Publisher's note

930.1 Archaeology

Barber, Nicola

Lost cities; by Nicola Barber. Capstone Raintree 2013 48 p. col. ill. (hardcover) $29.33; (paperback) $8.99

Grades: 5 6 7 8   **930.1**

1. Picture books for children 2. Extinct cities -- Juvenile literature 3. Legends -- Juvenile literature 4. Archaeology -- History -- Juvenile literature

ISBN 1410949524; 1410949591; 9781410949523; 9781410949592

    LC 2012012891

This book by Nicola Barber is part of the Treasure Hunters series and looks at lost cities. This entry "examines the search for lost cities and the important artefacts within them that can offer us an extraordinary window on to the past. . . . Cities covered in the book include Pompeii, Troy, the desert city of Ubar, and the Inca city of Machu Picchu." (Publisher's note)

Includes bibliographical references (p. 46-47) and index.

Tomb explorers; by Nicola Barber. Capstone Raintree 2013 48 p. ill. (mostly col.) (library) $29.33; (paperback) $8.99

Grades: 5 6 7 8   **930.1**

1. Tombs -- Juvenile literature 2. Antiquities -- Juvenile literature 3. Archaeology -- Juvenile literature 4. Treasure troves -- Juvenile literature 5. Archaeology -- History -- Juvenile literature

ISBN 1410949559; 9781410949554; 9781410949622

    LC 2012012894

This book by Nicola Barber "examines the hunt for and discovery of ancient tombs, and the valuable treasures they hold. . . . Part of the Treasure Hunters series, 'Tomb Explorers' offers a crosscurricular mix of science & technology and history & civilizations. . . .Tombs covered in the book include that of Tutankhamun, the Sumerian royal tombs of Ur, the Terracotta Army of ancient China, and the Mayan tombs of Palanque in the Mexican Rainforest, and the Oseberg ship burial." (Publisher's note)

Includes bibliographical references and index.

Compoint, Stephane
Buried treasures; uncovering secrets of the past. Abrams Books for Young Readers 2011 72p il $19.95
Grades: 5 6 7 8 **930.1**
1. Archeology 2. Antiquities 3. Ancient civilization
ISBN 978-0-8109-9781-3; 0-8109-9781-9
LC 2010021626

"Showcasing the work of a specialist in archaeological photography, this loosely themed album offers a broad range of eye candy for fans of ancient artifacts, fossils, remote natural locales, and rare animals. . . . Confined to captions and a few introductory paragraphs, the text supplies useful background. . . . The photos are . . . dramatically lit, sharply reproduced, and tellingly angled. . . . Casual browsers will consider this book a real find." Booklist

Croy, Anita
Exploring the past. Marshall Cavendish Benchmark 2010 48p il (Invisible worlds) $28.50
Grades: 4 5 6 7 **930.1**
1. Fossils 2. Archeology 3. Human origins 4. Prehistoric peoples 5. Ancient civilization
ISBN 978-0-7614-4194-6; 0-7614-4194-8

The narrative is "clear, well written, broken down into manageable pieces, and peppered with eye-opening facts. The numerous photographs are so phenomenal that they will inspire kids to read the text . . . so that they can wrap their minds around what they see." SLJ

Includes glossary and bibliographical references

Getz, David
★ **Frozen** man; illustrated by Peter McCarty. Holt & Co. 1994 68p il maps hardcover o.p. pa $10.99
Grades: 5 6 7 8 **930.1**
1. Mummies 2. Archeology 3. Prehistoric peoples 4. Italy -- Antiquities -- Juvenile literature
ISBN 0-8050-3261-4; 0-8050-4645-3 pa
LC 94-9109

"This is an account of the mummified stone-age corpse who was found in Austria in 1991. . . . Getz's generally well-organized information and smooth exposition makes the effort to understand the Iceman, as this book calls him, into an intriguing detective story. This could well stimulate the interest of kids who didn't think they liked science or archeology. Black-and-white drawings include useful maps and diagrams." Bull Cent Child Books

Includes glossary and bibliographical references

Hunter, Nick
Ancient treasures; by Nick Hunter; edited by Laura Knowles ... [et al.]; illustrated by Martin Bustamante. Raintree 2013 48 p. col. ill., col. maps (Treasure hunters) (hardcover) $29.33; (paperback) $8.99
Grades: 5 6 7 8 **930.1**
1. Archaeology -- Juvenile literature 2. Buried treasure -- Juvenile literature 3. Ancient civilization -- Juvenile

literature 4. Treasure troves -- Juvenile literature 5. Archaeology -- History -- Juvenile literature
ISBN 1410949508; 9781410949509; 9781410949578
LC 2012012757

"Part of the Treasure Hunters series, 'Ancient Treasures' offers a crosscurricular mix of science & technology and history. . . .Treasures covered in the book include the Roman Hoxne Hoard, the Anglo-Saxon Staffordshire Hoard, the extraordinary discoveries of the Rosetta Stone and Dead Sea Scrolls, and the South American treasures of Lake Guatavita. The book also looks at the motives for these searches, and the importance of responsible archaeology." (Publisher's note)

Includes bibliographical references (p. 46-47) and index.

Matthews, Rupert
Ancient mysteries. QEB Pub. 2011 32p il (Unexplained) lib bdg $28.50
Grades: 4 5 6 7 **930.1**
1. Legends 2. Ancient civilization 3. Curiosities and wonders
ISBN 978-1-59566-854-7; 1-59566-854-3
LC 2010014189

This discusses mysteries in the ancient world.

"This well-written and thoughtfully designed [book] features [an] engrossing [topic]. . . . Though the pages are profusely illustrated with large, well-reproduced photographs and drawings, the layout is not cluttered. This [book] just might inspire kids to seek out more in-depth materials." SLJ

Panchyk, Richard
Archaeology for kids; uncovering the mysteries of our past: 25 activities. Chicago Review Press 2001 146p il map pa $14.95
Grades: 5 6 7 8 **930.1**
1. Archeology 2. Antiquities 3. Ancient civilization 4. Archaeology 5. Antiquities -- Juvenile literature 6. Archaeology -- Juvenile literature 7. Archaeology -- Study and teaching -- Activity programs -- Juvenile literature
ISBN 1-55652-395-5
LC 2001-42134

Twenty five activities support an overview of the science of archaeology as well as some of the secrets it has revealed from ancient civilizations throughout the world

"Panchyk explains things clearly and vividly. . . . Illustrations are plentiful, and suggested activities are practical and illuminate the subject matter well." Booklist

Includes bibliographical references

931 Specific places

Ball, Jacqueline A.
★ **Ancient** China; archaeology unlocks the secrets of China's past. by Jacqueline Ball and Richard Levey, Robert Murowchick, consultant. National Geographic 2006 64p il (National Geographic investigates) hardcover o.p. lib bdg $27.90; $17.95
Grades: 5 6 7 8 **931**
1. China -- Civilization 2. China -- Antiquities
ISBN 9780792278566 lib bdg; 9780792277835

"This volume spotlights archaeological finds from Ancient China. . . . While the discussions of archaeology will hold readers' interest, the accompanying illustrations steal the show." Booklist

Cole, Joanna

Ms. Frizzle's adventures: Imperial China; illustrated by Bruce Degen. Scholastic Press 2005 39p il hardcover o.p. $16.95; pa $6.99

Grades: 2 3 4   **931**

1. China -- History 2. China -- Civilization

ISBN 0-590-10822-0; 0-590-10823-9 pa

Ms. Frizzle "has traded her Magic School Bus for a watch that functions as a time machine. . . . [She] leads three youngsters back a thousand years into China's past. . . . Ms. Frizzle and her fellow time travelers land in a farming village, where they learn that a poor rice harvest has left the farmers unable to pay their taxes. . . . Primary." (Horn Book)

"Readers will savor sidebars touting Chinese contributions to society, pore over Degen's delightfully cluttered compositions and lovely chinoiserie embellishments." Booklist

O'Connor, Jane

★ The **emperor's** silent army; terracotta warriors of Ancient China. Viking 2002 48p il $17.99

Grades: 4 5 6 7   **931**

1. Emperors 2. Shaanxi Sheng (China) -- Antiquities -- Juvenile literature 3. Terra-cotta sculpture, Chinese -- Qin-Han dynasties, 221 B.C.-220 A.D -- Juvenile literature

ISBN 0-670-03512-2

LC 2001-46900

Describes the archaeological discovery of thousands of life-sized terracotta warrior statues in northern China in 1974, and discusses the emperor who had them created and placed near his tomb

"This intriguing book is enhanced by beautiful illustrations—pictures of stone engravings, colorful paintings, drawings, and maps—while numerous photographs show the clay soldiers from different perspectives. . . . The author's writing style is entertaining, yet informative." Book Rep

Includes bibliographical references

Shuter, Jane

Ancient China; [by] Jane Shuter. Heinemann Library 2006 48p il map (Excavating the past) lib bdg $31.43

Grades: 4 5 6   **931**

1. Excavations (Archeology) -- China

ISBN 1-4034-5995-9

LC 2005009178

"Ancient China covers the region's history from the first single kingdom dynasty, Xia (2205 B.C.E. to 1700 B.C.E), to the conquering of China by Mongols in C.E.1279. Shuter includes a history of archaeology conducted by Westerners and by the Chinese government. Artifacts and a few well-preserved burial sites reveal lifestyles of the powerful and wealthy. Short chapters describe living conditions of the poor and of skilled workers as well." SLJ

Includes bibliographical references

932   Egypt to 640

Ancient Egypt; edited by Sherman Hollar. Britannica Educational Pub. in association with Rosen Educational Services 2011 87p il map (Ancient civilizations) lib bdg $31.70

Grades: 5 6 7 8   **932**

1. Egypt -- Civilization 2. Egypt -- History

ISBN 978-1-61530-523-0; 1-61530-523-8

LC 2011004714

This book provides "enough information about the development, way of life, accomplishments, and decline of [Ancient Egypt] without overwhelming readers. Maps; full-color illustrations and photographs, many full page; and sidebars provide additional focus. . . . The use of the Nile and its influence on the development of this civilization is emphasized. . . . The building of the great pyramids and the art of mummification are also mentioned. A detailed discussion of the everyday lives of the rich and the poor provide valuable insight." SLJ

Includes glossary and bibliographical references

Bolton, Anne

Pyramids and mummies. Simon & Schuster 2008 un il map $21.99

Grades: 3 4 5 6   **932**

1. Mummies 2. Pyramids

ISBN 978-1-4169-5873-4; 1-4169-5873-8

LC 2008-299284

"The illustrations are an alluring mix of gold, images from ancient walls, cutaway views, and dried-out bodies. Almost hidden beneath all the visual glamour is a . . . text that begins with the death(s) of Osiris, ends with a game of 'Asps and Ladders,' and in between touches on the preparation of mummies, the history and purposes of Egyptian pyramids, animal mummies, sphinxes, King Tut, and other related topics. All in all, an ephemeral but artfully designed showstopper." SLJ

Hartland, Jessie

★ **How** the sphinx got to the museum. Blue Apple Books 2010 un il $17.99

Grades: 2 3 4   **932**

1. Queens 2. Museums 3. Sphinxes (Mythology)

ISBN 978-1-609050-32-0; 1-609050-32-0

LC 2010-31603

How the seven-ton sphinx of the Pharaoh Hatshepsut got to the Metropolitan Museum of Art in New York City is described "with exhaustive, dizzying, yet crystal clear detail. . . . Before it's over we'll meet art movers, curators, conservators, riggers, registrars, retouchers, and more . . . . Eye-openers abound." Booklist

Hawass, Zahi A.

★ **Tutankhamun**; the mystery of the boy king. by Zahi Hawass. National Geographic 2005 64p il $17.95; lib bdg $27.90

Grades: 3 4 5 6   **932**

1. Kings

ISBN 0-7922-8354-6; 0-7922-8355-4 lib bdg

LC 2004-15002

"Hawass, director of excavations at the Giza pyramids and head of Egypt's archaeological council, . . . offers a solid summary . . . of the complex and controversial 18th dynasty in which Tut lived. . . . Black-and-white shots from the past join rich color photographs that almost glow. Especially marvelous is a stunning recreation, employing current reconstructive techniques, of what Tut might have looked like. . . . A first-rate investigation enriched by beautiful artwork." SLJ

Includes bibliographical references

Henzel, Cynthia Kennedy

Pyramids of Egypt. ABDO Pub. Co. 2011 32p il (Troubled treasures: world heritage sites) $25.65

Grades: 3 4 5   **932**

1. Pyramids

ISBN 978-1-61613-566-9; 1-61613-566-2

LC 2010021308

This "book describes in general terms [the Egyptian pyramids'] construction, . . . distinctive features, and history, as well as threats to its continued existence and both current and past restoration intitiatives. Revealing color photos taken from different heights and angles are supplemented by maps and by graphic reconstructions. . . . Henzel's distinctive approach gives this [book] unusual value for both assignment and general reading." SLJ

Includes glossary

Jestice, Phyllis G.

Ancient Egyptian warfare. Gareth Stevens 2010 32p il map (Ancient warfare) lib bdg $26

Grades: 3 4 5 6   **932**

1. Military art and science -- History 2. Greece -- History

ISBN 978-1-4339-1971-8 lib bdg; 1-4339-1971-0 lib bdg

LC 2009006189

Ancient Egyptian warfare "is presented in a well-organized, contextualized manner. The [author discusses] the overarching history of the times and then [gets] to specifics about weapons and military tactics. . . . A strong purchase for reports and pleasure reading." SLJ

Includes glossary and bibliographical references

Kennett, David

★ Pharaoh; life and afterlife of a God. Walker & Company 2008 48p il map $18.95; lib bdg $19.85

Grades: 3 4 5 6   **932**

1. Pharaohs -- Juvenile literature

ISBN 978-0-8027-9567-0; 0-8027-9567-6; 978-0-8027-9568-7 lib bdg; 0-8027-9568-4 lib bdg

LC 2007-24236

"This extraordinarily handsome [book] delves deeply into the various roles of the pharoah, and, in the process, gives readers a much fuller understanding of Egyptian life. . . . One of the best things about this is the way the narrative moves simply and logically from topics such as flooding to farming and trading. But as fine as the text is, it more than meets its match in the masterful artwork. . . . There is much to see here, and children will want to look at the book again and again." Booklist

Kerrigan, Michael

Egyptians. Marshall Cavendish Benchmark 2010 64p il (Ancients in their own words) $32.79

Grades: 5 6 7 8   **932**

ISBN 978-1-60870-064-6; 1-60870-064-X

Features "Numerous photographs provide visual interest, with text describing the images to give details and background. Translations of the writings offer primary sources to accompany the secondary material presented. . . . The text is interesting enough to read cover to cover while the table of contents' descriptive chapter titles and the comprehensive index enable the . . . [book] to be used for specific research." Libr Media Connect

Includes bibliographical references

Logan, Claudia

★ The 5,000-year-old puzzle; solving a mystery of Ancient Egypt. illustrated by Melissa Sweet. Farrar, Straus & Giroux 2001 41p il $17

Grades: 2 3 4   **932**

1. Excavations (Archeology) 2. Curators 3. Archaeologists 4. Excavations (Archeology) -- Egypt 5. Tombs -- Egypt -- Juvenile fiction 6. Jizah (Egypt) -- Antiquities -- Juvenile fiction

ISBN 0-374-32335-6

LC 00-60243

An account of Dr. George Reisner's 1925 discovery and excavation of a secret tomb in Giza, Egypt, based on archival documents and records, but told through the fictionalized experiences of a young boy named Will who accompanies his father on the dig.

"There's considerable value to the sidebar information . . . and the journal-style exposition of the excavation's painstaking pace. Snapshots and photographed artifacts from the expedition mingle with Sweet's golden acrylic and watercolor scenes, and readers who patiently sift through the fictional bits will be rewarded with an intriguing glimpse of an important excavation." Bull Cent Child Books

Malam, John

The Egyptians. PowerKids Press 2011 30p il map (Dig it: history from objects) lib bdg $25.25

Grades: 3 4 5   **932**

ISBN 978-1-4488-3283-5; 1-4488-3283-7

LC 2010023834

Uses artifacts and other archaeological evidence to describe daily life in ancient Egypt, including their homes and towns, clothes, rulers, religion, and how they fought in war.

"The information is well-written and easily understood, well suited to the curriculum and national standards. Website links are intriguing and students will enjoy adding this piece to their research." Libr Media Connect

Includes glossary and bibliographical references

Rubalcaba, Jill

★ Ancient Egypt; archaeology unlocks the secrets of Egypt's past. by Jill Rubalcaba. National Geographic 2007 64p il map (National Geographic investigates) $17.95; lib bdg $27.90

Grades: 5 6 7 8   **932**

1. Excavations (Archeology) -- Egypt

ISBN 0-7922-7784-8; 978-0-7922-7784-2; 0-7922-7857-7 lib bdg; 978-0-7922-7857-3 lib bdg

LC 2006032111

This describes how archeologists have learned about Ancient Egypt.

This offers "the beautiful photography and illustrations characteristic of the National Geographic Society, [a] well-written [text] and sidebars, and information on recent archaeological finds." SLJ

Includes bibliographical references

Sabuda, Robert

Tutankhamen's gift; written and illustrated by Robert Sabuda. Atheneum Pubs. 1994 un il $17; pa $6.99

Grades: K 1 2 3   932

1. Kings 2. Egypt -- Civilization -- Juvenile literature

ISBN 0-689-31818-9; 0-689-81730-4 pa

LC 93-5401

"His tutor foresees that little Tutankhamen's 'gift for the gods' will someday be revealed. That day comes sooner than expected, when the young boy becomes pharaoh after his brother's death and rebuilds the beautiful temples created by his father and destroyed by his brother. Bold pictures outlined in black against a background of painted, handmade Egyptian papyrus illustrate the book, and an afterword provides historical details." Horn Book Guide

Smith, Miranda

Ancient Egypt. Kingfisher 2010 48p (Navigators) $12.99

Grades: 4 5 6 7   932

1. Egypt -- Civilization

ISBN 978-0-7534-6429-8; 0-7534-6429-2

"Ancient Egypt opens with prominent pharaohs and continues with life at home, within a palace, and amidst the construction of a pyramid. Although it includes such typical subjects as religion, mummification, and tomb raiders, it also comprises female rulers, taxes, and extensive trading expeditions... a good first stop in the research process." Booklist

Stanley, Diane

★ Cleopatra; [by] Diane Stanley, Peter Vennema; illustrated by Diane Stanley. Morrow Junior Bks. 1994 un il map hardcover o.p. pa $7.99

Grades: 4 5 6 7   932

1. Queens

ISBN 0-688-10413-4; 0-688-10414-2 lib bdg; 0-688-15480-8 pa

LC 93-27032

This is a biography of the ancient Egyptian queen

"Lucid writing combines with carefully selected anecdotes, often attributed to the Greek historian Plutarch to create an engaging narrative. . . . Stanley's stunning, full-color gouache artwork is arresting in its large, well-composed images executed in flat Greek style." SLJ

Includes bibliographical references

Twist, Clint

Cleopatra; Queen of Egypt. by Clint Twist and Ian Andrew. Candlewick Press 2012 30 p. (reinforced) $19.99

Grades: 4 5 6   932

1. Queens 2. Egypt -- Civilization -- Juvenile literature

ISBN 0763660957; 9780763660956

LC 2012942304

This book by Clint Twist presents a biography of Egyptian ruler Cleopatra. It covers topics "such as her complicated relationships with both Julius Caesar and, later, Mark Antony. Her role in the Ptolemy family is described. . . . Illustrated flaps to lift and explore and sidebars offer up .

. . details about hairstyles, jewelry, battles, and religion." (School Library Journal)

Van Vleet, Carmella

Great Ancient Egypt projects you can build yourself. Nomad 2006 122p il (Build it yourself series) pa $14.95

Grades: 4 5 6   932

1. Handicraft 2. Egypt -- Civilization

ISBN 0-9771294-5-4

"The fascinating text in this collection of 30 projects is supplemented by sepia-colored illustrations or photos on each page. . . . The projects are tied to many aspects of this civilization, including the Nile River, agriculture, craftsmanship, pyramids, mummies, family, farming, bartering, the Egyptian calendar, Royal Library of Alexandria, temples, hieroglyphs, and more." SLJ

Includes bibliographical references

Weitzman, David L.

★ Pharaoh's boat; written and illustrated by David Weitzman. Houghton Mifflin Harcourt 2009 un il map $17

Grades: 4 5 6 7   932

1. Ships 2. Kings 3. Ships, Ancient -- Egypt -- Juvenile literature

ISBN 978-0-547-05341-7; 0-547-05341-X

LC 2008036081

"Weitzman recounts the construction of a boat made for the Pharaoh Cheops and discusses its rediscovery and restoration in the 20th century. He weaves the history, texts, mythology, and customs of ancient Egypt into an effective narrative. . . . The volume's stylized illustrations are inspired by the two-dimensional depictions from ancient Egyptian art. The paintings' earth tones, accentuated by bright greens and blues, are both appropriate for the subject matter and pleasing to the eye." SLJ

Whiting, Jim

Threat to ancient Egyptian treasures; by Jim Whiting. Mitchell Lane Publishers 2007 32p il (On the verge of extinction: crisis in the environment) lib bdg $25.70

Grades: 3 4 5   932

1. Egypt -- Antiquities

ISBN 978-1-58415-588-1

LC 2007000817

This describes dangers to ancient Egyptian archeological sites and artifacts, including sand storms, air pollution, flooding, and human activity.

"Short chapters, large font, and pronunciation guides to key words engage children doing research, but the depth of information is not compromised. . . . Colorful, up-close photographs are accompanied by satisfying explanatory captions." SLJ

Includes glossary and bibliographical references

935 Mesopotamia to 637 and Iranian Plateau to 637

Gruber, Beth

★ Ancient Iraq; archaeology unlocks the secrets of Iraq's past. by Beth Gruber; Tony Wilkinson, consultant.

National Geographic 2007 64p il map (National Geographic investigates) $17.95; lib bdg $27.90
Grades: 5 6 7 8   **935**
1. Excavations (Archeology) -- Iraq
ISBN 978-0-7922-5382-2; 978-0-7922-5383-9 lib bdg
LC 2006032109
This explores the "world of ancient Iraq, in the region once known as Mesopotamia, the cradle of civilization. Join scientists as they study the Citadel in northern Iraq; explore the ancient city of Nineveh; and see how ancient treasures help scientists reassemble the mosaic-like puzzle of Iraq's past." Publisher's note
Includes bibliographical references

Jestice, Phyllis G.
Ancient Persian warfare. Gareth Stevens 2010 32p il map (Ancient warfare) lib bdg $26
Grades: 3 4 5 6   **935**
1. Military art and science -- History
ISBN 978-1-4339-1973-2 lib bdg; 1-4339-1973-7 lib bdg
LC 2009006199
Ancient Persian warfare "is presented in a well-organized, contextualized manner. The [author discusses] the overarching history of the times and then [gets] into specifics about weapons and military tactics.... A strong purchase for reports and pleasure reading." SLJ
Includes glossary and bibliographical references

Kerrigan, Michael
Mesopotamians. Marshall Cavendish Benchmark 2010 64p il (Ancients in their own words) lib bdg $32.79
Grades: 5 6 7 8   **935**
1. Iraq -- Civilization
ISBN 978-1-60870-066-0; 1-60870-066-6
"Numerous photographs provide visual interest, with text describing the images to give details and background. Translations of the writings offer primary sources to accompany the secondary material presented. . . . The text is interesting enough to read cover to cover while the table of contents' descriptive chapter titles and the comprehensive index enable the . . . [book] to be used for specific research." Libr Media Connect
Includes bibliographical references

936   Europe north and west of Italian Peninsula to ca. 499

Aronson, Marc
★ **If** stones could speak; unlocking the secrets of Stonehenge. by Marc Aronson; with Mike Parker Pearson and the Riverside Project. National Geographic 2010 64p il map $17.95; lib bdg $26.90
Grades: 4 5 6 7   **936**
1. Archeology 2. Archaeologists 3. College teachers 4. Excavations (Archeology) -- Juvenile literature 5. Stonehenge -- England
ISBN 978-1-4263-0599-3; 1-4263-0599-0; 978-1-4263-0600-6 lib bdg; 1-4263-0600-8 lib bdg
"Aronson investigates the work of archaeologist Mike Parker Pearson and his controversial theory that Stonehenge is but one end of a memorial ritual pathway that would

have had an equivalent wood structure at the other end. . . . Time lines, resource lists, and photos of researchers at work add even more value to this informative, thought-provoking study. A uniquely perceptive look at how real science works." Booklist
Includes bibliographical references

Green, Jen
★ **Ancient** Celts; archaeology unlocks the secrets of the Celts' past. by Jen Green; Bettina Arnold, consultant. National Geographic 2008 64p il map (National Geographic investigates) $17.95; lib bdg $27.90
Grades: 4 5 6 7   **936**
1. Celts 2. Celtic civilization 3. Excavations (Archeology) -- Europe
ISBN 978-1-4263-0225-1; 1-4263-0225-8; 978-1-4263-0226-8 lib bdg; 1-4263-0226-6 lib bdg
LC 2007047836
This describes ancient Celtic civilization and how archeologists have found out about it.
"With excellent-quality photographs and a well-written text, this is a thorough presentation of the most up-to-date knowledge about this ancient European culture." SLJ
Includes glossary and bibliographical references

Millard, Anne
A street through time; written by Anne Millard; illustrated by Steve Noon. Revised ed. DK Pub. 2012 32p col il $17.99
Grades: 4 5 6 7   **936**
1. Cities and towns
ISBN 0-7894-3426-1
LC 98-3226
"The time-line construct is a useful demonstration for children, and the busy vistas would make a fine spring-board for encouraging students to create scenes of local history." Horn Book Guide

936.2   England to 410 and Wales to 410

Henzel, Cynthia Kennedy
Stonehenge. ABDO Pub. Co. 2011 32p il (Troubled treasures: world heritage sites) lib bdg $25.65
Grades: 3 4 5   **936.2**
1. Megalithic monuments 2. Stonehenge -- England
ISBN 978-1-61613-567-6; 1-61613-567-0
LC 2010021307
This "book describes in general terms [Stonehenge's] construction, . . . distinctive features, and history, as well as threats to its continued existence and both current and past restoration intitiatives. Revealing color photos taken from different heights and angles are supplemented by maps and by graphic reconstructions. . . . Henzel's distinctive approach gives this [book] unusual value for both assignment and general reading." SLJ
Includes glossary

937 Italian Peninsula to 476 and adjacent territories to 476

Ancient Rome; edited by Michael Anderson. Britannica Educational Pub. in association with Rosen Educational Services 2011 88p il map (Ancient civilizations) lib bdg $31.70

Grades: 5 6 7 8   **937**

1. Rome -- Civilization 2. Rome -- History
ISBN 978-1-61530-522-3; 1-61530-522-X

LC 2011004749

This book provides "enough information about the development, way of life, accomplishments, and decline of [Ancient Rome] without overwhelming readers. Maps; full-color illustrations and photographs, many full page; and sidebars provide additional focus. . . . [The book] discusses the military expertise of Caesar and Pompey and the winning of the Punic Wars that led to world domination. The Romans' genius in engineering is highlighted." SLJ

Includes glossary and bibliographical references

Beller, Susan Provost

Roman legions on the march; soldiering in the ancient Roman Army. by Susan Provost Beller. Twenty-First Century Books 2008 112p il map (Soldiers on the battlefront) lib bdg $33.26

Grades: 5 6 7 8   **937**

1. Soldiers -- Rome
ISBN 978-0-8225-6781-3

LC 2006037829

"The format is inviting with a variety of fonts at the beginning of each chapter, quotations, and a multitude of illustrations. . . . The text is clear and to the point, and chapters are divided into short topics." SLJ

Includes bibliographical references

Bingham, Jane

How people lived in ancient Rome. PowerKids Press 2009 30p il map (How people lived) lib bdg $25.25; pa $10.60

Grades: 4 5 6 7   **937**

1. Rome -- Social life and customs
ISBN 978-1-4042-4432-0 lib bdg; 1-4042-4432-8 lib bdg; 978-1-4358-2622-9 pa; 1-4358-2622-1 pa

LC 2007-40221

Describes everyday life among the ancient Romans, covering family life, marriage, leisure, education, clothing, food and drink, warfare, religion, and funerals

"Clear, readable narrative is supplemented by large color and b&w reproductions of Roman art and artifacts. . . . It will hold the attention of both readers and reasearchers, and is a good choice for collections that serve elementary and younger middle level students." Libr Media Connect

Includes bibliographical references

Deckker, Zilah

★ **Ancient** Rome; archaeology unlocks the secrets of Rome's past. by Zilah Deckker; Robert Lindley Vann, Consultant. National Geographic 2007 64p il map (National Geographic investigates) $17.95; lib bdg $27.90

Grades: 4 5 6 7   **937**

1. Archeology 2. Rome -- Antiquities 3. Rome --

Civilization
ISBN 978-1-4263-0128-5; 978-1-4263-0129-2 lib bdg

LC 2007024795

This describes what archeologists have learned about Ancient Rome

Includes glossary and bibliographical references

Deem, James M.

★ **Bodies** from the ash. Houghton Mifflin 2005 50p il $16

Grades: 4 5 6 7   **937**

1. Pompeii (Extinct city)
ISBN 0-618-47308-4

LC 2004-26553

"On August 24, 79 C.E., the long-silent Mt. Vesuvius erupted, and volcanic ash rained down on the 20,000 residents of Pompeii. This photo-essay explains what happened when the volcano exploded—and how the results of this disaster were discovered hundreds of years later. . . . [This offers an] enormous amount of information. . . . But the jewels here are the numerous . . . photographs, especially those featuring the plaster casts and skeletons of people in their death throes. . . . Excellent for browsers as well as researchers." Booklist

Hanel, Rachael

Gladiators. Creative Education 2008 48p il (Fearsome fighters) lib bdg $31.35

Grades: 4 5 6   **937**

1. Gladiators 2. Rome -- Civilization
ISBN 978-1-58341-535-1 lib bdg; 1-58341-535-1 lib bdg

LC 2006021842

This "recounts the brutality and cruelty of fighting for sport celebrated during Roman times. . . . [The book does] an adequate job of covering fighting techniques, weapons, and history. Photographs and archival reproductions enhance the [presentation]; sidebars provide additional information." Horn Book Guide

Includes glossary and bibliographical references

James, Simon

Ancient Rome; written by Simon James. rev ed.; DK Pub. 2008 72p il map (DK eyewitness books) $15.99

Grades: 4 5 6 7   **937**

1. Rome -- Civilization
ISBN 978-0-7566-3766-8; 0-7566-3766-X

LC 2008-276034

First published 1990 by Knopf

A photo essay documenting ancient Rome and the people who lived there as revealed through the many artifacts they left behind, including shields, swords, tools, toys, cosmetics, and jewelry

Includes glossary

Kerrigan, Michael

Romans. Marshall Cavendish Benchmark 2010 64p il (Ancients in their own words) lib bdg $32.79

Grades: 5 6 7 8   **937**

1. Rome -- Civilization
ISBN 978-1-60870-067-7; 1-60870-067-4

"Numerous photographs provide visual interest, with text describing the images to give details and background. Translations of the writings offer primary sources to accompany the secondary material presented. . . . The text is interesting enough to read cover to cover while the table of contents' descriptive chapter titles and the comprehensive index enable the . . . [book] to be used for specific research." Libr Media Connect

Includes bibliographical references

Lassieur, Allison

★ The **ancient** Romans; written by Allison Lassieur. Franklin Watts 2004 112p il map (People of the ancient world) lib bdg $30.50; pa $9.95

Grades: 5 6 7 8   937

1. Rome -- Civilization

ISBN 0-531-12338-3 lib bdg; 0-531-16742-9 pa

LC 2004-1955

"This attractive, thorough, and comprehensible book . . . offers a stellar introduction to life in ancient Rome." Booklist

Includes bibliographical references

Malam, John

The **Romans.** PowerKids Press 2011 30p il map (Dig it: history from objects) lib bdg $25.25

Grades: 3 4 5   937

1. Rome -- Civilization

ISBN 978-1-4488-3285-9; 1-4488-3285-3

LC 2010023832

This book about the Romans includes information about "homes and towns, daily life, clothing, religion, and entertainment. . . . The layout is crisp and the object illustrations and photographs, plus the 'What does it tell us' section provide visual understanding. These qualities will assist the teacher who needs to differentiate instruction. The information is well-written and easily understood, well suited to the curriculum and national standards. Website links are intriguing and students will enjoy adding this piece to their research." Libr Media Connect

Includes glossary and bibliographical references

Mann, Elizabeth

★ The **Roman** Colosseum; with illustrations by Michael Racz. Mikaya Press 1998 45p il (Wonders of the world) $19.95

Grades: 4 5 6   937

1. Amphitheaters -- Rome -- Juvenile literature 2. Rome (Italy) -- Antiquities -- Juvenile literature 3. Rome (Italy) -- Buildings, structures, etc -- Juvenile literature 4. Colosseum (Rome, Italy)

ISBN 0-9650493-3-7

LC 98-20060

Describes the building of the Colosseum in ancient Rome, and tells how it was used

This offers "a clear, well-written text and full-color drawings and paintings." SLJ

Includes glossary

Murrell, Deborah Jane

Gladiator; written by Deborah Murrell. QEB Pub. 2010 32p il map (QEB warriors) lib bdg $28.50

Grades: 4 5 6 7   937

1. Gladiators

ISBN 978-1-59566-736-6 lib bdg; 1-59566-736-9 lib bdg

LC 2009-3540

"Bold, comprehensible type and full-color and black-and-white illustrations; reproductions; and photographs will make this offering a hit with its target audience, including reluctant readers." SLJ

Includes glossary

Park, Louise

The **Roman** gladiators; by Louise Park and Timothy Love. Marshall Cavendish Benchmark 2009 32p il (Ancient and medieval people) $19.95

Grades: 4 5 6   937

1. Gladiators

ISBN 978-0-7614-4443-5; 0-7614-4443-2

This title has "a simple and elegant design with the proper balance of quality writing and quantity of information. . . . Handy time lines, well-chosen photos of ruins and artifacts, quality illustrations, inset 'Quick Facts,' and 'What You Should Know About' features will grab reluctant readers and captivate even those with short attention spans." SLJ

Includes glossary

Rice, Rob S.

Ancient Roman warfare. Gareth Stevens 2010 32p il map (Ancient warfare) lib bdg $26

Grades: 3 4 5 6   937

1. Military art and science -- History 2. Rome -- History

ISBN 978-1-4339-1974-9 lib bdg; 1-4339-1974-5 lib bdg

LC 2009006201

Ancient Roman warfare "is presented in a well-organized, contextualized manner. The [author discusses] the overarching history of the times and then [gets] into specifics about weapons and military tactics. . . . A strong purchase for reports and pleasure reading." SLJ

Includes glossary and bibliographical references

Riggs, Kate

Gladiators. Creative Education 2011 24p il (Great warriors) $24.25; pa $8.99

Grades: K 1 2   937

1. Gladiators

ISBN 978-1-60818-000-4; 1-60818-000-X; 978-0-89812-571-9 pa; 0-89812-571-5 pa

LC 2010019599

An introduction to the Roman warriors known as gladiators, including their history, lifestyle, weapons, and how they remain a part of today's culture through sports such as wrestling.

This title makes gladiators "accessible to students just beginning to read on their own. The text and design of the [book is] spare, and vocabulary words are introduced unobtrusively. . . . The concepts are simple, but introduced without oversimplification that might lead to misunderstandings. [This is an] excellent [introduction]—and fun to read aloud." SLJ

Includes glossary and bibliographical references

Sonneborn, Liz

Pompeii; by Liz Sonneborn. Twenty-First Century Books 2008 80p il map (Unearthing ancient worlds) lib bdg $30.60

Grades: 5 6 7 8   937

1. Excavations (Archeology) -- Italy 2. Pompeii

(Extinct city)
ISBN 978-0-8225-7505-4 lib bdg; 0-8225-7505-1 lib bdg
LC 2007022058

This describes the excavation of the Roman city buried in lava and ash when the volcano Mount Vesuvius erupted in A.D. 79.

This "clearly written [title is] illustrated with large photographs and period artwork, and the pages are broken up with text boxes featuring quotes and interesting anecdotes." SLJ

Includes glossary and bibliographical references

Ancient Rome; edited by Michael Anderson. Britannica Educational Pub. in association with Rosen Educational Services 2011 88p il map (Ancient civilizations) lib bdg $31.70
Grades: 5 6 7 8   937
1. Greece -- Civilization
ISBN 978-1-61530-522-3; 1-61530-522-X
LC 2011004749

This book provides "enough information about the development, way of life, accomplishments, and decline of [Ancient Rome] without overwhelming readers. Maps; full-color illustrations and photographs, many full page; and sidebars provide additional focus. . . . [The book] discusses the military expertise of Caesar and Pompey and the winning of the Punic Wars that led to world domination. The Romans' genius in engineering is highlighted." SLJ

Includes glossary and bibliographical references

938   Greece to 323

Ancient Greece; edited by Michael Anderson. Britannica Educational Pub. in association with Rosen Educational Services 2012 88p il (Ancient civilizations) lib bdg $31.70
Grades: 5 6 7 8   938
ISBN 978-1-61530-513-1; 1-61530-513-0
LC 2011000086

This book provides "enough information about the development, way of life, accomplishments, and decline of [Ancient Greece] without overwhelming readers. Maps; full-color illustrations and photographs, many full page; and sidebars provide additional focus. . . . The system of city-states is explained. Literature, art, and architecture and their lasting influence are described in detail." SLJ

Includes glossary and bibliographical references

Kerrigan, Michael
Greeks. Marshall Cavendish Benchmark 2010 64p il (Ancients in their own words) lib bdg $32.79
Grades: 5 6 7 8   938
1. Greece -- Civilization
ISBN 978-1-60870-065-3; 1-60870-065-8

"Numerous photographs provide visual interest, with text describing the images to give details and background. Translations of the writings offer primary sources to accompany the secondary material presented. . . . The text is interesting enough to read cover to cover while the table of contents' descriptive chapter titles and the comprehensive

index enable the . . . [book] to be used for specific research." Libr Media Connect
Includes bibliographical references

Malam, John
The **Greeks**. PowerKids Press 2011 30p il map (Dig it: history from objects) lib bdg $25.25
Grades: 3 4 5   938
ISBN 978-1-4488-3284-2; 1-4488-3284-5
LC 2010023833

This book about the ancient Greeks includes information about "homes and towns, daily life, clothing, religion, and entertainment. . . . The layout is crisp and the object illustrations and photographs, plus the 'What does it tell us' section provide visual understanding. These qualities will assist the teacher who needs to differentiate instruction. The information is well-written and easily understood, well suited to the curriculum and national standards. Website links are intriguing and students will enjoy adding this piece to their research." Libr Media Connect

Includes glossary and bibliographical references

McGee, Marni
★ **Ancient** Greece; archaeology unlocks the secrets of Greece's past. by Marni McGee; Michael Shanks, consultant. National Geographic 2007 64p il map (National Geographic investigates) $17.95; lib bdg $27.90
Grades: 5 6 7 8   938
1. Excavations (Archeology) -- Greece 2. Greece -- Civilization
ISBN 978-0-7922-7826-9; 0-7922-7826-7; 978-0-7922-7872-6 lib bdg; 0-7922-7872-0 lib bdg
LC 2006032108

This describes how archeologists have found out about Ancient Greek civilization

This offers "the beautiful photography and illustrations characteristic of the National Geographic Society, [a] well-written [text] and sidebars, and information on recent archaeological finds." SLJ

Includes bibliographical references

Park, Louise
The **Spartan** hoplites; by Louise Park and Timothy Love. Marshall Cavendish Benchmark 2009 32p il map (Ancient and medieval people) $19.95
Grades: 4 5 6   938
1. Soldiers 2. Sparta (Extinct city) 3. Athens (Greece) -- History
ISBN 978-0-7614-4449-7; 0-7614-4449-1
LC 2008-55779

This title has "a simple and elegant design with the proper balance of quality writing and quantity of information. . . . Handy time lines, well-chosen photos of ruins and artifacts, quality illustrations, inset 'Quick Facts', and 'What You Should Know About' features will grab reluctant readers and captivate even those with short attention spans." SLJ

Includes glossary

Reynolds, Susan
The **first** marathon: the legend of Pheidippides; by Susan Reynolds; illustrated by Daniel Minter. Albert Whitman & Company 2006 un il $16.95
Grades: 2 3 4   938
1. Marathon running 2. Marathon, Battle of, 490 B.C.

3. Runners (Athletes)
ISBN 978-0-8075-0867-1; 0-8075-0867-5

LC 2005024618

The author tells the "story of how the Greeks fought off the mighty Persian army on the plains of Marathon, and how the young long-distance runner Pheidippides ran 140 miles in 36 hours to Sparta to ask for help, then ran back without stopping, fought in the battle, ran to tell Athens of the victory, and died. Now marathons are named for his heroic run. The dramatic, full-color, double-page illustrations, with heavy black accents, show the strong, rhythmic movement of the brave young athlete, the battle scenes, and then runners across the world today." Booklist

Rice, Rob S.

Ancient Greek warfare. Gareth Stevens 2010 32p il map (Ancient warfare) lib bdg $26
Grades: 3 4 5 6   938
1. Military art and science -- History
ISBN 978-1-4339-1972-5 lib bdg; 1-4339-1972-9 lib bdg

LC 2009006198

Ancient Greek warfare "is presented in a well-organized, contextualized manner. The [author discusses] the overarching history of the times and then [gets] into specifics about weapons and military tactics. . . . A strong purchase for reports and pleasure reading." SLJ

Includes glossary and bibliographical references

Steele, Phillip

Ancient Greece; by Philip Steele. Kingfisher 2011 48 p. ill. (hardcover) $12.99
Grades: 4 5 6 7   938
1. Greece -- Civilization -- Juvenile literature
ISBN 0753465795; 9780753465790

In this "look at ancient Greece," author Philip Steele "offers young readers insight into the origins of all things Greek. Two page spreads cover Minoan civilization, the rise of the Mycenaean, war with Troy, the establishment of city-states, and the spread of the Hellenistic empire in a somewhat chronological order. Digital illustrations merge with historical artifacts, maps, works of art, and photographs." (Children's Literature)

939   Other parts of ancient world

Cline, Eric H.

★ Digging for Troy; from Homer to Hisarlik. [by] Jill Rubalcaba and Eric H. Cline; with illustrations by Sarah S. Brannen. Charlesbridge 2011 74p il map $17.95; pa $9.95
Grades: 5 6 7 8   939
1. Trojan War 2. Archaeologists -- Juvenile literature 3. Civilization, Mycenaean -- Juvenile literature 4. Excavations (Archaeology) -- Turkey -- Troy (Extinct city) -- Juvenile literature
ISBN 978-1-58089-326-8; 1-58089-326-0; 978-1-58089-327-5 pa; 1-58089-327-9 pa

LC 2010-07586

"Rubalcaba teams up with a noted archaeologist to make sense of the complicated, contradictory, contradictory history and remains of the Turkish site called Hisarlik, better

known as Troy. . . . The book begins with a brief but exciting retelling of the Trojan War . . . and goes on to profile Heinrich Schliemann. . . . After Schliemann, generations of archaeologists have excavated Hisarlik: along with the history of the excavations, readers are given an overview of technological developments in the field. . . . Source notes and an impressive bibliography attest to meticulous research and guide readers to journal articles, books, and online museum exhibits. Elegant illustrations mimicking Greek red-figure pottery are lovely and appropriate. Extraordinarily readable, gracefully laid out, and speckled with lines from The Iliad, this book will inspire young people interested in solving the mysteries of the past." SLJ

Includes bibliographical references

Sherrow, Victoria

★ Ancient Africa; archaeology unlocks the secrets of Africa's past. by Victoria Sherrow; James Denbow, consultant. National Geographic Society 2007 64p il map (National Geographic investigates) $17.95
Grades: 4 5 6 7   939
1. Africa -- Civilization
ISBN 978-0-7922-5384-6; 0-7922-5384-1

LC 2007277594

This describes archeological discoveries about ancient peoples of Africa including the Dogon people of Mali, the ancient city of Jenne-jeno, and the Kushite temples at Jebel Barkal.

Includes bibliographical references

940   History of specific continents, countries, localities in modern world; extraterrestrial worlds

Foster, Karen

Atlas of Europe. Picture Window Books 2008 32p il map (Picture Window Books world atlases) lib bdg $27.93
Grades: 2 3 4   940
1. Europe
ISBN 978-1-4048-3882-6 lib bdg; 1-4048-3882-1 lib bdg

This introduction to the geography of Europe offers maps and information about countries, landforms, bodies of water, climate, plants, animals, population, people and customs, places of interest, industries, transportation, and the Orient Express.

Includes glossary

Lyons, Mary E.

Feed the children first; Irish memories of the Great Hunger. edited by Mary E. Lyons. Atheneum Bks. for Young Readers 2002 43p il pbk. $22.99
Grades: 5 6 7 8   940
1. Famines 2. Ireland -- History
ISBN 9781442482920

LC 00-49606

The editor presents extracts from memoirs of the Irish famine period. Bibliography. "Intermediate, middle school." (Horn Book)

Lyons "compiles quotations from Irish citizens on the devastating effects of the potato famine that ravaged Ireland between 1845 and 1852." Publ Wkly

940.1 Early history to 1453

Adkins, Jan
★ **What** if you met a knight? [by] Jan Adkins, scribe and illuminator. Roaring Brook Press 2006 32p il $16.95
Grades: 3 4 5 6   **940.1**
1. Medieval civilization 2. Knights and knighthood
ISBN 1-59643-148-2; 978-1-59643-148-5
LC 2005-29163
"Adkins sets out to debunk some common misconceptions about knights, and he does so with style and wit. . . . Light in approach but quite informative, the text ably explains the feudal system, the business of knighthood, and the origins of legends such as King Arthur and dragons, and also discusses castles, arms, and the Crusades. Throughout the book, colorful, detailed illustrations and captions provide information even as they open windows on the medieval world." Booklist

Aliki
★ A **medieval** feast; written and illustrated by Aliki. Crowell 1983 un il hardcover o.p. pa $6.95
Grades: 2 3 4 5   **940.1**
1. Courts and courtiers 2. Medieval civilization 3. Dining -- History 4. Festivals -- History
ISBN 0-690-04246-9 lib bdg; 0-06-446050-9 pa
LC 82-45923
"In pictures of minute, charming detail and vibrant, translucent colors, Aliki takes us through the ritual of preparation and the enthusiastic consumption of a medieval feast served to a king and his retinue when they stop for a few days at Camdenton Manor. Not to be outdone by the art, the text has its own various facets. There is the fictional story set in type outside the art and there is within the paintings a collection of delightful historical, gastronomical, agricultural, and zoological facts printed by hand. And throughout the spendid whole are border decorations worthy of the great illuminated manuscripts." Child Book Rev Serv

Ashman, Linda
★ **Come** to the castle! a visit to a castle in thirteenth-century England. illuminated by S.D. Schindler. Roaring Brook Press 2009 un il $17.95
Grades: 3 4 5   **940.1**
1. Castles 2. Stories in rhyme 3. Medieval civilization
ISBN 978-1-59643-155-3; 1-59643-155-5
"Wit meets historical accuracy in a pitch-perfect mix of laugh-out-loud text and entertaining image." Kirkus

Boyer, Crispin
Everything castles; capture these facts, photos, and fun to be king of the castle! 2011 64p il (National Geographic kids) lib bdg $25.90; pa $12.95
Grades: 3 4 5 6   **940.1**
1. Castles 2. Medieval civilization
ISBN 978-1-4263-0804-8 lib bdg; 1-4263-0804-3 lib bdg; 978-1-4263-0803-1 pa; 1-4263-0803-5 pa
This describes the history of medieval castles and their inhabitants.
"Exploding with astounding full-color photographs and written in an appealing conversational tone, [this book is] for every kid. . . . The [text] will keep kids interested and turning pages to discover more and more facts. . . . [This]

compelling, browseable, and completely engrossing [title] will delight readers." SLJ
Includes glossary and bibliographical references

Corbishley, Mike
The **Middle** Ages; 3rd ed.; Chelsea House 2007 96p il map (Cultural atlas for young people) $35
Grades: 5 6 7 8   **940.1**
1. Middle Ages 2. Medieval civilization
ISBN 978-0-8160-6825-8; 0-8160-6825-9
First published 1989
Maps, charts, illustrations, and text explore the history and culture of the Middle Ages.
"The maps are excellent, precise, clear, and easy to read and understand, and the illustrations, particularly those of works of art, are wonderful. . . . This attractive volume provides an intriguing cross-cultural look at the medieval world. An excellent addition." SLJ
Includes glossary and bibliographical references

Durman, Laura
Castle life; by Laura Durman. Arcturus Pub. 2013 32 p. col. ill. (library) $28.50
Grades: 4 5 6   **940.1**
1. Castles -- Juvenile literature 2. Medieval civilization -- Juvenile literature
ISBN 1848585608; 9781848585607
LC 2011051440
In this book, author "[Laura] Durman presents young readers with a . . . view of what life was really like for everyday people in the Middle Ages. Bound by the strict societal system known as feudalism, peasants, knights, and nobles shared space . . . in castles. Readers take a room by room tour, learning how castles functioned both day-to-day, when under siege, and at times of feasting and banqueting." (Children's Literature)

Knights; by Laura Durman. Arcturus Pub. 2012 32 p. col. ill. (library) $28.50
Grades: 4 5 6   **940.1**
1. Picture books for children 2. Knights and knighthood -- Juvenile literature
ISBN 1848585616; 9781848585614
LC 2011051452
This book by Laura Durman is part of the Knights and Castles series and looks at knights. The "books cover a wide range of topics such as weapons, castle construction, food, religion, and the structure and hierarchy of society." Full-color photographs and illustrations are included. (School Library Journal)
Includes bibliographical references (p. 31) and index.

Galloway, Priscilla
★ **Archers,** alchemists, and 98 other medieval jobs you might have loved or loathed; art by Martha Newbigging. Annick Press 2003 96p il lib bdg $24.95; pa $14.95
Grades: 3 4 5 6   **940.1**
1. Medieval civilization 2. Occupations -- Juvenile literature
ISBN 1-55037-811-2 lib bdg; 1-55037-810-4 pa
"Galloway introduces medieval Europe from 1000 to 1500 not by recounting dates, wars, and rulers but by discussing the occupations available in the society. . . . The jaunty, cartoonlike ink drawings, brightened with color

washes, heighten the informal, upbeat tone of the informative text." Booklist

Includes bibliographical references

Helget, Nicole
    Barbarians; Nicole Helget. Creative Education 2012 48 p. (alk. paper) $35.65
Grades: 5 6 7 8   **940.1**
    1. Huns 2. Nomads 3. Vikings 4. Teutonic peoples 5. Classical civilization 6. Middle Ages -- Juvenile literature 7. Migrations of nations -- Juvenile literature
    ISBN 1608181820; 9781608181827
                                                    LC 2011035798
    This book by Nicole Lea Helget "focuses on the transient, adaptable Gelts, Franks, Goths, Huns, and Vikings, collectively known as 'barbarians,' and their differing warring skills against the Greek and Roman Empires." (Booklist) "Viewed as threats by the Romans in particular, the barbarian people were often co-opted or conquered and then integrated into the Empire. Eventually, as the Roman Empire waned, the pressure of nomadic barbarians proved too much to withstand and Rome fell." (Children's Literature)
    Includes bibliographical references and index

Kroll, Steven
    ★ **Barbarians!** illustrated by Robert Byrd. Dutton Children's Books 2009 48p il $18.99
Grades: 3 4 5   **940.1**
    1. Huns 2. Goths 3. Mongols 4. Vikings 5. Middle Ages
    ISBN 978-0-525-47958-1; 0-525-47958-9
                                                    LC 2008-39210
    "Kroll introduces four notable groups referred to by their enemies as barbarians: the Goths, the Huns, the Vikings, and the Mongols. . . . Showing clear differences among the four groups, the many detailed, energetic ink-and-watercolor illustrations show the barbarians at home and at war. . . . This handsome volume will fill a collection gap while providing warrior-loving browsers with an informative and brightly illustrated book to enjoy." Booklist

Langley, Andrew
    Medieval life; written by Andrew Langley; photographed by Geoff Brightling. rev ed; DK Pub. 2011 72p il (DK eyewitness books) lib bdg $19.99
Grades: 4 5 6 7   **940.1**
    1. Medieval civilization
    ISBN 9780756682828 lib bdg
    First published 1996 by Knopf
    An illustrated look at various aspects of life in medieval Europe, covering everyday life, religion, royalty, and more.

Park, Louise
    The **medieval** knights; by Louise Park and Timothy Love. Marshall Cavendish Benchmark 2009 32p il map (Ancient and medieval people) $19.95
Grades: 4 5 6   **940.1**
    1. Medieval civilization 2. Knights and knighthood
    ISBN 978-0-7614-4444-2; 0-7614-4444-0
                                                    LC 2008-55777
    This title has "a simple and elegant design with the proper balance of quality writing and quantity of information. . . . Handy time lines, well-chosen photos of ruins and artifacts, quality illustrations, inset 'Quick Facts', and 'What

You Should Know About' features will grab reluctant readers and captivate even those with short attention spans." SLJ
    Includes glossary

Riggs, Kate
    Knights. Creative Education 2011 24p il (Great warriors) $16.98; pa $8.99
Grades: K 1 2   **940.1**
    1. Medieval civilization 2. Knights and knighthood
    ISBN 978-1-60818-001-1; 1-60818-001-8; 978-0-89812-572-6 pa; 0-89812-572-3 pa
                                                    LC 2010019604
    An introduction to the European warriors known as knights, including their history, lifestyle, weapons, and how they remain a part of today's culture through books and films.
    This title makes knights "accessible to students just beginning to read on their own. The text and design of the [book is] spare, and vocabulary words are introduced unobtrusively. . . . The concepts are simple, but introduced without oversimplification that might lead to misunderstandings. [This is an] excellent [introduction] and fun to read aloud." SLJ
    Includes glossary and bibliographical references

Schlitz, Laura Amy
    ★ **Good** masters! Sweet ladies! voices from a medieval village. [by] Laura Amy Schlitz; illustrated by Robert Byrd. Candlewick Press 2007 85p il $19.99; pa $9.99
Grades: 5 6 7 8   **940.1**
    1. Monologues 2. Children's plays 3. Middle Ages -- Drama
    ISBN 978-0-7636-1578-9; 0-7636-1578-1; 978-0-7636-4332-4 pa; 0-7636-4332-7 pa
    Awarded the Newbery Medal, 2008
    A collection of short one-person plays featuring characters, between ten and fifteen years old, who live in or near a thirteenth-century English manor
    "Designed for performance and excellent for use in interdisciplinary history classrooms, the book offers students an incredibly approachable format for learning about the Middle Ages that makes the period both realistic and relevant. . . . Byrd's illustrations evoke the era and give dramatists ideas for appropriate costuming and props." SLJ

940.3 World War I, 1914-1918

Adams, Simon
    World War I; written by Simon Adams; photographed by Andy Crawford. rev ed.; DK Pub. 2007 72p il (DK eyewitness books) $15.99
Grades: 4 5 6 7   **940.3**
    1. World War, 1914-1918
    ISBN 978-0-7566-3007-2; 0-7566-3007-X
                                                    LC 2007279476
    First published 2001
    This look at World War I examines life in the trenches and the devastation of Europe by the Great War

Swain, Gwenyth
    World War I; an interactive history adventure. by Gwenyth Swain; consultant: Timothy Solie. Capstone Press

2012 112 p. ill. (some col.) (library) $31.32; (paperback) $6.95

Grades: 3 4 5 6 **940.3**

1. World War, 1914-1918 -- Juvenile literature
ISBN 1429679972; 9781429660204; 9781429679978
LC 2011033624

This book by Gwenyth Swain is part of the You Choose series. "At the bottom of many pages, you are asked to make a decision about what to do or where to go. Subsequent decisions take you to the adventure's end, at which point readers may choose to go back and begin again and find out where an alternate path might have led. ... [In] Belgium ... student nurses must decide whether to stay at their hospital or flee. Later, a British teen has to choose whether to enlist or wait." (Booklist)

Includes bibliographical references (p. 111) and index.

940.4   Military history of World War I

Beller, Susan Provost

The **doughboys** over there; soldiering in World War I. by Susan Provost Beller. Twenty-First Century Books 2008 112p il map (Soldiers on the battlefront) lib bdg $33.26

Grades: 5 6 7 8 **940.4**

1. World War, 1914-1918 2. Soldiers -- United States
ISBN 978-0-8225-6295-5 lib bdg; 0-8225-6295-2 lib bdg
LC 2006026249

The is an account of the U.S. soldiers who fought in Europe in the First World War.

"The format is inviting with a variety of fonts at the beginning of each chapter, quotations, and a multitude of illustrations. ... The text is clear and to the point, and chapters are divided into short topics." SLJ

Includes bibliographical references

Burleigh, Robert

Fly, Cher Ami, fly! the pigeon who saved the lost battalion. by Robert Burleigh; illustrated by Robert MacKenzie. Abrams Books for Young Readers 2008 un il $16.95

Grades: K 1 2 3 **940.4**

1. Pigeons 2. World War, 1914-1918
ISBN 978-0-8109-7097-7; 0-8109-7097-X

"Burleigh tells the true story of the last flight of a U.S. Army Signal Corps carrier pigeon, which took place in France during World War I. Cher Ami was the last hope for the 'Lost Battalion' of the 77th Division in the Battle of Argonne. ... Burleigh's short text clearly depicts the story's action, while MacKenzie's full-page golden-hued yet somber illustrations add to the account by showing the drama from a variety of perspectives." Booklist

Greenwood, Mark

The **donkey** of Gallipoli; a true story of courage in World War I. [by] Mark Greenwood; illustrated by Frane Lessac. Candlewick Press 2008 un il map $16.99

Grades: 2 3 4 **940.4**

1. Donkeys 2. Sailors 3. Soldiers 4. World War, 1914-1918 5. Gallipoli campaign, 1915
ISBN 978-0-7636-3913-6; 0-7636-3913-3
LC 2007032525

This is a "stirring picture book. ... In folk-art style, the paintings, in shades that reflect the heat of a sandy landscape, show the heroic soldier and the gentle animal amid the slaughter of war." Booklist

Murphy, Jim

★ **Truce**; the day the soldiers stopped fighting. Scholastic Press 2009 116p il map $19.99

Grades: 5 6 7 8 **940.4**

1. World War, 1914-1918 2. Christmas Truce, 1914 -- Juvenile literature 4. World War, 1914-1918 -- Armistices -- Juvenile literature 5. World War, 1914-1918 -- Campaigns -- Western Front -- Juvenile literature
ISBN 978-0-545-13049-3; 0-545-13049-2
LC 2008-40500

"By December 1918, the western front of World War I featured two parallel trenches stretching from the North Sea to the Alps. ... On Christmas Day, an informal peace broke out in many locations along the front. ... Murphy's excellent telling of this unusual war story begins with an account of the events that led to WWI and follows the shift in the soldiers' mind-sets. ... Printed in tones of sepia, the illustrations in this handsome volume include many period photos as well as paintings and maps. ... Well organized and clearly written, this presentation vividly portrays the context and events of the Christmas Truce." Booklist

Includes bibliographical references

940.53   World War II, 1939-1945

Adams, Simon

World War II; written by Simon Adams; photographed by Andy Crawford. rev ed.; DK Pub. 2007 72p il (DK eyewitness books) $16.99

Grades: 4 5 6 7 **940.53**

1. World War, 1939-1945
ISBN 978-0-7566-3008-9; 0-7566-3008-8
LC 2008273315

First published 2000

Provides a concise history of World War II including information about the Holocaust, the code-breaking Enigma, and the deadly V2 rocket

Adler, David A.

Hiding from the Nazis; illustrated by Karen Ritz. Holiday House 1997 un il $15.95; pa $6.95

Grades: 2 3 4 **940.53**

1. Holocaust survivors 2. Jews -- Netherlands 3. Holocaust, 1933-1945 4. World War, 1939-1945 -- Jews
ISBN 0-8234-1288-1; 0-8234-1666-6 pa
LC 96-38451

The true story of Lore Baer who as a four-year-old Jewish child was placed with a Christian family in the Dutch farm country to avoid persecution by the Nazis

"Adler includes a lot of factual information about the history of the time and about the people in the story, before and after the war. Ritz's realistic watercolors in warm shades of brown focus on the small girl whose childhood games of hide-and-seek become a terrifying reality." Booklist

Ambrose, Stephen E.

★ The **good** fight; how World War II was won. Atheneum Bks. for Young Readers 2001 96p il maps $19.95
Grades: 5 6 7 8	**940.53**
1. World War, 1939-1945 -- United States
ISBN 0-689-84361-5

LC 00-49600

"An excellent balance between the big picture and the humanizing details, well supported by fact boxes, tinted photographs, and battlefield maps that are both simple and clear. ... Ambrose's style is authoritative and warm." Booklist

Includes glossary and bibliographical references

Bachrach, Susan D.

★ **Tell** them we remember; the story of the Holocaust. Little, Brown 1994 109p il maps pa $15.99
Grades: 5 6 7 8	**940.53**
1. Holocaust, 1933-1945
ISBN 0-316-69264-6; 0-316-07484-5 pa

LC 93-40090

"Intended to extend the experience of the United States Holocaust Memorial Museum beyond its walls, this book reproduces some of its artifacts, photographs, maps, and taped oral and video histories. ... Bachrach makes the victims of Hitler's cruelty immediate to readers, showing that, like readers, they were individuals with hobbies and desires, friends and families. ... This is a very personal approach to Holocaust history and a very effective one." SLJ

Includes glossary and bibliographical references

Callery, Sean

★ **World** War II; Visual history of the world's darkest days. by Sean Callery. 1st ed. Scholastic 2013 105 p. ill. (some col.), col. maps (paperback) $15.99
Grades: 5 6 7 8	**940.53**
1. Military history -- Juvenile literature 2. World War, 1939-1945 -- Juvenile literature
ISBN 0545479754; 9780545479752

LC 2012285678

This book presents "World War II in a nutshell. The text is divided into five chapters: 'The Path to War,' 'Europe & the Atlantic War,' the Pacific theater, Africa & the Middle East, and the end of the war. Each section is divided into several two-page topics. The title page of each chapter asks three questions that are answered in the text. It is followed by a two-page time line with boxed information and vintage photos." (School Library Journal)

Finkelstein, Norman H.

Remember not to forget; a memory of the Holocaust. [by] Norman H. Finkelstein; illustrated by Lois and Lars Hokanson. Jewish Publication Society 2004 31p il pa $9.95
Grades: 4 5 6 7	**940.53**
1. Jews -- History 2. Holocaust, 1933-1945
ISBN 0-82760-770-9

LC 2004556462

A reissue of the title first published 1985 by Watts

"This spare, starkly illustrated book explains what the Holocaust was and how it is remembered on Yom Hashoa, Holocaust Remembrance Day. The explanation reaches back to the explusion of the Jews from Jerusalem in A.D. 70 and describes how Jews ... became targets of anti-Semitism, which culminated in the systematic murder of six million by

the Nazis in World War II. The tone is straightforward and matter-of-fact. Black-and-white woodcuts accompany the text with somber scenes reflective of the narrative." Booklist [review of 1985 edition]

Frank, Anne, 1929-1945

★ The **diary** of a young girl: the definitive edition; edited by Otto H. Frank and Mirjam Pressler; translated by Susan Massotty. Doubleday 1995 340p $29.95; pa $6.99
Grades: 6 7 8 9	**940.53**
1. Children 2. Diarists 3. Holocaust victims 4. Jews -- Netherlands 5. Holocaust, 1933-1945 66. World War, 1939-1945 -- Jews
ISBN 0-385-47378-8; 0-553-57712-3 pa

LC 94-41379

"This new translation of Frank's famous diary includes material about her emerging sexuality and her relationship with her mother that was originally excised by Frank's father, the only family member to survive the Holocaust." Libr J

Greenfeld, Howard

★ The **hidden** children. Ticknor & Fields Bks. for Young Readers 1993 118p il hardcover o.p. pa $9.99
Grades: 4 5 6 7	**940.53**
1. Jews -- Europe 2. Holocaust, 1933-1945 -- Personal narratives 3. World War, 1939-1945 -- Children -- Juvenile literature 4. World War, 1939-1945 -- Jews -- Rescue -- Juvenile literature ISBN 0-395-66074-2; 0-395-86138-1 pa

LC 93-20326

Describes the experiences of those Jewish children who were forced to go into hiding during the Holocaust and survived to tell about it

"Illustrated with black-and-white photographs, the moving stories and dramatic facts make inspiring, and often troubling, reading. A lovely, important book about heroism and survival." Horn Book Guide

Includes bibliographical references

Hodge, Deborah

Rescuing the children; the story of the kindertransport. Deborah Hodge. Tundra Books of Northern New York 2012 60 p. (hardcover) $17.95
Grades: 4 5 6	**940.53**
1. Holocaust, 1939-1945 2. Jewish children in the Holocaust 3. World War, 1939-1945 -- Children 4. World War, 1939-1945 -- Refugees 5. Child refugees -- Great Britain -- History
ISBN 1770492569; 9781770492561

LC 2011938776

This children's book, by Deborah Hodge, "tells the story of how ten thousand Jewish children were rescued out of Nazi Europe just before the outbreak of World War 2. They were saved by the Kindertransport--a rescue mission that transported the children (or Kinder) from Nazi-ruled countries to safety in Britain. The book includes real-life accounts of the children and is illustrated with archival photographs ... and original art by the Kinder commemorating their rescue." (Publisher's note)

Hurwitz, Johanna

Anne Frank: life in hiding; illustrated by Vera Rosenberry. Jewish Publ. Soc. 1988 62p il map $13.95

Grades: 3 4 5 **940.53**
1. Children 2. Diarists 3. Holocaust victims 4. Jews
-- Netherlands 5. Holocaust, 1933-1945 6. World War,
1939-1945 -- Jews
ISBN 0-8276-0311-8

LC 87-35263

The author "gives a concise explanation of the political
and economic background to the Holocaust and provides a
map of Europe and a chronology. She ably covers the events
of Anne's life before, during, and after the period covered by
the 'Diary of Anne Frank,' explaining the significance and
importance of the 'Diary' throughout the world." SLJ

Kacer, Kathy
Hiding Edith; a true story. Second Story 2006 120p
(Holocaust remembrance book for young readers) pa
$10.95
Grades: 4 5 6 7 **940.53**
1. Holocaust survivors 2. Jews -- France 3. Holocaust,
1933-1945
ISBN 1-897187-06-8
"Kacer recounts some extraordinary history: in Moissac,
France, under Nazi occupation, a French Jewish couple hid
100 Jewish refugee children—with the support of the townspeople. Kacer, who based her account on interviews, tells
the story of one child, Edith Schwalb. Captioned black-and-
white photos on almost every page show Edith at home in
Vienna before the war, then in Belgium, and then, separated
from her parents, living with the rescuers." Booklist

Levine, Karen
Hana's suitcase; a true story. Whitman, A. 2003 111p
il lib bdg $15.95
Grades: 4 5 6 7 **940.53**
1. Holocaust victims 2. Holocaust, 1933-1945 3.
Nové Město nad Metuji (Czech Republic) -- Biography
-- Juvenile literature 4. Holocaust, Jewish (1939-
1945) -- Czech Republic -- Nové Město nad Metuji
-- Biography -- Juvenile literature 5. Jewish children
in the Holocaust -- Czech Republic -- Nové Město nad
Metuji -- Biography -- Juvenile literature
ISBN 0-8075-3148-0

LC 2002-27439

First published 2002 in Canada
A biography of a Czech girl who died in the Holocaust,
told in alternating chapters with an account of how the curator of a Japanese Holocaust center learned about her life
after Hana's suitcase was sent to her
"The account, based on a radio documentary Levine did
in Canada . . . is part history, part suspenseful mystery, and
always anguished family drama, with an incredible climactic
revelation." Booklist

Meltzer, Milton
★ **Never** to forget: the Jews of the Holocaust. Harper
& Row 1976 217p maps hardcover o.p. pa $9.99
Grades: 6 7 8 9 **940.53**
1. Holocaust, 1933-1945
ISBN 0-06-446118-1 pa
"The mass murder of six million Jews by the Nazis dur-
ing World War II is the subject of this compelling history. In-
terweaving background information, chilling statistics, indi-

vidual accounts and newspaper reports, it provides an excellent introduction to its subject." Interracial Books Child Bull
Includes bibliographical references

★ **Rescue**: the story of how Gentiles saved Jews in the
Holocaust. Harper & Row 1988 168p maps hardcover
o.p. pa $9.99
Grades: 6 7 8 9 **940.53**
1. Holocaust, 1933-1945 2. World War, 1939-1945 --
Jews -- Rescue
ISBN 0-06-024210-8; 0-06-446117-3 pa

LC 87-47816

A recounting drawn from historic source material of the
many individual acts of heroism performed by righteous
gentiles who sought to thwart the extermination of the Jews
during the Holocaust
"This is an excellent portrayal of a difficult topic. Meltzer manages to both explain without accusing, and to laud
without glorifying. . . . The discussion of the complicated
relations between countries are clear, but not simplistic. An
impressive aspect of this book is its lack of didacticism."
Voice Youth Advocates
Includes bibliographical references

Mochizuki, Ken
★ **Passage** to freedom; the Sugihara story. written
by Ken Mochizuki; illustrated by Dom Lee; afterword by
Hiroki Sugihara. Lee & Low Bks. 1997 un il $15.95
Grades: 3 4 5 6 **940.53**
1. Diplomats 2. Humanitarians 3. Holocaust, 1933-
1945 4. World War, 1939-1945 -- Jews -- Rescue
ISBN 1-880000-49-0

LC 96-35359

"Lee's stirring mixed-media illustrations in sepia shades
are humane and beautiful. . . . The immediacy of the narrative will grab kids' interest and make them think." Booklist

Perl, Lila
Four perfect pebbles; a Holocaust story. by Lila Perl
and Marion Blumenthal Lazan. Greenwillow Bks. 1996
130p il $16.99; pa $5.99
Grades: 6 7 8 9 **940.53**
1. Holocaust survivors 2. Jews -- Germany 3.
Holocaust, 1933-1945 -- Personal narratives 4.
Holocaust, 1933-1945 -- Personal narratives -- Juvenile
literature
ISBN 0-688-14294-X; 0-380-73188-6 pa

LC 95-9752

"This book warrants attention both for the uncommon
experiences it records and for the fullness of that record. . .
. Quotes from Lazan's 87-year-old mother are invaluable—
her memories of the family's experiences afford Marion's
story a precision and wholeness rarely available to child survivors." Publ Wkly
Includes bibliographical references

Robbins, Trina
Lily Renée, escape artist; illustrated by Anne Timmons
and Mo Oh. Graphic Universe 2011 96p. chiefly col. ill.
$7.95
Grades: 4 5 6 7 8 **940.53**
1. Artists 2. Illustrators 3. Graphic novels 4. Jews --

Biography 5. Holocaust, 1933-1945 -- Graphic novels
ISBN 978-0-7613-6010-0; 0-7613-6010-7

LC 2011001084

Presents the story of Lily Renée Wilheim, the Jewish girl who escaped from the Nazis through the Kindertransport operation, leaving her parents behind and traveling alone to England, later becoming a comic book artist in New York.

"This comic-book biography of a Jewish girl's life under the Nazi jackboot and then as a refugee is low key and that much more profound for it. The panels are brightly lit, and the narrative is crisp, both of which serve to chillingly amplify the everyday banality of evil. . . . A fitting tribute." Kirkus

Rol, Ruud van der

Anne Frank, beyond the diary; a photographic remembrance. by Ruud van der Rol and Rian Verhoeven; in association with the Anne Frank House; translated by Tony Langham and Plym Peters; with an introduction by Anna Quindlen. Viking 1993 113p il map hardcover o.p. pa $10.99

Grades: 5 6 7 8   **940.53**
1. Children 2. Diarists 3. Holocaust victims 4. Jews -- Netherlands 5. Holocaust, 1933-1945 6. World War, 1939-1945 -- Jews 7. Holocaust, 1933-1945 -- Juvenile literature
ISBN 0-670-84932-4; 0-14-036926-0 pa

LC 92-41528

Original Dutch edition, 1992

Photographs, illustrations, and maps accompany historical essays, diary excerpts, and interviews, providing an insight to Anne Frank and the massive upheaval which tore apart her world

"Readers will become absorbed in the richness of the detail and careful explanation which revisit and expand the familiar, well-loved story." Horn Book

Rubin, Susan Goldman

The **flag** with fifty-six stars; a gift from the survivors of Mauthausen. illustrated by Bill Farnsworth. Holiday House 2005 39p il $16.95

Grades: 3 4 5   **940.53**
1. Jews -- Germany 2. Holocaust, 1933-1945 3. Flags -- United States 4. World War, 1939-1945 -- Germany
ISBN 0-8234-1653-4

LC 2004-47457

"In the spring of 1945, U.S. troops marched into the Mauthausen concentration camp in Austria to liberate surviving prisoners and were given an American flag that had been secretly made by a group of detainees there. This is an inspiring account of the camp, its survivors, and its liberators. . . . Nazi atrocities are muted here, but the sorrow, hunger, hopelessness, and, finally, optimism shine through in the pictures and in the text." SLJ

Includes bibliographical references

Ruelle, Karen Gray

★ The **grand** mosque of Paris; a story of how Muslims saved Jews during the Holocaust. by Karen Gray Ruelle and Deborah Durland DeSaix. Holiday House 2009 40p il $17.95

Grades: 3 4 5 6   **940.53**
1. Muslims 2. Jewish-Arab relations 3. Holocaust, 1933-1945 4. World War, 1939-1945 -- France 5.

World War, 1939-1945 -- Jews -- Rescue 6. Righteous Gentiles in the Holocaust -- Juvenile literature 7. World War, 1939-1945 -- Jews -- Rescue -- Juvenile literature 8. Holocaust, Jewish (1939-1945) -- France -- Juvenile literature
ISBN 978-0-8234-2159-6; 0-8234-2159-7

LC 2008-17209

"Although few documents remain, substantial evidence supports this fascinating and courageous story. . . . Realistic oil paintings complement the lengthy text. . . . A must read." Kirkus

Russo, Marisabina

★ **Always** remember me; how one family survived World War II. [by] Marisabina Russo. Atheneum Books for Young Readers 2005 un il $16.95

Grades: 3 4 5   **940.53**
1. Artists 2. Authors 3. Illustrators 4. Jews -- Germany 5. Children's authors 6. Holocaust, 1933-1945 7. Holocaust, Jewish (1939-1945) -- Juvenile literature ISBN 0-689-86920-7

LC 2004-4228

"Russo tells her Jewish family's story of Holocaust survival. She remembers herself as a small child visiting her grandmother, Oma, who tells Russo the family history with photos stretching back to Oma's youth and marriage before World War I. . . . Russo personalizes the history with photo-album entries printed on the endpapers, and her gouache illustrations, framed like photos, show the individuality and strength of family members." Booklist

Includes glossary

Samuels, Charlie

Home front; by Charlie Samuels. Brown Bear Books 2012 48 p. ill. (some col.) (library) $35.65

Grades: 5 6 7 8   **940.53**
1. Military history -- Juvenile literature 2. World War, 1939-1945 -- Juvenile literature 3. World War, 1939-1945 -- Social aspects -- Juvenile literature 4. World War, 1939-1945 -- Economic aspects -- Juvenile literature
ISBN 1936333228; 9781936333226

LC 2011007054

This book by Charlie Samuels is part of the World War II Sourcebook series and focuses on the home front. "Each page is illustrated. Little-known facts and, sometimes, direct narratives are presented with the information given to the reader. . . . Each book has the same timeline of World War II, maps of both the European and Pacific theaters, interesting biographical snapshots of people involved, and a list of websites that students may use to further explore World War II." (Library Media Connection)

Life under occupation; by Charlie Samuels. Brown Bear Books 2011 48 p. ill. (chiefly col.), col. maps (World War II sourcebook) (library) $35.65

Grades: 5 6 7 8   **940.53**
1. World War, 1939-1945 -- Juvenile literature 2. World War, 1939-1945 -- Occupied territories 3. World War, 1939-1945 -- Europe -- Juvenile literature 4. World War, 1939-1945 -- Atrocities -- Juvenile literature 5. World War, 1939-1945 -- Pacific Area -- Juvenile literature
ISBN 1936333260; 9781936333264

LC 2011007055

This book by Charlie Samuels, part of the World War II Sourcebook series, and focuses on life under occupation. "Each page is illustrated. Little-known facts and, sometimes, direct narratives are presented with the information given to the reader. . . . Each book has the same timeline of World War II, maps of both the European and Pacific theaters, . . . biographical snapshots of people involved, and a list of websites." (Library Media Connection)

Includes bibliographical references and index.

Taylor, Peter Lane

The **secret** of Priest's Grotto; a Holocaust survival story. [by] Peter Lane Taylor with Christos Nicola. Kar-Ben Pub. 2007 64p il map lib bdg $10.95; pa $8.95

Grades: 5 6 7 8 9 10 11 12   **940.53**

1. Caves 2. Jews -- Ukraine 3. Holocaust, 1933-1945 4. Jews -- Ukraine -- Juvenile literature 6. Holocaust survivors -- Juvenile literature

ISBN 978-1-58013-260-2 lib bdg; 1-58013-260-X lib bdg; 978-1-58013-261-9 pa; 1-58013-261-8 pa

LC 2006-21709

"This volume relays the tale of 38 Ukrainian Jews who sought refuge in a local cave to escape the invading Nazis in fall of 1942 and remained there for 344 days. . . . At once sobering and uplifting, this is an astounding story of survival, powerfully told." Publ Wkly

Thomson, Ruth

★ **Terezin**; voices from the Holocaust. Candlewick Press 2011 64p il $18.99

Grades: 5 6 7 8   **940.53**

1. Jews -- Czechoslovakia 2. Holocaust, 1933-1945 -- Personal narratives 4. Holocaust, Jewish (1939-1945) -- Juvenile literature

ISBN 0-7636-4963-5; 978-0-7636-4963-0

LC 2010-39164

"Between 1941 and 1945, Nazi Germany turned the small town of Terezín, Czechoslovakia, into a ghetto, and then into a transit camp for thousands of Jewish people. It was a 'show' camp, where inmates were forced to use their artistic talents to fool the world about the truth of gas chambers and horrific living conditions for imprisoned Jews. Here is their story, told through the firsthand accounts of those who were there." (Publisher's note) Index. "Grades five to eight." (Bull Cent Child Books)

"Two years after the Nazi invasion of Czechoslovakia, the small fortress village of Terezin was converted into a Jewish ghetto, and over the next four years, ten of thousands of Jews were transported there while in transit to death camps in the east. The history of Terezin is fascinating: the camp housed many noted artists. . . . Much of the art created at Terezin survived the Holocaust, and a generous sampling is included in this volume. Thomson opts to tell the story of Terezin almost entirely in the voices of those who lived there. . . . This is an accessible, carefully researched work that effectively uses primary-source material to make the experience of the Jews of Terezin come alive for today's students." Bull Cent Child Books

Includes glossary and bibliographical references

Warren, Andrea

★ **Surviving** Hitler; a boy in the Nazi death camps. HarperCollins Pubs. 2001 146p il hardcover o.p. pa $6.99

Grades: 5 6 7 8   **940.53**

1. Holocaust, 1933-1945 2. Gdynia (Poland) -- Biography -- Juvenile literature 3. Jewish children in the Holocaust -- Biography -- Juvenile literature 4. Holocaust, Jewish (1939-1945) -- Poland -- Gdynia -- Personal narratives -- Juvenile literature

ISBN 0-688-17497-3; 0-06-029218-0 lib bdg; 0-06-000767-2 pa

LC 00-38899

"Simply told, Warren's powerful story blends the personal testimony of Holocaust survivor Jack Mandelbaum with the history of his time, documented by stirring photos from the archives of the U.S. Holocaust Memorial Museum. . . . An excellent introduction for readers who don't know much about the history." Booklist

Includes bibliographical references

Wood, Douglas

★ **Franklin** and Winston; a Christmas that changed the world. illustrated by Barry Moser. Candlewick Press 2011 un il $16.99

Grades: 3 4 5   **940.53**

1. Governors 2. Statesmen 3. Historians 4. Presidents 5. Handicapped 6. Prime ministers 7. Memoirists 8. Philatelists 9. Cabinet members 10. Members of Parliament 11. Children of presidents 12. Nobel laureates for literature 13. World War, 1939-1945 -- Diplomatic history 14. World War, 1939-1945 -- Juvenile literature

ISBN 978-0-7636-3383-7; 0-7636-3383-6

LC 2008025456

"An engaging chronicle of the month that Roosevelt and Churchill spent together at the White House, forging an affectionate friendship as well as a world-changing alliance. . . . Wood's narrative effectively captures both the desperation of the times and how much Churchill and Roosevelt genuinely enjoyed each other's company. Moser's detailed watercolor illustrations likewise capture their robust personalities." Kirkus

Includes bibliographical references

940.54   Military history of World War II

Allen, Thomas B.

★ **Remember** Pearl Harbor; American and Japanese survivors tell their stories. foreword by Robert D. Ballard. National Geographic Soc. 2001 57p il maps $17.95

Grades: 5 6 7 8   **940.54**

1. Pearl Harbor (Oahu, Hawaii), Attack on, 1941 2. World War, 1939-1945 -- Personal narratives

ISBN 0-7922-6690-0

LC 2001-796

Personal accounts of the Japanese attack on Pearl Harbor, with background information.

"Eyewitness testimony of Japanese and American men and women from various backgrounds enriches this balanced treatment of World War II. . . . The first-person voices along with dozens of black-and-white photos and several full-color maps make this a draw for both browsers and World War II buffs." Booklist

Includes bibliographical references

Chrisp, Peter

World War II: fighting for freedom; the story of the conflict that changed the world 1939-1945. Scholastic 2010 63p il map $12.99

Grades: 4 5 6 7   **940.54**

1. World War, 1939-1945

ISBN 978-0-545-24984-3; 0-545-24984-8

Provides information and facts on events leading up to the war, important battles and campaigns, political and military leaders, and life on the home fronts.

"Fascinating photographs dominate each spread, but there are also maps, quotations, diagrams, and interesting text box features.... This book provides a solid overview of World War II, but it is the visual aspect that makes it stand out." Libr Media Connect

Includes glossary

De Capua, Sarah

The **Tuskegee** airmen; by Sarah E. De Capua. Child's World 2009 32p il map (Journey to freedom) lib bdg $28.50

Grades: 4 5 6   **940.54**

1. African American pilots 2. World War, 1939-1945 -- Aerial operations

ISBN 978-1-60253-138-3 lib bdg; 1-60253-138-2 lib bdg

LC 2008031939

Tuskegee "Airmen celebrates the pilots' extraordinary achievements by placing them within the context of their time, when segregation was common.... Personal accounts, historical photographs of training, news stories about the men's fighting ability, and records of successful missions help to explain the squadron's determination not only to fly but also to prove its proficiency and bravery.... The [book is] concise and direct, yet the writing remains sophisticated. Vibrant personal stories accompanied by striking photographs of historical figures and artifacts provide a sense of the subjects' hopes and dreams." SLJ

Includes glossary and bibliographical references

Drez, Ronald J.

★ **Remember** D-day; the plan, the invasion, survivor stories. National Geographic Books 2004 61p il map $17.95; lib bdg $27.90

Grades: 5 6 7 8   **940.54**

1. World War, 1939-1945 -- Campaigns -- France 2. World War, 1939-1945 -- Germany -- Juvenile literature 3. World War, 1939-1945 -- Campaigns -- France -- Normandy 4. World War, 1939-1945 -- Campaigns -- France -- Normandy -- Juvenile literature

ISBN 0-7922-6666-8; 0-7922-6965-9 lib bdg

LC 2003-17733

Discusses the events and personalities involved in the momentous Allied invasion of France on June 6, 1944

"This well-organized, clearly written account provides a solid overview for readers unfamiliar with the subject. A first-rate purchase." SLJ

Includes bibliographical references

Hama, Larry

★ The **battle** of Iwo Jima; guerilla warfare in the Pacific. by Larry Hama; illustrated by Anthony Williams. Rosen Pub. 2007 48p il map (Graphic battles of World War II) lib bdg $29.25

Grades: 5 6 7 8 9   **940.54**

1. Graphic novels 2. World War, 1939-1945 -- Graphic novels 3. Iwo Jima, Battle of, 1945 -- Graphic novels

ISBN 978-1-4042-0781-3 lib bdg; 1-4042-0781-3 lib bdg

LC 2006007645

"Using a graphic novel to introduce the battle for Iwo Jima makes it very accessible. Before the graphic-novel section of the book begins, Hama provides a short, informative background piece describing the run-up to World War II, the significance of the Japanese war machine, and the importance of the tiny island of Iwo Jima. Then the graphic novel, illustrated by Williams in camouflage colors, does a terrific job of examining the ups and downs of the battle as well as the horror of so many losses—on both sides." Booklist

Includes bibliographical references

Lawton, Clive

Hiroshima; the story of the first atom bomb. [by] Clive A. Lawton. Candlewick Press 2004 48p il map $18.99

Grades: 5 6 7 8   **940.54**

1. Atomic bomb 2. World War, 1939-1945 -- Japan

ISBN 0-7636-2271-0

LC 2004-45166

"Engaging text and powerful photographs are intricately woven together to make a long-lasting impact on readers." Libr Media Connect

Manning, Mick

Tail-end Charlie; [by] Mick Manning and Brita Granström. Frances Lincoln Children's Books 2009 un il $16.95

Grades: 3 4 5   **940.54**

1. World War, 1939-1945 -- Aerial operations 2. World War, 1939-1945 -- Juvenile literature

ISBN 978-1-84507-651-1; 1-84507-651-6

"The remembrances of Manning's father, a British Air Force gunner during World War II, are vividly presented through comic strips, watercolor-and-ink illustrations, and memorabilia such as ration books, postcards, and photographs.... Reluctant readers will be drawn to the graphic format and quickly engaged by the authentic voice." SLJ

Samuels, Charlie

Propaganda; by Charlie Samuels. Brown Bear Books 2011 48 p. ill. (chiefly col.), col. maps (library) $35.65

Grades: 5 6 7 8   **940.54**

1. World War, 1939-1945 -- Propaganda 2. World War, 1939-1945 -- Juvenile literature 3. World War, 1939-1945 -- Propaganda -- Juvenile literature

ISBN 1936333236; 9781936333233

LC 2011010241

This book by Charlie Samuels on propaganda is part of the World War II Sourcebook series. "Each page is illustrated. Little-known facts and, sometimes, direct narratives are presented with the information given to the reader.... Each book has the same timeline of World War II, maps of both the European and Pacific theaters, interesting biographical snapshots of people involved, and a list of websites that students may use to further explore World War II." (Library Media Connection)

Includes bibliographical references and index.

Soldiers; [Charlie Samuels] Brown Bear Books 2011 48 p. ill. (some col.), maps (col.) (World War II sourcebook)

Grades: 5 6 7 8 **940.54**

1. Soldiers -- Juvenile literature 2. World War, 1939-1945 -- Juvenile literature 3. Soldiers -- History -- 20th century -- Juvenile literature

ISBN 1936333244; 9781936333240

LC 2011007057

This book by Charlie Samuels, part of the World War II Sourcebook series, "Describes the life of a soldier in World War II, from recruitment efforts around the world, to the daily life during the fighting." (Publisher's note)

Includes bibliographical references (p. 47) and index

Spying and security; by Charlie Samuels. Brown Bear Books 2012 48 p. ill. (some col.) (World War II Sourcebook)

Grades: 5 6 7 8 **940.54**

1. Police -- History -- 20th century -- Juvenile literature 2. World War, 1939-1945 -- Secret service -- Juvenile literature 3. Spies -- History -- 20th century -- Juvenile literature 4. Espionage -- History -- 20th century -- Juvenile literature 5. World War, 1939-1945 -- Cryptography -- Juvenile literature

ISBN 1936333252; 9781936333257

LC 2011007058

This book by Charlie Samuels, part of the World War II Sourcebook, provides a history of spying and security for young readers. It "Describes the role spies and police played around the world during World War II, from controlling riots to gathering intelligence from the enemy." (Publisher's note)

Seiple, Samantha

Ghosts in the fog; the untold story of Alaska's WWII invasion. Scholastic 2011 221p il map $16.99

Grades: 5 6 7 8 **940.54**

1. World War, 1939-1945 -- Campaigns

ISBN 978-0-545-29654-0; 0-545-29654-4

LC 2011027821

"A little-known story from World War II shows the unique role played by a small group of military personal and native civilians in a remote region of the county. The role of Alaska in World War II following the attack on Pearl Harbor is not often told. . . . The story illuminates the cultural differences between the American and Japanese cultures at that time as well as the reluctance of the U.S. government to treat the native Alaskans as full citizens. The narrative is full of details, and . . . the text is supported by many photographs of those involved. Maps, including a strategic military map, increase the level of specificity." Kirkus

Includes bibliographical references

Stone, Tanya Lee

★ **Courage** has no color, the true story of the Triple Nickles; America's first black paratroopers. Tanya Lee Stone. Candlewick Press 2013 160 p. $24.99

Grades: 5 6 7 8 **940.54**

1. Parachute troops 2. World War, 1939-1945 3. African American soldiers

ISBN 0763651176; 9780763651176

LC 2012942315

This book tells the "untold story of the 555th Parachute Infantry Battalion, America's first black paratroopers." Enlisted black men "faced the tyranny of racial discrimination on the homefront. . . . When 1st Sgt. Walter Morris, whose men served as guards at The Parachute School at Fort Ben-

ning, saw white soldiers training to be paratroopers, he knew his men would have to train and act like them to be treated like soldiers." (Kirkus Reviews)

941 British Isles

Bean, Rachel

★ **United** Kingdom; [by] Rachel Bean; Robert Bennett and Michael Dunford, consultants. National Geographic 2007 64p il map (Countries of the world) lib bdg $28.50

Grades: 4 5 6 7 **941**

ISBN 978-1-4263-0126-1 lib bdg; 1-4263-0126-X lib bdg

LC 2007024750

This describes the geography, nature, history, people and culture, government and economy of the United Kingdom

"What helps [this book] stand out from the pack is [its] high-quality, rich photography. . . . The photos provide as much information as the [text]. . . . The writing is straightforward and solid." SLJ

Includes glossary and bibliographical references

Dillon, Patrick

The **story** of Britain from the Norman Conquest to the European Union; illustrated by P.J. Lynch. Candlewick Press 2011 341p il map $21.99

Grades: 5 6 7 8 **941**

ISBN 978-0-7636-5122-0; 0-7636-5122-2

LC 2010038883

"This well-written, thoughtfully illustrated volume [is] an indispensible tool for European history buffs." Horn Book Guide

Dunn, James

ABC UK; illustrated by Helen Bate. Frances Lincoln 2009 un il $16.95

Grades: K 1 2 3 **941**

1. Alphabet

ISBN 978-1-84507-696-2; 1-84507-696-6

"Featuring historical and cultural highlights of Great Britain (Giant's Causeway, punk music, vindaloo), each letter of the alphabet gets a uniquely stylized treatment in Bate's mixed media art. . . . The diversity of subjects makes it a prime pick for Anglophiles of all ages." Publ Wkly

Indovino, Shaina C.

United Kingdom; by Rae Simons and Shaina C. Indovino. Mason Crest Publishers 2012 64 p. col. ill., col. maps (library) $22.95

Grades: 5 6 7 8 **941**

1. Great Britain -- Juvenile literature

ISBN 1422222616; 9781422222614; 9781422222928

LC 2010051852

This book on the United Kingdom by Rae Simons and Shaina Carmel Indovino "covers Modern Issues, History and Government, The Economy, People and Culture, and Looking to the Future. . . Identical information on "The Formation of the European Union" appears in every book" in the series. (Library Media Connection) Also covered are "issues like immigration and the global financial crisis". (Publisher's note)

Includes bibliographical references (p. 60) and index.

941.5   Ireland

McQuinn, Colm

★ **Ireland**; [by] Anna and Colm McQuinn; Elizabeth Malcolm and John McDonagh, consultants. National Geographic 2008 64p il map (Countries of the world) lib bdg $27.90

Grades: 4 5 6 7   **941.5**

ISBN 978-1-4263-0299-2 lib bdg; 1-4263-0299-1 lib bdg

This describes the geography, nature, history, people and culture, government, and economy of Ireland.

Includes glossary and bibliographical references

Murphy, Patricia J.

Ireland; by Patricia J. Murphy. Benchmark Bks. 2003 48p il map (Discovering cultures) lib bdg $28.50

Grades: 2 3 4   **941.5**

ISBN 0-7614-1515-7

LC 2002-15303

Highlights the geography, people, food, schools, recreation, celebrations, and language of Ireland

"Illustrated with clear color photos [and] simply written." Horn Book Guide

Includes glossary and bibliographical references

941.508   1800-1899

Fradin, Dennis Brindell

The **Irish** potato famine; by Dennis Fradin. Marshall Cavendish Benchmark 2012 32 p. (library) $34.21

Grades: 5 6 7 8   **941.508**

1. Famines -- Juvenile literature 2. Ireland -- History -- Famine, 1845-1852 3. Escapes -- Ireland -- History -- 19th century -- Juvenile literature 4. Disaster victims -- Ireland -- History -- 19th century -- Juvenile literature

ISBN 1608704734; 9781608704736

LC 2010018788

This book, part of the Great Escapes series, focuses on the Irish Potato Famine. "Each book begins with an introduction to an individual who escaped, followed by the history of the precipitating events, the escape itself, and a follow-up on what happened after the escape. Each title includes a timeline, notes, and additional information on the topic." (Library Media Connection)

Includes bibliographical references and index.

942   England and Wales

Banting, Erinn

England; by Erinn Banting; edited by Sarah Cairns; illustrated by Jeff Crosby, Dianne Eastman, and David Wysotski. Revised ed. Crabtree Pub. Co. 2012 32 p. ill. (some col.) (library) $26.60; (paperback) $8.95; (ebook) $26.60

Grades: 4 5 6   **942**

1. Culture 2. England -- Juvenile literature

ISBN 0778798283; 9780778798286; 9780778798316; 9781427180056 pdf

LC 2012013776

This book by Erinn Banting is part of the Lands, Peoples and Cultural Series and looks at the culture of England. The books offer information about "folktales, sports, and history." Also included are "a table of contents, short glossary (words highlighted in test) and index." (Catholic Library World)

Includes index

Blashfield, Jean F.

England; by Jean F. Blashfield. Children's Press 2013 144 p. ill. (some col.), col. maps (library) $40.00

Grades: 4 5 6 7   **942**

1. England -- Juvenile literature

ISBN 9780531275429

LC 2012000503

This book by Jean F. Blashfield, part of the "Enchantment of the World" series, "describes the geography, history, economy, language, religions, culture, people, plants, and animals of England." (Publisher's note)

It includes "topics as recent as the 2012 Olympics and 2012 Grammy winners, as well as the latest royal wedding." (Children's Literature)

Includes bibliographical references (p. 134-135) and index.

Oxlade, Chris

A **visit** to England; [by] Chris Oxlade and Anita Ganeri. Heinemann Lib. 2003 32p il map (Visit to) lib bdg $22.79

Grades: 1 2 3 4   **942**

ISBN 1-4034-0965-X

LC 2002-7415

An introduction to the land and culture of England

This is "clear, concise, . . . reader-friendly, [and] informative. . . . Accurate, up-to-date material is supported by large, full-color photographs on each spread." SLJ

Includes glossary and bibliographical references

Platt, Richard

★ **London**; illustrated by Manuela Cappon. Kingfisher 2009 45p il (Through time) $16.95

Grades: 3 4 5   **942**

ISBN 978-0-7534-6255-3; 0-7534-6255-9

This "book explores the history of London from 'Neolithic camp' to the modern city it is today. . . . Cutaway views of various structures and concise but engaging text effectively capture the changing face of a city over time." Publ Wkly

Rubbino, Salvatore

★ A **walk** in London. Candlewick Press 2011 40p il $16.99

Grades: PreK K 1 2   **942**

ISBN 978-0-7636-5272-2; 0-7636-5272-5

LC 2010038769

"A mother and daughter get off a double-decker bus in central London for a day of sightseeing. . . . Playful yet realistic mixed-media illustrations, drawn from different perspectives, give the reader a real sense of what it's like to visit London. . . . Highly informative, visually stunning, and jam-packed with things for young readers to look at." Horn Book

942.05 Period of House of Tudor, 1485-1603

Hollihan, Kerrie Logan
Elizabeth I--the people's queen; her life and times: 21 activities. Chicago Review Press 2011 129p il pa $16.95
Grades: 4 5 6 7 8   **942.05**
    1. Queens
    ISBN 978-1-56976-349-0; 1-56976-349-6
                                        LC 2010047647
This is an interactive biography of Queen Elizabeth I.
"The writing is clear and suited to readers with no previous knowledge of the topic. The activities vary in difficulty, from reading The Faerie Queen, to creating a family coat of arms, to growing a knot garden. The book is well illustrated with black-and-white reproductions of portraits, engravings, and paintings depicting major events in the Tudors' lives. . . . This well-organized book succeeds at being interesting and scholarly at the same time." SLJ
    Includes bibliographical references

942.9 Wales

Hestler, Anna
Wales; [by] Anna Hestler and Jo-Ann Spilling. 2nd ed.; Marshall Cavendish Benchmark 2011 144p il map (Cultures of the world) lib bdg $42.79
Grades: 5 6 7 8   **942.9**
    ISBN 978-1-6087-0457-6; 1-6087-0457-2
                                        LC 2010030339
    First published 2001
    Provides information on the geography, history, wildlife, governmental structure, economy, cultural diversity, peoples, religion, and culture of Wales.
    "Plentiful color photographs accompany substantial amounts of information." Booklist
    Includes glossary and bibliographical references

943 Germany and neighboring central European countries

Indovino, Shaina C.
Germany; by Ida Walker and Shaina C. Indovino. Mason Crest Publishers 2013 64 p. ill. (some col.), col. maps (library) $22.95
Grades: 5 6 7 8   **943**
    1. Germany -- Juvenile literature 2. Germany -- Politics and government -- Juvenile literature
    ISBN 1422222438; 9781422222430
                                        LC 2010051291
    This book on Germany by Ida Walker and Shaina Carmel Indovino is part of the "Major European Nations" series, which "stresses the modern relationships, goals, and problems of the European Union. . . . Chapters begin with 'Modern Issues' and a brief summary of the country's history and government, followed by chapters on economy, people and culture, and 'Looking to the Future.' In addition, there is a time line and a few suggestions for finding out more." (School Library Journal)

Russell, Henry
    ★ Germany; [by] Henry Russell; Benedict Kork and

Antje Schlottmann, consultants. National Geographic 2007 64p il map (Countries of the world) lib bdg $27.90
Grades: 4 5 6 7   **943**
    ISBN 978-1-4263-0059-2
                                        LC 2007024677
    Describes the geography, nature, history, people and culture, government and economy of Germany.
    This "appealing [title has] wonderful photographs and maps. . . . The [book offers] reliable sources for country research, and the interesting and current material holds browsing potential as well." SLJ
    Includes glossary and bibliographical references

943.6 Austria and Liechtenstein

Grahame, Deborah A.
Austria; [by] Deborah Grahame. Marshall Cavendish Benchmark 2007 48p il map (Discovering cultures) lib bdg $28.50
Grades: 2 3 4   **943.6**
    ISBN 978-0-7614-1984-6 lib bdg; 0-7614-1984-5 lib bdg
                                        LC 2006011471
    An introduction to the geography, history, people, and culture of Austria
    Includes glossary and bibliographical references

Indovino, Shaina C.
Austria; by Jeanine Sanna and Shaina C. Indovino. Mason Crest Publishers 2012 64 p. col. ill., col. maps (library) $22.95
Grades: 5 6 7 8   **943.6**
    1. Austria -- History 2. Austria -- Juvenile literature
    ISBN 1422222322; 9781422222324
                                        LC 2010051075
    This book, part of the Major European Union Nations series, focuses on Austria. In "addition to history, the book details government, economy, culture, and prospects for the future. There is a glossary and an index and a nice chronology in the back of the book as well as a brief bibliography and a list of photo credits." (Children's Literature)
    Includes bibliographical references (p. 57) and index.

943.7 Czech Republic and Slovakia

Sioras, Efstathia
Czech Republic; [by] Efstathia Sioras and Michael Spilling. Marshall Cavendish Benchmark 2010 144p il map (Cultures of the world) lib bdg $42.79
Grades: 5 6 7 8   **943.7**
    ISBN 978-0-7614-4476-3 lib bdg; 0-7614-4476-9 lib bdg
                                        LC 2009003185
    This describes the geography, history, wildlife, governmental structure, economy, cultural diversity, peoples, religion, and culture of the Czech Republic
    Includes glossary and bibliographical references

943.710   Period of Republic, 1993-

Docalavich, Heather

Czech Republic; by Heather Docalavich and Shaina C. Indovino. Mason Crest Publishers 2013 64 p. col. ill, col. maps (library) \$344.25; (library) \$22.95; (ebook) \$28.95
Grades: 5 6 7 8   **943.710**
   1. Czech Republic -- Juvenile literature   2. European Union -- Juvenile literature
   ISBN 1422222373; 9781422222317 set;
9781422222379; 9781422222683; 9781422292648
                      LC 2010051083

This book by Heather Docalavich is part of the Major European Union Nations series and focuses on the Czech Republic. "The Czech Republic is one of the newest countries in the world. It's also new to the EU—it joined in 2004. People have lived in what we now call the Czech Republic for thousands of years, however. This land has a long history and is moving forward while dealing with challenges like the recent global recession." (Publisher's note)

Includes bibliographical references (p. 57-58, 63) and index.

943.8   Poland

Deckker, Zilah

   ★ Poland; [by] Zilah Deckker; Richard Butterwick and Iwona Sagan, consultants. National Geographic 2008 64p il map (Countries of the world) lib bdg \$27.90
Grades: 4 5 6 7   **943.8**
   ISBN 978-1-4263-0201-5
                      LC 2007047823
This describes the geography, nature, history, people and culture, government, and economy of Poland.

Includes glossary and bibliographical references

Docalavich, Heather

   Poland; by Healther Docalavich and Shaina C. Indovino. Mason Crest Publishers 2013 64 p. col. ill., col. maps (library) \$22.95
Grades: 5 6 7 8   **943.8**
   1. Poland -- Juvenile literature   2. European Union -- Juvenile literature
   ISBN 1422222543; 9781422222546
                      LC 2010051465
This book by Heather Docalavich and Shaina C. Indovino is part of the Major European Union Nations series and looks at Poland. "It joined the EU in 2004 . . . . For long time, Poland has been home to scientific thinkers, artists, and musicians. Today, it is one of the countries that have weathered the global recession the best, proving this nation's strength." (Publisher's note)

Includes bibliographical references and index

944   France and Monaco

Dubowski, Mark

   Discovery in the cave; by Mark Dubowski; illustrated by Bryn Barnard. Random House 2010 48 p. col. ill.
Grades: 1 2 3   **944**
   1. Caves   2. Prehistoric art   3. Cave drawings and paintings   4. Cave paintings -- France -- Montignac (Dordogne) -- Juvenile literature   5. Art, Prehistoric -- France -- Montignac (Dordogne) -- Juvenile literature   6. Magdalenian culture -- France -- Montignac (Dordogne) -- Juvenile literature
   ISBN 0375858938; 0375958932; 9780375858932; 9780375958939
                      LC 2009007099
This book tells the "true adventure story about the discovery of the Lascaux Cave. . . . In 1940, four teenage boys and a dog dropped themselves into a hole in the forest floor. Using a flaming grease gun as a torch, they ventured deep underground, eventually coming to a huge cave, the walls of which were covered with life-size paintings of animals. Whole herds of horses! Deer with horns as big as tree branches! Giant bison! The boys were amazed by their discovery. They'd stumbled upon the world's finest examples of prehistoric painting!" (Publisher's note)

Indovino, Shaina C.

   France; by Jeanine Sanna and Shaina C. Indovino. Mason Crest Publishers 2013 64 p. col. ill., col. maps (hardcover) \$22.95
Grades: 5 6 7 8   **944**
   1. France -- Juvenile literature
   ISBN 142222242X; 9781422222423
                      LC 2010051290
This book by Liz Sonneborn is part of the Enchantment of the World series and looks at France. It covers "history, government, geography, natural resources, economics, the arts, and culture. . . . Maps, charts, sidebars highlighting items of interest, a time line, and a 'Fast Facts' section add to the presentation." (School Library Journal)

Includes bibliographical references (p. 59) and index.

King, David C.

   Monaco; [by] David C. King. Marshall Cavendish Benchmark 2008 144p il map (Cultures of the world) lib bdg \$42.79
Grades: 5 6 7 8   **944**
   ISBN 978-0-7614-2567-0
                      LC 2006030238
This describes the geography, history, government, economy, environment, people, and culture of Monaco
   Includes glossary and bibliographical references

Sonneborn, Liz

   France; by Liz Sonneborn. Children's Press 2013 144 p. ill., maps (library) \$40
Grades: 5 6 7 8   **944**
   ISBN 0531256006; 9780531256008
                      LC 2012047113
   Includes bibliographical references (page 134) and index

Tidmarsh, Celia

   France. Sea-to-sea Publications 2009 32p il map (Facts about countries) lib bdg \$28.50
Grades: 3 4 5   **944**
   ISBN 978-1-59771-115-9 lib bdg; 1-59771-115-2 lib bdg
   Describes the geography, history, industries, education, government, and cultures of France
   "The attractive layout includes color photographs and charts of current statistics as well as maps illustrating main

farming regions, natural resources, or the literacy rates of girls and boys. The [text is] clear and succinct." SLJ

944.04   France since 1789

Riggs, Kate
The **French** Revolution. Creative Education 2009 48p il map (Days of change) lib bdg $32.80
Grades: 5 6 7 8   **944.04**
    ISBN 978-1-58341-734-8 lib bdg; 1-58341-734-6 lib bdg
                                        LC 2008009728
"With elegant design and mature prose, the Days of Change series is an ideal starting point for all manner of school projects. . . . The political pressures at the center of The French Revolution are difficult to dramatize, but Riggs carefully lays out the factions and civil disobedience that led to the Declaration of the Rights of Man and of The Citizen— and then the emperor's reign that overthrew everything." Booklist
    Includes bibliographical references

945   Italy, San Marino, Vatican City, Malta

Indovino, Shaina C.
    Italy; by Ademola O. Sadik and Shaina C. Indovino. Mason Crest Publishers 2013 64 p. ill. (col. ill.), maps (library) $22.95
Grades: 5 6 7 8   **945**
    1. Women in the workplace 2. Italy -- Juvenile literature
    ISBN 1422222489; 9781422222485
                                        LC 2010051333
    This book by Ademola O. Sadik and Shaina C. Indovino is part of the Major European Nations series and looks at Italy. "Chapters begin with "Modem Issues" and a brief summary of the country's history and government, followed by chapters on economy, people and culture, and 'Looking to the Future.'" The texts "liken Italy's treatment of the "Roma" (Gypsies) to the U.S. treatment of the American Indian; the social standing of Italy's women is examined." (School Library Journal)

Nivola, Claire A.
    ★ **Orani**; my father's village. Farrar Straus Giroux 2011 un il $16.99
Grades: 2 3 4   **945**
    1. Artists 2. Illustrators
    ISBN 978-0-374-35657-6; 0-374-35657-2
                                        LC 2009047598
"Nivola's charming primitive-style art works well in both the upclose images as well as in the broad landscape scenes that she loving captures. A book to inspire young writers and artists to interview and write about their own parents' (or grandparents') lives." SLJ

Sheehan, Sean
    Malta; by Sean Sheehan and Yong Jui Lin. 2nd ed. Marshall Cavendish Benchmark 2010 144 p. col. ill. (library) $47.07
Grades: 5 6 7 8   **945**
    1. Malta -- Juvenile literature 2. Culture -- Juvenile

literature
    ISBN 1608700240; 9781608700240
                                        LC 2010000733
    This book by Sean Sheehan is part of the Cultures of the World series and looks at Malta. The books in the series provide "broad overviews of each country's culture, geography, and history. The . . . texts discuss government, economy, people, lifestyles, religion, language, arts and leisure, festivals, and food." (School Library Journal)
    Includes bibliographical references (p. 142) and index.

946   Spain, Andorra, Gibraltar, Portugal

Augustin, Byron
    Andorra; by Byron D. Augustin. Marshall Cavendish Benchmark 2009 144p il map (Cultures of the world) lib bdg $42.79
Grades: 5 6 7 8   **946**
    ISBN 978-0-7614-3122-0 lib bdg; 0-7614-3122-5 lib bdg
                                        LC 2007040356
"Provides comprehensive information on the geography, history, governmental structure, economy, cultural diversity, peoples, religion, and culture of Andorra." Publisher's note
    Includes glossary and bibliographical references

Croy, Anita
    Spain. National Geographic 2010 64p il map (Countries of the world) lib bdg $27.90
Grades: 4 5 6 7   **946**
    ISBN 978-1-4263-0633-4 lib bdg; 1-4263-0633-4 lib bdg
    This describes the geography, nature, history, people and culture, government and economy of Spain
    "The information is substantial but not overwhelming. The [text is] clear, and the discussion points are well chosen. . . . [The text is] complemented with stunning photographs." SLJ
    Includes glossary and bibliographical references

Hanks, Reuel R.
    Spain; by Zoran Pavlovic and Reuel Hanks. Chelsea House 2006 104 p. col. ill., col. maps (library) $35.00; (hardcover) $35
Grades: 5 6 7 8   **946**
    1. Spain -- Juvenile literature 2. European Union -- Juvenile literature
    ISBN 9780791066973 out of print; 1617530476; 9781617530470
                                        LC 2006002218
    This book by Zoran Pavlovic is part of the Modern World Nations series and looks at Spain. "Although Spain is now part of a unified Europe, . . . it is also a land divided by a combination of its own history, ethnicity, and geography." This entry "offers readers a wealth of information about this nation, touching on a variety of topics such as Spanish geography, history, political evolution, and ethnic issues." (Publisher's note)
    Includes bibliographical references (p. 96) and index.

Indovino, Shaina C.
    Spain; by Rae Simons and Shaina C. Indovino. Mason

Crest Publishers 2013 64 p. col. ill., col. maps (library) $22.95

Grades: 5 6 7 8   **946**

1. Spain -- Juvenile literature 2. European Union -- Juvenile literature

ISBN 9781422222904; 1422222594; 9781422222591

LC 2010051847

This book by Rae Simons is part of the Major European Union Nations series and looks at Spain. "Spain has it all: beaches, modern cities, soaring architecture, mountains, and more. It has been a member of the EU since 1986. From the ancient Celts to the Moors to the Christian kings and queens, many people have influenced Spain. It has recently taken a step back in the current financial crisis, but this proud nation is slowly getting back on its feet." (Publisher's note)

946.9   Portugal

Deckker, Zilah

★ **Portugal**. National Geographic 2009 64p il map (Countries of the world) lib bdg $27.90

Grades: 4 5 6 7   **946.9**

ISBN 978-1-4263-0390-6 lib bdg; 1-4263-0390-4 lib bdg

LC 2009275584

This describes the geography, nature, history, people and culture, government and economy of Portugal

Includes glossary and bibliographical references

Etingoff, Kim

Portugal; by Kim Etingoff and Shaina C. Indovino. Mason Crest Publishers 2013 64 p. col. ill. (library) $22.95

Grades: 5 6 7 8   **946.9**

1. Portugal -- Juvenile literature 2. European Union -- Juvenile literature

ISBN 1422222551; 9781422222553

LC 2010051466

This book by Kim Etingoff and Shaina C. Indovino is part of the Major European Union Nations series and looks at Portugal. "Long ago, Portugal was one of the world's most powerful countries, as it explored and conquered places far from home. Today, it is a nation that has had some economic and social struggles, but also some triumphs. It joined the EU in 1986." (Publisher's note)

Tuminelly, Nancy

Cool holiday food art; easy recipes that make food fun to eat! ABDO Pub. Company 2010 32p il (Cool food art) lib bdg $25.65

Grades: 3 4 5   **946.9**

1. Food 2. Holiday cooking

ISBN 978-1-61613-365-8; 1-61613-365-1

LC 2010003476

Provides step-by-step instructions for creating holiday-themed food art, such as reindeer cookies, dreidel pretzels, and creepy popcorn balls; and includes tips on techniques.

"Photographs provide clear step-by-step instructions as well as images of the finished products." Horn Book Guide

Includes glossary

947   Russia and neighboring east European countries

Robinson, Anthony

Hamzat's journey; a refugee diary. by Anthony Robinson and AnneMarie Robinson; illustrated by June Allan. Frances Lincoln Books 2010 un il (Refugee diary) $17.95

Grades: 3 4 5   **947**

1. Refugees 2. Physically handicapped children

ISBN 978-1-84780-030-5; 1-84780-030-0

"In 2001, eight-year-old Hamzat stepped on a land mine on the way to school with two friends in Grozny, Chechnya. His friends died, but Hamzat survived with a shattered leg. In his spare, quiet first-person narrative, Hamzat describes the horrific struggle of civilians in wartime. . . . Clear, detailed back matter offers more facts about Chechnya's geography and long, troubled history, while occasional small, color family photos add even more immediacy." Booklist

Stanley, Diane

★ **Peter** the Great. Morrow Junior Bks. 1999 32p il $16

Grades: 4 5 6 7   **947**

1. Emperors

ISBN 0-688-16708-X

LC 98-45250

A reissue of the title first published 1986 by Four Winds Press

A biography of the tsar who began the transformation of Russia into a modern state in the late seventeenth-early eighteenth centuries

The author's "material is presented with a modicum of oversimplification and a plethora of details that are sure to fascinate children. But what really makes this biography shine are its breathtaking illustrations. The meticulously researched, vivid scenes of Russian life during Peter's reign—courts, countryside, architecture, costumes—are beautifully rendered." Publ Wkly

Yomtov, Nel

Russia; by Nel Yomtov. Children's Press 2012 144 p. col. ill., col. maps (library) $40

Grades: 5 6 7 8   **947**

1. Russia (Federation) -- Juvenile literature

ISBN 0531275450; 9780531275450

LC 2012000520

This children's book, by Nel Yomtov, describes the geography and culture of Russia as part of the "Enchantment of the World" series. The book includes "colourful photos . . . [with] views of foreign cities and landscapes," facts and statistics on "interesting people, places, and events" in Russian history, and "delicious, easy recipes [to] give readers the opportunity to experience foreign cuisine firsthand." (Publisher's note)

Includes bibliographical references and index

947.5   Caucasus

Dhilawala, Sakina

Armenia; [by] Sakina Dhilawala. 2nd ed.; Marshall Cavendish Benchmark 2008 144p il map (Cultures of the world) lib bdg $39.93

Grades: 5 6 7 8   947.5
    ISBN 978-0-7614-2029-3

                                LC 2007014890
    First published 1997
    "Provides comprehensive information on the geography,
history, wildlife, governmental structure, economy, cultural
diversity, peoples, religion, and culture of Armenia." Publisher's note
    Includes glossary and bibliographical references

947.7   Ukraine

Bassis, Volodymyr
    Ukraine; [by] Volodymyr Bassis & Sakina Dhilawala.
2nd ed.; Marshall Cavendish Benchmark 2008 144p il
map (Cultures of the world) lib bdg $42.79
Grades: 5 6 7 8   947.7
    ISBN 978-0-7614-2090-3

                                LC 2007019179
    First published 1997
    "Provides comprehensive information on the geography,
history, wildlife, governmental structure, economy, cultural
diversity, peoples, religion, and culture of Ukraine." Publisher's note
    Includes glossary and bibliographical references

947.93   Lithuania

Kagda, Sakina
    Lithuania; [by] Sakina Kagda & Zawiah Abdul Latif.
2nd ed.; Marshall Cavendish Benchmark 2008 144p il
map (Cultures of the world) lib bdg $42.79
Grades: 5 6 7 8   947.93
    ISBN 978-0-7614-2087-3

                                LC 2007016290
    First published 1997
    "Provides comprehensive information on the geography,
history, wildlife, governmental structure, economy, cultural
diversity, peoples, religion, and culture of Lithuania." Publisher's note
    Includes glossary and bibliographical references

947.96   Latvia

Barlas, Robert
    Latvia; [by] Robert Barlas and Winnie Wong. 2nd ed.;
Marshall Cavendish Benchmark 2010 144p il map (Cultures of the world) lib bdg $42.79
Grades: 5 6 7 8   947.96
    ISBN 978-0-7614-4857-0 lib bdg; 0-7614-4857-8
lib bdg

                                LC 2009046001
    First published 2000
    This offers information on the geography, history, wild-
life, governmental structure, economy, cultural diversity,
peoples, religion, and culture of Latvia
    Includes glossary and bibliographical references

947.98   Estonia

Spilling, Michael
    Estonia; 2nd ed.; Marshall Cavendish Benchmark
2010 142p il map (Cultures of the world) lib bdg $42.79
Grades: 5 6 7 8   947.98
    ISBN 978-0-7614-4846-4 lib bdg; 0-7614-4846-2
lib bdg

                                LC 2009021201
    First published 1999
    This describes the geography, history, wildlife, govern-
mental structure, economy, cultural diversity, peoples, religion, and culture of Estonia
    Includes glossary and bibliographical references

948   Scandinavia

Malam, John
    The **Vikings**. PowerKids Press 2011 30p il (Dig it:
History from objects) lib bdg $25.25
Grades: 3 4 5   948
    1. Vikings
    ISBN 978-1-4488-3286-6; 1-4488-3286-1
                                LC 2010023867
    This book about the Vikings includes information about
"homes and towns, daily life, clothing, religion, and entertainment. . . . The layout is crisp and the object illustrations
and photographs, plus the 'What does it tell us' section
provide visual understanding. These qualities will assist
the teacher who needs to differentiate instruction. The information is well-written and easily understood, well suited
to the curriculum and national standards. Website links are
intriguing and students will enjoy adding this piece to their
research." Libr Media Connect
    Includes glossary and bibliographical references

Park, Louise
    The **Scandinavian** Vikings; by Louise Park and Timo-
thy Love. Marshall Cavendish Benchmark 2009 32p il
map (Ancient and medieval people) $19.95
Grades: 4 5 6   948
    1. Vikings
    ISBN 978-0-7614-4445-9; 0-7614-4445-9
    This title has "a simple and elegant design with the
proper balance of quality writing and quantity of information. . . . Handy time lines, well-chosen photos of ruins and
artifacts, quality illustrations, inset 'Quick Facts', and 'What
You Should Know About' features will grab reluctant readers and captivate even those with short attention spans." SLJ
    Includes glossary

Raum, Elizabeth
    What did the Vikings do for me? Heinemann Library
2010 32p il map (Heinemann infosearch: linking past to
present) lib bdg $29; pa $7.99
Grades: 3 4 5   948
    1. Vikings
    ISBN 978-1-4329-3745-4 lib bdg; 1-4329-3745-6 lib
bdg; 978-1-4329-3752-2 pa; 1-4329-3752-9 pa
                                LC 2009039662
    "Children will likely know the Vikings primarily as ma-
rauding warriors, and although they won't stop thinking that

after reading this title, . . . they will also have a nicely balanced understanding of the other significant aspects and lasting impact of their civilization. Small chunks of text . . . . sit alongside a grab bag of digital illustrations, maps, paintings, and photographs." Booklist

Includes glossary and bibliographical references

948.5　Sweden

Docalavich, Heather

Sweden; by Heather Docalavich and Shaina C. Indovino. Mason Crest Publishers 2013 64 p. col. ill., col. maps (library) $22.95

Grades: 5 6 7 8　　　　　　　　　　　　　　　948.5

1. Sweden -- Juvenile literature　2. European Union -- Juvenile literature

ISBN 1422222608; 9781422222607; 9781422222911

LC 2010051848

This book by Heather Docalavich is part of the Major European Union Nations series and looks at Sweden. "A member of the EU since 1995, Sweden is one of the most stable and [peaceful] countries in the world. It takes caring for its people and the environment very seriously." The 2008-2009 financial crisis is discussed. (Publisher's note)

Includes bibliographical references (p. 57-58) and index

Grahame, Deborah A.

Sweden; [by] Deborah Grahame. Marshall Cavendish Benchmark 2007 48p il map (Discovering cultures) lib bdg $28.50

Grades: 2 3 4　　　　　　　　　　　　　　　948.5

ISBN 978-0-7614-1985-3 lib bdg; 0-7614-1985-3 lib bdg

LC 2006011474

An introduction to geography, history, government, and culture of Sweden

Includes glossary and bibliographical references

Phillips, Charles

★ Sweden; [by] Charles Phillips; Susan C. Brantly and Eric Clark consultants. National Geographic 2009 64p il map (Countries of the world) lib bdg $27.90

Grades: 4 5 6 7　　　　　　　　　　　　　　948.5

ISBN 978-1-4263-0389-0 lib bdg; 1-4263-0389-0 lib bdg

LC 2009275585

This describes the geography, nature, history, people & culture, and government & economy of Sweden

Includes glossary and bibliographical references

948.9　Denmark and Finland

Docalavich, Heather

Denmark; by Heather Docalavich and Shaina C. Indovino. Mason Crest Publishers 2013 64 p. col. ill., col. maps (hardcover) $22.95

Grades: 5 6 7 8　　　　　　　　　　　　　　948.9

1. Denmark -- Juvenile literature　2. European Union -- Juvenile literature

ISBN 1422222381; 9781422222386

LC 2010051090

This book by Heather Docalavich and Shaina Carmel Indovino is part of the Major European Union Nations series and focuses on Denmark. "Denmark is a peaceful northern country that joined the EU in 1973. From the Vikings to the modern day, Denmark has a long [history]. Today, Denmark is a very environmentally conscious nation with a lot going on. It also must figure out how to deal with issues of immigration and the global recession as it looks to the future." (Publisher's note)

Includes bibliographical references (p. 57) and index

948.97　Finland

Tan, Chung Lee

★ Finland; [by] Tan Chung Lee. 2nd ed.; Marshall Cavendish Benchmark 2007 144p il map (Cultures of the world) lib bdg $39.93

Grades: 5 6 7 8　　　　　　　　　　　　　　948.97

ISBN 978-0-7614-2073-6 lib bdg; 0-7614-2073-8 lib bdg

LC 2006015897

First published 1996

This provides "information on the geography, history, governmental structure, economy, cultural diversity, peoples, religion, and culture of Finland." Publisher's note

Includes glossary and bibliographical references

949.12　Iceland

McMillan, Bruce

Going fishing; written and photo-illustrated by Bruce McMillan. Houghton Mifflin Co. 2005 32p il $16

Grades: 2 3 4　　　　　　　　　　　　　　　949.12

1. Fishing

ISBN 0-618-47201-0

LC 2004-15506

"This narrative photo-essay follows a young boy from Reykjavik to the fishing village where his two grandfathers live. Each takes his grandson out on his own boat to catch a type of fish important to Iceland. . . . The clarity of the color photos brings the people, their surroundings, and the process of fishing sharply into focus. . . . A delightfully illustrated presentation of fishing, family, and, of course, Iceland." Booklist

Somervill, Barbara A.

Iceland; by Barbara A. Somervill. Children's Press 2013 144 p. ill., maps (library) $40

Grades: 5 6 7 8　　　　　　　　　　　　　　949.12

1. Iceland -- Juvenile literature　2. Icelandic language -- Juvenile literature

ISBN 0531256022; 9780531256022

LC 2012047117

This book by Barbara A. Somervill is part of the Enchantment of the World series and looks at Iceland. A discussion is offered of "how this land near the Arctic Circle came to be. . . . Maps and illustrations show the variety in the terrain and the areas of major geological activity. . . . Chapters [are] devoted to history, the economy, the government and the flora and fauna." (Children's Literature)

Includes bibliographical references (page 134) and index.

949.2   Netherlands

Docalavich, Heather

The **Netherlands**; by Heather Docalavich and Shaina Carmel Indovino. Mason Crest Publishers 2013 64 p. col. ill. (series hardcover) $344.25; (library) $22.95; (ebook) $28.95

Grades: 5 6 7 8   **949.2**

1. Netherlands -- Juvenile literature
ISBN 9781422222317; 9781422222539; 9781422222843; 9781422292716

LC 2010051464

This book on the Netherlands by Heather Docalvich and Shaina Carmel Indovino is part of the "Major European Union Nations" series. It presents an "overview of some of the successes and challenges that the Netherlands has faced and continues to face." Topics include "history, one on government, the economy, people and culture, and . . . global climate change." (Children's Literature)

Includes bibliographical references (p. 57-58, 63) and index.

949.304   Belgium-1909

Indovino, Shaina C.

Belgium; by Ida Walker and Shaina C. Indovino. Mason Crest Publishers 2012 64 p. col. ill., col. maps (library) $22.95

Grades: 5 6 7 8   **949.304**

1. Belgium
ISBN 1422222330; 9781422222331

LC 2010051078

This book, "part of the 'Modern World Nations' series, is an . . . introduction to the kingdom of Belgium. For middle school and high school readers, the chapters are descriptive of the physical features, the history, people, government, and economy. There is a chapter about the future of the nation as well as a description of life in the country today." (Children's Literature)

Includes bibliographical references and index.

949.35   Luxembourg

Sheehan, Patricia

Luxembourg; by Patricia Sheehan & Sakina Dhilawala. 2nd ed.; Marshall Cavendish Benchmark 2008 144p il map (Cultures of the world) lib bdg $42.79

Grades: 5 6 7 8   **949.35**

ISBN 978-0-7614-2088-0

LC 2007014891

First published 1997

Discusses the geography, history, government, economy, and customs of the smallest of the Benelux countries

Includes glossary and bibliographical references

949.4   Switzerland

Harris, Pamela K.

Welcome to Switzerland; by Pamela K. Harris and Brad Clemmons. Child's World 2008 32p il map (Welcome to the world) lib bdg $27.07

Grades: 1 2 3 4   **949.4**

ISBN 978-1-59296-980-7 lib bdg; 1-59296-980-1 lib bdg

LC 2007038146

This briefly describes the geography, history, people, and culture of Switzerland.

"Report writers and browsers will appreciate [this book]. . . . The captioned, color photographs have a balanced gender representation. Maps, fast facts, and recipes round out excellent offerings." SLJ

Includes glossary and bibliographical references

949.5   Greece

Etingoff, Kim

Greece; by Kim Etingoff and Shaina C. Indovino. Mason Crest Publishers 2013 64 p. ill. (library) $22.95

Grades: 5 6 7 8   **949.5**

1. Greece -- Juvenile literature 2. European Union -- Juvenile literature
ISBN 1422222446; 9781422222447; 9781422222751

LC 2010051304

This book by Kim Etingoff and Shaina C. Indovino is part of the Major European Union Nations series and looks at Greece. The series "stresses the modern relationships, goals, and problems of the European Union. . . . Chapters begin with 'Modem Issues' and a brief summary of the country's history and government, followed by chapters on economy, people and culture, and 'Looking to the Future.'" (School Library Journal)

Green, Jen

★ **Greece**; [by] Greg Anderson and Kostas Vlassopoulos, consultants. National Geographic 2009 64p il map (Countries of the world) lib bdg $27.90

Grades: 4 5 6 7   **949.5**

ISBN 978-1-4263-0470-5 lib bdg; 1-4263-0470-6 lib bdg

This describes the geography, nature, history, people and culture, government and economy of Greece

Includes glossary and bibliographical references

Heinrichs, Ann

Greece; by Ann Heinrichs. Children's Press 2012 144 p. col. ill., col. maps (library) $40

Grades: 5 6 7 8   **949.5**

1. Greece -- History -- Juvenile literature 2. Greece -- Civilization -- Juvenile literature
ISBN 0531275434; 9780531275436

LC 2012000519

This book, part of the Enchantment of the World series, focuses on Greece. The books in the series each feature 10 "chapters, several maps, a fast-facts section, and a few references to other sources, including a referral to a Scholastic website . . . . The chapters cover geography, natural environment, history, politics, people and culture." (School Library Journal)

Includes bibliographical references and index.

Vanvoorst, Jennifer Fretland

The **Byzantine** Empire; by Jenny Fretland VanVoorst. Compass Point Books 2013 48 p. ill. (chiefly col.), col. map (library) $28.65; (paperback) $8.95

Grades: 6 7 8   **949.5**

1. Byzantine Empire -- Civilization -- Juvenile literature
ISBN 075654565X; 0756545862; 9780756545659; 9780756545864

LC 2012001994

This children's nonfiction book, by Jennifer Fretland VanVoorst, profiles the Byzantine Empire as part of the "Exploring the Ancient World" series. "The Byzantine Empire, which thrived from 395 to 1453, was a fascinating place. Its people thought of themselves as Romans, spoke Greek, and hailed from all across Europe and Asia. . . . It was a Christian empire that preserved and developed Europe's intellectual heritage at a time when western Europe was in decline." (Publisher's note)

Includes bibliographical references (p. 46-47) and index.

949.65   Albania

Knowlton, MaryLee

Albania; by MaryLee Knowlton. Marshall Cavendish Benchmark 2005 144p il map (Cultures of the world) lib bdg $42.79

Grades: 5 6 7 8   **949.65**

ISBN 0-7614-1852-0

LC 2004-22236

An overview of the history, culture, peoples, religion, government, and geography of Albania

Includes glossary and bibliographical references

949.7   Serbia, Croatia, Slovenia, Bosnia and Hercegovina, Montenegro, Macedonia

Cooper, Robert

Croatia; [by] Robert Cooper and Michael Spilling. 2nd ed; Marshall Cavendish Benchmark 2011 144p il map (Cultures of the world) lib bdg $42.79

Grades: 5 6 7 8   **949.7**

ISBN 978-1-6087-0215-2; 1-6087-0215-4

LC 2010019626

First published 2001

Provides information on the geography, history, wildlife, governmental structure, economy, cultural diversity, peoples, religion, and culture of Croatia.

"Plentiful color photographs accompany substantial amounts of information." SLJ

Includes glossary and bibliographical references

Halilbegovich, Nadja

My childhood under fire; a Sarajevo diary. Kids Can Press 2006 120p il $14.95

Grades: 5 6 7 8   **949.7**

1. Yugoslav War, 1991-1995 2. Diarists 3. Pacifists
ISBN 1-55337-797-4

"In 1992, when the bombing started in Sarajevo, Halilbegovich, 12, kept a diary of her terrifying daily life under siege. Her terse vignettes replay the horror of her comfortable home torn apart." Booklist

Knowlton, MaryLee

Macedonia; by MaryLee Knowlton. Benchmark Books 2005 144p il map (Cultures of the world) lib bdg $42.79

Grades: 5 6 7 8   **949.7**

ISBN 0-7614-1854-7

LC 2004-22735

Describes the geography, history, government, economy, people, and culture of Macedonia

Includes glossary and bibliographical references

950   History of Asia

Law, Felicia

Atlas of Southwest and Central Asia. Picture Window Books 2008 32p il map (Picture Window Books world atlases) lib bdg $27.93; pa $7.95

Grades: 2 3 4   **950**

ISBN 978-1-4048-3884-0 lib bdg; 1-4048-3884-8 lib bdg; 978-1-4048-3892-5 pa; 1-4048-3892-9 pa

This introduction to the geography of Southwest and Central Asia offers maps and information about countries, landforms, bodies of water, climate, plants, animals, population, people and customs, places of interest, industries, transportation, and Mount Everest

Includes glossary

Atlas of the Far East and Southeast Asia. Picture Window Books 2008 32p il map (Picture Window Books world atlases) lib bdg $27.93; pa $7.95

Grades: 2 3 4   **950**

ISBN 978-1-4048-3883-3 lib bdg; 1-4048-3883-X lib bdg; 978-1-4048-3891-8 pa; 1-4048-3891-0 pa

This introduction to the geography of the Far East and Southeast Asia offers maps and information about countries, landforms, bodies of water, climate, plants, animals, population, people and customs, places of interest, industries, transportation, and the Pacific Islands

Includes glossary

951   China and adjacent areas

Demi, 1942-

The **great** voyages of Zheng He; by Demi. Shen's Books 2012 64 p. col. ill., col. map (hardcover) $21.95

Grades: 3 4 5   **951**

1. China -- History 2. Explorers -- China -- Biography -- Juvenile literature
ISBN 1885008457; 9781885008459

LC 2012000934

This book is "Demi's account of 15th-century Chinese explorer Zheng He," demonstrating the "dazzling wealth his fleet carried back to China: 'Precious ambergris used for medicine, cowrie shells, sapphires, rubies, oriental topaz, and Persian carpers filled the Forbidden City.' His 62 'Treasure Ships' were the largest the world had ever seen, but Zheng He also displayed a wealth of intellect and imagination that allowed him to embrace religious tolerance and open-mindedness." (Publishers Weekly)

Henzel, Cynthia Kennedy
Great Wall of China. ABDO Pub. Co. 2011 32p il (Troubled treasures: world heritage sites) $25.65
Grades: 3 4 5   **951**
1. Great Wall of China
ISBN 978-1-61613-565-2; 1-61613-565-4
LC 2010021309
This "book describes in general terms [the Great Wall of China's] construction, . . . distinctive features, and history, as well as threats to its continued existence and both current and past restoration intitiatives. Revealing color photos taken from different heights and angles are supplemented by maps and by graphic reconstructions. . . . Henzel's distinctive approach gives this [book] unusual value for both assignment and general reading." SLJ
Includes glossary

Keister, Douglas
To grandmother's house; a visit to old-town Beijing. Gibbs Smith, Publisher 2008 un $15.95
Grades: K 1 2 3 4   **951**
1. Bilingual books -- English-Chinese
ISBN 978-1-4236-0283-5; 1-4236-0283-8
LC 2007033167
"Through an engaging bilingual narrative and lovely, full-color photos, Zhang Yue gives readers a tour of her hometown, beautiful and historic Beijing. She starts the day with a visit to her grandmother in a hutong , or neighborhood, in the old part of the city. Along the way she introduces the sights and shops in a voice that is natural and interesting, inviting readers to experience all of the little details that make Beijing unique. The photographs wonderfully capture the splendor of the major monuments as well as the fascinating bustle of the outdoor markets." SLJ

Levy, Patricia
Tibet; [by] Patricia Levy & Don Bosco. 2nd ed.; Marshall Cavendish Benchmark 2007 144p il map (Cultures of the world) lib bdg $42.79
Grades: 5 6 7 8   **951**
ISBN 978-0-7614-2076-7 lib bdg; 0-7614-2076-2 lib bdg
LC 2006015826
First published 1996
This provides "information on the geography, history, wildlife, governmental structure, economy, diversity, peoples, religion, and culture of Tibet." Publisher's note
Includes glossary and bibliographical references

Lewin, Betsy, 1937-
★ Horse song; the Naadam of Mongolia. [by] Ted and Betsy Lewin. Lee & Low Books 2008 un il $19.95
Grades: 2 3 4 5   **951**
1. Nomads 2. Festivals 3. Horse racing
ISBN 978-1-58430-277-3; 1-58430-277-1
LC 2007025899
"In simple, captivating language, the Lewins describe their long journey. . . . Throughout, clearly presented cultural specifics mix with vivid sensory perceptions . . . but it's the color-washed sketches and beautiful full-page spreads . . . that will truly capture readers' attention." Booklist

Mara, Wil
People's Republic of China; by Wil Mara. Children's Press 2012 144 p. ill., maps (library) $40
Grades: 5 6 7 8   **951**
1. China -- Economic conditions 2. China -- Juvenile literature
ISBN 053125352X; 9780531253526
LC 2011011308
This book, part of the Enchantment of the World, offers an "introduction to China. The book covers geography, climate, history, language, different ethnic groups, religion, government structure, and the arts. Frequent text boxes and large, bright photographs add extra information and deeper context. There is a heavy focus on the Chinese economy and recent strides made in human rights." (School Library Journal)
Includes bibliographical references and index.

Marx, Trish
Elephants and golden thrones; inside China's Forbidden City. written by Trish Marx; photographs and photograph selection by Ellen B. Senisi; foreword by Li Ji. Abrams Books for Young Readers 2008 48p il $18.95
Grades: 4 5 6 7   **951**
1. Forbidden City (Beijing, China) 2. China
ISBN 978-0-8109-9485-0; 0-8109-9485-2
LC 2007-022413
Introduces Beijing's Forbidden City, recounting some of the most famous incidents from its past, and describing its rooms, their function, and some of the daily rituals of palace life.
The author "brings the Forbidden City to life by telling stories about six different royal inhabitants from Zhengde, 'one of the worst emperors in Chinese history,' to Puyi, who became a pawn of the invading Japanese. . . . Beautiful drawings and photographs, some provided by the Palace Museum and some taken for this book, lend color and provide additional information. Of particular note are the photos of the interiors of buildings, a number of which are not regularly open to the public." Booklist
Includes bibliographical references

Riehecky, Janet
China; by Janet Riehecky. Lerner Publications Company 2008 48p il (Country explorers) lib bdg $27.93
Grades: 2 3 4   **951**
ISBN 978-0-8225-7129-2
LC 2006036731
This introduction to China covers "all of the areas of interest to students, including animals, sports, foods, celebrations, storytime, and even a few words in the country's native language. Small amounts of information are surrounded by current photographs, maps, charts, and illustrations. . . . Sure to grab the attention of even reluctant readers." SLJ
Includes glossary and bibliographical references

Sis, Peter
★ Tibet; through the red box. Farrar, Straus & Giroux 1998 un il maps $25
Grades: 4 5 6 7   **951**
ISBN 0-374-37552-6
LC 97-50175
A Caldecott Medal honor book, 1999

"When Sis opens the red lacquered box that has sat on his father's table for decades, he finds the diary his father kept when he was lost in Tibet in the mid-1950s. The text replicates the diary's spidery handwriting, while the illustrations depict elaborate mazes and mandalas, along with dreamlike spreads that are filled with fragmented details of the father's and son's lives. . . . Impeccably designed and beautifully made, the book has a dreamlike quality that will keep readers of many ages coming back to find more in its pages." Booklist

951.05 Period of People's Republic, 1949-

Chen, Jiang Hong
Mao and me; the Little Red Guard. [by] Chen Jiang Hong; [translated by Claudia Zoe Bedrick] Enchanted Lion Books 2008 77p il $19.95
Grades: 3 4 5 **951.05**
1. Children -- China
ISBN 978-1-59270-079-0; 1-59270-079-9
LC 2008037650
Originally published in French
Chen's "picture book memoir of growing up during the Cultural Revolution is not easy to read, but stands out for its epic sweep and unflinching honesty. Rendered in large panels, his ink and wash paintings document everything from the making of dumplings to the public humiliation of cherished neighbors. . . . [This shows] excellence in representing political upheaval." Publ Wkly

Jiang, Ji-li
Red scarf girl; a memoir of the Cultural Revolution. foreword by David Henry Hwang. HarperCollins Pubs. 1997 285p $16.99; pa $6.99
Grades: 6 7 8 9 10 **951.05**
1. Authors 2. Businesspeople 3. Communism -- China
ISBN 0-06-027585-5; 0-06-446208-0 pa
LC 97-5089
"This is an autobiographical account of growing up during Mao's Cultural Revolution in China in 1966. . . . Jiang describes in terrifying detail the ordeals of her family and those like them, including unauthorized search and seizure, persecution, arrest and torture, hunger, and public humiliation. . . . Her voice is that of an intelligent, confused adolescent, and her focus on the effects of the revolution on herself, her family, and her friends provides an emotional focal point for the book, and will allow even those with limited knowledge of Chinese history to access the text." Bull Cent Child Books

951.25 Hong Kong

Kagda, Falaq
Hong Kong; [by] Falaq Kagda & Magdalene Koh. 2nd ed.; Marshall Cavendish Benchmark 2008 144p il map (Cultures of the world) lib bdg $42.79
Grades: 5 6 7 8 **951.25**
ISBN 978-0-7614-3034-6 lib bdg; 0-7614-3034-2 lib bdg
LC 2007048285
First published 1998

Surveys the geography, history, government, economy, and culture of Hong Kong
Includes glossary and bibliographical references

951.7 Mongolia

Pang, Guek-Cheng, 1950-
Mongolia; Pang Guek Cheng. Marshall Cavendish Benchmark 2010 144 p. col. ill., col. maps (Cultures of the world) (library) $42.79
Grades: 5 6 7 8 **951.7**
ISBN 9780761448495; 0761448497
LC 2009022643
This describes the geography, history, wildlife, governmental structure, economy, cultural diversity, peoples, religion, and culture of Mongolia
Includes bibliographical references and index.

951.9 Korea

Bowler, Ann Martin
All about Korea; stories, songs, crafts, and more. illustrated by Soosoonam Barg. Periplus Editions 2011 64p il $16.95
Grades: 3 4 5 6 **951.9**
ISBN 978-0-8048-4012-5; 0-8048-4012-1 (hardcover)
LC 2010040845
Introduces Korea, describing its history, culture, everyday life, food, sports, and holidays, as well as providing examples of Korean poems, songs, handicrafts, writing, legends, and folkore.
Includes bibliographical references

Cheung, Hyechong
K is for Korea; [by] Hyechong Chung, Prodeepta Das. Frances Lincoln 2008 un il $16.95
Grades: K 1 2 3 **951.9**
1. Alphabet
ISBN 978-1-84507-789-1; 1-84507-789-X
"This attractive book presents several aspects of Korea: its culture, traditional practices, national treasures, wildlife, food, and dress. Nicely designed pages showcase the excellent color photos. . . . Although other books speak more precisely of South Korea, North Korea, and the Korean peninsula, few are as accessible to primary-grade children as this one." Booklist

Santella, Andrew
The Korean War; by Andrew Santella. Compass Point Books 2007 48p il map (We the people) lib bdg $25.26; pa $8.95
Grades: 4 5 6 7 **951.9**
1. Korean War, 1950-1953
ISBN 978-0-7565-2027-4 lib bdg; 0-7565-2027-4 lib bdg; 978-0-7565-2039-7 pa; 0-7565-2039-8 pa
LC 2006006767
This "begins by explaining how North and South Korea became divided; the involvement of the United Nations and the United States; conflict between President Harry Truman and General Douglas MacArthur; eventual peace talks; and the division still occurring today. Accessible and straight-

forward, this book is an excellent one for the intended audience." SLJ

Includes bibliographical references

951.93 North Korea (People's Democratic Republic of Korea)

Kummer, Patricia K.

North Korea; by Patricia K. Kummer. Children's Press 2008 144p il map (Enchantment of the world, second series) lib bdg $38

Grades: 5 6 7 8 9   951.93

ISBN 978-0-531-18485-1 lib bdg; 0-531-18485-4 lib bdg

LC 2007025693

In this introduction to North Korea "geography is the focus, but Kummer also discusses ancient and recent history, . . . the economy, religion, sports, education, and more. Without discounting the rich culture, the book doesn't shy away from more sensitive issues. . . . The open design will draw readers, with clear type on thick, high-quality paper; numerous maps and color photos and spacious back matter are also included." Booklist

Includes bibliographical references

951.95 South Korea (Republic of Korea)

Ryan, Patrick

Welcome to South Korea; by Patrick Ryan. The Child's World 2008 32p il map (Welcome to the world) lib bdg $27.07

Grades: 1 2 3 4   951.95

ISBN 978-1-59296-978-4 lib bdg; 1-59296-978-X lib bdg

LC 2007036354

This briefly describes the geography, history, people, and culture of South Korea.

"Report writers and browsers will appreciate [this book]. . . . The captioned, color photographs have a balanced gender representation. Maps, fast facts, and recipes round out excellent offerings." SLJ

Includes glossary and bibliographical references

952 Japan

★ Art and life in rural Japan; Toho village through the eyes of its youth. Rolbin, Cyrus, editor. Next Generation Press 2011 176p il map $29.95; pa $24.95

Grades: 3 4 5 6   952

1. Country life -- Japan 2. Bilingual books -- English-Japanese

ISBN 978-0-9815595-4-4; 978-0-9815595-3-7 pa

"This gem of a book takes readers . . . into a small mountain community. . . . Simple, often poignant sentences in English and Japanese tell Toho's story, rich in history and culture. Stunning, full-color pictures capture verdant rice fields, jubilant school scenes, a lively festival, and expressive portraits of Toho's citizens. . . . A fascinating window into a vanishing way of life, this book holds appeal for both pleasure reading and reports." SLJ

Blumberg, Rhoda

★ Commodore Perry in the land of the Shogun. Lothrop, Lee & Shepard Bks. 1985 144p il map $21.99; pa $8.99

Grades: 5 6 7 8   952

1. Naval officers 2. Japan -- Foreign relations -- United States -- Juvenile literature 3. United States -- Foreign relations -- Japan -- Juvenile literature

ISBN 0-688-03723-2; 0-06-008625-4 pa

LC 84-21800

A Newbery Medal honor book, 1986

This "is a well-written story of Matthew Perry's expedition to open Japan to American trade and whaling ports. The account is sensitive to the extreme cultural differences that both the Japanese and Americans had to overcome. Especially good are the chapters and paragraphs explaining Japanese feudal society and culture. The text is marvelously complemented by the illustrations, almost all reproductions of contemporary Japanese art." SLJ

Includes bibliographical references

Moore, Willamarie

All about Japan; stories, songs, crafts, and more. illustrated by Kazumi Wilds. Tuttle Pub. 2011 63p il $16.95

Grades: 3 4 5 6   952

ISBN 978-4-8053-1077-9; 4-8053-1077-4

LC 2010040843

"In this treasure-trove of information, two children, one a Tokyo urbanite and the other from a rural village, introduce readers to their country and its culture, including geography, language, traditional arts, costume, etiquette, sports, and festivals. The dual narrators' conversational descriptions of their homes and daily routines will engage young readers while highlighting the differences between the Westernized big-city existence and the traditional way of life in Japan's countryside, deftly demonstrating the rich variety of lifestyles within this island nation. The scope of this book is remarkably comprehensive, covering almost anything a child would want to know." SLJ

Includes bibliographical references

Phillips, Charles

★ Japan; [by] Charles Phillips; Gil Latz and Kyohei Shibata, consultants. National Geographic 2007 64p il map (Countries on the world) lib bdg $27.90

Grades: 4 5 6 7   952

ISBN 1-4263-0029-8 lib bdg; 978-1-4263-0029-5 lib bdg

LC 2007296571

A basic overview of the history, geography, climate and culture of Japan.

This "clear, succinct [overview] will support assignments without overwhelming casual readers. . . . A good selection of recent, high quality color photographs gives the [book] visual appeal." SLJ

Includes glossary and bibliographical references

Riggs, Kate

Samurai. Creative Education 2011 24p il (Great warriors) $16.95; pa $8.99

Grades: K 1 2   **952**

   1. Samurai

   ISBN 978-1-60818-003-5; 1-60818-003-4; 978-0-
89812-574-0 pa; 0-89812-574-X pa

                   LC 2010019612

   A simple introduction to the Japanese warriors known as samurai, including their history, lifestyle, weapons, and how they remain a part of today's culture through the martial arts

   This title makes samurai "accessible to students just beginning to read on their own. The text and design of the [book is] spare, and vocabulary words are introduced unobtrusively. . . . The concepts are simple, but introduced without oversimplification that might lead to misunderstandings. [This is an] excellent [introduction] and fun to read aloud." SLJ

   Includes glossary and bibliographical references

Somervill, Barbara A.

   Japan; by Barbara A. Somervill. Children's Press 2012 144 p. ill., maps (library) $40

Grades: 5 6 7 8   **952**

   1. Japan -- Juvenile literature   2. Japan -- Social life and customs

   ISBN 0531253546; 9780531253540

                   LC 2011009503

   This book is part of the Enchantment of the World series and focuses on Japan. "Topics such as climate, wildlife, history, government, pop culture, and the arts are all addressed, providing a . . . look at Japan's past and present. With content revised considerably from previous editions, this book goes beyond facts and statistics to give readers an intimate glimpse at typical Japanese youth through fictionalized anecdotes detailing moments in their daily lives." (School Library Journal)

   Includes bibliographical references and index.

Takabayashi, Mari

   ★ **I** live in Tokyo; written & illustrated by Mari Takabayashi. Houghton Mifflin 2001 un il map $16

Grades: K 1 2 3   **952**

   ISBN 0-618-07702-2

                   LC 00-5964

   "Seven-year-old narrator Mimiko takes readers on a month-by-month tour of contemporary Tokyo, briefly describing one or two festivals, customs, or facets of life each month. The narrative remains consistently childlike throughout. . . . This book is a model of efficiency and elegance, cramming numerous details into a small space in a compact and attractive manner." Horn Book

953   Arabian Peninsula and adjacent areas

King, David C.

   ★ The **United** Arab Emirates; [by] David C. King. 2nd ed; Marshall Cavendish Benchmark 2008 144p il map (Cultures of the world) lib bdg $42.79

Grades: 5 6 7 8   **953**

   ISBN 978-0-7614-2565-6

                   LC 2006030237

   This describes the geography, history, government, economy, environment, people, and culture of the United Arab Emirates.

   Includes glossary and bibliographical references

953.3   Yemen

Hestler, Anna

   Yemen; by Anna Hestler and Jo-Ann Spilling. 2nd ed.; Marshall Cavendish Benchmark 2010 144p il map (Cultures of the world) lib bdg $42.79

Grades: 5 6 7 8   **953.3**

   ISBN 978-0-7614-4850-1 lib bdg; 0-7614-4850-0 lib bdg

                   LC 2009021200

   First published 1999

   This describes the geography, history, wildlife, governmental structure, economy, cultural diversity, peoples, religion, and culture of Yemen

   Includes glossary and bibliographical references

O'Neal, Claire

   We visit Yemen; by Claire O'Neal. Mitchell Lane Publishers 2012 63 p. ill. (chiefly col.), col. maps (library) $33.95; (ebook) $33.95

Grades: 4 5 6 7 8   **953.3**

   1. Yemen -- Description and travel -- Juvenile literature

   ISBN 1584159618; 1612281060; 9781584159612; 9781612281063

                   LC 2011016773

   This book on Yemen by Claire O'Neal is part of the "Your Land and My Land: The Middle East" series, which "provides an . . . introduction to the history and geography of several Middle Eastern and Southeast Asian countries from a tourist's perspective." Also included are a "recipe and a . . . craft project representing the country." (Booklist)

   Includes bibliographical references and index.

953.53   Oman

Ejaz, Khadija

   We visit Oman; by Khadija Ejaz. Mitchell Lane Publishers 2012 63 p. col. ill., col. maps (library) $33.95; (ebook) $33.95

Grades: 4 5 6 7 8   **953.53**

   1. Oman -- Description and travel -- Juvenile literature

   ISBN 1584159626; 1612281044; 9781584159629; 9781612281049

                   LC 2011000724

   This book on Oman by Khadija Ejaz is part of the "Your Land and My Land: The Middle East" series, which "provides an . . . introduction to the history and geography of several Middle Eastern and Southeast Asian countries from a tourist's perspective." Also included are a "recipe and a . . . craft project representing the country." (Booklist)

   Includes bibliographical references (p. 59-61) and index.

953.6 Persian Gulf States

Cooper, Robert
Bahrain; [by] Robert Cooper and Jo-Ann Spilling. 2nd ed.; Marshall Cavendish Benchmark 2011 144p il map (Cultures of the world) lib bdg $42.79
Grades: 5 6 7 8 **953.6**
ISBN 978-1-6087-0213-8; 1-6087-0213-8
LC 2010019621

First published 2000
Provides information on the geography, history, wildlife, governmental structure, economy, cultural diversity, peoples, religion, and culture of Bahrain.
Includes glossary and bibliographical references

Orr, Tamra
Qatar; [by] Tamra Orr. Marshall Cavendish Benchmark 2008 144p il map (Cultures of the world) lib bdg $42.79
Grades: 5 6 7 8 **953.6**
ISBN 978-0-7614-2566-3; 0-7614-2566-7
LC 2006033626

This describes the geography, history, government, economy, environment, people, and culture of Qatar
Includes glossary and bibliographical references

953.67 Kuwait

O'Shea, Maria
Kuwait; by Maria O'Shea and Michael Spilling. 2nd ed.; Marshall Cavendish Benchmark 2010 144p il map (Cultures of the world) lib bdg $42.79
Grades: 5 6 7 8 **953.67**
ISBN 978-0-7614-4479-4 lib bdg; 0-7614-4479-3 lib bdg
LC 2009007069

First published 1999
Provides information on the geography, history, wildlife, governmental structure, economy, cultural diversity, peoples, religion, and culture of Kuwait
Includes glossary and bibliographical references

Tracy, Kathleen
We visit Kuwait; by Kathleen Tracy. Mitchell Lane Publishers 2012 63 p. ill. (chiefly col.), col. maps (Your land and my land. The Middle East) (library bound) $33.95; (ebook) $33.95
Grades: 4 5 6 7 8 **953.67**
1. Kuwait -- Description and travel -- Juvenile literature
ISBN 1584159588; 1612281001; 9781584159582; 9781612281001
LC 2011002756

This book on Kuwait by Kathleen Tracy is part of the "Your Land and My Land: The Middle East" series, which "provides an . . . introduction to the history and geography of several Middle Eastern and Southeast Asian countries from a tourist's perspective." Also included are a "recipe and a . . . craft project representing the country." (Booklist)
Includes bibliographical references (p. 58-61) and index.

953.8 Saudi Arabia

Tracy, Kathleen
We visit Saudi Arabia; by Kathleen Tracy. Mitchell Lane Publishers 2011 63 p. col. ill., map (library) $33.95
Grades: 4 5 6 7 8 **953.8**
1. Persian Gulf region 2. Saudi Arabia -- Juvenile literature
ISBN 1584159634; 9781584159636
LC 2011000728

This book by Kathleen Tracy is part of the Social Studies series and looks at Saudi Arabia. "One of the most socially conservative countries on earth, Saudi Arabia is defined by Islam and ancient traditions. At the same time, its vast oil fields have helped build glistening, modern cities filled with world-class restaurants and designer shops." (Publisher's note)
Includes bibliographical references and index.

954 India and neighboring south Asian countries

Apte, Sunita
India. Children's Press 2009 48p il map (True book) lib bdg $26
Grades: 3 4 5 **954**
ISBN 978-0-531-16890-5 lib bdg; 0-531-16890-5 lib bdg
LC 2008014786

This "attractive [work covers] the geography, history, people, customs, and economy of [India]. . . . [The book has] large-size print and colorful pictures. [It] contains a section about current political challenges such as the recent terrorist attacks in Mumbai, India." SLJ
Includes glossary and bibliographical references

Arnold, Caroline
★ Taj Mahal; by Caroline Arnold and Madeleine Comora; illustrated by Rahul Bhushan. Carolrhoda Books 2007 un il lib bdg $17.95
Grades: 4 5 6 7 **954**
1. Emperors 2. Mogul Empire
ISBN 978-0-7613-2609-0 lib bdg; 0-7613-2609-X lib bdg
LC 2001006685

Recounts the love story behind the building of the Taj Mahal in India, discussing how it was constructed and providing information on Indian culture.
"The small, detailed paintings are . . . set on beautifully constructed pages resembling those of illuminated manuscripts. . . . The book is sumptuous in appearance and presents a bit of history not often told for children." SLJ

Dalal, A. Kamala
★ India; [by] A. Kamala Dalal; Ramesh C. Dhussa and Pradyumna P. Karan, consultants. National Geographic 2007 64p il map (Countries of the world) lib bdg $27.90
Grades: 4 5 6 7 **954**
ISBN 978-1-4263-0127-8 lib bdg; 1-4263-0127-8 lib bdg
LC 2007039552

This describes the geography, nature, history, people and culture, government and economy of India

"What helps [this book] stand out from the pack is [its] high-quality, rich photography. . . . The photos provide as much information as the [text]. . . . The writing is straightforward and solid." SLJ

Includes glossary and bibliographical references

Mann, Elizabeth

★ **Taj** Mahal; a story of love and empire. by Elizabeth Mann; with illustrations by Alan Witschonke. Mikaya 2008 47p il (Wonders of the world) $22.95

Grades: 4 5 6 7   **954**

1. Mogul Empire

ISBN 1-931414-20-3; 978-1-931414-20-3

LC 2008060054

This is a "dramatic retelling of the construction of the Taj Mahal. Mann begins with two pages of prose that relay the commonly told legend, but then proceeds to explode that legend with descriptive writing, colorful illustrations, ancient paintings, maps, and photographs." Booklist

Includes bibliographical references

954.03   Period of British rule, 1785-1947

Demi

★ **Gandhi**. Margaret K. McElderry Bks. 2001 un il $19.95

Grades: 3 4 5 6   **954.03**

1. Authors 2. Journalists 3. Passive resistance 4. Essayists 5. Pacifists 6. Memoirists 7. Political leaders 8. Writers on politics 9. Statesmen -- India -- Biography -- Juvenile literature 10. Nationalists -- India -- Biography -- Juvenile literature

ISBN 0-689-84149-3

LC 00-32911

"Beginning with Gandhi's failure as a student in India, this . . . biography traces Gandhi's life, from his first rallies against prejudice in South Africa to his remarkable victory over colonialism in India. . . . With extraordinarily detailed illustrations, decorated with gold leaf . . . and accessible, flowing text, veteran artist-author Demi reveals how a simple man who spun his own cloth became one of history's most important political and spiritual leaders." Booklist

McGinty, Alice B.

Gandhi. Amazon Childrens Pub 2013 40 p. (hardcover) $17.99

Grades: 1 2 3 4 5   **954.03**

1. Civil disobedience 2. India -- History -- 1765-1947, British occupation

ISBN 1477816445; 9781477816448

This children's picture book by Alice B. McGinty "tells . . . [the] present-tense story of Mohandas Gandhi's 24-day march to the sea in 1930 in search of freedom and peaceful change for the people of India. . . . His goal is to challenge 200 years of British rule by breaking the law prohibiting Indians from collecting salt from the sea." (Kirkus Reviews)

954.9   Other jurisdictions

NgCheong-Lum, Roseline

Maldives; 2nd ed.; Marshall Cavendish Benchmark 2011 144p il map (Cultures of the world) lib bdg $42.79

Grades: 5 6 7 8   **954.9**

ISBN 978-1-6087-0217-6; 1-6087-0217-0

LC 2010019746

First published 2001

Provides information on the geography, history, wildlife, governmental structure, economy, cultural diversity, peoples, religion, and culture of Maldives.

Includes glossary and bibliographical references

Taylor-Butler, Christine

Sacred mountain; Everest. Lee & Low Books 2009 48p il $19.95

Grades: 5 6 7 8   **954.9**

1. Sherpa (Nepalese people) -- Juvenile literature 2. Mountaineering -- Mount Everest (China and Nepal) -- Juvenile literature

ISBN 978-1-60060-255-9; 1-60060-255-X

LC 2008-30423

"The informative text is amply illustrated with well-chosen black-and-white and color photographs." SLJ

Includes glossary

954.91   Pakistan

Hinman, Bonnie

We visit Pakistan; by Bonnie Hinman. Mitchell Lane Publishers 2012 63 p. ill. (chiefly col.), col. maps (Your land and my land. The Middle East) (library) $33.95

Grades: 4 5 6 7 8   **954.91**

1. Pakistan -- Juvenile literature

ISBN 158415960X; 9781584159605

LC 2011030763

This book on Pakistan by Bonnie Hinman is part of the "Your Land and My Land: The Middle East" series, which "provides an . . . introduction to the history and geography of several Middle Eastern and Southeast Asian countries from a tourist's perspective." Topics such as "terrorism and al-Qaeda" are covered along with "descriptions of the country's history and attractions." Also included are a "recipe and a . . . craft project representing the country." (Booklist)

Includes bibliographical references (p. 59-61) and index.

Kwek, Karen

Pakistan; [written by Karen Kwek and Jameel Haque] Marshall Cavendish Benchmark 2010 48p il map (Welcome to my country) $19.95

Grades: 2 3 4 5   **954.91**

ISBN 978-1-60870-158-2; 1-60870-158-1

This is an introduction to Pakistan's culture, history, sports, religions, and foods.

"Beautifully illustrated. . . . The writing is clear. . . . [This title] will work well for reports and will be enjoyed by browsers." SLJ

Includes glossary and bibliographical references

Sonneborn, Liz

Pakistan; by Liz Sonneborn. Children's Press 2013

144 p. ill. (mostly col.), col. maps. (Enchantment of the world, second series) (library) $40

Grades: 5 6 7 8 **954.91**

1. Pakistan -- Juvenile literature 2. Pakistan -- Description and travel

ISBN 0531275442; 9780531275443

LC 2012000505

This book, by Liz Sonneborn, is part of the "Enchantment of the World" series. In it the author provides information and photographs showcasing the people, places and events surrounding the South Asian country of Pakistan. Contents include photographs of Pakistani cities and landscapes, statistics describing the nation's features, and traditional Pakistani recipes.

Includes bibliographical references and index

954.92 Bangladesh

March, Michael
Bangladesh. Sea-to-sea Publications 2009 32p il map (Facts about countries) $28.50

Grades: 3 4 5 **954.92**

ISBN 978-1-59771-113-5; 1-59771-113-6

Describes the geography, history, industries, education, government, and cultures of Bangladesh

"The attractive layout includes color photographs and charts of current statistics as well as maps illustrating main farming regions, natural resources, or the literacy rates of girls and boys. The [text is] clear and succinct." SLJ

Includes glossary

955 Iran

DiPrimio, Pete
We visit Iran; by Pete DiPrimio. Mitchell Lane Publishers 2012 63 p. col. ill., maps (library) $33.95

Grades: 4 5 6 7 8 **955**

1. Iran -- History 2. Iran -- Juvenile literature

ISBN 1584159545; 9781584159544

LC 2011016765

This book by Pete DiPrimio looks at Iran. "It is a Middle Eastern country with European (not Arabian) founders. It was the home of one of the ancient world's greatest empires, the Persian Empire. Its many ancient ruins include the palace complex of Persepolis, which was so big it took 150 years to finish. While the nation develops nuclear technology, its government—called an Islamic Republic—dictates people's lives, from the clothing they wear to the news they hear." (Publisher's note)

Includes bibliographical references and index.

Mara, Wil
Iran; [by] Wil Mara. Marshall Cavendish Benchmark 2007 48p il map (Discovering cultures) lib bdg $28.50

Grades: 2 3 4 **955**

ISBN 978-0-7614-1986-0 lib bdg; 0-7614-1986-1 lib bdg

LC 2006011476

An introduction to the geography, history, people, and culture of Iran

Includes glossary and bibliographical references

956.04 Middle East -- 1945-1980

Marx, Trish
★ **Sharing** our homeland; Palestinian and Jewish Children at summer Peace Camp. photographs by Cindy Karp. Lee & Low Books 2010 47p il $19.95

Grades: 3 4 5 6 **956.04**

1. Palestinian Arabs 2. Jewish-Arab relations

ISBN 978-158430-260-5; 1-58430-260-7

"Alya, an Israeli Palestinian girl in a Muslim family, chooses to wear a hijab. Yuval, an Israeli Jewish boy, lives in a moshav farming community. In this picture-book photo-essay, crisp color images show the kids at home and then having fun at Peace Camp, where they swim, make arts and crafts, and do other universal summer-camp activities. Field trips introduce some kids to places they've never been, including a museum, a kibbutz, and an Arab village. . . . Marx weaves in detailed history of the Holy Land, from ancient times to 1948 and the establishment of the Jewish state and then the 1967 War. Throughout, she is frank about the continuing violence and conflict, and a contemporary image shows that the tall West Bank safety wall is also a divider between cultures. Realistic and upbeat, this moves beyond stereotypes and notions of the 'other.'" Booklist

Senker, Cath
The **Arab**-Israeli conflict; [by] Cath Senker. new ed.; Arcturus Pub. 2008 48p il map (Timelines) lib bdg $32.80

Grades: 5 6 7 8 **956.04**

1. Israel-Arab conflicts

ISBN 978-1-84193-725-0 lib bdg; 1-84193-725-8 lib bdg

LC 2007-7547

First published 2005 by Smart Apple Media

This describes current conditions in Israel and the occupied territories and includes a history of major events and political developments.

"A complex situation is clearly explained. . . . [This is] well-illustrated. . . . Throughout, the tone is nonjudgmental." SLJ [review of 2005 edition]

Includes bibliographical references

956.1 Turkey

LaRoche, Amelia
We visit Turkey; by Amelia LaRoche. Mitchell Lane Publishers 2012 63 p. ill. (chiefly col.), col. maps (library) $33.95

Grades: 4 5 6 7 8 **956.1**

1. Turkey -- Description and travel -- Juvenile literature

ISBN 1584159561; 9781584159568

LC 2011030765

This book on Turkey by Amelia Laroche is part of the "Your Land and My Land: The Middle East" series, which "provides an . . . introduction to the history and geography of several Middle Eastern and Southeast Asian countries from a tourist's perspective." It "similarly mentions but does not dwell upon the rise of Islam and the hijab controversy." Also included are a "recipe and a . . . craft project representing the country." (Booklist)

Includes bibliographical references (p, 59-61) and index.

Shields, Sarah D.

★ Turkey; [by] Sarah Shields. National Geographic 2009 64p il map (Countries of the world) lib bdg $27.90

Grades: 4 5 6 7   **956.1**

ISBN 978-1-4263-0387-6 lib bdg; 1-4263-0387-4 lib bdg

LC 2009275583

This describes the geography, nature, history, people and culture, government and economy of Turkey

Includes glossary and bibliographical references

956.7 Iraq

Falvey, David

Letters to a soldier; by First Lieutenant David Falvey and Mrs. Julie Hutt's fourth-grade class. Marshall Cavendish Children 2009 un il $16.99

Grades: 3 4 5   **956.7**

1. Soldiers 2. Children's writings 3. Contractors 4. Army officers 5. Iraq War, 2003- -- Personal narratives

ISBN 978-0-7614-5637-7; 0-7614-5637-6

LC 2008050268

"While serving in Iraq in 2008, First Lieutenant David Falvey received a packet of letters from Julie Hutt's fourth-grade class in Roslyn, NY. The children's correspondences and drawings, paired with Falvey's thoughtful answers and photographs from his deployment, are reproduced in an inviting, child-friendly format." SLJ

Goldish, Meish

Baghdad pups. Bearport Pub. 2011 32p il (Dog heroes) lib bdg $25.27

Grades: 3 4 5   **956.7**

1. Dogs 2. Iraq War, 2003 -- Personal narratives

ISBN 978-1-6177-2150-2; 1-6177-2150-6

LC 2010035187

This book "explores how a special division of the Society for the Prevention of Cruelty to Animals International (SPCAI) has been rescuing dogs who have befriended service people in Iraq, despite the clear disapproval of the United States military, which has strict laws about removing property, including animals, from war zones. . . . [This book is] engaging not just because the content is so compelling, but also because the [author has] highlighted specific dogs currently working in [this field]. The use of real names and full-color photographs on every page, many contributed by the individuals who work with these dogs, makes reading [this book] a personal experience. . . . [An] excellent [introduction] to [this] new [development] in service-dog training." SLJ

Includes bibliographical references

Malhotra, Sonali

Iraq. Marshall Cavendish Benchmark 2010 48p il map (Welcome to my country) $19.99

Grades: 2 3 4 5   **956.7**

ISBN 978-1-60870-155-1; 1-60870-155-7

LC 2010006405

An overview of the history, geography, government, economy, language, people, and culture of Iraq.

"Beautifully illustrated. . . . The writing is clear. . . . [This title] will work well for reports and will be enjoyed by browsers." SLJ

Includes glossary and bibliographical references

O'Neal, Claire

We visit Iraq; by Claire O'Neal. Mitchell Lane Publishers 2012 63 p. ill. (chiefly col.), col. maps (library bound) $33.95

Grades: 4 5 6 7 8   **956.7**

1. Persian Gulf region 2. Iraq -- Juvenile literature

ISBN 1584159553; 9781584159551

LC 2011016771

This book by Claire O'Neal is part of the Social Studies series and looks at Iraq. "Iraq's Tigris and Euphrates rivers turned this Middle Eastern desert into the world's first farmland. Over six millenia, Iraq's civilizations have laid foundations for the rest of the world. They built great stone ziggurats and soaring mosques. They invented the wheel, the calendar, and the written word. With their riches, they also attracted war." (Publisher's note)

Includes bibliographical references (p. 59-61) and index.

Samuels, Charlie

★ Iraq; [by] Charlie Samuels; Sarah Shields and Shakir Mustafa, consultants. National Geographic 2007 64p il map (Countries of the world) lib bdg $27.90

Grades: 4 5 6 7   **956.7**

ISBN 978-1-4263-0061-5

LC 2007024675

This describes the geography, nature, history, people and culture, government and economy of Iraq.

Includes glossary and bibliographical references

Wilkes, Sybella

Out of Iraq; refugees' stories in words, paintings and music. Evans 2010 70p il map $17.99

Grades: 4 5 6 7   **956.7**

1. Refugees

ISBN 978-0-237-53930-6; 0-237-53930-6

"Provides an concise overview of events before and during the invasion, interspersed with first-person narratives of Iraqi refugees, gathered while Wilkes worked with the United Nations Refugee Agency in Syria. . . . Moving photographs and artwork, quotations from political figures, and accessible language form a harrowing window into lives rarely paid witness." Publ Wkly

956.92 Lebanon

Sheehan, Sean

Lebanon; [by] Sean Sheehan & Zawiah Abdul Latif. 2nd ed.; Marshall Cavendish Benchmark 2008 144p il map (Cultures of the world) lib bdg $42.79

Grades: 5 6 7 8   **956.92**

ISBN 978-0-7614-2081-1 lib bdg; 0-7614-2081-9 lib bdg

LC 2006101735

First published 1997

"Provides comprehensive information on the geography, history, wildlife, governmental structure, economy, cultural diversity, peoples, religion, and culture of Lebanon." Publisher's note

Includes bibliographical references

956.93 Cyprus

Spilling, Michael

Cyprus; [by] Michael Spilling and Jo-Ann Spilling. 2nd ed.; Marshall Cavendish Benchmark 2010 144p il map (Cultures of the world) lib bdg $42.79

Grades: 5 6 7 8 **956.93**

ISBN 978-0-7614-4855-6 lib bdg; 0-7614-4855-1 lib bdg

LC 2009045689

First published 2000

This offers information on the geography, history, wildlife, governmental structure, economy, cultural diversity, peoples, religion, and culture of Cyprus

Includes glossary and bibliographical references

956.94 Palestine; Israel

Bowden, Rob, 1973-

Jerusalem; [by] Rob Bowden. World Almanac Library 2006 48p il map (Great cities of the world) lib bdg $31

Grades: 3 4 5 6 **956.94**

ISBN 0-8368-5051-3

LC 2005043586

This describes the geography, cultures, work, play, history, and religions of Jerusalem

This is "attractive, informative . . . straightforward and objective." SLJ

Includes bibliographical references

Ellis, Deborah

Three wishes; Palestinian and Israeli children speak. Groundwood Bks. 2004 110p il map hardcover o.p. pa $9.99

Grades: 5 6 7 8 **956.94**

1. Palestinian Arabs 2. Israel-Arab conflicts

ISBN 0-88899-608-X; 0-88899-645-4 pa

"An excellent presentation of a confusing historic struggle, told within a palpable, perceptive and empathetic format." SLJ

Includes bibliographical references

Saul, Laya

We visit Israel; by Laya Saul. Mitchell Lane Publishers 2012 63 p. ill., maps (library) $33.95

Grades: 4 5 6 7 8 **956.94**

1. Israel -- Description and travel -- Juvenile literature

ISBN 158415957X; 9781584159575

LC 2011024706

This book on Israel by Laya Saul is part of the "Your Land and My Land: The Middle East" series, which "provides an . . . introduction to the history and geography of several Middle Eastern and Southeast Asian countries from a tourist's perspective. . . . 'We Visit Israel' is clearly written from a Jewish Israeli perspective, but Saul makes sure to mention areas of conflict and controversy." Also included

are a "recipe and a . . . craft project representing the country." (Booklist)

Includes bibliographical references (p. 60-61) and index.

Young, Emma

★ Israel; [by] Emma Young; Zvi Ben-Dor Benite, George Kanazi, and Aviva Halamish, consultants. National Geographic 2008 64p il map (Countries of the world) lib bdg $27.90

Grades: 4 5 6 7 **956.94**

ISBN 978-1-4263-0258-9 lib bdg; 1-4263-0258-4 lib bdg

This describes the geography, nature, history, people and culture, government, and economy of Israel.

Includes glossary and bibliographical references

958.1 Afghanistan

Ali, Sharifah Enayat

Afghanistan; by Sharifah Enayat Ali. 2nd ed.; Marshall Cavendish Benchmark 2006 144p il map (Cultures of the world) lib bdg $42.79

Grades: 5 6 7 8 **958.1**

ISBN 978-0-7614-2064-4 lib bdg; 0-7614-2064-9 lib bdg

LC 2005034789

First published 1995

This is "well organized, informative, and entertaining. . . . Excellent-quality full-color photographs and reproductions show the people, landforms, buildings, and everyday activities of [Afghanistan]." SLJ [review of 1995 edtion]

Includes glossary and bibliographical references

Bjorklund, Ruth

Afghanistan; by Ruth Bjorklund. Children's Press 2012 144 p. col. ill., col. maps (library) $40

Grades: 5 6 7 8 **958.1**

1. Afghanistan -- Juvenile literature 2. Afghanistan -- Description and travel

ISBN 0531253503; 9780531253502

LC 2011013627

This book by Ruth Bjorklund is part of the Enchantment of the World series and looks at Afghanistan. In each book, "colourful photos provide . . . views of foreign cities and landscapes," "sidebars highlight especially interesting people, places, and events," and "recipes give readers the opportunity to experience foreign cuisine firsthand." (Publisher's note)

Includes bibliographical references (p. 134-135) and index.

Fordyce, Deborah

Afghanistan; [written by Deborah Fordyce] Marshall Cavendish Benchmark 2010 48p il map (Welcome to my country) $19.95

Grades: 2 3 4 5 **958.1**

ISBN 978-1-60870-149-0; 1-60870-149-2

This is an introduction to Afghanistan's culture, history, sports, religions, and foods.

"Beautifully illustrated. . . . The writing is clear. . . . [This title] will work well for reports and will be enjoyed by browsers." SLJ

Includes glossary and bibliographical references

O'Brien, Tony

★ Afghan dreams; young voices of Afghanistan. by Tony O'Brien and Mike Sullivan; photographs by Tony O'Brien. Bloomsbury Children's Books 2008 69p il map $18.99; lib bdg $19.89

Grades: 3 4 5 6   **958.1**
1. Children -- Afghanistan 2. Teenagers -- Afghanistan 2. Documentary photography -- Juvenile literature 3. Teenagers -- Afghanistan -- Juvenile literature

ISBN 978-1-59990-287-6; 1-59990-287-7; 978-1-59990-321-7 lib bdg; 1-59990-321-0 lib bdg

LC 2008-07004

"This handsome photo-essay features contemporary Afghan children ranging in age from 8 to 18 years. They were asked about their families, lives, and hopes for the future. The young people's straightforward statements tell much about the devastating effects of decades of war." SLJ

Whitfield, Susan

Afghanistan; [by] Susan Whitfield; Thomas Barfield and Maliha Zulfacar, consultants. National Geographic 2008 64p il map (Countries of the world) lib bdg $27.90

Grades: 4 5 6 7   **958.1**
ISBN 978-1-4263-0256-5 lib bdg; 1-4263-0256-8 lib bdg

This describes the geography, nature, history, people and culture, government, and economy of Aghanistan.

Includes glossary and bibliographical references

958.4   Turkestan

King, David C.

Kyrgyzstan; [by] David C. King. Marshall Cavendish Benchmark 2005 144p il map (Cultures of the world) lib bdg $42.79

Grades: 5 6 7 8   **958.4**
ISBN 0-7614-2013-4

LC 2005001314

Describes the geography, history, government, economy, people, and culture of Kyrgyzstan

Includes glossary and bibliographical references

Pang, Guek-Cheng, 1950-

Kazakhstan; 2nd ed.; Marshall Cavendish Benchmark 2011 144p il map (Cultures of the world) lib bdg $42.79

Grades: 5 6 7 8   **958.4**
ISBN 978-1-6087-0455-2; 1-6087-0455-6

First published 2001

This offers information on the geography, history, wildlife, governmental structure, economy, cultural diversity, peoples, religion, and culture of Kazakhstan.

958.5   Turkmenistan

Knowlton, MaryLee

Turkmenistan; [by] MaryLee Knowlton. Marshall

Cavendish Benchmark 2006 144p il map (Cultures of the world) lib bdg $42.79

Grades: 5 6 7 8   **958.5**
ISBN 0-7614-2014-2

LC 2005006455

Describes the geography, history, government, economy, people, and culture of Turkmenistan

Includes glossary and bibliographical references

958.6   Tajikistan

Abazov, Rafis

Tajikistan; [by] Rafis Abazov. Marshall Cavendish Benchmark 2006 144p il map (Cultures of the world) lib bdg $42.79

Grades: 5 6 7 8   **958.6**
ISBN 0-7614-2012-6

LC 2005001166

Describes the geography, history, government, economy, people, and culture of the former Soviet republic of Tajikistan

Includes glossary and bibliographical references

959.3   Thailand

Morris, Ann

★ Tsunami; helping each other. by Ann Morris & Heidi Larson. Millbrook Press 2005 32p il map $15.95

Grades: 3 4 5   **959.3**
1. Indian Ocean earthquake and tsunami, 2004
ISBN 0-7613-9501-6

LC 2005-13616

The story of how one family in Thailand survived the tsunami of December 26, 2004, and, with the help of others, began to rebuild their lives.

"The brisk and straightforward text is enhanced by many excellent well-captioned color photos." Horn Book Guide

Rau, Dana Meachen

Thailand; [by] Dana Meachen Rau. Marshall Cavendish Benchmark 2007 48p il map (Discovering cultures) lib bdg $28.50

Grades: 2 3 4   **959.3**
ISBN 978-0-7614-1989-1 lib bdg; 0-7614-1989-6 lib bdg

LC 2006011475

An introduction to the geography, history, people, and culture of Thailand

Includes glossary and bibliographical references

959.4   Laos

Dalal, A. Kamala

★ Laos; [by] A. Kamala Dalal. National Geographic 2009 64p il (Countries of the world) lib bdg $27.90

Grades: 4 5 6 7   **959.4**
ISBN 978-1-4263-0388-3 lib bdg; 1-4263-0388-2 lib bdg

This describes the geography, nature, history, people and culture, and govenment and economy of Laos

Includes glossary and bibliographical references

959.5   Malaysia, Brunei, Singapore

Foo Yuk Yee

Malaysia; by Heidi Munan, Foo Yuk Yee, and Jo-Ann Spilling. 3rd ed. Marshall Cavendish Benchmark 2012 144 p. col. ill., col. maps (library) $47.07

Grades: 5 6 7 8   959.5

1. Culture -- Juvenile literature 2. Malaysia -- Juvenile literature

ISBN 1608707857; 9781608707850

LC 2011004468

This book by Heidi Munan is part of the Cultures of the World series and looks at Malaysia. The "geography, history, economy and culture are all covered . . . . . An entire chapter is devoted to the festivals, which are many because of the ethnic diversity of Malaysia. This is also made apparent in the section about food and manners, as the Muslims do not eat pork and the Hindus and Sikhs cannot eat beef, making it necessary to prepare various dishes for parties." (Children's Literature)

Includes bibliographical references and index.

959.57   Singapore

Layton, Leslie

Singapore; by Lesley Layton, Pang Guek Cheng,and Jo-Ann Spilling. 3rd ed. Marshall Cavendish Benchmark 2012 144 p. (library) $47.07

Grades: 5 6 7 8   959.57

1. Singapore -- Juvenile literature

ISBN 1608707873; 9781608707874

LC 2011004479

This book is part of the Cultures of the World series and looks at Singapore. "Singapore is a small but mighty nation. Thanks to its strategic position and the energy of its people—the Malays, and migrant Chinese, Indians, and Eurasians—it is now the world's number one airport and sea port, a regional financial center, a telecommunications hub, and a favored tourist destination." (Publisher's note)

Includes bibliographical references and index.

959.6   Cambodia

Sobol, Richard

The mysteries of Angkor Wat; exploring Cambodia's ancient temple. Candlewick Press 2011 42p il map (Traveling photographer) $17.99

Grades: 3 4 5 6   959.6

1. Temples 2. Angkor Wat

ISBN 978-0-7636-4166-5; 0-7636-4166-9

LC 2010041479

"This ancient temple, located in the jungles of Cambodia, has long been a source of mystery, reverence, and wonder. Sobol takes readers on a journey into the heart of the 1000-year-old ruins and presents a fascinating look at the history of the temple, the people who built it and worshipped

there, and the current culture surrounding it. A good amount of information is presented while keeping the text conversational and accessible for young people. . . . . The handsome book contains captioned color photographs on each page; they give interesting glimpses into the modern lives of the people living around this ancient site and a fascinating look at the ruins themselves." SLJ

Includes glossary

959.604   -1949

Sonneborn, Liz

The Khmer Rouge; by Liz Sonneborn. Marshall Cavendish Benchmark 2012 80 p. ill. (some col.), col. map (library) $34.21; (ebook) $34.21

Grades: 5 6 7 8   959.604

1. Dith Pran, 1942-2008 -- Juvenile literature 2. Genocide -- Cambodia -- Juvenile literature 3. Cambodia -- History -- 1975- -- Juvenile literature 4. Political atrocities -- Cambodia -- Juvenile literature 5. Journalists -- Cambodia -- Biography -- Juvenile literature 6. Political refugees -- Cambodia -- Biography -- Juvenile literature

ISBN 1608704742; 9781608704743; 9781608706952 pdf

LC 2011005595

This book "tells the story of Dith Pran, a Cambodian journalist and translator who provided support to Sydney Schanberg, a New York Times correspondent. . . . Sadly, when Schanberg evacuated, Pran was forced to remain behind where he fell into captivity. Over a three year period Dith Pran survived horrendous conditions but ultimately escaped and fled to Thailand. There, in a refugee camp, Pran was rescued by Schanberg and relocated to the United States." (Children's Literature)

Includes bibliographical references and index.

959.7   Vietnam

Green, Jen

Vietnam; [by] Jen Green. National Geographic 2008 64p il map (Countries of the world) lib bdg $27.90

Grades: 4 5 6 7   959.7

ISBN 978-1-4263-0202-2

LC 2007047832

This describes the geography, nature, history, people and culture, government, and economy of Vietnam.

Includes glossary and bibliographical references

Guile, Melanie

Culture in Vietnam; [by] Melanie Guile. Raintree 2005 32p il map lib bdg $29.29

Grades: 4 5 6 7   959.7

ISBN 1-4109-1135-7

LC 2004-16651

This "title includes a map and picture of the nation's flag as well as color photographs that bring to life the wide range of topics addressed. Two to four-page chapters briefly cover languages, history, people, religions, holidays and festivals, customs, minority groups, costumes and clothing, food, and arts and crafts, providing students with lots of cultural information. Text is well spaced in an overall neat and pleasing manner." SLJ

Includes bibliographical references

959.704 Vietnam ---1945

Skrypuch, Marsha Forchuk

Last airlift; a Vietnamese orphan's rescue from war. Marsha Forchuk Skrypuch. Pajama Press 2012 120 p.
Grades: 3 4 5 6   **959.704**
1. Orphans 2. Aeronautics -- Flights 3. International adoption 4. Evacuation of civilians -- Vietnam 5. Vietnam War, 1961-1975 -- Children
ISBN 098694954X; 9780986949548

This book "tells the story of the last Canadian airlift [from Vietnam] through the memories of one child, Son Thi Anh Tuyet. Nearly 8 years old, the sad-eyed girl . . . had lived nearly all her life in a Catholic orphanage." When "she and a number of the institution babies were taken away, placed on an airplane and flown to a new world. . . . she assumed that John and Dorothy Morris had chosen her to help with their three children; instead, she had acquired a family." (Kirkus Reviews)

959.8 Indonesia and East Timor

Cooper, Robert

Indonesia; by Gouri Mirpuri and Robert Cooper. 3rd ed. Marshall Cavendish Benchmark 2012 144 p. ill., maps (library) $47.07
Grades: 5 6 7 8   **959.8**
1. Indonesia -- History 2. Indonesia -- Juvenile literature 3. Indonesia/Juvenile literature
ISBN 1608707830; 9781608707836

LC 200128607

First published 1990

This "nonfiction book in the 'Cultures of the World' series presents a . . . story of the physical, social and historical characteristics of Indonesia. . . . Throughout the book, also, there are textboxes that add . . . information to the subject matter and include . . . drawings of native musical instruments, weapons, foods and other" things. (Children's Literature)

"The pictures are lush, with captions in tiny print offering much additional information. The text is written smoothly and readably, and it contains a substantial amount of information." Booklist

Includes bibliographical references and index.

960 History of Africa

Bowden, Rob, 1973-

★ **African** culture; [by] Rob Bowden and Rosie Wilson. Heinemann Library 2009 48p il map (Africa focus) $30; pa $8.99
Grades: 4 5 6   **960**
ISBN 978-1-4329-2440-9; 1-4329-2440-0; 978-1-4329-2445-4 pa; 1-4329-2445-1 pa

LC 2008-48310

This book "presents a clear and timely overview of the diverse and complex continent. The full-color photographs are of exceptional quality. [The] book also includes interesting fact boxes, sidebars, maps, and a time line. [It] focuses on traditions and how they are relevant for today. Highlights include family and daily life; religion, beliefs, and customs; and the performing and visual arts." SLJ

Includes bibliographical references

★ **Ancient** Africa; [by] Rob Bowden and Rosie Wilson. Heinemann Library 2008 48p il map (Africa focus) $30; pa $8.99
Grades: 4 5 6   **960**
ISBN 978-1-4329-2439-3; 1-4329-2439-7; 978-1-4329-2444-7 pa; 1-4329-2444-3 pa

LC 2008-48306

This book "presents a clear and timely overview of the diverse and complex continent. The full-color photographs are of exceptional quality. [The] book also includes interesting fact boxes, sidebars, maps, and a time line. . . . [It] begins with the origin of humankind and continues through the beginning of the slave trade in Europe and America. Early civilizations such as Egypt, ancient Ghana, the Mali Empire, Great Zimbabwe, and Kongo are represented. Invasions and explorations are discussed, as is slavery and colonialism." SLJ

Includes bibliographical references

★ **Changing** Africa; [by] Rob Bowden and Rosie Wilson. Heinemann Library 2009 48p il map (Africa focus) $30; pa $8.99
Grades: 4 5 6   **960**
ISBN 978-1-4329-2437-9; 1-4329-2437-0; 978-1-4329-2442-3 pa; 1-4329-2442-7 pa

LC 2008-48277

This book "presents a clear and timely overview of the diverse and complex continent. The full-color photographs are of exceptional quality. [The] book also includes interesting fact boxes, sidebars, maps, and a time line. . . . [It] presents recent positive and negative changes. The rise of poverty and slums is explored, as is the lowered life expectancy due to the spread of malaria and HIV/AIDS. Positive changes include the freedom that voting has brought." SLJ

Includes bibliographical references

★ **Modern** Africa; [by] Rosie Wilson and Rob Bowden. Heinemann Library 2009 48p il map (Africa focus) $30; pa $8.99
Grades: 4 5 6   **960**
ISBN 978-1-4329-2438-6; 1-4329-2438-9; 978-1-4329-2443-0 pa; 1-4329-2443-5 pa

This book "presents a clear and timely overview of the diverse and complex continent. The full-color photographs are of exceptional quality. [The] book also includes interesting fact boxes, sidebars, maps, and a time line. . . . [It] chronicles the history of colonial Africa to independence, and the changes that have arisen and continue to manifest themselves. Topics include apartheid and recent and ongoing violence in Rwanda, Darfur, and the Congo. While corrupt leaders continue to hamper Africa's attempts at advancement, the exportation of oil as well as aid from missionaries and international organizations are presented as hopes for the future." SLJ

Mooney, Carla

Amazing Africa; projects you can build yourself. illustrated by Megan Stearns. Nomad Press 2010 122p il (Build it yourself) pa $15.95

Grades: 4 5 6 7   960

1. Handicraft

ISBN 978-1-934670-41-5; 1-934670-41-3

"Casual and informative, this large, attractive, browsable paperback . . . offers a view of contemporary African life that reaches far beyond the usual scenery-and-wildlife tourists' perspective. Blending history, culture, and tradition with politics and life in both cities and rural areas, the chapters begin with a look at natural wonders and dangerous wildlife that will grab readers, then move on to historical discussions of humankind's birthplace and early civilizations. . . . The open design includes sketches on every page. . . . The craft projects [include making] your own Maasai beaded necklace, kente cloth, woven basket, galimoto doll, and . . . more." Booklist

Murray, Jocelyn

Africa; updated by Brian A. Stewart. 3rd ed.; Chelsea House 2007 96p il map (Cultural atlas for young people) $35

Grades: 5 6 7 8   960

ISBN 978-0-8160-6826-5; 0-8160-6826-7

First published 1990

Presents information on the history and various regions and cultures of Africa.

Includes glossary and bibliographical references

Musgrove, Margaret

★ Ashanti to Zulu: African traditions; pictures by Leo and Diane Dillon. Dial Bks. for Young Readers 1976 un il $21.99; pa $6.99

Grades: 3 4 5 6   960

1. Ethnology -- Africa

ISBN 0-8037-0357-0; 0-14-054604-9 pa

Awarded the Caldecott Medal, 1977

"In brief texts arranged in alphabetical order, each accompanied by a large framed illustration, the author introduces 'the reader to twenty-six African peoples by depicting a custom important to each.' . . . In most of the paintings the artists 'have included a man, a woman, a child, their living quarters, an artifact, and a local animal' and have, in this way, stressed the human and the natural ambience of the various peoples depicted." Horn Book

961.1   Tunisia

Brown, Roslind Varghese

Tunisia; [by] Roslind Varghese Brown & Michael Spilling. 2nd ed.; Marshall Cavendish Benchmark 2008 144p il map (Cultures of the world) lib bdg $42.79

Grades: 5 6 7 8   961.1

ISBN 978-0-7614-3037-7 lib bdg; 0-7614-3037-7 lib bdg

LC 2007050798

First published 1998

"Provides comprehensive information on the geography, history, wildlife, governmental structure, economy,

cultural diversity, peoples, religion, and culture of Tunisia." Publisher note

Includes glossary and bibliographical references

962   Egypt, Sudan, South Sudan

Heinrichs, Ann

The Nile. Marshall Cavendish Benchmark 2008 96p il map (Nature's wonders) lib bdg $24.95

Grades: 5 6 7 8   962

ISBN 978-0-7614-2854-1

LC 2007019187

"It's tough to make a river interesting, but this . . . does an admirable job of it. . . . Crisp, full-color photos and original artwork decorate nearly every page. . . . [This is a] well-thought-out natural history." Booklist

Includes glossary and bibliographical references

962.055   Egypt

Abouraya, Karen Leggett

★ Hands around the library; protecting Egypt's treasured books. by Susan L. Roth and Karen Leggett Abouraya; collages by Susan L. Roth. Dial Books for Young Readers 2012 40 p. (hardcover) $16.99

Grades: 1 2 3   962.055

1. Arab Spring, 2010- 2. Picture books for children 3. Cultural property -- Protection -- Juvenile literature 4. Libraries -- Egypt -- Alexandria -- Juvenile literature 5. Libraries -- Destruction and pillage -- Egypt -- Alexandria -- Juvenile literature

ISBN 0803737475; 9780803737471

LC 2011038198

Author Susan L. Roth's book shows the "days of the Arab Spring when Egyptians marched to bring down their government, [and] youthful demonstrators and library staff stood together to protect the Bibliotheca Alexandrina, contemporary counterpart to the Great Library of Alexandria, from vandalism. Roth's . . . collages capture these heady moments, blending photos, papers and fabrics to bring the people's positive actions and the building's intriguing facade together in a celebration of patriotism and libraries." (Kirkus Reviews)

962.4   Sudan and South Sudan

Brownlie, Ali

Sudan in our world; by Ali Brownlie Bojang. Smart Apple Media 2010 32p il (Countries in our world) lib bdg $28.50

Grades: 5 6 7 8   962.4

ISBN 978-1-59920-434-5 lib bdg; 1-59920-434-7 lib bdg

LC 2009052421

"Issues such as Civil War, fighting in Darfur, the government, and millions of displaced refugees continue to cripple the country and impede its advancement. While Sudan is rich in resources, its future remains uncertain. [This title]

will appeal to children interested in learning more about Africa and those needing factual information for reports." SLJ

Includes glossary and bibliographical references

Levy, Patricia

Sudan; [by] Patricia Levy and Zawiah Abdul Latif. 2nd ed.; Marshall Cavendish Benchmark 2008 144p il map (Cultures of the world) lib bdg $42.79

Grades: 5 6 7 8   962.4

ISBN 978-0-7614-2083-5 lib bdg; 0-7614-2083-5 lib bdg

LC 2006101725

Describes the geography, history, government, economy, people, lifestyle, religion, language, arts, leisure, festivals, and food of Sudan

Includes bibliographical references

963   Ethiopia and Eritrea

Gish, Steven

Ethiopia; [by] Steven Gish & Winnie Thay & Zawiah Abdul Latif. 2nd ed.; Marshall Cavendish Benchmark 2007 144p il map (Cultures of the world) lib bdg $42.79

Grades: 5 6 7 8   963

ISBN 978-0-7614-2025-5 lib bdg; 0-7614-2025-8 lib bdg

LC 2006020819

First published 1996

This provides "information on the geography, history, governmental structure, economy, cultural diversity, peoples, religion, and culture of Ethiopia." Publisher's note

Includes glossary and bibliographical references

963.5   Eritrea

NgCheong-Lum, Roseline

Eritrea; 2nd ed.; Marshall Cavendish Benchmark 2011 144p il map (Cultures of the world) lib bdg $42.79

Grades: 5 6 7 8   963.5

ISBN 978-1-6087-0454-5; 1-6087-0454-8

LC 2010035973

First published 2001

Provides information on the geography, history, wildlife, governmental structure, economy, cultural diversity, peoples, religion, and culture of Eritea.

"Plentiful color photographs accompany substantial amounts of information." SLJ

Includes glossary and bibliographical references

964   Morocco, Ceuta, Melilla, Western Sahara, Canary Islands

Seward, Pat

Morocco; [by] Pat Seward & Orin Hargraves. 2nd ed.; Marshall Cavendish Benchmark 2006 144p il map (Cultures of the world) lib bdg $42.79

Grades: 5 6 7 8   964

ISBN 0-7614-2051-7

LC 2005020782

First published 1995

Describes the geography, history, government, economy, people, and culture of Morocco

Includes glossary and bibliographical references

965   Algeria

Kagda, Falaq

Algeria; [by] Falaq Kagda & Zawiah Abdul Latif. 2nd ed.; Marshall Cavendish Benchmark 2008 144p il map (Cultures of the world) lib bdg $42.79

Grades: 5 6 7 8   965

ISBN 978-0-7614-2085-9 lib bdg; 0-7614-2085-1 lib bdg

LC 2007014888

First published 1997

"Provides comprehensive information on the geography, history, wildlife, governmental structure, economy, cultural diversity, peoples, religion, and culture of Algeria." Publisher's note

Includes glossary and bibliographical references

966.1   Mauritania

Blauer, Ettagale

Mauritania; [by] Ettagale Blauer & Jason Lauré. Marshall Cavendish Benchmark 2009 144p il map (Cultures of the world) lib bdg $42.79

Grades: 5 6 7 8   966.1

ISBN 978-0-7614-3116-9

This describes the geography, history, government, economy, environment, people, and culture of Mauritania

966.2   Mali, Burkina Faso, Niger

Blauer, Ettagale

Mali; [by] Ettagale Blauer & Jason Lauré. 2nd ed.; Marshall Cavendish Benchmark 2008 144p il map (Cultures of the world) lib bdg $42.79

Grades: 5 6 7 8   966.2

ISBN 978-0-7614-2568-7

First published 1997

This describes the geography, history, government, economy, environment, people, and culture of Mali

Includes glossary and bibliographical references

McKissack, Patricia C.

The royal kingdoms of Ghana, Mali, and Songhay; life in medieval Africa. [by] Patricia and Fredrick McKissack. Holt & Co. 1993 142p il maps hardcover o.p. pa $12.99

Grades: 5 6 7 8   966.2

ISBN 0-8050-4259-8 pa

LC 93-4838

Examines the civilizations of the Western Sudan which flourished from 700 to 1700 A.D., acquiring such vast wealth that they became centers of trade and culture for a continent

"The McKissacks are careful to distinguish what is known from what is surmised; they draw on the oral tradition, eyewitness accounts, and contemporary scholarship;

and chapter source notes discuss various conflicting views of events." Booklist

Includes bibliographical references

966.3   Senegal

Berg, Elizabeth

Senegal; by Elizabeth L. Berg and Ruth Lau. 2nd ed.; Marshall Cavendish Benchmark 2009 144p il map (Cultures of the world) lib bdg $42.79

Grades: 5 6 7 8   966.3

ISBN 978-0-7614-4481-7 lib bdg; 0-7614-4481-5 lib bdg

LC 2009007067

First published 1999

Describes the geography, history, wildlife, governmental structure, economy, cultural diversity, peoples, religion, and culture of Senegal

Includes glossary and bibliographical references

966.4   Sierra Leone

LeVert, Suzanne

Sierra Leone; [by] Suzanne LeVert. Marshall Cavendish Benchmark 2007 144p il map (Cultures of the world) lib bdg $42.79

Grades: 5 6 7 8   966.4

ISBN 978-0-7614-2334-8 lib bdg; 0-7614-2334-6 lib bdg

LC 2005035964

This provides "information on the geography, history, governmental structure, economy, cultural diversity, peoples, religion, and culture of Sierra Leone." Publisher's note

Includes glossary and bibliographical references

966.68   Côte d'Ivoire (Ivory Coast)

Sheehan, Patricia

Cote d'Ivoire; [by] Patricia Sheehan and Jacqueline Ong. 2nd ed.; Marshall Cavendish Benchmark 2010 144p il map (Cultures of the world) lib bdg $42.79

Grades: 5 6 7 8   966.68

ISBN 978-0-7614-4854-9 lib bdg; 0-7614-4854-3 lib bdg

LC 2009045688

First published 2000

This offers information on the geography, history, wildlife, governmental structure, economy, cultural diversity, peoples, religion, and culture of Cote d'Ivoire

Includes glossary and bibliographical references

966.7   Ghana

Levy, Patricia

Ghana; [by] Patricia Levy and Winnie Wong. 2nd ed.; Marshall Cavendish Benchmark 2010 144p il map (Cultures of the world) lib bdg $42.79

Grades: 5 6 7 8   966.7

ISBN 978-0-7614-4847-1 lib bdg; 0-7614-4847-0 lib bdg

First published 1999

Introduces the geography, history, government, economy, culture, and people of Ghana

Includes glossary and bibliographical references

966.9   Nigeria

Giles, Bridget

★ Nigeria; [by] Bridget Giles. National Geographic 2007 64p il map (Countries of the world) lib bdg $27.90

Grades: 4 5 6 7   966.9

ISBN 978-1-4263-0124-7

LC 2007024729

This describes the geography, nature, history, people and culture, government, and economy of Nigeria

"What helps [this book] stand out from the pack is [its] high-quality, rich photography. . . . The photos provide as much information as the [text]. . . . The writing is straightforward and solid." SLJ

Includes glossary and bibliographical references

Oluonye, Mary N.

Nigeria; by Mary N. Oluonye. Lerner Publications Company 2007 48p il map (Country explorers) lib bdg $27.93; pa $8.95

Grades: 2 3 4   966.9

ISBN 978-0-8225-7131-5 lib bdg; 978-0-8225-8509-1 pa

LC 2006035846

"With short, chatty sentences and a lively, contemporary color photo on every page, this title . . . gives a brief overview of the history, geography, and culture of Nigeria. . . . The current information is not oversimplified." Booklist

Onyefulu, Ifeoma

Ikenna goes to Nigeria. Frances Lincoln 2007 33p il map hardcover o.p. $16.95

Grades: K 1 2 3   966.9

ISBN 978-1-84507-585-9; 1-84507-585-4; 978-1-84507-960-4 pa; 1-84507-960-4 pa

"Onyefulu delivers another photo-essay filled with vivid, colorful photographs, accompanied by brief, clear text about the land, people, and culture of her native Nigeria. The text is narrated by the author's son. . . . An outline map of the country shows the location of the cities/towns/villages that Ikenna will visit during the course of his trip. . . . The clear images contain a wealth of detail and provide valuable visual insight into the people and culture." SLJ

967.11   Cameroon

Sheehan, Sean

Cameroon; [by] Sean Sheehan and Josie Elias. 2nd ed.; Marshall Cavendish Benchmark 2011 144p il map (Cultures of the world) lib bdg $42.79

Grades: 5 6 7 8   967.11

ISBN 978-1-6087-0214-5; 1-6087-0214-6

LC 2010019623

First published 2001

Provides information on the geography, history, wildlife, governmental structure, economy, cultural diversity, peoples, religion, and culture of Cameroon.

Includes glossary and bibliographical references

967.3 Angola

Sheehan, Sean

Angola; [by] Sean Sheehan and Jui Lin Yong. 2nd ed.; Marshall Cavendish Benchmark 2010 144p il map (Cultures of the world) lib bdg $42.79

Grades: 5 6 7 8   **967.3**

1. Angola

ISBN 978-0-7614-4845-7 lib bdg; 0-7614-4845-4 lib bdg

LC 2009021203

"Provides comprehensive information on the geography, history, wildlife, governmental structure, economy, cultural diversity, peoples, religion, and culture of Angola." Publisher's note

Includes glossary and bibliographical references

967.43 Chad

Kneib, Martha

Chad; [by] Martha Kneib. Marshall Cavendish Benchmark 2007 144p il map (Cultures of the world) lib bdg $42.79

Grades: 5 6 7 8   **967.43**

ISBN 978-0-7614-2327-0 lib bdg; 0-7614-2327-3 lib bdg

LC 2005027079

This provides "information on the geography, history, governmental structure, economy, cultural diversity, peoples, religion, and culture of Chad." Publisher's note

Includes glossary and bibliographical references

967.51 Democratic Republic of the Congo

Heale, Jay

Democratic Republic of the Congo; by Jay Heale and Yong Jui Lin. 2nd ed.; Marshall Cavendish Benchmark 2009 144p il map (Cultures of the world) lib bdg $42.79

Grades: 5 6 7 8   **967.51**

ISBN 978-0-7614-4478-7 lib bdg; 0-7614-4478-5 lib bdg

LC 2009003195

First published 1999

Describes the geography, history, government, economy, people, lifestyle, religion, languages, arts, leisure, festivals, and food of The Democratic Republic of the Congo

Includes glossary and bibliographical references

967.571 Rwanda

King, David C.

Rwanda; [by] David C. King. Marshall Cavendish

Benchmark 2007 144p il map (Cultures of the world) lib bdg $42.79

Grades: 5 6 7 8   **967.571**

ISBN 978-0-7614-2333-1 lib bdg; 0-7614-2333-8 lib bdg

LC 2005031817

This provides "information on the geography, history, governmental structure, economy, cultural diversity, peoples, religion, and culture of Rwanda." Publisher's note

Includes glossary and bibliographical references

967.61 Uganda

Barlas, Robert

Uganda; [by] Robert Barlas and Yong Jui Lin. 2nd ed.; Marshall Cavendish Benchmark 2010 144p il map (Cultures of the world) lib bdg $42.79

Grades: 5 6 7 8   **967.61**

ISBN 978-0-7614-4859-4 lib bdg; 0-7614-4859-4 lib bdg

LC 2009046002

First published 2000

This offers information on the geography, history, wildlife, governmental structure, economy, cultural diversity, peoples, religion, and culture of Uganda

Includes glossary and bibliographical references

967.62 Kenya

Williams, Karen Lynn

Beatrice's dream; a story of Kibera slum. photographs by Wendy Stone. Frances Lincoln 2011 il $17.95

Grades: 3 4 5 6   **967.62**

ISBN 978-1-84780-019-0; 1-84780-019-X

"Beatrice, a 13-year-old orphan who lives with her brother and his wife in a Kenyan slum, describes her current life and her hopes for the future. She touches on her 30-minute walks to school, her classes, and helping her brother in his shop. Vivid color photographs give readers a firsthand glimpse into a world about which they are likely to know nothing. . . . Although the book deals with difficult subject matter, it does so in an upbeat and positive way. . . . A unique and important addition." SLJ

967.73 Somalia

Hassig, Susan M.

Somalia; by Susan M. Hassig & Zawiah Abdul Latif. 2nd ed.; Marshall Cavendish Benchmark 2008 144p il map (Cultures of the world) lib bdg $42.79

Grades: 5 6 7 8   **967.73**

ISBN 978-0-7614-2082-8 lib bdg; 0-7614-2082-7 lib bdg

LC 2006102270

First published 1997

"Provides comprehensive information on the geography, history, wildlife, governmental structure, economy, cultural diversity, peoples, religion, and culture of Somalia." Publisher's note

Includes glossary and bibliographical references

967.8 Tanzania

Heale, Jay

Tanzania; by Jay Heale & Winnie Wong. 2nd ed.; Marshall Cavendish Benchmark 2009 144p il map (Cultures of the world) lib bdg $42.79

Grades: 5 6 7 8   **967.8**

ISBN 978-0-7614-3417-7 lib bdg; 0-7614-3417-8 lib bdg

LC 2008028802

First published 1998

"Provides comprehensive information on the geography, history, wildlife, governmental structure, economy, cultural diversity, peoples, religion, and culture of Tanzania." Publisher's note

Includes glossary and bibliographical references

967.9 Mozambique

King, David C.

Mozambique; [by] David C. King. Marshall Cavendish Benchmark 2007 144p il map (Cultures of the world) lib bdg $42.79

Grades: 5 6 7 8   **967.9**

ISBN 978-0-7614-2331-7 lib bdg; 0-7614-2331-1 lib bdg

LC 2006002302

This provides "information on the geography, history, wildlife, governmental structure, economy, cultural diversity, peoples, religion, and culture of Mozambique." Publisher's note

Includes glossary and bibliographical references

968   Republic of South Africa and neighboring southern African countries

Mace, Virginia

★ South Africa; [by] Virginia Mace; Kate Rowntree and Vukile Khumalo, consultants. National Geographic 2008 64p il map (Countries of the world) lib bdg $27.90

Grades: 4 5 6 7   **968**

ISBN 978-1-4263-0203-9

LC 2007047835

This describes the geography, nature, history, people and culture, government, and economy of South Africa.

"Through its numerous maps and standout photographs, this book provides a general overview of South Africa that will satisfy the basic needs of upper-elementary research paper writers." Horn Book Guide

Includes glossary and bibliographical references

968.06   Period as Republic, 1961-

Brownlie, Ali

South Africa in our world; [by] Ali Brownlie Bojang. Smart Apple Media 2010 32p il (Countries in our world) lib bdg $28.50

Grades: 5 6 7 8   **968.06**

ISBN 978-1-59920-444-4 lib bdg; 1-59920-444-4 lib bdg

LC 2009043163

This "contains relevant information presented in a visually appealing layout. Large colorful photographs inform readers about the past, present, and future of the country. . . . The book gives an honest view of apartheid, poverty, and government conflicts. At the same time, it is hopeful about recent changes, such as the hosting of the World Cup and the growing economy." SLJ

Includes glossary and bibliographical references

Cooper, Floyd

Mandela; from the life of the South African statesman. written and illustrated by Floyd Cooper. Philomel Bks. 1996 un il hardcover o.p. pa $6.99

Grades: 2 3 4   **968.06**

1. Presidents 2. Political prisoners 3. Political leaders 4. Human rights activists 5. Nobel laureates for peace

ISBN 0-399-22942-6; 0-698-11816-2 pa

LC 95-19639

"Cooper's oil paintings are infused with golden light. Elegant composition and subtle shifts in perspective add emotional value to the carefully focused account." SLJ

Includes bibliographical references

McDonough, Yona Zeldis

★ Peaceful protest: the life of Nelson Mandela; illustrations by Malcah Zeldis. Walker & Co. 2002 un il hardcover o.p. pa $8.95

Grades: 2 3 4 5   **968.06**

1. Presidents 2. Political prisoners 3. Political leaders 4. Human rights activists 5. Nobel laureates for peace 6. Presidents -- South Africa -- Biography -- Juvenile literature

ISBN 0-8027-8821-1; 0-8027-8823-8 lib bdg; 0-8027-8948-X pa

LC 2002-23462

A biography of the black South African leader who became a civil rights activist, political prisoner, and president of South Africa

This is an "easy-to-read but engaging biography. . . . Zeldis's brightly colored folk-art illustrations reflect her subject's life and struggle with candid simplicity." SLJ

Includes bibliographical references

Nelson, Kadir

★ Nelson Mandela; Kadir Nelson. Katherine Tegen Books 2013 40 p. (hardcover bdg.) $17.99

Grades: 1 2 3   **968.06**

1. Stories in rhyme 2. South Africa -- History 3. Mandela, Nelson, 1918- -- Juvenile literature

ISBN 0061783749; 9780061783746; 9780061783760

LC 2012025492

This illustrated children's book by illustrator Kadir Nelson is a biography in verse of Nelson Mandela. "It is the story of a young boy's determination to change South Africa and of the struggles of a man who eventually became the president of his country by believing in equality for people of all colors." (Publisher's note)

968.94   Zambia

Holmes, Timothy

Zambia; by Timothy Holmes & Winnie Wong. rev ed.; Marshall Cavendish Benchmark 2008 144p il map (Cultures of the world) lib bdg $42.79

Grades: 5 6 7 8   968.94

ISBN 978-0-7614-3039-1 lib bdg; 0-7614-3039-3 lib bdg

LC 2007050794

First published 1998

Describes the geography, history, government, economy, people, lifestyle, religion, language, arts, leisure, festivals, and food of Zambia

Includes glossary and bibliographical references

969.1   Madagascar

Heale, Jay

Madagascar; [by] Jay Heale & Zawiah Abdul Latif. 2nd ed.; Marshall Cavendish Benchmark 2008 144p il map (Cultures of the world) lib bdg $42.79

Grades: 5 6 7 8   969.1

ISBN 978-0-7614-3036-0 lib bdg; 0-7614-3036-9 lib bdg

LC 2007048288

First published 1998

"Provides comprehensive information on the geography, history, wildlife, governmental structure, economy, cultural diversity, peoples, religion, and culture of Madagascar." Publisher's note

Includes glossary and bibliographical references

970   History of North America

Foster, Karen

Atlas of North America. Picture Window Books 2008 32p il map (Picture Window Books world atlases) lib bdg $27.93; pa $7.95

Grades: 2 3 4   970

ISBN 978-1-4048-3885-7 lib bdg; 1-4048-3885-6 lib bdg; 978-1-4048-3893-2 pa; 1-4048-3893-7 pa

This introduction to the geography of North America offers maps and information about countries, landforms, bodies of water, climate, plants, animals, population, people and customs, places of interest, industries, transportation, and the Mississippi River

This book offers "well-organized, easy-to-access information. . . . Small photographs or colorful text boxes draw readers' attention to points of interest or fun facts. Maps and legends are simple, yet disseminate information clearly." SLJ

Includes glossary

970.004   North American native peoples

Andre, Julie-Ann

We feel good out here; by Julie-Ann Andre and Mindy Willett; photographs by Tessa Macintosh. Fitzhenry & Whiteside 2008 32p il (The land is our storybook) $16.95

Grades: 3 4 5 6   970.004

1. Native Americans -- Canada

ISBN 978-1-89725-233-8; 1-89725-233-1

This title focuses on the land and culture "of Canada's Northwest Territories and is replete with sharp and attractive full-color photographs. In [this book] a local woman describes her life with her husband and two daughters. Julie-Ann is a Canadian Ranger who studies business management but, more importantly, she is a student of Gwich'in language and culture. She was sent to a residential school at age seven and has spent the last 10 years reestablishing her people's traditional practices and beliefs. A boxed area, 'Our Words,' gives a few words in English and in Gwichya Gwich'in. . . . [This title provides] some useful information for reports and [is an] interesting [addition] for general reading." SLJ

Arnold, Caroline

★ The ancient cliff dwellers of Mesa Verde; photographs by Richard Hewett. Clarion Bks. 1992 64p il hardcover o.p. pa $7.95

Grades: 4 5 6 7   970.004

1. Pueblo Indians 2. Mesa Verde National Park (Colo.) -- Juvenile literature

ISBN 0-395-56241-4; 0-618-05149-X pa

LC 91-8145

Discusses the native Americans known as the Anasazi, who migrated to southwestern Colorado in the first century A.D. and mysteriously disappeared in 1300 A.D. after constructing extensive dwellings in the cliffs of the steep canyon walls

"A thorough and attractive introduction to the Anasazi people with outstanding photographs of the dramatic vistas and ceremonial chambers within this national park." SLJ

Includes glossary

Baylor, Byrd

★ When clay sings; illustrated by Tom Bahti. Scribner 1972 un il hardcover o.p. pa $6.99

Grades: 1 2 3 4   970.004

1. Pottery 2. Native American art 3. Native Americans -- Southwestern States

ISBN 0-684-18829-5; 0-689-71106-9 pa

A Caldecott Medal honor book, 1973

"A lyrical tribute to an almost forgotten time of the prehistoric Indian of the desert West presents broken bits of pottery from this ancient time. The designs and drawings, done in rich earth tones, are derived from prehistoric pottery found in the American Southwest." Read Ladders for Hum Relat. 6th edition

Bealer, Alex W.

Only the names remain; the Cherokees and the Trail of Tears. illustrated by Kristina Rodanas. Little, Brown 1996 79p il hardcover o.p. pa $6.99

Grades: 4 5 6   970.004

1. Cherokee Indians 2. Trail of Tears, 1838

ISBN 0-316-08519-7

A reissue with new illustrations of the title first published 1972

The author describes "the rise of the Cherokee Nation, with its written language, constitution, and republican form of government, and its tragic betrayal in the 1830s." Chicago Public Libr

Bjorklund, Ruth

The **Hopi**; by Ruth Bjorklund. Marshall Cavendish Benchmark 2009 48p il (First Americans) lib bdg $31.36
Grades: 2 3 4   970.004
1. Hopi Indians
ISBN 978-0-7614-3021-6 lib bdg; 0-7614-3021-0 lib bdg
LC 2007-33676
"Provides comprehensive information on the background, lifestyle, beliefs, and present-day lives of the Hopi people." Publisher's note
Includes glossary and bibliographical references

Bjornlund, Lydia D.

The **Trail** of Tears; the relocation of the Cherokee Nation. Lucent Books 2010 104p il map (American history) lib bdg $33.45
Grades: 5 6 7 8   970.004
1. Cherokee Indians 2. Native Americans -- Relocation 3. Trail of Tears, 1838
ISBN 978-1-4205-0211-4; 1-4205-0211-5
LC 2010001549
Describes the Federal government's seizure of Cherokee lands in Georgia and the forced migration of the Cherokee Nation to Oklahoma along the route that came to be known as the Trail of Tears.
This is "well written and [includes] primary sources, photographs, reproductions, and maps." SLJ
Includes bibliographical references

★ A Braid of lives; Native American childhood. edited by Neil Philip. Clarion Bks. 2000 81p il $20
Grades: 4 5 6 7   970.004
1. Native Americans
ISBN 0-395-64528-X
LC 00-21343
"This is an excellent choice for curriculum support and brief read-aloud material." Booklist
Includes bibliographical references

Bruchac, Joseph

★ The **Trail** of Tears; illustrated by Diana Magnuson. Random House 1999 46p il (Step into reading) hardcover o.p. pa $3.99
Grades: 2 3 4   970.004
1. Cherokee Indians 2. Trail of Tears, 1838 3. Cherokee Indians -- History 4. Native Americans -- Relocation 5. Trail of Tears, 1838 -- Juvenile literature 6. Cherokee Indians -- Relocation -- Juvenile literature 7. Indians of North America -- Southern States -- History 8. Cherokee Indians -- History -- 19th century -- Juvenile literature
ISBN 0-679-99052-6 lib bdg; 0-679-89052-1 pa
LC 98-36199
Recounts how the Cherokees, after fighting to keep their land in the nineteenth century, were forced to leave and travel 1200 miles to a new settlement in Oklahoma, a terrible journey known as the Trail of Tears
"Magnuson's colorful pictures, packed with people and action, are a little bright for the subject, but strong new readers will find that nonfiction can tell a powerful story." Booklist

Connolly, Sean

★ The **Americas** and the Pacific. Zak Books 2009 48p il map (History of the world) lib bdg $34.25
Grades: 4 5 6 7 8   970.004
1. Maoris 2. Aboriginal Australians 3. Native Americans -- History
ISBN 978-88-60981-61-5 lib bdg; 88-60981-61-1 lib bdg
LC 2008008404
"Artists' renderings show groups of people engaged in representative activities, but it's the reproductions of artifacts . . . that will pull readers and browsers most. . . . [This is an] engaging overview." Booklist
Includes bibliographical references

Cunningham, Kevin

The **Cheyenne**; [by] Kevin Cunningham and Peter Benoit. Children's Press 2011 48p il map (True books: American Indians) lib bdg $28; pa $6.95
Grades: 3 4 5   970.004
1. Cheyenne Indians
ISBN 978-0-531-20759-8 lib bdg; 0-531-20759-5 lib bdg; 978-0-531-29301-0 pa; 0-531-29301-7 pa
LC 2010049082
An introduction to the Cheyenne people, explaining who they are, reviewing the history of the Cheyenne, looking at how the Cheyenne lived, their beliefs, and rituals, and discussing the Council of Forty-Four.
Includes bibliographical references

The **Comanche**; [by] Kevin Cunningham and Peter Benoit. Children's Press 2011 48p il (True book: American Indians) lib bdg $28; pa $6.95
Grades: 3 4 5   970.004
1. Comanche Indians
ISBN 978-0-531-20770-3 lib bdg; 0-531-20770-6 lib bdg; 978-0-531-29312-6 pa; 0-531-29312-2 pa
LC 2010049081
This book "covers cultural basics such as diet, clothing, lifestyle, and child rearing for [the Comanche]. Relevant historical events are also covered simply and clearly, including a time line of highlights in each group's history. This balance between history and culture keeps the series dynamic and interesting. Photos, paintings, and drawings—as well as occasional contemporary illustrations—add visual interest to the well-designed package and keep the [title] from feeling formulaic. The [book] traces the historical changes in Comanche life and their causes, from the 1600s to the twentieth century." Booklist
Includes bibliographical references

The **Inuit**; [by] Kevin Cunningham and Peter Benoit. Children's Press 2011 48p il (True book: American Indians) lib bdg $28; pa $6.95
Grades: 3 4 5   970.004
1. Inuit
ISBN 978-0-531-20760-4 lib bdg; 978-0-531-29302-7 pa
LC 2010049080
This book "covers cultural basics such as diet, clothing, lifestyle, and child rearing for [the Inuit]. Relevant historical events are also covered simply and clearly, including a time line of highlights in each group's history. This balance between history and culture keeps the series dynamic and

interesting. Photos, paintings, and drawings-as well as occasional contemporary illustrations-add visual interest to the well-designed package and keep the [title] from feeling formulaic." Booklist

Includes bibliographical references

The **Navajo**; [by] Kevin Cunningham and Peter Benoit. Children's Press 2011 48p il map (True book: American Indians) lib bdg $28; pa $6.95

Grades: 3 4 5 **970.004**

1. Navajo Indians

ISBN 978-0-531-20762-8 lib bdg; 0-531-20762-5 lib bdg; 978-0-531-29304-1 pa; 0-531-29304-1 pa

LC 2010050837

An exploration of the Navajo Indians, discussing the nation's relationship with Spaniards and settlers, culture, crafts, and more.

The "balance between history and culture keeps the [book] dynamic and interesting. Photos, paintings, and drawings—as well as occasional contemporary illustrations—add visual interest to the well-designed package and keep the [title] from feeling formulaic." Booklist

Includes bibliographical references

The **Pueblo**; [by] Kevin Cunningham and Peter Benoit. Children's Press 2011 48p il map (True book: American Indians) lib bdg $28; pa $6.95

Grades: 3 4 5 **970.004**

1. Pueblo Indians

ISBN 978-0-531-20763-5 lib bdg; 0-531-20763-3 lib bdg; 978-0-531-29305-8 pa; 0-531-29305-X pa

LC 2010050838

An introduction to the Pueblo people, explaining who they are, reviewing the history of the Pueblo, examining key aspects of Pueblo culture, and looking at Pueblo traditions that continue into the twenty-first century.

Includes bibliographical references

The **Sioux**; [by] Kevin Cunningham and Peter Benoit. Children's Press 2011 48p il map (True book: American Indians) lib bdg $28; pa $6.95

Grades: 3 4 5 **970.004**

1. Teton Indians

ISBN 978-0-531-20768-0 lib bdg; 0-531-207684- lib bdg; 978-0-531-29310-2 pa; 0-531-29310-6 pa

LC 2010049083

An introduction to the Sioux people, explaining who they are, reviewing the history of the Sioux, telling the story of Little Bighorn, and examining key parts of Sioux culture.

Includes bibliographical references

The **Zuni**; [by] Kevin Cunningham and Peter Benoit. Children's Press 2011 48p il map (True book: American Indians) $28; pa $6.95

Grades: 3 4 5 **970.004**

1. Zuni Indians

ISBN 978-0-531-20761-1; 978-0-531-29303-4 pa

LC 2010050846

This book "covers cultural basics such as diet, clothing, lifestyle, and child rearing for [the Zuni]. Relevant historical events are also covered simply and clearly, including a time line of highlights in each group's history. This balance between history and culture keeps the [book] dynamic and

interesting. Photos, paintings, and drawings-as well as occasional contemporary illustrations-add visual interest to the well-designed package and keep the [title] from feeling formulaic." Booklist

Includes bibliographical references

De Capua, Sarah

The **Cheyenne**. Marshall Cavendish Benchmark 2007 47p il (First Americans) lib bdg $31.36

Grades: 2 3 4 **970.004**

1. Cheyenne Indians

ISBN 978-0-7614-2248-8 lib bdg; 0-7614-2248-X lib bdg

LC 2006011967

Provides information on the background, lifestyle, beliefs, and present-day lives of the Cheyenne people

Includes glossary and bibliographical references

The **Choctaw**; by Sarah De Capua. Marshall Cavendish Benchmark 2009 48p il (First Americans) lib bdg $31.36

Grades: 2 3 4 **970.004**

1. Choctaw Indians

ISBN 978-0-7614-3018-6 lib bdg; 0-7614-3018-0 lib bdg

LC 2007-33727

"Provides comprehensive information on the background, lifestyle, beliefs, and present-day lives of the Choctaw people." Publisher's note

Includes glossary and bibliographical references

The **Comanche**. Marshall Cavendish Benchmark 2007 47p il (First Americans) lib bdg $31.36

Grades: 2 3 4 **970.004**

1. Comanche Indians

ISBN 978-0-7614-2249-5 lib bdg; 0-7614-2249-8 lib bdg

LC 2006011975

Provides information on the background, lifestyle, beliefs, and present-day lives of the Comanche people

Includes glossary and bibliographical references

The **Menominee**. Marshall Cavendish Benchmark 2009 48p il (First Americans) lib bdg $31.36

Grades: 2 3 4 **970.004**

1. Menominee Indians

ISBN 978-0-7614-4131-1 lib bdg; 0-7614-4131-X lib bdg

LC 2008041999

Provides information on the background, lifestyle, beliefs, and present-day lives of the Menominee people

The **Shawnee**. Marshall Cavendish Benchmark 2007 48p il (First Americans) lib bdg $31.36

Grades: 2 3 4 **970.004**

1. Shawnee Indians

ISBN 978-0-7614-2682-0 lib bdg; 0-7614-2682-5 lib bdg

LC 2006034117

Provides information on the background, lifestyle, beliefs, and present-day lives of the Shawnee people

Includes glossary and bibliographical references

The **Shoshone**. Marshall Cavendish Benchmark 2007

48p il (First Americans) lib bdg $31.36

Grades: 2 3 4   **970.004**

  1. Shoshone Indians

  ISBN 978-0-7614-2683-7 lib bdg; 0-7614-2683-3 lib bdg

                         LC 2006034113

  Provides information on the background, lifestyle, beliefs, and present-day lives of the Shoshone people

  Includes glossary and bibliographical references

Dennis, Yvonne Wakim

  ★ **Children** of native America today; [by] Yvonne Wakim Dennis & Arlene Hirschfelder; with a foreword by Buffy Sainte-Marie. Charlesbridge Pub. 2003 64p il map lib bdg $19.95

Grades: 3 4 5 6   **970.004**

  1. Native Americans

  ISBN 1-57091-499-0

                         LC 2002-2272

  "This photo-essay features 25 of the more than 500 native cultures of the U.S. as well as a section on urban Indians. In this 'book of few words and many pictures,' the clear, captioned photographs speak eloquently of contemporary Native American young people. . . . An excellent resource for multicultural studies, this handsome album will also attract browsers." Booklist

  Includes glossary and bibliographical references

  ★ A **kid's** guide to native American history; more than 50 activities. by Yvonne Wakim Dennis and Arlene Hirschfelder. Chicago Review Press 2009 226p il pa $16.95

Grades: 3 4 5 6   **970.004**

  1. Games 2. Cooking 3. Handicraft 4. Native Americans -- History

  ISBN 978-1-55652-802-6 pa; 1-55652-802-7 pa

                         LC 2009015832

  "This two-in-one history and activity book does an excellent job of explaining Native American history in easy-to-understand language while stressing the differences between and diversity among tribes. The book is divided by region. . . . Activities are kid-friendly . . . and encourage exploration of the text. . . . Clear illustrations accompany each activity." SLJ

  Includes glossary and bibliographical references

Dolbear, Emily J.

  The **Iroquois**; [by] Emily J. Dolbear and Peter Benoit. Children's Press 2011 48p il map (True book: American Indians) lib bdg $28; pa $6.95

Grades: 3 4 5   **970.004**

  1. Iroquois Indians

  ISBN 978-0-531-20771-0 lib bdg; 0-531-20771-4 lib bdg; 978-0-531-29313-3 pa; 0-531-29313-0 pa

                         LC 2010049079

  This covers cultural basics of the Iroquois such as diet, clothing, lifestyle, and child rearing as well as relevant historical events.

  Includes bibliographical references

Ehrlich, Amy

  Wounded Knee: an Indian history of the American West; adapted for young readers by Amy Ehrlich from Dee Brown's Bury my heart at Wounded Knee. Holt & Co. 1974 202p il maps hardcover o.p. pa $13.95

Grades: 6 7 8 9   **970.004**

  1. Generals 2. Ghost dance 3. Apache Indians 4. Dakota Indians 5. Navajo Indians 6. Arapaho Indians 7. Cheyenne Indians 8. Sand Creek, Battle of, 1864 9. Indian chiefs 10. Civil engineers 11. Government officials 12. Native Americans -- Wars 13. Native Americans -- West (U.S.)

  ISBN 0-8050-2700-9 pa

  This book traces the plight of the Navaho, Apache, Cheyenne and Sioux Indians in their struggles against the white man in the West between 1860 and 1890. It recounts battles and their causes, participants, and consequences during this era

  "Some chapters [of the original] have been deleted, others condensed, and in some instances sentence structure and language have been simplified. The editing is good, and this version is interesting, readable, and smooth." SLJ

  Includes bibliographical references

Enzoe, Pete

  The **caribou** feed our soul; [by] Pete Enzoe and Mindy Willett; photographs by Tessa Macintosh. Fitzhenry & Whiteside 2011 26p il (The land is our storybook) $16.95

Grades: 3 4 5 6   **970.004**

  1. Caribou 2. Chipewyan Indians 3. Wildlife conservation

  ISBN 978-1-89725-267-3; 1-89725-267-6

                         LC 2010-9045793

  "This informative first-person narrative cleanly captures the Dénésôliné (Chipewyan) culture's dependence on and reverence for the caribou, the predominant symbol of the tribe's existence. . . . Enzoe, a Native spokesperson, teacher, and hunter, explains aspects of his tribe's daily life in the Northwest Territories. He speaks of the mysticism of the caribou and illustrates its importance in feeding and clothing the tribe. . . . The book is thoughtfully illustrated with a variety of engaging photographs of the area and its people, immersed in the daily goings-on of their lives. The aerial photography gives readers a grand view of the stunning geography." SLJ

  Includes glossary and bibliographical references

Freedman, Russell

  Indian chiefs. Holiday House 1987 151p il $24.95; pa $14.95

Grades: 6 7 8 9 10   **970.004**

  1. Kiowa Indians 2. Dakota Indians 3. Oglala Indians 4. Comanche Indians 5. Shoshone Indians 6. Shoshoni Indians 7. Nez Perce Indians 8. Centenarians 9. Indian chiefs 10. Nez Percé Indians 11. Native Americans -- Biography 12. Indians of North America -- Biography -- Juvenile literature

  ISBN 0-8234-0625-3; 0-8234-0971-6 pa

                         LC 86-46198

  This "book chronicles the lives of six renowned Indian chiefs, each of whom served as a leader during a critical period in his tribe's history. . . . The text relates information about the lives of each chief and aspects of Indian/white relationships that illuminate his actions. Interesting vignettes and quotations are well integrated into the narrative as are dramatic accounts of battles. While the tone of the text is nonjudgmental, an underlying sympathy for the Indians' situation is apparent." Horn Book

Includes bibliographical references

Goble, Paul

All our relatives; traditional Native American thoughts about nature. compiled and illustrated by Paul Goble. World Wisdom 2005 un il $15.95

Grades: 5 6 7 8   **970.004**

1. Native Americans 2. Philosophy of nature

ISBN 0-941532-77-1; 978-0-941532-77-8

LC 2005004285

"The pages of this book are chock-full of quotations, songs, and brief stories that exemplify Native American attitudes toward nature. . . . Black Elk, Standing Bear, Brave Buffalo, and others observe the importance of various animals and the sacred qualities of all living things. . . . The spaces between text blocks are filled with Goble's familiar illustrations based on traditional Native American designs and colors." SLJ

Includes bibliographical references

Hicks, Terry Allan

The **Chumash**; by Terry Allan Hicks. Marshall Cavendish Benchmark 2008 48p il map (First Americans) lib bdg $29.93

Grades: 2 3 4   **970.004**

1. Chumash Indians

ISBN 978-0-7614-2678-3 lib bdg; 0-7614-2678-7 lib bdg

LC 2006034101

This describes Chumash "history and culture, way of life, beliefs, present status, and future outlook. Colorful modern photographs appear throughout, as do paintings, photos, and maps. [The] volume includes a simple craft . . . as well as a Native recipe. . . . [The] book has a helpful, easy-to-read graphical time line. Clear writing and attractive [layout makes this book] accessible and appealing." SLJ

Includes glossary and bibliographical references

King, David C.

First people; an illustrated history of American Indians. DK Pub. 2008 192p il map $19.99

Grades: 5 6 7 8   **970.004**

1. Native Americans

ISBN 978-0-7566-4092-7; 0-7566-4092-X

"This rich pictorial work serves as an entertaining, informative, and visually appealing introduction to American Indian culture and history. Each of the seven chapters covers a different time period in chronological order. . . . The glossy photographs, colorful drawings, and easily accessible paragraphs . . . make for an easy-to-use overall package." SLJ

The **Haida**. Marshall Cavendish Benchmark 2007 48p il (First Americans) lib bdg $31.36

Grades: 2 3 4   **970.004**

1. Haida Indians

ISBN 978-0-7614-2250-1 lib bdg; 0-7614-2250-1 lib bdg

LC 2006011969

Provides information on the background, lifestyle, beliefs, and present-day lives of the Haida people

Includes glossary and bibliographical references

The **Huron**. Marshall Cavendish Benchmark 2007 48p il (First Americans) lib bdg $31.36

Grades: 2 3 4   **970.004**

1. Huron Indians

ISBN 978-0-7614-2251-8 lib bdg; 0-7614-2251-X lib bdg

LC 2006011970

Provides information on the background, lifestyle, beliefs, and present-day lives of the Huron people

Includes glossary and bibliographical references

The **Inuit**; [by] David C. King. Marshall Cavendish Benchmark 2008 48p il map (First Americans) lib bdg $31.36

Grades: 2 3 4   **970.004**

1. Inuit

ISBN 978-0-7614-2679-0 lib bdg; 0-7614-2679-5 lib bdg

LC 2006034111

This describes Inuit "history and culture, way of life, beliefs, present status, and future outlook. Colorful modern photographs appear throughout, as do paintings, photos, and maps. . . . [It] includes a simple craft . . . (soapstone carving) as well as a Native recipe . . . (fish soup). . . . [It] has a helpful, easy-to-read graphical time line. Clear writing and attractive [layout makes this book] accessible and appealing." SLJ

Includes glossary and bibliographical references

The **Mohawk**. Marshall Cavendish Benchmark 2009 48p il (First Americans) lib bdg $31.36

Grades: 2 3 4   **970.004**

1. Mohawk Indians

ISBN 978-0-7614-4132-8 lib bdg; 0-7614-4132-8 lib bdg

LC 2008042000

Provides information on the background, lifestyle, beliefs, and present-day lives of the Mohawk people.

Includes glossary and bibliographical references

The **Nez Perce**; by David C. King. Marshall Cavendish Benchmark 2008 48p il map (First Americans) lib bdg $31.36

Grades: 2 3 4   **970.004**

1. Nez Percé Indians

ISBN 978-0-7614-2680-6 lib bdg; 0-7614-2678-7 lib bdg

LC 2006034114

This describes Nez Perce "history and culture, way of life, beliefs, present status, and future outlook. Colorful modern photographs appear throughout, as do paintings, photos, and maps. [The] volume includes a simple craft . . . as well as a Native recipe. . . . [The] book has a helpful, easy-to-read graphical time line. Clear writing and attractive [layout makes this book] accessible and appealing." SLJ

Includes glossary and bibliographical references

The **Ojibwe**. Marshall Cavendish Benchmark 2007 45p il (First Americans) lib bdg $31.36

Grades: 2 3 4   **970.004**
  1. Ojibwa Indians
  ISBN 978-0-7614-2252-5 lib bdg; 0-7614-2252-8
lib bdg
            LC 2006011971
Provides information on the background, lifestyle, beliefs, and present-day lives of the Ojibwe people
Includes glossary and bibliographical references

The **Powhatan**. Marshall Cavendish Benchmark 2007 48p il (First Americans) lib bdg $31.36
Grades: 2 3 4   **970.004**
  1. Powhatan Indians
  ISBN 978-0-7614-2681-3 lib bdg; 0-7614-2681-7
lib bdg
            LC 2006034115
Provides information on the background, lifestyle, beliefs, and present-day lives of the Powhatan people
Includes glossary and bibliographical references

The **Seminole**. Marshall Cavendish Benchmark 2007 48p il (First Americans) lib bdg $31.36
Grades: 2 3 4   **970.004**
  1. Seminole Indians
  ISBN 978-0-7614-2253-2 lib bdg; 0-7614-2253-6
lib bdg
            LC 2006011977
Provides information on the background, lifestyle, beliefs, and present-day lives of the Seminole people
Includes glossary and bibliographical references

Kissock, Heather
  Apache; American Indian art and culture. [by] Heather Kissock and Jordan McGill. Weigl Publishers Inc. 2010 24p il (American Indian art and culture) lib bdg $25.70; pa $9.95
Grades: 2 3 4   **970.004**
  1. Apache Indians
  ISBN 978-1-60596-991-6 lib bdg; 1-60596-991-5 lib bdg; 978-1-60596-992-3 pa; 1-60596-992-3 pa
            LC 2010005331
Introduces the history, housing, clothing, agriculture, culture, art, and recipes of the Apache Indians.
This "provides early elementary students with an outstanding overview of the art and culture of [the Apache]. . . . Perfect for beginning readers, the content is straightforward and concise. Full-color up close photographs are integral to . . . [the] book, visually clarifying each idea and extending the text to aid in the student's understanding."
Libr Media Connect
  Includes glossary

  Caddo; [by] Heather Kissock and Rachel Small. Weigl Publishers Inc. 2011 24p il (American Indian art and culture) lib bdg $25.70; pa $9.95
Grades: 2 3 4   **970.004**
  1. Caddo Indians
  ISBN 978-1-60596-979-4 lib bdg; 1-60596-979-6 lib bdg; 978-1-60596-980-0 pa; 1-60596-980-X pa
            LC 2010005334
Highlights the traditional ways of the Caddo.
This "provides early elementary students with an outstanding overview of the art and culture of [the Caddo]. . . . Perfect for beginning readers, the content is straightfor-

ward and concise. Full-color up close photographs are integral to . . . [the] book, visually clarifying each idea and extending the text to aid in the student's understanding."
Libr Media Connect
  Includes glossary

  Cherokee; American Indian art and culture. [by] Heather Kissock and Rachel Small. Weigl Publishers Inc. 2011 24p il (American Indian art and culture) lib bdg $25.70; pa $9.95
Grades: 2 3 4   **970.004**
  1. Cherokee Indians
  ISBN 978-1-60596-994-7 lib bdg; 1-60596-994-X lib bdg; 978-1-60596-995-4 pa; 1-60596-995-8 pa
            LC 2010005335
Introduces the history, housing, clothing, agriculture, culture, art, and recipes of the Cherokee Indians
This "provides early elementary students with an outstanding overview of the art and culture of [the Cherokee Indians]. . . . Perfect for beginning readers, the content is straightforward and concise. Full-color up close photographs are integral to . . . [the] book, visually clarifying each idea and extending the text to aid in the student's understanding."
Libr Media Connect
  Includes glossary

  Comanche; American Indian art and culture. Weigl Publishers Inc. 2011 24p il (American Indian art and culture) lib bdg $25.70; pa $9.95
Grades: 2 3 4   **970.004**
  1. Comanche Indians
  ISBN 978-1-60596-988-6 lib bdg; 1-60596-988-5 lib bdg; 978-1-60596-989-3 pa; 1-60596-989-3 pa
            LC 2010005336
Introduces the history, housing, clothing, agriculture, culture, art, and recipes of the Comanche Indians
This "provides early elementary students with an outstanding overview of the art and culture of [the Comanche]. . . . Perfect for beginning readers, the content is straightforward and concise. Full-color up close photographs are integral to . . . [the] book, visually clarifying each idea and extending the text to aid in the student's understanding."
Libr Media Connect
  Includes glossary

  Tigua; [by] Heather Kissock and Jordan McGill. Weigl Publishers Inc. 2011 24p il (American Indian art and culture) lib bdg $25.70; pa $9.95
Grades: 2 3 4   **970.004**
  1. Tigua Indians
  ISBN 978-1-60596-982-4 lib bdg; 1-60596-982-6 lib bdg; 978-1-60596-983-1 pa; 1-60596-983-4 pa
            LC 2010005355
Introduces the history, housing, clothing, agriculture, culture, art, and recipes of the Tigua Indians.
This "provides early elementary students with an outstanding overview of the art and culture of [the Tigua Indians]. . . . Perfect for beginning readers, the content is straightforward and concise. Full-color up close photographs are integral to . . . [the] book, visually clarifying each idea and extending the text to aid in the student's understanding."
Libr Media Connect
  Includes glossary

McLeod, Tom

The **Delta** is my home; by Tom McLeod and Mindy Willett; photographs by Tessa Macintosh. Fitzhenry & Whiteside 2008 26p il (The land is our storybook) $16.95

Grades: 4 5 6 7   **970.004**

1. Native Americans -- Canada

ISBN 978-1-8972-5232-1; 1-8972-5232-3

"An 11-year-old boy who lives in the Mackenzie Delta region with his family tells about life there. His father is a renewable resource officer and has taught him how to hunt, fish, trap, and drive a boat. Readers also learn about his language, schooling, and clothing as well as the important role that storytelling plays in the culture. [This title provides] some useful information for reports and [is an] interesting [addition] for general reading." SLJ

McNeese, Tim

The **fascinating** history of American Indians; the age before Columbus. Enslow Publishers 2009 128p il map (America's living history) lib bdg $31.93

Grades: 5 6 7 8   **970.004**

1. Native Americans

ISBN 978-0-7660-2938-5 lib bdg; 0-7660-2938-7 lib bdg

"This thorough discussion of Native American life prior to Columbus's arrival combines theories of archaeologists, anthropologists, historians, and scientists to provide an engaging portrayal of the daily experiences of regional tribes. Based mostly on archaeological discoveries, the accessible text is supported by archival photographs, maps, and sidebars." Horn Book Guide

Includes glossary and bibliographical references

Molin, Paulette Fairbanks

American Indian stereotypes in the world of children; a reader and bibliography. 2nd ed; Scarecrow Press 1999 343p il hardcover o.p. pa $40.50

Grades: Adult Professional   **970.004**

1. Race awareness 2. Native Americans

ISBN 0-8108-3612-2; 0-8108-3613-0 pa

LC 98-49654

First published 1982

"This volume presents a collection of . . . articles detailing uses and abuses of Native American symbols, images, ideas, and stories that are directed at youth in the mass media. Toys, cartoons, textbooks, general reading, media portrayals, sports, logos, nicknames and more are discussed in stand-alone articles." Voice Youth Advocates

Includes bibliographical references

Murdoch, David Hamilton

North American Indian; written by David Murdoch; chief consultant, Stanley A. Freed; photographed by Lynton Gardiner. rev ed; DK Pubs. 2005 72p il (DK eyewitness books) $16.99; lib bdg $19.99

Grades: 4 5 6 7   **970.004**

1. Native Americans

ISBN 0-7566-1081-8; 0-7566-1082-6 lib bdg

First published 1995 by Knopf

This is a guide to the civilizations of North American Indians including full-color photographs of artifacts and descriptions ceremonies and customs.

Pokiak, James

Proud to be Inuvialuit; by James Pokiak and Mindy Willett; illustrated by Tessa Macintosh. Fitzhenry & Whiteside 2010 26p il pa $16.95

Grades: 3 4 5   **970.004**

1. Inuit 2. Native Americans -- Northwest Coast of North America

ISBN 1-89725-259-5; 978-1-89725-259-8

"Pokiak introduces his people, the Inuvialuit . . . to readers by having them meet his own family and their community of 900 people on the Arctic coast of Canada's Northwest Territories. Though they live in modern houses, have cell phones, and enjoy an indoor swimming pool, the people of Tuktoyaktuk still hunt beluga whales for subsistence as their ancestors did. . . . Text, illustrations, and captions work together well to present the Inuvialuit way of life. Illustrations include a large map and small paintings as well as many clear, color photos. . . . An informative introduction to an Inuit community today." Booklist

Terry, Michael Bad Hand

Daily life in a Plains Indian village, 1868. Clarion Bks. 1999 48p il map hardcover o.p. pa $9.95

Grades: 4 5 6 7   **970.004**

1. Native Americans -- Great Plains 2. Indians of North America -- Great Plains 3. Indians of North America -- Great Plains -- History -- Juvenile literature 4. Indians of North America -- Material culture -- Great Plains -- Juvenile literature 5. Indians of North America -- Great Plains -- Social life and customs -- Juvenile literature

ISBN 0-395-94542-9; 0-395-97499-2 pa

LC 98-32382

Depicts the historical background, social organization, and daily life of a Plains Indian village in 1868, presenting interiors, landscapes, clothing, and everyday objects

"The author presents short paragraphs of fascinating information accompanied by visuals that explain even more than the text." SLJ

Includes glossary

Zimmerman, Dwight Jon

Saga of the Sioux; an adaptation of Dee Brown's Bury My Heart at Wounded Knee. [adapted] by Dwight Jon Zimmerman. Henry Holt and Company 2011 208p il map $18.99

Grades: 5 6 7 8   **970.004**

1. Dakota Indians 2. Native Americans -- Wars

ISBN 978-0-8050-9364-3; 0-8050-9364-8

LC 2011004792

"Dwight Jon Zimmerman has created a masterful adaptation of Dee Brown's Bury My Heart at Wounded Knee, presenting late nineteenth century history from a Native American viewpoint. While Brown's book traces the fates of several Native American tribes in the western United States, Zimmerman's adaptation focuses solely on the Sioux. . . . Historical figures central to the narrative, both Native American and white, are portrayed as real people, rather than caricatures. Rather than simply describing what happened, the book looks at why it happened. Individuals' motivations, strengths, and flaws are all explored in relation to how historical events unfolded. The book includes numerous photographs, illustrations, and maps that aid understanding and create visual appeal. . . . This is a must-have addition to any United States history collection serving teens." Voice Youth Advocates

Includes glossary and bibliographical references

Zoe, Therese

Living stories; [by] Therese Zoe, Philip Zoe and Mindy Willett; photographs by Tessa Macintosh. Fitzhenry & Whiteside 2009 32p il (The land is our storybook) $16.95

Grades: 3 4 5 6   **970.004**

1. Native Americans -- Canada 2. Native Americans -- Folklore

ISBN 978-1-89725-244-4; 1-89725-244-7

"Therese Zoe is a Tlicho woman from Gamèti in the Northwest Territories. . . . [In this book she] shares her love for her community and translates the sacred stories and traditional wisdom of her brother-in-law, Philip Zoe, and his sister, Elizabeth Chocolate. . . . Join Tlicho young people, Shelinda, Forest, and Bradley, as they learn about making dry-fish, bows and arrows, and birchbark baskets; the practices of old-time healers; as well as the sacred stories that tell the history of the Tlicho people." Publisher's note

970.01   Historical periods

Bodden, Valerie

Columbus reaches the New World. Creative Education 2009 48p il (Days of change) lib bdg $32.80

Grades: 5 6 7 8   **970.01**

1. Explorers

ISBN 978-158341-732-4; 1-58341-732-X

LC 2008009163

"With elegant design and mature prose, the Days of Change series is an ideal starting point for all manner of school projects. . . . Columbus Reaches the New World intelligently explains the famous sailor's motivations for forging a new trade route. . . . Anti-Columbus Day sentiments are mostly relegated to sidebars, but Bodden doesn't surgarcoat the enslavement and death that followed discovery." Booklist

Includes bibliographical references

Demi

Columbus; by Demi. Marshall Cavendish 2012 64 p. ill. (hardcover) $19.99

Grades: 3 4 5 6   **970.01**

1. America -- Exploration -- Juvenile literature 2. Columbus, Christopher, 1451-1506 -- Juvenile literature 3. Explorers -- Spain -- Biography -- Juvenile literature 4. Explorers -- America -- Biography -- Juvenile literature

ISBN 0761461671; 9780761461678

LC 2011036019

This book on Christopher Columbus was written and illustrated by the children's book author Demi. "From his childhood in Italy to his death in Spain, this biography presents a detailed view of the explorer's life. . . .Columbus's faults and accomplishments are both presented, acknowledging that his drive to explore furthered Europeans' knowledge of other lands, but that his mistreatment of Native peoples devastated their lives and culture." (School Library Journal)

Englar, Mary

French colonies in America. Compass Point Books 2009 48p il (We the people) lib bdg $26.60

Grades: 4 5 6   **970.01**

1. French Americans 2. French Canadians

ISBN 978-0-7565-3839-2

LC 2008007209

This is a history of French exploration and colonization in North America.

This provides "solid background matter and [introduces] key people and vocabulary." SLJ

Gunderson, Jessica

Conquistadors; by Jessica Gunderson. Creative Education 2011 48 p. (alk. paper) $35.65

Grades: 5 6 7 8   **970.01**

1. United States -- History 2. Soldiers -- Juvenile literature 3. Military art and science -- History 4. Soldiers -- Spain -- History -- Juvenile literature 5. Military art and science -- History -- Juvenile literature

ISBN 1608181839; 9781608181834

LC 2011035799

Author Jessica Gunderson's book "covers the beginnings of the people, weaponry, war tactics, and famous leaders, and examines the current perception of the group in popular culture in an appealing, detailed, and evenhanded manner. Historical reproductions, primary documents, photographs, maps, and film stills appear throughout" the "explorations of history." (Publisher's note)

Includes bibliographical references and index

Harrison, David L.

Mammoth bones and broken stones; the mystery of North America's first people. with illustrations by Richard Hilliard and archaeological photographs. Boyds Mills Press 2010 48p il map $18.95

Grades: 4 5 6 7   **970.01**

1. Prehistoric peoples

ISBN 978-1-59078-561-4; 1-59078-561-4

LC 2009020247

"How and when the Western Hemisphere . . . came to be populated continues to be both mysterious and controversial for scientists. . . . Harrison does a good job setting the issue in context. He describes the earliest efforts to identify the original inhabitants of the continents, exploring the Clovis culture. . . . After clearly explaining how scholars decided that they were the first, he then lists the arguments against this hypothesis. . . . The narrative is aided by both photographs and original illustrations that imagine scenes from both the distant past and the field experiences." Kirkus

Includes glossary and bibliographical references

Hernandez, Roger E.

Early explorations: the 1500s. Marshall Cavendish Benchmark 2009 79p il map (Hispanic America) lib bdg $34.21

Grades: 4 5 6 7   **970.01**

1. Explorers 2. Southwestern States -- History

ISBN 978-0-7614-2937-1 lib bdg; 0-7614-2937-9 lib bdg

"Provides comprehensive information on the history of Spanish exploration in the United States." Publisher's note

Includes glossary and bibliographical references

Huey, Lois Miner

American archaeology uncovers the Vikings. Marshall Cavendish Benchmark 2009 64p il map (American archaeology) lib bdg $21.95

Grades: 4 5 6 7   970.01

1. Vikings -- North America   2. Excavations (Archeology) -- Canada   3. Excavations (Archeology) -- United States

ISBN 978-0-7614-4270-7 lib bdg; 0-7614-4270-7 lib bdg

LC 2008050266

This describes how archeologists have learned about the Vikings in America.

This is "both intriguing and engaging for young readers. . . . A welcomed addition to classroom and school libraries." Libr Media Connect

Includes glossary and bibliographical references

Lilly, Alexandra

Spanish colonies in America. Compass Point Books 2009 48p il map (We the people) lib bdg $26.60

Grades: 4 5 6   970.01

1. Explorers 2. Spaniards -- United States

ISBN 978-0-7565-3840-8 lib bdg; 0-7565-3840-8 lib bdg

LC 2008011727

This is a history Spanish exploration, conquest, and colonization in North America.

This provides "solid background matter and [introduces] key people and vocabulary." SLJ

Maestro, Betsy

★ **Exploration** and conquest; the Americas after Columbus, 1500-1620. [by] Betsy & Giulio Maestro. Lothrop, Lee & Shepard Bks. 1994 48p il maps hardcover o.p. pa $6.95

Grades: 2 3 4   970.01

ISBN 0-688-09268-3 lib bdg; 0-688-15474-3 pa

LC 93-48618

"The book's most outstanding feature is its full-color artwork. Large, double-page spreads give scope to dramatic landscapes, while smaller pictures on every page show events, places, and maps pertinent to the text. . . . This book provides a useful overview of the period." Booklist

★ The **discovery** of the Americas; by Betsy and Giulio Maestro. Lothrop, Lee & Shepard Bks. 1990 48p il maps hardcover o.p. pa $6.95

Grades: 2 3 4   970.01

1. America -- Exploration

ISBN 0-688-06837-5; 0-688-11512-8 pa

LC 89-32375

Discusses both hypothetical and historical voyages of discovery to America by the Phoenicians, Saint Brendan of Ireland, the Vikings, and such later European navigators as Columbus, Cabot, and Magellan

"The dazzlingly clean and accurate prose and the exhilarating beauty of the pictures combine for an extraordinary achievement in both history and art." SLJ

Mann, Charles C.

★ **Before** Columbus; the Americas of 1491. Atheneum Books for Young Readers 2009 117p il map $24.99

Grades: 5 6 7 8 9 10   970.01

1. Native Americans -- Origin 2. Native Americans -- History

ISBN 978-1-4169-4900-8; 1-4169-4900-3

LC 2009007691

Adapted from 1491, published 2006 by Knopf for adults

"Mann paints a superb picture of pre-Columbian America. In the process, he overturns the misconceived image of Natives as simple, widely scattered savages with minimal impact on their surroundings. Well-chosen, vividly colored graphics and photographs of mummies, pyramids, artifacts, and landscapes as well as the author's skillful storytelling will command the attention of even the most reluctant readers." SLJ

Includes glossary and bibliographical references

Markle, Sandra

Animals Christopher Columbus saw; an adventure in the New World. by Sandra Markle; illustrations by Jamel Akib. Chronicle Books 2008 46p il $16.99

Grades: 2 3 4   970.01

1. Explorers 2. Animals -- North America

ISBN 978-0-8118-4916-6; 0-8118-4916-3

LC 2006033623

This "concentrates less on Christopher Columbus and more on the location, habitat, and fauna found during his discovery of the Americas." Publisher's note

Includes glossary and bibliographical references

Mooney, Carla

Explorers of the New World; discover the golden age of exploration; with 22 projects. illustrated by Tom Casteel. Nomad 2011 120p il map (Build it yourself) pa $15.95 970.01

1. Explorers

ISBN 978-1-936313-44-0; 1-936313-44-8

Provides twenty-two step-by-step projects to help readers learn about the explorers that discovered America and their voyages.

"This informative, entertaining activity book takes readers on a fascinating voyage of their own. . . . Each chapter concludes with 'Make Your Own' activities that bring life to the history with instructions for the construction of a logbook, clay activities, recipes, games, etc. Some may require the assistance of an adult but are not complicated or time consuming." SLJ

Includes glossary and bibliographical references

Wyatt, Valerie

★ **Who** discovered America? with illustrations by Howie Woo. Kids Can Press 2008 40p il map $17.95; pa $8.95

Grades: 4 5 6   970.01

ISBN 978-1-55453-128-8; 1-55453-128-4; 978-1-55453-129-5 pa; 1-55453-129-2 pa

"With interesting sidebars and engaging illustrations and photos, this 'whodunit' of sorts describes, on a spread each, evidence for the journeys of various groups who discovered, or claimed to have discovered, [the North American] continent. . . . Wyatt writes clearly about how scientists unlock clues to how and when various groups could have made landfall. . . . Raising perhaps more questions than it answers, this book leaves it to readers to decide the solution to the mystery." SLJ

Includes glossary

970.02   North America, 1600-1699

Maestro, Betsy

★ The **new** Americans; colonial times, 1620-1689. illustrated by Giulio Maestro. Lothrop, Lee & Shepard Bks. 1998 48p il map hardcover o.p. pa $7.99
Grades: 2 3 4   **970.02**
ISBN 0-688-13448-3; 0-06-57572-7 pa
LC 95-19636

Traces the competition among the American Indians, French, English, Spanish, and Dutch for land, furs, timber, and other resources of North America

This is "accessibly written and meticulously illustrated. . . . Giulio Maestro's carefully detailed watercolor and color-pencil art includes maps, closely focused spot illustrations and dramatic spreads, which together provide a vivid picture of the century's pivotal events." Publ Wkly

971   Canada

Baker, Stuart

In the Arctic. Marshall Cavendish Benchmark 2010 32p il map (Climate change) lib bdg $19.95
Grades: 5 6 7 8   **971**
1. Greenhouse effect 2. Arctic regions
ISBN 978-0-7614-4437-4 lib bdg; 0-7614-4437-8 lib bdg
LC 2009-5767

The book about climate change in the Arctic "is perfectly organized for students. . . . Unique layout features serve as signposts and will help focus readers' attention. . . . [The book] features an outstanding chart of possible effects of global warming on the area in question, listing 'Possible Event,' 'Predicted Result,' and 'Impact' in short, bulleted statements." SLJ

Includes glossary

Bowers, Vivien

Hey Canada! by Vivien Bowers; illustrated by Milan Pavlovic. Tundra Books of Northern New York 2012 72 p. ill. (chiefly col.), maps (hardcover) $19.95
Grades: 3 4 5   **971**
1. Canada 2. Travelers 3. Voyages and travels
ISBN 1770492550; 9781770492554
LC 2011923470

This children's picture book by Vivien Bowers presents "a young traveler's . . . account of a quick province-by-province drive across Canada." The "9-year-old narrator [travels] to cities, roadside attractions and natural wonders from Cape Spear to Iqaluit." The book also provides information "about regional foods . . . . and other artifacts of European settlement." (Kirkus Reviews)

Coulter, Laurie

★ **Ballplayers** and bonesetters; one hundred ancient Aztec and Maya jobs you might have adored or abhorred.

[written] by Laurie Coulter; illustrated by Martha Newbigging. Annick Press 2008 96p il $25.95; pa $16.95
Grades: 4 5 6   **971**
1. Mayas 2. Aztecs 3. Aztecs -- Juvenile literature 4. Occupations -- Juvenile literature ISBN 978-1-55451-141-9; 1-55451-141-0; 978-1-55451-140-2 pa; 1-55451-140-2 pa

"Following a readable and humorous overview of the highly developed Aztec and Maya civilizations, this lively text lists 100 jobs that a young person might have held or aspired to during the Late Postclassic period in Mesoamerica (1350 to 1521). . . . Taken as a whole, the descriptions of the vocations yield a rich view of the culture, and the breezy text makes this as much a browsing as a reference title. The colorful cartoon illustrations enhance the text, adding just the right artistic complement." SLJ

Greenwood, Barbara

★ A **pioneer** sampler; the daily life of a pioneer family in 1840. illustrated by Heather Collins. Ticknor & Fields Bks. for Young Readers 1995 240p il hardcover o.p. pa $15
Grades: 4 5 6 7   **971**
1. Frontier and pioneer life   ISBN 0-395-71540-7; 0-395-88393-8 pa
LC 94-12829

First published 1994 in Canada with title: A pioneer story

"Using a combination of fiction and fact-filled supplementary commentary, with illustrations inspired by Garth Williams, the author tells the story of the Robertsons, a large, hardworking farm family. Good projects for school or home." N Y Times Book Rev

★ Junior Worldmark encyclopedia of the Canadian provinces; [Timothy L. Gall and Susan Bevan Gall, editors] 5th ed.; U.X.L 2007 294p il map $70
Grades: 5 6 7 8 9 10   **971**
1. Reference books 2. United States -- Encyclopedias
ISBN 978-1-4144-1060-9; 1-4144-1060-3
LC 2007003908

First published 1997

"Arranged by 40 . . . subheadings . . . this . . . resource provides . . . information on all of Canada's provinces and territories. [It includes] details on Canada's arts, climate, government, health, languages, notable persons, ethnic groups and . . . more." Publisher's note

Includes bibliographical references

Penn, Briony

The **kids** book of Canadian geography; written and illustrated by Briony Penn. Kids Can Press 2008 56p il map $19.95
Grades: 3 4 5 6   **971**
ISBN 978-1-55074-890-1; 1-55074-890-4

This "traces the continents' formation, touching on Canada's ancient landscapes, evolving climate, continent shaping and life on the land including human settlement, plus a geographical coast to coast tour and much more." Publisher's note

Sonneborn, Liz

Canada; by Liz Sonneborn. Children's Press 2012 144 p. col. ill.. col. maps (library) $40

Grades: 5 6 7 8   **971**

1. Canada -- Juvenile literature 2. Canada -- Social life and customs

ISBN 0531253511; 9780531253519

LC 2011011970

This book by Liz Sonneborn is part of the Enchantment of the World series and looks at Canada. The introduction focuses on Canadian Terry Fox. Sonneborn "covers geography, natural resources, environment, history, government, diversity, religions, culture, and everyday life. She includes details like 'poutine' (fries, cheese curds, and gravy) and 'Timmies' (a coffee and doughnut chain)." (School Library Journal)

Includes bibliographical references (p. 134) and index.

Walker, Sally M.

★ **Blizzard** of glass; the Halifax explosion of 1917. Henry Holt 2011 xii, 145p il $18.99

Grades: 5 6 7 8   **971**

1. World War, 1914-1918 -- Naval operations

ISBN 978-0-8050-8945-5; 0-8050-8945-4

LC 2011005914

"The text reads smoothly with unfamiliar words defined in the text. Illustrations consist of two full-page maps and numerous black-and-white photos. The final chapter revisits the featured families and their descendants, thus tying up the loose ends. . . . This tragic, but well-told story belongs in most collections." SLJ

Includes bibliographical references

Wallace, Mary

Inuksuk journey; an artist at the top of the world. Maple Tree Press 2008 64p il $24.95

Grades: 5 6 7 8   **971**

1. Inuit

ISBN 978-1-897349-26-7; 1-897349-26-2

"Nunavut, an Arctic territory in northern Canada, is a cold, open space where inuksuk, piles of stone in the shape of a person used to 'mark a family home, welcome guests, guide travelers, and ensure safe passage,' are commonly found. Wallace has developed a passion for these ancient messengers, and here she presents a journal of her week-long trek to Inuksugassait, a place where countless numbers of the stone markers stand. . . . Wallace includes personal photos, sketches, and comments that give readers an intimate portrait of life in this place. Over a dozen vibrant oil paintings depicting scenes from her journey are scattered throughout. . . . Readers will be fascinated by this firsthand account of true adventure." SLJ

Williams, Brian

★ **Canada**; [by] Brian Williams; Tom Carter and Ben Cecil, consultants. National Geographic 2007 64p il map (Countries of the world) lib bdg $27.90; pa $12.95

Grades: 4 5 6 7   **971**

ISBN 978-1-4263-0025-7 lib bdg; 978-1-4263-0573-3 pa

LC 2007296572

A basic overview of the history, geography, climate and culture of Canada

This "clear, succinct [overview] will support assignments without overwhelming casual readers. . . . A good

selection of recent, high-quality color photographs gives the [book] visual appeal." SLJ

Includes glossary and bibliographical references

971.01   Early history to 1763

Worth, Richard

New France, 1534-1763; featuring the region that now includes all or parts of Michigan, Minnesota, Wisconsin, Illinois, Indiana, Ohio, Pennsylvania, Vermont, Maine, and Canada from Manitoba to Newfoundland. by Richard Worth. National Geographic Society 2007 109p il map (Voices from colonial America) $21.95; lib bdg $32.90

Grades: 5 6 7 8   **971.01**

1. Canada -- History -- 0-1763 (New France) 2. Mississippi River valley -- History

ISBN 978-1-4263-0147-6; 1-4263-0147-2; 978-1-4263-0148-3 lib bdg; 1-4263-0148-0 lib bdg

LC 2007-29544

"Worth presents the history of the vast French colony known as New France. Clearly written, the book is studded with quotes from people living in the colony and illustrated with colorful paintings, prints, and maps from a variety of periods. . . . This nicely designed introduction to a historically significant area fills a gap in many colonial history series and library collections." Booklist

Includes bibliographical references

972   Mexico, Central America, West Indies, Bermuda

Apte, Sunita

The **Aztec** empire. Children's Press 2009 48p il map (True book) lib bdg $26; pa $6.95

Grades: 3 4 5   **972**

1. Aztecs

ISBN 978-0-531-25227-7 lib bdg; 0-531-25227-2 lib bdg; 978-0-531-24108-0 pa; 0-531-24108-4 pa

LC 2009000299

In this book the Aztec empire is "outlined for young readers with care and precision. . . . Loaded with access points such as captions, pull-outs, a time line, and a map, and with better-than-usual reproductions of well-chosen primary sources and art, the [book sports] a bright, peppy design. . . . [This book is] rigorous in distinguishing fact from theory, and conscientious about presenting competing theories where they exist." SLJ

Includes glossary and bibliographical references

Cooke, Tim

★ **Ancient** Aztec; archaeology unlocks the secrets of Mexico's past. National Geographic 2007 64p il map (National Geographic investigates) $17.95; lib bdg $27.90

Grades: 4 5 6 7   **972**

1. Aztecs 2. Excavations (Archeology) -- Mexico

ISBN 978-1-4263-0072-1; 1-4263-0072-7; 978-1-4263-0073-8 lib bdg; 1-4263-0073-5 lib bdg

LC 2007024813

This describes ancient Aztec origins, technology, major archeological sites, civilization, and connections to the present

"Pithy and appealing. . . . Aerial photos, time [line], informative sidebars, an interview with an archaeologist, and excellent maps augment rigorously supported [text] that [asks] and [answers] interesting questions." SLJ

Gruber, Beth

★ **Mexico**; [by] Beth Gruber; Gary S. Elbow and Jorge Zamora, consultants. National Geographic 2007 64p il map (Countries of the world) lib bdg $27.90; pa $12.95
Grades: 4 5 6 7   972
1. Mexico
ISBN 0-7922-7669-8 lib bdg; 1-4263-0566-4 pa
LC 2004026452

"This volume introduces Mexico's geography, history, wildlife, culture, and government. The many excellent color photos and maps are a striking feature of the series. . . . This will be a useful addition to many libraries." Booklist

Includes glossary and bibliographical references

Harris, Nathaniel

★ **Ancient** Maya; archaeology unlocks the secrets to the Maya's past. by Nathaniel Harris; Elizabeth Graham, consultant. National Geographic 2008 64p il map (National Geographic investigates) $17.95; lib bdg $27.90
Grades: 4 5 6 7   972
1. Mayas 2. Excavations (Archeology) -- Mexico
ISBN 978-1-4263-0227-5; 1-4263-0227-4; 978-1-4263-0228-2 lib bdg; 1-4263-0228-2 lib bdg
LC 2007047837

This describes ancient Mayan civilization and how archeologists found out about it.

Includes glossary and bibliographical references

★ Junior Worldmark encyclopedia of the Mexican states; [Timothy L. Gall and Susan Bevan Gall, editors] 2nd ed.; U.X.L,Thomson/Gale 2007 423p il map $70
Grades: 5 6 7 8 9 10   972
1. Reference books 2. Mexico
ISBN 978-1-4144-1112-5
LC 2007003906

First published 2004

"Arranged by 28 . . . subheadings . . . Junior Worldmark Encyclopedia of the Mexican States provides . . . information on each of Mexico's 31 states. Topics covered include climate, plants and animals, population and ethnic groups, religions, transportation, history, state and local governments, political parties, judicial system, economy, education, arts, media, tourism, sports, famous people and . . . more." Publisher's note

Includes bibliographical references

Kent, Deborah

Mexico; by Deborah Kent. Children's Press 2012 144 p. cil. ill., photographs (library) $40
Grades: 5 6 7 8   972
1. Mexico -- Juvenile literature 2. Culture -- Juvenile literature
ISBN 0531253554; 9780531253557
LC 2011010812

This book by Deborah Kent is part of the Enchantment of the World series and looks at Mexico. The books in the series offer 10 "chapters, several maps, a fast-facts section, and a few references to other sources, including a referral to a Scholastic website (new). The chapters cover geography,

natural environment, history, politics, people and culture." (School Library Journal)

Includes bibliographical references and index.

Kops, Deborah

Palenque; by Deborah Kops. Twenty-First Century Books 2008 80p il (Unearthing ancient worlds) lib bdg $30.60
Grades: 5 6 7 8   972
1. Mayas 2. Excavations (Archeology) -- Mexico
ISBN 978-0-8225-7504-7 lib bdg; 0-8225-7504-3 lib bdg
LC 2007021323

This describes the discovery of the ancient Mayan site of Palenque in 1840 by John Stephens and Frederick Catherwood, and the mid-20th century excavations of the site by Alberto Ruz Lhuillier, who discovered the tomb of the Mayan king Pakal, who died in 683 A.D., inside a pyramid

This "clearly written [title is] illustrated with large photographs and period artwork, and the pages are broken up with text boxes featuring quotes and interesting anecdotes." SLJ

Includes glossary and bibliographical references

Lourie, Peter

Hidden world of the Aztec. Boyds Mills Press 2006 48p il map $17.95
Grades: 4 5 6 7   972
1. Aztecs 2. Excavations (Archeology) -- Mexico
ISBN 978-1-59078-069-5; 1-59078-069-8

The author takes a "look at the Aztecs from the perspective of archaeological digs at the Great Temple in modern-day Mexico City and at the Pyramid of the Moon in Teotihuacan. . . . The writing style is clear, informative, and interesting." SLJ

Includes glossary and bibliographical references

McDaniel, Melissa

New Mexico; [by] Melissa McDaniel, Ettagale Blauer, and Jason Laure. 2nd ed.; Marshall Cavendish Benchmark 2008 144p il map (Celebrate the states) lib bdg $39.93
Grades: 4 5 6 7   972
ISBN 978-0-7614-2719-3; 0-7614-2719-8
LC 2007-9273

First published 1999

"Provides comprehensive information on the geography, history, wildlife, governmental structure, economy, cultural diversity, peoples, religion, and landmarks of New Mexico." Publisher's note

Includes bibliographical references

Streissguth, Thomas

Mexico; by Tom Streissguth. Lerner Publications Company 2008 48p il map (Country explorers) lib bdg $27.93; pa $8.95
Grades: 2 3 4   972
ISBN 978-0-8225-7130-8 lib bdg; 978-0-8225-8508-4 pa
LC 2006036726

This introduction to Mexico covers "all of the areas of interest to students, including animals, sports, foods, celebrations, storytime, and even a few words in the country's native language. Small amounts of information are surrounded

by current photographs, maps, charts, and illustrations. . .
. Sure to grab the attention of even reluctant readers." SLJ

Includes glossary and bibliographical references

972.81　Guatemala

Croy, Anita

★ **Guatemala**. National Geographic 2009 64p il map
(Countries of the world) lib bdg $27.90

Grades: 4 5 6 7　　　　　　　　　　　　　**972.81**

1. Guatemala

ISBN 978-1-4263-0471-2 lib bdg; 1-4263-0471-4
lib bdg

This describes the geography, nature, history, people and
culture, government and economy of Guatemala

Includes glossary and bibliographical references

Mann, Elizabeth

★ **Tikal**; the center of the Maya world. with illustrations by Tom McNeely. Mikaya Press 2002 47p il map
(Wonders of the world) $19.95

Grades: 4 5 6 7　　　　　　　　　　　　　**972.81**

1. Mayas -- Antiquities　2. Mayas -- Antiquities --
Juvenile literature

ISBN 1-931414-05-X

LC 2002-29599

A history of the Maya Indians in the city of Tikal, founded in 800 B.C.

"Mann's narrative flows smoothly, and frequent, full-
color illustrations . . . help to clarify the details mentioned in
the text." Booklist

Includes glossary

Ollhoff, Jim

Mayan and Aztec mythology; by Jim Ollhoff. ABDO
Publishing Company 2011 32p. ill. (The world of mythology) lib bdg $27.07

Grades: 5 6 7 8　　　　　　　　　　　　　**972.81**

1. Mythology　2. Mayas -- Folklore　3. Aztecs --
Folklore　4. Mayas -- Religion　5. Aztecs -- Religion

ISBN 978-1-61714-724-1; 1-61714-724-9;
9781617147241

LC 2010042976

This describes the history of myths of the Maya and
Aztecs, their meaning, and their gods and goddesses in-
cluding Itzamna, Xolotl, the Aztec feathered serpent god
Quetzalcoatl,and the Mayan rain god Chac.

"Ollhoff writes in a clear and engaging fashion, presenting complex issues in a way that will be easy for youngsters
to grasp. . . . The photographs and reproductions of art tie
directly to the [text]." SLJ

972.82　Belize

Jermyn, Leslie

Belize; [by] Leslie Jermyn and Yong Jui Lin. 2nd ed.;
Marshall Cavendish Benchmark 2012 144p il map (Cultures of the world) lib bdg $42.79

Grades: 5 6 7 8　　　　　　　　　　　　　**972.82**

1. Belize

ISBN 978-1-60870-452-1; 1-60870-452-1

LC 2010035966

Provides information on the geography, history, wildlife, governmental structure, economy, cultural diversity,
peoples, religion, and culture of Belize.

"The concise writing offers enough material for report
writers without overwhelming them. Numerous full-color
and black-and-white photos of interest, a clean layout, and
use of pastels to highlight headings and sidebars contribute
to the attractiveness of . . . [this presentation]." SLJ

Includes glossary and bibliographical references

972.83　Honduras

McGaffey, Leta

Honduras; [by] Leta McGaffey and Michael Spilling.
2nd ed.; Marshall Cavendish Benchmark 2010 144p il
map (Cultures of the world) lib bdg $42.79

Grades: 5 6 7 8　　　　　　　　　　　　　**972.83**

1. Honduras

ISBN 978-0-7614-4848-8 lib bdg; 0-7614-4848-9
lib bdg

LC 2009022642

First published 1999

"Provides comprehensive information on the geography,
history, wildlife, governmental structure, economy, cultural
diversity, peoples, religion, and culture of Honduras." Publisher's note

Includes glossary and bibliographical references

Shields, Charles J.

Honduras. Mason Crest Pubs. 2003 63p il map (Discovering Central America) lib bdg $19.95

Grades: 4 5 6 7　　　　　　　　　　　　　**972.83**

1. Honduras

ISBN 1-59084-096-8

LC 2002-9089

This describes the history, geography, and culture
of Honduras

This is "jam-packed with useful information. . . . [It con-
tains] straightforward writing, clearly titled chapters, high
quality color, and well-captioned photographs and graphics." Libr Media Connect

Includes glossary and bibliographical references

972.84　El Salvador

Foley, Erin

El Salvador; [by] Erin Foley, Rafiz Hapipi. 2nd ed.;
Benchmark Bks. 2005 144p il map (Cultures of the world)
lib bdg $42.79

Grades: 5 6 7 8　　　　　　　　　　　　　**972.84**

1. El Salvador

ISBN 0-7614-1967-5

LC 2005009360

First published 1994

This describes the geography, history, government, economy, environment, people, lifestyle, religion, language, arts, leisure, festivals, and food of El Salvador

Includes glossary and bibliographical references

972.85 Nicaragua

Kott, Jennifer
★ Nicaragua; [by] Jennifer Kott, Kristi Streiffert. 2nd ed.; Benchmark Bks. 2005 144p il map (Cultures of the world) lib bdg $42.79
Grades: 5 6 7 8   972.85
1. Nicaragua
ISBN 0-7614-1969-1
LC 2005009240

First published 1994
An illustrated overview of the geography, economy, history, government, politics, and culture of Nicaragua

Includes glossary and bibliographical references

972.86 Costa Rica

Foley, Erin
Costa Rica; [by] Erin Foley and Barbara Cooke. 2nd ed.; Marshall Cavendish Benchmark 2008 144p il map (Cultures of the world) lib bdg $42.79
Grades: 5 6 7 8   972.86
1. Costa Rica
ISBN 978-0-7614-2079-8 lib bdg; 0-7614-2079-7 lib bdg
LC 2006101736

First published 1997
This offers "information on the geography, history, wildlife, governmental structure, economy, cultural diversity, peoples, religion, and culture of Costa Rica." Publisher's note

Includes glossary and bibliographical references

972.87 Panama

Hassig, Susan M.
Panama; [by] Susan Hassig & Lynette Quek. 2nd ed.; Marshall Cavendish Benchmark 2007 144p il map (Cultures of the world) lib bdg $42.79
Grades: 5 6 7 8   972.87
1. Panama
ISBN 978-0-7614-2028-6 lib bdg; 0-7614-2028-2 lib bdg
LC 2006020824

First published 1996
This provides "information on the geography, history, wildlife, governmental structure, economy, cultural diversity, peoples, religion, and culture of Panama." Publisher's note

Includes glossary and bibliographical references

972.9 West Indies (Antilles) and Bermuda

Kras, Sara Louise
Antigua and Barbuda; [by] Sara Louise Kras. Marshall Cavendish Benchmark 2008 144p il map (Cultures of the world) lib bdg $42.79
Grades: 5 6 7 8   972.9
1. Antigua and Barbuda
ISBN 978-0-7614-2570-0
LC 2006031537

This describes the geography, history, government, economy, environment, people, and culture of Antigua and Barbuda

Includes glossary and bibliographical references

972.91 Cuba

Green, Jen
★ Cuba; [by] Jen Green; Damián Fernández and Alejandro de la Fuente, consultants. National Geographic 2007 64p il map (Countries of the world) lib bdg $27.90
Grades: 4 5 6 7   972.91
1. Cuba
ISBN 978-1-4263-0057-8
LC 2007026468

This describes the geography, nature, history, people & culture, government & economy of Cuba.

Includes glossary and bibliographical references

Sheehan, Sean
Cuba; [by] Sean Sheehan, Leslie Jermyn. 2nd ed.; Benchmark Bks. 2005 144p il map (Cultures of the world) lib bdg $42.79
Grades: 5 6 7 8   972.91
1. Cuba
ISBN 0-7614-1965-9
LC 2005009362

First published 1994
This describes the geography, history, government, economy, population, lifestyle, religion, language, arts, leisure, festivals, and food of Cuba

Includes glossary and bibliographical references

Stein, R. Conrad
Cuban Missile Crisis; in the shadow of nuclear war. Enslow Publishers 2009 128p il map (America's living history) lib bdg $31.93
Grades: 5 6 7 8   972.91
1. Cuban Missile Crisis, 1962
ISBN 978-0-7660-2905-7 lib bdg; 0-7660-2905-0 lib bdg
LC 2008-4703

"Discusses the Cuban missile crisis, a thirteen-day struggle between the United States and the Soviet Union, including the causes of the conflict, the leaders faced with important decisions, and the final resolution to avoid nuclear war." Publisher's note

Includes glossary and bibliographical references

Tracy, Kathleen
We visit Cuba. Mitchell Lane Publishers 2010 63p il (Your land and my land) lib bdg $33.95

Grades: 4 5 6 7   **972.91**
1. Cuba
ISBN 978-1-58415-890-5 lib bdg; 1-58415-890-5
lib bdg

LC 2010006558

"With an inviting format that includes bright color photos on every spread, this title . . . offers an appealing overview of Cuba's history, geography, culture and lifestyle, politics, economics, and more. . . . A good starting point for research as well as for personal interest." Booklist

Includes glossary and bibliographical references

972.92   Jamaica and Cayman Islands

Green, Jen
★ **Jamaica**; [by] Jen Green; David J. Howard and Joel Frater, consultants. National Geographic 2008 64p il map (Countries of the world) lib bdg $27.90
Grades: 4 5 6 7   **972.92**
1. Jamaica
ISBN 978-1-4263-0300-5 lib bdg; 1-4263-0300-9
lib bdg

This describes the geography, nature, history, people and culture, government, and economy of Jamaica.

Includes glossary and bibligraphical references

Sheehan, Sean
Jamaica; [by] Sean Sheehan & Angela Black. 2nd ed; Benchmark Books 2004 144p il map (Cultures of the world) lib bdg $42.79
Grades: 5 6 7 8   **972.92**
1. Jamaica
ISBN 0-7614-1785-0

LC 2004-7676

First published 1996
Introduces the geography, history, religion, government, economy, and culture of Jamaica

"An informative book with captivating pictures, a visually attractive layout, and flowing text. . . . A well-balanced and interesting look at one country's culture." SLJ

Includes glossary and bibliographical references

972.93   Dominican Republic

Foley, Erin
Dominican Republic; [by] Erin Foley & Leslie Jermyn. 2nd ed; Marshall Cavendish Benchmark 2005 144p (Cultures of the world) lib bdg $42.79
Grades: 5 6 7 8   **972.93**
1. Dominican Republic
ISBN 0-7614-1966-7
First published 1995

"The material is well organized in easily readable sections, accurately illustrated with well-placed, full-color photographs on every page." SLJ

972.94   Haiti

Aronin, Miriam
Earthquake in Haiti. Bearport Pub. 2011 32p il map (Code red) lib bdg $25.27
Grades: 4 5 6 7   **972.94**
1. Earthquakes 2. Haiti
ISBN 978-1-936088-66-9; 1-936088-66-5

LC 2010011126

Describes the devastating earthquake that occurred in Haiti on January 12, 2010.

"The text is written from the points of view of some of the people involved, including primary source direct quotes. Some of the pictures are necessarily graphic, which adds to the authenticity. . . . This title will be used for browsing as well as for reports." Libr Media Connect

Includes glossary and bibliographical references

Benoit, Peter
The **Haitian** earthquake of 2010. Children's Press 2011 48p il (True book: disasters) lib bdg $28; pa $6.95
Grades: 3 4 5   **972.94**
1. Earthquakes 2. Haiti
ISBN 978-0-531-25420-2 lib bdg; 0-531-25420-8;
978-0-531-26625-0 pa; 0-531-26625-7 pa

LC 2011007912

This book about the earthquake in Haiti in 2010 and its aftermath is "thoughtfully designed. . . . The information . . . is right on target: concise, accurate, and thorough. . . . The photographs . . . are especially effective at putting a human face on large-scale devastation." Booklist

Includes glossary and bibliographical references

Mara, Wil
Haiti; [by] Wil Mara. Marshall Cavendish Benchmark 2007 48p il map (Discovering cultures) lib bdg $28.50
Grades: 2 3 4   **972.94**
1. Haiti
ISBN 978-0-7614-1987-7 lib bdg; 0-7614-1987-X
lib bdg

LC 2006011473

An introduction to the geography, history, people, and culture of Haiti

Includes glossary and bibliographical references

NgCheong-Lum, Roseline, 1962-
Haiti; [by] Roseline Ng Cheong-Lum & Leslie Jermyn. 2nd ed; Marshall Cavendish Benchmark 2005 144p il map (Cultures of the world) lib bdg $42.79
Grades: 5 6 7 8   **972.94**
1. Haiti
ISBN 0-7614-1968-3
First published 1995
Describes the geography, history, government, economy, culture, peoples, and religion of Haiti

Includes glossary and bibliographical references

Oelschlager, Vanita
I came from the water; one Haitian boy's incredible tale of survival. VanitaBooks 2012 $8.95
Grades: K 1 2   **972.94**
1. Haiti 2. Orphans 3. Picture books for children
ISBN 0983290458; 9780983290452

In this book, Vanita Oelschlager "shares the real-life story of an eight-year-old Haitian boy who, as an infant, was packed into a basket during a catastrophic flood, rescued, and sent to a children's village, where he was named Moses. . . . Moses describes the priest who runs the village . . . and the new children who arrived after the great earthquake of 2012' 'I am one of the strong ones,' he says. 'I must help those who are not as strong.'" (Publishers Weekly)

Yomtov, Nel
Haiti; by Nel Yomtov. Children's Press 2012 144 p. col. ill. (library) $40
Grades: 5 6 7 8   972.94
1. Haiti
ISBN 0531253538; 9780531253533
LC 2011010048
This book is part of the Enchantment of the World series and focuses on Haiti. This series presents "factual information against a backdrop of brightly colored pictures and maps. . . . Each book provides a timeline, Fast Facts, and embassies." The books also include "brief chapters that follow real people in their daily lives." (Library Media Connection)
Includes bibliographical references and index.

972.95   Puerto Rico

DaSilva-Gordon, Maria
Puerto Rico; past and present. Rosen Central 2011 48p il map (The United States: past and present) lib bdg $26.50; pa $11.75
Grades: 3 4 5 6   972.95
1. Puerto Rico
ISBN 978-1-4358-9502-7 lib bdg; 1-4358-9502-9 lib bdg; 978-1-4358-9529-4 pa; 1-4358-9529-0 pa
LC 2010005891
This describes the history, culture, economy, and geography of the island of Puerto Rico.
Includes bibliographical references

Schwabacher, Martin
Puerto Rico; by Martin Schwabacher and Steve Otfinoski. 2nd ed.; Marshall Cavendish Benchmark 2010 144p il map (Celebrate the states) $42.79
Grades: 5 6 7 8   972.95
1. Puerto Rico
ISBN 978-0-7614-4734-4; 0-7614-4734-2
LC 2009007066
First published 2001
This offers information on the geography, history, wildlife, governmental structure, economy, cultural diversity, peoples, religion, and landmarks of Puerto Rico.
Includes bibliographical references

Stille, Darlene R.
Puerto Rico. Children's Press 2009 144p il map (America the beautiful, third series) lib bdg $39
Grades: 4 5 6 7   972.95
1. Puerto Rico
ISBN 978-0-531-18589-6; 0-531-18589-3
LC 2008000819

An introduction to the land, history, and people of Puerto Rico.
Includes glossary and bibliographical references

972.96   Bahama Islands

Hintz, Martin
The Bahamas; by Martin Hintz. Children's Press 2013 144 p. col. ill., col. maps (Enchantment of the world. Second series) (library) $40
Grades: 5 6 7 8   972.96
1. Bahamas -- Juvenile literature 2. Bahamas -- Description and travel
ISBN 0531275418; 9780531275412
LC 2012000513
This book, by Martin Hintz, is part of the "Enchantment of the World" series. In it the author provides information and photographs showcasing the people, places and events surrounding the Caribbean island chain of the Bahamas. Contents include photographs of Bahaman cities and landscapes, statistics describing the islands' features, and traditional Bahaman recipes.
Includes bibliographical references and index

972.98   Windward and other southern islands

Elias, Marie Louise
Barbados; [by] Marie Louise Elias and Josie Elias. 2nd ed.; Marshall Cavendish Benchmark 2010 144p il map (Cultures of the world) lib bdg $42.79
Grades: 5 6 7 8   972.98
1. Barbados
ISBN 978-0-7614-4853-2 lib bdg; 0-7614-4853-5 lib bdg
LC 2009044592
First published 2000
This offers information on the geography, history, wildlife, governmental structure, economy, cultural diversity, peoples, religion, and culture of Barbados
Includes glossary and bibliographical references

Orr, Tamra
Saint Lucia; [by] Tamra Orr. 2nd ed.; Marshall Cavendish Benchmark 2008 144p il map (Cultures of the world) lib bdg $42.79
Grades: 5 6 7 8   972.98
1. Saint Lucia
ISBN 978-0-7614-2569-4
First published 1997
This describes the geography, history, government, economy, environment, people, and culture of Saint Lucia
Includes glossary and bibliographical references

Pang, Guek-Cheng, 1950-
Grenada; 2nd ed.; Marshall Cavendish Benchmark 2011 144p il map (Cultures of the world) lib bdg $42.79
Grades: 5 6 7 8   972.98
1. Grenada
ISBN 978-1-6087-0216-9; 1-6087-0216-2
LC 2010019807
First published 2001

Provides information on the geography, history, wildlife, governmental structure, economy, cultural diversity,
peoples, religion, and culture of Grenada.

Includes glossary and bibliographical references

973   United States

Addasi, Maha

A **kid's** guide to Arab American history; more than 50
activities. by Yvonne Wakim Dennis and Maha Addasi. 1st
ed. Chicago Review Press 2013 xx, 204 p.p ill. (paperback) $16.95

Grades: 4 5 6 7   973

1. Arab Americans -- History 2. Arab Americans --
Social life and customs 3. Arab Americans -- History
-- Juvenile literature 4. Arab Americans -- History
-- Study and teaching -- Activity programs -- Juvenile
literature

ISBN 1613740174; 9781613740170

LC 2012035758

This book by Yvonne Wakim Dennis and Maha Addasi
"provides a contemporary as well as historical look at the
people and experiences that have shaped Arab American
culture. Each chapter focuses on a different group of Arab
Americans including those of Lebanese, Syrian, Palestinian,
Jordanian, Egyptian, Iraqi, and Yemeni descent and features
more than 50 fun activities that highlight their distinct arts,
games, clothing, and food." (Publisher's note)

America the Beautiful, third series. Children's Press 2007
52v il map lib bdg set $851.20

Grades: 4 5 6 7   973

1. United States

ISBN 978-0-531-20407-8 lib bdg; 0-531-20407-3
lib bdg

Replaces America the Beautiful, second series, published 1998-2001; Original series published 1987-1992

This series describes the geography, history, people,
economy, and government of each state

"Most students should be able to satisfy their information needs with these polished new editions, and the copious
extras and lively presentation will help keep them interested
too." Booklist

Armstrong, Jennifer

★ The **American** story; 100 true tales from American
history. illustrated by Roger Roth. Alfred A. Knopf 2006
358p il map $34.95; lib bdg $39.99

Grades: 4 5 6 7   973

1. United States -- History

ISBN 0-375-81256-3; 0-375-91256-8 lib bdg

LC 2005-34822

"This large, fully illustrated compendium features 100
stories, familiar and lesser known, drawn from America's
past and arranged in chronological order. . . . Thanks to writing that is consistently good and sometimes excellent, the
tales will certainly hold readers' attention, and brightening
nearly every page are lively drawings enhanced by watercolor washes." Booklist

Includes bibliographical references

Bockenhauer, Mark H.

★ **Our** fifty states; by Mark H. Bockenhauer and Stephen F. Cunha; foreword by former president Jimmy Carter.
National Geographic Society 2004 239p il map $25.95;
lib bdg $45.90

Grades: 4 5 6 7   973

1. Reference books 2. United States

ISBN 0-7922-6402-9; 0-7922-6992-6 lib bdg

LC 2004-1190

This "book is organized by regions: the Northeast,
Southeast, Midwest, Southwest, and West, with a map of
each region and a short history. Four pages are devoted to
each state and include basic facts and a map. The full-color
photographs are outstanding. Reproductions of archival illustrations depict four important events from each state's
history. The final sections offer a paragraph about each of the
territories and a page of facts and figures about the United
States." SLJ

Includes bibliographical references

Buckley, Susan

★ **Journeys** for freedom; a new look at America's
story. [by] Susan Buckley and Elspeth Leacock; illustrations by Rodica Prato. Houghton Mifflin Co. 2006 48p il
map $17

Grades: 4 5 6 7   973

1. United States -- History

ISBN 978-0-618-22323-7; 0-618-22323-1

LC 2004000974

This "history focuses on 20 individuals' quest for freedom across U.S. history. Some . . . will be familiar, but most
will not. The stories, both varied and fascinating, often go
beyond the personal. . . . Running along the bottom of each
double-page spread is a pictorial map keyed to the text. . . .
The authors make excellent use of primary sources. . . . As
powerful as it is useful." Booklist

Kids make history; a new look at America's story. [by]
Susan Buckley and Elspeth Leacock; Illustrations by Randy
Jones. Houghton Mifflin 2006 48p il $17

Grades: 4 5 6 7   973

1. United States -- History

ISBN 978-0-618-22329-9; 0-618-22329-0

LC 2005036309

"This book introduces 20 children in extraordinary
times, starting in 1607 with Pocahontas and ending in 2001
with 9/11 as experienced by high school senior Jukay Hsu.
Laura Ingalls Wilder; John Rankin, Jr.; and Susie Baker,
a young slave celebrating her independence in 1863, are
among those included. The text and the highly detailed
watercolor illustrations are married with numbers in small
red boxes keyed to both elements for clarification. . . . A
good browsing choice for children interested in American
history." SLJ

Cooper, Ilene

★ **Jack**; the early years of John F. Kennedy. by Ilene
Cooper. 1st ed. Penguin Group USA 2013 168 p. ill.
(paperback) $12.99

Grades: 5 6 7 8 9 10 11 12   973

1. Catholics 2. Presidents 3. Presidents -- United
States

ISBN 0147510317; 9780147510310

LC 2002075912

This book by Ilene Cooper offers a "portrait of [John F.] Kennedy's "youth and the forces that shaped it. . . . Readers discover what it was like for Jack to grow up under the paradoxical influences of privilege and prejudice. His father's wealth . . . couldn't remove the perceived taint of the family's Irish Catholic heritage . . . . To compensate, Joseph and Rose Kennedy pushed their children to excel at everything they did," leading to rivalry between Jack and his brother Joe. (Horn Book Magazine)

"Intelligent design and numerous fabulous, well-placed, and well-captioned black-and-white photographs enrich Cooper's clear prose. . . . This sensitive, well-researched biography will enhance any collection." Voice Youth Advocates

Includes bibliographical references and index.

Croy, Elden
   United States. National Geographic 2010 64p il map (Countries of the world) lib bdg $27.90
   Grades: 4 5 6 7   973
   1. United States
   ISBN 978-1-4263-0632-7 lib bdg; 1-4263-0632-6 lib bdg
This describes the geography, nature, history, people and culture, government and economy of the United States.

"The information is substantial but not overwhelming. The [text is] clear, and the discussion points are well chosen. . . . [The text is] complemented with stunning photographs." SLJ

Hoose, Phillip M.
   ★ We were there, too! young people in U.S. history. [by] Phillip Hoose. Farrar, Straus & Giroux 2001 264p il $28
   Grades: 5 6 7 8   973
   1. Youth 2. Children 3. Youth -- United States -- Biography -- Anecdotes -- Juvenile literature 4. Children -- United States -- Biography -- Anecdotes -- Juvenile literature
   ISBN 0-374-38252-2
                              LC 99-89052
Biographies of dozens of young people who made a mark in American history, including explorers, planters, spies, cowpunchers, sweatshop workers, and civil rights workers

"A treasure chest of history come to life, this is an inspired collection. . . . Because the book is packed with historical documents, evocatively illustrated . . . and full of eyewitness quotations, it should prove valuable to young historians and researchers." SLJ

Includes bibliographical references

Isaacs, Sally Senzell
   Colonists and independence. Kingfisher 2011 32p il map (All about America)
   Grades: 3 4 5 6   973
   1. United States -- History
   ISBN 0-7534-6513-2 pa; 0-7534-6581-7; 978-0-7534-6513-4 pa; 978-0-7534-6581-3
This book covers U.S. history from 1600 to 1800.

This "visually appealing [title] effectively [combines] paintings, engravings, primary documents, and photographs with cartoon illustrations. The eye-catching [layout includes] different font sizes, bold type, and text boxes to highlight different pieces of information. The content is interesting and pithy." SLJ

Includes glossary and bibliographical references

★ **It's** my state [series] Second ed.; Marshall Cavendish Benchmark 2010 18v il map lib bdg set $564.43
   Grades: 3 4 5   973
   1. United States
   ISBN 978-1-60870-044-8 group 1
   Series first published 2003-2007

"These information-packed updates will be great resources both for kids doing reports as well as for families who are planning a trip. . . . Each chapter is full of interesting facts, entertaining details, and fun quotes. The texts are accessible, straightforward, and clear, and are broken up on each page by a colorful photo, graph, time line, or map." SLJ

Johnston, Robert D.
   ★ The **making** of America; the history of the United States from 1492 to the present. Robert D. Johnston; with a foreword by Douglas Brinkley. Revised ed. National Geographic 2010 240 p. ill. (chiefly col.), col. maps (hardcover) $29.95; (library) $38.90
   Grades: 5 6 7 8   973
   1. United States -- History
   ISBN 9781426306631; 1426306636; 9781426306655; 1426306652
                              LC 2011401219
   First published 2002
   Includes bibliographical references (p. 226-234) and index.

"This energetically written and profusely illustrated history remains one of the top-drawer single-volume accounts of the founding and growth of the U.S. for middle grade students. The previous edition ended with 9/11; here, into the same page count, Johnston fits Hurricane Katrina, the wars in Iraq and Afghanistan, Barack Obama's election, and other major events." Booklist

King, David C.
   ★ **Children's** encyclopedia of American history. DK Pub. 2003 304p il map $29.99
   Grades: 5 6 7 8   973
   1. Reference books 2. United States -- History -- Encyclopedias
   ISBN 0-7894-8330-0
                              LC 2002-73388
   Full-color maps, photographs, and paintings illustrate a comprehensive reference guide to American history

"A visually enticing and textually fascinating survey." SLJ

★ **Junior** Worldmark encyclopedia of the states; [Timothy L. Gall and Susan Bevan Gall, editors] 5th ed.; Thomson Gale 2007 4v il map set $235
   Grades: 5 6 7 8 9 10   973
   1. Reference books
   ISBN 978-1-4144-1106-4 set; 1-4144-1106-5 set
                              LC 2007003910
   First published 1996
   This reference "includes facts and details on every state in the U.S., including the District of Columbia and U.S. dependencies. Entries cover the geography, history, politics, economy and other facts about each state. Alphabetically

arranged entries feature . . . subheadings for each state. . . .
An index of people, places and subjects [is included]." Publisher's note

Includes bibliographical references

Kuntz, Lynn

★ **Celebrate** the USA; hands-on history activities for kids. [by] Lynn Kuntz; illustrated by Mark A. Hicks. Gibbs Smith, Publisher 2007 80p il map pa $7.95

Grades: 3 4 5   973

1. United States -- History

ISBN 978-1-58685-846-9 pa; 1-58685-846-7 pa

LC 2006021953

This is a "fact-filled, fun-to-read compendium of American history and 25 related activities. . . . Many topics and fascinating facts are covered in brief, sometimes humorous explanations. Coverage includes the early immigrants, how America got its name, Native Americans, the 13 colonies, currency, songs, and holidays." SLJ

Leacock, Elspeth

★ **Journeys** in time; a new atlas of American history. [by] Elspeth Leacock and Susan Buckley; illustrations by Rodica Prato. Houghton Mifflin 2001 48p il maps $15; pa $6.95

Grades: 4 5 6 7   973

1. United States -- Historical geography

ISBN 0-395-97956-0; 0-618-31114-9 pa

LC 00-40803

Each double-page spread of this book "takes an individual who was part of a historic movement (such as the Underground Railroad or immigration) and gives a brief narrative outlining his or her circumstances. Added to the text are sequential numbers that indicate major events in each of the twenty journeys. A double-page location map traces the routes each took, using illustrative vignettes marked with corresponding numbers that reference the text." Horn Book

Leedy, Loreen

Celebrate the 50 states; written and illustrated by Loreen Leedy. Holiday House 1999 32p il maps hardcover o.p. pa $6.95

Grades: K 1 2 3   973

1. United States -- Miscellanea -- Juvenile literature

ISBN 0-8234-1431-0; 0-8234-1631-3 pa

LC 99-10986

Introduces statistics, emblems, notable cities, products, and other facts about the fifty states, United States territories, and Washington, D.C.

"Brightly colored and amusingly designed, this is a simple yet winning introduction to the U.S." Booklist

Moberg, Julia

Presidential pets; by Julia Moberg; illustrated by Jeff Albrecht. Charlesbridge Pub. 2012 95 p. col. ill. (reinforced) $14.95

Grades: 3 4 5   973

1. Presidents -- United States -- Juvenile literature 2. Presidents' pets -- United States -- Juvenile literature 3. Pets -- United States -- Juvenile literature 4. Presidents -- United States -- Biography -- Juvenile literature

ISBN 9781936140794

LC 2011047785

In this book by Julia Moberg readers "will discover that all our chief executives but one, from Washington to Obama, have owned a variety of pets -- and, in some cases, been owned by them. In addition to the familiar dogs, cats and birds, some unusual First Animals have included goats, mice, bears, zebras, hyenas, lions, snakes, rats and tigers. . . Brief details about each president's life and term [and] a 'Tell Me More!' feature with tidbits of trivia . . . supplement the pet facts." (Kirkus)

Pinkney, Andrea Davis

Hand in hand; ten Black men who changed America. by Andrea Davis Pinkney; paintings by Brian Pinkney. Disney/Jump at the Sun 2012 243 p. $19.99

Grades: 4 5 6 7   973

1. Biography 2. United States -- History 3. African Americans -- Biography 4. African Americans -- Biography -- Juvenile literature 5. African American men -- Biography -- Juvenile literature 6. Social change -- United States -- History -- Juvenile literature

ISBN 1423142578; 9781423142577

LC 2011051348

Coretta Scott King Author Book Award (2013)

Boston Globe-Horn Book Honor: Nonfiction (2013).

In this book, Andrea Davis Pinkney profiles "ten influential black men--including Frederick Douglass, W.E.B. Du Bois, Thurgood Marshall, Jackie Robinson, and Martin Luther King Jr." She presents "descriptions of each man's influence on civil rights, culture, art, or politics. . . . An examination of Barack Obama's life and presidential election carries readers into the present day, placing the achievements of those who came before him into perspective." (Publishers Weekly)

Includes bibliographical references and index.

Provensen, Alice

The **buck** stops here; the presidents of the United States. 20th anniversary ed.; Viking 2010 un il $18.99

Grades: 2 3 4   973

1. Presidents -- United States

ISBN 978-0-670-01252-7; 0-670-01252-1

First published 1990

"Provensen updates her compendium of presidential portraits to include Clinton, Bush, and Obama. Rhyming couplets serve as footers beneath detailed earth-toned watercolor illustrations that fill each page with miniature scenes featuring campaign slogans, historical events with time line dates, and major accomplishments and inopportune failures. . . . This is an excellent introduction to America's leaders." SLJ

Rubel, David

★ **Scholastic** encyclopedia of the presidents and their times; by David Rubel. Scholastic 1994 vii, 216 p.p ill. (some col.), col. maps (hardcover) $24.99

Grades: 5 6 7 8   973

1. Presidents -- United States -- Encyclopedias 2. United States -- History -- Juvenile literature 3. United States/Biography/Dictionaries 4. Presidents/United States/Dictionaries 5. Biography, Collective/Juvenile literature 6. United States/History/Juvenile literature 7. Children's literature/Works/Grades two through six 8. Children's literature/Works/Preschool through grade two 9. Presidents/United States/Dictionaries/Juvenile

literature

ISBN 0545499852; 9780545499859

LC 93011810

Includes index.

This book is an encyclopedia of the U.S. presidency. It "begins each president's entry with a list including birth and death dates, party, vice president, and nickname, and then describes key elements of each man's presidency. Short sidebars discuss famous people and events of the time." (Cobblestone Magazine)

An "examination of the political and personal lives of U.S. Presidents that begins with George Washington and ends halfway through Bill Clinton's current term in office." SLJ

Smith, David J.

★ **If** America were a village; a book about the people of the United States. written by David J. Smith; illustrated by Shelagh Armstrong. Kids Can Press 2009 32p il $18.95

Grades: 3 4 5   973

1. United States

ISBN 978-1-55453-344-2; 1-55453-344-9

This "offers a thought-provoking perspective on the people who make up America. Organized by overarching questions such as 'Where do we come from?' and 'What do we use?' the text illustrates the ethnic divisions, income levels and material consumption (among other categories) of Americans—were a theoretical village containing only 100 people. . . . Armstrong's cheerful, smudgy paintings balance the text's heaviness." Publ Wkly

Talbott, Hudson

★ **United** tweets of America; 50 state birds; their stories, their glories. [by] Hudson Talbott. G.P. Putnam's Sons 2008 un il $17.99

Grades: 3 4 5   973

1. State birds

ISBN 978-0-399-24520-6; 0-399-24520-0

LC 2007019419

"In this sly, comic, and irreverent book, loaded with hilarious puns and parodies about our 50 state birds, words and images deliver bits of history, folklore, and geography about each state. . . . Talbott's colored pencil and mixed-media illustrations ably combine the cartoon uproar with a sense of the individuality of the feathered creatures. . . . Clever, refeshing, and fun." Booklist

Tarrant-Reid, Linda

★ **Discovering** Black America; from the age of exploration to the twenty-first century. Linda Tarrant-Reid. Abrams Books for Young Readers 2012 xi, 244 p.p ill. (some col.), col. maps (hardcover) $29.95

Grades: 4 5 6   973

1. Blacks -- History 2. United States -- History -- 1775-1783, Revolution 3. United States -- History -- 1861-1865, Civil War -- Juvenile fiction 4. African Americans -- History -- Juvenile literature 5. African Americans -- Biography -- Juvenile literature

ISBN 9780810970984

LC 2011052201

Author Linda Tarrant-Reid presents a book on "African-American history, beginning with accounts of black explorers before the settlement of North America . . . [The book] includes major historical events . . . [such as] the American

Revolution . . . [and] the period following the Civil War and Reconstruction . . . The societal changes brought on by World War II and the civil rights movement [are presented] . . . [E]xchanges between Malcolm X and Martin Luther King . . . [and] the election of President Barack Obama and the challenges facing the first black president" are also described. (Kirkus)

Includes bibliographical references and index.

The **United** States: past and present [series] Rosen Central 2010 52v il map set $1,378

Grades: 3 4 5 6   973

1. United States

ISBN 978-1-4358-9573-7

"These attractive overviews cover the geography, history, government, economy, and famous people in each state. . . . The writing is clear, and facts are plainly stated. . . . Good-quality photos, portraits and relevant paintings illustrate the texts." SLJ

Yaccarino, Dan

Go, go America. Scholastic Press 2008 71p il map $17.99

Grades: 1 2 3 4   973

1. United States 2. Curiosities and wonders -- United States -- Juvenile literature

ISBN 0-439-70338-7; 978-0-439-70338-3

LC 2007-05733

"Readers accompany the fabulous Farley Family on their circuitous car and plane trip across the U.S., from Maine to Hawaii. Mom, Dad, Freddie, Fran, and Fido appear on each pastel-colored page chronicling the fun-filled activities available in each state and learning unusual facts. . . . Each fact is presented in a separate area of the page, with accompanying cartoon art, resulting in a busy but energetic layout. . . . The concluding pages list the states in alphabetical order and give their capitals, dates of statehood, rank in entering the Union, area, bird, flower, insect, tree, motto, and nickname. This book is loads of fun and is certain to stimulate interest in the U.S." SLJ

Yorinks, Adrienne

Quilt of states; quilts by Adrienne Yorinks; written by Adrienne Yorinks and 50 librarians from across the nation; librarian contributions compiled and edited by Jeanette Larson. National Geographic 2005 122p il $19.95

Grades: 5 6 7 8   973

1. United States -- History

ISBN 0-7922-7285-4

LC 2004-17796

"The United States is stitched together chronologically in this stunning book that features a quilted spread for each state. Yorinks enlisted a librarian from each state to contribute a short entry to point up a few significant facts that add to the tapestry of the emerging nation. . . . The quilted representations are not only artistically intricate and beautiful, but also informative. A handsome book to linger over and learn from." SLJ

973.09   Presidents -- United States

Bausum, Ann

★ **Our** Country's Presidents; All You Need to Know About the Presidents, From George Washington to Barack Obama. by Ann Bausum; foreword by President Barack Obama. 4th ed. National Geographic 2013 223 p. ill., maps (hardcover) $24.95

Grades: 5 6 7 8   **973.09**
  1. Presidents -- United States -- Encyclopedias 2. Presidents -- United States -- Juvenile literature
  ISBN 1426310897; 9781426310898

LC 2009290293

First published 2001

This book by Ann Bausum looks at U.S. presidents. The text shares "facts about the men's personal lives, humorous incidents, political backgrounds, records, struggles, battles, successes, what they are most famous for, events that occurred during their administrations, and memorable quotes." (School Library Journal)

"This exceedingly attractive offering is . . . chock-full of information, presented . . . in such an inviting manner that children will enjoy paging through, even if there's no school report looming. . . . Full of interesting tidbits as well as solid information." Booklist

Includes bibliographical references

Gherman, Beverly

First mothers; written by Beverly Gherman; illustrated by Julie Downing. Clarion Books 2012 60 p. col. ill. (hardcover) $17.99

Grades: 3 4 5   **973.09**
  1. Biography 2. Mother-child relationship 3. Presidents -- United States
  ISBN 0547223013; 9780547223018

LC 2012930747

Author Beverly Gherman presents information on the mothers of past U.S. presidents. "Franklin Pierce's mother loved to shock her Puritan neighbors in New Hampshire . . . William McKinley's mother snatched roses from a train car to carry to her son's inauguration. The mother of five-star general Dwight Eisenhower was a pacifist. These are among the details Gherman . . . unearths in this collection of profiles of the mothers of each of the U.S. presidents." (Publishers Weekly)

Rhatigan, Joe

White House kids; the perks, pleasures, problems, and pratfalls of the Presidents' children. Joe Rhatigan; with illustrations by Jay Shin. Charlesbridge Pub. 2012 96 p. ill. (chiefly col.) $14.95

Grades: 5 6 7 8   **973.09**
  1. Presidents -- United States -- Family 2. Presidents -- United States -- Children 3. Children of presidents -- United States 4. Children of presidents -- United States -- Biography
  ISBN 1936140802; 9781936140800

LC 2011045090

This book presents "an overview of the young occupants of the White House . . . [and] details the perks and downfalls of being a president's child. Information on pets, favorite games and activities . . . and education of presidential offspring is . . . presented. [Joe] Rhatigan explores the press's and the public's fascination with the children . . . as well as

the scrutiny and negative press endured by Amy Carter and Chelsea Clinton." (School Library Journal)

"An inviting collection of insightful, interesting and often wacky and weird facts and stories about U.S. presidents and their families." Kirkus

Includes bibliographical references and index

973.1   Early history to 1607

Hernandez, Roger E.

New Spain: 1600-1760s. Marshall Cavendish Benchmark 2009 79p il map (Hispanic America) lib bdg $34.21

Grades: 4 5 6 7   **973.1**
  1. Spaniards -- United States 2. Southwestern States -- History
  ISBN 978-0-7614-2936-4 lib bdg; 0-7614-2936-0 lib bdg

"Provides comprehensive information on the history of Spanish exploration in the United States." Publisher's note

Includes glossary and bibliographical references

973.2   Colonial period, 1607-1775

Fishkin, Rebecca Love

English colonies in America. Compass Point Books 2009 48p il map (We the people) lib bdg $26.60

Grades: 4 5 6   **973.2**
  ISBN 978-0-7565-3838-5

LC 2008007210

This is a history of English colonies in North America.

This provides "solid background matter and introduce key people and vocabulary." SLJ

Includes glossary and bibliographical references

Huey, Lois Miner

American archaeology uncovers the earliest English colonies. Marshall Cavendish Benchmark 2009 64p il map (American archaeology) lib bdg $31.36

Grades: 4 5 6 7   **973.2**
  1. Excavations (Archeology) -- United States
  ISBN 978-0-7614-4264-6 lib bdg; 0-7614-4264-2 lib bdg

LC 2008050259

This describes how archeologists have learned about the history of early English colonists in America at Jamestown, Popham Colony, and Roanoke

"Huey enthusiastically brings . . . [this era] to life through artifacts and field research. . . . [The volume begins with an] introduction that defines 'historical archaeology' and explains its value in terms simple enough for lower-elementary readers to comprehend, yet detailed enough for older children to enjoy, an approach followed in the remaining chapters. . . . Huey's focus on American history, which is broken down into small, manageable chunks, is sure to entice budding historians." SLJ

Includes glossary and bibliographical references

Mara, Wil

The **farmer**. Marshall Cavendish Benchmark 2010 48p il (Colonial people) lib bdg $29.93

Grades: 3 4 5 6   **973.2**
  1. Farm life -- United States
  ISBN 978-0-7614-4797-9; 0-7614-4797-0
                     LC 2009019580
This describes the life of a colonial farmer and his importance to the community, as well as everyday life, responsibilities, and social practices during that time.

"The type font, just slightly larger than usual, makes the text very visually appealing. . . . [The] book is liberally illustrated with artwork dating from the colonial period . . . [and] information boxes offer supplemental material." Libr Media Connect

Includes glossary and bibliographical references

McNeese, Tim
  Colonial America, 1543-1763. Chelsea House 2010 136p il map (Discovering U.S. history) $35
Grades: 5 6 7 8   **973.2**
  1. United States -- History -- 1600-1775, Colonial period
  ISBN 978-1-60413-349-3; 1-60413-349-X
                     LC 2008055170
This history of Colonial America "begins with a chapter on 'Rivals for North America' and ends with 'The Fight for the Ohio Country.' . . . [The] book has an excellent chronology; rich sidebars; and numerous well-captioned illustrations, maps, and photos that enhance the texts. [This book provides a] satisfying [introduction] to American history for students." SLJ

Includes glossary and bibliographical references

Tunis, Edwin
  ★ **Colonial** living; written and illustrated by Edwin Tunis. Johns Hopkins Univ. Press 1999 155p il pa $18.95
Grades: 5 6 7 8   **973.2**
  1. United States -- Social life and customs -- 1600-1775, Colonial period
  ISBN 0-8018-6227-2
                     LC 99-22591
A reprint of the title first published 1957 by World Pub. Co.

"Common everyday aspects of colonial living from 1564-1770 are highlighted by the detailed descriptions and numerous black and white illustrations of items such as tools, home furnishings, clothing, etc." N Y Public Libr. Ref Books for Child Collect

★ **Colonial** America and the Revolutionary War; the story of the people of the colonies, from early settlers to revolutionary leaders. Laurie Lanzen Harris, editor. Favorable Impressions 2009 399p il map (Biography for beginners) $49
Grades: 2 3 4 5   **973.2**
  1. Reference books 2. United States -- Biography 3. United States -- History -- 1600-1775, Colonial period 4. United States -- History -- 1775-1783, Revolution
  ISBN 978-1-931360-34-0; 1-931360-34-0
                     LC 2008-49193
"This volume is highly recommended for public and school library collections. The affordable price, well-organized basic information, and user-friendly format make it a valuable resource for young researchers." Booklist

Includes glossary

Voices from colonial America [series] National Geographic 2005 18v il map
Grades: 5 6 7 8   **973.2**
Each volume in this series describes the colonial history of a state illustrated with historical maps and reprints of period artwork, and includes excerpts from first-person accounts.

"Presented in clear, succinct text . . . this resource, containing a great deal of information, will be a welcome addition to history classes and a great source for report writers." Booklist [review of New Jersey volume]

Includes bibliographical references

973.3   Periods of Revolution and Confederation, 1775-1789

Adler, David A.
  ★ **B.** Franklin, printer. Holiday House 2001 126p il lib bdg $19.95
Grades: 4 5 6 7   **973.3**
  1. Authors 2. Diplomats 3. Inventors 4. Statesmen 5. Scientists 6. Writers on science 7. Members of Congress 8. Statesmen -- United States 9. Printers -- United States -- Biography -- Juvenile literature 10. Inventors -- United States -- Biography -- Juvenile literature 11. Statesmen -- United States -- Biography -- Juvenile literature 12. Scientists -- United States -- Biography -- Juvenile literature
  ISBN 0-8234-1675-5
                     LC 2001-24535
This "surveys Benjamin Franklin's life as a printer, a scientist, an inventor, a writer, and a statesman. . . . Throughout the book, details, anecdotes, and quotations bring the man's portrait into clearer focus, while period illustrations . . . help readers envision the background of his times." Booklist

Includes bibliographical references

Allen, Thomas B.
  Remember Valley Forge; patriots, Tories, and Redcoats tell their stories. [by] Thomas B. Allen. National Geographic 2007 61p il map $17.95; lib bdg $27.90
Grades: 5 6 7 8   **973.3**
  1. Generals 2. Presidents 3. United States -- History -- 1775-1783, Revolution 4. Valley Forge (Pa.) -- History
  ISBN 978-1-4263-0149-0; 978-1-4263-0150-6 lib bdg
                     LC 2007024821
The author "recounts here the activities of Washington and his soldiers during the winter of 1777-8, spent regrouping at Valley Forge, Pennsylvania. . . . Allen's strength is his attention to military details and strategies, but his account is clearly presented and succinctly written as well. . . . Illustrated with reproductions of period artwork, drawings, maps, and a few contemporary photographs." Booklist

Anderson, Laurie Halse
  ★ **Independent** dames; what you never knew about the women and girls of the American Revolution. by Laurie Halse Anderson; illustrated by Matt Faulkner. Simon & Schuster Books for Young Readers 2008 37p il $16.99
Grades: 3 4 5   **973.3**
  1. Women -- United States -- History 2. United States -- History -- 1775-1783, Revolution 3. Girls -- United

States -- History -- Juvenile literature 4. Women -- United States -- History -- Juvenile literature
ISBN 978-0-689-85808-6; 0-689-85808-6

LC 2007042643

"The stories of 22 'Revolutionary Grandmothers' take center stage in this well-illustrated volume. . . . Faulkner's ink-and-watercolor illustrations are exuberant, often amusing, and filled with crosshatching and dialogue balloons. The spreads are busy and information-packed, and readers will be both engaged by and educated about this critical period." SLJ

Includes bibliographical references

Blair, Margaret Whitman

Liberty or death; the surprising story of runaway slaves who sided with the British during the American Revolution. National Geographic 2010 64p il map lib bdg $27.90
Grades: 5 6 7 8   **973.3**
1. African American soldiers 2. Slavery -- United States 3. Freedmen -- Juvenile literature 4. Fugitive slaves -- Juvenile literature 5. African American loyalists -- Juvenile literature 6. African Americans -- History -- Juvenile literature
ISBN 978-1-4263-0590-0 lib bdg; 1-4263-0590-7 lib bdg

LC 2009-26853

"Blair provides a well-researched account of slaves in Virginia who, beginning in 1775, fled to the British. . . . Though told in a matter-of-fact tone, the story is often heartwrenching. . . . Colorful reproductions of period paintings, prints, and documents illustrate the clearly written text. . . . A fine and singular addition to American history collections." Booklist

Includes bibliographical references

Bobrick, Benson

★ Fight for freedom; the American Revolutionary War. Atheneum Books for Young Readers 2004 96p il map $22.95
Grades: 5 6 7 8   **973.3**
1. United States -- History -- 1775-1783, Revolution
ISBN 0-689-86422-1

LC 2003-25548

"This large-format volume profiles significant individuals and discusses the progress of the Revolutionary War. . . . Printed in color, most of the illustrations are period paintings and prints. . . . Students will find the book a well-organized and clearly written introduction to the war." Booklist

Includes glossary and bibliographical references

Brenner, Barbara

★ If you were there in 1776. Bradbury Press 1994 136p il $17.95
Grades: 3 4 5 6   **973.3**
1. United States -- History -- 1775-1783, Revolution
ISBN 0-02-712322-7

LC 93-24060

Demonstrates how the concepts and principles expressed in the Declaration of Independence were drawn from the experiences of living in America in the late eighteenth century, with emphasis given to how children lived on a New England farm, a Southern plantation, and the frontier

"The author's inclusion of details of how peoples' lives began to change as a result of the Revolution and her acces-

sible style are the selling points here. Both budding historians and report writers will find this title worth their time." SLJ

Includes bibliographical references

Brown, Don

★ Henry and the cannons; an extraordinary true story of the American Revolution. Don Brown. Roaring Brook Press 2013 32 p. (hardcover) $16.99
Grades: K 1 2 3 4   **973.3**
1. Picture books for children 2. United States -- History -- 1775-1783, Revolution 3. Military roads -- Massachusetts -- History -- 18th century
ISBN 1596432667; 9781596432666

LC 2012013450

This children's picture book recounts the difficulties faced by the American armies in the winter of 1775. "British soldiers occupy Boston, and the Americans have no way to dislodge them. Despite the seeming impossibility of transporting heavy cannons over snowy roads, across icy lakes and through forbidding forests, young Henry Knox, a bookseller and militia member, volunteered to get the job done." (Kirkus)

★ Let it begin here! April 19, 1775, the day the American Revolution began. Roaring Brook Press 2008 un il (Actual times) $17.95
Grades: 2 3 4   **973.3**
1. Concord (Mass.), Battle of, 1775 2. Lexington (Mass.), Battle of, 1775 3. United States -- History -- 1775-1783, Revolution
ISBN 978-1-59643-221-5; 1-59643-221-7

LC 2008-11221

"Brown distills the fairly complex story of the beginning of the American Revolution in a manner that deftly balances information and intrigue. . . . Equally impressive and vital to the success of this picture book are Brown's compositions which sometimes dramatically, sometimes whimsically intersect with the text. . . . [This is] rousing, accessible, and splendidly executed." Booklist

Carson, Mary Kay

Did it all start with a snowball fight? and other questions about the American Revolution. by Mary Kay Carson. Sterling Pub. Co., Inc. 2012 31 p. $12.95
Grades: 3 4 5   **973.3**
1. Boston Massacre, 1770 2. Picture books for children 3. United States -- History -- 1775-1783, Revolution
ISBN 1402796269; 9781402787348; 9781402796265

LC 2011019963

This children's book offers information about the American Revolution. "Starting with the Boston Massacre (the snowball fight in question) and ending with the Treaty of Paris, the facts are related in a question-and-answer format, in an arrangement that's more topical than chronological (though there is a . . . time line at the end). Each spread has one or two questions and answers on one side and a captioned, colorful full-page painting or cartoon on the other." (School Library Journal)

Includes bibliographical references and index

Crompton, Samuel Willard

The **Boston** Tea Party; colonists protest the British government. by Russell Freeman; illustrated by Peter Malone. Holiday House 2011 39 p. (hardcover) $17.95

Grades: 3 4 5   **973.3**

   1. Boston (Mass.) -- History 2. Boston Tea Party, 1773 -- Juvenile literature 3. United States -- History -- 1775-1783, Revolution -- Juvenile literature

   ISBN 9780823422661; 0823422666

                     LC 2010028726

This children's book, by Russell Freedman, illustrated by Peter Malone, tells the story of the Boston Tea Party. "[T]he Boston Tea Party of 1773 has come to stand for the determination of American colonists to control their own destinies." The book tells the events from "the arrival of the ships full of controversial taxed tea in Boston Harbor, through the . . . protest meetings at the Old South Church, to the . . . dumping 226 chests of fine tea into the harbor on December 16." (Publisher's note)

Includes bibliographical references and index.

Decker, Timothy

For liberty; the story of the Boston Massacre. Calkins Creek 2009 un il $17.95

Grades: 4 5 6   **973.3**

   1. Boston Massacre, 1770

   ISBN 978-1-59078-608-6; 1-59078-608-4

"This handsomely designed picture book begins the story of the Boston Massacre by filling in the background. . . . The book concludes with the soldiers' trial and their lawyer, John Adams, reflecting on the protection of liberty. . . . The book does quite a good job of conveying how the actions and emotions of those on both sides escalated toward violence and death. Using parallel lines, crosshatching, and other texturing effects, the black-and-white drawings hold attention. . . . A fine, balanced look at an important event." Booklist

Figley, Marty Rhodes

John Greenwood's journey to Bunker Hill; illustrated by Craig Orback. Millbrook Press 2010 48p il (History speaks: picture books plus reader's theater) lib bdg $27.93

Grades: 2 3 4   **973.3**

   1. Readers' theater 2. Bunker Hill (Boston, Mass.), Battle of, 1775

   ISBN 978-1-58013-673-0 lib bdg; 1-58013-673-7 lib bdg

                     LC 2009050063

This tells the story of fifteen-year-old John Greenwood, who fought at the Battle of Bunker Hill.

This "title begins with a well-illustrated narrative and concludes with a tip sheet for performing Reader's Theater as well as a list of characters, a script, and a pronunciation guide. . . . [This book will] make history come alive in a unique and interesting way." Libr Media Connect

Includes bibliographical references

Fleming, Thomas J.

Everybody's revolution; a new look at the people who won America's freedom. [by] Thomas Fleming. Scholastic Nonfiction 2006 96p il $19.99

Grades: 4 5 6 7   **973.3**

   ISBN 0-439-63404-0

                     LC 2005051814

A history of the American Revolution, focusing on the roles played by women, young people, and various ethnic groups.

"With an open layout and clean typeface, this clearly written title is attractive and inviting. . . . Fleming's sound offering is an excellent starting point for discussions of the implications of the Revolutionary War in terms of freedom for all people." SLJ

Includes glossary and bibliographical references

Fradin, Dennis B.

The **Boston** Tea Party; [by] Dennis Brindell Fradin. Marshall Cavendish Benchmark 2007 45p il map (Turning points in U.S. history) lib bdg $31.36

Grades: 3 4 5   **973.3**

   1. Boston Tea Party, 1773

   ISBN 978-0-7614-2035-4

                     LC 2006025344

Beginning with British debt for its colonial wars and ending with the battles of Lexington and Concord, this is an account of the American colonists' rebellion against taxes on British tea

Includes glossary and bibliographical references

The **Declaration** of Independence; [by] Dennis Brindell Fradin. Marshall Cavendish Benchmark 2007 45p il map (Turning points in U.S. history) lib bdg $31.36

Grades: 3 4 5   **973.3**

   1. United States -- Declaration of Independence 2. United States -- Politics and government -- 1775-1783, Revolution

   ISBN 978-0-7614-2129-0 lib bdg; 0-7614-2129-7 lib bdg

                     LC 2005016023

This "describes the unrest that led up to the signing of the famous document, how Jefferson composed it, and the uncertainty surrounding the vote for independence. . . . The clear, concise, and dynamic style of writing simplifies the information without dumbing it down. . . . The photos, paintings, and maps . . . add a wealth of information." SLJ

Includes glossary and bibliographical references

Let it begin here! Lexington & Concord: first battles of the American Revolution. [by] Dennis Brindell Fradin; illustrations by Larry Day. Walker & Co. 2005 un il maps $16.95; lib bdg $17.85

Grades: 2 3 4   **973.3**

   1. Concord (Mass.), Battle of, 1775 2. Lexington (Mass.), Battle of, 1775 3. Concord, Battle of, 1775 -- Juvenile literature 4. Lexington, Battle of, 1775 -- Juvenile literature

   ISBN 0-8027-8945-5; 0-8027-8946-3 lib bdg

                     LC 2004-49473

This is an "account of Paul Revere's actions on the night of April 18, 1775, and the battles in Lexington and Concord on the following day. . . . Well-composed double-page illustrations, ink drawings with watercolor and gouache, highlight the human drama implicit in the text." Booklist

Includes bibliographical references

★ The **signers**; the fifty-six stories behind the Declaration of Independence. [by] Dennis Brindell Fradin; illustrations by Michael McCurdy. Walker & Co. 2002 164p il map $22.95; lib bdg $23.85

Grades: 4 5 6 7 **973.3**

1. Statesmen -- United States 2. Statesmen -- United States -- Biography 3. United States -- Declaration of Independence 4. United States -- Politics and government -- 1775-1783, Revolution

ISBN 0-8027-8849-1; 0-8027-8850-5 lib bdg

LC 2002-66364

Profiles each of the fifty-six men who signed the Declaration of Independence, giving historical information about the colonies they represented. Includes the text of the Declaration and its history

"Fradin gives brief, fascinating glimpses into the people who have been overlooked as well as those with whom readers might be familiar. . . . An excellent resource for report writing." SLJ

Includes bibliographical references

Freedman, Russell

★ **Washington** at Valley Forge. Holiday House 2008 100p il map $24.95

Grades: 5 6 7 8 9 **973.3**

1. Generals 2. Presidents 3. Valley Forge (Pa.) -- History 4. United States -- History -- 1775-1783, Revolution

ISBN 978-0-8234-2069-8; 0-8234-2069-8

LC 2007-52467

NCTE Orbis Pictus Award honor book (2009)

"With his usual clarity of focus and keen eye for telling quotations, Freedman documents how Washington struggled to maintain morale despite hunger, near-nakedness, and freezing conditions. . . . Throughout, high-quality reproductions depict Washington among the men, and with the numerous other influential people who played crucial roles." Booklist

Freedman, Russell, 1929-

★ **Give** me liberty! the story of the Declaration of Independence. Holiday House 2000 90p il $24.95; pa $14.95

Grades: 5 6 7 8 9 10 **973.3**

1. United States -- Declaration of Independence 2. United States -- Politics and government -- 1775-1783, Revolution

ISBN 0-8234-1448-5; 0-8234-1753-0 pa

LC 99-57513

This book describes the events leading up to the Declaration of Independence as well as the personalities and politics behind its framing. Chronology. Annotated bibliography. Index. "Grades five to eight." (Bull Cent Child Books)

"Handsomely designed with a generous and thoughtful selection of period art, the book is dramatic and inspiring." Horn Book

Includes bibliographical references

Fritz, Jean

★ **Why** not, Lafayette? illustrated by Ronald Himler. Putnam 1999 87p il $16.99; pa $5.99

Grades: 5 6 7 8 **973.3**

1. Generals 2. Statesmen 3. Generals -- France -- Biography -- Juvenile literature 4. Generals -- United States -- Biography -- Juvenile literature 5. United States -- History -- Revolution, 1775-1783 -- Biography

-- Juvenile literature

ISBN 0-399-23411-X; 0-698-11882-0 pa

LC 98-31417

Traces the life of the French nobleman who fought for democracy in revolutions in both the United States and France

This biography is "chock-full of quotes, anecdotes, and wry humor." Booklist

Includes bibliographical references

Harness, Cheryl

The **revolutionary** John Adams; written and illustrated by Cheryl Harness. National Geographic Soc. 2003 39p il map $17.95; pa $7.95

Grades: 3 4 5 6 **973.3**

1. Presidents 2. Vice-presidents 3. Presidents -- United States

ISBN 0-7922-6970-5; 0-7922-5491-0 pa

LC 2002-11271

A biography of John Adams with emphasis on his role in the American Revolution

"Harness' warm, friendly, mixed-media illustrations, which range from full-color, double-page spreads to labeled diagrams to black-line silhouettes, will delight children, and quotes from Adams' letters, including many letters to his wife, Abigail, are a bonus. A fascinating book for young history buffs." Booklist

Includes bibliographical references

Herbert, Janis

★ The **American** Revolution for kids; a history with 21 activities. Chicago Review Press 2002 139p il pa $14.95

Grades: 4 5 6 **973.3**

1. United States -- History -- 1775-1783, Revolution

ISBN 1-55652-456-0

LC 2002-7938

Discusses the events of the American Revolution, from the hated Stamp Act and the Boston Tea Party to the British surrender at Yorktown and the writing of the Constitution. Activities include making a tricorn hat and discovering local history

"Achieving a good balance between textual material, illustration, and projects, the book immerses children in the milieu of these years. . . . The directions are detailed enough and adequately illustrated with pencil drawings to make them exciting and easy to follow." SLJ

Includes glossary and bibliographical references

Jules, Jacqueline

Unite or die; how thirteen states became a nation. illustrated by Jef Czekaj. Charlesbridge 2009 48p il $16.95; pa $7.95

Grades: 2 3 4 5 **973.3**

1. Constitutional history -- United States -- Juvenile literature 2. United States -- History -- 1783-1809

ISBN 1-58089-189-6; 1-58089-190-X pa; 978-1-58089-189-9; 978-1-58089-190-5 pa

LC 2008-07229

"Using the conceit of a school play, Unite or Die traces the challenges, conflicts, and compromises that shaped the United States Constitution and brought unity to the states. Ages nine to twelve." (Publisher's note)

"This presentation is written as if it were a school play about the 13 colonies becoming a nation. Told through colorful comic-book illustrations, it stars students dressed as states humorously explaining the path to the writing of the Constitution. The brief text is accompanied by speech balloons expressing the states' multiple, often competing, views. . . . The vividly colored spreads will hold the interest of even middle school students and would be useful to introduce how our form of government was created." SLJ

Includes bibliographical references

Kostyal, K. M.

1776; a new look at revolutionary Williamsburg. by K.M. Kostyal with the Colonial Williamsburg Foundation; photographs by Lori Epstein. National Geographic 2009 48p il $17.95; lib bdg $27.90

Grades: 4 5 6   **973.3**

1. Colonial Williamsburg (Williamsburg, Va.) 2. United States -- History -- 1775-1783, Revolution

ISBN 978-1-4263-0517-7; 1-4263-0517-6; 978-1-4263-0518-4 lib bdg; 1-4263-0518-4 lib bdg

LC 2009-18002

"Clear, distinctive photos add visual appeal to this short history of the American Revolution, written from the point of view of those living in Williamsburg, Virginia's capital in 1776. Kostyal blends political and social history into a readable account of the period, bolstered by informative sidebars, a chronology, and a closing note about the restoration of colonial Williamsburg. . . . The increasing inclusion of nonwhite colonists in the illustrations as well as the text is a welcome trend." Booklist

Includes bibliographical references

Leavitt, Amie Jane

The **Declaration** of Independence in translation; what it really means. by Amie Jane Leavitt. Capstone Press 2009 32p il (Fact finders. Kids' translations) lib bdg $23.93; pa $7.95

Grades: 3 4 5   **973.3**

1. United States -- Declaration of Independence 2. United States -- Politics and government -- 1775-1783, Revolution

ISBN 978-1-4296-1929-5 lib bdg; 1-4296-1929-5 lib bdg; 978-1-4296-2844-0 pa; 1-4296-2844-8 pa

LC 2008-3229

Provides "a nearly line-by-line translation that makes . . . the written word accessible and meaningful." SLJ

Includes glossary and bibliographical references

Maestro, Betsy

Liberty or death; the American Revolution, 1763-1783. illustrated by Giulio Maestro. HarperCollins 2005 64p il map (American story series) $15.99; lib bdg $16.89

Grades: 3 4 5 6   **973.3**

1. United States -- History -- 1775-1783, Revolution

ISBN 0-688-08802-3; 0-688-08803-1 lib bdg

LC 00-54042

The author and illustrator describe "the 20 years leading up to, and fighting, the American Revolution. A simple narrative, largely from the Colonists' perspective, touches on the major events, players, and ideas of the times, beginning with the Stamp Act and ending with Yorktown and the subsequent peace treaty. . . . Full-color ink, colored-pencil, and watercolor illustrations . . . grace the page in a pleasing,

uncluttered way. . . . This book serves as a good introductory overview." SLJ

A **new** nation; the United States, 1783-1815. illustrated by Giulio Maestro. HarperCollins Publishers 2009 64p il map (American story series) $17.99; lib bdg $18.89

Grades: 3 4 5 6   **973.3**

ISBN 978-0-688-16015-9; 0-688-16015-8; 978-0-688-16016-6 lib bdg; 0-688-16016-6 lib bdg

LC 2008-26947

"The Maestros . . . cover a jam-packed 32 years that saw the country more than double in population and, with the Lousiana Purchase, double in size. . . . The abundant pastel artwork breaks up the pages and provides nifty images of the times. . . . Interesting for history buffs, useful for researchers." Booklist

McNeese, Tim

Revolutionary America, 1764-1789; consulting editor, Richard Jensen. Chelsea House 2010 128p il map (Discovering U.S. history) $35

Grades: 5 6 7 8   **973.3**

1. United States -- History -- 1775-1783, Revolution

ISBN 978-1-60413-350-9; 1-60413-350-3

LC 2008-55179

"The information is accurate and easy to understand. Pictures are well placed, and primary sources are included. . . . The maps are well done and there are sidebars with additional information. . . . [This would be good] to have on hand for reports as it is well laid out and easy to use." Libr Media Connect

Includes glossary and bibliographical references

Micklos, John

The **brave** women and children of the American Revolution; [by] John Micklos, Jr. Enslow Publishers 2008 48p il (The Revolutionary War library) lib bdg $17.95

Grades: 3 4 5 6   **973.3**

1. Children -- United States 2. Women -- United States -- History

ISBN 978-0-7660-3019-0 lib bdg; 0-7660-3019-9 lib bdg

LC 2007048510

This describes the roles of women and children in the American Revolution, at home, in business, as spies and messengers, and on the battlefield.

This is "illustrated with historical engravings and photographs. . . . The many sidebars are informative. . . . The well-written text is studded with footnotes, and the appended time line is helpful." Booklist

Includes glossary and bibliographical references

Miller, Brandon Marie

Declaring independence; life during the American Revolution. by Brandon Marie Miller. Lerner Publications Co. 2005 112p il map (People's history) lib bdg $31.93

Grades: 5 6 7 8   **973.3**

1. United States -- History -- 1775-1783, Revolution 2. United States -- Social conditions

ISBN 0-8225-1275-0

LC 2004-17917

This describes the lives of American colonists in the late 1700s and the fight for independence from Great Britain with emphasis on "firsthand accounts, contemporary writings, and official documents. Miller does a good job of chronicling the history, presenting the information in a clear, concise, and well-organized manner." SLJ

Includes bibliographical references

Minor, Wendell

Yankee Doodle America; the spirit of 1776 from A to Z. [by] Wendell Minor. G.P. Putnam's Sons 2006 un il $16.99

Grades: 2 3 4   **973.3**

1. Alphabet 2. United States -- History -- 1775-1783, Revolution

ISBN 0-399-24003-9

          LC 2005025174

"In colonial America, the public houses served as the news hubs of their surrounding areas. . . . Using hand-carved replicas of the signs for these inns and taverns to share facts about the American Revolution, Minor, in concert with master woodworker John Reichling, has created an unusual alphabet book. . . . The factual material is correct, clearly stated, and intriguing." SLJ

Includes bibliographical references

Murphy, Jim

★ The **crossing**; how George Washington saved the American Revolution. Scholastic Press 2010 96p il map $21.99

Grades: 5 6 7 8   **973.3**

1. Generals 2. Presidents 3. Trenton (N.J.), Battle of, 1776

ISBN 978-0-439-69186-4; 0-439-69186-9

          LC 2009-11561

Murphy "again digs into the well of history, this time emerging with a well-researched, absorbing account of the early battles of the Revolutionary War with General George Washington at their center. Enhanced by numerous sepia maps of troop movements, prints, paintings, and portraits of prominent figures, the blow-by-blow narrative begins with the shots fired at Lexington and Concord in 1775 and continues until the tide-turning battles at Trenton and Princeton in early 1777." Publ Wkly

Includes bibliographical references

★ A **young** patriot; the American Revolution as experienced by one boy. Clarion Bks. 1996 101p il maps $16; pa $7.95

Grades: 5 6 7 8   **973.3**

1. Soldiers 2. United States -- History -- 1775-1783, Revolution -- Campaigns -- Juvenile literature

ISBN 0-395-60523-7; 0-395-90019-0 pa

          LC 93-38789

"Using Joseph Plumb Martin's first person account of his participation in the Revolutionary War as primary source material, Murphy intertwines this story of one teenager's life as a soldier with broader information about the Revolution, to put Martin's story in context. The handsome, informative, and fascinating look at American history is illustrated with many period reproductions." Horn Book Guide

Includes bibliographical references

Otfinoski, Steven

The **new** republic: 1760-1840s. Marshall Cavendish Benchmark 2009 79p il map (Hispanic America) lib bdg $23.95

Grades: 4 5 6 7   **973.3**

1. Latinos (U.S.) 2. Florida -- History and 3. Spaniards -- United States 4. Mexico -- History

ISBN 978-0-7614-2938-8 lib bdg; 0-7614-2938-7 lib bdg

          LC 2007-45958

"Provides comprehensive information on the history of the Spanish exploring the United States." Publisher's note

Includes glossary and bibliographical references

Rockwell, Anne F.

They called her Molly Pitcher; by Anne Rockwell; illustrated by Cynthia von Buhler. Knopf 2002 un il $16.95; lib bdg $17.99

Grades: 3 4 5   **973.3**

1. Soldiers 2. Revolutionaries 3. Monmouth, Battle of, Freehold, N.J., 1778 -- Juvenile literature 4. Revolutionaries -- United States -- Biography -- Juvenile literature 5. Women revolutionaries -- United States -- Biography -- Juvenile literature 6. United States -- History -- Revolution, 1775-1783 -- Biography -- Juvenile literature

ISBN 0-679-89187-0; 0-679-99187-5 lib bdg

          LC 2001-29422

A biography of the woman who was named a sergeant in the Continental Army by George Washington for her bravery in the Battle of Monmouth

"The language is inviting, the story, exciting. Von Buhler's illustrations, which appear crackled, as if they were painted during this period, make the book shine." SLJ

Sanders, Nancy I.

America's black founders; revolutionary heroes & early leaders with 21 activities. Chicago Review Press 2010 150p il $16.95

Grades: 4 5 6 7   **973.3**

1. African Americans -- History 2. United States -- History -- 1775-1783, Revolution

ISBN 978-1-55652-811-8; 1-55652-811-6

"This activity-based guide reveals how African Americans played crucial roles in helping the United States gain its independence. Sanders includes well-known figures such as Phillis Wheatley, Crispus Attucks, and James Forten in her narrative, but also enriches traditional accounts of the period by explaining the contributions of lesser-known patriots. . . . Most of the activities help make this period real to young people. . . . Sanders makes excellent use of primary sources." SLJ

Schanzer, Rosalyn

★ **George** vs. George; the American Revolution as seen from both sides. National Geographic 2004 60p il maps $16.95

Grades: 3 4 5 6   **973.3**

1. Generals 2. Presidents 3. Kings 4. United States -- History -- 1775-1783, Revolution

ISBN 0-7922-7349-4

          LC 2003-20843

This book explores how the characters and lives of King George III of England and George Washington affected he progress and outcome of the American Revolution. Bibliography. Index. "Grades four to six." (Bull Cent Child Books)

"A carefully researched, evenhanded narrative with well-crafted, vibrant, watercolor illustrations. . . . This is a lovely book, showing historical inquiry at its best." SLJ

Includes bibliographical references

Sheinkin, Steve

★ **King** George: what was his problem? everything your schoolbooks didn't tell you about the American Revolution. Roaring Brook Press 2008 195p il map $19.95
Grades: 4 5 6   **973.3**
   1. United States -- History -- 1775-1783, Revolution
ISBN 978-1-59643-319-9; 1-59643-319-1
           LC 2007-39999
First published 2005 in paperback by Summer Street Press, in series Storyteller's History, with title: The American Revolution

This history of the American Revolution "features many droll line drawings that suit the tone of the writing and source notes for the extensive quotes. Sheinkin clearly conveys the gravity of events during the Revolutionary period, but he also has the knack of bringing historical people to life and showing what was at stake for them as individuals as well as for the new nation. . . . Vivid storytelling makes this an unusually readable history book." Booklist

Includes bibliographical references

St. George, Judith

★ The **journey** of the one and only Declaration of Independence; illustrated by Will Hillenbrand. Philomel Books 2005 un il $16.99
Grades: 2 3 4   **973.3**
   ISBN 0-399-23738-0
           LC 2004-13567
This decribes how the Declaration of Independence was written and how the document was preserved and displayed throughout American history

"Readers will learn fascinating details. . . . Hillenbrand's lively mixed-media illustrations are a perfect match for the text, filling the pages with visual energy and humor. . . . This well-researched, readable, and well-illustrated book belongs on the shelves of all public and school libraries." SLJ

Includes bibliographical references

Winters, Kay

★ **Colonial** voices; hear them speak. [by] Kay Winters; illustrated by Larry Day. Dutton Children's Books 2008 un il map $17.99
Grades: 3 4 5 6   **973.3**
   1. Boston Tea Party, 1773
ISBN 978-0-525-47872-0; 0-525-47872-8
           LC 2007-28480
"Colonial Bostonians introduce themselves through free-verse vignettes that describe their work and their feelings about the current political situation. As errand boy Ethan moves about the city, he links the people together. . . . The watercolor and ink illustrations add humor and drama through shifting perspectives and well-detailed settings full of period details. . . . A unique presentation for all libraries." SLJ

Includes bibliographical references

973.4   Constitutional period, 1789-1809

Adler, David A.

A **picture** book of Thomas Jefferson; illustrated by John & Alexandra Wallner. Holiday House 1990 un il lib bdg $17.95; pa $6.95
Grades: 1 2 3   **973.4**
   1. Architects 2. Presidents 3. Vice-presidents 4. Essayists 5. Presidents -- United States 6. Biography, Individual -- Juvenile literature
ISBN 0-8234-0791-8 lib bdg; 0-8234-0881-7 pa
           LC 89-20076
Traces the life and achievements of the architect, bibliophile, president, and author of the Declaration of Independence

"The book includes an amazing amount of material. An appealing package with simple language and detailed drawings." Horn Book

Delano, Marfé Ferguson

Master George's people; George Washington, his slaves, and his revolutionary transformation. By Marfe Ferguson Delano. National Geographic 2013 64 p. (hardcover: alk. paper) $18.95
Grades: 4 5 6   **973.4**
   1. Slaves 2. Mount Vernon (Va.: Estate) 3. Slaves -- Virginia -- Mount Vernon (Estate)
ISBN 1426307594; 9781426307591; 9781426307607
           LC 2012024295
This book, by Marfé Ferguson Delano, explores the lives of the slaves owned by U.S. President George Washington at "his Virginia plantation, Mount Vernon. . . . [The book] gives us . . . portraits of cooks, overseers, valets, farm hands, and more . . . interwoven with an extraordinary examination of the conscience of the Father of Our Country." (Publisher's note)

Includes bibliographical references and index

Fradin, Dennis B.

★ **Duel!** Burr and Hamilton's deadly war of words. by Dennis Brindell Fradin; illustrated by Larry Day. Walker & Co. 2008 un il $16.95; lib bdg $17.85
Grades: 3 4 5 6   **973.4**
   1. Statesmen 2. Vice-presidents 3. Secretaries of the treasury 4. Burr-Hamilton Duel, Weehawken, N.J., 1804 -- Juvenile literature
ISBN 978-0-8027-9583-0; 0-8027-9583-8; 978-0-8027-9584-7 lib bdg; 0-8027-9584-6 lib bdg
           LC 2007-37994
"Even children who don't know much about Aaron Burr . . . and Alexander Hamilton . . . will be hooked by this dramatic picture-book account of their deadly quarrel. . . . When Fradin deals with the divisive politics, Day's ink, watercolor, and gouache illustrations ably show the body language as the enemies furiously confront one another. . . . The words and art humanize the history for children." Booklist

Harness, Cheryl

George Washington. National Geographic Soc. 2000 48p il $17.95
Grades: 3 4 5   **973.4**
   1. Generals 2. Presidents 3. Presidents -- United States

4. Presidents -- United States -- Biography
ISBN 0-7922-7096-7

LC 99-29920

Presents the life of George Washington, focusing on the Revolutionary War years and his presidency

"Detailed paintings, full of action and rich with color, portray Washington as well as important moments in American history. . . . This heavily illustrated biography serves as a good introduction to Washington." Booklist

Includes bibliographical references

Jurmain, Suzanne

★ The **worst** of friends; Thomas Jefferson, John Adams, and the true story of an American feud. illustrated by Larry Day. Dutton Children's Books 2011 32p il $16.99
Grades: 1 2 3   973.4
1. Architects 2. Presidents 3. Vice-presidents 4. Essayists 5. Presidents -- United States
ISBN 978-0-525-47903-1; 0-525-47903-1

LC 2011005190

"In zingy prose, Jurmain tells how Thomas Jefferson and John Adams 'were as different as pickles and ice cream.' . . . Yet she emphasizes that the two were best friends who worked together to shape America before parting ways when Jefferson backed the Republicans and Adams the Federalists. Entertaining anecdotes about both presidents' personal and political lives are energized by Day's lightly caricatured watercolor cartoons, which flesh out their personalities. . . . This entertaining and character-driven slice of history also offers a clear message about friendship." Publ Wkly

Includes bibliographical references

Kerley, Barbara

★ **Those** rebels, John and Tom; illustrated by Edwin Fotheringham. Scholastic Press 2012 il $17.99
Grades: 3 4 5   973.4
1. Architects 2. Presidents 3. Vice-presidents 4. Essayists 5. Presidents -- United States
ISBN 978-0-545-22268-6; 0-545-22268-0

LC 2011002131

"Kerley and Fotheringham . . . cleverly contrast two diverse founding fathers and early presidents, Thomas Jefferson and John Adams. Entertaining verse and droll illustrations parlay their differences and similarities into a lens through which to view the start of the American Revolution. . . . A playful tone also is reflected in the typeface, with certain phrases enlarged for shout-out emphasis, and in the caricatured artwork. Skillfully rendered and decidedly modern in a patriotic palette of red, white, blue, and brown, the digitally created scenes mirror and enhance the text's wit." Publ Wkly

Includes bibliographical references

McNeese, Tim

Early national America, 1790-1850. Chelsea House 2010 136p il map (Discovering U.S. history) $35
Grades: 5 6 7 8   973.4
1. United States -- History -- 1783-1865
ISBN 978-1-60413-351-6; 1-60413-351-1

LC 2009003679

McNeese "discusses the people, politics, economic conditions, and foreign affairs of [the U.S. from 1790 to 1850], objectively explaining how the attitudes, perceptions, and expectations of the American people and their leaders

shaped the development of the country. . . . Color period art and photos, maps, and cutaway drawings supplement the [text]." SLJ

Includes glossary and bibliographical references

Wallner, Alexandra

Abigail Adams; written and illustrated by Alexandra Wallner. Holiday House 2001 un il $17.95; pa $6.95
Grades: 1 2 3   973.4
1. Parents of presidents 2. Spouses of presidents 3. Presidents' spouses -- United States
ISBN 0-8234-1442-6; 0-8234-1942-8 pa

LC 00-23149

A biography of Abigail Adams, wife of second United States President John Adams, and a dedicated wife and mother who spoke up against slavery and for women's rights

"Full-page, colorful pictures in a folk-art style contribute greatly to the text, capturing the daily life, clothing, and household routines of the times." SLJ

973.5   United States -- 1809-1845

Fritz, Jean

The **great** little Madison. Putnam 1989 159p il hardcover o.p. pa $6.99
Grades: 5 6 7 8   973.5
1. Presidents 2. Members of Congress 3. Secretaries of state 4. Presidents -- United States
ISBN 0-399-21768-1; 0-698-11621-6 pa

LC 88-31584

"Small, soft-spoken, and by nature diffident, James Madison found it difficult to speak in the midst of controversy, but his zeal and his convictions in the struggle between Republicans and Federalists gave him confidence, and his successes brought him to the presidency. Fritz has given a vivid picture of the man and an equally vivid picture of the problems—especially the internal dissension—that faced the leaders of the new nation. . . . Notes by the author and a bibliography are appended." Bull Cent Child Books

973.7   Administration of Abraham Lincoln, 1861-1865

Adler, David A., 1947-

Harriet Tubman and the Underground Railroad; by David A. Adler. Holiday House 2013 140 p. ill. (hardcover) $18.95
Grades: 5 6 7 8   973.7
1. Underground Railroad -- Juvenile literature 2. African American women -- Biography -- Juvenile literature 3. Slaves -- United States -- Biography -- Juvenile literature
ISBN 0823423654; 9780823423651

LC 2012006582

This book, by David A. Adler, gives a biography of the ex-slave Harriet Tubman. "She escaped from her owners in Maryland on the Underground Railroad in 1849 and then fearlessly returned . . . to help guide . . . others to freedom as the most famous conductor of the Underground Railroad. . . . During and after the war, she helped hundreds of freed slaves begin new lives, and she later founded a home for elderly former slaves and became active in the women's suffrage movement." (Publisher's note)

Includes bibliographical references

Beller, Susan Provost

Billy Yank and Johnny Reb; soldiering in the Civil War. Twenty-First Century Books 2008 112p il map (Soldiers on the battlefront) lib bdg $33.26

Grades: 5 6 7 8   **973.7**

1. Soldiers -- United States 2. United States -- History -- 1861-1865, Civil War

ISBN 978-0-8225-6803-2 lib bdg; 0-8225-6803-9 lib bdg

LC 2006010240

First published 2000

Describes military life for the average soldier in the Civil War, including camp life, diseases, and conditions for the wounded and prisoners of war. Includes excerpts from first-person accounts, letters, and diaries

The author "presents a good deal of solid information in an interesting manner. . . . Good black-and-white reproductions, mainly of photographs from the 1860s, appear throughout the book." Booklist [review of 2000 ed]

Includes bibliographical references

Benoit, Peter

The **surrender** at Appomattox; by Peter Benoit. Children's Press 2012 64 p. chiefly col. ill., col. map (library) $30.00; (paperback) $8.95

Grades: 4 5 6   **973.7**

1. Appomattox Campaign, 1865 -- Juvenile literature 2. United States -- History -- 1861-1865, Civil War -- Peace -- Juvenile literature

ISBN 0531250415; 9780531250419; 9780531265666

LC 2011011967

This book by Peter Benoit, part of the "Cornerstones of Freedom" series, describes the events leading up to the end of the U.S. Civil War. It "sketches the events of the Battle of the Wilderness and the capture of Richmond as well as the meeting between [Ulysses S.] Grant and [Robert E.] Lee on April 9, 1865." (School Library Journal)

Includes bibliographical references (p. 61) and index.

A **Civil** War scrapbook; I was there too! History Colorado. Fulcrum Pub. 2012 64 p. ill. (some col.), maps (paperback) $14.95

Grades: 4 5 6 7 8   **973.7**

1. United States -- History -- 1861-1865, Civil War

ISBN 1555916686; 9781555916688

LC 2011042043

This book is "a multicultural Civil War history for children. The book . . . feature[es] chronological information" and "focus[es] on the different types of people and their place in the war. This . . . book emphasizes the roles of the children, women, minorities, and even pets that became mascots in the war." Also included are "historical photographs, drawings, maps, games, and primary quotes from children." (Publisher's Note)

Includes bibliographical references (p. 62-63) and index.

★ The **Civil** War: a visual history. DK Pub. 2011 360p il map $40

Grades: 5 6 7 8   **973.7**

1. United States -- History -- 1861-1865, Civil War

ISBN 978-0-7566-7185-3; 0-7566-7185-X

"A stunning, large-format pictorial history. The seven chapters are arranged chronologically, beginning with an overview of slavery in the United States, 1815 to 1860, and ending with a survey of the legacies of the conflict during the period 1865 to 1877. . . . Chapter introductions are followed by illustrated time lines and by short topical divisions that include biographies, maps, original documents or eyewitness accounts, illustrations, historical photographs, artifacts, and reproductions of paintings. Page layouts and the use of color are superb, and sidebars abound, adding to this extraordinary book." SLJ

Clinton, Catherine

★ **Hold** the flag high; illustrated by Shane W. Evans. Katherine Tegen Books 2005 un il $15.99; lib bdg $16.89

Grades: 2 3 4   **973.7**

1. Soldiers 2. African American soldiers 3. Postal employees 4. United States -- History -- 1861-1865, Civil War

ISBN 0-06-050428-5; 0-06-050429-3 lib bdg

LC 2003-11956

Describes the Civil War battle of Morris Island, South Carolina, during which Sargeant William H. Carney became the first African American to earn a Congressional Medal of Honor

"The story captures the fear and horror of battle as well as the bravery of the soldiers. . . . Evans' paintings convey the emotions of the characters as well as their actions." Booklist

Includes bibliographical references

Evans, Shane

★ **Underground**; [by] Shane W. Evans. Roaring Brook Press 2010 1 v. col. ill. $16.99

Grades: K 1 2   **973.7**

1. Abolitionists 2. Underground railroad 3. Slavery -- United States 4. Fugitive slaves -- Juvenile literature

ISBN 1596435380; 9781596435384

LC 2010007735

Coretta Scott King Award (Illustrators) (2012)

This picture book portrays fugitive slaves escaping to freedom through the Underground Railroad. "Preschool, primary." (Horn Book)

"Powerfully expressive imagery will sweep young viewers into this suspenseful journey along the Underground Railroad. Accompanied by a commentary of, usually, just two or three words per spread, the scenes track a small group of escapees stealing through darkness beneath a thin crescent moon. . . . Underscoring the sense of fear and urgency with broad, slanted strokes of thinly applied paint, Evans limns his hunched, indistinct figures in dark lines and adds weight with scribbled fill and jagged bits of paper or cloth. . . . Lengthier accounts of travel on the Underground Railroad abound, but few if any portray the experience with such compelling immediacy." Kirkus

Fradin, Dennis Brindell

★ The **price** of freedom; how one town stood up to slavery. by Judith Bloom Fradin & Dennis Brindell Fradin;

illustrated by Eric Velasquez. Walker & Co. 2013 48 p.
(hardback) $16.99

Grades: 1 2 3   **973.7**

1. Fugitive slaves -- Juvenile literature 2. Oberlin-
Wellington Rescue, 1858 -- Juvenile literature 3.
Underground railroad -- Ohio -- History -- Juvenile
literature 4. Quakers -- Ohio -- History -- 19th century
-- Juvenile literature 5. Fugitive slaves -- Ohio --
History -- 19th century -- Juvenile literature
ISBN 0802721664; 9780802721662; 9780802721679

LC 2012015781

This juvenile history book, by Dennis Brindell Fradin
and Judith Bloom Fradin, with illustrations by Eric Velasquez, describes how "an Ohio community successfully de-
fied the 1850 Fugitive Slave Act. In 1856, John Price and
two other Kentucky slaves crossed the Ohio River to freedom in Oberlin. . . . Two years later, when slave hunters
tracked him down and captured him, the citizens of the town
banded together to defend him." (Kirkus Reviews)

Friedman, Robin

The **silent** witness; a true story of the Civil War. illustrated by Claire A. Nivola. Houghton Mifflin Co. 2005
un il $16

Grades: K 1 2 3   **973.7**

1. United States -- History -- 1861-1865, Civil War 2.
Virginia -- History
ISBN 0-618-44230-8

LC 2004-1013

"Young Lula McLean watched the Civil War begin and
end: General Beauregard used her family's Virginia home as
his headquarters, and Lee surrendered at their second home.
The finely executed, primitive-like paintings accentuate the
idea that this war was an intimate part of everyday life in the
South, and the small telling details show a personal side of
the war." Horn Book Guide

Gregory, Josh

Gettysburg; by Josh Gregory. Children's Press 2012
64 p. chiefly col. ill. (library) $30.00; (paperback) $8.95

Grades: 4 5 6   **973.7**

1. Gettysburg (Pa.), Battle of, 1863 -- Juvenile literature
ISBN 0531250342; 9780531250341; 9780531265598

LC 2011010751

In this book on the 1863 Battle of Gettysburg, "[Josh]
Gregory takes his readers back to the precursor events that
set the stage for this meeting engagement pitting General
[Robert E.] Lee's Army of Northern Virginia against General
[George] Meade's oft times defeated Union Army of the Po-
tomac. In the end the efforts of Lee's seemingly indomitable
veterans were not enough to overcome the forces of fate and
tactics." (Children's Literature)

Includes bibliographical references (p. 61) and index.

Hernandez, Roger E.

The **Civil** War, 1840s-1890s. Marshall Cavendish
Benchmark 2008 80p il map (Hispanic America) lib bdg
$34.21

Grades: 4 5 6 7   **973.7**

1. Latinos (U.S.) 2. Hispanic Americans 3. United
States -- History -- 1861-1865, Civil War
ISBN 978-0-7614-2939-5 lib bdg; 0-7614-2939-5
lib bdg

LC 2007049525

Discusses Hispanic participation during the Civil War

Includes glossary and bibliographical references

Holzer, Harold

The **president** is shot! the assassination of Abraham
Lincoln. Boyds Mills Press 2004 181p il $17.95

Grades: 5 6 7 8   **973.7**

1. Lawyers 2. Presidents 3. State legislators 4.
Members of Congress 5. Lincoln, Abraham, 1809-1865
-- Assassination
ISBN 1-56397-985-3

"A page-turner of a text, a fascinating array of photos
and archival illustrations, and an event that changed the
course of history: all these elements combine in this strong,
highly readable book." Booklist

Includes bibliographical references

Huey, Lois Miner

American archaeology uncovers the Underground Railroad. Marshall Cavendish Benchmark 2009 64p il map
(American archaeology) lib bdg $21.95

Grades: 4 5 6 7   **973.7**

1. Abolitionists 2. Underground railroad 3. Slavery
-- United States 4. Excavations (Archeology) -- United
States
ISBN 978-0-7614-4267-7 lib bdg; 0-7614-4267-7
lib bdg

LC 2009003168

This describes how archeologists have learned about the
history of the Underground Railroad.

This is "both intriguing and engaging for young readers.
. . . A welcomed addition to classroom and school libraries."
Libr Media Connect

Includes glossary and bibliographical references

Isaacs, Sally Senzell

The **Civil** War; Sally Senzell Isaacs. Kingfisher 2011
32 p. ill., map (hardcover) $19.89

Grades: 3 4 5 6   **973.7**

1. United States -- History -- 1861-1865, Civil War
ISBN 0753466937; 9780753466933

LC 2011049248

This book is part of the "All About America" series
which "covers the most important periods in the history of a
burgeoning nation, from Colonists and Independence to The
Civil War, and from Cowboys and the Wild West to the early
inhabitants, the Native Americans." In this volume, readers
learn about the American Civil War. (Publisher's note)

Jordan, Anne Devereaux

The **Civil** War; by Anne Devereaux Jordan; with Virginia Schomp. Marshall Cavendish Benchmark 2007 72p
il (Drama of African-American history) lib bdg $34.21

Grades: 5 6 7 8   **973.7**

1. African Americans -- History 2. United States --
History -- 1861-1865, Civil War
ISBN 978-0-7614-2179-5 lib bdg; 0-7614-2179-3
lib bdg

LC 2006012472

Describes the role of African Americans during the Civil
War (1861-1865)

Includes glossary and bibliographical references

Kostyal, K. M.

1862, Fredericksburg; a new look at a bitter Civil War battle. National Geographic 2011 48p (National Geographic kids)

Grades: 3 4 5 6   **973.7**

1. United States -- History -- 1861-1865, Civil War
ISBN 1-4263-0835-3; 1-4263-0836-1 lib bdg; 978-1-4263-0835-2; 978-1-4263-0836-9 lib bdg

LC 2011011798

Details the Civil War battle of Fredericksburg, Virginia, and profiles some of the key figures involved in what was a decisive victory for the Confederacy.

"Realistic, full-color pictures of modern-day re-enactors mix with clear language to bring the action to life. The text is interspersed with personal accounts. . . . Brief chapters tell the war's story from the perspective of what happened at Fredericksburg in a concise manner. . . . A valuable resource for classrooms, libraries, and travelers to Fredericksburg and the surrounding area." SLJ

Landau, Elaine

Fleeing to freedom on the Underground Railroad; the courageous slaves, agents, and conductors. Twenty-First Century Books 2006 88p il map (People's history) lib bdg $26.60

Grades: 5 6 7 8   **973.7**

1. Abolitionists 2. Underground railroad 3. Slavery -- United States
ISBN 978-0-8225-3490-7 lib bdg; 0-8225-3490-8 lib bdg

LC 2005020358

"Landau discusses the history of slavery in the United States, slave life, the Underground Railroad, and the leaders, both black and white, of antislavery organizations. Three chapters outline specifics of slaves' escapes. . . . An outstanding feature of this book is the use of primary sources and quotes from former slaves, contemporary newspaper accounts, and reminiscences of escaped slaves. . . . Excellent historical photographs and illustrations enhance the text." SLJ

Includes bibliographical references

McNeese, Tim

The **Civil** War era, 1851-1865; consulting editor, Richard Jensen. Chelsea House 2010 144p il map (Discovering U.S. history) $35

Grades: 5 6 7 8   **973.7**

1. United States -- History -- 1861-1865, Civil War
ISBN 978-1-60413-352-3; 1-60413-352-X

LC 2009-3660

"The information is accurate and easy to understand. Pictures are well placed, and primary sources are included. . . . The maps are well done and there are sidebars with additional information. . . . [This would be good] to have on hand for reports as it is well laid out and easy to use." Libr Media Connect

Includes glossary and bibliographical references

McPherson, James M.

★ **Fields** of fury; the American Civil War. Atheneum Bks. for Young Readers 2002 96p il map $22.95

Grades: 5 6 7 8   **973.7**

1. United States -- History -- 1861-1865, Civil War
ISBN 0-689-84833-1

LC 2001-46048

Examines the events and effects of the American Civil War

"McPherson writes with authority, offering a broad overview as well as many details and anecdotes that give his account a human dimension. . . . The many fine illustrations include period photographs, paintings, prints, some excellent maps." Booklist

Includes glossary and bibliographical references

Murphy, Jim

★ The **boys'** war; Confederate and Union soldiers talk about the Civil War. Clarion Bks. 1990 110p il hardcover o.p. pa $8.95

Grades: 5 6 7 8 9 10   **973.7**

1. United States -- History -- 1861-1865, Civil War -- Juvenile literature
ISBN 0-89919-893-7; 0-395-66412-8 pa

LC 89-23959

This book includes diary entries, personal letters, and archival photographs to describe the experiences of boys, sixteen years old or younger, who fought in the Civil War.

"An excellent selection of more than 45 sepia-toned contemporary photographs augment the text of this informative, moving work." SLJ

Includes bibliographical references

★ The **long** road to Gettysburg. Clarion Bks. 1992 116p il maps $17; pa $7.95

Grades: 5 6 7 8 9 10   **973.7**

1. Gettysburg (Pa.), Battle of, 1863 2. United States -- History -- 1861-1865, Civil War
ISBN 0-395-55965-0; 0-618-05157-0 pa

LC 90-21881

Describes the events of the Battle of Gettysburg in 1863 as seen through the eyes of two actual participants, nineteen-year-old Confederate lieutenant John Dooley and seventeen-year-old Union soldier Thomas Galway. Also discusses Lincoln's famous speech delivered at the dedication of the National Cemetery at Gettysburg

The author "uses all of his fine skills as an information writer—clarity of detail, conciseness, understanding of his age group, and ability to find the drama appealing to readers—to frame a well-crafted account of a single battle in the war." Horn Book

Includes bibliographical references

★ A **savage** thunder; Antietam and the bloody road to freedom. Margaret K. McElderry Books 2009 103p il map $17.99

Grades: 5 6 7 8 9   **973.7**

1. Generals 2. Governors 3. Antietam (Md.), Battle of, 1862 4. College presidents 5. Presidential candidates 6. Antietam, Battle of, Md., 1862 -- Juvenile literature
ISBN 978-0-689-87633-2; 0-689-87633-5

LC 2008-32738

"Murphy provides readers with a lucid and compelling narrative, drawn mainly from firsthand accounts. . . . Replete with excellent-quality archival photos, reproductions, and maps, this is an outstanding account of a battle." SLJ

Includes bibliographical references

Norwich, Grace

I am Harriet Tubman; by Grace Norwich; illustrated by Ute Simon. Scholastic 2013 127 p. ill. (paperback) $5.99

Grades: 3 4 5   973.7

1. Slavery -- United States

ISBN 0545484367; 9780545484367

This book is part of the I Am series and focuses on Harriet Tubman, "the legendary Underground Railroad conductor. Prefaced by a time line and a page introducing important individuals to the story, [Grace] Norwich's narrative provides information as well as insight into how that information has come down to us. . . . . Tubman's early life in slavery is . . . described, as are her brave efforts to escape." (Booklist)

Raatma, Lucia

The Underground Railroad; by Lucia Raatma. Children's Press 2011 64 p. col. ill. (library) $30.00; (paperback) $8.95

Grades: 4 5 6   973.7

1. Fugitive slaves -- Juvenile literature 2. Underground Railroad -- Juvenile literature 3. Fugitive slaves -- United States -- History -- 19th century -- Juvenile literature 4. Antislavery movements -- United States -- History -- 19th century -- Juvenile literature

ISBN 0531250431; 9780531250433; 9780531265680

LC 2011009493

This book by Lucia Raatma is part of the Cornerstones of Freedom series and looks at the Underground Railroad. The entry "explains how the system worked, the journey, and important people who guided slaves such as Harriet Tubman and Levi and Catherine White Coffin of Indiana, who helped about 2,000 slaves reach freedom." (School Library Journal)

Includes bibliographical references (p. 61) and index.

Rossi, Ann

Freedom struggle; the anti-slavery movement in America 1830-1865. National Geographic 2005 40p il (Crossroads America) $12.95; lib bdg $21.90

Grades: 4 5 6   973.7

1. Abolitionists 2. Slavery -- United States

ISBN 0-7922-7828-3; 0-7922-8061-X lib bdg

LC 2003-19824

This discusses the Abolitionist Movement in the United States, profiling some of its leaders and its role in the Civil War.

"Period photographs, drawings, and cartoons; primary-source material; and biographical content make [this] introductory [title] interesting and accessible." SLJ

Includes glossary

Sheinkin, Steve

★ Two miserable presidents; everything your school-books didn't tell you about the Civil War. illustrated by Tim Robinson. Roaring Brook Press 2008 246p il $19.95

Grades: 4 5 6 7   973.7

1. United States -- History -- 1861-1865, Civil War

ISBN 978-1-59643-320-5; 1-59643-320-5

LC 2007-33115

"Chatty and accessible, this book does double duty: it introduces Civil War history for readers who don't know much about it and supplies browsable commentary for those familiar with the big picture. . . . [Sheinkin's] fast-paced narrative is broken into short, tersely titled vignettes." Booklist

Includes bibliographical references

Stark, Ken

Marching to Appomattox; the footrace that ended the Civil War. [by] Ken Stark. G.P. Putnam's Sons 2009 un il $17.99

Grades: 3 4 5   973.7

1. Generals 2. Presidents 3. Appomattox Campaign, 1865 4. College presidents

ISBN 978-0-399-24212-0; 0-399-24212-0

LC 2008012551

"The beginning of April 1865 was a pivotal time in the Civil War. Following a defeat at Richmond, VA, the Confederate forces tried to outrun the Union troops and get to waiting reinforcements in North Carolina. Instead, Lee's men ended up trapped by General Grant's army. The week culminated with Lee's surrender at Appomattox Court House. Stark frames this war vignette effectively for young readers. . . . The illustrations are a great strength. Rendered in watercolor, the inclusion of gouache and casein gives the hues a vividness and depth not always associated with the medium." SLJ

Includes bibliographical references

Turner, Ann Warren

Abe Lincoln remembers; [by] Ann Turner; pictures by Wendell Minor. HarperCollins Pubs. 2001 un il hardcover o.p. pa $6.99

Grades: K 1 2 3   973.7

1. Lawyers 2. Presidents 3. State legislators 4. Members of Congress 5. Presidents -- United States 6. Presidents -- United States -- Biography -- Juvenile literature

ISBN 0-06-027577-4; 0-06-027578-2 lib bdg; 0-06-051107-9 pa

LC 98-50937

A simple description of the life of Abraham Lincoln, presented from his point of view

"Turner's free-verse reminiscence gracefully ties images and themes from Lincoln's youth to those of his adult years. . . . Minor's well-composed paintings, best seen from a little distance, effectively portray the man as he ages." Booklist

Weber, Jennifer L.

Summer's bloodiest days; the Battle of Gettysburg as told from all sides. foreword by James M. McPherson. National Geographic 2010 61p il map $17.95; lib bdg $27.90

Grades: 5 6 7 8   973.7

1. Gettysburg (Pa.), Battle of, 1863

ISBN 978-1-4263-0706-5; 1-4263-0706-3; 978-1-4263-0707-2 lib bdg; 1-4263-0707-1 lib bdg

"This colorful book tells of the Battle of Gettysburg, a dramatic event that becomes even more compelling because the text is laced with pertinent quotes from those who were there. Weber's vivid, pithy writing packs a great deal of information and many anecdotes into a relatively short account. . . . Many battle maps, short, informative sidebars, and the use of modern realistic paintings and photos of artifacts as well as period photographs . . . illustrate the book." Booklist

Includes bibliographical references

Williams, Carla

The Underground Railroad. Child's World 2009 32p il (Journey to freedom) lib bdg $28.50

Grades: 4 5 6 **973.7**
1. Underground railroad 2. Slavery -- United States
ISBN 978-1-60253-139-0 lib bdg; 1-60253-139-0
lib bdg
LC 2008031946

"Underground Railroad describes how this secret system worked and introduces key figures. Williams discusses relevant laws and amendments as well as the advent and conclusion of the Civil War. The facts, presented through stories, historical news accounts, and biographical sketches of Harriet Tubman and Levi Weeks, capture the desperation of the enslaved as well as the abolitionists' commitment to them. The [book is] concise and direct, yet the writing remains sophisticated. Vibrant personal stories accompanied by striking photographs of historical figures and artifacts provide a sense of the subjects' hopes and dreams." SLJ

Includes glossary and bibliographical references

973.8   United States -- Reconstruction period, 1865-1901

Howell, Brian
The US Civil War and Reconstruction. Cherry Lake Pub. 2011 il (Language arts explorer: history digs) $18.95; pa $14.95
Grades: 3 4 5 6 **973.8**
1. Reconstruction (1865-1876)
ISBN 978-1-61080-201-7; 978-1-61080-289-5 pa
LC 2011015126

"This compact volume is narrated by an unnamed child, who is helping a museum curator set up a Civil War museum. The first boxes that the narrator unpacks hold documents and exhibits about slavery. Each day, the child learns more about the origins of the war, its battles, and Reconstruction. Through simply told prose in first person, the book provides a great deal of information presented in ways that kids can understand. It also gives solid background in how research is done. . . . Photographs and numerous reproductions of historical documents add to the usefulness of this slim book." Booklist

McNeese, Tim
The Gilded Age and Progressivism, 1891-1913; Tim McNeese; consulting editor, Richard Jensen. Chelsea House 2010 136 p. ill. (some col.) (Discovering U.S. history) (library) $35.00
Grades: 5 6 7 8 **973.8**
1. Progressivism (United States politics) 2. -- History -- 19th century -- Juvenile literature 3. Progressivism (United States politics) -- History -- 19th century -- Juvenile literature 4. Progressivism (United States politics) -- History -- 20th century -- Juvenile literature
ISBN 1604133554; 9781604133554
LC 2009015012

McNeese "discusses the people, politics, economic conditions, and foreign affairs of [the U.S. from 1891 to 1913], objectively explaining how the attitudes, perceptions, and expectations of the American people and their leaders shaped the development of the country. . . . Color period art and photos, maps, and cutaway drawings supplement the [text]." SLJ

Includes bibliographical references and index.

Sanders, Nancy I.
Frederick Douglass for kids; his life and times with 21 activities. Nancy I. Sanders. Chicago Review Press 2012 ix, 145 p.p ill. (paperback) $16.95; (ebook) $11.99; (prebind) $25.95
Grades: 5 6 7 **973.8**
1. Biography 2. Slavery -- History 3. African Americans -- Biography 4. Abolitionists -- United States -- Biography -- Juvenile literature 5. African American abolitionists -- Biography -- Juvenile literature 6. Antislavery movements -- United States -- Study and teaching -- Activity programs 7. Antislavery movements -- United States -- History -- 19th century -- Juvenile literature
ISBN 1569767173; 9781569767177; 9781613743560; 9781451774788
LC 2011050092

Author Nancy I. Sanders presents information on Frederick Douglass. "Born on a plantation, he later escaped slavery and helped others to freedom via the Underground Railroad. In time he became a bestselling author, an outspoken newspaper editor, a brilliant orator, a tireless abolitionist, and a brave civil rights leader. He was famous on both sides of the Atlantic in the years leading up to the Civil War, and when war broke out, Abraham Lincoln invited him to the White House for counsel and advice." (Publisher's note)

Includes bibliographical references (p. 136-137) and index.

Stroud, Bettye
The Reconstruction era; by Bettye M. Stroud with Virginia Schomp. Marshall Cavendish Benchmark 2007 70p il (Drama of African-American history) lib bdg $34.21
Grades: 5 6 7 8 **973.8**
1. Reconstruction (1865-1876) 2. African Americans -- History
ISBN 978-0-7614-2181-8 lib bdg; 0-7614-2181-5 lib bdg
LC 2006012149

"Traces the history of Reconstruction, from the end of the Civil War in 1865 to 1877, when federal troops were removed from the South." Publisher's note

Includes glossary and bibliographical references

Todras, Ellen H.
Wagon trains and settlers. Kingfisher 2011 32p il (All about America) $19.89; pa $9.99
Grades: 3 4 5 6 **973.8**
1. Frontier and pioneer life 2. Overland journeys to the Pacific
ISBN 978-0-7534-6583-7; 0-7534-6583-3; 978-0-7534-6511-0 pa; 0-7534-6511-6 pa

This describes westward migration and pioneer life in the United States in the 19th century.

This "visually appealing [title] effectively [combines] paintings, engravings, primary documents, and photographs with cartoon illustrations. The eye-catching [layout includes] different font sizes, bold type, and text boxes to highlight different pieces of information. The content is interesting and pithy." SLJ

Includes glossary and bibliographical references

Walker, Paul Robert

★ **Remember** Little Bighorn; Indians, soldiers, and scouts tell their stories. [by] Paul Robert Walker; [foreword by John A. Doerner] National Geographic Society 2006 61p il map $17.95; lib bdg $27.90

Grades: 5 6 7 8   **973.8**

1. Little Bighorn, Battle of the, 1876

ISBN 0-7922-5521-6; 0-7922-5522-4 lib bdg

LC 2005030929

This "volume gives an almost blow-by-blow account of the famous battle that came to be known as Custer's Last Stand. Walker concentrates on the battle itself, fought on the Great Plains in 1876, and the book includes diagrams of each side's tactics. . . . Walker's exhaustive research . . . [brings] together the conflicting viewpoints of the whites and the Lakota Sioux, Cheyenne, and Arapaho fighters, documenting everything in source notes. The handsome book design, with thick paper, clear type, maps, stirring photos, and archival images, will attract readers to the battle story and then start them thinking about lasting historical issues." Booklist

Includes bibliographical references

973.9   United States -- 1901-

Sandler, Martin W.

★ The **Dust** Bowl through the lens; how photography revealed and helped remedy a national disaster. Walker & Co. 2008 96p il map $15.99; lib bdg $20.89

Grades: 5 6 7 8   **973.9**

1. Dust storms 2. Documentary photography 3. Documentary photography -- Juvenile literature 4. Dust Bowl Era, 1931-1939 -- Juvenile literature

ISBN 978-0-8027-9547-2; 0-8027-9547-1; 978-0-8027-9548-9 lib bdg; 0-8027-9548-X lib bdg

LC 2008-55979

"This excellent photo-essay traces the history of the Dust Bowl from its causes to its resolution. In tandem, Sandler treats the role of the budding field of photojournalism. Forty-four spreads feature a page of clear, direct text with a large, well-reproduced image, many of which are set on color pages. . . . Seldom has the connection between the arts and the general quality of life been made so clear. The text deals equally with those who fled the decimated Bread Basket for California and those who waited out the devastation and dust. Throughout, the use of primary sources is superb, with quotations from affected citizens, the photojournalists themselves, political and entertainment figures, and writers, giving a multifaceted picture of a seminal time in United States history." SLJ

973.91   1901-1953

Bingham, Jane

The **Great** Depression; the Jazz Age, Prohibition, and the Great Depression, 1921-1937. Chelsea House 2011 il (A cultural history of women in America) $35

Grades: 5 6 7 8   **973.91**

1. Great Depression, 1929-1939 2. Women -- United States 3. Women -- United States -- History

ISBN 978-1-60413-933-4; 1-60413-933-1

LC 2010044889

An "eye-catching [layout] with good use of color, photographs, and informative sidebars, many of which use primary-source quotations, are the highlights of [this] appealing [volume]. . . . After a succinct overview of contemporary events, the chapters describe women's lives at home, at work, in education, in politics, in the arts, and their role in the general culture. . . . [This book] surveys an era after women won the right to vote and when the nation's economic crash placed new hardships on families." SLJ

Includes glossary and bibliographical references

Corrigan, Jim

The **1900s** decade in photos; a decade of discovery. Enslow Publishers 2010 64p il (Amazing decades in photos) lib bdg $27.93

Grades: 4 5 6 7   **973.91**

1. United States -- History -- 20th century

ISBN 978-0-7660-3129-6 lib bdg; 0-7660-3129-2 lib bdg

LC 2008042900

This highlights the important world, national, and cultural developments of the 1900s.

This is illustrated with "large, well-chosen black-and-white and color photos. . . . Captions provide specific information about the photos and supplement, rather than repeat, information in the [narrative]. Attractive and readable, this . . . will be popular with browsers and beginning researchers." SLJ

Includes glossary and bibliographical references

The **1910s** decade in photos; a decade that shook the world. Enslow Publishers 2010 64p il (Amazing decades in photos) lib bdg $27.93

Grades: 4 5 6 7   **973.91**

1. United States -- History -- 20th century

ISBN 978-0-7660-3130-2 lib bdg; 0-7660-3130-6 lib bdg

LC 2008042902

This highlights the important world, national, and cultural developments of the decade 1910-1919, including the sinking of the Titanic, the establishment of the Boy Scouts and Girl Scouts, immigration, income tax, Hollywood feature films, World War I, the Lusitania sinking, and more.

Includes glossary and bibliographical references

The **1920s** decade in photos; the Roaring Twenties. Enslow Publishers 2010 64p il (Amazing decades in photos) lib bdg $27.93

Grades: 4 5 6 7   **973.91**

1. United States -- History -- 20th century

ISBN 978-0-7660-3131-9 lib bdg; 0-7660-3131-4 lib bdg

LC 2008042903

This highlights the important world, national, and cultural developments of the decade 1920-1929, including Prohibition, jazz music, women's suffrage, the rise of Mussolini, flappers fashions, the KKK, U.S. Presidents Harding and Coolidge, the Teapot Dome Scandal, the rise of the Nazi Party, and more.

Includes glossary and bibliographical references

Stanley, George Edward

An **emerging** world power (1900-1929) [by] George E. Stanley. World Almanac Library 2005 48p il (Primary source history of the United States) lib bdg $30

Grades: 5 6 7 8   **973.91**

1. United States -- History -- 20th century

ISBN 0-8368-5828-X

                            LC 2004-61501

The author describes United States politics and foreign relations in the 1920s.

"Stanley explains and connects events utilizing clear language and a blending of text, images, and primary accounts. . . . Well-organized, highly attractive." SLJ

Includes bibliographical references

973.917   Administration of Franklin Delano Roosevelt, 1933-1945

Cooney, Barbara

★ **Eleanor**. Viking 1996 un il $15.99; pa $6.99

Grades: K 1 2 3   **973.917**

1. Diplomats 2. Columnists 3. Humanitarians 4. Social activists 5. Spouses of presidents 6. United Nations officials

ISBN 0-670-86159-6; 0-14-055583-8 pa

                            LC 96-7723

"There are many biographies of Eleanor Roosevelt but this one is special. Not only does it boast Cooney's artwork, but it also gets to the heart of a young girl, which in many ways is as interesting as Roosevelt's later, well-known accomplishments." Booklist

Cooper, Michael L.

★ **Dust** to eat; drought and depression in the 1930's. Clarion Books 2004 81p il map hardcover o.p. $15

Grades: 4 5 6 7   **973.917**

1. Droughts 2. Migrant labor 3. Great Depression, 1929-1939 4. Depressions -- 1929 -- Juvenile literature

ISBN 0-618-15449-3

                         LC 2003-17807

This book begins "with the 1929 stock market crash that ushered in the Great Depression and {continues} with the severe drought in the Midwest, known as the Dust Bowl." (Publisher's note) Index. "Grades six to nine." (Bull Cent Child Books)

This includes "lots of stunning black-and-white archival photos and a clear, spacious text that draws on eloquent eyewitness reports—including comments from John Steinbeck and Woody Guthrie. . . . This is an excellent historical account." Booklist

Includes bibliographical references

Corrigan, Jim

The **1930s** decade in photos; Depression and hope. Enslow Publishers 2010 64p il (Amazing decades in photos) lib bdg $27.93

Grades: 4 5 6 7   **973.917**

1. Great Depression, 1929-1939 2. United States -- History -- 20th century

ISBN 978-0-7660-3132-6 lib bdg; 0-7660-3132-2 lib bdg

                         LC 2008042904

This highlights the important world, national, and cultural developments of the decade 1930-1939, including the Great Depression, the Lindbergh kidnapping, the administration of FDR, the New Deal, jazz and swing music, the rise of Nazism, the repeal of Prohibition and more.

Includes glossary and bibliographical references

The **1940s** decade in photos; a world at war. Enslow Publishers 2010 64p il (Amazing decades in photos) lib bdg $27.93

Grades: 4 5 6 7   **973.917**

1. World War, 1939-1945 2. United States -- History -- 20th century

ISBN 978-0-7660-3133-3 lib bdg; 0-7660-3133-0 lib bdg

                         LC 2008042910

This covers the important world, national, and cultural developments of the decade 1940-1949, focusing on World War II.

This is illustrated with "large, well-chosen black-and-white and color photos. . . . Captions provide specific information about the photos and supplement, rather than repeat, information in the [narrative]. Attractive and readable, this . . . will be popular with browsers and beginning researchers." SLJ

Includes glossary and bibliographical references

Freedman, Russell

★ **Eleanor** Roosevelt; a life of discovery. Clarion Bks. 1993 198p il hardcover o.p. pa $11.95

Grades: 5 6 7 8 9 10   **973.917**

1. Diplomats 2. Columnists 3. Humanitarians 4. Social activists 5. Spouses of presidents 6. United Nations officials 7. Presidents' spouses -- United States

ISBN 0-89919-862-7; 0-395-84520-3 pa

                         LC 92-25024

A Newbery Medal honor book, 1994

"This impeccably researched, highly readable study of one of this country's greatest First Ladies is nonfiction at its best. . . . Approximately 140 well-chosen black-and-white photos amplify the text." Publ Wkly

Includes bibliographical references

★ **Franklin** Delano Roosevelt. Clarion Bks. 1990 200p il hardcover o.p. pa $9.95

Grades: 5 6 7 8 9 10   **973.917**

1. Governors 2. Presidents 3. Handicapped 4. Philatelists 5. Presidents -- United States

ISBN 0-89919-379-X; 0-395-62978-0 pa

                         LC 89-34986

The author "traces the personal and public events in a life that led to the formation of one of the most influential and magnetic leaders of the twentieth century." Horn Book

Includes bibliographical references

Garland, Sherry

Voices of the dust bowl; by Sherry Garland; illustrated by Judith Hierstein. Pelican Pub. Co. 2011 p. cm. un il

Grades: 4 5 6   **973.917**

1. Great Plains -- History 2. Droughts -- United States 3. Dust Bowl Era, 1931-1939 -- Juvenile literature 4. Farmers -- Great Plains -- History -- 20th century -- Juvenile literature 5. Droughts -- Great Plains -- History -- 20th century -- Juvenile literature 6. Dust storms

-- Great Plains -- History -- 20th century -- Juvenile
literature
ISBN 9781589809642

LC 2011002670

This book, by Sherry Garland, presents "[v]oices from
those who lived through the largest environmental catastrophe in American history. From 1931 to 1940, a combination
of drought and soil erosion destroyed the fragile ecology and
economy of the Great Plains." Illustrations are given along
with accounts such as "a farmer's wife, a banker, and a child
who had never seen rain." (Publisher's note)
Includes bibliographical references

McNeese, Tim
The **Great** Depression, 1929-1940; consulting editor
Richard Jensen. Chelsea House 2010 136p il map (Dis-
covering U.S. history) $35
Grades: 5 6 7 8   **973.917**
1. Economic conditions 2. Great Depression, 1929-
1939
ISBN 978-1-60413-357-8; 1-60413-357-0

LC 2009-22090

"The information is accurate and easy to understand.
Pictures are well placed, and primary sources are included.
. . . The maps are well done and there are sidebars with ad-
ditional information. . . . [This would be good] to have on
hand for reports as it is well laid out and easy to use." Libr
Media Connect
Includes glossary and bibliographical references

973.92   United States -- 1953-2001

Corrigan, Jim
The **1990s** decade in photos; the rise of technology.
Enslow Publishers 2010 64p il (Amazing decades in pho-
tos) lib bdg $27.93
Grades: 4 5 6 7   **973.92**
1. World history -- 20th century 2. United States --
History -- 20th century
ISBN 978-0-7660-3138-8 lib bdg; 0-7660-3138-1
lib bdg

LC 2008054648

This highlights the important world, national, and cul-
tural developments of the decade 1990-1999, including
Operation Desert Storm in 1991, race riots in Los Angeles,
the election of President Clinton, the 1993 bombing of the
World Trade Center, the Human Genome Project, the end of
Apartheid, massacres in Bosnia and Rwanda, the Oklahoma
City bombing, the O.J. Simpson murder trial, the Columbine
High School shootings, and more
Includes glossary and bibliographical references

McNeese, Tim
Modern America, 1964-present; consulting editor,
Richard Jensen. Chelsea House 2010 144p il map (Dis-
covering U.S. history) $35
Grades: 5 6 7 8   **973.92**
1. United States -- History -- 20th century
ISBN 978-1-60413-361-5; 1-60413-361-9

"Through a good balance of social and political topics,
McNeese capably covers a diverse range of subjects in [this]
volume. . . . Modern America discusses civil rights, terror-

ism, and Barack Obama's first year as president. [The] book
has an excellent chronology; rich sidebars; and numerous
well-captioned illustrations, maps, and photos that enhance
the [text]. [This book provides a] satisfying [introduction] to
American history for students." SLJ
Includes glossary and bibliographical references

973.921   Administration of Dwight David Eisenhower, 1953-1961

Corrigan, Jim
The **1950s** decade in photos; the American decade. Enslow Publishers 2010 64p il (Amazing decades in photos)
lib bdg $27.93
Grades: 4 5 6 7   **973.921**
1. United States -- History -- 20th century
ISBN 978-0-7660-3134-0 lib bdg; 0-7660-3134-9
lib bdg

LC 2008042994

This highlights the important world, national, and cul-
tural developments of the decade 1950-1959, including the
Korean War, McCarthyism, the Baby Boom generation, the
execution of the Rosenbergs, the Beat Generation, the polio
epidemic and vaccine, the Montgomery Bus Boycott, the
Suez Crisis, the beginning of rock music, the launching of
Sputnik, and the Cuban Revolution
Includes glossary and bibliographical references

973.922   Administration of John Fitzgerald Kennedy, 1961-1963

Adler, David A.
A **picture** book of John F. Kennedy; illustrated by Rob-
ert Casilla. Holiday House 1991 un il $16.95; pa $6.95
Grades: 1 2 3   **973.922**
1. Presidents 2. Senators 3. Members of Congress 4.
Presidents -- United States
ISBN 0-8234-0884-1; 0-8234-0976-7 pa

LC 90-23589

Depicts the life and career of John F. Kennedy
"Adler presents a brief, clearly written text that provides
basic information about his subject in an appealing format. .
. . Casilla's watercolors are full-color copies of famous photographs." SLJ

973.923   Administration of Lyndon Baines Johnson, 1963-1969

Corrigan, Jim
The **1960s** decade in photos; love, freedom, and flower
power. Enslow Publishers 2010 64p il (Amazing decades
in photos) lib bdg $27.93
Grades: 4 5 6 7   **973.923**
1. United States -- History -- 20th century
ISBN 978-0-7660-3135-7 lib bdg; 0-7660-3135-7
lib bdg

LC 2008042996

This highlights the important world, national, and cultural developments of the decade 1960-1969, including the

U-2 spy plane, the election and assassination of JFK, the beginnings of manned space exploration, the Bay of Pigs invasion, the Vietnam War, the Cuban Missile Crisis, the British invasion in rock music, the Civil Rights movement, the Six-Day War in the Middle East, the assassinations of RFK and Martin Luther King, and Hippie culture

Includes glossary and bibliographical references

973.924   Administration of Richard Milhous Nixon, 1969-1974

Corrigan, Jim
The **1970s** decade in photos; protest and change. Enslow Publishers 2010 64p il (Amazing decades in photos) lib bdg $27.93
Grades: 4 5 6 7   **973.924**
   1. United States -- History -- 20th century
   ISBN 978-0-7660-3136-4 lib bdg; 0-7660-3136-5
   lib bdg
                                                LC 2008042998
This highlights the important world, national, and cultural developments of the decade 1970-1979, including protests against the Vietnam War, terrorist airplane hijackings, the thawing of the Cold War, the deaths of rock musicians Jimi Hendrix, Janice Joplin, and Jim Morrison, the attack at the Munich Olympics, Watergate and the resignation of President Nixon, Three Mile Island, and more.

Includes glossary and bibliographical references

973.927   Administration of Ronald Reagan, 1981-1989

Corrigan, Jim
The **1980s** decade in photos; the triumph of democracy. Enslow Publishers 2010 64p il (Amazing decades in photos) lib bdg $27.93
Grades: 4 5 6 7   **973.927**
   1. World history -- 20th century 2. United States -- History -- 20th century
   ISBN 978-0-7660-3137-1 lib bdg; 0-7660-3137-3
   lib bdg
                                                LC 2008052627
This highlights the important world, national, and cultural developments of the decade 1980-1989, including the 1980 Winter Olympics, the presidency of Ronald Reagan, the Iran hostage crisis, the Space Shuttle, MTV, the War on Drugs, AIDS, the rise of the computer, fashion, the Chernobyl nuclear disaster, the Iran-Contra Affair, the massacre in Tiananmen Square, the fall of the Berlin Wall, and the U.S. invasion of Panama

Includes glossary and bibliographical references

973.93   United States--2001-

Corrigan, Jim
The **2000s** decade in photos; a new millennium. Enslow Publishers 2010 64p il (Amazing decades in photos) lib bdg $27.93

Grades: 4 5 6 7   **973.93**
   1. World history -- 21st century
   ISBN 978-0-7660-3139-5 lib bdg; 0-7660-3139-X
   lib bdg
                                                LC 2008054644
This highlights the important world, national, and cultural developments of the first decade of the 21st century, including the disputed presidential election of 2000, the attacks of September 11, 2001, the Iraq War, digital technology and gadgets, the drop in stock market prices of internet companies, steroid use in sports, the Space Shuttle disaster of 2003, the tsunami of 2004, Hurricane Katrina, the massacre at Virginia Tech, the energy crisis, and the 2008 presidential election

Includes glossary and bibliographical references

973.931   Administration of George W. Bush, 2001-2009

Benoit, Peter
September 11 we will never forget; by Peter Benoit. Children's Press 2012 64 p. col. ill., col. map (ornerstones of freedom) (library) $30.00; (paperback) $8.95
Grades: 4 5 6 7   **973.931**
   1. September 11 terrorist attacks, 2001 -- Juvenile literature 2. Terrorism -- United States -- Juvenile literature 3. September 11 Terrorist Attacks, 2001 -- Juvenile literature
   ISBN 0531250407; 9780531250402; 9780531265659
                                                LC 2011009586
This book presents an "overview of the events of September 11, 2001 and the impact the day continues to have on present day life.... Boxed text adds information about international reaction, and the life of Osama Bin Laden, and other topics throughout the book..... The immediate emergency responses at each site are described as well as government actions such as immediate grounding of planes . . . and military initiatives in the Middle East." (Children's Literature)

Includes bibliographical references (p. 61) and index.

Brown, Don
   ★ **America** is under attack; September 11, 2001: the day the towers fell. Roaring Brook Press 2011 un il $16.99
Grades: 2 3 4   **973.931**
   1. Terrorism 2. September 11 terrorist attacks, 2001 3. War on terrorism
   ISBN 978-1-5964-3694-7; 1-5964-3694-8
                                                LC 2010045417
"Brown's compelling narrative chronologically recounts the morning's events in a tone both straightforward and compassionate, without resorting to sensationalism. Brown's watercolor illustrations, covering most of each spread, mirror this voice, conveying the day's chaos and despair without unnecessarily frightening readers." SLJ

Burgan, Michael
   George W. Bush; Michael Burgan. Marshall Cavendish Benchmark 2012 112 p. $34.21
Grades: 5 6 7 8   **973.931**
   1. Terrorism 2. Presidents -- United States 3. Presidents

-- United States -- Biography -- Juvenile literature
ISBN 1608701840; 9781608701841

LC 2010014801

This book "in the 'Presidents and Their Times' series
provides . . . information about George W. Bush and how
he handled critical situations (e.g., domestic spying vis-a-vis
telephone records to highlight the difficulty battling terrorism and the effect of Bush's response to Hurricane Katrina).
. . . Personal information is also provided about his early
years, including his marriage to Laura, entry into politics,
relationships with other family members, a decision to stop
drinking, and his choice to become a Christian fundamen-
talist." Also included are "color and older black and white
photos" and back matter such as "a timeline, chapter notes
with complete citations, a glossary, books and websites for
additional information, bibliography (books, articles, media), and index." (Children's Literature)

Includes bibliographical references and index

Fradin, Dennis B.

September 11, 2001; by Dennis Brindell Fradin. Marshall Cavendish Benchmark 2009 47p il map (Turning
points in U.S. history) lib bdg $21.95

Grades: 3 4 5   **973.931**

1. September 11 terrorist attacks, 2001 2. War on
terrorism
ISBN 978-0-7614-4259-2 lib bdg; 0-7614-4259-6
lib bdg

LC 2008038267

This book provides "accurate, nonsensationalized information in [a] well-organized, clearly written, and politically
neutral [text]. The photos are crisp, and, due to the subject
matter, heartrending." SLJ

Includes glossary and bibliographical references

973.932   Administration of Barack Obama, 2009-

Staake, Bob

The **First** Pup; the real story of how Bo got to the
White House. Feiwel and Friends 2010 un il $16.99

Grades: 1 2 3   **973.932**

1. Dogs 2. Lawyers 3. Presidents 4. Senators 5. State
legislators 6. Nobel laureates for peace 7. Presidents
-- United States -- Family
ISBN 978-0-312-61346-4; 0-312-61346-6

Weatherford, Carole Boston

First pooch; the Obamas pick a pet. Illustrated by Amy
Bates. Marshall Cavendish 2009 un il $16.99

Grades: PreK K 1 2   **973.932**

1. Dogs 2. Presidents 3. Presidents -- United States
-- Family
ISBN 978-0-7614-5636-0; 0-7614-5636-8

LC 2009006117

"This brief, lighthearted chronicle of the Obama family's search for a suitable puppy to fulfill candidate Obama's
promise to his daughters focuses on Malia and Sasha. But it
also brings in information about promises made by previous
presidents, various breeds of dogs that lived in the White
House, whimsical duties of a first dog. . . . Lively watercolor,
pencil, and gouache illustrations featuring a smiling Obama
family happy in their endeavors, portraits of select past presidents, and a lineup of adorable potential first pooches add to
the telling." Booklist

Zeiger, Jennifer

Barack Obama; by Jennifer Zeiger. Children's Press
2012 64 p. ill. (chiefly col.), col. map (library binding)
$30.00; (paperback) $8.95

Grades: 4 5 6   **973.932**

1. Presidents -- United States -- Biography 2. Racially
mixed people -- United States -- Biography 3. Presidents
-- United States -- Biography -- Juvenile literature 4.
Racially mixed people -- United States -- Biography --
Juvenile literature
ISBN 0531230503; 0531281507; 9780531230503;
9780531281505

LC 2011031124

This book presents a "nonfiction account of President
[Barack]Obama's life for middle school students. . . . The
book includes many color photographs of the President as a
young boy and young adult. It gives the details of his life in
Indonesia and Hawaii and traces his career up to the 2012 re-
election campaign. His education is a focus of the biography
and there is ample discussion of his educational career and
how it has helped to shape him into the man he is today."
(Children's Literature)

Includes bibliographical references (p. 61) and index.

974   Specific states of United States

Rylant, Cynthia, 1954-

★ **Appalachia**; the voices of sleeping birds. illustrated
by Barry Moser. Harcourt Brace Jovanovich 1991 21p il
$17; pa $6

Grades: 4 5 6 7   **974**

1. Appalachian region
ISBN 0-15-201605-8; 0-15-201893-X pa

LC 90-36798

"Taking her subtitle from a passage by James Agee, the
author conveys with a marvelous economy of words the
essence of the very special part of America where she was
raised. A poetic text projects emotion as well as information.
. . . Moser's watercolors capture the scene perfectly. . . . The
book is a treasure—simply a beautiful combination of text
and art." Horn Book

974.1   Maine

Dornfeld, Margaret

Maine; by Margaret Dornfeld and Joyce Hart. 2nd ed.;
Marshall Cavendish Benchmark 2010 144p il map (Celebrate the states) lib bdg $42.79

Grades: 5 6 7 8   **974.1**

ISBN 978-0-7614-4726-9; 0-7614-4726-1

LC 2009002583

This offers information on the geography, history, wildlife, governmental structure, economy, cultural diversity,
peoples, religion, and landmarks of Maine.

Includes bibliographical references

Heinrichs, Ann

Maine; by Ann Heinrichs. Children's Press 2008 144p il map (America the beautiful, third series) lib bdg $38

Grades: 4 5 6 7   **974.1**

  ISBN 978-0-531-18575-9; 0-531-18575-3

                                              LC 2007-302

Describes the history, geography, ecology, people, economy, cities, and sights of the state of Maine.

  Includes glossary and bibliographical references

Peterson, Judy Monroe

Maine; past and present. Rosen Central 2011 48p il map (The United States: past and present) lib bdg $26.50; pa $11.75

Grades: 3 4 5 6   **974.1**

  ISBN 978-1-4358-9484-6 lib bdg; 1-4358-9484-7 lib bdg; 978-1-4358-9511-9 pa; 1-4358-9511-8 pa

                                              LC 2009048769

Presents the history, geography, government, economy, and people of Maine, as well as general facts about the state.

  Includes glossary and bibliographical references

974.2   New Hampshire

Auden, Scott

New Hampshire, 1603-1776; [by] Scott Auden; with Alan Taylor, consultant. National Geographic Society 2007 109p il map (Voices from colonial America) $21.95; lib bdg $32.90

Grades: 5 6 7 8   **974.2**

  1. New Hampshire -- History

  ISBN 978-1-4263-0034-9; 1-4263-0034-4; 978-1-4263-0035-6 lib bdg; 1-4263-0035-2 lib bdg

                                              LC 2006-36055

Provides a look at the long and changing colonial history of the state of New Hampshire through a review of its borders, founding fathers, motto, and more, complete with archival images, period maps, and various first-person accounts.

Offers "thorough, well-documented information about the struggles and successes of early non-native settlers [in New Hampshire]. . . . Many reproductions of period illustrations (both color and sepia) and some photos of archival documents and maps enhance the text." Horn Book Guide

  Includes bibliographical references

Ciarleglio, Lauren

New Hampshire; past and present. Rosen Central 2011 48p il map (The United States: past and present) lib bdg $26.50; pa $11.75

Grades: 3 4 5 6   **974.2**

  ISBN 978-1-4358-9489-1 lib bdg; 1-4358-9489-8 lib bdg; 978-1-4358-9516-4 pa; 1-4358-9516-9 pa

                                              LC 2009053334

Presents the history, geography, government, economy, and people of New Hampshire, as well as general facts about the state.

  Includes bibliographical references

Kent, Deborah

New Hampshire. Children's Press 2010 144p il map (America the beautiful, third series) lib bdg $39

Grades: 4 5 6 7   **974.2**

  ISBN 978-0-531-18501-8; 0-531-18501-X

                                              LC 2008048940

Takes readers on a tour of New Hampshire, describing the state's history, culture, land, economy, government, and sights, and including unique facts, color maps and photos, the state song, suggested activities, lists of famous people, cultural institutions, and annual events, and other resources.

  Includes glossary and bibliographical references

Otfinoski, Steven

New Hampshire; [by] Steve Otfinoski. 2nd ed.; Marshall Cavendish Benchmark 2008 144p il map (Celebrate the states) lib bdg $39.93

Grades: 4 5 6 7   **974.2**

  ISBN 978-0-7614-2718-6; 0-7614-2718-X

                                              LC 2007-9944

First published 1999

"Provides comprehensive information on the geography, history, wildlife, governmental structure, economy, cultural diversity, peoples, religion, and landmarks of New Hampshire." Publisher's note

  Includes bibliographical references

974.3   Vermont

Heinrichs, Ann

Vermont. Children's Press 2010 144p il map (America the beautiful, third series) lib bdg $39

Grades: 4 5 6 7   **974.3**

  ISBN 978-0-531-18506-3; 0-531-18506-0

                                              LC 2008007241

Presents an introduction to the geography, natural resources, history, economy, important sites, daily life, and people of Vermont.

  Includes glossary and bibliographical references

Sommers, Michael

Vermont; past and present. Rosen Central 2011 48p il map (The United States: past and present) lib bdg $26.50; pa $11.75

Grades: 3 4 5 6   **974.3**

  ISBN 978-1-4358-9498-3 lib bdg; 1-4358-9498-7 lib bdg; 978-1-4358-9525-6 pa; 1-4358-9525-8 pa

                                              LC 2009053185

Presents the history, geography, government, economy, and people of Vermont, as well as general facts about the state.

  Includes bibliographical references

974.4   Massachusetts

Bjorklund, Ruth

Massachusetts; [by] Ruth Bjorklund, Stephanie Fitzgerald. 2nd ed.; Marshall Cavendish Benchmark 2010 90p il map (It's my state!) lib bdg $31.36

Grades: 3 4 5   **974.4**

  ISBN 978-1-6087-0053-0; 1-6087-0053-4

                                              LC 2010003927

First published 2003

Surveys the history, geography, government, and economy of the state of Massachusetts as well as the diverse ways of life of its people

Freedman, Jeri

Massachusetts; past and present. Rosen Central 2010 48p il map (The United States: past and present) lib bdg $26.50; pa $11.50

Grades: 3 4 5 6   **974.4**

ISBN 978-1-4358-5294-5 lib bdg; 1-4358-5294-X lib bdg; 978-1-4358-5586-1 pa; 1-4358-5586-8 pa

LC 2008-54229

Presents the history, geography, government, economy, and people of Massachusetts, as well as general facts about the state.

Includes glossary and bibliographical references

Fritz, Jean

★ **Who's** that stepping on Plymouth Rock? illustrated by J. B. Handelsman. Coward, McCann & Geoghegan 1975 30p il hardcover o.p. pa $6.99

Grades: 2 3 4   **974.4**

1. Plymouth Rock

ISBN 0-698-20325-9; 0-698-11681-X pa

"Both a delightful story and a perceptive commentary on how the mythmaking process works in American history." N Y Times Book Rev

Krensky, Stephen

What's the big idea? four centuries of innovation in Boston. [by] Stephen Krensky. Charlesbridge 2008 64p il lib bdg $18.95; pa $9.95

Grades: 4 5 6   **974.4**

1. Boston (Mass.) -- History

ISBN 978-1-58089-310-7 lib bdg; 1-58089-310-4 lib bdg; 978-1-58089-311-4 pa; 1-58089-311-2 pa

LC 2006021255

This "title combines a short history of Boston with brief biographies of some of the city's major figures in diverse fields. . . . Each page includes a well-captioned illustration, many in color, and the book is effectively laid out, making for pleasant browsing. . . . Teachers and students . . . will find some well-presented and useful information here." Booklist

Includes bibliographical references

LeVert, Suzanne

Massachusetts; by Suzanne LeVert and Tamra B. Orr. 2nd ed.; Marshall Cavendish Benchmark 2009 144p il map (Celebrate the states) lib bdg $42.79

Grades: 4 5 6 7   **974.4**

ISBN 978-0-7614-3005-6; 0-7614-3005-9

First published 2000

"Provides comprehensive information on the geography, history, wildlife, governmental structure, economy, cultural diversity, peoples, religion, and landmarks of Massachusetts." Publisher's note

Includes glossary and bibliographical references

Sewall, Marcia

★ The **pilgrims** of Plimoth; written and illustrated by Marcia Sewall. Atheneum Pubs. 1986 48p il hardcover o.p. pa $6.99

Grades: 3 4 5 6   **974.4**

1. Pilgrims (New England colonists) 2. Pilgrims (New

England colonists) -- Juvenile literature

ISBN 0-689-31250-4; 0-689-80861-5 pa

LC 86-3362

"Translating narrative and descriptive details into visual images, the illustrations accompany every page of text, occasionally overspreading double pages for panoramic effects. Combining subtle, modulating color with a spiritual as well as an actual luminosity, the paintings—done in gouache—are vibrant with the daily pulse of life among an energetic, enterprising people." Horn Book

Trueit, Trudi Strain

Massachusetts; by Trudi Strain Trueit. Children's Press 2008 144p il map (America the beautiful, third series) lib bdg $38

Grades: 4 5 6 7   **974.4**

ISBN 978-0-531-18561-2; 0-531-18561-3

LC 2006-39235

Describes the history, geography, ecology, people, economy, cities, and sights of the state of Massachusetts.

Includes glossary and bibliographical references

Waters, Kate

Sarah Morton's day; a day in the life of a pilgrim girl. photographs by Russ Kendall. Scholastic 1989 32p il hardcover o.p. pa $5.99

Grades: 2 3 4   **974.4**

1. Pilgrims (New England colonists) 2. Pilgrims (New England colonists) -- Juvenile literature

ISBN 0-590-42634-6; 0-590-47400-6 pa

LC 88-35581

Text and photographs of Plimouth Plantation follow a pilgrim girl through a typical day as she milks the goats, cooks and serves meals, learns her letters, and adjusts to her new stepfather

Includes glossary

974.5   Rhode Island

Burgan, Michael

Rhode Island. Children's Press 2009 144p il map (America the beautiful, third series) $39

Grades: 4 5 6 7   **974.5**

ISBN 978-0-531-18590-2; 0-531-18590-7

LC 2007037178

Presents an introduction to the geography, natural resources, history, economy, important sites, daily life, and people of Rhode Island.

Includes glossary and bibliographical references

Furgang, Adam

Rhode Island; past and present. Rosen Central 2011 48p il map (The United States: past and present) lib bdg $26.50; pa $11.95

Grades: 3 4 5 6   **974.5**

ISBN 978-1-4358-9494-5 lib bdg; 1-4358-9494-4 lib bdg; 978-1-4358-9521-8 pa; 1-4358-9521-5 pa

LC 2010001451

Presents the history, geography, government, economy, and people of Rhode Island, as well as general facts about the state.

Includes bibliographical references

Klein, Ted

Rhode Island; by Ted Klein. 2nd ed.; Marshall Cavendish Benchmark 2008 144p il map (Celebrate the states) lib bdg $39.93

Grades: 4 5 6 7   **974.5**

ISBN 978-0-7614-2560-1; 0-7614-2560-8

LC 2006-36490

First published 1999

"Provides comprehensive information on the geography, history, wildlife, governmental structure, economy, cultural diversity, peoples, religion, and landmarks of Rhode Island." Publisher's note

Includes bibliographical references

974.6   Connecticut

Burgan, Michael

Connecticut; [by] Michael Burgan, Stephanie Fitzgerald. 2nd ed.; Marshall Cavendish Benchmark 2010 90p il map (It's my state) lib bdg $31.36

Grades: 3 4 5   **974.6**

ISBN 978-1-6087-0047-9; 1-6087-0047-X

LC 2010003917

First published 2003

Surveys the history, geography, government, economy, and people of Connecticut.

Connecticut, 1614-1776. National Geographic Society 2007 109p il map (Voices from colonial America) $21.95; lib bdg $32.90

Grades: 5 6 7 8   **974.6**

ISBN 978-1-4263-0068-4; 1-4263-0068-9; 978-1-4263-0069-1 lib bdg; 1-4263-0069-7 lib bdg

LC 2007-3123

A history of Connecticut from its beginning as an English colony to 1788 when it became the fifth state.

Offers " thorough, well-documented information about the struggles and successes of early colonial settlers and settlements. . . . Many reproductions of period illustrations and some photographs of period documents and maps with relevant captions are included." Horn Book Guide

Includes bibliographical references

Kent, Zachary

Connecticut; by Zachary Kent. Children's Press 2008 144p il map (America the beautiful, third series) lib bdg $38

Grades: 4 5 6 7   **974.6**

ISBN 978-0-531-18571-1; 0-531-18571-0

LC 2007-2328

Describes the history, geography, ecology, people, economy, cities, and sights of the state of Connecticut.

Includes glossary and bibliographical references

La Bella, Laura

Connecticut; past and present. Rosen Central 2011 48p il map (The United States: past and present) lib bdg $26.50; pa $11.75

Grades: 3 4 5 6   **974.6**

ISBN 978-1-4358-9478-5 lib bdg; 1-4358-9478-2 lib bdg; 978-1-4358-9505-8 pa; 1-4358-9505-3 pa

LC 2010000401

Presents the history, geography, government, economy, and people of Connecticut, as well as general facts about the state.

Includes glossary and bibliographical references

974.7   New York

Bial, Raymond

★ Tenement; immigrant life on the Lower East Side. Houghton Mifflin 2002 48p il $16

Grades: 4 5 6 7   **974.7**

1. Poor 2. Immigrants -- United States 3. Tenement-houses -- Juvenile literature 4. Immigrants -- New York (N.Y.) -- History -- Juvenile literature

ISBN 0-618-13849-8

LC 2002-00407

Presents a view of New York City's tenements during the peak years of foreign immigration, discussing living conditions, laws pertaining to tenements, and the occupations of their residents

"The writing is particularly clear and sharp. Calling upon and quoting the writing of reformer Jacob Riis (and featuring his compelling photographs), Bial explains simply, yet engagingly, what tenement life was like. . . . Along with Riis' photographs, Bial provides some of his own, taken at the Lower East Side Tenement Museum in New York City." Booklist

Includes bibliographical references

Burgan, Michael

New York, 1609-1776; [by] Michael Burgan; with Timothy J. Shannon, consultant. National Geographic Society 2006 109p il map (Voices from colonial America) $21.95; lib bdg $32.90

Grades: 5 6 7 8   **974.7**

1. New York (State) -- History

ISBN 978-0-7922-6390-6; 0-7922-6390-1; 978-0-7922-6860-4 lib bdg; 0-7922-6860-1 lib bdg

LC 2005-22033

Presents a brief history of colonial New York, from 1609 to 1776, and contains illustrations, historical maps, and first-person accounts from explorers, Native Americans, and colonists on early settlements.

Includes bibliographical references

Elish, Dan

New York; [by] Dan Elish and Stephanie Fitzgerald. 2nd ed.; Marshall Cavendish Benchmark 2010 90p il map (It's my state!) lib bdg $31.36

Grades: 3 4 5   **974.7**

ISBN 978-1-6087-0056-1; 1-6087-0056-9

LC 2010003916

First published 2003

Surveys the history, geography, and economy of New York State, as well as the diverse ways of life of its people.

Englar, Mary

Dutch colonies in America. Compass Point Books 2009 48p il map (We the people) lib bdg $26.60

Grades: 4 5 6 **974.7**
1. Dutch Americans
ISBN 978-0-7565-3837-8

LC 2008007211

This is a history of Dutch exploration and colonization in North America.

This provides "solid background matter and [introduces] key people and vocabulary." SLJ

Includes glossary and bibliographical references

Glaser, Linda
★ **Emma's** poem; the voice of the Statue of Liberty. with paintings by Claire A. Nivola. Houghton Mifflin Books for Children 2010 un il $17
Grades: K 1 2 3 **974.7**
1. Statue of Liberty (New York, N.Y.)
ISBN 0-547-17184-6; 978-0-547-17184-5

LC 2009026924

This is an account of how the poet and social reformer Emma Lazarus came to write the sonnet, 'The New Colossus,' now on the pedestal of The Statue of Liberty. The text of the poem is appended. "Primary." (Horn Book)

"The art and words are moving in this picture book, which pairs free verse with detailed, full-page paintings in watercolor, ink, and gouache to tell the history behind Lazarus' famous inscription on the Statue of Liberty." Booklist

Huey, Lois Miner
American archaeology uncovers the Dutch colonies. Marshall Cavendish Benchmark 2009 64p il map (American archaeology) lib bdg $21.95
Grades: 4 5 6 7 **974.7**
1. Dutch Americans 2. Excavations (Archeology) -- United States
ISBN 978-0-7614-4263-9 lib bdg; 0-7614-4263-4 lib bdg

LC 2008050187

This describes how archeologists have learned about the history of Dutch settlers in America

"The text is quite chatty in this attractive title. . . . An inviting design with clear type includes several paintings of the period by a modern artist as well as maps and photos of excavation sites." Booklist

Includes glossary and bibliographical references

Maestro, Betsy
The **story** of the Statue of Liberty; [by] Betsy & Giulio Maestro. Lothrop, Lee & Shepard Bks. 1986 39p il hardcover o.p. pa $5.95
Grades: K 1 2 3 **974.7**
1. Artists 2. Sculptors 3. Statue of Liberty (New York, N.Y.)
ISBN 0-688-08746-9 pa

LC 85-11324

"Although Maestro simplifies the story—including only the most important people's names, for example—she still presents an accurate account of what happened. The exceptional drawings are visually delightful—primarily in the blue-green range, although they are in full color—and cover most of every page. Human figures—workers, tourists—are included in many drawings, indicating the statue's tremendous scale. Further, the drawings involve viewers through the use of unusual perspectives and angles and by placing the statue in scenes of city life." SLJ

Includes bibliographical references

Mann, Elizabeth
Statue of Liberty; a tale of two countries. with illustrations by Alan Witschonke. Mikaya Press 2011 47p il map (Wonders of the world) $22.95
Grades: 4 5 6 7 **974.7**
1. Artists 2. Authors 3. Lawyers 4. Sculptors 5. National monuments 6. Children's authors 7. Fairy tale writers 8. Members of Parliament
ISBN 978-1-931414-43-2; 1-931414-43-2

"The story of how Lady Liberty was conceived, constructed and bestowed makes a compelling tale. Pointing to the disparate long-term outcomes of the American and French revolutions to explain why the U.S. system of government became so admired in France, Mann takes the statue from Edouard Laboulaye's pie-in-the-sky proposal at a dinner party in 1865 to the massive opening ceremonies in 1886. . . . Witschonke supplements an array of period photos and prints with full-page or larger painted reconstructions of Bartholdi's studio and workshop, of the statue's piecemeal creation and finally of the Lady herself, properly copper colored as she initially was, presiding of New York's crowded harbor. As she still does." Kirkus

Includes bibliographical references

Marrin, Albert
★ **Flesh** & blood so cheap; the Triangle fire and its legacy. Alfred A. Knopf 2011 182p il map $19.99; lib bdg $22.99
Grades: 5 6 7 8 **974.7**
1. Fires 2. Italian Americans 3. Jews -- United States 4. Labor -- United States 5. Industrial safety -- Juvenile literature
ISBN 978-0-375-86889-4; 0-375-86889-5; 978-0-375-96889-1 lib bdg; 0-375-96889-X lib bdg

LC 2010-21533

"Published to coincide with the centennial anniversary of the 1911 fire that erupted in the Triangle Shirtwaist Factory, this powerful chronicle examines the circumstances surrounding the disaster, which resulted in the deaths of 146 workers, mostly young Italian and Jewish women. . . . B&W photographs and illustrations reveal immigrant families' impoverished living environments, while testimonials describe the 'humiliating' work rules and unsafe conditions of factories like Triangle. . . . A concluding description of a Bangladeshi garment factory fire in 2010 offers contemporary parallels. Marrin's message that protecting human dignity is our shared responsibility is vitally resonant." Publ Wkly

Includes bibliographical references

McKendry, Joe
One Times Square; a century of change at the crossroads of the world. written & illustrated by Joe McKendry. David R. Godine 2011 64 p. ill. (chiefly col.), col. maps (hardcover: alk. paper) $19.95
Grades: 4 5 6 **974.7**
1. Times Square (New York, N.Y.) -- History -- Juvenile literature
ISBN 156792364X; 9781567923643

LC 2011027379

This children's book by Joe McKendry "takes readers on a journey through 100 years of shifts and changes to . . . Times Square. . . . Beginning in 1904 when the 'New York Times' headquarters was built and forever changed the name of this small plot of land, McKendry accompanies the text with a . . . painting of the Square from a specific point of view. . . . as buildings and technology sprout and change." (Kirkus)

Includes bibliographical references and index.

Melmed, Laura Krauss

New York, New York; the Big Apple from A to Z. illustrated by Frané Lessac. HarperCollins Pub. 2005 un il $16.99; lib bdg $17.89; pa $6.99

Grades: K 1 2 3   **974.7**

1. Alphabet 2. New York (N.Y.)

ISBN 0-06-054674-6; 0-06-054876-2 lib bdg; 0-06-054877-0 pa

"From the American Museum of Natural History to the Bronx Zoo, each letter is accompanied by a peppy eight-line poem as well as multiple sidebars, factoids, and tidbits about the sights described. Melmed brilliantly touches on all the major sights of NYC." SLJ

Mills, J. Elizabeth

New York; past and present. Rosen Central 2010 48p il map (The United States: past and present) lib bdg $26.50; pa $11.75

Grades: 3 4 5 6   **974.7**

1. New York (State)

ISBN 978-1-4358-5285-3 lib bdg; 1-4358-5285-0 lib bdg; 978-1-4358-5568-7 pa; 1-4358-5568-X pa

LC 2008054256

Presents the history, geography, government, economy, and people of New York, as well as general facts about the state.

Includes bibliographical references

Murphy, Jim

The **giant** and how he humbugged America; by Jim Murphy. Scholastic Press 2012 112 p. (hardcover: alk. paper) $19.99

Grades: 5 6 7 8   **974.7**

1. Relics 2. Sculpture 3. Impostors and imposture 4. Cardiff giant -- Juvenile literature 5. Forgery of antiquities -- New York (State) -- Cardiff -- Juvenile literature

ISBN 0439691842; 9780439691840

LC 2011036798

In this book, "[Jim] Murphy traces the checkered career of the 'Cardiff Giant,' a 10-foot-long stone figure unearthed in 1869 in an upstate New York farmyard. The giant was a national sensation until its unmasking as a hoax a few months later. Almost from the outset, both educated and popular opinion was divided over whether the figure was a fossilized human or a carving, an ancient relic or a modern 'humbug.' Murphy shows how the controversy itself fueled the giant's notoriety." (Booklist)

Includes bibliographical references and index

Platt, Richard

New York City; an illustrated history of the Big Apple. illustrated by Manuela Cappon. Kingfisher 2010 45p il map (Through time) $16.99

Grades: 4 5 6 7   **974.7**

1. New York (N.Y.)

ISBN 978-0-7534-6416-8; 0-7534-6416-0

This is a history of New York City from its Native American origins to the present.

"In this magnificently illustrated work, historical happenings and intriguing offshoots are showcased like stars on Broadway. . . . A wealth of information in an engaging format." Booklist

Rappaport, Doreen

★ **Lady** Liberty; a biography. illustrated by Matt Tavares. Candlewick Press 2008 un il $17.99

Grades: 2 3 4 5   **974.7**

1. Statue of Liberty (New York, N.Y.)

ISBN 978-0-7636-2530-6; 0-7636-2530-2

LC 2007-40723

This presents the story of the Statue of Liberty including "its conception and construction in France, the efforts to raise funds on both sides of the Atlantic, preparations for her arrival in New York, and the celebration culminating in her unveiling in 1886. Rappaport tells the story in a series of free-verse poems representing the reflections of individuals. . . . The first-person narratives effectively convey the personal significance the statue has had for many people. Large in scale and monumental in effect, the watercolor, ink, and pencil illustrations . . . offer often beautiful views of her many-faceted story." Booklist

Includes bibliographical references

Schomp, Virginia

New York; [by] Virginia Schomp. 2nd ed.; Benchmark Books 2006 144p il map (Celebrate the states) lib bdg $39.93

Grades: 4 5 6 7   **974.7**

1. New York (State)

ISBN 978-0-7614-1738-5; 0-7614-1738-9

LC 2004-853

First published 1997

This book about New York covers "standard facts: geography, history, government, economy, landmarks, and regions. . . . [It is] attractively illustrated with clear maps, charts, and pie graphs. Photos and reproductions of original documents add to overall effectiveness. . . . . Excellent additions for reports or general interest." SLJ

Includes bibliographical references

Shea, Pegi Deitz

★ **Liberty** rising; the story of the Statue of Liberty. illustrated by Wade Zahares. Henry Holt 2005 un il $17.95

Grades: 2 3 4   **974.7**

1. Artists 2. Sculptors 3. Statue of Liberty (New York, N.Y.)

ISBN 0-8050-7220-9

LC 2004-24279

In this account of the building of the Statue of Liberty "Shea introduces the size and scale of creating such a large object. . . . Each step in the process . . . is told in simple text. . . . The book is easy to read, with three-quarter spreads of illustration and single columns of text. The stylized graphic art is fairly realistic with bold colors and unusual angles to create a sense of excitement." SLJ

Includes bibliographical references

Somervill, Barbara A.

New York; by Barbara A. Somervill. Children's Press 2008 144p il map (America the beautiful, third series) lib bdg $38

Grades: 4 5 6 7 **974.7**

ISBN 978-0-531-18565-0; 0-531-18565-6

LC 2006101742

Describes the history, geography, ecology, famous people, economy, cities, and sights of the state of New York.

Includes glossary and bibliographical references

Talbott, Hudson

★ **River** of dreams; the story of the Hudson River. G. P. Putnam's Sons 2009 un il map $17.99

Grades: 4 5 6 7 **974.7**

ISBN 978-0-399-24521-3; 0-399-24521-9

Talbott offers a "compelling blend of political and natural history in this beautifully illustrated celebration of the Hudson River. Combining delicate watercolor-and-pencil illustrations with accessible text, the spreads move briskly through the Hudson's River's history." Booklist

Vila, Laura

★ **Building** Manhattan. Viking 2008 un il $16.99

Grades: K 1 2 3 **974.7**

1. Manhattan (New York, N.Y.) 2. New York (N.Y.) -- History

ISBN 978-0-670-06284-3; 0-670-06284-7

LC 2007-38119

"Tracing the growth of Manhattan from a time 'before maps or words were used' to the present day, . . . author/artist Vila employs many lenses—geography, sociology, politics, ethnography. Likewise, her radiantly dramatic mural-like paintings present a wide range of visual styles and approaches. . . . While her paintings are lavish, it takes her only one pithy sentence on each spread to convey both a specific moment and a sense of history and human ambitions." Publ Wkly

974.8 Pennsylvania

Hart, Joyce

Pennsylvania; [by] Joyce Hart and Richard Hantula. 2nd ed.; Marshall Cavendish Benchmark 2010 90p il map (It's my state!) lib bdg $31.36

Grades: 3 4 5 **974.8**

1. Pennsylvania -- Juvenile literature.

ISBN 978-1-6087-0058-5; 1-6087-0058-5

LC 2010003931

First published 2004

Surveys the history, geography, government, and economy of Pennsylvania, as well as the diverse ways of life of its people

Hasan, Heather

Pennsylvania; past and present. Rosen Central 2010 48p il map (The United States: past and present) lib bdg $26.50; pa $11.50

Grades: 3 4 5 6 **974.8**

ISBN 978-1-4358-5291-4 lib bdg; 1-4358-5291-5 lib bdg; 978-1-4358-5580-9 pa; 1-4358-5580-9 pa

LC 2008-54214

Presents the history, geography, government, economy, and people of Pennsylvania, as well as general facts about the state.

Includes glossary and bibliographical references

Magaziner, Henry J.

★ **Our** Liberty Bell; by Henry Jonas Magaziner; illustrated by John O'Brien. Holiday House 2007 32p il $15.95; pa $5.95

Grades: 2 3 4 **974.8**

1. Liberty Bell

ISBN 978-0-8234-1892-3; 0-8234-1892-8; 978-0-8234-2081-0 pa; 0-8234-2081-7 pa

LC 2004054196

"Written with clarity and verve. . . . O'Brien's imaginative and sometimes witty ink drawings illustrate with finesse." Booklist

Includes glossary and bibliographical references

Peters, Stephen

Pennsylvania; by Stephen Peters and Joyce Hart. 2nd ed.; Marshall Cavendish Benchmark 2009 144p il map (Celebrate the states) lib bdg $42.79

Grades: 4 5 6 7 **974.8**

ISBN 978-0-7614-3403-0; 0-7614-3403-8

LC 2008-8032

First published 2000

"Provides comprehensive information on the geography, history, wildlife, governmental structure, economy, cultural diversity, peoples, religion, and landmarks of Pennsylvania." Publisher's note

Includes bibliographical references

Somervill, Barbara A.

Pennsylvania. Children's Press 2009 144p il map (America the beautiful, third series) lib bdg $39

Grades: 4 5 6 7 **974.8**

ISBN 978-0-531-18588-9; 0-531-18588-5

LC 2007031121

Presents an introduction to the geography, natural resources, history, economy, important sites, daily life, and people of Pennsylvania.

Includes glossary and bibliographical references

Staton, Hilarie

Independence Hall. Chelsea Clubhouse 2010 48p il (Symbols of American freedom) $30

Grades: 3 4 5 **974.8**

1. Independence Hall (Philadelphia, Pa.) 2. Philadelphia (Pa.) 3. United States -- Politics and government -- 1775-1783, Revolution

ISBN 978-1-60413-521-3; 1-60413-521-2

LC 2009-12824

This book about Independence Hall in Phildelphia "provides nearly as much information as a guided tour by a park ranger. [It begins] with the story of how the place came to be, and where it fits into U.S. history. Information boxes offer additional background and some surprising facts. . . . The final chapter shows the landmark today and includes maps and photographs of the visitors' center and some of the things individuals might see or do while visiting the site. Much information is packed into [this] slim [book]. Excellent . . . for state reports or to complement U.S. history units." SLJ

Includes glossary

974.9 New Jersey

Doak, Robin S.

New Jersey 1609-1776; y. [by] Robin Doak with Brendan McConville. National Geographic 2005 109p il map (Voices from colonial America) $21.95; lib bdg $32.90

Grades: 5 6 7 8   **974.9**

1. Georgia -- History
ISBN 978-0-7922-6385-2; 0-7922-6385-5; 978-0-7922-6680-8 lib bdg; 0-7922-6680-3 lib bdg

LC 2004-26242

"This book gives detailed descriptions of family life and working in a Colonial village and the fight for independence. It also includes information about the Native people, early settlers, and first developments. . . . Paintings, maps, woodcuts, portraits, and reproductions accompany the well-written text. . . . An excellent resource." SLJ

Includes bibliographical references

Kent, Deborah

New Jersey; by Deborah Kent. Children's Press 2008 144p il map (America the beautiful, third series) lib bdg $38

Grades: 4 5 6 7   **974.9**

ISBN 978-0-531-18564-3; 0-531-18564-8

LC 2006100058

Describes the history, geography, ecology, people, economy, cities, and sights of the state of New Jersey.

Includes glossary and bibliographical references

King, David C.

New Jersey; [by] David C. King and William A. McGeveran, Jr. 2nd ed.; Marshall Cavendish Benchmark 2010 90p il map (It's my state!) lib bdg $31.36

Grades: 3 4 5   **974.9**

ISBN 978-1-6087-0055-4; 1-6087-0055-0

LC 2010003910

First published 2004

Surveys the history, geography, government, and economy of New Jersey as well as the diverse ways of life of its people

Mattern, Joanne

New Jersey; past and present. Rosen Central 2010 48p il map (The United States: past and present) lib bdg $26.50; pa $11.75

Grades: 3 4 5 6   **974.9**

ISBN 978-1-4358-3525-2 lib bdg; 1-4358-3525-5 lib bdg; 978-1-4358-8500-4 pa; 1-4358-8500-7 pa

LC 2009026985

Presents the history, geography, government, economy, and people of New Jersey, as well as general facts about the state.

Includes bibliographical references

Moragne, Wendy

New Jersey; by Wendy Moragne and Tamra B. Orr. 2nd ed.; Marshall Cavendish Benchmark 2009 144p il map (Celebrate the states) lib bdg $39.93

Grades: 4 5 6 7   **974.9**

ISBN 978-0-7614-3006-3; 0-7614-3006-7

LC 2007-38642

First published 2000

"Provides comprehensive information on the geography, history, wildlife, governmental structure, economy, cultural diversity, peoples, religion, and landmarks of New Jersey." Publisher's note

Includes bibliographical references

975.1 Delaware

King, David C.

Delaware; [by] David C. King, Brian Fitzgerald. 2nd ed.; Marshall Cavendish Benchmark 2010 90p il map (It's my state) lib bdg $31.36

Grades: 3 4 5   **975.1**

ISBN 978-1-6087-0048-6; 1-6087-0048-8

LC 2010003920

Surveys the history, geography, government, and economy of Delaware as well as the diverse ways of life of its people.

Price, Karen

Delaware, 1638-1776; [by] Karen Hossell, with Karin Wulf, consultant. National Geographic Society 2006 109p il map (Voices from colonial America) $21.95; lib bdg $32.90

Grades: 5 6 7 8   **975.1**

ISBN 978-0-7922-6408-8; 0-7922-6408-8; 978-0-7922-6864-2 lib bdg; 0-7922-6864-4 lib bdg

LC 2006-13444

"The text is . . . written in full paragraphs, making up chronological chapters. These are divided into topical sections, which are clearly marked by large headings. This lovely, calm layout is liberally sprinkled with primary source illustrations, including reproductions of period maps, pamphlets, paintings, and drawings. . . . An essential purchase for schools with a colonies research project . . . and for the public libraries that support their communities." Voice Youth Advocates

Includes bibliographical references

Schuman, Michael

Delaware; by Michael Schuman and Marlee Richards. 2nd ed.; Marshall Cavendish Benchmark 2009 144p il map (Celebrate the states) lib bdg $42.79

Grades: 4 5 6 7   **975.1**

ISBN 978-0-7614-3399-6; 0-7614-3399-6

LC 2008-5369

First published 2000

"Provides comprehensive information on the geography, history, wildlife, governmental structure, economy, cultural diversity, peoples, religion, and landmarks of Delaware." Publisher's note

Includes bibliographical references

Wolny, Philip

Delaware; past and present. Rosen Central 2010 48p il map (The United States: past and present) lib bdg $26.50; pa $11.75

Grades: 3 4 5 6　　**975.1**

ISBN 978-1-4358-3526-9 lib bdg; 1-4358-3526-3 lib bdg; 978-1-4358-8502-8 pa; 1-4358-8502-3 pa

LC 2009024554

Presents the history, geography, government, economy, and people of Delaware, as well as general facts about the state.

Includes glossary and bibliographical references

975.2　Maryland

Blashfield, Jean F.

Maryland; by Jean F. Blashfield. Children's Press 2008 144p il map (America the beautiful, third series) lib bdg $38

Grades: 5 6 7 8　　**975.2**

ISBN 978-0-531-18576-6; 0-531-18576-1

LC 2007-12699

Describes the history, geography, ecology, people, economy, cities, and sights of the state of Maryland.

Includes glossary and bibliographical references

Doak, Robin S.

Maryland, 1634-1776. National Geographic 2007 105p il map (Voices from colonial America) $21.95; lib bdg $32.90

Grades: 5 6 7 8　　**975.2**

ISBN 978-1-4263-0143-8; 1-4263-0143-x; 978-1-4263-0144-5 lib bdg; 1-4263-0144-8 lib bdg

LC 2007-27886

Offers "thorough, well-documented information about the struggles and successes of early colonial settlers and settlements. . . . Many reproductions of period illustrations and some photographs of period documents and maps with relevant captions are included." Horn Book Guide

Includes bibliographical references

Friddell, Claudia

★ Goliath; hero of the great Baltimore fire. illustrated by Troy Howell. Sleeping Bear Press 2010 un il (True stories) $17.95

Grades: K 1 2 3 4 5　　**975.2**

1. Fire 2. Horses 3. Fire fighting 4. Working animals 5. Baltimore (Md.) -- History

ISBN 978-1-58536-455-8; 1-58536-455-X

LC 2009036941

"The Great Baltimore Fire of 1904 was one of the most destructive in U.S. history. Friddell brings the event to life through the true story of a huge horse from Engine Company 15. Goliath bore the full brunt of an explosion and then heroically pulled an entire fire rig to safety by himself. The text builds suspense. . . . Howell's expressive, sepia-toned illustrations interplay with the text to keep readers in the moment. Exciting, historically accurate, and visually appealing." SLJ

Includes glossary and bibliographical references

Mattern, Joanne

Maryland; past and present. Rosen Central 2010 48p il map (The United States: past and present) lib bdg $26.50; pa $11.75

Grades: 3 4 5 6　　**975.2**

ISBN 978-1-4358-3519-1 lib bdg; 1-4358-3519-0 lib bdg; 978-1-4358-8488-5 pa; 1-4358-8488-4 pa

LC 2009025517

Presents the history, geography, government, economy, and people of Maryland, as well as general facts about the state.

Includes glossary and bibliographical references

Otfinoski, Steven

Maryland; [by] Steven Otfinoski, Andy Steinitz. 2nd ed.; Marshall Cavendish Benchmark 2010 90p il map (It's my state) lib bdg $31.36

Grades: 3 4 5　　**975.2**

ISBN 978-1-6087-0052-3; 1-6087-0052-6

LC 2010003929

First published 2003

Surveys the history, geography, government, and economy of Maryland as well as the diverse ways of life of its people

Pietrzyk, Leslie

Maryland; by Leslie Rauth and Martha Kneib. 2nd ed.; Marshall Cavendish Benchmark 2008 144p il map (Celebrate the states) lib bdg $39.93

Grades: 4 5 6 7　　**975.2**

ISBN 978-0-7614-3004-9; 0-7614-3004-0

LC 2007-29497

First published 2000

"Provides comprehensive information on the geography, history, wildlife, governmental structure, economy, cultural diversity, peoples, religion, and landmarks of Maryland." Publisher's note

Includes bibliographical references

975.3　District of Columbia (Washington)

Elish, Dan

Washington, D.C. by Dan Elish. 2nd ed.; Marshall Cavendish Benchmark 2007 144p il map (Celebrate the states) lib bdg $39.93

Grades: 4 5 6 7　　**975.3**

ISBN 978-0-7614-2352-2; 0-7614-2352-4

LC 2006-13838

First published 1998

"Provides comprehensive information on the geography, history, wildlife, governmental structure, economy, cultural diversity, peoples, religion, and landmarks of Washington, D.C." Publisher's note

Includes bibliographical references

Kenney, Karen Latchana

The White House; illustrated by Judith A. Hunt. Magic Wagon 2011 32p il (Our nation's pride) lib bdg $28.50

Grades: 2 3 4　　**975.3**

1. White House (Washington, D.C.)

ISBN 978-1-61641-154-1; 1-61641-154-6

LC 2010014010

In this title about the White House "the author describes how the land was chosen, how the White House was built, the fact in burned down in 1814 and was rebuilt in 1817, and that it takes 570 buckets of white paint to cover the outside. . . . The full-color artwork not only explains the text but also gives the most photographic renderings of the [topic]." SLJ

Kent, Deborah

Washington, D.C. Children's Press 2010 144p il map (America the beautiful, third series) lib bdg $39

Grades: 4 5 6 7   **975.3**

ISBN 978-0-531-18593-3; 0-531-18593-1

LC 2008019546

Discusses the geography, history, people, government, economy, and recreation of Washington, D.C.

Includes glossary and bibliographical references

★ **Our** White House; looking in, looking out. created by The National Children's Book and Literacy Alliance; introduction by David McCullough. Candlewick Press 2008 241p il $29.99

Grades: 5 6 7 8   **975.3**

1. White House (Washington, D.C.) 2. Short stories -- Collections -- Juvenile literature 3. Presidents -- United States -- Family -- Juvenile literature

ISBN 0-7636-2067-X; 978-0-7636-2067-7

This is a collection of essays, personal accounts, historical fiction, and poetry devoted to the history of the White House. Index. "Age ten and up." (N Y Times Book Rev)

"The White House is the focus of this handsome, large-format compendium of writings, both factual and fictional, and illustrations. . . . Poems and essays, stories and memoirs—all combine to create a mosaic of impressions of the house's residents and visitors and of the important events that occurred there. . . . The often-spectacular, beautifully reproduced on glossy paper, is particularly striking." Booklist

Rinaldo, Denise

White House Q & A. Smithsonian/Collins 2008 47p il (Smithsonian Q & A) lib bdg $16.99; pa $7.99

Grades: 3 4 5   **975.3**

1. Presidents -- United States 2. White House (Washington, D.C.)

ISBN 978-0-06-089966-0 lib bdg; 0-06-089966-2 lib bdg; 978-0-06-089965-3 pa; 0-06-089965-4 pa

LC 2006102994

"The history and functions of the presidential residence are unveiled in the typical series format. The questions are organized so that the story of the White House unfolds logically—first with a definition of what it is, how it came to be, some of its history, how to visit, special rooms, and, of course, a look at how the first families live. Anecdotes are plentiful and child-centered. . . . The elegant page layout includes full-color, full-bleed illustrations from Smithsonian archives and some presidential libraries." SLJ

Includes glossary and bibliographical references

Sonneborn, Liz

District of Columbia; past and present. Rosen Central 2011 48p il map (The United States: past and present) lib bdg $26.50; pa $11.75

Grades: 3 4 5 6   **975.3**

ISBN 978-1-4358-9501-0 lib bdg; 1-4358-9501-0 lib bdg; 978-1-4358-9528-7 pa; 1-4358-9528-2 pa

LC 2009053986

This describes life in the U.S. capitol city, Washington D.C.

Includes glossary and bibliographical references

975.4   West Virginia

Byers, Ann

West Virginia; past and present. Rosen Central 2011 48p il map (The United States: past and present) lib bdg $26.50; pa $11.75

Grades: 3 4 5 6   **975.4**

ISBN 978-1-4358-9499-0 lib bdg; 1-4358-9499-5 lib bdg; 978-1-4358-9526-3 pa; 1-4358-9526-6 pa

LC 2010002514

Presents the history, geography, government, economy, and people of West Virginia, as well as general facts about the state.

Includes bibliographical references

Hoffman, Nancy

West Virginia; [by] Nancy Hoffman and Joyce Hart. 2nd ed.; Marshall Cavendish Benchmark 2007 144p il map (Celebrate the states) lib bdg $39.93

Grades: 4 5 6 7   **975.4**

ISBN 978-0-7614-2562-5; 0-7614-2562-4

LC 2006-29393

First published 1999

Relates the history and describes the geographic features, places of interest, government, industry, environmental concerns, and life of the people of West Virginia.

Includes bibliographical references

975.5   Virginia

Chorao, Kay

D is for drums; a Colonial Williamsburg ABC. [by] Kay Chorao. Harry N. Abrams 2004 un il $16.95

Grades: K 1 2 3   **975.5**

1. Alphabet 2. Colonial Williamsburg (Williamsburg, Va.)

ISBN 0-8109-4927-X

LC 2003-25793

"Chorao has created a large, visually charming, and fact-rich look at Colonial Williamsburg. Endpaper maps of the city's streets show everything from a shoemaker's shop to the Governor's Palace. Each page in between displays a huge capital letter decorated with drawings that showcase an alliterative list of words. . . . Chorao selected items to foster chuckles and amazement. Her pen-and-ink and watercolor drawings of children and animals add energy to the stunning layouts." SLJ

Demarest, Chris L.

Arlington; the story of our nation's cemetery. written and illustrated by Chris Demarest. Roaring Brook Press/ Flash Point 2010 un il $17.99

Grades: 3 4 5 6   **975.5**

1. Arlington National Cemetery (Va.)

ISBN 978-1-59643-517-9; 1-59643-517-8

"This handsome volume presents the history of Arlington National Cemetery. [It tells and illustrates] the story with quiet dignity. . . . Demarest writes clearly, organizes the information well, and illustrates the story in nicely composed, sometimes luminous paintings." Booklist

Kent, Deborah

Virginia. Children's Press 2008 144p il map (America the beautiful, third series) lib bdg $39

Grades: 4 5 6 7   **975.5**

ISBN 978-0-531-18581-0; 0-531-18581-8

LC 2007028463

Presents an introduction to the geography, natural resources, history, economy, important sites, daily life, and people of Virginia.

Includes glossary and bibliographical references

King, David C.

Virginia; [by] David C. King and Stephanie Fitzgerald. 2nd ed.; Marshall Cavendish Benchmark 2010 90p il map (It's my state!) lib bdg $31.36

Grades: 3 4 5   **975.5**

ISBN 978-1-6087-0060-8; 1-6087-0060-7

LC 2010003933

First published 2005

Surveys the history, geography, economy, and people of Virginia

Lange, Karen E.

★ **1607**; a new look at Jamestown. photography by Ira Block. National Geographic 2007 48p il $17.95; lib bdg $27.90

Grades: 3 4 5 6   **975.5**

1. Jamestown (Va.) -- History 2. Virginia -- History 3. United States -- History -- 1600-1775, Colonial period

ISBN 1-4263-0012-3; 1-4263-0013-1 lib bdg

LC 2006-05824

"In 1994, scientists unearthed important new evidence about the original Jamestown fort. The work . . . has changed many established ideas about the early settlers. 1607 incorporates these findings and offers a fascinating look at archaeology in action. Color photographs of costumed interpreters and recreated buildings from the Jamestown Settlement living-history museum depict both English and Native American ways of life." SLJ

Pobst, Sandy

Virginia, 1607-1776; [by] Sandy Pobst with Kevin D. Roberts, consultant. National Geographic Society 2005 109p il map (Voices from colonial America) $21.95; lib bdg $32.90

Grades: 5 6 7 8   **975.5**

1. Virginia -- History

ISBN 978-0-7922-6388-3; 0-7922-6388-X; 978-0-7922-6771-3 lib bdg; 0-7922-6771-0 lib bdg

LC 2005-8885

"This title discusses the colony's founding, life on the Tidewater plantations, the struggles to survive, and the desire for independence. Full of period maps; portraits; photographs; and first-person accounts from masters and slaves, explorers, Native Americans, servants, and other residents,

this is narrative nonfiction at its best. . . . An excellent resource." SLJ

Includes bibliographical references

Porterfield, Jason

Virginia; past and present. Rosen Central 2009 48p il map (The United States: past and present) lib bdg $26.50; pa $11.50

Grades: 3 4 5 6   **975.5**

ISBN 978-1-4358-5289-1 lib bdg; 1-4358-5289-3 lib bdg; 978-1-4358-5576-2 pa; 1-4358-5576-0 pa

LC 2008-54403

Presents the history, geography, government, economy, and people of Virginia, as well as general facts about the state.

Includes glossary and bibliographical references

975.6   North Carolina

Cannavale, Matthew C.

North Carolina, 1524-1776; by Matthew C. Cannavale; with Patrick Griffith, consultant. National Geographic Society 2007 109p il map (Voices from colonial America) $21.95; lib bdg $32.90

Grades: 5 6 7 8   **975.6**

ISBN 978-1-4263-0032-5; 1-4263-0032-8; 978-1-4263-0033-2 lib bdg; 1-4263-0033-6 lib bdg

LC 2006-36004

A history of colonial North Carolina.

Includes bibliographical references

Fritz, Jean

★ The **Lost** Colony of Roanoke; illustrated by Hudson Talbott. G.P. Putnam's Sons 2004 58p il map $16.99

Grades: 3 4 5 6   **975.6**

ISBN 0-399-24027-6

LC 2002-152000

Describes the English colony of Roanoke, which was founded in 1585, and discusses the mystery of its disappearance.

"Talbott's softly colored watercolor illustrations . . . are at once detailed and impressionistic. Clever touches of humor abound. . . . Fritz has scored again, making history breathe while showing both historians and archaeologists at their reconstructive best." SLJ

Gaines, Ann

North Carolina; [by] Ann Graham Gaines and Andy Steinitz. 2nd ed.; Marshall Cavendish Benchmark 2010 90p il map (It's my state!) lib bdg $31.36

Grades: 3 4 5   **975.6**

ISBN 978-1-6087-0057-8; 1-6087-0057-7

LC 2010003930

First published 2003

Surveys the history, geography, government, and economy of North Carolina as well as the diverse ways of life of its people

Heinrichs, Ann

North Carolina. Children's Press 2009 144p il map (America the beautiful, third series) lib bdg $39

Grades: 4 5 6 7 **975.6**
ISBN 978-0-531-18566-7; 0-531-18566-4
LC 2007039773

Presents an introduction to the geography, natural resources, history, economy, important sites, daily life, and people of North Carolina.

Includes glossary and bibliographical references

Lew, Kristi
North Carolina; past and present. Rosen Central 2011 48p il map (The United States: past and present) lib bdg $26.50; pa $11.75
Grades: 3 4 5 6 **975.6**
ISBN 978-1-4358-9491-4 lib bdg; 1-4358-9491-X lib bdg; 978-1-4358-9518-8 pa; 1-4358-9518-5 pa
LC 2009054264

Presents the history, geography, government, economy, and people of North Carolina, as well as general facts about the state.

Includes glossary and bibliographical references

Miller, Lee
Roanoke; the mystery of the Lost Colony. Scholastic Nonfiction 2007 112p il map $18.99
Grades: 4 5 6 7 **975.6**
1. Roanoke Island (N.C.) -- History
ISBN 0-439-71266-1; 978-0-439-71266-8
LC 2005-51820

"Miller, author of Roanoke: solving the mystery of the Lost Colony (2001), here reprises for a young audience her historical theory that a certain man sabotaged the expedition eventually known as the Lost Colony. . . . Miller does an exceptional job of preseneting the Native American culture and viewpoint. . . . This handsomely designed book features one or two illustrations on each spread, many in color, including reproductions or period drawings, paintings, and maps, as well as modern photos of sites and wildlife." Booklist

Includes bibliographical references

Reed, Jennifer
Cape Hatteras National Seashore; adventure, explore, discover. [by] Jennifer Reed. MyReportLinks.com Books 2008 128p il map (America's national parks) lib bdg $33.27
Grades: 5 6 7 8 **975.6**
1. Cape Hatteras National Seashore (N.C.)
ISBN 978-1-59845-086-6 lib bdg; 1-59845-086-7 lib bdg
LC 2006102321

This "informative, well-written book contains a physical description of the park; a summary of its history including the Native peoples of the area; activities such as hiking trails, campsites, and visitor centers; information about the park's plants, animals, and weather; full-color photographs; and numerous approved links available through the publisher's Web page. . . . Thorough, useful, and appealing, this . . . is a great update for collections." SLJ

Includes glossary and bibliographical references

Shirley, David
North Carolina; by David Shirley and Joyce Hart. 2nd ed.; Marshall Cavendish Benchmark 2010 144p il map (Celebrate the states) lib bdg $43.79

Grades: 5 6 7 8 **975.6**
ISBN 978-0-7614-4729-0; 0-7614-4729-6
LC 2009007139

First published 2001

This offers information on the geography, history, wildlife, governmental structure, economy, cultural diversity, peoples, religion, and landmarks of North Carolina.

Includes bibliographical references

975.7   South Carolina

Doak, Robin S.
South Carolina, 1540-1776; by Robin Doak with Robert Olwell. National Geographic Society 2007 109p il map (Voices from colonial America) $21.95; lib bdg $32.90
Grades: 5 6 7 8 **975.7**
1. South Carolina -- History
ISBN 978-1-4263-0066-0; 1-4263-0066-2; 978-1-4263-0067-7 lib bdg; 1-4263-0067-0 lib bdg
LC 2007-3120

A history of South Carolina from its beginning as an English colony to 1788 when it became the eighth state.

Offers "thorough, well-documented information about the struggles and successes of early colonial settlers and settlements. . . . Many reproductions of period illustrations and some photographs of period documents and maps with relevant captions are included" Horn Book Guide

Includes bibliographical references

Harmon, Dan
South Carolina; past and present. [by] Daniel E. Harmon. Rosen Central 2011 48p il (The United States: past and present) lib bdg $26.50; pa $11.75
Grades: 3 4 5 6 **975.7**
ISBN 978-1-4358-9495-2 lib bdg; 1-4358-9495-2 lib bdg; 978-1-4358-9522-5 pa; 1-4358-9522-3 pa
LC 2010002586

Presents the history, geography, government, economy, and people of South Carolina, as well as general facts about the state.

Includes bibliographical references

Hoffman, Nancy
South Carolina; by Nancy Hoffman and Joyce Hart. 2nd ed.; Marshall Cavendish Benchmark 2010 144p il map (Celebrate the states) lib bdg $42.79
Grades: 5 6 7 8 **975.7**
ISBN 978-0-7614-4034-5; 0-7614-4034-8
LC 2008038266

First published 2001

This offers information on the geography, history, wildlife, governmental structure, economy, cultural diversity, peoples, religion, and landmarks of South Carolina.

Includes bibliographical references

Somervill, Barbara A.
South Carolina. Children's Press 2009 144p il map (America the beautiful, third series) lib bdg $39
Grades: 4 5 6 7 **975.7**
ISBN 978-0-531-18591-9; 0-531-18591-5
LC 2007031030

Presents an introduction to the geography, natural resources, history, economy, important sites, daily life, and people of South Carolina.

Includes glossary and bibliographical references

975.8   Georgia

Doak, Robin S.
Georgia, 1521-1776. National Geographic Society 2006 109p il map (Voices from colonial America) $21.95; lib bdg $32.90

Grades: 5 6 7 8   **975.8**
ISBN 978-0-7922-6389-0; 0-7922-6389-8; 978-0-7922-6858-1 lib bdg; 0-7922-6858-X lib bdg
LC 2005-22141

Provides a history of Georgia from the arrival of European explorers in the sixteenth century to its becoming a state in 1788.

Includes bibliographical references

Otfinoski, Steven
Georgia; 2nd ed.; Marshall Cavendish Benchmark 2010 144p il map (Celebrate the states) lib bdg $42.79

Grades: 5 6 7 8   **975.8**
ISBN 978-0-7614-4031-4; 0-7614-4031-3
LC 2008041711

First published 2001

This offers information on the geography, history, wildlife, governmental structure, economy, cultural diversity, peoples, religion, and landmarks of Georgia.

Includes bibliographical references

Prentzas, G. S.
Georgia; by G.S. Prentzas. Children's Press 2008 144p il map (America the beautiful, third series) lib bdg $38

Grades: 4 5 6 7   **975.8**
ISBN 978-0-531-18572-8; 0-531-18572-9
LC 2007-8256

Describes the history, geography, ecology, people, economy, cities, and sights of the state of Georgia.

Includes glossary and bibliographical references

Watson, Stephanie
Georgia; past and present. Rosen Central 2010 48p il map (The United States: past and present) lib bdg $26.50; pa $11.50

Grades: 3 4 5 6   **975.8**
ISBN 978-1-4358-5292-1 lib bdg; 1-4358-5292-3 lib bdg; 978-1-4358-5582-3 pa; 1-4358-5582-5 pa
LC 2008-54225

Presents the history, geography, government, economy, and people of Georgia, as well as general facts about the state.

Includes glossary and bibliographical references

975.9   Florida

Cannavale, Matthew C.
Florida, 1513-1821; [by] Matthew C. Cannavale with Robert Olwell, consultant. National Geographic 2006 109p

il map (Voices from colonial America) $21.95; lib bdg $32.90

Grades: 5 6 7 8   **975.9**
ISBN 978-0-7922-6409-5; 0-7922-6409-6; 978-0-7922-6866-6 lib bdg; 0-7922-6866-0 lib bdg
LC 2006-20505

Offers "thorough, well-documented information about the struggles and successes of early nonnative settlers [in Florida]. . . . Many reproductions of period illustrations (both color and sepia) and some photos of archival documents and maps enhance the text." Horn Book Guide

Includes bibliographical references

George, Jean Craighead
★ Everglades; paintings by Wendell Minor. HarperCollins Pubs. 1995 un il hardcover o.p. pa $6.95

Grades: 2 3 4   **975.9**
1. Everglades (Fla.) -- Juvenile literature 2. Everglades National Park (Fla.) -- Juvenile literature
ISBN 0-06-021228-4; 0-06-446194-7 pa
LC 92-9517

"The story and the art create a mystical tale that flows from a serene start to a powerful conclusion." SLJ

Hart, Joyce
Florida; [by] Perry Chang and Joyce Hart. 2nd ed.; Marshall Cavendish Benchmark 2007 144p il map (Celebrate the states) lib bdg $39.93

Grades: 4 5 6 7   **975.9**
ISBN 978-0-7614-2348-5; 0-7614-2348-6
LC 2006-8174

First published 1998

"Provides comprehensive information on the geography, history, wildlife, governmental structure, economy, cultural diversity, peoples, religion, and landmarks of Florida." Publisher's note

Includes bibliographical references

Hess, Debra
Florida; [by] Debra Hess, Lori P. Wiesenfeld. 2nd ed.; Marshall Cavendish Benchmark 2010 90p il map (It's my state) lib bdg $31.36

Grades: 3 4 5   **975.9**
ISBN 978-1-6087-0049-3; 1-6087-0049-6
LC 2010003922

First published 2003

Surveys the history, geography, government, and economy of Florida as well as the diverse ways of life of its people

Jankowski, Susan
Everglades National Park; adventure, explore, discover. [by] Susan Jankowski. MyReportLinks.com Books 2009 128p il map (America's national parks) lib bdg $33.27

Grades: 5 6 7 8   **975.9**
1. Everglades National Park (Fla.)
ISBN 978-1-59845-091-0 lib bdg; 1-59845-091-3 lib bdg
LC 2007-38262

This "informative, well-written book contains a physical description of the park; a summary of its history including the Native peoples of the area; activities such as hiking trails, campsites, and visitor centers; information about the park's plants, animals, and weather; full-color photographs;

and numerous approved links available through the publisher's Web page. . . . Thorough, useful, and appealing, this . . . is a great update for collections." SLJ

Includes glossary and bibliographical references

Orr, Tamra

Florida; by Tamra B. Orr. Children's Press 2008 144p il map (America the beautiful, third series) lib bdg $38

Grades: 4 5 6 7 **975.9**

ISBN 0-531-18558-3; 978-0-531-18558-2

LC 2006100102

Describes the history, geography, ecology, people, economy, cities, and sights of the state of Florida.

Includes glossary and bibliographical references

Sawyer, Sarah

Florida; past and present. Rosen Central 2010 48p il map (The United States: past and present) lib bdg $26.50; pa $11.50

Grades: 3 4 5 6 **975.9**

ISBN 978-1-4358-5288-4 lib bdg; 1-4358-5288-5 lib bdg; 978-1-4358-5574-8 pa; 1-4358-5574-4 pa

LC 2008-54223

Presents the history, geography, government, economy, and people of Florida, as well as general facts about the state.

Includes glossary and bibliographical references

Turner, Glennette Tilley

★ Fort Mose; and the story of the man who built the first free black settlement in Colonial America. Abrams Books for Young Readers 2010 42p il map $18.95

Grades: 5 6 7 8 **975.9**

1. Army officers 2. Slavery -- United States 3. Fort Mose site (Fla.) 4. United States -- History -- 1600-1775, Colonial period 5. Fugitive slaves -- Juvenile literature 6. African Americans -- History -- Juvenile literature

ISBN 978-0-8109-4056-7; 0-8109-4056-6

LC 2009-52205

"In the 18th century, some Africans escaped slavery in England's southern colonies to find freedom in the Spanish colony of Florida. As a leader of St. Augustine's community, African-born Francisco Menendez helped establish Fort Mose, the first free black community on North American soil. Turner does an excellent job of explaining how the residents of Fort Mose probably blended African, English, and Spanish traditions to create a unique—and uniquely American—culture." SLJ

Includes glossary and bibliographical references

976.1 Alabama

Heos, Bridget

Alabama; past and present. Rosen Central 2010 48p il map (The United States: past and present) lib bdg $26.50; pa $11.75

Grades: 3 4 5 6 **976.1**

ISBN 978-1-4358-3518-4 lib bdg; 1-4358-3518-2; 978-1-4358-8486-1 pa; 1-4358-8486-8 pa

LC 2009021850

Presents the history, geography, government, economy, and people of Alabama, as well as general facts about the state.

Includes bibliographical references

Parks, Rosa

★ Rosa Parks: my story; by Rosa Parks with Jim Haskins. Dial Bks. 1992 192p il $17.99; pa $6.99

Grades: 5 6 7 8 **976.1**

1. African American women 2. Civil rights activists 3. African Americans -- Civil rights 4. African American women -- Biography

ISBN 0-8037-0673-1; 0-14-130120-1 pa

LC 89-1124

Rosa Parks describes her early life and experiences with race discrimination, and her participation in the Montgomery bus boycott and the civil rights movement

"A remarkable story, a record of quiet bravery and modesty, a document of social significance, a taut drama told with candor." Bull Cent Child Books

Shirley, David

Alabama; by David Shirley and Joyce Hart. 2nd ed.; Marshall Cavendish Benchmark 2009 144p il map (Celebrate the states) lib bdg $39.93

Grades: 4 5 6 7 **976.1**

ISBN 978-0-7614-3397-2; 0-7614-3397-X

LC 2008-4601

First published 2000

"Provides comprehensive information on the geography, history, wildlife, governmental structure, economy, cultural diversity, peoples, religion, and landmarks of Alabama." Publisher's note

Includes bibliographical references

Somervill, Barbara A.

Alabama; by Barbara A. Somervill. Children's Press 2008 144p il map (America the beautiful, third series) lib bdg $38

Grades: 4 5 6 7 **976.1**

ISBN 978-0-531-18556-8; 0-531-18556-7

LC 2006-37697

Describes the history, geography, ecology, people, economy, cities, and sights of the state of Alabama.

Includes glossary and bibliographical references

976.2 Mississippi

Casil, Amy Sterling

Mississippi; past and present. Rosen Central 2011 48p il map (The United States: past and present) lib bdg $26.50; pa $11.75

Grades: 3 4 5 6 **976.2**

ISBN 978-1-4358-9485-3 lib bdg; 1-4358-9485-5; 978-1-4358-9512-6 pa; 1-4358-9512-6 pa

LC 2009054262

Presents the history, geography, government, economy, and people of Mississippi, as well as general facts about the state.

Includes glossary and bibliographical references

Dell, Pamela
   Mississippi. Children's Press 2008 144p il map (America the beautiful, third series) lib bdg $39
   Grades: 4 5 6 7   **976.2**
      ISBN 978-0-531-18563-6; 0-531-18563-X
                                                LC 2006101965
   Presents an introduction to the geography, natural resources, history, economy, important sites, daily life, and people of Mississippi.
   Includes glossary and bibliographical references

Shirley, David
   Mississippi; [by] David Shirley and Patricia K. Kummer. Marshall Cavendish Benchmark 2008 144p il map (Celebrate the states) lib bdg $39.93
   Grades: 4 5 6 7   **976.2**
      ISBN 978-0-7614-2717-9; 0-7614-2717-1
                                                LC 2007-7868
   First published 1999
   "Provides comprehensive information on the geography, history, wildlife, governmental structure, economy, cultural diversity, peoples, religion, and landmarks of Mississippi." Publisher's note
   Includes bibliographical references

976.3   Louisiana

Benoit, Peter
   Hurricane Katrina. Children's Press 2011 48p il (True book: disasters) lib bdg $28; pa $6.95
   Grades: 3 4 5   **976.3**
      1. Hurricane Katrina, 2005
      ISBN 978-0-531-25421-9 lib bdg; 0-531-25421-6; 978-0-531-26626-7 pa; 0-531-26626-5 pa
                                                LC 2011007145
   This book about Hurricane Katrina in 2005 and its aftermath is "thoughtfully designed. . . . The information . . . is right on target: concise, accurate, and thorough. . . . The photographs . . . are especially effective at putting a human face on large-scale devastation." Booklist
   Includes glossary and bibliographical references

Bjorklund, Ruth
   Louisiana; [by] Ruth Bjorklund, Andy Steinitz. 2nd ed.; Marshall Cavendish Benchmark 2010 90p il map (It's my state) lib bdg $31.36
   Grades: 3 4 5   **976.3**
      ISBN 978-1-6087-0051-6; 1-6087-0051-8
                                                LC 2010003925
   Surveys the history, geography, government, and economy of Louisiana, as well as the diverse ways of life of its people.

Freedman, Jeri
   Louisiana; past and present. Rosen Central 2011 48p il map (The United States: past and present) lib bdg $26.50; pa $11.75
   Grades: 3 4 5 6   **976.3**
      ISBN 978-1-4358-9483-9 lib bdg; 1-4358-9483-9 lib bdg; 978-1-4358-9510-2 pa; 1-4358-9510-X pa
                                                LC 2010001616

Presents the history, geography, government, economy, and people of Louisiana, as well as general facts about the state.
   Includes glossary and bibliographical references

Lassieur, Allison
   Louisiana; by Allison Lassieur. Children's Press 2008 144p il map (America the beautiful, third series) lib bdg $38
   Grades: 4 5 6 7   **976.3**
      ISBN 978-0-531-18560-5; 0-531-18560-5
                                                LC 2007-300
   Describes the history, geography, ecology, people, economy, cities, and sights of the state of Louisiana.
   Includes glossary and bibliographical references

Worth, Richard
   Louisiana, 1682-1803. National Geographic Society 2005 109p il map (Voices from colonial America) $21.95; lib bdg $32.90
   Grades: 5 6 7 8   **976.3**
      1. Louisiana -- History
      ISBN 978-0-7922-6544-3; 0-7922-6544-0; 978-0-7922-6850-5 lib bdg; 0-7922-6850-4 lib bdg
                                                LC 2005-16225
   This "history of Louisiana begins in 1682 when Sieur de La Salle claimed the region for France. After that time, the region was governed under several different flags, including France, Spain, and Great Britain. . . . Thomas Jefferson purchased the land for the United States in 1803." Publisher's note
   Includes bibliographical references

976.4   Texas

Altman, Linda Jacobs
   Texas; [by] Linda Jacobs Altman and Tea Benduhn. 2nd ed.; Marshall Cavendish Benchmark 2010 80p il map (It's my state) $31.36
   Grades: 3 4 5   **976.4**
      ISBN 978-1-6087-0059-2; 1-6087-0045-3
                                                LC 2010003932
   First published 2003
   This provides a broad overview of the state of Texas, from a concise geography and detailed history to a discussion of its government and economy. Also provided are many key facts, figures, people, and dates; information about state symbols, plants, animals, products, and resources; a calendar of state events; and a historical time line.

Chemerka, William R.
   Juan Seguin; Tejano leader. William R. Chemerka; illustrations by Don Collins. Bright Sky Press 2012 64 p. ill. $16.95
   Grades: 3 4 5 6   **976.4**
      1. Texas -- History 2. Political activists 3. Soldiers -- Texas -- Biography -- Juvenile literature 4. Politicians -- Texas -- Biography -- Juvenile literature
      ISBN 1933979798; 9781933979793
                                                LC 2011052720
   This book is a biography of Texan Juan Seguin by William R. Chemerka. Despite "having been forced to flee to

Mexico and die in obscurity, Tejano Juan Seguin is recognised as a Texas hero. From his family's early support of settlers such as Stephen F. Austin to his years in the Texas Senate and as mayor of Bexar, this biography celebrates the life of Juan Seguin and his . . . efforts in securing Texas' independence." (WorldCat)

Fradin, Dennis B.
The **Alamo**; [by] Dennis Brindell Fradin. Marshall Cavendish Benchmark 2007 45p il map (Turning points in U.S. history) lib bdg $29.93
Grades: 3 4 5   **976.4**
1. Alamo (San Antonio, Tex.) 2. Texas -- History
ISBN 978-0-7614-2127-6 lib bdg; 0-7614-2127-0 lib bdg
LC 2005016022
This "includes the background to the battle, as well as an account of its aftermath and some information on famous combatants. . . . The clear, concise, and dynamic style of writing simplifies the information without dumbing it down. . . . The photos, paintings, and maps . . . add a wealth of information." SLJ
Includes glossary and bibliographical references

Green, Carl R.
Sam Houston; courageous Texas hero. by William R. Sanford and Carl R. Green. Enslow Publishers 2013 48 p. ill., map (library) $21.26; (paperback) $7.95
Grades: 5 6 7 8   **976.4**
1. Picture books for children 2. Governors -- Texas -- Biography -- Juvenile literature 3. Legislators -- United States -- Biography -- Juvenile literature
ISBN 0766040097; 9780766040090; 9781464400926
LC 2011051265
This book, part of the Courageous Heroes of the American West series, looks at Sam Houston. "One of the founders of Texas, Sam Houston served the state as governor and senator—but he is most remembered as an American hero" for defeating the Mexican army. "Surprising the Mexican troops with their bold attack, . . . the fiery Texans rallied to an overwhelming victory, claiming their independence." (Publisher's note)
Includes bibliographical references (p. 47) and index.

Melmed, Laura Krauss
Heart of Texas; a Lone Star ABC. Illustrated by Frané Lessac. Collins 2009 un il $17.99; lib bdg $18.89
Grades: 1 2 3 4   **976.4**
1. Alphabet 2. Texas
ISBN 978-0-06-114283-3; 0-06-114283-2; 978-0-06-114285-7 lib bdg; 0-06-114285-9 lib bdg
LC 2008026948
"From Alamo to Ziller Park, Melmed and Lessac provide a tour of places to visit, people to know, and historic events to remember about Texas. Each entry begins with an eight-line poem with an impeccable rhythmic beat that slips off the tongue for reading aloud. . . . [Lessac's] detailed and colorful folk art perfectly conveys the multicultural panorama of the second-largest state." Booklist

Nagle, Jeanne
Texas; past and present. [by] Jeanne Nagle. Rosen Central 2010 48p il map (The United States: past and present) lib bdg $26.50; pa $11.50

Grades: 3 4 5 6   **976.4**
ISBN 978-1-4358-5287-7 lib bdg; 1-4358-5287-7 lib bdg; 978-1-4358-5572-4 pa; 1-4358-5572-8 pa
LC 2008-50962
Presents the history, geography, government, economy, and people of Texas, as well as general facts about the state.
Includes glossary and bibliographical references

Somervill, Barbara A.
Texas. Children's Press 2009 144p il map (America the beautiful, third series) lib bdg $39
Grades: 4 5 6 7   **976.4**
ISBN 978-0-531-18580-3; 0-531-18580-X
LC 2007017787
Presents an introduction to the geography, natural resources, history, economy, important sites, daily life, and people of Texas.
Includes glossary and bibliographical references

Spradlin, Michael P.
Texas Rangers; legendary lawmen. [by] Michael P. Spradlin; illustrations by Roxie Munro. Walker & Co. 2008 un il $16.95; lib bdg $17.85
Grades: 2 3 4   **976.4**
1. Frontier and pioneer life
ISBN 978-0-8027-8096-6; 0-8027-8096-2; 978-0-8027-8097-3 lib bdg; 0-8027-8097-0 lib bdg
LC 2007020139
"This picture-book account of the nearly 200-year history of the Texas Rangers begins in 1823. . . . The bulk of the book covers the 1800s, when the Rangers fought Indian tribes; participated in the war against Mexico; and defended settlers from bank robbers, cattle rustlers, and horse thieves. . . . There is a brief section on modern Rangers. . . . Munro's colorful illustrations provide a look at the lawmen, depict the action and locales, and portray the changing times. They're sure to entice youngsters and keep them turning the pages." SLJ

Teitelbaum, Michael
Texas, 1527-1836. National Geographic Society 2005 109p il map (Voices from colonial America) $21.95; lib bdg $32.90
Grades: 5 6 7 8   **976.4**
ISBN 978-0-7922-6387-6; 0-7922-6387-1; 978-0-7922-6682-2 lib bdg; 0-7922-6682-X lib bdg
LC 2005-11450
"Presents the history of Texas, including life in Spanish Texas, the arrival of American settlers, and The Texas Republic and statehood." Publisher's note
Includes bibliographical references

Wade, Mary Dodson
Henrietta King, la patrona; by Mary Dodson Wade; illustrated by Bill Farnsworth. Bright Sky Press 2012 23 p. $16.95
Grades: 4 5 6 7   **976.4**
1. Women ranchers -- Biography 2. Women philanthropists -- Biography 3. King Ranch (Tex.) -- Juvenile literature 4. Ranchers -- Texas -- Biography -- Juvenile literature 5. Women ranchers -- Texas -- Biography -- Juvenile literature 6. Philanthropists -- Texas -- Biography -- Juvenile literature 7. Women philanthropists -- Texas -- Biography -- Juvenile

literature
ISBN 1933979631; 9781933979632

LC 2011052721

This book by Mary Dodson Wade "examines the . . . life of one of Texas's foremost frontier women and philanthropists, Henrietta Maria Morse Chamberlain King. . . . Henrietta accompanied her missionary father on his travels and later settled with her husband Richard King in the untamed frontiers of the south Texas gulf coast. . . . Under her stewardship, the family ranch went from . . . $500,000 in debt at her husband's death to a debt-free enterprise of more than one million acres." (Publisher's note)

Walker, Paul Robert
★ **Remember** the Alamo; Texians, Tejanos, and Mexicans tell their stories. by Paul Robert Walker. National Geographic 2007 61p il map $17.95; lib bdg $27.90
Grades: 5 6 7 8　　　　　　　　　　　　　　**976.4**
1. Alamo (San Antonio, Tex.) 2. Texas -- History
ISBN 978-1-4263-0010-3; 978-1-4263-0011-0 lib bdg

LC 2006034497

"Opening with clear context about why tensions between Texas residents and the Mexican government were brought to a head, the book then chronicles events directly leading to the siege of the Alamo and its immediate aftermath, following up with an epilogue on the decisive battle of San Jacinto 10 months later. Bringing the history to life is a healthy selection of dramatic, modern paintings along with plenty of archival drawings, maps, and old photos." Booklist
Includes bibliographical references

Winter, Jonah
Born and bred in the Great Depression. Schwartz & Wade Books 2011 un il $17.99
　　　　　　　　　　　　　　　　　　　976.4
1. Great Depression, 1929-1939 2. Texas
ISBN 978-0-375-86197-0; 0-375-86197-1

LC 2009048809

Jonah Winter offers an "account of his father's hardscrabble Depression-era childhood. He softens the rough edges and sees the beauty of the East Texas country where Grandpa Winter lives with his wife and eight children. Directly addressing his father in second-person narration, Winter pulls no punches about the humiliation Grandpa Winter faced to keep his family fed. . . . Winters writing is thoughtful and deeply felt. Root's portraits of the boy's solitary exploration convey the force of Winter's message about 'learning to love those things/ that didn't cost a single penny.'" Publ Wkly

976.6　Oklahoma

Baldwin, Guy
Oklahoma; by Guy Baldwin and Joyce Hart. 2nd ed.; Marshall Cavendish Benchmark 2009 144p il map (Celebrate the states) lib bdg $42.79
Grades: 5 6 7 8　　　　　　　　　　　　　**976.6**
ISBN 978-0-7614-4032-1; 0-7614-4032-1

LC 2008044261

First published 2001

This offers information on the geography, history, wildlife, governmental structure, economy, cultural diversity, peoples, religion, and landmarks of Oklahoma.
Includes bibliographical references

Dorman, Robert L.
Oklahoma; past and present. Rosen Central 2011 48p il map (The United States: past and present) lib bdg $26.50; pa $11.75
Grades: 3 4 5 6　　　　　　　　　　　　　**976.6**
ISBN 978-1-4358-9493-8 lib bdg; 1-4358-9493-6 lib bdg; 978-1-4358-9520-1 pa; 1-4358-9520-7 pa

LC 2010002591

Presents the history, geography, government, economy, and people of Oklahoma, as well as general facts about the state.
Includes bibliographical references

Orr, Tamra
Oklahoma; by Tamra B. Orr. Children's Press 2008 144p il map (America the beautiful, third series) lib bdg $38
Grades: 4 5 6 7　　　　　　　　　　　　　**976.6**
ISBN 978-0-531-18567-4; 0-531-18567-2

LC 2007-4774

Describes the history, geography, ecology, people, economy, cities and sights of the state of Oklahoma.
Includes glossary and bibliographical references

976.7　Arkansas

Altman, Linda Jacobs
Arkansas; [by] Linda Jacobs Altman, Ettagale Blauer, and Jason Laure. 2nd ed.; Marshall Cavendish Benchmark 2009 144p il map (Celebrate the states) lib bdg $42.79
Grades: 4 5 6 7　　　　　　　　　　　　　**976.7**
ISBN 978-0-7614-3001-8; 0-7614-3001-6
First published 2000
"Provides comprehensive information on the geography, history, wildlife, governmental structure, economy, cultural diversity, peoples, religion, and landmarks of Arkansas." Publisher's note
Includes bibliographical references

Levy, Janey
Arkansas; past and present. Rosen Central 2011 48p il map (The United States: past and present) lib bdg $26.50; pa $11.75
Grades: 3 4 5 6　　　　　　　　　　　　　**976.7**
ISBN 978-1-4358-9476-1 lib bdg; 1-4358-9476-6 lib bdg; 978-1-4358-9504-1 pa; 1-4358-9504-5 pa

LC 2009052310

Presents the history, geography, government, economy, and people of Arkansas, as well as general facts about the state.
Includes glossary and bibliographical references

Prentzas, G. S.
Arkansas. Children's Press 2009 144p il map (America the beautiful, third series) lib bdg $39

Grades: 4 5 6 7   **976.7**

ISBN 978-0-531-18596-4; 0-531-18596-6

LC 2007044423

Presents an introduction to the geography, natural resources, history, economy, important sites, daily life, and people Arkansas.

Includes glossary and bibliographical references

976.8   Tennessee

Barrett, Tracy

Tennessee; by Tracy Barrett. 2nd ed.; Marshall Cavendish Benchmark 2006 144p il map (Celebrate the states) lib bdg $39.93

Grades: 4 5 6 7   **976.8**

ISBN 978-0-7614-2151-1; 0-7614-2151-3

LC 2005-24055

First published 1998

"Provides comprehensive information on the geography, history, wildlife, governmental structure, economy, cultural diversity, peoples, religion, and landmarks of Tennessee." Publisher's note

Includes bibliographical references

Graham, Amy

Great Smoky Mountains National Park; adventure, explore, discover. [by] Amy Graham. MyReportLinks.com Books 2009 128p il map (America's national parks) lib bdg $33.27

Grades: 5 6 7 8   **976.8**

1. Great Smoky Mountains National Park (N.C. and Tenn.) 2. National parks and reserves -- United States

ISBN 978-1-59845-093-4 lib bdg; 1-59845-093-X lib bdg

LC 2007-13456

This "informative, well-written book contains a physical description of the park; a summary of its history including the Native peoples of the area; activities such as hiking trails, campsites, and visitor centers; information about the park's plants, animals, and weather; full-color photographs; and numerous approved links available through the publisher's Web page. . . . Thorough, useful, and appealing, this . . . is a great update for collections." SLJ

Includes glossary and bibliographical references

Green, Carl R.

Davy Crockett; courageous hero of the Alamo. by William R. Sanford and Carl R. Green. Rev. ed. Enslow Publishers 2013 48 p. col. ill., map (library) $21.26; (paperback) $7.95

Grades: 5 6 7 8   **976.8**

1. Alamo (San Antonio, Tex.) -- History -- Siege, 1836 2. Pioneers -- Tennessee -- Biography -- Juvenile literature 3. Legislators -- United States -- Biography -- Juvenile literature

ISBN 0766040054; 9780766040052; 9781464400865

LC 2011037749

This book by William Sanford is part of the Courageous Heroes of the American West series and focuses on Davy Crockett. "The courageous Texans chose to defend the fort in San Antonio against more than two thousands Mexican soldiers. . . . Although his brave deeds at the Alamo made

him legendary, Crockett had already gained fame as a hunter, soldier, and U.S. Congressman." (Publisher's note)

Includes bibliographical references (p. 47) and index.

Somervill, Barbara A.

Tennessee. Children's Press/Scholastic 2010 144p il map (America the beautiful, third series) lib bdg $39 **976.8**

ISBN 978-0-531-18504-9; 0-531-18504-4

LC 2008000505

Presents an introduction to the geography, natural resources, history, economy, important sites, daily life, and people of Tennessee.

Includes glossary and bibliographical references

976.9   Kentucky

Barrett, Tracy

Kentucky; [by] Tracy Barrett. 2nd ed.; Marshall Cavendish Benchmark 2008 144p il map (Celebrate the states) lib bdg $39.93

Grades: 4 5 6 7   **976.9**

ISBN 978-0-7614-2715-5; 0-7614-2715-5

LC 2007-6388

First published 1999

"Provides comprehensive information on the geography, history, wildlife, governmental structure, economy, cultural diversity, peoples, religion, and landmarks of Kentucky." Publisher's note

Includes bibliographical references

Cook, C.

Kentucky; past and present. [by] Colleen Ryckert Cook. Rosen Central 2011 48p il map (The United States: past and present) lib bdg $26.50; pa $11.95

Grades: 3 4 5 6   **976.9**

ISBN 978-1-4358-9482-2 lib bdg; 1-4358-9482-0 lib bdg; 978-1-4358-9509-6 pa; 1-4358-9509-6 pa

LC 2010002507

Presents the history, geography, government, economy, and people of Kentucky, as well as general facts about the state.

Includes bibliographical references

Green, Carl R.

Daniel Boone; courageous frontiersman. by William R. Sanford and Carl R. Green. Enslow Publishers 2013 48 p. col. ill., map (library) $21.26; (paperback) $7.95

Grades: 5 6 7 8   **976.9**

1. Frontier and pioneer life -- United States -- Juvenile literature 2. Pioneers -- Kentucky -- Biography -- Juvenile literature 3. Frontier and pioneer life -- Kentucky -- Juvenile literature

ISBN 076604002X; 9780766040021; 9781464400858; 9781464509926; 9781464609923

LC 2011037736

This book by William Sanford is part of the Courageous Heroes of the American West series and focuses on Daniel Boone. "Through the untamed wilderness, Daniel Boone marched forward. He was leading a group of workers to carve out the Wilderness Road. Over hills, through dense forests, along stony paths, and fending off American Indian attacks, Boone never quit. He opened the way for thou-

sands of settlers to move west, establishing the settlement of Boonesborough in 1775." (Publisher's note)
Includes bibliographical references (p. 47) and index.

Santella, Andrew
Kentucky; by Andrew Santella. Children's Press 2008 144p il map (America the beautiful, third series) lib bdg $38
Grades: 4 5 6 7 **976.9**
ISBN 978-0-531-18574-2; 0-531-18574-5
LC 2007-4803
Describes the history, geography, ecology, people, economy, cities, and sights of the state of Kentucky.
Includes glossary and bibliographical references

977 North central United States

Kummer, Patricia K.
The **Great** Lakes; [by] Patricia K. Kummer. Marshall Cavendish Benchmark 2008 96p il map (Nature's wonders) lib bdg $35.64
Grades: 5 6 7 8 **977**
ISBN 978-0-7614-2853-4 lib bdg; 0-7614-2853-4 lib bdg
LC 2007019728
"Provides comprehensive information on the geography, history, wildlife, peoples, and environmental issues of the Great Lakes." Publisher's note
Includes glossary and bibliographical references

977.1 Ohio

Lew, Kristi
Ohio; past and present. Rosen Central 2010 48p il map (The United States: past and present) lib bdg $26.50; pa $11.50
Grades: 3 4 5 6 **977.1**
ISBN 978-1-4358-5286-0 lib bdg; 1-4358-5286-9 lib bdg; 978-1-4358-5570-0 pa; 1-4358-5570-1 pa
LC 2008-54234
Presents the history, geography, government, economy, and people of Ohio, as well as general facts about the state.
Includes glossary and bibliographical references

Sherrow, Victoria
Ohio; [by] Victoria Sherrow. 2nd. ed.; Marshall Cavendish Benchmark 2008 144p il map (Celebrate the states) lib bdg $39.93
Grades: 4 5 6 7 **977.1**
ISBN 978-0-7614-2558-8; 0-7614-2558-6
LC 2006-34103
First published 1999
"Provides comprehensive information on the geography, history, wildlife, governmental structure, economy, cultural diversity, peoples, religion, and landmarks of Ohio." Publisher's note
Includes bibliographical references

Stille, Darlene R.
Ohio. Children's Press 2009 144p il map (America the beautiful, third series) lib bdg $39

Grades: 4 5 6 7 **977.1**
ISBN 978-0-531-18579-7; 0-531-18579-6
LC 2007037177
Presents an introduction to the geography, natural resources, history, economy, important sites, daily life, and people of Ohio.
Includes glossary and bibliographical references

977.2 Indiana

Brezina, Corona
Indiana; past and present. Rosen Central 2010 48p il map (The United States: past and present) lib bdg $26.50; pa $11.75
Grades: 3 4 5 6 **977.2**
ISBN 978-1-4358-3521-4 lib bdg; 1-4358-3521-2; 978-1-4358-8492-2 pa; 1-4358-8492-2 pa
LC 2009023685
Presents the history, geography, government, economy, and people of Indiana, as well as general facts about the state.
Includes bibliographical references

Stille, Darlene R.
Indiana. Children's Press 2009 144p il map (America the beautiful, third series) lib bdg $39
Grades: 4 5 6 7 **977.2**
ISBN 978-0-531-18582-7; 0-531-18582-6
LC 2007043670
Presents an introduction to the geography, natural resources, history, economy, important sites, daily life, and people of Indiana.
Includes glossary and bibliographical references

977.3 Illinois

Burgan, Michael
Illinois; by Michael Burgan. Children's Press 2008 144p il map (America the beautiful, third series) lib bdg $38
Grades: 4 5 6 7 **977.3**
ISBN 978-0-531-18559-9; 0-531-18559-1
LC 2006-36020
Describes the history, geography, ecology, people, economy, cities, and sights of the state of Illinois.
Includes glossary and bibliographical references

Hurd, Owen
Chicago history for kids; triumphs and tragedies of the Windy city, includes 21 activities. [by] Owen Hurd. Chicago Review Press 2007 182p il map $14.95
Grades: 5 6 7 8 **977.3**
1. Chicago (Ill.) -- History
ISBN 978-1-55652-654-1; 1-55652-654-7
LC 2006031807
"This attractive overview begins with geography and moves to the colorful stories that characterize the city. Hurd tapped local experts and collections, using primary and secondary sources and the responses of young readers to craft this engaging resource. . . . Excellent-quality photos, maps, illustrations, or boxed facts appear on every page." SLJ
Includes bibliographical references

Mattern, Joanne

Illinois; past and present. Rosen Central 2010 48p il map (The United States: past and present) lib bdg $26.50; pa $11.50

Grades: 4 5 6   **977.3**

ISBN 978-1-4358-5284-6 lib bdg; 1-4358-5284-2 lib bdg; 978-1-4358-5566-3 pa; 1-4358-5566-3 pa

LC 2008-50577

Presents the history, geography, government, economy, and people of Illinois, as well as general facts about the state.

Includes glossary and bibliographical references

Murphy, Jim

★ The **great** fire. Scholastic 1995 144p il maps $16.95; pa $12.99

Grades: 5 6 7 8 9 10   **977.3**

1. Fires -- Chicago (Ill.) 2. Chicago (Ill.) -- History

ISBN 0-590-47267-4; 0-439-20307-4 pa

LC 94-9963

Newbery honor book, 1996

"Firsthand descriptions by persons who lived through the 1871 Chicago fire are woven into a gripping account of this famous disaster. Murphy also examines the origins of the fire, the errors of judgment that delayed the effective response, the organizational problems of the city's firefighters, and the postfire efforts to rebuild the city. Newspaper lithographs and a few historical photographs convey the magnitude of human suffering and confusion." Horn Book Guide

Includes bibliographical references

Price-Groff, Claire

Illinois; [by] Claire Price-Groff, Elizabeth Kaplan. 2nd ed.; Marshall Cavendish Benchmark 2010 90p il map (It's my state) lib bdg $31.36

Grades: 3 4 5   **977.3**

ISBN 978-1-6087-0050-9; 1-6087-0050-X

LC 2010003923

First published 2003

Surveys the history, geography, government, and economy of Illinois as well as the diverse ways of life of its people

977.4   Michigan

Brill, Marlene Targ

Michigan; by Marlene Targ Brill. 2d ed.; Marshall Cavendish Benchmark 2007 144p il map (Celebrate the states) lib bdg $39.93

Grades: 4 5 6 7   **977.4**

ISBN 978-0-7614-2351-5; 0-7614-2351-6

LC 2006-8181

First published 1998

"Provides comprehensive information on the geography, history, wildlife, governmental structure, economy, cultural diversity, peoples, religion, and landmarks of Michigan." Publisher's note

Includes bibliographical references

Levy, Janey

Michigan; past and present. Rosen Central 2010 48p il map (The United States: past and present) lib bdg $26.50; pa $11.75

Grades: 3 4 5 6   **977.4**

ISBN 978-1-4358-3523-8 lib bdg; 1-4358-3523-9 lib bdg; 978-1-4358-8496-0 pa; 1-4358-8496-5 pa

LC 2009028025

Presents the history, geography, government, economy, and people of Michigan, as well as general facts about the state.

Includes glossary and bibliographical references

Raatma, Lucia

Michigan; by Lucia Raatma. Children's Press 2008 144p il map (America the beautiful, third series) lib bdg $38

Grades: 4 5 6 7   **977.4**

ISBN 978-0-531-18562-9; 0-531-18562-1

LC 2006100708

Describes the history, geography, ecology, people, economy, cities, and sights of the state of Michigan.

Includes   glossary,   filmography   and bibliographical references

977.5   Wisconsin

Blashfield, Jean F.

Wisconsin; by Jean F. Blashfield. Children's Press 2008 144p il map (America the beautiful, third series) lib bdg $38

Grades: 4 5 6 7   **977.5**

ISBN 978-0-531-18568-1; 0-531-18568-0

LC 2006102490

Describes the history, geography, ecology, famous people, economy, cities and sights of the state of Wisconsin.

Includes glossary and bibliographical references

Dornfeld, Margaret

Wisconsin; [by] Margaret Dornfeld and Richard Hantula. 2nd ed.; Marshall Cavendish Benchmark 2010 90p il map (It's my state!) lib bdg $31.36

Grades: 3 4 5   **977.5**

ISBN 978-1-6087-0062-2; 1-6087-0062-3

LC 2010003937

First published 2003

Surveys the history, geography, economy, and people of Wisconsin.

Heos, Bridget

Wisconsin; past and present. Rosen Central 2010 48p il map (The United States: past and present) lib bdg $26.50; pa $11.50

Grades: 3 4 5 6   **977.5**

ISBN 978-1-4358-5293-8 lib bdg; 1-4358-5293-1 lib bdg; 978-1-4358-5584-7 pa; 1-4358-5584-1 pa

LC 2009-3906

Includes glossary and bibliographical references

977.6   Minnesota

Brill, Marlene Targ

Minnesota; [by] Marlene Targ Brill and Elizabeth Kaplan. 2nd ed.; Marshall Cavendish Benchmark 2010 90p il map (It's my state!) lib bdg $31.36

Grades: 3 4 5   **977.6**

  ISBN 978-1-6087-0054-7; 1-6087-0054-2

                         LC 2010003909

  First published 2004

  Surveys the history, geography, government, and economy of Minnesota as well as the diverse ways of life of its people

Harmon, Dan

  Minnesota; past and present. [by] Daniel E. Harmon. Rosen Central 2010 48p il map (The United States: past and present) lib bdg $26.50; pa $11.75

Grades: 3 4 5 6   **977.6**

  ISBN 978-1-4358-3524-5 lib bdg; 1-4358-3524-7 lib bdg; 978-1-4358-8498-4 pa; 1-4358-8498-1 pa

                         LC 2009028024

  Presents the history, geography, government, economy, and people of Minnesota, as well as general facts about the state.

  Includes glossary and bibliographical references

Schwabacher, Martin

  Minnesota; [by] Martin Schwabacher and Patricia K. Kummer. 2nd ed.; Marshall Cavendish Benchmark 2008 144p il map (Celebrate the states) lib bdg $39.93

Grades: 4 5 6 7   **977.6**

  ISBN 978-0-7614-2716-2; 0-7614-2716-3

                         LC 2007-2895

  First published 1999

  "Provides comprehensive information on the geography, history, wildlife, governmental structure, economy, cultural diversity, peoples, religion, and landmarks of Minnesota." Publisher's note

  Includes bibliographical references

977.7   Iowa

Blashfield, Jean F.

  Iowa. Children's Press 2010 144p il map (America the beautiful, third series) lib bdg $39

Grades: 4 5 6 7   **977.7**

  ISBN 978-0-531-18599-5; 0-531-18599-0

                         LC 2008004841

  Presents an introduction to the geography, natural resources, history, economy, important sites, daily life, and people of Iowa.

  Includes glossary and bibliographical references

Freedman, Jeri

  Iowa; past and present. Rosen Central 2010 48p il map (The United States: past and present) lib bdg $26.50; pa $11.75

Grades: 3 4 5 6   **977.7**

  ISBN 978-1-4358-3517-7 lib bdg; 1-4358-3517-4 lib bdg; 978-1-4358-8485-4 pa; 1-4358-8485-X pa

                         LC 2009024564

  Presents the history, geography, government, economy, and people of Iowa, as well as general facts about the state.

  Includes bibliographical references

Morrice, Polly Alison

  Iowa; by Polly Morrice and Joyce Hart. 2nd ed.; Mar-

shall Cavendish Benchmark 2007 144p il map (Celebrate the states) lib bdg $39.93

Grades: 4 5 6 7   **977.7**

  ISBN 978-0-7614-2350-8; 0-7614-2350-8

                         LC 2006-13620

  First published 1998

  "Provides comprehensive information on the geography, history, wildlife, governmental structure, economy, cultural diversity, peoples, religion, and landmarks of Iowa." Publisher's note

  Includes bibliographical references

977.8   Missouri

Bennett, Michelle

  Missouri; by Michelle Bennett and Joyce Hart. 2nd ed.; Marshall Cavendish Benchmark 2010 144p il map (Celebrate the states) lib bdg $42.79 **977.8**

  ISBN 978-0-7614-4727-6; 0-7614-4727-X

                         LC 2009005754

  First published 2001

  This offers information on the geography, history, wildlife, governmental structure, economy, cultural diversity, peoples, religion, and landmarks of Missouri.

  Includes bibliographical references

Blashfield, Jean F.

  Missouri. Children's Press 2009 144p il map (America the beautiful, third series) lib bdg $39

Grades: 4 5 6 7   **977.8**

  ISBN 978-0-531-18585-8; 0-531-18585-0

                         LC 2007035320

  Presents an introduction to the geography, natural resources, history, economy, important sites, daily life, and people of Missouri.

  Includes glossary and bibliographical references

Bullard, Lisa

  The **Gateway** Arch. Lerner Publications 2010 32p il map (Lightning Bolt Books. Famous places) lib bdg $25.26

Grades: 2 3 4   **977.8**

  1. Monuments 2. Gateway Arch (Saint Louis, Mo.)

  ISBN 978-0-8225-9406-2; 0-8225-9406-4

                         LC 2008-30640

  Discusses the history, design, and construction of the Gateway Arch in Saint Louis, Missouri.

  This book uses "high-quality photos, illustrations, maps, and diagrams. . . . Readers will enjoy learning about [the Gateway Arch] . . . and the challenges of building and maintaining large structures." SLJ

  Includes glossary and bibliographical references

Roza, Greg

  Missouri; past and present. Rosen Central 2010 48p il map (The United States: past and present) lib bdg $26.50; pa $11.75

Grades: 3 4 5 6   **977.8**

  ISBN 978-1-4358-3520-7 lib bdg; 1-4358-3520-4; 978-1-4358-8490-8 pa; 1-4358-8490-6 pa

                         LC 2009025520

Presents the history, geography, government, economy, and people of Missouri, as well as general facts about the state.

Includes bibliographical references

978 Western United States

Adler, David A.
A **picture** book of Sacagawea; illustrated by Dan Brown. Holiday House 2000 un il $16.95; pa $6.95
Grades: 1 2 3   **978**
  1. Shoshoni Indians 2. Interpreters 3. Guides (Persons) 4. Native Americans -- Biography
  ISBN 0-8234-1485-X; 0-8234-1665-8 pa
                                    LC 99-37135
A biography of the Shoshone woman who joined the Lewis and Clark Expedition
"The narrative is clear, direct, and never fictionalized. . . . The soft watercolor art is more successful in depicting landscapes than human figures." Booklist
Includes bibliographical references

Burgan, Michael
The **Arapaho**. Marshall Cavendish Benchmark 2009 48p il map (First Americans) lib bdg $31.36
Grades: 2 3 4   **978**
  1. Arapaho Indians
  ISBN 978-0-7614-3017-9 lib bdg; 0-7614-3017-2 lib bdg
                                    LC 2007-33675
Provides information on the background, lifestyle, beliefs, and present-day lives of the Arapaho people
Includes glossary and bibliographical references

Croy, Anita
Ancient Pueblo; archaeology unlocks the secrets of America's past. by Anita Croy; J. Jefferson Reid, consultant. National Geographic 2007 64p il map (National Geographic investigates) $17.95; lib bdg $27.90
Grades: 4 5 6 7   **978**
  1. Archeology 2. Pueblo Indians 3. Southwestern States -- Antiquities
  ISBN 978-1-4263-0130-8; 978-1-4263-0131-5 lib bdg
                                    LC 2007024800
This describes the prehistoric sites of the American Southwest, and what archeologists have learned from them about the lives of ancient Pueblo peoples.
Includes glossary and bibliographical references

Freedman, Russell
★ The **life** and death of Crazy Horse; drawings by Amos Bad Heart Bull. Holiday House 1996 166p il maps $22.95
Grades: 5 6 7 8 9 10   **978**
  1. Oglala Indians 2. Indian chiefs 3. Native Americans -- Biography
  ISBN 0-8234-1219-9
                                    LC 95-33303
A biography of the Oglala Indian leader who relentlessly resisted the white man's attempt to take over Indian lands.

This is "a compelling biography that is based on primary source documents and illustrated with pictographs by a Sioux band historian." Voice Youth Advocates
Includes bibliographical references

Friedman, Mel
The **Oregon** Trail. Children's Press 2010 il map (True book) lib bdg $26; pa $6.95
Grades: 3 4 5   **978**
  1. Oregon Trail 2. Frontier and pioneer life 3. Overland journeys to the Pacific
  ISBN 978-0-531-20584-6; 0-531-20584-3; 978-0-531-21247-9 pa; 0-531-21247-5 pa
                                    LC 2009014186
This introduction to the Oregon Trail provides "readers with clear explanations, maps, illustrations, time lines, and engaging reproductions of primary resources. [This] volume contains eye-catching quick facts; illustrations and photographs are representative of regional Native Americans, pioneers, and explorers. This is ideal material for reports on the Westward expansion." SLJ
Includes bibliographical references

George-Warren, Holly
The **cowgirl** way; hats off to America's women of the West. Houghton Mifflin Books for Children 2010 112p il $18
Grades: 4 5 6 7   **978**
  1. Cowhands 2. Women -- West (U.S.) 3. Cowgirls -- Western States -- Juvenile literature 4. Women -- United States -- History -- Juvenile literature
  ISBN 978-0-618-73738-3; 0-618-73738-3
"With ample dynamic photos and lively quotes throughout, George-Warren presents a thoroughly absorbing overview of the history of cowgirls up to the present. . . . Famous figures such as Belle Starr, Calamity Jane, and Annie Oakley are discussed in brief, but the real delights here are the anecdotes on lesser-known figures such as Lucille Mulhall, the first woman to be dubbed a cowgirl in print. . . . The introduction of women as rodeo and trick riders and their contributions to the sports in the 1920s and '30s are covered in fascinating detail, as are the film and singing sensations of the 1940s and '50s." SLJ

Green, Carl R.
Buffalo Bill Cody; courageous wild west showman. by William R. Sanford and Carl R. Green. Enslow Publishers 2013 48 p. ill., map (library) $21.26; (paperback) $7.95
Grades: 5 6 7 8   **978**
  1. Buffalo Bill's Wild West Show 2. Frontier and pioneer life -- West (U.S.) 3. Pioneers -- West (U.S.) -- Biography -- Juvenile literature 4. Entertainers -- United States -- Biography -- Juvenile literature
  ISBN 0766040070; 9780766040076; 9781464400902
                                    LC 2011031052
This book by William Sanford and Carl R. Green is part of the "Courageious Heroes of the American West" series. It presents a biography of Buffalo Bill Cody, who "had many jobs--Pony Express rider, scout, soldier, buffalo hunter. But he was most famous for entertaining audiences with his Wild West show. Many Americans and others around the world

could not travel to see the real Wild West, so Buffalo Bill Brought it to them." (Publisher's note)

Includes bibliographical references (p. 47) and index.

Calamity Jane; courageous wild west woman. by William R. Sanford and Carl R. Green. Enslow Publishers 2013 48 p. ill., map (library) $21.26; (paperback) $7.95

Grades: 5 6 7 8   978

1. Cowgirls -- Juvenile literature 2. Pioneers -- West (U.S.) -- Biography -- Juvenile literature 3. Women pioneers -- West (U.S.) -- Biography -- Juvenile literature

ISBN 0766040100; 9780766040106; 9781464400933

LC 2011033840

This book by William Sanford is part of the Courageous Heroes of the American West series and focuses on Calamity Jane. "The truth and myth are difficult to separate in the wild life of Calamity Jane. An independent spirit, she never stayed in one place for long. She worked as a gold prospector, bullwhacker, nurse, and had many other jobs, Calamity Jane refused to conform to the typical roles of a nineteenth-century woman." (Publisher's note)

Includes bibliographical references (p. 47) and index.

Sacagawea; courageous American Indian guide. by William R. Sanford and Carl R. Green. Enslow Publishers 2013 48 p. ill., map (library) $21.26

Grades: 5 6 7 8   978

1. Native Americans -- United States 2. Shoshoni women -- Biography -- Juvenile literature 3. Shoshoni Indians -- Biography -- Juvenile literature

ISBN 0766040062; 9780766040069

LC 2011048291

This book, part of the Courageous Heroes of the American West series, looks at Sacagawea. "Throughout Lewis and Clark's journey in the uncharted American West, this young America Indian woman proved to be an invaluable member of the expedition. Sacagawea served as translator and guide, all while caring for her infant son." (Publisher's note)

Includes bibliographical references (p. 47) and index.

Zebulon Pike; courageous Rocky Mountain explorer. by William R. Sanford and Carl R. Green. Enslow Publishers 2013 48 p. ill. (library) $21.26; (paperback) $7.95

Grades: 5 6 7 8   978

1. Exploration -- Juvenile literature 2. Explorers -- West (U.S.) -- Biography -- Juvenile literature

ISBN 1464400954; 9780766040120; 9781464400957

LC 2011051629

This book by William R. Sanford is part of the Courageous Heroes of the American West series and looks at Zebulon Pike. "After the United States purchased the Louisiana Territory in 1803, the young nation needed brave pioneers to explore this vast uncharted land. Zebulon Pike . . . led an expedition across rolling prairies before arriving at the towering mountains" and being the first to explore the southern Rocky Mountains. (Publisher's note)

Includes bibliographical references (p. 47) and index.

Grupper, Jonathan

Destination: Rocky Mountains. National Geographic Soc. 2001 31p il $16.95

Grades: 3 4 5 6   978

1. Natural history -- West (U.S.) 2. Rocky Mountains

ISBN 0-7922-7722-8

LC 00-55926

"A hypothetical trek up the Rocky Mountains provides the framework for . . . information about its animals and the vegetation that sustains them at elevations beyond fourteen thousand feet. Each animal—from huge grizzly bear to tiny pika—has a double-page spread, lavishly illustrated with well-chosen color photographs. The text and graphics work well together." Horn Book Guide

Huey, Lois Miner

American archaeology uncovers the westward movement. Marshall Cavendish Benchmark 2009 64p il map (American archaeology) lib bdg $21.95

Grades: 4 5 6 7   978

1. Historical geography 2. Frontier and pioneer life -- West (U.S.) 3. Excavations (Archeology) -- United States

ISBN 978-0-7614-4265-3 lib bdg; 0-7614-4265-0 lib bdg

LC 2009003167

This describes how archeologists have learned about the history of the American West.

"The visually pleasing . . . [book is] replete with maps, paintings, and photographs, all appropriately placed and thoughtfully captioned. . . . Huey's focus on American history, which is broken down into small, manageable chunks, is sure to entice budding historians." SLJ

Includes glossary and bibliographical references

King, David C.

★ **Pioneer** days; discover the past with fun projects, games, activities, and recipes. Wiley 1997 118p il (American kids in history) pa $12.95

Grades: 3 4 5 6   978

1. Cooking 2. Handicraft 3. Frontier and pioneer life -- West (U.S.)

ISBN 0-471-16169-1

LC 96-37495

This book is an "assortment of history, culture, crafts, and stories to teach about the daily life of the pioneers. . . . [Crafts and recipes include] air-dried flowers, toys and games, homemade soda pop, johnny-cakes, and various holiday ornaments. The author's research is evident, and the presentation of the activities and recipes is so engaging that the book will appeal to a wide audience." SLJ

Includes glossary and bibliographical references

Nelson, Maria

The **life** of Sacagawea; Maria Nelson. Gareth Stevens Pub. 2012 24 p. ill. (chiefly col.) (library binding) $22.60; (paperback) $8.15

Grades: 2 3 4   978

1. Native American women 2. United States -- History 3. Native Americans -- Biography 4. Shoshoni women -- Biography -- Juvenile literature 5. Shoshoni Indians -- Biography -- Juvenile literature

ISBN 9781433963575; 9781433963599

LC 2011035145

Author Maria Nelson presents information on "one of the most famous Native Americans in US history--Sacagawea. Though much of her life remains a mystery, this book will explore the story of the . . . woman who helped Lewis and Clark explore the American West. . . . [Nelson also includes] a timeline of important events [for children.]" (Publisher's note)

Includes bibliographical references (p. 23) and index.

Norwich, Grace

I am Sacagawea. Scholastic 2012 128 p. ill., map
Grades: 2 3 4   978
 1. Native Americans -- United States 2. Shoshoni women -- Biography -- Juvenile literature 3. Shoshoni Indians -- Biography -- Juvenile literature
ISBN 0545405742; 9780545405744

Author Grace Norwich's biography of "Shoshoni Indian Sacagawea, known for guiding the Lewis and Clark expedition across the western half of the United States from 1804 to 1806," discusses "her childhood and kidnapping by the Hidatsa tribe, her marriage to Toussaint Charbonneau, and the mystery surrounding her death." (yabookscentral.com)

Includes bibliographical references (pages 124-125) and index.

Olson, Tod

How to get rich on a Texas cattle drive; afterword by Marc Aronson; illustrations by Scott Allred & Gregory Proch. National Geographic 2010 47p il map $18.95
Grades: 4 5 6 7   978
 1. Cowhands 2. Frontier and pioneer life -- West (U.S.)
ISBN 978-1-4263-0524-5; 1-4263-0524-9

"This book provides one of the better true-to-life insider accounts of what happens on a cattle drive: why the cattle are being driven, where they're being driven to and from, and the multitude of daily chores and unforeseen obstacles along the way. Period photos and artwork, as well as original drawings, make for a lively design, and an ongoing ledger keeps track of the main character's mostly modest finances." Booklist

★ How to get rich on the Oregon Trail; my adventures among cows, crooks & heroes on the road to fame and fortune. [illustrations by Scott Allred & Gregory Proch; afterword by Marc Anonson] National Geographic 2009 47p il (How to get rich) $18.95; lib bdg $27.90
Grades: 4 5 6 7   978
 1. Oregon Trail 2. Frontier and pioneer life 3. Overland journeys to the Pacific 4. Frontier and pioneer life -- Juvenile literature 5. Overland journeys to the Pacific -- Juvenile literature
ISBN 978-1-4263-0412-5; 1-4263-0412-9; 978-1-4263-0413-2 lib bdg; 1-4263-0413-7 lib bdg

"The action follows young Will Reed and his family as they set off from Illinois to find their fortune along the 2,000-mile Oregon Trail. . . . Informing Will's impish sketches and wry journal entries is a wealth of information about life along the trail. . . . An ongoing ledger calculates the family's balance as it fluctuates from $10.70 to $3,021.70, but it's clear that this journey is more about survival than riches. The illustrations, historical anecdotes, and run-ins with everyone from the Mormons to escaped slaves to Abraham Lincoln form a perfect blend of history and humbuggery." Booklist

Patent, Dorothy Hinshaw

The horse and the Plains Indians; a powerful partnership. Dorothy Hinshaw Patent; photographs by William Munoz. Clarion Books 2012 xiii, 98 p.p ill. (chiefly col.) $17.99
Grades: 4 5 6 7 8   978
 1. Horses 2. Domestic animals 3. Native Americans -- Great Plains 4. Horses -- Great Plains -- History -- Juvenile literature 5. Human-animal relationships -- Great Plains -- History -- Juvenile literature 6. Indians of North America -- Domestic animals -- Great Plains -- Juvenile literature
ISBN 9780547125510
          LC 2011025954

This book explores the relationship between Plains Indians and horses. The "Plains Indians and the horse were not always inseparable. Once, Native Americans used dogs to help carry their goods, and even after the Spaniards introduced the horse to the Americas," the Spanish hoarded the valuable animals. But "soon horses escaped from Spanish settlements, and Native Americans quickly learned how valuable the horse could be as a hunting mount, beast of burden, and military steed." (Publisher's note)

Includes bibliographical references (p. [94]) and index

Perritano, John

The Lewis and Clark Expedition. Children's Press 2010 48p il (True book) lib bdg $26; pa $6.95
Grades: 3 4 5   978
 1. Explorers 2. Territorial governors 3. Lewis and Clark Expedition (1804-1806)
ISBN 978-0-531-20582-2 lib bdg; 0-531-20582-7 lib bdg; 978-0-531-21245-5 pa; 0-531-21245-9 pa
          LC 2009014183

This introduction to the Lewis and Clark Expedition provides "elementary readers with clear explanations, maps, illustrations, time lines, and engaging reproductions of primary resources. [This] volume contains eye-catching quick facts; illustrations and photographs are representational of regional Native Americans, pioneers, and explorers. This is ideal material for reports on the Westward expansion." SLJ

Includes bibliographical references

Scott, Ann Herbert

★ Cowboy country; pictures by Ted Lewin. Clarion Bks. 1993 un il hardcover o.p. pa $6.95
Grades: K 1 2 3   978
 1. Cowhands 2. Cowhands -- Juvenile literature 3. Ranch life -- Juvenile literature
ISBN 0-395-57561-3; 0-395-76482-3 pa
          LC 92-24499

An "old buckaroo" tells how he became a cowboy, what the work was like in the past, and how this life has changed

The author "succinctly captures the laconic speaking rhythms and distinctive jargon of her subject. . . . Lewin's . . . well-lit watercolors suggest the affability of the weathered narrator and the awe of the boy with him." Publ Wkly

Sheinkin, Steve

★ Which way to the wild West? everything your schoolbooks didn't tell you about America's westward expansion. illustrated by Tim Robinson. Roaring Brook Press 2009 260p il map $19.95

Grades: 5 6 7 8   **978**
1. Frontier and pioneer life -- West (U.S.)
ISBN 978-1-59643-321-2; 1-59643-321-3

Presents the greatest adventures of America's Westward expansion, from the Louisiana Purchase and the gold rush to the Indian wars and life of the cowboy, as well as the everyday happenings that defined living on the frontier

"An engaging storyteller, the author uses humor and little-known anecdotes to make such subjects as Manifest Destiny, the Mexican-American War, the Gold Rush and Custer's Last Stand entertaining for readers. His chatty, informal style . . . will appeal to young readers turned off to history by stale textbooks. Robinson's cartoons complement the text. . . . An accessible and engaging historical overview." Kirkus

Includes bibliographical references

Staton, Hilarie
Cowboys and the wild West. Kingfisher 2011 32p il map (All about America)
Grades: 3 4 5 6   **978**
1. Cowhands 2. Frontier and pioneer life -- West (U.S.)
ISBN 0-7534-6510-8 pa; 0-7534-6582-5; 978-0-7534-6510-3 pa; 978-0-7534-6582-0

This is a history of cowboys and the American West from the early 1800s to around 1890.

This "visually appealing [title] effectively [combines] paintings, engravings, primary documents, and photographs with cartoon illustrations. The eye-catching [layout includes] different font sizes, bold type, and text boxes to highlight different pieces of information. The content is interesting and pithy." SLJ

Includes glossary and bibliographical references

Waldman, Stuart
The **last** river; John Wesley Powell & the Colorado River Exploration Expedition. by Stuart Waldman; illustrated by Gregory Manchess. Mikaya Press 2005 47p il map (Great explorers book) $19.95
Grades: 3 4 5 6   **978**
1. Explorers 2. Geologists 3. West (U.S.) -- Exploration 4. Colorado River (Colo.-Mexico)
ISBN 1-931414-09-2

     LC 2005041580
"In 1869 the Colorado River Exploring Expedition set forth from Green River City led by John Wesley Powell, a one-armed explorer who was determined to reach the Colorado's canyons to study their geology. . . . Waldman relates their story clearly in the main text, while occasional sidebars carry short excerpts from the men's journals and letters. Illustrations include clear nineteenth-century photos as well as handsome full and double-page paintings. . . . Rich in color, strong in composition, and beautifully executed, these often-dramatic paintings bring the story to life." Booklist

Includes bibliographical references

Yasuda, Anita
Explore the wild west! Anita Yasuda; illustrated by Alex Kim. Nomad Press 2012 92 p. ill. (paperback) $12.95; (prebind) $21.95; (ebook) $9.99
Grades: 3 4 5   **978**
1. West (U.S.) -- History 2. Frontier and pioneer life

-- West (U.S.) 3. United States -- History -- 19th century
ISBN 1936749718; 9781936749713; 9781451777307; 9781936749720

Author Anita Yasuda presents "a fun and educational journey through time [that] invites young readers to experience the spirit of the Wild West . . . [Yasuda provides a history of] Wild West legends, gold miners, settlers and frontier towns, Native American and cowboy cultures, cattle drives, and the peacekeepers and lawbreakers . . . [The book also includes fun facts, trivia, jokes, and riddles." (Publisher's note)

978.1   Kansas

Bailey, Diane
Kansas; past and present. Rosen Central 2011 48p il map (The United States: past and present) lib bdg $26.50; pa $11.75
Grades: 3 4 5 6   **978.1**
ISBN 9781435894815 lib bdg; 1-4358-9481-2 lib bdg; 978-1-4358-9508-9 pa; 1-4358-9508-8 pa
     LC 2010000816
Presents the history, geography, government, economy, and people of Kansas, as well as general facts about the state.
Includes bibliographical references

Bjorklund, Ruth
Kansas; by Ruth Bjorklund and Trudi Strain Trueit. 2nd ed.; Marshall Cavendish Benchmark 2009 144p il map (Celebrate the states) lib bdg $42.79
Grades: 4 5 6 7   **978.1**
ISBN 978-0-7614-3400-9; 0-7614-3400-3
     LC 2008-5537
"Provides comprehensive information on the geography, history, wildlife, governmental structure, economy, cultural diversity, peoples, religion, and landmarks of Kansas." Publisher's note
Includes bibliographical references

Cannarella, Deborah
Kansas. Children's Press 2009 144p il map (America the beautiful, third series) lib bdg $39
Grades: 4 5 6 7   **978.1**
ISBN 978-0-531-18583-4; 0-531-18583-4
     LC 2007028461
Presents an introduction to the geography, natural resources, history, economy, important sites, daily life, and people of Kansas.
Includes glossary and bibliographical references

978.2   Nebraska

Bjorklund, Ruth
Nebraska; [by] Ruth Bjorklund and Marlee Richards. 2nd ed.; Marshall Cavendish Benchmark 2010 144p il map (Celebrate the states) $42.79
Grades: 5 6 7 8   **978.2**
ISBN 978-0-7614-4732-0; 0-7614-4732-6
"Every school library should purchase this." Voice Youth Advocates

Bringle, Jennifer

Nebraska; past and present. Rosen Central 2011 48p il map (The United States: past and present) lib bdg $26.50; pa $11.75

Grades: 3 4 5 6   **978.2**

ISBN 978-1-4358-9487-7 lib bdg; 1-4358-9487-1 lib bdg; 978-1-4358-9514-0 pa; 1-4358-9514-2 pa

LC 2010002545

Presents the history, geography, government, economy, and people of Nebraska, as well as general facts about the state.

Includes bibliographical references

Heinrichs, Ann

Nebraska; by Ann Heinrichs. Children's Press 2008 144p il map (America the beautiful, third series) lib bdg $38

Grades: 4 5 6 7   **978.2**

ISBN 978-0-531-18577-3; 0-531-18577-X

LC 2007-6720

Describes the history, geography, ecology, people, economy, cities, and sights of the state of Nebraska.

Includes glossary and bibliographical references

978.3   South Dakota

Burgan, Michael

South Dakota. Children's Press 2010 144p il map (America the beautiful, third series) lib bdg $39

Grades: 4 5 6 7   **978.3**

ISBN 978-0-531-18503-2; 0-531-18503-6

LC 2008002299

Takes readers on a tour of South Dakota, describing the state's history, culture, land, economy, government, and sights, and including unique facts, color maps and photos, the state song, suggested activities, lists of famous people, cultural institutions, and annual events, and other resources.

Includes glossary and bibliographical references

Kenney, Karen Latchana

Mount Rushmore; illustrated by Judith A. Hunt. Magic Wagon 2011 32p il (Our nation's pride) lib bdg $28.50

Grades: 2 3 4   **978.3**

1. Mount Rushmore National Memorial (S.D.)

ISBN 978-1-61641-153-4; 1-61641-153-8

LC 2010014009

This book "tells of the sculptor who came to work on the carving, how men were lowered on special harnesses to do the work, and how dynamite specialists and drillers prepared the mountain. . . . The full-color artwork not only explains the text but also gives almost photographic renderings of the [topic]." SLJ

Petersen, Christine

South Dakota; past and present. Rosen Central 2011 48p il (The United States: past and present) lib bdg $26.50; pa $11.75

Grades: 3 4 5 6   **978.3**

ISBN 978-1-4358-9496-9 lib bdg; 1-4358-9496-0 lib bdg; 978-1-4358-9523-2 pa; 1-4358-9523-1 pa

LC 2010002584

Presents the history, geography, government, economy, and people of South Dakota, as well as general facts about the state.

Includes glossary and bibliographical references

Thomas, William

Mount Rushmore; by William David Thomas. Chelsea Clubhouse 2010 48p il (Symbols of American freedom) $30

Grades: 3 4 5   **978.3**

ISBN 978-1-60413-515-2; 1-60413-515-8

LC 2009-13027

This book about Mount Rushmore "provides nearly as much information as a guided tour by a park ranger. [It begins] with the story of how the place came to be, and where it fits into U.S. history. Information boxes offer additional background and some surprising facts, such as . . . the origin of the name of Mount Rushmore. The final chapter shows the landmark today and includes maps and photographs of the visitors' center and some of the things individuals might see or do while visiting the site. Much information is packed into [this] slim [book]. Excellent . . . for state reports or to complement U.S. history units." SLJ

Includes glossary

978.4   North Dakota

Lewis, Mark J.

North Dakota; past and present. Rosen Central 2011 48p il map (United States: past and present) lib bdg $26.50; pa $11.75

Grades: 3 4 5 6   **978.4**

ISBN 978-1-4358-9492-1 lib bdg; 1-4358-9492-8 lib bdg; 978-1-4358-9519-5 pa; 1-4358-9519-3 pa

LC 2010002697

This describes the geography, history, government, economy, and famous people of North Dakota.

Includes bibliographical references

McDaniel, Melissa

North Dakota; by Melissa McDaniel and Sara Louise Kras. 2nd ed.; Marshall Cavendish Benchmark 2010 144p il map (Celebrate the states) lib bdg $42.79

Grades: 5 6 7 8   **978.4**

ISBN 978-0-7614-4733-7; 0-7614-4733-4

LC 2009002584

First published 2001

This offers information on the geography, history, wildlife, governmental structure, economy, cultural diversity, peoples, religion, and landmarks of North Dakota.

Includes bibliographical references

Stille, Darlene R.

North Dakota. Children's Press 2010 144p il map (America the beautiful, third series) lib bdg $39

Grades: 4 5 6 7   **978.4**

ISBN 978-0-531-18502-5; 0-531-18502-8

LC 2008011282

Presents an introduction to the geography, natural resources, history, economy, important sites, daily life, and people of North Dakota.

Includes glossary and bibliographical references

978.6 Montana

Bennett, Clayton

Montana; by Clayton Bennett and Wendy Mead. 2nd ed.; Marshall Cavendish Benchmark 2010 144p il map (Celebrate the states) $42.79

Grades: 5 6 7 8   **978.6**

ISBN 978-0-7614-4731-3; 0-7614-4731-8

LC 2009007939

First published 2001

This offers information on the geography, history, wildlife, governmental structure, economy, cultural diversity, peoples, religion, and landmarks of Montana.

Includes bibliographical references

Porterfield, Jason

Montana; past and present. Rosen Central 2011 48p il map (The United States: past and present) lib bdg $26.50; pa $11.75

Grades: 3 4 5 6   **978.6**

ISBN 978-1-4358-9486-0 lib bdg; 1-4358-9486-3 lib bdg; 978-1-4358-9513-3 pa; 1-4358-9513-4 pa

LC 2010000415

Presents the history, geography, government, economy, and people of Montana, as well as general facts about the state.

Includes bibliographical references

Stein, R. Conrad

Montana. Children's Press 2010 144p il map (America the beautiful, third series) lib bdg $39

Grades: 4 5 6 7   **978.6**

ISBN 978-0-531-18500-1; 0-531-18500-1

LC 2008000823

Takes readers on a tour of Montana, describing the state's history, culture, land, economy, government, and sights, and including unique facts, color maps and photos, the state song, suggested activities, lists of famous people, cultural institutions, and annual events, and other resources.

Includes glossary and bibliographical references

978.7 Wyoming

Baldwin, Guy

Wyoming; [by] Guy Baldwin and Joyce Hart. 2nd ed.; Marshall Cavendish Benchmark 2008 144p il map (Celebrate the states) lib bdg $39.93

Grades: 4 5 6 7   **978.7**

ISBN 978-0-7614-2563-2; 0-7614-2563-2

LC 2007-19560

First publsihed 1999

"Provides comprehensive information on the geography, history, wildlife, governmental structure, economy, cultural diversity, peoples, religion, and landmarks of Wyoming." Publisher's note

Includes bibliographical references

Byers, Ann

Wyoming; past and present. Rosen Central 2011 48p il map (The United States: past and present) lib bdg $26.50; pa $11.75

Grades: 3 4 5 6   **978.7**

ISBN 978-1-4358-9500-3 lib bdg; 1-4358-9500-2 lib bdg; 978-1-4358-9527-0 pa; 1-4358-9527-4 pa

LC 2010002519

Presents the history, geography, government, economy, and people of Wyoming, as well as general facts about the state.

Includes glossary and bibliographical references

Prentzas, G. S.

Wyoming. Children's Press 2010 144p il map (America the beautiful, third series) lib bdg $39

Grades: 4 5 6 7   **978.7**

ISBN 978-0-531-18508-7; 0-531-18508-7

LC 2008016789

Takes readers on a tour of Wyoming, describing the state's history, culture, land, economy, government, and sights, and including unique facts, color maps and photos, the state song, suggested activities, lists of famous people, cultural institutions, and annual events, and other resources.

Includes glossary and bibliographical references

978.8 Colorado

Altman, Linda Jacobs

Colorado; [by] Linda Jacobs Altman, Stephanie Fitzgerald. 2nd ed.; Marshall Cavendish Benchmark 2010 90p il map (It's my state) $31.36

Grades: 3 4 5   **978.8**

ISBN 978-1-6087-0046-2; 1-6087-0046-1

LC 2010003903

Surveys the history, geography, government, and economy of Colorado as well as the diverse ways of life of its people.

Heos, Bridget

Colorado; past and present. Rosen Central 2011 48p il map (The United States: past and present) lib bdg $26.50; pa $11.75

Grades: 3 4 5 6   **978.8**

ISBN 978-1-4358-9477-8 lib bdg; 1-4358-9477-4 lib bdg; 978-1-4358-9530-0 pa; 1-4358-9530-4 pa

LC 2010000419

Presents the history, geography, government, economy, and people of Colorado, as well as general facts about the state.

Includes glossary and bibliographical references

Lowery, Linda

★ Aunt Clara Brown; official pioneer. illustrations by Janice Lee Porter. Carolrhoda Bks. 1999 48p il (On my own biography) lib bdg $19.93; pa $5.95

Grades: 2 3 4   **978.8**

1. Slaves 2. African American women 3. Frontier and pioneer life 4. Pioneers 5. African American women -- Biography 6. Central City (Colo.) -- Biography -- Juvenile literature 7. Frontier and pioneer life -- Colorado -- Juvenile literature 8. Women pioneers -- Colorado -- Biography -- Juvenile literature 9. Free African Americans -- Colorado -- Biography -- Juvenile literature 10. African American women pioneers --

Colorado -- Biography -- Juvenile literature
ISBN 1-57505-045-5 lib bdg; 1-57505-416-7 pa
LC 98-24259

A biography of the freed slave who made her fortune in Colorado and used her money to bring other former slaves there to begin new lives

"The well-defined primitivist shapes, canvas-y textures, and muted earth tones of the illustrations perfectly evoke the roughness of the terrain and the historical period, as well as the powerful basic emotions motivating the characters. The straightforward text allows the facts speak for themselves. . . . A good story and a solid resource." Bull Cent Child Books

Quigley, Mary
Mesa Verde; [by] Mary Quigley. Heinemann Library 2006 48p il (Excavating the past) lib bdg $31.43
Grades: 4 5 6 **978.8**
1. Native Americans -- Antiquities 2. Excavations (Archeology) -- United States
ISBN 1-4034-5997-5
LC 2005009179

"Mesa Verde explains how these ancient people reached North and South America using the land bridge and settled down to farm in the Four Corners area. Quigley uses the term Ancestral Puebloans rather than the sometimes derogatory Anasazi and explains why. She describes the daily lives of the people and includes current theories about why they may have abandoned this site. Activities and discoveries by the Wetherill brothers and other archaeologists as well as cultural information from modern-day people bring knowledge about the ancients up to date. This [is an] excellent title." SLJ
Includes bibliographical references

Somervill, Barbara A.
Colorado; by Barbara A. Somervill. Children's Press 2008 144p il map (America the beautiful, third series) lib bdg $38
Grades: 4 5 6 7 **978.8**
ISBN 978-0-531-18570-4; 0-531-18570-2
LC 2007-301

Describes the history, geography, ecology, people, economy, cities, and sights of the state of Colorado.
Includes glossary and bibliographical references

978.9 New Mexico

Brezina, Corona
New Mexico; past and present. Rosen Central 2011 48p il map (The United States: past and present) lib bdg $26.50; pa $11.75
Grades: 3 4 5 6 **978.9**
ISBN 978-1-4358-9490-7 lib bdg; 1-4358-9490-1; 978-1-4358-9517-1 pa; 1-4358-9517-7 pa
LC 2010003059

Presents the history, geography, government, economy, and people of New Mexico, as well as general facts about the state.
Includes bibliographical references

Burgan, Michael
New Mexico. Children's Press 2008 144p il map (America the beautiful, third series) lib bdg $39
Grades: 4 5 6 7 **978.9**
ISBN 978-0-531-18578-0; 0-531-18578-8
LC 2007007728

Presents an introduction to the geography, natural resources, history, economy, important sites, daily life, and people of New Mexico.
Includes glossary and bibliographical references

979 Great Basin and Pacific Slope region of the United States

Ray, Deborah Kogan
Paiute princess; the story of Sarah Winnemucca. Deborah Kogan Ray. Frances Foster Books, Farrar Straus Giroux 2011 48 p. col. ill., col. map $17.99
Grades: 3 4 5 **979.004**
1. Paiute Indians 2. Native American women 3. Paiute women -- Biography -- Juvenile literature 4. Paiute Indians -- Biography -- Juvenile literature 5. American literature -- Indian authors -- Biography -- Juvenile literature 6. Women political activists -- West (U.S.) -- Biography -- Juvenile literature 7. Indians of North America -- Civil rights -- History -- 19th century -- Juvenile literature
ISBN 0374398976; 9780374398972
LC 2009046090

This book is a biography of Sarah Winnemucca, who was "[b]orn into the Northern Paiute tribe of Nevada in 1844" and who "straddled two cultures: the traditional life of her people, and the modern ways of her grandfather's white friends." Her skill with languages "made her a great leader." The book includes "illustrations and . . . backmatter, including hand-drawn maps, a chronology, archival photographs, an author's notes, and additional resource information." (Publisher's note)
Includes bibliographical references

979.1 Arizona

Brezina, Corona
Arizona; past and present. Rosen Central 2010 48p il map (The United States: past and present) lib bdg $26.50; pa $11.75
Grades: 3 4 5 6 **979.1**
ISBN 978-1-4358-3516-0 lib bdg; 1-4358-3516-6 lib bdg; 978-1-4358-8483-0 pa; 1-4358-8483-3 pa
LC 2009017004

Presents the history, geography, government, economy, and people of Arizona, as well as general facts about the state.
Includes glossary and bibliographical references

McDaniel, Melissa
Arizona; by Melissa McDaniel and Wendy Mead. 2nd ed.; Marshall Cavendish Benchmark 2009 144p il map (Celebrate the states) lib bdg $39.93

Grades: 4 5 6 7   **979.1**
ISBN 978-0-7614-3398-9; 0-7614-3398-8
LC 2008-6212
First published 2000

"Provides comprehensive information on the geography, history, wildlife, governmental structure, economy, cultural diversity, peoples, religion, and landmarks of Arizona." Publisher's note

Includes bibliographical references

Somervill, Barbara A.

Arizona; by Barbara A. Somervill. Children's Press 2008 144p il map (America the beautiful, third series) lib bdg $38

Grades: 4 5 6 7   **979.1**
ISBN 978-0-531-18595-7; 0-531-18595-8
LC 2007-37923

Presents an introduction to the geography, natural resources, history, economy, important sites, daily life, and people of Arizona.

"This title in the America the Beautiful series is also a fun read, with a chatty style, open design, and color photos, maps, screens, and charts on just about every spread." Booklist

Includes glossary and bibliographical references

979.2   Utah

Ching, Jacqueline

Utah; past and present. Rosen Central 2011 48p il map (The United States: past and present) lib bdg $26.50; pa $11.75

Grades: 3 4 5 6   **979.2**
ISBN 978-1-4358-9497-6 lib bdg; 1-4358-9497-9 lib bdg; 978-1-4358-9524-9 pa; 1-4358-9524-X pa
LC 2010002493

Presents the history, geography, government, economy, and people of Utah, as well as general facts about the state.

Includes bibliographical references

Kent, Deborah

Utah. Children's Press 2009 144p il map (America the beautiful, third series) $39

Grades: 4 5 6 7   **979.2**
ISBN 978-0-531-18592-6; 0-531-18592-3
LC 2007051225

Presents an introduction to the geography, natural resources, history, economy, important sites, daily life, and people of Utah.

Includes glossary and bibliographical references

Stefoff, Rebecca

Utah; by Rebecca Stefoff and Wendy Mead. 2nd ed.; Marshall Cavendish Benchmark 2010 144p il map (Celebrate the states) lib bdg $42.79

Grades: 5 6 7 8   **979.2**
ISBN 978-0-7614-4035-2; 0-7614-4035-6
LC 2008040026

This offers information on the geography, history, wildlife, governmental structure, economy, cultural diversity, peoples, religion, and landmarks of Utah.

Includes bibliographical references

979.3   Nevada

Heinrichs, Ann

Nevada; by Ann Heinrichs. Children's Press 2008 144p il map (America the beautiful, third series) lib bdg $38

Grades: 4 5 6 7   **979.3**
ISBN 978-0-531-18586-5; 0-531-18586-9
LC 2006-39526

Describes the history, geography, ecology, people, economy, cities, and sights of the state of Nevada.

Includes glossary and bibliographical references

Roza, Greg

Nevada; past and present. Rosen Central 2011 48p il map (The United States: past and present) lib bdg $26.50; pa $11.75

Grades: 3 4 5 6   **979.3**
ISBN 978-1-4358-9488-4 lib bdg; 1-4358-9488-X; 978-1-4358-9515-7 pa; 1-4358-9515-0 pa
LC 2010001980

Presents the history, geography, government, economy, and people of Nevada, as well as general facts about the state.

Includes bibliographical references

Stefoff, Rebecca

Nevada; 2nd ed.; Marshall Cavendish Benchmark 2010 144p il map (Celebrate the states) lib bdg $42.79

Grades: 5 6 7 8   **979.3**
ISBN 978-0-7614-4728-3; 0-7614-4728-8
LC 2009007137

This offers information on the geography, history, wildlife, governmental structure, economy, cultural diversity, peoples, religion, and landmarks of Nevada.

Includes bibliographical references

979.4   California

Brown, Don

★ Gold! Gold from the American River! Roaring Brook Press 2011 un il map (Actual times) $17.99

Grades: 2 3 4   **979.4**
1. Frontier and pioneer life -- California 2. California -- Gold discoveries
ISBN 978-1-59643-223-9; 1-59643-223-3
LC 2010-14375

"Brown here takes a look at the 1849 California gold rush. [This is written] with easygoing prose and revealing quotes from forty-niners and historians alike. . . . The inventive page compositions and scratchy watercolor cartoon figures carry small, telling dramas . . . and sweeping landscapes come into full relief, bringing not only visual context but a sense of playfulness to the book." Booklist

Includes bibliographical references

Burgan, Michael

California; [by] Michael Burgan, William McGeveran. 2nd ed.; Marshall Cavendish Benchmark 2010 80p il map (It's my state) lib bdg $31.36

Grades: 3 4 5 **979.4**

ISBN 978-1-6087-0045-5; 1-6087-0045-3

LC 2010003902

Surveys the history, geography, government, and economy of California as well as the diverse ways of life of its people.

Calabro, Marian

★ The **perilous** journey of the Donner Party. Clarion Bks. 1999 192p il maps $20

Grades: 5 6 7 8 **979.4**

1. Donner party 2. Overland journeys to the Pacific 3. Survival 4. Donner Party 5. Donner Party -- Juvenile literature 6. Frontier and pioneer life -- West (U.S.) 7. Pioneer children -- West (U.S.) -- History -- 19th century -- Juvenile literature

ISBN 0-395-86610-3

LC 98-29610

Uses materials from letters and diaries written by survivors of the Donner Party to relate the experiences of that ill-fated group as they endured horrific circumstances on their way to California in 1846-47

"Calabro's offering is a fine addition to the Donner Party canon and particularly well suited to its young audience, for whom the story of hardship and survival will be nothing short of riveting. . . . From the haunting cover with its lonely campfire to the recounting of a survivors' reunion, this is a page-turner." Booklist

Includes bibliographical references

Doak, Robin S.

California, 1542-1850; by Robin Doak; Andres Resendez, consultant. National Geographic Society 2006 109p map il (Voices from colonial America) $21.95; lib bdg $32.90

Grades: 5 6 7 8 **979.4**

1. California -- History

ISBN 978-0-7922-6391-3; 0-7922-6391-X; 978-0-7922-6861-1 lib bdg; 0-7922-6861-X lib bdg

LC 2005-30920

"The text is not written in sound bites but in full paragraphs, making up chronological chapters. These are divided into topical sections, which are clearly marked by large headings. This lovely, calm layout is liberally sprinkled with primary source illustrations, including reproductions of period maps, pamphlets, paintings, and drawings. . . . An essential purchase for schools with a colonies research project . . . and for the public libraries that support their communities." Voice Youth Advocates

Includes bibliograhical references

Krensky, Stephen

Lizzie Newton and the San Francisco earthquake; illustrated by Jeremy Tugeau. Millbrook Press 2010 48p il (History speaks: picture books plus reader's theater) lib bdg $27.93

Grades: 2 3 4 **979.4**

1. Earthquakes 2. Readers' theater 3. San Francisco (Calif.) -- History

ISBN 978-0-8225-9031-6 lib bdg; 0-8225-9031-X lib bdg

LC 2009049597

Ten-year-old Lizzie Newton, having helped take her grandmother to the hospital after the 1906 San Francisco earthquake, sets off on her own to find her parents. Includes a readers' theater script and performance tips.

This "title begins with a well-illustrated narrative and concludes with a tip sheet for performing Reader's Theater as well as a list of characters, a script, and a pronounciation guide. . . . [This book will] make history come alive in a unique and interesting way." Libr Media Connect

Includes bibliographical references

La Bella, Laura

California; past and present. Rosen Central 2010 48p il map (The United States: past and present) lib bdg $26.50; pa $11.50

Grades: 3 4 5 6 **979.4**

ISBN 978-1-4358-5290-7 lib bdg; 1-4358-5290-7 lib bdg; 978-1-4358-5578-6 pa; 1-4358-5578-7 pa

LC 2008-55151

Presents the history, geography, government, economy, and people of California, as well as general facts about the state.

Includes glossary and bibliographical references

Olson, Tod

★ **How** to get rich in the California Gold Rush; an adventurer's guide to the fabulous riches discovered in 1848 . . . illustrations by Scott Allred; afterword by Marc Aronson. National Geographic 2008 47p il map (How to get rich) $16.95; lib bdg $25.90

Grades: 4 5 6 7 **979.4**

1. Gold mines and mining 2. Prospecting -- Juvenile literature 4. Frontier and pioneer life -- California 5. Gold mines and mining -- Juvenile literature 6. Frontier and pioneer life -- Juvenile literature

ISBN 1-4263-0315-7; 1-4263-0316-5 lib bdg; 978-1-4263-0315-9; 978-1-4263-0316-6 lib bdg

LC 2008-19601

This is a personal account of the California Gold Rush from the point-of-view of the fictitious character Thomas Hartley. "Grades four to seven." (Bull Cent Child Books)

This "deftly blends story with history to not only give readers an understanding of a gold rush but also to provide a lighthearted and engaging entry point into frontier life. . . . Period lithographs are reproduced alongside original illustrations. . . . A ledger on each page tracks the young men's finances in a genuinely exciting way, adding a sly element of math to this well-conceived and compulsively appealing book." Booklist

Includes bibliographical references

Orr, Tamra

California; by Tamra B. Orr. Children's Press 2008 144p il map (America the beautiful, third series) lib bdg $38

Grades: 4 5 6 7 **979.4**

ISBN 978-0-531-18557-5; 0-531-18557-5

LC 2006-36021

Describes the history, geography, ecology, people, economy, cities, and sights of the state of California.

Includes glossary and bibliographical references

Ryan, Pam Munoz

Our California; by Pam Munoz Ryan; illustrated by Rafael Lopez. Charlesbridge 2008 un il $17.95; pa $7.95

Grades: PreK K 1 2   **979.4**

ISBN 978-1-58089-116-5; 978-1-58089-117-2 pa

"A whirlwind loop tour whisks readers through the Golden State, starting with the beaches of San Diego, heading up to L.A. and beyond to Gold Country, then swinging down through Yosemite (depicted in a stunning nighttime vertical spread) and Death Valley before ending up poolside at Palm Springs. . . . López's illustrations, paintings rendered on wood and sometimes distressed, remain fresh and surprising as he finds ways to express wonder and affection. . . . This title is virtually certain to inspire California dreamin' in readers of all ages." Publ Wkly

Walker, Paul Robert

Gold rush and riches. Kingfisher 2011 32p il map (All about America)

Grades: 3 4 5 6   **979.4**

1. Frontier and pioneer life -- California 2. California -- Gold discoveries 3. California -- History

ISBN 0-7534-6512-4 pa; 0-7534-6584-1; 978-0-7534-6512-7 pa; 978-0-7534-6584-4

This book looks at California and its neighboring states starting in 1848, with the discovery of gold and other precious metals.

This "visually appealing [title] effectively [combines] paintings, engravings, primary documents, and photographs with cartoon illustrations. The eye-catching [layout includes] different font sizes, bold type, and text boxes to highlight different pieces of information. The content is interesting and pithy." SLJ

Includes glossary and bibliographical references

Yep, Laurence, 1948-

The **lost** garden; Laurence Yep. 1st Beech Tree ed. Beech Tree Books 1996 xi, 116 p.p ill. (paperback) $6.99

Grades: 5 6 7 8   **979.4**

1. Authors 2. Novelists 3. College teachers 4. Authors, American 5. Children's authors 6. Young adult authors 7. Chinese Americans -- Biography

ISBN 9780688137014 reprint; 0688137016

LC 95053801

First published 1991 by Julian Messner

The author describes how he grew up as a Chinese American in San Francisco and how he came to use his writing to celebrate his family and his ethnic heritage

"The writing is warm, wry, and humorous. . . . The Lost Garden will be welcomed as a literary autobiography for children and, more, a thoughtful probing into what it means to be an American." SLJ

Zuehlke, Jeffrey

The **Golden** Gate Bridge. Lerner Publications 2010 32p il map (Lightning bolt books. Famous places) lib bdg $25.26

Grades: 2 3 4   **979.4**

1. Golden Gate Bridge (San Francisco, Calif.)

ISBN 978-0-8225-9407-9; 0-8225-9407-2

LC 2008-30641

Describes the Golden Gate Bridge that connects Marin County to the city of San Francisco, including information about its history, design, and construction.

This book uses "high-quality photos, illustrations, maps, and diagrams. . . . Readers will enjoy learning about [the

Golden Gate Bridge] . . . and the challenges of building and maintaining large structures." SLJ

Includes glossary and bibliographical references

979.5   Oregon

Kent, Deborah

Oregon. Children's Press 2008 144p il map (America the beautiful, third series) lib bdg $39

Grades: 4 5 6 7   **979.5**

ISBN 978-0-531-18587-2; 0-531-18587-7

LC 2007038691

Presents an introduction to the geography, natural resources, history, economy, important sites, daily life, and people of Oregon.

Includes glossary and bibliographical references

Roza, Greg

Oregon; past and present. Rosen Central 2010 48p il map (The United States: past and present) lib bdg $26.50; pa $11.75

Grades: 3 4 5 6   **979.5**

ISBN 978-1-4358-3515-3 lib bdg; 1-4358-3515-8 lib bdg; 978-1-4358-8480-9 pa; 1-4358-8480-9 pa

LC 2009016193

Presents the history, geography, government, economy, and people of Oregon, as well as general facts about the state.

Includes bibliographical references

979.6   Idaho

Kent, Deborah

Idaho. Children's Press 2010 144p il map (America the beautiful, third series) lib bdg $39

Grades: 4 5 6 7   **979.6**

ISBN 978-0-531-18598-8; 0-531-18598-2

LC 2008005647

Takes readers on a tour of Idaho, describing the state's history, culture, land, economy, government, and sights, and including unique facts, color maps and photos, the state song, suggested activities, lists of famous people, cultural institutions, and annual events, and other resources.

Includes glossary and bibliographical references

Stanley, John

Idaho; past and present. Rosen Central 2011 48p il map (The United States: past and present) lib bdg $26.50; pa $11.75

Grades: 3 4 5 6   **979.6**

ISBN 978-1-4358-9480-8 lib bdg; 1-4358-9480-4 lib bdg; 978-1-4358-9507-2 pa; 1-4358-9507-X pa

LC 2009049391

Presents the history, geography, government, economy, and people of Idaho, as well as general facts about the state.

Includes glossary and bibliographical references

Stefoff, Rebecca

Idaho; by Rebecca Stefoff. 2nd ed.; Marshall Cavendish Benchmark 2008 144p il map (Celebrate the states) lib bdg $39.93

Grades: 4 5 6 7 **979.6**
ISBN 978-0-7614-3003-2; 0-7614-3003-2
LC 2007-29496

First published 2000

"Provides comprehensive information on the geography, history, wildlife, governmental structure, economy, cultural diversity, peoples, religion, and landmarks of Idaho." Publisher's note

Includes bibliographical references

979.7 Washington

Harmon, Dan

Washington; past and present. [by] Daniel E. Harmon. Rosen Central 2010 48p il map (The United States: past and present) lib bdg $26.50; pa $11.50

Grades: 3 4 5 6 **979.7**
ISBN 978-1-4358-5295-2 lib bdg; 1-4358-5295-8 lib bdg; 978-1-4358-5588-5 pa; 1-4358-5588-4 pa
LC 2008-54236

Presents the history, geography, government, economy, and people of Washington, as well as general facts about the state.

Includes glossary and bibliographical references

Jankowski, Susan

Olympic National Park; adventure, explore, discover. [by] Susan Jankowski. MyReportLinks.com Books 2009 128p il map (America's national parks) lib bdg $33.27

Grades: 5 6 7 8 **979.7**
1. Olympic National Park (Wash.)
ISBN 978-1-59845-092-7 lib bdg; 1-59845-092-1 lib bdg
LC 2007-17341

This "informative, well-written book contains a physical description of the park; a summary of its history including the Native peoples of the area; activities such as hiking trails, campsites, and visitor centers; information about the park's plants, animals, and weather; full-color photographs; and numerous approved links available through the publisher's Web page. . . . Thorough, useful, and appealing, this . . . is a great update for collections." SLJ

Includes glossary and bibliographical references

Otfinoski, Steven

Washington; [by] Steven Otfinoski and Tea Benduhn. 2nd ed.; Marshall Cavendish Benchmark 2010 90p il map (It's my state!) lib bdg $31.93

Grades: 3 4 5 **979.7**
ISBN 978-1-6087-0061-5; 1-6087-0061-5
LC 2010003935

First published 2003

Surveys the history, geography, economy, and people of the state of Washington.

Stefoff, Rebecca

Washington; [by] Rebecca Stefoff. 2nd ed.; Marshall Cavendish Benchmark 2008 144p il map (Celebrate the states) lib bdg $39.93

Grades: 4 5 6 7 **979.7**
ISBN 978-0-7614-2561-8; 0-7614-2561-6
LC 2006-32436

First published 1999

"Provides comprehensive information on the geography, history, wildlife, governmental structure, economy, cultural diversity, peoples, religion, and landmarks of Washington." Publisher's note

Includes bibliographical references

979.8 Alaska

Mattern, Joanne

Alaska; past and present. Rosen Central 2011 48p il map (The United States: past and present) lib bdg $26.50; pa $11.75

Grades: 3 4 5 6 **979.8**
ISBN 978-1-4358-9475-4 lib bdg; 1-4358-9475-8 lib bdg; 978-1-4358-9503-4 pa; 1-4358-9503-7 pa
LC 2009046615

This describes the history, culture, geography and people of Alaska.

Includes bibliographical references

Miller, Debbie S.

Big Alaska; journey across America's most amazing state. illustrations by Jon Van Zyle. Walker 2006 un il map $17.95; lib bdg $18.85

Grades: 2 3 4 **979.8**
ISBN 978-0-8027-8069-0; 0-8027-8069-5; 978-0-8027-8070-6 lib bdg; 0-8027-8070-9 lib bdg
LC 2005-24086

"Miller's text follows a bald eagle's flight across Alaska, beginning with Admiralty Island and circling back to the Chilkat Bald Eagle Preserve. . . . Zyle's acrylic paintings perfectly suit the grandeur of the subject. . . . Back matter includes Alaska Facts, State Symbols, Climate Records, and Alaska's Special Places, which has additional information on the locations described in the text. . . . The book . . . is a special treasure both for readers already interested in the subject and newcomers." SLJ

Includes bibliographical references

Orr, Tamra

Alaska; by Tamra B. Orr. Children's Press 2008 144p il map (America the beautiful, third series) lib bdg $38

Grades: 4 5 6 7 **979.8**
ISBN 978-0-531-18569-8; 0-531-18569-9
LC 2007-22220

Describes the history, geography, ecology, people, economy, cities, and sights of the state of Alaska.

Includes glossary and bibliographical references

980 History of South America

Foster, Karen

Atlas of South America. Picture Window books 2008 32p il map (Picture Window Books world atlases) lib bdg $27.93

Grades: 2 3 4 **980**
1. South America
ISBN 978-1-4048-3887-1 lib bdg; 1-4048-3887-2 lib bdg

This introduction to the geography of South America offers maps and information about countries, landforms, bodies of water, climate, plants, animals, population, people and customs, places of interest, industries, transportation, and Lake Titicaca.

Includes glossary

Gorrell, Gena K.

★ In the land of the jaguar; South America and its people. illustrated by Andrej Krystoforski. Tundra Books 2007 149p il $22.95

Grades: 5 6 7 8 9   **980**

1. South America

ISBN 978-0-88776-756-2

"This beautifully designed volume, with an engaging narrative, combines a highly informative overview of the continent with country-by-country detail. . . . The spacious design includes big maps, clear type on thick paper, and small, beautiful, fully captioned illustrations." Booklist

981   Brazil

Berkenkamp, Lauri

Discover the Amazon; the world's largest rainforest. illustrated by Blair Shedd. Nomad Press 2008 90p il map pa $16.95

Grades: 4 5 6 7   **981**

1. Amazon River valley 2. Rain forests -- Juvenile literature 2. Rain forest ecology -- Juvenile literature

ISBN 978-1-9346702-7-9 pa; 1-9346702-7-8 pa

"Berkenkamp's introduction to the [Amazon] river basin incorporates maps, drawings, and photos in various shades of green and brown on recycled paper.' The conversational style provides a 'you are there' feeling, conveying information and anecdotes while stressing outdoor survival skills. . . . Even readers who never travel to Amazonia will appreciate the region's complexity and significance after perusing this book." SLJ

Deckker, Zilah

★ Brazil; [by] Zilah Deckker; David Robinson and Joao Cezar de Castro Rocha, consultants. National Geographic 2008 64p il (Countries of the world) lib bdg $27.90

Grades: 4 5 6 7   **981**

1. Brazil

ISBN 978-1-4263-0298-5 lib bdg; 1-4263-0298-3 lib bdg

This describes the geography, nature, history, people and culture, government, and economy of Brazil.

Includes glossary and bibliographical references

982   Argentina

Lourie, Peter

Tierra del Fuego; a journey to the end of the earth. Boyds Mills Press 2002 47p il map $19.95

Grades: 4 5 6 7   **982**

1. Tierra del Fuego (Argentina and Chile)

ISBN 1-56397-973-X

LC 2001-96395

The author describes his travels in Tierra del Fuego and provides historical background on the area

"Lourie's smooth, first-person narrative mixes history, adventure, and personal insights, while glorious photographs of the remarkable land at the southernmost point of the world enhance his travelogue. . . . Highly informative for reports, this fascinating account will also appeal to young readers with wanderlust." SLJ

983   Chile

Rau, Dana Meachen

Chile. Marshall Cavendish Benchmark 2007 48p il map (Discovering cultures) lib bdg $28.50

Grades: 2 3 4   **983**

1. Chile

ISBN 978-0-7614-1988-4 lib bdg; 0-7614-1988-8 lib bdg

An introduction to the geography, history, people, and culture of Chile

Includes glossary and bibliographical references

984   Bolivia

Pateman, Robert

Bolivia; [by] Robert Pateman & Marcus Cramer. 2nd ed.; Marshall Cavendish Benchmark 2006 144p il map (Cultures of the world) lib bdg $42.79

Grades: 5 6 7 8   **984**

1. Bolivia

ISBN 978-0-7614-2066-8 lib bdg; 0-7614-2066-5 lib bdg

LC 2006002425

First published 1995

This is "well organized, informative, and entertaining. . . . Excellent-quality full-color photographs and reproductions show the people, landforms, buildings, and everyday activities." SLJ

Includes bibliographical references

985   Peru

Calvert, Patricia

★ The ancient Inca; written by Patricia Calvert. Franklin Watts 2004 128p il (People of the ancient world) lib bdg $30.50; pa $9.95

Grades: 5 6 7 8   **985**

1. Incas

ISBN 0-531-12358-8 lib bdg; 0-531-16740-2 pa

LC 2004-1956

This "well-written, attractive [title has] extensive collections of quality color photographs of ruins and artifacts." SLJ

Includes bibliographical references

Gruber, Beth

★ Ancient Inca; archaeology unlocks the secrets of the Inca's past. by Beth Gruber; Johan Reinhard, consultant. National Geographic 2007 64p il map (National Geographic investigates) $17.95; lib bdg $27.90

Grades: 5 6 7 8 **985**

1. Incas 2. Excavations (Archeology) -- Peru
ISBN 978-0-7922-7827-6; 978-0-7922-7873-3 lib bdg
LC 2006032104

This describes how archeologists have found out about ancient Incan civilization.

This offers "the beautiful photography and illustrations characteristic of the National Geographic Society, [a] well-written [text] and sidebars, and information on recent archaeological finds." SLJ

Includes bibliographical references

Krebs, Laurie

Up and down the Andes; a Peruvian festival tale. [by] Laurie Krebs, Aurelia Fronty. Barefoot Books 2008 un il $16.99

Grades: K 1 2 3 **985**

1. Inti Raymi Festival 2. Festivals -- Peru 3. Native Americans -- Peru
ISBN 978-1-84686-203-8; 1-84686-203-5
LC 2008020722

This is a "picture book about the Peruvian Inti Raymi Festival as children travel from all over southern Peru, by bus, train, boat, mule, and truck, to the city of Cusco to celebrate with feasting and fun in their traditional costumes. The simply rhyming text and the bright, clear, beautiful unframed acrylic paintings express a strong sense of the rich traditions that are still part of contemporary life." Booklist

Lewin, Ted

★ Lost city; the discovery of Machu Picchu. Philomel Bks. 2003 un il $16.99

Grades: 2 3 4 **985**

1. Machu Picchu (Peru)
ISBN 0-399-23302-4
LC 2002-4461

In 1911, Yale professor Hiram Bingham discovers a lost Incan city with the help of a young Peruvian boy

"The language is graceful and uncomplicated, weaving in bits of background history along the way. . . . Full-page watercolors spreads of the stunning vistas and thick forests contrast with dark, intimate views of Bingham inside homes and walking along walled city streets. . . . An exciting, eye-catching story." Booklist

Newman, Sandra

The Inca empire. Children's Press 2009 48p il map (True book) lib bdg $26; pa $6.95

Grades: 3 4 5 **985**

1. Incas
ISBN 978-0-531-25228-4 lib bdg; 0-531-25228-0 lib bdg; 978-0-531-24109-7 pa; 0-531-24109-2 pa
LC 2009000293

In this book the Inca civilization is "outlined for young readers with care and precision. . . . Loaded with access points such as captions, pull-outs, a time line, and a map, and with better-than-usual reproductions of well-chosen primary sources and art, the [book sports] a bright, peppy design. . . [This book is] rigorous in distinguishing fact from theory, and conscientious about presenting competing theories where they exist." SLJ

986.1   Colombia

Croy, Anita

★ Colombia; [by] Anita Croy; Ulrich Oslender and Mauricio Pardo, consultants. National Geographic 2008 64p il map (Countries of the world) lib bdg $27.90

Grades: 4 5 6 7 **986.1**

1. Colombia
ISBN 978-1-4263-0257-2 lib bdg; 1-4263-0257-6 lib bdg

This describes the geography, nature, history, people and culture, government, and economy of Colombia

Includes glossary and bibliographical references

De Capua, Sarah

Colombia. Benchmark Bks. 2004 48p il maps (Discovering cultures) lib bdg $28.50

Grades: 2 3 4 **986.1**

1. Colombia
ISBN 0-7614-1715-X
LC 2003-8128

Highlights the geography, people, food, schools, recreation, celebrations, and language of Colombia

Includes glossary and bibliographical references

986.6   Ecuador

Foley, Erin

Ecuador; [by] Erin L. Foley & Leslie Jermyn. 2nd ed.; Marshall Cavendish Benchmark 2006 144p il map (Cultures of the world) lib bdg $42.79

Grades: 5 6 7 8 **986.6**

1. Ecuador
ISBN 0-7614-2050-9
LC 2005022671

First published 1995

This briefly describes Ecuador's "history, government, economy, and geography. . . . Particularly useful is the information on religion, the arts, food, leisure activities, and social roles. The [book has] great visual appeal with excellent full-color photographs on every page. [It] is especially successful in explaining social and economic hierarchies within the country." SLJ

Includes glossary and bibliographical references

Henzel, Cynthia Kennedy

Galapagos Islands. ABDO Pub. Co. 2011 32p il (Troubled treasures: world heritage sites) $25.65

Grades: 3 4 5 **986.6**

1. Galapagos Islands
ISBN 978-1-61613-563-8; 1-61613-563-8
LC 2010021311

This "book describes in general terms [the Galapagos Islands'] . . . creation, distinctive features, and history, as well as threats to its continued existence and both current and past restoration initiatives. Revealing color photos taken from different heights and angles are supplemented by maps and by graphic reconstructions. . . . Henzel's distinctive approach gives this [book] unusual value for both assignment and general reading." SLJ

Includes glossary

Kras, Sara Louise

The **Galapagos** Islands; [by] Sara Louise Kras. Marshall Cavendish Benchmark 2008 96p il map (Nature's wonders) lib bdg $35.64

Grades: 5 6 7 8   **986.6**

1. Galapagos Islands

ISBN 978-0-7614-2856-5 lib bdg; 0-7614-2856-9 lib bdg

LC 2007020416

"Provides comprehensive information on the geography, history, wildlife, peoples, and environmental issues of the Galapagos Islands." Publisher's note

Includes glossary and bibliographical references

988.1   Guyana

Jermyn, Leslie

Guyana; by Leslie Jermyn and Winnie Wong. Marshall Cavendish Benchmark 2010 144 p. col. ill., col. maps (library) $47.07

Grades: 5 6 7 8   **988.1**

1. Guyana -- Juvenile literature

ISBN 1608700232; 9781608700233

LC 2010000724

This book by Leslie Jermyn is part of the Cultures of the World series and looks at the South American nation of Guyana. "Touching upon everything from its history to religion to architecture, this book . . . highlights the country's rich diversity and unique qualities. With a population that includes many different ethnic groups, the author . . . examines the contributions of each to Guyana's development and to its present culture." (Children's Literature)

Includes bibliographical references (p.142) and index.

989.2   Paraguay

Jermyn, Leslie

Paraguay; [by] Leslie Jermyn and Yong Jui Lin. 2nd ed.; Marshall Cavendish Benchmark 2010 144p il map (Cultures of the world) lib bdg $42.79

Grades: 5 6 7 8   **989.2**

1. Paraguay

ISBN 978-0-7614-4858-7 lib bdg; 0-7614-4858-6 lib bdg

LC 2009046495

First published 2000

This offers information on the geography, history, wildlife, governmental structure, economy, cultural diversity, peoples, religion, and culture of Paraguay

Includes glossary and bibliographical references

989.5   Uruguay

Jermyn, Leslie

Uruguay; by Leslie Jermyn and Winnie Wong. 2nd ed.; Marshall Cavendish Benchmark 2009 144p il map (Cultures of the world) lib bdg $42.79

Grades: 5 6 7 8   **989.5**

1. Uruguay

ISBN 978-0-7614-4482-4 lib bdg; 0-7614-4482-3 lib bdg

LC 2009007127

First published 1999

Provides information on the geography, history, wildlife, governmental structure, economy, cultural diversity, peoples, religion, and culture of Uruguay

Includes glossary and bibliographical references

993   New Zealand

Jackson, Barbara

★ **New** Zealand; [by] Barbara Jackson; Vaughan Wood and Simon Milne, consultants. National Geographic 2008 64p il map (Countries of the world) lib bdg $27.90

Grades: 4 5 6 7   **993**

1. New Zealand

ISBN 978-1-4263-0301-2 lib bdg; 1-4263-0301-7 lib bdg

This describes the geography, nature, history, people and culture, government, and economy of New Zealand.

Smelt, Roselynn

New Zealand; by Roselynn Smelt. 2nd ed.; Marshall Cavendish Benchmark 2009 128p il map (Cultures of the world) lib bdg $42.79

Grades: 5 6 7 8   **993**

1. New Zealand

ISBN 978-0-7614-3415-3 lib bdg; 0-7614-3415-1 lib bdg

LC 2008028792

First published 1998

"Provides comprehensive information on the geography, history, wildlife, governmental structure, economy, cultural diversity, peoples, religion, and culture of New Zealand." Publisher's note

Includes glossary and bibliographical references

994   Australia

Arnold, Caroline

★ **Uluru,** Australia's Aboriginal heart; photographs by Arthur Arnold. Clarion Books 2003 64p il $16

Grades: 5 6 7 8   **994**

1. Aboriginal Australians 2. Australian aborigines -- Australia -- Uluru National Park -- Juvenile literature

ISBN 0-618-18181-4

LC 2002-15542

Describes Uluru, formerly known as Ayers Rock, in Australia's Uluru-Kata Tjuta National Park, its plant and animal life, and the country's Aboriginal people for whom the site is sacred

"The book's greatest accomplishment . . . is to give readers a sense of the ongoing spiritual importance of Uluru to the Anangu, who have lived around it for 10,000 years. Clear, colorful photos of Uluru and its surroundings appear on nearly every page, illustrating the text with beauty and finesse." Booklist

Foster, Karen

Atlas of Australia. Picture Window Books 2008 32p il map (Picture Window Books world atlases) lib bdg $27.93
Grades: 2 3 4   **994**

1. Australia

ISBN 978-1-4048-3881-9 lib bdg; 1-4048-3881-3 lib bdg

This introduction to the geography of Australia offers maps and information about landforms, bodies of water, climate, plants, animals, population, people and customs, places of interest, industries, transportation, and the Great Barrier Reef.

This book offers "well-organized, easy-to-access information. . . . Small photographs or colorful text boxes draw readers' attention to points of interest or fun facts. Maps and legends are simple, yet disseminate information clearly." SLJ

Includes glossary

Rau, Dana Meachen

Australia. Sea-to-Sea Publications 2009 32p il map (Facts about countries) lib bdg $28.50
Grades: 3 4 5   **994**

1. Australia

ISBN 978-1-59771-112-8 lib bdg; 1-59771-112-8 lib bdg

LC 2008004630

Describes the geography, history, industries, education, government, and cultures of Australia

"The attractive layout includes color photographs and charts of current statistics as well as maps illustrating main farming regions, natural resources, or the literacy rates of girls and boys. The [text is] clear and succinct." SLJ

Includes glossary

Turner, Kate

★ **Australia**; [by] Kate Turner; Elaine Stratford and Joseph Powell, consultants. National Geographic 2007 64p il map (Countries of the world) lib bdg $27.90
Grades: 4 5 6 7   **994**

1. Australia

ISBN 978-1-4263-0055-4

Describes the geography, nature, history, people and culture, government and economy of Australia

This "appealing [title has] wonderful photographs and maps. . . . [This book is a] reliable [source] for country research, and the interesting current material hold browsing potential as well." SLJ

Includes glossary and bibliographical references

995.3   Papua New Guinea

Gascoigne, Ingrid

Papua New Guinea; [by] Ingrid Gascoigne. 2nd ed.; Marshall Cavendish Benchmark 2009 144p il map (Cultures of the world) lib bdg $42.79
Grades: 5 6 7 8   **995.3**

1. Papua New Guinea

ISBN 978-0-7614-3416-0 lib bdg; 0-7614-3416-X lib bdg

LC 2008028794

First published 1998

"Provides comprehensive information on the geography, history, wildlife, governmental structure, economy, cultural diversity, peoples, religion, and culture of Papua New Guinea." Publisher's note

Includes glossary and bibliographical references

996   Polynesia and other Pacific Ocean islands

NgCheong-Lum, Roseline

Tahiti; [by] Roseline NgCheong-Lum. 2nd ed.; Marshall Cavendish Benchmark 2008 144p il map (Cultures of the world) lib bdg $42.79
Grades: 5 6 7 8   **996**

1. Tahiti

ISBN 978-0-7614-2089-7

LC 2007014901

"Provides comprehensive information on the geography, history, wildlife, governmental structure, economy, cultural diversity, peoples, religion, and culture of Tahiti." Publisher's note

Includes glossary and bibliographical references

996.9   Hawaii and neighboring north central Pacific Ocean islands

Feeney, Stephanie

Sun and rain; exploring seasons in Hawaii. University of Hawaii Press 2008 un il $13.95
Grades: K 1 2 3   **996.9**

1. Rain 2. Seasons 3. Hawaii 4. Sun

ISBN 978-0-8248-3088-5; 0-8248-3088-1

LC 2008272547

"Readers learn that Hawaii has only two seasons: wet and dry. Easy-to-read text and large, inviting photographs show the changing seasons and explain how humans, animals, and plants are affected. . . . Back matter includes additional information for adults." Horn Book Guide

Kent, Deborah

Hawaii; by Deborah Kent. Children's Press 2008 144p il map (America the beautiful, third series) lib bdg $38
Grades: 4 5 6 7   **996.9**

ISBN 978-0-531-18573-5; 0-531-18573-7

LC 2007-5705

Describes the history, geography, ecology, people, economy, cities, and sights of the state of Hawaii.

Includes glossary and bibliographical references

Mattern, Joanne

Hawaii; past and present. Rosen Central 2011 48p il map (The United States: past and present) lib bdg $26.50; pa $11.75
Grades: 3 4 5 6   **996.9**

ISBN 978-1-4358-9479-2 lib bdg; 1-4358-9479-0 lib bdg; 978-1-4358-9506-5 pa; 1-4358-9506-1 pa

LC 2009050544

Presents the history, geography, government, economy, and people of Hawaii, as well as general facts about the state.

Includes glossary and bibliographical references

998 Arctic islands and Antarctica

Bledsoe, Lucy Jane
★ **How** to survive in Antarctica; written and photographed by Lucy Jane Bledsoe. Holiday House 2006 101p il map $16.95
Grades: 5 6 7 8   998
1. Antarctica
ISBN 0-8234-1890-1
LC 2004-60639
"Bledsoe, who made three trips to study Antarctica, bases her informal, chatty narrative on her thrilling adventure, bringing close the amazing science and geography as well as the gritty facts of human survival in the frigid environment. . . . Bledsoe's own black-and-white photos . . . will grab students across the curriculum." Booklist
Includes glossary

Foster, Karen
Atlas of the Poles and Oceans. Picture Window Books 2008 32p il map (Picture Window Books world atlases) lib bdg $27.93
Grades: 2 3 4   998
1. Ocean 2. Antarctica 3. Arctic regions
ISBN 978-1-4048-3886-4 lib bdg; 1-4048-3886-4 lib bdg
This introduction to the geography of the Arctic, Antarctic, and the oceans offers maps and information about plants, animals, people, and protecting the environment.
Includes glossary

Goodman, Susan
★ **Life** on the ice; [by] Susan E. Goodman; with photographs by Michael J. Doolittle. Millbrook Press 2006 32p il lib bdg $22.60
Grades: 3 4 5   998
ISBN 978-0-7613-2775-2 lib bdg; 0-7613-2775-4 lib bdg
LC 2005-06141
"Excellent photos, often captioned with fascinating facts . . . accompany this text." Horn Book Guide

Lourie, Peter
Arctic thaw; the people of the whale in a changing climate. Boyds Mills Press 2007 47p il map $17.95
Grades: 5 6 7 8   998
1. Inupiat 2. Whaling 3. Human ecology 4. Greenhouse effect 5. Inupiat -- Juvenile literature 6. Human ecology -- Alaska -- Juvenile literature
ISBN 978-1-59078-436-5; 1-59078-436-7
LC 2006-20045
"A somewhat sobering, yet upbeat examination of the probable effects of global warming on the culture of the Iñupiaq whale hunters of Alaska's North Slope. . . . [Lourie's] lively, straightforward text describes the mixture of traditional and modern ways of the present-day Iñupiaq, as well as the work of [Paul] Shepson and his team to record weather and climate changes and to predict what effect they will have locally and globally." SLJ
Includes bibliographical references

Markle, Sandra
Animals Robert Scott saw; an adventure in Antarctica. Chronicle Books 2008 45p il (Explorers) $16.99

Grades: 2 3 4 5   998
1. Explorers 2. Animals -- Antarctica 3. Animals -- Juvenile literature 4. Antarctica -- Exploration
ISBN 978-0-8118-4918-0; 0-8118-4918-X
LC 2006-20920
"Well illustrated with acrylic paintings and archival photos, this volume . . . traces the two Antarctic expeditions of English explorer Robert Falcon Scott, who reached the South Pole with his companions in 1912, 35 days after Amundsen's Norwegian expedition. The story may be Scott's, but the focus continually turns to animals. . . . Children fascinated by both explorers and animals are the natural audience for this." Booklist
Includes glossary and bibliographical references

Thompson, Gare
Roald Amundsen and Robert Scott race to the South Pole; by Gare Thompson. National Geographic 2007 48p il (National Geographic history chapters) lib bdg $17.90
Grades: 2 3 4   998
1. Explorers 2. Antarctica -- Exploration
ISBN 978-1-4263-0187-2
LC 2007007898
This "presents the dramatic, tragic story of the South Pole's dueling explorers. . . . Crisp, informatively captioned photographs, some presumably taken by the doomed men, lend immediacy to the facts." Booklist

Wade, Rosalyn
Polar worlds. Simon & Schuster Books for Young Readers 2011 64p il (Insiders) $16.99
Grades: 4 5 6 7   998
1. Antarctica 2. Arctic regions
ISBN 978-1-4424-3275-8; 1-4424-3275-6
This "takes a look at the nether regions of the globe in this browser-friendly resource. . . . 'Introducing' opens with a geographic look at the Arctic and Antarctic regions, then moves on to the related topics of icebergs, plant and animal life, exploration, survival measures, and environmental threats. The 'In Focus' section zeroes in on 12 specific animals found in polar regions. . . . Each spread is dominated by a sharply rendered, often dramatic digital illustration. . . . A fine introduction to the world's deep freezers." Booklist

E EASY BOOKS

Ackerman, Karen
Song and dance man; illustrated by Stephen Gammell. Knopf 1988 un il lib bdg $17.99; pa $6.99
Grades: K 1 2 3   E
1. Entertainers -- Fiction 2. Grandfathers -- Fiction
ISBN 0-394-99330-6 lib bdg; 0-679-81995-9 pa
LC 87-3200
Awarded the Caldecott Medal, 1989
The illustrator "captures all the story's inherent joie de vivre with color pencil renderings that fairly leap off the pages." Booklist

Ackerman, Peter
The lonely phone booth; illustrations by Max Dalton. Godine 2010 un il $16.95

Grades: 2 3 4   E
  1. Telephones -- Fiction
  ISBN 978-1-56792-414-5; 1-56792-414-X
       LC 2010-09372

"On the corner of West End Avenue and 100th Street in Manhattan there stands an old-fashioned phone booth, a superfluous fixture in our cell-phone world. This lonely phone booth, however, enjoys a happy ending after an electric storm shuts down the city. Finding their cell phones dead but the landlines in working order, a grateful neighborhood rallies to save the booth after a city crew threatens to haul it to the dump. Ackerman injects humor into the tale through a bevy of characters. . . . Dalton adds wit and color with illustrations that are a combination of individual vignettes and full-page images. A well-paced story." SLJ

Adams, Diane
  I can do it myself! written by Diane Adams; illustrated by Nancy Hayashi. Peachtree Publishers 2009 un il $15.95
Grades: PreK K   E
  1. Stories in rhyme 2. Bedtime -- Fiction
  ISBN 978-1-56145-471-6; 1-56145-471-0
       LC 2008031117

Emily Pearl is a big girl who insists on doing everything for herself until evening, when having someone help her get ready for bed is nice

"Hayashi's cheerful watercolors vary in size from spreads to small vignettes and help give the story just the right pace. . . . This tale is told in a fresh, yet familiar way." SLJ

Adams, Sarah
  Dave & Violet. Frances Lincoln 2011 il $17.95
Grades: PreK K 1 2   E
  1. Dragons -- Fiction 2. Friendship -- Fiction
  ISBN 978-1-84780-052-7; 1-84780-052-1

"Violet's best friend Dave has a hard time fitting in. Not only is he a dragon, Dave is also shy. Violet, a little girl, takes him to the park to meet her friends, who have never seen a dragon before. They approach him amiably, but Dave gets very nervous. He turns bright orange, and a huge flame gushes from his mouth. . . . Adams' illustrations, like her story, are simple and direct; the lino prints have bold outlines and bright colors, and eggplant-shaped, mop-topped Dave has a goofy appeal. A fitting fable for the very young about friendship and diversity." Kirkus

  Gary and Ray. Frances Lincoln Children's Books 2010 un il $17.95
Grades: PreK K 1 2   E
  1. Birds -- Fiction 2. Gorillas -- Fiction 3. Friendship -- Fiction
  ISBN 978-1-84507-955-0; 1-84507-955-8

Gary the gorilla is lonely because he has no friends and there are no other gorillas around, but then he meets a friendly bird called Ray.

"The charming illustrations, vibrantly colored lino prints, will be a draw to many readers. . . . The sweet story about the yearning for companionship will resonate will many as well." Booklist

Addasi, Maha
  Time to pray; Arabic translation by Nuha Albitar; illustrated by Ned Gannon. Boyds Mills Press 2010 un il $17.95
Grades: 1 2 3 4   E
  1. Islam -- Fiction 2. Prayer -- Fiction 3. Muslims -- Fiction 4. Grandmothers -- Fiction 5. Bilingual books -- English-Arabic
  ISBN 978-1-59078-611-6; 1-59078-611-4
       LC 2010005090

When young Yasmin goes for a visit, her grandmother teaches her a Muslim's daily prayers, makes special prayer clothes, and gives a gift that will help Yasmin remember when to pray. Includes facts about prayer customs.

"This is a beautifully woven tale of grandparent affection and spiritual development. Gannon's illustrations present a warm and authentic balance of Islamic geometric designs and Arab architecture and culture. . . . Familiarizing Islamic prayer through realistic fiction makes this a fine choice for most collections." SLJ

  The **white** nights of Ramadan; [by] Maha Addasi; illustrated by Ned Gannon. Boyds Mills Press 2008 un il $16.95
Grades: 1 2 3 4   E
  1. Muslims -- Fiction 2. Ramadan -- Fiction
  ISBN 978-1-59078-523-2; 1-59078-523-1
       LC 2008002637

"This story is centered around Girgian, a Muslim celebration observed mostly in the Arabian Gulf states during the middle of the month of Ramadan. When Noor, who lives in Kuwait, sees the almost-full moon rise, she knows it's time to prepare for the festival. The family makes candy from honey, sugar, and nuts to share with the children in the neighborhood, wrapping it with cellophane and colorful bows. . . . Shimmering with moonlit hues, the attractive illustrations are done in a style that reflects one of many Muslim cultures. A helpful author's note and glossary are appended. An excellent choice for units on diversity and multiculturalism." SLJ

Addy, Sharon
  Lucky Jake; illustrated by Wade Zahares. Houghton Mifflin 2006 un il $17
Grades: PreK K 1 2   E
  1. Pigs -- Fiction 2. Gold mines and mining -- Fiction
  ISBN 0-618-47286-X; 978-0-618-47286-4
       LC 2005-03917

While panning for gold with his Pa, Jake adopts a pig that he names Dog.

"Using pastels in deep and heavy hues, solid shapes, and unusual perspectives, he provides images that roll breathtakingly across the pages. . . . An intriguing mix of old-fashioned storytelling and cutting-edge art." Booklist

Adler, David A., 1947-
  The **Babe** & I; written by David A. Adler; illustrated by Terry Widener. Harcourt Brace & Co. 1999 un il $17; pa $7
Grades: K 1 2 3   E
  1. Baseball players 2. Depressions -- 1929 3. Moneymaking projects 4. Great Depression, 1929-1939

-- Fiction 5. Depressions -- 1929 -- Juvenile fiction
ISBN 0-15-201378-4; 0-15-205026-4 pa

LC 97-37580

While helping his family make ends meet during the Depression by selling newspapers, a boy meets Babe Ruth

"Widener's illustrations evoke the ambiance of the period in this book that is carefully paced and remarkable for its unified focus." Horn Book Guide

It's time to sleep, it's time to dream; illustrated by Kay Chorao. Holiday House 2009 un il $16.95
Grades: PreK K   **E**
1. Bedtime -- Fiction 2. Seasons -- Fiction
ISBN 978-0-8234-1924-1; 0-8234-1924-X

LC 2008022570

A parent lulls a child to sleep with visions of soft spring breezes, lazy summer days, cool autumn winds, and moonlit winter nights

"Chorao's gouache-and-watercolor illustrations lend a new-fashioned slant to a bedtime book. . . . The softly infused color pictures pair well with the spare text. . . . Kids will be drawn to the comforting cover image of a cute tyke cuddling his toy bunny." Booklist

Millions, billions & trillions; understanding big numbers. by David A. Adler; illustrated by Edward Miller. 1st ed. Holiday House 2012 32 p. col. ill. (hardcover) $17.95
Grades: 2 3 4   **E**
1. Counting 2. Picture books for children 3. Number concept -- Juvenile literature 4. Billion (The number) -- Juvenile literature 5. Million (The number) -- Juvenile literature 6. Trillion (The number) -- Juvenile literature
ISBN 0823424030; 9780823424030

LC 2011044752

In this book, David A. Adler and Edward Miller "put giant numbers into perspective by using familiar frames of reference and by appealing to readers' imaginations: 'How many ice cream sundaes would one billion dollars buy? At five dollars a sundae, you could buy one thousand sundaes every day for more than five hundred years.' Real-world examples (New York City has a population of over eight million people) combine with more fanciful ways to conceptualize these quantities.'" (Publishers Weekly)

★ **Young** Cam Jansen and the dinosaur game; illustrated by Susanna Natti. Viking 1996 32p il (Viking easy-to-read) $13.99; pa $3.99
Grades: K 1 2 3   **E**
1. Mystery fiction
ISBN 0-670-86399-8; 0-14-037779-4 pa

LC 95-46463

"At Jane's birthday party, everyone guesses the number of toy dinosaurs in a big jar. Jennifer 'the Camera' Jansen's photographic memory helps her nab Robert, who has cheated in order to win all the dinosaurs. Observant readers can follow Cam's reasoning and solve the mystery, too." Horn Book Guide

Other easy-to-read titles about Cam Jansen are:
Young Cam Jansen and the 100th day of school mystery (2009)
Young Cam Jansen and the baseball mystery (1999)
Young Cam Jansen and the double beach mystery (2002)
Young Cam Jansen and the ice skate mystery (1998)

Young Cam Jansen and the library mystery (2001)
Young Cam Jansen and the lions' lunch mystery (2007)
Young Cam Jansen and the lost tooth (1997)
Young Cam Jansen and the Molly shoe mystery (2008)
Young Cam Jansen and the missing cookie (1996)
Young Cam Jansen and the new girl mystery (2004)
Young Cam Jansen and the pizza shop mystery (2000)
Young Cam Jansen and the speedy car mystery (2010)
Young Cam Jansen and the substitute mystery (2005)
Young Cam Jansen and the zoo note mystery (2003)

Adler, Victoria
★ **All** of baby, nose to toes; pictures by Hiroe Nakata. Dial Books for Young Readers 2009 un il $14.99
Grades: PreK   **E**
1. Stories in rhyme 2. Infants -- Fiction 3. Infants -- Juvenile literature
ISBN 978-0-8037-3217-9; 0-8037-3217-1

LC 2008-30971

Rhyming text celebrates everything about a beloved baby, from eyes to toes

"Adler's sunny poem and Nakata's ebullient watercolors demonstrate not only a baby's exploratory joy but also the palpable delight a baby brings to a family." Publ Wkly

Baby, come away; pictures by David Walker. Farrar Straus Giroux 2011 un il $16.99
Grades: PreK K 1   **E**
1. Stories in rhyme 2. Animals -- Fiction 3. Infants -- Fiction
ISBN 978-0-374-30480-5; 0-374-30480-7

LC 2010036234

A bird, a cat, a dog, and a fish each imagines an ideal day spent with a baby.

"This offering is destined to become a cherished favorite. [It has] utterly charming paintings. . . . Full of rhyme, alliteration, and playful wording, the text lends itself to group reading or one-on-one sharing equally well." SLJ

Adoff, Arnold
★ **Black** is brown is tan; pictures by Emily Arnold McCully. HarperCollins Pubs. 2002 un il $17.99; pa $6.99
Grades: PreK K 1 2   **E**
1. Family life -- Fiction 2. Racially mixed people -- Fiction
ISBN 0-06-028776-4; 0-06-443644-6 pa

LC 00-44864

A newly illustrated edition of the title first published 1973
Describes in verse a family with a brown-skinned mother, white-skinned father, two children, and their various relatives

"Children everywhere will love the simple, joyful rhythmic words in Adoff's signature 'shaped speech' style, with McCully's beautiful dancing watercolors." Booklist

Agee, Jon
Milo's hat trick; story and pictures by Jon Agee. Hyperion Bks. for Children 2001 un il $15.95
Grades: PreK K 1 2   **E**
1. Bears 2. Magicians 3. Magic tricks
ISBN 0-7868-0902-7

In the busy city, there are lots of people with hats. But there is only one guy with a bear in his hat. That's Milo The Magician

"Agee's bold, angular pencil-and-paint illustrations drive this warm story about perseverance, luck, and courage." Booklist

Mr. Putney's quacking dog. Michael Di Capua Books 2010 un il $16.95
Grades: PreK K 1   E
  1. Puns -- Fiction 2. Riddles, Juvenile
  ISBN 978-0-545-16203-6; 0-545-16203-3
"Clue-packed pictures add to the fun. Agee fills out the spreads with thick-lined, soft-colored, comedic pictures. A great choice for fans of punnery." SLJ

My rhinoceros. Scholastic 2011 un il $16.95
Grades: PreK K 1   E
  1. Pets -- Fiction 2. Rhinoceros -- Fiction
  ISBN 978-0-545-29441-6; 0-545-29441-X
"Adopting a rhinoceros, in and of itself, would be absurd enough for most storytellers. For Agee, . . . it is simply the first in a series of weird narrative curveballs. . . . When two bank robbers attempt a getaway, using a hot-air balloon and a hang-glider, does the rhinoceros prove its mettle, springing into superheroic action and demonstrating a third, even more surprising ability. Agee's deadpan voice and blocky, India-ink-and-watercolor pictures play into the inherent oddity of the story." Publ Wkly

Nothing. Hyperion Books for Children 2007 un il $16.99
Grades: K 1 2 3   E
  1. Selling -- Fiction 2. Humorous fiction
  ISBN 978-0-7868-3694-9; 0-7868-3694-6
                             LC 2007-25191
When Suzie Gump, the richest lady in town, walks into Otis's empty antique shop and insists on buying nothing, she starts a fad that has everyone buying nothing and emptying their homes and stores to make room for it—until Suzie realizes things have gone too far.
"In illustrations that possess a timeless air, Agee contrasts cluttered, patterned spaces with airy rooms, outlines chunky, geometric areas with firm charcoal lines and tints broad surfaces with transparent watercolor wash. . . . This timely parable is certainly something worth having." Publ Wkly

★ **Terrific**; story and pictures by Jon Agee. Hyperion Books for Children 2005 un il $15.95
Grades: PreK K 1 2   E
  1. Parrots -- Fiction 2. Shipwrecks -- Fiction
  ISBN 0-7868-5184-8
                             LC 2004-117133
"Terrific," says Eugene when he wins an all-expenses-paid cruise to Bermuda. "I'll probably get a really nasty sunburn." But Eugene's luck is much worse than that. His ship sinks, and he ends up stranded on a tiny island with a talking parrot.
"With pithy humor and a knack for comic timing, Agee has created a character who will endear himself to readers despite his curmudgeonly exterior and posturing. . . . The cartoon illustrations feature strong lines and soft colors that contrast wonderfully with the story line." SLJ

★ **Why** did the chicken cross the road? [by] Jon Agee . . . [et al.] Dial Books for Young Readers 2006 un il $16.99
Grades: 1 2 3 4   E
  1. Chickens -- Fiction 2. American wit and humor -- Juvenile literature
  ISBN 0-8037-3094-2
                             LC 2005-16196
"What is perhaps the world's most tired joke becomes fresh and inspired in this lively collection of work by well-known contemporary children's book artists. On each double-page spread, a different contributor offers a new, illustrated punch line to the title question. . . . Lots of fun for young children, this collection, which demonstrates the impressive artistic range and talent featured in today's picture books, will also attract older art students and children's book enthusiasts." Booklist

The **retired** kid. Hyperion Books for Children 2008 un il $16.99
Grades: K 1 2 3   E
  1. Old age -- Fiction 2. Retirement -- Fiction
  ISBN 978-1-4231-0314-1; 1-4231-0314-9
                             LC 2007-41998
Although he enjoys some aspects of his retirement, eight-year-old Brian gains a new perspective on his job of being a child after spending time in Florida's Happy Sunset Retirement Community
"Agee's gentle story about juvenile job dissatisfaction is filled with witty verbal and visual flourishes . . . that will have kids—and their grandparents—chuckling from start to finish." Booklist

Ahlberg, Allan

Hooray for bread; Allan Ahlberg, illustrated by Bruce Ingman. Candlewick Press 2013 32 p. ill. (reinforced) $15.99
Grades: PreK K 1   E
  1. Bread -- Juvenile fiction
  ISBN 0763663115; 9780763663117
                             LC 2012942661
In this children's story, by Allan Ahlberg, illustrated by Bruce Ingman, "early in the morning the baker bakes a delicious loaf of bread. So delicious, in fact, that by the time the sun goes down it has been gobbled up! Who eats it all? . . . The baker's wife eats some toast for breakfast, and the baker's son gets a cheese and ham sandwich for lunch. And let's not forget the dog! As the loaf gets smaller, slice by slice and crumb by crumb, everyone eats their fill." (Publisher's note)

Previously; [by] Allan Ahlberg; [illustrated by] Bruce Ingman. Candlewick Press 2007 un il $16.99
Grades: PreK K 1 2   E
  1. Fairy tales 2. Nursery rhymes
  ISBN 978-0-7636-3542-8; 0-7636-3542-1
                             LC 2006-51831
The adventures of various nursery rhyme and fairy tale characters are retold in backward sequence with each tale interrelated to the other. Includes Goldilocks, Jack and the beanstalk, Jack and Jill, the frog prince, Cinderella, and the gingerbread man.

"The jazzy, colorful pictures display substantive variety. . . . Children will delight in this energetic, amusing, and very approachable tale." SLJ

★ The **baby** in the hat; written by Allan Ahlberg; illustrations by Andre Amstutz. Candlewick Press 2008 un il $16.99
Grades: K 1 2   E
1. Seafaring life -- Fiction
ISBN 978-0-7636-3958-7; 0-7636-3958-3
LC 2007-52029
Catching a baby in his hat sets off a series of adventures for a young nineteenth-century English boy as he becomes a sea captain and finds a surprising mate.
"Ahlberg and Amstutz . . . overlook few opportunities for humor in this tall tale. . . . Witty, detailed gouaches dotted with dialogue balloons lend a theatricality to the picaresque tale." Publ Wkly

The **runaway** dinner; [by] Allan Ahlberg and [illustrated by] Bruce Ingman. Candlewick Press 2006 un il $15.99; pa $6.99
Grades: PreK K 1 2   E
1. Dining -- Fiction
ISBN 978-0-7636-3142-0; 0-7636-3142-6; 978-0-7636-3893-1 pa; 0-7636-3893-5 pa
LC 2005058126
A young boy named Banjo Cannon always eats a sausage for dinner, until the night that his sausage—and the rest of his meal—runs away
"With a plot timed faster than fast food and illustrations that keep pace, this picture book about a dinner that literally runs away is a comic treat." Publ Wkly

The **shopping** expedition; illustrated by André Amstutz. Candlewick Press 2005 un il $16.99
Grades: PreK K 1   E
1. Shopping -- Fiction 2. Imagination -- Fiction
ISBN 0-7636-2586-8
LC 2003-69674
A routine shopping trip becomes a grand adventure in the eyes of a little girl
"Amstutz's richly colored illustrations have a painterly look, often with visible brush strokes, that really suits the imaginative subject matter. The repetitive phrase keeps the pace of the story going and works well for reading aloud." SLJ

Ahlberg, Allan, 1938-
★ The **pencil**; [illustrated by] Bruce Ingman. Candlewick Press 2008 un il $16.99
Grades: PreK K 1 2   E
1. Drawing -- Fiction
ISBN 978-0-7636-3894-8; 0-7636-3894-3
LC 2007-51885
A lonely pencil timidly draws a boy, a dog, and other items but soon faces a problem as his creations begin demanding changes, and when he draws an eraser to make them happy, the real trouble begins.
"Both clever and suspenseful, this surefire delight tells the story of a pencil who must deal with the consequences of his inventions. . . . The book's comical, unexpected plot and wry narrator keep the story fresh throughout." Publ Wkly

Ahlberg, Janet
The **jolly** postman; or other people's letters. [by] Janet and Allan Ahlberg. Little, Brown Books for Young Readers 2001 un il $17.99
Grades: PreK K 1 2   E
1. Fairy tales 2. Stories in rhyme 3. Letters -- Fiction 4. Postal service -- Fiction
ISBN 978-0-316-12644-1; 0-316-12644-6
A reissue of the title first published 1986
A Jolly Postman delivers letters to several famous fairy-tale characters such as the Big Bad Wolf, Cinderella, and the Three Bears. Each letter may be removed from its envelope page and read separately.
"The story of the postman's travels is told in charming verse; the pictures are delightful, full of clever detail; and the results are frequently hilarious." Publ Wkly

Aigner-Clark, Julie
You are the best medicine; [by] Julie Aigner Clark; illustrated by Jana Christy. Balzer + Bray 2010 un il $16.99
Grades: PreK K 1 2   E
1. Sick -- Fiction 2. Cancer -- Fiction 3. Mother-child relationship -- Fiction
ISBN 978-0-06-195644-7; 0-06-195644-9
A mother who has cancer gently informs her child of what the effects will be, and reminds her little one of all the special times they have shared, and will continue to share, even while she undergoes treatment.
"Here's a much-needed book, and one that's done with lots of love. . . . Soft-edge illustrations, tender in feel and comforting in color, add sweetness." Booklist

Ain, Beth
Starring Jules (as herself) Beth Ain; illustrated by Anne Keenan Higgins. Scholastic Press 2013 160 p. (hardcover) $14.99
Grades: 2 3 4 5   E
1. Acting -- Juvenile fiction 2. Friendship -- Juvenile fiction 3. Acting -- Fiction 4. Schools -- Fiction 5. Auditions -- Fiction 6. Friendship -- Fiction 7. Elementary schools -- Fiction 8. Elementary schools -- Juvenile fiction 9. Acting -- Auditions -- Juvenile fiction
ISBN 0545443520; 9780545443524
LC 2012017678
This children's story, by Beth Ain, is the first book in the "Starring Jules" series. "Seven-year-old Jules has been asked to audition for a television commercial. But she needs help. . . . But Jules is in the middle of a mean fight with her former best friend, Charlotte. . . . But with the opportunity of a lifetime four days away, Jules doesn't have the time to stay angry with Charlotte." (Kirkus Reviews)

Ainsworth, Kimberly
Hootenanny! a festive counting book. illustrated by Jo Brown. Little Simon 2011 un il $12.99
Grades: PreK K   E
1. Counting 2. Owls -- Fiction 3. Parties -- Fiction
ISBN 978-1-4424-2273-5; 1-4424-2273-4; 978-1-4424-3490-5 e-book; 1-4424-3490-2 e-book
LC 2011006557
"Five owls help youngsters learn to count from one to five as they get ready for a party at the top of an old oak tree. . . . The text is printed in a large, easy-to-read font with each numeral highlighted in a different color. The bright spreads

feature a rainbow of colors, smiling characters, and some humorous details. With its jazzy vocabulary and cheerful illustrations, the book lives up to its title." SLJ

Akbarpour, Ahmad

Good night, Commander; pictures by Morteza Zahedi; translated by Shadi Eskandani and Helen Mixter. Groundwood Books 2010 un il $17.95

Grades: 3 4 5   E

    1. Iran-Iraq War, 1980-1988 -- Fiction 2. Physically handicapped children -- Fiction

    ISBN 978-0-88899-989-4; 0-88899-989-5

"This picture book with difficult concepts could possibly be used with younger students who need a fiction bridge to their own reality. This is a brief and powerful story about the impact of war on the youngest inhabitants of the country." Libr Media Connect

Akin, Sara Laux

Three scoops and a fig; written by Sara Laux Akin; illustrated by Susan Kathleen Hartung. Peachtree Publishers 2010 un il $15.95

Grades: PreK K   E

    1. Food -- Fiction 2. Family life -- Fiction 3. Restaurants -- Fiction

    ISBN 1-56145-522-9; 978-1-56145-522-5

                     LC 2009024519

Tired of always being told she is too little to help in the busy kitchen of her family's Italian restaurant, Sofia is inspired by a storm and a fig tree to come up with a delicious recipe of her own. Includes facts about the foods mentioned in the story.

"This title enlivens the well-traveled territory with a graceful, satisfying text, filled with repetitive lines that read aloud well, and endearing, uncluttered line-and-watercolor pictures." Booklist

Alalou, Ali

The butter man; [by] Elizabeth Alalou and Ali Alalou; illustrated by Julie Klear Essakalli. Charlesbridge 2008 un il lib bdg $14.95

Grades: K 1 2 3   E

    1. Morocco -- Fiction

    ISBN 978-1-58089-127-1 lib bdg; 1-58089-127-6 lib bdg

                     LC 2007-02278

While Nora waits for the couscous her father is cooking to be finished, he tells her a story about his youth in the High Atlas Mountains of Morocco. Includes author's note and glossary

The authors "write in descriptive language that speaks directly to children. . . . The folk-art paintings, created by a textile designer, feature whimsical characters and cozy domestic scenes, while the ochre, gold, and rust palette evokes the feeling of the dusty, sunlit landscape." Booklist

Alborough, Jez

    ★ **Duck** in the truck. HarperCollins Pubs. 2000 un il hardcover o.p. pa $7.95; bd bk $8.99

Grades: PreK K 1   E

    1. Trucks 2. Animals 3. Stories in rhyme

    ISBN 0-06-028685-7; 1-933605-76-6 pa; 978-1-929132-83-6 bd bk; 1-929132-83-2 bd bk

                     LC 99-60934

"A rhyming text relates the troubles of a duck whose truck gets stuck in the muck. . . . The art makes the most of the story's physical comedy, with exaggerated humor and an engaging animal cast, including a frog, a sheep, and a goat who all come to help out." Horn Book Guide

    Other titles about Duck are:

    Captain Duck (2003)

    Duck's key, where can it be (2005)

    Fix-it Duck (2002)

    Hit the ball Duck (2006)

    Super Duck (2009)

Some dogs do. Candlewick Press 2003 un il $15.99

Grades: PreK K 1 2   E

    1. Dogs 2. Flight 3. Schools 4. Individuality 5. Stories in rhyme 6. Parent and child

    ISBN 0-7636-2201-X

                     LC 2002-41760

When Sid tries to convince his doggy classmates that he flew to school, they do not believe him.

"Done in gouache, the illustrations glow with bright colors. . . . A wonderful addition to any library and a great choice for storytime." SLJ

Super Duck. Kane/Miller Book Publishers 2009 un il $15.95

Grades: K 1 2   E

    1. Stories in rhyme 2. Ducks -- Fiction 3. Superheroes -- Fiction

    ISBN 978-1-933605-89-0; 1-933605-89-8

    First published 2008 in the United Kingdom

"After reading Super Duck, Duck dons a cape and mask and tries a variety of ways to get Goat's kite up in the air. His friends patiently let him try his own ideas, like using a truck to fly the kite, before coming up with their own conventional solutions. Finally the superhero comes through with an unexpected maneuver. Alborough's short, amusing rhyming couplets keep the text moving along fluidly, making the book a good choice for storytimes. . . . All in all, this funny book is about friendship-the protagonist is allowed his individuality, but is supported when things don't work out. A gem." SLJ

Tall. Candlewick Press 2005 un il $15.99

Grades: PreK K 1 2   E

    1. Size -- Fiction 2. Chimpanzees -- Fiction

    ISBN 0-7634-2784-4

                     LC 2004-062941

Illustrations and just a few words depict how various jungle animals help Bobo the chimp to feel that he is tall.

"Bobo embodies an impressive range of identifiable emotions. Alborough's adept pen-and-gouache illustrations make each feeling and point of view crystal clear. . . . A must-have title for any children who have ever felt less than enchanted with their diminutive status." SLJ

    Other titles about Bobo the chimp are:

    Hug (2000)

    Yes (2006)

Where's my teddy? Candlewick Press 1992 un il hardcover o.p. pa $6.99

Grades: PreK K   E

    1. Stories in rhyme 2. Bears -- Fiction 3. Teddy bears

-- Fiction

ISBN 1-5640-2048-7; 1-5640-2280-3 pa

When a small boy named Eddie goes searching for his lost teddy in the dark woods, he comes across a gigantic bear with a similar problem.

"Alborough's verse adroitly employs kid-pleasing rhythms and repetitions, while his watercolor, crayon and pencil drawings underscore the broad comedy of this perfectly satisfying scenario of scary fun." Publ Wkly

Yes. Candlewick Press 2006 un il $15.99
Grades: PreK K 1   E

1. Chimpanzees -- Fiction

ISBN 978-0-7636-3183-3; 0-7636-3183-3

When Mama tells Bobo the chimp that it is bath time he says "yes," but when she says "bedtime" he says "no."

"The text, consisting predominantly of yes and no, appears in word bubbles, and bright gouache pictures, full-page and vertical panels, present lively depictions of expressions and verbal and nonverbal interactions." Booklist

The **gobble** gobble moooooo tractor book. Kane Miller 2010 un il $15.99
Grades: PreK K   E

1. Sheep -- Fiction 2. Sounds -- Fiction 3. Tractors -- Fiction 4. Farm life -- Fiction 5. Domestic animals -- Fiction

ISBN 978-1-935279-66-2; 1-935279-66-1

While Farmer Dougal is sleeping, Sheep convinces the other farm animals to take a ride on his tractor and imitate the different noises that it makes.

"With simple, sprightly, repetitive text, this amusing story invites lively, participatory read-alouds. The cheerful color illustrations incorporate playful fonts and depict the expressive animals in humorously contrasting scenes." Booklist

Alda, Arlene

Did you say pears? Tundra Books 2006 31p il $16.95
Grades: K 1 2 3   E

1. English language -- Homonyms

ISBN 0-88776-739-7

"A marvelously imaginative pairing (sorry) of homonyms (words that sound alike but have different meanings and the same spelling) and homophones (words that sound alike but have different meanings and different spellings), wrapped up in a rhyme of amazingly few words and terrific offbeat photographs." Booklist

Hello, good-bye. Tundra Books 2009 un il $16.95
Grades: PreK K   E

1. Opposites

ISBN 978-0-88776-900-9; 0-88776-900-4

"Exceptionally fine color photographs bring clarity as well as beauty to this book of opposites. Alda . . . creates images that are striking in themselves and meaningful when paired with their opposites. . . . This offers plenty of opportunities for interaction between young children and those reading to them." Booklist

Here a face, there a face. Tundra 2008 un il $14.95
Grades: PreK K 1 2 3   E

1. Face 2. Stories in rhyme

ISBN 0-88776-845-8; 978-0-88776-845-3

"A simple rhyming text leads children from page to page and photo to photo in the discovery of 'faces' in ordinary objects. Each page has a short line of the verse and a color photograph of a manmade or natural object with facial characteristics. The photographs are clearly focused and cropped so that viewers can zoom in on the countenance. The subjects include buildings, a kitchen pot, a tree, mailboxes, and more. Youngsters will delight in finding the eyes, noses, and mouths." SLJ

Iris has a virus; [by] Arlene Alda; illustrated by Lisa Desimini. Tundra Books 2008 un il $18.95
Grades: PreK K 1 2   E

1. Sick -- Fiction 2. Viruses -- Fiction

ISBN 978-0-88776-844-6; 0-88776-844-X

"Alda sensitively captures a kid's viewpoint on illness. . . . The straightforward text is enlivened with occasional . . . rhyming couplets. . . . The colorful paper-collage illustrations incorporate whimsical perspectives and scenarios." Booklist

Alderson, Brian

Thumbelina; [by] Hans Christian Andersen; retold by Brian Alderson; illustrated by Bagram Ibatoulline. Candlewick Press 2009 un il $17.99
Grades: 1 2 3 4   E

1. Authors 2. Novelists 3. Dramatists 4. Fairy tales 5. Children's authors 6. Short story writers

ISBN 978-0-7636-2079-0; 0-7636-2079-3

LC 2008-27721

A tiny girl no bigger than a thumb is stolen by a great ugly toad and subsequently has many adventures and makes many animal friends, before finding the perfect mate in a warm and beautiful southern land.

"This retelling of Andersen's classic tale remains close to the original. . . . Alderson retells these adventures and misadventures with a wry wit, moving the plot quickly through each scene. . . . Ibatoulline's illustrations are lavishly composed in watercolor and gouache." Bull Cent Child Books

Alexander, Claire

★ **Lucy** and the bully; by Claire Alexander. Albert Whitman & Co. 2008 un il $16.99
Grades: PreK K 1 2   E

1. School stories 2. Animals -- Fiction 3. Bullies -- Fiction

ISBN 978-0-8075-4786-1; 0-8075-4786-7

LC 2008001340

When a mean classmate in preschool wrecks Lucy's artwork, she discovers that they can be friends once he stops being jealous of her.

"Alexander's child-friendly watercolors beautifully convey a range of emotions. An excellent note to parents and teachers discusses bullying and ways to combat it." Booklist

Small Florence, piggy pop star. Albert Whitman & Co. 2010 un il $16.99
Grades: PreK K 1   E

1. Pigs -- Fiction 2. Shyness -- Fiction 3. Singers -- Fiction ISBN 978-0-8075-7455-3; 0-8075-7455-4

LC 2009-23624

Florence, a young pig, is too shy to sing in front of her sisters but gathers her courage at a singing competition when they lose their nerve.

"Working mostly in midnight blues and spotlight yellows—and piggy pink, of course—Alexander's . . . spots, multiple panels, and three-quarter page spreads add flash to the pages. . . . Many laughs will find Florence lots of fans." Publ Wkly

Alexander, Kwame

Acoustic Rooster and his barnyard band; written by Kwame Alexander; illustrated by Tim Bowers. Sleeping Bear Press 2011 il $15.95

Grades: K 1 2 3   E

1. Stories in rhyme 2. Contests -- Fiction 3. Musicians -- Fiction 4. Jazz music -- Fiction 5. Domestic animals -- Fiction

ISBN 978-1-58536-688-0; 1-58536-688-9

LC 2010053709

Acoustic Rooster forms a jazz band with Duck Ellington, Bee Holliday, and Pepe Ernesto Cruz to compete in the annual Barnyard Talent Show against such greats as Thelonius Steer, Mules Davis, and Ella Finchgerald. Includes glossary, notes on the characters and songs, and jazz timeline.

This is a "delightful picture book. . . . The large illustrations are done in bold colors and have humorous, jazzy details." SLJ

Alexander, Lloyd

The **fortune** -tellers; illustrated by Trina Schart Hyman. Dutton Children's Bks. 1992 un il hardcover o.p. pa $6.99

Grades: K 1 2 3   E

1. Fortune telling -- Fiction

ISBN 0-525-44849-7; 0-14-056233-8 pa

LC 91-30684

A carpenter goes to a fortune teller and finds the predictions about his future coming true in an unusual way

"Alexander's rags-to-riches story combines universal elements of the trickster character and the cumulative disaster tale. Hyman's pictures set it all in a vibrant community in Cameroon, West Africa. . . . The energetic, brilliantly colored paintings are packed with people and objects that swirl around the main characters. . . . With its ups and downs, this is a funny, playful story that evokes the irony of the human condition." Booklist

Alexander, Martha G.

Max and the dumb flower picture; [by] Martha Alexander with James Rumford. Charlesbridge 2009 un il $9.95

Grades: PreK K 1 2   E

1. School stories 2. Artists -- Fiction 3. Mother's Day -- Fiction

ISBN 978-1-58089-156-1; 1-58089-156-X

LC 2008007251

Despite his teacher's entreaties that it would be perfect for Mother's Day, Max refuses to color in the same flower picture as the rest of the class

"Before her death in 2006, Alexander . . . left her manuscript and sketches in the hands of James Rumford. . . . The tender result honors both Alexander and the children for whom she wrote for 40 years. . . . The soft sketches are color washed digitally and by hand, and with Rumford's collaboration, still bear Alexander's simple, expressive style." Publ Wkly

Aliki

All by myself! written and illustrated by Aliki. HarperCollins Pubs. 2000 un il $14.95; lib bdg $14.89; pa $6.99

Grades: K 1 2 3   E

1. Autonmy (Psychology) 2. Self-reliance -- Pictorial works

ISBN 0-06-028929-5; 0-06-028930-9 lib bdg; 0-06-446253-2 pa

LC 99-51672

A child shows all the things he has learned to do all on his own

"Aliki's colorful illustrations closely match the moods and energy levels of a five- or six-year-old. . . . The text has a hand-printed appearance, large and easy to read. . . . A good choice for story-hours and beginning readers." SLJ

★ **Painted** words: Marianthe's story one. Greenwillow Bks. 1998 un il $16.99; lib bdg $17.89

Grades: K 1 2 3   E

1. School stories 2. Immigrants -- Fiction

ISBN 0-688-15661-4; 0-688-15662-2 lib bdg

LC 97-34653

Two separate stories, the first telling of Mari's starting school in a new land, and the second describing village life in her country before she and her family left in search of a better life

"In simple, understated language, Aliki has captured the emotions and experiences of many of today's children. Colored-pencil and crayon illustrations in soft primary and secondary colors reinforce the mood of the text." SLJ

★ **Push** button. Greenwillow Books 2010 un il $16.99; lib bdg $17.89

Grades: PreK   E

1. Stories in rhyme 2. Play -- Fiction

ISBN 978-0-06-167308-5; 0-06-167308-0; 978-0-06-167309-2 lib bdg; 0-06-167309-9 lib bdg

LC 2008047690

A little boy who loves pushing buttons of all kinds ends up with such a sore finger that he must play with other things.

"Against the clean white backgrounds, Aliki's familiar style of mixing pencils, watercolors, ink, and markers give the tousle-headed protagonist a vivid, crayon-colored expressiveness. . . . Rhyming text and sound effects add wry touches." Booklist

Quiet in the garden; written and illustrated by Aliki. Greenwillow Books 2009 un il lib bdg $18.89

Grades: PreK K   E

1. Animals -- Fiction 2. Gardens -- Fiction 3. Gardens -- Juvenile literature

ISBN 978-0-06-155207-6; 0-06-155207-0; 978-0-06-155208-3 lib bdg; 0-06-155208-9 lib bdg

LC 2008-12641

Sitting quietly in his garden, a little boy observes the eating habits of birds, bugs, butterflies, and other small animals. Includes instructions on how to make your own garden and a detailed illustration of plants typically found in a garden.

"With spare words and a balance of line and color against white backgrounds framed with lacey branches, Aliki deftly portrays the benefits of observing nature." SLJ

We are best friends. Greenwillow Bks. 1982 un il hardcover o.p. $16.99; pa $5.99

Grades: PreK K 1 2   E

1. Friendship -- Fiction

ISBN 0-688-00822-4; 0-688-07037-X pa

LC 81-6549

When Robert's best friend Peter moves away, both are unhappy, but they learn that they can make new friends and still remain best friends

"Brightly lit pictures in cheerful primary colors portray with just a stroke of the pen the misery of losing a friend who must move away and the tentative beginnings of a new companionship. . . . Details of school and home abound in the lively pictures." Horn Book

★ A **play's** the thing; written and illustrated by Aliki. HarperCollins 2005 32p il $16.99; lib bdg $17.89

Grades: K 1 2 3   E

1. School stories 2. Theater -- Fiction

ISBN 0-06-074355-7; 0-06-074356-5 lib bdg

LC 2004-22101

When Miss Brilliant's class puts on a performance of "Mary had a little lamb," all the children are eager to participate except for the uncooperative José—until Miss Brilliant assigns him the role of teacher. "Primary." (Horn Book)

"When Miss Brilliant's class decides to put on a fractured version of [Mary Had a Little Lamb], José must learn to work with his classmates and overcome his antisocial tendencies. . . . This is . . . the type of work that children will be drawn to again and again because they recognize their world so aptly captured in both word and art. Each time they revisit, they will find something new in the colorful cartoon illustrations." SLJ

The **two** of them; written and illustrated by Aliki. Greenwillow Bks. 1979 un il hardcover o.p. pa $6.99

Grades: PreK K 1 2   E

1. Death -- Fiction 2. Grandfathers -- Fiction

ISBN 0-688-07337-9 pa

LC 79-10161

Describes the relationship of a grandfather and his granddaughter from her birth to his death

"The eloquent illustrations in muted full color and the smaller soft-pencil drawings show the life the two shared as well as the tenderness and pure pleasure implicit in their relationship." Horn Book

Alko, Selina

Every-day dress-up. Alfred A. Knopf 2011 un il $16.99; lib bdg $19.99

Grades: PreK K 1   E

1. Week -- Fiction 2. Women -- Fiction 3. Costume -- Fiction 4. Imagination -- Fiction

ISBN 978-0-375-86092-8; 0-375-86092-4; 978-0-375-96092-5 lib bdg; 0-375-96092-9 lib bdg

LC 2010001604

A young girl imagines her own future as she puts on costumes and pretends to be great women from history, including Amelia Earhart, Lucille Ball, and Eleanor Roosevelt.

All the great women "are introduced in a fun way with minimal text. Humorous, detailed gouache and collage illustrations will hold children's attention and spark their imagination." SLJ

Allard, Harry

★ **Miss** Nelson is missing! [by] Harry Allard, James Marshall. Houghton Mifflin 1977 32p il $16; pa $5.95

Grades: PreK K 1 2   E

1. School stories 2. Teachers -- Fiction

ISBN 0-395-25296-2; 0-395-40146-1 pa

LC 76-55918

"Humor and suspense fill the pages of [this book]." Christ Sci Monit

Other titles about Miss Nelson are:

Miss Nelson has a field day (1985)

Miss Nelson is back (1982)

Allegra, Mike

Sarah gives thanks; how Thanksgiving became a national holiday. by Mike Allegra; illustrated by David Gardner. Albert Whitman & Co. 2012 32 p. col. ill.

Grades: 2 3 4   E

1. Thanksgiving Day -- History -- Juvenile fiction 2. Thanksgiving Day -- History -- Juvenile literature

ISBN 080757239X; 9780807572399

LC 2011034161

This book by Mike Allegra, illustrated by David Gardner, tells the story of Sarah Josepha Hale, who "dedicated her life to making Thanksgiving a national holiday, all while raising a family and becoming a groundbreaking writer and women's magazine editor . . . [d]uring the nineteenth century. . . . Sarah Hale's . . . story, accompanied by . . . watercolor illustrations, tells the tale of one woman who wouldn't take no for an answer." (Publisher's note)

Allen, Debbie

Dancing in the wings; pictures by Kadir Nelson. Dial Bks. for Young Readers 2000 un il $16.99; pa $6.99

Grades: PreK K 1 2   E

1. Ballet 2. Teasing 3. Self-confidence 4. Ballet -- Fiction 5. African Americans -- Fiction

ISBN 0-8037-2501-9; 0-14-250141-7 pa

LC 99-462181

Sassy tries out for a summer dance festival in Washington, D.C., despite the other girls' taunts that she is much too tall

"Allen's dialogue is realistic, and Nelson's illustrations of the predominantly African-American cast ably capture Sassy's love of dance and her lively personality." Horn Book Guide

Allen, Elanna

★ **Itsy** Mitsy runs away. Atheneum Books for Young Readers 2011 un il $16.99

Grades: PreK K 1 2   E

1. Runaway children -- Fiction 2. Father-daughter relationship -- Fiction

ISBN 978-1-4424-0671-1; 1-4424-0671-2

LC 2010004418

When Mitsy decides to run away, her father helps her pack.

"Mitsy may be itsy, but she has no shortage of energy or determination. She's also a sartorial standout, wearing lime green, dinosaur-style footie/hoodie pajamas and bright orange goggles. . . . Allen . . . has a breezy drawing style and a cheery disdain for logic reminiscent of 1950s-era cartoons. . . . Yet the freewheeling art stays anchored by Allen's very funny text, which combines rhythmic, cumulative passages with Mitsy's irreverent, precocious voice." Publ Wkly

Allen, Jonathan

I'm not Santa! Hyperion Books for Children 2008 un il $14.99

Grades: PreK K   E

1. Owls -- Fiction 2. Rabbits -- Fiction 3. Christmas -- Fiction 4. Santa Claus -- Fiction

ISBN 978-1-4231-1300-3; 1-4231-1300-4

When Baby Hare mistakes Baby Owl for Santa Claus, it takes a visit from St. Nick himself to straighten things out.

"With almost no background illustration, the two cartoon-style characters face off from opposite pages, their growing frustration evident in their body language. . . . This will . . . have appeal for children at the stage where Christmas is all about Santa sightings." Booklist

I'm not scared! Hyperion Books for Children 2007 un il $14.99

Grades: PreK K   E

1. Fear -- Fiction 2. Owls -- Fiction 3. Animals -- Fiction

ISBN 978-0-7868-3722-9

When Baby Owl takes his stuffed Owly out for a walk in the moonlit woods, he insists that he is not afraid of the other animals that keep popping up and making them jump.

"The cartoon illustrations are painted in dusky hues with black outlines, and the glossy quality of the light-infused colors makes the art look like animation cels. . . . The expressive visuals, brief text, and protagonist's believably childlike behavior are just right for young audiences." SLJ

The little rabbit who liked to say moo. Boxer Books 2008 un il $14.95

Grades: PreK K 1   E

1. Sound -- Fiction 2. Animals -- Fiction 3. Rabbits -- Fiction

ISBN 978-1-905417-78-0; 1-905417-78-0

"Little Rabbit likes to say 'moo,' because rabbits don't have a big noise. The little creature also likes to say 'baa,' 'oink,' 'heehaw,' and 'quack,' and gets the other young farm animals to join the refrain until a surprise ending reveals the bunny's favorite sound. The illustrations are large, uncluttered, simple, and bold, made of black lines and computer air-brushed color. . . . With its large print and natural repetition, this cumulative tale will be useful for building early literacy skills." SLJ

Alsdurf, Phyllis

★ It's milking time; by Phyllis Alsdurf; illustrations by Steve Johnson & Lou Fancher. Random House 2012 40 p. col. ill. (hardcover) $16.99

Grades: K 1 2 3   E

1. Milk -- Juvenile fiction 2. Farms -- Juvenile fiction 3. Farm life -- Juvenile fiction 4. Milk supply -- Juvenile fiction 5. Father-daughter relationship -- Juvenile fiction 6. Cows -- Fiction 7. Milking -- Fiction 8. Farm life -- Fiction 9. Fathers and daughters -- Fiction

ISBN 0375869115; 9780375869112; 9780375899935; 9780375969119

LC 2010047772

In this children's book by Phyllis Alsdurf, illustrated by Steve Johnson and Lou Fancher, "a little girl and her father

begin the evening milking. They work side by side, fanning out beds of straw, bringing in the cows, and hooking up the milkers. . . . The fresh dairy product isn't just for them--other families will buy their milk, butter, and cheese at stores and farmers' markets near and far, connecting the little girl's farm to the world beyond." (Publisher's note)

Alter, Anna

Abigail spells. Alfred A. Knopf 2009 un il $16.99; lib bdg $19.99

Grades: K 1 2   E

1. Friendship -- Fiction 2. Spelling bees -- Fiction

ISBN 978-0-375-85617-4; 0-375-85617-X; 978-0-375-95617-1 lib bdg; 0-375-95617-4 lib bdg

LC 2008024529

George helps his best friend Abigail practice for the city spelling bee, then cheers her up when she makes a mistake.

"Alter's folk-style acrylics done in warm, muted shades beautifully complement this steady-paced, conversational story." SLJ

Disappearing Desmond. Alfred A. Knopf 2010 un il $17.99

Grades: K 1 2 3   E

1. School stories 2. Cats -- Fiction 3. Rabbits -- Fiction 4. Shyness -- Fiction 5. Friendship -- Fiction

ISBN 0375866841; 9780375866845; 978-0-375-86684-5; 0-375-86684-1

Desmond the cat is so skilled at disappearing that sometimes even his teacher cannot find him but when he meets Gloria the rabbit, a new student at school, his attitude slowly changes.

"This low-key story of how friendship can support and encourage others will be a welcome addition for most libraries." SLJ

A photo for Greta. Alfred A. Knopf 2011 un il $16.99; lib bdg $19.99

Grades: PreK K 1   E

1. Rabbits -- Fiction 2. Photographers -- Fiction 3. Father-daughter relationship -- Fiction

ISBN 978-0-375-85618-1; 0-375-85618-8; 978-0-375-95618-8 lib bdg; 0-375-95618-2 lib bdg

LC 2010036001

"Greta, a young rabbit, loves her father, a photographer who 'travels all around the world taking pictures of very important people.' Admiring the framed pictures he's taken . . . she wishes to be famous and photo-ready herself. . . . Alter displays notable sensitivity to children's insecurities and doubts, while providing reassurance of their worth. Her acrylics have a comforting sturdiness, and readers who similarly take pride in their parents' professions, even as they miss them in their absence, will relate both to Greta's role-playing when her father is away and their tender time together when he comes home." Publ Wkly

Altes, Marta

My grandpa; by Marta Altes. Abrams Books for Young Readers 2013 32 p. ill. (reinforced) $15.95

Grades: PreK K 1   E

1. Picture books for children 2. Senile dementia -- Juvenile fiction 3. Bears -- Fiction 4. Old age -- Fiction

5. Grandfathers -- Fiction
ISBN 1419705881; 9781419705885

LC 2012015616

This children's picture book is "narrated by a young bear whose grandfather is exhibiting signs of advanced age and dementia. The simple text uses single sentences that vacillate between the joy of the pair's loving bond and the young bear's honest look at Grandpa's decline." (School Library Journal)

Alvarez, Julia

A **gift** of gracias; the legend of Altagracia. written by Julia Alvarez; illustrated by Beatriz Vidal. Knopf 2005 un il $15.95; lib bdg $17.99
Grades: K 1 2 3   E
1. Saints -- Fiction 2. Oranges -- Fiction
ISBN 0-375-82425-1; 0-375-92425-6 lib bdg
Maria's family is almost forced to leave their farm on the new island colony, until a mysterious lady appears in Maria's dream

"Rich in cultural authenticity and brimming with the magical realism that is characteristic of Hispanic literature, this elegantly woven tale introduces the legend of Our Lady of Altagracia, the patron saint of the Dominican Republic. . . . With an exquisite use of watercolor and gouache, Vidal has painted colorful, yet warm illustrations that add depth to the story." SLJ

Amado, Elisa

Tricycle; [by] Elisa Amado; [illustrated by] Alfonso Ruano. Groundwood Books/House of Anansi Press 2007 un il $17.95
Grades: 1 2 3 4   E
1. Theft -- Fiction 2. Friendship -- Fiction 3. Social classes -- Fiction 4. Truthfulness and falsehood -- Fiction
ISBN 978-0-88899-614-5; 0-88899-614-4
"This book tells of rich and poor from the viewpoint of young Margarita, who climbs a tree on her rich family's estate and sees the shacks on the other side of the hedge, where her friend Rosario lives. Margarita watches as Rosario and her brother take her tricycle, but she doesn't say anything about it, even when her mother's lunch guests spew prejudice. . . . The text is spare, and the richly colored acrylic art . . . is just on the edge of magical realism. Although there is no overt message, there is much to talk about." Booklist

What are you doing? pictures by Manuel Monroy. Groundwood Books/House of Anansi Press 2011 un il $16.95
Grades: PreK K 1 2   E
1. Books and reading -- Fiction 2. Books and reading -- Juvenile literature
ISBN 978-1-55498-070-3; 1-55498-070-4
"Everywhere Chepito goes in his little village, there are people reading. He questions the readers on their motives . . . and receives a variety of responses. . . . When he starts school, he's drawn to the classroom's big shelf of books. . . . He takes one home to share with his sister, who then asks him why he wants to read to her. . . . Monroy's digitally enhanced colored pencil and watercolor illustrations offer simple renderings of Chepito's conversations around town. . . . This is a thoughtful offering for soon-to-be literates that

just may get them thinking about the power of reading." Bull Cent Child Books

Amato, Mary

The **chicken** of the family; illustrated by Delphine Durand. G.P. Putnam's Sons 2007 un il $16.99
Grades: PreK K 1 2   E
1. Sisters -- Fiction 2. Chickens -- Fiction
ISBN 0-399-24196-5; 978-0-399-24196-3

LC 2006-03606

When her older sisters tease her into believing that she is actually a chicken, Henrietta runs off to a farm to be among her own kind.

The "storytelling is set off brilliantly by Durand's . . . off-kilter, kid-like cartooning. Packed with funny details and small plots . . . the art, like the story, delivers grade-AA comedy." Publ Wkly

Ander

Me and my bike; [written & illustrated by] Ander. Heryin Books 2008 un il $16.95
Grades: 2 3 4 5   E
1. Wishes -- Fiction 2. Bicycles -- Fiction
ISBN 978-0-9787550-2-7; 0-9787550-2-2

LC 2007005817

A child wants nothing more than a new bicycle, and it seems the wish might come true with some help from the magic lamp that once made Grandpa grow up really fast

"The book has the feel of a graphic novel. The sketchy cartoon illustrations done on heavy stock are full of movement and changes in perspective, and they carry much of the storytelling and humor. This is a beautifully understated, often amusing meditation on being resilient, appreciating what you have, and still sustaining hope for something better." SLJ

Andersen, Hans Christian, 1805-1875

The **emperor's** new clothes; designed and illustrated by Virginia Lee Burton. Houghton Mifflin 2004 44p il $16
Grades: K 1 2 3   E
1. Fairy tales
ISBN 0-618-34421-7
A reissue of the edition first published 1949
Weavers convince the vain emperor that the clothing they make for him can only be seen by those who are not fools, but only the child recognizes the truth

"Burton's sense of pageantry sets forth in beautiful colors the magnificence of the Emperor's domain and entourage; her sense of humor brings out rightly the ridiculous situation with all its implications." Horn Book Guide

★ The **nightingale**; [by] Hans Christian Andersen; adapted and illustrated by Jerry Pinkney. Phyllis Fogelman Bks. 2002 un il $16.99
Grades: 2 3 4   E
1. Authors 2. Novelists 3. Dramatists 4. Fairy tales 5. Children's authors 6. Short story writers 7. Nightingales -- Fiction
ISBN 0-8037-2464-0

LC 2001-47601

Despite being neglected by the emperor for a jewel-studded bird, the little nightingale revives the dying ruler with its beautiful song. A retelling set in Morocco

This "is a pleasing version of the classic, fresh in its interpretation but true to the spirit of the original. . . . Each double-page spread is illuminated by artwork that glows with rich colors and teems with lively details. Done in graphic, gouache, and watercolor, the large, gracefully composed illustrations feature a profusion of patterns." Booklist

The **nightingale**; illustrated by Pirkko Vainio. North South Books 2011 un il $16.95
Grades: K 1 2 3   E
1. Nightingales -- Fiction
ISBN 978-0-7358-4029-4; 0-7358-4029-6
Though the emperor banishes the nightingale in preference of a jeweled mechanical imitation, the little bird remains faithful and returns years later when the emperor is near death and no one else can help him.
"A fresh version of Andersen's tender tale is illustrated with delicate watercolors. . . . This retelling, first published in Switzerland . . . is straightforward, allowing the soft, muted artwork to accent the details and ambiance." Kirkus

★ **Thumbeline**; illustrated by Lisbeth Zwerger; translated by Anthea Bell. North-South Bks. 2000 un il hardcover o.p. pa $6.95
Grades: K 1 2 3   E
1. Fairy tales
ISBN 0-7358-1213-6; 0-7358-2236-0 pa
LC 99-57073
A reissue of 1985 edition published by Picture Book Studio
The adventures of a tiny girl no bigger than a thumb and her many animal friends
"The book's squarish design . . . draws the reader's attention to the exceptional art. Lovely, lean, lithe lines combine with a palette of tawny earth tones to create a minimalist world redolent with grace and rich with imagination." Horn Book Guide

The **ugly** duckling; [illustrated by] Pirkko Vainio. NorthSouth 2009 un il $16.95
Grades: PreK K 1 2   E
1. Fairy tales 2. Ducks -- Fiction 3. Swans -- Fiction
ISBN 978-0-7358-2226-9; 0-7358-2226-3
"Andersen's timeless story is lovingly revisited in this modest yet engaging retelling. With the sound and feel of a classic in the very best sense, the familiar tale has been reworked but not oversimplified, making it particularly appealing for children who might be too young for some of the harsher elements of the original. But what makes this version particularly appealing is the lovely watercolor artwork, which, like the text, exudes a feeling of tradition and familiarity." SLJ

Anderson, AnnMarie
★ The **Nutcracker**; pictures by Alison Jay. Dial Books for Young Readers 2010 un il $16.99
Grades: K 1 2 3   E
1. Fairy tales 2. Christmas -- Fiction 3. Ballet -- Stories, plots, etc.
ISBN 978-0-8037-3285-8; 0-8037-3285-6
LC 2009051657
After rescuing her Christmas nutcracker from an army of angry toys, Marie and her brother are rewarded by the nutcracker, now a prince, with a fantastic nighttime journey

to a realm of dancing fairies, beautiful palaces, and wonderful things to eat.
"Jay's delicate crackle-varnish oil paintings—equal parts elegant and whimsical-distinguish this edition of Hoffman's Nutcracker, based on Balanchine's staging of the ballet. . . . Jay's gleaming marzipan palace, pink spun-sugar trees, and peppermint-stick gates are the stuff of holiday visions, indeed" Publ Wkly

Anderson, Brian
The **Prince's** new pet. Roaring Brook Press 2011 il $16.99
Grades: K 1 2 3   E
1. Pets -- Fiction 2. Color -- Fiction 3. Princes -- Fiction
ISBN 978-1-59643-357-1; 1-59643-357-4
LC 2010036798
In a gray and colorless kingdom, the Prince receives an unusual, colorful new pet called a wooglefoof for his birthday.
"Fans of Tim Burton's films will love the stylized artwork and the oh-so-dreary palette. To keep it visually interesting, Anderson plays with the design by adding insets that pop off the page despite the shared palette. . . . Careful readers will chuckle at the wordplay." SLJ

Anderson, Derek
Story County; here we come! Orchard Books 2011 un il $16.99
Grades: PreK K   E
1. Farms -- Fiction 2. Domestic animals -- Fiction
ISBN 978-0-545-16844-1; 0-545-16844-9
LC 2010-12094
A farmer and his animal friends—Dog, Pig, Chicken, and Miss Cow—join forces to build a farm that they can all enjoy.
"This book's loose aesthetic features characters composed of boldly outlined geometric shapes, splashy colors, and confident brushwork. Chronicled in punchy, dialogue-driven prose, the friends' slapdash process lends itself to amusing scenes." Publ Wkly

Anderson, Laurie Halse
The **hair** of Zoe Fleefenbacher goes to school; illustrated by Ard Hoyt. Simon & Schuster Books for Young Readers 2009 un il $16.99
Grades: K 1 2   E
1. School stories 2. Hair -- Fiction
ISBN 978-0-689-85809-3; 0-689-85809-4
LC 2007045161
A young girl's talented but untamed tresses do not impress her strict first-grade teacher, who has rules for everything, including hair.
"Anderson's narrative sparkles with exuberant language and exaggerated humor. Hoyt's buoyant cartoons, done in pen and ink and watercolors, are filled with flowing lines and comical touches." SLJ

Anderson, Peggy Perry
Chuck's band. Houghton Mifflin 2008 32p il $16
Grades: PreK K 1 2   E
1. Stories in rhyme 2. Bands (Music) -- Fiction 3.

Domestic animals -- Fiction

ISBN 978-0-618-96506-9; 0-618-96506-8

LC 2007021728

Chuck and his barnyard friends form a band, but they have trouble finding an instrument for Fat Cat Pat to play, since all the cat wants to do is sleep all day.

"The short, rhyming phrases of the text roll along in a pleasing way. . . . Bold lines, bright colors, and crayon textures come together to create scenes that are vivid and easy for young children to 'read.'" Booklist

Chuck's truck; by Peggy Perry Anderson. Houghton Mifflin 2006 un il $16

Grades: PreK K 1 2   E

1. Stories in rhyme 2. Trucks -- Fiction 3. Domestic animals -- Fiction

ISBN 0-618-66836-5; 978-0-618-66836-6

LC 2005020870

When too many barnyard friends climb in to go to town, Chuck's truck breaks down, but Handyman Hugh knows just what to do.

"Filled with rhyming language, this story will be a boon for beginning readers who will easily identify the rhyming words. . . . Anderson uses a crayon-resist technique to great effect, and the pictures are filled with dimension and texture. The bright colors are vibrant and energetic." SLJ

Another title about Chuck is:

Chuck's band (2008)

Joe on the go; [by] Peggy Perry Anderson. Houghton Mifflin 2007 32p il $16

Grades: PreK K 1 2   E

1. Stories in rhyme 2. Play -- Fiction 3. Frogs -- Fiction 4. Family reunions -- Fiction

ISBN 978-0-618-77331-2; 0-618-77331-2

LC 2006009771

Joe the frog wants to be on the go, but even at a family reunion he is out of luck, as everyone says they are too busy, or he is too fast, too slow, too big, or too small to go with them, until Grandma invites him to go with her on a special outing.

"Illustrated with bright, boisterous line-and-watercolor pictures, the simple rhyming text . . . will draw story hour listeners as well as beginning readers to a scenario they may recognize." Booklist

Other titles about Joe the frog are:

Time for bed, the babysitter said (1987)

To the tub (1996)

Out to lunch (1998)

Let's clean up (2002)

Andreae, Giles, 1966-

I love my mommy; [by] Giles Andreae and [illustrated by] Emma Dodd. Hyperion/Disney 2011 un il $12.99

Grades: PreK   E

1. Mother-child relationship -- Fiction

ISBN 978-1-4231-4327-7; 1-4231-4327-2

First published 2010 in the United Kingdom with title: I love my mummy

"This appealing oversize book has a rhyming text and a huggable-looking toddler who clutches a purple toy duck. He lists some of the reasons he loves his mother. . . . The bright illustrations are set against pastel backgrounds with close-ups of the child and Mom outlined in black. . . . This is

a tale oft told, but with its cheerful, familiar scenarios, it will be a hit at storytimes." SLJ

Andreasen, Dan

The **baker's** dozen; [by] Dan Andreasen. Henry Holt 2007 un il $16.95

Grades: PreK K   E

1. Counting 2. Stories in rhyme 3. Baking -- Fiction

ISBN 978-0-8050-7809-1; 0-8050-7809-6

LC 2006031372

The reader is invited to count from one to thirteen as a jolly baker makes delectable treats from one mouthwatering eclair to twelve luscious cupcakes, and serves them to invited guests

This offers "a simple rhyme and clear, mouthwatering illustrations." Booklist

The **giant** of Seville; a tall tale based on a true story. Abrams Books for Young Readers 2007 un il $15.95

Grades: K 1 2 3   E

1. Giants 2. Army officers 3. Circus performers

ISBN 978-0-8109-0988-5; 0-8109-0988-X

LC 2006-13579

"Seville, Ohio, is so quiet that you can 'hear the corn grow' until a giant comes to town. Nearly eight feet tall, Captain Martin Van Buren is searching for a friendly community in which to settle down. Seville's residents welcome him, but accommodating a guest of his stature proves difficult. . . . An endnote introduces the historical people and events that inspired the story, and Andreasen extends the tale's old-fashioned feel in detailed, color-washed ink drawings of townspeople in nineteenth-century dress." Booklist

The **treasure** bath. Henry Holt and Co. 2009 un il $16.99

Grades: PreK   E

1. Stories without words 2. Baths -- Fiction 3. Imagination -- Fiction

ISBN 978-0-8050-8686-7; 0-8050-8686-2

LC 2008-38224

A wordless picture book in which a young boy explores a creature-filled world beneath the bubbles in his bathtub

"Andreasen borrows motifs from comic-book art—extra gleam on objects, squared-off, blunt-cut hair and the humans' doll-like postures—and combines them with Disney-esque cheer to create amiable scenarios with just a hint of irony." Publ Wkly

Andrews, Julie

The **very** fairy princess; by Julie Andrews & Emma Walton Hamilton; [illustrations by Christine Davenier] Little, Brown Books for Young Readers 2010 un il $16.99

Grades: PreK K 1 2   E

1. Princesses -- Fiction

ISBN 978-0-316-04050-1; 0-316-04050-9

LC 2009-19307

Despite her scabby knees and dirty fingernails, Geraldine knows that she is a princess inside and shows it through her behavior at home and in school.

"Davenier's whimsical ink-and-colored-pencil illustrations enchant. . . . The mother-daughter team successfully demonstrates an understanding of that magical stage of childhood in which determination, desire and dreams can transform reality." Kirkus

Another title about Geraldine is:
The very fairy princess takes the stage (2011)

Angleberger, Tom

★ **Crankee** Doodle; by Tom Angleberger; illustrations by Cece Bell. Clarion Books 2013 32 p. ill. (hardcover) $16.99

Grades: PreK K 1   E

1. Picture books for children 2. Historical fiction -- Juvenile fiction 3. Humorous stories 4. Ponies -- Fiction 5. Mood (Psychology) -- Fiction
ISBN 0547818548; 9780547818542

LC 2012001346

In this children's picture book, "when a colonial-era Yankee announces that he's bored, his pony suggests the pair could go to town. 'Town?' replies the man. 'No way. I hate going to town. There are too many people in town.' For each subsequent nudge from the pony . . . , the Yankee has a long-winded and highly opinionated rant against the idea." (Publishers Weekly)

Anholt, Laurence

Cezanne and the apple boy. Barron's 2009 un il
Grades: PreK K 1   E

1. Artists 2. Painters 3. Artists -- Fiction 4. Father-son relationship -- Fiction
ISBN 0-7641-6282-9; 978-0-7641-6282-4

Paul's father, the artist Paul Cézanne has been away from home for so long that the boy hardly recognizes his father when he returns. But the two soon become fast friends. The local townspeople laugh at the artist's pictures. But young Paul likes the art. An influential art dealer comes from Paris the lives of the artist and his son change dramatically.

"Evocative, realistic illustrations mix with reproductions of Cézanne works and, along with the young character, will draw kids into this enjoyable, informative portrayal of Cézanne as both a father and an influential artist." Booklist

Anno, Mitsumasa

★ **Anno's** counting book. Crowell 1977 un il $17.99; lib bdg $18.89; pa $6.99
Grades: PreK K 1   E

1. Counting 2. Stories without words 3. Seasons -- Fiction
ISBN 0-690-01287-X; 0-690-01288-8 lib bdg; 0-06-443123-1 pa

LC 76-28977

Original Japanese edition, 1975

"A distinctive, beautifully conceived counting book in which twelve full-color doublespreads show the same village and surrounding countryside during different hours (by the church clock) and months. Both the seasons and community changes are studied, as such components of the scene as flowers, trees, animals, people, and buildings increase from one to twelve." LC. Child Books, 1977

Antle, Bhagavan

Suryia swims!: the true story of how an orangutan learned to swim; Bhagavan "Doc" Antle, with Thea Feldman; photographs by Barry Bland. Henry Holt 2012 32 p. (hc) $16.99

Grades: 1 2 3   E

1. Swimming 2. Orangutan -- Juvenile literature 3. Animal behavior -- Juvenile literature 4. Swimming --

Fiction 5. Orangutan -- Fiction 6. Wildlife refuges -- Fiction 7. Orangutan -- Juvenile fiction
ISBN 0805093176; 9780805093179

LC 2011029047

This book, by Bhagavan Antle, illustrated by Barry Bland, narrated by Thea Feldman, describes an episode in the life of the orangutan Suryia. "Suryia is not your average orangutan. In the first book about him, . . . Suryia found an unusual best friend: a dog named Roscoe. Now Suryia jumps into an unusual new hobby: swimming! Orangutans don't swim; it doesn't come naturally to them. But Suryia shows that adventures await those who are willing to try something new." (Publisher's note)

Appelt, Kathi

★ **Bats** around the clock; illustrated by Melissa Sweet. HarperCollins Pubs. 2000 un il $15.99; lib bdg $16.89
Grades: PreK K 1 2   E

1. Bats 2. Time 3. Rock music 4. Stories in rhyme 5. Clocks and watches 6. Bats -- Fiction 7. Rock music -- Fiction
ISBN 0-688-16469-2; 0-688-16470-6 lib bdg

LC 99-15502

Click Dark hosts a special twelve-hour program of American Bat Stand where the bats rock and roll until the midnight hour ends.

"The rhymes are delightful and the narrative jives right along." SLJ

Other titles about the bats are:
The bat jamboree (1996)
Bats on parade (1999)

Brand-new baby blues; words by Kathi Appelt; illustrations by Kelly Murphy. HarperCollins Publishers 2010 un il $16.99

Grades: PreK K 1 2   E

1. Stories in rhyme 2. Infants -- Fiction 3. Siblings -- Fiction
ISBN 978-0-06-053233-8; 0-06-053233-5; 978-0-06-053234-5 lib bdg; 0-06-053234-3 lib bdg

LC 2008-05796

The arrival of a new little brother has his big sister singing the blues.

"Funny and concise, the rollicking rhyme bounces along, accepting the frustration natural to the situation, while gently allowing the girl's love of and appreciation for her brother. . . . The process is complemented by the illustrations, which modulate in palette from angry blues and greens to sunny yellows, while serene compositions replace off-kilter ones. Older brothers and sisters will easily identify with this jaunty heroine and profit from her realizations—an excellent choice for a new older sibling." Kirkus

Oh my baby, little one; pictures by Jane Dyer. Harcourt Brace & Co. 2000 un il $16; pa $3.99

Grades: PreK K   E

1. Love 2. Stories in rhyme 3. Mother and child 4. Mother-child relationship -- Fiction
ISBN 0-15-200041-0; 0-15-206031-6 pa

LC 99-6363

"The light, bright pictures will charm young listeners, who will find this book best enjoyed while cuddled up next to Mama." Booklist

Applegate, Katherine

The **buffalo** storm; illustrated by Jan Ormerod. Clarion Books 2007 32p il $16

Grades: 2 3 4   E

1. Fear -- Fiction 2. Grandmothers -- Fiction 3. Frontier and pioneer life -- Fiction 4. Overland journeys to the Pacific -- Fiction

ISBN 978-0-618-53597-2; 0-618-53597-7

LC 2006-15661

When Hallie and her parents join a wagon train to Oregon and leave her grandmother behind, Hallie must learn to face the storms that frighten her so, as well as other, newer fears, with just her grandmother's quilt to comfort her.

"Ormerod's . . . textured watercolors and pastels employ billowy swaths of color to suggest the vastness of the setting. . . . Vivid imagery makes this lyrical tale an accessible, fresh addition to the children's pioneer genre as it tackles themes of change, courage and home." Publ Wkly

Armand, Glenda

Love twelve miles long; illustrated by Colin Bootman. Lee & Low Books 2011 il $17.95

Grades: K 1 2   E

1. Slaves 2. Authors 3. Abolitionists 4. Memoirists 5. Slavery -- Fiction 6. Mother-son relationship -- Fiction

ISBN 978-1-60060-245-0; 1-60060-245-2

LC 2011014275

In 1820s Maryland, Frederick's mother, who is a slave on a different plantation, walks twelve miles each way for a nighttime visit with her son, during which she recounts what each mile of the journey represents. Based on the childhood of Frederick Douglass.

"Armand's debut reveals a poignant conversation between young Frederick and his mother, paired with Bootman's arresting and emotive paintings. . . . Bootman . . . deftly uses candlelight and moonlight to give his art a lovely iridescence, and presents intimate portraits of mother and son." Pub Wkly

Armstrong, Jennifer

Magnus at the fire; illustrated by Owen Smith. Simon & Schuster Books for Young Readers 2005 un il $15.95

Grades: PreK K 1 2   E

1. Horses -- Fiction 2. Fire fighting -- Fiction

ISBN 0-689-83922-7

LC 2004-11487

When the Broadway Fire House acquires a motorized fire engine, Magnus the fire horse is not ready to retire.

A "stirring historical story. . . . Impressive oil paintings in vibrant colors capture the drama of firefighting in the 1800s." SLJ

★ **Once** upon a banana; illustrated by David Small. Simon & Schuster Books for Young Readers 2006 un il $16.95

Grades: PreK K 1 2   E

1. Stories without words 2. City and town life -- Fiction

ISBN 0-689-84251-1; 978-0-689-84251-1

LC 2005-08567

"A street juggler's pet monkey runs off and steals a deli's outdoor stall. . . . The monkey tosses the banana peel on the sidewalk, thus triggering a book-long, slapstick-rich chase that covers an entire city center and ensnares a cavalcade of characters. . . . Small's loose yet precise ink lines and watercolor wash seem ideal for these crowded streets where anarchy abounds. . . . The pages overflow with enough pratfalls and comic asides to reward many readings." Publ Wkly

Armstrong, Matthew S.

Jane and Mizmow; by Matthew S. Armstrong. Harper 2011 il

Grades: PreK K 1   E

1. Monsters -- Fiction 2. Friendship -- Fiction

ISBN 0061177199; 9780061177194

LC 2010012628

Jane and her best friend, a monster named Mizmow, are best friends in spite of their differences, and nothing can keep them apart.

"A palette of fall colors mirrors the warmth of their friendship, while the expressive faces of the two characters reinforce both mood and action. Emerging readers will be able to read much of the simple text, but the illustrations really tell the tale. . . . A solid choice that youngsters will enjoy time and time again." SLJ

Arnold, Caroline

Wiggle and Waggle; [by] Caroline Arnold; illustrated by Mary Peterson. Charlesbridge 2007 48p il lib bdg $12.95; pa $5.95

Grades: K 1 2   E

1. Worms -- Fiction 2. Gardens -- Fiction 3. Friendship -- Fiction

ISBN 978-1-58089-306-0 lib bdg; 978-1-58089-307-4 pa

LC 2006020948

Two worms who are best friends have fun together as they tunnel their way through a garden. Includes facts on how worms help plants grow

"The artwork, done in earth tones, of course, features two goofy, google-eyed worms. Good quality paper and an attractive design add to the book's pick-me-up quotient." Booklist

Arnold, Marsha Diane

Prancing, dancing Lily; pictures by John Manders. Dial Books for Young Readers 2004 un il

Grades: PreK K 1 2   E

1. Dance 2. Self-realization 3. Cows 4. Dance -- Fiction 5. Cattle -- Fiction

ISBN 0803728239

LC 2002-5852

Lily will someday be the "bell cow," leading her herd, but because her prancing and dancing only disrupts their order, she travels the world looking for the right place and dance for her

"Arnold's amusing characters and clever text come to life through Manders's comical cartoon illustrations." SLJ

Arnold, Tedd

Dirty Gert; by Tedd Arnold. Holiday House 2013 40 p. (hardcover) $16.95

Grades: K 1 2 3   E

1. Stories in rhyme 2. Trees -- Juvenile fiction 3. Humorous fiction -- Juvenile fiction 4. Humorous stories 5. Trees -- Fiction

ISBN 0823424049; 9780823424047

LC 2012006578

This children's story, by Tedd Arnold, follows a girl who becomes a tree. "Gert loves dirt. . . . Then one day while making mud pies in the rain, Gert becomes reorganized: she grows branches, leaves and roots. Gert is delighted . . . until camera crews televise her, botanists analyze her, and Hollywood tries to immortalize her. The child is traumatized! But Mom and Dad know what to do to protect their offbeat plant-child." (Publisher's note)

Green Wilma, frog in space. Dial Books for Young Readers 2009 un il $16.99

Grades: K 1 2   E

1. Stories in rhyme 2. Frogs -- Fiction 3. Space flight -- Fiction 4. Extraterrestrial beings -- Fiction
ISBN 978-0-8037-2698-7; 0-8037-2698-8
LC 2008039497

Green Wilma the frog is mistaken for an alien child and taken on a trip through space.

This is written "in perfect rhyme. . . . The illustrations explode across the pages with frantic innocence. . . . To say that the pictures complement the text is like declaring that the Sun complements the Earth. Children will adore Wilma." SLJ

Another title about Green Wilma is:
Green Wilma (1993)

Hi, Fly Guy! Scholastic 2005 30p il $5.99; pa $3.99

Grades: PreK K 1 2   E

1. Pets -- Fiction 2. Flies -- Fiction
ISBN 0-439-63903-4; 0-439-85311-7 pa; 978-0-439-63903-3; 978-0-439-85311-8 pa
LC 2004-20553

When Buzz captures a fly to enter in The Amazing Pet Show, his parents and the judges tell him that a fly cannot be a pet, but Fly Guy proves them wrong. "Grades one to three." (Bull Cent Child Books)

"Suitably wacky cartoon art accompanies the text, which is simple enough for beginning readers." Publ Wkly

Other titles in this series are:
Super Fly Guy (2006)
Shoo Fly Guy (2006)
There was an old lady who swallowed Fly Guy (2007)
Fly high, Fly Guy (2008)
Hooray for Fly Guy! (2008)
I spy Fly Guy! (2009)
Fly Guy meets Fly Girl! (2010)
Buzz Boy and Fly Guy (2010)
Fly Guy vs. the flyswatter! (2011)
Ride, Fly Guy, ride! (2012)

The **twin** princes; [by] Tedd Arnold. Dial Books for Young Readers 2006 un il $16.99

Grades: K 1 2   E

1. Twins -- Fiction 2. Princes -- Fiction 3. Chickens -- Fiction
ISBN 0-8037-2696-1
LC 2005013300

Two chicken princes who are twins take part in a contest to determine which one will inherit the throne.

"With his signature verve [Arnold] . . . folds a satisfying brainteaser into an original folktale. . . . The problem and its solution are clearly presented, and there are plenty of clever touches to engage kids and grownups alike." Booklist

Arnosky, Jim

At this very moment. Dutton Children's Books 2011 un il $16.99

Grades: K 1 2   E

1. Stories in rhyme 2. Nature -- Fiction 3. Animals -- Fiction
ISBN 978-0-525-42252-5; 0-525-42252-8
LC 2010037711

Identifies some of the things happening in nature while one goes about an ordinary day, such as a shark circling a reef while one brushes one's teeth, or puffins eating fresh-caught fish while one eats dinner.

"With a gentle rhythm, unforced rhymes and near rhymes and perfect pacing, this bedtime story encourages children to think, dream and wonder about the lives of animals in the wild." Kirkus

★ **Babies** in the bayou; [by] Jim Arnosky. G. P. Putnam's Sons 2007 un il $16.99

Grades: PreK K   E

1. Wetlands 2. Animal babies
ISBN 978-0-399-22653-3; 0-399-22653-2
LC 2006011910

There are many babies in the bayou, and even though they might have sharp white teeth, hard shells, webbed feet, or quick claws, their mothers still need to protect them.

"This is a wonderful resource to use with children to illuminate the ways of nature; it's economical and rhythmic in text, and beautifully and clearly illustrated. Arnosky uses simple language and a repeated refrain to describe the animals that live in a lush Southern environment." SLJ

Dolphins on the sand; by Jim Arnosky. G.P. Putnam's Sons 2008 un il $16.99

Grades: PreK K 1 2   E

1. Dolphins -- Fiction 2. Wildlife conservation -- Fiction
ISBN 978-0-399-24606-7; 0-399-24606-1
LC 2007045384

A dozen dolphins, led by their eldest member and her youngster, become stranded on a sandbar and must be helped to safety by humans.

This "juxtaposes a straightforward narrative with particularly colorful paintings. . . . Arnosky reflects the simple beauty of the dolphins of the dolphins' happy existance in tropical pinks, oranges, and aquas, moving to a more somber palette of grays and blacks as danger sets in. He includes all manner of flora and fauna in his illustrative arc." Booklist

Gobble it up! a fun song about eating. Scholastic Press 2008 un il $16.99

Grades: PreK K 1 2   E

1. Children's songs 2. Stories in rhyme 3. Food -- Songs 4. Food -- Fiction 5. Animals -- Songs 6. Animals -- Fiction 7. Animals -- Food -- Juvenile literature
ISBN 978-0-439-90362-2; 0-439-90362-9
LC 2007-29510

"This book takes a direct look at different animals and what they eat. It works well as a picture book, telling readers that if they were wild raccoons, or crocodiles, or great white sharks, they would 'gobble up' crawdads, or ducklings, or fishes. The catchy song sung by the author on the accompanying CD adds the element of fun that's advertised. Recognizable, true-to-life acrylic illustrations . . . . fill the spreads." SLJ

Grandfather Buffalo; [by] Jim Arnosky. G.P. Putnam's Sons 2006 un il $16.99
Grades: PreK K 1 2   E
1. Bison -- Fiction 2. Old age -- Fiction
ISBN 0-399-24169-8
LC 2005003535
When Grandfather Buffalo, the oldest bull of the herd, trails behind the group, he finds that he is joined by a newborn calf.
"Arnosky's signature artwork, which beautifully evokes the western landscape, is especially effective showing the buffalo closeup, and the writer-artist's respect for nature is clearly reflected in the simple, poignant story." Booklist

I'm a turkey! Scholastic Press 2009 un il $16.99
Grades: PreK K 1   E
1. Stories in rhyme 2. Turkeys -- Fiction
ISBN 978-0-439-90364-6; 0-439-90364-5
LC 2008-38335
"Arnosky's illustrations manage to be both autumnal and bright. . . . Arnosky gives [the birds] personality and charm." Booklist

Slow down for manatees. G. P. Putnam's Sons 2009 un il $16.99
Grades: PreK K 1   E
1. Manatees -- Juvenile literature
ISBN 978-0-399-24170-3; 0-399-24170-1
LC 2008-47983
Injured by a passing motorboat, a pregnant manatee is rescued and taken to an aquarium to recover and have her baby in a safe environment.
"Text and art work in tandem to present a portrait of a gentle, innocent creature. . . . A solid addition to naturalist Arnosky's oeuvre." Publ Wkly

Aronson, Billy
The **chicken** problem; Jennifer Oxley & Billy Aronson. Random House 2012 25 p. col. ill. (hardcover) $16.99; (library) $16.99
Grades: PreK K   E
1. Picture books for children 2. Chickens -- Juvenile fiction 3. Chickens -- Fiction 4. Counting -- Fiction 5. Farm life -- Fiction 6. Problem solving -- Fiction
ISBN 0375869891; 9780375869891; 9780375969898
LC 2011031249
In this children's picture book by Jennifer Oxley, "Peg (a girl) and her pal Cat (a cat) are getting ready 'to have a perfect picnic with a pig' when they realize that they've cut one too many pieces of pie. Cat retrieves a little chicken (for the little piece of pie) from the nearby chicken coop, but she leaves the door to the coop wide open. . . . Peg and Cat eventually manage to return the errant poultry to the coop." (Bulletin of the Center for Children's Books)

Arrigan, Mary
★ **Mario's** Angels; a story about the artist Giotto. written by Mary Arrigan; illustrated by Gillian McClure. Frances Lincoln 2006 un il $15.95

Grades: PreK K 1 2   E
1. Artists 2. Painters 3. Sculptors 4. Architects 5. Angels -- Fiction 6. Artists -- Fiction
ISBN 1-84507-404-1
"Mario, an exuberant boy, visits the artist [Giotto] as he works on his fresco Nativity in Padua. . . . When the artist is at a loss about how to fill the sky, Mario suggests angels. . . . The gentle text is matched by light, airy colors and feathery movement in the art. The cherubic Mario is full of life and will seem very real to readers." SLJ

Aruego, Jose
★ The **last** laugh; [by] Jose Aruego & Ariane Dewey. Dial Books for Young Readers 2006 un il $12.99
Grades: PreK K 1 2   E
1. Stories without words 2. Ducks -- Fiction 3. Snakes -- Fiction
ISBN 0-8037-3093-4
LC 2005-48461
A wordless tale in which a clever duck outwits a bullying snake
"In comic-strip panels, Aruego and Deweys signature pen-and-ink and gouache art is droll and accessible. . . . Young readers will find the format and the karmic justice of this story appealing." SLJ

Asch, Frank
The **Daily** Comet; boy saves Earth from giant octopus. written by Frank Asch; illustrated by Devin Asch. Kids Can Press 2010 un il $16.95
Grades: K 1 2 3   E
1. Octopuses -- Fiction 2. Journalists -- Fiction 3. Father-son relationship -- Fiction
ISBN 978-1-55453-281-0; 1-55453-281-7
When Hayward Palmer accompanies his father, a reporter for the sensationalistic Daily Comet, on a "Go to Work with a Parent Day," he has a rational explanation for all the weird and wacky things they encounter until he finally comes face to face with an enormous octopus.
"The dialogue is brisk, and visual quotes from Hollywood abound; Devin Asch's digital illustrations portray Hayward's father as a Gregory Peck look-alike and his photographer sidekick is an Elvis clone; dozens of other retro elements whirl at high speed. . . . It's a strangely believable tall tale." Publ Wkly

Happy birthday, Moon. Simon & Schuster Books for Young Readers 2000 un il pa $6.99
Grades: PreK K 1   E
1. Bears -- Fiction 2. Birthdays -- Fiction
ISBN 978-0-689-83544-5; 0-689-83544-2
First published 1982 by Prentice Hall
Bear travels to the highest mountaintop to find out what to give the Moon for its birthday and discovers a delightful surprise—the Moon has the same birthday as Bear. Or so it seems.
Other titles in this series are:
Mooncake (1983)
Moongame (1984)
Moonbear's shadow (1985)

Like a windy day; [by] Frank Asch & Devin Asch. Harcourt 2002 un il $16; pa $7

Grades: PreK K   E
1. Winds 2. Winds -- Fiction
ISBN 0-15-216376-X; 0-15-206403-6 pa

LC 2001-5260

A young girl discovers all the things the wind can do, by playing and dancing along with it

Written "in a poetic text. . . . The brief story is filled with action verbs. . . . The exciting pen-and-ink illustrations were colorized in Adobe Photoshop. Broad and sweeping spreads are filled with movement." SLJ

Mrs. Marlowe's mice; written by Frank Asch; illustrated by Devin Asch. Kids Can Press 2007 un il $17.95
Grades: 2 3 4   E
1. Cats -- Fiction 2. Mice -- Fiction
ISBN 978-1-55453-022-9

Mrs. Marlowe, a cat, secretly cares for the large family of mice who live with her, until one day, suspicious officers from the Department of Catland Security search the premises.

"Carefully detailed period dress and furnishings add a genteel air to the digital picture-book art. . . . Children will have a quiet, compassionate new hero." Booklist

The **sun** is my favorite star. Harcourt 2001 un il $15; pa $7
Grades: PreK K 1   E
ISBN 0-15-202127-2; 0-15-206397-8 pa

LC 98-46383

Celebrates a child's love of the sun and the wondrous ways in which it helps the earth and the life upon it

"Asch strikes just the right tone for his audience. . . . With colors as warm as a summer day, he creates a series of large-scale illustrations that reflect the direct unaffected tone of the writing." Booklist

Ashburn, Boni

I had a favorite dress; pictures by Julia Denos. Abrams 2011 un il $16.95
Grades: PreK K 1 2   E
1. Clothing and dress -- Fiction
ISBN 978-1-4197-0016-3; 1-4197-0016-2

"When the unnamed narrator's favorite dress is suddenly a size too small, she is not a happy camper; she wears that dress every Tuesday, which is her favorite day of the week. Then her mother transforms the too-small dress into the perfect shirt. As the child's favorite day of the week changes so does her garment as she grows out of it. It becomes a tank top . . . a skirt . . . a scarf . . . socks . . . a hair bow . . . and, finally, a picture of the original dress by the narrator herself. . . . Some of Ashburn's text is playfully placed in and around the art to good effect. . . . Denos's multimedia illustrations, a combination of collages, watercolors, and graphite and colored pencil artwork, reinforce the narrator's vibrant personality and the amazing transformations of the dress while capturing the action and emotion of the story." SLJ

Over at the castle; illustrated by Kelly Murphy. Abrams 2010 un il $15.95
Grades: PreK K 1 2   E
1. Counting 2. Stories in rhyme 3. Castles -- Fiction 4. Dragons -- Fiction 5. Middle Ages -- Fiction
ISBN 978-0-8109-8414-1; 0-8109-8414-8

"The familiar rhythm of the folk song Over in the Meadow finds a new setting as over at the castle, on the hill in the sun, an old mother dragon tries to teach her little dragon patience as they laze about near a castle. . . . Richly textured paintings in subtle hues that fit the medieval period convey the chores of the occupants of the castle, and comedic touches throughout . . . deepen the story and will have children flipping back through the pages." Booklist

Asher, Sandy

Here comes Gosling! illustrations by Keith Graves. Philomel Books 2009 un il $16.99
Grades: PreK K   E
1. Geese -- Fiction 2. Animals -- Fiction 3. Infants -- Fiction
ISBN 978-0-399-25085-9; 0-399-25085-9

LC 2008032613

Froggie and Rabbit host a picnic for Goose and Gander's new baby, but when the guest of honor starts to cry, Froggie finds a way to cheer her up

"Graves's quirky cartoon illustrations, created in bold-colored acrylic, ink, and pencil, combine full-bleed spreads with spot illustrations, keeping the story flowing. . . . The characters are oddly appealing with their expressive faces, long necks, and short, round bodies. Asher perfectly captures her young protagonist's emotions, and preschoolers will easily empathize with him." SLJ

Ashman, Linda

★ **Babies** on the go; illustrated by Jane Dyer. Harcourt 2003 un il $16
Grades: PreK K 1   E
1. Animal babies 2. Animal locomotion 3. Animals -- Infancy 4. Parental behavior in animals 5. Animal locomotion -- Juvenile literature 6. Animals -- Infancy -- Juvenile literature 7. Parental behavior in animals -- Juvenile literature
ISBN 0-15-201894-8

LC 2002-6310

Illustrations and rhyming text show how different animals carry their babies when they are on the move

"The large, soft watercolor illustrations and rhyming text make this celebration of parent/child love a natural for toddler storytime, and it's also perfect for one-on-one sharing." SLJ

Castles, caves, and honeycombs; illustrated by Lauren Stringer. Harcourt 2001 un il $16
Grades: PreK K 1   E
1. Home 2. Animals 3. Stories in rhyme 4. Dwellings 5. Animals -- Habitations
ISBN 0-15-202211-2

LC 99-50801

Describes some of the unique places where animals build their homes such as in a heap of twigs, on a castle tower, in a cave, or in the hollow space inside a tree

"The concise text and womb-like illustrations convey the feelings of love, safety, and security that a home should have." Horn Book Guide

Creaky old house; A topsy-turvy tale of a real fixer-upper. illustrated by Michael Chesworth. Sterling 2009 un il $14.95

Grades: K 1   **E**
   1. Stories in rhyme 2. Houses -- Fiction 3. Family
life -- Fiction
   ISBN 978-1-4027-4461-7; 1-4027-4461-7
                               LC 2008037836
   A large family gets into an increasingly complicated
home repair situation when the doorknob falls off a door
   "The clever, rhyming text bounces along with a perfect
cadence. The ink, watercolor, and pencil illustrations enhance the telling, and readers will take great pleasure in poring over the many amusing details." SLJ

   M is for mischief; an A to Z of naughty children. illustrated by Nancy Carpenter. Dutton Children's Books 2008
un il $16.99
Grades: K 1 2   **E**
   1. Alphabet 2. Stories in rhyme 3. Children's poetry
   4. Alphabet -- Juvenile literature
   ISBN 0-525-47564-8; 978-0-525-47564-4
                               LC 2007-28491
   A rhyme for each letter of the alphabet describes the
misbehavior of a child, from Angry Abby to Zany Zelda.
"Grades three to five." (Bull Cent Child Books)
   "Each eight-line rhyme in this energetic title has fun with
the sounds of words, as well as their slapstick meaning. . . .
Though the words are the wonderful winners here, Carpenter's rambunctious watercolor-and-collage pictures provide
excellent comedic support." Booklist

   ★ **Mama's** day; [illustrated by] Jan Ormerod. Simon
& Schuster Books for Young Readers 2006 un il $15.95
Grades: PreK K 1   **E**
   1. Stories in rhyme 2. Mother-child relationship --
Fiction
   ISBN 0-689-83475-6
                               LC 00-45063
   In rhyming text, mothers and their babies are described
sharing in a variety of activities, from playing at the ocean to
reading books and taking a bath
   "Ashman's skillful verse and Ormerod's cozy ink-and-
gouache artwork improve upon many other picture-book
fulminations on mother love. A lilting line of verse appears
on each spread, illustrated by a neatly framed scene of a
different mother-child pair (including a demure image of
breastfeeding) as well as a crew of charming, multicultural
babies." Booklist

   No dogs allowed! [illustrated by] Kristin Sorra. Sterling
2011 un il $14.95
Grades: PreK K 1   **E**
   1. Dogs -- Fiction 2. Pets -- Fiction 3. Animals --
Fiction 4. Restaurants -- Fiction
   ISBN 978-1-4027-5837-9; 1-4027-5837-5
   When Alberto turns away people with pets from his
restaurant, they gather in the street and buy treats from a
street vendor.
   "Digital artwork with plenty of captivating details essentially tells this story; the only text appears in speech bubbles
and changing restaurant signage. . . . This lively picture book
is a good choice for one-on-one sharing; the details in the

art could serve as a visual stimulus to initiate conversations
about what is happening." SLJ

   Rain! written by Linda Ashman; illustrated by Christian
Robinson. Houghton Mifflin Books for Children 2013 32
p. col. ill. (reinforced) $16.99
Grades: PreK K 1   **E**
   1. Rain -- Juvenile fiction 2. Picture books for children
   3. Neighbors -- Fiction 4. Mood (Psychology) -- Fiction
   5. Rain and rainfall -- Fiction
   ISBN 054773395X; 9780547733951
                               LC 2011042039
   This children's picture book is set on a rainy day. "Two
strangers have very different views about the weather: one
is an elderly man who grumbles and complains throughout
the day, and the other is a little boy who makes the most of
the puddles on the sidewalk. When they meet at the Rain
or Shine Café, the child finds himself momentarily brought
down by the man's sullen demeanor until a mix-up with their
hats brings out the old man's smile and optimism." (School
Library Journal)

   ★ **Samantha** on a roll; pictures by Christine Davenier.
Farrar, Straus & Giroux 2011 un il $16.99
Grades: K 1 2   **E**
   1. Stories in rhyme 2. Roller skating -- Fiction
   ISBN 978-0-374-36399-4; 0-374-36399-4
   "Samantha decides to try out her roller skates for the
first time, despite her mother's admonition to wait. She likes
skating so much in the house that she hungers for the wide
open spaces of the great outdoors. She sneaks outside, and
the fun begins. . . . The rhyming text makes this delightful
story tons of fun to read aloud. Davenier's illustrations aptly
capture the action with bold colors and plenty of lines indicating motion." SLJ

   Stella, unleashed; notes from the doghouse. illustrated
by Paul Meisel. Sterling Pub. Co. 2008 40p il $14.95
Grades: K 1 2   **E**
   1. Stories in rhyme 2. Dogs -- Fiction 3. Family life
-- Fiction
   ISBN 978-1-4027-3987-3; 1-4027-3987-7
                               LC 2007036499
   The family dog describes her life in a series of rhymes.
   "Ashman aptly captures life with a pup, balancing the
sweet (lap naps) with the sour (shedding). . . . Meisel's realistic acrylic, gouache, and pencil illustrations are filled with
a variety of people and pups. . . . This collection of rhymes is
ideal for family read-alouds." SLJ

   To the beach! illustrated by Nadine Bernard Westcott.
Harcourt 2005 un il $16
Grades: PreK K 1 2   **E**
   1. Beaches -- Fiction 2. Family life -- Fiction
   ISBN 0-15-216490-1
                               LC 2003-19444
   A family keeps forgetting the things they need to take
to the beach
   "Rhyming text and bouncy and boldly colored illustrations in acrylic on watercolor paper capture the frenzy surrounding this hilarious . . . family. A rip-roaring fun read-
aloud." SLJ

When I was king; by Linda Ashman; illustrated by David McPhail. HarperCollins 2008 un il $16.99; lib bdg $17.89

Grades: PreK K 1   E

1. Stories in rhyme 2. Infants -- Fiction 3. Brothers -- Fiction

ISBN 978-0-06-029051-1; 0-06-029051-X; 978-0-06-029052-8 lib bdg; 0-06-029052-8 lib bdg

LC 2005017868

A young boy describes how he is no longer "king" now that there is a new baby in the house, but then his family helps him enjoy the change

This is an "expertly rhymed story. . . . McPhail's charming illustrations perfectly capture the narrator's mood in his facial expressions and body language. Ashman's verses, lettered in a child-friendly font that varies in size, are perfect for reading aloud." SLJ

Asper-Smith, Sarah

Have you ever seen a smack of jellyfish? an alphabet book. Sasquatch Books 2010 un il $16.95

Grades: PreK K   E

1. Animals 2. Alphabet

ISBN 978-1-57061-687-7; 1-57061-687-6

"Asper-Smith's background in graphic design is evident in this ABC book devoted to collective nouns. Crisp, eye-popping silhouettes put the animals' shapes . . . in high relief. A murder of crows perches on a tree's spindly blue branches against a neon green sky . . . while the yellow-on-pink victim of a 'scourge of mosquitoes' makes their descriptor feel all the more apt. Clean design, attention to detail, and intriguing animal selections . . . make this an elegant primer." Publ Wkly

I would tuck you in; Sarah Asper-Smith. Sasquatch Books 2012 32 p. $16.99

Grades: K 1 2   E

1. Picture books for children 2. Bedtime -- Juvenile fiction 3. Animal behavior -- Juvenile literature 4. Love -- Fiction 5. Mother and child -- Fiction 6. Animals -- Alaska -- Fiction 7. Animals -- Infancy -- Fiction

ISBN 1570618445; 9781570618444

LC 2012032054

This children's picture book features drowsy animals alongside scientific explanations of animal behavior. "Each two-page spread features an illustration of an adult/child animal pair and a sweet, nonrhyming promise . . . . The feel-good sentiment is then explained in scientific terms via smaller text at the bottom of the page." (Booklist)

Aston, Dianna Hutts

★ **Dream** something big; the story of the Watts Towers. Dial Books for Young Readers 2011 un il $16.99

Grades: K 1 2 3   E

1. Artists 2. Folk artists

ISBN 978-0-8037-3245-2; 0-8037-3245-7

LC 2010028797

"Aston pays tribute to the creative genius of an Italian immigrant and tile worker who, in the 1920s, begins a unique project on his Watts, Calif., property that takes 34 years to complete. Simon Rodia uses only rebar, cement, broken tiles, shells, and other found items to build towering spires, some almost a hundred feet tall, decorated with mosaic designs. A fictional neighbor girl, Marguerite, provides lyrical first-person narration as she watches the towers take shape throughout her childhood. The subject lends itself perfectly to the collage illustrations. Employing mostly paper, but also bits of pottery, cloth, clay and string, Roth stunningly recreates bold, stylized versions of the towers. This book beautifully illuminates a little-known story of imagination and perseverance that resulted in a national landmark." Publ Wkly

★ **Moon** over Star; pictures by Jerry Pinkney. Dial Books for Young Readers 2008 un il $17.99

Grades: PreK K 1 2 3   E

1. Farm life -- Fiction 2. African Americans -- Fiction 3. Space flight to the moon -- Fiction

ISBN 978-0-8037-3107-3; 0-8037-3107-8

LC 2007050703

Coretta Scott King honor book for illustration, 2009

On her family's farm in the town of Star, eight-year-old Mae eagerly follows the progress of the 1969 Apollo 11 flight and moon landing and dreams that she might one day be an astronaut, too.

"Spaced vertically in phrases like free verse alongside the large illustrations, the text combines dignity and immediacy in a clean, spare telling of events. Pinkney's evocative artwork, created using graphite, ink, and watercolor, depicts a black family captivated, and perhaps subtly changed, by the moon landing in 1969." Booklist

An **orange** in January; [by] Dianna Hutts Aston; illustrated by Julie Maren. Dial Books for Young Readers 2007 un il $16.99

Grades: PreK K 1   E

1. Oranges -- Fiction

ISBN 978-0-8037-3146-2

LC 2006014488

An orange begins its life as a blossom where bees feast on the nectar, and reaches the end of its journey, bursting with the seasons inside it, in the hands of a child.

This is a "poetic tale. . . . Like the text, the glowing acrylic paintings are artfully simple and make beautiful use of color." SLJ

Auch, Mary Jane

Beauty and the beaks; a Turkey's cautionary tale. [by] Mary Jane and Herm Auch. Holiday House 2007 un il $16.95; pa $6.95

Grades: K 1 2 3   E

1. Turkeys -- Fiction 2. Chickens -- Fiction 3. Thanksgiving Day -- Fiction

ISBN 978-0-8234-1990-6; 0-8234-1990-8; 978-0-8234-2164-0 pa; 0-8234-2164-3 pa

LC 2006049468

When Lance, a very pretentious turkey, arrives on the farm and boasts that he is the only bird invited to a special feast, no hen is impressed, but when Beauty learns that Lance is the main course, she convinces the others to save him

"Wonderfully creative handmade characters and sets are the highlight of this over-the-top chicken tale. . . . The author made chicken mannequins with polymer eyes, beaks, and shoes, as well as wool wings and yarn feathers. Her husband designed the sets, built them, and photographed the images, adjusting their size. A humorous story about dressing a turkey, but not in the usual manner." SLJ

The **plot** chickens; by Mary Jane and Herm Auch. Holiday House 2009 un il $16.95
Grades: PreK K 1 2 **E**
1. Chickens -- Fiction 2. Authorship -- Fiction 3. Books and reading -- Fiction
ISBN 978-0-8234-2087-2; 0-8234-2087-6
LC 2007011234

Henrietta the chicken loves to read so much that she decides to write a book herself, but first no one will publish a book written by a chicken, and then, when she publishes it herself and it gets a terrible review in "The Corn Book," Henrietta is devastated

"The illustrations, a combination of oil paints and digital technology, are bold and colorful. . . . A droll chicken with a repeating line adds to the humor. This offering works on two levels. It's a funny picture book that could be used as a manual on writing." SLJ

Averbeck, Jim
Except if. Atheneum Books for Young Readers 2011 un il $12.99
Grades: PreK K 1 **E**
1. Eggs -- Fiction 2. Animals -- Fiction 3. Reasoning -- Juvenile literature
ISBN 978-1-4169-9544-9; 1-4169-9544-7
LC 2009-52489

An egg is just an egg, except if, after hatching it becomes something else.

"Averbeck's simple shapes are outlined in pastel, a coloring-book style nicely suited to the deadpan narration. . . . It's a book in which the action unfolds in the mind as much as it does on the page." Publ Wkly

★ **In** a blue room; [by] Jim Averbeck; illustrated by Trica Tusa. Harcourt 2008 un il $16
Grades: PreK K 1 2 **E**
1. Color -- Fiction 2. Bedtime -- Fiction 3. Mother-daughter relationship -- Fiction
ISBN 978-0-15-205992-7; 0-15-205992-X
LC 2006034453

Alice wants everything in her bedroom to be blue before she falls asleep

"Prose and pictures partner each other effortlessly all the way to the last page." Publ Wkly

Avi
Silent movie; Avi, the author; C.B. Mordan, the illustrator. Atheneum Bks. for Young Readers 2002 un il $16.95
Grades: K 1 2 3 **E**
1. Immigrants -- Fiction 2. Silent films -- Fiction
ISBN 0-689-84145-0
LC 2001-33025

In the early years of the twentieth century, a Swedish family encounters separation and other hardships upon immigrating to New York City until the son is cast in a silent movie, in a picture book that evokes an actual silent movie

"Clear, beautiful ink-on-clayboard illustrations; white type on thick, glossy black paper; and cinematic lighting effects combine to evoke the historical period." Booklist

Avraham, Kate Aver
What will you be, Sara Mee? illustrated by Anne Sibley O'Brien. Charlesbridge 2010 un il $16.95; pa $7.95
Grades: PreK K 1 **E**
1. Parties -- Fiction 2. Siblings -- Fiction 3. Birthdays -- Fiction 4. Korean Americans -- Fiction
ISBN 978-1-58089-210-0; 1-58089-210-8; 978-1-58089-211-7 pa; 1-58089-211-6 pa
LC 2009-1708

At her Tol, the first birthday party, Sara Mee plays the traditional Korean prophecy game—Toljabee—while her extended family and friends watch.

"The illustrations are ink brush line with watercolor and done in vibrant colors. The love among family and friends is evident in these pictures, depicting their joy about this important event." SLJ

Axtell, David
We're going on a lion hunt; [illustrated by] David Axtell. Holt & Co. 2000 un il $15.95
Grades: PreK K 1 2 **E**
1. Lions -- Fiction
ISBN 0-8050-6159-2
LC 98-47507

First published 1999 in the United Kingdom

Two girls set out bravely in search of a lion, going through long grass, a swamp, and a cave before they find what they're looking for

"Axtell takes a storytime classic to the African savanna. . . . [His] sun-soaked, impressionistic oil paintings offer beautiful landscapes and engaging details. . . . Large figures on the page make this a good choice for storytimes as well as lap times." SLJ

Aylesworth, Jim
Little Bitty Mousie; [by] Jim Aylesworth; illustrated by Michael Hague. Walker 2007 un il $16.95; lib bdg $17.85
Grades: PreK K 1 **E**
1. Alphabet 2. Stories in rhyme 3. Mice -- Fiction
ISBN 978-0-8027-9637-0; 0-8027-9637-0; 978-0-8027-9638-7 lib bdg; 0-8027-9638-9 lib bdg
LC 2007002366

Little Bitty Mousie sneaks into a house one night and discovers many tantalizing new things, as well as one very scary thing.

"The alphabet-related words are in boldface, the bouncy rhymes are fun, and the cute periodic refrain . . . will encourage listener participation. . . . Enchanting, vividly colored pictures, created in pencil and then digitally colored, set the sweet miss mouse in the middle of realistic, detailed close-ups of familiar household objects." Booklist

Old black fly; illustrations by Stephen Gammell. Holt & Co. 1992 un il $16.95; pa $6.95
Grades: K 1 2 3 **E**
1. Alphabet 2. Stories in rhyme 3. Flies -- Fiction
ISBN 0-8050-1401-2; 0-8050-3924-4 pa
LC 91-26825

Rhyming text and illustrations follow a mischievous old black fly through the alphabet as he has a very busy bad day landing where he should not be

Aylesworth's "snappy couplets constitute a waggish presentation of a basic concept. . . . Gammell's paintings are exuberant splashes of mayhem—rainbows of splattered hues from which truly memorable characters emerge. His appropriately bug-eyed (and cross-eyed) fly and gap-toothed humans sporting crazy hairdos provide a level of dementia that children will relish." Publ Wkly

★ The **full** belly bowl; illustrated by Wendy Halperin. Atheneum Bks. for Young Readers 1998 un il $16.95
Grades: K 1 2 3   E
   1. Fairy tales
   ISBN 0-689-81033-4
                                                           LC 98-14052
In return for the kindness he showed a wee small man, a very old man is given a magical bowl that causes problems when it is not used properly

"From the dainty pictures on the endpapers to the stunning artwork inside, this book is a feast for the eyes. The story . . . is just as good, smoothly blending folktale conventions with touches of magic and a dusting of comedy." Booklist

Ayres, Katherine

   Up, down, and around; [by] Katherine Ayres; illustrated by Nadine Bernard Westcott. Candlewick Press 2007 un il $16.99
Grades: PreK K 1   E
   1. Stories in rhyme 2. Gardening -- Fiction
   ISBN 978-0-7636-2378-4; 0-7636-2378-4
                                                         LC 2006049576
"This picture book depicts a bustling kitchen garden. Two children help a man with planting, watering, and harvesting vegetables, while a dog, a cat, and a rabbit observe the fun. All around them, snails, caterpillars, birds, bugs, and worms creep, crawl, fly, climb, dig, and generally cavort about. . . . The ink-and-watercolor illustrations offer plenty of details for children to explore. . . . The short verses create a quick pace and an upbeat tempo throughout." Booklist

Baasansuren, Bolormaa

   My little round house; adapted by Helen Mixter. Groundwood Books 2009 un il $18.95
Grades: K 1 2 3   E
   1. Infants -- Fiction 2. Family life -- Fiction
   ISBN 978-0-88899-934-4; 0-88899-934-8
"The little round house of the title is a large tent, or ger, home to the nomadic people of Mongolia. In a spare first-person narrative, baby Jilu recounts his first year and introduces readers to the rhythm of his loving family's nomadic life. . . . Attractive full-page gouache illustrations by the Mongolian writer/illustrator Baasansuren show the round house's interior as well as the characters' clothes, including elaborate details such as painted woodwork, embroidery, and the texture of fabrics." SLJ

Bachelet, Gilles

   My cat, the silliest cat in the world; written and illustrated by Gilles Bachelet. Abrams 2006 un il $16.95
Grades: PreK K 1 2   E
   1. Cats -- Fiction 2. Elephants -- Fiction
   ISBN 0-8109-4913-X; 978-0-8109-4913-3
                                                         LC 2005-27837
"While the text is a completely conventional list of a cat's habits, the very, very, large cat in the pictures is, in fact, an elephant. The straight-faced humor becomes all the fun-

nier because Bachelet captures a cat's peculiar postures and behavior exactly. The paintings are filled with visual wit." Horn Book Guide
   Another title about the silliest cat is:
   When the silliest cat was small (2007)

   When the silliest cat was small; written and illustrated by Gilles Bachelet. Abrams Books for Young Readers 2007 un il $16.95
Grades: PreK K 1 2   E
   1. Cats -- Fiction 2. Elephants -- Fiction
   ISBN 978-0-8109-9415-7; 0-8109-9415-1
                                                         LC 2007001198
Unaware that his pet cat is actually an elephant, the author describes how he selected his "kitten" and recounts their first days together at home.

   "Coming to a satisfying and hilarious conclusion, this story has colorful pen-and-ink illustrations." SLJ

Badescu, Ramona

   Pomelo begins to grow; illustrated by Benjamin Chaud; translated from French by Claudia Bedrick. Enchanted Lion Books 2011 un il $16.95
Grades: 1 2 3   E
   1. Growth -- Fiction 2. Elephants -- Fiction
   ISBN 978-1-59270-111-7; 1-59270-111-6
                                                         LC 2010053472
When his favorite dandelion looks surprisingly small, Pomelo the garden elephant discovers that he is growing and then wonders about the mysterious process called growth.

   "The author and illustrator demonstrate a brilliant marriage of text and illustration. Chaud's charming paintings of Pomelo in his landscape of dandelions, strawberries, and smiling potatoes—set simply against oversize white pages—breathe life and humor into Badescu's big-picture questions, while playing with scale." SLJ

   Pomelo explores color; Ramona Badescu; [illustrated by] Benjamin Chaud. Enchanted Lion Books 2012 120 p.
Grades: K 1 2   E
   1. Color -- Juvenile fiction 2. Emotions -- Juvenile literature 3. Color -- Fiction 4. Elephants -- Fiction
   ISBN 1592701264; 9781592701261
                                                         LC 2012022766
This children's book by Ramona Badescu and illustrated by Benjamin Chaud "is all about exploration and the experience of seeing color anew. . . . Pomelo discovers colors in all their nuance. He encounters the infinite white of falling snow, the hypnotizing red of love, and the shadowy blue of the unknown. The colors describe our concrete world, but also reflect emotional states, as well as the curious, oddball sensibility of our dear Pomelo." (Publisher's note)

Bae, Hyun-Joo

   ★ **New** clothes for New Year's Day. Kane/Miller 2007 un il $15.95
Grades: K 1 2 3   E
   1. New Year -- Fiction 2. Clothing and dress -- Fiction
   ISBN 978-1-933605-29-6
A young Korean girl describes the new clothes that she will be wearing to celebrate the new year.

   "Simple words and inventively composed pictures depict each step in donning the elaborate, traditional costume. . . . Bae's delicate illustrations move smoothly between depictions of mishaps as the child wrestles with troublesome accessories and grand, wordless portraits." Booklist

Baehr, Patricia Goehner

Boo Cow; illustrated by Margot Apple. Charlesbridge 2010 un il $14.95

Grades: K 1 2   E

1. Ghost stories 2. Cattle -- Fiction 3. Chickens -- Fiction 4. Farm life -- Fiction

ISBN 978-1-58089-108-0; 1-58089-108-X

LC 2008-25333

When Mr. and Mrs. Noodleman start a chicken farm, they are terrorized by a ghostly cow that seems to be keeping the hens from laying any eggs, but upon further investigation they discover the real culprit.

"A mix of mystery and hilarity, Baehr's . . . story is made far from frightening by Apple's . . . soft pencil illustrations, as well as an ending that will leave children assured of Boo Cow's gentle nature." Publ Wkly

Baek, Matthew J.

Panda and polar bear; by Matthew J. Baek. Dial Books for Young Readers 2009 un il $16.95

Grades: PreK   E

1. Bears -- Fiction 2. Friendship -- Fiction 3. Polar bear -- Fiction 4. Giant panda -- Fiction

ISBN 978-0-8037-3359-6; 0-8037-3359-3

LC 2008046231

Curious to know what lies beyond his wintry world, a polar bear goes exploring, falls into a mud puddle, and is mistaken for a panda by a new playmate

"The simple, lively text folds in light humor as it delivers a positive message about appreciating differences and finding commonalities, themes that are reflected in the soft watercolor illustrations." Booklist

Baeten, Lieve

The **curious** Little Witch. North-South 2010 un il $16.95

Grades: PreK K 1 2   E

1. Witches -- Fiction

ISBN 978-0-7358-2305-1; 0-7358-2305-7

First published 1992

"A young blonde witch and her cat decide to investigate a house, but the witch's broomstick breaks. As she explores the house, flaps reveal each of the residents: the Music Witch, who creates 'sublime' sounds; the Kitchen Witch, who prepares delicious food; and the Bedroom Witch, with soporific powers. Luckily, the Tinkering Witch is able to fix her broom-while adding rocket power. The cozy, cluttered details on every floor lend the book warmth and charm." Publ Wkly

Other titles about Little Witch are:

Up and away with the Little Witch (2011)

Happy Birthday, Little Witch (2011)

Bailey, Linda

Stanley's little sister; written by Linda Bailey; illustrated by Bill Slavin. Kids Can Press 2010 un il $17.95

Grades: K 1 2   E

1. Cats -- Fiction 2. Dogs -- Fiction

ISBN 978-1-55453-487-6; 1-55453-487-9

Baker, Barbara

★ **Digby** and Kate and the beautiful day; pictures by Marsha Winborn. Dutton Children's Bks. 1998 48p il hardcover o.p. pa $3.99

Grades: PreK K 1 2   E

1. Cats -- Fiction 2. Dogs -- Fiction 3. Best friends -- Fiction

ISBN 0-525-45855-7; 0-14-240035-4 pa

Digby the dog and Kate the cat disagree about many things but they remain best friends

"The artwork . . . together with the cheerful stories make up good, light fare for beginning readers." Horn Book Guide

Other titles about Digby and Kate are:

Digby and Kate (1988)

Digby and Kate 1 2 3 (2004)

Digby and Kate again (1989)

One Saturday evening; pictures by Kate Duke. Dutton Children's Books 2007 48p il hardcover o.p. $13.99

Grades: K 1 2 3   E

1. Bears -- Fiction 2. Family life -- Fiction

ISBN 978-0-525-47103-5; 0-525-47103-0

LC 2006-24785

On a Saturday evening, the members of a bear family busy themselves with cleaning up the kitchen, taking baths, and reading.

"The chapter structure and short, basic sentences are well tuned to newly confident readers, and the reassuringly familiar scenarios, nicely extended in Duke's expressive ink-and-watercolor pictures, will draw children into the cozy nighttime mayhem." Booklist

Another title about the bear family is:

One Saturday morning (1994)

Baker, Jeannie

Home. Greenwillow Books 2004 un il $15.99

Grades: PreK K 1 2   E

1. City and town life 2. Stories without words

ISBN 0-06-623935-4

LC 2003-49287

A wordless picture book that observes the changes in a neighborhood from before a girl is born until she is an adult, as it first decays and then is renewed by the efforts of the residents

"Baker uses natural materials to create detailed, arresting collages that tell a story in which words are superfluous. Children can pore over these pages again and again and make fresh discoveries with each perusal." SLJ

★ **Mirror**. Candlewick Press 2010 un il $18.99

Grades: PreK K 1 2   E

1. Stories without words 2. Markets -- Fiction

ISBN 978-0-7636-4848-0; 0-7636-4848-5

LC 2009-50391

In Sydney, Australia, and in Morocco, two boys and their families have a day of shopping. Readers are invited to compare illustrations in two wordless stories that are intended to be read one from left to right and the other from right to left.

"Baker's entrancing collages, packed with visual information and created with fabric, sand, vegetation, and other unusual materials, have the power to bring back child and adult viewers for infinite 'readings.' Perfectly spectacular." Kirkus

Where the forest meets the sea; story and pictures by Jeannie Baker. Greenwillow Bks. 1988 un il $16

Grades: PreK K 1 2   **E**

    1. Rain forests -- Fiction

    ISBN 0-688-06363-2

         LC 87-7551

First published 1987 in the United Kingdom

On a camping trip in an Australian rain forest with his father, a young boy thinks about the history of the plant and animal life around him and wonders about their future

The illustrations "are relief collages 'constructed from a multitude of materials, including modeling clay, papers, textured materials, preserved natural materials, and paints.' Integrated by the artist's vision, the collages create three-dimensional effects on two-dimensional pages drawing the reader into each scene as willing observer and explorer." Horn Book

Window. Greenwillow Bks. 1991 un il lib bdg $17.89

Grades: PreK K 1 2   **E**

    1. Stories without words 2. Human ecology -- Fiction

    ISBN 0-688-08918-6

         LC 90-3922

"Filled with marvelous detail, the textured collages make an affecting statement about the erosion of the planet Earth." SLJ

Baker, Keith

Hickory dickory dock; [by] Keith Baker. Harcourt 2007 un il $16

Grades: PreK K 1 2   **E**

    1. Stories in rhyme 2. Animals -- Fiction 3. Clocks and watches -- Fiction

    ISBN 978-0-15-205818-0; 0-15-205818-4

         LC 2006003257

"The nursery rhyme 'Hickory Dickory Dock' gets new life as it goes through 12 hours of the day. . . . As each hour chimes, another creature appears, often completing an action initiated in the previous spread. . . . With a bouncy, easy-to-enjoy text and child-appealing collage-style pictures, this is a book that will work well one-on-one or with groups." Booklist

Just how long can a long string be!? Arthur A. Levine Books 2009 un il hardcover o.p. $16.99

Grades: PreK K 1 2   **E**

    1. Stories in rhyme 2. Children's poetry 3. Ants -- Fiction 4. Birds -- Fiction

    ISBN 978-0-545-08661-5; 0-545-08661-2; 978-0-545-08662-2 pa; 0-545-08662-0 pa

         LC 2008027344

Be it tied to a balloon, or kite, or hanging a picture, or stringing a banjo or a mop, a bird explains to an ant how long a string needs to be

"By using pale overlapping images, Baker creates a sense of movement in many of the illustrations. A palette of pastels captures the beauty of spring. . . . [This is a] lovely book . . . for a fine spring storytime." SLJ

  ★ **LMNO** peas. Beach Lane Books 2010 un il $16.99

Grades: PreK K 1 2   **E**

    1. Alphabet 2. Stories in rhyme 3. Occupations --

Fiction

    ISBN 978-1-4169-9141-0; 1-4169-9141-7

         LC 2009012672

Busy little peas introduce their favorite occupations, from astronaut to zoologist.

"With its digital illustrations' luminous colors, buoyant spirit, and engaging characters, this handsome picture book is definitely worth a second look, even in the overcrowded field of alphabet books." Booklist

  ★ **Meet** Mr. and Mrs. Green. Harcourt 2004 71p il hardcover o.p. pa $5.95

Grades: K 1 2   **E**

    1. Alligators -- Fiction

    ISBN 0-15-204954-1; 0-15-204955-X pa

         LC 2001-1955

First published 2002

A loving alligator couple enjoy going camping, eating pancakes, and visiting the county fair

"The acrylic illustrations have a loud, oversized presence that is complemented by the strong text." SLJ

Other titles about Mr. and Mrs. Green are:

Lucky days with Mr. and Mrs. Green (2005)

More Mr. and Mrs. Green (2004)

On the go with Mr. and Mrs. Green (2006)

  ★ **No** two alike. Beach Lane Books 2011 un il $16.99

Grades: PreK K 1   **E**

    1. Stories in rhyme 2. Birds -- Fiction 3. Winter -- Fiction

    ISBN 978-1-4424-1742-7; 1-4424-1742-0

         LC 2010044659

Follows a pair of birds on a snowflake-filled journey through a winter landscape, where everything everywhere, from branches and leaves to forests full of trees, is unique.

"Brief rhyming couplets, printed in large type and each requiring a page turn for completion, describe the birds' discoveries. . . . The engaging, digitally rendered avian characters stand out against the wintry landscape, and their many antics as they navigate their surroundings will sustain readers' interest." SLJ

Potato Joe; [by] Keith Baker. Harcourt 2008 un il $16

Grades: PreK K 1   **E**

    1. Nursery rhymes 2. Counting -- Fiction

    ISBN 978-0-15-206230-9; 0-15-206230-0

         LC 2007005930

Potato Joe leads the other spuds from the familiar nursery rhyme, "One Potato, Two Potato," in various activities, from a game of tic-tac-toe to a rodeo.

"The fuzzy-edged, childlike illustrations were done in Adobe Photoshop and complement the bouncy tone of the text. This will be fun to share, and even young children will soon have the rhyme committed to memory." SLJ

Balian, Lorna

Humbug witch; [by] Lorna Balian. Star Bright Books 2003 un il $12.95

Grades: PreK K 1 2   **E**

    1. Witches -- Fiction

    ISBN 1-932065-32-6

         LC 2003-16979

A reissue of the title first published 1965 by Abingdon Press

Despite looking the part, a little witch cannot seem to do the things that witches are supposed to do.

This is a "warm-hearted, conversational story.... [Illustrated with] friendly ink drawings in black, red, and yellow." Horn Book Guide

Balouch, Kristen

Feelings. Little Simon 2011 un il bd bk $6.99
Grades: PreK   E
1. Board books for children 2. Animals -- Fiction 3. Emotions -- Fiction
ISBN 978-1-4424-1199-9; 1-4424-1199-6

"Familiar animals convey common emotions through body language and facial expressions. A lion's frown, curled-in tail, and droopy mane communicate his sadness, . . . while a crocodile with a sly smile is feeling sneaky about planning a surprise.... Vivid colors, relatable examples, and a compact trim size should appeal to toddlers." Publ Wkly

★ The **little** little girl with the big big voice. Little Simon 2011 un il $12.99
Grades: PreK K 1   E
1. Play -- Fiction 2. Voice -- Fiction 3. Friendship -- Fiction
ISBN 1-4424-0808-1; 978-1-4424-0808-1

A loud little girl has trouble finding a jungle friend to play with because of her booming voice, until at last, she meets the one jungle animal whose roar is louder than hers. "Preschool." (Horn Book)

"Exuberant, stylized illustrations in bright pink, peach, coral, lime, orange and lemon effectively portray this girl and her energy.... Young readers can practically hear this little, little girl's big, big voice from where they're sitting, and most pre-schoolers will know exactly how she feels." Kirkus

Bancroft, Bronwyn

Kangaroo and crocodile; my big book of Australian animals. Bronwyn Bancroft. Little Hare Books 2011 48 p. (hbk) $19.99
Grades: 1 2 3   E
1. Animals -- Australia 2. Picture books for children 3. Animals -- Australia -- Juvenile literature
ISBN 1921714255; 9781921714252

LC 2012405708

This children's picture book looks at Australian animals. "Most of the double-page spreads feature two often-related animals (bottlenose dolphin and great white shark, for instance), although a few . . . concentrate on one animal. There are also several spreads with four different animals." (Kirkus)

W is for wombat; my first Australian word book. Little Hare 2010 un il bd bk $8.99
Grades: PreK   E
1. Alphabet 2. Board books for children 3. Animals -- Australia
ISBN 978-1-921541-17-9 bd bk; 1-921541-17-2 bd bk

"This ABC book features Australian Aboriginal motifs. Creatures like a koala, platypus, and quokka are thickly outlined in paint and decorated with multicolored dots, making

them resemble ornate masks, while a river, sun, and tree take on an elemental quality. It's an aesthetically striking guide to Australian wildlife." Publ Wkly

Bandy, Michael S.

White water; [by] Michael S. Bandy and Eric Stein; illustrated by Shadra Strickland. Candlewick Press 2011 40p il $16.99
Grades: K 1 2 3   E
1. Segregation -- Fiction 2. African Americans -- Fiction
ISBN 978-0-7636-3678-4; 0-7636-3678-9

LC 2010040343

After tasting the warm, rusty water from the fountain designated for African Americans, a young boy questions why he cannot drink the cool, refreshing water from the 'Whites Only' fountain. Based on a true experience co-author Michael S. Bandy had as a boy.

"Strickland's watercolor-and-ink illustrations extend the story.... Inspirational in tone, this is a strong introduction for young listeners and readers to the American Civil Rights movement." Kirkus

Bang, Molly

All of me! a book of thanks. Blue Sky Press 2009 un il $16.99
Grades: PreK K   E
1. Human body -- Fiction
ISBN 978-0-545-04424-0; 0-545-04424-3

LC 2008-49692

A celebration of how the body's parts work together, from hands and eyes to lips and heart, allowing one to exist in the wondrous universe. Includes instructions for making a book.

"Bang's artwork incorporates cut paper and fabric, photographed elements, red crayon, and paints.... Unusual, uneven, creative, and challenging." Booklist

★ **When** Sophie gets angry--really, really angry. Blue Sky Press (NY) 1999 un il $16.99; pa $6.99
Grades: PreK K 1   E
1. Anger -- Fiction
ISBN 0-590-18979-4; 0-439-59845-1 pa

LC 97-42209

A Caldecott Medal honor book, 2000

"The text is appropriately brief, for it is Bang's double-page illustrations, vibrating with saturated colors, that reveal the drama of the child's emotions." SLJ

★ The **paper** crane. Greenwillow Bks. 1985 un il $16.99; pa $6.99
Grades: K 1 2 3   E
ISBN 0-688-04108-6; 0-688-07333-6 pa

LC 84-13546

"Every detail of the restaurant interior, from the strawberries on the cake to the floral centerpieces, is a delight to the eye and imagination.... The book successfully blends Asian folklore themes with contemporary Western characterization." Horn Book

Bang-Campbell, Monika

Little Rat makes music; [by] Monika Bang-Campbell; illustrated by Molly Bang. Harcourt 2007 un il $15

Grades: 1 2 3   E
   1. Rats -- Fiction 2. Music -- Fiction 3. Violins --
Fiction
   ISBN 978-0-15-205305-5; 0-15-205305-0
                   LC 2005-27536
   Little Rat loves the violin but hates to practice, until
her teacher suggests she perform a duet with one of the advanced students at the holiday concert.
   "The jewel-toned watercolor-and-gouache artwork will
help keep readers engaged. A realistic and meaningful look
at the satisfying results of hard work and perseverance." SLJ

   Little Rat rides; illustrated by Molly Bang. Harcourt
2004 un il $15
Grades: 1 2 3   E
   1. Horsemanship -- Fiction
   ISBN 0-15-204667-4
                   LC 2003-4985
   Little Rat overcomes her fear and learns to ride a horse,
just like her daddy did when he was young
   "The simple text flows smoothly. . . . Bang-Campbell
skillfully captures a young child's perspective. . . . Done in
pencil, gouache, and watercolor, the vibrant illustrations add
detail to the narrative and reflect its emotional content." SLJ

Banks, Kate

   ★ **And** if the moon could talk; pictures by Georg Hallensleben. Foster Bks. 1998 un il $15
Grades: PreK K 1 2   E
   1. Night -- Fiction 2. Bedtime -- Fiction
   ISBN 0-374-30299-5
                   LC 97-29770
   As evening progresses into nighttime, the moon looks
down on a variety of nocturnal scenes, including a child getting ready for bed
   "The deeply saturated tones of the lovely, impressionistic oil paintings perfectly match the somnolent feeling of
the text." SLJ

   Baboon; pictures by Georg Hallensleben. Farrar, Straus
& Giroux 1997 un il $14
Grades: PreK K 1 2   E
   1. Baboons -- Fiction
   ISBN 0-374-30474-2
                   LC 96-20888
   Original French edition, 1994
   "Visible brush-strokes give texture to the impressionistic
paintings, and adept lighting evokes sunlight and shadow.
The simple, eloquent text is as subtly understated." Horn
Book Guide

   ★ **Close** your eyes; pictures by Georg Hallensleben.
Foster Bks. 2002 un il $16
Grades: PreK K 1   E
   1. Sleep -- Fiction 2. Dreams -- Fiction 3. Tigers
-- Fiction
   ISBN 0-374-31382-2
                   LC 99-46430
   A mother tiger entices her child to sleep by telling of all
that can been seen with one's eyes closed
   "Banks' language will delight young children with its
delicious rhythms, patterned sounds, and the mystery in the
poetic imagery. . . . Hallensleben's thick, expressive brush
strokes occasionally blur shapes and details, but the vividly

colored dreamscapes . . . will capture young imaginations
and reassure children who . . . harbor secret fears of falling
asleep." Booklist

   Fox; pictures by Georg Hallensleben. Farrar, Straus and
Giroux 2007 un il $16
Grades: PreK K 1 2   E
   1. Foxes -- Fiction
   ISBN 0-374-39967-0; 978-0-374-39967-2
                   LC 2005-47701
   A baby fox anticipates the time when he can go out
alone, but first his parents must teach him the ways of
the wilderness.
   "Hallensleben handles outdoor scenes with finesse,
and his signature scuffed layers of brushwork mesh with
Banks's evocative prose." Publ Wkly

   ★ **Max's** words; pictures by Boris Kulikov. Farrar,
Straus and Giroux 2006 un il $16
Grades: PreK K 1 2   E
   1. Storytelling -- Fiction 2. English language -- Fiction
   3. Collectors and collecting -- Fiction
   ISBN 978-0-374-39949-8; 0-374-39949-2
   When Max cuts out words from magazines and newspapers, collecting them the way his brothers collect stamps and
coins, they all learn about words, sentences, and storytelling
   "Imaginative, softly colored illustrations reveal the gathered words scattered all over the pages. . . . This tale pays
homage to the written word and may get children thinking
about cutting and pasting their own stories or creating concrete poetry." SLJ
   Other titles about Max are:
   Max's dragon (2008)
   Max's castle (2011)

   Monkeys and dog days; pictures by Tomek Bogacki.
Farrar, Straus and Giroux 2008 48p il $14.95
Grades: 1 2 3   E
   1. Dogs -- Fiction 2. Pets -- Fiction 3. Brothers --
Fiction 4. Chimpanzees -- Fiction
   ISBN 0-374-35029-9; 978-0-374-35029-1
                   LC 2007060726
   When Max and Pete get a new dog, they learn that taking
care of a pet is not as easy as they thought.
   "The story, divided into four chapters, includes a sprin-
kling of fun facts about dogs and emphasizes important les-
sons about responsibility, loyalty, and cooperation. Muted
pastel illustrations show the brothers and their new pet." SLJ

   Monkeys and the universe; pictures by Tomek Bogacki. Farrar, Straus & Giroux 2009 48p il (Monkey
reader) $14.95
Grades: K 1 2   E
   1. Monkeys -- Fiction 2. Brothers -- Fiction 3.
Astronomy -- Fiction
   ISBN 978-0-374-35028-4; 0-374-35028-0
                   LC 2006048401
   Max and his older brother Pete learn about stars,
planets, and galaxies when their father takes them to an
astronomical observatory.
   "Bogacki's illustrations, with soft colors and blurry
lines, convey gentle feelings even amidst brotherly discord.

Banks does a fine job combining facts with story." Horn Book Guide

Another title about Max and Pete is:
Monkeys and dog days (2008)

That's Papa's way; pictures by Lauren Castillo. Farrar, Straus and Giroux 2009 un il $16.95
Grades: PreK K 1   E
1. Fishing -- Fiction 2. Father-daughter relationship -- Fiction
ISBN 978-0-374-37445-7; 0-374-37445-7
LC 2007045475
When a father and daughter go fishing together, each does certain things his own way, and both have a wonderful day.

"The illustrations in pastel and ink are perfect for conveying the sense of calm that the story requires. The full-bleed spreads show the expanse of the water and the pines, and the depiction of the wildlife is just detailed enough to be naturalistic." SLJ

This baby; pictures by Gabi Swiatkowska. Farrar, Straus and Giroux 2010 il $16.99
Grades: PreK K 1 2   E
1. Infants -- Fiction 2. Siblings -- Fiction
ISBN 978-0-374-37514-0; 0-374-37514-3
LC 2009009299
While waiting for it to be born, a young child wonders what its new sibling will be like.

"Swiatkowska . . . pivots easily between the real and the magical . . . [and] Banks . . . acknowledges the gravity of children's thoughts and the depth of their love; it's a quiet, idiosyncratic celebration of new life." Publ Wkly

What's coming for Christmas? pictures by Georg Hallensleben. Farrar, Straus and Giroux 2009 un il $15.99
Grades: PreK K 1   E
1. Christmas -- Fiction 2. Domestic animals -- Fiction
3. Christmas stories -- Juvenile literature
ISBN 978-0-374-39948-1; 0-374-39948-4
LC 2008-20753
While a farm family bustles about, preparing for the arrival of Christmas, they do not notice the great anticipation spreading among the animals, who know that something very special is on its way.

"The muted colors and quality of Hallensleben's illustrations create a dreamlike feeling, matched by the quiet, lyrical text, with its simple, repeated refrains that create a mounting sense of mysterious expectation." Kirkus

The **bear** in the book; Kate Banks; pictures by Georg Hallensleben. Frances Foster Books 2012 36 p. $16.99
Grades: PreK K 1 2   E
1. Bears -- Juvenile Fiction 2. Bedtime -- Juvenile fiction 3. Hibernation -- Juvenile fiction 4. Bears -- Fiction 5. Bedtime -- Fiction 6. Reading -- Fiction 7. Hibernation -- Fiction
ISBN 0374305919; 9780374305918
LC 2011036691
In this children's book by Kate Banks, illustrated by Georg Hallensleben, "it's time for bed, and a little boy chooses his favorite book for his mother to read to him. The bear in the book is preparing for his own deep slumber, hibernating through the winter while humans and other animals explore the snowy landscape around him. Just when the bear wakes up to greet the spring, the boy drifts off to sleep. . . . This bedtime read . . . will carry young readers through the seasons." (Publisher's note)

The **cat** who walked across France; pictures by Georg Hallensleben. Farrar, Straus and Giroux 2004 un il $16
Grades: PreK K 1 2   E
1. Cats -- Fiction
ISBN 0-374-39968-9
LC 2002-25091
After his owner dies, a cat wanders across the countryside of France, unable to forget the home he had in the stone house by the edge of the sea

"Banks uses simple, lovely words to tell the elemental story of an outcast's journey home. . . . The paintings are exquisite . . . but what kids will like best is the cat's adventure and the loving welcome he receives." Booklist

The **eraserheads**; pictures by Boris Kulikov. Farrar, Straus and Giroux 2010 un il $16.99
Grades: PreK K 1 2   E
1. Adventure fiction 2. Drawing -- Fiction
ISBN 978-0-374-39920-7; 0-374-39920-4
LC 2008024144
Three eraserheads that live with a boy in the land of pencils, paper, rulers, numbers, letters, and drawings become trapped in one of his pictures while trying to correct mistakes

"Kulikov combines loving attention to detail . . . with beguiling portraits of the erasers in various attitudes of dismay and distress. In the story's dueling realities, the 'real life' sections of the spreads feature three-dimensional figures, while the boy's drawings are done in gawky crayon." Publ Wkly

★ The **night** worker; pictures by Georg Hallensleben. Farrar, Straus & Giroux 2000 un il $16
Grades: PreK K 1 2   E
1. Work 2. Night
ISBN 0-374-35520-7
LC 99-27595
Alex wants to be a "night worker" like his father who goes to work at a construction site after Alex goes to bed

"Banks' elegant, simple words and poetic images and rhythms evoke the book's exciting activity and the secure comfort Alex feels with his father. With thick brush strokes and deep, satisfying primary and earth colors, Hallensleben's paintings extend the story's balance of exhilarating intensity and reassuring calm." Booklist

Bansch, Helga
Brava, mimi! NorthSouth 2010 un il $16.95
Grades: PreK K 1 2   E
1. Mice -- Fiction 2. Acting -- Fiction 3. Dancers -- Fiction 4. Singing -- Fiction 5. Theater -- Fiction
ISBN 978-0-7358-2322-8; 0-7358-2322-7
"Mimi the mouse wants to be on stage, but she doesn't think she is talented or beautiful enough. As she seeks advice and lessons from friends, she prepares herself for an audition. . . . The scale of the illustrations portray the size of Mimi in comparison to her environment. Budding ballerinas will recognize the tutus on the cover; this is sure to

delight all who love to read about performing in theater."
Libr Media Connect

I want a dog! North-South 2009 un il $16.95
Grades: K 1 2   E
1. Dogs -- Fiction
ISBN 978-0-7358-2255-9; 0-7358-2255-7

"A dog is all young Lisa yearns for, but whether whee-
dles or tantrums, the parental answer is the same: 'Our apartment is still too small for a dog.' Finally, the clever girl puts
up signs in the park asking for a dog to borrow, whereupon
Mr. Lewis shows up at her door with sausagy hound Rollo.
. . . Bausch writes with a dry humor even as the text effectively conveys Lisa's longing, and the solution is both a
reasonable and creative one." Bull Cent Child Books

Odd bird out; translated from the German by Monika
Smith. Gecko Press 2011 il $17.95
Grades: K 1 2   E
1. Ravens -- Fiction
ISBN 978-1-8774-6708-0; 1-8774-6708-1

Robert is different from all other ravens. He is a happy
bird. But when he laughs and tells jokes, the other birds
don't like it at all. Nor do they like his colorful clothes and
they hold their ears when he tries to sing.

"The conversational text is paired with paintings that
perfectly capture the raven's nature. Who knew birds could
have so many facial expressions and disapproving postures?
In his wildly colored outfits and high-heeled shoes, Robert
shines amid the status quo." SLJ

Banyai, Istvan

The **other** side. Chronicle Books 2005 un il $15.95
Grades: K 1 2 3   E
1. Stories without words
ISBN 0-8118-4608-3

LC 2004-63448

"This is a challenging book, one that allows for creative
speculation. The graphite-rendered artwork is quirky as well
as infinitely interesting." SLJ

Barasch, Lynne

First come the zebra. Lee & Low Books 2009 un il
$18.95 E
1. Masai (African people) -- Fiction 2. Kikuyu (African
people) -- Fiction
ISBN 978-1-60060-365-5; 1-60060-365-3

LC 2008053717

When two young Kenyan boys, one Maasai and one Kikuyu, first meet, they are hostile toward each other based
on traditional rivalries, but after they suddenly have to work
together to save a baby in danger, the boys begin to discover
what they have in common

"Heartfelt storytelling and strong research combine to
offer a universal message with a unique setting. The clear,
light-filled illustrations are expressive and create a sense
of place. A lovely, hopeful story that manages to convey its
message with minimal didacticism." SLJ

Includes bibliographical references

Barclay, Jane

Proud as a peacock, brave as a lion; illustrated by Renné Benoit. Tundra Books 2009 un il $18.95

Grades: PreK K 1 2   E
1. Memory -- Fiction 2. Veterans -- Fiction 3.
Grandfathers -- Fiction 4. World War, 1939-1945 --
Fiction
ISBN 978-0-88776-951-1; 0-88776-951-9

"A small boy has fun with his grandfather as they page
through an old photo album, and Poppa tells how, at age 17,
he lied about his age so that he could join the army. Small
photos in sepia shades evoke the past. . . . Opposite the wartime photos, large, bright, unframed pictures in watercolor
and gouache show the boy and Poppa in the present, talking
about the soldier's feelings—proud as a peacock, pretending
to be brave as a lion—and the lively animal images in the
words are also part of the pictures. . . . The blend of grim
reality, heroic battle, and playful fantasy will speak to kids."
Booklist

Bardhan-Quallen, Sudipta

Chicks run wild; [by] Sudipta Bardhan; illustrated by
Ward Jenkins. Simon & Schuster Books for Young Readers
2011 un il
Grades: PreK K 1   E
1. Stories in rhyme 2. Bedtime -- Fiction 3. Chickens
-- Fiction 4. Mother-child relationship -- Fiction
ISBN 1-4424-0673-9; 978-1-4424-0673-5

When her little chicks refuse to settle down for the night,
Mama decides to surprise them with an unusual request.

"The pencil and digitally painted illustrations carry the
folksy tale in an able fashion. An entertaining selection for
bedtime." SLJ

Hampire! illustrated by Howard Fine. Balzer & Bray
2011 un il $16.99
Grades: PreK K   E
1. Stories in rhyme 2. Vampires -- Fiction 3. Domestic
animals -- Fiction
ISBN 978-0-06-114239-0; 0-06-114239-5

LC 2009011750

Duck cannot sleep because he is hungry, but while he is
preparing a snack the Hampire, who roams the barnyard at
night sinking his fangs into food, is creeping near.

"The creepy cadence of the rhyme scheme will take a
few practice runs before sharing it in storytime. Fine is a
master of painted porcine grins. . . . A deliciously macabre
choice for a not-too-spooky classroom read-aloud." SLJ

The **hog** prince; illustrated by Jason Wolff. Dutton
Children's Books 2009 un il $16.99
Grades: K 1 2   E
1. Fairy tales 2. Pigs -- Fiction
ISBN 978-0-525-47900-0; 0-525-47900-7

LC 2008-13888

On the advice of a mixed-up fairy, Eldon the hog tries to
achieve his princely ambitions by kissing the perfect mate.

"The large acrylic illustrations are perfect for the story.
The animal faces are expressive and the backgrounds are
lush. This is a great read-aloud that cheerfully fractures
many fairy tales all at once." SLJ

Bardoe, Cheryl

The **ugly** dinosaur; a prehistoric tale. illustrated by
Doug Kennedy. Abrams Books for Young Readers 2011
un il $16.95

Grades: PreK K 1   E
>1. Ducks -- Fiction 2. Dinosaurs -- Fiction
>ISBN 978-0-8109-9739-4; 0-8109-9739-8
>
>LC 2010021624

In this take on "The Ugly Duckling," a tyrannosaurus rex is hatched in a nest of ducklings. Includes facts about dinosaurs.

"Kennedy's cartoonish watercolors nicely balance the ugly 'duckling's' good intentions with his slightly threatening appearance and clumsiness, helping readers empathize with him. . . . A sure winner for those dino-hungry readers." Kirkus

Includes bibliographical references

Barner, Bob
> ★ **Bug** safari. Holiday House 2004 un il $16.95
Grades: PreK K 1 2   E
>1. Insects 2. Ants -- Fiction 3. Insects -- Fiction 4. Insects -- Juvenile literature
>ISBN 0-8234-1707-7
>
>LC 2003-56619

"The bright, cut-paper collages will appeal to the youngest bug lovers, but the funny, dramatically told story is tailored to a more sophisticated young entomologist." Booklist

Barnett, Mac
Billy Twitters and his big blue whale problem; Mac Barnett, author; Adam Rex, illustrator. Disney/Hyperion Books 2009 un il $16.99
Grades: PreK K 1 2   E
>1. School stories 2. Whales -- Fiction 3. Family life -- Fiction
>ISBN 978-0-7868-4958-1; 0-7868-4958-4
>
>LC 2009-11203

When Billy Twitters' mother follows through on her threat to buy him a blue whale if he refuses to obey, he finds himself the owner of an enormous pet that he must take with him everywhere, which does not make him popular at school.

"Young readers will likely enjoy the ridiculous premise, and the many whale facts worked seamlessly into the tale." SLJ

> ★ **Extra** yarn; written by Mac Barnett; illustrated by Jon Klassen. Balzer & Bray 2012 il $16.99
Grades: PreK K 1 2   E
>1. Yarn -- Fiction 2. Magic -- Fiction 3. Knitting -- Fiction
>ISBN 978-0-06-195338-5; 0-06-195338-5
>
>LC 2010015945

Caldecott Honor Book (2013)

With a supply of yarn that never runs out, Annabelle knits for everyone and everything in town until an evil archduke decides he wants the yarn for himself.

"Klassen . . . uses inks, gouache and colorized scans of a sweater to create a stylized, linear design of dark geometric shapes against a white background. . . . Barnett . . . maintains a folkloric narrative that results in a traditional story arc complete with repetition, drama and a satisfying conclusion. A quiet story of sharing with no strings attached." Kirkus

Guess again! illustrated by Adam Rex. Simon & Schuster Books for Young Readers 2009 un il $16.99

Grades: 1 2 3 4   E
>1. Stories in rhyme 2. Picture puzzles -- Juvenile literature
>ISBN 978-1-4169-5566-5; 1-4169-5566-6
>
>LC 2008-12882

"A rhymed text joins with hinting illustrations to encourage readers to fill in the last word of the verse. A page turn, however, unveils an answer that's an absurd breach of expectation. . . . The confounding of expectations is pleasingly goofy. . . . Rex partners the rhyme with robust and solid gouache scenes that are comedic in their own right. . . . This would be particularly useful as a quick pick for reluctant readers, who'll warm to the combination of corniness and sophistication in the satirically unguessable guessing game." Bull Cent Child Books

Mustache! illustrations by Kevin Cornell. Disney/Hyperion Books 2011 un il $16.99
Grades: 1 2 3   E
>1. Kings and rulers -- Fiction 2. Personal appearance -- Fiction
>ISBN 978-1-4231-1671-4; 1-4231-1671-2
>
>LC 2011008462

When extremely good-looking King Duncan builds more and more tributes to his handsome face, neglecting kingdom projects and repairs, his loyal subjects find a mustachioed solution.

"The large cartoon illustrations, mostly spreads, are framed in gold with a peacock motif along the bottom. The brief, humorous text appears in scrolls superimposed on the paintings. . . . This royal romp of a story contains some subtle messages behind the hilarity." SLJ

Oh no! Not again! (or how I built a time machine to save history) (or at least my history grade) written by Mac Barnett; illustrated by Dan Santat. Disney-Hyperion 2012 40 p. col. ill. $17.99
Grades: K 1 2 3   E
>1. Belgium -- Fiction 2. Time travel -- Fiction 3. Picture books for children 4. Humorous stories 5. Cave dwellers -- Fiction 6. Cave paintings -- Fiction
>ISBN 1423149122; 9781423149125
>
>LC 2011011111

In this book, part of the "Oh No!" series "[Mac] Barnett's overachiever has a new dilemma: Her history test is returned with one point off for an incorrect answer. Noting that 'Belgium' is not the country where the oldest prehistoric cave paintings exist . . . she builds a time machine to alter history. After a few glitches . . . she finds her Belgian cavemen. . . . The duo gives the transporter a spin while the frustrated scholar decorates the cave herself." (Kirkus Reviews)

> ★ **Oh** no!, or, How my science project destroyed the world; written by Mac Barnett; illustrated by Dan Santat. Disney Hyperion Books 2010 un il $16.99
Grades: K 1 2   E
>1. Robots -- Fiction 2. Science projects -- Fiction
>ISBN 978-1-4231-2312-5; 1-4231-2312-3
>
>LC 2010004516

After winning the science fair with the giant robot she has built, a little girl realizes that there is a major problem.

"Santat's brilliantly hued digital illustrations are the perfect foil for Barnett's almost-wordless tale of a science project gone awry. . . . . Comic-book, picture-book and movie styles come together in a well-designed package that includes a movie poster on the reverse side of the jacket, an old-time computation book as the inside cover and detailed scientific drawings on the endpapers. . . . A must-have." Kirkus

Barrett, Judi

Cloudy with a chance of meatballs; written by Judi Barrett and drawn by Ron Barrett. Aladdin Paperbacks 1982 un il pa $6.99

Grades: PreK K 1 2   **E**

     1. Food -- Fiction 2. Weather -- Fiction

     ISBN 0-689-70749-5

                      LC 87-29643

     First published 1978

     Life is delicious in the town of Chewandswallow where it rains soup and juice, snows mashed potatoes, and blows storms of hamburgers—until the weather takes a turn for the worse.

     ★ **Never** take a shark to the dentist and other things not to do; [by] Judi Barrett; illustrated by John Nickle. Atheneum Books for Young Readers 2007 un il $16.99

Grades: PreK K 1 2   **E**

     1. Animals -- Fiction

     ISBN 978-1-4169-0724-4; 1-4169-0724-6

                     LC 2006000153

     A list of things one should not do with various animals, such as "hold hands with a lobster".

     "Nickle, working in hyper-detailed acrylics, enhances the comical phrases with surreal imagery. . . . Kids will revel in the absurd humor." Publ Wkly

     Santa from Cincinnati; Judi Barrett; illustrated by Kevin Hawks. Atheneum Books for Young Readers 2012 p. cm.

Grades: K 1 2 3   **E**

     1. Christmas -- Juvenile fiction 2. Santa Claus -- Juvenile fiction 3. Humorous fiction -- Juvenile fiction 4. Christmas -- Fiction 5. Santa Claus -- Fiction

     ISBN 9781442429932; 9781442429949

                     LC 2011050810

     This children's book, by Judi Barrett, illustrated by Kevin Hawkes, tells the story of Santa Claus' childhood. "His first words were 'ho ho ho!' By five he was wearing a fake beard and mustache, and could rarely be found without his favorite stuffed reindeer. . . . Despite this, his parents went to great lengths to keep the normalcy in his life. . . . But there was no stopping Santa from being Santa, and one winter, he began to make his lists." (Publisher's note)

Barrett, Mary Brigid

Shoebox Sam; illustrated by Frank Morrison. Zonderkidz 2011 un il $15.99

Grades: K 1 2   **E**

     1. Shoes -- Fiction 2. Christian life -- Fiction 3. Homeless persons -- Fiction

     ISBN 978-0-310-71549-8; 0-310-71549-0

     On Saturdays, Delia and Jesse help Shoebox Sam, who teaches them about charity and love by not only repairing shoes for paying customers, but also giving poor and homeless people the dignity—and footwear—they need.

"Even in quieter poses, Morrison's bright-eyed, rubber-limbed figures look like they are dancing, and they perfectly reflect the lively sounds and rhythms of Barrett's language." Booklist

Barretta, Gene

Timeless Thomas; how Thomas Edison changed our lives. Gene Barretta. Henry Holt 2012 37 p.

Grades: 2 3 4   **E**

     1. Inventions -- History 2. Inventions -- Juvenile literature 3. Inventions -- History -- Juvenile literature

     ISBN 0805091084; 9780805091083

                     LC 2011034057

     In this children's book, by Gene Barretta, the life and inventions of Thomas Edison are described. "Edison is most famous for inventing the incandescent lightbulb, but at his landmark laboratories in Menlo Park & West Orange, New Jersey, he also developed many other staples of modern technology. Despite many failures, Edison persevered. And good for that, because it would be very difficult to go through a day without using one of his life-changing inventions." (Publisher's note)

     Includes bibliographical references

     Zoola Palooza; a book of homographs. Henry Holt 2011 un il $16.99

Grades: K 1 2   **E**

     1. Animals -- Fiction 2. Concerts -- Fiction 3. Musicians -- Fiction 4. English language -- Homonyms

     ISBN 0-8050-9107-6; 978-0-8050-9107-6

                     LC 2010025833

     Playing a variety of musical instruments, an all-animal touring concert group introduces words that are spelled the same but sound differently and have different meanings, such as tear (to cry) and tear (to rip).

     "While teachers are sure to reach for this entertaining resource again and again, the humor, illustrations, wordplay and story are strong enough that casual readers will pick this up, chuckle and even . . . learn." Kirkus

Barron, T. A.

Ghost hands; a story inspired by Patagonia's Cave of the Hands. illustrated by William Low. Philomel Books 2011 un il $18.99

Grades: PreK K 1   **E**

     1. Courage -- Fiction 2. Native Americans -- Fiction 3. Cave drawings and paintings -- Fiction

     ISBN 978-0-399-25083-5; 0-399-25083-2

                     LC 2010010648

     Auki, a young member of the Tehuelche tribe in Patagonia, wants to prove himself as a hunter but when he sets out on his own to face the puma, he stumbles upon a sacred cave and its guardian.

     "As in Barron and Low's previous collaboration . . . tightly connected visuals and text provoke curiosity and awe about a phenomenon at once mysterious and accessible." Kirkus

Barry, Frances

Duckie's ducklings; a one-to-ten counting book. Candlewick 2005 un il $7.99

Grades: PreK K   **E**

     1. Counting 2. Ducks -- Fiction

     ISBN 0-7636-2514-0

Duckie is ready to take the family for a swim. But where are her ducklings? Turn the shaped pages to find out!

"Barry's uncluttered paper collages are excellent. The elemental shapes and vivid, saturated colors nicely fit the book's handsome design." Booklist

Bartlett, T. C.

Tuba lessons; illustrated by Monique Felix. Creative Editions 2009 un il $25.65

Grades: PreK K 1   E

1. Stories without words 2. Animals -- Fiction 3. Musical instruments -- Fiction

ISBN 978-1-56846-209-7; 1-56846-209-3

LC 2009-3834

First published 1997 by Harcourt, Brace and Company

While walking through the woods on his way to his tuba lesson, a boy becomes sidetracked by all the animals that want to hear him play.

"This text is not only for storytimes, but can be used as a catalyst to get young readers and writers to create their own words to enhance the imaginative, playful illustrations. Friendship, music and the journey are the themes in this picture tale." Libr Media Connect

Bartoletti, Susan Campbell

★ **Naamah** and the ark at night. Candlewick Press 2011 un il $16.99

Grades: PreK K 1 2   E

1. Lullabies 2. Stories in rhyme 3. Children's poetry 4. Night -- Fiction 5. Animals -- Fiction 6. Noah's ark -- Fiction 7. Noah's ark -- Juvenile literature

ISBN 978-0-7636-4242-6; 0-7636-4242-8

LC 2010040398

"Bartoletti shapes his verse form into a gentle litany . . . centerd on Naamah's lulling song. . . . Meade's watercolor collages are a fine complement. . . . A lovely lullaby, in a beautiful, masterfully integrated book." Horn Book

Barton, Byron

★ **Dinosaurs,** dinosaurs. Crowell 1989 un il $16.99; lib bdg $17.89; pa $6.99; bd bk $7.99

Grades: PreK K   E

1. Dinosaurs 2. Dinosaurs -- Fiction

ISBN 0-694-00269-0; 0-690-04768-1 lib bdg; 0-06-443298-X pa; 0-694-400625-4 bd bk

LC 88-22938

This book examines the many different kinds of dinosaurs, big and small, those with spikes and those with long, sharp teeth

"Barton conveys the primordial sense of excitement that draws children to these beasts. . . . The endpapers identify the creatures by scientific name and pronunciation. Barton wisely keeps his text simple, describing dinosaurs only by size and physical features." SLJ

★ **My** car. Greenwillow Bks. 2001 un il $14.95; pa $6.99; bd bk $7.99

Grades: PreK K   E

1. Automobiles 2. Automobiles -- Fiction

ISBN 0-06-029624-0; 0-06-029625-9 lib bdg; 0-06-058940-X pa; 0-06-056045-2 bd bk

LC 00-50334

Sam describes in loving detail his car and how he drives it

"The chunky blocks of color and minimalist text will withstand countless readings." Publ Wkly

Barton, Chris

★ **Shark** vs. train; by Chris Barton & [illustrated by] Tom Lichtenheld. Little, Brown 2010 un il $16.99

Grades: PreK K 1   E

1. Sharks -- Fiction 2. Railroads -- Fiction

ISBN 978-0-316-00762-7; 0-316-00762-5

LC 2009-17961

A shark and a train compete in a series of contests on a seesaw, in hot air balloons, bowling, shooting baskets, playing hide-and-seek, and more.

"This is a genius concept. . . . Lichtenheld's . . . watercolor cartoons have a fluidity and goofy intensity that recalls Mad magazine, while Barton . . . gives the characters snappy dialogue throughout." Publ Wkly

Bartone, Elisa

★ **Peppe** the lamplighter; illustrations by Ted Lewin. Lothrop, Lee & Shepard Bks. 1993 un il $17.99; pa $6.99

Grades: K 1 2 3   E

1. Italian Americans -- Fiction

ISBN 0-688-10268-9; 0-688-15469-7 pa

LC 92-1397

A Caldecott Medal honor book, 1994

Peppe's father is upset when he learns that Peppe has taken a job lighting the gas street lamps in his New York City neighborhood

"Peppe's quiet quest for familial respect and pleasure in his work is touching and rhythmically written. The early-American city scenes are dark but have a nice period luminescence in the myriad street and table lamps, and the earth-toned watercolors lend the bustling streets and interiors of Little Italy an air both somber and lively." Bull Cent Child Books

Bartram, Simon

Bob's best ever friend. Templar Books 2009 un il $16.99

Grades: K 1 2   E

1. Dogs -- Fiction 2. Astronauts -- Fiction 3. Friendship -- Fiction

ISBN 978-0-7636-4425-3; 0-7636-4425-0

"Bob, an astronaut who travels daily from Earth to the Moon to entertain tourists, is lonely: there are no visitors this Tuesday and his friends have gone off to Pluto. The next day, he begins to look for a 'best-ever friend' and decides that it could be a pet. One day he sees something amazing pop out of a crater: a dog. Bartram's detailed acrylics give readers comic relief while Bob is on his quest. . . . The artwork is reminiscent of books from the 1950s and is done in electric blues, yellows, and reds." SLJ

Another title about Bob is:

Man on the moon (2002)

Baruzzi, Agnese

The **true** story of Little Red Riding Hood; [by] Agnese Baruzzi and Sandro Natalini. Templar Books 2009 un il $14.99

Grades: K 1 2 3   E

1. Fairy tales 2. Pop-up books

ISBN 978-0-7636-4427-7

"In this fractured fairy tale, the wolf asks for help rehabilitating his reputation. Little Red Riding Hood's advice (become a vegetarian) works—for a while. The book overflows with lift-the-flaps; envelopes with tiny letters inside and a fabric shower curtain and apron are also included. The boldly colored naive-style paintings are enhanced by collage elements, including rickrack borders." Horn Book Guide

Base, Graeme

★ The **Jewel** Fish of Karnak. Abrams Books for Young Readers 2011 un il

Grades: K 1 2 3   E

1. Magic -- Fiction 2. Thieves -- Fiction 3. Kings and rulers -- Fiction

ISBN 1-4197-0086-3; 978-1-4197-0086-6

LC 2010050080

Two thieves, caught stealing from an Egyptian market, are brought before the Cat Pharaoh, who agrees to pardon them if they bring back a treasure that was stolen from her, without taking anything else and without getting the precious Jewel Fish wet.

Base "doesn't disappoint his sleuthing fans, providing decodable hieroglyphic messages on painted stone tablets across the bottom of each spread. This tale packs in plenty of puzzle solving and Egyptology amid the boldly animated scenes; the illustrations' exquisite details—right down to the comical facial expressions of the bumbling thieves—tell much of the story." Publ Wkly

Uno's garden. Abrams Books for Young Readers 2006 un il $19.95

Grades: 2 3 4   E

1. Counting 2. Nature -- Fiction 3. Pollution -- Fiction

ISBN 978-0-8109-5473-1; 0-8109-5473-7

LC 2006-13208

Uno builds a home and garden in the magnificent forest among the playful puddlebuts and feathered frinklepods, but as the place becomes more and more popular, it is overtaken by tourists and buildings until the forest and animals seem to disappear altogether.

"Providing plenty of opportunity for seek-and-find fun, the vibrant art also visually reinforces the progressive change. . . . This is both a visual treasure trove and a cautionary yet hopeful tale of environmental awareness and responsibility." Booklist

The **legend** of the Golden Snail. Abrams Books for Young Readers 2010 un il $19.95

Grades: PreK K 1 2   E

1. Adventure fiction 2. Ships -- Fiction 3. Snails -- Fiction 4. Imagination -- Fiction 5. Seafaring life -- Fiction

ISBN 978-0-8109-8965-8; 0-8109-8965-4

LC 2010002394

Wilbur loves the legend of the Golden Snail, an enchanted galleon, and vows to become its next master.

"A fantastical nautical adventure unwinds seamlessly in Base's . . . sumptuous, large-format picture book. . . . Base's art steers the journey, alternating between action scenes and spectacular seascapes. . . . This is a beguiling excursion for adventurers of any age." Publ Wkly

Basher, Simon

★ **ABC** Kids. Kingfisher Books 2011 un il $17.99

Grades: PreK K   E

1. Alphabet

ISBN 978-0-7534-6495-3; 0-7534-6495-0

"This ABC book provides a stylish introduction to the alphabet while building vocabularies. [Basher's] chunky cartoon illustrations are front and center, joined by heavily alliterative sentences. . . . Full-bleed pastel backdrops give the book the feel of a cheerily illustrated sheaf of construction paper; with inventive vocab on left-hand pages opposite pages focusing on one stand-alone image, . . . the book is appropriate for both beginning and developing readers. Smart fun." Publ Wkly

Go! go! Bobo: colors. Kingfisher 2011 un il bd bk $6.99

Grades: PreK   E

1. Color 2. Board books for children

ISBN 978-0-7534-6493-9; 0-7534-6493-4

Bouncy Bobo can't sit still. He just has to bounce his way across the pages of this book, painting everything he sees. From yellow ducks, to blue butterflies, orange carrots, pink piggies, red roses, and green apples.

"A great title in encourage toddlers' interactive play. . . . Kids will want to move from the book to the real world and name the colors all around them." Booklist

Bass, L. G.

Boom boom go away! by Laura Geringer; illustrated by Bagram Ibatoulline. Atheneum 2010 un il $15.99

Grades: PreK K 1   E

1. Toys -- Fiction 2. Music -- Fiction 3. Bedtime -- Fiction

ISBN 978-0-689-85093-6; 0-689-85093-X

"Each time a parent tells a boy to go to bed, the toys in his room delay the process by playing their instruments and saying they can't be disturbed. . . . The rhythmical text has an appealing cadence and a catchy refrain. Ibatoulline's watercolor and acrylic-gouache spreads of the child's room are wonderfully designed." SLJ

Bastedo, Jamie

Free as the wind; saving the horses of Sable Island. illustrated by Susan Tooke. Red Deer Press 2007 32p il (Northern lights books for children) hardcover o.p. pa $10.95

Grades: K 1 2   E

1. Horses -- Fiction 2. Islands -- Fiction

ISBN 978-0-88995-350-5; 0-88995-350-3; 978-0-88995-446-5 pa; 0-88995-446-1 pa

In the 1960s, the wild horses of Sable Island in Nova Scotia were to be sold and auctioned off, many of them to be slaughtered for dog meat. School children from across Canada wrote to the Prime Minister pleading with him to have the horses returned and to save them from certain death. This fictional account follows young Lucas Beauregard, son of the retiring superintendent of Sable Island, as he befriends and then plots to save Gem, one of the horses.

"The writing style of this well-told story draws readers into the urgency of the horses' situation. The plot develops quickly. Tooke's realistic, painterly artwork follows the story line well and places readers on the island." SLJ

Bastianich, Lidia

Nonna's birthday surprise; Lidia Bastianich. Running Press Kids 2013 60 p. (hardcover) $16.95

Grades: K 1 2 3   E

1. Birthdays -- Juvenile fiction 2. Farm life -- Juvenile fiction

ISBN 0762446552; 9780762446551

LC 2012944237

In this children's story, by Lidia Bastianich, illustrated by Renée Graef, "It's Nonna Mima's birthday, and Nonna Lidia and her grandkids are determined to throw her a surprise feast! While planning the evening's menu, Nonna Lidia shares her memories of growing up on the farm during each season of the year, gardening her own fruits and vegetables, and being surrounded by animals of all kinds." (Publisher's note)

Bataille, Marion

10. Roaring Brook Press 2011 un il $14.99

Grades: 1 2 3 4 5   E

1. Numbers 2. Pop-up books

ISBN 978-1-59643-682-4; 1-59643-682-4

"Housed within a shiny red slipcase, this minimalist counting book can be viewed in multiple ways. By turning the pages once from left to right, readers can count from '01' to '10,' the black numerals appearing on the left side of each white spread. By proceeding through the book and unfolding each page twice, however, the numbers transform—the top of the '2' swivels, losing its base to become a '9,' for example—so readers can count down to '01.' . . . the sleek construction should appeal to pop-up fans of any age." Publ Wkly

★ **ABC3D**. Roaring Brook Press 2008 un il $19.95

Grades: 1 2 3 4 5   E

1. Alphabet 2. Toy and movable books 3. Pop-up books

ISBN 978-1-59643-425-7; 1-59643-425-2

LC 2008-08933

"From the lenticular cover to the jazzy use of a red, white and black color scheme, this hand-size French alphabet book is as stylish as a pop-up can be. Letters here not only pop up, they move and transform. . . . Many letters are three-dimensional (i.e., the legs of H are hollow paper rectangles), and gain extra glamour from high-contrast backgrounds (white on black; red or black on white). A-plus for drama and innovation." Publ Wkly

Bateman, Teresa

April foolishness; illustrated by Nadine Bernard Westcott. Albert Whitman & Co. 2004 un il $15.95

Grades: PreK K 1 2   E

1. Farm life 2. Grandparents 3. April Fools' Day 4. Stories in rhyme 5. Farm life -- Fiction 6. April Fools' Day -- Fiction

ISBN 0-8075-0404-1

LC 2004-825

"Bateman's verse prances along in a pleasing way, never sounding a false note or tripping over its metric feet. Bright with colorful washes, Westcott's ink drawings illustrate the action with equal lightness and grace. . . . Zany and inventive, the artwork amplifies the story's humor." Booklist

Harp o' gold; illustrated by Jill Weber. Holiday House 2001 un il $16.95

Grades: K 1 2 3   E

1. Fairy tales 2. Harp -- Fiction 3. Musicians -- Fiction

ISBN 0-8234-1523-6

LC 99-18821

A poor musician who dreams of riches and fame trades his beloved but worn harp for one made of gold, but when he becomes famous he finds that something is missing "Acrylic paintings rendered in a blue-green palette with flat tilty perspectives complement this bittersweet cautionary tale set in an Irish-looking countryside." Horn Book Guide

★ **Keeper** of soles; illustrated by Yayo. Holiday House 2006 un il $16.95

Grades: K 1 2 3   E

1. Death -- Fiction 2. Shoes -- Fiction 3. Shoemakers -- Fiction

ISBN 0-8234-1734-4

LC 2004-52297

When Death comes for a shoemaker's soul, he outwits him by making shoes for him, giving him soles instead of souls.

"Bateman pairs the cadences of a traditional folktale with contemporary humor. The scenes are imbued with suspense without being macabre. Yayo's full-bleed acrylics provide large expanses of rich, layered colors as foils for the smaller, whimsical details." SLJ

Paul Bunyan vs. Hals Halson; the giant lumberjack challenge! illustrated by C.B. Canga. Albert Whitman 2011 un il $16.99

Grades: PreK K 1 2   E

1. Tall tales 2. Bunyan, Paul (Legendary character)

ISBN 978-0-8075-6367-0; 0-8075-6367-6

LC 2010025881

Hals Halson, who is nearly as tall as the legendary Paul Bunyan, strides into a logging camp determined to prove himself the greatest lumberjack in North America, despite Paul's attempts at friendship.

"Bateman's simple, smooth text has fun with the inherently faulty credibility of tall-tale narrators. . . . Canga's slickly textured, digital compositions find the humor in Paul's and Hals' outsize proportions while highlighting their everyday emotions." Booklist

Bates, Janet Costa

Seaside dream; illustrated by Lambert Davis. Lee & Low Books 2010 un il $17.95

Grades: K 1 2   E

1. Gifts -- Fiction 2. Birthdays -- Fiction 3. Grandmothers -- Fiction

ISBN 978-1-60060-347-1; 1-60060-347-5

LC 2009-17049

At a birthday celebration on the beach, Cora gives her grandmother a special gift and encourages her to make a trip back to her home country, Cape Verde.

"This poignant tale of a special relationship between a young girl and her grandmother showcases the joy of gift giving as well as the importance of family connections. . . . Color-drenched illustrations in deep-blue tones effectively evoke the summery coastal setting." Booklist

Battersby, Katherine

Squish Rabbit. Viking 2011 un il $12.99

Grades: PreK K   E

1. Size -- Fiction 2. Rabbits -- Fiction 3. Friendship -- Fiction 4. Loneliness -- Fiction

ISBN 978-0-670-01267-1; 0-670-01267-X

LC 2010042227

A lonely little rabbit wants to make a friend.

"Battersby's expert, ample distribution of white space provides room on each page for readers to luxuriate in her impressive, evocative ink, watercolor and collage illustrations—and to absorb a small rabbit's feelings. Rough papers and textured fabrics add depth, creating an almost tactile reading experience.... Minimal, moving and adorable, little Squish makes a big impression." Kirkus

Battut, Eric

Little Mouse's big secret. Sterling 2011 un il $12.95

Grades: PreK K   E

1. Mice -- Fiction 2. Trees -- Fiction 3. Apples -- Fiction 4. Animals -- Fiction

ISBN 978-1-4027-7462-1; 1-4027-7462-1

LC 2010019689

Little Mouse refuses to reveal his secret despite being questioned by his friends.

"The urge to hoard treats is a common one, and Battut's . . . brisk, spare treatment of the problem has the feel of a classic. . . . Elemental text and artwork effectively convey the lesson about Mouse's best-laid plans, while his obliviousness to the tree's growth provides suspense and satisfaction." Publ Wkly

★ The **fox** and the hen. Boxer 2010 un il $16.95

Grades: PreK K   E

1. Eggs -- Fiction 2. Foxes -- Fiction 3. Domestic animals -- Fiction

ISBN 978-1-907152-02-3; 1-907152-02-4

"Henrietta Hen lays her first egg and innocently trades it to Red Fox for a worm. The other farm animals quickly tell her that she must get her precious egg back and go with her to make the trade. . . . Each time Red Fox refuses and thinks of a new way to eat the egg. . . . Henrietta finds an enormous stone that her friends paint white, and Red Fox eagerly trades her egg for this bigger one. . . . The animals are outlined in thick, black line and dabs of white highlight the vibrant red and orange palette. . . . With great economy, Battut gives each animal an expressive face and moves the story to a satisfying conclusion." SLJ

Bauer, Marion Dane

One brown bunny; text by Marion Dane Bauer; illustrated by Ivan Bates. Orchard Books 2009 32p il $14.99

Grades: PreK K   E

1. Stories in rhyme 2. Play -- Fiction 3. Animals -- Fiction 4. Rabbits -- Fiction 5. Friendship -- Fiction

ISBN 978-0-439-68010-3; 0-439-68010-7

LC 2006102289

"A bright-eyed little bunny looks for playmates to share a sunny day in this engaging, energetic counting rhyme. Coupled with Bates's bright, dynamic illustrations that place a curious, slightly rumpled protagonist in an inviting forest landscape, the text bounces along cheerfully." Kirkus

Thank you for me! illustrated by Kristina Stephenson. Simon & Schuster Books for Young Readers 2010 un il $14.99

Grades: PreK K 1   E

1. Human body -- Fiction

ISBN 978-0-689-85788-1; 0-689-85788-8

LC 2006023872

Rhythmic text enumerates what various body parts can do, including hands to clap and a body to twirl, then expresses thanks for each of those parts—and for the whole.

"Bauer's lilting text matches the jubilant energy in Stephenson's watercolor rainbow palette." SLJ

The **longest** night; illustrated by Ted Lewin. Holiday House 2009 un il $17.95

Grades: K 1 2 3   E

1. Night -- Fiction 2. Winter -- Fiction 3. Animals -- Fiction

ISBN 978-0-8234-2054-4; 0-8234-2054-X

LC 2008022575

One very long night, a crow, a moose, and a fox all claim they can bring back the sun, but the wind knows that only one little creature has what is needed to end the darkness.

"This stunningly crafted tale, written in the language of the storyteller, realistically pictures, in both words and paintings, the phenomenon that is the winter solstice. . . . There is plenty of moonlight in Lewin's watercolor paintings created with just blue, brown, and green." SLJ

Bauer, Marion Dane, 1938-

In like a lion, out like a lamb; illustrated by Emily Arnold McCully. Holiday House 2011 un il $16.95

Grades: PreK K 1 2   E

1. Stories in rhyme 2. Lions -- Fiction 3. Sheep -- Fiction 4. Spring -- Fiction

ISBN 0-8234-2238-0; 978-0-8234-2238-8

LC 2010007892

"In Bauer's capable hands, the age-old simile of March coming in like a lion and going out like a lamb is made quite literal. . . . While the text provides the skeleton, McCully's pen, ink and watercolor illustrations truly bring the old song to life. Her lion is a wonderful cross between a fierce foe . . . and a party pooper. . . . Meanwhile, the lamb is a perfect ball of fluff. . . . A good addition to the spring shelf, it is sure to find its way, roaring and bleating, to classrooms studying similes." Kirkus

Bean, Jonathan

★ At **night.** Farrar, Straus and Giroux 2007 un il $15

Grades: PreK K 1   E

1. Night -- Fiction 2. Sleep -- Fiction 3. City and town life -- Fiction

ISBN 0-374-30446-7; 978-0-374-30446-1

LC 2006-48403

Boston Globe-Horn Book Award: Picture Book (2008)

A sleepless city girl imagines what it would be like to get away from snoring family members and curl up alone with one's thoughts in the cool night air under wide-open skies.

"The artist supplies luminous aerial scenes of the roof garden amid a friendly, well-lit cityscape. . . . The story breathes reassurance and adventure at the same time." Publ Wkly

★ **Building** our house; Jonathan Bean. Farrar, Straus
and Giroux 2013 48 p. (reinforced) $17.99

Grades: 1 2 3   E

1. Houses 2. House construction 3. Picture books for
children 4. Building -- Fiction 5. Dwellings -- Design
and construction -- Fiction

ISBN 0374380236; 9780374380236

                      LC 2007027681

Boston Globe-Horn Book Award: Picture Book (2013).

In this children's picture book, Jonathan Bean tells the
story of his "back-to-the-land parents, who built his childhood home in the 1970s. . . . Frontmatter depicts [the fam-
ily] packing and leaving the city, Ensuing spreads detail
how they live in a trailer on their new property while slowly
building the house: setting the corners of the foundation;
digging out the basement; gathering rocks and using them in
the foundation; measuring, marking and cutting timber for
the frame; and so on." (Kirkus)

"The watercolor-and-ink illustrations invite close examination for narrative details such as these while also providing ample visual information about construction." Kirkus

Beard, Alex

Monkey see monkey draw. Abrams Books for Young
Readers 2010 un il $16.95

Grades: PreK K 1   E

1. Play -- Fiction 2. Monkeys -- Fiction 3. Elephants
-- Fiction

ISBN 978-0-8109-8970-2; 0-8109-8970-0

Elephant leads a troupe of monkeys into a cave they
have been afraid to explore, and after admiring the paintings
found on the walls they make their own art with mud, squabbling over whose painting is best until Elephant explains that
this is not a game to win or lose.

"Bold, imaginative and very comical pen, ink and watercolor illustrations rely on line, color, pattern and thumbprints
to produce surreal, gangly blue monkeys frenetically cavorting and clambering across the pages. . . . Beard aptly conjures the look and feel of prehistoric cave paintings, inspiring readers to create their own. Wild and wonderful." Kirkus

The **jungle** grapevine. Abrams Books for Young Readers 2009 un il $16.95

Grades: K 1 2 3   E

1. Animals -- Fiction 2. Communication -- Fiction

ISBN 978-0-8109-8001-3; 0-8109-8001-0

                      LC 2008046197

When Turtle makes an off-hand remark to Bird at the
watering hole one day, Bird's misunderstanding starts a series of rumors that stirs up the other animals.

"Young children will easily understand the moral of the
story. This book will be constantly circulating, thanks to the
dialogue, storyline, and artwork." Libr Media Connect

Beaty, Andrea

Artist Ted; Andrea Beaty; illustrated by Pascal Lemaitre. Margaret K. McElderry Books 2012 32 p.

Grades: PreK K 1   E

1. Artists -- Fiction 2. Friendship -- Fiction 3. Creative
ability -- Fiction 4. Artists' materials -- Fiction 5.
Imagination -- Juvenile fiction 6. Humorous stories 7.

Schools -- Fiction 8. Imagination -- Fiction

ISBN 9781416953746

                      LC 2010027936

This book is "as much about making friends as about artistic inspiration. . . . The . . . narrative explains how Ted decides to become an artist and recounts his creativity in making his own materials. Meanwhile, . . . illustrations outlined
in thick black . . . show him dismantling curtain ties for the
"paintbrush" and painting on the walls with condiments. At
school, Ted's art isn't always received well. His caricatures
of the principle . . . provoke exactly the expected reaction.
. . . After some misguided attempts to make friends, all is
resolved when the students join forces to create a giant mural
with the message 'Welcome Friends.'" (Booklist)

Doctor Ted; [illustrated by] Pascal Lemaitre. Atheneum Books for Young Readers 2008 32p il $14.99

Grades: PreK K 1   E

1. Bears -- Fiction 2. Physicians -- Fiction 3.
Imagination -- Fiction

ISBN 978-1-4169-2820-1; 1-4169-2820-0

                      LC 2006-03191

After bumping his knee one morning, Ted the bear cub
decides to become a doctor, but he has only one problem—
he has no patients!

This is "a breezy story about pretend play that's laugh-
out-loud funny. . . . The pictures' chunky ink lines and almost neon-like digital colors give every page plenty of
punch." Publ Wkly

Another title about Ted is:

Firefighter Ted (2009)

Firefighter Ted; by Andrea Beaty and [illustrated by]
Pascal Lemaitre. Margaret K. McElderry Books 2009 un
il $15.99

Grades: PreK K 1   E

1. School stories 2. Imagination -- Fiction 3. Fire
fighters -- Fiction

ISBN 978-1-4169-2821-8; 1-4169-2821-9

                      LC 2008-31904

When Ted awakens to the smell of smoke and cannot
find a firefighter, he decides to become one for the day,
much to the dismay of his mother, neighbors, principal,
and classmates.

"Lemaitre's brilliant colors fairly jump off the pages.
Capitalizing on the understated tone, his characters brim
with personality and the scenes tell the real story. Sure to fire
up kids' imaginations while tickling their funny bones at the
same time." Kirkus

When giants come to play; written by Andrea Beaty; illustrated by Kevin Hawkes. Abrams Books for Young Readers 2006 un il $16.95

Grades: PreK K 1 2   E

1. Play -- Fiction 2. Giants -- Fiction

ISBN 0-8109-5759-0

                      LC 2005-32243

"A delightful romp, full of imagination, told in lyrical
prose. . . . Large, full-page illustrations in charcoal pencils
and acrylics depict the oversize, affable playmates and diminutive girl." SLJ

Beaumont, Karen

★ **Baby** danced the polka; pictures by Jennifer Plecas. Dial Books for Young Readers 2004 un il $12.99

Grades: PreK K 1 2   E

    1. Infants -- Fiction

    ISBN 0-8037-2587-6

"What a happy, rollicking baby. And what a rolling, rhythmic text. . . . The sprightly pen-and-watercolor artwork bears a very strong resemblance to the work of Helen Oxenbury." Booklist

Doggone dogs! pictures by David Catrow. Dial Books for Young Readers 2008 un il $16.99

Grades: PreK K   E

    1. Counting 2. Stories in rhyme 3. Dogs -- Fiction

    ISBN 978-0-8037-3157-8; 0-8037-3157-4

                        LC 2007008620

Ten unruly dogs get loose at obedience school, and when they are captured by the dog-catcher, they work together to effect their escape and return home.

"The minimal rhyming text is paired with Catrow's exuberant, comic, pencil and watercolor illustrations. The frenetic, goofy-looking dogs of various sizes and breeds romping through the park are sure to bring smiles to young faces." SLJ

Duck, duck, goose! a coyote's on the loose! illustrated by Jose Aruego and Ariane Dewey. HarperCollins Pubs. 2004 un il $15.95; lib bdg $16.89

Grades: PreK K 1 2   E

    1. Domestic animals 2. Stories in rhyme 3. Coyote 4. Animals -- Fiction

    ISBN 0-06-050802-7; 0-06-050804-3 lib bdg

                        LC 2003-8734

Several farm animals try to evade a coyote that they think is dangerous

"Aruego and Dewey use bold paints as varied as a child's imagination to color their comically rendered farmyard animals. A suspenseful romp that will strike a chord with children." SLJ

★ **I** ain't gonna paint no more! illustrated by David Catrow. Harcourt 2005 un il $16

Grades: PreK K 1 2   E

    1. Stories in rhyme 2. Painting -- Fiction

    ISBN 0-15-202488-3

                      LC 2003-27739

"Catrow splashes color all over, uses white space cleverly, and includes playful flourishes. . . . Elongated figures and exaggerated expressions match the silly tone of the story. . . . With rhymes that invite audience participation and scenes that draw the eye, this is a strong storytime choice." SLJ

Move over, Rover; [by] Karen Beaumont; illustrated by Jane Dyer. Harcourt 2006 un il $16

Grades: PreK K 1 2   E

    1. Stories in rhyme 2. Dogs -- Fiction 3. Rain -- Fiction 4. Animals -- Fiction

    ISBN 978-0-15-201979-2; 0-15-201979-0

                      LC 2005014557

When a storm comes, Rover expects to have his doghouse all to himself but finds that various other animals, including a skunk, come to join him.

This offers "marvelously textured watercolor-and-acrylic illustrations. . . . The repetition of key phrases, the rhythmic text, and the cumulative structure of the narrative make this book an ideal read-aloud." SLJ

★ **No** sleep for the sheep! illustrated by Jackie Urbanovic. Houghton Mifflin Harcourt 2011 un il $16.99

Grades: PreK K 1   E

    1. Stories in rhyme 2. Sleep -- Fiction 3. Sounds -- Fiction 4. Domestic animals -- Fiction

    ISBN 978-0-15-204969-0; 0-15-204969-X

                      LC 2009007978

A sheep wants nothing but to go to sleep in the big red barn on the farm, but each time he closes his eyes, another animal moos or neighs or peeps to come in.

"Beaumont's playful, repetitive text, with its loud animal sounds, will have children chanting along to the beat." Kirkus

Shoe -la-la! illustrated by Leuyen Pham. Scholastic Press 2011 un il $16.99

Grades: PreK K   E

    1. Stories in rhyme 2. Shoes -- Fiction

    ISBN 978-0-545-06705-8; 0-545-06705-7

                      LC 2010007848

Four girls go in search of the perfect pair of party shoes.

"The sparkly jacket is an irresistible draw, depicting the girls vamping in dress-up clothes and high heels, as are the humorously expressive, cartoonlike illustrations rendered in full-color with lots of girl-pleasing pink and purple. Pure fun." SLJ

Where's my t-r-u-c-k? pictures by David Catrow. Dial Books for Young Readers 2011 un il $16.99

Grades: PreK K 1   E

    1. Stories in rhyme 2. Dogs -- Fiction 3. Toys -- Fiction 4. Trucks -- Fiction 5. Lost and found possessions -- Fiction

    ISBN 978-0-8037-3222-3; 0-8037-3222-8

                      LC 2010045689

"This peppy picture book relates in rhyming verse the story of a boy's expansive search for his favorite toy—a riding truck. . . . A raucous and rotund dog finally digs a huge hole and reveals the treasure, which lies amid other items, including an iPod and a set of false teeth. Beaumont's refrain promises that listeners will know how to spell 'truck' by tale's end and is perfectly paced for expressive pauses and exclamations. Catrow's jam-packed pencil and watercolor scenes are masterworks of detail and humor." SLJ

Who ate all the cookie dough? [by] Karen Beaumont; illustrated by Eugene Yelchin. Henry Holt and Company 2008 un il $16.95

Grades: PreK K 1   E

    1. Stories in rhyme 2. Animals -- Fiction 3. Lost and found possessions -- Fiction

    ISBN 978-0-8050-8267-8; 0-8050-8267-0

                      LC 2007012733

Kanga and her friends try to discover who ate all of her cookie dough

"Infectious repetitive rhyming verse, eye-catching gouache illustrations with ample white space, and a lift-

the-flap surprise combine to create a joyful tale." Horn
Book Guide

Bechtold, Lisze

Sally and the purple socks; [by] Lisze Bechtold.
Philomel Books 2008 un il $15.99

Grades: PreK K 1   E

1. Size -- Fiction 2. Clothing and dress -- Fiction

ISBN 978-0-399-24734-7; 0-399-24734-3

LC 2007023649

When her tiny purple socks start to expand, Sally turns
them into a scarf and then curtains, but things soon get out
of hand.

"The quirky, playful, and ultimately warm illustrations,
coupled with the simple text and a plot with just the right
amount of suspense, make the book spot-on for sharing with
young audiences." Booklist

Beck, Andrea

Pierre Le Poof! written and illustrated by Andrea Beck.
Orca Book Publishers 2009 un il $19.95

Grades: PreK K 1 2   E

1. Dogs -- Fiction

ISBN 978-1-55469-028-2; 1-55469-028-5

"Lapdog Pierre Le Poof, 'a pedigreed pooch,' lives a
pampered life with Miss Murphy but longs to frolic with the
dogs in the park. At a practice session for a dog championship, Pierre makes his escape . . . but soon longs for the
comforts of home. . . . Dog and owner bear a strong resemblance to each other in airy ink-and-watercolor pictures that
delightfully go for the laughs." Booklist

Other titles about Pierre are:

Pierre's friends (2010)

Pierre in the air! (2011)

Beck, Scott

Monster sleepover! Abrams Books for Young Readers
2009 un il $14.95

Grades: K 1 2   E

1. Parties -- Fiction 2. Monsters -- Fiction

ISBN 978-0-8109-4059-8; 0-8109-4059-0

LC 2009-00317

Doris throws a slumber party for Ben and her other monster friends, complete with games, snacks, and an effort to
stay up all night.

"Bright, acrylic paintings enhance the lively tone. Beck's
silly sense of humor will delight young readers." SLJ

Becker, Bonny

A **visitor** for Bear; illustrated by Kady MacDonald
Denton. Candlewick Press 2008 un il $16.99

Grades: PreK K 1 2   E

1. Mice -- Fiction 2. Bears -- Fiction 3. Friendship
-- Fiction

ISBN 978-0-7636-2807-9; 0-7636-2807-7

LC 2006-51850

Bear's efforts to keep out visitors to his house are undermined by a very persistent mouse.

This offers "watercolor, ink and gouache illustrations in
a soft color palette. . . . The characters are highly expressive
. . . and the dramatic text will lend itself to reading aloud."
Booklist

Other titles about Bear are:

A birthday for Bear (2009)

A bedtime for Bear (2010)

The sniffles for Bear (2011)

Becker, Helaine

Juba this, juba that; illustrated by Ron Lightburn. Tundra 2011 il $17.95

Grades: PreK K   E

1. Cats -- Fiction 2. Fairs -- Fiction

ISBN 978-0-88776-975-7; 0-88776-975-6

"This modern-day version of a traditional African chant
imagines an adventure that happens one evening when a
dark-skinned boy follows a yellow cat to the fair. They laugh
at their reflections in the House of Mirrors, take a spooky
fun-house ride, and generally have a wonderful time before
returning home to bed. Becker's simple rhyme plays with
opposites and is just right for clapping and bouncing along.
Lightburn's lively illustrations perfectly capture the joy of
the nighttime escapade and extend the story." SLJ

Becker, Suzy

★ **Manny's** cows; the Niagara Falls tale. written and
illustrated by Suzy Becker. HarperCollins 2006 un il lib
bdg $16.89

Grades: PreK K 1 2   E

1. Cattle -- Fiction 2. Vacations -- Fiction

ISBN 978-0-06-054152-1; 0-06-054152-0; 978-0-06-
054153-8 lib bdg; 0-06-054153-9 lib bdg

LC 2005-14508

For his summer vacation, Manny takes his five hundred
cows to Niagara Falls.

"The over-the-top story, full of fun and laced with amusing visual and verbal details, . . . is accompanied by occasional sidebar facts about dairy cattle. The cows' outrageous
comments and antics are bolstered by free-spirited ink drawings brightened with color." Booklist

Bedford, David, 1969-

The **way** I love you. Simon & Schuster Books for
Young Readers 2005 un il $12.95

Grades: PreK K   E

1. Dogs -- Fiction

ISBN 0-689-87625-4

LC 2004-3964

First published 2004 in Australia with title: I love

A little girl celebrates all of the ways she loves her puppy.

"Loose charcoal lines provide texture and motion, while
splashes of pastel-hued watercolors keep the pictures warm
and cozy. . . . The simple language and clean, colorful artwork make this book just right for the youngest pet lovers."
SLJ

Bee, William

And the train goes. . . . Candlewick Press 2007 un il
$15.99

Grades: PreK K   E

1. Sounds -- Fiction 2. Parrots -- Fiction 3. Railroads
-- Fiction

ISBN 978-0-7636-3248-9; 0-7636-3248-1

LC 2006-43857

As assorted passengers comment on their train ride, and
the train itself goes "Clickerty click, clickerty clack," the
station parrot is carefully listening to every sound

"Filled with sound effects galore, this rollicking read-
aloud is perfect for transportation storytimes. . . . The train

and the characters' clothing are depicted in glossy colors and covered with flat floral patterns and other graphic designs. . . . There are many details for children to pore over." SLJ

Beil, Karen Magnuson

Jack's house; illustrated by Mike Wohnoutka. Holiday House 2008 un il $16.95

Grades: PreK K 1 2   E

  1. Dogs -- Fiction 2. House construction -- Fiction

  ISBN 978-0-8234-1913-5; 0-8234-1913-4

                 LC 2007014978

Cumulative text reveals who was really responsible for the house that Jack claims to have built, and all of the trucks involved, from the bulldozer used to clear the land to the van that brought a hammock for the back yard

"A wonderful twist on an age-old rhyme. . . . Wohnoutka's full-page acrylic paintings are large scale, but are also full of small details for readers to enjoy. . . . This beguiling book will be a hit both at storytimes and in circulating collections." SLJ

Beiser, Tim

Bradley McGogg, the very fine frog; illustrated by Rachel Berman. Tundra Books 2009 un il $19.99

Grades: PreK K 1 2   E

  1. Stories in rhyme 2. Food -- Fiction 3. Frogs -- Fiction

  ISBN 978-0-88776-864-4; 0-88776-864-4

Bradley McGogg the frog "discovers that his cupboard is empty and goes in search of something for lunch. Miss Mousie offers him rye crackers and cheese, while Herr Bear and Herr Hare invite him to dine on carrots covered in honey. . . . Unable to accept the other animals' favorite foods and still hungry, Brad drags himself back home. To his delight, he discovers an infestation of bugs in his hollowed-out log and sits down to a delectable feast. . . . The sophisticated rhyming text is accompanied by subdued watercolor and gouache illustrations. . . . Each animal's face is imbued with character and personality." SLJ

Miss Mousie's blind date; by Tim Beiser; illustrated by Rachel Berman. Tundra Books of Northern New York 2012 24 p. col. ill. (hardcover) $17.95

Grades: K 1 2 3   E

  1. Mice -- Juvenile fiction 2. Self-acceptance -- Juvenile fiction 3. Dating (Social customs) -- Juvenile fiction

  ISBN 1770492518; 9781770492516

                 LC 2011938763

In this children's story, written by Tim Beiser with illustrations by Rachel Berman, "when Miss Mousie is shopping at the mole's deli, her heart stops at the sight of [a] rakish . . . water rat, who . . . calls her fat, which brings tears to her eyes and sends her to bed for a day. What brings her out of sadness is an anonymous invitation to dinner. . . . But the would-be suitor is not Matt the water rat; it's the kind mole who owns the deli." (Kirkus Reviews)

Bell, Cece

Itty bitty. Candlewick Press 2009 un il $9.99

Grades: PreK K 1   E

  1. Dogs -- Fiction 2. Size -- Fiction

  ISBN 978-0-7636-3616-6; 0-7636-3616-9

"Where does a tiny dog find just the right decor for his hollowed-out-bone house? Why, the 'teeny-weeny depart-

ment' at a huge store downtown, of course! Such is the premise of this sweet and silly picture book that introduces a sunny pup of small size but big personality. . . . Bell's . . . crisp acrylic and ink artwork features blocks of color and simple stylized shapes on grainy, speckled backgrounds." Publ Wkly

Rabbit and Robot; the sleepover. Cece Bell. Candlewick 2012 56 p. (hardback) $14.99

Grades: K 1 2   E

  1. Children's stories 2. Negotiation -- Fiction 3. Friendship -- Juvenile fiction 4. Humorous stories 5. Robots -- Fiction 6. Rabbits -- Fiction 7. Friendship -- Fiction 8. Sleepovers -- Fiction

  ISBN 0763654752; 9780763654757

                 LC 2011048365

Theodor Seuss Geisel Honor Book (2013)

This "book's four chapters . . . correspond to the plan for [Rabbit and Robot's] eagerly anticipated sleepover: make pizza, watch TV, play Go Fish, go to bed. But it's a list Rabbit generated without consulting his friend, so negotiations . . . are the order of the day. . . . Robot wants to play Old Maid in addition to Go Fish; Rabbit insists it's 'not on the list.' Robot . . . insists on taking apart Rabbit's furniture to get his favorite topping, nuts and bolts." (Publishers Weekly)

Belloc, Hilaire

Jim who ran away from his nurse and was eaten by a lion; a cautionary tale. pictures by Mini Grey. Alfred A. Knopf 2010 un il $19.99

Grades: 2 3 4   E

  1. Stories in rhyme 2. Pop-up books 3. Zoos -- Fiction 4. Lions -- Fiction

  ISBN 978-0-375-85970-0; 0-375-85970-5

Text originally published 1907; A newly illustrated edition of the title first published 1987 by Little Brown; this edition first published 2009 in the United Kingdom

Jim runs away from his nurse at the zoo and he is eaten by a lion.

"Grey's artwork is gorgeous and bold. . . . Fold-outs, pop-ups and lift-up flaps contribute to the over-the-top element that makes even little Jim's bloody, chewed-off head seem not as horrific as it might. . . . All but the most sensitive children (over eight) will laugh . . . especially if the book is read aloud with an English accent." Kirkus

Belton, Robyn

Herbert; the true story of a brave sea dog. Candlewick Press 2010 un il $15.99

Grades: PreK K 1 2   E

  1. Sea stories 2. Dogs -- Fiction

  ISBN 978-0-7636-4741-4; 0-7636-4741-1

                 LC 2009-46538

Herbert, a beloved, small dog who lives near the sea in New Zealand, sets out one fine day with his boy Tim's father on a boat that is beset by a sudden storm, which washes Herbert overboard.

"Belton's beautiful watercolor illustrations bring to life the dangerously changeable weather at sea without making it too scary. Reproductions of newspaper articles and letters about the incident, as well as Herbert's 'Iron Dog' medal, appear on the endpapers. These real-life documents give readers a fascinating taste of the true story behind the book and provide a nice balance to Belton's dreamy illustrations." Booklist

Bemelmans, Ludwig, 1898-1962

★ **Madeline**; story and pictures by Ludwig Bemelmans. Viking 1985 un il $17.99; pa $7.99

Grades: PreK K 1 2   E

1. Stories in rhyme

ISBN 0-670-44580-0; 0-14-056439-X pa

A reissue of the title first published 1939 by Simon & Schuster

A Caldecott Medal honor book, 1940

"Madeline is a nonconformist in a regimented world—a Paris convent school. This rhymed story tells how she made an adventure out of having appendicitis." Hodges. Books for Elem Sch Libr

Other titles about Madeline are:

Madeline and the bad hat (1957)

Madeline and the gypsies (1959)

Madeline in London (1961)

Madeline's Christmas (1985)

Madeline's rescue (1985)

Benchley, Nathaniel

★ A **ghost** named Fred; pictures by Ben Shecter. Harper & Row 1968 un il (I can read mystery book) lib bdg $17.89

Grades: K 1 2   E

1. Ghost stories

ISBN 0-06-020474-5

"More humorous than scary . . . this is a pleasing and acceptable ghost story for beginning readers." Booklist

Bennett, Kelly

Dad and Pop; an ode to fathers & stepfathers. illustrated by Paul Meisel. Candlewick Press 2010 un il $15.99

Grades: PreK K 1 2   E

1. Fathers -- Fiction 2. Stepfathers -- Fiction 3. Father-daughter relationship -- Fiction

ISBN 978-0-7636-3379-0; 0-7636-3379-8

"A cheerful girl explains that Dad and Pop are different in many ways, but the same in their love for her. . . . Dad is the girl's biological father and . . . Pop is her step-father. . . . This is a positive and playful portrayal of a blended family. . . . Expressive faces and gentle humor add charm to the pictures." SLJ

Your daddy was just like you; illustrated by David Walker. G. P. Putnam's Sons 2010 un il $16.99

Grades: PreK K 1   E

1. Fathers -- Fiction 2. Grandmothers -- Fiction

ISBN 978-0-399-24798-9; 0-399-24798-X

LC 2008053644

A grandmother describes to her grandson how his father was just like him when he was a child, never wanting to take a bath, fearing the dark, and swooping through the house in a cape and mask.

"Characters' facial expressions and body language successfully capture emotions, actions, and reactions. . . . The humorous text is in perfect sync with the simple illustrations." SLJ

Your mommy was just like you; illustrated by David Walker. G. P. Putnam's Sons 2011 un il $16.99

Grades: PreK K   E

1. Mothers -- Fiction 2. Grandmothers -- Fiction

ISBN 978-0-399-24798-9; 0-399-24798-X

"A grandmother looks at an old photo album with her granddaughter, telling her stories about her mother when she was little. . . . The illustrations are soft and gentle, complementing each milestone mentioned in the story. Perfect for intergenerational sharing." SLJ

Bently, Peter

★ **King** Jack and the dragon. Dial Books for Young Readers 2011 un il $17.99

Grades: PreK K   E

1. Stories in rhyme 2. Play -- Fiction 3. Imagination -- Fiction

ISBN 978-0-8037-3698-6; 0-8037-3698-3

LC 2011001273

"Bently's verse never misses a beat, and Oxenbury shifts between monochromatic, engraving-like drawings and pale watercolors; the images feel as if they were drawn from a classic fairy tale book and contemporary life simultaneously. It's an enchanting tribute to both full-throttle pretend play and the reassurance of a parent's embrace." Publ Wkly

Berger, Carin

Forever friends. Greenwillow Books 2010 un il $16.99; lib bdg $17.89

Grades: PreK K   E

1. Birds -- Fiction 2. Rabbits -- Fiction 3. Seasons -- Fiction 4. Friendship -- Fiction

ISBN 978-0-06-191528-4; 0-06-191528-9; 978-0-06-191529-1 lib bdg; 0-06-191529-7 lib bdg

LC 2009-18758

In the spring, a blue bird awakens a rabbit and invites him to play, and they enjoy every day together until it is time for the bird to fly south for the winter, with a promise to return again next spring.

"Berger's superb, stylized cut-paper collage illustrations, constructed from lined and graph paper and magazines, depict sylvan landscapes with graceful curves and airy compositions that echo the simplicity and gentleness of the tale. A reassuring, poetic story that will give young children much to ponder any time of the year." Booklist

★ **OK** go. Greenwillow Books 2009 un il $17.99; lib bdg $18.89

Grades: K 1 2 3   E

1. Automobiles -- Fiction 2. Environmental protection -- Fiction

ISBN 978-0-06-157666-9; 0-06-157666-2; 978-0-06-157669-0 lib bdg; 0-06-157669-7 lib bdg

LC 2008-14681

In this almost wordless picture book, car drivers stuck in traffic under smoggy skies seek "greener" alternatives to driving, including riding bicycles, walking, and playing

"Berger's simple environmental message is delivered through clever, innovative illustrations that make her point without being didactic. Idiosyncratic creatures decked out in fabric pieces, buttons, and tall imaginative hats sail along in even more idiosyncratic vehicles that are variously colored and decorated with stickers and decals." SLJ

The **little** yellow leaf. Greenwillow Books 2008 un il $16.99; lib bdg $17.89

Grades: PreK K 1 2   **E**
1. Trees -- Fiction 2. Autumn -- Fiction 3. Leaves -- Fiction
ISBN 978-0-06-145223-9; 0-06-145223-8; 978-0-06-145224-6 lib bdg; 0-06-145224-6 lib bdg
LC 2007-39191

A yellow leaf is not ready to fall from the tree when autumn comes, but finally, after finding another leaf still on the tree, the two let go together.

"In Berger's eye-catching collage illustrations, pieced background papers in shades of yellow, green, blue, and beige show off stylized forms of naked tree branches, leaves, and sun created by clipping and pasting (sometimes tiny) segments of various papers—faded, lined ledger, and graph paper; colored and printed magazine pages—and adding touches of paint." SLJ

Berger, Joe
Bridget Fidget and the most perfect pet! Dial Books for Young Readers 2009 un il $16.99
Grades: PreK K   **E**
1. Pets -- Fiction 2. Ladybugs -- Fiction
ISBN 978-0-8037-3405-0; 0-8037-3405-0
LC 2009011528
First published 2008 in the United Kingdom with title: Bridget Fidget

Bridget has always wanted a pet unicorn named Thunderhooves, so when a box is delivered to her door she is sure that is what is inside.

"Bridget Fidget is the timeless cartoon poppet, dreaming, dashing, fussing, laughing, dragging her remarkably expressive stuffed animal everywhere. . . . The cartoon illustrations . . . are so joyfully kinetic that viewers are left breathless." SLJ

Berger, Lou
Dream dog; by Lou Berger; illustrated by David J. Catrow. 1st ed. Schwartz & Wade Books 2013 40 p. ill. (hardcover) $17.99; (library) $20.99
Grades: PreK K 1 2   **E**
1. Dogs -- Juvenile fiction 2. Picture books for children 3. Imaginary playmates -- Juvenile fiction 4. Dogs -- Fiction 5. Imagination -- Fiction 6. Fathers and sons -- Fiction
ISBN 0375866558; 9780375866555; 9780375966552
LC 2011048582
In this children's picture book, "Harry wants a dog, but Dad has allergies. So Harry puts on his X-35 Infra-Rocket Imagination Helmet and conjures up his own perfect pet, a dream dog named Waffle. This new pet is huge and fuzzy, all light blue and white like cumulous clouds, and only Harry can see him. Waffle and Harry become best pals, with Harry's dad playing along with the idea of the imaginary dog. . . . When Dad's allergies suddenly improve, he brings home a real dog." (Kirkus Reviews)

The **elephant** wish; by Lou Berger; illustrated by Ana Juan. Schwartz & Wade Books 2008 un il $16.99; lib bdg $19.99
Grades: PreK K 1 2   **E**
1. Wishes -- Fiction 2. Elephants -- Fiction 3. Family

life -- Fiction
ISBN 978-0-375-83962-7; 0-375-83962-3; 978-0-375-93962-4 lib bdg; 0-375-93962-8 lib bdg
LC 2007034329
Soon after wishing that an elephant will come and take her away from her too-busy parents, Eliza's fondest desire comes true but her journey is observed by ninety-seven-year-old Adelle, who once made the same wish

"Berger threads shimmers of lighthearted whimsy through this obscure tale, creating a fantasy with deep resonance. Juan matches the slightly melancholic tone with dark, swirly images that are dense and dreamy." Booklist

Berger, Samantha
Martha doesn't say sorry! illustrated by Bruce Whatley. Little, Brown and Co. 2009 un il $15.99
Grades: PreK K 1 2   **E**
1. Otters -- Fiction
ISBN 978-0-316-06682-2; 0-316-06682-6
LC 2008-16769
Young Martha learns that she must apologize for her bad behavior if she wants people to cooperate with her.

"The watercolor and colored pencil artwork encapsulates Martha's girliness, her better-than-thou attitude and her internal struggle with her conscience. Whatley's representation of body language and facial expression powerfully complement the text. An enjoyable introduction to what could be a new beloved character." Kirkus
Another title about Martha is:
Martha doesn't share (2010)

Bergman, Mara
Lively Elizabeth! what happens when you push; illustrated by Cassia Thomas. Albert Whitman 2010 un il
Grades: PreK K 1 2   **E**
1. School stories
ISBN 0807547026; 9780807547021
Describes a chain reaction that is caused by Elizabeth pushing her classmate Joe.

"The text is placed in and around the illustrations for maximum effect. . . . Thomas's illustrations make the whole thing work. The action is clear, as are the consequences of that ill-fated push. The myriad children wear wacky costumes, have expressive faces, and are awash in detail that makes multiple readings a joy." SLJ

Snip snap! what's that? illustrated by Nick Maland. Greenwillow Books 2005 un il $15.99
Grades: PreK K 1 2   **E**
1. Alligators -- Fiction
ISBN 0-06-077754-0
LC 2004-13420
Three siblings are frightened by the wide mouth, long teeth, and strong jaws of the alligator that has crept up the stairs—until they decide they have had enough

"Using elements of rhythm and rhyme as well as an enjoyably predictable question-and-answer refrain, the text maintains a playful tone beneath the scary details. . . . Expressive line drawings, brightened with watercolor washes, illustrate the story with wit and style." Booklist

Yum yum! What fun! written by Mara Bergman; illustrated by Nick Maland. Greenwillow Books 2009 un il $17.99

Grades: PreK K 1 2   E

1. Stories in rhyme 2. Animals -- Fiction

ISBN 978-0-06-168860-7; 0-06-168860-6

LC 2008012640

A series of animals sneaks into the house, looking for something to eat

"Enticing rhymes and onomatopoeia make each animal intruder's entrance the read-aloud equivalent of a star turn. . . . Treats usually disappear quickly, but this one will last through repeated readings." Publ Wkly

Bergren, Lisa Tawn

God found us you; art by Laura J. Bryant. HarperCollins Children's Books 2009 un il $10.99

Grades: PreK K 1   E

1. Foxes -- Fiction 2. Adoption -- Fiction 3. Christian life -- Fiction

ISBN 978-0-06-113176-9; 0-06-113176-8

LC 2008016216

When Little Fox asks his mother to tell his favorite story, Mama Fox recounts the day he arrived in her life, from God to her arms

"Bryant's delicate illustrations in pastel shades augment the heartfelt message of Bergren's simple story. . . . This woodland tale answers many questions adopted children may ask their parents." SLJ

Bergstein, Rita M.

Your own big bed; by Rita M. Bergstein; illustrated by Susan Kathleen Hartung. Viking 2008 un il $15.99

Grades: PreK K 1   E

1. Beds -- Fiction 2. Growth -- Fiction

ISBN 978-0-670-06079-5; 0-670-06079-8

LC 2007-17902

Introduces how different animals and even human babies grow from being newly-hatched or born, through being carried everywhere, to having their own special place to sleep.

"The absence of the anxiety, whining, or excuses common to books of this ilk is refreshing. . . . This sweet book provides a gentle, matter-of-fact introduction to a sometimes-difficult transition." SLJ

Berkes, Marianne Collins

Over in the forest; come and take a peek. by Marianne Berkes; illustrated by Jill Dubin. Dawn Publications 2012 32 p. (hardback) $16.95

Grades: PreK K 1 2   E

1. Counting 2. Stories in rhyme 3. Forest animals -- Poetry 4. Nature -- Juvenile literature 5. Forest animals -- Fiction 6. Animals -- Infancy -- Fiction

ISBN 9781584691624; 9781584691631; 158469162X

LC 2011030879

This nature book by Marianne Berkes allows children to "follow the tracks of ten woodland animals. . . . Children learn the ways of forest animals to the rhythm of 'Over in the Meadow' as they leap like a squirrel, dunk like a raccoon, and pounce like a fox. They . . . also count the babies and search for ten hidden forest animals. . . . Marianne [also] provides [multiple] ideas for activities and curriculum extensions about forest animals, literature, and writing." (Publisher's note)

Over in the jungle; a rainforest rhyme. by Marianne Berkes; illustrated by Jeanette Canyon. Dawn Publications 2007 un il $16.95; pa $8.95

Grades: PreK K 1 2 3   E

1. Counting 2. Rain forest animals

ISBN 1-58469-091-7; 1-58469-092-5 pa

LC 2006030962

"Another variation on the familiar song, this one enumerates some of the unusual fauna of the rain forest. It not only spotlights some of the animals . . . but also offers pertinent information on the habitat. Berkes describes the different layers of the rainforest and its importance to our global ecology, and suggests movement activities for children to act out the rhyme. The unusual and colorful illustrations are made with polymer clay and then photographed, giving them a three-dimensional look." SLJ

Berne, Jennifer

Calvin can't fly; the story of a bookworm birdie. illustrated by Keith Bendis. Sterling 2010 un il $14.95

Grades: PreK K 1 2   E

1. Birds -- Fiction 2. Books and reading -- Fiction

ISBN 978-1-4027-7323-5; 1-4027-7323-4

LC 2009050797

A young starling chooses to read books when his cousins are learning to fly, and the knowledge he acquires comes in handy when a hurricane threatens the flock's migration.

"The irresistible story of a proud bookworm will put smiles on the faces of readers of all ages. . . . The illustrations are wildly original and full of funny details." Kirkus

Berner, Rotraut Susanne

In the town all year 'round. Chronicle Books 2008 un il $16.99

Grades: PreK K 1 2   E

1. Stories without words 2. Year -- Fiction 3. Seasons -- Fiction 4. City and town life -- Fiction

ISBN 978-0-8118-6474-9; 0-8118-6474-X

LC 2008012860

Originally published in German in 4 vols.

"This oversize identification book . . . opens by introducing a cast of characters for children to find as they explore eight different scenes throughout each of the seasons. Myriad details of people, places, and events, colorfully drawn in cartoon style, will have youngsters examining the pages for hours." Booklist

Bernheimer, Kate

The **girl** in the castle inside the museum; [illustrated by] Nicoletta Ceccoli. Schwartz & Wade Books 2008 un il $16.99; lib bdg $19.99

Grades: K 1 2 3   E

1. Castles -- Fiction 2. Museums -- Fiction

ISBN 978-0-375-83606-0; 978-0-375-83606-7 lib bdg

LC 2006-101854

"In an eclectic toy museum, children are drawn to a snow globe where it is said that, if they look hard enough, they can see the little girl who lives in the castle therein. To their delight, she is visible, as is her entire enchanted world. The girl is lonely when the museum empties, and she dreams of other children visiting her. . . . Using media as varied as clay sculpture and photography, Ceccoli has created a world that beckons young readers inside. . . . This unusual book will jump-start the imaginations of all who are lucky enough to enter it." SLJ

Berry, Lynne

★ **Duck** skates; illustrated by Hiroe Nakata. Henry Holt and Co. 2005 un il $15.95

Grades: PreK K   E

1. Stories in rhyme 2. Snow -- Fiction 3. Ducks -- Fiction

ISBN 978-0-8050-7219-8; 0-8050-7219-5

LC 2004-22176

Five little ducks skate, romp, and play in the snow.

"The illustrations follow the text exactly, allowing children to count the ducks engaged in each activity. The watercolor-and-ink pictures convey the playfulness in warm, cozy tones, and a surprising amount of expression is conveyed in simple lines." SLJ

Other titles about these ducks are:

Duck dunks (2008)

Duck tents (2009)

Ducking for apples (2010)

What floats in a moat? by Lynne Berry; illustrated by Matthew Cordell. 1st ed. Simon & Schuster Books for Young Readers 2013 48 p. col. ill. (hardcover) $17.99

Grades: K 1 2 3   E

1. Floating bodies -- Juvenile literature 2. Science -- Experiments -- Juvenile literature 3. Goats -- Fiction 4. Stories in rhyme 5. Chickens -- Fiction 6. Floating bodies -- Fiction

ISBN 1416997636; 9781416997634

LC 2010002844

This children's book by Lynne Berry is "inspired by Archimedes' principle. "Archie . . . the goat and Skinny the hen need to deliver three barrels of buttermilk to the queen . . . in her moated castle. Rejecting the drawbridge in the name of 'Science!' they embark on a process of trial and error to float the barrels across the moat." (Kirkus Reviews)

Berry, Matt

Up on Daddy's shoulders; by Matt Berry; illustrated by Lucy Corvino. Scholastic 2006 un il $6.99

Grades: PreK K 1 2   E

1. Size -- Fiction 2. Father-son relationship -- Fiction

ISBN 0-439-67045-4

LC 2005023626

While riding on his father's shoulders, a young boy feels taller than everything in his house, his neighborhood, and the world.

"Corvino's sunny paintings fill each double-page spread. . . . Easy on the eyes and ears, this title's rhythm and attractiveness make it a fine read-aloud choice." Booklist

Bertrand, Diane Gonzales

Adelita and the veggie cousins; illustrations by Christina Rodriguez; Spanish translation by Gabriela Baeza Ventura. Pinata Books/Arte Publico Press 2011 il

Grades: PreK K 1   E

1. School stories 2. Vegetables -- Fiction 3. Bilingual books -- English-Spanish

ISBN 1-55885-699-4; 978-1-55885-699-8

LC 2010054521

On her first day at a new school, Adelita makes new friends through a lesson on vegetables, including

how some vegetables are 'cousins' because they share certain characteristics.

"The dual message of nutrition and diversity will probably find its place in today's curriculum and can certainly augment units on food, language and culture." Kirkus

Bertrand, Lynne

★ **Granite** baby; pictures by Kevin Hawkes. Farrar, Straus and Giroux 2005 un il $16

Grades: PreK K 1 2   E

1. Tall tales 2. Infants -- Fiction

ISBN 0-374-32761-0

LC 2002-192882

Five talented New Hampshire sisters try to care for a baby that one of them has carved out of granite.

"Together with Bertrand's rollicking text, Hawkes' broad double-page paintings make this ideal for sharing with groups." Booklist

Beskow, Elsa

Princess Sylvie. 2011 il $17.95

Grades: PreK K 1   E

1. Dogs -- Fiction 2. Rabbits -- Fiction 3. Princesses -- Fiction 4. Father-daughter relationship -- Fiction

ISBN 978-086315-813-1; 0-86315-813-7

First published 1934

Princess Sylvie persuades her father, the king, to leave the palace gardens and walk in the woods. The king is unsure. What might be in the woods? Then Sylvie's dog Oskar runs off after a long-eared hare and Sylvie's adventures begin.

"The bear looks like a very large teddy, the 'wild' wood is spacious and airy and Sylvie never loses her tiny crown or musses her dress. . . . Old-fashioned in all the senses of the word, but quite charming in its art-deco shapes and vintage colors." Kirkus

Best, Cari

Beatrice spells some lulus and learns to write a letter; by Cari Best; illustrated by Giselle Potter. Margaret Ferguson Books 2013 40 p. ill. (reinforced) $16.99

Grades: K 1 2 3   E

1. Spelling -- Juvenile fiction 2. Grandparent-grandchild relationship -- Juvenile fiction

ISBN 0374399042; 9780374399047

LC 2012015337

This children's picture book by Cari Best "tell[s] the story of a girl named Beatrice whose initially rocky relationship with spelling (she spells her name ABCTERIE) turns into a full-fledged romance. Although Beatrice's family doesn't share her interest in spelling ('Leo had his ant farm, June had gymnastics, and her parents had their music'), she discovers a fellow word lover in her grandmother." (Publishers Weekly)

Easy as pie; [pictures by Melissa Sweet] Farrar, Straus and Giroux 2010 un il $16.99

Grades: K 1 2 3   E

1. Pies -- Fiction 2. Baking -- Fiction

ISBN 0-374-39929-8; 978-0-374-39929-0

LC 2008-16803

Jacob watches his favorite television show, Baking with Chef Monty, and bakes a beautiful peach pie, which he gives to his parents on their anniversary. "Ages six to nine." (Bull Cent Child Books)

"With pencil and watercolor illustrations done in a palette of soft colors, Sweet captures the warmth and security Jacob feels in the kitchen. . . . Important themes abound—love, security, cooperation, warmth, respect—and somehow all are tied to the simple acts of cooking and eating together. A delicious book for all collections." SLJ

Goose's story; pictures by Holly Meade. Farrar, Straus & Giroux 2002 un il hardcover o.p. pa $6.99
Grades: PreK K 1 2   E
1. Canada goose 2. People with disabilities
ISBN 0-374-32750-5; 0-374-40032-6 pa
                                                    LC 2001-27285
A young girl finds a Canada goose with a badly injured foot and looks for her each day to see how she is doing
"Holly Meade's animated paper collage enhances Best's poignant story. . . . Best tells the story from the girl's point of view, and her language is appropriately childlike and empathetic." Horn Book

★ **Sally** Jean, the Bicycle Queen; pictures by Christine Davenier. Farrar, Straus and Giroux 2005 un il $16
Grades: PreK K 1 2   E
1. Cycling -- Fiction 2. Bicycles -- Fiction
ISBN 0-374-36386-2
                                                    LC 2004-40461
When Sally Jean outgrows her beloved bicycle, Flash, she experiments with various ideas for acquiring a new, bigger one.
"Davenier's ink-and-watercolor illustrations are light and airy and convey a variety of emotions and delightful details. Sally Jean is a real charmer, and children will appreciate her resourcefulness and tenacity." SLJ

Shrinking Violet; illustrated by Giselle Potter. Farrar, Straus & Giroux 2001 un il $16
Grades: PreK K 1 2   E
1. Schools 2. Theater 3. School stories 4. Bashfulness 5. Theater -- Fiction
ISBN 0-374-36882-1
                                                    LC 99-88966
Violet, who is very shy and hates for anyone to look at her in school, finally comes out of her shell when she is cast as Lady Space in a play about the solar system and saves the production from disaster
"In wry, well-paced prose, Best . . . tells a good-natured story. . . . Potter's charming, signature-style illustrations, filled with wacky angles and proportions, rich colors, and slightly nostalgic details, extend the story's drama and warmth." Booklist

★ **Three** cheers for Catherine the Great! illustrated by Giselle Potter. Sunburst ed.; Farrar, Straus and Giroux 2003 un il pa $7.99
Grades: PreK K 1 2   E
1. Gifts -- Fiction 2. Parties -- Fiction 3. Birthdays -- Fiction 4. Grandmothers -- Fiction 5. Russian Americans -- Fiction
ISBN 0-374-47551-2
                                                    LC 2002040804
First published 1999 by DK Pub.

Sara's Russian grandmother has requested that there be no presents at her seventy-eighth birthday party so Sara must think of a gift from her heart.
"In lively, lyrical prose, Best celebrates a special family relationship, and conveys the unique challenges and joys of an immigrant's new life. . . . Potter's festive, whimsical artwork is an irresistible play of vibrant colors and patterns, filled with rich detail and diverse, expressive characters." Booklist
Another title about Sara and her grandmother is:
When Catherine the Great and I were eight! (2003)

What's so bad about being an only child? [by] Cari Best; pictures by Sophie Blackall. Farrar, Straus and Giroux 2007 un il $16
Grades: PreK K 1 2   E
1. Pets -- Fiction 2. Only child -- Fiction
ISBN 0-374-39943-3; 978-0-374-39943-6
                                                    LC 2005-51232
Rosemary Emma Angela Lynette Isabel Iris Malone grows tired of being an only child, but eventually finds a way to feel less alone.
"Kids should applaud this self-reliant, spunky heroine." Publ Wkly

Bevis, Mary Elizabeth
Wolf song; [by] Mary Bevis; illustrated by Consie Powell. Raven Productions 2007 un il $18.95; pa $12.95
Grades: K 1 2 3   E
1. Uncles -- Fiction 2. Wolves -- Fiction
ISBN 978-0-9794202-0-7; 978-0-9794202-1-4 pa
                                                    LC 2007027953
At twilight, Nell and her Uncle Walter go into the north woods, hoping to hear—and join—the howling of the wolves. Includes facts about wolves and howling expeditions.
"The text and illustrations both convey the wonder and mystery of nature." SLJ

Biedrzycki, David
Ace Lacewing, bug detective: the big swat. Charlesbridge 2010 un $16.95
Grades: K 1 2   E
1. Mystery fiction 2. Insects -- Fiction
ISBN 978-1-57091-747-9; 1-57091-747-7

Me and my dragon. Charlesbridge 2011 un il $16.95; pa $7.95
Grades: PreK K   E
1. Pets -- Fiction 2. Dragons -- Fiction
ISBN 978-1-58089-278-0; 1-58089-278-7; 978-1-58089-279-7; 1-58089-279-5 pa
A child tells all the reasons a small, fire-breathing dragon would make an excellent pet, and the ways to take proper care of it.
"The Adobe Photoshop artwork abounds with expressions of surprise and alarm when others see the dragon. . . . While the brief text is a boon for early readers, this clever, funny book will delight young dragon lovers at storytimes." SLJ

Biggs, Brian
Everything goes in the air; Brian Biggs; edited by Donna Bray. 1st ed. Balzer + Bray 2012 56 p. col. ill. (hardcover) $14.99

Grades: PreK K 1   E
  1. Air travel -- Fiction 2. Transportation -- Fiction 3.
Voyages and travels -- Juvenile fiction
  ISBN 0061958107; 9780061958106
                       LC 2012942240
Author Brian Biggs presents an interactive book about
things that fly. "Jets and blimps and helicopters and gliders!
Balloons and biplanes too! Everything goes! Zoom along
with Henry and his parents as they take off on an airborne
journey and learn about all kinds of flying vehicles. . . . [The
book includes] mini-story lines, seek-and-find activities, . . .
[and] cutaways." (Publisher's note)

Bildner, Phil

  ★ The **Hallelujah** Flight; illustrated by John Holyfield. G.P. Putnam's Sons 2010 un il $16.99
Grades: K 1 2 3   E
  1. Air pilots 2. Mechanics (Persons) 3. Flight -- Fiction
4. Air pilots -- Fiction 5. African Americans -- Fiction
  ISBN 978-0-399-24789-7; 0-399-24789-0
                       LC 2009-10362
In 1932, James Banning, along with his co-pilot Thomas
Allen, make history by becoming the first African Americans to fly across the United States, relying on the generosity
of people they meet in the towns along the way who help
keep their 'flying jalopy' going.
  "Based on both fictional and nonfiction sources, the story is briskly told in Allen's voice, with plenty of imagined
dialogue. Holyfield's gorgeous . . . paintings are done on textured backgrounds in a palette of blues and browns." Kirkus

  ★ **Shoeless** Joe & Black Betsy; illustrated by C.F.
Payne. Simon & Schuster Bks. for Young Readers 2002
un il $17
Grades: K 1 2 3   E
  1. Baseball players 2. Baseball -- Fiction
  ISBN 0-689-82913-2
                       LC 99-40563
Shoeless Joe Jackson, said by some to be the greatest
baseball player ever, goes into a hitting slump just before
he is to start his minor league career, so he asks his friend to
make him a special bat to help him hit
  This is "told in a folksy, Southern voice, with many of
the stylistic elements of a tall tale. . . . The mixed-media illustrations are layered and rich in texture, qualities that add
depth and drama." SLJ

  Turkey Bowl; [by] Phil Bildner; illustrated by C.F.
Payne. Simon & Schuster Books for Young Readers 2008
un il $15.99
Grades: 1 2 3   E
  1. Snow -- Fiction 2. Football -- Fiction 3. Family life
-- Fiction 4. Thanksgiving Day -- Fiction
  ISBN 9780-689-87896-1; 0-689-87896-6
                       LC 2005020139
Ethan looks forward to the Thanksgiving Day when he
and his friends are finally old enough to play in the annual
family football game, but that day arrives full of snow and
icy roads
  "Payne's muted, full-color illustrations capture the disappointment and joy the characters experience and feature
plenty of gridiron action. Perfect for reading aloud at holiday

time, this lively story will resonate year-round with sports
fans." SLJ

  The **greatest** game ever played; a football story. by
Phil Bildner; illustrated by Zachary Pullen. Putnam's Sons
2006 un il $16.99
Grades: K 1 2 3   E
  1. Football -- Fiction 2. Father-son relationship --
Fiction
  ISBN 0-399-24171-X
                       LC 2005025177
"The New York Giants are Sam and his father's favorite
baseball team until they move west. Sam misses the team,
but most of all he misses spending time with Pop, who has
forsaken sports—despite Sam's breathless discovery of a
football team with the same name. When Sam is given tickets to the 1958 NFL championship game, he and Pop go together. . . . The father-son relationship . . . is realistically
portrayed. . . . The energy of the paintings perfectly matches
Bildner's lively text." Booklist

Billingsley, Franny

  ★ **Big** Bad Bunny; story by Franny Billingsley; art by
G. Brian Karas. Atheneum Books for Young Readers 2008
un il $16.99
Grades: PreK K 1   E
  1. Mice -- Fiction 2. Mother-child relationship --
Fiction
  ISBN 978-1-4169-0601-8; 1-4169-0601-0
                       LC 2006-32754
When Baby Boo-Boo, a mouse dressed in a bunny suit,
becomes lost in the forest, his mother follows the sound of
his cries to locate him.
  Billingsley "extends her plot with satisfying onomata-
poeia; the oversize format, too, marks this for a readaloud.
Karas . . . strategically deploys mixed-media to render the
id-gone-wild scenes with comic abandon." Publ Wkly

Bingham, Kelly

  ★ **Z** is for Moose; by Kelly Bingham; illustrations by
Paul O. Zelinsky. Greenwillow Books 2012 32 p.
Grades: PreK K 1 2   E
  1. Moose -- Fiction 2. Zebras -- Fiction 3. Children's
stories 4. Alphabet -- Fiction 5. Books and reading
-- Fiction 6. Humorous stories 7. Behavior -- Fiction
  ISBN 9780060799847; 9780060799854
                       LC 2011002148
In this illustrated children's book, "[c]lipboard-bearing
Zebra is in charge of getting the players on and off the
stage in an item-by-item alphabetical pageant. . . . [Then]
the excited Moose . . . pops onto the stage for D, leaving
the distressed Duck fluttering in frustration. . . . Moose then
tantrums through the rest of the book, . . . defacing other
subjects with crayoned-on antlers and claiming . . . that R
and S are also for Moose." (Bulletin of the Center for Children's Books)

Birdsall, Jeanne

  ★ **Flora's** very windy day; illustrated by Matt Phelan.
Clarion Books 2010 un il $16
Grades: K 1 2   E
  1. Winds -- Fiction 2. Siblings -- Fiction
  ISBN 978-0-618-98676-7; 0-618-98676-6
                       LC 2008-56061

When a big wind blows her annoying little brother away, Flora decides to save him despite the many tempting offers she gets for him from, among others, a cloud, an eagle, the man in the moon, and the wind itself.

"This is a gem of a book that will resonate with older siblings everywhere." SLJ

Birtha, Becky
★ **Grandmama's** pride; illustrated by Colin Bootman. Albert Whitman 2005 un il $16.95
Grades: K 1 2 3   E
1. Segregation -- Fiction 2. Grandmothers -- Fiction 3. African Americans -- Fiction
ISBN 0-8075-3028-X
LC 2005003991
While on a trip in 1956 to visit her grandmother in the South, six-year-old Sarah Marie experiences segregation for the first time, but discovers that things have changed by the time she returns the following year.

"The strong, sensitive writing is enhanced by beautiful watercolor paintings filled with chips of light." SLJ

★ **Lucky** beans; illustrated by Nicole Tadgell. Albert Whitman 2010 un il $16.99
Grades: 1 2 3   E
1. Beans -- Fiction 2. Mathematics -- Fiction 3. African Americans -- Fiction 4. Great Depression, 1929-1939 -- Fiction
ISBN 978-0-8075-4782-3; 0-8075-4782-4
During the Great Depression, an African American boy named Marshall uses lessons learned in arithmetic class to figure out how many beans are in a jar to win his mother a sewing machine.

"Math and wry comedy mix in this lively historical story. . . . The expressive watercolor paintings show both the racism that Marshall and his family endure as well as his final triumph, and Tadgell folds in humor." Booklist

Bitterman, Albert
Fortune cookies; illustrated by Chris Raschka. Beach Lane Books 2011 un il $14.99
Grades: PreK K   E
1. Fortune telling -- Fiction
ISBN 978-1-4169-6814-6; 1-4169-6814-8
LC 2008-20158
Seven fortune cookies foretell a child's fortunes for each day of the week.

"A tidy, perfectly paced story with subtle grace and a kernel of wisdom." Publ Wkly

Bjorkman, Steve
Dinosaurs don't, dinosaurs do. Holiday House 2011 un il (I like to read) $14.95
Grades: PreK K 1   E
1. Dinosaurs -- Fiction 2. Etiquette -- Fiction
ISBN 978-0-8234-2355-2; 0-8234-2355-7
LC 2010032832
This book "deftly [combines] text and art to create a positive experience for new readers. [It is] larger than typical easy readers, leaving plenty of room for uncluttered, colorful cartoon illustrations and clear, large fonts. . . . Björkman uses repetitive text and playful pictures to introduce appropriate behavior. 'Dinosaurs don't run here' is demonstrated by a dismayed dinosaur in front of glassware falling from a

china cabinet; opposite, 'Dinosaurs do run here' shows two smiling creatures running through a playground. . . . [This title has] similar-sounding vowels and consonants, popular sight words, and short, simple sentences with clear punctuation, making [it a] successful [entry] in the beginning-reader canon." SLJ

Black, Michael Ian
Chicken cheeks; illustrated by Kevin Hawkes. Simon & Schuster Books for Young Readers 2009 un il $15.99
Grades: PreK K 1 2   E
1. Stories in rhyme 2. Animals -- Fiction
ISBN 978-1-4169-4864-3; 1-4169-4864-3
LC 2007-16872
This "features the hind quarters of animals, complete with silly names for them. . . . The closeup, color-saturated illustrations—which are at the same time obviously hilarious and sneakily deadpan—tell a story. A brown bear stands poised atop a ladder, gazing thoughtfully up the skinny trunk of a tall, branch-free tree. He grabs a duck and sets it on his head. . . . Sixteen animals later, children can only laugh helplessly at the absurd ladder of animals balanced parallel to the tree trunk. . . . Filled with visual jokes and amusing details, ChickenCheeks is a lot more than a list of words for kids to snicker at." SLJ

★ **A pig** parade is a terrible idea; illustrated by Kevin Hawkes. Simon & Schuster Books for Young Readers 2010 un il $16.99
Grades: PreK K 1 2   E
1. Pigs -- Fiction 2. Parades -- Fiction
ISBN 978-1-4169-7922-7; 1-4169-7922-0
LC 2008-51562
Explains precisely why, although it may sound like a good idea, gathering hundreds of pigs to march in a parade through one's hometown is inadvisable.

"If this book's arch-toned text wasn't flat-out funny enough, Hawkes' deliciously down-and-dirty art takes the concept to a whole other level." Booklist

The **purple** kangaroo; illustrated by Peter Brown. Simon & Schuster Books for Young Readers 2010 un il $16.99
Grades: PreK K 1 2   E
1. Telepathy -- Fiction 2. Imagination -- Fiction
ISBN 978-1-4169-5771-3; 1-4169-5771-5
LC 2008003534
After asking the reader to think of something spectacular, the narrator sets out to prove his ability to read minds by describing a preposterous situation and characters.

"The engaging artwork features muted acrylic paintings punctuated by the computer-generated monkey narrating each page. A silly, fun romp that kids will ask for again and again." SLJ

Blackaby, Susan
★ **Brownie** Groundhog and the February fox; illustrated by Carmen Segovia. Sterling 2010 un il $16.99
Grades: PreK K 1   E
1. Foxes -- Fiction 2. Winter -- Fiction 3. Marmots -- Fiction
ISBN 978-1-4027-4336-8; 1-4027-4336-X

Brownie the groundhog encounters a fox while waiting for winter to be over, and through clever maneuvering—and tasty snacks—the two become friends.

"Segovia's acrylic paints and inks elevate the simple-seeming story, truly driving home the bone-penetrating chill of a typical February day. Blackaby is as tricky as her heroine, economically developing two distinct and likable characters and delivering plenty of chuckles and wordplay. Elegant." Kirkus

Blackall, Sophie

★ **Are** you awake? Henry Holt 2011 un il $12.99
Grades: PreK K 1   E
    1. Night -- Fiction 2. Bedtime -- Fiction 3. Mother-son relationship -- Fiction
    ISBN 978-0-8050-7858-9; 0-8050-7858-4
                      LC 2010026946

Persistent young Edward has many questions for his sleepy mother, many of which are answered, "Because it's night time."

Blackall's "palette starts out gray, warming to sunlit yellow as the bedside clock hands rotate and dawn breaks. Dialogue moves from speech balloons to type and back again, while watercolor panels offer affectionate closeups of Edward, his mother, and night scenes from their apartment window. Edward's antics hit the mark. . . . while Blackall's arch voice . . . makes this a solid candidate for the favorites pile." Publ Wkly

Blackford, Andy

Bill's bike; illustrated by Hannah Wood. Crabtree Pub. Co. 2011 21p il (Tadpoles) lib bdg $21.27; pa $6.95
Grades: PreK K 1   E
    1. Wheels -- Fiction 2. Bicycles -- Fiction
    ISBN 978-0-7787-0575-8 lib bdg; 0-7787-0575-7 lib bdg; 978-0-7787-0586-4 pa; 0-7787-0586-2 pa
                      LC 2010052360

"Bill starts off with four wheels on his bike but finds that he only needs two. . . . The [story is] gently funny with supportive illustrations that offer a solid structure within which kids can begin to read on their own. . . . [This book offers] characters with personality and scenes full of action." SLJ

The **hungry** little monkey; illustrated by Gabriele Antonini. Crabtree Pub. Co. 2011 21p il (Tadpoles) lib bdg $21.27; pa $6.95
Grades: PreK K 1   E
    1. Animals -- Fiction 2. Monkeys -- Fiction
    ISBN 978-0-7787-0581-9 lib bdg; 0-7787-0581-1 lib bdg; 978-0-7787-0592-5 pa; 0-7787-0592-7 pa
                      LC 2010052367

"A little monkey gets advice from the other animals on how to eat his banana, . . . but the right answer eventually comes from his mother. The [story is] gently funny with supportive illustrations that offer a solid structure within which kids can begin to read on their own. . . . [This book offers] characters with personality and scenes full of action." SLJ

Blackstone, Stella

Bear's birthday; [illustrations by] Debbie Harter. Barefoot Books 2011 un il pa $6.99; bd bk $6.99
Grades: PreK   E
    1. Counting 2. Stories in rhyme 3. Bears -- Fiction 4.

Parties -- Fiction 5. Birthdays -- Fiction
    ISBN 978-1-84686-515-2 pa; 1-84686-515-8 pa; 978-1-84686-516-9 bd bk; 1-84686-516-6 bd bk
                      LC 2010041171

Bear celebrates his birthday with a party, games, and ten balloons.

"The busy scenes with bright geometrics and patterns promise many fun readings." SLJ

My granny went to market; a round-the-world counting rhyme. written by Stella Blackstone; illustrated by Christopher Corr. Barefoot Books 2005 un il $16.99
Grades: PreK K 1 2   E
    1. Counting 2. Stories in rhyme 3. Grandmothers -- Fiction 4. Voyages and travels -- Fiction
    ISBN 1-84148-792-9
                      LC 2004-17394

A child's grandmother travels around the world, buying things in quantities that illustrate counting from one to ten.

"The brightly colored gouache illustrations have the feel of Mexican folk art, and endpaper maps route Granny's travels, with a one-page legend showing her purchases—from one carpet to 10 llamas. A cheery, global shopping trip, fun to read alone and also useful in the classroom." Booklist

Octopus opposites; written by Stella Blackstone; illustrated by Stephanie Bauer. Barefoot Books 2010 un il $16.99 E
    1. Opposites 2. Stories in rhyme 3. Animals -- Fiction
    ISBN 978-1-84686-328-8; 1-84686-328-7
                      LC 2008051071

Creatures big and small introduce pairs of opposites.

"The text is accompanied by vivid, appealing acrylic drawings surrounded by textured borders, with backgrounds painted in thick strokes. An attractive, useful concept book." SLJ

Blackwood, Freya

★ **Ivy** loves to give. Arthur A. Levine Books 2010 un il $15.99
Grades: PreK K 1   E
    1. Gifts -- Fiction
    ISBN 978-0-545-23467-2; 0-545-23467-0
    First published 2009 in Australia

Ivy loves to give presents, and although they are not always appropriate, they are always given with enthusiasm and generosity.

Blackwood's "text—five sentences total—is brilliant in its economy, empathy, and pacing; the same can be said for the subtle and slyly funny family characterizations of her delicate pencil and watercolor drawings, rendered on a creamy white backdrop with minimal propping." Publ Wkly

Blake, Robert J.

Little devils. Philomel Books 2009 un il $16.99
Grades: PreK K 1 2   E
    1. Tasmanian devils -- Fiction
    ISBN 978-0-399-24322-6; 0-399-24322-4
                      LC 2008048106

When their mother fails to return one night, three Tasmanian Devil cubs venture out of their den in search of food and, by doing what Tasmanian Devils are supposed to do, manage to save their mother from a trap.

"Blake loads his light-filled paintings with natural details and realistic expressions. . . . He makes the story heartwarming and accessible without anthropomorphizing the animals." SLJ

Painter and Ugly. Philomel Books 2011 un il $16.99
Grades: K 1 2 3   E
1. Dogs -- Fiction 2. Friendship -- Fiction 3. Sled dog racing -- Fiction
ISBN 978-0-399-24323-3; 0-399-24323-2
                                    LC 2010005395
Painter and Ugly, two sled dogs who are inseparable best friends, are put on different teams for the Junior Iditarod, but they manage to find their way back to one another for the big race.

"Blake paints the dogs' heavy coats and eager faces in painstaking detail, and does a notably good job of narrating from a dog's point of view. His portrait of this specialized world will lure even those who have never been part of it." Publ Wkly

Blake, Stephanie

I don't want to go to school! written and illustrated by Stephanie Blake. Random House 2009 un il $12.99; lib bdg $15.99
Grades: PreK K   E
1. School stories 2. Rabbits -- Fiction
ISBN 978-0-375-85688-4; 0-375-85688-9; 978-0-375-95688-1 lib bdg; 0-375-95688-3 lib bdg
                                    LC 2008011256
Original French edition 2007
Simon the rabbit does not want to go to his first day of school, but by the time his mother comes to take him home, he is having such a good time that he does not want to leave

"This title has a standard premise that is instantly understandable and reassuring, and the naive-style art, rendered in bold outlines and primary colors, is appealing and expressive." Booklist
Another title about Simon the Rabbit is:
A deal's a deal (2011)

Blechman, Nicholas

Night light; Nicholas Blechman. Scholastic 2013 48 p. ill. (reinforced) $16.99
Grades: PreK K 1   E
1. Counting 2. Picture books for children 3. Light -- Fiction 4. Stories in rhyme 5. Vehicles -- Fiction
ISBN 0545462630; 9780545462631
                                    LC 2012024221
This children's picture book is "a counting book about big vehicles . . . with an extra . . . twist. [Nicholas Btechman] invites readers to identify the vehicles with a turn-the-page guessing game. First, spreads of pure black show only the vehicles' distinctive signature of lights. '1 light, shining bright?' reads the first black spread, a small, die-cut circle on the right side creating a single white dot. A page turn uncovers the answer: 'train.'" (Publishers Weekly)

Blessing, Charlotte

New old shoes; written by Charlotte Blessing; illustrated by Gary R. Phillips. Pleasant St. Press 2009 un il $16.95

Grades: K 1 2   E
1. Shoes -- Fiction
ISBN 978-0-9792035-6-5; 0-9792035-6-2
"This story is narrated by a pair of red sneakers and follows their journey from their first home with a young boy in America to children in Africa. . . . The color-saturated illustrations provide a vibrant background to this touching story." SLJ

Blexbolex

★ **People**; [translated by Claudia Bedrick] Enchanted Lion Books 2011 il $19.95
Grades: K 1 2   E
1. Occupations -- Fiction
ISBN 978-1-59270-110-0; 1-59270-110-8
                                    LC 2011001132
Explores, through brief text and illustrations, various sorts of people, the jobs they do, and the connections among them.

"German artist Blexbolex's captivating silk-screens explore human archetypes using a 1960s-era design aesthetic. Powder-blue type identifies each figure. As with its predecessor, the book's brilliance lies in the intriguing ways in which the images mimic, challenge, and inform one another. . . . Readers will form new associations and make new discoveries upon each revisiting." Publ Wkly

★ **Seasons**; translated by Claudia Bedrick. Enchanted Lion Books 2010 un il $19.95
Grades: K 1 2   E
1. Seasons -- Fiction
ISBN 978-1-59270-095-0; 1-59270-095-0
                                    LC 2010001114
Original French edition, 2009
Explores, through brief text and illustrations, various aspects of each season of the year.

"This thick volume is both beautiful and intriguing—artist's portfolio, concept book, and word book rolled into one. The words, in huge, vividly pink block capitals, caption full pages and spreads for which seasons are the organizing principle. . . . These sophisticated images are sure to stimulate creative thought." Horn Book

Bley, Anette

And what comes after a thousand? Kane/Miller 2007 un il $15.95
Grades: PreK K 1 2   E
1. Death -- Fiction 2. Friendship -- Fiction 3. Bereavement -- Fiction
ISBN 978-1-933605-27-2
"This tender tale about intergenerational friendship, love, and loss tells of the cozy relationship between a young girl and an old, hard-of-hearing man. . . . After he dies, she must learn to deal with her pain and feelings of abandonment. The closeness of the characters is portrayed in heartwarming illustrations. . . . This universal story will speak to many readers." SLJ

Bliss, Harry

★ **Bailey**. Scholastic 2011 un il $16.99
Grades: PreK K 1 2   E
1. School stories 2. Dogs -- Fiction
ISBN 978-0-545-23344-6; 0-545-23344-5
                                    LC 2010045096

Although he is a dog, Bailey goes to school where his canine abilities enliven an ordinary day.

"Deceptively simple cartoon illustrations belie the brilliance of the story. . . . From the facial expressions to the titles of the books Bailey reads, no opportunity is lost for fleshing out this character; and laughs abound on every page." SLJ

Bloch, Serge
Butterflies in my stomach and other school hazards; by Serge Bloch. Sterling Pub. Co. 2008 un il $12.95
Grades: PreK K 1 2   E
1. School stories 2. English language -- Idioms -- Fiction
ISBN 978-1-4027-4158-6; 1-4027-4158-8
LC 2007-43372
On the first day of school, a student is confused by many of the phrases that are used, such as when the librarian says not to open a can of worms, or when the teacher says he expects the class to be busy bees doing their homework.

"Bloch's simple though imaginative pictures and clean visual style invite discussion of the deeper meanings of these oft-used phrases, making this an ideal book for the classroom or for one-on-one sharing." SLJ

Snowed under and other Christmas confusions. Sterling 2011 il $12.95
Grades: PreK K 1   E
1. Christmas -- Fiction
ISBN 978-1-4027-7131-6; 1-4027-7131-2
LC 2010037056
A snow storm the day before Christmas causes a boy many worries, which are not helped by such confusing phrases as "Don't be a wet blanket" and "That's the way the cookie crumbles."

"The illustrations are creatively composed with effective use of white space, shadows and perspective along with motion and sight gags. As all kids know, 'time flies when you're having fun,' even on Christmas Eve. This is more fun than a barrel of monkeys." Kirkus

Blomgren, Jennifer
Where do I sleep? a Pacific Northwest lullabye. illustrated by Andrea Gabriel. Sasquatch Bks. 2001 un il $15.95
Grades: PreK K 12   E
1. Sleep 2. Lullabies 3. Stories in rhyme 4. Sleep -- Fiction 5. Animals -- Fiction 6. Animals -- Infancy
ISBN 1-57061-258-7
LC 2001-20940
Rhyming text describes some of the young animals— from a gray wolf pup and a horned puffin to a cougar kit and a small brown bat—as they settle down to sleep.

"Kids get an opportunity to practice map skills, learn about new animals, find out why Alaska's summer days are so long, and add such unfamiliar words as tundra to their vocabulary. . . . Gabriel's gorgeous artwork reflects the beauty and diversity of the wildlife and landscape." Booklist

Bloom, Suzanne
Feeding friendsies. Boyds Mills Press 2011 un il $16.95

Grades: PreK K   E
1. Play -- Fiction 2. Gardens -- Fiction
ISBN 978-1-59078-529-4; 1-59078-529-0
Baby and friends are busy in the garden making lunch that includes puddle-water soup, mud pie, and dandelion-and-dirt dessert.

"Bloom's sunny, naive watercolor illustrations show the children joyfully playing in the dirt while a shaggy dog and a black cat watch with curiosity. . . . This celebration of imaginative, outdoor fun is a tasty treat." SLJ

A **mighty** fine time machine. Boyds Mills Press 2009 un il $16.95
Grades: PreK K 1   E
1. Play -- Fiction 2. Boxes -- Fiction 3. Animals -- Fiction 4. Imagination -- Fiction
ISBN 978-1-59078-527-0; 1-59078-527-4
LC 2008-28043
An aardvark, an anteater, and an armadillo attempt to travel back in time when they turn a big box into a time machine.

"The colored pencil-and-gouache illustrations add warmth and humor to the story. Bloom's whimsical word choice will further draw children into the story and have them rooting for the friends' success." Booklist

★ A **splendid** friend, indeed; written and illustrated by Suzanne Bloom. Boyds Mills Press 2005 un il $15.95
Grades: PreK K 1   E
1. Geese -- Fiction 2. Friendship -- Fiction 3. Polar bear -- Fiction
ISBN 1-59078-286-0
LC 2004-10780
When a studious polar bear meets an inquisitive goose, they learn to be friends.

"The cool palette of the pastel illustrations, consisting of shades of blue and white and touches of violet, sets a quiet, friendly tone, and the animals' priceless expressions tell all. The gentle humor will elicit giggles." SLJ
Other titles about Bear and Goose are:
Treasure (2007)
What about Bear? (2010)

Blue, Rose
Ron's big mission; [by] Rose Blue and Corinne J. Naden; illustrated by Don Tate. Dutton Childrens Books 2009 un il $16.99
Grades: K 1 2 3   E
1. Astronauts 2. Physicists 3. Libraries -- Fiction 4. Segregation -- Fiction 5. African Americans -- Fiction 6. Books and reading -- Fiction
ISBN 978-0-525-47849-2; 0-525-47849-3
LC 2007050563
One summer day in 1959, nine-year-old Ron McNair, who dreams of becoming a pilot, walks into the Lake City, South Carolina, public library and insists on checking out some books, despite the rule that only white people can have library cards. Includes facts about McNair, who grew up to be an astronaut

"Vibrant illustrations portray a cozy small town. . . . Tate's figures feature oversized heads with very expressive faces that vividly convey well-meant kindness and the frustrations of injustice. . . . This will make a good choice for reading aloud and discussing." Booklist

Bluemle, Elizabeth

Dogs on the bed; illustrated by Anne Wilsdorf. Candlewick Press 2008 un il $15.99

Grades: PreK K 1 2   E

1. Dogs -- Fiction 2. Bedtime -- Fiction 3. Family life -- Fiction

ISBN 978-0-7636-2608-2; 0-7636-2608-2

"As bedtime begins . . . everyone—Mom, Dad, two kids, and six dogs—falls asleep in the same big bed. Throughout the night, the pets do what they do best: sleep sideways, bark at things no one else can hear, and whine to go out, and then in. . . . The exuberant, rhyming text delights the ear as the hilarious illustrations engage the eye in this kid and dog-friendly tale." SLJ

★ How do you wokka-wokka? illustrated by Randy Cecil. Candlewick Press 2009 un il $15.99

Grades: PreK K 1   E

1. Stories in rhyme 2. Dance -- Fiction

ISBN 978-0-7636-3228-1; 0-7636-3228-7

LC 2008-27715

A young boy who likes to "wokka-wokka, shimmy-shake, and shocka-shocka" gathers his neighbors together for a surprise celebration.

"The sketchy, full-color oil illustrations in muted colors feature cartoon children cavorting alternately against stark white backgrounds or cityscapes as they join a giant block party. This bouncy book is a joy as a read-aloud." SLJ

Blume, Judy

★ The Pain and the Great One; illustrations by Irene Trivas. rev format ed; Atheneum Books for Young Readers 2002 un il $17.95; pa $6.99

Grades: K 1 2 3   E

1. Siblings -- Fiction

ISBN 0-689-85507-9; 0-440-40967-5 pa

First published 1984 by Bradbury Press

A six-year-old (The Pain) and his eight-year-old sister (The Great One) see each other as troublemakers and the best-loved in the family

"Young readers, depending on their position within the family, will readily identify with either character and may learn empathy for the other. Used in a group, this will provide much healthy discussion. . . . Trivas' vibrant colors add depth and humor to a valuable book on sibling relationships." SLJ

Blumenthal, Deborah

The blue house dog; illustrated by Adam Gustavson. Peachtree 2010 un il $15.95

Grades: K 1 2 3   E

1. Dogs -- Fiction

ISBN 978-1-56145-537-9; 1-56145-537-7

"After his owner dies, Bones [a dog] roams the streets until young Cody acknowledges his grief over losing his own pet and persuades Bones to trust him. Perceptive art and emotive, free verse-style text work well together." Booklist

Bodeen, S. A.

★ Elizabeti's doll; illustrated by Christy Hale. Lee & Low Bks. 1998 un il $15.95

Grades: K 1 2 3   E

1. Dolls 2. Siblings -- Fiction

ISBN 1-880000-70-9

LC 98-13086

When a young Tanzanian girl gets a new baby brother, she finds a rock, which she names Eva, and makes it her baby doll

"Vibrant patterns and soft watercolor backgrounds evoke a sense of place and familial love." SLJ

Other titles about Elizabeti are:

Elizabeti's school (2002)

Mama Elizabeti (2000)

A small, brown dog with a wet, pink nose; by Stephanie Stuve-Bodeen; [illustrations by Linzie Hunter] Little Brown Books for Young Readers 2009 un il $16.99

Grades: K 1 2   E

1. Dogs -- Fiction 2. Parent-child relationship -- Fiction

ISBN 978-0-316-05830-8; 0-316-05830-0

LC 2008039298

Amelia will stop at nothing to convince her parents to let her adopt a very special dog.

"The concepts are complicated but clear, and Hunter's patterned illustrations are appropriately unpredictable, with nearly every page design different from the last. Plenty for kids to pore over." Booklist

Boelts, Maribeth

Before you were mine; story by Maribeth Boelts; pictures by David Walker. Putnam 2007 un il $15.99

Grades: PreK K 1 2   E

1. Dogs -- Fiction

ISBN 978-0-399-24526-8; 0-399-24526-X

LC 2006-20525

A young boy imagines what his rescued dog's life might have been like before he adopted him.

"Cozy, soft-edged pictures of an adorable dog characterize this warmhearted book. . . . The pastel illustrations use a variety of layouts to infuse the story with emotion." Booklist

Dogerella; illustrated by Donald Wu. Random House 2008 48p il (Step into reading) lib bdg $11.99; pa $3.99

Grades: 1 2 3   E

1. Fairy tales 2. Dogs -- Fiction

ISBN 978-0-375-93393-6 lib bdg; 0-375-93393-X lib bdg; 978-0-375-83393-9 pa; 0-375-83393-5 pa

LC 2007-15229

With the help of her fairy dogmother, Dogerella attends Princess Bea's ball where she competes with other dogs to become the princess's royal pet

"The combination of dozens of dogs, an earnest princess and a touch of magic add up to a charming whole." Kirkus

Those shoes; [by] Maribeth Boelts; illustrated by Noah Z. Jones. Candlewick Press 2007 un il $15.99; pa $6.99

Grades: K 1 2 3   E

1. Shoes -- Fiction 2. Grandmothers -- Fiction

ISBN 978-0-7636-2499-6; 0-7636-2499-3; 978-0-7636-4284-6 pa; 0-7636-4284-3 pa

LC 2006-51839

Jeremy, who longs to have the black high tops that everyone at school seems to have but his grandmother cannot afford, is excited when he sees them for sale in a thrift shop and decides to buy them even though they are the wrong size.

"Jones mixed-media, digitally assembled pictures cleverly capture how thoroughly the shoe craze permeates every aspect of Jeremy's life. . . . Boelts and Jones create a work with broad appeal." Bull Cent Child Books

Bogan, Paulette

★ **Goodnight** Lulu. Bloomsbury Children's Bk. 2003 un il hardcover o.p. pa $6.95

Grades: PreK K 1 2   E

1. Bedtime -- Fiction 2. Chickens -- Fiction

ISBN 1-58234-803-0; 1-58234-983-5 pa

LC 2002-27825

When her mother tucks her in for the night, Lulu the chicken worries what would happen if a bear or a tiger or an alligator should come in during the night

This is a "funny, original, and reassuring tale. . . . The saturated watercolor and ink spreads deftly capture the night's ominous as well as cozy qualities." Horn Book Guide

Another title about Lulu is:

Lulu the big little chick (2009)

Lulu the big little chick. Bloomsbury Children's Books 2009 un il $16.99

Grades: PreK K 1 2   E

1. Size -- Fiction 2. Chickens -- Fiction 3. Mother-child relationship -- Fiction

ISBN 978-1-59990-343-9; 1-59990-343-1

LC 2008-36222

When Lulu gets tired of being told she is too little to do things, she decides to go far, far away.

"Vibrant watercolor-and-ink double-page spreads seamlessly blend shades to create a natural gleam. This comic feature clucks in with a vengeance." Kirkus

Bogart, Jo Ellen

Big and small, room for all; illustrated by Gillian Newland. Tundra Books 2009 un il $18.95

Grades: PreK K 1 2   E

1. Size -- Fiction 2. Size -- Juvenile literature

ISBN 978-0-88776-891-0; 0-88776-891-1

"A young girl sitting on a low tree branch views the vast mountains, sky, and fields around her. As the book progresses, realistic watercolor illustrations show the universe, the solar system, and a mountain range, as the spare text labels each concept in comparison to the size of the one before it. . . . Youngsters will delight in the awe-inspiring illustrations. . . . Word choice is highly suitable for the earliest independent readers." SLJ

Boisrobert, Anouck

Popville; [by] Anouck Boisrobert & Louis Rigaud. Roaring Brook Press 2010 un il lib bdg $16.99

Grades: K 1 2 3   E

1. Stories without words 2. Pop-up books 3. City and town life -- Fiction 4. Cities and towns -- Juvenile literature

ISBN 1-59643-593-3 lib bdg; 978-1-59643-593-3 lib bdg

Successive pop-up scenes show the progress as a rural area is built up into a busy city. "Ages four to eight." (N Y Times Book Rev)

"Using crisp, appealing pop-ups in a long, thin binding, [this book] chronicles a city's evolution from a bucolic, perhaps lonely, country church to an urban landscape. . . .

'Popville' has a clever central mechanism that tells the story quietly: a window cut out right through the book allows all the successive buildings to stay popped up even when the pages turn. The artwork is uncluttered and stylized, using muted, solid colors with a fabric-like texture to create clean geometric shapes." New York Times

Boldt, Claudia

Odd dog; written and illustrated by Claudia Boldt. North-South Books 2012 32 p. $16.95

Grades: PreK K 1 2   E

1. Dogs -- Fiction 2. Apples -- Fiction 3. Sharing -- Fiction 4. Picture books for children 5. Friendship -- Juvenile fiction

ISBN 0735840687; 9780735840683

In this children's picture book, Peanut, the titular odd dog, "does not care for bones; rather, he is obsessed with apples. His covetousness leads to paranoia, as he worries neighbor-dog Milo is plotting to steal his prized possessions. . . . He comically attempts to save the juiciest of apples from an oblivious Milo. . . . In the end, Peanut learns that Milo, like most dogs, only likes bones, emotionally freeing the pensive pup and opening up his world to friendship." (Kirkus Reviews)

Boldt, Mike

123 versus ABC; by Mike Boldt. Harper, an imprint of HarperCollinsPublishers 2013 32 p. (hardcover) $17.99

Grades: K 1 2 3   E

1. Alphabet 2. Numbers -- Juvenile fiction 3. Alphabet -- Juvenile fiction 4. Counting 5. Humorous stories 6. Alphabet -- Fiction 7. Numbers, Natural -- Fiction

ISBN 0062102990; 9780062102997

LC 2012025494

This book, written by Mike Boldt, asks "which is more important, numbers or letters? Numbers and letters, the colorful characters in this story, compete to be the stars of this book. Their debate escalates when funny animals and props arrive—starting with 1 alligator, 2 bears, and 3 cars." (Publisher's note)

Bond, Felicia

Big hugs, little hugs. Philomel Books 2012 un il $16.99

Grades: PreK K   E

1. Animals -- Fiction 2. Hugging -- Fiction

ISBN 978-0-399-25614-1; 0-399-25614-8

LC 2010053139

"This jubilant ode to the joys of hugging boldly announces its message on the first page: 'Everyone hugs all over the world.' What follows are tidy snippets of text that declare what animals like to hug, . . . as well as where, how, and when this hugging takes place. Bond . . . works in torn and cut-paper collage, her cheerful animal families showing various happy emotions. . . . The book's many whimsical touches should prove both comforting and entertaining." Publ Wkly

Bonsall, Crosby Newell

★ **Mine's** the best; newly il ed; HarperCollins Pubs. 1996 32p il (My first I can read book) lib bdg $16.89; pa $3.99

Grades: K 1 2   E

1. Balloons -- Fiction 2. Friendship -- Fiction

ISBN 0-06-027091-8 lib bdg; 0-06-444213-6 pa

LC 95-12405

A newly illustrated edition of the title first published 1973

Two little boys meet at the beach, each sure that his balloon is better

"The playful illustrations tell their own story; the extremely brief text (not to mention the head start provided by the two initial wordless spreads) will give new readers a sense of accomplishment." Horn Book Guide

★ **Who's** afraid of the dark? by Crosby Bonsall. Harper & Row 1980 32p il (Early I can read book) lib bdg $16.89; pa $3.99

Grades: K 1 2   E

1. Fear -- Fiction 2. Night -- Fiction

ISBN 0-06-020599-7 lib bdg; 0-06-444071-0 pa

LC 79-2700

"A little boy describes to a friend the nighttime fears of his dog Stella. Stella shivers in the dark, he claims; she sees shapes and hears scary sounds. The doubting but sympathetic friend offers a suggestion—hug Stella in the night and comfort her until her fears go away. . . . The illustrations in shades of light blue and brown are filled with as much life and warmth as ever." Horn Book

★ The **case** of the hungry stranger; by Crosby Bonsall. HarperCollins Pubs. 1992 64p il (I can read book) hardcover o.p. pa $3.99

Grades: K 1 2 3   E

1. Mystery fiction

ISBN 0-06-020571-7 lib bdg; 0-06-444026-5 pa

LC 91-13345

A reissue of the title first published 1963. This edition has full color illustrations

Wizard and his friends are clueless when they are sent on the trail of a blueberry pie thief, until Wizard hits on a plan that is sure to nab the sweet-toothed pilferer

This offers "suspense and humor." Horn Book

Other titles in this series are:

The case of the cat's meow (1965)

The case of the double cross (1980)

The case of the dumb bells (1966)

The case of the scaredy cats (1971)

★ The **day** I had to play with my sister; story and pictures by Crosby Bonsall. newly il ed; HarperCollins Pubs. 1999 32p il (My first I can read book) hardcover o.p. pa $3.99

Grades: K 1 2   E

1. Siblings -- Fiction

ISBN 0-06-028181-2; 0-06-444253-5 pa

LC 98-20342

A newly illustrated edition of the title first published 1972

A young boy becomes very frustrated when he tries to teach his little sister to play hide-and-seek

"The extremely simple text . . . is one with which children can readily identify. . . . The realistic atmosphere makes Bonsall's book an excellent addition to the very early reading shelves." SLJ

Bonwill, Ann

Naughty toes; illustrated by Teresa Murfin. Tiger Tales 2011 un il $15.95

Grades: K 1 2   E

1. Dance -- Fiction 2. Sisters -- Fiction

ISBN 978-1-58925-103-8; 1-58925-103-2

Chloe and Belinda are sisters, but they couldn't be more different. Belinda is a born dancer and the star of Madame Mina's dance class. Chloe is . . . not. Madame Mina thinks that Chloe has "naughty toes." But Mr. Tiempo, the class pianist, thinks otherwise.

"The mixed-media illustrations are fun and free, capturing Chloe's nature and attitude. Great as a read-aloud, for a guidance lesson on self-esteem, or even on sibling rivalry." SLJ

Bootman, Colin

Steel pan man of Harlem. Carolrhoda Books 2009 un il lib bdg $16.95

Grades: K 1 2 3   E

1. Rats -- Fiction 2. Steel drum (Musical instrument) -- Fiction

ISBN 978-0-8225-9026-2 lib bdg; 0-8225-9026-3 lib bdg

LC 2008039654

A mysterious man appears in Harlem and promises to rid the city of its rats by playing the steel pan drum

Bootman "triumphs with this gorgeously moody, thoroughly cinematic retelling of the Pied Piper of Hamelin. . . . The oil paintings conjure up a gritty, workaday world where magic has taken hold." Publ Wkly

Borden, Louise

The **A** + custodian; illustrated by Adam Gustavson. Margaret K. McElderry Books 2004 un il $15.95

Grades: K 1 2 3   E

1. School stories 2. Janitors -- Fiction

ISBN 0-689-84995-8

LC 2002-12029

The students and teachers at Dublin Elementary School make banners, posters, and signs for their school custodian to show how much they appreciate him and all the work he does

"The simple, unrhymed poetic words and the realistic oil paintings create a strong sense of a diverse school community and a man in flannel shirt and worn leather shoes." Booklist

A. Lincoln and me; illustrated by Ted Lewin. Scholastic 1999 un il hardcover o.p. pa $5.99

Grades: K 1 2 3   E

1. Lawyers 2. Presidents 3. State legislators 4. Members of Congress 5. Self-perception -- Fiction

ISBN 0-590-45714-4 pa

LC 98-51921

With the help of his teacher, a young boy realizes that he not only shares his birthday and similar physical appearance with Abraham Lincoln, but that he is like him in other ways as well

"Borden's text flows nicely, creating imagery of the physical presence of the man. Lewin's distinctive watercolors lend style and substance to the book, producing a treat for the eyes." SLJ

Big brothers don't take naps; art by Emma Dodd. Margaret K. McElderry Books 2011 un il $16.99
Grades: PreK K 1   E
  1. Infants -- Fiction 2. Brothers -- Fiction 3. Siblings -- Fiction
  ISBN 978-1-4169-5503-0; 1-4169-5503-8
"Nicholas admires and pays great attention to everything his big brother does. . . . James is a patient teacher and role model for his younger sibling. . . . When the two boys work together on a list of names for a 'special event' to take place in June, the older boy lets his brother make the definitive choice. Of course, the surprise is a baby sister, which makes Nicholas a big brother himself. Bright pastel, digitally rendered illustrations span autumn, winter, and spring and show the brothers and their ever-present dogs in a loving, noncompetitive relationship." SLJ

Good luck, Mrs. K! written by Louise Borden; illustrated by Adam Gustavson. Margaret K. McElderry Bks. 1999 un il hardcover o.p. pa $6.99
Grades: K 1 2 3   E
  1. School stories 2. Cancer -- Fiction 3. Schools -- Fiction 4. Teachers -- Fiction
  ISBN 0-689-82147-6; 0-689-85119-7 pa
                             LC 97-50553
"A truly endearing story. Gustavson's watercolor illustrations exude all of the warmth and vibrancy of Borden's words." SLJ

The **John** Hancock Club; written by Louise Borden; illustrated by Adam Gustavson. Margaret K. McElderry Books 2007 un il $16.99
Grades: 1 2 3   E
  1. School stories 2. Handwriting -- Fiction
  ISBN 1-4169-1813-2
                           LC 2005033171
Third-grader Sean McFerrin wants to be part of the good penmanship club, but it all depends on how well he learns the new cursive writing
"Gustavson's expressive paintings underscore the individuality of the characters and create a realistic school setting for the story. A fine picture book on a childhood rite of passage." Booklist

Off to first grade; illustrated by Joan Rankin. Margaret K. McElderry Books 2008 un il $16.99
Grades: PreK K 1   E
  1. School stories
  ISBN 978-0-689-87395-9; 0-689-87395-6
                           LC 2005-02320
Each member of a first grade class, as well as their teacher, principal, and a bus driver, expresses excitement, worry, or hope as the first day of school begins.
"The sequence is gentle yet genuinely perceptive in its documentation of the varying responses to the dramatic transition from home to school." Bull Cent Child Books

Boswell, Addie K.
  The **rain** stomper. Marshall Cavendish 2008 un il $16.99
Grades: PreK K 1 2   E
  1. Rain -- Fiction 2. Parades -- Fiction
  ISBN 978-0-7614-5393-2; 0-7614-5393-8

When it begins to rain and storm on the day of her big parade, Jazmin stomps, shouts, and does all she can think of to drive the rain away.
"Velasquez's large oils impart a sense of the girl's disappointment as well as the feel of a driving rain and eventual pleasure. Large letters in white, black, or red and in different sizes emphasize the sounds and rhythm of the rain and thunder. . . . A delightful read-aloud that deals with making the best of a disappointing situation." SLJ

Bottner, Barbara
  Bootsie Barker bites; illustrated by Peggy Rathmann. Putnam 1992 un il $17.99; pa $5.99
Grades: K 1 2 3   E
  1. Bullies -- Fiction
  ISBN 0-399-22125-5; 0-698-11427-2 pa
                           LC 91-12182
"Bottner's tone is a model of simplicity and matter-of-factness, sometimes droll but never coy. Rathmann's neon-bright, full-color artwork extends the emotional tenor and the humor of the text." Booklist
Another title about Bootsie is:
Bootsie Barker ballerina (1997)

★ **Miss** Brooks loves books (and I don't) story by Barbara Bottner; illustrations by Michael Emberley. Alfred A. Knopf 2010 un il $17.99; lib bdg $20.99
Grades: PreK K 1 2   E
  1. School stories 2. Librarians -- Fiction 3. Books and reading -- Fiction
  ISBN 978-0-375-84682-3; 0-375-84682-4; 978-0-375-94682-0 lib bdg; 0-375-94682-9 lib bdg
                           LC 2009-02305
A first-grade girl who does not like to read stubbornly resists her school librarian's efforts to convince her to love books until she finds one that might change her mind.
"Children will delight in Emberley's spirited watercolor and ink renderings of literary favorites. . . . Bottner's deadpan humor and delicious prose combine with Emberley's droll caricatures to create a story sure to please those who celebrate books—and one that may give pause to those who don't (or who work with the latter)." SLJ

Pish and Posh wish for fairy wings; by Barbara Bottner and Gerald Kruglik; pictures by Barbara Bottner. Katherine Tegen Books 2006 47p il (I can read!) hardcover o.p. pa $3.99
Grades: K 1 2   E
  1. Magic -- Fiction 2. Fairies -- Fiction
  ISBN 978-0-06-051419-8; 0-06-051419-1; 978-0-06-051420-4 lib bdg; 0-06-051420-5 lib bdg; 0-06-051421-3 pa
                           LC 2005-22862
Best friends and beginner fairies Pish and Posh receive encouragement from the Monster Under the Bed as they each try to make four wise wishes in order to earn their wings
"This book scores a hit with two well-defined characters. . . . Bottner's humorous illustrations convey the action well. The characters . . . are delightfully drawn and full of expression." SLJ

Raymond and Nelda; written by Barbara Bottner; illustrated by Nancy Hayashi. Peachtree 2007 un il $15.95

Grades: PreK K 1   E
1. Friendship -- Fiction
ISBN 1-56145-394-3

LC 2006024277

Raymond and Nelda have always been the very best of
friends, and when they have a falling out they are both so
miserable that Florence, their mail carrier, helps them get
past their pride and hurt feelings to make up

"In Hayashi's clear watercolor, pen, and colored-pencil
illustrations, the plump, awkward characters wear clothes
and act like children, their body language as expressive of
their anger and longing as their words." Booklist

★ An **annoying** ABC; illustrated by Michael Emberley. Alfred A. Knopf 2011 un il $17.99; lib bdg $20.99
Grades: PreK K 1 2   E
1. Alphabet 2. School stories
ISBN 978-0-375-86708-8; 0-375-86708-2; 978-0-375-
96708-5 lib bdg; 0-375-96708-7 lib bdg; 978-0-375-
98469-3 e-book

LC 2011011843

"Adelaide annoys Bailey when she runs at him wearing
her tiger costume, scaring him and causing him to let the
gerbil out of its cage. So begins a rollicking preschool/early
elementary romp featuring kids who appear in alphabetical
order with a corresponding action. . . . The hilarity lies in
the illustrations, typical Emberley style, done in mechanical
pencil and watercolors. . . . One read-through will simply not
be enough to enjoy all the fun." Kirkus

Boudreau, Helene
I dare you not to yawn; Helene Boudreau, illustrated
by Serge Bloch. Candlewick Press 2013 32 p. (reinforced)
$15.99
Grades: PreK K 1   E
ISBN 9780763650704

LC 2012942415

Bourguignon, Laurence
Heart in the pocket; by Laurence Bourguignon; illus-
trated by Valerie d'Heur. Eerdmans Books for Young Read-
ers 2008 un il $16.50
Grades: PreK K 1 2   E
1. Kangaroos -- Fiction 2. Mother-child relationship
-- Fiction
ISBN 978-0-8028-5343-1; 0-8028-5343-9

LC 2007049348

A baby kangaroo is reluctant to leave the comfort of his
mother's pocket, where he is safe and warm and can always
hear her heartbeat, until he finds out that her heart is not
actually in her pocket.

"The gentle, well-crafted text is sweet, but not overly so.
The watercolor illustrations have a soft palette dominated
by yellowish tans and light blues, and expressively portray a
wise and loving mother with her shy, slightly fearful child."
SLJ

Boutignon, Beatrice
Not all animals are blue; a big book of little differences.
Kane/Miller 2009 un il $15.95
Grades: PreK K 1 2   E
1. Animals 2. Individual differences -- Juvenile
literature
ISBN 978-1-933605-96-8; 1-933605-96-0

Boutignon "invites readers to examine five animals on
one side of the spread, read five descriptive sentences on the
other, and determine which sentence describes which animal. Working in pencil and watercolor, Boutignon confers
on her creatures an elegance that they maintain even when
they are wearing flippers or their umbrellas are being blown
inside-out. . . . Children won't have any trouble matching
words to pictures." Publ Wkly

Bowen, Anne
I know an old teacher; story by Anne Bowen; pictures
by Stephen Gammell. Carolrhoda Books 2008 un il lib
bdg $16.95
Grades: K 1 2 3   E
1. School stories 2. Stories in rhyme 3. Pets -- Fiction
4. Teachers -- Fiction
ISBN 978-0-8225-7984-7; 0-8225-7984-7

LC 2007-42631

In this take on the well-known cumulative rhyme, a
teacher inadvertently swallows a flea, then follows it with
an assortment of classroom pets while her students look on
in surprise.

"Bowen's rhymes will have kids rolling in the aisles between their desks, and Gammell's spiky mixed-media illustrations are fittingly absurd." Horn Book Guide

Boyer, Cecile
Woof, meow, tweet-tweet. Seven Footer Kids 2011
un il $15.95
Grades: PreK K 1   E
1. Cats -- Fiction 2. Dogs -- Fiction 3. Birds -- Fiction
ISBN 978-1-934734-60-5; 1-934734-60-8

Presents a humorous account of the differences between
dogs, cats, and birds, from the sounds they make, how they
behave, and what happens when they all meet.

"The book's unique juxtaposition of text, clean graphic
images, and font changes might also encourage older readers, noting its text-as-art or perhaps a few new vocabulary
words. . . . This simple yet cleverly executed story can be
used in multiple ways in various classes and individual settings." SLJ

Boyle, Bob
Hugo and the really, really, really long string. Random
House 2010 un il $15.99; lib bdg $18.99
Grades: PreK K 1 2   E
1. Stories in rhyme 2. Animals -- Fiction
ISBN 978-0-375-83423-3; 0-375-83423-0; 978-0-375-
93423-0 lib bdg; 0-375-93423-5 lib bdg

LC 2006016303

Hugo follows a mysterious red string through his town,
collecting a series of new friends along the way, all of
them knowing that something special must be at the end of
the string.

"This is a great story that can lead to a discussion of
friends and neighborhoods. Written in rhyme, it is an entertaining story. The geometric style used in the artwork will
be familiar to students as Boyle is the author/illustrator who
created the Nick Jr. television show, WOW! WOW! Wub-
bzy!" Libr Media Connect

Boynton, Sandra
★ **Happy** Hippo, angry Duck; a book of moods. Little
Simon 2011 un il $5.99

Grades: PreK K   **E**

1. Board books for children 2. Animals -- Fiction 3. Emotions -- Fiction

ISBN 978-1-4424-1731-1; 1-4424-1731-5

"With her familiar brand of gentle absurdity, Boynton creates similes that ascribe moods to various animals. . . . Part of the book's pleasure is that Boynton doesn't rely on clichéd animal personifications. . . . Even kids in the stoniest of moods will feel the effect of this pick-me-up." Publ Wkly

Bradby, Marie

★ **Momma,** where are you from? illustrated by Chris K. Soentpiet. Orchard Bks. 2000 un il $16.95

Grades: K 1 2 3   **E**

1. City and town life 2. Afro-Americans 3. Mother and child 4. African Americans -- Fiction 5. Mother-daughter relationship -- Fiction

ISBN 0-531-30105-2

LC 99-23068

Momma describes the special people and surroundings of her childhood, in a place where the edge of town met the countryside, in a time when all the children at school were brown.

"Soentpiet's detailed, beautifully lit paintings freeze the mother's vivid memories, culminating in a dreamy, gray-toned montage of all the previous scenes. Children will be inspired by the mother's eloquent, proud answer to her daughter's essential question." Booklist

★ **More** than anything else; story by Marie Bradby; pictures by Chris K. Soentpiet. Orchard Bks. 1995 un il $15.95

Grades: K 1 2 3   **E**

1. Slaves 2. Authors 3. Educators 4. Memoirists 5. Nonfiction writers 6. Civil rights activists 7. African Americans -- Fiction 8. Books and reading -- Fiction

ISBN 0-531-09464-2

LC 94-48804

Nine-year-old Booker works with his father and brother at the saltworks, but dreams of the day when he'll be able to read.

"An evocative text combines with well-crafted, dramatic watercolors to provide a stirring, fictionalized account of the early life of Booker T. Washington." Horn Book

Bradford, Wade

Why do I have to make my bed? or, a history of messy rooms. illustrations by Johanna Van der Sterre. Tricycle Press 2011 un il $16.99

Grades: K 1 2   **E**

1. Home economics -- Fiction 2. Mother-son relationship -- Fiction

ISBN 978-1-58246-327-8; 1-58246-327-1

When a boy asks his mother why he must make his bed, she tells him a story about his ancestors who posed the same question through the centuries, going all the way back to a caveboy and his mother.

"While playing up the timelessness and universality of the human condition (at least as far as chores are concerned), the text and pictures underscore the evolving demands and trappings of domestic life. With its clever premise, keenly observed visual comedy, and easygoing pedagogy . . . this book deserves a place next to the Magic School Bus series." Publ Wkly

Bradley, Kimberly Brubaker

Ballerino Nate; illustrated by R.W. Alley. Dial Books for Young Readers 2006 un il $16.99

Grades: PreK K 1 2   **E**

1. Ballet -- Fiction 2. Sex role -- Fiction

ISBN 0-8037-2954-5

LC 2004-17822

After seeing a ballet performance, Nate decides he wants to learn ballet but he has doubts when his brother Ben tells him that only girls can be ballerinas.

"Bradley writes smoothly and insightfully about Nate's experiences. . . . Alley's watercolor-and-pencil contributions, portraying an entirely canine universe, capture both the warm family dynamics and Nate's zooming, irrepressible energy. " Booklist

The **perfect** pony; [by] Kimberly Brubaker Bradley; pictures by Shelagh McNicholas. Dial Books for Young Readers/Penguin Group 2007 un il $16.99

Grades: K 1 2   **E**

1. Horses -- Fiction

ISBN 0-8037-2851-4; 978-0-8037-2851-6

LC 2004024071

While searching for a sleek, fast, and spirited pony to own, a young girl comes to realize that the "perfect" pony is actually very different.

"McNicholas' realistic watercolor illustrations are completely in step with the understated text and the experience itself." Booklist

Braeuner, Shellie

The **great** dog wash; illustrated by Robert Neubecker. Simon & Schuster Books for Young Readers 2009 un il $15.99

Grades: PreK K 1   **E**

1. Stories in rhyme 2. Cats -- Fiction 3. Dogs -- Fiction

ISBN 978-1-4169-7116-0; 1-4169-7116-5

Rhyming text welcomes the reader to a dog wash that goes awry when someone brings their cat.

"Braeuner's sprightly, humorous rhymes are well paired with Neubecker's unfussy black-outlined digital illustrations." Horn Book Guide

Brallier, Jess M.

Tess's tree; pictures by Peter H. Reynolds. Harper 2009 un il $16.99

Grades: PreK K 1   **E**

1. Trees -- Fiction 2. Bereavement -- Fiction

ISBN 978-0-06-168752-5; 0-06-168752-9

LC 2009014580

When nine-year-old Tess invites her friends, family, and neighbors to celebrate her beloved maple tree's life before it must be cut down, she learns that it has meant a lot to other people, as well.

"Reynolds's soft watercolor vignettes extend the quiet story. Wispy lines portray a subtle vulnerability; washes of muted blue effectively provide emotional depth as Tess survives grief's powerful storm." Kirkus

Brannen, Sarah S.

Uncle Bobby's wedding; [by] Sarah S. Brannen. G. P. Putnam's Sons 2008 32p il $15.99

Grades: PreK K 1 2   **E**

1. Uncles -- Fiction 2. Weddings -- Fiction 3. Guinea

pigs -- Fiction 4. Homosexuality -- Fiction
ISBN 978-0-399-24712-5; 0-399-24712-2

LC 2007-16550

Chloë the guinea pig is jealous and sad when her favorite uncle announces that he will be getting married, but as she gets to know Jamie better and becomes involved in planning the wedding, she discovers that she will always be special to Uncle Bobby—and to Uncle Jamie, too.

"Warmly affectionate watercolor and graphite illustrations accompany this genial story of same-sex marriage." Horn Book Guide

Braun, Sebastien

★ **Back** to bed, Ed! Peachtree Publishers 2010 un il $15.95

Grades: PreK K 1   E

1. Mice -- Fiction 2. Sleep -- Fiction 3. Bedtime -- Fiction 4. Parent-child relationship -- Fiction
ISBN 978-1-56145-518-8; 1-56145-518-0

First published 2009 in the United Kingdom

Ed the mouse will not sleep in his own bed, until eventually his exasperated and tired parents find a way to keep him from joining them in the middle of the night.

"Braun's clean illustrations in India ink with markers and colored pencils are bright and bold. . . . They show all the emotions of the characters and many interesting details. . . . The simple text works in tandem with the illustrations to produce a great story that's fun to read." SLJ

Meeow and the big box. Boxer Books 2009 un il lib bdg $12.95

Grades: PreK   E

1. Cats -- Fiction 2. Play -- Fiction 3. Imagination -- Fiction
ISBN 978-1-906250-86-7 lib bdg; 1-906250-86-3 lib bdg

"Braun shows a wide-eyed black cat in a red scarf playing with a box. The omniscient narrator carries on a one-way dialogue, describing imaginative Meeow's actions and intentions as he transforms the box into a bright red fire engine. . . . The book is simple and direct, and pulls together all the ingredients (box, red paint, green scissors) in the same methodical way that toddlers hard at work would. Uncluttered pages and primary colors make this a highly attractive book, as does the tactile jacket that allows readers to stroke fuzzy Meeow." SLJ

Other titles about Meeow are:
Meeow and the little chairs (2009)
Meeow and the pots and pans (2010)
Meeow and the blue table (2010)

On our way home. Boxer 2009 un il $14.95

Grades: PreK K   E

1. Bears -- Fiction 2. Father-child relationship -- Fiction
ISBN 978-1-906250-59-1; 1-906250-59-6

"With unadorned, heartfelt prose and idyllic images, Braun . . . conveys just how wonderful it feels to spend a day alone with Daddy. . . . Braun's acrylic pictures strike a lovely balance, as he places his genial, naïf-styled characters within majestically scaled landscapes." Publ Wkly

The **ugly** duckling. Boxer Books 2010 il (A Story House book) lib bdg $16.95

Grades: PreK K   E

1. Authors 2. Novelists 3. Dramatists 4. Fairy tales 5. Ducks -- Fiction 6. Swans -- Fiction 7. Children's authors 8. Short story writers
ISBN 978-1-907152-04-7; 1-907152-04-0

A retelling of Hans Christian Andersen's tale of the ugly little duckling who grows up to become a beautiful swan.

"This text presents the highlights of the story in a straightforward fashion that perserves the formal feel of the original. . . . The expressive pictures, though rendered with ink and colored pencil, have the careful lines and bold edges that give them the feel of woodcuts. . . . The large format, combined with bright, bold illustrations and simplified language, makes this ideal for storytime sharing." SLJ

Breathed, Berke

Pete & Pickles; [by] Berkeley Breathed. Philomel Books 2008 un il $17.99

Grades: 2 3 4   E

1. Pigs -- Fiction 2. Elephants -- Fiction 3. Friendship -- Fiction
ISBN 978-0-399-25082-8; 0-399-25082-4

LC 2007-50044

When Pickles the elephant turns his life upside-down, Pete the pig comes to realize that a perfectly predictable, practical, and uncomplicated life is not always preferable.

"This heartwarming tale is packed with adventure, imagination, and the all-important message of accepting differences. The illustrations alternate from naturalistic renderings of fantastical scenarios to flat compositions reminiscent of traditional comic strips." SLJ

Breen, Steve

Stick; [by] Steve Breen. Dial Books For Young Readers 2007 un il $16.99

Grades: PreK K 1 2 3   E

1. Frogs -- Fiction 2. Dragonflies -- Fiction
ISBN 978-0-8037-3124-0

LC 2006046318

An independent young frog goes on a wild adventure when he accidentally gets carried away by a dragonfly.

"Breen generates plenty of fun and suspense in the skillfully rendered, animated pictures." Booklist

Violet the pilot; [by] Steve Breen. Dial Books for Young Readers 2008 un il $16.99

Grades: K 1 2 3   E

1. Dogs -- Fiction 2. Air pilots -- Fiction
ISBN 978-0-8037-3125-7

LC 2007022367

Young Violet's only friend is her dog, Orville, until one of her homemade flying machines takes her to the rescue of a Boy Scout troop in trouble.

"An engaging story of a spunky girl who follows her dreams. . . . Done in watercolors, acrylics, and Photoshop, the lively cartoon artwork evokes a nostalgic setting. Violet's various inventions are clever and amusing." SLJ

Brendler, Carol

Winnie Finn, worm farmer. Farrar Straus Giroux 2009 un il $15.99

Grades: PreK K 1 2   E
    1. Worms -- Fiction
    ISBN 978-0-374-38440-1; 0-374-38440-1

LC 2008004255

Winnie Finn raises earthworms, which help her neighbors win prizes at the county fair. Includes instructions on making a worm farm.

"Nimble lines and cool colors depict the energy of the active outdoor scenes. Humorous details abound through animated expressions. . . . Winnie's spunky, good-natured heart anchors a gentle and entertaining read." SLJ

Includes bibliographical references

Brennan, Eileen
    Dirtball Pete. Random House 2010 un il $15.99; lib bdg $18.99
Grades: K 1 2 3   E
    1. School stories 2. Theater -- Fiction 3. Cleanliness -- Fiction
    ISBN 978-0-375-83425-7; 0-375-83425-7; 978-0-375-93425-4 lib bdg; 0-375-93425-1 lib bdg

LC 2006022433

"It's tough to make a book sardonic and heartwarming at the same time, but Brennan nails it." Publ Wkly

Brennan, Rosemarie
    Willow; written by Denise Brennan Nelson and Rosemarie Brennan; illustrated by Cyd Moore. Sleeping Bear Press 2008 un il $16.95
Grades: K 1 2 3   E
    1. Art -- Fiction 2. Painting -- Fiction 3. Imagination -- Fiction
    ISBN 978-1-58536-342-1; 1-58536-342-1

LC 2007034588

In art class, neatness, conformity, and imitation are encouraged, but when Willow brings imagination and creativity to her projects, even straight-laced Miss Hawthorn is influenced

"Soft-toned watercolors contrast colorful, autumn trees with all-the-same green ones. . . . Expressive faces show wonderment and joy as teacher and students discover . . . the intese power of imagination." SLJ

"Another title about Willow is:
Willow and the snow day dance (2011)

Brennan-Nelson, Denise
    Willow and the Snow Day Dance; written by Denise Brennan-Nelson; illustrated by Cyd Moore. Sleeping Bear Press 2011 un il $16.95
Grades: K 1 2 3   E
    1. Moving -- Fiction
    ISBN 978-1-58536-522-7; 1-58536-522-X

LC 2010030381

When Willow's family moves to a new home, she makes friends with all of the neighbors, even unsmiling Mr. Larch, through her letters inviting each to be as generous as she is.

"Brimming with details, Moore's cheerful pictures capture Willow's outsize personality." Publ Wkly

Brenner, Barbara
    Good morning, garden; illustrated by Denise Ortakales. Northword Press 2004 un il $15.95

Grades: K 1 2 3   E
    1. Stories in rhyme 2. Gardens -- Fiction
    ISBN 1-55971-888-9

Upon entering a garden one morning, a child greets the flowers, plants, insects, and animals there.

"The alliterative tone and subtle rhyme scheme continue throughout this joyful celebration. . . . Ortakales works with sculpted paper to convey the depth and detail of a garden replete with luscious plants and friendly creatures." SLJ

    ★ **Wagon** wheels; story by Barbara Brenner; pictures by Don Bolognese. newly il ed; HarperCollins Pubs. 1993 64p il (I can read book) hardcover o.p. pa $3.99
Grades: K 1 2   E
    1. African Americans -- Fiction 2. Frontier and pioneer life -- Fiction
    ISBN 0-06-444052-4 pa

LC 92-18780

A newly illustrated edition of the title first published 1978

Shortly after the Civil War a black family travels to Kansas to take advantage of the free land offered through the Homestead Act

"The based-on-fact story . . . is as fascinating as ever. Beautifully narrated with sensitivity, compassion, and just the right amount of suspense, and featuring new full-color illustrations." Horn Book Guide

Brenner, Tom
    And then comes Halloween; illustrated by Holly Meade. Candlewick Press 2009 un il $16.99
Grades: PreK K 1 2   E
    1. Autumn -- Fiction 2. Halloween -- Fiction 3. Halloween -- Juvenile literature
    ISBN 978-0-7636-3659-3; 0-7636-3659-2

"When autumn arrives, a group of suburban children and their parents rake leaves, carve pumpkins, decorate yards and porches, and make Halloween costumes. The big day comes at last, and the children go trick-or-treating. . . . The descriptions beautifully evoke the feeling of fall. . . . The watercolor and collage art contributes to the autumnal mood, and the varied perspectives and page design make the story more dynamic. The text and illustrations are a perfect complement to one another." SLJ

Brett, Jan
    The **3** little dassies. Putnam 2010 un il $17.99
Grades: PreK K 1 2   E
    1. Eagles -- Fiction 2. Dassies -- Fiction 3. Lizards -- Fiction
    ISBN 978-0-399-25499-4; 0-399-25499-4

"Brett's sumptuous retelling of 'The Three Little Pigs' is set in southern Africa and stars three small guinea-pig-like creatures that live in rock crevices in the Namib desert. The three dassies, garbed in traditional African dresses and turbans, are harassed by an eagle, who, like the wolf in the traditional tale, wants them for supper. . . . On the side panels another story develops with a brightly dressed lizard, the Agama Man, who is intent on rescuing the little creatures. Children will enjoy following both stories and will linger on each page following the exacting detail of the setting. . . . This tale will captivate children and introduce a setting and animals unfamiliar to most of them." SLJ

The **Easter** egg. G.P. Putnam's Sons 2010 un il
$17.99
Grades: PreK K   E
  1. Eggs -- Fiction 2. Easter -- Fiction 3. Rabbits --
Fiction 4. Contests -- Fiction
  ISBN 978-0-399-25238-9; 0-399-25238-X
                           LC 2009-08234
  Hoppi the bunny wants to win the egg-decorating contest
so the Easter Bunny will choose him to help distribute Easter
eggs, but instead, while everyone else is working on their
decorations, he finds himself guarding an egg that has fallen
from a robin's nest.
  "Brett's large watercolors include a few visual puns . .
. and lots of woodland detail. . . . A satisfying, gentle tale
whose text and images can be enjoyed multiple times over."
Booklist

  Gingerbread friends; [by] Jan Brett. G.P. Putnam's
Sons 2008 un il $17.99
Grades: PreK K 1 2   E
  1. Cookies -- Fiction 2. Friendship -- Fiction
  ISBN 978-0-399-25161-0; 0-399-25161-8
                         LC 2007042829
  Lonely Gingerbread Baby, having set out to find a friend,
enters a bakery where he tries to talk to different cookies and
other figures, but winds up leading a crowd back to his house
on a chase similar to the one in the familiar tale.
  "Brett's highly detailed, luscious illustrations do a fine
job telling this story for nonreaders, while readers and listeners will enjoy Gingerbread Baby's energy and enthusiasm."
SLJ

  Home for Christmas. G. P. Putnam's Sons 2011 un
il $17.99
Grades: PreK K   E
  1. Christmas stories 2. Trolls -- Fiction 3. Christmas
-- Fiction 4. Family life -- Fiction
  ISBN 978-0-399-25653-0; 0-399-25653-9
                         LC 2010045002
  Rollo the troll is tired of chores, but after spending time
on the tundra with various animal families, from owls to
moose, he realizes that he wants to be home for Christmas
even if that means behaving himself.
  "Set in the mountains of Sweden, the book introduces
a cast of naturalistic woodland animals, portrayed in intricate detail in Brett's watercolor and gouache paintings. . . .
The reformed Rollo's homecoming, just in time for Christmas celebrations, is foregone yet no less heartwarming."
Publ Wkly

  ★ **Honey** . . . honey . . . lion! a story from Africa. G.P.
Putnam's Sons 2005 un il $16.99
Grades: PreK K 1 2   E
  1. Badgers -- Fiction 2. Honeyguides (Birds) -- Fiction
  ISBN 0-399-24463-8
                         LC 2005-00449
  After working together to obtain honey, the African honey badger always shares it with his partner, the honeyguide
bird, until one day when the honey badger becomes greedy
and his feathered friend decides to teach him a lesson.

  "Brett has created another lush winner with beautifully
detailed illustrations of the animals and a clear, fast-paced
story." SLJ

  On Noah's ark. Putnam 2003 un il $16.99
Grades: K 1 2 3   E
  1. Animals 2. Noah's ark 3. Grandfathers
  ISBN 0-399-24028-4
                         LC 2003-1281
  Noah's granddaughter helps him bring the animals onto
the ark, calm them down, and get them to sleep
  "The words are basic and effective; it's the detailed watercolors of the animals that are the real attraction here. In
precise brushstrokes and vivid colors, Brett creates incredibly textured feathers and fur." Booklist

  ★ The **hat**. Putnam 1997 un il $16.95
Grades: PreK K 1 2   E
  1. Animals -- Fiction 2. Hedgehogs -- Fiction 3.
Clothing and dress -- Fiction
  ISBN 0-399-23101-3
                         LC 96-54015
  When Lisa hangs her woolen clothes in the sun to air
them out for winter, the hedgehog, to the amusement of the
other animals, ends up wearing a stocking on his head
  This story "has charm and humor. . . . The setting is the
Danish countryside (detailed down to the moss on a tree) on
a day when the first snow begins to fall, and Brett conveys
the season with such loving spirit that children will almost
wish for winter." Booklist

Breznak, Irene
  Sneezy Louise; written by Irene Breznak; illustrated by
Janet Pedersen. Random House 2009 un il $15.99; lib
bdg $18.99
Grades: PreK K 1   E
  1. Sneezing -- Fiction
  ISBN 978-0-375-85169-8; 0-375-85169-0; 978-0-375-
95169-5 lib bdg; 0-375-95169-5 lib bdg
                         LC 2007026720
  When Louise wakes up with itchy eyes, a wheezy throat,
and a sneezy nose, she just knows it is not going to be a very
good day
  "Breezy watercolors with lots of free-flowing lines and
action not only set the tone but also add energetic zest to this
story." Booklist

Briant, Ed
  Don't look now. Roaring Brook Press 2009 un il
$16.95
Grades: PreK K 1   E
  1. Brothers -- Fiction
  ISBN 978-1-59643-345-8; 1-59643-345-0
                         LC 2008-49330
  "For two young brothers, playtime in the backyard
quickly becomes rivalry time. . . . As the conflict rises, so
do the boys, literally, and they sail skyward into a fantasy
land. . . . Escape requires working together creatively. . . .
The story's real and fantasy worlds come to life in vibrant illustrations, laid out in detailed panels and full-page pictures,
peppered with occasional word and thought bubbles. Clever,
fast paced, and entertaining." Booklist

If you lived here you'd be home by now. Roaring Brook Press 2009 un il $17.99
Grades: PreK K 1 2   E
   1. Stories without words 2. Leaves -- Fiction 3. Animals -- Fiction
   ISBN 978-1-59643-420-2; 1-59643-420-1
   "Crisp colors and bold outlines make the illustrations sing, and tell the story without any words. The linear time line is easy to follow." SLJ

Bridges, Shirin Yim
   ★ **Mary** Wrightly, so politely; by Shirin Bridges; illustrated by Maria Monescillo. Houghton Mifflin Harcourt 2013 32 p. (reinforced) $16.99
Grades: PreK K   E
   1. Etiquette -- Fiction 2. Assertiveness (Psychology) -- Fiction
   ISBN 9780547342481
                      LC 2012019633
   "Every child will enjoy joining in on this book's irresistible refrain... Understated and sunny." Kirkus

   ★ **Ruby's** wish; illustrated by Sophie Blackall. Chronicle Bks. 2002 un il $15.95
Grades: K 1 2 3   E
   1. Sex role -- Fiction 2. Education -- Fiction
   ISBN 0-8118-3490-5
                      LC 2001-7406
   In China, at a time when few girls are taught to read or write, Ruby dreams of going to the university with her brothers and male cousins
   "This true story about Bridges' own grandmother has a gentle momentum. . . . Blackall's gouache illustrations have a quietly historical air, their palette subtly shaded with smoky inks and highlighted with touches of brilliant red." Bull Cent Child Books

   The **Umbrella** Queen; illustrations by Taeeun Yoo. Greenwillow Books 2008 un il $16.99; lib bdg $17.89
Grades: K 1 2 3   E
   1. Painting -- Fiction 2. Umbrellas and parasols -- Fiction
   ISBN 978-0-06-075040-4; 0-06-075040-5; 978-0-06-075041-1 lib bdg; 0-06-075041-3 lib bdg
                             LC 2005-35730 In a village in Thailand where everyone makes umbrellas, young Noot dreams of painting the most beautiful one and leading the annual parade as Umbrella Queen, but her unconventional designs, depicting elephants instead of flowers and butterflies, displease her parents.
   "Yoo's orange, green, and black colored linoleum prints wonderfully establish the tone for the story, which is related through gracefully told text." SLJ

Briggs, Raymond
   ★ The **snowman**. Random House 1978 un il $17; pa $6.99; bd bk $4.99
Grades: PreK K 1 2   E
   1. Stories without words 2. Snow -- Fiction 3. Dreams -- Fiction
   ISBN 0-394-83973-0; 0-394-88466-3 pa; 0-375-81067-6 bd bk
                      LC 78-55904

   "The pastel-toned pencil-and-crayon pictures in their neat rectangular frames will hold the attention of primary 'readers.'" SLJ

Bright, Paul
   The **not** -so-scary Snorklum; [illustrations by] Jane Chapman. Good Books 2011 un il $16.99
Grades: PreK K 1   E
   1. Fear -- Fiction 2. Animals -- Fiction 3. Mythical animals -- Fiction
   ISBN 978-1-56148-728-8; 1-56148-728-7
                      LC 2011007764
   First published in the United Kingdom
   As the scary Snorklum stomps home to his cave, he encounters a mole, a rabbit, and a badger, who see through his attempts to frighten them.
   "Brisk and bright, yet subtle in its message." Kirkus

Brimner, Larry Dane
   Trick or treat, Old Armadillo; illustrated by Dominic Catalano. Boyds Mills Press 2010 un il $16.95
Grades: K 1 2 3   E
   1. Animals -- Fiction 2. Halloween -- Fiction 3. Armadillos -- Fiction 4. Spanish language -- Vocabulary
   ISBN 978-1-59078-758-8; 1-59078-758-7
                      LC 2010004342
   On Halloween, Old Armadillo sits inside his little house waiting for his friends to come trick-or-treating.
   "Brimner infuses this tale with humor and Southwestern flavor. Spanish words are sprinkled throughout and defined in a glossary at the beginning of the book. . . . Catalano's dark pastel illustrations work well with the text." SLJ
   Another title about Old Armadillo is:
   Merry Christmas, Old Armadillo (1995)

Brisson, Pat
   I remember Miss Perry; illustrated by Stéphane Jorisch. Dial Books for Young Readers 2006 un il $16.99
Grades: K 1 2 3   E
   1. School stories 2. Death -- Fiction 3. Teachers -- Fiction 4. Bereavement -- Fiction
   ISBN 0-8037-2981-2
                      LC 2004-24070
   When his teacher, Miss Perry, is killed in a car accident, Stevie and his elementary school classmates take turns sharing memories of her, especially her fondest wish for each day.
   "The delicate pen-and-ink, watercolor, and gouache illustrations reflect the varied emotions evoked by this treasured individual." SLJ

   Tap -dance fever; illustrated by Nancy Cote. Boyds Mills Press 2004 un il $15.95
Grades: K 1 2 3   E
   1. Tap dancing -- Fiction
   ISBN 1-59078-290-9
                      LC 2004-14575
   Annabelle Applegate will not stop tap-dancing no matter what the frustrated citizens of Fiddlers Creek do to make her quit
   "A deliciously tall tale with an appealing young heroine, the story of Annabelle's troubles and triumph reads aloud well. Just as amusing are Cote's fanciful watercolor-and-

gouache paintings of a multicultural, rural community." Booklist

Broach, Elise

Gumption! with pictures by Richard Egielski. Atheneum Books for Young Readers 2010 un il $16.99
Grades: PreK K   E
1. Uncles -- Fiction 2. Animals -- Fiction 3. Jungles -- Fiction
ISBN 978-1-4169-1628-4; 1-4169-1628-8
LC 2008-49048
"Peter is thrilled when his uncle Nigel invites him on an expedition in search of a rare African gorilla, but making it through the jungle involves lots of challenges. Nigel leads the way, surmounting each obstacle . . . but Egielski's ink-and-watercolor illustrations show a parallel story. As Nigel charges ahead, Peter is swept along by a succession of wild animals. . . . Egielski plays up the comedy with clever, small details, and Broach's repetitive text, with its occasionally vocabulary, is well suited for dramatic read-alouds." Booklist

When dinosaurs came with everything; written by Elise Broach; illustrated by David Small. Atheneum Books for Young Readers 2006 un il $16.99
Grades: PreK K 1 2   E
1. Dinosaurs -- Fiction 2. Mother-son relationship -- Fiction
ISBN 978-0-689-86922-8; 0-689-86922-3
LC 2005-11612
Although his mother is a little worried, a young boy is delighted to discover that every shop in town is giving away real dinosaurs to their customers.
"Small's sketchy, tongue-in-cheek watercolor-and-ink artwork perfectly captures the boy's exuberance, the dinosaurs' mass, and the hubbub that a city full of these reptiles would create." SLJ

Brokamp, Elizabeth

The **picky** little witch; illustrated by Marsha Riti. Pelican 2011 il $16.99
Grades: PreK K 1 2   E
1. Witches -- Fiction 2. Halloween -- Fiction
ISBN 978-1-58980-882-9; 1-58980-882-7
LC 2011004655
Mama Witch tries to get her daughter to eat some Halloween soup before going out to trick-or-treat, but Picky Little Witch finds many reasons to refuse. Includes a recipe for soup.
"This humorous story has dialogue that contains an occasional rhyme and characters that resemble humans except for their pale green skin." SLJ

Brooks, Erik

Polar opposites; written and illustrated by Erik Brooks. Marshall Cavendish 2010 un il $16.99
Grades: PreK K 1   E
1. Opposites 2. Penguins -- Fiction 3. Polar bear -- Fiction
ISBN 978-0-7614-5685-8; 0-7614-5685-6
LC 2009005214
Ambrose, a polar bear, and Zina, a penguin, are very different but they can still find ways to meet in the middle

"The cheerful pencil, charcoal, and watercolor illustrations brim with energy and engaging details. . . . A natural for storytimes or as a lapsit." Booklist

Brooks, Susie

Get into Art! Enjoy Great Art--then Create Your Own! by Susie Brooks. Kingfisher 2013 31 p. col. ill. (hardcover) $14.99
Grades: 3 4 5 6 7   E
1. Art -- Guidebooks 2. Art -- Juvenile literature 3. Picture books for children
ISBN 0753470586; 9780753470589
For this book, Susie Brooks' "goal is to convince her readers that art is not just something one observes, but rather something that one does. Using a topic beloved by many kids—animals—she presents 13 works by famous artists, each of which incorporates animals into its subject and theme. Each reproduced masterpiece occupies its own two-page spread, and Brooks explores one major art technique for each." (Bookstlist)

Brown, Alan

Love -a-duck; by Alan James Brown; illustrated by Francesca Chessa. Holiday House 2010 un il $16.95
Grades: PreK K 1 2   E
1. Toys -- Fiction 2. Baths -- Fiction 3. Ducks -- Fiction
ISBN 978-0-8234-2263-0; 0-8234-2263-1
After falling out of the window and spending an unforgettable day outdoors, a plastic duck is returned home safely, just in time for little Jane's bath.
"Cheerful, bright illustrations help relate this humorous escapade. Call-and-response portions of the book will engage young listeners." SLJ

Brown, Calef

Boy wonders. Atheneum Books for Young Readers 2011 un il $16.99
Grades: K 1 2   E
1. Stories in rhyme 2. Questions and answers
ISBN 978-1-4169-7877-0; 1-4169-7877-1
LC 2010020976
A young boy's questions lead to more and more questions, but there do not seem to be any answers.
"The connotations of everyday words and sayings are pondered and turned inside out and upside down in this wholly original paeon to intellectual curiosity. . . . The artist's trademark stylized illustrations, flat, hip, and jazzy, are rendered in a palette of predominantly blue/green/yellow acrylics." SLJ

Pirateria; the wonderful plunderful pirate emporium. written and illustrated by Calef Brown. Atheneum Books for Young Readers 2012 304 p. col. ill. (hardcover) $16.99
Grades: PreK K 1 2   E
1. Stories in rhyme 2. Pirates -- Fiction 3. Picture books for children 4. Stores, Retail -- Fiction
ISBN 141697878X; 9781416978787
LC 2011034023
This rhyming children's book "extols the virtues of the Pirateria," a "one-stop shop [that] carries everything from 'solid maple walking planks' to 'fresh lime quinine/to ward off the scurvy' to eye patches in colors such as 'plunder plum' and 'cannonball black.' However, Pirateria is more

than just a store: it provides night classes in subjects such as chart reading, smuggling molasses, and spyglass making." (School Library Journal)

Brown, Heather

The **robot** book. Accord Pub. 2010 un il bd bk $16.99

Grades: PreK K   E

1. Board books for children 2. Robots -- Fiction

ISBN 978-0-7407-9725-5 bd bk; 0-7407-9725-5 bd bk

"'A robot is made of so many parts,' begins this modest board book with movable components. Each spread focuses on a specific feature of a humble red robot that looks very DIY. . . . It's an elegantly simple design with care paid to every detail." Publ Wkly

Brown, Jeff

★ **Flat** Stanley; by Jeff Brown; illustrated by Scott Nash. HarperCollins Pubs. 2006 un il $16.99

Grades: K 1 2 3   E

ISBN 978-0-06-112904-9; 0-06-112904-6

LC 2006019547

Based on the original Flat Stanley by Jeff Brown c1964

A bulletin board falls on Stanley while he is sleeping, and he finds that being flat has its advantages

"Full-page, cartoon illustrations in watercolor and crayon enhance the story while remaining true to the original. This version of an old favorite will introduce a beloved character to a new generation of younger children." SLJ

Brown, Lisa

How to be. HarperCollins Pubs. 2006 un il $15.99

Grades: PreK K 1   E

1. Animals -- Fiction 2. Conduct of life -- Fiction

ISBN 0-06-054635-2

LC 2005-15147

"A girl and a younger boy take turns imitating different animals, including a bear, a snake, and a dog. . . . The final chapter, How to be a PERSON, shows both children embodying all the positive characteristics of the critters with the animals shadowing their actions. . . . The spare text matches the black-and-white drawings, supplemented with well-placed smatterings of bright paint." SLJ

Vampire boy's good night. Harper 2010 un il $16.99

Grades: PreK K 1 2   E

1. Witches -- Fiction 2. Vampires -- Fiction 3. Halloween -- Fiction

ISBN 978-0-06-114011-2; 0-06-114011-2

When Morgan, a young vampire, and his witchy friend Bela set out one night to see if human children really exist, they find themselves at a Halloween party.

"The use of speech balloons adds to the intimacy of Brown's detail-rich scenes, and the absence of parental figures contributes to an exultant mood. The lyrical, understated prose and clever outsider's perspective on the holiday might make this a new seasonal favorite." Publ Wkly

Brown, Marc Tolon

Arthur's nose; 25th aniversary limited edition. [by] Marc Brown. Little, Brown and Company 2001 un il $15.95

Grades: PreK K 1 2   E

1. Nose -- Fiction 2. Aardvark -- Fiction

ISBN 0-316-11884-2

LC 00-106832

A reissue of the title first published 1976

Unhappy with his nose, Arthur the aardvark visits the rhinologist to get a new one. In this edition "Brown shows the evolution of his drawings of Arthur from 1976 to the present, along with a sidebar of 'Fun Facts,' . . . followed by a photo gallery of Brown's family with some pretty clear correlations between the author's relatives and Arthur's. Aspiring writers and artists also get a peek at the original manuscript and sketches for Arthur's Nose." Publ Wkly

Other titles about Arthur are:

Arthur babysits (1992)

Arthur goes to camp (1982)

Arthur, it's only rock 'n roll (2002)

Arthur meets the president (1991)

Arthur writes a story (1996)

Arthur's April Fool (1983)

Arthur's baby (1987)

Arthur's birthday (1989)

Arthur's chicken pox (1994)

Arthur's Christmas (1985)

Arthur's computer disaster (1997)

Arthur's eyes (1979)

Arthur's family vacation (1993)

Arthur's first sleepover (1994)

Arthur's Halloween (1982)

Arthur's new puppy (1993)

Arthur's perfect Christmas (2000)

Arthur's pet business (1990)

Arthur's teacher trouble (1986)

Arthur's Thanksgiving (1983)

Arthur's tooth (1985)

Arthur's TV trouble (1995)

Arthur's underwear (1999)

Arthur's valentine (1980)

Authur turns green (2011)

★ **D.W.** all wet; [by] Marc Brown. Little, Brown 1988 un il hardcover o.p. pa $5.95

Grades: PreK K 1 2   E

1. Beaches -- Fiction 2. Aardvark -- Fiction 3. Siblings -- Fiction

ISBN 0-316-11268-2; 0-316-11077-9 pa

LC 87-15752

"A simple, even predictable vignette, but entertaining nonetheless because of Brown's warm pictures." Booklist

Other titles about D.W. are:

D.W. flips (1987)

D.W. go to your room! (1999)

D.W. rides again (1993)

D.W. the picky eater (1995)

D.W. thinks big (1993)

D.W.'s guide to perfect manners (2006)

D.W.'s guide to preschool (2003)

D.W.'s library card (2001)

D.W.'s lost blankie (1998)

D.W.'s library card; [by] Marc Brown. Little, Brown 2001 un il $14.95; pa $5.99

Grades: PreK K 1 2   E

1. Aardvark 2. Libraries 3. Books and reading 4.
Aardvark -- Fiction 5. Siblings -- Fiction 6. Brothers
and sisters 7. Libraries -- Fiction 8. Books and reading
-- Fiction

ISBN 0-316-11013-2; 0-316-73820-4 pa

LC 00-42805

After finally getting her first library card, Arthur's
little sister D.W. tries to check out her favorite book, with
humorous results.

Brown, Margaret Wise

★ **Another** important book; pictures by Chris Raschka.
HarperCollins Pubs. 1999 un il $15.99; lib bdg $16.89

Grades: PreK K 1   E

1. Counting 2. Stories in rhyme 3. Growth -- Fiction
4. Children -- Growth -- Pictorial works -- Juvenile
fiction 5. Identity (Psychology) -- Pictorial works --
Juvenile fiction

ISBN 0-06-026282-6; 0-06-026283-4 lib bdg

LC 98-7212

Illustrations and simple rhyming text describe how a
child grows from ages one through six

"Raschka assigns each age group a geometric shape: a
simple circle represents age one, pairs of stacked squares
indicate two, a five-pointed star signifies five and so on. . . .
It's a pleasure to hear the organic rhythms of Brown's prose
. . . and Raschka paints in boisterous surprises." Publ Wkly

Big red barn; pictures by Felicia Bond. newly il ed;
Harper & Row 1989 un il $16.99; lib bdg $17.89; bd
bk $7.99

Grades: PreK K 1 2   E

1. Stories in rhyme 2. Animals -- Fiction 3. Farm life
-- Fiction

ISBN 0-06-020748-5; 0-06-020749-3 lib bdg; 0-694-
00624-6 bd bk

LC 85-45814

A newly illustrated edition of the title first published 1956

Rhymed text and illustrations introduce the many different animals that live in the big red barn

"The large illustrations are somewhat stylized, but still
have a strong sense of detail and reality. The bright colors
will attract young readers. The short text on each page is
superimposed on the picture, but always in a way that is easy
to read. Children will enjoy studying each of the pages as the
day progresses from early morning to night." SLJ

Doctor Squash, the doll doctor; illustrated by David
Hitch. Golden Books 2010 un il $17.99; lib bdg $20.99

Grades: PreK K 1   E

1. Dolls -- Fiction 2. Physicians -- Fiction

ISBN 978-0-375-84800-1; 0-375-84800-2; 978-0-375-
95623-2 lib bdg; 0-375-95623-9 lib bdg

A revised and newly illustrated edition of the title first
published 1952

"When dolls are sick or in pain, there's really only one
doctor to call: the good Doctor Squash, who attends to their
every need. . . . And when the doc falls ill, the dolls take care
of him in return. . . . Playing doctor with dolls never falls out
of style, and Hitch's retro style and modern toy updates work
overtime to ensure that this book becomes a classic all over
again. Entertaining and charming." Kirkus

★ **Goodnight** moon; by Margaret Wise Brown; pictures by Clement Hurd. rev ed; HarperCollins Publishers
2005 un il $17.99

Grades: PreK K   E

1. Stories in rhyme 2. Bedtime -- Fiction 3. Rabbits
-- Fiction

ISBN 978-0-06-077585-8; 0-06-077585-8

LC 2005281602

A reissue of the title first published 1947

A little bunny bids goodnight to all the objects in his
room before falling asleep

"Rhythmic, gently lulling words combined with warm
and equally lulling pictures make this beloved classic an
ideal bedtime book." Christ Sci Monit

Goodnight moon ABC; an alphabet book. based on the
book by Margaret Wise Brown; pictures by Clement Hurd.
Harper 2010 un il $16.99

Grades: PreK K   E

1. Alphabet 2. Bedtime -- Fiction

ISBN 978-0-06-189484-8; 0-06-189484-2

"Familiar objects in the classic story are arranged in alphabetical order and accompanied by upper and lowercase
letters in the original style and palette. . . . Endpapers show
the entire alphabet being investigated by two mice. The book
conveys the timeless appeal of the original, and the literacy
skill building will appeal to adults." SLJ

Sleepy ABC; illustrated by Karen Katz. HarperCollinsPublishers 2010 un il $16.99; lib bdg $17.89

Grades: PreK   E

1. Alphabet 2. Stories in rhyme 3. Bedtime -- Fiction

ISBN 978-0-06-128863-0; 0-06-128863-2; 978-0-06-
128865-4 lib bdg; 0-06-128865-9 lib bdg

LC 2008051781

Simple rhymes for each letter of the alphabet are illustrated with an array of toddlers and babies saying goodnight.

"Katz's interpretation of Brown's text . . . is joyful and
energetic and features her trademark, round-faced, multicultural children, rendered in collage-like art. . . . Likely to be
just what little not-yet-sleeping beauties will want." Booklist

★ **Two** little trains; pictures by Leo and Diane Dillon.
HarperCollins Pubs. 2001 un il $15.95; lib bdg $15.89;
pa $6.99

Grades: PreK K 1 2   E

1. Railroads -- Trains 2. Railroads -- Fiction

ISBN 0-06-028376-9; 0-06-028377-7 lib bdg; 0-06-
443568-7 pa

LC 00-40798

A newly illustrated edition of the title first published
1949 by Scott

Two little trains, one streamlined, the other old-fashioned, puff, puff, puff, and chug, chug, chug, on their
way West

"The rhythms, the word sounds and the resonant echo of
folk song set up a veritable hypnotic chant. . . . [The] soft-
grained paintings . . . are beautifully composed in both form
and color. A handsome reinterpretation." Booklist

★ **Where** have you been? pictures by Leo and Diane
Dillon. HarperCollins 2004 un il $15.99; lib bdg $16.89

Grades: PreK K 1   E
  1. Animals 2. Stories in rhyme 3. Animals -- Fiction
ISBN 0-06-028378-5; 0-06-028379-3 lib bdg
                         LC 2003-49981

A newly illustrated edition of the title first published 1952 by Crowell

In rhyming verse, various animals tell where they have been.

"Children fond of call-and-response will enjoy this humorous nursery rhyme. . . . The illustrations are as lively as they are charming, and have enough detail to keep children interested." SLJ

A **child's** good morning book; illustrated by Karen Katz. newly illustrated ed.; HarperCollins 2009 un il $17.99; lib bdg $18.89

Grades: PreK   E
  1. Animals -- Fiction 2. Morning -- Fiction
ISBN 978-0-06-128864-7; 0-06-128864-0; 978-0-06-128861-6 lib bdg; 0-06-128861-6 lib bdg
                       LC 2008000786

A newly illustrated edition of the title first published 1952

As the sun rises, birds, horses, rabbits, flowers, bugs, and finally children get up to start their day.

"Katz has reinterpreted the text in her warm and rounded style. . . . Brightly colored patterns and use of collage add interest to each page. This book has been popular over the years." SLJ

★ The **fierce** yellow pumpkin; story by Margaret Wise Brown; pictures by Richard Egielski. HarperCollins Pubs. 2003 un il $15.99; lib bdg $16.89

Grades: PreK K 1   E
  1. Pumpkin 2. Halloween 3. Jack-o-lanterns 4. Pumpkin -- Fiction
ISBN 0-06-024479-8; 0-06-024481-X lib bdg
                       LC 2002-8338

A little pumpkin dreams of the day when he will be a big, fierce, yellow pumpkin who frightens away the field mice as the scarecrow does

"Egielski's artwork features subtle shadings and interesting juxtapositions of colors. . . . The story rolls along smoothly with a clear plot line and some nice phrasing." Booklist

The **little** island; with illustrations by Leonard Weisgard. Doubleday Bks. for Young Readers 2003 un il $14.95

Grades: PreK K 1 2   E
  1. Islands -- Fiction
ISBN 0-385-74640-7

A reissue of the title first published 1946 under the pseudonym Golden MacDonald

Awarded the Caldecott Medal, 1947

There was a little island in the ocean and his book is about how the seasons and the storm and the day and night changed it, how the lobsters and seals and gulls and everything else lived on it, and what the kitten who came to visit found out about it

The **little** scarecrow boy; pictures by David Diaz. newly il ed; HarperCollins Pubs. 1998 un il $15.99; lib bdg $16.89; pa $6.99

Grades: PreK K 1 2   E
  1. Scarecrows -- Fiction
ISBN 0-06-026284-2; 0-06-026290-7 lib bdg; 0-06-77891-1 pa
                       LC 97-32558

Early one morning, a little scarecrow whose father warns him that he is not fierce enough to frighten a crow goes out into the cornfield alone

"Diaz provides wonderful illustrations for a story Brown wrote in the 1940s. . . . Brown's masterful use of repetition and rhythm creates a fine read-aloud story. The warm watercolor illustrations incorporate straw and patchwork." SLJ

★ The **runaway** bunny; pictures by Clement Hurd. HarperCollins Publishers 2005 un il $16.99; lib bdg $17.89

Grades: PreK K   E
  1. Rabbits -- Fiction
ISBN 0-06-077582-3; 0-06-077583-1 lib bdg

A reissue, with some illustrations redrawn, of the title first published 1942

"The text has the simplicity of a folk tale and the illustrations are black and white or double page drawings in startling colour." Ont Libr Rev

Brown, Monica

Chavela and the Magic Bubble; illustrated by Magaly Morales. Clarion Books 2010 un il $16

Grades: K 1 2 3   E
  1. Magic -- Fiction 2. Chewing gum -- Fiction 3. Grandmothers -- Fiction 4. Mexican Americans -- Fiction
ISBN 978-0-547-24197-5; 0-547-24197-6
                       LC 2009015819

When Chavela blows a bubble with a strange new gum, she floats away to Mexico, where her great-grandfather once worked harvesting the tree sap that makes gum chewy.

"Kids will want to chew their own bubblegum as they listen to this exciting, magical journey, handsomely illustrated in brilliantly colored double-page spreads." Booklist

Waiting for the BiblioBurro; illustrations by John Parra. Tricycle Press 2011 un il $16.99; lib bdg $19.99

Grades: PreK K 1   E
  1. Reading teachers 2. Libraries -- Fiction 3. Elementary school teachers 4. Books and reading -- Fiction
ISBN 978-1-58246-353-7; 1-58246-353-0; 978-1-58246-398-8 lib bdg; 1-58246-398-0 lib bdg
                       LC 2010024183

When a man brings to a remote village two burros, Alfa and Beto, loaded with books the children can borrow, Ana's excitement leads her to write a book of her own as she waits for the BiblioBurro to return. Includes glossary of Spanish terms and a note on the true story of Columbia's BiblioBurro and mobile libraries in other countries.

"Parra's naïve-styled acrylics brim with scenes of country life. A palette of salmon pinks and turquoise and sky blues, painted on board, give the book a roughhewn, handmade quality and an innocent, childlike appeal." Publ Wkly

Brown, Peter

★ **Children** make terrible pets. Little, Brown 2010 un il $16.99

Grades: PreK K 1   E
1. Pets -- Fiction 2. Bears -- Fiction
ISBN 978-0-316-01548-6; 0-316-01548-2

LC 2010-04982

When Lucy, a young bear, discovers a boy lost in the woods, she asks her mother if she can have him as a pet, only to find him impossible to train. "Ages three to six." (N Y Times Book Rev)

"Appealing and humorous, with a lesson to boot!" SLJ
Another title about Lucy the bear is:
You will be my friend! (2011)

Chowder; [by] Peter Brown. Little, Brown 2006 un il $15.99
Grades: PreK K 1 2   E
1. Dogs -- Fiction
ISBN 978-0-316-01180-8; 0-316-01180-0

LC 2005035616

Chowder the bulldog has never fit in with the other neighborhood canines, but he sees a chance to make friends with the animals at the local petting zoo

"The tongue-in-cheek humor melds delightfully with Brown's distinctive acrylic-and-pencil artwork." Booklist
Another title about Chowder is:
The fabulous bouncing Chowder (2007)

Mr. Tiger goes wild; written and illustrated by Peter Brown. Little Brown & Co 2013 48 p. ill. (reinforced) $18
Grades: PreK K 1 2   E
1. Picture books for children 2. Tigers -- Juvenile fiction 3. Tigers -- Fiction 4. Etiquette -- Fiction 5. City and town life -- Fiction 6. Self-actualization (Psychology) -- Fiction
ISBN 0316200638; 9780316200639

LC 2012048429

In this children's picture book, "Mr. Tiger lives a peaceable, if repressed, life alongside other anthropomorphic animals in a monochromatic, dreadfully formal little town." He finally gets tired of being respectable and starts embracing "a quadruped stance." Then he "sheds his clothing, runs away to the wilderness, roars and generally runs amok. But" he "comes to miss his friends, his city and his home, and so he returns to find 'that things were beginning to change.'" (Kirkus Reviews)

You will be my friend! Little, Brown 2011 un il $16.99
Grades: PreK K 1   E
1. Bears -- Fiction 2. Animals -- Fiction 3. Friendship -- Fiction
ISBN 978-0-316-07030-0; 0-316-07030-0

LC 2011009709

Lucy, a young bear, starts her day determined to make a new friend but her enthusiasm leads to all sorts of problems until, just as she is about to give up, an unexpected friend finds her.

This "features an earth-tone palette, pencil illustrations, cut-paper voice bubbles, and hand-lettered display type; Lucy's wilderness is thoroughly domesticated. . . . Readers won't miss the message that friendship is something that happens in its own time." Publ Wkly

★ The **curious** garden. Little, Brown 2009 un il
Grades: K 1 2 3   E
1. Gardens -- Fiction 2. City and town life -- Fiction
ISBN 0-316-01547-4; 978-0-316-01547-9

LC 2008029165

Liam discovers a hidden garden and with careful tending spreads color throughout the gray city.

This "is a quiet but stirring fable of urban renewal, sure to capture imaginations. . . . In Brown's utopian vision, the urban and the pastoral mingle to joyfully harmonious effect." Publ Wkly

The **fabulous** bouncing Chowder; [by] Peter Brown. Little, Brown 2007 un il $15.99
Grades: PreK K 1 2   E
1. Dogs -- Fiction 2. Camps -- Fiction 3. Trampolines and trampolining -- Fiction
ISBN 978-0-316-01179-2

When Chowder goes off to the Fabu Pooch Boot Camp, he has trouble fitting in until, at the Fabu Pooch Pageant, he discovers his real talent as a trampoline artist.

"The sturdy artwork, in acrylic-and-pencil on board, goes for humor. . . . This combines lots of wit with lots of energy." Booklist

Brown, Ruth
Gracie the lighthouse cat. Andersen Press USA 2011 un il $16.95
Grades: K 1 2 3   E
1. Cats -- Fiction 2. Storms -- Fiction 3. Shipwrecks -- Fiction 4. Lighthouses -- Fiction
ISBN 978-0-7613-7454-1; 0-7613-7454-X

LC 2010032950

"Gracie, a cat whose home is in a lighthouse, relaxes alongside her little kitten while in the background Grace, the lighthouse keeper's daughter, spots a ship in trouble on the rocks. The two stories about bravery during a raging storm in 1838 unfold simultaneously. Gracie's story is described in the text, while the human drama is portrayed primarily in the artwork. Attractive, painterly renditions of the treacherous sea as well as the emotional features on the faces of the animals will draw children into the suspenseful tale." SLJ

★ A **dark,** dark tale; story and pictures by Ruth Brown. Dial Bks. for Young Readers 1981 un il hardcover o.p. pa $6.99
Grades: PreK K 1 2   E
1. Cats -- Fiction
ISBN 0-14-054621-9 pa

"The book's mysterious power is engendered by the illustrations of weed-choked gardens and abandoned, echoing halls, of mullioned windows and blowing curtains." Time

Brown, Stephanie Gwyn
Bang! Boom! Roar! a busy crew of dinosaurs. by Nate Evans and Stephanie Gwyn Brown; illustrated by Christopher Santoro. Harpercollins Childrens Books 2012 40 p. (trade bdg.) $15.99
Grades: PreK K 1   E
1. Alphabet -- Fiction 2. Picture books for children 3. Dinosaurs -- Juvenile fiction 4. Alphabet 5. Stories in rhyme 6. Building -- Fiction 7. Dinosaurs -- Fiction 8. Playgrounds -- Fiction 9. Construction workers --

Fiction

ISBN 0060879602; 9780060879600; 9780060879624

LC 2009005244

In this book by Nate Evans, "[a] teeming dino crew in hard hats and safety vests create organized if frenetic chaos on a mucky construction . . . [A] swarm of grimacing, toothy cartoon monsters convert a trash-filled empty lot into an urban playground. . . . Whether peeking out of a port-a-potty . . . [or] racing lumbering earth movers . . . the well-larded laborers are easily identifiable . . . . [a]long with the aforementioned hidden alphabet." (Kirkus)

Brown, Tameka Fryer

Around our way on neighbors' day; illustrated by Charlotte Riley-Webb. Abrams 2010 un il $16.95

Grades: PreK K 1 2   E

1. African Americans -- Fiction 2. City and town life -- Fiction

ISBN 978-0-8109-8971-9; 0-8109-8971-9

"As an African American girl bounces around her urban neighborhood celebrating Neighbors' Day, when everyone comes together for celebration and community bonding, she shares her energetic and enthusiastic observations. . . . The acrylic art is saturated with rich color, energetic movement, and abstract figures and shapes, all reminiscent of Jacob Lawrence's art. Most scenes are double-page spreads that, together with the words, demonstrate the size and diversity of a joyful world." Booklist

Browne, Anthony

Little Beauty. Candlewick Press 2008 un il $16.99

Grades: PreK K 1 2 3   E

1. Cats -- Fiction 2. Zoos -- Fiction 3. Gorillas -- Fiction 4. Sign language -- Fiction

ISBN 978-0-7636-3959-4; 0-7636-3959-1

LC 2007051887

When a gorilla who knows sign language tells his keepers that he is lonely, they bring him a small kitten and he names her Beauty

Browne "tells a picture-book story with exquisitely detailed art that blends magic and realism." Booklist

★ **Me** and you. Farrar Straus Giroux 2010 un il

Grades: PreK K 1 2 3   E

1. Fairy tales 2. Bears -- Fiction 3. Social classes -- Fiction

ISBN 0-374-34908-8; 978-0-374-34908-0

Original French edition 2009

In this retelling of "The Three Bears, Goldilocks is a modern-day have-not, while the three bears are haves; their stories unfold separately and receive distinct visual treatments. . . . Primary." (Horn Book) Originally published in France in 2009 under the title Une autre histoire.

This "is a work that's both playfully interpretive and interestingly thought-provoking at a youthful level, raising some easily discussable questions." Bull Cent Child Books

★ **My** brother; [by] Anthony Browne. Farrar, Straus & Giroux 2007 un il $16

Grades: PreK K 1   E

1. Brothers -- Fiction

ISBN 978-0-374-35120-5; 0-374-35120-1

LC 2006050262

"To the younger brother, the older one is coolness personified. . . . Browne . . . takes this universal theme of sibling idolatry and interprets it visually with economy and verve." Booklist

★ **My** dad. Farrar, Straus & Giroux 2001 un il $16

Grades: PreK K 1 2   E

1. Fathers 2. Fathers -- Fiction

ISBN 0-374-35101-5

LC 00-37951

First published 2000 in the United Kingdom

A child describes the many wonderful things about "my dad," who can jump over the moon, swim like a fish, and be as warm as toast

"The offhand affection is genuinely moving as well as funny." Booklist

★ **My** mom. Farrar, Straus & Giroux 2005 un il $16; pa $6.95

Grades: PreK K 1 2   E

1. Mothers -- Fiction

ISBN 0-374-35098-1; 0-374-40026-1 pa

LC 2004-47173

A child describes the many wonderful things about "my mom," who can make anything grow, roar like a lion, and be as comfy as an armchair

"Browne's paintings hold attention, whether depicting images true to life or flights of fancy, and the honesty of the narrator's emotions and Mom's devotion shine through." Booklist

Piggybook. Knopf 1986 un il hardcover o.p. pa $7.99

Grades: PreK K 1 2   E

1. Mothers -- Fiction 2. Family life -- Fiction

ISBN 0-679-80837-X pa

LC 86-3008

When Mrs. Piggott unexpectedly leaves one day, her demanding family begins to realize just how much she did for them

"As in most of Browne's art, there is more than a touch of irony and visual humor here, bringing off the didactic with a light touch and turning the lesson into satire." Bull Cent Child Books

Silly Billy. Candlewick Press 2006 un il $15.99

Grades: PreK K 1 2   E

1. Dolls -- Fiction 2. Worry -- Fiction

ISBN 0-7636-3124-8

LC 2005-55305

To help with his anxiety, Billy uses the worry dolls his grandmother recommends, but he finds that they do not quite solve his problem.

"The pictures are amazing. In counterpoint to the monochromatic worry scenes are pictures so vivid and colorful they ease concern and spread cheer with each turn of the page." Booklist

★ **Voices** in the park. DK Ink 1998 un il hardcover o.p. pa $7.99

Grades: PreK K 1 2   E

1. Dogs -- Fiction 2. Parks -- Fiction 3. Gorilla --

Fiction

ISBN 978-0-7894-8191-7 pa; 978-0-7894-2522-5

LC 97-48730

"A simple outing is described by two parents and two children, each with a different point of view and emotional outlook. Intriguing illustrations of the gorilla characters and surreal touches add layers of visual humor." SLJ

Browning, Diane

★ **Signed,** Abiah Rose; written & illustrated by Diane Browning. Tricycle Press 2009 un il $15.99

Grades: 1 2 3   E

1. Artists -- Fiction 2. Sex role -- Fiction 3. Frontier and pioneer life -- Fiction

ISBN 978-1-58246-311-7; 1-58246-311-5

LC 2009-22172

In pioneer days, a young girl who is a talented artist is encouraged to paint portraits, Bible scenes, and other pictures, but told never to sign her work, either because it would be a sign of pride or because artists are expected to be men.

"In an engaging narrative, Abiah Rose tells of her experiences. . . . In Browning's pleasing colored-pencil-and-acrylic illustrations, the formal composition and decorative elements are reminiscent of folk art, while the softer, more natural depiction of the characters is all her own." Booklist

Broyles, Anne

Priscilla and the hollyhocks; [by] Anne Broyles; illustrated by Anna Alter. Charlesbridge 2008 un il $15.95

Grades: 2 3 4   E

1. Slavery -- Fiction 2. Native Americans -- Fiction 3. African Americans -- Fiction

ISBN 978-1-57091-675-5

LC 2007002281

A young African American girl is sold away from her mother as a slave, and then later is sold to a Cherokee Indian, but eventually she is bought by a white man who not only sets her free, but adopts her into his family of fifteen children. Based on a true story; includes instructions for making a hollyhock doll.

"Told in descriptive language accompanied by engaging acrylic paintings, this fictionalized story about a real child . . . offers a unique perspective on slavery." SLJ

Bruchac, Joseph

Crazy Horse's vision; illustrated by S.D. Nelson. Lee & Low Bks. 2000 un il pa $9.95

Grades: K 1 2 3   E

1. Indian chiefs 2. Oglala Indians -- Fiction 3. Dakota Indians -- Kings and rulers

ISBN 9781584302827

LC 99-47451

This is "a fictionalized account of the early life of Lakota leader Crazy Horse. . . . Grades three to six." (Bull Cent Child Books)

"Bruchac has created a memorable tale about Crazy Horse's childhood. . . . In beautiful illustrations inspired by the ledger book style of the Plains Indians, Sioux artist Nelson fills the pages with both action and quiet drama." Booklist

My father is taller than a tree; illustrated by Wendy Halperin. Dial Books for Young Readers 2010 un il $16.99

Grades: PreK K 1   E

1. Stories in rhyme 2. Children's poetry 3. Father-son relationship -- Fiction 4. Fathers and sons -- Juvenile literature

ISBN 978-0-803-73173-8; 0-803-73173-6

LC 2009-3608

Describes, in rhyming text and illustrations, the many different ways fathers and sons interact with one another.

"Short, simple rhymes are highlighted by Halperin's wonderfully expressive, soft yet colorful crayon and pencil drawings. . . . A charming celebration of fathers, dads, pops, papas, and pas." SLJ

Bruel, Nick

Little red bird; by Nick Bruel. Roaring Brook Press 2008 un il $16.95

Grades: PreK K 1 2   E

1. Stories in rhyme 2. Birds -- Fiction

ISBN 978-1-59643-339-7; 1-59643-339-6

LC 2007-13198

After escaping from her cage to see the world, a little red bird finds it difficult to decide whether to stay free or to go home and never fly again.

"The rhyming narrative, . . . is appealingly bouncy and will draw children through the small hero's exciting peregrinations until the final page, which hints at a satisfying conclusion while leaving room to wonder." Booklist

Bruel, Robert O.

Bob and Otto; pictures by Nick Bruel. Roaring Brook Press 2007 un il $15.95

Grades: PreK K 1 2   E

1. Worms -- Fiction 2. Friendship -- Fiction 3. Butterflies -- Fiction 4. Caterpillars -- Fiction

ISBN 978-1-59643-203-1; 1-59643-203-9

LC 2006012008

Otto the worm is shocked to discover that his best friend Bob is actually a caterpillar who emerges one day as a butterfly.

"Along with the engaging story, the science in the illustrations and text is quite accurate; there are rich, not-to-be missed visual details." Horn Book

Bruins, David

The **legend** of Ninja Cowboy Bear; illustrated by Hilary Leuny. Kids Can Press 2009 un il $16.95

Grades: PreK K 1 2   E

1. Bears -- Fiction 2. Ninja -- Fiction 3. Cowhands -- Fiction

ISBN 978-1-55453-486-9; 1-55453-486-0

The ninja, the cowboy and the bear do everything together. But when a contest among themselves leads to resentment, they soon learn that the only way to stop disagreeing is to be considerate of their differences and appreciate one another.

"Readers can take the story a step further with the Ninja Cowboy Bear Game, which is strongly reminiscent of Rock Paper Scissors. The digital-cartoon illustrations are set in comic panels; the art and the occasional Japanese word bubble give the story an anime feel. A fun purchase with a solid message." SLJ

Other titles in this series are:

The way of the ninja (2010)

The call of the cowboy (2011)

Brun-Cosme, Nadine

★ **Big** Wolf & Little Wolf; illustrated by Olivier Tallec. Enchanted Lion Books 2009 un il $16.95

Grades: PreK K 1   E

1. Wolves -- Fiction 2. Loneliness -- Fiction

ISBN 978-1-5927-0084-4; 1-5927-0084-5

LC 2008054040

ALA ALSC Batchelder Award Honor Book (2010)

Big Wolf has always lived alone at the top of a hill under a tree, so when a little wolf suddenly arrives one day, he does not know what to think.

"Tallec's colorful illustrations play off the quiet dignity of the text, revealing emotion through the characters' stances and expressions, employing a sketchy painting style that brims with light." SLJ

Other titles about Big Wolf & Little Wolf are:

Big Wolf & Little Wolf, the little leaf that wouldn't fall (2009)

Big Wolf & Little Wolf, such a beautiful orange! (2011)

Big Wolf & Little Wolf, such a beautiful orange! [illustrated by] Oliver Tallec; [translated by Claudia Bedrick] Enchanted Lion Books 2011 un il $16.95

Grades: PreK K 1   E

1. Worry -- Fiction 2. Wolves -- Fiction 3. Friendship -- Fiction

ISBN 978-1-59270-106-3; 1-59270-106-X

LC 2010051981

When Little Wolf does not return after chasing an orange that Big Wolf has tossed to him, Big Wolf begins to worry about all the things that might have happened to his friend.

"Tallec's beautifully composed spreads, rich with blues, greens, and yellows, are a marvel of soft, richly applied hues and dark swaths of color for contrast, and the two characters, formed with a lithe roundedness and sense of vitality, will engage readers." SLJ

Big Wolf & Little Wolf, the little leaf that wouldn't fall; [illustrated by] Olivier Tallec; [translated by Claudia Bedrick] Enchanted Lion Books 2009 un il $16.95

Grades: PreK K 1   E

1. Leaves -- Fiction 2. Wolves -- Fiction 3. Friendship -- Fiction

ISBN 978-1-59270-088-2; 1-59270-088-8

LC 2009-27594

When Big Wolf decides to surprise Little Wolf in the dead of winter by fetching a little leaf from an otherwise bare tree, both of them are rewarded in different ways by Big Wolf's effort.

"Drawn with long, bold pencil stroke, Big Wolf looms hugely over Little Wolf and would have a fierce, wild look did Tallec not add subtle cues of dress and posture to hint at his gentle nature." Kirkus

Brunhoff, Jean de

★ The **story** of Babar, the little elephant; translated from the French by Merle S. Haas. Random House 1937 47p il $15.95; lib bdg $17.99

Grades: PreK K 1 2   E

1. Elephants

ISBN 0-394-80575-5; 0-394-90575-X lib bdg

Original French edition, 1931; this is a reduced format version of the 1933 United States edition

"Babar runs away from the jungle and goes to live with an old lady in Paris, where he adapts quickly to French amenities. Later he returns to the jungle and becomes king. Much of the charm of the story is contributed by the author's gay pictures." Hodges. Books for Elem Sch Libr

Other titles about Babar are:

Babar and Father Christmas (1940)

Babar and his children (1938)

Babar the king (1935)

Bonjour, Babar (2000)

Travels of Babar (1934)

Brunhoff, Laurent de

Babar's Celesteville games. Abrams Books for Young Readers 2011 un il $18.95

Grades: PreK K 1 2   E

1. Love -- Fiction 2. Sports -- Fiction 3. Elephants -- Fiction

ISBN 978-1-4197-0006-4; 1-4197-0006-5

"Olympics-style games have come to Celesteville, and Babar's children ('now grown up') watch various animals compete. When an elephant pole vaulter from Mirza catches Flora's eye, the games become a backdrop for their courtship. . . . De Brunhoff incorporates modern details into his gentle, ink-outlined watercolors. . . . The athletic, romantic, and cross-cultural themes make this an unusual but satisfying addition to the beloved series." Publ Wkly

Bruss, Deborah

Book! book! book! illustrated by Tiphanie Beeke. Levine Bks. 2001 un il $15.95

Grades: PreK K 1   E

1. Libraries 2. Animal sounds 3. Domestic animals 4. Books and reading 5. Books and reading -- Fiction

ISBN 0-439-13525-7

LC 99-59758

When the children go back to school, the animals on the farm are bored, so they go into the library in town trying to find something to do

"Soft, naive watercolor paintings illustrate the satisfying story, which, with its witty conclusion, will be a sure winner at story time." Horn Book Guide

Bryant, Jennifer

Abe's fish; a boyhood tale of Abraham Lincoln. by Jen Bryant; illustrated by Amy June Bates. Sterling 2009 un il $15.95

Grades: PreK K 1 2   E

1. Lawyers 2. Presidents 3. State legislators 4. Members of Congress 5. Presidents -- United States -- Fiction

ISBN 978-1-4027-6252-9; 1-4027-6252-6

LC 2008028597

Young Abe Lincoln learns the meaning of selflessness and freedom when he encounters a soldier on a country road and gives up his prized possession: a fish he caught for the family's evening meal. Includes author's note on the early life of the sixteenth president.

"Bates's lively watercolors have rich detail, depicting Abe as a boy in a coonskin hat, still too small to lift his father's ax. The full-spread, sepia-toned paintings capture his rustic lifestyle, the Kentucky landscape, and the reactions of Abe's family to his generosity." SLJ

Includes bibliographical references

Buck, Nola

A **Christmas** goodnight; illustrated by Sarah Jane Wright. Katherine Tegen Books 2011 un il $12.99; lib bdg $13.89

Grades: PreK K   E

1. Stories in rhyme 2. Christmas stories 3. Bedtime -- Fiction 4. Christmas -- Fiction

ISBN 978-0-06-166491-5; 0-06-166491-X; 978-0-06-166492-2 lib bdg; 0-06-166492-8 lib bdg

Illustrations and rhyming text portray characters from the Nativity story, from doves in the stable to the wise men, as they go to sleep on Christmas Eve.

"The double-page-spread format makes this a fine read-aloud for a group of little ones, but it's also a cozy choice as a December bedtime story. A terrific introduction for preschoolers who are just learning about the Nativity story." Kirkus

Buckley, Michael

Kel Gilligan's daredevil stunt show; semiprofessional daredevil. pictures by Dan Santat; written by Michael Buckley. Abrams Books for Young Readers 2012 35 p. (alk. paper) $16.95

Grades: PreK K 1   E

1. Vegetables -- Fiction 2. Picture books for children 3. Toilet training -- Fiction 4. Humorous stories 5. Courage -- Fiction

ISBN 141970379X; 9781419703799

LC 2012001285

In his debut children's picture book, Michael Buckley tells the story of "a child who just loves danger. . . . [Protagonist Kel Gilligan] earnestly recollects his past triumphs in pictures designed to look like freeze frames of his life," discussing the times he successfully ate his broccoli and used the toilet. (School Library Journal)

Budnitz, Paul

The **hole** in the middle; illustrated by Aya Kakeda. Disney/Hyperion Books 2011 un il $16.99

Grades: PreK K 1   E

1. Friendship -- Fiction

ISBN 978-1-4231-3761-0; 1-4231-3761-2

LC 2010036236

Morgan was born with a big hole through his middle that gives him a strange, empty feeling all of the time, but when his good friend Yumi becomes ill, he finds that helping her makes him feel whole.

"The colorful, cheerful spreads depict all sorts of amusements and feature whimsical details that add to the brief text. . . . Focusing on the needs of others is a time-honored solution for those dissatisfied with their own lot in life; here is a motivating parable for contemporary kids." Kirkus

Buehner, Caralyn

Fanny's dream; pictures by Mark Buehner. Dial Bks. for Young Readers 1996 un il $16.99; pa $6.99

Grades: K 1 2 3   E

1. Marriage -- Fiction 2. Farm life -- Fiction

ISBN 0-8037-1496-3; 0-14-250060-7 pa

LC 94-31910

Fanny Agnes is a sturdy farm girl who dreams of marrying a prince, but when her fairy godmother doesn't show up, she decides on a local farmer instead

"Fanny Agnes is a delight: a feminist with a wry sense of humor, she balances her dreams with common sense and a loving heart. What's more, there's plenty for youngsters to enjoy in the robust, bucolic pictures, which seem almost to jump off the page." Booklist

★ **Snowmen** at night; pictures by Mark Buehner. Phyllis Fogelman Bks. 2002 un il $15.99

Grades: PreK K 1 2   E

1. Stories in rhyme 2. Snowmen 3. Snow -- Fiction

ISBN 0-8037-2550-7

LC 2001-33517

Snowmen play games at night when no one is watching

The "text has bouncy rhymes, but it's the artwork that is spectacular. Acrylic-over-oil paintings feature fat, happy snowpeople who practically jump—or sled—off the pages." Booklist

Other titles about the snowmen are:

Snowmen at Christmas (2005)

Snowmen all year (2010)

★ **Superdog**; the heart of a hero. illustrated by Mark Buehner. HarperCollins 2004 un il $15.99; lib bdg $16.89

Grades: PreK K 1 2   E

1. Dogs -- Fiction

ISBN 0-06-623620-7; 0-06-623621-5 lib bdg

LC 2002-3540

Tired of being overlooked because he is so small, a big-hearted dog named Dexter transforms himself into a superhero

"Solid shapings, surprising perspectives, and thick paints in dynamic colors combine for artwork that practically jumps off the page. There's plenty of wit, too." Booklist

Buhler, Cynthia von

But who will bell the cats? Houghton Mifflin Books for Children 2009 un il $16

Grades: K 1 2   E

1. Bats -- Fiction 2. Cats -- Fiction 3. Mice -- Fiction 4. Princesses -- Fiction 5. Fables -- Juvenile literature

ISBN 978-0-618-99718-3; 0-618-99718-0

LC 2008050165

While a princess spoils her eight cats, a mouse and his friend, a brown bat, live on scraps in the castle cellar, but Mouse decides to place bells on the cats necks so that he and Brown Bat might live comfortably, as well. Includes the Aesop fable on which the story is based.

"Dark, complicated mixed-media illustrations bring a humorously creepy feel to the tale." Horn Book

Buitrago, Jairo

★ **Jimmy** the greatest! Jairo Buitrago; Rafael Yockteng, illustrator; Elisa Amado, translator. Groundwood Books/House of Anansi Press 2012 48 p. ill. $18.95

Grades: K 1 2 3   E

1. Boxing -- Fiction 2. Poverty -- Fiction 3. Picture books for children

ISBN 1554981786; 9781554981786

In this book, "[w]ide-eyed Jimmy lives in a ramshackle, tin-roofed village, painted by [illustrator Rafael] Yockteng . . . . Jimmy finds out about Muhammad Ali from a boxful of old newspapers and, galvanized, starts training in the local gym. 'He wasn't thinking about what he didn't have anymore. . . . He didn't need much stuff to run.' . . . But it's

Jimmy's trainer, Don Apolinar, who leaves for the big city, while Jimmy stays behind; he ends up coaching kids at the gym." (Publishers Weekly)

Bulla, Clyde Robert

★ The **chalk** box kid; illustrated by Thomas B. Allen. Random House 1987 un il hardcover o.p. pa $3.99
Grades: K 1 2 3   E
ISBN 0-394-99102-8; 0-394-89102-3 pa

LC 87-4683

"Bulla manages a poignant depth within the confines of simple style and narrative. Understated and easy to read, this nevertheless tackles problems that are not easy to solve without exercising the imagination." Bull Cent Child Books

Bunting, Eve

Baby can; [by] Eve Bunting; illustrated by Maxie Chambliss. Boyds Mills Press 2007 un il $15.95
Grades: PreK   E
1. Growth -- Fiction 2. Infants -- Fiction 3. Brothers -- Fiction
ISBN 978-1-59078-322-1

LC 2006011485

Every time his family gets excited over something Baby James can do, big brother Brendan demonstrates that he can do even better, from burping to rolling over to walking

"The watercolor illustrations match the light touch of the spare text." Booklist

The **Banshee**; illustrated by Emily Arnold McCully. Clarion Books 2009 un il $16
Grades: K 1 2 3   E
1. Fear -- Fiction 2. Family life -- Fiction 3. Superstition -- Fiction
ISBN 978-0-618-82162-4; 0-618-82162-7

LC 2008-14581

When Terry wakes up in the middle of the night to horrible screeching, he thinks the Banshee has come to pay his family a visit.

"This picture book creates a convincing story of bravery in the face of vividly imagined danger. Not a word is wasted in the first-person text, and the ink-and-watercolor illustrations show Terry's emotions with clarity and sensitivity." Booklist

Butterfly house; illustrated by Greg Shed. Scholastic Press 1999 un il $17.99
Grades: K 1 2 3   E
1. Stories in rhyme 2. Butterflies -- Fiction 3. Grandfathers -- Fiction
ISBN 0-590-84884-4

LC 98-16349

With the help of her grandfather, a little girl makes a house for a larva and watches it develop before setting it free, and every summer after that butterflies come to visit her

"Shed's gouache-on-canvas paintings evoke feelings of warmth and nostalgia suited to the quiet story. Earth tones predominate, especially the browns and oranges found in this species. Appended with directions for raising a butterfly." Booklist

Cheyenne again; illustrated by Irving Toddy. Clarion Bks. 1995 un il $16; pa $5.95

Grades: K 1 2 3   E
1. School stories 2. Cheyenne Indians -- Fiction
ISBN 0-395-70364-6; 0-618-19465-7 pa

LC 94-43287

Young Bull, "a young Cheyenne boy tells how he's taken from his parents on the reservation in the late 1880s and sent to a boarding school, where he's forced to learn white ways. . . . This is a picture book for older readers, a grim story of painful separation and forced assimilation. . . . The short, spare lines of free verse are illustrated by double-page-spread oil and acrylic paintings that contrast the open landscape with the stiffness of figures forced into uniform and regimentation." Booklist

Christmas cricket; illustrated by Timothy Bush. Clarion Bks. 2002 32p il $15
Grades: K 1 2 3   E
1. Crickets 2. Christmas 3. Crickets -- Fiction 4. Christmas -- Fiction
ISBN 0-618-06554-7

LC 2001-55266

On Christmas Eve, a little cricket finds its way into a house where its singing is thought to be the voice of an angel

"Bush's watercolor pictures celebrate the story's cheerful warmth while their varying sizes and shapes create a cinematic effect that cleverly captures both the rhythm of the text and a cricket's kinetic spirit." Booklist

Dandelions; illustrated by Greg Shed. Harcourt Brace & Co. 1995 un hardcover o.p. pa $7
Grades: K 1 2 3   E
1. Family life -- Fiction 2. Frontier and pioneer life -- Fiction
ISBN 0-15-200050-X; 0-15-202407-7 pa

LC 94-27104

"Like the dandelions she plants on the roof of their Nebraska soddie, Zoe believes that the transplanting of her family will 'take,' despite the difficult transition. Young Zoe's narration conveys both youthful confidence and fear as the family work to adjust to their new life. Gouache illustrations effectively portray the vast, sun-drenched prairie and complement the text." Horn Book Guide

★ **Fly** away home; illustrated by Ronald Himler. Clarion Bks. 1991 32p il $16; pa $6.99
Grades: K 1 2 3   E
1. Airports -- Fiction 2. Homeless persons -- Fiction
ISBN 0-395-55962-6; 0-395-66415-2 pa

LC 90-42353

A homeless boy who lives in an airport with his father, moving from terminal to terminal and trying not to be noticed, is given hope when he sees a trapped bird find its freedom

"Himler's quiet paintings echo the economy and the touching quality of the story, which is all the more effective in depicting the plight of the homeless because it is so low-keyed." Bull Cent Child Books

Girls A to Z; illustrated by Suzanne Bloom. Boyds Mills Press 2002 un il $15.95
Grades: PreK K 1 2   E
1. Alphabet 2. Occupations
ISBN 1-56397-147-X

Girls with names ranging from Aliki to Zoe imagine themselves in various fun and creative professions

"Bunting has created a winning alphabet book that is playful, inventive, and (coincidentally) politically correct. Accompanied by Bloom's exuberant watercolor portraits." SLJ

Hey diddle diddle; illustrated by Mary Ann Fraser. Boyds Mills Press 2011 un il $16.95

Grades: PreK K　　　　　　　　　　　　　　　　E

1. Stories in rhyme 2. Animals -- Fiction 3. Musicians -- Fiction

ISBN 978-1-59078-768-7; 1-59078-768-4

In this variation on the traditional nursery rhyme, the cat plays the fiddle, the cow plays the silver trombone, and other animals play other musical instruments and join in a band, which is revealed in the end to be a music box wound by a small child.

"Pure whimsy . . . is what [Bunting] delivers here. . . . Fraser's accompanying artwork is cheery and saturated, the colors running from cool to hot. . . . The music made here will be in a sing-along read-aloud, with accompanying guffaws to mark the time." Kirkus

★ **How** many days to America? a Thanksgiving story. illustrated by Beth Peck. Clarion Bks. 1988 un il lib bdg $16; pa $5.95

Grades: K 1 2 3　　　　　　　　　　　　　　　　E

1. Refugees -- Fiction 2. Thanksgiving Day -- Fiction

ISBN 0-89919-521-0 lib bdg; 0-395-54777-6 pa

LC 88-2590

Refugees from an unnamed Caribbean island embark on a dangerous boat trip to America where they have a special reason to celebrate Thanksgiving

"Bunting's simple tale focuses on the hardships of the journey and on the American ideals of freedom and safety. She wisely leaves aside the issues of politics in the homeland or in this country. Her prose is poetically spare. . . . Peck's richly colored crayon drawings yield added enjoyment. . . . A poignant story and a thought-provoking discussion starter." SLJ

Hurry! hurry! illustrated by Jeff Mack. Harcourt 2007 un il $16

Grades: PreK K 1　　　　　　　　　　　　　　　　E

1. Eggs -- Fiction 2. Chickens -- Fiction 3. Domestic animals -- Fiction

ISBN 978-0-15-205410-6; 0-15-205410-3

LC 2005021120

All the animals of the barnyard community hurry to greet their newest member, who is just pecking his way out of an egg

"The sweet story is filled with movement and excitement. . . . Acrylic spreads are bright and cheerful." SLJ

Jin Woo; illustrated by Chris K. Soentpiet. Clarion Bks. 2001 30p il $16

Grades: K 1 2 3　　　　　　　　　　　　　　　　E

1. Adoption 2. Brothers 3. Korean Americans 4. Adoption -- Fiction 5. Brothers -- Fiction 6. Korean Americans -- Fiction

ISBN 0-395-93872-4

LC 00-38408

Davey is dubious about having a new adopted brother from Korea, but when he finds out that his parents still love him, he decides that having a baby brother will be fine

"Soentpiet's watercolors are suffused with light and perfectly capture the characters' expressions. . . . The story's emotional veracity will speak to any new sibling." SLJ

Little Bear's little boat; illustrated by Nancy Carpenter. Clarion Bks. 2003 32p il $12

Grades: PreK K 1 2　　　　　　　　　　　　　　　　E

1. Size 2. Bears 3. Growth 4. Boats and boating 5. Bears -- Fiction 6. Growth -- Fiction 7. Animals -- Infancy

ISBN 0-395-97462-3

LC 2001-37233

When Little Bear can no longer fit into his boat he finds someone else who can use it

"This is a sensitive, affecting story about growing up and leaving favorite things behind, with charming ink-and-paint illustrations that echo the spare clarity of the words." Booklist

Mouse island; [by] Eve Bunting; illustrated by Dominic Catalano. Boyds Mills Press 2008 un il $15.95

Grades: PreK K 1 2　　　　　　　　　　　　　　　　E

1. Cats -- Fiction 2. Mice -- Fiction 3. Islands -- Fiction

ISBN 978-1-59078-447-1; 1-59078-447-2

LC 2007-17558

Mouse enjoys living on his island but feels that something is missing from his life until the day he performs a daring rescue and acquires an unlikely friend.

"Illustrations in grays, greens, and blues, sometimes stormy, sometimes placid, provide the backdrop for this tale of camaraderie." Horn Book Guide

My robot; by Eve Bunting; illustrated by Dagmar Fehlau. Harcourt, Inc. 2006 un il (Green Light readers) $12.95; pa $3.95

Grades: K 1 2　　　　　　　　　　　　　　　　E

1. Robots -- Fiction

ISBN 0-15-205593-2; 0-15-205617-3 pa

LC 2005006936

Cecil the robot is good at playing tag, leading the school band, and performing tricks with the dog, but there is one important thing he does best of all.

"Fehlau's bright, stylized illustrations have a festive feel and infuse the fantastical situations with lighthearted fun." Booklist

My special day at Third Street School; illustrated by Suzanne Bloom. Boyds Mills Press 2004 un il $15.95; pa $9.95

Grades: K 1 2 3　　　　　　　　　　　　　　　　E

1. School stories 2. Authors -- Fiction

ISBN 1-59078-745-5; 1-59078-745-5 pa

A school visit from children's book author Amanda Drake brings a day full of fun.

"Just as Bunting's writing captures the action and the children's emotions in a convincing way, Bloom's gouache, colored pencil, and crayon artwork illustrates the contemporary classroom setting and the children's body language to perfection." Booklist

One candle; illustrated by K. Wendy Popp. HarperCollins Pubs. 2002 un il hardcover o.p. pa $6.99

Grades: K 1 2 3   E
1. Hanukkah 2. Concentration camps 3. Jews -- Fiction 4. Hanukkah -- Fiction 5. Holocaust, 1933-1945 -- Fiction
ISBN 0-06-028115-4; 0-06-028116-2 lib bdg; 0-06-008560-6 pa

LC 2001-47205

Every year a family celebrates Hanukkah by retelling the story of how Grandma and her sister managed to mark the day while in a German concentration camp

"Popp invests her art with all the emotion of Bunting's heartfelt text. . . . A gentle but forthright opening for discussion about the Holocaust." Booklist

★ **One** green apple; illustrated by Ted Lewin. Clarion Books 2006 un il $16

Grades: K 1 2 3   E
1. School stories 2. Apples -- Fiction 3. Muslims -- Fiction 4. Immigrants -- Fiction
ISBN 0-618-43477-1

LC 2005011378

While on a school field trip to an orchard to make cider, a young immigrant named Farah gains self-confidence when the green apple she picks perfectly complements the other students' red apples

"Young readers will respond as much to Bunting's fine first-person narrative as to Lewin's double-page, photorealistic watercolors." Booklist

Our library; by Eve Bunting; illustrated by Maggie Smith. Clarion Books 2008 32p il $16

Grades: K 1 2   E
1. Raccoons -- Fiction 2. Libraries -- Fiction 3. Books and reading -- Fiction
ISBN 978-0-618-49458-3; 0-618-49458-8

LC 2006009519

A raccoon and his friends go to great lengths to make sure they will always have a library from which to borrow books.

"Bunting's style has a graceful simplicity, descriptive enough to be evocative without overwhelming. . . . Smith's watercolor and acrylic illustrations are charming and should have most children longing to enter the buttercup-yellow library with the grass-green door. An excellent vehicle for discussing the importance of libraries, books, reading, and teamwork." SLJ

Pirate boy; illustrated by Julie Fortenberry. Holiday House 2011 un il $16.95

Grades: PreK K   E
1. Pirates -- Fiction 2. Imagination -- Fiction 3. Mother-son relationship -- Fiction
ISBN 978-0-8234-2321-7; 0-8234-2321-2

LC 2010029446

As Colin imagines himself in a series of adventures beginning with joining a pirate crew, his mother assures him that she will always be there to help if he needs her.

"Layers of color and heavily worked figures give Fortenberry's . . . digital art a thick, substantial feel. . . . The book

reads like a conversation Bunting . . . might once have had with one of her own children; it's a warmhearted portrait of an endlessly patient parent, ready to help her child work through his fears and desires." Publ Wkly

★ **Pop's** bridge; written by Eve Bunting; illustrated by C. F. Payne. Harcourt, Inc. 2006 un il $17

Grades: 1 2 3 4   E
1. Fathers -- Fiction
ISBN 0-15-204773-5

LC 2004-23774

Robert and his friend Charlie are proud of their fathers, who are working on the construction of San Francisco's Golden Gate Bridge.

"Distinguished by its lovely, understated text and Payne's lavish and affectionate mixed-media pictures, this picture book does a quietly successful job of humanizing one of the most important feats of civil engineering in American history." Booklist

★ **Smoky** night; written by Eve Bunting; illustrated by David Diaz. Harcourt Brace & Co. 1994 un il $17; pa $7

Grades: K 1 2 3   E
1. Riots -- Fiction 2. Korean Americans -- Fiction 3. African Americans -- Fiction
ISBN 0-15-269954-6; 0-15-201884-0 pa

LC 93-14885

Awarded the Caldecott Medal, 1995

When the Los Angeles riots break out in the streets of their neighborhood, Daniel and his mother, African Americans, make friends with Mrs. Kim, a Korean grocer from across the street

"Thick black lines border vibrant acrylic paintings. . . . Diaz places these dynamic paintings on collages of real objects that, for the most part, reinforce the narrative action. . . . Both author and illustrator insist on a headlong confrontation with the issue of rapport between different races, and the result is a memorable, thought-provoking book." Horn Book

So far from the sea; illustrated by Chris K. Soentpiet. Clarion Bks. 1998 30p il $16; pa $7.99

Grades: K 1 2 3   E
1. Japanese Americans -- Fiction 2. Japanese Americans -- Juvenile fiction 3. Manzanar War Relocation Center -- Fiction 4. Japanese Americans -- Evacuation and relocation, 1942-1945 -- Fiction
ISBN 0-395-72095-8; 0-547-23752-9 pa

LC 97-28176

When seven-year-old Laura and her family visit Grandfather's grave at the Manzanar War Relocation Center, the Japanese American child leaves behind a special symbol

"Soentpiet's impressionistic watercolors perfectly complement Bunting's evocative text." SLJ

Someday a tree; illustrated by Ronald Himler. Clarion Bks. 1993 un il hardcover o.p. pa $6.95

Grades: K 1 2 3   E
1. Trees -- Fiction 2. Pollution -- Fiction
ISBN 0-395-61309-4; 0-395-76478-5 pa

LC 92-24074

Alice, her parents, and their neighbors try to save an old oak tree that has been poisoned by pollution

"Himler's soft, realistic watercolors spread over double pages and complement the sensitive, poetic mood of the story." SLJ

That's what leprechauns do; illustrated by Emily Arnold McCully. Clarion Books 2005 32p il $16
Grades: K 1 2 3　　　　　　　　　　　　　　E
1. Leprechauns -- Fiction
ISBN 0-618-35410-7
When leprechauns Ari, Boo, and Col need to place the pot of gold at the end of the rainbow, they cannot help getting into mischief along the way.
"McCully graces this lighthearted story with her characteristically expressive and charming watercolors that eloquently capture the verdant beauty of the Irish countryside and the irrepressible personalities." SLJ

★ **Tweak,** tweak; illustrated by Sergio Ruzzier. Clarion Books 2011 40p il $14.99
Grades: PreK K 1　　　　　　　　　　　　　E
1. Elephants -- Fiction　2. Mother-child relationship -- Fiction
ISBN 978-0-618-99851-7; 0-618-99851-9
　　　　　　　　　　　　　　　LC 2010024651
While out for a walk, Mama Elephant answers her child's questions about a monkey, a frog, a songbird, a butterfly, and a crocodile, all the while teaching about Little Elephant too.
"Young children will enjoy following Little Elephant's fantasies, depicted in the uncluttered, double-page spreads, all the way to the story's climax, which celebrates what Little Elephant really is, as well as the big, strong creature she will grow up to be. Along with imaginative silliness, the nurturing parent-child tenderness is the core of the story." Booklist

Walking to school; by Eve Bunting; illustrated by Michael Dooling. Clarion Books 2008 32p il $16
Grades: 2 3 4　　　　　　　　　　　　　　E
1. Prejudices -- Fiction
ISBN 978-0-618-26144-4; 0-618-26144-3
"The book does an excellent job of presenting the situation from a child's perspective without demonizing either side. . . . Dooling's oil-on-canvas illustrations are realistic enough to resemble stills from documentary footage." SLJ

★ The **Wall**; illustrated by Ronald Himler. Clarion Bks. 1990 un il $16; pa $5.95
Grades: K 1 2 3　　　　　　　　　　　　　E
1. Vietnam Veterans Memorial (Washington, D.C.) -- Fiction
ISBN 0-395-51588-2; 0-395-62977-2 pa
　　　　　　　　　　　　　　　LC 89-17429
"A father and his young son come to the Vietnam Veterans Memorial to find the name of the grandfather the boy never knew. This moving account is beautifully told from a young child's point of view; the watercolors capture the impressive mass of the wall of names as well as the poignant reactions of the people who visit there." Horn Book Guide

The **Wednesday** surprise; illustrated by Donald Carrick. Clarion Bks. 1989 un il lib bdg $16; pa $5.95

Grades: K 1 2 3　　　　　　　　　　　　　E
1. Reading -- Fiction　2. Grandmothers -- Fiction
ISBN 0-89919-721-3　lib bdg; 0-395-54776-8 pa
　　　　　　　　　　　　　　　LC 88-12117
"Bunting's writing is simple and warm and direct. . . . Carrick's pictures echo the warmth, especially in the faces of the family, painted in realistically detailed watercolors with a careful attention to familial resemblance. A gentle charmer." Bull Cent Child Books

Will it be a baby brother? illustrated by Beth Spiegel. Boyd Mills Press 2010 un il $16.95
Grades: PreK K　　　　　　　　　　　　　E
1. Infants -- Fiction　2. Siblings -- Fiction
ISBN 978-1-59078-439-6; 1-59078-439-1
A little boy is certain that his expectant mother will give birth to a baby brother.
"The large, bright, watercolor-and-ink cartoon-style pictures skillfully convey the boy's feelings. . . . This warm, reassuring story is about a child's fear of displacement as much as his longing for a sibling just like him." Booklist

You were loved before you were born; [by] Eve Bunting & [illustrated by] Karen Barbour. Blue Sky Press 2008 un il $16.99
Grades: PreK　　　　　　　　　　　　　　E
1. Love -- Fiction　2. Family life -- Fiction
ISBN 978-0-439-04061-7; 0-439-04061-2
　　　　　　　　　　　　　　　LC 2007-9703
A mother shares with her child all the ways in which family members and friends were loving and welcoming before the child was even born
"A marvelous integration of color, image and verbal rhythm sure to delight and to become a must-purchase for newborns and their parents." Kirkus

★ The **bones** of Fred McFee; illustrated by Kurt Cyrus. Harcourt 2002 un il hardcover o.p. pa $6
Grades: K 1 2 3　　　　　　　　　　　　　E
1. Stories in rhyme　2. Halloween -- Fiction
ISBN 0-15-202004-7; 0-15-205423-5 pa
　　　　　　　　　　　　　　　LC 2001-2414
A toy skeleton at Halloween provides menace and mystery
"The story, told in rhyme keeps readers on the edge of their seats. . . . Cyrus's detailed, realistic illustrations, done in scratchboard and watercolor, are appropriately dark and are a perfect complement to the subtly scary mood of the text." SLJ

The **memory** string; pictures by Ted Rand. Clarion Bks. 2000 32p il $15
Grades: K 1 2 3　　　　　　　　　　　　　E
1. Girls　2. Memory　3. Stepmothers　4. Grief in children　5. Memory -- Fiction　6. Stepmothers -- Fiction
ISBN 0-395-86146-2
　　　　　　　　　　　　　　　LC 99-42771
While still grieving for her mother and unable to accept her stepmother, Laura clings to the memories represented by forty-three buttons on a string
"Rand's realistic artwork concentrates on the faces of the family and the emotions that cross them. Some children will find this touches them very deeply." Booklist

Bunting, Eve, 1928-

Big Bear's big boat; by Eve Bunting; illustrated by Nancy Carpenter. Clarion Books 2013 32 p. (hardcover) $12.99

Grades: PreK K 1   E

1. Bears -- Juvenile Fiction 2. Boats and boating -- Juvenile fiction 3. Bears -- Fiction 4. Boats and boating -- Fiction

ISBN 0618585370; 9780618585373

LC 2012003974

In this book by Eve Bunting "Big Bear outgrew his little boat, so he is building himself a big boat and can't wait till he's rowing, fishing, and relaxing in it. When his friends start suggesting improvements, Big Bear obligingly follows their advice. To his dismay, his big boat is turning out all wrong. It's because he hasn't followed his own dream, and he knows exactly how to fix it." (Publisher's note)

Frog and friends; written by Eve Bunting; illustrated by Josee Masse. Sleeping Bear Press 2011 37p il (I am a reader!)

Grades: 1 2   E

1. Frogs -- Fiction 2. Ponds -- Fiction 3. Animals -- Fiction 4. Friendship -- Fiction

ISBN 1-58536-548-3; 1-58536-689-7 pa; 978-1-58536-548-7; 978-1-58536-689-7 pa

LC 2010053706

Frog and his friends are alarmed by a strange object that appears on his pond, share a thoughtful—if scratchy—gift, and meet a hippopotamus that has run away from the zoo.

"This clever beginning reader is divided into three chapters. . . . Repetition, white space, and a large font help prepare children for tackling a smattering of more challenging vocabulary. Bright cartoon illustrations provide some picture clues. Readers will enjoy feeling superior to Frog and his friends." SLJ

★ **Have** you seen my new blue socks? by Eve Bunting; illustrated by Sergio Ruzzier. Clarion Books 2013 32 p. (hardcover) $16.99

Grades: PreK K 1   E

1. Stories in rhyme 2. Ducks -- Juvenile fiction 3. Lost and found possessions -- Juvenile fiction 4. Ducks -- Fiction 5. Socks -- Fiction 6. Animals -- Fiction 7. Lost and found possessions -- Fiction

ISBN 0547752679; 9780547752679

LC 2012012192

This rhyming children's book, by Eve Bunting, illustrated by Sergio Ruzzier, "spin[s] the tale of a small duck who waddles through the countryside, forlornly searching for his blue socks. . . . Finally, a sharp-eyed peacock sees a bit of blue peeking out of duck's lace-up shoes and the mini-mystery is solved!" (Publisher's note)

My dog Jack is fat; illustrated by Michael Rex. Marshall Cavendish Children 2011 un il $16.99

Grades: PreK K 1   E

1. Dogs -- Fiction 2. Weight loss -- Fiction

ISBN 978-0-7614-5809-8; 0-7614-5809-3

LC 2010018271

Carson does his best to help his dog, Jack, lose weight, with unexpected results.

"This appealing take on a common problem has understated, smooth writing and colorful, digitally rendered cartoons enlivened by Rex's characteristic humor." SLJ

Burell, Sarah

Diamond Jim Dandy and the sheriff; illustrated by Bryan Langdo. Sterling Pub. 2010 un il $14.95

Grades: K 1 2   E

1. Infants -- Fiction 2. Rattlesnakes -- Fiction

ISBN 978-1-4027-5737-2; 1-4027-5737-9

LC 2008013767

When a friendly and talented rattlesnake slithers into Dustpan, Texas, he must prove his value to the residents of the town before the sheriff will allow him to stay.

"This charming tale has bright, appealing, kid-friendly illustrations. The lively dialogue combined with the satisfying ending will serve as an excellent storytime read-aloud." SLJ

Burgess, Mark

Where teddy bears come from; written by Mark Burgess; illustrated by Russell Ayto. Peachtree 2009 un il $16.95

Grades: PreK K 1 2   E

1. Wolves -- Fiction 2. Teddy bears -- Fiction

ISBN 978-1-56145-487-7; 1-56145-487-7

LC 2008052705

When Little Wolf cannot fall asleep, he decides that he needs a teddy bear and goes into the woods to see if he can find out where to get one.

"This charming story plays with the conventions of familiar nursery tales. . . . With its lively, bold watercolors filled with humorous details, this tale is likely to be a storytime hit." SLJ

Burkert, Rand

★ **Mouse** & Lion; [by] Aesop; retold by Rand Burkert; picutres by Nancy Ekholm Burkert. Michael di Capua Books 2011 un il $17.95

Grades: 2 3 4 5 6   E

1. Fables 2. Mice -- Fiction 3. Lions -- Fiction

ISBN 978-0-545-10147-9; 0-545-10147-6

This is "a book rich with [Nancy Ekholm Burkert's] signature meticulous brush lines, compelling display of color, and carefully delineated detail. Each page offers dramatic delight that extends the story. In an unusual but fascinating variation on the Aesop tale, Rand Burkert places Mouse at center stage. . . . The illustrations for this spirited tale are nothing less than spectacular. . . . Choosing the Aha Hills (between Botswana and Namibia) for her setting, the artist imbues the scenes with the fauna and flora of this region." SLJ

Burleigh, Robert

Clang-clang! Beep-beep! listen to the city. illustrated by Beppe Giacobbe. Simon & Schuster Books for Young Readers 2009 un il $14.99

Grades: PreK K 1   E

1. Stories in rhyme 2. Noise -- Fiction 3. Sound -- Fiction 4. Sound -- Juvenile literature 5. City and town life -- Fiction 6. Cities and towns -- Juvenile literature

ISBN 978-1-4169-4052-4; 1-4169-4052-9

LC 2007-45844

From morning until night, a city is filled with such sounds as the roars and snores of a subway ride, the flutters and coos of pigeons, and the shouts and beeps of drivers in traffic

"The rhymes that accompany the story are short but evocative. . . . The artist uses a vivid mix of primary and secondary colors to set the stage." SLJ

Good-bye, Sheepie; illustrated by Peter Catalanotto. Marshall Cavendish 2010 un il $16.99
Grades: K 1 2   E
1. Dogs -- Fiction 2. Death -- Fiction 3. Father-son relationship -- Fiction
ISBN 978-0-7614-5598-1; 0-7614-5598-1
LC 2009-5955
A father teaches his young son about death and remembrance as he buries their beloved dog.

"Catalanotto's gentle watercolor-and-gouache paintings give off a yellow glow suggestive of warm sunshine on an autumn day, and are well suited to Burleigh's quiet text." Booklist

Burn, Doris
Andrew Henry's meadow; Doris Burn. Philomel Books 2012 48 p. ill. $14.99
Grades: K 1 2   E
1. Picture books for children 2. Runaway children -- Juvenile fiction 3. Building -- Fiction 4. Self-acceptance -- Fiction
ISBN 0399256083; 9780399256080
LC 2011017476
First published by Coward, McCann (1965)
In this children's picture book reissue, "Andrew Henry has two younger brothers, who are always together, and two older sisters, who are always together. But Andrew Henry is in the middle—and he's always with himself. He doesn't mind this very much, because he's an inventor. But when Andrew Henry's family doesn't appreciate him or his inventions, he decides it's time to run away." (Publisher's note)

Burningham, John
Edwardo; the horriblest boy in the whole wide world. Alfred A. Knopf 2006 un il $16.99; lib bdg $19.99
Grades: PreK K 1 2 3   E
ISBN 978-0-375-84053-1; 0-375-84053-2; 978-0-375-94053-8 lib bdg; 0-375-94053-7 lib bdg
LC 2006-03681
Each time he does something a little bit bad, Edwardo is told that he is very bad and soon his behavior is awful, but when he accidentally does good things and is complimented, he becomes much, much nicer.

"Fans of Burningham will delight in his witty, winsome pictures, so full of animation and expression." SLJ

★ **It's** a secret. Candlewick Press 2009 un il $16.99
Grades: PreK K 1   E
1. Cats -- Fiction 2. Night -- Fiction
ISBN 978-0-7636-4275-4; 0-7636-4275-4
Boston Globe-Horn Book Award honor book: Picture Book (2010)
"Marie Elaine wonders what her cat, Malcolm, does at night that causes him to sleep all day. When she goes down to the kitchen late one night and finds him all dressed up to go out, she asks to come along. . . . He takes her and her

neighbor Norman to a secret cat party on the rooftops, where they dance, feast, and meet the queen of the cats. Burningham's signature sketchy mixed-media illustrations are a good fit for the dreamlike story, as is the off-kilter logic of the text." SLJ

John Patrick Norman McHennessy; the boy who was always late. Alfred A. Knopf 2008 un il $16.99
Grades: PreK K 1 2   E
1. School stories 2. Teachers -- Fiction 3. Truthfulness and falsehood -- Fiction
ISBN 978-0-375-85220-6; 0-375-85220-4
First published 1987 by Crown Publishers
A teacher regrets his decison to disbelieve a student's outlandish excuses for being tardy.

"Burningham uses mixed media here to create boldly-colored illustrations which do a marvelous job of reinforcing the text. The storyline is a simple one, but it is filled with irony." SLJ

Mr. Gumpy's motor car. Crowell 1976 un il lib bdg $18.89
Grades: PreK K 1 2   E
1. Animals -- Fiction 2. Automobiles -- Fiction
ISBN 0-690-00799-X
LC 75-4582
First published 1973 in the United Kingdom
"The strength here is in the rural simplicity and in the colorful illustrations of amiable animals, the countryside in sunshine and under lowering clouds. Those things and the bold type which carries words and phrases for the reader to chew on and roll around on the tongue." N Y Times Book Rev

★ **Mr.** Gumpy's outing. Holt & Co. 1971 un il $17.95; pa $7.99; bd bk $6.95
Grades: PreK K 1 2   E
1. Animals -- Fiction
ISBN 0-8050-0708-3; 0-8050-1315-6 pa; 0-8050-6629-2 bd bk
First published 1970 in the United Kingdom
"Mr. Gumpy is about to go off for a boat ride and is asked by two children, a rabbit, a cat, a dog, and other animals if they may come. To each Mr. Gumpy says yes, if—if the children don't squabble, if the rabbit won't hop, if the cat won't chase the rabbit or the dog tease the cat, and so on. Of course each does exactly what Mr. Gumpy forbade, the boat tips over, and they all slog home for tea in friendly fashion." Sutherland. The Best in Child Books
Another title about Mr. Gumpy is:
Mr. Gumpy's motor car (1976)

★ **There's** going to be a baby; [illustrated by] Helen Oxenbury. Candlewick Press 2010 un il $16.99
Grades: PreK K 1   E
1. Infants -- Fiction 2. Siblings -- Fiction 3. Imagination -- Fiction
ISBN 978-0-7636-4907-4; 0-7636-4907-4
LC 2009-51509
A young boy imagines what life will be like when his new sibling arrives.

"The handsome, clear-lined images may seem retro at first, but the crispness acts as a containing presence for displacement fears and a source of narrative momentum—all the while allowing Oxenbury to exercise the full power of her visual image." Publ Wkly

Burton, Virginia Lee, 1909-1968

Katy and the big snow; story and pictures by Virginia Lee Burton. Houghton Mifflin 1943 32p il $16; pa $6.95
Grades: PreK K 1   E
   1. Snow -- Fiction 2. Tractors -- Fiction
   ISBN 0-395-18155-0; 0-395-18562-9 pa

"Katy was a beautiful red crawler tractor. In summer she wore a bulldozer to push dirt with. In winter she wore a snowplow. She was big and strong and the harder the job the better she liked it. When the Big Snow covered the city of Geoppolis like a thick blanket, Katy cleared the city from North to South and East to West." Ont Libr Rev

★ Mike Mulligan and his steam shovel; story and pictures by Virginia Lee Burton. Houghton Mifflin 1939 un il $16; pa $6.95
Grades: PreK K 1   E
   1. Steam-shovels -- Fiction
   ISBN 0-395-16961-5; 0-395-25939-8 pa

"One of the most convincing personifications of a machine ever written. Lively pictures, dramatic action, and a satisfying conclusion." Adventuring with Books. 2d edition

★ The little house; story and pictures by Virginia Lee Burton. Houghton Mifflin 1942 40p il $14.95; pa $5.95
Grades: PreK K 1   E
   1. Houses -- Fiction 2. City and town life -- Fiction
   ISBN 0-395-18156-9; 0-395-25938-X pa
   Awarded the Caldecott Medal, 1943

"The little house was very happy as she sat on the quiet hillside watching the changing seasons. As the years passed, however, tall buildings grew up around her, and the noise of city traffic disturbed her. She became sad and lonely until one day someone who understood her need for twinkling stars overhead and dancing apple blossoms moved her back to just the right little hill." Child Books Too Good to Miss

Butler, Dori Hillestad

My grandpa had a stroke; written by Dori Hillestad Butler; illustrated by Nicole Wong. Magination Press 2007 31p il $14.95; pa $8.95
Grades: K 1 2   E
   1. Stroke -- Fiction 2. Fishing -- Fiction 3. Grandfathers -- Fiction
   ISBN 978-1-59147-806-5; 1-59147-806-5; 978-1-59147-807-2 pa; 1-59147-807-3 pa
                      LC 2006034528

"Ryan loves spending Saturdays fishing with his grandfather. But when Grandpa suffers a stroke, everything changes. . . . The book, illustrated in soft-edged watercolors, ends on a hopeful note. . . . With quiet prose, this covers most of the emotional and practical hurdles faced by both patient and child." Booklist

Butler, John

Bedtime in the jungle; [written and illustrated by John Butler] Peachtree 2009 un il $16.95
Grades: PreK K   E
   1. Counting 2. Stories in rhyme 3. Animals -- Fiction

   4. Bedtime -- Fiction
   ISBN 978-1-56145-486-0; 1-56145-486-9
                      LC 2008040592

As dusk falls in the jungle, animal babies and their parents prepare for bedtime

"What distinguishes this title is its stunning illustrations. . . . The animals are depicted in their natural settings in soothing shades that are sure to bring about the calm that encourages sleep. A lovely addition." SLJ

Butler, M. Christina

The smiley snowman; illustrations by Tina Macnaughton. Good Books 2010 un il $16.99
Grades: PreK K   E
   1. Snow -- Fiction 2. Bears -- Fiction 3. Foxes -- Fiction 4. Rabbits -- Fiction
   ISBN 978-1-56148-696-0; 1-56148-696-5
                      LC 2010004916

A bear, a fox, and a rabbit build a snowman, but their efforts to keep it happy and warm almost bring about its demise.

"Silvery blue-green glitter makes the snowman appear to twinkle. And as the lovable animal friends play in the snowy woods, they make winter seem cozy and fun. This book would be a pleasant read-aloud for a winter-themed storytime." SLJ

Button, Lana

Willow's whispers; illustrated by Tania Howells. Kids Can Press 2010 il $16.95
Grades: PreK K 1   E
   1. Voice -- Fiction
   ISBN 978-1-55453-280-3; 1-55453-280-9

Buxton, Jane

The littlest llama; by Jane Buxton; illustrated by Jenny Cooper. Sterling 2008 un il $9.95
Grades: K 1 2   E
   1. Stories in rhyme 2. Play -- Fiction 3. Llamas -- Fiction
   ISBN 978-1-4027-5277-3; 1-4027-5277-6
                      LC 2007036396

High in the Andes Mountains, the littlest llama wants to play but his mother, sisters, gran, and aunt are busy, and so he leaves the herd to seek a playmate and finds adventure, instead.

"The descriptive rhyming text will make a lively read-aloud, while the beautiful, intricately detailed color illustrations extend each scenario." Booklist

Buzzeo, Toni

Adventure Annie goes to kindergarten; illustrated by Amy Wummer. Dial Books for Young Readers 2010 un il $16.99
Grades: PreK K 1   E
   1. School stories
   ISBN 978-0-8037-3358-9; 0-8037-3358-5

"Adventure Annie approaches her first day of kindergarten with gusto. In her enthusiasm, she proceeds to break the first two Kindergarten Gold Star Rules—'Respect our classroom and everything in it' and 'Make good decisions' by painting the classroom hamster cage and sneaking out to the jungle gym. She redeems herself, however, when she is asked to find two lost helpers. . . . Annie's good intentions, optimism, and curiosity make her a likable character and an excellent one to dispel fears for incoming kindergartners. Rendered in pencil and bright watercolors, the cheerful cartoon art, which occupies most of each page, will delight Annie's fans." SLJ

Adventure Annie goes to work; illustrated by Amy Wummer. Dial 2009 un il lib bdg $16.99
Grades: PreK K 1   E
1. Superheroes -- Fiction 2. Lost and found possessions -- Fiction
ISBN 978-0-8037-3233-9; 0-8037-3233-3

When she goes to work with her mother on a Saturday, Adventure Annie uses her own special methods to help find a missing report.

"The bright, full-color pencil and watercolor pictures are set against ample white space and show the warm relationship between mother and daughter. This is an office adventure that children will want to experience and a heroine they'll love meeting." SLJ

Another title about Adventure Annie is:
Adventure Annie goes to kindergarten (2010)

Inside the books; readers and libraries around the world. Toni Buzzeo; illustrations by Jude Daly. Upstart Books 2012 32 p. col. ill. (hardcover) $17.95
Grades: K 1 2   E
1. Libraries -- Juvenile nonfiction 2. Stories in rhyme 3. Libraries -- Fiction 4. Bookmobiles -- Fiction 5. Books and reading -- Fiction
ISBN 1602130582; 9781602130586
                                                  LC 2011287827

This children's book by Toni Buzzeo and illustrated by Jude Daly presents a "gentle homage to books and libraries. . . . [Buzzeo] reminds us of the extraordinary possibilities that lie inside every book and introduces us to many unique places these treasures can be found." (Publisher's note)

★ **One** cool friend; pictures by David Small. Dial Books for Young Readers 2012 32 p. (reinforced) $16.99
Grades: K 1 2   E
1. Pets -- Juvenile fiction 2. Penguins/Juvenile fiction 3. Father-son relationship -- Juvenile fiction 4. Penguins -- Fiction 5. Etiquette -- Fiction 6. Father-son relationship -- Fiction
ISBN 0803734131; 9780803734135
                                                  LC 2011021637
Caldecott Honor Book (2013)

In this book, "[a]fter Elliott convinces his father to allow him to bring home a penguin (Dad thinks he means a toy) from the aquarium, he sets Magellan (named after the explorer who discovered the species) up in style, creating an ice rink in his bedroom using a wading pool, the garden hose, and the lowest air-conditioning setting. Elliott reads up on his new pet, . . . feeds him anchovy pizza, and lets him hang out in the freezer and the bathtub." (Bulletin of the Center for Children's Books)

Penelope Popper, book doctor; illustrations by Jana Christy. Upstart Books 2011 un il $17.95
Grades: 1 2 3   E
1. Libraries -- Fiction 2. Books -- Conservation and restoration -- Fiction
ISBN 978-1-60213-054-8; 1-60213-054-X
                                                  LC 2011283516

In all corners of the library, there are books that need care and Penelope immediately dedicates herself to learning how to mend them.

"The upbeat narrative is . . . enlivened by cheerful illustrations depicting Penelope, an earnest girl with red hair and freckles, in her bright and pleasant classroom and school library. With its soft edges and palette of springtime colors, each painting reflects the positive tone of the story." SLJ

Ready or not, Dawdle Duckling; illustrated by Margaret Spengler. Dial Books for Young Readers 2005 un il $15.99
Grades: PreK K   E
1. Ducks -- Fiction 2. Animals -- Fiction
ISBN 0-8037-2959-6
                                                  LC 2003026423

After a few tries and with some help from friends, Dawdle Duckling finds the best way to hide while playing hide-and-seek with his mother and siblings.

"Spengler's compositions, her interplay of color and light, and her gift for conveying individuality in an unfailingly upbeat manner—all of these elements (plus enchanting details like duck-couture boaters and bonnets) transform a simple story into an excellent choice that is tailor-made for preschoolers." SLJ

Byars, Betsy Cromer

Boo's surprise; [by] Betsy Byars; illustrated by Erik Brooks. Henry Holt and Co. 2009 45p il $15.99
Grades: K 1 2   E
1. Siblings -- Fiction 2. Dinosaurs -- Fiction 3. Imagination -- Fiction
ISBN 978-0-8050-8817-5; 0-8050-8817-2
                                                  LC 2008048849
Boo finds an egg that hatches into a new dinosaur.

"Lively black-and-white drawings extend the fun, with a climactic double-page illustration at the end of each chapter." Booklist

★ **The Golly** sisters go West; by Betsy Byars; pictures by Sue Truesdell. Harper & Row 1986 64p il (I can read book) lib bdg $16.89; pa $3.99
Grades: K 1 2   E
1. Entertainers -- Fiction 2. Frontier and pioneer life -- Fiction
ISBN 0-06-020884-8 lib bdg; 0-06-444132-6 pa
                                                  LC 84-48474
May-May and Rose, the singing, dancing Golly sisters, travel west by covered wagon, entertaining people along the way

"The dialogue and antics are convincingly like those of rivalrous young siblings anywhere on the block. The story lines are cleverer than much easy-to-read fare, and the old-West setting adds flair. The accompanying watercolors, too, add a generous dollop of humor." Bull Cent Child Books
Other titles about the Golly sisters are:
The Golly sisters ride again (1994)
Hooray for the Golly sisters! (1990)

Bynum, Eboni

Jamari's drum; [by] Eboni Bynum and Roland Jackson; pictures on glazed tiles by Baba Wagué Diakité. Groundwood Books 2004 un il $16.95

Grades: K 1 2 3   E

   1. Drums -- Fiction 2. Volcanoes -- Fiction

   ISBN 0-88899-531-8

When Jamari forgets to heed Baba Mdogo's warning to play the drum in the village every day, he narrowly averts disaster from a volcano.

"The beautifully executed, folk-style artwork swirls with bold lines and bright patterns, incorporating backgrounds that blend earth tones with the blues and purples of the sky. . . . This book makes an excellent read-aloud." SLJ

Bynum, Janie

Kiki's blankie. Sterling Pub. 2009 un il $14.95

Grades: PreK   E

   1. Monkeys -- Fiction 2. Blankets -- Fiction 3. Lost and found possessions -- Fiction

   ISBN 978-1-4027-5910-9; 1-4027-5910-X

           LC 2008-26837

Kiki the monkey has many daring adventures with her polka-dot 'blankie,' but when it sails away without her and lands above a sleeping crocodile, she may not be brave enough to come to the rescue.

"Brightly colored, uncluttered illustrations are set on large areas of white space, making the objects and action easy for young children to find and follow. Preschoolers will relate to Kiki, her blankie attachment, and to her energy and creative play." SLJ

Byrne, John

Donald & Benoit; written and illustrated by John Patrick Byrne. Rizzoli 2011 un il $17.95

Grades: 2 3 4 5   E

   1. Cats -- Fiction 2. Drums -- Fiction

   ISBN 978-0-7893-2084-1; 0-7893-2084-3

"Benoît, the son of a sailor, and Donald, his new kitten, live in an idyllic fishing village. . . . When Benoît's father, Jean-Kiki, disappears at sea and they're left to support themselves, Donald's love of drumming and the timely help of a library book . . . wins him resounding professional triumph—which Jean-Kiki reappears in time to enjoy. With a nod to early cubism, Byrne paints bulky, curvy figures whose swoops and angles have the rhythmic energy of Donald's drums; their impact is heightened by the book's large trim size. Dreamy, melancholy hand-lettering and graceful design add even more charm." Publ Wkly

Cabral, Olga

The seven sneezes; illustrated by Bruce Ingman. Golden Books 2009 unp il

Grades: PreK K 1 2   E

   1. Animals -- Fiction 2. Sneezing -- Fiction

   ISBN 9780375835940; 9780375935947 lib bdg

A newly illustrated edition of the title first published 1948

What happens when the local rag man sneezes? The kitten's ears end up on the bunny. The bunny's ears end up on the kitten. The dog meows, the cat barks. But with a little concentration—and a lot of pepper—the rag man tries to sneeze everything right

"At the conclusion of this sweet tale, one feels fully satisfied, as a topsy-turvy situation is resolved and order

is regained. First published in 1948, this version preserves the original charm of Cabral's text and introduces Ingman's fresh illustrations, which combine splashes of bright color with simple line drawings." SLJ

Cabrera, Jane

Here we go round the mulberry bush. Holiday House 2010 un il $16.95

Grades: PreK   E

   1. Day -- Fiction 2. Dogs -- Fiction

   ISBN 978-0-8234-2288-3; 0-8234-2288-7

           LC 2009048137

"This old favorite gets a sprightly new workout in Cabrera's adorable offering. The duo going around the mulberry bush 'on a cold and frosty morning' is a small spotted puppy and an even younger sibling. Lots of verses are added to the familiar refrain. . . . A fun read-aloud, or more aptly put, read-along, because children will want to pick up on the chant." Booklist

★ If you're happy and you know it. Holiday House 2005 un il hardcover o.p. board book $7.95

Grades: PreK K   E

   1. Songs 2. Animals -- Fiction

   ISBN 0-8234-1881-2; 978-0-8234-2227-2 board book

           LC 2004-47264

An elephant, a monkey, and a giraffe join other animals to sing different verses of this popular song that encourages everyone to express their happiness through voice and movement.

"Cheerful painterly pictures in a kaleidoscope of colors enhance the jovial mood of the song." SLJ

Kitty's cuddles. Holiday House 2007 26p il $16.95

Grades: PreK   E

   1. Cats -- Fiction 2. Animals -- Fiction

   ISBN 978-0-8234-2066-7

Cat tries out hugs from all different animals but finds he likes the hug from his baby brother the best

"Cabrera's trademark eye-catching, lush colors are used to full advantage on every page. . . . Youngsters will be riveted by the bold pictures and find comfort in Kitty's predictable exploits." SLJ

★ Mommy, carry me please! Holiday House 2006 un il $16.95

Grades: PreK K   E

   1. Animals -- Fiction 2. Mother-child relationship -- Fiction

   ISBN 0-8234-1935-5

           LC 2004048862

"On each spread of this warm lapsit book, a baby animal asks its mother to carry me please. Each mother accommodates by transporting the youngster in that animals special way: lemur under its belly, kangaroo in a pouch, tiger in its mouth, crocodile in teeth, penguin on its feet, and so on until the cozy ending when a human child is carried in the mothers arms. The art features Cabrera's trademark breezy, blocky, and bold animals in bright and energetic colors that focus childrens eye and attention." SLJ

One, two, buckle my shoe. Holiday House 2009 un il $16.95

Grades: PreK   E
1. Counting 2. Stories in rhyme 3. Animals -- Fiction
4. Parties -- Fiction 5. Birthdays -- Fiction
ISBN 978-0-8234-2230-2; 0-8234-2230-5
LC 2008055303
Four chicks have fun hiding while Rabbit and Mommy
Hen prepare a party for the little pigs' birthday.
Cabrera's "version of this familiar schoolyard song
takes readers all the way up through the number 20. . . .
The lively images, thick with paint strokes, create a cheerful
atmosphere. Additionally, the opening challenge to find four
small chicks on each spread will keep readers entertained as
they read along." Publ Wkly

Twinkle, twinkle, little star; by Jane Cabrera. 1st
American ed. Holiday House 2012 1 v. (unpaged) ill.
(hardcover) $16.95
Grades: PreK K 1   E
ISBN 9780823425198
LC 2011044969

Cadena, Beth
Supersister; illustrated by Frank W. Dormer. Clarion
Books 2009 un il $16
Grades: K 1 2   E
1. Pregnancy -- Fiction 2. Mother-daughter relationship
-- Fiction
ISBN 978-0-547-01006-9; 0-547-01006-0
LC 2008-11618
A young girl does all kinds of things around the house
to help her pregnant mother, proud that when the new baby
comes she is going to be 'a super sister.'
"Lively yet thoughtful text and bright, funny illustrations
combine beautifully to settle into a pleasing conclusion: a
supersister dream that features a superbrother. Highly rec-
ommended for children with siblings on the way." Kirkus

Cadow, Kenneth M.
Alfie runs away; pictures by Lauren Castillo. Frances
Foster Books 2010 un il $16.99
Grades: PreK K   E
1. Runaway children -- Fiction 2. Mother-son
relationship -- Fiction
ISBN 978-0-374-30202-3; 0-374-30202-2
LC 2008024146
Told he must give up his favorite, now too-small, shoes,
Alfie leaves home, but not before his mother persuades him
to take all of the things he might need while he is gone
"Castillo's . . . spreads, comfortingly rendered in muted
colors, are just right for Cadow's even-tempered narration."
Publ Wkly

Calhoun, Mary
★ **Cross**-country cat; illustrated by Erick Ingraham.
Morrow 1979 un il hardcover o.p. pa $6.99
Grades: K 1 2 3   E
1. Cats -- Fiction
ISBN 0-688-22186-6; 0-698-06519-8 pa
LC 78-31718
When he becomes lost in the mountains, Henry, a cat
with the unusual ability of walking on two legs finds his way
home on cross-country skis
"Only the careful blending of skills by a talented author
and illustrator could turn such a farfetched plot into a warm,

rich, and rewarding story. The realistic illustrations seem to
be enveloped in a glowing light and invite the reader to step
right into the story." Child Book Rev Serv
Other titles about Henry the cat are:
Blue-ribbon Henry (1999)
Henry the Christmas cat (2004)
Henry the sailor cat (1994)
High-wire Henry (1991)
Hot-air Henry (1981)

Cali, Davide
I love chocolate; illustrated by Evelyn Daviddi. Tundra
Books 2009 un il $12.95
Grades: PreK K   E
1. Chocolate -- Fiction
ISBN 0-88776-912-8; 978-0-88776-912-2
Original Italian edition 2001
"'Why do I love chocolate?' a boy asks as he is about to
take a colossal bite of a candy bar. He then lists all the reasons: it crunches and melts, and it can make bad times better.
. . . The text captures the essence of chocolate—its varying
incarnations and textures—and it will leave everyone sali-
vating. In addition to being a great candidate for programs,
the book has potential as an easy reader as well. The art has
a European flair." SLJ

The **bear** with the sword; illustrated by Gianluca Foli.
Wilkins Farago 2010 un il $15.99
Grades: K 1 2 3   E
1. Bears -- Fiction 2. Animals -- Fiction
ISBN 978-0-9806-0704-8; 0-9806-0704-3
A bear with a powerful sword goes out into the forest
to chop down all of the trees and build on his impregnable
home fort. After it is washed away by a flood, he sets out on
a journey to find and punish the creature responsible. After
accusing an array of unusual creatures, he finally arrives at
the truth: the flood was caused by someone with a sword
who chopped down all the trees.
"This title features inventive, whimsical mixed-media illustrations that combine black-lined and colored figures, as
well as spacious, white backgrounds. An intriguing offering
that will open up discussion." Booklist

The **enemy**; a book about peace. written by Davide
Cali and illustrated by Serge Bloch. Schwartz & Wade
Books 2009 un il $15.99; lib bdg $18.99
Grades: 1 2 3 4   E
1. War stories 2. Soldiers -- Fiction
ISBN 978-0-375-84500-0; 0-375-84500-3; 978-0-375-
93752-1 lib bdg; 0-375-93752-8 lib bdg
LC 2007047974
After watching an enemy for a very long time during
an endless war, a soldier finally creeps out into the night to
the other man's hole and is surprised by what he finds there.
"Bloch pairs pen-and-ink cartoons with collage elements
like family photos, and gives readers a bird's-eye view from
which to observe the men's similarities. The point will not
be lost on readers." Publ Wkly

Calmenson, Stephanie
Jazzmatazz! by Stephanie Calmenson; illustrated by
Bruce Degen. HarperCollinsPublishers 2008 un il $16.99;
lib bdg $17.89

Grades: PreK K 1   E
1. Stories in rhyme 2. Mice -- Fiction 3. Animals -- Fiction 4. Musicians -- Fiction 5. Jazz music -- Fiction
ISBN 978-0-06-077289-5; 0-06-077289-1; 978-0-06-077290-1 lib bdg; 0-06-077290-5 lib bdg
LC 2007009133

When a mouse scurries into a house and starts to play jazz music, other animals join in, one by one, each using his or her own particular talent

"This cheerful book . . . is full of color and sound. . . . Degen fills the white space . . . with colorful zigzags, curlicues, stars, and other patterns to show how the music is connecting and joining all of the characters together." SLJ

Late for school! by Stephanie Calmenson; illustrated by Sachiko Yoshikawa. Carolrhoda Books 2008 un il lib bdg $16.95
Grades: K 1 2   E
1. School stories 2. Stories in rhyme 3. Teachers -- Fiction 4. Transportation -- Fiction
ISBN 978-1-57505-935-8 lib bdg; 1-57505-935-5 lib bdg
LC 2007034776

When Mr. Bungles the teacher oversleeps, he goes to great lengths, trying every form of transportation he can find to get to school on time.

"Cartoon characters in scenes of collage and mixed media follow Mr. Bungles's efforts to watch the clock and avoid breaking his own rule, 'Never, ever, ever be late for school!' A colorful selection for all libraries." SLJ

Calvert, Pam
  Multiplying menace; the revenge of Rumpelstiltskin. illustrated by Wayne Geehan. Charlesbridge Pub. 2006 32p il $16.95; pa $6.95
Grades: 3 4 5 6   E
1. Fairy tales 2. Multiplication -- Fiction
ISBN 1-57091-889-9; 1-57091-890-2 pa
LC 2004-23072

Ten years after being tricked, Rumpelstiltskin returns to the royal family to wreak vengeance using multiplication. Includes nonfiction math notes about multiplying by whole numbers and by fractions.

"Calvert has created an interesting vehicle for teaching children about the differences between multiplying with whole numbers and multiplying with fractions. . . . Calvert has written an enjoyable teaching tool, and Geehan's luminous and expressive paintings are perfect for this fairy-tale world." SLJ

Princess Peepers; illustrated by Tuesday Mourning. Marshall Cavendish 2008 un il $16.99
Grades: K 1 2 3   E
1. Eyeglasses -- Fiction 2. Princesses -- Fiction
ISBN 978-0-7614-5437-3; 0-7614-5437-3
LC 2007022134

When the other princesses make fun of her for wearing glasses, Princess Peepers vows to go without, but after several mishaps—one of which is especially coincidental—she admits that she really does need them if she wants to see.

"Mourning's graphite and digital/collage illustrations combine figures in traditional costumes from different eras with lush backgrounds. The palette of pinks keeps the emphasis on sweet, even when some of the characters are not.

Princess Peepers will circulate well and bring laughs during storytimes." SLJ

Another title about Princess Peepers is:
Princess Peepers picks a pet (2011)

Princess Peepers picks a pet; illustrated by Tuesday Mourning. Marshall Cavendish 2011 un il
Grades: K 1 2 3   E
1. Pets -- Fiction 2. Dragons -- Fiction 3. Eyeglasses -- Fiction 4. Princesses -- Fiction
ISBN 0-7614-5815-8; 978-0-7614-5815-9
LC 2010010056

When Princess Peepers loses her glasses, she mistakes a dragon for a unicorn and enters it in the pet show at the Royal Academy for Perfect Princesses.

"Peepers' personality comes through loud and clear. . . . Digital painting and graphite merge with bold collage images to glossy effect, and elongated limbs provide a whimsical nuance. It's a light regal romp." Kirkus

Campbell, Bebe Moore
  Stompin' at the Savoy; [by] Bebe Moore Campbell; illustrated by Richard Yarde. Philomel Books 2006 un il $16.99
Grades: K 1 2 3   E
1. Dance -- Fiction 2. Jazz music -- Fiction 3. African Americans -- Fiction
ISBN 0-399-24197-3
LC 2005025044

On the night of her jazz dance recital Mindy feels too nervous to go, until a magical drum whisks her away to the Savoy Ballroom in Harlem where she finds her "happy feet"

"Rhythmic gouache and pastel paintings depicting swinging dancers and jiving musicians perfectly complement the lyrical energy and magical realism of the cadenced prose." SLJ

Campbell, Eileen
  Charlie and Kiwi; illustrated by Peter H. Reynolds. Atheneum Books for Young Readers 2011 un il $16.99
Grades: PreK K 1 2   E
1. School stories 2. Birds -- Fiction 3. Evolution -- Fiction 4. Grandfathers -- Fiction 5. Space and time -- Fiction 6. Evolution (Biology) -- Juvenile literature
ISBN 978-1-4424-2112-7; 1-4424-2112-6
LC 2010042905

Charlie, who wants to explain to his classmates why the kiwi is so different from other birds, follows his stuffed friend Kiwi on a journey through time on which one of his ancestors helps him understand how the kiwi—and all birds—evolved.

"The story's fast-paced narrative and cartoon vignettes do a commendable job of explaining how small adaptations over time lead to evolution." Booklist

Campbell, Nicola I.
  Shi-shi-etko; pictures by Kim La Fave. Groundwood Books 2005 un il $16.95
Grades: K 1 2 3   E
1. Native Americans -- Fiction
ISBN 0-88899-659-4

"This is a moving story set in Canada about the practice of removing Native children from their villages and sending them to residential schools to learn the English language and culture. . . . Shi-shi-etko counts down her last four days before going away. . . . The vivid, digital illustrations rely on a red palette, evoking not only the land but also the sorrow of the situation and the hope upon which the story ultimately ends." SLJ

Campbell, Rod

Dear zoo; a pop-up book. Little Simon 2005 un il $12.95

Grades: PreK K   E

1. Pop-up books 2. Animals -- Fiction

ISBN 0-689-87751-X

First published as a board book in the United Kingdom 1982; first published as a pop-up book 2004 in the United Kingdom

Each animal arriving from the zoo as a possible pet fails to suit its prospective owner, until just the right one is found.

Cannon, A. E.

Sophie's fish; by A.E. Cannon; illustrated by Lee White. Viking 2012 32p.

Grades: PreK K 1 2   E

1. Pets -- Fiction 2. Fishes -- Fiction 3. Children's stories 4. Picture books for children 5. Humorous stories 6. Worry -- Fiction

ISBN 9780670012916

LC 2011016227

In this picture book, "[w]hen schoolmate Sophie asks Jake to care for her fish, Yo-Yo, for a weekend, he agrees, because '[h]ow hard can it be to babysit a fish?' But while waiting for Yo-Yo to arrive, Jake begins to worry. 'What kind of snacks do fish like to eat?' he frets. [Illustrator Lee] White presents a massive Strawberry Worm Cake as a possible fish snack; standing atop the highest layer, Jake offers a slice to a laughing blue fish he finds sitting upright on a wire chair. The fish is as big as Jake. Next, Jake wonders, '[w]hat if Yo-Yo wants to play a game?' Here, the portrayed fish is several times Jake's size, dressed as a pirate and riding an enormous rubber ducky." (Kirkus)

Cannon, Janell

★ **Crickwing**; written and illustrated by Janell Cannon. Harcourt 2000 un il $16; pa $7

Grades: K 1 2 3   E

1. Ants 2. Insects 3. Cockroaches 4. Forest insects 5. Ants -- Fiction 6. Cockroaches -- Fiction

ISBN 0-15-201790-9; 9780152050610

LC 99-50456

A lonely cockroach named Crickwing has a creative idea that saves the day for the leaf-cutter ants when their fierce forest enemies attack them

"An amusing tale lightly rooted in natural history. . . . Cannon's illustrations skillfully blur the line between fact and fancy." Publ Wkly

★ **Stellaluna**. Harcourt Brace Jovanovich 1993 un il $17

Grades: K 1 2 3   E

1. Bats -- Fiction

ISBN 0-15-280217-7

LC 92-16439

After she falls headfirst into a bird's nest, a baby bat is raised like a bird until she is reunited with her mother

"Cannon's delightful story is full of gentle humor. . . . [She] provides good information about bats in the story, amplifying it in two pages of notes at the end of the book. Her full-page colored-pencil-and-acrylic paintings fairly glow." Booklist

Cantrell, Charlie

A **friend** for Einstein; the smallest stallion. by Charlie Cantrell and Rachel Wagner. Disney/Hyperion 2011 un il $16.99

Grades: PreK K 1 2   E

1. Dogs -- Fiction 2. Size -- Fiction 3. Horses -- Fiction

ISBN 978-1-4231-4563-9; 1-4231-4563-1

"With hooves the size of quarters, Einstein, a mini miniature horse, is the smallest horse ever born. . . . Einstein is not tall enough to keep up with other equines, even his fellow miniature horses. The fascinating facts lead into a fictional story line as the presumably lonely horse searches for a playmate. . . . Einsten meets a dog named Lilly . . . who is just his size. Although Lilly and Einstein are actual friends, children will care less about the reality of their meeting and more about this unusual horse and the color photographs. . . . No doubt little Einstein will appeal to big hearts everywhere." Booklist

Caple, Kathy

Duck & Company. Holiday House 2007 32p il $14.95; pa $4.95

Grades: K 1 2   E

1. Rats -- Fiction 2. Ducks -- Fiction 3. Booksellers and bookselling -- Fiction

ISBN 978-0-8234-1993-7; 0-8234-1993-2; 978-0-8234-2125-1 pa; 0-8234-2125-2 pa

LC 2006-12118

Rat and Duck run a bookshop and work to find the right book for each of their customers.

"There are tons of visual clues embedded in the ink and gouache illustrations to help burgeoning readers. . . . Young readers will appreciate both the humor and the diversity of the five included tales." Bull Cent Child Books

Another title about Duck and Rat is:

Duck & Company Christmas (2011)

Duck & Company Christmas. Holiday House 2011 il $14.95

Grades: K 1 2   E

1. Animals -- Fiction 2. Christmas -- Fiction

ISBN 978-0-8234-2239-5; 0-8234-2239-9

LC 2010029574

Duck and Rat's bookstore is busy as Christmas approaches and all the animals buy gifts and celebrate with their friends.

"The droll humor and quietly amusing holiday preparations have the flavor of the Frog and Toad stories, with the same comforting sense of a kind and reassuring world. Understated illustrations in gouache and ink are filled with tiny, humorous details and clever costumes for the animal characters." Kirkus

The **friendship** tree. Holiday House 2000 48p il (Holiday House reader) lib bdg $15.95

Grades: K 1 2   E

1. Sheep -- Fiction 2. Trees -- Fiction 3. Friendship

-- Fiction
ISBN 0-8234-1376-4

LC 98-39043

This book "includes four little stories about trees. Best friends Blanche and Otis are sheep who live next door to each other and share their sorrows and joys. . . . The line-and-watercolor illustrations reflect the sweet, gentle tone of the text with the soft, pastel shades." Booklist

Capucilli, Alyssa

★ **Biscuit's** new trick; story by Alyssa Satin Capucilli; pictures by Pat Schories. HarperCollins Pubs. 2000 24p il (My first I can read book) $12.95; lib bdg $15.89; pa $3.99

Grades: PreK K 1 2   E
1. Dogs -- Fiction 2. Biscuit (Fictitious character) -- Pictorial works -- Juvenile fiction
ISBN 0-06-028067-0; 0-06-028068-9 lib bdg; 0-06-444308-6 pa

LC 99-23004

"While his owner tries to teach him to fetch a ball, Biscuit the dog chews his bone or chases the cat—that is, until the ball lands in a mud puddle. . . . The simple language . . . and playful watercolor illustrations make this an appealing choice for beginning readers." Horn Book Guide

Other titles about Biscuit are:
Bathtime for Biscuit (1998)
Biscuit (1996)
Biscuit and the baby (2005)
Biscuit and the lost teddy bear (2011)
Biscuit finds a friend (1997)
Biscuit goes to school (2002)
Biscuit visits the big city (2006)
Biscuit wants to play (2001)
Biscuit wins a prize (2004)
Biscuit's big friend (2003)
Biscuit's day at the farm (2007)
Biscuit's picnic (1998)
Happy birthday, Biscuit! (1999)
Hello, Biscuit! (1998)

Katy duck is a caterpillar; by Alyssa Satin Capucilli; illustrated by Henry Cole. Simon & Schuster 2009 un il $14.99

Grades: PreK K 1 2   E
1. Dance -- Fiction 2. Ducks -- Fiction 3. Caterpillars -- Fiction
ISBN 978-1-4169-6061-4; 1-4169-6061-9

Katy Duck is disappointed when she is cast as a caterpillar in the Spring dance recital.

"Cole's illustrations aptly convey Katy's expressions of joy and disappointment, as well as her exuberant energy." SLJ

Pedro's burro; story by Alyssa Satin Capucilli; pictures by Pau Estrada. HarperCollinsPublishers 2007 32p il (I can read!) $15.99; lib bdg $16.89

Grades: PreK K 1   E
1. Donkeys -- Fiction
ISBN 978-0-06-056031-7; 0-06-056031-2; 978-0-06-056032-4 lib bdg; 0-06-056032-0 lib bdg

LC 2006036323

Pedro and his papa go to the market to look for the perfect burro

"This winning story is enhanced by Estrada's colorful, inviting illustrations. . . . Featuring repetition and humor, the simple story is set in large type with ample white space." SLJ

Carbone, Elisa

★ **Heroes** of the surf; by Elisa Carbone. Viking 2012 40 p.

Grades: 2 3 4   E
1. Shipwrecks -- Fiction 2. Rescue work -- Fiction 3. Picture books for children 4. New Jersey -- History -- Fiction
ISBN 0670063126; 9780670063123

LC 2011012218

The book is "based on a true story of shipwreck and rescue . . . with narration by Anthony, a venturesome lad whose penchant for playing pirates helps him through the harrowing event" aboard the steamship Pliny, which was wrecked in a storm near New Jersey in 1882. Elisa Carbone describes Anthony's rescue with his friend Pedro from the sinking ship: "'I swing out into open space. Below me, waves crash and twist like angry snakes. Will the ropes hold?' Illustrator Nancy Carpenter depicts the scene with "a seagoing palette of blue, gray, brown and ochre, crosshatched in black." (Kirkus)

Carbone, Elisa Lynn

★ **Night** running; how James escaped with the help of his faithful dog; based on a true story. [by] Elisa Carbone; illustrated by E.B. Lewis. Alfred A. Knopf 2008 un il $16.99; lib bdg $19.99

Grades: 2 3 4   E
1. Dogs -- Fiction 2. Slavery -- Fiction 3. African Americans -- Fiction
ISBN 0-375-82247-X; 978-0-375-82247-6; 0-375-92247-4 lib bdg; 978-0-375-92247-3 lib bdg

LC 2003014502

A runaway slave makes a daring escape to freedom with the help of his faithful hunting dog, Zeus. Based on the true story of James Smith's journey from Virginia to Ohio in the mid-1800s.

"The watercolor paintings beautifully evoke the sun-drenched cotton fields. Deep purples and rich, dark greens capture the moonlit night. . . . A vividly realized narrative, based on a true story." SLJ

Carle, Eric

★ **10** little rubber ducks. HarperCollins 2005 un il $21.99; bd bk $11.99

Grades: PreK K 1 2   E
1. Counting 2. Toys -- Fiction
ISBN 0-06-074075-2; 0-06-074078-7 bd bk

LC 2004-1420

When a storm strikes a cargo ship, ten rubber ducks are tossed overboard and swept off in ten different directions. Based on a factual incident

"Carle's signature cut-paper collages burst with color, texture, light, and motion, delighting the eye and bringing out the text's nuances." SLJ

★ **Do** you want to be my friend? Crowell 1971 un il $17.99; lib bdg $18.89; pa $6.99; bd bk $7.99

Grades: PreK K   **E**
1. Stories without words 2. Mice -- Fiction
ISBN 0-690-24276-X; 0-690-01137-7 lib bdg; 0-06-443127-4 pa; 0-694-00709-9 bd bk
"Good material for discussion and guessing games. . . . The pictures tell an amusing story and they are good to look at as well." Times Lit Suppl

★ **Mister** Seahorse. Philomel Books 2004 un il $17.99; bd bk $8.99
Grades: PreK K 1   **E**
1. Fishes 2. Sea horses 3. Father and child 4. Fishes -- Fiction 5. Fathers -- Fiction
ISBN 0-399-24269-4; 978-0-399-25490-1 bd bk
         LC 2003-17125
After Mrs. Seahorse lays her eggs on Mr. Seahorse's belly, he drifts through the water, greeting other fish fathers who are taking care of their eggs
"With each encounter comes a delightful surprise: an acetate overlay camouflages the sea creatures as Mister Seahorse passes by. . . . Awash with the wonders of undersea life, this is a stunning, ingeniously conceived lesson in nature as well as a celebration of fatherly affection." Booklist

Papa, please get the moon for me. Simon & Schuster Books for Young Readers 1991 un il $6.99
Grades: PreK K 1   **E**
ISBN 0-8870-8177-0
         LC 91014561
First published 1986 by Picture Book Studio
Monica's father fulfills her request for the moon by taking it down after it is small enough to carry, but it continues to change in size. Some pages fold out to display particularly large pictures.
This is "drawn in thick, brilliant brushstrokes of blues and greens and reds that dazzle the eye. . . . A splendid introduction to the monthly lunar cycle, this is also a wondrous work of art that will stand up to countless readings." Publ Wkly

★ **Slowly,** slowly, slowly, said the sloth. Philomel Bks. 2002 un il $16.99; pa $7.99
Grades: PreK K 1   **E**
1. Sloths -- Fiction 2. Animals -- Fiction
ISBN 0-399-23954-5; 0-14-240847-6 pa
         LC 2002-16057
Challenged by the other jungle animals for its seemingly lazy ways, a sloth living in a tree explains the many advantages of his slow and peaceful existence
"Carle's art is at its best with a brightly colored selection of painted tissue-paper collage that captures 25 rain-forest denizens." SLJ

★ **Where** are you going? To see my friend! [by] Eric Carle & Kazuo Iwamura. Orchard Bks. 2003 un il $19.95
Grades: PreK K 1   **E**
1. Animals -- Fiction 2. Friendship -- Fiction 3. Bilingual books -- English-Japanese
ISBN 0-439-41659-0
         LC 2002-70396
Original Japanese edition, 2001
This "bilingual picture book is told in dialogue, with rebuslike symbols used to identify speakers. It details an energetic romp with a dog, cat, rooster, goat, rabbit, and a child, all of whom become friends. Carle's familiar collage technique is employed in the book's first half, while Iwamura's gentle watercolor illustrations, combined with the Japanese text, make up the second half. . . . An irresistible, spirited ode to friendship." SLJ

★ The **artist** who painted a blue horse. Philomel Books 2011 un il $17.99
Grades: PreK K 1   **E**
1. Artists 2. Painters 3. Color -- Fiction 4. Animals -- Fiction 5. Artists -- Fiction 6. Painting -- Fiction
ISBN 978-0-399-25713-1; 0-399-25713-6
         LC 2011000662
Rather than use the same old colors, a child paints animals and objects in a variety of different hues. Includes biographical information about the German painter Franz Marc, who created unconventional animal paintings in the early 1900s.
"While Carle's creatures are constructed from his familiar, brilliantly colored painted-paper shapes, it is the strength and sinew of their forms that impresses. . . . An homage to Marc becomes testimony to Carle's gifts, too. A short afterword about Marc's life is included." Publ Wkly

★ The **grouchy** ladybug. HarperCollins Pubs. 1996 un il $17.99; lib bdg $18.89; pa $7.99; bd bk $8.99
Grades: PreK K 1   **E**
1. Ladybugs -- Fiction
ISBN 0-06-027087-X; 0-06-027088-8 lib bdg; 0-06-443450-8 pa; 0-694-01320-X bd bk
         LC 95-26581
A reissue of the title first published 1977 by Crowell
A grouchy ladybug, looking for a fight, challenges everyone she meets regardless of their size or strength
"The finger paint and collage illustrations—as bold as the feisty hero—are satisfyingly placed on pages sized to suit the successive animals that appear. . . . Tiny clocks show the time of each enjoyable encounter, with the sun rising and setting as the action proceeds." SLJ

★ A **house** for Hermit Crab. Picture Bk. Studio 1988 un il $18.99; pa $7.99; bd bk $8.99
Grades: PreK K 1   **E**
1. Crabs -- Fiction
ISBN 0-88708-056-1; 0-689-84894-3 pa; 0-689-87064-7 bd bk
         LC 87-29261
"The bright illustrations in Carle's familiar style, which seems particularly suited to undersea scenes, and the cumulative story are splendid." Horn Book

★ The **mixed** -up chameleon. Crowell 1984 un il $17.99; lib bdg $18.89; pa $6.99; bd bk $8.99
Grades: PreK K 1   **E**
1. Chameleons -- Fiction
ISBN 0-690-04396-1; 0-690-04397-X lib bdg; 0-06-443162-2 pa; 0-694-01147-9 bd bk
         LC 83-45950
A revised and newly illustrated edition of the title first published 1975
The author "has replaced the heavy-lined, childlike, scrawled colors with crisp, appealing collages and has

streamlined the text. The cutaway pages have been retained, and none of the humor has been lost. The simpler text results in a smoother flow, and children will enjoy the resulting repetition." Booklist

★ The **very** busy spider. Philomel Bks. 1984 un il $21.99; bd bk $11.99; oversized bd bk $15.99
Grades: PreK K 1   E
   1. Spiders -- Fiction
   ISBN 0-399-21166-7; 0-399-21592-1 pa; 0-399-22919-1 bd bk; 978-0-399-25601-1 oversized bd bk
           LC 84-5907

The farm animals try to divert a busy little spider from spinning her web, but she persists and produces a thing of both beauty and usefulness

This book "has a disarming ingenuousness and a repetitive structure that will capture the response of pre-school audiences. Of special note is the book's use of raised lines for the spider, its web, and an unsuspecting fly. Both sighted and blind children will be able to follow the action with ease." Booklist

★ The **very** clumsy click beetle. Philomel Bks. 1999 un il $22.99
Grades: PreK K 1   E
   1. Toy and movable books 2. Animals -- Fiction 3. Beetles -- Fiction 4. Sound effects books 5. Clumsiness -- Fiction 6. Sound effects books -- Specimens
   ISBN 0-399-23201-X
           LC 97-33417

A clumsy young click beetle learns to land on its feet with encouragement from various animals and a wise old beetle. An electronic chip with a built-in battery creates clicking sounds to accompany the story

"Done in colored tissue-paper collage, the illustrations burst from the pages and are charmingly rendered. . . . A well-crafted story, joyfully illustrated." SLJ

★ The **very** hungry caterpillar. Philomel Bks. 1981 un il $21.99; bd bk $10.99
Grades: PreK K 1   E
   1. Caterpillars -- Fiction
   ISBN 0-399-20853-4; 0-399-22690-7 bd bk
   First published 1970 by World Publishing Company

"This caterpillar is so hungry he eats right through the pictures on the pages of the book—and after leaving many holes emerges as a beautiful butterfly on the last page." Best Books for Child, 1972

★ The **very** lonely firefly. Philomel Bks. 1995 un il $22.99; bd bk $11.99
Grades: PreK K 1   E
   1. Fireflies -- Fiction
   ISBN 0-399-22774-1; 0-399-23427-6 bd bk
           LC 94-27827

A lonely firefly goes out into the night searching for other fireflies

"The illustrations are painted cut-paper collages, designed to draw the eye to the page. This is a compelling accomplishment." SLJ

★ The **very** quiet cricket. Philomel Bks. 1990 un il $22.99; bd bk $12.99

Grades: PreK K 1   E
   1. Crickets -- Fiction
   ISBN 0-399-21885-8; 0-399-22684-7 bd bk
           LC 89-78317

A very quiet cricket who wants to rub his wings together and make a sound as do so many other animals finally achieves his wish

"The text is skillfully shaped; the illustrations convey energy and immediacy; and, in a surprise ending, a microchip inserted in the last page replicates the cricket's chirp." Horn Book Guide

Carling, Amelia Lau
   ★ **Mama** & Papa have a store; story and pictures by Amelia Lau Carling. Dial Bks. for Young Readers 1998 un il $16.99
Grades: K 1 2 3   E
   1. Chinese -- Fiction 2. Retail trade -- Fiction 3. Stores, Retail -- Fiction 4. Family life -- Guatemala -- Fiction
   ISBN 0-8037-2044-0
           LC 97-10217

A little girl describes what a day is like in her parents' Chinese store in Guatemala City

"Carling's lovingly detailed watercolors in candy-box colors illustrate [the author's] memories. . . . A pleasant family story that should enrich library collections, especially those looking for multicultural themes." SLJ

Carlson, Nancy L.
   ★ **Get** up and go! by Nancy Carlson. Viking 2006 un il $15.99
Grades: PreK K   E
   1. Exercise 2. Pigs -- Fiction 3. Rabbits -- Fiction
   ISBN 0-670-05981-1
           LC 2005003864

Text and illustrations encourage readers, regardless of shape or size, to turn off the television and play games, walk, dance, and engage in sports and other forms of exercise.

"Bright and sassy, the clearly delineated drawings with vivid washes provide a light, sometimes-comical tone that makes the lessons easier to take. With a short, simple text and a cheerful look, this will suit preschool and kindergarten teachers looking for an accessible book on exercise." Booklist

   Henry and the Valentine surprise; [by] Nancy Carlson. Viking 2008 un il $15.99
Grades: PreK K 1 2   E
   1. School stories 2. Mice -- Fiction 3. Animals -- Fiction 4. Teachers -- Fiction 5. Valentine's Day -- Fiction
   ISBN 978-0-670-06267-6; 0-670-06267-7
           LC 2008001283

When Henry the mouse and his first-grade classmates notice a heart-shaped box on their teacher's desk the day before Valentine's Day, they try to find out if he has a girlfriend.

"Told with mounting suspense, this mystery has a delightful and satisfying conclusion. Brightly colored comic illustrations portray the excitement at school as the special day approaches." SLJ
   Other titles about Henry are:
   Henry's show and tell (2004)
   Henry's 100 days of kindergarten (2005)
   Henry's amazing imagination! (2008)

Start saving, Henry! (2009)

Henry and the bully (2010)

I like me! [by] Nancy Carlson. Viking Kestrel 1988 un
il lib bdg $16.99; pa $6.99

Grades: PreK K 1   E

1. Pigs -- Fiction

ISBN 0-670-82062-8 lib bdg; 0-14-050819-8 pa

LC 87-32616

By admiring her finer points and showing that she can
take care of herself and have fun even when there's no one
else around, a charming pig proves the best friend you can
have is yourself

This book is "visually interesting, with sturdy animals
drawn in a deliberately artless style. Simple shapes, strong
lines, and clear colors, with lots of pattern mixing, show
what is not described in the minimal text. The text is hand-
lettered." SLJ

Another title about this pig is:

ABC I like me! (1997)

Carlstrom, Nancy White

Climb the family tree, Jesse Bear! illustrated by Bruce
Degen. Simon & Schuster Books for Young Readers 2004
un il $16.99

Grades: PreK K   E

1. Bears 2. Family reunions 3. Stories in rhyme 4.
Bears -- Fiction 5. Family reunions -- Fiction

ISBN 0-689-80701-5

LC 2001-20579

Jesse Bear experiences the excitement of a family reunion filled with grandparents, aunts, uncles, and cousins
and lots of food, games, and storytelling.

"Rhyming couplets keep the story moving along quickly
from one happy scene to the next, while the ink drawings,
brightened with colorful washes, reflect the genial tone of
the words." Booklist

It's your first day of school, Annie Claire. Abrams
Books for Young Readers 2009 un il $15.95

Grades: PreK K   E

1. School stories 2. Stories in rhyme 3. Dogs -- Fiction
4. Mother-daughter relationship -- Fiction

ISBN 978-0-8109-4057-4; 0-8109-4057-4

LC 2009-2124

Annie Claire the puppy, excited but nervous about her
first day of school, is reassured by her mother, whose love
always goes with her.

"Sweet, gentle illustrations pair with reassuring text."
Booklist

★ **Jesse** Bear, what will you wear? illustrations by
Bruce Degen. Macmillan 1986 un il $16.95; pa $6.99;
bd bk $7.99

Grades: PreK K   E

1. Stories in rhyme 2. Bears -- Fiction

ISBN 0-02-717350-X; 0-689-80623-X pa; 0-689-
80930-1 bd bk

LC 85-10610

"The big, cheerful watercolor paintings show the baby
bear in loving relation to his family and world. Without
crossing the line into sentimentality, this offers a happy, humorous soundfest that will associate reading aloud with a
sense of play." Bull Cent Child Books

Other titles about Jesse Bear are:

Better not get wet, Jesse Bear (1988)

Climb the family tree, Jesse Bear (2004)

Guess who's coming, Jesse Bear (1998)

Happy birthday, Jesse Bear (1994)

How do you say it today, Jesse Bear? (1992)

It's about time, Jesse Bear, and other rhymes (1990)

Let's count it out, Jesse Bear (1996)

What a scare, Jesse Bear! (1999)

Where is Christmas, Jesse Bear? (2000)

Carluccio, Maria

I'm 3! look what I can do. Henry Holt 2010 un il
$10.99

Grades: PreK   E

1. Growth -- Fiction 2. Siblings -- Fiction

ISBN 978-0-8050-8313-2; 0-8050-8313-8

"The accomplishments of two young siblings are presented, from morning to night. Short, declarative sentences
announce, 'I can sleep in my bed,' 'I can eat with my fork
and spoon,' 'I can try different foods.' At preschool, the
twins 'read,' paint, and demonstrate social skills such as
sharing. At the end of the day they put on their pajamas and
kiss their family good night. The bright, cheery digital collages have an eye-catching variety of textures and patterns.
An exuberant celebration of three-year-old milestones." SLJ

The **sounds** around town; by Maria Carluccio. Barefoot Books 2008 un il $16.99

Grades: PreK   E

1. Stories in rhyme 2. Day -- Fiction 3. Sound --
Fiction 4. City and town life -- Fiction

ISBN 978-1-905236-28-2; 1-905236-28-X

LC 2007025044

Reveals many things a child might hear during the day,
from the singing of birds at dawn to the soft sounds of sleep.

"The text is alive with onomatopoeia, and the visually
stimulating cut-paper collages provide myriad sources of the
sounds to share and enjoy." Horn Book Guide

Carr, Jan

Greedy Apostrophe; a cautionary tale. by Jan Carr; illustrated by Ethan Long. Holiday House 2007 un il $16.95

Grades: K 1 2 3   E

1. Punctuation -- Fiction

ISBN 978-0-8234-2006-3; 0-8234-2006-X

LC 2006012114

"All the punctuation marks stumble into the Hiring Hall
one morning, sipping cocoa and discussing their job prospects. Each receives an important assignment, even Greedy
Apostrophe, who has a well-deserved reputation for his bad
attitude. . . . Students are asked to be vigilant and to take
Greedy away from all the places where he inserts himself but
doesn't really belong. With jazzy colors and cartoon-style
characters, the upbeat artwork gives personality to the inanimate while underscoring the witty, vivacious tone of the
text." Booklist

Carrer, Chiara

Otto Carrotto; written and illustrated by Chiara Carrer.
Eerdmans Books for Young Readers 2011 un il $15.99

Grades: K 1 2   E
1. Carrots -- Fiction 2. Rabbits -- Fiction
ISBN 978-0-8028-5393-6; 0-8028-5393-5
LC 2010049546
Otto the rabbit decides to eat nothing but carrots, causing unexpected consequences.

"Sophisticated readers will pore over the thumbnail drawings and speech bubbles within the intricate collage illustrations, and the boldface text emphasizing repetitive words adds visual interest." SLJ

Carrick, Carol
   ★ **Patrick's** dinosaurs; pictures by Donald Carrick. Clarion Bks. 1983 un il lib bdg $16; pa $5.95
Grades: PreK K 1 2   E
1. Brothers -- Fiction 2. Dinosaurs -- Fiction
ISBN 0-89919-189-4 lib bdg; 0-89919-402-8 pa
LC 83-2049
When his older brother talks about dinosaurs during a visit to the zoo, Patrick is afraid, until he discovers they all died millions of years ago.

"The Carricks do a particularly good job of creating an impressive array of creatures both in text and illustrations—realistic pencil drawings washed in muted greens, browns and oranges." SLJ
   Other titles about Patrick's dinosaurs are:
   Patrick's dinosaurs on the Internet (1999)
   What happened to Patrick's dinosaurs? (1986)

Carter, David A.
   600 black spots. Little Simon 2007 un il $19.99
Grades: 2 3 4 5 6   E
1. Puzzles 2. Counting 3. Toy and movable books 4. Pop-up books
ISBN 1-4169-4092-8; 978-1-4169-4092-0
In this pop-up book, readers are encouraged to search for the black spots throughout the pages

"This is both simple and stunning. . . . It takes a sophisticated artistic taste to appreciate the modern-art-style creations. . . . Older children will have an interesting time interpreting the artwork and marveling at the skill involved in the construction." Booklist

   Blue 2; a pop-up book for children of all ages. Little Simon 2006 un il $10.95
Grades: 2 3 4 5 6   E
1. Puzzles 2. Pop-up books
ISBN 1-4169-1781-0
Each page contains an original piece of artwork that challenges the reader to find the a blue 2.

"Mobiles pop from the pages and readers spin pinwheels and pull tabs to find each elusive numeral two. Another enchanting creation from the inventive paper engineer." Publ Wkly

   Hide and Seek. Harry N Abrams Inc 2012 20 p. (hardcover) $25
Grades: K 1 2 3 4 5   E
1. Paper crafts 2. Stories in rhyme 3. Picture books for children
ISBN 1849761019; 9781849761017
This pop-up book "offers six . . . new constructs—each hiding a handful of small cutouts or printed shapes to find. . . . Tallies along the margins invite viewers to spot a 'yel-

low splat, a red vine, a car and a star. / . . . A sleepy head, in bed, with a red thread on his forehead' and like prizes. These are attached to, dangling from or hidden within the bursts of paper swirls, interlocking mazes and geometrical structures that rise up as each spread opens." (Kirkus)

   Lots of bots; a counting pop-up book. Random House/Corey 2011 un il $14.99
Grades: PreK K 1   E
1. Counting 2. Stories in rhyme 3. Pop-up books 4. Robots -- Fiction
ISBN 978-0-375-86509-1; 0-375-86509-8
This is "a counting book that introduces an eclectic cast of specialized robots that sport antennae, springs, wheels, pincers, and other handy apparatuses. Using a question-and-answer format to count up to 10, the book asks energetic, reader-directed questions like 'Who makes you happy when you are sad?' with the answers appearing in verse. . . . Carter's quirky robots . . . should have effortless appeal for the preschool audience." Publ Wkly

   ★ **One** red dot; a pop-up book for children of all ages. Little Simon 2005 un il $19.95
Grades: 2 3 4 5 6   E
1. Puzzles 2. Counting 3. Pop-up books
ISBN 0-689-87769-2
Original Italian edition 2004
"A graphically bold pop-up book that entices readers to find the one red dot that is hidden on each paper sculpture. Going from 1 to 10, Carter creates a visual hide-and-seek game, ranging from flip-flop flaps to fluttering flicker clickers that really click to orbs that tower above the page. Bold primary colors and a silver-black text give the book a very slick, modern feel." SLJ

   White noise; a pop-up book for children of all ages. Little Simon 2009 un il $22.99
Grades: 2 3 4 5 6   E
1. Pop-up books 2. Noise -- Fiction
ISBN 978-1-4169-4094-4; 1-4169-4094-4
"Each spread, designed to make crackly, crinkly, creaky, tinkling or snapping noises as the pages are turned, evokes children's construction-paper cutouts. . . . Carter's creations are akin to fireworks displays, each building in pyrotechnical intensity until the most impressive burst at the end." NY Times Book Rev

   Yellow square; a pop-up book for children of all ages. Little Simon 2008 un il $19.99
Grades: 2 3 4 5 6   E
1. Pop-up books
ISBN 978-1-4169-4093-7; 1-4169-4093-6
"A yellow square hides in plain sight in or within the paper engineering on each spread; sometimes, the creation of the yellow square is entirely up to the reader. On the first spread, for example, that square exists only when the reader peers through a die-cut while holding the book at the correct angle-in other words, perspective is everything. Captions are variously enigmatic . . . or childlike. . . . Carter confines himself to primary colors, black and white; even with this palette, he alludes to a number of artists, among them Agam, . . . Christo, . . . Miro, and Calder. . . . Not all the spreads are equally impressive, but the best are dazzlers." Publ Wkly

Casanova, Mary

Some dog! pictures by Ard Hoyt. Farrar, Straus & Giroux 2007 un il $16

Grades: PreK K 1 2   E

1. Dogs -- Fiction

ISBN 0-374-37133-4; 978-0-374-37133-3

LC 2004053262

A stray dog moves into George's formerly peaceful home, dazzling the man and woman of the house with lively tricks and antics that just leave George exhausted

"The watercolor-and-pencil illustrations perfectly capture the exuberance and spirit of this tale." SLJ

Utterly otterly day; by Mary Casanova; illustrated by Ard Hoyt. Simon & Schuster Books for Young Readers 2008 un il $16.99

Grades: PreK K 1   E

1. Stories in rhyme 2. Otters -- Fiction

ISBN 978-1-4169-0868-5; 1-4169-0868-4

LC 2007041428

After a day out on his own, Little Otter realizes that he still needs his family no matter how big he grows

"The pen-and-ink-and-watercolor illustrations . . . emphasize the quick, exciting movement of the forest's animals, while the text hops with made-up rhyming words. . . . The adventurous otter and his caring family prove fairly irresistible." Booklist

Another title about Little Otter and his family is:

Utterly Otter night (2011)

Utterly otterly night; illustrated by Ard Hoyt. Simon & Schuster Books for Young Readers 2011 il $16.99

Grades: PreK K 1   E

1. Otters -- Fiction

ISBN 978-1-4169-7562-5; 1-4169-7562-4

LC 2010026429

While out playing with his family one night, Little Otter shows that he knows what to do when danger is near.

"Hoyt's pen-and-ink illustrations wonderfully convey the playfulness and innocence of Little Otter, his every emotion worn on his sleeve. Casanova's onomatopoeic phrases punctuate the action with infectious glee." Kirkus

The **day** Dirk Yeller came to town; illustrated by Ard Hoyt. Farrar, Straus and Giroux 2011 un il $16.99

Grades: PreK K 1 2   E

1. Tall tales 2. Libraries -- Fiction 3. Books and reading -- Fiction

ISBN 978-0-374-31742-3; 0-374-31742-9

"Dangerous outlaw Dirk Yeller looms into town . . . terrifying even the tumbleweeds. . . . Only one small boy, the narrator of the tale, stands up to Dirk and leads him to, of all places, the public library. . . . The sandy-hued illustrations are packed with details and humor. . . . Hoyt's marvelous caricatures are worth thousands of words, making this hilarious tall tale not only a plug for books and reading but an outsized winner." Kirkus

Casarosa, Enrico

La Luna; story and illustrations by Enrico Casarosa, words by Kiki Thorpe. Disney Press 2012 40 p. $14.99

Grades: PreK K 1   E

1. Moon -- Juvenile fiction 2. Picture books for children

3. Intergenerational relations -- Fiction

ISBN 1423137663; 9781423137665

This children's book is based on a "Pixar film with an Academy Award nomination for Best Animated Short. . . . [T]hree characters, a boy, his hugely mustachioed father and his hugely bearded grandfather take their little boat, La Luna, out. . . . This family's job is to clean up the moon. . . . A huge star crashes into the moon, and while his father and grandfather argue about how to deal with it, the boy taps it. The star breaks into . . . tiny stars, and the three sweep them all up." (Kirkus)

Case, Chris

Sophie and the next-door monsters. Walker 2008 un il $15.99; lib bdg $16.89

Grades: PreK K 1 2   E

1. Monsters -- Fiction

ISBN 978-0-8027-9756-8; 0-8027-9756-3; 978-0-8027-9757-5 lib bdg; 0-8027-9757-1 lib bdg

LC 2007-49133

When new neighbors move in next door to Sophie, she is startled—and afraid—to discover that they are monsters.

"This is an offbeat delight. The humans matter-or-factness about the monsters' monstrousness intensifies the humor, and the lively text begs to be read aloud. Case layers colors and uses lots of scratchy hatchwork lines and brushwork to accent the figures and objects in his ink, watercolor, and gouache art." Bull Cent Child Books

Caseley, Judith

★ **On** the town; a community adventure. Greenwillow Bks. 2002 un il $15.95; lib bdg $15.89

Grades: PreK K 1 2   E

1. Community life -- Fiction

ISBN 0-06-029584-8; 0-06-029585-6 lib bdg

LC 2001-23896

Charlie and his mother walk around the neighborhood doing errands so that Charlie can write in his notebook about the people and places that make up his community

"Written from a child's perspective, the story has a cheerful tone and enough variety to keep the expedition interesting. The lively ink, watercolor, and colored-pencil illustrations are full of intriguing details." Booklist

Castella, Krystina

Discovering nature's alphabet; [by] Krystina Castella and Brian Boyl. Heyday Books 2005 un il $15.95

Grades: 1 2 3 4   E

1. Alphabet 2. Natural history

ISBN 1-59714-021-X

LC 2005017857

"Castella and Boyl have assembled a portfolio of photographs of natural objects that form individual letters of the alphabet. From beaches to deserts, they discovered letters large and small in vines and flowers, tree trunks and seedpods. The minimal text urges readers to undertake such explorations to find their own hidden patterns." SLJ

Includes bibliographical references

Castellucci, Cecil

Grandma's gloves; illustrated by Julia Denos. Candlewick Press 2010 un il $15.99

Grades: PreK K 1 2   E

1. Death -- Fiction 2. Gardening -- Fiction 3.

Grandmothers -- Fiction

ISBN 978-0-7636-3168-0; 0-7636-3168-X

LC 2009015139

When her grandmother, a devoted gardener, dies, a little girl inherits her gardening gloves and feels closer to her memory.

"Castellucci's narrative details give voice to the perspicacity of a sensitive child—the smells, gestures, and alterations of experience that are noticed but rarely articulated. Denos's watercolor, pencil, and digital collage illustrations are bright and charming." SLJ

Castillo, Lauren

Melvin and the boy. Henry Holt 2011 un il $16.99

Grades: PreK K 1   E

1. Pets -- Fiction 2. Turtles -- Fiction

ISBN 978-0-8050-8929-5; 0-8050-8929-2

LC 2010038103

When a boy finds a turtle basking in the sun at the park he thinks he has found the perfect pet, but the turtle only seems happy at bath time. Includes facts about turtles.

"Castillo's . . . gently outlined drawings help to soften a potentially disappointing situation. . . . The boy's parents offer surprising support, allowing their son to bring Melvin home from the park, but the decision to return Melvin is the boy's own. . . . It's an honest account of a small, manageable failure, with a lemonade-from-lemons moment at the end." Publ Wkly

Caswell, Deanna

Train trip; written by Deanna Caswell; illustrated by Dan Andreasen. Disney Hyperion 2011 un il $16.99

Grades: PreK K   E

1. Railroads -- Fiction

ISBN 978-1-4231-1837-4; 1-4231-1837-5

"A young boy sets off on a solo train trip. As he climbs aboard, he takes in the new sights and sounds. . . . The staccato stop and start iambic verse mimics the rhythm of the train. . . . At the final station, he finds his grandmother waiting. Andreasen's cartoon illustrations have a sentimental, homespun appeal. The anthropomorphized train has a wide, smiling face and even the whistle has goggle eyes and gives a friendly toot. . . . The excitement of the journey rings true." SLJ

Catalanotto, Peter

Emily's art. Atheneum Bks. for Young Readers 2001 un il $16

Grades: PreK K 1   E

1. Artists 2. Contests 3. Artists -- Fiction 4. Winning and losing 5. Contests -- Fiction

ISBN 0-689-83831-X

LC 00-29293

Emily paints four pictures and enters one in the first-grade art contest, but the judge interprets Emily's entry as a rabbit instead of a dog

"Filled with touches of humor and authentically childlike emotions, this book explores the subjectivity of opinion and the importance of personal conviction." Horn Book Guide

Question Boy meets Little Miss Know-It-All. Atheneum Books for Young Readers 2012 il $16.99

1. Curiosity -- Juvenile fiction 2. Humorous fiction

ISBN 978-1-4424-0670-4; 1-4424-0670-4

LC 2011000496

A curious boy with non-stop questions meets a girl who seems to know all the answers.

Catchpool, Michael

The cloud spinner; by Michael Catchpool; illustrations by Alison Jay. Alfred A. Knopf 2012 32 p.

Grades: K 1 2 3   E

1. Fairy tales 2. Clouds -- Fiction 3. Weaving -- Fiction 4. Kings and rulers -- Fiction 5. Conservation of natural resources -- Juvenile fiction 6. Kings, queens, rulers, etc. -- Fiction

ISBN 9780375870118; 9780375970115; 9780375987397

LC 2011000894

In this book, a "young boy spins clouds into thread, . . . then weaves the thread into cloth. . . . [The] king . . . requests a scarf from the boy, then goes on to demand more and more clothing. . . . [The] king's daughter has been paying attention, and when the king's greedy consumption . . . results in the disappearance of all the clouds and . . . rain, she brings the clothes back to the spinner so that they can be reverted to clouds." (Bulletin of the Center for Children's Books)

Cate, Annette LeBlanc

The magic rabbit; [by] Annette LeBlanc Cate. Candlewick Press 2007 un il $15.99

Grades: K 1 2 3   E

1. Rabbits -- Fiction 2. Magicians -- Fiction 3. Lost and found possessions -- Fiction

ISBN 978-0-7636-6685-9; 978-0-7636-2672-3; 0-7636-2672-4

LC 2007022789

When Bunny becomes separated from Ray, a magician who is his business partner and friend, he follows a crowd to a park where he has a lovely afternoon, and after the people leave and darkness falls, the lonely and frightened Bunny finds a glittering trail of hope

"Embellished only with the gold of 'glittering stars,' Cate's black-and-white drawings perfectly evoke an urban setting in this tale of lost and found." SLJ

Cates, Karin

★ The Secret Remedy Book; a story of comfort and love. illustrated by Wendy Anderson Halperin. Orchard Bks. 2003 un il $16.95

Grades: K 1 2 3   E

1. Aunts -- Fiction

ISBN 0-439-35226-6

LC 2002-35475

Although Lolly loves to visit her Auntie Zep's house, she feels homesick when she actually gets there, and so Auntie Zep retrieves the Secret Remedy Book from an old trunk

"This wonderfully warm and satisfying story is paired with Halperin's lovely illustrations. Her trademark details and patterns abound, with softened edges, muted colors, and quiet landscapes." SLJ

Catrow, David

Best in Show. Orchard Books 2011 un il (Max Spaniel) $6.99

Grades: K 1 2   E
  1. Dogs -- Fiction
ISBN 978-0-545-12277-1; 0-545-12277-5

                  LC 2010047442

Max Spaniel outperforms all of the other entrants in a dog show.

"The hilarity of the artwork makes this easy reader shine. . . . The short, simple sentences, only one or two per page, and daffy drawings are a bouncy mix that will have new readers turning the pages." SLJ

  Dinosaur hunt. Orchard Books 2009 un il (Max Spaniel) $6.99
Grades: K 1 2   E
  1. Dogs -- Fiction 2. Dinosaurs -- Fiction
ISBN 978-0-545-05748-6; 0-545-05748-5

                  LC 2008-30144

Max Spaniel searches for dinosaurs in his back yard.

"Washed with colors, the exaggerated, cartoonlike drawings create a zany mood that energizes and extends the deadpan text." Booklist

  Other titles about Max Spaniel are:
  Funny lunch (2010)
  Best in show (2011)

  Funny lunch. Scholastic 2010 un (Max Spaniel) $6.99
Grades: K 1 2   E
  1. Cats -- Fiction 2. Dogs -- Fiction 3. Restaurants -- Fiction
ISBN 978-0-545-05747-9

"Dog Max Spaniel becomes a 'great chef,' but when a tour bus driver orders 'one hundred pizzas with everything,' Max knows he's in over his head. The humorous text with numerous puns is easy to read. Zany, exuberant watercolor illustrations expand the story." Horn Book Guide

Catusanu, Mircea
  The **strange** case of the missing sheep. Viking 2009 un il $16.99
Grades: PreK K 1   E
  1. Dogs -- Fiction 2. Sheep -- Fiction 3. Wolves -- Fiction 4. Superheroes -- Fiction
ISBN 978-0-670-01131-5; 0-670-01131-2

                  LC 2009-12358

When ten sheep go missing in the Dark Forest, Super Sheep Dog Doug comes to the rescue.

"Catusanu's cracked sense of humor and accomplished skills as an illustrator make for a strong authorial debut—readers won't be able to stop giggling." Publ Wkly

Cauley, Lorinda Bryan
  Clap your hands. Putnam 1992 un il hardcover o.p. pa $6.99; bd bk $7.99
Grades: PreK K   E
  1. Stories in rhyme 2. Animals -- Fiction
ISBN 0-399-22118-2; 0-698-11428-0 pa; 0-399-237100 bd bk

                  LC 91-12863

Rhyming text instructs the listener to find something yellow, roar like a lion, give a kiss, tell a secret, spin in a circle, and perform other playful activities along with the human and animal characters pictured

"The illustrations feature glowing colors and make good use of Cauley's gift for characterization. . . . Some parts of the book would be fun as action rhymes for preschool story time." Booklist

Cave, Kathryn
  One child, one seed; a South African counting book. photographs by Gisèle Wulfsohn. Holt & Co. 2003 un il $16.95
Grades: PreK K 1 2   E
  1. Pumpkin 2. Counting
ISBN 0-8050-7204-7

                  LC 2002-24098

"Children count from 1 to 10 with Nothando as she plants a pumpkin seed that grows to bear fruit for a delicious stew. . . . In a harmonious partnership of narrative and crisp, beautifully composed photographs that show the individuality of each person, readers get a glimpse into the life of an extended family living in a rural South African community. . . . The recipe for isijingi, the pumpkin stew, is included as are some basic geographical facts and a simple map. The writing has good rhythm, and reads aloud well." SLJ

Cazet, Denys
  Elvis the rooster almost goes to heaven. HarperCollins Pubs. 2003 48p il (I can read book) lib bdg $16.89
Grades: K 1 2   E
  1. Roosters -- Fiction
ISBN 978-0-06-000501-6; 0-06-000501-7

                  LC 2002-14416

Elvis the rooster thinks he has died when he fails to crow at the rising of the sun but the chickens find a way to restore his cluck

"Cazet's writing is filled with quirky characters, simple wordplay, and gentle humor. The cartoon artwork perfectly reflects the tone of the text." SLJ

  Another title about Elvis the rooster is:
  Elvis the rooster and the magic words (2004)

  Minnie and Moo and the haunted sweater; [by] Denys Cazet. HarperCollinsPublishers 2007 45p il (I can read!) $15.99; lib bdg $16.89
Grades: 1 2 3   E
  1. Cattle -- Fiction 2. Birthdays -- Fiction
ISBN 978-0-06-073016-1; 0-06-073016-1; 978-0-06-073017-8 lib bdg; 0-06-073017-X lib bdg

                  LC 2006036246

Minnie and Moo want to give special presents to the Farmer for his birthday, but something goes awry when Moo knits him a sweater.

This is "an outlandishly hilarious romp. . . . Nonstop action and a clever plot place this title at the top of the list for young readers ready for a slightly more complex story." SLJ

  ★ **Minnie** and Moo, wanted dead or alive. HarperCollinsPublishers 2006 47p il (I can read book) hardcover o.p. lib bdg $16.89; pa $3.99
Grades: 1 2 3   E
  1. Cattle -- Fiction 2. Thieves -- Fiction
ISBN 0-06-073010-2; 978-0-06-073010-9; 0-06-073011-0 lib bdg; 978-0-06-073011-6 lib bdg; 978-0-06-073012-3 pa; 0-06-073012-9 pa

                  LC 2005-14526

Trying to help Mr. Farmer with his finances, Minnie and Moo (dressed in trenchcoats, ties, and gray fedoras) go to the bank to ask for money and are mistaken for the Bazooka sisters, dangerous outlaws. "Preschool, primary." (Horn Book)

"Cazet's watercolor illustrations of cows dressed as gangsters and cows driving a tractor extend the story's absurd humor and will help move emerging readers through eight chapters of text." Booklist

★ **Will** you read to me? story and pictures by Denys Cazet. Atheneum Books for Young Readers 2007 un il $16.99

Grades: PreK K 1 2   E

1. Pigs -- Fiction 2. Books and reading -- Fiction

ISBN 978-1-4169-0935-4; 1-4169-0935-4

LC 2005024144

Hamlet enjoys reading books and writing poetry, not playing in the mud and fighting over supper like the other pigs, but he finally finds someone who appreciates him just as he is

"Kids will enjoy the uproarious pigsty scenes. . . . But Cazet's simple poetry and soft-toned watercolor-and-colored-pencil spreads also show the beauty of the quiet night . . . and the farm community in solitude. This is not only a celebration of reading but also a moving story about not fitting in, even at home." Booklist

★ The **octopus**; Grandpa Spanielson's Chicken pox stories, story #1. HarperCollins 2005 46p il (I can read!) $15.99; lib bdg $16.89

Grades: PreK K 1 2   E

1. Dogs -- Fiction 2. Octopuses -- Fiction 3. Chickenpox -- Fiction

ISBN 0-06-051088-9; 0-06-051089-7 lib bdg

LC 2003-26557

Grandpa Spanielson helps his favorite grandpup to avoid scratching his chicken pox by telling how he once had to fight off an octopus during a terrible storm.

"Beginning readers will love the humor, action, and compassion in this story, brought to life in the fun-filled text and superb cartoon illustrations." SLJ

Other titles in Grandpa Spanielson's Chicken pox series are:

A snout for chocolate (2006)

The shrunken head (2007)

The **shrunken** head; Grandpa Spanielson's chicken pox stories: story #3. HarperCollinsPublishers 2007 48p il (I can read!) $15.99; lib bdg $16.89

Grades: PreK K 1 2   E

1. Dogs -- Fiction 2. Sick -- Fiction 3. Grandparents -- Fiction 4. Storytelling -- Fiction

ISBN 978-0-06-073013-0; 0-06-073013-7; 978-0-06-073014-7 lib bdg; 0-06-073014-5 lib bdg

LC 2006-00583

As Barney continues to recover from the chicken pox, Grandpa tells him the story of how Dr. Storkmeyer's head was shrunk during a jungle expedition.

This is "a rollicking tall tale; the hilarious cartoon drawings of the dogs dancing around their cauldron of vile green stuff and the boxes with silly dialogue throughout will make children laugh." SLJ

A **snout** for chocolate; Grandpa Spanielson's chicken pox stories: story #2. by Denys Cazet. HarperCollinsPublishers 2006 47p il (I can read!) hardcover o.p. pa $4.99

Grades: PreK K 1 2   E

1. Dogs -- Fiction 2. Sick -- Fiction 3. Grandparents -- Fiction 4. Storytelling -- Fiction

ISBN 978-0-06-051093-0; 0-06-051093-5; 978-0-06-051094-7 lib bdg; 0-06-051094-3 lib bdg; 978-0-06-051095-4 pa; 0-06-051095-1 pa

LC 2004030197

"One seldom sees a beginning reader with such strong characters and an equally appealing plot—Cazet has created both, added hilarious illustrations, and made a neat little package for all to enjoy." SLJ

Cech, John

The **nutcracker**; based on the story by E.T.A. Hoffmann; retold by John Cech; illustrated by Eric Puybaret. Sterling 2009 un il $17.95

Grades: 2 3 4 5   E

1. Fairy tales 2. Christmas -- Fiction

ISBN 978-1-4027-5562-0; 1-4027-5562-7

LC 2008043084

In this retelling of the original 1816 German story, Godfather Drosselmeier gives young Marie a nutcracker for Christmas, and she finds herself in a magical realm where she saves a boy from an evil curse

"This beautifully illustrated rendition . . . is wordier than some picture-book adaptations. . . . The language is accessible, though, and lustrous, richly colored paintings cover half, sometimes more, of nearly every spread, providing valuable visual breaks." Booklist

The **princess** and the pea; by Hans Christian Andersen; retold by John Cech; illustrated by Bernhard Oberdieck. Sterling Pub. 2007 un il $14.95

Grades: K 1 2 3   E

1. Authors 2. Novelists 3. Dramatists 4. Fairy tales 5. Children's authors 6. Short story writers

ISBN 978-1-4027-3065-8; 1-4027-3065-9

LC 2006007033

A girl proves that she is a real princess by feeling a pea through twenty mattresses and twenty featherbeds. Includes historical notes about Hans Christian Anderson and the original fairy tale.

"Cech's fluid text sparkles in this well-crafted retelling. . . . The illustrations, created with colored pencils, pastels, and acrylics, glow with lustrous yellow-gold, blue, and green tones." SLJ

Cecil, Randy

Duck; [by] Randy Cecil. Candlewick Press 2008 un il $15.99

Grades: PreK K 1   E

1. Ducks -- Fiction

ISBN 978-0-7636-3072-0

LC 2007040407

Duck happily raises a duckling that has wandered into the amusement park where she is a carousel animal, but finds that she cannot teach what she herself has always longed to do—fly—and sets out to find real ducks to instruct him

"Cecil's illustrations . . . are done in oils. Duck, with her bright, striped scarf, stands out against soft green and gold hues. Many of the paintings are in circles of various sizes on a white background with a gold frame. . . . A beautifully realized friendship story with a happy ending." SLJ

Celenza, Anna Harwell

Duke Ellington's Nutcracker suite; illustrated by Don Tate. Charlesbridge 2011 il lib bdg $19.95

Grades: K 1 2 3   E

1. Pianists 2. Composers 3. Jazz musicians 4. Band leaders 5. Music arrangers 6. Jazz music -- Fiction 7. Jazz musicians -- Fiction 8. African Americans -- Fiction

ISBN 978-1-57091-700-4; 1-57091-700-0

LC 2010023060

Tells the story of how jazz composer and musician Duke Ellington, along with Billy Strayhorn, created his jazz composition based on Tchaikovsky's famous Nutcracker Suite ballet.

"This fictionalization of Ellington and Strayhorn's daring collaboration is well told, and the illustrations convey the hip, cool feeling of the time. An author's note provides more information, and a CD of the piece is included." SLJ

Gershwin's Rhapsody in Blue; [by] Anna Harwell Celenza; illustrated by JoAnn E. Kitchel. Charlesbridge 2006 un il $19.95

Grades: 1 2 3 4   E

1. Composers 2. Music -- Fiction 3. Composers -- Fiction

ISBN 978-1-57091-556-7; 1-57091-556-3

LC 2005006009

In January of 1924, a twenty-six-year-old pianist, George Gershwin, finds himself slated to compose, in only five weeks, a concerto that defines "American music," and the result is his masterpiece, Rhapsody in Blue.

"Celenza's tale, complete with invented dialogue, brings the composer to life. . . . An author's note contains Gershwin's words describing the rhythm of the train ride that freed his mental block. . . . Kitchel's sensitivity to this source material is especially evident in her spread of multifaceted patterns and images. . . . An accompanying CD features Gershwin himself (courtesy of a piano roll)." SLJ

Chabon, Michael

★ The **astonishing** secret of Awesome Man; illustrated by Jake Parker. Balzer + Bray 2011 un il $17.99

Grades: K 1 2   E

1. Family life -- Fiction 2. Imagination -- Fiction 3. Superheroes -- Fiction

ISBN 978-0-06-191462-1; 0-06-191462-2

LC 2010041192

A young superhero describes his awesome powers, which he then demonstrates as various foes arrive on the scene.

"Chabon's first picture book discharges delectable language. . . . Things are more likely to skloosh and skarunch than not. Verbiage like this nudges the story into read-aloud territory, and children will be swooping around the room as they listen. But if they stop long enough to peek at the pages, they'll enjoy the way Parker kicks it up another notch with hyperkinetic, hypercolored comic-book action scenes." SLJ

Chaconas, Dori

★ **Cork** & Fuzz; illustrated by Lisa McCue. Viking 2005 32p il (Viking easy-to-read) $13.99

Grades: K 1 2   E

1. Muskrats -- Fiction 2. Opossums -- Fiction 3. Friendship -- Fiction

ISBN 0-670-03602-1

LC 2004-13613

A possum and a muskrat become friends despite their many differences.

"The story's repeated words and entire sentences will help beginning readers feel successful. McCue's endearing drawings add personality and humor to the animals' faces. An excellent addition to easy-reader collections." SLJ

Other titles about Cork & Fuzz are:

Cork & Fuzz: short and tall (2006)

Cork & Fuzz: good sports (2007)

Cork & Fuzz: the collectors (2008)

Cork & Fuzz: finder's keepers (2009)

Cork & Fuzz: the babysitters (2010)

Cork & Fuzz: the swimming lesson (2011)

Don't slam the door! illustrated by Will Hillenbrand. Candlewick Press 2010 un il $15.99

Grades: PreK K 1 2   E

1. Stories in rhyme 2. Doors -- Fiction 3. Animals -- Fiction

ISBN 978-0-7636-3709-5; 0-7636-3709-2

LC 2009015254

A cumulative, rhyming tale of a slamming door which wakes a cat, setting into motion an absurd chain of events and resulting in chaos.

"The author's bouncy couplets are rhythmically consistent all the better for reading aloud. Hillenbrand's mixed-media illustrations with characteristic domestic details and expressive faces on both animal and human figures are a spot-on match to the narrative." SLJ

Hurry down to Derry Fair; illustrated by Gillian Tyler. Candlewick Press 2011 un il

Grades: PreK K 1 2   E

1. Stories in rhyme 2. Fairs -- Fiction 3. Family life -- Fiction

ISBN 0-7636-3208-2; 978-0-7636-3208-3

LC 2010038704

Eager to go on the rides at the county fair, Dinny Brown helps his parents finish their chores.

"The watercolor-and-ink images are rendered in muted greens and browns, like spring, and they contain every toy or pet a preschooler might want. . . . Even the homely interiors and details will fascinate." Kirkus

Mousie love; illustrated by Josee Masse. Bloomsbury U.S.A. Children's Books 2009 un il $16.99; lib bdg $17.89

Grades: K 1 2   E

1. Love -- Fiction 2. Mice -- Fiction

ISBN 978-1-59990-111-4; 1-59990-111-0; 978-1-59990-368-2 lib bdg; 1-59990-368-7 lib bdg

LC 2008-39888

After falling in love at first sight, Tully the mouse strives to prove his devotion to Frill every day—while avoiding the cat—but never gives her a chance to respond to his marriage proposal

"Masse's bright, cheerful acrylic-and-gel illustrations complement the text . . . [and] courtship vignettes alternate with humorous, action-packed chase scenes from a mouse-eye perspective. Mousie love triumphs through adversity in this fetching little romance." Kirkus

Chall, Marsha Wilson

One pup's up; story by Marsha Wilson Chall; art by Henry Cole. Margaret K. McElderry Books 2010 un il $16.99

Grades: PreK K   E

    1. Counting 2. Stories in rhyme 3. Dogs -- Fiction

    ISBN 978-1-416-97960-9; 1-416-97960-3

                     LC 2009-03172

Rhyming text counts off ten puppies as they awaken one by one, chase and bounce around the house, eat kibble and get washed, then fall back to sleep.

"With its lively tone and large-scale art that, thanks to ample white space, focuses exclusively on the dogs, this is a winning choice for reading aloud at story hour or lap time." Publ Wkly

Pick a pup; [by] Marsha Chall; illustrated by Jed Henry. Margaret K. McElderry Books 2011 un il $16.99

Grades: PreK K 1   E

    1. Stories in rhyme 2. Dogs -- Fiction 3. Pets -- Fiction 4. Grandmothers -- Fiction

    ISBN 978-1-4169-7961-6; 1-4169-7961-1

After observing different types of dogs in his neighborhood, Sam and Gram go to the local pet shelter to choose a puppy.

"Terrific for sharing, with bouncing and memorable phrasing and appealing, energetic illustrations, this sweet and satisfying tale showcases the charm and special qualities of dogs as well as the tenderness of a grandparent-grandchild relationship." Kirkus

Chamberlain, Margaret

Please don't tease Tootsie. Dutton 2008 un il $16.99

Grades: PreK K 1 2   E

    1. Stories in rhyme 2. Pets -- Fiction

    ISBN 978-0-525-47982-6; 0-525-47982-1

"Tootsie, a disgruntled red cat, is arching her back and glowering at the little girl who is cheerfully threatening to spray her with a hose. On succeeding pages, readers meet a number of animals under siege by naughty preschoolers. The text consists of brief, alliterative entreaties to mend their ways. . . . The illustrations are droll and stylized, featuring expressive cartoon animals on fields of bright color or flamboyant Art Nouveau patterns." SLJ

Chandra, Deborah

★ **George** Washington's teeth; written by Deborah Chandra & Madeleine Comora; pictures by Brock Cole. Farrar, Straus & Giroux 2003 un il $16

Grades: PreK K 1 2   E

    1. Teeth 2. Generals 3. Presidents 4. Tooth loss -- United States -- Anecdotes -- Juvenile literature

    ISBN 0-374-32534-0

                     LC 2002-25086

A rollicking rhyme portrays George Washington's lifelong struggle with bad teeth. A timeline taken from diary entries and other nonfiction sources follows

This is written "with wit, verve, and a generous amount of sympathy for poor Washington and his dental woes. . . .

Illustrator Cole is at his absolute best here, totally at ease with human gesture and expression." Booklist

Chapman, Jane

I'm not sleepy! Jane Chapman. Good Books 2012 32 p. col. ill. (hardcover: alk. paper) $16.99

Grades: PreK K 1   E

    1. Grandmothers -- Fiction 2. Owls -- Juvenile fiction 3. Bedtime -- Juvenile fiction 4. Owls -- Fiction 5. Bedtime -- Fiction

    ISBN 1561487651; 9781561487653

                     LC 2012000185

In author Jeffrey Frank's book, "a little owlet employs a big bag of tricks when Grandma tries to get him to settle down to sleep." Grandma comes "up with a plan. She will go to sleep, and Mo, after putting her to bed, can play to his heart's content. Mo is delighted, but he finds that the effort of arranging a nest for Grandma and flying down to get her bedtime snack has made him...sleepy." (Kirkus Reviews)

Charest, Emily MacLachlan

Before you came; by Patricia MacLachlan & Emily MacLachlan Charest; illustrated by David Diaz. Katherine Tegen Books 2011 un il $16.99; lib bdg $17.89

Grades: PreK K 1   E

    1. Mother-child relationship -- Fiction

    ISBN 978-0-06-051234-7; 0-06-051234-2; 978-0-06-051235-4 lib bdg; 0-06-051235-0 lib bdg

A mother relates how she spent time before her child arrived, then passes on a gift of days paddling a red canoe, reading in a pillow-filled hammock until dark, and watching the moon rise at night.

"Iridescent light, tropical colors, and entwined, nature-themed patterns distinguish Caldecott Medalist Diaz's . . . lavish art, which is the bedrock of this resplendent book. . . . Details of their mothers' and fathers' lives before they became parents are a constant source of fascination for children, and this talented team celebrates the 'before', while emphasizing (and reassuring) that the 'now' is even better." Publ Wkly

Charles, Veronika Martenova

The birdman; illustrated by Annouchka Gravel Galouchko & Stéphan Daigle. Tundra Books 2006 un il $17.95

Grades: K 1 2 3   E

    1. Birds -- Fiction 2. Bereavement -- Fiction

    ISBN 978-0-88776-740-1; 0-88776-740-0

"In the crowded streets of Calcutta, Nobi, a tailor, works hard to support his family. Then his wife and children are killed. . . . After weeks of immobilizing anguish, Nobi buys some caged birds at the market, sets them free, and finds some of his weighty sorrow released. . . . Charles, who based her vivid, poetic text on a true story (explained in a lengthy afterword), is frank about the pain of loss, but focuses on the uplifting message that acts of kindness can ease grief. The illustrators extend the story's spirit-healing themes in vibrant folk-art paintings, gloriously patterned with flowers, Hindu symbols, and soaring birds." Booklist

Charlip, Remy

Fortunately; written and illustrated by Remy Charlip. Aladdin Books 1993 un il pa $6.99

Grades: PreK K 1   E
  1. Chance -- Fiction 2. Travel -- Fiction
  ISBN 0-689-71660-5; 978-0-689-71660-7

                          LC 92-22794
  First published 1964 by Four Winds Press
  Good and bad luck accompany Ned from New York to
Florida on his way to a surprise party.

  ★ A **perfect** day; [by] Remy Charlip. Greenwillow
Books 2007 un il $16.99; lib bdg $17.89
Grades: PreK K 1 2   E
  1. Stories in rhyme 2. Father-son relationship -- Fiction
  ISBN 0-06-051972-X; 0-06-051973-8 lib bdg

                          LC 2004-52350
  A father and son's "perfect day consists of doing ordinary things—going for a walk, picnicking with friends,
watching the clouds, reading books.... The simple illustrations resemble something a youngster might draw, and the
palette of soft pastel colors supports the story's comforting
atmosphere and the love between these two.... Charlip has
crafted a cozy story that is a perfect example of parent and
child bonding." SLJ

Chast, Roz
  ★ **Too** busy Marco. Atheneum Books for Young Read-
ers 2010 un il $16.99
Grades: PreK K 1 2   E
  1. Birds -- Fiction 2. Bedtime -- Fiction
  ISBN 978-1-4169-8474-0; 1-4169-8474-7

                          LC 2009052481
  "Cartoonist Chast brings her affectionate, anxious line
and fascination with the eccentrically ordinary to an original
riff on bedtime avoidance." Horn Book

Chen, Chih-Yuan
  ★ **Guji** Guji. Kane/Miller 2004 un il $15.95
Grades: PreK K 1 2   E
  1. Ducks -- Fiction 2. Crocodiles -- Fiction
  ISBN 1-929132-67-0
  Crocodile Guji Guji, who was raised by a family of
ducks, meets three crocodiles who tell him that he was not
a duck. When the crocodiles ask Guji Guji to help them trap
the ducks he saves the duck family.
  "This beautifully written story has much to say about
appreciating families and differences.... Chen's unique
illustrations are compelling.... The rich blues and earth
tones and dramatic page layouts create moving scenes, but
the quirky details and characters' expressions are hilarious."
SLJ

  On my way to buy eggs; written and illustrated by
Chih-Yuan Chen. Kane/Miller 2003 un il hardcover o.p.
pa $7.99
Grades: PreK K 1 2   E
  1. Imagination -- Juvenile fiction
  ISBN 1-929132-49-2; 1-933605-41-3 pa

                          LC 2002-117381
  First published 2001 in Taiwan
  "A young girl's errand to the store turns into a sensory
adventure.... After a make-believe game with the shopkeeper and more adventures along the way, Shau-yu returns
home to her loving dad. The story is basic, but the simple
words and phrases easily show Shau-yu's delight in trans-

forming small things. The earth-tone colors in the crisp
paper-and-pencil collages are as quiet as the story." Booklist

Chen, Yong
  A **gift.** Boyds Mills Press 2009 un il $16.95
Grades: K 1 2 3   E
  1. Aunts -- Fiction 2. Uncles -- Fiction 3. Chinese New
  Year -- Fiction 4. Chinese Americans -- Fiction
  ISBN 978-1-59078-610-9; 1-59078-610-6

                          LC 2009012794
  Amy receives a gift for the Chinese New Year from her
aunt and uncles who live far away in China.
  "Chen's text is spare but, combined with her luscious
watercolors, evokes a vivid portrait of rural Chinese culture." SLJ

Cherry, Lynne
  How Groundhog's garden grew. Blue Sky Press (NY)
2003 un il $15.95
Grades: PreK K 1 2   E
  1. Gardening 2. Squirrels 3. Vegetable gardening 4.
  Woodchuck 5. Marmots -- Fiction
  ISBN 0-439-32371-1

                          LC 2002-3428
  Squirrel teaches Little Groundhog how to plant and tend
a vegetable garden
  The author "tells a charming and also informative story
about plants, gardening, and environmental respect. Her
beautiful, full-color illustrations—realistic and wonderfully
detailed—often incorporate spot-art borders of labeled seedlings and plants, highlighting a diverse array of wildlife."
Booklist

  ★ The **great** kapok tree; a tale of the Amazon rainforest. Harcourt Brace Jovanovich 1990 un il $16; pa $7
Grades: K 1 2 3   E
  1. Rain forests -- Fiction
  ISBN 0-15-200520-X; 0-15-202614-2 pa

                          LC 89-2208
  The many different animals that live in a great kapok tree
in the Brazilian rainforest try to convince a man with an ax
of the importance of not cutting down their home
  "A carefully researched picture book.... Cherry captures the Amazonian proportions of the plants and animals
that live there by using vibrant colors, intricate details, and
dramatic perspectives.... The writing is simple and clear."
Booklist

  The **sea,** the storm, and the mangrove tangle. Farrar,
Straus and Giroux 2004 un il $16
Grades: K 1 2 3   E
  1. Ecology 2. Marine animals 3. Caribbean Area 4.
  Mangrove swamps 5. Ecology -- Fiction 6. Wetlands
  -- Fiction 7. Marine animals -- Fiction
  ISBN 0-374-36482-6

                          LC 2002-29705
  A seed from a mangrove tree floats on the sea until it
comes to rest on the shore of a faraway lagoon where, over
time, it becomes a mangrove island that shelters many birds
and animals, even during a hurricane.
  "Cherry paints lustrous, detailed scenes that, together
with her accessible narrative, will spark children's interest in
a magnificent, endangered ecosystem." Booklist

Chessa, Francesca

Holly's red boots; [by] Francesca Chessa. Holiday House 2008 un il $16.95

Grades: PreK K 1   E

1. Snow -- Fiction 2. Color -- Fiction 3. Shoes -- Fiction

ISBN 978-0-8234-2158-9; 0-8234-2158-9

LC 2007-35516

Holly wants to play in the snow and needs her red boots, so she and her cat Jasper search the house for anything red.

"The bright, childlike art uses multiple perspectives and bold swatches of color to portray the freckled preschooler, her patient mom, and the chaotic house search." SLJ

Chichester-Clark, Emma

Little Miss Muffet counts to ten. Andersen Press 2010 un il pa $9.99

Grades: K 1 2   E

1. Counting 2. Stories in rhyme 3. Animals -- Fiction 4. Nursery rhymes -- Fiction

ISBN 978-1-84270-955-9; 1-84270-955-0

"The text is spot-on as Clark keeps the rhyming pattern of the original nursery rhyme and makes it her own. . . . The whimsical illustrations show plenty of activity as the number of characters increases, but they never descend into overwhelming busyness and many invite closer inspection. Perfect for storytime or individual sharing." SLJ

Melrose and Croc: an adventure to remember. Walker & Co. 2008 un il $16.95; lib bdg $17.85

Grades: PreK K 1 2   E

1. Dogs -- Fiction 2. Birthdays -- Fiction 3. Crocodiles -- Fiction

ISBN 978-0-8027-9774-2; 0-8027-9774-1; 978-0-8027-9775-9 lib bdg; 0-8027-9775-X lib bdg

LC 2007-037146

A friendly crocodile receives the best birthday present ever when he rescues his dear companion, Melrose the dog, during a storm at sea

"This simple story, set in a European seaside village, celebrates two caring individuals who think only of one another. Its gentle, affectionate message and expressive illustrations are a wonderful, reassuring way to lull any child into a peaceful sleep in which all is right with the world." SLJ

Other titles about Melrose and Croc are:

Melrose and Croc: a Christmas to remember (2006)

Melrose and Croc beside the sea (2009)

Melrose and Croc find a smile (2009)

Melrose and Croc: friends for life (2009)

Melrose and Croc go to town (2009)

Piper; [written and illustrated by] Emma Chichester Clark. Eerdmans Books for Young Readers 2007 un il $17

Grades: PreK K 1 2   E

1. Dogs -- Fiction

ISBN 978-0-8028-5314-1

LC 2006008548

A young dog runs away from its cruel master, but finds a new home after saving the life of an old woman

"Both honorable and adorable, Piper will inspire strong reactions from kids, and Clark's always-impressive watercolors effectively capture both the happy and the dark moments of the tale." Booklist

Child, Lauren

But, excuse me, that is my book; Lauren Child. Dial Books for Young Readers 2005 un il $16.99

Grades: PreK K 1 2   E

1. Siblings -- Fiction 2. Libraries -- Fiction 3. Books and reading -- Fiction

ISBN 0-8037-3096-9

LC 2005-10389

When Lola's favorite book is not on the library's shelf, her older brother, Charlie, tries to find another book she will enjoy.

"The story flows at a comfortable pace, and the language is easy to comprehend. The collage artwork is charming." SLJ

I am not sleepy and I will not go to bed. Candlewick Press 2001 un il $16.99

Grades: PreK K 1 2   E

1. Animals 2. Bedtime 3. Bedtime -- Fiction 4. Siblings -- Fiction

ISBN 0-7636-1570-6

LC 00-66682

Charlie helps Lola get ready for bed, despite the tigers, whales, and other animals that serve as obstacles.

"The illustrations and text are appealingly quirky and lively. The exuberant colors and patterns provide visual stimuli, and the varied fonts and sizes of the text and clever layout of the mixed-media artwork are sure to please." SLJ

★ **I** am too absolutely small for school. Candlewick 2004 un il $16.99; pa $6.99

Grades: PreK K 1 2   E

1. School stories 2. Siblings -- Fiction

ISBN 0-7636-2403-9; 0-7636-2887-5 pa

LC 2003-65576

When Lola is worried about starting school, her older brother Charlie reassures her

"The children's relationship is refreshingly noncombative. . . . Incorporating photos, fabric, and appealingly childlike cartoon renderings of the siblings, the mixed-media illustrations are a visual treat of color and texture." SLJ

Other titles about Lola and Charlie are:

But excuse me that is my book (2006)

I am not sleepy and I will not go to bed (2001)

I will never not eat a tomato (2000)

Say cheese (2007)

Slightly invisible (2011)

Snow is my favorite and my best (2006)

I will never not ever eat a tomato. Candlewick Press 2000 un il $16.99

Grades: PreK K 1 2   E

1. Food -- Fiction 2. Siblings -- Fiction

ISBN 0-7636-1188-3

LC 99-57573

Lola, a fussy eater, decides to sample the carrots after her brother Charlie convinces her that they are really orange twiglets from Jupiter

"Child has created two likable, winsome siblings with spunk and imagination. . . . Child's mixed-media artwork (primitive cartoon characters, photographs, fabric swatches, and wallpaper remnants) enhances the innocent tone of the book." SLJ

Say cheese! characters created by Lauren Child; [text based on the script written by Samantha Hill; illustrations from the TV animation produced by Tiger Aspect]. Dial Books for Young Readers 2007 un il $16.99
Grades: PreK K 1 2   E
1. Siblings -- Fiction 2. Photography -- Fiction
ISBN 978-0-80373-095-3
LC 2006102579
"Lola is excited about her first-ever school photo. Charlie cautions that she must stay tidy and clean. . . . True to her nature, Lola makes a mess. . . . Child's collages combine graphically imposed read objects with simply drawn characters and are colored with funky patterns that emphasize their childlike quality." Booklist

Snow is my favorite and my best. Dial Books for Young Readers 2006 un il $16.99
Grades: PreK K 1 2   E
1. Snow -- Fiction 2. Siblings -- Fiction
ISBN 0-8037-3174-4
LC 2006-05427
"Lola is enthralled with snow. . . . Too soon, however, the snow melts, and Lola is bereft, leaving Charlie to explain that snow is special and snow every day could be a drag. . . . Lola's exuberance is made manifest on every page. Child puts a simply shaped, almost scrawled pair of siblings against jellybean-bright backgrounds, and ingeniously decorates everything with collage." Booklist

Who wants to be a poodle I don't. Candlewick Press 2009 un il $16.99
Grades: PreK K 1 2   E
1. Dogs -- Fiction
ISBN 978-0-7636-4610-3; 0-7636-4610-5
LC 2009003659
Tired of being a pampered poodle dressed in a little pink poncho, Trixie Twinkle Toes sets off in search of dangerous and daring adventures.
"Young readers will sympathize with Trixie and savor the details of her posh urban existence. . . . Child's . . . collages contain all the action Trixie's life lacks, sizzling with dizzying colors and patterns; her sentences lead adventurous lives of their own, curlicuing, shrinking, growing and spiraling into muddy puddles." Publ Wkly

Chinn, Karen
Sam and the lucky money; illustrated by Cornelius Van Wright, and Ying-Hwa Hu. Lee & Low Bks. 1995 un il hardcover o.p. pa $7.95
Grades: PreK K 1 2   E
1. Chinese New Year -- Fiction 2. Chinese Americans -- Fiction
ISBN 1-880000-13-X; 1-880000-53-9 pa
LC 94-11766
"The illustrators masterfully combine Chinatown's exotic setting with the universal emotions of childhood through expressive portraits of the characters." SLJ

Chocolate, Debbi
El barrio; illustrated by David Diaz. Henry Holt 2009 un il $16.95

Grades: PreK K 1 2   E
1. Community life -- Fiction 2. City and town life -- Fiction 3. Hispanic Americans -- Fiction
ISBN 978-0-8050-7457-4; 0-8050-7457-0
LC 2008013422
A young boy explores his vibrant Latino neighborhood, with its vegetable gardens instead of lawns, Nativity parades, quinceanera parties, and tejana and salsa music.
"Thick lines surround the woodcut-like artwork imbued with a rainbow of glowing colors. Fascinating mixed-media collages (toy skulls, rocks, beads, shells) border each spread. The whole is an exuberant cacophony of colors and sights." Booklist

Chodos-Irvine, Margaret
Best best friends; [by] Margaret Chodos-Irvine. Harcourt 2006 un il $16
Grades: PreK K 1   E
1. School stories 2. Birthdays -- Fiction 3. Friendship -- Fiction
ISBN 0-15-205694-7
LC 2005002251
Mary and Clare do everything together at preschool, but Mary's birthday celebration puts a strain on the girls' friendship.
"In spot-on words and crisp, gaily patterned prints, the [author-illustrator] captures the unselfconscious affection and quicksilver shifts in mood that characterize preschool friendships." Booklist

★ **Ella** Sarah gets dressed. Harcourt 2003 un il $16; bd bk $10.95
Grades: PreK K 1   E
1. Clothing and dress -- Fiction
ISBN 0-15-216413-8; 0-15-206486-9 bd bk
LC 2002-5097
A Caldecott Medal honor book, 2004
Despite the advice of others in her family, Ella Sarah persists in wearing the striking and unusual outfit of her own choosing
"With minimal words and her signature art marked by bright, bold prints, Chodos-Irvine perfectly captures a universal childhood struggle." Booklist

Choldenko, Gennifer
Louder, Lili; [by] Gennifer Choldenko; illustrated by S.D. Schindler. G.P. Putnam's Sons 2007 un il $16.99
Grades: PreK K 1 2   E
1. School stories 2. Friendship -- Fiction
ISBN 978-0-399-24252-6
LC 2007007511
Lili is so shy that her voice is never heard in class until the day a good friend needs her help
"This engaging story is well written and even poetic. Lili is a well-developed character, and her growth is believable. The warm, energetic illustrations highlight the elements of humor in the story." SLJ

A **giant** crush; illustrated by Melissa Sweet. G.P. Putnam's Sons 2011 un il $16.99
Grades: PreK K 1 2   E
1. School stories 2. Rabbits -- Fiction 3. Shyness --

Fiction 4. Valentine's Day -- Fiction
ISBN 978-0-399-24352-3; 0-399-24352-6
LC 2009040110

"Jackson, a young rabbit, has a giant crush on Cami, a bunny in his class, but he's too shy to tell her he likes her. Instead, he leaves her a flower, candy, and a giant valentine. . . . Sweet's watercolor, gouache, and mixed-media illustrations are sunny and expressive, and bring the characters and their world to life. The lighthearted pictures are a perfect match for the breezy text." SLJ

Choung, Euh-Hee
Minji's salon. Kane Miller 2008 un il $15.95
Grades: PreK   E
1. Dogs -- Fiction 2. Beauty shops -- Fiction
ISBN 978-1-933605-67-8; 1-933605-67-7
"When Minji's mother heads to the beauty salon, Minji pretends to be her dog's hairdresser. . . . The simply charming story of a young girl using her imagination is accompanied by delightful artwork." Booklist

Christelow, Eileen
★ **Five** little monkeys jumping on the bed; retold and illustrated by Eileen Christelow. Clarion Bks. 1989 un il $15; pa $5.95; bd bk $11.99
Grades: PreK K 1 2   E
1. Counting 2. Monkeys -- Fiction
ISBN 0-89919-769-8; 0-395-55701-1 pa; 0-547-13176-3 bd bk
LC 88-22839

A counting book in which one by one the five little monkeys jump on the bed only to fall off and bump their heads
"Squiggling, swirling lines of color capture the sense of unbridled motion as the monkeys bounce and, one by one, topple from the bed. After all five bandaged youngsters finally fall asleep, a relaxed mama gratefully retires to her room . . . to bounce on 'her' bed. An amusingly presented counting exercise." Booklist

Other titles about the five little monkeys are:
Don't wake up Mama! (1992)
Five little monkeys go shopping (2007)
Five little monkeys play hide and seek (2004)
Five little monkeys reading in bed (2011)
Five little monkeys sitting in a tree (1991)
Five little monkeys wash the car (2000)
Five little monkeys with nothing to do (1996)

Letters from a desperate dog; [by] Eileen Christelow. Clarion Books 2006 32p il $16
Grades: PreK K 1 2   E
1. Dogs -- Fiction
ISBN 978-0-618-51003-0; 0-618-51003-6
LC 2005032744

Feeling misunderstood and unappreciated by her owner, Emma the dog asks for advice from the local canine advice columnist.
"This is a delightful romp, and Christelow shows Emma's story off to great advantage in an oversize format with comic-book-style watercolor art." Booklist
Another title about Emma the dog is:
The desperate dog writes again (2010)

The **desperate** dog writes again. Clarion Books 2010 32p il $16.99

Grades: PreK K 1 2   E
1. Dogs -- Fiction
ISBN 978-0-547-24205-7; 0-547-24205-0
When a new girlfriend comes between Emma the dog and her owner George, Emma e-mails "Ask Queenie," an advice column for dogs having problems with difficult humans.
"Christelow's bright, cartoon-like illustrations in comic-book panels humorously display the antics while dialogue bubbles abet easy reading. Pitch perfect for those children adjusting to a new person in their lives." Kirkus

Christensen, Bonnie
★ **Plant** a little seed; Bonnie Christensen. Roaring Brook Press 2012 32 p.
Grades: 2 3 4 5   E
1. Seeds -- Fiction 2. Seasons -- Fiction 3. Gardening -- Fiction 4. Picture books for children 5. Community gardens -- Fiction
ISBN 159643550X; 9781596435506
LC 2011005202

In this picture book, "a girl narrates the cycle of working a community-garden plot over three productive seasons. She and her friend (a boy) plan, plant, tend and harvest fruits, veggies and flowers. . . . [Bonnie] Christensen's pictures . . . convey visual affirmations of friendship, cooperation and patience through changing seasons. Basic biological facts about plants, arranged on seed packets scattered across a final page, are reinforced visually throughout." (Kirkus Reviews)

Christian, Cheryl
Witches; illustrated by Wish Williams. Star Bright Books 2011 24p il pa $5.95
Grades: PreK   E
1. Stories in rhyme 2. Witches -- Fiction 3. Halloween -- Fiction
ISBN 978-1-59572-283-6; 1-59572-283-1
LC 2010050909

"Children dressed as witches are gathered around a kitchen table putting all sorts of food from the cupboards and refrigerator in a giant black cauldron. This image sets the scene for a very simple story of children (or witches) getting ready for their Halloween outing. The whimsical and vibrant colors in Williams's pictures make this story great fun to view and help to move the rhyming text forward." SLJ

Church, Caroline
One more hug for Madison; by Caroline Jayne Church. Orchard Books 2010 un il lib bdg $16.99
Grades: PreK K   E
1. Mice -- Fiction 2. Bedtime -- Fiction 3. Mother-child relationship -- Fiction
ISBN 978-0-545-16179-4 lib bdg; 0-545-16179-7 lib bdg
LC 2008-52691

Madison the mouse keeps asking her patient mother for just one more thing before she goes to sleep.

One smart goose; [by] Caroline Jayne Church. Orchard Books 2005 un il $16.95
Grades: PreK K 1 2   E
1. Foxes -- Fiction 2. Geese -- Fiction
ISBN 0-439-68765-9
First published 2003 in the United Kingdom

A goose who likes to wash in a muddy pond is teased by the other geese, until they realize that he is the only one not chased by the fox

"The clever story will hold the attention of young children, but the illustrations are the book's most striking feature. Bold black lines define the forms of the geese, the fox, and the setting, while textured papers, buts of smudgy print, and collage elements enrich the simple compositions." Booklist

Cinderella

Cinder Edna; by Ellen Jackson; illustrated by Kevin O'Malley. Lothrop, Lee & Shepard Bks. 1994 un il $16.99; pa $5.99

Grades: PreK K 1 2   E

1. Fairy tales

ISBN 0-688-12322-8; 0-688-16295-9 pa

LC 92-44160

Cinderella and Cinder Edna, who live with cruel stepmothers and stepsisters, have different approaches to life; and, although each ends up with the prince of her dreams, one is a great deal happier than the other

"O'Malley's full-page, full-color illustrations are exuberant and funny. Ella is suitably bubble-headed and self-absorbed while Edna is plain, practical, and bound to enjoy life." SLJ

Claflin, Willy

The **uglified** ducky; a Maynard Moose tale. [by] Willy Claflin; illustrated by James Stimson. August House/Little-Folk 2008 un il $18.95

Grades: K 1 2 3   E

1. Fairy tales

ISBN 978-0-87483-858-9; 0-87483-858-4

LC 2008000974

Resets Hans Christian Andersen's tale. The ugly duckling, in the Northern Piney Woods of Alaska, where a baby moose is raised by a family of ducks who try to teach him to waddle, quack, and fly but cannot see his true beauty.

"Stimson's colorful illustrations are a riot, featuring stylized shapes, funny expressions, and animated scenes. A CD of the story performed hilariously by Claflin is delightful. This fresh, lively story is laugh-out-loud funny." SLJ

Clarke, J.

Stuck in the mud; [by] Jane Clarke; illustrations by Garry Parsons. Walker Pub. Co. 2008 un il $16.95

Grades: PreK K 1   E

1. Stories in rhyme 2. Chickens -- Fiction 3. Domestic animals -- Fiction

ISBN 978-0-8027-9758-2; 0-8027-9758-X

LC 2007032179

"One morning, a hen awakens to find a chick missing from her brood. She spots him in the middle of a patch of 'mucky mud,' assumes he is trapped, and clucks hysterically until her friends come to help pull him out. One by one, the rescuers also become mired in the muck. . . . Bright paintings in solid colors and simple, yet expressive cartoon animals are well suited to very young listeners." SLJ

Clayton, Dallas

An **awesome** book! Dallas Clayton. Harper 2012 64 p. (trd. bdg.) $16.99

Grades: PreK K 1 2   E

1. Stories in rhyme 2. Creative thinking 3. Dreams -- Fiction

ISBN 0062114689; 9780062114686

LC 2011935482

Author and illustrator Dallas Clayton presents a children's picture book about imagination and dreams demonstrated through monsters.

Cleary, Beverly

The **hullabaloo** ABC; illustrated by Ted Rand. rev ed; Morrow Junior Bks. 1998 un il $17.99

Grades: PreK K 1 2   E

1. Alphabet 2. Stories in rhyme 3. Noise -- Fiction 4. Farm life -- Fiction

ISBN 0-688-15182-5

LC 97-6457

A revised and newly illustrated edition of the title first published 1960 by Parnassus Press

An alphabet book in which two children demonstrate all the fun that is to be had by making and hearing every kind of noise as they dash about on the farm

"Rand's expert watercolor illustrations on crisp white backgrounds bring the action to life with just the slightest touch of nostalgia." SLJ

Cleland, Jo

Getting your zzzzs; Jo Cleland; [edited by] Precious McKenzie. Rourke Pub. 2012 24 p. $22.79

Grades: K 1 2   E

1. Sleep 2. Children's songs 3. Picture books for children

ISBN 1618100858; 9781618100856

LC 2011944395

This children's book from Jo Cleland is part of the "Sing and Read: Healthy Habits series, which sets healthful reminders to familiar tunes." Here, the tune of "If You're Happy and You Know It" is used to remind children about the immune system-boosting effects of getting enough sleep. (Booklist)

Clement, Nathan

★ **Drive**; [by] Nathan Clement. Front Street 2008 un il $16.95

Grades: PreK K   E

1. Trucks -- Fiction 2. Fathers -- Fiction

ISBN 978-1-59078-517-1

LC 2007037469

In brief text with illustrations, a boy describes his father's work as a truck driver

"Working in big, streamlined shapes; flat, bright colors; and shiny, airbrushed-like surfaces, [Clement] evokes a deco-esque world. . . . Unusual and often cinematic perspectives . . . plunge readers into the action and give the compositions a red-blooded energy." Publ Wkly

Job site. Boyds Mills Press 2011 un il

Grades: PreK K 1   E

1. Building -- Fiction 2. Vehicles -- Fiction

ISBN 1-59078-769-2; 978-1-59078-769-4

"Over the course of a day on the job, a burly construction foreman, referred to only as 'Boss,' makes good on his name and bosses around a bulldozer, excavator, dump truck, and other vehicles. . . . Featuring . . . bold digital artwork, . . . this book . . . makes excellent use of perspective to play up the machines' immensity and power." Publ Wkly

Clements, Andrew

Circus family dog; illustrated by Sue Truesdell. Clarion Bks. 2000 32p il $16

Grades: PreK K 1 2   E

1. Circus animals 2. Dogs -- Fiction 3. Circus -- Fiction

ISBN 0-395-78648-7

LC 99-52657

Grumps is content to do his one trick in the center ring at the circus, until a new dog shows up and steals the show—temporarily

"The combination of Clements's impeccable storyteller pacing and Truesdell's creative and whimsical cartoons create a reading and visual experience second only to actually being at the circus. The illustrator uses a mixture of watercolors with pen and ink to bring the action to life in vibrant colors." SLJ

The **handiest** things in the world; photographs by Raquel Jaramillo. Atheneum 2010 un il $16.99

Grades: PreK K 1 2   E

1. Stories in rhyme 2. Hand -- Fiction

ISBN 978-1-416-96166-6; 1-416-96166-6

"This unusual concept book looks at all the things that hands can do and the tools that help do them better. On a typical double-page spread, two short rhyming sentences are paired with photos. The first shows a child's hands performing a job, while the next shows them using a tool. . . . In the first picture, a girl untangles her hair with her fingers; in the next, with a comb. . . . Excellent color photos of different children engaged in everyday activities enhance the book's appeal." Booklist

Cleminson, Katie

Cuddle up, goodnight. Disney Hyperion Books 2011 un il $15.99

Grades: PreK K   E

1. Stories in rhyme 2. Day -- Fiction 3. Toddlers -- Fiction

ISBN 978-1-4231-3844-0; 1-4231-3844-9

LC 2010004890

First published 2010 in the United Kingdom with title: Wake up!

Follows, in rhymed text and illustrations, a little boy's activities from the time he wakes up in the morning until he goes to bed at night.

"Boldly outlined illustrations effectively employ spare brush strokes and soft-shaded colors to playfully depict characters, objects, and irrepressibly goofy experiences, such as a hippo slurping spaghetti at the table. . . . Children will enjoy the unexpected antics as well as the reassuring sense of a daily routine." Booklist

Clifton-Brown, Holly

Annie Hoot and the knitting extravaganza. Andersen Press USA 2010 un il $16.95

Grades: PreK K 1 2   E

1. Owls -- Fiction 2. Knitting -- Fiction

ISBN 978-0-7613-6444-3; 0-7613-6444-7

Annie Hoot, an owl, loves to knit, but the other owls in the woods will not wear the clothes she makes for them so she goes off in search of other animals that will appreciate her knitwear.

"The exuberant and joyful tale about finding one's bliss is accompanied by watercolor illustrations full of whimsical details." Horn Book Guide

Cline-Ransome, Lesa

Light in the darkness; a story about how slaves learned in secret. by Lesa Cline-Ransome; illustrations by James E. Ransome. Disney/Jump at the Sun Books 2013 40 p. $16.99

Grades: 2 3 4   E

1. Books and reading -- Juvenile fiction 2. Slavery -- United States -- Juvenile fiction 3. African Americans -- History -- Juvenile fiction 4. Reading -- Fiction 5. Slavery -- Fiction 6. Learning -- Fiction 7. African Americans -- Fiction

ISBN 1423134958; 9781423134954

LC 2012001834

This children's story, by Lesa Cline-Ransome, illustrated by James E. Ransome, is a historical story of 19th century life in slavery. "Rosa and her mama go to school . . . in the dark of night, silently, afraid that any noise they hear is a patroller on the lookout for escaped slaves. . . . If the Master catches them, it'll mean a whipping--one lash for each letter. No matter how slow and dangerous the process might be, Rosa is determined to learn, and pass on her learning to others." (Publisher's note)

Cobb, Jane

What'll I do with the baby-o? Nursery rhymes, songs and stories for babies. Jane Cobb; illustrated by Kathryn Shoemaker. Black Sheep Press 2012 255 p. ill. (paperback) $39.95; (ebook) $29.95

Grades: Adult Professional   E

1. Children's libraries 2. Children's literature 3. Infants -- Development 4. Early childhood education

ISBN 0969866615; 9780969866619; 9780969866640

This book by Jane Cobb presents "rhymes, songs, and stories . . . to engage . . . babies throughout their first two years of development. All of the activities recommended encourage bonding, fun, and brain and emotional development. . . . This resource contains . . . chapters on a baby's brain, early language, and literacy development; program planning and presentation tips; 350 rhymes and songs arranged by type . . . and other resources and bibliographies for further reading." (Publisher's note)

"Extensive preliminary chapters cover such things as identifying the audience, considering the developmental needs of the babies, and selecting and teaching the rhymes and books. The remainder of the book contains thoughtful suggestions of specific rhymes and songs, as well as comments to use with parents. . . . A musical CD provides samples of songs. . . . This book is a must-have for those embarking upon 'Baby and Me' or 'Mother Goose'-type programs." SLJ

Cobb, Rebecca

★ **Missing** mommy; Rebecca Cobb. Henry Holt and Co. 2013 32 p. (hardcover) $16.99

Grades: K 1 2   E

1. Mother-son relationship 2. Bereavement -- Juvenile fiction 3. Death -- Fiction 4. Grief -- Fiction 5.

Mothers -- Fiction
ISBN 0805095071; 9780805095074

LC 2011052417

This children's book, by Rebecca Cobb, "explores the many emotions a bereaved child may experience, from anger and guilt to sadness and bewilderment. Ultimately, [the story] focuses on the positive--the recognition that the child is not alone but still part of a family that loves and supports him." (Publisher's note)

"Told from a young child's point of view, Cobb's moving story respectfully explores the complex emotions a little one may experience while grieving the loss of a parent. ... The artwork, done in a primary palette, skillfully emulates the innocence of a child's drawings... Accessible and tender, this story gives young children a voice and shows how to hold the memory of a loved one close." Kirkus

Cocca-Leffler, Maryann

Princess K.I.M. and the lie that grew. Albert Whitman & Co. 2009 32p $16.99
Grades: PreK K 1 2   E
1. Truthfulness and falsehood -- Fiction
ISBN 978-0-8075-4178-4; 0-8075-4178-8

LC 2008-28056

After new girl Kim tells her classmates she is from a royal family, her lie grows and grows.

"The brightly colored artwork brings the story to life. ... Varying layouts effectively convey the action." SLJ

Another title about Kim is:
Princess Kim and too much truth (2011)

Princess Kim and too much truth. Albert Whitman 2011 un il $16.99
Grades: PreK K 1 2   E
1. School stories 2. Honesty -- Fiction
ISBN 978-0-8075-6618-3; 0-8075-6618-7

LC 2010024275

Kim, who has decided always to tell the truth, tells her Dad that the pancakes are rubbery, her teacher that her baby is ugly, and her Grandma that her new necklace looks the the slimy rocks at the bottom of the fish tank.

"The story, with its lighthearted illustrations, provides good examples of the if-you-can't-say-something-nice principle." Horn Book Guide

Rain brings frogs; a little book of hope. Harper 2011 un il $9.99
Grades: PreK K 1   E
1. Hope -- Fiction 2. Happiness -- Fiction
ISBN 978-0-06-196106-9; 0-06-196106-X

"Nate sees everything in a positive light. When Charlie says, 'Keep Out!'/Nate says, 'Room for All.' When Mom says, 'I Hate Rain.' Nate says, 'Rain Brings Frogs!' Green frog endpapers enhance the cheerful colors and cartoonlike characters surrounded by plenty of white space. The font is large, and the narrative waves through the pages showing action and movement." SLJ

A **vacation** for Pooch; Maryann Cocca-Leffler. Christy Ottaviano Books 2013 32 p. (hardcover) $16.99
Grades: K 1 2 3   E
1. Dogs -- Juvenile fiction 2. Girls -- Juvenile fiction 3. Vacations -- Juvenile fiction 4. Dogs -- Fiction 5.

Vacations -- Fiction
ISBN 0805091068; 9780805091069

LC 2012011271

This children's story, by Maryann Cocca-Leffler, follows a girl and her pet dog going on separate vacations. Violet is "going on vacation to sunny Florida. She packed her bag very carefully. . . ." Pooch is "going on vacation to Grandpa's snowy farm. Violet packed his bag very carefully, too. . . . When their bags get mixed up, Violet thinks Pooch's vacation will be miserable. But Pooch is having a grand old time, so all is very well!" (Publisher's note)

Cochran, Bill

My parents are divorced, my elbows have nicknames, and other facts about me; illustrated by Steve Björkman. HarperCollins 2009 un il $17.99; lib bdg $18.89
Grades: K 1 2 3   E
1. Divorce -- Fiction
ISBN 978-0-06-053942-9; 0-06-053942-9; 978-0-06-053943-6 lib bdg; 0-06-053943-7 lib bdg

While describing his not-so-weird life with his divorced parents, a young boy also describes some other things about himself that could be considered weird.

"This story uses humor to help children cope with the issue of divorce. ... Ted has a believable voice that children will recognize. ... The colorful cartoons add to the upbeat nature of the story and make a serious subject a little easier to swallow." SLJ

Codell, Esmé Raji

Fairly fairy tales; illustrated by Elisa Chavarri. Aladdin 2011 un il
Grades: PreK K 1   E
1. Fairy tales 2. Books and reading -- Fiction
ISBN 1-4169-9086-0; 978-1-4169-9086-4

LC 2009-16475

This book reimagines six familiar fairy tales. "Ages four to seven." (Bull Cent Child Books)

"In this fanciful collection, Codell takes six familiar fairy tales, lists three known attributes for each . . . then throws in a novel element . . . which provides impetus for a fanciful revisioning depicted in the following spread. ... It's a great gimmick, and the 'what if?' approach to fairy tales offers heaps of potential for classroom projects and discussions. ... Chavarri's splashy, digitally rendered illustrations are most notable for their attention to detail: the wordless alternative-story spreads are chock full of minutiae that add considerable humor to the simple text." Bull Cent Child Books

Coerr, Eleanor

The **Josefina** story quilt; pictures by Bruce Degen. Harper & Row 1986 64p il (I can read book) hardcover o.p. pa $3.99
Grades: K 1 2 3   E
1. Quilts -- Fiction 2. Overland journeys to the Pacific -- Fiction
ISBN 0-06-021348-5; 0-06-444129-6 pa

LC 85-45260

While traveling west with her family in 1850, a young girl makes a patchwork quilt chronicling the experiences of the journey and reserves a special patch for her pet hen Josefina

"The story makes the history go down easily, and an author's note at the end fills in facts about the western trip and the place of quilts as pioneer diaries. The charcoal and blue/yellow wash illustrations are clear and natural. . . . A good introduction to historical fiction that children can read for themselves." SLJ

The **big** balloon race; pictures by Carolyn Croll. Harper & Row 1981 62p il (I can read book) hardcover o.p. pa $3.99

Grades: K 1 2   E
  1. Balloons -- Fiction
  ISBN 0-06-444053-2 pa

LC 80-8368

The author "recounts the winning of a hydrogen balloon race by Carlotta Myers, a famous aeronaut, and her stowaway daughter Ariel. Balloon facts are slipped naturally and painlessly into the story, which moves cogently along. The novel subject matter, straightforward mother-daughter relationship, and clear composition of the orange, blue and gray illustrations . . . make for a high-flying new look at a piece of the past." SLJ

Coffelt, Nancy
Catch that baby! illustrated by Scott Nash. Aladdin 2011 un il $16.99

Grades: PreK K   E
  1. Baths -- Fiction 2. Infants -- Fiction 3. Family life -- Fiction
  ISBN 978-1-4169-9148-9; 1-4169-9148-4

LC 2009-34934

Everyone from Mom to Grandpa joins the chase when baby Rudy decides he does not want to get dressed after his bath.

"Ebullient in tone and sassy in spirit, this is a romp where both family and action seem quite real." Booklist

★ **Fred** stays with me; illustrated by Tricia Tusa. Little, Brown 2007 un il $16.99

Grades: PreK K 1 2   E
  1. Dogs -- Fiction 2. Divorce -- Fiction
  ISBN 0-316-88269-0

LC 2005-07973

Boston Globe-Horn Book Award honor book: Picture Book (2008)

A child describes how she lives sometimes with his mother and sometimes with his father, but his dog is his constant companion.

"Coffelt and Tusa have teamed up to create a charming book that meshes text and illustrations seamlessly. . . . Tusa uses gold and brown hues with occasional splashes of red to create a warm tone." SLJ

Cohen, Barbara
★ **Molly's** pilgrim; illustrated by Daniel Mark Duffy. Lothrop, Lee & Shepard Bks. 1998 un il $17.99; pa $3.95

Grades: K 1 2 3   E
  1. School stories 2. Jews -- Fiction 3. Schools -- Fiction 4. Immigrants -- Fiction 5. Thanksgiving Day -- Fiction 6. Russian Americans -- Fiction 7. Jews -- United States -- Fiction 8. Emigration and immigration -- Fiction 9. Jews -- United States -- Juvenile fiction
  ISBN 0-688-16279-7; 0-688-16280-0 pa

LC 98-9227

A newly illustrated edition of the title first published 1983

Told to make a Pilgrim doll for the Thanksgiving display at school, Molly is embarassed when her mother tries to help her out by creating a doll dressed as she herself was dressed before leaving Russia to seek religious freedom

Cohen, Caron Lee
Broom, zoom! illustrated by Sergio Ruzzier. Simon & Schuster Books for Young Readers 2010 un il $12.99

Grades: PreK K 1   E
  1. Brooms -- Fiction 2. Goblins -- Fiction 3. Witches -- Fiction
  ISBN 978-1-4169-9113-7; 1-4169-9113-1

LC 2009000581

One beautiful, starry night, a little witch wants to go for a ride on a broom but first she must help a little monster clean up a mess.

"The text is simple enough for beginning readers, as the characters speak in one and two-word sentences. The illustrations were digitally created in flat, singular colors. . . . . Although Witch and Monster give the story a Halloween feel, it is a simple tale of cooperation and friendship, and youngsters will respond to it as such." SLJ

Cohen, Deborah Bodin
Engineer Ari and the sukkah express; illustrated by Shahar Kober. Kar-Ben Pub. 2010 p. cm. il lib bdg $17.95; pa $7.95

Grades: PreK K 1 2   E
  1. Jews -- Fiction 2. Sukkot -- Fiction 3. Railroads -- Fiction
  ISBN 978-0-7613-5126-9 lib bdg; 0-7613-5126-4 lib bdg; 978-0-7613-5128-3 pa; 0-7613-5128-0 pa

LC 2009001876

Nachshon, who was afraid to swim; a Passover story. by Deborah Bodin Cohen; illustrations by Jago. Kar-Ben Pub. 2009 un il lib bdg $17.95; pa $8.95

Grades: 1 2 3 4   E
  1. Fear -- Fiction 2. Jews -- Fiction 3. Courage -- Fiction 4. Slavery -- Fiction 5. Passover -- Fiction
  ISBN 978-0-8225-8764-4 lib bdg; 0-8225-8764-5 lib bdg; 978-0-8225-8765-1 pa; 0-8225-8765-3 pa

LC 2007048359

When the Israelites flee Egypt, Nachshon exhibits great courage by being the first to step into the Red Sea, even though he cannot swim.

"The digitally prepared, mixed-media illustrations utilize muted yellow, orange, and brown tones to depict the sweltering heat of the desert and bright blue and green tones to illustrate the celebration of freedom. They complement and enhance the text marvelously. A wonderful, unique addition." SLJ

Cohen, Miriam
★ **First** grade takes a test; by Miriam Cohen; illustrated by Ronald Himler. Star Bright Books 2006 un il $15.95; pa $5.95

Grades: PreK K 1 2   E
  1. School stories 2. Examinations -- Fiction
  ISBN 978-1-59572-054-2; 1-59572-054-5; 978-1-59572-055-9 pa; 1-59572-055-3 pa

LC 2006020488

A revised and newly illustrated edition of the title first published 1980 by Greenwillow Bks.

"One day the first-graders are given a special multiple-choice test by the principal. Some kids find the questions puzzling. Then, suddenly, time's up. Anna Maria announces, 'That was easy.' But many kids are confused and upset, and 'You're a dummy!' echoes through the class, which only settles down when the kindly teacher reminds the children of all the things they do understand. . . . Cohen's sensitivity to children's feelings and reactions really shows here. . . . Himler's loose-lined, pencil-and-watercolor pictures skillfully use body language and facial expressions to chart the children's emotional highs and lows." Booklist

My big brother; art by Ronald Himler. Star Bright 2005 un il $15.95
Grades: K 1 2 3   E
1. Brothers -- Fiction 2. Soldiers -- Fiction 3. Family life -- Fiction
ISBN 1-59572-007-3
                                        LC 2004-16056
When his big brother leaves to become a soldier, a boy does what he can to take his place in the family.
"This quiet picture book packs a strong emotional wallop. Himler's artwork, pencil with watercolor washes, sensitively depicts each character's emotions through body language and facial expressions." Booklist

★ **Will** I have a friend? by Miriam Cohen; illustrated by Ronald Himler. Star Bright Books 2009 un il $15.95
Grades: PreK K 1   E
1. School stories 2. Friendship -- Fiction
ISBN 978-1-59572-069-6; 1-59572-069-3
                                        LC 2008036957
A newly illustrated edition of the title first published 1967 by Macmillan
Jim's anxieties on his first day of school are happily forgotten when he makes a new friend.
The art is "fresh and new. . . . Himler's soft watercolors are . . . contemporary in look, with touches like a recycle mark on the trash bin. . . . Great for combating new-kid-in-school blues." Booklist

Cohn, Diana
Namaste! illustrated by Amy Cordova; with an Afterward by Ang Rita Sherpa of the Mountain Institute. SteinerBooks 2009 un il $17.95
Grades: K 1 2   E
ISBN 978-0-88010-625-2; 0-88010-625-5
                                        LC 2009003216
Whenever Nima meets someone on her long walk to the market village in Nepal, she brings her hands together with her fingers almost touching her chin, bows her head slightly, and says "Namaste," which means "the light in me meets the light in you." Includes information on the geography, culture, and people of Nepal
"The vibrant folk-art illustrations showing the details of Nima's life in her village support the simple story perfectly. This beautiful book will appeal to primary readers and make an ideal addition to multicultural collections." SLJ

Colato Lainez, Rene
My shoes and I; illustrations by Fabricio Vanden Broeck. Boyds Mills Press 2010 un il $16.95
Grades: K 1 2 3   E
1. Shoes -- Fiction 2. Travel -- Fiction 3. Immigrants

-- Fiction 4. Father-son relationship -- Fiction
ISBN 978-1-59078-385-6; 1-59078-385-9
                                        LC 2008-30003
As Mario and his Papa travel from El Salvador to the United States to be reunited with Mama, Mario's wonderful new shoes help to distract him from the long and difficult journey.
"Vanden Broeck's color-drenched illustrations on weathered backgrounds add immediacy and detail. This moving, heartfelt tale of courage and perseverance will be embraced by a wide audience of readers, young and old." SLJ

Playing loteria; illustrated by Jill Arena. Luna Rising 2005 un il hardcover o.p. pa $6.95
Grades: PreK K 1 2   E
1. Games -- Fiction 2. Grandmothers -- Fiction 3. Mexican Americans -- Fiction 4. Bilingual books -- English-Spanish
ISBN 0-87358-881-9; 978-0-87358-919-2 pa; 0-87358-919-X pa
A boy has a good time attending a fair with his grandmother in San Luis de La Paz, Mexico, as she teaches him Spanish words and phrases and he teaches her English.
"This is a warm and reassuring story of a boy's involvement not only with his family but also his culture. The prose flows easily in both English and Spanish. [This is illustrated with] spirited primitive acrylics." SLJ

The **Tooth** Fairy meets El Raton Perez; illustrations by Tom Lintern. Tricycle Press 2010 un il $15.99; lib bdg $18.99
Grades: PreK K 1   E
1. Mice -- Fiction 2. Teeth -- Fiction 3. Fairies -- Fiction 4. Mexican Americans -- Fiction
ISBN 978-1-58246-296-7; 1-58246-296-8; 978-1-58246-342-1 lib bdg; 1-58246-342-5 lib bdg
                                        LC 2009-16782
When Miguel loses a tooth, two legendary characters come to claim it—one who is responsible for collecting teeth in the United States and one who has collected the teeth of the boy's parents and grandparents.
"Lainez's creative story approaches the topic of cultural identity with humor and grace, while newcomer Lintern's colored pencil illustrations give it a sense of nocturnal whimsy." Publ Wkly

Cole, Brock
★ **Buttons**. Farrar, Straus & Giroux 2000 un il hardcover o.p. $16
Grades: K 1 2 3   E
1. Humorous stories 2. Fathers and daughters 3. Father-daughter relationship -- Fiction
ISBN 0-374-31001-7; 0-374-41013-5 pa
                                        LC 99-27162
When their father eats so much that he pops the buttons off his britches, each of his three daughters tries a different plan to find replacements
"A delectable tall tale. . . . Cole's narrative has a humorous lilt that's as much fun as his rollicking illustrations." Horn Book Guide

★ **Good** enough to eat. Farrar, Straus & Giroux 2007 un il $16

Grades: K 1 2 3   E

1. Fairy tales 2. Orphans -- Fiction 3. Homeless persons -- Fiction

ISBN 978-0-374-32737-8; 0-374-32737-8

LC 2006-37368

When an Ogre comes to town demanding a bride, the mayor sacrifices the homeless girl with no name that everyone thinks is a pest and a bother, but she finds a way to outwit them all.

The illustrations offer "lively line and delicate use of color. The cadenced language and blithe illustrations work perfectly together. . . . With the structure of a fairy tale and the freshness of an original story, Good Enough to Eat is satisfying fare indeed." Horn Book

★ **Larky** Mavis. Farrar, Straus & Giroux 2001 un il $16

Grades: K 1 2 3   E

1. Babies 2. Infants -- Fiction

ISBN 0-374-34365-9

LC 00-51419

Having found a tiny baby in a peanut shell, Larky Mavis calls him Heart's Delight and carries him around as he grows bigger, to the confusion and anger of the adults around her

"The prose is lyrical, peppered with quaint speech patterns and lively dialogue that is a delight to read aloud. . . . The rumpled, animated line-and-watercolor illustrations extend the charming story beyond his tightly constructed prose." SLJ

★ The **money** we'll save. Farrar Straus & Giroux 2011 un il $16.99

Grades: K 1 2   E

1. Christmas stories 2. Turkeys -- Fiction 3. Christmas -- Fiction 4. Apartment houses -- Fiction

ISBN 978-0-374-35011-6; 0-374-35011-6

LC 2010037760

In nineteenth-century New York City, when Pa brings home a young turkey in hopes of saving money on their Christmas dinner, his family faces all sorts of trouble—and expense—in their tiny apartment.

"The cleverly constructed text is full of understated humor and witty dialogue, with a satisfying conclusion describing the family's simple but happy Christmas celebration. Cole's loose watercolor-and-ink illustrations skillfully evoke the old-fashioned setting and busy life of a New York tenement community." Kirkus

Cole, Henry

★ **On** Meadowview Street; [by] Henry Cole. Greenwillow Books 2007 un il $17.99; lib bdg $18.89

Grades: K 1 2 3   E

1. Nature -- Fiction 2. Meadows -- Fiction 3. Suburban life -- Fiction

ISBN 978-0-06-056481-0; 0-06-056481-4; 978-0-06-056482-7 lib bdg; 0-06-056482-2 lib bdg

LC 2006023761

Upon moving to a new house, young Caroline and her parents encourage wildflowers to grow and birds and animals to stay in their yard, which soon has the whole suburban street living up to its name

"Cole's understated watercolors match the tale's gentle tone." Booklist

On the way to the beach. Greenwillow Bks. 2003 un il $16.99

Grades: PreK K 1 2   E

1. Nature 2. Nature -- Fiction 3. Ecology -- Fiction 4. Senses and sensation -- Fiction

ISBN 0-688-17515-5

LC 2002-23537

On a walk through the woods and a marsh to the seashore, the reader is encouraged to notice all sorts of plants, animals, insects, and shells

"Each locale . . . is gloriously depicted in a three-page foldout that is entered through a die-cut. . . . The outstanding realistic acrylic illustrations depict the scenes in an almost three-dimensional perspective. . . . This beautiful, interactive book encourages discussion, develops observation skills, and provides a learning experience that will bring children closer to nature." SLJ

Trudy. Greenwillow Books 2009 un il $17.99; lib bdg $18.89

Grades: PreK K 1 2   E

1. Snow -- Fiction 2. Goats -- Fiction

ISBN 978-0-06-154267-1; 0-06-154267-9; 978-0-06-154268-8 lib bdg; 0-06-154268-7 lib bdg

LC 2007-47641

It seems as though Trudy the goat knows when to expect snow, but it turns out that she is really expecting something completely different.

"Cole's acrylic paintings are rounded and soft. They juxtapose muted, earth-toned colors of the environment with the bright, primary colors of manmade objects. . . . The steady pace of the text combined with its loosely repetitive structure creates a calm, reassuring mood, making the book an excellent bedtime read." SLJ

★ **Unspoken**; a story from the Underground Railroad. by Henry Cole. Scholastic Press 2012 40 p. (hardcover: alk. paper) $16.99

Grades: 2 3 4 5   E

1. Fugitive slaves -- Juvenile fiction 2. Underground railroad -- Juvenile fiction 3. United States -- History -- 1861-1865, Civil War -- Juvenile fiction 4. Fugitive slaves -- Fiction 5. African Americans -- Fiction 6. Underground Railroad -- Fiction

ISBN 0545399971; 9780545399975

LC 2011043583

In this worldless picture book about the Underground Railroad by Henry Cole, "a farm child and a fugitive [slave] make an unspoken connection" during the American "Civil War. Going about her chores after watching a detachment of mounted soldiers beneath a Confederate flag trot by, the child is startled and fearful to realize that someone is hiding in a pile of cornstalks in the storehouse. . . . She courageously ventures out by herself, carrying small gifts of food." (Kirkus Reviews)

The **littlest** evergreen. Katherine Tegen Books 2011 un il $16.99; lib bdg $18.89

Grades: PreK K 1 2   E

1. Trees -- Fiction 2. Christmas stories 3. Christmas trees -- Fiction 4. Conservation of natural resources --

Fiction

ISBN 978-0-06-114619-0; 0-06-114619-6; 978-0-06-114620-6 lib bdg; 0-06-114620-X lib bdg

LC 2008022630

"The littlest evergreen, Cole's narrator, is dug out of the earth . . . by men searching for Christmas trees. They forgo using their chainsaw on it, believing it 'too small to make much of a tree,' but a young family purchases it and, after Christmas, replants the pine, which thrives. . . . Preschool, primary." (Horn Book)

"Told from the perspective of a small evergreen, this tale begins with the narrator as a sprout and continues through the seasons until men come with their chainsaws. Luckily, the tree's size saves it from being cut down. . . . Taken to a Christmas tree lot, it is taken home by a family where it is decorated with ornaments and begins to feel loved. After a few weeks, the evergreen is replanted in the yard, where it grows big and strong. Illustrations are of a contemporary setting with nature's beauty brought forth through the lush greenery. A fine Christmas choice with an environmental message." SLJ

Collard, Sneed B.

Butterfly count; illustrated by Paul Kratter. Holiday House 2002 un il $16.95

Grades: K 1 2 3   E

1. Prairies 2. Butterflies 3. Wildlife conservation 4. Butterfly watching 5. Prairies -- Fiction 6. Butterflies -- Fiction 7. Wildlife conservation -- Fiction

ISBN 0-8234-1607-0

LC 2001-24114

Amy and her mother look for a very special butterfly while attending the annual Fourth of July Butterfly Count at a prairie restoration site. Includes factual information about butterflies and how to attract and watch them

"A gentle family story with an environmental message. . . . Soft watercolor illustrations of prairie grasses, plants, and butterflies quietly illuminate this tranquil tale." SLJ

Collier, Bryan

★ **Uptown**. Holt & Co. 2000 un il $16.95

Grades: K 1 2 3   E

1. African Americans -- Fiction

ISBN 0-8050-5721-8

LC 99-31774

Coretta Scott King Award for illustration

A tour of the sights of Harlem, including the Metro-North Train, brownstones, shopping on 125th Street, a barber shop, summer basketball, the Boy's Choir, and sunset over the Harlem River

"Collier's evocative watercolor-and-collage illustrations create a unique sense of mood and place. Bold color choices for text as well as background pages complement engagingly detailed pictures of city life." SLJ

Collins, Pat Lowery

The **Deer** watch; Pat Lowery Collins, illustrated by David Slonim. Candlewick Press 2013 32 p. ill. (reinforced) $15.99

Grades: K 1 2 3   E

1. Deer -- Juvenile fiction 2. Father-son relationship -- Juvenile fiction

ISBN 0763648906; 9780763648909

LC 2012942667

In this children's story, by Pat Lowery Collins, illustrated by David Slonim, "a father promises his young son that this summer they will see a deer. They set out over the dunes, through the marsh, and into the woods, searching for a white-flag tail or a set of leaping legs. But deer are hard to find, especially if your feet want to dance and your nose tickles until you sneeze." (Publisher's note)

Collins, Ross

Dear Vampa; written and illustrated by Ross Collins. Katherine Tegen Books 2009 un il $16.99

Grades: K 1 2   E

1. Letters -- Fiction 2. Vampires -- Fiction

ISBN 978-0-06-135534-9; 0-06-135534-8

LC 2008-22631

A young vampire writes a letter to his grandfather bemoaning his new neighbors

"Collins's . . . black, angular vampires lace the comedy with a drop of real creepiness. . . . Young vampire fans will enjoy (and perhaps be secretly relieved by) the vampires' beleaguered state." Publ Wkly

Doodleday. Albert Whitman 2011 un il $16.99

Grades: PreK K   E

1. Drawing -- Fiction 2. Mother-son relationship -- Fiction

ISBN 978-0-8075-1683-6; 0-8075-1683-X

LC 2010-31128

First published in the United Kingdom

Despite his mother's warning, young Harvey draws on Doodleday, but when his drawings come to life in frightening ways, only his mother can help.

"Collins brings to life the always intriguing notion of art brought to life, giving it a movie-blockbuster level of entertaining disaster. Spare, exclamatory text keeps the focus squarely on the action. . . . Any kid who's put crayon to paper will relish the notion that there's having waiting to be caused thereby." Bull Cent Child Books

Colon, Edie

Good-bye, Havana! Hola, New York! illustrated by Raúl Colón. Simon & Schuster Books for Young Readers 2011 un il $16.99

Grades: PreK K 1   E

1. Immigrants -- Fiction 2. Cuban Americans -- Fiction

ISBN 978-1-4424-0674-2; 1-4424-0674-7; 9781442406742; 1442406747

LC 2010020932

When Fidel Castro's government takes over their restaurant in 1960, six-year-old Gabriella and her parents move from Cuba to New York City.

"In his signature, almost pointillist style, Raúl Colón's earth-toned artwork imbues the story with a comforting texture and warmth, closely depicting the clothing, hair, and décor of the era. The dialogue is smoothly rendered in Spanish and English, and many Spanish words are defined on the final page. This gentle look back at an important time will also speak to contemporary children whose families are starting anew in the United States." Publ Wkly

Comden, Betty

What's new at the zoo? by Betty Comden and Adolph Green; illustrations by Travis Foster; with an introduction by Phyllis Newman. Blue Apple Books 2011 un il $16.99

Grades: K 1 2 3   E
1. Songs 2. Animals -- Songs
ISBN 978-1-60905-088-7; 1-60905-088-6

LC 2011019080

Presents the lyrics to a song from the Broadway musical, 'Do Re Mi,' in which animals in an overcrowded zoo beg to be let out while accidentally stepping on one anothers trunks, quills, and toes.

"With fun lift-the-flap details and tummy-tickling rhymes, this book will appeal to fans of slapstick humor. The cartoon illustrations really bring the silliness to life." SLJ

Compestine, Ying Chang
★ **Boy** dumplings; illustrated by James Yamasaki. Holiday House 2009 un il $16.95
Grades: PreK K 1 2   E
1. Ghost stories 2. Cooking -- Fiction
ISBN 978-0-8234-1955-5; 0-8234-1955-X

LC 2006050064

When a hungry ghost threatens to gobble up a plump little boy, the boy tricks the ghost by convincing him to prepare an elaborate recipe first.

"In keeping with the tale's brisk pacing and light tone, Yamasaki depicts the beaming, succulent boy and the menacing but increasingly beleaguered ghost with particularly comical faces in his cartoon illustrations. . . . [This is a] crowd-pleaser." Booklist

★ The **runaway** rice cake; pictures by Tungwai Chau. Simon & Schuster Bks. for Young Readers 2001 un il $16.95
Grades: K 1 2 3   E
1. Generosity 2. Chinese New Year 3. Chinese New Year -- Fiction
ISBN 0-689-82972-8

LC 99-462168

After chasing the special rice cake, Nian Gao, that their mother has made to celebrate the Chinese New Year, three poor brothers share it with an elderly woman and have their generosity richly rewarded

"Compestine's engaging tale brims with intriguing details of the traditions that surround the holiday. . . . Chau makes a splash with vibrant acrylics whose textured surface and controlled, sophisticated blending of shades mimic the look of pastels." Publ Wkly

★ The **runaway** wok; a Chinese New Year tale. illustrated by Sebastià Serra. Dutton Children's Books 2011 un il $16.99
Grades: K 1 2 3   E
1. Magic -- Fiction 2. Chinese New Year -- Fiction
ISBN 978-0-525-42068-2; 0-525-42068-1

LC 2010013473

On Chinese New Year's Eve, a poor man who works for the richest businessman in Beijing sends his son to market to trade their last few eggs for a bag of rice, but instead he brings home an empty—but magic—wok that changes their fortunes forever. Includes information about Chinese New Year and a recipe for fried rice.

"Inspired by the Danish folktale, The Talking Pot, Compestine's . . . jaunty story takes place long ago in Beijing, which Serra . . . portrays as a bustling, cheerful village. . . . The sight of the insouciant wok carrying away the miserly family . . . will make kids snicker. They'll also chime

in, since the wok's refrain begs for audience participation." Publ Wkly

Conahan, Carolyn
The **big** wish. Chronicle Books 2011 il $16.99
Grades: PreK K 1   E
1. Wishes -- Fiction
ISBN 978-0-8118-7040-5; 0-8118-7040-5

LC 2010027353

When Molly's neighbor, Pie, tries to mow down her dandelions, Molly insists that dandelions aren't weeds they're wishes in the making! Molly is convinced that if she grows enough dandelions she can make the world's biggest wish ever, a world record!

"Conahan's whimsical watercolors, full of swirl and movement, complement her gentle fable of community harmony. Quirky and full of heart." Kirkus

Connor, Leslie
Miss Bridie chose a shovel; illustrated by Mary Azarian. Houghton Mifflin 2004 un il $16
Grades: K 1 2 3   E
1. Immigrants -- Fiction
ISBN 0-618-30564-5

LC 2003-12290

Miss Bridie emigrates to America in 1856 and chooses to bring a shovel, which proves to be a useful tool throughout her life.

"Azarian's sturdy woodcuts are an excellent choice to illustrate daily life in mid-nineteenth-century America, and her pictures catch some of the emotions that the text shies away from. . . . This is a simple pleasure that will be truly appreciated by those old enough to understand the message." Booklist

Conway, David
Lila and the secret of rain; [by] David Conway; illustrated by Jude Daly. Frances Lincoln Children's 2007 un il $16.95
Grades: PreK K 1 2   E
1. Rain -- Fiction 2. Droughts -- Fiction
ISBN 978-1-84507-407-4; 1-84507-407-6

Lila's village in Kenya is experiencing a terrible drought. When Lila's grandfather tells her the secret of rain, she sets off on her own to save her village.

"This quiet story offers inspiration and hope. . . . The illustrations are quite lovely. A huge orange sun in a brilliant blue sky dominates most pages. The prominence of the brown baked earth intensifies the unwanted result of the lack of rain. . . . This story will work well both as a read-aloud and for sharing one-on-one." SLJ

The **great** nursery rhyme disaster; illustrated by Melanie Williamson. Tiger Tales 2009 un il $15.95
Grades: PreK K 1 2   E
1. Nursery rhymes -- Fiction
ISBN 978-1-58925-080-2; 1-58925-080-X

First published 2008 in the United Kingdom

Little Miss Muffet is bored. So she goes off to find a new nursery rhyme to be in. No rhyme seems quite right for Little Miss Muffet. Suddenly life with a scary little spider doesn't seem so bad after all.

"Witty prose and updated interpretations are complemented by Williamson's exuberant illustrations. Colorful, comical, and energetic, the characters race through the pages to the story's end." SLJ

The **most** important gift of all; illustrated by Karin Littlewood. Gingham Dog Press 2006 un il $15.95
Grades: K 1 2 3   E
    1. Love -- Fiction 2. Infants -- Fiction 3. Siblings -- Fiction
ISBN 0-7696-4618-2
"Ama is excited when her baby brother is born, and like all the people of her Kenyan village, she wants to bring him a gift. Because Grandma tells her that love is the most important gift of all, the small girl goes in search of it. . . . The beautiful blend of the traditional storytelling pattern and contemporary realism is expressed in Littlewood's double-page spreads." Booklist

Cook, Lisa Brodie
Peanut butter and homework sandwiches; illustrated by Jack E. Davis. G.P. Putnam's Sons 2011 un il $16.99
    Grades: K 1   E
    1. School stories 2. Homework -- Fiction 3. Teachers -- Fiction 4. Family life -- Fiction
ISBN 978-0-399-24533-6; 0-399-24533-2
         LC 2010026221
When his teacher is out sick for a week, Martin MacGregor has a difficult time with the homework assigned by the substitute teacher.
"Davis' toothy cartoon characters are wonderfully expressive, especially the hapless Martin. The bright color and humorous situations are certain to keep readers' attention as they try to guess what could possibly happen to Martin next." Kirkus

Cooke, Trish
Full, full, full of love; illustrated by Paul Howard. Candlewick Press 2003 un il hardcover o.p. pa $3.99
Grades: PreK K 1   E
    1. Grandmothers 2. African Americans 3. Dinners and dining 4. Grandmothers -- Fiction 5. African Americans -- Fiction
ISBN 0-7636-1851-9; 0-7636-3883-8 pa
         LC 2001-43761
For young Jay Jay, Sunday dinner at Gran's house is full of hugs and kisses, tasty dishes, all kinds of fishes, happy faces, and love
"Howard's generous, full-bleed illustrations capture the loving, bountiful spirit of a big family meal with a colorful palette and expressive eyes and smiles." Booklist

Coombs, Kate
The **secret** -keeper; story by Kate Coombs; paintings by Heather M. Solomon. Atheneum Books for Young Readers 2006 un il $16.95
Grades: 1 2 3 4   E
    1. Fairy tales
ISBN 0-689-83963-4
         LC 2003-24695
The people of Maldinga and the surrounding area bring their deep, dark secrets to Kalli, who keeps them all safe until they become too much for her to bear.
"This original fairy tale is elegantly and tenderly told. . . . Solomon's watercolor and oil paintings are lushly colored.

. . . The intricate details . . . slow and eye and invite repeated viewings." Bull Cent Child Books

Cooney, Barbara
Chanticleer and the fox; adapted and illustrated by Barbara Cooney. Crowell 1958 un il $16.99; lib bdg $17.89; pa $7.99
Grades: K 1 2 3   E
    1. Poets 2. Fables 3. Authors 4. Foxes -- Fiction
ISBN 0-690-18561-8; 0-690-18562-6 lib bdg; 0-06-443087-1 pa
Adaptation of the Nun's Priest's Tale from the Canterbury Tales. Verso of title page
    Awarded the Caldecott Medal, 1959
This adaptation "retains the spirit of the original in its telling and in the beautiful, strongly colored illustrations softened by detailed lines. . . . [It] will be excellent for reading aloud to children." Libr J

Cooper, Elisha
★ **Beach**. Orchard Books 2006 un il $16.99
Grades: PreK K 1 2   E
    1. Beaches -- Fiction 2. Seashore -- Fiction
ISBN 0-439-68785-3
         LC 2005-20195
Women, men, boys, and girls spend a day at the beach enjoying a variety of activities on the sand and in the water.
"Cooper opens with a gorgeous stretch of sand in sun-flecked, amber-white watercolors. . . . His fondness for his subject is evident and infectious." SLJ

Bear dreams. Greenwillow Books 2006 un il $16.99; lib bdg $17.89
Grades: PreK K 1 2   E
    1. Bears -- Fiction 2. Sleep -- Fiction
ISBN 0-06-087428-7; 0-06-087429-5 lib bdg
After a bear cub persuades his friends to play with him instead of hibernating, he gets very tired and falls asleep
"The watercolor-and-pencil illustrations softly portray the transition from fall to winter as well as from wakefulness to slumber. . . . This quiet book with its dreamlike quality is ideal for bedtime sharing." SLJ

Beaver is lost. Schwartz & Wade Books 2010 un il $17.99; lib bdg $20.99
Grades: PreK K 1   E
    1. Beavers -- Fiction
ISBN 978-0-375-85765-2; 0-375-85765-6; 978-0-375-95765-9 lib bdg; 0-375-95765-0 lib bdg
         LC 2009-24915
A lost beaver looks for the way home.
"Beaver's saga unfolds entirely through Cooper's splendid watercolor-and-pencil illustrations. . . . Stunning in their simplicity, these pictures speak a thousand words." Kirkus

★ **Farm**. Orchard Books 2010 un il $17.99
Grades: K 1 2 3   E
    1. Farm life -- Fiction 2. Farm life -- Juvenile literature
ISBN 0-545-07075-9; 978-0-545-07075-1
         LC 2009-04342
This book describes the activities on a family farm from the spring when preparations for planting begin to the autumn when the cats grow winter coats and the cold rains begin to fall. "Ages five to nine." (Bull Cent Child Books)

"Working in his signature style of loosely rendered figures and simple compositions in pencil and watercolor, Cooper combines beautiful expansive views of the farm . . . with small, individual images. . . . Filled with sensory details, the brief text has a poetic, stripped-down simplicity that matches the stark images and will read aloud well." Booklist

★ **Homer**; Elisha Cooper. Greenwillow Books 2012 32 p. col. ill. (trade bdg.) $16.99

Grades: PreK K 1 2   E

1. Dogs -- Fiction 2. Family -- Fiction 3. Picture books for children 4. Contentment -- Fiction 5. Human-animal relationships -- Fiction

ISBN 0062012487; 9780062012487

LC 2011013453

This picture book tells the story of "an aging yellow Lab named Homer . . . [and his] love for his family. . . . At daybreak Homer is already lying on the front porch. . . . As the family members . . . pass by Homer on their way out, they all invite him to come along to play in the water, dig in the sand or bike to the store. Homer replies to each in turn that he is happy to stay right there on the porch. . . . Homer finally curl[s] up in a cozy armchair for the night, content because 'I have everything I want.'" (Kirkus Reviews)

★ **Magic** thinks big. Greenwillow Books 2004 un il $14.99; lib bdg $15.89

Grades: PreK K 1 2   E

1. Cats -- Fiction

ISBN 0-06-058164-6; 0-06-058165-4 lib bdg

LC 2003-12566

A cat sits in the doorway and tries to decide whether to go inside where he might get fed again, go outside where he might have an adventure, or stay where he is.

"The simple text is full of dry humor and whimsy. The dreamy pencil-and-watercolor illustrations are a pleasing mixture of soft colors and thick lines." SLJ

A **good** night walk. Orchard Books 2005 un il $16.99

Grades: PreK K 1 2   E

1. Bedtime -- Fiction 2. Walking -- Fiction

ISBN 0-439-68783-7

LC 2004-23571

The reader is taken on a journey through a neighborhood and shown the sights, sounds, and smells as evening approaches.

"The clear, unfussy compositions echo the poetic words' soothing, elemental sounds . . . which beautifully capture the soft, slowdown rhythms of dusk. Children will find much that's cozy, reassuring, and familiar in the scenes, . . . depicted in luminous watercolors and firmly penciled shapes" Booklist

Cooper, Floyd

Max and the tag-along moon; Floyd Cooper. Philomel Books 2012 32 p. ill. (reinforced) $16.99

Grades: PreK K 1   E

1. Picture books for children 2. Grandparent-grandchild relationship -- Juvenile fiction 3. Grandfathers -- Fiction

ISBN 0399233423; 9780399233425

LC 2011049784

In this children's picture book, "it's hard to leave Granpa's house, but he has a promise for young Max" the 'big fine moon' in the sky 'will always shine for you . . . on and

on!' Granpa seems right for most of the 'swervy-curvy' trip home. . . . Then storm clouds turn the sky dark," and Max begins to worry. "When moon reappears, Max has a deeper understanding of what Granpa's promise means: love, like the moon's light, goes 'on and on.'" (Publishers Weekly)

★ **Willie** and the All-Stars; [by] Floyd Cooper. Philomel Books 2008 un il $16.99

Grades: PreK K 1   E

1. Baseball -- Fiction 2. Race relations -- Fiction 3. African Americans -- Fiction

ISBN 978-0-399-23340-1; 0-399-23340-7

LC 2007042101

In 1934 Chicago, Willie sees a game between the Negro League All-Star team and the Major League All-Stars, and realizes that his dream of becoming a professional baseball player could come true.

"By looking at race relations through the prism of baseball, Cooper will draw readers. . . . The soft-focus sepia-touched artwork, vintage Cooper, is a nice mix of action and nostalgia." Booklist

Cooper, Helen

Delicious! Farrar, Straus and Giroux 2007 un il $16

Grades: PreK K 1 2   E

1. Cats -- Fiction 2. Ducks -- Fiction 3. Cooking -- Fiction 4. Squirrels -- Fiction

ISBN 978-0-374-31756-0; 0-374-31756-9

LC 2006-938789

"Disaster has struck the pumpkin patch—no ripe pumpkins for the animals' favorite dish. The friends decide to make something new to eat, but Duck is unwilling to try either fish soup, mushroom soup, or beet soup (especially offensive because it is pink). Cat tries to trick Duck by mixing a combination of veggies and ingredients that result in a broth that is the exact color of pumpkin soup. . . . The story has universal appeal. . . . The illustrations are warm and rustic, and the layout does an excellent job of mixing full-page portraits and white space." SLJ

★ **Dog** biscuit. Farrar Straus Giroux 2009 un il $16

Grades: PreK K 1   E

1. Dogs -- Fiction 2. Imagination -- Fiction

ISBN 978-0-374-31812-3; 0-374-31812-3

LC 2008-24124

"One day, while Bridget is at Mrs. Blair's house being looked after, she eats a biscuit she finds in the shed—a dog biscuit. Mrs. Blair jokes that she will 'go bowwow and turn into a dog,' and Bridget begins to believe it. . . . A handsome and thoughtfully done layout uses different fonts and sizes for the text, and Cooper's illustrations alternate quiet, ordinary scenes with wild scenes of Bridget's imagination. . . . This is a beautiful and imaginative book for anyone who loves a good story." SLJ

★ **Pumpkin** soup. Farrar, Straus & Giroux 1999 un il hardcover o.p. pa $6.95

Grades: PreK K 1 2   E

1. Cats -- Fiction 2. Ducks -- Fiction 3. Cooking -- Fiction 4. Squirrels -- Fiction

ISBN 0-374-36164-9; 0-374-46031-0 pa

LC 98-18677

First published 1998 in the United Kingdom

The Cat and the Squirrel come to blows with the Duck in arguing about who will perform what duty in preparing their pumpkin soup, and they almost lose the Duck's friendship when he decides to leave them

"Cooper serves up a well-rounded tale told with story-teller's cadences. . . . Rich autumn colors and enchanting details on large spreads and spot illustrations embellish characterizations and setting." SLJ

Other titles about Cat, Squirrel and Duck are:
A pipkin of pepper (2005)
Delicious! (2007)

A **pipkin** of pepper. Farrar Straus Giroux 2005 un il $16
Grades: PreK K 1 2   E
1. Cats -- Fiction 2. Ducks -- Fiction 3. Squirrels -- Fiction 4. City and town life -- Fiction
ISBN 0-374-35953-9
LC 2004-060003
While making pumpkin soup, three friends discover they have no salt and go to the city to buy some, but while Cat and Squirrel head straight to the salt store, Duck pauses at a pepper shop, then fears he will never see his friends again.

"Readers will be reassured by this beguiling rendition of a common childhood experience. The rich coloration and expressive representations of the characters raise this story above the ordinary." SLJ

Cooper, Ilene
The **golden** rule; by Ilene Cooper; illustrated by Gabi Swiatowska. Abrams Books for Young Readers 2007 un il $16.95
Grades: K 1 2 3   E
1. Conduct of life -- Fiction
ISBN 978-0-8109-0960-1; 0-8109-0960-X
LC 2006013333
Grandpa explains that the golden rule is a simple statement on how to live that can be practiced by people of all ages and faiths, then helps his grandson figure out how to apply the rule to his own life.

"The rich, golden paintings and large format reinforce the importance of the topic. . . . Swirling patterns of animal shapes and symbols from various traditions are reminders that the topic is as abstract as the art, with much room for interpretation. This is less a story than a discussion starter, and teachers, parents, and religious leaders will welcome it as a clear introduction to an important subject." SLJ

Copp, Jim
Jim Copp, will you tell me a story? three uncommonly clever tales. as told by Jim Copp; illustrated by Lindsay duPont. Harcourt 2008 54p il $17.95
Grades: 2 3 4   E
1. Short stories 2. Stories in rhyme
ISBN 978-0-15-206331-3; 0-15-206331-5
LC 2007033969
"This collection contains three short stories that were originally recordings by Copp, who died in 1999. The humorous tales, some rhyming, have definite kid appeal. In the first, feisty Kate Higgins refuses to take her medicine and suffers the consequences in the morning. . . . [In] 'Miss Goggins and the Gorilla,' . . . a fourth-grade class is saved from a cruel teacher by a visitor in a gorilla suit. In the last story, forgetful Martha Matilda O'Toole has to keep return-

ing home to get school supplies she's left behind—until her teacher reminds her that it is Sunday. . . . DuPont's pen-and-ink and watercolor illustrations are a perfect match for the quirky stories. . . . Copp's narration on the accompanying CD are a refreshing contrast to the commercialized sound of much of today's children's music." SLJ

Cora, Cat
A **suitcase** surprise for Mommy; pictures by Joy Allen. Dial Books for Young Readers 2011 un il $16.99
Grades: PreK K   E
1. Mother-son relationship -- Fiction
ISBN 978-0-8037-3332-9; 0-8037-3332-1
Mommy must travel for business, and Zoran is not happy—he will miss her too much! But what if he gives Mommy one of his special things to take with her so that she will have a part of him with her when she goes?

"The story's concepts and emotions ring true and are accessibly related through the descriptive narrative, which is filled with realistic dialogue and interactions. . . . The brightly colored, cartoon-style, gouache-and-pencil illustrations include many playful touches that reinforce the comforting tone." Booklist

Cordell, Matthew
★ **Another** brother; written and illustrated by Matthew Cordell. Feiwel and Friends 2012 un il $16.99
Grades: PreK K 1 2   E
1. Sheep -- Fiction 2. Brothers -- Fiction 3. Family life -- Fiction
ISBN 978-0-312-64324-9; 0-312-64324-1
LC 2011001135
Davy the sheep wishes he had time alone with his parents, as he did before his twelve brothers came along and started imitating his every move, but when his wish comes true Davy misses playing with the youngsters.

"This is not just another new-baby book: Cordell's humorous text and mischievously silly, expressive cartoon art will have readers bleating to read it again and again." Kirkus

Trouble gum. Feiwel & Friends 2009 un il $16.99
Grades: K 1 2 3   E
1. Pigs -- Fiction 2. Brothers -- Fiction 3. Chewing gum -- Fiction
ISBN 978-0-312-38774-7; 0-312-38774-1
Playing indoors with his little brother on a rainy day, a rambunctious young pig causes a ruckus and then breaks his mother's three chewing gum rules.

"The simple story line and liberal use of white space open plenty of opportunities for Cordell's winsome art to generate laughs. Even better are the sound effects bouncing around each page." Booklist

Corderoy, Tracey
The **little** white owl; illustrated by Jane Chapman. Good Books 2010 un il $16.99
Grades: PreK K 1   E
1. Owls -- Fiction 2. Imagination -- Fiction 3. Storytelling -- Fiction
ISBN 978-1-56148-693-9; 1-56148-693-0
"Living all alone in a snowy landscape under a starry sky, a little white owl imagines himself as a knight or as a rocket, blasting off to the moon. Those empowering fantasies inspire him to take off one day . . . until he reaches a

group of big beautiful owls in bright-jewel colors. . . . After he tells the snotty birds his magical stories, . . . they are . . . smitten. . . . [The book offers] tropically hued, textured illustrations. . . . Young children will recognize the pain of loneliness, the power of solitude, and the bliss of imaginative play." Booklist

Cordsen, Carol Foskett

★ **Market** day; illustrated by Douglas B. Jones. Dutton Children's Books 2008 un il $16.99

Grades: PreK K 1   E

1. Stories in rhyme 2. Cattle -- Fiction 3. Markets -- Fiction 4. Farm life -- Fiction

ISBN 978-0-525-47883-6; 0-525-47883-3

LC 2007-28489

The Benson family is so busy preparing for their day at a farmers' market that they not only forget to feed the cow, they leave the farmyard gate open and the hungry cow follows them, making a mess of the market.

"It's not often that words and art mesh as well as they do here. . . . The retro-style artwork . . . mixes striking compositions with tints of glowing peach, vegetable green, honey yellow, and other luscious colors. A delightful read-aloud." Booklist

Corey, Shana

Monster parade; a sticker reader. illustrated by Will Terry. Random House 2009 24p il (Step into reading) lib bdg $11.99; pa $3.99

Grades: PreK K 1   E

1. Stories in rhyme 2. Monsters -- Fiction 3. Halloween -- Fiction

ISBN 0-375-85638-2 pa; 978-0-375-95638-6 lib bdg; 0-375-95638-7 lib bdg; 978-0-375-85638-9 pa

LC 2008009718

Children dressed in monster costumes attend a community party, march in a Halloween parade, and go trick-or-treating.

"The bouncy rhymes, featuring kid-pleasing monster noises, encourage participation. With soft, friendly illustrations showing rounded, silly costumes, this is a decidedly non-scary holiday celebration." Horn Book Guide

Players in pigtails; illustrated by Rebecca Gibbon. Scholastic Press 2003 un il $16.95

Grades: K 1 2 3   E

1. Baseball -- Fiction 2. Sex role -- Fiction

ISBN 0-439-18305-7

LC 2002-3445

Katie Casey, a fictional character, helps start the All-American Girls Professional Baseball League, which gave women the opportunity to play professional baseball while America was involved in World War II

"Kids, both girls and boys, will revel in the energy and joy Corey packs into her story. Gibbon's pictures look straight out of the 1940s, with vintage details and an evocative color palette. They also possess a winsome charm that plays nicely with the text." Booklist

Cosentino, Ralph

Superman: the story of the man of steel; written and illustrated by Ralph Cosentino; Superman created by Jerry Siegel & Joe Shuster. Viking 2010 33p il $16.99

Grades: 1 2 3   E

1. Superman (Fictional character) 2. Superheroes -- Fiction

ISBN 978-0-670-06285-0; 0-670-06285-5

"Cosentino acquaints the youngest readers with a comic-book legend. . . . Cosentino presents snapshots that provide a groundwork for understanding Supe's endless print, TV, and movie iterations. Thick-lined new-retro cartoon art in startling primary colors sets off the . . . block-jawed hero. . . . A flashback follows his escape from Krypton, and his boyhood with the Kents features many beloved touchstones. . . . The lineup of his Daily Planet cohorts . . . is followed by the evildoers, who get one double-page spread apiece: Luthor, Metallo, Braniac, and Bizarro." Booklist

Wonder Woman; the story of the Amazon princess. written and illustrated by Ralph Cosentino. Viking 2011 un il $16.99

Grades: 1 2 3   E

1. Wonder Woman (Fictitious character) 2. Superheroes -- Fiction

ISBN 978-0-670-06256-0; 0-670-06256-1

LC 2010024540

Wonder Woman tells how she came to be the protector of humankind, who her enemies are, and how she keeps her identity secret.

"The bold retro artwork has vivid colors and thick black outlines. It's a mix that will work well for the intended audience." SLJ

Cossi, Olga

Pemba Sherpa; Olga Cossi; illustrated by Gary Bernard. Odyssey Books 2009 32p $15.95

Grades: PreK K 1 2   E

1. Siblings -- Fiction 2. Gender role -- Fiction 3. Tibet (China) -- Fiction 4. Himalaya Mountains -- Fiction

ISBN 9780976865582

LC 2009934415

This book take place "[i]n a Himalayan village in Tibet, [where] a young boy rises before dawn to collect firewood. His younger sister, Yang Ki, longs to join him in his task, which is part of the training to be a Sherpa, but the boy scoffs: it isn't girls' work. One morning, . . . Yang Ki disregards her brother's . . . command to stay home, follows him along the steep mountain path, and saves his life when he loses his footing. When Yang Ki carries his heavy load of firewood home, the villagers are astonished, and she . . . grow[s] up to be a famous guide. . . . [T]his . . . story . . . embeds specifics of Tibetan culture as it captures a child's . . . feelings of frustration when she is . . . underestimated, her determination, and her final pleasure when she triumphs." (Booklist)

Costello, David

I can help; [by] David Hyde Costello. Farrar, Straus & Giroux 2010 un il $12.99

Grades: PreK   E

1. Animals -- Fiction 2. Helping behavior -- Fiction

ISBN 978-0-374-33526-7; 0-374-33526-5

LC 2005044321

When a duck gets lost and a monkey helps him find his way, it starts a chain reaction in which all the young animals help each other solve their problems.

"The ink-and-watercolor artwork features simply drawn, brightly colored focal characters set against landscaped backgrounds.... Spare, repetitive text and attractive artwork make this an ideal story hour choice for even the squirmiest group." Booklist

Cote, Genevieve

Me and you. Kids Can Press 2009 un il $16.95
Grades: PreK K   E
1. Pigs -- Fiction 2. Rabbits -- Fiction
ISBN 978-1-55453-446-3; 1-55453-446-1

"A rabbit and a pig decide they want to trade places with one another, so they use art supplies and other items at hand to transform themselves accordingly.... Children will identify with the animals' playful, imaginative antics.... Fans of dress up and creative play, especially, will relate to the story. Moreover, the mixed-media artwork evokes children's drawings and paintings." SLJ

Another title about this rabbit and pig is:
Without out (2011)

Without you. Kids Can 2011 un il
Grades: PreK K   E
1. Pigs -- Fiction 2. Rabbits -- Fiction 3. Friendship -- Fiction
ISBN 1554536200; 9781554536207

"After falling out over a spilled wagon of toys, a fussy bunny and an exuberant piggy explore all the things they can do without each other—and gradually realize that life is much sweeter when it's shared with one another. This gently humorous, charmingly illustrated look at the ups and downs of friendship is a book you won't want to do without." SLJ

Cotten, Cynthia

Rain play; [by] Cynthia Cotten; illustrated by Javaka Steptoe. Henry Holt & Co. 2008 un il $16.95
Grades: PreK K 1 2   E
1. Stories in rhyme 2. Play -- Fiction 3. Rain -- Fiction 4. African Americans -- Fiction
ISBN 978-0-8050-6795-8; 0-8050-6795-7
LC 2007012734

Most people leave the park when rain begins to fall, while others enjoy the sights, sounds, and feel of the cool water—until thunder and lightening come near

"The text is written in rhythmic two-line rhymes.... Steptoe's cut-paper collages are filled with texture and motion. Facial features rendered in paint show the joy that the youngsters feel.... These African-American kids exuberantly jump, splash, run, and puddle-stomp all around the playground." SLJ

This is the stable; illustrated by Delana Bettoli. Holt 2006 un il lib bdg $16.95
Grades: PreK K 1 2   E
1. Stories in rhyme 2. Children's poetry 3. Christmas -- Poetry -- Juvenile literature
ISBN 0-8050-7556-9
LC 2005-19904

Recalls, in rhyming text and illustrations, the Nativity story, from the brown and dusty stable to the star shining brightly above.

"This lovely picture book combines beautiful artwork and a seamless, thoughtful ... style.... The rhyme is sweet but never forced. Bettoli uses a mixture of pastels, primary colors, and earth tones." SLJ

Cottin, Menena

★ The **black** book of colors; by Menena Cottin and Rosana Faria; translated by Elisa Amado. Groundwood/Anansi Books 2008 un il $17.95
Grades: 1 2 3 4   E
1. Blind -- Fiction 2. Color -- Fiction 3. Color -- Juvenile literature
ISBN 978-0-88899-873-6; 0-88899-873-2
Original Spanish edition 2006

"With entirely black pages and a bold white text, this is not your typical color book. Meant to be experienced with the fingers instead of the eyes, this extraordinary book allows sighted readers to experience colors the way blind people do: through the other senses. The text, in both print and Braille, presents colors through touch ... taste ... smell ... and sound.... Faria's distinctive illustrations present black shapes embossed on a black background for readers to feel instead of see.... Fascinating, beautifully designed, and possessing broad child appeal, this book belongs on the shelves of every school or public library committed to promoting disability awareness and accessibility." SLJ

Cottringer, Anne

Eliot Jones, midnight superhero; illustrated by Alex T. Smith. Tiger Tales 2009 un il $15.95; pa $7.95
Grades: PreK K 1 2   E
1. Superheroes -- Fiction
ISBN 978-1-58925-083-3; 1-58925-083-4; 978-1-58925-416-9 pa; 1-58925-416-3 pa

"By day, Eliot is a quiet boy who likes to read, but when the clock strikes midnight, he becomes a superhero. ... Eliot's adventures are fast-paced and exciting. A variety of fonts are used, making the text feel integrated into the action-packed illustrations. Done in vibrant pastel hues, the collage-style spreads match the tone of each adventure and include many details that youngsters will enjoy exploring." SLJ

Cousins, Lucy

★ **Hooray** for fish! Candlewick Press 2005 un il $14.99; $8.99
Grades: PreK K 1   E
1. Fishes -- Fiction
ISBN 0-7636-2741-0; 978-0-7636-3918-1

Little Fish has all sorts of fishy friends in his underwater home, but loves one of them most of all

"This winning title ... features ... bright hues and cheerful, childlike creatures. The stars here are fish, and Cousins matches a gloriously decorated assortment of them with rhyming text that encourages children to look carefully and think about similarities and differences." Booklist

★ **I'm** the best. Candlewick Press 2010 un il $14.99
Grades: PreK K 1   E
1. Dogs -- Fiction 2. Animals -- Fiction 3. Friendship -- Fiction
ISBN 978-0-7636-4684-4; 0-7636-4684-9

When Dog's constant boasting makes his friends sad, they find a way to teach him what it means to be a good friend.

"The book's large format gives plenty of range for Cousins' naive, expressive pencil-and-ink illustrations. From the exuberant text to the bold, colorful artwork, a joyous spirit pervades this picture book and its fallible yet lovable protagonist." Booklist

Maisy goes to preschool. Candlewick Press 2009 un il $12.99
Grades: PreK   E
  1. School stories 2. Mice -- Fiction
ISBN 978-0-7636-4254-9; 0-7636-4254-1

"Maisy is confident and acquainted with the routines of preschool. She clearly has no separation issues. She hangs up her coat, joins in making music, listens to a story, and so on. Throughout the day, the young mouse and her friends have a good time. As always, Cousins's bright color illustrations are simple and appealing." SLJ

Other titles about Maisy are:
Doctor Maisy (2001)
Happy birthday Maisy (2008)
Maisy at the beach (2001)
Maisy at the fair (2001)
Maisy at the farm (2008)
Maisy bakes a cake (2009)
Maisy big, Maisy small (2007)
Maisy, Charlie, and the wobbly tooth (2009)
Maisy cleans up (2002)
Maisy dresses up (1999)
Maisy drives the bus (2000)
Maisy goes camping (2005)
Maisy goes on vacation (2010)
Maisy goes shopping (2001)
Maisy goes swimming (1990)
Maisy goes to bed (2006)
Maisy goes to school (2008)
Maisy goes to the city (2011)
Maisy goes to the hospital (2007)
Maisy goes to the library (2005)
Maisy goes to the museum (2009)
Maisy loves you (2000)
Maisy makes lemonade (2002)
Maisy takes a bath (2000)
Maisy's ABC (2008)
Maisy's amazing book of big words (2007)
Maisy's amazing big book of learning (2011)
Maisy's animals (2007)
Maisy's bedtime (1999)
Maisy's big flap book (2007)
Maisy's book of things that go (2010)
Maisy's Christmas day (2008)
Maisy's favorite animals (2001)
Maisy's morning on the farm (2001)
Maisy's nature walk (1999)
Maisy's pool (2008)
Maisy's show (2010)
Sweet dreams, Maisy (2007)
Vroom, vroom Maisy (2008)
What are you doing, Maisy? (2003)
Where are Maisy's friends? (2000)
Where is Maisy? (2007)

Coville, Bruce
  Hans Brinker; inspired by the novel by Mary Mapes Dodge; retold by Bruce Coville; illustrated by Laurel Long. Dial Books for Young Readers 2007 un il $16.99
Grades: 3 4 5   E
  1. Siblings -- Fiction 2. Ice skating -- Fiction
ISBN 978-0-8037-2868-4
                  LC 2006027109

A Dutch brother and sister work toward two goals, finding the doctor who can restore their father's memory and winning the competition for the silver skates.

"The story's climax . . . is unglamorous yet satisfying. . . . The book's highlight is Long's glowing oil paintings, which are equally effective in illustrating Holland's snowy, glittering landscape and the story's warmer, more intimate family moments." Horn Book

Cowell, Cressida
  ★ **That** rabbit belongs to Emily Brown; written by Cressida Cowell; illustrated by Neal Layton. Hyperion Books for Children 2006 un il hardcover o.p. $16.99
Grades: PreK K 1 2   E
  1. Play -- Fiction 2. Toys -- Fiction 3. Rabbits -- Fiction
ISBN 978-1-4231-0645-6; 1-4231-0645-8
                  LC 2006-49046

Emily defends her stuffed rabbit from the naughty queen who is determined to acquire it any way she can. "Ages four to seven." (Bull Cent Child Books)

"The wacky illustrations, done in collage, pen and ink, and watercolor, perfectly depict the joy and energy of the companions' playtime activities. The exuberant text makes use of various fonts and cartoon-bubble dialogue." SLJ

Cowen-Fletcher, Jane
  Hello puppy! Candlewick Press 2010 un il $12.99
Grades: PreK K 1   E
  1. Dogs -- Fiction
ISBN 978-0-7636-4303-4; 0-7636-4303-3

A child spends time with her new puppy, learning what it means when puppy yawns, stretches, and sniffs.

"The simple sentences are paired with cozy pastel illustrations. The youngster explores the puppy's behavior indoors and out with a special emphasis on play and fun. The story gives young readers a good sense of the responsibility of taking care of a pet." SLJ

Cox, Judy
  Carmen learns English; illustrated by Angela N. Dominguez. Holiday House 2010 un il $16.95
Grades: PreK K 1 2   E
  1. School stories 2. Sisters -- Fiction 3. Immigrants -- Fiction 4. English language -- Fiction 5. Mexican Americans -- Fiction 6. Spanish language -- Vocabulary
ISBN 978-0-8234-2174-9; 0-8234-2174-0
                  LC 2008048462

"Older sister Carmen tells Lupita, who is about to enter kindergarten, about her first day of school, when she could speak only Spanish. She recalls other children teasing her about saying the wrong words or mocking her accent. Yet with a kind teacher's help, Carmen mastered English well enough to teach her new language to Lupita and then to begin to use it at school, where classmates learn Spanish from her. Dominguez's . . . paintings convey a childlike energy and effectively express Carmen's moods. This charming celebration of bilingualism captures both the fears and delights of learning a new tongue." SLJ

Cinco de Mouse-O! illustrated by Jeffrey Ebbeler. Holiday House 2010 un il $16.95
Grades: PreK K 1 2   E
1. Mice -- Fiction 2. Cinco de Mayo -- Fiction
ISBN 978-0-8234-2194-7; 0-8234-2194-5
LC 2008048463
Mouse enjoys the sights and smells of Cinco de Mayo despite being trailed by a determined cat.
"A brief introductory note explains the significance of the holiday, but Cox focuses on the day's celebratory activities, illustrated in Ebbeler's exuberant pictures." Booklist

Go to sleep, Groundhog! illustrated by Paul Meisel. Holiday House 2004 un il $16.95
Grades: PreK K 1 2   E
1. Marmots -- Fiction 2. Groundhog Day -- Fiction
ISBN 0-8234-1645-3
LC 2002-24124
When Groundhog is unable to sleep, he experiences autumn and winter holidays he never knew about, and then he finally falls asleep before Groundhog Day
"An endnote discussing the tradition of using critters as meteorologists makes this a useful as well as a charming answer to the scarcity of engaging material on Groundhog Day." Booklist

Haunted house, haunted Mouse; illustrated by Jeffrey Ebbeler. Holiday House 2011 un il $16.95
Grades: PreK K 1 2   E
1. Mice -- Fiction 2. Halloween -- Fiction
ISBN 0823423158; 9780823423156; 978-0-8234-2315-6; 0-8234-2315-8
LC 2010025312
When three costumed trick-or-treaters come to Mouse's door, he crawls into one of their candy-filled bags to see what Halloween is all about.
"Cox keeps readers turning pages with fast-paced action in her descriptive text. Ebbeler contributes plenty for the eye to feast upon in his bountiful acrylic-on-paper scenes. Readers will delight in the cast of costumed characters populating the pages and get a true feel for Mouse's perspective in both exciting and slightly dire situations." Kirkus

My family plays music; illustrated by Elbrite Brown. Holiday House 2003 un il $17.95
Grades: PreK K 1 2 3   E
1. Musicians -- Fiction 2. Family life -- Fiction 3. Musical instruments -- Fiction
ISBN 0-8234-1591-0
LC 00-44903
A musical family with talents for playing a variety of instruments enjoys getting together to celebrate
"The paper-cut illustrations vibrate with color and—almost—with sound. The multiracial family with its rainbow of skin tones is not only a lovely multicultural statement but also a vivid reflection of contemporary families and musical tastes." Booklist

One is a feast for Mouse; a Thanksgiving tale. illustrated by Jeffrey Ebbeler. Holiday House 2008 un il $16.95; pa $6.95
Grades: PreK K 1 2   E
1. Cats -- Fiction 2. Mice -- Fiction 3. Thanksgiving Day -- Fiction
ISBN 978-0-8234-1977-7; 0-8234-1977-0; 978-0-8234-2231-9 pa; 0-8234-2231-3 pa
LC 2007-13972
On Thanksgiving Day while everyone naps, Mouse spots one pea, a perfect feast, but he cannot help adding all of the fixings—until Cat spots him
"Whimsical, large-scale illustrations drawn in acrylics, pastels, and colored pencils are a perfect complement to the story. Plenty of action and humor as well as a thoroughly satisfying ending make this a wonderful holiday read-aloud." SLJ
Other titles about Mouse are:
Cinco de Mouse-O! (2010)
Haunted house, haunted Mouse (2011)

Coxe, Molly
Benjamin and Bumper to the rescue; photographs by Olivier Toppin. BraveMouse Books 2010 un il $17.95
Grades: PreK K 1 2   E
1. Animals -- Fiction
ISBN 978-0-9819697-1-8; 0-9819697-1-8

Coy, John
Hoop genius; how a desperate teacher and a rowdy gym class invented basketball. by John Coy; illustrated by Joe Morse. Carolrhoda Books 2013 32 p. (reinforced) $16.95
Grades: 2 3 4 5 6   E
1. Basketball 2. Picture books for children 3. Basketball -- United States -- History -- Juvenile literature
ISBN 0761366172; 9780761366171
LC 2011021235
This children's picture book looks at the invention of basketball. "In 1891, a teacher named James Naismith invented a game that was destined to become a national sensation. The boys' gym class at his school was particularly rowdy. He needed to find an indoor activity for the energetic lads that was fun, but not too rough. Inspired by a favorite childhood game, he stayed up late one night typing the rules of his new game." The class was captivated and the game's popularity spread. (School Library Journal)

★ **Strong** to the hoop; illustrations by Leslie Jean-Bart. Lee & Low Bks. 1999 un il hardcover o.p. pa $8.95
Grades: 2 3 4 5   E
1. African Americans 2. Basketball -- Fiction
ISBN 1-880000-80-6; 1-58430-178-3 pa
LC 98-33264
Ten-year-old James tries to hold his own and prove himself on the basketball court when the older boys finally ask him to join them in a game
"Coy's text moves with all the free-wheeling speed of playground ball. . . . Best of all, though, are Jean-Bart's collage-style illustrations, produced by combining Polaroid photographs and scratchboard drawings." Booklist

Craig, Lindsey
Dancing feet! illustrations by Marc Brown. Knopf 2010 un il $16.99

Grades: PreK   E

  1. Stories in rhyme 2. Dance -- Fiction 3. Animals -- Fiction

  ISBN 978-0-375-86181-9; 0-375-86181-5

"Children are asked to guess who's dancing across a spread by looking at clues in the artwork and listening to the rhymes. . . . Brown uses hand-painted paper collage and primary shapes to create all of the happy dancers. A surprise pairing of partners ends this cheerful story and acts as a motivator to get children moving." SLJ

Farmyard beat; illustrations by Marc Brown. Alfred A. Knopf 2011 un il $15.99; lib bdg $18.99

Grades: PreK K   E

  1. Stories in rhyme 2. Bedtime -- Fiction 3. Domestic animals -- Fiction

  ISBN 978-0-375-86455-1; 0-375-86455-5; 978-0-375-96455-8 lib bdg; 0-375-96455-X lib bdg

                        LC 2010016123

The sounds of the farm animals create a lively beat that keep Farmer Sue, the chicks, sheep, and other farm animals awake.

"The repetition, rhythm, and sounds of the words are a big part of the fun in this picture book and will have toddlers chanting along." Booklist

Crews, Donald

  ★ **Harbor**. Greenwillow Bks. 1982 un il hardcover o.p. pa $6.99

Grades: PreK K 1   E

  1. Ships 2. Harbors

  ISBN 0-688-00862-3 lib bdg; 0-688-07332-8 pa

                        LC 81-6607

This book "is an exciting, educational and beautiful show-and-tell. . . . The full-page, full-color paintings will delight children." Publ Wkly

  ★ **Night** at the fair; pictures and words by Donald Crews. Greenwillow Bks. 1998 un il $17.99

Grades: PreK K 1 2   E

  1. Fairs -- Fiction 2. Night -- Fiction

  ISBN 0-688-11483-0

                       LC 96-48780

Nighttime is a wonderful time to enjoy the lights, the games, and the rides at a fair

"Each borderless double-page spread bursts with color and light and action and noise. . . . A minimal text acts for the most part as captioning or clues us in to what's coming next in this truly spectacular visual experience." Horn Book Guide

  ★ **Parade**. Greenwillow Bks. 1983 un il hardcover o.p. pa $6.99

Grades: PreK K 1   E

  1. Parades

  ISBN 0-688-01996-X lib bdg; 0-688-06520-1 pa

                       LC 82-20927

Illustrations and brief text present the various elements of a parade-the spectators, street vendors, marchers, bands, floats, and the cleanup afterwards.

The author/illustrator's "refined poster-art approach to evoking an event works again here. . . . A polished assem-

bly of crisp shapes, effective compositions, and pure, bright color." Booklist

  ★ **Sail** away. Greenwillow Bks. 1995 un il $17.99; pa $6.99

Grades: PreK K 1   E

  1. Sailing -- Fiction

  ISBN 0-688-11053-3; 0-688-17517-1 pa

                        LC 94-6004

A family takes an enjoyable trip in their sailboat and watches the weather change throughout the day

"To read any Crews book is to be immersed in sights and sounds vividly rendered and perfectly phrased, and this book proves no exception. The paintings move and swell; the words are haiku-like in their efficiency and implication." Horn Book

  ★ **School** bus. Greenwillow Bks. 1984 un il $16.99; lib bdg $17.89; pa $6.99; bd bk $7.99

Grades: PreK K 1   E

  1. School stories 2. Buses -- Fiction

  ISBN 0-688-02807-1; 0-688-02808-X lib bdg; 0-688-12267-1 pa; 0-694-01690-X bd bk

                        LC 83-18681

Follows the progress of school buses as they take children to school and bring them home again

"The author-artist cleverly avoids monotony in his subject matter by using different size buses and a pleasing variety of background, perspectives, and the directions in which they travel. . . . The . . . yellow of the buses provides both a unifying element and a contrast for the cheerful colors of the children's clothing and for the bustle of city streets." Horn Book

  ★ **Shortcut**. Greenwillow Bks. 1992 un il $17.99; lib bdg $18.89; pa $6.99

Grades: K 1 2   E

  1. Railroads -- Fiction 2. African Americans -- Fiction

  ISBN 0-688-06436-1; 0-688-06437-X lib bdg; 0-688-813576-5 pa

                        LC 91-36312

Children taking a shortcut by walking along a railroad track find excitement and danger when a train approaches

"The story . . . is a perfect foil for the artist's masterful renderings of trains. . . . Scenes portraying the frightened children are equally effective in this out of the ordinary drama set forth with uncommon artistry." Publ Wkly

Ten black dots; rev ed; Greenwillow Bks. 1986 un il $16.99; lib bdg $17.89; pa $6.99; bd bk $7.99 E

  1. Counting 2. Stories in rhyme

  ISBN 0-688-06067-6; 0-688-06068-4 lib bdg; 0-688-13574-9 pa; 978-0-06-185779-9 bed bk

                        LC 85-14871

A revision of the title first published 1968

"In this basic counting book . . . large black dots appear as an integral part of each illustrated subject. For example, 'Five dots can make buttons on a coat . . . or the port-holes of a boat.' This simple concept succeeds admirably through the bold, flat colors and briskly delineated graphics of Crews' illustrations." Booklist

  ★ **Truck**. Greenwillow Bks. 1980 un il $16.99; lib

bdg $17.89; pa $6.99; bd bk $7.99

Grades: PreK K 1   E

1. Trucks 2. Stories without words 3. Trucks -- Fiction

ISBN 0-688-80244-3; 0-688-84244-5 lib bdg; 0-688-10481-9 pa; 0-688-15597-9 bd bk

LC 79-19031

A Caldecott Medal honor book, 1981

"Although there is no text, the story is far from wordless; trucks, buses, and vans are emblazoned with letters and emblems, the streets are lined with familiar traffic signs, and a truck stop is festooned with advertisements in neon lights. . . . [This is] an imaginative, almost pop-art view of mobile America." Horn Book

Crews, Nina

Below. Henry Holt 2006 un il $16.95

Grades: PreK K 1 2   E

1. Toys -- Fiction 2. Imagination -- Fiction

ISBN 0-8050-7728-6; 978-0-8050-7728-5

LC 2005-12128

"Crews uses digitally manipulated photos and line drawings along with brief text to relate the adventures of Jack and his action-figure toy, Guy. . . . One day Guy falls through a hole in the stairs. . . . The child uses his crane and other action figures to effect a rescue. . . . This story . . . will surely inspire young readers to see everyday objects in a new light." SLJ

Another title about Guy is:

Sky-high Guy (2010)

Sky-high Guy. Henry Holt 2010 un il $16.99

Grades: PreK K 1 2   E

1. Play -- Fiction 2. Toys -- Fiction 3. Brothers -- Fiction 4. Imagination -- Fiction

ISBN 978-0-8050-8764-2; 0-8050-8764-8

LC 2009012218

Jack likes to play with his action figure Guy without the interference of his little brother Gus, but when Guy gets stuck in a tree, Gus is the perfect companion to help Jack rescue him.

"The authenticity of Crew's illustrations makes it easy for readers to access Jack's imagination. . . . Threats are depicted as white line drawings over color photographs that blend reality and imagination perfectly." SLJ

Crimi, Carolyn

Dear Tabby; illustrated by David Roberts. Harper 2011 un il $16.99

Grades: PreK K 1 2   E

1. Cats -- Fiction 2. Animals -- Fiction 3. Journalists -- Fiction

ISBN 978-0-06-114245-1; 0-06-114245-X

LC 2007041935

A feline advice columnist assists other animals with their problems, such as a parrot whose owners complain that he talks too much, a groundhog who feels the pressure of predicting the weather, and a cat who objects to being pampered.

"Roberts' playful artwork provides many details that extend and enhance Crimi's clever text." Booklist

Rock 'n' roll Mole; pictures by Lynn Munsinger. Dial Books for Young Readers 2011 il $16.99

Grades: PreK K 1   E

1. Musicians -- Fiction 2. Rock music -- Fiction 3.

Moles (Animals) -- Fiction

ISBN 978-0-8037-3166-0; 0-8037-3166-3

LC 2010028796

Mole has a "rock-and-roll soul" and the groupies to prove it, but when his friend Pig organizes a talent show, Mole's stagefright may prevent him from performing.

"Munsinger's charming band of characters includes a break-dancing pig, a skateboarding raccoon, and a trio of swooning chicks. The watercolor illustrations are full of witty details." SLJ

Cronin, Doreen

Bounce; illustrated by Scott Menchin. Atheneum Books for Young Readers 2007 un il $14

Grades: PreK K 1   E

1. Dogs -- Fiction

ISBN 978-1-4169-1627-7; 1-4169-1627-X

LC 2005-37128

"Readers are invited to jump, hop, leap, and bounce balls off their noses and toes along with the playful pooch. Rhymes weave in and out of the pen-and-ink and digitally colored spreads. The cartoon art is eye-catching and as playful as the text." SLJ

★ **Click,** clack, moo; cows that type. pictures by Betsy Lewin. Simon & Schuster Bks. for Young Readers 2000 un il $15

Grades: PreK K 1 2   E

1. Cows 2. Cattle -- Fiction 3. Farm life -- Fiction

ISBN 0-689-83213-3

LC 97-29718

A Caldecott Medal honor book, 2001

When Farmer Brown's cows find a typewriter in the barn they start making demands, and go on strike when the farmer refuses to give them what they want

"A laugh-out-loud look at life on a very funny farm. . . . Lewin's hilarious cartoons deftly capture the farmer's exasperation and the animals' sheer determination." SLJ

Other titles about Farmer Brown's animals are:

Giggle, giggle, quack (2002)

Click, clack, quackity quack (2005)

Click, clack, splish, splash (2006)

Dooby, dooby, moo (2006)

Thump, quack, moo (2008)

★ **Diary** of a fly; pictures by Harry Bliss. Joanna Cotler Books 2007 un il $15.99; lib bdg $16.89

Grades: PreK K 1 2   E

1. Flies -- Fiction

ISBN 978-0-06-000156-8; 0-06-000156-9; 978-0-06-000157-5 lib bdg; 0-06-000157-7 lib bdg

LC 2006-36064

A young fly discovers, day by day, that there is a lot to learn about being an insect, including the dangers of flyswatters and that heroes come in all shapes and sizes.

"The attention to detail . . . and a lively layout that has a comic-book vibe are sure to appeal." SLJ

★ **Diary** of a spider; pictures by Harry Bliss. Joanna Cotler Books 2005 un il $15.99; lib bdg $16.89

Grades: PreK K 1 2   E

1. Spiders -- Fiction

ISBN 0-06-000153-4; 0-06-000154-2 lib bdg

LC 2004-11549

A young spider discovers, day by day, that there is a lot to learn about being a spider, including how to spin webs and avoid vacuum cleaners.

"The amusing pen-and-ink and watercolor cartoons, complete with funny asides in dialogue balloons, expand the sublime silliness of some of the scenarios." SLJ

★ **Diary** of a worm; pictures by Harry Bliss. Harper-Collins Pubs. 2003 un il $15.99; lib bdg $16.89
Grades: PreK K 1 2   E
  1. Worms -- Fiction
  ISBN 0-06-000150-X; 0-06-000151-8 lib bdg
                                          LC 2002-7949
A young worm discovers, day by day, that there are some very good and some not so good things about being a worm in this great big world

"Bliss's droll watercolor illustrations are a marvel. He gives each worm an individual character with a few deft lines. . . . Inventive and laugh-out-loud funny, this worm's-eye view of the world will be a sure-fire hit." Publ Wkly

★ **Duck** for President; illustrated by Betsy Lewin. Simon & Schuster Books for Young Readers 2004 un il $15.95
Grades: PreK K 1 2   E
  1. Ducks 2. Elections 3. Ducks -- Fiction 4. Politics, Practical 5. Elections -- Fiction
  ISBN 0-689-86377-2
                                          LC 2003-21923
When Duck gets tired of working for Farmer Brown, his political ambition eventually leads to his being elected President.

"Lewin's characteristic humorous watercolors with bold black outlines fill the pages with color and jokes. Cronin's text is hilarious for kids and adults and includes a little math and quite a bit about the electoral process." SLJ

Stretch; illustrated by Scott Menchin. Atheneum Books for Young Readers 2009 un il $15.99
Grades: PreK K 1   E
  1. Stories in rhyme 2. Dogs -- Fiction 3. Yoga -- Fiction 4. Animals -- Fiction
  ISBN 978-1-416-95341-8; 1-416-95341-8
                                          LC 2007044476
"The potbellied canine from Wiggle (2005) and Bounce (2007) learns a new move in this colorful definition (and re-definition) of the word stretch. . . . Our doggie narrator leads a mixed-species yoga session. . . . Fine, sharp illustrations of the dog and other animals are combined with photographic elements . . . and the result is playful and wildly colorful." Booklist

★ **Wiggle**; art by Scott Menchin. Atheneum Books for Young Readers 2005 un il $12.95
Grades: PreK K 1   E
  1. Stories in rhyme 2. Dogs -- Fiction
  ISBN 0-689-86375-6
                                          LC 2004-3326
"A spotted dog on the cover, vigorously working a hula hoop, leads children through a wiggling world. . . . The de-lightful cartoon-style, ink-and-watercolor artwork is high-lighted by tidbits of collage. . . . Every candy-colored page features the funny, frenetic dog involved in some furious

activity, and the sense of motion and movement is palpable each time." Booklist
  Other titles about this dog are:
  Bounce (2007)
  Stretch (2009)

Crosby, Jeff
  Wiener wolf. Hyperion Books 2011 32p il $15.99
Grades: PreK K 1   E
  1. Dogs -- Fiction 2. Pets -- Fiction 3. Wolves -- Fiction
  ISBN 978-1-4231-3983-6; 1-4231-3983-6
Weiner Dog's life of leisure has lost its bite. So when he hears the call of the wild one day, he answers! Thus Weiner Dog becomes Weiner Wolf.

"Crosby employs an array of techniques in his visual storytelling, from the way Wiener Dog appears to run right out of spot illustrations to the hilarious contrast between the turtleneck sweater wearing dog and the slavering wolves. This wiener's a winner." Publ Wkly

Crow, Kristyn
  Bedtime at the swamp. HarperCollins Children's 2008 un il $16.99
Grades: PreK K 1 2   E
  1. Bedtime -- Fiction 2. Mothers -- Fiction 3. Monsters -- Fiction 4. Wetlands -- Fiction
  ISBN 978-0-06-083952-9; 0-06-083952-X
It's bedtime at the swamp—except somebody's not ready. Somebody's still splashing in the water and the mud. Is there a monster on the loose?

"Lively, colorful cartoon characters set in inky black or deep blue moonlit scenes and offset by crisp, white pages add energy and suspense to the story. The repetitive chorus, a simple rhyming story line that will draw readers in, and the perennial appeal of books that are just 'scary' enough make this title an appropriate addition." SLJ

★ **Cool** Daddy Rat; [by] Kristyn Crow; illustrated by Mike Lester. Putnam 2008 un il $16.99
Grades: PreK K 1 2   E
  1. Stories in rhyme 2. Rats -- Fiction 3. Musicians -- Fiction 4. Jazz music -- Fiction
  ISBN 978-0-399-24375-2; 0-399-24375-5
                                          LC 2006020533
A young rat hides in his father's bass case and tags along as he plays and scats around the big city.

This "hip ode to jazz (and scat in particular) will sweep up its audience in its catchy beat as kinetic cartoon art adds verve and wit. . . . Lester's . . . computer-assisted watercolor illustrations in a heady palette show characters seemingly in perpetual motion." Publ Wkly

The **middle**-child blues; illustrated by David Catrow. G.P. Putnam's Sons 2009 un il $16.99
Grades: K 1 2   E
  1. Children's songs 2. Stories in rhyme 3. Siblings -- Fiction 4. Birth order -- Fiction 5. Blues music -- Fiction
  ISBN 978-0-399-24735-4; 0-399-24735-1
                                          LC 2008-30591
A boy named Lee sings about all the miserable aspects of being a middle child.

"Catrow's trademark pencil and watercolor illustrations are perfect for this story. Heads are oversized, and facial expressions exaggerated. The colorful illustrations dance all over the pages. This book is a winner." SLJ

Crowley, Ned

Nanook & Pryce; gone fishing. pictures by Larry Day. HarperCollinsPublishers 2009 un il $16.99
Grades: PreK K 1 2   E
1. Stories in rhyme 2. Adventure fiction 3. Friendship -- Fiction 4. Marine animals -- Fiction 5. Voyages and travels -- Fiction
ISBN 978-0-06-133641-6; 0-06-133641-6; 978-0-06-133642-3 lib bdg; 0-06-133642-4 lib bdg
                                                    LC 2008032095
Parka-clad friends Nanook and Pryce and their dog Yukon encounter many different types of ocean life and adventure on an unexpected voyage.

"Crowley's perfectly rhymed narrative about an accidental adventure is both minimal and evocative, and Day's watercolor and line illustrations turn some very funny text into a hilarious book." SLJ

Crowther, Robert

Amazing pop-up trucks. Candlewick Press 2011 il $17.99
Grades: PreK K   E
1. Trucks 2. Pop-up books
ISBN 978-0-7636-5587-7; 0-7636-5587-2
"Crowther offers formidable pop-ups of a car transporter, a cement mixer, a monster truck, a 'rubbish' truck, and truck trains. Each spread contains a description of the featured vehicle and its primary function, while flaps offer photographs along with additional information about how the trucks operate. . . . The brightly colored vehicles, which include working door/window flaps, and real-life details should give truck enthusiasts a gratifying peek into the world of big rigs." Publ Wkly

★ **Opposites**. Candlewick Press 2005 un il $12.99
Grades: PreK K 1   E
1. Opposites
ISBN 0-7636-2783-6
"Each page features a word and readers must take some action—pulling a tab or turning a wheel—to discover its opposite. The pictures incorporate easy-to-understand examples in creative ways. . . . Warmly colored backgrounds and simply rendered images keep kids' attention focused on the task at hand, and the volume's sturdy pages and reinforced tabs will survive lots of use." SLJ

The **most** amazing hide-and-seek alphabet book. Candlewick Press 2010 un il $12.99
Grades: PreK K 1   E
1. Alphabet 2. Animals -- Fiction
ISBN 978-0-7636-5030-8; 0-7636-5030-7
First published 1999
This "pull-the-tab [book features a] clean, attractive [cover] and sturdy paper-on-board construction. The solid black letters . . . on white pages reveal colorful creatures when tabs are pulled and animals peek out. [The book is] cleverly designed and visually appealing." Horn Book Guide

The **most** amazing hide-and-seek numbers book. Candlewick Press 2010 un il $12.99
Grades: PreK K 1   E
1. Numbers 2. Animals -- Fiction
ISBN 978-0-7636-5029-2; 0-7636-5029-3
First published 1999
This "pull-the-tab [book features a] clean, attractive [cover] and sturdy paper-on-board construction. The solid black . . . numbers on white pages reveal colorful creatures when tabs are pulled and animals peek out. [The book is] cleverly designed and visually appealing." Horn Book Guide

Croza, Laurel

I know here; pictures by Matt James. Groundwood Books 2010 un il $18.95
Grades: K 1 2 3   E
1. Moving -- Fiction
ISBN 978-0-88899-923-8; 0-88899-923-2
Boston Globe-Horn Book Award: Picture Book (2010)
A tale about a young girl whose family moves from the forests of northeastern Saskatchewan to a strange new place called "Toronto."

"James's vividly colored, naive-style scenes capture the bright intensity of the child's inner and outer landscapes and also the unaffected way in which she observes them. Good for sharing." Kirkus

Cruise, Robin

Bartleby speaks! pictures by Kevin Hawkes. Farrar, Straus and Giroux 2009 un il $16.99
Grades: PreK K 1   E
1. Growth -- Fiction 2. Family life -- Fiction 3. Grandfathers -- Fiction
ISBN 978-0-374-30514-7; 0-374-30514-5
                                                    LC 2008-17235
As he grows from infancy to three-years of age, Bartleby Huddle remains quiet, not speaking a word, until the day Grampy Huddle arrives and discovers the solution

"Hawkes accompanies Cruise's gently pointed text with characteristically comic line-and-color cartoons, varying vignettes with full and double-page spreads that focus readers' attention exactly where it needs to be, modulating noise and silence through artful pacing. A sweetly underscored paean to the beauty of quiet." Kirkus

Little Mama forgets; illustrated by Stacey Dressen-McQueen. Farrar, Straus and Giroux 2006 32p il $16
Grades: PreK K 1 2   E
1. Memory -- Fiction 2. Family life -- Fiction 3. Grandmothers -- Fiction 4. Mexican Americans -- Fiction
ISBN 0-374-34613-5
                                                    LC 2004-40462
Although her Mexican-American grandmother now forgets many things, Luciana finds that she still remembers the things that are important to the two of them. Includes glossary of Spanish words used

"The story is bittersweet, but Lucy's ability to look on the bright side, and the obvious love that she and Little Mama share, wrap the events in affection and warmth. Dressen-McQueen's artwork is outstanding. . . . The Mexican family . . . comes alive in pictures that show the vibrancy of the happy household." Booklist

Crum, Shutta

Dozens of cousins; by Shutta Crum; illustrated by David Catrow. Clarion Books 2013 32 p. col. ill. (reinforced) $16.99

Grades: PreK K 1 2   E

1. Family reunions -- Fiction 2. Cousins -- Juvenile fiction 3. Cousins -- Fiction 4. Behavior -- Fiction

ISBN 061815874X; 9780618158744

LC 2012005010

This book, written by Shutta Crum and illustrated by David Catrow, focuses on an "annual family reunion, and . . . dozens of cousins are running wild. They hug fluttering aunts and soft-spoken elders, play in the creek, shimmy up trees [and] take 'double-dog dares.' Hilarious side stories unfold in Catrow's . . . colorful, chaotic spreads that gambol and splash with comical caricatures of grinning kinfolk large and small." (Publisher's note)

★ Mine! story by Shutta Crum; pictures by Patrice Barton. Knopf 2011 un il $16.99

Grades: PreK   E

1. Infants -- Fiction 2. Siblings -- Fiction

ISBN 978-0-375-86711-8; 0-375-86711-2

A preschooler "and an enthralled baby are placed in a room with a collection of toys and a bemused canine observer. . . . The preschooler quickly lays claim to everything in sight. . . . The discovery of the dog's water dish turns the story into a giddy, soppy free-for-all that culminates in the baby taking its (presumed) first steps to tackle the preschooler, while shrieking 'MINE' in utter adoration. Crum . . . uses only the title word . . . but the various inflections speak volumes about the comic dynamics of sharing. . . . [Barton's] dizzyingly expressive digitized pencil sketches seem to be everywhere at once, continually reframing the action to make sure readers savor every gleefully anarchic moment." Publ Wkly

★ Thunder-Boomer! illustrated by Carol Thompson. Clarion Books 2009 32p il $16

Grades: PreK K 1 2   E

1. Farm life -- Fiction 2. Family life -- Fiction 3. Thunderstorms -- Fiction

ISBN 978-0-618-61865-1; 0-618-61865-1

LC 2008-10478

A farm family scurries for shelter from a violent thunderstorm that brings welcome relief from the heat and also an unexpected surprise.

"Thompson's illustrations, done in pastels, ink, and watercolor, are full of motion and capture the sensations. . . . The free-verse storytelling is light, airy, and perfectly matched to the drawings." SLJ

Crummel, Susan Stevens

★ The Little Red Pen; written by Janet Stevens and Susan Stevens Crummel; illustrated by Janet Stevens. Harcourt Children's Books 2011 un il $16.99

Grades: PreK K 1 2   E

1. School stories 2. Office equipment and supplies -- Fiction

ISBN 978-0-15-206432-7; 0-15-206432-X

LC 2010009062

When a little red pen accidentally falls into the waste basket while trying to correct papers all by herself, the other classroom supplies must cooperate to rescue her.

"Steven's humor-filled watercolors are busy and active, especially since each character is a familiar object with its own personality, facial and body expressions, color, and even typeface. . . . A rollicking read-aloud." Horn Book

Ten-Gallon Bart beats the heat; illustrated by Dorothy Donohue. Marshall Cavendish 2010 il $17.99

Grades: K 1 2 3   E

1. Dogs -- Fiction 2. Animals -- Fiction 3. Blizzards -- Fiction

ISBN 978-0-7614-5634-6

LC 2009006342

Tired of the blistering heat in Dog City, Ten-Gallon Bart departs for the frozen north, where he gets lost in a blizzard.

Cummings, Pat

Harvey Moon, museum boy; written and illustrated by Pat Cummings. HarperCollinsPublishers 2008 un il $16.99; lib bdg $17.89

Grades: PreK K 1 2   E

1. Stories in rhyme 2. Lizards -- Fiction 3. Museums -- Fiction 4. African Americans -- Fiction

ISBN 978-0-688-17889-5; 0-688-17889-8; 978-0-06-057861-9 lib bdg; 0-06-057861-0 lib bdg

LC 2004030056

When Harvey and his pet lizard Zippy go on a school field trip, Zippy gets loose in the museum and they have a harrowing adventure

"A lively read-aloud." Booklist

Another title about Harvey Moon is:

Clean your room, Harvey Moon (1991)

Cummings, Phil

Boom bah! [text by Phil Cummings; illustrations by Nina Rycroft] Kane Miller 2010 un il $15.99

Grades: PreK K   E

1. Music -- Fiction 2. Orchestra -- Fiction 3. Domestic animals -- Fiction

ISBN 1-935279-22-X; 978-1-935279-22-8

First published 2008 in Australia

After a tiny mouse taps a cup with a spoon and creates a noise, everyone wants to join in. Follow the band as it gathers and grows from a solo perfomance to an explosive, full-scale orchestra.

"Cummings's minimal text moves along in clipped phrases, punctuated by onomatopoeic effects, creating a splendid read-aloud chant. Rycroft's buoyant watercolors, arranged gracefully against expansive white space, add zest. Even the youngest readers should be able to handle the simple text and catch the rhythm." Kirkus

Cummings, Troy

Giddy-up, daddy! written and illustrated by Troy Cummings. 1st ed. Random House Inc. 2013 40 p. col. ill. (library) $19.99; (hardcover) $16.99

Grades: PreK K 1 2   E

1. Picture books for children 2. Father-child relationship -- Juvenile fiction 3. Play -- Fiction 4. Humorous stories 5. Imagination -- Fiction 6. Father and child -- Fiction

ISBN 0375971297; 9780375971297; 9780307978561

LC 2012009236

In this children's picture book, the "childhood game of 'horsey' leaps into outlandish territory as a bespectacled, bald, and very accommodating father eagerly bounds about with his daughter and diapered son riding on his back. . . . When two horse rustlers lure Dad away with sugar cubes, it's up to the kids to rescue him from the rodeo, after which their adventures take them to the Kentucky Derby, a polo match, the circus, and exotic—Canada." (Publishers Weekly)

The **eensy** weensy spider freaks out (big time!) written and illustrated by Troy Cummings. Random House 2010 un il $16.99; lib bdg $19.99

Grades: 1 2 3   E
1. Fear -- Fiction 2. Spiders -- Fiction 3. Ladybugs -- Fiction
ISBN 978-0-375-86582-4; 0-375-86582-9; 978-0-375-96582-1 lib bdg; 0-375-96582-3 lib bdg

Frightened after the scary waterspout incident, the Eensy Weensy Spider needs some encouragement from her friend the ladybug before she will try climbing again.

"The lively text and whimsical, cartoon-style illustrations include periodic word balloons . . . that advance the story line. The vibrant settings and expressive insects have a retro flair, while the varying perspectives add to the fun." Booklist

Cumpiano, Ina

Quinito's neighborhood; story Ina Cumpiano; illustrations by José Ramirez. Children's Book Press 2005 22p il $16.95

Grades: PreK K 1 2   E
1. Occupations -- Fiction 2. Bilingual books -- English-Spanish
ISBN 0-89239-209-6

Quinito not only knows everyone in his neighborhood, he also knows that each person in his community has a different, important occupation

"Ramírez's vibrant acrylic-on-canvas paintings bring this community to life, the primitive forms fairly bursting from the book's pages with their deep hues and sense of emotional warmth. The simple text, equally good in both English and Spanish, is in a font that resembles a child's printing." SLJ

Another title about Quinito is:
Quinito, day and night (2008)

Cunnane, Kelly

★ **Chirchir** is singing. Schwartz & Wade Books 2011 un il $17.99

Grades: PreK K 1 2   E
1. Singing -- Fiction 2. Family life -- Fiction
ISBN 978-0-375-86198-7; 0-375-86198-X

This book, set in Kenya, is "given depth by lyrical prose. . . . Chirchir tries but fails to help her elders and is sent away time after time. . . . Not until Chirchir finds her baby brother, Kip-rop, crying untended does she discover a task she can do as well as the grownups. In an afterword, Cunnane explains that Chirchir is a member of the Kalenjin tribe; the story contains a great deal of information about Kalenjin life, language, customs, and Kenyan flora and fauna. . . . Daly's . . . softly shaded acrylics have much to teach, too. . . . Images of security, dependability, and plenty offer a fresh picture of African life." Publ Wkly

★ **For** you are a Kenyan child; [by] Kelly Cunnane; art by Ana Juan. Atheneum Books for Young Readers 2005 un il $16.95

Grades: PreK K 1 2   E
ISBN 0-689-86194-X
LC 2004-17060

From rooster crow to bedtime, a Kenyan boy plays and visits neighbors all through his village, even though he is supposed to be watching his grandfather's cows.

This story is told "through vivid, descriptive text. . . . The brilliant, colorful, and humorous illustrations stand out against the white backgrounds and are large enough for group viewing. A gentle story about family, responsibility, and a curious little boy." SLJ

Curtis, Gavin

★ The **bat** boy & his violin; illustrated by E.B. Lewis. Simon & Schuster Bks. for Young Readers 1998 un il hardcover o.p. pa $7.99

Grades: K 1 2 3   E
1. Baseball 2. Negro leagues 3. African Americans 4. Violin 5. Fathers and sons 6. Baseball -- Fiction 7. Violinists -- Fiction 8. African Americans -- Fiction 9. Father-son relationship -- Fiction
ISBN 0-689-80099-1; 0-689-84115-9 pa
LC 97-25417

Reginald is more interested in practicing his violin than in his father's job managing the worst team in the Negro Leagues, but when Papa makes him the bat boy and his music begins to lead the team to victory, Papa realizes the value of his son's passion

"Lewis's soft watercolor illustrations portray the characters with depth and beauty, resulting in a very special book." SLJ

Curtis, Jamie Lee

★ **Big** words for little people; illustrated by Laura Cornell. Joanna Cotler Books 2008 un il $16.99; lib bdg $17.89

Grades: PreK K 1   E
1. Stories in rhyme 2. Conduct of life -- Fiction
ISBN 978-0-06-112759-5; 0-06-112759-0; 978-0-06-112760-1 lib bdg; 0-06-112760-4 lib bdg
LC 2008011856

A big sister teaches her younger siblings some important words, like "responsibility," "perseverance," and "respect"

"Curtis once again demonstrates her trademark sensibility for childhood's simultaneously awkward and silly moments while focusing on the positive values learned from these experiences. Cornell keeps the tone ever lighthearted with her charmingly busy illustrations." SLJ

★ **I'm** gonna like me; letting off a little self-esteem. illustrated by Laura Cornell. HarperCollins Pubs. 2002 un il $16.99; lib bdg $17.89

Grades: PreK K 1 2   E
1. Self-esteem 2. Conduct of life 3. Stories in rhyme
ISBN 0-06-028761-6; 0-06-028762-4 lib bdg
LC 2002-1300

"Though the message is both catchy and effective in its delivery, it's Cornell's humorous, detailed, ink-and-watercolor illustrations that give this volume true pizzazz." Publ Wkly

★ **Is** there really a human race? illustrated by Laura Cornell. Joanna Cotler Books 2006 un il $16.99; lib bdg $17.89

Grades: PreK K 1 2   E

1. Stories in rhyme 2. Conduct of life -- Fiction 3. Philosophy -- Juvenile literature

ISBN 978-0-06-075346-7; 0-06-075346-3; 978-0-06-075348-1 lib bdg; 0-06-075348-X lib bdg

LC 2006-00274

While thinking about life as a race, a child wonders whether it is most important to finish first or to have fun along the way.

"Curtis writes so very well, in infectious toe-tapping poetic form, of the inner thoughts and worries that children struggle with all too frequently. . . . Cornell's ink-and-color wash cartoons are a perfect match to Curtis's lilting text." SLJ

My mommy hung the moon; a love story. [by] Jamie Lee Curtis & Laura Cornell. HarperCollins 2010 un il $16.99

Grades: PreK K 1   E

1. Stories in rhyme 2. Mothers -- Fiction

ISBN 978-0-06-029016-0; 0-06-029016-1

A hardworking mother's extraordinary accomplishments are listed by her devoted child.

"This is a lively homage to mothers that children and parents alike will enjoy." Booklist

★ **Tell** me again about the night I was born; illustrated by Laura Cornell. HarperCollins Pubs. 1996 un il $16.99; pa $5.99; bd bk $7.99

Grades: PreK K 1 2   E

1. Infants -- Fiction 2. Adoption -- Fiction

ISBN 0-06-024528-X; 0-06-443581-4 pa; 0-694-01215-7 bd bk

LC 95-5412

"The young female narrator asks her adoptive parents to 'tell me again' the story of her birth and introduction into the family she is now a part of. . . . The humorous, cartoon-style pictures by Laura Cornell . . . are a perfect visual counterpart to the text." Horn Book

Cushman, Doug

Christmas Eve good night. Henry Holt 2011 un il $12.99

Grades: PreK K 1   E

1. Stories in rhyme 2. Christmas stories 3. Bedtime -- Fiction 4. Christmas -- Fiction

ISBN 978-0-8050-6603-6; 0-8050-6603-9

LC 2010038058

On Christmas Eve, animals at the North Pole, gingerbread men, robots, and more say good night to their mommas, papas, and buddies.

"Cushman's watercolor-and-ink illustrations are full of witty details and hints about the conclusion, but it is his dramatic pacing and skilled balance between art and text that makes this Christmas offering sparkle." Kirkus

Dirk Bones and the mystery of the haunted house; story and pictures by Doug Cushman. HarperCollinsPublishers 2006 31p il (I can read book) $15.99; lib bdg $16.89

Grades: K 1 2   E

1. Ghost stories 2. Mystery fiction

ISBN 978-0-06-073764-1; 0-06-073764-6; 978-0-06-073765-8 lib bdg; 0-06-073765-4 lib bdg

LC 2005019484

"Daily Tombs" newspaper reporter Dirk Bones, who also happens to be a skeleton, investigates when a family of ghosts fears that they are being haunted.

"Cushman's illustrations are delightfully silly and spirited; his hilarious plot will please youngsters who often claim that they want horror but are relieved to get humor instead." SLJ

Another title about Dirk Bones is:

Dirk Bones and the mystery of the missing books (2009)

Dirk Bones and the mystery of the missing books; story and pictures by Doug Cushman. HarperCollinsPublishers 2009 30p il (I can read!) $16.99

Grades: K 1 2   E

1. Mystery fiction 2. Skeleton -- Fiction 3. Books and reading -- Fiction

ISBN 978-0-06-073768-9; 0-06-073768-9

LC 2008031437

Investigative reporter Dirk Bones sets out to discover who is stealing books in the town of Ghostly.

"Dirk Bones and the other ghastly inhabitants of Ghostly are fresh and attractive characters. . . . The book's design has the comfort of beginning readers in mind, and the simple sentences and dialogue are clear and well supported." SLJ

Halloween goodnight. Henry Holt & Co. 2010 un il $12.99

Grades: PreK K 1   E

1. Bedtime -- Fiction 2. Monsters -- Fiction 3. Halloween -- Fiction

ISBN 978-0-8050-8928-8; 0-8050-8928-4

On Halloween night, monsters, from hairy werewolves on the moors to scaly swamp creatures in a black lagoon, say goodnight to their mommies and daddies.

"The watercolor and ink drawings are colorful and clever. . . . The delightful illustrations make these seasonal monsters not-so-scary for very young readers. This book will fly off your holiday shelves." SLJ

★ **Inspector** Hopper; story and pictures by Doug Cushman. HarperCollins Pubs. 2000 64p il (I can read book) hardcover o.p. pa $3.99

Grades: K 1 2   E

1. Insects 2. Mystery fiction 3. Insects -- Fiction 4. Mystery and detective stories

ISBN 0-06-028382-3; 0-06-028383-1 lib bdg; 0-06-444260-8 pa

LC 99-30878

Inspector Hopper and his perpetually hungry assistant McBugg solve three mysteries for their insect friends

"Beginning readers will find a familiar structure, natural language, compelling plot, supporting illustrations, and engaging characters. . . . The light watercolors define the characters as soft-boiled while slyly playing on stereotypes out of film noir." Horn Book Guide

Another title about Inspector Hopper is:
Inspector Hopper's mystery year (2003)

Mystery at the Club Sandwich; written and illustrated by Doug Cushman. Clarion Books 2004 un il $15
Grades: K 1 2 3   E
1. Animals 2. Elephants 3. Peanut butter 4. Mystery fiction 5. Lost and found possessions 6. Animals -- Fiction 7. Elephants -- Fiction 8. Mystery and detective stories
ISBN 0-618-41969-1

LC 2004-537

When Lola, famous singer at the Club Sandwich, loses her lucky marbles, elephant detective Nick Trunk, lover of peanut butter, takes the case

"Readers will guess the villain early on but that won't interfere with their enjoyment of the droll story, which is greatly enhanced by delightful illustrations. Cushman uses black watercolor washes, colored pencil, and pastel against a stark white background, suggesting the silver nitrate photographs and popular black-and-white movies of the gumshoe era." SLJ

Pigmares; porcine poems of the silver screen. Doug Cushman. Charlesbridge 2012 40 p. col. ill.
Grades: 2 3 4   E
1. Pigs -- Poetry 2. Children's poetry 3. Monsters -- Poetry 4. Swine -- Juvenile poetry 5. Children's poetry, American
ISBN 1580894011; 9781580894012

LC 2011025703

This book of children's poems by Doug Cushman "versifies classic movie and literary monsters in 18 single-page poems with accompanying movie-poster-inspired watercolor illustrations starring, of course, pigs rather than people. Plants from outer space (Pigweed), the Yeti (Abominable Snow Pig) and Pig Kong all enjoy the spotlight in turn. All entries are rhymed . . . and each has a humorous twist beyond the punny titles." (Kirkus)

Cutbill, Andy
The **cow** that laid an egg; [by] Andy Cutbill; illustrated by Russell Ayto. HarperCollins Publishers 2008 un il $16.99
Grades: PreK K 1 2   E
1. Eggs -- Fiction 2. Cattle -- Fiction 3. Chickens -- Fiction
ISBN 978-0-06-137295-7; 0-06-137295-1
First published 2006 in the United Kingdom
Marjorie the cow "has no special talents like the rest of the herd, so the chickens hatch a plan. One morning, Marjorie shrieks, 'I've laid an egg!' . . . The bovine endures the taunts of the suspicious cows and the support of the ever-present, silent chickens, until the egg finally hatches a chick with an astonishing 'moo' voice. Cutbill's writing is spare and amusing, and Ayto's goofy, mixed-media collages are a perfect match." SLJ

Another title about Marjorie the cow is:
The cow that was the best moo-ther (2009)

The **cow** that was the best moo-ther; by Andy Cutbill; illustrated by Russell Ayto. HarperCollinsPublishers 2009 un il $17.99

Grades: PreK K 1 2   E
1. Cattle -- Fiction 2. Mothers -- Fiction 3. Chickens -- Fiction 4. Contests -- Fiction
ISBN 978-0-06-166472-4; 0-06-166472-3

LC 2008010083

Although her baby hatched from an egg and looks suspiciously like a chick, Marjorie the cow proudly enters her in the "beautiful baby cow" contest.

"Ayto's busy cartoon illustrations match the off-kilter humor of the story." SLJ

Cutler, Jane
Guttersnipe; pictures by Emily Arnold McCully. Farrar Straus Giroux 2009 un il $16.95
Grades: K 1 2 3   E
1. Jews -- Fiction 2. Poverty -- Fiction 3. Immigrants -- Fiction
ISBN 978-0-374-32813-9; 0-374-32813-7

LC 2007034417

In Canada early in the twentieth century, Ben, the youngest in a family of Jewish immigrants struggling to make ends meet, decides to help out but when a hat maker gives him a chance, disaster strikes and Ben nearly loses hope.

"Detailed watercolors reflect Ben's exhilaration and evoke the early-twentieth-century setting of this unusual story based on true events." Horn Book Guide

★ **Rose** and Riley; pictures by Thomas F. Yezerski. Farrar Straus Giroux 2005 48p il $15
Grades: PreK K 1 2   E
1. Friendship -- Fiction
ISBN 0-374-36340-4

LC 2003-54887

Together, Rose, a vole, and Riley, a groundhog, figure out how to prepare for the possibility of rain, how to celebrate un-birthdays, and what to do with worries.

"Soft pastel illustrations add to the warmth of the text while repetition eases the decoding. A sweet, thoughtful offering with two memorable characters." SLJ

Another title about Rose and Riley is:
Rose and Riley come and go (2005)

Cuyler, Margery
100th day worries; illustrated by Arthur Howard. Simon & Schuster Bks. for Young Readers 2000 un il $16
Grades: K 1 2   E
1. Counting 2. School stories 3. Worry -- Fiction 4. Schools -- Fiction
ISBN 0-689-82979-5

LC 98-52887

Jessica worries about collecting 100 objects to take to class for the 100th day of school

"Energetic pen-and-ink squiggles and bright watercolors fill the pages with round-eyed figures and striped, dotted, and floral patterns as the groups of objects are described and counted." Booklist

Other titles about Jessica are:
Stop, drop, and roll (2001)
Hooray for Reading Day! (2008)
Bullies never win (2009)

Bullies never win; illustrated by Arthur Howard. Simon & Schuster Books for Young Readers 2009 un il $16.99

Grades: K 1 2   **E**

1. Worry -- Fiction 2. Bullies -- Fiction 3. Friendship -- Fiction

ISBN 978-0-689-86187-1; 0-689-86187-7

LC 2007045251

First-grader Jessica worries about everything Brenda the bully might tease her about, until the day she has had enough and discovers a new way to deal with Brenda.

"Entertaining pen-and-ink and watercolor illustrations clearly illuminate the take while deftly revealing the characters' variety of emotions." SLJ

Guinea pigs add up; illustrated by Tracey Campbell Pearson. Walker Books for Young Readers 2010 un il $16.99

Grades: PreK K 1   **E**

1. School stories 2. Stories in rhyme 3. Pets -- Fiction 4. Guinea pigs -- Fiction 5. Mathematics -- Fiction

ISBN 978-0-8027-9795-7; 0-8027-9795-4

"After a teacher announces that a new animal is coming, his young students imagine a giraffe, an elephant, and a snake. What they find, though, is a guinea pig, and the students enjoy petting and feeding him. Because he is lonely, they get him a playmate, who gives birth to three babies, and the numbers start growing. . . . The pen-and-ink, watercolor, and acrylic-gouache pictures show the classroom chaos. . . . The arithmetic exercises—addition, subtraction, multiplication—are woven into the story, and there are surprises right up to the end." Booklist

Hooray for Reading Day! by Margery Cuyler; illustrated by Arthur Howard. Simon & Schuster Books for Young Readers 2008 un il $15.99

Grades: K 1 2   **E**

1. School stories 2. Dogs -- Fiction 3. Worry -- Fiction 4. Reading -- Fiction

ISBN 978-0-689-86188-8; 0-689-86188-5

LC 2007005191

First-grader Jessica, a big worrier, is especially afraid that she will make a mistake when she is reading in front of her class and parents on Reading Theater Day, but after lots of practice reading to her dog Wiggles, she performs perfectly.

"Cuyler ackowledges Jessica's insecurity and shows a practical solution while offering bits of humor along the way. Amusing cartoon-style ink drawings with colorful washes help create the right tone for this encouraging picture book." Booklist

Monster mess! [by] Margery Cuyler; illustrated by S.D. Schindler. Margaret K. McElderry Books 2008 40p il $14.99

Grades: PreK K 1   **E**

1. Stories in rhyme 2. Monsters -- Fiction 3. Cleanliness -- Fiction

ISBN 0-689-86405-1; 978-0-689-86405-6

LC 2005-012762

A monster sneaks into a boy's room and cleans up while the boy is asleep.

"The watercolor illustrations at times show only part of the creature as its head or other body parts extend off the page. . . . Rhyming, repetitive text and whimsical images whirl on the pages, making this a fun read-aloud." SLJ

Princess Bess gets dressed; illustrated by Heather Maione. Simon & Schuster Books for Young Readers 2009 un il $15.99

Grades: PreK K 1   **E**

1. Stories in rhyme 2. Princesses -- Fiction 3. Clothing and dress -- Fiction

ISBN 978-1-4169-3833-0; 1-4169-3833-8

LC 2007-25915

A fashionably dressed princess reveals her favorite clothes at the end of a busy day.

This "story brims over with little-girl appeal. Princess Bess [is] depicted in debut artist Maione's zesty ink-and-watercolor art. . . . The well-crafted rhymes roll easily off the tongue; Maione's droll pictures, balancing fashion-loving detail with Bess's brio, are a skillful accompaniment." Publ Wkly

Skeleton hiccups; illustrated by S.D. Schindler. Margaret K. McElderry Books 2002 un il $14.95; pa $6.99

Grades: PreK K 1   **E**

1. Ghost stories 2. Hiccups -- Fiction 3. Skeleton -- Fiction

ISBN 0-689-84770-X; 1-4169-0276-7 pa

LC 2001-44121

Ghost tries to help Skeleton get rid of the hiccups

"This simple story begs to be read aloud. . . . Schindler's gouache, watercolor, and ink pictures make the most out of each situation, instilling humor in every scene." SLJ

Stop, drop, and roll; illustrated by Arthur Howard. Simon & Schuster Bks. for Young Readers 2001 un il $16

Grades: K 1 2   **E**

1. Worry 2. Fire prevention 3. Safety 4. Worry -- Fiction 5. Fire prevention -- Fiction 6. Safety education -- Fiction

ISBN 0-689-84355-0

LC 2001-20803

Jessica, who worries about everything from her spelling homework to remembering to fill her dog's water dish, learns that fire safety begins with extinguishing her fears.

"The large, cartoon illustrations, done in watercolor and ink, lighten the tone and feature a child with wide, round eyes worrying her way through her life and agonizing over her performance." SLJ

Tick tock clock; pictures by Robert Neubecker. HarperCollins Children's Books 2012 il (My first I can read) $16.99; pa $3.99

Grades: PreK K 1   **E**

1. Stories in rhyme 2. Time -- Fiction 3. Twins -- Fiction 4. Sisters -- Fiction 5. Grandmothers -- Fiction

ISBN 978-0-06-1363092-; 0-06-136309-X; 978-0-06-136311-5 pa; 0-06-136311-1 pa

LC 2008051780

"Grandma spends a busy day with her twin granddaughters in a day filled with action, rhythm and rhyme. . . . Neubecker's sunny illustrations, in rich reds, yellows and greens, perfectly reflect the spare, very easy-to-read text. Each illustration is set on a white, unframed background and is set apart from the text, making it nicely legible. The repetition of words . . . helps beginning readers build confidence." Kirkus

The **bumpy** little pumpkin; illustrated by Will Hillenbrand. Scholastic Press 2005 un il $15.95
Grades: PreK K 1 2　　　　　　　　　E
1. Pumpkin -- Fiction
ISBN 0-439-52835-6

LC 2004-12179

Little Nell chooses an unusual pumpkin for her Halloween jacko-lantern, despite her big sisters' criticisms

"Cuyler's infectious, repetitive text, with its recurrent use of BIG, is perfectly paced for participatory read-alouds, and Hillenbrand's cheery, whimsical mixed-media illustrations show Little Nell's perspective." Booklist

Another title about Little Nell is:
The biggest, best snowman (1998)

The **little** dump truck; illustrated by Bob Kolar. Henry Holt and Co. 2009 un il $12.99
Grades: PreK K 1　　　　　　　　　E
1. Stories in rhyme 2. Trucks -- Fiction
ISBN 978-0-8050-8281-4; 0-8050-8281-6

LC 2008036811

A happy little dump truck, driven by Hard Hat Pete, hauls stones, rocks, and debris from a construction site to a landfill.

"The digital artwork will appeal to young children, who will look for the face depicted on each of the various trucks. The endpapers show all of the vehicles that play a part in the illustrations. The heavy-duty pages are perfect for curious youngsters. Preschoolers will love this book." SLJ

Cyrus, Kurt
★ **Big** rig bugs. Walker 2010 un il $16.99; lib bdg $17.89
Grades: PreK K 1　　　　　　　　　E
1. Stories in rhyme 2. Insects -- Fiction 3. Construction workers -- Fiction
ISBN 978-0-8027-8674-6; 0-8027-8674-X; 978-0-8027-8688-3 lib bdg; 0-8027-8688-X lib bdg

"Digital illustrations explore perspective as a crew of insects joins together to clean up a construction worker's littered tuna-fish sandwich. Rhymed couplets . . . feature creatures such as an ant, a weevil, a pickleworm, an earwig, and a dragonfly. The oversize views of bugs will delight many children, as will the construction analogy." SLJ

★ **Tadpole** Rex; by Kurt Cyrus. Harcourt 2008 un il $16
Grades: K 1 2 3　　　　　　　　　E
1. Stories in rhyme 2. Frogs -- Fiction 3. Growth -- Fiction 4. Dinosaurs -- Fiction
ISBN 978-0-15-205990-3; 0-15-205990-3

LC 2006033825

A tiny primordial tadpole grows into a frog, feeling just as strong and powerful as the huge tyrannosaurus rex that stomps through the mud

"The rhyming text is image-rich, informational, and fun to read aloud. . . . Cyrus's oversize artwork conveys information spectacularly. . . . Created in scratchboard and then colored digitally, the illustrations are luminous and striking." SLJ

★ The **voyage** of Turtle Rex; written and illustrated by Kurt Cyrus. Harcourt Children's Books 2011 $16.99

Grades: PreK K 1 2　　　　　　　　　E
1. Stories in rhyme 2. Sea turtles -- Fiction 3. Marine animals -- Fiction 4. Prehistoric animals -- Fiction
ISBN 978-0-547-42924-3; 0-547-42924-X; 054742924X; 9780547429243

LC 2010019226

"A tiny prehistoric ancestor to modern sea turtles hatches from a buried egg, scuttles across a beach into the sea, survives multiple hazards to grow into a mighty two-ton Archelon and then in season returns to shore to lay a clutch of her own. Injecting plenty of drama into his beach and sunlit undersea scenes with sudden close-ups and changes of scale, the illustrator vividly captures the hatchling's vulnerability. . . . . . Like it's subject, the rhymed text moves with grand deliberation, carrying the primeval story line to a clever transition between that ancient era and ours." Kirkus

Czekaj, Jef
Call for a new alphabet. Charlesbridge 2011 un il lib bdg $12.95; pa $5.95
Grades: K 1 2 3　　　　　　　　　E
1. Alphabet -- Fiction 2. English language -- Fiction
ISBN 978-1-58089-228-5 lib bdg; 1-58089-228-0 lib bdg; 978-1-58089-229-2 pa; 1-58089-229-9 pa

LC 2010007534

Tired of being near the end of the alphabet, starting few words, and being governed by grammar rules, X calls for a vote on a new Alphabet Constitution, then dreams of how life would be if he became a different letter.

"Written with sly wit and wordplay that will appeal to the target audience, this little book delves into constitutional government as well as spelling rules. . . . The upbeat text and brightly colored, cartoon-like illustrations propel the story, while the personified letters' grievances will draw a sympathetic response from children struggling with the order of letters as they learn to read." Booklist

Cat secrets. Balzer + Bray 2011 un il $16.99
Grades: PreK K 1　　　　　　　　　E
1. Cats -- Fiction 2. Cats -- Juvenile literature
ISBN 978-0-06-192088-2; 0-06-192088-6

LC 2009-49424

Important secrets about how best to live a cat's life will be revealed only to those who can prove that they are genuine cats.

"Although the appeals for reader interaction may make for a rowdy read-aloud, Czekaj cleverly slows the book's pace at the end by demanding that readers take a catnap. It's easy to see this one being read just before preschool naptime." Publ Wkly

Hip & Hop, don't stop. Disney/Hyperion 2010 un il $16.99
Grades: K 1 2　　　　　　　　　E
1. Rabbits -- Fiction 2. Turtles -- Fiction 3. Contests -- Fiction 4. Rap music -- Fiction
ISBN 978-1-4231-1664-6; 1-4231-1664-X

LC 2009-20022

A fast rabbit named Hip and a slow turtle named Hop defy convention when they team up to win a rap music contest in spite of their differences.

"Speech balloons and short rhymes are seamlessly incorporated into the story line. Red text means read fast and green text means read slowly. . . . The bright colors and engaging characters will grab children's attention." SLJ

Oink-a-doodle-moo; written and illustrated by Jef Czekaj. Balzer + Bray 2012 32 p. (tr. bdg.) $16.99

Grades: PreK K 1   E

1. Games -- Fiction 2. Picture books for children 3. Domestic animals -- Juvenile fiction 4. Humorous stories 5. Animal sounds -- Fiction 6. Domestic animals -- Fiction

ISBN 0062060112; 9780062060112

LC 2011010065

This barnyard story "is propelled by an old-fashioned game of telephone. 'I have a secret,' a bubble-gum pink pig whispers, hoof to mouth, to a blank-eyed rooster: 'Oink. Pass it on.' The rooster, in turn, relays an 'Oink-a-doodle-doo' to a cow, whose 'Oink-a-doodle-moo' becomes a frog's 'Oink-a-ribbit-moo,' and so on." (Publishers Weekly)

D'Amico, Carmela

Ella the Elegant Elephant; by Carmela & Steven D'Amico. Arthur A. Levine Books 2004 un il $16.95

Grades: PreK K 1 2   E

1. Hats 2. Schools 3. Teasing 4. Elephants 5. School stories 6. Hats -- Fiction 7. Moving, Household 8. Elephants -- Fiction

ISBN 0-439-62792-3

LC 2003-28081

Ella is nervous about the first day of school in her new town, but wearing her grandmother's good luck hat makes her feel better—until the other students tease her and call her names.

"Combining a fairy-tale quality with elements in story and setting that will be familiar to children, this has a charming protagonist, as well as lovely, whimsical art, in a soft rich palette. . . . The text is simple, descriptive, and often lively, making a good read-aloud." Booklist

Other titles about Ella are:

Ella takes the cake (2005)

Ella sets the stage (2006)

Ella sets sail (2008)

Suki, the very loud bunny; [by] Carmela & Steven D'Amico. Dutton Children's Books 2011 un il $16.99

Grades: PreK K 1   E

1. Noise -- Fiction 2. Rabbits -- Fiction

ISBN 978-0-525-42230-3; 0-525-42230-7

LC 2010013470

Unlike most bunnies, Suki loves shouting and playing in the mud, but when she disobeys her mother and leaves the burrow one day, her loud voice is what saves her.

"Appealing for reading in a lap but also well suited to storytimes, this tale of a bunny whose most troublesome traits save the day will ring true with children who have ever been scolded for being noisy or curious." SLJ

D'Aulaire, Ingri

Foxie; the singing dog. [by] Ingri and Edgar Parin d'Aulaire. New York Review Books 2007 un il (New York Review Books children's collection) $14.95

Grades: K 1 2   E

1. Dogs -- Fiction

ISBN 978-1-59017-264-3; 1-59017-264-7

LC 2007-27028

First published 1949

A lost dog's luck makes him fat and famous, but when given a chance he proves he still thinks there is no place like home.

"Foxie's adventures are illustrated in delightful color." Horn Book Guide

The **two** cars; [by] Ingri & Edgar Parin d'Aulaire. New York Review Books 2007 un il (The New York Review children's collection) $14.95

Grades: PreK K 1   E

1. Fables 2. Automobiles -- Fiction

ISBN 978-1-59017-234-6; 1-59017-234-5

LC 2007-2636

First published 1955 by Doubleday

On a magic moonlit night, the sleek, shiny automatic new car and the beat-up old car with many miles on its speedometer go for a drive to see which car is the best.

"A modern adaptation of The Tortoise and the Hare, in which safe and courteous driving wins the day. Delicate pencil illustrations and a plot delivered at a pace fit for a turnpike should prove as enchanting to today's automotively inclined children as when the book was first published in 1955." Pub Wkly

Da Costa, Deborah

Hanukkah moon; [illustrated by] Gosia Mosz. Kar-Ben Pub. 2007 un il lib bdg $17.95; pa $7.95

Grades: PreK K 1 2   E

1. Jews -- Fiction 2. Aunts -- Fiction 3. Hanukkah stories 4. Hanukkah -- Fiction 5. Rosh Hodesh -- Fiction 6. Mexican Americans -- Fiction

ISBN 978-1-58013-244-2 lib bdg; 1-58013-244-8 lib bdg; 978-1-58013-245-9 pa; 1-58013-245-6 pa

LC 2006-27430

When Isobel visits her Aunt Luisa, who has just arrived from Mexico, she celebrates Hanukkah with a dreidel-shaped piñata and learns how to celebrate Rosh Hodesh, the women's holiday of the new moon

This is "a valuable contribution to the canon of holiday literature. . . . Mosz's mixed-media pictures . . . feature a cast of doe-eyed, stylized characters golden as Hanukkah lights against the deep purple of moonless night." Bull Cent Child Books

DaCosta, Barbara

★ **Nighttime** Ninja; by Barbara DaCosta; illustrated by Ed Young. Little, Brown 2012 32 p. (hardback) $16.99

Grades: PreK K 1   E

1. Ninja -- Fiction 2. Suspense fiction 3. Picture books for children 4. Bedtime -- Fiction 5. Imagination -- Fiction

ISBN 031620384X; 9780316203845

LC 2012005492

This children's picture book features a "ninja, a black silhouette, [who] breaks into a house and makes his way silently toward some unknown object: 'He crept down the twisting moonlit hallway, and knelt in the dark shadows, listening.' Suddenly, a huge mother-shaped shadow flicks the light on, and the ninja is revealed as a boy sneaking into the kitchen for ice cream." (Publishers Weekly)

Daddo, Andrew

Goodnight, me; [by] Andrew Daddo; illustrations by Emma Quay. Bloomsbury Children's Books 2007 un il $11.95
Grades: PreK E
1. Bedtime -- Fiction 2. Orangutan -- Fiction
ISBN 978-1-59990-153-4; 1-59990-153-6
LC 2007002613
A baby orangutan says goodnight to each and every part of himself until sleep finally comes

"This delightful book has a quiet cadence. . . . Using a mix of pencil, acrylic paints, and watercolors, Quay has created uncluttered spreads that focus on the highlighted body parts. The colors are as soothing as the gentle text." SLJ

Dahl, Michael

Nap time for Kitty; illustrated by Oriol Vidal. Picture Window Books 2011 un il (Hello genius) bd bk $7.99
Grades: PreK E
1. Board books for children 2. Cats -- Fiction 3. Sleep -- Fiction
ISBN 978-1-4048-5216-7; 1-4048-5216-6
LC 2010032115
"Toddlers will see themselves in this kitten who just doesn't want to take a nap. When Mama calls him in, he has been busy ogling a bird—and leaping into the birdbath. . . . The cute cats have a slightly stylized and digitized look. Minimal text and plenty of action are just right for the intended age group." Booklist

Daly, Cathleen

★ **Prudence** wants a pet. Roaring Brook Press 2011 un il $16.99
Grades: PreK K 1 E
1. Pets -- Fiction
ISBN 978-1-59643-468-4; 1-59643-468-6
LC 2010022001
"Small pen-and-ink and watercolor illustrations on a white background reveal a time progression in vignettes that are spread across the pages. The humorous consequences of Prudence's experiments make this a lighthearted read about never giving up on one's dreams." SLJ

Daly, Jude

Sivu's six wishes; a Taoist tale. retold and illustrated by Jude Daly. Eerdmans Books for Young Readers 2010 un il
Grades: K 1 2 E
1. Taoism -- Fiction 2. Wishes -- Fiction 3. Happiness -- Fiction 4. Stonecutting -- Fiction 5. Folklore -- Juvenile literature
ISBN 0-8028-5369-2; 978-0-8028-5369-1
LC 2010001619
Sivu, an African stonecarver, is not paid well for his work, but through his wishes to become more powerful and live as different people, like the mayor, and things, like the wind, he discovers where real power lies.

"Daly's stylized art, in a rich, clear palette, is quietly stunning. . . . Repetition in both text . . . and art . . . helps make the story easy to follow, and the modern embellishments never obscure its meaning." Horn Book

Daly, Niki

★ **Pretty** Salma; a Red Riding Hood story from Africa. Clarion Books 2007 29p $16

Grades: K 1 2 3 E
1. Fairy tales 2. Folklore -- Juvenile literature
ISBN 978-0-618-72345-4; 0-618-72345-5
LC 2006-04249
In this version of "Little Red Riding Hood," set in Ghana, a young girl fails to heed Granny's warning about the dangers of talking to strangers.

"The cartoon-style paintings capture the sights and flavor of the setting and add dimension and humorous details to this modern version of a timeless tale." SLJ

A **song** for Jamela; story and pictures by Niki Daly. Frances Lincoln Children's Books 2010 un il $16.95
Grades: K 1 2 E
1. Singers -- Fiction 2. Celebrities -- Fiction 3. Beauty shops -- Fiction
ISBN 978-1-84507-871-3; 1-84507-871-3
It is summer vacation and Jamela is bored, until her Aunt Beauty asks her to come and help her get her hair salon ready for a special client, who turns out to be "Afro-Idols" contestant Miss Bambi Chaka Chaka.

"Daly's humorous and colorful illustrations reflect everyday South African scenes from a child's point of view. The illustrations [are made] utilizing digital art." SLJ
Other titles about Jamela are:
Jamela's dress (1999)
What's cooking Jamela? (2001)
Where's Jamela? (2004)
Happy birthday, Jamela! (2006)

★ **Welcome** to Zanzibar Road; story and pictures by Niki Daly. Clarion Books 2006 31p il $16
Grades: PreK K 1 2 E
1. Chickens -- Fiction 2. Elephants -- Fiction
ISBN 0-618-64926-3
LC 2005021758
After moving into the house on Zanzibar Road that her neighbors helped her build, Mama Jumbo the elephant decides to share it with Little Chico the chicken.

"Through his warm, expressive watercolors, Daly teaches readers about some of the important things in life—friendship, family, and how to make a house into a home. Details abound, and the animals' patterned clothing adds texture and variety to the pages." SLJ

Danneberg, Julie

The **big** test; illustrated by Judy Love. Charlesbridge 2011 un il $16.95; pa $6.95
Grades: K 1 2 E
1. School stories
ISBN 1580893600; 1580893619 pa; 9781580893602; 9781580893619 pa; 978-1-58089-360-2; 1-58089-360-0; 978-1-58089-361-9 pa; 1-58089-361-9 pa
Mrs. Hartwell is concerned that preparing her students to take the Big Test is only making them nervous, and so she thinks of a way to help them relax.

"Mrs. Hartwell's students . . . are not sure they can deal with the Big Test. . . . The kids worry and get headaches, stomachaches, and other maladies. On Thursday, Mrs. Hartwell lines up her class and marches them down the hall to the library. The sign on the door says, 'Library Closed: Students Testing.' But inside it's a test party. The students get to play and relax and eat. This works so well that no one is sick anymore and they breeze through the actual Big Test on

Friday. The illustrations, done in ink and transparent dyes on watercolor paper, are priceless. The children's faces clearly express all the agony that the situation requires." SLJ

Monet paints a day; Julie Danneberg; illustrated by Caitlin Heimerl. Charlesbridge 2012 48 p. col. ill. (reinforced) $15.95
Grades: 2 3 4   E
  1. Plein-air painting -- Juvenile literature 2. Impressionism (Art) -- Juvenile literature
  ISBN 1442435798; 9781580892407
                     LC 2011025789
This book by Julie Danneburg is "written in the voice of the artist and drawn from the letters of the noted French Impressionist Claude Monet. . . . One day, so absorbed in painting as much as he could within a seven-to-15-minute window . . . Monet was actually swept away by a high tide, supplies and all. . . . [Danneburg] integrates details from Monet's letters and minifacts about Impressionism and the exciting practice of plein-air painting." (Kirkus)

Danticat, Edwidge
  ★ **Eight** days; a story of Haiti. pictures by Alix Delinois. Orchard Books 2010 un il
Grades: K 1 2 3   E
  1. Play -- Fiction 2. Earthquakes -- Fiction 3. Imagination -- Fiction
  ISBN 0-545-27849-X; 978-0-545-27849-2
                     LC 2010035981
Junior tells of the games he played in his mind during the eight days he was trapped in his house after the devastating January 12, 2010 earthquake in Haiti. Includes author's note about Haitian children before the earthquake and her own children's reactions to the disaster.
This is illustrated with "beautiful, bright artwork, in acrylics, pastel, and collage. . . . The narrative's powerful rhythm echoes the Genesis Creation story, giving it even more gravity. . . . Never too sentimental, the story works because of the clear presence of great sadness and loss." Booklist

Danziger, Paula
  ★ **It's** Justin Time, Amber Brown; illustrated by Tony Ross. Putnam 2001 48p il (A is for Amber) $12.99; pa $3.99
Grades: K 1 2 3   E
  1. Time 2. Birthdays 3. Clocks and watches 4. Best friends 5. Time -- Fiction 6. Birthdays -- Fiction 7. Clocks and watches -- Fiction
  ISBN 0-399-23470-5; 0-698-11907-X pa
                     LC 99-89396
Unlike her best friend Justin, Amber Brown loves to measure time and hopes to receive a watch on her seventh birthday
"The illustrations capture the mood of the story, which is playful and spirited. Beginning readers will enjoy sharing Amber's pre-birthday anticipation and older readers may want to go back and see the early years of the characters they know and love." SLJ
  Other easy-to-read titles about Amber Brown are:
  Get ready for second grade, Amber Brown (2002)
  It's a fair day, Amber Brown (2002)
  Orange you glad it's Halloween, Amber Brown (2005)
  Second grade rules, Amber Brown (2004)

What a trip, Amber Brown (2001)

Darbyshire, Kristen
  Put it on the list. Dutton Children's Books 2009 un il $16.99
Grades: PreK K 1   E
  1. Week -- Fiction 2. Memory -- Fiction 3. Shopping -- Fiction 4. Family life -- Fiction
  ISBN 978-0-525-47906-2; 0-525-47906-6
                     LC 2007-28490
"A family of anthropomorphized chickens keeps running out of household staples. Mom tells everyone to put the needed items on the shopping list that's posted on the refrigerator, but they ignore the directive and just complain when supplies run out. . . . The chickens are depicted as stick figures with large round heads. The gouache illustrations are spare, with ink outlines and solid-colored backgrounds. An amusing cautionary tale for families everywhere." SLJ

Darrow, Sharon
  Yafi's family; an Ethiopian boy's journey of love, loss, and adoption. by Linda Pettitt and Sharon Darrow; illustrated by Jan Spivey Gilchrist. Amharic 2010 un il
Grades: PreK K 1 2   E
  1. Adoption -- Fiction 2. Family life -- Fiction
  ISBN 0-979748-14-3; 978-0-979748-14-1
"With his new family in America, Yafi, six, remembers when they first came to his orphanage in Ethiopia. . . . Mom remembers too. . . . They talk about his first mother, who died, and his grandma Elsa, who raised him until she could no longer care for him. . . . Gilchrist's beautiful sepia-toned portraits depict the love Yafi feels for his American family and also his warm remembrances of his birth family. Both words and pictures effectively convey the strong familial ties." Booklist

Daugherty, James Henry
  ★ **Andy** and the lion; by James Daugherty. Viking 1938 un il hardcover o.p. pa $6.99
Grades: PreK K 1 2   E
  1. Lions -- Fiction
  ISBN 0-14-050277-7 pa
  A Caldecott Medal honor book, 1939
A modern picture story of Androcles and the lion in which Andy, who read a book about lions, was almost immediately plunged into action. The next day he met a circus lion with a thorn in his paw. Andy removed the thorn and earned the lion's undying gratitude
"This is a tall tale for little children. It is typically American in its setting and its fun. The large full page illustrations are in yellow, black and white and the brief, hand-lettered text on the opposite page is clear and readable." Libr J

Davies, Jacqueline
  ★ **Tricking** the Tallyman; illustrated by S. D. Schindler. Alfred A. Knopf 2009 un il $17.99; lib bdg $20.99
Grades: 1 2 3 4   E
  1. Census -- Fiction
  ISBN 978-0-375-83909-2; 0-375-83909-7; 978-0-375-93909-9 lib bdg; 0-375-93909-1 lib bdg
                     LC 2007-45488
In 1790, the suspicious residents of a small Vermont town try to trick the man who has been sent to count their population for the first United States Census.

"This lively, engaging picture book is an outstanding introduction to the concept of census taking and its role in the implementation of the new United States Constitution. . . . Schindler's exceptional illustrations, mainly in earth tones, depict indoor and outdoor scenes that are full of activity. . . . Charming and humorous." SLJ

The **night** is singing; illustrations by Kyrsten Brooker. Dial Books for Young Readers 2006 un il $16.99
Grades: PreK K 1   E
1. Stories in rhyme 2. Night -- Fiction 3. Sound -- Fiction
ISBN 0-8037-3004-7; 978-0-8037-3004-5
LC 2004-14161
Rhyming text tells of lullabies that can be heard in the sounds of the night, such as a radiator's hiss, a cat's shadowboxing, and a rainstorm's drumming

This is a "perfect bedtime read. . . . Attractive, full-page folk-art illustrations that combine collage and oil paint on gessoed watercolor paper lend an old-fashioned charm." SLJ

Davies, Matt
Ben rides on; Matt Davies. 1st ed. Roaring Brook Press 2013 32 p. (reinforced) $16.99
Grades: PreK K 1 2 3   E
1. Picture books for children 2. Bullies -- Juvenile fiction 3. Bullies -- Fiction 4. Stealing -- Fiction 5. Conduct of life -- Fiction 6. Bicycles and bicycling -- Fiction
ISBN 1596437944; 9781596437944
LC 2012013101
In this children's picture book, when "Adrian Underbite takes Ben's bicycle for a joyride and hurtles off a cliff, Ben leans over the edge and sees Adrian clinging to a tiny branch. 'How extraordinarily terrible,' Ben thinks, though his toothy grin conveys quite another emotion. But Ben's conscience smites him, and he goes back to rescue Adrian." (Publishers Weekly)

Davies, Nicola, 1958-
Outside your window; a first book of nature. Nicola Davies; illustrated by Mark Hearld. Candlewick Press 2012 105 p. il
Grades: K 1 2   E
1. Nature poetry 2. Nature -- Fiction
ISBN 076365549X; 9780763655495
LC 2011046637
This book of poetry has as its subject "the seasons. . . . The year starts with spring (featuring aspects such as "Bulbs," "Lambs' Tails," and "Planting Seeds") and goes on through summer (a bird's "Summer Song," a farm's "Making Hay") and on to fall ("Acorn," "Harvest," "Berry Picking") and finally winter ("Winter Trees," "Snow Song"). The verses, in different forms ranging from prose poems (including craft instructions) to tightly metered rhymes, . . . offer . . . observations ("In the morning, you'll find the snow has kept a diary/ of things that happened when you were asleep" "Snow Song") or invit[e] humor (one of the "Five Reasons to Keep Chickens" is "They look very silly when they are taking a dust bath")." (Bulletin of the Center for Children's Books)

What happens next? Nicola Davies, illustrated by Marc Boutavant. Candlewick Press 2012 24 p. $9.99

Grades: PreK K 1   E
1. Animal behavior -- Juvenile fiction 2. Animals -- Juvenile literature 3. Toy and movable books -- Specimens
ISBN 076366264X; 9780763662646
LC 2012942306
This "lift-the-flap book reveals surprises in the animal kingdom. A hungry chameleon spies a juicy grasshopper. Turn the half-page. His long tongue shoots out to catch it. Going on, [Nicola] Davies presents other unexpected animal behaviors. . . . The final spread in this sequencing exercise offers a matching game to remind young viewers of the actions described." (Kirkus Reviews)

★ **White** owl, barn owl; illustrated by Michael Foreman. Candlewick Press 2007 29p il $16.99; pa $6.99
Grades: PreK K 1 2 3   E
1. Owls -- Fiction 2. Owls -- Juvenile literature
ISBN 978-0-7636-3364-6; 0-7636-3364-X; 978-0-7636-4143-6 pa; 0-7636-4143-X pa
"Simple facts about the hunting and nesting habits of barn owls intertwine with the story of two humans who put a nesting box for them high in a tree. Narrated by a girl whose grandfather explains owl behavior as the two watch for avian visitors in the evenings, the story also contains insets of information bits. Well-chosen design elements move both fiction and fact along with clarity and ease. . . . Foreman's artwork includes lovely watercolor and pastel paintings of the birds." SLJ

Who lives here? Nicola Davies, illustrated by Marc Boutavant. Candlewick Press 2012 24 p. $9.99
Grades: PreK K 1   E
1. Animals -- Habitations -- Juvenile literature 2. Toy and movable books -- Specimens
ISBN 0763662631; 9780763662639
LC 2012942307
In this children's book by Nicola Davies, illustrated by Marc Boutavant, readers can "lift the flaps and learn about animal life. . . . The jungle is warm and steamy. What kind of animal might live there, a snow goose or a sloth? What about a still, cool pond -- could that be home for a howler monkey? Find out why meerkats like dry sunny grasslands (hint: they like to dig holes to hide in) or why clown fish feel right at home in a coral reef." (Publisher's note)

Davis, Anne
No dogs allowed! words and pictures by Anne Davis. HarperCollins Children's Books 2011 un il $16.99
Grades: PreK K 1 2   E
1. Cats -- Fiction 2. Dogs -- Fiction 3. Friendship -- Fiction
ISBN 978-0-06-075353-5; 0-06-075353-6
LC 2010007028
Bud the cat is not happy when his feline companion Gabby befriends a dog.

"Charming illustrations add humor, and young readers will note small details. . . . The kindness-wins-out theme is perfect for storytime." Booklist

Davis, Aubrey
Kishka for Koppel; illustrated by Sheldon Cohen. Orca Book Publishers 2011 il $19.95

Grades: K 1 2 3   E
  1. Jews -- Fiction 2. Wishes -- Fiction
  ISBN 978-1-55469-299-6; 1-55469-299-7

"In this Jewish retelling of the Grimm Brothers' 'Three Wishes,' Koppel finds a wish-granting meat grinder. The junk man and his wife, Yetta, dream of all the riches they'll wish for, but inevitably they end up wishing for kishka (a kind of sausage), and subsequently wishing it onto and off Koppel's nose. All ends well as the meat grinder points out how lucky they are to have each other (plus a delicious kishka). The naive, folksy cartoon illustrations are expressive and lend a lighthearted air with their varying perspectives and bright acrylic colors. The storytelling is lively and humorous." SLJ

Davis, David
  Fandango stew; illustrated by Ben Galbraith. Sterling Pub. 2011 un il
Grades: PreK K 1 2   E
  1. Folklore
  ISBN 1402765274; 9781402765278

                LC 2010004775

Penniless Slim and his grandson Luis ride into the unwelcoming western town of Skinflint, and manage to rustle up a delicious meal for all its citizens out of one lone bean.

"Witty illustrations featuring warm tones and amusing details effectively complement the text. Either alone or paired with a traditional version, this will make for an appealing read and an even better read-aloud, especially when audiences join in on the chorus: 'Chili's good,/ so is barbecue,/ but nothing's finer than/ fandango stew!'" Libr Media Connect

Davis, Jill
  The **first** rule of little brothers; illustrated by Sarah McMenemy. Alfred A. Knopf 2008 un il $16.99; lib bdg $19.99
Grades: PreK K 1   E
  1. Brothers -- Fiction
  ISBN 978-0-375-84046-3; 0-375-84046-X; 978-0-375-94046-0 lib bdg; 0-375-94046-4 lib bdg

                LC 2007-44314

A young boy learns that, while his little brother's constant mimicking may be annoying, it is also a sign of admiration.

"Davis makes her point—siblings can drive eachother crazy but also have fun together—credibly and sympathetically with plenty of humor as well. . . . McMenemy's mixed-media art (which looks to incorporate watercolor, ink, and torn paper collage) is sunny and vivid, with lots of crisp white space surrounding the brightly colored figures and backgrounds." Bull Cent Child Books

Davis, Katie
  Little Chicken's big day; [by] Katie Davis and Jerry Davis. Margaret K. McElderry Books 2011 un il $14.99
Grades: PreK K   E
  1. Chickens -- Fiction 2. Mother-child relationship -- Fiction
  ISBN 978-1-4424-1401-3; 1-4424-1401-4

                LC 2010011826

Little Chicken is tired of being told what to do by Big Chicken, but when they become separated he misses all of the clucking.

"Done in bold lines, simple shapes, and bright colors, the chunky poultry are set against unadorned, mainly white backgrounds. . . . This look at a busy mom and preschooler perfectly echoes a child's experience." SLJ

Day, Alexandra
  Carl and the puppies; story and pictures by Alexandra Day. Square Fish 2011 un il (My readers) $15.99; pa $3.99
Grades: PreK K 1   E
  1. Dogs -- Fiction
  ISBN 978-0-312-62482-8; 0-312-62482-4; 978-0-312-62483-5 pa; 0-312-62483-2 pa

"Carl dog-sits three active pups. Large print, controlled vocabulary, simple sentences and story [arc], supportive pictures, and plentiful white space make [this] a good choice for the newest readers." Horn Book Guide

  ★ **Carl's** sleepy afternoon. Farrar, Straus and Giroux 2005 un il $12.95
Grades: PreK K 1   E
  1. Dogs -- Fiction
  ISBN 0-374-31088-2

Carl's owners have many errands to do and expect Carl to sleep the entire afternoon. Instead, Carl the rottweiler roams the town assisting many people in their daily chores

"The entertaining story is told through the gently detailed, warmly realistic paintings." SLJ

Other titles about Carl are:
Carl and the baby duck (2011)
Carl and the puppies (2011)
Carl goes shopping (1990)
Carl goes to daycare (1993)
Carl makes a scrapbook (1994)
Carl's afternoon in the park (1991)
Carl's birthday (1995)
Carl's Christmas (1990)
Carl's masquerade (1992)
Carl's snowy afternoon (2009)
Carl's summer vacation (2008)
Follow Carl (1998)
Good dog, Carl (1985)

  Frank and Ernest. Green Tiger Press 2010 un il $15.95
Grades: PreK K 1 2   E
  1. Bears -- Fiction 2. Elephants -- Fiction 3. Restaurants -- Fiction
  ISBN 978-1-59583-424-9; 1-59583-424-9

                LC 2010010747

A reissue of the title first published 1988 by Scholastic
An elephant and a bear take over a diner and find out about responsibility and food language.

"Day's mock-dignified illustrations, lush and attractive, add dimension to the entertaining story. A diner glossary is included to aid comprehension." Horn Book Guide

Another title about Frank and Ernest is:
Frank and Ernest play ball (2011)

  Frank and Ernest play ball. Green Tiger Press 2011 un il $15.95
Grades: PreK K 1 2   E
  1. Bears -- Fiction 2. Baseball -- Fiction 3. Elephants

-- Fiction

ISBN 978-1-59583-438-6; 1-59583-438-9

LC 2010048046

A reissue of the title first published 1990 by Scholastic

With the help of a baseball dictionary so they can learn the necessary language, an elephant and a bear take over the management of a baseball team.

"Sports fans will enjoy the text with its in-the-know lingo. . . . Day's play-it-straight paintings—except for the elephant and bear in the infield—convey much of the spirit of baseball." Horn Book Guide

Good dog, Carl. Simon & Schuster Children's Publishing 2010 un il $9.99; pa $6.99

Grades: PreK K 1   E

1. Stories without words 2. Dogs -- Fiction 3. Infants -- Fiction

ISBN 978-1-4424-1660-4; 1-4424-1660-2; 978-0-689-81771-7 pa; 0-689-81771-1 pa

A reissue of the title first published 1985

Lively and unusual things happen when Carl the dog is left in charge of the baby.

Day, Nancy Raines

On a windy night; illustrated by George Bates. Abrams Books for Young Readers 2009 un il $16.95

Grades: PreK K 1   E

1. Stories in rhyme 2. Fear -- Fiction 3. Halloween -- Fiction

ISBN 978-0-8109-3900-4; 0-8109-3900-2

LC 2008-52532

On a windy Halloween night as a boy is returning home through the woods after trick-or-treating, he hears scary noises behind him.

Bates's "pen-and-ink drawings push and pull, creating scariness with forceful hatching and eerie lighting. . . . There's enough Halloween fright to satisfy adventurous young readers, and a comforting ending for those with jangled nerves." Publ Wkly

De Groat, Diane

Ants in your pants, worms in your plants! (Gilbert goes green) Harper 2011 un il $16.99

Grades: K 1 2 3   E

1. School stories 2. Opossums -- Fiction 3. Earth Day -- Fiction 4. Environmental protection -- Fiction

ISBN 978-0-06-176511-7; 0-06-176511-2

LC 2010009396

Gilbert seems to be the only one in his class who cannot think of any ideas for an Earth Day project.

"The cartoon illustrations add detail to the story, and fans of Gilbert and friends will enjoy reading about their Earth-friendly plans." SLJ

April Fool! watch out at school! [by] Diane de Groat. HarperCollinsPublishers 2009 un il $17.99; lib bdg $18.89

Grades: K 1 2 3   E

1. School stories 2. Picture puzzles 3. Practical jokes -- Fiction 4. April Fools' Day -- Fiction

ISBN 978-0-06-143042-8; 0-06-143042-0; 978-0-06-143043-5 lib bdg; 0-06-143043-9 lib bdg

LC 2008012797

On April Fools' Day, Gilbert is unhappy that everyone is tricking him and he is unable to get them back, but then he thinks of a great way to fool his best friend. Includes tricks hidden in the illustrations for the reader to find.

"Children will find it easy to sympathize with gullible yet sometimes cagy Gilbert. . . . And they'll enjoy studying the colorful illustrations for the many sight gags that go unmentioned in the text." Booklist

Gilbert, the surfer dude; 1st ed.; HarperCollinsPublishers 2009 31p il (I can read!) $16.99

Grades: K 1 2   E

1. Surfing -- Fiction 2. Opossums -- Fiction

ISBN 978-0-06-125211-2; 0-06-125211-5

LC 2008020222

Gilbert the opossum imagines himself as Surfer Dude on a fun-filled day at the beach.

Good night, sleep tight, don't let the bedbugs bite! SeaStar Bks. 2002 un il hardcover o.p. pa $6.99

Grades: K 1 2 3   E

1. Camps -- Fiction

ISBN 1-58717-128-7; 1-58717-129-5 lib bdg; 0-06-134061-8 pa

LC 2001-49863

Gilbert is excited about staying overnight at Camp Hi-Dee-Ho, until he hears about the legendary camp ghost

"The animal characters look and act convincingly childlike, and deGroat gets the thrills and (slight) chills of a first overnight camping experience just right." Horn Book

Happy Birthday to you, you belong in a zoo. Morrow Junior Bks. 1999 un il hardcover o.p. $15; pa $6.99

Grades: K 1 2 3   E

1. Gifts -- Fiction 2. Friendship -- Pictorial works -- Juvenile fiction 3. Gilbert (Fictitious character) -- Pictorial works -- Juvenile fiction

ISBN 0-688-16544-3; 0-688-16545-1 lib bdg; 0-06-001029-0 pa

LC 98-44722

Before Lewis's birthday party, Gilbert's mother wisely substitutes a toy for the frying pan Gilbert wants to give Lewis

"Both story and watercolor pictures excel at capturing the anguish that children often feel as they try to learn the social game." Booklist

Jingle bells, homework smells. HarperCollins Publishers 2000 un il hardcover o.p. pa $6.99

Grades: K 1 2 3   E

1. School stories 2. Snow -- Fiction 3. Animals -- Fiction 4. Homework -- Fiction 5. Christmas -- Fiction

ISBN 0-688-17543-0; 0-688-17544-9 lib bdg; 978-0-688-17545-0 pa; 0-688-17545-7 pa

LC 99-50291

Gilbert forgets to do his homework over the weekend because he is busy playing in the snow and getting ready for Christmas, but then he comes up with a solution at the last minute

"The Christmas season makes a warm, colorful backdrop, which is reflected in the watercolor artwork." Booklist

Last one in is a rotten egg! [by] Diane de Groat. HarperCollins 2007 un il $15.99; lib bdg $16.89

Grades: K 1 2 3   E

1. Easter -- Fiction 2. Cousins -- Fiction

ISBN 978-0-06-089294-4; 0-06-089294-3; 978-0-06-089295-1 lib bdg; 0-06-089295-1 lib bdg

LC 2006021474

When Gilbert and Lola's cousin Wally comes to visit for Easter, he learns a lesson about being greedy during the annual Easter egg hunt.

"Pastel, cartoon-style watercolor illustrations depict the activities while revealing the small town's populace made up of raccoons, porcupines, rabbits, cats, and dogs. Children will relate to the story, which imparts a gentle lesson on how to be a friend." SLJ

Liar, liar, pants on fire. SeaStar Books 2003 un il hardcover o.p. pa $6.99

Grades: K 1 2 3   E

1. Honesty 2. Schools 3. Theater 4. School stories 5. Self-confidence 6. Theater -- Fiction 7. Truthfulness and falsehood -- Fiction

ISBN 978-15871-7214-4; 978-0-8118-5453-5 pa

Gilbert is nervous about portraying George Washington in front of the class, and he feels even worse when he cannot find his main prop.

"This entertaining tale provides good discussion material and should be a winner at storytime." SLJ

Mother, you're the best! (but Sister, you're a pest!) by Diane deGroat. 1st ed.; HarperCollins Children's Books 2008 un il $16.99; lib bdg $17.89

Grades: K 1 2 3   E

1. Mothers -- Fiction 2. Siblings -- Fiction 3. Mother's Day -- Fiction

ISBN 978-0-06-123899-4; 0-06-123899-6; 978-0-06-123900-7 lib bdg; 0-06-123900-3 lib bdg

LC 2007009134

Gilbert wants to do something special for his mother on Mother's Day, but first he must stop his sister, Lola, from being the center of attention.

"Full-bleed, large-scale illustrations convey the intermittently disgruntled and longsuffering hero's moods. . . . This is a winning addition." Publ Wkly

No more pencils, no more books, no more teacher's dirty looks! HarperCollins 2006 un il lib bdg $18.89; pa $6.99

Grades: K 1 2 3   E

1. School stories 2. Friendship -- Fiction

ISBN 978-0-06-079115-5 lib bdg; 0-06-079115-2 lib bdg; 978-0-06-079116-2 pa; 0-06-079116-0 pa

LC 2005008783

Gilbert and his first-grade classmates are nervous about their performance on the last day of school, curious about the awards they will receive, sad to be leaving their teacher, and excited about summer vacation.

"The bright, cheery watercolor illustrations, with their sizeable cast of lovable, expressive characters, will draw youngsters into Gilbert's comfortable small-town suburban environment." Booklist

Roses are pink, your feet really stink. Morrow Junior Bks. 1996 un il $15; pa $6.99

Grades: K 1 2 3   E

1. School stories 2. Valentine's Day -- Fiction

ISBN 0-688-13604-4; 0-688-13605-2; 0-688-15220-1 pa

LC 94-43774

On Valentine's Day, Gilbert brings a tin of homemade cookies and his original nice or nasty poems to school

"The winning touch here is de Groat's . . . characteristically buoyant watercolor art, which features an amiable crew of assorted animals." Publ Wkly

★ **Trick** or treat, smell my feet. Morrow Junior Bks. 1998 un il hardcover o.p. pa $4.95

Grades: K 1 2 3   E

1. Siblings -- Fiction 2. Halloween -- Fiction 3. Costume -- Juvenile fiction 4. Schools -- Juvenile fiction 5. Halloween -- Juvenile fiction 6. Brothers and sisters -- Juvenile fiction

ISBN 0-688-15766-1; 0-688-15767-X lib bdg; 0-688-17061-7 pa

LC 97-32916

"De Groat's funny watercolor pictures capture the various animal creatures' very human expressions and body language." Booklist

Other titles about Gilbert are:

Ants in your pants, worms in your plants! (2011)

April fool!, watch out at school! (2009)

Brand-new pencils, brand-new books (2005)

Good night, sleep tight, don't let the bedbugs bite! (2002)

Happy birthday to you, you belong in the zoo (1999)

Jingle, bells, homework smells (2000)

Last one in is a rotten egg! (2007)

Liar, liar, pants on fire (2003)

Mother, you are the best! (2008)

No more pencils, no more books, no more teacher's dirty looks! (2006)

Roses are pink, your feet really stink (1996)

We gather together--now please get lost! (2001)

We gather together--now please get lost! SeaStar Bks. 2001 un il $15.95; lib bdg $15.88; pa $6.95

Grades: K 1 2 3   E

1. School stories 2. Thanksgiving Day -- Fiction

ISBN 1-58717-096-5; 1-58717-095-7 lib bdg; 0-8118-5055-2 pa

LC 2001-34407

At Thanksgiving time, Gilbert the opossum gets stuck with Philip as his partner on class trip to Pilgrim Town

"DeGroat's watercolor illustrations add charm and humor to the straightforward text." SLJ

De Paola, Tomie, 1934-

Four friends at Christmas. Aladdin 2009 un il $12.99

Grades: PreK K 1 2   E

1. Frogs -- Fiction 2. Animals -- Fiction 3. Christmas -- Fiction 4. Friendship -- Fiction

ISBN 978-1-4169-9175-5; 1-4169-9175-1

A reissue of the edition published 2002; previously published 1977, in different form, as the chapter entitled Winter in Four Stories for Four Seasons

Mister Frog has slept through Christmas every year and is determined to celebrate this one with his three best friends. But when he takes a short nap that turns into a very long sleep, he wakes up late on Christmas Eve, and there's no one to celebrate with!

"The tale of Frog's first Christmas is charming in its simplicity. The four animal friends' unique personalities come through in dePaola's trademark cozy illustrations." Horn Book Guide

★ **Guess** who's coming to Santa's for dinner? written and illustrated by Tomie dePaola. Putnam's 2004 un il $16.99

Grades: PreK K 1 2   E
1. Christmas 2. Family life 3. Santa Claus 4. Hospitality 5. Humorous stories 6. Christmas -- Fiction 7. Family life -- Fiction 8. Santa Claus -- Fiction
ISBN 0-399-24271-6

        LC 2003-26638
A houseful of relatives turns "Mrs. C." and Santa's Christmas into a string of surprises, from the arrival of a pet polar bear to Cousin James B.'s flaming plum pudding.

"The part comic strip-style format cleverly reflects the busy, everyone-talk-at-once hum of a big family gathering and serves up plenty of funny asides. Warm and wonderful as Christmas cake fresh out of the oven, dePaola's softly hued, rounded illustrations shine with holiday spirit." Booklist

★ **Jamie** O'Rourke and the pooka. Putnam 2000 un il $16.99; pa $6.99

Grades: PreK K 1 2 3   E
1. Goblins 2. Laziness
ISBN 0-399-23467-5; 0-698-11974-X pa

        LC 99-22469
While his wife is away, lazy Jamie O'Rourke relies on a pooka to clean up the messes that he and his friends make

"DePaola's cozy, colorful illustrations are a good match for the lighthearted, rhythmic text." Horn Book Guide

Meet the Barkers; Morgan and Moffat go to school. written and illustrated by Tomie dePaola. Putnam 2001 un il $13.99; pa $5.99

Grades: PreK K 1 2   E
1. Dogs 2. Twins 3. Schools 4. School stories 5. Dogs -- Fiction 6. Twins -- Fiction 7. First day of school 8. Brothers and sisters
ISBN 0-399-23708-9; 0-14-250083-6 pa

        LC 00-55355
Bossy Moffie (a dog) and her quiet twin brother Morgie both enjoy starting school, especially getting gold stars and making new friends

"Genuinely expressive, lovable characters, depicted in warm tones on handmade watercolor paper, make this a great read-aloud." SLJ

Other titles about the Barkers are:
Boss for a day (2001)
Hide-and-seek all week (2001)
A new Barker in the house (2002)
Trouble in the Barkers' class (2003)

★ **Nana** Upstairs & Nana Downstairs; written and illustrated by Tomie dePaola. Putnam 1998 un il $16.99; pa $6.99

Grades: PreK K 1 2   E
1. Death -- Fiction 2. Grandmothers -- Fiction
ISBN 0-399-23108-0; 0-698-11836-7 pa

        LC 96-31908
A newly illustrated edition of the title first published 1973

"The illustrations are vintage dePaola, and the warm palette conveys the boy's love for his elderly relatives." Horn Book Guide

Now one foot, now the other. G. P. Putnam's Sons 2005 un il $14.99; pa $7.99

Grades: PreK K 1 2   E
1. Stroke -- Fiction 2. Grandfathers -- Fiction
ISBN 0-399-24259-7; 0-14-240104-8 pa
A newly illustrated edition of the title first published 1981

When his grandfather suffers a stroke, Bobby teaches him to walk, just as his grandfather had once taught him.

"The illustrations have been digitally colorized in this welcome new edition." Horn Book Guide

Pascual and the kitchen angels; written and illustrated by Tomie dePaola. G.P. Putnam 2004 un il hardcover o.p. pa $5.99

Grades: PreK K 1 2   E
1. Angels -- Fiction 2. Cooking -- Fiction 3. Christian life -- Fiction
ISBN 0-399-24214-7; 0-14-240536-1 pa

        LC 2003-8521
Pascual, a boy blessed by angels at his birth, receives divine help when the Franciscan monks make him their cook

"Acrylic illustrations with soft pastel backgrounds show Pascual as a little boy. . . . The winsome paintings capture his serene spirituality as he and the creatures lift their voices toward heaven. Simple, well-chosen words reflect the youngster's sincere love for God and all of His creatures." SLJ

★ **Stagestruck**; written and illustrated by Tomie dePaola. G.P. Putnam's Sons 2005 un il $16.99

Grades: PreK K 1 2   E
1. School stories 2. Theater -- Fiction
ISBN 0-399-24338-0

        LC 2004-9261
Although Tommy fails to get the part of Peter Rabbit in the kindergarten play, he still finds a way to be the center of attention on stage

"The gently delivered lesson at the end does not dampen the fun of watching this aspiring thespian get carried away. . . . With its warm palette, rounded shapes, and clarity of expression, dePaola's signature style makes Tommy's world an inviting place to visit." Booklist

★ **Strega** Nona: an old tale. Simon & Schuster 1988 un il $18.99; pa $7.99

Grades: PreK K 1 2   E
1. Witches -- Fiction
ISBN 0-671-66283-X; 0-671-66606-1 pa

        LC 88-11438
A reissue of the title first published 1975 by Prentice-Hall

A Caldecott Medal honor book, 1976

"Tomie de Paola has used simple colors, simple line, and medieval costume and architecture in his spaciously composed humorous pictures." Bull Cent Child Books

Other titles about Strega Nona are:
Big Anthony and the magic ring (1979)
Big Anthony: his story (1998)
Brava, Strega Nona (2008)
Merry Christmas, Strega Nona (1986)
Strega Nona: her story (1996)
Strega Nona meets her match (1993)
Strega Nona takes a vacation (2000)
Strega Nona's gift (2011)
Strega Nona's harvest (2009)
Strega Nona's magic lessons (1982)

The **art** lesson; written and illustrated by Tomie de-Paola. Putnam 1989 un il hardcover o.p. pa $5.99
Grades: PreK K 1 2   E
1. Art -- Fiction
ISBN 0-399-21688-X; 0-698-11572-4 pa
LC 88-27617
Having learned to be creative in drawing pictures at home, young Tommy is dismayed when he goes to school and finds the art lesson there much more regimented
This is "engrossing reading. DePaola's characteristic bright illustrations complement and enliven his tale of growing up." Horn Book

The **baby** sister; written and illustrated by Tomie de-Paola. Putnam 1996 un il $16.99; pa $5.99
Grades: PreK K 1 2   E
1. Infants -- Fiction 2. Siblings -- Fiction 3. Grandmothers -- Fiction
ISBN 0-399-22908-6; 0-698-11773-5 pa
LC 94-37218
"Tommy's mother is expecting a baby. Tommy helps get the baby's room ready and longs for a sister with a red ribbon in her hair. He's thrilled when the baby is a girl, but while his mother is away in the hospital, his Italian grandmother comes to stay, and he finds it hard to get along with her. . . . Simple lines and warm colors convey the affection in the extended family and the special closeness between Tommy and his parents." Booklist

★ The **night** of Las Posadas; written and illustrated by Tomie dePaola. Putnam 1999 un il $15.99; pa $6.99
Grades: K 1 2 3   E
1. Saints 2. Christmas -- Fiction 3. Posadas (Social custom) -- Fiction
ISBN 0-399-23400-4; 0-698-11901-0 pa
LC 98-36405
At the annual celebration of Las Posadas in old Santa Fe, the husband and wife slated to play Mary and Joseph are delayed by car trouble, but a mysterious couple appear who seem perfect for the part
"DePaola's talent for crafting folktales is honed to near-perfection, and his pages glow with the soft sun-washed hues of the Southwest." Publ Wkly

★ The **song** of Francis; [by] Tomie dePaola. G.P. Putnam's Sons 2009 un il $16.99
Grades: PreK K 1 2   E
1. Saints 2. Birds -- Fiction 3. Saints -- Fiction 4. Writers on religion
ISBN 978-0-399-25210-5; 0-399-25210-X
LC 2008018578

Francis, the Little Poor One, is so filled with the love of God that he bursts into song, and he is joined by birds of every color.
"De Paola's tropical-hued collages convey the magic of this religious interpretation in an appealing way." SLJ

De Regniers, Beatrice Schenk
★ **May** I bring a friend? illustrated by Beni Montresor. Atheneum Pubs. 1964 un il hardcover o.p. pa $7.99
Grades: PreK K   E
1. Animals -- Fiction
ISBN 0-689-20615-1; 0-689-71353-3 pa
Awarded the Caldecott Medal, 1965
"Rich color and profuse embellishment adorn an opulent setting. Absurdities and contrasts are so imaginatively combined in a hilarious comedy of manners that the merriment can be enjoyed on several levels." Horn Book

De Roo, Elena
The **rain** train; illustrated by Brian Lovelock. Candlewick Press 2011 un il $15.99
Grades: PreK K   E
1. Rain -- Fiction 2. Night -- Fiction 3. Railroads -- Fiction
ISBN 978-0-7636-5313-2; 0-7636-5313-6
LC 2010039174
A young boy watches and listens as the Rain Train takes him on a ride past city lights, over rivers, and through tunnels one rainy night.
"De Roo's rhyming, lyrical text never derails; the onomatopoeic verse rolls rhythmically along, both lulling listeners and moving the action forward. . . . Lovelock's misty watercolor and ink illustrations, dominated by dusky purples and blues, convey the excitement of a special nighttime journey." Horn Book

De Seve, Randall
The **Duchess** of Whimsy; an absolutely delicious fairy tale. [by] Randall de Seve; [illustrated by] Peter de Seve. Philomel Books 2009 un il $17.99
Grades: PreK K 1   E
1. Fairy tales
ISBN 978-0-399-25095-8; 0-399-25095-6
LC 2009-2637
The Duchess of Whimsy has absolutely no interest in the Earl of Norm until he makes a sandwich that causes her to look at him in an entirely different way
"Pages burst to life with rich colors whenever the duchess appears and then become comically dull whenever the earl shows up. With a romantic story and smooth art, this charming picture book will appeal to sophisticated young readers who will find the happily-ever-after whimsically ordinary." Booklist

★ The **toy** boat; [by] Randall DeSeve; [illustrated by] Loren Long. Philomel Books 2007 un il $16.99
Grades: PreK K   E
1. Toys -- Fiction 2. Boats and boating -- Fiction
ISBN 978-0-399-24374-5
LC 2006026281
A toy boat gets separated from its owner and has an adventure on the high seas
"The streamlined text is straightforward, letting the amazing art do much of the work. Long's acrylic, hyper-

realistic pictures, awash with many shades of blue, are so substantial they seem to be molded from clay." Booklist

De Smet, Marian

I have two homes; Marian De Smet; [illustrated by] Nynke Talsma. Clavis 2011 32 p. col. ill. $15.95

Grades: PreK K 1 2   E

1. Divorce -- Fiction 2. Picture books for children 3. Children of divorced parents -- Juvenile fiction

ISBN 1605371025; 9781605371023

In this children's picture book, "Nina's parents have divorced, and she is dealing with the changes in her life . . . . When they decide to have separate homes, Nina notices changes in their behavior toward her. She misbehaves in an attempt to get their attention but they are often preoccupied. She talks about missing each parent while she is in the home of the other. . . . She finally concludes that her parents aren't happy with each other but they are happy with her." (School Library Journal)

DeFelice, Cynthia C.

★ **Old** Granny and the bean thief; pictures by Cat Bowman Smith. Farrar, Straus and Giroux 2003 un il $16

Grades: K 1 2 3   E

1. Thieves -- Fiction 2. Grandmothers -- Fiction

ISBN 0-374-35614-9

LC 2002-20770

After a thief steals Old Granny's beans while she is asleep at night, she gets some surprising help with catching him.

"The down-home narrative is folksy and fun to read aloud. . . . Smith uses a Southwestern palette in her cartoon-style paintings." SLJ

★ **One** potato, two potato; pictures by Andrea U'Ren. Farrar, Straus and Giroux 2006 un il $16

Grades: K 1 2 3   E

1. Magic -- Fiction 2. Potatoes -- Fiction

ISBN 978-0-374-35640-8; 0-374-35640-8

LC 2004-47217

A very poor, humble couple live so simple a life they share everything, until the husband discovers a pot with magical powers buried under the very last potato in the garden.

"U'Ren's large pen-and-gouache illustrations infuse the couple's grim situation with humor. . . . An entertaining tale." SLJ

DeGroat, Diane

Brand -new pencils, brand-new books. HarperCollins Publishers 2005 il lib bdg $16.89

Grades: K 1 2 3   E

1. School stories

ISBN 0-06-072615-6

LC 200404179

Gilbert's excitement over starting first grade turns to worry that the teacher will be mean, the work too hard, and his classmates too unfriendly, but throughout the day there are pleasant surprises.

"With its charming, detailed watercolor illustrations, this story has significant child appeal." SLJ

DePalma, Mary Newell

Bow-wow wiggle waggle; written and illustrated by Mary Newell DePalma. Eerdmans Books for Young Readers 2012 32 p. col. ill. (reinforced: alk. paper) $14.00

Grades: PreK K 1 2   E

1. Dogs -- Fiction 2. Animals -- Fiction 3. Picture books for children 4. Stories in rhyme

ISBN 0802854087; 9780802854087

LC 2011035827

This story is "told exclusively with onomatopoetic narrative and watercolor illustrations." In it, "a boy and his dog encounter other animals while playing outdoors," including a cat, a frog, a butterfly, and other animals. "Geese chase them from the pond, a snake and then rabbits appear from under the bushes, and the dog wanders off from the boy to chase a cat." (School Library Journal)

The **Nutcracker** doll. Arthur A. Levine Books 2007 un il $16.99

Grades: K 1 2   E

1. Ballet -- Fiction

ISBN 0-439-80242-0; 978-0-439-80242-0

LC 2006-16466

Kepley, a young ballerina, gets to play a flower doll in a professional production of "The Nutcracker."

"Airy pen-and-wash illustrations convey moments both large and small. The text thoughtfully keeps the spotlight on the young dancer's feelings." Horn Book Guide

Uh-oh! William B. Eerdmans 2011 un il

Grades: PreK K 1   E

1. Dinosaurs -- Fiction

ISBN 0-8028-5372-2; 978-0-8028-5372-1

LC 2010048403

"A young dinosaur gets himself into all kinds of trouble in this clever, nearly wordless book. The little terror is jumping on the couch, which leads to knocking over his siblings' blocks and a plant. This begins a chain of events that culminates in an overflowing dishwasher washing the youngster out the window. . . . The plot is humorously appealing, if deceptively sophisticated. Despite the lack of text, it is likely to appeal most to older preschoolers and early elementary children who will understand the humor." SLJ

A **grand** old tree. Arthur A. Levine Books 2005 un il $16.99

Grades: K 1 2 3   E

1. Trees -- Fiction

ISBN 0-439-62334-0

"For many years a tree flourishes. . . . After the old tree dies, it still provides a home to animals and insects as it slowly decomposes. . . . Neither sentimental nor unfeeling, this appealing picture book offers an appreciation of the cycle of life through a story that is accessible to young children." Booklist

The **perfect** gift. Arthur A. Levine Books 2010 un il $16.99

Grades: PreK K 1   E

1. Gifts -- Fiction 2. Animals -- Fiction 3. Parrots -- Fiction 4. Grandmothers -- Fiction 5. Books and reading -- Fiction

ISBN 978-0-545-15402-4; 0-545-15402-2

LC 2009006769

Lori the lorikeet wants to give her grandmother a present, but after dropping her beautiful red berry into the river, she and her friends must try to retrieve the berry or find another gift.

"While DePalma uses delightfully expressive, rhythmic language to tell her accessible tale, her acrylic illustrations are the standout." SLJ

Deacon, Alexis

Beegu. Farrar, Straus & Giroux 2003 un il $16
Grades: PreK K 1 2   E
  1. Extraterrestrial beings -- Fiction
ISBN 0-374-30667-2

LC 2002-192738

A small creature from space finds no welcome on Earth, until she meets a group of children on a playground

"Beegu's black outline and solid yellow center evoke a celestial simplicity. . . . The accomplished artwork underscores the children's easy acceptance of Beegu and highlights the book's uplifting message that acts of kindness have lasting effects." Publ Wkly

★ A **place** to call home; Alexis Deacon; illustrated by Viviane Schwarz. Candlewick Press 2011 1 v. col. ill. $15.99
Grades: PreK K 1   E
  1. Adventure fiction 2. Hamsters -- Fiction 3. Picture books for children 4. Voyages and travels -- Fiction 5. Home -- Fiction 6. Brothers -- Fiction
ISBN 0-7636-5360-8; 9780763653606

LC 2010040125

This book tells the story of "hamsterlike creatures bumbling across a junkyard . . . [as] they embark on a search for a new home. They cross an ocean (readers can see it's a puddle), a 'desert,' and make their way to the edge of the world--the top of an old dryer. In [various] scenes, . . . [illustrator Viviane] Schwarz's . . . furry animals squabble, fret, and cheer each other on; in sequential panels, their running commentary appears in word balloons above their heads. When the junkyard dog grabs one of them, they balk, . . . but taking courage from all they've done so far, they tackle the dog and rescue their sibling." (Publishers Weekly)

"In scenes bursting with physical comedy, Schwarz's . . . furry animals squabble, fret, and cheer each other on; in sequential panels, their running commentary appears in word balloons above their heads. . . . While the creatures may trip over themselves, blundering through their tiny lives not knowing quite where they are headed, Deacon . . . and Schwarz never put a foot wrong. Children will clamor for repeats." Publ Wkly

Degen, Bruce

★ **Jamberry**; story and pictures by Bruce Degen. Harper & Row 1983 un il $17.99; pa $7.99; bd bk $7.99
Grades: PreK K 1 2   E
  1. Stories in rhyme 2. Berries -- Fiction
ISBN 0-06-021416-3; 0-06-443068-5 pa; 0-694-00651-3 bd bk

LC 82-47708

"Berries and jam are roundly celebrated in a lilting rhyme that, coupled with the jaunty colored pictures, makes it . . . a good pick for sharing one on one, or fun to read aloud as a poetry introduction." Booklist

Degman, Lori

1 zany zoo. Simon & Schuster Books for Young Readers 2010 un il $15.99
Grades: PreK K 1   E
  1. Counting 2. Stories in rhyme 3. Zoos -- Fiction 4. Animals -- Fiction
ISBN 978-1-4169-8990-5; 1-4169-8990-0

LC 2009003776

When one fearless fox grabs the zookeeper's keys and opens all the cages, increasing numbers of animals behave in most unusual ways.

"Kids will enjoy hearing the catchy rhymes read multiple times. Digital cartoon images, made to appear like hand-drawn ink sketches, capture the swift movement and playful mood." SLJ

Delessert, Etienne

Big and Bad; [by] Etienne Delessert. Houghton Mifflin 2008 32p il $17
Grades: 1 2 3 4   E
  1. Cats -- Fiction 2. Pigs -- Fiction 3. Wolves -- Fiction 4. Animals -- Fiction
ISBN 978-0-618-88934-1; 0-618-88934-5

LC 2007019291

In this variation on the classic tale of the three little pigs, two clever cats decide to rid their locale of a vicious wolf whose hunger threatens the entire planet, and enlist the help of assorted animals to build houses for the bait—three exquisitely pink pigs.

"Surreal watercolor and colored-pencil scenes are rendered in the artist's signature earthy tones against white backgrounds. . . . Delessert's direct, sophisticated language and unnerving closeups of the 'marauding' felines and their predator are not for the faint of heart, but the message—that the powerless can reverse their fortunes if they unite and use their wits—will resonate with many readers." SLJ

Moon theater. Creative Editions 2009 un il $17.95
Grades: K 1 2 3   E
  1. Theater -- Fiction
ISBN 978-1-56846-208-0; 1-56846-208-5

LC 2008-53991

To prepare for the moon's nightly rising, a young stagehand performs such tasks as dressing the birds in long dark coats, training wild dogs to howl, and watering the stars.

"Delessert's distinctive, sophisticated style and a dark palette evoke a nighttime theme that turns the onset of evening into a theatrical production. . . . Inventive and dramatic, this has more child appeal than usual from Delessert; although other man-in-the-moon tales exist, they wane alongside this numinous performance." Booklist

Demarest, Chris L.

All aboard! a traveling alphabet. concept by Chris L. Demarest; illustrated by Bill Mayer. Simon & Schuster 2008 un il $17.99
Grades: PreK K 1 2   E
  1. Alphabet 2. Travel -- Fiction 3. Travel -- Juvenile literature
ISBN 978-0-689-85249-7; 0-689-85249-5

LC 2006103006

An alphabet book provides a presentation of the common structures one sees and uses while getting from place to place, using such images as an 'O' for a looped overpass and a 'B' to denote the arches of a bridge.

"Mayer is a master of airbrush and bold design, using striking perspectives and dynamic angles, often evoking a strong sense of motion in this homage to travel posters of the 1920s." Horn Book Guide

Demas, Corinne

Always in trouble; written by Corinne Demas & pictures by Noah Z. Jones. Scholastic Press 2009 un il $16.99
Grades: K 1 2 3   E
1. Dogs -- Fiction
ISBN 978-0-545-02453-2; 0-545-02453-6
LC 2007-36079
Even after attending obedience school, Emma's dog Toby misbehaves until she takes him back to become a "specially trained dog."

"The story is great for reading aloud, but the many humorous details in the cartoon-style illustrations make it fun for individual reading as well. Text, illustration, and design all work together to create a delightful story." SLJ

Halloween surprise; illustrated by R.W. Alley. Walker & Co. 2011 un il $12.99
Grades: PreK K 1 2   E
1. Cats -- Fiction 2. Costume -- Fiction 3. Halloween -- Fiction
ISBN 978-0-8027-8612-8; 0-8027-8612-X
LC 2010043434
Lily tries many different costumes before she creates the perfect one for surprising her father on Halloween.

"The soft, orange-hued drawings done in pencil, watercolor, and gouache are appropriate for the season and full of activity. . . . Children will enjoy the Lily's imagination and the reactions of her kittens as she creates several costumes from materials she finds around her house. The just-right size of the book; plentiful white space; and large, clean font make this a good choice for beginning readers." SLJ

Pirates go to school; illustrated by John Manders. Orchard Books 2011 un il $16.99
Grades: K 1 2   E
1. School stories 2. Stories in rhyme 3. Pirates -- Fiction
ISBN 978-0-545-20629-7; 0-545-20629-4
LC 2010031394
A rhyming tale of pirates who go to school accompanied by their parrots, learn arithmetic and letters, and want to hear sea stories at storytime.

"Boldly colored scenes in watercolor, gouache, and colored pencil are paired with a nonthreatening ensemble, introducing imaginative readers to a typical school day. . . . A humorous read and a general purchase for most libraries." SLJ

Saying goodbye to Lulu; illustrated by Ard Hoyt. Little, Brown 2004 un il hardcover o.p. pa $6.99
Grades: PreK K 1 2   E
1. Dogs 2. Pets 3. Death 4. Grief 5. Dogs -- Fiction
6. Death -- Fiction 7. Bereavement -- Fiction
ISBN 0-316-70278-1; 0-316-04749-X pa
LC 2003-44690
When her dog Lulu dies, a girl grieves but then continues with her life

"Hoyt's expressive illustrations, ink-and-colored-pencil drawings washed with watercolors, reflect the tone of the text and show the child's sadness without sentimentality. . . . A sensitive, hopeful portrayal." Booklist

Valentine surprise; [by] Corinne Demas; illustrations by R. W. Alley. Walker & Co. 2008 un il $12.95
Grades: PreK K 1   E
1. Valentine's Day -- Fiction 2. Mother-daughter relationship -- Fiction
ISBN 978-0-8027-9664-6; 0-8027-9664-8
LC 2007020143
A little girl tries to create the perfect heart-shaped valentine for her mother on Valentine's Day.

"The language is simple enough for beginning readers, and the story will also work well for group sharing. The typeface changes to reflect the adjective relating to each valentine. Cartoon illustrations in pencil, watercolor, and gouache show Lily in a frenzy of activity." SLJ

Another title about Lily is:
Halloween surprise (2011)

Demers, Dominique

Today, maybe; illustrated by Gabrielle Grimard; translated by Sheila Fischman. Orca Book Publishers 2011 un il $19.95
Grades: K 1 2 3   E
1. Fairy tales
ISBN 978-1-55469-400-6; 1-55469-400-0
"A little girl lives alone in a small house in a big forest, where she waits for someone. She doesn't know for whom she waits, nor why. . . . Then a parade of strangers arrives. . . . The girl sends them off . . . explaining that she is waiting for someone else. And, at last, that someone comes. . . . [This] is a work of clever, poetic sweetness, with familiar folktale imagery giving way to tender surprise." Booklist

Demi

★ The **boy** who painted dragons; [by] Demi. Margaret K. McElderry Books 2007 un il $21.99
Grades: 1 2 3 4   E
1. Artists -- Fiction 2. Courage -- Fiction 3. Dragons -- Fiction
ISBN 978-1-4169-2469-2; 1-4169-2469-8
LC 2005033679
Ping, a painter of dragons—of which he is secretly afraid—is challenged to seek the truth, find the truth, and dare to be true

"Each page contains paintings of gilt-colored creatures and swatches of delicate Chinese silk brocade. The colors range from rich purples and vibrant reds to cool blues and muted beiges. . . . An elegantly told tale, enhanced by exquisite illustrations." SLJ

★ The **emperor's** new clothes; a tale set in China. Margaret K. McElderry Bks. 2000 un il $19.95
Grades: K 1 2 3   E
1. Authors 2. Novelists 3. Dramatists 4. Fairy tales
5. Children's authors 6. Short story writers
ISBN 0-689-83068-8
LC 99-24883
In this retelling of Hans Christian Andersen's tale, two rascals sell a vain Chinese emperor an invisible suit of clothes

"Demi's retelling is lucid, graceful, and true to the original. . . . Figures are delicately outlined; they are painted with flat, jewel-like colors and metallic gold and set against subtly patterned grounds that resemble silk damask. . . . A lovely and meticulously wrought rendition." Horn Book Guide

The **girl** who drew a phoenix; [by] Demi. Margaret K. McElderry Books 2008 un il $21.99

Grades: 1 2 3   E

1. Drawing -- Fiction 2. Phoenix (Mythical bird) -- Fiction
ISBN 978-1-4169-5347-0; 1-4169-5347-7

LC 2007015411

A young Chinese girl acquires the qualities of the miraculous phoenix—wisdom, clear sight, generosity, and right judgment—by practicing drawing the mythical bird

"Created in paint, ink, and Chinese silk brocade, swirling images of phoenixes with long, feathery tails fill the pages, including elegant horizontal foldouts." Booklist

The **greatest** power. Margaret K. McElderry Bks. 2004 un il $19.95

Grades: K 1 2 3   E

1. Power (Social sciences) -- Fiction
ISBN 0-689-84503-0

LC 2002-10869

Long ago, a Chinese emperor challenges the children of his kingdom to show him the greatest power in the world, and all are surprised at what is discovered

"The text and the handsomely designed, richly colored artwork, which is touched with gold leaf, are set within a circular motif that reinforces the idea of eternity. As usual, Demi ably combines striking artwork and a meaningful story, with quiet dignity and wisdom." Booklist

The **magic** pillow; written and illustrated by Demi. Margaret K. McElderry Books 2008 un il $19.99

Grades: K 1 2   E

1. Magic -- Fiction 2. Dreams -- Fiction
ISBN 978-1-4169-2470-8; 1-4169-2470-1

LC 2006-029213

A poor young boy in China yearns for wealth and power, until a magician gives him a magic pillow that brings dreams of what would happen if his wishes came true.

"Demi's dainty, jewel-like art is the perfect vehicle for this story, adoped from a Shen Jiji story. Rendered in traditional Chinese paints and inks and framed in her characteristic gold borders." Booklist

Dempsey, Kristy

Me with you; illustrated by Christopher Denise. Philomel Books 2009 un il $16.99

Grades: PreK K 1   E

1. Stories in rhyme 2. Bears -- Fiction 3. Grandfathers -- Fiction
ISBN 978-0-399-25017-0; 0-399-25017-4

LC 2008-11751

A little girl bear describes her relationship with her beloved grandfather.

"While the rhyming text is delightful, it is the lush, computer-generated illustrations and the two cozy, endearing characters that children will treasure. The enticing, picturesque scenes will make readers want to climb right into the pages to participate in each charming episode." Booklist

Mini racer; illustrated by Bridget Strevens-Marzo. Bloomsbury USA Children's Books 2011 un il $16.99; lib bdg $17.89

Grades: PreK K 1   E

1. Stories in rhyme 2. Racing -- Fiction 3. Animals -- Fiction 4. Vehicles -- Fiction
ISBN 978-1-59990-170-1; 1-59990-170-6; 978-1-59990-591-4 lib bdg; 1-59990-591-4 lib bdg

LC 2010006950

Animals in a variety of fanciful vehicles, including a snail on a skateboard and rabbits in a carrot-car, race over a difficult course with a suspenseful and surprising outcome.

"Dempsey's rapid text helps spur readers to keep the pages turning. . . . Full of zooming action and fender-bender drama, it has definite appeal for youngsters." Kirkus

Surfer Chick; by Kristy Dempsey; illustrated by Henry Cole. Abrams Books for Young Readers 2012 32 p.

Grades: PreK K 1 2 3   E

1. Stories in rhyme 2. Picture books for children 3. Surfing -- Juvenile fiction 4. Chickens -- Juvenile fiction 5. Father-daughter relationship -- Juvenile fiction 6. Surfing -- Fiction 7. Chickens -- Fiction 8. Roosters -- Fiction 9. Fathers and daughters -- Fiction
ISBN 1419701886; 9781419701887

LC 2011031798

This children's rhyming picture book tells a story with extensive use of surfing slang of a chicken father and his young daughter "who take to the beach so she can finally learn how to surf." The daughter learns perseverance and how to face new discouraging challenges. "At first Chick's mood is foul as she struggles through some [difficult] waters, but soon she is catching waves on her own board and even doing . . . just like her . . . dad!" (Publisher's note)

Dempsey, Sheena

Bye -bye baby brother! Sheena Dempsey. Candlewick Press 2013 32 p. (reinforced) $15.99

Grades: PreK K 1 2   E

1. Imagination -- Juvenile fiction 2. Sibling rivalry -- Juvenile fiction
ISBN 0763662410; 9780763662417

LC 2012942659

In this children's story, by Sheena Dempsey, "Ruby loves nothing more than playing, especially with Mom. But Mom is always so busy with Oliver, Ruby's baby brother . . . and Ruby is tired of waiting. . . . Maybe if Ruby puts her imagination to work, she can invent a way to make Oliver disappear to a place far, far away. Or would it be even more fun if she and Mom climbed aboard and went along for the ride?" (Publisher's note)

Denise, Anika

Bella and Stella come home; [illustrated] by Christopher Denise. Philomel Books 2010 un il $16.99

Grades: PreK K 1 2   E

1. Moving -- Fiction 2. Imaginary playmates -- Fiction
ISBN 978-0-399-24243-4; 0-399-24243-0

"Bella, an endearing girl with a big imagination and lots of personality, is nervous about moving to a new home. Fortunately, her trusted stuffed elephant, Stella, who looms large and lifelike in the child's mind, remains at her side through the upcoming uncertainties. . . . The sweet narrative, told from Bella's point of view, perfectly captures the little girl's psyche. The story is enhanced by luminous, almost photographic illustrations drawn in shades of pink, ivory, and gold." SLJ

Pigs love potatoes; illustrated by Christopher Denise. Philomel Books 2007 un il $15.99

Grades: PreK K   E

1. Counting 2. Stories in rhyme 3. Pigs -- Fiction 4. Cooking -- Fiction

ISBN 978-0-399-24036-2; 0-399-24036-5

LC 2006-20975

A counting book in which increasing numbers of pigs arrive and are recruited to help as Mamma cooks potatoes.

"Charming acrylic and charcoal pictures of a cozy household and a happy family will have wide appeal." SLJ

Derby, Sally

No mush today; by Sally Derby; illustrated by Nicole Tadgell. Lee & Low 2008 un il $16.95

Grades: PreK   E

1. Infants -- Fiction 2. Siblings -- Fiction 3. African Americans -- Fiction

ISBN 978-1-60060-238-2; 1-60060-238-X

"Nonie, a young African-American girl, sits at the breakfast table with her parents and a wailing baby, sulking: 'Not gonna eat my mush. Not gonna eat it!' I say. 'Squishy, yucky, yellow stuff-mush is baby food.' She puts on her shiny black shoes, and, with her chin poked out, stomps off to live with Grandma (next door). . . . The spare text deftly conveys Nonie's reactions and emotions, which are clearly reflected in Tadgell's realistic, folksy watercolors sweeping across double pages." SLJ

Derom, Dirk

Pigeon and Pigeonette; [text by] Dirk Derom; [illustrations by] Sarah Verroken. Enchanted Lion Books 2009 un il $16.95

Grades: K 1 2   E

1. Flight -- Fiction 2. Pigeons -- Fiction 3. Friendship -- Fiction 4. Handicapped -- Fiction

ISBN 978-1-59270-087-5; 1-59270-087-X

LC 2009-20779

An old, blind pigeon and a young, deformed pigeon become friends as they persevere in their quest to fly.

"The bold woodcuts and limited color palette convey the setting of the woods throughout the seasons. The boot-wearing pigeons are stylized and encourage closer examination. This is a story of overcoming odds and obstacles, and, despite an occasional adult tone, it delivers a positive and important message." SLJ

Derrick, David G.

Animals don't, so I won't! by David G. Derrick. Immedium 2012 36 p. (hardcover) $15.95

Grades: PreK K 1   E

1. Conduct of life -- Fiction 2. Animal behavior -- Juvenile fiction 3. Mother-child relationship -- Fiction 4. Behavior -- Fiction 5. Imagination -- Fiction 6. Mother and child -- Fiction 7. Animals -- Habits and

behavior -- Fiction

ISBN 159702029X; 9781597020299

LC 2011052797

Author David G. Derrick, Jr. presents a "knowledgeable mother turns the tables on her balky son by pointing out what animals DO. . . . Animal-loving Ben likes to pretend he's wild himself. He won't clean his room until his mother reminds him that as a beetle, he'll have to clean up elephant dung. He pretends to be a penguin that won't eat his lasagna until his mother pretends to barf up fish for him. And so forth . . . [When the story is about to end with] baby chimps rocking in their bedtime nests, there's a surprise: Dawn comes early for roosters." (Kirkus)

Desrosiers, Sylvie

Hocus Pocus. Kids Can Press 2011 un il

Grades: PreK K 1   E

1. Stories without words 2. Dogs -- Fiction 3. Rabbits -- Fiction

ISBN 1-55453-577-8; 978-1-55453-577-4

"This wordless book features a Wile E. Coyote vs. Road Runner-like battle between a rabbit, Hocus Pocus, and a hapless canine. Mr. Magic arrives home one day with a bag of peanuts, greens, and carrots. When he and his pooch settle down for a nap, his rabbit decides to bolt from the magic hat he left on the bureau. . . . The digitally rendered illustrations are suggestive of '60s cartoon storyboards. The drawings are colorful, and the amusing facial expressions and antics of Dog and Hocus Pocus will appeal to children." SLJ

Devlin, Jane

Hattie the bad; [pictures by] Joe Berger. Dial Books for Young Readers 2010 un il $16.99

Grades: PreK K 1   E

1. Good and evil -- Fiction

ISBN 978-0-8037-3447-0; 0-8037-3447-6

LC 2009-09281

A little girl tries to be good but soon discovers that being bad is ever so much more fun.

"Berger's zesty, orange-splashed illustrations hum with energy and comic hyperbole, in perfect sync with the text. . . . This is a romp worth reading time and again." Publ Wkly

Dewan, Ted

One true bear. Walker 2009 un il $14.99

Grades: 1 2 3   E

1. Teddy bears -- Fiction

ISBN 978-0-8027-8495-7; 0-8027-8495-X

LC 2009001807

A brave teddy bear puts his fur on the line when he goes to live with a boy who has a long history of destroying his toys.

"Wonderfully rich and detailed illustrations clearly show an active, rambunctious boy who is also capable of some quiet time with his bear. The placement of the text in and around the illustrations reinforces how well they complement one another." SLJ

Dewdney, Anna

Llama, llama red pajama; by Anna Dewdney. Viking 2005 un il $15.99

Grades: PreK K   E

1. Stories in rhyme 2. Llamas -- Fiction 3. Bedtime

-- Fiction 4. Mother-child relationship -- Fiction
ISBN 0-670-05983-8

LC 2004-25149

At bedtime, a little llama worries after his mother puts him to bed and goes downstairs.

"Dewdney gives a wonderfully fresh twist to a familiar nighttime ritual with an adorable bugeyed baby llama, staccato four-line rhymes, and page compositions that play up the drama. The simple rhymes call out for repeating." Booklist

Other titles about Llama are:

Llama Llama mad at Mama (2007)

Llama Llama misses Mama (2009)

Llama Llama holiday drama (2010)

Llama Llama home with Mama (2011)

Nobunny's perfect; by Anna Dewdney. Viking Childrens Books 2008 32p il $12.99
Grades: PreK K 1   E
1. Stories in rhyme 2. Rabbits -- Fiction 3. Etiquette -- Fiction
ISBN 978-0-670-06288-1; 0-670-06288-X

LC 2007-24008

Bunnies, who slurp their juice, forget to say "please," and bite their friends, learn about good manners.

"Dewdney's straightforward text, written in short sentences and rhyme, flows well. Full-color artwork effectively captures the facial expressions, conveys the bunnies' changing emotions, and recreates the activity described in the text." SLJ

Roly Poly pangolin. Viking 2010 un il $16.99
Grades: PreK K   E
1. Stories in rhyme 2. Shyness -- Fiction 3. Pangolins -- Fiction
ISBN 978-0-670-01160-5; 0-670-01160-6

"In this short rhyming story, a small pangolin is afraid of new experiences, including meeting other animals. When he hears an unexpected sound, he runs off in a panic, trips, and rolls into a tight ball to keep himself safe. . . . Dewdney has created a lovable childlike character with whom most preschoolers can easily identify. Textured full-bleed pages interspersed with some small action drawings on white space convey movement. Expressive closeup illustrations aptly portray Roly Poly's feelings." SLJ

Dewey, Ariane

Splash! [by] Ariane Dewey and Jose Aruego. Harcourt 2001 un il (Green Light readers) $10.95; pa $3.95
Grades: PreK K 1 2   E
1. Bears 2. Fishing 3. Clumsiness 4. Bears -- Fiction 5. Fishing -- Fiction
ISBN 0-15-216256-9; 0-15-216262-3 pa

LC 00-9723

Two clumsy bears join in fishing fun at the river

"This combines big, silly ink-and-watercolor pictures with two or three lines of text on each page. New readers will enjoy the slapstick . . . and the sounds of such words as splash and slip add to the fun of the story." Booklist

Dewey, Jennifer

Once I knew a spider; [by] Jennifer Owens Dewey; illustrated by Jean Cassels. Walker & Co. 2002 un il $16.95; lib bdg $17.85

Grades: PreK K 1 2   E
1. Spiders 2. Orb weavers 3. Spiders -- Fiction 4. Orb weavers -- Juvenile fiction
ISBN 0-8027-8700-2; 0-8027-8701-0 lib bdg

LC 2001-26345

An expectant mother watches as an orb weaver spider spins a web, lays her eggs, and stays with them over the winter

An "eloquent meditation on the cycle of life. The muted tones of Cassels's . . . austere interiors and the detailed paintings of the spider's behavior complement the calm, contemplative tone of the journal-like text." Publ Wkly

DiCamillo, Kate

★ **Great** joy; illustrated by Bagram Ibatoulline. Candlewick Press 2007 un il $16.99
Grades: PreK K 1 2   E
1. Christmas -- Fiction 2. Homeless persons -- Fiction
ISBN 978-0-7636-2920-5; 0-7636-2920-0

LC 2007-29934

Just before Christmas, when Frances sees a sad-eyed organ grinder and his monkey performing near her apartment, she cannot stop thinking about them, wondering where they go at night, and wishing she could do something to help.

"The plotline is simplicity itself, and the text lacks any sentimentality or fluff, allowing the acrylic paintings . . . to enrich and expand the story." SLJ

★ **Louise**; the adventures of a chicken. written by Kate DiCamillo; pictures by Harry Bliss. Joanna Cotler Books 2008 un il $17.99; lib bdg $18.89
Grades: PreK K 1 2   E
1. Adventure fiction 2. Pirates -- Fiction 3. Chickens -- Fiction
ISBN 978-0-06-075554-6; 0-06-075554-7; 978-0-06-075555-3 lib bdg; 0-06-075555-5 lib bdg

LC 2008-20091

Longing for adventure, intrepid Louise the chicken leaves her comfortable nest and goes to sea.

"DiCamillo's brisk, comic narrative crackles with read-aloud savoriness, and her respect for Louise makes the book all the funnier. . . . Bliss creates a thrilling sense of place and puts his wide-eyed heroine front and center. An enlarged format does justice to the details in the art—and to the grand sweep of the storytelling." Publ Wkly

DiPucchio, Kelly S.

★ **Crafty** Chloe; illustrated by Heather Ross. Atheneum Books for Young Readers 2012 il $16.99
Grades: PreK K 1 2   E
1. Gifts -- Fiction 2. Birthdays -- Fiction 3. Handicraft -- Fiction
ISBN 978-1-4424-2123-3; 1-4424-2123-1

LC 2010042811

Chloe is very good at sewing and crafts and when her best friend's birthday approaches, she creates a fabulous gift but also saves the day for a classmate who had been unkind to her.

"DiPucchio is to be commended for providing a simple and strong story with a loving solution that will surprise readers. Strong pacing and fanciful illustrations full of happy yellow highlights capture a delightfully determined and winning child." Kikus

Gilbert Goldfish wants a pet; by Kelly DiPucchio; pictures by Bob Shea. Dial Books for Young Readers 2011 un il $16.99

Grades: PreK K 1   E

1. Pets -- Fiction 2. Fishes -- Fiction 3. Animals -- Fiction 4. Goldfish -- Fiction

ISBN 978-0-8037-3394-7; 0-8037-3394-1

LC 2010028806

Gilbert has everything a goldfish could want except a pet of his own, but none of the animals who come near his fishbowl seem quite right until Fluffy, with his long tail and whiskers, appears.

"The clever text stands on its own, but Shea's bold, expressive illustrations elevate this title to a higher plane. Wavy orange endpapers establish the watery setting and bright palette. Gilbert exudes emotion. . . . Gilbert Goldfish is a perfect choice for storytime and bedtime." SLJ

DiSalvo, DyAnne

Uncle Willie and the soup kitchen. Morrow Junior Bks. 1991 un il hardcover o.p. pa $5.99

Grades: K 1 2 3   E

1. Uncles -- Fiction 2. Poverty -- Fiction

ISBN 0-688-15285-6 pa

LC 90-6375

A boy spends the day with Uncle Willie in the soup kitchen where he works preparing and serving food for the hungry

"The color-pencil and wash illustrations observe . . . [a] balance between attracting the viewer with softly blended colors and avoiding the sentimentality of glamorizing an essentially sad situation. Without sacrifice of story, the total effect leaves young listeners with new considerations of society and social service, a theme too often neglected in picture books." Bull Cent Child Books

A **castle** on Viola Street. HarperCollins Pubs. 2001 un il $16.95; lib bdg $16.89

Grades: K 1 2 3   E

1. Dwellings 2. Houses -- Fiction

ISBN 0-688-17690-9; 0-688-17691-7 lib bdg

LC 00-40889

A hardworking family gets their own house at last by joining a community program that restores old houses

"DiSalvo-Ryan shares an uplifting story of the importance and impact of community pride and support. . . . The colorful gouache, pen, and pencil pictures are folksy and warm." Booklist

A **dog** like Jack. Holiday House 1999 un il hardcover o.p. $17.95

Grades: K 1 2 3   E

1. Dogs -- Fiction 2. Pets -- Fiction 3. Death -- Fiction 4. Grief -- Fiction

ISBN 0-8234-1369-1; 0-8234-1680-1 pa

LC 97-41949

After a long life of chasing squirrels, licking ice cream cones, and loving his adoptive family, an old dog comes to the end of his days

"Thoughtful words and tender pictures beautifully convey the special relationship between a young boy and his dog." Booklist

DiTerlizzi, Angela

Say what? illustrated by Joey Chou. Beach Lane Books 2011 un il $15.99

Grades: PreK K 1   E

1. Stories in rhyme 2. Animal communication 3. Parent-child relationship -- Fiction

ISBN 978-1-4169-8694-2; 1-4169-8694-4

In simple rhyming verse, explores the meaning of sounds exchanged between animal parents and their offspring.

"With bright, vivid colors, endearing animals, and plenty of delightful details, this picture book is sure to find an appreciative audience." SLJ

DiTerlizzi, Tony

Jimmy Zangwow's out-of-this-world, moon pie adventure. Simon & Schuster Bks. for Young Readers 2000 un il $16; pa $4.99

Grades: PreK K 1 2   E

1. Space flight to the moon -- Fiction

ISBN 0-689-80076-2; 0-689-87830-3 pa

LC 98-16602

When Jimmy's mother won't let him have any moon pies for a snack, he takes a trip to the moon to get some

"The dialogue includes quirky sayings like 'Holy macaroni!' and 'Jumping june bugs!,' which young readers will relish. Large double-page watercolor, gouache, and colored-pencil illustrations enhance the story." SLJ

Diakite, Penda

★ **I** lost my tooth in Africa; by Penda Diakité and Baba Wagué Diakité; illustrated by Baba Wagué Diakité. Scholastic Press 2006 un il $16.99

Grades: PreK K 1 2 3   E

1. Teeth -- Fiction 2. Chickens -- Fiction 3. Family life -- Fiction

ISBN 0-439-66226-5

LC 2004-01933

While visiting her father's family in Mali, a young girl loses a tooth, places it under a calabash, and receives a hen and a rooster from the African Tooth Fairy.

"The vivid ceramic-tile illustrations expand the text, revealing a range of animals, houses, and greenery. At the end are the words to Grandma's Good Night Song, the recipe for African Onion Sauce, and a glossary of Bambara words, all of which add to the authentic feel of the story." SLJ

Dickinson, Rebecca

Over in the hollow; illustrated by Stephan Britt. Chronicle Books 2009 un il $15.99

Grades: PreK K 1 2   E

1. Counting 2. Stories in rhyme 3. Monsters -- Fiction 4. Halloween -- Fiction

ISBN 978-0-8118-5035-3; 0-8118-5035-8

LC 2009000955

A counting book that features a variety of spooky Halloween creatures, from one spider to thirteen ghosts.

"The rhyme and rhythm flow well, making this a good choice for reading aloud. The mixed-media illustrations have a retro cartoon feel and are spooky, but not scary—just like the text." SLJ

Diesen, Deborah

The **pout** -pout fish; illustrated by Dan Hanna. Farrar, Straus & Giroux 2008 un il $16

Grades: PreK K 1   E
1. Stories in rhyme 2. Fishes -- Fiction 3. Marine animals -- Fiction

ISBN 978-0-374-36096-2; 0-374-36096-0

LC 2007-60730

The pout-pout fish believes he only knows how to frown, even though many of his friends suggest ways to change his expression, until one day a fish comes along that shows him otherwise.

"The bouncy rhythm is appealing [and] . . . the cartoon illustrations of undersea life are bright and clean and the protagonist's exaggerated expressions are entertaining. The layout is attractive, and the three-panel sequences showing the fish moping around during the refrain are especially well done." SLJ

Another title about the pout-pout fish is:
The pout-pout fish in the big-big dark (2010)

The **pout** -pout fish in the big-big dark; pictures by Dan Hanna. Farrar Straus Giroux 2010 un il $16.99
Grades: PreK K 1   E
1. Stories in rhyme 2. Fishes -- Fiction 3. Marine animals -- Fiction 4. Lost and found possessions -- Fiction

ISBN 978-0-374-30798-1; 0-374-30798-9

LC 2009-13601

Mr. Fish feels nervous venturing deep in the sea to look for Ms. Clam's lost pearl until Miss Shimmer helps him conquer his fear of the dark.

"The playful, rhyming verse is well matched with Hanna's funny cartoon illustrations. . . . A buoyant tale." SLJ

Diggs, Taye
Chocolate me! illustrated by Shane W. Evans. Feiwel and Friends 2011 40p il $16.99
Grades: PreK K 1 2   E
1. Race relations -- Fiction 2. African Americans -- Fiction

ISBN 978-0-312-60326-7; 0-312-60326-6

The boy is teased for looking different than the other kids. His skin is darker, his hair curlier. He tells his mother he wishes he could be more like everyone else. And she helps him to see how beautiful he really, truly is.

"The cartoonlike illustrations are done in bold colors. . . . With its universal themes of wanting to fit in, self-acceptance, and self-esteem, this read-aloud offering is sure to strike a chord with many young readers/listeners, and on a variety subjects, not just race." SLJ

Dipucchio, Kelly
Clink; manufactured by Kelly DiPucchio and [illustrated by] Matthew Myers. Balzer & Bray 2011 un il
Grades: PreK K 1   E
1. Robots -- Fiction

ISBN 006192928X; 9780061929281

While newer, fancier robots are quickly purchased, Clink, an old-fashioned robot who can only make toast and music, gathers dust and feels downhearted until a young boy enters the shop looking for something special.

"The witty text, occasionally interspersed with colorful onomatopoeic robot-centric words . . . is ideal for reading aloud. . . . Myer's paintings . . . burst with loud colors and an energy that's perfect for a store—and story—full of bopping robots and smiling clientele." Horn Book

Grace for president; written by Kelly DiPucchio; pictures by LeUyen Pham. Hyperion Books for Children 2008 un il $15.99
Grades: K 1 2 3   E
1. Elections -- Fiction

ISBN 0-7868-3919-8; 978-0-7868-3919-3

When Grace discovers that there has never been a female U.S. president, she decides to run for school president.

"The illustrations are colorful, and depict the various aspects of political campaigns. While the readership of this title is elementary students, Social Studies teachers at upper levels might consider this as a good way to introduce a concept that isn't always easily understood. This is a timely title, with a likeable heroine." Libr Media Connect

Ditchfield, Christin
Cowlick! by Christin Ditchfield; illustrated by Rosalind Beardshaw. Random House 2007 un il $14.99; lib bdg $17.99
Grades: PreK K 1   E
1. Hair -- Fiction 2. Cattle -- Fiction

ISBN 0-375-83540-7; 0-375-93540-1 lib bdg

This offers "appealingly rich and textured paintings. . . . The short, lively text makes this fun for sharing aloud." SLJ

Shwatsit! illustrated by Rosalind Beardshaw. Golden Books 2009 un il $15.99
Grades: PreK K 1   E
1. Siblings -- Fiction 2. Toddlers -- Fiction

ISBN 978-0-375-84181-1; 0-375-84181-4

As Baby points at everything in sight, she has just one thing to say: "Shwatsit!" But what on earth does it mean? Finally, her older brother solves the mystery.

"The well-designed, expressive illustrations expand on the rhyming text by showing the toddler throughout her day." SLJ

Divakaruni, Chitra Banerjee, 1956-
Grandma and the great gourd; a Bengali folk tale. retold by Chitra Divakaruni; illustrated by Susy Waters. Roaring Brook Press 2013 32 p. (hardcover) $17.99
Grades: PreK K 1 2   E
1. Fairy tales 2. Picture books for children 3. Folklore -- India -- Bengal 4. Bengali (South Asian people) -- Folklore

ISBN 1596433787; 9781596433786

LC 2012001392

This children's picture book sets a retelling of "Little Red Riding Hood" in India, "where the forest hides a fox, a bear, and a tiger. Grandma talks the three predators out of eating her during her first trip ("I'll be a lot fatter on my way back from my daughter's house because she's such a good cook"), but she has to innovate on her way back. Grandma rolls herself home in a giant gourd, singing cheerfully," and continues to elude the predators. (Publishers Weekly)

Dobbins, Jan
Driving my tractor; [text by] Jan Dobbins; [illustrations by] David Sim. Barefoot Books 2009 un il $16.99
Grades: PreK K   E
1. Counting 2. Stories in rhyme 3. Color -- Fiction 4.

Tractors -- Fiction 5. Domestic animals -- Fiction

ISBN 978-1-84686-358-5; 1-84686-358-9

LC 2008051065

The reader is invited to count the animal passengers riding in a tractor traveling on a bumpy road.

"This tale is ideal for storytime with its rhyming text, fun sounds, and refrain, 'Chug, chug, clank, clank, toot! It's a very busy day.' This is a jolly read-aloud, and the accompanying CD with a jazzy version adds to the charm, with both an instrumental track and SteveSongs (of PBS fame) singing the text." SLJ

Docherty, Thomas

Big scary monster. Candlewick Press 2010 un il

Grades: PreK K   E

1. Fear -- Fiction 2. Monsters -- Fiction 3. Self-perception -- Fiction

ISBN 978-0-7636-4787-2; 0-7636-4787-X

LC 2009047397

Big Scary Monster learns some surprising things about himself when he goes down his mountain to find the creatures he has frightened away.

"The full-spread watercolor illustrations in deep colors add to the 'scary' element of the story. . . . The style of these pictures will give young readers an early lesson in perspective. Great as a read-aloud, this book will engage young monster lovers." SLJ

Little boat. Templar Books 2009 un il $15.99

Grades: PreK K   E

1. Boats and boating -- Fiction

ISBN 978-0-7636-4428-4; 0-7636-4428-5

Setting off into the big, wide world, Little Boat runs into treacherous waters, turbulent tides, and seafaring friends. After all his nautical adventures, he finds out that he's no longer such a little boat.

"This simple story of friendship and self-esteem is beautifully illustrated in ink-and-watercolor paintings with a wistful, nostalgic flavor." Booklist

To the beach. Templar Books 2009 un il $15.99

Grades: PreK K 1   E

1. Imagination -- Fiction 2. Voyages and travels -- Fiction

ISBN 978-0-7636-4429-1; 0-7636-4429-3

"A boy packs up all of the necessary gear for a day at the beach, like goggles, snorkel, flippers, bathing suit, and, of course, a big yellow inner tube. The only problem is: it's raining. His imagination then takes over as he secures an airplane, a sailboat, a truck, a camel, and some sand, and finally arrives at the sea. . . . This clever book is complemented by beautiful ink and watercolor drawings of the landscapes that the boy has created. The simple narrative encourages youngsters to think for themselves and never to limit the places their imaginations will take them." SLJ

Dockray, Tracy

The **lost** and found pony; illustrated by Paul Bachem. Feiwel and Friends 2011 85p il $16.99

Grades: PreK K 1 2   E

1. Horses -- Fiction

ISBN 978-0-312-59259-2; 0-312-59259-0

"The little pony at the heart of this surprisingly affecting story is thrilled when he becomes a little girl's perfect birthday present. He loves jumping and running with her on his back—until the day he encounters a jump too high. The little girl falls, and he is declared too small for her. Her parents sell him to the circus, where he brings joy to thousands of children, but he never forgets his first owner. When the circus closes down and he is sold at auction, who should buy him but the little girl, now an adult and running a stable of her own. . . . The simple, straightforward narrative in the pony's voice, combined with Dockray's soft, expressive watercolor and ink illustrations, makes it truly heartwarming." SLJ

Dodd, Emma

Foxy; Emma Dodd. Harper 2012 40 p. (trade bdg.) $14.99

Grades: PreK K 1   E

1. Foxes -- Fiction 2. Magic -- Fiction 3. Picture books for children 4. First day of school -- Fiction

ISBN 0062014196; 9780062014191

LC 2010045555

In this children's picture book, "Emily cannot go to sleep because she is worried that she won't have all the things she needs for . . . school. Her friend, Foxy, is sure that he can help her with his magic tail, and . . . waves it at Emily's every wish--only, the tail doesn't always work as he hopes. Emily needs a pencil and Foxy's . . . tail produces a penguin. . . . However, second tries work better, and so Emily goes to sleep with all her supplies in her book pack." (School Library Journal)

I am small. Cartwheel Books 2011 il $8.99

Grades: PreK K   E

1. Penguins -- Fiction

ISBN 978-0-545-35370-0; 0-545-35370-X

"A penguin chick ponders the big, fast, long, steep world around him and notes how small he is in comparison. But when he is with his mother, he knows he is safe. . . . The simple text and easy-to-read block printing make this a good choice for beginning readers. Dodd uses a palette of black, white, and slate blue with touches of silver to evoke the freezing Antarctic habitat." SLJ

★ **I** don't want a cool cat! Little, Brown 2010 un il $15.99

Grades: PreK K 1   E

1. Cats -- Fiction

ISBN 978-0-316-03674-0; 0-316-03674-9

A little girl "knows what she does not want: 'A stuffy cat. A huffy, over-fluffy cat.' . . . The true-to-life hilarity of the text commands attention, especially when mixed with such smart art. With a combination of paint and collage, the images have a three-dimensional feel as they sit on their smooth, candy-colored backgrounds. . . . Combine the art with the pithy text, and you've got a book that's perfect to read aloud to groups." Booklist

I don't want a posh dog! Little, Brown 2009 un il $15.99

Grades: PreK K 1   E

1. Stories in rhyme 2. Dogs -- Fiction

ISBN 978-0-316-03390-9; 0-316-03390-1

LC 2008002229

First published 2008 in the United Kingdom

A girl describes in rhyming text the types of dogs she does not want, and finally arrives at a dog that she can call her own

"The rhymes are clever and succinct, and the simple line art incorporates photo elements . . . that lend the right touch of surrealism." Booklist

I love bugs. Holiday House 2010 un il $16.95
Grades: PreK K 1 2　　　　　　　　　　　　**E**
　　1. Insects -- Fiction 2. Spiders -- Fiction 3. Insects -- Juvenile literature
　　ISBN 978-0-8234-2280-7; 0-8234-2280-1
　　　　　　　　　　　　　　　LC 2009-32814
"The text juggles sounds and rhymes skillfully. . . . Varied in composition, palette, and scale, the illustrations have great vitality. . . . Easy to see from a distance, this would be an excellent choice for group sharing." Booklist

Just like you; [by] Emma Dodd. Dutton Children's Books 2008 un il $10.99
Grades: PreK　　　　　　　　　　　　　　**E**
　　1. Stories in rhyme 2. Bears -- Fiction 3. Father-son relationship -- Fiction
　　ISBN 978-0-525-47933-8; 0-525-47933-3
　　　　　　　　　　　　　　　LC 2007019208
A baby bear describes the ways in which he wants to be like his father when he grows up.

"This warm, honest tribute to a child's love for a caring adult is almost flawless in its execution. Dodd's minimalist illustrations feature big, simple shapes with thick black outlines and blocks of complementary contrasting colors. . . . The sentiment comes across in just a few easy words at a time. . . . A sweet, soothing selection for bedtime sharing." SLJ

Meow said the cow. Arthur A. Levine Books 2011 un il $16.99
Grades: PreK K 1　　　　　　　　　　　　**E**
　　1. Stories in rhyme 2. Magic -- Fiction 3. Domestic animals -- Fiction
　　ISBN 978-0-545-31861-7; 0-545-31861-0
　　　　　　　　　　　　　　　LC 2010034247
A noisy rooster causes a disgruntled cat to cast a magic spell that creates confusion among the other farm animals.

"The rollicking text is paired with large, colorful digitally produced art that has the kinetic animals fairly popping off the spreads." SLJ

No matter what; [by] Emma Dodd. Dutton Children's Books 2008 un il $10.99
Grades: PreK　　　　　　　　　　　　　　**E**
　　1. Stories in rhyme 2. Elephants -- Fiction 3. Parent-child relationship -- Fiction
　　ISBN 978-0-525-47932-1; 0-525-47932-5
　　　　　　　　　　　　　　　LC 2007019207
In rhyming text, a baby elephant is assured of being loved unconditionally.

"Each phrase is supported by a stylized African landscape in muted colors, but with bright touches. . . . The young elephant is simply rendered, too, and quite charming. The art, and the padded cover with metallic accents, is appealing, and the comforting text is perfect for toddlers." SLJ

What pet to get? [by] Emma Dodd. Arthur A. Levine Books 2008 un il $16.99
Grades: PreK K 1 2　　　　　　　　　　　**E**
　　1. Pets -- Fiction
　　ISBN 0-545-03570-8
　　　　　　　　　　　　　　　LC 2007010106
Jack's mother agrees that he may have a pet, but when he suggests everything from an elephant to a tyranosaurus rex, she must explain why each would be less than ideal

"Filling in her thick black outlines with a mixture of digitally manipulated textures and densely saturated colors, Dodd . . . creates a daffy, winning cast of googly-eyed creatures whose ids run rampant." Publ Wkly

Dodds, Dayle Ann
　　Minnie's Diner; a multiplying menu. illustrated by John Manders. Candlewick Press 2004 un il hardcover o.p. pa $6.99
Grades: K 1 2 3　　　　　　　　　　　　**E**
　　1. Stories in rhyme 2. Restaurants -- Fiction 3. Multiplication -- Fiction
　　ISBN 0-7636-1736-9; 0-7636-3313-5 pa
　　　　　　　　　　　　　　　LC 2002-34756
Rhyming tale of five boys and their father who forget about their chores on the farm to enjoy Minnie's good cooking, each requesting double what the previous one ordered

"Told in jaunty rhymes with varied type sizes for emphasis, this funny story is illustrated with colorful cartoons done in gouache. Children will appreciate the humor and groan with delight when they recognize the math pattern." SLJ

　　Teacher's pets; illustrated by Marylin Hafner. Candlewick Press 2006 un il $15.99
Grades: PreK K 1 2　　　　　　　　　　**E**
　　1. School stories 2. Pets -- Fiction
　　ISBN 0-7636-2252-4
A teacher invites her students to bring their pets in each Monday for sharing day, but by the end of the year, she has a classroom full of "forgotten" animals.

"This gentle and humorous story has charming watercolor illustrations that reinforce the emotions of the children, the animals, and, of course, the warmhearted teacher." SLJ

　　Where's Pup? pictures by Pierre Pratt. Dial Bks. for Young Readers 2003 un il $12.99
Grades: PreK K 1　　　　　　　　　　　**E**
　　1. Dogs 2. Circus 3. Clowns 4. Stories in rhyme 5. Toy and movable books 6. Dogs -- Fiction 7. Circus -- Fiction 8. Clowns -- Fiction 9. Toy and movable books -- Specimens
　　ISBN 0-8037-2744-5
　　　　　　　　　　　　　　　LC 2002-588
A circus clown's search for his partner leads him to the top of an acrobatic pyramid, found by unfolding the book's final page

"Relying on a jeweled palette of acrylic reds and oranges, the images are simple yet arresting and show the action from varying perspectives. A visually exciting charmer." SLJ

　　The **prince** won't go to bed; pictures by Kyrsten Brooker. Farrar, Straus & Giroux 2007 un il $16
Grades: PreK K 1 2　　　　　　　　　　**E**
　　1. Stories in rhyme 2. Bedtime -- Fiction 3. Princes

-- Fiction
ISBN 0-374-36108-8; 978-0-374-36108-2

LC 2005051234

When the young prince refuses to go to bed, assorted members of the royal household offer their ideas on exactly what he needs, but it is his sister, Princess Kate, who learns the truth.

Dodd's "rhymed text abounds with the kind of repetitions in structure and language that make children want to join in. . . . The fonts grow larger and Brooker's hilarious, cock-eyed collages ever more frantic with each repetition." Publ Wkly

Doerrfeld, Cori

Penny loves pink. Little, Brown 2011 un il $15.99
Grades: PreK K 1   E
1. Color -- Fiction 2. Infants -- Fiction 3. Siblings -- Fiction
ISBN 978-0-316-05458-4; 0-316-05458-5

LC 2010008632

A little girl who loves pink more than anything must learn to accept the color blue when her baby brother arrives.

"The illustrations are bright and lively. . . . A sweet, satisfying story." SLJ

Dokas, Dara

Muriel's red sweater; illustrations by Bernadette Pons. Dutton Children's Books 2009 un il $16.99
Grades: PreK K 1   E
1. Gifts -- Fiction 2. Animals -- Fiction 3. Birthdays -- Fiction 4. Clothing and dress -- Fiction
ISBN 978-0-525-47962-8; 0-525-47962-7

LC 2008020605

"Unbeknownst to duck Muriel, her sweater is unraveling as she delivers invitations to her birthday party. Luckily, her friends have already been working on the perfect present: a new sweater. The cheery illustrations do a good deal of storytelling; readers can spot hints about the new sweater and chuckle at the uses Muriel's friends find for yarn from the old one." Horn Book Guide

Dominguez, Angela

Let's go, Hugo! story and pictures by Angela Dominguez. Dial Books for Young Readers 2013 40 p. col. ill. (hardcover) $16.99
Grades: PreK K   E
1. Fear -- Fiction 2. Birds -- Fiction 3. Artists -- Fiction
ISBN 9780803738645

LC 2012003561

Domney, Alexis

Splish, splat! written by Alexis Domney; illustrated by Alice Crawford. Second Story Press 2011 un il $15.95
Grades: PreK K 1   E
1. Deaf -- Fiction 2. Painting -- Fiction 3. Sign language -- Fiction
ISBN 978-1-897187-88-3; 1-897187-88-2

"Colin is having nightmares in his yolk-colored room. As he sleeps, eggs over easy zoom around like alien spaceships. It is time for a new paint job, and his mother opts for professionals to do the work. She gets the message relay number of Deaf painters and, via an interpreter, makes an appointment. Whereas this could simply be a didactic picture book on Deaf and hearing etiquette, the humor imbued

makes it a delightful story about the joy of communication. The unique collage illustrations add warmth and render the two women painters in realistic signing stances." SLJ

Don, Lari

Little Red Riding Hood; Lari Don; illustrated by Celia Chauffrey. Barefoot Books 2012 32 p. $16.99
Grades: K 1 2 3   E
1. Fairy tales 2. Wolves -- Juvenile fiction 3. Children and strangers -- Juvenile fiction 4. Folklore
ISBN 1846867665; 9781846867668

LC 2012009603

In this book by Lari Don, "Little Red Riding Hood loves to visit her Granny's cottage in the forest. Her mother warns her to go straight to Granny's, but when she meets a handsome grey wolf, she doesn't see the harm in stopping for a chat." (Publisher's note) "Although the two leading ladies are gobbled up, legs last, the hunter comes to the rescue. He is rewarded with cakes, Granny learns to lock her door, and Red 'never turned round to talk to strangers again.'" (School Library Journal)

Donaldson, Julia

One Ted falls out of bed; illustrated by Anna Currey. Henry Holt 2006 un il $15.95
Grades: PreK K 1 2   E
1. Counting 2. Stories in rhyme 3. Toys -- Fiction 4. Teddy bears -- Fiction
ISBN 978-0-8050-7787-2; 0-8050-7787-1

LC 2005-12173

"In this rhythmic counting book, a sleeping child's teddy bear falls out of bed and can't climb back up. Three mice invite him to play, racing four cars, counting five stars, sipping tea with six dolls, and so on. . . . The toys in the airy illustrations that sweep across the pages are packed with personality. Perfect for storytimes or one-on-one lapsits, this book can be counted on for a gentle, cozy read." SLJ

Stick Man; illustrated by Axel Scheffler. Arthur A. Levine Books 2009 un il $16.99
Grades: PreK K 1   E
1. Stories in rhyme 2. Christmas -- Fiction 3. Santa Claus -- Fiction
ISBN 978-0-545-15761-2; 0-545-15761-7

LC 2008-48323

First published 2008 in the United Kingdom

Stick Man ends up far away from his family tree when he is fetched by a dog, thrown by a child, used as a snowman's arm, and even put on a fire, but finally Santa Claus steps in to make sure that Stick Man and his family have a joyous Christmas.

"Scheffler's engaging illustrations, Donaldson's irresistible rhyming text and repeated refrains make this a winning read-aloud that will stick around long after the holiday season." Kirkus

Tyrannosaurus Drip; [by] Julia Donaldson; [illustrations by] David Roberts. Feiwel and Friends 2008 un il $16.95
Grades: K 1 2   E
1. Stories in rhyme 2. Dinosaurs -- Fiction
ISBN 978-0-312-37747-2; 0-312-37747-9

LC 2007-40511

A duckbilled dinosaur, accidentally raised by fierce tyrannosauruses who would eat duckbills if only they could reach them, tries to be like his "family" but finally gives up, runs away, and finds a real home with others of his kind.

"The dinosaurs are rendered in an Art Deco-influenced style, and the lines roll off the tongue like the rhymes of Dr. Seuss. Children will enjoy the repetitive lilt, and adults will appreciate how naturally it reads. Expressive characters enhance the humor, and the limited palette helps emphasize just how different the creatures' worlds are. An enjoyable group read-aloud." SLJ

What the ladybug heard; illustrated by Lydia Monks. Henry Holt and Company 2010 un il $16.99

Grades: PreK K 1   E

1. Stories in rhyme 2. Sounds -- Fiction 3. Thieves -- Fiction 4. Ladybugs -- Fiction 5. Domestic animals -- Fiction

ISBN 978-0-8050-9028-4; 0-8050-9028-2

LC 2009005266

First published 2009 in the United Kingdom

Although much quieter than the farm animals that moo, cluck, or oink, a gentle ladybug is instrumental in foiling a plan to steal the farm's prize-winning cow.

"Filled with drama, lively action, and a large supporting cast of characters, this is a mini play more than a fully fleshed story. The appealing and brightly colored collage illustrations, rhyming text, and assorted animal sounds make it a natural for individual or group read-alouds." Booklist

Where's my mom? illustrated by Axel Scheffler. Dial Books for Young Readers 2008 un il $16.99

Grades: PreK K   E

1. Stories in rhyme 2. Animals -- Fiction 3. Monkeys -- Fiction 4. Butterflies -- Fiction

ISBN 978-0-8037-3228-5; 0-8037-3228-7

LC 2007005236

A butterfly tries to help a lost young monkey find its mother in the jungle, meeting many different animals along the way.

"The bouncy rhyming couplets will charm children. . . . Bold cartoon illustrations on full spreads in bright jungle colors feature a host of expressive insects and creatures." SLJ

The **fish** who cried wolf; [by] Julia Donaldson & Axel Scheffler. Arthur A. Levine Books 2008 un il $15.99

Grades: PreK K 1 2   E

1. Stories in rhyme 2. Fishes -- Fiction 3. Storytelling -- Fiction

ISBN 978-0-439-92825-0; 0-439-92825-7

LC 2007-12308

Tiddler the fish is always telling tall tales about why he is late for school, but when he is actually caught in a net and taken far from home, it is his stories that help him find his way back.

"Donaldson's rhyming text is crisp and clean, leaving plenty of metaphorical room for Scheffler's expansively imagined art." Publ Wkly

Donaldson, Julia, 1948-

The **Highway** Rat; a tale of stolen snacks. by Julia Donaldson and illustrated by Axel Scheffler. 1st American ed. Arthur A. Levine Books 2013 32 p. (reinforced) $16.99

Grades: PreK K 1 2   E

1. Theft -- Juvenile fiction 2. Picture books for children 3. Rats -- Fiction 4. Stories in rhyme 5. Animals -- Fiction 6. Robbers and outlaws -- Fiction

ISBN 0545477581; 9780545477581

LC 2012009889

This children's picture book is the tale "of a swashbuckling rat with mask and cape who stops hapless travelers and takes their food at sword point. . . . A brave duck in a red kerchief lures the thief to a distant cave, supposedly full of biscuits and buns. While he follows the echoes of his own voice deeper and deeper into the dark, the duck jumps on Rat's horse and takes the stolen food back to her hungry friends." (School Library Journal)

Donofrio, Beverly

Mary and the mouse, the mouse and Mary; by Beverly Donofrio; illustrated by Barbara McClintock. Schwartz & Wade Books 2007 un il $16.99

Grades: PreK K 1   E

1. Mice -- Fiction 2. Friendship -- Fiction

ISBN 978-0-375-83609-1

LC 2006030980

While Mary, a girl whose family lives in a big house, is learning things at school, a young mouse whose family lives in a small house within the big one is learning the same things at her school, and when the two eventually meet they become friends

"The telling is clean, the parallel structure of the tale is pleasing, and McClintock's warm, precisely drawn ink, gouache, and watercolor artwork will fascinate children and adults alike." Booklist

Donovan, Jane Monroe

Small, medium & large; [written and illustrated by] Jane Monroe Donovan. Sleeping Bear Press 2010 un il $15.95

Grades: PreK K 1   E

1. Stories without words 2. Gifts -- Fiction 3. Christmas -- Fiction

ISBN 978-1-58536-447-3; 1-58536-447-9

"A girl who has just moved to a new house mails a letter to Santa, and on Christmas Day her wishes appear under the tree in three appropriately sized boxes–a cat, a dog, and a miniature horse. The new friends play in the snow, make Christmas cookies, and finally snuggle in bed together after a long, wonderful day. This wordless story [is] told in full and half-page illustrations. . . . It's a sure bet that this supersweet yet cozy story will have kids adding 'a cat, a dog, and a horse–REAL ones' to their Christmas lists." SLJ

Doodler, Todd H.

What color is Bear's underwear? Blue Apple Books 2011 il bd bk $9.99

Grades: PreK K   E

1. Color 2. Stories in rhyme 3. Board books for children 4. Bears -- Fiction 5. Underwear -- Fiction

ISBN 978-1-60905-096-2; 1-60905-096-7

LC 2011018924

Bear wears different colored underwear for every day of the week.

"It's about as an irreverently silly guide to colors as one could want." Publ Wkly

Doremus, Gaetan

Bear despair; Gaetan Doremus. Enchanted Lion Books 2012 32 p. (alk. paper) $14.95
Grades: PreK K 1 2   E
1. Bears -- Juvenile Fiction 2. Theft -- Juvenile fiction 3. Teddy bears -- Juvenile fiction
ISBN 1592701256; 9781592701254

LC 2012931209

This book by Gaetan Doreumus, part of the Stories Without Words series, was designated a 2012 "New York Times" Best Illustrated Children's Book. "[B]ear is napping when his teddy bear is taken by a fox who leads him on a merry chase. . . . Since neither animal is particularly good at conflict resolution, bear swallows the fox whole. As he searches, bear is taunted by a series of creatures that play keep-away with his toy. Furious, bear swallows each one." (Children's Literature)

Empty Fridge; by Gaetan Doremus. Trafalgar Square Books 2013 40 p. ill. (hardcover) $19.99
Grades: PreK K 1   E
1. Food -- Juvenile fiction 2. Sharing -- Juvenile fiction 3. Neighbors -- Juvenile fiction
ISBN 0987109936; 9780987109934

In this picture book by Gaetan Doremus,"the many and varied occupants of an apartment house in a French city have been . . . so busy . . . that . . .no one has remembered to buy any food! In a . . . chain of visits, each . . . character makes a trip up to the next floor to explore how they can pool the paltry ingredients they have scavenged to make a meal that everyone can share. . . . A cozy quiche-baking party ensues." (Kirkus Reviews)

Dormer, Frank W.

Socksquatch; words and pictures by Frank W. Dormer. Henry Holt 2010 un il $14.99
Grades: PreK K 1   E
1. Monsters -- Fiction
ISBN 978-0-8050-8952-3; 0-8050-8952-7

LC 2009-27413

Socksquatch tries to find a sock to warm his cold foot.

"The palette contrasts warm-toned monsters with soothing backgrounds of aqua or plain white, and Dormer uses scrawled ink motion and texture lines to great effect to add movement and dimension to the artwork. While youngsters will definitely enjoy listening to this one in a crowd, don't be surprised if they borrow it afterwards to reenact with a friend." Bull Cent Child Books

The obstinate pen; Frank W. Dormer. Henry Holt 2012 32 p. (hardcover: alk. paper) $16.99
Grades: K 1 2 3   E
1. Writing -- Fiction 2. Picture books for children 3. Bad behavior -- Juvenile fiction 4. Pens -- Fiction 5. Obstinacy -- Fiction
ISBN 0805092951; 9780805092950

LC 2010031794

In this children's story, by Frank W. Dormer, a pen writes what it wants instead of what the writer decides. The pen "speaks the truth to a series of self-involved townsfolk" after it is delivered to Uncle Flood and then passes from person

to person through the town, correcting and insulting all who try to use it. (Kirkus)

Dorros, Alex

Numero uno; by Alex Dorros and Arthur Dorros; illustrated by Susan Guevara. Abrams Books for Young Readers 2007 un il $16.95
Grades: K 1 2 3   E
1. Spanish language -- Vocabulary
ISBN 0-8109-5764-7

Tired of listening to strong Hercules and smart Socrates constantly argue over who is more important to their village, the townspeople devise a test to settle the question once and for all.

"The battle between brains and brawn is entertainingly pitched here. . . . The Spanish dialogue is simple . . . and punctuates the story-hour-ready text with verve. Guevara's tropically accented pastoral oil paintings provide contrast to the often slapstick goings-on but also do their share of storytelling." Horn Book

Dorros, Arthur

★ Abuela; illustrated by Elisa Kleven. Dutton Children's Bks. 1991 un il $16.99; pa $7.99
Grades: PreK K 1 2   E
1. Flight -- Fiction 2. Imagination -- Fiction 3. Grandmothers -- Fiction 4. Hispanic Americans -- Fiction
ISBN 0-525-44750-4; 0-14-056225-7 pa

LC 90-21459

While riding on a bus with her grandmother, a little girl named Rosalba imagines that they are carried up into the sky and fly over the sights of New York City

"Each illustration is a masterpiece of color, line, and form that will mesmerize youngsters. . . . The smooth text, interpresed with Spanish words and phrases, provides ample context clues, so the glossary, while helpful, is not absolutely necessary." Booklist

Another title about Rosalba and her grandmother is: Isla (1995)

Julio's magic; collages by Ann Grifalconi. HarperCollins 2005 32p il $15.99; lib bdg $16.89
Grades: PreK K 1 2   E
1. Wood carving -- Fiction
ISBN 0-06-029004-8; 0-06-029005-6 lib bdg

LC 2004-6616

A young artist in a Mexican village discovers the power of friendship when he helps his mentor win a prestigious wood-carving contest

"Grifalconi's photorealistic collages capture the texture, color, and feel of village life. This book will be excellent for art and social studies classrooms. . . . It is also a compassionate intergenerational story." SLJ

Mama and me; pictures by Rudy Gutierrez. Rayo 2011 un il $16.99; lib bdg $17.89
Grades: PreK K 1 2   E
1. Mother's Day -- Fiction 2. Spanish language -- Vocabulary 3. Mother-daughter relationship -- Fiction
ISBN 0-06-058160-3; 0-06-058161-1 lib bdg; 978-0-06-058160-2; 978-0-06-058161-9 lib bdg

A girl and her mother spend a day together gardening, making cookies, and visiting a neighbor. Includes Spanish words interspersed in the text.

"The first person point of view and smooth integration of informal Spanish terms and phrases provide a comfortable intimacy with the characters, and the vibrant magic realism of the full-page spreads includes elements of street art." Booklist

Papa and me; by Arthur Dorros; illustrated by Rudy Gutierrez. HarperCollinsPublishers 2008 un il $16.99; lib bdg $17.89

Grades: PreK K   E
1. Hispanic Americans -- Fiction 2. Spanish language -- Vocabulary 3. Father-son relationship -- Fiction
ISBN 978-0-06-058156-5; 978-0-06-058157-2 lib bdg
LC 2007011868

A Pura Belpre Illustrator Award honor book, 2009

"From the time they wake up in the morning, a Latino boy and his father have fun. . . . The simple words, in both Spanish and English, and the bright, exuberant unframed double-page pictures celebrate the loving connection between parent and child. . . . The big, swirling circles in the artwork embrace the characters within the widening arcs of sky and waves." Booklist

Doughty, Rebecca

Oh no! Time to go! a book of goodbyes. Schwartz & Wade 2009 un il $15.99; lib bdg $18.99

Grades: PreK K 1 2   E
1. Stories in rhyme 2. Family life -- Fiction
ISBN 978-0-375-84981-7; 0-375-84981-5; 978-0-375-95696-6 lib bdg; 0-375-95696-4 lib bdg
LC 2008022462

A young boy presents the different ways his family members and others say goodbye, then describes the worst goodbye he ever experienced.

"Opaque, brightly colored illustrations outlined in black ink are rendered in a spare, stylized manner. . . . This satisfying tale conveys an important truth about how life's goodbyes often lead to new hellos." SLJ

Dowdy, Linda Cress

All kinds of kisses; [illustrated] by Priscilla Lamont. Cartwheel Books 2010 un il bd bk $8.99

Grades: PreK   E
1. Stories in rhyme 2. Board books for children 3. Kissing -- Fiction
ISBN 978-0-545-14599-2 bd bk; 0-545-14599-6 bd bk
LC 2010010215

Simple, rhyming text explores different kinds of kisses.

"The padded cover, Lamont's dusky palette, and Dowdy's simple rhymes convey a cozy, loving world, making this a ready choice for easing into bedtime." Publ Wkly

Downing, Julie

No hugs till Saturday; [by] Julie Downing. Clarion Books 2008 31p il lib bdg $16

Grades: PreK K 1   E
1. Week -- Fiction 2. Dragons -- Fiction 3. Hugging

-- Fiction 4. Mother-son relationship -- Fiction
ISBN 978-0-618-91078-6 lib bdg; 0-618-91078-6 lib bdg
LC 2007010030

When Felix the dragon declares that there will be no hugs, snuggles, or super squeezes for a whole week, both he and his mama have a hard time.

"The soft-edged paintings show a lovable green dragon and humorously depict his antics. . . . Featuring a believably childlike protagonist, a cozy parent-child relationship, and a satisfying resolution, it is a delightfully warmhearted choice for most collections." SLJ

Dowson, Nick

Tracks of a panda; illustrated by Yu Rong. Candlewick Press 2007 un il $16.99

Grades: PreK K 1 2   E
1. Giant panda -- Fiction 2. Pandas -- Juvenile literature
ISBN 978-0-7636-3146-8; 0-7636-3146-9
LC 2006051836

A mother panda teaches her cub how to survive in their mountain habitat but as the sound of villagers clearing the forest approaches, she knows they must look for a new home.

"The mother panda's endearing facial features—beautifully rendered in black and white in contrast to the delicate watercolor backgrounds of green, blue, brown, and gray—may well elicit an adoring squeal or two. . . . Dowson leaves the reader with the uncertainty of this pair's future and, on a larger scale, the survival of the species as a whole." Horn Book

Doyen, Denise

★ **Once** upon a twice; illustrated by Barry Moser. Random House Children's Books 2009 un il $16.99; lib bdg $19.99

Grades: PreK K 1   E
1. Nonsense verses 2. Stories in rhyme 3. Mice -- Fiction 4. Conduct of life -- Fiction
ISBN 978-0-375-85612-9; 0-375-85612-9; 978-0-375-95612-6 lib bdg; 0-375-95612-3 lib bdg
LC 2008011125

"Doyen's utterly sound and alive story is paired with the perfect illustrator, whose deft touch provides all the eeriness that it begs for. . . . With gloriously nonsensical words and phrases . . . the author manages to get the point across that there is much to fear in the night. . . . This wonderful book is a marvelous read-aloud that children will want to hear again and again." SLJ

Doyle, Malachy

Get happy; illustrated by Caroline Uff. Walker & Co. 2011 un il $15.99

Grades: PreK K   E
1. Stories in rhyme 2. Happiness -- Fiction
ISBN 978-0-8027-2271-3; 0-8027-2271-7
LC 2010031000

Simple, rhyming text urges the reader to be happy by making such choices as teasing less and tickling more, or groaning less and giggling more.

"With a short, powerful text and endearing, recognizable children, this book is an excellent discussion starter for the youngest children." Booklist

Doyle, Roddy

Her mother's face; by Roddy Doyle; illustrated by Freya Blackwood. Arthur A. Levine Books 2008 un il $16.99

Grades: K 1 2 3   E

1. Mothers -- Fiction 2. Bereavement -- Fiction

ISBN 978-0-439-81501-7; 0-439-81501-0

LC 2007043660

Siobhan and her father continue to feel sad in the years following the death of Siobhan's mother, until Siobhan follows the advice of a mysterious woman

"The storytelling flows gracefully between the naturalistic details . . . and the magical encounter. Blackwood . . . magnifies Doyle's optimism in her limpid watercolor and charcoal art." Publ Wkly

Dragonwagon, Crescent

All the awake animals are almost asleep; written by Crescent Dragonwagon; illustrated by David McPhail. Little, Brown 2012 40 p. $16.99

Grades: PreK   E

1. Sleep -- Fiction 2. Animals -- Fiction 3. Picture books for children 4. Alphabet 5. Stories in rhyme 6. Bedtime -- Fiction

ISBN 0316070459; 9780316070454

LC 2011042734

Author Crescent Dragonwagon "introduces a familiar bedtime battle of wills between a child who resists slumber and a mother trying to lull him to sleep. This introductory section adopts a rhythmic, rhyming text . . . [and e]nsuing pages go through the alphabet using alliterative language to describe animals going to sleep, from" antelopes to zebras. (Kirkus)

Drescher, Henrik

McFig & McFly; a tale of jealousy, revenge, and death (with a happy ending) [by] Henrik Drescher. Candlewick Press 2008 40p il $17.99

Grades: K 1 2 3   E

1. Building -- Fiction

ISBN 978-0-7636-3386-8; 0-7636-3386-0

LC 2007-32345

As neighbors McFig and McFly compete to see who can outdo the other in additions to their cottages, they become so involved that they do not realize McFig's daughter and McFly's son have grown up and fallen in love.

"Drescher achieves balance to this outlandish story by swathing his pages in creamy aqua and rosy hues, and using his recognizable rough-line drawings to delineate the characters and buildings. . . . For readers who enjoy the offbeat, this story is sure to generate a laugh." SLJ

Drummond, Allan

Liberty! Farrar, Straus & Giroux 2002 un il pa $6.95

Grades: K 1 2 3   E

1. Freedom 2. Statue of Liberty (New York, N.Y.) 3. Statue of Liberty National Monument (N.Y. and N.J.) -- Juvenile fiction

ISBN 0-374-34385-3; 0-374-44397-1 pa

LC 2001-18777

"Drummond tells the story of October 28, 1886, the day the Statue of Liberty was first unveiled in New York harbor. A boy, whose name is now lost, is on the ground, ready to signal Bartholdi, the statue's sculptor, to release the tricolor veil that covers the Lady of Liberty's face. . . . This is an unusual offering. Drummond takes a kernel of history . . . and turns it into both a thoughtful lesson and a visual pageant. Scenes of the construction of France's gift to the U.S. are shown in finely wrought, energetic, pen-and-wash images that swirl through the text." Booklist

Drummond, Ree

Charlie the ranch dog; illustrations by Diane deGroat. HarperCollins 2011 un il $16.99

Grades: PreK K 1 2   E

1. Dogs -- Fiction 2. Ranch life -- Fiction

ISBN 978-0-06-199655-9; 0-06-199655-6

LC 2010018435

While Charlie, a sleepy basset hound, tells about the busy life of a ranch dog, his best friend Suzie, a Jack Russell terrier, is getting the work done.

"Charlie seems unaware of the impish chipmunk that deGroat, with characteristic humor, sneaks into each spread. Her paintings drolly portray the discrepancy between reality and Charlie's perceptions of his day. . . . Kids should find it irresistible." Publ Wkly

Dubosarsky, Ursula

The **terrible** plop; pictures by Andrew Joyner. Farrar, Straus and Giroux 2009 un il $15.95

Grades: PreK K   E

1. Stories in rhyme 2. Fear -- Fiction 3. Animals -- Fiction 4. Courage -- Fiction 5. Rabbits -- Fiction

ISBN 978-0-374-37428-0; 0-374-37428-7

LC 2008043323

When a mysterious sound sends the whole forest running away in fear, only the littlest rabbit is courageous enough to discover what really happened.

"Basic, fun rhymes and repetitive, excitable text lend themselves to reading aloud, and the recurring appearance of the word PLOP provides an explosive entree for children to chime in while soaking up Joyner's bouyant mixed-media artwork. In addition, kids will appreciate the easy absurdity of the situation, enjoy the role-reversal in the end, and maybe even come away knowing that most things aren't so scary once you look a little closer." Booklist

Dubuc, Marianne

Animal masquerade; Marianne Dubuc. Kids Can Press 2012 120 p.

Grades: PreK K 1   E

1. Animals -- Fiction 2. Costume -- Fiction 3. Picture books for children

ISBN 1554537827; 9781554537822

In this children's picture book, "[i]t's time for the animal masquerade, and lion begins considering his costume. He settles on . . . an elephant. But what will the elephant be? A parrot. And which costume will the parrot choose? A turn of the page reveals all. Simple text, translated from French, accompanies . . . colored-pencil illustrations of an assortment of animals in and out of costume on white backgrounds. . . . For the most part, each spread features an animal in disguise." (Kirkus)

In front of my house; translated from the French by Yvette Ghione. Kids Can Press 2010 un il $18.95

Grades: PreK K 1 2   **E**
  1. Imagination -- Fiction
  ISBN 978-1-55453-641-2; 1-55453-641-3

"In an excursion that starts and ends with a little house on a hill, a child's imagination soars, moving from a rosebush and a bird outside to discover things 'behind the window' and 'in my room,' including a book of fairy tales in which a dragon, a frog prince, and the Big Bad Wolf dwell, as well as the Abominable Snowman, a werewolf, a ghost, and a vampire. Finally, the adventure leads into outer space. . . . While this small picture book is thick, the childlike text is brief. . . . Its size is perfect for one-on-one interaction, and youngsters will enjoy the twists and turns of the trip. . . . The illustrations, rendered in pencil crayon, are appropriately simple. . . . This little gem has everything." SLJ

Duffy, Carol Ann
  The **gift**; [text] by Carol Ann Duffy and [illustrations] by Rob Ryan. Barefoot Books 2010 un il $16.99
Grades: 2 3 4   **E**
  1. Wishes -- Fiction
  ISBN 978-1-84686-355-4; 1-84686-355-4

After meeting a magical old woman in a clearing in the woods and trading her daisy chain for the granting of a wish, a little girl grows into a young woman and the clearing begins to fill with the loveliest flowers, the most fragrant herbs, and the most perfect stones.

"This original tale is told in simple language and has a clarity and beauty all its own. Ryan's silhouette illustrations are created using hand-cut paper that is painted and photographed, a technique that makes effective use of color and shadows." Booklist

Duke, Kate
  Ready for pumpkins; Kate Duke. Knopf Books for Young Readers 2012 40 p. col. ill.
Grades: K 1 2   **E**
  1. Gardens -- Juvenile fiction 2. Pumpkin -- Juvenile fiction 3. Gardening -- Juvenile Fiction 4. Pumpkin -- Fiction 5. Gardening -- Fiction 6. Guinea pigs -- Fiction
  ISBN 0375870687; 9780307974549; 9780375870682; 9780375970689
                    LC 2011044615

In this children's book by Kate Duke "Hercules, a classroom guinea pig, has a revelation when he watches the first graders grow plants from seeds. He wants to grow things, too! And during summer vacation (spent with the teacher's dad), he gets his chance. With the help of a friendly rabbit, Herky prepares the soil, carefully plants pumpkin seeds, and waits. . . . [I]n October, the teacher's dad arrives with a big pumpkin for her class--that just mysteriously grew in his yard!" (Publisher's note)

Dumbleton, Mike
  Cat; written by Mike Dumbleton; illustrated by Craig Smith. Kane/Miller 2008 un il $15.95
Grades: PreK K   **E**
  1. Cats -- Fiction
  ISBN 978-1-933605-73-9; 1-933605-73-1
  First published 2007 in Australia

As a cat navigates the perils of the outside world, it and its prey all find things to be thankful for

"The humor is elucidated in the richly colored green- and brown-tinged gouache and pen-and-ink illustrations that move the action along from one episode to another." Horn Book Guide

Dumont, Jean-François
  The **chickens** build a wall; written and illustrated by Jean Francois Dumont. Eerdmans Books for Young Readers 2013 33 p. ill. (reinforced) $16.00
Grades: PreK K 1   **E**
  1. Walls -- Fiction 2. Chickens -- Fiction 3. Toleration -- Fiction 4. Domestic animals -- Fiction
  ISBN 9780802854223
                    LC 2012038991

Dunbar, Joyce
  Oddly. Candlewick Press 2009 un il $16.99
Grades: K 1 2   **E**
  1. Love -- Fiction 2. Friendship -- Fiction
  ISBN 978-0-7636-4274-7; 0-7636-4274-6

"Patrick Benson's ink-and-watercolor illustrations make this existential questioning pleasant to witness, delivering three appealing imaginary beasts in a quietly bizarre landscape. . . . Dunbar's text is concise and lively, with many memorable touches." Booklist

  The **monster** who ate darkness; illustrated by Jimmy Liao. Candlewick Press 2008 un il $16.99
Grades: PreK K 1   **E**
  1. Fear -- Fiction 2. Night -- Fiction 3. Bedtime -- Fiction 4. Monsters -- Fiction
  ISBN 978-0-7636-3859-7; 0-7636-3859-5
                    LC 2008-928826

"Under Jo-Jo's bed lurks a 'tiny speck of a monster' with a 'big empty feeling.' This endearingly unscary creature discovers a taste for darkness and eats up even the dimmest corners of the room. . . . Jo-Jo, who is normally afraid of the dark, can't fall asleep in the endless daylight. As the compassionate monster cradles the little boy in his arms and soothes him with a lullaby, the evening shades return. Liao's digitally enhanced pen and watercolor illustrations humorously capture the mayhem caused by lack of darkness." SLJ

Dunbar, Polly
  Dog Blue. Candlewick Press 2004 un il hardcover o.p. pa $7.99
Grades: PreK K 1 2   **E**
  1. Dogs -- Fiction
  ISBN 0-7636-2476-4; 0-7636-3881-1 pa
                    LC 2003-65223

Bertie, who loves the color blue and really wants a dog, finally gets his wish even though the dog he meets is white with black spots

"Dunbar makes clever use of page turns, unfolding the story in pithy, alliterative prose. . . . In the end, the wish fulfillment is gratifying, but it's Bertie's ingenious self-sufficiency that truly resonates." Booklist

  ★ **Penguin**. Candlewick Press 2007 un il $15.99
Grades: PreK K   **E**
  1. Toys -- Fiction 2. Penguins -- Fiction
  ISBN 0-7636-3404-2

"A pajama-clad toddler opens his present to find a toy penguin. Much to Ben's chagrin, the bird doesn't say any-

thing, no matter how hard the boy tries to engage it. . . .
It isn't until a blue lion chomps on the child that Penguin
jumps into action and rescues his new pal. . . . The attractive,
spare illustrations in mixed media are focused and centered
on a white background." SLJ

Where's Tumpty? Candlewick Press 2009 un il
$12.99
Grades: PreK   E
1. Animals -- Fiction 2. Elephants -- Fiction 3.
Friendship -- Fiction
ISBN 978-0-7636-4273-0; 0-7636-4273-8
"After several unsuccessful attempts at hiding, Tumpty
the elephant is able to trick his friends into thinking he has
disappeared. . . . There are many amusing situations involv-
ing Tilly, a little girl, and her animal friends. . . . The back-
ground consists of a variety of muted tones, which contrast
with the brighter mixed-media drawings. The illustrations
are whimsical and detailed. . . . Young children and begin-
ning readers are sure to gravitate to this delightful story that
celebrates the joy of friendship." SLJ
Other titles about Tilly and her friends are:
Doodle bites (2009)
Good night, Tiptoe (2009)
Happy Hector (2008)
Hello, Tilly (2008)
Pretty Pru (2009)

Dunklee, Annika
★ **My** name is Elizabeth! written by Annika Dunklee;
illustrated by Matthew Forsythe. Kids Can Press 2011 un
il $14.95
Grades: PreK K 1 2   E
1. Personal names -- Fiction
ISBN 978-1-55453-560-6; 1-55453-560-3
Elizabeth is not not amused when people insist on using
nicknames like "Lizzy" and "Beth." She bears her frustration in silence until an otherwise ordinary autumn day, when
she discovers her power to change things once and for all.
"Forsythe's restrained color palette and expressive line
contribute to his brilliant rendering of Elizabeth's character,
and his whimsical inclusion of a pet duck (unmentioned in
the text) adds another layer of idiosyncratic delight." Kirkus

Dunn, Todd
We go together! by Todd Dunn; illustrated by Miki
Sakamoto. Sterling 2007 un il $12.95
Grades: PreK K   E
1. Stories in rhyme 2. Vocabulary -- Fiction
ISBN 978-1-4027-3260-7; 1-4027-3260-0
                   LC 2006023425
A rhyming picture book with pairs of things that go
together exceptionally well, like horse and wagon and fire
and dragon.
"Using very readable pictures and predictable scheme,
children will easily finish the lines. . . . The colorful illustrations are uncomplicated, yet interesting enough to encourage
conversation." SLJ

Dunrea, Olivier
Bear Noel. Farrar, Straus & Giroux 2000 un il hardcover o.p. pa $5.95
Grades: PreK K 1 2   E
1. Bears 2. Animals 3. Christmas 4. Bears -- Fiction

5. Animals -- Fiction 6. Christmas -- Fiction
ISBN 0-374-39990-5; 0-374-40001-6 pa
                   LC 99-27600
The animals of the North Woods react with excitement
as they hear Bear Noel coming to bring them Christmas
"Dunrea beautifully creates the effect of falling snow
throughout the pictures and uses a limited palette of browns,
grays, and greens with flashes of fox red to lend a celebratory feel." Booklist

A **Christmas** tree for Pyn. Philomel Books 2011 un
il $16.99
Grades: PreK K   E
1. Trees -- Fiction 2. Christmas stories 3. Christmas
-- Fiction 4. Father-daughter relationship -- Fiction
ISBN 978-0-399-24506-0; 0-399-24506-5
                   LC 2010041653
Little Pyn finally persuades her gruff father to find the
perfect Christmas tree in the snowy forest and, after bringing
it home, decorates it with him.
Dun-rea's "talent for capturing a mood of majestic stillness in snowy landscapes shines yet again, as does his skill
at creating cozy, rustic details—bushy fur coats and boots,
tree-stump beds, a stone hearth—that suggest a mythical
time. Pyn and Papa's warming relationship is one to celebrate any time of year." Publ Wkly

Gideon; Olivier Dunrea. Houghton Mifflin Books for
Children 2012 1 v. (unpaged) col. ill.
Grades: K 1 2 3   E
1. Geese -- Fiction 2. Children's stories 3. Picture
books for children 4. Domestic animals -- Fiction 5.
Animals -- Fiction
ISBN 9780618436613
                   LC 2010044359
This children's book tells the story of "Gideon, 'a small,
ruddy gosling who likes to play,' [who] joins Gossie and
the other goslings on Dunrea's farm. Always on the move,
Gideon chases a piglet, plays 'tag-the-mole,' leaps over a
frog, and listens to bees buzzing in their hive—always with
his octopus toy in tow. No naps for Gideon, no matter what
mother goose says, but a day of barnyard shenanigans has a
way of tiring out a gosling." (Publishers Weekly)

Gideon and Otto; Olivier Dunrea. Houghton Mifflin
Harcourt 2012 1 v. (unpaged) col. ill.
Grades: K 1 2 3   E
1. Children's stories 2. Friendship -- Fiction 3. Picture
books for children 4. Domestic animals -- Fiction 5.
Toys -- Fiction 6. Geese -- Fiction 7. Rabbits -- Fiction
ISBN 9780618436620
                   LC 2010045844
This children's book tells the story of "Gideon [who] is
a 'small ruddy gosling who likes to play. All day.' . . . After climbing to the top of a haystack and snuggling down
in the straw, sleepiness wins out. In Gideon and Otto, children meet the gosling's favorite friend. When the toy octopus goes missing, a search of the leaf pile and pond ensues.
Otto's triumphant return is on the back of a turtle." (SLJ)

★ **Gossie**. Houghton Mifflin 2002 un il $9.95

Grades: PreK K 1   **E**
  1. Geese -- Fiction
ISBN 0-618-17674-8

                               LC 2002-214

Gossie is a gosling who likes to wear bright red boots every day, no matter what she is doing, and so she is heartbroken the day the boots are missing and she can't find them anywhere. "Ages two to four." (Bull Cent Child Books)

The succinct text uses "repetition and predictability with great skill and will therefore work equally well with early independent readers and preschoolers. . . . The illustrations, focused against restful white space, are spare and expressive, models of composition and clarity." Horn Book

Other titles about Gossie and her friends are:
BooBoo (2004)
Gossie & Gertie (2002)
Merry Christmas, Ollie (2008)
Ollie (2003)
Ollie the stomper (2003)
Ollie's Easter eggs (2010)
Ollie's Halloween (2010)
Peedie (2004)

  ★ **It's** snowing! Farrar, Straus & Giroux 2002 un il hardcover o.p. pa $6.99
Grades: PreK K 1   **E**
  1. Snow -- Fiction 2. Infants -- Fiction 3. Mothers -- Fiction
ISBN 0-374-39992-1; 0-312-60216-2 pa
                               LC 00-42172

A mother shares the magic of a snowy night with her baby

"The gentle, rhythmical rocking of the text conveys a reassuring message that's beautifully supported by Dunrea's spare, snow-dappled gouache illustrations." Horn Book

Jasper & Joop; Olivier Dunrea. Houghton Mifflin Books for Children 2013 32 p. col. ill. (reinforced) $9.99
Grades: PreK K 1   **E**
  1. Geese -- Fiction 2. Friendship -- Fiction
ISBN 9780547867625
                               LC 2012018964

Little Cub; Olivier Dunrea. Philomel 2012 32 p. (hardback) $16.99
Grades: PreK K 1 2   **E**
  1. Adoption -- Fiction 2. Bears -- Juvenile Fiction 3. Picture books for children 4. Bears -- Fiction 5. Loneliness -- Fiction 6. Foster home care -- Fiction
ISBN 039924235X; 9780399242359
                               LC 2012015126

In this book, "Little Cub is sad and lonely. He has no one to take care of him, teach him how to catch fish, help him get honey, and be with him during the long dark nights. Old Bear is sad and lonely. He has no one to teach, share his food with, and keep him company during the long dark nights. One day he finds Little Cub . . . . Old Bear names him, takes him home, feeds him, puts him to bed, tells him a story, and the rest is history." (School Library Journal)

Merry Christmas, Ollie! [by] Olivier Dunrea. Houghton Mifflin 2008 un il $12.95

Grades: PreK K 1   **E**
  1. Geese -- Fiction 2. Christmas -- Fiction 3. Santa Claus -- Fiction
ISBN 978-0-618-53242-1; 0-618-53242-0
                             LC 2004025126

On Christmas Eve, Ollie and the other goslings anxiously await the arrival of Father Christmas Goose.

"First-time readers and those already familiar with Dunrea's goslings will be delighted by this simple story. . . . Remaining true to his uncomplicated watercolor style, Dunrea maintains an element of charm to Ollie's waiting, depicting his impatience as sweet and subdued." SLJ

  ★ **Old** Bear and his cub. Philomel Books 2010 un il $16.99
Grades: PreK K 1 2   **E**
  1. Bears -- Fiction 2. Parent-child relationship -- Fiction
ISBN 978-0-399-24507-7; 0-399-24507-3
                             LC 2008-00663

Although they love each other, Old Bear and his little Cub have a tug of war over which one knows best in a variety of situations.

"The adult-child give-and-take in this charming bedtime story will be quite familiar and is bound to bring smiles to both ages. Simplicity at its best." Kirkus

Ollie's Halloween. Houghton Mifflin Books for Children 2010 un il $12.99
Grades: PreK K 1   **E**
  1. Stories in rhyme 2. Geese -- Fiction 3. Halloween -- Fiction
ISBN 978-0-618-53241-4; 0-618-53241-2
                             LC 2009-49699

Dressed in their costumes, Ollie and his siblings go out on Halloween night and have a scary but fun adventure.

"As with the previous titles starring this gosling crew, Dunrea's ink and watercolor images beget an understandable and cozy world, this time with just a hint of spookiness and autumnal gloom." Publ Wkly

Dunston, Marc
  The **magic** of giving; illustrated by Katie Cantrell; foreword by Wally Amos. Pelican 2010 32p il $16.99
Grades: K 1 2   **E**
  1. School stories 2. Contests -- Fiction 3. Magic tricks -- Fiction
ISBN 978-1-58980-805-8; 1-58980-805-3
                             LC 2010014648

Little Marc is determined to win his school's talent contest and use the prize money to buy Thanksgiving dinner for his neighbors, but first he must pick a talent and master it.

"The positive, uplifting message encourages children to read and develop their talents not to just help themselves, but to help others. Cantrell's illustrations are bright and sunny and feature a multigenerational, multiethnic cast of characters. The foreward is written by literacy advocate Wally Amos. Literacy awareness is stressed below the storyline on each page with the placement of vocabulary development tools." Libr Media Connect

Durand, Hallie
  Mitchell's license; illustrated by Tony Fucile. Candlewick Press 2011 un il $15.99

Grades: PreK K 1   E

1. Bedtime -- Fiction 2. Father-son relationship -- Fiction

ISBN 978-0-7636-4496-3; 0-7636-4496-X

LC 2010039181

Mitchell never wants to go to bed until, at the age of three years, nine months, and five days he gets his license so that he can drive there—at least until he and the car have a disagreement about what fuel goes in the tank.

"Durmand's text will appeal to the active and car obsessed, but Fucile's masterful illustrations, full of expressive characters, great physical comedy and wonderful warmth, will engage readers young and old. . . . An incredibly entertaining ride." Kirkus

Durango, Julia

Angels watching over me; adapted by Julia Durango; illustrated by Elisa Kleven. Simon & Schuster Books for Young Readers 2007 un il $16.99

Grades: PreK K 1 2   E

1. Stories in rhyme 2. Day -- Fiction 3. Angels -- Fiction

ISBN 978-0-689-86252-6; 0-689-86252-0

"Rhyming couplets take a child from sunrise to sunset, imagining all the ways . . . that the angels send their vigilant protection. . . . The melody of the language and its reverence for the natural world are sure to spark interest. Kleven's mixed-media compositions—watercolor, ink, collage and colored pencil—convey an appropriately dream-in-flight feeling." Publ Wkly

Cha -cha chimps; illustrated by Eleanor Taylor. Simon & Schuster Books for Young Readers 2006 un il $15.95

Grades: PreK K 1   E

1. Stories in rhyme 2. Dance -- Fiction 3. Chimpanzees -- Fiction

ISBN 0-689-86456-6

In this counting book, "10 little chimps sneak out of their tree house to go dancing at Mambo Jambas, where a pig band plays music all night long. . . . The rhymes roll easily off the tongue, making the text fun to read aloud. . . . Done in watercolor and pencil, the illustrations are bright and lively." SLJ

Go -go gorillas; illustrated by Eleanor Taylor. Simon & Schuster Books for Young Readers 2010 un il $15.99

Grades: PreK K 1   E

1. Stories in rhyme 2. Gorillas -- Fiction 3. Transportation -- Fiction

ISBN 978-1-4169-3779-1; 1-4169-3779-X

LC 2007045160

Summoned to the Great Gorilla Villa by King Big Daddy to meet the newest member of their family, ten gorillas arrive on time using various forms of transportation, including hot-air balloon, taxicab, and pogo stick.

"Durango and Taylor present a bouncy book that will keep little ones counting. . . . The watercolor art, with pictures big enough for groups, has the same sprightly spirit as the text." Booklist

Pest fest; by Julia Durango; illustrated by Kurt Cyrus. Simon & Schuster 2007 un il lib bdg $16.99

Grades: PreK K 1 2   E

1. Insects -- Fiction

ISBN 978-0-689-85569-6

In beauty, talent and skills, the housefly can't compete with other bugs. But as a pest he is a winner. Book shows beetle, firefly, cricket, cicada, housefly and spider.

"The rhyming verses capture amusing verbal jousting among the insects. Cyrus's watercolor and colored-pencil illustrations offer stunning closeups of the contestants, showing lush views of the streamside setting from their down-to-earth perspective." SLJ

Durant, Alan

I love you, Little Monkey; by Alan Durant; illustrated by Katharine McEwen. Simon & Schuster Books for Young Readers 2007 un il $15.99

Grades: PreK K   E

1. Love -- Fiction 2. Monkeys -- Fiction

ISBN 978-1-4169-2481-4; 1-4169-2481-7

First published 2006 in the United Kingdom

"Little Monkey gets into mischief when Big Monkey is too busy to play with him. . . . Little Monkey fears that he is no longer loved when he is sent to bed for punishment, but is reassured that Big Monkey loves him always, even when naughty. . . . The familiar message is always on target for small children. . . . Lively cartoon drawings in watercolor and pencil depict the mischievous animals at play in a colorful jungle setting." SLJ

Duval, Kathy

The **Three** Bears' Halloween; by Kathy Duval; illustrated by Paul Meisel. Holiday House 2007 un il $16.95

Grades: PreK K 1   E

1. Bears -- Fiction 2. Halloween -- Fiction

ISBN 978-0-8234-2032-2; 0-8234-2032-9

LC 2006012120

Is it a witch or a blonde little girl hiding in the bushes of the spooky house when the three bears go trick or treating?

This is a "delightfully presented story, rich with folk-art warmth and whimsical humor." SLJ

Duvoisin, Roger

★ **Petunia**; fiftieth anniversary edition; Knopf 2000 un il $15.95; pa $6.99

Grades: PreK K 1   E

1. Geese -- Fiction 2. Books and reading -- Fiction

ISBN 0-394-90865-7; 0-394-90865-1 lib bdg; 0-440-41754-6 pa

A reissue of the title first published 1950

Petunia, the goose, learns that possessing knowledge involves more than just carrying a book around under her wing

"Duvoisin's energetic drawings perfectly capture Petunia's growing arrogance." Horn Book Guide

DwellStudio (Firm)

Good morning, toucan; by DwellStudio. Blue Apple Books 2011 un il bd bk $8.99

Grades: PreK   E

1. Board books for children 2. Morning -- Fiction 3. Rain forest animals -- Fiction

ISBN 978-1-60905-085-6; 1-60905-085-1

LC 2010046649

Simple text invites the reader to look under lift-up flaps to find various creatures as they awaken in the rain forest.

This is "engaging. . . . [This] visually appealing [book features a] very basic [layout] and graphic-style illustrations that resemble Colorforms, which allow youngsters to focus on the guessing game in [the] book." SLJ

Goodnight, owl; by DwellStudio. Blue Apple Books 2011 un il bd bk $8.99

Grades: PreK   E
1. Board books for children 2. Night -- Fiction 3. Bedtime -- Fiction 4. Forest animals -- Fiction
ISBN 978-1-60905-083-2; 1-60905-083-5
           LC 2010046819

Simple text invites the reader to look under lift-up flaps to find various creatures as they go to sleep at night in the forest.

This is "engaging. . . . [This] visually appealing [book features a] very basic [layout] and graphic-style illustrations that resemble Colorforms, which allow youngsters to focus on the guessing game in [the] book." SLJ

Dyer, Sarah
   Batty. Frances Lincoln Children's Books 2011 un il $16.95

Grades: PreK K 1 2   E
1. Bats -- Fiction 2. Zoos -- Fiction 3. Animals -- Fiction
ISBN 978-1-84780-084-8; 1-84780-084-X

"Batty is a zoo-dwelling, long-eared bat. . . . Zoo visitors tend to drift past Batty toward the more popular, talented animals; he tries hanging out with the eager-to-groom gorillas and the raucous birds in the aviary . . . but he doesn't fit in. . . . The spreads in which Batty watches the other animals are upside-down, as a hanging bat would see them, with intervening spreads right-side-up—an entertaining way of representing Batty's point of view. . . . Dyer's understated humor, both in her text and artwork, makes for a winning take on the be-true-to-yourself theme." Publ Wkly

Monster day at work. Frances Lincoln 2010 un il
Grades: PreK K 1   E
1. Monsters -- Fiction
ISBN 1-84780-069-6; 978-1-84780-069-5

Little monster spends a day at work with his father.

"Wide-set eyes, squat statures and two horns that look like party hats worn askew make these monsters anything but scary, Detailed spreads filled with other oddball creatures and quirky touches . . . complete this offbeat monster landscape." Kirkus

Eastman, P. D.
   ★ **Are** you my mother? written and illustrated by P. D. Eastman. Beginner Bks. 1960 63p il $8.99; lib bdg $12.99; bd bk $4.99

Grades: PreK K 1   E
1. Birds -- Fiction 2. Bilingual books -- English-Spanish 3. Mother-child relationship -- Fiction
ISBN 0-394-80018-4; 0-394-90018-9 lib bdg; 0-679-89047-5 bd bk

"A small bird falls from his nest and searches for his mother. He asks a kitten, a hen, a dog, a cow, a boat, [and] a plane . . . 'Are you my mother?' Repetition of words and phrases and funny pictures are just right for beginning readers." Chicago. Public Libr

Eaton, Maxwell
   ★ **Best** buds; [by] Maxwell Eaton III. Alfred A. Knopf 2007 un il (The adventures of Max and Pinky) $12.99; lib bdg $14.99

Grades: PreK K 1   E
1. Pigs -- Fiction 2. Friendship -- Fiction
ISBN 978-0-375-83803-3; 0-375-83803-1; 978-0-375-93803-0 lib bdg; 0-375-93803-6 lib bdg
           LC 2006-02037

Best friends Max and Pinky the pig have an adventure together every Saturday, but one week Max looks everywhere and cannot find Pinky.

"The book is offbeat, irreverent, and affectionate, contrasting the pared-down simplicity of the main text with cheerful dialogue in the speech balloons and the sturdy simplicity of of the flat-planed, digitally colored art with the eccentric actions they depict." Horn Book

Other titles about Max and Pinky are:
Superheroes (2007)
The mystery (2008)

Two dumb ducks. Alfred A. Knopf 2010 un il $12.99; lib bdg $15.99

Grades: PreK K 1 2   E
1. Anger -- Fiction 2. Ducks -- Fiction 3. Gulls -- Fiction 4. Bullies -- Fiction
ISBN 978-0-375-84576-5; 0-375-84576-3; 978-0-375-94576-2 lib bdg; 0-375-94576-8 lib bdg
           LC 2010-04959

Steve and Carl, two ducks, decide to get even when the seagulls call them "dumb."

This "is utterly genuine in both its humor and pain; Eaton's bold cartooning and dead-pan, economic storytelling make every page a treat." Publ Wkly

Edgemon, Darcie
   Seamore, the very forgetful porpoise; by Darcie Edgemon; illustrated by J. Otto Seibold. HarperCollinsPublishers 2008 un il hardcover o.p. lib bdg $17,89

Grades: K 1 2 3   E
1. Memory -- Fiction 2. Whales -- Fiction 3. Porpoises -- Fiction 4. Friendship -- Fiction
ISBN 978-0-06-085075-3; 0-06-085075-2; 978-0-06-085076-0 lib bdg; 0-06-085076-0 lib bdg
           LC 2007010906

Seamore is a very forgetful porpoise and when neither notes to himself nor string around his fins help, he decides to search for his missing memory

This is "effervescent. . . . The straightforward story is buoyed by the polychrome exuberance of Seibold's unmistakable computer-generated illustrations." Booklist

Edwards, David
   The **pen** that Pa built; by David Edwards; illustrations by Ashley Wolff. Tricycle Press 2007 un il $14.95

Grades: PreK K 1 2   E
1. Stories in rhyme 2. Wool -- Fiction 3. Sheep -- Fiction 4. Weaving -- Fiction
ISBN 978-1-58246-153-3; 1-58246-153-8
           LC 2006101994

A cumulative, illustrated tale describing the process of raising sheep and using their wool to make warm woolen blankets.

"The language is pleasant and the rhymes clever. What really works here are Wolff's highly textured gesso-and-gouache illustrations." Booklist

Edwards, Michelle

★ **Papa's** latkes; illustrated by Stacey Schuett. Candlewick Press 2004 un il $15.99
Grades: PreK K 1 2   E
1. Jews -- Fiction 2. Hanukkah -- Fiction 3. Bereavement -- Fiction
ISBN 0-7636-0779-7

LC 00-69801

On the first Hanukkah after Mama died, Papa and his two daughters try to make latkes and celebrate without her.
"The poignant text with touches of humor is nicely matched with warm and richly colored oil paintings. . . . A touching and uplifting story." SLJ

Edwards, Pamela Duncan

Jack and Jill's treehouse; illustrated by Henry Cole. Katherine Tegen Books 2008 un il $16.99; lib bdg $17.89
Grades: PreK K 1   E
1. Birds -- Fiction 2. Building -- Fiction 3. Tree houses -- Fiction
ISBN 978-0-06-009077-7; 0-06-009077-4; 978-0-06-009078-4 lib bdg; 0-06-009078-2 lib bdg

A cumulative tale about Jack and Jill who build a treehouse, as a pair of robins make their own home in the same tree.
"Color, spirit, and a sense of satisfaction fill the soft illustrations, which depict idyllic days spent in outdoor amusement. . . . The large images lend themselves well to group sharing, and the text includes small rebus pictures of each added item, allowing listeners to chant along." SLJ

Princess Pigtoria and the pea; illustrated by Henry Cole. Orchard Books 2010 un il $16.99
Grades: PreK K 1   E
1. Fairy tales 2. Pigs -- Fiction 3. Princesses -- Fiction
ISBN 978-0-545-15625-7; 0-545-15625-4

LC 2008-52693

To make her pigsty of a palace picturesque again, penniless Princess Pigtoria tries to get the pompous porker Prince Proudfoot to propose marriage.
"Fun for listeners and readers alike. . . The scale of the artwork make this a good choice for storytime." Booklist

Some smug slug; illustrated by Henry Cole. HarperCollins Pubs. 1996 32p il $17.99; pa $6.99
Grades: PreK K 1 2   E
1. Animals -- Fiction 2. Slugs (Mollusks) -- Fiction
ISBN 0-06-024789-4; 0-06-443502-4 pa

LC 94-18682

"A slug senses a slope and saunters on up, against the advice of a sparrow, a spider, and a skink, among others, and meets with a sudden, spontaneous demise. Such is the life of a slug told with a multitude of common and not so common 'S' words. . . . Realistically detailed, earth-toned illustrations focus attention on each scene. . . . This slug is so appealing and full of personality that it will certainly garner sympathy." SLJ

While the world is sleeping; illustrated by Dan Kirk. Orchard Books 2010 un il lib bdg $16.99

Grades: PreK K 1   E
1. Stories in rhyme 2. Night -- Fiction 3. Animals -- Fiction 4. Bedtime -- Fiction
ISBN 978-0-545-01756-5; 0-545-01756-4

LC 2007040283

A sleepy child is flown through the night sky to see foxes hunting, rabbits playing, raccoons scrounging, and other animals that are active while people sleep.
"Kirk's illustrations are big and bold, featuring the shimmering light of the moon, animals whose every hair seems distinct, and playful faux-Rousseau forests. The book's mix of the realistic and fantastic seems like a perfect prelude to dream time." Booklist

The **leprechaun's** gold; illustrated by Henry Cole. Katherine Tegen Books 2004 un il $15.99; lib bdg $16.89; pa $6.99
Grades: K 1 2 3   E
1. Greed 2. Leprechauns 3. Harp 4. Musicians -- Fiction 5. Leprechauns -- Fiction
ISBN 0-06-623974-5; 0-06-623975-3 lib bdg; 0-06-443878-3 pa

LC 2002-3150

A leprechaun intervenes with gold and magic when a greedy, boastful young harpist gains an unfair advantage for a royal harping contest
"Cole's imaginative illustrations are a good match for the story, displaying both realism and fantasy. . . . An appealing tale that need not be limited to St. Patrick's Day storytime." Booklist

★ The **mixed** -up rooster; written by Pamela Duncan Edwards; illustrated by Megan Lloyd. Katherine Tegen Books 2006 un il lib bdg $16.89
Grades: PreK K 1 2   E
1. Chickens -- Fiction 2. Roosters -- Fiction
ISBN 978-0-06-028999-7; 0-06-028999-6; 978-0-06-029000-9 lib bdg; 0-06-029000-5 lib bdg

LC 2005014401

Ned the rooster is fired from his job because he cannot wake up in the morning, but he restores his reputation after discovering his usefulness as a night bird
"This lighthearted story is written in an uncomplicated, comical style and has vibrant illustrations that are full of personality and charm." SLJ

The **neat** line; scribbling through Mother Goose. illustrated by Diana Cain Bluthenthal. Katherine Tegen Books 2004 un il hardcover o.p. lib bdg $16.89
Grades: PreK K 1 2   E
1. Nursery rhymes -- Fiction
ISBN 0-06-623970-2; 0-06-623971-0 lib bdg

LC 2002-153424

A young scribble matures into a neat line, then wriggles into a book of nursery rhymes where he transforms himself into different objects to assist the characters he meets there
This is a "brilliantly creative romp. . . . The large cartoon paintings . . . are appropriately outlined with thick, bold lines and are framed by book pages on either side." SLJ

The **old** house; [by] Pamela Duncan Edwards; illustrated by Henry Cole. Dutton Children's Books 2007 un il $16.99; pa $6.99

Grades: PreK K 1   E
1. Houses -- Fiction
ISBN 978-0-525-47796-9; 0-14-241480-8 pa
LC 2006102950

An old empty house feels sorry for itself because it has no family living inside, but with the help of some good friends, its dreams come true

"Edwards colloquial text is accessible for young readers to tackle on their own and would make a lively read-aloud. Cole's energetic cartoon-style artwork gives oodles of personality to this house waiting to shine." SLJ

Edwards, Wallace
Uncle Wally's old brown shoe; Wallace Edwards. Orca Book Publishers 2012 32 p. (hardcover) $19.95
Grades: 3 4 5   E
1. Shoes -- Juvenile fiction 2. Picture books for children 3. Animals -- Juvenile fiction
ISBN 1459801547; 9781459801547; 9781459801554
LC 2012935414

The protagonist of this book by Wallace Edwards "is a tiger, resplendent in red-and-white-striped pyjamas and a solitary brown oxford. His missing shoe has all the fun in this story, as it is driven by a kitten, who is tickled by a pig in a fancy hat, who is chased by a limber frog on stilts, who well, you get the idea. Eventually, the reader is treated to the revelation of how the shoe has come to pass through the possession of a menagerie of animals." (Quill & Quire)

Eeckhout, Emmanuelle
There's no such thing as ghosts! Kane/Miller 2008 un il $13.95
Grades: PreK K 1   E
1. Ghost stories
ISBN 978-1-933605-91-3; 1-933605-91-X

"Eager to explore a neighborhood haunted house, a diminutive boy grabs his butterfly net and sets out to catch a ghost. . . . The joke is that readers see the adorable, playful spirits that cavort, tease, and go about their ghostly business, invisible to the boy. Through a simple palette of black, white, yellow, and pink, Eeckhout uses plenty of white space, full spreads, silhouettes, and small vignettes to great advantage." SLJ

Egan, Tim
Dodsworth in London; written and illustrated by Tim Egan. Houghton Mifflin Harcourt 2009 un il $15
Grades: K 1 2   E
1. Ducks -- Fiction 2. Voyages and travels -- Fiction
ISBN 978-0-547-13816-9; 0-547-13816-4
LC 2008-40464

Despite a dart-throwing episode at a local pub and a case of mistaken identity, Dodsworth and his mischievous duck companion receive a royal invitation to stay at Buckingham Palace during their trip to London.

"As usual, Egan's wit is as sharp as the fashion sense of the assorted animals populating his droll ink-and-watercolor illustrations." Horn Book

★ Dodsworth in New York; written and illustrated by Tim Egan. Houghton Mifflin 2007 un il $15

Grades: K 1 2   E
1. Ducks -- Fiction 2. Voyages and travels -- Fiction
ISBN 978-0-618-77708-2; 0-618-77708-3
LC 2006-34522

When Dodsworth sets out for adventure, including a stop in New York City before going to Paris, London, and beyond, he does not expect a crazy duck to stow away in his suitcase and lead him on a merry chase.

"Egan favors a palette of golds and clay-browns, and draws pillowy shapes in a gentle, never rigid line. . . . Egan keeps the hijinks low-key, preferring long pauses and slow burns to nutty slapstick." Publ Wkly

Other titles about Dodsworth are:
Dodsworth in Paris (2008)
Dodsworth in London (2009)
Dodsworth in Rome (2011)

Dodsworth in Paris; written and illustrated by Tim Egan. Houghton Mifflin Co. 2008 un il $15
Grades: K 1 2   E
1. Ducks -- Fiction 2. Voyages and travels -- Fiction
ISBN 978-0-618-98062-8; 0-618-98062-8
LC 2007-47732

When Dodsworth and the duck vacation in Paris, they have a grand time despite running out of money and accidentally riding their bicycles in the Tour de France.

"An out-of-the-ordinary offering for new readers that moves them to new places, both literally and literarily." Booklist

Dodsworth in Rome; written and illustrated by Tim Egan. Houghton Mifflin Harcourt 2011 un il $14.99
Grades: K 1 2   E
1. Ducks -- Fiction 2. Voyages and travels -- Fiction
ISBN 978-0-547-39006-2; 0-547-39006-8
LC 2010007024

Dodsworth and his duck companion have a lovely time in Rome, even though the duck tries to improve the ceiling of the Sistine Chapel and takes all the coins from the Trevi Fountain.

"Egan's understated, hilarious travelogue continues." Kirkus

The pink refrigerator; [by] Tim Egan. Houghton Mifflin 2007 un il $16
Grades: K 1 2   E
1. Mice -- Fiction
ISBN 978-0-618-63154-4; 0-618-63154-2
LC 2006009816

Dodsworth the mouse does as little work as he can, collecting items from a junkyard and placing them in his thrift store for sale, until he happens upon a pink refrigerator that spurs him to do much more with his life.

"The ink-and-watercolor art mirrors the laid-back tone of the narrative. . . . This offbeat tale is perfect for reading aloud, but will also be appreciated as a read-alone and lapsit." SLJ

Egielski, Richard
★ Captain Sky Blue. Michael Di Capua Books 2010 un il $17.95
Grades: PreK K 1 2   E
1. Adventure fiction 2. Toys -- Fiction 3. Christmas -- Fiction 4. Air pilots -- Fiction 5. Christmas stories

-- Juvenile literature

ISBN 978-0-545-21342-4; 0-545-21342-8

Jack's best toy pal is Captain Sky Blue, a pilot. After a thunderstorm separates Sky and his buddy, Sky is abducted by a whale, then left alone to wander a frigid ocean floor until he chances upon a very special place, a place where he's been before.

Egielski "is in top form in this story.... From start to finish, it has the feel of an old-fashioned adventure. . . . Egielski's boldly outlined artwork lends the story a cinematic scope. . . . Airplane-obsessed readers will be thrilled with the aeronautical jargon Sky uses." Publ Wkly

The **sleepless** little vampire. Arthur A. Levine Books 2011 un il $16.99
Grades: PreK K 1   E
1. Bedtime -- Fiction 2. Vampires -- Fiction
ISBN 978-0-545-14597-8; 0-545-14597-X
LC 2010032096

A young vampire, unable to sleep, tries to figure out whether it is the howling of a werewolf, the clacking of skeletons, or something else that is keeping him awake.

"The book closes on a satisfying note, with everyone safe and sound. Egielski's watercolor/ink paintings are superbly executed, with strong colors and bold, expressive lines." SLJ

Ehlert, Lois

Boo to you! Beach Lane Books 2009 un il $17.99
Grades: PreK K 1   E
1. Stories in rhyme 2. Cats -- Fiction 3. Mice -- Fiction
4. Parties -- Fiction
ISBN 978-1-4169-8625-6; 1-4169-8625-1
LC 2008-44352

When the neighborhood cat tries to crash the mice's harvest party, the mice have a plan to scare the intruder away

"Ehlert's use of paper, fruit, seeds, and string is labyrinthine enough to have young children tracing their routes, and so vivid they'll want to touch the page to make sure it's not real." Booklist

★ **Circus**. HarperCollins Pubs. 1992 un il $17.99
Grades: PreK K 1   E
1. Circus -- Fiction 2. Animals -- Fiction
ISBN 0-06-020252-1
LC 91-12067

Leaping lizards, marching snakes, a bear on the high wire, and others perform in a somewhat unusual circus

"The book approximates a light show in visual intensity, with neon-bright illustrations set against black or bold backgrounds. . . . The sprightly rhythm of Ms. Ehlert's text complements her Day-Glo palette. Echoing a ringmaster's speech, she's afraid of neither alliteration . . . nor hyperbole." N Y Times Book Rev

★ **Hands**; growing up to be an artist. Harcourt 2004 un il $14.95
Grades: PreK K 1 2   E
1. Handicraft 2. Creative ability 3. Toy and movable books 4. Parent and child 5. Toy and movable books -- Specimens
ISBN 0-15-205107-4
LC 2004-1237

A reformatted edition of the title first published 1997

When a child works alongside her parents doing carpentry, sewing, and gardening, she thinks of being an artist as well when she grows up

This edition offers "slightly reworked trimmings, but keeps the same die-cut pages—in the shapes of scissors, seed packets and more—as well as a 'paint box' that opens." Publ Wkly

★ **Leaf** Man. Harcourt 2005 un il $16
Grades: PreK K 1 2   E
1. Winds -- Fiction 2. Leaves -- Fiction
ISBN 0-15-205304-2
LC 2004-9981

A man made of leaves blows away, traveling wherever the wind may take him.

This is an "eye-popping book. . . . Scalloped edgings on the tops of the pages, cut at varying heights, artfully give the effect of setting the action against a three-dimensional landscape." Booklist

★ **Lots** of spots. Beach Lane Books 2010 un il $17.99
Grades: PreK K 1   E
1. Animals 2. Children's poetry 3. Animals -- Juvenile literature 4. Camouflage (Biology) -- Juvenile literature
ISBN 978-1-4424-0289-8; 1-4424-0289-X
LC 2009034361

"Each of the 50 featured creatures in Ehlert's . . . offering sports distinctive markings. . . . Each spread freatures a beautiful collage illustration of an animal, accompanied by a poem of four, short, catchy lines. . . . Children will enjoy paging through and identifying the multitude of brilliantly hued animals that make up this visual zoo." Booklist

★ **Market** day; a story told with folk art. written and designed by Lois Ehlert. Harcourt 2000 un il $17; pa $7
Grades: PreK K 1 2   E
1. Stories in rhyme 2. Markets -- Fiction 3. Farm life -- Fiction 4. Markets -- Pictorial works -- Juvenile fiction
ISBN 0-15-202158-2; 0-15-216820-6 pa
LC 99-6252

On market day, a farm family experiences all the fun and excitement of going to and from the farmers' market

"The very young will enjoy the spare, simple rhymes. . . . All ages will appreciate the illustrations, comprising images of folk art, primitive art, and textiles from around the world. An annotated inventory of the featured items is included." Horn Book Guide

Oodles of animals. Harcourt 2008 un il $17
Grades: PreK K 1 2   E
1. Stories in rhyme 2. Children's poetry 3. Animals -- Fiction 4. Animals -- Juvenile literature
ISBN 978-0-15-206274-3; 0-15-206274-2
LC 2007-17018

Short, easy to read rhymes reveal what is unique about various animals, from ape to wolf.

"The artist uses scissors, pinking shears, and a hole punch to transform brightly colored papers into squares, rectangles, triangles, circles, diamonds, half circles, ovals, hearts, and teardrops of different sizes, which she then fashions into a menagerie guaranteed to spark readers' imaginations. Each creature is coupled with a short, humorous poem that is sure to delight." SLJ

★ **Pie** in the sky. Harcourt 2004 un il $16

Grades: PreK K 1 2   E
1. Pies 2. Trees 3. Cherry 4. Pies -- Fiction 5. Father and child 6. Cherries -- Fiction
ISBN 0-15-216584-3

LC 2003-4986

A father and child watch the cherry tree in their back yard, waiting until there are ripe cherries to bake in a pie. Includes a recipe for cherry pie

"The vibrant collage illustrations, made with an eclectic combination of materials—from paint and handmade papers to sheet metal, wires, and tree branches—celebrate the colors and simplified shapes of birds, insects, the cherry tree, and, yes, kitchen implements." Booklist

★ **Planting** a rainbow; written and illustrated by Lois Ehlert. Harcourt Brace Jovanovich 1988 un il $17; pa $7; bd bk $6.95

Grades: PreK K 1   E
1. Flowers -- Fiction 2. Gardening -- Fiction
ISBN 0-15-262609-3; 0-15-262610-7 pa; 0-15-204633-X bd bk

LC 87-8528

A mother and daughter plant a rainbow of flowers in the family garden

"The stylized forms of the plants are clearly and beautifully designed, and the primary, blazing colors of the blossoms dazzle in their resplendence. The minimal text, in very large print, is exactly right to set off the glorious illustrations, making a splendid beginning book of colors and flowers cleverly arranged for young readers." Horn Book

★ **Top** cat. Harcourt Brace & Co. 1998 un il $17; pa $7

Grades: PreK K 1 2   E
1. Stories in rhyme 2. Cats -- Fiction
ISBN 0-15-201739-9; 0-15-202425-5 pa

LC 97-8818

The top cat in a household is reluctant to accept the arrival of a new kitten but decides to share various survival secrets with it

"Ehlert creates a memorable cat duo in her trademark cut-paper collage style. . . . Children and other feline fans will quickly warm to this spunky story of rivalry and acceptance." Publ Wkly

★ **Wag** a tail; [by] Lois Ehlert. Harcourt, Inc. 2007 un il $16

Grades: PreK K 1 2   E
1. Stories in rhyme 2. Dogs -- Fiction
ISBN 978-0-15-205843-2

LC 2006013318

Assorted graduates of the Bow Wow School meet at a farmers market and a dog park, where most of them remember their obedience training.

"This simple story has a rhythmic, jazzy quality that begs to be read aloud. . . . Collages composed of brightly colored buttons and scraps of paper stand out on vivid green backgrounds." SLJ

Ehlert, Lois, 1934-
★ **Rrralph**. Beach Lane Books 2011 32p il $17.99

Grades: PreK K 1 2 3   E
1. Dogs -- Fiction
ISBN 1-4424-1305-0; 978-1-4424-1305-4

LC 2010006866

The narrator describes discovering how Ralph the dog can talk, appropriately saying words such as "roof," "rough," "bark," and "wolf."

"Created with realia as well as painted and textured papers, the three-dimensional collage illustrations feature zippers for Ralph's mouth, a metal pop-top for his nose, buttons for the bird's eyes, and actual bark for the tree's trunk. The pages, colored in hot-pink, grass-green, and pumpkin, magnify the visual energy of the artwork and graphics. . . . With its appealing jacket art, clever text, and vibrant illustrations, this amusing picture book is a pleasure to read aloud." Booklist

Ehrhardt, Karen
★ **This** Jazz man; pictures by R. G. Roth. Harcourt 2006 un il $16

Grades: K 1 2 3   E
1. Counting 2. Stories in rhyme 3. Jazz musicians -- Fiction 4. African Americans -- Fiction
ISBN 0-15-205307-7

LC 2004-21094

Presents an introduction to jazz music and nine well-known jazz musicians, set to the rhythm of the traditional song, "This Old Man." Includes brief facts about each musician.

"The candy-colored collages burst from the pages, making this addition just right as an up-tempo introduction for youngest music lovers." Publ Wkly

Ehrlich, Amy
Baby Dragon; [by] Amy Ehrlich; illustrated by Will Hillenbrand. Candlewick Press 2008 un il $16.99

Grades: PreK K 1 2   E
1. Animals -- Fiction 2. Dragons -- Fiction 3. Mother-child relationship -- Fiction
ISBN 978-0-7636-2840-6; 0-7636-2840-9

LC 2007051883

All day, Baby Dragon turns down other animals' offers to go play or find a snack while he waits for his mother to return for him, but at nightfall, he agrees to go with Crocodile to find her

"Hillenbrand's illustrations, done with ink, colored pencil, finger paint, gouache, and collage, and digitally manipulated, bring to life Baby Dragon's misty tropical forest where water buffaloes wander and storks splash in the river." SLJ

★ **Thumbelina**; by Hans Christian Andersen; retold by Amy Ehrlich; [illustrated by Susan Jeffers] Dutton Children's Books 2005 32p il $16.99

Grades: K 1 2 3   E
1. Authors 2. Novelists 3. Dramatists 4. Fairy tales 5. Children's authors 6. Short story writers
ISBN 0-525-47508-7

LC 2004028979

A reissure of the edition published 1979 by Dial Books for Young Readers

A retelling of Hans Christian Andersen's classic fairy tale about a girl who is only one inch tall.

"This sumptuous picture book version the classic Andersen story has been an adapted text that shows some softening of the tale's harsher edges. . . . [Readers will] be caught up in the action as depicted in Jeffers' striking, pastel-dominated pictures." Booklist

★ The **girl** who wanted to dance; by Amy Ehrlich; illustrated by Rebecca Walsh. Candlewick Press 2009 un il $17.99
Grades: 2 3 4   E
  1. Fairy tales 2. Dance -- Fiction 3. Loss (Psychology) -- Fiction
  ISBN 978-0-7636-1345-7; 0-7636-1345-2

"Both a haunting fairy tale and a parable for families separated by divorce or death, this lyrically rendered story also presents art as a vehicle for transcending pain. . . . Working in a representational style, Walsh . . . adds lush paintings of an idealized old world, and her nighttime scenes glow." Publ Wkly

Ehrlich, Fred
  Does an elephant take a bath? pictures by Emily Bolan. Blue Apple Books 2005 un il (Early experiences) lib bdg $13.50; pa $5.95
Grades: PreK K   E
  1. Baths 2. Animals 3. Cleanliness
  ISBN 1-59354-111-2 lib bdg; 1-59354-123-5 pa

"The humor is just right for the audience . . . and, like the text, the uncluttered illustrations . . . are both informative and amusing." Horn Book Guide
  Other titles in the Early experiences series are:
  Does a baboon sleep in a bed? (2005)
  Does a chimp wear clothes? (2005)
  Does a hippo say ahh? (2006)
  Does a lion brush? (2005)
  Does a panda go to school? (2006)
  Does a pig flush? (2005)
  Does a seal smile? (2006)
  Does a tiger open wide? (2006)
  Does a yak get a haircut? (2006)

Ehrlich, H. M.
  ★ **Louie's** goose; illustrated by Emily Bolam. Houghton Mifflin 2000 un il $15
Grades: PreK K 1   E
  1. Toys 2. Geese 3. Beaches 4. Toys -- Fiction 5. Beaches -- Fiction
  ISBN 0-618-03023-9
                       LC 99-28566

While spending the summer at the beach with his parents, Louie has a wonderful time playing with his toy goose and even rescues her from a big wave

"This true-to-life look at a preschooler growing more independent is low-key and natural. . . . Bolam's sunny paintings capture the seashore experience of a charming, lovable family." Booklist
  Another title about Louie is:
  Gotcha, Louie! (2002)

Eichenberg, Fritz
  Ape in a cape; an alphabet of odd animals. Harcourt Brace & Co. 1952 un il hardcover o.p. pa $8

Grades: PreK K 1   E
  1. Animals 2. Alphabet
  ISBN 0-15-607830-9 pa
  A Caldecott Medal honor book, 1953

"The skill of a craftsman distinguishes this picture book illustrated with bold and lively drawings printed in three colors." N Y Public Libr

Eitzen, Ruth
  Tara's flight; [by] Ruth Eitzen; illustrated by Allan Eitzen. Boyds Mills Press 2008 un il $16.95
Grades: K 1 2 3   E
  1. Birds -- Fiction 2. Noah's ark -- Fiction 3. Grandfathers -- Fiction
  ISBN 978-1-59078-563-8
                   LC 2007018815

Aram, a grandson of Noah, is responsible for taking care of the birds on the ark, including his pet dove Tara, who becomes the first creature to leave after the flood

"Decorated with cut-paper pictures of flying white birds, the endpapers celebrate the dove as the elemental peace symbol then and now." Booklist

Elffers, Joost
  Do you love me? [by] Joost Elffers + Curious Pictures. Bowen Press 2009 un il $14.99
Grades: PreK K 1   E
  1. Stories in rhyme 2. Love -- Fiction
  ISBN 978-0-06-166799-2; 0-06-166799-4
                   LC 2008005939

Playful creatures called Snuzzles explore the idea of unconditional love

"The gentle, rhyming text is the straightforward stuff of bedtime rituals. But while the questions are expected, the answers feel fresh. . . . Set against high-contrast, single-color backgrounds, the action takes place at close range, so that just their heads, or parts of their heads, are visible." Publ Wkly

Elkin, Mark
  Samuel's baby; illustrations by Amy Wummer. Tricycle Press 2010 un il $15.99
Grades: PreK K 1   E
  1. School stories 2. Infants -- Fiction 3. Siblings -- Fiction
  ISBN 978-1-58246-301-8; 1-58246-301-8
                   LC 2009-7548

Samuel announces during show-and-tell that he is having a baby and soon his kindergarten classmates are expecting everything from twins to puppies, but while Samuel teaches them how to hold and diaper a newborn, he has some qualms about becoming a big brother.

"A standout original title among new-baby picture books. . . . Wummer's pencil and watercolor illustrations effectively utilize facial expressions to communicate voice and personality." SLJ

Ellery, Amanda
  If I were a jungle animal; illustrated by Tom Ellery. Simon & Schuster Books for Young Readers 2009 un il $15.99
Grades: PreK K 1   E
  1. Animals -- Fiction 2. Baseball -- Fiction 3.

Imagination -- Fiction
ISBN 978-1-4169-3778-4; 1-4169-3778-1

While playing baseball, a boy wonders what it would be like to be different jungle animals.

"Amanda Ellery's tale is simple but delicious, and accessible to very young readers. Husband Tom's expressive, Bill Peet-esque illustrations-in colored pencil, pen and ink-are all they should be: funny, original and so lively they virtually jump off the page." Kirkus

Elliot, David

Henry's map; by David Elliot. Philomel Books 2013 40 p. ill. (reinforced) $16.99

Grades: PreK K 1 2   E
1. Farms -- Juvenile fiction 2. Picture books for children 3. Maps -- Fiction 4. Pigs -- Fiction 5. Farm life -- Fiction 6. Domestic animals -- Fiction
ISBN 0399160728; 9780399160721

LC 2012035391

This children's picture book stars a very organized pig named Henry, who "decries the messy state of the farm. . . . Henry decides to draw a map to sort things out and, armed with pencil and paper, makes his way across the barnyard. All the animals are excited to be included, falling in line behind the earnest cartographer." His efforts are less than successful, however, and ultimately all the animals stay where they were originally, "to the relief of all concerned." (Publishers Weekly)

Elliott, David

Finn throws a fit; illustrated by Timothy Basil Ering. Candlewick Press 2009 un il $16.99; pa $6.99

Grades: PreK K 1   E
1. Anger -- Fiction
ISBN 978-0-7636-2356-2; 0-7636-2356-3; 978-0-7636-5604-1 pa; 0-7636-5604-6 pa

LC 2008-21174

A cranky toddler has an enormous tantrum.

"Elliott . . . and Ering . . . operate like the left and right hands of a single comic mind; each tongue-in-cheek line of text is deftly countered with raw charcoal scrawls, wild strokes of paint and crazed scribbles. Small readers will giggle at the realization of their angry feelings—complete with rippling lengths of toilet paper, floods of tears and flying crockery—while parents will blanch at the brilliant exposition of the power their children hold over them." Publ Wkly

Knitty Kitty; illustrated by Christopher Denise. Candlewick Press 2008 un il $16.99

Grades: PreK K 1 2   E
1. Cats -- Fiction 2. Winter -- Fiction
ISBN 978-0-7636-3169-7; 0-7636-3169-8

LC 2007-52160

Knitty Kitty is knitting a scarf, a hat, and some mittens for her kittens, but when night falls and the snow comes down, the kittens request a blanket to keep them warm Knitty Kitty has a better idea.

"The full-bleed illustrations in acrylic and ink portray an idyllic cottage in a snow-covered countryside. Inside the warmth is made evident with soft golds, browns, and touches of soft color here and there." SLJ

★ **On** the farm; [by] David Elliott; illustrated by Holly Meade. Candlewick Press 2008 un il $16.99; pa $6.99

Grades: PreK K 1 2   E
1. Domestic animals
ISBN 978-0-7636-3322-6; 0-7636-3322-4; 978-0-7636-5591-4 pa

LC 2007060857

"Elliott looks at a rooster, a cow, a pony, a dog, sheep, a barn cat, a goat, a pig, a snake, bees, a bull, a turtle, a duck, a hen, and a rabbit in verses that are rich in vocabulary and, for the most part, written in rhyme. Large, black typeface mirrors the black lines in Meade's beautiful, color woodblock prints that superbly reflect the mood and action in the poetry." SLJ

One little chicken; a counting book. by David Elliott; illustrated by Ethan Long. Holiday House 2007 un il $16.95

Grades: PreK K   E
1. Counting 2. Dance -- Fiction 3. Chickens -- Fiction
ISBN 978-0-8234-1983-8

LC 2006037046

"For each number up to 10, funny flapping fowls dance up a storm of different steps—from the hula to the cha cha. . . . The computer-generated cartoon art adds shimmy to the text, with egg-eyed pullets wearing silly attire and equally silly expressions." Booklist

What the grizzly knows; [by] David Elliott; illustrated by Max Grafe. Candlewick Press 2008 un il $16.99

Grades: PreK K   E
1. Stories in rhyme 2. Bears -- Fiction 3. Teddy bears -- Fiction
ISBN 978-0-7636-2778-2; 0-7636-2778-X

LC 2007052158

When night falls magical things begin to happen to Teddy, taking the reader on an adventure around the countryside and seeing the world through the senses of a bear

"The simple, rhyming text is paired with noteworthy, realistically rendered watercolor art that glows with a dreamlike quality. . . . An engaging fantasy." Booklist

Elliott, Laura

A **string** of hearts; by Laura Malone Elliott; illustrations by Lynn Munsinger. Katherine Tegen Books 2010 un il $16.99; lib bdg $17.89

Grades: PreK K 1   E
1. Valentine's Day -- Fiction
ISBN 978-0-06-000085-1; 0-06-000085-6; 978-0-06-000086-8 lib bdg; 0-06-000086-4 lib bdg

Sam's friend Mary Ann helps him make a special valentine for Tiffany, but when Tiffany does not even notice it, Sam realizes who is really special. Includes facts about the history of Valentine's Day.

"The cheery artwork illustrating this heartwarming love triangle shows fluffy, well-dressed animals in bright colors. Their expressive faces mirror the emotions explored in the narrative. A lovely Valentine story about the real meaning of friendship." SLJ

Elliott, Rebecca

★ **Just** because. Trafalgar 2011 un il $14.99

Grades: K 1 2 3   E
1. Love -- Fiction 2. Siblings -- Fiction 3. Handicapped -- Fiction
ISBN 978-0-7459-6267-2; 0-7459-6267-X

Toby describes all the fun he has with Clemmie, his beloved big sister who "can't walk, talk, [or] move around much."

"An endearing and enduring picture book about sibling love. . . . Clemmie's wheelchair plays only a minor role in this story. . . . The double-page spreads burst forth in vibrant colors and energetic streaks and swirls. . . . Full of unconditional love, this is a must-have title." Kirkus

Zoo girl; Rebecca Elliott. Lion Children's 2012 26 p. col. ill $14.99
Grades: PreK K 1   E
1. Zoos -- Fiction 2. Orphans -- Fiction 3. Picture books for children 4. Adopted children -- Fiction 5. Families -- Fiction 6. Loneliness -- Fiction 7. Zoos -- Juvenile fiction 8. Families -- Juvenile fiction 9. Loneliness -- Juvenile fiction
ISBN 0745963234; 9780745963235
LC 2012392527
This children's picture book is the story of a "lonely orphan girl [who] finds her true friends within the walls of the zoo. . . . While the other children play on the swing set and slide outside the orphanage, she sits huddled on the grass far away from them. But the mere sight of the animals at the zoo brings a big smile to her face." After a night where she is accidentally left behind at the zoo, she is adopted by "the pair of zoo workers who find her." (Kirkus)

Elliott, Zetta
Bird; illustrated by Shadra Strickland. Lee & Low Books Inc. 2008 un il $18.95
Grades: 2 3 4 5   E
1. Novels in verse 2. Death -- Fiction 3. Drawing -- Fiction 4. Drug abuse -- Fiction 5. Family life -- Fiction 6. African Americans -- Fiction
ISBN 978-1-60060-241-2; 1-60060-241-X
LC 2007-49039
Bird, an artistic young African American boy, expresses himself through drawing as he struggles to understand his older brother's drug addiction and death, while a family friend, Uncle Son, provides guidance and understanding

"This picture book tells a poignant story. . . . A complicated weaving of impressive watercolor, gouache, charcoal and ink drawings amplifies the metaphors and action of the poetic text as it combines black-and-white with color." Publ Wkly

Ellis, Sarah
Ben over night; illustrated by Kim LaFave. Fitzhenry & Whiteside 2005 un il $16.95
Grades: PreK K 1   E
1. Fear -- Fiction
ISBN 1-55041-807-6
"Little Ben loves to play at his friend Peter's house across the street, but every time he tries to sleep over, he wakens in the night and chickens out. His supportive parents suggest that he take his flashlight and security blanket, but nothing works until his big sister comes up with more imaginative ideas. Ellis tells Ben's story with economy and understanding. . . . With fresh colors and energetic line work, the apparently digital illustrations do a good job of expressing the characters' emotions as well as defining their actions." Booklist

Elvgren, Jennifer Riesmeyer
Josias, hold the book; [by] Jennifer Riesmeyer Elvgren; illustrated by Nicole Tadgell. Boyds Mills Press 2006 un il $15.95
Grades: PreK K 1 2   E
1. Education -- Fiction 2. Gardening -- Fiction
ISBN 1-59078-318-2
LC 2005024989
Each day Chrislove, who lives in Haiti, asks his friend Josias when he will "hold the book," or join them at school, but Josias can only think of tending the bean garden so that his family will have enough food

"Elvgren has crafted a matter-of-fact snapshot of rural Haitian life. Tadgells muted watercolor spreads set the tone and enhance the text. Emotions are clearly depicted, giving the characters added dimension and believability." SLJ

Elwell, Peter
Adios, Oscar! a butterfly fable. The Blue Sky Press 2009 un il $16.99
Grades: K 1 2   E
1. Moths -- Fiction 2. Caterpillars -- Fiction 3. Books and reading -- Fiction
ISBN 978-0-545-07159-8; 0-545-07159-3
LC 2007050842
Despite his friends' teasing, Oscar the caterpillar studies to prepare for becoming a butterfly and migrating to Mexico, so when things do not turn out as he expects, he is still able to make his dream come true.

"This charming story about loving oneself and pursuing one's dreams sends an important message to children without being preachy or pedantic. The bright colors and cartoon-style illustrations enhance its ebullient, optimistic tone." SLJ

Elya, Susan Middleton
Adios, tricycle; illustrated by Elisabeth Schlossberg. G. P. Putnam's Sons 2009 un il $16.99
Grades: PreK K   E
1. Stories in rhyme 2. Growth -- Fiction 3. Cycling -- Fiction 4. Garage sales -- Fiction 5. Hispanic Americans -- Fiction 6. Spanish language -- Vocabulary
ISBN 978-0-399-24522-0; 0-399-24522-7
LC 2008006562
Even though he has outgrown his tricycle, a young pig hides it at his family's yard sale until just the right smaller child comes along.

"Peppy, rhyming text filled with Spanish vocabulary words tells this entertaining, supportive story. . . . Schlossberg's pastel illustrations capture the mixed emotions in scenes of the diverse animal characters." Booklist

★ **Bebe** goes shopping; illustrated by Steven Salerno. Harcourt 2006 un il $16
Grades: PreK K 1   E
1. Stories in rhyme 2. Infants -- Fiction 3. Shopping -- Fiction 4. Spanish language -- Vocabulary
ISBN 0-15-205426-X
Rhyming text describes a trip to the grocery store for a mamá and her baby boy. Includes Spanish words.

"Almost all the words can be understood from the context or from the pictures. . . . Using gouache, watercolors, colored inks, and pencils, Salerno evokes the hip, retro style of 1950s cartoon-style advertisements. . . . Salerno is also a master at getting motion into his pictures, and his spreads rumble and tumble." Booklist

Another title about Bebé is:

Bebé goes to the beach (2008)

Cowboy Jose; illustrated by Tim Raglin. Putnam's 2005 un il $15.99
Grades: PreK K 1 2   E

1. Stories in rhyme 2. Cowhands -- Fiction 3. Spanish language -- Vocabulary
ISBN 0-399-23570-1

LC 2003-26636

A poor cowboy enters a rodeo to win a date from a pretty señorita, but afterwards wonders if he should spend his winnings on the girl, who is only interested in the money, or on his trusty horse, whose encouragement helped him win.

"Elya's engaging text features snappy rhymes and plenty of contextual clues for the Spanish words that appear in bold type. . . . Raglin's watercolor-and-colored-pencil artwork features bright south-of-the-border colors and characters in traditional dress to accentuate the story's Mexican setting." SLJ

★ **F** is for fiesta; illustrated by G. Brian Karas. G.P. Putnam's Sons 2006 un il $11.99
Grades: PreK K 1 2   E

1. Alphabet 2. Birthdays 3. Stories in rhyme 4. Spanish language -- Vocabulary
ISBN 0-399-24225-2

LC 2004-20478

A rhyming book that outlines the preparations for and celebration of a young boy's birthday, with Spanish words for each letter of the alphabet translated in a glossary.

"At their best, Elya's verses bounce as easily between languages as they did in Oh, No, Gotta Go! (2003), which was also buoyantly illustrated by Karas." Booklist

Fairy trails; a story told in English and Spanish. illustrated by Mercedes McDonald. Bloomsbury Children's Books 2005 un il $17.99
Grades: PreK K 1 2   E

1. Fairy tales 2. Stories in rhyme 3. Spanish language -- Vocabulary
ISBN 1-58234-927-4

Miguel and Maria meet various fairy tale characters as they walk to their aunt's house. Includes some Spanish words

"Done in pastels, the warm and colorful illustrations have an appealing folk-art quality. . . . A glossary of the Spanish words is included, but the rhyming text provides ample context clues so that the story is accessible to non-Spanish speakers. Overall, Fairy Trails would be a great storytime choice for both bilingual and English-only audiences." SLJ

N is for Navidad; by Susan Middleton Elya and Merry Banks; illustrated by Joe Cepeda. Chronicle Books 2007 un il $14.95
Grades: PreK K 1   E

1. Alphabet 2. Stories in rhyme 3. Christmas -- Fiction 4. Hispanic Americans -- Fiction 5. Spanish language -- Vocabulary
ISBN 978-0-8118-5205-0; 0-8118-5205-9

LC 2006008169

A rhyming book that outlines the preparations for and celebration of the Christmas season, with Spanish words for each letter of the alphabet translated in a glossary.

"Cepeda's lively paintings take a colorful, dynamic look at a warm Latino neighborhood celebration of the holiday season. . . . This book has potential to provide a springboard for discussion of holiday traditions while keeping children entertained visually." SLJ

No more, por favor; pictures by David Walker. G.P. Putnam's Sons 2010 un il $16.99
Grades: PreK K 1 2   E

1. Stories in rhyme 2. Food -- Fiction 3. Rain forest animals -- Fiction 4. Spanish language -- Vocabulary
ISBN 978-0-399-24766-8; 0-399-24766-1

LC 2008048411

Rain forest parents come up with a solution when all their children become picky eaters at the same time. Spanish words interspersed in the rhyming text are defined in a glossary.

"Walker's acrylic paintings in rich, primary rainforest colors add appeal to the bouncy, sometimes uneven rhyme. Kids with picky palates will appreciate the message and discover new tasty options while training their tongues with morsels of Spanish." Kirkus

Oh no, gotta go! illustrated by G. Brian Karas. Putnam 2003 un il $14.99
Grades: PreK K 1 2   E

1. Stories in rhyme 2. Bathrooms -- Fiction 3. Spanish language -- Vocabulary
ISBN 0-399-23493-4

LC 2002-17703

As soon as she goes out for a drive with her parents, a young girl needs to find a bathroom quickly. Text includes some Spanish words and phrases

"The unexpected rhyming of the English and boldface Spanish words give the rhythmic text an ebullient humor enhanced by Karas' understated gouache, acrylic, pencil, and collage illustrations." Bull Cent Child Books

Another title is:

Oh no, gotta go! #2 (2007)

Emberley, Barbara

Night's nice; [by] Barbara and Ed Emberley. Little, Brown Children 2008 un il $12.99
Grades: PreK K   E

1. Night -- Fiction
ISBN 978-0-316-06623-5; 0-316-06623-0
First published 1962 by Doubleday Books

Moonlit treetops, city lamps aglow, bright fireworks bursting in a dark July sky, and other wondrous illuminated evening sights are captured in a colorful picture book with a die-cut moon and silver foil title type on the cover.

"An inviting exploration of the wonders of nighttime. . . . Thin, sketchlike black line drawings, awash in sumptuous jewel-toned colors, work in tandem with this soothing tale sure to diminish night frights for youngsters concerned about the dark." SLJ

Emberley, Ed

Ed Emberley's bye-bye, big bad bullybug! Little, Brown & Co. 2007 un il $10.99

Grades: PreK K 1 2   E
1. Bullies -- Fiction 2. Insects -- Fiction 3. Monsters -- Fiction
ISBN 978-0-316-01762-6; 0-316-01762-0

LC 2006-15423
Die-cut pages reveal "a mean and scary 'Big Bad Bully-bug' from outer space who threatens to bite, pinch, and tickle itty-bitty baby bugs. Luckily for the small fliers, a human with a huge sneaker is willing to do away with the pink-polka-dotted meanie. The cobolt blue backgrounds create a grand contrast for the electric greens, oranges, and yellows." SLJ

★ Go away, big green monster! Little, Brown 1992 un il $10.99
Grades: PreK K 1   E
1. Fear -- Fiction 2. Bedtime -- Fiction 3. Monsters -- Fiction
ISBN 0-316-23653-5

LC 9206231
"Using die-cut, black pages, the book begins with the monster's 'two big yellow eyes' glowing through round holes. Each flip of a page displays more features shining in electric colors through new holes—'a long blue nose/ a big red mouth with sharp white teeth/ two little squiggly ears . . .,' and so on—until the narrator announces, 'You don't scare me! So GO AWAY scraggly purple hair .. .,' and dismisses the monster page by page, feature by feature, like the departing Cheshire Cat." (Booklist) "Preschool." (SLJ)
"In the first half of this fear-dispelling book, graphically distinctive die-cut pages reveal, bit by bit, a monster with 'sharp white teeth' and 'scraggly purple hair.' The process is then reversed as the text commands each scary feature to 'go away,' until there is nothing at all left of the monster but a black page instructing 'Don't Come Back! Until I say so.' Entertaining and empowering for young children." Horn Book Guide

Mice on ice; by Rebecca Emberley and Ed Emberley. Holiday House 2012 32 p. (I like to read) (hardcover) $14.95
Grades: K 1 2   E
1. Ice skating -- Fiction 2. Cats -- Juvenile fiction 3. Mice -- Juvenile fiction 4. Cats -- Fiction 5. Mice -- Fiction 6. Stories in rhyme
ISBN 0823425762; 9780823425761

LC 2011038812
Authors and illustrators Rebecca Emberley and Ed Emberley present a children's rhyming book about a cat and some mice ice-skating. "Mice skate on ice. As they skate, their blades leave lines that depict a cat. Magically, the cat appears, colorful, graphic, and three-dimensional. What happens next? Why, the cat and the mice skate together!" (Publisher's note)

Thanks, Mom! Little, Brown 2003 un il $11.95
Grades: PreK K 1   E
1. Mice 2. Cheese 3. Animals 4. Mice -- Fiction 5. Mother and child 6. Animals -- Fiction
ISBN 0-316-24022-2

LC 2001-50715

Kiko the mouse finds some delicious cheese and gets help from his mother when a group of various animals tries to take it
"Using sunny yellow highlights and creatures constructed from bold, geometric shapes, Emberley creates an exciting, chaotic chase with sparse text and an impressive sense of graphic design." SLJ

Where's my sweetie pie? LB Kids 2010 un il $7.99
Grades: PreK   E
1. Stories in rhyme 2. Board books for children
ISBN 978-0-316-01891-3; 0-316-01891-0
"The book's title becomes a refrain for the short, rhyming text, encouraging kids to lift the flap and discover what's hidden. . . . Bold and colorful, the simple forms that make up the digital illustrations show up clearly against the white backgrounds. . . . As rewarding as a good game of peeka-boo." Booklist

Emberley, Rebecca
★ If you're a monster and you know it; by Rebecca Emberley & Ed Emberley. Orchard Books 2010 un il $16.99
Grades: PreK K 1   E
1. Monsters -- Fiction
ISBN 978-0-545-21829-0; 0-545-21829-2
"In this rollicking interpretation of 'If You're Happy and You Know It,' brightly colored, digitally created monsters . . . run amok, wriggling and roaring, stomping and twitching. The never-frightening creatures are rendered in eye-popping psychedelic colors against a flat black background and feature horns. antennae, claws, teeth and any number of eyes. . . . This will be a favorite with adults and children alike, allowing for both imaginative play and a raucous but structured outpouring of energy." Kirkus

Ten little beasties; [by] Rebecca Emberley and Ed Emberley. Roaring Brook Press 2011 un il $12.99
Grades: PreK K 1   E
1. Counting 2. Monsters -- Fiction
ISBN 978-1-59643-627-5; 1-59643-627-1

LC 2010028118
"Begin with one weird and wacky, black-and-white beastie, then add an additional, but very different-looking one, to each subsequent page, and you have the Emberleys' newest offering, done with their inimitable twist and style. . . . Each creature is fantastical and geometric, but with a splotch of color to add to the exotic designs each one sports. Each spread is of a different vibrant color." SLJ

★ There was an old monster! [by] Rebecca, Adrian, & Ed Emberley. Orchard Books 2009 un il lib bdg $16.99
Grades: PreK K   E
1. Songs 2. Monsters -- Fiction
ISBN 978-0-545-10145-5; 0-545-10145-X

LC 2008007191
In this variation on the traditional cumulative rhyme, a monster swallows ants, a lizard, a bat, and other creatures to try to cure a stomach ache than began when he swallowed a tick.
"Individual readers will pore over the illustrations and enjoy the repetition in the text while the large pictures make this a natural to share with groups. With the song provided

as a free download at the publisher's Web site, this jazzy crowd-pleaser will have kids begging for repeat reads." SLJ

★ The **ant** and the grasshopper; Rebecca Emberley and Ed Emberley. Roaring Brook Press 2012 32 p. (alk. paper) $16.99

Grades: PreK K 1 2 3   E

1. Fables 2. Ants -- Juvenile fiction 3. Grasshoppers -- Juvenile fiction 4. Ants -- Fiction 5. Insects -- Fiction 6. Grasshoppers -- Fiction 7. Bands (Music) -- Fiction

ISBN 1596434937; 9781596434936

LC 2011033800

This children's story, by Rebecca Emberley, illustrated by Ed Emberley, retells the fable of the ant and the grasshopper. "While hard at work on her chores, an ant hears the wonderful clickety click chirrup of music coming from the distance. Although she knows she should focus on the task at hand, she can't help but explore the joyful noise!" (Publisher's note)

The **lion** and the mice; by Rebecca Emberley and Ed Emberley. Holiday House 2011 un il (I like to read picture book) $14.95

Grades: PreK K 1 2   E

1. Mice -- Fiction 2. Size -- Fiction 3. Lions -- Fiction

ISBN 978-0-8234-2357-6; 0-8234-2357-3

LC 2010044205

"Aesop's lion and mouse (or mice, as this case has it) have never looked more stylish. . . . A wacky-hued lion sleeps. But when a tiny mouse, resplendent in olive-green heels and a tuft of electric-blue fur, finds herself next to the lion, he wakes up. The wry narrator intones . . . 'Uh-oh.' But . . . the lion lets the mouse go, with the mouse squeaking in reply, 'One day I will help you.' . . . The mouse returns, with the help of many fashion-forward rodent friends, and fits a key into a never-before-seen padlock. . . . Fantastic visual fun." Kirkus

Emmett, Jonathan

Leaf trouble; illustrated by Caroline Jayne Church. Chicken House 2009 un il $16.99

Grades: PreK K 1 2   E

1. Autumn -- Fiction 2. Leaves -- Fiction 3. Squirrels -- Fiction

ISBN 978-0-545-16070-4; 0-545-16070-7

LC 2009008268

A young squirrel panics when the leaves on his tree change color and fall, but he feels better when his mother tells him about autumn.

"The colorful and endearing ink illustrations, placed in a layered collage using a variety of textures and perspectives, are a delight." SLJ

The **best** gift of all; illustrated by Vanessa Cabban. Candlewick Press 2008 un il $15.99

Grades: K 1 2   E

1. Gifts -- Fiction 2. Animals -- Fiction 3. Moles (Animals) -- Fiction

ISBN 978-0-7636-3860-3; 0-7636-3860-9

LC 2007-52214

Mole has not seen his friend Rabbit for days because it has been raining, and when he decides to tunnel to her home, he accidentally meets Squirrel and Hedgehog, who would like to visit her, as well

"Children will enjoy this simple tale of friendship. Cabban's cuddly animals drawn in a palette of soft, autumn watercolors reinforce the warm and fuzzy feeling of Emmett's story. A pleasant selection for fall storytimes and a good choice for beginning readers." SLJ

The **princess** and the pig; by Jonathan Emmett; illustrated by Poly Bernatene. Bloomsbury Distributed to the trade by Macmillan 2011 32 p. col. ill. (hardcover) $16.99

Grades: PreK K 1 2 3 4   E

1. Humorous fiction 2. Pigs -- Juvenile fiction 3. Princesses -- Juvenile fiction 4. Pigs -- Fiction 5. Humorous stories 6. Princesses -- Fiction

ISBN 0802723349; 9780802723345

LC 2010049549

In this children's picture book by Jonathan Emmett, "There's been a terrible mix-up in the royal nursery. Priscilla the princess has accidentally switched places with Pigmella, the farmer's new piglet. The kindly farmer and his wife believe it's the work of a good witch, while the ill-tempered king and queen blame the bad witch. . . . While Priscilla grows up on the farm, poor yet very happy, things don't turn out quite so well for Pigmella." (Publisher's note)

Enderle, Judith Ross

Smile, Principessa! by Judith Ross Enderle and Stephanie Jacob Gordon; illustrated by Serena Curmi. Margaret K. McElderry Books 2007 un il $16.99

Grades: PreK K 1   E

1. Infants -- Fiction 2. Siblings -- Fiction 3. Photography -- Fiction

ISBN 978-1-4169-1004-6; 1-4169-1004-2

LC 2005012761

A sister is jealous when her baby brother starts getting all the attention in the family photographs

"Featuring characters in snazzy attire, the acrylic and pencil illustrations are delightful. . . . An engaging take on a common family situation." SLJ

Endle, Kate

Bunny Rabbit in the sunlight; [by] Kate Endle & Casper Babypants. Sasquatch Books 2011 il bd bk $9.99

Grades: PreK   E

1. Board books for children 2. Animals -- Fiction

ISBN 978-1-57061-749-2; 1-57061-749-X

"Eye-catching collages depict gentle animals whose habitats are brightened by different light sources. . . . Endle varies her compositions with warm and cool colors; visual textures suggest smoothness of glass and the roughness of gravel. When it's time to turn off the lights, readers will likely request a rereading. A recording by Babypants (aka Chris Ballew, lead singer for the Presidents of the United States of America) is available for download." Publ Wkly

Endrulat, Harry

A **bear** in war; [by] Stephanie Innes & Harry Endrulat; illustrated by Brian Deines. Key Porter Books 2009 un il $19.95

Grades: 1 2 3   E

1. Teddy bears 2. World War, 1914-1918 3. Father-daughter relationship 4. Soldiers -- Canada

ISBN 1-55470-097-3; 978-1-55470-097-4

"In Quebec during World War I, Aileen Rogers sent her cherished teddy bear overseas to protect her father, a medic, on the front lines. The bear . . . is the narrator. With sensitivity, he describes his experiences. . . . When Lawrence Browning Rogers is killed at the battle of Passchendaele, his uniform, his medal of bravery, and Teddy are sent to his family. [This is illustrated with] Deines's evocative, softly focused pastel illustrations. . . . Inspired by true events, the book includes archival photographs of the Rogers family, a newspaper clipping from 1916, and the Canadian government's report of Lieutenant Rogers's death. A moving remembrance." SLJ

English, Karen

★ **Hot** day on Abbott Avenue; illustrated by Javaka Steptoe. Clarion Books 2004 32p il $15
Grades: PreK K 1 2   E
1. Summer -- Fiction 2. Friendship -- Fiction 3. Rope skipping -- Fiction 4. African Americans -- Fiction
ISBN 0-395-98527-7
LC 2002-09043
After having a fight, two friends spend the day ignoring each other, until the lure of a game of jump rope helps them to forget about being mad.
"Steptoe's found-object and cut-paper collages highlight facial features and depict oppressive summertime weather to perfection. . . . English's simple narrative consists mostly of two to three sentences per page and ends on a gratifying note." SLJ

★ **Speak** to me; (and I will listen between the lines) pictures by Amy June Bates. Farrar Straus Giroux 2004 un il $16
Grades: 2 3 4 5   E
1. Schools 2. School stories 3. African Americans -- Fiction
ISBN 0-374-37156-3
LC 2002-192895
Describes events of one day at a San Francisco Bay Area school as perceived by different second-graders, from the observations of first to arrive on the playground to the walk home.
"English's rich descriptions and insights bring readers into the world of six inner-city . . . students. . . . Bates's watercolor-and-ink illustrations capture the characters' expressions and moods vividly." SLJ

★ The **baby** on the way; pictures by Sean Qualls. Farrar, Straus and Giroux 2005 un il $16
Grades: PreK K 1 2   E
1. Infants -- Fiction 2. Childbirth -- Fiction 3. Grandmothers -- Fiction 4. African Americans -- Fiction
ISBN 0-374-37361-2
LC 2003-49047
Jamal, a young African American boy, asks his grandmother if she was ever a baby, she tells him the story of how she was born.
"The intimate artwork, in earth colors with pencil-thin line details, shows the loving bond between family members stretching back in time and into the future." Booklist

Ericsson, Jennifer A.

A **piece** of chalk; by Jennifer A. Ericsson; illustrated by Michelle Shapiro. Roaring Brook Press 2007 un il $16.95

Grades: PreK K 1   E
1. Drawing -- Fiction
ISBN 978-1-59643-057-0; 1-59643-057-5
LC 2006032178
A little girl creates a colored chalk drawing on her driveway
"This simple, sunny offering captures the delight and escape a child finds in art. . . . The words and rhythms read like poetry, but there are no bouncy rhymes to distract from the story's quiet joy. Shapiro effectively mirrors the girl's art with a childlike style and an appealing palette of bright, opaque colors, muted with chalk white." Booklist

★ **Whoo** goes there? illustrated by Bert Kitchen. Roaring Brook Press 2009 un il $17.99
Grades: K 1 2 3   E
1. Owls -- Fiction 2. Night -- Fiction 3. Animals -- Fiction
ISBN 978-1-59643-371-7; 1-59643-371-X
"Finding food involves a long night of waiting and listening that's also filled with disappointment for a handsome owl. . . . Ericsson uses a simple repetitive scheme to introduce an array of small animals that travel through the owl's moonlit world. . . . Kitchen's naturalistic paintings are set in attractive alternating sets. . . . The predictive text and handsome pictures are just right for reading with preschoolers." SLJ

Ernst, Lisa Campbell

The **Gingerbread** Girl. Dutton Children's Books 2006 un il $16.99
Grades: PreK K 1 2   E
1. Fairy tales
ISBN 0-525-47667-9; 978-0-525-47667-2
LC 2006004193
Like her older brother, the Gingerbread Boy, who was eventually devoured by a fox, the Gingerbread Girl eludes the many people who would like to eat her but also has a plan to escape her sibling's fate.
"Ernst's familiar art . . . utilizes the oversize format to best advantage, with large characters leaping out of their frames." Booklist

The **Gingerbread** Girl goes animal crackers. Dutton Childrens Books 2011 un il $16.99
Grades: PreK K 1 2   E
1. Foxes -- Fiction 2. Cookies -- Fiction 3. Birthdays -- Fiction
ISBN 978-0-525-42259-4; 0-525-42259-5
LC 2011005244
The Gingerbread Girl, who once escaped the fox that devoured her brother, must now try to save from a similar fate the animal crackers she received as a birthday gift.
"Ernst's pastel palette is well-suited to this lively story of 'Animal Crackers gone wild,' which, with words like 'menagerie' and 'brouhaha,' scattered throughout, offers a bit of a vocabulary lesson, too." Publ Wkly

Round like a ball! by Lisa Campbell Ernst. Blue Apple Books 2008 un il $15.95 E
ISBN 978-1-934706-01-5; 1-934706-01-9
Everyone tries to guess what is round and warm and cold and strong and fragile, until they finally realize it is Earth

"The clues are placed in large letters on the left side of a double-page spread, encircling progressively larger cutout circles. The cutout on each successive page offers a glimpse of the next article guessed. When the pages are flipped, a rainbow of cutout circles, large and small, is created on the previous page. . . . The distinctive illustrations, the guessing element, and the showstopping foldout of the Earth will work well for individual or group viewing." Booklist

Sam Johnson and the blue ribbon quilt. Lothrop, Lee & Shepard Bks. 1983 32p il lib bdg $17.89; pa $6.99
Grades: K 1 2 3   E
1. Quilts -- Fiction 2. Sex role -- Fiction
ISBN 0-688-01517-4 lib bdg; 0-688-11505-5 pa
LC 82-9980
While mending the awning over the pig pen, Sam discovers that he enjoys sewing the various patches together but meets with scorn and ridicule when he asks his wife if he could join her quilting club
The illustrations "bring an old-timey, bucolic scene to life and show steps in an equal-rights issue." Publ Wkly

Snow surprise; 1st Green Light Readers ed.; Harcourt 2008 un il $12.95; pa $3.95
Grades: 1 2 3   E
1. Snow -- Fiction 2. Siblings -- Fiction
ISBN 978-0-15-206553-9; 0-15-206553-9; 978-0-15-206559-1 pa; 0-15-206559-8 pa
LC 2007-42343
Joan makes a surprise for her little brother, Ben, but in the end, she is the one who is surprised.

Sylvia Jean, scout supreme. Dutton Children's Books 2010 un il $16.99
Grades: PreK K 1 2   E
1. Pigs -- Fiction 2. Costume -- Fiction 3. Scouts and scouting -- Fiction
ISBN 978-0-525-47873-7; 0-525-47873-6
LC 2009017919
Sylvia Jean disguises herself in order to assist a neighbor who does not want her enthusiastic help, but she still might be the only one in her Pig Scout Troop who will not earn a Good Deed Badge.
"Expressive faces enhance the gentle narrative; thin lines indicate a quiet vulnerability. Ernst's scenes feature her signature pastel palette even as humorous details advance the energetic tale." Kirkus
Another title about Sylvia Jean is:
Sylvia Jean, drama queen (2005)

Zinnia and Dot. Viking 1992 un il $16.99; pa $5.99
Grades: PreK K 1 2   E
1. Chickens -- Fiction
ISBN 0-670-83091-7; 0-14-054199-3 pa
LC 91-36178
Zinnia and Dot, self-satisfied hens who bicker constantly about who lays better eggs, put aside their differences to protect a prime specimen from a marauding weasel.
"Ernst has an easy storytelling style and a flair for grouchy dialogue that clucks to be read aloud, and her line-and-wash paintings, lighted with gentle yellow tones, warm the comedy." Bull Cent Child Books

The **turn** -around upside-down alphabet book. Simon & Schuster Books for Young Readers 2004 un il $15.95
Grades: PreK K 1 2   E
1. Alphabet 2. Toy and movable books 3. Toy and movable books -- Specimens 4. English language -- Alphabet -- Juvenile literature
ISBN 0-689-85685-7
LC 2003-16318
"With touches of humor and a great deal of creativity, Ernst fashioned this book out of cut paper and surrounded each block with a thick black border that sets off white words. Children will enjoy tilting the pages to see the transformations and will be motivated to come up with ideas of their own." SLJ

Esbaum, Jill
Stanza; illustrated by Jack E. Davis. Harcourt Children's Books 2009 un il $16
Grades: PreK K 1 2   E
1. Stories in rhyme 2. Dogs -- Fiction 3. Poetry -- Fiction 4. Contests -- Fiction
ISBN 978-0-15-205998-9; 0-15-205998-9
LC 2007051078
Stanza the dog and his two rotten brothers terrorize the streets by day, but at night Stanza secretly writes poetry.
"The message, though well seasoned, is refreshed by lively characterizations of Stanza, his brothers, and the people around them. Children will delight in the details that are often hidden on the page. Rhyming verse makes this an especially fine read-aloud, but the real fun is in upclose scrutiny of the illustrations." SLJ

To the big top; [by] Jill Esbaum; pictures by David Gordon. Farrar Straus Giroux 2008 un il $16.95
Grades: PreK K 1 2   E
1. Circus -- Fiction 2. Friendship -- Fiction
ISBN 0-374-39934-4; 978-0-374-39934-4
LC 2006053530
When the circus comes to the small town of Willow Grove in the early 1900s, best friends Benny and Sam enjoy an exciting day helping set up the tent, admiring the various animals, and anticipating the big show.
"Gordon's joyful illustrations capture the appeal traveling entertainers had for small-town residents of the early twentieth century. . . . Esbaum . . . provides a nostalgic trip down memory lane that will give children . . . a good idea of what it was like back then." Booklist

Tom's tweet; illustrated by Kyle M. Stone. Alfred A. Knopf 2010 il $16.99; lib bdg $19.99
Grades: PreK K 1   E
1. Cats -- Fiction 2. Birds -- Fiction
ISBN 978-0-375-85171-1; 0-375-85171-2; 978-0-375-95171-8 lib bdg; 0-375-95171-7 lib bdg
LC 2009017262
When a cat finds a bedraggled baby bird that has fallen from its nest, an unlikely friendship develops between the two.
"Esbaum's tweet tale will have listeners in stitches (especially the wormy bits), and Santat's Photoshopped cartoon illustrations of bulky Tom and the goggle-eyed tweets are as expressive as they are goofy. Totally tweet-rific." Kirkus

Escoffier, Michael

Rabbit and the Not-So-Big-Bad Wolf; by Michaël Escoffier; illustrated by Kris Di Giacomo. Holiday House 2013 32 p.

Grades: PreK K   E

1. Wolves -- Fiction 2. Rabbits -- Fiction

ISBN 9780823428137

LC 2012027931

Eszterhas, Suzi

Brown bear; by Suzi Eszterhas. Frances Lincoln Children's Books 2012 32 p. ill. (hardcover) $15.99

Grades: K 1 2   E

1. Brown bear -- Juvenile literature

ISBN 1847803024; 9781847803023

This book, part of the Eye on the Wild series, "introduces two little brown bears, . . . and follows them for several years as they grow up and become independent. First seen as cubs closely guarded by their mother, the sisters . . . play fight, and nap under her watchful eye. After more than two years of teaching them how to hunt for food and protect themselves, their mother leaves. They hibernate together before going their separate ways to start families of their own." (Booklist)

Ets, Marie Hall

Play with me; story and pictures by Marie Hall Ets. Viking 1955 31p il hardcover o.p. pa $5.99

Grades: PreK K   E

1. Animals -- Fiction

ISBN 0-14-050178-9 pa

A Caldecott Medal honor book, 1956

On a sunny morning in the meadow an excited little girl tries to catch the meadow creatures and play with them. But, one by one, they all run away. Finally, when she learns to sit quietly and wait, there is a happy ending

The "pictures done in muted tones of brown, gray and yellow . . . accurately reflect the little girl's rapidly changing moods of eagerness, bafflement, disappointment and final happiness." N Y Times Book Rev

Evans, Cambria

Bone soup. Houghton Mifflin 2008 un il lib bdg $16

Grades: K 1 2 3   E

1. Monsters -- Fiction 2. Halloween -- Fiction

ISBN 978-0-618-80908-0 lib bdg; 0-618-80908-2 lib bdg

LC 2008001862

The skeletal Finnigin tricks a town's witches, ghouls, and zombies into helping him make soup

"Even the zombies are lovable in Evans's charming Halloween-themed rendition of 'Stone Soup.' . . . Seasoned with sprightly, luminescent watercolors and the perfect dose of gross-out factor, this tale has all the right ingredients for a hearty storytime." SLJ

Evans, Freddi Williams

★ **Hush** harbor; praying in secret. illustrated by Erin Bennett Banks. Carolrhoda Books 2008 un il lib bdg $16.95

Grades: K 1 2 3   E

1. Slavery -- Fiction 2. Religion -- Fiction 3. Christian life -- Fiction 4. African Americans -- Fiction

ISBN 978-0-8225-7965-6 lib bdg; 0-8225-7965-0 lib bdg

LC 2007-34777

While Simmy watches for danger from high in a tree, other slaves gather in a hidden spot in the woods to sing and pray together in their own way, risking their lives in pursuit of religious freedom. Includes historical facts about hush, or brush, arbors and the churches that grew from them

This is "a moving narrative. . . . Illustrated with extremely stylized pictures that don't prettify their subjects, this captures some of the fear and horror associated with slavery." Booklist

Evans, Kristina

What's special about me, Mama? words by Kristina Evans; pictures by Javaka Steptoe. Hyperion 2011 un il $16.99

Grades: PreK K   E

1. African Americans -- Fiction 2. Mother-child relationship -- Fiction

ISBN 978-0-7868-5274-1; 0-7868-5274-7

A child wonders what exactly makes him unique. Mama lists her son's many good traits, from physical attributes to behavior. He dismisses each quality as just a little thing, until Mama explains that there is nothing little about love.

"Evans's dialogue swings with an easy back-and-forth rhythm between a mother and her son, and Steptoe's collage illustrations, in deep rich colors, effectively position the characters, harmoniously connecting the two. . . . A heartfelt, comforting tale." SLJ

Evans, Lezlie

Who loves the little lamb? illustrated by David McPhail. Disney-Hyperion Books 2010 un il $15.99

Grades: PreK   E

1. Stories in rhyme 2. Animals -- Fiction 3. Mother-child relationship -- Fiction

ISBN 978-1-4231-1659-2; 1-4231-1659-3

LC 2009015896

Rhyming text reveals that, although baby animals are not always perfect, their mothers love them and help them through difficult moments.

"This has two things going for it that set it apart: Evans' uncommonly clever text and artwork by McPhail. . . . What's so terrific about this . . . is the motherly diversity shown in the art." Booklist

Evans, Michael

Poggle and the treasure. Egmont 2011 il $16.99

Grades: PreK K   E

1. Dragons -- Fiction

ISBN 978-1-4052-4811-2; 1-4052-4811-4

"Poggle is a teddy-bearish blue dragon with a best friend named Henry, who's equally cuddly but of a less determinate species. Inhabiting a cheery world that's given depth and texture by crayon-y black shading, Poggle lives at the beach. . . . It's an ideal setting for making important discoveries, like a mysterious pink egg that the duo uncovers while playing pirates. . . . Evans deftly sidesteps treacle and spins out his stories with a light and distinctly British touch; a few novelty elements . . . provide additional interest. Sweet, expressive, and reassuring." Publ Wkly

Evans, Shane W.

We march; Shane W. Evans. Roaring Brook Press 2012 32 p.

Grades: PreK K 1 2 3   **E**

1. Family -- Juvenile fiction 2. Civil rights demonstrations -- Juvenile fiction 3. African Americans -- Civil rights -- Juvenile fiction 4. African Americans -- Fiction 5. March on Washington for Jobs and Freedom, Washington, D.C., 1963 -- Fiction 6. March on Washington for Jobs and Freedom, Washington, D.C., 1963 -- Juvenile fiction

ISBN 9781596435391

LC 2010046862

This illustrated children's book tells the story of "[a]n African-American family [which] awakens before dawn to prepare for the historic March on Washington in August, 1963. In this . . . companion to 'Underground' (2011), [author and illustrator Shane W.] Evans captures a pivotal event in the struggle for equality and civil rights in America. The family joins neighbors to pray at their church, paint signs and travel by bus to Washington. They walk and sing and grow tired but "are filled with hope" as they stand together at the Washington Monument to listen to Dr. King speak of dreams and freedom. . . . The March has become synonymous with Dr. King's . . . speech, but Evans reminds readers that ordinary folk were his determined and courageous audience." (Kirkus)

Everitt, Betsy

Mean soup. Harcourt Brace Jovanovich 1992 un il hardcover o.p. pa $8

Grades: PreK K 1 2   **E**

1. Anger -- Fiction 2. Cooking -- Fiction

ISBN 0-15-253146-7; 0-15-200227-8 pa

LC 91-15244

Horace feels really mean at the end of a bad day, until he helps his mother make Mean Soup

"The text features short sentences and easy but effective vocabulary, so the story bubbles with a building excitement. Everitt's . . . stylized paintings and bold palette—hot pinks, purples and black predominate—convey all of the feisty emotion of a frustrated youngster." Publ Wkly

Eversole, Robyn Harbert

East Dragon, West Dragon; story by Robyn Eversole; pictures by Scott Campbell. Atheneum Books for Young Readers 2012 un il $16.99

Grades: PreK K 1 2   **E**

1. Dragons -- Fiction 2. Prejudices -- Fiction

ISBN 978-0-689-85828-4; 0-689-85828-0

LC 2010039609

East Dragon and West Dragon are suspicious of one another although they have never met, but when the western king is captured in the Eastern Kingdom and West Dragon goes to rescue him, they find they have much in common.

"Eversole's spare narrative mixes tongue-in-cheek exaggeration, childhood fears and adventure, inspiring Campbell to contrast the rough and the refined, designing detailed watercolor worlds brimming with humor and beauty. This primer on friendship wrapped in hijinks is paced for maximum pleasure." Kirkus

Ewart, Claire

Fossil; [by] Claire Ewart. Walker 2004 un il $16.89;

lib bdg $17.85

Grades: PreK K 1 2

1. Fossils 2. Pterosaurs 3. Stories in rhyme 4. Fossils -- Fiction 5. Pterosaurs -- Fiction

ISBN 0-8027-8890-4; 0-8027-8891-2 lib bdg

LC 2003-53469

Upon finding a special stone, a child imagines the life of a pterosaur, the ancient flying reptile that lived, died, and was fossilized into that stone. Includes facts about fossils and how they are formed.

"Ewart's inviting text and dramatic artwork work nicely together to describe the fossilization process in an engrossing way." SLJ

Includes bibliographical references

Fackelmayer, Regina

The gifts; illustrated by Christa Unzner. North-South Books 2009 un il $16.95

Grades: K 1 2 3   **E**

1. Gifts -- Fiction 2. Christmas -- Fiction 3. Christmas stories -- Juvenile literature

ISBN 978-0-7358-2265-8; 0-7358-2265-4

"Mia buys a turkey for dinner, gifts for her dog and cat, a hat for herself, and a Christmas tree. Stopping to help an old man who has slipped on the ice, she leaves her tree outdoors. . . . The story is written with clarity and restraint. . . . The sensitive artwork includes a delicately spattered effect that textures all the illustrations and works particularly well in the snowy outdoor scenes." Booklist

Fagan, Cary

Book of big brothers; pictures by Luc Melanson. Groundwood Books 2010 un il $18.95

Grades: PreK K 1 2   **E**

1. Brothers -- Fiction

ISBN 978-0-88899-977-1; 0-88899-977-1

"In this fictionalized story, the author reminisces about what it was like to live with two older brothers. The trio will make readers giggle with delight as the boys' escapades, teasing, and love capture the warmth and fireworks of sibling dynamics. The 1970s retro-style illustrations reflect the mood and tone, and color choices accent the setting, creating a shared story from the past. . . . This fresh approach to fraternal relationships makes a welcome purchase." SLJ

Ella May and the wishing stone; illustrated by Geneviève Côté. Tundra Books 2011 un il $17.95

Grades: PreK K 1 2   **E**

1. Wishes -- Fiction 2. Friendship -- Fiction

ISBN 978-1-77049-225-7; 1-77049-225-9

Ella May finds a stone and makes a wish on it, then refuses to share it with friends who then turn against her, but she finds a way to win them back.

"Fagan believably captures the delicate balance of friendship in the very young and lets the story [play] out with welcome complexity. Côté's illustrations are simple without being cartoonish, demonstrating the same warm understanding of childhood." Kirkus

Mr. Zinger's hat; Cary Fagan. Tundra Books of Northern New York 2012 32 p. (hardcover) $17.95

Grades: K 1 2   **E**

1. Imagination -- Juvenile fiction 2. Storytelling --

Juvenile fiction

ISBN 1770492534; 9781770492530

LC 2011938764

In this children's book, by Cary Fagan and illustrated by Dusan Petricic, "when old Mr. Zinger's windblown hat lands atop young Leo, the elder's suggestion . . . leads the pair to make up a tale about a rich but bored lad who offers half his possessions to anyone who can cheer him up. . . . Zinger then departs, leaving Leo to continue playing alone . . . until a new friend named Sophie shows up to share both the ball and the creation of a brand new story." (Kirkus Reviews)

Falconer, Ian

★ **Olivia**; written and illustrated by Ian Falconer. Atheneum Bks. for Young Readers 2000 un il $17.99; bd bk $7.99

Grades: PreK K 1 2   E

1. Pigs 2. Behavior 3. Pigs -- Fiction

ISBN 0-689-82953-1; 0-689-87472-3 bd bk

LC 99-24003

A Caldecott Medal honor book, 2001

Whether at home getting ready for the day, enjoying the beach, or at bedtime, Olivia is a young pig who has too much energy for her own good. "Ages three to seven." (Christ Sci Monit)

"The spacious design of the book; the appeal of the strong, clever art; and the humor that permeates every page make this a standout. . . . Falconer . . . renders Olivia's world in charcoal with dollops of red brightening the pages." Booklist

Other titles about Olivia are:

Olivia . . . and the missing toy (2003)

Olivia forms a band (2006)

Olivia goes to Venice (2010)

Olivia helps with Christmas (2007)

Olivia saves the circus (2001)

Olivia and the fairy princesses; Ian Falconer. Atheneum Books for Young Readers 2012 40 p. (hardback) $17.99

Grades: PreK K 1 2   E

1. Pigs -- Fiction 2. Princesses -- Fiction 3. Professions -- Fiction 4. Individuality -- Fiction

ISBN 1442450274; 9781442450271; 9781442450288

LC 2011053046

In this book, the piglet Olivia is "suffering from an identity crisis. While all the other girls she knows, and even some of the boys, dress as ruffled pink princesses for parties and desperately want to be fairy princess ballerinas, Olivia's aspirations are more" unique. Dressed like choreographer Martha Graham, "Olivia explains that she is 'trying to develop a more stark, modern style'...Her ultimate choice is quintessentially Olivia." (Kirkus Reviews)

"Fans will be pleased with this addition to the series." (Booklist)

Olivia goes to Venice; written and illustrated by Ian Falconer. Atheneum Books for Young Readers 2010 un il $17.99

Grades: PreK K 1 2   E

1. Pigs -- Fiction 2. Vacations -- Fiction

ISBN 978-1-4169-9674-3; 1-4169-9674-5

LC 2010009589

On a family vacation in Venice, Olivia indulges in gelato, rides in a gondola, and finds the perfect souvenir. "Ages three to seven." (N Y Times Book Rev)

"The contrast between the antic lines of the charcoal and gouache paintings superimposed over gorgeous color photographs provides much hilarity. . . . Falconer's understated text is both witty and subtle." Publ Wkly

Falkenstern, Lisa

A **dragon** moves in; written and illustrated by Lisa Falkenstern. Marshall Cavendish Children 2011 il $16.99; ebook $16.99

Grades: PreK K   E

1. Houses -- Fiction 2. Dragons -- Fiction 3. Rabbits -- Fiction 4. Hedgehogs -- Fiction

ISBN 978-0-7614-5947-7; 0-7614-5947-2; 978-0-7614-5995-8 e-book; 0-7614-5995-2 e-book

LC 2011001122

When Rabbit and Hedgehog bring home a newly-hatched dragon they all have a wonderful time together, but soon the dragon baby grows too big for their house.

"Falkerstern's oils have depth and warmth, and, though her animals are anthropomorphized, they're closer in authenticity to nature photos than cartoons. Gentle country concoction, two parts Beatrix Potter and one part Cressida Cowell." Kirkus

Faller, Regis

★ The **adventures** of Polo. Roaring Brook Press 2006 75p il $16.95

Grades: PreK K 1 2 3   E

1. Stories without words 2. Dogs -- Fiction

ISBN 978-1-59643-160-7; 1-59643-160-1

LC 2005055261

Polo the dog sets out from his home and enjoys many adventures, including sailing his boat on top of a whale, roasting hot dogs over a volcano, and taking a ride in a spaceship built from a mushroom.

"Young readers will be charmed by this hound, and be awed by his ingenuity. Somewhat similar to a graphic-novel format, this wordless picture book contains bold, colorful, cartoon panels that are sure to captivate even the most finicky youngster." SLJ

Other titles about Polo are:

Polo: the runaway book (2006)

Polo and the magic flute (2009)

Polo and Lily (2009)

Polo and the dragon (2009)

Polo and the magician (2009)

Falwell, Cathryn

David's drawings; story and pictures by Cathryn Falwell. Lee & Low Bks. 2001 un il hardcover o.p. pa $8.95

Grades: PreK K 1 2   E

1. Drawing 2. Friendship 3. School stories 4. Drawing -- Fiction 5. Friendship -- Fiction 6. African Americans -- Fiction

ISBN 1-58430-031-0; 1-58430-261-5 pa

LC 2001-16450

A shy African American boy arriving at a new school makes friends with his classmates by drawing a picture of a tree

"The cut-paper-and-fabric collages are a good choice for the story. . . . Both theme and execution make this a fine choice for classroom read-alouds." Booklist

Gobble, gobble. Dawn Publications 2011 un il
Grades: PreK K 1   E
  1. Stories in rhyme
  ISBN 1-58469-148-4; 1-58469-149-2 pa; 978-1-58469-148-8; 978-1-58469-149-5 pa
                                    LC 2011011698
"After discovering a flock of turkeys in her yard in the spring, Jenny continues to watch them thoughout the year. With simple text, mostly rhyming couplets, the young nature watcher describes the turkeys' appearance and behavior as they nest and raise their young in the woods nearby. . . . Falwell augments her multimedia (cut and torn paper and found natural materials) images with overlaid block prints. Leaf prints add further texture. These charming illustrations also show other animals. . . . The author includes suggestions for artwork and other activities." Kirkus

Pond babies. Down East 2011 un il $15.95
Grades: PreK K 1   E
  1. Ponds -- Fiction 2. Animals -- Fiction
  ISBN 978-0-89272-920-3; 0-89272-920-1
                                    LC 2010043117
"This offering focuses on creatures that live in or near ponds, with a human child included at the end. A simple question-and-answer format presents a single physical characteristic of each one and then inquires, 'Whose baby is this?' Children will quickly catch on to the pattern and the idea that a page turn is necessary to learn the answer. Whether it is white spots that indicate a fawn or a wiggly tail to represent a tadpole, Falwell's colorful collages incorporate the given features. . . . The soft hues of the illustrations evoke the wonder of springtime." SLJ

★ **Scoot!** Greenwillow Books 2008 un il $16.99; lib bdg $17.89
Grades: PreK K 1 2   E
  1. Stories in rhyme 2. Ponds -- Fiction 3. Turtles -- Fiction
  ISBN 978-0-06-128882-1; 0-06-128882-9; 978-0-06-128883-8 lib bdg; 0-06-128883-7 lib bdg
                                    LC 2007-18355
Six silent turtles sit still as stones on a log, as energetic movement by the other animals in the pond happens all around them
  "Extraordinary paper collages accompany a high-spirited romp. . . . Strong, predictable rhymes bounce across the pages. . . . Unusual, lively words extend vocabulary." SLJ

Shape capers; [by] Cathryn Falwell. Greenwillow Books 2007 un il $16.99; lib bdg $17.89
Grades: PreK K   E
  1. Stories in rhyme 2. Shape -- Fiction 3. Imagination -- Fiction
  ISBN 978-0-06-123699-0; 978-0-06-123700-0 lib bdg
                                    LC 2006043061
A group of children shakes shapes out of a box and discovers the fun of using circles, squares, triangles, semicircles, rectangles, and their imaginations

This is a "bright, playful book, illustrated in whimsical cut-paper collage." Booklist

★ **Turtle** splash! countdown at the pond. Greenwillow Bks. 2001 un il $15.95; lib bdg $15.89
Grades: PreK K 1 2   E
  1. Turtles 2. Counting 3. Stories in rhyme 4. Turtles -- Fiction
  ISBN 0-06-029462-0; 0-06-029463-9 lib bdg
                                    LC 00-30918
As they are startled by the activities of other nearby creatures, the number of turtles on a log in a pond decreases from ten to one
  "The rhyming, alliterative text is energized with a rolling rhythm, suspense, and vivid, descriptive words. . . . Evocative woodland scenes spring to life with well-defined animals that are described in a final appended section." Booklist

Fancher, Lou
  Star climbing; by Lou Fancher; paintings by Steve Johnson and Lou Fancher. Laura Geringer Books 2006 un il hardcover o.p. lib bdg $16.89
Grades: PreK K   E
  1. Stars -- Fiction 2. Bedtime -- Fiction 3. Imagination -- Fiction 4. Constellations -- Fiction
  ISBN 978-0-06-073901-0; 0-06-073901-0; 978-0-06-073902-7 lib bdg; 0-06-073902-9 lib bdg
                                    LC 2005005048
When he cannot sleep, a little boy imagines himself on a nighttime journey across the sky where he can run and dance with star constellations
  "Ethereal, textured paintings accompany Fancher's rhythmic, lyrical poem." Publ Wkly

Farber, Norma
  How the hibernators came to Bethlehem; by Norma Farber; illustrated by Barbara Cooney. Walker 2006 un il $9.95
Grades: K 1 2 3   E
  1. Animals -- Fiction 2. Christmas -- Fiction 3. Hibernation -- Fiction
  ISBN 0-8027-9610-9
  A reissue of the title first published 1980
The Star of Bethlehem awakens the winter-sleeping creatures, such as Bear, Badger, and Raccoon, to send them to visit a newborn baby.
  "The simple, unabashed realism of Cooney's art . . . along with Farber's respectful text, celebrates the hibernators as part of a divine plan." Horn Book Guide

Farley, Robin
  Mia and the too big tutu; pictures by Aleksey and Olga Ivanov. HarperCollins 2010 32p il (I can read) $16.99; pa $3.99
Grades: PreK K 1   E
  1. Cats -- Fiction 2. Ballet -- Fiction
  ISBN 978-0-06-173302-4; 0-06-173302-4; 978-0-06-173301-7 pa; 0-06-173301-6 pa
                                    LC 2010021960
Mia the kitten is so excited about her first day of ballet class that she accidentally brings her big sister's tutu instead of her own.
  "Large, colorful illustrations and an easy-to-read typeface make [this book] visually appealing." SLJ

Farmer, Jacqueline

Valentine be mine; Jacqueline Farmer; illustrated by Megan Halsey and Sean Addy. Charlesbridge 2013 32 p. (reinforced) $17.95; (paperback) $7.95
Grades: 1 2 3   E
1. Valentine's Day -- Juvenile literature
ISBN 1580893902; 9781580893893; 9781580893909
LC 2011049504

This children's book, by Jacqueline Farmer, discusses the history of Valentine's Day. "Influenced by kings, poets, and religious customs, Valentine's Day has changed over the centuries from its origins in ancient Rome. Readers of all ages will learn the history of Valentine's Day as well as its past and present traditions in this informative dual-level text." (Publisher's note)

Farooqi, Musharraf

The **cobbler's** holiday, or, why ants don't have shoes; illustrated by Eugene Yelchin. Roaring Brook Press 2008 un il $16.95
Grades: K 1 2 3   E
1. Ants -- Fiction 2. Shoes -- Fiction 3. Fashion -- Fiction
ISBN 978-1-59643-234-5; 1-59643-234-9
LC 2007044046

At a time when every ant has at least fifteen pairs of shoes and disputes over footwear are common, the one and only ant cobbler decides to take some time off, which leads to many tears until the Red Ant provides an elegant solution.

This is "a dainty, droll fable. . . . Farooqi builds scenarios ripe with comedy. . . . Yelchin . . . contributes decorative initial caps and a modish Jazz Age aesthetic; his spiky-looking ant flappers and dandies sport ritzy top hats and beaded caps, tailored and fur-collared coats, monocles and, of course, elaborate footwear." Publ Wkly

Farrell, Darren

Doug-Dennis and the flyaway fib; words and pictures by Darren Farrell. Dial Books for Young Readers 2010 un il $16.95
Grades: K 1 2   E
1. Sheep -- Fiction 2. Circus -- Fiction 3. Honesty -- Fiction 4. Friendship -- Fiction 5. Truthfulness and falsehood -- Fiction
ISBN 978-0-8037-3437-1; 0-8037-3437-9
LC 2009-12141

Having fibbed about stealing his best friend's popcorn at the circus, Doug-Dennis the sheep finds himself carried far away to a place filled with lies and liars of all sorts and must discover a way to return.

"Sharp-edged irony and wacky cartoon visuals provide newcomer Farrell's moral tale with some serious wattage. . . . Despite the antifib message, the fibs are where all the entertainment is ('I invented the inter-web,' declares a spider), and the ethically unsteady Doug-Dennis has plenty of Homer Simpson–like appeal." Publ Wkly

Faulkner, Matt

A **taste** of colored water. Simon & Schuster 2008 un il $16.99
Grades: K 1 2 3   E
1. Cousins -- Fiction 2. Civil rights demonstrations -- Fiction 3. African Americans -- Segregation -- Fiction
ISBN 978-1-4169-1629-1; 1-4169-1629-6

In the 1960s two cousins hear of a water fountain labelled "Colored" and imagine a multicolored drink, but they discover the true meaning of the sign when they encounter a Civil Rights demonstration.

"Watercolors decorated with ink crosshatching ably contrast the sweet pastoral fun the children experience with their sudden, terrifying wake up. Faulkner's personal note about his growing up in the north, where segregation was not official but prejudice was always there, will spark discussion." Booklist

Fearnley, Jan

Martha in the middle; [by] Jan Fearnley. Candlewick Press 2008 40p il $16.99
Grades: PreK K 1   E
1. Mice -- Fiction 2. Frogs -- Fiction 3. Siblings -- Fiction 4. Family life -- Fiction
ISBN 978-0-7636-3800-9; 0-7636-3800-5

Martha, a young mouse with a sensible big sister and a cute little brother, begins to feel invisible and decides to run away, but at the end of the garden she meets a wise frog who points out just how special the middle can be.

"Fearnley's nimble use of line and uncluttered watercolors focus on character and plenty of action. . . . Witty details . . . ramp up the fun." Publ Wkly

Milo Armadillo. Candlewick Press 2009 un il $15.99
Grades: PreK K 1 2   E
1. Toys -- Fiction 2. Armadillos -- Fiction
ISBN 978-0-7636-4575-5; 0-7636-4575-3
LC 2009004231

When no one can find a pink, fluffy rabbit to give to Tallulah for her birthday, her grandmother knits her a pink, fluffy 'thing' that they name Milo Armadillo, which proves to be a great present.

"Mixed-media collages pay homage to all things handmade by incorporating worked yarn and fabric into the illustrations. This candy-colored picture book tells a simple, sweet story about learning to love what you have." SLJ

Mr. Wolf's pancakes; [by] Jan Fearnley. Tiger Tales 2001 un il $15.95; pa $6.95
Grades: PreK K 1 2 3   E
1. Fairy tales 2. Wolves -- Fiction
ISBN 1-58925-004-4; 1-58925-354-X pa
LC 2001-834

First published 1999 in the United Kingdom

"Mr. Wolf seeks assistance from his neighbors, but Chicken Little, Wee Willy Winkle, the Gingerbread Man, Little Red Riding Hood and the Three Little Pigs all nastily refuse. Of course, when Mr. Wolf eventually whips up the pancakes all by himself, they demand a share of his culinary creation. Mr. Wolf . . . lets the marauders into the kitchen- and then gobbles them all up. . . . Chipper watercolors depict a sunny storybook town. . . . A gleeful twist on a nursery staple." Publ Wkly

Another title about Mr. Wolf is:
Mr. Wolf and the three bears (2002)

Feelings, Muriel

★ **Jambo** means hello; Swahili alphabet book. pictures by Tom Feelings. Dial Bks. for Young Readers 1981 un il hardcover o.p. pa $6.99

Grades: PreK K 1 2   **E**
1. Alphabet 2. Swahili language
ISBN 0-14-054652-1 pa
A Caldecott Medal honor book, 1975

"Integrated totally in feeling and mood, the book has been engendered by an intense personal vision of Africa—one that is warm, all-enveloping, quietly strong and filled with love." Horn Book

★ **Moja** means one; Swahili counting book. pictures by Tom Feelings. Dial Bks. for Young Readers 1971 un il hardcover o.p. pa $6.99
Grades: PreK K 1 2   **E**
1. Counting 2. Swahili language
ISBN 0-14-054662-6 pa
A Caldecott Medal honor book, 1972

"A short introduction explaining the importance of Swahili and providing a map of the areas in which it is spoken expands the book's use beyond the preschool level of the text into the first three school grades." SLJ

Feiffer, Jules

★ **Bark,** George. HarperCollins Pubs. 1999 un il $15.99
Grades: PreK K 1 2   **E**
1. Dogs 2. Animal sounds 3. Dogs -- Fiction 4. Humorous stories
ISBN 0-06-205185-7

"Feiffer's characters are unforgettable, the text is brief and easy to follow, and the pictures burst with the sort of broad physical comedy that a lot of children just love." Booklist

Feiffer, Kate

But I wanted a baby brother! illustrated by Diane Goode. Simon & Schuster Books for Young Readers 2010 un il $16.99
Grades: PreK K 1   **E**
1. Infants -- Fiction 2. Siblings -- Fiction 3. Family life -- Fiction
ISBN 978-1-4169-3941-2; 1-4169-3941-5

Oliver Keaton wants a baby brother more than anything but when he gets a baby sister instead, he sets out with his dog Chaplin to trade his sister for the perfect baby brother.

"Both text and breezy cartoon illustrations are laced with humor, making this an excellent choice for reading aloud. . . . Feiffer's book is a cut above many of its kind." Booklist

Double pink; illustrated by Bruce Ingman. Simon & Schuster Books for Young Readers 2005 un il $15.95
Grades: PreK K 1   **E**
1. Color -- Fiction
ISBN 0-689-87190-0
LC 2004--06582

Madison covers and surrounds herself with her favorite color, pink, until the day her mother has trouble finding her.

"Feiffer's simple text reads easily, and Ingman's playful acrylic-and-ink paintings take a light approach to this look at childhood obsession." SLJ

Henry, the dog with no tail; illustrated by Jules Feiffer. Simon & Schuster Books for Young Readers 2007 un il $16.99

Grades: PreK K 1 2   **E**
1. Dogs -- Fiction
ISBN 978-1-4169-1614-7; 1-4169-1614-8
LC 2006-13418

Envious of the other dogs that have tails, Henry goes in search of a tail of his own, but in the end he decides he is happy the way he is.

"Feiffer's story features droll humor, wonderfully outlandish plot twists, and a satisfying journey of self-discovery. . . . The charcoal and watercolor illustrations use loose lines and color splashes to convey the action and capture the characters' personalities." SLJ

★ **My** mom is trying to ruin my life; [by] Kate Feiffer; illustrated by Diane Goode. Simon & Schuster Books for Young Readers 2009 un il $16.99
Grades: PreK K 1 2   **E**
1. Father-daughter relationship -- Fiction 2. Mother-daughter relationship -- Fiction
ISBN 978-1-4169-4100-2; 1-4169-4100-2
LC 2007045351

A young girl describes all the ways in which her mother and father conspire to ruin her life

"Feiffer and Goode . . . give the old chestnut of a story line an urbane sheen. . . . [Goode's] watercolor vignettes are gems of wry intelligence and comic understatement." Publ Wkly

★ **My** side of the car; illustrated by Jules Feiffer. Candlewick Press 2011 un il $16.99
Grades: PreK K 1 2   **E**
1. Rain -- Fiction 2. Automobile travel -- Fiction 3. Father-daughter relationship -- Fiction
ISBN 978-0-7636-4405-5; 0-7636-4405-6
LC 2010039184

Sadie and her father have been planning a trip to the zoo for a long time but something always gets in the way, so when they finally start out and her father sees some raindrops, Sadie insists there is no rain on her side of the car.

"Feiffer's sweet and loopy watercolor-and-pencil drawings follow Sadie's imaginings and explanations for wet car windows. . . . Sadie's cheerful sass and her father's obvious respect for and indulgence of the force of her imagination make this a keeper." Publ Wkly

President Pennybaker; [by] Kate Feiffer; illustrated by Diane Goode. Simon & Schuster Books for Young Readers 2008 un il $16.99
Grades: PreK K 1 2   **E**
1. Politics -- Fiction
ISBN 978-1-4169-1354-2; 1-4169-1354-8
LC 2007004815

Tired of the unfairness of life, young Luke Pennybaker decides to run for president, with his dog Lily as his running mate

"Deadpan narration allows the absurdity of the premise to carry the day, with plenty of help from the illustrations. Goode's breezy watercolors set just the right tone. . . . The humor is deftly understated, both visually and verbally, making this an amusing and appealing send-up of politics and children's chores." SLJ

Feldman, Eve

★ **Billy** and Milly, short and silly! written by Eve Feldman; pictures by Tuesday Mourning. G.P. Putnam's Sons 2009 un il $16.99
Grades: PreK K 1 2　　　　　　　　　　　　　　E
　　1. Stories in rhyme
　　ISBN 978-0-399-24651-7; 0-399-24651-7
　　　　　　　　　　　　　　　　LC 2008-26143
"This picture book presents 13 short rhyming stories about Billy and Milly. Most of them are four words long; some, only three. Every word in each selection rhymes. . . . The bright cartoon illustrations done in mixed-media collage are the keys to understanding the stories and the humor. . . . Both clever and slapstick, this book can be read for pleasure or used as a jumping-off point for thinking about rhyme, language, and story." SLJ

Feldman, Thea

Harry Cat and Tucker Mouse: Harry to the rescue! Square Fish 2011 47p (My readers) $15.99; pa $3.99
Grades: 1 2 3　　　　　　　　　　　　　　　E
　　1. Cats -- Fiction 2. Mice -- Fiction
　　ISBN 978-0-312-62507-8; 0-312-62507-3; 978-0-312-62509-2 pa; 0-312-62509-X pa
Tucker Mouse spotted a lost penny in the shoeshine store, so he ran in to get it for his collection. Now the store is closed up tight, and Tucker is trapped. Can Harry Cat find a way to get him out?

Harry Cat and Tucker Mouse: Tucker's beetle band. Square Fish 2011 47p il (My readers) $15.99; pa $3.99
Grades: 1 2 3　　　　　　　　　　　　　　　E
　　1. Cats -- Fiction 2. Mice -- Fiction 3. Beetles -- Fiction 4. Crickets -- Fiction 5. Bands (Music) -- Fiction
　　ISBN 978-0-312-62575-7; 0-312-62575-8; 978-0-312-62576-4 pa; 0-312-62576-6 pa
"Tucker Mouse, Harry Cat, and Chester Cricket contend with a beetle rock band disturbing their sleep under Times Square. The band is practicing to win the Battle of the Bug Bands competition and travel the country. . . . The Ivanovs' intricate ink and watercolor illustrations reflect the charm of Garth Williams's characters and original setting but add many details including varied visual perspectives and characters that exude facial and kinesthetic expression. . . . This well-told tale will appeal to the many young readers and their friends whose family members are in bands, and it serves as a wonderful introduction to the beloved characters in George Selden's The Cricket in Times Square." SLJ
　　Other titles in this series are:
　　Harry Cat and Tucker Mouse: Harry to the rescue! (2011)
　　Harry Cat and Tucker Mouse: Starring Harry! (2011)

Harry Cat and Tucker Mouse: starring Harry. Square Fish 2011 32p (My readers) $15.99; pa $3.99
Grades: K 1 2　　　　　　　　　　　　　　　E
　　1. Cats -- Fiction 2. Mice -- Fiction 3. Theater -- Fiction 4. Friendship -- Fiction
　　ISBN 978-0-312-68168-5; 978-0-312-68169-2 pa
　　　　　　　　　　　　　　　　LC 2010048674
Harry Cat loves the theater, but when he becomes the star of a Broadway play he and his best friend Tucker Mouse miss one another terribly.

Fenton, Joe

What's under the bed? written and illustrated by Joe Fenton. Simon & Schuster for Young Readers un il $15.99
Grades: PreK K 1 2　　　　　　　　　　　　　E
　　1. Stories in rhyme 2. Fear -- Fiction 3. Bedtime -- Fiction
　　ISBN 978-1-4169-4943-5; 1-4169-4943-7
When Fred lays down his head, he imagines there is something monstrous under his bed.
　　"The narrative is accessible, using uncomplicated rhymes. . . . The brooding illustrations would be more unnerving if Fred, diminutive in outsize glasses, weren't so adorably disarming." Horn Book Guide

Ferber, Brenda A.

The **yuckiest**, stinkiest, best Valentine ever; by Brenda A. Ferber; pictures by Tedd Arnold. Dial Books for Young Readers 2012 32 p. col. ill. (hardcover) $16.99
Grades: PreK K 1 2　　　　　　　　　　　　　E
　　1. Love -- Fiction 2. Valentine's Day 3. Valentine's Day -- Fiction
　　ISBN 0803735057; 9780803735057
　　　　　　　　　　　　　　　　LC 2011047668
In this children's picture book, "Leon makes a very special valentine for his crush, Zoey Maloney, but the valentine has a mind and life of its own. The valentine tells Leon not to tell Zoey that he loves her. In a gingerbread man-like fashion, the valentine dashes out of the house with Leon running after it. During the chase, Leon and the valentine come across different groups of kids who share their opinions about Leon's declaration of love." (Children's Literature)

Fern, Tracey E.

★ **Buffalo** music; illustrated by Lauren Castillo. Clarion Books 2008 31p il $16
Grades: 1 2 3 4　　　　　　　　　　　　　　E
　　1. Teachers 2. Conservationists 3. Ranchers 4. Bison -- Fiction 5. Frontier and pioneer life -- Fiction
　　ISBN 978-0-618-72341-6; 0-618-72341-2
　　　　　　　　　　　　　　　　LC 2007-18435
After hunters kill off the buffalo around her Texas ranch, a woman begins raising orphan buffalo calves and eventually ships four members of her small herd to Yellowstone National Park, where they form the beginnings of newly thriving buffalo herds. Based on the true story of Mary Ann Goodnight and her husband Charles; includes author's note about her work, with websites and a bibliography.
　　"Fern's lyrical text and Castillo's folk-style artwork beautifully capture the era and events. Done in warm, earthy hues, the mixed-media illustrations depict a rugged landscape of grays and browns speckled with touches of color-wildflowers or bright blooms on a tree." SLJ

★ **Pippo** the Fool; [by] Tracey E. Fern; illustrated by Pau Estrada. Charlesbridge 2009 un il $15.95
Grades: 1 2 3　　　　　　　　　　　　　　　E
　　1. Artists 2. Sculptors 3. Architects
　　ISBN 978-1-57091-655-7; 1-57091-655-1
　　　　　　　　　　　　　　　　LC 2007002283
In fifteenth-century Florence, Italy, a contest is held to design a magnificent dome for the town's cathedral, but when Pippo the Fool claims he will win the contest, everyone laughs at him. Based on the true story of Filippo Brunelleschi.

This is "told with a great deal of charm and buttressed by understated humor. . . . Estrada's timeless art highlights Florence's orange-roofed architecture and colorfully attired citizens." Booklist

Fernandes, Eugenie

Kitten's summer; [by] Eugenie Fernandes. Kids Can Press 2011 un il $14.95

Grades: PreK   E

1. Stories in rhyme 2. Cats -- Fiction 3. Summer -- Fiction

ISBN 978-1-55453-342-8; 1-55453-342-2

"As rain begins to fall, Kitten dashes home. . . . Using rhyming couplets, the text tracks her progress and the critters she passes by. . . . Fernandes's clay, acrylic paint, and mixed-media collage artwork creates a unique look for the forest and its denizens. There is a tremendous amount of detail and charm in these realistic vignettes." SLJ

Other titles about Kitten are:
Kitten's autumn (2010)
Kitten's spring (2010)
Kitten's winter (2011)

Finchler, Judy

★ Miss Malarkey leaves no reader behind. Walker & Company 2006 un il $16.95; lib bdg $17.85

Grades: K 1 2 3   E

1. School stories 2. Teachers -- Fiction 3. Books and reading -- Fiction

ISBN 978-0-8027-8084-3; 0-8027-8084-9; 978-0-8027-8085-0 lib bdg; 0-8027-8085-7 lib bdg

LC 2005037182

Miss Malarkey vows to find each of her students a book to love by the end of the school year, but one video-game loving boy proves to be a challenge. "O'Malley's illustrations, done in markers and colored pencils, enhance the text with expressive pictures. . . . A must-have for all libraries." SLJ

Other titles about Miss Malarkey are:
Congratulations, Miss Malarkey! (2009)
Miss Malarkey doesn't live in Room 10 (1995)
Miss Malarkey won't be in today (1998)
Miss Malarkey's field trip (2004)
Testing Miss Malarkey (2000)
You're a good sport, Miss Malarkey (2002)

Fine, Edith Hope

Armando and the blue tarp school; [by] Edith Hope Fine & Judith Pinkerton Josephson; illustrated by Hernan Sosa. Lee & Low 2007 un il lib bdg $16.95

Grades: K 1 2 3   E

1. School stories 2. Poverty -- Fiction

ISBN 978-1-58430-278-0

"This poignant picture book . . . is based on a true story. . . . [It is illustrated with] clear, unframed, double-page pictures in watercolor and ink with thick white outlines. . . . Without melodrama, Armando's story shows what poverty means and the hope that things can change." Booklist

Fischer, Scott M.

Jump! [by] Scott Fischer. Simon & Schuster Books for Young Readers 2010 un il $14.99

Grades: PreK K   E

1. Stories in rhyme 2. Fear -- Fiction 3. Animals

-- Fiction

ISBN 978-1-4169-7884-8; 1-4169-7884-4

LC 2008025861

From bugs and frogs to alligators and whales, frightened animals always move out of the way of a larger opponent.

"With simple, rhyming text and action-packed artwork, this picture book will appeal to young preschoolers. . . . Even after kids have figured out what is coming, they will enjoy the animals' shifts in power roles, all depicted in lively drawings, rendered in thick black lines and strong, bright colors against blank white space." Booklist

Fisher, Aileen Lucia

The story goes on; illustrated by Mique Moriuchi. Roaring Brook Press 2004 un il $16.95

Grades: PreK K 1 2   E

1. Stories in rhyme 2. Food chains (Ecology)

ISBN 1-59643-037-0

LC 2003-18143

An illustrated poem about the cycle of life—bug eats plant, frog eats bug, snake eats frog, hawk eats snake, and so on

"With bright colors, rhyming text, and collage illustrations, this circular tale points out the interdependence of life. . . . This offering is a visual treat and an engaging opportunity to introduce the cycle of life to young readers." SLJ

Fisher, Carolyn

The Snow Show; with Chef Kelvin. producer, Carolyn Fisher. Harcourt 2008 un il $17

Grades: K 1 2 3   E

1. Snow -- Fiction 2. Cooking -- Fiction 3. Snow -- Juvenile literature 4. Television programs -- Fiction

ISBN 978-0-15-206019-0; 0-15-206019-7

LC 2007031724

A cooking show goes on location to the North Pole to demonstrate the recipe for making snow.

"The visually dynamic, digitally created art features lettering that helps tell the story. . . . Fisher includes collage, dialogue asides, arrows, onomatopoeic descriptors, and fact boxes, yet maintains clarity, cohesion, and purpose." SLJ

Fisher, Valorie

Everything I need to know before I'm five. Schwartz & Wade 2011 un il $17.99; lib bdg 20.99

Grades: PreK K 1   E

1. Color 2. Numbers 3. Seasons 4. Alphabet 5. Concepts 6. Geometry 7. Opposites

ISBN 978-0-375-86865-8; 0-375-86865-8; 978-0-375-96865-5 lib bdg; 0-375-96865-2 lib bdg

LC 2010031265

Fisher "gives preschoolers a leg up on need-to-know information in this energetic collection. In candy-colored multimedia collages, . . . she presents such topics as weather, seasons, and numbers up to 20. . . . Considering all the titles on just one of these topics, these vintage/tacky photo-spreads are worth several books in one, even as they display the vast potential in rummage sales and vending machines." Publ Wkly

My big brother. Atheneum Bks. for Young Readers 2002 un il $15.95

Grades: PreK K 1   E

1. Brothers 2. Brothers -- Fiction

ISBN 0-689-84327-5

LC 2001-22947

Photographs and simple text depict a big brother from the point of view of his baby sibling

"The design is clean and strong, and the colors, textures, and lines all lead the eye to the important parts of the story. Together the text and the pictures tell a funny, very tender story of sibling relationships." Booklist

Fitzpatrick, Marie-Louise

There. Roaring Brook Press 2009 un il $17.95

Grades: K 1 2   E

1. Questions and answers 2. Growth -- Fiction

ISBN 978-1-59643-087-7; 1-59643-087-7

LC 2008-54266

A young girl asks questions about growing up as she walks over rolling hills, climbs a ladder up to the stars, and meets a dragon.

This "is a book for rumination, a rare permission to ask the unanswerable questions. The thoughts that propel it and the images that illuminate it make this volume a small wonder for children." SLJ

Flack, Marjorie

Ask Mr. Bear. Macmillan 1958 un il $15.95; pa $6.99

Grades: PreK K 1   E

1. Animals -- Fiction 2. Birthdays -- Fiction

ISBN 0-02-735390-7; 0-02-043090-6 pa

First published 1932

Danny did not know what to give his mother for a birthday present, so he set out to ask various animals—the hen, the duck, the goose, the lamb, the cow and others, but he met with very little success until he met Mr. Bear

This "will have a strong appeal to very young children because of its repetition, its use of the most familiar animals, its gay pictures and the cumulative effect of the story." N Y Times Book Rev

Flaherty, Alice

The **luck** of the Loch Ness monster; a tale of picky eating. [by] A. W. Flaherty; illustrated by Scott Magoon. Houghton Mifflin 2007 un il $16

Grades: K 1 2 3   E

1. Ocean travel -- Fiction 2. Loch Ness monster -- Fiction

ISBN 978-0-618-55644-1; 0-618-55644-3

LC 2006026083

"A girl is traveling alone to visit her grandmother in Scotland. . . . She tosses her dreaded morning oatmeal overboard, only to attract the attention of a tiny sea worm that gobbles it up and immediately quadruples in size. . . . This pourquoi tale about how the Loch Ness Monster came to be has a lot of imagination and wonderful storytelling techniques. Dark, cartoonlike watercolors exhibit an excellent use of perspective." SLJ

Fleischman, Paul

★ The **Matchbox** diary; Paul Fleischman, illustrated by Bagram Ibatoulline. Candlewick Press 2013 40 p. $16.99

Grades: 1 2 3 4 5   E

1. Memory -- Juvenile fiction 2. Diaries -- Juvenile fiction 3. Immigrants -- United States -- Juvenile fiction

ISBN 0763646016; 9780763646011

LC 2012942613

In this children's story, by Newbery Medalist Paul Fleischman and illustrated by Bagram Ibatoulline, "when a little girl visits her great-grandfather at his curio-filled home, she chooses an unusual object to learn about: an old cigar box. What she finds inside surprises her: a collection of matchboxes making up her great-grandfather's diary. . . . Together they tell of his journey from Italy to a new country, before he could read and write." (Publisher's note)

Sidewalk circus; presented by Paul Fleischman and Kevin Hawkes. Candlewick Press 2004 un il $15.99

Grades: PreK K 1 2 3   E

1. Circus 2. City and town life 3. Stories without words 4. Circus -- Fiction 5. City and town life -- Fiction

ISBN 0-7636-1107-7

LC 2002-74168

"As posters advertising the world-renowned Garibaldi circus are put up along a busy city block, a girl waiting for a bus watches the circus of everyday life unfold. There is no actual text to the book, just the words of store signs, a scrolling theater marquee, and the show bills. What the girl imagines is revealed through the playful shadows of the people on the street and the corresponding circus flyers. . . . Hawkes's richly colored acrylic paintings sustain interest and pacing throughout the book. . . . This delightful book will fascinate children and help them to see their world with new eyes." SLJ

★ **Weslandia**; illustrated by Kevin Hawkes. Candlewick Press 1999 un il $15.99; pa $5.99

Grades: K 1 2 3   E

1. Plants -- Fiction 2. Gardening -- Fiction 3. Civilization -- Fiction

ISBN 0-7636-0006-7; 0-7636-1052-6 pa

LC 98-30240

Wesley's garden produces a crop of huge, strange plants which provide him with clothing, shelter, food, and drink, thus helping him create his own civilization and changing his life

"This story about a nonconformist creating his own reality resonates with imagination and humor. . . . His natural creativity is reflected in Hawkes' vivid recreations of Wesley's altered environment, lush illustrations that have a realistic whimsy." Bull Cent Child Books

The **animal** hedge; illustrated by Bagram Ibatoulline. Candlewick Press 2003 un il $16.99

Grades: K 1 2 3   E

1. Animals -- Fiction 2. Farmers -- Fiction

ISBN 0-7636-1606-0

LC 2002-23751

A newly illustrated edition of the title first published 1983 by Dutton

After being forced to sell the animals he loves, a farmer cuts his hedge to look like them and teaches his sons about following their hearts

"Ibatoulline's watercolor-and-gouache illustrations, inspired by 19th-century American folk-art paintings, are the perfect complement to this simple allegory." SLJ

The **birthday** tree; illustrated by Barry Root. Candlewick Press 2008 un il $16.99

Grades: K 1 2 3   E

  1. Trees -- Fiction

  ISBN 978-0-7636-2604-4

LC 2007-32344

A newly illustrated edition of the title first published 1979 by Harper & Row

When Jack goes to sea, his parents watch as the tree planted at his birth reflects his fortunes and misfortunes

"Precisely worded and fluid in the telling, the story has a timeless quality that is echoed in the expressive watercolor artwork." Booklist

Fleming, Candace

  ★ **Boxes** for Katje; pictures by Stacey Dressen-McQueen. Farrar, Straus & Giroux 2003 un il $16

Grades: K 1 2 3   E

  1. World War, 1939-1945 -- Fiction

  ISBN 0-374-30922-1

LC 2002-20027

After a young Dutch girl writes to her new American friend in thanks for the care package sent after World War II, she begins to receive increasingly larger boxes

The story is "moving, and Dressen-McQueen's lively illustrations, in colored pencil, oil pastel, and acrylic, pack lots of color, pattern, and historical details onto every expansive page." Booklist

  ★ **Clever** Jack takes the cake; written by Candace Fleming; illustrated by G. Brian Karas. Schwartz & Wade Books 2010 un il

Grades: K 1 2 3   E

  1. Fairy tales 2. Cake -- Fiction 3. Birthdays -- Fiction 4. Princesses -- Fiction 5. Storytelling -- Fiction

  ISBN 0375849793; 0375956972 lib bdg;
  9780375849794; 9780375956973 lib bdg

LC 2009030030

A poor boy named Jack struggles to deliver a birthday present worthy of the princess. "Ages five to eight." (Bull Cent Child Books)

"Jack accidentally receives an invitation to the princess's birthday party. He . . . bakes a wonderful cake. On his way to the castle, the cake is slowly demolished by crows, a troll, a spooky forest, a dancing bear, and even a palace guard, until the only present Jack has to offer . . . is the story of the cake's demise. . . . This entertaining adventure is packed with action. Karas's scratchy gouache and pencil cartoon illustrations are as detail-rich as the text itself." SLJ

  ★ **Imogene's** last stand; written by Candice Fleming; illustrated by Nancy Carpenter. Schwartz & Wade Books 2009 un il $16.99; lib bdg $19.99

Grades: K 1 2   E

  1. United States -- History -- Fiction

  ISBN 978-0-375-83607-7; 0-375-83607-1; 978-0-375-93607-4 lib bdg; 0-375-93607-6 lib bdg

LC 2008-22458

Enamored of history, young Imogene Tripp tries to save her town's historical society from being demolished in order to build a shoelace factory.

"Fleming's sense of small-town space is impeccable; Carpenter's pen-and-ink art enjoyably scribbly; and the historical facts and quotes that bookend the story are just the thing to get new Imogenes fired up." Booklist

  ★ **Muncha!** Muncha! Muncha! illustrated by G. Brian Karas. Atheneum Bks. for Young Readers 2002 un il $16; lib bdg $18.63

Grades: PreK K 1 2   E

  1. Rabbits -- Fiction 2. Gardening -- Fiction

  ISBN 0-689-83152-8; 0-689-93652-X lib bdg

LC 99-24882

After planting the garden he has dreamed of for years, Mr. McGreely tries to find a way to keep some persistent bunnies from eating all his vegetables

"Fleming's text is lilting and deftly paced, with sound effects . . . strategically and enjoyably employed. . . . Karas' mixed-media (gouache, acrylic, and pencil) illustrations offer a cornucopia of plot-enriching details." Bull Cent Child Books

Another title about Mr. Greely and the bunnies is:
Tippy-tippy-tippy-hide! (2007)

  ★ **Oh,** no! Candace Fleming; [illustrations by Eric Rohmann] Schwartz & Wade Books 2012 40 p. $17.99

Grades: PreK K 1 2   E

  1. Rescue work -- Fiction 2. Jungle animals -- Fiction 3. Picture books for children 4. Stories in rhyme 5. Animals -- Fiction

  ISBN 0375842713; 9780375842719; 9780375945571

LC 2009045564

In this book, when a "frog falls into a deep hole . . . , a . . . mouse, . . . loris, . . . sun bear, and . . . monkey all tumble down after him during unsuccessful rescue attempts. . . . The animals face a lurking tiger eager to snack on the helpless group," who, in the end, is himself caught in the hole, seeking help. (School Library Journal)

Papa's mechanical fish; by Candace Fleming; pictures by Boris Kulikov. 1st ed. Margaret Ferguson Books 2013 40 p. ill. (chiefly col.) (reinforced) $16.99

Grades: 2 3 4   E

  1. Picture books for children 2. Submarines -- Juvenile fiction 3. Inventors -- Fiction 4. Family life -- Fiction 5. Submarines (Ships) -- Fiction

  ISBN 0374399085; 9780374399085

LC 2012029659

This children's picture book "profiles a would-be inventor and his indulgent family. Out fishing one day, daughter and narrator Virena happens to ask, "Papa . . . have you ever wondered what it's like to be a fish?'" At this, her "inspired father races for his workshop. To a refrain of 'Clink! Clankety-bang! Thump-whirrrr!' Papa sets to building a series of submarines, which he tests in Lake Michigan." (Publishers Weekly)

Seven hungry babies; illustrated by Eugene Yelchin. Atheneum Books for Young Readers 2010 un il $16.99

Grades: PreK K 1   E

1. Stories in rhyme 2. Birds -- Fiction
ISBN 978-1-4169-5402-6; 1-4169-5402-3

LC 2008-53481

A mother bird frantically tries to keep her seven baby birds fed.

"Fleming's playful text features endearments that will tickle listeners . . . and a rhythm that sweeps the story along. The fresh gouache illustrations are awash in blues and white with fire-bright red and yellow birds and feature expressive faces on the avian stars." SLJ

Sunny Boy! the life and times of a tortoise. pictures by Anne Wilsdorf. Farrar, Straus and Giroux 2005 un il $16
Grades: PreK K 1 2   E

1. Turtles -- Fiction
ISBN 0-374-37297-7

LC 2004-40451

In this fictionalized account, Sunny Boy, a 100-year-old tortoise, describes various events in his long life including the dangerous barrel ride over Niagara Falls that he takes with his daredevil owner on July 5, 1930

"This saga makes for wildly entertaining reading. . . . The comical cartoon narrative . . . enhances the textual flow of the story. Not to be missed is the author's fascinating historical note." SLJ

★ **This** is the baby; pictures by Maggie Smith. Farrar, Straus and Giroux 2004 un il $16.50
Grades: PreK K 1   E

1. Stories in rhyme 2. Infants -- Fiction 3. Clothing and dress -- Fiction
ISBN 0-374-37486-4

LC 2002-70941

A cumulative rhyme enumerating all the items of clothing that go on the baby who hates to be dressed, from the diaper often a mess to the jacket woolen and plaid.

"Smith's naive and rosy-cheeked characters, cozy textures, and crayon-box colors are a perfect accompaniment to Fleming's well-constructed, cumulative, 'House That Jack-Built' patterned story that positively insists on reader interaction." SLJ

The **hatmaker's** sign; a story. by Benjamin Franklin; retold by Candace Fleming; illustrated by Robert Andrew Parker. Orchard Bks. 1998 un il $16.95; lib bdg $17.99
Grades: K 1 2 3   E

1. Authors 2. Diplomats 3. Inventors 4. Statesmen 5. Architects 6. Presidents 7. Scientists 8. Vicepresidents 9. Essayists 10. Writers on science 11. Members of Congress
ISBN 0-531-30075-7; 0-531-33075-3 lib bdg

LC 97-27596

To heal the hurt pride of Thomas Jefferson as Congress makes changes to his Declaration of Independence, Benjamin Franklin tells his friend the story of a hatmaker and his sign

"Based on an anecdote in The Papers of Thomas Jefferson, the story has a folktale-like quality that lends itself to being read aloud. The illustrations give dimension to the characters and a sense of times past." Horn Book Guide

Fleming, Denise

★ **Beetle** bop. Harcourt 2007 un il $16

Grades: PreK K   E

1. Stories in rhyme 2. Beetles -- Fiction
ISBN 978-0-15-205936-1

LC 2006-09756

Illustrations and rhyming text reveal the great variety of beetles and their swirling, humming, crashing activities.

"Fleming creates a vibrant exciting portrait of oftenoverlooked creatures. Here she uses expertly crafted fiber collage to celebrate beetles, and both words and pictures vibrate with the relentless energy of the subject." Booklist

Buster. Holt & Co. 2003 un il $16.95; pa $6.95
Grades: PreK K 1 2   E

1. Cats -- Fiction 2. Dogs -- Fiction
ISBN 0-8050-6279-3; 0-8050-8757-5 pa

LC 2002-10857

Buster the dog thinks his perfect life is spoiled when Betty the cat comes to live with him, until he learns not to be afraid of cats

"Fleming's trademark handmade-paper artwork is awash with vibrant colors and dazzling details." SLJ

Another title about Buster is:

Buster goes to Cowboy Camp (2008)

Buster goes to Cowboy Camp. Henry Holt 2008 un il $16.95
Grades: PreK K 1 2   E

1. Dogs -- Fiction 2. Camps -- Fiction
ISBN 978-0-8050-7892-3; 0-8050-7892-4

LC 2007-12368

When Buster the dog's owner goes away for a few days, he sends Buster to Sagebrush Kennels for Cowboy Camp, where Buster is homesick at first, but then has fun herding balls into the corral, gathering sticks for a campfire, and making wanted posters with his pawprints.

"This sweet, simple story is steeped in the stuff of the Wild West. . . . Fleming extracts remarkable expression from her signature paper-pulp illustrations." Booklist

★ **Lunch**. Holt & Co. 1993 un il $17.99; pa $7.99; bd bk $7.95
Grades: PreK K 1   E

1. Color 2. Mice -- Fiction
ISBN 0-8050-1636-8; 0-8050-4646-1 pa; 0-8050-5696-3 bd bk

LC 92-178

"Fleming continues to work in the medium of handmade paper built from layers of colored pulp that has been forced through a stencil. A huge typeface and the judicious use of large blocks of bold, solid color give this book a fresh look. Delectable fun, and, with its simple yet engaging plot, sure to be requested over and over by the youngest readers." Horn Book

★ **Mama** cat has three kittens. Holt & Co. 1998 un il $17.95; pa $7.95
Grades: PreK K 1   E

1. Cats -- Fiction 2. Animals -- Infancy -- Fiction
ISBN 0-8050-5745-5; 0-8050-7162-8 pa

LC 98-12249

While two kittens copy everything their mother does, their brother naps

"Fleming's kittens, created by pouring colored cotton pulp through hand-cut stencils, are large and bold and set against colorful backdrops. An excellent choice for reading aloud to groups." SLJ

★ **Pumpkin** eye. Holt & Co. 2001 un il $16.99; pa $7.95

Grades: PreK K 1   E

1. Halloween 2. Stories in rhyme 3. Halloween -- Fiction

ISBN 0-8050-6681-0; 0-8050-7635-2 pa

LC 00-44850

Simple rhymes describe the sights, sounds, and smells of Halloween

"Fleming's homemade paper landscapes set off their midnight-blue—well, probably eight-o'clock blue—backdrops with glowing orange and white accents as well as with the rainbow of colors represented in the trick-or-treaters' costumes. . . . This will be just the shivery ticket for kids looking to move from Halloween giggles to genuine spookiness." Bull Cent Child Books

★ **Sleepy,** oh so sleepy. Henry Holt and Company 2010 un il $16.99

Grades: PreK   E

1. Animals -- Fiction 2. Bedtime -- Fiction 3. Mother-child relationship -- Fiction

ISBN 978-0-8050-8126-8; 0-8050-8126-7

LC 2009006151

Depicts a number of animal babies sleeping as a mother puts her own baby to bed.

"Formed using Fleming's signature medium of 'pulp painting,' which simultaneously creates the image and the paper that bears it, and accented with pastel pencil, the large-scale illustrations are bold in form and rich in color. With mesmerizing words rolling along, this large-format book does its job so well that it's hard to repress a contented yawn when the story winds down to its quiet ending." Booklist

★ **Time** to sleep. Holt & Co. 1997 un il $17.95; pa $7.95

Grades: PreK K 1   E

1. Winter -- Fiction 2. Animals -- Fiction 3. Hibernation -- Fiction

ISBN 0-8050-3762-4; 0-8050-6767-1 pa

LC 96-37553

When Bear notices that winter is nearly here he hurries to tell Snail, after which each animal tells another until finally the already sleeping Bear is awakened in his den with the news

"Fleming's simple text is ripe with astute observations of the natural world and animal behavior. . . . Fleming's 'pulp painting' style results in lushly textured handmade paper compositions saturated with earthy browns, reds and golds." Publ Wkly

★ The **cow** who clucked. Henry Holt 2006 un il $16.95

Grades: PreK K 1 2   E

1. Cattle -- Fiction 2. Animals -- Fiction

ISBN 978-0-8050-7265-5; 0-8050-7265-9

LC 2005-22676

When a cow loses her moo, she searches to see if another animal in the barn has it

"The gentle inside jokes, the animal sounds, and the repetitive phrase constitute only a fraction of this book's appeal. Fleming is, after all, a thrilling illustrator whose pulp-painting technique brings subtlety and texture to densely colored art. . . . The layers of subtle humor and visual splendor are truly impressive." SLJ

★ The **everything** book. Holt & Co. 2000 64p il $18.95

Grades: PreK K   E

1. Literature 2. Children's literature

ISBN 0-8050-6292-0

LC 99-53626

Fleming offers an illustrated introduction to such concepts as colors, shapes, numbers, animals, food, and seasons. "Ages two to five." (N Y Times Book Rev)

"The book includes everything needed to make it an anthology of preschool interests and concerns. . . . The very attractive illustrations, done in Fleming's characteristic bold and energetic style, were produced by pouring cotton pulp through hand-cut stencils, the result being simple forms that are attractively textured, with edges that are just fuzzy enough to look soft and friendly." SLJ

★ The **first** day of winter. Henry Holt and Co. 2005 un il $16.95

Grades: PreK K 1   E

1. Snow -- Fiction 2. Winter -- Fiction

ISBN 0-8050-7384-1

LC 2004-22181

A snowman is built and is given special gifts to put on by his best friend each day for ten days with cumulative items of gifts

"Fleming captures the tranquility and light of snowy days with her unique artistic style. Her paper-pulp and stencil illustrations depict a winter wonderland in which vibrant striped scarves, blue mittens, and red hats provide the color in a white, uncluttered landscape. . . . Quietly told and thoughtfully illustrated." SLJ

Fleming, Denise, 1950-

Shout! Shout it out! Henry Holt 2011 40p il $16.99

Grades: PreK K   E

1. Alphabet 2. Counting 3. Mice -- Fiction 4. Vocabulary -- Fiction

ISBN 978-0-8050-9237-0; 0-8050-9237-4

LC 2010011691

Mouse invites the reader to shout out what he or she knows as they review numbers, letters, and easy words.

"Fleming brings new dimension to her signature pulp-painting technique, using swatches of patterned paper collage and marker accents on her figures. . . . Children just learning their colors, animals, and ABCs will be invigorated, and those who have already mastered these basics will still enjoy the top-of-their lungs review." Publ Wkly

Fletcher, Ashlee

My dog, my cat. Tanglewood Press 2011 un il $13.95

Grades: PreK K 1   E
1. Cats -- Fiction 2. Dogs -- Fiction
ISBN 978-1-933718-22-4; 1-933718-22-6;
1933718226; 9781933718224

LC 2010032919

A child points out the differences between a dog and a cat, but finds something they have in common, as well.

"Fletcher outlines the friendly blue dog and orange cat in thick, dark lines and surrounds each picture with a wide squiggly frame. The trim size, simple text, predictable story pattern, and obvious picture clues make this book a fine choice for beginning readers." SLJ

Fletcher, Ralph

The **Sandman**; [by] Ralph Fletcher; illustrated by Richard Cowdrey. Henry Holt and Company 2008 un il $16.95
Grades: PreK K 1 2   E
1. Sleep -- Fiction 2. Bedtime -- Fiction 3. Dragons -- Fiction
ISBN 978-0-8050-7726-1; 0-8050-7726-X

LC 2007002831

A tiny little man discovers that sand made from a dragon's scale will send him to dreamland, and begins carrying this magical sand to children each night to give them the gift of sleep

"Fletcher's smoothly written story flows in a thoroughly plausible way and is beautifully served by Cowdrey's vibrant acrylic paintings." SLJ

Fletcher, Susan

Dadblamed Union Army cow; [by] Susan Fletcher; illustrated by Kimberly Bulcken Root. Candlewick Press 2007 un il $16.99
Grades: 2 3 4 5   E
1. Cattle -- Fiction
ISBN 978-0-7636-2263-3; 0-7636-2263-X

LC 2006051833

During the Civil War, a devoted cow follows her owner when he joins the Union Army and, despite all his efforts to send her home, stays with him and his regiment until the end of the war. Based on a true story

"Root's pencil and watercolor drawings vividly render the Civil War landscape. . . . A terrific read-aloud, and a marvelous approach to history." Publ Wkly

Flood, Nancy Bo

Cowboy up! ride the navajo rodeo. Nancy Bo Flood. WordSong 2013 48 p. (hardcover) $17.95
Grades: 1 2 3 4 5   E
1. Rodeos -- Juvenile literature 2. Navajo Indians -- Juvenile literature
ISBN 1590788931; 9781590788936

LC 2012949009

This book looks at the "history and tradition of the Navajo rodeo" through a day-in-the-life account. "Short narrative poems accompany each spread, recounting the anticipation, determination, danger, and excitement of the day. . . . An announcer guides readers through the book (and each individual event) page by page." (School Library Journal)

Flora, James

The **day** the cow sneezed; story and pictures by James Flora. Enchanted Lion Books 2010 un il $16.95

Grades: K 1 2 3   E
1. Tall tales 2. Cattle -- Fiction 3. Animals -- Fiction 4. Sneezing -- Fiction
ISBN 978-1-59270-097-4; 1-59270-097-7

LC 2010025866

First published 1957 by Harcourt, Brace & World, Inc

A cow sneezes and sets off a series of ridiculous events.

"Flora's illustrations are rich and varied. It doesn't take long to read the text, but children will spend hours with the pictures." Horn Book Guide

Florian, Douglas

★ **Shiver** me timbers; Douglas Florian; illustrated by Robert Neubecker. Beach Lane Books 2012 32 p.
Grades: 2 3 4   E
1. Pirates -- Poetry 2. Pirates -- Juvenile poetry
ISBN 1442413212; 9781442413214

LC 2010048963

In this collection of "pirate poems and paintings" for children by Douglas Florian, illustrated by Robert Neubecker, "readers will meet scoundrels, scalawags, and scurvy dogs (human and canine). They'll partake in battles, treasure hunts, and some pirate-style grub (flounder, anyone?)" (Publisher's note)

Flournoy, Valerie

The **patchwork** quilt; pictures by Jerry Pinkney. Dial Bks. for Young Readers 1985 un il $16.99
Grades: K 1 2 3   E
1. Quilts -- Fiction 2. Family life -- Fiction 3. African Americans -- Fiction
ISBN 0-8037-0097-0

LC 84-1711

Coretta Scott King Award for illustration

Using scraps cut from the family's old clothing, Tanya helps her grandmother and mother make a beautiful quilt that tells the story of her Afro-American family's life

"Plentiful full-page and double-page paintings in pencil, graphite and watercolor are vivid yet delicately detailed. . . . Giving a sense of dramatization to the text, . . . the illustrations provide just the right style and mood for the story." SLJ

Foggo, Cheryl

Dear baobab; written by Cheryl Foggo; illustrated by Qin Leng. Second Story 2011 il $15.95
Grades: K 1 2 3   E
1. Trees -- Fiction 2. Orphans -- Fiction 3. Immigrants -- Fiction 4. Africans -- United States -- Fiction
ISBN 978-1-8971-8791-3; 1-8971-8791-2

"Maiko used to live in a village in Africa. He misses his home and the 2000-year-old baobab tree beneath which he and other village children sat. . . . Now, since the death of his parents, the lonely child lives in what appears to be a North American city. . . . He likes to sit on the stone steps outside his red brick house where a little spruce tree has sprung up. . . . When its roots begin to threaten the foundation of the house, something needs to be done. . . . The tree is moved and replanted elsewhere, just as Maiko has been. Leng's colorful, cartoonlike watercolor illustrations impart a sense of warmth and emotion to this story of a child's bewildering sense of loss and loneliness, as well as new beginnings." SLJ

Fogliano, Julie

★ **And** then it's spring; Julie Fogliano; illustrated by Erin E. Stead. Roaring Brook Press 2012 32 p.

Grades: PreK K 1   E

1. Seeds -- Fiction 2. Spring -- Fiction 3. Gardening -- Fiction 4. Picture books for children 5. Gardens -- Fiction

ISBN 9781596436244

LC 2010049379

This picture book is about a boy who gardens and explores the seasonal changes of "spring. . . . Amid the brown "all around," he plants seeds, and he waits hopefully for the miracle of their growth; he trudges through in the rain and squelches out in the post-rain puddles to check, but there's no sign of progress. As the weeks of waiting go by and the earth remains stubbornly brown, the boy fears that disaster ("maybe it was the birds . . . or maybe it was the bears and all that stomping") has befallen his would-be crop. Eventually, though, spring, real spring, comes, greening up the earth and sprouting the young gardener's young seedlings." (Bulletin of the Center for Children's Books)

If you want to see a whale; Julie Fogliano; Erin E. Stead. 1st ed. Roaring Brook Press 2013 32 p. ill. (hardcover) $16.99

Grades: PreK K 1   E

1. Patience -- Juvenile fiction 2. Whale watching -- Juvenile literature 3. Patience -- Fiction 4. Whale-watching -- Fiction

ISBN 1596437316; 9781596437319

LC 2012012988

This children's book by Julie Fogliano presents a "story about a boy, his animal friends (a basset hound and a bird) and practicing patience. Whale watching requires lots of resolve to avoid distractions like birds, roses, pirate ships, clouds, pelicans and so on. . . . The poem's unresolved ellipses at the conclusion suggest an unending whale hunt, but [illustrator Erin] Stead's final two images silently deliver what we've been waiting for." (Kirkus Reviews)

Foley, Greg

I miss you Mouse. Viking 2010 un il $12.99

Grades: PreK K   E

1. Mice -- Fiction 2. Bears -- Fiction 3. Friendship -- Fiction

ISBN 978-0-670-01238-1; 0-670-01238-6

After receiving a special note from her friend Bear, Mouse searches everywhere for Bear because she has something important to tell him.

"The simple illustrations are as endearing as Mouse and Bear themselves. . . . The sweetness of the characters, their obvious fondness for one another, and the message of friendship freshen the story." SLJ

Purple Little Bird. Balzer + Bray 2011 un il $14.99

Grades: PreK K 1 2   E

1. Birds -- Fiction 2. Color -- Fiction 3. Houses -- Fiction 4. Animals -- Fiction 5. Happiness -- Fiction

ISBN 978-0-06-200828-2; 0-06-200828-5

LC 2010030617

Purple Little Bird leaves his almost-perfect purple home in search of a better place, but although Brown Bear, Yellow Camel, and others live in very nice places, none is quite right for him.

"The economical text packs in a surprising amount. . . . Foley uses a crayon palette to good effect, with warm hues and quick strokes that color outside the friendly cartoon lines and fill the page. . . . Satisfying for the very youngest." Kirkus

Thank you Bear; by Greg Foley. Viking 2007 un il $15.99

Grades: PreK K   E

1. Mice -- Fiction 2. Bears -- Fiction 3. Boxes -- Fiction 4. Gifts -- Fiction

ISBN 978-0-670-06165-5

LC 2006016881

Despite the criticism of others, a bear finds the perfect gift for his mouse friend

"Bear's journey from euphoria to doubt to euphoria again is gently rendered. . . . Pastels provide the backdrop for the text, while Bear and his detractors stand in contrast on a white page, carrying the story with their expressions and body language." SLJ

Other titles about Bear are:

Don't worry Bear (2008)

Good luck Bear (2009)

I miss you Mouse (2010)

★ **Willoughby** & the lion. Bowen Press 2009 un il $17.99; lib bdg $18.89

Grades: PreK K 1 2   E

1. Lions -- Fiction 2. Magic -- Fiction 3. Wishes -- Fiction 4. Friendship -- Fiction

ISBN 978-0-06-154750-8; 0-06-154750-6; 978-0-06-154751-5 lib bdg; 0-06-154751-4 lib bdg

LC 2008000430

When Willoughby moves to a new house far away from his friends, he meets an enchanted lion who shows him what is truly important in life

Foley "scores points for unique visual presentation in this sumptuously produced, two-color book, instantly distinguished by its heavily embossed jacket. . . . With every wish, the ratio of gold to gray increases and Foley's compositions, mingling line drawings with digitally manipulated b&w photos, become more complex. . . . The elegant combination of the two basic colors boosts the visual impact exponentially." Publ Wkly

Another title about Willoughby is:

Willoughby & the moon (2010)

Folgueira, Rodrigo

Ribbit! written by Rodrigo Folguiera; illustrated by Poly Bernatene. Alfred A. Knopf 2013 32 p. (library) $18.99

Grades: PreK K 1   E

1. Pigs -- Fiction 2. Animals -- Fiction 3. Friendship -- Fiction

ISBN 9780307981462; 9780307981479; 9780307981509

LC 2012012718

Ford, Bernette

★ **First** snow; illustrated by Sebastien Braun. Holiday House 2005 un il $16.95

Grades: PreK K 1 2   E

1. Snow -- Fiction 2. Night -- Fiction 3. Rabbits --

Fiction
ISBN 0-8234-1937-1

LC 2004-55257

A family of young rabbits goes into a meadow at night to explore and play in winter's first snow.

"Ford's text has a poetic rhythm that emphasizes the senses as the rabbits explore their wintry world. . . . Braun's illustrations . . . are particularly engaging and complement the story wonderfully." SLJ

No more blanket for Lambkin. Boxer Books 2009 un il $12.95

Grades: PreK   E

1. Ducks -- Fiction 2. Sheep -- Fiction 3. Blankets -- Fiction 4. Friendship -- Fiction

ISBN 978-1-906250-28-7; 1-906250-28-6

"One day Lambkin's friend Ducky comes to visit and decides that they should play laundry day, immediately zeroing in on her friend's much-loved and rather-soiled blanket. Lambkin is none too happy, but she decides it is worth it to play with Ducky. Once the blanket is washed, it's cleaner, but it's also smaller and has some holes. Lambkin is upset, but Ducky surprises her by turning the blanket into a little toy lamb. This is a good story to read to young children when it is nearing the time to give up their blankets. . . . The overall feel is one of gentleness, from the soft style of illustrations to the tone of the dialogue between the two friends." SLJ

No more bottles for Bunny! [by] Bernette Ford and [illustrations by] Sam Williams. Sterling Pub. 2007 un il $12.95

Grades: PreK   E

1. Pigs -- Fiction 2. Ducks -- Fiction 3. Growth -- Fiction 4. Rabbits -- Fiction 5. Bottle feeding -- Fiction

ISBN 978-1-905417-34-6; 1-905417-34-9

LC 2007006856

Bunny gives up his bottle so he can have tea and cookies just like the big kids

"This tough topic is handled subtly but the point is made. Complementing this endearing tale are expressive, bright watercolor illustrations with black outlines that make them jump out from the page." SLJ

No more diapers for Ducky! [by] Bernette Ford and [illustrations by] Sam Williams. Sterling Pub. 2006 un il $12.95

Grades: PreK   E

1. Ducks -- Fiction 2. Toilet training -- Fiction

ISBN 1-905417-08-X

When Piggy can't come out to play because he is using the potty, Ducky decides it's time for him to learn to use the potty too.

"The interaction between these toddlers and their implicit support of one another is charming. The dynamic characters, done in thick charcoal outlines and watercolor, are set against a white background." SLJ

Ford, Christine

Ocean's child; by Chistine Ford and Trish Holland; illustrated by David Diaz. Golden Books 2009 un il $15.99; lib bdg $18.99

Grades: PreK K 1 2   E

1. Inuit -- Fiction 2. Bedtime -- Fiction 3. Marine

animals -- Fiction

ISBN 978-0-375-84752-3; 0-375-84752-9; 978-0-375-95752-9 lib bdg; 0-375-95752-9 lib bdg

"As an Inuit mother paddles her baby home at dusk, she identifies baby ocean animals as they prepare for night. . . . The language is warm and assuring bedtime fare with two free-verse lines introducing each animal, followed by a refrain. . . . Close inspection of mother and child's parkas reveal delicate indigenous designs. . . . The soothing flow of rhythmic language and elegant images creates a serenity just right for bedtimes." Booklist

Fore, S. J.

Read to Tiger; illustrated by R.W. Alley. Viking 2010 un il $15.99

Grades: PreK K 1   E

1. Noise -- Fiction 2. Tigers -- Fiction 3. Books and reading -- Fiction

ISBN 978-0-670-01140-7; 0-670-01140-1

LC 2009-35147

A little boy who wants to read his book keeps being distracted by a tiger who is busy chomping on gum, growling, and practicing karate kicks.

"Fore and Alley play with sound effects and comic expressions, which will please a read-aloud audience. The spare ink drawings expand on Tiger's amusing antics." SLJ

Another title about Tiger is:

Tiger can't sleep (2006)

Foreman, Jack

Say hello; [by] Jack & Michael Foreman. Candlewick Press 2008 un il $15.99

Grades: PreK K 1 2   E

1. Stories in rhyme 2. Dogs -- Fiction 3. Friendship -- Fiction

ISBN 978-0-7636-3657-9; 0-7636-3657-6

"A simple story about loneliness and the power of friendliness. Spare charcoal, pastel, and colored pencil drawings illustrate [this book]." SLJ

Foreman, Mark

Grandpa Jack's tattoo tales; [by] Mark Foreman. Farrar, Straus & Giroux 2007 un il $16

Grades: PreK K 1 2   E

1. Sea stories 2. Tattooing -- Fiction 3. Grandfathers -- Fiction 4. Storytelling -- Fiction

ISBN 978-0-374-32768-2; 0-374-32768-8

LC 2006040853

Chloe loves to spend time at her grandparents' restaurant, where she gets to hear Grandpa Jack's stories about the many tattoos that commemorate events in his life at sea

The illustrations are "done in bright crisp watercolors . . . and the pictures are filled with minute details. . . . Children will relish this amusing tall tale and delight in its visual elements." SLJ

Foreman, Michael

Fortunately, unfortunately. Andersen Press 2011 un il $16.95

Grades: PreK K 1 2   E

1. Adventure fiction

ISBN 0-7613-7460-4; 978-0-7613-7460-2

LC 2010032952

On his way to return his grandmother's umbrella, Milo has a series of unlikely adventures, some more fortunate than others.

"Brightly colored, cartoon-style characters (some large but not too ominous) cavorting across the oversize pages convey the lively action. These eye-catching illustrations and the briskly paced text make this a natural for group sharing." Booklist

Mia's story; a sketchbook of hopes and dreams. Candlewick Press 2006 un il $15.99
Grades: 1 2 3   E
   1. Dogs -- Fiction 2. Flowers -- Fiction
   ISBN 0-7636-3063-2
                       LC 2005-53183
"Mia's father harvests scrap metal from the nearby dump and sells it in the city. When Mia's dog Poco disappears one winter day, she rides a horse into the mountains to look for him, gathers some flowering plants she has never seen before, and brings them back to her village, where they change the landscape and her fortunes for the better. . . . This unusual book offers an engaging story, graceful illustrations, and a rare glimpse of a child's life in contemporary Chile." Booklist

The **littlest** dinosaur's big adventure; written and illustrated by Michael Foreman. Walker & Co. 2009 un il $16.99
Grades: PreK K 1 2   E
   1. Size -- Fiction 2. Dinosaurs -- Fiction
   ISBN 978-0-8027-9545-8; 0-8027-9545-5
                       LC 2008-40297
The littlest dinosaur discovers the advantages of being small as he frolics among the lily pads with his new frog friends, and then bravely finds his way home after getting lost in the woods

"Foreman's soft and gentle cartoon-style illustrations are tailored for young eyes and hearts. Sharing the book aloud will invite discussion as Foreman leaves readers a well-marked trail for inference and reflection, while the twists and turns of the plot will keep even the youngest audiences riveted." SLJ

Another title about the littlest dinosaur is:
The littlest dinosaur (2008)

Foreman, Michael, 1938-
   Friends; Michael Foreman. Lerner Pub. Group 2012 32 p. (trade hard cover: alk. paper) $16.95
Grades: PreK K 1   E
   1. Picture books for children 2. Animal behavior -- Juvenile fiction 3. Conduct of life -- Juvenile fiction 4. Cats -- Fiction 5. Fishes -- Fiction 6. Friendship -- Fiction
   ISBN 1467703176; 9781467703178
                       LC 2011051456
Author Michael Foreman presents a picture book on the relationship between a goldfish and a cat. "Bubble is a goldfish who swims around and around unhappily in his tank. Cat is his friend and wishes he could show him the world. One day, Cat has an idea to set Bubble free. But is Bubble ready to swim off into the world and leave his friend behind?" (Publisher's note)

Forler, Nan
   Bird child. Tundra Books 2009 un il $19.95
Grades: K 1 2 3   E
   1. Bullies -- Fiction 2. Friendship -- Fiction
   ISBN 978-0-88776-894-1; 0-88776-894-6
"Silently, Eliza observes new girl Lainey's ostracism due to her unusual appearance, watching as the bullying increases, refraining from intervention when Lainey is brutally pushed in the snow. The authentic voice portrays bullying's devastating impact. . . . Eliza's mother gently guides her daughter to a moral decision. The symbolism of flight is woven through the narrative. Thisdale's vibrant mixed-media art plays with dominance and size in its compositions; drawings, paintings and digital images add layers of context. . . . This is a sensitive account through an empowered youngster's eyes." Kirkus

Formento, Alison
   These bees count! Alison Formento; illustrated by Sarah Snow. Albert Whitman & Co. 2012 32 p.
Grades: PreK K 1 2   E
   1. Counting 2. Field trips 3. Bees -- Juvenile literature 4. Beekeeping -- Juvenile literature 5. Bees -- Fiction 6. Honeybee -- Fiction 7. Beekeepers -- Fiction 8. School field trips -- Fiction 9. Human-animal communication -- Fiction
   ISBN 0807578681; 9780807578681
                       LC 2011008567
This children's story by Alison Formento, illustrated by Sarah Snow, provides a lesson both in basic counting and in the ecological importance of bees. "How do bees count? The bees at the Busy Bee Farm buzz through the sky as one big swarm, fly over two waving dandelions, find three wild strawberries dripping tasty nectar" As the children in Mr. Tate's class listen, they learn how bees work to produce honey and make food and flowers grow. Bees count--they're important to us all." (Publisher's note)

This tree counts! illustrated by Sarah Snow. Albert Whitman 2010 un il $16.99
Grades: PreK K 1 2   E
   1. Counting 2. Trees -- Fiction 3. Ecology -- Fiction
   ISBN 978-0-8075-7890-2; 0-8075-7890-8
As Mr. Tate's class prepares to plant saplings, they hear the giant oak tree in their schoolyard tell about all the animal life it supports.

"Snow's collage illustrations add texture and natural beauty to the story. . . . The picture of the industrious kids working together in the grassy field under a bright blue sky epitomizes the story's theme of cooperation and friendship." SLJ

Forward, Toby
   What did you do today? the first day of school. illustrated by Carol Thompson. Clarion Books 2004 29p il $15
Grades: PreK K 1   E
   1. School stories 2. Mother-child relationship -- Fiction
   ISBN 0-618-49586-X
                       LC 2004-2467
A child describes the events of the first day of school, from making sandwiches for lunch to holding a parent's hand on the walk home

"The parallels between a child's day at school and his mother's day at work are shown with insight and love in this cleverly designed book. . . . Thompson varies her pen-and-watercolor illustrations in surprising and eye-catching ways." Booklist

Fox, F. G.

Jean Laffite and the big ol' whale; pictures by Scott Cook. Farrar, Straus & Giroux 2003 un il $16

Grades: K 1 2 3   E

1. Tall tales 2. Whales -- Fiction

ISBN 0-374-33669-5

LC 99-43733

When a huge white whale gets stuck between the banks of the Mississippi River causing the water to stop flowing, Jean Laffite finds a way to get the river moving again

"This rollicking good yarn is brought to life with Cook's warm, glowing oil paintings full of action and humor." SLJ

Fox, Lee

Ella Kazoo will not brush her hair; illustrated by Jennifer Plecas. Walker & Co. 2010 un il $15.99; lib bdg $16.89

Grades: PreK K 1   E

1. Stories in rhyme 2. Hair -- Fiction

ISBN 978-0-8027-8836-8; 0-8027-8836-X; 978-0-8027-8755-2 lib bdg; 0-8027-8755-X lib bdg

LC 2009-13329

First published 2007 in Australia

A little girl refuses to brush her hair until it becomes so unruly that it takes over everything.

"Plecas's creative illustrations bring out quirky Ella and her story of stubbornness. The use of rhyme and its overall energy make this book a terrific read-aloud. . . . This book will definitely find fans in libraries serving the young and the young at heart." Libr Media Connect

Fox, Mem

Good night, sleep tight; written by Mem Fox; illustrated by Judy Horacek. Orchard Books 2013 32 p. ill. (reinforced) $16.99

Grades: PreK   E

1. Nursery rhymes -- Fiction 2. Storytelling -- Juvenile fiction 3. Nursery rhymes 4. Stories in rhyme 5. Bedtime -- Fiction 6. Babysitters -- Fiction 7. Bedtime -- Juvenile fiction 8. Babysitters -- Juvenile fiction

ISBN 0545533708; 9780545533706

LC 2012032174

In this book, written by Mem Fox and illustrated by Judy Horacek, Bonnie and Ben's favorite babysitter tells them nursery rhymes at bedtime--including "It's raining! It's pouring! The old man is snoring"; "This little piggy went to market"; and more. Bonnie and Ben enjoy the stories so much that they don't want to go to sleep; they want to hear each one again! Instead the babysitter tells them new nursery rhymes until, finally, all three of them fall fast sleep." (Publisher's note)

★ Hattie and the fox; illustrated by Patricia Mullins. Bradbury Press 1987 un il $16.95; pa $6.99

Grades: PreK K 1 2   E

1. Foxes -- Fiction 2. Chickens -- Fiction

ISBN 0-02-735470-9; 0-689-71611-7 pa

LC 86-18849

First published 1986 in Australia

"Bright, whimsical tissue collage and crayon illustrations add zest to this simple cumulative tale, and reveal more action than is expressed by the text alone." SLJ

★ Hello baby! illustrated by Steve Jenkins. Beach Lane Books 2009 un il $15.99

Grades: PreK K 1   E

1. Stories in rhyme 2. Animals -- Fiction 3. Infants -- Fiction 4. Animals -- Infancy -- Juvenile literature

ISBN 978-1-4169-8513-6; 1-4169-8513-1

LC 2008-34421

A baby encounters a variety of young animals, including a clever monkey, a hairy warthog, and a dusty lion cub, before discovering the most precious creature of all.

This "has all the marks of a lap-sit classic. . . . While Fox is cooing as only she can, Jenkins . . . works his usual magic with cut paper. In many of his large-scale closeups . . . his subjects' big, expressive eyes seem locked in a gaze with the reader." Publ Wkly

Hunwick's egg; illustrated by Pamela Lofts. Harcourt 2005 un il $16

Grades: PreK K 1 2   E

1. Bandicoots -- Fiction

ISBN 0-15-216318-2

LC 2003-16385

When a wild storm sends a beautiful egg to Hunwick the bandicoot's burrow, he decides to give it a home and become its friend.

"This slightly offbeat story . . . is accompanied by glowing watercolor pencil illustrations in orange, pink, and violet tones that showcase the flora and fauna of the Australian landscape, adding an interesting element to this charming title." SLJ

★ Koala Lou; illustrated by Pamela Lofts. Harcourt Brace Jovanovich 1989 un il $16.95; pa $6.99

Grades: PreK K 1 2   E

1. Koalas -- Fiction

ISBN 0-15-200502-1; 0-15-200076-3 pa

LC 88-26810

First published 1988 in Australia

"A reassuring story for the child who feels neglected when siblings arrive." Child Book Rev Serv

Let's count goats! illustrated by Jan Thomas. Beach Lane Books 2010 un il $16.99

Grades: PreK K   E

1. Counting 2. Stories in rhyme 3. Goats -- Fiction

ISBN 978-1-4424-0598-1; 1-4424-0598-8

LC 2009-41627

The reader is invited to count goats of many shapes, sizes, hobbies, and professions.

"The traditional counting format receives a charming update as playfully expressive goats mimic human behavior. . . . Fox, an early-literacy specialist to the core, gets each rhyme just right. . . . Thomas's trademark digital spreads provide punch through chunky, dark outlines and zany off-kilter expressions. . . . These wacky goats guarantee a goofy good time." Kirkus

Night noises; written by Mem Fox; illustrated by Terry Denton. Harcourt Brace Jovanovich 1989 un il $16; pa $6

Grades: PreK K 1 2   E

1. Night -- Fiction 2. Sleep -- Fiction

ISBN 0-15-200543-9; 0-15-257421-2 pa

LC 89-2162

Old Lily Laceby dozes by the fire with her faithful dog Butch Aggie at her feet as strange night noises herald a surprising awakening

"With an almost joltingly bright palette . . . Denton has divided up many of the double-page spreads into three scenes: the main one depicting Lily Laceby and Butch Aggie in various stages of alertness, another showing the chronology of Lily's life, and the third cleverly revealing clues to the mysterious activity outdoors. The text, in Mem Fox's Houdini-like hands, reads beautifully—the language, pacing, tension, and sparks of excitement absolutely at one with the artwork." Horn Book

★ **Sleepy** bears; illustrated by Kerry Argent. Harcourt Brace & Co. 1999 un il $16; pa $6

Grades: PreK K 1 2   E

1. Stories in rhyme 2. Bears -- Fiction 3. Sleep -- Fiction 4. Bedtime -- Fiction 5. Mother and child -- Fiction

ISBN 0-15-202016-0; 0-15-216542-8 pa

LC 98-42640

"Mother Bear tucks in her six cubs, sending them off on dreamy adventures. Baxter dreams of pirates, Bella of the circus, Winifred of the jungle, Tosca of kingdoms, Ali of divine foods, and Baby Bear of moonbeams. . . . The rhymes are well written, and the charming pictures, done in gouache, watercolor, and colored pencil, are full of funny details." SLJ

Sophie; illustrated by Aminah Brenda Lynn Robinson. Harcourt Brace & Co. 1994 un il hardcover o.p. pa $7

Grades: PreK K 1 2   E

1. Grandfathers -- Fiction 2. African Americans -- Fiction

ISBN 0-15-277160-3; 0-15-201598-1 pa

LC 94-1976

First published 1989 in Australia

"The artwork is rich, expressionist, heavily lined oil. . . . The oversized hands depicted in many drawings exemplify the handholding theme, and the sunny hues of earth and garden convey with warmth a loving and extended African-American family." Bull Cent Child Books

★ **Ten** little fingers and ten little toes; [illustrations by] Helen Oxenbury. Harcourt 2008 un il $16

Grades: PreK K   E

1. Stories in rhyme 2. Infants -- Fiction

ISBN 978-0-15-206057-2; 0-15-206057-X

LC 2007-10692

Rhyming text compares babies born in different places and in different circumstances, but they all share the commonality of ten little fingers and ten little toes.

"Given their perfect cadences, the rhymes feel as if they always existed in our collective consciousness and were simply waiting to be written down. . . . Oxenbury . . . once again makes multiculturalism feel utterly natural and chum-

my. As her global brood of toddlers grows . . . readers can savor each addition both as beguiling individualist and giggly, bouncy co-conspirator." Publ Wkly

Tough Boris; illustrated by Kathryn Brown. Harcourt Brace & Co. 1994 un il $16; pa $6

Grades: PreK K 1 2   E

1. Parrots -- Fiction 2. Pirates -- Fiction

ISBN 0-15-289612-0; 0-15-201891-3 pa

LC 92-8015

Boris von der Borch is a tough pirate but he weeps when his parrot dies

"The text is deceptively simple, but the observant child will quickly fill in the details, aptly provided in the illustrations. The reassuring message, although understated, is clear and effective." Horn Book Guide

Two little monkeys; Mem Fox; illustrated by Jill Barton. Beach Lane Books 2010 32 p.

Grades: PreK K 1   E

1. Stories in rhyme 2. Picture books for children 3. Monkeys -- Juvenile fiction 4. Leopards -- Juvenile fiction 5. Leopard -- Fiction 6. Monkeys -- Fiction

ISBN 1416986871; 9781416986874

LC 2009021995

This preschool children's rhyming picture book by Mem Fox, illustrated by Jill Barton, follows two monkeys hiding from a predator "[w]ith the . . . rhythm of a nursery-school finger game. . . .[T]he text . . . [tells] this story of two little monkeys and their escapades on the plains. Playing among the high grasses and dirt, Cheeky and Chee are frightened by something prowling and take refuge in a nearby tree. . . . Hidden in the landscape are hints of the action to come: a tail in the grass or leopard spots in the brush." (Kirkus)

Where is the green sheep? [by] Mem Fox and [illustrated by] Judy Horacek. Harcourt 2004 un il $15

Grades: PreK K 1 2   E

1. Stories in rhyme 2. Sheep -- Fiction

ISBN 0-15-204907-X

LC 2003-4990

A story about many different sheep, and one that seems to be missing.

"Until the lost sheep turns up, children will have fun with the other sheep that make an appearance and perhaps, unbeknownst to them, also get lessons in colors and comparisons. . . . In this neat and satisfying wedding of text and art, the squat, square format uses wool-white backgrounds to display much of the amusing pen-and-watercolor pictures." Booklist

Where the giant sleeps; [by] Mem Fox; pictures by Vladimir Radunsky. Harcourt 2007 un il $16

Grades: PreK K 1 2   E

1. Stories in rhyme 2. Sleep -- Fiction 3. Bedtime -- Fiction

ISBN 978-0-15-205785-5

LC 2006020539

Illustrations and rhyming text portray the different residents of fairyland and where each one goes to sleep.

"The paintings and multifaceted structure of the book inventively translate the puckish text, conjuring misty visions of magical realms." Publ Wkly

The **goblin** and the empty chair; [illustrated by] Leo & Diane Dillon. Beach Lane Books 2009 un il $17.99
Grades: K 1 2 3   E
   1. Monsters -- Fiction
ISBN 978-1-4169-8585-3; 1-4169-8585-9
                          LC 2008041862
A goblin who for many years has been hiding himself so that he does not frighten anyone finally finds a family
"The all-star team of Fox and the Dillons brings poise and sensitivity to this folksy tale of the pitfalls of self-perception. . . . The ink-and-watercolors are rigidly confined to uniform frames, but even these frames are ornately festooned with not-so-monstrous faces, further developing the story's theme." Booklist

A **particular** cow; [by] Mem Fox; illustrated by Terry Denton. Harcourt 2006 un il $16
Grades: PreK K 1 2   E
   1. Cattle -- Fiction
ISBN 0-15-200250-2
                          LC 2004030060
"When a cow decides to take her usual Saturday constitutional, she accidentally steps through a clothesline and ends up with a pair of bloomers covering her head. Unable to see and running off in a panic, the poor bovine wreaks havoc. . . . The story is told with a dry wit and an economy of words, and the illustrations interpret the action with panache." SLJ

Fox, Paula
   Traces. Front Street 2008 un il $16.95
Grades: K 1 2 3   E
   1. Nature -- Fiction
ISBN 978-1-932425-43-7; 1-932425-43-8
                          LC 2006-11739
Looks at the traces left behind by a turtle on the sand, a jet in the sky, and even a long-gone dinosaur in loose soil.
Fox "gives the book an energetic and distilled poetry. . . . The charming medallion sun, torn-paper clouds and watercolor ribbon of the horizon found on these spreads all feel like the naive and studious work of a dedicated seven-year-old. . . . The pictures are much fun and fit the story perfectly." Publ Wkly

Fox, Tamar
   No baths at camp; by Tamar Fox; illustrated by Natalia Vasquez. Kar-Ben Pub. 2013 32 p. col. ill. (reinforced) $17.95
Grades: PreK K 1 2   E
   1. Baths -- Fiction 2. Camps -- Fiction 3. Sabbath -- Fiction 4. Jews -- United States -- Fiction
ISBN 9780761381204
                          LC 2012009498

Frame, Jeron Ashford
   ★ **Yesterday** I had the blues; illustrations by R. Gregory Christie. Tricycle Press 2003 un il $14.95
Grades: K 1 2 3   E
   1. Emotions -- Fiction 2. Family life -- Fiction 3.

African Americans -- Fiction
ISBN 1-58246-084-1
                          LC 2002-155295
A young African American boy ponders a variety of emotions and how different members of his family experience them, from his own blues to his father's grays and his grandmother's yellows
"Vibrant acrylic-and-gouache spreads give rhythm and meaning to this child's interpretation of everyday life, his neighborhood, and his family. The illustrations effectively express each individual's mood and beautifully capture the cultural and artistic aspects of the family's life, while the expressive text is engaging." SLJ

Franceschelli, Christopher
   (oliver) Lemniscaat 2011 un il bd bk $12.95
Grades: PreK K   E
   1. Board books for children 2. Eggs -- Fiction 3. Chickens -- Fiction
ISBN 978-1-9359-5401-9; 1-9359-5401-6
First published in Holland
In this board book, Oliver the egg can't do much but roll from one side to the other, until a miracle happens and he becomes a chick.
This book "contains crisp, attractive text and drawings, using space, light, and dark elegantly. Small children will delight in pulling open the sturdy pages and experiencing Oliver's transformation over and over." SLJ

Franco, Betsy
   Bird songs; a backwards counting book. [by] Betsy Franco; [illustrated by] Steve Jenkins. Margaret K. McElderry Books 2006 un il $16.99
Grades: PreK K 1 2   E
   1. Counting 2. Day -- Fiction 3. Birds -- Fiction 4. Birdsongs -- Fiction
ISBN 0-689-87777-3; 978-0-689-87777-3
                          LC 2004-25056
Throughout the day and into the night various birds sing their songs, beginning with the woodpecker who taps a pole ten times and counting down to the hummingbird who calls once.
"In his vivid, realistic-looking collages, Jenkins uses accurate textures and colors for each species, and creates the appearance of depth, light, and warmth. . . . The writing is lyrical and engaging, and quick 'feathery facts' about the creatures are appended." SLJ

   Double play! monkeying around with addition. illustrations by Doug Cushman. Tricycle Press 2011 un il $15.99; lib bdg $18.99
Grades: PreK K 1   E
   1. Addition 2. School stories 3. Stories in rhyme 4. Play -- Fiction 5. Monkeys -- Fiction
ISBN 978-1-58246-384-1; 1-58246-384-0; 978-1-58246-396-4 lib bdg; 1-58246-396-4 lib bdg
                          LC 2010024347
Monkey friends Jill and Jake play together at recess, and each game they play provides practice in doubling. Each page displays the matching addition problem.
"The large watercolor illustrations show a joyous romp. . . . Young students will enjoy the book for its play aspect, not realizing that the math lesson is built into it." SLJ

Pond circle; illustrated by Stefano Vitale. Margaret K. McElderry Books 2009 un il $16.99

Grades: PreK K 1 2 3   E

1. Animals -- Fiction 2. Ecology -- Fiction 3. Pond ecology -- Fiction 4. Ponds -- Juvenile literature 5. Food chains (Ecology) -- Fiction 6. Food chains (Ecology) -- Juvenile literature

ISBN 978-1-4169-4021-0; 1-4169-4021-9

LC 2008016268

In the pond by Anna's house, a food chain begins with algae which is eaten by a mayfly nymph which is eaten by a beetle which is eaten by a bullfrog.

"Vitale's rich, colorful oil-on-wood illustrations are as poetic as the text in their depiction of the natural world. . . . A clear, child-friendly look at ecology." SLJ

Frank, John

How to catch a fish; by John Frank; illustrated by Peter Sylvada. Roaring Brook Press 2007 un il $17.95

Grades: K 1 2   E

1. Stories in rhyme 2. Fishing -- Fiction

ISBN 978-1-59643-163-8; 1-59643-163-6

LC 2006032184

Rhyming text and illustrations describe the ways fish are caught in various locations around the world

"The handsome, full-page oil paintings are rendered in an impressionistic style that evokes the atmospheres of watery, misty, aquatic environments. . . . Resonating poetic vignettes spawn a glinting, striking catch." Booklist

Franson, Scott E.

Un-brella. Roaring Brook Press 2007 un il $15.95

Grades: PreK K   E

1. Stories without words 2. Magic -- Fiction 3. Weather -- Fiction 4. Umbrellas and parasols -- Fiction

ISBN 978-1-59643-179-9; 1-59643-179-2

LC 2006047658

In this wordless book, a little girl uses her magic umbrella to give her the weather she wants, regardless of what the conditions really are outside.

"The crisp, clean pictures have bright colors, exceptional detail, fun patterns, sly repetition, and heaps of whimsy." SLJ

Fraser, Mary Ann

Heebie-Jeebie Jamboree. Boyds Mills Press 2011 un il

Grades: PreK K 1   E

1. Siblings -- Fiction 2. Festivals -- Fiction 3. Halloween -- Fiction

ISBN 1-59078-857-5; 978-1-59078-857-8

"Dressed as a witch and a ghost, Sam and Daphne pull tickets out of thin air to the Heebie-Jeebie Jamboree on Halloween night. They are treated to a magical, good time. . . . Then, in the midst of the festivities, Sam goes missing. . . . The full-bleed illustrations in vibrant colors feature Halloween creatures of all sorts (but none frightening), and the pages are packed with action and energy. Children will love poring over the many details." SLJ

Pet shop lullaby. Boyds Mills Press 2009 un il $16.95

Grades: PreK K   E

1. Pets -- Fiction 2. Animals -- Fiction 3. Bedtime

-- Fiction

ISBN 978-1-59078-618-5; 1-59078-618-1

LC 2009019661

When the pet store closes for the night, a hamster's activities keep the other animals awake as they try to think of some way to put him to sleep.

"Fraser's tale is brief and to the point, and the comical gouache illustrations infuse energy into the telling. Fun touches abound." SLJ

Another title about the pet shop is:

Pet shop follies (2010)

Frasier, Debra

★ **On** the day you were born. Harcourt Brace Jovanovich 1991 un il $16

Grades: K 1 2 3 4   E

1. Childbirth

ISBN 0-15-302160-8

LC 90-36816

This combination of text and paper-collage graphics depicts the earth's preparation for, and celebration of, the birth of a newborn baby

"The text reads like unrhymed poetry, and both parents and educators will find themselves wanting to share this book over and over with individuals and with groups. A three-page appendix that includes miniature versions of each spread elaborates on natural phenomena for older readers—migrating animals, spinning Earth, rising tide, falling rain, growing trees, and more." SLJ

★ **A birthday** cake is no ordinary cake; written and illustrated by Debra Frasier. Harcourt 2006 un il $16

Grades: PreK K 1 2   E

1. Cake -- Fiction 2. Year -- Fiction 3. Birthdays -- Fiction

ISBN 978-0-15-205742-8; 0-15-205742-0

A lyrical recipe using the changes in the natural world to explain to a child the time that passes between one birthday and the next. Includes recipe for more traditional birthday cake.

"Pop-off-the-page, vibrant-colored cut-paper collage illustrations capture the fanciful and factual concepts." SLJ

A fabulous fair alphabet. Beach Lane Books 2010 un il $16.99

Grades: PreK K 1   E

1. Alphabet 2. Fairs -- Fiction

ISBN 978-1-4169-9817-4; 1-4169-9817-9

LC 2009038329

Letters of the alphabet in various graphic styles accompany words associated with fairs.

"Despite the flat graphic style, the pages seem to sparkle and blink with the bright lights of a midway. The endpapers are bold collages of photos of signs at fairs. As alphabet books go, this one is delightful. As graphic art goes, it's alive with evocative, almost magical examples." SLJ

Frazee, Marla

★ **Boot** & Shoe; Marla Frazee. Beach Lane Books 2012 40 p. (hardcover) $16.99

Grades: PreK K 1 2   E

1. Dogs -- Juvenile fiction 2. Solitude -- Juvenile fiction 3. Squirrels -- Juvenile fiction 4. Dogs -- Fiction 5.

Solitude -- Fiction
ISBN 1442422475; 9781442422476

LC 2011035990

In this children's picture book by Marla Frazee "Two adorably floppy dogs confront unexpected change.... Boot and Shoe were born into the same litter, and now they live in the same house. . . . But they spend their days apart--Boot on the back porch because he's a back porch kind of dog, and Shoe on the front porch because he's a front porch kind of dog. . . . Then a crazy neighborhood squirrel arrives . . . and everything goes topsy-turvy!" (Publisher's note)

★ **Roller** coaster. Harcourt 2003 un il
Grades: PreK K 1 2   E
1. Roller coasters
ISBN 0-15-204554-6

LC 2002-7805

Twelve people set aside their fears and ride a roller coaster, including one who has never done so before. "Ages three to seven." (Christ Sci Monit)

"Frazee does an extraordinary job of conveying motion by the placement of her images, her use of white space, bright colors, and swooshing speed lines. . . . What will keep children coming back for extra looks, however, is Frazee's clever, dramatic depiction of the 12 riders and their wildly and amusingly different reactions to the stomach-churning experience." Booklist

★ **Santa** Claus, the world's number one toy expert. Harcourt 2005 $16
Grades: PreK K 1 2   E
1. Christmas -- Fiction 2. Santa Claus -- Fiction
ISBN 0-15-204970-3; 0152049703

LC 2004005228

Santa Claus has his own ways of knowing more about children and toys than anyone else in the world. "Ages four to eight." (Bull Cent Child Books)

"Frazee, a master at creating scenes and moods in her energetic drawings and spare text, fills these pages with details and vignettes that readers will want to explore repeatedly." SLJ

★ **Walk** on! a guide for babies of all ages. Harcourt, Inc. 2006 un il $16
Grades: PreK K 1 2   E
1. Infants -- Fiction 2. Walking -- Fiction 3. Infants -- Juvenile literature
ISBN 0-15-205573-8

LC 2004-29895

"In this how-to for little ones, a baby learns to walk for the first time. . . . The pencil-and-gouache art has the delightful feel of self-help pamphlets from an earlier era. . . . This is one of those rare books that speaks to crawling and walking babies who like to look at pictures of creatures like themselves, preschoolers who enjoy stories about what they were like when they were little, and older children and adults who will appreciate the wry humor." SLJ

★ The **boss** baby. Beach Lane Books 2010 un il $16.99
Grades: PreK K 1   E
1. Infants -- Fiction
ISBN 978-1-4424-0167-9; 1-4424-0167-2

From the moment he arrives, it is obvious that the new baby is boss and he gets whatever he wants, from drinks made-to-order around the clock to his executive gym.

"Cartoon vignettes in pencil-streaked gouache hum with a funky, retro style seen in sleek furnishings and the '50s fashions of the accommodating but increasingly exhausted parents. . . . Clever and empathetic." Publ Wkly

★ A **couple** of boys have the best week ever; [by] Marla Frazee. Harcourt 2008 32p il $16
Grades: K 1 2 3   E
1. Beaches -- Fiction 2. Vacations -- Fiction 3. Friendship -- Fiction 4. Grandparents -- Fiction
ISBN 978-0-15-206020-6

LC 2006-25781

A Caldecott Medal honor book, 2009

Friends James and Eamon enjoy a wonderful week at the home of Eamon's grandparents during summer vacation. "Ages six to nine." (Bull Cent Child Books)

"After Eamon enrolls in nature camp, he spends nights with his grandparents, Bill and Pam, at their beach cottage. Eamon's friend James joins the sleepover. . . . Humorous contradictions arise between the hand-lettered account . . . and voice-bubble exchanges between the boys. . . . Frazee's narrative resembles a tongue-in-cheek travel journal, with plenty of enticing pencil and gouache illustrations of the characters knocking about the shoreline." Publ Wkly

Frazier, Craig
Bee & Bird. Roaring Brook Press 2011 un il $16.99
Grades: PreK K 1   E
1. Adventure fiction 2. Stories without words 3. Bees -- Fiction 4. Birds -- Fiction 5. Travel -- Fiction
ISBN 978-1-59643-660-2; 1-59643-660-3

LC 2010013012

In this wordless picture book, a bumblebee and a bird embark on a travel adventure.

Frazier "uses perspective to great advantage in creating mystery and drawing readers into the story. . . . The vividly colored artwork will immediately snag young readers' attention; the perplexing views will entice them into the plot; and subtle clues . . . will help them make sense of the details in subsequent viewings." Booklist

★ **Hank** finds inspiration; [by] Craig Frazier. Roaring Brook Press 2008 un il $16.95
Grades: K 1 2   E
1. Snakes -- Fiction
ISBN 978-1-59643-358-8; 1-59643-358-2

LC 2007047919

Hank the snake and his human friend, Stanley, each go to the city in search of inspiration, but Hank's journey is a failure until he returns home

"Frazier's crisp graphics draw the eye to varied perspectives with bold splashes of color and sharply defined silhouettes and shadings. An 'inspired' addition for all libraries." SLJ

Lots of dots. Chronicle Books 2010 un il
Grades: PreK K 1   E
1. Stories in rhyme 2. Shape -- Fiction
ISBN 0811877159; 9780811877152

Circular shapes are spotted in familiar objects and everyday situations. Buttons are dots. Wheels are dots. Stars are dots. Ladybugs have dots and so do the fried eggs on your plate. Lots of dots!

"Frazier maintains an upbeat tone with tight rhyme and meter throughout; with the exception of one night scene, with dots for stars, the backgrounds are plain white, giving the pages a freshly washed, contemporary feel." Publ Wkly

Frederick, Heather Vogel

Babyberry pie; [illustrations by] Amy Schwartz. Harcourt Children's Books 2010 un il $16.99

Grades: PreK K 1   **E**
1. Stories in rhyme 2. Bedtime -- Fiction 3. Infants -- Fiction

ISBN 978-0-15-205927-9; 0-15-205927-X

In illustrations and rhyming text, gives the recipe for making "babyberry pie," from picking a baby from the babyberry tree and popping him in the tub to putting powdered sugar on his nose and toes and tucking him into pie crust covers.

"Schwartz brings out her best with these vivid gouache and pen-and-ink illustrations of a family getting a toddler ready for bed. . . . Frederick's rhyming text, repetition, and wordplay amplify the fun in this yummy mix of old-fashioned cozy and modern setting." SLJ

Hide-and-squeak; illustrated by C.F. Payne. Simon & Schuster Books for Young Readers 2011 un il $16.99

Grades: PreK K 1   **E**
1. Stories in rhyme 2. Mice -- Fiction 3. Bedtime -- Fiction 4. Father-child relationship -- Fiction

ISBN 978-0-689-85570-2; 0-689-85570-2

LC 2008039648

A mouse baby leads his father on a merry game of hide-and-squeak at bedtime.

"Payne's settings, amplifying the baby mouse's inexhaustible energy and giddy transgressiveness, while buoying Frederick's . . . rock solid, somewhat quaint rhymes. . . . The spreads are small masterpieces of composition, yet they never feel static; rather, it's as if someone has hit the pause button to briefly allow readers to savor the image's beauty before the story continues on its rollicking way to the bedtime wrap-up." Publ Wkly

Freedman, Claire

Gooseberry Goose; illustrated by Vanessa Cabban. Tiger Tales 2003 un il $15.95

Grades: PreK K 1 2   **E**
1. Geese 2. Winter 3. Forest animals 4. Geese -- Fiction 5. Winter -- Fiction 6. Animals -- Fiction

ISBN 1-58925-030-3

LC 2003-12960

As Gooseberry Goose practices flying on a beautiful fall morning, his friends are preparing for winter, causing Gooseberry to wonder if there is something else he should be doing

"The text is brought to life through the illustrations, which are loose and lovely. Vibrant red and gold leaves enliven the pages. Gooseberry is a bundle of expression. . . . Readers will be captivated by this irrepressible gosling's infectious charm." SLJ

Freedman, Deborah

★ **Blue** chicken. Viking 2011 un il $15.99

Grades: PreK K 1   **E**
1. Chickens -- Fiction 2. Farm life -- Fiction 3. Domestic animals -- Fiction

ISBN 978-0-670-01293-0; 0-670-01293-9

LC 2011001502

An enterprising chicken attempts to help an artist paint the barnyard and accidentally turns the whole picture blue.

"Watercolor washes and splashes, from pale blue to dark, create wonderful, wet patterns; their liquid edges contrast alluringly with fine pencil lines and shadings. . . . Delicate and durable, visually sophisticated yet friendly: simply exquisite." Kirkus

Freeman, Don

★ **Corduroy**; 40th anniversary edition; Viking Press 2008 32p il $19.99

Grades: PreK K 1   **E**
1. Teddy bears -- Fiction

ISBN 978-0-670-06336-9; 0-670-06336-3

A reissue of the title first published 1968

A toy bear in a department store wants a number of things, but when a little girl finally buys him he finds what he has always wanted most of all. This edition includes copies of letters and the original manuscript.

"The art and story are direct and just right for the very young who like bears and escalators." Book World

Another title about Corduroy is:

A pocket for Corduroy (1978)

Earl the squirrel. Viking 2005 un il $15.99

Grades: PreK K 1   **E**
1. Squirrels -- Fiction

ISBN 0-670-06019-4

LC 2005-03929

Earl the squirrel learns to gather acorns on his own.

"The pictures are full of energy and detail, and Earl is both cheeky and endearing. . . . The story is gentle, innocent, and funny." SLJ

Quiet! there's a canary in the library; by Don Freeman. Viking Children's Books 2007 un il $15.99

Grades: PreK K 1   **E**
1. Animals -- Fiction 2. Libraries -- Fiction

ISBN 978-0-670-06230-0; 0-670-06230-8

LC 2006-37904

A reissue of the title first published 1969 by Golden Gate

Cary imagines a special day at the library when she invites only animals and birds to browse.

"Freeman contrasts more detailed drawings of the actual library with childlike crayoned depictions of Cary's daydreamed adventures." Horn Book Guide

Freeman, Martha

Mrs. Wow never wanted a cow; by Martha Freeman; illustrated by Steven Salerno. Random House 2006 un il (Beginner books) $8.99; lib bdg $11.99

Grades: K 1 2   **E**
1. Cats -- Fiction 2. Dogs -- Fiction 3. Cattle -- Fiction

ISBN 0-375-83418-4; 0-375-93418-9 lib bdg

LC 2005006000

When Mrs. Wow takes in a stray cow, her lazy dog and cat hope to train the new household member to catch mice and intimidate the mailman

"The mostly one-syllable words with regular phonetic patterns are spare and natural, and Salerno's brightly colored cartoon illustrations amplify the text's humor." SLJ

Freeman, Tor

Olive and the big secret; Tor Freeman. Candlewick Press 2012 32 p. $15.99

Grades: PreK K 1 2   E

ISBN 076366149X; 9780763661496

LC 2012938740

French, Jackie

Christmas wombat; by Jackie French; illustrated by Bruce Whatley. Clarion Books 2012 32 p. (hardback) $16.99

Grades: PreK K 1 2   E

1. Holidays -- Fiction 2. Animals -- Juvenile literature 3. Human-animal relationship -- Fiction 4. Diaries -- Fiction 5. Wombats -- Fiction 6. Christmas -- Fiction 7. Wombats -- Juvenile fiction

ISBN 0547868723; 9780547868721

LC 2011052112

Author Jackie French's story centers on a wombat. "A bearlike Australian animal, the wombat likes to sleep, hide in holes and eat. This wombat especially likes to eat carrots, and the . . . plot focuses on the wombat's intensive search for more and more carrots." The book "describes the wombat's activities and its discovery of carrots set out for some 'strange creatures' (Santa's reindeer). The wombat chomps every carrot in sight, stows away in Santa's sleigh and beats the reindeer to their carrot treats at stops around the world." (Kirkus Reviews)

Diary of a baby wombat; written by Jackie French; illustrated by Bruce Whatley. Clarion Books 2010 un il $16.99

Grades: PreK K 1 2   E

1. Wombats -- Fiction

ISBN 978-0-547-43005-8; 0-547-43005-1

LC 2009050452

Through a week of diary entries, a wombat describes his life of sleeping, playing, and helping his mother look for a bigger hole in which to make their home.

"Economy of voice is reflected in the understated illustrations. . . . This will be read over and over, providing new laughs each time." Horn Book

★ **Diary** of a wombat; illustrated by Bruce Whatley. Clarion Bks. 2003 un il $14

Grades: PreK K 1 2   E

1. Wombats -- Fiction

ISBN 0-618-38136-8

LC 2003-829

First published 2002 in Australia

In his diary, a wombat describes his life of eating, sleeping, and getting to know some new human neighbors

The story is presented in "simple sentences and hilarious yet realistic acrylic illustrations. . . . Whatley gives a sublime balance of the adorable charm of the creature, along with its drawbacks as an acquaintance." SLJ

Another title about the wombat is:

Diary of a baby wombat (2010)

Pete the sheep-sheep; illustrated by Bruce Whatley. Clarion Books 2005 32p il $14

Grades: PreK K 1 2   E

1. Dogs -- Fiction 2. Sheep -- Fiction

ISBN 0-618-56862-X

LC 2004-30935

First published 2004 in Australia with title: Pete the sheep

The sheep-shearers in Shaggy Gully all have a sheep dog, but the new guy Shaun uses an extremely polite sheep named Pete.

"Cleanly designed illustrations work well with French's understated text. Strong lines focus attention on the expressive characters." Horn Book Guide

French, Vivian

The **Daddy** Goose treasury; as told to Vivian French; illustrated by AnnaLaura Cantone . . . [et al.] Scholastic 2006 93p il $18.99

Grades: K 1 2 3   E

1. Nursery rhymes -- Fiction

ISBN 0-439-79608-3

"French includes 12 untold stories that give background and context for such familiar rhymes as Little Miss Muffet, Georgie Porgie, Old King Cole, and Hickory, Dickory, Dock. . . . Four European illustrators contribute lively, colorful, and witty illustrations that adeptly articulate the cozy narratives." SLJ

★ **Yucky** worms; illustrated by Jessica Ahlberg. Candlewick Press 2010 28p il $16.99; pa $6.99

Grades: PreK K 1 2   E

1. Worms -- Fiction 2. Gardening -- Fiction 3. Grandmothers -- Fiction 4. Earthworms -- Juvenile literature

ISBN 978-0-7636-4446-8; 0-7636-4446-3; 978-0-7636-5817-5 pa

LC 2009-17307

While helping Grandma in the garden, a child learns about the important role of the earthworm in helping plants grow.

"The cheerful pencil-and-gouache artwork shows scenes both above and below the ground and weaves facts into each image, as well as humorous cartoon speech bubbles. . . . Friendly and interactive, this is a great choice for sharing at home and in the classroom." Booklist

Freymann, Saxton

★ **Fast** food; written and illustrated by Saxton Freymann. Arthur A. Levine Books 2006 32p il $12.99

Grades: PreK K 1 2 3   E

1. Transportation

ISBN 0-439-11019-X

"This picture book takes a theme (here, transportation) and illustrates it with exceptionally clear color photos of ephemeral, sometimes whimsical sculptures created from fruits and vegetables. As quietly witty as its title, the book is narrated by a little mushroom man who suggests different ways of getting about. . . . The playful text gallops along smoothly in rhymed couplets, while the illustrations work their inimitable charm." Booklist

★ **Food** for thought; the complete book of concepts for growing minds. written and illustrated by Saxton Freymann. Arthur A. Levine Books 2005 61p il $14.95

Grades: PreK K 1 2 3   E

1. Alphabet 2. Concepts 3. Counting

ISBN 0-439-11018-1

This "covers basic shapes, colors, numbers, letters, and opposites—all introduced through images of artfully manipulated fruits and vegetables. . . . The simple, clean design is ideal for demonstrating the concepts. . . . But it's the playful, wonderfully clever transformation of familiar foods that will win an audience." Booklist

Friedlaender, Linda K.

Look! look! look! by Nancy Elizabeth Wallace with Linda K. Friedlaender; illustrated by Nancy Elizabeth Wallace. Marshall Cavendish 2006 un il $16.95

Grades: K 1 2 3   E

1. Art -- Fiction 2. Mice -- Fiction

ISBN 978-0-7614-5282-9; 0-7614-5282-6

LC 2005016934

Three mice "borrow" a postcard which is a reproduction of a painting, and from it they learn about color, pattern, line, and shape. Includes instructions for making and sending a postcard.

This picture book tells the story of three mice exploring a sculpture exhibit in a museum. "Three frisky mice, sensibilities honed by an exposure to painting in [Linda K. Friedlaender's] 'Look! Look! Look!' (2006), give 3-D art a similarly close once over. The story is centered on an abstract work in slate by Barbara Hepworth in the Yale Center for British Art (where Friedlaender is a curator), but it features sharp color photos of 20 other sculptures from as many eras and cultures." (Kirkus)

"This is not only an amusing, creative story, but also an adventure into art that encourages originality while inspiring creativity." SLJ

Friedman, Caitlin

How do you feed a hungry giant? a munch-and-sip pop-up book. illustrated by Shaw Nielsen. Workman 2011 un il $18.95

Grades: PreK K 1 2   E

1. Pop-up books 2. Giants -- Fiction

ISBN 978-0-7611-5752-6; 0-7611-5752-2

"A gentle giant clothed in patchwork clothing appears in a boy's front yard carrying a sign that says, 'Food Please.' The giant gobbles an entire pizza, slurps up 15 bottles of chocolate milk from a kiddie pool, and consumes 197 cookies, but remains hungry. Luckily, the boy's mother is willing to help. The well-integrated interactive elements—popups, tabs, and flaps—add an extra touch of fun to this lighthearted story." Publ Wkly

Friedman, Darlene

Star of the Week; a story of love, adoption, and brownies with sprinkles. story by Darlene Friedman; illustrations by Roger Roth. HarperCollins 2009 un il $17.99; lib bdg $18.89

Grades: PreK K 1 2 3   E

1. School stories 2. Adoption -- Fiction 3. Chinese Americans -- Fiction

ISBN 978-0-06-114136-2; 0-06-114136-4; 978-0-06-114137-9 lib bdg; 0-06-114137-2 lib bdg

LC 2008-22581

As her turn to be "Star of the Week" in her kindergarten class approaches, Cassidy-Li puts together a poster with pictures of her family, friends, and pets, and wonders about her birthparents in China.

"Roth's vibrant illustrations capture the personality of Cassidy-Li, the six-year-old narrator who tells her story in unaffected language that will appeal to children." SLJ

Friedman, Ina R.

How my parents learned to eat; illustrated by Allen Say. Houghton Mifflin 1984 30p il hardcover o.p. pa $6.99

Grades: K 1 2 3   E

1. Dining -- Fiction

ISBN 0-395-35379-3; 0-395-44235-4 pa

LC 83-18553

An American sailor courts a Japanese girl and each tries, in secret, to learn the other's way of eating

"The illustrations have precise use of line and soft colors, and the composition is economical. A warm and gentle story of an interracial family." Bull Cent Child Books

Friend, Catherine

Eddie the raccoon; illustrated by Wong Herbert Yee. Candlewick Press 2004 40p il (Brand new readers) hardcover o.p. pa $5.99

Grades: K 1 2   E

1. Raccoons -- Fiction

ISBN 0-7636-2331-8; 0-7636-2334-2 pa

LC 2003-69717

"Pleasant watercolors . . . provide ample visual clues to the accompanying sentence—usually comprising four or five basic vocabulary words. . . . Each setup packs a gently humorous punch that's easy enough for children to grasp and sweet enough to make their adult helpers chuckle." Booklist

The **perfect** nest; illustrated by John Manders. Candlewick Press 2007 un il $16.99

Grades: K 1 2   E

1. Cats -- Fiction 2. Chickens -- Fiction

ISBN 978-0-7636-2430-9; 0-7636-2430-6

LC 2006047518

Jack the cat gets much more than he bargained for when he decides to build the perfect nest to attract the perfect chicken

This is "highly comical yet heartwarming tale. . . . Manders's gouache illustrations are a perfect complement to the text." SLJ

Friester, Paul

Owl howl; [illustrated by] Philippe Goossens; [English translation by Erica Stenfalt] NorthSouth Books 2011 un il (Tuff books) pa $6.95

Grades: PreK K   E

1. Owls -- Fiction 2. Forest animals -- Fiction

ISBN 978-0-7358-4017-1; 0-7358-4017-2

"In response to a little owl's howling, various forest animals take turns trying to determine the problem and stop her tears. The bulbous-eyed owl is uncommonly sympathetic thanks to Goossens's illustrations on sturdy, glossy pages. When the owl is back under her mom's wings, readers will exhale with relief—before they grin at the punch line." Horn Book Guide

Frisch, Aaron

A **night** on the range; written by Aaron Frisch; illustrated by Chris Sheban. Creative Editions 2010 un il $25.65

Grades: K 1 2 3   E
1. Fear -- Fiction 2. Camping -- Fiction 3. Cowhands -- Fiction 4. Imagination -- Fiction
ISBN 978-1-56846-205-9; 1-56846-205-0
LC 2008016595
"Young cowboy-wannabe Cole daydreams about roping strays and hunting down rustlers. He's beyond excited for his first camping experience—that is, until it gets dark. . . . Dreamy, expansive illustrations distinguish between Cole's wild imagination and his reality—a suburban backyard—in this well-done ode to self-fulfillment." Horn Book Guide

Fucile, Tony
★ **Let's** do nothing! Candlewick Press 2009 un il $16.99; pa $6.99
Grades: PreK K 1 2   E
1. Imagination -- Fiction
ISBN 978-0-7636-3440-7; 0-7636-3440-9; 978-0-7636-5269-2 pa
LC 2008-935654
"Frankie and Sal are bored . . . and now there is nothing—which is exactly what they will attempt to do for ten whole seconds. In a series of increasingly hilarious spreads, the two boys . . . are deterred everytime by Frankie's overactive imagination. . . . The imagined scenes employ vibrant color, in effective contrast with the reality sequences. . . . Fucile's figures, ink line with acrylic paints, . . . have a retro touch in their period hues and springy drafting." Bull Cent Child Books

Fuge, Charles
Astonishing animal ABC. Sterling 2011 un il $14.95
Grades: PreK K 1   E
1. Alphabet 2. Stories in rhyme
ISBN 978-1-4027-8645-7; 1-4027-8645-X
An alphabet book featuring rhyming text and all sorts of animals.
"The rhyming text is abundant with adjectives and alliteration. Fuge's animals communicate a variety of emotions (fear, happiness and worry), but when they gather together to see the animal that starts with the letter Z zoom past them, they all look surprised. Readers will likely express a similar sentiment." SLJ

Fuller, Sandy Ferguson
My cat, coon cat; illustrated by Jeannie Brett. Islandport 2011 il $17.95
Grades: PreK K 1 2   E
1. Stories in rhyme 2. Cats -- Fiction
ISBN 978-1-934031-32-2; 1-934031-32-1
When a young girl moves into a new home, she slowly wins the affection of a shy Maine coon cat, as he meets the girl's kitten, chases dragonflies, and explores the neighborhood.
"The illustrations are full of color and character, capturing with equal charm the bucolic background and the winsome feline. . . . Any reader who has ever known the love of a cat will find much to relate to in this cozy book." SLJ

Funke, Cornelia Caroline
Princess Pigsty; by Cornelia Funke; illustrated by Kerstin Meyer; translated by Chantal Wright. Chicken House/Scholastic 2007 un il $16.99

Grades: K 1 2   E
1. Fairy tales 2. Princesses -- Fiction
ISBN 0-439-88554-X
LC 2006006294
"Sick of her pampered existence, Princess Isabella tosses aside her tiara, declaring, 'I want to get dirty!' The outraged king prescribes tours of duty in the kitchens and pigsty, but Isabella merely revels in the good, honest work and good, honest mess. . . . Most kids will relate to her spirit of rebellion, especially as embodied in Meyer's ebullient watercolors of the beaming, disheveled girl." Booklist

★ The **princess** knight; by Cornelia Funke; illustrations by Kerstin Meyer; translated by Anthea Bell. Chicken House/Scholastic 2004 un il $15.95
Grades: PreK K 1 2   E
1. Princesses -- Fiction 2. Knights and knighthood -- Fiction
ISBN 0-439-53630-8
Original German edition 2001
"Raised by a widowed king, Princess Violetta is put through the same paces (swordplay, riding, jousting) as her older, brawnier brothers. Her practice pays off when her father holds a tournament—with Violetta as the grand prize—and she handily scuttles his plans. Bell translates Funke's story from the German with aplomb . . . and Meyer's effervescent line-and-watercolor artwork, as funny as it is lovely, stretches across each spread in horizontal strips." Booklist

The **wildest** brother; [by] Cornelia Funke; illustrated by Kerstin Meyer; translated by Oliver Latsch. The Chicken House/Scholastic 2006 un il $16.99
Grades: PreK K 1 2   E
1. Siblings -- Fiction
ISBN 0-439-82862-7
When it comes to protecting his big sister, Anna, young Ben is as brave as a lion. But when the day is over and darkness falls, Ben suddenly doesn't feel quite so brave. Sometimes, he realizes, it's Anna who does the protecting
"Wright's wonderfully expressive acrylic paintings elevate this simple glimpse of sibling play into something special. The animated scenes, filled with Ben's imagined foes, perfectly capture the wild-eyed, physical fun." Booklist

Fusco Castaldo, Nancy
★ **Pizza** for the queen; by Nancy Castaldo; illustrated by Mélisande Potter. Holiday House 2005 un il $16.95
Grades: PreK K 1 2 3   E
1. Pizza -- Fiction 2. Cooking -- Fiction
ISBN 0-8234-1865-0
LC 2004-58134
In 1889 Napoli, Italy, Raffaele Esposito prepares a special pizza for Queen Margherita. Based on a true story. Includes a recipe.
"The richly toned, detailed illustrations . . . extend the action and the sense of history in busy scenes in the kitchen and on the picturesque streets." Booklist

Fyleman, Rose, 1877-1957
Mice; Rose Fyleman; illustrated by Lois Ehlert. Beach Lane Books 2012 p. cm.
Grades: PreK K 1   E
1. Stories in rhyme 2. Mice -- Juvenile fiction 3.

Picture books for children 4. Mice -- Fiction
ISBN 9781442456846; 9781442456860

LC 2011020555

In this book, "a 1932 poem from [Rose] Fyleman (1877–1957) serves as a springboard for [Lois] Ehlert's" artwork. As "the mice scamper across the pages ('They nibble things they shouldn't touch') Ehlert labels the items they find, turning the story into an introduction to art supplies, household items, and food items that range from mangos and avocadoes to cereal and desserts." (Publishers Weekly)

Gag, Wanda

★ **Millions** of cats. Putnam 2004 un il $13.99
Grades: PreK K 1   E
1. Cats -- Fiction
ISBN 0-399-23315-6

A reissue of the title first published 1928 by Coward-McCann

A Newbery Medal honor book, 1929

It is "a perennial favorite among children and takes a place of its own, both for the originality and strength of its pictures and the living folktale quality of its text." NY Her Trib Books

Gaiman, Neil

Crazy hair; illustrated by Dave McKean. HarperCollins Publishers 2009 un il $18.99; lib bdg $19.89
Grades: PreK K 1 2 3   E
1. Stories in rhyme 2. Hair -- Fiction
ISBN 978-0-06-057908-1; 0-06-057908-0; 978-0-06-057909-8 lib bdg; 0-06-057909-9 lib bdg

LC 2008012791

Bonnie encounters all sorts of exotic animals and marvelous things inside a man's crazy hair.

This is a "chaotic picture book popping with bright collage and multimedia imagery. . . . Each page is a veritable feast for the eyes, with frazzled clumps of hair competing for attention with outlandish elements. . . . There's something a little unsettling and unhinged about the imagery, just on the safe side of nightmarish; but the text, for the most part, is delightful and glib." Booklist

Instructions; written by Neil Gaiman; illustrated by Charles Vess. Harper 2010 un il $14.99; lib bdg $15.89
Grades: 1 2 3 4   E
1. Poetry 2. Voyages and travels -- Poetry
ISBN 978-0-06-196030-7; 0-06-196030-6; 978-0-06-196031-4 lib bdg; 0-06-196031-4 lib bdg

The poem first published 2000 in A Wolf at the Door published by Simon & Schuster

Go on a journey to unknown, but strangely familiar, lands and then travel home again.

"Vess's compositions are distinguished by elegant, winding lines-gnarled vines, plumes of smoke, dragon tails-and intimate frames that evoke moments of gentle wisdom. Young readers should relish the chimerical vision while older Gaiman fans should grasp the underlying suggestion that the compass used to navigate fairy tales can also guide us in the real world." Publ Wkly

The **dangerous** alphabet; by Neil Gaiman; illustrated by Gris Grimly. HarperCollinsPublishers 2008 un il $17.99; lib bdg $18.89

Grades: 2 3 4 5   E
1. Stories in rhyme 2. Pirates -- Fiction 3. Alphabet -- Fiction 4. Monsters -- Fiction 5. Alphabet -- Juvenile literature
ISBN 978-0-06-078333-4; 0-06-078333-8; 978-0-06-078334-1 lib bdg; 0-06-078334-6 lib bdg

LC 2007-10893

As two children and their pet gazelle sneak out of the house in search of treasure, they come across a world beneath the city that is inhabited with monsters and pirates.

"A sophisticated, interactive alphabet tale in which even the letters break the expected pattern. . . . Skillful narrative and visual storytelling combine to present a complex adventure that unravels through multilayered text and illustrations, challenging readers to ponder the numerous levels of plot. . . . The gothic illustrations, done in sepia tones and faded color washes, ensure that readers remain riveted throughout the story." SLJ

The **wolves** in the walls; written by Neil Gaiman; illustrated by Dave McKean. HarperCollins Pubs. 2003 un il $16.99
Grades: 2 3 4   E
1. Wolves -- Fiction
ISBN 0-380-97827-X

LC 2002-192194

Lucy is sure there are wolves living in the walls of her house, although others in her family disagree, and when the wolves come out, the adventure begins

"Gaiman's text rings with energetic confidence and an inviting tone. . . . McKean . . . expertly matches the tale's funny-scary mood . . . against shadow-filled backdrops that blend paint, digital manipulation and photography, his stylized human figures look right at home. His pen-and-inks of the wolves . . . suggest that they inhabit a world apart—or perhaps unreal?" Publ Wkly

Gaiman, Neil, 1960-

Chu's day; Neil Gaiman, Adam Rex; [edited by] Rosemary Brosnan. HarperCollins 2013 32 p. (hardcover bdg.) $17.99
Grades: PreK   E
1. Mystery fiction 2. Sneezing -- Fiction 3. Picture books for children
ISBN 0062017810; 9780062017819

LC 2012942557

In this children's picture book, "[Neil] Gaiman builds suspense from the . . . opening sentence ('When Chu sneezed, bad things happened')." Trips to a dusty library and a diner with peppery air make "Chu's anxious parents ask, 'Are you going to sneeze?' . . . That evening, under a big top . . . , Chu cannot resist, and his true power is revealed." (Publishers Weekly)

Gal, Susan

Day by day; Susan Gal. Alfred A. Knopf 2012 40 p. col. ill. (hardback) $16.99
Grades: PreK K 1 2   E
1. Pigs -- Fiction 2. Family -- Fiction 3. Picture books for children 4. Family life -- Fiction 5. Neighborhoods -- Fiction
ISBN 037586959X; 9780375869594; 9780375969591; 9780375984334

LC 2011042371

In this children's picture book, "[a]cross a golden prairie, a family of pigs heads west. Their small actions grow in significance as bricks become a house, beloved paraphernalia create a home, neighbors are welcomed and friendships begin." Through daily hard work, "a community is built" and at the end of the book, the pigs gather "under a festive tree at twilight to enjoy the bounty they have grown." (Kirkus)

★ **Night** lights. Alfred A. Knopf 2009 un il $14.99; lib bdg $17.99
Grades: PreK K 1   E
1. Light -- Fiction 2. Night -- Fiction
ISBN 978-0-375-85862-8; 0-375-85862-8; 978-0-375-95862-5 lib bdg; 0-375-95862-2 lib bdg
LC 2008-50909
While preparing for bedtime, a little girl and her dog note all the different kinds of lights that brighten up the night, from headlights to moonlight.
"An appropriately dark palette complements the 15 types of illumination named in this nearly wordless story. Young children will enjoy poring over the rich details in the cozy charcoal and digital collage spreads as they learn to read the simple text." SLJ

Please take me for a walk. Alfred A. Knopf 2010 un il $15.99; lib bdg $18.99
Grades: PreK K 1   E
1. Dogs -- Fiction
ISBN 0375858636; 0375958630 lib bdg; 9780375858635; 9780375958632; 978-0-375-85863-5; 0-375-85863-6; 978-0-375-95863-2 lib bdg; 0-375-95863-0 lib bdg
A dog gives many good reasons it likes to go for a walk—to chase away the neighbor's cat, to greet people on the street, to watch guys shooting hoops, and to feel the wind lifting its ears.
"Gal celebrates the joys of perambulating the neighborhood in simple sentences and mixed-media collage illustrations featuring expressive canines and humans, as well as inventive details." Booklist

Galbraith, Kathryn Osebold
Arbor Day square; written by Kathryn Galbraith; illustrated by Cyd Moore. Peachtree Publishers 2010 un $16.95
Grades: K 1 2 3   E
1. Trees -- Fiction 2. Arbor Day -- Fiction 3. Frontier and pioneer life -- Fiction 4. Father-daughter relationship -- Fiction
ISBN 978-1-56145-517-1; 1-56145-517-2
LC 2009017017
In the mid-nineteenth century, as young Katie and her father help plant and tend trees in their booming frontier town, she doubts that the spindly saplings will ever grow big. Includes facts about Arbor Day.
"Galbraith's poetic text and Moore's soft watercolor and colored-pencil illustrations recreate those spring days on the prairie when planting trees was cause for celebration." SLJ

Boo, bunny! [by] Kathryn O. Galbraith; illustrated by Jeff Mack. Harcourt 2008 un il $16
Grades: PreK K   E
1. Stories in rhyme 2. Fear -- Fiction 3. Rabbits --

Fiction 4. Halloween -- Fiction
ISBN 978-0-15-216246-7; 0-15-216246-1
LC 2007021426
Two small bunnies face their fears while trick-or-treating on Halloween night
"With very simple, shivery rhyme and bright shapes on black double-page spreads, this picture book brings toddlers the creepy fun of Halloween." Booklist

Gall, Chris
Dear fish; written and illustrated by Chris Gall. Little, Brown 2006 un il $16.99
Grades: 1 2 3 4   E
1. Fishes -- Fiction 2. Beaches -- Fiction
ISBN 0-316-05847-5; 978-0-316-05847-6
LC 2005-03828
One afternoon at the beach, a small boy puts an invitation to the fish to come for a visit in a bottle and throws it into the ocean, and the results are unprecedented.
"The text has a rich vocabulary. . . . Boldly colored illustrations combine clay-engraved art with digital effects to give the pages a three-dimensional look. Readers who enjoy poring over pictures that are layered with meaning on both the literal and figurative levels will find much to explore here." SLJ

★ **Dinotrux**. Little, Brown 2009 un il $16.99
Grades: PreK K 1 2   E
1. Trucks -- Fiction 2. Dinosaurs -- Fiction
ISBN 978-0-316-02777-9; 0-316-02777-4
LC 2008-27531
Millions of years ago, the prehistoric ancestors of today's trucks, such as garbageadon, dozeratops, and craneosaurus, roamed the Earth until they rusted out and became extinct.
"Blending the endless appeal of dinosaurs and trucks in one hilarious volume, this title will be hard to keep on the shelves." SLJ

Revenge of the Dinotrux; Chris Gall. Little, Brown & Co 2012 32 p.
Grades: PreK K 1 2   E
1. Picture books for children 2. Trucks -- Juvenile fiction 3. Dinosaurs -- Juvenile fiction 4. Mythical animals -- Juvenile fiction 5. Trucks -- Fiction 6. Behavior -- Fiction 7. Imaginary creatures -- Fiction
ISBN 0316132888; 9780316132886
LC 2011025118
This picture book by Chris Gall is a sequel to his earlier children's book "Dinotrux!" in which the metal dinosaurs escape from their museum. "Exploding through the dino-museum's wall in the wake of a particularly stressful Kindergarten Day, enraged Tyrannosaurus Trux rolls off to climb a skyscraper. . . . Further chaos threatens when they burst out again, though, taking along the children who have introduced them to the wonders of (truck) books and other reading." Gall illustrates the dinotrux as "towering massively atop heavy-duty tires, with wide, headlight eyes and toothy maws agape." (Kirkus)

★ **Substitute** Creacher. Little, Brown 2011 un il $16.99
Grades: K 1   E
1. School stories 2. Stories in rhyme 3. Monsters --

Fiction 4. Teachers -- Fiction

ISBN 978-0-316-08915-9; 0-316-08915-X

LC 2010019758

Mr. Creacher, a multi-tentacled substitute teacher, warns his prankish students not to misbehave, recounting rhyming cautionary tales of the weird, spooky, and unexpected.

Gall "illustrates in explosive, cinematic panels; retro Ben-Day dot patterns allude to classic funnies. If the dire warnings fail to inspire repentance, Mr. Creacher's dilemma—and a conclusion that breaks the spell—may warm the cold hearts of defiant substitute baiters." Publ Wkly

There's nothing to do on Mars; written and illustrated by Chris Gall. Little, Brown 2008 un il $16.99

Grades: PreK K 1 2   E

1. Science fiction

ISBN 978-0-316-16684-3; 0-316-16684-7

LC 2006025290

After moving to Mars with his family, Davey complains of being bored until he begins exploring the planet with his dog Polaris and discovers a most unusual "treasure"

"The illustrations, created with an engraving technique, are precisely drawn and appropriately painted in scorching reds and oranges. . . . Amusing details . . . extend the text and play off the deadpan humor." SLJ

Gammell, Stephen

★ **Mudkin.** Carolrhoda Books 2011 un il

Grades: PreK K 1   E

1. Play -- Fiction 2. Rain -- Fiction 3. Imagination -- Fiction

ISBN 0-7613-5790-4 lib bdg; 978-0-7613-5790-2 lib bdg

LC 2010026373

While playing outside on a rainy day, a little girl peers into a puddle and sees Mudkin, who invites her to become his queen.

"Kids love mud, and here's a picture book that positively revels in all its gleefully gloppy glory. . . . The girl has a few lines of dialogue, but Mudkin's responses are all a scrawl of indecipherable brown smears, offering a neat chance for kids to engage and fill in their own ideas for what he's saying. But what will really bring on the squeals is the joyfully messy watercolors that look composed of thick, overhand tosses of mud splatters and heartily ground-in grass stains." Booklist

Once upon MacDonald's farm; rev format ed; Simon & Schuster Bks. for Young Readers 2000 un il $15

Grades: PreK K 1 2   E

1. Animals 2. Farm life 3. Humorous stories 4. Animals -- Fiction 5. Farm life -- Fiction

ISBN 0-689-82885-3

LC 99-30691

First published 1981 by Four Winds Press

MacDonald tries farming with exotic circus animals, but has better luck with his neighbor's cow, horse, and chicken—or does he?

"The accomplished, shaded pencil drawings are well suited to this slyly humorous tale with an unexpected twist." Horn Book Guide

Gannij, Joan

Topsy-turvy bedtime; by Joan Levine; illustrated by Tony Auth. Candlewick 2008 un il $14.99

Grades: PreK K 1   E

1. Bedtime -- Fiction 2. Parent-child relationship -- Fiction

ISBN 978-0-7636-3008-9; 0-7636-3008-X

"Arathusela hates going to bed. Her parents are exhausted by day's end, so they reverse roles with her. . . . Kids will appreciate the tables-turned humor ('You forgot to sing us a song') and the reasuring resolution. Auth has a light touch; his watercolors display the particular coziness of domestic life at night." Horn Book Guide

Gantos, Jack

★ **Rotten** Ralph; written by Jack B. Gantos; illustrated by Nicole Rubel. Houghton Mifflin 1976 un il lib bdg $16; pa $7.95

Grades: PreK K 1 2   E

1. Cats -- Fiction

ISBN 0-395-24276-2 lib bdg; 0-395-29202-6 pa

The "bright watercolor scenes . . . capturing Ralph's demonic meanness and his family's chagrin are a perfect complement to the text." SLJ

Other titles about Rotten Ralph are:

Back to school for Rotten Ralph (1998)

Best in show for Rotten Ralph (2005)

Happy birthday Rotten Ralph (1990)

The nine lives of Rotten Ralph (2009)

Not so Rotten Ralph (1994)

Practice makes perfect for Rotten Ralph (2002)

Rotten Ralph helps out (2001)

Rotten Ralph's rotten Christmas (1984)

Rotten Ralph's rotten romance (1997)

Rotten Ralph's show and tell (1989)

Rotten Ralph's trick or treat! (1986)

Three strikes for Rotten Ralph (2011)

Wedding bells for Rotten Ralph (1999)

Worse than rotten, Ralph (1978)

Garcia, Emma

Tap tap bang bang. Boxer Books 2010 un il $16.95

Grades: PreK K   E

1. Tools -- Fiction 2. Sounds -- Fiction 3. Building -- Fiction

ISBN 978-1-907152-00-9; 1-907152-00-8

"A lively introduction to tools and the sounds that they make. . . . They all work together to make a bright, cherry-red go-kart. . . . Garcia's artwork is clear and colorful, and all of the tools stand out against the stark white backgrounds. . . . There are plenty of opportunities to stretch vocabulary with these building-tool words." SLJ

Garden, Nancy

Molly's family; pictures by Sharon Wooding. Farrar Straus Giroux 2004 un il $16

Grades: PreK K 1 2   E

1. Family 2. Schools 3. School stories 4. Lesbian mothers 5. Lesbians -- Fiction 6. Family life -- Fiction

ISBN 0-374-35002-7

LC 2002-29784

When Molly draws a picture of her family for Open School Night, one of her classmates makes her feel bad because he says she cannot have a mommy and a momma

"By tying this specific household to the general diversity within all families, Garden manages to celebrate them all.

The soft colored-pencil drawings with their many realistic details depict a room full of active kindergartners." SLJ

Garland, Michael

Grandpa's tractor. Boyds Mills Press 2011 un il $16.95

Grades: PreK K 1   E

1. Farm life -- Fiction 2. Grandfathers -- Fiction

ISBN 978-1-59078-762-5; 1-59078-762-5

Grandpa Joe brings his grandson Timmy back to the site of the family farm, where the old house and a ramshackle barn still stand. The visit evokes many memories for Grandpa Joe, which he shares with Timmy.

"Garland's artistic genius has never been shown to such advantage as in this book. . . . The text . . . complements the vivid and folksy digitally enhanced artwork. . . . The pictures and text together compose a loving tribute to the heyday of small farms in America." SLJ

Super snow day: seek and find. Dutton Children's Books 2010 un il $16.99

Grades: PreK K 1 2 3   E

1. Picture puzzles 2. Literary recreations 3. Snow -- Fiction 4. Aunts -- Fiction

ISBN 978-0-525-42245-7; 0-525-42245-5

LC 2009-53245

When a heavy snowfall causes schools and businesses to close, Tommy follows a series of notes from his Aunt Jeanne as he explores the frozen landscape, makes new friends, and participates in winter sports. Artwork includes over 200 objects for the reader to find and count.

"Garland's computer-generated illustrations are eye-catching and surreal. . . . They're characterized by bright colors, Claymation-style figures, and an admirable restraint when it comes to clutter." SLJ

Garland, Michael, 1952-

Fish had a wish; by Michael Garland. Holiday House 2012 24p

Grades: PreK K 1 2   E

1. Fishes -- Fiction 2. Wishes -- Fiction 3. Children's stories 4. Picture books for children 5. Animals -- Fiction 6. Contentment -- Fiction 7. Self-acceptance -- Fiction

ISBN 9780823423941

LC 2010050124

In this children's picture book, "Fish has a wish to be some creature other than what he is: a bird, so he can fly high in the sky; a turtle, so he can nap on a sunny rock; a skunk, so he can make a big stink; or a bobcat, a bee, a beaver, a butterfly or a snake. But when a mayfly lands on the water, Fish eats it in one bite and declares: 'That was so good! . . . I wish to stay a fish.' . . . The double-page spreads have wood-grain backgrounds . . . evok[ing] Fish's woodland pond environment." (Kirkus)

Garland, Sarah

Eddie's garden; and how to make things grow. Frances Lincoln 2004 40p il hardcover o.p. pa $8.95

Grades: K 1 2   E

1. Gardening 2. Siblings -- Fiction 3. Gardening -- Fiction

ISBN 1-8450-7015-1; 978-1-8450-7089-2 pa

"Watching their mother dig in her garden, Eddie and his little sister, Lily, ask for their own. During the next few months, Eddie plants seeds, waters them, helps Lily, watches their plants grow, hunts slugs, harvests vegetables, and eats the home-grown produce. Bits of humor in the telling and appealing visual elements such as a bean-pole teepee will help keep children involved in the story. This book ends with four helpful pages explaining how to grow 'Eddie's plants,' such as carrots, nasturtiums, and sunflowers, as well as discussing soil, seeds, pests, hazards, and gardening indoors and in containers. . . . This picture book offers plenty of genial details in the bright, engaging colored artwork." Booklist

Eddie's kitchen; and how to make good things to eat. Frances Lincoln 2008 un il $16.95

Grades: K 1 2   E

1. Cooking -- Fiction 2. Birthdays -- Fiction 3. Grandfathers -- Fiction

ISBN 978-1-84507-58-0; 1-84507-88-9

"Grandad phones at 2 p.m., sings happy birthday to himself, and then announces, 'I'll see you at six o'clock for my birthday party.' Mum is horrified; the date has completely slipped her mind. But with a lot of help from her kids, capable Eddie and mischievous toddler Lily, she plans the meal, assembles the ingredients, . . . cooks a festive dinner and finally sits down by the fire. . . . Garland cleverly weaves some playful patterns into the smoothly written story. . . . The accessible pictures convey an atmosphere of warmth and cheerful dishevelment. Readers will find recipes for the special dinner at the end of the book; the steps are clearly described, and the dishes look nutritious and tasty." SLJ

Eddie's toolbox; and how to make and mend things. Frances Lincoln 2011 un il $17.95

Grades: K 1 2   E

1. Tools -- Fiction 2. Friendship -- Fiction

ISBN 978-1-84780-053-4; 1-84780-053-X

"Eddie is hoping a boy his age will move in next door, but when he sees the new family unpack, he notices that the only child is a girl his younger sister's age. When the two families meet . . . the two girls form an instant bond. . . . Tilly's dad asks him if he'd like to help him with chores that need to be done. . . . Tom teaches him how to use a saw, a hammer, and a screwdriver. . . . Soon, the two families are completing projects together. . . . This is a lovely story about friendship between neighbors. Garland's watercolor illustrations show scenes in which everyone is helping one another. These two families make lending a hand look fun and rewarding." SLJ

Other titles about Eddie are:

Eddie's kitchen (2004)

Eddie's garden (2008)

Garland, Sherry

The **buffalo** soldier; by Sherry Garland; illustrated by Ronald Himler. Pelican Pub. Co. 2006 un il $15.95

Grades: 2 3 4   E

1. African American soldiers -- Fiction

ISBN 978-1-58980-391-6

LC 2006012484

Realizing that his future lies in owning land, not just being free, a young man raised as a slave becomes a buffalo soldier—a member of an all-black cavalry regiment formed to protect white settlers from Indians, bandits, and outlaws, and that later fought in the Spanish American War. Includes historical note

"Himler's vibrant illustrations capture the broad vistas of western landscape, the excitement of horseback pursuit, and the hardships of the work, at the same time conveying respect for the loyal soldiers who endured it all." Booklist

Includes bibliographical references

Gary, Meredith

Sometimes you get what you want; art by Lisa Brown; words by Meredith Gary. HarperCollinsPublishers 2008 un il $16.99; lib bdg $17.89

Grades: PreK K   E

1. School stories 2. Siblings -- Fiction 3. Conduct of life -- Fiction

ISBN 978-0-06-114015-0; 978-0-06-114016-7 lib bdg

LC 2007041933

A brother and sister spend a day in preschool learning lessons about boundaries, such as that it is sometimes okay to make a lot of noise, but at other times one must be quiet.

"Gary's concise text conveys an important life lesson about the need to balance fun, responsibility, and respect for others. . . . Appealing illustrations depict each scenario and keep the tone light. Background scenery, props, and adult characters are portrayed in black lines and white and gray shades, while the children are fully fleshed out with a variety of skin tones and bright-hued clothing." SLJ

Garza, Xavier

Juan and the Chupacabras; by Xavier Garza; illustrations by April Ward; Spanish translation by Carolina Villarroel. Pinata Books 2006 un il $15.95

Grades: K 1 2 3   E

1. Monsters -- Fiction 2. Grandfathers -- Fiction 3. Bilingual books -- English-Spanish

ISBN 978-1-55885-454-3; 1-55885-454-1

After hearing about their grandfather's boyhood encounter with the Chupacabras, a green, winged creature with glowing eyes, Juan and his cousin Luz decide to find out if the story could be true.

"The English and Spanish texts appear on the same page, separated by a narrow illustration. The full-page illustration moves the action along nicely. An excellent choice for storytime and classroom sharing." SLJ

Gauch, Patricia Lee

Aaron and the Green Mountain Boys; pictures by Margot Tomes. Boyds Mills Press 2005 64p il $16.95; pa $9.95

Grades: K 1 2   E

ISBN 1-59078-335-2; 1-59078-354-9 pa

A reissue of the title first published 1972 by Coward, McCann & Geohegan

In 1777 nine-year-old Aaron would rather help the Green Mountain Boys fight the British than stay home and bake bread for them.

★ **Tanya** and the red shoes; illustrated by Satomi Ichikawa. Philomel Bks. 2002 un il $16.99

Grades: PreK K 1 2   E

1. Dancers 2. Sisters 3. Ballet dancing 4. Ballet

-- Fiction

ISBN 0-399-23314-8

LC 2001-33916

"Tanya confides her dreams of dancing en pointe like the dancer in the movie The Red Shoes. She finally gets her wish but discovers that the seemingly effortless beauty of the dance requires much work (and produces many blisters). The use of the present tense underscores the conversational tone, adding verisimilitude matched by Ichikawa's marvelously agile, expressive illustrations." Horn Book

Other titles about Tanya are:

Bravo Tanya (1992)

Dance Tanya (1989)

Presenting Tanya the Ugly Duckling (1999)

Tanya and the magic wardrobe (1997)

Gauch, Sarah

Voyage to the Pharos; illustrated by Roger Roth. Viking 2009 un il $16.99

Grades: 1 2 3   E

1. Sea stories 2. Lighthouses -- Fiction

ISBN 978-0-670-06254-6; 0-670-06254-5

LC 2009012345

A young boy in ancient times embarks on an adventurous sea voyage to Alexandria, Egypt, home of the famous Pharos Lighthouse.

"Large-scale illustrations capture the drama of the events to full effect. . . . Roth varies his palette to increase the intensity of the perilous scenes and to highlight the joy of surviving unharmed." SLJ

Gay, Marie-Louise

Caramba and Henry. Groundwood Books 2011 $17.95

Grades: PreK K 1   E

1. Cats -- Fiction 2. Flight -- Fiction 3. Siblings -- Fiction

ISBN 978-1-55498-097-0; 1-55498-097-6; 9781554980970; 1554980976

"Caramba, a zebra-striped cat who lives in a world where cats can fly, has always wanted a brother—but not the one he gets. Henry screams and cries all of the time and, unlike Caramba, Henry isn't having any trouble flying. To Caramba's chagrin, his mother puts him in charge of making sure Henry's fledgling flights don't end in disaster. . . . Gay's watercolors, laced with feathery pencil lines, bring warmth to this fresh spin on a story about learning how to be an older sibling." Publ Wkly

Another title about Caramba is:

Caramba (2005)

★ **Roslyn** Rutabaga and the biggest hole on earth; by Marie-Lou Gay. Groundwood Books/House of Anansi Press 2010 un il $18.95

Grades: PreK K   E

1. Rabbits -- Fiction 2. Father-daughter relationship -- Fiction

ISBN 978-0-88899-994-8; 0-88899-994-1

"The whimsical illustrations, created on Kraft paper and handmade Japanese paper with watercolor, acrylic, pastels, aquarelle crayons, pencil, and collage, are busy without being overdone. Imaginative and adventurous children will identify with Roslyn in this simple, fun story." SLJ

★ **When** Stella was very very small. Groundwood
Books 2009 un il $16.95
Grades: PreK K 1 2   E
    1. Size -- Fiction 2. Growth -- Fiction
    ISBN 978-0-88899-906-1; 0-88899-906-2
"Stella explores her vantage points from each developmental stage to date. As a crawler, she's eye to eye with a
turtle. . . . A goldfish and dog phase follow. Gay's sensitivity
to the rich inner life of childhood flows into her art and language. . . . Gay's mixed-media scenes dance with the energy
of scribbled butterflies on the walls, teetering objects, and a
blanket-turned-turban. . . . Subtle and sweet, yet full of life
and humor, the child's world is a place kids will want to visit
again and again." SLJ
    Other titles about Stella are:
    Stella, star of the sea (1999)
    Stella, queen of the snow (2000)
    Stella, fairy of the forest (2002)
    Stella, princess of the sky (2004)

Geeslin, Campbell
    ★ **Elena's** serenade; written by Campbell Geeslin; il-
lustrated by Ana Juan. Atheneum Books for Young Readers
2004 un il $16.95
Grades: K 1 2 3   E
    1. Sex role -- Fiction 2. Glassblowing -- Fiction
    ISBN 0-689-84908-7
                             LC 2002-3233
In Mexico a little girl disguised as a boy sets out for
Monterrey determined to master the art of glassblowing, and
in the process, experiences self-discovery along the way
    "The story flows well and Spanish words are smoothly
incorporated into the text. The alluring acrylic-and-crayon
illustrations have a stylized folk-art quality that helps to set
the stage for the tale." SLJ

Geisert, Arthur
    Country road ABC; an illustrated journey through
America's farmland. Houghton Mifflin Harcourt 2010 un
il $17
Grades: K 1 2 3   E
    1. Alphabet 2. Farm life -- Fiction 3. Farms -- Juvenile
literature 4. Alphabet -- Juvenile literature
    ISBN 978-0-547-19469-1; 0-547-19469-2
                             LC 2009045450
Arthur Geisert takes readers on a literal journey following a real road in Iowa through the ins and outs of America's farmland.
    "Pastoral charm is not Geisert's aim: . . . he begins with
'A is for ammonia fertilizer.' His finely worked etchings,
colored in muted shades, sweep across a sprawl of fields
and roads. . . . Much visual information about farming is provided for lovers of tractors and farm animals, but it's more
than a simple picture book; it's a deeply personal account."
Publ Wkly

    Hogwash. Houghton Mifflin 2008 32p il $16
Grades: K 1 2 3   E
    1. Stories without words 2. Pigs -- Fiction 3. Machinery
-- Fiction 4. Cleanliness -- Fiction
    ISBN 978-0-618-77332-9; 0-618-77332-0
                             LC 2007-21731

Illustrations without words depict the enormous and
complicated contraption that Mama Pig uses to get her little
piglets clean.
    This is illustrated with "intricately detailed colored etch-
ings. . . . A master of the 'page turn,' only Geisert could
take a one-word title and create such an engaging scenario."
Booklist

    ★ **Ice**. Enchanted Lion Books 2011 un il $14.95
Grades: K 1 2   E
    1. Stories without words 2. Ice -- Fiction 3. Pigs
-- Fiction
    ISBN 978-1-59270-098-1; 1-59270-098-5
                             LC 2010-942321
This wordless tale depicts a community of pigs that suffer from the heat and go in search of ice despite the odds
against them.
    "This is an especially satisfying Geisert title, because
the task is essential for the pigs' survival and they carry it
off with such élan. And the air-schooner, a charming marriage of sailing and balloon technology, is a standout among
Geisert's many contraptions." Publ Wkly

    ★ **Lights** out. Houghton Mifflin Co. 2005 32p il $16
Grades: 1 2 3 4   E
    1. Pigs -- Fiction 2. Bedtime -- Fiction 3. Inventions
-- Fiction
    ISBN 0-618-47892-2
                             LC 2005-00555
Told by his parents that his light must be out at eight
o'clock, a young piglet who is afraid of the dark devises an
ingenious solution to the problem.
    "Fans of roller-coaster construction, marble runs, and
contraption-like machines will be immediately engaged, and
the problem-solving humor is for everyone. The fine lines
and small scale of Geisert's color art work perfectly to give
an effect that is intimate, energetic, and delightful." SLJ

    Thunderstorm; Arthur Geisert. 1st ed. Enchanted
Lion Books 2013 32 p. (hardcover) $17.95
Grades: PreK K 1 2   E
    1. Farm life -- Juvenile literature 2. Thunderstorms
-- Juvenile literature
    ISBN 1592701337; 9781592701339
                             LC 2012952191
This picture book by Arthur Geisert "follows the course
of a storm through midwestern farm country minute-by-
minute, hour-by-hour, from late morning into late afternoon." (Publisher's note) "Cutaway views show the interiors
of buildings and, in the ground below, the burrows of rabbits
and foxes. The story follows a single farming family driving
a red pickup truck hauling a trailer-load of hay; timestamps
('3:00 pm') are the only text." (Publishers Weekly)

Genechten, Guido van
    Kai -Mook. Clavis Pub. 2011 il $16.95
Grades: PreK K   E
    1. Zoos -- Fiction 2. Animals -- Fiction 3. Elephants
-- Fiction
    ISBN 978-1-60537-096-5; 1-60537-096-7
    "When a baby elephant is born, all the animals are smit-
ten. . . . Each creature takes a turn to point out similarities
with the new baby and all declare her 'cute.' At last the new
baby says, 'I AM NOT CUTE,'. . . 'I AM KAI-MOOK!' The

friendly collage and pastel cartoon-style animals are just right for toddlers and preschoolers. . . . Bright-eyed, smiling faces and interesting texturing provide visual appeal that earns this book a spot among the pack of baby-in-the-jungle tales." SLJ

No ghost under my bed. Clavis Pub. 2010 un il $17.95
Grades: PreK K 1 2   E
   1. Fear -- Fiction 2. Bedtime -- Fiction 3. Penguins -- Fiction 4. Father-child relationship -- Fiction
   ISBN 978-1-60537-069-9; 1-60537-069-X

When a little penguin named Jake becomes afraid of strange noises in his room at night, he calls his father to check out the situation, and when everything from the curtain to the wardrobe and toy box has been checked, Jake feels comforted that all of the ghosts are gone and prepares to sleep.

   "This story is kept lighthearted with the addition of animated stuffed animals and humorous illustrations of Jake's father looking for ghosts. . . . Told mostly through dialogue between parent and child, this picture book starring two charming penguins dispels bedtime fears by replacing them with belief in a father's love." SLJ

George, Jean Craighead
   ★ Goose and Duck; illustrated by Priscilla Lamont. Laura Geringer Books 2008 48p il (I can read!) $16.99; lib bdg $17.89
Grades: PreK K 1 2   E
   1. Ducks -- Fiction 2. Geese -- Fiction
   ISBN 978-0-06-117076-8; 0-06-117076-3; 978-0-06-117077-5 lib bdg; 0-06-117077-1 lib bdg
                                                         LC 2006-21715

A young boy becomes the "mother" to a goose, who becomes "mother" to a duck, as they learn about the rhythms of nature together.

   "Lamont's colorful illustrations combine sensitive line work with appealing color washes. . . . The clearly written story is well suited to beginning readers and, as a read-aloud." Booklist

Luck; the story of a sandhill crane. by Jean Craighead George; paintings by Wendell Minor. Laura Geringer Books 2006 un il $16.99; lib bdg $17.89
Grades: 1 2 3   E
   1. Cranes (Birds) -- Fiction
   ISBN 0-06-008201-1; 0-06-008202-X lib bdg
                                                         LC 2004-15628

A young sandhill crane, Luck, finds his place in the ancient crane migration from northern Canada to the Platte River

   "Minor's beautifully painted spreads of Luck, including many pictures of the birds in flight, increase the sense of awe that the birds' miraculous journey inspires. A fine title to prompt discussion about local wildlife." Booklist

Morning, noon, and night; paintings by Wendell Minor. HarperCollins Pubs. 1999 un il $16.99; lib bdg $17.89
Grades: K 1 2 3   E
   1. Day -- Fiction 2. Animals -- Fiction
   ISBN 0-06-023628-0; 0-06-023629-9 lib bdg
                                                         LC 97-28796

Each day as the sun makes its dawn-to-dusk journey from the Eastern seaboard to the Pacific coast, the animals perform their daily activities

   This offers "rhythmic, lyrical text. . . . Minor's lushly detailed paintings capture the beauty of both animals and landscape, elucidating the subtle journey the book makes from east coast to west." Horn Book Guide

Nutik, the wolf pup; illustrated by Ted Rand. HarperCollins Pubs. 2001 un il hardcover o.p. lib bdg $18.89
Grades: K 1 2 3   E
   1. Inuit -- Fiction 2. Wolves -- Fiction 3. Eskimos -- Fiction 4. Eskimos -- Juvenile fiction 5. Brothers and sisters -- Fiction
   ISBN 0-06-028164-2; 0-06-028165-0 lib bdg
                                                         LC 99-10501

When his older sister Julie brings home two small wolf pups, Amaroq takes care of the one called Nutik and grows to love it, even though Julie tells him it cannot stay

   "Rand's realistic paintings establish the Alaska setting and capture the affection between boy and pup. . . . First told in Julie's Wolf Pack (1997), the story is skillfully telescoped into a picture book with heart-tugging appeal." Booklist

   Another title about Nutik and Amaroq is:
   Nutik & Amaroq play ball (2001)

George, Kristine O'Connell
   Hummingbird nest; a journal of poems. illustrated by Barry Moser. Harcourt 2004 un il $16
Grades: 2 3 4   E
   1. Stories in rhyme 2. Hummingbirds -- Fiction
   ISBN 0-15-202325-9
                                                         LC 99-50909

When a mother hummingbird builds a nest on a family's porch, they watch and record her actions and the birth and development of her fledglings.

   "Moser's quiet, exquisitely detailed pictures show the people watching and the small, delicate creatures. . . . The long, beautifully written notes with astonishing facts about hummingbirds make this a fine choice for both language arts and science classes." Booklist

Up! illustrated by Hiroe Nakata. Clarion Books 2005 32p il $15
Grades: PreK K   E
   1. Stories in rhyme 2. Father-daughter relationship -- Fiction
   ISBN 0-618-06489-3
                                                         LC 2004-10729

Rhyming text and illustrations animate the feeling of "up" as experienced by a little girl with her father.

   "Nakata's airy, spirited watercolors beautifully expand on the words' carefree, physical elation with skewed angles, glorious fruit-juice colors, and leaping, tumbling toys and figures." Booklist

George, Lindsay Barrett
   ★ Inside mouse, outside mouse. Greenwillow Books 2004 un il $15.99; lib bdg $16.89
Grades: PreK K 1 2   E
   1. Mice 2. Mice -- Fiction
   ISBN 0-06-000466-5; 0-06-000467-3 lib bdg
                                                         LC 2003-48497

Two mice, one who sleeps inside the house in a clock and one who sleeps outside the house in a stump, follow complicated but strangely parallel paths and meet each other at a window.

"The pictures are packed with interesting details just waiting to be explored. The simple text . . . . compares and contrasts the animals' environments and lifestyles. The overall effect is mesmerizing" SLJ

Maggie's ball. Greenwillow Books 2010 un il $16.99
Grades: PreK K　　　　　　　　　　　　　　　　E
1. Dogs -- Fiction
ISBN 978-0-06-172166-3; 0-06-172166-2
LC 2008052482

When Maggie the dog goes searching for her missing ball, she finds a lot of different things—including a new friend.

"The illustrations are bright and big, as is the minimal text, making the oversize book a winner for preschool storytimes as well as for individual perusings where the ample small details will fascinate children." SLJ

That pup! Greenwillow Books 2011 un il $16.99
Grades: PreK　　　　　　　　　　　　　　　　E
1. Dogs -- Fiction 2. Squirrels -- Fiction
ISBN 978-0-06-200413-0; 0-06-200413-1
LC 2010012641

After having fun digging up acorns, a little dog decides to bury them all again.

"There is a real story here about taking things that don't belong to you and putting things right after a misunderstanding, right on target for younger preschoolers. Gouache illustrations of the appealing puppy and concerned squirrel use simple layouts and lots of white space." Kirkus

George, Lucy M.
Back to school Tortoise; written by Lucy M. George; illustrated by Merel Eyckerman. Albert Whitman 2011 un il $15.99
Grades: PreK K 1　　　　　　　　　　　　　　E
1. School stories 2. Turtles -- Fiction 3. Teachers -- Fiction
ISBN 978-0-8075-0510-6; 0-8075-0510-2
LC 2010046344

Summer is over and Tortoise must summon the courage to go back to school.

"The precisely worded text and amiable mixed-media illustrations work well together. An empathetic read-aloud choice, this book offers a welcome antidote for first-day-of-school jitters." Booklist

George, William T.
Box Turtle at Long Pond; pictures by Lindsay Barrett George. Greenwillow Bks. 1989 un il $17.99
Grades: PreK K 1 2　　　　　　　　　　　　　E
1. Turtles -- Fiction
ISBN 0-688-08184-3
LC 88-18787

On a busy day at Long Pond, Box Turtle searches for food, basks in the sun, and escapes a raccoon

"A beautifully illustrated book that introduces a pond environment. . . . The reader learns of other plants, animals, and insects that inhabit the pond." Sci Child
Other titles about Long Pond are:

Beaver at Long Pond (1988)
Christmas at Long Pond (1992)
Fishing at Long Pond (1991)

Geras, Adèle
★ **Little** ballet star; by Adèle Geras; pictures by Shelagh McNicholas. Dial Books for Young Readers 2008 un il $16.99
Grades: PreK K 1 2　　　　　　　　　　　　　E
1. Aunts -- Fiction 2. Ballet -- Fiction
ISBN 978-0-8037-3237-7; 0-8037-3237-6

Tilly is thrilled when she gets to see her aunt perform in the ballet, "The Sleeping Beauty," especially because she gets to go backstage and even on the stage itself.

"This picture book will charm aspiring young dancers. The large format allows plenty of space for the expressive pencil illustrations, tinted with washes in pastel shades." Booklist
Another book about about Tilly is:
Time for ballet (2004)

Gerber, Carole
Leaf jumpers; [illustrated by] Leslie Evans. Charlesbridge 2004 32p il $16.95; pa $6.95
Grades: PreK K 1 2　　　　　　　　　　　　　E
1. Autumn 2. Leaves 3. Trees -- Juvenile literature 4. Leaves -- Juvenile literature
ISBN 1-57091-497-4; 1-57091-498-2 pa
LC 2003-15846

Illustrations and rhyming text describe different leaves and the trees from which they fall

"Gerber's poetic text describes colors, shapes, and characteristics with an abundance of similes and metaphors. . . . Evans' vibrant hand-colored linoleum prints feature scenes of a brother and sister with the family dog enjoying traditional fall activities." Booklist

Seeds, bees, butterflies, and more! poems for two voices. poems by Carole Gerber; illustrated by Eugene Yelchin. 1st ed. Henry Holt and Co. 2013 32 p. col. ill. (reinforced) $17.99
Grades: 2 3 4　　　　　　　　　　　　　　　E
1. Nature poetry 2. Children's poetry
ISBN 0805092110; 9780805092110
LC 2012011490

This book by Carole Gerber presents a "collection of nature- and spring-themed poems designed to be recited by two readers. The poems' alternating parts are differentiated by color, with multicolored phrases intended to be read in unison." They contain "information about flowers, berries, bugs, and more, as well as topics including germination and pollination." (Publishers Weekly)

Gerdner, Linda
Grandfather's story cloth; written by Linda Gerdner and Sarah Langford; illustrated by Stuart Loughridge. Shen's Books 2008 29p il $16.95
Grades: 2 3 4　　　　　　　　　　　　　　　E
1. Quilts -- Fiction 2. Grandfathers -- Fiction 3. Laotian Americans -- Fiction 4. Alzheimer's disease -- Fiction 5. Hmong (Asian people) -- Fiction 6. Bilingual books -- English-Hmong
ISBN 978-1-885008-34-3; 1-885008-34-1

Ten-year-old Chersheng helps his beloved grandfather cope with his failing memory, brought on by Alzheimer's disease, by showing him the story quilt Grandfather made after fleeing his homeland, Laos, during wartime.

"The English and Hmong texts face paintings that express the many moods of the characters. Endpapers and the back cover feature numerous geometric patterns that are common in Hmong handicrafts. . . . [The book includes] background information on Alzheimer's disease and the Hmong refugees and their story cloths. . . . A strong family story about difficult social issues relevant to today's society." SLJ

Gerritsen, Paula

Nuts; [by] Paula Gerritsen. Front Street 2006 un il $15.95

Grades: PreK K 1 2   E
1. Mice -- Fiction 2. Nuts -- Fiction 3. Storms -- Fiction
ISBN 1-932425-66-7

LC 2005021491

Original Dutch edition 2005

Mouse braves many dangers while trying to collect nuts before winter sets in, including a sudden storm that first brings her disappointment, then a delightful surprise

"The words are well chosen and the repeated refrain will delight readers. The pencil-and-pastel illustrations are charming, displaying the textures and colors of fall and the foreboding energy of the storm." SLJ

Gershator, Phillis

★ Listen, listen; [by] Phillis Gershator; [illustrated by] Alison Jay. Barefoot Books 2007 un il $16.95

Grades: K 1 2 3   E
1. Stories in rhyme 2. Sound -- Fiction 3. Nature -- Fiction 4. Seasons -- Fiction
ISBN 978-1-84686-084-3

LC 2006100351

Illustrations and rhyming text explore the sights and sounds of nature in each season of the year.

"Jay's magical and occasionally eerie crackle-glaze oil paintings furnish a visual feast. The text is built around a series of rhyming, gentile directives to attune one's ears." Publ Wkly

Moo, moo, brown cow, have you any milk? illustrated by Giselle Potter. Random House Children's Books 2011 32p il $16.99; lib bdg $19.99

Grades: PreK K 1   E
1. Stories in rhyme 2. Bedtime -- Fiction 3. Domestic animals -- Fiction
ISBN 978-0-375-86744-6; 0-375-86744-9; 978-0-375-96744-3 lib bdg; 0-375-96744-3 lib bdg

LC 2010018767

Through rhyming text, farm animals are asked if they have items needed to prepare for a snack and bedtime, such as wool for a blanket, down for a pillow, and milk to drink.

"Gershator uses rhyme and the melodic rhythm of 'Baa, Baa, Black Sheep' in her dialogue, making the tale fit for either singing or speaking. Potter uses soft colors for day and rich cobalt and chocolate for night in her folksy paintings." SLJ

Sky sweeper; pictures by Holly Meade. Farrar, Straus & Giroux 2007 un il $16

Grades: 1 2 3 4   E
1. Work -- Fiction 2. Gardens -- Fiction 3. Buddhism -- Fiction
ISBN 978-0-374-37007-7; 0-374-37007-9

LC 2005-49762

Despite criticism for his lack of "accomplishments," Takiboki finds contentment sweeping flower blossoms and raking the sand and gravel in the monks' temple garden. Includes a note on the art and beauty of Japanese gardens

"This is a complex, challenging story. . . . But Meade's beautiful collage illustrations of the earthly garden and glorious afterlife greatly enhance the story's accessibility and will help kids get closer to the text's religious and philosophical themes." Booklist

Who's awake in springtime? [by] Phillis Gershator and Mim Green; illustrated by Emilie Chollat. Henry Holt & Co. 2010 un il $16.99

Grades: PreK K 1 2   E
1. Stories in rhyme 2. Spring -- Fiction 3. Animals -- Fiction 4. Bedtime -- Fiction
ISBN 978-0-8050-6390-5; 0-8050-6390-0

LC 2009009224

Describes, in rhymed cumulative text and illustrations, how various young animals and one small human prepare for sleep at the end of a spring day.

"This cumulative tale is simple and accessible by young readers. . . . Adults who share this book with children can engage the students with the rhythmic text, and repetition throughout the book begs for call-backs and other participation activities. . . . Chollat's illustrations offer bold colors and clear lines and strongly support the story." Libr Media Connect

Who's in the forest? [illustrations by] Jill McDonald. Barefoot Books 2010 un il bd bk $14.99

Grades: PreK K   E
1. Stories in rhyme 2. Board books for children 3. Forest animals -- Fiction
ISBN 978-1-84686-476-6; 1-84686-476-3

LC 2010009438

"Simple rhymes tell listeners that the deep and dark forest is home to bears, foxes, squirrels, and all types of birds. The collage illustrations are colorful and childlike, and every other page has a cutout circle that highlights a particular animal. . . . Toddlers, especially, will love the rhyming couplets and enjoy finding the creatures revealed with each page turn of this large-format board book." SLJ

Gerstein, Mordicai, 1935-

★ A book. Roaring Brook 2009 un il

Grades: PreK K 1 2   E
1. Authorship -- Fiction 2. Books and reading -- Fiction
ISBN 1-59643-251-9; 978-1-59643-251-2

"Among a family who lives in a book, the youngest daughter is the only one who doesn't have a story to belong to, so she sets out among fairy tales, adventures, mysteries, histories, science fiction, and others to track down her story." (Publisher's note) "Grades two to four." (Bull Cent Child Books)

"This charming story follows a young girl and her family who live in a book, . . . though she doesn't know what kind of story her book is. . . . She dashes though spreads that take her into nursery rhymes, on the trail of a mystery, across pirate waters, and even into outer space before she ultimately decides to write her own story, which is, of course, this story. . . . The concept is executed with . . . cleverness and gentleness." Booklist

★ **Carolinda** clatter! Roaring Brook Press 2005 un il $16.95
Grades: PreK K 1 2 3   E
1. Fairy tales 2. Giants -- Fiction
ISBN 1-59643-063-X
LC 2004-24258
The excessively quiet town of Pupickton and the sleeping lovesick giant upon which it was built, are both awakened by the joyful noise of a little girl's songs.
"Gerstein tells his whimsical tale with direct humor, and his lovely paint-and-ink illustrations extend the comedy." Booklist

Leaving the nest. Farrar, Straus and Giroux 2007 un il $16
Grades: K 1 2 3   E
1. Cats -- Fiction 2. Birds -- Fiction 3. Growth -- Fiction 4. Squirrels -- Fiction
ISBN 978-0-374-34369-9; 0-374-34369-1
LC 2005-51228
The lives of a baby jaybird, a young girl, a kitten, and a small squirrel intersect as they venture out into the world.
"Using dialogue bubbles to reveal conversations and thoughts, Gerstein's realistic illustrations set the backyard stage and choreograph the frenzied acts of the drama, adding touches of humor without diminishing the tension." Booklist

Minifred goes to school. HarperCollins 2009 un il $17.99
Grades: PreK K 1 2   E
1. School stories 2. Cats -- Fiction 3. Animals -- Fiction
ISBN 978-0-06-075889-9; 0-06-075889-9; 978-0-06-075890-5 lib bdg; 0-06-075890-2 lib bdg
LC 2008-13861
When Mr. Portly finds a kitten, he and his wife raise her like a child, but unlike a typical child, Minifred the kitten does not like to follow rules at home or at school.
"Gerstein matches the story's lighthearted mood with action-packed scenes, using playful colors, caricatured figures, and sometimes multiple scenes per page, increasing the sense of action." SLJ

Sparrow Jack. Frances Foster Bks. 2003 un il $16
Grades: PreK K 1 2 3   E
1. Photographers 2. Sparrows -- Fiction 3. Immigrants -- Fiction
ISBN 0-374-37139-3
LC 2001-23829
In 1868, John Bardsley, an immigrant from England, brought one thousand sparrows from his home country back to Philadelphia, where he hoped they would help save the trees from the inch-worms that were destroying them
"Though a few imaginative liberties are taken with the facts, Gerstein's cheerful tale is based on a true story. The humor of his whimsically witty text is beautifully captured

and expanded by drawings that are filled with comic action and droll details." Booklist

★ The **white** ram; a story of Abraham and Isaac. Holiday House 2006 un il $16.95
Grades: 1 2 3 4   E
1. Prophets 2. Sheep -- Fiction 3. Biblical characters 4. Rosh ha-Shanah -- Fiction
ISBN 0-8234-1897-9; 978-0-8234-1897-8
LC 2005-46001
A white ram, made on the sixth day of creation, waits patiently in the garden of Eden until the time is right, then runs to save a certain child in fulfillment of God's plan.
"This stunningly illustrated picture book is based on a Midrash. . . . The art, done in pen and ink, oils, and colored pencil, is mesmerizing. [This is told] with a captivating use of language along with true drama." SLJ

Ghigna, Charles
Barn storm; by Charles Ghigna and Debra Ghigna; illustrated by Diane Greenseid. Random House 2010 32p il (Step into reading) lib bdg $12.99; pa $3.99
Grades: 1 2 3   E
1. Stories in rhyme 2. Farm life -- Fiction 3. Tornadoes -- Fiction
ISBN 978-0-375-96114-4 lib bdg; 0-375-96114-3 lib bdg; 978-0-375-86114-7 pa; 0-375-86114-9 pa
LC 2009033321
When a tornado touches down in a pond on Farmer Brown's property, it sets off a chain of events among the barnyard animals that soon has every creature displaced, but not unhappy
"The Ghignas' silly rhymes bounce along; Greenseid's textured illustrations will elicit giggles." Horn Book Guide

Gibfried, Diane
Brother Juniper; illustrated by Meilo So. Clarion Books 2006 un il $16
Grades: K 1 2 3   E
1. Saints 2. Clergy -- Fiction 3. Writers on religion
ISBN 0-618-54361-9; 978-0-618-54361-8
LC 2005-10038
Worried about having left the overly-generous Brother Juniper in charge of their chapel when they went out to preach, Father Francis of Assisi and the other friars are not prepared for what they find upon their return.
"Filled with delicate details and gentle humor, the accomplished watercolor paintings add greatly to the book's appeal. . . . This is an excellent choice to open discussion about generosity." SLJ

Giff, Patricia Reilly
Watch out, Ronald Morgan! illustrated by Susanna Natti. Viking Kestrel 1985 24p il hardcover o.p. pa $5.99
Grades: PreK K 1 2   E
1. School stories 2. Eyeglasses -- Fiction
ISBN 0-14-050638-1 pa
LC 84-19623
Ronald has many humorous mishaps until he gets a pair of eyeglasses. Includes a note for adults about children's eye problems
"Told in a forthright manner but with appreciation for children's candor, the book's dialogue rings true with catchy humor. . . . Natti's illustrations show the characters to be

bright, colorful informal figures who move with the text." SLJ

Other titles about Ronald Morgan are:
Good luck, Ronald Morgan (1996)
Happy birthday, Ronald Morgan! (1986)
Ronald Morgan goes to bat (1988)
Ronald Morgan goes to camp (1995)
Today was a terrible day (1980)

Gilani-Williams, Fawsia

★ **Nabeel's** new pants; an Eid tale. retold by Fawzia Gilani-Williams; illustrations by Proiti Roy. Marshall Cavendish Children 2010 un il $15.99
Grades: K 1 2 3   E
1. Muslims -- Fiction 2. Id al-Adha -- Fiction 3. Family life -- Fiction
ISBN 978-0-7614-5629-2; 0-7614-5629-5
First published 2007 in India
"Turkish shoemaker Nabeel buys Eid gifts for his family. . . . The shopkeeper also persuades Nabeel to buy himself new pants, but the pants are too long. His wife, mother, and daughter are all too busy cooking for Eid to shorten his pants, so he cuts a few inches off himself. Later, the women in the house feel guilty and each secretly trims the pants more. . . . Roy's cheerful gouache, watercolor, and ink illustrations show the bonds among family members as they follow their traditions together. Kids will laugh right along with the loving characters." Booklist
Includes glossary

Gilchrist, Jan Spivey

My America; illustrations by Ashley Bryan and Jan Spivey Gilchrist; poem by Jan Spivey Gilchrist. HarperCollins Pubs. 2007 un il $16.99; lib bdg $17.89
Grades: PreK K 1 2   E
ISBN 978-0-06-079104-9; 0-06-079104-7; 978-0-06-079105-6 lib bdg; 0-06-079105-5 lib bdg
LC 2006029867
"This unusual tribute celebrates America's diversity in its landscapes, both urban and rural, its wildlife, but most of all its people. . . . Both Bryan and Gilchrist illustrate the poem in alternating spreads: his signature color swirls work in tandem with her muted, blue-toned tableaux and faces. . . . The words have the potential for choral reading or dramatization." Booklist

Gilman, Grace

Dixie; pictures by Sarah McConnell. HarperCollins 2011 30p il (I can read!) $16.99; pa $3.99
Grades: PreK K 1   E
1. School stories 2. Dogs -- Fiction 3. Theater -- Fiction
ISBN 978-0-06-171914-1; 0-06-171914-5; 978-0-06-171913-4 pa; 0-06-171913-7 pa
LC 2010015979
Dixie the puppy plays with Emma every day after school until Emma starts memorizing her lines for the school play.
This "should make for a successful experience for the brand-new reader. The simple sentences are accompanied by uncluttered, realistic, brightly colored paintings that complement the story and provide clues to help the reader decipher the text." Booklist

Ginsburg, Mirra

Good morning, chick; by Mirra Ginsburg, adapted from a story by Korney Chukovsky; pictures by Byron Barton. Greenwillow Bks. 1980 un il hardcover o.p. pa $6.99
Grades: PreK K   E
1. Chickens -- Fiction
ISBN 0-688-84284-4 lib bdg; 0-688-08741-8 pa
LC 80-11352
"Based upon a tale by the great Russian poet and storyteller, the totally childlike picture book for the very young employs an engaging device: The text, illustrated with a bright vignette, appears on each of the left-hand pages; then, after pausing briefly and leading the eye to the right, a sentence runs to completion on the opposite page with two words contained in a large storytelling picture done in bold, brilliant color." Horn Book

★ **The chick** and the duckling; translated [and adapted] from the Russian of V. Suteyev; pictures by Jose & Ariane Aruego. Macmillan 1972 un il hardcover o.p. pa $6.99
Grades: PreK K   E
1. Ducks -- Fiction 2. Chickens -- Fiction
ISBN 0-689-71226-X pa
"The sunny simplicity of the illustrations is just right for a slight but engaging text, and they add a note of humor that is a nice foil for the bland directness of the story." Bull Cent Child Books

Giovanni, Nikki

★ **The grasshopper's** song; an Aesop's fable revisited. by Nikki Giovanni; illustrated by Chris Raschka. Candlewick Press 2008 44p il $16.99
Grades: K 1 2 3   E
1. Ants -- Fiction 2. Trials -- Fiction 3. Grasshoppers -- Fiction
ISBN 978-0-7636-3021-8; 0-7636-3021-7
Every year the Grasshoppers sing and play their instruments and the Ants work in rhythm to the music. But when winter comes, the Ants turn their backs on the Grasshoppers, and Jimmy Grasshopper finds this unfair. He's hired Robin, Robin, Robin, and Wren to sue Abigail and Nestor Ant for what he deserves—R-E-S-P-E-C-T—and a one-half share of the harvest. But will a jury of his peers agree about the worth of art?
"To illustrate Giovanni's detailed and insightful prose, Raschka . . . creates evocative, earth-tone watercolors that suggest camouflage." Publ Wkly

Glaser, Linda

Hoppy Hanukkah! illustrated by Daniel Howarth. Albert Whitman 2009 un il $15.99
Grades: PreK K   E
1. Hanukkah stories 2. Rabbits -- Fiction 3. Hanukkah -- Fiction 4. Family life -- Fiction
ISBN 978-0-8075-3378-9; 0-8075-3378-5
LC 2008-55696
Two young bunnies learn about the customs of Hanukkah from their parents and grandparents before they light the menorahs, eat potato latkes, and play dreidel.
"Howarth's soft, bright illustrations of an extended floppy-eared family offer details of a Judaic home in this gentle introduction to the rituals of a traditional celebration

that young families can follow as they create a Hanukkah atmosphere in their own homes." Kirkus

Hoppy Passover! illustrated by Daniel Howarth. Albert Whitman 2011 un il $15.99
Grades: PreK K   E
1. Jews -- Fiction 2. Rabbits -- Fiction 3. Passover -- Fiction
ISBN 978-0-8075-3380-2; 0-8075-3380-7
LC 2010024111
Two young bunnies learn about the customs of the Passover seder from their parents and grandparents as they all celebrate the holiday meal.
"Howarth's cozy and colorful illustrations portray a warm and loving family enjoying this holiday and passing their traditions along to a new generation." Booklist
Another title about this rabbit family is:
Hoppy Hanukkah! (2009)

Our big home; an Earth poem. illustrated by Elisa Kleven. Millbrook Press 2000 un il $23.90; pa $7.95
Grades: K 1 2 3   E
1. Nature
ISBN 0-7613-1650-7; 0-7613-1776-7 pa
LC 99-45775
Describes the water, air, soil, sky, sun, and more shared by all living creatures on Earth
"A joyful celebration of the Earth. . . . Kleven's colorful artwork is full of subtle detail. . . . The artist uses an effective mix of media, from collage to chalk, to portray depth of scenes and vibrancy of detail." SLJ

Glass, Beth Raisner
Blue -ribbon dad; illustrated Margie Moore. Harry N Abrams Inc. 2011 un il $14.95
Grades: PreK K 1   E
1. Fathers -- Fiction 2. Squirrels -- Fiction
ISBN 978-0-8109-9727-1; 0-8109-9727-4
"A young squirrel hustles to get a surprise ready before his father comes home. While working on an arts-and-crafts project that necessitates glue, glitter, sequins, stickers, and more, the squirrel reflects on everything his father does for him. . . . Moore's delicately outlined watercolors mirror the coziness of the text." Publ Wkly

Glass, Eleri
The **red** shoes; by Eleri Glass; illustrated by Ashley Spires. Simply Read 2008 un il $16.95
Grades: PreK K 1 2   E
1. Shoes -- Fiction 2. Shopping -- Fiction
ISBN 978-1-894965-78-1; 1-894965-78-7
"Shopping for shoes, a little girl knows that her mother will pick the practical, very dull, lace-ups. Even the palette that Spires uses is dark and drab, and the child's body language screams disappointment. But when she gets to the store, she sees the most wonderful pair of red shoes and wants them more than anything. . . . This sweet story will appeal to little girls who count shoes as something very important indeed." SLJ

Gleeson, Libby
★ **Clancy** & Millie, and the very fine house; [illustrated by] Freya Blackwood. Little Hare Books 2009 un il $16.99

Grades: 1 2   E
1. Moving -- Fiction
ISBN 978-1-921541-19-3; 1-921541-19-9
LC 2010399372
"Australians Gleeson and Blackwood . . . portray with sensitivity a small boy's ambivalence about moving to a new house. . . . Blackwood exaggerates the building's imposing exterior and its rooms, with towering walls, windows that seem miles away, and chilly gray expanses of floor, emphasizing the enormity of the move for Clancy. . . . Though the story deals with a particular childhood dilemma, Clancy's feelings are conveyed with a dignity that should appeal to a wide audience." Publ Wkly

★ **Half** a world away; by Libby Gleeson; illustrated by Freya Blackwood. Arthur A. Levine Books 2007 un il hardcover o.p. $15.99
Grades: PreK K 1 2   E
1. Moving -- Fiction 2. Friendship -- Fiction
ISBN 0-439-88977-4; 0-439-88978-2 pa
LC 2006007712
When Louie's best friend Amy moves to the other side of the world, Louie must find a way to reconnect with her
"Blackwood's tender, realistic watercolors reinforce the friends' sweet closeness and magic. . . . Subtle, direct, and profound." Booklist

The **great** bear; [illustrations by Armin Greder] Candlewick Press 2011 il $16.99
Grades: PreK K 1   E
1. Bears -- Fiction 2. Freedom -- Fiction
ISBN 978-0-7636-5136-7; 0-7636-5136-2
LC 2010040288
A bear imprisoned in a medieval circus is forced to perform night after night before a mocking crowd, but she finally can no longer stand the torment and determines to set herself free.
"Greder's darkly beautiful charcoal-and-pastel illustrations carry the weight of the storytelling . . . and are abetted by a unique design. . . . Subtle—yet spectacular and deeply moving" Kirkus

Glenn, Sharlee Mullins
Just what Mama needs; [by] Sharlee Glenn; illustrated by Amiko Hirao. Harcourt 2008 un il lib bdg $16
Grades: PreK K 1 2   E
1. Dogs -- Fiction 2. Week -- Fiction 3. Imagination -- Fiction
ISBN 978-0-15-205759-6; 0-15-205759-5
LC 2005-25440
Abby the dog assumes a different identity for each day of the week until Sunday, when she is just herself.
"Glenn's descriptive text and use of onomatopoeia provide an ideal read-aloud [and] . . . Hirao's collage and colored-pencil art, expressed on a variety of paper surfaces, alternates stark views as Abby introduces a costume, followed by busy scenes of her imagination and the real-life labors. . . . There's something to please nearly everyone in this tale." SLJ

Gliori, Debi
No matter what. Harcourt Brace & Co. 1999 un il $16; bd bk $6.95

Grades: PreK K 1   E
  1. Stories in rhyme 2. Foxes -- Fiction 3. Parent-child
relationship -- Fiction
ISBN 0-15-202061-6; 0-15-206343-9 bd bk
                              LC 98-47277

Small, a little fox, seeks reassurance that Large will always provide love, no matter what

"Gliori's whimsical illustrations use warm, inviting color to invoke the same sense of emotional security as the rhyming text." Booklist

Stormy weather; written and illustrated by Debi Gliori. Walker & Co. 2009 un il $15.99; lib bdg $16.89
Grades: PreK K   E
  1. Stories in rhyme 2. Foxes -- Fiction 3. Animals
-- Fiction 4. Bedtime -- Fiction 5. Mother-child
relationship -- Fiction
ISBN 978-0-8027-9419-2; 0-8027-9419-X; 978-0-
8027-9422-2 lib bdg; 0-8027-9422-X lib bdg
                            LC 2008043523

As nighttime approaches, a baby fox and his mother imagine all the different animals around the world preparing for bed and falling asleep.

"The story's lulling pace enhances the quiet bedtime read-aloud. . . . Watercolor-and-ink spreads utilize warm earth tones within the family homes to contrast the sometimes threatening outside elements or cool night backdrops. Nimble lines support the comforting images, and swirling designs and twinkling stars add unique details." SLJ

What's the time, Mr. Wolf? by Deb Gliori. Walker 2012 32 p.
Grades: PreK K 1   E
  1. Time -- Juvenile fiction 2. Wolves -- Juvenile
fiction 3. Characters and characteristics in literature 4.
Characters in literature -- Fiction
ISBN 0802734324; 9780802734327
                            LC 2012014710

This book by Debi Gliori is "told from the point of view of Mr. Wolf on his birthday. Four and twenty black birds wake him up at seven o'clock, tweeting, 'What's the time, Mr. Wolf?' . . . Little Red Riding Hood, Hickory Dickory Dock . . . Humpty Dumpty, and other favorite nursery rhyme characters make an appearance in the text and/or pictures. Mr. Wolf's day is not going well until six o'clock when his friends surprise him with a birthday party." (School Library Journal)

The **trouble** with dragons; [by] Debi Gliori. Walker & Co. 2008 un il $16.99; lib bdg $17.89
Grades: PreK K 1   E
  1. Stories in rhyme 2. Dragons -- Fiction 3.
Environmental protection -- Fiction 4. Conservation of
natural resources -- Fiction
ISBN 978-0-8027-9789-6; 0-8027-9789-X; 978-0-
8027-9790-2 lib bdg; 0-8027-9790-3 lib bdg
                            LC 2008005389

When dragons cut down too many trees, blow out too much hot air, and do other environmental damage, the future looks grim, but other animals advise them on how to mend their ways and save the planet

This "is magical, thanks to the playful artwork and bouncy rhymes. Though the text sticks to the basics of taking care

of the Earth, the illustrations offer fodder for discussion." SLJ

Global Fund for Children (Organization)
  American babies; developed by the Global Fund for Children. Charlesbridge 2010 un il $6.95
Grades: PreK   E
  1. Infants 2. Board books for children
ISBN 978-1-58089-280-3; 1-58089-280-9

"This appealing board book offers 17 closeup photos of babies. . . . [It] has a brief text, really a single sentence divided into phrases. . . . From the Hawaiian child on the cover to the African-American girl on the last page, all the babies pictured are beyond early infancy. Their expressive faces and emotions are as varied as their family backgrounds, surroundings, and activities. . . . The pleasing layout places each colorful, full-page photo opposite a page with a slightly smaller photo and large-type text on its bright, solid-color border." Booklist

  Global babies; developed by the Global Fund for Children. Charlesbridge 2007 un il $6.95
Grades: PreK   E
  1. Infants 2. Board books for children
ISBN 978-1-58089-174-5

This board book offers color photographs of babies from 17 cultures around the world.

Goble, Paul
  Beyond the ridge; story and illustrations by Paul Goble. Bradbury Press 1989 un il hardcover o.p. pa $6.99
Grades: 2 3 4   E
  1. Native Americans -- Fiction
ISBN 0-689-71731-8 pa
                            LC 87-33113

At her death an elderly Plains Indian woman experiences the afterlife believed in by her people, while the surviving family members prepare her body according to their custom

"Goble's illustrations—in a double spread of gray rocks, smoothly surfaced in a skyscape of flying vultures—make a dignified context for a moving, direct discussion of death." Bull Cent Child Books

  Death of the iron horse; story and illustrations by Paul Goble. Bradbury Press 1987 un il hardcover o.p. pa $7.99
Grades: K 1 2 3   E
  1. Railroads -- Fiction 2. Cheyenne Indians -- Fiction
ISBN 0-689-71686-9 pa
                            LC 85-28011

The author "has taken several accounts of the 1867 Cheyenne attack of a Union Pacific freight train . . . and combined them into a story from the Indians' viewpoint. As the Cheyenne Prophet Sweet Medicine had foretold, strange hairy people were invading the land, killing women and children and driving off the horses. Descriptions of the iron horse inspired curiosity and fear in the young braves who decided to go out and protect their village from this new menace. Keeping fairly close to actual Indian accounts, Goble presents the braves' bold attack on the train, glossing over the deaths of the train crew." SLJ

Godden, Rumer

The **story** of Holly & Ivy; [by] Rumer Godden; [pictures by] Barbara Cooney. Viking 2006 31p il $17.99
Grades: K 1 2 3   E
1. Dolls -- Fiction 2. Christmas stories 3. Orphans -- Fiction 4. Christmas -- Fiction
ISBN 0-670-06219-7; 978-0-670-06219-5

First published 1957; a reissue of the newly illustrated edition published 1985

Orphaned Ivy finds her Christmas wish fulfilled with the help of a lonely couple and a doll named Holly.

"Texturally rich and evocatively wintry, this reissue is timeless." Horn Book Guide

Godwin, Laura

★ **Happy** and Honey; written by Laura Godwin; pictures by Jane Chapman. Margaret K. McElderry Bks. 2000 un il (Happy Honey) $12.95
Grades: PreK K 1   E
1. Cats 2. Dogs 3. Play 4. Cats -- Fiction 5. Dogs -- Fiction
ISBN 0-689-83406-3

LC 99-46923

Honey the cat is determined to play with Happy the dog, even though he is trying to sleep

"The text is short and effective, and the delightful acrylic paintings, which are set against an expanse of white space, center on Happy and Honey, keeping children as focused on the goings-on as does the just-right text." Booklist

Other titles about Happy and Honey are:
The best fall of all (2002)
Happy Christmas, Honey (2002)
Honey helps (2000)

One moon, two cats; illustrated by Yoko Tanaka. Atheneum Books for Young Readers 2011 un il $16.99
Grades: PreK K 1   E
1. Stories in rhyme 2. Cats -- Fiction 3. Country life -- Fiction 4. City and town life -- Fiction
ISBN 978-1-4424-1202-6; 1-4424-1202-X

LC 2009053697

Two cats, one in the city and one in the country, chase mice before going to sleep.

"The brief, rhymed text changes size to match the rhythms of the cats' adventures, and the rich acrylic paintings create an air of nighttime mystery. An ably told and atmospheric romp." SLJ

Goembel, Ponder

Animal fair; adapted and illustrated by Ponder Goembel. Marshall Cavendish Children 2010 un il $12.99
Grades: PreK K 1   E
1. Stories in rhyme 2. Animals -- Fiction
ISBN 978-0-7614-5642-1; 0-7614-5642-2

LC 2009005937

"Based on the children's song Animal Fair, Goembel's adaptation adroitly posits the wild imaginings of a child: what might go on at a fair apparently run by animals? The answer is nonsense, as virtually nothing the animals do makes a whit of sense. That, of course, is what will make young listeners squeal with glee. The text is wonderfully wordy and tied to an irresistible rhythm. . . . Goembel's ink and acrylic-wash artwork has an appealing orderliness to it." Booklist

Going, K. L.

Dog in charge; by K.L. Going; illustrated by Dan Santat. Dial Books for Young Readers 2012 40 p. col. ill. (hardcover) $16.99
Grades: PreK K 1 2   E
1. Cats -- Fiction 2. Dogs -- Fiction 3. Picture books for children 4. Cats -- Juvenile fiction 5. Dogs -- Juvenile fiction
ISBN 0803734794; 9780803734791

LC 2011035211

This is "Printz-winner [K.L.] Going['s] . . . picture-book debut." It's a "saga of a tutu-wearing bulldog who is the designated cat-sitter while the humans are at the store. Once the car leaves the driveway, five cats of varying breeds skedaddle from the sofa to spill milk, stir up fireplace ash, empty the hamper, disrupt a vanity, and more. Dog worries that their raucous acting out will reflect badly on him: 'Would he still be a good Dog, a smart Dog, the very best Dog?' His idea to entice good behavior with kibbles disappears with his own hunger. As he naps, the cats remember that they love Dog and bring the house back to perfect order as the family arrives." (School Library Journal)

Gold, August

★ **Thank** you, God, for everything; by August Gold; illustrated by Wendy Anderson Halperin. G.P. Putnam's Sons 2009 un il $16.99
Grades: PreK K 1 2   E
1. God -- Fiction 2. Religious life -- Fiction
ISBN 978-0-399-24049-2; 0-399-24049-7

LC 2008016801

As Daisy watches her parents thanking God everyday, she begins to look at everything around her and realizes she is also thankful for many things.

Gold's "goal here is to 'show young readers how to develop their own thankful eyes.' Both she and artist Halperin do that beautifully in this story. . . . In her signature softly colored style . . . Halperin takes everyday doings and elevates them." Booklist

Goldfinger, Jennifer P.

My dog Lyle. Clarion Books 2007 un il $16
Grades: PreK K 1 2   E
1. Dogs -- Fiction
ISBN 978-0-618-63983-0; 0-618-63983-7

LC 2006-07146

A child provides an ever-increasing list of characteristics that make Lyle a very special dog, despite appearances.

"The lively text matches perfectly with the vibrant, playful illustrations, done in bold, richly hued acrylics and oils." SLJ

Goldin, Barbara Diamond

Cakes and miracles; a Purim tale. [illustrated by] Jaime Zollars. Marshall Cavendish 2010 un il $17.99
Grades: PreK K 1   E
1. Jews -- Fiction 2. Blind -- Fiction 3. Purim -- Fiction
ISBN 978-0-7614-5701-5; 0-7614-5701-1

A revised and newly illustrated edition of the title first published 1991

Young, blind Hershel finds that he has special gifts he can use to help his mother during the Jewish holiday of Purim. Includes author's notes about the holiday and its origins

"Edited significantly from the 1991 edition, the new text is more accessible to a younger audience and works better as a read-aloud. Rich, full-spread illustrations in collage and acrylic paint warmly depict the Eastern European shtetl setting with expression and dimension." SLJ

Goldin, David

Meet me at the art museum; a whimsical look behind the scenes. by David Goldin. Abrams Books for Young Readers 2012 33 p. (hardback) $18.95

Grades: K 1 2 3   E

1. Museums 2. Picture books for children 3. Art museums -- Juvenile literature

ISBN 1419701878; 9781419701870

LC 2012019355

In this book, an "anthropomorphized name tag named Daisy gives a discarded 'Admit One' ticket stub (named Stub) a tour of an art museum—doing the same for readers in the process. . . . As Daisy guides Stub through the galleries, she discusses the museum's layout, operations (including security systems and temperature controls), and various staff responsibilities, from conservators to archivists." (Publishers Weekly)

Includes bibliographical references and index

Goldman, Judy

Uncle monarch and the Day of the Dead; [by] Judy Goldman; illustrated by Rene King Moreno. Boyds Mills Press 2008 un il $16.95

Grades: K 1 2 3   E

1. Death -- Fiction 2. Uncles -- Fiction 3. Butterflies -- Fiction 4. All Souls' Day -- Fiction 5. Spanish language -- Vocabulary

ISBN 978-1-59078-425-9; 1-59078-425-1

LC 2007049322

Upon the death of her beloved Tio Urbano, who has taught her that monarch butterflies are the souls of the dead, young Lupita gains a deeper understanding of Dia de los Muertos, the Day of the Dead, as it is observed in rural Mexico. Includes glossary of Spanish terms and facts about the Day of the Dead

"This lovely picture book effectively blends a poignant story about losing a beloved relative with a lucid description of Día de Muertos. . . . [This features] lovely, bright-hued colored-pencil illustrations. . . . Spanish words are integrated into the text." SLJ

Goldstone, Bruce

Awesome autumn; Bruce Goldstone. 1st ed. Henry Holt and Co. 2012 48 p. ill. (hardcover) $16.99

Grades: K 1 2   E

1. Climate 2. Seasons -- Encyclopedias 3. Autumn -- Juvenile literature

ISBN 0805092102; 9780805092103

LC 2011029043

This book is an educational resource for learning about the Autumn season. "Leaves change color. Animals fly south or get ready to hibernate. People harvest crops and dress up as scary creatures for Halloween. . . . With . . . photographs, . . . explanations, and . . . craft ideas, Bruce Goldstone has created a[n] . . . exploration of autumn." (Publisher's note)

Golenbock, Peter

ABC's of baseball; by Peter Golenbock; illustrated by Dan Andreasen. Dial Books for Young Readers 2012 48 p. col. ill. (reinforced) $16.99

Grades: 3 4 5   E

1. Alphabet -- Juvenile literature 2. Baseball -- Juvenile literature

ISBN 0803737114; 9780803737112

LC 2011021928

In this book, "[Peter] Golenbock defines several baseball terms and phrases for each letter of the alphabet, the entries and their definitions appearing in . . . sidebars that let [illustrator Dan] Andreasen's artwork take center stage. Figures like Babe Ruth and Alexander Cartwright . . . are mentioned alongside terms like 'bases loaded,' 'fielder's choice,' 'line drive' and 'southpaw,' which all receive brief definitions." (Publishers Weekly)

Golson, Terry

Tillie lays an egg; [by] Terry Golson; with photographs by Ben Fink. Scholastic Press 2009 un il $16.99

Grades: PreK K 1 2   E

1. Chickens -- Fiction

ISBN 978-0-545-00537-1; 0-545-00537-X

LC 2008011737

In search of the perfect place to lay her egg, Tillie the chicken leaves the barnyard and explores the farmhouse

"The photographed scenes are packed with Golson's own chicken-motif treasures—glassware, tins, vintage board games—and invite close exploration. Text and photos appear in bordered boxes; these are set against pastel wallpapers with country patterns—a pleasant contrast to Fink's crisp photography. . . . Full of charm." Publ Wkly

Gonzalez, Maya Christina

★ **My** colors, my world. Children's Book Press 2007 23p il $16.95

Grades: PreK K 1 2   E

1. Color -- Fiction 2. Deserts -- Fiction 3. Hispanic Americans -- Fiction 4. Bilingual books -- English-Spanish

ISBN 978-0-89239-221-6; 0-89239-221-5

LC 2007005297

A Pura Belpré Award honor book, 2008

Maya, who lives in the dusty desert, opens her eyes wide to find the colors in her world, from Papi's black hair and Mami's orange and purple flowers to Maya's red swing set and the fiery pink sunset

Goode, Diane

★ **Thanksgiving** is here! HarperCollins Pubs. 2003 un il $15.99; lib bdg $16.89

Grades: PreK K 1 2   E

1. Family life -- Fiction 2. Thanksgiving Day -- Fiction 3. Thanksgiving Day -- Juvenile literature

ISBN 0-06-051588-0; 0-06-051589-9 lib bdg

LC f002-151781

A family gathers to celebrate Thanksgiving at Grandma's house

"The humorously detailed, pen-and-ink and watercolor, cartoon artwork is exuberant, mischievous, and full of surprises. This Thanksgiving book has something for everyone." SLJ

The **most** perfect spot; by Diane Goode. HarperCollins 2006 un il $16.99; lib bdg $17.89

Grades: PreK K 1 2   E

1. Parks -- Fiction 2. Mother-son relationship -- Fiction
ISBN 0-06-072697-0; 0-06-072698-9 lib bdg

LC 2004030058

"Young Jack wants to go on a picnic with his mother and thinks that he knows the perfect spot in Prospect Park. Maybe it is, but getting there is fraught with problems. . . . When the rain begins to pour down, Mama and Jack decide there's only one perfect spot for a picnic—back home. . . . Goode's art was inspired by the early years of the last century.... Full of amusing details and nice touches . . . this book will sustain more readings than one might expect." Booklist

Goodhart, Pippa

Three little ghosties; illustrated by AnnaLaura Cantone. Bloomsbury Children's Books 2007 un il $16.95

Grades: PreK K 1 2   E

1. Ghost stories 2. Stories in rhyme
ISBN 978-1-58234-711-0; 1-58234-711-5

LC 2007-02610

Three mischievous ghosts love scaring little children, until the children decide to take matters into their own hands.

"Goodhart's engagingly silly rhymes are paired with mixed-media illustrations that use dark and spooky colors but feature goofy-looking ghosts." Horn Book

Goodrich, Carter

★ **Say** hello to Zorro! Simon & Schuster Books for Young Readers 2010 un il $15.99

Grades: PreK K 1   E

1. Dogs -- Fiction
ISBN 978-1-4169-3893-4; 1-4169-3893-1

LC 2009-11484

Mister Bud, the family dog, has a satisfying routine to his life, but when another dog joins the family and disrupts his schedule, Mister Bud must learn to adapt.

"Goodrich has a delightfully economical and humorous voice: trim yet filled with barely contained emotion—kind of like a dog. . . . And the artwork is arresting, done in watercolors of enormous personality and quality." Kirkus

The **hermit** crab. Simon & Schuster Books for Young Readers 2009 un il $16.99

Grades: K 1 2 3   E

1. Crabs -- Fiction 2. Marine animals -- Fiction
ISBN 978-1-4169-3892-7; 1-4169-3892-3

LC 2007045240

Absorbed in his search for food, a shy hermit crab, disguised in a fancy new shell, inadvertently rescues a flounder caught beneath a trap and wins the admiration of the other marine animals.

"The personal tone engages the audience, bringing immediacy to the plot, and serves as a warm contrast to the cool illustrations. Goodrich's colored pencil and watercolor spreads predominately feature greens and blues to convey the watery depth of the sea." SLJ

Gorbachev, Valeri

★ **Christopher** counting; [by] Valeri Gorbachev. Philomel Books 2008 un il $15.99

Grades: PreK K 1   E

1. Animals -- Fiction 2. Rabbits -- Fiction 3. Counting

-- Fiction
ISBN 978-0-399-24629-6

LC 2007023642

When Christopher Rabbit learns to count in school, he enjoys it so much that he counts everything in sight, including how many baskets his friends make when they play basketball and how many peas and carrots are on his plate.

"The simplicity of this charming story is what sets it apart from others that aim to introduce this concept. The text's deliberate pace is a perfect match for the pen, ink, and watercolor illustrations." SLJ

Dragon is coming! Harcourt Children's Books 2009 un il $16

Grades: PreK K 1 2   E

1. Fear -- Fiction 2. Mice -- Fiction 3. Clouds -- Fiction
4. Animals -- Fiction 5. Thunderstorms -- Fiction
ISBN 978-0-15-205196-9; 0-15-205196-1

LC 2006101580

Mouse frightens all of the animals she sees by shouting that a dragon is going to eat the sun, and then come after them.

"While the story is familiar, Gorbachev's illustrations revive it with delightful details and humorous poses." SLJ

Molly who flew away. Philomel Books 2009 un il $16.99

Grades: PreK K 1 2   E

1. Mice -- Fiction 2. Fairs -- Fiction 3. Animals -- Fiction 4. Balloons -- Fiction
ISBN 978-0-399-25211-2; 0-399-25211-8

LC 2008-32607

Molly the mouse buys so many balloons for all her animal friends at the fair, she gets carried away into the air.

"Pen-and-ink and watercolor illustrations carry this simple friendship story along to the climactic end. Molly's flight is especially well shown, with a double-page spread with three ascending panels followed by a bird's eye view of the frightened mouse high over the scenery and her friends running to the rescue down below." Booklist

Another title about Molly is:
What's the big idea, Molly? (2010)

★ **Ms.** Turtle the babysitter. HarperCollins Pubs. 2005 64p il (I can read book) hardcover o.p. pa $3.99

Grades: PreK K 1 2   E

1. Frogs -- Fiction 2. Turtles -- Fiction 3. Babysitters
-- Fiction
ISBN 0-06-058073-9; 0-06-058074-7 lib bdg; 0-06-058075-5 pa

LC 2004-6234

Ms. Turtle babysits for three little frogs when their parents go out for the evening

"Beginning readers will enjoy this chapter-style book. . . . The pen-and-ink and watercolor cartoons seamlessly complement the text. The expressions on the faces of these endearing frogs are priceless." SLJ

Shhh! Philomel Books 2011 un il $16.99

Grades: PreK K 1   E

1. Play -- Fiction 2. Noise -- Fiction 3. Sleep -- Fiction

4. Brothers -- Fiction
ISBN 978-0-399-25429-1; 0-399-25429-3

LC 2010041652

A little boy tries hard to be quiet while his little brother takes a nap.

"The illustrations, done in watercolors, gouache, and ink, are cheerfully rendered in soft tones that capture the calm, then playful, actions in the story. This is a fine book about how a child should behave while a younger sibling is asleep." SLJ

★ **That's** what friends are for. Philomel Books 2005 un il $15.99
Grades: PreK K 1 2   E
1. Pigs -- Fiction 2. Goats -- Fiction 3. Friendship -- Fiction
ISBN 0-399-23966-9

LC 2004-18118

When Goat finds his friend Pig crying, he imagines all the terrible things that might have happened to cause his distress

"The book is a warm display of friendship and a caution against unnecessary worry. Soft-colored drawings supply details for the simple text." Horn Book Guide

★ **Turtle's** penguin day; [by] Valeri Gorbachev. Alfred A. Knopf 2008 un il $16.99; lib bdg $19.99
Grades: PreK K 1   E
1. School stories 2. Animals -- Fiction 3. Turtles -- Fiction 4. Penguins -- Fiction
ISBN 978-0-375-84374-7; 0-375-84374-4; 978-0-375-94564-9 lib bdg; 0-375-94564-4 lib bdg

LC 2007037078

After hearing a bedtime story about penguins, Turtle dresses as a penguin for school and soon the entire class is having a penguin day.

"Cheerful watercolors and expressive line art imbue the matter-of-fact narrative with personality. . . . This nurturing tale celebrates the inspiration and information found in books, the invention bubbling up from a child who is read to, and the quality of learning that is possible when a teacher seizes the moment." SLJ

Two little chicks. NorthSouth Books 2011 un il (Tuff books) $6.95
Grades: PreK   E
1. Fear -- Fiction 2. Chickens -- Fiction 3. Playgrounds -- Fiction
ISBN 978-0-7358-4018-8; 0-7358-4018-0
First published 2001 with title: Chicken chickens

When two little chicks go to the playground for the very first time, everything looks scary—the seesaw, the merry-go-round, the swings, even the slide. But it takes just one slide down to turn two frightened little chicks into two brave little chicks.

"The new 'Tuff Books' edition of the story . . . sports a smaller trim size and glossy, heavy paper suitable for young hands." Horn Book Guide

What's the big idea, Molly? Philomel Books 2010 un il $16.99
Grades: PreK K 1 2   E
1. Mice -- Fiction 2. Gifts -- Fiction 3. Animals --

Fiction 4. Seasons -- Fiction 5. Turtles -- Fiction 6. Birthdays -- Fiction 7. Books and reading -- Fiction
ISBN 978-0-399-25428-4; 0-399-25428-5

Molly Mouse and her friends struggle to come up with ideas for birthday gifts for their friend Turtle and decide to make a book about the four seasons.

"Written and illustrated with verve and affection, this . . . features a sympathetic protagonist. . . . A fitting tribute to the art of storytelling." Booklist

The **missing** chick. Candlewick Press 2009 un il $15.99
Grades: PreK K 1   E
1. Ducks -- Fiction 2. Chickens -- Fiction
ISBN 978-0-7636-3676-0; 0-7636-3676-2

"Mother Hen and her seven chicks are hanging the laundry one sunny morning when neighborly Mrs. Duck observes that one chick is missing. Goat, Sheep, and Dog help to search the premises before being joined by the firefighters and the police on the ground and in helicopters. Amid all this noisy commotion, the missing chick wakes up from its napping spot in the laundry basket. . . . The story's simple premise, just-enough page-turning tension, and comical watercolor and ink illustrations add up to a gentle and satisfying tale that will hold up to repeated readings." SLJ

Gore, Leonid
Danny's first snow; by Leonid Gore. Atheneum 2007 un il $16.99
Grades: PreK K   E
1. Snow -- Fiction 2. Rabbits -- Fiction 3. Imagination -- Fiction
ISBN 1-4169-1330-0

When he ventures outside to experience his first snowfall, a young rabbit discovers that his world has greatly changed.

"The exquisite illustrations in this story . . . will delight young readers. . . . Gore achieves remarkable shapes and surfaces, with green pines transformed into bears that gradually melt away as the day advances." Publ Wkly

Mommy, where are you? [by] Leonid Gore. Atheneum Books for Young Readers 2009 un il $16.99
Grades: PreK K 1   E
1. Mice -- Fiction 2. Mother-child relationship -- Fiction
ISBN 978-1-4169-5505-4; 1-4169-5505-4

LC 2008-25994

A little mouse wakes up one day and, when he cannot find his mother, goes in search of her.

"Gore skillfully provides both repetition and variety for his audience, so both young listeners and their adults will find the story engaging as well as easy to follow. . . . Acrylic illustrations are simply composed, and the layered colors . . . and textured application of the paint . . . add pleasing depth and sophistication to the images." Bull Cent Child Books

When I grow up. Scholastic Press 2009 un il $16.99
Grades: PreK   E
1. Growth -- Fiction 2. Father-son relationship -- Fiction
ISBN 978-0-545-08597-7; 0-545-08597-7

LC 2008014313

At his drawing table on a rainy day, a boy imagines all the ways in which different things might grow up, and comes to the conclusion that he will grow up to be just like his dad.

"The simple and poetic artwork was done in acrylic and mixed media on die-cut pages. . . . The exploration of his world gives this father-and-son selection a refreshing take on a familiar theme." SLJ

Worms for lunch? Scholastic Press 2011 un il $16.99
Grades: PreK K   E
 1. Food -- Fiction 2. Animals -- Fiction 3. Animals -- Food -- Juvenile literature
ISBN 0-545-24338-6; 978-0-545-24338-4
          LC 2010004023

In this picture book, readers "follow a curious worm through die-cut pages to discover what different animals like to eat for lunch. 'Who on earth would eat worms for lunch?' the curious little leaf-loving worm wants to know... Not the mouse who likes cheese. Not the little girl, who loves spaghetti and ice cream! Not the cow, nor the bee, nor the monkey... But when a fish reveals what he most desires for lunch, . . . our little worm goes quickly on his way." (Publisher's note) "Preschool." (Horn Book)

"In this entertaining primer about what animals like to eat, Gore's bright acrylic paintings are reminiscent of the artwork of Carle and Lionni in their simplicity, textures, and whimsical humor. . . . The clever and effective die-cuts will easily keep readers' interest." Publ Wkly

The **wonderful** book. Scholastic Press 2010 un il
Grades: PreK K 1   E
 1. Forest animals -- Fiction 2. Books and reading -- Fiction
ISBN 0-545-08598-5; 978-0-545-08598-4
          LC 2009026348

When various forest animals discover a mysterious object in the woods, they each use it for a different purpose, until a boy reads stories from it, much to the animals' delight. "Ages three to five." (Bull Cent Child Books)

"Unpretentious watercolor-and-ink illustrations on textured paper suit well, because both text and pictures have a light, unfussy vibe—even while puns lurk unstated, such as the fox treating sheets of paper as bedsheets. Children just beginning to recognize books as objects will appreciate the animals' confusion and their own advanced understanding." Kirkus

Gormley, Greg
 ★ **Dog** in boots; illustrated by Roberta Angaramo. Holiday House 2011 un il $17.95
Grades: PreK K 1   E
 1. Dogs -- Fiction 2. Shoes -- Fiction
ISBN 978-0-8234-2347-7; 0-8234-2347-6
          LC 2010029889

After reading "Puss in Boots," an adventurous dog sets out to find the perfect pair of shoes to suit his every need.

"Children will identify with Dog's good-natured struggle through trial and error, fall in love with the evocative and funny illustrations and laugh out loud at the satisfying ending. A truly enjoyable selection and a nice follow-up to a favorite fairy tale, just right for reading aloud." Kirkus

Gourley, Robbin
 ★ **Bring** me some apples and I'll make you a pie; a story about Edna Lewis. Clarion Books 2009 45p il $16
Grades: PreK K 1 2   E
 1. Cooks 2. Food -- Fiction 3. Cookbook writers 4. Cooking -- Fiction 5. Farm life -- Fiction 6. Family life -- Fiction 7. African Americans -- Fiction
ISBN 978-0-618-15836-2; 0-618-15836-7
          LC 2007-46978

Edna and members of her family gather fruits, berries, and vegetables from the fields, garden, and orchard on their Virginia farm and turn them into wonderful meals. Includes facts about the life of Edna Lewis, a descendant of slaves who grew up to be a famous chef, and five recipes.

"The cheery watercolor spreads follow Edna and various relatives . . . from spring to first snow. . . . Folk sayings or songs accompany mention of each new food. . . . Dynamic paintings, increasingly lush as summer intensifies, add vigor." Publ Wkly

Gow, Nancy
 Ten big toes and a prince's nose; illustrated by Stephen Costanza. Sterling Pub. 2010 un il $14.95
Grades: PreK K 1 2   E
 1. Stories in rhyme 2. Princes -- Fiction 3. Princesses -- Fiction
ISBN 978-1-4027-6396-0; 1-4027-6396-4
          LC 2008031835

A lovely princess with enormous feet and a charming prince with a huge nose meet on a ski lift and, while their flaws are hidden, fall in love.

"Told in chatty rhyme, . . . this cleverly plotted tale conveys its message . . . with aplomb. The saturated colors and folk-like feel of the artwork are just right for this jaunty tale." Kirkus

Gower, Catherine
 Long -Long's New Year; a story about the Chinese spring festival. illustrated by He Zhihong. Tuttle 2005 un il $16.95
Grades: K 1 2 3   E
 1. Grandfathers -- Fiction 2. Chinese New Year -- Fiction
ISBN 0-8048-3666-3
          LC 2004-111580

"Gower's simple, appealing story aptly captures the details of the festival as well as specifics of Chinese life. Zhihong's softly colored, detailed drawings on tan rice paper evoke both the bustle of a preholiday marketplace as well as the gentle warmth shared by grandfather and grandchild." SLJ

Graber, Janet
 Muktar and the camels. Henry Holt and Co. 2009 un il $16.99
Grades: K 1 2 3   E
 1. School stories 2. Camels -- Fiction 3. Orphans -- Fiction 4. Refugees -- Fiction
ISBN 978-0-8050-7834-3; 0-8050-7834-7
          LC 2008038217

Muktar, an eleven-year-old refugee living in a Kenyan orphanage, dreams of tending camels again, as he did with his nomadic family in Somalia, and has a chance to prove himself when a traveling librarian with an injured camel arrives at his school.

"Muktar longs to live the life that is in his blood, and Graber tells his story well. . . . Mack's oil-on-canvas paintings evoke the sun and dust of Kenya, giving readers an impression of the landscape." SLJ

Graham, Bob

★ **April** and Esme, tooth fairies. Candlewick Press 2010 un il $16.99
Grades: PreK K 1 2   E
  1. Teeth -- Fiction 2. Fairies -- Fiction 3. Sisters -- Fiction
  ISBN 978-0-7636-4683-7; 0-7636-4683-0
On their first assignment, two young tooth fairy sisters journey by night into the huge world of humans to collect Daniel Dangerfield's tooth and fly it safely home.

"Young audiences will linger over the detailed illustrations that bring to life Graham's gentle tale." Horn Book

Dimity Dumpty; the story of Humpty's little sister. Candlewick Press 2006 un il $15.99
Grades: PreK K 1 2   E
  1. Eggs -- Fiction 2. Circus -- Fiction 3. Siblings -- Fiction 4. Nursery rhymes -- Fiction
  ISBN 0-7636-3078-0
                                        LC 2005-55306
Humpty Dumpty's little sister is too shy to be part of her family's circus act, but she finds courage when her brother needs her help.

"The full-color watercolor illustrations are a delight. . . . The language is lyrical . . . and makes a perfect read-aloud." SLJ

★ **How** to heal a broken wing. Candlewick Press 2008 un il $16.99
Grades: PreK K 1 2   E
  1. Birds -- Fiction 2. Rescue work -- Fiction
  ISBN 978-0-7636-3903-7; 0-7636-3903-6
                                        LC 2007-40622
When Will finds a bird with a broken wing, he takes it home and cares for it, hoping in time it will be able to return to the sky.

This is a "sparsely worded story. . . . Graham breaks his watercolor-and-ink cartoons into full-bleed spreads and large and small comics-like panels, enabling him to dwell on each moment of tender loving care and to preach patience." Publ Wkly

Let's get a pup, said Kate. Candlewick Press 2001 un il hardcover o.p. pa $6.99
Grades: PreK K 1 2   E
  1. Dogs 2. Pets 3. Animal shelters 4. Dog adoption 5. Dogs -- Fiction 6. Animal shelters -- Fiction
  ISBN 0-7636-1452-1; 0-7636-2193-5 pa
                                        LC 00-57208
When Kate and her parents visit the animal shelter, an adorable puppy charms them, but it is very hard to leave an older dog behind

"Bob Graham's cozy watercolors, lightly held in place by loose, sketchy outlines, contribute to this story's feelings of warmth, family, and belonging." Horn Book

Another title about Kate and her dog is:

"The trouble with dogs . . . " said Dad (2007)

★ **Oscar's** half birthday. Candlewick Press 2005 un il $16.99
Grades: PreK K 1 2   E
  1. Birthdays -- Fiction 2. Family life -- Fiction 3. Racially mixed people -- Fiction
  ISBN 0-7636-2699-6
                                        LC 2004-57041
"A mixed-race family sets out for a picnic in the park to celebrate baby Oscar's half birthday. . . . The warm, expressive illustrations show a family apartment in which a mop, shoes, and toys all share floor space. . . . This is an effortlessly multicultural story, full of the joy of childhood, family, and community." SLJ

A **bus** called Heaven; written and illustrated by Bob Graham. Candlewick Press 2012 40p. ill. $16.99
Grades: PreK K 1   E
  1. Friendship 2. Neighborhood 3. Buses -- Fiction
  ISBN 978-0-7636-5893-9
                                        LC 2011278839
This book tells the story of "[a] city neighborhood" which "takes shape around an abandoned school bus." (Kirkus) The bus "becomes a hub of activity. People come together to hold meetings, play games and share stories. . . . But one day a tow truck arrives and threatens to take away not just the bus, but everything everyone has worked so hard to create. . . . This is . . . [a] story about friendship, the strength of a community and a little girl who . . . comes into her own." (Publisher's note)

Gralley, Jean

The **moon** came down on Milk Street; written and illustrated by Jean Gralley. Holt 2004 un il $16.95
Grades: PreK K 1 2   E
  1. Stories in rhyme 2. Rescue work -- Fiction
  ISBN 0-8050-7266-7
When the moon comes down in pieces, different helpers work to set things right again, including the Fire Chief, rescue workers, and helper dogs.

"Gralley presents a perceptive look at how individuals react to an unexpected crisis. . . . Done in gouache and mixed media, the large, uncluttered illustrations on white backgrounds contribute to the gentle nature of the story." SLJ

Gramatky, Hardie

Little Toot; pictures and story by Hardie Gramatky. G.P. Putnam's Sons 2007 86p il $17.99
Grades: PreK K   E
  1. Tugboats -- Fiction
  ISBN 978-0-399-24713-2; 0-399-24713-0
First published 1939
Little Toot the tugboat conquers his fear of rough seas when he singlehandedly rescues an ocean liner during a storm

"Mr. Gramatky tells his story with humor and enjoyment, giving, too, a genuine sense of the water front in both pictures and story." Horn Book

Grambling, Lois G.

T. Rex and the Mother's Day hug; by Lois G. Grambling; illustrated by Jack E. Davis. HarperCollins 2008 un il $16.99; lib bdg $17.89

Grades: K 1 2   E

1. Dinosaurs -- Fiction 2. Mother's Day -- Fiction
ISBN 978-0-06-053126-3; 0-06-053126-6; 978-0-06-053127-0 lib bdg; 0-06-053127-4 lib bdg

LC 2007-6882

Eager to do something special for Mother's Day, T. Rex decides to surprise his mother by decorating her car.

"Davis's jaunty cartoon illustrations bring these less-than-extinct dinosaurs alive. This fun read-aloud will tickle young children as they prepare for Mother's Day themselves." SLJ

Other titles in this series are:
Here comes T. Rex Cottontail (2007)
T. Rex trick-or-treats (2005)

Grandits, John

★ **Ten** rules you absolutely must not break if you want to survive the school bus; illustrated by Michael Allen Austin. Clarion Books 2011 32p il $16.99
Grades: K 1 2   E

1. School stories 2. Buses -- Fiction 3. Brothers -- Fiction
ISBN 978-0-618-78822-4; 0-618-78822-0

Before Kyle rides a school bus for the first time, his older brother gives him a list of rules he must follow but after breaking every single one the first day, Kyle discovers the rule his brother left out.

"Austin's acrylic artwork is amazingly lifelike. He is at his best when he illustrates scenes from Kyle's vivid imagination, which has a tendency toward the metaphor. Kyle's every thought and feeling are manifest on the page. . . . Worthy of being shelved next to Jon Scieszka's funniest." Kirkus

The **travel** game; illustrated by R. W. Alley. Clarion Books 2009 32p il $16
Grades: K 1 2 3   E

1. Aunts -- Fiction 2. Games -- Fiction 3. Tailoring -- Fiction 4. Imagination -- Fiction 5. Polish Americans -- Fiction
ISBN 978-0-618-56420-0; 0-618-56420-9

LC 2005017646

To avoid a nap, Tad plays his favorite quiet game with his aunt and together their imaginations take them from their home in Buffalo, New York, to Hong Kong.

"Alley's cheery and busy street, home, and shop scenes in ink, watercolor, and acrylic are filled with the sorts of details that are fully appreciated over multiple readings. Children will be charmed by the warmth and humor of Grandits's wonderful tribute to family memories and the power of imagination." SLJ

Grandpre, Mary

The **sea** chest; illustrated by Mary GrandPré. Dial Bks. for Young Readers 2002 un il $16.99
Grades: K 1 2 3   E

1. Islands 2. Sisters 3. Lighthouses 4. Rescues 5. Islands -- Fiction 6. Sisters -- Fiction 7. Lighthouses -- Fiction
ISBN 0-8037-2703-8

LC 2001-28255

A young girl listens as her great-aunt, a lighthouse keeper's daughter, tells of her childhood living on a Maine island, and of the infant that washed ashore after a storm

"GrandPré's oil paintings create the dramatic effects of the story. . . . This lovely book has an intimacy that is enhanced by reading it aloud." SLJ

Granstrom, Brita

Baby knows best; illustrated by Brita Granström. Little, Brown 2002 un il $15.95
Grades: PreK K 1 2   E

1. Stories in rhyme 2. Infants -- Fiction
ISBN 0-316-60580-8

LC 00-107325

First published 2001 in the United Kingdom

"The rhyming text is short and fun, and Granström's colorful watercolor illustrations get the point across." Booklist

Grant, Judyann

★ **Chicken** said, Cluck! by Judyann Ackerman Grant; pictures by Sue Truesdell. HarperCollins 2008 32p il (My first I can read book) $16.99; lib bdg $17.89
Grades: K 1 2   E

1. Chickens -- Fiction 2. Gardening -- Fiction 3. Grasshoppers -- Fiction
ISBN 978-0-06-028723-8; 0-06-028723-3; 978-0-06-028724-5 lib bdg; 0-06-028724-1 lib bdg

LC 2001-24016

A Geisel Award honor book, 2009

Earl and Pearl do not want Chicken's help in the garden, until a swarm of grasshoppers arrives and her true talent shines

"This easy reader has short sentences, a variety of verb tenses, and vowel and consonant blends and digraphs. . . . Emergent readers may chime in with their own 'Shoo, Shoos' and 'Cluck, Cluck.' The funny, expressive pen-and-ink drawings support the reading with simple clarity." SLJ

Grant, Karima

Sofie and the city; [by] Karima Grant; illustrated by Janet Montecalvo. Boyds Mills Press 2006 un il $15.95
Grades: PreK K 1 2   E

1. Friendship -- Fiction 2. Immigrants -- Fiction 3. African Americans -- Fiction 4. City and town life -- Fiction
ISBN 1-59078-273-9

LC 2005020116

When Sofie calls her grandmother in Senegal on Sundays, she complains about the ugliness of the city she now lives in, but her life changes when she makes a new friend

"Told in simple language, with dialogue matching that of a child learning English, the text and art show how upsetting any move can be and how it feels to be small in a large and unfamiliar place." SLJ

Graves, Keith

Chicken Big. Chronicle Books 2010 un il $16.99
Grades: PreK K 1 2   E

1. Size -- Fiction 2. Chickens -- Fiction
ISBN 978-0-8118-7237-9; 0-8118-7237-8

"Compared to panicky Chicken Little, Chicken Big is unflappable. . . . This newborn towers over four fellow chickens, who decide he must be an elephant. . . . When something drops on the smallest hen, she yelps 'The sky is falling!' Chicken Big calmly says, 'It's only an acorn. They're actually quite tasty.' He is equally placid and helpful when the ditsy chickens freak out over the rain and wind.

. . . Graves . . . renders his fowl in a palette of gray-blue, taupe, and wheat yellow, with exuberant voice bubbles that highlight the ridiculousness of the smaller chickens' assertions." Publ Wkly

Gravett, Emily

Blue chameleon. Simon & Schuster Books for Young Readers 2011 un il $16.99
Grades: PreK K 1   E
  1. Chameleons -- Fiction 2. Friendship -- Fiction
  ISBN 1-4424-1958-X; 978-1-4424-1958-2

Chameleon can turn himself into anything and appear to fit in anywhere, but it seems that neither the swirly snail, the green grasshopper nor the striped sock want to be friends. Will he ever find someone to talk to? Someone just like him?

"Gravett's art charms; colored pencil lines on rough paper give the pages warmth, and the chameleon's 'disguises' repay attention as readers spot similarities to and differences from the things the chameleon mimics." Publ Wkly

★ **Dogs**. Simon & Schuster 2010 un il $15.99
Grades: PreK K 1   E
  1. Opposites 2. Stories in rhyme 3. Dogs -- Fiction
  ISBN 978-1-4169-8703-1; 1-4169-8703-7

"In minimal, rhyming text, an unidentified narrator describes its favorite kinds of dogs . . . and, along the way, offers a subtle lesson in the meaning of opposites. Expressive pencil drawings, overlaid with soft washes of watercolor on creamy stock, waggishly animate more than a dozen varieties of dogs. . . . The pacing of the simple text and scale of the drawings lend this title equally well to preschool storytimes, lap-sharing, and emergent-reader[s]." SLJ

★ **Little** Mouse's big book of fears. Simon & Schuster Books for Young Readers 2008 un il $17.99
Grades: K 1 2 3   E
  1. Fear -- Fiction 2. Mice -- Fiction
  ISBN 978-1-4169-5930-4; 1-4169-5930-0
                          LC 2008-61104
First published 2007 in the United Kingdom with title: Emily Gravett's big book of fears

Little Mouse draws pictures of some of the many things he is afraid of, including creepy crawlies, sharp knives, and having accidents, and provides the correct scientific name for each of his fears

"Spare text and delightful illustrations chronicle this nervous rodent's journey. . . . The striking mixed-media art captures the humorous adventures of the white mouse and his red pencil." SLJ

Meerkat mail. Simon & Schuster Books for Young Readers 2007 un il $17.99
Grades: PreK K 1   E
  1. Meerkats -- Fiction
  ISBN 978-1-4169-3473-8; 1-4169-3473-1
                          LC 2007001569
Through a series of flip-up postcards addressed to his family, Sunny Meerkat documents his travels as he searches for the perfect place for him to live.

"Gravett neatly incorporates facts about meerkats, mongooses, and their habitats. She employs a spare narrative, allowing Sunny's postcards to tell most of the story through both the character's distinctive voice and each post card's illustrations." Horn Book

★ **Monkey** and me. Simon & Schuster 2008 un il $15.99
Grades: PreK K   E
  1. Toys -- Fiction 2. Animals -- Fiction 3. Imagination -- Fiction
  ISBN 978-1-4169-5457-6; 1-4169-5457-0

"A little girl pretends that she and her adored stuffed monkey fit right in with tribes of penguins, kangaroos, bats, elephants and . . . monkeys. A catchy refrain sets up each scenario. . . . Working in pencil and watercolor, with a palette limited to red, black and brown, Gravett . . . portrays the action in a series of exuberant spot sketches set against a white sweep." Publ Wkly

★ **Orange** pear apple bear. Simon & Schuster Books for Young Readers 2007 un il $12.99
Grades: PreK K   E
  1. Bears -- Fiction 2. Color -- Fiction 3. Shape -- Fiction
  ISBN 978-1-4169-3999-3; 1-4169-3999-7
                          LC 2006-17964
A "bear changes color and shape as he balances, juggles, and eventually eats the three pieces of fruit before loping off. The front endpapers show oranges, green pears, and green apples with rosy tinges in a line leading readers into the simple and appealing story. . . . Beautiful, softly hued watercolor illustrations loosely outlined in black pen and ink are delightful." SLJ

★ **Spells**. Simon & Schuster Books for Young Readers 2009 un il $16.99
Grades: K 1 2 3 4   E
  1. Frogs -- Fiction 2. Magic -- Fiction
  ISBN 978-1-4169-8270-8; 1-4169-8270-1
                          LC 2008-941243
"A small green frog stumbles on a book of spells, . . . tries to turn himself into a handsome prince, but suffers a series of glitches. Frog transforms himself into a snake, bird, rabbit and other creatures before getting it right. . . . The five pages that show Frog's new forms are cut in half horizontally, and children will delight in turning the half-pages, reading the new spells that appear on the left side of each spread and seeing the combined creatures that emerge (a half-prince, half-newt "prewt," for instance)." Publ Wkly

Wolf won't bite! Emily Gravett. Simon & Schuster Books for Young Readers 2012 32 p.
Grades: PreK K   E
  1. Pigs -- Juvenile fiction 2. Circus -- Juvenile fiction 3. Picture books for children 4. Wolves -- Juvenile fiction 5. Pigs -- Fiction 6. Circus -- Fiction 7. Wolves -- Fiction
  ISBN 1442427639; 9781442427631
                          LC 2011000773
In this illustrated children's book by Emily Gravett, "three pigs have captured a wild wolf, and now he's the star of their little circus production as the ringmaster gloatingly presents his patient submission: "I can stand him on a stool! I can dress him in a bow. . . I can ride him like a horse but WOLF WON'T BITE!" When the trio attempts to place

their heads "between his mighty jaws," however, they have tried the wolf's patience too far (. . . not to a fatal degree, as the endpapers show the wolf pursuing the three with a bit of the ringmaster pig's jacket in his mouth)." (Bulletin of the Center for Children's Books)

Wolves; [by] Emily Grrrabbett [i.e. Gravett] Simon & Schuster Books for Young Readers 2006 un il $15.95
Grades: 1 2 3   E
    1. Wolves -- Fiction 2. Rabbits -- Fiction 3. Books and reading -- Fiction
    ISBN 978-1-4169-1491-4; 1-4169-1491-9
                LC 2005027540
When a young rabbit checks out a library book about wolves, he learns much more about their behavior than he wanted to know
"This imaginative, cleverly designed story unfolds in a delectable blend of spare text and eloquent multimedia illustrations." SLJ

★ The **odd** egg. Simon & Schuster Books for Young Readers 2009 un il $15.99
Grades: PreK K 1   E
    1. Eggs -- Fiction 2. Birds -- Fiction 3. Ducks -- Fiction 4. Alligators -- Fiction
    ISBN 978-1-4169-6872-6; 1-4169-6872-5
                LC 2008-61108
Duck is trying to hatch the oddest egg of all.
"Using visual suspense and few words, Gravett depicts an alligator bursting from the shell, snapping its jaws and scattering the naysayers. . . . A witty salute to both nature and nurture." Publ Wkly

★ The **rabbit** problem. Simon & Schuster Books for Young Readers 2010 un il $17.99
Grades: K 1 2   E
    1. Counting 2. Months -- Fiction 3. Rabbits -- Fiction 4. Seasons -- Fiction 5. Family life -- Fiction
    ISBN 978-1-4424-1255-2; 1-4424-1255-0
                LC 2010009751
In Fibonacci's Field, Lonely and Chalk Rabbit meet, snuggle together, and then spend a year trying to cope with their ever-increasing brood and the seasonal changes that bring a new challenge each month. Presented in calendar format with one pop-up illustration and other special features.
"Whimsical ideas proliferate as fast as rabbits in Gravett's splendid sendup of Fibonacci's query. . . . The only drawback to Graver's delicious creation is that the moving parts and magnificent final pop-ups are likely to fall prey to small hands. Solution: purchase a duplicate." Publ Wkly

Gray, Libba Moore
★ **My** mama had a dancing heart; illustrated by Raúl Colón. Orchard Bks. 1995 un il hardcover o.p. pa $6.99
Grades: K 1 2 3   E
    1. Dance -- Fiction 2. Seasons -- Fiction 3. Mother-daughter relationship -- Fiction
    ISBN 0-531-09470-7; 0-531-08770-0 lib bdg; 0-531-07142-1 pa
                LC 94-48802
"In spring, summer, fall and winter, a mother leads her young daughter in dancing a celebratory ballet, a hymn to the season. When the girl is older, she is a ballerina and remembers that her mother gave her a dancing heart. . . .

Colón's etched watercolors in earth and muted jewel tones give the book an old-fashioned ambiance. . . . Gray's writing lends itself to reading aloud, but independent readers will also enjoy it." SLJ

Gray, Luli
★ **Ant** and Grasshopper; written by Luli Gray; illustrated by Giuliano Ferri. Margaret K. McElderry Books 2011 un il $16.99
Grades: K 1 2   E
    1. Ants -- Fiction 2. Grasshoppers -- Fiction
    ISBN 1-4169-5140-7; 978-1-4169-5140-7
"Industrious Ant and pesty, music-loving Grasshopper move beyond Aesop's pointed lesson on negligence to a quite different moral as Gray further develops their relationship in this engaging, extended story. . . . Ferri expands the fun in fulsome watercolor scenes of Ant's glowing home and the changing seasons beyond his door and windows. The sturdy comic insects . . . have expressive eyes and body language. . . . The old tale has a new implied moral about empathy and friendship as the two unlikely fellows learn to care for each other. . . . The humorous, fluent telling and pictures would pair well with terse Aesop versions and stand on their own, offering especially nice read-aloud fare." SLJ

Green, Alison
The **fox** in the dark; illustrated by Deborah Allwright. Tiger Tales 2010 un il $15.95
Grades: PreK K 1   E
    1. Fear -- Fiction 2. Foxes -- Fiction 3. Animals -- Fiction
    ISBN 978-1-58925-091-8; 1-58925-091-5
Rabbit, Duck, Mouse and Lamb squish into Rabbit's house to hide from Fox.
"Allwright's warm and comforting mixed-media illustrations are full of soft lines and earth tones, which balance the threat felt by the animals and make Rabbit's home a safe haven. Young children will squeal every time they hear the knock at the door, but will be relieved by the gentle ending." SLJ

Green, Dan
Wild alphabet; an A to zoo pop-up book. [by] Dan Green, [illustrated by] Mike Haines and Julia Frohlich. Kingfisher 2010 un il $19.99
Grades: PreK K 1 2   E
    1. Animals 2. Alphabet 3. Pop-up books
    ISBN 978-0-7534-6472-4; 0-7534-6472-1
"On each spare, uncluttered spread, a short poem, a small color photo, and a creative paper construction introduce a different animal for each letter of the alphabet. . . . The letters are clearly presented, opening this to a broad audience of both new ABC learners and elementary students, who will appreciate the whimsical, action-filled verse and artistry in the images." Booklist

Greenberg, David
Crocs! by David T. Greenberg; illustrated by Lynn Munsinger. Little, Brown 2008 un il $16.99
Grades: K 1 2 3   E
    1. Stories in rhyme 2. Crocodiles -- Fiction
    ISBN 978-0-316-07306-6; 0-316-07306-7
                LC 2006020571

Having moved from the city to a tropical island to escape such horrifying creatures as bugs and cats, a boy encounters a horde of friendly crocodiles, who drink Tabasco sauce, get tangled in dental floss, and turn the house into a swamp

"The zany illustrations—done in mixed-media, soft-palette watercolors with pen and ink—use plenty of white space and add humor and charm to the perfect-pitch verses." SLJ

Enchanted lions; by David T. Greenberg; illustrated by Kristina Swarner. Dutton Children's Books 2009 un il $16.99

Grades: PreK K 1 2   E
   1. Stories in rhyme 2. Constellations -- Fiction 3. Outer space -- Exploration -- Fiction
   ISBN 978-0-525-47938-3; 0-525-47938-4
                      LC 2008-34215

One evening, Rose climbs on the back of an enchanted lion who takes her on a tour of outer space, where they race with Monoceros the unicorn, pass by Pegasus and Pisces, and are rescued from a black hole by Cetus the whale.

"The gentle, rhyming text and the mottled, softly colored scratchboardlike illustrations work together to convey a quiet, calm tone for this heavenly romp." Booklist

Greenfield, Eloise
   Africa dream; illustrated by Carole Byard. Crowell 1977 un il hardcover o.p. pa $6.99

Grades: PreK K 1 2   E
   ISBN 0-690-04776-2 lib bdg; 0-06-443277-7 pa
                      LC 77-5080

Coretta Scott King Award for text
"As ethereal as the title implies, this sparsely worded prose-poem relates the benign dream experience of a young child who transports her mind to 'Long-ago Africa.'" Booklist

   Grandpa's face; illustrated by Floyd Cooper. Philomel Bks. 1988 un il lib bdg $16.99; pa $6.99

Grades: PreK K 1 2   E
   1. Actors -- Fiction 2. Grandfathers -- Fiction
   ISBN 0-399-21525-5 lib bdg; 0-399-22106-9 pa
                      LC 87-16729

"Tamika fears that her grandfather, an actor, is incapable of loving her when she sees him practicing a cruel expression. The young girl's turmoil and its resolution are keenly felt through evocative text and striking pictures." SLJ

Gregorich, Barbara
   Waltur paints himself into a corner and other stories; by Barbara Gregorich; illustrated by Kristin Sorra. Houghton Mifflin 2007 un il $15

Grades: K 1 2 3   E
   1. Bears -- Fiction 2. Animals -- Fiction 3. Proverbs -- Fiction
   ISBN 978-0-618-74796-2; 0-618-74796-6
                  LC 2006102370

Walter the bear learns more lessons from his friend Matilda, such as "do not put the cart before the horse" and "let sleeping dogs lie."

"Gregorich creates some deliciously sticky, comical situations. . . . Sorra's pen-and-ink and watercolor artwork is a lively mix of spread and panels." Booklist

   Another title about Walter is:
   Walter buys a pig in a poke and other stories (2006)

Gregory, Nan
   Pink; [illustrated by] Luc Melanson. Groundwood 2007 32p il $17.95

Grades: PreK K 1 2   E
   1. Dolls -- Fiction
   ISBN 978-0-88899-781-4

Vivi loves the color pink. She is working and saving her money in order to buy a pink doll from the store. How does she feel when the doll is sold to someone else?

"Gregory writes with precision and creates apt, sometimes surprising phrases that capture the characters' feelings. Melanson's painterly, digitally assisted pictures create a distinctive look though the elongated forms and faces of the characters." Booklist

Gretz, Susanna
   ★ **Riley** and Rose in the picture. Candlewick Press 2005 un il $16.99

Grades: PreK K 1 2   E
   1. Cats -- Fiction 2. Dogs -- Fiction 3. Friendship -- Fiction
   ISBN 0-7636-2681-3
                  LC 2004-54569

On a rainy day Reilly the dog and Rosa the cat decide to stay indoors and draw a picture together but have trouble agreeing on how to do it

"The lively text is read-aloud friendly, incorporating child-familiar dialogue, interactions, and humor. The colorful gouache art is charming, too, filling the pages with expressive characters and distinctive childlike artwork that perfectly matches the story." Booklist

Grey, Mini
   Egg drop. Alfred A. Knopf 2009 un il $16.99; lib bdg $19.99

Grades: 1 2 3   E
   1. Eggs -- Fiction 2. Flight -- Fiction
   ISBN 978-0-375-84260-3; 0-375-84260-8; 978-0-375-94260-0 lib bdg; 0-375-94260-2 lib bdg
                  LC 2008-24534

Tragedy strikes when an egg, eager to fly like birds, airplanes, and insects, steps off of a tall tower.

"The mixed-media and collage full-color art is quirky and inventive with multiple perspectives, and imbues the Egg with personality." SLJ

   ★ **Three** by the sea. Alfred A. Knopf 2011 un il $17.99; lib bdg $20.99

Grades: K 1 2   E
   1. Cats -- Fiction 2. Dogs -- Fiction 3. Mice -- Fiction 4. Foxes -- Fiction 5. Happiness -- Fiction 6. Friendship -- Fiction 7. Cooperation -- Fiction
   ISBN 978-0-375-86784-2; 0-375-86784-8; 978-0-375-96784-9 lib bdg; 0-375-96784-2 lib bdg
                  LC 2010004084

First published 2010 in the United Kingdom

Cat, Dog, and Mouse live together contentedly in a cottage by the sea, dividing the work between them, until A. Stranger, Esq., a fox from the Winds of Change company, arrives and stirs up trouble.

This is "a beguiling little parable. . . . The artwork is standard-issue outstanding for Grey, with creative dollops of collage, endearing animal characters, and detail-strewn settings. . . . [The] complex resolution . . . refreshingly eschews any simple message." Booklist

Traction Man and the beach odyssey; Mini Grey. Alfred A. Knopf 2012 32 p.
Grades: PreK K 1 2   E
1. Toys -- Juvenile fiction 2. Dolls -- Juvenile fiction 3. Beaches -- Juvenile fiction 4. Toys -- Fiction 5. Beaches -- Fiction 6. Brooms and brushes -- Fiction 7. Action figures (Toys) -- Fiction
ISBN 0375969527; 9780375869525; 9780375969522; 9780375983641
      LC 2011020102
In this children's book by Mini Grey, "the action-figure star . . .Traction Man and his trusty sidekick, Scrubbing Brush, are brought to the beach by their boy owner. They explore an underwater world of crabs and cockles, defend their picnic lunch from a hungry dog, and get swept out to sea by a vigorous wave. They're rescued by a girl and squirreled away in a sand castle, where they meet two towering sirens called the Dollies." (Booklist)

★ **Traction** Man is here! Knopf 2005 un il $15.95; lib bdg $17.99
Grades: PreK K 1 2   E
1. Toys -- Fiction 2. Imagination -- Fiction 3. Superheroes -- Fiction 4. Superheroes (Fictional characters) -- Fiction
ISBN 0-375-83191-6; 0-375-93191-0 lib bdg
      LC 2004-4452
Traction Man, a boy's courageous action figure, has a variety of adventures with Scrubbing Brush and other objects in the house
And "imaginative and very funny romp. . . . The angular, full-color art sweeps across the pages and perfectly animates the antics of Traction Man and his enemies." SLJ

★ The **adventures** of the dish and the spoon. Knopf 2006 un il $16.95; lib bdg $18.99
Grades: PreK K 1 2   E
1. Tableware -- Fiction 2. Nursery rhymes -- Fiction
ISBN 0-375-83691-8; 0-375-93691-2 lib bdg
      LC 2005017548
Having run away together, the Dish and the Spoon from the nursery rhyme "The Cat and the Fiddle" become vaudeville stars before turning to a life of crime
"The narrative is packed with tongue-in-cheek humor. The rich art mingles paint with collage, featuring framed scenes and a palette of lush browns dotted with primary reds and blues." Bull Cent Child Books

Gribnau, Joe
Kick the cowboy; illustrated by Adrian Tans. Pelican Pub. Co. 2009 un il $15.95
Grades: PreK K 1 2   E
1. Tall tales 2. Cowhands -- Fiction
ISBN 978-1-58980-605-4; 1-58980-605-0
      LC 2009-3950
A cowboy named Kick becomes a mean braggart, driving away all of his friends and terrorizing the people of his Texas town, until a no-nonsense little girl named Belle helps him to mend his ways.
"Gribnau has a real winner here. . . . This above average story will be a real hit with both kids and storytellers. . . .

Tans' illustrations are terrific, making the reader really want to see what happens next. This is a fantastic children's story. . . . Highly Recommended." Libr Media Connect

Grifalconi, Ann
★ **Ain't** nobody a stranger to me; illustrated by Jerry Pinkney. Hyperion/Jump at the Sun 2007 un il $16.99
Grades: K 1 2 3   E
1. Slavery -- Fiction 2. Grandfathers -- Fiction 3. African Americans -- Fiction 4. Underground railroad -- Fiction
ISBN 978-0-7868-1857-0
This story spotlights both the loving rapport between a girl and her grandfather, and the story of his family's escape to freedom.
"Pinkney's watercolor double-paged spreads contrast the sepia-toned gloom of slavery and hiding with the abundant light-filled apple orchard today. . . . Caught by the action, children will hear Finger's shining words across time, race, and generations." Booklist

★ The **village** that vanished; illustrated by Kadir Nelson. Dial Bks. for Young Readers 2002 un il $16.99
Grades: 1 2 3 4   E
1. Escapes -- Fiction 2. Slave trade -- Fiction 3. Yao (African people) -- Fiction
ISBN 0-8037-2623-6
      LC 00-38416
In southeastern Africa, a young Yao girl and her mother find a way for their fellow villagers to escape approaching slave traders
"This story celebrating resourcefulness, quick thinking, and community solidarity may inspire and empower readers. Nelson's pencil drawings enhanced with oil paints are wonderfully evocative of place, mood, posture, and expression." SLJ

Griffin, Kitty
The **ride**; the legend of Betsy Dowdy. illustrated by Marjorie Priceman. Atheneum Books for Young Readers 2010 un il $16.99
Grades: 1 2 3   E
ISBN 978-1-4169-2816-4; 1-4169-2816-2
"The year is 1775, and teenage Betsy Dowdy secretly sets off on an all-night horseback journey to alert colonial militia to the British advance upon her North Carolina island home. . . . Swirls of deep royal and swaths of magenta evoke the eerie nighttime setting. . . . Griffin's . . . direct yet descriptive narrative recounts the calamities that befall Betsy, while the characters' cartoon styling lessens the tension. Priceman's . . . trademark freeflowing lines speed the story's momentum." Publ Wkly

Griffin, Molly Beth
Loon baby; illustrated by Anne Hunter. Houghton Mifflin Harcourt 2011 un il $16.99
Grades: PreK K 1 2   E
1. Loons -- Fiction 2. Animals -- Fiction
ISBN 978-0-547-25487-6; 0-547-25487-3
      LC 2010006770
A baby loon, afraid that his mother will not return, sets out on his own to find his way across a stormy lake to their home in the great north woods.

This offers "simple text . . . [and] loosely rendered watercolors in blues, greens and grays textured with pen-and-ink cross hatch. . . . Guaranteed to hit the mark with anyone who's ever felt lost and alone." Kirkus

Griffith, Helen V.

Moonlight; by Helen V. Griffith; illustrations by Laura Dronzek. Greenwillow Books 2012 1 v. (unpaged) col. ill. Grades: PreK K **E**

1. Stories in rhyme 2. Dreams -- Fiction 3. Rabbits -- Fiction 4. Picture books for children
ISBN 9780062032850; 9780062032867

LC 2011002149

This children's picture book "tell[s] the . . . story of a rabbit who--too sleepy to wait for the moon to appear--hops into his safe, grass-lined burrow. He dreams of a sky full of veggies, strawberries, and tender flowers, until the moon's buttery light seeps into his burrow, 'spatters him with moondrops/shakes him out of bed--' and draws him out into the bright, flowery field to dance. What Rabbit does not see is the small gray mouse outside his burrow, a raccoon family watching from their hollow tree, and a deer and fawn asleep in the moonlit grass." (School Libr J)

Griffiths, Andy

★ The **big** fat cow that goes kapow; illustrated by Terry Denton. Feiwel & Friends 2009 123p $14.99 Grades: 2 3 4 **E**

1. Animals -- Fiction
ISBN 978-0-312-36788-6; 0-312-36788-0
First published 2008 in Australia

In these ten easy-to-read stories there is a mixed-up cow that says "miaow," a mole called Noel who plays rock 'n' roll in a hole, and a boy named Mike who rides a bike with a very big spike

"Broad slapstick humor and galloping, Seuss-like rhymes are just part of the reason this . . . has strong child appeal. Denton's funny illustrations are full of action, and his use of stick figures and stink lines makes the book look as though it had been illustrated by a cheeky but talented kid." SLJ

The **cat** on the mat is flat; [by] Andy Griffiths; illustrated by Terry Denton. Feiwel & Friends 2007 166p il pa $9.95 Grades: 2 3 4 **E**

1. Stories in rhyme 2. Animals -- Fiction
ISBN 978-0-312-36787-9

This "innovative book for beginning readers collects nine short, intentionally silly snippets propelled by kid-pleasing, tongue-tripping verse. In the title tale, a cat sitting on a mat decides to chase a rat, who grabs a baseball bat. . . . Other protagonists also encounter tongue-in-cheek adversity. . . . Denton's edgy, stick-figure-filled sketches enhance the zaniness factor and the offbeat, ironic humor." Publ Wkly

Grigsby, Susan

In the garden with Dr. Carver; illustrated by Nicole Tadgell. Albert Whitman 2010 un il $16.99 Grades: 2 3 4 **E**

1. Botanists 2. Gardening -- Fiction 3. African Americans -- Fiction
ISBN 978-0-8075-3630-8; 0-8075-3630-X

Sally is a young girl living in rural Alabama in the early 1900s, a time when people were struggling to grow food in soil that had been depleted by years of cotton production. One day, Dr. George Washington Carver shows up to help the grownups with their farms and the children with their school garden.

"Concepts like composting and planting are well conveyed through Sally's descriptive, sometimes lyrical narrative. . . . The colorful watercolor illustrations, featuring soft touches and historical details, depict the rural setting and expressive characters." Booklist

Grimes, Nikki

Oh, brother! [by] Nikki Grimes; illustrations by Mike Benny. 1st ed.; Greenwillow Books 2008 un il $16.99; lib bdg $17.89 Grades: 2 3 4 **E**

1. Brothers -- Fiction 2. Remarriage -- Fiction 3. Stepfamilies -- Fiction 4. Hispanic Americans -- Fiction
ISBN 978-0-688-17294-7; 0-688-17294-6; 978-0-688-17295-4 lib bdg; 0-688-17295-4 lib bdg

LC 2005035645

Xavier is unhappy when his mother remarries and he suddenly has a new stepbrother, as well as a stepfather, in his home.

"Snappy language and varied rhyme schemes energize Grimes's . . . verses. . . . Benny . . . intersperses surreal illustrations with more realistic scenes. . . . The art and poems capture and memorably convey a range of emotions." Publ Wkly

Grindley, Sally

It's my school; [by] Sally Grindley; illustrations by Margaret Chamberlain. Walker & Company 2006 un il $15.95; lib bdg $16.85 Grades: PreK K 1 2 **E**

1. School stories 2. Siblings -- Fiction
ISBN 978-0-8027-8086-7; 0-8027-8086-5; 978-0-8027-8087-4 lib bdg; 0-8027-8087-3 lib bdg

LC 2005037181

Tom is not happy that his younger sister, Alice, is starting kindergarten at his school

"The large illustrations . . . are depicted in soft pastel hues, capturing the siblings' facial expressions and the varying degress of emotion. . . . This is a new take on first-day-of-school stories, and a realistic choice to help children share their lives with a younger sibling." SLJ

Groom, Juliet

Silent night; [illustrated by] Tim Warnes. Good Books 2010 un il $16.99 Grades: PreK K 1 2 **E**

1. Songs 2. Carols 3. Bears -- Fiction
ISBN 978-1-56148-697-7; 1-56148-697-3

LC 2010004919

"This new interpretation of the beloved Christmas carol focuses on an enchanting pair of bears, a parent and cub. The text retains the familiar beginning and then moves on to new words celebrating the beauty of the mountain setting at night under a full moon, as well as peace among the animals and love between parent and child. . . . Warnes masterfully illustrates the charismatic bears, with intimate views of parent and child in close harmony with nature." Kirkus

Guback, Georgia

Luka's quilt. Greenwillow Bks. 1994 un il $16.99; lib bdg $13.93

Grades: K 1 2 3   E

1. Quilts -- Fiction 2. Grandmothers -- Fiction

ISBN 0-688-12154-3; 0-688-12155-1 lib bdg

LC 93-12241

When Luka's grandmother makes a traditional Hawaiian quilt for her, she and Luka disagree over the colors it should include

"Eye-catching collages of brightly painted papers, the illustrations express the characters' emotions and show a delight in the Hawaiian landscape and traditions. . . . An involving story that's all the more satisfying because the ending offers no mere emotional patch up but a real solution." Booklist

Gudeon, Adam

Me and Meow. Harper 2011 il

Grades: PreK K   E

1. Cats -- Fiction 2. Play -- Fiction

ISBN 0061998214; 9780061998218

LC 2010003095

A little girl and her cat enjoy a full day of playing together.

"The primitive figures are expertly posed and arranged with simple props on color-saturated spreads to reflect the joy and devotion the companions share. Children as young as two years will appreciate the brevity, rhythm, onomatopoeia, and repetition in the text. . . . Me and Meow may inspire children to talk about a special friend and events in their day." SLJ

Guest, Elissa Haden

Harriet's had enough; illustrated by Paul Meisel. Candlewick Press 2009 un il $15.99

Grades: PreK K 1 2   E

1. Raccoons -- Fiction 2. Family life -- Fiction

ISBN 978-0-7636-3454-4; 0-7636-3454-9

"Harriet refuses to pick up her toys, and her mother is angry. When she tells her grandmother and father that she will run away because 'Mama's mean', they explain that everyone has chores to complete. Grandma succinctly explains, 'That's life, honey-bun.' . . . Harriet's shifting emotions are conveyed through her varied expressions. Intricate strokes add depth and texture to this raccoon family. Soft watercolor, acrylic, and gouache illustrations suit the subject." SLJ

★ Iris and Walter; written by Elissa Haden Guest; illustrated by Christine Davenier. Harcourt 2000 43p il $15; pa $5.95

Grades: K 1 2   E

1. Friendship 2. Country life 3. City and town life 4. Friendship -- Fiction 5. Country life -- Fiction 6. City and town life -- Fiction 7. Iris (Fictitious character: Guest) -- Fiction 8. Walter (Fictitious character: Guest) -- Fiction

ISBN 0-15-202122-1; 0-15-216442-1 pa

LC 99-6242

When Iris moves to the country, she misses the city where she formerly lived; but with the help of a new friend named Walter, she learns to adjust to her new home

"Christine Davenier's exuberant pen-and-ink drawings reveal all the delightful things Iris discovers with Walter. .

. . An easy-to-read chapter book . . . just right for children ready to step up their skills." Booklist

Other titles about Iris and Walter are:

Iris and Walter and Baby Rose (2002)

Iris and Walter and Cousin Howie (2003)

Iris and Walter and the birthday party (2006)

Iris and Walter and the field trip (2005)

Iris and Walter and the substitute teacher (2004)

Iris and Walter, lost and found (2004)

Iris and Walter, the school play (2003)

Iris and Walter, the sleepover (2002)

Iris and Walter, true friends (2001)

Guidone, Thea

Drum city; illustrations by Vanessa Newton. Tricycle Press 2010 un il $15.99

Grades: PreK K 1 2   E

1. Stories in rhyme 2. Drums -- Fiction

ISBN 978-1-58246-308-7; 1-58246-308-5

"Leaning against a tree and beating a kettle with a spoon and whisk, a smiling young drummer seems to be in the zone, mesmerized by his own beats. An exuberant, multicultural crowd quickly gathers, and as hundreds and hundreds of kid drummers march down the streets, they turn the heads of the ho-hum passersby. . . . Guidone's steadily rhythmic, rhyming text captures the allure of a beating drum, and Newton's catchy illustrations echo the cadences of people at work." Booklist

Guthrie, James

★ Last song; a poem. illustrated by Eric Rohmann. Roaring Brook Press 2010 un il $10.99

Grades: PreK K   E

1. Stories in rhyme 2. Squirrels -- Fiction 3. Family life -- Fiction

ISBN 978-1-59643-508-7; 1-59643-508-9

"Rohmann tenderly interprets a 30-word poem by Scotsman James Guthrie in this attractive offering with a small, easily held trim size and a die-cut cover. One bright day, two squirrels bounce out of their tree to frolic in the meadow, but after the sky darkens, they return home again, where another, parental squirrel awaits them. The watercolor artwork is warm and sweet but never cloying, and it pairs well with the rhythm of the poem. . . . The brevity and calmness of the words make this a good just-one-more book at bedtime, and the depictions of the circle of family love and the cycle of the day will inspire many just-one-more kisses before the lights go out." Booklist

Guy, Ginger Foglesong

★ Fiesta! pictures by Rene King Moreno. Greenwillow Bks. 1996 un il $15.99

Grades: PreK K 1 2   E

1. Counting 2. Parties -- Fiction 3. Bilingual books -- English-Spanish

ISBN 0-688-14331-8

LC 95-35848

"Three children begin with una canasta (one basket) and proceed to fill it with scrumptious candies, trinkets, and toys in preparation for a Mexican fiesta. . . . A simple bilingual text provides numbers in English and Spanish. The soft-edged full-color illustrations done in pencils, pastels, and watercolors have a subtle folkloric quality." SLJ

★ **Perros!** Perros! Dogs! Dogs! a story in English and Spanish. by Ginger Foglesong Guy; pictures by Sharon Glick. Greenwillow Books 2006 un il $15.99; lib bdg $16.89

Grades: PreK K 1 2   E

1. Opposites 2. Dogs -- Fiction 3. Bilingual books -- English-Spanish

ISBN 978-0-06-083574-3; 0-06-083574-5; 978-0-06-083575-0 lib bdg; 0-06-083575-3 lib bdg

This "title makes use of a wide array of breeds to demonstrate the concept of opposites. The story begins with a girl waking up in her bedroom. . . . As she looks out her window, an excited pack of dogs runs by. Big dog. Little dog. . . .Where are they going? . . . What the book lacks in plot development it makes up for in the sheer exuberance of the watercolor cartoons. A must for dog lovers and a good choice for beginning readers in either language." SLJ

Haas, Jessie

Sugaring; pictures by Jos. A. Smith. Greenwillow Bks. 1996 un il $17.99

Grades: PreK K 1 2   E

1. Horses -- Fiction 2. Maple sugar -- Fiction 3. Grandfathers -- Fiction

ISBN 0-688-14200-1

LC 95-38139

Nora wants to find a way to give the horses a special treat for helping her grandfather and her gather sap to make maple syrup

"The realistic watercolor illustrations effectively capture the scenes; color and texture are skillfully used to depict the cold, hard job of gathering the sap and the hot steamy atmosphere of the sugar house." SLJ

Haas, Rick de

Peter and the winter sleepers. NorthSouth Books 2011 un il $16.95

Grades: PreK K 1 2   E

1. Snow -- Fiction 2. Animals -- Fiction 3. Lighthouses -- Fiction

ISBN 978-0-7358-4033-1; 0-7358-4033-4

"When a huge snowstorm hits, sounds of scratching bring Peter to the door of the lighthouse where he and his grandmother live. First one animal and then another is trapped in the deep snow and seeking shelter. Peter and Grandma invite them in, letting them sleep (except the nocturnal ones) in boxes set up along the stairs. . . . The story is simply told, yet charming. The illustrations are also inviting, and characters have expressive faces and animated movements." SLJ

Haber, Tiffany Strelitz

The **monster** who lost his mean; Tiffany Strelitz Haber; illustrated by Kirstie Edmunds. Henry Holt 2012 36 p. (hc) $16.99

Grades: PreK K 1 2   E

1. Picture books for children 2. Monsters -- Juvenile fiction 3. Stories in rhyme 4. Monsters -- Fiction 5. Conduct of life -- Fiction 6. Self-acceptance -- Fiction

ISBN 0805093753; 9780805093759

LC 2011029046

In this children's picture book, "monsters are characterized . . . as Mean, Observant, Noisy, Super Strong, Tough-to-please, Envious, and Remarkable, but what happens if the letter M for Mean is missing? The multicolored monster crew of Monsterwood won't tolerate the chartreuse mutant, not even while eating eyeball soup. Try as he might to find the M and be mean . . ., Onster's behavior is altered. A new identity brings an array of friends that leave footprints on his heart." (Children's Literature)

Hacohen, Dean

★ **Tuck** me in! [by] Dean Hacohen & Sherry Scharschmidt. Candlewick Press 2010 un $9.99

Grades: PreK   E

1. Animals -- Fiction 2. Bedtime -- Fiction

ISBN 0-7636-4728-4; 978-0-7636-4728-5

"In a gentle, rhythmic nighttime chant, an unseen narrator asks, 'Who needs to be tucked in?' The next page reveals a pop-eyed cartoon baby animal, head on a pillow against a field of white. Readers turn a half-page which is revealed as a blanket and the baby is tucked in. The opposite page, night blue with yellow stars, displays the text 'Good night, baby' and the next request for who needs tucking. . . . The animals are rendered digitally in a sketchy, jazzy style with swaths of bright color. Youngsters will delight in covering the babies and chanting the text in this book that will be re-read endlessly as a comfy prelude to bedtime." SLJ

Haddon, Mark

★ **Footprints** on the Moon; illustrated by Christian Birmingham. Candlewick Press 2009 un il $16.99

Grades: K 1 2 3   E

1. Space flight to the moon -- Fiction 2. Space flight to the moon -- Juvenile literature

ISBN 978-0-7636-4440-6; 0-7636-4440-4

First published 1996 in the United Kingdom with title: The sea of tranquillity

A man remembers his boyhood fascination with the Moon and the night mankind first bounced through the dust in the Sea of Tranquillity.

"Birmingham's nostalgia-tinged illustrations have a dreamlike quality and provide readers a glimpse into both the boy's and astronauts' separate worlds until, in a wonderful spread, both worlds join as a third tiny astronaut is seen bouncing on the Moon with Armstrong and Aldrin. The pairing of text and art creates a wonderful read-aloud." SLJ

Hader, Berta

The **big** snow; by Berta and Elmer Hader. Macmillan 1948 un il $18.99; pa $7.99

Grades: PreK K 1   E

1. Winter -- Fiction 2. Animals -- Fiction

ISBN 0-02-737910-8; 0-689-71757-1 pa

Awarded the Caldecott Medal, 1949

This book shows "the birds and animals which come for the food put out by an old couple after a big snow." Hodges. Books for Elem Sch Libr

Hafner, Marylin

M & M and the bad news babies; pictures by Marylin Hafner. Puffin Books 1985 46p il pa $4.99

Grades: K 1 2   E

1. Twins -- Fiction 2. Babysitters -- Fiction

ISBN 0-14-031851-8

LC 84-16557

Mandy and Mimi discover a way to make the unruly twins for whom they babysit into perfect angels.

Hajdusiewicz, Babs Bell

Sputter, sputter, sput! by Babs Bell; illustrated by Bob Staake. HarperCollins 2008 un il $16.99; lib bdg $17.89

Grades: PreK K   E

1. Stories in rhyme 2. Automobiles -- Fiction

ISBN 978-0-06-056222-9; 0-06-056222-6; 978-0-06-056223-6 lib bdg; 0-06-056223-4 lib bdg

A driver happily cruising in his car sputters out of gas, refills his tank, and zooms right out of town.

"Staake's vibrant, computer-generated geometric art perfectly complements the playfulness of the simple, rhyming text. Certain to be a favorite among toddler vehicle enthusiasts." SLJ **Hakala, Marjorie**

Mermaid dance; by Marjorie Rose Hakala; illustrated by Mark Jones. Blue Apple 2009 un il $16.99

Grades: PreK K 1 2   E

1. Summer solstice -- Fiction 2. Mermaids and mermen -- Fiction

ISBN 978-1-934706-47-3; 1-934706-47-7

LC 2008042595

On the first night of summer when high tide brings the ocean to the edge of the forest, woodland animals watch mermaids frolicking under a full moon.

"Jones's pastel illustrations show the dreamlike festivities both above and below water. A magical fantasy to celebrate the summer solstice." SLJ

Hale, Bruce

Snoring Beauty; written by Bruce Hale; illustrated by Howard Fine. Harcourt 2008 un il $16

Grades: PreK K 1 2   E

1. Fairy tales 2. Dragons -- Fiction

ISBN 978-0-15-216314-3; 0-15-216314-X

LC 2006022950

"Princess Marge, daughter of King Gluteus and Queen Esophagus, who is nearly doomed by an irate fairy to homicide by a pie wagon, has the harsh sentence modified by another ('half-deaf') fairy, Tintinnitus. The princess will become a sleeping dragon and will 'one day' be awakened by 'a quince.' . . . Enriched by Fine's large, double-page watercolor paintings . . . ; a repetitive refrain ('Yada, yada, hippity-hop'); and those cacophonous snores, this fantastic story is a delightful treat that begs to be read aloud." SLJ

Hale, Nathan

The **twelve** bots of Christmas. Walker & Company 2010 un il $14.99; lib bdg $15.89

Grades: PreK K 1 2   E

1. Robots -- Songs 2. Christmas -- Songs 3. Carols -- Juvenile literature 4. Christmas stories -- Juvenile literature

ISBN 978-0-8027-2237-9; 0-8027-2237-7; 978-0-8027-2238-6 lib bdg; 0-8027-2238-5 lib bdg

LC 2010009541

In this variation on the folk song "The Twelve Days of Christmas," Robo-Santa gives gifts that consist of electronic gear, including a cartridge in a gear tree, three wrench hens, and nine droids a-dancing.

"The brightly colored digital artwork pays subtle homage to everything from Star Wars to Dr. Who and rewards careful study with fun details." SLJ

Hall, Bruce Edward

Henry and the kite dragon; illustrated by William Low. Philomel Books 2004 un il $15.99

Grades: K 1 2 3 4   E

1. Kites -- Fiction 2. Chinese Americans -- Fiction 3. Italian Americans -- Fiction

ISBN 0-399-23727-5

LC 2003-16381

In New York City in the 1920s, the children from Chinatown go after the children from Little Italy for throwing rocks at the beautiful kites Grandfather Chin makes, not realizing that they have a reason for doing so.

The author "tells an engaging story about a vibrant community, which is beautifully captured in Low's detailed, dramatic paintings." Booklist

Hall, Donald

Ox -cart man; pictures by Barbara Cooney. Viking 1979 un il $16.99; pa $6.99

Grades: K 1 2 3   E

1. New England -- Fiction

ISBN 0-670-53328-9; 0-14-050441-9 pa

LC 79-14466

Awarded the Caldecott Medal, 1980

"The stunning combination of text and illustrations, suggesting early American paintings on wood, depict the countryside through which [the farmer] travels, the jostle of the marketplace, and the homely warmth of family life." Horn Book

Hall, Michael, 1941-

★ **Cat** tale; Michael Hall. Greenwillow Books 2012 40 p. col. ill. (trade ed.) $16.99

Grades: PreK K 1   E

1. Cats -- Juvenile fiction 2. Picture books for children 3. Puns -- Juvenile literature 4. Cats -- Fiction 5. Stories in rhyme 6. Imagination -- Fiction

ISBN 0061915165; 9780061915161

LC 2011033654

In this story, three cats "try to keep up with . . . wordplay as [Michael] Hall . . . explores verbal puns. The . . . text is reinforced by . . . illustrations . . . . Each line ends with a . . . thump: 'They flee a steer. / They steer a plane. / They plane a board. / They board a train.' A huge, blue steer sends the cats dashing into a blobby purple plane. 'They plane a board' explains the verb 'to plane' with vivid red curls of wood; two cats do carpentry" while the third talks to the train driver. (Publishers Weekly)

My heart is like a zoo. Greenwillow Books 2010 un il

Grades: PreK K 1   E

1. Stories in rhyme 2. Love -- Fiction 3. Animals -- Fiction

ISBN 0-06-191510-6; 0-06-191511-4 lib bdg; 978-0-06-191510-9; 978-0-06-191511-6 lib bdg

LC 2009017818

Depicts in rhyming text how love can be many different things, such as eager as a beaver, steady as a yak, or silly as a seal.

"The bold digital collages of zoo animals in this debut picture book are clear and bright, and the simple rhymes about feelings will have preschoolers savoring the words, joining in, and pointing at every playful zoo scene, each featuring one animal per page." Booklist

★ **Perfect** square. Greenwillow Books 2011 un il $16.99
Grades: PreK K 1 2   E
  1. Shape -- Fiction 2. Square -- Fiction 3. Happiness -- Fiction 4. Color -- Juvenile literature 5. Geometry -- Juvenile literature
ISBN 978-0-06-191513-0; 0-06-191513-0
                    LC 2010004104

A perfect square that is perfectly happy is torn into pieces, punched with holes, crumpled, and otherwise changed but finds in each transformation that it can be something new, and just as happy.

"This near-perfect concept book incorporates an imaginative exploration of colors, a nice assortment of vivid words, and the tranformational possibilities of a simple-seeming square.... Just right for toddlers, but also for those ready for the abstract theme of inventive self-empowerment: a book to revisit often, and with delight." Horn Book

Hallowell, George
  Wagons ho! by George Hallowell and Joan Holub; illustrated by Lynne Avril. Albert Whitman 2011 il $16.99
Grades: K 1 2   E
  1. Moving -- Fiction 2. Automobile travel -- Fiction 3. Overland journeys to the Pacific -- Fiction
ISBN 978-0-8075-8612-9; 0-8075-8612-9
                    LC 2010050422

Compares the experiences of Jenny Johnson and Katie Miller as their families move from Missouri to Oregon, one in 1846 and one in 2011.

"Carefully chosen facts make contrasts and similarities easy to comprehend.... Readers will relate to the travel activities and smile at the humor in the pen-and-ink and watercolor drawings. Together, the art and text make a good introduction to the Westward Movement." SLJ

Hamanaka, Sheila
  Grandparents song. HarperCollins Pubs. 2003 un il $15.99; lib bdg $16.89
Grades: 1 2 3 4   E
  1. Ethnicity 2. Grandparents 3. Multiculturalism 4. Stories in rhyme 5. Grandparents -- Fiction 6. Racially mixed people -- Fiction
ISBN 0-688-17852-9; 0-688-17853-7 lib bdg
                    LC 00-47952

In verse "a young girl recounts the roots of her family tree. Fondly and respectfully, she describes her grandparents—one American Indian, one Irish, one Mexican, and one a descendent of African slaves. Beautifully rendered in calligraphy, the text is clean, simple, and lilting.... Filled with magnificent texture, Hamanaka's oil paintings are substantial and striking." SLJ

Hamilton, K. R.
  ★ **Police** officers on patrol; by Kersten Hamilton; pictures by R. W. Alley. Viking 2009 un il $15.99
Grades: PreK   E
  1. Stories in rhyme 2. Police -- Fiction
ISBN 978-0-670-06315-4; 0-670-06315-0
                    LC 2008023240

"Sergeant Santole dispatches Officers Mike, Jan, and Carl to spots around town that require their expertise. Mike in his police car attends to a broken traffic light, Jan on horseback reconnects a small child with his mom, and Carl runs to a crime scene.... The hilarious cartoon illustrations effectively convey excitement and brisk movement.... Preschoolers will be reassured that special people are there to assist in a variety of circumstances and see that their jobs require all kinds of cool tools." SLJ

  ★ **Red** Truck; by Kersten Hamilton; illustrated by Valeria Petrone. Viking Childrens Books 2008 un il $15.99
Grades: PreK K   E
  1. Stories in rhyme 2. Buses -- Fiction 3. Trucks -- Fiction
ISBN 978-0-670-06275-1
                    LC 2007-22902

When a school bus gets stuck in the mud, Red Truck the tow truck saves the day by pulling it out.

"Strong, flowing lines and highly simplified forms create a certain retro look in the digital artwork.... With a well-crafted text spiced with sound effects, this appealing picture book is highly recommended for reading aloud to the truck-loving crowd." Booklist

Hamilton, Virginia
  Wee Winnie Witch's Skinny; an original African American scare tale. engravings by Barry Moser. Blue Sky Press 2004 un il $16.95
Grades: 2 3 4 5   E
  1. Witches -- Fiction 2. African Americans -- Fiction
ISBN 0-590-28880-6
                    LC 00-67999

James Lee and Uncle Big Anthony become victims of Wee Winnie Witch, who takes them on a ride up into the sky, but Mama Granny saves them.

This "is a wonderful horror story that draws on traditional beliefs about witches.... Moser's framed, colored wood engravings do a great job of bringing the wild, shivery adventure close to home, their black backgrounds and strong lines lit with garish Halloween images in green and red." Booklist

Hamlisch, Marvin, 1944-2012
  Marvin makes music; Marvin Hamlisch; illustrated by Jim Madsen. Dial Books for Young Readers 2012 32 p. (hardcover) $17.99
Grades: 2 3 4   E
  1. Anxiety 2. Picture books for children 3. Pianists -- Fiction 4. Composers -- Fiction
ISBN 0803737300; 9780803737303
                    LC 2011052317

This book, by Marvin Hamlisch, illustrated by Jim Madsen, is the "story of [the author,] ... who, at the age of six, was ... accepted into the Juilliard School.... Marvin loves to play the piano and compose his own songs. But performing music over and over that's composed by some old guys ... just gives him knots in his stomach. When ... he has an audition with the most prestigious music school, how can Marvin overcome his nerves and get swept away by the music?" (Publisher's note)

Hamm, Mia

Winners never quit! illustrated by Carol Thompson. HarperCollins 2004 un il $15.99; lib bdg $16.89

Grades: PreK K 1 2   E

1. Soccer 2. Soccer -- Fiction

ISBN 0-06-074050-7; 0-06-074051-5 lib bdg

"Mia's favorite sport is soccer but she hates losing. In fact, she dislikes it so much that she quits in the middle of a game. . . . Mia learns quickly that there will be times when she will score a goal and those when she will not, but playing the game is the most fun of all. Bright, energetic cartoons depict the child's ups and downs." SLJ

Hammill, Matt

Sir Reginald's logbook. Kids Can Press 2008 un il $17.95

Grades: K 1 2 3   E

1. Adventure fiction 2. Imagination -- Fiction

ISBN 978-1-55453-202-5; 1-55453-202-7

"Sir Reginald is on a mission to find the Lost Tablet of Illusion. Readers will quickly realize, with the help of Hammill's illustrations, that his dangerous and mysterious quest into the deepest jungle is happening in his imagination. In actuality, he is only searching his home and yard for a missing TV remote control. . . . Hammill's keen sense of humor abounds in both the text and art." SLJ

Hanson, Warren

Bugtown Boogie; illustrated by Steve Johnson and Lou Fancher. Laura Geringer Books 2008 un il $16.99; lib bdg $17.89

Grades: PreK K 1 2   E

1. Stories in rhyme 2. Dance -- Fiction 3. Insects -- Fiction 4. Parties -- Fiction

ISBN 978-0-06-059937-9; 0-06-059937-5; 978-0-06-059938-6 lib bdg; 0-06-059938-3 lib bdg

LC 2006029207

While strolling home through the woods one evening, a young boy happens upon a rollicking dancing party in Bugtown

This is written "in jazzy rhyming couplets. . . . Vibrant hues and frenetic energy suffuse the artwork." SLJ

The **Sea** of Sleep; illustrations by Jim LaMarche. Scholastic Press 2010 un il $16.99

Grades: PreK K 1   E

1. Ocean -- Fiction 2. Sleep -- Fiction 3. Otters -- Fiction 4. Bedtime -- Fiction

ISBN 978-0-439-69735-4; 0-439-69735-2

LC 2009032602

This "bedtime story follows an otter and its mother on a journey in the Sea of Sleep. They see the moon, myriad examples of marine life, and the personified sea herself. . . . Hanson's musician roots show in the text, which reads very much like lyrics, including a repeating chorus. . . . Young audiences . . . will appreciate the lilting, poetic language. The illustrations are done in restful blues and purples befitting a bedtime story." SLJ

Hardin, Melinda

Hero dad; [illustrations by] Bryan Langdo. Marshall Cavendish 2010 un il $12.99

Grades: PreK K 1 2   E

1. Soldiers -- Fiction 2. Heroes and heroines -- Fiction

3. Father-child relationship -- Fiction

ISBN 978-0-7614-5713-8; 0-7614-5713-5

A child demonstrates that while Dad differs from a traditional superhero, as an American soldier he is a superhero of a different kind.

"Langdo's watercolor-and-pencil illustrations have an appealing simplicity and texture, almost as if made by the boy narrator himself. . . . An important message, delivered with effective straightforwardness and an abundance of heart." Kirkus

Hardy, Aurelia

Dancers of the World; by Aurelia Hardy; illustrated by Sybile; edited by Rebecca Frazer, translated by Susan Allen Maurin. Innovative Logistics Llc 2013 32 p. ill. (hardcover) $19.95

Grades: 3 4 5   E

1. Dogs -- Juvenile literature 2. Dance -- Juvenile literature

ISBN 2733812335; 9782733812334

In this book by Aurelia Hardy, "fifteen young women worldwide enthusiastically describe the dance form they love and practice. Each one talks about the music, the steps, and the dance's history, and imagines herself in a particular role. In some cases, she describes a real performance. The styles vary greatly--ballet, ballroom, folk, Kabuki, Senegalese, Flamenco, Tahitian, etc." (School Library Journal)

Harley, Bill

Dirty Joe, the pirate; a true story. words by Bill Harley; pictures by Jack E. Davis. HarperCollinsPublishers 2008 un il $16.99; lib bdg $17.89

Grades: PreK K 1 2   E

1. Stories in rhyme 2. Pirates -- Fiction 3. Clothing and dress -- Fiction

ISBN 978-0-06-623780-0; 0-06-623780-7; 978-0-06-623781-7 lib bdg; 0-06-623781-5 lib bdg

LC 2007018377

Dirty Joe and his pirate crew terrorize the seven seas in their quest for dirty socks, but they meet their match in Stinky Annie, whose favorite loot is pilfered underwear

"Davis's balloon-headed, goofy characters are just right for the tale. The chaotic full-color pictures are jam-packed with pirates and dirty laundry. The crews, dressed in a hilarious mishmash of styles, will have readers poring over the pages to spot amusing details." SLJ

Harper, Charise Mericle

Gigi in the big city. Random House 2010 un il $12.99

Grades: K 1 2   E

1. City and town life -- Fiction

ISBN 978-0-375-84235-1; 0-375-84235-7

"With an arsenal of flaps, mini-booklets, and wheels, Harper demonstrates the possibilities cities have to offer, as readers follow Gigi on a solo journey through a lively metropolis. Harper balances traditionally girly activities (shoe shopping! makeovers!) with basic information about art, literature, and more (one wheel rotates through birthstones, art movements, and mythical creatures; another simply lets Gigi try different hairstyles). Cheerful cartoons, surprises aplenty, and a smart design will keep young urbanites occupied." Publ Wkly

Henry's heart. Henry Holt 2011 un il $16.99 **E**
1. Dogs -- Fiction 2. Heart -- Fiction 3. Family life -- Fiction
ISBN 978-0-8050-8989-9; 0-8050-8989-6
LC 2010040321

When Henry falls in love with a puppy but his father will not buy it for him, his heart reacts strangely. Includes facts about the heart's role within the body.

"Harper's acrylic-and-collage artwork with its filled-in stick figures is a perfect match for the irreverent humor of the text." Kirkus

Includes bibliographical references

Mimi and Lulu; three sweet stories: one forever friendship. Balzer & Bray 2009 un il $16.99
Grades: PreK K 1 **E**
1. Friendship -- Fiction
ISBN 978-0-06-175583-5; 0-06-175583-4

Mimi and Lulu are best friends despite liking different colors and they love playing together, whether it's pretending to be on a phone or about princesses.

"The dramatic, fuming stand-offs and the fun when things turn around are playfully illustrated in the bright scenes of the cartoonish, animal-like figures, set against spacious white pages. A solid offering to add to the picture-book friendship canon." Booklist

Pink me up. Alfred A. Knopf 2010 un il $16.99; lib bdg $19.99
Grades: PreK K 1 **E**
1. Color -- Fiction 2. Father-daughter relationship -- Fiction
ISBN 978-0-375-85607-5; 0-375-85607-2; 978-0-375-95607-2 lib bdg; 0-375-95607-7 lib bdg
LC 2009-23168

When Mama is too sick to go to the Pink Girls Pink-nic with Violet, Daddy offers to take her place but, first, he needs to "pink-up" his clothes.

"Rendered in acrylics, the illustrations are humorous and lively." SLJ

★ **When** Randolph turned rotten. Alfred A. Knopf 2007 un il $16.99; lib bdg $19.99
Grades: K 1 2 3 **E**
1. Geese -- Fiction 2. Beavers -- Fiction 3. Friendship -- Fiction
ISBN 978-0-375-84071-5; 978-0-375-94071-2 lib bdg
LC 2006-30572

Best friends Randolph, a beaver, and Ivy, a goose, do everything together until Ivy is invited to a girls-only birthday sleepover party and Randolph, full of bad feelings, tries to spoil her fun

This is "irreverent and fun thanks to Harper's exaggerated situations and signature art, with its brightly colored backgrounds and charmingly simple figures." Booklist

The **power** of cute. Robin Corey Books 2011 un il $10.99
Grades: PreK K **E**
1. Size -- Fiction 2. Courage -- Fiction 3. Monsters -- Fiction
ISBN 978-0-375-85965-6; 0-375-85965-9

In this picture book with lift-the-flaps, pull-tabs, and simple pop-ups, a small teddy bear-like superhero claims he is unafraid of a monster because of his "power of cute."

Harper "knows a thing or two about cute; now she shows it's about being more than a pretty face." Publ Wkly

Harper, Dan
★ **Sit,** Truman! illustrated by Cara Moser & Barry Moser. Harcourt 2001 un il hardcover o.p. pa $6.99
Grades: PreK K 1 2 **E**
1. Dogs 2. Dogs -- Fiction
ISBN 0-15-202616-9; 0-15-205068-X pa
LC 00-9298

A busy day in the life of Truman the big dog includes walks, play time, and a little dog named Oscar

"Harper's minimal text and the Mosers' watercolor paintings are perfectly paired. Slobbery canine Truman is both exasperating and lovable." SLJ

Harper, Jamie
Miles to go. Candlewick Press 2010 un il $12.99
Grades: PreK **E**
1. Automobiles -- Fiction
ISBN 978-0-7636-3598-5; 0-7636-3598-7

Although concerned about a broken horn, young Miles makes his way to preschool in his very own car, with Mom close at hand.

"The rosy-cheeked Miles marvelously embodies the exuberance, imagination and passions of a preschool boy. The block-print, watercolor, ink and cut-paper illustrations create a feast of colors and textures without being overbusy." Kirkus

Harper, Lee
The **Emperor's** cool clothes; written and illustrated by Lee Harper. Marshall Cavendish Children's 2011 il $16.99
Grades: PreK K 1 2 **E**
1. Authors 2. Novelists 3. Dramatists 4. Fairy tales 5. Children's authors 6. Short story writers
ISBN 978-0-7614-5948-4; 0-7614-5948-0
LC 2010024234

Two rascally weavers convince the emperor they are making clothing that will make him look "cool" and will let him know who else is "cool," as well, but when he wears them during the Royal Parade, a child cries out that the emperor has nothing on. Includes author's note about the story's origins.

"Humorous details are scattered throughout, some seemingly for the benefit of adult audiences. He uses bright colors in his watercolor-and-pencil artwork and ably conveys the sad fact that the emperor's clothes, no matter how nice, cannot mask his lack of cool. The visual humor makes this a winner, and adults will appreciate the easy segue into conversations about honesty and what defines 'cool' that are sure to follow." Kirkus

Snow! Snow! Snow! Simon & Schuster Books for Young Readers 2009 un il $14.99
Grades: K 1 2 3 4 **E**
1. Dogs -- Fiction 2. Snow -- Fiction 3. Sledding -- Fiction 4. Father-son relationship -- Fiction
ISBN 978-1-4169-8454-2; 1-4169-8454-2
LC 2008051985

A dog father and his two sons spend a perfect day sledding together.

"Harper's watercolor illustrations are simple, yet effective. Readers get a good sense of the cold, crisp snow and billowing clouds, and the characters' faces are expressive." SLJ

Harrington, Janice N.

Busy-busy Little Chick; Janice Harrington; pictures by Brian Pinkney. Farrar Straus Giroux 2013 32 p. (hardcover) $15.99

Grades: PreK K 1   E

1. Birds -- Juvenile fiction 2. Picture books for children 3. Chickens -- Fiction 4. Perseverance (Ethics) -- Fiction
ISBN 0374347468; 9780374347468

LC 2012004871

This children's picture book is "based on a fable of the Nkundo people of Central Africa" about being self-reliant. Mama Nsoso's chicks need a new, warmer nest, but Mama keeps getting distracted by food and doesn't build one. It's up to "persistent, industrious Little Chick" to help. He works "alone and in secret on a new nest for the family. . . . When the nest is ready, Little Chick invites his brothers and sisters in for a good night's rest." (Kirkus Reviews)

Going north; pictures by Jerome Lagarrigue. Farrar, Straus and Giroux 2004 un il $16

Grades: 2 3 4 5   E

1. Moving -- Fiction 2. African Americans -- Fiction
ISBN 0-374-32681-9

A young African American girl and her family leave their home in Alabama and head for Lincoln, Nebraska, where they hope to escape segregation and find a better life.

"Lagarrigue's paintings are subdued but powerful and well-suited to Harrington's somber, poetic narrative voice." SLJ

★ The chicken -chasing queen of Lamar County; pictures by Shelley Jackson. Farrar, Straus and Giroux 2007 un il $16

Grades: K 1 2 3   E

1. Chickens -- Fiction 2. Farm life -- Fiction 3. African Americans -- Fiction
ISBN 0-374-31251-6; 978-0-374-31251-0

LC 2005-52768

A young farm girl tries to catch her favorite chicken, until she learns something about the hen that makes her change her ways.

"Both words and pictures elevate a simple story about a girl's sly barnyard game into a rollicking, well-told delight." Booklist

Harris, Joe

The belly book; [written and illustrated] by Joe Harris. Random House Children's Books 2008 un il (Beginner books) $8.99; lib bdg $12.99

Grades: PreK K 1   E

1. Stories in rhyme 2. Stomach -- Fiction
ISBN 978-0-375-84340-2; 0-375-84340-X; 978-0-375-94340-9 lib bdg; 0-375-94340-4 lib bdg

LC 2006016630

Bellies can be used for many things, such as dancing the hula and resting your cup, but it is important to feed them healthy foods, too

"This beginning reader has vibrant illustrations, ample white space, and just two to four lines of simple text per page. . . . [This is a] funny, fast-moving, and original romp." SLJ

Harris, John

Jingle bells; how the holiday classic came to be. written by John Harris; illustrated by Adam Gustavson. Peachtree 2011 un il $16.95

Grades: K 1 2   E

1. Clergy 2. Songs 3. Christmas stories
ISBN 978-1-56145-590-4; 1-56145-590-3

LC 2010052274

Tells the story of how, in Savannah, Georgia, in 1857 James Lord Pierpont sat down to write a song for his congregation's Thanksgiving program and, homesick for the cold New England weather he remembered, came up with an enduring classic.

"The oil painting illustrations do right by the story . . . capturing the atmosphere of a community willing to stick together as they journey against the grain, whether that means bringing snow somehow to the South or standing by an unpopular belief." SLJ

Harris, Robie H.

★ Goodbye, Mousie; illustrated by Jan Ormerod. Margaret K. McElderry Bks. 2001 un il hardcover o.p. pa $6.99

Grades: PreK K   E

1. Mice 2. Pets 3. Death 4. Grief 5. Mice -- Fiction 6. Death -- Fiction
ISBN 0-689-83217-6; 0-689-87134-1 pa

LC 99-89167

A boy grieves for his dead pet Mousie, helps to bury him, and begins to come to terms with his loss

"Ormerod's honest pictures, black-pencil line drawings with watercolor washes on buff-colored paper, capture the emotions of the situation and chronicle the boy's move from disbelief to acceptance. . . . This covers all the bases of a frequently asked-for subject." Booklist

I am not going to school today; illustrated by Jan Ormerod. Margaret K. McElderry Bks. 2003 un il $16.95

Grades: PreK K 1 2   E

1. Schools 2. School stories 3. First day of school
ISBN 0-689-83913-8

LC 00-48053

A little boy decides to skip his very first day of school, because on the first day one doesn't know anything, but on the second, one knows everything

"Children with first-day jitters will take comfort in this story. . . . Ormerod's colorful, expressive illustrations capture a child's anxiety and the warmth of family with equal success." Booklist

★ Mail Harry to the moon! [illustrated by] Michael Emberley. Little, Brown and Co. 2008 un il $16.99

Grades: PreK K 1 2   E

1. Infants -- Fiction 2. Siblings -- Fiction
ISBN 978-0-316-15376-8; 0-316-15376-1

LC 2007-48369

Harry's older brother, unhappy that the new baby seems to have taken over, dreams up imaginative ways to get rid of him.

"Harris and Emberley . . . are old hands at striking the right balance between comic Sturm and Drang and genuine poignancy, and their considerable talents make this otherwise familiar tale feel fresh and funny—and psychologically true." Publ Wkly

Maybe a bear ate it! by Robie Harris; illustrated by Michael Emberley. Orchard Books 2007 un il lib bdg $15.99
Grades: PreK K 1 2   E
1. Animals -- Fiction 2. Bedtime -- Fiction 3. Books and reading -- Fiction
ISBN 978-0-439-92961-5
LC 2006102373
At bedtime, a young boy who cannot find his favorite book imagines the various creatures that might have taken it from him
"Plain white backgrounds allow Emberley, who obviously knows how toddlers move and react, to concentrate closely on his character, whose every beautifully calibrated movement and feeling blasts out across the page." Booklist

★ **Who's** in my family? all about our families. Robie H. Harris; illustrated by Nadine Bernard Westcott. Candlewick 2012 40 p.
Grades: 1 2 3   E
1. Family life -- Juvenile literature 2. Zoos -- Fiction 3. Families -- Fiction 4. Brothers and sisters -- Fiction
ISBN 0763636312; 9780763636319
LC 2011046668
In this book, by Robie H. Harris, "[j]oin Nellie and Gus and their family . . . for a day at the zoo, where they see animal families galore! To top off their day, Nellie and Gus invite friends and relatives for a fun dinner at home. . . . [D]epicting families of many configurations, this engaging story interweaves conversations between the siblings and a matter-of-fact text, making it clear to every child that whoever makes up your family, it is perfectly normal." (Publisher's note)

★ The **day** Leo said I hate you; illustrated by Molly Bang. Little, Brown and Co. 2008 un il $16.99
Grades: PreK K 1 2   E
1. Love -- Fiction 2. Anger -- Fiction 3. Mother-son relationship -- Fiction
ISBN 978-0-316-06580-1; 0-316-06580-3
LC 2007-48371
Leo, upset he has been hearing the word "no" all day, lets three words slip out that he wishes he could take back.
The hero is "evoked via vibrant collages of photos and cut paper." Publ Wkly

Harris, Teresa E.
Summer Jackson: grown up; illustrated by AG Ford. Katherine Tegen Books 2011 un il $16.99
Grades: PreK K 1 2   E
1. Parent-child relationship -- Fiction
ISBN 978-0-06-185757-7; 0-06-185757-2
LC 2010-15962
Seven-year-old Summer Jackson wants to be a grown-up, starting right now.

"Ford's charming and humorous cartoon illustrations are liberally sprinkled throughout the book, ranging from three pictures on a page to full-page images. Although predictable, this story should have wide appeal." SLJ

Harris, Trudy
Say something, Perico; illustrated by Cecilia Rebora. Millbrook Press 2011 un il lib bdg $21.27
Grades: PreK K   E
1. Parrots -- Fiction 2. Bilingualism -- Fiction 3. Spanish language -- Fiction
ISBN 978-0-7613-5231-0; 0-7613-5231-7
LC 2011001114
Perico is a Spanish-speaking parrot who lives in a pet store, and although he works very hard to earn a new home, buyers keep returning him until the bird, now bilingual, finds the perfect owner. Includes Spanish glossary and pronunciation guide.
"The text is well assisted by Rebora's bright, wide-eyed illustrations, which bring out the humor and frustration of Perico's search for a home." Booklist

Tally cat keeps track; illustrated by Andrew N. Harris. Millbrook Press 2011 31p il lib bdg $22.60
Grades: K 1 2 3   E
1. Counting 2. Stories in rhyme 3. Cats -- Fiction 4. Friendship -- Fiction 5. Mathematics -- Fiction
ISBN 978-0-7613-4451-3; 0-7613-4451-9
LC 2009049586
Alley cat Tally McNally loves to tally and loves to win, but when his competitive streak gets him into trouble, he has to rely on his friends for help.
"The illustrations depict a bunch of street savvy, hip cats with great facial expressions. . . . This concept book would work equally well in the classroom or at storytime." SLJ

The **clock** struck one; a time-telling tale. written by Trudy Harris; illustrations by Carrie Hartman. Millbrook Press 2009 31p il (Math is fun) lib bdg $16.95
Grades: K 1 2   E
1. Stories in rhyme 2. Time -- Fiction 3. Animals -- Fiction 4. Clocks and watches -- Fiction
ISBN 978-0-8225-9067-5 lib bdg; 0-8225-9067-0 lib bdg
LC 2008041583
Rhyming text expands on the nursery rhyme, "Hickory Dickory Dock," as a cat chases the mouse up the clock, followed by other animals, until midnight arrives and the tired creatures fall asleep. Includes facts about clocks and basic information about telling time
"The animated romp's peppy verse and colorful art capture the comical bedlam with flair. . . . An entertaining addition to beginning time-telling lessons." Booklist

Harrison, David L.
A **monster** is coming! illustrated by Hans Wilhelm. Random House 2011 32p il (Step into reading) lib bdg $12.99; pa $3.99
Grades: PreK K 1   E
1. Fear -- Fiction 2. Food -- Fiction 3. Animals -- Fiction
ISBN 978-0-375-96677-4 lib bdg; 0-375-96677-3; 978-0-375-86677-7 pa; 0-375-86677-9 pa
LC 2010014513

When Inchworm overhears Mama Bug tell Baby Bug that she eats like a monster, he cries out in fear and sets off a chain reaction of animals trying to hide from the horrible beast they believe is coming.

"Beginning readers who crave suspense will be drawn to this gentle spin on the 'Chicken Little' motif. . . . Wilhelm's expressive, cheerfully colored cartoon illustrations reflect the fact that there is nothing to fear and provide a lot of picture clues to help decode the clever, descriptive text." SLJ

Harrison, Joanna

Grizzly dad. David Fickling Books 2009 un il $16.99; lib bdg $19.99

Grades: PreK K 1   E

1. Bears -- Fiction 2. Father-son relationship -- Fiction
ISBN 978-0-385-75173-5; 0-385-75173-7; 978-0-385-75174-2 lib bdg; 0-385-75174-5 lib bdg

LC 2007049461

First published 2008 in the United Kingdom

One morning Dad wakes up in such a bad mood that he turns into a bear

This "combines appealing text told from the children's point of view with hilarious illustrations that will ring true to parents and caregivers." Booklist

Harshman, Marc

Only one neighborhood; by Marc Harshman & Barbara Garrison; illustrated by Barbara Garrison. Dutton Children's Books 2007 un il $15.99

Grades: PreK K 1 2   E

1. City and town life -- Fiction
ISBN 978-0-525-47468-5

LC 2006035908

Explores a neighborhood that has only one of several kinds of buildings, but within each there are many things, such as different kinds of breads in the bakery, then shows that the neighborhood itself is just one of many in a world united by a single wish

"Like the best celebrations of unity, this picture book is about the exciting diversity that enriches everyone, and the collagraph illustrations, in warm colors, establish the details and the connections." Booklist

Hartfield, Claire

Me and Uncle Romie; a story inspired by the life and art of Romare Bearden. paintings by Jerome Lagarrigue. Dial Bks. for Young Readers 2002 un il $16.99

Grades: 2 3 4   E

1. Uncles 2. Artists 3. African Americans 4. Uncles -- Fiction 5. Artists -- Fiction 6. African Americans -- Fiction
ISBN 0-8037-2520-5

LC 99-41390

A boy from North Carolina spends the summer in New York City visiting the neighborhood of Harlem, where his uncle, collage artist Romare Bearden, grew up. Includes a biographical sketch of Bearden and instructions on making a story collage

This is a "vibrant, evocative picture book. . . . Lagarrigue's lush, acrylic illustrations with collage elements recall the tones, brush strokes, and mixture of media that saturate Bearden's groundbreaking work." SLJ

Hartland, Jessie

Night shift. Bloomsbury Children's Books 2007 un il $16.95; lib bdg $17.85

Grades: PreK K 1 2   E

1. Night -- Fiction 2. Occupations -- Fiction 3. Night -- Juvenile literature 4. Occupations -- Juvenile literature
ISBN 978-1-59990-025-4; 1-59990-025-4; 978-1-59990-138-1 lib bdg; 1-59990-138-2 lib bdg

LC 2006-102092

Late at night after children have gone to bed, people who work the night shift, like street sweepers, window dressers, newspaper printers, road workers, and donut bakers, are doing their jobs.

"Quirky gouache paintings capture the mood of this alternative world with its vibrant life. . . . Text and illustrations are equally unique." SLJ

Harvey, Jeanne

My hands sing the blues; Romare Bearden's childhood journey. illustrated by Elizabeth Zunon. Marshall Cavendish 2011 40p il

Grades: K 1 2 3   E

1. Artists 2. Stories in rhyme 3. Artists -- Fiction 4. Blues music -- Fiction
ISBN 0-7614-5810-7; 978-0-7614-5810-4

In Harlem, New York City, artist Romare Bearden follows the rhythms of blues music as he recalls his North Carolina childhood while painting, cutting, and pasting to make art.

"The talented Zunon's pictures intriguingly combine realistic faces, stylized landscapes and photo-collage that pays homage to Bearden's art. . . . The interplay of poetic and visual metaphor makes for a striking presentation; adults who can appreciate and chant the bluesy poem as well as sensitively interpret the pictures together with children are the ideal collaborators in savoring this intriguing work." Kirkus

Harvey, Matt

Shopping with Dad; [by] Matt Harvey and [illustrated by] Miriam Latimer. Barefoot Books 2008 un il $16.99

Grades: PreK K 1 2   E

1. Stories in rhyme 2. Shopping -- Fiction 3. Father-daughter relationship -- Fiction
ISBN 978-1-84686-172-7; 1-84686-172-1

LC 2007042763

A little girl and her father have a wonderful time in the grocery store until she nearly knocks over a display, then while trying her best to be good she lets out a big sneeze that results in chaos.

"The cartoon mixed-media illustrations depict a lively hubbub amid plenty of color. . . . Funny and warmhearted, this story will be enjoyed one-on-one and handy in classrooms." SLJ

Haseley, Dennis

Twenty heartbeats; [illustrated by] Ed Young. Roaring Brook Press 2008 un il $16.95

Grades: 2 3 4 5   E

1. Horses -- Fiction 2. Artists -- Fiction
ISBN 978-1-59643-238-3; 1-59643-238-1

LC 2007-13202

After waiting for decades for the portrait of his prize horse to be finished, an angry rich man decides to confront the artist.

"Based on a literary anecdote, the story, like its subject, contains only what is essential. Haseley's minimalist text leaves plenty of room for Young's marvelous collages to set the scene and develop the characters." SLJ

Hassett, Ann

Too many frogs; by Ann and John Hassett. Houghton Mifflin Harcourt 2011 un il $16.99

Grades: PreK K 1   **E**

1. Frogs -- Fiction

ISBN 978-0-547-36299-1; 0-547-36299-4

LC 2010006783

With rapidly increasing numbers of frogs coming out of her basement, Nana Quimby asks assorted neighborhood children for help, but finally it is up to her to come up with a solution.

"Delicious to look at—with its explosion of acrobatic frogs, its primitivist-detail décor, its confectionery colors— and a treat to listen to." Horn Book

Hatsue Nakawaki

Wait! wait! by Hatsue Nakawaki; illustrated by Komako Sakai; translated from the Japanese by Yuki Kaneko. 1st American ed. Enchanted Lion Books 2013 24 p. ill. (hardcover) $14.95

Grades: PreK   **E**

1. Animals -- Juvenile fiction 2. Parent-child relationship -- Juvenile fiction 3. Animals -- Fiction 4. Parent and child -- Fiction

ISBN 1592701388; 9781592701384

LC 2013011003

This book by Hatsue Nawaki "follows a young child's discovery of other creatures. This discovery comes with the recognition that while other creatures can suddenly appear they can also go away and disappear just as quickly. But the delightful appearance of a dad and his playful swoop of his toddler up onto his shoulders will remind little ones that the people who love them will always be there and will never, ever not come back." (Publisher's note)

Haughton, Chris

Little owl lost. Candlewick Press 2010 un il $14.99

Grades: PreK K   **E**

1. Owls -- Fiction 2. Mothers -- Fiction 3. Forest animals -- Fiction

ISBN 978-0-7636-5022-3; 0-7636-5022-6

While his mother is away finding food, a newborn owl falls out of his nest and anxiously tries to find her, receiving help from various forest animals.

"Haughton's pitch-perfect use of language flows smoothly to the satisfying end. The pencil and digitally rendered illustrations, which have the feel of a mix of woodblock and cut-paper collage, are done in intense, saturated colors of olive, red, orange, fuchsia, blue, and yellow." SLJ

Havill, Juanita

Call the horse Lucky; illustrated by Nancy Lane. Gryphon Press 2010 un il $15.95

Grades: K 1 2 3   **E**

1. Horses -- Fiction

ISBN 978-0-940719-10-1; 0-940719-10-X

"A girl helps a neglected horse in this heartfelt picture book about animal rescue. Bike riding in the country with her grandmother, Mel sees a despondent pinto alone in a corral. When she realizes that the horse is too skinny and moves painfully, her grandmother calls the Humane Society. Lucky, as Mel names him, is taken to a veterinarian and ultimately to a horse therapy ranch where he will live and work. Havill's conversational text keeps the story moving along swiftly without being hindered by a lot of detail, thus keeping the didacticism at a minimum. Lane's watercolor paintings deftly convey the emotions of both the horse and Mel." SLJ

★ **Jamaica's** find; illustrations by Anne Sibley O'Brien. Houghton Mifflin 1986 32p il $16; pa $6.95

Grades: PreK K 1 2   **E**

1. Toys -- Fiction 2. African Americans -- Fiction

ISBN 0-395-39376-0; 0-395-45357-7 pa

LC 85-14542

"This is a pleasant picture book with warm, expressive pictures and an appealing story line that encourages values clarification." Interracial Books Child Bull

Other titles about Jamaica are:

Brianna, Jamaica, and the Dance of Spring (2002)

Jamaica and Brianna (1993)

Jamaica and the substitute teacher (1999)

Jamaica is thankful (2009)

Jamaica tag-along (1989)

Jamaica's blue marker (1995)

Just like a baby; [by] Juanita Havill; [illustrated by] Christine Davenier. Chronicle Books 2009 un il $15.99

Grades: PreK K 1   **E**

1. Infants -- Fiction 2. Family life -- Fiction

ISBN 978-0-8118-5026-1; 0-8118-5026-9

LC 2008021971

Delighted by the arrival of baby Ellen, extended family members describe their plans for the young one, from becoming a fisherman to playing the saxophone, but baby Ellen prefers other activities.

"Lively dialogue and an upbeat refrain enhance the spare text. Davenier's watercolor-and-ink illustrations seamlessly blend colors; bursts of rosy reds lead to an arresting presentation." Kirkus

Hawkes, Kevin

The wicked big toddlah. Alfred A. Knopf 2007 un il $16.99; lib bdg $19.99

Grades: PreK K 1 2   **E**

1. Size -- Fiction 2. Infants -- Fiction

ISBN 978-0-375-82427-2; 0-375-82427-8; 978-0-375-92427-9 lib bdg; 0-375-92427-2 lib bdg

LC 2006-32209

A year in the life of a baby in Maine who is just like any other baby except that he is gigantic.

"Each lush spread . . . uses space and perspective to particular advantage. . . . The many bits of visual humor will keep youngsters poring back and forth over the pages." SLJ

Another title about the wicked big toddlah is:

The wicked big toddlah goes to New York (2011)

The wicked big toddlah goes to New York. Alfred A. Knopf 2011 un il $16.99; lib bdg $19.99

Grades: PreK K 1 2   **E**
  1. Size -- Fiction 2. Missing children -- Fiction
  ISBN 978-0-375-86188-8; 0-375-86188-2; 978-0-375-
  96189-2 lib bdg; 0-375-96189-5 lib bdg
                                        LC 2009-48258
A Maine couple and their gigantic toddler take a trip to
New York City, where despite his size, the 'wicked big toddlah' becomes lost.
  "Hawkes pairs caricaturish sketches of Toddie with gorgeous blue summer skies and skillful renderings of iconic
landmarks." Publ Wkly

Hayes, Geoffrey
  Benny and Penny in Lights out! a Toon book. by
Geoffrey Hayes. Toon Books 2012 32 p. ill. (reinforced)
$12.95
Grades: K 1 2   **E**
  1. Mice -- Fiction 2. Siblings -- Fiction 3. Picture
  books for children 4. Graphic novels 5. Bedtime --
  Fiction 6. Brothers and sisters -- Fiction
  ISBN 1935179209; 9781935179207
                                        LC 2011050927
This children's picture book follows mouse brother and
sister Benny and Penny. Penny is getting ready for bed, but
"her restless big brother interrupts obnoxiously with warnings about the Boogey Mouse, loud belches and other distractions. When Benny realizes that he's left his prized pirate hat in the backyard, though, Penny braves the Boogey
Mouse to follow him . . . and prod him into reclaiming it
from the spooky, dark playhouse." (Kirkus)

  A **poor** excuse for a dragon. Random House Children's
Books 2011 47p il (Step into reading) $12.99; lib bdg
$14.99; pa $3.99
Grades: K 1 2   **E**
  1. Dragons -- Fiction
  ISBN 978-0-375-87180-1; 0-375-87180-2; 978-0-375-
  96867-9 lib bdg; 0-375-96867-9 lib bdg; 978-0-375-
  86867-2 pa; 0-375-86867-4 pa; 978-0-375-89938-6
  e-book
                                        LC 2010025000
When Fred the dragon leaves home he learns that he is
not very good at roaring or breathing fire and swallowing
people only makes him ill, but with help from a witch, a giant, and a wise boy he finds his true calling.
  "Entertaining black-line and colored pencil cartoon
drawings enliven this Kuklapolitan-esque cast. Part-slap-
stick, part-fairy tale, the gently humorous plot has enough
twists and turns to keep newly independent readers engaged." SLJ

Hayes, Karel
  The **summer** visitors. Down East 2011 un il $16.95
Grades: K 1 2 3   **E**
  1. Bears -- Fiction 2. Summer -- Fiction
  ISBN 978-0-89272-918-0; 0-89272-918-X
                                        LC 2011014445
During the summer a family of bears enjoys the comforts
of life at a cottage by a lake, alongside the human visitors.
  "The book is almost wordless. The humorous illustra-
tions, done in pen and ink, cleverly highlight the puzzled
family's expressions. Children will enjoy being in on the

joke as they watch the bears' antics. A fine vacation choice,
especially for one-on-one sharing." SLJ

  The **winter** visitors; by Karel Hayes. Down East
Books 2007 un il $15.95
Grades: K 1 2 3   **E**
  1. Bears -- Fiction 2. Houses -- Fiction 3. Winter
  -- Fiction
  ISBN 978-0-89272-750-6
                                        LC 2007014051
When the summer visitors leave in the fall, a family of
bears moves into the vacation cottage to spend the winter.
  "Just five sentences of simple text, spread throughout
the book, are a perfect accompaniment to the delightful pen-
and-ink and watercolor artwork." SLJ

Hayes, Sarah
  Dog day; by Sarah Hayes; illustrated by Hannah Broad-
way. Farrar Straus and Giroux 2008 un il $16.95
Grades: PreK K 1 2   **E**
  1. School stories 2. Dogs -- Fiction 3. Teachers --
  Fiction
  ISBN 978-0-374-31810-9; 0-374-31810-7
Ben and Ellie's class has a new teacher, and it's a dog
named Riff!
  "Colorful full-page illustrations add to the doggone good
fun. The placement of the illustrations and text lets readers'
eyes scamper across the page." SLJ

Hays, Anna Jane
  Kindergarten countdown; written by Anna Jane Hays;
illustrated by Linda Davick. Alfred A. Knopf 2007 un il
$8.99; lib bdg $11.99
Grades: PreK K   **E**
  1. Counting 2. School stories 3. Stories in rhyme
  ISBN 978-0-375-84252-8; 978-0-375-94252-5 lib bdg
                                        LC 2006024249
Rhyming text follows an excited little girl as she counts
down the days before the start of kindergarten
  "Both the rhyming verse and the pictures are filled with
humor and energy. . . . The computer-generated illustrations
are detailed and vibrant." SLJ

  ★ **Ready,** set, preschool! illustrated by True Kelley.
Knopf 2005 30p il $16.95; lib bdg $18.99
Grades: PreK   **E**
  1. School stories
  ISBN 0-375-82519-3; 0-375-92519-8 lib bdg
A collection of simple stories, poems, and picture games
designed to prepare children for preschool
  "With lots of cheerfully illustrated rhymes, stories, and
interactive games, this big picture book is an excellent title
to prepare kids for preschool." Booklist

  Smarty Sara; by Anna Jane Hays; illustrated by Sylvie
Wickstrom. Random House 2008 32p il (Step into reading) lib bdg $11.99; pa $3.99
Grades: K 1 2   **E**
  1. Stories in rhyme 2. Diaries -- Fiction
  ISBN 978-0-375-95054-4 lib bdg; 0-375-95054-0 lib
  bdg; 978-0-375-83512-4 pa; 0-375-83512-1 pa
                                        LC 2007-11068

Everywhere Sara goes she brings along her journal where she jots notes, makes lists, draws pictures and maps, writes poems, and plans a big surprise for her friends.

"The casual, rhyming text has fun with the sound of words as well as their meaning, and the colorful, relaxed pictures, in thick line and watercolor, add to the celebration of reading and writing—not as a duty, but as play." Booklist

Hazen, Barbara Shook

★ **Digby**; story by Barbara Shook Hazen; pictures by Barbara J. Phillips-Duke. HarperCollins Pubs. 1996 32p il (I can read book) hardcover o.p. lib bdg $15.89; pa $4.99
Grades: K 1 2   E
1. Dogs -- Fiction 2. Old age -- Fiction
ISBN 0-06-026253-2; 0-06-026254-0 lib bdg; 0-06-444239-X pa
LC 95-1689
"A boy wants the family dog to play ball, but his big sister explains that Digby is too old now to run and catch. . . . The story of aging and of time passing is told in very simple conversation . . . and the bright contemporary pictures show the bond between the African American brother and sister and their beloved pet." Booklist

Heap, Sue

Danny's drawing book; by Sue Heap. Candlewick Press 2008 un il $9.99
Grades: PreK K 1   E
1. Zoos -- Fiction 2. Animals -- Fiction 3. Drawing -- Fiction 4. Imagination -- Fiction
ISBN 978-0-7636-3654-8; 0-7636-3654-1
LC 2007040402
On a trip to the zoo with his friend Ettie, Danny draws pictures of some animals, who then lead the two on an imaginary adventure to Africa and back

This is a "charming picture book, illustrated in a childlike style. . . . Heap's colorful acrylic paintings and pencil sketches differentiate between reality and fantasy, but young children will easily recognize that . . . there's plenty of overlap between the worlds." Booklist

Hector, Julian

The **Gentleman** Bug. Atheneum Books for Young Readers 2010 un il $16.99
Grades: PreK K 1   E
1. Insects -- Fiction 2. Books and reading -- Fiction
ISBN 978-1-4169-9467-1; 1-4169-9467-X
LC 2009-13177
Teased because he likes to spend all of his time reading, the Gentleman Bug decides to change in order to catch the eye of the new Lady Bug in the garden, but she is not impressed until he goes back to being himself.

"Hector's crisp, utterly charming watercolor-and-colored pencil illustrations have a classic, timeless feel, and the spectacularly detailed scenes, which demand close-up viewing, do the bulk of the storytelling." Booklist

The **Little** Matador; words and pictures by Julian Hector. Hyperion Books for Children 2008 un il $15.99
Grades: PreK K 1 2   E
1. Artists -- Fiction 2. Bullfights -- Fiction
ISBN 978-1-4231-0779-8; 1-4231-0779-9
LC 2007042072

A young matador who would rather draw pictures than fight bulls finds a new way to entertain the townsfolk

"The old-time setting is well conveyed through illustrations using muted colors for the most part, with the hero in a bright red matador's outfit. The succinct text is enriched by numerous visual touches that help tell the story." SLJ

Hegamin, Tonya

★ **Most** loved in all the world; illustrated by Cozbi Cabrera. Houghton Mifflin 2009 un il $17
Grades: PreK K 1 2   E
1. Slavery -- Fiction 2. African Americans -- Fiction 3. Mother-daughter relationship -- Fiction
ISBN 0-618-41903-9; 978-0-618-41903-6
LC 2004-13189
Even though Mama is an agent on the Underground Railroad, in order to help others she must remain a slave, but she teaches her daughter the value of freedom through a gift of love and sacrifice.

Cabrera's "broad sweeping paintings—filled with shadowy images, occasionally bordering on the abstract, with some pages merely washes of color—add a deeper note of somberness to the spare text, told in a child's voice." Publ Wkly

Heide, Florence Parry

Always listen to your mother; [by] Florence Parry Heide & Roxanne Heide; pictures by Kyle M. Stone. Disney/Hyperion Books 2010 un il $15.99
Grades: K 1 2   E
1. Monsters -- Fiction
ISBN 978-1-4231-1395-9; 1-4231-1395-0
LC 2010004519
When a new neighbor moves in next door, Ernest's mother, who always insists that he obey all the rules, encourages them to play together every day.

"Young readers will love the contrast in colors from Vlapid's bright and cheery home and the neighbors' dark gray home. This book creates a great opportunity to talk about following directions and how to make chores fun." Libr Media Connect

★ The **day** of Ahmed's secret; [by] Florence Parry Heide & Judith Heide Gilliland; illustrated by Ted Lewin. Lothrop, Lee & Shepard Bks. 1990 un il $16; pa $6.99
Grades: 1 2 3 4   E
ISBN 0-688-08894-5; 0-688-14023-8 pa
LC 90-52694
"Ahmed has monumental news to share with his family, but first he must complete the age-old duties of a butagaz boy, delivering cooking gas to customers all over Cairo. . . . Enhanced by Lewin's distinguished photorealistic watercolors, the sights, sounds, and smells of the exotic setting come to life. . . . At home at last, surrounded by his loving family, Ahmed demonstrates his newly acquired facility, proudly writing his name in Arabic." SLJ

The **one** and only Marigold; written by Florence Parry Heide; illustrated by Jill McElmurry. Schwartz & Wade Books 2009 un il $16.99; lib bdg $19.99
Grades: PreK K 1 2   E
1. Monkeys -- Fiction 2. Friendship -- Fiction 3.

Family life -- Fiction 4. Hippopotamus -- Fiction
ISBN 978-0-375-84031-9; 0-375-84031-1; 978-0-375-
94051-4 lib bdg; 0-375-94051-0 lib bdg

LC 2007-37840

Relates the misadventures of Marigold the monkey, who
does not agree with anyone, as she shops with her mother
for a coat, becomes interested in a new hobby, finds a way to
"bug" her best friend, Maxine (a hippo), and imaginatively
copes with finding the right outfit for the first day of school

"As depicted in McElmurry's . . . stylish spreads, a blend
of up-to-the-minute humor and nostalgic, folklike patterning, Marigold has a long prehensile tail and spiky rust-col-
ored hair that she sometimes wears in topknots. Heide . . .
introduces a stubborn, potentially maddening character, but
Marigold's sunny disposition and creativity make up for her
mischief." Publ Wkly

★ **Princess** Hyacinth; (the surprising tale of a girl who
floated) illustrated by Lane Smith. Schwartz & Wade Books
2009 un il $17.99; lib bdg $20.99
Grades: PreK K 1 2   E
1. Princesses -- Fiction
ISBN 978-0-375-84501-7; 0-375-84501-1; 978-0-375-
93753-8 lib bdg; 0-375-93753-6 lib bdg

LC 2008-39923

Princess Hyacinth is bored and unhappy sitting in her
palace every day because, unless she is weighed down by
specially-made clothes, she will float away, but her days are
made brighter when kite-flying Boy stops to say hello.

"The quirky oil and watercolor illustrations seamlessly
match Heide's wry, understated text." Publ Wkly

★ **Sami** and the time of the troubles; [by] Florence
Parry Heide & Judith Heide Gilliland; illustrated by Ted
Lewin. Clarion Bks. 1992 un il $16; pa $6.95
Grades: 1 2 3 4   E
1. Family life -- Fiction
ISBN 0-395-55964-2; 0-395-72085-0 pa

LC 91-14343

A ten-year-old Lebanese boy in Beirut goes to school,
helps his mother with chores, plays with his friends, and
lives with his family in a basement shelter when bombings
occur and fighting begins on his street

This is "a powerful, poignant book. Heide and Gillil-
and's lyrically written, haunting story makes clear that war
threatens not only physical existence but affects the human
spirit as well. Lewin's watercolor illustrations capture contemporary Beirut with stunning clarity and drama." SLJ

Heide, Iris van der

A **strange** day; [by] Iris van der Heide; illustrations by
Marijke ten Cate. Lemniscaat 2007 un il $15.95
Grades: K 1 2   E
1. Letters -- Fiction
ISBN 978-1-932425-94-9; 1-932425-94-2

LC 2006029265

Original Dutch edition 2006

Upset when an important letter does not arrive in the
mail as expected, Jack wanders through the park not even
noticing what he is doing and becomes an unwitting hero

"Dutch artist ten Cate's landscapes may be delicate and
winsome, but they also brim with scenes of farce and slapstick. . . . It all adds up to a clever comedy of coincidences

and misadventures, with ample rewards for attentive youngsters." Publ Wkly

Heilbroner, Joan, 1929-

A **pet** named Sneaker; by Joan Heilbroner; illustrated
by Pascal Lemaitre. Random House Children's Books 2013
48 p. (Beginner books) (library binding) $12.99
Grades: K 1 2   E
1. Snakes as pets -- Juvenile fiction 2. Snakes as pets
-- Fiction
ISBN 0375971165; 9780307975805; 9780375971167;
9780375981128

LC 2011047340

This children's book by Joan Heilbroner presents "the
story of a pet-store snake who longs for a real home. When
he is finally adopted by Pete . . . Sneaker not only proves
himself a good pet, but proves to be a good student (sneaking into school with Pete and learning to read and write);
a good citizen (saving a drowning toddler at a community
pool); and a goodwill ambassador for the entire animal kingdom (inspiring the community to open the pool to all animals)!" (Publisher's note)

Heiligman, Deborah

Cool dog, school dog; illustrated by Tim Bowers. Marshall Cavendish Children 2009 un il $15.99
Grades: PreK K 1   E
1. School stories 2. Stories in rhyme 3. Dogs -- Fiction
ISBN 978-0-7614-5561-5; 0-7614-5561-2

LC 2008029398

When Tinka the dog follows her owner to school and
creates havoc, the children discover a way to let her stay in
the classroom and help.

"Bowers's vivid acrylic illustrations are full of expression. . . . Youngsters will like learning with each turn of the
page just what makes this dog so special." SLJ

Helakoski, Leslie Hebert

Big chickens; [by] Leslie Helakoski; illustrated by
Henry Cole. Dutton Children's Books 2006 un il $15.99
Grades: PreK K 1 2   E
1. Fear -- Fiction 2. Chickens -- Fiction
ISBN 0-525-47575-3

LC 2005003282

While trying to escape from a wolf, four frightened
chickens keep getting themselves into the very predicaments
they are trying to avoid

"Bright pictures convey the comic events with an exaggerated style just right for the story line. There's a satisfying
amount of silliness that will leave children giggling." SLJ

Other titles about the big chickens are:
Big chickens fly the coop (2008)
Big chickens go to town (2009)

Fair cow; written and illustrated by Leslie Helakoski.
Marshall Cavendish 2010 un il $16.99
Grades: PreK K 1 2   E
1. Pigs -- Fiction 2. Cattle -- Fiction
ISBN 978-0-7614-5684-1; 0-7614-5684-8

LC 2009004789

Effie the cow dreams of winning a blue ribbon at the
state fair, while her best friend Petunia the pig advises her
to give up all that she truly enjoys in order to prepare for
the big day.

"The acrylic on paper illustrations are large, bright, and humorous. The animals' faces are quite expressive. . . . This book will work well for storytimes about barnyard antics and for those always-be-yourself lessons. Besides that, it's just plain fun." SLJ

Helfer, Ralph
World's greatest lion; Ralph Helfer; illustrated by Ted Lewin. Philomel Books 2012 40 p.
Grades: 2 3 4   E
    1. Lions 2. Mascots 3. Animals in motion pictures 4. Zamba (Lion) -- Juvenile literature 5. Lion -- California -- Los Angeles -- Biography -- Juvenile literature 6. Animal trainers -- California -- Los Angeles -- Biography -- Juvenile literature 7. Animals in motion pictures -- California -- Los Angeles -- Biography -- Juvenile literature
    ISBN 039925417X; 9780399254178
                      LC 2011020681
This children's picture book, by Ralph Helfer, "opens in Zambia, where a woman in a safari camp rescues an orphaned lion cub and names him Zamba. . . . Animal behaviorist [Ralph] Helfer . . . brings the lion to his animal sanctuary in California. . . . He eventually becomes sufficiently gentle to star in Hollywood films. Zamba's heroism emerges in the book's final episode, in which he saves Helfer and the sanctuary animals during a flash flood." (Publishers Weekly)

Heller, Linda
How Dalia put a big yellow comforter inside a tiny blue box; and other wonders of tzedakah. illustrations by Stacey Dressen McQueen. Tricycle Press 2011 un il $16.99; lib bdg $19.99
Grades: K 1 2   E
    1. Jews -- Fiction 2. Charity -- Fiction 3. Judaism -- Fiction 4. Siblings -- Fiction
    ISBN 978-1-58246-378-0; 1-58246-378-6; 978-1-58246-402-2 lib bdg; 1-58246-402-2 lib bdg; 978-1-58246-382-7 e-book; 1-58246-382-4 e-book
                      LC 2010024325
After learning about the Jewish tradition of tzedakah boxes, Dalia shares her knowledge with her younger brother, Yossi, by telling him what her savings can help to provide for someone in need. Includes a note about the history and customs of tzedakah boxes.
"Dressen-McQueen's fully developed summer scenes in acrylic and oil pastel provide a vivid complement to the often-page-filling text, their naive, folk quality bringing great quantities of love and warmth to the tale." Kirkus

Today is the birthday of the world; by Linda Heller; illustrated by Allison Jay. Dutton Children's Books 2009 un il $16.99
Grades: PreK K 1   E
    1. God -- Fiction 2. Animals -- Fiction 3. Birthdays -- Fiction
    ISBN 978-0-525-47905-5; 0-525-47905-8
                      LC 2008-34216
On the birthday of the world, all of God's creatures pass before Him as He asks whether each has been the best giraffe, or bee, or child they could be, helping to make the world a better place.
Heller's "repeating form lends the soothing tone of a lullaby, well-matched by Jay's . . . bucolic scenes. . . . Readers

will be left feeling connected to the larger world, as one of the 'dear little helpers' God praises." Publ Wkly

Helmore, Jim
Oh no, monster tomato! illustrated by Karen Wall. Egmont 2011 un il pa $8.99
Grades: K 1 2   E
    1. Plants -- Fiction 2. Siblings -- Fiction 3. Tomatoes -- Fiction
    ISBN 978-1-4052-4741-2; 1-4052-4741-X
"Marvin is the smallest child in his family, but when the Great Grislygust Grow-off comes around, he is determined to produce the tastiest tomatoes and win. His brother and sister bait and tease him . . . but he has a potion and a few songs up his sleeve. He grows a plant so large that it shoots its tomatoes—they are the size of beach balls—at his mean siblings. . . . Helmore uses alliteration to make the story sing . . . and the rollicking words dance across the pages. Wall's vibrant, cartoon-style, collage illustrations can seem as fast-growing as Marvin's plant." SLJ

Helquist, Brett
  ★ **Bedtime** for bear. Harper 2010 un il $16.99
Grades: PreK K 1   E
    1. Bears -- Fiction 2. Winter -- Fiction 3. Bedtime -- Fiction 4. Hibernation -- Fiction
    ISBN 978-0-06-050205-8; 0-06-050205-3
Just after the first snowfall, Bear is ready to go to sleep until spring but his friends encourage him to spend one last day playing with them.
"Helquist's sumptuous paintings and expansive sense of visual comedy make this otherwise familiar hibernation tale a keeper. . . . Reader's will want to jump right into these pages and join in the fun—and they'll close the book agreeing that Bear has truly earned his zzzzs." Publ Wkly

Hemingway, Edward
Bump in the night; [by] Edward Hemingway. G.P. Putnam's Sons 2008 un il $15.99
Grades: PreK K 1 2   E
    1. Bedtime -- Fiction 2. Monsters -- Fiction
    ISBN 978-0-399-24761-3; 0-399-24761-0
                      LC 2007013812
After Billy goes to bed one night he hears a scary noise, which, upon investigation turns out to be nothing but a sweet little monster named Bump.
"This lively story meets nighttime fears head-on with the right mix of silliness and reassurance. . . . The acrylic-on-wood illustrations create the perfect mood for this appealing bedtime story." SLJ

Henderson, Kathy
  ★ **Look** at you! a baby body book. illustrated by Paul Howard. Candlewick Press 2006 un il $15.99
Grades: PreK   E
    1. Infants -- Fiction 2. Human body -- Fiction 3. Infants -- Juvenile literature 4. Body, Human -- Juvenile literature
    ISBN 0-7636-2745-3
                      LC 2005-50792
This "commemorates a small child's amazing feats, from crawling to clapping to exploring food with their entire bodies. . . . The oversize pencil-and-watercolor illustrations are

warm and soft, with perfectly captured body movements and facial expressions." SLJ

Henkes, Kevin, 1960-

★ **Birds**; illustrated by Laura Dronzek. Greenwillow Books 2009 un il $17.99; lib bdg $18.89

Grades: PreK K 1 2   E

1. Birds -- Fiction 2. Birds -- Juvenile literature
ISBN 978-0-06-136304-7; 0-06-136304-9; 978-0-06-136305-4 lib bdg; 0-06-136305-7 lib bdg

LC 2007-45084

Fascinated by the colors, shapes, sounds, and movements of the many different birds she sees through her window, a little girl is happy to discover that she and they have something in common.

"Henkes' spare, direct words have a lyrical magic, while Dronzek's bright acrylic paintings, in saturated primary color and heavy black outlines, reflect the text's plain elegance while carrying an exuberant energy all their own." Booklist

★ **Chester's** way. Greenwillow Bks. 1988 un il $16.99; lib bdg $17.89; pa $6.99

Grades: PreK K 1 2   E

1. Mice -- Fiction
ISBN 0-688-07607-6; 0-688-07608-4 lib bdg; 0-688-15472-7 pa

LC 87-14882

The mice Chester and Wilson share the same exact way of doing things, until Lilly moves into the neighborhood and shows them that new ways can be just as good

"Henkes' charming cartoons are drawn with pen-and-ink, washed over with cheerful watercolors. They give witty expressions to his characters." SLJ

★ **Chrysanthemum**. Greenwillow Bks. 1991 un il $16.99; lib bdg $17.89; pa $6.99

Grades: PreK K 1 2   E

1. School stories 2. Mice -- Fiction 3. Personal names -- Fiction
ISBN 0-688-09699-9; 0-688-09700-6 lib bdg; 0-688-814732-1 pa

LC 90-39803

Chrysanthemum, a mouse, loves her name, until she starts going to school and the other children make fun of it

"The text, precise and evocative, uses contrast and repetition to achieve rhythm and balance; the illustrations are forthright yet delicately colored, remarkable for the agility of the fine line which creates setting and characters." Horn Book

★ A **good** day. Greenwillow Books 2007 un il $16.99; lib bdg $17.89; bd bk $7.99

Grades: PreK K 1   E

1. Board books for children 2. Animals -- Fiction
ISBN 978-0-06-114018-1; 0-06-114018-X; 978-0-06-114019-8 lib bdg; 0-06-114019-8 lib bdg; 978-0-06-185778-2 bd bk; 0-06-185778-5 bd bk

LC 2005-35923

A bird, a fox, a dog, and a squirrel overcome minor setbacks to have a very good day

"This story works well in every way. As precise, unaffected, and easy for a young child to understand as the text,

the illustrations feature forms cleanly defined with thick black lines and brightened with watercolors." Booklist

★ **Jessica**. Greenwillow Bks. 1989 un il $16.99; lib bdg $17.89; pa $6.99

Grades: PreK K 1 2   E

1. Imaginary playmates -- Fiction
ISBN 0-688-07829-X; 0-688-07830-3 lib bdg; 0-688-15847-1 pa

LC 87-38087

"A shy preschooler insists that her friend Jessica is not imaginary—and, in the end, she's absolutely correct. Henkes' depiction of play-alone and play-together time brims with buoyant camaraderie in this upbeat story of friendship fulfilled." SLJ

★ **Julius,** the baby of the world. Greenwillow Bks. 1990 un il $16.99; lib bdg $16.89; pa $5.99

Grades: PreK K 1 2   E

1. Mice -- Fiction
ISBN 0-688-08943-7; 0-688-08944-5 lib bdg; 0-688-14388-1 pa

LC 88-34904

"Magically, Henkes conveys a world of expressions and a wide range of complex emotions with a mere line or two upon the engaging mousey faces of Lilly and her family. A reassuring, funny book for all young children who suffer from new-sibling syndrome." SLJ

★ **Kitten's** first full moon. Greenwillow Books 2004 un il $17.99; lib bdg $16.89

Grades: PreK K 1   E

1. Cats 2. Cats -- Fiction 3. Animals -- Infancy
ISBN 0-06-058828-4; 0-06-058829-2 lib bdg

LC 2003-12564

Awarded the Caldecott Medal, 2005

When Kitten mistakes the full moon for a bowl of milk, she ends up tired, wet, and hungry trying to reach it

"Done in a charcoal and cream-colored palette, the understated illustrations feature thick black outlines, pleasing curves, and swiftly changing expressions that are full of nuance. The rhythmic text and delightful artwork ensure storytime success." SLJ

★ **Lilly's** purple plastic purse. Greenwillow Bks. 1996 un il $17.99; lib bdg $18.89

Grades: PreK K 1 2   E

1. School stories 2. Mice -- Fiction
ISBN 0-688-12897-1; 0-688-12898-X lib bdg

LC 95-25085

"Lilly loves everything about school. . . . But most of all, she loves her teacher, Mr. Slinger. . . . The little mouse will do anything for him—until he refuses to allow her to interrupt lessons to show the class her new movie-star sunglasses, three shiny quarters, and purple plastic purse. Seething with anger, she writes a mean story about him and places it in his book bag at the end of the day. . . . Rich vocabulary and just the right amount of repetition fuse perfectly with the watercolor and black-pen illustrations. . . . Clever dialogue and other funny details will keep readers looking and laughing." SLJ

Another title about Lilly is:

Lilly's big day (2006)

★ **Little** white rabbit. Greenwillow Books 2011 un il $16.99; lib bdg $17.89
Grades: PreK K   E
1. Rabbits -- Fiction 2. Imagination -- Fiction
ISBN 978-0-06-200642-4; 0-06-200642-8; 978-0-06-200643-1 lib bdg; 0-06-200643-6 lib bdg
LC 2010011602
"The colored-pencil-and-acrylic art combines thick outlines with vibrant hues, here mostly in a soothing palette of green that fits the nature setting and the comforting tone." Booklist

★ **My** garden. Greenwillow Books 2010 un il $17.99; lib bdg $18.89
Grades: PreK K 1   E
1. Gardens -- Fiction 2. Imagination -- Fiction 3. Gardening -- Juvenile literature
ISBN 978-0-06-171517-4; 0-06-171517-4; 978-0-06-171518-1 lib bdg; 0-06-171518-2 lib bdg
LC 2008-42364
After helping her mother weed, water, and chase the rabbits from their garden, a young girl imagines her dream garden complete with jellybean bushes, chocolate rabbits, and tomatoes the size of beach balls
This is rendered with "thick outlines; boldly applied, ice-cream parlor colors; and simple declarative sentences. . . . [This book is] an enjoyable tour of an imaginary place and will plant creativity in young minds." Booklist

★ **Old** Bear. Greenwillow Books 2008 un il $17.99; lib bdg $18.89
Grades: PreK   E
1. Bears -- Fiction 2. Dreams -- Fiction 3. Seasons -- Fiction 4. Hibernation -- Fiction
ISBN 978-0-06-155205-2; 0-06-155205-4; 978-0-06-155206-9 lib bdg; 0-06-155206-2 lib bdg
LC 2007-35965
Boston Globe-Horn Book Award honor book: Picture Book (2009)
When Old Bear falls asleep for the winter, he has a dream that he is a cub again, enjoying each of the four seasons.
"Every word, line, color choice, and composition element feels essential and fits beautifully into a common theme. . . . The elemental words and graceful pacing make this a perfect read-aloud. . . . [The illustrations are] rendered in bold outlines and color washes." Booklist

★ **Owen**. Greenwillow Bks. 1993 un il $17.99; lib bdg $16.89
Grades: PreK K 1 2   E
1. Blankets -- Fiction
ISBN 0-688-11449-0; 0-688-11450-4 lib bdg
LC 92-30084
A Caldecott Medal honor book, 1994
Owen's parents try to get him to give up his favorite blanket before he starts school, but when their efforts fail, they come up with a solution that makes everyone happy
This is "imbued with Henkes's characteristically understated humor, spry text and brightly hued watercolor-and-ink pictures." Publ Wkly

★ **Penny** and her doll; by Kevin Henkes. Greenwillow Books 2012 32 p. $12.99
Grades: K 1 2   E
1. Mice -- Fiction 2. Dolls -- Fiction 3. Personal names -- Fiction 4. Picture books for children 5. Family life -- Fiction 6. Names, Personal -- Fiction
ISBN 0062081993; 9780062081995 (trade bdg.))
LC 2011030043
In this children's picture book, Penny the mouse "is delighted to receive a doll from her grandmother ('I love her already,' Penny tells her mother and father separately). But Penny faces a quandary when it comes to naming her doll. As her mother and father attend to 'the babies,' they offer suggestions, but nothing feels right until Penny stops thinking so hard and lets the name come to her." (Publishers Weekly)

★ **Penny** and her marble; by Kevin Henkes. Greenwillow Books 2012 48 p. $12.99
Grades: PreK K 1 2   E
1. Mice -- Juvenile fiction 2. Lost and found possessions -- Juvenile fiction 3. Mice -- Fiction 4. Marbles -- Fiction 5. Lost and found possessions -- Fiction
ISBN 0062082035; 9780062082039; 9780062082046
LC 2012000708
In this children's book, written and illustrated by Kevin Henkes, the question of ownership is explored when a mouse finds a marble and discovers the lesson of finding objects which aren't yours. "When Penny spots a marble in Mrs. Goodwin's front yard, she picks it up, puts it in her pocket, and takes it home. . . . but does the marble really belong to Penny?" (Publisher's note)
"Henkes continues to plumb the emotional world of childhood as few author/illustrators can... Another gem." Kirkus

Penny and her song; by Kevin Henkes. Greenwillow Books 2012 32 p.
Grades: PreK K 1 2   E
1. Mice -- Fiction 2. Songs -- Fiction 3. Children's stories 4. Singing -- Fiction 5. Family life -- Fiction
ISBN 9780062081957; 9780062081964
LC 2011002154
In this book, "after dinner is done, Penny[, a mouse,] sings her song for her family. They like it so much that they ask her to sing it again, then join her in singing and, on a fourth round, put on silly costumes while belting the tune. In the end, it turns out that Penny's song helped the babies to fall asleep, as they have both dozed off in their basket." (Bulletin of the Center for Children's Books)

★ **Sheila** Rae, the brave. Greenwillow Bks. 1987 un il $16.99; lib bdg $17.89; pa $6.99
Grades: PreK K 1 2   E
1. Mice -- Fiction
ISBN 0-688-07155-4; 0-688-07156-2 lib bdg; 0-688-14738-0 pa
LC 86-25761
"Bouncy watercolors in spring-like colors with some pen-and-ink detailing highlight Sheila Rae's bravado in an engaging and amusing way, and Henkes provides Sheila Rae, Louise, and their school friends with highly expressive faces." SLJ

★ **So** happy! pictures by Anita Lobel. Greenwillow
Books 2005 un il $15.99; lib bdg $16.89
Grades: PreK K 1 2   E
    1. Seeds -- Fiction 2. Flowers -- Fiction 3. Rabbits
-- Fiction
ISBN 0-06-056483-0; 0-06-056484-9 lib bdg
"Lobel's vigorous artwork, a riot of color that pays hom-
age to Van Gogh, locates events in a sun-toasted, south-of-
the-border landscape, and captures the rhythm of Henkes'
splitting, braided narratives in triptychs alternating with co-
hesive scenes." Booklist

★ **Wemberly** worried. Greenwillow Bks. 2000 un il
lib bdg $16.89
Grades: PreK K 1 2   E
    1. Mice 2. Worry 3. Schools 4. School stories 5.
Nursery schools 6. Mice -- Fiction 7. Worry -- Fiction
8. First day of school
ISBN 0-688-17028-5
                    LC 99-34341
A mouse named Wemberly, who worries about everything, finds that she has a whole list of things to worry about
when she faces the first day of nursery school.
    The author combines "good storytelling, careful char-
acterization, and wonderfully expressive artwork to create
an entertaining and reassuring picture book that addresses a
common concern." SLJ

Hennessy, B. G.
    ★ **Because** of you; [by] B.G. Hennessy; illustrated by
Hiroe Nakata. Candlewick Press 2005 un il $15.99
Grades: PreK K 1   E
    1. Kindness -- Fiction 2. Conduct of life -- Fiction
ISBN 0-7636-1926-4
                  LC 2004-45168
"'Because of you,' Hennessy writes, 'there is one more
person who will grow and learn,' but also 'one more person
who can teach others.' . . . In an empowering conclusion,
Hennessy widens the child's sphere of influence, seeing the
'small and precious' acts at home as the first step toward
world peace—an ambitious goal made less daunting by
Nakata's billowy, cotton candy-hued watercolors of smiling characters exchanging gestures of help and affection."
Booklist

Henrichs, Wendy
    When Anju loved being an elephant; written by Wendy
Henrichs; illustrated by John Butler. Sleeping Bear Press
2011 il
Grades: K 1 2 3   E
    1. Elephants -- Fiction
ISBN 1-58536-533-5; 978-1-58536-533-3
                 LC 2010053708
Anju the Asian elephant recalls her childhood in Sumatra, and the American circuses and zoos in which she toiled
for fifty years, when she is loaded into a trailer truck and
taken to a sanctuary. Includes advice on helping elephants
and 'Elephant Q&A'.
    "Butler's realistic paintings in acrylic and colored pen-
cil deliver a soft, hazy muted quality that provides balance
to the gentle and often lyrical narration, which highlights
Anju's flashback memories of her childhood life with fellow young elephant Lali. . . . This heartfelt, humane vignette

provides just the right details to appeal to animal-loving
children." Kirkus

Henson, Heather
    Grumpy Grandpa; written by Heather Henson; illus-
trated by Ross MacDonald. Atheneum Books for Young
Readers 2009 un il $16.99
Grades: K 1 2   E
    1. Fishing -- Fiction 2. Old age -- Fiction 3. Country
life -- Fiction 4. Grandfathers -- Fiction
ISBN 978-1-4169-0811-1; 1-4169-0811-0
                 LC 2008-21543
Jack's grandfather is always grumpy, and a bit scary,
too, but during a visit to the country house where "Grumpy
Grandpa" lives with the brave Aunt Ellie and Uncle Wilbur,
Jack learns that his grandfather was once very different.
    "MacDonald's wonderful watercolors have his typical
'50s look, and include comic scenes. . . . The pictures are
a great match for the text, where the modern elements sit
comfortably alongside the old-fashioned ones." SLJ

    ★ **That** Book Woman; pictures by David Small. Ath-
eneum Books for Young Readers 2008 un il $16.99
Grades: K 1 2 3   E
    1. Librarians -- Fiction
ISBN 978-1-4169-0812-8; 1-4169-0812-9
                 LC 2007-18156
A family living in the Appalachian Mountains in the
1930s gets books to read during the regular visits of the
"Book Woman"—a librarian who rides a pack horse through
the mountains, lending books to the isolated residents.
    "Complementing Cal's authentically childlike thoughts,
Small's deft, rough-edged lines and masterful watercolors
convey even more than Henson's carefully honed text."
Horn Book

Heo, Yumi
    Ten days and nine nights; an adoption story. Schwartz
& Wade Books 2009 un il $16.99; lib bdg $19.99
Grades: PreK K 1 2   E
    1. Sisters -- Fiction 2. Adoption -- Fiction 3. Family
life -- Fiction 4. Korean Americans -- Fiction
ISBN 978-0-375-84718-9; 0-375-84718-9; 978-0-375-
94715-5 lib bdg; 0-375-94715-9 lib bdg
                 LC 2007044073
A young girl eagerly awaits the arrival of her newly-
adopted sister from Korea, while her whole family prepares.
    "The exquisite oil, pencil, and collage illustrations dove-
tail with the quiet, simple tone of the text." SLJ

Heos, Bridget
    Mustache baby; Bridget Heos; [illustrations by] Joy
Ang. Clarion Books 2013 40 p. col. ill. (hardcover)
$16.99
Grades: PreK K 1 2   E
    1. Mustaches -- Juvenile fiction 2. Bad behavior
-- Juvenile fiction 3. Humorous stories 4. Babies --
Fiction 5. Behavior -- Fiction 6. Mustaches -- Fiction
ISBN 0547773579; 9780547773575
                 LC 2012008155
In this children's picture book by Bridget Heos, "[w]hen
Baby Billy is born with a mustache, his family takes it in
stride. They are reassured when he nobly saves the day in
imaginary-play sessions as a cowboy or cop. . . . But as time

passes, their worst fears are confirmed when little Billy's mustache starts to curl up at the ends in a suspiciously villainous fashion. Sure enough, 'Billy's disreputable mustache led him into a life of dreadful crime.'" (Publisher's note)

Herman, Charlotte

First rain; illustrated by Kathryn Mitter. Albert Whitman 2010 un il $16.99

Grades: 1 2 3   E

1. Rain -- Fiction 2. Grandmothers -- Fiction

ISBN 978-0-8075-2453-4; 0-8075-2453-0

When Abby moves with her family to Israel, she misses her grandmother and during the dry Israeli summer, she remembers the fun they used to have splashing in puddles together

"Besides being a realistic look at another culture, this well-written book is heartwarming and reassuring." SLJ

Herman, Emily

★ **Hubknuckles**; illustrated by Deborah Kogan Ray. Crown Pubs. 2010 un il $14.99; lib bdg $17.99

Grades: PreK K 1 2   E

1. Ghost stories 2. Halloween -- Fiction

ISBN 978-0-517-55646-7; 0-517-55646-4; 978-0-375-96687-3 lib bdg; 0-375-96687-0 lib bdg

A reissue of the title first published 1985

Lee, certain that the Halloween ghost that visits her family is just a trick played by her mother or father, decides one year to go outside and dance with Hubknuckles the ghost.

"Ray's black-and-white drawings of family scenes and costumed children playing Halloween games are warm and friendly, while her pictures o the spectral dance add just the right touch of mystery to the story." Horn Book Guide

Hernandez, Leeza

Dog gone! Leeza Hernandez. G.P. Putnam's Sons 2012 40 p. (hardcover) $15.99

Grades: PreK K 1 2   E

1. Dogs -- Fiction 2. Pets -- Juvenile fiction 3. Picture books for children 4. Lost and found possessions -- Fiction

ISBN 0399254471; 9780399254475

LC 2011013408

In this picture book, a "dog acts up at home and is reprimanded by his human. He runs away, gets lost wandering the streets, and meets a rough crowd of street cats and dogs. They are friendly to him and become envious when the boy comes to find him, using a big flashlight in the pouring rain. As the boy and dog reunite, there are lots of big hugs and sloppy kissing. The two fall asleep together in the boy's bed that night." (School Library Journal)

Herold, Maggie Rugg

★ A **very** important day; illustrated by Catherine Stock. Morrow Junior Bks. 1995 un il $17.99

Grades: K 1 2 3   E

1. Immigrants -- Fiction 2. Naturalization -- Fiction

ISBN 0-688-13065-8

LC 94-16647

Two-hundred nineteen people from thirty-two different countries make their way to downtown New York in a snowstorm to be sworn in as citizens of the United States

"After the first quiet, gray-tone painting . . . this book bursts forth in a riot of color and activity. . . . A glossary sup-

plies guidance for pronouncing names, and a clear, nicely detailed overview of the process of naturalization rounds things out. Pictures and story combine to make the joy of the day contagious." Booklist

Hesse, Karen

★ **Come** on, rain! pictures by Jon J. Muth. Scholastic Press 1999 un il $15.95

Grades: PreK K 1 2   E

1. Summer 2. African Americans 3. Rain -- Fiction 4. Rain and rainfall 5. Summer -- Fiction 6. Mothers and daughters

ISBN 0-590-33125-6

LC 98-11575

A young girl eagerly awaits a coming rainstorm to bring relief from the oppressive summer heat

"Beautifully drafted watercolor paintings illustrate the lyrical text, creating a wonderful sense of atmosphere." Horn Book Guide

★ **Spuds**; by Karen Hesse; illustrated by Wendy Watson. Scholastic Press 2008 un il $16.99

Grades: PreK K 1 2   E

1. Potatoes -- Fiction 2. Siblings -- Fiction 3. Country life -- Fiction 4. Great Depression, 1929-1939 -- Fiction

ISBN 978-0-439-87993-4; 0-439-87993-0

LC 2007-24046

Maybelle, Jack, and Eddie want to help Ma by putting something extra on the table, so they set out in the dark to take potatoes from a nearby field, but when they arrive home and empty their potato sacks, they are surprised by what they see.

"This beautifully crafted picture book features panoramic landscapes and intimate pictures. Watson's pencil, ink, watercolor, and gouache illustrations, warmly rendered in earth tones, capture the small figures trudging along under a huge full moon. . . . This sweetly understated affirmation of hard work and honesty, neighborliness and family love, will resonate with a wide audience." SLJ

★ The **cats** in Krasinski Square; illustrated by Wendy Watson. Scholastic Press 2004 un il $16.95

Grades: 2 3 4 5   E

1. Cats -- Fiction 2. Jews -- Fiction 3. Holocaust, 1933-1945 -- Fiction 4. Jews -- Persecutions -- Poland -- Warsaw -- Juvenile fiction 5. Warsaw (Poland) -- History -- Warsaw Ghetto Uprising, 1943 -- Juvenile fiction

ISBN 0-439-43540-4

LC 2003-27775

Two Jewish sisters, escapees of the infamous Warsaw ghetto, devise a plan to thwart an attempt by the Gestapo to intercept food bound for starving people behind the dark Wall.

"In luminous free verse [this] book tells a powerful story. . . . In bold black lines and washes of smoky gray and ochre, Watson's arresting images echo the pared-down language as well as the hope that shines like glints of sunlight on Kraskinski Square." Booklist

Hest, Amy

★ **Charley's** first night; Amy Hest, Helen Oxenbury. Candlewick Press 2012 32 p. $15.99

Grades: PreK K 1   **E**
1. Dogs -- Juvenile fiction 2. Pets -- Juvenile fiction 3. Human-animal relationship -- Juvenile fiction
ISBN 0763640557; 9780763640552

                       LC 2012942295

In this children's picture book by Amy Hest, "on Charley's first night, Henry carries his new puppy . . . . all the way to his house. . . . Henry's parents are very clear about who will be walking and feeding Charley. . . . They are also very clear about where Charley will be sleeping . . . the kitchen. But when the crying starts in the middle of the night, Henry knows right away that it's Charley! And it looks like his parents' idea . . . may have to change." (Publisher's note)

★ **Guess** who, Baby Duck! illustrated by Jill Barton. Candlewick 2004 un il $15.99
Grades: PreK K   **E**
1. Ducks -- Fiction 2. Grandfathers -- Fiction
ISBN 0-7636-1981-7

"Baby Duck has a cold and Grampa comes to visit, bringing a 'cheering-up present,' an album of her baby photos. Together they look at pictures of her on the day she was born, after her first bath, taking her first steps, and on her first birthday. She feels better and draws a picture of Grampa kissing her cheek, which is just what he does. . . . Barton's watercolor-and-pencil art is as warm and playful as Baby Duck herself." SLJ

Other titles about Baby Duck are:
Baby Duck and the bad eyeglasses (1996)
In the rain with Baby Duck (1995)
Make the team, Baby Duck (2003)
Off to school, Baby Duck (1999)
You're the boss, Baby Duck (1997)

Kiss good night; illustrated by Anita Jeram. Candlewick Press 2001 un il $15.99
Grades: PreK K   **E**
1. Bears 2. Bedtime 3. Bears -- Fiction 4. Bedtime -- Fiction
ISBN 0-7636-0780-0

                       LC 00-41372

Even after a story, being tucked in, and warm milk, Sam the bear is not ready to go to sleep until his mother kisses him good-night

"This is an enchanting little story, with homey illustrations that add to its appeal." SLJ

Other titles about Sam the bear are:
Don't you feel well, Sam? (2002)
You can do it, Sam (2003)

★ **Little** Chick; illustrated by Anita Jeram. Candlewick Press 2009 un il $17.99
Grades: PreK K   **E**
1. Aunts -- Fiction 2. Chickens -- Fiction
ISBN 978-0-7636-2890-1; 0-7636-2890-5

                    LC 2008-935296

"Old-Auntie the hen, endlessly patient, marvelously kind, helps Little Chick deal with frustration in three stories. As depicted in Jeram's . . . watercolor washes, Old-Auntie's feathered bulk dwarfs Little Chick, and her gestures . . . are infused with tenderness. Old-Auntie helps Little Chick deal with her eagerness to harvest the carrot she planted; helps Little Chick endure the long wait until her kite finally flies;

and assures Little Chick that the star in the night sky that she wants is better off staying just where it is. . . . Hest's . . . light humor and Jeram's visual charm work . . . harmoniously together." Publ Wkly

★ **Mr.** George Baker; illustrated by Jon J. Muth. Candlewick Press 2004 un il hardcover o.p. pa $6.99
Grades: K 1 2 3   **E**
1. Old age -- Fiction 2. Reading -- Fiction 3. Friendship -- Fiction 4. African Americans -- Fiction
ISBN 0-7636-1233-2; 0-7636-3308-9 pa

Harry sits on the porch with Mr. George Baker, an African American who is one hundred years old but can still dance and play the drums, waiting for the school bus that will take them both to the class where they are learning to read.

This is "beautifully illustrated in subtle watercolors. Hest's understated, unhurried poetry echoes the syncopated rhythms of music. . . . Her book is a simple, sweet, moving portrait of a natural friendship between seniors and children." Booklist

★ **When** you meet a bear on Broadway; pictures by Elivia Savadier. Farrar, Straus and Giroux 2009 un il $16.99
Grades: PreK K 1   **E**
1. Bears -- Fiction 2. Mother-child relationship -- Fiction
ISBN 978-0-374-40015-6; 0-374-40015-6

                    LC 2008026053

When a little bear becomes separated from its mother in New York, a sympathetic child explains the proper steps that must be taken to reunite them.

"The repetitive beat in the sly, humorous words make this a perfect read-aloud, although the irresistible nuances in Savadier's artwork . . . are best viewed at close range." Booklist

★ The **dog** who belonged to no one; by Amy Hest; illustrated by Amy Bates. Abrams Books for Young Readers 2008 un il $15.95
Grades: PreK K 1   **E**
1. Dogs -- Fiction
ISBN 978-0-8109-9483-6; 0-8109-9483-6

                    LC 2007012763

The hard-working daughter of two bakers and a perfectly nice stray dog live lonely lives in the same town, until they meet one very stormy day.

"The pencil and watercolor illustrations, featuring a palette of golden earth tones, echo the gentle sentiment of the narrative. Lia in her blue dress, pinafore, and jaunty cap and the bright-eyed little dog evoke tender sympathy." SLJ

The **purple** coat; pictures by Amy Schwartz. Four Winds Press 1986 un il hardcover o.p. pa $6.99
Grades: PreK K 1 2   **E**
1. Coats -- Fiction 2. Grandfathers -- Fiction
ISBN 0-02-743640-3; 0-689-71634-6 pa

                    LC 85-29186

"The artwork is full color, and the deep shades and vibrant colors (especially that purple) are arresting. The numerous details and patternings catch the eye and make for pictures that can be looked at over and over; each time the story's satisfying conclusion rings sweetly true." Booklist

Heyward, DuBose

The **country** bunny and the little gold shoes; as told to Jenifer; pictures by Marjorie Flack. Houghton Mifflin 1939 un il lib bdg $15; pa $5.95

Grades: PreK K   E

1. Easter -- Fiction 2. Rabbits -- Fiction

ISBN 0-395-15990-3 lib bdg; 0-395-18557-2 pa

This is an Easter story for young readers which grew out of a story the author has told and retold to his young daughter. It is of the little country rabbit who wanted to become one of the five Easter bunnies, and how she managed to realize her ambition

"It is really imaginative and well written. . . . The colored pictures are just right too." New Yorker

Hicks, Barbara Jean

Jitterbug jam; pictures by Alexis Deacon. Farrar, Straus and Giroux 2005 un il $16

Grades: K 1 2 3   E

1. Monsters -- Fiction

ISBN 0-374-33685-7

LC 2004-46981

First published 2004 in the United Kingdom

Grandpa Boo-Dad not only believes that Bobo has seen a pink-skinned boy with orange fur on his head hiding under the bed, he knows exactly how a little monster can scare off such a horrible creature

"Printed on luxurious, buff-colored paper, Deacon's line-and-watercolor artwork unites cleverly altered Victorian decorative elements . . . with the striking, varied design of contemporary graphic novels. . . . Hicks' folksy, slightly off-kilter language . . . keeps the sense of an exotic, alternate reality watertight." Booklist

Monsters don't eat broccoli; illustrated by Sue Hendra. Alfred A. Knopf 2009 un il $16.99; lib bdg $19.99

Grades: K 1 2   E

1. Stories in rhyme 2. Food -- Fiction 3. Monsters -- Fiction

ISBN 978-0-375-85686-0; 0-375-85686-2; 978-0-375-95686-7 lib bdg; 0-375-95686-7 lib bdg

LC 2008-24536

Illustrations and rhyming text reveal how imagination can spice up even the healthiest meal

"With a toe-tapping beat and loud, splashy spreads, this paean to mealtime chaos will charm small monsters everywhere. . . . Too much fun to limit to kids who don't like broccoli." Publ Wkly

Hill, Isabel

Building stories; Isabel Hill. Star Bright Books 2012 40p. ill. (some col.) $17.95

Grades: 2 3 4   E

1. Buildings 2. City and town life 3. Stories in rhyme

ISBN 9781595722805; 9781595722799

LC 2010050860

"Rhyming text and photographs of icons on buildings invite the reader to guess what was done or made in each building originally. Includes "stories characters and plots" of the buildings, as well as their settings." (Publisher's note)

"The sharp, clear pictures of the ornaments appear opposite those of the exterior and interior of the buildings on which they are found. . . . [This is a] good resource." SLJ

Hill, Susan

Ruby's perfect day; pictures by Margie Moore. HarperCollins 2006 32p il (I can read!) $15.99; lib bdg $16.89

Grades: PreK K 1 2   E

1. Raccoons -- Fiction

ISBN 978-0-06-008982-5; 0-06-008982-2; 978-0-06-008983-2 lib bdg; 0-06-008983-0 lib bdg

LC 2005-14516

When Ruby Raccoon wants to share a perfectly sunny day with her busy woodland friends, she discovers that perfect days can be spent all by yourself.

This "book is perfect for beginning readers. A simple plot and good sentence structure provide repetition without being simplistic, and Ruby is indeed appealing." SLJ

Hill, Susanna Leonard

April Fool, Phyllis! illustrated by Jeffrey Ebbeler. Holiday House 2011 un il

Grades: K 1 2 3   E

1. Snow -- Fiction 2. Marmots -- Fiction 3. Riddles -- Fiction 4. Maple sugar -- Fiction 5. April Fools' Day -- Fiction 6. Weather forecasting -- Fiction

ISBN 0-8234-2270-4; 978-0-8234-2270-8

LC 2010019878

When Punxsutawney Phyllis forecasts a blizzard on April Fools' Day—the same day as the Spring Treasure Hunt—the other groundhogs are convinced that Phyllis is pulling a prank. Includes information of the origins of April Fools' Day and how it is celebrated around the world.

"Warm acrylics, saturated in rich golden tones and creamy tans, offer a cozy look into this furry family's den. . . . Funny details abound. . . . Here's a lighthearted romp that highlights an often overlooked holiday." Kirkus

Can't sleep without sheep; illustrated by Mike Wohnoutka. Walker & Co. 2010 un il $16.99; lib bdg $17.89

Grades: PreK K 1 2   E

1. Sheep -- Fiction 2. Sleep -- Fiction 3. Animals -- Fiction 4. Bedtime -- Fiction

ISBN 978-0-8027-2066-5; 0-8027-2066-8; 978-0-8027-2067-2 lib bdg; 0-8027-2067-6 lib bdg

LC 2009054215

When counting sheep does not help Ava fall asleep and the sheep complain that they are exhausted, they send in replacements, including cows, horses, penguins, and pigs, but none prove satisfactory.

"Hill's words are simple and effective, and leave room for the art to tell the story. . . . A book that is delightful for the eyes and soothing to the ears, Can't Sleep Without Sheep will quickly become a bedtime favorite." SLJ

Not yet, Rose; written by Susanna Leonard Hill; illustrated by Nicole Rutten. Eerdmans Books for Young Readers 2009 un il $16.50

Grades: PreK K   E

1. Infants -- Fiction 2. Hamsters -- Fiction 3. Siblings -- Fiction 4. Imagination -- Fiction

ISBN 978-0-8028-5326-4; 0-8028-5326-9

LC 2008031736

While impatiently waiting for the birth of a new baby brother or sister, Rose the hamster imagines the things they will do together and how her life will change.

"Rutten's cheery watercolor illustrations, depicting the hamsters' life in their cozy country cottage and later in the hospital, are infused with subtle, appropriate humor. With its thoughtful text and playful art, this book gently helps older siblings confidently adjust to their new roles." SLJ

Punxsutawney Phyllis; illustrated by Jeffrey Ebbeler. Holiday House 2005 un il $16.95

Grades: K 1 2 3   E
1. Marmots -- Fiction 2. Sex role -- Fiction 3. Groundhog Day -- Fiction
ISBN 0-8234-1872-3
LC 2003-67641

Although she can predict the weather much better than the boys in her family, no one thinks that Phyllis the groundhog has a chance of replacing the aging Punxsutawney Phil when Groundhog Day's official groundhog retires

"Details about the origins of Groundhog Day and Punxsutawney Phil are appended. Ebbeler's full-bleed acrylic illustrations show an exuberant Phyllis skipping through a brook, sunbathing, and munching on berries." SLJ

Another title about Punxsutawney Phyllis is:
April fool, Phyllis! (2011)

Hillenbrand, Will
Cock-a-doodle Christmas! by Will Hillenbrand. Marshall Cavendish 2007 un il $16.99

Grades: PreK K 1   E
1. Roosters -- Fiction 2. Christmas -- Fiction 3. Farm life -- Fiction
ISBN 978-0-7614-5354-3
LC 2006030236

Long ago in the town of Bethlehem, young Harold the rooster keeps failing to wake the other farm animals in the morning, but when a young woman gives birth to a very special baby in the stable, Harold is finally able to crow loudly and help spread the good news

"The text, matter-of-fact and unsentimental, reads like a folktale, making this an excellent story to read aloud, and the gouache, ink, and collage illustrations depict a humble but colorful farm." SLJ

Kite day; a Bear and Mole book. Will Hillenbrand. Holiday House 2012 32 p.

Grades: PreK K 1   E
1. Bears -- Fiction 2. Kites -- Fiction 3. Storms -- Fiction 4. Moles (Animals) -- Fiction 5. Picture books for children 6. Birds -- Fiction
ISBN 9780823416035
LC 2011007269

In this children's picture book, "Bear . . . and his friend Mole work together to construct a lovely yellow [kite] which soars . . . until a storm hits and snaps the kite's string. The two friends rush to extricate their storm-battered creation from a tree but change their minds when they see where it has landed: right above a nest of baby birds, who are now sheltered by its cover." (Bulletin of the Center for Children's Books)

★ **Louie!** Philomel Books 2009 un il $16.99

Grades: PreK K 1 2   E
1. Pigs -- Fiction 2. Artists -- Fiction 3. Drawing -- Fiction
ISBN 978-0-399-24707-1; 0-399-24707-6
LC 2008-19453

Louie the pig loves to draw but it gets him thrown out of every school he attends, so he goes to live with his aunt and uncle who help him realize he has a wonderful talent.

"Using the bare-bones outline of Ludwig Bemelmans's childhood, Hillenbrand brings to life the experience of countless children whose creativity sets them apart in structured environments, especially school. . . . Hillenbrand's gloriously colored, superbly executed illustrations—collages, fingerpaintings, gouache, inks, pencils—magnetically draw readers from page to page." SLJ

Spring is here! Holiday House 2011 un il $16.95

Grades: PreK K 1   E
1. Bears -- Fiction 2. Spring -- Fiction 3. Moles (Animals) -- Fiction
ISBN 978-0-8234-1602-8; 0-8234-1602-X
LC 2010018883

Excited that spring has finally arrived, Mole tries—unsuccessfully—to wake up Bear, but then he comes up with the perfect plan.

"The repetition, ample onomatopoeia, and tender tone of the spare text, combined with heavily textured mixed-media renderings of this gentle pair of pals, create a sunny welcome to the season." Publ Wkly

Hills, Tad
★ **Duck** & Goose; written and illustrated by Tad Hills. Schwartz & Wade Books 2006 un il $14.95; lib bdg $17.99

Grades: PreK K   E
1. Ducks -- Fiction 2. Geese -- Fiction
ISBN 0-375-83611-X; 0-375-93611-4 lib bdg
LC 2005010849

Duck and Goose learn to work together to take care of a ball, which they think is an egg

"While the narrative is fairly straightforward and has touches of childlike humor throughout, it's the bright and colorful artwork that will attract youngsters' attention. The cartoon-style oil paintings set against soft-focus, almost impressionistic backgrounds keep Duck and Goose center stage, and their expressions are priceless." SLJ

Other titles about Duck and Goose are:
Duck, duck, goose (2007)
Duck & Goose, 1, 2, 3 (2008)
What's up, Duck?: a book of opposites (2008)
Duck & Goose, how are you feeling? (2009)
Duck & Goose find a pumpkin (2009)
Duck & Goose: it's time for Christmas (2010)

How Rocket learned to read. Schwartz & Wade Books 2010 un il

Grades: PreK K 1   E
1. Dogs -- Fiction 2. Birds -- Fiction 3. Reading -- Fiction
ISBN 0-375-85899-7; 0-375-95899-1 lib bdg; 978-0-375-85899-4; 978-0-375-95899-1 lib bdg
LC 2008051015

A little yellow bird teaches Rocket the dog how to read by first introducing him to the "wondrous, mighty, gorgeous alphabet."

The author "offers up an appealing picture of the learning-to-read process. . . . Hills' oil-paint and colored-pencil illustrations nicely capture both the sweetness of pupil and tutor and the prettiness of the changing seasons." Booklist

★ **Rocket** writes a story; Tad Hills. Schwartz & Wade 2012 40 p. col. ill. (hardback) $17.99
Grades: PreK K 1 2   E
1. Dogs -- Fiction 2. Authorship -- Fiction 3. Picture books for children 4. Owls -- Fiction 5. Birds -- Fiction 6. Books and reading -- Fiction
ISBN 0375870865; 9780307974914; 9780375870866; 9780375970863
LC 2011041233

In this book, "Rocket sniffs out . . . new words in his environment," and his bird friend "helps him create a . . . word tree. Now Rocket searches for ideas for his own story in which he can use his word collection. . . . It's not all smooth sailing; he writes, crosses out, and draws pictures, alternately wagging his tail and growling" but his "finished story wins rave reviews." (Kirkus Reviews)

Himmelman, John
10 little hot dogs. Marshall Cavendish 2010 un $12.99
Grades: PreK K 1   E
1. Counting 2. Dogs -- Fiction
ISBN 978-0-7614-5797-8; 0-7614-5797-6
LC 2009042307

One by one, ten excitable dachshunds pile onto a chair.
"Every page has a watercolor scene of the same chair and the changing number of lively dogs. This book will work well as a read-aloud with small groups, though the engaging puppies will encourage closer examination." SLJ

★ **Chickens** to the rescue. H. Holt 2006 un il $16.95
Grades: PreK K 1 2   E
1. Days -- Fiction 2. Chickens -- Fiction 3. Farm life -- Fiction
ISBN 978-0-8050-7951-7; 0-8050-7951-3
LC 2005-20044

Six days a week the chickens help the Greenstalk family and their animals recover from mishaps that occur on the farm, but they need one day to rest

"The simplicity of the text allows the sheer brilliance of the colored-pencil and watercolor illustrations to shine through. The details in each rescue scene will have everyone laughing." SLJ

Other titles in this series are:
Pigs to the rescue (2010)
Cows to the rescue (2011)

Cows to the rescue. Henry Holt 2011 un il $16.99
Grades: PreK K 1 2   E
1. Cattle -- Fiction 2. Farm life -- Fiction
ISBN 978-0-8050-9249-3; 0-8050-9249-8
LC 2010036880

After helping the Greenstalk family get to the county fair, the cows busy themselves finding solutions to many other problems that arise during the day.

"The pencil and watercolor illustrations are packed with plenty of personality and have enough detail to keep

kids turning the pages to learn the outcome. Children will, of course, pipe up with the refrain 'Cows to the Rescue!' in group readings and during lapsits, and the mad antics of these friendly and very game rescuers will delight them." SLJ

Frog in a bog. Charlesbridge 2004 un il $15.95; pa $6.95
Grades: K 1 2 3   E
1. Marshes -- Fiction 2. Bog ecology -- Juvenile literature
ISBN 1-57091-517-2; 1-57091-518-0 pa
LC 2003-3737

"Himmelman leads children through natural events that occur on a typical day in a bog, beginning with a frog hopping into some moss. . . . Throughout, readers are introduced to plant, insect, and animal names that may not be commonly known and the idea that some events trigger others. Some classification lessons are included at the end of the book. The watercolor illustrations are definitely a draw: the effect is soft and delicate. Detail is beautifully rendered. . . . This book will have broad appeal." SLJ

Includes bibliographical references

Katie loves the kittens. Henry Holt & Co. 2008 un il $16.95
Grades: PreK K 1 2 3   E
1. Cats -- Fiction 2. Dogs -- Fiction 3. Friendship -- Fiction
ISBN 978-0-8050-8682-9; 0-8050-8682-X

When Sara Ann brings home three little kittens, Katie the dog's enthusiasm frightens the kittens away, until she learns that quiet patience is sometimes needed to begin a friendship.

"Himmelman's charming watercolor-and-ink illustrations depict a character sure to earn the affection of young readers. Katie's expressive movements make both her excitement and her dismay palpable and adorable." SLJ

Hindley, Judy
★ **Baby** talk; a book of first words and phrases. illustrated by Brita Granström. Candlewick Press 2006 un il $15.99
Grades: PreK   E
1. Stories in rhyme 2. Infants -- Fiction
ISBN 0-7636-2971-5

Rhyming text describes the the activities in a baby's day and the words he says while going to the playground, eating dinner, and taking a bath.

"Hindley's unfussy rhyme offers on-target opportunities for concept development: low, high, bye, out. Granström's festive gouache-and-pencil cartoons shine." SLJ

Hines, Anna Grossnickle
★ **1,** 2, buckle my shoe. Harcourt 2008 un il $16
Grades: PreK   E
1. Counting 2. Nursery rhymes
ISBN 978-0-15-206305-4; 0-15-206305-6
LC 2007007022

A child learns to count with the help of a classic nursery rhyme

"The popular verse, included in numerous collections of nursery rhymes, gets the star treatment in this delightful picture book. Illustrated entirely with quilt patches festooned with buttons, the ditty bounces along in bursts of color." SLJ

Daddy makes the best spaghetti. Clarion Bks. 1986 un il hardcover o.p. pa $5.95; bd bk $5.95
Grades: PreK K 1 2   E
1. Father-son relationship -- Fiction
ISBN 0-89919-794-9 pa; 0-395-98036-4 bd bk
LC 85-13993
"Corey and his father enjoy a close relationship that is aptly demonstrated in picture and story. He teases Corey and they spend time together doing things such as shopping for groceries and making a pot of spaghetti or being silly at bath time and getting ready for bed. Hines' simple but warm pencil drawings play out the scenes by capitalizing on the incidents described in the text; the strong sense of family (Mother is here too) is evident." Booklist

I am a Tyrannosaurus. Tricycle Press 2011 un il $12.99; lib bdg $15.99
Grades: PreK K   E
1. Dinosaurs -- Fiction 2. Imagination -- Fiction
ISBN 978-1-58246-413-8; 1-58246-413-8; 978-1-58246-414-5 lib bdg; 1-58246-414-6 lib bdg
LC 2010024181
A boy mimics the actions of several different dinosaurs as he imagines he is one of them.
"Set against bright backdrops, Hines's digital illustrations focus on the boy, and in scenes where he appears with the various dinos, his poses mimic theirs. Kids are sure to follow suit." Publ Wkly

I am a backhoe. Tricycle Press 2010 un il $12.99
Grades: PreK K   E
1. Play -- Fiction 2. Trucks -- Fiction
ISBN 978-1-58246306-3; 1-58246306-9
LC 2009007534
A young boy imagines himself to be different types of trucks as he plays in the sand.
"Richly colored, digitally enhanced spreads depict the boy at play, intermingled with illustrations of the actual vehicles. The text is set in white and includes plenty of action words. This is a worthy choice for preschoolers and kindergarteners with a big appetite for truck books." SLJ

Hoban, Lillian

★ **Arthur's** Christmas cookies; words and pictures by Lillian Hoban. Harper & Row 1972 63p il (I can read book) hardcover o.p. pa $3.99
Grades: PreK K 1 2   E
1. Christmas -- Fiction 2. Chimpanzees -- Fiction
ISBN 0-06-022368-5 lib bdg; 0-06-444055-9 pa
The characters are chimpanzees but "are endearingly like human children. . . . The Christmas setting is appealing, the plot has problem, conflict, and solution yet is not too complex for the beginning independent reader, and the simplicity and humor make the book an appropriate one for reading aloud to preschool children also." Bull Cent Child Books
Other titles about Arthur are:
Arthur's back to school day (1996)
Arthur's birthday party (1999)
Arthur's camp-out (1993)
Arthur's funny money (1981)
Arthur's great big valentine (1989)

Arthur's Halloween costume (1984)
Arthur's Honey Bear (1974)
Arthur's loose tooth (1985)
Arthur's pen pal (1976)
Arthur's prize reader (1978)

Silly Tilly's Thanksgiving dinner; story and pictures by Lillian Hoban. Harper & Row 1990 63p il (I can read book) hardcover o.p. pa $3.99
Grades: PreK K 1 2   E
1. Animals -- Fiction 2. Moles (Animals) -- Fiction 3. Thanksgiving Day -- Fiction
ISBN 0-06-022423-1 lib bdg; 0-06-444154-7 pa
LC 89-29287
Forgetful Silly Tilly Mole nearly succeeds in ruining her Thanksgiving dinner, but her animal friends come to the rescue with tasty treats
"Watercolors in vibrant autumn hues accentuate this comedy of errors with quirky characterizations and fine brushwork." Booklist
Other titles about Silly Tilly are:
Silly Tilly and the Easter Bunny (1987)
Silly Tilly's valentine (1998)

Hoban, Russell

★ **Bedtime** for Frances; pictures by Garth Williams. HarperCollins Pubs. 1995 31p il $16.99; lib bdg $17.89; pa $6.99
Grades: PreK K 1   E
1. Badgers -- Fiction 2. Bedtime -- Fiction
ISBN 0-06-027106-X; 0-06-027107-8 lib bdg; 0-06-443451-6 pa
LC 94-43809
A reissue of the title first published 1960
"The soft humorous pictures of these lovable animals in human predicaments are delightful." Horn Book
Other titles about Frances are:
A baby sister for Frances (1964)
A bargain for Frances (1970)
Best friends for Frances (1969)
A birthday for Frances (1968)
Bread and jam for Frances (1964)

Rosie's magic horse; Russell Hoban, illustrated by Quentin Blake. Candlewick Press 2013 40 p. $15.99
Grades: PreK K 1 2   E
1. Dreams -- Juvenile fiction 2. Picture books for children
ISBN 0763664006; 9780763664008
LC 2012942392
In this children's picture book, "Rosie finds a discarded ice-pop stick and adds it to the others collected in her cigar box. . . . The sticks discuss what they can be without their ice pops. 'Maybe a horse,' muses" one. "Meanwhile, Rosie overhears her parents say that they can't pay their bills. Longing to help, she falls asleep and dreams of Stickerino, a flying, talking horse that gallops out of the cigar box and takes her on a treasure hunt. The next morning, Rosie surprises her dad with . . . gold." (Booklist)

Hoban, Tana

★ **Black** on white. Greenwillow Bks. 1993 un il bd bk $5.99

Grades: PreK   E
1. Board books for children
ISBN 0-688-11918-2

LC 92-18897

Black illustrations against a white background depict such objects as an elephant, butterfly, and leaf

This board book features "the stunning, sophisticated photography of Tana Hoban. . . . Simply the best for babies." Horn Book Guide

★ **Is** it red? Is it yellow? Is it blue? an adventure in color. Greenwillow Bks. 1978 un il lib bdg $17.99; pa $6.99
Grades: PreK K   E
1. Size 2. Color 3. Shape
ISBN 0-688-84171-6 lib bdg; 0-688-07034-5 pa

LC 78-2549

Illustrations and brief text introduce colors and the concepts of shape and size

"The wordless book is simply designed and opens the eye to the marvelous world of color; each stark-white page contains one photograph which nearly fills it. In the bottom margin the predominant colors in the photograph are indicated by a row of corresponding circles." Horn Book

Over, under & through, and other spatial concepts. Macmillan 1973 un il hardcover o.p. pa $8.99
Grades: PreK K   E
1. Vocabulary
ISBN 0-02-744820-7; 1-4169-7541-1 pa

In brief text and photographs, the author depicts several spatial concepts—over, under, through, on, in, around, across, between, beside, below, against, and behind

"Children who are confused by these concepts may need help understanding that many of the pictures illustrate more than one concept. However, both the photographs and the format, with the words printed large on broad yellow bands at the beginning of each section, are uncluttered and appealing." Booklist

★ **White** on black. Greenwillow Bks. 1993 un il bd bk $6.99 E
1. Board books for children
ISBN 0-688-11919-0

LC 92-20092

In this board book, white illustrations against a black background depict such objects as a horse, baby bottle, and sailboat

"Hoban's compositions are so supple and her layouts so well balanced that she casts a kind of spell." Publ Wkly

Hobbie, Holly
★ **Everything** but the horse; a childhood memory. Little, Brown 2010 un il $16.99
Grades: PreK K 1 2   E
1. Horses -- Fiction 2. Farm life -- Fiction 3. Country life -- Fiction
ISBN 978-0-316-07019-5; 0-316-07019-X

LC 2010006907

When Holly's family moves from the city to a farm, she longs to get a horse for her birthday. Based on events in the author's childhood.

"The simple artwork, done in pen-and-ink and watercolor, beautifully depicts a time when life for a young farm girl was filled with rustic barns, fields, and delightful animals,

while her heartwarming text conveys a sense of innocence and dreams." SLJ

Gem; Holly Hobbie. Little, Brown & Co. 2012 32 p.
Grades: PreK   E
1. Girls -- Fiction 2. Toads -- Fiction 3. Spring -- Fiction 4. Gardens -- Fiction 5. Picture books for children
ISBN 0316203343; 9780316203340

This picture book "explores the wonders of spring through the eyes of a toad that survives the perils and pleasures of its trek to a country garden, where he encounters the author's granddaughter, Hope. Opening with a letter explaining how Hope's discovery of a toad named Gem inspired her to 'tell the story of Gem's spring journey,' [Holly] Hobbie wordlessly chronicles this odyssey in . . . watercolor, pen and ink illustrations. A palette of fresh greens and yellows heralds springtime, while varying frame sizes and perspectives allow readers to view the . . . toad's cross-country ramble from multiple angles." (Kirkus)

Toot & Puddle; 10th anniversary ed.; Little, Brown Books for Young Readers 2007 un il $16.99; pa $6.99
Grades: PreK K 1 2   E
1. Pigs -- Fiction 2. Voyages and travels -- Fiction
ISBN 978-0-316-16702-4; 0-316-16702-9; 978-0-316-08080-4 pa; 0-316-08080-2 pa
A reissue of the title first published 1997

Toot and Puddle pigs are best friends with very different interests, so when Toot spends the year travelling around the world, Puddle enjoys receiving his postcards.

"In Hobbie's expert watercolors are dozens of inventive touches. . . . The book and its heroes are endearing." Kirkus

Toot & Puddle: let it snow. Little, Brown & Co. 2007 un il $16.99
Grades: PreK K 1 2   E
1. Pigs -- Fiction 2. Snow -- Fiction 3. Gifts -- Fiction 4. Christmas -- Fiction 5. Friendship -- Fiction
ISBN 978-0-316-16686-7; 0-316-16686-3

Toot and Puddle celebrate Christmas and learn that the best kind of present for the best kind of friend is one that shows just how much you care.

"Hobbie infuses her holiday story of devoted friendship with cozy language . . . all evoked in Hobbie's signature watercolor illustrations." Horn Book

Other titles about Toot & Puddle are:
Toot & Puddle (1997)
Toot & Puddle: a present for Toot (1998)
Toot & Puddle: you are my sunshine (1999)
Toot & Puddle: Puddle's ABC (2000)
Toot & Puddle: I'll be home for Christmas (2001)
Toot & Puddle: top of the world (2002)
Toot & Puddle: charming Opal (2003)
Toot & Puddle: the new friend (2004)
Toot & Puddle: the one and only (2006)

Hoberman, Mary Ann
I like old clothes; by Mary Ann Hoberman; illustrations by Patrice Barton. Alfred A. Knopf 2012 32 p. (hard cover) $16.99
Grades: PreK K 1   E
1. Play -- Fiction 2. Picture books for children 3.

Clothing and dress -- Fiction 4. Stories in rhyme
ISBN 0375869514; 9780375869518; 9780375969515

LC 2010038292

This children's picture book was "[o]riginally published by Knopf in 1976 (with illustrations by Jacqueline Chwast)," using a poem from "Children's Poet Laureate Mary Ann Hoberman" as its text. The story features a "protagonist who likes old clothes for their 'history' and 'mystery.'" In the update, "[i]llustrator Patrice Barton" offers illustrations of a "little girl and her younger brother playing dress-up, making crafts, and happily treasuring their hand-me-downs." (Barnes and Noble)

★ You read to me, I'll read to you; very short fairy tales to read together (in which wolves are tamed, trolls are transformed, and peas are triumphant) illustrated by Michael Emberley. Little, Brown 2004 32p il $16.95
Grades: K 1 2 3   E
1. Fairy tales
ISBN 0-316-14611-0

LC 2003-47445

"The two voices join seamlessly together to create a truly delightful reading ensemble. Emberley's humorous illustrations feature expressive characters drawn in pen, watercolor, and pastel." SLJ

The two sillies; illustrated by Lynne Cravath. Harcourt 2000 un il $16
Grades: PreK K 1 2   E
1. Stories in rhyme 2. Cats -- Fiction 3. Mice -- Fiction
ISBN 0-15-202221-X

LC 98-51844

"When Silly Lilly admires Sammy's cat and asks how to get one, he gives her step-by-step instructions that seem to make no sense at all. . . . Short sentences use mono-syllabic words and rhyme to great effect. The brightly colored cartoon-style art adds just the right touch of exaggerated humor." Horn Book Guide

Hodges, Margaret
The wee Christmas cabin; retold by Margaret Hodges; illustrated by Kimberly Bulcken Root. Holiday House 2009 un il $16.95
Grades: K 1 2 3   E
1. Christmas stories 2. Fairies -- Fiction 3. Christmas -- Fiction
ISBN 978-0-8234-1528-1; 0-8234-1528-7

LC 00044877

A tinker's child who grows up helping everyone in her Irish village is rewarded in her old age with a cabin built by fairies on Christmas Eve.

"Hodges' elegant prose doesn't spell out exactly what happens to Oona, allowing children's imaginations to fill in the rest, and preserving the wonder of the story. Delicate watercolor paintings emphasize the cool dark blues and greens of wintry Ireland against the warm golds and reds of the cheery cabin's hearth." Booklist

Hodgkins, Fran
Who's been here? a tale in tracks. illustrated by Karel Hayes. Down East 2008 un il $15.95

Grades: PreK K 1 2   E
1. Dogs -- Fiction 2. Animal tracks -- Fiction
ISBN 978-0-89272-714-8; 0-89272-714-4

LC 2008015756

"Three children follow golden retriever Willy into the snowy outdoors, seeing not only his paw prints but also those animals he's tracked. Delicate illustrations of snow-covered forest include accurate animal tracks and woodsy borders. The spare text uses repetition effectively in this book for nature lovers." Horn Book Guide

Hodgkinson, Jo
The talent show. Andersen 2011 un il $16.95
Grades: PreK K 1   E
1. Stories in rhyme 2. Size -- Fiction 3. Birds -- Fiction 4. Animals -- Fiction
ISBN 0761374876; 9780761374879; 978-0-7613-7487-9; 0-7613-7487-6

LC 2010032965

A tiny red bird wants very much to win the upcoming talent show, but first he must prove that being small does not mean having little talent.

"The rhyming text and dynamic scenes in vivid colors keep the tale rocking. Panels in various sizes are simple compositions that encourage focus on the personalities depicted. From the crooning moose to the singing hippo in a boa, the illustrations don't miss a beat of humor." SLJ

Hodgkinson, Leigh
Limelight Larry. Tiger Tales 2011 un il $15.95
Grades: PreK K 1   E
1. Peacocks -- Fiction 2. Books and reading -- Fiction
ISBN 978-1-58925-102-1; 1-58925-102-4

Limelight Larry the peacock is delighted when he finds an empty book— he can be the star of the story! Then a whole host of storybook characters arrive and Larry, much to his outrage, is pushed out of the limelight.

"Prereaders should be captivated by this cacophony of type and images, and they will certainly identify with the willful peacock." Kirkus

Smile! Balzer & Bray 2010 un il $16.99
Grades: PreK K 1   E
1. Family life -- Fiction
ISBN 978-0-06-185269-5; 0-06-185269-4

LC 2009-14277

A little girl searches all over the house for the smile that seems to have deserted her.

"The childlike illustrations are done in bright colors with collage elements, occasional labels, and sometimes with sound effects. . . . Sunny's imagination enriches her search." SLJ

Hodson, Sally
Granny's clan; a tale of wild orcas. by Sally Hodson; illustrated by Ann Jones. Dawn Publications 2012 32 p. (hardback) $16.95
Grades: 2 3 4   E
1. Killer whales -- Fiction
ISBN 1584691719; 9781584691716; 9781584691723

LC 2011049431

In this book, Sally Hodson offers a "glimpse into the real world of a Pacific Northwest killer whale family or pod. Also known as an orca, 100-year-old granny and her family (the J-pod) interact with one another, just as humans do. Granny teaches her children, grandchildren and great-grandchildren, how and where to locate food, play nicely, avoid danger, sing orca songs, and coexist with people." (Children's Literature)

Hoff, Syd

Danny and the dinosaur; story and pictures by Syd Hoff. Harper & Row 1958 64p il (I can read book) $16.99; pa $3.99

Grades: PreK K 1 2   E
1. Dinosaurs -- Fiction
ISBN 0-06-022465-7; 0-06-444002-8 pa

"The bold, humorous, colored pictures convey the imaginative story. . . . Because of the simple vocabulary and sentence structure, first-graders can actually read this story." Libr J

Another title about Danny and the dinosaur is:
Happy birthday, Danny and the dinosaur! (1995)

Oliver; story and pictures by Syd Hoff. HarperCollins Pubs. 2000 64p il (I can read book) lib bdg $17.89; pa $3.99

Grades: PreK K 1 2   E
1. Circus 2. Elephants 3. Circus -- Fiction 4. Elephants -- Fiction
ISBN 0-06-028709-8 lib bdg; 0-06-444272-1 pa

LC 99-25591

A newly illustrated edition of the title first published 1960
Oliver the elephant looks elsewhere for employment after learning that the circus already has enough elephants

"One of the most warm-hearted and appealing easy-to-read books available." SLJ

Sammy the seal; story and pictures by Syd Hoff. newly il ed; HarperCollins Pubs. 2000 64p il (I can read book) $16.99; lib bdg $16.89; pa $3.99

Grades: PreK K 1 2   E
1. Zoos -- Fiction 2. Humorous stories 3. Seals (Animals) -- Fiction
ISBN 0-06-028545-1; 0-06-028546-X lib bdg; 0-06-444270-5 pa

LC 99-13805

A newly illustrated edition of the title first published 1959
Anxious to see what life is like outside the zoo, Sammy the seal explores the city, goes to school, and plays with the children but decides that there really is no place like home

"Happy adventures told in entertaining colored cartoon-like drawings and in simple vocabulary and short sentences which first graders can read with a minimum of help." Booklist

The **littlest** leaguer; story and pictures by Syd Hoff. HarperCollins Childrens Books 2008 48p il (I can read!) $16.99; pa $3.99

Grades: PreK K 1 2   E
1. Baseball -- Fiction
ISBN 978-0-06-053772-2; 0-06-053772-8; 978-0-06-053774-6 pa; 0-06-053774-4 pa

A reissue of the title first published 1976
Littlest of all the little leaguers, Harold has a hard time finding some way to really help his team.

"Hoff's ability to tell an interesting story with a minimum of words is unsurpassed." Horn Book Guide

Hoffman, Mary

★ **Amazing** Grace; pictures by Caroline Binch. Dial Bks. for Young Readers 1991 un il $16.99

Grades: K 1 2 3   E
1. Theater -- Fiction 2. African Americans -- Fiction
ISBN 0-8037-1040-2

LC 90-25108

Although her classmates say that she cannot play Peter Pan in the school play because she is black and a girl, Grace discovers that she can do anything she sets her mind to do

"Gorgeous watercolor illustrations portraying a determined, talented child and her warm family enhance an excellent text and positive message of self-affirmation. Grace is an amazing girl and this is an amazing book." SLJ

Other picture book titles about Grace are:
Boundless Grace (1995)
Grace at Christmas (2011)
Princess Grace (2008)

Grace at Christmas; illustrated by Cornelius Van Wright and Ying-Hwa Hu. Dial Books for Young Readers 2011 il $17.99

Grades: K 1 2 3   E
1. Christmas -- Fiction 2. Family life -- Fiction 3. African Americans -- Fiction
ISBN 978-0-8037-3577-4; 0-8037-3577-4

LC 2011004571

When her grandmother takes in a stranded family at Christmas, Grace is reluctant to share her favorite holiday with strangers, even though the visiting family includes a "real live ballerina."

"Hoffman's empathetic storytelling and Van Wright and Hu's naturalistic illustrations make the most of Grace's abundant humor and personality." Publ Wkly

The **color** of home; pictures by Karin Littlewood. Phyllis Fogelman Bks. 2002 un il $15.99

Grades: K 1 2 3   E
1. Refugees -- Fiction 2. Immigrants -- Fiction 3. Somali Americans -- Juvenile fiction
ISBN 0-8037-2841-7

LC 2001-7393

Hassan, newly-arrived in the United States and feeling homesick, paints a picture at school that shows his old home in Somalia as well as the reason his family had to leave

"Readers gain a realistic child's perspective on what it is like to be forced to emigrate from a war-torn country. . . . Littlewood's impressionistic watercolor illustrations . . . beautifully convey Hassan's sadness, fear, and ultimate happiness." SLJ

Hogan, Jamie

Seven days of Daisy. Down East 2012 un il $14.95

Grades: PreK K   E
1. Islands -- Fiction 2. Grandmothers -- Fiction
ISBN 978-0-89272-919-7; 0-89272-919-8

"Counting down the days before Nana comes to visit her island home, young Daisy describes how she fills her time. Sailing, tea parties at the shore, rocking in the hammock, and playing tag all make the wait a bit less tedious. When Nana arrives, Daisy is ready to tell her about her various activities. . . . The simple sentences and childlike focus stay true to the narrator. . . . The realistic charcoals and pastels offer texture, and colors vary to reflect moods and times of day." SLJ

Hogrogian, Nonny

Cool cat. Roaring Brook Press 2009 un il $17.99
Grades: PreK K 1 2   **E**

1. Stories without words 2. Cats -- Fiction 3. Animals -- Fiction 4. Painting -- Fiction
ISBN 978-1-59643-429-5; 1-59643-429-5

"A vacant lot strewn with garbage is transformed by an artistic and imaginative black cat in this wordless picture book. Using paints and brushes from his wooden art box, the feline covers his drab surroundings with leaves and sky, enlisting the help of some birds and woodland creatures that take up brushes to add flowers, trees, and a pond. . . . Simple, almost childlike art in the lush colors of summer combines with brilliant composition to tell the story. . . . Both visually and conceptually, this is a gem." SLJ

Holabird, Katharine

★ **Angelina** Ballerina; story by Katharine Holabird; illustrations by Helen Craig. Viking 2006 un il $12.99
Grades: PreK K 1 2   **E**

1. Mice -- Fiction 2. Ballet -- Fiction
ISBN 0-670-06026-7

A reissue of the title first published 1983 by Potter

Angelina the mouse loves to dance and wants to become a ballerina more than anything else in the world.

"Touches of humor, attention to detail, a feel for dance and truly anthropomorphic mice make the illustrations a major part of the book." Child Book Rev Serv

Other titles about Angelina are:
Angelina and Alice (1987)
Angelina and Henry (2002)
Angelina and the princess (1984)
Angelina and the royal wedding (2010)
Angelina at the fair (1985)
Angelina on stage (1986)
Angelina, star of the show (2008)
Angelina's baby sister (1991)
Angelina's Christmas (1985)
Angelina's Halloween (2000)

Hole, Stian

★ **Garmann's** summer. Eerdmans Books for Young Readers 2008 un il $17.50
Grades: 1 2 3   **E**

1. Fear -- Fiction 2. Aunts -- Fiction 3. Summer -- Fiction 4. Old age -- Fiction 5. Family life -- Fiction
ISBN 978-0-8028-5339-4; 0-8028-5339-0

Original Norwegian edition, 2006

Now that summer is nearly over, Garmann is afraid of starting school. He asks his elderly aunts, and his father, and his mother what they are afraid of.

"The illustrations, spacious, quirky mosaic collages comprising photos, old-fashioned etchings, and wallpaper samples are utterly without a trace of sentimentality. In a feat of deceptive simplicity, Hole has crafted an elegant, fanciful, wholly poetic exploration of the nature of fear and the strength and hope required to conquer it." Booklist

Another title about Garmann is:
Garmann's street (2010)

Holmberg, Bo R.

A **day** with Dad; illustrations by Eva Eriksson. Candlewick Press 2008 un il $15.99

Grades: K 1 2 3   **E**

1. Divorce -- Fiction 2. Father-son relationship -- Fiction
ISBN 978-0-7636-3221-2; 0-7636-3221-X

LC 2007034228

Tim waits with excitement for a train to bring his father, who lives in another town, then spends an entire day with him, doing all of their favorite things, until it is time for Dad to catch the train home.

"Eriksson's unfussy colored-pencil illustrations are a good match for Holmberg's straightforward text. . . . This gentle, poignant story offers comfort to readers in similar circumstances and leaves them with a hopeful message." Horn Book

Holmes, Janet A.

Have you seen Duck? [by] Janet A. Holmes and [illustrated by] Jonathan Bentley. Scholastic 2011 un il $8.99
Grades: PreK K   **E**

1. Toys -- Fiction 2. Lost and found possessions -- Fiction
ISBN 978-0-545-22488-8; 0-545-22488-8

LC 2010-20587

"Holmes offers a fresh spin on an old favorite—the child who can't be away from his stuffed animal. Here that child is the towheaded narrator, and the stuffie, a small yellow duck. But in the boy's mind, it's Duck who needs him. . . . The light, airy ink-and-watercolor artwork, brightened by yellows, keeps its focus on the boy and his duck. Perhaps not as dramatic as Knuffle Bunny (2004) but every bit as moving." Booklist

Holmes, Mary Tavener

A **giraffe** goes to Paris; by Mary Tavener Holmes and John Harris; illustrated by Jon Cannell. Marshall Cavendish 2010 31p il $16.95
Grades: K 1 2 3   **E**

1. Giraffes -- Fiction 2. Voyages and travels -- Fiction
ISBN 978-0-7614-5595-0; 0-7614-5595-7

LC 2009-19047

Recounts the 1827 journey of a young giraffe named Belle, a gift from the Pasha of Egypt to King Charles X of France, as she makes her way by boat and land to Paris, accompanied by her devoted caretaker, Atir.

"Loopy handwritten script is used for emphasis . . . while old maps, photographs, and potraits supplement Cannell's watercolor-and-ink drawings. . . . This is history for children as it ought to be written." Publ Wkly

Holt, Kimberly Willis

The **adventures** of Granny Clearwater & Little Critter; illustrated by Laura Huliska-Beith. Henry Holt and Company 2010 un il $16.99
Grades: K 1 2 3   **E**

1. Tall tales 2. Grandmothers -- Fiction 3. Frontier and pioneer life -- Fiction
ISBN 978-0-8050-7899-2; 0-8050-7899-1

LC 2009-27418

"When the Clearwaters start their journey west in a covered wagon, a mishap separates Granny and her grandson Little Critter from the others. They travel across the scorching-hot prairie in an effort to find their missing family members. . . . This is a wonderful tall tale, told with plenty of humor and enhanced by colorful collage illustrations. . . . A rip-roaring yarn." SLJ

Holub, Joan

Apple countdown; by Joan Holub; illustrated by Jan Smith. Albert Whitman & Co. 2009 un il $16.99

Grades: PreK K 1 2   E
1. Counting 2. School stories 3. Stories in rhyme 4. Apples -- Fiction

ISBN 978-0-8075-0398-0; 0-8075-0398-3

LC 2008031705

Rhyming text describes a school field trip to an apple orchard, where the students count down all the things they see, from twenty nametags to one apple pie.

"The vibrant watercolor illustrations are dominated by primary colors, and the excitement shows on the smiling faces of the students." SLJ

Spring is here! a story about seeds. by Joan Holub; illustrated by Will Terry. Aladdin 2008 un il (Ready-to-read: Ant hill) hardcover o.p. pa $3.99

Grades: PreK K 1   E
1. Stories in rhyme 2. Ants -- Fiction 3. Seeds -- Fiction 4. Gardening -- Fiction

ISBN 978-1-4169-5132-2; 1-4169-5132-6 lib bdg; 978-1-4169-5131-5 pa; 1-4169-5131-8 pa

LC 2007-17677

In autumn, the little friends from Ant Hill find and plant some seeds, then patiently wait until spring to enjoy the plants that appear.

"The very few words of rhyming text on each spread are supplemented by the book's funny illustrations, which fill the pages and are integral to helping tell the stories. The rhymes and picture clues will help even the newest readers decipher these simplest of tales." Horn Book Guide

Zeus and the thunderbolt of doom; Joan Holub, Suzanne Williams. Aladdin, Simon and Schuster 2012 100 p. (paperback) $5.99; (hardcover) $15.99

Grades: 3 4 5   E
1. Greek mythology -- Graphic novels 2. Gods and goddesses -- Graphic novels 3. Zeus (Greek deity) -- Graphic novels

ISBN 1442457872; 9781442452633; 9781442457874

LC 2012939508

Authors Joan Hollub and Suzanne Williams present a children's story. "After 10-year-old Zeus is plucked from his childhood cave in Crete by armed 'Cronies' of the Titan king, Cronus, he is rescued by harpies. He then finds himself in a Grecian temple where he acquires a lightning bolt with the general personality of a puppy and receives hints of his destiny from an Oracle with fogged eyeglasses. Recaptured and about to be eaten by Cronus, Zeus hurls the bolt down the Titan's throat--causing the king to choke and . . . barf up several previously eaten Olympians." (Kirkus)

The **garden** that we grew; pictures by Hiroe Nakata. Viking 2001 un il (Viking easy-to-read) $13.99

Grades: K 1 2   E
1. Pumpkin 2. Gardening 3. Stories in rhyme 4. Pumpkin -- Fiction 5. Gardening -- Fiction

ISBN 0-670-89799-X

LC 00-10966

Children plant pumpkin seeds, water and weed the garden patch, watch the pumpkins grow, pick them, and enjoy them in various ways

"The text blossoms with the ample warmth, light, and gentle sense of humor in the pictures." Horn Book

Hood, Susan

Pup and Hound hatch an egg; written by Susan Hood; illustrated by Linda Hendry. Kids Can Press 2007 32p il (Kids can read) $14.95; pa $3.95

Grades: PreK K 1   E
1. Stories in rhyme 2. Dogs -- Fiction 3. Turtles -- Fiction

ISBN 978-1-55337-974-4; 1-55337-974-8; 978-1-55337-975-1 pa; 1-55337-975-6 pa

"Pup finds an egg in the grass and tries to return it to Duck and then Mother Hen. Both mothers deny ownership, and when the egg eventually hatches, it turns out to be a baby turtle—a new friend for Pup and Hound. [The book has] appealing characters and all of the requisites for a successful beginning reader. . . . Bouncy rhymes add to the fun." SLJ

Other titles about Pup and Hound are:
Pup and Hound (2004)
Pup and Hound at sea (2006)
Pup and Hound catch a thief (2007)
Pup and Hound in trouble (2005)
Pup and Hound lost and found (2006)
Pup and Hound move in (2004)
Pup and Hound play copycats (2007)
Pup and Hound scare a ghost (2007)
Pup and Hound stay up late (2005)

Hooks, Bell

Grump groan growl; illustrated by Chris Raschka. Hyperion Books for Children 2008 un il $16.99

Grades: PreK K 1   E
1. Emotions -- Fiction

ISBN 978-0-7868-0816-8; 0-7868-0816-0

LC 2007022312

Rhythmic text exposes a bad mood on the prowl, and advises the reader not to hide, but to let those feelings be

"Expressionistic art and economical poetry combine smoothly to create an inspiring model of self-control. . . . Thick, almost tactile lines of paint are slathered onto the pages with gusto, capturing a feeling of movement and strong emotion." SLJ

Hooks, Gwendolyn

Pet costume party; a Pet Club story. illustrated by Mike Byrne. Stone Arch Books 2011 31p il (Stone Arch readers) lib bdg $21.32; pa $3.95

Grades: K 1 2   E
1. Pets -- Fiction 2. Fishes -- Fiction 3. Parties -- Fiction 4. Halloween -- Fiction

ISBN 978-1-4342-2513-9 lib bdg; 1-4342-2513-5 lib bdg; 978-1-4342-3053-9 pa; 1-4342-3053-8 pa

LC 2010036339

"Andy and his pet goldfish are having a Halloween party and need costumes. They move through various choices but the fact that Nibbles can't talk complicates matters. . . . Byrne's vibrant cartoon drawings offer gentle humor to Hooks's giggle-worthy story. Basic vocabulary combined with dialogue and slightly more complex sentence structures will help stretch beginning readers while keeping them engaged with the familiar. An excellent addition to most collections." SLJ

Hopgood, Tim
   Wow! said the owl. Farrar, Straus and Giroux 2009 un il $14.95
Grades: PreK K 1   E
   1. Day -- Fiction 2. Owls -- Fiction 3. Color -- Fiction 4. Night -- Fiction
   ISBN 978-0-374-38518-7; 0-374-38518-1
                     LC 2008044038
A curious little owl decides to stay awake to find out how the things he sees at night look during the daytime.
   "Collage-style illustrations done in simple, bright shapes show little owl in her tree while the changing colors and perspectives keep each page turn 'WOW!'-worthy. . . . Straightforward and flowing, this title makes a satisfying introduction to the colors of the day." SLJ

Hopkins, Lee Bennett, 1938-
   Full moon and star; illustrated by Marcellus Hall. Abrams Books for Young Readers 2011 un il $16.95
Grades: PreK K 1 2   E
   1. Stars -- Fiction 2. Theater -- Fiction 3. Authorship -- Fiction 4. Friendship -- Fiction
   ISBN 978-1-4197-0013-2; 1-4197-0013-8
"This winsome tale is just another preschool story of cooperation. Yet the focus on playwriting and performance, complete with script formatting and special punctuation, sets a new stage for this common tale. Perfect for budding thespians, this book in three acts would make an excellent springboard for classroom explorations of drama." Kirkus

Hopkinson, Deborah
   ★ Abe Lincoln crosses a creek; a tall, thin tale (introducing his forgotten frontier friend) pictures by John Hendrix. Schwartz & Wade Books 2008 un il $16.99; lib bdg $19.99
Grades: K 1 2 3   E
   1. Lawyers 2. Presidents 3. State legislators 4. Members of Congress 5. Friendship -- Fiction
   ISBN 978-0-375-83768-5; 0-375-83768-X; 978-0-375-93768-2 lib bdg; 0-375-93768-4 lib bdg
                     LC 2007-35149
In Knob Creek, Kentucky, in 1816, seven-year-old Abe Lincoln falls into a creek and is rescued by his best friend, Austin Gollaher.
   "Hopkinson has created a lively, participatory tale that will surely stand out. . . . Hendrix's illustrations have a naive and rustic flavor that's in perfect harmony with the gravelly, homespun narrator's voice." SLJ

   ★ Apples to Oregon; being the (slightly) true narrative of how a brave pioneer father brought apples, peaches, pears, plums, grapes, and cherries (and children) across the plains. illustrated by Nancy Carpenter. Atheneum Books for Young Readers 2004 un il map $15.95
Grades: 1 2 3 4   E
   1. Tall tales 2. Fruit culture -- Fiction 3. Frontier and pioneer life -- Fiction 4. Overland journeys to the Pacific -- Fiction
   ISBN 0-689-84769-6
                     LC 2001-22949

A pioneer father transports his beloved fruit trees and his family to Oregon in the mid-nineteenth century. Based loosely on the life of Henderson Luelling
   "Carpenter's oil paintings are filled with vivid shades that reflect the changing scenery. Amusing details abound, and the slightly exaggerated humor of the pictures is in perfect balance with the tone of the text." SLJ

   ★ Billy and the rebel; based on a true Civil War story. illustrated by Brian Floca. Atheneum Books for Young Readers 2002 44p il map (Ready-to-read) $14.95
Grades: 1 2 3 4   E
   1. Gettysburg (Pa.), Battle of, 1863 -- Fiction
   ISBN 0-689-83964-2
                     LC 2001-22982
During the Battle of Gettysburg in 1863, a mother and son shelter a young Confederate deserter. Includes a historical note on the incident.
   "Based on the real William Bayly and his mother, Harriet Hamilton Bayly, [this book] . . . allows beginning readers and researchers some insight into life during the Civil War. Full-page, full-spread, and spot art, executed mainly in shades of yellow and tan, add detail and expression to this story of courage and an unlikely friendship." SLJ

   ★ From slave to soldier; based on a true Civil War story. illustrated by Brian Floca. Atheneum Books for Young Readers 2005 44p il $14.95
Grades: 1 2 3   E
   1. Slaves 2. Soldiers 3. Slavery -- Fiction 4. African American soldiers -- Fiction
   ISBN 0-689-83965-8
A boy who hates being a slave joins the Union Army to fight for freedom, and proves himself brave and capable of handling a mule team when the need arises
   This is written "in simple sentences for those who have just begun to read proficiently. . . . Short chapters and detailed watercolors aid the transition to more difficult text, while an exciting plot . . . keeps readers interested." SLJ

   Girl wonder; a baseball story in nine innings. with pictures by Terry Widener. Atheneum Bks. for Young Readers 2003 un il $16.95
Grades: 1 2 3 4   E
   1. Baseball -- Fiction
   ISBN 0-689-83300-8
                     LC 99-47052
In the early 1900s, Alta Weiss, a young woman who knows from an early age that she loves baseball, finds a way to show that she can play, even though she is a girl
   "Hopkinson tells her story with practiced skill—vivid details, lively language, varied pacing. . . . The illustrations are . . . broad, somewhat exaggerated, but conveying much emotion and narrative content." Horn Book

   Knit your bit; a World War One story. by Deborah Hopkinson; illustrated by Steven Guarnaccia. G.P. Putnam's Sons 2013 32 p. $16.99
Grades: 1 2 3 4   E
   1. Historical fiction 2. Knitting -- Fiction 3. Picture books for children 4. Sex role -- Fiction 5. World War, 1914-1918 -- United States -- Fiction 6. World War,

1914-1918 -- New York (State) -- New York -- Fiction
ISBN 039925241X; 9780399252419

LC 2012009635

This children's picture book offers a "story highlighting a patriotic civilian initiative during WWI. After Pop goes overseas, Mikey scoffs at helping Mama and his sister knit clothing for soldiers . . . . But after his teacher announces a knitting competition to benefit soldiers (based on an actual 'Knit-In' held in New York City's Central Park in 1918), Mikey and two friends accept a boys vs. girls challenge to win the knitting bee." (Publishers Weekly)

★ **Sky** boys; how they built the Empire State Building. [by] Deborah Hopkinson & James E. Ransome. Schwartz & Wade Books 2006 un il $16.95
Grades: K 1 2 3 4   E
  1. Building -- Fiction
  ISBN 0-375-83610-1

LC 2005010852

In 1931, a boy and his father watch as the world's tallest building, the Empire State Building, is constructed, step-by-step, near their Manhattan home.

"Crisp, lyrical free verse and bold paintings celebrate the skill and daring of those who constructed the Empire State Building. . . . Ransome's powerful acrylic paintings show the building in all stages of construction, and includes the workers' perilous views. A unique, memorable title." Booklist

★ **Sweet** Clara and the freedom quilt; paintings by James Ransome. Knopf 1993 un il hardcover o.p. pa $6.99
Grades: K 1 2 3 4   E
  1. Quilts -- Fiction 2. Slavery -- Fiction
  ISBN 0-679-82311-5; 0-679-92311-X lib bdg; 0-679-87472-0 pa

LC 91-11601

Clara, a young slave, stitches a quilt with a map pattern which guides her to freedom in the North

"The smooth, optimistic, first-person vernacular of the story is ably accompanied by Ransome's brightly colored, full-page paintings." Horn Book Guide

Another title about Clara is:
Under the quilt of night (2001)

★ A **band** of angels; a story inspired by the Jubilee Singers. illustrated by Raúl Colón. Atheneum Bks. for Young Readers 1999 un il hardcover o.p. pa $7.99
Grades: 1 2 3 4   E
  1. Pianists 2. Choral conductors 3. Gospel music -- Fiction 4. African Americans -- Fiction
  ISBN 0-689-81062-8; 0-689-84887-0 pa

LC 96-20011

Based on the life of Ella Sheppard Moore. The daughter of a slave forms a gospel singing group and goes on tour to raise money to save Fisk University

"Lilting prose, poignant historical details and arresting portraits of trailblazing singers lost in song contribute to this triumphant tale." Publ Wkly

The **humblebee** hunter; pictures by Jen Corace. Disney Hyperion Books 2010 un il $16.99

Grades: K 1 2   E
  1. Naturalists 2. Travel writers 3. Bees -- Fiction 4. Writers on science
  ISBN 978-1-4231-1356-0; 1-4231-1356-X

LC 2009-33987

On a beautiful day, some of Charles Darwin's many children help him study humblebees (bumblebees) in the garden at their home in the English countryside.

"The delicate, stylized illustrations, outlined in black and washed in natural shades of green and brown with spots of color, depict an amiable country Victorian household. . . . [This is an] inspiring read-aloud." SLJ

Hoppe, Paul
  Hat. Bloomsbury U.S.A Children's Books 2009 un il $14.99
Grades: PreK K 1   E
  1. Hats -- Fiction 2. Imagination -- Fiction 3. Lost and found possessions -- Fiction
  ISBN 978-1-59990-247-0; 1-59990-247-8; 978-1-59990-248-7 lib bdg; 1-59990-248-6 lib bdg

LC 2008-22357

When Henry finds a hat he is very excited by its possibilities, but becomes worried when he thinks that the hat might belong to someone else

"The text is simple but imaginative. The illustrations bring each imagined scenario to life, and the ink drawings have a slightly retro feel with their subdued colors. The story lends itself to being read aloud, and the red hat pops off the pages." SLJ

The **woods**. Chronicle Books 2011 un il $16.99
Grades: PreK K 1   E
  1. Boys -- Fiction 2. Fear -- Fiction 3. Toys -- Fiction 4. Animals -- Fiction 5. Bedtime -- Fiction
  ISBN 978-0-8118-7547-9; 0-8118-7547-4

LC 2010039393

"The refrain—'we weren't scared at all. Until...'—sets a comfortable pattern, and the fuzzy watercolors on thick creamy stock enhance the coziness of the tale. . . . Hoppe's delightfully quirky monsters enhance this pleasant tonic for bedtime fears." Kirkus

Horáček, Petr
  ★ **Choo** choo. Candlewick Press 2008 un il $5.99
Grades: PreK   E
  1. Board books for children 2. Railroads -- Fiction
  ISBN 978-0-7636-3477-3; 0-7636-3477-8

"Horácek's cheerful acrylic collage artwork shines in this small, beautifully designed board book about a train that carries cars full of smiling children to the beach. From the sound effects that begin the single line on each spread . . . to the shaped pages that emphasize the curve of mountains or the spikes of treetops, this book begs for interaction." Booklist

  Look out, Suzy Goose. Candlewick Press 2008 un il $14.99
Grades: PreK K 1 2   E
  1. Geese -- Fiction 2. Animals -- Fiction
  ISBN 978-0-7636-3803-0; 0-7636-3803-X

"Suzy Goose . . . finds herself feeling dissatisfied with her life. The incessant honking of her fellow geese sends her flip-flopping to the woods to find a quiet respite. . . . Soon she is unwittingly pursued by a fox, a wolf, and a bear—tip-toeing, creeping, and padding behind her. . . . Visually stimulating mixed-media illustrations, including textured paints and paper collage, evoke those fundamental emotions often found in stories involving the fabled 'woods.' . . . Despite its mildly scary content, this book is amusing, relatively short, and overall suitable for younger children." SLJ

One spotted giraffe; a counting pop-up book. Petr Horáček. Candlewick 2012 20 p. (hardback) $18.95

Grades: PreK   E
1. Counting 2. Toy and movable books 3. Numerals -- Juvenile fiction 4. Pop-up books 5. Animals -- Fiction 6. Numerals -- Fiction 7. Pop-up books -- Specimens
ISBN 0062234897; 9780763661571

LC 2011048376

This pop-up book by Petr Horacek is aimed at helping children "identify animals, count them, and discover numerals. . . . Spreads filled with realistic depictions of colorful creatures -- everything from pandas to lemurs -- entice readers to count the animals, then flip the flap to reveal a corresponding pop-up numeral. And then the surprise: the numeral looks just like the animal -- fur, spots, stripes, and all!" (Publisher's note)

★ **Silly** Suzy Goose. Candlewick Press 2006 un il $14.99

Grades: PreK K 1 2   E
1. Geese -- Fiction 2. Lions -- Fiction
ISBN 0-7636-3040-3

Suzy longs to be different from all the other geese, but learns that imitating a lion may not be the best way to express her individuality.

"Created in mixed media, the art jumps off the pages, a fitting verb for a clever, clever book, alive in every way." Booklist

Other titles about Suzy Goose are:
Look out, Suzy Goose (2008)
Suzy Goose and the Christmas star (2009)

Suzy Goose and the Christmas star. Candlewick Press 2009 un il $15.99

Grades: PreK K 1 2   E
1. Geese -- Fiction 2. Stars -- Fiction 3. Christmas -- Fiction 4. Christmas stories -- Juvenile literature
ISBN 978-0-7636-4487-1; 0-7636-4487-0

Silly Suzy Goose tries to get a star from the sky to put on the Christmas tree.

"The full-spread mixed-media illustrations depicting a textured snowy landscape against a starry night sky contrast with the friendly and determined figure of Suzy, with her orange beak glowing and her tiny eyes on the prize. Quiet and sweet–a fine choice for both storytime and family sharing." SLJ

Horning, Sandra

Chicks! by Sandra Horning; illustrated by Jon Goodell. Random House 2013 32 p. (Step into Reading. Step 1) (trade pbk.) $3.99

Grades: PreK K 1   E
1. Chickens -- Juvenile fiction 2. Animal babies -- Juvenile literature 3. Chickens -- Fiction 4. Animals

-- Infancy -- Fiction
ISBN 0307932214; 9780307932211; 9780375971174; 9780375981142

LC 2011050438

In this children's book by Sandra Horning, "when a family brings home chicks from a local farm, they must do everything they can to make sure their feathered friends thrive in their new environment. With the help of their knowledgeable parents, the children provide the baby chicks with food, water, warmth, and proper shelter." (Publisher's note)

The **giant** hug; illustrated by Valeri Gorbachev. Knopf 2005 un il $15.95; lib bdg $17.99

Grades: PreK K 1 2   E
1. Pigs -- Fiction 2. Grandmothers -- Fiction 3. Postal service -- Fiction
ISBN 0-375-82477-4; 0-375-92477-9 lib bdg

LC 2003-25883

When Owen the pig sends a real hug to his grandmother for her birthday he inadvertently brings cheer to the postal workers as they pass the hug along

"Gorbachev's cast of animal characters, drawn with a . . . sense of whimsy, are well chosen to emphasize the relevant personality traits." Booklist

Horowitz, Dave

Twenty-six pirates; by Dave Horowitz. Nancy Paulsen Books 2013 32 p. col. ill. (reinforced) $16.99

Grades: PreK K 1   E
1. Pirates -- Juvenile fiction 2. Alphabet -- Juvenile fiction
ISBN 9780399257773

LC 2012023866

This children's book by Dave Horowitz presents "an alphabetical parade of pirates -- by name! . . . Each pirate receives a full-page portrait that depicts him (they are all boys) engaged in the behavior described. Pirate Lee, who needs to pee, quivers outside the head, hands over his crotch. Pirate Quaid, who is not afraid, nevertheless looks a little dubious as giant octopus tentacles loom. Pirate Tony, who is fall of baloney, happily munches a sandwich." (Kirkus Reviews)

Twenty-six princesses. Putnam 2008 un il $15.99

Grades: PreK K 1 2   E
1. Alphabet 2. Fairy tales 3. Princesses -- Fiction
ISBN 978-0-399-24607-4; 0-399-24607-X

LC 2007-13233

Twenty-six princesses, one for each letter of the alphabet, go to a party at the prince's castle.

"Horowitz has a light, witty touch, and the text is rich with puns. The words and the pictures play off one another perfectly, encouraging children to pore over each humorously detailed portrait." SLJ

Includes bibliographical references

Horrocks, Anita

Silas' seven grandparents; story by Anita Horrocks; illustrations by Helen Flook. Orca Book Publishers 2010 un il $19.95

Grades: PreK K   E
1. Family life -- Fiction 2. Grandparents -- Fiction
ISBN 978-1-55143-561-9; 1-55143-561-9

Silas' Seven Grandparents is a fun and loving story about having multiple sets of grandparents and stepgrandparents.

When Silas' parents go away on a business trip, all seven grandparents invite Silas to stay with them. How can he choose one without hurting the others' feelings?

"The deftly drawn water-based ink illustrations reflect the story's upbeat tone and portray the widely diverse grandparents in ways that make them distinctive." Booklist

Horse, Harry

Little Rabbit lost. Peachtree Pubs. 2002 un il $15.95; bd bk $9.95

Grades: PreK K 1   E

1. Rabbits 2. Birthdays 3. Amusement parks 4. Lost children 5. Rabbits -- Fiction 6. Birthdays -- Fiction
ISBN 1-56145-273-4; 1-56145-345-5 bd bk

LC 2002-2697

On his birthday Little Rabbit thinks that he is now a big rabbit, until he gets lost at the Rabbit World amusement park

"The lovely ink-and-watercolor illustrations are filled with clever details kids will enjoy—carrot-shaped paddleboats and bunny roller-coaster cars. Children will welcome this charming story." Booklist

Other titles about Little Rabbit are:
Little Rabbit goes to school (2004)
Little Rabbit runaway (2005)
Little Rabbit's Christmas (2007)
Little Rabbit's new baby (2008)

Horstman, Lisa

Squawking Matilda. Marshall Cavendish Children 2009 un il $17.99

Grades: PreK K 1 2   E

1. Aunts -- Fiction 2. Chickens -- Fiction 3. Farm life -- Fiction
ISBN 978-0-7614-5463-2; 0-7614-5463-2

LC 2008003657

Mae likes starting projects but never seems to finish them, and so when Aunt Susan asks her to take care of a feisty chicken Mae is soon distracted, then must find a way to make up for her neglect before Aunt Susan's visit.

"Handcrafted puppets wearing cheery clothing are posed, photographed, and digitally colored to give this charming selection a down-to-earth quality that matches the story perfectly." SLJ

Horvath, David

What dat? the great big Uglydoll book of things to look at, search for, point to, and wonder about. Random House 2011 il $14.99

Grades: PreK K 1 2 3   E

1. Puzzles 2. Vocabulary
ISBN 978-0-375-86434-6; 0-375-86434-2

"Horvath and Kim have created a word book featuring the Uglyverse. Each spread has bright, labeled cartoon illustrations, and brief paragraphs ask readers to find different things on each page. The scenarios, while full, are not too busy, so the items are easy to find and the labels are easy to read. The scenes are funny, and some jokes are obviously intended for an older audience.... These jokes will be easily passed over by younger children as they are buried within the scenes. The popularity of the toys combined with the fun of a look-and-find word book should make this a popular choice." SLJ

Hosford, Kate

Infinity and me; written by Kate Hosford; illustrations by Gabi Swiatkowska. Carolrhoda Books 2012 32 p. (lib. bdg.: alk. paper) $16.95

Grades: K 1 2 3 4 5   E

1. Infinity 2. Mathematics 3. Picture books for children 4. Schools -- Fiction 5. Infinity -- Fiction 6. Grandmothers -- Fiction
ISBN 0761367268; 9780761367260

LC 2011044746

In this book, protagonist "Uma's struggle with the meaning of infinity offers readers a[n] . . . introduction to the mathematical concept. When little Uma gazes at the vast night sky and wonders how many stars are there, she asks, 'How could I even think about something as big as infinity?' When friends, her grandmother, the school cook and the music teacher offer creative ways of describing infinity, Uma ends up feeling rather overwhelmed." (Kirkus Reviews)

Houston, Gloria

Miss Dorothy and her bookmobile; illustrated by Susan Condie Lamb. Harper 2010 un il $16.99

Grades: K 1 2   E

1. Librarians -- Fiction 2. Bookmobiles -- Fiction 3. Country life -- Fiction 4. Books and reading -- Fiction
ISBN 978-0-06-029155-6; 0-06-029155-9

LC 2005-18630

Dorothy has always wanted to work in a library like the red brick one of her girlhood, but after moving to rural North Carolina she discovers that the type of library is less important than the books and the people who read them.

"Beautiful, soft landscapes of the rugged terrain throughout the seasons serve as a backdrop for this charming story of a librarian on the go." SLJ

The **year** of the perfect Christmas tree; an Appalachian story. pictures by Barbara Cooney. Dial Bks. for Young Readers 1988 un il $15.99; pa $6.99

Grades: K 1 2 3   E

1. Christmas -- Fiction
ISBN 0-8037-0299-X; 0-14-055827-2 pa

LC 87-24551

"It's 1918 in the mountains of North Carolina, and the custom in the village is for one family to select and donate the Christmas tree each year. In the spring Ruthie and her father select a perfect balsam high on a rocky crag. Then Father goes to war. Still, on Christmas Eve the tree is in the church and Ruthie plays the angel. The winning illustrations perfectly match the tone of this affecting story, which comes from the author's family." NY Times Book Rev

Hovland, Henrik

★ **John** Jensen feels different; by Henrik Hovland; illustrated by Torill Kove; translated by Don Bartlett. Eerdmans Books for Young Readers 2012 33 p. col. ill. (alk. paper) $16

Grades: PreK K 1 2   E

1. Picture books for children 2. Crocodiles -- Juvenile fiction 3. Crocodiles -- Fiction 4. Individuality -- Fiction
ISBN 0802853994; 9780802853998

LC 2011022446

This children's picture book follows John Jensen, "a well-dressed, well-mannered crocodile living a civilized life in the human world" who worries constantly about being different. "When John Jensen trips and falls after binding up his bulky tail in a futile attempt to conceal it, he meets Dr. Field, whose huge ears and long trunk mean he knows a thing or two about being different. . . . John Jensen realizes that his tail—and his differentness in general—are all a question of attitude." (Publishers Weekly)

Howard, Arthur

Hoodwinked. Harcourt 2001 un il $16

Grades: PreK K 1   E

1. Pets 2. Witches 3. Pets -- Fiction 4. Witches -- Fiction

ISBN 0-15-202656-8

LC 00-8318

Mitzi, a young witch, searches for a creepy pet, but finds that a cute kitten is perfect for her

"The pictures are perfect for this lively story—lots of fangs and slimy, scaly, weird, and wiggly outlines fill the pages." SLJ

Howard, Elizabeth Fitzgerald

★ **Aunt** Flossie's hats (and crab cakes later) paintings by James Ransome. 10th anniversary ed; Clarion Books 2001 31p il $16; pa $6.95

Grades: K 1 2 3   E

1. Hats -- Fiction 2. Aunts -- Fiction 3. African Americans -- Fiction

ISBN 0-618-12038-6; 0-395-72077-X pa

LC 00-65757

A reissue of the title first published 1991

Sara and Susan share tea, cookies, crab cakes, and stories about hats when they visit their favorite relative, Aunt Flossie.

"This is an affecting portrait of a black American family. . . . Howard's quiet, sure telling is well matched by Ransome's art-elegant, expressive oil paintings that convey warmth, joy, tenderness and love." Publ Wkly

★ **Virgie** goes to school with us boys; illustrated by E.B. Lewis. Simon & Schuster Bks. for Young Readers 1999 un il $17.99; pa $7.99

Grades: K 1 2 3   E

1. African Americans 2. African Americans -- Fiction 3. African Americans -- Juvenile fiction

ISBN 0-689-80076-2; 0-689-87793-5 pa

LC 97-49406

In the post-Civil War South, a young African American girl is determined to prove that she can go to school just like her older brothers

"The story is a superb tribute to the author's great aunt, the inspiration for this book. . . . Lewis's watercolor illustrations capture the characters with warmth and dignity." SLJ

Howe, James

★ **Brontorina**; illustrated by Randy Cecil. Candlewick Press 2010 un il $15.99

Grades: PreK K 1 2   E

1. Ballet -- Fiction 2. Dinosaurs -- Fiction

ISBN 978-0-7636-4437-6; 0-7636-4437-4

"Initially turned away from Madame Lucille's Dance Academy for Boys and Girls because she is an enormous dinosaur, Brontorina counters, 'But in my heart I am a ballerina.' . . . Text and illustrations work beautifully together

in this witty fantasy. . . . In Cecil's arresting oil paintings, the tawny orange dinosaur stands out boldly against slate blue or white backgrounds, and the unusual texture of the paint creates a distinctive effect." Booklist

★ **Horace** and Morris but mostly Dolores; written by James Howe; illustrated by Amy Walrod. Atheneum Bks. for Young Readers 1999 un il $16; pa $6.99

Grades: PreK K 1 2   E

1. Mice -- Fiction 2. Clubs -- Fiction 3. Sex role -- Fiction 4. Friendship -- Fiction

ISBN 0-689-31874-X; 0-689-85675-X pa

LC 96-17645

"Three adventure-loving mice are best friends until gender stereotypes separate them, driving Horace and Morris into a rowdy boys-only clubhouse while Dolores reluctantly goes off to join the ultra-ladylike Cheese Puffs. The bold artwork suits the book's lively protest against conformity." Horn Book Guide

Other titles about Horace, Morris, and Dolores are:

Horace and Morris join the chorus (but what about Dolores?) (2002)

Horace and Morris say cheese (which makes Dolores sneeze!) (2009)

★ **Houndsley** and Catina; illustrated by Marie-Louise Gay. Candlewick Press 2006 36p il $14.99

Grades: PreK K 1 2   E

1. Cats -- Fiction 2. Dogs -- Fiction 3. Friendship -- Fiction

ISBN 0-7636-2404-7

LC 2005-50187

Houndsley, a dog, and Catina, a cat, run into trouble when they decide to prove that they are the best at cooking and writing, respectively.

"The lively, brisk writing is wonderfully extended in Gay's airy watercolor-and-pencil illustrations." Booklist

Other titles about Houndsley and Catina are:

Houndsley and Catina and the birthday surprise (2006)

Houndsley and Catina and the quiet time (2008)

Houndsley and Catina plink and plunk (2009)

Kaddish for Grandpa in Jesus' name, amen; [Illustrated by] Catherine Stock. Atheneum Books for Young Readers 2004 un il $16.95

Grades: K 1 2 3   E

1. Judaism 2. Christianity 3. Grandfathers 4. Funeral rites and ceremonies 5. Death -- Fiction 6. Judaism -- Fiction 7. Christianity -- Fiction 8. Grandfathers -- Fiction 9. Death -- Religious aspects 10. Funeral rites and ceremonies -- Fiction

ISBN 0-689-80185-8

LC 2002-11569

Five-year-old Emily tries to understand her grandfather's death by exploring the Christian and Jewish rituals that her family practices during and after his funeral

"The soft watercolor illustrations, done in pastel colors, are a perfect accompaniment to the story. This book is a good vehicle to explain the rituals of death to children." SLJ

★ **Pinky** and Rex; illustrated by Melissa Sweet. Atheneum Pubs. 1990 38p il $15; pa $3.99

Grades: K 1 2   **E**
1. Toys -- Fiction 2. Museums -- Fiction 3. Friendship
-- Fiction
ISBN 0-689-31454-X; 0-689-82348-7 pa

LC 89-30786

"Sweet's gently washed, jovial illustrations reflect the unpretentious sincerity of Rex and Pinky's relationship, while Howe's readable text blending natural dialogue with narrative, is divided into individual chapters." Booklist

Other titles about Pinky and Rex are:

Pinky and Rex and the bully (1996)
Pinky and Rex and the double-dad weekend (1995)
Pinky and Rex and the just-right pet (2001)
Pinky and Rex and the mean old witch (1991)
Pinky and Rex and the new baby (1993)
Pinky and Rex and the new neighbors (1997)
Pinky and Rex and the perfect pumpkin (1998)
Pinky and Rex and the school play (1998)
Pinky and Rex and the spelling bee (1991)
Pinky and Rex get married (1990)
Pinky and Rex go to camp (1992)

Howe, James, 1946-
Otter and odder; James Howe; illustrated by Chris Raschka. 1st ed. Candlewick Press 2012 40 p. ill. (reinforced) $14
Grades: 2 3 4   **E**
1. Otters -- Juvenile fiction 2. Picture books for children 3. Love -- Fiction 4. Fishes -- Fiction 5. Otters -- Fiction
ISBN 076364174X; 9780763641740

LC 2010048213

In this story, while Otter is hunting for food, "he realizes something unlikely has happened: 'I am in love with my food source.' Myrtle (as Otter hears the fish's name of Gurgle) has fallen for Otter as well, but despite their love the two can't make it work: 'I am no longer sure a fish can love an otter . . . when the way of the otter is to eat fish.' Fortunately, a wise beaver introduces Otter to vegetarianism, and the two 'lived happily ever after.'" (Bulletin of the Center for Children's Books)

Howland, Naomi
★ **Latkes,** latkes, good to eat; a Chanukah story. Clarion Bks. 1999 31p il $16; pa $5.95
Grades: PreK K 1 2   **E**
1. Fairy tales 2. Jews -- Fiction 3. Magic -- Fiction 4. Hanukkah -- Fiction 5. Jews -- Russia -- Fiction
ISBN 0-395-89903-6; 0-618-49295-X pa

LC 97-50616

In an old Russian village, Sadie and her brothers are poor and hungry until an old woman gives Sadie a frying pan that will make potato pancakes until it hears the magic words that make it stop

"Howland effectively sets her story in a Russian shtetl, using words, intonation, and especially pictures. Working in gouache and colored pencil, she offers a snowy landscape peopled with Jewish villagers who work hard and celebrate harder." Booklist

Princess says goodnight; illustrated by David Small. HarperCollins 2010 un il $16.99; lib bdg $17.89
Grades: PreK K 1 2   **E**
1. Stories in rhyme 2. Bedtime -- Fiction 3. Princesses

-- Fiction
ISBN 978-0-06-145525-4; 0-06-145525-3; 978-0-06-145526-1 lib bdg; 0-06-145526-1 lib bdg
Rhyming text presents what a princess might do between leaving the ball and saying goodnight.

"Sweet and disarmingly infectious without being cloying, this is a bedtime story full of joy and imagination." Publ Wkly

Hubbell, Patricia
Airplanes; soaring! diving! turning! by Patricia Hubbell; illustrated by Megan Halsey and Sean Addy. Marshall Cavendish Children 2008 un il $16.99
Grades: PreK K 1 2   **E**
1. Stories in rhyme 2. Airplanes -- Fiction
ISBN 978-0-7614-5388-8; 0-7614-5388-1

LC 2007011721

Illustrations and rhyming text celebrate different kinds of airplanes and what they can do

"This picture book features . . . animated, whimsical art that will delight young would-be jet-setters. . . . The lively, descriptive prose . . . incorporates peppy sounds that amp up the energy that's echoed in the vibrant illustrations." Booklist

★ **Boats**; speeding! sailing! cruising! illustrated by Megan Halsey and Sean Addy. Marshall Cavendish 2009 un il $17.99
Grades: PreK K 1 2   **E**
1. Stories in rhyme 2. Boats and boating -- Juvenile literature
ISBN 978-0-7614-5524-0; 0-7614-5524-8

LC 2007-49522

Illustrations and rhyming text celebrate different kinds of boats and what they can do.

"The tight, surprisingly informative rhyming text works so well because it pairs with art that shows off each of these boats to best advantage. The fun part comes in the way the design and the mixed-media art . . . come together." Booklist

Cars; rushing! honking! zooming! illustrated by Megan Halsey and Sean Addy. Marshall Cavendish Children 2006 un il $14.99
Grades: PreK K 1   **E**
1. Stories in rhyme 2. Automobiles -- Fiction
ISBN 978-0-7614-5296-6; 0-7614-5296-6
Illustrations and rhyming text celebrate different kinds of cars and what they can do

"The rhyming text rolls smoothly along. . . . Color heightens the appeal of the clip art, stamps, etchings, maps, and original drawings, which come together in the paper-collage illustrations." Booklist

Firefighters! speeding! spraying! saving! illustrated by Viviana Garofoli. Marshall Cavendish 2007 un il $14.99; bd bk $7.99
Grades: PreK K 1   **E**
1. Stories in rhyme 2. Board books for children 3. Fire fighters -- Fiction
ISBN 978-0-7614-5337-6; 0-7614-5337-7; 978-0-7614-5615-5 bd bk; 0-7614-5615-5 bd bk
"The tale begins with the 'Clang! Clang! Clang!' of the alarm. The firefighters rush to get dressed and board their truck, along with Spot, the firehouse Dalmatian. Brief, pul-

sating, rhythmic text follows across the pages. . . . The digital, cartoon-style artwork is simple. Done in vibrant hues of predominately primary colors." SLJ

Horses; Trotting! Prancing! Racing! illustrated by Joe Mathieu. Marshall Cavendish Children 2011 il $17.99
Grades: PreK K 1   E
1. Stories in rhyme 2. Horses -- Fiction
ISBN 978-0-7614-5949-1; 0-7614-5949-9; 978-0-7614-5997-2 e-book

LC 2010044929

"A simple, rhyming text introduces readers to horses—the different breeds, their abilities in providing transportation, and all else they do. . . . Lovely, action-packed illustrations done in watercolors and colored pencils highlight the different hues and patterns found on the horses' coats. . . . This is an excellent addition for any collection, and it will extend knowledge about transportation that isn't manmade." SLJ

My first airplane ride; by Patricia Hubbell; illustrated by Nancy Speir. Marshall Cavendish 2008 un il $16.99
Grades: PreK K 1   E
1. Stories in rhyme 2. Airplanes -- Fiction
ISBN 978-0-7614-5436-6; 0-7614-5436-5
"Short, rhyming phrases record the events as a boy takes his first plane ride. Every incident along the way is chronicled here: packing, driving to the airport, getting boarding passes, going through security in stocking feet, waiting at the gate, etc. . . . The level of detail is well calibrated to the target audience. . . . Colorful and reassuring." Booklist

Police: hurrying! helping! saving! Marshall Cavendish Children 2008 un il $14.99
Grades: PreK K 1   E
1. Stories in rhyme 2. Police -- Fiction
ISBN 978-0-7614-5421-2; 0-7614-5421-7
Illustrations and rhyming text celebrate police officers and what they do.
"A picture book with a rhyming text, bright colors, and plenty of action." SLJ

Shaggy dogs, waggy dogs; illustrated by Donald Wu. Marshall Cavendish 2011 un il $17.99
Grades: PreK K 1 2   E
1. Dogs -- Fiction
ISBN 978-0-7614-5957-6; 0-7614-5957-X
"An assortment of lovable-looking pooches is pictured in this charming ode to man's best friend. In perfect rhyme, Hubbell describes the canines by their characteristics rather than breeds: shaggy, waggy, thin, saggy, shy, bold, pretty, puppies, full-grown, and more. Next she offers a litany of the things dogs are good at doing. . . . Wu's detailed illustrations drawn with colored pencil over acrylic vividly depict the different textures of each animal's fur as it engages in typical doggie pastimes. Children who love animals will adore this fetching book." SLJ

Snow happy! Tricycle Press 2010 un il $15.99
Grades: PreK K 1   E
1. Stories in rhyme 2. Snow -- Fiction
ISBN 978-1-58246-329-2; 1-58246-329-8

"A rollicking verse about the joys of playing in the snow. Lively children and their parents and grandparents enjoy a day of sledding, making snow angels, building igloos, even shoveling. Hubbell's meter is bouncy. . . . The artwork matches the upbeat mood of the text. . . . The simple watercolor characters are full of activity." SLJ

Hubbell, Will
Pumpkin Jack; written and illustrated by Will Hubbell. Whitman, A. 2000 un il $15.95
Grades: PreK K 1 2 3   E
1. Pumpkin 2. Halloween 3. Jack-o-lanterns 4. Pumpkin -- Fiction 5. Halloween -- Fiction
ISBN 0-8075-6665-9

LC 00-8282

After Halloween, Tim discards Jack, his jack-o'-lantern, in the garden and during the following year it sprouts, blooms, and grows new pumpkins
"Satisfying and surprisingly varied in approach and perspective, Hubbell's colored pencil drawings illustrate the simple story in a series of well-imagined scenes." Booklist

Huckabee, Mike
Can't wait till Christmas; [illustrated by Jed Henry] G. P. Putnam's Sons 2010 un il $17.99
Grades: PreK K 1   E
1. Gifts -- Fiction 2. Siblings -- Fiction 3. Christmas -- Fiction
ISBN 978-0-399-25539-7; 0-399-25539-7
Mike is so eager to open his Christmas gifts that he convinces his older sister, Pam, to unwrap and play with them in advance, but when Christmas morning arrives they are unhappy about what they have done.
"Huckabee's lighthearted cautionary tale is buoyed by zippy digital illustrations that convey both its humor and warmth." Publ Wkly

Hucke, Johannes
Pip in the Grand Hotel; illustrated by Daniel Müller. North-South 2009 un il $16.95
Grades: PreK K 1 2   E
1. Mice -- Fiction 2. Hotels and motels -- Fiction
ISBN 978-0-7358-2225-2; 0-7358-2225-5
Originally published in Sweden
Mary has a new pet, a mouse named Pip. When she opens the lid to his box, Pip is off straight into the Grand Hotel. The reader can search for Pip in the pictures.
"This lively escapade is heightened by ellipses at the end of each spread, which create dramatic page turns. As the children race through this bustling high-end hotel, Müller's detail-filled watercolor illustrations truly bring the caper to life." SLJ

Hudes, Quiara Alegria
Welcome to my neighborhood! a barrio ABC. illustrated by Shino Arihara. Arthur A. Levine Books 2010 un il $16.99
Grades: PreK K   E
1. Alphabet 2. Stories in rhyme 3. City and town life -- Fiction 4. Hispanic Americans -- Fiction
ISBN 978-0-545-09424-5; 0-545-09424-0
"An expressive girl takes a friend on a poetic tour of her inner-city neighborhood. 'E is for the echo of the elevated train./ F is for the fire hydrant spraying summer rain.'

Chalky, gouache washes capture both the vital and gently dilapidated elements of city life. . . . The subtle presence of the girl's personal narrative and her nuanced understanding of what makes her neighborhood home set this ABC book apart." Publ Wkly

Huget, Jennifer LaRue

How to clean your room in 10 easy steps; illustrated by Edward Koren. Schwartz & Wade Books 2009 un il $16.99; lib bdg $19.99

Grades: K 1 2　　　　　　　　　　　　　　　**E**
　　1. Home economics -- Fiction
　　ISBN 978-0-375-84410-2; 0-375-84410-4; 978-0-375-96410-7 lib bdg; 0-375-96410-X lib bdg
　　　　　　　　　　　　　　　　LC 2008-48824

A young girl provides unique advice on how to tidy a bedroom.

"Children and their adults are in for a treat with this new showcase for Koren's illustrations. His wry, bushy, squiggly style is well-matched by Huget's puckish and not entirely serious advice. . . . Good for great giggles-and at the end, she promises even more awesome advice on fixing your hair." Kirkus

Thanks a LOT, Emily Post! written by Jennifer LaRue Huget; illustrated by Alexandra Boiger. Schwartz & Wade Books 2009 un il $16.99; lib bdg $19.99

Grades: K 1 2 3　　　　　　　　　　　　　　**E**
　　1. Novelists 2. Advice columnists 3. Mothers -- Fiction 4. Etiquette -- Fiction 5. Conduct of life -- Fiction
　　ISBN 978-0-375-83853-8; 0-375-83853-8; 978-0-375-93853-5 lib bdg; 0-375-93853-2 lib bdg
　　　　　　　　　　　　　　　　LC 2008004994

When a mother instructs her children to behave according to Emily Post's rules of etiquette, they respond by insisting that Mother follow the rules, as well. Includes information about Post and selected items from her 1922 book.

"Written with clarity and wit. . . . The fresh, expressive watercolors dramatize events through distinctive characters playing out sometimes-chaotic scenes full of energy, elegance, and entertaining details." Booklist

The **best** birthday party ever; illustrated by LeUyen Pham. Schwartz & Wade Books 2011 un il $16.99; lib bdg $19.99

Grades: PreK K 1 2　　　　　　　　　　　　　**E**
　　1. Parties -- Fiction 2. Birthdays -- Fiction
　　ISBN 978-0-375-84763-9; 0-375-84763-4; 978-0-375-95763-5 lib bdg; 0-375-95763-4 lib bdg
　　　　　　　　　　　　　　　　LC 2009-28010

A child plans an elaborate birthday party and eagerly counts the months, days, hours, and minutes before the celebration.

"Pham's watercolor illustrations perfectly capture the frivolity of the little girl's imagination. . . . Young birthday enthusiasts will readily identify with the considerable thought and energy involved in getting ready for the big day." Bull Cent Child Books

Hughes, Shirley

Alfie and the big boys. Bodley Head 2007 un il $17.95

Grades: PreK K 1　　　　　　　　　　　　　　**E**
　　1. School stories 2. Friendship -- Fiction
　　ISBN 978-0-370-32884-3; 0-370-32884-1

Alfie and his friends wish they could play with the bigger boys and one day they get a chance

This "sensitively portrays children's emotional lives through everyday events in familiar settings. Ink drawings, brightened with washes and strokes of color, have the narrative power to tell the basic story on their own. But the book is richer for the inclusion of a straightforward text." Booklist

★ **Annie** Rose is my little sister. Candlewick Press 2003 un il $15.99

Grades: PreK K 1 2　　　　　　　　　　　　**E**
　　1. Siblings -- Fiction
　　ISBN 0-7636-1959-0
　　　　　　　　　　　　　　　　LC 2002-67695

Alfie describes all the things that he and his younger sister Annie Rose do together

"Few artists have recreated the young child's body language and surroundings as faithfully as Hughes. The gouache-and-oil pastel illustrations teem with well-observed details." Booklist

★ The **Christmas** Eve ghost. Candlewick Press 2010 un il $15.99

Grades: K 1 2 3　　　　　　　　　　　　　　**E**
　　1. Laundry -- Fiction 2. Christmas -- Fiction 3. Prejudices -- Fiction 4. Single parent family -- Fiction 5. Christmas stories -- Juvenile literature
　　ISBN 978-0-7636-4472-7; 0-7636-4472-2
　　　　　　　　　　　　　　　　LC 2009051506

In 1930s Liverpool, England, Bronwen and Dylan live with their widowed mother, who works long hours doing other people's washing, and even though she sometimes must leave the children alone in the house, she cautions them not to speak to the O'Rileys next door, who go to a different church.

"A mixture of full-page and spot illustrations in watercolor and ink creates a nostalgic atmosphere. . . . The overall theme of the budding friendship between families of different faiths is subtly and effectively presented." Kirkus

★ **Don't** want to go! Candlewick Press 2010 un il $16.99

Grades: PreK K　　　　　　　　　　　　　　**E**
　　1. Babysitters -- Fiction
　　ISBN 978-0-7636-5091-9; 0-7636-5091-9
　　　　　　　　　　　　　　　　LC 2010011454

Lily's mother is sick and her father must go to work, but she does not want to stay with a babysitter, even if it means playing with cute baby Sam, sweet little dog Ringo, and fun big brother Jack.

Hughes's "unadorned narration exudes empathy for the dislocated Lily. . . . And her densely textured, saturated gouache images . . . make a strong case that the right people can make any situation feel homey. . . . Lily's gradual acceptance of the situation unfolds naturally and believably." Publ Wkly

Ella's big chance; a Jazz-Age Cinderella. [by] Shirley Hughes. Simon & Schuster Books for Young Readers 2004 un il $16.95

Grades: K 1 2 3 E
1. Fairy tales
ISBN 0-689-87399-9

LC 2003-27274

In this version of the Cinderella tale set in the 1920s, Ella has two men courting her—the handsome Duke of Arc and Buttons the delivery boy

"Hughes's gouache-and-pen-line illustrations exhibit her usual meticulous attention to detail. . . . This insightful retelling also offers a fascinating visual peek at a glamorous time." SLJ

Jonadab and Rita. Red Fox 2011 il pa $11.99
Grades: PreK K 1 E
1. Toys -- Fiction 2. Magic -- Fiction 3. Fairies -- Fiction
ISBN 978-1-86-230313-3; 1-86-230313-4

Jonadab is a very special toy donkey who can fly. But Minnie has so many other toys that often Jonadab and his friend Rita the mouse find themselves sad and lonely and left behind in the toy box. One moonlit night, tired of being ignored, Jonadab flies away and joins a magical fairy feast. But then he can't get back in to Minnie's room.

"Colorful illustrations cover half of each page while the text is set off in rectangular boxes highlighted with small black pen-and-ink sketches featuring characters from the tale. . . . This quiet fantasy will be welcomed by [Hughes'] many fans." SLJ

Olly and me 1 2 3. Candlewick Press 2009 un il $16.99
Grades: PreK K 1 2 E
1. Counting 2. Siblings -- Fiction
ISBN 978-0-7636-4016-3; 0-7636-4016-6

LC 2008-934556

"Hughes warms up this counting book with appealing characters and colorful action scenes. On the first page, which begins with a big numeral 1 and one large dot, a little girl named Katie introduces herself. On the next, with the numeral 2 and and two large dots, she is joined by her baby brother, Olly. . . . On the pages that follow, more family members, friends, neighbors, and pets join the siblings. . . . The line drawings depict characters with a certain air of rumpled reality that makes Hughes' artwork so endearing and enduring." Booklist

Hughes, Ted, 1930-1998
My brother Bert; pictures by Tracey Campbell Pearson. Farrar, Straus & Giroux 2009 un il $16.95
Grades: PreK K 1 E
1. Stories in rhyme 2. Children's poetry 3. Pets -- Fiction 4. Animals -- Fiction 5. Siblings -- Fiction
ISBN 978-0-374-39982-5; 0-374-39982-4

LC 2007034415

Illustrations and rhyming text portray a hobby gone awry, as Bert's collection of exotic pets seems on the verge of breaking into a quarrel, and perhaps a rumpus, as well.

"Full of action, merriment, and wit, the pictures will occupy children with always one more thing to see. . . . Dizzying and delightful." Booklist

Hughes, Vi
Once upon a bathtime. Tradewind Books 2010 un il $17.95

Grades: PreK K 1 E
1. Baths -- Fiction
ISBN 978-1-896580-5-48; 1-896580-5-48

As a child takes a bath and gets ready for bed, characters from fairy tales accompany the child.

"This picture book is told in simple, elegant verse and illustrated with paper-cut collage artwork." SLJ

Huneck, Stephen
★ **Sally** goes to the beach; written and illustrated by Stephen Huneck. Abrams 2000 un il $17.95
Grades: PreK K 1 E
1. Dogs 2. Beaches 3. Dogs -- Fiction 4. Beaches -- Fiction 5. Dogs -- Juvenile fiction
ISBN 0-8109-4186-4

LC 99-28421

Sally, a black Labrador retriever, goes to the beach, where she enjoys various activities with other visiting dogs

"The playful pup's enjoyment is conveyed through a simple but engaging text and beautiful, full-page woodblock prints." SLJ

Other titles about Sally are:
Sally goes to the mountains (2001)
Sally goes to the farm (2002)
Sally goes to the vet (2004)
Sally's snow adventure (2006)
Sally gets a job (2008)
Sally's great balloon adventure (2010)

Hunt, Julie
Precious Little; [by] Julie Hunt & Sue Moss; pictures by Gaye Chapman. Allen & Unwin 2011 un il $16.99
Grades: K 1 2 3 E
1. Circus -- Fiction 2. Acrobats and acrobatics -- Fiction
ISBN 978-1-74175-147-5; 1-74175-147-0

LC 2011290332

"A tatterdemalion heroine wearing rags and stars falls into a dream hole and flies through the heavens. Precious Little works for the Light Fantastics, watching the contortionists, Knots-RUs, and the fire-eaters, Flambé and the Infernos, but longing to fly. Her friends Fat Chance and Tough Luck draw a wire across the 'lucky dip,' and she begins to cross it. . . . The text swirls and makes loop-the-loops all over the pages, necessitating constant turning, all the better to pore over the spectacular art. . . . Children (and adults) can be lost for a long and pleasurable time amid the sparkles." Kirkus

Hurd, Edith Thacher
★ **Johnny** Lion's book; pictures by Clement Hurd. new ed.; HarperCollins Pubs. 2001 63p il (I can read book) hardcover o.p. pa $3.99
Grades: PreK K 1 E
1. Lions 2. Books and reading 3. Lions -- Fiction 4. Animals -- Infancy
ISBN 0-06-029334-9 lib bdg; 0-06-444297-7 pa

A reissue of the title first published 1965

When his parents go out hunting, Johnny Lion stays home and experiences exciting adventures reading a book about a baby lion who goes out into the world and gets lost

"A subtle boost for the joys of reading in a story with engaging illustrations." Booklist

Other titles about Johnny Lion are:
Johnny Lion's bad day (1970)

Johnny Lion's rubber boots (1972)

Hurd, Thacher

★ **Art** dog. HarperCollins Pubs. 1996 un il $15.99;
pa $6.99

Grades: PreK K 1 2   E

1. Dogs -- Fiction 2. Artists -- Fiction
ISBN 0-06-024424-0; 0-06-443489-3 pa

LC 95-31092

When the Mona Woofa is stolen from the Dogopolis Museum of Art, a mysterious character who calls himself Art Dog tracks down and captures the thieves

"This is exuberantly drawn by Hurd, who has imbued Art Dog with the flash and dash every artist feels at times; but Hurd also captures the shyness that comes with displaying your art. Kids will respond not just to the pictures but also to a story that does as well with characters as with plot." Booklist

Bad frogs. Candlewick Press 2009 un il $15.99
Grades: PreK K 1 2   E

1. Frogs -- Fiction
ISBN 978-0-7636-3253-3; 0-7636-3253-8

"Hurd's bad frogs—170 of them—revel in mischievous conduct and generate chaos wherever they go. Whether jumping in muck, slurping ice cream, burping at the dinner table, fighting with toothbrushes, or skateboarding down stair railings, the delightfully green, yellow-tinged characters prance across the pages in an array of costumes, entertaining viewers with their antics. The artwork gleams with Hurd's shiny bright colors, and his swinging text, presented in bold purple, trumpets the frogs' badness as they romp through the action-packed illustrations." SLJ

Mama don't allow; starring Miles and the Swamp Band. Harper & Row 1984 un il hardcover o.p. pa $5.99
Grades: PreK K 1 2   E

1. Alligators -- Fiction 2. Bands (Music) -- Fiction
ISBN 0-06-022690-0 lib bdg; 0-06-443078-2 pa

LC 83-47703

Miles and the Swamp Band have the time of their lives playing at the Alligator Ball, until they discover the menu includes Swamp Band soup

"The multi-colored full-spread watercolor illustrations are stunningly bright and full of movement, far outpacing the story line in energy and imagination." SLJ

The **weaver**; pictures by Elisa Kleven. Farrar Straus Giroux 2010 un il $16.99
Grades: PreK K 1 2   E

1. Dreams -- Fiction 2. Weaving -- Fiction
ISBN 978-0-374-38254-4; 0-374-38254-9

LC 2008028533

High above the world, a weaver spins thread from such things as clouds, dyes it with colors from the sky and grass, and weaves a cloth filled with the emotions she sees throughout the day to make a blanket of dreams.

"The fanciful illustrations reflect the story's sense of celebration, portraying children, their families, and friends sharing small but significant moments in a kaleidoscope of springtime colors. Tiny characters of all nationalities enjoy life in a sun-drenched landscape while the gentle weaver and her adorable gray kitten watch from above. This dreamy story offers a reassuring message of love and security." SLJ

Hurst, Carol Otis

Rocks in his head; pictures by James Stevenson. Greenwillow Bks. 2001 un il $15.99; lib bdg $15.89
Grades: PreK K 1 2   E

1. Depressions -- 1929 2. Rocks -- Collectors and collecting 3. Rocks -- Collection and preservation
ISBN 0-06-029403-5; 0-06-029404-3 lib bdg

LC 00-56197

Hurst "recounts the story of her father, an avid rock collector from the time he was a boy. . . . Dominated by earth tones, Stevenson's artwork convincingly evokes both the personality of this endearing protagonist and the period in which he lived." Publ Wkly

★ **Terrible** storm; [illustrated by] S. D. Schindler. Greenwillow Books 2007 un il $16.99; lib bdg $17.89
Grades: K 1 2 3   E

1. Blizzards -- Fiction 2. Grandfathers -- Fiction
ISBN 978-0-06-009001-2; 0-06-009001-4; 978-0-06-009002-9 lib bdg; 0-06-009002-2 lib bdg

LC 2005-35731

"Humor is everywhere, but the funniest pictures show the men shoveling out of the snow, passing one another through the drifts. This lively, clever story, based on a real storm, neatly captures both the oddities of nature and how differing natures view the same event." Booklist

Hurwitz, Johanna

New shoes for Silvia; illustrated by Jerry Pinkney. Morrow Junior Bks. 1993 un il $17.99; lib bdg $16.89
Grades: PreK K 1 2   E

1. Shoes -- Fiction
ISBN 0-688-05286-X; 0-688-05287-8 lib bdg

LC 92-40868

Silvia receives a pair of beautiful red shoes from her Tia Rosita and finds different uses for them until she grows enough for them to fit

"This simple story, told in spare prose, speaks universally to the imagination and emotions. Pinkney's spirited watercolors animate the narrative and are large enough for group sharing." SLJ

Husband, Amy

Dear teacher. Sourcebooks Jabberwocky 2010 un il pa $8.99
Grades: K 1 2   E

1. School stories 2. Letters -- Fiction
ISBN 978-1-4022-4268-7 pa; 1-4022-4268-9 pa

"Each vertical, double-page spread in this inventive title is a letter from young Michael to his new teacher explaining why he may be late for the first day of school. . . . The wild, colorful illustrations show the imaginative play, and kids with back-to-school panic will find comic relief in these over-the-top scenes." Booklist

Hutchins, H. J.

Mattland; story by Hazel Hutchins and Gail Herbert; art by Dušan Petričić. Annick Press 2008 un il $19.95; pa $8.95
Grades: K 1 2   E

1. Moving -- Fiction 2. Friendship -- Fiction 3. Imagination -- Fiction
ISBN 978-1-55451-121-1; 1-55451-121-6; 978-1-55451-120-4 pa; 1-55451-120-8 pa

"Matt finds himself in yet another new home. Surrounded by an uninspiring landscape and lacking friends, he begins to poke at the mud outside his house. He quickly notices in his marks the beginning of a landscape. Bit by bit, a miniature world unfolds before Matt. . . . When a rainstorm threatens to flood the newly created 'Mattland,' helping hands appear to route the current safely away. Petričić's understated watercolors are an essential counterpart to Hutchins and Herbert's mature narrative. . . . The illustrator skillfully leads readers from gray, nondescript images to a detailed world brimming with color." SLJ

Hutchins, Pat

 1 hunter. Greenwillow Bks. 1982 un il hardcover o.p. pa $6.99
Grades: PreK K 1 2   **E**
 1. Counting 2. Animals -- Fiction
 ISBN 0-688-00614-0; 0-688-06522-8 pa

          LC 81-6352
"Humorous illustrations done in a flat, clear style make an outstanding counting book." Horn Book

 ★ **Rosie's** walk. Macmillan 1968 un il $16.95; pa $6.99
Grades: PreK K 1   **E**
 1. Foxes -- Fiction 2. Chickens -- Fiction
 ISBN 0-02-745850-4; 0-02-043750-1 pa

"Rosie the hen goes for a walk around the farm and gets home in time for dinner, completely unaware that a fox has been hot on her heels every step of the way. The viewer knows, however, and is not only held in suspense but tickled by the ways in which the fox is foiled at every turn by the unwitting hen. A perfect choice for the youngest." Booklist

 Ten red apples. Greenwillow Bks. 2000 un il $17.99; lib bdg $18.89
Grades: PreK K 1   **E**
 1. Apples 2. Counting 3. Animal sounds 4. Domestic animals 5. Stories in rhyme 6. Apples -- Fiction 7. Domestic animals -- Fiction
 ISBN 0-688-16797-7; 0-688-16798-5 lib bdg

          LC 99-25065
In rhyming verses, one animal after another neighs, moos, oinks, quacks and makes other appropriate sounds as each eats an apple from the farmer's tree

"A concept book that blends rhyming, counting, repetition, and animal sounds into a charming, folksy story. . . . The gouache paintings are bright and clear." SLJ

 ★ **We're** going on a picnic! Greenwillow Bks. 2002 un il $15.95; lib bdg $15.89
Grades: PreK K 1 2   **E**
 1. Ducks -- Fiction 2. Chickens -- Fiction
 ISBN 0-688-16799-3; 0-688-16800-0 lib bdg

          LC 00-62225
"With an understated humor infusing both narrative and pictures, Hutchins successfully pulls off the child-pleasing contrivance of letting readers in on the secret." Publ Wkly

 ★ The **doorbell** rang. Greenwillow Bks. 1986 un il $15.99; lib bdg $16.89; pa $5.99

Grades: PreK K 1 2   **E**
 1. Cookies -- Fiction 2. Division -- Fiction
 ISBN 0-688-05251-7; 0-688-05252-5 lib bdg; 0-688-09234-9 pa

          LC 85-12615
"Bright, joyous, dynamic, this wonderfully humorous piece of realism for the young is presented simply but with style and imagination." Horn Book

Hyde, Heidi Smith

 Feivel's flying horses; illustrated by Johanna van der Sterre. Kar-Ben Pub. 2010 un il lib bdg $17.95; pa $7.95
Grades: PreK K 1 2   **E**
 1. Jews -- Fiction 2. Carousels -- Fiction 3. Immigrants -- Fiction 4. Wood carving -- Fiction
 ISBN 978-0-7613-3957-1; 0-7613-3957-4; 978-0-7613-3959-5 pa; 0-7613-3959-0 pa

         LC 2008033480
A Jewish immigrant who is saving money to bring his wife and children to join him in America creates ornate horses for a carousel on Coney Island, one for each member of his family.

"Watercolor illustrations with ink lines illustrate the immigrant experience on New York's Lower East Side in the late 1800s and help bring to life the magic of Coney Island." SLJ

Ichikawa, Satomi

 ★ **Come** fly with me; [by] Satomi Ichikawa. Philomel Books 2008 un il $15.99
Grades: PreK K 1   **E**
 1. Dogs -- Fiction 2. Toys -- Fiction 3. Airplanes -- Fiction
 ISBN 978-0-399-24679-1

         LC 2007023643
Woggy and Cosmos, a toy dog and a toy airplane, go on an adventure in Paris.

"The adventure element is perfectly keyed to the age group. . . . The charming watercolors with their everchanging scenes and skies will pull [children] in." Booklist

 La La Rose. Philomel Books 2004 un il $15.99
Grades: PreK K 1 2   **E**
 1. Gardens -- Fiction 2. Lost and found possessions -- Fiction
 ISBN 0-399-24029-2

         LC 2002-15366
La La Rose, a young girl's stuffed rabbit, gets lost in Luxembourg Gardens in Paris.

"Ichikawa's ink-and-watercolor paintings are a wonderful mix of action and thoughtfulness, sweetness and subtlety that extend the story and give it life past a first reading. . . . A very satisfying story that also captures the magic and excitement of a special place." Booklist

 My father's shop. Kane/Miller 2006 un il $15.95
Grades: K 1 2 3   **E**
 1. Roosters -- Fiction 2. Rugs and carpets -- Fiction 3. Father-son relationship -- Fiction
 ISBN 1-929132-99-9

"When given a flawed carpet, Mustafa . . . drums up business for his merchant father by attracting first a similarly colored rooster, then numerous trourists who crow in their own languages: 'Co-co-ri-co!' 'Qui-qui-ri-qui!' and

'Cock-a-doodle-do!' The multicultural message is light and the humor contagious. Bright scenes of the crowded Moroccan marketplace amplify the story." Horn Book Guide

My little train. Philomel Books 2010 un il $15.99
Grades: PreK K 1   E
1. Toys -- Fiction 2. Animals -- Fiction 3. Railroads -- Fiction
ISBN 978-0-399-25453-6; 0-399-25453-6
A little train goes for a ride, taking all the stuffed animals where they want to go.
"Ichikawa's soft watercolors reveal destinations that are ripped from kids' playtime imaginations. . . . Repeated animal noises and train sounds encourage readers to lend their voices to this whimsical read-aloud." Publ Wkly

My pig Amarillo. Philomel Bks. 2003 un il $15.99
Grades: PreK K 1 2   E
1. Pets 2. Pigs 3. Kites 4. Pigs -- Fiction
ISBN 0-399-23768-2
LC 2002-7318
Original French edition, 2002
Pablito, a Guatemalan boy whose pet pig Amarillo has disappeared, uses a kite to send him a message that he still loves him
"Ichikawa uses her Guatemalan setting very effectively, but she also wraps the story in universal emotions: love, longing, grief, hope. The pen-and-watercolor artwork brings children close to all facets of Pablito's story." Booklist

Idle, Molly

Flora and the flamingo; by Molly Idle. Chronicle Books 2013 44 p. col. ill. (reinforced) $16.99
Grades: PreK K 1   E
1. Stories without words 2. Dance -- Juvenile fiction 3. Picture books for children 4. Dance -- Fiction 5. Flamingos -- Fiction 6. Flamingos -- Juvenile fiction 7. Human-animal relationships -- Fiction 8. Human-animal relationships -- Juvenile fiction
ISBN 1452110069; 9781452110066
LC 2012014608
"In this . . . wordless picture book with interactive flaps, [by Molly Idle,] Flora and her graceful flamingo friend explore the trials and joys of friendship through an elaborate synchronized dance. With a twist, a turn, and even a flop, these unlikely friends learn at last how to dance together in perfect harmony." (Publisher's note)

Tea Rex; by Molly Idle. Viking 2013 40 p. ill. (hardcover) $16.99
Grades: PreK K 1   E
1. Afternoon teas -- Juvenile fiction 2. Humorous fiction -- Juvenile fiction 3. Tyrannosaurus Rex -- Juvenile fiction 4. Humorous stories 5. Parties -- Fiction 6. Dinosaurs -- Fiction 7. Etiquette -- Fiction 8. Tyrannosaurus rex -- Fiction
ISBN 0670014303; 9780670014309
LC 2012016443
This children's story, by Molly Idle, describes a tea party between children and a Tyrannosaurus rex. "Some tea parties are for grown-ups. Some are for girls. But this tea party is for a very special guest. And it is important to follow some rules . . . like providing comfortable chairs, and good conversation, and yummy food. But sometimes that is not

enough for special guests, especially when their manners are more Cretaceous than gracious." (Publisher's note)

Il Sung Na

★ **Snow** rabbit, spring rabbit; a book of changing seasons. Alfred A. Knopf 2011 un il $15.99; lib bdg $18.99
Grades: PreK K 1   E
1. Winter -- Fiction 2. Animals -- Fiction 3. Rabbits -- Fiction 4. Seasons -- Juvenile literature 5. Animal behavior -- Juvenile literature
ISBN 0-375-86786-4; 0-375-96786-9 lib bdg; 978-0-375-86786-6; 978-0-375-96786-3 lib bdg
LC 2010-09361
First published 2010 in the United Kingdom with title: A book of winter
While other animals migrate, hibernate, or stay busy all winter, a little white rabbit watches.
"Complex and ethereal at the same time, Na's digitally manipulated spreads feature collage, stenciling, and finger painting over thickly daubed backgrounds; the pages teem with interest and texture." Publ Wkly

Imai, Ayano

Chester. Minedition 2007 un il $16.99
Grades: PreK K   E
1. Dogs -- Fiction
ISBN 978-0-698-40062-7
"Chester, a black-and-white dog with a serious mein, loves his family, but they seem to have forgotten about him. Unhappy, he puts his doghouse on his head and leaves. . . . Imai . . . has produced a small gem. The story . . . is illustrated in delicate watercolors that nonetheless project force both in action and emotion." Booklist

Ingalls, Ann

The **little** piano girl; by Ann Ingalls & Maryann Macdonald; illustrated by Giselle Potter. Houghton Mifflin Books for Children 2010 un il
Grades: K 1 2 3   E
1. Pianists 2. Composers 3. Jazz musicians 4. Pianists -- Fiction 5. Jazz musicians -- Fiction 6. Jazz -- Juvenile literature 7. African American musicians -- Fiction 8. Biography, Individual -- Juvenile literature
ISBN 0-618-95974-2; 978-0-618-95974-7
LC 2008040457
This story depicts the life of the American pianist and composer. "Grades one to five." (SLJ)
Potter's "gouache paintings provide a vivid portrait of industrial Pittsburgh at the beginning of the 20th century, yet have an iconic quality too. Ingalls and MacDonald provide a touching memorial to a jazz great who is not a household name—a valuable contribution." Publ Wkly

Ingman, Bruce

When Martha's away. Candlewick Press 2010 un il $16.99
Grades: PreK K 1 2   E
1. Cats -- Fiction
ISBN 978-0-7636-5135-0; 0-7636-5135-4
A reissue of the title first published 1995 by Houghton Mifflin
Martha's cat reveals that he does not sleep all day, as she believes, but rather has a very busy schedule of activities.

"With humor and sponaneity, the large, spacious illustrations combine line drawings, simple shapes, and bright textured colors." Horn Book Guide

Intriago, Patricia
★ **Dot**. Farrar Straus Giroux 2011 un il $14.99
Grades: PreK K 1   E
1. Opposites
ISBN 978-0-374-31835-2; 0-374-31835-2
LC 2010019816
"Even two and three-year-olds will make astute observations. . . . Children will encounter ample ways to interact with this incredibly elegant, clever, and delightful concept book." SLJ

Isaacs, Anne
★ **Dust** Devil; illustrated by Paul O. Zelinsky. Schwartz & Wade 2010 un il $17.99
Grades: K 1 2 3   E
1. Tall tales 2. Frontier and pioneer life -- Fiction
ISBN 0-375-86722-8; 978-0-375-86722-4
Having moved to Montana from Tennessee in the 1830s, fearless Angelica Longrider—also known as Swamp Angel—changes the state's landscape, tames a wild horse, and captures some desperadoes.
"Isaac's far-fetched tall tale is again paired with Zelinsky's stunning American-primitive paintings, framed by the wood upon which they are painted. . . . Zelinsky's action-packed panoramas capture Angel's Paul Bunyanlike strength. . . . Isaacs wraps her narrative in exaggeration that will have kids howling." Publ Wkly

Pancakes for supper! illustrated by Mark Teague. Scholastic Press 2006 un il $15.99
Grades: PreK K 1   E
1. Animals -- Fiction 2. New England -- Fiction
ISBN 0-439-64483-6
LC 2005-14532
In the backwoods of New England, a young girl cleverly fends off the threats of wild animals by trading her clothes for her safety.
"Isaacs's clever, respectful take on an iconic tale is testament to its appeal. Teague's pictures are brilliant, cinematic full-bleed oil-paint dramas that capture the essence of a nascent New England spring." SLJ

★ **Swamp** Angel; illustrated by Paul O. Zelinsky. Dutton Children's Bks. 1994 un il $16.99; pa $6.99
Grades: K 1 2 3   E
1. Tall tales 2. Frontier and pioneer life -- Fiction
ISBN 0-525-45271-0; 0-14-055908-6 pa
LC 93-43956
A Caldecott Medal honor book, 1995
Along with other amazing feats, Angelica Longrider, also known as Swamp Angel, wrestles a huge bear, known as Thundering Tarnation, to save the winter supplies of the settlers in Tennessee
"Isaacs tells her original story with the glorious exaggeration and uproarious farce of the traditional tall tale and with its typical laconic idiom—you just can't help reading it aloud. . . . Zelinsky's detailed oil paintings in folk-art style are exquisite, framed in cherry, maple, and birch wood grains." Booklist
Another title about Swamp Angel is:

Dust Devil (2010)

Isadora, Rachel
Bea at ballet; Rachel Isadora. Nancy Paulsen Books 2012 32 p. col. ill. (hardcover) $12.99
Grades: PreK K 1   E
1. Ballet -- Fiction 2. Picture books for children 3. Dance -- Study and teaching -- Fiction 4. Ballet dancing -- Fiction
ISBN 0399254099; 9780399254093
LC 2011046803
This children's picture book offers a "primer" about ballet for preschool children. The illustrations "present the preschoolers in black, white, and gray line with bursts of color in wardrobe and accessories, which [author Rachel Isadora] explains piece by piece, for each gender. The class instruction includes labels for the barre, mirror, piano, the five classic positions, and four foot movements (point, flex, flat, relevé)." (School Library Journal)

★ **Ben's** trumpet. Greenwillow Bks. 1979 un il $17.99; pa $6.99
Grades: PreK K 1 2   E
1. Musicians -- Fiction 2. African Americans -- Fiction
ISBN 0-688-80194-3; 0-688-10988-8 pa
LC 78-12885
A Caldecott Medal honor book, 1980
This is the story of Ben, a boy whose dream is to be a jazz trumpeter but who is too poor to own an instrument until a real musician, remembering his own dreams, puts one into the boy's hands
"The art is astonishingly varied in its brilliant recreation—in the margins, in the urban backgrounds—of the commercial art of the 20's and 30's." N Y Times Book Rev

Happy belly, happy smile. Harcourt Children's Books 2009 un il $16
Grades: PreK K 1   E
1. Restaurants -- Fiction 2. Grandfathers -- Fiction 3. Chinese Americans -- Fiction
ISBN 978-0-15-206546-1; 0-15-206546-6
LC 2008046221
Sitting in the kitchen of his grandfather's Chinese restaurant, a young boy enjoys watching the chefs and waiters prepare and serve mouth-watering dishes
"Isadora's characteristic collage-and-oil illustrations [are] attractive as always. . . . This brief bite of Chinese cuisine will add flavor to cuisine-themed story hours." Booklist

★ **Max**; story & pictures by Rachel Isadora. Macmillan 1976 un il hardcover o.p. pa $5.99
Grades: PreK K 1 2   E
1. Ballet -- Fiction 2. Baseball -- Fiction
ISBN 0-02-043800-1 pa
LC 76-9088
Max "is the star of his baseball team. On a Saturday morning, he has time to spare before his game and accepts (with some hidden disdain) the invitation of his sister, Lisa, to watch her ballet class in action. Max is surprised to find himself interested and happy to join the students at their teacher's suggestion. . . . The experience pays off at the ball park where Max hits a home run. Now he warms up for the game each week at Lisa's dancing class. The pictures are an ebullient combination of grace and comedy, with the leggy

students dipping and soaring, in contrast to Max in his uniform." Publ Wkly

Peekaboo bedtime. G.P. Putnam's Sons 2008 un il $16.99

Grades: PreK   E

1. Bedtime -- Fiction 2. Toddlers -- Fiction

ISBN 978-0-399-24384-4; 0-399-24384-4

LC 2007-34814

A toddler plays peekaboo with parents, grandparents, toys, and the moon while getting ready for bed.

"The pastel illustrations are a delight, a visual celebration of family. . . . Perfect for laptime sharing or calm story hours." Kirkus

Say hello! G.P. Putnam's Sons 2010 un il $16.99

Grades: PreK K 1   E

1. City and town life -- Fiction 2. Language and languages -- Fiction

ISBN 978-0-399-25230-3; 0-399-25230-4

LC 2009011318

A little girl greets people in her neighborhood in many different languages.

"The text is paired down to essentials and the striking collage-style illustrations are colorful and dynamic. Richly patterned with oil paints as well as printed patterns, the cut-paper shapes show up vividly against the white backgrounds." Booklist

Uh-oh! Harcourt 2008 un il $16

Grades: PreK   E

1. Toddlers -- Fiction 2. African Americans -- Fiction

ISBN 978-0-15-205765-7; 0-15-205765-X

LC 2006039652

As an African American toddler keeps getting into mischief throughout the day, the reader is invited to discover what the trouble is with each page-turn and to say "uh-oh."

This offers "homey, vibrantly colored pastel illustrations. . . . Young listeners . . . [will] get a charge from each thrilling descent into disarray." Horn Book

The **ugly** duckling; written by Hans Christian Andersen; retold and illustrated by Rachel Isadora. G.P. Putnam's Sons 2009 un il $16.99

Grades: 1 2 3 4   E

1. Authors 2. Novelists 3. Dramatists 4. Fairy tales 5. Ducks -- Fiction 6. Swans -- Fiction 7. Children's authors 8. Short story writers

ISBN 978-0-399-25029-3; 0-399-25029-8

LC 2008036514

In this retelling of the Ugly Duckling, set on the African continent, the duckling spends an unhappy year ostracized by the other animals before he grows into a beautiful swan.

"What shines in this telling are the illustrations, all collage spreads executed in oil on palette paper and printed paper. . . . Isadora's brilliant colors and broad brushstrokes beautifully capture the unnamed African setting." SLJ

Isol

It's useful to have a duck; It's useful to have a boy. Groundwood Books 2009 un il $10

Grades: PreK K 1 2 3   E

1. Board books for children 2. Ducks -- Fiction

ISBN 978-0-88899-927-6; 0-88899-927-5

"Why on earth is it useful to have a duck? In a series of accordioned spreads on yellow board, a little boy reveals the answers, accompanied by swift line sketches that illustrate them. . . . The verso, on blue board, . . . is titled It's Useful to Have a Boy, [and] the identical images receive a very different gloss in the duck's voice. . . . Do not be deceived by the simple-looking board format: This is not for babies. Rather, it challenges children who have accepted the initial premise with developmentally appropriate narcissism to regard the world from the opposite perspective. Gently mind-bending, this playful Mexican import, packaged in a slipcase, will get readers thinking." Kirkus

Petit, the monster; words and pictures by Isol; translated by Elisa Amado. Groundwood Books 2010 un il $16.95

Grades: PreK K   E

1. Good and evil -- Fiction

ISBN 978-0-88899-947-4; 0-88899-947-X

"Poor Petit is a little confused: sometimes he's a good boy and sometimes he's a bad boy, and that's a hard contradiction to work out. . . . Argentinian author-illustrator Isol touches imaginatively on the challenging complexities of behavioral morality, and the book gains special traction from going into failed intentions and contrary correlations . . . while keeping the concept easily kid-accessible. Isol's quirky illustrations feature pencil and oil pastels . . . while computer planes of color fill in figures and backgrounds. . . . Kids will appreciate this playful approach to one of their biggest moral conundrums." Bull Cent Child Books

Isop, Laurie

How do you hug a porcupine? illustrated by Gwen Millward. Simon & Schuster Books for Young Readers 2011 il $15.99

Grades: PreK K 1   E

1. Stories in rhyme 2. Animals -- Fiction 3. Hugging -- Fiction 4. Porcupines -- Fiction

ISBN 978-1-4424-1291-0; 1-4424-1291-7

LC 2010006941

A child figures out the best way to hug a porcupine as he watches his friends hug other animals.

"The spare, interactive text and clear, uncluttered illustrations . . . make this a natural for group sharing." Booklist

Ives, Penny

★ **Celestine,** drama queen. Arthur A. Levine Books 2009 un il $16.99

Grades: PreK K   E

1. Ducks -- Fiction 2. Theater -- Fiction

ISBN 978-0-545-08149-8; 0-545-08149-1

Celestine the duck is sure that she is destined for stardom, but when her big break comes, she is temporarily stricken with stage fright.

Celestine "captures the essence of children, their emotions, and how they cope. Adorable, annoying, and utterly childlike, Celestine is appealingly portrayed in Ives' funny, sunny watercolors." Booklist

Iwai, Melissa

★ **Soup** day. Henry Holt 2010 un il $12.99

Grades: PreK K 1 2   E

1. Soups -- Fiction 2. Cooking -- Fiction 3. Vegetables

-- Fiction 4. Mother-daughter relationship -- Fiction
ISBN 978-0-8050-9004-8; 0-8050-9004-5

LC 2009029314

A mother and daughter spend a snowy day together buying and preparing vegetables, assembling ingredients, and playing while their big pot of soup bubbles on the stove. Includes a recipe for "Snowy Day Vegetable Soup."

"With economical text and vivid, multitextured collages whose upbeat charm belies their sophistication, the process of preparing the dish unfolds. In one spread, Iwai cleverly offers lessons about numbers, colors, sizes, textures, and what various vegetables look like. . . . . A perfect meal and a perfect book." SLJ

Iwamatsu, Atushi Jun

Crow Boy; [by] Taro Yashima. Viking 1955 37p il lib bdg $17.99; pa $5.99

Grades: PreK K 1 2   E

1. School stories

ISBN 0-670-24931-9 lib bdg; 0-14-050172-X pa

A Caldecott Medal honor book, 1956

"A moving story interpreted by the author's distinctive illustrations, valuable for human relations and for its picture of Japanese school life." Hodges. Books for Elem Sch Libr

Umbrella; [by] Taro Yashima. Viking 1958 30p il $16.99; pa $6.99

Grades: PreK K 1   E

1. Umbrellas and parasols -- Fiction

ISBN 0-670-73858-1; 0-14-050240-8 pa

A Caldecott Medal honor book, 1959

In this simple tale, young children "will be carried along by their identification with the actions of this very real little girl. . . . . The beauty of the book makes this worthwhile." Horn Book

Iwamura, Kazuo

Bedtime in the forest. North-South Books 2010 un il $16.95

Grades: PreK K   E

1. Owls -- Fiction 2. Bedtime -- Fiction 3. Squirrels -- Fiction

ISBN 978-0-7358-2310-5; 0-7358-2310-3

Original Japanese edition 1982

Mick, Mack, and Molly, three young squirrels, find themselves awake and wanting to play all night like the owl children and learn that they should be going to bed instead.

"This unpretentious story with lovely art and endearing animals will be enjoyed by young children." SLJ

Jackson, Alison

Desert Rose and her highfalutin hog; illustrated by Keith Graves. Walker & Co. 2009 un il $16.99; lib bdg $17.89

Grades: K 1 2 3   E

1. Tall tales 2. Animals -- Fiction

ISBN 978-0-8027-9833-6; 0-8027-9833-0; 978-0-8027-9834-3 lib bdg; 0-8027-9834-9 lib bdg

LC 2009000206

Upon finding a large gold nugget on her pig farm, Desert Rose sets out to buy the biggest, fattest hog in Texas to enter in the state fair, but first she must get the hog to Laredo and every animal she asks for help is just as "ornery" as the hog

"The cartoon style of the acrylic illustrations accentuates the alliterative text. Youngsters will laugh out loud." SLJ

Thea's tree; [by] Alison Jackson; illustrated by Janet Pedersen. Dutton Children's Books 2008 un il $15.99

Grades: K 1 2 3   E

1. Plants -- Fiction 2. Science projects -- Fiction

ISBN 978-0-525-47443-2; 0-525-47443-9

LC 2007-5220

Thea Teawinkle plants an odd, purple, bean-shaped seed in her backyard for her class science project, with astonishing results that even the experts she writes to—including a botanist, an arborist, a museum curator, and a symphony director—cannot offer any explanations for.

"Pedersen's energetic, full-page watercolor illustrations capture the hilarious consequences of Thea's growing crisis." SLJ

The **ballad** of Valentine; illustrated by Tricia Tusa. Dutton Children's Bks. 2001 un il $16.99; pa $6.99

Grades: K 1 2 3   E

1. Valentines 2. Stories in rhyme 3. Valentines -- Fiction

ISBN 0-525-46720-3; 0-14-240400-4 pa

LC 2001-42737

An ardent suitor tries various means of communication, from smoke signals to Morse code to skywriting, in order to get his message to his Valentine

"Tusa uses sketchy, wispy lines to create loads of droll details that are both funny and subtle. . . . Jackson and Tusa make perfect harmony here—the cadence and rhythm of text and the watercolor artwork are right on pitch." Booklist

Jackson, Shelley

★ **Mimi's** Dada Catifesto. Clarion Books 2009 41p il $17

Grades: 1 2 3 4   E

1. Cats -- Fiction 2. Dadaism -- Fiction

ISBN 978-0-547-12681-4; 0-547-12681-6

LC 2008-39486

In Zurich, Switzerland, an artistic cat finds the perfect owner in fellow Dadaist, Mr. Dada. Author's note provides background on the Dadaist art movement.

"Children . . . may not know much about the artistic movement Dada but . . . all (well perhaps not all) becomes clear through Jackson's zingy text and wildly inventive art. . . . With pictures inspired by many artists, including Marcel Duchamp, it's the art that will get kids to sit up and take notice. A mix of collage, fantastical and realistic drawings, and offbeat design work, the illustrations are played against a variety of fonts and typefaces, designed to keep the reader off balance." Booklist

Jacobs, Paul DuBois

Fire drill; [by] Paul DuBois Jacobs and Jennifer Swender; illustrated by Huy Voun Lee. Henry Holt and Company 2010 un il $15.99

Grades: PreK K 1   E

1. School stories 2. Stories in rhyme 3. Fire drills -- Fiction 4. Safety education -- Fiction

ISBN 978-0-8050-8953-0; 0-8050-8953-5

LC 2009005268

In this story told in brief rhyming text, students in a class follow the proper procedures during a fire drill.

"Simple rhyming text paired with colorful, upbeat art offer children an accessible overview of fire-drill rules... . Appealing, cheerful illustrations in elemental shapes and colors and vibrant patterns portray the multicultural group and familiar school settings." Booklist

Jadoul, Emile
Good night, Chickie. Eerdmans Books for Young Readers 2011 un il $13.99
Grades: PreK K   E
1. Bedtime -- Fiction 2. Chickens -- Fiction 3. Parent-child relationship -- Fiction
ISBN 978-0-8028-5378-3; 0-8028-5378-1
LC 2010024985
Mother Hen reassures Chickie, and Chickie's bunny, that she is nearby and keeping watch over them at bedtime.
"Jadoul is a minimalist, but his big, rounded shapes, thick ink outlines, forceful brushstrokes, and expanses of bright colors do more visual and emotional work than a truckload of detail. . . . Jadoul strikes the right balance between flattering kids' independence and acknowledging their uncertainties." Publ Wkly

Jahn-Clough, Lisa
Felicity & Cordelia; a tale of two bunnies. Farrar Straus and Giroux 2010 un il $16.99
Grades: PreK K 1   E
1. Rabbits -- Fiction 2. Balloons -- Fiction 3. Friendship -- Fiction 4. Voyages and travels -- Fiction
ISBN 978-0-374-32300-4; 0-374-32300-3
LC 2009016143
Felicity Rose and Cordelia Bean are best friends, but they are separated when Felicity wants to go on a hot air balloon trip and Cordelia does not want to accompany her.
"Jahn-Clough's illustrations are, as ever, childlike, winsome, and boldly colored. Her story . . . reinforces the importance and interdependence of distinct personalities as well as the beauty of real friendship." SLJ

Little Dog; by Lisa Jahn-Clough. Houghton Mifflin 2006 un il $16
Grades: PreK K   E
1. Dogs -- Fiction 2. Artists -- Fiction
ISBN 978-0-618-57405-6; 0-618-57405-0
LC 2005020455
A lonely stray dog befriends a struggling artist, transforming her art and both their lives.
"The minimal text is accompanied by simple, childlike artwork, framed in and accented by heavy, black brush strokes." SLJ

Jalali, Reza
Moon watchers; Shirin's Ramadan miracle. illustrated by Anne Sibley O'Brien. Tilbury 2010 un il
Grades: 2 3 4   E
1. Muslims -- Fiction 2. Ramadan -- Fiction 3. Siblings -- Fiction 4. Family life -- Fiction
ISBN 0884483215; 9780884483212
Nine-year-old Shirin wants to join her family and other Muslims in fasting for Ramadan but is told she is too young, and so she seeks other ways to participate including, perhaps, getting along better with her older brother, Ali.
"O'Brien's watercolor illustrations evoke a culturally authentic Persian-American aesthetic, depicting warm char-

acters in a family setting. An explanation of Ramadan and Eid is given in the back matter. This is another wonderful contribution to the slowly increasing collection of fictional books on the observance of Ramadan and a great resource for librarians and teachers." SLJ

James, Simon
★ **Baby** Brains. Candlewick Press 2004 un il $15.99; pa $6.99
Grades: PreK K 1 2   E
1. Infants -- Fiction
ISBN 0-7636-2507-8; 0-7636-3682-7 pa
LC 2003-65528
Even though the new baby of Mr. and Mrs. Brains is very intelligent, they realize that he is still just a baby
"This tongue-in-cheek tale will tickle the funny bones of young listeners. The loose and playful lines of the watercolor-and-ink illustrations are used judiciously and to great effect." SLJ
Other titles about Baby Brains are:
Baby Brains superstar (2005)
Baby Brains and RoboMom (2008)

George flies south. Candlewick Press 2011 un il $16.99
Grades: PreK K   E
1. Birds -- Fiction 2. Flight -- Fiction
ISBN 978-0-7636-5724-6; 0-7636-5724-7
LC 2010049468
George does not feel ready to learn to fly, leave his nest, and go south with the other birds, despite his mother's encouragement, but when a strong autumn wind gets hold of the nest, he may have no choice.
This is an "understated yet action-packed story. . . . Beige and pale blue dominate the subtle palette of James's . . . minimalist ink and watercolor pictures, arranged in square and rectangular panels, full-page scenarios, and—when George at last takes flight—a sprawling double-page vista." Publ Wkly

Little One Step. Candlewick Press 2003 un il $15.99; bd bk $6.99
Grades: PreK K 1   E
1. Ducks -- Fiction 2. Brothers -- Fiction
ISBN 0-7636-2070-X; 0-7636-3520-0 bd bk
LC 2002-71407
As three duckling brothers cross forest and field to return to their mother, the older ones encourage the youngest by teaching him a game that earns him the name of Little One Step
"Abundant white space surrounds the line drawings suffused with buttery yellow and peach watercolor tones. . . . This satisfying tale about perseverance will find an eager audience at storytimes, on a parent's lap, and with independent readers." SLJ

Nurse Clementine; Simon James. Candlewick Press 2013 40 p. (reinforced) $15.99
Grades: PreK K   E
ISBN 9780763663827
LC 2012942668
In this picture book, "young Clementine is thrilled with the nurse's kit she receives for her birthday, so pleased that she starts work immediately when her father bangs his toe on

a door, bandaging his leg from toe to knee and admonishing him to keep the bandage on for a week. Her mom gets similar treatment for a headache, and Clementine eagerly waits for her risk-taking little brother, Tommy, to require her medical skills." (Bulletin of the Center for Children's Books)

Jane, Pamela

Little goblins ten; written by Pamela Jane; illustrated by Jane Manning. Harper 2011 un il $16.99; lib bdg $17.89

Grades: K 1 2   **E**

1. Counting 2. Stories in rhyme 3. Monsters -- Fiction 4. Halloween -- Fiction

ISBN 978-0-06-176798-2; 0-06-176798-0; 978-0-06-176800-2 lib bdg; 0-06-176800-6 lib bdg

LC 2010010169

Ghouls, goblins, ghosts, witches, and other scary creatures cavort in the forest on Halloween, introducing the numbers one through ten.

"Numerous titles interpreting 'Over in the Meadow' have been published, but trust the team of Jane and Manning to conjure up an impressive new vision in time for Halloween. Set in a fantastical land dominated by watery blues, greens and grays and punctuated by warm reds and yellows, Manning's tale presents ethereal ghosts, country-bumpkin werewolves, parading mummies, screeching witches, happy bats and boogieing skeletons that readers will instantly want to have as friends. . . . Truly satisfying." Kirkus

Janni, Rebecca

Every cowgirl needs a horse; illustrations by Lynne Avril. Dutton Children's Books 2010 un il $16.99

Grades: PreK K 1   **E**

1. Cycling -- Fiction 2. Cowhands -- Fiction 3. Birthdays -- Fiction 4. Imagination -- Fiction

ISBN 978-0-525-42164-1; 0-525-42164-5

LC 2009-12278

Nellie Sue, who fancies herself a real cowgirl, wants a horse for her birthday, but she discovers that a brand new bicycle—her first—takes almost as much taming as a filly.

"The bright, sketchy, watercolor and ink illustrations are suffused with pinks and purples and capture a child who tries to live up to cowgirl ideals of helping others, looking on the bright side, and being strong. The lesson on dealing positively with disappointment is gently delivered." SLJ

Another title about Nellie Sue is:

Every cowgirl needs dancing boots (2011)

Every cowgirl needs dancing boots; illustrated by Lynne Avril. Dutton Children's Books 2011 un il $16.99

Grades: PreK K 1   **E**

1. Dance -- Fiction 2. Cowhands -- Fiction 3. Imagination -- Fiction

ISBN 978-0-525-42341-6; 0-525-42341-9

LC 2010037712

Nellie Sue hopes to make friends with her new neighbors by hosting a hoedown in her barn, but wonders if the 'glitter girls' will be able to dance in their ballet slippers, rather than in dancing boots like hers.

"Avril's line-and-watercolor cartoons keep the visual tone light. . . . A passel of fun activities—dancing, crafting, biking and dress up—are tucked into Janni's tonic tale of imagination and optimism." Kirkus

Janovitz, Marilyn

Baby baby baby! Sourcebooks 2010 un il bd bk $7.99

Grades: PreK   **E**

1. Stories in rhyme 2. Board books for children 3. Infants -- Fiction

ISBN 978-1-4022-4414-8 bd bk; 1-4022-4414-2 bd bk

"Nine stanzas of appealing verse show a baby playing with family members and pets, taking a bath, and going to bed. . . . [This board book's] bouncy verses will hold young children's attention with rhythm, rhyme, repeated phrases, and references to familiar things. . . . The digital artwork illustrates the cheerful characters in squiggly, black line drawings brightened with bold patterns and colors." Booklist

Jarka, Jeff

Love that kitty; the story of a boy who wanted to be a cat. Henry Holt 2010 un il $12.99

Grades: PreK K 1   **E**

1. Cats -- Fiction 2. Imagination -- Fiction

ISBN 978-0-8050-9053-6; 0-8050-9053-3

Tired of being an ordinary boy, Peter decides to become a cat.

"Jarka draws each character and setting with only a few well-placed lines filled in with bright solid colors. Peter's quirky confidence contrasts hilariously with his parents' bewilderment." SLJ

Love that puppy! the story of a boy who wanted to be a dog. Henry Holt 2009 un il $12.95

Grades: PreK K 1   **E**

1. Dogs -- Fiction 2. Imagination -- Fiction

ISBN 978-0-8050-8741-3; 0-8050-8741-9

LC 2008018333

When his parents want him to change back into a human boy, Peter the dog comes up with a novel solution.

"Jarka's colorful comic-strip-style illustrations drive the humor with one visual joke after another. . . . Children will appreciate both the absurdity of Peter's behavior and Jarka's delivery." SLJ

Another title about Peter is:

Love that kitty (2010)

Jarrett, Clare

★ Arabella Miller's tiny caterpillar; [by] Clare Jarrett. Candlewick Press 2008 un il $16.99

Grades: PreK K 1 2   **E**

1. Butterflies -- Fiction 2. Caterpillars -- Fiction

ISBN 978-0-7636-3660-9; 0-7636-3660-6

Arabella Miller finds a tiny caterpillar and watches and cares for it until it becomes a butterfly

This is "an engaging, exceptional picture book. . . . Based on the verse about Little Arabella Miller, the story arc is simple but the charm lies in the sketchy, pencil-and-paper collage illustrations." Booklist

Javaherbin, Mina

★ Goal! illustrated by A.G. Ford. Candlewick Press 2010 un il $16.99; pa $6.99

Grades: 2 3 4   **E**

1. Soccer -- Fiction 2. Bullies -- Fiction 3. Friendship

-- Fiction
ISBN 0763645710; 9780763645717; 9780763658229

LC 2008047266

In a dangerous alley in a township in South Africa, the strength and unity which a group of young friends feel while playing soccer keep them safe when a gang of bullies arrives to cause trouble.

"Illustrations rendered in oil are impressive. Large and colorful action shots, many full spread, keep the story moving at a quick pace." SLJ

Javernick, Ellen

The **birthday** pet; illustrated by Kevin O'Malley. Marshall Cavendish 2009 un il $16.99

Grades: PreK K 1 2   E

1. Stories in rhyme 2. Pets -- Fiction 3. Turtles -- Fiction 4. Birthdays -- Fiction
ISBN 978-0-7614-5522-6; 0-7614-5522-1

LC 2008010740

Danny can have a pet for his birthday and he knows exactly what he wants, but the other members of his family think differently.

"The colorful, animated illustrations incorporate exaggerated close-ups, unusual perspectives, and witty details that extend the humor in the words. Young readers and listeners will enjoy the simple, well-paced, rhyming text." Booklist

Jay, Alison

★ **1** 2 3; a child's first counting book. Dutton Children's Books 2007 un il $15.99; bd bk $9.99

Grades: PreK K 1 2   E

1. Counting
ISBN 978-0-525-47836-2; 978-0-525-42165-8 bd bk

LC 2006035905

"Jay takes readers on an enchanted journey from 1 to 10 and back again, with help from fairy tale figures. A quartet of self-satisfied frog princes impressively embody the number 4, while a plate of gingerbread men . . . represent the number 6. . . . The pictures are a wonder to behold: Jay's flattened perspectives, gently faded colors, crackle-glaze finishes and lean, angular characterizations vaguely evoke the dreamy, ambiguous narrative qualities of medieval art." Publ Wkly

★ **ABC**: a child's first alphabet book. Dutton Children's Bks. 2003 un il hardcover o.p. bd bk $9.99

Grades: PreK K 1 2   E

1. Alphabet
ISBN 0-525-46951-6; 0-525-47524-9 bd bk

LC 2003-45218

In this alphabet book, a is for apple and z is for zoo

"This imaginative alphabet book offers visual clues to track and a story to tease out in its beautiful paintings. . . . Older children will flip from page to page, finding the simple story, drawing connections, and naming the letter-related objects. Younger ones can simply enjoy the delightful paintings with their crackle-glazed folk art look and touches of humor." Booklist

Red green blue; a first book of colors. Dutton Children's Books 2010 un il $16.99

Grades: PreK K 1   E

1. Stories in rhyme 2. Color -- Fiction 3. Nursery

rhymes -- Fiction
ISBN 978-0-525-42303-4; 0-525-42303-6

LC 2009-25098

Characters from nursery rhymes populate this tale, which highlights the colorful aspects of the familiar poems. Includes a key to the nursery rhymes referenced in the story.

"There are numerous opportunities for discussing colors, but as ever, it's Jay's luminous images that steal the show." Publ Wkly

Welcome to the zoo. Dial 2008 un il $16.99

Grades: PreK K 1 2   E

1. Stories without words 2. Zoos -- Fiction 3. Animals -- Fiction
ISBN 978-0-8037-3177-6; 0-8037-3177-9

"Jay creates a zoo without the usual barriers between the animals and their visitors. . . . The oil paintings reward close attention with amusing visual details and small wordless dramas that carry through from page to page. . . . Polished yet playful, this nearly wordless picture book is a engaging choice." Booklist

Jeffers, Oliver

The **Hueys** in The new sweater; Oliver Jeffers. Philomel Books 2012 32 p.

Grades: PreK K 1 2   E

1. Children's stories 2. Sweaters -- Juvenile fiction 3. Individuality -- Juvenile fiction 4. Sweaters -- Fiction 5. Individuality -- Fiction
ISBN 0399257675; 9780399257674

LC 2011048399

In this children's story by Oliver Jeffers ,"each Huey looks the same, thinks the same, and does the same exact things. So you can imagine the chaos when one of them has the idea of knitting a sweater! It seems like a good idea at the time--he is quite proud of it, in fact--but it does make him different from the others. So the rest of the Hueys, in turn, decide that they want to be different too! How? By knitting the exact same sweater, of course!" (Publisher's note)

★ **Stuck**. Philomel Books 2011 un il $16.99

Grades: PreK K   E

1. Kites -- Fiction
ISBN 978-0-399-25737-7; 0-399-25737-3

LC 2011016349

When Floyd's kite gets stuck in a tree, he tries to knock it down with increasingly larger and more outrageous things.

This is "an exuberantly absurd tale. . . . Jeffers . . . pictures the extravagant accumulation in abstract pencil-and-gouache doodles, with hand-lettered text to set a conversational tone." Publ Wkly

This moose belongs to me; Oliver Jeffers. Philomel Books 2012 32 p.

Grades: PreK K 1 2   E

1. Pets -- Juvenile fiction 2. Moose -- Juvenile fiction 3. Human-animal relationship -- Juvenile fiction 4. Pets -- Fiction 5. Moose as pets -- Fiction
ISBN 9780399161032

LC 2012020373

This children's picture book by Oliver Jeffers tells the "tale of a boy and his moose. Wilfred is a boy with rules. He lives a very orderly life. . . . There is, however, one rule that Wilfred's pet has difficulty following: Going whichever way Wilfred wants to go. Perhaps this is because Wilfred's pet doesn't quite realize that he belongs to anyone. . . . Fortunately, the two manage to work out a compromise." (Publisher's note)

★ **Up** and down. Philomel Books 2010 un il $16.99
Grades: PreK K 1   E
    1. Flight -- Fiction 2. Penguins -- Fiction 3. Friendship -- Fiction
ISBN 978-0-399-25545-8; 0-399-25545-1
                         LC 2010011358

Even though the penguin and the boy are close friends and do many things together, the penguin decides that he wants to fly and he wants to do it on his own.

"Serene white backdrops highlight brilliant compositional choices, while full-page spreads of unconfined color depict dramatic moments with subtle force. Children will intuit, absorb and appreciate this soothing book's heart—the fast, offbeat friendship that makes it so singular and appealing." Kirkus

Another title about Penguin and the boy is:
Lost and found (2006)

The **great** paper caper; [by] Oliver Jeffers. Philomel Books 2009 un il $17.99
Grades: PreK K   E
    1. Trees -- Fiction 2. Animals -- Fiction
ISBN 978-0-399-25097-2; 0-399-25097-2
                         LC 2008026192

When tree branches begin disappearing and paper airplanes are left in their place, the forest creatures carry out an investigation to find the culprit who has been stealing their homes.

"Managed forestry is the theme of this book that features folk-art-style animals with funny little stick legs. The mixed-media illustrations nicely complement the spare yet eloquent text." SLJ

The **heart** and the bottle. Philomel Books 2010 un il $17.99
Grades: PreK K 1   E
    1. Death -- Fiction 2. Emotions -- Fiction 3. Bereavement -- Fiction
ISBN 978-0-399-25452-9; 0-399-25452-8

After safeguarding her heart in a bottle hung around her neck, a girl finds the bottle growing heavier and her interest in things around her becoming smaller.

The "artwork is the sweetness in this bittersweet story. . . . While the subject of loss always has the potential to unsettle young readers, most should find this quietly powerful treatment of grief moving." Publ Wkly

The **incredible** book eating boy; by Oliver Jeffers. Philomel Books 2007 un il $16.99
Grades: PreK K 1 2 3   E
    1. Food -- Fiction 2. Books and reading -- Fiction
ISBN 978-0-399-24749-1
                         LC 2006026279

Henry loves to eat books, until he begins to feel quite ill and decides that maybe he could do something else with the books he has been devouring

"The simple cartoon illustrations twinkle with humor and feeling. Done in paint and pencil on smart backdrops—

pages from old books—the pictures set the stage for the quirky story." SLJ

The **way** back home; [by] Oliver Jeffers. Philomel Books 2008 un il $16.99
Grades: PreK K 1 2   E
    1. Space flight -- Fiction 2. Extraterrestrial beings -- Fiction
ISBN 978-0-399-25074-3; 0-399-25074-3
                         LC 2007029570

Stranded on the moon after his extraordinary airplane takes him into outer space, a boy meets a marooned young Martian with a broken spacecraft, and the two new friends work together to return to their respective homes

"The charm of this story is how completely it maintains a childlike perspective. . . . This approach continues in the watercolor, graphite, and collage artwork. Figures consist of circle heads, box bodies, and stick legs; the backgrounds are flat colors with a few scribbled-in clouds or puffs of exhaust. Humorous details abound." SLJ

Jeffers, Susan
    My Chincoteague pony. Hyperion Books for Children 2008 un il $16.99
Grades: PreK K 1 2 3   E
    1. Horses -- Fiction
ISBN 1-4231-0023-9; 978-1-4231-0023-2

Julie's "fondest wish is to have a pony of her own. The child convinces her farm-dwelling parents to take her to Chincoteague Island for Pony Penning Day so that she can bid in the auction. Unfortunately, she is continually outbid and realizes that the money she's earned won't be enough. Then one pony is returned and several people in the crowd pitch in to make her dream come true. . . . The lovely illustrations capture Julie's love of horses, the beauty of the ponies, and the excitement of the roundup." SLJ

The **Nutcracker**; [retold and illustrated by] Susan Jeffers. HarperCollinsPublishers 2007 un il $16.99; lib bdg $17.89
Grades: K 1 2   E
    1. Fairy tales 2. Toys -- Fiction 3. Magic -- Fiction 4. Christmas -- Fiction
ISBN 978-0-06-074386-4; 0-06-074386-7; 978-0-06-074387-1 lib bdg; 0-06-074387-5 lib bdg
                         LC 2007012489

An abridged version of the story of Marie Stahlbaum, who helps break the spell on her toy nutcracker and watches him change into a handsome prince

"Children who love the traditional Christmas ballet will enjoy this romantic illustrated edition. . . . The illustrations communicate the beauty and the emotional quality of the ballet." SLJ

Jenkins, Emily
    Daffodil, crocodile; pictures by Tomek Bogacki. Farrar, Straus & Giroux 2007 un il $16
Grades: PreK K 1 2   E
    1. Sisters -- Fiction 2. Triplets -- Fiction 3. Imagination -- Fiction
ISBN 978-0-374-39944-3; 0-374-39944-1
                         LC 2005-40163

Tired of being one of three look-alike sisters that no one can tell apart, Daffodil puts on a papier mâché crocodile head and has her own individual adventures

"Daffodil's words and actions ring kidlike and true. . . . Colorful art, whimsical and expressive, fills the pages with fanciful patterns, perspectives, and details." Booklist

Five creatures; pictures by Tomek Bogacki. Foster Bks. 2001 un il $16; pa $5.95
Grades: K 1 2 3   E
1. Cats 2. Family life 3. Cats -- Fiction 4. Family life -- Fiction
ISBN 0-374-32341-0; 0-374-42328-8 pa
LC 00-28771

In words and pictures, a girl describes the three humans and two cats that live in her house, and details some of the traits that they share

"This clever, multilayered book is as much for sharing and getting little ones on the path to deductive reasoning as it is for reading. . . . The text encourages readers to be observant. . . . Bogacki's colored chalk art . . . is childlike in the best possible way—immediate, identifiable, and executed with soft colors and simple shapes." Booklist

Lemonade in winter; a book about two kids counting money. Emily Jenkins; illustrated by G. Brian Karas. Schwartz & Wade Books 2012 40 p. $16.99
Grades: PreK K 1 2   E
1. Siblings -- Fiction 2. Picture books for children 3. Entrepreneurship/Juvenile literature 4. Winter -- Fiction
ISBN 0375858830; 9780375858833; 9780375958830
LC 2010024135

In this children's picture book, "two young entrepreneurs, Pauline and John-John, ignore the naysayers (their parents) and set up a lemonade stand smack dab on the snowy sidewalk. The lemonade, limeade--and lemon-limeade--are ready. But there are no customers to be seen. Pauline and John-John aren't discouraged. Instead, they improvise by singing a catchy jingle, turning cartwheels to attract attention, decorating their stand and, finally, having a half-price sale." (Kirkus Reviews)

"This quirky tale is a boon for young entrepreneurs, who will enjoy looking at the humorous details in the pictures as much as working out the math after each sale. Abounding with teaching possibilities

Skunkdog; pictures by Pierre Pratt. Farrar, Straus and Giroux 2008 un il $16.95
Grades: K 1 2 3   E
1. Dogs -- Fiction 2. Skunks -- Fiction
ISBN 0-374-37009-5; 978-0-374-37009-1
LC 2005-54701

Dumpling, a lonely dog with no sense of smell, moves with his family to the country and makes a new friend who takes some getting used to.

"Jenkins uses a lot of detail and repetition. Pratt's sunlit illustrations are done in oils and portray a white dog with an elongated nose and a furiously wagging black tail who complements the black-and-white skunk. Children will instantly relate to the pup's skunk encounters. . . . Important themes of loneliness, tolerance, friendship, and family emerge from this funny story." SLJ

★ **That** new animal; pictures by Pierre Pratt. Farrar, Straus and Giroux 2005 un il $16
Grades: PreK K 1 2   E
1. Dogs -- Fiction 2. Infants -- Fiction
ISBN 0-374-37443-0
LC 2003-44058

The lives of two dogs change after a new animal, a baby, comes to their house.

"Both the author and illustrator demonstrate wonderful insight into pet psychology and family dynamics, and the elongated style of the vibrantly colored artwork strikes just the right note of humor and whimsy." SLJ

Water in the park; a book about water and the times of the day. Emily Jenkins. 1st ed. Schwartz & Wade Books 2013 40 p. ill. (hardcover) $16.99; (library) $19.99
Grades: PreK K 1   E
1. Parks -- Juvenile literature 2. Water -- Juvenile literature 3. Parks -- Fiction 4. Water -- Fiction
ISBN 0375870024; 9780375870026 trade; 9780375970023
LC 2011050243

This children's picture book, by Emily Jenkins, illustrated by Stephanie Graegin, shows the readers "from the first orange glow on the water in the pond, to the last humans and animals running home from an evening rain shower, . . . a day-in-the-life of a city park, and the playground within it." (Publisher's note)

Jenkins, Steve
★ **Move!** [written by Steve Jenkins and Robin Page; illustrated by Steve Jenkins] Houghton Mifflin 2006 un il $16; bd bk $7.99
Grades: PreK K   E
1. Animal locomotion 2. Animals -- Juvenile literature 3. Animal locomotion -- Juvenile literature
ISBN 0-618-64637-X; 0-547-24000-7 bd bk
LC 2005-19082

In this "book illustrated with cut and torn-paper collages, animals leap, swim, slide, swing, and waddle. Each spread contains one action word and two animals for whom that behavior is typical. . . . Jenkins uses brief phrases as captions and provides a well-written, concise appendix. . . . This book is gorgeous and educational." SLJ

Jennings, Sharon
A **Chanukah** Noel; a true story. written by Sharon Jennings; illustrated by Gillian Newland. Second Story Press 2010 un il $15.95
Grades: K 1 2   E
1. Jews -- Fiction 2. Hanukkah stories 3. Christmas stories 4. Christmas -- Fiction
ISBN 978-1-897187-74-6; 1-897187-74-2

A young Jewish girl is fascinated by the traditions of Christmas when her family moves to a small town in France.

Jessell, Tim
Falcon; by Tim Jessell. Random House Inc 2012 40 p. (trade: alk. paper) $17.99; (library) $20.99
Grades: 1 2 3   E
1. Falcons 2. Flight -- Fiction 3. Falcons -- Fiction 4. Imagination -- Fiction
ISBN 0375868666; 9780375868665; 9780375968662
LC 2011012758

This book looks at falcons, inviting "readers to imagine taking wing. In a series of . . . paintings, [Tim] Jessell provides a bird's-eye view of the raptor in flight, as well as sweeping panoramas that show how it interacts with landscapes as diverse as mountains, sea cliffs, and skyscrapers." (School Library Journal)

Jesset, Aurore

Loopy; by Aurore Jesset; illustrated by Barbara Korthues. North-South 2008 un il $16.95; pa $7.95

Grades: PreK K 1   E

1. Toys -- Fiction 2. Lost and found possessions -- Fiction

ISBN 978-0-7358-2175-0; 0-7358-2175-5; 978-0-7358-2261-0 pa; 0-7358-2261-1 pa

"A child leaves her favorite toy at the doctor's office and ponders its fate should they fail to be reunited 'RIGHT NOW!' On each spread, Jesset's speculation about the beloved stuffed animal's current state is matched with Korthues's Tim Burton-esque illustrations rendered in vibrant colors, often muted to depict the nighttime setting. The simple, rhythmic prose recalls a small child's inner dialogue or storytelling voice." SLJ

Ji Zhaohua

No! that's wrong! [by] Zhaohua Ji and Cui Xu. Kane Miller Book Pub. 2008 un il $15.95

Grades: PreK K 1 2   E

1. Animals -- Fiction 2. Rabbits -- Fiction 3. Clothing and dress -- Fiction

ISBN 978-1-933605-66-1; 1-933605-66-9

"A rabbit has a humorous encounter with a pair of red underpants. Rabbit's not sure how to wear the mysterious garment and tries it on as a hat. He offers the hat in turn to eight different animals until a donkey straightforwardly inquires why the rabbit is wearing underpants on his head. . . . The cartoon-style artwork and the text, consisting primarily of dialogue, work well together. . . . This entertaining picture book stimulates a bit of creative thinking and problem solving." SLJ

Jimenez, Francisco

The **Christmas** gift: El regalo de Navidad; illustrated by Claire B. Cotts. Houghton Mifflin 2000 un il $15; pa $6.99

Grades: K 1 2 3   E

1. Christmas 2. Migrant labor 3. Mexican Americans 4. Christmas -- Fiction 5. Migrant labor -- Fiction 6. Mexican Americans -- Fiction 7. Bilingual books -- English-Spanish

ISBN 0-395-92869-9; 0-547-13364-2 pa

LC 99-26224

When his family has to move again a few days before Christmas in order to find work, Panchito worries that he will not get the ball he has been wanting

"This story, a version of which appeared in Jiménez's . . . TheCircuit, is presented here in a bilingual picture book format with an excellent Spanish text. . . . Mural-like illustrations soulfully depict the hard life and strong people of the migrant labor camps." Horn Book Guide

Jocelyn, Marthe

Eats; [by] Marthe Jocelyn; [illustrations by] Tom Slaughter. Tundra Books 2007 un il $15.95; bd bk $7.95

Grades: PreK K 1 2   E

1. Animals -- Food

ISBN 978-0-88776-820-0; 978-0-88776-988-7 bd bk

"Painted paper cuts in jewel colors graphically portray the principal foods eaten by 14 different animals. . . . Using bold, simple, brightly colored shapes . . . [and] placing them on backgrounds of equally bold contrasting colors, the animals and their dinners are easily identified and, thus, will have instant kid appeal." SLJ

★ Ones and twos; by Marthe Jocelyn and Nell Jocelyn. Tundra Books 2011 un il $15.95

Grades: PreK K 1   E

1. Numbers 2. Stories in rhyme 3. Birds -- Fiction 4. Friendship -- Fiction

ISBN 978-1-77049-220-2; 1-77049-220-8

"Deceptively simple text accompanied by highly textured, patterned, and colorful collages invite children to consider number relationships, opening with the spread 'One birds, two eggs. One girl, two legs.' The rhyming couplets, akin to terse verse, trace both bird and girl throughout the day. . . . Operating on two levels as a concept book that also tells a story, this delightful picture book will draw readers for many repeat visits." Booklists

Over under; [illustrated by] Tom Slaughter. Tundra Books 2005 un il $15.95; bd bk $7.95

Grades: PreK   E

1. Opposites

ISBN 0-88776-708-7; 0-88776-790-7 bd bk

"Minimal rhyming text and cut-paper illustrations of animals in six basic colors introduce opposites: e.g. 'big' and 'small' are represented by a black elephant and mouse on a vibrant red background." Horn Book Guide

★ Same same; Tom Slaughter, illustrator. Tundra Books 2009 un il $15.95; bd bk $7.95

Grades: PreK K 1   E

1. Concepts 2. Classification -- Juvenile literature

ISBN 978-0-88776-885-9; 0-88776-885-7; 978-0-88776-987-0 bd bk; 0-88776-987-X bd bk

"Jocelyn and Slaughter . . . strikingly introduce the concept of classification. Slaughter's graphic cut-paper compositions command attention with their paintbox-bright colors. The first spread, for example, shows an apple, a blue-and-green planet Earth and a tambourine. . . 'Round things,' reads the caption. The next pages show the tambourine again, now with a guitar and a bird. This spread is captioned 'things that make music.' Always carrying forward one of the three objects from the previous spread, Jocelyn delivers the vital lesson that everyday objects fall into many categories. The concept is clear and the delivery attractive." Publ Wkly

Johnson, Angela

★ I dream of trains; illustrated by Loren Long. Simon & Schuster Bks. for Young Readers 2003 un il $16.95

Grades: K 1 2 3   E

1. Locomotive engineers 2. Railroads -- Fiction 3. African Americans -- Fiction

ISBN 0-689-82609-5

LC 98-52886

The son of a sharecropper dreams of leaving Mississippi on a train with the legendary engineer Casey Jones

"Long's moody acrylic paintings, mainly in subdued tones, are a sterling accompaniment to the book's provocative prose." SLJ

Just like Josh Gibson; written by Angela Johnson; illustrated by Beth Peck. Simon & Schuster Books for Young Readers 2004 un il $15.95; pa $6.99
Grades: K 1 2 3   E
   1. Baseball -- Fiction 2. Grandmothers -- Fiction 3. African Americans -- Fiction
   ISBN 0-689-82628-1; 1-4169-2728-X pa
                        LC 2001-49531
A young girl's grandmother tells her of her love for baseball and the day they let her play in the game even though she was a girl.
"Johnson tempers what could have been a sentimental tale with Grandmama's contagious enthusiasm and sense of empowerment, and her text has a baseball announcer's suspenseful rhythm. . . . Peck's angular pastels . . . skillfully capture the nostalgic sports action and celebration." Booklist

Lottie Paris lives here; illustrated by Scott Fischer. Simon & Schuster Books for Young Readers 2011 un il $16.99
Grades: PreK K 1 2   E
   1. Parks -- Fiction 2. Houses -- Fiction
   ISBN 978-0-689-87377-5; 0-689-87377-8
Relates a day in the life of a little girl who lives with her Papa Pete in a house across from a park.
"Lottie Paris is an exuberant, imaginative, and mischievous girl. . . . Fischer's large gouache images created with brayer, linocut, stamping, airbrush, sandpaper and brush line are endearing. . . . A universal story told through the eyes of a vivacious youngster." SLJ

Wind flyers; illustrated by Loren Long. Simon & Schuster 2006 un il $16.99
Grades: K 1 2 3   E
   1. Air pilots -- Fiction 2. African Americans -- Fiction 3. World War, 1939-1945 -- Fiction
   ISBN 0-689-84879-X
"In spare, poetic lines, a young African American boy introduces his great-great-uncle, who was a Tuskegee airman. . . . Johnson introduces the history in oblique, pared-down words. . . . Long's acrylics beautifully extend the evocative words." Booklist

The **day** Ray got away; illustrated by Luke LaMarca. Simon & Schuster 2010 un il $16.99
Grades: PreK K 1 2   E
   1. Parades -- Fiction 2. Balloons -- Fiction
   ISBN 978-0-689-87375-1; 0-689-87375-1
"In this lighthearted story, the fateful morning begins when Ray wakes up with a smile (he always does) and announces to his fellow balloons, 'Today is the day.' The parade begins the same as usual, until Ray makes his break and havoc ensues. Cheerful acrylic cartoon illustrations elevate the understated story, adding foreshadowing, drama, and much humor." SLJ

Johnson, Crockett
   ★ **Harold** and the purple crayon. Harper & Row 1955 un il $15.99; lib bdg $15.89; pa $6.99

Grades: PreK K   E
   1. Drawing -- Fiction
   ISBN 0-06-022935-7; 0-06-022936-5 lib bdg; 0-06-443022-7 pa
"As Harold goes for a moonlight walk, he uses his purple crayon to draw a path and the things he sees along the way, then draws himself back home." Hodges. Books for Elem Sch Libr
   Other titles about Harold are:
   Harold's ABC (1963)
   Harold's circus (1959)
   Harold's fairy tale (1986)
   Harold's trip to the sky (1957)
   A picture for Harold's room (1960)

Johnson, D. B., 1944-
Magritte's marvelous hat; a picture book. by D.B. Johnson. Houghton Mifflin Harcourt 2012 32 p.
Grades: K 1 2 3 4   E
   1. French painting 2. Hats -- Fiction 3. Dogs -- Juvenile fiction 4. Picture books for children 5. Magic -- Fiction 6. Painting, French -- Fiction
   ISBN 9780547558646
                        LC 2011012242
This picture book "recasts René Magritte as a dapper, blue-eyed hound and incorporates the painter's surreal iconography. . . . The black bowler hat (a familiar, recurrent image in Magritte's paintings) is characterized as a playful muse, engaging the artist in frisky games on walks." Author/illustrator D.B. Johnson depicts the story with "surreal elements," including "four see-through acetate pages . . . [that] transform adjacent spreads," and images inspired by famous Magritte paintings. (Kirkus

Johnson, David
Snow sounds; an onomatopoeic story. [by] David A. Johnson. Houghton Mifflin Company 2006 un il $16
Grades: PreK K 1   E
   1. Snow 2. Sound
   ISBN 978-0-618-47310-6; 0-618-47310-6
                        LC 2006-00333
A nearly-wordless book in which a young boy, eager to reach a much-anticipated holiday party on time, listens to the sounds of the shovels, snow plow, and other equipment used to clear his way.
"Full-bleed watercolor spreads capture the light of a wintry morning perfectly. . . . This accomplished offering has a variety of uses and will appeal to a wide age range." SLJ

Johnson, Dinah
   ★ **Black** magic; illustrated by R. Gregory Christie. Henry Holt and Co. 2010 un il $15.99
Grades: PreK K 1 2   E
   1. Black 2. African Americans -- Fiction
   ISBN 978-0-8050-7833-6; 0-8050-7833-9
                        LC 2009-9219
"This expressive book combines well-matched text and pictures to pay tribute to the myriad qualities of blackness. Buoyant yet reflective, Johnson's . . . free-flowing verse presents an imaginative girl's musings on the essence of black, which she sees as containing multitudinous, even oppositional, dimensions. . . . With vibrant colors offsetting velvety black images, Christie's . . . acrylic gouache illus-

trations playfully tweak perspective and scale, echoing the verse's energy and fluidity. " Publ Wkly

Johnson, Donald B.

★ **Henry** hikes to Fitchburg; [by] D. B. Johnson. Houghton Mifflin 2000 un il $16; pa $6.95
Grades: PreK K 1 2   E
1. Bears 2. Nature 3. Authors 4. Naturalists 5. Essayists 6. Pacifists 7. Bears -- Fiction 8. Nature -- Fiction 9. Writers on nature 10. Nonfiction writers 11. Walking -- Fiction
ISBN 0-395-96867-4; 0-618-73749-9 pa
LC 99-35302
While his friend works hard to earn the train fare to Fitchburg, Henry the bear walks the thirty miles through woods and fields, enjoying nature and the time to think great thoughts. Includes biographical information about Henry David Thoreau

"This splendid book works on several levels. Johnson's adaption of a paragraph taken from Thoreau's Walden (set down in an author's note) illuminates the contrast between materialistic and naturalistic views of life without ranting or preaching. His illustrations are breathtakingly rich and filled with lovingly rendered details." Booklist

Other titles about Henry the bear are:
Henry builds a cabin (2002)
Henry climbs a mountain (2003)
Henry works (2004)
Henry's night (2009)

Johnson, Lindsay Lee

Ten moonstruck piglets; illustrated by Carll Cneut. Clarion Books 2011 un il $16.99
Grades: PreK K 1 2   E
1. Counting 2. Stories in rhyme 3. Pigs -- Fiction
ISBN 0-618-86866-6; 978-0-618-86866-7
LC 2010-05443
On the night of the full moon, ten piglets go out adventuring while their mother is fast asleep. "Ages four to seven." (Bull Cent Child Books)

"The precise yet playful verse sets the tone and creates the story's structure. Cneut's acrylic paintings give individual traits to the piglets, create a magical moonlit setting, and brilliantly transform it when the moon disappears. . . . An amusing romp and a great opportunity to practice counting from 1 to 10." Booklist

Johnson, Paul Brett

★ **On** top of spaghetti; written and illustrated by Paul Brett Johnson; with lyrics by Tom Glazer. Scholastic Press 2006 un il $15.99
Grades: PreK K 1 2   E
1. Songs 2. Children's songs 3. Dogs -- Fiction 4. Animals -- Fiction 5. Meatballs -- Fiction
ISBN 0-439-74944-1
LC 2005-14311
"Expanding on the popular song, Johnson spins the tale of Yodeler Jones, a hound dog who serves nothing but meatballs and spaghetti at his dining establishment. When business begins to slow, Yodeler concocts a brand-new meatball, but before he can taste it, someone sneezes. . . . With original text printed in black and the lyrics sprinkled throughout in color, this story successfully marries the two. The loony illustrations, full of color and movement, effectively capture the zaniness." SLJ

Johnston, Lynn

Farley follows his nose; story by Lynn Johnston & Beth Cruikshank; illustrations by Lynn Johnston. Bowen Press 2009 un il $17.99
Grades: PreK K 1   E
1. Dogs -- Fiction 2. Smell -- Fiction
ISBN 978-0-06-170234-1; 0-06-170234-X
LC 2008-24713
Farley the dog follows his nose from one good smell to another all over town.

"Big-eyed, energetic Farley and his 'sniff snorfle SNUFF' nose will be a big hit with storytimers, and it won't matter a bit that they're too young to recognize the characters. A great addition to storytimes on baths, senses and dogs." Kirkus

Johnston, Tony

★ **Levi** Strauss gets a bright idea or; the positively true and unfabricated story of a pair of pants. written by Tony Johnston; illustrated by Stacy Innerst. Houghton Mifflin Harcourt 2011 il $16.99
Grades: PreK K 1 2   E
1. Tall tales 2. Jeans (Clothing) -- Fiction 3. Clothing industry executives 4. Clothing and dress -- Fiction 5. Gold mines and mining -- Fiction
ISBN 978-0-15-206145-6; 0-15-206145-2
LC 2010043402
Retells, in tall-tale fashion, how Levi Strauss went to California during the Gold Rush, saw the need for a sturdier kind of trouser, and invented jeans.

"Johnston creates an unrepentantly exaggerated version of events that is sure to entertain, offering more factual information about Strauss in an author's note. Using a bright idea of his own, Innerst . . . chronicles the raucous action in acrylic paintings on a canvas of, yes, old Levi's jeans. The denim's texture provides an appropriately rugged tone to the colorful proceedings." Kirkus

★ **My** abuelita; written by Tony Johnston; illustrated by Yuyi Morales; photographed by Tim O'Meara. Harcourt Children's Books 2009 un il $16
Grades: 1 2 3   E
1. Grandmothers -- Fiction 2. Storytelling -- Fiction 3. Spanish language -- Vocabulary
ISBN 978-0-15-216330-3; 0-15-216330-1
ALA ALSC Belpre Illustrator Medal Honor Book (2010)
"A boy describes the morning routine he shares with his grandmother as she prepares for work. Flights of fancy enliven the tasks of bathing, eating breakfast, and dressing. When the pair arrive at her workplace, readers discover that Abuelita is a storyteller—a calling that her grandson shares. Spanish words are sprinkled throughout, often followed by brief definitions. . . . Johnston effectively engages young readers' interest. . . . Morales's bold, innovative illustrations brilliantly reinforce the text. . . . Characters molded from polymer clay are dressed in brightly patterned fabrics and placed among images that evoke Mexican art." SLJ

Uncle Rain Cloud; illustrated by Fabricio Vanden Broeck. Charlesbridge Pub. 2001 un il $15.95; pa $7.95

Grades: PreK K 1 2   E
1. Uncles 2. English language 3. Mexican Americans
4. Uncles -- Fiction 5. English language -- Fiction 6.
Mexican Americans -- Fiction
ISBN 0-88106-371-1; 0-88106-372-X pa
LC 99-54195

Carlos tries to help his uncle, who is frustrated and angry
at his inability to speak English, adjust to their new home in
Los Angeles

"Brisk pacing, sympathetic characters, and clear prose
that uses embedded Spanish words effectively make a winner. VandenBroeck's acrylic and colored-pencil illustrations
flesh out the narrative in soft, bright colors enhanced by dramatic shading." SLJ

Jonas, Ann
Round trip. Greenwillow Bks. 1983 un il $15.99;
pa $5.99
Grades: PreK K 1 2   E
1. City and town life -- Fiction
ISBN 0-688-01772-X; 0-688-09986-6 pa
LC 82-12026

Black and white illustrations and text record the sights
on a day trip to the city and back home again to the country.
The trip to the city is read from front to back and the return
trip, from back to front, upside down

"Although one or two pictures too easily suggest their
upside-down images and the device is occasionally strained,
the author-artist displays a fine sense of graphic design and
balance, and pictorial beauty is never sacrificed for mere
cleverness." Horn Book

★ **Splash!** Greenwillow Bks. 1995 un il $16.99;
pa $6.99
Grades: PreK K 1 2   E
1. Counting 2. Animals -- Fiction
ISBN 0-688-11051-7; 0-688-15284-8 pa
LC 94-4110

A little girl's turtle, fish, frogs, dog, and cat jump in and
out of a backyard pond, constantly changing the answer to
the question "How many are in my pond?"

"A clever concept book with physical humor and exciting acrylic paintings that capture the heat and drama of a
sunny summer day." Booklist

The **quilt.** Greenwillow Bks. 1984 un il $16.99
Grades: PreK K 1 2   E
1. Quilts -- Fiction
ISBN 0-688-03825-5
LC 83-25385

"The intricate illustrations in Jonas's book can be described only in superlatives. Backed by a length of golden-
yellow calico imprinted with small red flowers, a quilt fashioned from squares in a variety of colors is the prize shown
to readers by a dear little girl." Publ Wkly

Jones, Sally Lloyd
★ **How** to be a baby--by me, the big sister; [by] Sally
Lloyd-Jones and [illustrated by] Sue Heap. Schwartz &
Wade Books 2007 un il $15.99; lib bdg $18.99

Grades: PreK K 1 2   E
1. Infants -- Fiction 2. Siblings -- Fiction
ISBN 0-375-83843-0; 978-0-375-83843-9; 0-375-
93843-5 lib bdg; 978-0-375-93843-6 lib bdg
LC 2006-02469

"A worldly wise big sister . . . reads from a book she has
written for her new sibling. She itemizes a long list of things
that babies cannot do. . . . Although she tends to focus on the
negatives, in the end the unnamed protagonist admits that
babies have some uses. . . . Heap uses acrylic paint, crayon,
and felt-tip pen in a pleasing palette of pinks, blues, and yellows to enhance the story with childlike charm." SLJ

Other titles about this character are:
How to get married by me, the bride (2009)
How to get a job by me, the boss (2011)

The **ultimate** guide to grandmas and grandpas; by
Sally Lloyd-Jones; illustrated by Michael Emberley. Harp-
erCollinsPublishers 2008 un il $14.99; lib bdg $15.89
Grades: PreK K 1 2 3   E
1. Family life -- Fiction 2. Grandparents -- Fiction
ISBN 978-0-06-075687-1; 0-06-075687-X; 978-0-06-
075688-8 lib bdg; 0-06-075688-8 lib bdg
LC 2007020880

"In this story about how children should treat their elders, grandparents and grandchildren representing all kinds
of animal species play together, enjoy snacks, take trips, tell
stories, snuggle, and share secrets. Lloyd-Jones's text is both
charming and tongue-in-cheek. . . . Emberley's enchanting
illustrations mirror each character's personality." SLJ

Joosse, Barbara
Lovabye dragon; text by Barbara Joosse; illustrations
by Randy Cecil. Candlewick 2012 32 p. (hardback) $15.99
Grades: PreK K 1 2   E
1. Dragons -- Fiction 2. Picture books for children 3.
Friendship -- Juvenile fiction 4. Friendship -- Fiction 5.
Princesses -- Fiction
ISBN 0763654086; 9780763654085
LC 2011046647

In this children's picture book, "[w]hen the tears of a
young princess trickle onto a dragon, a sweet friendship is
born. . . . [Barbara] Joosse creates a friendship born out of
loneliness and tears between a young princess who longs for
a dragon and a friendly dragon who dreams of a girl for a
friend." (Kirkus)

Joosse, Barbara M.
Friends (mostly) by Barbara Joosse; illustrated by To-
maso Milian. Greenwillow Books 2010 un il $16.99
Grades: K 1 2 3   E
1. Friendship -- Fiction
ISBN 978-0-06-088222-8; 0-06-088222-0
LC 2009-34951

Henry and Ruby are best friends forever, even though
they do not always get along.

"This title provides an excellent springboard for conversations about friendship. . . . Joosse uses some of the text
in a dialogue format, the characters responding as if they
were being interviewed, providing this picture book with a
pre-chapter-book feel. Sections are loosely separated by a
rhyme. Lively watercolor illustrations express the children's
moods and provide vibrancy to the theme." SLJ

Higgledy -piggledy chicks; by Barbara Joosse; pictures by Rick Chrustowski. Greenwillow Books 2010 un il $16.99; lib bdg $17.89

Grades: PreK K 1 2   E

1. Chickens -- Fiction

ISBN 978-0-06-075042-8; 0-06-075042-1; 978-0-06-075043-5 lib bdg; 0-06-075043-X lib bdg

LC 2007047594

Banty Hen keeps her seven new baby chicks safe, even though they like to go exploring.

"Chrustowski's illustrations—done in colorful torn-paper collages—effectively capture the energy of the roaming and curious chicks. Readers will delight in counting the seven chicks on each spread and in predicting what danger might be hiding on the following page." Booklist

★ **Hot** city; by Barbara Joosse; illustrated by R. Gregory Christie. Philomel Books 2004 un il $16.99

Grades: PreK K 1 2   E

1. Summer -- Fiction 2. Libraries -- Fiction 3. African Americans -- Fiction 4. City and town life -- Fiction

ISBN 0-399-23640-6

LC 2002-1254

Mimi and her little brother Joe escape from home and the city's summer heat to read and dream about princesses and dinosaurs in the cool, quiet library.

"This eloquently told story is boldly illustrated with evocative acrylic paintings in shades of orange, red, and yellow." SLJ

★ **Papa,** do you love me? illustrated by Barbara Lavallee. Chronicle Books 2005 un il $15.95

Grades: PreK K   E

1. Masai (African people) -- Fiction 2. Father-son relationship -- Fiction

ISBN 0-8118-4265-7

LC 2003-17344

When a Masai father in Africa answers his son's questions, the boy learns that his father's love for him is unconditional.

"Echoing the soothing rhythm of the poetic narrative, Lavallee's graceful watercolors feature a harmoniously balanced palette." Publ Wkly

Please is a good word to say; by Barbara Joosse; pictures by Jennifer Plecas. Philomel Books 2007 un il $12.99

Grades: PreK K 1 2   E

1. Etiquette -- Fiction

ISBN 978-0-399-24217-5

LC 2006034508

Harriet gives examples of polite words and expressions to use in various social situations to make them more pleasant.

"Joosse's effective use of speech bubbles in various fonts, in addition to the main text, makes for especially interesting and amusing reading. Plecas's ink-and-watercolor cartoons imbue the already spirited commentary with personality, dimension, and even more energy." SLJ

Roawr! illustrated by Jan Jutte. Philomel Books 2009 un il $16.99

Grades: PreK K   E

1. Bears -- Fiction

ISBN 978-0-399-24777-4; 0-399-24777-7

LC 2008-16907

When Liam hears a load roar in the middle of the night, he must use all his ingenuity to protect his sleeping mother from a hungry bear.

"This adrenaline-charged romp is, first and foremost, exciting. Jutte's lively cartoon artwork contrasts muted night colors to form powerful images." SLJ

Sleepover at gramma's house; illustrated by Jan Jutte. Philomel Books 2010 un il $17.99

Grades: PreK K 1   E

1. Elephants -- Fiction 2. Grandmothers -- Fiction

ISBN 978-0-399-25261-7; 0-399-25261-4

LC 2009-31549

A little girl and her grandmother have a rollicking good time during a sleepover.

"Jutte's illustrations are jam-packed full of details. Readers get a clear sense of the child's excitement and activity level, but they will never lose sight of the relationship being celebrated. The colors in the ink, watercolor and acrylic illustrations lend the artwork a retro feel, and the elephants may remind many readers of Babar." Kirkus

Wind-wild dog; written by Barbara Joosse; illustrated by Kate Kiesler. Henry Holt and Company 2006 un il $16.95

Grades: K 1 2 3   E

1. Dogs -- Fiction

ISBN 978-0-8050-7053-8; 0-8050-7053-2

LC 2005020055

Ziva, a "wind-wild" young sled dog, decides whether to stay with the man who has trained her or to run free with the wolves and wind

"In spare, precise prose, Ziva's story drives with understated dramatic tension toward a satisfying conclusion. Kiesler's oil paintings capture the clean beauty of the rural Alaska setting as well as the unique qualities of Ziva and the man." Booklist

Jordan, Deloris

★ **Salt** in his shoes; Michael Jordan in pursuit of a dream. by Deloris Jordan with Roslyn M. Jordan; illustrated by Kadir Nelson. Simon & Schuster Bks. for Young Readers 2000 un il $16.95; pa $7.99

Grades: 2 3 4   E

1. Size 2. Basketball 3. Baseball players 4. Olympic athletes 5. Basketball players

ISBN 0-689-83371-7; 0-689-83419-5 pa

LC 00-20539

"This readable and entertaining story will delight the superstar's fans. Nelson's illustrations bring the right blend of vivid color, realism, and personality." SLJ

Jordan, Sandra

★ **Mr.** and Mrs. Portly and their little dog Snack; pictures by Christine Davenier. Farrar Straus Giroux 2009 un il $16.99

Grades: PreK K 1 2   E

1. Art -- Fiction 2. Dogs -- Fiction

ISBN 978-0-374-35089-5; 0-374-35089-2

LC 2007046663

Snack is a very happy puppy when Mrs. Portly adopts him but when persnickety Mr. Portly returns from a fishing trip, he banishes Snack to a doghouse until their mutual love of art, and a thief, bring them together.

"Davenport's ink-and-watercolor drawings are a delightful mix of sizes and shapes. . . . Exuding warmth, both narrative and pictures transcend the basic plotline, turning this into an irresistible offering." Booklist

Joubert, Beverly

African animal alphabet; by Beverly and Dereck Joubert. National Geographic 2011 48p il (National Geographic little kids) $16.95
Grades: PreK K 1 2   E
   1. Alphabet 2. Animals -- Africa
   ISBN 978-1-4263-0781-2; 1-4263-0781-0

"This alphabet book features vivid photographs of African animals. Readers will recognize a cheetah, elephant, and lion, but this husband-and-wife naturalist team also highlights unsung species like the tsessebe, the umbrette, and the dung beetle. . . . Appended animal facts and a glossary for words like 'vociferous' underscore the book's dual focus on diverse animal characteristics and language development." Publ Wkly

Joyce, William

★ Dinosaur Bob and his adventures with the family Lazardo; new ed; HarperCollins Pubs. 1995 un il $16.99
Grades: K 1 2 3   E
   1. Dinosaurs -- Fiction
   ISBN 0-06-021074-5
                     LC 94-19100
A revised and enlarged edition of the title first published 1988

"The Lazardo family goes on safari to Africa where they find a dinosaur. They name him Bob and take him back to Pimlico Hills. . . . Bob soon becomes famous because he can play the trumpet, dance, and most importantly play baseball." Child Book Rev Serv [review of 1988 edition]

★ George shrinks; story and pictures by William Joyce. Harper & Row 1985 un il $16.99; pa $6.99
Grades: K 1 2 3   E
   1. Fantasy fiction 2. Body size 3. Size -- Fiction
   ISBN 0-06-023070-3; 0-06-443129-0 pa
                     LC 83-47697
"The colorful illustrations, executed with painstaking attention to detail, create a surreal landscape from an ordinary breakfast-cereal world, as familiar objects become monumental structures through which the diminutive George moves with panache." Horn Book

★ The Man in the Moon; edited by Laura Geringer Books. Atheneum Books for Young Readers 2011 un il (Guardians of childhood) $17.99
Grades: K 1 2 3   E
   1. Fantasy fiction
   ISBN 978-1-4424-3041-9; 1-4424-3041-9
                  LC 2010053985
When a newly orphaned baby in the moon makes friends with the children of Earth, he begins to shine as brightly as possible to ward off their fears.

This "is a rich, cinematic brew of steampunk fancies. [Joyce's] sumptuous spreads are crowded with rotund telescopes, Jules Verne rocket ships, and sherbet-bearing robots, all painted in a superb palette of indigo and gold. . . . Joyce combines elemental fairyland themes . . . into a tale that's warm and fuzzy, swashbuckling, and dazzling inventive all at the same time." Publ Wkly

A day with Wilbur Robinson; by William Joyce. Laura Geringer Books 2006 un il $16.99
Grades: PreK K 1 2   E
   1. Family life -- Fiction 2. Eccentrics and eccentricities -- Fiction
   ISBN 978-0-06-089098-8; 0-06-089098-3
                  LC 2005037287
An expanded version of the title published 1990

While spending the day in the Robinson household, Wilbur's best friend joins in the search for Grandfather Robinson's missing false teeth and meets one wacky relative after another

"The real fun is in the tension between the deadpan words and the fantastical pictures. . . . Save this for small groups, which will most appreciate the wondrous visual details." Booklist

The fantastic flying books of Mr. Morris Lessmore; William Joyce. Atheneum Books for Young Readers 2012 56 p. (hardback) $17.99
Grades: PreK K 1 2 3   E
   1. Fantasy 2. Libraries -- Fiction 3. Books and reading -- Fiction
   ISBN 1442457023; 9781442457027; 9781442464896
                  LC 2012004465
This children's picture book "follows a dreamy bibliophile named Morris Lessmore, who loses his cherished book collection to a cataclysmic storm. . . . After meeting a 'lovely lady . . . being pulled along by a festive squadron of flying books,' Morris finds an abandoned library whose books are alive and whose covers beat like the wings of birds. They flutter around him protectively, watch as he starts writing again, and care for him as he ages." (Publishers Weekly)

"The message-heavy narrative is lifted by Joyce's superb artwork, presenting nostalgic, picket-fence scenes with a modeled, dimensional feel built on the animation but given a lustrous polish for the printed page." Booklist

Juan, Ana

The Night Eater; by Ana Juan. Arthur A. Levine Books 2004 un il $16.95
Grades: K 1 2 3   E
   1. Night -- Fiction
   ISBN 0-439-48891-5
                  LC 2003-20197
The Night Eater, who brings each new day by gobbling up the darkness, decides he is too fat and stops eating, with dire consequences

"The sense of magic realism in this story is matched by in Juan's richly colored acrylic-and-wax paintings. . . . This delightful tale will definitely appeal to children's imaginations." SLJ

The pet shop revolution. Arthur A. Levine Books 2011 un il
Grades: 1 2 3   E
   1. Pets -- Fiction 2. Animals -- Fiction 3. Animal

rescue -- Fiction

ISBN 0-545-12810-2; 978-0-545-12810-0

LC 2010051325

Everyone is afraid of Mr. Walnut, the scowling owner of the biggest pet store in the city, who sells all kinds of animals to rich customers from out of town, but when Mina's pet rabbit goes missing she vows to do something about it.

"This intriguing and thought-provoking tale skillfully illustrates the benevolence that is born when one walks in the shoes of another. It may also generate some activist thinking among young readers. . . . Juan's beautifully stylized and deeply expressive acrylic and colored pencil drawings perfectly capture the somber tone that prevails throughout most of the book." SLJ

Judge, Lita

Pennies for elephants. Hyperion Books for Children 2009 un il $16.99

Grades: PreK K 1 2   E

1. Zoos -- Fiction 2. Elephants -- Fiction

ISBN 978-1-4231-1390-4; 1-4231-1390-X

"In 1914, the children of Boston raised $6,000 to buy three trained elephants for the Franklin Park Zoo. But told through the eyes of siblings (and fund-raisers) Dorothy and Henry, the story expands into an inspired celebration of kid power. . . . Dollops of historical flavor abound, with watercolors of knickers-clad boys and streets bustling with people, horses and horseless carriages. Warm sepia tones lend atmosphere." Publ Wkly

Red hat; Lita Judge. Atheneum Books for Young Readers 2013 40 p. (hardcover) $16.99

Grades: PreK K 1 2   E

1. Hats -- Juvenile fiction 2. Picture books for children 3. Forest animals -- Juvenile fiction 4. Hats -- Fiction 5. Forest animals -- Fiction 6. Animals -- Infancy -- Fiction

ISBN 1442442328; 9781442442320; 9781442442337

LC 2012002600

In this children's picture book story, by Lita Judge, "it's spring-cleaning time now, so the child washes the red hat and hangs it out to dry. . . . When the critters spy the hat pinned to the line, . . . an energetic game of keep-away breaks out, with the accompanying sounds and exclamations of pursuit and merriment. . . . [Until] the animals' realiz[e] that the hat is now just one long red strand of yarn with a white pompom on the end." (Kirkus)

★ **Red** sled. Atheneum Books for Young Readers 2011 un il $16.99

Grades: PreK K 1 2   E

1. Sounds -- Fiction 2. Sledding -- Fiction 3. Forest animals -- Fiction

ISBN 978-1-4424-2007-6; 1-4424-2007-3

LC 2010033264

At night, a host of woodland creatures plays with a child's red sled.

"The premise of this book is simple; the execution is anything but. . . . Pencil and watercolor spreads create a basic wintry mountain environment, but the stars of the show are the expressive animals. Their childlike delight in each dynamic scene brings a sense of excitement to the story. The text consists entirely of sound effects, laid out on the page in varying font sizes to evoke a sense of movement." SLJ

Jules, Jacqueline

Duck for Turkey Day; illustrated by Kathyrn Mitter. Albert Whitman 2009 un il $16.99

Grades: K 1 2 3   E

1. School stories 2. Thanksgiving Day -- Fiction 3. Vietnamese Americans -- Fiction

ISBN 978-0-8075-1734-5; 0-8075-1734-8

LC 2008055537

When Tuyet finds out that her Vietnamese family is having duck rather than turkey for Thanksgiving dinner, she is upset until she finds out that other children in her class did not eat turkey either.

"Mitter's acrylic illustrations, in clear bright colors and simple shapes, capture the warmth of the holiday bustle and the affection among family members." Booklist

Juster, Norton

★ **Neville**; [illustrations by G. Brian Karas] Schwartz & Wade Books 2011 un il $17.99; lib bdg $20.99

Grades: PreK K 1 2   E

1. Moving -- Fiction

ISBN 978-0-375-86765-1; 0-375-86765-1; 978-0-375-96765-8 lib bdg; 0-375-96765-6 lib bdg

LC 2010024119

When a boy and his family move to a new house, he devises an ingenious way to meet people in the neighborhood.

This is an "emotionally authentic tale. . . . Karas's melancholy illustrations brighten and expand as the mood improves; small, quiet type sets the sullen tone, until colorful hand-lettered display type implies the children's collective chatter. . . . Juster . . . identifies a common, stressful situation, and Karas handles the drama with compassion." Publ Wkly

★ The **hello**, goodbye window; story by Norton Juster; pictures by Chris Raschka. Hyperion Books for Children 2005 un il $15.95

Grades: PreK K 1 2   E

1. Grandparents -- Fiction

ISBN 0-7868-0914-0

Awarded the Caldecott Medal, 2006

"The window in Nanna and Poppy's kitchen is no ordinary window—it is the place where love and magic happens. . . . The first-person text is both simple and sophisticated, conjuring a perfectly child-centered world. . . . Using a bright rainbow palette of saturated color, Raschka's impressionistic, mixed-media illustrations portray a loving, mixed-race family." SLJ

Another title about Nanna and Poppy and their granddaughter is:

Sourpuss and Sweetie Pie (2008)

★ The **odious** Ogre; story by Norton Juster; pictures by Jules Feiffer. Michael Di Capua Books 2010 un il $17.95

Grades: K 1 2 3   E

1. Fairy tales 2. Monsters -- Fiction

ISBN 978-0-545-16202-9; 0-545-16202-5

An ogre "rampages through the countryside, terrorizing (and eating) the residents with impunity. Until, that is, he is utterly 'confounded, overcome, and undone' by the unexpected kindness and friendly advice of a young woman. . . . Kids might not pick up on all of the philosophical overtones, but they're sure to enjoy Juster's rich wordplay and happily ridiculous story and Feiffer's wonderfully scratchy and energetic watercolors." Kirkus

Kain, Karen

The **Nutcracker**; paintings by Rajka Kupesic. Tundra Books 2005 un il $18.95

Grades: K 1 2 3   E

1. Fairy tales 2. Christmas -- Fiction

ISBN 0-88776-696-X

This is a "striking staging of the classic ballet. . . . The narrative reads smoothly, but it's the art that steals the show. Peopled with doll-like folk-art figures, Kupesic's full-page illustrations . . . are intense with luminous colors." Booklist

Kalan, Robert

★ **Jump,** frog, jump! pictures by Byron Baron. Greenwillow Books 1995 un il $16.99; pa $6.99

Grades: PreK K 1   E

1. Stories in rhyme 2. Frogs -- Fiction

ISBN 0-688-13954-X; 0-688-09241-1 pa

A reissue of the title first published 1981

"When a frog catches a fly, he sets off a chain of predators. . . . The title answers the repeated refrain 'How did the frog get away?' and children will soon be chanting along with this cumulative tale enhanced by Barton's folk-art-style illustrations." Publ Wkly

Kanevsky, Polly

Sleepy boy; illustrated by Stephanie Anderson. Atheneum Books for Young Readers 2006 un il $15.95

Grades: PreK K   E

1. Bedtime -- Fiction 2. Father-son relationship -- Fiction

ISBN 0-689-86735-2

Unable to fall asleep, a little boy lying next to his father experiences the various sensations of his body and remembers a lion cub he saw that day at the zoo

"Simple, physical words and full-page, unframed, sepia-toned watercolor-and-charcoal images combine to create a portrait of blissful intimacy between a toddler and his father." Booklist

Kanninen, Barbara J.

A **story** with pictures; story by Barbara Kanninen; pictures by Lynn Rowe Reed. Holiday House 2007 un il $16.95

Grades: PreK K 1 2   E

1. Authorship -- Fiction 2. Illustration of books -- Fiction

ISBN 978-0-8234-2049-0; 0-8234-2049-3

LC 2006019535

An author forgets to give her manuscript to an illustrator who begins to paint whatever she herself wants, making the author a character in the book, along with a meddlesome duck and other creatures

Reed's "mixed-media compositions expertly contain the antic action. . . . The artist renders the characters in a childlike style, painting them with skewered proportions and in gumdrop-colored clothes, and enhances her spreads with collage elements. . . . Readers will enjoy the wild ride." Publ Wkly

Kaplan, Bruce Eric

★ **Monsters** eat whiny children. Simon & Schuster Books for Young Readers 2010 un il $15.99

Grades: PreK K 1   E

1. Cooking -- Fiction 2. Monsters -- Fiction 3. Siblings -- Fiction

ISBN 978-1-4169-8689-8; 1-4169-8689-8

LC 2008-50434

Henry and Eve, having ignored their father's warning, are kidnapped by monsters who eat whiny children, but while increasing numbers of monsters argue over how to prepare them, the siblings begin to play nicely. Includes a recipe for cucumber sandwiches.

"For those who like their picture books with a little edge and offbeat humor, this is a surefire hit. . . . Kaplan's minimalist cartoon illustrations bring to mind Quentin Blake's work and complement the humorous, quirky text with its askew frames, thick black lines, and color accents." SLJ

Kaplan, Michael B.

Betty Bunny didn't do it; written by Michael B. Kaplan; illustrated by Stéphane Jorisch. Dial Books for Young Readers 2013 32 p. (hardcover) $16.99

Grades: PreK K 1 2   E

1. Honesty 2. Rabbits -- Juvenile fiction 3. Conduct of life -- Juvenile fiction 4. Blame -- Fiction 5. Honesty -- Fiction 6. Rabbits -- Fiction 7. Behavior -- Fiction 8. Family life -- Fiction

ISBN 0803738587; 9780803738584

LC 2012014367

In this children's book, by Michael Kaplan, illustrated by Stephanie Jorisch, "the value of honesty as seen through the eyes of a . . . precocious preschooler. When Betty Bunny breaks a lamp, she blames it on the Tooth Fairy. Blaming someone else for something she had done seems like such a good idea to Betty Bunny. . . . But when a vase gets broken, everyone blames Betty Bunny, and no one believes her when she says that she really didn't do it." (Publisher's note)

★ **Betty** Bunny loves chocolate cake; pictures by Stephane Jorisch. Dial Books for Young Readers 2011 un il $16.99

Grades: PreK K 1   E

1. Cake -- Fiction 2. Food -- Fiction 3. Rabbits -- Fiction 4. Family life -- Fiction

ISBN 978-0-8037-3407-4; 0-8037-3407-7

LC 2010-28799

From her first bite, young Betty Bunny likes chocolate cake so much that she claims she will marry it one day, and she has trouble learning to wait patiently until she can have her next taste.

"Readers will delight in feeling older and wiser than Betty, and both Jorisch . . . and debut talent Kaplan demonstrate a sure handle on feisty modern family dynamics." Publ Wkly

Karas, G. Brian

The **Village** Garage. Henry Holt and Company 2010 un il $16.99

Grades: PreK K 1 2 3   E

1. Garages -- Fiction 2. Seasons -- Fiction 3. City and town life -- Fiction

ISBN 0-8050-8716-8; 978-0-8050-8716-1

LC 2009009223

Throughout the seasons the workers at the Village Garage are busy taking care of the town and its residents.

"Adding bits of fun along the way, the simple text explains [the workers'] tasks without too much detail. Nicely varied in composition, the appealing pencil, gouache, and acrylic illustrations offer wonderfully childlike depictions of the workers and their machines." Booklist

Kargman, Jill

Pirates & Princesses; by Jill Kargman & Sadie Kargman; illustrated by Christine Davenier. Dutton Childrens Books 2011 il $16.99

Grades: PreK K 1 2   E

1. School stories 2. Play -- Fiction 3. Sex role -- Fiction 4. Friendship -- Fiction 5. Kindergarten -- Fiction

ISBN 978-0-525-42229-7; 0-525-42229-3

LC 2011005191

Ivy and Fletch have been best friends since they were born but now, at age five, the boys in their kindergarten play Pirates at recess while the girls play Princesses, and the duo is split apart.

"The mother-and-daughter team tells the story, but it's Davenier's energetic pencil-and-watercolor illustrations that give the story its heart. . . . Though the story ends as expected, it's nice to see that they figure out things for themselves, with no adult intervention, giving young readers some good ideas for when gender roles exert themselves in school. Teachers especially will turn to this good-natured story; it will help open up a discussion about friendship that many children will profit from." Kirkus

Kasbarian, Lucine

The greedy sparrow; an Armenian tale. illustrated by Maria Zaikina. Marshall Cavendish 2011 un il $17.99

Grades: PreK K 1 2   E

1. Birds -- Fiction 2. Folklore -- Armenia

ISBN 978-0-7614-5821-0; 0-7614-5821-2

LC 2010-18172

A sparrow who is treated kindly by strangers repays each act of kindness with a trick to get more. Will the sparrow's greed get the best of him?

"Zaikina's expressive portrayals of both animal and human characters, rendered in bold outline and rich color, beautifully convey the tale's goofy fun. Her use of wax and oil paint in a kind of scratchboard technique smartly blends folk and cartoon styles." SLJ

Kasza, Keiko

★ My lucky day. Putnam 2003 un il $15.99; pa $5.99

Grades: PreK K 1 2   E

1. Pigs 2. Foxes 3. Pigs -- Fiction 4. Foxes -- Fiction

ISBN 0-399-23874-3; 0-14-240456-X pa

LC 2001-57874

When a young pig knocks on a fox's door, the fox thinks dinner has arrived, but the pig has other plans

"Kasza's gouache art is as buoyant and comical as her narrative." Publ Wkly

Ready for anything. G.P. Putnam's Sons 2009 un il $16.99

Grades: PreK K 1 2   E

1. Ducks -- Fiction 2. Worry -- Fiction 3. Raccoons

-- Fiction

ISBN 978-0-399-25235-8; 0-399-25235-5

LC 2008033615

Raccoon is nervous about all of the things that could spoil a picnic, from bees to dragons, until Duck convinces him that surprises can be fun.

"The characters' dialogue is lively and fun to read aloud; Kasza's affable gouache illustrations spotlight action and emotions." Horn Book

★ The dog who cried wolf; [by] Keiko Kasza. G.P. Putnam's Sons 2005 un il $15.99; pa $6.99

Grades: K 1 2 3   E

1. Dogs -- Fiction 2. Wolves -- Fiction

ISBN 0-399-24247-3; 0-14-241305-4 pa

LC 2004-24737

Tired of being a house pet, Moka the dog moves to the mountains to become a wolf but soon misses the comforts of home.

"With an effective variety of page layouts, the expressive pen-and-watercolor pictures show [Moka] dashing off on his adventures. . . . Thanks to excellent pacing, children will get caught up in the childlike Moka's emotions." SLJ

★ The wolf's chicken stew. Putnam 1987 un il $16.99; pa $6.99

Grades: K 1 2 3   E

1. Wolves -- Fiction 2. Chickens -- Fiction

ISBN 0-399-21400-3; 0-399-22000-9 pa

LC 86-12303

"Kasza combines quivery line and shaded color to turn Wolf and Chicken into scuptural forms. Landscape images are treated similarly. . . . Wolf is comically and suspensefully visualized, making the flimflamming refrains sound just right." Wilson Libr Bull

Kato, Yukiko

In the meadow; illustrated by Komako Sakai. Enchanted Lion Books 2011 un il $16.99

Grades: PreK   E

1. Sound -- Fiction 2. Nature -- Fiction 3. Meadows -- Fiction

ISBN 978-1-59270-108-7; 1-59270-108-6

LC 2010051988

A little girl named Yu hears the sounds of nature all around her when she follows a butterfly into a meadow.

This is illustrated with "expressionistic acrylic and oil-pencil illustrations in a palette of soft greens, browns, and blues. . . . With her fascination with nature and her first steps into independence and back again, Yu is a relatable, believable preschooler; and illustrator Sakai . . . eloquently captures the facial expressions and postures of the very young." Horn Book

Katz, Alan

Stalling; illustrated by Elwood H. Smith. Margaret K. McElderry Books 2010 un il $16.99

Grades: PreK K 1 2   E

1. Stories in rhyme 2. Bedtime -- Fiction

ISBN 978-1-4169-5567-2; 1-4169-5567-4

"Katz's exuberent, ebulliently punctuated tale is enhanced by Smith's humorous art. Cartoon drawings intermixed with digitally collaged items create a visual rhythm for the catchy rhyme." Kirkus

Katz, Bobbi

Nothing but a dog; illustrated by Jane Manning. Dutton Children's Books 2010 un il $16.99

Grades: PreK K 1 2   E

1. Dogs -- Fiction

ISBN 978-0-525-47858-4; 0-525-47858-2

LC 2009017918

"A young girl wishes for a dog while she engages in everyday activities, exclaiming that once the longing for a pup sets in, nothing stops it. Each page gives examples of other kinds of fun . . . but 'a dog is something else.' Subtle images of canines appear in the delightful watercolor illustrations. . . . This is a sweet addition to the child/pet genre." SLJ

Katz, Karen

My first Chinese New Year; [by] Karen Katz. H. Holt 2004 un il $14.95

Grades: PreK K   E

1. Chinese New Year -- Fiction 2. Chinese Americans -- Fiction

ISBN 0-8050-7076-1

LC 2003-23488

In this "picture book, a young girl prepares for and celebrates the Chinese New Year with her extended family. . . . The tale radiates warmth. . . . The collage illustrations, cut from paper with colorful Asian designs, also include paint and other media to capture the joyful celebrants." SLJ

My first Ramadan; [by] Karen Katz. Henry Holt & Co. 2007 un il $14.95

Grades: PreK K   E

1. Muslims -- Fiction 2. Ramadan -- Fiction

ISBN 978-0-8050-7894-7; 0-8050-7894-0

LC 2006030768

"A young Muslim boy describes the ways his family celebrates the holy month of Ramadan, explaining some of the rituals and symbols of the holiday. Straightforward, easy-to-read text and bright, friendly collage and mixed-media illustrations make this a solid, approachable resource." Horn Book Guide

Now I'm big; Karen Katz. Margaret K. McElderry Books 2013 32 p. (hardcover) $15.99

Grades: PreK   E

1. Babies -- Fiction 2. Growth -- Fiction

ISBN 9781416935476

LC 2011047256

In this picture book, "a multiracial cast of children who note ways they've grown up from babyhood to toddlers/preschoolers. 'I used to be a baby,' the first speaker begins, setting up a pattern: on each spread, the verso lists something the child did as a baby ('When I was a baby, I had to wear diapers') while the recto offers a contrasting ability of the older child ('NOW I'M BIG! I can wear real underpants and poo in the toilet')." (Bulletin of the Center for Children's Books)

Princess Baby; [by] Karen Katz. Schwartz & Wade Books 2008 un il $14.99; lib bdg $17.99

Grades: PreK   E

1. Nicknames -- Fiction 2. Princesses -- Fiction

ISBN 978-0-375-84119-4; 0-375-84119-9; 978-0-375-94119-1 lib bdg; 0-375-94119-3 lib bdg

LC 2007001913

A little girl does not like any of the nicknames her parents have for her she wants to be called by her "real" name, Princess Baby

"Katz has drawn the human and stuffed-animal characters with perfectly rounded heads, and she uses other softly curving lines in rendering motions. . . . The [predominant] color is fuchsia, while other bright hues complement the rosy tones. . . . Toddlers will ask for repeated readings of this cheerful view of a youngster's world." SLJ

Other titles about Princess Baby are:

Princess Baby, night-night (2009)

Princess Baby on the go! (2010)

Ten tiny babies; [by] Karen Katz. Margaret K. McElderry Books 2008 un il $14.99

Grades: PreK K 1   E

1. Counting 2. Stories in rhyme 3. Infants -- Fiction

ISBN 978-1-4169-3546-9; 1-4169-3546-0

LC 2007-36061

Babies from one to ten enjoy a bouncy, noisy, jiggly day until they are finally fast asleep at night

"The second half of every couplet is split by a page turn, providing a gentle tease that encourages readers to flip the page and complete the rhyme. Ideally suited for read-aloud in both cadence and content." Publ Wkly

Katz, Susan

ABC, baby me! by Susan B. Katz; illustrated by Alicia Padrón. Robin Corey Books 2010 un il bd bk $7.99

Grades: PreK   E

1. Alphabet 2. Board books for children 3. Infants -- Fiction

ISBN 978-0-375-86679-1 bd bk; 0-375-86679-5 bd bk

"This alphabet book is comprised of activities and actions that are presented from the perspective of several babies. For each letter, a simple scene features a child and caregiver from 'Adore me' to 'Zzzz, I'm fast asleep.' The soft-focus watercolor and pencil artwork is done in a predominately pastel palette. The text is simple with a lilting rhyme scheme that will encourge reading aloud." SLJ

Kay, Verla

Covered wagons, bumpy trails; illustrated by S.D. Schindler. Putnam 2000 un il $15.99

Grades: K 1 2 3   E

1. Stories in rhyme 2. Frontier and pioneer life -- Fiction 3. Overland journey to the Pacific -- Fiction 4. Overland journeys to the Pacific -- Fiction

ISBN 0-399-22928-0

LC 96-37478

Illustrations and simple rhyming text follow a family as they make the difficult journey by wagon to a new home across the Rocky Mountains

"Schindler handsomely augments the clip-clop rhyme with sweeping vistas and close-up views of the wagons, animals, and people through various stages of the journey." Horn Book Guide

Hornbooks and inkwells; illustrated by S.D. Schindler. G.P. Putnam's Sons 2011 32p il $16.99

Grades: PreK K   E

1. School stories 2. Stories in rhyme 3. Frontier and

pioneer life -- Fiction
ISBN 978-0-399-23870-3; 0-399-23870-0

LC 2010-13070

John Paul and his older brother Peter spend a year attending a one-room schoolhouse on the frontier.

"In both text and illustrations, the light narrative element is engaging. . . . Schindler's well-composed watercolor-and-gouache paintings offer appealing glimpses of a period that seems distant while portraying the characters as individuals behaving in ways that are wholly recognizable." Booklist

Keane, Dave

Daddy Adventure Day; illustrated by Sue Ramá. Philomel Books 2011 un il $15.99
Grades: PreK K   E
1. Baseball -- Fiction 2. Father-son relationship -- Fiction
ISBN 978-0-399-24627-2; 0-399-24627-4

LC 2010024077

Daddy Adventure Days are always special, and this one, featuring a boy's first visit to a baseball stadium, is no exception.

"Ramá's watercolor and digital collage illustrations capture the warm relationship between the wide-eyed boy and his ever-patient dad. . . . A satisfying story about spending time with loved ones." SLJ

Sloppy Joe; illustrated by Denise Brunkus. Harper 2009 un il $16.99; lib bdg $17.89
Grades: PreK K 1 2   E
1. Cleanliness -- Fiction
ISBN 978-0-06-171020-9; 0-06-171020-2; 978-0-06-171021-6 lib bdg; 0-06-171021-0 lib bdg

LC 2008020212

Sloppy Joe determines to do everything he can to surprise his family by becoming Neat Joe.

"The illustrations are hilarious. This charming picture book is a wonderful choice for most libraries." SLJ

Keats, Ezra Jack

Apt. 3. Viking 1999 un il hardcover o.p. pa $6.99
Grades: PreK K 1 2   E
1. Blind -- Fiction 2. Brothers -- Fiction 3. People with disabilities 4. Apartment houses -- Fiction 5. City and town life -- Fiction
ISBN 0-670-88342-5; 0-14-056507-8 pa

LC 98-41043

A reissue of the title first published 1971 by Macmillan
On a rainy day two brothers try to discover who is playing the harmonica they hear in their apartment building

"The well-paced text is illustrated with shadowy paintings that capably convey both the dingy surroundings and the brothers' affection." Horn Book Guide

Hi, cat! Viking 1999 un il $15.99
Grades: PreK K 1 2   E
1. Cats 2. African Americans 3. Cats -- Fiction 4. African Americans -- Fiction
ISBN 0-670-88546-0

LC 98-37764

A reissue of the title first published 1970 by Macmillan
This book "tells the story of Peter's friend Archie and the inquisitive, nondescript, half-grown alley cat that tags after him and manages to make a shambles out of the boys'

street carnival. The text provides an adequate framework for Keats's bold bright paintings of a lively city neighborhood." Horn Book Guide

Another title about Archie is:
Pet show! (1972)

Louie. Viking 2004 un il pa $6.99
Grades: PreK K 1 2   E
1. Puppets and puppet plays -- Fiction
ISBN 978-0-14-240080-7 pa; 0-14-240080-7 pa

LC 2003-11378

First published 1975 by Greenwillow Books
Susie and Roberto's puppet show is temporarily interrupted when Louis becomes fascinated by one of the puppets

"This story is illustrated with the same glowing colors . . . and with some of the postercollage that is the artist's trademark. The aura is touching without being maudlin, the writing simple and informal." Sutherland. The Best in Child Books

Other titles about Louie are:
Louie's search (1980)
Regards to the man in the moon (1981)
The trip (1978)

★ **Over** in the meadow; [written and] illustrated by Ezra Jack Keats. Viking 1999 un il $16.99; pa $6.99
Grades: PreK K 1 2   E
1. Counting 2. Nursery rhymes 3. Animals -- Poetry
ISBN 0-670-88344-1; 0-14-056508-6 pa

LC 98-47037

A reissue of the title first published 1971 by Four Winds Press

An old nursery poem introduces animals and their young and the numbers one through ten

"The book features Keats's illustrations that show animals in lively characteristic activity." Horn Book Guide

★ **The snowy** day. Viking 1962 31p il lib bdg $16.99; pa $5.99; bd bk $6.99
Grades: PreK K 1 2   E
1. Snow -- Fiction
ISBN 0-670-65400-0 lib bdg; 0-14-050182-7 pa; 0-670-86733-0 bd bk
Awarded the Caldecott Medal, 1963

A small "boy's ecstatic enjoyment of snow in the city is shown in vibrant pictures. Peter listens to the snow crunch under his feet, makes the first tracks in a clean patch of snow, makes angels and a snowman. At night in his warm bed he thinks over his adventures, and in the morning wakens to the promise of another lovely snowy day." Moorachian. What is a City?

Other titles about Peter are:
Goggles (1969)
A letter to Amy (1968)
Peter's chair (1967)
Whistle for Willie (1964)

Keller, Holly

★ **Geraldine's** blanket. Greenwillow Bks. 1984 un il hardcover o.p. pa $5.99
Grades: PreK K 1 2   E
1. Blankets -- Fiction
ISBN 0-688-07810-9 pa

LC 83-14062

"Simply but wonderfully expressive line drawings washed with pastel colors capture the gentleness and humor of the story." SLJ

Other titles about Geraldine are:

Geraldine and Mrs. Duffy (2000)

Geraldine first (1996)

Geraldine's baby brother (1994)

Geraldine's big snow (1988)

Merry Christmas, Geraldine (1997)

Grandfather's dream. Greenwillow Bks. 1994 un il $16.99

Grades: PreK K 1 2   E

1. Grandfathers -- Fiction 2. Cranes (Birds) -- Fiction

ISBN 0-688-12339-2

LC 93-18186

After the end of the war in Vietnam, a young boy's grandfather dreams of restoring the wetlands of the Mekong delta, hoping that the large cranes that once lived there will return

"Keller uses simple, direct storytelling and vivid watercolor and ink illustrations to present a complex theme in a story of hope and rebirth." Horn Book Guide

★ **Help!** a story of friendship. Greenwillow Books 2007 un il $16.99; lib bdg $17.89

Grades: PreK K 1 2   E

1. Fear -- Fiction 2. Animals -- Fiction 3. Friendship -- Fiction

ISBN 978-0-06-123913-7; 0-06-123913-5; 978-0-06-123914-4 lib bdg; 0-06-123914-3 lib bdg

LC 2006-32116

Mouse hears a rumor that snakes do not like mice and while trying to avoid his former friend, Snake, he falls into a hole from which neither Hedgehog, Squirrel, nor Rabbit can help him out

"This story has the simplicity of a fable. The appealing art is done in collographs, which are printed collages, and watercolors." SLJ

Miranda's beach day. Greenwillow Books 2009 un il $17.99; lib bdg $18.89

Grades: PreK K   E

1. Beaches -- Fiction 2. Mother-daughter relationship -- Fiction

ISBN 978-0-06-158298-1; 0-06-158298-0; 978-0-06-158300-1 lib bdg; 0-06-158300-6 lib bdg

LC 2008012645

Miranda and Mama spend a fun day at the beach building castles and catching sand crabs, and Miranda learns that just like the sand and the sea, she and her mother will always be together

"Attractive illustrations in watercolors and printed collages on well-designed spreads capture the children's activities and the vastness of the sand and sea. This is a disarmingly simple and reassuring selection." SLJ

Nosy Rosie; [by] Holly Keller. Greenwillow Books 2006 un il $16.99; lib bdg $17.89

Grades: PreK K 1 2   E

1. Foxes -- Fiction 2. Smell -- Fiction 3. Personal names -- Fiction

ISBN 978-0-06-078758-5; 0-06-078758-9; 978-0-06-078759-2 lib bdg; 0-06-078759-7 lib bdg

LC 2005022183

Rosie the fox's excellent sense of smell is good for finding things, but she stops using it after everyone begins to call her "Nosy Rosie"

"Keller takes on the subject of name calling in a gentle, simple, and compassionate manner. . . . The heartfelt dialogue poignantly conveys the little fox's hurt feelings and reads aloud perfectly. The colorful mixture of robust watercolors and simple black lines touchingly reveals each character's attitude through expressive body movement." SLJ

Pearl's new skates. Greenwillow Books 2005 24p il $15.99

Grades: PreK K 1 2   E

1. Ice skating -- Fiction

ISBN 0-06-056280-3

LC 2004-576

Pearl's birthday skates have a single blade and learning to use them is harder than she expects

"With her pitch-perfect text and uncluttered watercolor-and-ink pictures . . . Keller tells a tender story about accepting the failures and frustrations that come with learning something new." Booklist

Keller, Laurie

★ **Do** unto otters; (a book about manners) by Laurie Keller. Henry Holt 2007 un il $16.95

Grades: PreK K 1 2   E

1. Otters -- Fiction 2. Rabbits -- Fiction 3. Etiquette -- Fiction

ISBN 978-0-8050-7996-8; 0-8050-7996-3

LC 2006030505

Mr. Rabbit wonders if he will be able to get along with his new neighbors, who are otters, until he is reminded of the golden rule

"From the gleeful title pun to the kenetic illustrations, this clever book . . . introduces the golden rule with irresistible humor." Booklist

The **scrambled** states of America talent show. Henry Holt 2008 un il $16.95

Grades: PreK K 1 2   E

ISBN 978-0-8050-7997-5; 0-8050-7997-1

LC 2007-40907

The states decide to get together and put on a show featuring their particular talents. Also includes facts about the history and geography of the states.

"The snappy dialogue flows effortlessly, the personalities are as winning as ever, and the pictures' energy never flags. It's e pluribus boffo." Publ Wkly

Kelley, Ellen A.

My life as a chicken; as told to Ellen A. Kelley; pictures by Michael Slack. Harcourt, Inc. 2007 un il $16

Grades: PreK K 1 2   E

1. Stories in rhyme 2. Chickens -- Fiction

ISBN 0-15-205306-2; 978-0-15-205306-2

LC 2005020051

After escaping the frying pan, Pauline the chicken has an adventure that includes pirates, a typhoon, and a balloon ride before landing happily in a petting zoo.

"Slack's digital mixed-media illustrations are wacky and cartoonish, and the text ripples with big, impressive words befitting the exaggerated nature of Pauline's adventures." SLJ

Kelley, Marty

★ **Twelve** terrible things. Tricycle Press 2008 un il $15.99

Grades: 1 2 3 4   **E**

1. Courage -- Fiction 2. Monsters -- Fiction

ISBN 978-1-58246-229-5; 1-58246-229-1

LC 2007-46795

Grownups who wax nostalgic about their youth are given a visual tour through twelve terrible experiences of childhood, including bedtime monsters and "atomic wedgies."

"Realistic, double-page watercolor illustrations use a clever first-person perspective to render readers the victims of horrors such as a cheek-pinching lady, an over-the-top birthday clown, and a hairy-moled lunch lady. . . . Minimal text and detailed artwork combine to convey a macabre humor that is bound to ensnare even the most hesitant of readers." SLJ

Kelley, True

Dog who saved Santa. Holiday House 2008 un il $16.95

Grades: PreK K 1 2   **E**

1. Dogs -- Fiction 2. Christmas -- Fiction 3. Santa Claus -- Fiction

ISBN 978-0-8234-2120-6; 0-8234-2120-1

LC 2007-041180

With the help of his take-charge dog Rodney and a self-help video, young Santa Claus mends his lazy and irresponsible ways.

"The cartoon artwork, done in acrylic, watercolors, and colored pencils, captures the endearing pup's antics and will give readers the giggles." SLJ

Kellogg, Steven

★ **Best** friends; story and pictures by Steven Kellogg. Dial Bks. for Young Readers 1986 un il $16.99; pa $6.99

Grades: PreK K 1 2   **E**

1. Friendship -- Fiction

ISBN 0-8037-0099-7; 0-14-054607-3 pa

LC 85-15971

Kathy feels lonely and betrayed when her best friend Louise goes away for the summer and has a wonderful time

"The watercolor and ink illustrations are appealingly bright and magical. Kathy and Louise's daydreams are vividly and flamboyantly portrayed, with 'reality' just as attractively pictured." SLJ

The **Pied** Piper's magic. Dial Books for Young Readers 2009 un il $16.99

Grades: PreK K 1   **E**

1. Fairy tales 2. Rats -- Fiction 3. Magic -- Fiction

ISBN 978-0-8037-2818-9; 0-8037-2818-2

LC 2008-12267

In a story loosely based on The Pied Piper of Hamelin, an elf acquires from a miserable witch a magic pipe that allows him to transform things, including the mean-spirited Grand Duke who rules over a rat-infested town.

"Kellogg depicts the magic-making in bright, buoyant mixed media spreads that show streams of colorful text and corresponding animals pouring from the mouth of the pipe. . . . Far sunnier than the original, this slightly educational adaptation (thanks to the built-in spelling lessons within) should please parents and kids alike." Publ Wkly

★ **Pinkerton,** behave! story and pictures by Steven Kellogg. Dial Books for Young Readers 2002 un il $17.99; pa $6.99

Grades: PreK K 1 2   **E**

1. Dogs -- Fiction

ISBN 0-8037-2722-4; 0-14-230007-1 pa

A reissue of the title first published 1979

"Kellogg wittily captures expressions and movements of animal and human, wisely allowing the focal humor to emanate through the faces and action." Booklist

Other titles about Pinkerton are:

A penguin pup for Pinkerton (2001)

Prehistoric Pinkerton (1987)

A Rose for Pinkerton (1981)

Tallyho, Pinkerton (1982)

★ The **missing** mitten mystery; story and pictures by Steven Kellogg. Dial Bks. for Young Readers 2000 un il $15.99; pa $6.99

Grades: PreK K 1 2   **E**

1. Lost and found possessions 2. Mittens 3. Lost and found possessions -- Fiction

ISBN 0-8037-2566-3; 0-14-230192-2 pa

LC 99-54777

First published 1974 with title: The mystery of the missing red mitten

Annie searches the neighborhood for her red mitten, the fifth she's lost this winter

"Kellogg really outdoes himself with pictures that are filled with good cheer, warm spirits, and happy daydreams. . . . A book that's upbeat and touching by turns." Booklist

Kelly, Mij

Where giants hide; illustrated by Ross Collins. Sourcebooks/Jabberwocky 2010 un il

Grades: PreK K 1 2   **E**

1. Imagination -- Fiction 2. Voyages and travels -- Fiction

ISBN 1-4022-4270-0; 978-1-4022-4270-0

"A girl, convinced that all the world's magic has leaked away, is sad because she can't find any giants, fairies, goblins, unicorns, dragons, or genies. . . . By reading the pictures, young children will enjoy the visual joke and find satisfaction in figuring out the mismatch between the girl's narration and what is actually happening. The whimsical, detailed illustrations, dominated by bright red, yellow, and turquoise, add humor and capture the subtle message of the story" SLJ

Kelly, Sheila M.

Yummy! good food makes me strong. by Shelley Rotner and Sheila M. Kelly; photographs by Shelley Rotner. Holiday House 2013 32 p. col. ill. (reinforced) $16.95

Grades: 1 2 3   **E**

1. Food -- Juvenile literature 2. Children -- Nutrition -- Juvenile literature 3. Nutrition -- Juvenile literature

ISBN 082342426X; 9780823424269

LC 2012016564

This book by Shelley Rotner presents "color photos of children eating nourishing foods with enjoyment and helping to prepare them. The youngsters are shown in various indoor and outdoor settings, sometimes displaying brightly colored fruits and vegetables. Throughout, text boxes with nutrition tips are clearly meant for adults. The end page includes a handful of additional recommendations . . . and a ChooseMyPlate.gov diagram." (School Library Journal)

Kelsey, Elin

You are stardust; Elin Kelsey, Soyeon Kim. Owlkids Books 2012 32 p. $18.95

Grades: 1 2 3   E

    1. Nature -- Juvenile literature 2. Human beings -- Juvenile literature

    ISBN 1926973356; 9781926973357

                  LC 2011943505

This book by Elin Kelsey, illustrated by Soyeon Kim, "begins by introducing the idea that every tiny atom in our bodies came from a star that exploded long before we were born. From its opening pages, the book suggests that we are intimately connected to the natural world; it compares the way we learn to speak to the way baby birds learn to sing, and the growth of human bodies to the growth of forests." (Publisher's note)

Kempter, Christa

Wally and Mae; by Christa Kempter; illustrated by Frauke Weldin. North-South 2008 un il $16.95

Grades: PreK K 1 2   E

    1. Bears -- Fiction 2. Rabbits -- Fiction 3. Friendship -- Fiction

    ISBN 978-0-7358-2208-5; 0-7358-2208-5

"A capricious bear named Mae befriends a sensible rabbit named Wally, and this unlikely pair shares an idyllic cottage in the woods. . . . Both of the animals are depicted with tenderness. The colors are bright and many of the scenes show one or both of the characters in full action." SLJ

When Mama can't sleep; illustrated by Natascha Rosenberg. NorthSouth Books 2011 un il (Tuff books) $6.95

Grades: PreK   E

    1. Bedtime -- Fiction 2. Family life -- Fiction

    ISBN 978-0-7358-4015-7; 0-7358-4015-6

When worries keep Mama, Papa, and Max awake, they crawl into bed together with Max's teddy bear for comfort.

"The vibrant speads are filled with color, and the heavy, glossy paper will withstand toddler destruction. Comforting, soothing, and sure to be a hit." SLJ

Kenah, Katharine

    The **best** seat in second grade; story by Katharine Kenah; pictures by Abby Carter. HarperCollins Pubs. 2005 48p il (I can read book) $15.99; lib bdg $16.89; pa $3.99

Grades: K 1 2   E

    1. School stories 2. Hamsters -- Fiction

    ISBN 0-06-000734-6; 0-06-000735-4 lib bdg; 0-06-000736-2 pa

                  LC 2004-178

Sam's favorite thing about second grade is the class pet, a hamster named George Washington, so when the class goes on a field trip to a science museum, Sam cannot resist bringing George along

"Kenah has created an appealing cast of characters whose actions ring true. . . . Carter's watercolor illustrations add to the story's appeal." Booklist

    Other titles about this second grade are:

    The best teacher in second grade (2006)

    The best chef in second grade (2007)

Kent, Jack

There's no such thing as a dragon. Golden Book 2005 un il hardcover o.p. pa $6.99

Grades: PreK K 1 2   E

    1. Dragons -- Fiction

    ISBN 0-375-83208-4; 0-375-85137-2 pa

                  LC 2004-6123

    First published 1975 by Western Pub.

"When Billy Bixbee wakes up and finds a dragon in his room, his mother tells him there is no such thing. The neglected dragon grows larger and larger, eventually walking off with the house, and the Bixbee family is forced to admit his existence. Practically a classic. . . for its neat story line and humorous cartoons of expressively surprised characters." Horn Book Guide

Kerby, Mona

    ★ **Owney,** the mail-pouch pooch; pictures by Lynne Barasch. Farrar, Straus and Giroux 2008 un il $16.95

Grades: K 1 2 3   E

    1. Dogs -- Fiction 2. Postal service -- Fiction 3. Voyages and travels -- Fiction

    ISBN 0-374-35685-8; 978-0-374-35685-9

                  LC 2006-47605

In 1888, Owney, a stray terrier puppy, finds a home in the Albany, New York, post office and becomes its official mascot as he rides the mail train through the Adirondacks and beyond, criss-crossing the United States, into Canada and Mexico, and eventually traveling around the world by mail boat in 132 days.

"The author does an excellent job of introducing readers to the late-19th century and the system used by the postal service to send mail both nationally and internationally via horse-pulled wagons, trains, and steamships. . . . Barasch's ink and watercolor illustrations complement the narrative with period details. A pair of sepia-toned photographs at the end of the book adds to the authenticity of the tale." SLJ

    Another title about Owney is:

    The further adventures of a lucky dog: Owney, U.S. rail mail mascot (2009)

Kerley, Barbara

    You and me together; moms, dads, and kids around the world. with a note by Marian Wright Edelman. National Geographic 2005 32p il $16.95; lib bdg $25.90

Grades: PreK K 1 2   E

    1. Parent-child relationship 2. Family -- Juvenile literature 3. Parent and child -- Juvenile literature

    ISBN 0-7922-8297-3; 0-7922-8298-1 lib bdg

"Using a simple rhyming text, Kerley captures the essence of childhood's special moments, accompanied by superb full-color photos. . . . Diverse cultures in various locations around the world are represented. . . . Children and parents engage in activities such as playing an instrument, taking a walk, making a meal, fishing, and dancing. . . . This book is an excellent tool for raising awareness of cultural differences and similarities." SLJ

Kerr, Judith

One night in the zoo. Kane Miller 2010 un il $15.99
Grades: PreK K   E
  1. Counting 2. Stories in rhyme 3. Children's poetry
  4. Zoos -- Fiction 5. Magic -- Fiction 6. Animals
  -- Fiction
ISBN 978-1-935279-37-2; 1-935279-37-8

One magical night an elephant jumped in the air and
flew. Wild antics, high spirits and silly games of the other
zoo animals also occur. Will anyone find out?

"Kerr's softly shaded pencil drawings depict the beasts
and birds with all the charm of friendly animal characters
come to life. Fresh and simple." Booklist

Kessler, Cristina

The **best** beekeeper of Lalibela; a tale from Africa. by
Cristina Kessler; illustrated by Leonard Jenkins. Holiday
House 2006 un il $16.95
Grades: K 1 2 3   E
  1. Sex role -- Fiction 2. Beekeeping -- Fiction
ISBN 978-0-8234-1858-9; 0-8234-1858-8
                                          LC 2005046217

In the Ethiopian mountain village of Lalibela a young
girl named Almaz determines to find a way to be a beekeeper
despite being told that is something only men can do

"Jenkins follows the ups and downs of Almaz's labor in
deep-hued, mixed-media scenes spread richly across double
pages. . . . Kessler includes well-chosen details about the
beekeeping project and a few words from the local Amharic
and Tigringna languages." SLJ

Kessler, Leonard P.

★ **Here** comes the strikeout; newly il ed.; HarperCollins Pubs. 1992 64p il (I can read book) hardcover o.p.
pa $3.99
Grades: K 1 2   E
  1. Baseball -- Fiction
ISBN 0-06-023156-4; 0-06-444011-7 pa
                                           LC 91-14717

A revised and newly illustrated edition of the title first
published 1965

This "concerns a boy who can't hit a baseball until he
follows the advice of a friend. 'Lucky helmets won't do it.
Lucky bats won't do it. Only hard work will do it.' . . . A
winner." Booklist

★ **Kick,** pass, and run; story and pictures by Leonard
Kessler. newly il ed; HarperCollins Pubs. 1996 64p il (I
can read book) hardcover o.p. pa $3.99
Grades: K 1 2   E
  1. Football -- Fiction
ISBN 0-06-027105-1; 0-06-444210-1 pa
                                            LC 95-6185

A newly illustrated edition of the title first published 1966

"After a group of animal friends watches a boys' football
team play, they are eager to have their own game. An apple
serves as a ball until Frog eats it; a paper-bag football works
until Duck kicks and pops it. The game is kept alive when
a real football from the boys' game sails into the animals'
midst. [A] simply told story with plenty of sports action."
Horn Book Guide

★ **Last** one in is a rotten egg; newly il ed; HarperCollins Pubs. 1999 64p il (I can read book) hardcover o.p.
pa $3.99
Grades: K 1 2   E
  1. Swimming -- Fiction
ISBN 0-06-028485-4; 0-06-444262-4 pa
                                           LC 98-50882

A newly illustrated edition of the title first published 1969

After Freddy is pushed into deep water by a couple of
toughs, he decides to learn to swim

"This lively . . . sports story has been newly illustrated
with a multicultural cast in a New York City neighborhood."
Booklist

Ketteman, Helen

Goodnight, Little Monster; illustrated by Bonnie
Leick. Marshall Cavendish 2010 un il $16.99
Grades: PreK K   E
  1. Stories in rhyme 2. Bedtime -- Fiction 3. Monsters
  -- Fiction 4. Mother-child relationship -- Fiction
ISBN 978-0-7614-5683-4; 0-7614-5683-X
                                          LC 2009002185

Rhyming text describes a mother guiding her young
monster through bedtime preparations, such as howling at
the moon, snacking on worm juice and beetle bread, and
choosing a bedtime story.

"While the text is quite fun to read, it is the watercolor
illustrations that steal the show. Each page is filled with kid-
friendly monster details." SLJ

Swamp song; illustrated by Ponder Goembel. Marshall
Cavendish Children 2009 un il $17.99
Grades: PreK K 1 2   E
  1. Stories in rhyme 2. Animals -- Fiction 3. Marshes
  -- Fiction
ISBN 978-0-7614-5563-9; 0-7614-5563-9
                                          LC 2008013810

Down in the swamp where the cypress grows, the animals all come out to enjoy the day.

"The sunny illustrations are done with colored ink lines
and acrylic wash paint against mostly white backgrounds. . .
. Children will be tapping their toes with Old Man Gator and
creating their own cacophony of swamp sounds as they learn
about the inhabitants of this habitat." SLJ

The **three** little gators; illustrated by Will Terry. Albert
Whitman 2009 un il $16.99
Grades: K 1 2 3   E
  1. Folklore 2. Alligators -- Folklore
ISBN 978-0-8075-7824-7; 0-8075-7824-X
                                          LC 2008028085

In this adaptation of the traditional folktale, three little
gators each build their house in an east Texas swamp, hoping
for protection from the Big-bottomed Boar.

"Ketteman's retelling, including a sassy Texas twang,
makes the story hilarious and bright. . . . Terry's illustrations
work well with the story. The colors are vibrant yet ominous
and swampy." SLJ

Khan, Hena

★ **Night** of the Moon; a Muslim holiday story. illustrated by Julie Paschkis. Chronicle Books 2008 un il
$16.99

Grades: PreK K 1 2   E
1. Islam -- Fiction 2. Muslims -- Fiction 3. Ramadan -- Fiction 4. Id al-Adha -- Fiction 5. Pakistani Americans -- Fiction
ISBN 978-0-8118-6062-8; 0-8118-6062-0

LC 2007024962

"A new moon is in the sky, and Yasmeen, identified on the jacket as a seven-year-old Pakistani-American, knows that it is time for the holidays of Ramadan and Eid. . . . Paschkis, borrowing from the arabesque motifs and jeweled colors of Islamic art, portrays the Muslim community as warm, welcoming and multiethnic. . . . Sweet and visually striking, this is a good choice both for children who celebrate these holidays and for others seeking a bridge to their culture." Publ Wkly

Khan, Rukhsana
★ **Big** red lollipop; illustrated by Sophie Blackall. Viking 2010 un il lib bdg $16.99
Grades: PreK K 1 2   E
1. Parties -- Fiction 2. Sisters -- Fiction 3. Birthdays -- Fiction 4. Pakistani Americans -- Fiction
ISBN 978-0-670-06287-4 lib bdg; 0-670-06287-1 lib bdg

LC 2009-22676

"Khan is of Pakistani descent, and this tale of clashing cultural customs is based on an incident from her childhood. The story (and its lesson) comes to like in Blackall's spot-on illustrations. . . . This is an honest, even moving, commentary on sisterly relationships." Booklist

★ **Silly** chicken; illustrated by Yunmee Kyong. Viking 2005 un il $15.99
Grades: K 1 2 3   E
1. Chickens -- Fiction
ISBN 0-670-05912-9

LC 2004-15830

In Pakistan, Rani believes that her mother loves their pet chicken Bibi more than she cares for her, until the day that a fluffy chick appears and steals Rani's own affections.

"This picture book clearly depicts a child's jealousy. . . . Kyong . . . paints in a naive style, using fresh, warm colors. A pleasing book with an unusual setting." Booklist

Killen, Nicola
Not me! Egmont USA 2010 un il $13.99
Grades: PreK K 1   E
1. Cleanliness -- Fiction
ISBN 978-1-4052-4829-7; 1-4052-4829-7

Not one member of a group of friends admits to having made a big mess, or offers to pitch in to clean it up.

"The illustrations and typeface will melt hearts and delight and inspire potato-printing young readers. The simple, expressive shapes, mostly in muted tones with dapples of red to keep things cheery, are utterly fresh and warm, and the textures feel organic. Children will delight in this sweet-natured picture book." SLJ

Kimmel, Elizabeth Cody
Glamsters; written by Elizabeth Cody Kimmel; illustrated by Jackie Urbanovic. Hyperion Books for Children 2008 un il $16.99

Grades: K 1 2   E
1. Hamsters -- Fiction
ISBN 978-1-4231-1148-1; 1-4231-1148-6

LC 2008029692

Harriet the hamster is desperate to be adopted, so she gives her sister Patricia and herself glamorous makeovers in hopes they will get more attention when Hamster World has its huge annual sale

"The story is filled with clever details and laugh-out-loud humor, but the underlying message of self-acceptance is an important one for children to hear." SLJ

My penguin Osbert; illustrated by H. B. Lewis. Candlewick Press 2004 un il $16.99; pa $6.99
Grades: PreK K 1 2   E
1. Gifts 2. Penguins 3. Christmas 4. Penguins -- Fiction 5. Christmas -- Fiction
ISBN 0-7636-1699-0; 0-7636-5730-1 pa

LC 2003-40981

When a boy finally gets exactly what he wants from Santa, he learns that owning a real penguin may not have been a good idea after all

"Kimmel sneaks some sly humor into the well-told, nicely paced story, and Lewis' artwork, executed in watercolor and pastels and enhanced with digital renderings, has a soft look, colored in marshmallow tints." Booklist

Another title about Osbert the penguin is:
My penguin Osbert in love (2009)

The **top** job; by Elizabeth Cody Kimmel; illustrated by Robert Neubecker. Dutton Children's Books 2007 un il $16.99; pa $6.99
Grades: K 1 2 3   E
1. Occupations -- Fiction 2. Father-daughter relationship -- Fiction
ISBN 978-0-525-47789-1; 0-525-47789-6; 978-0-14-241424-8 pa; 0-14-241424-7 pa

LC 2006039770

On Career Day, a young girl entertains the class with a description of her father's exciting job as light bulb changer at the top of the Empire State Building.

"The pacing and rhythm of the text is impeccable. . . . The stylized, cartoon-style illustrations, rendered in clear colors and bold black outlines, nicely extend the plot." Booklist

Kimmel, Eric A.
★ The **Golem's** latkes; adapted by Eric A. Kimmel; illustrated by Aaron Jasinski. Marshall Cavendish Children 2011 un il $17.99
Grades: K 1 2   E
1. Rabbis 2. Jews -- Fiction 3. Hanukkah -- Fiction 4. Household employees -- Fiction
ISBN 978-0-7614-5904-0; 0-7614-5904-9

LC 2010020008

Rabbi Judah Loew ben Bezalel visits the Emperor, leaving a new housemaid to prepare for his Hanukkah party, but returns to find that she has misused the clay man he created. Includes historical and cultural notes.

"Kimmel's storytelling is effective in its use of suspense, humor, trope and repetition, making a fine read-aloud holiday treat." Kirkus

★ **Joha** makes a wish; a Middle Eastern tale. adapted by Eric A. Kimmel; illustrated by Omar Rayyan. Marshall Cavendish Children 2010 un il $17.99

Grades: 1 2 3   E

1. Wishes -- Fiction

ISBN 978-0-7614-5599-8; 0-7614-5599-X

LC 2009006334

An original story, based on the Joha tales of the Arabic-speaking world, in which a hapless man finds a wishing stick that brings him nothing but bad luck. Includes an author's note about the history of Joha tales.

"Kimmel's well-paced text smoothly builds events and dialogue, leaving the character interpretation to the comic portrayals in Rayyan's energetic watercolors." SLJ

Little Britches and the rattlers; by Eric A. Kimmel; illustrated by Vincent Nguyen. Marshall Cavendish Children 2008 un il $16.99

Grades: PreK K 1 2   E

1. Cowhands -- Fiction 2. Rattlesnakes -- Fiction

ISBN 978-0-7614-5432-8; 0-7614-5432-2

LC 2007030155

As Little Britches, in her best attire, starts for the rodeo in town, she is waylaid by several rattlesnakes wanting to do her harm, but with some quick thinking she finds a way to outsmart them all

"Kimmel's little yarn makes good use of early counting concepts and introduces some western lingo in a leisurely repetitive structure. . . . Nguyen's artwork complements the glib silliness." Booklist

Rip Van Winkle's return; adapted and retold by Eric A. Kimmel from Rip Van Winkle by Washington Irving; pictures by Leonard Everett Fisher. Farrar, Straus and Giroux 2007 un il $17

Grades: 1 2 3 4   E

ISBN 978-0-374-36308-6; 0-374-36308-0

LC 2005042922

A man who sleeps for twenty years in the Catskill Mountains wakes to a much-changed world

"Kimmel and Fisher take on an American literary treasure and make it accessible to young children. . . . The drama is nicely played out with Fisher's solid, strategically placed figures." Booklist

Stormy's hat; just right for a railroad man. pictures by Andrea U'Ren. Farrar, Straus and Giroux 2008 un il $16.95

Grades: PreK K 1 2   E

1. Hats -- Fiction 2. Sewing -- Fiction 3. Railroads -- Fiction

ISBN 0-374-37262-4; 978-0-374-37262-0

LC 2005-51233

As Stormy, a railroad engineer, searches for the perfect hat—one that will not blow off, get too hot, or shade his eyes too much—his wife, Ida, becomes increasingly annoyed that he will not let her help. Includes a historical note about the real Stormy and Ida Kromer.

"U'Ren's vibrant paintings capture the palette and motion of Midwestern landscapes and city scenes. . . . With a snappy, high-interest story and connections to hats, history,

trains, gender equality, and industrialism, this book is a gem for libraries and classrooms." SLJ

★ **Zigazak!** a magical Hanukkah night. illustrated by Jon Goodell. Doubleday Bks. for Young Readers 2001 un il $15.95; lib bdg $19.99

Grades: K 1 2 3   E

1. Jews -- Fiction 2. Magic -- Fiction 3. Hanukkah -- Fiction

ISBN 0-385-32652-1; 0-385-90004-X lib bdg

LC 98-46269

Two evil spirits wreak havoc on the town of Brisk's Hanukkah celebration, until the town's wise rabbi puts a stop to their mischief

"The text is safely boxed away from the devilry in double-page spreads in which intricately detailed art realistically depicts the furnishings, clothing, facial features, and even the townspeople's pets. Storytellers will have fun with the surprise ending." Booklist

The **mysterious** guests; a Sukkot story. by Eric A. Kimmel; illustrated by Katya Krenina. Holiday House 2008 un il $16.95

Grades: K 1 2 3   E

1. Jews -- Fiction 2. Sukkot -- Fiction 3. Brothers -- Fiction

ISBN 978-0-8234-1893-0; 0-8234-1893-6

LC 2007-43208

Three mysterious guests appear at generous but impoverished Ezra's table on Sukkot and bless him, while they bring curses upon his rich but selfish brother Eben.

This is "a lyrically rendered tale. . . . Krenina's stylized, harvest-toned acrylics and thoughtful, dark-eyed characters evoke a world where the everyday and mystical are intertwined, and righteousness is clear-cut." Publ Wkly

The **three** little tamales; by Eric A. Kimmel; illustrated by Valeria Docampo. Marshall Cavendish 2009 un il $17.99

Grades: K 1 2 3   E

1. Fairy tales 2. Wolves -- Fiction 3. Hispanic Americans -- Fiction

ISBN 978-0-7614-5519-6; 0-7614-5519-1

LC 2008010738

In this variation of 'The Three Little Pigs' set in the Southwest, three little tamales escape from a restaurant before they can be eaten, and set up homes in the prairie, cornfield, and desert.

"Docampo's oil-on-paper illustrations add dimension to the story and bring the three little tamales to life. An excellent addition to collections of fairy-tale retellings." Booklist

Kimmelman, Leslie

★ **Everybody** bonjours! by Leslie Kimmelman; illustrated by Sarah McMenemy. Alfred A. Knopf 2008 un il $16.99; lib bdg $19.99

Grades: PreK K   E

1. Stories in rhyme

ISBN 978-0-375-84443-0; 978-0-375-94443-7 lib bdg

LC 2007006899

"On vacation with her parents . . . and little brother, a girl embraces her role as tourist, savoring all the places where one can say 'Bonjour': On a barge trip down the Seine, at the top of the Tour Eiffel and Notre Dame, in a chic boutique. .

.. McMenemy's ... mixed-media images, mostly full-page scenes of classic locations, are a stylish yet timeless mélange of fauvist whimsy and affectionate reportage." Publ Wkly

In the doghouse; an Emma and Bo story. by Leslie Kimmelman; illustrated by True Kelley. Holiday House 2006 30p il (Holiday House reader) $14.95
Grades: K 1 2   E
1. Dogs -- Fiction 2. Vacations -- Fiction
ISBN 0-8234-1882-0

LC 2004047466

When the Lewis family goes on vacation to the lake, Emily gets mad at her best friend Bo, the family dog, so he runs away to look for a new best friend
"Kimmelman writes with simplicity and wit, affectionately portraying the main characters' flaws, feelings, and pride. Kelley's cartoonlike ink drawings, brightened with colorful washes, have a carefree air that suits the vacation setting and the tone of the story." Booklist

Mind your manners, Alice Roosevelt! written by Leslie Kimmelman and illustrated by Adam Gustavson. Peachtree Publishers 2009 un il $16.95
Grades: K 1 2 3   E
1. Governors 2. Presidents 3. Vice-presidents 4. Socialites 5. Children of presidents 6. Nobel laureates for peace 7. Presidents -- United States -- Fiction
ISBN 978-1-5614-5492-1; 1-5614-5492-3

LC 2008052837

A brief, fictionalized account of what life was like for Theodore Roosevelt during his political career, with his oldest daughter, Alice, a strong-willed and somewhat wild young woman, who loved to do things that shocked the public, even when she lived in the White House
"Gustavson's energetic oil paintings do justice to Alice's shocking escapades, and parts of the text . . . are cleverly incorporated into the art." Booklist

The **three** bully goats; illustrated by Will Terry. Albert Whitman 2011 un il $16.99
Grades: PreK K 1   E
1. Goats -- Fiction 2. Bullies -- Fiction
ISBN 0-8075-7900-9; 978-0-8075-7900-8

LC 2010024274

Billy goat brothers Gruff, Ruff, and Tuff are bullies who rule their meadow, but when they cross Little Ogre's bridge and are mean to the baby animals on the other side, they are in for a surprise.
"Terry's brilliantly colored acrylics have a soft, out-of-focus look to them, but there is no mistaking the grouchy looks and mean personalities of his Bully Goats. . . . Kimmelman's version stands out even from other nontraditional versions, since the ogre/troll is the good guy and the goats are the villains. A good springboard for both bullying conversations and problem-solving sessions." Kirkus

Kimura, Ken
999 Frogs Wake Up; by Ken Kimura; illustrated by Yasunari Murakami. NorthSouth 2013 48 p. $17.95
Grades: PreK K 1   E
1. Sleep -- Juvenile fiction 2. Frogs -- Juvenile literature
ISBN 073584108X; 9780735841086

In this children's book, by Ken Kimura, illustrated by Yasunari Murakami, "it's springtime in the swamp! As 999

young frogs awaken, they panic to find that all of the other animals are still asleep. First they wake the biggest frog . . . then the tortoise, the lizard, and the ladybugs. But when they hop down a hole and all pull together, they find someone they don't want to wake--a big, long snake." (Publisher's note)

★ **999** tadpoles. NorthSouth Books 2011 un $16.95
Grades: PreK K 1   E
1. Frogs -- Fiction 2. Hawks -- Fiction
ISBN 978-0-7358-4013-3; 0-7358-4013-X
Original Japanese edition, 2003
"This well-paced journey, with just enough tension to keep young listeners engaged, will be a solid storytime choice." Kirkus

Kinerk, Robert
Clorinda; illustrated by Steven Kellogg. Simon & Schuster Bks. for Young Readers 2003 un il $15.95; pa $6.99
Grades: PreK K 1 2   E
1. Stories in rhyme 2. Ballet -- Fiction 3. Cattle -- Fiction
ISBN 0-689-86449-3; 1-4169-3964-4 pa

LC 2003-4559

Defying the odds, Clorinda the cow follows her dream of becoming a ballet dancer
"As fine a mix of story and message as this is, it's the irrepressible art that makes this book shine. Kellogg is at the top of his game, finding the humor in every line." Booklist
Another title about Clorinda is:
Clorinda takes flight (2007)

King, Dedie
I see the sun in Afghanistan; illustration by Judith Inglese. Satya House Pub. 2011 40p il $12.95
Grades: PreK K 1   E
1. Family life -- Fiction 2. Bilingual books -- English-Dari
ISBN 978-0-9818720-8-7; 0-9818720-8-5
"This simple story follows a young Afghani girl from sunrise to sunset. Living in Bamiyan, a relatively safe city, Habiba fetches water, attends school, and anticipates the arrival of her cousins, who have lost their home because of the war. The story captures the flavor of the culture, and the love and support of this close family is evident. The story is written in both English and Dari (Afghan Farsi), and an author's note provides supplemental information. Inglese's watercolor and collage illustrations are well composed, and color and pattern add richness and texture." SLJ

King, Stephen Michael
Leaf; ideas, sound effects, and pictures. Roaring Brook 2009 un il $14.95
Grades: K 1 2   E
1. Dogs -- Fiction 2. Hair -- Fiction 3. Dreams -- Fiction
ISBN 978-1-59643-503-2; 1-59643-503-8
"A mopheaded child faces a momlike figure with scissors in her hands—definitely time for a haircut. The child, however, has other ideas and runs out to frolic in the grass. . . . Wonderful squiggly line, patches of green and brown, gold and blue and fabulous use of negative white space make this a joy to reread." Kirkus

Mutt dog! words and pictures by Stephen Michael King. Harcourt 2005 un il $16
Grades: PreK K 1 2   E
1. Dogs -- Fiction 2. Homeless persons -- Fiction
ISBN 0-15-205561-4
First published 2004 in Australia
A lonely dog finally finds a home after he makes friends with a woman who works at a homeless shelter.
"The presentation is well done, and the gentle pen-and-ink and watercolor cartoons tell the story beautifully. . . . The book's oversize format and clear wash illustrations on white backgrounds make this a good choice for storytimes." SLJ

You. Greenwillow Books 2011 un il $14.99
Grades: PreK K 1 2   E
1. Birds -- Fiction 2. Rabbits -- Fiction 3. Friendship -- Fiction
ISBN 978-0-06-206014-3
        LC 2010032237
Reveals the world as a colorful, musical, and exciting place where the most special thing of all is a best friend.
King "draws a pup with gravity-defying ears whose best chum is a tiny orange bird; together, they cavort through this free-verse paean to friendship. With curlicue lines and gentle watercolor tints, King creates a winning series of scenarios to accompany his text. . . . The text is good-tempered and reassuring, but it's King's pocket-size, whimsical characters that will endear his creation to readers." Publ Wkly

King-Smith, Dick
The **twin** giants; [by] Dick King-Smith; illustrated by Mini Grey. Candlewick Press 2008 67p il $16.99
Grades: K 1 2 3   E
1. Twins -- Fiction 2. Giants -- Fiction
ISBN 978-0-7636-3529-9; 0-7636-3529-4
Two twin giants do everything together, including looking for the perfect wives.
"This handsomely designed volume offers an original story accompanied by droll illustrations." Booklist

Kinney, Jessica
The **pig** scramble; written by Jessica Kinney; illustrated by Sarah S. Brannen. Islandport Press 2011 un il $17.95
Grades: PreK K 1   E
1. Pigs -- Fiction 2. Fairs -- Fiction 3. Brothers -- Fiction 4. Contests -- Fiction
ISBN 978-1-934031-61-2; 1-934031-61-5
"August is County Fair time in New England, and Clarence, the youngest of three brothers, is looking forward to the Pig Scramble, which involves 10 children and one wily piglet. . . . Clarence thinks that he can be the best, winning the contest and the pig. The story and illustrations match perfectly—they are both timeless and evocative of yesteryear. Brannen's watercolors are detailed. . . . The illustrations are many sizes, keeping the story flowing, and Brannen's pigs are bristly, adorable, and full of life." SLJ

Kinsey-Warnock, Natalie
★ **Nora's** ark; illustrated by Emily Arnold McCully. HarperCollins 2005 un il $15.99; lib bdg $16.89
Grades: K 1 2 3   E
1. Floods -- Fiction 2. Farm life -- Fiction 3.

Grandparents -- Fiction
ISBN 0-688-17244-X; 0-06-029517-1 lib bdg
        LC 2004-3444
During the Vermont flood of 1927, a girl and her grandparents share their new hilltop house with neighbors and animals.
This is a "well-told tale, based on an incident from the author's life. . . . [A] stunning picture is the wild, rainy scene showing houses bobbing along as the water pours down." Booklist

Kirk, Connie Ann
Sky dancers; illustrations by Christy Hale. Lee & Low Books 2004 un il $16.95
Grades: 1 2 3 4   E
1. Mohawk Indians -- Fiction 2. Steel construction -- Fiction 3. Father-son relationship -- Fiction
ISBN 1-58430-162-7
        LC 2004-1885
John Cloud, a Mohawk boy, lives in upstate New York, but he goes to visit his father who is working on the Empire State Building
"Rich, sunlit gouache illustrations establish the 1930s setting for this well-told story." Horn Book Guide

Kirk, Daniel
Honk honk! Beep beep! words and pictures by Daniel Kirk. Disney/Hyperion Books 2010 un il $15.99
Grades: PreK K   E
1. Stories in rhyme 2. Toys -- Fiction 3. Vehicles -- Fiction
ISBN 978-1-4231-2486-3; 1-4231-2486-3
        LC 2010010275
When a toy father and son set out early one morning for a cross-country drive in their jeep, they see all sorts of vehicles and pick up diverse passengers along the way.
"Bright colors, a rhythmic text, and an imaginative premise make this a winner for kids just starting to find fun in books. . . . The spacious layout and oversize typeface make the story accessible to the youngest readers and listeners, who will want to call out the noisy refrain." Booklist

Keisha Ann can! [by] Daniel Kirk. G.P. Putnam's Sons 2008 un il $15.99
Grades: PreK K 1 2   E
1. School stories 2. Stories in rhyme
ISBN 978-0-399-24179-6; 0-399-24179-5
        LC 2007-034815
Keisha Ann is proud of all the things she can do during her day at school.
The "rhyming text . . . is catchy and upbeat. . . . Gouache paintings done in a striking, childlike style are filled with motion and color. . . . The images are clear and crisp, making the book ideal for sharing aloud. The story ends on a positive, all-inclusive note." SLJ

★ **Library** mouse. Abrams Books for Young Readers 2007 32 p. col. ill. $15.95; $15.95
Grades: K 1 2 3   E
1. Mice -- Fiction 2. Libraries -- Fiction 3. Authorship -- Fiction
ISBN 0810993465; 9780810993464
        LC 2006031851

"In a rainbow of colors, the art, which features a slightly flattened perspective, ranges from small oval pictures of Sam busily sharpening pencils with his teeth to full-page views of the busy library.... This is ready-made to introduce a classroom writing activity.... This is fun, fun, fun." Booklist

A **friend's** tale; Daniel Kirk. Abrams Books for Young Readers 2009 32 p. col. ill.

Grades: K 1 2 3   E
   1. Mice -- Fiction 2. Authorship -- Fiction 3. Friendship -- Fiction 4. Libraries -- Fiction 5. Bashfulness -- Fiction
   ISBN 0810989271; 9780810989276

LC 2008024686

In this book, "Sam, the perky creative mouse hero of 'Library Mouse,' returns. The Writers and Illustrators Club's next project at the library is to be a joint one. Each author is to collaborate with an illustrator.... One night, busy researching his next story, Sam falls asleep. He must hide when the children start arriving, and he leaves his notebook behind. Tom finds it. Suspicious, the boy follows inky footprints to Sam's mouse hole and realizes that the mysterious author must be a mouse. When Tom leaves cheese and a cracker for him, Sam hopes that the boy will forget about him. Instead, Tom is inspired to write a story about shy Sam. He leaves the story by the mouse hole, and Sam surprises Tom by illustrating it. Together, they keep the secret of Sam's identity." (Children's Literature)

Kirk, David, 1955-
   Oh So Tiny Bunny; David Kirk. Feiwel & Friends 2013 40 p. $16.99

Grades: PreK K   E
   1. Size -- Juvenile fiction 2. Dreams -- Juvenile fiction 3. Rabbits -- Juvenile fiction
   ISBN 1250016886; 9781250016881

This children's book, by David Kirk, follows a small rabbit who dreams of being larger. "During the day, Oh So Tiny Bunny is very, very small. But at night, he dreams of being . . . as big as a dragon, or even a mountain! At first, that's fine, but then he feels lonely. There's no one to share it with. Are there no other bunnies so big as him? . . . In this book David Kirk reminds us that sometimes . . . it's not so bad being small." (Publisher's note)

Kirk, Katie
   Eli, no! Abrams Books for Young Readers 2011 un il $14.95

Grades: PreK K 1   E
   1. Dogs -- Fiction
   ISBN 978-0-8109-8964-1; 0-8109-8964-6

Eli is a sweet black dog with a knack for getting into huge messes. He makes his disastrous way through the house and the yard, at every turn disobeying his owners.

"There is a retro feel to the minimalist, bold illustrations that match the simple rhyming story.... Amusing details ... make this a fun read-aloud for small groups and lapsits." SLJ

Kirsch, Vincent X.
   Forsythia & me. Farrar Straus Giroux 2011 un il $16.99

Grades: PreK K 1   E
   1. Friendship -- Fiction
   ISBN 978-0-374-32438-4; 0-374-32438-7

LC 2009-53233

Chester has always been in awe of his best friend's accomplishments, but when she becomes ill, he discovers that he is capable of doing amazing things to entertain her while she is bed-ridden.

"The young audience will welcome the wild, imaginative play and the story of loyal friendship, all captured in the winsome ink, watercolor, and pencil illustrations." Booklist

Natalie & Naughtily. Bloomsbury Children's Books 2008 un il $16.99; lib bdg $17.89

Grades: K 1 2 3   E
   1. Twins -- Fiction 2. Sisters -- Fiction 3. Department stores -- Fiction
   ISBN 978-1-59990-269-2; 1-59990-269-9; 978-1-59990-320-0 lib bdg; 1-59990-320-2 lib bdg

LC 2007-51098

Natalie and Naughtily Nopps live above their family's department store and love to play there, but one particularly busy day they discover that 'helping' is even better than playing.

"Readers will pore over the intricately detailed watercolor and pencil illustrations of each floor of the department store while chuckling over the girls' ideas of helpfulness." Horn Book Guide

Two little boys from Toolittle Toys. Bloomsbury 2010 un $16.99; lib bdg $17.89

Grades: PreK K 1 2 3   E
   1. Play -- Fiction 2. Toys -- Fiction 3. Brothers -- Fiction
   ISBN 978-1-59990-428-3; 1-59990-428-4; 978-1-59990-429-0 lib bdg; 1-59990-429-2 lib bdg

LC 2009034583

The Toolittle Toy Company makes toys that children like to play with by making toys that like to play with children.

"Kirsch offers a clever story about the nature and rewards of play, and children will enjoy poring over the wild details of fanciful toys in the watercolor-and-pencil scenes, which culminate in a Toolittle Toy Company catalog at the back of the book." Booklist

Kirwan, Wednesday
   Minerva the monster. Sterling 2008 un il $14.95

Grades: PreK K 1 2   E
   1. Monsters -- Fiction 2. Family life -- Fiction
   ISBN 978-1-4027-5718-1; 1-4027-5718-2

LC 2007043376

Feeling out of sorts, Minerva pretends to be a monster, but after realizing that monsters do not eat cookies, read stories, or sleep in nice warm beds, she decides to rejoin her family.

"The gouache and colored-pencil illustrations are crisp, bright, and full of mischief, much like Minerva herself. This book will be a hit with readers." SLJ

Another title about Minerva is:
   Nobody notices Minerva (2007)

Kitamura, Satoshi
   Stone Age boy. Candlewick Press 2007 32p il $15.99

Grades: K 1 2 3 **E**

1. Stone Age -- Fiction 2. Prehistoric peoples -- Fiction
ISBN 978-0-7636-3474-2; 0-7636-3474-3

LC 2007025614

"A boy walking in the woods finds himself falling . . . through time and space, landing in the Stone Age. He befriends a girl named Om and learns about prehistoric society by watching her people make fire, prepare food, use tools, and celebrate a successful hunt. . . . Kitmaura makes Om's society come alive. . . . Sentences are concise and easy to read. . . . The well-designed pages make effective use of white space." Horn Book

Kladstrup, Kristin

★ The **gingerbread** pirates; illustrated by Matt Tavares. Candlewick Press 2009 un il $16.99

Grades: K 1 2 3 **E**

1. Cookies -- Fiction 2. Pirates -- Fiction 3. Christmas -- Fiction
ISBN 978-0-7636-3223-6; 0-7636-3223-6

LC 2007-23171

When Jim's gingerbread pirate, Captain Cookie, comes alive, the tasty treat prepares to battle Santa Claus, who likes to eat cookies on Christmas Eve.

"An exciting story and full-page, dramatically composed paintings depicting harrowing adventures with a mouse, a cat, and the crew imprisoned in a cookie jar make this a good holiday read-aloud." SLJ

Klassen, Jon

★ **I** want my hat back. Candlewick Press 2011 un il $15.99

Grades: PreK K 1 2 **E**

1. Hats -- Fiction 2. Bears -- Fiction 3. Animals -- Fiction 4. Lost and found possessions -- Fiction
ISBN 978-0-7636-5598-3; 0-7636-5598-8

LC 2010042793

"Digitally manipulated ink paintings show a slow-witted bear. . . . Unadorned lines of type, printed without quotation marks of attributions, parallel the sparse lines Klassen uses for the forest's greenery. . . . [Klassen creates] skillful characterizations. . . . Each animal emerges fully realized." Publ Wkly

★ **This** is not my hat; Jon Klassen. Candlewick Press 2012 40 p. col. ill. $15.99

Grades: K 1 2 3 **E**

1. Hats -- Juvenile fiction 2. Theft -- Juvenile fiction 3. Fishes -- Juvenile fiction
ISBN 0763655996; 9780763655990

LC 2012942300

Randolph Caldecott Medal (2013).

In this children's story, written and illustrated by Jon Klassen, a fish steals a hat from a larger fish. "When a tiny fish shoots into view wearing a round blue topper (which happens to fit him perfectly), trouble could be following close behind. So it's a good thing that enormous fish won't wake up. And even if he does, it's not like he'll ever know what happened." (Publisher's note)

Klausmeier, Jesse

★ **Open** this little book; by Jesse Klausmeier; illustrated by Suzy Lee. Chronicle Books 2013 40 p. (alk. paper) $16.99

Grades: PreK K 1 2 **E**

1. Toy and movable books 2. Books and reading -- Juvenile fiction 3. Board books 4. Color -- Fiction 5. Animals -- Fiction 6. Colors -- Juvenile fiction 7. Animals -- Juvenile fiction 8. Books and reading -- Fiction
ISBN 0811867838; 9780811867832

LC 2012002129

Boston Globe-Horn Book Honor: Picture Book (2013).

This children's book, by Jesse Klausmeier, illustrated by Suzy Lee, features a series of nested smaller books within itself. The story revolves around a group of animals which each individually read about other animals reading more books until the end where they close their books and find another. The book gives tribute and attention to the joys of reading, colors, and friendship.

Kleven, Elisa

Welcome home, Mouse. Tricycle Books 2010 un il $15.99; lib bdg $18.99

Grades: PreK K 1 **E**

1. Mice -- Fiction 2. Houses -- Fiction 3. Elephants -- Fiction
ISBN 978-1-58246-277-6; 1-58246-277-1; 978-1-58246-364-3 lib bdg; 1-58246-364-6 lib bdg

Stanley the elephant, who is very clumsy, accidentally smashes Mouse's house, then promises to try to make a new one.

"The fascinating illustrations made from watercolors, ink, pastels, and colored pencils feature two simply drawn plump gray elephants and a small tan mouse placed on intricately assembled collage backgrounds. . . . Using one's imagination, repairing a mistake, and making a new friend are some of the themes contained in this charming story." SLJ

★ The **apple** doll; [by] Elisa Kleven. Farrar, Straus & Giroux 2007 un il $16

Grades: PreK K 1 2 **E**

1. School stories 2. Dolls -- Fiction 3. Apples -- Fiction
ISBN 978-0-374-30380-8; 0-374-30380-0

LC 2006040981

Lizzy is scared to start school, so she makes a doll out of an apple from her favorite tree to take with her on the first day and keep her company. Includes instructions for making an apple doll

"Kleven's lovely mixed-media collage illustrations . . . are filled with eye-catching detail and activity. A sweet story about accepting change, working together, and forming new friendships." SLJ

The **friendship** wish. Dutton Childrens Books 2011 un il $17.99

Grades: PreK K 1 2 **E**

1. Dogs -- Fiction 2. Angels -- Fiction 3. Moving -- Fiction 4. Animals -- Fiction 5. Friendship -- Fiction
ISBN 978-0-525-42374-4; 0-525-42374-5

LC 2011005248

Foley the dog has trouble making friends when he moves to a new home, but after an angel visits him in a dream, Foley's neighbors come to hear about the experience and they all begin to share their talents in hopes the angel will return.

Kleven "deftly interweaves fantastic and familiar elements, and kids will recognize how imagination, support, and shared activities can inspire fun and connection. The lively, lyrical prose is illustrated with colorful, intricate mixed-media artwork that includes droll details that invited close viewing." Booklist

Kling, Kevin

Big little brother; illustrations by Chris Monroe. Borealis Books 2011 il $17.95

Grades: PreK K 1 2   E

1. Size -- Fiction 2. Brothers -- Fiction

ISBN 978-0-87351-844-4; 0-87351-844-6

LC 2011018586

A four-year-old boy explains that his little brother is bigger than he is, follows him everywhere, and is annoying, but his presence becomes indispensible when bullies are around.

"Monroe's minimalist, boldly hued cartoons carefully and humorously depict the action. Big Brother's emotional ups and downs are subtly expressed, while Little Brother mostly maintains an even-tempered smile. A sweet-natured tale about negotiating sibling dynamics that is as comforting as a hug." Kirkus

Klinting, Lars

What do you want? [translated from the Swedish by Maria Lundin] Groundwood Books/House of Anansi Press 2006 un il $15.95; board book $7.95

Grades: PreK   E

1. Board books for children 2. Wishes -- Fiction

ISBN 0-88899-636-5; 978-0-88899-988-7 board book

Original Swedish edition 2003

"This diminutive book is mesmerizing in its calm simplicity. Cream-colored pages provide the backdrop to clear, precise color illustrations that are executed with artistic aplomb." SLJ

Klise, Kate

Grammy Lamby and the secret handshake; Kate Klise; illustrated by M. Sarah Klise. Henry Holt 2012 32 p. (hc) $16.99

Grades: K 1 2   E

1. Storms -- Fiction 2. Grandmothers -- Fiction 3. Picture books for children 4. Sheep -- Fiction 5. Repairing -- Fiction 6. Neighborliness -- Fiction

ISBN 0805093133; 9780805093131

LC 2011028532

This is the tale of "Grammy Lamby who arrives for a visit and swoops down on her little grandson Larry. Larry learns her secret handshake is meant to let him know Grammy loves him but he is more than a little intimidated by her. She's very energetic and a trifle overbearing," which "leaves Larry waiting for her visits to end. However, when a terrible storm descends and leaves the house in shambles, Grammy Lamby stays for a month, energetically fixing things." (Children's Literature)

★ **Shall** I knit you a hat? a Christmas yarn. illustrated by M. Sarah Klise. H. Holt 2004 un il $16.95; pa $6.99

Grades: PreK K 1 2   E

1. Hats 2. Rabbits 3. Knitting 4. Christmas 5. Domestic animals 6. Hats -- Fiction 7. Animals -- Fiction 8. Rabbits -- Fiction 9. Christmas -- Fiction

ISBN 0-8050-7318-3; 0-312-37139-X pa

LC 2003-22497

When Mother Rabbit knits a warm winter hat for Little Rabbit, he likes it so much that he suggests they make hats for all of their friends as Christmas gifts

"The acrylic artwork glows with humor and radiates warmth." Booklist

Other titles about Little Rabbit are:

Why do you cry?: not a sob story (2006)

Imagine Harry (2007)

Little Rabbit and the night mare (2008)

Little Rabbit and the Meanest Mother on Earth (2010)

★ **Stand** straight, Ella Kate; the true story of a real giant. pictures by M. Sarah Klise. Dial Books for Young Readers 2010 un il $16.99

Grades: K 1 2 3   E

1. Giants 2. Giants -- Fiction

ISBN 978-0-8037-3404-3; 0-8037-3404-2

A fictionalized biography of Ella Kate Ewing, born in 1872, who was eight feet tall by the age of seventeen and who became financially independent by traveling the country for nearly twenty years appearing at museums, exhibitions, and in circus shows.

"The story is well told in straightforward prose with lots of dialogue, and Ella's strength of character shines through. The stylized acrylic illustrations add much to the text, using bright colors and emphasizing Ella's height from various perspectives." SLJ

Kloske, Geoffrey

Once upon a time, the end; (asleep in 60 seconds) by Geoffrey Kloske and Barry Blitt. Atheneum Books for Young Readers 2005 25p il $15.95

Grades: PreK K 1 2   E

1. Fairy tales 2. Bedtime -- Fiction

ISBN 0-689-86619-4

A tired father takes only a few sentences to tell a number of classic tales in order to get the persistent listener to fall asleep.

"Blitt's ink-and-watercolor illustrations are amusing, with fine lines and soothing colors underscoring the comedy in the characters and situations." SLJ

Knapman, Timothy

Guess what I found in Dragon Wood? by Timothy Knapman; illustrated by Gwen Millward. Bloomsbury Children's Books 2008 un il $16.95

Grades: PreK K 1 2   E

1. Dragons -- Fiction

ISBN 978-1-59990-190-9; 1-59990-190-0

LC 2007018847

A young dragon finds a boy and introduces him to his family, friends, and teacher, but it is clear that the boy would like to return to his faraway home

"Executed with humor and cozy, scaly charm. . . . The tidy linework in the line-and-watercolor art adds a certain comic formality to the dragonworld." Bull Cent Child Books

Mungo and the spiders from space; illustrated by Adam Stower. Dial Books for Young Readers 2008 un il $16.99

Grades: PreK K 1 2   E

1. Science fiction 2. Comic books, strips, etc. -- Fiction

ISBN 978-0-8037-3277-3; 0-8037-3277-5

First published 2007 in the United Kingdom

"Mungo discovers the last page is missing from his secondhand picture book; how will he learn what happens to Captain Galacticus and Gizmo? Mungo himself provides the ending when, suddenly, he is pulled into the book and saves the universe. The brightly colored comic-book format, busy with rocket ships, space creatures, and humorous details, weaves Mungo's story into this metafictional adventure." Horn Book Guide

Knapp, Ruthie

★ **Who** stole Mona Lisa? illustrations by Jill McElmurry. Bloomsbury Children's Books 2010 un il $17.99; lib bdg $18.89

Grades: K 1 2 3   E

1. Artists 2. Painters 3. Scientists 4. Writers on science 5. Art thefts -- Fiction 6. Art -- History -- Juvenile literature

ISBN 978-1-59990-058-2; 1-59990-058-0; 978-1-59990-549-5 lib bdg; 1-59990-549-3 lib bdg

LC 2010005512

Tells the story of the famous Leonardo Da Vinci portrait known as the Mona Lisa, including its 1911 theft from the Louvre in Paris, from the point of view of the subject of the painting. Includes an author's note with facts about the painting.

"The engaging, rhythmic-but-not-rhyming text fuses deliciously with McElmurry's marvelous artwork—its flat, decorative style, skewed head angles, strong lines and rich gouache colors echo both illuminated manuscripts and the Sienese school of painting. . . . A gem." Kirkus

Kneen, Maggie

Chocolate moose. Dutton Children's Books 2011 un il $16.99

Grades: PreK K 1   E

1. Mice -- Fiction 2. Moose -- Fiction 3. Baking -- Fiction

ISBN 978-0-525-42202-0; 0-525-42202-1

LC 2010013464

When a chocolate-loving moose goes to work in Mrs. Mouse's bakery he does not fit in very well, but Mrs. Mouse discovers that he has other useful talents.

"This is a winsome offering, illustrated in soft-edged shapes and pastel colors. . . . The baby mice are delighted with Moose, and children will be too." Booklist

Knowlton, Laurie Lazzaro

A **young** man's dance; [by] Laurie Knowlton; paintings by Layne Johnson. Boyds Mills Press 2006 un il $15.95

Grades: K 1 2 3   E

1. Old age -- Fiction 2. Grandmothers -- Fiction 3. Alzheimer's disease -- Fiction

ISBN 1-59078-259-3

LC 2005021138

Grandma Ronnie's grandson has a hard time adjusting to her needing a wheelchair, living in a nursing home, and not recognizing him when he comes to visit her

"Swirling, dancing colors, both muted and sunny, accompany this lyrical story. . . . Oil paintings reveal clear, expressive faces on soft, fluid backgrounds that breathe action." SLJ

Knudsen, Michelle

Argus; illustrated by Andrea Wesson. Candlewick

Press 2011 un il $15.99

Grades: PreK K 1 2   E

1. School stories 2. Dragons -- Fiction 3. Chickens -- Fiction 4. Science -- Experiments -- Fiction

ISBN 978-0-7636-3790-3; 0-7636-3790-4

LC 2010-38721

Sallie's class is supposed to be raising chicks as a science project, but although Argus, the large, green, scaly creature that hatches from her egg, causes all sorts of trouble she worries about him when he disappears.

Wesson's "watercolors of the tubby Argus are wonderfully goofy. . . . Knudsen . . . never overplays her hand, but lets the story's laughs unfold naturally from the characters and circumstances. Her grasp of the life of the elementary school classroom is spot-on." Publ Wkly

Bugged! illustrated by Blanche Sims. Kane Press 2008 32p il (Science solves it!) pa $5.95

Grades: 1 2 3   E

1. Mosquitoes -- Fiction

ISBN 978-1-57565-259-7 pa; 1-57565-259-5 pa

LC 2007026567

Tired of being covered in itchy mosquito bites, Riley uses science to investigate why mosquitoes are more attracted to him than to his friends.

"Clear and simple sentences, colorful realistic illustrations, and diverse characters all contribute to this appealing easy reader. . . . Riley's activities serve as a great model of the research process as well as the scientific method." SLJ

★ **Library** lion; [by] Michelle Knudsen; illustrated by Kevin Hawkes. Candlewick Press 2006 un il $15.99; pa $6.99

Grades: PreK K 1 2   E

1. Lions -- Fiction 2. Libraries -- Fiction

ISBN 978-0-7636-2262-6; 0-7636-2262-1; 978-0-7636-3784-2 pa; 0-7636-3784-X pa

LC 2006042578

A lion starts visiting the local library but runs into trouble as he tries to both obey the rules and help his librarian friend

"Hawkes's deft acrylic-and-pencil pictures have appeal for generations of library lovers. They are rich with expression, movement, and detail. . . . This winsome pairing of text and illustration is a natural for storytime and a first purchase for every collection." SLJ

Kockere, Geert De

★ **Willy**; illustrated by Carll Cneut. Eerdmans Books for Young Readers 2011 un il $14

Grades: K 1 2   E

1. Elephants -- Fiction

ISBN 978-0-8028-5395-0; 0-8028-5395-1

LC 2010049545

Willy the elephant has everything an elephant should have, from four sturdy legs to a tail with a little brush on the end.

"It is the unexpected turn that De Kockere takes at the story's end that is the showstopper. Suddenly we are all Willy, in one great inclusive hug." Kirkus

Kohara, Kazuno

★ **Ghosts** in the house! [by] Kazuno Kohara. Roaring Brook Press 2008 un il $12.95

Grades: PreK K 1   **E**

1. Ghost stories 2. Witches -- Fiction

ISBN 978-1-59643-427-1; 1-59643-427-9

LC 2008018204

Tired of living in a haunted house, a young witch captures, washes, and turns her pesky ghosts into curtains and a tablecloth

"Kohara's wonderfully distinctive art, all orange and black, has the look of woodcuts. . . . A must-have for Halloween." Booklist

Here comes Jack Frost. Roaring Brook Press 2009 un il $12.99

Grades: PreK K 1   **E**

1. Winter -- Fiction

ISBN 978-1-59643-442-4; 1-59643-442-2

"A young boy has nobody to play with until a frosty figure named Jack appears. . . . All the boy has to do to ensure more fun is never mention anything warm. . . . The artwork is divine, beginning with the glittered jacket cover. . . . The simple yet creatively rendered shapes are all icy blues and snowy whites. . . . The artful design . . . is what will draw repeat viewers, young and old." Booklist

Kohuth, Jane

Duck sock hop; by Jane Kohuth; illustrated by Jane Porter. Dial Books for Young Readers 2012 32 p. col. ill. (hardcover) $16.99

Grades: PreK K 1   **E**

1. Ducks -- Fiction 2. Stories in rhyme 3. Picture books for children 4. Dance -- Fiction 5. Socks -- Fiction

ISBN 0803737122; 9780803737129

LC 2011029969

This children's picture book "stars a crew of dancing ducks whose webby feet are made even happier by donning all kinds of sprightly socks . . . . No matter that socks prove more of a hindrance than a help when it comes to dancing (the sock hop results in 'big duck flops!' and trips to the first-aid station); at book's end, the dancers are back at the Duck Sock Shop to pick up new pairs for the next soiree." (Publishers Weekly)

Ducks go vroom; illustrated by Viviana Garofoli. Random House 2011 31p il (Step into reading) lib bdg $12.99; pa $3.99

Grades: PreK K 1   **E**

1. Stories in rhyme 2. Ducks -- Fiction 3. Noise -- Fiction

ISBN 978-0-375-96567-8 lib bdg; 0-375-96567-X lib bdg; 978-0-375-86560-2 pa; 0-375-86560-8 pa

LC 2010002695

Relates three silly ducks' rather impolite visit to their Auntie Goose's house, introducing simple action and noise words.

"Concentrated colored backgrounds add to the visual appeal of the pages, which have either black or white text and bright cartoon illustrations. . . . A solid choice for libraries needing entry-level readers." SLJ

Kolanovic, Dubravka

Everyone needs a friend. Price Stern Sloan 2010 il $9.99

Grades: PreK K 1   **E**

1. Mice -- Fiction 2. Wolves -- Fiction 3. Friendship -- Fiction

ISBN 978-0-8431-9918-5; 0-8431-9918-0

Jack the wolf has been wishing for a friend, but Walter the dormouse may not be the right choice.

"This simple story is rendered in bright oil pastels, with thoughtful background details that give the illustrations a cozy feel. A tale of friendship that will fit nicely into most collections." SLJ

Kolar, Bob

Big kicks. Candlewick Press 2008 un il $16.99

Grades: PreK K 1 2   **E**

1. Bears -- Fiction 2. Soccer -- Fiction 3. Animals -- Fiction

ISBN 978-0-7636-3390-5; 0-7636-3390-9

"Biggie Bear's soccer-playing friends appear at his doorstep . . . begging him to join them. . . . Biggie is a jazz fan who collects stamps. . . . Despite his athletic shortcomings, the score is tied until the bear bends over to grasp a rare stamp on the ground and heads the ball into the net for the winning goal. . . . Kolar's soccer story is just rollicking enough for listeners. . . . Digital cartoons of rounded figures with exaggerated features are brightly hued and presented in detailed scenes that are balanced with less complex spreads." SLJ

Konagaya, Kiyomi

Beach feet; by Kiyomi Konagaya; illustrated by Masamitsu Saito. Enchanted Lion Books 2012 32 p. (hardback) $14.95

Grades: PreK K 1   **E**

1. Beaches -- Fiction 2. Picture books for children 3. Foot -- Fiction

ISBN 9781592701216

LC 2011052465

In this "installment in the 'Being in the World' series, Japanese collaborators [Kiyomi] Konagaya and [Masamitsu] Saito offer a[n] . . . account of a day in the life of a child at the beach. Cover art depicts . . . toes scrunching down into the sand, and the book opens to a first-person, stream-of-consciousness text detailing the child's seaside experience. It's never clear whether this child is a boy or a girl, but this doesn't matter, as from page to page those feet from the cover art feel the heat of sun-baked sand, the coolness of the ocean waters, and the hard pressure of a seashell underfoot. . . . [N]arration delivers the child's experiences in brief snippets of text that" describe the child's "experiences of the surroundings." (Kirkus)

Konnecke, Ole

Anton can do magic. Gecko Press 2011 il $17.95

Grades: PreK K 1 2   **E**

1. Magicians -- Fiction

ISBN 978-1-8774-6737-0; 1-8774-6737-5

"Young Anton dons a magician's turban and sets off to prove that he can make things disappear. Because his too-large turban keeps slipping down over his eyes, a few things do indeed go missing. . . . This story is told with a spare, easy-to-read text; it's the illustrations that tell the true story and add much humor." SLJ

Kono, Erin Eitter

Hula lullaby; [by] Erin Eitter Kono. Little, Brown 2005 un il $15.99

Grades: PreK K 1 2   E

1. Bedtime -- Fiction 2. Mother-child relationship -- Fiction

ISBN 0-316-73591-4

LC 2004-10270

Against the backdrop of a beautiful Hawaiian landscape, a young girl cuddles and sleeps in her mother's lap

"The rhyming text becomes almost hypnotic as night deepens around the two and, finally, the girl falls asleep. Glowing with warm colors, which seem all the more brilliant in the night scenes, the gouache-and-pencil illustrations create an idyllic vision of Hawaiian culture." Booklist

Kontis, Alethea

Alpha oops! the day Z went first. [by] Alethea Kontis; illustrated by Bob Kolar. Candlewick Press 2006 un il $15.99

Grades: K 1 2   E

1. Alphabet -- Fiction

ISBN 978-0-7636-2728-7; 0-7636-2728-3

LC 2006042310

Chaos ensues when Z thinks that its time for him to go first in the alphabet for a change

"Reflecting the letters' saucy ways, the colorful, stylized artwork dramatizes the action and offers bits of comic byplay for the observant. An alphabet book with attitude." Booklist

★ **AlphaOops!**: H is for Halloween; illustrated by Bob Kolar. Candlewick Press 2010 un il $15.99

Grades: K 1 2 3   E

1. Alphabet 2. Halloween -- Fiction 3. Alphabet -- Juvenile literature

ISBN 978-0-7636-3966-2; 0-7636-3966-4

LC 2009-14827

While putting on a Halloween pageant, the alphabet mixes things up with some spooky, and funny, results.

"Kontis's text is rhythmic and comical, and readers who are comfortable with the alphabet will delight in the silliness of this story. Kolar's illustrations are imbued with a sense of nighttime theater magic, and the slightly muted jewel-tone hues set the scene perfectly. A winsome union of humorous text and art." SLJ

Kooser, Ted, 1939-

Bag in the wind; illustrated by Barry Root. Candlewick 2010 un il

Grades: 1 2 3   E

1. Bags -- Fiction 2. Landfills -- Fiction 3. Recycling -- Fiction

ISBN 0-7636-3001-2; 978-0-7636-3001-0

One cold, spring morning, an ordinary grocery bag begins blowing around a landfill, then as it travels down a road, through a stream, and into a town, it is used in various ways by different people, many of whom do not even notice it.

"The muted, dappled colors of Root's gouache and watercolor illustrations are a perfect complement to Kooser's lengthy, meditative passages. . . . An excellent opener for discussions about creative reuse and recycling." Booklist

Kornell, Max

Bear with me. Putnam 2011 un il $15.99

Grades: PreK K 1   E

1. Bears -- Fiction 2. Family life -- Fiction

ISBN 978-0-399-25257-0; 0-399-25257-6

LC 2010-23202

A boy at first is angry when his parents suddenly welcome a giant bear named Gary into their family, but eventually he and Gary learn to get along.

"The pleasant watercolor, ink, and acrylic illustrations are expertly drawn, with an interesting use of outlining, perspectives, and layout. . . . . This charming offering can be enjoyed even by those whose families are staying just the way they are." SLJ

Kostecki-Shaw, Jenny Sue

My travelin' eye; [by] Jenny Sue Kostecki-Shaw. Henry Holt 2008 un il $16.95

Grades: K 1 2   E

1. Eye -- Fiction 2. Vision -- Fiction

ISBN 978-0-8050-8169-5; 0-8050-8169-0

LC 2007007224

Jenny Sue loves that her "travelin' eye" lets her see the world in a special way, and so she is not happy when her teacher suggests that her parents take her to an opthamologist to fix the lazy eye

"Bright colors and patterns warm the realistic story, while graphics-style artwork gives a since of [Jenny] Sue's vision." Booklist

Same, same, but different. Henry Holt 2011 un il $16.99

Grades: PreK K 1 2   E

1. Friendship -- Fiction

ISBN 978-0-8050-8946-2; 0-8050-8946-2

LC 2010030121

Pen pals Elliott and Kailash discover that even though they live in different countries—America and India—they both love to climb trees, own pets, and ride school buses.

"The imaginative multimedia illustrations, drawn in an animated, childlike style, add vibrant color and rich details to the story. Kostecki-Shaw presents a meaningful message of inclusivity in this engaging title." SLJ

Koster, Gloria

The **Peanut** -Free Cafe; illustrated by Maryann Cocca-Leffler. Whitman, A. 2006 un il $16.95

Grades: K 1 2 3   E

1. School stories 2. Allergy -- Fiction 3. Peanuts -- Fiction

ISBN 0-8075-6386-2

When a new classmate has a peanut allergy and has to sit in a special area of the lunchroom, Simon reconsiders his love for peanut butter.

"The cartoon-style art is fun, with some moments of exaggerated drama, as when Grant demonstrates what would happen to him if he ate just one peanut." Booklist

Kraegel, Kenneth

King Arthur's very great grandson; by Kenneth Kraegel. Candlewick 2012 40 p. (hardback) $15.99

Grades: PreK K 1 2   E

1. Dragons -- Fiction 2. Picture books for children 3. Knights and knighthood -- Fiction 4. Animals, Mythical

-- Fiction 5. Adventure and adventurers -- Fiction
ISBN 076365311X; 9780763653118

LC 2011046646

In this book, "Henry Alfred Grummorson, the great-great-great-great-great-great-great grandson of Arthur, King of Britain, goes in search of adventure. First, he challenges a fire-breathing Dragon that simply blows smoke rings. He announces his presence to the giant Cyclops who, instead of fighting, engages him in a staring contest. . . . Travelling far in search of a worthy adversary, his search leads him past the winged Griffin (who offers a game of chess) to the sea monster Leviathan. Has he finally found something worthy of a fight? . . . Despite the determined lack of conflict, Henry still manages to find a treasure he didn't know he was seeking." (Kirkus)

Krall, Dan

The **great** lollipop caper; Dan Krall. 1st ed. Simon & Schuster Books for Young Readers 2013 48 p. col. ill. (hardcover) $16.99

Grades: PreK K 1 2   E

1. Lollipops -- Juvenile fiction 2. Humorous fiction -- Juvenile fiction 3. Humorous stories 4. Pickles -- Fiction 5. Lollipops -- Fiction 6. Contentment -- Fiction
ISBN 1442444606; 9781442444607; 9781442444614

LC 2012004041

In this children's story, by Dan Krall, "Mr. Caper . . . wants the children of the world to love him--just as much as they love the sweet, saccharine Lollipop. And thus a plot is hatched: Caper-flavored lollipops are dispatched throughout the world . . . and everything goes horribly wrong. Will Mr. Caper find a way to repair the havoc he's wreaked by over-reaching? Maybe, if Lollipop helps save the day!" (Publisher's note)

Includes bibliographical references and index

Krasnesky, Thad

I always, always get my way; illustrated by David Parkins. Flashlight 2009 un il $16.95

Grades: PreK K 1 2   E

1. Family life -- Fiction
ISBN 978-0-9799746-4-9; 0-9799746-4-X

"Three-year-old Emmy wreaks havoc on her entire household. . . . Krasnesky tells the story with flowing rhyme that accommodates the humor of the plot and heightens Parkins's comical cartoon illustrations." SLJ

That cat can't stay! illustrated by David Parkins. Flashlight 2010 il $16.95

Grades: K 1 2   E

1. Cats -- Fiction
ISBN 978-0-9799746-5-6; 0-9799746-5-8

Kraus, Robert

★ **Whose** mouse are you? pictures by José Aruego. 30th anniversary ed.; Simon & Schuster Books for Young Readers 2000 un il $17.95

Grades: PreK K   E

1. Stories in rhyme 2. Mice -- Fiction
ISBN 0-689-84052-7

A reissue of the title first published 1970 by Macmillan

A lonely little mouse has to be resourceful in order to bring his family back together

"This is an absolute charmer of a picture book, original, tender, and childlike. The rhyming text is so brief, so catchy, and so right that a child will remember the words after one or two readings, and the large, uncluttered illustrations are gay and appealing." Booklist

Other titles about the mouse and his family are:
Come out and play, little mouse (1987)
Mouse in love (2000)
Where are you going, little mouse? (1986)

Krause, Ute

Oscar and the very hungry dragon. NorthSouth Books 2010 un il $16.95

Grades: PreK K 1 2   E

1. Cooking -- Fiction 2. Dragons -- Fiction
ISBN 978-0-7358-2306-8; 0-7358-2306-5

Original German edition, 2007

"When the earth trembles, the villagers at the bottom of the hill know it's time to send the dragon a princess to eat. One day, unfortunately, no princess is available; a child is the next best thing. Village elder Mr. Ballymore holds a lottery and young Oscar . . . is selected. . . . Packed with wit that never descends into camp and illustrated with verve and style in ink-and-watercolor cartoons, Krause's substantial, self-translated fractured fairy tale delights on every level." Kirkus

Krauss, Ruth

And I love you; illustrated by Steven Kellogg. Scholastic Press 2010 un il $16.99

Grades: PreK K 1   E

1. Cats -- Fiction 2. Love -- Fiction 3. Parent-child relationship -- Fiction
ISBN 978-0-439-02459-4; 0-439-02459-5

LC 2010009003

A newly illustrated edition of Big and Little, published 1987

Simple, rhythmic text follows a mother cat and her kitten as they discover the love of big forests for little trees, big skies for little skyscrapers, and parents for their children.

"With lots to look at, talk about and wonder over, this imaginative flight of fancy might also find a place in elementary art or creative-writing classes. Surprisingly and pleasantly offbeat." Kirkus

★ **Bears**; story by Ruth Krauss; pictures by Maurice Sendak. HarperCollins Pubs. 2005 un il $14.95

Grades: PreK   E

1. Bears -- Fiction
ISBN 0-06-027994-X

A newly illustrated edition of the title first published 1948

"The 27-word text is full of possibility: 'Bears—Under chairs—Washing hairs—Giving stares—Collecting fares—.' . . . Sendak sets a full-color story in motion on the cover. In a scene both familiar and fresh, a boy in a wolf suit snuggles his stuffed bear in a themed room where the object of his affection is replicated on every conceivable surface. . . . Sure to spark laughter and original wordplay, this is the marriage of two masters." SLJ

The **backward** day; story by Ruth Krauss; pictures by Marc Simont. New York Review Children's Collection 2007 un il (New York Review Children's Collection) $14.95

Grades: PreK K 1   E

1. Family -- Fiction 2. Morning -- Fiction

ISBN 978-1-59017-237-7; 1-59017-237-X

LC 2007-6747

A reissue of the title first published 1950 by Harper

Having decided that it is backward day, a boy dresses himself first in his coat, last in his socks, and continues in that way with the cooperation of his family.

"The silliness is enhanced by Simont's bold three-color illustrations showing everyone playing along. The universality of Krauss's work assures that a new generation will want to celebrate backward day." Horn Book Guide

★ The **carrot** seed; pictures by Crockett Johnson. Harper & Row 1945 un il $14.99; pa $5.99; bd bk $6.99

Grades: PreK K   E

1. Gardening -- Fiction

ISBN 0-06-023350-8; 0-06-443210-6 pa; 0-06-443210-6 bd bk

Simple text and picture show how the faith of a small boy, who planted a carrot seed, was rewarded

"Crockett Johnson's pictures are perfect and the brief text is just right." Book Week

★ The **growing** story; by Ruth Krauss; illustrated by Helen Oxenbury. HarperCollins 2000 un il $16.99; lib bdg $17.89

Grades: PreK K   E

1. Growth -- Fiction

ISBN 0-06-024716-9; 0-06-024717-7 lib bdg

LC 97-42822

A newly illustrated edition of the title first published 1947

A little boy worries throughout the summer that he's not getting bigger, but at the end of the season he tries on his winter clothes and realizes that he has grown.

"The story gets right to a child's experiences as it expresses both wondering and wonderment. This comes out beautifully in art that captures the affection between a boy and his hardworking mother who makes a bountiful place of the land they farm." Booklist

A **very** special house; by Ruth Krauss; pictures by Maurice Sendak. HarperCollins 1981 un il $16.95

Grades: PreK K   E

1. Imagination -- Fiction

ISBN 0-06-028638-5

LC 2002511422

A reissue of the title first published 1953

A Caldecott Medal honor book, 1954

"The very special house is a house which exists in the imagination of a small boy—a house where the chairs are for climbing, the walls for writing on, and the beds for jumping on; a house where a lion, a giant, or a dead mouse is welcome, and where nobody ever says stop. Told in a chanting rhythm that demands participation by the reader; the imaginary characters, objects, and doings are pictured in line drawings almost as a child would scribble them while the real little boy stands out boldly in bright blue overalls." Booklist

Krebs, Laurie

The **Beeman**; [text by] Laurie Krebs; [illustrations by] Valeria Cis. Barefoot Books 2008 un il $16.99

Grades: PreK K 1 2   E

1. Stories in rhyme 2. Bees -- Fiction 3. Grandfathers -- Fiction

ISBN 978-1-84686-146-8; 1-84686-146-2

A newly illustrated edition of the title first published 2002 by National Geographic

In rhyming text, a child describes the work Grandpa does to take care of honeybees and harvest the honey they make.

"This charming book is visually enticing and just plain fun to read. . . . The acrylic illustrations are done in predominantly muted, pastel shades with occasional touches of bright colors." SLJ

Krensky, Stephen

Hanukkah at Valley Forge; illustrated by Greg Harlin. Dutton Children's Books 2006 un il $17.99

Grades: 1 2 3 4   E

1. Generals 2. Presidents 3. Jews -- Fiction 4. Hanukkah -- Fiction

ISBN 0-525-47738-1

During the Revolutionary War, a Jewish soldier from Poland lights the menorah on the first night of Hanukkah and tells General George Washington the story of the Maccabees and the miracle that Hanukkah celebrates. Based on factual events.

"Harlin's evocative paintings are rich with period details that successfully bring the settings to life. A well-told story." Booklist

★ **How** Santa got his job; illustrated by S.D. Schindler. Simon & Schuster Bks. for Young Readers 1998 un il hardcover o.p.; pa $6.99

Grades: PreK K 1 2   E

1. Humorous stories 2. Occupations -- Fiction 3. Santa Claus -- Fiction 4. Santa Claus -- Juvenile fiction

ISBN 0-689-80697-3; 0-689-84668-1 pa

LC 97-23474

This "peek at Santa's resume reveals how various odd jobs, like chimney sweep and mail carrier, helped prepare him for his world-famous career. . . . [Schindler's] intricate pen-and-watercolor illustrations make Santa's evolution from boyish redhead to the familiar heavy-set, snowy-bearded character a joy to watch." Publ Wkly

Another title about Santa by this author and illustrator is: How Santa lost his job (2001)

Noah's bark; illustrated by Roge. Carolrhoda Books 2010 un il lib bdg $16.95

Grades: K 1 2   E

1. Sounds -- Fiction 2. Animals -- Fiction 3. Biblical characters 4. Noah's ark -- Fiction

ISBN 978-0-8225-7645-7; 0-8225-7645-7

LC 2007010022

Noah is distracted by animals making whatever sound comes into their heads while he is trying to build, then pilot, the ark, and so he devises a way for each animal to choose only one sound.

"The stylized, brushstroked paintings are embellished with highlighted sound effects and subtle comic expressions. Inventive and sure to elicit a boatload of giggles." Booklist

★ **Play** ball, Jackie! illustrated by Joe Morse. Millbrook Press 2011 un il lib bdg $16.95

Grades: 2 3 4 5   E
1. Baseball players 2. Army officers 3. Baseball
-- Fiction 4. Race relations -- Fiction 5. African
Americans -- Fiction
ISBN 978-0-8225-9030-9; 0-8225-9030-1
                                        LC 2010027270
On April 15, 1947, Matt Romano and his father watch
the Brooklyn Dodgers season-opener, during which Jackie
Robinson, a twenty-eight-year-old rookie, breaks the "color
line" that had kept black men out of Major League baseball.
Includes facts about Jackie Robinson's life and career.
"Morse's dramatically grained, exaggerated artwork
plays up the intensity of the era's racial tensions and the dy-
namism of the game, while Krensky adeptly moves between
the action on Ebbets Field and Matty's conversations with
his father. An intimate and powerful account of a historic
day," Publ Wkly

Sisters of Scituate Light; by Stephen Krensky; illustrated by Stacey Schuett. Dutton Children's Books 2008
un il $16.99
Grades: 1 2 3   E
1. Sisters -- Fiction 2. Lighthouses -- Fiction 3. War
of 1812 -- Fiction
ISBN 978-0-525-47792-1; 0-525-47792-6
                                        LC 2007028297
In 1814, when their father leaves them in charge of the
Scituate lighthouse outside of Boston, two teenaged sisters
devise a clever way to avert an attack by a British warship
patrolling the Massachusetts coast
"Krensky's fine telling is well matched by Schuett's illustrations, which are especially effective in capturing the
colors of the sea and sky." Booklist

Spark the firefighter; by Stephen Krensky; illustrated
by Amanda Haley. Dutton Childrens Books 2008 un il
$16.99
Grades: PreK K 1   E
1. Fear -- Fiction 2. Dragons -- Fiction 3. Fire fighters
-- Fiction
ISBN 978-0-525-47887-4; 0-525-47887-6
                                        LC 2007050565
Spark's fear of fire has kept him from being a proper
dragon, so he takes a job with the Hardscrabble volunteer
fire department in hopes of conquering his fear
"Simply told with bright cartoon pictures and a dragon
to hold interest, the . . . story teaches fire safety in an appealing way." SLJ

★ **Too** many leprechauns; (or how that pot o' gold got
to the end of the rainbow) illustrated by Dan Andreasen.
Simon & Schuster Books for Young Readers 2007 un il
$12.99
Grades: K 1 2 3   E
1. Leprechauns -- Fiction
ISBN 0-689-85112-X
                                        LC 2005-20659
Finn O'Finnegan returns home after a year in Dublin
and when he finds his village taken over by leprechauns,
he must devise a way to get them to leave without making
them angry.

"The well-paced story moves along smoothly, enhanced
by Andreasen's handsome oil paintings, which picture the
setting and characters with equal verve and charm." Booklist

Krilanovich, Nadia
Chicken, chicken, duck! Tricycle Press 2011 un il
$16.99
Grades: PreK K   E
1. Ducks -- Fiction 2. Games -- Fiction 3. Sounds --
Fiction 4. Domestic animals -- Fiction
ISBN 978-1-58246-385-8; 1-58246-385-9
                                        LC 2010010773
"A feisty white duck coordinates an impressive stunt
amid lots of barnyard noise in Krilanovich's rhythmic
book for very young readers. Paintings of the duck with
outstretched wings suggest her cheerleader role directing a
flock of chickens, a cat, a dog, and assorted other barnyard
animals as they prepare to form a Flying Wallendas-style
pyramid. The animals appear in tight close-up against clean
white pages; they'd look clinical if not for their obvious excitement, the intensity of their interactions, and the painterly
attention Krilanovich . . . devotes to their feathers, whiskers,
black noses, and furry tails." Publ Wkly

Moon child; illustrations by Elizabeth Sayles. Tricycle
Press 2010 un il $15.99; lib bdg $18.99
Grades: PreK K 1   E
1. Animals -- Fiction 2. Bedtime -- Fiction
ISBN 978-1-58246-325-4; 1-58246-325-5; 978-1-
58246-366-7 lib bdg; 1-58246-366-2 lib bdg
                                        LC 2009032304
"Various animal babies interact with the full moon in this
quiet charmer. Otter playfully 'catches' it in order to give
the orb a big hug, a raccoon plays with the reflection of its
light, and an owl smiles at the stars and pretends she can
balance the moon on the tip of her nose. There is very little
text—only one sentence per spread—but it works well for
this subject matter and mood. Sayles has primarily used dark
blue and brown pastels with acrylic ink to set the tone for
this peaceful night where all is well. Sweet dreams are sure
to follow. Perfect for bedtime or evening storytimes." SLJ

Krishnaswami, Uma
Monsoon; pictures by Jamel Akib. Farrar, Straus & Giroux 2003 un il $16
Grades: K 1 2 3   E
1. Monsoons -- Fiction
ISBN 0-374-35015-9
                                        LC 2001-54753
A child in India describes waiting for the monsoon rains
to arrive and the worry that they will not come
"Krishnaswami's poetic text rides faithfully on the
child's sensibilities. . . . Akib's impressionistic, pastel illustrations make stunning use of extreme perspectives." SLJ

★ **Out** of the way! Out of the way! story, Uma Krish-
naswami; pictures, Uma Krishnaswamy. Groundwood
Books/House of Anansi Press 2012 28 p. col. ill. $17.95
Grades: K 1 2 3   E
1. India -- Fiction 2. Picture books for children 3.
Rural development -- Fiction
ISBN 1554981301 Groundwood Books;
9781554981304 Groundwood Books

In this picture book, "[a] boy in India sees a baby tree growing by the side of a dusty path, and, because he protects it, it flourishes throughout his lifetime despite the changes to the landscape around him." The illustrations "depict the path [by the tree] turning into a lane, then a street, then a road, signaling the rapid development that transforms the landscape from a quiet, sleepy village into a busy town. Meanwhile, the boy grows into a man, and the tree becomes a meeting place for local people." (Kirkus)

Kroll, Steven
The **Hanukkah** mice; by Steven Kroll; illustrated by Michelle Shapiro. Marshall Cavendish Children 2008 un il $14.99
Grades: PreK K 1 2   E
1. Mice -- Fiction 2. Hanukkah -- Fiction
ISBN 978-0-7614-5428-1; 0-7614-5428-4
LC 2007035003
A family of mice enjoys the doll house and furnishings that Rachel receives as gifts on the eight nights of Hanukkah
"This book would make a wonderful addition to any holiday collection, and will most likely become a new holiday classic that will be cherished by students for years to come." Libr Media Connect

Stuff! reduce, reuse, recycle. illustrated by Steve Cox. Marshall Cavendish 2009 un il $16.99
Grades: PreK K 1 2   E
1. Rats -- Fiction 2. Recycling -- Fiction 3. Recycling (Waste, etc.) -- Juvenile literature
ISBN 978-0-7614-5570-7; 0-7614-5570-1
LC 2008-12915
Pinch is a pack rat who does not want to give up the possessions that are cluttering his house, but when he finally is persuaded to sell them at a neighborhood tag sale, he discovers the beauty of recycling. Includes tips on "reducing, reusing, and recycling."
"The bright, bold colors convey the friendly tone of the story and ably show the movement from cluttered to clean as Pinch relinquishes his possessions. An admirable introduction to beginning environmentalism for a young audience." Kirkus

Kroll, Virginia L.
Everybody has a teddy; [by] Virginia Kroll; illustrated by Sophie Allsopp. Sterling Pub. 2007 un il $12.95
Grades: PreK K   E
1. Stories in rhyme 2. Teddy bears -- Fiction
ISBN 978-1-4027-3580-6; 1-4027-3580-4
LC 2006005154
A child describes teddy bears owned by other children, from Joshy's giant grizzly to the floppy bear Poppy's grandmother made from socks.
"This light, gentle offering celebrates individuality. . . . The text rolls along with the infectious, easy rhyme and rhythm of a children's song. . . . Cheerful illustrations capture the happy hum of a multicultural classroom filled with kids who paint, play, and look at books." Booklist

Krosoczka, Jarrett J.
Ollie the purple elephant. Knopf 2011 un il $16.99
Grades: PreK K   E
1. Elephants -- Fiction
ISBN 978-0-375-86654-8; 0-375-86654-X

"With bright, friendly acrylic art . . . the author offers a fast-paced and surreal tale with twists aplenty. After Mr. McLaughlin makes good on a silly promise that comes back to bite him ('that should they ever come across a purple elephant, they could keep him'), the McLaughlin family makes room for Ollie. . . . Good times and floor-shaking dance parties follow, upsetting the family cat and the downstairs neighbor, who collude to remove the unwanted pachyderm. . . . Krosoczka's story feels tailor-made for story time, thanks to kid-pleasing plot elements, . . . emphatic prose, . . . and emotive art." Publ Wkly

Krupinski, Loretta
Snow dog's journey. Dutton Children's Books 2010 un il $16.99
Grades: PreK K 1 2   E
1. Dogs -- Fiction 2. Love -- Fiction 3. Snow -- Fiction
ISBN 978-0-525-42246-4; 0-525-42246-3
LC 2009-53237
Anna builds a dog of snow, which the Frost King admires and takes away with him, but when Anna's love and faith eventually reunite her with Snow Dog, they each get their fondest wish.
"Krupinski's delightful tale blends fantasy and reality in a familiar, shape-shifting animal story. . . . The softly textured illustrations smoothly convey the characters' individual perspectives and emotions." Booklist

Kruusval, Catarina
Franny's friends. R & S Books 2008 un il $16
Grades: PreK   E
1. Play -- Fiction 2. Toys -- Fiction 3. Imagination -- Fiction
ISBN 978-91-29-66836-0; 91-29-66836-0
"Franny is a sweet little girl who plans a picnic for her seven stuffed animals. The simple outing runs into trouble when the two smallest guests, Itty Bitty Kitty and Little Heddy, fall into a hole and can't get out. . . . Kruusval's pastel-shaded illustrations capture the story's charm. . . . Each animal is drawn with a liveliness that will seem wholly believable to a young child engaged in imaginative play." SLJ

Kubler, Annie
Humpty Dumpty; illustrated by Annie Kubler. Child's Play 2010 un il (Baby board books) bd bk $4.99
Grades: PreK   E
1. Nursery rhymes 2. Board books for children
ISBN 978-1-84643-339-9 bd bk; 1-84643-339-8 bd bk
"Kubler sets the familiar nursery rhyme in a jolly daycare setting peopled with a multiethnic cast of toddlers. . . . This is a splendid, slightly larger-than-usual contribution that is sure to see many repeated readings." Kirkus

Kulka, Joe
★ **Wolf's** coming! [by] Joe Kulka. Carolrhoda Books 2007 un il lib bdg $15.95
Grades: PreK K 1   E
1. Wolves -- Fiction 2. Animals -- Fiction
ISBN 978-1-57505-930-3 lib. bdg; 1-57505-930-4 lib bdg
LC 2006013865
"The simple rhyming text describes the various ways in which the denizens of the forest prepare for Wolf's imminent

arrival.... Saturated with color, the cartoonlike illustrations depict characters that are more human than animal, but will likely appeal to young children." SLJ

Kulling, Monica

In the bag! Margaret Knight wraps it up. Monica Kulling. Tundra Books of Northern New York 2011 32 p. ill. (Great idea) (hardcover) $17.95

Grades: K 1 2 3 4   E

   1. Women inventors 2. Picture books for children 3. Inventors

ISBN 1770492399; 9781770492394

LC 2010938592

This children's picture book is a "portrait of [Margaret] Knight [that] chronicles her process in inventing the machine that made the flat-bottomed paper bag and, at the age of 12, the shuttle cover for cotton-mill machinery." It points out "the trouble facing female inventors in the 1800s." (School Library Journal)

   This is written "in clean, straightforward prose.... [The text is] paired with Parkin's detailed and handsome pen-and-ink illustrations." Publ Wkly

Kumin, Maxine, 1925-

Oh, Harry! illustrated by Barry Moser. Roaring Brook Press 2011 un il $16.99

Grades: PreK K   E

   1. Stories in rhyme 2. Horses -- Fiction

ISBN 978-1-59643-439-4; 1-59643-439-2

LC 2010024837

Harry the Horse excels at calming skittish equines in Adams & Son's show-horse barn, but he faces a different challenge when mischievous six-year-old Algernon Adams the Third arrives.

   "Moser uses vibrant watercolors from multiple perspectives against dramatic white backgrounds to convey animal personality and movement in an uncluttered way. His Harry grins and rolls his eyes in ways that, like the text, are fanciful but grounded in reality.... Good fun for the preschool set and slightly beyond." Kirkus

Kupfer, Wendy

Let's hear it for Almigal. Handfinger Press 2012 32 p. $16.99

Grades: PreK K 1   E

   1. Cochlear implants 2. Picture books for children

ISBN 0983829403; 9780983829409

This children's picture book follows deaf Amigal, who wants "to hear every single sound in the whole entire universe," so her "doctor suggests cochlear implants.... The book gently covers Almigal's trip to the hospital for the operation and the importance of handling the implants carefully.... The implants successfully help Almigal hear all the things she'd been missing." (Kirkus)

Kurtz, Jane

Faraway home; illustrated by E.B. Lewis. Harcourt Brace & Co. 2000 un il $16

Grades: PreK K 1 2   E

   1. African Americans -- Fiction 2. Father-daughter relationship -- Fiction 3. Ethiopians -- United States -- Pictorial works -- Juvenile fiction 4. Immigrants --

United States -- Pictorial works -- Juvenile fiction

ISBN 0-15-200036-4

LC 96-47664

Desta's father, who needs to return briefly to his Ethiopian homeland, describes what it was like for him to grow up there

   "Lewis captures the lyricism and rich imagery of the text with his evocative, realistic watercolors." SLJ

Water hole waiting; by Jane and Christopher Kurtz; illustrated by Lee Christiansen. Greenwillow Bks. 2002 un il $15.95; lib bdg $15.89

Grades: PreK K 1 2   E

   1. Animals -- Fiction 2. Monkeys -- Fiction

ISBN 0-06-029850-2; 0-06-029851-0 lib bdg

LC 2001-23040

A thirsty monkey waits as the larger animals drink from the water hole on the African savanna

   "Richly colored pastel drawings and precise, surprising word choices make this story a natural for sharing with a group." SLJ

Kushner, Lawrence

In God's hands; [by] Lawrence Kushner and Gary Schmidt; illustrated by Matthew J. Baek. Jewish Lights Pub. 2005 un il $16.99

Grades: K 1 2 3   E

   1. Jews -- Fiction 2. Prayer -- Fiction 3. Miracles -- Fiction

ISBN 1-58023-224-8

LC 2005001669

While contemplating their problems in a synagogue, Jacob and David, one man rich, the other poor, come to realize their role in making miracles happen. Inspired by an ancient legend.

   "This lovely piece of bookmaking combines a good tale with a strong, easily understood message. Baek's artwork, set against buff-colored pages and highlighted in shades of blue, uses a variety of angles, placements, and design elements to invite interest." Booklist

Kuskin, Karla

Green as a bean. Laura Geringer Books 2007 un il $16.99; lib bdg $17.89

Grades: PreK K 1 2   E

   1. Stories in rhyme

ISBN 978-0-06-075332-0; 0-06-075332-3; 978-0-06-075334-4 lib bdg; 0-06-075334-X lib bdg

LC 2005017881

First published 1960 with title: Square as a house

   Questions in verse about the many things you could be if you were square or soft or loud or red or small or fat or fierce or dark

   This "is sure to inspire loud crowd participation.... Lines in expertly modulated rhyme and meter ... are nicely extended in Iwai's bright, fanciful acrylic paintings." Booklist

I am me. Simon & Schuster Bks. for Young Readers 2000 un il $14.95

Grades: PreK K   E

   1. Identity -- Fiction 2. Family life -- Fiction

ISBN 0-689-81473-9

LC 98-7911

After being told how she resembles other members of her family, a young girl states positively and absolutely that she is "NO ONE ELSE BUT ME"

"The illustrations set the story during a family trip to the beach, and in Wolcott's brightly colored double-page spreads, all the rhythmic curves . . . show the natural connections around us, the loving family embrace across generations, and the child's exuberant energy as her own individual self." Booklist

★ **So** what's it like to be a cat? Atheneum Books for Young Readers 2005 un il $15.95; pa $6.99
Grades: PreK K 1 2   E
1. Cats -- Fiction
ISBN 0-689-84733-5; 0-689-85930-9 pa
LC 2003-27338
A cat answers a young child's questions about such things as how much and where it sleeps, and whether or not it likes living with people.

"Lewin's charming, uncluttered watercolors extend the spare poetry's precise wit with swooping bold lines that beautifully capture both characters' movements and moods." Booklist

A **boy** had a mother who bought him a hat. Harper 2010 un il $16.99
Grades: PreK K 1   E
1. Stories in rhyme 2. Children's poetry 3. Mother-son relationship -- Fiction
ISBN 978-0-06-075330-6; 0-06-075330-7
A newly illustrated edition of the title first published 1976
After a boy's mother buys him a hat, she buys him a mouse, shoes, boots, skis, mask, cello, and an elephant-none of which he is ever without.

This "showcases the late poet's mastery of verse and her acute awareness of both children's sense of humore and the value they place on special belongings. . . . Hawkes' pictures . . . . are skillfully executed and include some hidden surprises." Booklist

Kvasnosky, Laura McGee
Really truly Bingo; [by] Laura McGee Kvasnosky. Candlewick Press 2008 un il $15.99
Grades: PreK K 1   E
1. Dogs -- Fiction 2. Imaginary playmates -- Fiction
ISBN 978-0-7636-3210-6; 0-7636-3210-4
LC 2007-40103
When Bea wants to play, her busy mother tells her to use her imagination—outside—and soon Bea and a talking dog, Bingo, are getting into all kinds of mischief.

"This book, with its child-sized problem and child-sized solution, is a fresh take on imaginary friends." Horn Book Guide

★ **Zelda** and Ivy, the runaways. Candlewick Press 2006 42p il $14.99; pa $4.99
Grades: PreK K 1 2   E
1. Foxes -- Fiction 2. Sisters -- Fiction
ISBN 0-7636-2689-9; 978-0-7636-2689-1; 0-7636-3061-6 pa; 978-0-7636-3061-4 pa
LC 2005-54282
In three short stories, fox sisters Zelda and Ivy run away from home, bury a time capsule, and take advantage of some creative juice.

"Bright, expressive cartoon illustrations complement the fine writing in this beginning reader." SLJ
Other titles about Zelda and Ivy are:
Zelda and Ivy (1998)
Zelda and Ivy and the boy next door (1999)
Zelda and Ivy one Christmas (2000)
Zelda and Ivy: keeping secrets (2009)
Zelda and Ivy: the big picture (2010)

Zelda and Ivy: the big picture. Candlewick Press 2010 42p $14.99; pa $4.99
Grades: PreK K 1 2   E
1. Foxes -- Fiction 2. Camping -- Fiction 3. Sisters -- Fiction 4. Detectives -- Fiction
ISBN 978-0-7636-4180-1; 0-7636-4180-4; 978-0-7636-5645-4 pa; 0-7636-5645-3 pa
LC 2010007545
After fox sisters Zelda and Ivy and their best friend Eugene watch the new Secret Agent Fox movie, they are inspired to do some detective work then practice their new skills when rain threatens their campout plans.

"The distinctive gouache resist illustrations add lots of humorous details and textual clues for beginning readers. A wonderful addition to the series for existing fans or new readers." SLJ

Kwon, Yoon-Duck
My cat copies me. Kane/Miller 2007 un il $15.95
Grades: PreK K 1 2   E
1. Cats -- Fiction
ISBN 978-1-933605-26-5
Original Korean edition, 2005
"Kwon tells the story of a little girl and her cat. The pet may act coy and shy when the child seeks its affection, but when she turns away, the feline begins to follow her and mimics her actions. . . . . The bright, colorful illustrations feature light gray outlining and accents that add a luminous quality and increase the imaginative nature of the drawings." SLJ

La Chanze
Little diva; illustrated by Brian Pinkney. Feiwel and Friends 2010 un il $16.99
Grades: PreK K   E
1. Theater -- Fiction 2. Mother-daughter relationship -- Fiction
ISBN 978-0-312-37010-7; 0-312-37010-5
"LaChanze, a star of stage and screen herself, supplies a peek at the life of a Broadway performer in this enticing story about a girl's dream of one day conquering the Great White Way. Nena relates her activities from morning to night as she works as a 'D.I.T.—Diva inTraining.' After trying on her mother's clothes, dancing and singing about the house, and watching her mother practice her yoga, the two spend the afternoon at the theater, where the woman is the star. . . . Pinkney catches the mood with sprawling thick black lines and swirling soft hues of pink, lavender, blue, and tawny, bringing a breezy lightness that fits this upbeat tale." SLJ

LaFaye, A.
Walking home to Rosie Lee; illustrated by Keith D. Shepherd. Cinco Puntos Press 2011 il $16.95
Grades: 2 3 4   E
1. Slavery -- Fiction 2. African Americans -- Fiction

3. Voyages and travels -- Fiction 4. Mother-son relationship -- Fiction

ISBN 978-1-933693-97-2; 1-933693-97-5

LC 2010037397

At the end of the Civil War, young Gabe meets many other former slaves getting a feel for freedom whose kindness helps him in his quest to find his mother, who was sold away.

This "is distinguished by a vivid narrative voice and page-turning suspense. . . . Shepherd contributes big, dramatic spreads, thickly painted and filled with the blues of night and the yellow light of fires and lanterns." Publ Wkly

LaMarche, Jim

Lost and found. Chronicle Books 2009 un il $17.99

Grades: PreK K 1   E

1. Short stories 2. Dogs -- Fiction 3. Lost and found possessions -- Fiction

ISBN 978-0-8118-6401-5; 0-8118-6401-4

LC 2008-23009

"In the first story, Anna's retriever Molly leads the way home after the girl runs off in anger and gets lost; in the second, Jules enjoys a happy reunion with his pet Ginger after the scruffy dog disappears in the woods. Jack finds a husky named Yuki, whose owner gives Jack's single mother a fresh start in the final tale. . . . LaMarche's gentle artwork distinguishes this collection, gracefully rendering the special bond between dogs and children. . . . The soft colors of autumn unite the stories visually, and the pages are full of activity." Publ Wkly

Up; by Jim LaMarche. Chronicle Books 2006 un il $16.95

Grades: PreK K 1 2   E

1. Whales -- Fiction 2. Fishing -- Fiction 3. Psychokinesis -- Fiction

ISBN 978-0-8118-4445-1; 0-8118-4445-5

LC 2005029793

Tired of being called Mouse and staying home while his brother helps on their father's fishing boat, Daniel proves himself when a problem arises that he can solve using his newly-developed, extraordinary talent.

"The soft acrylics capture the low light, palpable chill, and blue-gray color scheme of Daniel's fishing village. This is an inspiring and (yes) uplifting title about pursuing one's own talents and possibilities." SLJ

★ The raft. Lothrop, Lee & Shepard Bks. 2000 un il $15.99; pa $6.99

Grades: 2 3 4 5   E

1. Rivers 2. Animals 3. Grandmothers 4. Rafting (Sports) 5. Animals -- Fiction 6. Grandmothers -- Fiction 7. Rafting (Sports) -- Fiction

ISBN 0-688-13977-9; 0-06-443856-2 pa

LC 99-35546

Reluctuant Nicky spends a wonderful summer with Grandma who introduces him to the joy of rafting down the river near her home and watching the animals along the banks

"LaMarche introduces young readers to a visually resplendent, magical world. . . . Nicky's descriptive first-person narration supports the radiant, expressive illustrations." SLJ

LaReau, Kara

Rabbit & Squirrel; a tale of war & peas. [by] Kara LaReau; Scott Magoon. Harcourt 2008 un il $16

Grades: K 1 2 3   E

1. Rabbits -- Fiction 2. Gardening -- Fiction 3. Squirrels -- Fiction

ISBN 978-0-15-206307-8; 0-15-206307-2

LC 2006-101618

Rabbit and Squirrel are neighbors who never even say hello until someone starts damaging their gardens, and then they blame one another and start a fight that continues even after they meet the real culprit.

"The textured, earth-tone illustrations assist in identifying the real garden grabber [and] . . . both text and illustration suggest the bickering may become wearisome and the two may actually become friends." Libr Media Connect

LaRochelle, David

1 +1; illustrated by Brenda Sexton. Sterling Pub. Co. 2010 un il

Grades: K 1 2   E

1. Mathematics -- Fiction

ISBN 1-4027-5995-9; 978-1-4027-5995-6

"This clever concept book asks children to take a fresh look at simple addition. Are there times when one plus one can equal three and not two? Yes—if you add one unicorn and one goat, you get three horns. Can one plus one ever equal five? Yes, because when you add one set of triplets and one set of twins, you get five babies. After sharing the numerous examples provided, children can be asked to stretch their imaginations and come up with their own quirky equations. Sexton's brightly colored digitally rendered cartoonlike illustrations are not only cheerful and attractive, but they also provide subtle clues." SLJ

How Martha saved her parents from green beans; by David LaRochelle; illustrated by Mark Fearing. Dial Books for Young Readers 2013 32 p. (hardcover) $16.99

Grades: K 1 2 3   E

1. Food -- Juvenile fiction 2. Beans -- Juvenile fiction 3. Humorous fiction -- Juvenile fiction 4. Beans -- Fiction 5. Food habits -- Fiction 6. Parent and child -- Fiction

ISBN 0803737661; 9780803737662

LC 2012014361

In this juvenile story, by David LaRochelle, illustrated by Mark Fearing, "Martha hates green beans. When some mean, green bandits stroll into town, anyone who ever said 'Eat your green beans' is in big trouble. But when the beans kidnap Martha's parents, Martha is forced to take action. She can think of only one way to stop the villainous veggies from taking over her town, and it's not pretty . . . or tasty." (Publisher's note)

★ The end; story by David LaRochelle; illustrations by Richard Egielski. Arthur A. Levine Books 2007 un il hardcover o.p. $16.99

Grades: PreK K 1 2 3   E

1. Fairy tales

ISBN 978-0-439-64011-4; 0-439-64011-3; 978-0-439-64012-1 pa; 0-439-64012-1 pa

LC 2005-24044

When a princess makes some lemonade, she starts a chain of events involving a fire-breathing dragon, one hundred rabbits, a hungry giant, and a handsome knight

"Turning the standard fairy-tale formula on its head, LaRochelle begins his story at the end. . . . The hand-lettered text, enclosed in streaming banners, consists of terse, declarative statements that are lavishly expounded upon by the illustrations." SLJ

★ The **haunted** hamburger and other ghostly stories; illustrated by Paul Meisel. Dutton Children's Books 2011 un il $16.99

Grades: K 1 2 3   E

1. Ghost stories 2. Bedtime -- Fiction 3. Siblings -- Fiction 4. Storytelling -- Fiction

ISBN 978-0-525-42272-3; 0-525-42272-2

LC 2010038179

Father Ghost tells Franny and Frankie Ghost three scary bedtime stories: The Scary Baby, The Haunted Hamburger, and The Big Bad Granny

"Meisel's charming watercolor and ink cartoon illustrations keep the tone light and augment the tongue-in-cheek humor. Smartly written with plenty of unexpected twists, this book is sure to become a year-round bedtime favorite." SLJ

Labatt, Mary

Pizza for Sam; written by Mary Labatt; illustrated by Marisol Sarrazin. Kids Can Press 2003 32p il (Kids can read) $14.95; pa $3.95

Grades: PreK K 1 2   E

1. Dogs -- Fiction 2. Food -- Fiction

ISBN 1-55337-329-4; 1-55337-331-6 pa

"Sam the dog watches eagerly as [her] owners set out cakes, cookies, and pies for a party. . . . Sam's presented with traditional dog food, but [she] turns up [her] snout, preferring to go hungry . . . until a pizza arrives and he finds [her] perfect puppy chow. Winsome pastel illustrations combine with a few large-type sentences per page in an attractive, uncluttered layout. The basic, repetitive text is filled with action, noise, and enough suspense and silliness to engage new readers." Booklist

Other titles about Sam are:

A friend for Sam (2003)

A parade for Sam (2005)

Sam at the seaside (2006)

Sam finds a monster (2004)

Sam gets lost (2004)

Sam goes next door (2006)

Sam goes to school (2004)

Sam's first Halloween (2003)

Sam's snowy day (2005)

Lacamara, Laura

★ **Floating** on Mama's song; illustrated by Yuyi Morales. Katherine Tegen Books 2010 un il $16.99

Grades: K 1 2 3   E

1. Mothers -- Fiction 2. Singing -- Fiction 3. Bilingual books -- English-Spanish

ISBN 978-0-06-084368-7; 0-06-084368-3

Anita, a seven-year-old girl, is amazed when her mother's singing suddenly begins to make her listeners float, but Grandma says she must stop, making Mama terribly sad until her daughter makes her smile again.

"Lacámara's debut weaves together a stirring Caribbean tale inspired by her Cuban roots and her mother's opera singing. Both the English and Spanish versions of the story are fun and easy to read, and also well translated. The fusion of Morales's collage illustrations, with bright energetic colors, large warm brown characters, and real photographs interspersed with digitally enhanced foliage, will help children's imaginations take flight." SLJ

Lacombe, Benjamin

Cherry and Olive; [by] Benjamin Lacombe. Walker & Co. 2007 un il $16.95

Grades: PreK K 1 2   E

1. Dogs -- Fiction 2. Friendship -- Fiction

ISBN 978-0-8027-9707-0; 0-8027-9707-5; 978-0-8027-9708-7 lib bdg; 0-8027-9708-3 lib bdg

LC 2007006671

Orginial French edition 2006

Cherry, a shy girl who longs for a friend, falls in love with a lost puppy at the shelter where her father works and names the dog Olive.

"The illustrations are somewhat stylized. . . . The artist's palette is dark and rich in the beginning but lightens as Cherry's world expands. . . . This title will be particularly useful . . . anywhere . . . where lonely children might need some help fitting in with others." SLJ

Lakritz, Deborah

Say hello, Lily; illustrated by Martha Aviles. Kar-Ben Pub. 2010 un il lib bdg $17.95; pa $7.95

Grades: PreK K 1 2   E

1. Old age -- Fiction 2. Shyness -- Fiction

ISBN 978-0-7613-4511-4 lib bdg; 0-7613-4511-6 lib bdg; 978-0-7613-4512-1 pa; 0-7613-4512-4 pa

LC 2009001873

Lily wants to go with her mother to visit the people who live at Shalom Home, an assisted living facility, but when they arrive she suddenly feels very shy.

"Pencil-and-gouache illustrations brightly delineate an elder community of kind, thoughtful faces. . . . A gentle and satisfying introduction to a senior residential situation." Kirkus

Lamb, Albert

Tell me the day backwards. Candlewick Press 2011 un il $15.99

Grades: PreK K   E

1. Day -- Fiction 2. Bears -- Fiction 3. Bedtime -- Fiction 4. Mother-son relationship -- Fiction

ISBN 978-0-7636-5055-1; 0-7636-5055-2

LC 2010039177

"Gentle storytelling and a clever concept set this bedtime book apart from the pack. . . . McPhail's always playful and evocative illustrations set against a beautiful countryside perfectly capture this original way of remembering a day's events. An exceptional idea and a truly fine follow through." Kirkus

The **abandoned** lighthouse; [illustrated by David McPhail] Roaring Brook Press 2011 un il $15.99

Grades: PreK K 1   E

1. Dogs -- Fiction 2. Bears -- Fiction 3. Friendship -- Fiction 4. Lighthouses -- Fiction 5. Boats and boating

-- Fiction

ISBN 978-1-59643-525-4; 1-59643-525-9

LC un

A bear, followed by a boy and his dog, use a rowboat to float to an abandoned lighthouse where they all spend the day fishing, cooking their catch, and then joining together to make the lighthouse work again.

"Strikingly evocative of the craggy New England coastline and infused with light—from the sun, moon, and lighthouse—McPhail's quaint, jewel-toned paintings anchor the story. The accessible sentences, early-reader trim size, and slightly mysterious setting and adventure are just right for newly independent readers." Publ Wkly

Laminack, Lester L.

Three hens and a peacock; written by Lester L. Laminack; illustrated by Henry Cole. Peachtree 2011 un il $15.95

Grades: PreK K 1 2   E

1. Dogs -- Fiction 2. Chickens -- Fiction 3. Peacocks -- Fiction 4. Farm life -- Fiction 5. Happiness -- Fiction

ISBN 978-1-56145-564-5; 1-56145-564-4

LC 2010031989

When life on the Tucker farm is disrupted by the arrival of a peacock, whose shrieking and strutting bring many welcome visitors, the hens complain that they are doing all of the work until the hound suggests a trade.

"Laminack's tale of barnyard envy is a fine addition to farm fables, but it's Cole's signature watercolor, ink, and pencil cartoon illustrations that charm here." Kirkus

Lamorisse, Albert

The **red** balloon. Doubleday 1957 un il $16.95; pa $12.95

Grades: PreK K 1 2   E

1. Balloons -- Fiction

ISBN 0-385-00343-9; 0-385-14297-8 pa

Original French edition, 1956

"The chief feature of this book is the stunning photographs, many in color, which were taken during the filming of the French movie of the same name. A little French schoolboy Pascal catches a red balloon which turns out to be magic. The streets of Paris form a backdrop for a charming story and superb photographs." Libr J

Lamstein, Sarah Marwil

A **big** night for salamanders; [by] Sarah Marwil Lamstein; art by Carol Benioff. Boyds Mills Press 2010 un il $17.95

Grades: K 1 2 3   E

1. Salamanders -- Fiction

ISBN 978-1-9324-2598-7; 1-9324-2598-5

"One spring evening . . . spotted salamanders emerge from their winter burrows and make their way to a vernal pool. . . . Young Evan and his parents . . . carry salamanders across the road and even stop cars to ask drivers to slow down and watch out for their amphibian neighbors. . . . The dual text offers Evan's story in plain type and information about salamanders in italics. Readers intrigued by salamanders will learn plenty here and more in the back matter. . . . The gouache paintings add color and drama to this informative picture book." Booklist

Includes glossary and bibliographical references

Landman, Tanya

Mary's penny; written by Tanya Landman; illustrated by Richard Holland. Candlewick Press 2010 un il $15.99

Grades: K 1 2   E

1. Farms -- Fiction 2. Sex role -- Fiction

ISBN 978-0-7636-4768-1; 0-7636-4768-3

A farmer learns that the best man for the job of farm manager is a girl, as his clever daughter bests his brawny sons in a competition.

"The illustrations make this humorous read-aloud even more enjoyable." Libr Media Connect

Landolf, Diane Wright

★ **What** a good big brother! by Diane Wright Landolf; paintings by Steve Johnson & Lou Fancher. Random House 2009 un il $16.99; lib bdg $19.99

Grades: PreK K 1 2   E

1. Infants -- Fiction 2. Siblings -- Fiction 3. Family life -- Fiction

ISBN 978-0-375-84258-0; 0-375-84258-6; 978-0-375-94258-7 lib bdg; 0-375-94258-0 lib bdg

LC 2006015181

Cameron is always ready to help when his baby sister cries, whether by handing wipes to his father during a diaper change or finding the nursing pillow for his mother, until one day, when no one else can stop Sadie's tears, her big brother succeeds and gets a wonderful reward

Landolf's "simple, descriptive writing should go a long way in alleviating . . . the anxieties of newly minted sibling rivalry. Johnson and Fancher . . . offer a stunning visual counterpoint with their most luxuriant work to date." Publ Wkly

Landry, Leo

Grin and bear it. Charlesbridge 2011 48p il lib bdg $12.95

Grades: K 1 2 3   E

1. Bears -- Fiction 2. Comedians -- Fiction 3. Forest animals -- Fiction

ISBN 978-1-57091-745-5; 1-57091-745-0

LC 2010033633

Will stage fright prevent a very funny bear from becoming a stand-up comedian?

"A deft balance of punchy, dialogue-driven text and expressive, appealingly naïf pencil-and-watercolor pictures make this well suited to newly independent readers. With humor and subtlety, Landry's words and art impart a smart message about partnership, ingenuity, and pursuing one's goals." Publ Wkly

Space boy; written and illustrated by Leo Landry. Houghton Mifflin Company 2007 un il $16

Grades: PreK K 1   E

1. Bedtime -- Fiction 2. Family life -- Fiction 3. Space flight to the moon -- Fiction

ISBN 978-0-618-60568-2; 0-618-60568-1

LC 2006-26081

Having decided not to go to bed because his home is too noisy, Nicholas flies his spaceship to the Moon, where he enjoys a snack, takes a moonwalk, and enjoys the quiet—until he realizes what he is missing at home.

"Simple lines and shapes become much more in the bright watercolor-and-pen paintings. . . . Kids who love outer space and rockets will adore this quiet, imaginative adventure." SLJ

Landstrom, Lena

A **hippo's** tale; [by] Lena Landström; translated by Joan Sandin. R&S Books 2007 un il $15

Grades: PreK K 1 2　　　　　　　　　　E

1. Hippopotamus -- Fiction

ISBN 978-91-29-66603-8; 91-29-66603-1

Original Swedish edition 1993

Deep in the middle of Africa, Mrs. Hippopotamus enjoys having quiet time all to herself, especially when bathing. But then a monkey shows up and disturbs her solitude.

"This quiet picture book manages to convey a wide range of human emotions through its hippo heroine. . . . The text is simple, and Landstrom's paintings create a pleasing setting and expressive characters with a minimum of fuss." Booklist

Other titles in this series are:

The little hippo's adventure (2002)

The new hippos (2003)

Lane, Adam J. B.

Stop thief! Adam J.B. Lane. Roaring Brook Press 2012 32 p.

Grades: PreK K 1 2 3 4　　　　　　　　E

1. Toys -- Juvenile fiction 2. Thieves -- Juvenile fiction 3. Adventure fiction -- Juvenile fiction 4. Growth -- Fiction 5. Robbers and outlaws -- Fiction 6. Adventure and adventurers -- Fiction

ISBN 159643693X; 9781596436930

LC 2011013505

In this children's book, by Adam J. B. Lane, "[o]n the first night that Randall tries to sleep like a big boy, without dear, stuffed Mr. Pigglesworth, he becomes restless. Climbing out of bed, . . . he encounters a thick-necked stranger with the pig in hand. . . . He reels through a zoo, chocolate factory, natural-history museum, and carnival. The . . . chase . . . is traceable with a finger due to the trail of arrow and dash marks on a series of maplike spreads." (School Library Journal)

Langdo, Bryan

Tornado Slim and the magic cowboy hat. Marshall Cavendish un il

Grades: K 1 2　　　　　　　　　　　　E

1. Tall tales 2. Cowhands -- Fiction

ISBN 0-7614-5962-6; 978-0-7614-5962-0

A coyote gives Tornado Slim at magic hat that stops tornadoes, floods, and fires.

"Colloquially told, with an epistolary twist, this Western tall tale of guileless cowboy Slim, who finds himself thrust into the role of a hero, packs a lot of charm. . . . Langdo's jaunty, energetic pictures employ highlighted circles to zoom in for the occasional telling closeup." Kirkus

Larsen, Andrew

The **imaginary** garden; [by] Andrew Larsen; [illustrated] by Irene Luxbacher. Kids Can Press 2009 un il $16.95

Grades: PreK K 1 2　　　　　　　　　　E

1. Gardens -- Fiction 2. Imagination -- Fiction 3. Grandfathers -- Fiction

ISBN 978-1-55453-279-7; 1-55453-279-5

"Theo's Poppa's new apartment has no garden, and the windy balcony does not promise to be a good growing spot. But Theo proposes an imaginary garden, and she and her grandfather begin to fill a large blank canvas with a stone wall for the vines to climb on, early springtime flowers, and a visiting robin. . . . The lively artwork is rendered in pen and ink and multimedia collage. The warmth of the grandparent/grandchild relationship is evident." SLJ

Lasky, Kathryn

Marven of the Great North Woods; written by Kathryn Lasky; illustrated by Kevin Hawkes. Harcourt Brace & Co. 1997 un il hardcover o.p. pa $7

Grades: K 1 2 3　　　　　　　　　　　E

1. Jews -- Fiction 2. Lumber and lumbering -- Fiction

ISBN 0-15-200104-2; 0-15-216826-5 pa

LC 96-2334

When his Jewish parents send him to a Minnesota logging camp to escape the influenza epidemic of 1918, ten-year-old Marven finds a special friend

"Inspired by her father's childhood, Lasky's handsomely crafted picture book is also a captivating survival story. . . . Contributing to the book's vivid sense of time and place are Hawkes' graphically accomplished paintings." Booklist

Poodle and Hound; illustrated by Mitch Vane. Charlesbridge 2009 48p il $12.95

Grades: 1 2 3 4　　　　　　　　　　　E

1. Dogs -- Fiction 2. Friendship -- Fiction

ISBN 978-1-58089-322-0; 1-58089-322-8

LC 2008025343

In three adventures, Hound and Poodle discover how much they enjoy each other's company, in spite of, or maybe because of, their differences.

"The lively prose, in large, well-spaced print, provides an entertaining, accessible celebration of friendship. . . . The colorful, watercolor-and-ink illustrations incorporate word balloons and amusing, whimsical details." Booklist

Latimer, Alex

The **boy** who cried ninja; written and illustrated by Alex Latimer. Peachtree 2011 un il $15.95

Grades: PreK K 1 2　　　　　　　　　　E

1. Honesty -- Fiction

ISBN 978-1-56145-579-9; 1-56145-579-2

LC 2010034688

A young boy named Tim is accused of lying when he tells his parents that a ninja ate the last piece of cake and a sunburned crocodile landed on the roof, so he figures out a way to prove that he is telling the truth.

"Latimer has created offbeat digitally colored drawings brimming with quirky, diverse perspectives and hilarious details." SLJ

Laval, Thierry

★ **Colors**. Chronicle Books 2011 un il bd bk $6.99

Grades: PreK　　　　　　　　　　　　E

1. Color 2. Board books for children

ISBN 978-0-8118-7952-1; 0-8118-7952-6

LC 2010035582

Original French edition 2009

"This zesty book about colors offers genuine surprises. Each page features a flap with a die-cut shape that lets readers view the color and texture beneath. . . . Many of the revealed objects are thematically linked to the main scene. . . . Laval delivers the thrills that a peek-a-boo book should with his charmingly eccentric compositions." Publ Wkly

Lawrence, John

★ **This** little chick. Candlewick Press 2002 un il $15.99; bd bk $6.99

Grades: PreK   E

1. Chickens 2. Animal sounds 3. Domestic animals 4. Stories in rhyme 5. Animals -- Infancy 6. Chickens -- Fiction 7. Domestic animals -- Fiction

ISBN 0-7636-1716-4; 0-7636-2882-4 bd bk

LC 2001-35633

A little chick shows that he can make the sounds of the animals in his neighborhood

"The silly farce and raucous noises will . . . delight toddlers, and Lawrence coaxes plenty of character from his boisterous, woodcut animal characters." Booklist

Lawson, Dorie McCullough

Tex; a book for little dreamers. Trafalgar Square Books 2011 un il $15.95

Grades: PreK K   E

1. Cowhands -- Fiction 2. Ranch life -- Fiction

ISBN 978-1-57076-501-8; 1-57076-501-4

LC 2011014775

"Through full-color photographs, each one accompanied by a short sentence or phrase, Lawson tells the story of Luke, a boy who becomes 'Tex' in his dreams each night. He has all sorts of ranch duties like riding horses, digging irrigation trenches, checking the fence, and riding the tractor, and he relaxes for a bit in the pasture. The full-page photos will delight all cowhand enthusiasts." SLJ

Lazo Gilmore, Dorina K.

★ **Cora** cooks pancit; written by Dorina Lazo Gilmore; illustrated by Kristi Valiant. Shen's Books 2009 un il $17.95

Grades: PreK K 1 2 3   E

1. Cooking -- Fiction 2. Filipino Americans -- Fiction

ISBN 978-1-885008-35-0; 1-885008-35-X

LC 2008045836

When all her older siblings are away, Cora's mother finally lets her help make pancit, a Filipino noodle dish. Includes recipe for pancit.

"Clear expository prose explains how to perform kitchen tasks. . . . These scenes effectively model how adults can introduce children to cooking. The simple, direct style also makes the book equally well suited as a read-aloud and for newly independent readers. The artwork nicely complements the text, as Valiant's warm hues of gold, red, and orange highlight the family's loving relationship." SLJ

Lazo, Caroline Evensen

Someday when my cat can talk; by Caroline Lazo; illustrated by Kyrsten Brooker. Schwartz & Wade Books 2008 un il $16.99; lib bdg $19.99

Grades: K 1 2   E

1. Stories in rhyme 2. Cats -- Fiction 3. Imagination -- Fiction 4. Voyages and travels -- Fiction

ISBN 978-0-375-83754-8; 0-375-83754-X; 978-0-375-93754-5 lib bdg; 0-375-93754-4 lib bdg

LC 2006101809

A girl imagines what her cat would tell her about its exotic travels to such places as the foggy English coast, Spanish bullfights, and an art gallery in Monmartre, France. Includes facts about the places mentioned

"Brooker's illustrations, rendered in collage and oil paint, have the look and feel of a scrapbook. . . . . 'The Facts Behind the Story' presents some tidbits about some of the locales, but they seem unnecessary after such a fanciful journey. Rather, the book should be enjoyed as the whimsical daydream that it is." SLJ

Le Guin, Ursula K.

★ **Cat** dreams; illustrations by S.D. Schindler. Orchard Books 2009 un il lib bdg $16.99

Grades: PreK K 1   E

1. Stories in rhyme 2. Cats -- Fiction 3. Dreams -- Fiction

ISBN 978-0-545-04216-1 lib bdg; 0-545-04216-X lib bdg

LC 2008-46299

Presents a feline dreamland where it rains mice, all the dogs have run away, and a big bowl of kibbles and cream is waiting

"Easy rhyming text will be quickly memorized, but the realistic, full-bleed watercolor illustrations will keep youngsters turning the pages. A perfect fit for storytimes on cats, naps and dreams." Kirkus

Leaf, Munro

★ **The** story of Ferdinand; illustrated by Robert Lawson. Viking 1936 un il $17.99; pa $6.99

Grades: PreK K 1 2   E

1. Bulls -- Fiction 2. Bullfights -- Fiction

ISBN 0-670-67424-9; 0-14-050234-3 pa

"The drawings picture not only Ferdinand but Spanish scenes and characters as well." N Y Public Libr

Leathers, Philippa

The **Black** rabbit; Philippa Leathers. Candlewick Press 2013 40 p. (reinforced) $14

Grades: PreK K 1 2   E

1. Children's stories 2. Picture books for children 3. Rabbits -- Juvenile fiction 4. Shades and shadows -- Juvenile fiction

ISBN 076365714X; 9780763657147

LC 2012942317

In this children's book by Philippa Leathers, part of the Junior Library Guild Selection series, "rabbit has a problem. There's a large black rabbit chasing him. No matter where he runs--behind a tree, over the river--the shadowy rabbit follows. Finally in the deep, dark wood, Rabbit loses his nemesis--only to encounter a real foe!" (Publisher's note)

Lechner, John

Sticky Burr: adventures in Burrwood Forest; [by] John Lechner. Candlewick Press 2007 un il $15.99; pa $6.99

Grades: K 1 2 3   E

1. Insects -- Fiction 2. Forests and forestry -- Fiction

ISBN 978-0-7636-3054-6; 0-7636-3054-3; 978-0-7636-3567-1 pa; 0-7636-3567-7 pa

LC 2006049575

Sticky Burr is on the verge of being kicked out of his village in Burrwood Forest because he is not prickly enough to suit some of the other burrs, but when the village is attacked by wild dogs, Sticky Burr and his friends come to the rescue.

"Written in graphic-novel style, the lively and sometimes punny dialogue leads young readers through Sticky's exciting escapades. . . . The illustrations are simple, colorful, and easy to follow." SLJ

Another title about Stick Burr is:

Sticky Burr: the prickly peril

The **clever** stick. Candlewick Press 2009 un il $14.99
Grades: K 1 2 3   E
1. Drawing -- Fiction 2. Communication -- Fiction
ISBN 978-0-7636-3950-1; 0-7636-3950-8
                                        LC 2008024230

"A clever stick longs to express himself but can't find a way to make his thoughts understood. Discouraged, he drags himself home and discovers that the lines he creates in the sand make shapes and even pictures. . . . Lechner's gently funny ink and watercolor pictures convey the story's meaning." Horn Book Guide

Lee, Ho Baek

While we were out. Kane/Miller 2003 un il $15.95
Grades: PreK K 1 2   E
1. Rabbits -- Fiction
ISBN 1-929132-44-1
                                        LC 2002-112325

"A white rabbit who lives on the patio notices that his family has gone to Grandma's, leaving the house empty. Now the house is hers. Simple line-and-wash pictures alternating with radiant full-page paintings follow the rabbit as she indulges in a multitude of obviously long-held wishes. . . . This Korean import is amusing, yes, but there is also a delicacy and intelligence that pervades the tale. A definite cut above." Booklist

Lee, Mark

★ **Twenty** big trucks in the middle of the street; by Mark Lee; illustrated by Kurt Cyrus. Candlewick Press 2013 32 p. col. ill. (reinforced) $15.99
Grades: PreK K   E
1. Trucks -- Juvenile fiction 2. City traffic -- Juvenile fiction
ISBN 076365809X; 9780763658090
                                        LC 2012943654

In this children's picture book by Mark Lee, "an ice cream truck breaking down in 'the middle of our street' is a dream come true for many a kid--not to mention the ensuing traffic jam that strands 20 trucks of every shape and purpose. But one boy has something bigger in mind than licking a cone or being a spectator: he wants to solve the problem. That takes some persistence, but he eventually wins over the crowd with a solution that's literally right in front of them." (Publishers Weekly)

Lee, Spike

Giant steps to change the world; [by] Spike and Tonya Lewis Lee; illustrated by Sean Qualls. Simon & Schuster Books for Young Readers 2011 un il $16.99
Grades: PreK K 1 2 3   E
1. Conduct of life -- Fiction
ISBN 978-0-689-86815-3; 0-689-86815-4
                                        LC 2009-27622

"In plainspoken free verse directed right to kids, this title introduces individuals who took 'giant steps to make the world a better place.' . . . Rendered in paint, pencil, and collage, the artwork, featuring often-faceless figures, leaves space for young people to imagine their own stories and, like the poems, will inspire many children to match the pictures with the famous names and find out more." Booklist

Lee, YJ

The **little** moon princess; written and illustrated by YJ Lee. HarperCollins 2010 un il $16.99
Grades: K 1 2   E
1. Stars -- Fiction 2. Sparrows -- Fiction 3. Princesses -- Fiction
ISBN 978-0-06-154736-2; 0-06-154736-0
                                        LC 2009-9294

With the help of a friendly sparrow, the Little Moon Princess, who is afraid of the dark, uses the jewels on the surface of her moon to light up the sky.

"Lee's stunning use of watercolor and ink creates the illusion of light, and her art offers readers a breathtaking view of the night sky. A lovely read-aloud." SLJ

Leedy, Loreen

Crazy like a fox; a simile story. written and illustrated by Loreen Leedy. Holiday House 2008 un il lib bdg $16.95; pa $6.95
Grades: K 1 2   E
1. Foxes -- Fiction 2. Parties -- Fiction 3. Birthdays -- Fiction 4. English language -- Idioms
ISBN 978-0-8234-1719-3 lib bdg; 0-8234-1719-0 lib bdg; 978-0-8234-2248-7 pa; 0-8234-2248-7 pa
                                        LC 2007-051016

"Rufus, a spunky fox in suspenders, rudely startles his friend Babette, a lamb, by roaring 'like...a lion.' She gets 'mad...as a hornet' and chases him, and he eventually leads her to her surprise birthday party. Leedy relates this narrative entirely through similes. Her illustrations emphasize the comparisons as each protagonist is amusingly transformed from one object into another. . . . [Leedy's] vivid illustrations, filled with movement and wide-eyed creatures, will entertain readers." SLJ

The **great** graph contest; written and illustrated by Loreen Leedy. Holiday House 2005 32p il $16.95; pa $6.95
Grades: 1 2 3   E
1. Graphic methods 2. Frogs -- Fiction 3. Snails -- Fiction 4. Lizards -- Fiction
ISBN 0-8234-1710-7; 0-8234-2029-9 pa
                                        LC 2003-62549

Gonk the toad, Chester the snail, and Beezy the lizard hold a contest to see who can make better graphs

"A splashy and colorful offering designed to inform and entertain. . . . The lively text, delivered in large type and contained in dialogue and thought balloons, is engaging and well supported by the vivid, cartoon illustrations." SLJ

Lehman, Barbara

Museum trip. Houghton Mifflin 2006 un il $15
Grades: K 1 2 3   E
1. School stories 2. Stories without words 3. Art museums -- Fiction
ISBN 0-618-58125-1
                                        LC 2005052840

In this wordless picture book, a boy imagines himself inside some of the exhibits when he goes on a field trip to an art museum.

"The sturdiness and clarity of the ink-lined, watercolor-and-gouache art juxtaposes wonderfully with the story's airy world of imagination." Booklist

Rainstorm. Houghton Mifflin 2007 un il $16
Grades: PreK K 1 2   E
1. Stories without words 2. Play -- Fiction
ISBN 978-0-618-75639-1; 0-618-75639-6
                                         LC 2006-49318

In this wordless picture book, a boy finds a mysterious key which leads him on an adventure one rainy day.

"Lehman provides purely colored, precisely rendered artwork that capably captures both adventures and emotions." Booklist

Trainstop. Houghton 2008 un il $16
Grades: PreK K 1 2   E
1. Stories without words 2. Railroads -- Fiction 3. Imagination -- Fiction
ISBN 0-618-75640-X

In this wordless picture book, a young girl takes a train and makes a stop at a most unusual place where she has an important task to perform.

Lehman "demonstrates her extraordinary knack for storytelling sans words. . . . Gouache, watercolor, and ink illustrations reveal a bleak cityscape and adults dressed in muted tones—all in pointed contrast to the girl's head-to-toe multicolored outfit. . . . Lehman's true talent is her spot-on depiction of a young child's capacity for criss-crossing the real with the imaginary." Horn Book

★ The **red** book. Houghton Mifflin 2004 un il $12.95
Grades: K 1 2 3   E
1. Stories without words 2. Books and reading -- Fiction
ISBN 0-618-42858-5
A Caldecott Medal honor book, 2005

This "wordless book tells the complex story of a reader who gets lost, literally, in a little book that has the magic to move her to another place. . . . Done in watercolor, gouache, and ink, the simple, streamlined pictures are rife with invitations to peek inside, to investigate further, and—like a hall of mirrors—reflect, refract, repeat, and reveal. Lehman's story captures the magical possibility that exists every time readers open a book." SLJ

★ The **secret** box. Scholastic Press 2011 un il $15.99
Grades: PreK K 1   E
1. Stories without words 2. Boys -- Fiction 3. Photography -- Fiction
ISBN 978-0-547-23868-5; 0-547-23868-1

"Here, three boys discover a box in the top floor of their urban boarding school that holds decades-old sepia photographs of a schoolboy, a postcard, and a map leading to a location on the coast. Picking out features of the old landscape amid the built-up, modern city around them, the boys make their way to a boardwalk amusement park, where they find the schoolboy of the photograph with a crowd of children who presumably have made the same trip. . . . A provocative example of the complexity that can be conveyed using only pictures." Publ Wkly

Leist, Christina
Jack the bear. Simply Read Books 2009 un il $16.95
Grades: K 1 2   E
1. Bears -- Fiction 2. Kindness -- Fiction 3. Friendship -- Fiction
ISBN 978-1-894965-97-2; 1-894965-97-3

"It is an earnest message, and Leist spells it out explicitly, but the warmth in the words will hit home with the target audience. The sketchy watercolor-and-crayon illustrations are printed on recycled brown bags, and the visible creases and folded handles add to the book's distinctive look." Booklist

Lendroth, Susan
Ocean wide, ocean deep; illustrated by Raúl Allén. Tricycle Press 2007 un il $15.99
Grades: K 1 2 3   E
1. Stories in rhyme 2. Sailors -- Fiction 3. Family life -- Fiction
ISBN 978-1-58246-232-5; 1-58246-232-1
                                         LC 2007-18619

In nineteenth-century New England, a young girl watches her baby brother learn to walk and talk while waiting for Papa's return from the sea after he joins the China trade and sails to foreign lands.

"In Allén's American picture book debut, he channels the soft-edged realism and absorption with light shared by 19th-century American painters to create an atmosphere of foreboding. . . . Children in the contemporary equivalent of the narrator's situation—a son or daughter anxious about an absent parent's wellbeing—will appreciate both the distance afforded by the period setting and the comfort of the melodic language and happy ending." Publ Wkly

Lerman, Josh
How to raise Mom and Dad; instructions from someone who figured it out. illustrated by Greg Clarke. Dutton Children's Books 2009 un il $16.99
Grades: K 1 2   E
1. Parents -- Fiction
ISBN 978-0-525-47870-6; 0-525-47870-1
                                         LC 2008-13886

Advice on how to manipulate your parents in order to avoid eating vegetables, extend your bedtime, or get a puppy.

"The gouache illustrations are as joyful as the text. . . . This is a manual every child will want to read." SLJ

Lester, Alison
Noni the pony; Alison Lester. Beach Lane Books 2013 32 p. (hardback) $15.99
Grades: PreK K 1   E
1. Stories in rhyme 2. Horses -- Juvenile fiction 3. Friendship -- Juvenile fiction 4. Ponies -- Fiction
ISBN 144245959X; 9781442459595; 9781442459601
                                         LC 2012004907

This rhyming children's book, by Alison Lester, introduces readers to "Noni, the friendliest, funniest, and friskiest pony you—ll ever meet! When she's not racing and chasing with her best pals Dave Dog and Coco the Cat, she's busy making sure they feel cozy and loved. Because Noni isn't just heaps of fun--she's a great friend, too." (Publisher's note)

★ **Running** with the horses. North South Books 2011 un il $16.95

Grades: 2 3 4   **E**
  1. Horses -- Fiction 2. World War, 1939-1945 -- Fiction
  3. Father-daughter relationship -- Fiction
  ISBN 0-7358-4002-4; 978-0-7358-4002-7
  First published 2009 in Australia
  "Lester crafts a believable wartime adventure. . . . The
illustrations, predominately black-and-white drawings layered between photographic and colored-pencil back- and
foregrounds, make the historical contemporary." Kirkus

Lester, Helen
  ★ **Hooway** for Wodney Wat; illustrated by Lynn Mun-
singer. Houghton Mifflin 1999 32p il $16; pa $5.95
Grades: PreK K 1 2   **E**
  1. School stories 2. Bullies -- Fiction 3. Rodents --
Fiction 4. Schools -- Fiction 5. Speech disorders --
Fiction
  ISBN 0-395-92392-1; 0-618-21612-X pa
                                        LC 98-46149
  All his classmates make fun of Rodney because he can't
pronounce his name, but it is Rodney's speech impediment
that drives away the class bully.
  "Munsinger's watercolor with pen-and-ink illustrations
positively bristle with humor and each rat, mouse, hamster,
and capybara is fully realized as both rodent and child." SLJ
  Another title about Rodney is:
  Wodney Wat's wobot (2011)

  Tacky's Christmas; written by Helen Lester; illustrated
by Lynn Munsinger. Houghton Mifflin Harcourt 2010 un
il $16.99
Grades: PreK K 1 2   **E**
  1. Penguins -- Fiction 2. Christmas -- Fiction
  ISBN 978-0-547-17208-8; 0-547-17208-7
                                        LC 2010000954
  Goodly, Lovely, Angel, Neatly, Perfect, and Tacky the
penguin are having a wonderful Christmas, complete with
an unusual tree, when Tacky's odd behavior saves them from
a group of hunters.
  "The comical illustrations, silly mistaken-identity concept and the impossibly dim hunters' comments all add up to
a funny, entertaining read." Kirkus

  Three cheers for Tacky; illustrated by Lynn Munsinger.
Houghton Mifflin 1994 32p il $16; pa $5.95
Grades: PreK K 1 2   **E**
  1. Contests -- Fiction 2. Penguins -- Fiction 3.
Cheerleading -- Fiction
  ISBN 0-395-66841-7; 0-395-82-740-X pa
                                        LC 93-14342
  This "is a smooth, fun read. Munsinger's full-color il-
lustrations are charming and subtle." SLJ
  Other titles about Tacky are:
  Tacky the penguin (1988)
  Tacky in trouble (1998)
  Tacky and the emperor (2000)
  Tackylocks and the three bears (2002)
  Tacky and the winter games (2005)
  Tacky goes to camp (2009)
  Tacky's Christmas (2010)

  Wodney Wat's wobot; written by Helen Lester; illustrated by Lynn Munsinger. Houghton Mifflin Books for
Children 2011 un il $16.99

Grades: PreK K 1 2   **E**
  1. School stories 2. Robots -- Fiction 3. Speech
disorders -- Fiction
  ISBN 978-0-547-36756-9; 0-547-36756-2
                                        LC 2010044363
  When Wodney Wat, who cannot pronounce the letter R,
gets a talking robot for his birthday, it turns out to be more
than just a fun gift.
  "Wodney is a wonderfully quirky character with whom
many children will connect. Munsinger's illustrations are
joyful and humorous." SLJ

  The **sheep** in wolf's clothing; illustrated by Lynn Munsinger. Houghton Mifflin 2007 32p il $16
Grades: PreK K 1 2   **E**
  1. Sheep -- Fiction 2. Wolves -- Fiction 3. Clothing
and dress -- Fiction
  ISBN 978-0-618-86844-5; 0-618-86844-5
                                        LC 2007-00644
  Clothing is important to Ewetopia, but her carefully-
chosen wolf outfit fails to impress the other sheep at the
Woolyones' costume ball until a real wolf appears dressed as
a sheep, mistakes her for his mother, and throws a tantrum
when she outsmarts him.
  "The playful illustrations, suffused with expression and
shades of pink, show sheep outfitted in tutus and an Elvis
costume, and the wolf having a tantrum. Lester follows a
familiar format in this clever tale." SLJ

Lester, Helen, 1936-
  Happy birdday, Tacky! written by Helen Lester; il-
lustrated by Lynn Munsinger. Houghton Mifflin Books for
Children 2013 32 p. col. ill. (reinforced) $16.99
Grades: PreK K 1 2   **E**
  1. Penguins/Juvenile fiction 2. Birthdays -- Juvenile
fiction 3. Dance -- Fiction 4. Parties -- Fiction 5.
Penguins -- Fiction 6. Birthdays -- Fiction
  ISBN 0547912285; 9780547912288
                                        LC 2012014847
  This children's picture book is part of the Tacky the Penguin series. Here, "everyone is deep into preparations for
Tacky's Birdday Party. This includes baking, practicing the
special song and making a whole slew of cards for their decidedly odd friend." However, the party goes awry due to
Tacky's strange habits and another penguin's injury. Can the
party be saved? (Kirkus)

Lester, J. D.
  Daddy calls me doodlebug; illustrations by Hiroe Na-
kata. Robin Corey Books 2010 un il $7.99
Grades: PreK   **E**
  1. Board books for children 2. Animals -- Fiction 3.
Father-child relationship -- Fiction
  ISBN 978-0-375-85830-7; 0-375-85830-X
  Describes the reasons why animal fathers give nick-
names to their children based on their characteristics and
love for the child.

  Grandma calls me gigglepie; illustrations by Hiroe
Nakata. Robin Corey Books 2011 un il bd bk $7.99
Grades: PreK   **E**
  1. Board books for children 2. Animals -- Fiction 3.
Grandmothers -- Fiction
  ISBN 978-0-375-85904-5; 0-375-85904-7

"Sprightly watercolors explore the special relationship between grandmothers and their grandchildren. . . . In rhyming couplets, animals share the terms of endearment given to them by their grandmas. . . . Readers for whom a grandparent is a primary caregiver should especially value this buoyant affirmation of affection." Publ Wkly

Mommy calls me monkeypants; illustrations by Hiroe Nakata. Robin Corey Books 2009 un il $7.99
Grades: PreK   E
1. Board books for children 2. Animals -- Fiction 3. Mother-child relationship -- Fiction
ISBN 978-0-375-84502-4; 0-375-84502-X
"Through several spreads, each with a different bright background color, animals and insects say their nicknames as they swing, play, chirp, and bounce with their mothers, ending with the girl in bed saying 'Mommy calls me Monkeypants . . . because she loves me so.' The pictures capture the lighthearted mood of the couplets exactly and together they create a perfect foray into toddler territory." SLJ

Lester, Julius
★ **Black** cowboy, wild horses; a true story. [by] Julius Lester, Jerry Pinkney. Dial Bks. 1998 un il $18.99
Grades: 2 3 4   E
1. Horses 2. African Americans 3. Cowboys 4. Mustang 5. Horses -- Fiction 6. Cowhands -- Fiction 7. African Americans -- Fiction
ISBN 0-8037-1787-3
LC 97-25210
A black cowboy is so in tune with wild mustangs that they accept him into the herd, thus enabling him singlehandedly to take them to the corral
This story is told in "vivid, poetic prose. . . . Pinkney's magnificent earth-toned paintings bring to life the wild beauty of the horses and the western plains." Horn Book Guide

Sam and the tigers; a new telling of Little Black Sambo. pictures by Jerry Pinkney. Dial Bks. for Young Readers 1996 un il $16.99; pa $6.99
Grades: K 1 2 3   E
1. Tigers -- Fiction
ISBN 0-8037-2028-9; 0-14-056288-5 pa
LC 95-43080
A boy named Sam, who lives in the land of Sam-sam-sa-mara, gives his new school clothes to tigers who threaten to eat him, but he re-claims them when the tigers chase one another until they turn into butter
"The rolling, lilting narrative is a model of harmony, clarity, and meticulously chosen detail. . . . Pinkney's lively pencil-and-watercolor illustrations sprawl extravagantly across double spreads and are smoothly integrated with the narrative." SLJ

Leuck, Laura
I love my pirate papa; [by] Laura Leuck; illustrated by Kyle M. Stone. Harcourt 2007 un il $16
Grades: PreK K 1 2   E
1. Pirates -- Fiction 2. Father-son relationship -- Fiction
ISBN 978-0-15-205664-3
LC 2006009240
A pirate's son shares the things he loves about his father, including climbing the mast together to yell "Land ho" and sharing the booty when they find buried treasure.

This is written "in well cadenced, rhyming verses. . . . The stylized acrylic paintings, using exaggeration and comical details effectively, create one dramatic double-page scene after another." Booklist

★ **One** witch; illustrations by S.D. Schindler. Walker & Co. 2003 un il hardcover o.p. pa $6.95
Grades: K 1 2   E
1. Counting 2. Stories in rhyme 3. Witches -- Fiction 4. Halloween -- Fiction
ISBN 0-8027-8860-2; 0-8027-7729-5 pa
LC 2002-191049
A witch goes around to her fiendish friends—from two cats to ten werewolves—to gather the ingredients to make gruesome stew for her party
"Eerie yet amusing illustrations and a romping, rhyming text add up to fun in this Halloween counting book. Schindler's ink-and-watercolor artwork is a fine fit for Leuck's action-packed, easy-to-read text." SLJ

Levert, Mireille
The **princess** who had almost everything; [text by] Mireille Levert; [illustrations by] Josée Masse. Tundra Books 2008 un il $19.95
Grades: K 1 2 3   E
1. Fairy tales 2. Princesses -- Fiction
ISBN 978-0-88776-887-3; 0-88776-887-3
"A princess' parents do everything to make their daughter happy. But Alicia keeps yelling, 'I'M BORED!' . . . When she decides she wants a prince, her parents promise her hand in marriage to anyone who can keep their daughter from tedium. . . . Dramatic angular illustrations in an earth-tone palette let the viewer see the world from contrasting perspectives. . . . The message of the importance of creativity come through loud and clear." Booklist

A **wizard** in love; [written by] Mireille Levert; [illustrated by] Marie Lafrance. Tundra Books 2009 un il $17.95
Grades: PreK K 1 2   E
1. Magic -- Fiction 2. Noise -- Fiction 3. Witches -- Fiction
ISBN 978-0-88776-901-6; 0-88776-901-2
Original French edition published 2007 in Canada
Hector, a retired wizard, lives happily and quietly with his cat, Poison, in a dilapidated house at the edge of the forest, until a noisy new neighbor moves into the abandoned house across the road, and things are never the same again.
"Both verbally and visually entirely funny . . . this offbeat import is a sophisticated treat.." Kirkus

Levine, Arthur A.
★ **Monday** is one day; illustrated by Julian Hector. Scholastic Press 2011 un il $16.99
Grades: PreK K 1   E
1. Counting 2. Stories in rhyme 3. Day -- Fiction 4. Week -- Fiction 5. Family life -- Fiction
ISBN 978-0-439-78924-0; 0-439-78924-9
LC 2009011575
A rhyming countdown of the days of the week as families find ways to spend time together while waiting for the weekend.
"Hector's grinning cartoon-style illustrations are delightful, based in reality but accented with unexpected color.

. . . But the book's greatest accomplishment might be its cross section of middle America: white, black, old, young, white-collar, blue-collar, straight, and gay. . . . It's that rare book perceptive enough to recognize that the random moments are those we treasure most." Booklist

Levine, Ellen

★ Henry's freedom box; illustrated by Kadir Nelson. Scholastic Press 2007 un il $16.99

Grades: 1 2 3　　　　　　　　　　　　　　　　　E

1. Slaves 2. Magicians 3. Abolitionists 4. Slavery -- Fiction 5. African Americans -- Fiction 6. Underground railroad -- Fiction

ISBN 0-439-77733-X

LC 2006-09487

A Caldecott Medal honor book, 2008

A fictionalized account of how in 1849 a Virginia slave, Henry "Box" Brown, escapes to freedom by shipping himself in a wooden crate from Richmond to Philadelphia.

"According to the flap copy, an antique lithograph of Brown inspired Nelson's paintings, which use crosshatched pencil lines layered with watercolors and oil paints. . . . Transcending technique is the humanity Nelson imbues in his characters." Booklist

Levine, Gail Carson

Betsy Red Hoodie; illustrated by Scott Nash. HarperCollins Publishers 2010 un il $16.99; lib bdg $17.89

Grades: K 1 2　　　　　　　　　　　　　　　　　E

1. Sheep -- Fiction 2. Wolves -- Fiction 3. Grandmothers -- Fiction

ISBN 978-0-06-146870-4; 0-06-146870-3; 978-0-06-146871-1 lib bdg; 0-06-146871-1 lib bdg

LC 2008-27456

In this variation of "Little Red Riding Hood," Betsy Red Hoodie goes to visit her grandma with her friend Zimmo the wolf and her flock of sheep, but Zimmo, her mother, and her grandma have a surprise planned.

"Nash stages the shenanigans in an attractive country landscape, supporting Levine's light tone with comical pen drawings. . . . Good read-aloud fun." Horn Book

Betsy who cried wolf; illustrated by Scott Nash. HarperCollins Pubs. 2002 un lib bdg $16.89

Grades: PreK K 1 2　　　　　　　　　　　　　　　E

1. Sheep -- Fiction 2. Wolves -- Fiction 3. Shepherds -- Fiction

ISBN 0-06-028763-2; 0-06-028764-0 lib bdg

LC 00-54032

Betsy, a serious young shepherd, finds that there is more than one way to keep a wolf from eating her sheep

"Nash's cartoonlike illustrations, with their clean lines, crisp colors, and folk-art touches, add considerably to the story." SLJ

Levis, Caron

Stuck with the Blooz; Caron Levis; illustrated by Jon Davis. Harcourt Children's Books 2012 40 p. $16.99

Grades: K 1 2 3　　　　　　　　　　　　　　　　E

1. Melancholy 2. Emotions -- Juvenile fiction 3. Monsters -- Juvenile fiction 4. Sadness -- Fiction 5. Monsters -- Fiction

ISBN 0547745605; 9780547745602

LC 2011041938

This children's book, by Caron Lewis, illustrated by Jon Davis, asks "What do you do when you're feeling blue--especially when your mood takes the form of a drippy, oozy monster called the Blooz? Do you ignore it? Do you ask it lots of questions? Do you give it an ice-pop and hope it goes away? Through trial and error, the child in this story discovers that while it may not be easy, it's not impossible to shake the Blooz." (Publisher's note)

Leviton, Michael

My first ghost; illustrated by Stephanie Buscema; text by Margaret Miller & Michael Leviton. 1st ed. Disney/Hyperion Books 2012 40 p.

Grades: PreK K 1 2　　　　　　　　　　　　　　　E

1. Wit and humor 2. Picture books for children 3. Ghosts -- Juvenile literature 4. Ghosts -- Fiction

ISBN 1423119495; 9781423119494

LC 2011017596

This children's picture book, by Maggie Miller and Michael Leviton, illustrated by Stephanie Buscema, "comes with a free ghost! But, like any pet, ghosts need special care and attention. . . . [The book] teaches kids everything they need to know about taking care of their very own ghost. . . . [A]uthors Miller and Leviton offer humorous tips on feeding, grooming, and ghostly games which are complemented by . . . illustrations." (Publisher's note)

Levy, Janice

Gonzalo grabs the good life; written by Janice Levy; illustrated by Bill Slavin. Eerdmans Books for Young Readers 2009 un il $17.50

Grades: K 1 2 3　　　　　　　　　　　　　　　　E

1. Wealth -- Fiction 2. Roosters -- Fiction

ISBN 978-0-8028-5328-8; 0-8028-5328-5

LC 2008009998

When Gonzalo the rooster wins the lottery, he leaves his job at the farm in search of the good life.

"Acrylic illustrations on gessoed paper animate the humor with fine-feathered cleverness, adding wry details. . . . A vocabulary list defines the six Spanish words sprinkled throughout. This is beak-in-cheek fun with an underlying message." Booklist

Lewin, Betsy

Where is Tippy Toes? [written and] illustrated by Betsy Lewin. Atheneum Books for Young Readers 2010 un il $16.99

Grades: PreK K　　　　　　　　　　　　　　　　E

1. Stories in rhyme 2. Cats -- Fiction

ISBN 978-1-4169-3808-8; 1-4169-3808-7

LC 2009-24455

Although everyone can see how Tippy Toes, a mischievous cat, spends his days, only one knows where he goes after dark.

"Oversize watercolors outlined in a thick black line add humor to the text . . . and the bright hues seen in the flowers, sun, and cat's fur enhance the changing backgrounds. Rhyming sentences come together with the turn of a page and continue to the satisfying page turn at the end. This cat's sun up to sun down routine makes an excellent choice for those looking for a new bedtime story." SLJ

Lewin, Betsy, 1937-

★ **Puffling** patrol; Ted and Betsy Lewin. Lee & Low Books 2012 56 p. (hardcover: alk. paper) $19.95

Grades: 2 3 4   E

  1. Puffins 2. Heimaey (Iceland) 3. Birds -- Protection 4. Children and animals 5. Wildlife rescue -- Iceland -- Heimaey (Westman Islands) 6. Atlantic puffin -- Infancy -- Iceland -- Heimaey (Westman Islands)

  ISBN 1600604242; 9781600604249

LC 2011032248

In this book, "husband and wife team Ted and Betsy Lewin detail their visit to the island of Heimaey (off the coast of Iceland). They accompany two child members of the 'Puffling Patrol' (who rescue newly hatched puffins that become disoriented and lost on their way to the sea) and observe as the children find, care for, and release the baby pufflings." (Bulletin of the Center for Children's Books)

★ **You** can do it! by Betsy Lewin. 1st ed. Holiday House 2013 32 p. (I like to read) (reinforced) $14.95

Grades: K 1 2   E

  1. Racing -- Juvenile fiction 2. Crocodiles -- Juvenile fiction 3. Self-confidence -- Juvenile fiction 4. Racing -- Fiction 5. Alligators -- Fiction 6. Self-confidence -- Fiction

  ISBN 0823425223; 9780823425228

LC 2011051992

This children's book, by Caldecott Honor-winning illustrator Betsy Lewin, is part of the "I Like to Read" series. "'Can I do it?' wonders the little crocodile when he sees a sign for Sunday's big swimming race. A mean, bigger crocodile tells him he cannot win, but the little crocodile's friend helps him train and tells him more than once that he can indeed succeed. On the day of the big race, the little crocodile is ready to prove himself." (Publisher's note)

"Limited, repetitive text invites new readers to adopt the same spirit of determination about reading that the protagonist alligator does about swimming... Lewin's restrained watercolor-and-ink artwork matches the control of the text... while delivering engaging and expressive characters. Subtle shifts in the placement of speech balloons provide humor while helping children decode. A winner of an early reader." Kirkus

Lewis, J. Patrick

Big is big (and little, little) a book of contrasts. by J. Patrick Lewis; illustrated by Bob Barner. Holiday House 2007 un il $16.95

Grades: PreK K 1   E

  1. Opposites 2. Animals -- Poetry

  ISBN 978-0-8234-1909-8; 0-8234-1909-6

LC 2005050341

"Wordplay meets playful art in this clever look at opposites. Lewis's bouncy verse and Barner's rollicking illustrations show the contrasts between various animals. . . . Done in a combination of cut-paper collage, bright pastels, and bold black line, Barner's animals cavort against vivid backgrounds." SLJ

Face bug; by J. Patrick Lewis; illustrated by Kelly Murphy; photographs by Frederic B. Siskind. WordSong 2013 36 p. ill. (reinforced) $16.95

Grades: 3 4 5   E

  1. Insects -- Poetry

  ISBN 1590789253; 9781590789254

LC 2012943510

This book by J. Patrick Lewis "combines poetry, line drawings and scientific facts. . . . A collection of small bugs . . . visits the Face Bug Museum, where they learn to drill like a carpenter bee, experience the stinkbug's stench, sip on nectar at the snack bar and measure the speed of the green darner dragonfly. The insects on display at the 'museum' . . . are portrayed in . . . full-color micrographs by renowned nature photographer [Frederic B.] Siskind." (Kirkus Reviews)

The **Fantastic** 5 & 10[cents] store; a rebus adventure. words by J. Patrick Lewis; pictures by Valorie Fisher. Schwartz & Wade Books 2010 un il $17.99; lib bdg $20.99

Grades: PreK K 1 2   E

  1. Riddles 2. Stories in rhyme 3. Department stores -- Fiction

  ISBN 978-0-375-85878-9; 0-375-85878-4; 978-0-375-95878-6 lib bdg; 0-375-95878-9 lib bdg

LC 2008048827

Rhymed text, featuring rebuses, describes the wonders of the store run by Mr. Nickel and Mrs. Dime.

"The rebuses appear opposite each image on yellowing lined paper, straight from a vintage school notebook, and for those having trouble guessing, the full text of the rhymes appears at the end of the book. Good, old-fashioned fun, with a surprise ending that reveals Benny's talent for public relations." Publ Wkly

World Rat day; J. Patrick Lewis, illustrated by Anna Raff. Candlewick Press 2013 40 p. (reinforced) $15.99

Grades: K 1 2 3   E

  ISBN 9780763654023

LC 2012942612

The **kindergarten** cat; illustrated by Ailie Busby. Schwartz & Wade Books 2009 un il $16.99; lib bdg $19.99

Grades: PreK K   E

  1. School stories 2. Stories in rhyme 3. Cats -- Fiction

  ISBN 978-0-375-84475-1; 0-375-84475-9; 978-0-375-98807-3 lib bdg; 0-375-98807-6 lib bdg

LC 2008006691

A stray cat finds a happy home in a kindergarten classroom.

"Lewis's verse is sweetly complemented by Busby's mixed-media illustrations. Her fat, scruffy orange tiger cat brims with personality, her cartoony roundness matching that of the children neatly. Broad paint strokes accented with swift pencil scribbles lend energy throughout." Kirkus

The **snowflake** sisters; illustrated by Lisa Desimini. Atheneum Bks. for Young Readers 2003 un il $16.95

Grades: K 1 2 3   E

  1. Snow 2. Santa Claus 3. Stories in rhyme 4. Snow -- Fiction

  ISBN 0-689-85029-8

LC 2002-6138

Two snowflakes named Crystal and Ivory travel on Santa's sleigh and make their way through the wintry sky until they become part of a snowboy in Central Park

"The setting is New York City, captured through witty collage illustrations that make use of such materials as rice paper, maps, newsprint, and Scrabble letters. Lewis's elegant and fluid rhymed text offers surprises on every page." SLJ

Lewis, Jill

Don't read this book! illustrated by Deborah Allwright. Tiger Tales 2010 un il $15.95

Grades: 2 3 4   E

1. Fairy tales

ISBN 978-1-58925-094-9; 1-58925-094-X

The king frantically rides throughout his kingdom trying to piece together fragments of his story.

"The collage pictures in blazing colors are just right for scenes of the king threatening to put the reader in the dungeon if he does not go away. . . . Not for the usual picture-book fairy-tale crowd, this is for readers who already know the classic stories and will enjoy the parodies and rebellious chaos, especially their own defiance just by turning the pages." Booklist

Lewis, Kevin

Not inside this house! illustrated by David Ercolini. Orchard Books 2011 un il $16.99

Grades: PreK K   E

1. Stories in rhyme 2. Animals -- Fiction 3. Explorers -- Fiction 4. Mother-son relationship -- Fiction

ISBN 978-0-439-43981-7; 0-439-43981-7

LC 2010033233

Rhyming text follows a young explorer as he discovers bugs and then increasingly larger creatures, brings them home to learn about them, and is warned by his mother that each is unwelcome.

"The precisely composed ink drawing, painting, and Photoshop illustrations, which set the tale in the halcyon age when men wore hats and women donned aprons, add an odd-fashioned charm and much humor to the story." SLJ

Lewis, Kim

Good night, Harry. Candlewick Press 2004 un il $15.99

Grades: PreK   E

1. Toys 2. Sleep 3. Bedtime 4. Elephants 5. Friendship 6. Sleep -- Fiction 7. Bedtime -- Fiction 8. Elephants -- Fiction

ISBN 0-7636-2206-0

LC 2002-41468

First published 2003 in the United Kingdom

When Harry, a toy elephant, has trouble sleeping, his friends help him.

"Lewis's meticulous illustrations were rendered in colored pencil and pastel, and the vivid, warm textures of the toys are sure to be appreciated by children. . . . This is a gentle book with illustrations that hum, and a bedtime story that's as warm as it is irresistible." SLJ

Other titles about Harry are:

Here we go Harry (2005)

Hooray for Harry (2006)

My friend Harry (1997)

Lewis, Paeony

No more yawning! by Paeony Lewis; illustrated by Brita Granström. Chicken House/Scholastic 2008 un il $16.99

Grades: PreK K   E

1. Toys -- Fiction 2. Sleep -- Fiction 3. Bedtime -- Fiction

ISBN 0-545-02957; 978-0-545-02957-5

Florence and her toy monkey Arnold try to fall asleep but Florence's big yawns keep them awake. Includes tips for falling asleep.

"Florence's childlike voice carries this charming story, and the repetition of her excuses . . . adds humor, as do her crayon drawings, which frequently appear superimposed on the watercolor-and-pencil scenes." Booklist

Lewis, Rose A.

Every year on your birthday; written by Rose Lewis; illustrated by Jane Dyer. Little, Brown 2007 un il $16.99

Grades: PreK K 1 2   E

1. Adoption -- Fiction 2. Birthdays -- Fiction 3. Mother-daughter relationship -- Fiction

ISBN 978-0-316-52552-7; 0-316-52552-9

LC 2006026467

Each year on the birthday of her adopted Chinese daughter, a mother recalls the moments they have shared, from the first toy to the friends left behind in China

"Expressive watercolors evoke vivid memories. . . . By story's end, readers see a matured parent, secure in her love for her child." Publ Wkly

I love you like crazy cakes; written by Rose Lewis; illustrated by Jane Dyer. Little, Brown 2000 un il $14.95; bd bk $6.99

Grades: PreK K 1 2   E

1. Adoption 2. Babies 3. Infants -- Fiction 4. Adoption -- Fiction 5. Intercountry adoption

ISBN 0-316-52538-3; 0-316-52576-6 bd bk

LC 99-34175

A woman describes how she went to China to adopt a special baby girl. Based on the author's own experiences

"Dyer's simple watercolor layouts with expressive characters make this a calming read, befitting the gentle affection in the text." SLJ

Lexau, Joan M.

Come back, cat; by Joan L. Nodset; pictures by Steven Kellogg. Harper Collins Childrens Books 2008 un il $16.99; lib bdg $17.89

Grades: PreK K 1 2   E

1. Cats -- Fiction

ISBN 978-0-06-028081-9; 0-06-028081-6; 978-0-06-028082-6 lib bdg; 0-06-028082-4 lib bdg

LC 2007041937

A newly illustrated edition of Come here cat, published 1973

A stray cat and a little girl have their problems getting acquainted.

"This picture book, originally published in two colors and out of print for many years, has been reissued with Kellogg's full-color, mixed-media illustrations. Color is used quite effectively. . . . The text, which consists exclusively of the child's dialogue, is both fresh and timeless." SLJ

Who took the farmer's [hat]? [by] Joan L. Nodset; pictures by Fritz Siebel. Harper & Row 1963 un il lib bdg $17.89; pa $6.99

Grades: PreK K   E

1. Animals -- Fiction

ISBN 0-06-024566-2 lib bdg; 0-06-443174-6 pa

"Away flew the farmer's hat. In his search for it he found that his hat could be many things to many animals including, most permanently, a bird's nest." Publ Wkly

Liao, Jimmy

The **sound** of colors; a journey of imagination. [by] Jimmy Liao; English text adapted by Sarah L. Thomson. Little, Brown 2006 un il $16.99

Grades: K 1 2 3 4   E

1. Blind -- Fiction

ISBN 0-316-93992-7

LC 2004-025100

"A young girl's eyesight began slipping away a year ago. With her white cane in hand, she ventures on a subway trip using her imagination to take herself and readers on a journey. . . . Poetic, lyrical language is used in this translation from Chinese. The girl is strong and admirable. . . . Liao's watercolor illustrations invite readers to take time, slow down, and pore over the details." SLJ

Lichtenheld, Tom

★ **Bridget's** beret. Henry Holt and Company 2010 un il $16.99

Grades: K 1 2   E

1. Hats -- Fiction 2. Artists -- Fiction 3. Drawing -- Fiction

ISBN 978-0-8050-8775-8; 0-8050-8775-3

LC 2009-12220

When Bridget loses the beret that provides her with artistic inspiration like other great artists, she thinks she will never be able to draw again.

"This smart, saucy book, with its spacious cartoon-style art, is both a spur to artistic endeavor and a message about inspiration and hard work. Yet the motivations are cocooned by a crackin' good tale and tempered by a full-faceted heroine." Booklist

Cloudette. Henry Holt 2011 un il $16.99

Grades: PreK K 1   E

1. Rain -- Fiction 2. Size -- Fiction 3. Clouds -- Fiction

ISBN 978-0-8050-8776-5; 0-8050-8776-1

LC 2010011688

Cloudette, the littlest cloud, finds a way to do something big and important as the other clouds do.

"Sprinkled with punny jokes, Lichtenheld's polished spreads show Cloudette as a simple, scalloped-edged puff who looks mighty dejected as she tries to be useful. . . . Neatly constructed and nicely pitched, the message of self-reliance comes through as clear as a cloudless day." Publ Wkly

★ **E** -mergency. Chronicle Books 2011 il $16.99

Grades: 1 2 3   E

1. Alphabet -- Fiction 2. English language -- Spelling -- Fiction

ISBN 978-0-8118-7898-2; 0-8118-7898-8

LC 2010053591

"Though some of the jokes will be clear only to older brothers and sisters, readers who are in the thick of learning spelling rules will pore over the pages. Comprehensive, witty entertainment from A to Z." Publ Wkly

★ **Exclamation** mark; Amy Krouse Rosenthal, Tom Lichtenheld. Scholastic Press 2013 56 p. (reinforced) $17.99

Grades: PreK K 1 2   E

1. Self-acceptance -- Juvenile fiction 2. Identity (Psychology) -- Juvenile fiction

ISBN 0545436796; 9780545436793

LC 2012936803

This children's book, by Amy Krouse Rosenthal, illustrated by Tom Lichtenheld, is a story about an exclamation point that learns to be comfortable with its own identity, different from all the other periods around it. "It's not easy being seen. Especially when you're NOT like everyone else. Especially when what sets you apart is YOU. Sometimes we squish ourselves to fit in. We shrink. Twist. Bend. Until--!--a friend shows the way to endless possibilities." (Publisher's note)

Lies, Brian

Bats at the beach; written and illustrated by Brian Lies. Houghton Mifflin 2006 un il $16

Grades: PreK K 1 2   E

1. Bats -- Fiction 2. Beaches -- Fiction

ISBN 978-0-618-55744-8; 0-618-55744-X

LC 2005010757

On a night when the moon can grow no fatter, bats pack their moon-tan lotion and baskets of treats and fly off for some fun on the beach.

"The acrylic paintings capture a moonlit night's deep shadows and reinforce the exuberant rhyming text." Horn Book Guide

Other titles about the bats are:

Bats at the library (2008)

Bats at the ballgame (2010)

Lieshout, Maria van

Bloom! a little book about finding love. written and illustrated by Maria van Lieshout. Feiwel and Friends 2008 un il $12.95

Grades: PreK K 1   E

1. Love -- Fiction 2. Pigs -- Fiction 3. Friendship -- Fiction 4. Butterflies -- Fiction

ISBN 978-0-312-36913-2; 0-312-36913-1

LC 2007-33411

Bloom, a pig who prefers flowers to mud puddles, falls in love with a flying flower," but when the butterfly leaves she is brokenhearted until a friend gives her a reason to smile again.

"Van Lieshout's loosely drawn pen and ink illustrations, mostly on stark white pages, wring Oscar-winning expressions from the slenderest curves and squiggles. The minimalist text begins before the title page, when Bloom's faithful friend urges her to join him playing in a puddle. . . . This paper-overboard book's stylish design and small square format designate it as a natural for Valentine's Day." Publ Wkly

Tumble; a little book about having it all. written and illustrated by Maria van Lieshout; designed by Molly Leach. Feiwel & Friends 2010 un il $12.99

Grades: PreK K 1   E

1. Polar bear -- Fiction

ISBN 978-0-312-54859-9; 0-312-54859-1

When three little bears find a red toy to play with and Tumble claims it for his own, this proves to be not such a good idea.

"This title gently reminds youngsters about the rewards of sharing. . . . The pencil, ink, and watercolor artwork is digitally enhanced and done in van Lieshout's expressive trademark style. . . . A perfect choice for a wintertime story-hour or one-on-one sharing." SLJ

Light, Steve

Trains go; Steve Light. Chronicle Books 2012 16 p. (board) $8.99

Grades: 1 2 3   E
1. Board books for children 2. Sounds -- Juvenile literature 3. Locomotives -- Juvenile literature 4. Board books 5. Railroad trains -- Fiction 6. Railroad trains -- Juvenile fiction
ISBN 0811879429; 9780811879422

LC 2011008004

This children's story, by Steve Light, describes different types of trains and their sounds. "All aboard! Take a trip on eight noisy trains as they huff, puff, and toot-toot their way through this . . . board book!" Trains described include steam engines, diesel trains, and magnetic high-speed commuter rails. (Publisher's note)

Zephyr takes flight; Steve Light. Candlewick 2012 40 p. (hardcover) $16.99

Grades: PreK K 1   E
1. Flight -- Juvenile fiction 2. Imagination -- Juvenile fiction 3. Adventure fiction -- Juvenile fiction 4. Flight -- Fiction
ISBN 076365695X; 9780763656959

LC 2011046669

This children's story, by Steve Light, follows "a clever girl's flight of fancy in a whimsical ode to free spirits, inventiveness, and flying pigs. Zephyr is a girl who loves airplanes . . . and hopes one day to fly one of her own. But when Gramma, Daddy, and Mom are too busy to play airplane with her, Zephyr's excess enthusiasm gets her sent to her room--where she discovers a secret door that leads to the most wondrous place she's ever seen!" (Publisher's note)

Light, Steven

★ The Christmas giant. Candlewick Press 2010 un il $15.99

Grades: PreK K 1   E
1. Giants -- Fiction 2. Christmas -- Fiction 3. Christmas stories -- Juvenile literature
ISBN 978-0-7636-4692-9; 0-7636-4692-X

When two best friends, a giant and an elf, grow Christmastown's holiday tree, disaster strikes.

"The pen, ink, and pastel artwork is truly lovely. Muted colors and swirly lines evoke old-fashioned folk art while retaining a fresh cartoon whimsy. . . . The story itself is sweet and economically told, capturing not only the spirit of Christmas, but also of friendship, persistence, and resourcefulness." SLJ

Lillegard, Dee

Tiger, tiger; illustrated by Susan Guevara. Putnam 2002 un il $16.99

Grades: PreK K 1
1. Magic -- Fiction 2. Tigers -- Fiction
ISBN 0-399-22633-8

LC 2002-272

A bored young boy uses a magic feather to form a tiger, and then must use the feather to save his village when the tiger gets hungry

"The suspenseful story reaches a dramatic climax, made all the more vivid by Guevara's highly charged artwork." Booklist

Lin, Grace

Bringing in the New Year; [by] Grace Lin. Alfred A. Knopf 2008 un il $15.99; lib bdg $18.99

Grades: PreK K 1 2   E
1. Chinese New Year 2. Chinese New Year -- Fiction 3. Chinese Americans -- Fiction
ISBN 978-0-375-83745-6; 0-375-83745-0; 978-0-375-93745-3 lib bdg; 0-375-93745-5

LC 2007011687

A Chinese American family prepares for and celebrates the Lunar New Year. End notes discuss the customs and traditions of Chinese New Year.

"The lustrous gouache illustrations are saturated with bold primary colors and deftly convey the joyousness of the festivities. . . . A wonderful and much-needed addition to Chinese New Year literature." SLJ

★ Dim sum for everyone! written and illustrated by Grace Lin. Knopf 2001 un il $14.95; pa $6.99

Grades: K 1 2 3   E
1. Food habits -- China 2. Restaurants -- Fiction 3. Dinners and dining -- China 4. Chinese Americans -- Fiction
ISBN 0-375-81082-X; 0-440-41770-8 pa

LC 00-34813

A child describes the various little dishes of dim sum that she and her family enjoy on a visit to a restaurant in Chinatown

"Lin's paintings are graphically striking. They combine a simplicity of form and design with a delight of patterning that appears in clothing and in backgrounds. . . . Like the pleasures of dim sum, this is a compact treat." Booklist

Kite flying. Knopf 2002 un il hardcover o.p. pa $6.99

Grades: K 1 2 3   E
1. Kites 2. Kites -- Fiction 3. Kites -- Juvenile literature
ISBN 0-375-81520-1; 0-553-11254-6 pa

LC 2001-33456

"A Chinese girl describes how the members of her family come together to make and fly a dragon kite. . . . The overall simplicity is effective and appealing, and the spare text is accentuated by bright gouache illustrations, in colorful shapes and painted fabric patterns." Booklist

Olvina flies; written and illustrated by Grace Lin. Holt & Co. 2003 un il $15.95

Grades: PreK K 1 2   E
1. Fear 2. Pigs 3. Chickens 4. Voyages and travels 5. Fear -- Fiction 6. Pigs -- Fiction 7. Voyages and travels -- Fiction
ISBN 0-8050-6711-6

LC 2002-8090

When Olvina, a chicken, receives an invitation to the annual Bird Convention in Hawaii, Will the pig and a fellow passenger help her to overcome her fear of flying

"The reassuring story gets a madcap twist from the artwork. Lin's jelly-bean-colored artwork, executed in gouache, finds humor in the small details." Booklist

Another title about Olvina is:

Olvina swims (2007)

Thanking the moon; celebrating the Mid-Autumn Moon Festival. Alfred A. Knopf 2010 un il $16.99; lib bdg $19.99

Grades: PreK K 1 2 E

1. Food -- Fiction 2. Mid-autumn Day -- Fiction
ISBN 978-0-375-86101-7; 0-375-86101-7; 978-0-375-96101-4 lib bdg; 0-375-96101-1 lib bdg

LC 2009052349

Each member of a Chinese family contributes to the celebration of the Mid-Autumn Moon Festival.

"Lin fashions a child-friendly introduction to the mid-autumn harvest moon festival with engagingly simple text and colorful, oversize gouache illustrations. . . . The writing is concise and accessible, and an author's note adds further information on the holiday and its significance. The inviting nocturnal landscapes are vivid with interesting details" SLJ

Lin, Grace, 1974-

★ **Ling** & Ting: not exactly the same! Little, Brown 2010 43p il

Grades: K 1 2 E

1. Twins -- Fiction 2. Sisters -- Fiction
ISBN 031602452X; 9780316024525

"Sticking together through everything from getting haircuts and preparing dumplings to practicing magic tricks and using chopsticks, identical twin sisters Ling and Ting display distinctive differences in personality and preference despite their similar looks." (Publisher's note) "Primary." (Horn Book)

"Sisters Ling and Ting may be twins, but that doesn't mean they're 'exactly the same,' no matter what everyone says upon first meeting them. Children will come to their own conclusions after reading the six short, interconnected stories that make up this pleasing book for beginning readers. . . . Framed with narrow borders, the paintings illustrate the stories with restrained lines, vivid colors, and clarity." Booklist

Lindbergh, Reeve

Homer, the library cat; illustrated by Anne Wilsdorf. Candlewick Press 2011 un il

Grades: PreK K 1 E

1. Stories in rhyme 2. Cats -- Fiction 3. Libraries -- Fiction
ISBN 0-7636-3448-4; 978-0-7636-3448-3

LC 2010048130

A cat's quiet life is disrupted one day when a window is broken, and after several frustrating attempts to find a suitable place, he winds up in the perfect spot.

"Lindbergh's simple rhyming text makes a good match with Wilsdorf's exuberant ink-and-watercolor artwork, which captures all the fun of a cat on the loose." Booklist

My hippie grandmother; illustrated by Abby Carter. Candlewick Press 2003 un il $15.99

Grades: K 1 2 3 E

1. Stories in rhyme 2. Hippies -- Fiction 3. Grandmothers -- Fiction
ISBN 0-7636-0671-5

LC 00-37964

A young girl describes all the things she likes about her grandmother, including the purple bus she drives, growing vegetables, picketing City Hall, and playing the banjo

"A wonderful, poetic portrait. . . . Carter's colorful watercolor-and-gouache illustrations capture the happy mood of the verse." SLJ

Lindenbaum, Pija

Mini Mia and her darling uncle; translated by Elizabeth Kallick Dyssegaard. Farrar, Straus & Giroux 2007 un il $16

Grades: PreK K 1 2 E

1. Uncles -- Fiction 2. Homosexuality -- Fiction
ISBN 978-91-29-66734-9; 91-29-66734-8

LC 2006-93704

"The 'darling uncle' of this . . . title is a gay man, but Lindenbaum . . . focuses not on his identity but on his niece Ella's resentment of his new partner. . . . Lindenbaum paints Uncle Tommy's fabulous shirts and retro furniture with verve, and her pacing is sure. . . . The emotions stay true." Publ Wkly

Lindgren, Astrid

Goran's great escape; translated by Polly Lawson; illustrated by Marit Törnqvist. Floris 2011 il $17.95

Grades: PreK K 1 2 E

1. Bulls -- Fiction 2. Easter -- Fiction 3. Farm life -- Fiction
ISBN 978-0-86315-793-6; 0-86315-793-9

Original Swedish edition published 1950 as part of a story collection; first English language edition published 1991 with title: The day Adam got mad

"Years ago in Sweden, on an Easter morning, Goran the bull escaped from his barn and might still be at large if 7-year-old Karl hadn't come by and offered to scratch his head. This charming story . . . gets new life with Lawson's translation, which smoothes and slightly modernizes the English. . . . Törnqvist's meticulous watercolor illustrations again complement the story. . . . There are lovely touches of humor. . . . From a beloved author, a tiny gem for reading aloud or reading alone." Kirkus

Lindgren, Barbro

Julia wants a pet; [by] Barbro Lindgren & [illustrated by] Eva Eriksson; translated by Elisabeth Kallick Dyssegaard. R & S Books 2003 un il $15

Grades: K 1 2 E

1. Pets -- Fiction
ISBN 91-29-65940-X

Original Swedish edition 2002

"On the lookout for a much-wished-for pet—preferably one that will fit in her baby carriage—Julia darts through town. . . . Lindgren's bracingly straightforward prose makes Julia's yearning and perversity feel immediate and authentic. . . . While Eriksson's brown-and-yellow-toned pictures may seem subdued at first glance, the earthtone colors and subtle pencil textures ground the heroine in the real world, while her yellow tutu and red baby carriage add playful tones." Publ Wkly

Lindsey, Kat

Sweet potato pie; by Kathleen D. Lindsey; illustrated by Charlotte Riley-Webb. Lee & Low Books 2003 un il $16.95; pa $7.95

Grades: K 1 2 3   E

1. Pies 2. Farm life 3. Family life 4. African Americans 5. Pies -- Fiction 6. Farm life -- Fiction 7. Moneymaking projects 8. Family life -- Fiction 9. African Americans -- Fiction

ISBN 1-58430-061-2; 1-60060-277-0 pa

LC 2002-30164

During a drought in the early 1900s, a large loving African American family finds a delicious way to earn the money they need to save their family farm

"Lindsey's down-home storytelling quality is charming. . . . The artwork's broad, energetic strokes and strong color palette sweep children into this tasty tale, and the included pie recipe makes the experience complete." Booklist

Lionni, Leo

Alexander and the wind-up mouse; by Leo Lionni. Alfred A. Knopf 2006 un il $16.99; lib bdg $18.99; pa $6.99

Grades: PreK K 1 2   E

1. Mice -- Fiction

ISBN 0-394-80914-9; 0-394-90914-3 lib bdg; 0-394-82911-5 pa

A reissue of the title first published 1969 by Pantheon Books

A Caldecott Medal honor book, 1970

The author's "collage illustrations are dazzling in their color and bold design and contribute to a beautiful and appealing picture book." Booklist

★ **Fish** is fish. Alfred A. Knopf 2005 un il $15.95

Grades: PreK K 1 2   E

1. Frogs -- Fiction 2. Fishes -- Fiction

ISBN 0-394-80440-6

A reissue of the title first published 1970 by Pantheon Bks.

The frog tells the fish all about the world above the sea. The fish, however, can only visualize it in terms of fish-people, fish-birds and fish-cows.

"The story is slight but pleasantly and simply told, the illustrations are page-filling, deft, colorful, and amusing." Bull Cent Child Books

★ **Frederick**. Pantheon Bks. 1967 un il $16.95; lib bdg $18.99; pa $5.99

Grades: PreK K 1 2   E

1. Mice -- Fiction

ISBN 0-394-81040-6; 0-394-91040-0 lib bdg; 0-394-82614-0 pa

"This captivating book . . . sings a hymn of praise to poets in a gentle story that is illustrated with gaiety and charm." Saturday Rev

★ **Inch** by inch. Alfred A. Knopf 2010 un il $16.99; lib bdg $19.99

Grades: PreK K 1 2   E

1. Birds -- Fiction 2. Measurement -- Fiction 3. Caterpillars -- Fiction

ISBN 978-0-375-85764-5; 0-375-85764-8; 978-0-375-95764-2 lib bdg; 0-375-95764-2 lib bdg

LC 2009-1767

A reissue of the title first published 1960 by Astor-Honor

A Caldecott Medal honor book, 1961

To keep from being eaten, an inchworm measures a robin's tail, a flamingo's neck, a toucan's beak, a heron's legs, and a nightingale's song.

"This is a book to look at again and again. The semi-abstract forms are sharply defined, clean and strong, the colors subtle and glowing, and the grassy world of the inchworm is a special place of enchantment." N Y Times Book Rev

★ **Little** blue and little yellow; a story for Pippo and Ann and other children. 50th anniversary ed.; Alfred A. Knopf 2009 un il $15.99; lib bdg $18.99

Grades: PreK K 1 2   E

1. Color -- Fiction 2. Friendship -- Fiction

ISBN 978-0-375-86013-3; 0-375-86013-4; 978-0-375-96013-0 lib bdg; 0-375-96013-9 lib bdg

LC 2008035932

A reissue of the title first published 1959 by Astor-Honor

A little blue spot and a little yellow spot are best friends, and when they hug each other they become green.

"So well are the dots handled on the pages that little blue and little yellow and their parents seem to have real personalities. It should inspire interesting color play and is a very original picture book by an artist." N Y Her Trib Books

Six crows; a fable. Alfred A. Knopf 2010 un il $16.99; lib bdg $19.99

Grades: PreK K 1 2   E

1. Owls -- Fiction 2. Crows -- Fiction 3. Farm life -- Fiction

ISBN 978-0-375-84550-5; 0-375-84550-X; 978-0-375-94550-2 lib bdg; 0-375-94550-4 lib bdg

A reissue of the title first published 1988

An owl helps a farmer and some crows reach a compromise over the rights to the wheat crop.

"This brief, simple story works on a literal level as well as on a metaphoric one. It is illustrated with Lionni's usual handsome, colorful collages which project well for reading aloud to groups." SLJ

★ **Swimmy**. Pantheon Bks. 1973 un il $16; pa $5.99

Grades: PreK K 1 2   E

1. Fishes -- Fiction

ISBN 0-394-81713-3; 0-394-82620-5 pa

"To illustrate his clever, but very brief story, Leo Lionni has made a book of astonishingly beautiful pictures, full of undulating, watery nuances of shape, pattern, and color." Horn Book

Lipson, Eden Ross

Applesauce season; illustrated by Mordicai Gerstein. Roaring Brook Press 2009 un il $17.99

Grades: PreK K 1 2   E

1. Apples -- Fiction 2. Family life -- Fiction

ISBN 978-1-59643-216-1; 1-59643-216-0

"Flavored with family tradition and spiced with Gerstein's cheerful illustrations, this account of one family's love of applesauce hits the spot. . . . In a crowded orchard of apple books, this one stands out for home or school apple and/or family-tradition projects. Applesauce recipe appended." Kirkus

Lithgow, John

★ **Micawber**; illustrated by C.F. Payne. Simon &

Schuster Bks. for Young Readers 2002 un il $17.95; pa $6.99

Grades: PreK K 1 2   E

1. Stories in rhyme 2. Artists -- Fiction 3. Squirrels -- Fiction

ISBN 0-689-83341-5; 0-689-83542-6 pa

LC 2001-20919

Micawber, a squirrel fascinated by art, leaves the Metropolitan Museum of Art with an art student, secretly uses her supplies to make his own paintings, and starts his own art museum atop Central Park's carousel

"The rhymed text sparkles with pleasing sounds. . . . Lithgow's reading on the CD is brimming with texture and playful pomposity. The mixed-media illustrations depict an utterly fetching protagonist displaying a range of moods and poses." SLJ

Little, Jean

★ **Emma's** yucky brother; story by Jean Little; pictures by Jennifer Plecas. HarperCollins Pubs. 2001 63p il (I can read book) hardcover o.p. pa $3.99

Grades: PreK K 1 2   E

1. Adoption -- Fiction 2. Siblings -- Fiction

ISBN 0-06-028348-3; 0-06-444258-6 pa

LC 99-34515

Emma finds out how hard it is to be a big sister when her family adopts a four-year-old boy named Max

"Heartfelt and honest. . . . Little's simple words and Plecas' clear, expressive line-and-watercolor illustrations tell an intense story." Booklist

Other titles about Emma are:

Emma's magic winter (1998)

Emma's strange pet (2003)

Littlewood, Karin

Immi's gift; written and illustrated by Karin Littlewood. Peachtree 2010 un il $15.95

Grades: K 1 2   E

1. Inuit -- Fiction 2. Fishing -- Fiction

ISBN 978-1-56145-545-4; 1-56145-545-8

Day after day in the frozen north, a young Inuit girl catches brightly-colored objects while ice fishing and uses them to decorate her igloo, until the ice begins to melt and she drops in a gift of her own before leaving for the season.

"A fur-clad Inuit girl searches for the brightest objects she can find in a 'frozen white world,' rendered in smudgy watercolor and gouache with colored pencil detailing. Ice fishing, she finds a painted wooden bird, followed by an orange starfish, a green leaf, and a purple feather, which she uses to adorn her igloo. . . . It's a story with a quiet magic and beauty." Publ Wkly

Litwin, Eric

Pete the cat: I love my white shoes. Harper 2010 un il $16.99

Grades: PreK K 1 2   E

1. Cats -- Fiction 2. Color -- Fiction 3. Shoes -- Fiction

ISBN 978-0-06-190622-0; 0-06-190622-0

First published 2008 by Blue Whiskey Press

Pete the Cat goes walking down the street wearing his brand-new white shoes. Along the way, his shoes change from white to red to blue to brown to WET as he steps in piles of strawberries, blueberries, and other big messes! But

no matter what color his shoes are, Pete keeps movin' and groovin' and singing his song . . . because it's all good.

Liu, Jae Soo

Yellow umbrella; written and illustrated by Jae Soo Liu. Kane/Miller 2002 un il $19.95

Grades: PreK K 1   E

1. Stories without words 2. Umbrellas and parasols -- Fiction

ISBN 1-929132-36-0

A story, in pictures and music, of children on their way to school on a rainy day

"Originally published in South Korea, the volume is both delicate and handsome. . . . The joyful hues multiply with each successive spread. Composer Dong Il Sheen gracefully glides between rhythms throughout the 15 tracks here [on the CD] . . . maintaining an overall happy tone." Publ Wkly

Livingston, Myra Cohn

Calendar; by Myra Cohn Livingston; illustrated by Will Hillenbrand. Holiday House 2007 un il $16.95

Grades: PreK K 1 2   E

1. Months -- Poetry

ISBN 978-0-8234-1725-4; 0-8234-1725-5

LC 2006012145

"'January shivers / February shines / March blows off the winter ice / April makes / the mornings nice . . .' First published in 1959 in the collection Wide Awake and Other Poems, this simple poem by the late Livingston gets its own picture book here with a lively double-page spread for each month of the year. The bright, clear, mixed-media artwork— ink, acrylic, gouache, and collage—extends the words." Booklist

Liwska, Renata

★ **Little** panda; written and illustrated by Renata Liwska. Houghton Mifflin Co. 2008 un il $12.95

Grades: PreK K 1 2   E

1. Giant panda -- Fiction

ISBN 978-0-618-96627-1; 0-618-96627-7

LC 2007047735

A grandfather tells his grandson an unlikely story about a panda and how it escapes from the tiger that wants to eat it.

"In every word, readers can hear the wise, wry voice of a narrator who knows how to hold a child's attention. The illustrations, a combination of pencil and soft digital color, evoke the simplicity of traditional Chinese art and underscore the intimacy of the book's small format." SLJ

★ **Red** wagon. Philomel Books 2011 un il $16.99

Grades: PreK K   E

1. Play -- Fiction 2. Work -- Fiction

ISBN 978-0-399-25237-2; 0-399-25237-1

LC 2010005393

When Lucy gets a new red wagon she wants to play with it immediately, but first she must use it to bring vegetables home from the market for her mother.

"Liwska's story stays true to the way children see the world, gives the gentlest of pushes toward cooperation, and offers respite from suburban anxiety and busyness." Publ Wkly

Ljungkvist, Laura

★ **Follow** the line; words and art by Laura Ljungkvist. Viking 2006 un il $16.99

Grades: PreK K 1 2   E

1. Counting

ISBN 0-670-06049-6

LC 2005-22701

Invites the reader to visit a wide variety of places and count different objects found in each, from fire hydrants in a big city in the morning, through starfish in the ocean during the day, to babies sleeping in a country village at night.

"An entrancing counting game with a search through detailed art, this title doubles as a vocabulary builder for the youngest readers and includes shapes, colors, and patterns in the search." SLJ

Other titles in this series are:

Follow the line through the house (2007)

Follow the line around the world (2008)

Follow the line to school (2011)

Follow the line to school. Viking Childrens Books 2011 il $16.99

Grades: PreK K 1 2   E

1. School stories

ISBN 978-0-670-01226-8; 0-670-01226-2

LC 2010041039

"This outing takes readers on a tour of a school, as a black line forms words and objects in bright scenes with crisp collages and lots of prompts to engage children. The line trails into 'the science corner,' where readers learn a bit about animals, before heading into a modish library, the art room . . . , the cafeteria, and outdoors for recess. Ljungkvist covers all the basic elements of an ordinary school day, and the story's interactive elements highlight the underlying message about the joys of learning." Publ Wkly

Lloyd, Jennifer

Looking for loons; [by] Jennifer Lloyd; Kirsti Anne Wakelin, illustrator. Simply Read Books 2007 un il $16.95

Grades: PreK K 1 2 3   E

1. Loons -- Fiction 2. Family life -- Fiction

ISBN 978-1-894965-54-5

"It's a beautiful September morning, and Patrick awakens when the dim sunlight hits his pillow. He gets out of bed and reaches for his 'cozy housecoat' and binoculars. . . . His patient persistence is rewarded . . . when a group of loons flies into view and lands on the lake. . . . This gentle story is illustrated with warm, muted watercolors that are evocative of unhurried and carefree mornings on a lake in the country." SLJ

Lloyd, Sam

Doctor Meow's big emergency. Henry Holt & Co. 2008 un il (Whoops-a-daisy world) $14.95

Grades: PreK K 1 2   E

1. Cats -- Fiction 2. Hospitals -- Fiction 3. Physicians -- Fiction

ISBN 978-0-8050-8819-9; 0-8050-8819-9

First published 2007 in the United Kingdom

"At Kiss-It-Better Hospital, busy Dr. Meow, a cat wearing a pink coat and stethoscope, receives an emergency call from Tom Cat, who has fallen from a tree after a leap toward Mr. Bird. . . . The cartoon-style animal characters and the spare, animated text, filled with sound effects, make for a

light and lively read that doesn't downplay the discomfort of being injured and scared. Vibrant, page-spanning illustrations . . . incorporate playful details." Booklist

Mr. Pusskins and Little Whiskers; another love story. 1st U.S. ed.; Atheneum Books for Young Readers 2008 un il $15.99

Grades: PreK K 1 2   E

1. Cats -- Fiction

ISBN 978-1-4169-5796-6; 1-4169-5796-0

LC 2007031911

When Emily brings home a little kitten to be best friends with Mr. Pusskins, the older cat does not appreciate the gesture.

"The combination of bold colors, highly expressive characters, and slightly off-kilter illustrations will pull children in and keep them wanting more." SLJ

Another title about Mr. Pusskins is:

Mr. Pusskins: a love story (2007)

Lloyd-Jones, Sally

How to get a job by me, the boss; [written by] Sally Lloyd-Jones and [illustrated by] Sue Heap. Schwartz & Wade Books 2011 un il $17.99; lib bdg $20.99

Grades: PreK K 1 2   E

1. Occupations -- Fiction

ISBN 978-0-375-86664-7; 0-375-86664-7; 978-0-375-96664-4 lib bdg; 0-375-96664-1 lib bdg

LC 2009050696

The narrator knows all about how to get a job, and she walks readers through the whole process: from deciding what you want to be all the way to acing the interview.

"The illustrations are perfectly rendered in childlike acrylic paint and crayons and show the fun details of imaginative play on a rainy day." SLJ

Song of the stars; a Christmas story. illustrated by Alison Jay. Zonderkidz 2011 il $15.99

Grades: PreK K 1   E

1. Nature -- Fiction 2. Animals -- Fiction

ISBN 978-0-310-72291-5; 0-310-72291-8

LC 2011006762

Nature and the animal kingdom celebrate the birth of Jesus, while most people do not even notice that a miracle has occurred.

"A subtle, yet satisfying story. . . . Lloyd-Jones's lyrical language . . . and repetitive refrains make the text suitable for reading aloud. Jay's signature-style, crackle-varnish paintings are bright and effective in conveying a sense of eager anticipation and movement among the animals." SLJ

Lobel, Anita

★ **Hello,** day! Greenwillow Books 2008 un il $16.99; lib bdg $17.89

Grades: PreK   E

1. Animals -- Fiction 2. Morning -- Fiction

ISBN 978-0-06-078765-3; 0-06-078765-1; 978-0-06-078766-0 lib bdg; 0-06-078766-X lib bdg

LC 2007-18361

Various animals greet the sunrise in their own unique voices, except for the owl who welcomes the night.

"The luxuriantly hued, playfully textured portraits will rivet preschoolers and invite them to make animal sounds of their own; the minimal text, set in big, friendly type, may also encourage some simple word recognition." Publ Wkly

★ **Nini** here and there. Greenwillow Books 2007 un il lib bdg $17.89

Grades: PreK K 1 2   E

   1. Cats -- Fiction 2. Moving -- Fiction

   ISBN 0-06-078767-8; 0-06-078768-6 lib bdg

                  LC 2005-22186

Fearing at first that her family is going on vacation without her, Nini the cat ends up traveling with her owners to their new home.

"The artwork makes this picture book an endearing delight. Irresistible Nini steals the show in full-page portraits painted with Lobel's usual sensitivity in watercolor and gouache." Booklist

   Another title about Nini is:

   Nini lost and found (2010)

★ **Nini** lost and found. Alfred A. Knopf 2010 un il $15.99; lib bdg $20.99

Grades: PreK K 1   E

   1. Cats -- Fiction 2. Lost and found possessions -- Fiction

   ISBN 978-0-375-85880-2; 0-375-85880-6; 978-0-375-95880-9 lib bdg; 0-375-95880-0 lib bdg

                  LC 2008048721

Nini Cat enjoys her outdoor adventure until she ventures too far and cannot find her way home.

"Told with an elegant simplicity that children will appreciate, . . . this is filled with Lobel's endearing watercolor-and-gouache artwork. . . . A wonderful read-aloud." Booklist

★ **One** lighthouse, one moon. Greenwillow Bks. 2000 40p il hardcover o.p. pa $6.99

Grades: PreK K 1 2   E

   1. Counting 2. Days -- Fiction 3. Months -- Fiction

   ISBN 0-688-15539-1; 0-06-000537-8 pa

                  LC 98-50790

This is a "three-part introduction to days, seasons, colors, counting, and other basics. The first section pictures a little girl's feet as they journey through a week, with a different colored shoe marking each day's activity. . . . The second section shows Nini the cat in postcard-size images that reflect those from the 12 months of the year. The title section presents the numbers 1 through 10 in serene images of shoreline activity. . . . The simple phrases are lyrical in places, and Lobel's beautiful paintings, with their rich patterns and textures, luxurious detail, and sophisticated palette, will inspire children to linger over the pages and connect new words with images." Booklist

Lobel, Arnold

★ **Frog** and Toad are friends. Harper & Row 1970 64p il (I can read book) $16.99; lib bdg $17.89; pa $3.99

Grades: K 1 2   E

   1. Frogs -- Fiction 2. Toads -- Fiction 3. Friendship -- Fiction

   ISBN 0-06-023957-3; 0-06-023958-1 lib bdg; 0-06-444020-6 pa

   A Caldecott Medal honor book, 1971

Here are five stories . . . which recount the adventures of two best friends—Toad and Frog. The stories are: Spring; The story; A lost button; A swim; The letter

The stories are told "with humor and perception. Illustrations in soft green and brown enhance the smooth flowing and sensitive story." SLJ

Other titles about Frog and Toad are:

Days with Frog and Toad (1979)

Frog and Toad all year (1976)

Frog and Toad together (1972)

★ **Grasshopper** on the road. Harper & Row 1978 62p il (I can read book) lib bdg $17.89; pa $3.99

Grades: K 1 2   E

   1. Animals -- Fiction 2. Grasshoppers -- Fiction

   ISBN 0-06-023962-X lib bdg; 0-06-444094-X pa

                  LC 77-25653

"The contemporary version of the fable of the ant and the grasshopper is told in a repetitive I-Can-Read text and extended in three-color illustrations which delicately capture the grasshopper's microcosmic world view." Horn Book

Ming Lo moves the mountain; written and illustrated by Arnold Lobel. Greenwillow Bks. 1982 un il hardcover o.p. pa $5.99

Grades: K 1 2 3   E

   1. Houses -- Fiction 2. Mountains -- Fiction

   ISBN 0-688-10995-0 pa

                  LC 81-13327

"An original tale utilizing folkloric motifs, the book is Chinese-like rather than Chinese, for the artist has created an imagined landscape. The setting, shown in flowing lines and tones of delicate watercolors, provides a source of inspiration drawn from an ancient artistic tradition; particularly effective in conveying a sense of distance are the panoramic double-page spreads." Horn Book

★ **Mouse** soup. Harper & Row 1977 63p il (I can read book) $15.99; lib bdg $16.89; pa $3.99

Grades: K 1 2   E

   1. Mice -- Fiction

   ISBN 0-06-023967-0; 0-06-023968-9 lib bdg; 0-06-444041-9 pa

                  LC 76-41517

"An artistic triumph with enough suspense, humor and wisdom to hold any reader who has a trace of curiosity and compassion. . . . The little one triumphs over the big one, and every child will rejoice. The exquisite wash drawings in mousey shades of grays, blues, greens and golds, have enough humor and pathos to exact repeated scrutiny. Like the stories, they improve with each reading." N Y Times Book Rev

★ **Mouse** tales. Harper & Row 1972 61p il (I can read book) $15.99; lib bdg $16.89; pa $3.99

Grades: K 1 2   E

   1. Mice -- Fiction

   ISBN 0-06-023941-7; 0-06-023942-5 lib bdg; 0-06-444013-3 pa

   Papa Mouse tells seven bedtime stories, one for each of his sons

"The illustrations have soft colors and precise, lively little drawings of the imaginative and humorous events in the stories. The themes are familiar to children: cloud shapes, wishing, a tall and a short friend who observe-and greet-natural phenomena on a walk, taking a bath, et cetera." Bull Cent Child Books

★ **On** Market Street; pictures by Anita Lobel; words by Arnold Lobel. Greenwillow Bks. 1981 un il $16.99; lib bdg $17.89; pa $6.99

Grades: K 1 2 3   E
 1. Alphabet 2. Stories in rhyme 3. Shopping -- Fiction
 ISBN 0-688-80309-1; 0-688-84309-3 lib bdg; 0-688-08745-0 pa

LC 80-21418

A Caldecott Medal honor book, 1982

"The artist has adapted the style of old French trade engravings, infusing it with a wonderful sense of color and detail. . . . Arnold Lobel's words ring of old rhymes, but it is these intricate, lovely drawings that take the day, and truly make it brighter." N Y Times Book Rev

★ **Owl** at home. Harper & Row 1982 64p il (I can read book) lib bdg $16.89; pa $3.99

Grades: K 1 2   E
 1. Owls -- Fiction
 ISBN 0-06-023949-2 lib bdg; 0-06-444034-6 pa

Five stories describe the adventures of a lovably foolish owl

"A child reader or listener in a kind of one-upmanship over wide-eyed tufted Owl will bristle with anxiety to have him perceive what causes two bewildering bumps under the blanket at the foot of his bed. The best scope for Lobel's inventiveness in drawing is, however, the opening episode where 'poor old' Winter makes a pushy entry into Owl's home. Muted browns and greys are countered by an animation that fully reveals Owl's distresses and contentments." Wash Post Child Book World

★ **Small** pig; story and pictures by Arnold Lobel. Harper & Row 1969 63p il (I can read book) lib bdg $16.89; pa $3.99

Grades: K 1 2   E
 1. Pigs -- Fiction
 ISBN 0-06-023932-8 lib bdg; 0-06-444120-2 pa

This "is the story of a pig who, finding the clean farm unbearable, runs away to look for mud—and ends up stuck in cement. His facial expressions alone are worth the price of the book; the illustrations, in blue, green, and gold, are a perfect complement to the story. Humor, adventure, and short, simple sentences provide a real treat for beginning readers." SLJ

★ **Uncle** Elephant. Harper & Row 1981 62p il (I can read book) lib bdg $16.89; pa $3.99

Grades: K 1 2   E
 1. Uncles -- Fiction 2. Elephants -- Fiction
 ISBN 0-06-023980-8 lib bdg; 0-06-444104-0 pa

LC 80-8944

Uncle Elephant takes care of his nephew whose parents are lost at sea. This book describes the way they lived together until the parents are rescued and little elephant rejoins them

"Nine gentle stories for the beginning independent reader; the soft grey, peach, and green tones of the deft pictures are an appropriate echo of the mood." Bull Cent Child Books

A **treeful** of pigs; pictures by Anita Lobel. Greenwillow Bks. 1979 un il lib bdg $17.89

Grades: K 1 2 3   E
 1. Pigs -- Fiction 2. Farm life -- Fiction
 ISBN 0-688-84177-5

LC 78-1810

"The framed, full-color illustrations, characterized by intricately detailed designs in costumes and setting, are as elaborate as the diction is simple. The total effect, however, is one of unity." Horn Book

Lobel, Gillian

 Moonshadow's journey; illustrated by Karin Littlewood. Albert Whitman & Co. 2009 un il $16.99

Grades: K 1 2 3 4   E
 1. Death -- Fiction 2. Swans -- Fiction 3. Grandfathers -- Fiction 4. Birds -- Migration -- Fiction
 ISBN 978-0-8075-5273-5; 0-8075-5273-9

LC 2009000004

When his beloved grandfather is killed in a storm while leading the swan flock south for the winter, Moonshadow is reassured by his father that the flock will go on with Grandfather always in their hearts

"Lobel skillfully moves the plot forward while creating appropriate character development for Moonshadow. . . . Littlewood's combination of watercolors and gouache on textured paper of light and dark hues adds to the moods and movement of the book. The pictures capture the elements of nature in both harsh and calm circumstances." SLJ

Loewen, Nancy

 The **last** day of kindergarten; illustrated by Sachiko Yoshikawa. Marshall Cavendish 2011 un il $16.99

Grades: PreK K   E
 1. School stories 2. Kindergarten -- Fiction
 ISBN 978-0-7614-5807-4; 0-7614-5807-7

LC 2010001225

As she prepares for her graduation ceremony, a first grader-to-be remembers her enjoyable year in kindergarten.

"Included in the text are excellent discussion questions that focus on summer plans and first-grade privileges. Yoshikawa's irresistibly sweet illustrations are perfect for children ready to emerge from the kindergarten cocoon and rejoice in their achievements." SLJ

Logan, Bob

 The **Sea** of Bath. Sourcebooks Jabberwocky 2010 un il $16.99

Grades: PreK K   E
 1. Toys -- Fiction 2. Baths -- Fiction 3. Boats and boating -- Fiction
 ISBN 978-1-4022-4185-7; 1-4022-4185-2

"A ship captain, commander of the S.S. Rubb A. Dubb, navigates 'a curious sea indeed!' Full of unusual creatures (e.g., rubber duckies) and unpredictable conditions (e.g., bubbles), the setting makes itself known to readers as a bathtub. . . . Logan's eye-pleasing illustrations of animated-looking bath toys support a satisfying preschooler-friendly text." Horn Book Guide

Logue, Mary

 ★ **Sleep** like a tiger; written by Mary Logue and illustrated by Pamela Zagarenski. Houghton Mifflin Harcourt 2012 40 p. $16.99

Grades: PreK K 1 2   **E**
  1. Sleep -- Juvenile fiction   2. Tigers -- Juvenile fiction   3. Bedtime -- Juvenile fiction   4. Sleep -- Fiction   5. Bedtime -- Fiction   6. Animals -- Sleep behavior -- Fiction
  ISBN 0547641028; 9780547641027
                   LC 2011044881
  Caldecott Honor Book (2013)
  This picture book features a "little girl" whose "wise parents sidestep her protestation of not being sleepy ('They nodded their heads and said she didn't have to go to sleep. But she had to put her pajamas on'), but once she's in bed she starts a new delaying tactic, inquiring about sleeping habits in the animal kingdom. After exploring the sleep habits of bats, whales, and tigers, she's inspired enough by their snoozes to fall asleep herself." (Bulletin of the Center for Children's Books)

London, Jonathan
  ★ **Baby** whale's journey; illustrated by Jon Van Zyle. Chronicle Bks. 1999 un il $15.95; pa $6.95
Grades: K 1 2 3   **E**
  1. Whales -- Fiction   2. Sperm whale -- Pictorial works -- Juvenile fiction   3. Animals -- Infancy -- Pictorial works -- Juvenile fiction
  ISBN 0-8118-2496-9; 0-8118-5761-1 pa
                   LC 99-13020
  Off the Pacific coast of Mexico, a baby sperm whale is born, feeds, speaks to her mother in clicks, and spends her days diving, spy-hopping, lob-tailing, and rolling as she grows and learns the ways of the sea
  This book offers "London's lyrical text and Van Zyle's dramatic paintings dominated by blues and purples. . . . An informative afterword supplies additional facts about sperm whales, and a reader's guide offers thoughtful ideas for discussion of both the scientific and poetic aspects of the text." Horn Book Guide

  Froggy builds a tree house; illustrated by Frank Remkiewicz. Viking 2011 un il $16.99
Grades: PreK K 1 2   **E**
  1. Frogs -- Fiction   2. Animals -- Fiction   3. Building -- Fiction   4. Friendship -- Fiction   5. Tree houses -- Fiction
  ISBN 978-0-670-01222-0; 0-670-01222-X
                   LC 2011010983
  Froggy and his friends build a treehouse, while avoiding help from his little sister, Frogilina.

  Froggy goes to Hawaii; illustrated by Frank Remkiewicz. Viking 2010 un il $15.99
Grades: PreK K 1 2   **E**
  1. Frogs -- Fiction   2. Vacations -- Fiction
  ISBN 978-0-670-01221-3; 0-670-01221-1
                   LC 2010007323
  When Froggy goes on vacation to Hawaii, he is too excited to pay much attention to his parents.

  Froggy learns to swim; illustrated by Frank Remkiewicz. Viking 1995 un il $15.99; pa $5.99
Grades: PreK K 1 2   **E**
  1. Frogs -- Fiction   2. Swimming -- Fiction
  ISBN 0-670-85551-0; 0-14-055312-6 pa
                   LC 94-43077

Froggy is afraid of the water until his mother, along with his flippers, snorkle, and mask, help him learn to swim
  "Vivid watercolor cartoons add the humor, showing the comical facial expressions and hilarious beachwear. Froggy's childlike dialogue and the sound words—'zook! zik!'; 'flop flop . . . splash!'—make this story a wonderful readaloud." SLJ
  Other titles about Froggy are:
  Froggy bakes a cake (2000)
  Froggy builds a treehouse (2011)
  Froggy eats out (2001)
  Froggy gets dressed (1992)
  Froggy goes to bed (2000)
  Froggy goes to camp (2008)
  Froggy goes to Hawaii (2011)
  Froggy goes to school (1996)
  Froggy goes to the doctor (2002)
  Froggy plays in the band (2002)
  Froggy plays T-Ball (2007)
  Froggy plays soccer (1999)
  Froggy's baby sister (2003)
  Froggy's best Christmas (2000)
  Froggy's day with Dad (2004)
  Froggy's first kiss (1998)
  Froggy's Halloween (1999)
  Froggy's sleepover (2005)
  Let's go, Froggy! (1994)

  I'm a truck driver; illustrated by David Parkins. Henry Holt 2010 26p il $12.99
Grades: PreK K 1   **E**
  1. Stories in rhyme   2. Trucks -- Fiction
  ISBN 978-0-8050-7989-0; 0-8050-7989-0
                   LC 2009009220
  "This is a wonderful picture book about trucks. . . . On every other spread, a girl and a boy take turns driving each of the vehicles. The trucks are described in rhyming couplets. . . . The alternating voices of the children help to enhance the rhythm and rhyme of the story. . . . The acrylic illustrations are vibrant, cartoonlike, and friendly." SLJ

  A **plane** goes ka-zoom! illustrated by Denis Roche. Henry Holt & Co. 2010 un il $15.99
Grades: PreK   **E**
  1. Airplanes -- Fiction
  ISBN 978-0-8050-8970-7; 0-8050-8970-5
  "Simple enough for toddlers, the rhythmic, rhyming text comments on what planes do as well as how they look, sound, and move. . . . The naive gouache paintings invite kids to stop along the way and talk about who's doing what in each colorful illustration. A engaging choice." Booklist

  A **train** goes clickety-clack; by Jonathan London; illustrated by Denis Roche. Henry Holt 2007 un il $15.95
Grades: PreK K   **E**
  1. Stories in rhyme   2. Railroads -- Fiction
  ISBN 978-0-8050-7972-2; 0-8050-7972-6
                   LC 2006030765
  Easy-to-read, rhyming text describes the sounds of, and uses for, different kinds of trains

"Brief sentences and bright gouache artwork in primary hues capture the excitement and attraction of trains. The text is filled with appealing rhythms and rhymes." SLJ

★ A **truck** goes rattley-bumpa; illustrated by Denis Roche. Henry Holt and Co. 2005 un il $14.95
Grades: PreK K   E
1. Stories in rhyme 2. Trucks -- Fiction
ISBN 0-8050-7233-0
             LC 2004-22174
"Short, rhyming couplets tell about a variety of trucks: what they look like, what sounds they make, where they go, and what they do. Meanwhile, childlike gouache paintings clearly illustrate the brief sentences or phrases on each page." Booklist

Long, Ethan
  Bird & Birdie in a fine day. Ten Speed Press 2010 un il $14.99
Grades: PreK K 1   E
1. Birds -- Fiction 2. Friendship -- Fiction
ISBN 978-1-5824-6321-6; 1-5824-6321-2
"Three separate stories introduce two bug-eyed cartoon birds (Bird is blue, while Birdie, who is yellow, sports eyelashes and a pink ribbon) interacting over the course of a day. In 'A Beautiful Morning,' they meet, exchange pleasantries, are briefly separated by a storm, and happily join up again. In 'A Wonderful Afternoon,' Bird tries to concentrate on getting a worm out of the ground but is distracted by Birdie. In 'A Marvelous Night,' Birdie can't get comfortable in her nest until Bird helps out. . . . The fetching Bird and Birdie will hit the right note with many preschoolers and beginning readers." Booklist

The **Croaky** Pokey! Holiday House 2011 un il $14.95
Grades: PreK K 1   E
1. Frogs -- Fiction
  ISBN 978-0-8234-2291-3; 0-8234-2291-7
"Inspired by a tasty-looking dragonfly, a group of frogs decides to perform their own version of the Hokey Pokey. The first part of the song is familiar ('Put your right hand in...'), but each verse is intended to end with a snack: 'Hop the Croaky Pokey/ As we chase a fly around./ Right in the froggy's mouth!/ Whap!') The problem is, not a single member of the froggy chorus can catch the fly. . . . Long . . . has a gift for conveying manic, obsessive personalities . . . and he has found a great match in a song of relentless, rote cheeriness." Publ Wkly

Max & Milo go to sleep! by Heather & Ethan Long. Aladdin 2013 32 p. (hardcover edition) $14.99
Grades: PreK K 1 2   E
1. Bedtime -- Juvenile fiction 2. Brothers -- Juvenile fiction 3. Humorous fiction -- Juvenile fiction 4. Humorous stories 5. Beavers -- Fiction 6. Bedtime -- Fiction 7. Brothers -- Fiction
ISBN 1442451432; 9781442451438
             LC 2012011458
This children's story, by Heather Long and Ethan Long, follows "Max and Milo, two . . . beaver brothers who make going to sleep an up-all-night adventure. Milo can't get to sleep, . . . but no matter what helpful sleeping tip Max suggests, Milo turns it riotously on its head and is as far from

rest as ever. Will Milo finally get to sleep? Will he ever stop driving Max crazy?" (Publisher's note)

My dad, my hero. Sourcebooks Jabberwocky 2011 un il $12.99
Grades: PreK K 1   E
1. Father-son relationship -- Fiction
ISBN 978-1-4022-4239-7; 1-4022-4239-5
A child describes his dad, who may not have super powers, but is still wonderful.
"Powered by a Roy Lichtenstein meets Sunday funnies aesthetic and a self-effacing sense of humor, Long's story is sincere without being saccharine—which dads will appreciate." Publ Wkly

One drowsy dragon. Orchard Books 2010 un il $16.99
Grades: PreK K 1 2   E
1. Counting 2. Stories in rhyme 3. Noise -- Fiction 4. Sleep -- Fiction 5. Dragons -- Fiction
ISBN 978-0-545-16557-0; 0-545-16557-1
             LC 2009032861
As one dragon tries to take a nap, his ten little dragons, in increasing numbers, disturb his sleep by making milk shakes, screaming at scary movies, and playing loud games.
"The digital art features clean lines and distinct colors. . . . Big round eyes and slightly goofy expressions lend an air of silliness to the cartoon figures. . . . A solid storytime choice that covers several popular picture-book topics, including counting, colors, dragons, and bedtime." SLJ

Up, tall and high; Ethan Long. G.P. Putnam's Sons 2012 p. cm.
Grades: K 1 2 3   E
1. Vocabulary 2. Birds -- Fiction 3. Altitudes -- Fiction
ISBN 9780399256110
             LC 2011003291
Theodor Seuss Geisel Award (2013)
This children's picture book presents "three tiny tales of a flock of bird buddies. 'I Am Tall' centers on boasting about stature . . . 'I Can Go High' finds the birds outdoing each other on altitude attempts . . . In 'I Am Up,' two birds 'up' in a nest collapse the branch and are now decidedly 'down,' until their friends arrive to help them 'up' on their feet again . . . each tale's punchline is delivered with a visual gag revealed with a lifted or pulled flap." (Bulletin of the center for Children's Books)

Long, Loren
  ★ **Otis**. Philomel Books 2009 un il $17.99; board bk $8.99
Grades: PreK K 1 2   E
1. Tractors -- Fiction 2. Farm life -- Fiction
ISBN 978-0-399-25248-8; 0-399-25248-7; 978-0-399-25600-4 board bk; 0-399-25600-8 board bk
             LC 2008-50020
When a big new yellow tractor arrives, Otis the friendly little tractor is cast away behind the barn, but when trouble occurs Otis is the only one who can help.
"Long's gouache and pencil artwork is stunning with a red and cream main character against a sepia-toned monochromatic background. The overall effect is nostalgic and comforting." SLJ

Otis and the tornado. Philomel Books 2012 il $17.99

Grades: PreK K 1 2   **E**

1. Tractors -- Fiction 2. Farm life -- Fiction 3. Tornadoes -- Fiction 4. Domestic animals -- Fiction

ISBN 978-0-399-25477-2; 0-399-25469-2

LC 2010036770

When a tornado threatens his farm, Otis the tractor must try to save the animals, including an unfriendly bull.

"Long's sepia-tinged, rolling croplands evoke Dust Bowl paintings and photos, and Otis's heroism is steeped in old-fashioned Americana, from 1930s picture books to 1960s TV dramas." Publ Wkly

Long, Melinda

★ **How** I became a pirate; written by Melinda Long; illustrated by David Shannon. Harcourt 2003 un il $16

Grades: K 1 2 3   **E**

1. Pirates -- Fiction

ISBN 0-15-201848-4

LC 2002-6308

"Jeremy spies a pirate ship. When he's asked to join its crew, he can't resist. On board, he does all sorts of fun pirate stuff. . . . But, alas, Jeremy soon discovers, there's no goodnight kiss or bedtime story, so there's something to be said for home. . . . The rollicking tale is a charmer, with a lively, witty, first-person narrative, highly expressive characters, and farcical elements. . . . Shannon's acrylic art is marvelously animated, with bright, bold colors and extraordinary details." Booklist

Another title about Jeremy is:

Pirates don't change diapers (2007)

Long, Sylvia

Sylvia Long's Thumbelina. Chronicle Books 2010 un $17.99

Grades: 1 2 3 4   **E**

1. Authors 2. Novelists 3. Dramatists 4. Fairy tales 5. Children's authors 6. Short story writers

ISBN 978-0-8118-5522-8; 0-8118-5522-8

LC 2009-04369

A tiny girl no bigger than a thumb is stolen by a great ugly toad and subsequently has many adventures and makes many animal friends, before finding the perfect mate in a warm and beautiful southern land.

"While following the familiar story line of Hans Christian Andersen's original, Long effectively condenses the narrative and gives a contemporary touch to the wording. . . . Thumbelina's adventures with the beautifully drawn toad, beetles, mouse, mole, and swallow unfold in jewel-like colors, defined textures, and well-imagined details to complete the surroundings." SLJ

Longstreth, Galen Goodwin

Yes, let's; by Galen Goodwin Longstreth; illustrated by Maris Wicks. Tanglewood Publishing 2013 32 p. (hardcover) $15.95

Grades: PreK K 1 2   **E**

1. Stories in rhyme 2. Camping -- Juvenile fiction 3. Family life -- Juvenile fiction 4. Family life -- Fiction 5. Outdoor life -- Fiction

ISBN 1933718870; 9781933718873

LC 2012045312

This children's book, by Galen Goodwin Longstreth, illustrated by Maris Wicks, is "about a family's camping trip." Activities such as driving, singing, taking pictures and hik-

ing are all included. "The . . . rhyming text is enhanced by comical illustrations. . . . This little book serves as a loving tribute to family togetherness." (Publisher's note)

Look, Lenore

★ **Brush** of the gods; by Lenore Look; illustrated by Meilo So Sandford. 1st ed. Schwartz & Wade Books 2013 40 p. ill. (hardcover) $17.99; (library) $20.99

Grades: K 1 2 3   **E**

1. Picture books for children 2. Artists -- Fiction 3. Painting -- Fiction

ISBN 0375870016; 9780375870019; 9780375970016

LC 2012006442

In this children's picture book, Lenore Look "blends mystical realism and biography to create a magical portrait of one of ancient China's famous artists, Wu Daozi. As a boy during the T'ang Dynasty in the seventh century, Daozi is unable to conform in calligraphy class. . . . Later known for his dynamic murals, Daozi paints subjects so realistically they seem to come alive." (Publishers Weekly)

★ **Henry's** first-moon birthday; illustrated by Yumi Heo. Atheneum Bks. for Young Readers 2001 un il $16

Grades: PreK K 1 2   **E**

1. Babies -- Fiction 2. Infants -- Fiction 3. Grandmothers -- Fiction 4. Chinese Americans -- Fiction 5. Brothers and sisters -- Fiction

ISBN 0-689-82294-4

LC 98-21626

Jen helps her grandmother with preparations for the traditional Chinese celebration to welcome her new baby brother

"The words are clear and basic as well as creative . . . and Jen's chatty narration infuses the book with the cozy immediacy that's beautifully picked up in Heo's swirling paint-and-paper collages." Booklist

★ **Love** as strong as ginger; illustrated by Stephen T. Johnson. Atheneum Pubs. 1999 un il $15

Grades: PreK K 1 2   **E**

1. Work -- Fiction 2. Grandmothers -- Fiction 3. Chinese Americans -- Fiction

ISBN 0-689-81248-5

LC 96-43459

A Chinese American girl comes to realize how hard her grandmother works to fulfill her dreams when they spend a day together at the grandmother's job cracking crabs

"Inspired by the author's memories of her grandmother, this gentle story is carefully and precisely told. . . . Johnson's expressive pastel-and-watercolor illustrations are rendered in muted colors and set within wide, softly colored margins." SLJ

Polka Dot Penguin Pottery; illustrated by Yumi Heo. Schwartz & Wade Books 2011 un il $16.99

Grades: PreK K 1 2   **E**

1. Artists -- Fiction 2. Pottery -- Fiction 3. Authorship -- Fiction 4. Chinese Americans -- Fiction

ISBN 978-0-375-86332-5; 0-375-86332-X

A visit to a pottery shop and the encouragement of family and friends not only provide Aspen the opportunity to paint something beautiful, they also help her get past her writer's block.

"Naïve-style oil, pencil, and collage illustrations are unpredictably laid out in a top-to-bottom format rather than side-to-side. The girl's frustration and eventual pleasure as she works through her writer's and painter's blocks are revealed in single-page and full-spread pictures. Good motivation for children who need to activate their artistic side." SLJ

★ **Uncle** Peter's amazing Chinese wedding; illustrated by Yumi Heo. Atheneum Books for Young Readers 2006 un il $16.95
Grades: PreK K 1 2   E
    1. Uncles -- Fiction 2. Weddings -- Fiction 3. Chinese Americans -- Fiction
    ISBN 0-689-84458-1
                    LC 2002-10740
    Jenny, a Chinese American girl, describes the festivities of her uncle's Chinese wedding and the customs behind them.
    "Heo's child-inspired illustrations contribute to the story's strong appeal with lively colors, perspectives, and details that accentuate both Jenny's feelings and the wedding traditions. A delightful invitation to learn more about Chinese traditions." SLJ

Lopez, Mario
    Mario and baby Gia; [illustrations by Maryn Roos] Celebra Childrens Books 2011 il $17.99
Grades: PreK K   E
    1. Cousins -- Fiction 2. Infants -- Fiction 3. Birthdays -- Fiction 4. Babysitters -- Fiction 5. Family life -- Fiction
    ISBN 978-0-451-23417-9; 0-451-23417-0
                    LC 2011005235
    Unable to find anyone to play with, Mario agrees to help his Nana by watching cousin Gia, but caring for the toddler is challenging and Mario is near the end of his rope when he gets a reminder that spending time with family is a gift.
    "Roos continues the commercial-looking cartoon-style illustrations from the earlier Mario book, which work well with the story, particularly during Mario's stories. A good choice for children with younger siblings and cousins, especially Latinos." Kirkus
    Another title about Mario is:
    Mud tacos (2009)

Lopez, Susana
    The **best** family in the world; [illustrated by] Ulises Wensell. Kane Miller un il $15.99
Grades: PreK K 1 2   E
    1. Orphans -- Fiction 2. Adoption -- Fiction 3. Family life -- Fiction
    ISBN 978-1-935279-47-1; 1-935279-47-5
    Carlota is anxiously awaiting the arrival of the family who is adopting her. She imagines that they might be astronauts, pastry chiefs or even pirates. And then Carlota finds out that the Lopez family is the best family in the world.
    "The telling is clear and lively, while the artwork glows with warmth and light. . . . A lovely, thought-provoking picture book to share and discuss." Booklist

Lorbiecki, Marybeth
    Paul Bunyan's sweetheart; written by Marybeth Lorbiecki; illustrated by Renee Graef. Sleeping Bear Press 2007 un il $16.95
Grades: 1 2 3 4   E
    1. Tall tales 2. Bunyan, Paul (Legendary character) 3.

Love -- Fiction 4. Nature -- Fiction 5. Environmental protection -- Fiction
    ISBN 1-58536-289-1; 978-1-58536-289-9
                    LC 2006026583
    When legendary logger Paul Bunyan falls in love with Lucette Diana Kensack, he will do whatever it takes to win her heart, including trying to restore the Minnesota environment to its previous condition as part of Lucette's "love test."
    "The prose is just right for the genre. . . . The paintings extend the story's humorous images, while firmly placing the action in a mythical time." SLJ

Lord, Cynthia
    Happy birthday, Hamster; pictures by Derek Anderson. Scholastic Press 2011 un il $16.99
Grades: PreK K 1   E
    1. Dogs -- Fiction 2. Hamsters -- Fiction 3. Birthdays -- Fiction 4. Friendship -- Fiction
    ISBN 978-0-545-25522-6; 0-545-25522-8
                    LC 2010018989
    Follows Hamster and his friend Dog as they prepare for a birthday party.
    "Those who miss the clues the first time, should enjoy being privy to them upon rereading." Publy Wkly

    Hot rod hamster; pictures by Derek Anderson. Scholastic Press 2010 un il lib bdg $16.99
Grades: PreK K 1   E
    1. Dogs -- Fiction 2. Mice -- Fiction 3. Hamsters -- Fiction 4. Automobiles -- Fiction 5. Automobile racing -- Fiction
    ISBN 978-0-545-03530-9 lib bdg; 0-545-03530-9 lib bdg
                    LC 2009-03930
    A hamster, with the help of a canine junkyard dealer and his mouse assistants, builts a hot rod and drives it in a race against some very large dogs.
    This "is a rollicking, roaring read. In addition to the rhymed text punctuated by questions, the characters talk in speech balloons that move the story along without breaking the flow. Anderson's fluffy, jaunty illustrations are as full of energy as the rhymes." Kirkus

Lord, Janet
    ★ **Albert** the Fix-it Man; story by Janet Lord; pictures by Julie Paschkis. Peachtree 2008 un il $15.95
Grades: PreK K 1 2   E
    1. Repairing -- Fiction 2. Community life -- Fiction
    ISBN 978-1-56145-433-4
                    LC 2007-29465
    A cheerful repairman fixes squeaky doors, leaky roofs, and crumbling fences for his neighbors, who return the kindness when he catches a terrible cold
    "Lord's rhythmic, simple text is perfectly cadenced for reading aloud, while Paschkis' cheerful illustrations, filled with scrolling designs and smiling friends, reinforce the sense of the close, busy community working together." Booklist

    Here comes Grandma! [by] Janet Lord; illustrated by Julie Paschkis. Henry Holt and Co. 2005 un il $12.95

Grades: PreK K 1   E
  1. Grandmothers -- Fiction 2. Transportation -- Fiction
ISBN 0-8050-7666-2

LC 2004-22179

Grandma is coming to visit and she will use any possible method of transport, including a horse and a hot air balloon, to get there

"The simple, rhythmic text suits the mood of the story, and the vivid gouache illustrations have a warm, folklike quality." SLJ

Where is Catkin? written by Janet Lord; illustrated by Julie Paschkis. Peachtree Publishers 2010 un il $16.95
Grades: PreK K 1   E
  1. Cats -- Fiction 2. Animals -- Fiction
ISBN 978-1-56145-523-2; 1-56145-523-7

"In this picture-book hide-and-seek game, feline Catkin jumps off young Amy's lap and goes hunting into the grass, by a pond, through rocks, and up a tree, looking for Cricket, then Frog, Mouse, Snake, and Bird. Where are they? Children will enjoy searching through the busy, bright, stylized pictures in ink and gouache and pointing to the creatures hiding where Catkin doesn't see them." Booklist

Lord, John Vernon
  The **giant** jam sandwich; story and pictures by John Vernon Lord, with verses by Janet Burroway. Houghton Mifflin 1973 32p il lib bdg $17; pa $6.95; bd bk $6.99
Grades: K 1 2 3   E
  1. Stories in rhyme 2. Wasps -- Fiction
ISBN 0-395-16033-2 lib bdg; 0-395-44237-0 pa;
0-547-15077-6 bd bk
First published 1972 in the United Kingdom

"Highly amusing in the details of John Vernon Lord's illustrations. . . . The figures are deliciously grotesque, their expressions wickedly accurate and the colours cheerfully vivid." Jr Bookshelf

Lorig, Steffanie
  Such a silly baby! by Steffanie and Richard Lorig; illustrated by Amanda Shepherd. Chronicle Books 2008 un il $15.99
Grades: PreK   E
  1. Stories in rhyme 2. Animals -- Fiction 3. Infants -- Fiction
ISBN 978-0-8118-5134-3; 0-8118-5134-6

LC 2007-13135

Rhyming text and illustrations follow the adventures of a baby who on excursions to the zoo, the circus, or the farm manages to get switched with an animal.

"Each time [the baby] greets Mom again, he adds a new phrase learned from his animal friends, for a cumulative festival of animal sounds that storytime listeners will love. Shepherd's bright, wildly cartoonlike oil paintings perfectly reflect the wackiness of the text." SLJ

Loth, Sebastian
  Clementine. North-South 2011 un il $14.95
Grades: PreK K 1 2   E
  1. Shape -- Fiction 2. Worms -- Fiction 3. Snails -- Fiction
ISBN 978-0-7358-4009-6; 0-7358-4009-1

Clementine the snail loves all things round and dreams of flying to the moon. Her earthworm friend Paul helps her

fly a rocket in orbit around the Earth, and she discovers that the Earth is round too.

"Loth's illustrations carry the weight of the offbeat story, featuring rich colors, beautiful compositions and a cinematic sense of movement." Kirkus

Remembering Crystal. NorthSouth 2010 un il $14.95
Grades: PreK K 1 2   E
  1. Death -- Fiction 2. Ducks -- Fiction 3. Turtles -- Fiction 4. Friendship -- Fiction
ISBN 978-0-7358-2300-6; 0-7358-2300-6

Zelda is a young duck that lives in the garden. Her friend Crystal is a turtle who is growing old. The two do many things together. One day Crystal is not in the garden. But friendship never dies.

"This gets high points for the simplicity of the text . . . and the handsomeness of the design. Buff, mottled pages serve as the background for illustrations that are elegant in their spareness. . . . Despite the somber subject, moments of humor escape into the art. . . . This story of a final friendship touches the heart." Booklist

Zelda the Varigoose; Sebastian Loth. NorthSouth Books 2012 32 p. $15.95
Grades: PreK K   E
  1. Geese -- Fiction 2. Imagination -- Fiction 3. Picture books for children
ISBN 0735840768; 9780735840768

This children's picture book is about Zelda the goose who "enjoys changing her persona as she allows her imagination to take flight. The left side of each spread features a digitalized photo of the habitat of a different creature. Opposite, Zelda becomes a different animal through the assistance of an overlay. . . . After the little bird transforms into a "Chamelegoose,' a 'Goosquid,' and so on, she is also perfectly content to just be herself." (School Library Journal)

Lottridge, Celia Barker
  One watermelon seed. Fitzhenry & Whiteside 2008 un il $17.95
Grades: PreK K 1 2   E
  1. Counting 2. Gardening -- Fiction
ISBN 978-1-55455-034-0; 1-55455-034-3
First published 1986 by Oxford University Press

"Numbers, colors, and gardening are combined in this vividly illustrated counting book. The story starts as Max and Josephine plant a garden, first 1 watermelon seed, then 2 pumpkin seeds, and so on all the way to 10. The phrase, 'and they grew' follows mention of each new set of seeds. The graphic-style illustrations depict the seedlings as they grow. . . . The vibrant colors and closeup views of the produce make it look delicious and irresistible." SLJ

Lotu, Denize
  ★ **Running** the road to ABC; by Denizé Lauture; illustrated by Reynold Ruffins. Simon & Schuster Bks. for Young Readers 1996 un il hardcover o.p. pa $6.99
Grades: PreK K 1 2   E
  1. School stories
ISBN 0-689-80507-1; 0-689-83165-X pa

LC 95-38290

A Coretta Scott King honor book for illustration, 1997

Long before the sun even thinks of rising the Haitian children run to school where they learn the letters, sounds, and words of their beautiful books

"The rich lyrical language used by the author, a Haitian poet, creates a strong sense of place. . . . The lush, green country and sense of hope are reflected and enhanced by stylized, warmly detailed gouache paintings." Horn Book

Loupy, Christophe

Hugs and kisses; [by] Christophe Loupy, Eve Tharlet; translated by J. Alison James. North-South Bks. 2001 un il $15.95; bd bk $6.95

Grades: PreK   E
1. Kissing 2. Dogs -- Fiction 3. Animals -- Fiction
ISBN 0-7358-1484-8; 0-7358-2019-8 bd bk

LC 2001-42595

Original German edition published 2001 in Switzerland

Hugs the puppy sets out to collect lots of wonderful kisses from his animal friends, but in the end he discovers that the best kiss of all is the one he gets from his loving mother

"With fur that seems real enough to touch, a sunny disposition, and sweet manners, Hugs is a real charmer." Booklist

Low, William

★ **Machines** go to work in the city; William Low. 1st ed. Henry Holt and Company 2012 48 p.

Grades: PreK K   E
1. Vehicles -- Juvenile fiction 2. Cities & towns -- Juvenile fiction 3. Lift-the-flap books -- Specimens 4. Machinery -- Juvenile literature 5. Cities and towns -- Juvenile literature
ISBN 0805090509; 9780805090505

LC 2011029045

This children's book by William Low focuses on "Trains, planes, trucks and cranes and the people who make them work [and] keep the city moving. . . . Low presents each vehicle, with an appropriate onomatopoetic sound, in two double-page spreads wherein a simply stated question is posed with the answer appearing on a gate-fold that enlarges the view even further." (Kirkus)

Lowell, Susan

The **elephant** quilt; stitch by stitch to California! pictures by Stacey Dressen-McQueen. Farrar, Straus and Giroux 2008 un il $16.95

Grades: K 1 2 3   E
1. Quilts -- Fiction 2. Overland journeys to the Pacific -- Fiction
ISBN 0-374-38223-9; 978-0-374-38223-0

LC 2005-51227

Lily Rose and Grandma stitch a quilt that tells the story of their family's journey from Missouri to California by covered wagon in 1859.

"Dramatic, mixed-media paintings portray majestic landscapes and frontier dangers, as well as moments of family merriment. An earthly color palette and brightly patterned quilt pieces add warmth and vibrancy to the 'bodacious' journey." Booklist

Lowry, Lois

★ **Crow** call; illustrated by Bagram Ibatoulline. Scholastic Press 2009 un il $16.99

Grades: 1 2 3 4   E
1. Crows -- Fiction 2. Hunting -- Fiction 3. Veterans

-- Fiction 4. Father-daughter relationship -- Fiction
ISBN 978-0-545-03035-9; 0-545-03035-8

LC 2008-30158

Nine-year-old Liz accompanies the stranger who is her father, just returned from the war, when he goes hunting for crows in Pennsylvania farmland.

"Beautifully written. . . . Lowry's narrative, dense with sensory details, is based on her own life's events. Fittingly, Ibatoulline's muted, earth-toned palette is reminiscent of vintage, faded photographs." Kirkus

Lucas, David

The **Skeleton** pirate; David Lucas. Candlewick Press 2013 30 p. ill. (reinforced) $15.99

Grades: PreK K 1 2   E
1. Picture books for children 2. Pirates -- Juvenile fiction
ISBN 0763661074; 9780763661076

LC 2012942674

This children's picture book, by David Lucas, follows "the Skeleton Pirate . . . , and he'll never be beaten! That is, until he gets beaten by an unruly bunch of pirates and is thrown overboard. Down in the depths of the sea, he is rescued by a beautiful mermaid, only to be swallowed by a whale. But the whale has a tummy ache from all the other things he has swallowed--like a golden ship full of treasure." (Publisher's note)

Something to do. Philomel Books 2009 un il $14.99

Grades: PreK K   E
1. Bears -- Fiction 2. Imagination -- Fiction 3. Parent-child relationship -- Fiction
ISBN 978-0-399-25247-1; 0-399-25247-9

LC 2009-1821

A parent and child bear must use their imaginations to find something to do.

"Young readers will instantly relate to the richly textured crayon drawings, which illustrate the expressiveness of the story and complement its softness with their deceptively simple, fuzzy-edged forms. . . . This stands out as a unique work because of its emotionally simple charm." Kirkus

The **robot** and the bluebird. Farrar, Straus and Giroux 2008 un il $16.95

Grades: PreK K 1 2   E
1. Birds -- Fiction 2. Robots -- Fiction
ISBN 978-0-374-36330-7; 0-374-36330-7

LC 2007026930

A broken robot makes a home for a cold, tired bluebird trying to fly south for the winter, and eventually he carries the bird to a warmer climate while she rests in the cavity where his heart used to be.

"In characteristically elaborate, warmly lit illustrations, Lucas uses sharp geometrical forms as the basis for his urban scenes; against this backdrop, the bird's more organic form is a welcome contrast. . . . This book's genuine sweetness will easily win over readers." SLJ

Lucke, Deb

Sneezenesia. Clarion Books 2010 un il $17

Grades: K 1 2   E
1. Sneezing -- Fiction
ISBN 978-0-547-33006-8; 0-547-33006-5

Young Zack sneezes so hard, over and over, that he sneezes all memories out of his head, leaving everything he once knew standing before him, trying to figure out how to get back inside.

"The artwork, done in paint, collage, and Photoshop, jumps off the page and adds pace and animation to the story. The supermarket mothers are worth a giggle with their retro outfits and accessories. This funny read-aloud could be paired with any version of 'I Know an Old Lady Who Swallowed a Fly' for a rousing storytime." SLJ

The **boy** who wouldn't swim. Clarion Books 2008 31p il $16

Grades: K 1 2 3   E
1. Fear -- Fiction 2. Siblings -- Fiction 3. Swimming -- Fiction
ISBN 978-0-618-91484-5; 0-618-91484-6
LC 2007-22120

One very hot summer, Eric Dooley watches his younger sister go from her first swimming lesson all the way to the diving board, while his fear of the water keeps him from joining her and the rest of the people of Clermont County in the pool.

"This fear-of-swimming tale is ideal for kids who are afraid to take that first step. . . . Hot summer yellows and cool watery blues abound in the gouache illustrations, which are filled with action and humor." SLJ

Ludwig, Trudy
Better than you; illustrations by Adam Gustavson. Tricycle Press 2011 un il $15.99; lib bdg $18.99

Grades: PreK K 1 2   E
1. Friendship -- Fiction
ISBN 978-1-58246-380-3; 1-58246-380-8; 978-1-58246-407-7 lib bdg; 1-58246-407-3 lib bdg
LC 2010033224

Tyler's friend Jake continually boasts about his abilities, making Tyler feel bad about himself until his Uncle Kevin and new neighbor Niko help him see that Jake is the one with the problem.

"Focusing on a subject not often written about for children, Ludwig's story may be helpful to youngsters dealing with braggarts. . . . Well-executed paintings are appealing and portray the characters' emotions clearly." SLJ

Luebs, Robin
Please pick me up, Mama! Atheneum Books for Young Readers 2009 un il $15.99

Grades: PreK   E
1. Stories in rhyme 2. Raccoons -- Fiction 3. Mother-child relationship -- Fiction
ISBN 978-1-4169-7977-7; 1-4169-7977-8
LC 2007052679

A baby raccoon spends the day with its mother enjoying many different experiences, from dressing up the cat to splashing and clapping.

"Warm autumn hues—rich, buttery oranges and crisp, apple greens—permeate the soft acrylic illustrations. Thick brush strokes in blacks, creams and browns naturally blend, adding depth to bushy tails and loving faces. . . . This small selection has both sweetness and spunk." Kirkus

Lum, Kate
What! cried Granny; an almost bedtime story. pictures by Adrian Johnson. Dial Bks. for Young Readers 1999 un il hardcover o.p. pa $6.99

Grades: K 1 2 3   E
1. Beds -- Fiction 2. Bedtime -- Fiction 3. Grandmothers -- Fiction
ISBN 0-8037-2382-2; 0-14-230092-6 pa
LC 98-19642

First published 1998 in the United Kingdom with title: What!

This "combines the deadpan and the surreal in wild words and neon-colored acrylic illustrations." Booklist

Lumry, Amanda
Safari in South Africa; by Amanda Lumry and Laura Hurwitz; illustrated by Sarah McIntyre. Scholastic 2008 32p il map (Adventures of Riley) $16.99; pa $6.99

Grades: 1 2 3 4   E
1. Game reserves 2. Animals -- Africa 3. Wildlife conservation -- Fiction
ISBN 978-0-545-06827-7; 0-545-06827-4; 978-0-545-06826-0 pa; 0-545-06826-6 pa
First published 2003 by Eaglemont Press

Riley travels with his Uncle Max to check on the animal population at a South African game reserve.

"Combining whimsical cartoons and striking photographs of animals in the bush, this title is a marvelous intermingling of adventure and science. . . . Boxes presenting significant facts about the animals appear next to their photographs." SLJ

Other titles in this series are:
Amazon River rescue (2004)
Dolphins in danger (2009)
Mission to Madagascar (2005)
Operation Orangutan (2007)
Polar bear puzzle (2008)
Project Panda (2008)
Riddle of the reef (2009)
South Pole penguins (2008)
Tigers in Terai (2009)

Lund, Deb
Monsters on machines; [by] Deb Lund; illustrated by Robert Neubecker. Harcourt 2008 un il $16

Grades: PreK K 1 2   E
1. Stories in rhyme 2. Monsters -- Fiction 3. Construction workers -- Fiction 4. Construction equipment -- Fiction
ISBN 978-0-15-205365-9; 0-15-205365-4
LC 2006037393

Construction crew monsters arrive on the scene with tractors, cranes, and grader machines, and after a gruesome site is created as their routine, they straighten it up and leave everything clean.

"The India-ink drawings colored digitally in neon-bright hues exude a jazzy, busy look that brings to life the chaos that results when monsters and machines meet." SLJ

Lunde, Darrin
Monkey colors; Darrin Lunde; illustrated by Patricia J. Wynne. Charlesbridge 2011 48 p. col. ill.

Grades: PreK K 1 2   E
1. Color 2. Monkeys 3. Picture books for children 4.

Monkeys -- Color -- Juvenile literature
ISBN 1570917418; 9781570917417; 9781570917424
LC 2011000669

In this children's picture book, "[Darrin] Lunde and [Patricia] Wynne describe 12 monkey species in simple sentences. The monkeys are grouped into three categories: four whose fur is a single all-over color (yellow, red, brown, orange); four who have colorful features or stripes; and four whose colors vary with sex or age or gender or who are truly multicolored." (Kirkus)

Lunde, Stein Erik

My father's arms are a boat; Stein Erik Lunde; [illustrated by] Oyvind Torseter; [translated by Kari Dickson] Enchanted Lion Books 2013 40 p. (hardback) $15.95
Grades: K 1 2 3   E
1. Death -- Fiction 2. Emotions -- Fiction 3. Father-son relationship -- Fiction 4. Fathers and sons -- Fiction
ISBN 1592701248; 9781592701247
LC 2012022767

In author Stein Erik Lunde's book, "it's quieter than it's ever been. Unable to sleep, a young boy climbs into his father's arms. Feeling the warmth and closeness of his father, he begins to ask about the birds, the foxes...and whether his mother will ever wake up. Even in the face of absence and loss, the cycles of life continue unabated. We know in the end everything will somehow be all right." (Publisher's note)

Luthardt, Kevin

Peep! Peachtree Pubs. 2003 un il $15.95
Grades: PreK K   E
1. Pets 2. Ducks 3. Stories without words 4. Pets -- Fiction 5. Ducks -- Fiction
ISBN 1-56145-046-4
LC 2002-35910

"With just a dozen-plus words, Luthardt tells the story of a young boy's attachment to a duckling ('peep!') who grows up into a duck ('quack!') and grows away from the boy ('it's time'; 'bye bye'). . . . The book's strength is the directness and speed with which art and minimal text tell the story. Pastel and mixed-media illustrations are on colored paper, which imparts warmth and a pleasing texture." Horn Book

Luxbacher, Irene

Mattoo, let's play! written and illustrated by Irene Luxbacher, Kids Can Press 2010 un il $16.95
Grades: PreK K 1   E
1. Cats -- Fiction 2. Play -- Fiction
ISBN 978-1-55453-424-1; 1-55453-424-0

"Highly imaginative Ruby wants to play with Mattoo, her 'shy' cat, who shuns her attempts at entertainment. As the child crashes and clangs pots and pans, or jumps up and down on her bed . . . readers will understand his 'shyness.' . . . This clever, unique tale illustrates how 'play' can be fun for humans but not so great for pets. Ruby is delightful, full of creativity and imagination. The use of acrylic ink and collage makes for stunning illustrations." SLJ

Lynn, Sarah

Tip -Tap Pop; illustrated by Valeria Docampo. Marshall Cavendish 2010 un il $17.99
Grades: PreK K 1   E
1. Dance -- Fiction 2. Old age -- Fiction 3. Grandfathers

-- Fiction
ISBN 978-0-7614-5712-1; 0-7614-5712-7

Emma and Pop have been tap dancing together since before she could talk, but Pop becomes very forgetful and can no longer dance until one special day when he hears Emma's steps and they find a way for him to join in.

"Short text and attention-grabbing words combine with colorful gouache and pencil illustrations. . . . With Docampo's inclusion of a gramophone, bowties, and suspenders, Tip-Tap Pop has a nostalgic feel and leisurely pace. A first purchase." SLJ

Lyon, George Ella

My friend, the starfinder; by George Ella Lyon; pictures by Stephen Gammell. Atheneum Books for Young Readers 2008 un il $16.99
Grades: PreK K 1 2   E
1. Storytelling -- Fiction
ISBN 978-1-4169-2738-9; 1-4169-2738-7
LC 2006032026

A child relates some of the wondrous tales told by an old man who once found a falling star and stood at the end of a rainbow.

This is a "sumptuously illustrated book. . . . Text and art are sure to evoke wonder in young readers." Publ Wkly

Trucks roll! words by George Ella Lyon; art by Craig Frazier. Atheneum Books for Young Readers 2007 un il $14.99
Grades: PreK   E
1. Stories in rhyme 2. Children's poetry 3. Trucks -- Fiction
ISBN 978-1-4169-2435-7; 1-4169-2435-3
LC 2006-10811

Illustrations and simple, rhyming text reveal many different—and sometimes silly—items that trucks can haul.

"Solid, up-to-date information about a major preschool enthusiasm is leavened with lively verse and touch of whimsey." Horn Book

You and me and home sweet home; illustrated by Stephanie Anderson. Atheneum Books for Young Readers 2009 un il $17.99
Grades: PreK K 1 2 3   E
1. Houses -- Fiction 2. Building -- Fiction 3. Volunteer work -- Fiction 4. African Americans -- Fiction
ISBN 978-0-689-87589-2; 0-689-87589-4
LC 2008010414

Third-grader Sharonda and her mother help volunteers from their church to build the house that will be their very own.

"Sharonda narrates in clean, simple prose. . . . Varied in composition and perspective, the watercolor-and-pastel-pencil illustrations center on the nicely individualized characters . . . and readers will share Sharonda's quiet glow of happiness at the end." Booklist

The pirate of kindergarten; illustrated by Lynne Avril. Atheneum Books for Young Readers 2010 un il $16.99
Grades: PreK K 1 2   E
1. School stories 2. Vision disorders -- Fiction
ISBN 978-1-4169-5024-0; 1-4169-5024-9

Ginny's eyes play tricks on her, making her see everything double, but when she goes to vision screening at school and discovers that not everyone sees this way, she learns that her double vision can be cured.

"Lyon's short, descriptive sentences set up the situation deftly, and Avril's astute chalk, pencil, and acrylic drawings of 'two of everything' provide a vivid window into Ginny's pretreatment world." SLJ

Lyon, Tammie

Olive and Snowflake; written and illustrated by Tammie Lyon. Marshall Cavendish Children 2011 il
Grades: PreK K 1   **E**
  1. Dogs -- Fiction
ISBN 0761459553; 9780761459552; 9780761460695 e-book
          LC 2011001124

When her parents threaten to send away the dog if he cannot learn to behave, Olive is worried they will both be sent to live with a new family.

"Bold text and vibrant cartoon-style illustrations make this a great read-aloud or lap read. Children will delight in the happy ending and will appreciate this simple tale of love, responsibility, and growing up." SLJ

Lyons, Kelly Starling

Ellen's broom; Kelly Starling Lyons; illustrated by Daniel Minter. G. P. Putnam's Sons 2012 32 p.
Grades: K 1 2 3   **E**
  1. Brooms -- Fiction 2. Picture books for children 3. Reconstruction (1865-1876) -- Fiction 4. Slaves -- Emancipation -- Juvenile fiction 5. Marriage customs and rites -- Juvenile fiction 6. Slavery -- Fiction 7. Marriage -- Fiction 8. African Americans -- Fiction 9. Brooms and brushes -- Fiction 10. Reconstruction (U.S. history, 1865-1877) -- Fiction
ISBN 9780399250033
          LC 2011047101
Coretta Scott King Illustrator Honor Book (2013)

This picture book, "[s]et during Reconstruction, . . . [is] based on a historical event, [and] opens with a preacher's announcement to his black congregation that "all former slaves living as husband and wife shall be registered and seen as married in the eyes of the law." Young Ellen doesn't quite understand what this means until her mother explains to her that during slavery, slave couples like Ellen's mother and father were only allowed "broom weddings," wherein couples would jump over a broom. . . . Ellen grabs the marriage broom, . . . decorates it with flowers, and hands it to her parents during the[ir] ceremony. . . . [T]he story touches . . . on how formerly enslaved people . . . found . . . ways to celebrate their freedoms during . . . Reconstruction." (Bulletin of the Center for Children's Books)

Hope's gift; Kelly Starling Lyons; illustrated by Don Tate. G.P. Putnam's Sons 2012 32 p. (hardcover) $16.99
Grades: 1 2 3   **E**
  1. Slaves -- Emancipation -- Juvenile fiction 2. United States -- History -- 1861-1865, Civil War -- Juvenile fiction 3. Slavery -- Fiction 4. African Americans -- Fiction 5. Emancipation Proclamation -- Fiction
ISBN 0399160019; 9780399160011
          LC 2012014587

In this children's story, by Kelly Starling Lyons, illustrated by Don Tate, "it's 1862. . . . Hope's father . . . decides to join the Union army to fight for freedom. He slips away one tearful night, leaving Hope, . . . with only a conch shell for comfort. . . . But then Lincoln finally does it: on January 1, 1863, he issues the Emancipation Proclamation, freeing the slaves, and a joyful Hope finally spies the outline of a familiar man standing on the horizon." (Publisher's note)

Maass, Robert

A is for autumn. Henry Holt 2011 un il $16.99
Grades: PreK K 1 2   **E**
  1. Alphabet 2. Autumn -- Fiction
ISBN 978-0-8050-9093-2; 0-8050-9093-2
          LC 2010040333

Photographs and simple text present a variety of things seen in the fall.

"Vivid photography brings the autumn season to life in an alphabet book with thoughtful descriptions of nature, changing weather, and leisure activities. . . . Maass delivers a vibrant tribute to Autumn." Publ Wkly

MacDonald, Ross

★ **Another** perfect day. Millbrook Press 2002 un il hardcover o.p. pa $6.95
Grades: PreK K 1 2   **E**
  1. Heroes and heroines -- Fiction
ISBN 0-7613-1595-0; 1-59643-079-6 pa
          LC 2002-18798

What started out as another perfect day for Jack the superhero performing heroic feats suddenly goes awry

"With a beefy hero and graphics inspired by 1930-40s comic books, this impeccably designed volume features a forthright text that comically counterpoints a livelier tale told through the pictures." Publ Wkly

Another title about Jack is:
Bad baby (2005)

MacHale, D. J.

The **monster** princess; written by D.J. MacHale; illustrated by Alexandra Boiger. Aladdin Paperbacks 2010 un il $17.99
Grades: PreK K   **E**
  1. Stories in rhyme 2. Monsters -- Fiction 3. Princesses -- Fiction 4. Self-acceptance -- Fiction
ISBN 978-1-4169-4809-4; 1-4169-4809-0
          LC 2008037933

Unhappy with her life in a dark cave, Lala longs to live like the princesses far, far above but after venturing into their world, she finds contentment at home.

"A potentially didactic story . . . is saved by a wry text . . . and endearing illustrations. . . . The resolution satisfies." Booklist

MacLachlan, Patricia, 1938-

All the places to love; paintings by Mike Wimmer. HarperCollins Pubs. 1994 un il $16.99; lib bdg $17.89
Grades: K 1 2 3   **E**
  1. Farm life -- Fiction 2. Family life -- Fiction
ISBN 0-06-021098-2; 0-06-021099-0 lib bdg
          LC 92-794

A young boy describes the favorite places that he shares with his family on his grandparents' farm and in the nearby countryside

Wimmer's "paintings beautifully convey the splendor of nature, as well as the deep affection binding three generations. This inspired pairing of words and art is a timeless, uplifting portrait of rural family life." Publ Wkly

★ **Bittle**; by Patricia MacLachlan & Emily MacLachlan; illustrations by Dan Yaccarino. Joanna Cotler Books 2004 un il hardcover o.p. lib bdg $16.89
Grades: PreK K 1 2   E
  1. Cats 2. Dogs 3. Pets 4. Babies
  ISBN 0-06-000961-6; 0-06-000962-4 lib bdg
                       LC 2003-2357
Nigel the cat and Julia the dog think they will have no use for the new baby in their house, but after awhile they realize that they have come to love her
"The colors are bright, the lines simple. . . . The authors cleverly highlight the changes a new baby brings to a home, and the animals' growing affection for Bittle is humorous and heartwarming." SLJ

Lala salama; a Tanzanian lullaby. illustrated by Elizabeth Zunon. Candlewick Press 2011 il $16.99
Grades: PreK K 1   E
  1. Lullabies 2. Family life -- Fiction 3. Mother-child relationship -- Fiction
  ISBN 978-0-7636-4747-6; 0-7636-4747-0
                     LC 2010040465
A mother relates the events of a peaceful day along the banks of Lake Tanganyika to her baby, wrapped up and ready for sleep.
"Zunon's lush, softly textured oil paintings on watercolor paper reflect the warmth of the African setting and emotion-imbued prose. . . . Share this with preschoolers who may enjoy a peek into another culture's family life or keep at hand for the tired child, who will most appreciate this quietly sentimental offering." Kirkus

Painting the wind; by Patricia MacLachlan & Emily MacLachlan; illustrated by Katy Schneider. J. Cotler Bks. 2003 un il $15.99; pa $7.99
Grades: K 1 2 3   E
  1. Artists 2. Islands 3. Painting
  ISBN 0-06-029798-0; 0-06-443825-2 pa
                     LC 2001-47549
Several artists who paint different things, with different kinds of paint, and at different times of the day, all paint the same island that they visit each summer
"The gentle prose pairs well with handsome artwork that evokes warm, strong sensory impressions through a combination of thick brushwork, texture, and a vibrant color palette." Booklist

Your moon, my moon; a grandmother's words to a faraway child. illustrated by Bryan Collier. Simon & Schuster Books for Young Readers 2011 un il $16.99
Grades: PreK K 1 2   E
  1. Grandmothers -- Fiction
  ISBN 978-1-4169-7950-0; 1-4169-7950-6
                     LC 2008050451
Although their homes are different, a grandmother in New England and her loving grandson in Africa share the same moon.
"Collier's vibrant illustrations are a blend of watercolor and his trademark collage. This is a wonderful book to contrast different lifestyles." SLJ

MacLennan, Cathy
  ★ **Chicky** chicky chook chook. Boxer 2007 un il $12.95; bd bk $7.95
Grades: PreK K 1   E
  1. Stories in rhyme 2. Bees -- Fiction
  ISBN 978-1-905417-40-3; 1-905417-40-3; 978-1-906250-55-3 bd bk; 1-906250-55-3 bd bk
Chicks, chickens, cats, and bees on a farm enjoy an active, busy day playing, snoozing, and getting drenched in a thunderstorm before finally going to sleep at night
"This rambunctious story has an onomatopoeic rhyming text that children will love to hear again and again. . . . Inspired by the art and culture of her native Zimbabwe, MacLennan dabs, swirls, and sponges bright splashes of paint on brown butcher paper." SLJ

MacLeod, Doug
  Heather Fell in the Water; by Doug MacLeod; illustrated by Craig Smith. Independent Pub Group 2013 32 p. ill. (hardcover) $16.99
Grades: PreK K   E
  1. Picture books for children 2. Swimming -- Juvenile fiction
  ISBN 1742376487; 9781742376486
In this children's picture book, "everywhere Heather goes, from farms to art galleries, she falls in the water. As a result, her parents make her wear water wings at all times, even in bed. Then one day they determine that their child needs to learn how to swim. Unsurprisingly, Heather is frightened, convinced that the water dislikes her. But she climbs into the shallow end of a pool with her mother and father," and finds that she loves the water and it loves her. (School Library Journal)

Macaulay, David
  Why the chicken crossed the road. Houghton Mifflin 1987 31p il lib bdg $16
Grades: 3 4 5   E
  1. Chickens -- Fiction
  ISBN 0-395-44241-9 lib bdg
                     LC 87-2908
"A ridiculous chicken sets off a circular story involving a herd of cows, a bridge, a train, a robber, the fire department and some hydrangeas. Chaos. The illustrations are suitably wild—painted with brilliant color and almost palpable energy." N Y Times Book Rev

Maccarone, Grace
  ★ **Miss** Lina's ballerinas; illustrated by Christine Davenier. Feiwel and Friends 2010 un il $16.99
Grades: PreK K 1   E
  1. Stories in rhyme 2. Ballet -- Fiction
  ISBN 0-312-38243-X; 978-0-312-38243-8
                     LC 2009-49367
Ballet instructor Miss Lina has a solution when her eight students, who always dance in pairs, are distraught when a ninth girl joins the class.
"The rhymic rhyming text flows beautifully throughout the book. . . . Davenier's free-spirited drawings and color washes add a sense of music as well as movement to the scenes." Booklist
  Another title about Miss Lina is:
  Miss Lina's ballerinas and the prince (2011)

Macdonald, Suse

Alphabet animals; a slide-and-peek adventure. Little Simon 2008 un il $12.99

Grades: PreK K   E

1. Alphabet 2. Board books for children 3. Animals -- Fiction

ISBN 978-1-4169-5045-5; 1-4169-5045-1

"A note to parents explains that this book is a guessing game in which animals and birds are drawn in the shapes of letters and children are encouraged to identify them. Each page presents one critter, set against a bright backdrop, with a pullout panel that reveals the letter represented along with the name of that particular animal. The color combinations are eye-catching and the images are appealing. . . . This is a clever way to help children learn the alphabet and reinforce pre-reading skills." SLJ

Circus opposites; an interactive extravaganza. Little Simon 2010 un il $11.99

Grades: PreK K 1 2   E

1. Opposites 2. Circus -- Fiction

ISBN 978-1-4169-7154-2; 1-4169-7154-8

"Macdonald's crisp trademark paper collages are the main event, as she uses the sights of the circus to explore the concept of opposites. Readers kick things off by pulling a tab to let 11 clowns 'out' of a tiny yellow car. They can also literally turn a clown's frown upside down. . . . The elaborate costumes and variety of interactive elements should prove kid-pleasing." Publ Wkly

Fish, swish! splash, dash! Little Simon 2007 un il $8.99

Grades: PreK K 1 2   E

1. Counting 2. Stories in rhyme 3. Fishes -- Fiction

ISBN 978-1-4169-3605-3; 1-4169-3605-X

Follow the leader and count the fish that live beneath the sea. Turn the book upside-down and count again.

"Vivid hues, clean visual elements, and simple language combine to create a successful and eye-catching concept book." SLJ

Machado, Ana Maria

What a party! Ana Maria Machado, illustrated by Helene Moreau. Groundwood Books 2013 32 p. ill. (hardcover) $18.95

Grades: PreK K 1 2   E

1. Cooking -- Juvenile fiction 2. Children's parties -- Juvenile fiction

ISBN 1554981689; 9781554981687

This children's book, by Ana Maria Machado, illustrated by Helene Moreau, warns that "if it is just a few days until your birthday, and your mother says you can invite anyone you like to come over to play, be careful! . . . In a celebration of neighbors and diversity, an open-ended party invitation results in a raucous gathering of children, pets, and parents (plus salsa dancers and a reggae band!), all feasting on food from all over the world." (Publisher's note)

Mack, Jeff

Good news, bad news; Jeff Mack. Chronicle Books 2012 40 p. (alk. paper) $16.99

Grades: PreK K 1   E

1. Rain -- Fiction 2. Picnics -- Fiction 3. Picture books for children 4. Optimism -- Fiction 5. Pessimism --

Fiction

ISBN 1452101108; 9781452101101

LC 2011016710

In this book, "[w]hen optimistic Rabbit and unlucky Mouse go on a picnic, there is plenty of good news and bad news. Some good news-umbrella, apples, cake, cave. Some bad news-rain, worms, bees, bear. Unfortunately, all the bad seems to happen to Mouse, who eventually has a hissy fit that makes Rabbit cry. But as the sun breaks through the clouds, Mouse makes it all better with a peace offering of the picnic basket and a hug" (School Library Journal)

Hippo and Rabbit in 3 more tales: brave like me. Scholastic Inc. 2011 32p pa $3.99

Grades: K 1 2   E

1. Fear -- Fiction 2. Courage -- Fiction 3. Rabbits -- Fiction 4. Hippopotamus -- Fiction

ISBN 978-0-545-28360-1; 0-545-28360-4

Hippo is scared of everything. He worries his balloon will pop and make a big noise. He's nervous about taking a bath. And he is so very afraid of spiders. Rabbit tells him not to worry—to just be brave, like him.

Hush little polar bear; [by] Jeff Mack. Roaring Brook Press 2008 un il $16.95

Grades: PreK K   E

1. Stories in rhyme 2. Adventure fiction 3. Dreams -- Fiction 4. Bedtime -- Fiction 5. Polar bear -- Fiction

ISBN 978-1-59643-368-7; 1-59643-368-X

LC 2007044049

A little girl invites her plush polar bear to dream of all of the places where sleeping bears go, from the high seas to a starry desert and back home

"The richly textured spreads are bright and imaginative, perfectly complementing the simple, lyrical text." SLJ

Mackall, Dandi Daley

First day; illustrated by Tiphanie Beeke. Harcourt 2003 un il $16

Grades: PreK K   E

1. School stories 2. Stories in rhyme

ISBN 0-15-216577-0

LC 2002-933

The first day of school starts out filled with doubt, but after facing fear of the big kids, reciting the alphabet with ease, and learning about recess, a child can't help but look forward to day two.

"The rhyming text gives the story a sweet, singsong quality. . . . The softly colored, reassuring art works well with the simple text that is set on pastel backgrounds." SLJ

Listen to the silent night; illustrated by Steve Johnson and Lou Fancher. Dutton Childrens Books 2011 un il $16.99

Grades: PreK K 1   E

1. Stories in rhyme 2. Noise -- Fiction 3. Sound -- Fiction 4. Christmas stories

ISBN 978-0-525-42276-1; 0-525-42276-5

LC 2011005243

Rhyming text reveals many sounds heard on the night of Jesus' birth, such as the flapping of Joseph's sandals as he walks into Bethlehem, the lowing of a cow in the stable, and the flutter of angels' wings as they proclaim the news.

"Johnson and Fancher's lovely artwork is filled with warm welcoming colors and highly textured details. A noisy account of the miraculous night." SLJ

Macken, JoAnn Early

Baby says moo! written by JoAnn Early Macken; illustrated by David Walker. Disney Hyperion Books 2011 un il lib bdg $15.99

Grades: PreK   E

1. Stories in rhyme 2. Sounds -- Fiction 3. Animals -- Fiction 4. Infants -- Fiction

ISBN 978-1-4231-3400-8 lib bdg; 1-4231-3400-1 lib bdg

LC 2009-52504

A cumulative, rhyming tale of a baby who sees many animals while out with her family, only one of which makes her favorite sound.

"The rhyming text reads smoothly, and the acrylic illustrations are childlike and cheerful, making the book exactly right for toddlers." SLJ

★ **Waiting** out the storm; illustrated by Susan Gaber. Candlewick Press 2010 un il $15.99

Grades: PreK K 1 2   E

1. Stories in rhyme 2. Rain -- Fiction 3. Storms -- Fiction 4. Mother-child relationship -- Fiction

ISBN 978-0-7636-3378-3; 0-7636-3378-X

LC 2008030746

A mother reassures her child about the wind, lightning, and thunder when a storm passes through.

"The text creates a natural-sounding rhythm and flow of dialogue. . . . Gaber's captivating artwork, combining watercolor, pencil, and charcoal with digital renderings, is simultaneously strong and delicate." Booklist

Mackintosh, David

Marshall Armstrong is new to our school. Abrams 2011 il

Grades: PreK K 1 2   E

1. School stories 2. Parties -- Fiction 3. Birthdays -- Fiction 4. Friendship -- Fiction

ISBN 1-4197-0036-7; 978-1-4197-0036-1

Marshall Armstrong is new to school and definitely stands out from the crowd, with his pale skin, perpetual hats, and special "space food" lunches that come in silver wrappers. He doesn't play sports, and he doesn't watch television. So when he invites everyone in class over for his birthday party, it's sure to be a disaster. Or is it?

"Macintosh's beautifully underplayed text and genial drawings manage to be empathic to both the leery narrator and the serenely outré object of his misapprehension." Publ Wkly

Maclear, Kyo

Spork; written by Kyo Maclear; illustrated by Isabelle Arsenault. Kids Can Press 2010 un il $16.95

Grades: PreK K 1 2   E

1. Cutlery -- Fiction 2. Prejudices -- Fiction 3. Identity (Psychology) -- Fiction 4. Racially mixed people -- Fiction

ISBN 978-1-55337-736-8; 1-55337-736-2

His mum is a spoon. His dad is a fork. And he's a bit of both. He's Spork! The spoons think he's too pointy, while the forks find him too round.

"Maclear's text feels nearly effortless. The inanimate-object identification . . . pairs brilliantly with Arsenault's melding of mixed media and digital art. . . . A sublime little parable." Kirkus

Madison, Alan

★ **Velma** Gratch & the way cool butterfly; written by Alan Madison; illustrated by Kevin Hawkes. Schwartz & Wade Books 2007 un il $16.99; lib bdg $19.99

Grades: PreK K 1 2   E

1. School stories 2. Sisters -- Fiction 3. Butterflies -- Fiction

ISBN 978-0-375-83597-1; 978-0-375-93597-8 lib bdg

LC 2006030978

Velma starts first grade in the shadow of her memorable older sisters, and while her newfound interest in butterflies helps her to stand out, it also leads to an interesting complication

"With humorous wordplay and electric cartoon art, this is an uplifting and way-cool look at one child's metamorphosis." SLJ

Madrigal, Antonio Hernandez

Erandi's braids; written by Antonio Hernandez Madrigal; illustrated by Tomie dePaola. Putnam 1999 un il $15.99; pa $6.99

Grades: K 1 2 3   E

1. Hair -- Fiction 2. Mothers and daughters -- Fiction

ISBN 0-399-23212-5; 0-698-11885-5 pa

LC 97-49631

In a poor Mexican village, Erandi surprises her mother by offering to sell her long, beautiful hair in order to raise enough money to buy a new fishing net

"This tale of love and sacrifice is based on an actual Mexican practice in the 1940s and 50s. The facial expressions in dePaola's warm illustrations add to the poignancy of the story." Horn Book Guide

Mahy, Margaret, 1936-2012

★ **Bubble** trouble; illustrated by Polly Dunbar. Clarion Books 2009 37p il $16

Grades: PreK K 1   E

1. Stories in rhyme 2. Bubbles -- Fiction

ISBN 978-0-547-07421-4; 0-547-07421-2

LC 2008-07244

Boston Globe-Horn Book Award: Picture Book (2009)

Mabel blows a bubble that captures Baby and wafts him away, resulting in a wild chase that involves the whole neighborhood.

"Mahy is a master at creating verse that is as light and airy as the baby's bubble. Filled with lovely Briticisms, alliterative nonsense words, double, triple and internal rhymes, it's meant to be read aloud. . . . Dunbar's joyous watercolor-and-cut-paper illustrations are wonderfully expressive, a visual treat moving apace with the text." Kirkus

The **man** from the land of Fandango; Margaret Mahy; illustrations by Polly Dunbar. Clarion Books 2012 32 p. (hardback) $16.99

Grades: PreK K 1 2   E

1. Picture books for children 2. Imagination -- Juvenile fiction 3. Adventure fiction -- Juvenile fiction 4. Stories

in rhyme 5. Imagination -- Fiction

ISBN 0547819889; 9780547819884

LC 2011052109

In this children's book by Margaret Mahy, illustrated by Polly Dunbar, "two children paint Mr. Fandango to life, and together the trio has a tremendous adventure with baboons and bisons, dinosaurs and kangaroos . . . [in] a playful imaginary world. . . . Even the lines of type curve and tango." (Publisher's note)

Mair, J. Samia

The **perfect** gift; illustrated by Craigh Howarth. Kube Pub. 2010 29p il $8.95

Grades: 1 2 3 4   E

1. Gifts -- Fiction 2. Muslims -- Fiction 3. Id al-Adha -- Fiction 4. Family life -- Fiction

ISBN 978-0-86037-438-1; 0-86037-438-6

Sarah is sad because she cannot find an Eid gift for her mother, so she takes a walk along the secret path in the woods that always makes her feel better. There she finds the first flower of spring—God's perfect gift to the world. Leaving her gift in its place to share with her entire family, Sarah grows in her understanding and appreciation of nature and what it means to live in submission to God.

"Howarth's watercolor illustrations effectively portray a contemporary Muslim family living in North America or Europe. This realistic picture book, one of the few stories on Eid-ul-Adha, is a solid purchase for many collections." SLJ

Mak, Kam

★ **My** Chinatown; one year in poems. HarperCollins Pubs. 2002 un il $16.95

Grades: 2 3 4   E

1. Chinese Americans 2. Immigrants -- Fiction 3. Emigration and immigration

ISBN 0-06-029190-7; 0-06-029191-5 lib bdg

LC 2001-16686

A boy adjusts to life away from his home in Hong Kong, in the Chinatown of his new American city

"Extraordinary photo-realistic paintings and spare, free-verse poems bring New York's Chinatown to life in this picture book with appeal to a wide age group." Booklist

Malaspina, Ann

★ **Heart** on fire; Susan B. Anthony votes for president. by Ann Malaspina; illustrated by Steve James. Albert Whitman & Co. 2012 32 p. col. ill. (hardcover) $16.99

Grades: 2 3 4   E

1. Elections 2. Voter registration 3. Women's rights -- History 4. Election law -- New York (State) -- Criminal provisions 5. Trials (Political crimes and offenses) -- New York (State) -- Juvenile literature 6. Women -- Suffrage -- United States -- History -- 19th century -- Juvenile literature

ISBN 080753188X; 9780807531884

LC 2011034179

Author Ann Malaspina tells the story of Susan B. Anthony. "On November 5, 1872, Susan B. Anthony made history--and broke the law--when she voted in the US presidential election, a privilege that had been reserved for men. She was arrested, tried, and found guilty . . . It wasn't until 1920 that women were granted the right to vote, but the civil rights victory would not have been possible without Susan

B. Anthony's leadership and passion to stand up for what was right." (Publisher's note)

"Incisive storytelling and luminous oil paintings make for a memorable, important read." SLJ

Includes bibliographical references.

Maloney, Peter

★ **One** foot two feet; an exceptional counting book. [by] Peter Maloney & Felicia Zekauskas. G.P. Putnam's Sons 2011 un il $12.99

Grades: PreK K   E

1. Counting 2. English language -- Grammar

ISBN 978-0-399-25446-8; 0-399-25446-3

LC 2010028172

"Preschoolers will enjoy pointing at the pictures and turning the pages in this simple, interactive counting book that is also a game of wordplay. Along with the numbers, the spreads introduce the vocabulary changes from single to plural nouns. Each brightly colored page has a central cut-out window of a single object, beginning with one foot. Turn the page, and there are two feet. . . . The playful cartoon pictures on thick paper with lots of white space will draw kids with the humorous details." Booklist

Mandel, Peter

Jackhammer Sam; illustrated by David Catrow. Roaring Brook Press 2011 un il $16.99

Grades: PreK K 1 2   E

1. Stories in rhyme 2. Construction workers -- Fiction

ISBN 978-1-59643-034-1; 1-59643-034-6

LC 2010036341

A jackhammer operator boasts about his loud, sidewalk-blasting skills.

"The sing-song text is punctuated by onomatopoeia and nonsense words, and it is as loud and brash as the illustrations or, for that matter, a jackhammer." Horn Book

Manning, Maurie

Kitchen dance; by Maurie J. Manning. Clarion Books 2008 un il $16

Grades: PreK K 1   E

1. Dance -- Fiction 2. Bedtime -- Fiction 3. Family life -- Fiction 4. Hispanic Americans -- Fiction

ISBN 978-0-618-99110-5; 0-618-99110-7

LC 2007036838

"Drawn from their beds by noises downstairs, the narrator and her little brother, Tito, peer into the kitchen to find that their parents have turned dinner cleanup into a rambunctious, Latin-flavored song and dance number. . . . As the rounded, sculptural bodies of the couple move about the kitchen with humor and grace, the illustrations take on a cinematic sense of motion and space." Publ Wkly

Manning, Maurie J.

Laundry day; by Maurie J. Manning. Houghton Mifflin Harcourt 2012 40 p.

Grades: K 1 2 3 4   E

1. Scarves 2. Picture books for children 3. City and town life -- Fiction 4. Lost and found possessions -- Fiction 5. New York (N.Y.) -- History -- Fiction 6. Graphic novels 7. Neighborhoods -- Fiction 8. Tenement houses -- Fiction

ISBN 0547241968; 9780547241968

LC 2010043252

This picture book depicts the events of "one windy day [when] a young shoeshine boy makes a world of new friends. Unable to make a sale, he looks up to see a long, bright-red scarf drifting down to him as he sits dejectedly on the curb. The story of his search for the owner is told with dialogue balloons in comic-book style. Text and illustrations are mutually dependent as one panel follows another, moving the story along. . . . [Maurie J.] Manning's . . . detailed digital pencil, watercolor and pastel drawings depict an unnamed but unmistakable turn-of-the-20th-century New York City. Laundry whips in the wind, and busy people on every floor of the buildings are shown from multiple perspectives." (Kirkus)

Manning, Mick

Snap! [by] Mick Manning, [illustrated by] Brita Granström. Frances Lincoln 2006 un il $14.95
Grades: PreK K 1 2   E
1. Food chains (Ecology) -- Fiction
ISBN 1-84507-408-4

This "story looks at the food chain, first by introducing a fly who is gobbled up by a frog, who is, in turn, guzzled by a duckling, who is, in turn, eaten by a pike, etc. . . . The comical conclusion is perfect for the younger set, but even the older kids will enjoy the drama in these pages. The bold colorful cartoons are inviting; the text is simple." SLJ

Mannis, Celeste Davidson

One leaf rides the wind; counting in a Japanese garden. by Celeste Davidson Mannis, pictures by Susan Kathleen Hartung. Viking 2002 un il $15.99; pa $6.99
Grades: PreK K 1 2   E
1. Haiku 2. Counting 3. Gardens -- Poetry
ISBN 0-670-03525-4; 0-14-240195-1 pa
LC 2002-1024

In this collection of haiku poems, a young girl walks through a Japanese garden and discovers many delights, from one leaf to ten stone lanterns. Includes notes about Japanese religion and philosophy

"The book as a whole is elegantly and respectfully presented and the counting aspect is especially well crafted, capturing the meandering focus of a small child. Mannis's simple verses are complemented by Hartung's pleasing and evocative pen-and-ink and watercolor art." SLJ

Manushkin, Fran

The belly book; illustrated by Dan Yaccarino. Feiwel and Friends 2011 il $16.99
Grades: PreK K   E
1. Stories in rhyme 2. Abdomen
ISBN 978-0-312-64958-6; 0-312-64958-4

"A meditation on the middle for beginning readers and younger listeners supports some appealingly merry illustrations. Manushkin's rhyming text is an invitation to a general celebration of abdomens—readers' own or other peoples', and occasionally those of beasts and birds. . . . The art . . . is the real treat here, Yaccarino's clever, energetic, lighthearted illustration. . . . His playful full-page gouaches zip nimbly from thought to thought and invest the whole with a generous dollop of whimsy." Kirkus

How Mama brought the spring; [by] Fran Manushkin; illustrated by Holly Berry. Dutton 2008 un il $16.99

Grades: K 1 2 3   E
1. Spring -- Fiction 2. Cooking -- Fiction 3. Family life -- Fiction
ISBN 978-0-525-42027-9; 0-525-42027-4
LC 2007-05217

A mother in Chicago tells her daughter how Grandma used to make a special surprise on the freezing cold winter mornings in Belarus—so special that it seemed to bring spring with it.

"This tale is filled with rich language and imagery. The illustrations fill the page with great detail and show images of the Russian culture. A recipe for cheese blintzes is included. This book would be a great addition." Libr Media Connect

★ The Shivers in the fridge; illustrated by Paul O. Zelinsky. Dutton Children's Books 2006 un il $16.99
Grades: PreK K 1 2   E
1. Magnets -- Fiction 2. Refrigeration -- Fiction
ISBN 0-525-46943-5
LC 2006-03867

One-by-one, the members of the Shivers family disappear from the inside of their chilly refrigerator home

"The story's humor is matched by Zelinsky's inventive artwork, which picks up on the wit and slyness of the text." Booklist

Marceau, Fani

★ Panorama; a foldout book. [illustrated by] Joëlle Jolivet. Abrams Books for Young Readers 2009 un il $19.95
Grades: 1 2 3   E
1. Toy and movable books 2. Travel -- Fiction 3. Voyages around the world -- Fiction 4. Voyages and travels -- Juvenile literature
ISBN 978-0-8109-8332-8; 0-8109-8332-X
LC 2008022166

Original French edition 2007

Illustrations and simple text invite the reader to visit different places around the world, then to view the same scenes at night on the reverse of the fanfolded page.

This is a "stunning travelogue. . . . Each oversize page is grounded by a poetic fragment evoking each locale. . . . A faint ecological bent further enriches the descriptions. But the main event is the alternately dizzying and mysterious black-and-white woodcut illustrations. They can be flipped through like an ordinary book, though the full impact is felt only through unfurling all 15 pages so that they lay flat in a seamless panorama." Booklist

Marcellino, Fred

I, crocodile. HarperCollins Pubs. 1999 un il hardcover o.p. pa $6.99
Grades: 1 2 3 4   E
1. Emperors 2. Crocodiles -- Fiction
ISBN 0-06-205168-7; 0-06-008859-1 pa

"The text is reportorial in tone, a perfect complement to the extravagant, expressive illustrations. . . . A sophisticated picture book, this is one publication with appeal to many different audiences." Horn Book

Marciano, John Bemelmans

Madeline at the White House; story and pictures by John Bemelmans Marciano. Viking Children's Books 2011 un il $17.99

Grades: PreK K 1   **E**
1. Stories in rhyme 2. Easter -- Fiction 3. Orphans -- Fiction 4. Presidents -- Fiction
ISBN 978-0-670-01228-2; 0-670-01228-9
LC 2010025110
Madeline and the other orphans of the vine-covered house in Paris spend Easter at the White House visiting with the President's daughter.

"Based on an idea Bemelmans was working on at the time of his 1962 death, grandson Marciano has done a credible job copying the rhythms and artistic style of the originals." Booklist

Marcus, Kimberly
Scritch-scratch a perfect match; illustrated by Mike Lester. G.P. Putnam's Sons 2011 un il $16.99
Grades: PreK K   **E**
1. Stories in rhyme 2. Dogs -- Fiction 3. Fleas -- Fiction
ISBN 978-0-399-25004-0; 0-399-25004-2
LC 2008-30482
When a flea lands on a stray dog, it starts a chain of events that ends with the dog happily adopted by a pet-loving man.

"Abundant motion lines, copious scrawled hatch and crosshatch details, and heaps of sly character humor . . . all work together to support the playful text. Those who like their friendship tales with a touch of chaos will gladly take a bite out of this mischievous offering." Bull Cent Child Books

Mariconda, Barbara
Sort it out! illustrated by Sherry Rogers. Sylvan Dell 2008 un il $16.95; pa $8.95
Grades: PreK K 1 2   **E**
1. Rats -- Fiction 2. Collectors and collecting -- Fiction
ISBN 978-1-934359-11-2; 1-934359-11-4; 978-1-934359-32-7 pa; 1-934359-32-7 pa
"When Pack rat comes home with a cart full of stuff—a locket, a book, an umbrella, a pinecone, and many more random items—his mother admonishes him to sort it all out and put it away. Packy does just that, cleverly sorting things with like characteristics such as where they're found, their color, shape, etc. . . . The illustrations are brightly colored, large, and very clear. Careful readers will notice a subplot in the pictures and find satisfaction in seeing its resolution on the final page. In addition, the rhyming text prompts them to guess the word that defines each collection. Back matter has activities to extend the experience." SLJ

Ten for me; illustrated by Sherry Rogers. Sylvan Dell 2011 il $16.95; pa $8.95
Grades: 2 3 4   **E**
1. Stories in rhyme 2. Butterflies -- Fiction 3. Mathematics -- Fiction
ISBN 978-1-60718-074-6; 1-60718-074-X; 978-1-60718-085-2 pa; 1-60718-085-5 pa
"Rose and Ed learn much more than expected on their butterfly hunt. . . . Each day is seen as a double-page spread of the duo hunting in field and garden. As Rose's totals grow, Ed's shrink. The totals in the text are mirrored in a tally of 'Butterflies Captured and Released' in the illustrations. . . . An excellent rhyming tale that doubles as math lesson and triples as a butterfly-biology primer." Kirkus

Marino, Gianna
One too many; a seek & find counting book. Chronicle Books 2010 un il
Grades: PreK K 1 2   **E**
1. Counting 2. Animals -- Fiction
ISBN 0-8118-6908-3; 978-0-8118-6908-9
Children count from one jumping flea to twelve frisky animals until, at last, they reach one too many.

"Marino's naturalistic illustrations are done in gouache in this remarkable counting book. . . . Young readers will find much to discover as they revisit the book time after time." SLJ

Zoopa; an animal alphabet. Chronicle Books 2005 un il $14.95
Grades: PreK K 1 2   **E**
1. Animals 2. English language -- Alphabet -- Juvenile literature
ISBN 0-8118-4789-6
LC 2004-63449
"A bowl of tomato soup is the vehicle for introducing the letters of the alphabet and their corresponding animals. Beginning with a playful ant and an orange-and-purple butterfly, two to three animals and their first letters are introduced on each spread. As the menagerie multiplies, the creatures move around the pages, sometimes interacting with humorous results. . . . The playful gouache illustrations depict the colorful crew having as much fun as readers will surely have identifying them." SLJ

Markes, Julie
Good thing you're not an octopus! story by Julie Markes; pictures by Maggie Smith. HarperCollins Pubs. 2001 un il $14.95; pa $6.99
Grades: PreK K   **E**
1. Animals 2. Self-acceptance
ISBN 0-06-028465-X; 0-06-443586-5 pa
LC 99-37139
"A boy who complains about getting dressed, riding in his car seat, and more is answered with funny worst-case scenarios: 'You don't like to take a nap? It's a good thing you're not a bear. If you were a bear, you would have to nap all winter long!' The tone is silly, and the cheerful illustrations convey the absurdity in the text." Horn Book Guide

Shhhhh! Everybody's sleeping; illustrated by David Parkins. HarperCollins 2005 un il $14.99; lib bdg $15.89
Grades: PreK K 1   **E**
1. Sleep 2. Bedtime 3. Stories in rhyme
ISBN 0-06-053790-6; 0-06-053791-4 lib bdg
LC 2003-27854
A young child is encouraged to go to sleep by the thought of everyone else sleeping, from teacher to baker to postman

"The text satisfyingly moves along while the artwork soars. . . . Glowing with warm colors in subdued hues, the sturdy pictures stretch wide across double-page spreads, offering surprisingly energetic, varied compositions." Booklist

Markle, Sandra, 1946-
Butterfly tree; written by Sandra Markle; illustrated by Leslie Wu. Peachtree 2010 32 p. ill.
Grades: K 1 2   **E**
1. Clouds -- Fiction 2. Monarch butterflies 3. Lake Erie -- Fiction 4. Butterflies -- Fiction 5. Picture books

for children

ISBN 1561455393; 9781561455393

LC 2009040526

In this picture book, "[a] black rain that becomes a mysterious orange cloud over Lake Erie is the beginning for of a magical encounter with monarch butterflies for Jilly, her dog, Fudge, and her mother. Veteran nature-writer [Sandra] Markle . . . offers a gentle free-verse narrative based on a never-to-be-forgotten experience from her own Ohio childhood. . . . At first, Jilly is worried, hesitant about following the cloud into the woods with her mother, wanting to turn back. [In illustrator Leslie] Wu's hazy pastel paintings . . . the monarchs explode from the tree where they were resting and Jilly realizes what they are. . . . Author's notes, a map showing monarch migration and a list of books and websites for further exploration add . . . information." (Kirkus)

"What looks dark and indistinct closeup shows surprisingly well at a distance; the text reads aloud smoothly, suiting this especially well for use with a group. Author's notes, a map showing monarch migration and a list of books and websites for further exploration add helpful information. Even collections with many monarch titles will want to add this one for its masterful evocation of a child's sense of wonder at the natural world." Kirkus

Includes bibliographical references

★ **Family** pack; illustrated by Alan Marks. Charlesbridge 2011 un il lib bdg $15.95

Grades: K 1 2 3 **E**

1. Wolves -- Fiction

ISBN 978-1-58089-217-9 lib bdg; 1-58089-217-5 lib bdg

LC 2010-07548

A young wolf, taken from her pack in Canada to Yellowstone National Park, struggles alone to master the skills of hunting and survival until she finds a lone male and begins a new pack with him.

"Without a hint of anthropomorphism but with vivid, poetic language, [Markle] shows readers the wolves bound only by nature. . . . The illustrator's watercolors add drama and energy. . . . An excellent story for wolf-lovers and a welcome addition to elementary-school science shelves." Kirkus

Race the wild wind; a story of the Sable Island horses. Sandra Markle; paintings by by Layne Johnson. Walker 2011 1 v. (unpaged) $17.99

Grades: K 1 2 3 **E**

1. Horses -- Fiction 2. Wild horses -- Fiction 3. Wild horses -- Juvenile fiction

ISBN 978-0-8027-9766-7; 0-8027-9766-0; 9780802797667; 9780802797674

LC 2010036013

"After being lowered into the frigid Atlantic by a schooner, a young stallion and his equine companions swim to Sable Island in this poetic tale that imagines how wild horses first came to live on this isolated island off of Nova Scotia. . . . Dramatic oil spreads depict his survival and transformation from domestic to wild horse amid this beautiful yet harsh environment." Booklist

Includes bibliographical references

Snow school; Sandra Markle; illustrated by Alan Marks. Charlesbridge 2013 32 p. (reinforced) $16.95

Grades: PreK K 1 2 **E**

1. Snow leopard -- Juvenile literature 2. Animal behavior -- Juvenile literature 3. Learning in animals -- Juvenile literature 4. Snow leopard -- Infancy -- Juvenile literature

ISBN 1580894100; 9781580894104

LC 2012000790

In this children's book, by Sandra Markle, illustrated by Alan Marks, "readers are introduced to twin snow leopard cubs and their mother from the Hindu Kush mountains of Pakistan. . . . Text and . . . watercolor illustrations lead readers through the struggles these snow leopards face from finding food to bearing harsh weather conditions and the lessons the young cubs learn as they prepare for a life on their own, out from underneath the watchful, caring eye of their mother." (Publisher's note)

Includes bibliographical references

What If You Had Animal Teeth? by Sandra Markle; illustrated by Howard McWilliam. Scholastic 2013 32 p. ill. (paperback) $3.99

Grades: K 1 2 **E**

1. Teeth -- Juvenile literature 2. Comparative anatomy -- Juvenile literature

ISBN 0545484383; 9780545484381

In this book by Sandra Markle, readers "explore what it would be like if their own front teeth were replaced by those of a different animal. Featuring a dozen animals (beaver, great white shark, narwhal, elephant, rattlesnake, naked mole rat, hippopotamus, crocodile, and more), this book explores how different teeth are especially adapted for an animal's survival. At the end of the book, children will discover why their own teeth are just right for them." (Publisher's note)

Marlow, Layn

★ **Hurry** up and slow down; [by] Layn Marlow. Holiday House 2009 un il $16.95

Grades: PreK K 1 **E**

1. Bedtime -- Fiction 2. Rabbits -- Fiction 3. Turtles -- Fiction 4. Books and reading -- Fiction

ISBN 978-0-8234-2178-7; 0-8234-2178-3

LC 2008010796

First published 2008 in the United Kingdom

Hare likes to hurry through the day, unlike Tortoise, but manages to slow down for his favorite bedtime story

"This delightful spinoff of 'The Tortoise and the Hare' follows a typical day in the lives of these two friends. . . . The illustrations of Hare, Tortoise, their animal companions, and their environment are rounded and softly colored, creating a comforting world for young children. An endearing story that will no doubt become a bedtime favorite." SLJ

Marsalis, Wynton, 1961-

Squeak! rumble! whomp! whomp! whomp! a sonic adventure. Wynton Marsalis; illustrated by Paul Rogers. Candlewick 2012 40 p. (hardback) $15.99

Grades: PreK K 1 **E**

1. Music -- Juvenile fiction 2. Sound -- Juvenile fiction 3. Neighborhood -- Juvenile fiction 4. Sound -- Fiction

5. Neighborhoods -- Fiction

ISBN 9780763639914; 0763639915

LC 2011048367

This children's book, by Wynton Marsalis, illustrated by Paul Rogers, explores various sounds in everyday life in a neighborhood. "What's that sound? The back door squeee-aks open, sounding like a noisy mouse nearby--eeek, eeeek, eeeek! Big trucks on the highway rrrrrrumble, just as hunger makes a tummy grrrrumble." (Publisher's note)

Marshall, Edward

★ **Fox** and his friends; pictures by James Marshall. Dial Bks. for Young Readers 1982 56p il (Dial easy-to-read) hardcover o.p. pa $3.99

Grades: K 1 2   E

1. Foxes -- Fiction

ISBN 0-14-037007-2 pa

LC 81-68769

"The sibling exchanges and situations are comically true to life. . . . The red, green and black illustrations . . . pick the story up and add character embellishment and humor." SLJ

Other titles about Fox are:

Fox in love (1982)

Fox on wheels (1983)

Fox at school (1983)

Fox all week (1984)

Foc on the job (1988)

Fox be nimble (1990)

Fox outfoxed (1992)

Fox on stage (1993)

★ **Space** case; pictures by James Marshall. Dial Bks. for Young Readers 1980 un il hardcover o.p. pa $6.99

Grades: PreK K 1 2   E

1. Science fiction 2. Halloween -- Fiction

ISBN 0-8037-8005-2; 0-14-054704-5 pa

LC 80-13369

"The open ending of the brief story is as satisfying as it is original, for the small space traveler is thoroughly childlike in its insouciance, curiosity, and concern for self-gratification. The text is an economical, tongue-in-cheek accompaniment to the various levels of humor depicted in the illustrations." Horn Book

Three by the sea; pictures by James Marshall. Dial Bks. for Young Readers 1981 48p il (Dial easy-to-read) hardcover o.p. pa $3.99

Grades: K 1 2   E

1. Storytelling -- Fiction

ISBN 0-14-037004-8 pa

"The mild lunacy of the illustrations (an almost vertical hill, a neatly striped cat) with their ungainly, comical figures is nicely matched with the bland directness of the writing. This is good-humored and amusing." Bull Cent Child Books

Other titles about Spider, Sam, and Lolly are:

Four on the shore (1985)

Three up a tree (1986)

Marshall, James

★ **George** and Martha; written and illustrated by James Marshall. Houghton Mifflin 1972 46p il lib bdg $16; pa $6.95

Grades: PreK K 1 2   E

1. Friendship -- Fiction 2. Hippopotamus -- Fiction

ISBN 0-395-16619-5 lib bdg; 0-395-19972-7 pa

In these five short episodes which include a misunderstanding about split pea soup, invasion of privacy and a crisis over a missing tooth, two not very delicate hippopotamuses reveal various aspects of friendship

"The pale pictures of these creatures and their adventures—in yellows, pinks, greens, and grays—capture the directness and humor of the stories." Horn Book

Other titles about George and Martha are:

George and Martha back in town (1984)

George and Martha encore (1973)

George and Martha, one fine day (1978)

George and Martha rise and shine (1976)

George and Martha round and round (1988)

George and Martha, tons of fun (1980)

★ **Swine** Lake; [pictures by] Maurice Sendak. HarperCollins Pubs. 1999 un il $16.95

Grades: PreK K 1 2   E

1. Pigs 2. Ballet 3. Wolves 4. Pigs -- Fiction 5. Ballet -- Fiction 6. Wolves -- Fiction

ISBN 0-06-205171-7

LC 98-73253

A hungry wolf attends a performance of Swine Lake, performed by the Boarshoi Ballet, intending to eat the performers, but he is so entranced by the story unfolding that he forgets about his meal

"Both Marshall and Sendak are cleverly comic here . . . the text shines. Sendak's art captures the nuance as well as all the humor of the story." Booklist

Marshall, Linda Elovitz

Talia and the rude vegetables; illustrated by Francesca Assirelli. Kar-Ben 2011 un il lib bdg $16.95

Grades: PreK K 1 2   E

1. Jews -- Fiction 2. Gardening -- Fiction 3. Vegetables -- Fiction 4. Rosh ha-Shanah -- Fiction

ISBN 978-0-7613-5217-4; 0-7613-5217-1

LC 2010020301

City-girl Talia misunderstands her grandmother's request that she go to the garden for "root vegetables" for a Rosh Hashanah stew but manages to find some she thinks are rude, as well as a good use for the rest she harvests. Includes a recipe for Rude Vegetable Stew.

"This laugh-out-loud title keeps the little jokes coming. . . . Quirky, cool-palette color illustrations by Italian artist Assirelli perfectly convey the whimsical narrative." Publ Wkly

Martin, Amy

Symphony city; written and illustrated by Amy Martin. McSweeney's 2011 un il $17.95

Grades: 2 3 4 5   E

1. Music -- Fiction 2. Sounds -- Fiction 3. City and town life -- Fiction

ISBN 978-1-936365-39-5; 1-936365-39-1

A young girl, lost in a big city, makes her way home by following the rich and vibrant music of the streets.

"The story is told visually through the gradual outpouring of color; the division of space in surprising vertical and horizontal lines, with cityscape backgrounds like blueprints; and colors layered as if silk-screened. . . . The economical text is a paean to music. . . . Craftsmanship reigns in this title. A flock of birds embossed in gold flies from the back to the front of the textured orange binding, and the jacket folds out into a two-sided poster. A perfect book for music lovers and bibliophiles." SLJ

Martin, Bill, 1916-2004

Baby Bear, Baby Bear, what do you see? by Bill Martin, Jr.; pictures by Eric Carle. Henry Holt & Co. 2007 un il $16.95; My first reader ed. $8.99

Grades: PreK K   E

1. Stories in rhyme 2. Bears -- Fiction

ISBN 978-0-8050-8336-1; 0-8050-8336-7; 978-0-8050-9291-2 My first reader ed.

LC 2006037769

Illustrations and rhyming text portray a young bear searching for its mother and meeting many North American animals along the way

"Creative action words and renderings of the various creatures in motion give the book a pleasing energy, while Mama Bear's obvious delight at finding her cub provides an endearing poignancy. [An] elegant balance of art, text, emotion and exposition." Publ Wkly

Barn dance! by Bill Martin, Jr. and John Archambault; illustrated by Ted Rand. Holt & Co. 1986 un il $16.95; pa $6.95

Grades: PreK K 1 2   E

1. Stories in rhyme 2. Dance -- Fiction 3. Country life -- Fiction

ISBN 0-8050-0089-5; 0-8050-0799-7 pa

LC 86-14225

Unable to sleep on the night of a full moon, a young boy follows the sound of music across the fields and finds an unusual barn dance in progress

"The bouncy rhyme will be a pleasure for listeners and tellers as they pick up the twang and the barn-dance beat. Rand's raucous two-page watercolor spreads are as spirited as the story poem." Booklist

★ A **beasty** story; [written by] Bill Martin, Jr. & [illustrated by] Steven Kellogg. Harcourt Brace & Co. 1999 un il $16; pa $7

Grades: PreK K 1 2   E

1. Stories in rhyme 2. Mice -- Fiction 3. Color -- Fiction

ISBN 0-15-201683-X; 0-15-216560-6 pa

LC 97-49519

A group of mice venture into a dark, dark woods where they find a dark brown house with a dark red stair leading past other dark colors to a spooky surprise

"A rhymed narrative tells the story along the top of the pages, with the mice commenting in rhymed conversation as they move through the adventure. The silly resolution will appeal to young children. . . . Kellogg's lively ink-and-watercolor art strikes just the right note for the gently suspenseful story." Booklist

★ **Brown** bear, brown bear what do you see? pictures by Eric Carle. Holt & Co. 1992 un il $16.99; bd bk $7.95; $8.99

Grades: PreK K   E

1. Stories in rhyme 2. Color -- Fiction 3. Animals

-- Fiction

ISBN 0-8050-1744-5; 0-8050-4790-5 bd bk; 978-0-8050-9244-8 My first reader ed.; 0-8050-9244-7 My first reader ed.

LC 91-29115

A newly illustrated edition of the title first published 1967 by Holt, Rinehart & Winston

A chant in which a variety of animals, each one a different color, answers the question, "What do you see?"

"Carle's large, brilliantly colored animals set against a white background make the book perfect for sharing with a group of preschoolers, while Martin's repetitious text is eminently chantable—a boon for beginning readers." Horn Book

★ **Chicka** chicka 1, 2, 3; [by] Bill Martin, Jr. & Michael Sampson; illustrated by Lois Ehlert. Simon & Schuster Books for Young Readers 2004 un il $15.95

Grades: PreK K 1   E

1. Counting 2. Stories in rhyme

ISBN 0-689-85881-7

LC 2003-19106

Numbers from one to one hundred climb to the top of an apple tree in this rhyming chant.

"The chanting rhyme and eye-popping images have a contagious energy youngsters will find irresistible." Booklist

★ **Chicka** chicka boom boom; [by] Bill Martin, Jr. and John Archambault; illustrated by Lois Ehlert. anniversary edition; Beach Lane Books 2009 un il $17.99   E

1. Alphabet 2. Stories in rhyme

ISBN 978-1-4169-9091-8; 1-4169-9091-7

LC 2009-626

A reissue of the title first published 1989

An alphabet rhyme/chant that relates what happens when the whole alphabet tries to climb a coconut tree.

"Ehlert's illustrations-bold, colorful shapes-are contained by broad polka-dotted borders, like a proscenium arch through which the action explodes. Tongue-tingling, visually stimulating, with an insistent repetitive chorus of 'chicka chicka boom boom,' the book demands to be read again and again and again." Horn Book

★ The **ghost**-eye tree; by Bill Martin, Jr. and John Archambault; illustrated by Ted Rand. Holt & Co. 1985 un il $16.95; pa $6.95

Grades: K 1 2 3   E

1. Ghost stories 2. Fear -- Fiction

ISBN 0-8050-0208-1; 0-8050-0947-7 pa

LC 85-8422

"On a dark and ghostly night a brother and sister are sent to fetch a pail of milk from the other end of town. They must pass the fearful ghost-eye tree, old and horribly twisted, looking like a monster, with a gap in the branches where the moon shines through like an eye. . . . The story is rhythmically told, sometimes rhyming, always moving ahead, sharp with the affectionate teasing of the brother and sister. The realistic watercolor illustrations are superb—strong, striking, very dark, with highlights of moonlight and lantern light that cast a spooky, scary spell. A splendidly theatrical book for storytelling and reading aloud." Horn Book

Kitty cat, kitty cat, are you waking up? by Bill Martin Jr. & Michael Sampson; illustrated by Laura J. Bryant. Marshall Cavendish 2008 un il $14.99
Grades: PreK K 1   E
   1. Stories in rhyme 2. Cats -- Fiction
   ISBN 978-0-7614-5438-0; 0-7614-5438-1
               LC 2007041987
Kitty Cat is distracted by many things as she gets ready for school in the morning

This is a "delightfully comic rhyming book. . . . A tiny mouse serves as an interested observer in each watercolor, until he becomes prey, and then a very relieved escapee, as the kitten is finally swept off to school." Booklist

Kitty cat, kitty cat, are you going to sleep? by Bill Martin Jr. and Michael Sampson; illustrated by Laura J. Bryant. Marshall Cavendish Children's 2011 un il $15.99
Grades: PreK K   E
   1. Stories in rhyme 2. Cats -- Fiction 3. Bedtime -- Fiction
   ISBN 978-0-7614-5946-0; 0-7614-5946-4
               LC 2010025274
A young cat is distracted by many things while getting ready for bed at night.

"A simple rhyming exchange alternates between parent and child as it playfully follows the usual bedtime routine and stall tactics. . . . Adorable colored pencil and watercolor illustrations support the conversation and take Kitty from wide awake to sleeping sooo tight. The soft palette and simple details have the perfect calming effect." SLJ

★ **Knots** on a counting rope; by Bill Martin, Jr. and John Archambault; illustrated by Ted Rand. Holt & Co. 1987 un il $16.95; pa $6.95
Grades: K 1 2 3   E
   1. Blind -- Fiction 2. Grandfathers -- Fiction 3. Native Americans -- Fiction
   ISBN 0-8050-0571-4; 0-8050-5479-0 pa
               LC 87-14858
A different version of the title illustrated by Joe Smith was published in 1966

"The powerful spare poetic text is done full justice by Rand's fine full-color illustrations, which capture both the drama and brilliance of vast southwestern space and the intimacy of starlit camp-fire scenes." Booklist

Panda bear, panda bear, what do you see? by Bill Martin Jr.; pictures by Eric Carle. Henry Holt & Co. 2003 un il $15.95; bd bk $7.95; My first reader ed. $8.99
Grades: PreK K   E
   1. Stories in rhyme 2. Animals -- Fiction 3. Endangered species -- Fiction
   ISBN 0-8050-1758-5; 0-8050-8078-3 bd bk; 978-0-8050-9292-9 My first reader ed.
               LC 2002-10855
Illustrations and rhyming text present ten different endangered animals

"The pictures, featuring animals strolling, splashing, and soaring, are brilliant lessons in the application of color, shape, form, and texture. . . . A fine read-aloud with a subtle, yet clear, message." Booklist

★ **Ten** little caterpillars; [by] Bill Martin Jr.; illustrated by Lois Ehlert. Beach Lane Books 2011 40p il
Grades: PreK K   E
   1. Stories in rhyme 2. Caterpillars -- Fiction
   ISBN 1-4424-3385-X; 978-1-4424-3385-4
               LC 2011002156
A newly illustrated edition of the title first published 1967

Illustrations and rhyming text follow ten caterpillars as one wriggles up a flower stem, another sails across a garden pool, and one reaches an apple leaf, where something amazing happens.

"Martin's caterpillar counting rhyme has been given new life with gorgeous and bold watercolor collages from . . . Ehlert. . . . This is a graphically sumptuously book, but the lesson is clear: nature is one tough town." Publ Wkly

★ **Trick** or treat? [by] Bill Martin, Jr. and Michael Sampson; illustrated by Paul Meisel. Simon & Schuster Bks. for Young Readers 2002 un il hardcover o.p. pa $6.99
Grades: PreK K 1 2   E
   1. Candy 2. Magic 3. Halloween 4. Magic -- Fiction 5. Halloween -- Fiction
   ISBN 0-689-84968-0; 1-4169-0262-7 pa
               LC 2002-70646
A child has a wonderful time collecting treats from the wacky neighbors until Magic Merlin decides that a trick would be more fun

"Meisel's cartoon illustrations take full advantage of the topsy-turvy story, adding lots of comic holiday detail to keep little ones alert. The fun is in the pictures, and the challenge is in figuring out the visual joke and the backward names." Booklist

Martin, David
  Christmas tree; illustrated by Melissa Sweet. Candlewick Press 2009 un il bd bk $5.99
Grades: PreK   E
   1. Board books for children 2. Trees -- Fiction 3. Christmas -- Fiction
   ISBN 978-0-7636-3030-0 bd bk; 0-7636-3030-6 bd bk
At Christmastime, a tree from the outside comes inside, just waiting to be decorated

This "attractive board [book features] simple, [a] clear [concept] and delightful pencil-and-watercolor illustrations enhanced with patterned fabric swatches." SLJ

  Hanukkah lights; illustrated by Melissa Sweet. Candlewick Press 2009 un il bd bk $5.99
Grades: PreK   E
   1. Board books for children 2. Hanukkah -- Fiction
   ISBN 978-0-7636-3029-4 bd bk; 0-7636-3029-2 bd bk
Children celebrate Hanukkah by lighting candles, eating latkes, spinning a dreidel, and giving presents

This "attractive board [book features] simple, clear concepts and delightful pencil-and-watercolor illustrations enhanced with patterned fabric swatches." SLJ

  Peep and Ducky; David Martin, illustrated by David Walker. Candlewick Press 2013 32 p. (reinforced) $14.99

Grades: PreK K   **E**
1. Stories in rhyme 2. Play -- Juvenile fiction 3. Friendship -- Juvenile fiction
ISBN 0763650390; 9780763650391

LC 2012942391

In this children's book, by David Martin, illustrated by David Walker, "when Peep goes to the playground with his mommy and runs into Ducky and his daddy, the result is definitely lucky. In . . . rhyming verse, the two encounter the usual highs and lows of playground adventures. . . . After a long bout of play, it's time to go home, but the two don't whine, promising instead to play together another time." (Kirkus)

Piggy and Dad go fishing; illustrated by Frank Remkiewicz. Candlewick Press 2005 un il $14.99
Grades: PreK K 1 2   **E**
1. Pigs -- Fiction 2. Fishing -- Fiction 3. Father-son relationship -- Fiction
ISBN 0-7636-2506-X

LC 2004-51941

When his dad takes Piggy fishing for the first time and Piggy ends up feeling sorry for the worms and the fish, they decide to make some changes.

"The summery watercolor-and-pencil cartoon illustrations clue listeners into Piggy's emotions and create a bit of tension in the nicely paced story." Horn Book Guide

Other titles about Piggy and Dad are:
Piggy and Dad (2001)
Piggy and Dad play (2002)

Martin, Jacqueline Briggs

Grandmother Bryant's pocket; pictures by Petra Mathers. Houghton Mifflin 1996 48p il hardcover o.p. pa $5.95
Grades: K 1 2 3   **E**
1. Fear -- Fiction 2. Grandmothers -- Fiction
ISBN 0-395-68984-8; 0-618-03309-2 pa

LC 94-31309

"Appealingly structured in one-and two-page chapters, the book is illustrated with watercolor paintings. Executed in naive style, the artwork has an unassuming sweetness." Booklist

On Sand Island; illustrated by David Johnson. Houghton Mifflin 2003 un il $16
Grades: 1 2 3   **E**
1. Islands -- Fiction
ISBN 0-618-23151-X

LC 2002-5090

In 1916 on an island in Lake Superior, Carl builds himself a boat by bartering with the other islanders for parts and labor

"Martin's simple, poetic text deftly balances small, revealing details about the island's characters and Carl's life with the particulars of boat building. . . . The illustrations . . . capture the lake's translucent light and the story's nostalgic mood in expert, geometric line drawings washed with watery blue-green and sunset-orange colors." Booklist

Martin, Rafe

Will's mammoth; illustrated by Stephen Gammell. Putnam 1989 un il $16.99

Grades: K 1 2 3   **E**
1. Mammoths -- Fiction
ISBN 0-399-21627-8

LC 88-11651

"Gammell's depiction of a child's rich imagination is illustrated in vivid colors. The fantasy spreads use winter whites and blues as background for subtly individualized animals who move energetically across the pages." Booklist

Martin, Ruth

Moon dreams; illustrated by Olivier Latyk. Templar Books 2010 un il $15.99
Grades: PreK K 1   **E**
1. Day -- Fiction 2. Night -- Fiction 3. Dreams -- Fiction
ISBN 978-0-7636-5012-4; 0-7636-5012-9

LC 2010003808

Published in the United Kingdom with title: Where on earth is the moon?

Luna, who loves to look at the moon, wonders where it goes during the day.

"Latyk's lush artwork, well-executed and incredibly tasteful, is a visual treat. Composed of graphic shapes in a retro-cool style, the digital illustrations flow with Martin's words as the story progresses. . . . A lovely, slumberous story." Kirkus

Martin, Steve

The **alphabet** from A to Y with bonus letter, Z! by Steve Martin & [illustrated by] Roz Chast. Doubleday/Flying Dolphin Press 2007 un il $17.95; lib bdg $17.95
Grades: K 1 2 3   **E**
1. Alphabet 2. Stories in rhyme
ISBN 978-0-385-51662-4; 978-0-385-52377-6 lib bdg

LC 2006102543

Presents a rhyming couplet featuring each letter of the alphabet, with such characters as David the dog-faced boy, who dons a derby despite being dirty, and Victor, whose frequent victories have made him vainglorious

"Martin and Chast show their mettle as each other's wacky sidekicks. . . . [A] peculiar and funny book." Publ Wkly

Martins, Isabel Minhós

My neighbor is a dog; Isabel Minhos Martins. Owlkids Books 2013 32 p. $16.95
Grades: K 1 2   **E**
1. Dogs -- Juvenile fiction 2. Picture books for children
ISBN 1926973682; 9781926973685

LC 2012943001

In this children's picture book, apartment building residents "are shocked when a blue dog moves into a vacant apartment. 'My parents thought it was very strange to have a dog as a neighbor,' says the young narrator. 'They said he would leave his hair all over the place . . .' (Meanwhile, the dog's habits actually involve reading the newspaper and playing saxophone.) Additional animals move in, but while the girl befriends them, her parents are having none of it." (Publishers Weekly)

"Stylish and understated, this argument for tolerance is a welcome one." Kirkus

Marzollo, Jean

Help me learn numbers 0-20; photographs by Chad Phillips. Holiday House 2011 un il $15.95

Grades: PreK K   E

1. Numbers 2. Counting

ISBN 978-0-8234-2334-7; 0-8234-2334-4

LC 2010029892

"Marzollo and Phillips team up for an idiosyncratic and eye-catching counting book featuring photographic compositions of miscellaneous objects including vintage toy cars, Dalmatian figurines, and rubber finger-puppet monsters. In one spread, 10 glass animals are clustered atop white steps, while the verse hints at the answer. . . . The playful displays suggest that number sense isn't just a classroom tool, but a way in which to explore and engage with one's environment." Publ Wkly

Ten little Christmas presents. Scholastic 2008 un il pa $9.99

Grades: PreK K   E

1. Counting 2. Stories in rhyme 3. Gifts -- Fiction 4. Animals -- Fiction 5. Christmas -- Fiction 6. Santa Claus -- Fiction

ISBN 978-0-545-02791-5 pa; 0-545-02791-8 pa

LC 2007-21572

A counting-down book in which ten forest animals find unexpected Christmas presents, left for them by a Secret Santa

"Toddlers will like the simple, rhyming story and the sketchy, childlike illustrations, and preschoolers will like the reverse counting game. Teachers and librarians will find this a good fit for story hours about counting or Christmas presents." Kirkus

Mason, Margaret H.

These hands. Houghton Mifflin Harcourt 2011 un il $16.99

Grades: PreK K 1 2 3   E

1. Hand -- Fiction 2. Grandfathers -- Fiction 3. African Americans -- Fiction 4. African Americans -- Civil rights -- Fiction

ISBN 978-0-547-21566-2; 0-547-21566-5

LC 2010006782

"Cooper's signature style of softly blurred illustrations in sepia shades shows the bonds in a loving family. . . . The story's roots in rarely told history will widen the audience of this moving title to older readers, too." Booklist

Mathers, Petra

★ **Lottie's** new beach towel. Atheneum Bks. for Young Readers 1998 un il hardcover o.p. pa $6.99

Grades: PreK K 1 2   E

1. Towels -- Fiction 2. Beaches -- Fiction 3. Chickens -- Fiction

ISBN 0-689-81606-5; 0-689-84441-7 pa

LC 97-6689

Lottie the chicken has a number of adventures at the beach, during which her new towel, a gift from her friend Herbie the duck, comes in handy.

"Pure fun, with a resourceful, big-hearted main character; humor in both text and pictures; and a good story, elegantly shaped." Horn Book

Other titles about Lottie and Herbie are:

A cake for Herbie (2000)

Herbie's secret Santa (2002)

Lottie's new friend (1999)

Matsuoka, Mei

★ **Footprints** in the snow. Henry Holt & Co. 2008 un il $16.95

Grades: PreK K 1 2 3   E

1. Wolves -- Fiction 2. Storytelling -- Fiction

ISBN 978-0-8050-8792-5; 0-8050-8792-3

Wolf is feeling offended and indignant: All the wolves he's ever read about are nasty, scary, and greedy! To set the record straight he decides to write a story about a nice wolf. But will his wolfish instincts get the better of him after all?

"Both plot and pictures . . . take a surprising turn, which will delight young readers. Replete with visual allusions to popular wold stories, the folk-art style illustrations set up the scenario for this story-within-stories." Booklist

Matthews, Tina

Out of the egg. Houghton Mifflin 2007 un il $12.95

Grades: K 1 2 3   E

1. Animals -- Fiction 2. Chickens -- Fiction

ISBN 978-0-618-73741-3; 0-618-73741-3

LC 2006-09812

When the barnyard animals who refused to help her plant and tend a seed ask to play under the "great green whispery tree" that Little Red Hen grew, she says no, but her chick thinks that answer is mean.

"This gritty, sharply graphic woodcut version of the time-honored tale sets our feathered friend and her slothful sidekicks squarely in the present. . . . Matthews's hand-painted Japanese woodblock illustrations, black and white and red all over—with, of course, an important touch of green—are striking editorial panoramas." SLJ

Matthies, Janna

★ **The Goodbye** Cancer garden; illustrated by Kristi Valiant. Albert Whitman 2011 un il $16.99

Grades: K 1 2 3   E

1. Cancer -- Fiction 2. Gardens -- Fiction 3. Gardening -- Fiction 4. Family life -- Fiction

ISBN 978-0-8075-2994-2; 0-8075-2994-X

LC 2010024069

When a mother is diagnosed with breast cancer, she and her family plant a garden and watch it grow through the seasons as she undergoes treatments and gets better.

"Smoothly told in a reassuringly matter-of-fact and understated way. . . . Details about the treatment and the woman's physical reactions to it are worked in unobtrusively. . . . Realistic emotions like her general sadness or Janie's brother's dismay at his mom's baldness are included, but are downplayed. The sketchy illustrations are tender and sweet. . . . An uplifting, hopeful story, well told and beautifully illustrated." SLJ

Mayer, Mercer

★ **A boy,** a dog, and a frog. Dial Bks. for Young Readers 1967 un il hardcover o.p. $6.99

Grades: PreK K 1   E

1. Stories without words 2. Frogs -- Fiction

ISBN 0-8037-2880-8

"Without the need for a single word, humorous, very engaging pictures tell the story of a little boy who sets forth with his dog and a net on a summer day to catch an enterprising and personable frog. Even very young preschoolers will 'read' the tiny book with the greatest satisfaction and pleasure." Horn Book

Other titles in this series are:

A boy, a dog, a frog, and a friend (1971)
Frog goes to dinner (1974)
Frog on his own (1973)
Frog, where are you? (1969)
One frog too many (1975)

Octopus soup. Marshall Cavendish Children 2011 un il $16.99

Grades: PreK K 1 2   E

1. Stories without words 2. Animals -- Fiction 3. Octopuses -- Fiction
ISBN 978-0-7614-5812-8; 0-7614-5812-3
                                                  LC 2010021232

An octopus struggles with misadventure when he leaves home but is relieved to know how and where to find a safe haven.

"The artist's signature cartoons are colorful, whimsical, and entertaining. Mayer continues to enchant." SLJ

★ **There's** a nightmare in my closet. Dial Bks. for Young Readers 1968 un il $16.99; pa $6.99

Grades: PreK K 1   E

1. Fear -- Fiction
ISBN 0-8037-8682-4; 0-14-054712-6 pa

"Childhood fear of the dark and the resulting exercise in imaginative exaggeration are given that special Mercer Mayer treatment in this dryly humorous fantasy. Young children will easily empathize with the boy and can be comforted by his experience." SLJ

Another title about this boy is:

There's an alligator under my bed (1987)

Too many dinosaurs. Holiday House 2011 un il $16.95

Grades: PreK K 1   E

1. Pets -- Fiction 2. Dinosaurs -- Fiction
ISBN 978-0-8234-2316-3; 0-8234-2316-6
                                                  LC 2010029442

A little boy really wants a dog, but instead he gets dinosaurs!

"Mayer's colloquial text and unmistakable illustrative style are both present here. The illustrations are full-page or cutouts surrounded by white space and done in rich colors. The text is placed in and around them to good effect. Plenty of background details spice up the very funny scenes for observant readers, and wild action and chases abound." SLJ

The **bravest** knight; story and pictures by Mercer Mayer. Dial Books for Young Readers 2007 un il $16.99

Grades: PreK K 1 2   E

1. Play -- Fiction 2. Knights and knighthood -- Fiction
ISBN 978-0-8037-3206-3
                                                  LC 2006021321

First published 1968 by Dial Press with title: Terrible Troll

A little boy imagines the adventures he would have if he lived a thousand years ago and was the squire of a bold knight who fought dragons and trolls.

"Funny details abound in every picture. . . . This fresh version of an old favorite should find a place in all picture-book collections." SLJ

Mayo, Margaret

Choo choo clickety-clack! written by Margaret Mayo; illustrated by Alex Ayliffe. Carolrhoda Books 2005 un il lib bdg $14.95

Grades: PreK K   E

1. Noise -- Fiction 2. Transportation -- Fiction
ISBN 1-57505-819-7
                                                  LC 2004-11976

First published 2004 in the United Kingdom

Rhythmic sounds imitate trains, planes, and other busy transports that come and go

"Short and snappy, four lines of text encapsulate the excitement that comes with getting in a car, sailing on a lake, or floating in a hot-air balloon. The graphic-style artwork is executed in a melange of pure colors." Booklist

Roar! [by] Margaret Mayo & [illustrated by] Alex Ayliffe. Carolrhoda Books 2007 un il lib bdg $15.95

Grades: PreK K 1   E

1. Animals -- Fiction
ISBN 978-0-7613-9473-0
                                                  LC 2006029853

First published 2006 in the United Kingdom

Text and pictures describe the things which different kinds of animals like to do

"The creatures each get a spread with a rhythmic, fun-to-read narrative. . . . The malleable lines of type stretch with the giraffes, wave with the hippos, and jump with the kangaroos. Ayliffe's illustrations have bright, bold colors and simple, but effective depictions of the animals and landscapes that fairly leap off the pages." SLJ

Zoom, rocket, zoom! by Margaret Mayo; illustrated by Alex Ayliffe. Walker Books for Young Readers 2012 32 p. $16.99

Grades: PreK K 1 2   E

1. Stories in rhyme 2. Outer space -- Exploration 3. Astronauts -- Juvenile literature 4. Space vehicles -- Juvenile literature 5. Astronauts -- Fiction 6. Space vehicles -- Fiction
ISBN 0802727905; 9780802727909; 9780802727916
                                                  LC 2011024959

This children's picture book by Margaret Mayo "introduces youngsters to the jobs various space vehicles do and to the astronauts that explore outer space. . . . Lunar modules and moon buggies allow them to explore the moon. And space stations are a home away from home for astronauts who need to work in space. Mayo also devotes pages to unmanned space vehicles, including satellites, robotic spacecraft and rovers, all the while explaining in simple language what each does." (Kirkus Reviews)

Mayr, Diane

Run, Turkey run; [by] Diane Mayr; illustrated by Laura Rader. Walker Pub. Co. 2007 un il $15.95; lib bdg $16.85

Grades: PreK K 1 2   E

1. Turkeys -- Fiction 2. Thanksgiving Day -- Fiction
ISBN 978-0-8027-9630-1; 0-8027-9630-3; 978-0-8027-9631-8 lib bdg; 0-8027-9631-1 lib bdg
                                                  LC 2006036190

The day before Thanksgiving, Turkey tries to disguise himself as other animals in order to avoid being caught by the farmer.

"This fast-paced romp is as much fun to read as it is to listen to. . . . The illustrations are light and humorous." SLJ

Mazer, Norma Fox

Has anyone seen my Emily Greene? [by] Norma Fox Mazer; illustrated by Christine Davenier. Candlewick Press 2007 un il $15.99

Grades: PreK K 1 2   E

1. Stories in rhyme 2. Play -- Fiction 3. Father-daughter relationship -- Fiction

ISBN 978-0-7636-1384-6; 0-7636-1384-3

LC 2006051828

Emily decides to play hide and seek when her father calls her for lunch

This is a "picture-book romp that reads with the hand-clapping, foot-stomping rhythm of a rowdy folk song and includes lots of sound effects that kids will want to shout out loud. Davenier's sweeping ink lines, dabbed with watercolors, match the energy in the rhyming words." Booklist

McAlister, Caroline

Brave Donatella and the Jasmine thief; illustrated by Donald Hendricks. Charlesbridge 2010 un il $16.95

Grades: 1 2 3   E

1. Princes 2. Love -- Fiction 3. Middle Ages -- Fiction

ISBN 978-1-57091-729-5; 1-57091-729-9

In sixteenth-century Florence, in what would become Italy, Antonio and Donatella flee the wrath of Duke Cosimo de Medici from whom Antonio has stolen a sprig of jasmine, and they use that rare plant to make a fresh start. Includes facts about the duke and Italian history.

"The illustrations have a soft quality to them and fit the time period perfectly. . . . This story could be used in a world history class for older students, as well as in a class studying legends around the world. And of course, it can be read aloud to younger students." Libr Media Connect

McAllister, Angela

Little Mist; illustrated by Sarah Fox-Davies. Alfred A. Knopf 2011 un il $16.99; lib bdg $19.99

Grades: PreK K 1   E

1. Snow leopard -- Fiction

ISBN 978-0-375-86788-0; 0-375-86788-0; 978-0-375-96788-7 lib bdg; 0-375-96788-5 lib bdg

LC 2010-28822

Little Mist, a young snow leopard, is filled with wonder when his mother introduces him to the world for the first time.

"Young readers will be lulled by the incantatory quality of the text and drawn to the snow leopards, who look as friendly and welcoming as they do dignified." SLJ

My mom has x-ray vision; illustrated by Alex T. Smith. Tiger Tales 2011 un il $15.95; pa $7.95

Grades: PreK K 1 2   E

1. Mothers -- Fiction 2. Superheroes -- Fiction

ISBN 978-1-58925-097-0; 1-58925-097-0; 978-1-58925-428-2 pa; 1-58925-428-7 pa

"Matthew is certain that his mother has superhuman abilities. She might have 'ordinary hair, ordinary clothes, and a nice smile,' but she also seems to have x-ray vision.

So Matthew decides to test his hypothesis. He disobeys her request to bring in the groceries and hides in a closet, waiting to see if she knows where he is. . . . Matthew's logical thought processes pull youngsters along through bright full-page cartoons with visual details like the dragon in his fantasies or a superhero costume hanging on the clothesline while font changes add emphasis. . . . Young readers will recognize this puzzled child's analysis of an age-old mystery." SLJ

Yuck! That's not a monster! illustrated by Alison Edgson. Good Books 2010 un il $16.99

Grades: PreK K   E

1. Monsters -- Fiction 2. Parent-child relationship -- Fiction

ISBN 978-1-56148-683-0; 1-56148-683-3

LC 2009-33696

As Mr. and Mrs. Monster's three eggs begin to hatch, they happily welcome the first two ugly little monsters to come out, but are shocked and disappointed when they see what pops out of their last egg.

"The large format and brightly colored cartoons lend themselves well to group sharing. Edgson's monsters are like plush toys with coy expressions, more funny than fierce. McAllister offers fresh descriptions touched with humor." SLJ

McBratney, Sam

★ **Guess** how much I love you; illustrated by Anita Jeram; paper engineering by Corina Fletcher. pop-up edition; Candlewick Press 2011 un il $19.99

Grades: PreK K   E

1. Pop-up books 2. Love -- Fiction 3. Rabbits -- Fiction

ISBN 978-0-7636-5378-1; 0-7636-5378-0

First published 1995

During a bedtime game, every time Little Nutbrown Hare demonstrates how much he loves his father, Big Nutbrown Hare gently shows him that the love is returned even more

"It's hard to believe that a pop-up wasn't the creators' original intention, so seamlessly do moveable parts dovetail into this modern classic's storyline. . . . The figures here move on every page, and with an unusually graceful naturalism to boot. . . . All of Little Nutbrown Hare's hops, stretches and small gestures serve the poetically spare text. . . . The book is available in just about every format—but this is the perfect one." Kirkus

When I'm big; illustrated by Anita Jeram. Candlewick 2007 un il bd bk $7.99

Grades: PreK   E

1. Board books for children 2. Growth -- Fiction 3. Rabbits -- Fiction

ISBN 978-0-7636-3546-6 bd bk

Little Nutbrown Hare loves playing in the spring, when everything is growing and changing, but what will a little brown hare grow into?

"Jeram's sunny ink-and-watercolor illustrations—sprightly spot art and spreads—offer subtle yet solid reinforcement of the text." Publ Wkly

McCall, Bruce

Marveltown. Farrar, Straus and Giroux 2008 un il $16.95

Grades: PreK K 1 2   E

1. Science fiction 2. Robots -- Fiction 3. Inventions

-- Fiction

ISBN 978-0-374-39925-2; 0-374-39925-5

LC 2006-38250

Marveltown's adults are outstanding inventors, but when their best engineers create giant but stupid robots that threaten the town, it is the children's outrageous creations that save the day.

"The boldly colored, nostalgic-looking illustrations depict the action with detail, vitality, and humor and will easily grab readers' attention." SLJ

McCarthy, Mary

★ A **closer** look. Greenwillow Books 2007 un il $16.99; lib bdg $17.89

Grades: PreK K 1 2   E

1. Nature -- Fiction 2. Visual perception -- Juvenile literature

ISBN 978-0-06-124073-7; 0-06-124073-7; 978-0-06-124074-4 lib bdg; 0-06-124074-5 lib bdg

LC 2006-29459

Detailed collage illustrations accompanied by simple text present expanding views of familiar objects in nature, such as a bug and a flower.

"Rendered from handmade papers and collage, the bold artwork is elegant and eye-catching. The broad lines, simple graphic images, and textured details suit the magnified perspectives, while the more expansive scenes are beautifully composed." SLJ

McCarthy, Meghan

Daredevil; by Meghan McCarthy. 1st ed. Simon & Schuster Books for Young Readers 2013 48 p. col. ill. (reinforced) $16.99

Grades: K 1 2   E

1. Women air pilots 2. Skelton, Betty, 1926-2011 3. Air pilots -- United States -- Biography -- Juvenile literature 4. Women air pilots -- United States -- Biography -- Juvenile literature 5. Automobile racing drivers -- United States -- Biography -- Juvenile literature 6. Women automobile racing drivers -- United States -- Biography -- Juvenile literature

ISBN 1442422629; 9781442422629

LC 2012023603

This biographical "portrait of Betty June Skelton (1926-2011) reveals a woman who embodies a 'need for speed.'. . . She was obsessed with flying from an early age, and she made the newspapers for a solo flight on her 16th birthday--never mind that her father had already plopped her into a cockpit four years earlier. . . . Skelton went on to break records on land, sea, and air, and she even had a shot at becoming the first woman in space." (Publishers Weekly)

McCarty, Peter

Chloe; Peter McCarty. Balzer + Bray 2012 40 p.

Grades: PreK K   E

1. Play -- Fiction 2. Rabbits -- Fiction 3. Siblings -- Fiction 4. Television -- Fiction 5. Family life -- Fiction 6. Brothers and sisters -- Fiction

ISBN 0061142913; 9780061142918; 9780061142925

LC 2011019346

In this picture book, a bunny tries to get her siblings to "put on a monster show in a big, cardboard box or pop bubble wrap at rapid-fire speed. After a new television ruins "family fun time," Chloe, the middle bunny in a brood of 21,

tries to pull her brothers and sisters from its glowing grip. . . . [Author Peter] McCarty says simply and directly to middle children everywhere, "Chloe was in the middle." . . . A bustling dinner scene shows the family nibbling on every kind of spring veggie. . . . Fashion (eyeglasses, dresses, shirts) and minute tweaks in expression individualize each rabbit. . . . McCarty captures the tensile ties strung among siblings, parents, genders and ages in every household." (Kirkus)

★ **Henry** in love. Balzer & Bray 2009 un il $16.99; lib bdg $17.89

Grades: PreK K 1   E

1. School stories 2. Cats -- Fiction 3. Love -- Fiction 4. Rabbits -- Fiction

ISBN 978-0-06-114288-8; 0-06-114288-3; 978-0-06-114289-5 lib bdg; 0-06-114289-1 lib bdg

LC 2009-14412

On the first day of school, Henry the cat vies for the attention of the most amazing girl in class, Chloe Rabbit.

"This gentle, pitch-perfect romance will have readers hearts thumping with the thrill of first love." Publ Wkly

★ **Hondo** and Fabian. Holt & Co. 2002 un il $16.95 pa $6.95

Grades: PreK K 1 2

1. Cats -- Fiction 2. Dogs -- Fiction

ISBN 0-8050-6352-8; 0-312-36747-3 pa

LC 2001-188

A Caldecott Medal honor book, 2003

Hondo the dog gets to go to the beach and play with h friend Fred, while Fabian the cat spends the day at home

"McCarty's staccato text, one line to a page, captures lot of action in a few words, but it is the pencil-on-wate color-paper art that makes this so arresting. Each careful shaded picture, in muted tones, has a smooth, solid look Booklist

Another title about Hondo and Fabian is:

Fabian escapes (2007)

Jeremy draws a monster. Henry Holt 2009 un $16.99 E

1. Drawing -- Fiction 2. Monsters -- Fiction

ISBN 978-0-8050-6934-1; 0-8050-6934-8

LC 2008-3681

A young boy who spends most of his time alone in hi bedroom makes new friends after the monster in his drawing becomes a monstrous nuisance.

"The finely rendered pen-and-ink and watercolor illustrations skillfully delineate characters and objects. . . . [This is] top-notch." Booklist

★ **Moon** plane; written and illustrated by Peter McCarty. Henry Holt 2006 un il $16.95

Grades: PreK K   E

1. Flight -- Fiction 2. Airplanes -- Fiction

ISBN 978-0-8050-7943-2; 0-8050-7943-2

LC 2005016244

A young boy looks at a plane in the sky and imagines flying one all the way to the moon

"Using pencils, McCarty creates soft-edged, silvertone artwork notable for its elegant simplicity. . . . McCarty catches both the way children's imaginations work and the connections they make." Booklist

T is for terrible; written and illustrated by Peter Mc-Carty. Henry Holt 2004 un il $15.95; pa $6.99

Grades: PreK K 1   E

1. Dinosaurs -- Fiction

ISBN 0-8050-7404-X; 0-312-38423-8 pa

LC 2003-18246

A tyrannosaurus rex explains that he cannot help it that he is enormous and hungry and is not a vegetarian.

"Filled with textured lines and soft shading, the artwork glows with warmth and vitality. This beautifully formatted and well-conceived offering has creamy ivory pages that frame the subtle illustrations and spare text." SLJ

McClatchy, Lisa

Dear Tyrannosaurus Rex; illustrated by John Manders. Random House 2010 un il $16.99; lib bdg $19.99

Grades: PreK K 1 2   E

1. Parties -- Fiction 2. Birthdays -- Fiction 3. Dinosaurs -- Fiction

ISBN 978-0-375-85608-2; 0-375-85608-0; 978-0-375-95608-9 lib bdg; 0-375-95608-5 lib bdg

LC 2009005038

Enamored of dinosaurs, Erin writes a letter inviting a real one to her sixth birthday party.

"Enthusiastic descriptions of games, treats, the cake, party favors, etc., are accompanied by large cartoonlike illustrations featuring the T. rex as if he were in attendance. Each spread is filled with humor. . . . Perfect for reading aloud." SLJ

McClements, George

★ **Dinosaur** Woods; can seven clever critters save their forest home? Beach Lane Books 2009 un il $16.99

Grades: PreK K 1 2   E

1. Animals -- Fiction 2. Dinosaurs -- Fiction 3. Endangered species -- Fiction 4. Environmental protection -- Fiction

ISBN 978-1-4169-8626-3; 1-4169-8626-X

LC 2008-33084

To save their homes from being destroyed by developers, a fanciful group of endangered animals constructs a fearsome dinosaur.

"This title's generous trim size, cleanly rendered illustrations, and fast-paced text are perfect for group read-alouds or one-on-one sharing." SLJ

Night of the Veggie Monster. Bloomsbury Children's Books 2008 un il $14.95; lib bdg $15.85

Grades: K 1 2 3   E

1. Food -- Fiction 2. Family life -- Fiction

ISBN 978-1-59990-061-2; 1-59990-061-0; 978-1-59990-234-0 lib bdg; 1-59990-234-6 lib bdg

LC 2007017850

Every Tuesday night, while his parents try to enjoy their dinner, a boy turns into a monster the moment a pea touches his lips

"Illustrations are a creative medley of photographed realia . . . cut-out brown paper . . . and simple pastel lines and textural elements, . . . resulting in a spare vigor that nicely supports the textual humor." Bull Cent Child Books

Ridin' dinos with Buck Bronco; as told to George Mc-Clements. Harcourt 2007 un il $16

Grades: PreK K 1 2   E

1. Cowhands -- Fiction 2. Dinosaurs -- Fiction

ISBN 978-0-15-205989-7

LC 2006006175

Buck Bronco teaches how to care for and ride a variety of strange dinosaurs.

"Bright, goofy mixed-media collage illustrations demonstrate the cowboy's instructions and will have dinosaur fans chuckling." SLJ

McClintock, Barbara

★ **Adele** & Simon. Farrar, Straus & Giroux 2006 un il $16

Grades: PreK K 1 2   E

1. Siblings -- Fiction 2. Lost and found possessions -- Fiction

ISBN 0-374-38044-9

LC 2002-35311

When Adele walks her little brother Simon home from school he loses one more thing at every stop: his drawing of a cat at the grocer's shop, his books at the park, his crayons at the art museum, and more.

"Set in Paris during the early 20th century, this simple story is the basis for some remarkable illustrations. McClintock's pen-and-ink with watercolor technique has the feel of illustrated children's books from that period. . . . A beautiful example of bookmaking, with plenty to charm children, this is a visual delight." SLJ

Another title about Adele and Simon is:

Adele & Simon in America (2008)

★ **Dahlia.** Farrar, Straus & Giroux 2002 un il $16

Grades: PreK K 1   E

1. Dolls -- Fiction

ISBN 0-374-31678-3

LC 2001-18778

"Charlotte doesn't want a doll for a playmate. . . . She prefers to climb trees, make mud pies, and dig in the dirt. When her Aunt Edme sends her a doll that's dressed in lace, ribbons, and gloves, Charlotte wrinkles her nose and informs the doll that there will be no tea parties or riding in 'frilly prams!' . . . McClintock tells an engaging story about an unusual character. . . . In her trademark delicate pen-and-ink outline art—filled with soft watercolors—McClintock delightfully juxtaposes spirited Charlotte within the old-fashioned setting." Booklist

McCloskey, Robert, 1914-2003

★ **Blueberries** for Sal. Viking 1948 54p il $16.99; pa $7.99

Grades: PreK K 1 2   E

1. Bears -- Fiction

ISBN 0-670-17591-9; 0-14-050169-X pa

A Caldecott Medal honor book, 1949

"The author-artist tells what happens on a summer day in Maine when a little girl and a bear cub, wandering away from their blueberry-picking mothers, each mistakes the other's mother for its own. The Maine hillside and meadows are real and lovely, the quiet humor is entirely childlike, and there is just exactly the right amount of suspense for small children." Wis Libr Bull

Another title about Sal is:

One morning in Maine (1952)

Lentil. Viking 1940 un il $18.99; pa $5.99

Grades: PreK K 1 2   E

1. Harmonicas -- Fiction

ISBN 0-670-42357-2; 0-14-050287-4 pa

Picture-story book about a small boy who could not sing, but who could work wonders on a simple harmonica, especially on the day when the great Colonel Carter returned to his home town

"Big, vigorous, amusing pictures in black-and-white, with an Ohio small-town background." New Yorker

★ **Make** way for ducklings. Viking 1941 un il $17.99; pa $7.99

Grades: PreK K 1 2   E

1. Ducks -- Fiction

ISBN 0-670-45149-5; 0-14-056434-9 pa

Awarded the Caldecott Medal, 1942

"There are some very beautiful drawings in this book." Horn Book

★ **Time** of wonder. Viking 1957 63p il $18.99; pa $6.99

Grades: K 1 2 3   E

ISBN 0-670-71512-3; 0-14-050201-7 pa

Awarded the Caldecott Medal, 1958

"A summer on an island in Maine is described through the simple everyday experiences of children, but also reveals the author's deep awareness of an attachment to all the shifting moods of season and weather, and the salty, downright character of the New England people." Top News

McClure, Nikki

Apple; Nikki McClure. Abrams Appleseed 2012 40 p. $12.95

Grades: PreK K 1   E

1. Apples 2. Plants -- Growth 3. Picture books for children

ISBN 9781419703782

LC 2011052130

This picture book by cut-paper artist Nikki McClure "follows the life of an apple throughout the year, demonstrating the cyclical patterns in nature. . . . [R]eaders will . . . follow[. . .] the journey of the bright red apple—the only splash of color in the otherwise black-and-white illustrations—as it travels from tree, to harvest, to snack, to compost, and finally to sprout. A single word complements each illustration, urging early readers to reflect on each stage in the apple's life." (Amazon.com)

How to be a cat; Nikki McClure. Abrams Books for Young Readers 2013 40 p. $16.95

Grades: PreK K 1   E

1. Cats 2. Picture books for children 3. Cats -- Fiction 4. Animals -- Infancy -- Fiction

ISBN 1419705288; 9781419705281

LC 2012021633

This children's picture book from Nikki McClure includes cut-paper illustrations that "show nothing more than cats being cats, with a single word describing each of their actions." Words illustrated include "stretch," "wait," "find," "feast," and "dream." (Publishers Weekly)

Mama, is it summer yet? Abrams Books for Young Readers 2010 un il $17.95

Grades: PreK K 1   E

1. Summer -- Fiction 2. Mother-son relationship -- Fiction

ISBN 978-0-8109-8468-4; 0-8109-8468-7

"Repetition of this book's title question ties together responses and scenes of a child and his mother as they wait for warmer weather. . . . The days pass with a graceful swirl as the most delicate of paper-cuts detail budding trees, squirrels nesting, soft earth for seedlings, young ducklings following their mother, swallows circling overhead, and blossoming trees, culminating in the anticipated delight of summer berries. . . . Simple black paper contrasts with a light, neutral background, highlighting spare use of digitally added color accents; solid-color sheets underscore the repeated text. . . . Children will appreciate the simple sentences and lyrical verse that relate the seasonal passing of time." SLJ

McCourt, Frank

Angela and the baby Jesus; illustrated by Raúl Colón. Simon & Schuster Books for Young Readers 2007 un il $17.99

Grades: K 1 2 3   E

1. Christmas -- Fiction 2. Christmas stories -- Juvenile literature

ISBN 978-1-4169-3789-0; 1-4169-3789-7

"The six-year-old heroine is McCourt's mother, Angela, who is disturbed that the Baby Jesus must be cold as he lies outside in a Nativity scene. . . . Angela steals the baby so she get hime home and warm him in her bed. . . . McCourt writes with the lilt of the Irish and the ability to get inside a child's mind. . . . Painted with a glow that comes from street lamps or candlelight, Colon's artwork showcases the warmth that a caring family radiates." Booklist

McCue, Lisa

Quiet Bunny. Sterling 2009 un il $14.95

Grades: PreK K   E

1. Sounds -- Fiction 2. Rabbits -- Fiction

ISBN 978-1-4027-5719-8; 1-4027-5719-0

LC 2008-32903

Quiet Rabbit enjoys listening to the night song of the other animals every evening and wishes he could join them, but no matter how hard he tries he is unable to copy their sounds.

"The text is full of onomatopoeic words, often incorporated into the illustrations, creating a pleasing link between story and picture." SLJ

Other titles about Quiet Bunny are:

Quiet Bunny's many colors (2011)

Quiet Bunny & Noisy Puppy (2011)

McCully, Emily Arnold

★ **Beautiful** warrior; the legend of the nun's kung fu. Levine Bks. 1998 un il $18.95

Grades: 1 2 3 4   E

1. Kung fu -- Fiction 2. Sex role -- Fiction 3. Martial arts -- Fiction

ISBN 0-590-37487-7

LC 97-3823

"Born near the end of the Ming Dynasty, a girl grows up to become a fighting nun, renowned for her martial arts. Later, when a timid village girl asks for help in deterring her loutish husband-to-be, the nun teaches her kung fu so she can save herself. The story is intriguing, and the watercolors . . . are filled with dramatic motion." Horn Book Guide

The **bobbin** girl. Dial Bks. for Young Readers 1996 un il $15.99

Grades: 3 4 5   E

   1. Strikes -- Fiction 2. Factories -- Fiction ISBN 0-8037-1827-6

LC 95-6997

Rebecca, a ten-year-old bobbin girl working in a textile mill in Lowell, Massachusetts, in the 1830s, must make a difficult decision—will she participate in the first workers' strike in Lowell?

"McCully weaves historical facts and fictional characters into an intriguing story. The author's note details the background, incidents, and people who inspired the book. Beautifully composed watercolor paintings give a vivid impression of America in the 1830s and bring the period to life." Booklist

★ **First** snow. HarperCollins Publishers 2004 un il $15.99

Grades: PreK K   E

   1. Mice 2. Snow 3. Sledding 4. Grandparents ISBN 0-06-623852-8

LC 2003-44971

A timid little mouse discovers the thrill of sledding in the first snow of the winter.

"First published as a wordless picture book in 1985, First Snow is back with a brief text, enhanced illustrations, and a larger trim size. . . . This new edition has brighter, deeper colors. . . . Full of exuberance and excitement." SLJ

   Other titles about this young mouse are:

   Picnic (2003)

   School (2005)

★ The **grandma** mix-up; story and pictures by Emily Arnold McCully. Harper & Row 1988 63p il (I can read book) hardcover o.p. pa $5.99

Grades: PreK K 1 2   E

   1. Grandmothers -- Fiction ISBN 0-06-444150-4 pa

LC 87-29378

Young Pip doesn't know what to do when two very different grandmothers come to baby sit, each with her own way of doing things

"McCully's two-color, line-and-wash drawings emphasize the personality differences by consciously flouting stereotypes: Pip's laid-back Grandma Sal has white hair and glasses, while his strict Grandma Nan dresses like a teenager. Choice of words and sentence length will make the sly humor easy for beginning readers to grasp." Booklist

   Other titles about Pip and his grandmothers are:

   Grandmas at bat (1993)

   Grandmas at the lake (1990)

★ **Mirette** on the high wire. Putnam 1992 un il hardcover o.p. pa $6.99

Grades: K 1 2 3   E

   1. Tightrope walking -- Fiction ISBN 0-399-22130-1; 0-698-11443-4 pa

LC 91-36324

Awarded the Caldecott Medal, 1993

Mirette learns tightrope walking from Monsieur Bellini, a guest in her mother's boarding house, not knowing that he is a celebrated tightrope artist who has withdrawn from performing because of fear

"With a rich palette of deep colors, the artist immerses the reader in 19th-century Paris. Colorful theatrical personalities . . . fill the glowing interiors with robust life. And the exterior scenes . . . are filled with the magic of a Paris night when anything can happen. . . . An exuberant and uplifting picture book." N Y Times Book Rev

   Other titles about Mirette and Bellini are:

   Mirette & Bellini cross Niagra Falls (2000)

   Starring Mirette and Bellini (1997)

★ The **secret** cave; discovering Lascaux. Farrar Straus Giroux 2010 un il $16.99

Grades: 1 2 3 4   E

   1. Prehistoric art -- Fiction 2. Cave drawings and paintings -- Fiction

   ISBN 978-0-374-36694-0; 0-374-36694-2

"This mesmerizing look at the discovery of the prehistoric cave paintings of Lascaux invites today's readers to experience the wonder of the event. McCully has written and drawn a stunning fictionalized account based on historical records and interviews. The endpapers entice with the rendering of the maps of the caves, and soft wide watercolor strokes capture the essence of the prehistoric art. . . . The Caldecott winner gets the emotions of the secret decent for buried treasure just right." Kirkus

   Includes bibliographical references

Squirrel and John Muir. Farrar Straus Giroux 2004 un il $16

Grades: K 1 2 3   E

   1. Authors 2. Naturalists 3. Writers on nature 4. Frontier and pioneer life -- California

   ISBN 0-374-33697-0

LC 2003-45511

In the early 1900s, a wild little girl nicknamed Squirrel meets John Muir, later to become a famous naturalist, when he arrives at her parents' hotel in Yosemite Valley seeking work and knowledge about the natural world.

"The afterword explains how this fictionalized retelling of an actual relationship reveals much about the compelling founder of the Sierra Club. . . . McCully's sure watercolors capture the stunning natural beauty of the area and provide a majestic backdrop for the small figure of Squirrel." SLJ

   Includes bibliographical references

★ **Wonder** horse. Henry Holt and Company 2010 un il $16.99

Grades: K 1 2 3   E

   1. Slaves 2. Veterinarians 3. Animal trainers 4. Horses -- Fiction 5. African Americans -- Fiction 6. Horses -- Juvenile literature

   ISBN 978-0-8050-8793-2; 0-8050-8793-1

LC 2009006208

A fictionalized account of Bill "Doc" Key, a former slave who became a veterinarian, trained his horse, Jim Key, to recognize letters and numbers and to perform in skits around the country, and moved the nation toward a belief in treating animals humanely. Includes an author's note.

"McCully's storytelling is as sensitive, engaging, and well paced as her brightly colored, expressive artwork." Booklist

Includes bibliographical references

McDermott, Gerald
  Creation. Dutton Children's Bks. 2003 un il $16.99
Grades: 2 3 4   E
  1. Creation -- Fiction
ISBN 0-525-46905-2
The author's meditation on the creation story based on Genesis I of Hebrew Bible. In it man and woman are created last to be the keepers of all this beauty
  "McDermott casts the story of creation in strong poetic text and sweeping vibrant views. . . . Sumptuous, rhythmic, and mystical, this book is arresting and evocative." SLJ

Papagayo; the mischief maker. written and illustrated by Gerald McDermott. Harcourt Brace Jovanovich 1992 un il hardcover o.p. pa $8
Grades: 2 3 4   E
  1. Parrots -- Fiction
ISBN 0-15-259465-5; 0-15-259464-7 pa
                                          LC 91-40364
A reissue of the title first published 1980 by Windmill Bks. Papagayo, the noisy parrot, helps the night animals save the moon from being eaten up by the moon dog
  "McDermott's original story assumes folktale proportions. . . . Art for the story is striking; deep tropical colors seem intensified by glossy page surfaces, and they nearly vibrate against the intermittent deep-blue backdrop of a night sky." Booklist

McDonald, Megan
  Ant and Honey Bee; a pair of friends at Halloween. illustrated by G. Brian Karas. new ed.; Candlewick Press 2010 44p il $14.99
Grades: K 1 2   E
  1. Ants -- Fiction 2. Bees -- Fiction 3. Costume -- Fiction 4. Halloween -- Fiction 5. Friendship -- Fiction
ISBN 978-0-7636-4662-2; 0-7636-4662-8
                                       LC 2009021485
A new edition of Ant and Honey Bee: what a pair! published 2005
  Best friends Ant and Honey Bee, who think of themselves as quite a pair, become matching home appliances on Halloween.
  "With its open format, large type, judious use of repetition, and plentiful, narrative-laden mixed-media illustrations, this book functions well both as a picture book and an easy reader." Horn Book Guide

Hen hears gossip; illustrated by Joung Un Kim. HarperCollins 2008 un il $17.99; lib bdg $17.89
Grades: PreK K   E
  1. Gossip -- Fiction 2. Animals -- Fiction
ISBN 978-0-06-113876-8; 0-06-113876-2; 978-0-06-113877-5 lib bdg; 0-06-113877-0 lib bdg
                                       LC 2007027137
When Hen overhears some news on the farm, she runs to tell Duck, who tells another animal, and as the gossip is repeated from one animal to the next, it becomes unrecognizable
  "The simple prose incorporates capitals and punctuation that offer guidance for animated read-alouds. The colorful,

mixed-media collages . . . blend bold, blocky shapes with vivid, intricate patterns and textures. Children will enjoy the farcical fun." Booklist

It's picture day today! illustrated by Katherine Tillotson. Atheneum Books for Young Readers 2009 un il $16.99
Grades: PreK K   E
  1. School stories 2. Artists' materials -- Fiction
ISBN 978-1-4169-2434-0; 1-4169-2434-5
                                       LC 2007-46435
A classroom of art supplies gathers for their picture day.
  "Tillotson's collage work, both creative and endearingly clunky, will awaken the inner cutter-and-paster in almost any young child. An ideal book to pair with a craft session." Booklist

McDonnell, Christine
  Dog wants to play; illustrated by Jeff Mack. Viking Children's Books 2009 un il $15.99
Grades: PreK K   E
  1. Dogs -- Fiction 2. Play -- Fiction
ISBN 978-0-670-01126-1; 0-670-01126-6
                                       LC 2009001955
Dog is eager to have fun, but no one in the barnyard will play with him except one special friend.
  "Textured, sun-kissed painted images put bounce into the simple story and capture Dog's realistic body poses." Booklist

  ★ **Goyangi** means cat; Christine McDonnell; pictures Steve Johnson & Lou Fancher. Viking Children's Books 2011 1 v. (unpaged) $16.99
Grades: PreK K 1 2   E
  1. Cats -- Fiction 2. Home -- Fiction 3. Adoption -- Fiction 4. Korean Americans -- Fiction 5. Intercountry adoption -- Fiction
ISBN 978-0-670-01179-7; 0-670-01179-7; 9780670011797
                                       LC 2010043325
An understanding cat helps a young Korean girl named Soo Min adjust to her new home and adopted family in America.
  "Soft-focus collage-and-paint illustrations show the family members getting to know one another. . . . Korean words in hanja (characters) incorporated into the pictures' backgrounds and the presence of Korean words in the Western alphabet interspersed throughout the text make this an excellent choice to share with children like Soo Min. . . . A sensitive portrayal of international adoption, authentically and realistically done." Kirkus

McDonnell, Patrick
  ★ **South**; [by] Patrick McDonnell. Little, Brown and Co. 2008 un il $14.99
Grades: PreK K 1 2   E
  1. Stories without words 2. Cats -- Fiction 3. Birds -- Fiction
ISBN 978-0-316-00509-8; 0-316-00509-6
                                       LC 2007048373
Mooch the cat helps a lonely bird find its flock, which has flown south for the winter
  "McDonnell's comfort with unfilled expanses, his beautifully balanced compositions, and the nature of his brush-

work evoke the feel of traditional Chinese art. Tan recycled paper provides warmth in keeping with this tender, compact story." SLJ

★ The **monsters'** monster; Patrick McDonnell. Little, Brown 2012 40 p. $16.99
Grades: PreK   E
  1. Monsters -- Fiction   2. Conduct of life -- Fiction   3. Behavior -- Fiction
  ISBN 0316045470; 9780316045476
                   LC 2011042742

In this children's picture book by Patrick McDonnell, a National Parenting Publications Award Silver Winner, a trio of monsters "bicker about who is the most impressive monster." When they decide to create "'the biggest, baddest monster EVER!'" they discover that "they cannot change their creation's pleasant nature . . . and learn that respectful, mannerly companionship can lead to fulfilling and sunny results." (Kirkus Reviews)

McElligott, Matthew
  ★ **Bean** thirteen. G. P. Putnam's Sons 2007 un il lib bdg $15.99
Grades: K 1 2 3   E
  1. Insects -- Fiction   2. Division -- Fiction
  ISBN 978-0-399-24535-0 lib bdg; 0-399-24535-9 lib bdg
                   LC 2006-26295

Two bugs, Ralph and Flora, try to divide thirteen beans so that the unlucky thirteenth bean disappears, but they soon discover that the math is not so easy.

"Done in pen and ink with digital effects, the cartoon illustrations feature bright hues and slightly off-kilter perspectives that will appeal to children. Youngsters will undoubtedly enjoy this funny tale; teachers will truly appreciate the connections it makes to their curriculum and the use of manipulatives in math." SLJ

  Even monsters need haircuts. Walker & Co. 2010 un il $16.99
Grades: PreK K 1   E
  1. Monsters -- Fiction   2. Barbers and barbershops -- Fiction
  ISBN 978-0-8027-8819-1; 0-8027-8819-X

At night under a full moon, a child operates a barber shop with a monstrous clientele.

"With the distinctive combination of the freakish and the humdrum, it's a good candidate for the stack of battered bedtime favorites." Publ Wkly

  ★ The **lion's** share; [by] Matt McElligott. Walker & Co. 2009 un il $16.99; lib bdg $17.89
Grades: PreK K 1 2   E
  1. Ants -- Fiction   2. Lions -- Fiction   3. Etiquette -- Fiction   4. Mathematics -- Fiction
  ISBN 978-0-8027-9768-1; 0-8027-9768-7; 978-0-8027-9769-8 lib bdg; 0-8027-9769-5 lib bdg
                   LC 2008013358

Ant is honored to receive an invitation to lion's annual dinner party, but is shocked when the other guests behave rudely and then accuse her of thinking only of herself.

"McElligott's digitally touched ink-and-watercolor artwork combines expressive animal characters with clear groupings of objects that illustrated the embedded arithmetic

exercises. While the story will find an obvious place in early elementary math or character education units, the lively illustrations amplify the story's slapstick humor and will easily entertain story hour crowds." Booklist

McElmurry, Jill
  Mario makes a move; Jill McElmurry. Schwartz & Wade Books 2012 32 p. (glb) $19.99
Grades: K 1   E
  1. Dance -- Fiction   2. Squirrels -- Fiction   3. Picture books for children
  ISBN 0375968547; 9780375868542; 9780375968549
                   LC 2011011014

In this children's picture book, "Mario is a frenetic squirrel whose 'amazing' acrobatic high jinks impress his family but not his . . . friend Isabelle. Not only does she put down his best trick, but she also comes up with a more impressive one of her own and points out that everyone can have special moves. Crushed, Mario abandons his beloved but no longer unique hobby . . . . Isabelle persuades him to return to his spiffy move-making. Teaming up, they teach each other new stunts." (School Library Journal)

McEvoy, Anne
  Betsy B. Little; by Anne McEvoy; illustrated by Jacqueline Rogers. HarperCollinsPublishers 2009 un il $17.99; lib bdg $18.89
Grades: PreK K 1 2   E
  1. Stories in rhyme   2. Size -- Fiction   3. Ballet -- Fiction   4. Giraffes -- Fiction
  ISBN 978-0-06-059337-7; 0-06-059337-7; 978-0-06-059338-4 lib bdg; 0-06-059338-5 lib bdg
                   LC 2008010569

Betsy the giraffe longs to be a ballerina, so when her dance class does not work out, she discovers another way to make her dreams come true

"The rhyming text is fairly smooth and has a satisfying ending. . . . Watercolor illustrations show Betsy's uniqueness and awkwardness with sympathy and wit." SLJ

McGhee, Alison
  Always; illustrated by Pascal Lemaitre. Simon & Schuster Books for Young Readers 2009 un il $15.99
Grades: PreK K 1   E
  1. Dogs -- Fiction
  ISBN 978-1-4169-7481-9; 1-4169-7481-4
                   LC 2008-42624

A loyal dog promises to protect his young mistress and her home from any danger.

"Succinct, funny and, in its way, action-packed, this is written in the universal language of affection—only the stonyhearted could withstand its charms." Publ Wkly

  ★ **Bye**-bye, crib; illustrated by Ross MacDonald. Simon & Schuster Books for Young Readers 2008 un il $16.99
Grades: PreK   E
  1. Beds -- Fiction   2. Growth -- Fiction
  ISBN 978-1-4169-1621-5; 1-4169-1621-0
                   LC 2006-10583

A big boy and his best stuffed friend seek the courage to move to a gigantic new bed.

"MacDonald's evocative art . . . employs the comic-book conventions, visual wit, and pulp-art palette fans know and love, and the animation in both the text and the pictures turns what might have been a ho-hum tale of trepidation into a proactive adventure with a winsome wee hero." SLJ

Little boy; [by] Alison McGhee and [illustrated by] Peter H. Reynolds. Atheneum Books for Young Readers 2008 un il $15.99
Grades: PreK K 1   E
1. Father-son relationship -- Fiction
ISBN 978-1-4169-5872-7; 1-4169-5872-X
LC 2007029625
A father reflects on how the future depends upon the all of the little things in his son's world, from his yellow drinking cup to a big cardboard box
"There is ample white space around the charming pen, ink, and watercolor illustrations. The artwork bursts with energy. . . . The straightforward text, written from the dad's perspective, recounts the simple things that are important to his child." SLJ

Making a friend; illustrated by Marc Rosenthal. Atheneum Books for Young Readers 2011 40p il $16.99
Grades: K 1 2   E
1. Snow -- Fiction 2. Seasons -- Fiction 3. Friendship -- Fiction
ISBN 978-1-4169-8998-1; 1-4169-8998-6
LC 2010041661
When the snow falls, a young boy makes a snowman that becomes his friend until the seasons change
This is written "in minimal but evocative text. . . . This gentle story offers [an] opportunity to discuss the cycle of love, loss, and emotional renewal. The digitally manipulated pencil illustrations have a retro look. . . . A simple but deeply nuanced story that should resonate with children." SLJ

Mrs. Watson wants your teeth; story by Alison McGhee; pictures by Harry Bliss. Harcourt 2004 un il $16; pa $6
Grades: K 1 2 3   E
1. School stories 2. Teeth -- Fiction 3. Teachers -- Fiction
ISBN 0-15-204931-2; 0-15-206348-X pa
LC 2003-21267
A first grader is frightened on her first day of school after hearing a rumor that her teacher is a 300-year-old alien with a purple tongue who steals baby teeth from her students.
"McGhee has the pulse of this blue-ribbon worrier. . . . Bliss's watercolor and black-ink illustrations feature distinctive, large-eyed classmates and a number of humorous toothy references on the walls in the hall and in the classroom." SLJ

★ **Only** a witch can fly; illustrated by Taeeun Yoo. Feiwel and Friends 2009 un il $16.99
Grades: K 1 2   E
1. Stories in rhyme 2. Flight -- Fiction 3. Witches -- Fiction
ISBN 978-0-312-37503-4; 0-312-37503-4
LC 2008-28542
A young girl wants to fly like a witch on a broom, and one special night, through enormous effort and with the help of her brother, her black cat, and an owl, she fulfills her dream.

"Yoo's illustrations are linoleum block prints done in shades of green and brown with black and white details, adding a wonderful simplicity to this beautiful story." Libr Media Connect

So many days; with illustrations by Taeeun Yoo. Atheneum Books for Young Readers 2010 un il $15.99
Grades: PreK K 1   E
1. Conduct of life -- Fiction 2. Parent-child relationship -- Fiction
ISBN 978-1-4169-5857-4; 1-4169-5857-6
LC 2008038300
Through rhythmic text, a parent reflects on the options and opportunities possible in a beloved child's future.
"This book seamlessly pairs lyrical text and digitally manipulated linocut illustrations in a philosophical offering that encourages youngsters to face life head on." SLJ

Song of middle C; illustrated by Scott Menchin. Candlewick Press 2009 un il $16.99
Grades: K 1 2 3   E
1. Fear -- Fiction 2. Pianists -- Fiction
ISBN 978-0-7636-3013-3; 0-7636-3013-6
"One little girl uses imagination, bravado and her lucky underwear to overcome a colossal case of stage fright. She has practiced 'Dance of the Wood Elves' diligently [on the piano]. . . . When she steps confidently onto the stage, however, she totally forgets everything she rehearsed. . . . The only note she can manage is Middle C, so she plays it in several different ways with gusto, verve and true artistry, earning great applause. McGhee . . . employs a first-person narration to tell the story in direct, vivid, fast-paced colloquial language. Menchin's digitally colored pen-and-ink cartoons are remarkably detailed while appearing deceptively simple and childlike." Kirkus

A **very** brave witch; [by] Alison McGhee; [illustrated by] Harry Bliss. Simon & Schuster Books for Young Readers 2006 un il lib bdg $12.95
Grades: PreK K 1 2   E
1. Witches -- Fiction 2. Halloween -- Fiction
ISBN 0-689-86730-1
"A friendly young witch describes what she likes most about Halloween. . . . After boarding her broom, she zooms in a circle, becomes dizzy, and crashes near some trick-or-treaters. She soon discovers that a brave witch and a brave human girl dressed as a witch are not so very different. . . . The chatty text appears in dialogue balloons. Done in black ink and watercolor, the cartoon artwork captures the holiday's spirit with crisp fall colors and amusing details." SLJ

McGinley, Phyllis
A **year** without a Santa Claus; illustrated by John Manders. Marshall Cavendish 2010 un il $16.99
Grades: PreK K 1 2   E
1. Christmas -- Fiction 2. Santa Claus -- Fiction
ISBN 978-0-7614-5799-2; 0-7614-5799-2
A newly illustrated edition of the title first published 1957 by Lippincott
"This newly illustrated edition maintains all of the original's read-aloud charm while accentuating its playfulness with Mander's vibrant gouache and pencil illustrations." Horn Book Guide

McGinness, Suzanne

My bear Griz. Frances Lincoln Children's Books 2011
un il $17.95
Grades: PreK K   E
    1. Bears -- Fiction 2. Teddy bears -- Fiction
    ISBN 978-1-84780-113-5; 1-84780-113-7

Billy has a bear called Griz. A Grizzly Bear. And the two
friends have all kinds of wonderful adventures together. Is
he a real Grizzly Bear or a teddy bear? Well, that's for every
reader to decide.

"A bear of imposing presence provides safety and joy in
this visually distinctive debut. . . . Griz is striking, drawn in
densely hatched and layered pen lines of browns and blacks,
too big to fit on the page yet dominating the space. . . .
Backgrounds are abstract, mellow watercolor, balancing the
energetic lines of Griz's fur. . . . A winner for read-alouds,
whether in groups or one-on-one." Kirkus

Eliza's kindergarten surprise; illustrated by Nancy
Speir. Marshall Cavendish 2007 un il $14.99
Grades: PreK K   E
    1. School stories 2. Mother-daughter relationship --
Fiction
    ISBN 978-0-7614-5351-2; 0-7614-5351-2
                        LC 2006022415

On her first day of school, Eliza fills her pocket with objects—buttons, a pebble, a napkin, and a piece of yarn—that
remind her of her mother, whom she misses very much

"McGinty avoids overly sweet clichés with a strong
concept and smooth telling, and Speir's cartoonlike illustrations balance scenes showing Eliza's anguish with brightly
colored views of a welcoming classroom and pictures of a
loving mother and daughter that reinforce the warm, reassuring words." Booklist

    Another title about Eliza is:
    Eliza's kindergarten pet (2010)

McGowan, Michael

Sunday is for God; illustrated by Lou Fancher and
Steve Johnson. Schwartz & Wade Books 2010 un il
$17.99; lib bdg $20.99
Grades: 1 2 3   E
    1. Church -- Fiction 2. Family life -- Fiction 3. African
Americans -- Fiction 4. Sunday -- Juvenile literature
    ISBN 978-0-375-84188-0; 0-375-84188-1; 978-0-375-
94591-5 lib bdg; 0-375-94591-1 lib bdg
                        LC 2008-48828

"It's Sunday morning and a young African American
boy knows what that means: 'Sunday is for God. That's what
Momma says.' . . . McGowan unleashes a wealth of sensory
details. . . . Johnson and Facher's artwork . . . gets a lift from
its textured mix of acrylic and collage. . . . A tender reflection
of many children's Sunday experience." Booklist

McGrath, Barbara Barbieri

Teddy bear counting; illustrated by Tim Nihoff.
Charlesbridge 2010 il lib bdg $16.95; pa $7.95 E
    1. Color 2. Shape 3. Counting 4. Stories in rhyme 5.
Teddy bears -- Fiction
    ISBN 978-1-58089-215-5 lib bdg; 978-1-58089-216-
2 pa
                        LC 2008025339

Teddy bears introduce numbers from one to twelve, as
well as colors and shapes.

The **little** red elf; illustrated by Rosalinde Bonnet.
Charlesbridge 2009 un il lib bdg $14.95
Grades: PreK K 1   E
    1. Fairies -- Fiction 2. Christmas -- Fiction 3. Folklore
-- Juvenile literature
    ISBN 978-1-58089-236-0; 1-58089-236-1
                        LC 2008-25340

In this version of "The Little Red Hen," set at the North
Pole, a penguin and a hare refuse to help an elf plant, grow,
and decorate an evergreen tree but nevertheless expect to
open the presents found under its branches on Christmas Day.

"The acrylic and ballpoint-pen illustrations are full of
childlike humor, depicting cute North Pole characters who
look like toys themselves. This is that rare beast—an endearing holiday book without a hint of treacle." SLJ

McGrory, Anik

Kidogo; [by] Anik McGrory. Bloomsbury Children's
Books 2005 un il $15.95
Grades: PreK K 1   E
    1. Size -- Fiction 2. Elephants -- Fiction
    ISBN 1-58234-974-6
                        LC 2004-54729

Sure that he is the smallest creature on earth, a young
elephant leaves home and journeys over woodlands, rivers,
and plains searching for someone even smaller than he is

"The poetic text is perfectly matched with pencil-and-
watercolor illustrations that depict a warm and lovely
home." SLJ

    Another title about Kidogo is:
    Quick, slow, mango! (2010)

McGuirk, Leslie

★ **If** rocks could sing. Tricycle Press 2011 un il
$15.99; lib bdg $18.89
Grades: PreK K 1 2   E
    1. Alphabet 2. Rocks -- Fiction
    ISBN 1-58246-370-0; 1-58246-395-6 lib bdg; 978-1-
58246-370-4; 978-1-58246-395-7 lib bdg
                        LC 2010019206

"This unique alphabet book features photos of ocean-
sculpted rocks lovingly collected over the course of a decade by the author. McGuirk amassed a complete alphabet of
letter-shaped rocks, which she pairs with other humorously
representational geologic findings. She puts the emphasis
on the rocks themselves, employing simple text, solid backgrounds, and spare, yet engaging layouts to showcase her
finds. . . . Sure to spark imaginative rock-finding hunts and
found-object art projects, this quirky title will earn its place
in any picture-book collection." SLJ

McKee, David

Elmer and the hippos. Andersen un il $16.95
Grades: PreK K 1 2   E
    1. Hippopotamus -- Fiction
    ISBN 978-0-7613-6442-9; 0-7613-6442-0

McKissack, Pat, 1944-

The **all**-I'll-ever-want Christmas doll; written by Patricia C. McKissack; illustrated by Jerry Pinkney. Schwartz &
Wade Books 2007 1 v. (unpaged) col. ill.

Grades: PreK K 1 2 3 4 5   E
1. Dolls -- Fiction 2. Sisters -- Fiction 3. Christmas -- Fiction 4. Sharing -- Fiction 5. African Americans -- Fiction 6. Depressions -- 1929 -- Fiction
ISBN 9780375836152

LC 2006030981

In this children's book, a recipient of a starred review by "Booklist" and "Kirkus Reviews" in 2007, "[i]t's Christmas and Nella is beside herself with excitement! She and her sisters have been given a real gift—a beautiful Baby Betty doll. But it's hard to share something you've waited your whole seven-year-old life for, and Nella grabs the doll for herself. It isn't long before she discovers that a doll can't do the fun things she and her sisters do together. So, as Christmas day fades, Nella shares it with her sisters." (Publisher's note)

★ **Flossie** & the fox; pictures by Rachel Isadora. Dial Bks. for Young Readers 1986 un il $15.99
Grades: K 1 2 3   E
1. Foxes -- Fiction 2. African Americans -- Fiction
ISBN 0-8037-0250-7

LC 86-2024

A wily fox notorious for stealing eggs meets his match when he encounters a bold little girl in the woods who insists upon proof that he is a fox before she will be frightened

"The watercolor and ink illustrations, with realistic figures set on impressionistic backgrounds, enliven this humorous and well-structured story which is told in the black language of the rural south." SLJ

★ **Goin'** someplace special; [illustrated by] Jerry Pinkney. Atheneum Bks. for Young Readers 2001 un il $16; pa $6.99
Grades: K 1 2 3   E
1. Libraries -- Fiction 2. Segregation -- Fiction 3. African Americans -- Fiction
ISBN 0-689-81885-8; 1-4169-2735-2 pa

LC 99-88258

Coretta Scott King Award for illustration

In segregated 1950s Nashville, a young African American girl braves a series of indignities and obstacles to get to one of the few integrated places in town: the public library

"Pinkney's watercolor paintings are lush and sprawling as they evoke southern city streets and sidewalks as well as Tricia Ann's inner glow. . . . This book carries a strong message of pride and self-confidence as well as a pointed history lesson." Booklist

★ **Mirandy** and Brother Wind; illustrated by Jerry Pinkney. Knopf 1988 un il $17; pa $6.99
Grades: K 1 2 3   E
1. Dance -- Fiction 2. Winds -- Fiction 3. African Americans -- Fiction
ISBN 978-0-394-88765-4; 0-394-88765-4; 978-0-679-88333-3 pa; 0-679-88333-9 pa

LC 87-349

A Caldecott Medal honor book, 1989
Coretta Scott King Award for illustration

"Ms. McKissack and Mr. Pinkney's ebullient collaboration captures the texture of rural life and culture 40 years after the end of slavery." N Y Times Book Rev

★ **Precious** and the Boo Hag; [by] Patricia C. McKissack and Onawumi Jean Moss; illustrated by Kyrsten Brooker. Atheneum Books for Young Readers 2004 un il $16.95
Grades: K 1 2 3   E
1. Monsters -- Fiction 2. African Americans -- Fiction
ISBN 0-689-85194-4

LC 2002-1571

Home alone with a stomachache while the family works in the fields, a young girl faces up to the horrifying Boo Hag that her brother warned her about.

"With the grand feel of a folktale, this lively story speaks to choosing right in a world full of temptation and peril. . . . Expressive and fluid, Brooker's mixed-media art, comical yet scary, too, pops from the pages." Booklist

McLeod, Heather
Kiss me! (I'm a prince!) illustrated by Brooke Kerrigan. Fitzhenry & Whiteside 2011 un il $18.95
Grades: K 1 2   E
1. Fairy tales 2. Frogs -- Fiction 3. Princes -- Fiction
ISBN 978-1-55455-161-3; 1-55455-161-7

"This clever variation on the classic 'Frog Prince' features a modern girl wearing a red ball cap, a striped T-shirt, purple pants, and red sneakers. She is carrying a basketball, ready to shoot hoops, when a little green frog with a crown on his head wants a kiss to become a prince. . . . The uncluttered artwork uses a pastel palette and makes good use of white space. Whether read independently or shared at storytime, this breezy tale of a frog who comes to value being a boy as much as being a prince will elicit smiles." SLJ

McLerran, Alice
Roxaboxen; illustrated by Barbara Cooney. Lothrop, Lee & Shepard Bks. 1991 un il $16.99; pa $6.99
Grades: K 1 2 3   E
1. Imagination -- Fiction
ISBN 0-688-07592-4; 0-06-052633-5 pa

LC 89-8057

A hill covered with rocks and wooden boxes in the desert becomes an imaginary town named Roxaboxen for Marian, her sisters, and their friends

"A celebration of the transforming magic of the imagination, the story was inspired by McLerran's mother's reminiscences of her childhood in Yuma, Arizona. . . . The story, told as though from the memory of a Roxaboxenite, brings their play to life through concrete details and a spare, understated style. Equally vivid, Cooney's full-color artwork evokes the striking variety of colors and moods found in the desert landscape." Booklist

McLimans, David
★ **Gone** wild; an endangered animal alphabet. Walker & Company 2006 un il $16.95; lib bdg $17.85
Grades: 1 2 3 4   E
1. Animals 2. Alphabet 3. Endangered species 4. Endangered species -- Juvenile literature 5. English language -- Alphabet -- Juvenile literature
ISBN 978-0-8027-9563-2; 978-0-8027-9564-9 lib bdg; 0-8027-9563-3; 0-8027-9564-1 lib bdg

LC 2006-44702

A Caldecott Medal honor book, 2007

"Although organized as a conventional alphabet book, the letters here are far from ordinary. McLimans has created a black-and-white iconic representation of 26 endangered animals, and his art is striking. . . . The arresting graphics and clean design will hold viewers' attention and create interest in the topic." SLJ

Includes bibliographical references

McMillan, Bruce

★ **How** the ladies stopped the wind; illustrated with paintings by Gunnella. Houghton Mifflin 2007 32p il $16
Grades: K 1 2 3   E
1. Sheep -- Fiction 2. Trees -- Fiction 3. Winds -- Fiction 4. Chickens -- Fiction
ISBN 978-0-618-77330-5; 0-618-77330-4
LC 2007-04207

The women of one village in Iceland decide to plant trees to stop the powerful winds that make it difficult even to go for a walk, but first they must find a ways to prevent sheep from eating all of their saplings, while encouraging chickens to fertilize them.

"The team that made stars of a group of Icelandic ladies in The Problem with Chickens returns for another winning round. . . . Gunnella's flat, deadpan oil portraits of the ladies, their polka-dot aprons and their hapless chickens are inherently funny, and every page contains another visual poke in the ribs." Publ Wkly

★ The **problem** with chickens; illustrated with paintings by Gunnella. Houghton Mifflin 2005 32p il $16
Grades: K 1 2 3   E
1. Chickens -- Fiction
ISBN 0-618-58581-8
LC 2005-01225

When women in an Icelandic village buy chickens to lay eggs for them to use, the chickens follow them, adopting human ways and forgetting their barnyard roots, until the ladies hatch a clever plan.

"The playful text is both silly and joyous, without a wasted word. Gunnella's enchanting oil paintings are full of childlike humor and saturated with appealing primary colors." SLJ

McMullan, Kate

★ **Bulldog's** big day; pictures by Pascal Lemaitre. Orchard Books 2011 un il $16.99
Grades: PreK K   E
1. Dogs -- Fiction 2. Animals -- Fiction 3. Occupations -- Fiction
ISBN 0-545-17155-5; 978-0-545-17155-7
LC 2010-26235

While looking for a job, Bulldog tries being a firefighter, a window washer, a sign painter, and a bookseller before finding just the right job for himself. "Ages four to seven." (Bull Cent Child Books)

"The illustrations were created in pen and ink, colored in Adobe Photoshop. . . . There are five or six scenes per spread. Everything is outlined in a thin black line and colored in flat hues. There's a lot to look at on each page, and children will enjoy poring over all the details." SLJ

★ **I** stink! [by] Kate & Jim McMullan. HarperCollins Pubs. 2002 un il $15.95; lib bdg $15.89; pa $6.99

Grades: PreK K 1 2   E
1. Refuse and refuse disposal
ISBN 0-06-029848-0; 0-06-029849-9 lib bdg; 0-06-443836-8 pa
LC 00-54229

A big city garbage truck makes its rounds, consuming everything from apple cores and banana peels to leftover ziti with zucchini

"Kate McMullan creates an automotive beast whose narrative style reeks of personality, and Jim McMullan's renderings are a perfect match, coaxing steely features into flexible, expressive shapes." Bull Cent Child Books

★ **I'm** bad; [by] Kate & Jim McMullan. Joanna Cotler Books 2008 un il $16.99; lib bdg $17.89
Grades: PreK K 1   E
1. Dinosaurs -- Fiction
ISBN 978-0-06-122971-8; 0-06-122971-7; 978-0-06-122972-5 lib bdg; 0-06-122972-5 lib bdg
LC 2007032020

A hungry Tyrannosaurus rex searches for food in the prehistoric forest but is thwarted in its attempts to find something to eat

"The high-energy illustrations and macho narrator's words create a rowdy, crowd-pleasing whole. Children will delight in the dinosaur's wild expressions and the dynamic text, filled with comic-book sound effects." Booklist

★ **I'm** big! [by] Kate & Jim McMullan. Balzer + Bray 2010 un il $16.99; lib bdg $17.89
Grades: PreK K 1   E
1. Dinosaurs -- Fiction
ISBN 978-0-06-122974-9; 0-06-122974-1; 978-0-06-122975-6 lib bdg; 0-06-122975-X lib bdg

A young Sauropod encounters friends and foes while searching for his pack, who left while he was oversleeping.

"This tale of a young dinosaur finding his inner power is told through childlike vernacular with varying type sizes and colors to emphasize mood. The full-color watercolor illustrations feature plenty of action and multiple perspectives. . . . Perfect as a read-aloud or a read-alone." SLJ

★ **I'm** dirty! [by] Kate & Jim McMullan. Joanna Cotler Books 2006 un il $16.99; lib bdg $17.89
Grades: PreK K 1 2   E
1. Cleanliness -- Fiction 2. Construction equipment -- Fiction
ISBN 978-0-06-009293-1; 0-06-009293-9; 978-0-06-009294-8 lib bdg; 0-06-009294-7 lib bdg
LC 2005-17919

A busy backhoe loader describes all the items it hauls off a lot and all the fun it has getting dirty while doing so

"With its saucy tone and dynamic color cartoon illustrations, this picture book exudes energy." SLJ

I'm mighty! [by] Kate & Jim McMullan. Joanna Cotler Bks. 2003 un il $17.99
Grades: PreK K 1 2   E
1. Tugboats -- Fiction
ISBN 0-06-009290-4
LC 2002-7948

A little tugboat shows how he can bring big ships into the harbor even though he is small

"The tugboat that narrates this picture book tells his story with more than a splash of moxie. Strong ink drawings define the harbor setting from a variety of perspectives and show the emotions of the anthropomorphic figures of boats and trucks, while color brightens the scenes and heightens the drama." Booklist

Pearl and Wagner; five days till summer. by Kate McMullan; pictures by R.W. Alley. Penguin Group USA 2012 47 p. col. ill. (hardcover) $14.99

Grades: K 1 2   E

1. Robots -- Juvenile fiction 2. Friendship -- Juvenile fiction 3. Science -- Exhibitions -- Juvenile fiction 4. Mice -- Fiction 5. Animals -- Fiction 6. Rabbits -- Fiction 7. Schools -- Fiction 8. Teachers -- Fiction

ISBN 9780803735897

LC 2011039844

In this children's book by Kate McMullan "Pearl, a hardworking rabbit, and Wagner, a daydreaming mouse . . . build a robot together, impress a judge at the science fair, and tell each other the truth at all times. But friendship isn't always easy. Sometimes a robot doesn't turn out quite the way it's supposed to, and sometimes a pair of new green boots can cause a fight. Through it all, Pearl and Wagner show that they know how to make up and stay good friends no matter what." (Publisher's note)

★ **Pearl** and Wagner: one funny day. Dial Books for Young Readers 2009 40p (Dial easy-to-read) $14.99

Grades: K 1 2   E

1. School stories 2. Mice -- Fiction 3. Animals -- Fiction 4. Rabbits -- Fiction 5. April Fools' Day -- Fiction

ISBN 978-0-8037-3085-4; 0-8037-3085-3

LC 2008007699

ALA ALSC Geisel Award Honor Book (2010)

April Fools' Day is not a happy one for Wagner the mouse because his best friend, Pearl the rabbit, and other children and adults at school keep tricking him.

"Alley's expressive ink-and-watercolor illustrations portray Wagner's shifting emotions with clarity and finesse." Booklist

Other titles about Pearl and Wagner are:

Pearl and Wagner: two good friends (2003)
Pearl and Wagner: three secrets (2004)
Pearl and Wagner: four eyes (2010)

McNamara, Margaret

How many seeds in a pumpkin? illustrated by G. Brian Karas. Schwartz & Wade Books 2007 un il $14.99

Grades: K 1 2   E

1. School stories 2. Size -- Fiction 3. Pumpkin -- Fiction 4. Counting -- Fiction

ISBN 978-0-375-84014-2; 0-375-84014-1; 978-0-375-94014-9 lib bdg; 0-375-94014-6 lib bdg

LC 2006-16866

Charlie, the smallest child in his first grade class, is amazed to discover that of the three pumpkins his teacher brings to school, the tiniest one has the most seeds.

"Karas's characteristic watercolor illustrations done in a fall palette depict a diverse, modern classroom full of warm and humorous details. . . . This enjoyable story, sprinkled

with math and science lessons, should be a first-purchase consideration." SLJ

The **three** little aliens and the big bad robot; written by Margaret McNamara; illustrated by Mark Fearing. Schwartz & Wade Books 2011 un il $16.99; lib bdg $19.99

Grades: PreK K 1 2   E

1. Robots -- Fiction 2. Siblings -- Fiction 3. Extraterrestrial beings -- Fiction 4. Outer space -- Exploration -- Fiction

ISBN 978-0-375-86689-0; 0-375-86689-2; 978-0-375-96689-7 lib bdg; 0-375-96689-7 lib bdg

LC 2010050153

Three aliens set off to find a new planet for themselves but soon Bork and Gork have forgotten all of their mother's good advice and only Nklxwcyz builds a home safe enough to withstand the Big Bad Robot.

"With its broad humor and a knowing wink to folktale conventions, this delightful reworking of 'The Three Little Pigs' has potential to become a crowd-pleasing favorite. . . . Fearing's hand-drawn cartoon illustrations rendered digitally with collage techniques offer bugeyed, green aliens and an enjoyable mix of science and playful details." SLJ

The **whistle** on the train; [by] Margaret McNamara; illustrated by Richard Egielski; paper engineering by Gene Vosough. Hyperion 2008 un il $18.99

Grades: PreK   E

1. Songs 2. Pop-up books 3. Railroads -- Fiction

ISBN 978-0-7868-4890-4; 0-7868-4890-1

"Here's a great concept, handsomely executed. Take a song known to virtually every preschooler, 'The Wheels on the Bus,' and update it with a vehicle much more widely adored by this group, a train, then soup it up with lavish but resilient paper engineering. Involving plenty of repetition, McNamara's lyrics are easy to learn. . . . The pop-ups, mostly stationary, are multidimensional renderings of Egielski's cheery cartoons." Publ Wkly

McNaughton, Colin

★ **Not** last night but the night before; illustrated by Emma Chichester Clark. Candlewick Press 2009 un il $16.99

Grades: PreK K 1 2   E

1. Fairy tales 2. Stories in rhyme 3. Parties -- Fiction 4. Birthdays -- Fiction 5. Nursery rhymes -- Fiction

ISBN 978-0-7636-4420-8; 0-7636-4420-X

"Rhyming, repetitive text tells of a boy who reluctantly welcomes a parade of nursery-rhyme characters into his home. Everyone from the man in the moon to Little Miss Muffet bursts through the entryway wearing party clothes and carrying presents. . . . Colorful pencil and acrylic illustrations alternate between scallop-edged vignettes and full-bleed scenes rife with excitement. Preschoolers will enjoy the predictability of this tale." SLJ

Once upon an ordinary school day; story by Colin McNaughton; pictures by Satoshi Kitamura. Farrar, Straus & Giroux 2005 un il $16

Grades: K 1 2   E

1. School stories 2. Teachers -- Fiction 3. Imagination -- Fiction

ISBN 0-374-35634-3

LC 2004-105656

First published 2004 in the United Kingdom

"An ordinary boy awakens to an ordinary school day. The story opens with drab scenes depicted in shades of gray that turn to Technicolor several pages in, with the arrival of a new teacher in a yellow suit. . . . Deftly rendered cartoon drawings convey the expressive gestures and transformation of the characters and scenes. . . . An excellent selection to start the creative juices flowing or to enliven an ordinary day." SLJ

McNelly McCormack, Caren

The **fiesta** dress; a quinceanera tale. illustrated by Martha Aviles. Marshall Cavendish 2009 un il $17.99
Grades: K 1   E
1. Sisters -- Fiction 2. Family life -- Fiction 3. Hispanic Americans -- Fiction 4. Quinceañera (Social custom) -- Fiction
ISBN 978-0-7614-5467-0; 0-7614-5467-5
LC 2008-10781

While Eva and her family prepare for her quinceanera, no one is paying attention to her younger sister, but when the dog gets out of the laundry room and steals Eva's sash, her little sister comes to the rescue.

"Aviles incorporates a warm palette of roses, aquas, deep oranges and springy greens to illustrate the story; her acrylic and watercolor compositions have a somewhat old fashioned feel. . . . There is abundant joy in this tale of a big extended family preparing for an exciting event, and audience members will relish being included." Bull Cent Child Books

McPhail, David

Pig Pig meets the lion; David McPhail. Charlesbridge 2012 32p.
Grades: PreK K   E
1. Lions -- Fiction 2. Children's stories 3. Picture books for children 4. English language -- Prepositions -- Fiction 5. English language -- Prepositions -- Juvenile fiction
ISBN 9781580893589
LC 2011009031

This book "starring . . . Pig Pig begins wordlessly on the pre-title page and continues onto the opening pages, as a lion escapes from a zoo and climbs up the tree outside Pig Pig's bedroom window. From there, the friendly lion enters Pig Pig's room, much to the delight of Pig Pig, who jumps '"out" of bed' and runs '"down" the stairs,' followed by the lion. Pig Pig and the lion continue their romp through the house, unbeknownst to his ever-distracted mother, and though Pig Pig longs to keep the lion, it must skedaddle when the zookeepers show up on the doorstep on the book's closing endpapers. There's a manifestly educational bent to this escapade, as prepositions are printed in boldfaced type." (Bulletin of the Center for Children's Books)

Waddles; by David McPhail. Abrams Books for Young Readers 2011 un il $15.95
Grades: PreK K 1 2   E
1. Ducks -- Fiction 2. Raccoons -- Fiction 3. Friendship -- Fiction
ISBN 0-8109-8415-6; 978-0-8109-8415-8
LC 2010023699

Waddles, a very plump and furry raccoon, helps his best friend Emily, a duck, hatch and raise her ducklings, and discovers what makes him truly happy.

"McPhail's ink-and-watercolor illustrations elevate the familiar story of mismatched, devoted friends, coaxing expertly drawn emotion from his endearing characters." Booklist

McPhail, David M.

Big Brown Bear's up and down day; [written and illustrated by] David McPhail. Harcourt 2003 un il $16; pa $6
Grades: PreK K 1 2   E
1. Rats -- Fiction 2. Bears -- Fiction
ISBN 0-15-216407-3; 0-15-205684-X pa
LC 2002-15854

Big Brown Bear is visited by a rat who wants to use one of his slippers for a bed

"A warm and gentle story. . . . Beautiful watercolor and pen-and-ink paintings make the most of the size difference between the characters and help to create real personalities by capturing the emotions they experience." SLJ

Other titles about Big Brown Bear are:
Big Brown Bear goes to town (2006)
Big Brown Bear's birthday surprise (2007)

Big Pig and Little Pig; [by] David McPhail. Harcourt 2003 un il (Green light readers) $11.95; pa $3.95
Grades: PreK K 1   E
1. Pigs -- Fiction
ISBN 978-0-15-204818-1; 0-15-204818-9; 978-0-15-204857-0 pa; 0-15-204857-X pa
A reissue of the title first published 2001

Big Pig and Little Pig enjoy spending time together, though they take different approaches to the same task

"McPhail's signature illustrations fill each page as he once again successfully manages to transfer human emotions to his lovable cartoon pigs. Well-chosen vocabulary and repetition of words make this story a suitable choice for those just learning to read." SLJ

Boy, Bird, and Dog; by David McPhail. Holiday House 2011 il (I like to read picture book) $14.95
Grades: PreK K 1 2   E
1. Dogs -- Fiction 2. Birds -- Fiction 3. Tree houses -- Fiction
ISBN 978-0-8234-2346-0; 0-8234-2346-8
LC 2010029435

In this story for beginning readers, Boy, Bird, and Dog have lots of fun in their tree house.

"The story is told in the sparest of language. . . . It reads smoothly with a clear plot, likable characters and an interesting setting. . . . McPhail's signature watercolor-and-ink illustrations are large scale with soft edges. The action and characters are well defined and appealing." Kirkus

★ **Drawing** lessons from a bear; [by] David McPhail. Little, Brown 2000 un il $14.95
Grades: PreK K 1   E
1. Bears -- Fiction 2. Artists -- Fiction
ISBN 0-316-56345-5
LC 98-54966

A bear explains how he became an artist, first experimenting with simple drawings, then continuing to draw both things around him and things in his imagination. Includes tips for drawing

"This gentle story combines a humorous tone with warm, cozy watercolors to create inspiration for budding artists." SLJ

★ **Emma** in charge; by David McPhail. Dutton Children's Books 2005 un il $12.99
Grades: PreK K 1   E
1. Play -- Fiction 2. Bears -- Fiction
ISBN 0-525-47411-0

LC 2004-21580
Emma the bear pretends that she and her dolls spend a day at school.

"McPhail's watercolors are . . . expressive and winsome . . . and the short sentences, printed in bold type, are just right for read-alouds or for emerging readers to follow along." Booklist
Other titles about Emma are:
Emma's pet (1985)
Emma's vacation (1987)
Fix-it (1984)

Mole music; written and illustrated by David McPhail. Holt & Co. 1999 un il $15.95; pa $7.99
Grades: PreK K 1 2   E
1. Music -- Fiction 2. Violins -- Fiction 3. Moles (Animals) -- Fiction
ISBN 0-8050-2819-6; 0-8050-6766-3 pa

LC 98-21318
Feeling that something is missing in his simple life, Mole acquires a violin and learns to make beautiful, joyful music

"McPhail's delicate watercolor-and-ink illustrations work with the simple text to create a lyrical celebration of music and musicians." Booklist

No! Roaring Brook Press 2009 un il $16.95
Grades: K 1 2 3   E
1. War stories 2. Stories without words 3. Bullies -- Fiction
ISBN 978-1-59643-288-8; 1-59643-288-8

LC 2008054607
"In this dark, nearly wordless allegory, the power of a single word ripples outward, stopping a bully, an army, a war. . . . McPhail's . . . delicately tinted crosshatching gives poignancy to the violence the boy witnesses without minimizing it. The idea of taking effective action without fighting is a powerful one, and children and adults alike will find that McPhail's images linger." Publ Wkly

Pig Pig returns; [by] David McPhail. Charlesbridge 2011 un il lib bdg $15.95
Grades: PreK K 1   E
1. Pigs -- Fiction 2. Aunts -- Fiction 3. Uncles -- Fiction 4. Vacations -- Fiction 5. Automobile travel -- Fiction
ISBN 978-1-58089-356-5; 1-58089-356-2

LC 2010023528
Initially reluctant to leave his mother and cat, Pig Pig spends his summer vacation road tripping with his Aunt Wilma and Uncle Fred across the country in their teal-green camper.

"The line-and-watercolor art is drawn with sweetness and humor. Many kids (and adults) will see their mixed feelings about travel here." Booklist

★ **Sylvie** & True; [by] David McPhail. Farrar, Straus, & Giroux 2007 31p il lib bdg $15
Grades: PreK K 1 2   E
1. Snakes -- Fiction 2. Rabbits -- Fiction 3. Friendship -- Fiction
ISBN 978-0-374-37364-1 lib bdg; 0-374-37364-7 lib bdg

LC 2006048979
In four vignettes, Sylvie the rabbit and her friend True, a giant water snake, share a small apartment in a big city, cook, go bowling, and have a good time together

The scenarios are "simple . . . occasioning affectionate dialogue and terrific sight gags. . . . [This is a] charmer." Publ Wkly

Water boy; [by] David McPhail. Abrams Books for Young Readers 2007 un il $15.95
Grades: PreK K 1 2   E
1. Magic -- Fiction 2. Water -- Fiction
ISBN 978-0-8109-1784-2; 0-8109-1784-X

LC 2006013578
Fascinated by the fact that humans are made mostly of water, a boy develops an unusual relationship with it once he stops being afraid.

"Beautifully written, illustrated, and designed, this small gem of a book calls to be opened, touched, and read from its texturally and visually appealing cover . . . to the rich, color-drenched pictures of the real and the fantastic inside." SLJ

Weezer changes the world; [by] David McPhail. Beach Lane Books 2009 un il $15.99
Grades: PreK K 1   E
1. Dogs -- Fiction
ISBN 978-1-4169-9000-0; 1-4169-9000-3

LC 2009005537
After an ordinary puppyhood, Weezer develops extraordinary skills that make him a major influence in the world.

"McPhail's amusing tale will inspire young children to consider how they can make the world a better place, and his droll ink-and-watercolor illustrations reinforce the book's simple but powerful message." Booklist

The **teddy** bear; written and illustrated by David McPhail. Holt & Co. 2002 un il $15.95; pa $7.99
Grades: PreK K 1 2   E
1. Teddy bears -- Fiction 2. Homeless persons -- Fiction
ISBN 0-8050-6414-1; 0-8050-7882-7 pa

LC 2001-1500
"By accident a boy leaves his beloved bear in a diner. A homeless man finds it in the garbage and loves the bear as much as the boy did. Then one day the boy sees the bear on a park bench and joyfully grabs it. But when he recognizes the lonely man's sorrow at losing his friend, the child returns the toy. . . . It works because McPhail's beautiful soft-toned watercolor pictures with detailed ink cross-hatching tell the elemental story of shelter and love through the child's eyes." Booklist

McQuinn, Anna

Lola at the library; [by] Anna McQuinn; illustrated by Rosalind Beardshaw. Charlesbridge 2006 un il lib bdg $15.95; pa $6.95

Grades: PreK K 1 2   E

1. Libraries -- Fiction 2. Books and reading -- Fiction

ISBN 978-1-58089-113-4 lib bdg; 1-58089-113-6 lib bdg; 978-1-58089-142-4 pa; 1-58089-142-X pa

LC 2005019620

Published in the United Kingdom with title: Layla loves the library

Every Tuesday Lola and her mother visit their local library to return and check out books, attend story readings, and share a special treat

"Simple text and large, bright acrylic illustrations of this engaging African-American child make this selection just right for sharing" SLJ

"Another title about Lola is:

Lola loves stories (2010)

My friend Jamal; by Anna McQuinn; illustrated by Ben Frey. Annick 2008 un il (My friend) lib bdg $17.95; pa $8.95

Grades: K 1 2 3   E

1. Friendship -- Fiction 2. Immigrants -- Fiction 3. Africans -- United States -- Fiction

ISBN 978-1-55451-123-5 lib bdg; 1-55451-123-2 lib bdg; 978-1-55451-122-8 pa; 1-55451-122-4 pa

"Joseph describes his friendship with Jamal, a boy whose family immigrated to the United States from Somalia. . . . He discusses their similarities . . . as well as their differences. . . . The lively, brightly colored collages consist of original photographs of the main characters and stock photos of food or objects with thickly painted outlines and accents added. Both text and pictures project an energetic, friendly tone." SLJ

My friend Mei Jing; text by Anna McQuinn; artwork by Ben Frey; photography by Irvin Cheung. Annick Press 2009 un il (My friend) $17.95; pa $8.95

Grades: K 1 2 3   E

1. Friendship -- Fiction 2. African Americans -- Fiction 3. Chinese Americans -- Fiction

ISBN 978-1-55451-153-2; 1-55451-153-4; 978-1-55451-152-5 pa; 1-55451-152-6 pa

"In this large, colorful book, a Nigerian-American second-grader tells the story of her best friend from school, who is Chinese-American. The girls share a love of arts and crafts, dressing up, and a desire to become veterinarians. Monifa describes aspects of Mei Jing's culture. . . . The story's authentic voice comes from simple declarative sentences. . . . The brightly colored collages combine photographs of the girls' heads and hands with their cartoon bodies and depict them as they work with clay in arts and crafts at school or walk through an outdoor market with Mei Jing's grandma." SLJ

The **sleep** sheep; [by] Anna McQuinn and [illustrated by] Hannah Shaw. Chicken House 2010 un il $17.99

Grades: PreK K 1   E

1. Sheep -- Fiction 2. Sleep -- Fiction 3. Bedtime

-- Fiction

ISBN 978-0-545-23145-9; 0-545-23145-0

LC 2009051481

When Sylvie cannot fall asleep and her mother suggests that she try counting sheep, the sheep do not cooperate.

"The cartoon pen-and-ink drawings paint vivid scenes of Sylvie's imagination and are flush with fun details. Readers will linger over each page. . . . The Sleep Sheep moves along at a rapid clip and with enough humor to be successful read-aloud." SLJ

Meade, Holly

★ **If** I never forever endeavor. Candlewick Press 2011 un il $15.99

Grades: PreK K 1 2   E

1. Birds -- Fiction 2. Flight -- Fiction

ISBN 978-0-7636-4071-2; 0-7636-4071-9

LC 2010-39182

"To fly or not to fly is the question for a little bird weighing the pros and cons of launching into the unknown. . . . Meade effectively uses rhyme . . . onomatopoeia . . . and repetition to accentuate the fledgling's inner conflict. . . . Stunning collages of textured linoleum block prints and watercolors span double-page spreads. . . . An irresistible invitation to test those wings and fly." Kirkus

Inside, inside, inside; written and illustrated by Holly Meade. Marshall Cavendish 2005 un il $16.95

Grades: PreK K 1 2   E

1. Games -- Fiction 2. Siblings -- Fiction

ISBN 0-7614-5125-0

LC 2004-19321

Noah and Jenny play a game in which they place one item inside another, over and over, until they place it all in the shower, then imagine and draw the shower inside the house, inside the neighborhood, and all the way to the solar system

"Meade cheerfully mixes cut-paper collage and watercolor, and sprinkles many homey details into the large and small scenes. . . . The messy game is fun, and the concept draws a useful lesson from creative play." SLJ

★ **John** Willy and Freddy McGee. Marshall Cavendish 1998 un il hardcover o.p. pa $5.95

Grades: PreK K 1 2   E

1. Guinea pigs -- Fiction

ISBN 0-7614-5033-5; 0-7614-5143-9 pa

LC 97-50362

Two guinea pigs escape from their safe but boring cage and have an adventure in the tunnels of the family's pool table

"Zesty cut-paper collages track all of the details of this funny outing." SLJ

Meadows, Michelle

Hibernation station; illustrated by Kurt Cyrus. Simon and Schuster Books for Young Readers 2010 un il $16.99

Grades: PreK K 1 2   E

1. Stories in rhyme 2. Sleep -- Fiction 3. Animals -- Fiction

ISBN 978-1-4169-3788-3; 1-4169-3788-9

LC 2008042141

"The hibernation train, fashioned of hollow logs, is filled with all sorts of animals. . . . On its way to the station, it hits a few snags: crowded conditions, leakage from a stream, and a lack of snacks and pillows. As the snow falls heavier and heavier, the bears in charge manage to get everyone squared away..... The enjoyable rhyming text provides the perfect platform for the wonderful illustrations that accompany it. Cyrus blends realistic depictions of the animals with just the right anthropomorphic touches." SLJ

Piggies in pajamas; Michelle Meadows; illustrated by Ard Hoyt. 1st ed. Simon & Schuster Books for Young Readers 2012 32 p. col. ill. (hardcover) $15.99
Grades: PreK K 1   E
1. Stories in rhyme 2. Pigs -- Juvenile fiction 3. Bedtime -- Juvenile fiction
ISBN 1416949828; 9781416949824
LC 2010024472
In this children's story, by Michelle Meadows, illustrated by Ard Hoyt, "after Mama has put her kids to bed, she settles in to make some phone calls. But she keeps hearing things from upstairs. Could her little piggies be jumping on the bed or playing dress-up instead of sleeping? But every time Mama goes up to check on them, they are all tucked in . . . until the noises begin again!" (Publisher's note)

Piggies in the kitchen; illustrated by Ard Hoyt. Simon & Schuster 2011 un il $14.99
Grades: PreK K 1   E
1. Stories in rhyme 2. Pigs -- Fiction 3. Baking -- Fiction
ISBN 978-1-4169-3787-6; 1-4169-3787-0
"Five little porkers and their father wave Mama off one bright, sunny day as she leaves the house. Daddy goes to cut the grass while his children enthusiastically descend upon the kitchen. Rhyming couplets filled with onomatopoeia tell the tale of the frenetic piglets making a mess plus a pleasant surprise for their mother. Pen-and-ink with watercolor illustrations in pastel hues humorously reveal the raucous goings-on." SLJ

Meddaugh, Susan
★ **Cinderella's** rat. Houghton Mifflin 1997 32p il $15; pa $5.95
Grades: PreK K 1 2   E
1. Fairy tales 2. Rats -- Fiction
ISBN 0-395-86833-5; 0-618-12540-X pa
LC 97-2156
One of the rats that was turned into a coachman by Cinderella's fairy godmother saves his rat sister's life, but an inept magician turns her into a girl who says "woof."
"The telling is a perfect example of a successful fractured fairy tale, with switched point of view. . . . The buoyant line drawings capture the whimsy." SLJ

★ **Harry** on the rocks. Houghton Mifflin 2003 32p il hardcover o.p. pa $6.95
Grades: PreK K 1 2   E
1. Eggs 2. Dragons 3. Islands 4. Shipwrecks 5. Shipwrecks -- Fiction
ISBN 0-618-27603-3; 0-618-84068-0 pa
LC 2002-9740
Harry and his boat become stranded on an island, where he discovers an egg which hatches into a strange lizard with wings

This is "a well-paced, cleanly wrought piece of storytelling. The cheerful watercolor and colored-pencil art has a sturdy matter-of-factness that makes the fantasy endearingly domestic." Bull Cent Child Books

★ **Hog**-eye. Houghton Mifflin 1995 32p il hardcover o.p. pa $5.95
Grades: PreK K 1 2   E
1. Pigs -- Fiction 2. Wolves -- Fiction
ISBN 0-395-74276-5; 0-395-93746-9 pa
LC 95-3951
Meddaugh presents a "story within a story as a piglet tells her family how she was caught by a wolf and nearly made into soup. Seeing that her captor is illiterate . . . she reads him a recipe that sends him on a wild wolf chase." SLJ

★ **Martha** speaks. Houghton Mifflin 1992 un il hardcover o.p. pa $6.99
Grades: PreK K 1 2   E
1. Dogs -- Fiction
ISBN 0-395-63313-3; 0-395-72952-1 pa
LC 91-48455
Problems arise when Martha, the family dog, learns to speak after eating alphabet soup
"Good-natured and amusing, with cheerful illustrations of the delightfully stocky Martha and her amazed family." Horn Book
Other titles about Martha are:
Martha and Skits (2000)
Martha and Skits out West (2011)
Martha blah blah (1996)
Martha calling (1994)
Martha walks the dog (1998)
Perfectly Martha (2004)

The **best** place. Houghton Mifflin 1999 un il $15
Grades: PreK K 1 2   E
1. Views -- Fiction 2. Wolves -- Fiction 3. Animals -- Fiction 4. Behavior -- Fiction
ISBN 0-395-97994-3
LC 98-50184
After traveling around the world to make sure that the view from his screen porch is the best, an old wolf tries drastic measures to get his house back from the rabbit family that had bought it
"Meddaugh combines understated humor with her expressive watercolor illustrations to produce a delightful book." SLJ

The **witch's** walking stick. Houghton Mifflin 2005 32p il $16
Grades: K 1 2 3   E
1. Magic -- Fiction 2. Witches -- Fiction
ISBN 0-618-52948-9
LC 2004-17509
When a witch loses her magic walking stick, which has been used over the years to grant hundreds of miserable wishes, she tricks a young girl into finding and returning it, with unexpected results.
"Illustrated with watercolor and ink in a style that will put readers in mind of William Steig, Meddaugh's dry, quirky tale of the little guy triumphing over adversity will have children smiling and cheering." SLJ

Medearis, Angela Shelf

Seven spools of thread; a Kwanzaa story. illustrated by Daniel Minter. Whitman, A. 2001 un il $15.95; pa $6.95

Grades: K 1 2 3   **E**

1. Kwanzaa 2. Brothers 3. Conduct of life 4. Blacks -- Ghana 5. Blacks -- Fiction 6. Kwanzaa -- Fiction 7. Brothers -- Fiction

ISBN 0-8075-7315-9; 0-8075-7316-7 pa

LC 00-8101

When they are given the seemingly impossible task of turning thread into gold, the seven Ashanti brothers put aside their differences, learn to get along, and embody the principles of Kwanzaa. Includes information on Kwanzaa, West African cloth weaving, and instructions for making a belt

"Well-paced, the story incorporates the Kwanzaa values without spelling them out too much. Minter's attractively composed, dramatic painted linocuts, with strong community images and lively, silhouetted figures, root the story in a sun-drenched, magical landscape." Booklist

Medina, Meg

Tia Isa wants a car. Candlewick Press 2011 un il $15.99

Grades: K 1 2   **E**

1. Aunts -- Fiction 2. Money -- Fiction 3. Automobiles -- Fiction 4. Family life -- Fiction 5. Hispanic Americans -- Fiction

ISBN 978-0-7636-4156-6; 0-7636-4156-1

LC 2010040128

"Always true to the child's viewpoint, the story shows how hard it is to be separated from loved ones and how long it can take to reunite, and the lively, unframed illustrations in pencil, watercolor, and ink extend the sense of warmth and longing." Booklist

Meinderts, Koos

On My Street; Koos Meinderts, illustrated by Annette Fienieg. Lemniscaat USA 2013 32 p. ill. (hardcover) $12.95

Grades: PreK K   **E**

1. Neighbors -- Juvenile fiction 2. Neighborhood -- Juvenile fiction

ISBN 1935954245; 9781935954248

In this children's book, by Koos Meinderts, illustrated by Annette Fienieg, characters created by the illustrator are presented in one story. "For every child born to one of her friends, Annette Fienieg used to make a colorfully decorated teeshirt, with a character you would fall in love with. Now it is time to introduce those creations--Mrs. McQueen Fifi LaPointe, Johnny Deck, Lightfingers Louie and more--to a wider audience." (Publisher's note)

Meisel, Paul

See me dig; by Paul Meisel. Holiday House 2013 32 p. (I like to read) (hardcover) $14.95

Grades: PreK K 1   **E**

1. Dogs -- Juvenile fiction 2. Pirates -- Juvenile fiction 3. Dogs -- Fiction

ISBN 0823427439; 9780823427437

LC 2012016549

This children's story, by Paul Meisel, is part of the "I Like to Read" series. "A crew of happy dogs dig merrily in the dirt. But the groundhogs, mice, and moles don't like it. The animals chase the dogs away to another digging

spot. This time the dogs dig up a box--a treasure chest-- from which ghostly pirates emerge. The dogs are on the run again!" (Publisher's note)

See me run. Holiday House 2011 un il $14.95

Grades: PreK K 1   **E**

1. Dogs -- Fiction 2. Parks -- Fiction

ISBN 978-0-8234-2349-1; 0-8234-2349-2

LC 2010029445

"Cartoon drawings done in acrylic ink, pen and colored pencils offer a variety of dog breeds; eyes are wide and tongues hang out in their expressive faces as they frolic through the pale green, grassy park. Formatted in a larger trim than the usual early reader, this imaginary rumpus is just right for beginners to successfully read and reread." Kirkus

Meister, Cari

My pony Jack; illustrated by Amy Young. Viking 2005 32p il (Viking easy-to-read) $13.99

Grades: PreK K 1 2   **E**

1. Stories in rhyme 2. Horses -- Fiction

ISBN 0-670-05917-X

LC 2004-21417

Easy-to-read, rhyming text follows Lacy as she spends a day with her pony, giving him exercise, grooming him, and feeding him oats and hay.

"The book has an attractive format, with colorful cartoon artwork and a small amount of text on each page. . . . A solid addition to easy-reader collections." SLJ

Other titles about Jack the pony are:

My pony Jack at riding lessons (2005)

My pony Jack at the horse show (2006)

★ **Tiny's** bath; illustrated by Rich Davis. Viking 1998 un il (Viking easy-to-read) hardcover o.p. pa $3.99

Grades: PreK K 1   **E**

1. Dogs -- Fiction 2. Baths -- Fiction

ISBN 0-670-87962-2; 0-14-130267-4 pa

LC 98-3844

Tiny is a very big dog who loves to dig, and when it is time for his bath, his owner has trouble finding a place to bathe him

"In this book for the least sophisticated beginning readers, each sentence appears on a single line, and only one sentence appears on a page. Illustrations mirror text, providing clues that support readers as they decipher both words and events. Add Tiny to the roll call of great dogs in children's literature." Horn Book Guide

Other titles about Tiny are:

Tiny goes camping (2006)

Tiny goes to the library (2000)

Tiny on the farm (2008)

Tiny the snow dog (2001)

When Tiny was tiny (1999)

Melanson, Luc

Topsy -Turvy Town. Tundra Books 2010 un il $17.95

Grades: PreK K   **E**

1. Imagination -- Fiction

ISBN 978-0-88776-920-7; 0-88776-920-9

Original French language edition published 2004 in Canada

A boy lives in a town where it rains broccoli that crunches when it lands on the tops of umbrellas, where police officers march to a very different beat, where you can go fishing in your living room or even juggle a wildcat before bedtime.

"This highly imaginative tale is told in simple text with outstanding illustrations. Round-headed humans and buildings with harlequin faces abound, as well as a menagerie of animals reminiscent of classic wooden toys." SLJ

Melling, David

Don't worry, Douglas! Tiger Tales 2011 il $12.95
Grades: PreK K 1   E
1. Hats -- Fiction 2. Bears -- Fiction 3. Gifts -- Fiction
4. Animals -- Fiction
ISBN 978-1-58925-106-9; 1-58925-106-7

"Douglas the bear loves the fuzzy orange hat that his father gives him, but when the hat snags on a branch, it turns into a 'long string of spaghetti.' Douglas's friends offer suggestions—the sheep try to wind it into a ball, a cow demonstrates how it can still be worn like a wig—but when it starts to rain, Douglas takes Rabbit's advice to tell his father the truth about what happened. Melling's artwork brims with physical comedy as he delivers his message about coming clean with sensitivity and good humor." Publ Wkly

"Another title about Douglas is:
Hugless Douglas (2010)

Hugless Douglas. Tiger Tales 2010 un il $15.95
Grades: PreK K 1   E
1. Bears -- Fiction 2. Hugging -- Fiction
ISBN 978-1-58925-098-7; 1-58925-098-2

"Melling gives new meaning to the phrase, 'a big bear hug' with this tale of a cub who sets off one morning in search of that special feeling he needs. A gigantic boulder is too heavy to hug and a tree trunk is too splintery. Douglas knows that a hug feels comfy, and he is not having an easy time locating one. Colorful illustrations enhance the humor." SLJ

★ The **Scallywags**. Barron's 2006 un il $14.99
Grades: K 1 2 3   E
1. Wolves -- Fiction 2. Animals -- Fiction 3. Etiquette -- Fiction
ISBN 0-7641-5991-7

"This hilarious story is accompanied by equally lively and humorous pictures that fill the pages with images worthy of close perusal." SLJ

Melmed, Laura Krauss

Hurry! Hurry! Have you heard? illustrated by Jane Dyer. Chronicle Books 2008 un il $16.99
Grades: PreK K 1 2   E
1. Stories in rhyme 2. Birds -- Fiction 3. Animals -- Fiction
ISBN 978-0-8118-4225-9

LC 2007021062

A small bird, her heart filled with love, hurries from her perch above the manger to spread the news to creatures of the field and forest that a child, to whom all are precious, has been born.

"This contemporary-set Nativity story, featuring seasonally clad but otherwise realistic-looking animals, has energy and movement." Horn Book Guide

Meltzer, Lynn

The **construction** crew; illustrated by Carrie Eko-Burgess. Henry Holt 2011 un il $12.99
Grades: PreK K   E
1. Stories in rhyme 2. Tools -- Fiction 3. Trucks -- Fiction 4. Building -- Fiction 5. Construction equipment -- Fiction
ISBN 978-0-8050-8884-7; 0-8050-8884-9

LC 2010039763

A construction crew tears down an old building and builds a new house in its place.

"Truck and construction fans will find an energetic exploration of both in this square-format volume. . . . Crisp, electric digital illustrations spotlight vehicles, construction equipment, and workers who resemble fleshed-out Lego characters. . . . The rhyming text offers variations on the same question ('Tons of dirt/ And lots of muck/ What do we need?/ DUMP TRUCK!'), . . . a narrative device that will have children shouting out the answers in no time." Publ Wkly

Melvin, Alice

Counting birds; written and illustrated by Alice Melvin. Tate 2010 un il $14.50
Grades: K 1 2   E
1. Counting 2. Day -- Fiction 3. Birds -- Fiction
ISBN 978-1-85437-855-2; 1-85437-855-4

"This is a charming counting book, replete with lilting text and exquisite illustrations. Beginning at dawn with one cockerel, the narration moves through the day and into the evening, counting birds from 1 to 20. . . . The text, which is composed in couplets, counts birds both inside and outside a stately country house. . . . In her bright and cheerful illustrations, Melvin employs geometric designs and patterns that bring to mind the warmth and comfort of a favorite quilt." SLJ

Menchin, Scott

What if everything had legs? Candlewick Press 2010 un il $15.99
Grades: PreK K 1   E
1. Imagination -- Fiction
ISBN 978-0-7636-4220-4; 0-7636-4220-7

LC 2010038719

Feeling too tired to walk the rest of the way home, a little girl wonders why the house cannot have legs to come to her and her mother, then imagines what else would change if everything had legs.

"The simple text and wacky, hybrid illustrations of objects sprouting legs (and arms) combine for an entertaining read-aloud that will engage young children and stir up their own creative juices." SLJ

Meng, Cece

I will not read this book; written by Cece Meng; illustrated by Joy Ang. Clarion Books 2011 32p il $15.99
Grades: K 1 2   E
1. Books and reading -- Fiction
ISBN 978-0-547-04971-7; 0-547-04971-4

LC 2010043175

A child adamantly refuses to read a book, regardless of the increasingly outrageous circumstances that might occur.

"Oh, yes, you will read this book. You'll be reeled in by the feisty, angular, frequently exciting digital illustrations, not to mention that confrontational title." Booklist

Merlin, Christophe
Under the hood; [by] Merlin. Candlewick Press 2011 il $14.99
Grades: PreK   E
  1. Animals -- Fiction 2. Automobiles -- Fiction
  ISBN 978-0-7636-5535-8; 0-7636-5535-X
                                                  LC 2010042743
A mechanic welcomes the reader to his garage where he will try to fix his car, but first needs help in finding his friends, Mouse, Crocodile, and Bird under lift-up flaps and fold-out pages.
"The large, humorous illustrations are done in vivid hues set against cream-colored backgrounds. Children will delight in the mystery of what lies beneath all those flaps." SLJ

Merz, Jennifer J.
Playground day! by Jennifer J. Merz. Clarion Books 2007 un il $16
Grades: PreK K 1   E
  1. Stories in rhyme 2. Play -- Fiction 3. Animals -- Fiction
  ISBN 978-0-618-81696-5
                                                  LC 2006039215
Children play on the playground, imitating animals from bunnies and squirrels to elephants and penguins.
"The cut- and torn-paper collages are filled with color, depth, and texture, making the pages come alive." SLJ

Meschenmoser, Sebastian
  ★ **Waiting** for winter. Kane Miller 2009 un il $15.99
Grades: PreK K 1 2   E
  1. Snow -- Fiction 2. Forest animals -- Fiction
  ISBN 978-1-935279-04-4; 1-935279-04-1
                                                  LC 2009-922111
Deer has told Squirrel how wonderful snow is. But Squirrel gets bored with the wait. With his friend Hedgehog they pass the time by singing and waking Bear. Soon things are falling from the sky, but they aren't snow. But eventually they find what snow is.
"The illustrations are deftly drawn in colored pencils, complete with sketching lines that give the renderings depth and maturity. . . . This is a beautiful title to share with children on a lap or with a small group." SLJ

Meserve, Jessica
  Bedtime without Arthur; illustrated by Jessica Meserve. Andersen Press USA 2009 un il $16.95
Grades: K 1 2   E
  1. Fear -- Fiction 2. Bedtime -- Fiction 3. Siblings -- Fiction 4. Teddy bears -- Fiction
  ISBN 978-0-7613-5497-0; 0-7613-5497-2
Arthur, Bella's very special bear, protects her from monsters while she sleeps, but when Arthur goes missing one night, Bella makes an interesting discovery.

Meshon, Aaron
  ★ **Take** me out to the Yakyu; Aaron Meshon. Atheneum Books for Young Readers 2013 40 p. (hardcover) $15.99

Grades: PreK K 1   E
  1. Picture books for children 2. Baseball -- Juvenile fiction 3. Grandfathers -- Juvenile fiction 4. Baseball -- Fiction 5. Grandfathers -- Fiction 6. Racially mixed people -- Fiction
  ISBN 1442441771; 9781442441774; 9781442441781
                                                  LC 2011050907
In this children's book by Aaron Meshon readers can "join one little boy and his family for two ballgames--on opposite sides of the world! Come along with one little boy and his grandfathers, one in America and one in Japan, as he learns about baseball and its rich, varying cultural traditions." (Publisher's note)

Metaxas, Eric
  It's time to sleep, my love (a lullabye) illustrated by Nancy Tillman. Feiwel and Friends 2008 un il $16.95; bd bk $7.99
Grades: PreK K   E
  1. Lullabies 2. Stories in rhyme 3. Animals -- Fiction 4. Bedtime -- Fiction
  ISBN 978-0-312-38371-8; 0-312-38371-1; 978-0-312-67336-9 bd bk; 0-312-67336-1 bd bk
                                                  LC 2008028550
At bedtime, birds, bees, fishes, and other creatures urge their tired children to go to sleep
"Mextaxas' words set the sleepy-time tone with lulling sounds, repetition, and rhythms in short lines that read like poetry. . . . Tillman combines vibrantly colored photos and textured paintings in digital collages of the detailed animals." Booklist

Metropolitan Museum of Art (New York, N.Y.)
  ★ **Museum** shapes. Little, Brown 2005 un il $16.99
Grades: PreK K 1 2   E
  1. Shape 2. Art appreciation
  ISBN 0-316-05698-7
"The concept is simple; what makes this book so wonderful is the art, which is varied in content, style, medium, culture, and period, and is beautifully reproduced." SLJ

Metzger, Steve, 1949-
  ★ **Detective** Blue; illustrated by Tedd Arnold. Orchard Books 2011 un il $16.99
Grades: PreK K 1 2   E
  1. Mystery fiction 2. Nursery rhymes -- Fiction
  ISBN 0545172861; 9780545172868
"Metzger and Arnold display a consistent wit on every page, tucking in manifold nursery rhyme references for readers to tease out. Children will enjoy recognizing familiar stories, as well as the satisfying surprise conclusion." Publ Wkly

Meyers, Susan
  Bear in the air; illustrated by Amy Bates. Abrams Books for Young Readers 2010 il $15.95
Grades: PreK K 1   E
  1. Stories in rhyme 2. Adventure fiction 3. Teddy bears -- Fiction 4. Lost and found possessions -- Fiction
  ISBN 978-0-8109-8398-4; 0-8109-8398-2
When a teddy bear is lost by the child who loves him, the bear begins an adventurous journey to get back home again.
"Words are almost unnecessary as the pencil and watercolor illustrations, in appealing beach tones of blue, brown,

and tan, tell the story of the lost, bewildered-looking bear and his surprising journey. . . . A sweet story that will capture the imaginations of young children." SLJ

★ **Everywhere** babies; illustrated by Marla Frazee. Harcourt 2001 un il $16; bd bk $6.95
Grades: PreK K 1   E
1. Infants 2. Stories in rhyme 3. Babies
ISBN 0-15-202226-0; 0-15-205315-8 bd bk
LC 99-6288
Describes babies and the things they do from the time they are born until their first birthday

"The rhythmic rhyming text hums along pleasantly. . . . The many moods, expressions, and body movements of babies are faithfully, gracefully rendered in the pencil drawings, and brightened with watercolors in rather muted hues." Booklist

★ **Kittens!** Kittens! Kittens! by Susan Meyers; illustrated by David Walker. Abrams Books for Young Readers 2007 un il $15.95
Grades: PreK K   E
1. Cats -- Fiction
ISBN 978-0-8109-1218-2; 0-8109-1218-X
LC 2006013575
Illustrations and rhyming text portray kittens as they go from nestling newborns to proud, independent, and ready to have kittens of their own.

"Cheerful rhymes, with the title used as a satisfying refrain, are expanded on by Walker's acrylic artwork in soft-toned, thickly applied colors that have the look of sunny chalks." Booklist

Michalak, Jamie
Joe and Sparky, superstars! illustrated by Frank Remkiewicz. Candlewick Press 2011 37p il $15.99
Grades: K 1 2   E
1. Turtles -- Fiction 2. Giraffes -- Fiction 3. Friendship -- Fiction
ISBN 978-0-7636-4578-6; 0-7636-4578-8
LC 2009006425
When Joe the giraffe and his friend Sparky, a turtle, see a television talent show, Joe tries to find Sparky's talent so that they can compete.

"The font is large and at times changes in appearance to reflect emotion and sound. Michalak and Remkiewicz have written another enjoyable book about two friends who bring out the best in each other." SLJ

Michelin, Linda
Zuzu's wishing cake. Houghton Mifflin Company 2006 un il $16
Grades: PreK K 1   E
1. Gifts -- Fiction 2. Friendship -- Fiction
ISBN 978-0-618-64640-1; 0-618-64640-X
When Zuzu smiles at the new boy next door and he does not smile back, she makes him a series of gifts that she thinks he needs.

"Zuzu does not understand the language [the new boy's] mother speaks, and the cross-cultural connection is a quiet addition to the warm story. Johnson . . . uses bright, bouncy collage-type pictures to show the fun of making exciting gifts and making a friend." Booklist

Michelson, Richard
Across the alley; [by] Richard Michelson; illustrated by E. B. Lewis. G. P. Putnam's Sons 2006 un il $16.99
Grades: K 1 2 3   E
1. Jews -- Fiction 2. Baseball -- Fiction 3. Friendship -- Fiction 4. Violinists -- Fiction 5. African Americans -- Fiction
ISBN 0-399-23970-7
LC 2005032656
Jewish Abe's grandfather wants him to be a violinist while African-American Wille's father plans for him to be a great baseball pitcher, but it turns out that the two boys are more talented when they switch hobbies.

"The poignancy of two boys who can be friends only at night is revealed brilliantly in both text and rich watercolor art." SLJ

★ **Busing** Brewster; illustrated by R. G. Roth. Knopf 2010 un il $16.99
Grades: 1 2 3   E
1. School stories 2. African Americans -- Fiction 3. School integration -- Fiction
ISBN 978-0-375-83334-2; 0-375-83334-X; 978-0-375-93334-9 lib bdg; 0-375-93334-4 lib bdg
LC 2009-22626
Bused across town to a school in a white neigborhood of Boston in 1974, a young African American boy named Brewster describes his first day in first grade. Includes historical notes on the court-ordered busing.

"This title will make a good addition for libraries that want to strengthen their picture book collection by adding material on this period in the African-American experience." Libr Media Connect

Miché, Mary
Nature's patchwork quilt; understanding habitats. by Mary Miché; illustrated by Consie Powell. Dawn Publications 2012 32 p.
Grades: 1 2 3   E
1. Nature -- Juvenile literature 2. Habitat (Ecology) -- Juvenile literature 3. Natural history -- Juvenile literature 4. Nature study -- Activity programs -- Juvenile literature
ISBN 1584691697; 9781584691693; 9781584691709
LC 2011048064
This children's book by Mary Miché "presents [natural] habitats while introducing environmental vocabulary: interdependence, niche, food chain, adaptations, biodiversity, deforestation and domestication, among others. . . . [W]ater-color quilts of different patterns dominate Powell's double-page compositions. A large center scene is surrounded by tiny blocks that each house lifelike depictions of the plants and animals that make up a habitat: forest, desert, ocean, rainforest, etc." (Kirkus)
Includes bibliographical references

Micklethwait, Lucy
★ **I** spy: an alphabet in art; devised & selected by Lucy Micklethwait. Greenwillow Bks. 1992 un il $19.99; pa $10.99
Grades: K 1 2 3   E
1. Alphabet 2. Art appreciation
ISBN 0-688-11679-5; 0-688-14730-5 pa
LC 91-42212

Presents objects for the letters of the alphabet through paintings by such artists as Magritte, Picasso, Botticelli, and Vermeer

"The author's stated intention of introducing young children to fine art, her choice of paintings, the handsome book design, and the quality of paper and reproduction take this beyond the usual alphabet book." Booklist

Other titles in this series are:

I spy a freight train: transportation in art (1996)

I spy a lion: animals in art (1994)

I spy colors in art (2007)

I spy shapes in art (2004)

I spy two eyes: numbers in art (1993)

Middleton, Charlotte

Nibbles: a green tale. Marshall Cavendish Children 2010 un il $17.99

Grades: PreK K 1 2   E

1. Dandelions -- Fiction 2. Guinea pigs -- Fiction 3. Plant conservation -- Fiction

ISBN 978-0-7614-5791-6; 0-7614-5791-7

"A guinea pig loves dandelions, just like everyone else in his town. The plants are eaten for breakfast, lunch, dinner, and all snacks in between until they slowly disappear. . . . Luckily Nibbles discovers a lone dandelion survivor growing under his bedroom window. With great patience and the help of a library book, he cares for his secret treasure until it has a full head of billowy white seeds. Then . . . he blows the precious seeds all over Dandeville. . . . Middleton's tale of overconsuming and scarcity is direct but not preachy. . . . The text is simple and age appropriate, but the mixed-media illustrations steal the show." SLJ

Middleton, Julie

Are the dinosaurs dead, Dad? written by Julie Middleton; illustrated by Russell Ayto. Peachtree Publishers 2013 32 p. ill. (reinforced) $16.95

Grades: K 1 2   E

1. Museums -- Juvenile fiction 2. Dinosaurs -- Juvenile fiction 3. Father-child relationship -- Juvenile fiction 4. Dinosaurs -- Fiction 5. Father and child -- Fiction

ISBN 156145690X; 9781561456901

LC 2012025716

"This story follows Dave and his dad to a natural history museum, where dinosaurs on exhibit come alive when Dad's back is turned, winking at Dave, tickling him, and attempting to snag a bite of his burger. Dave's dad dismisses questions . . . with the classic parental response, 'It's just your imagination.' But when a Tyrannosaurus rex follows the pair out of the exhibit and lets loose with an ear-splitting roar, Dad changes his mind at a dead run." (School Library Journal)

Miles, Victoria

Old Mother Bear; by Victoria Miles; illustrated by Molly Bang. Chronicle Books 2007 un il $16.95

Grades: 1 2 3 4   E

1. Bears -- Fiction 2. Grizzly bear -- Juvenile literature

ISBN 978-0-8118-5033-9; 0-8118-5033-1

LC 2006011651

A twenty-four-year-old grizzly bear gives birth to her last litter of cubs, then spends three years teaching them what they need to know to survive in their southern British Columbia home before they go off on their own. In-

cludes facts about grizzlies and the Khutzeymateen Grizzly Bear Sanctuary.

"The detailed zoology facts are the gripping story in this realistic picture book, which is based on true events and illustrated in beautifully textured, closeup, oil-and-chalk artwork by . . . artist Bang." Booklist

Milgrim, David

Amelia makes a movie; by David Milgrim. G.P. Putnam's Sons 2008 un il $16.99

Grades: K 1 2   E

1. Stories in rhyme 2. Siblings -- Fiction 3. Motion pictures -- Production and direction -- Fiction

ISBN 978-0-399-24670-8

LC 2007018389

Ably assisted by her younger brother Drew, Amelia makes a home video, from writing a script and casting herself as the star to hearing the reviews after their big premiere.

"Each time Amelia calls, 'Action,' Milgrim switches from full-page illustrations to framed comics panels. He works in digital media, yet his draftsmanship suggests traditional pen-and-ink. . . . An entertaining and practical how-to." Publ Wkly

Eddie gets ready for school. Cartwheel Books 2011 un il $8.99

Grades: PreK K 1   E

1. School stories 2. Mother-son relationship -- Fiction

ISBN 978-0-545-27329-9; 0-545-27329-3

LC 2010016779

As young Eddie goes through his checklist to get ready for school, his mother does not agree with all of his choices.

"Big, bold cartoons make their lighthearted tug-of-war the center of attention, as grinning Eddie sheepishly responds to the amended checklist. . . . Readers accustomed to chasing the bus with one shoe on will relate." Publ Wkly

My dog, Buddy. Scholastic 2008 un il pa $3.99

Grades: K 1 2   E

1. Dogs -- Fiction 2. Family life -- Fiction

ISBN 978-0-545-03593-4 pa; 0-545-03593-7 pa

LC 2007-22795

Mom, Dad, and brother Pete all try to get Buddy to obey, but only one family member understands how to communicate with the mischievous canine.

"Digitally created art suggests line and watercolor in its smooth planes of color neatly bordered by slightly off-kilter lines. . . . Packed with pithy humor, sly irreverence, and rampant usefulness, this is a beginning reader's best friend." Bull Cent Child Books

★ **Santa** Duck. G.P. Putnam's Sons 2008 un il lib bdg $16.99

Grades: PreK K 1 2   E

1. Ducks -- Fiction 2. Animals -- Fiction 3. Christmas -- Fiction 4. Santa Claus -- Fiction

ISBN 978-0-399-25018-7; 0-399-25018-2

LC 2007-43162

When Nicholas Duck, wearing a Santa hat and coat he found on his doorstep, goes looking for Santa to tell him what he wants for Christmas, all the other animals mistake him for Mr. Claus.

"Nicholas's silliness and frustration will appeal to youngsters as will the simple message. Milgrim's charming digital ink and oil pastel illustrations use a successful mix of narrative text and cartoon balloons to move the story along at a brisk pace." SLJ

Another title about Santa Duck is:
Santa Duck and his merry helpers (2010)

Santa Duck and his merry helpers. G.P. Putnam's Sons 2010 un il $12.99
Grades: PreK K 1 2   E
1. Ducks -- Fiction 2. Christmas -- Fiction 3. Santa Claus -- Fiction 4. Christmas stories -- Juvenile literature
ISBN 978-0-399-25473-4; 0-399-25473-0

It's Christmastime, so Nicholas Duck puts on his Santa's helper suit and proudly starts gathering wish lists for Santa. But this year, Nicholas's little brothers and sister want to help.

"A multifaceted plot and some succinct lessons are skillfully conveyed in just a few pages, with the funny dialogue contained in speech balloons within the holiday-bright, cartoon-style illustrations." Kirkus

Time to get up, time to go. Clarion Books 2006 32p il $15
Grades: PreK K   E
1. Stories in rhyme 2. Day -- Fiction 3. Dolls -- Fiction
ISBN 0-618-51998-X; 978-0-618-51998-9
LC 2005011359

"From early morning to bedtime, a boy whirls through his day's activities, taking care of his stuffed blue doll. . . . Milgrim's digital oil-paint illustrations have muted, pleasant shades with the figures crisply outlined in black. They work well with the minimal text, in which not a word is wasted." SLJ

Milich, Zoran
City 1 2 3. Kids Can Press 2005 un il $15.95; pa $6.95
Grades: PreK K 1 2   E
1. Counting
ISBN 1-55337-540-8; 1-55453-163-2 pa

Photographs of objects such as skyscrapers, bags of leaves, fire trucks, and taxis illustrate numbers from 1 to 10

"An excellent, well-constructed concept book. . . . The superb pictures feature not only the required number of items, but the corresponding numeral as well." SLJ

City colors. Kids Can Press 2004 un il $14.95; pa $5.95
Grades: PreK K 1 2   E
1. Color
ISBN 1-55337-542-4; 1-55337-981-0 pa

This is a collection of color photographs of objects found in cities such as a red bus, a blue warehouse wall, and a yellow highway cone, a green swing, an orange cylindrical curb block, and a purple playground stool.

This is "a dazzling . . . concept book. . . . Precise partial photos inspire speculation on each verso with the recto revealing the complete image." SLJ

Millen, C. M.
The **ink** garden of brother Theophane; illustrated by Andrea Wisnewski. Charlesbridge 2010 un il $17.95

Grades: 1 2 3 4   E
1. Stories in rhyme 2. Monks -- Fiction 3. Middle Ages -- Fiction 4. Illumination of books and manuscripts -- Fiction
ISBN 978-1-58089-179-0; 1-58089-179-9

In medieval Ireland, Theophane's boredom with his duties as a scribe distracts the other monks, but when he is sent to the kitchens he discovers that he can make inks of many colors from plants, allowing the others to illustrate their work. Includes facts about the history of monasteries, scriptoriums, and illuminated manuscripts.

"Written in rhythmic, rhyming, and rear-rhyming verse, the simple story unfolds in a satisfying way, accompanied by short poems inspired by the writings of Irish monks. The richly detailed illustrations were created by using a papercut design to print bold, black lines and brightening the pictures with watercolors." Booklist

Miller, Pat
Squirrel's New Year's resolution; illustrated by Kathi Ember. Albert Whitman & Co. 2010 un il $16.99
Grades: PreK K 1   E
1. New Year -- Fiction 2. Squirrels -- Fiction 3. Forest animals -- Fiction
ISBN 978-0-8075-7591-8; 0-8075-7591-7
LC 2009-49305

Squirrel cannot think of a New Year's resolution until she realizes that by helping her friends, she has made one after all.

"The simple dialogue and predictable plot make this a good read-aloud, and the brightly colored, acrylic cartoons are full of fun details and expression, giving the woodland creatures anthropomorphic characteristics." SLJ

Miller, Sara Swan
★ **Three** more stories you can read to your dog; illustrated by True Kelley. Houghton Mifflin 2000 un il $14; pa $5.95
Grades: PreK K 1 2   E
1. Dogs 2. Dogs -- Fiction
ISBN 0-395-92293-3; 0-618-15244-X pa
LC 99-39880

Stories addressed to dogs and written from a dog's point of view, featuring such topics as going to the vet, making friends with a rocklike creature, and getting a bath

"The witty, believable portrayal of canine thoughts and behavior will amuse readers. . . . True Kelley's lively ink-and-watercolor illustrations brighten every page." Booklist
Other titles in this series are:
Three more stories you can read to your cat (2002)
Three stories you can read to your cat (1997)
Three stories you can read to your dog (1995)
Three stories you can read to your teddy bear (2004)

Miller, William
★ **Night** golf; illustrated by Cedric Lucas. Lee & Low Bks. 1999 un il hardcover o.p. pa $8.95
Grades: K 1 2 3   E
1. Golf -- Fiction 2. Prejudices -- Fiction 3. Afro-Americans -- Fiction 4. African Americans -- Fiction 5. Afro-Americans -- Juvenile fiction
ISBN 1-880000-79-2; 1-58430-056-6 pa
LC 98-47168

Despite being told that only whites can play golf, James becomes a caddy and is befriended by an older African American man who teaches him to play on the course at night

"Gentle paste and pencil illustrations support this quietly powerful story." Horn Book Guide

★ **Rent** party jazz; illustrated by Charlotte Riley-Webb. Lee & Low Bks. 2001 un il $16.95; pa $7.95

Grades: K 1 2 3   E

1. Jazz 2. Jazz music -- Fiction

ISBN 1-58430-025-6; 1-60060-344-0 pa

LC 2001-16449

When Sonny's mother loses her job in New Orleans during the Depression, Smilin' Jack, a jazz musician, tells him how to organize a rent party to raise the money they need

"Miller uses folksy dialogue to tell the story that celebrates both community and the uplifting power of music. Evocative artwork, done in broad, swirling strokes, fills pages with color and motion." Booklist

Millman, Isaac

★ **Moses** goes to school. Farrar, Straus & Giroux 2000 un il $16

Grades: PreK K 1 2   E

1. Deaf 2. Schools 3. Sign language 4. School stories 5. Hearing impaired 6. Deaf -- Fiction 7. First day of school 8. People with disabilities 9. Sign language -- Fiction

ISBN 0-374-35069-8

LC 99-40582

Moses and his friends enjoy the first day of school at their special school for the deaf and hard of hearing, where they use sign language to talk to each other

"Child-friendly cartoon illustrations do a marvelous job of emphasizing the normalcy and charm of these youngsters. . . . The double-page layouts nicely accommodate the primary pictorial action along with written text and ASL inserts. . . . [This is a] great contribution to children's education about disabilities that also succeeds as effective storytelling in its own right." SLJ

Other titles about Moses are:

Moses goes to a concert (1998)

Moses goes to the circus (2003)

Moses sees a play (2004)

Mills, Claudia

★ **Gus** and Grandpa and the two-wheeled bike; pictures by Catherine Stock. Farrar, Straus & Giroux 1999 47p il hardcover o.p. pa $7.99

Grades: K 1 2 3   E

1. Cycling -- Fiction 2. Grandfathers -- Fiction 3. Bicycles and bicycling -- Fiction

ISBN 0-374-32821-8; 0-374-42816-6 pa

LC 97-44203

Gus doesn't want to give up the training wheels on his bike, even for a new five-speed bicycle, until Grandpa helps him learn how to get along without them

"Mills conveys strong sentiment without a trace of mawkishness, and Stock's illustrations in loose line and watercolor augment the story of this childhood rite of passage expressively." Horn Book Guide

Other titles about Gus and Grandpa are:

Gus and Grandpa (1997)

Gus and Grandpa and show-and-tell (2000)

Gus and Grandpa and the Christmas cookies (1997)

Gus and Grandpa and the Halloween costume (2002)

Gus and Grandpa and the piano lesson (2004)

Gus and Grandpa at basketball (2001)

Gus and Grandpa at the hospital (1998)

Gus and Grandpa go fishing (2003)

Gus and Grandpa ride the train (1998)

Milord, Susan

Happy 100th day! illustrated by Mary Newell DePalma. Scholastic Press 2011 37p il $16.99

Grades: PreK K 1 2   E

1. School stories 2. Birthdays -- Fiction 3. Books and reading -- Fiction

ISBN 978-0-439-88281-1; 0-439-88281-8

LC 2010009848

"Graham is a reluctant student at the start of the new school year. His irritability is compounded by the fact that his teacher is gung-ho about the 100th day, an event that just happens to fall on Graham's birthday, threatening to overshadow his own celebration. In addition Miss Currier assigns everyone a 100th day goal; Graham's is to complete 100 books despite the fact that he is a 'lousy' reader. In timeline fashion, Milord shows his progress. DePalma's delightful cartoon illustrations perfectly capture the boy's frustration and eventual pride, and the pages are chock-full of graphic elements that mirror the wall art and teaching tools of a typical first-grade classroom." SLJ

Love that baby! written and illustrated by Susan Milord. Houghton Mifflin 2005 un il $7.95

Grades: PreK K 1   E

1. Infants -- Fiction

ISBN 0-618-56323-7

LC 2004-25119

"Each folded-over page poses a situation to ponder, while the unfolded spread beneath it suggests what to do next. A drawing of a . . . child . . . is accompanied by the words: 'Baby is hungry,' while the picture of father . . . gives the advice, 'Feed that baby!' Other pages offer suggested actions to take if the baby is napping, hiding, scared, sad, or sleepy. Simple drawings, soft colors in offbeat combinations, and a variety of patterns give this simple picture book visual appeal, while the lift-the-flap game will make it enjoyable for toddlers to revisit again and again." Booklist

Milway, Katie Smith

One hen; how one small loan made a big difference. written by Katie Smith Milway; illustrated by Eugenie Fernandes. Kids Can Press 2008 32p il $18.95

Grades: 2 3 4   E

1. Eggs -- Fiction 2. Loans -- Fiction 3. Chickens -- Fiction

ISBN 978-1-55453-028-1; 1-55453-028-8

"In Ghana, young Kojo has a business idea, borrowing a small bit of money from his mother to purchase a hen, intending to sell her extra eggs at the market. Slowly his income grows so that he can not only pay his mother back but he can also buy more hens; eventually, he has enough money to go back to school. . . . [This gains] power from its modeling on a real Ghanian entrepeneur, Kwabena Darko. . . . The beneficial effects of small loans and small projects are thoughtfully and carefully explained in the extensive text.

. . . Acrylic illustrations, vivid and lively with an emphasis on sunny hues and warm earthtones, balance out the large blocks of text." Bull Cent Child Books

Includes glossary

Minarik, Else Holmelund

★ **Little** Bear; pictures by Maurice Sendak. Harper & Row 1957 63p il (I can read book) $16.95; lib bdg $17.89; pa $3.95

Grades: PreK K 1 2   E

1. Bears -- Fiction

ISBN 0-06-024240-X; 0-06-024241-8 lib bdg; 0-06-444004-4 pa

The pictures "depict all the warmth of feeling and the special companionship that exists between a small child and his mother." Publ Wkly

Other titles about Little Bear are:

Father Bear comes home (1959)

A kiss for Little Bear (1968)

Little Bear's friend (1960)

Little Bear's visit (1961)

Little Bear and the Marco Polo (2010)

★ **No** fighting, no biting! pictures by Maurice Sendak. Harper & Row 1958 62p il (I can read book) lib bdg $17.89; pa $3.95

Grades: PreK K 1 2   E

1. Alligators -- Fiction

ISBN 0-06-024291-4 lib bdg; 0-06-444015-X pa

"A young lady who is unable to read in peace because of two children squabbling beside her tells them a story about two little alligators whose fighting and biting almost lead to disastrous consequences with a big hungry alligator. Children are sure to accept and enjoy the lesson in this little adventure tale and be amused by the expressive old-fashioned drawings." Booklist

Minor, Wendell

My farm friends. G.P. Putnam's Sons 2011 un il $16.99

Grades: PreK K   E

1. Stories in rhyme 2. Farm life -- Fiction 3. Domestic animals -- Fiction

ISBN 0399244778; 9780399244773

LC 2010014793

Simple, rhyming text describes the characteristics of different farm animals. Includes 'Farm friends fun facts' and books and websites for further reading.

"Drawing on childhood memories of his family's Illinois farm, Minor celebrates farm animals—furry, feathered, hairy, and woolly—with warm watercolor-and-gouache artwork and cozy, playful rhymes that young children will love to hear many times over." Booklist

Miranda, Anne

★ **To** market, to market; written by Anne Miranda; illustrated by Janet Stevens. Harcourt Brace & Co. 1997 un il $16; pa $7

Grades: PreK K 1 2   E

1. Stories in rhyme 2. Animals -- Fiction

ISBN 0-15-200035-6; 0-15-216398-0 pa

LC 95-26326

"Patterned, staccato verses tell the zany tale, but it is Stevens's wonderfully wild illustrations that bring it to life." SLJ

Miron, Marie-Charlotte

My Little Handbook of Experiments; Physics, Water and Light, Ecology. by Marie-Charlotte Miron and Melanie Perez; illustrated by Vincent Hubert and Sandrine Lamour; translated by Susan Allen Maurin. Innovative Logistics Llc 2012 144 p. ill. (hardcover) $12.95

Grades: 2 3 4   E

1. Science -- Experiments 2. Science -- Study and teaching

ISBN 2733821474; 9782733821473

This book packs a "collection of science activities into three sections. . . . The unspecified 'Sciences' section is . . . approximately 18 activities including color, electricity and magnets, plus photography, astronomy, meteorology, and more. 'Water and Light' and 'Ecology' are" also included. (School Library Journal)

Mitchell, Margaree King

★ **Uncle** Jed's barbershop; illustrated by James Ransome. Simon & Schuster Bks. for Young Readers 1993 un il hardcover o.p. pa $6.99

Grades: PreK K 1 2   E

1. Uncles -- Fiction 2. African Americans -- Fiction 3. Barbers and barbershops -- Fiction

ISBN 0-671-76969-3; 0-689-81913-7 pa

LC 91-44148

Despite serious obstacles and setbacks Sarah Jean's Uncle Jed, the only black barber in the county, pursues his dream of saving enough money to open his own barbershop

"The author's convivial depictions of family life are enhanced by Ransome's . . . spirited oil paintings, which set the affectionate intergenerational cast against brightly patterned walls and crisp, leaf-strewn landscapes." Publ Wkly

When grandmama sings; illustrated by James Ransome. HarperCollins/Amistad 2011 un il $16.99

Grades: 2 3 4   E

1. Singers -- Fiction 2. Jazz music -- Fiction 3. Segregation -- Fiction 4. Grandmothers -- Fiction 5. Race relations -- Fiction 6. African Americans -- Fiction

ISBN 978-0-688-17563-4; 0-688-17563-5

"Set in the segregated South of the 1950s, Mitchell's poignant story features eight-year-old Belle and her loving, stalwart African-American family. When Grandmama, who can't read but whose singing voice captures the hearts of all who hear her, joins a jazz band for a tour of the South, Belle pleads to go along. . . . She experiences firsthand the difficulties her people face: hotels marked 'White Only,' diners that refuse them service, police who search their cars and luggage for no reason. . . . Ransome's full-page images, rich in color and feeling, portray the landscapes of the South and the individual emotions of the characters with equal aplomb." SLJ

Mitchell, Stephen

The **ugly** duckling; retold by Stephen Mitchell; illustrated by Steve Johnson and Lou Fancher. Candlewick Press 2008 un il $16.99

Grades: K 1 2 3   E

1. Authors 2. Novelists 3. Dramatists 4. Fairy tales

5. Swans -- Fiction 6. Children's authors 7. Short story writers

ISBN 978-0-7636-2159-9

LC 2007-34235

An ugly duckling spends an unhappy year ostracized by the other animals before he grows into a beautiful swan.

"Mitchell retells the familiar story, preserving just enough of the character of Andersen's narrative voice to give his adaptation a tart, bracing flavor.... Johnson and Fancher's lacy, luminous art, rich with underwaterlike greens, gives [the swan's transformation] all the visual splendor it deserves." Horn Book

Miura, Taro

★ **Tools**. Chronicle Books 2006 un il $15.95
Grades: PreK K 1   E
1. Tools

ISBN 978-0-8118-5519-8; 0-8118-5519-8

LC 2005-34057

"Miura shows a distinctive set of tools on a double-page spread, identifying items such as a clamp, a saw, and nails. A turn of the page reveals the worker using them. Prereading children will enjoy identifying the tools, but their biggest challenge will be guessing the occupation represented. ... The guessing-game aspect adds an element of fun to this beautifully designed and distinctively illustrated book." Booklist

Mobin-Uddin, Asma

★ The **best** Eid ever; [by] Asma Mobin-Uddin; illustrated by Laura Jacobsen. Boyds Mills Press 2007 un il $16.95
Grades: K 1 2 3   E
1. Muslims -- Fiction 2. Id al-Adha -- Fiction 3. Grandmothers -- Fiction 4. Pakistani Americans -- Fiction

ISBN 978-1-59078-431-0; 1-59078-431-6

LC 2006037945

Eid is the Islamic holiday that marks the end of Ramadan. In this story, young Aneesa meets two girls at the prayer hall dressed in ill-fitting clothes and discovers they are refugees. Aneesa comes up with a plan to make this the best Eid ever

"This is a heartwarming tale of a child's generosity, and Jacobsen's illustrations flesh out the warmth and tenderness of the characters' interaction." SLJ

A **party** in Ramadan; illustrated by Laura Jacobsen. Boyds Mills Press 2009 un il $16.95
Grades: K 1 2 3   E
1. Muslims -- Fiction 2. Parties -- Fiction 3. Ramadan -- Fiction

ISBN 978-1-59078-604-8; 1-59078-604-1

LC 2008-43890

"With lively pastel-and-pencil artwork, this warm picture book shows and tells the observance and meaning of Ramadan through the viewpoint of a Muslim child. Leena is happy to be invited to her friend's birthday party, although it turns out that the event is on a day during Ramadan when Leena plans to fast with her family.... The blend of the upbeat with challenging moments will spark discussion, and a final note fills in more about the holy month." Booklist

Mochizuki, Ken

★ **Baseball** saved us; written by Ken Mochizuki; illustrated by Dom Lee. Lee & Low Bks. 1993 un il $16.95; pa $6.95
Grades: K 1 2 3   E
1. Baseball -- Fiction 2. Prejudices -- Fiction 3. World War, 1939-1945 -- Fiction 4. Japanese Americans -- Evacuation and relocation, 1942-1945 -- Fiction

ISBN 1-880000-01-6; 1-880000-19-9 pa

LC 92-73215

A Japanese American boy learns to play baseball when he and his family are forced to live in an internment camp during World War II, and his ability to play helps him after the war is over

"Fences and watchtowers are in the background of many of Lee's moving illustrations, some of which were inspired by Ansel Adams' 1943 photographs of Manzanar.... The baseball action will grab kids—and so will the personal experience of bigotry." Booklist

Heroes; written by Ken Mochizuki; illustrated by Dom Lee. Lee & Low Bks. 1995 un il hardcover o.p. pa $6.95
Grades: K 1 2 3   E
1. Prejudices -- Fiction 2. Japanese Americans -- Fiction

ISBN 1-880000-16-4; 1-880000-50-4 pa

LC 94-26541

"The book is a powerful exploration of the cruelty children can inflict upon one another and of the confusion and pain borne by the target of such unthinking racism." Horn Book

Modarressi, Mitra

Taking care of Mama. G.P. Putnam's Sons 2010 un il $16.99
Grades: PreK K 1 2   E
1. Stories in rhyme 2. Sick -- Fiction 3. Raccoons -- Fiction 4. Family life -- Fiction

ISBN 978-0-399-25216-7; 0-399-25216-9

LC 2009011315

When Mama raccoon gets sick, Papa and the kids wear themselves out doing the cooking and cleaning for the day.

"The watercolor scenes ... capture cozy family chaos, while the smooth text make this a good read-aloud choice." Booklist

Moerbeek, Kees

★ **Count** 1 to 10. Abrams 2011 un il
Grades: K 1 2 3 4   E
1. Counting 2. Pop-up books

ISBN 0-8109-9644-8; 978-0-8109-9644-1

LC 2010928779

"A showpiece of popup design features the numbers one through 10 worked into multileveled constructs of dazzling virtuosity. Made fro brightly colored digits floating over contrasting monochromatic backgrounds ... the pop-ups range from a die-cut '1' that rotates into place and a pair of '2's folding out from behind a screen to phalanxes of '9's and '10's floating up as thier spreads open.... Every opening provides initial surprises, plenty of angles and spaces to explore and a rich visual experience."

Mol, Sine van

Meena; illustrated by Carianne Wijffels. Eerdmans Books for Young Readers 2011 un il $17

Grades: 1 2 3   E

1. Fear -- Fiction 2. Old age -- Fiction 3. Prejudices -- Fiction 4. Grandmothers -- Fiction

ISBN 978-0-8028-5394-3; 0-8028-5394-3

LC 2010049547

The children of Fly Street fear and taunt their neighbor Meena, thinking she is a witch, but when they meet her granddaughter and taste her red currant pie, they learn the truth.

"Simple sentences and a lot of dialogue will appeal to emerging readers. Wijffels uses childlike line drawings to show the youngsters' fevered imaginings. . . . Collage elements, children's art, and blue line drawings on uncluttered white space give the story unexpected depth." SLJ

Mollel, Tololwa M.

★ My rows and piles of coins; illustrated by E. B. Lewis. Clarion Bks. 1999 32p il $15

Grades: K 1 2 3   E

1. Money -- Fiction 2. Bicycles -- Fiction 3. Bicycles and bicycling -- Fiction

ISBN 0-395-75186-1

LC 98-21586

A Coretta Scott King honor book for illustration, 2000

A Tanzanian boy saves his coins to buy a bicycle so that he can help his parents carry goods to market, but then he discovers that in spite of all he has saved, he still does not have enough money

"The story is natural and never excessively moralistic. The fluid, light-splashed watercolor illustrations lend a sense of place and authenticity." SLJ

Monari, Manuela

Zero kisses for me! illustrated by Virginie Soumagnac. Tundra Books 2010 un il $12.95

Grades: PreK K   E

1. Kissing -- Fiction 2. Parent-child relationship -- Fiction

ISBN 978-1-77049-208-0; 1-77049-208-9

"A little one goes on strike against kisses. . . . Told mostly in a loving dialogue between mother and child, the language and syntax are true to life and utterly believable. Soumagnac's cartoon-style illustrations are a perfect match. . . . This is a sit-on-your-lap, kiss-and-hug read-aloud." Kirkus

Monfreid, Dorothee de

Dark night. Random House Children's Books 2009 un il $14.99; lib bdg $17.99

Grades: PreK K 1 2   E

1. Fear -- Fiction 2. Night -- Fiction 3. Animals -- Fiction

ISBN 978-0-375-85687-7; 0-375-85687-0; 978-0-375-95687-4 lib bdg; 0-375-95687-5 lib bdg

LC 2008011257

Original French edition, 2007

When he wanders into the forest at night, Felix, terrified by the ferocious animals he sees, finds refuge in an unusual underground house.

"De Monfreid's watercolor-and-ink illustrations are simple, charming, and extraordinarily expressive, making this a lovely book to add to any collection." SLJ

Monjo, F. N.

★ The drinking gourd; a story of the Underground Railroad. pictures by Fred Brenner. newly il ed.; HarperCollins Pubs. 1993 62p il (I can read book) pa $3.99

Grades: K 1 2 3   E

1. Underground railroad -- Fiction

ISBN 0-06-444042-7 pa

LC 92-10823

First published 1970

Set in New England in the decade before the Civil War. For mischievous behavior in church, Tommy is sent home to his room, but wanders instead into the barn. There he discovers that his father is helping runaway slaves escape to Canada

"The simplicity of dialogue and exposition, the level of concepts, and the length of the story [makes] it most suitable for the primary grades reader. The illustrations are deftly representational, the whole a fine addition to the needed body of historical books for the very young." Bull Cent Child Books

Monroe, Chris

Monkey with a tool belt. Carolrhoda 2008 un il lib bdg $16.95

Grades: K 1 2 3   E

1. Tools -- Fiction 2. Monkeys -- Fiction

ISBN 978-0-8225-7631-0; 0-8225-7631-7

LC 2007-10020

Clever monkey Chico Bon Bon builds lots of things with his many tools, and when he is captured by an organ grinder, he uses them to help him escape and get back home.

"Slightly edgy, highly detailed comics-style art will have readers poring over the pages. . . . Not only gadget jockeys will enjoy this visually polished tale." Publ Wkly

Other titles about Chico are:

Monkey with a tool belt and the noisy problem (2009)

Monkey with a tool belt and the seaside shenanigans (2011)

★ Sneaky sheep. Carolrhoda Books 2010 un il lib bdg $16.95

Grades: PreK K 1 2   E

1. Sheep -- Fiction

ISBN 978-0-7613-5615-8 lib bdg; 0-7613-5615-0 lib bdg

LC 2009040852

Blossom and Rocky, two sneaky and not very bright sheep, keep trying to get away from the rest of the flock, in spite of the dangers they encounter.

"Monroe's pen-and-ink and watercolor illustrations are entertaining; kids will enjoy following Rocky and Blossom's antics both in and out of panels." SLJ

Montes, Marisa

★ Los gatos black on Halloween; illustrated by Yuyi Morales. Henry Holt and Company 2006 un il $16.95

Grades: PreK K 1 2   E

1. Stories in rhyme 2. Halloween -- Fiction 3. Spanish language -- Vocabulary

ISBN 978-0-8050-7429-1; 0-8050-7429-5

LC 2005-20049

A Pura Belpré Author Award honor book, 2008

Easy to read, rhyming text about Halloween night incorporates Spanish words, from las brujas riding their broomsticks to los monstruos whose monstrous ball is interrupted by a true horror.

"Montes smoothly incorporates Spanish terms into a rhythmic poem. . . . The full-bleed paintings create a creepy mood with curving lines, fluid textures, and dusky hues. . . . The pictures are eerie enough to tingle spines, but the effect is leavened with bits of humor." SLJ

Montijo, Rhode

The **Halloween** Kid. Simon & Schuster 2010 un il $12.99

Grades: PreK K 1 2   **E**

1. Cowhands -- Fiction 2. Halloween -- Fiction

ISBN 978-1-4169-3575-9; 1-4169-3575-4

The brave and trusty Halloween Kid saves trick-or-treaters from a crowd of sweet-stealing Goodie Goblins.

"This rollicking story projects a delightfully retro style and sensibility, aided by black, white, and orange brush-and-ink illustrations. . . . A treat for storytime as well as for independent reading and a must for Halloween picture-book collections." SLJ

Moore, Eva

Lucky Ducklings; by Eva Moore; illustrations by Nancy Carpenter. Orchard Books 2013 32 p. (hardcover: alk. paper) $16.99

Grades: K 1 2 3   **E**

1. Animal rescue 2. Ducks -- Fiction 3. Animal babies -- Juvenile fiction 4. Rescues -- Fiction 5. Animals -- Infancy -- Fiction

ISBN 0439448611; 9780439448611

LC 2012002444

Author Eva Moore presents a children's picture book on ducks. "Early one morning, Mama Duck takes her babies for a walk. They follow safely behind her as they leave their pond, waddle through the park, and stop in the little sunlit town's parking lot for yummy breakfast. But one by one, Mama's little ducklings get separated when they disappear into the slats of the town's storm drain." Moore describes "how three firemen and a pickup truck rush to their rescue." (Publisher's note)

Moore, Genevieve

Catherine's story; illustrated by Karin Littlewood. Frances Lincoln Children's 2010 un il $17.95

Grades: 1 2 3   **E**

1. Handicapped -- Fiction

ISBN 978-1-84507-655-9; 1-84507-655-9

"Catherine, who wears leg braces, has a special walk and a special way of clapping her hands (so quietly, no one ever hears them). Her cousin Frances thinks she can walk like Catherine but when she tries, she falls over. When she says that Catherine can't talk, Catherine's dad says, 'lots and lots of people talk . . . too much . . . Catherine listens—really, really hard.' Catherine is loved and valued. . . . The lovely watercolor illustrations capture joy and optimism. With subtlety and grace, they perfectly depict a child with disabilities." SLJ

Moore, Inga

A **house** in the woods. Candlewick Press 2011 il $16.99

Grades: PreK K 1   **E**

1. Building -- Fiction 2. Friendship -- Fiction 3. Forest

animals -- Fiction 4. House construction -- Fiction

ISBN 978-0-7636-5277-7; 0-7636-5277-6

LC 2010050827

Two Little Pigs whose small homes in the woods have been accidentally destroyed by Bear and Moose decide to build a house they can all share, and with the help of Beaver Builders they soon have a fine new home.

"The gentle arc of the story about a warm friendship is perfectly echoed by the large, detailed illustrations. The pencil, pastel, and wash art is full of autumn colors and delicate touches and details that bring the woods and the animals to life." SLJ

Moore, Jodi

When a dragon moves in; written by Jodi Moore; illustrated by Howard McWilliam. Flashlight Press 2011 un il $16.95

Grades: PreK K 1   **E**

1. Beaches -- Fiction 2. Dragons -- Fiction 3. Family life -- Fiction 4. Imagination -- Fiction

ISBN 978-0-979974-67-0; 0-979974-67-4

"While enjoying a day at the beach with his family, a boy builds a perfect sand castle and a dragon promptly moves in toting a well-worn suitcase. The youngster can't believe his luck while the rest of the family can't believe him. Mischief blamed on the dragon eventually gets the child in trouble. . . . While the text is fun, the story is truly told through the comical illustrations. The friendly red dragon's expressions are hilarious. . . . This story of a runaway imagination will make for an entertaining storytime as well as an enjoyable one-on-one read." SLJ

Moore, Patrick

The **mighty** street sweeper. Holt & Co. 2006 un il $15.95

Grades: PreK K   **E**

1. Trucks 2. Street cleaning 3. Trucks -- Juvenile literature 4. Street cleaning -- Juvenile literature

ISBN 0-8050-7789-8

"This picture book compares and contrasts the utilitarian street sweeper with a grader, snowplow, bulldozer, and other trucks. While it may not be the largest, most powerful, or fastest machine, it performs an important job. Bright, simple cartoon illustrations of squirrels, cats, dogs, and other animals driving the vehicles are paired with the straightforward text. . . . This offering will delight young truck lovers." SLJ

Mora, Pat

Abuelos; story by Pat Mora; pictures by Amelia Lau Carling. Groundwood Books 2008 un il $18.95

Grades: PreK K 1 2   **E**

1. Winter -- Fiction 2. Hispanic Americans -- Fiction

ISBN 978-0-88899-716-6; 0-88899-716-7

Mora "introduces the intriguing midwinter New Mexican festival of 'los abuelos' in this playful tale. The narrator, Amelia, is about to experience the spooky-sounding tradition for the first time, and Papá offers reassurances. . . . Played by costumed villagers in scary masks, the abuelos chase the children around bonfires; when one snatches her brother, Amelia grabs the abuelo's mask, only to discover her uncle beneath it. Carling's . . . watercolor and pastel illustrations impart Amelia's apprehension as well as family togetherness." Publ Wkly

★ **Book** fiesta! celebrate Children's Day/Book Day. illustrated by Rafael Lopez. HarperCollins 2009 un il $17.99

Grades: PreK K 1 2 3   **E**
   1. Books and reading -- Fiction 2. Bilingual books -- English-Spanish

   ISBN 978-0-06-128877-7; 0-06-128877-2

   ALA ALSC Belpre Illustrator Medal (2010)

   "Mora encourages teachers, parents, and librarians to celebrate Children's Day/Book Day and includes ideas for observing the festivities. Written in English and Spanish, the text shows children reading in a variety of places, going to the library, listening to stories, and enjoying books. López's acrylic illustrations fill the pages with color. His upbeat iconic style shows how much fun this celebration can be." SLJ

★ **Dona** Flor; a tall tale about a giant woman with a great big heart. illustrated by Raul Colón. Knopf 2005 un il $15.99; lib bdg $17.99

Grades: K 1 2 3   **E**
   1. Tall tales 2. Pumas -- Fiction 3. Giants -- Fiction

   ISBN 0-375-82337-9; 0-375-92337-3 lib bdg

Doña Flor, a giant woman with a big heart, sets off to protect her neighbors from what they think is a dangerous animal, but soon discovers the tiny secret behind the huge noise.

"A charming tall tale. . . Colón uses his signature mix of watercolor washes, etching, and litho pencils for the art. There is great texture and movement on each page in the sunbaked tones of the landscape." SLJ

★ **Gracias**; Thanks. ilustraciones por John Parra; traducción por Adriana Domínguez; illustrations by John Parra; translation by Adriana Dominguez. Lee & Low Books 2009 un il

Grades: PreK K 1 2   **E**
   1. Hispanic Americans -- Fiction 2. Racially mixed people -- Fiction 3. Bilingual books -- English-Spanish

   ISBN 1600602584; 9781600602580

                       LC 2009013060

   ALA ALSC Belpre Illustrator Medal Honor Book (2010)

   In this bilingual picture book, a young boy says thank you for many things in his life. "Primary." (Horn Book)

"From the sun waking him up in the morning to a cricket chirping him to sleep at night, a young boy gives thanks for the many things and people who enrich his life. These blessings are remarkable for their childlike imagination and fresh imagery. . . . The bilingual format features Spanish on the left-hand page and English on the right. . . . Parra's vivid acrylic illustrations have the feel of folk-art woodcuts and whimsically portray the details of the boy's world." Booklist

Here, kitty, kitty; illustrated by Maribel Suarez. Rayo 2008 un il (My family, mi familia) $14.99; lib bdg $15.89

Grades: PreK K   **E**
   1. Cats -- Fiction 2. Bilingual books -- English-Spanish

   ISBN 978-0-06-085044-9; 0-06-085044-2; 978-0-06-085045-6 lib bdg; 0-06-085045-0 lib bdg

"This joyful picture book tells a lively story of a young girl who gets a shy new kitten that hides and makes trouble. With English and Spanish text on each double-page spread, the line-and-watercolor pictures show the loving family as the kitten hides under the sofa, under sister's bed, in a flowerpot, until finally the soft friend snuggles up on the girl's lap." Booklist

Tomas and the library lady; illustrated by Raúl Colón. Knopf 1997 un il $17; pa $6.99

Grades: K 1 2 3   **E**
   1. Poets 2. Authors 3. Novelists 4. Essayists 5. College teachers 6. Libraries -- Fiction 7. College administrators 8. Migrant labor -- Fiction 9. Books and reading -- Fiction 10. Mexican Americans -- Fiction

   ISBN 0-679-80401-3; 0-375-80349-1 pa

                     LC 89-37490

While helping his family in their work as migrant laborers far from their home, Tomás finds an entire world to explore in the books at the local public library

"Mora's story is based on a true incident in the life of the famous writer Tomás Rivera, the son of migrant workers who became an education leader and university president. . . . Colón's beautiful scratchboard illustrations, in his textured, glowingly colored, rhythmic style, capture the warmth and the dreams that the boy finds in the world of books." Booklist

Uno, dos, tres: one, two, three; illustrated by Barbara Lavallee. Clarion Bks. 1996 43p il hardcover o.p. pa $6.95

Grades: PreK K 1 2   **E**
   1. Counting 2. Stories in rhyme 3. Bilingual books -- English-Spanish

   ISBN 0-395-67294-5; 0-618-05468-5 pa

                     LC 94-15337

"Two girls search a Mexican market for gifts for their mother's birthday in this counting book in both English and Spanish. . . . Cheerful stylized paintings in muted reds, blues, and yellows depict designs from Mexican art and use pattern to highlight the number sequence." Horn Book Guide

Wiggling pockets. Rayo 2009 un il (My family, mi familia) $12.99

Grades: PreK K   **E**
   1. Frogs -- Fiction 2. Family life -- Fiction 3. Bilingual books -- English-Spanish

   ISBN 978-0-06-085047-0; 0-06-085047-7

"When Danny comes to the table with wiggling pockets, Mom and Dad ask what he has in them. Four frogs jump out and cause minor chaos. The simple text in both English and Spanish and the warm illustrations portray a loving family." Horn Book Guide

Morales, Melita

Jam & honey; illustrations by Laura J. Bryant. Tricycle Press 2011 un il $15.99

Grades: PreK K 1   **E**
   1. Stories in rhyme 2. Bees -- Fiction

   ISBN 978-1-58246-299-8; 1-58246-299-2

Tells the story of a young girl and a honeybee who learn to coexist peacefully in the same garden as they go about their respective tasks.

"Simple, bouncing rhymes switch from the child's viewpoint . . . to the bee's voice. . . . The whimsical, uncluttered watercolor-and-pencil illustrations show each character busy at first, then scared of the other, and finally safe and satisfied on their way home." Booklist

Morales, Yuyi

★ **Just** in case; a trickster tale and Spanish alphabet book. Roaring Brook Press 2008 un il $16.95

Grades: 1 2 3   E

1. Ghost stories 2. Gifts -- Fiction 3. Alphabet -- Fiction 4. Birthdays -- Fiction 5. Spanish language -- Alphabet -- Juvenile literature

ISBN 978-1-59643-329-8; 1-59643-329-9

LC 2007-44061

Awarded the Pura Belpre Illustrator Award, 2009

A Pura Belpre Author Award honor book, 2009

As Senor Calavera prepares for Grandma Beetle's birthday he finds an alphabetical assortment of unusual presents, but with the help of Zelmiro the Ghost, he finds the best gift of all.

"Luminous, jewel-tone spreads chronicle the collection of gifts and pay homage to a rich Mexican culture. . . . Part ghost story and part alphabet book, this trickster tale transcends both. Librarians will want to share it for the beautiful language, the spirited artwork, and the rightness of the ending." SLJ

Little Night. Roaring Brook Press 2006 un il $16.95

Grades: PreK K   E

1. Sky -- Fiction 2. Night -- Fiction 3. Bedtime -- Fiction 4. Mother-daughter relationship -- Fiction

ISBN 978-1-59643-088-4; 1-59643-088-5

LC 2006011571

At the end of a long day, Mother Sky helps her playful daughter, Little Night, to get ready for bed

"Morales has created a sumptuous feast of metaphors in her text: a bathtub filled with falling stars, a dress crocheted from clouds. The equally splendid illustrations effectively convey each of the images and heighten the comfort and serenity inspired by the text." Booklist

Niño wrestles the world; Yuyi Morales. 1st ed. Roaring Brook Press 2013 40 p. ill. (hardcover) $16.99

Grades: PreK K 1 2 3   E

1. Picture books for children 2. Wrestling -- Juvenile fiction 3. Monsters -- Fiction 4. Wrestling -- Fiction 5. Imagination -- Fiction 6. Brothers and sisters -- Fiction

ISBN 1596436042; 9781596436046

LC 2012012989

In this children's picture book, "playing alone in his room, Niño dons his Lucha Libre mask and lets his imagination take flight. (According to an endnote, Lucha Libre is a dramatic form of professional wrestling followed by fans in Mexico.) The young hero is then ready to take on an eclectic cast of monstrous opponents. Spurred on by chanting crowds, the boy handily defeats the Guanajuato Mummy (La Momia de Guanajuato), Olmec Head (Cabeza Olmeca), and the Weeping Woman (La Llorona)." (School Library Journal)

Morgan, Sally

Me and my dad; [by] Sally Morgan and Ezekiel Kwaymullina; illustrated by Matt Ottley. Little Hare Books 2011 un il $16.99

Grades: PreK K 1   E

1. Fear -- Fiction 2. Birds -- Fiction 3. Beaches -- Fiction 4. Father-son relationship -- Fiction

ISBN 978-1-921541-81-0; 1-921541-81-4

"During an action-filled day at the beach, a boy recounts everything his father isn't afraid of. . . . Making dynamic use of perspective and scale, Ottley shows the boy's father laughing as a skyscraper-high sandcastle tumbles down on him, flexing his bicep while a surging wave threatens to swallow him up, and confidently swimming amid transparent jellyfish to unhook a fishing line. There's a cartoonish sense of playfulness throughout, right up to the final scene in which the father's sole, improbable fear—seagulls—is revealed, giving the boy a chance to be the brave one." Publ Wkly

Sam's bush journey; [by] Sally Morgan and Ezekiel Kwaymullina; illustrated by Bronwyn Bancroft. Little Hare Books 2010 un il $15.99; pa $8.99

Grades: PreK K 1   E

1. Grandmothers -- Fiction 2. Aboriginal Australians -- Fiction

ISBN 978-1-921541-04-9; 1-921541-04-0; 978-1-921541-72-8 pa; 1-921541-72-8 pa

"Living in Australia, Sam's grandmother loves the bush that surrounds her house. On their long walks into the gum forest to the waterhole, spiky shrubs scratch the boy's legs and mosquitoes bite him. Though Nanna tells him about the many good things there, Sam would be happy if they all disappeared. One night he dreams of wandering in the bush lost and alone. Remembering what Nanna has told him, he finds edible berries when his stomach grumbles and shelter in a hollow gum tree during a storm. . . . Stunning illustrations feature thick black outlines and intricate patterns, evoking the Aboriginal culture of the book's creators. The story can be read independently, and the vivid illustrations will nurture an appreciation of the ecology of the Australian bush." SLJ

Morpurgo, Michael

Mirror. Seven Footer Kids 2010 un il $15.95

Grades: PreK K 1 2   E

1. Mirrors -- Fiction

ISBN 978-1-934734-39-1; 1-934734-39-X

In this wordless book "a small girl sits in the corner of a spread, her isolation and loneliness underscored by her head-down, hunkered-over posture as well as the austere palette . . . and stark white backdrop. Her mood . . . changes to surprise when she catches sight of her likeness in a mirror . . . and eventually transforms into playful exuberance as she makes faces at and dances with her reflected double. . . . A blank spread provides a narrative beat, and when the action resumes, the child's reflection no longer parallels her movements, taking on a life of its own. Enraged, the protagonist seems to push at the mirror, which shatters. . . . Lee's illustrations cut to the core to express deep-seated feelings." SLJ

★ **Wave**. Chronicle Books 2008 un il $15.99

Grades: PreK K   E

1. Stories without words 2. Ocean -- Fiction 3. Beaches -- Fiction

ISBN 978-0-8118-5924-0; 0-8118-5924-X

LC 2007-62026

A wordless picture book that shows a little girl's first experiences at the beach, as she goes from being afraid of the roaring waves to playing on the shore while gulls soar overhead.

"A panoramic trim size beautifully supports the expansiveness of the beach. . . . Loosely rendered charcoal and acrylic images curl and flow like water and reflect playfulness, especially in the facial and bodily expressions of the child and seagulls. . . . A simple, well-crafted story." SLJ

Morris, Jackie

I am cat; by Jackie Morris. Frances Lincoln Children's Books 2013 32 p. ill. (hardcover) $17.99

Grades: 1 2 3 4   E

1. Cats -- Poetry 2. Picture books for children

ISBN 1847801358; 9781847801357

In this children's picture book, "Cat, curled tight on a round tasseled pillow, sleeps and dreams. The tabby's poetic musings accompany . . . watercolor paintings of 10 great cats." Among the cats included are the Siberian tiger, the cheetah, and the lynx. "Cat also dreams of the Scottish wildcat on the verge of extinction and the regal Amur leopard, its 'thick coat coloured like leaves in autumn,/ almost the last' of its kind." (School Library Journal)

Morris, Richard T.

Bye-bye, baby! by Richard Morris; illustrated by Larry Day. Walker & Co. 2009 un il $16.99; lib bdg $17.89

Grades: PreK   E

1. Infants -- Fiction 2. Siblings -- Fiction

ISBN 978-0-8027-9772-8; 0-8027-9772-5; 978-0-8027-9773-5 lib bdg; 0-8027-9773-3 lib bdg

LC 2008044318

Felix does not like his new baby sister and thinks his parents should take her back, until a trip to the zoo makes him realize that she might not be as bad as he thought.

"Outstanding illustrations are done in pen, ink, watercolor, and gouache. The characters' expressions and body language could tell this story alone, but wonderfully enhance the strong and simple text." SLJ

Morrow, Barbara Olenyik

Mr. Mosquito put on his tuxedo; illustrated by Ponder Goembel. Holiday House 2009 un il $16.95

Grades: K 1 2 3   E

1. Stories in rhyme 2. Bears -- Fiction 3. Insects -- Fiction 4. Mosquitoes -- Fiction

ISBN 978-0-8234-2072-8; 0-8234-2072-8

LC 2007025486

Mr. Mosquito saves the insect ball from an intruding bear.

"The abundant and rhyming text is only half of this story; the illustrations tell the rest. Using lush colors befitting a royal ball and excellent attention to detail, Goembel brings this idiosyncratic tale to life." SLJ

A **good** night for freedom; illustrated by Leonard Jenkins. Holiday House 2004 un il $16.95

Grades: K 1 2 3   E

1. Slavery 2. Abolitionists 3. Fugitive slaves 4. Underground railroad 5. Slavery -- Fiction 6. Underground railroad -- Fiction 7. Underground railroad -- Juvenile fiction

ISBN 0-8234-1709-3

LC 2002-192207

Hallie discovers two runaway slaves hiding in Levi Coffin's home and must decide whether to turn them in or help them escape to freedom. Includes historical notes on the Underground Railroad and abolitionists Levi and Catharine Coffin.

"The well-written text smoothly blends fact and fiction. . . . Jenkins's mixed-media illustrations capture the emotions of the characters as well as the details of pre-Civil War life." SLJ

Includes bibliographical references

Morstad, Julie

How to. Simply Read Books 2013 36 p. (hardcover) $16.95

Grades: PreK K 1   E

1. Picture books for children

ISBN 1897476574; 9781897476574

This children's picture book by Julie Morstad "explores whimsical ways of doing a host of different tasks, including 'how to wonder,' 'how to see the breeze,' and 'how to be brave.'" (Publisher's note) "Morstad explores topics of interest to children, from 'staying close' (two girls sharing one braid) to disappearing—a scene in which meaning comes first from the curtained image; the text is nearly invisible." (Kirkus)

Mortensen, Denise Dowling

Bug patrol; by Denise Dowling Mortensen; illustrated by Cece Bell. Clarion Books 2012 32 p. col. ill. (hardcover) $16.99

Grades: PreK K 1 2   E

1. Stories in rhyme 2. Police -- Juvenile Fiction 3. Insects -- Juvenile fiction 4. Police -- Fiction 5. Insects -- Fiction

ISBN 0618790241; 9780618790241

LC 2011041586

In this children's book, by Denise Dowling Mortensen, illustrated by Cece Bell, "bugs are a misbehaving bunch, so Captain Bob, insect cop, has a busy beat. The beetles are using their bug mobiles like bumper cars, the roaches are protesting for better housing . . . , and the crickets are up late, partying. Can Captain Bob keep the peace and maintain law and order?" (Publisher's note)

Good night engines; illustrated by Melissa Iwai. Clarion Bks. 2003 32p il $15

Grades: PreK K   E

1. Bedtime 2. Vehicles 3. Stories in rhyme 4. Bedtime -- Fiction 5. Vehicles -- Fiction

ISBN 0-618-13537-5

LC 2002-155215

Rhyming verses describe how a variety of vehicles, from locomotives to eighteen-wheelers to automobiles, wind down for a night of rest

"The story is as smooth and easy as a familiar lullaby. . . . Iwai's acrylic, full-page spreads match the quiet text." SLJ

A companion to this volume is:

Wake up engines (2007)

Mortimer, Anne

Pumpkin cat; written & illustrated by Anne Mortimer. Katherine Tegen Books 2011 un il $14.99; lib bdg $15.89

Grades: PreK K 1   E

1. Cats -- Fiction 2. Mice -- Fiction 3. Pumpkin -- Fiction

ISBN 978-0-06-187485-7; 0-06-187485-X; 978-0-06-187486-4 lib bdg; 0-06-187486-8 lib bdg

"One morning in May, Cat wondered, 'How do pumpkins grow?' 'I know,' said Mouse. 'And I will show you how.' Mouse proceeds to guide Cat through the various steps and stages, one phase featured on each spread, until October arrives and they are rewarded with a large orange pumpkin. . . . Mortimer has masterfully captured the texture of her subjects—the softness of the animals' fur, the scratchiness of burlap bags, the silkiness of delicate flower petals, etc. . . . A lovely addition that should be popular in any season." SLJ

Mortiz, Dianne

Hush little beachcomber; illustrated by Holly McGee. Kane Miller 2011 un il $14.99

Grades: PreK K 1   E

1. Stories in rhyme 2. Seashore -- Fiction

ISBN 978-1-935279-81-5; 1-935279-81-5

"'Hush, Little Baby' receives a bright makeover, with seagulls and sand pies replacing mockingbirds and diamond rings. Repetitive phrases may mirror the soothing lullaby's format, but this blissful beach day opens with a more enthusiastic call for action. . . . The cheerful voice remains optimistic throughout. . . . The lilting text naturally progresses through each experience. . . . Pastel spreads flash with smudges of golden color, with their hazy hues dominating each page, the brief rhyming text highlighting each featured activity." Kirkus

Morton, Carlene

The **library** pages; illustrated by Valeria Docampo. UpstartBooks 2010 un il $17.95

Grades: K 1 2 3   E

1. School stories 2. Libraries -- Fiction

ISBN 978-1-60213-045-6; 1-60213-045-0

While Mrs. Heath, the school librarian, is on maternity leave, the library pages put all the thin books together, shelve the books by color, mend them with duct tape, cut pictures out of encyclopedias, shelve every third book with the pages pointing out, and borrow books without checking them out.

"Docampo's colorful combination of manual and digital illustrations sets a perfectly mood for this story. This is an entertaining read-aloud, a humorous joke, and an excellent starter for library orientation." SLJ

Moser, Lisa

Cowboy Boyd and Mighty Calliope; by Lisa Moser; illustrated by Sebastiaan Van Doninck. 1st ed. Random House Inc 2013 40 p. ill. (hardcover) $17.99; (library) $20.99; (ebook) $53.97

Grades: PreK K 1   E

1. Picture books for children 2. Rhinoceros -- Juvenile fiction 3. Cowboys -- Fiction 4. Ranch life -- Fiction 5. Rhinoceroses -- Fiction

ISBN 0375870563; 0375970568; 9780375870569; 9780375970566; 9780375980794

LC 2012025379

In this picture book, "Rancher Rose and her hired hands are skeptical when Cowboy Boyd and his unusual mount arrive for a job at the Double R Ranch. As it happens, Calliope is a sensitive and affectionate rhinoceros—though she is not a very good ranch horse. Each task that she attempts ends in failure and, unsurprisingly, the very night that Rancher Rose tells Boyd and Calliope to 'roll on,' a situation arises where only her unique talents can provide a happy ending." (School Library Journal)

Kisses on the wind; illustrated by Kathryn Brown. Candlewick Press 2009 un il $15.99

Grades: K 1 2 3   E

1. Moving -- Fiction 2. Grandmothers -- Fiction 3. Frontier and pioneer life -- Fiction

ISBN 978-0-7636-3110-9; 0-7636-3110-8

LC 2008-53490

Young Lydia struggles to say goodbye to her grandmother as her parents finish packing their wagon for the long journey to Oregon in the nineteenth century.

"Moser and Brown tell a wise, gentle story about goodbyes. . . . The fluid watercolors amplify the story's mood of transition." Booklist

Perfect Soup; illustrated by Ben Mantle. Random House 2010 un il $16.99; lib bdg $19.99

Grades: PreK K 1 2   E

1. Mice -- Fiction 2. Snow -- Fiction 3. Soups -- Fiction

ISBN 978-0-375-86014-0; 0-375-86014-2; 978-0-375-96014-7 lib bdg; 0-375-96014-7 lib bdg

LC 2009052846

Murray the mouse goes into town for the carrot he needs to make Perfect Soup, and soon finds himself with a chain of favors that will work only if a friendly snowman can help him gets things started

"Mantle's illustrations cheer, comedically maximizing Murray's diminutive size and adding gently whimsical touches." Kirkus

Railroad Hank; by Lisa Moser; illustrations by Benji Davies. Random House Children's Books 2012 40 p. col. ill. (trade) $16.99

Grades: PreK K 1 2   E

1. Farm life -- Fiction 2. Railroads -- Juvenile fiction 3. Humorous fiction -- Juvenile fiction 4. Humorous stories 5. Railroad trains -- Fiction

ISBN 0375868496; 9780375868498; 9780375968495

LC 2011030231

In this children's story, by Lisa Moser, illustrated by Benji Davies, "Railroad Hank is headed up the mountain in his . . . little train to see Granny Bett. . . . Along the way, he stops to talk to Missy May, Country Carl, Cinnamon Cobbler, and Reel-'Em-In Sam. Each friend offers up something to cheer Granny Bett. . . . By the time he reaches the mountaintop, his train is bursting with crazy cargo! And Granny Bett has a great idea for what to do with it all." (Publisher's note)

"Moser's folksy writing style is paired well with Davies's perky acrylic illustrations... This satisfying, good-humored picture book sends a worthy message about looking after other people." SLJ

★ Squirrel's world; illustrated by Valeri Gorbachev. Candlewick Press 2007 44p il $14.99; pa $4.99

Grades: 1 2 3   E

1. Animals -- Fiction 2. Squirrels -- Fiction \

ISBN 978-0-7636-2929-8; 0-7636-2929-4; 978-0-7636-4088-0 pa; 0-7636-4088-3 pa

LC 2007-60859

Squirrel's well-meaning attempts to help his forest friends do not always turn out as planned.

"Gorbachev's loosely hatched linework provides appealing informal texture to the forest clan, and his illustrations offer plenty of decoding clues for novices. . . . Early independent readers will revel in the abundant repetition." Bull Cent Child Books

Moses, Will

Mary and her little lamb; the true story behind the nursery rhyme. Philomel Books 2011 36p il $17.99

Grades: 1 2 3   E

1. School stories 2. Sheep -- Fiction 3. Farm life -- Fiction

ISBN 978-0-399-25154-2; 0-399-25154-5

LC 2010037445

In 1810s Massachusetts, young Mary Elizabeth Sawyer nurses a sickly lamb back to health and becomes the subject of a famous nursery rhyme. Includes facts about the real Mary, John Roulstone who wrote the rhyme, and Lowell Mason who set it to music.

"Moses's rich oil paintings, rendered in his characteristic folk-art style, beautifully depict rural 19th-century life. They include spreads, framed pictures with images of books and hens in the margins, and vignettes accompanying the lengthy text." SLJ

Moss, Lloyd

★ **Zin!** zin! zin! a violin; illustrated by Marjorie Priceman. Simon & Schuster Bks. for Young Readers 1995 un il $17.95; pa $6.99

Grades: K 1 2 3   E

1. Counting 2. Stories in rhyme 3. Musical instruments

ISBN 0-671-88239-2; 0-689-83524-8 pa

LC 93-37902

A Caldecott Medal honor book, 1996

"Rhyming couplets present 10 instruments and their characteristics. . . . In the process of adding instruments, the book teaches the names of musical groups up to a chamber group of 10 as well as the categories into which the instruments fall: strings, reeds, and brasses. Amazingly, Moss conveys this encyclopedic information while keeping the poem streamlined and peppy. Priceman's sprightly, sunny hued gouache paintings should take a bow, too." Booklist

Moss, Miriam

A **babysitter** for Billy Bear; [by] Miriam Moss; pictures by Anna Currey. Dial Books for Young Readers 2008 un il $16.99

Grades: PreK K   E

1. Bears -- Fiction 2. Worry -- Fiction 3. Babysitters -- Fiction

ISBN 978-0-8037-3269-8; 0-8037-3269-4

LC 2007017212

"Billy and his best friend, a small stuffed rabbit, experience their first night with a babysitter while Mama goes to her pottery class. . . . The gentle watercolor pictures perfectly match the story of the teddy bearish youngster and his Mama-bear-type babysitter." SLJ

Moss, Peggy

One of us; illustrated by Penny Weber. Tilbury House 2010 un il $16.95

Grades: 1 2 3   E

1. School stories 2. Moving -- Fiction 3. Friendship

-- Fiction 4. Individualism -- Fiction

ISBN 978-0-88448-322-9; 0-88448-322-3

Roberta is welcomed by different groups on her first day at a new school, only to be told she does not fit in with them for some reason, but by the next day, members of each group have begun to see that they do not have to be alike in every way.

"Expressive eyes, happy faces, and rosy cheeks are indicative of the engaging illustrations that complement this winning color picture book. It can be used to supplement guidance lessons, welcome new students, or just as a fun discussion after a read-aloud session." Libr Media Connect

Most, Bernard

ABC T-Rex. Harcourt Brace & Co. 2000 un il $14; pa $6

Grades: PreK K 1   E

1. Alphabet 2. Dinosaurs -- Fiction 3. Dinosaurs -- Pictorial works -- Juvenile literature 4. Dinners and dining -- Pictorial works -- Juvenile literature 5. English language -- Alphabet -- Pictorial works -- Juvenile literature

ISBN 0-15-202007-1; 0-15-205028-0 pa

LC 98-51128

A young T-Rex loves his ABCs so much that he eats them up, experiencing on each letter a word that begins with that letter

"Heavy black lines define the cartoonlike drawings, brightened with a colorful palette emphasizing shades of green, purple, and orange. Fun for alphabetically inclined preschoolers." Booklist

★ **Whatever** happened to the dinosaurs? written and illustrated by Bernard Most. Harcourt Brace Jovanovich 1984 un il hardcover o.p. pa $4.95

Grades: PreK K 1   E

1. Dinosaurs -- Fiction

ISBN 0-15-295295-0; 0-15-295296-9 pa

LC 84-3779

"A hilarious book, sure to be popular for individual reading or with groups." Child Book Rev Serv

Moulton, Mark Kimball

The **very** best pumpkin; written by Mark Kimball Moulton; illustrated by Karen Hillard Good. Simon & Schuster Books for Young Readers 2010 un il $12.99

Grades: PreK K 1   E

1. Autumn -- Fiction 2. Pumpkin -- Fiction 3. Friendship -- Fiction

ISBN 978-1-4169-8288-3; 1-4169-8288-4

LC 2008046639

While Peter carefully tends a special pumpkin on his grandparents' farm, quiet Meg watches from her new home next door.

"Illustrations, rendered in watercolors mottled by instant coffee and bleach, are full of life and happy moments. The iconic symbols of the season—falling leaves, acorns, ripe apples—help provide an idyllic autumnal setting for the appealing friendship story." Booklist

Moundlic, Charlotte

The **scar**; [illustrations by Olivier Tallec] Candlewick Press 2011 il $14.99

Grades: K 1   E
1. Death -- Fiction 2. Mothers -- Fiction 3. Bereavement
-- Fiction
ISBN 978-0-7636-5341-5; 0-7636-5341-1
LC 2010042792

When his mother dies, a little boy is angry at his loss but
does everything he can to hold onto the memory of her scent,
her voice, and the special things she did for him, even as he
tries to help his father and grandmother cope.

"Rendered in pencil and wash in a limited palette of reds
and yellows, simple illustrations stress the boy's distress and
isolation while powerfully conveying his progression from
anger and fear to sadness and acceptance. A sympathetic exploration of the stages of grief through the eyes of one little
boy." Kirkus

Mozelle, Shirley
Zack's alligator and the first snow; story by Shirley
Mozelle; pictures by James Watts. Harper 2011 32p il (I
can read!) $16.99; pa $3.99
Grades: PreK K 1 2   E
1. Snow -- Fiction 2. Alligators -- Fiction
ISBN 978-0-06-147370-8; 0-06-147370-7; 978-0-06-
147372-2 pa; 0-06-147372-3 pa
LC 2008034359

Zack and Bridget, his alligator keychain that grows into
a fun-loving, full-sized alligator when it gets wet, enjoy the
day playing in the snow, ice-fishing, and sledding.

"Watts' softly-colored illustrations reflect the joy and
exuberance that snow brings, while Bridget's innocence is
charming. . . . Simple sentences and vocabulary and a lively
story make this just right for developing readers." Kirkus

Other titles about Zack's alligator are:
Zack's alligator (1989)
Zack's alligator goes to school (1994)

Muir, Leslie
The **little** bitty bakery; illustrations by Betsy Lewin.
Disney-Hyperion Books 2011 il $16.99
Grades: PreK K 1   E
1. Stories in rhyme 2. Cake -- Fiction 3. Mice --
Fiction 4. Birthdays -- Fiction 5. Bakers and bakeries
-- Fiction
ISBN 978-1-4231-1640-0; 1-4231-1640-2
LC 2011012267

When a pastry chef works straight through her birthday
with no time for birthday cake, some industrious mice make
good use of her kitchen and bake a delicious surprise.

"This delightful read-aloud, with its enticing cover featuring an array of sparkling baked goods, works well on
many levels. Muir's sweet, engaging story is sprinkled with
French words throughout, and Lewin's charming cartoon
art, in nighttime shades of blue and purple, uses thick and
thin brush lines to capture the action." SLJ

Muldrow, Diane
We planted a tree; illustrated by Bob Staake. Golden
Books 2010 un il $17.99; lib bdg $20.99
Grades: PreK K 1 2   E
1. Trees -- Fiction 2. Growth -- Fiction 3. Ecology
-- Fiction
ISBN 978-0-375-86432-2; 0-375-86432-6; 978-0-375-
96432-9 lib bdg; 0-375-86432-6 lib bdg
LC 2009000394

"A family in Brooklyn plants a tree in their small backyard; turn the page and a Kenyan family plants a tree on
the bare African savannah. Then in Paris, Tokyo, and more
places across the globe, each newly planted tree grows up, as
the children in the family do. Muldow weaves some science
into the lines. . . . Illustrating the simple poetry are clean-
lined digital illustrations that show the botany details and
celebrate the connections between plants and people, present
and long-term, across time and space." Booklist

Munari, Bruno
Bruno Munari's zoo; [by] Bruno Munari. Chronicle
Books 2005 un il $17.95
Grades: PreK K   E
1. Zoos 2. Animals
ISBN 0-8118-4830-2
LC 2004-21214

A reissue of the title first published 1963 by
World Publishing

Illustrations and brief text introduce more than twenty
zoo animals, including a rhinoceros that is always ready
to fight and a peacock that struts proudly because he is
the peacock.

"A stunning picture book of birds and beasts original in
design, brilliant with color, and touched with humor." Booklist

Munro, Roxie
Circus. Chronicle Books 2006 un il $15.95
Grades: PreK K 1 2   E
1. Puzzles 2. Stories in rhyme 3. Circus -- Fiction
ISBN 0-8118-5209-1

Flaps open to reveal circus acts, from astounding acrobats to elegant elephants, and rhyming text lists objects hidden within each performance

"The detailed ink and watercolor illustrations are bold
and lively." Horn Book Guide

★ **Go!** go! go! with more than 70 flaps to uncover &
discover. Sterling 2009 un il $15.95
Grades: PreK K 1 2   E
1. Fires -- Fiction
ISBN 978-1-4027-3773-2; 1-4027-3773-4

Gatefolds, layers of lift-the-flaps and complex fold-outs
take the reader on a race of a fire truck to battle a blaze, to
gallop to the finish line on the favorite horse and riding the
race course in a car.

This is a "fascinating picture book. . . . Text is kept to a
minimum while full-spread artwork carries the story. . . . The
full-color illustrations are loaded with pertinent details." SLJ

Muntean, Michaela
★ **Do** not open this book! illustrated by Pascal LeMaitre. Scholastic Press 2006 un il $15.99
Grades: PreK K 1 2   E
1. Pigs -- Fiction 2. Authorship -- Fiction 3. Books and
reading -- Fiction
ISBN 0-439-69839-1

As Pig tries to write a book, he chastises the reader who
keeps interrupting him by turning the pages.

"Along with hand lettering Muntean's text, LeMaitre
contributes bright, comics-style pictures that clarify the
occasionally dizzying concepts. . . . Children will be . . .
enraptured by the irreverent, interactive premise and will

emerge with a fresh understanding of the powerful qualities of words." Booklist

Murphy, Claire Rudolf

Marching with Aunt Susan; Susan B. Anthony and the fight for women's suffrage. written by Claire Rudolf Murphy; illustrated by Stacey Schuett. Peachtree 2011 un il $16.95

Grades: 1 2 3 4   E

1. Suffragists 2. Abolitionists 3. Sex role -- Fiction 4. Women's rights -- Fiction 5. Women -- Suffrage -- Fiction

ISBN 978-1-56145-593-5; 1-56145-593-8

LC 2011002703

Not allowed to go hiking with her father and brothers because she is a girl, Bessie learns about women's rights when she attends a suffrage rally led by Susan B. Anthony.

"Schuett's somewhat impressionistic gouache paintings effectively capture the time and place and convey the emotionally charged tenor of the campaign. The endnotes, accompanied by photographs, provide factual material about the real Bessie Keith Pond, Anthony, and the suffrage movement, especially in California." SLJ

Murphy, Mary

★ **I** kissed the baby. Candlewick Press 2003 un il hardcover o.p. bd bk $6.99

Grades: PreK K 1   E

1. Ducks -- Fiction 2. Animals -- Fiction

ISBN 0-7636-2122-6; 0-7636-2443-8 bd bk

LC 2002-31419

Various animals tell how they saw, fed, sang to, tickled, and kissed the new duckling

"Murphy makes creative use of color on the edges of the black-and-white pages, until the duckling appears in a splash of vibrant yellow, and the text changes to hot pink. This is an ideal book for little eyes and ears, for text, illustrations, and design meld perfectly." SLJ

A **Kiss** like this; Mary Murphy. Candlewick Press 2012 32 p. $12.99

Grades: PreK K   E

1. Animals -- Juvenile fiction 2. Kissing -- Juvenile fiction 3. Parent-child relationship -- Juvenile fiction

ISBN 0763661821; 9780763661823

LC 2012942308

In this children's picture book by Mary Murphy, "split-page flaps reveal ... a silly series of animal kisses. ... Each spread features a vibrantly hued child/parent pair of creatures, including giraffes, mice, fish, bees, elephants, owls and bunnies. The black, smudgy hand-lettered text describes the different kinds of kisses. ... Each phrase ends with an ellipsis prompting readers to flip the half page to reveal 'like this!' and an eyes-closed buss." (Kirkus Reviews)

Murphy, Stuart J.

Emma's friendwich. Charlesbridge Pub. 2010 un il (I see I learn) $14.95; pa $6.95

Grades: PreK K   E

1. Animals -- Fiction 2. Friendship -- Fiction

ISBN 978-1-58089-450-0; 1-58089-450-X; 978-1-58089-451-7 pa; 1-58089-451-8 pa

LC 2009027784

After moving to a new home, Emma makes friends with the girl next door. Includes questions about the text and notes to parents about visual learning.

"Murphy folds his educational points into a warm standalone story, and the cheerful, uncluttered, jellybean-colored spreads clearly illustrate friend-making steps." Booklist

Freda is found. Charlesbridge 2011 un il (I see I learn) $14.95; pa $6.95

Grades: PreK K   E

1. School stories 2. Animals -- Fiction 3. Missing children -- Fiction

ISBN 978-1-58089-462-3; 1-58089-462-3; 978-1-58089-463-0 pa; 1-58089-463-1 pa

On a field trip, Freda is separated from her class, but she remembers just what to do. Includes questions about the text and a note to parents about visual learning.

The book has "vibrant, playful illustrations featuring animated characters that reinforce the story [line]. The highlighted text and expanded captions convey the action." SLJ

★ **Leaping** lizards; illustrated by JoAnn Adinolfi. HarperCollins Pubs. 2005 33p il (MathStart) hardcover o.p. pa $4.99

Grades: 1 2 3   E

1. Addition 2. Counting 3. Stories in rhyme 4. Lizards -- Fiction

ISBN 0-06-000130-5; 0-06-000132-1 pa

LC 2004-22470

"This book introduces the multiples of five, as lizards of different colors travel through the pages on unicycles, a hot-air balloon, an airplane, and other modes of transport, while a green snake looks on. Finally, the number 50 is reached, and lizards explode in all directions. ... An intelligent blending of white space and colors make each double-page spread visually stand out. A box on one side of each page helps children keep track of the multiplying lizards, and a closing section offers adults a few more ideas for easy math education." Booklist

Same old horse; illustrated by Steve Björkman. HarperCollins Pubs. 2005 31p il (Mathstart) hardcover o.p. pa $4.99

Grades: K 1 2 3   E

1. Horses -- Fiction

ISBN 0-06-055770-2; 0-06-055771-0 pa

Hankie wants to be unpredictable, but the other horses are sure he'll always be the same old Hankie. Someone's in for a surprise in this story about making predictions

This "is a lively story that encourages kids to work with numbers to find out what happens next. Bjorkman's clear, funny ink-and-watercolor pictures show horses in a barnyard acting just like children on a school playground." Booklist

Write on, Carlos! illustrated by Tim Jones. Charlesbridge 2011 un il $14.95; pa $6.95

Grades: PreK K   E

1. Literacy -- Fiction 2. Personal names -- Fiction

ISBN 978-1-58089-464-7; 1-58089-464-X; 978-1-58089-465-4 pa; 1-58089-465-8 pa

LC 2010023522

With his mother's help, Carlos learns to write his name, as some of his friends can do.

This book has "vibrant, playful illustrations featuring animated characters that reinforce the story [line]. The highlighted text and expanded captions convey the action." SLJ

Murphy, Yannick

Baby Polar; illustrated by Kristen Balouch. Clarion Books 2009 un il $16 **E**
1. Storms -- Fiction 2. Polar bear -- Fiction 3. Mother-child relationship -- Fiction
ISBN 978-0-618-99850-0; 0-618-99850-0
LC 2008011619

Even though his mother warns him of a coming storm, Baby Polar goes outside to play, but when he cannot see his own paw he realizes that he now faces danger.

"The illustrations are digitally produced and beautifully designed. Stylized white snowflakes and polar bear figures set against a blue gray background convey well the icy coldness of the storm. . . . The book's reassuring conclusion offers a satisfying story for that audience, as well as an introduction to polar bears and their Arctic world." SLJ

Murray, Alison

★ **Apple** pie ABC. Disney Hyperion 2011 un il $16.99
Grades: PreK K **E**
1. Alphabet 2. Dogs -- Fiction 3. Pies -- Fiction
ISBN 978-1-4231-3694-1; 1-4231-3694-2

"It all starts with 'A apple pie' in this terse, alphabetically organized story: a towheaded little girl, accompanied by her loyal pooch, bakes that pie, cools it, then dishes out a piece for herself. And that's when her dog develops his obssession: he tries to get at the treat. . . . The illustrations, retro-touched digital art with a strong graphic sensibility and a hearkening back to block prints, take this neat concept and joyously gallop with it." Bull Cent Child Books

Little mouse; Alison Murray. 1st U.S. ed. Disney-Hyperion Books 2013 32 p. ill. (reinforced) $16.99
Grades: PreK **E**
1. Picture books for children 2. Animals -- Juvenile fiction 3. Mother-daughter relationship -- Juvenile fiction 4. Nicknames -- Fiction 5. Mother and child -- Fiction
ISBN 1423143302; 9781423143307
LC 2012006147

In this book, "Mommy sometimes calls her daughter little mouse, which amuses the spirited child because her self-perception is that she's strong as an ox and brave as a lion and that she can howl like a wolf. But when bedtime nears and the sprightly child gets sleepy, she is more than happy to curl up in her mother's arms and be that little mouse." (Kirkus)

One two that's my shoe! Alison Murray. Disney-Hyperion Books 2012 32 p.
Grades: PreK **E**
1. Counting 2. Stories in rhyme 3. Dogs -- Juvenile fiction 4. Picture books for children 5. Dogs -- Fiction 6. Animals -- Infancy -- Fiction
ISBN 1423143299; 9781423143291
LC 2011013171

This preschool children's story, written and illustrated by Alison Murray, is a rhyming picture book describing a "mischievous puppy [who] runs off with his owner's shoe, it's a race from one to ten to get it back again!" (Publisher's note) Each page illustrates an exercise of counting household objects, animals, or landscape pieces. "The brief, rhymed text is . . . placed to allow viewers time to count the teddy bears, flowers, etc., along the way." (Kirkus Reviews)

Murray, Laura

The **gingerbread** man loose in the school; illustrated by Mike Lowery. G. P. Putnam's 2011 il $16.99
Grades: PreK K 1 **E**
1. School stories 2. Stories in rhyme 3. Cookies -- Fiction
ISBN 978-0-399-25052-1; 0-399-25052-2
LC 2009006642

A gingerbread man searches all over the school for the group of children that made him and then left him behind.

"With a little practice to get the beats just right, the text can be easily read aloud, and youngsters can be invited to chime in on the refrain: 'I'm the Gingerbread Man/and I'm trying to find,/the children who made me,/but left me behind.' A variety of fonts is used to indicate differences between speakers and the narration. The cartoon illustrations are primitive in style, but suit the story to a tee." SLJ

Murray, Marjorie Dennis

Halloween night; by Marjorie Dennis Murray; illustrations by Brandon Dorman. Greenwillow Books 2008 un il $16.99; lib bdg $17.89
Grades: K 1 2 3 **E**
1. Stories in rhyme 2. Parties -- Fiction 3. Monsters -- Fiction 4. Halloween -- Fiction
ISBN 978-0-06-135186-0; 0-06-135186-5; 978-0-06-135187-7 lib bdg; 0-06-135187-3 lib bdg
LC 2007027686

Loosely based on "The Night Before Christmas," this rhyming story tells of a group of animals, monsters, and witches who prepare such a frightening Halloween party that their expected trick-or-treaters all run away.

"Murray's smooth rhyming text combines well with Dorman's vibrant and extraordinarily detailed digital art, with surprises on every page. This is an energetic romp with a satisfying conclusion that will be a fun read-aloud." SLJ

Muth, Jon J.

Zen ghosts. Scholastic Press 2010 un il $17.99
Grades: K 1 2 3 **E**
1. Siblings -- Fiction 2. Halloween -- Fiction 3. Giant panda -- Fiction 4. Storytelling -- Fiction 5. Zen Buddhism -- Fiction
ISBN 978-0-439-63430-4; 0-439-63430-X
LC 2009-31236

On Halloween night, Stillwater the giant panda tells Karl, Addy, and Michael a spooky and unusual story. Based on a Zen koan.

"Haunting in multiple senses of the word, this tale should captivate thoughtful readers, as Muth's watercolors convey a world of infinite possibility and gentle enchantment." Publ Wkly

★ **Zen** shorts; illustrated by Jon Muth. Scholastic Press 2005 un il $16.95
Grades: K 1 2 3 **E**
1. Bears -- Fiction 2. Giant panda -- Fiction 3.

Storytelling -- Fiction 4. Zen Buddhism -- Fiction
ISBN 0-439-33911-1

LC 2003-20471

A Caldecott Medal honor book, 2006

When Stillwater the panda moves into the neighborhood, the stories he tells to three siblings teach them to look at the world in new ways.

This "is both an accessible, strikingly illustrated story and a thought-provoking mediation." Booklist

Other titles about Stillwater the panda are:

Zen ties (2008)

Zen ghosts (2010)

Myers, Christopher

★ **Black** cat. Scholastic Press 1999 un il $16.95
Grades: PreK K 1 2   E

1. Cats -- Fiction 2. City and town life -- Fiction
ISBN 0-590-03375-1

LC 98-28609

A Coretta Scott King honor book for illustration, 2000

A black cat wanders through the streets of a city

"With striking photo-collages enhanced with gouache and ink, this book captures the gritty beauty of the city." Horn Book Guide

Wings. Scholastic Press 2000 un il $16.95
Grades: K 1 2 3   E

1. Flight -- Fiction 2. Classical mythology -- Fiction
ISBN 0-590-03377-8

LC 99-87389

"Myers retells the myth of Icarus through the story of Ikarus Jackson, the new boy on the block, who can fly above the rooftops and over the crowd. In this contemporary version, the winged kid nearly falls from the sky . . . because jeering kids in the schoolyard and repressive adults don't like his being different and try to break his soaring spirit. . . . Myers' beautiful cut-paper collages are eloquent and open." Booklist

Myers, Tim

Basho and the river stones; illustrations by Oki S. Han. Marshall Cavendish 2004 un il $16.95
Grades: K 1 2 3   E

1. Foxes 2. Poets 3. Poetry 4. Authors 5. Foxes -- Fiction 6. Poetry -- Fiction
ISBN 0-7614-5165-X

LC 2003-26245

Tricked by a fox into giving up his share of cherries, a famous Japanese poet is inspired to write a haiku and the fox, ashamed of his actions, must devise another trick to set things right

"Han's expressive watercolors, with an unusual variety of perspectives, keep the story lively. A clever original fable." Booklist

Another title about Basho by this author and illustrator is:

Basho and the fox (2000)

Myers, Walter Dean, 1937-

Looking for the easy life; illustrated by Lee Harper. Harper 2010 un il $16.99
Grades: K 1 2 3   E

1. Work -- Fiction 2. Animals -- Fiction 3. Monkeys

-- Fiction 4. Conduct of life -- Fiction
ISBN 978-0-06-054375-4; 0-06-054375-2; 978-0-06-065476-1 lib bdg; 0-06-054376-0 lib bdg

LC 2008-34360

Five monkeys go in search of the easy life, but find that "easy ain't always good" and "a little work ain't always bad."

"Myers . . . offers deft characterizations and quick retorts . . . and Harper's . . . animals grin and flirt engagingly. . . . Myers demonstrates a profound talent for kid-pleasing humor—it's a story-time natural." Publ Wkly

★ **Looking** like me; illustrated by Christopher Myers. Egmont USA 2009 un il
Grades: 1 2 3   E

1. Family life -- Fiction 2. African Americans -- Fiction
ISBN 1-60684-001-0; 1-60684-041-X lib bdg; 978-1-60684-001-6; 978-1-60684-041-2 lib bdg

LC 2009-14640

Jeremy sets out to discover all of the different people that make him who he is, including brother, son, writer, and runner. "Grades two to four." (Bull Cent Child Books)

"The innovative art and design represent different identities with colorful silhouettes placed against photos of people, places, and icons. . . . This very contemporary work is encouraging, energetic, and inspired." Booklist

★ **Patrol**; an American soldier in Vietnam. collages by Ann Grifalconi. HarperCollins Pubs. 2002 un il hardcover o.p. lib bdg $16.89; pa $6.99
Grades: 3 4 5 6   E

1. Soldiers 2. Vietnamese Conflict, 1961-1975 3. Vietnam War, 1961-1975 -- Fiction 4. African American soldiers -- Fiction
ISBN 0-06-028363-7; 0-06-028364-5 lib bdg; 0-06-073159-1 pa

LC 00-35009

A frightened American soldier faces combat in the lush forests of Vietnam and sees a young enemy soldier who is as frightened as he is

The story is told "in free verse that is at once ethereal and white-knuckle tense. . . . Grifalconi's intricate paper and photo collages juxtapose snips of explosion smoke, snapshot images of fleeing villagers, and paper constructions of burning huts against a landscape that approaches fantasy in its lush beauty." Bull Cent Child Books

★ The **blues** of Flats Brown; illustrated by Nina Laden. Holiday House 2000 un il $16.95; pa $6.95
Grades: 1 2 3 4   E

1. Dogs 2. Blues (Music) 3. Dogs -- Fiction 4. Blues music -- Fiction
ISBN 0-8234-1480-9; 0-8234-1679-8 pa

LC 99-16695

To escape an abusive master, a junkyard dog named Flats runs away and makes a name for himself from Mississippi to New York City playing blues on his guitar

"The narrator's vernacular, rhythmic and easy-rolling, has the feel of a timeless legend, and the vibrant, jewel-toned illustrations, dominated by moody, bittersweet, tonal variations of blue, are filled with rich detail, expressive characters, and fantastic landscapes." Booklist

Na, Il Sung

★ **Hide** & seek; by Il Sung Na. Alfred A. Knopf 2012 32 p.

Grades: PreK K   **E**

1. Games -- Fiction 2. Rain forests -- Fiction 3. Picture books for children 4. Rain forest animals -- Fiction 5. Animals -- Fiction 6. Elephants -- Fiction 7. Chameleons -- Fiction 8. Hide-and-seek -- Fiction
ISBN 0375870784; 9780307974600; 9780375870781; 9780375970788

LC 2011021740

This picture book describes the action when "a group of animals plays a rainforest game of hide-and-seek," as the elephant counts and the flamingo, giraffe, rhino, and others find hiding places. Il Sung Na's artwork depicts a "tie-dyed rainforest awash in reds, yellows, greens and blues" and uses a "fusion of painterly textures, soft patterns and fine outlines . . . with dappled colors that shine like light through a leaf." (Kirkus)

A **book** of sleep. Alfred A. Knopf 2009 un il $15.99; lib bdg $18.99; bd bk $6.99

Grades: PreK K 1   **E**

1. Owls -- Fiction 2. Sleep -- Fiction 3. Animals -- Fiction
ISBN 978-0-375-86223-6; 0-375-86223-4; 978-0-375-96223-3 lib bdg; 0-375-96223-9 lib bdg; 978-0-375-86618-0 bd bk; 0-375-86618-3 bhd bk

LC 2008-47865

First published 2007 in the United Kingdom with title: Zzzz: a book of sleep

While other animals sleep at night, some quietly and others noisily, some alone and others huddled together, a wide-eyed owl watches.

"Na's textural images recall the lightheartedness and limpid charm of Paul Klee. . . . It's the rare picture book that, upon arrival, feels as though it has been around for years already; Na's belongs to this group." Publ Wkly

The **thingamabob**. Alfred A. Knopf 2010 un il $15.99; lib bdg $18.99

Grades: PreK K   **E**

1. Elephants -- Fiction 2. Umbrellas and parasols -- Fiction
ISBN 978-0-375-86106-2; 0-375-86106-8; 978-0-375-96106-9 lib bdg; 0-375-96106-2 lib bdg

LC 2009003120

First published 2008 in the United Kingdom

An elephant finds a "thingamabob" and experiments until he discovers what to do with it.

"Sumptuous colors and swirling textures turn this slight, silly story into a visual feast, buoyed by a handful of great sight gags and the hands-down adorableness of the animals." Booklist

Nakagawa, Chihiro

★ **Who** made this cake? text and English translation by Chihiro Nakagawa; illustrations by Junji Koyose. Front Street 2008 un il $16.95

Grades: PreK K 1   **E**

1. Cake -- Fiction 2. Size -- Fiction 3. Baking -- Fiction 4. Construction equipment -- Fiction
ISBN 978-1-59078-595-9; 1-59078-595-9

LC 2008003070

While a boy and his parents go for an outing, little people invade the house and use their big construction equipment to bake a cake.

"The understated text is almost unnecessary, as the pictures easily tell the story and then some. . . . Truck fans will naturally pore over every busy, action-filled scene." Horn Book

Namioka, Lensey

The **hungriest** boy in the world; illustrated by Aki Sogabe. Holiday House 2001 un il $16.95

Grades: K 1 2 3   **E**

1. Hunger 2. Hunger -- Fiction
ISBN 0-8234-1542-2

LC 00-25142

After swallowing the Hunger Monster, Jiro begins eating everything in sight, until his family finds a way to lure the monster out of Jiro's stomach

"The story is told economically but with wit and humor. Sogabe's illustrations, created using cut paper over rice paper that has been colored by airbrush or watercolor, complement the text with their elegant simplicity." SLJ

Napoli, Donna Jo, 1948-

★ **Albert**; illustrated by Jim LaMarche. Silver Whistle Bks. 2001 un il $16; pa $7

Grades: K 1 2 3   **E**

1. Birds -- Fiction 2. Birds -- Nests -- Fiction
ISBN 0-15-201572-8; 0-15-205249-6 pa

LC 97-7089

One day when Albert is at his window, two cardinals come to build a nest in his hand, an event that changes his life

"Napoli has written a pleasing modern fairy tale, transformed into a picture book by LaMarche's appealing, shaded pencil drawings." Booklist

★ The **crossing**; [illustrated by Jim Madsen] Atheneum Books for Young Readers 2011 un il $16.99

Grades: K 1 2   **E**

1. Trappers 2. Fur traders 3. Interpreters 4. Guides (Persons) 5. Native Americans -- Fiction 6. Shoshoni Indians -- Fiction 7. Overland journeys to the Pacific -- Fiction
ISBN 978-1-4169-9474-9; 1-4169-9474-2

LC 2010-08368

In 1805, Sacagawea, a woman of the Shoshoni tribe, helps Meriwether Lewis and William Clark find a passage to the West Coast, in this story told through the eyes of the baby boy on Sacagawea's back.

"Short, poetic descriptions of the landscape and journey . . . close with onomatopoetic phrases that refer to the many animals they meet during the journey. . . . Madsen's . . . full-bleed full and half-spread digital artwork is rendered in warm, earthy hues, shot through with tiny, crackling lines that give the images an aura of old oil paintings. . . . A refreshing new angle on a familiar story of American history." Publ Wkly

Earth shook; a Persian tale. illustrations by Gabi Swiatkowska. Hyperion Books for Children 2009 un il $15.99

Grades: K 1 2 3   **E**

1. Animals -- Fiction 2. Earthquakes -- Fiction
ISBN 978-1-4231-0448-3; 1-4231-0448-X

"In this Persian-inspired tale (based on a 2003 earthquake in Bam, Iran), Parisa desperately seeks the company of another human being when her village is destroyed. She knocks on door after door, but hostile animals now occupy any still-standing homes. . . . Swiatkowska's extraordinary artwork—textured oil paintings, decorative designs, splendid palette and artfully spare compositions—adds power and beauty to the poetic text that echoes Rumi. A gorgeous, discussion-provoking read-aloud." Kirkus

The **Wishing** Club; a story about fractions. Henry Holt 2007 un il $16.95

Grades: 1 2 3   E

1. Wishes -- Fiction 2. Siblings -- Fiction 3. Fractions -- Fiction

ISBN 978-0-8050-7665-3; 0-8050-7665-4

LC 2006030767

When four siblings wish on a star, each gets only a fraction of what he or she wanted, but when they combine their wishes, they just might get a whole new pet.

"Napoli's story moves smoothly between the magic of wishes granted and the reality of working with fractions. . . . Currey's watercolor-and-ink illustrations evoke summer nights when barefoot youngsters lean on porch railings and look at the stars." SLJ

Nargi, Lela

★ The **Honeybee** Man; illustrated by Kyrsten Brooker. Schwartz & Wade Books 2011 un il $17.99; lib bdg $20.99

Grades: PreK K 1 2   E

1. Bees -- Fiction 2. Beekeeping -- Fiction

ISBN 978-0-375-84980-0; 0-375-84980-7; 978-0-375-95695-9 lib bdg; 0-375-95695-6 lib bdg

LC 2009044216

Fred, a beekeeper whose hives are on the roof of his Brooklyn, New York, apartment building, tends his bees and distributes their honey to his neighbors. Includes facts about bees and beekeepers.

"Copious details are carefully woven into descriptions of Fred's day-today activities. . . . In sunny, oil-and-collage compositions, Brooker . . . captures the bustle of sidewalks and storefronts, as well as the serenity of Fred's rooftop and a green expanse of park. She also does a fine job demonstrating the steps of collecting honey. . . . Kids should find this easygoing blend of fiction and fact fascinating." Publ Wkly

Nascimbeni, Barbara

Animals and their families; Barbara Nascimbeni. Owlkids Books, Inc. 2012 72 p. ill. (hardcover) $17.95

Grades: K 1 2   E

1. Animal behavior 2. Animals -- Juvenile literature 3. Animal babies -- Juvenile literature

ISBN 1926973321; 9781926973326

LC 2011935958

Parents' Choice Awards - Picture Books: 2012

Author Barbara Nascimbeni's book helps children "explore the animal kingdom . . . . A new creature is introduced in silhouette, while the facing page shows that same creature in its natural habitat, playing with, caring for, or teaching its young. All members of the animal family--male and female, adult and baby--are illustrated in warm colors and identified by the proper term. Small bits of text share the sound each animals makes, where it lives, and what it eats with young readers." (Publisher's note)

Nayar, Nandini

What should I make? illustrations by Proiti Roy. Tricycle Press 2009 un il $12.99

Grades: PreK K 1   E

1. Cooking -- Fiction 2. Imagination -- Fiction 3. East Indians -- Fiction 4. Mother-son relationship -- Fiction

ISBN 978-1-58246-294-3; 1-58246-294-1

LC 2008-42803

While his mother makes chapatis (Indian flat bread), Neeraj transforms a piece of dough into different animals.

"Warm-toned illustrations keep attention centered squarely on mother and son. A recipe is included." Horn Book Guide

Nazoa, Aquiles

A **small** Nativity; by Aquiles Nazoa; illustrated by Ana Palmero Cáceres; translated by Hugh Hazelton. Groundwood Books 2007 44p il $9.95

Grades: 1 2 3   E

ISBN 0-88899-839-2

"Venezuelan poet Nazoa's unadorned retelling of the Nativity story offers a homely approach to the familiar tale. . . . Palmero Cáceres illustrates this humble text with devotional pictures inspired by medieval illuminated manuscripts. Her richly colored art successfully combines traditional symbols of Christianity with images of Latin American flora and fauna." Horn Book

Nedwidek, John

Ducks don't wear socks; by John Nedwidek; illustrated by Lee White. Viking Childrens Books 2008 un il $15.99

Grades: PreK K 1 2   E

1. Ducks -- Fiction

ISBN 978-0-670-06136-5; 0-670-06136-0

LC 2007023122

Emily, a serious girl, meets a duck who helps her see the more humorous side of life.

"White's colorful illustrations bring the story's humor to life. The cartoon style allows the creature's wackiness to shine while providing visual clues for those just beginning to read independently. A lighthearted lesson on the benefits of laughter, this is just plain fun." SLJ

Nelson, Marilyn

★ **Snook** alone; illustrated by Timothy Basil Ering. Candlewick Press 2010 48p il $16.99

Grades: 1 2 3   E

1. Dogs -- Fiction 2. Monks -- Fiction 3. Islands -- Fiction

ISBN 978-0-7636-2667-9; 0-7636-2667-8

LC 2009-49040

"Snook is a rat terrier who lives with a monk on an island hermitage. . . . He gleefully munches rats while his companion works and prays. This simple, wonderful life is interrupted when a storm strands Snook on a tiny nearby atoll. Nelson writes in delicate stanzas of effortless poetry. . . . Ering's acrylic-and-ink artwork fades from the bright palette of the monk's abode to a nearly two-tone earthiness and creates a style both realistic and emotional. . . . The final reuniting is sudden yet as genuine as everything else about the book." Booklist

Nelson, Vaunda Micheaux

★ **Who** will I be, Lord? illustrated by Sean Qualls. Random House 2009 un il $16.95; lib bdg $19.99
Grades: PreK K 1 2   **E**
  1. Family life -- Fiction 2. Occupations -- Fiction 3. African Americans -- Fiction 4. Family -- Juvenile literature
ISBN 978-0-375-84342-6; 0-375-84342-6; 978-0-375-94342-3 lib bdg; 0-375-94342-0 lib bdg

                  LC 2008035186

"An African-American girl looking to the future has a broad range of relatives to emulate—a banjo-playing mailman, a housewife who broke the color barrier, a pool shark, and a burger-flipping aspiring jazzman. Nelson's rhythmic and colloquial first-person narrative introduces the characters not only in terms of the jobs they hold, but also the kind of people they are. . . . Qualls's mixed-media illustrations combine muted and bright elements and feature full-spread renditions of each relative at home or work, followed by a page showing surreal floating heads of the girl and the featured role model as she repeats the title's query. Nelson shows respect for all the ways people live and work." SLJ

Nelson-Schmidt, Michelle

Cats, cats! Kane Miller 2011 un il pa $5.99
Grades: PreK K 1   **E**
  1. Cats -- Fiction
ISBN 978-1-61067-042-5; 1-61067-042-6
"After initially establishing that cats . . . are everywhere, [this] title presents nine different types. . . . Timid, nosy, stubborn, sad-these are animals as defined by a set of descriptors that children might recognize in themselves. . . . Text set against plenty of white space, with a few sophisticated words to challenge youngsters, make [this a] good [choice] for emerging readers. The bright, crisp illustrations are cheerful and attractive. . . . [This book is] also useful as [an introduction] to adjectives." SLJ

Dogs, Dogs! Kane Miller 2011 un il pa $5.99
Grades: PreK K 1   **E**
  1. Dogs -- Fiction
ISBN 978-1-61067-041-8; 1-61067-041-8
"After initially establishing that . . . dogs are everywhere, [this] title presents nine different types. . . . Timid, nosy, stubborn, sad-these are animals as defined by a set of descriptors that children might recognize in themselves. . . . Text set against plenty of white space, with a few sophisticated words to challenge youngsters, make [this a] good [choice] for emerging readers. The bright, crisp illustrations are cheerful and attractive. . . . [This book is] also useful as [an introduction] to adjectives." SLJ

Nesbitt, Kenn

More bears! illustrated by Troy Cummings. Sourcebooks/Jabberwocky 2010 un il $12.99
Grades: PreK K 1   **E**
  1. Bears -- Fiction 2. Authors -- Fiction
ISBN 978-1-4022-3835-2; 1-4022-3835-5
When an author starts writing, children yell that they want more bears in the story.
"Cummings's smooth, digitally rendered artwork does the job admirably. There is strong color on every page, and the bears are infused with zaniness and fun. The participa-tory refrain of 'More Bears' will bring this selection to life at storytimes." SLJ

Nesquens, Daniel

My tattooed dad; [by] Daniel Nesquens; & [illustrated by] Magicomora; translated by Elisa Amado. Groundwood Books 2011 un il $18.95
Grades: 3 4 5   **E**
  1. Fathers -- Fiction 2. Tattooing -- Fiction
ISBN 978-1-55498-109-0; 1-55498-109-3
"Loved without judgment despite his frequent absences, this larger-than-life figure dotes on his family while at home, cooking, gardening, and filling the space with his incredible stories. Like The Illustrated Man, his manifold tattoos provide a springboard for the narrative. . . . Magicomora's cameos and full spreads, a combination of folk art and caricatures, are drawn with pencil and colored digitally on backgrounds simulating antique wood, replete with stains and cracks. Not for the faint of heart, Nesquens's highly original anecdotes, narrated jointly by father and son in an aura of mystery, will be appreciated by fans of magical realism." SLJ

Ness, Evaline

★ **Sam,** Bangs & Moonshine; written and illustrated by Evaline Ness. Holt & Co. 1966 un il $17.95; pa $6.95
Grades: PreK K 1 2   **E**
  1. Imagination -- Fiction
ISBN 0-8050-0314-2; 0-8050-0315-0 pa
Awarded the Caldecott Medal, 1967
"In this unusually creative story the fantasy in which many, many children indulge is presented in a realistic and sympathetic context. The illustrations in ink and pale color wash (mustard, grayish-aqua) have a touching realism, too. This is an outstanding book." SLJ

Neubecker, Robert

What little boys are made of; by Robert Neubecker. Balzer + Bray 2012 32 p.
Grades: PreK K 1 2   **E**
  1. Boys -- Fiction 2. Play -- Fiction 3. Stories in rhyme 4. Imagination -- Fiction 5. Picture books for children
ISBN 9780062023551

                  LC 2011016612

In this children's picture book, the "half-pint hero imagines his way through most boys' obsessions. Astronaut, sports star, knight, dinosaur-tamer--they're all there, presented in action-packed, energetic illustrations. . . . Each verse begins with the boy and his toys in a plain and simple environment. But in resolving the verse ('That's what little boys are made of') . . . visually complex, full spreads are offered, giving readers insight into the boy's rollicking fantasies. . . . The illustrator also pays homage to a certain visual aesthetic for each of the youth's adventures." (Kirkus) "By the end, the text speculates that a boy's makeup consists of sugar and spice or puppy-dogs' tails but decides ultimately on snuggles and love." (School Libr J)

★ **Wow!** America! Hyperion Books for Children 2006 un il $16.99
Grades: PreK K 1 2   **E**
  1. United States -- Description and travel
ISBN 0-7868-3816-7

                  LC 2005-44735

"This companion to Wow! City! follows country girl Izzy on another journey, this time with her little sister and dog. Each spread reveals a location in the U.S. . . . Each spread also contains brief informational text. The drawings are as energetic as the exclamation-enhanced text." Horn Book Guide

Wow! Ocean! Disney/Hyperion Books 2011 un il
Grades: PreK K 1 2   **E**
1. Ocean -- Fiction 2. Beaches -- Fiction 3. Ocean -- Juvenile literature 4. Marine animals -- Juvenile literature
ISBN 1-4231-3113-4; 978-1-4231-3113-7
"When Izzy and her sister Jo travel from the mountains to the ocean they find a wealth of things to be excited about." (Publisher's note) "Preschool." (Horn Book)
"Izzy visits a beach with her family. Izzy's exclamations appear in colorful, chalky font in the borders ('Wow! Beach!'), as she and her sister peer at a treasure trove of shells and tide pool species; plunge underwater to swim and scuba dive among rays, whales, and sharks (all labeled for readers); and have a tea party on the ocean floor next to a sunken pirate ship. Foldout spreads, an abundance of whimsical details, and bold artwork that lives up to Izzy's repeated 'wows' make this a rewarding mix of fact and fancy." Publ Wkly

★ **Wow!** city! Hyperion 2004 un il $16.99
Grades: PreK K 1 2   **E**
1. City and town life -- Fiction
ISBN 0-7868-0951-5
Two-year-old toddler Izzy goes on a trip with her father and experiences in what she sees in the hustling-and-bustling, gigantic, crowded, loud, and colorful city.
"Drawn in India ink and vividly colored on a Macintosh computer using Adobe Photoshop, the illustrations are full of life, action, and detail." SLJ

★ **Wow!** school! Hyperion Books for Children 2007 un il $16.99
Grades: PreK K 1   **E**
1. School stories
ISBN 0-7868-3896-5; 978-0-7868-3896-7
LC 2006-49569
Izzy finds many things to be excited about on the first day of school.
"The bold, crayonlike lines of Neubecker's India-ink drawings contrast pleasingly with the computer-generated color. This is a wonderful book for sharing with groups of emergent readers, who will enjoy chiming along, and it is well suited to the attention spans of children just beginning preschool or kindergarten." SLJ

Nevius, Carol
Building with Dad; by Carol Nevius; illustrated by Bill Thomson. Marshall Cavendish 2006 un il $16.99
Grades: PreK K 1 2   **E**
1. Stories in rhyme 2. Building -- Fiction 3. Construction equipment -- Fiction 4. Father-son relationship -- Fiction
ISBN 978-0-7614-5312-3; 0-7614-5312-1
LC 2005027311
A father and his young child watch the construction of the new school, from the bulldozing of earth and mix-

ing of the concrete for the foundation to the hanging of the new sign.
This is an "energetic picture book with visual punch. . . . The spreads spill down the page vertically, rather than horizontally, for maximum impact. . . . Thomson uses full color, and his photo-realistic paintings bring viewers close up to, sometimes even under, giant machines." Booklist

★ **Karate** hour; illustrated by Bill Thomson. Marshall Cavendish 2004 un il $14.95
Grades: PreK K 1 2   **E**
1. Karate 2. Stories in rhyme 3. Karate -- Fiction
ISBN 0-7614-5169-2
LC 2003-27122
Rhyming text portrays the exuberance of an hour of karate class. Includes nonfiction information at end
Nevius "deftly captures the excitement and energy of the experience as well as the discipline and commitment required to rise in rank. Thomson's realistic mixed-media artwork is a standout, using light, shadow, and perspective in a variety of interesting ways." SLJ

Soccer hour; illustrated by Bill Thomson. Marshall Cavendish 2010 un il $16.99
Grades: PreK K 1 2   **E**
1. Stories in rhyme 2. Soccer -- Fiction
ISBN 978-0-7614-5689-6; 0-7614-5689-9
LC 2009014112
Pictures and rhyming text describe the drills and scrimmages of a team at soccer practice.
"This book offers a winning combination of rhyming couplets and striking artwork to describe an hour of practice among boys and girls. While the text reads in bursts of active statements . . . the extraordinary illustrations are the essence of the book. Thomson uses acrylics and colored pencils to create realistic paintings that almost resemble sepia photographs." SLJ

Newberry, Clare Turlay
April's kittens. HarperCollins Pubs. 1993 32p il $16.99
Grades: PreK K 1 2   **E**
1. Cats -- Fiction
ISBN 0-06-024400-3
A reissue of the title first published 1940
A Caldecott Medal honor book, 1941
"Though old-fashioned, the story of a small girl's yearning to keep both a mother cat and one of her kittens still speaks to pet owners young and old. Newberry's simple, charcoal drawings of the felines are as elegant and endearing as ever." Horn Book

Marshmallow; story and pictures by Clare Turlay Newberry. rev ed.; HarperCollinsPublishers 2008 un il $16.99; lib bdg $17.89; pa $6.99
Grades: K 1 2   **E**
1. Cats -- Fiction 2. Rabbits -- Fiction
ISBN 978-0-06-072486-3; 0-06-072486-2; 978-0-06-072487-0 lib bdg; 0-06-072487-0 lib bdg; 978-0-06-072488-7 pa; 0-06-072488-9 pa
LC 2007-30888
First published 1942
A Caldecott Medal honor book, 1943

A cat who is used to being the center of attention learns to share his home with a rabbit

Newbery, Linda
★ Posy! illustrated by Catherine Rayner. Atheneum Books for Young Readers 2009 un il $16.99
Grades: PreK K   E
  1. Stories in rhyme 2. Cats -- Fiction
ISBN 978-1-4169-7112-2; 1-4169-7112-2
                   LC 2008-03807
Posy the kitten has lots of adventures catching spiders, swiping crayons, tangling yarn, and cuddling
"Rendered in watercolor pencil crayons, acrylic, and India inks, [Posy] sometimes dominates the broad cream-colored spreads or divides a page into several vignettes with her actions. . . . While grownups, particularly cat lovers, will be charmed by the stylized art, children will notice in the kitten's daily activities much of what interests them." SLJ

Newcome, Zita
Head, shoulders, knees, and toes; and other action counting rhymes. Candlewick Press 2002 60p il $15.99
Grades: PreK K   E
  1. Poetry 2. Counting 3. Finger play 4. Nursery rhymes 5. Children's poetry 6. Counting-out rhymes
ISBN 0-7636-1899-3
                   LC 2002-17508
A collection of approximately fifty nursery and counting rhymes, most accompanied by fingerplays or other activities
"Each page includes the words of one rhyme and energetic watercolor-and-colored pencil illustrations of kids in action. . . . This is exercise and play as well as a lively celebration of the sound and beat of words in the nonsense rhymes that live on." Booklist

Newgarden, Mark
★ Bow-Wow bugs a bug; [by] Mark Newgarden and Megan Montague Cash. Harcourt 2007 un il $12.95
Grades: K 1 2 3   E
  1. Stories without words 2. Dogs -- Fiction 3. Insects -- Fiction
ISBN 978-0-15-205813-5
                   LC 2006-11026
A wordless picture book about a persistent terrier who follows a bug through his neighborhood.
"The clever circular plot is funny, quirky, and even suspenseful. . . . The simple, bold, expressive illustrations, outlined with heavy black line, challenge viewers to follow the visual story line and sequences of events." SLJ
  Other titles about Bow-Wow are:
  Bow-Wow naps by number (2007)
  Bow-Wow orders lunch (2007)
  Bow-Wow attracts opposites (2008)
  Bow-Wow hears things (2008)
  Bow-Wow 12 months running (2009)
  Bow-Wow's colorful life (2009)

Newman, Jeff
★ Hand book. Simon & Schuster Books for Young Readers 2011 il $15.99
Grades: PreK K 1 2   E
  1. Stories in rhyme 2. Hand -- Fiction 3. Growth

-- Fiction
ISBN 978-1-4169-5013-4; 1-4169-5013-3
                   LC 2010007017
Follows a person's journey through life, focusing on the hands and what they do, from babyhood to adulthood when a new pair of hands comes into existence.
"Telegraphic verse and line drawings celebrate the many things hands can do. . . . Newman challenges readers to consider their hands as intricate and capable tools, instruments of emotion, creation, and tenderness; children will almost certainly see them with new respect." Publ Wkly

The boys; written by Jeff Newman; illustrated by Jeff Newman. Simon & Schuster Books for Young Readers 2009 un il $15.99
Grades: 1 2 3   E
  1. Stories without words 2. Old age -- Fiction 3. Shyness -- Fiction 4. Baseball -- Fiction
ISBN 978-1-4169-5012-7; 1-4169-5012-5
                   LC 2007-47985
A shy boy, seeking the courage to play baseball with the other children in a park, is coaxed out of his shell by some "old timers" sitting nearby who, in turn, discover they are still in the game.
"Employing sly visual humor, Newman . . . presents the narrative in sketchy, retro-flavored gouache brushstrokes on a white background. This is a quirky book, but sensitive readers will appreciate the child's shyness and the men's efforts to help him remember what it means to be a kid." Publ Wkly

Newman, Leslea
Daddy, papa, and me; illustrated by Carol Thompson. Tricycle Press 2009 un il bd bk $7.99
Grades: PreK   E
  1. Board books for children 2. Homosexuality -- Fiction 3. Father-child relationship -- Fiction
ISBN 978-1-58246-262-2 bd bk; 1-58246-262-3 bd bk
  ALA GLBTRT Stonewall Book Award Honor Book (2010)
"A smiling tot describes his role within a nurturing two-dad family. . . . Thompson provides warm, mixed-media illustrations of the happy trio against clean white backgrounds as they play and keep house together. . . . It gives children with single-sex parents validation of their family structures in a healthy, positive way." Kirkus

Donovan's big day. Tricycle Press 2011 un il $15.99; lib bdg $18.99
Grades: PreK K   E
  1. Stories in rhyme 2. Lesbians -- Fiction 3. Weddings -- Fiction 4. Mother-son relationship -- Fiction
ISBN 978-1-58246-332-2; 1-58246-332-8; 978-1-58246-392-6 lib bdg; 1-58246-392-1 lib bdg
                   LC 2009048488
"Plain and poetic, the swiftly flowing free verse perfectly captures the day's excitement, as does Dutton's digitally touched gouache artwork. . . . A welcome addition to the still short shelf of picture books featuring same-sex parents." Booklist

Miss Tutu's star; illustrated by Carey Armstrong-Ellis. Abrams 2010 un il $16.95

Grades: PreK K 1 2   E
   1. Ballet -- Fiction
   ISBN 978-0-8109-8396-0; 0-8109-8396-6

Young Selena, who would rather twirl than walk, begins to study ballet and, after years of practice and a great deal of encouragement from Miss Tutu, finally makes her stage debut.

"Armstrong-Ellis's gouache and colored-pencil illustrations add comic touches. . . . The protagonist is a likable character with lots of heart. Many children will recognize themselves in this agreeable offering." SLJ

   ★ **Mommy,** mama, and me; illustrated by Carol Thompson. Tricycle Press 2009 un il (My family tree) bd bk $7.99
Grades: PreK   E
   1. Board books for children 2. Lesbians -- Fiction 3. Mother-child relationship -- Fiction
   ISBN 978-1-58246-263-9 bd bk; 1-58246-263-1 bd bk

ALA GLBTRT Stonewall Book Award Honor Book (2010)

"A curly-haired toddler . . . celebrates 'mommy' and 'mama,' and the activities and tender moments they share. . . . The bright colors . . . and pleasing verse offer a simple lesson about love that same-sex parents should embrace." Publ Wkly

The **best** cat in the world; written by Lesléa Newman; illustrated by Ronald Himler. Eerdmans Books for Young Readers 2004 un il $16; pa $8
Grades: K 1 2 3   E
   1. Cats 2. Grief 3. Cats -- Fiction 4. Death -- Fiction
   ISBN 0-8028-5252-1; 0-8028-5294-7 pa
                          LC 2003-13028

A young boy deals with the loss of his beloved cat Charlie, eventually accepting the arrival of another, very different cat.

"Himler's warm pencil-and-watercolor illustrations generously fill the pages. They portray the casually clad characters with tenderness and contrast the shape of the old and sick animal with that of the young and playful one. . . . For comfort and catharsis, Newman's fine story is the cat's pajamas." SLJ

A **fire** engine for Ruthie; illustrated by Cyd Moore. Clarion Books 2004 32p il $16
Grades: PreK K 1 2   E
   1. Play -- Fiction 2. Sex role -- Fiction 3. Grandmothers -- Fiction
   ISBN 0-618-15989-4
                          LC 2003-22791

Ruthie's Nana suggests playing tea party and fashion show during their visit, but Ruthie is much more interested in the vehicles that a neighbor boy is playing with as they pass his house each day.

"This book hits the mark on three solid counts—a real story, good pacing, and deliciously full artwork that has its own momentum." Booklist

Newman, Patricia

   Nugget on the flight deck; illustrated by Aaron Zenz. Walker & Co. 2009 un il $16.99; lib bdg $17.89

Grades: 1 2 3   E
   1. Air pilots -- Fiction 2. Aircraft carriers -- Fiction
   ISBN 978-0-8027-9735-3; 0-8027-9735-0; 978-0-8027-9736-0 lib bdg; 0-8027-9736-9 lib bdg
                       LC 2008044673

Aboard an aircraft carrier, a lieutenant introduces a new aviator to the 'lingo' and layout before taking him on a practice dogfight.

"Military jargon appears in boldface in the text and is defined in a separate pictorial area on each spread. Colored-pencil illustrations show many essential components of the carrier and the planes that take off and land on its deck. . . . Anyone interested in planes will appreciate the high level of information provided in an attractive, accessible format." SLJ

   Includes bibliographical references

Nez, John A.

   Cromwell Dixon's Sky-Cycle; [by] John Abbott Nez. G.P. Putnam's Sons 2009 un il $16.99
Grades: 2 3 4 5   E
   1. Air pilots 2. Flight -- Fiction 3. Inventors -- Fiction 4. Air pilots -- Fiction
   ISBN 978-0-399-25041-5; 0-399-25041-7
                       LC 2008026140

In 1907 Columbus, Ohio, fourteen-year-old Cromwell Dixon, aided by his mother, begins building the flying bicycle he has invented to enter in the St. Louis Air Ship Carnival. Includes facts about Dixon's life as an aviation pioneer.

"Through both text and pictures, Nez conveys a warm mother-son relationship. . . . Detailed watercolor paintings with tremendous kid appeal take readers back in time. . . . [This book tells] a fascinating story." Booklist

   Includes bibliographical references

Niemann, Christoph

   Pet dragon; a story about adventure, friendship, and Chinese characters. by Christoph Niemann. Greenwillow Books 2008 un il $16.99; lib bdg $17.89
Grades: K 1 2 3   E
   1. Chinese language 2. Dragons -- Fiction 3. Witches -- Fiction
   ISBN 978-0-06-157776-5; 0-06-157776-6; 978-0-06-157777-2 lib bdg; 0-06-157777-4 lib bdg

When Lin's beloved pet dragon disappears, she searches for him far and wide until a witch helps her to reach the dragon's new home. Introduces a different Chinese character on each step of Lin's adventure.

"The book is clever. Its purpose is to introduce the Chinese language, and it succeeds admirably. Each page contains one or more Chinese characters, which appear not only at the bottom with the English translation, but also superimposed on the drawings. . . . The stylized illustrations are jaunty and appealing, and the use of red, a color representing good fortune in China, visually unifies the tale from beginning to end. Playful and humorous." SLJ

   ★ **Subway**. Greenwillow Books 2010 un il $16.99; lib bdg $17.89
Grades: PreK K 1 2   E
   1. Stories in rhyme 2. Subways -- Fiction
   ISBN 978-0-06-157779-6; 0-06-157779-0; 978-0-06-157780-2 lib bdg; 0-06-157780-4 lib bdg
                       LC 2009-18756

"This colorful, vivacious, child-centered title began with a post on Niemann's blog, Abstract City, in which he describes a day of riding the subway with his two sons just for fun. The artist uses thick gouache paint to render his characters as standard pictograms, akin to those on city signs, with curved edges for hands and feet, and the technique creates a chalky texture that looks like correction fluid. . . . A sure hit with most youngsters, especially those who are transfixed by trains." SLJ

That's how! Greenwillow Books 2011 un il $16.99
Grades: PreK K 1   E
1. Vehicles -- Fiction 2. Imagination -- Fiction
ISBN 978-0-06-201963-9; 0-06-201963-5
LC 2010017216
"A boy entertains his friend with cleverly imagined ideas about how a number of vehicles work. When she asks about a truck, he responds, 'Hmmm. . . let me think.' A flip of the page shows a yellow lion pedaling a bicyclelike chain and gears inside a black truck. . . . The freighter is run by an octopus winding a whale's tale, the steamroller by a bird tickling two bears, and so forth. . . . The mixed-media digital illustrations are saturated full-bleed spreads. . . . Boy, girl, animals, and vehicles are all done in bold colors and have a cartoonish, childlike sensibility. The large trim size, popular topic, and brightly colored artwork will work well in storytimes. . . . A surefire hit." SLJ

The **police** cloud. Schwartz & Wade Books 2007 un il $15.99; lib bdg $17.99
Grades: PreK K 1   E
1. Clouds -- Fiction 2. Police -- Fiction
ISBN 0-375-83963-1; 978-0-375-83963-4; 0-375-93963-6 lib bdg; 978-0-375-93963-1 lib bdg
LC 2006-06415
A small cloud that has always dreamed of becoming a police officer discovers that he might not be suited to the job.
"The computer-enhanced illustrations have a very simple, bold graphic design and feature basic colors. . . . The illustrations do such a good job of telling the story, the concise text is almost unnecessary." Booklist

Nikola-Lisa, W.
Magic in the margins; a medieval tale of bookmaking. by W. Nikola-Lisa; illustrated by Bonnie Christensen. Houghton Mifflin 2007 un il $17
Grades: 1 2 3 4   E
1. Artists -- Fiction 2. Orphans -- Fiction 3. Apprentices -- Fiction 4. Middle Ages -- Fiction 5. Illumination of books and manuscripts -- Fiction
ISBN 978-0-618-49642-6; 0-618-49642-4
LC 2006017060
At a medieval monastery, orphaned Simon, who is apprenticing in illumination, dreams of the day he can create his own pictures, but finds he must first complete a strange and unusual assignment that Father Anselm has given him.
"Many kids . . . will be drawn in by the appealing story of a child's empowerment and the glimpse of the medieval world. Christensen extends the story with strong, clear scenes, bordered by botanical patterns and executed in ink and egg-tempura pigments." Booklist

Setting the turkeys free; written by W. Nikola-Lisa; illustrated by Ken Wilson-Max. Jump at the Sun/Hyperion Books for Children 2004 un il $15.99
Grades: PreK K 1   E
1. Foxes 2. Artists 3. Turkeys 4. Thanksgiving Day 5. Foxes -- Fiction 6. Artists -- Fiction 7. Turkeys -- Fiction
ISBN 0-7868-1952-9
LC 2003-50928
When a sly, hungry fox threatens a flock of turkeys, the young artist who drew the birds must find a way to save them.
"Right at a preschooler's level, the artwork . . . has humor as well as momentum. . . . This clever mixing of art and a spot-on text provides a fun story as well as a surefire craft idea that kids will want to try." Booklist

Nobisso, Josephine
Francis woke up early; illuminations, Maureen Hyde. Gingerbread House 2011 un il $17.95; pa $9.95
Grades: K 1 2 3   E
1. Saints 2. Saints -- Fiction 3. Wolves -- Fiction 4. Writers on religion 5. Farm life -- Fiction
ISBN 978-0-940112-20-9; 0-940112-20-5; 978-0-940112-22-3 pa; 0-940112-20-5 pa
LC 2011015539
Imagines a moment in the boyhood of Saint Francis of Assisi, in which he befriends a wild she-wolf by sharing with her his breakfast, gathered on his family's farm.
"A beautiful marriage of author, illustrator, and subject. . . . Hyde's work . . . perfectly captures early morning light in 13th-century Assisi. The bordered paintings are filled with tender detail. . . . This exquisite book will make peaceful family reading." Publ Wkly

Noble, Trinka Hakes
★ The **day** Jimmy's boa ate the wash; pictures by Steven Kellogg. Dial Bks. for Young Readers 1980 un il $16.99; pa $6.99
Grades: PreK K 1 2   E
1. School stories 2. Snakes -- Fiction 3. Farm life -- Fiction
ISBN 0-8037-1723-7; 0-8037-0094-6 pa
LC 80-15098
"The illustrations, which depict disgruntled chickens, expressive pigs, and smiling cats as well as other individualized animal and human characters, show the artist's flair for humorous detail." Horn Book
Other titles about Jimmy's boa are:
Jimmy's boa and the big splash birthday bash (1989)
Jimmy's boa and the bungee jump slam dunk (2003)
Jimmy's boa bounces back (1984)

The **last** brother; a Civil War tale. illustrated by Robert Papp. Sleeping Bear Press 2006 un il $17.95
Grades: 2 3 4 5   E
1. Brothers -- Fiction 2. Gettysburg (Pa.), Battle of, 1863 -- Fiction
ISBN 1-58536-253-0
Eleven-year-old Gabe enlists in the Union Army in Pennsylvania along with his older brother Davy and, as bugler, does his best to protect Davy during the Battle of Gettysburg.

This "story resonates with courage and fear, love and loyalty. . . . The well-rendered paintings are hauntingly detailed and place readers right in the action." SLJ

Nolan, Dennis

★ **Sea** of dreams. Roaring Brook Press 2011 il $16.99
Grades: PreK K 1   E
1. Stories without words 2. Beaches -- Fiction
ISBN 978-1-59643-470-7; 1-59643-470-8
LC 2010037815
A wordless picture book featuring a sandcastle that takes on a life of its own.
"Nolan's enchanting artwork creates a gorgeous, wordless nautical fantasy infused with the thrill of life-or-death adventure. . . . Readers will never look at the beach the same way." Publ Wkly

Nolen, Jerdine

★ **Big** Jabe; illustrations by Kadir Nelson. Lothrop, Lee & Shepard Bks. 2000 un il hardcover o.p. pa $6.99
Grades: K 1 2 3   E
1. Slavery -- Fiction 2. African Americans -- Fiction
3. Plantation life -- United States -- Juvenile fiction
4. Slaves -- Emancipation -- United States -- Juvenile fiction
ISBN 0-688-13662-1; 0-06-054061-3 pa
LC 99-38001
Momma Mary tells stories about a special young man who does wondrous things, especially for the slaves on the Plenty Plantation
"Nolen recounts her original tale with a light touch and lyrical voices that add depth and resonance to its imagery and serious overtones. The gouache and watercolor illustrations convey both the lush summer and the rigorous life of the slaves. This powerful story will be particularly effective shared aloud." Horn Book Guide

Christmas in the time of Billy Lee; illustrated by Barry Moser. Disney/Jump at the Sun Books 2010 un il $16.99
Grades: PreK K 1   E
1. Wishes -- Fiction 2. Christmas -- Fiction 3. Imaginary playmates -- Fiction
ISBN 978-0-7868-1871-6; 0-7868-1871-9
When Ellie makes three wishes and begins to believe in the magic of Christmas, all kinds of miracles occur, from broken tree lights twinkling again, to angel shapes appearing in snow, to the biggest of all: a baby brother arriving soon.
"The acknowledgment of money troubles and other concerns makes the magic feel all the sweeter, as Moser's bucolic winter landscapes and cozy portraits convey a hushed wonderment and warm family bonds." Publ Wkly

Harvey Potter's balloon farm; [illustrated by] Mark Buehner. Lothrop, Lee & Shepard Bks. 1994 un il $16.99; lib bdg $15.93; pa $5.99
Grades: PreK K 1 2   E
1. Tall tales 2. Balloons -- Fiction 3. Farm life -- Fiction
ISBN 0-688-07887-7; 0-688-07888-5 lib bdg; 0-688-15845-5 pa
LC 91-38129
"Harvey Potter's unusual crop is balloons—which grow just like corn on long, sturdy stalks. Harvey Potter himself is not at all unusual, and his friend, a young African-American

girl, is determined to uncover the secret of his curious harvest. The story is lively, but of even greater attraction are the vivid, air-brushed illustrations of balloons with expressive faces in every size, color, and shape." Horn Book Guide

★ **Hewitt** Anderson's great big life; illustrated by Kadir Nelson. Simon & Schuster Books for Young Readers 2005 un il $16.95
Grades: PreK K 1 2   E
1. Size -- Fiction 2. Giants -- Fiction
ISBN 0-689-86866-9
LC 98-14039
When tiny Hewitt is born into a family of giants, everyone learns that sometimes small is best of all.
"Nelson's funny, larger-than-life oil paintings warmly depict this African-American family and give readers a real sense of gigantic proportions. . . . Told in colorful language that begs to be read aloud, this humorous, oversize book offers a gentle look at accepting others as they are." SLJ

Pitching in for Eubie; illustrated by E.B. Lewis. Amistad 2007 un il $16.99; lib bdg $17.89
Grades: PreK K 1 2   E
1. Sisters -- Fiction 2. Family life -- Fiction 3. African Americans -- Fiction 4. Money-making projects for children -- Fiction
ISBN 978-0-688-14917-8; 978-0-06-056960-0 lib bdg
LC 2007-06995
Lily tries to find a way to pitch in and help her family make enough money to send her older sister, Eubie, to college
"Imbued with warmth, Nolen's . . . story about a family working together toward a common goal will appeal to many audiences. . . . Each painting helps advance the action and delineate the characters." Publ Wkly

Raising dragons; illustrated by Elise Primavera. Silver Whistle Bks. 1998 un il $16; pa $7
Grades: PreK K 1 2   E
1. Dragons -- Fiction 2. Farm life -- Fiction 3. Friendship -- Fiction
ISBN 0-15-201288-5; 0-15-216536-3 pa
LC 95-43307
A farmer's young daughter shares numerous adventures with the dragon that she raises from infancy
"Nolen's chimerical text meets its match in Primavera's imaginative and bold illustrations." Horn Book Guide

★ **Thunder** Rose; illustrated by Kadir Nelson. Harcourt 2003 un il $16; pa $7
Grades: K 1 2 3   E
1. Tall tales 2. African Americans -- Fiction
ISBN 0-15-216472-3; 0-15-206006-5 pa
LC 2002-12287
Unusual from the day she is born, Thunder Rose performs all sorts of amazing feats, including building fences, taming a stampeding herd of steers, capturing a gang of rustlers, and turning aside a tornado
"Nolen and Nelson offer up a wonderful tale of joy and love, as robust and vivid as the wide West. The oil, watercolor, and pencil artwork is outstanding." SLJ

Norac, Carl

My daddy is a giant; illustrated by Ingrid Godon. Clarion Books 2005 29p il $16

Grades: PreK K 1 2   **E**

1. Father-son relationship -- Fiction

ISBN 0-618-44399-1

LC 2004-12093

A little boy's father seems so large to him that he needs a ladder to cuddle him and birds nest in his father's hair

"The simple premise captures the little boy's idolization of his dad well. . . . With the man so large that he often has to bend his head or crouch down to fit onto the page, and the full-bleed spreads overflowing the book, these pictures will engage even the children in the last row of storytime." SLJ

My mommy is magic; by Carl Norac; illustrated by Ingrid Godon. Clarion Books 2007 29p il $16

Grades: PreK K   **E**

1. Mothers -- Fiction

ISBN 978-0-618-75766-4; 0-618-75766-X

LC 2006007149

First published 2006 in the United Kingdom with title: My mummy is magic

A child lists things a mommy does, such as chasing monsters away, that show she is magic, even if she does not have a wand or magic hat

"Godon's pastel-and-paint, full-bleed spreads in gentle hues exude warmth. They complement the text and the resulting mood is sweet without being cloying." SLJ

Swing Cafe; translated from the French by Jacob Homel; illustrated by Rebecca Dautremer. The Sacred Mountain 2010 un il $16.95

Grades: K 1 2 3   **E**

1. Insects -- Fiction 2. Crickets -- Fiction 3. Jazz music -- Fiction

ISBN 978-2-923163-62-8; 2-923163-62-1

"Norac's story stars a Brazilian jazz-singing cricket named Zaz who dreams of New York City. The death of her butterfly friend Miro releases her; she hops a ride in a flowered hat, befriends a blue fly, and arrives at last at the Swing Cafe. Zaz and the other characters are portrayed as stylish humans with just a trace of their insect nature. . . . Dautremer's visual imagination taps the subconscious brilliantly. . . . Norac's writing is equally arresting. . . . An enclosed CD supplies cherished jazz gems from Ellington, Calloway, Fitzgerald, and more, which accompany a lovely audio recording of the story. Intelligent, poetic, and provocative entertainment." Publ Wkly

Nordqvist, Sven

Tomtes' Christmas porridge; translated by Polly Lawson. Floris 2011 il $17.95

Grades: PreK K 1 2   **E**

1. Christmas -- Fiction

ISBN 978-0-86315-824-7; 0-86315-824-2

"Nordqvist's amusing watercolor-and-ink illustrations are full of distinct personalities and tiny details in costumes and settings. . . . A charming and sprightly story with the flavor of a traditional tale." Kirkus

Norman, Kimberly

I know a wee piggy; by Kim Norman; pictures by Henry Cole. Dial Books for Young Readers 2014 32 p. col. ill. (hardcover) $16.99

Grades: PreK K 1   **E**

1. Pigs -- Fiction 2. Picture books for children 3. Animals -- Color -- Fiction 4. Color -- Fiction 5. Stories in rhyme 6. Agricultural exhibitions -- Fiction

ISBN 0803737351; 9780803737358

LC 2011029977

This children's book is the story of a "little piggy [who] has escaped from his owner and is running riot through the county fair, getting covered in gunk, globs, and other stuff representing nine colors: brown from the muddy pig pen, red from the tomato canning display, yellow from the broken yolks in the chicken coop . . . and so forth. By the time the wee piggy proudly wins a blue ribbon," he's very dirty indeed. Author Kimberly E. Norman's text riffs on the folk song "I Know an Old Lady." (Publishers Weekly)

"The star's earnestness is irresistible, and both text and pictures are rich and energetic." (Booklist)

Ten on the sled; by Kim Norman; illustrated by Liza Woodruff. Sterling 2010 un il $14.95

Grades: PreK K 1   **E**

1. Counting 2. Stories in rhyme 3. Animals -- Fiction 4. Sledding -- Fiction

ISBN 978-1-4027-7076-0; 1-4027-7076-6

LC 2009-11501

Animals fall off a speeding sled one by one until only a lonely caribou is left, chasing a giant snowball that has engulfed the falling animals.

"What with animal identification, counting, vocabulary building and print awareness all scaffolded on a can't-lose rhyme, this one's a keeper." Kirkus

North, Sherry

Champ's story; dogs get cancer too! Sylvan Dell 2010 un il $16.95; pa $8.95

Grades: 1 2 3   **E**

1. Dogs -- Fiction 2. Cancer -- Fiction

ISBN 978-1-60718-077-7; 1-60718-077-4; 978-1-60718-088-3 pa; 1-60718-088-X pa

"While practicing for the upcoming agility show, Cody notices a lump on his dog's belly, which turns out to be cancer. The treatment is similar to what a human endures, and Cody is filled with worry for his pet. Champ is able to participate in the show, but it is Cody who has trouble when he trips and hurts his ankle. Now it's Champ's turn to take care of Cody, and she proves she is a real champion. Children will have empathy for both characters. . . . A sincere, caring story told with a straightforward, honest approach." SLJ

Noullet, Georgette

Bed hog; illustrated by David Slonim. Marshall Cavendish 2011 un il $12.99

Grades: PreK K   **E**

1. Dogs -- Fiction 2. Sleep -- Fiction

ISBN 978-0-7614-5823-4; 0-7614-5823-9

LC 2010008089

"Every night, Bailey, the family dog, travels from room to room trying to find a comfortable place to sleep. Although his owners call him a 'bed hog,' readers will see early on that the pup is not the one taking up all the space. . . . Gentle humor and spare wording with repetitive phrasing will allow pre-readers to retell the simple tale after hearing it once. The colorful cartoonlike illustrations in acrylic and charcoal will put a smile on the face of any family member who frequently finds a dog sleeping in the bed." SLJ

Novak, Matt

A **wish** for you. Greenwillow Books 2010 un il $16.99

Grades: PreK K   E

1. Stories in rhyme 2. Infants -- Fiction 3. Family life -- Fiction

ISBN 978-0-06-155202-1; 0-06-155202-X

LC 2008052485

"In this bouncy story, a man and woman meet, court, marry, and prepare for their new baby. . . . Half-page pictures zip through scenes of preparation for the infant's arrival. Then, when the baby joins them on their vacation adventures. . . . Novak's soft-edged digitally enhanced artwork perfectly portrays the merry mood of his pudgy characters. This is a great choice for cozy sharing with a beloved child." SLJ

Novesky, Amy

Georgia in Hawaii; when Georgia O'Keeffe painted what she pleased. written by Amy Novesky; illustrated by Yuyi Morales. Houghton Mifflin Harcourt 2012 40 p.

Grades: K 1 2 3 4   E

1. Painting -- Fiction 2. Flowers in art -- Fiction 3. Hawaii -- History -- Fiction 4. Artists -- Fiction 5. Obstinacy -- Fiction

ISBN 9780152054205

LC 2010043401

This book tells how in "1939, Georgia O'Keefe was commissioned by the Hawaiian Pineapple Company (later Dole Pineapple) to create two paintings to promote and market pineapple juice. She spent nine weeks traveling around the islands. . . . During that time, she decided she did not want to paint the way the pineapple company wanted her to paint, and they rejected some of the art she created. She discovered and fell in love with the lush greenery and flowers and waterfalls and all the beauty Hawaii had to offer, but she refused to paint a pineapple. . . . After the Hawaiian Pineapple Company airlifted a pineapple plant to her in New York, she agreed to paint what she would call "Pineapple Bud," which became part of their advertising campaign." (International Reading Association)

★ **Me,** Frida; illustrated by David Diaz. Abrams Books for Young Readers 2010 un il $16.95

Grades: K 1 2 3   E

1. Artists 2. Painters 3. Artists -- Fiction 4. Women artists -- Fiction

ISBN 978-0-8109-8969-6; 0-8109-8969-7

Pura Belpré Award honor book (Illustrator), 2011

Artist Frida Kahlo finds her own voice and style when her famous husband, Diego Rivera, is commissioned to paint a mural in San Francisco, California, in the 1930s and she finds herself exploring the city on her own.

"Overflowing with compelling imagery, . . . the story also incorporates the motif of Kahlo as a tiny bird. . . Vibrant spreads feature backdrops of warm colors dripping into cooler ones (and vice versa). . . . Diaz's . . . overlapping complementary colors add a gorgeous yet slightly unsettling

visual element, his intense hues and folk/naive style recalling Kahlo's work." Publ Wkly

Noyes, Deborah

★ **Red** butterfly; how a princess smuggled the secret of silk out of China. illustrated by Sophie Blackall. Candlewick Press 2007 un il $16.99

Grades: 1 2 3   E

1. Silkworms -- Fiction 2. Princesses -- Fiction

ISBN 978-0-7636-2400-2; 0-7636-2400-4

LC 2006-52931

In long-ago China, as a young princess prepares to leave her parents' kingdom to travel to far-off Khotan where she is to marry the king, she decides to surreptitiously take with her a precious reminder of home.

"Noyes' graceful text includes allusions to nature and the shifting seasons in a style reminiscent of Chinese poetry. . . . [This is illustrated with] beautiful, ink-and-watercolor illustrations in rich, jewel colors." Booklist

Numberman, Neil

Do not build a Frankenstein! Greenwillow Books 2009 un il $16.99

Grades: K 1   E

1. Moving -- Fiction 2. Monsters -- Fiction

ISBN 978-0-06-156816-9; 0-06-156816-3

LC 2008-20751

A boy warns his new neighbors of the trouble that comes with building a monster, including having to move to a different town in hopes of escaping his creation

"Numberman is a nimble, funny writer, and he opts for showing rather than telling, his naif watercolors scoring a punch line every time." Publ Wkly

Numeroff, Laura Joffe

Beatrice doesn't want to; illustrated by Lynn Munsinger. Candlewick Press 2004 un il $15.99; pa $6.99

Grades: PreK K 1 2   E

1. Libraries 2. Brothers and sisters 3. Libraries -- Fiction 4. Books and reading -- Fiction

ISBN 0-7636-1160-3; 0-7636-3843-9 pa

LC 2002-73908

A newly illustrated edition of the title first published 1981 by Watts

On the third afternoon of going to the library with her brother Henry, Beatrice finally finds something she enjoys doing.

"Done in watercolor, ink, and pencil and featuring floppy-eared canine characters, the expressive illustrations perfectly capture the humor of the text." SLJ

The **Chicken** sisters; by Laura Numeroff; pictures by Sharleen Collicott. HarperCollins Pubs. 1997 un il $15.99; pa $6.95

Grades: PreK K 1 2   E

1. Wolves -- Fiction 2. Sisters -- Fiction 3. Chickens -- Fiction

ISBN 0-06-026679-1; 0-06-443520-2 pa

LC 96-30297

"Violet, Poppy, and Babs, the chicken sisters, possess talents that annoy the neighbors until a threatening wolf moves into the neighborhood. The illustrations achieve a captivating sense of texture that adds immediacy to the humorous story." Horn Book Guide

★ **If** you give a mouse a cookie; by Laura Numeroff; illustrated by Felicia Bond. Harper & Row 1985 un il $15.99; lib bdg $16.89

Grades: PreK K 1   E
    1. Mice -- Fiction
    ISBN 0-06-024586-7; 0-06-024587-5 lib bdg

LC 84-48343

Relating the cycle of requests a mouse is likely to make after you give him a cookie takes the reader through a young child's day

"Children love to indulge in supposition or to ask 'what will happen if . . .?' and here there is a long, satisfying chain of linked and enjoyably nonsensical causes and effects. . . . The illustrations, neatly drawn, spaciously composed, and humorously detailed, extend the story just the way picture book illustrations should." Bull Cent Child Books

Other titles in this series are:
If you give a cat a cupcake (2008)
If you give a dog a donut (2011)
If you give a moose a muffin (1991)
If you give a pig a pancake (1998)
If you give a pig a party (2005)
If you take a mouse to school (2002)
If you take a mouse to the movies (2000)

The **Jellybeans** and the big Book Bonanza. Abrams 2010 il $15.95

Grades: PreK K 1 2   E
    1. School stories 2. Animals -- Fiction 3. Friendship -- Fiction 4. Books and reading -- Fiction
    ISBN 978-0-8109-8412-7; 0-8109-8412-1

"Anna and her friends Emily, Nicole, and Bitsy remain, like the candies, 'differenct flavors [that] go well together.' When their class has a Book Bonanza, book-loving Anna is excited, but her friends' expressions suggest they would rather be doing other things. Luckily, the librarian helps each Jellybean find the perfect book. . . . The characters sweetly express friendship dynamics in a group setting." Publ Wkly

The **Jellybeans** and the big camp kickoff; [by] Laura Numeroff, Nate Evans; illustrated by Lynn Munsinger. Abrams Books for Young Readers 2011 un il $16.95

Grades: PreK K 1 2   E
    1. Camps -- Fiction 2. Animals -- Fiction 3. Friendship -- Fiction
    ISBN 978-0-8109-9765-3; 0-8109-9765-7

LC 2010023698

When four friends with different talents and abilities go to summer camp together, they use their strengths to make camp fun for all.

"Though it's a simple story, readers who value their close friendships should appreciate how the girls encourage one another to succeed." Publ Wkly

Otis & Sydney and the best birthday ever; illustrated by Dan Andreasen. Abrams Books for Young Readers 2010 un il $16.95

Grades: PreK K 1 2   E
    1. Bears -- Fiction 2. Parties -- Fiction 3. Birthdays

-- Fiction 4. Friendship -- Fiction
    ISBN 978-0-8109-8959-7; 0-8109-8959-X

LC 2009-47199

Otis plans a surprise party for his best friend, Sydney, and although he has put the wrong date on the invitations and no one else comes, the two still have a wonderful time together.

Andreasen's "digitally colored pen and ink art echoes the old-fashioned tenor of Numeroff's . . . story; strong hatching for shading and texture leads the eye and gives the bears' fur a dapper, well-groomed quality. . . . The honeyed story never strays far from its warm and fuzzy core." Publ Wkly

Ponyella; [by] Laura Numeroff and Nate Evans; pictures by Lynn Munsinger. Disney/Hyperion Books 2011 un il $16.99

Grades: PreK K 1   E
    1. Fairy tales 2. Horses -- Fiction
    ISBN 978-1-4231-0259-5; 1-4231-0259-2

LC 2010-23406

Ponyella's dream of showing Princess Penelope her tricks at the pony championship comes true with the help of her fairy godmare.

"Cinderella gets a peppy makeover in this pony tale. . . . The frillier moments in Munsinger's pastel-dominated paintings are offset by lightly comedic particulars. . . . A sweet, playful adaptation." Publ Wkly

When sheep sleep; by Laura Numeroff; illustrated by David McPhail. Abrams Books for Young Readers 2006 un il $15.95

Grades: PreK K 1 2   E
    1. Counting 2. Stories in rhyme 3. Sleep -- Fiction 4. Animals -- Fiction 5. Bedtime -- Fiction
    ISBN 0-8109-5469-9

LC 2005022544

Rhyming text suggests other options when one tries to count sheep but discovers that they are all asleep.

"McPhail's charming watercolor-and-ink illustrations are infused with warmth and are a lovely complement to the gentle, rhyming lullaby." SLJ

Would I trade my parents? by Laura Numeroff; illustrated by James Bernardin. Abrams Books for Young Readers 2009 un il $16.95

Grades: PreK K 1 2   E
    1. Parents -- Fiction
    ISBN 978-0-8109-0637-2; 0-8109-0637-6

LC 2008030381

A young boy considers what is special about all of his friends' parents, and realizes that his own are the most wonderful of all.

"The illustrations are large and clear, made with acrylics and a digital paint program. They simply illustrate the text. . . . This is a straightforward retelling of a common childhood exercise in wishful thinking." SLJ

Nutt, Robert

Amy's light; written and illustrated by Robert Nutt. Dawn 2010 un il (Sharing nature with children) $16.95; pa $8.95

Grades: K 1 2   E
    1. Stories in rhyme 2. Fear -- Fiction 3. Fireflies

-- Fiction

ISBN 978-1-58469-128-0; 1-58469-128-X; 978-1-58469-129-7 pa; 1-58469-129-8 pa

A young girl discovers a light in nature that helps her overcome her fear of the dark. Includes an author's note about fireflies.

"Told in lyrical poetry, the author has created the magic of lightning bugs. His photo-illustrations capture Amy's fear, delight and joy." Libr Media Connect

Nyeu, Tao

Bunny days. Dial Books for Young Readers 2010 un il $16.99

Grades: PreK K   E

1. Bears -- Fiction 2. Goats -- Fiction 3. Rabbits -- Fiction

ISBN 978-0-8037-3330-5; 0-8037-3330-5

LC 2009-23060

As a pair of busy goats inadvertently cause trouble for six bunnies, their neighbor Bear comes to the rescue.

"Nyeu's illustrations are silk-screened using water-based ink. . . . The simple language and layout of the book make it suitable for beginning readers." SLJ

Squid and Octopus; friends for always. Tao Nyeu. Dial Books for Young Readers 2012 40 p. col. ill. (hardcover) $16.99

Grades: PreK K 1 2   E

1. Squids -- Fiction 2. Octopuses -- Fiction 3. Friendship -- Juvenile fiction 4. Friendship -- Fiction 5. Best friends -- Fiction

ISBN 0803735650; 9780803735651

LC 2011033194

This children's picture book presents "four stories about the relationship between two eccentric sea creatures. When Squid knits socks for his multiple limbs and Octopus tells him they wear mittens, not socks, the buddies argue. Next, Squid is sad to have lost the X-ray vision bestowed while dreaming--and his status as 'Super Squid.' . . . Octopus then mistakes a cowboy boot for a hat; finally, the duo reads a fortune about everlasting friendship." (Kirkus Reviews)

O Flatharta, Antoine

★ **Hurry** and the monarch; illustrated by Meilo So. Knopf 2005 un il $14.95; pa $7.99

Grades: K 1 2   E

1. Turtles -- Fiction 2. Butterflies -- Fiction

ISBN 0-375-83003-0; 0-385-73719-X pa

LC 2004-15984

Hurry the tortoise befriends a monarch butterfly when she stops in his garden in Wichita Falls, Texas, during her migration from Canada to Mexico. Includes facts about monarch butterflies

"Veined with a tracery of inked details, So's subtle watercolors reference both Asian nature-painting traditions and the limited palette of artwork in the early days of color printing. Together with its informative afterword, this is a particularly attractive, affecting introduction to the wonder of species diversity and the elegant continuum of life." Booklist

O'Callahan, Jay

★ **Raspberries!** [illustrated by] Will Moses. Philomel Books 2009 un il $17.99

Grades: K 1 2 3   E

1. Baking -- Fiction 2. Raspberries -- Fiction

ISBN 978-0-399-25181-8; 0-399-25181-2

LC 2008048085

Once a famous baker but now down on his luck, Simon makes a living selling eggs until he is given some very special raspberry plants.

"Faithful to narrative details, the energetic folk-art style illustrations capture the personalities, exuberance, and flavor of a story that celebrates a persevering, kindhearted entrepreneur." Booklist

O'Connell, Rebecca

Danny is done with diapers; a potty ABC. illustrated by Amanda Gulliver. Albert Whitman & Co. 2010 un il $16.99

Grades: PreK   E

1. Alphabet 2. Toilet training -- Fiction

ISBN 978-0-8075-1466-5; 0-8075-1466-7

"This book gently encourages, commends, and celebrates 26 youngsters who are in the process of being toilet trained. It begins 'A is for Accident, Adam had an accident. It's all right Adam.' Sweet, brightly colored acrylic illustrations discreetly show the kids using a potty chair or a toilet, washing hands, and pulling on clothing, with only a few bare bottoms revealed. . . . Written at a young child's level of understanding, this title will be useful in showing toddlers how others have accomplished this feat." SLJ

The **baby** goes beep; pictures by Ken Wilson-Max. Albert Whitman 2010 un il bd bk $7.99

Grades: PreK   E

1. Board books for children 2. Sound -- Fiction 3. Infants -- Fiction 4. Parent-child relationship -- Fiction

ISBN 978-0-8075-0508-3 bd bk; 0-8075-0508-0 bd bk

LC 2010002094

First published 2003 by Roaring Book Press

A baby makes various sounds as he explores the world around him.

"Wilson-Max's heavy black outlines and bright, thickly applied colors provide the perfect definition for the images. This pink baby (with a tuft of black hair) is clearly the best thing that ever happened to this set of parents, and this book is one of the best things to happen to those babies lucky enough to encounter it." Kirkus

O'Connor, Jane

Fancy Nancy; pictures by Robin Preiss Glasser. HarperCollins 2006 un il $17.99; lib bdg $17,89

Grades: PreK K   E

1. Family life -- Fiction 2. Clothing and dress -- Fiction

ISBN 0-06-054209-8; 0-06-054210-1 lib bdg

LC 2004-28662

A young girl who loves fancy things helps her family to be fancy for one special night. "Ages four to seven." (N Y Times Book Rev)

"For Nancy, there's no such thing as too, too much; she loves her frilly bedroom, her lace-trimmed socks, and her pen with a plume. Nancy teaches her family how to be fancy, too. . . . Nancy's perky narrative, in short, simple sentences, incorporates some 'fancy' vocabulary for kids to absorb (stupendous, posh), along with a sense of the rewards of a family doing things together. The cheerfully colored art is aptly exuberant, a riotous blending of color and pattern and action." Booklist

Other titles about Fancy Nancy are:

Fancy Nancy and the posh puppy (2007)
Fancy Nancy and the boy from Paris (2008)
Fancy Nancy at the museum (2008)
Fancy Nancy: Bonjour, butterfly (2008)
Fancy Nancy's favorite fancy words (2008)
Fancy Nancy sees stars (2009)
Fancy Nancy: poison ivy expert (2009)
Fancy Nancy: explorer extraordinaire! (2009)
Fancy Nancy tea parties (2009)
Fancy Nancy: the dazzling book report (2009)
Fancy Nancy: splendiferous Christmas (2009)
Fancy Nancy: poet extraordinaire! (2010)
Fancy Nancy: the 100th day of school (2010)
Fancy Nancy: ooh la la! It's beauty day (2010)
Fancy Nancy and the delectable cupcakes (2010)
Fancy Nancy and the fabulous fashion boutique (2010)
Fancy Nancy: aspiring artist (2011)
Fancy Nancy: stellar stargazer (2011)

★ **Ready,** set, skip! illustrated by Ann James. Viking 2007 un il $15.99; pa $6.99

Grades: PreK K   E
   1. Stories in rhyme 2. Mother-daughter relationship -- Fiction
   ISBN 978-0-670-06216-4; 978-0-14-241423-1 pa
                   LC 2006-08632

A little girl cannot skip until her mother shows her a special trick.

"Exuberant color and black line illustrations on a white background depict the actions with élan and convey the special camaraderie between girl and dog and mother and daughter." SLJ

The **perfect** puppy for me; by Jane O'Connor and Jessie Hartland; illustrated by Jessie Hartland. Viking 2003 un il $15.99

Grades: PreK K 1 2   E
   1. Dogs 2. Pets 3. Dogs -- Fiction
   ISBN 0-670-03614-5
                   LC 2002-15568

While waiting to get his very own puppy, a young boy spends time with various dogs and describes what the different breeds are like

"Each page is jam-packed with good advice, useful information, and bright and cleverly detailed paintings that successfully reflect the pertinent traits of the different canines." SLJ

O'Hair, Margaret

   My kitten; illustrated by Tammie Lyon. Marshall Cavendish Childrens 2011 un il $15.99

Grades: PreK   E
   1. Stories in rhyme 2. Cats -- Fiction
   ISBN 978-0-7614-5811-1; 0-7614-5811-5
                   LC 2009052902

Brief rhyming text and illustrations show a kitten's activities, from dreaming in the sunlight to playing with a ball of yarn.

This is "toe-tapping and easy to read. . . . The watercolor-and-colored-pencil illustrations are both spot and full-bleed,

and they match the action of the text wonderfully. . . . Repeated readings will be required." Kirkus

   My pup; by Margaret O'Hair; illustrated by Tammie Lyon. Marshall Cavendish 2008 un il $14.99; bd bk $7.99

Grades: PreK   E
   1. Stories in rhyme 2. Dogs -- Fiction
   ISBN 978-0-7614-5389-5; 0-7614-5389-X; 978-0-7614-5644-5 bk bk; 0-7614-5644-9 bd bk
                   LC 2007011719

"Bouncy text and simple rhyming couplets take readers through a day in the life of a little girl and her pet as they play in the mud, enjoy a car ride, get in the way of the cat, go for a walk, and finally cuddle up together in bed. . . . Children will delight in the expressive, brightly colored gouache and pencil spreads of a smiling, round-faced youngster with large, oval animal-print glasses and her pup." SLJ

O'Hora, Zachariah

   No fits, Nilson! by Zachariah OHora. Dial Books for Young Readers 2013 32 p. ill. (reinforced) $16.99

Grades: PreK K 1   E
   1. Picture books for children 2. Temper tantrums -- Juvenile fiction 3. Gorilla -- Fiction 4. Behavior -- Fiction
   ISBN 0803738528; 9780803738522
                   LC 2012021514

In this children's picture book, "Amelia helps a 9-foot blue gorilla named Nilson avoid tantrums by repeatedly reminding him, 'No fits, Nilson!' . . . Illustrations depict age-old meltdown triggers: a toppled block tower, uncooperative sneakers that just (eeergh!) won't get (oof!) on your feet and boring grownup errands." (Kirkus Reviews)

   Stop snoring, Bernard. Henry Holt & Co. 2011 un il $16.99

Grades: PreK K 1 2   E
   1. Zoos -- Fiction 2. Sleep -- Fiction 3. Otters -- Fiction 4. Animals -- Fiction 5. Snoring -- Fiction
   ISBN 978-0-8050-9002-4; 0-8050-9002-9

Bernard the otter snores so loudly that he keeps all of the otters at the zoo awake during naptime and Grumpy Giles tells Bernard to move his snoring somewhere else!

Ohora's "bright, flat paintings, saturated in the limited palette of red, teal, gold, gray, and black, convey depths of emotion in simple strokes and heavy outlines. Jaunty compositions, with animal characters busting out of the frames, make for audacious humor, and hand-painted lettering signifying Bernard's snoring and the animals' admonitions adds visual zing." Booklist

O'Malley, Kevin

   ★ **Animal** crackers fly the coop. Walker & Co. 2010 un il $16.99; lib bdg $17.89

Grades: 2 3 4   E
   1. Animals -- Fiction 2. Comedians -- Fiction
   ISBN 978-0-8027-9837-4; 0-8027-9837-3; 978-0-8027-9838-1 lib bdg; 0-8027-9838-1 lib bdg
                   LC 2009018188

In this humorous take-off of 'The Bremen Town Musicians,' four animals that aspire to make it big as comedians leave their owners and seek their fortunes.

"Full of puns, this . . . is clever, well executed, and loaded with laughs. O'Malley's expressive black-line illustrations over deep-hued colors bring the large images of the animals and robbers up-front on the page, increasing the interaction with his audience and enhancing the humor." SLJ

Captain Raptor and the moon mystery; illustrations by Patrick O'Brien. Walker & Co. 2005 un il $16.95; lib bdg $17.85

Grades: PreK K 1 2 3 4   E
1. Graphic novels 2. Science fiction 3. Science fiction graphic novels 4. Dinosaurs -- Fiction 5. Dinosaurs -- Graphic novels
ISBN 0-8027-8935-8; 0-8027-8936-6 lib bdg
LC 2004-53624

When something lands on one of the moons of the planet Jurassica, Captain Raptor and his spaceship crew go to investigate

"An action-packed science-fiction romp starring a cast of dinosaur characters. . . . Presented in comic-book style, this story blends an eye-catching layout with a quick-moving plot, tongue-in-cheek humor, and an imaginative setting." SLJ

Another title about Captain Raptor is:
Captain Raptor and the space pirates (2007)

Captain Raptor and the space pirates; [by] Kevin O'Malley and Patrick O'Brien; illustrations by Patrick O'Brien. Walker & Co. 2007 un il $16.95; lib bdg $17.85

Grades: 1 2 3   E
1. Science fiction 2. Pirates -- Fiction 3. Dinosaurs -- Fiction
ISBN 978-0-8027-9571-7; 0-8027-9571-4; 978-0-8027-9572-4 lib bdg; 0-8027-9572-2 lib bdg
LC 2006101182

Captain Raptor and the crew of the Megatooth are called back into action to save the planet Jurassica from rogue space pirates.

This "comes alive with O'Brien's watercolor and gouache illustrations. The action moves quickly in small frames dense with realistic dinosaurs in armor and the inner workings of spaceships." SLJ

★ **Gimme** cracked corn and I will share. Walker & Co. 2007 un il $16.95; lib bdg $17.85

Grades: 2 3 4   E
1. Chickens -- Fiction
ISBN 978-0-8027-9684-4; 0-8027-9684-2; 978-0-8027-9685-1 lib bdg; 0-8027-9685-0 lib bdg
LC 2007-03706

Chicken dreams about a treasure and sets off on a dangerous journey to find it

"Fans of corny humor and 'punny yolks' will welcome this tale. . . . The unique illustrations are a combination of pen, ink, and Photoshop." SLJ

Lucky leaf. Walker & Co. 2004 un il hardcover o.p. pa $6.95

Grades: PreK K 1 2   E
1. Leaves -- Fiction
ISBN 0-8027-8924-2; 0-8027-8925-0 lib bdg; 0-8027-9647-8 pa
LC 2003-68868

After his mother tells him to stop playing video games and go outside, a young boy tries to catch the last leaf on a tree, thinking it will bring him luck

"Done in pen and ink and colored in PhotoShop, the illustrations feature crisp, vibrant colors that create a vivid setting. . . . The story is told through spare, but effective, dialogue presented in speech bubbles." SLJ

Once upon a royal superbaby; written and illustrated by Kevin O'Malley; illustrated by Carol Heyer & Scott Goto. Walker & Co. 2010 un il lib bdg $17.89; $16.99

Grades: K 1 2 3   E
1. Infants -- Fiction 2. Authorship -- Fiction 3. Imagination -- Fiction 4. Superheroes -- Fiction 5. Kings and rulers -- Fiction
ISBN 978-0-8027-2165-5 lib bdg; 0-8027-2165-6 lib bdg; 978-0-8027-2164-8; 0-8027-2164-8
LC 2009054216

Cooperatively writing a story for school, a girl imagines a king and queen who have a baby named Sweet Piper who can talk to birds, while a boy names the baby Sweet Viper and gives him super-strength, cool wrestling moves, and a motorcycle and sunglasses.

"The boy and the girl are illustrated by O'Malley. Goto and Heyer's hyperrealistic art functions well to depict the imaginations of the narrators; and children of both genders will relate to the ongoing debate between the boy and girl." SLJ

O'Neill, Alexis
★ **Estela's** swap; illustrated by Enrique O. Sanchez. Lee & Low Bks. 2002 un il hardcover o.p. pa $7.95

Grades: K 1 2 3   E
1. Flea markets 2. Conduct of life 3. Mexican Americans 4. Music box 5. Moneymaking projects 6. Mexican Americans -- Fiction
ISBN 1-58430-044-2; 1-60060-253-3 pa
LC 2001-38785

A young Mexican American girl accompanies her father to a swap meet, where she hopes to sell her music box for money for dancing lessons

"This is a warm, nicely paced story about sharing and bartering that's filled with sensory descriptions of the vibrant open market. The textured acrylics capture the hum and bustle of the stalls." Booklist

O'Neill, Catharine
Annie and Simon. Candlewick Press 2008 57p il $15.99

Grades: 1 2   E
1. Dogs -- Fiction 2. Siblings -- Fiction
ISBN 978-0-7636-2688-4; 0-7636-2688-0
LC 2006-47521

Recounts four adventures of Annie, her big brother, Simon, and their dog, Hazel.

"Annie and Simon's four stories collected here will ring true for most newly independent readers. The watercolor illustrations of the two and their bark-full dog Hazel are full of humor and detail. . . . O'Neill's first solo effort in some years is well worth adding to the first-chapter-book collection." Kirkus

Oakley, Graham

The **church** mouse. Kane Miller 2010 un il $16.99 E
1. Cats -- Fiction 2. Mice -- Fiction 3. Church -- Fiction

ISBN 978-1-935279-69-3; 1-935279-69-6

A reissue of the title first published 1972 by Atheneum

Arthur, a lonely mouse living in a church with only Sampson, a friendly, sleepy cat, for company devises a plan to get all the mice in town to move in with him.

"The cover of this reissue is different from the 1972 original, but inside can be found the same detailed illustrations and child appealing events (e.g., mid-sermon melees, burglars, acrobatics)." Horn Book Guide

Obed, Ellen Bryan

★ **Who** would like a Christmas tree? illustrated by Anne Hunter. Houghton Mifflin Books for Children 2009 un il $16

Grades: 1 2 3 E
1. Trees -- Fiction 2. Months -- Fiction 3. Nature -- Fiction 4. Animals -- Fiction 5. Christmas -- Fiction 6. Christmas trees -- Juvenile lterature

ISBN 978-0-547-04625-9; 0-547-04625-1

LC 2008052302

Describes the flora and fauna that inhabit a Christmas tree farm throughout the year and use the growing trees for a variety of purposes. Includes section on how the farmer takes care of the farm through the year.

"Though presented as a Christmas book, this informative introduction to the different animals inhabiting a Maine tree plantation can be enjoyed year round. . . . The charming watercolor and ink illustrations are rendered in naturalistic fashion using nature's hues and cross-hatching techniques for shading and depth. . . . An excellent resource for getting youngsters enthused about nature." SLJ

Oberman, Sheldon

The **always** prayer shawl; illustrated by Ted Lewin. Boyds Mills Press 1994 un il $15.95; pa $10.95

Grades: 1 2 3 4 E
1. Jews -- Fiction 2. Immigrants -- Fiction

ISBN 1-878093-22-3; 1-59078-332-8 pa

This story "tells of the Jewish boy Adam, growing up in a shtetl, whose life drastically changes when famine and chaos in old Russia force his parents to immigrate to America. At parting, Adam's beloved grandfather gives the boy a gift, a prayer shawl . . . which was presented to the grandfather by his grandfather. . . . The watercolors are abundantly detailed and wonderfully expressive. . . . The pictures enrich the tranquil telling . . . as it movingly depicts how memory and tradition add texture and richness to our lives." Booklist

Ochiltree, Dianne

Molly, by golly! the legend of Molly Williams, America's first female firefighter. Dianne Ochiltree; illustrated by Kathleen Kemly. Boyds Mills Press 2012 32 p. ill. (reinforced) $16.95

Grades: 2 3 4 E
1. Fire fighters -- Juvenile literature 2. Fire fighting -- Juvenile literature

ISBN 1590787218; 9781590787212

LC 2012933452

This children's book by Diane Ochiltree tells the story of Molly Williams, "The first American female firefighter

[and] an African-American cook in the first quarter of the 19th century. . . . Molly cooked for Mr. Aymar, who was also a volunteer firefighter for the Oceanus Engine Company No. 11. A heavy snowstorm and a wave of influenza laid many of the volunteers low, so Molly . . . put on a leather helmet and gloves and worked beside the men . . . until finally the blaze was out." (Kirkus Reviews)

Odanaka, Barbara

Crazy day at the Critter Cafe; illustrated by Lee White. Margaret K. McElderry Books 2009 un il $16.99

Grades: K 1 2 E
1. Stories in rhyme 2. Animals -- Fiction 3. Restaurants -- Fiction

ISBN 978-1-4169-3914-6; 1-4169-3914-8

A quiet morning in a roadside cafe turns to chaos when a bus breaks down and a managerie of noisy, rude animals enters, demanding to be fed.

"The rhymed text emphasizes the zany sound effects as the mixed-media illustrations comically exaggerate the scenes. Kids will giggle over the heightened food mess the animals leave behind." Booklist

Oelschlager, Vanita

A **tale** of two daddies; illustrated by Kristin Blackwood and Mike Blanc. Vanita 2010 il $15.95

Grades: PreK K 1 2 E
1. Homosexuality -- Fiction 2. Father-daughter relationship -- Fiction

ISBN 9780981971452; 0981971458

Ofanansky, Allison

Harvest of light; by Allison Ofanansky; photos by Eliyahu Alpern. Kar-Ben Pub. 2008 un il (Nature in Israel) lib bdg $15.95

Grades: 1 2 3 E
1. Jews -- Fiction 2. Olives -- Fiction 3. Hanukkah -- Fiction

ISBN 978-0-8225-7389-0 lib bdg; 0-8225-7389-X lib bdg

LC 2007-43133

"In this wonderfully different Hanukkah book, an Israeli family harvests olives to be processed into the oil. The daughter provides a simple narrative, which is clearly written and accompanied by full-color photographs depicting each step in the process from gathering and sorting the olives to pressing them and using the oil to light the menorah. Resonating with familial warmth and a shared purpose, this is a fine offering." SLJ

Sukkot treasure hunt; photographs by Eliyahu Alpern. Kar-Ben 2009 un il (Nature in Israel) $15.95

Grades: PreK K 1 2 E
1. Jews -- Fiction 2. Sukkot -- Fiction

ISBN 978-0-8225-8763-7; 0-8225-8763-7

LC 2008-31202

In Israel, a young girl and her family go on a scavenger hunt to find the 'four species' they will use in their celebration of the Jewish holiday, Sukkot. Includes facts about plants named in the story.

"Straightforward first-person text and clear photographs encourage readers to join the family on their search for palm, willow, myrtle, and etrog." Horn Book Guide

What's the buzz? honey for a sweet new year. photographed by Eliyahu Alpern. Kar-Ben 2011 il (Nature in Israel) lib bdg $15.95

Grades: K 1 2 3   E

1. School stories 2. Bees -- Fiction 3. Honey -- Fiction 4. Rosh ha-Shanah -- Fiction

ISBN 978-0-7613-5640-0; 0-7613-5640-1

LC 2010026181

A class in Israel tours a farm to learn how honey is made and used to celebrate the Jewish New Year, Rosh Hashanah.

"Ofanansky and Alpern offer a fresh take on Rosh Hashanah. . . . Color photographs and a running narrative combine to produce an easy-to-grasp book that is about science but also about culture." Publ Wkly

Offill, Jenny

11 experiments that failed; written by Jenny Offill; pictures by Nancy Carpenter. 2011 un il $16.99

Grades: PreK K 1 2   E

1. Science -- Experiments -- Fiction

ISBN 978-0-375-84762-2; 0-375-84762-6

"The curious and mischief-minded heroine from 17 Things I'm Not Allowed to Do Anymore turns her attention to the scientific method. A typical experiment: 'Question: Do dogs like to be covered in glitter? Hypothesis: Dogs like everything.' Offill's matter-of-fact recounting . . . make for very funny reading and allow Carpenter to go all out with her collages, which create especially lively depictions of the protagonist's misadventures." Publ Wkly

★ **17** things I'm not allowed to do anymore. Schwartz & Wade Books 2006 un il $15.99

Grades: PreK K 1 2   E

1. Behavior -- Fiction

ISBN 0-375-83596-2

LC 2005-16414

A young girl lists the sixteen things she is not allowed to do anymore, including not being able to make ice after freezing a fly in one of the cubes.

"Ingenious artwork—a flawless marriage of digital imagery and pen-and-ink—is indisputably the focus of this winning title." SLJ

Another title about this girl is:

11 experiments that failed (2011)

Ogburn, Jacqueline K.

The **bake** shop ghost; illustrated by Marjorie Priceman. Houghton Mifflin 2005 un il $16; pa $6.99

Grades: K 1 2 3   E

1. Ghost stories 2. Cake -- Fiction 3. Bakers and bakeries -- Fiction

ISBN 0-618-44557-9; 0-547-07677-0 pa

Miss Cora Lee Meriweather haunts her bake shop after her death, until Annie Washington, the new shop owner, makes a deal with her.

"Priceman's illustrations are charming, with dashes of color and humor and a sense of action in each one. . . . This is a delightful story with a satisfying conclusion." SLJ

The **magic** nesting doll; illustrated by Laurel Long. Dial Bks. 2000 un il $16.99

Grades: K 1 2 3   E

1. Fairy tales

ISBN 0-8037-2414-4

LC 98-34397

After her grandmother dies, Katya finds herself in a kingdom where the Tsarvitch has been turned into living ice and she uses the magic nesting dolls her babushka had given her to try to break the curse

"The writings is filled with description and poetic images. . . . Created using oil paints on paper primed with gesso, the illustrations are alive with detail and reminiscent of the miniaturist style used in Russian decorative items." SLJ

Ohi, Ruth

Chicken, pig, cow and the class pet. Annick Press 2011 un il lib bdg $19.95; pa $6.95

Grades: PreK K 1 2   E

1. School stories 2. Toys -- Fiction 3. Hamsters -- Fiction

ISBN 1-55451-346-4 pa; 978-1-55451-347-5 lib bdg; 1-55451-347-2 lib bdg; 978-1-55451-346-8 pa

"Three toys take an unexpected field trip. Huddled in close quarters, Cow, Pig and Chicken try to dissect the sounds around them. Readers see that their temporary housing (a makeshift Popsicle-stick barn) confines them to a classroom while their beloved young owner enjoys her day at school. The friends' introduction to the imposing class pet, dubbed Furface by the anxious critters, leads to some wacky interactions. . . . Humorous watercolors splashed against open white backgrounds extend the visual humor, depicting the classroom environment from a toy's-eye point of view." Kirkus

Oldland, Nicholas

★ **Big** bear hug. Kids Can Press 2009 un il $16.95

Grades: PreK K   E

1. Bears -- Fiction 2. Trees -- Fiction 3. Hugging -- Fiction

ISBN 978-1-55453-464-7; 1-55453-464-X

A bear who loves to hug everything meets a human who is about to chop down a tree, and the bear must make a decision on how to save his forest.

"Oldland's rustic-styled digital artwork looks like a hip flannel pajama print . . . and his pictures play sly comic foil to the earnest text." Publ Wkly

The **busy** beaver. Kids Can Press 2011 un il

Grades: PreK K 1   E

1. Animals -- Fiction 2. Beavers -- Fiction

ISBN 1554537495; 9781554537495

A "busy but careless beaver spends his days following random impulses, . . . and leaving in his wake a devastated forest filled with stumps, half-nibbled trees and injured, homeless animals. But then one day the beaver finds himself on the wrong side of a falling tree, which as it turns out, is just the thing to knock some sense into him. After reflecting on his behavior, he decides to make some changes. Soon, the now wiser and gentler beaver is getting down to the business of making things right, much to the delighted surprise of his forest friends." (Publisher's note) "Ages three to five." (Quill Quire)

"Beaver's exuberance for his work leads to careless accidents for a bear, moose, and bird's nest, and eventually for himself. . . . Beaver realizes he has a great deal for which to atone. He exercises, reads a how-to book, and practices apologies. His return is greeted by fear until he shows his newfound consideration with gifts and kind deeds. . . . The comic Photoshop illustrations have a stop-action effect and creative attention to detail." SLJ

Making the moose out of life. Kids Can Press 2010 un il $16.95

Grades: PreK K 1 2   E
1. Moose -- Fiction 2. Friendship -- Fiction
ISBN 978-1-55453-580-4; 1-55453-580-8

"Mild-mannered Moose never joins his friends when they go puddle jumping, kite flying, or skiing. . . . When he sets out alone in a sailboat, he . . . is washed away to a deserted island. It's here that he learns how to fend for himself and he meets a new friend, a tortoise named Tuesday. . . . When Moose is rescued by a cruise ship, he embraces shipboard life, taking part in all of the activities. Finally, he returns to his former friends and is now ready to join them and have some fun. . . . The illustrations are in muted outdoorsy colors of brown, green, and blue with a contemporary folk-art look. . . . Charming and simply told." SLJ

Olshan, Matthew
The **mighty** Lalouche; Matthew Olshan; illustrated by Sophie Blackall. Schwartz & Wade Books 2012 40 p. (hardcover) $17.99; (library) $20.99

Grades: PreK K 1 2   E
1. Boxing -- Juvenile fiction 2. Letter carriers -- Juvenile fiction 3. Boxing -- Fiction 4. Letter carriers -- Fiction
ISBN 0375862250; 9780375862250; 9780375962257
LC 2010031825

This children's story, by Matthew Olshan, illustrated by Sophie Blackall, begins "in Paris, France, [where] there lived a humble postman named Lalouche. He was small, but his hands were nimble, his legs were fast, and his arms were strong. When his job was replaced by an electric car, he turned to boxing to support himself and his pet finch, Genevieve." (Publisher's note)

Olson, Julie
Tickle, tickle! itch, twitch! written and illustrated by Julie Olson. Marshall Cavendish 2010 un il $12.99

Grades: PreK K   E
1. Mice -- Fiction 2. Marmots -- Fiction
ISBN 978-0-7614-5714-5; 0-7614-5714-3

Gus the groundhog desperately needs to scratch his back after a mouse tickles him with a feather, but the stick, bush, and log he tries to scratch against are not what they appear to be.

"Olson has created a book that just begs to be read aloud. . . . This story is simple and repetitive, allowing for audience participation and many different storytelling techniques such as reader's theater or flannel-board retelling. Young children will enjoy the simple and silly humor and the bright, colorful illustrations that fill the pages." SLJ

Olson-Brown, Ellen
Ooh la la polka dot boots; illustrations by Christiane Engel. Tricycle Press 2010 il $14.99

Grades: PreK   E
1. Stories in rhyme 2. Clothing and dress -- Fiction
ISBN 9781582462875; 1582462879
LC 2009007547

Illustrations and brief rhyming text sing the praises of polka dot boots, which add panache to any outfit.

Omololu, Cynthia Jaynes
When it's six o'clock in San Francisco; a trip through time zones. illustrated by Randy DuBurke. Clarion Books 2009 31p il map $16

Grades: K 1 2 3   E
1. Time -- Fiction
ISBN 978-0-618-76827-1; 0-618-76827-0
LC 2007012721

When Jared wakes up in San Francisco at six o'clock in the morning, children in other parts of the world are doing other things, like going to school in Buenos Aires, Argentina, playing soccer in London, England, and eating dinner in Lahore, Pakistan, because of the difference in time zones around the globe. Includes factual material about telling time and time zones.

"The diversity and connections across the globe are the story, with warm, colorful, individual portraits that move beyond cultural stereotypes. . . . This is a great choice for science classes and for today's international families." Booklist

Onishi, Satoru
★ **Who's** hiding? Kane/Miller 2007 31p il $14.95

Grades: PreK K 1 2   E
1. Puzzles 2. Animals -- Fiction 3. Animals -- Juvenile literature 4. Visual perception -- Juvenile literature
ISBN 978-1-933605-24-1

"Eighteen simply drawn, brightly colored animals are laid out in the same order on each spread. . . . The first spread shows the creatures and their names and asks, Who is hiding? The next spread shows all of them except for the reindeer who is invisible except for his antlers. This question alternates with others. . . . This is a clever puzzle book for caregivers and young children to share and to learn animals, colors, concepts." SLJ

Oppel, Kenneth
★ The **king's** taster; paintings by Steve Johnson & Lou Fancher. HarperCollinsPublishers 2008 un il $17.99; lib bdg $18.89

Grades: K 1 2 3   E
1. Diet -- Fiction 2. Dogs -- Fiction 3. Food -- Fiction 4. Kings and rulers -- Fiction
ISBN 978-0-06-075372-6; 0-06-075372-2; 978-0-06-075373-3 lib bdg; 0-06-075373-0 lib bdg
LC 2008000779

The royal chef takes Max the dog, the royal taster, on several international journeys to find a dish for the land's pickiest king.

"The mixed-media illustrations are deliciously capricious with clever collage details. . . . Kids will relish this comic culinary calamity." Booklist

Orloff, Karen Kaufman
★ **I** wanna iguana; illustrated by David Catrow. Putnam 2004 un il $15.99

Grades: PreK K 1 2   E
1. Pets 2. Letters 3. Iguanas as pets 4. Pets -- Fiction

5. Mothers and sons 6. Iguanas -- Fiction
ISBN 0-399-23717-8

LC 2002-10895

Alex and his mother write notes back and forth in which Alex tries to persuade her to let him have a baby iguana for a pet.

"This funny story is told through an amusing exchange of notes. . . . Featuring his signature cartoon characters, Catrow's illustrations provide a hilarious extension of the text." SLJ

Another title about Alex is:
I wanna new room (2010)

I wanna new room; illustrated by David Catrow. Putnam 2010 un il $16.99
Grades: PreK K 1 2   E
1. Infants -- Fiction 2. Letters -- Fiction 3. Brothers -- Fiction 4. Family life -- Fiction
ISBN 978-0-399-25405-5; 0-399-25405-6

LC 2009040106

Through a series of brief letters to his parents, Alex presents all the reasons why he should not have to share a room with his younger brother

"The slapstick, sibling anger, and crowding issues are all spot-on." Booklist

Ormerod, Jan

Ballet sisters: the duckling and the swan. Scholastic 2007 32p il $5.99
Grades: PreK K 1 2   E
1. Ballet -- Fiction 2. Sisters -- Fiction 3. Imagination -- Fiction
ISBN 978-0-439-82281-7; 0-439-82281-5

LC 2006-02575

Sylvie and her older sister dance their way through make-believe adventures that include princesses, fairy queens, swans, and ducklings.

"The language . . . is clear, concise, and descriptive— essential qualities for beginning readers. The watercolor illustrations place the girls and their mother on a clean white background, which effectively highlights the expressive detail in their faces and postures." SLJ

Another title about Sylvie and her sister is:
Ballet sisters: the newest dancer (2008)

If you're happy and you know it! [by] Jan Ormerod, Lindsey Gardiner. Star Bright Books 2003 un il $15.95; pa $5.95
Grades: PreK   E
1. Stories in rhyme 2. Animals -- Fiction
ISBN 1-932065-07-5; 1-932065-10-5 pa

LC 2002-13692

A little girl and various animals sing their own versions of this popular rhyme

"Delightful, colorful animal figures cavort through the pages of this book that puts a twist on the familiar song. . . . The action on each spread gives the story a great deal of energy and the backgrounds are washes of color, from dark pink to yellow to blue." SLJ

★ **Lizzie** nonsense; a story of pioneer days. Clarion Books 2005 32p il lib bdg $15

Grades: PreK K 1 2   E
1. Family life -- Fiction 2. Imagination -- Fiction
ISBN 0-618-57493-X lib bdg

LC 2004-26642

First published 2004 in Australia

"Lizzie lives with her mother, father, and baby brother in a small, isolated house in the Australian bush. Her father has taken his sandalwood into town to sell and will be gone for weeks. Lizzie passes the lonely days by indulging in flights of fancy. . . . The text is simple yet evocative . . . while the skillfully rendered watercolors bring the unique setting to life." SLJ

Miss Mouse's day. HarperCollins Pubs. 2001 un il hardcover o.p. lib bdg $14.89
Grades: PreK   E
1. Day 2. Mice 3. Day -- Fiction 4. Mice -- Fiction
ISBN 0-688-16333-5; 0-688-16334-3 lib bdg

LC 99-27641

"The illustrations, in panels of varying sizes, brim with pattern, detail, and bright splashes of color. . . . Ormerod delightfully and realistically illustrates the challenges of energetic toddlerhood." Booklist

Another title about Miss Mouse is:
Miss Mouse takes off (2001)

Orr, Wendy

The **princess** and her panther; illustrated by Lauren Stringer. Simon & Schuster 2010 un il $16.99
Grades: K 1 2   E
1. Fear -- Fiction 2. Camping -- Fiction 3. Sisters -- Fiction 4. Panthers -- Fiction 5. Princesses -- Fiction
ISBN 978-1-4169-9780-1; 1-4169-9780-6

LC 2009034359

A brave princess and a panther who tries to be brave cross the desert together and settle into a red silk tent, in which they listen to "leaf-snakes," an "owl-witch," and other frightening creatures until the princess frightens them away.

"Deep-hued, textured acrylics ably reflect the imaginative story's drama and its nighttime setting." Horn Book Guide

Osborne, Mary Pope

★ **New** York's bravest; paintings by Steve Johnson & Lou Fancher. Knopf 2002 un il $15.95; pa $6.99
Grades: PreK K 1 2   E
1. Fire fighters 2. Fire fighters -- Fiction
ISBN 0-375-82196-1; 0-375-83841-4 pa

LC 2002-455

Tells of the heroic deeds of the legendary New York firefighter, Mose Humphreys

"Boldly executed art supports the tall-tale flavor of a story that is both powerful and humane." Booklist

Otoshi, Kathryn

★ **One**. KO Kids Books 2008 un il $16.95
Grades: PreK K 1   E
1. Counting 2. Color -- Fiction 3. Bullies -- Fiction 4. Courage -- Fiction
ISBN 0972394648; 9780972394642

Blue is a quiet color. Red's a hothead who likes to pick on Blue. Yellow, Orange, Green, and Purple don't like what they see, but what can they do? When no one speaks up, things get out of hand—until One comes along and shows all the colors how to stand up, stand together, and count.

"The use of colors and numbers gives the story a much-needed universality. . . . Otoshi cleverly offers a way to talk to very young children about the subject of bullying, even as she helps put their imaginations to work on solutions." Booklist

★ **Zero**. Ko Kids Books 2010 un il $17.95
Grades: PreK K 1   **E**
   1. Counting 2. Courage -- Fiction
   ISBN 978-0-9723946-3-5; 0-9723946-3-X

Zero, dismayed by her big, empty, roundness, tries to force herself into the shape of the much-admired One, but must finally accept that she can only be Zero.

"What could have been a pedestrian just-be-yourself tale is distinguished by Otoshi's simple and lucid text, judicious use of white space, and a voice that stays sincere without becoming overly moralistic." Publ Wkly

Owen, Karen
I could be, you could be; [text by] Karen Owen; [illustrations by] Barroux. Barefoot Books 2009 un il $16.99
Grades: PreK K 1   **E**
   1. Stories in rhyme 2. Imagination -- Fiction
   ISBN 978-1-84686-405-6; 1-84686-405-4
                LC 2008039825

"A boy and a girl make believe they are everything from astronauts to animals in the jungle. Each spread has a rhyming couplet that begins either with 'I' or 'You.' . . . This simple formula and clear writing make the story accessible for listeners who love to play pretend games as well as for beginning readers. Barroux's eye-catching acrylic and pencil illustrations are filled with vibrant color and evoke a joyful feeling." SLJ

Pace, Anne Marie
Vampirina ballerina; Anne Marie Pace; illustrated by LeUyen Pham. Disney Hyperion Books 2012 40 p. $14.99
Grades: PreK K   **E**
   1. Ballet -- Fiction 2. Vampires -- Fiction 3. Picture books for children 4. Ballet dancing -- Fiction
   ISBN 1423157532; 9781423157533
                LC 2011026660

In this children's picture book, "a pale little vampire with tiny fangs and a black cape enrolls in an evening class at Madame Sang's Dance Studio. . . . Vampirina does her best to fit in" with the other girls. "The aspiring ballerina practices and practices until she is ready for her debut. On the big night, she dons her costume, overcomes stage fright, and takes a well-earned bow after the performance." (School Library Journal)

Pak, Soyung
Dear Juno; illustrated by Susan Kathleen Hartung. Viking 1999 un il hardcover o.p. pa $5.99
Grades: PreK K 1 2   **E**
   1. Letters -- Fiction 2. Grandmothers -- Fiction 3. Korean Americans -- Fiction
   ISBN 0-670-88252-6; 0-14-230017-9 pa
                LC 98-43408

Although Juno, a Korean American boy, cannot read the letter he receives from his grandmother in Seoul, he understands what it means from the photograph and dried flower

that are enclosed and decides to send a similar letter back to her

"The handsome layout, featuring ample white space and illustrations that cover anywhere from one page to an entire spread, perfectly suit the gentle, understated tone of the text." SLJ

Pal, Erika
Azad's camel. Frances Lincoln Children's Books 2010 un il $17.95
Grades: PreK K 1 2   **E**
   1. Camels -- Fiction 2. Orphans -- Fiction
   ISBN 1-84507-982-5; 978-1-84507-982-6

In a big Arabian city, an orphan boy is forced to work as a camel jockey—a dangerous job he doesn't like. But a new friendship and a magical escape into the desert are about to change his life .

"Pal's striking illustrations in watercolor and ink position sharply delineated characters in the foreground against soft, blurry desert backgrounds. Her heart-tugging tale also folds in a succint social-studies lesson, and a brief afterword explains the controversial 'sport' of camel racing." Kirkus

Palatini, Margie
Bad boys get henpecked! illustrated by Henry Cole. Katherine Tegen Books 2009 un il $17.99; lib bdg $18.89
Grades: PreK K 1 2   **E**
   1. Wolves -- Fiction 2. Chickens -- Fiction
   ISBN 978-0-06-074433-5; 0-06-074433-2; 978-0-06-074434-2 lib bdg; 0-06-074434-0 lib bdg
                LC 2008-11771

Bad boy wolves Willy and Wally try to get a chicken dinner by disguising themselves as the Handy-Dandy Lupino Brothers and going to work for a hen in need of household help.

"With its fast-paced language and witty narrative paired with lively alliteration and puns, the Bad Boys' latest tale will entertain and capture youngsters' imaginations. Cole deftly expresses humor and the power of understatement in his pencil and watercolor illustrations. Expressive facial expressions and body language tell all." SLJ

Boo -hoo moo; illustrated by Keith Graves. Katherine Tegen Books 2009 un il $17.99; lib bdg $18.89
Grades: K 1 2   **E**
   1. Cattle -- Fiction 2. Farm life -- Fiction
   ISBN 978-0-06-114375-5; 0-06-114375-8; 978-0-06-114376-2 lib bdg; 0-06-114376-6 lib bdg
                LC 2007024417

When Hilda Mae Heifer's trademark 'moo' starts sounding even worse, the other animals decide she is lonely and hold auditions to find her some singing partners.

"Palatini's prose is poetic, quirky, inventive, and just plain fun. . . . Graves escalates the sophisticated silliness with his wacky, superbly crafted, almost 3D illustrations." SLJ

Earthquack! illustrated by Barry Moser. Simon & Schuster Bks. for Young Readers 2002 un il $15.95; pa $6.99
Grades: PreK K 1 2   **E**
   1. Animals 2. Domestic animals 3. Humorous stories

4. Domestic animals -- Fiction
ISBN 0-689-84280-5; 1-4169-0260-0 pa

LC 2001-31302

When Chucky Ducky feels the earth beneath him grumble and rumble, he runs to alert the other barnyard animals to the coming earthquake, but just as a wily weasel is about to take advantage of their fears, the true source of the rumbling is revealed

"Moser captures the essence of Weasel's dark determination as well as the bug-eyed hysteria of the farm animals in his expressive graphite and transparent watercolor illustrations. . . . Palatini's text is funny, with contemporary dialogue, puns, and a fast-paced narrative rich in rhythm and alliteration." SLJ

Goldie and the three hares; illustrated by Jack E. Davis. Katherine Tegen Books 2010 un il $16.99
Grades: K 1 2 3   E
1. Fairy tales 2. Rabbits -- Fiction
ISBN 978-0-06-125314-0; 0-06-125314-6

LC 2008036910

When Goldilocks, running from the three bears, falls down a rabbit hole and hurts her foot, a family of hares tries to help but she proves to be a very loud, demanding, and tenacious guest.

"The zingy prose begs for full-throttled performance . . . and there are plenty of visual laughs in both the Hares' wide-eyed, innocent dismay and Goldilocks' overweening narcissism." Publ Wkly

Gorgonzola; a very stinkysaurus. by Margie Palatini; illustrated by Tim Bowers. Katherine Tegen Books 2008 un il $16.99; lib bdg $17.89
Grades: PreK K 1 2   E
1. Birds -- Fiction 2. Smell -- Fiction 3. Dinosaurs -- Fiction 4. Cleanliness -- Fiction
ISBN 978-0-06-073897-6; 0-06-073897-9; 978-0-06-073898-3 lib bdg; 0-06-073898-7 lib bdg

LC 2006002191

When Gorgonzola the dinosaur learns that everyone runs from him to avoid his smell, rather than out of fear, he is grateful to the little bird who shows him how to brush his teeth and wash

"The over-the-top illustrations of the grossed-out dinosaurs . . . will bring belly laughs to children and inspiration to the grownups who have to wrestle them into the bathtub or dentist's chair. Witty dialogue and an effective layout get the personal hygiene message across without being preachy or didactic." SLJ

Hogg, Hogg & Hog. Simon & Schuster Books for Young Readers 2011 un il $15.99
Grades: PreK K 1 2   E
1. Pigs -- Fiction 2. Fashion -- Fiction 3. Domestic animals -- Fiction 4. City and town life -- Fiction
ISBN 1-4424-0322-5; 978-1-4424-0322-2

LC 2009053646

Three pigs achieve success in the big city by making oinking the ultimate in fashion, but their fresh, new idea captures the attention of some friends from back on the farm.

"Palatini's smart storytelling bustles with all the ringing phones and over-the-top bluster of 'big business' speech. Attentive text design places the emphasis in all the right places,

making this a fun read-aloud. . . . Palatini has created a hilariously relatable tale by including all the old barnyard favorites. . . . Quirky illustrations rendered digitally and mainly in pinks, lavenders, and grays suit this unusual story." SLJ

Piggie pie! illustrated by Howard Fine. Clarion Bks. 1995 un il $15; pa $5.95
Grades: PreK K 1 2   E
1. Pigs -- Fiction 2. Wolves -- Fiction 3. Witches -- Fiction
ISBN 0-395-71691-8; 0-395-86618-9 pa

LC 94-19726

"Gritch the Witch sets out for Old MacDonald's Farm to get herself a meal of plump piggies. Alerted, however, . . . the swine hastily don sheep, cow, and other barnyard disguises and fool her. . . . The still-hungry Gritch is persuaded to give up by a Big Bad Wolf . . . and the two go off for lunch, each picturing the other made into a sandwich. . . The exuberant illustrations are colorful and action-filled. Greedy (but not too bright) witch and wolf both get what they deserve in this thoroughly enjoyable romp." SLJ

★ **Three** French hens; a holiday tale. illustrations by Richard Egielski. Hyperion Books for Children 2005 un il $15.99
Grades: PreK K 1 2   E
1. Foxes -- Fiction 2. Christmas stories 3. Chickens -- Fiction 4. Christmas -- Fiction
ISBN 0-7868-5167-8

"The three French hens from the familiar Christmas song are sent by a Parisian lady to her boyfriend, Philippe Renard, in New York. Alas, the hens wind up in lost mail, and when they can't find Philippe in the phone book, they think perhaps they should translate his name: Phil Fox. They find Phil Fox, but he's a downtrodden fox living in the Bronx. . . . [This] is so much fun, it's hard to imagine an artist milking more laughs from it than Egielski. . . . Something really fresh for the holiday season." Booklist

★ **The cheese**; paintings by Steve Johnson and Lou Fancher. Katherine Tegan Books 2007 un il $16.99; lib bdg $17.89
Grades: K 1 2 3   E
1. Nursery rhymes -- Fiction
ISBN 978-0-06-052630-6; 0-06-052630-0; 978-0-06-052631-3 lib bdg; 0-06-052631-9 lib bdg

LC 2006-18163

After they all agree to ignore the story of "The Farmer in the Dell," the rat, cat, dog, child, farmer, and his wife have a party featuring the tempting hunk of cheese.

"The folk-art quality of the illustrations is rich with country colors—barn reds, field greens, and earthy yellows, and the cartoon animals are funny and expressive. A smattering of words and music from the song is worked in effectively on most pages, and the full lyrics are printed on the last page." SLJ

The **three** silly billies; illustrated by Barry Moser. Simon & Schuster Books for Young Readers 2005 un il $15.95

Grades: PreK K 1 2   **E**
   1. Goats -- Fiction
   ISBN 0-689-85862-0

LC 2002-155835

Three billy goats, unable to cross a bridge because they cannot pay the toll, form a car pool with The Three Bears, Little Red Riding Hood, and Jack of beanstalk fame to get past the rude Troll.

"Painted in cheery watercolors, Moser's figures are in contemporary dress and pop out from the white backgrounds. There is plenty of visual humor. . . . Palatini's hip and punny text is fun to read aloud." SLJ

Pallotta, Jerry
   Ocean counting; odd numbers. illustrated by Shennen Bersani. Charlesbridge 2004 un il $16.95; pa $6.95
Grades: PreK K 1   **E**
   1. Counting 2. Marine animals 3. Counting -- Juvenile literature 4. Marine animals -- Juvenile literature
   ISBN 0-88106-151-4; 0-88106-150-6 pa

LC 98-46035

"Bersani's bright, realistic colored-pencil illustrations will lure readers into perusing the factoid-loaded, simple, conversational text. . . . This book offers a colorful, engaging, and intriguing slant on the technique of counting." SLJ

Pamintuan, Macky
   Twelve haunted rooms of Halloween. Sterling Children's Books 2011 un il $14.95
Grades: PreK K 1   **E**
   1. Counting 2. Ghost stories 3. Picture puzzles 4. Stories in rhyme 5. Halloween -- Fiction
   ISBN 978-1-4027-7935-0; 1-4027-7935-6

A small bear journeys through a haunted house as rhyming text encourages readers to find and count holiday inspired items that have been hidden by the silly monsters.

"What raises this title above other books of this type . . . is the 'I Spy' type format. Each picture includes all of the items mentioned previously along with the new addition, and readers are invited to search each spread to find them. Children will want to pore over the not-too-scary pictures until they find every creature mentioned in the rhyme." SLJ

Panahi, H. L.
   Bebop Express; illustrated by Steve Johnson and Lou Fancher. Laura Geringer Books 2005 un il $15.99
Grades: K 1 2 3   **E**
   1. Stories in rhyme 2. Railroads -- Fiction 3. Jazz music -- Fiction
   ISBN 0-06-057190-X

LC 2003-24244

A rollicking rhythmic express train takes passengers on a jazzy journey that celebrates the United States and its unique musical culture.

"The intricate collages use old photographs and vintage fabrics to obtain a unique look. Teeming with life, the art visually complements the noisy text." Booklist

Pancheri, Jan
   Brother William's year; a monk at Westminster Abbey. Frances Lincoln 2010 36p il $17.95
Grades: 2 3 4   **E**
   1. Year -- Fiction 2. Monks -- Fiction 3. Middle Ages

-- Fiction
   ISBN 978-1-84507-953-6; 1-84507-953-1

"Narrated by a fourteenth-century monk, this lightly informative picture book takes readers through his activities during 12 months at Westminster Abbey. . . . Written and illustrated by the current head gardener at Westminster Abbey, this attractive picture book captures the rhythm of a monastery year." Booklist

Panzieri, Lucia
   The **kindhearted** crocodile; by Lucia Panzieri; illustrated by AntonGionata Ferrari. Holiday House 2013 24 p. (hardcover) $16.95
Grades: PreK K 1 2   **E**
   1. Pets -- Juvenile fiction 2. Crocodiles -- Juvenile fiction 3. Crocodiles as pets -- Fiction
   ISBN 0823427676; 9780823427673

LC 2012025486

This children's story, by Lucia Panzieri, illustrated by Anton Gionata Ferrari, follows "a crocodile with the kindest of hearts that was gentle and sensitive, and dreamed of one day being a beloved pet in a happy family. Through the magic of a picture book and with an irrepressible desire to please, this ferocious-looking crocodile that tidies toys, washes dishes, and even fights monsters in bad dreams makes his own dream come true." (Publisher's note)

Parenteau, Shirley
   Bears on chairs; illustrated by David Walker. Candlewick Press 2009 un il $15.99
Grades: PreK K   **E**
   1. Stories in rhyme 2. Bears -- Fiction
   ISBN 978-0-7636-3588-6; 0-7636-3588-X

LC 2008-937035

Four bears are happily seated on four chairs until Big Brown Bear shows up and demands a seat.

"Between the unerringly positive approach to a common early-childhood dilemma and the can't miss rhyme, this volume will likely find its place on many a daycare shelf." Kirkus

Parish, Herman
   Amelia Bedelia bakes off; pictures by Lynn Sweat. Greenwillow Books 2010 64p il (An I can read book) $17.99
Grades: K 1 2   **E**
   1. Cake -- Fiction 2. Baking -- Fiction 3. Contests -- Fiction 4. Household employees -- Fiction
   ISBN 978-0-06-084358-8; 0-06-084358-6

Literal-minded housekeeper Amelia Bedelia lends a hand at the bakery and enters a cakemaking contest, with unexpected results.

   Amelia Bedelia's first Valentine; illustrated by Lynne Avril. Greenwillow Books 2009 un il $16.99; lib bdg $17.89
Grades: PreK K 1   **E**
   1. School stories 2. Family life -- Fiction 3. Valentine's Day -- Fiction
   ISBN 978-0-06-154458-3; 0-06-154458-2; 978-0-06-154459-0 lib bdg; 0-06-154459-0 lib bdg

LC 2009009050

Literal-minded even as a child, Amelia Bedelia muddles through Valentine's Day with her heart on her sleeve, trying to make sense of strange greetings at school and home, and ever on the look-out for the arrows of Cupid.

Amelia Bedelia's "ingenuous spirit will continue to capture hearts." Publ Wkly

Amelia Bedelia's first apple pie; pictures by Lynne Avril. Greenwillow Books 2010 un il $16.99; lib bdg $17.89

Grades: PreK K 1   E

1. Pies -- Fiction 2. Apples -- Fiction 3. Baking -- Fiction 4. Grandparents -- Fiction
ISBN 978-0-06-196409-1; 0-06-196409-3; 978-0-06-196410-7 lib bdg; 0-06-196410-7 lib bdg
         LC 2010009379

While visiting her grandparents, literal-minded Amelia Bedelia finally learns, despite some mishaps, how to bake an apple pie.

"Children will find the humor relevant and funny. The illustrations flow well with the text." SLJ

Other titles about Amelia Bedelia as a child are:
Amelia Bedelia's first day of school (2009)
Amelia Bedelia's first valentine (2009)
Amelia Bedelia's first field trip (2011)

Amelia Bedelia's first field trip; pictures by Lynne Avril. Greenwillow Books 2011 un il $16.99; lib bdg $17.89

Grades: PreK K 1   E

1. School stories 2. Farms -- Fiction
ISBN 978-0-06-196413-8; 0-06-196413-1; 978-0-06-196414-5 lib bdg; 0-06-196414-X lib bdg
         LC 2010034175

Amelia Bedelia goes with her class to visit a farm, where her literal-mindedness causes confusion along with some laughs.

"Avril's gouache-and-black-pencil illustrations are filled with bright color, personality and, of course, that brand of humor that is all Amelia Bedelia." Kirkus

Go west, Amelia Bedelia! pictures by Lynn Sweat. Greenwillow Books 2011 64p il $17.99; lib bdg $18.89

Grades: K 1 2   E

1. Ranch life -- Fiction
ISBN 978-0-06-084361-8; 0-06-084361-6; 978-0-06-084362-5 lib bdg; 0-06-084362-4 lib bdg
         LC 2010012429

Amelia Bedelia visits her uncle's dude ranch and makes herself at home on the range, getting all tied up (by her own lasso) and stopping a stampede (with only her own two hands)!

Parish, Peggy

★ **Amelia** Bedelia; pictures by Fritz Siebel. Newly illustrated I can read ed.; HarperCollins 1992 63p il (I can read book) $16.99; lib bdg $17.89; pa $3.99

Grades: K 1 2   E

1. Household employees -- Fiction
ISBN 0-06-020186-X; 0-06-020187-8 lib bdg; 0-06-444155-5 pa
         LC 91010163

A newly illustrated edition of the title first published 1963

A literal-minded housekeeper causes chaos in the Rogers household when she attempts to make sense of some instructions.

Other titles in this series are:
Thank you, Amelia Bedelia (1993)
Good driving, Amelia Bedelia (1995) by Herman Parish
Come back, Amelia Bedelia (1995)
Amelia Bedelia and the surprise shower (1995)
Play ball, Amelia Bedelia (1996)
Bravo, Amelia Bedelia (1997) by Herman Parish
Amelia Bedelia 4 mayor (1999) by Herman Parish
Calling Doctor Amelia Bedelia (2002) by Herman Parish
Amelia Bedelia, bookworm (2003) by Herman Parish
Amelia Bedelia and the Christmas list (2003) by Herman Parish
Amelia Bedelia goes camping (2003) by Herman Parish
Happy haunting, Amelia Bedelia (2004) by Herman Parish
Amelia Bedelia, rocket scientist (2005) by Herman Parish
Be my valentine, Amelia Bedelia (2005) by Herman Parish
Amelia Bedelia under construction (2006) by Herman Parish
Amelia Bedelia's masterpiece (2007) by Herman Parish
Amelia Bedelia and the cat (2008) by Herman Parish
Amelia Bedelia talks turkey (2008) by Herman Parish
An Amelia Bedelia celebration [Contents: Amelia Bedelia
Good work, Amelia Bedelia
Good driving, Amelia Bedelia
Bravo, Amelia Bedelia] (2009)
Amelia Bedelia bakes off (2010) by Herman Parish
Go west, Amelia Bedelia! (2011) by Herman Parish

An Amelia Bedelia celebration; four stories tall. [by] Peggy Parish & Herman Parish; [illustrated by] Lynn Sweat & Fritz Siebel. Greenwillow Books 2009 214p il $19.99

Grades: PreK K 1 2   E

1. Household employees -- Fiction
ISBN 978-0-06-171030-8; 0-06-171030-X
         LC 2008043826

Four previously published stories featuring the extremely literal-minded Amelia Bedelia, with related activities and recipes. Includes CD.

Park, Barbara

Junie B. Jones and the stupid smelly bus; illustrated by Denise Brunkus. Random House 1992 69p il lib bdg $11.99; pa $4.99

Grades: 1 2 3   E

1. School stories
ISBN 0-679-92642-9 lib bdg; 0-679-82642-4 pa
         LC 91-51104

In her own words, a young girl describes her feelings about starting kindergarten and what she does when she decides not to ride the bus home

"Brunkus's occasional black-and-white pencil illustrations are appealing and reinforce the mood of the text. Junie B. is a real character; she talks a lot, is funny without knowing it, and honest to a fault." SLJ

Park, Frances

Good -bye, 382 Shin Dang Dong; [by] Frances and Ginger Park; illustrated by Yangsook Choi. National Geographic Soc. 2002 un il $16.95

Grades: K 1 2 3   E

1. Moving, Household 2. Immigrants -- Fiction 3.

Koreans -- United States
ISBN 0-7922-7985-9

LC 2001-2976

Jangmi finds it hard to say goodbye to relatives and friends, plus the food, customs, and beautiful things of her home in Korea, when her family moves to America

"The oil paintings done in a simple, childlike style are formally framed with white space. . . . Children will find the details of cultural differences and the immigrant experience well evoked." SLJ

Park, Linda Sue

★ **Bee** -bim bop! illustrated by Ho Baek Lee. Clarion Books 2005 32p il $15; pa $6.99
Grades: PreK K 1 2   E
    1. Stories in rhyme 2. Cooking -- Fiction 3. Korean Americans -- Fiction
ISBN 0-618-26511-2; 0-547-07671-1 pa

LC 2003027697

"Playful, cartoonlike drawings portray a round-faced girl helping her mother. . . . The illustrations . . . are very appealing. . . . The rhyme works well. A recipe follows the story." SLJ

★ The **firekeeper's** son; illustrated by Julie Downing. Clarion Books 2004 37p il $16; pa $6.99
Grades: 1 2 3 4   E
    1. 1. Korea -- Fiction
ISBN 0-618-13337-2; 0-547-23769-3 pa

LC 2002-13917

In eighteenth-century Korea, after Sang-hee's father injures his ankle, Sang-hee attempts to take over the task of lighting the evening fire which signals to the palace that all is well. Includes historical notes.

"Park's command of place, characterization, and language is as capable and compelling in this picture book as it is in her novels. . . . [This offers] lyrical prose and deftly realized watercolors and pastels." SLJ

Park, Linda Sue, 1960-

★ The **third** gift. Clarion Books 2011 il $16.99
Grades: K 1 2   E
    1. Magi -- Fiction 2. Father-son relationship -- Fiction
ISBN 978-0-547-20195-5; 0-547-20195-8;
9780547201955; 0547201958

LC 2010050819

"The hyperrealistic acryl-gouache illustrations depict the sandy beige hues and nuanced textures of a dry and inhospitable land, contrasting with the smooth skin and rounded cheeks of the young boy and his loving relationship with his father. This gorgeous picture book sheds thoughtful light on a fascinating facet of the Christmas story." SLJ

Parker, Marjorie Blain

A **paddling** of ducks; animals in groups from A to Z. written by Marjorie Blain Parker; illustrated by Joseph Kelly. Kids Can Press 2010 il $16.95
Grades: PreK K 1   E
    1. Animals 2. Alphabet
ISBN 978-1-55337-682-8; 1-55337-682-X

"This ABC book provides a delightfully offbeat introduction to collective nouns, featuring groups of animals at a Riviera-like resort locale with palm trees and a seaside Ferris wheel. . . . Even better than learning some of the unusual

ways to refer to multiple animals is the way Kelly's soft-focus oil and acrylic paintings riff on the terms themselves. . . . The anthropomorphic animals feel anatomically authentic, but with exaggerated joie de vivre to spare." Publ Wkly

Parker, Michael

You are a star! Michael Parker; illustrations by Judith Rossell. Walker 2012 40 p. (hardback) $16.99
Grades: PreK K 1 2 3   E
    1. Fear -- Juvenile fiction 2. Stars -- Juvenile fiction 3. Bedtime -- Juvenile fiction 4. Stars -- Fiction 5. Astronomy -- Fiction 6. Life (Biology) -- Fiction
ISBN 0802728413; 9780802728418; 9780802728425

LC 2011050073

In this children's bedtime story, by Michael Parker, illustrated by Judith Rossell, "readers take a journey through the night sky to the moment a star is born. Starting as a fire in the sky that explodes into millions of pieces, stars eventually become part of Earth with all the living things on it-meaning that everyone has a little bit of stardust inside them." (Publisher's note)

Parkhurst, Carolyn

★ **Cooking** with Henry and Elliebelly; illustrations by Dan Yaccarino. Feiwel and Friends 2010 un il $16.99
Grades: PreK K 1   E
    1. Cooking -- Fiction 2. Siblings -- Fiction 3. Imagination -- Fiction
ISBN 978-0-312-54848-3; 0-312-54848-6

LC 2009050247

Five-year-old Henry, along with his two-year-old sister, pretend to make waffles on a make-believe television show.

"The entire story is written in dialogue and the sibling relationship is presented with skill. . . . The pure adventure of creative play and experimentation will be a treat for any reader. . . . Yaccarino has created characters and an environment that grab readers' attention and won't let go." SLJ

Parot, Annelore

Kimonos. Chronicle Books 2011 un il
Grades: PreK K 1   E
    1. Dolls -- Fiction
ISBN 145210493X; 9781452104935

LC 2011008003

Original French edition 2009

Inspired by traditional Japanese dolls, this story introduces readers to the Kokeshis' kimonos and hair-dos as well as Japanese culture. Contains die-cut pages, flaps and gatefolds.

"Sharp-eyed children will enjoy poring over the pages again and again. Scenes that evoke everyday life in Japan . . . add delightfully authentic cultural texture, while lift-the-flap and die-cut panels enhance the book's interactivity." SLJ

Partridge, Elizabeth

Oranges on Golden Mountain; illustrated by Aki Sogabe. Dutton Children's Bks. 2001 un il hardcover o.p. pa $6.99
Grades: K 1 2 3   E
    1. Chinese Americans 2. Immigrants -- Fiction 3. Emigration and immigration 4. Chinese Americans -- Fiction
ISBN 0-525-46453-0; 0-14-250033-X pa

LC 99-462287

When hard times fall on his family, Jo Lee is sent from China to San Francisco, where he helps his uncle fish and dreams of being reunited with his mother and sister

"The spirited story is beautifully written. . . . The striking, skillful paper-cut illustrations . . . create a vivid sense of place and do much to explain and extend the story's action." Booklist

Paschkis, Julie

Mooshka; written and illustrated by Julie Paschkis. Peachtree Publishers 2012 35 p.
Grades: PreK K 1   E
1. Magic -- Fiction 2. Quilts -- Fiction 3. Infants -- Fiction 4. Sisters -- Fiction 5. Picture books for children 6. Babies -- Fiction 7. Sharing -- Fiction
ISBN 9781561456208

LC 2011020463

In this picture book, "Karla loves her quilt, and Mooshka makes Karla feel safe, brightening dark days. Made by Karla's grandmother from scraps of old fabric, Mooshka is unusual because it talks to Karla, telling her the stories behind each piece of the quilt. . . . When Karla's life changes--her mother's bulging belly is a hint of baby Hannah's arrival--Mooshka goes strangely silent. . . . Soon, both children curl up under the quilt with Karla retelling the family stories." (Horn Book Magazine)

Paterson, Katherine

★ **Brother** Sun, Sister Moon; Saint Francis of Assisi's Canticle of the Creatures. retold by Katherine Paterson; illustrated by Pamela Dalton. Chronicle Books 2011 un il
Grades: PreK K 1   E
1. Nature -- Fiction 2. Prayer -- Fiction
ISBN 0-8118-7734-5; 978-0-8118-7734-3

LC 2010035120

Reimagines Francis of Assisi's 1224 prayer of praise in celebration of God's gifts throughout the universe.

"As Paterson expresses thankfulness to God for various forces of creation . . . debut artist Dalton offers delicately detailed, loosely symmetrical cut-paper tableaus, set against black backdrops and framed by birds' nests, willow trees, vines, and branches." Publ Wkly

Patricelli, Leslie

Be quiet, Mike! Candlewick Press 2011 un il $14.99
Grades: PreK K 1 2   E
1. Stories in rhyme 2. Drums -- Fiction 3. Noise -- Fiction 4. Monkeys -- Fiction 5. Musicians -- Fiction
ISBN 978-0-7636-4477-2; 0-7636-4477-3

LC 2010044814

Monkey Mike is reprimanded for making noise when he taps pencils and clangs trash cans until he sees a drum set in the music store and puts his hands-on talents to work in a most impressive way.

"This rhythmic, rhyming romp about a youngster who must drum is illustrated with bold lines and colors in acrylic that suggest a jazzy ease. The bright, ever-changing background hues keep the focus on Mike and the onomatopoeic words scattered throughout the story." SLJ

★ **Higher!** higher! Candlewick Press 2009 un il $15.99; bd bk $6.99

Grades: PreK K 1   E
1. Play -- Fiction 2. Imagination -- Fiction
ISBN 978-0-7636-3241-0; 0-7636-3241-4; 978-0-7636-4433-8 bd bk; 0-7636-4433-1 bd bk
Boston Globe-Horn Book Award honor book: Picture Book (2009)

"As an adult pushes a pigtailed girl in a striped sweater and socks on a swing, the child calls out: 'Higher! Higher!' The ride gradually takes her from a giraffe's-eye view, to a mountaintop, to an airplane, and finally high enough to trade high fives with a one-eyed, green alien. . . . The repetitive text is ideal for new readers, and the cartoon paintings, though spare, provide plenty of room for imagination." SLJ

Potty. Candlewick Press 2010 un il $6.99
Grades: PreK   E
1. Board books for children 2. Toilet training -- Fiction
ISBN 978-0-7636-4476-5; 0-7636-4476-5

LC 2009-49045

Baby, a toddler, decides to use the potty for the first time.

This "appealing [book features] simple text, bright acrylic illustrations, and [an] everyday [situation] that [is] certain to engage the very young." SLJ

Tubby. Candlewick Press 2010 un il $6.99
Grades: PreK   E
1. Board books for children 2. Baths -- Fiction 3. Infants -- Fiction
ISBN 978-0-7636-4567-0; 0-7636-4567-2

LC 2009-49046

Baby loves playing during bath time.

This "appealing [book features] simple text, bright acrylic illustrations, and [an] everyday [situations] that [is] certain to engage the very young." SLJ

The **birthday** box. Candlewick Press 2007 un il $15.99; bd bk $6.99
Grades: PreK   E
1. Boxes -- Fiction 2. Birthdays -- Fiction 3. Imagination -- Fiction
ISBN 978-0-7636-2825-3; 0-7636-2825-5; 978-0-7636-4449-9 bd bk; 0-7636-4449-8 bd bk

LC 2006-49084

"A child wearing only a diaper and a striped party hat gets a present from Grandma. . . . The toddler takes off the wrapping paper . . . and discovers A big brown box! A box is full of possibilities and this child lets imagination reign. . . . Patricelli's simple, first-person narration is refreshing. With bold black outlines, the acrylic paintings are rudimentary but nonetheless expressive and endearing." SLJ

Patten, Brian

The **big** snuggle-up; [written by] Brian Patten & [illustrated by] Nicola Bayley. Kane Miller 2011 un il
Grades: PreK K 1   E
1. Stories in rhyme 2. Animals -- Fiction 3. Scarecrows -- Fiction
ISBN 1-61067-036-1; 978-1-61067-036-4

It all started with the scarecrow coming into the house out of the snow and bringing with him the mouse that lived up his sleeve. But it wasn't only these two who were looking for a warm place to snuggle up!

"The text is printed in a large, easy-to-read font on a cream-colored background and surrounded by Bayley's colored pencil and crayon illustrations. The art is meticulously crafted, with attention given to every hair and whisker. . . . A lovely book about sharing and compassion." SLJ

Pattison, Darcy S.

19 girls and me; [by] Darcy Pattison; illustrated by Steven Salerno. Philomel Books 2006 un il $16.99

Grades: PreK K 1 2   **E**

1. School stories 2. Sex role -- Fiction
ISBN 0-399-24336-4

LC 2005020501

John Hercules is worried about being the only boy in his kindergarten class, but after the first week he stops worrying.

"The mixed-media illustrations include wild color combinations and dizzying perspectives that provide the backdrops for the children, drawn in a stylishly simple but endearing cartoon style." SLJ

The **journey** of Oliver K. Woodman; written by Darcy Pattison; illustrated by Joe Cepeda. Harcourt 2003 un il $16; pa $6.99

Grades: K 1 2 3   **E**

1. Travel -- Fiction
ISBN 0-15-202329-1; 0-15-206118-5 pa

LC 2001-5320

Oliver K. Woodman, a man made of wood, takes a remarkable journey across America, as told through the postcards and letters of those he meets along the way

"The boldly colored, textured illustrations were made with oils over an acrylic under-painting on boards. . . . A fresh, unusual tale." SLJ

Another title about Oliver K. Woodman is:
Searching for Oliver K. Woodman (2005)

Patz, Nancy

Babies can't eat kimchee! by Nancy Patz & [illustrated by] Susan L. Roth. Bloomsbury Children's Books 2007 un il $16.95

Grades: PreK K 1 2   **E**

1. Infants -- Fiction 2. Sisters -- Fiction 3. Korean Americans -- Fiction
ISBN 1-59990-017-3

A baby sister must wait to grow up before doing big sister things, such as ballet dancing and eating spicy Korean food.

This book's "Korean-American perspective and mixed-media collage illustrations set the title apart. . . . The illustrations use just the right colors and lines to capture the child's changing emotions." SLJ

Paul, Ann Whitford

Count on Culebra; go from 1 to 10 in Spanish. Holiday House 2008 un il $16.95

Grades: PreK K 1   **E**

1. Counting 2. Iguanas -- Fiction 3. Rattlesnakes -- Fiction 4. Desert animals -- Fiction 5. Spanish language -- Vocabulary
ISBN 978-0-8234-2124-4; 0-8234-2124-4

LC 2007017303

When Iguana stubs her toe and cannot make her popular candies known as cactus butter dulces, Culebra the rattlesnake finds a cure that introduces the Spanish words for the numbers from one to ten.

"The well-paced story exudes a charming silliness and invites participation. Bright cartoon-style illustrations,

rendered in gouache and colored pencil, nicely depict the foolishness and are large enough for group sharing. . . . The introduction of Spanish words and counting concepts along with the appealing art and offbeat story make this a treat." Booklist

Fiesta fiasco; illustrated by Ethan Long. Holiday House 2007 un il $16.95

Grades: PreK K 1 2 3   **E**

1. Gifts -- Fiction 2. Rabbits -- Fiction 3. Desert animals -- Fiction 4. Spanish language -- Vocabulary
ISBN 0-8234-2037-X; 978-0-8234-2037-7

LC 2006-12112

When shopping for Culebra's birthday, Conejo convinces his friends Iguana and Tortuga to buy all the wrong presents. Includes a glossary of Spanish words used.

"A fiery palette enlivens the simple cartoon artwork set in the desert. The scenes are fun to look at." SLJ

Other titles about these characters are:
Mañana Iguana (2004)
Tortuga in trouble (2009)

If animals kissed good night-- [by] Ann Whitford Paul; pictures by David Walker. Farrar, Straus and Giroux 2008 un il $16.95

Grades: PreK K 1   **E**

1. Stories in rhyme 2. Animals -- Fiction 3. Kissing -- Fiction 4. Parent-child relationship -- Fiction
ISBN 0-374-38051-1; 978-0-374-38051-9

LC 2006051108

Rhyming text explores what would happen if animals kissed like humans do, from a slow kiss between a sloth and her cub to a mud-happy kiss from a hippo calf to his father

Walker "gets great emotional mileage from his rounded, stuffed toy-like shapes, velvety colors, and tiny dot eyes; the characters radiate unconditional love. There's a lot to go 'Ahhhh' over." Publ Wkly

Snail's good night; by Ann Whitford Paul; illustrated by Rosanne Litzinger. Holiday House 2008 32p il $14.95

Grades: PreK K 1   **E**

1. Snails -- Fiction 2. Bedtime -- Fiction
ISBN 978-0-8234-1912-8; 0-8234-1912-6

LC 2007-614

When Snail realizes that his friends are going to bed, he begins a very long, very slow slide to wish them all good night.

"Created using watercolor, gouache, and colored pencil, the fanciful artwork features mild-mannered animal characters and a benevolent moon shining down on the world. . . . The large type and short sentences make this gently amusing story just right for beginning readers." Booklist

Word builder; illustrated by Kurt Cyrus. Simon & Schuster Books for Young Readers 2009 un il $16.99

Grades: PreK K 1   **E**

1. Authorship -- Fiction
ISBN 978-1-4169-3981-8; 1-4169-3981-4

LC 2007045244

Text explains how putting letters into words, words into sentences, sentences into paragraphs, and paragraphs into chapters ends up creating a book

"This oversize book uses direct language and terrific artwork to show children how literal and figurative construction works. . . . The art, rendered in pencil and digital color, seems almost three-dimensional and will fascinate readers." Booklist

Payne, Emmy

Katy No-Pocket; pictures by H. A. Rey. Houghton Mifflin 1944 un il lib bdg $17; pa $5.95
Grades: PreK K 1 2   E
  1. Animals -- Fiction 2. Kangaroos -- Fiction
  ISBN 0-395-17104-0 lib bdg; 0-395-13717-9 pa
Katy Kangaroo was most unfortunately unprovided with a pocket in which to carry her son Freddy. She asked other animals with no pockets how they carried their children but none of their answers seemed satisfactory. Finally a wise old owl advised her to try to find a pocket in the City, and so off she went and in the City she found just what she and Freddy needed

Peacock, Carol Antoinette

Mommy far, Mommy near; an adoption story. written by Carol Antoinette Peacock; illustrated by Shawn Brownell. Whitman, A. 2000 un il $16.99
Grades: PreK K 1 2   E
  1. Adoption -- Fiction 2. Chinese Americans -- Fiction
  3. Mother-child relationship -- Fiction
  ISBN 0-8075-5234-8
                                          LC 99-36108
Elizabeth, who was born in China, describes the family who has adopted her and tries to sort out her feelings for her mother back in China

"The situation is handled sensitively by the author, who writes from personal experience. . . . The faces deftly show the strong emotional bond between adoptive mother and daughter." Horn Book Guide

Pearce, Emily Smith

Slowpoke; illustrated by Scot Ritchie. Boyds Mills Press 2010 39p il $16.95
Grades: K 1 2 3   E
  1. Speed -- Fiction 2. Family life -- Fiction
  ISBN 978-1-59078-705-2; 1-59078-705-6
                                          LC 2009033955
After pokey Fiona attends Speed School, where she learns to wash dishes, brush her teeth, and clean her room at the same time, she decides to demonstrate to her family the value of sometimes doing things more slowly.

"The text is interspersed with black-and-white illustrations that do a stellar job of conveying both leisure and frenzy. A clever early reader with challenging vocabulary and some food for thought to boot." Kirkus

Pearce, Philippa

The **squirrel** wife; illustrated by Wayne Anderson. Candlewick Press 2007 un il $16.99
Grades: K 1 2 3   E
  1. Fairy tales 2. Fairies -- Fiction 3. Brothers -- Fiction
  4. Squirrels -- Fiction 5. Forests and forestry -- Fiction
  ISBN 978-0-7636-3551-0; 0-7636-3551-0
                                          LC 2006052454
As a reward for saving the life of one of the feared green people, Jack acquires a beautiful and loving squirrel wife, knowledgeable in the secrets of the forest.

"Anderson's mixed-media illustrations strengthen the story's connections while amplifying the sense of enchantment with images of the elfin, lime-colored folk and the forest scenes, rendered in feathery strokes and an earthy green palette of moss and mushrooms. An intriguing, atmospheric offering." Booklist

Pearle, Ida

A **child's** day; an alphabet of play. Harcourt 2008 un il $12.95
Grades: PreK K   E
  1. Alphabet 2. Play -- Fiction 3. Play -- Juvenile literature
  ISBN 978-0-15-206552-2; 0-15-206552-0
                                          LC 2007-33966
"This simple, attractive alphabet of action words and pictures depicts children engaged in play and other activities. . . . The design is particularly effective. Large, colorful cut-paper collages of multiethnic children feature interesting patterns that stand out against solid backgrounds." SLJ

Pearson, Debora

Sophie's wheels; by Debora Pearson; art by Nora Hilb. Annick Press 2006 un il lib bdg $18.95; pa $6.95
Grades: PreK   E
  1. Growth -- Fiction 2. Wheels -- Fiction
  ISBN 978-1-55451-038-2 lib bdg; 1-55451-038-4 lib bdg; 978-1-55451-037-5 pa; 1-55451-037-6 pa
"The language is descriptive. . . . The text is accompanied by simple, soft-washed watercolor illustrations. . . . This [is a] satisfying, peaceful tale." SLJ

Pearson, Susan

How to teach a slug to read; illustrated by David Slonim. Marshall Cavendish Children's 2011 un il $16.99
Grades: PreK K 1 2   E
  1. Reading -- Fiction 2. Slugs (Mollusks) -- Fiction
  ISBN 978-0-7614-5805-0; 0-7614-5805-0
                                          LC 2010-24289
Provides simple, step-by-step instructions for teaching a slug how to read, including using Mother Slug rhymes, helping your slug sound out words, and making vocabulary lists.

"The two main slug characters are portrayed both affectionately and creatively. The literary references are fast and furious . . . and, fortunately, very accessible to current listeners. . . . Slonim's acrylic-and-charcoal illustrations have a pleasantly informal silliness, with rough, sketchy charcoal lines partnering with the paint." Bull Cent Child Books

We're going on a ghost hunt; by Susan Pearson; illustrated by S.D. Schindler. Marshall Cavendish 2012 32 p. (hardcover) $16.99
Grades: K 1 2 3   E
  1. Children's poetry 2. Picture books for children 3. Ghost stories -- Juvenile fiction 4. Ghosts -- Fiction 5. Adventure and adventurers -- Fiction
  ISBN 0761463070; 9780761463078; 9780761463085
                                          LC 2011031815
In this children's picture book, the "familiar cadence and words associated with 'We're Going on a Bear Hunt' are giving a seasonal twist by [Susan] Pearson. These kids are heading off on a ghost hunt. . . . But when they reach the graveyard and a ghost appears, their courage wavers and they make a fast trip back home retracting their steps

through the woods, across the stream, cornfield and swamp to race into their beds." (Children's Literature)

Pearson, Tracey Campbell

★ **Bob.** Farrar, Straus & Giroux 2002 un il $16; pa $6.95

Grades: PreK K 1 2   **E**
  1. Animals -- Fiction 2. Roosters -- Fiction
  ISBN 0-374-39957-3; 0-374-40871-8 pa

LC 2001-40439

While looking for someone to teach him how to crow, a rooster learns to sound like many different animals and finds that his new skills come in handy

"The droll, repetitious text, perfect for reading aloud, is delightfully complemented by bright, lively watercolor illustrations." SLJ

Myrtle. Farrar, Straus and Giroux 2004 un il $15

Grades: PreK K 1 2   **E**
  1. Mice -- Fiction 2. Aunts -- Fiction
  ISBN 0-374-35157-0

LC 2003-44059

With the help of her favorite Aunt Tizzy, Myrtle learns to overcome her fear of the mean next-door neighbor.

"Pearson uses a fruit-colored palette with lots of design work to showcase her delightful mouse characters, brimming with personality." Booklist

Pedersen, Janet

Houdini the amazing caterpillar; [by] Janet Pedersen. Clarion Books 2008 30p il $16

Grades: PreK K 1 2   **E**
  1. School stories 2. Butterflies -- Fiction 3. Caterpillars -- Fiction
  ISBN 978-0-618-89332-4; 0-618-89332-6

A caterpillar does amazing tricks, like making leaves disappear and shedding its skin, and finally it performs the most amazing trick of all. Includes facts about the life cycle of the monarch butterfly.

"Big, clear artwork in watercolors and liquid inks shows the smiling, hungry little caterpillar basking in the attention from a teacher and pupils. . . . The fantasy and the realism make the nature story fun for home and classroom." Booklist

Peet, Bill

Big bad Bruce. Houghton Mifflin 1977 38p il $17; pa $8.95

Grades: PreK K 1 2   **E**
  1. Bears -- Fiction 2. Witches -- Fiction
  ISBN 0-395-25150-8; 0-395-32922-1 pa

LC 76-62502

Bruce, a bear bully, never picks on anyone his own size until he is diminished in more ways than one by a small but very independent witch

"The language of the text is almost musical, with lots of words used for the sheer pleasure or appropriateness of their sounds. The illustrations are colorful and amusing." Child Book Rev Serv

Huge Harold; written and illustrated by Bill Peet. Houghton Mifflin 1961 un il hardcover o.p. pa $8.95

Grades: PreK K 1 2   **E**
  1. Stories in rhyme 2. Rabbits -- Fiction
  ISBN 0-395-18449-5; 0-395-32923-X pa

This story, "told in rhyming couplets and colored drawings, is action filled and laughable." Booklist

The **whingdingdilly**; written and illustrated by Bill Peet. Houghton Mifflin 1970 60p il $17; pa $9.95

Grades: PreK K 1 2   **E**
  1. Dogs -- Fiction 2. Witches -- Fiction
  ISBN 0-395-24729-2; 0-395-31381-3 pa

"Scamps, the dog, wants to be a horse, but a well-meaning witch turns him into a Whingdingdilly with the hump of a camel, zebra's tail, giraffe's neck, elephant's front legs and ears, rhinoceros' nose, and reindeer's horns." Adventuring With Books. 2d edition

Peete, Holly Robinson

My brother Charlie; written by Holly Robinson Peete and Ryan Elizabeth Peete with Denene Millner; pictures by Shane W. Evans. Scholastic Press 2010 un il

Grades: 1 2 3 4   **E**
  1. Twins -- Fiction 2. Autism -- Fiction 3. Siblings -- Fiction
  ISBN 0-545-09466-6; 978-0-545-09466-5

LC 2009005589

A girl tells what it is like living with her twin brother who has autism and sometimes finds it hard to communicate with words, but who, in most ways, is just like any other boy. Includes authors' note about autism

"The authors, a mother-daughter team, based this story on personal experience. Evans's bright, mixed-media illustrations skillfully depict the family's warmth and concern." SLJ

Pelham, David

★ **Trail**; paper poetry. Little Simon/Simon & Schuster Books for Young Readers 2007 un il $26.99

Grades: 1 2 3 4   **E**
  1. Pop-up books 2. Snails -- Fiction
  ISBN 978-1-4169-4894-0

In five pop-up spreads a silver line of poetry on white paper follows a small snail through its day, from roots and leaf on the forest floor to a pond at sunset. Pelham lays the verse out on a paper wheel that must be turned to be read in its entirety.

Pelley, Kathleen T.

Magnus Maximus, a marvelous measurer; [pictures by] S.D. Schindler. Farrar Straus Giroux 2010 un il $16.99

Grades: K 1 2   **E**
  1. Counting -- Fiction 2. Measurement -- Fiction
  ISBN 978-0-374-34725-3; 0-374-34725-5

LC 2006-51714

As the town's official measurer, Magnus Maximus is consumed with measuring and counting everything and everyone, missing out on life's simple pleasures, until one day when he breaks his glasses.

"Children will enjoy the humor in this eccentric's ever-increasing obsession. Fine ink lines and muted watercolors fill the illustrations with small details, add humor, and complete the story. The art firmly places it in the Victorian era, a time of scientific exploration. The style perfectly captures the focus of the marvelous measurer and his scientific obsession." SLJ

Raj, the bookstore tiger; illustrated by Paige Keiser. Charlesbridge 2011 un il lib bdg $15.95

Grades: K 1 2 3   E

1. Cats -- Fiction 2. Tigers -- Fiction 3. Books and reading -- Fiction

ISBN 978-1-58089-230-8; 1-58089-230-2

LC 2010007585

When a new manager brings Snowball, a grouchy cat, to the shop where Raj and his owner live and work, Snowball informs Raj that he is not the tiger everyone believes him to be.

"The lively, descriptive narrative will provide an entertaining read-aloud, while the cheery watercolor-and-pencil illustrations feature expressive feline and human characters. . . . A whimsical title with a positive message." Booklist

Pendziwol, Jean

Marja's skis; [by] Jean E. Pendziwol; pictures by Jirina Marton. Groundwood 2007 un il $17.95

Grades: 1 2 3   E

1. Skiing -- Fiction 2. Fathers -- Fiction 3. Immigrants -- Fiction 4. Lumber and lumbering -- Fiction

ISBN 978-0-88899-674-9

"Marja can hardly wait to be big and strong enough to help with Father's horses and attend school. . . . But after her father dies . . . being strong seems too hard. One day . . . Marja sees someone who has fallen through the ice and . . . she finds the courage to help him. . . . Evocative oil-pastels illustrate the text. . . . A simply told, emotionally resonant tale." Booklist

Penn, Audrey

Chester Raccoon and the acorn full of memories; illustrated by Barbara L. Gibson. Tanglewood 2009 un il $16.95

Grades: K 1 2 3   E

1. Death -- Fiction 2. Memory -- Fiction 3. Raccoons -- Fiction 4. Bereavement -- Fiction 5. Forest animals -- Fiction 6. Mother-child relationship -- Fiction

ISBN 978-1-933718-29-3; 1-933718-29-3

LC 2009013734

After his mother explains why his classmate is not returning to school, she teaches Chester Raccoon how to make a memory.

"Simple, direct dialogue demonstrates the love between this mother and child. Bright, stylized illustrations on high-gloss pages depict the animals with human emotions, convey warmth, and reinforce the text." SLJ

A **bedtime** kiss for Chester Raccoon; illustrated by Barbara Gibson. Tanglewood 2011 il $7.95

Grades: PreK   E

1. Stories in rhyme 2. Board books for children 3. Fear -- Fiction 4. Bedtime -- Fiction 5. Raccoons -- Fiction

ISBN 978-1-933718-52-1; 1-933718-52-8

LC 2010046711

"As Chester Raccoon nestles into his lair, he begins to imagine frightening creatures in the light that streams across his bedroom. . . . The ink and watercolor illustrations are realistic and reassuringly expressive. . . . Designed for younger children, this board book features rounded corners, rhyming couplets, and a simpler text than the earlier books in the series. It should find an audience in most public libraries." SLJ

Other titles about Chester Raccoon are:

Chester Raccoon and the acorn full of memories (2009)

Chester Raccoon and the big bad bully (2008)

The kissing hand (2006)

Pennypacker, Sara

Pierre in love; pictures by Petra Mathers. Orchard Books 2007 un il $16.99

Grades: K 1 2   E

1. Love -- Fiction 2. Mice -- Fiction 3. Rabbits -- Fiction

ISBN 0-439-51740-0

Feeling "bloopy and love-swoggled" in the presence of Catherine, the elegant ballet teacher, a humble fisherman tries to muster the courage to reveal his affection for her.

"Subtleties abound, and the emotions may affect adults more than children. But the purity of the love will touch children, too, and both the words and the art are delightful." Booklist

★ **Sparrow** girl; illustrated by Yoko Tanaka. Hyperion 2009 un il $16.99

Grades: 1 2 3 4   E

1. Birds -- Fiction 2. Sparrows -- Fiction

ISBN 978-1-4231-1187-0; 1-4231-1187-7

LC 2009-6758

When China's leader declares war on sparrows in 1958, everyone makes loud noise in hopes of chasing the hungry birds from their land except for Ming-Li, a young girl whose compassion and foresight prevent a disaster

"Pennypacker strikes a suitably moralistic tone and tells her story with rich, descriptive detail. Tanaka matches the somber elegance of the text with opaque, folk-inspired paintings in a subdued palette. An author's note explains the difficult facts behind the story." Booklist

Perez, Amada Irma

My diary from here to there; story, Amada Irma Pérez; illustrations, Maya Christina Gonzalez. Children's Bk. Press 2002 un il $16.95

Grades: 2 3 4   E

1. Immigrants -- Fiction 2. Mexican Americans -- Fiction 3. Bilingual books -- English-Spanish

ISBN 0-89239-175-8

LC 2001-58251

A young girl describes her feelings when her father decides to leave their home in Mexico to look for work in the United States

"The diary entries, written in conversational English and Spanish, resonate with the tensions of the experience. . . . The full-page, bright acrylic paintings complement the text, with the blocky primitive forms adding a reassuring note to the whole." SLJ

★ **My** very own room; story by Amada Irma Pérez; illustrations by Maya Christina Gonzalez. Children's Bk. Press 2000 30p il $16.95

Grades: PreK K 1 2   E

1. Family life 2. Mexican Americans 3. Bedrooms 4. Family life -- Fiction 5. Mexican Americans -- Fiction 6. Bilingual books -- English-Spanish 7. Spanish language materials -- Bilingual

ISBN 0-89239-164-2

LC 00-20769

With the help of her family, a resourceful Mexican American girl realizes her dream of having a space of her own to read and to think

"Gonzalez' palette is replete with joyfully exuberant colors; rich magentas, purples, and blues contrast with the warm golds of faces and arms, and the dark eyes and hair offer further contrast with the backgrounds and skin colors. Pérez based this story on her own life . . . and the text . . . exudes a comfortably familiar, accessible voice." Bull Cent Child Books

Perez, L. King

First day in grapes; illustrated by Robert Casilla. Lee & Low Bks. 2002 un il $16.95

Grades: K 1 2 3   E

1. Schools 2. Migrant labor 3. School stories 4. Mexican Americans 5. Self confidence 6. First day of school 7. Migrant labor -- Fiction 8. Mexican Americans -- Fiction

ISBN 1-58430-045-0

LC 2001-38787

When Chico starts the third grade after his migrant worker family moves to begin harvesting California grapes, he finds that self confidence and math skills help him cope with the first day of school

This story "sheds light on the life of migrant children in a poignant, balanced manner. . . . The watercolor, colored-pencil, and pastel illustrations bring warmth and color to this portrait of life in rural California." SLJ

Pericoli, Matteo

Tommaso and the missing line. Alfred A. Knopf 2008 un il $15.99; lib bdg $18.99

Grades: K 1 2 3   E

1. Drawing -- Fiction 2. Lost and found possessions -- Fiction

ISBN 978-0-375-84102-6; 0-375-84102-4; 978-0-375-94102-3 lib bdg; 0-375-94102-9 lib bdg

When Tommaso discovers that a line is missing from his favorite drawing, he goes looking for it all around town and notices many lines he never saw before.

Pericoli "demonstrates remarkable draftsmanship and a vivid eye for detail and perspective; the mostly black-and-white pictures combine the elegant extravagance of architectural engravings with the playfulness and spontaneity of a great doodle. The Italian setting adds to the charm. . . . The design is striking. . . . Facing each illustration, the text drops out from solid orange; the effect is eye-popping." Publ Wkly

The **true** story of Stellina. Knopf 2006 un il $15.95; lib bdg $17.99

Grades: PreK K 1 2   E

1. Artists 2. Authors 3. Finches 4. Architects 5. Illustrators 6. Children's authors 7. Birds -- Juvenile literature

ISBN 0-375-83273-4; 0-375-93273-9 lib bdg

The true story of a baby finch rescued and raised by the author and his wife when no zoo would take the abandoned bird fallen from her nest onto a busy street in the middle of New York City.

"A precise linguistic lyricism is at play. . . . The art is sophisticated and spare, but utterly accessible." Booklist

Perkins, Lynne Rae

★ **Pictures** from our vacation. Greenwillow Books 2007 un il $16.99; lib bdg $17.89

Grades: K 1 2 3   E

1. Vacations -- Fiction 2. Photography -- Fiction 3. Family reunions -- Fiction

ISBN 978-0-06-085097-5; 0-06-085097-3; 978-0-06-085098-2 lib bdg; 0-06-085098-1 lib bdg

LC 2006-49256

Given a camera that takes and prints tiny pictures just before leaving for the family farm in Canada, a young girl records a vacation that gets off to a slow start, but winds up being a family reunion filled with good memories.

"Using many overhead perspectives and with an eye for small details, [Perkins] offers watercolors that beautifully capture all that is real about family vacations: boredom, disappointment, fun, and love." Booklist

Snow music. Greenwillow Bks. 2003 un il $15.99

Grades: PreK K 1   E

1. Snow -- Fiction 2. Sound -- Fiction

ISBN 0-06-623956-7

LC 2002-192758

When a dog gets loose from the house on a snowy day, his owner searches for him and experiences the sounds of various animals and things in the snow

"With whispery, musical words and detailed, soft-focus images that depict typical winter scenes, this gentle book gives children a sense of what snow is." SLJ

★ The **cardboard** piano. Greenwillow Books 2008 un il $17.99; lib bdg $18.89

Grades: PreK K 1 2   E

1. Pianos -- Fiction 2. Friendship -- Fiction

ISBN 978-0-06-154265-7; 0-06-154265-2; 978-0-06-154266-4 lib bdg; 0-06-154266-0 lib bdg

LC 2007-39194

When Debbie tries to interest Tina in playing the piano by creating a cardboard keyboard, they find not only does it not have the same appeal but also that they do not need to share everything to be best friends.

"Perkins engages her young audience on three levels: the straightforward yet emotionally complex text; conversational asides in word balloons that develop characterization; and intricate pen-and-ink and watercolor illustrations. . . . Perkins presents the delicate nature of friendship without patronizing." Horn Book

Perl, Erica S.

Dotty; illustrated by Julia Denos. Abrams Books for Young Readers 2010 un il $16.95

Grades: PreK K 1   E

1. School stories 2. Imaginary playmates -- Fiction 3. Teacher-student relationship -- Fiction

ISBN 978-0-8109-8962-7; 0-8109-8962-X

Ida's imaginary friend, Dotty, is tied to her with a blue string and when Ida's classmates tease her about Dotty, Ida is surprised to discover that her teacher carries a red string with her wherever she goes.

"Denos's illustrations subtly show the characters and the seasons changing, and the pressures of growing up. The text is best suited for one-on-one reading as the pictures have hidden nuggets of information for those who look carefully. This enjoyable tale of maturing at one's own pace and on one's own terms will resonate with children and parents alike." SLJ

Perlman, Janet

The **delicious** bug. Kids Can Press 2009 un il $16.95
Grades: PreK K 1 2 3   E

1. Insects -- Fiction 2. Chameleons -- Fiction
ISBN 978-1-55337-996-6; 1-55337-996-9

"With a flick of the tongue, two hungry chameleons catch the same bumblebug. Neither is willing to let go, and they have a knockdown-dragout fight to claim the snack. Eventually they realize, thanks to some equally hungry crocodiles, how much they need each other. The snappy story . . . is accompanied by cartoony digital illustrations bordered by panel drawings." Horn Book Guide

Perlman, Willa

Good night, world; illustrated by Carolyn Fisher. Beach Lane Books 2011 il $16.99
Grades: PreK K   E

1. Stories in rhyme 2. Bedtime -- Fiction
ISBN 978-1-4424-0197-6; 1-4424-0197-4
LC 2009053078

Rhyming text bids goodnight to the world and everything that is in it, including stars, streams, animals, and roads.

"The evocative rhyme scans perfectly. . . . Each verse is grandly illustrted with a large, double-page painting. Fisher's multicolored, textured paintings match the expansive tone of the book with a wide palette of swirling colors and layed details." SLJ

Perret, Delphine

The **Big** Bad Wolf Goes on Vacation; Delphine Perret. Sterling 2013 64 p. (hardcover) $12.95
Grades: K 1 2 3   E

1. Picture books for children 2. Summer -- Juvenile fiction 3. Voyages and travels -- Juvenile fiction 4. Humorous stories 5. Wolves -- Fiction 6. Vacations -- Fiction 7. Grandfathers -- Fiction 8. Characters in literature -- Fiction
ISBN 1402786336; 9781402786334
LC 2012009933

This book is Delphine Perret's sequel to "The Big Bad Wolf and Me" and "again stars Louis and his wolf friend, Bernard." Here, Louis and Bernard go on a summer trip with Louis's Grandpa. "During their travels, the three enjoy lunch in a park when they can't take Bernard into a restaurant, come upon a herd of odiferous cows blocking the roadway, and stop to stretch their legs near woods. Arriving at the seaside, Louis and Bernard partake of plenty of interactive seaside fun." (School Library Journal)

The **Big** Bad Wolf and me; [by] Delphine Perret. Sterling Pub. 2006 un il $9.95
Grades: K 1 2 3   E

1. Wolves -- Fiction
ISBN 978-1-4027-3725-1; 1-4027-3725-4
LC 2005031460

Original French edition 2005

When the Big Bad Wolf is mistaken for a dog, he comes to live in a boy's closet and eat chocolate chip cookies.

"Told in witty, thumbnail-size line drawings accompanied by brief text in very small type. . . . The story's humor, absurdity, and heart will please a wide readership." Booklist

Perrin, Martine

Look who's there! Albert Whitman 2011 un il
Grades: PreK   E

1. Stories in rhyme 2. Board books for children 3. Animals -- Fiction
ISBN 080757676X; 9780807576762
LC 2010037841

Original French edition 2005

Text and images on die-cut pages lead the reader to discover the hiding places of a variety of animals in the water and near the shore.

This is a "striking hide-and-seek book. . . . A stylish presentation." Publ Wkly

What do you see? Albert Whitman 2011 un il
Grades: PreK   E

1. Board books for children 2. Animals -- Fiction
ISBN 0807567124; 9780807567128
LC 2010037477

Original French editiion 2005

Text and images on die-cut pages lead the reader to discover the hiding places of a variety of small animals.

"Kids will appreciate the objects profiled: boots, buckets, bibs, cribs, and the like." Booklist

Perry, Andrea

The **Bicklebys'** birdbath; illustrated by Roberta Angaramo. Atheneum 2010 un il $16.99
Grades: PreK K 1 2   E

1. Stories in rhyme
ISBN 978-1-4169-0624-7; 1-4169-0624-X

A cumulative rhyme in the style of "The House That Jack Built," describing the antics that occur when a mailman lands in a birdbath causing it to break.

"This jaunty cumulative tale has a pleasingly playful complexity, both in the wording and in its sense of time. Perry concocts a rhythmic text with unexpected twists and turns, and rather than moving the story forward, it works backward. . . . Sweetly clever." Kirkus

Peterkin, Allan

The **flyaway** blanket; illustrated by Emmeline Pidgen. Magination Press 2011 un il $14.95; pa $9.95
Grades: PreK K 1 2   E

1. Blankets -- Fiction 2. Mother-child relationship -- Fiction
ISBN 978-1-4338-1047-3; 1433810476; 978-1-4338-1046-6 pa; 1-4338-1046-8 pa
LC 2011011079

"In a sensitive lullaby, a small boy and his mother hang the laundry to dry on the clothesline, as she sings, 'time to fly, touch the sky, fly up, high up, wave goodbye.' Jake doesn't want to let go of his comforting blue blanket, but his mother assures him that it will soon be dry. As they sit together in the sun, Jake falls asleep, and a gust of wind sends the blanket sailing. . . . Pidgen's cheerful artwork is reassuring, with a bright palette, loose, sweeping lines, and plenty of attention on mother-child tenderness, human and animal alike. The message about attachment, security, and sometimes letting go is conveyed subtly and organically." Publ Wkly

Peters, Lisa Westberg

★ **Cold** little duck, duck, duck; pictures by Sam Williams. Greenwillow Bks. 2000 un il $15.99

Grades: PreK K 1   **E**

1. Stories in rhyme 2. Ducks -- Fiction 3. Spring -- Fiction 4. Ducks -- Pictorial works -- Juvenile fiction 5. Spring -- Pictorial works -- Juvenile fiction

ISBN 0-688-16178-2

LC 99-29880

Early one spring a little duck arrives at her pond and finds it still frozen, but not for long

"The poetic text, well served by expressive watercolors, is set in a large black typeface (inviting letter and word recognition); colorful and playful typefaces are used for the rhythmic three-word refrains." Horn Book Guide

Frankie works the night shift; illustrated by Jennifer Taylor. Greenwillow Books 2010 un il $16.99

Grades: PreK K   **E**

1. Counting 2. Cats -- Fiction 3. Night -- Fiction

ISBN 978-0-06-009095-1; 0-06-009095-2

LC 2008012644

In this counting book, Frankie the cat's night prowling causes a ruckus, waking sleeping neighbors who do not share Frankie's love of the "night shift."

"Peters's spare text, full of exclamatory statements in the second half . . . moves the story forward with energy and speed, but Taylor's artwork is the showstopper, creating a surreal environment for Frankie's nocturnal adventures." Publ Wkly

Petersen, David

Snowy Valentine; written and illustrated by David Petersen. Harper 2011 un il $14.99

Grades: PreK K 1   **E**

1. Love -- Fiction 2. Gifts -- Fiction 3. Rabbits -- Fiction 4. Forest animals -- Fiction 5. Valentine's Day -- Fiction

ISBN 978-0-06-146378-5; 0-06-146378-7

LC 2009027197

Jasper Bunny spends a snowy Valentine's Day visiting his forest friends in hopes of finding the perfect gift for his beloved Lilly.

"Petersen's whimsical, full-bleed illustrations with Victorian-pattern details add warmth and gentle humor to the story. . . . The timeless quality of the theme and perfect cast of supporting characters make this valentine story a head (or at least two rabbit ears) above the rest." SLJ

Pfister, Marcus

Questions, questions; [translated by NordSud Verlag; English adaptation by Marcus Pfister and Susan Pearson] NorthSouth 2011 un il $16.95

Grades: PreK K   **E**

1. Nature 2. Questions and answers

ISBN 978-0-7358-4000-3; 0-7358-4000-8

First published in Switzerland

Questions on nature.

"Pfister has created images as pithy as they are poignant, boldly graphic and dramatically cropped against white backgrounds. A blue-headed songbird is reminiscent of Asian watercolor; a storm cloud looks like it's been fashioned from salt dough; falling leaves seem cut from pieces of thickly tufted carpet. Although each was created using the same painted paper method (explained on the final page), the results are as varied as the questions." Publ Wkly

Snow puppy. North-South 2011 il $16.95

Grades: PreK K 1   **E**

1. Dogs -- Fiction 2. Snow -- Fiction 3. Christmas -- Fiction

ISBN 978-0-7358-4031-7; 0-7358-4031-8

A puppy is lost in the snowy woods and needs to make his way home.

"Rascal is a big-nosed scamp, full of curiosity and joy. Pfister's scenes are speckled throughout with the falling snow, wintry whites contrasting with the forest browns. This nicely captures a puppy's (or a child's) distractibility." Kirkus

Pham, LeUyen

★ **All** the things I love about you; written and illustrated by LeUyen Pham. Balzer + Bray 2010 un il $16.99

Grades: PreK K 1 2   **E**

1. Love -- Fiction 2. Mother-son relationship -- Fiction

ISBN 978-0-06-199029-8; 0-06-199029-9

LC 2009054255

A mother relates some of the many things that she loves about her young son.

"In capturing the goofy spontaneity of affection and everyday family life without a whiff of treacle, Pham proves once again that she's among the most natural and gifted illustrators working today." Publ Wkly

Phillipps, Julie C.

★ **Wink**: the ninja who wanted to be noticed. Viking Children's Books 2009 un il $15.99

Grades: K 1 2 3   **E**

1. School stories 2. Ninja -- Fiction

ISBN 978-0-670-01092-9; 0-670-01092-8

LC 2008-23238

Although ninjas should be silent and use stealth, Wink finds his enthusiasm gets him into trouble with his teacher until he finds the perfect way to express both traits.

"The story's oft-told message of acceptance has been invigorated with originality and humor. The collage-style illustrations often appear to have a three-dimensional effect and Wink practically bounds off the pages with barely contained energy." SLJ

Another title about Wink is:

Wink: the ninja who wanted to nap (2011)

Wink: the ninja who wanted to nap; by J.C. Phillipps. Viking 2011 un il $15.99

Grades: K 1 2 3   **E**

1. Fame -- Fiction 2. Ninja -- Fiction 3. Sleep -- Fiction

ISBN 978-0-670-01192-6; 0-670-01192-4

LC 2010025107

Wink loves being the most famous ninja in Japan but when he needs a nap his fans will not leave him alone, and so he seeks guidance from his former teacher, Master Zutsu.

"Phillipps offers wit aplenty in cut-paper compositions that match Wink's boundless energy and bravado. Even when sleepy, her hero demands to be noticed." Publ Wkly

Pichon, Liz

Penguins. Orchard Books 2008 un il lib bdg $12.99

Grades: PreK K   **E**
1. Zoos -- Fiction 2. Cameras -- Fiction 3. Penguins
-- Fiction
ISBN 978-0-545-02215-6 lib bdg; 0-545-02215-0
lib bdg
LC 2007-40419
Penguins at the zoo have an exciting afternoon when one
finds a camera left behind by a visitor.

"The cartoon style of these pastel illustrations is as light
and playful as the text. The sweet faces show a lot of expression, while the aqua and purple backgrounds highlight their
antics." SLJ

The **three** horrid little pigs; by Liz Pichon. Tiger Tales
2008 un il $15.95
Grades: PreK K 1 2   **E**
1. Pigs -- Fiction 2. Wolves -- Fiction
ISBN 978-1-58925-077-2; 1-58925-077-X
When their mother sends them packing, three pigs find
despicable ways to find new accommodations, but when the
big, friendly wolf tries to show them the error of their ways,
the pigs respond by huffing and puffing.

"The lively narrative, printed in playfully arranged text
of varying size, is well suited for spirited read-alouds, as are
the colorful illustrations that add to the hilarity with expressive characters. Children will enjoy the clever twist on a familiar story." Booklist

Pien, Lark
★ **Mr.** Elephanter. Candlewick Press 2010 un il
$14.99
Grades: PreK K   **E**
1. Nannies -- Fiction 2. Elephants -- Fiction
ISBN 978-0-7636-4409-3; 0-7636-4409-9
LC 2010-07577
From early morning until sunset, beloved Mr. Elephant-
er takes care of the rambunctious youngsters of the El-
ephantery, preparing their breakfast, taking them to the park,
tucking them in for naps, and joining them at play.

"The simple story will speak to youngsters, and Pien's
clever wording captures the humor in daily life. The sketchy
watercolor illustrations portray both movement and story
well." SLJ

Pilkey, Dav
★ The **paperboy**; story and paintings by Dav Pilkey.
Orchard Bks. 1996 un il $16.95; pa $6.99
Grades: PreK K 1 2   **E**
1. Newspaper carriers -- Fiction
ISBN 0-531-09506-1; 0-531-07139-1 pa
LC 95-30641
A Caldecott Medal honor book, 1997
"The palette of the artwork is rich and inviting, and
an emphasis is put on balance and geometric form, giving
solidity to this celebration of routine. A meditative evoca-
tion of the extraordinary aspects of ordinary living." Horn
Book Guide

Pinder, Eric
If all the animals came inside; by Eric Pinder; illustrated by Marc Brown. Little, Brown and Company 2012 40 p.
Grades: PreK K 1 2   **E**
1. Home -- Fiction 2. Stories in rhyme 3. Animals

-- Fiction 4. Picture books for children
ISBN 0316098833; 9780316098830
LC 2011020100
In this picture book, a "young boy imagines the riot that
would ensue if his house were overrun with wild animals. . .
. The hodgepodge of animals ranges from forest chipmunks
and savanna giraffes to Australian kangaroos and even an
octopus. And they all come with mischief in mind. . . . From
ruining the furniture and eating all the food to taking up the
comfiest places, they would eventually leave no room for the
boy and his family, relegating them to sleeping outside. And
in fact, the boy wisely decides in the end that, as much fun
as all the animals might be, he will be satisfied with just his
cat and dog." (Kirkus)

Pinfold, Levi
Black dog; Levi Pinfold. Candlewick Press 2012 32
p. ill. (hardcover) $15.99
Grades: PreK K 1 2   **E**
1. Dogs -- Fiction 2. Fear -- Fiction 3. Picture books
for children 4. Family life -- Fiction
ISBN 0763660973; 9780763660970
LC 2011048380
Boston Globe-Horn Book Honor: Picture Book (2013).
This book tells how "when the Hope family wakes up
one morning, they're stunned to see 'a black dog the size
of an elephant' outside their house. . . . The youngest Hope,
known as Small, fearlessly marches out to meet the humongous pooch. Singing a taunting rhyme, she entices him to
chase her, darting under the bridge, through the playground
slide, and back home through the cat flap in the door. With
each obstacle negotiated, the dog shrinks somewhat, until . .
. he clearly has become the new house pet." (Bulletin of the
Center for Children's Books)

★ The **Django**. Templar Books 2010 un il $16.99
Grades: K 1 2   **E**
1. Banjos -- Fiction 2. Gypsies -- Fiction 3. Musicians
-- Fiction 4. Imaginary playmates -- Fiction
ISBN 978-0-7636-4788-9; 0-7636-4788-8
A young Gypsy boy named Jean has an imaginary friend,
Django, who keeps getting him in trouble and eventually is
"sent away," but whenever Jean plays the banjo he continues
to feel close to Django. Inspired by the life of jazz musician
Django Reinhardt; includes facts about his life.

"Fish-eyed perspectives and generous detailing almost
suck readers' gazes into Pinfold's exotic and pastoral artwork. Once in, children will revel in the bouncy rhythms and
nonsense words sprinkled throughout the fun-to-read-and-
hear narrative." Booklist

Pinkney, Andrea Davis
★ **Boycott** blues; how Rosa Parks inspired a nation.
illustrations by Brian Pinkney. Greenwillow Books 2008
un il $16.99; lib bdg $17.89
Grades: 1 2 3 4   **E**
1. Civil rights activists 2. African Americans -- Fiction
3. Boycotts -- Juvenile literature 4. African Americans
-- Civil rights -- Juvenile literature
ISBN 978-0-06-082118-0; 0-06-082118-3; 978-0-06-
082119-7 lib bdg; 0-06-082119-1 lib bdg
LC 2006-38273
Illustrations and rhythmic text recall the December,
1955, bus boycott in Montgomery, Alabama.

"Color and movement are vibrant components in this extraordinary book. . . . Text and illustration work in perfect sync. Andrea Pinkney chose the rhythm of the blues as cadence for the guitar-strumming hound-dog narrator. . . . The evocative text is bolstered by Brian Pinkney's perceptive vision. . . . Against electric blues and greens diffused with streaks of black line, Pinkney's artwork rivets the eye." SLJ

Includes bibliographical references

★ **Peggony** -Po; a whale of a tale. illustrated by Brian Pinkney. Jump at the Sun/Hyperion Books for Children 2006 un il $16.99

Grades: K 1 2 3   E

1. Tall tales 2. Whales -- Fiction 3. Whaling -- Fiction 4. African Americans -- Fiction

ISBN 0-7868-1958-8

LC 2005047537

Peggony-Po, carved out of wood by his father, a one-legged whaler, determines to catch the huge whale that ate his father's leg.

"Told with humor and verve, this [is a] rollicking tall tale. . . . The illustrations brim with activity and energy." SLJ

Pinkney, Jerry

★ **Rikki** -tikki-tavi; by Rudyard Kipling; adapted and illustrated by Jerry Pinkney. Morrow Junior Bks. 1997 un il $16.99; pa $6.99

Grades: 1 2 3 4   E

1. Poets 2. Authors 3. Novelists 4. Memoirists 5. Cobras -- Fiction 6. Children's authors 7. Short story writers 8. Mongooses -- Fiction 9. Nobel laureates for literature

ISBN 0-688-14320-2; 0-06-058785-7 pa

LC 96-51194

This is a retelling of the story from Rudyard Kipling's The jungle book in which a mongoose saves an English boy and his family from cobras in their garden in India

"Dramatic in content, sensitive in line, and rich with color, the illustrations in this picture book make full use of the broad, double-page spreads. Children who are not familiar with the story will be captivated; those who have had the story read to them before will find new things to shiver over." Booklist

★ **Twinkle,** twinkle, little star. Little, Brown Books 2011 un il $16.99

Grades: PreK   E

1. Nursery rhymes 2. Stars -- Fiction 3. Chipmunks -- Fiction

ISBN 978-0-316-05696-0; 0-316-05696-0

"The song 'Twinkle, Twinkle, Little Star' proves lines of text for this imaginative picture book, in which a little chipmunk emerges from the safety of its burrow to discover the natural world. . . . This appropriate theme for young children finds expression in a series of vividly imagined, gracefully composed, and beautifully detailed illustrations, created using pencil, watercolors, and colored pencils. . . . This evocative picture book offers a rewarding reading experience at bedtime, or any time." Booklist

★ The **lion** & the mouse. Little, Brown Books for Young Readers 2009 un il $16.99

Grades: PreK K 1 2   E

1. Fables 2. Authors 3. Folklore 4. Stories without

words 5. Storytellers 6. Fables -- Juvenile literature 7. Folklore -- Juvenile literature

ISBN 978-0-316-01356-7; 0-316-01356-0

LC 2008-43852

Boston Globe-Horn Book Award honor book: Picture Book (2010)

Awarded the Caldecott Medal (2010)

In this wordless retelling of an Aesop fable, an adventuresome mouse proves that even small creatures are capable of great deeds when he rescues the King of the Jungle.

Young readers will be drawn "into watercolors of . . . detail and splendor. Pinkney's soft, multihued strokes make everything in the jungle seem alive. . . . His luxuriant use of close-ups humanizes his animal characters without idealizing them." Booklist

The **little** match girl; [by] Hans Christian Andersen; adapted and illustrated by Jerry Pinkney. Phyllis Fogelman Books 1999 un il hardcover o.p. pa $6.99

Grades: 1 2 3 4   E

1. Authors 2. Novelists 3. Dramatists 4. Fairy tales 5. Children's authors 6. Short story writers

ISBN 0-8037-2314-8; 0-14-230188-4 pa

LC 99-13814

The wares of the poor little match girl illuminate her cold world, bringing some beauty to her brief, tragic life

"A faithful retelling of a classic tale. . . . The story's haunting death imagery . . . may disturb the very young, but ultimately Pinkney's vision proves as transcendent as Andersen's." Publ Wkly

★ The **ugly** duckling; [by] Hans Christian Andersen; adapted and illustrated by Jerry Pinkney. Morrow Junior Bks. 1999 un il $16.99; lib bdg $17.89

Grades: 1 2 3 4   E

1. Authors 2. Novelists 3. Dramatists 4. Fairy tales 5. Swans -- Fiction 6. Children's authors 7. Short story writers

ISBN 0-688-15932-X; 0-688-15933-8 lib bdg

LC 98-23604

A Caldecott Medal honor book, 2000

An ugly duckling spends an unhappy year ostracized by the other animals before he grows into a beautiful swan

"This is an elegantly accessible retelling, with illustrations full of lively, emotive animals and the kind of vigorous movement that young children are bound to find appealing." Bull Cent Child Books

Pinkney, Sandra L.

Read and rise; photographs by Myles C. Pinkney; foreword by Maya Angelou. Scholastic 2006 un il $15.99

Grades: PreK K 1   E

1. Reading 2. African American children

ISBN 0-439-30929-8

Photographs and poetic text celebrate reading as a means of encouraging African American children to pursue their dreams

"Powerful verbs match the vivid portrayal of children succeeding." SLJ

Pinkwater, Daniel Manus

★ **Beautiful** Yetta; the Yiddish chicken. by Daniel Pinkwater; illustrated by Jill Pinkwater. Feiwel and Friends 2010 un il $16.99

Grades: PreK K 1 2   E
   1. Parrots -- Fiction 2. Chickens -- Fiction 3.
Spanish language -- Vocabulary 4. Yiddish language
-- Vocabulary
   ISBN 978-0-312-55824-6; 0-312-55824-4
   "With wry humor, this multilingual picture book tells
the story of a brave chicken, Yetta. Determined that she will
not be soup, she escapes from a delivery crate and runs into
the streets of Brooklyn. . . . She saves a little green parrot
from a pouncing cat, and the wild parrots who witness the
act welcome her and show her how to find food. Yetta speaks
Yiddish (gevahlt!), and her speech is printed in both Hebrew
and English alphabets with the English translation. The rich
language mix does not stop there, though. The parrots speak
Spanish, and their dialogue, shown in italics, includes a pronunciation guide. A warm twist on the immigration story
that celebrates the richness of urban diversity." Booklist

   I am the dog; by Daniel Pinkwater; illustrated by Jack
E. Davis. Harper 2010 un il $16.99
Grades: PreK K 1   E
   1. Dogs -- Fiction
   ISBN 978-0-06-055505-4; 0-06-055505-X
   Jacob the boy trades places with Max the dog.
   "This amiable and impressive walk for Pinkwater breez-
ily showcases his skill as a comic storyteller. . . . Davis keeps
the dry humor right up on the surface, the tone bright . . . but
not frantic." Kirkus

Pinkwater, Daniel Manus, 1941-
   Bear in love; by Daniel Pinkwater; illustrations by Will
Hillenbrand. 1st ed. Candlewick Press 2012 40 p. col. ill.
(reinforced) $15.99
Grades: PreK K 1 2   E
   1. Bears -- Fiction 2. Friendship -- Fiction 3. Picture
books for children 4. Humorous stories 5. Rabbits
-- Fiction
   ISBN 0763645699; 9780763645694
                        LC 2011046620
   This picture book is the story of an "impulsive, happy-
go-lucky bear [who] keeps finding carrots on a flat rock outside his cave, left by some anonymous well-wisher. After
days of this, the bear places honeycomb on the rock as a lure
. . . , and pretty soon there's a full-scale war of random acts
of kindness going on." (Publishers Weekly)

   ★ **Bear's** picture; written by Daniel Pinkwater; illustrated by D. B. Johnson. Houghton Mifflin Company 2008
un il $16
Grades: K 1 2 3   E
   1. Bears -- Fiction 2. Painting -- Fiction
   ISBN 978-0-618-75923-1; 0-618-75923-9
                        LC 2007-15149
   A newly illustrated editition of the title first published
1972 by Holt, Rinehart and Winston
   A bear continues to paint what he likes despite criticism
from two passing gentlemen.
   This is "a quirky, sardonic, and highly entertaining view
of what makes art. . . . Johnson . . . provides . . . fabulous
mixed-media artwork, including paper sculptures that add
both angular dimension and a wry touch to the simple story."
Booklist

Piper, Watty
   ★ The **little** engine that could; illustrated by Loren
Long. Philomel 2005 un il $17.99
Grades: PreK K 1 2   E
   1. Toys -- Fiction 2. Railroads -- Fiction
   ISBN 0-399-24467-0
   A newly illustrated edition of the title first published
1930 by Grosset & Dunlap
   Although she is not very big, the Little Blue Engine agrees to try to pull a stranded train full of toys over
the mountain.
   "Grand in scale but cozy in effect, the impressive acrylic
paintings use subtle strokes of rich colors to create a series
of narrative scenes large enough to be clearly visible back
to the last row of storytime or classroom. . . . This edition
provides a brilliant new setting that many readers will prefer
to the original picture book." Booklist

Piven, Hanoch
   My best friend is as sharp as a pencil; and other funny
classroom portraits. Schwartz & Wade 2010 un il $17.99
Grades: K 1 2 3   E
   1. Portraits -- Fiction
   ISBN 0375853383; 9780375853388; 978-0-375-
85338-8; 0-375-85338-3
   "Vibrant portraits in words and realia-collage illustrations, purportedly created by the child narrator in anticipation of her grandmother's inevitable questions about school,
will delight readers. One double-page spread gives each new
character's traits, expressed in several verbal metaphors . . .
and in photos of objects. . . . On the next spread, a painting
incorporating those objects forms an eye-catching, idiosyncratic portrait."
   "Vibrant portraits in words and realia-collage illustrations, purportedly created by the child narrator in anticipation of her grandmother's inevitable questions about school,
will delight readers. One double-page spread gives each new
character's traits, expressed in several verbal metaphors . . .
and in photos of objects. . . . On the next spread, a painting
incorporating those objects forms an eye-catching, idiosyncratic portrait." Booklist

   My dog is as smelly as dirty socks; and other funny
family portraits. Schwartz & Wade 2007 un il $16.99;
lib bdg $18.99
Grades: PreK K 1 2   E
   1. Portraits -- Fiction 2. Family life -- Fiction 3.
Family -- Juvenile literature
   ISBN 978-0-375-84052-4; 0-375-84052-4; 978-0-375-
94052-1 lib bdg; 0-375-94052-9 lib bdg
                        LC 2006-21936
   A young girl draws a family portrait, then makes it more
accurate by adding common objects to show aspects of each
member's personality, such as her father's playfulness, her
mother's sweetness, and her brother's strength
   "Childlike line drawings are paired with the more creative portraits, in which representational objects are glued
on gouache-and-watercolor backgrounds to make the figures. Children will get caught up in this playful, fun, creative, and easy-to-do art concept and will want to follow
through with their own creations." Booklist

Platt, Cynthia

A **little** bit of love; illustrated by Hannah Whitty. Tiger Tales 2011 il $15.95

Grades: PreK K   E

1. Food -- Fiction 2. Love -- Fiction 3. Mice -- Fiction 4. Baking -- Fiction 5. Mother-child relationship -- Fiction

ISBN 978-1-58925-095-6; 1-58925-095-8

"Small Mouse is tired of plain old cheese and crumbs and wants something new and sweet to eat, so her mother takes her on a journey, gathering ingredients to make something out of love. . . . Together they make a pie, and the youngster understands how good things are made with a mother's love. This is a sweet story that not only teaches a child how a pie is made, but also how each ingredient comes from nature. . . . The colors in the art are soft but sunny, making this a cozy read. The loving facial expressions between the mice are endearing." SLJ

Platt, Mary

The **Scoop** on Poop; Lifting the lid on the science of poo and wee. by Mary & Richard Platt; illustrated by John Kelly. Kingfisher 2012 48 p. ill. (chiefly col.) (hardcover) $15.99; (paperback) $7.99

Grades: 4 5 6   E

1. Feces -- Juvenile literature 2. Urine -- Juvenile literature

ISBN 0753468867; 0753469235; 9780753468869; 9780753469231

This children's picture book by Richard Platt looks at bodily waste. "'Gathering Gold' is about manure as fertilizer," while "'Garden Growers' is a bit about that as well. There are also two-page spreads on 'Pooper Paper,' (making paper from waste), 'Scent or Stink,' 'Dangerous Dung,'" and "'Backside Buffet,' which notes worldwide dishes that include poop and pee." (Booklist)

Player, Micah

Chloe, instead; by Micah Player. Chronicle Books 2012 32 p. (alk. paper) $15.99

Grades: PreK K 1 2   E

1. Picture books for children 2. Sisters -- Juvenile fiction 3. Family life -- Juvenile fiction 4. Sisters -- Fiction 5. Individuality -- Fiction 6. Individuality in children -- Juvenile fiction

ISBN 0811878651; 9780811878654

LC 2011012717

This children's book, by Micah Player, follows "Molly[, who] always dreamed of having a sister who is just like her. But she got Chloe, instead. These two sisters are nothing alike: Molly loves to color with crayons. Chloe prefers the taste of wax. . . . Molly is frustrated! But then she realizes that maybe sisters aren't the ones next to you on the piano bench, they're the ones dancing to the music you play!" (Publisher's note)

Plecas, Jennifer

Pretend! Philomel Books 2011 un il $15.99

Grades: PreK K 1   E

1. Imagination -- Fiction 2. Father-son relationship -- Fiction

ISBN 978-0-399-23430-9; 0-399-23430-6

LC 2010-19288

A father and son embark on an imaginary adventure and discover how much they love each other.

"The breezy writing and lighthearted watercolor cartoons make this father-son bonding story fly by; with occasional reminders of where Jimmy and Dad really are, readers gain a full appreciation for the powers of the boy's imagination." Publ Wkly

Plourde, Lynn

Dino pets go to school; illustrated by Gideon Kendall. Dutton Children's Books 2011 il $16.99

Grades: PreK K   E

1. School stories 2. Stories in rhyme 3. Pets -- Fiction 4. Dinosaurs -- Fiction

ISBN 978-0-525-42232-7; 0-525-42232-3

LC 2010038065

A boy brings various dinosaurs to school, but discovers that neither the loudest, nor the tallest, nor the smartest is suited to the classroom. Includes facts about dinosaurs.

"Exuberant illustrations bring a sense of whimsy to the story. The facial expressions are both comical and endearing. Children will love the dino baseball game at the conclusion." SLJ

Field trip day; illustrated by Thor Wickstrom. Dutton Children's Books 2010 un il $16.99

Grades: PreK K 1 2   E

1. School stories 2. Farm life -- Fiction

ISBN 978-0-525-47994-9; 0-525-47994-5

Today is Field Trip Day at school, and everyone in Mrs. Shepherd's class is excited to visit Fandangle's Farm, especially Juan, who loves to explore. But Juan just might be too good at exploring, and Mrs. Shepherd and the chaperones have trouble keeping track of him!

"This good-natured story . . . will appeal to children, especially those who adore farm animals. The watercolor-and-ink cartoons are lively and depict a diverse class that lauds thinking and questioning over strict rule-keeping." SLJ

Grandpappy snippy snappies; illustrated by Christopher Santoro. HarperCollinsPublishers 2009 un il $17.99

Grades: PreK K 1 2   E

1. Stories in rhyme 2. Farmers -- Fiction 3. Clothing and dress -- Fiction

ISBN 978-0-06-028050-5; 0-06-028050-6

LC 2001-24328

When things go wrong around his farm Grandpappy sets them right with a snap of his suspenders, but Grandmammy is in trouble and the suspenders are all worn out

"This whimsical tale of an everyday hero has a rhyming text and lively illustrations. . . . Santoro's digital mixed-media illustrations animate the tale in a wonderful way. Together the cartoon and realistic elements add depth, detail, and humor to the tale." SLJ

A **mountain** of mittens; [by] Lynn Plourde; illustrated by Mitch Vane. Charlesbridge 2007 un il $15.95; pa $7.95

Grades: PreK K 1   E

1. Clothing and dress -- Fiction 2. Lost and found possessions -- Fiction

ISBN 978-1-57091-585-7; 978-1-57091-466-9 pa

LC 2006021253

Molly's parents try various methods to help her remember her mittens but nothing seems to work.

"Readers will chuckle as they recognize what a problem mateless mittens can become. Vane's watercolor-and-ink drawings have a jaunty air." Booklist

Pochocki, Ethel

The **blessing** of the beasts; by Ethel Pochocki; illustrated by Barry Moser. Paraclete Press 2007 39p il $18.95
Grades: K 1 2 3   E
1. Skunks -- Fiction 2. Animals -- Fiction 3. Religion -- Fiction 4. Cockroaches -- Fiction
ISBN 978-1-55725-502-0; 1-55725-502-4
LC 2007002231

Martin the skunk and Francesca the cockroach wend their way across the city to attend the blessing of the animals celebration on the Feast of St. Francis at the Cathedral of St. John the Divine.

This is a "a delightful fantasy. . . . Cats and dogs are the usual celebrants at the real service; here they are joined by lions, bears, and falcons. . . . Funny, sly, and noble, the animal pictures range from amusing takeoffs to moving tributes." Booklist

Polacco, Patricia

Babushka's doll. Simon & Schuster Bks. for Young Readers 1990 un il hardcover o.p. pa $6.95
Grades: K 1 2 3   E
1. Dolls -- Fiction
ISBN 0-671-68343-8; 0-689-80255-2 pa
LC 89-6122

"Polacco's distinctive artwork interprets the story with style and verve. Using pencil, marker, and paint, she creates a series of varied compositions, highlighting muted shades with an occasional flare of bright colors and strong patterns. . . . A good, original story, illustrated with panache." Booklist

Bun Bun Button. G. P. Putnam's Sons 2011 il $17.99
Grades: PreK K 1   E
1. Toys -- Fiction 2. Grandmothers -- Fiction 3. Lost and found possessions -- Fiction
ISBN 978-0-399-25472-7; 0-399-25472-2
LC 2010047740

Paige Darling loves the stuffed rabbit her grandmother has made for her, but when she ties a helium-filled balloon to Bun Bun Button the toy gets loose and goes floating away, and it may take some Darling luck to bring her home.

"Brimming with nostalgia, heartfelt sentimentality, and eccentricity, this portrait of a tight-knit intergenerational bond will charm Polacco enthusiasts with its old-fashioned tone and bright illustrations. Even when she is illustrating a picture of a grandmother reading to her granddaughter, Polacco fills the pages with tumbling action, familial warmth, and love." Publ Wkly

★ **Chicken** Sunday. Philomel Bks. 1992 un il $16.99; pa $6.99
Grades: K 1 2 3   E
1. Jews -- Fiction 2. Easter -- Fiction 3. Friendship -- Fiction 4. African Americans -- Fiction
ISBN 0-399-22133-6; 0-698-11615-1 pa
LC 91-16030

To thank old Eula for her wonderful Sunday chicken dinners, her two grandsons and their friend, a girl who has

"adopted" her since her own "babushka" died, sell decorated eggs and buy her a beautiful Easter hat

"Without being heavy-handed, Polacco's text conveys a tremendous pride of heritage as it brims with rich images from her characters' African American and Russian Jewish cultures. Her vibrant pencil-and-wash illustrations glow— actual family photographs have been worked into several spreads." Publ Wkly

★ **G** is for goat. Philomel Bks. 2003 un il $16.99; pa $6.99; bd bk $6.99
Grades: PreK K 1 2   E
1. Goats 2. Alphabet 3. Stories in rhyme
ISBN 0-399-24018-7; 0-14-240550-7 pa; 0-399-24530-8 bd bk
LC 2002-11551

A rhyming celebration of goats and their antics, from A to Z

"The charming animals will energize any storytime. . . . The pencil-and-watercolor illustrations against white backgrounds steal the spotlight, with charming details." SLJ

★ **Ginger** and Petunia; [by] Patricia Polacco. Philomel Books 2007 un il $16.99
Grades: K 1 2 3   E
1. Pigs -- Fiction
ISBN 978-0-399-24539-8
LC 2006024878

When her beloved Ginger, a piano-playing socialite and very snappy dresser, makes a last-minute trip to London not knowing her housesitter has cancelled, Petunia the pig does more than fend for herself, she becomes Ginger.

"Polacco's comic portrayal of pampered pet and attentive owner is spot-on—and her characteristic watercolor illustrations highlight both characters' sense of fashion and joie de vivre. . . . A delight from start to finish." Booklist

In our mothers' house. Philomel Books 2009 un il $17.99
Grades: 1 2 3 4   E
1. Mothers -- Fiction 2. Adoption -- Fiction 3. Lesbians -- Fiction 4. Family life -- Fiction
ISBN 978-0-399-25076-7; 0-399-25076-X
LC 2008-32615

"The oldest of three adopted children recalls her childhood with mothers Marmee and Meema, as they raised their African American daughter, Asian American son, and Caucasian daughter in a lively, supportive neighborhood. . . . The energetic illustrations in pencil and marker, . . . teem with family activities and neighborhood festivity." Booklist

★ **John** Philip Duck. Philomel Books 2004 un il $16.99
Grades: K 1 2 3   E
1. Ducks -- Fiction 2. Hotels and motels -- Fiction
ISBN 0-399-24262-7

During the Depression, a young Memphis boy trains his pet duck to do tricks in the fountain of a grand hotel and ends up becoming the Duck Master of the Peabody Hotel

"This is Polacco at the height of her form in terms of both text and illustration. The story moves smoothly from start to finish and has a refreshing air of innocence. The artwork is simply beautiful as the artist orchestrates a harmonious symphony of color." SLJ

★ The **Lemonade** Club; [by] Patricia Polacco. Philomel Books 2007 un il $16.99
Grades: 2 3 4   E
1. School stories 2. Cancer -- Fiction 3. Teachers -- Fiction 4. Friendship -- Fiction
ISBN 978-0-399-24540-4
LC 2007011440

When Marilyn and her teacher, Miss Wichelman, both get cancer, they encourage each other and, aided by medical treatments and support from friends, they get better. Based on a true story.

"Polacco continues to draw from rich family experiences to weave satisfying, inspirations stories. . . . Pencil-and-marker illustrations in Polacco's usual free style gently convey the emotions." Booklist

★ **Mr.** Lincoln's way. Philomel Bks. 2001 un il $16.99
Grades: K 1 2 3   E
1. Birds 2. Bullies 3. Schools 4. Prejudices 5. School stories 6. School principals 7. Prejudices -- Fiction
ISBN 0-399-23754-2
LC 00-66939

When Mr. Lincoln, "the coolest principal in the whole world," discovers that Eugene, the school bully, knows a lot about birds, he uses this interest to help Eugene overcome his intolerance

"The book may be useful to schools in need of a springboard for discussion of the topic and is graced with impressive watercolors." SLJ

Mrs. Katz and Tush. Doubleday Books for Young Readers 1992 un il $16.99; lib bdg $19.99; pa $6.99
Grades: K 1 2 3   E
1. Jews -- Fiction 2. Friendship -- Fiction 3. African Americans -- Fiction
ISBN 0-553-08122-5; 0-385-90650-1 lib bdg; 0-440-40936-5 pa
LC 91-18710

A long-lasting friendship develops between Larnel, a young African-American, and Mrs. Katz, a lonely, Jewish widow, when Larnel presents Mrs. Katz with a scrawny kitten without a tail

"Polacco has used loving details in both words and art work to craft a moving and heartfelt story of a friendship that reaches across racial and generational differences." Horn Book

My rotten redheaded older brother. Simon & Schuster Bks. for Young Readers 1994 un il $17.95; pa $6.99
Grades: PreK K 1 2 3   E
1. Siblings -- Fiction
ISBN 0-671-72751-6; 0-689-82036-4 pa
LC 93-13980

"Featuring an obnoxious, freckle-faced, bespectacled boy and a comforting, tale-telling grandmother, this autobiographical story is as satisfying as a warm slice of apple pie. Patricia can't quite understand how anyone could possibly like her older brother Richard. Whether picking blackberries or eating raw rhubarb, he always manages to outdo her, rub-

bing it in with one of his 'extra-rotten, weasel-eyed, greeny-toothed grins.' When their Bubbie teaches Patricia to wish on a falling star, she knows just what to ask for." SLJ

★ **Oh,** look! Philomel Books 2004 un il $16.99
Grades: PreK K 1 2   E
1. Goats -- Fiction
ISBN 0-399-24223-6

Three goats visit a fair but run home after they seem to encounter a troll.

"In this colorful picture book, the . . . author transfers the rhythms and movement of the traditional bear-hunt chant to safer ground. . . . Polacco's signature pencil-and-watercolor paintings cascade across the pages, creating festive scenes and bright hues." SLJ

★ **Pink** and Say. Philomel Bks. 1994 un il $16.99
Grades: 2 3 4   E
1. Friendship -- Fiction 2. African American soldiers -- Fiction
ISBN 0-399-22671-0
LC 93-36340

Say Curtis describes his meeting with Pinkus Aylee, a black soldier, during the Civil War, and their capture by Southern troops

"Polacco pulls out all the stops in this heart-wrenching tale . . . which has been passed through several generations of the author's family. . . . Polacco's signature line-and-watercolor paintings epitomize heroism, tenderness, and terror. . . . Unglamorized details of the conventions and atrocities of the Civil War target readers well beyond customary picture book age." Horn Book

★ **Rechenka's** eggs; written and illustrated by Patricia Polacco. Philomel Bks. 1988 un il lib bdg $16.99; pa $6.99
Grades: K 1 2 3   E
1. Eggs -- Fiction 2. Geese -- Fiction 3. Easter -- Fiction
ISBN 0-399-21501-8 lib bdg; 0-698-11385-3 pa
LC 87-16588

An injured goose rescued by Babushka, having broken the painted eggs intended for the Easter Festival in Moscva, lays thirteen marvelously colored eggs to replace them, then leaves behind one final miracle in egg form before returning to her own kind

"Polacco achieves optimal dramatic contrast by using bold shapes against uncluttered white space and by contrasting rich colors and design details with faces in black and white." Bull Cent Child Books

Someone for Mr. Sussman; [by] Patricia Polacco. Philomel Books 2008 un il $16.99
Grades: 2 3 4   E
1. Grandmothers -- Fiction 2. Jews -- United States -- Fiction 3. Dating (Social customs) -- Fiction
ISBN 978-0-399-25075-0; 0-399-25075-1
LC 2008000660

Although she is the best matchmaker in the neighborhood, Jerome's Bubbie has a hard time finding a match for the fussy Mr. Sussman.

"The author brings in homey, Fiddler on the Roof syntax . . . along with words like 'oy' and 'farklempt,' illustrating the story in her signature style of comfortable caricatures and broad strokes. A good-natured spirit percolates throughout." Publ Wkly

★ **Thank** you, Mr. Falker. Philomel Bks. 1998 un il $16.99

Grades: K 1 2 3   **E**

   1. Reading -- Fiction 2. Teachers -- Fiction 3. Self-perception -- Fiction 4. Learning disabilities -- Fiction

   ISBN 0-399-23166-8

                LC 97-18685

   At first, Trisha loves school, but her difficulty learning to read makes her feel dumb, until, in the fifth grade, a new teacher helps her understand and overcome her problem

   "Young readers struggling with learning difficulties will identify with Trisha's situation and find reassurance in her success. Polacco's gouache-and-pencil compositions deftly capture the emotional stages—frustration, pain, elation—of Trisha's journey." Publ Wkly

   When lightning comes in a jar. Philomel Bks. 2002 un il $16.99; pa $6.99

Grades: 2 3 4   **E**

   1. Family life -- Fiction 2. Grandmothers -- Fiction 3. Family reunions -- Fiction

   ISBN 0-399-23164-1; 0-14-240350-4 pa

                LC 2001-45925

   A young girl describes the family reunion at her grandmother's house, from the food and baseball and photos to the flickering fireflies on the lawn

   "The watercolor-and-pencil illustrations, skillfully composed on the pages, expressively sketch the characters. . . . This autobiographical story will convey the joys of family." Booklist

   The **butterfly**. Philomel Bks. 2000 un il $16.99; pa $7.99

Grades: 2 3 4   **E**

   1. Jews -- Fiction 2. World War, 1939-1945 -- Fiction 3. Jews -- France -- Juvenile fiction 4. World War, 1939-1945 -- France -- Juvenile fiction 5. France -- History -- German occupation, 1940-1945 -- Juvenile fiction

   ISBN 0-399-23170-6; 0-14-241306-2 pa

                LC 99-30038

   During the Nazi occupation of France, Monique's mother hides a Jewish family in her basement and tries to help them escape to freedom

   "Polacco's use of color has never been more effective. . . . The bold pattern and heightened color of the insect provides a counterpoint to the equally dynamic black-on-red swastikas. Convincing in its portrayal of both the disturbing and humanitarian forces of the time." SLJ

   ★ The **keeping** quilt; rev format ed; Simon & Schuster Bks. for Young Readers 1998 un il $17.95; pa $6.99

Grades: K 1 2 3   **E**

   1. Jews -- Fiction 2. Quilts -- Fiction 3. Emigration and immigration -- Fiction

   ISBN 0-689-82090-9; 0-689-84447-6 pa

                LC 97-47690

   A reissue of the title first published 1988

   A homemade quilt ties together the lives of four generations of an immigrant Jewish family, remaining a symbol of their enduring love and faith

   "Jewish customs and the way they've shifted through the years are portrayed unobtrusively in the story, which is illustrated in sepia pencil, except for the quilt, which sparks every page with its strong colors." Booklist

   ★ The **trees** of the dancing goats. Simon & Schuster Bks. for Young Readers 1996 un il hardcover o.p. pa $6.99

Grades: K 1 2 3   **E**

   1. Jews -- Fiction 2. Hanukkah -- Fiction 3. Christmas -- Fiction

   ISBN 0-689-80862-3; 0-689-83857-3 pa

                LC 95-26670

   "On the family farm in Michigan, Trisha and Richard watch as Babushka and Grampa prepare for Hanukkah in their native Russian way. . . . When scarlet fever debilitates their neighbors, Trisha's whole family pitches in to make and deliver holiday dinners and Christmas trees." Publ Wkly

Polhemus, Coleman

   The **crocodile** blues; [by] Coleman Polhemus. Candlewick Press 2007 un il $16.99

Grades: PreK K   **E**

   1. Stories without words 2. Eggs -- Fiction 3. Crocodiles -- Fiction

   ISBN 978-0-7636-3543-5; 0-7636-3543-X

                LC 2006051848

   A wordless tale in which a man and his pet cockatoo discover, much to their dismay, the true nature of the egg they bring home from the store

   "Youngsters will laugh at both the story line and the characters depicted in this zany book. The simple royal blue and black silhouettes capture the feeling of the dark night, and the bright yellow of the daylight offers a realistic contrast." SLJ

Politi, Leo

   Emmet. Getty Publications 2009 un il $16.95

Grades: PreK K 1 2   **E**

   1. Dogs -- Fiction

   ISBN 978-0-89236-992-8; 0-89236-992-2

   A reissue of the title first published 1971 by Scribner

   Emmet, one of the many stray dogs taken in by old Mr. Winkel, was always the troublemaker of the lot. Mr. Winkel's neighbors are ready to call the dogcatcher when the rascally dog saves the grocer's shop from a fire set by a prowler.

   Juanita. Getty Publications 2009 un il $16.95

Grades: K 1 2 3   **E**

   1. Easter -- Fiction 2. Birthdays -- Fiction 3. Mexican Americans -- Fiction

   ISBN 978-0-89236-991-1; 0-89236-991-4

   A reissue of the title first published 1948 by Scribner

   A Caldecott honor book, 1949

   Juanita, a Mexican girl of Olvera Street in Los Angeles, brings the dove she received for her birthday to the Blessing of the Animals on the day before Easter.

   "The pictures in soft colors have a warmth and tenderness." Horn Book

Pedro, the angel of Olvera Street. Getty Publications 2009 un il $14.96

Grades: K 1 2 3   **E**

1. Christmas -- Fiction 2. Mexican Americans -- Fiction

ISBN 978-0-89236-990-4; 0-89236-990-6

A reissue of the title first published 1946 by Scribner

A Caldecott Medal honor book, 1947

Little Pedro, who sings like an angel, is allowed to lead the Christmas procession, known as La Posada, through the old Mexican section of downtown Los Angeles.

"Beguiling both in text and in the pictures with their soft, rich colors." Bookmark

Song of the swallows. Getty Publications 2009 un il $16.98

Grades: 2 3 4   **E**

1. Missions -- Fiction 2. Swallows -- Fiction

ISBN 978-0-89236-989-8; 0-89236-989-2

A reissue of the title first published 1949 by Scribner

Awarded the Caldecott Medal, 1950

Sad when the swallows leave for the winter, young Juan prepares to welcome them back to the old California Mission at Capistrano on St. Joseph's Day the next spring.

This is a "tender poetic story... Lovely pictures in soft colors bring out the charm of the southern California landscape and the melody of the swallow song adds to the feeling of Spring." Horn Book

Pomerantz, Charlotte

The **chalk** doll; pictures by Frané Lessac. Lippincott 1989 30p il hardcover o.p. pa $6.99

Grades: K 1 2 3   **E**

1. Dolls -- Fiction 2. Mother-daughter relationship -- Fiction

ISBN 0-06-443333-1 pa

LC 88-872

"The stylized illustrations by the West Indian artists Frané Lessac are primitive in bright, oscillating colors, evoking poverty in a tropical paradise as well as mother-daughter affection in a well-appointed home." N Y Times Book Rev

Poole, Amy Lowry

★ The **pea** blossom; retold and illustrated by Amy Poole. Holiday House 2005 un il hardcover o.p. pa $6.95

Grades: K 1 2 3   **E**

1. Authors 2. Novelists 3. Dramatists 4. Fairy tales 5. Children's authors 6. Short story writers

ISBN 0-8234-1864-2; 0-8234-2018-3 pa

LC 2003-67544

In a garden near Beijing, five peas in a shell grow and wait to discover what fate has in store for them.

"Choosing to set her version in Beijing, China, Poole illustrates her simple, elegant prose with watercolors on rice paper that are clearly reminiscent of Chinese paintings." Booklist

Portis, Antoinette

Kindergarten diary; as told to Antoinette Portis by me, Annalina. Harper 2010 un il $12.99; lib bdg $14.89

Grades: PreK K   **E**

1. School stories

ISBN 978-0-06-145691-6; 0-06-145691-8; 978-0-06-145692-3 lib bdg; 0-06-145692-6 lib bdg

"Imaginative, spirited Annalina narrates a month of days in her life, beginning with the day before she starts kindergarten. . . . Realistic and gorgeously patterned collage items outlined in black are mingled with simple paintings to create an explosion of color, shape, and texture. The narrative and illustrations are gently funny and filled with little details and jokes." SLJ

★ **Not** a box. HarperCollins 2007 un il $12.99; lib bdg $14.89

Grades: PreK K   **E**

1. Boxes -- Fiction 2. Rabbits -- Fiction 3. Imagination -- Fiction

ISBN 978-0-06-112322-1; 0-06-112322-6; 978-0-06-112323-8 lib bdg; 0-06-112323-4 lib bdg

LC 2006002477

To an imaginative bunny, a box is not always just a box.

"The spare, streamlined design and the visual messages about imagination's power will easily draw young children, who will recognize their own flights of fantasy." Booklist

★ **Not** a stick. HarperCollinsPublishers 2008 un il $12.99; lib bdg $14.89

Grades: PreK K   **E**

1. Pigs -- Fiction 2. Play -- Fiction 3. Imagination -- Fiction

ISBN 978-0-06-112325-2; 0-06-112325-0; 978-0-06-112326-9 lib bdg; 0-06-112326-9 lib bdg

LC 2007-14475

An imaginative young pig shows some of the many things that a stick can be.

"Portis's simple color palette and playful drawings with never a line out of place represent the best in children's illustration." SLJ

Princess Super Kitty. Harper 2011 il $14.99

Grades: K 1 2   **E**

1. Imagination -- Fiction

ISBN 978-0-06-182725-9; 0-06-182725-8

LC 2010032230

Maggie, a little girl with a huge imagination, becomes a cat, a superhero, a princess, and more in the course of a day.

"This girl is bouncy, delightful and not to be easily typed or contained. Bold lines and solid colors—not overly dominated by pink—surrounded by plenty of empty space keep the focus firmly on the girl and her props. Readers and listeners both bold and retiring will find much to like in this charming depiction of a child with a strong sense of self and confidence in her imaginative makeovers." Kirkus

★ A **penguin** story. HarperCollins 2009 un il $17.99; lib bdg $18.89

Grades: PreK K 1 2   **E**

1. Color -- Fiction 2. Penguins -- Fiction

ISBN 978-0-06-145688-6; 0-06-145688-8; 978-0-06-145689-3 lib bdg; 0-06-145689-6 lib bdg

LC 2008020210

Edna the penguin tries to find something in her surroundings that is not black, white, or blue.

"This gentle tribute to dreamers crackles with quiet humor, and the art's limited palette both parallels the plot and lends the book a classic feel. Portis's ability to convey emotion and character through the slightest change in Edna's beady eyes and flippers is extraordinary, and the interplay of the text and pictures nears perfection. A delightful story, delightfully told." SLJ

Portnoy, Mindy Avra

Tale of two Seders; illustrated by Valeria Cis. Kar-Ben Pub. 2010 32p il lib bdg $17.95; pa $7.95

Grades: PreK K 1 2   E

1. Jews -- Fiction 2. Divorce -- Fiction 3. Passover -- Fiction 4. Family life -- Fiction

ISBN 978-0-8225-9907-4; 0-8225-9907-4; 978-0-8225-9931-9 pa; 0-8225-9931-7 pa

LC 2008033570

After her parents' divorce, a young girl experiences a variety of Passover seders. Includes recipes and facts about Passover.

"Cis's delightful acrylic paintings beautifully complement the text. . . . [This is a] realistic, contemporary story." SLJ

Potter, Beatrix

The story of Miss Moppet. Warne 2002 32p il $6.99

Grades: PreK K 1 2 3   E

1. Cats -- Fiction 2. Mice -- Fiction

ISBN 0-7232-4790-0

First published 1906

Miss Moppet is a kitten who uses her wiles to capture a curious mouse. But her trickery amounts to naught when she herself is outwitted

Other titles about Moppet's brother Tom and sister Mittens are:

The complete adventures of Tom Kitten and his friends (1984)

The roly-poly pudding (1908)

The tale of Tom Kitten (1935)

★ The tailor of Gloucester. Warne 2002 56p il $6.99

Grades: PreK K 1 2 3   E

1. Mice -- Fiction 2. Christmas -- Fiction 3. Tailoring -- Fiction

ISBN 0-7232-4772-2

First published in 1903

"A read-aloud classic in polished style, perfectly complemented by the author's exquisite watercolor illustrations." Hodges. Books for Elem Sch Libr

★ The tale of Jemima Puddle-duck. Warne 2002 56p il $6.99; bd bk $6.99

Grades: PreK K 1 2 3   E

1. Ducks -- Fiction

ISBN 0-7232-4778-1; 0-7232-6434-1 bd bk

First published 1908

"Jemima Puddle-duck's obstinate determination to hatch her own eggs, makes a story of suspense and sly humor." Toronto Public Libr. Books for Boys & Girls

★ The tale of Mr. Jeremy Fisher. Warne 2002 56p il $6.99

Grades: PreK K 1 2 3   E

1. Frogs -- Fiction

ISBN 0-7232-4776-5

First published 1906

A frog fishing from his lilly pad boat doesn't catch any fish, but one catches him

★ The tale of Mrs. Tiggy-Winkle. Warne 2002 56p il $6.99

Grades: PreK K 1 2 3   E

1. Hedgehogs -- Fiction

ISBN 0-7232-4775-7

First published 1905

Lucie visits the laundry of Mrs. Tiggy-Winkle, a hedgehog, and finds her lost handerchiefs

The tale of Mrs. Tittlemouse. Warne 2002 56p il $6.99

Grades: PreK K 1 2 3   E

1. Mice -- Fiction

ISBN 0-7232-3470-1

First published 1910

The story of a little mouse's funny house, the visitors she has there, and how she finally rids herself of the untidy, messy ones

★ The tale of Peter Rabbit. Warne 2002 69p il $6.99

Grades: PreK K 1 2 3   E

1. Rabbits -- Fiction

ISBN 0-7232-4770-6

First published 1903

All about the famous rabbit family consisting of Flopsy, Mopsy, Cotton-tail and especially Peter Rabbit who disobeys Mother Rabbit's admonishment not to go into Mr. McGregor's garden

"Distinctive writing and a strong appeal to a small child's sense of justice and his sympathies make this an outstanding story. The water color illustrations add charm to the narrative by their simplicity of detail and delicacy of color." Child Books Too Good to Miss

Other titles about Peter Rabbit and his family are:

The tale of Benjamin Bunny (1904)

The tale of Mr. Tod (1912)

The tale of the flopsy bunnies (1909)

★ The tale of Pigling Bland. Warne 2002 80p il $6.99

Grades: PreK K 1 2 3   E

1. Pigs -- Fiction

ISBN 0-7232-4784-6

First published 1913

"Pigling's story ends happily with a perfectly lovely little black Berkshire pig called Pigwig." Toronto Public Libr. Books for Boys & Girls

★ The tale of Squirrel Nutkin. Warne 2002 56p il $6.99

Grades: PreK K 1 2 3   E

1. Squirrels -- Fiction

ISBN 0-7232-4771-4

First published 1903

Each day the squirrels gather nuts, Nutkin propounds a riddle to Mr. Brown, the owl, until impertinent Nutkin, overestimating Mr. Brown's patience, gets his due

★ The tale of Timmy Tiptoes. Warne 2002 56p il $6.99

Grades: PreK K 1 2 3 **E**
1. Squirrels -- Fiction
ISBN 0-7232-4781-1
First published 1911

An innocent squirrel accused of stealing nuts is forced down a hole in a tree, where he meets a friendly chipmunk

★ The **tale** of two bad mice. Warne 2002 56p il $6.99

Grades: PreK K 1 2 3 **E**
1. Mice -- Fiction
ISBN 0-7232-4774-9
First published 1904

"Two mischievous little mice pilfer a doll's house to equip their own. They are caught and finally make amends for what they have done. Perfectly charming illustrations and a most enticing tale." Adventuring With Books. 2d edition

Pow, Tom
Tell me one thing, Dad; illustrated by Ian Andrew. Candlewick Press 2004 un il $15.99

Grades: PreK K 1 2 3 **E**
1. Bedtime 2. Bedtime -- Fiction 3. Fathers and daughters 4. Father-daughter relationship -- Fiction
ISBN 0-7636-2474-8

LC 2003-65272

Molly and her father play a bedtime game that shows how much they love each other

"The sharp yet simple text avoids the obvious, going for interesting images. . . . The watercolor-and-ink artwork . . . brims with whimsy in both design and execution." Booklist

Poydar, Nancy
Fish school. Holiday House 2009 un il $16.95

Grades: PreK K 1 2 **E**
1. School stories 2. Goldfish -- Fiction 3. Marine aquariums -- Fiction
ISBN 978-0-8234-2140-4; 0-8234-2140-6

LC 2008022576

Charlie tries to educate his pet goldfish by taking him to school and to the aquarium on a class trip. Includes tips on the care and feeding of goldfish.

"Filled with lively and amusing details, this is a good choice for one-on-one or independent reading." SLJ

No fair science fair. Holiday House 2011 32p il $14.95

Grades: K 1 2 **E**
1. School stories 2. Birds -- Fiction 3. Science projects -- Fiction
ISBN 978-0-8234-2269-2; 0-8234-2269-0

LC 2010023224

As the judging of his class's science fair approaches, Otis has trouble even thinking of an idea but once he has built a bird feeder he is determined to make some good observations, no matter how long it takes.

"A great book for sharing with classes on many levels, this is both a good primer for science fairs and for skills such as being a good friend, appreciating differences and persistence." Kirkus

★ The **biggest** test in the universe. Holiday House 2005 un il $16.95

Grades: K 1 2 3 **E**
1. School stories 2. Examinations -- Fiction
ISBN 0-8234-1944-4

Sam and his classmates dread Friday, the day they are to take the infamous Big Test.

"Enlivened by colorful and humorous illustrations depicting the students' worries, this book is fun and cheerful, as well as unique in its subject." SLJ

Preller, James
Mighty Casey; by James Preller; illustrated by Matthew Cordell. Feiwel and Friends 2008 un il $16.95

Grades: K 1 2 3 **E**
1. Stories in rhyme 2. Baseball -- Fiction
ISBN 978-0-312-36764-0; 0-312-36764-3

LC 2007-47331

The Delmar Dogs baseball team is terrible, especially Casey Jenkins, but with a little bit of faith in themselves, they finally manage to win a game.

"Set against ample white space, Cordell's endearingly geeky kids take center stage. . . . It's hard to envision a reader who won't take to these underdogs." Publ Wkly

★ A **pirate's** guide to first grade; illustrated by Greg Ruth. Feiwel and Friends 2010 un il $16.99

Grades: PreK K 1 **E**
1. School stories 2. Pirates -- Fiction 3. Imagination -- Fiction
ISBN 978-0-312-36928-6; 0-312-36928-X

"Throughout his first day of first grade, a young boy describes his everyday actions in briny pirate terms, from breakfasting on grub in the galley to meeting Cap'n Silver (his new teacher) and walking the plank (seesaw) at recess. Each sharply rendered, full-color scene shows a crew of imagined pirates, differentiated in gray-toned drawings, who follow the boy and provide friendly company throughout the day. Young would-be buccaneers facing their own first-day jitters will enjoy this droll title." Booklist

Prelutsky, Jack
★ The **wizard**; by Jack Prelutsky; illustrations by Brandon Dorman. Greenwillow Books 2007 un il $16.99; lib bdg $17.89

Grades: K 1 2 3 **E**
1. Stories in rhyme 2. Magic -- Fiction
ISBN 978-0-06-124076-8; 978-0-06-124077-5 lib bdg

The verse originally appeared in the 1976 collection Nightmares: Poems to Trouble Your Sleep

An illustrated, rhyming tale of a wicked wizard and his evil deeds, as he uses "elemental sorcery" to change a bullfrog into a series of objects, from a flea to a flame.

"The illustrator's digital artwork has all the burnished lushness and radiance of oil paintings. . . . Dorman proves his mettle as a marvelous visual storyteller." Publ Wkly

Preus, Margi
The **Peace** Bell; illustrated by Hideko Takahashi. Henry Holt and Co. 2008 un il $16.95

Grades: K 1 2 3 **E**
1. Bells -- Fiction 2. Peace -- Fiction 3. New Year -- Fiction 4. Friendship -- Fiction 5. Grandmothers -- Fiction
ISBN 978-0-8050-7800-8; 0-8050-7800-2

LC 2007040897

Yoko's grandmother tells about how the bell in their town that would ring on New Year's Eve is given up during the war for scrap metal, finds its way back to their village, and becomes known as the Peace Bell.

"The simple plot is clearly developed with descriptive language, and an author's note provides more historical details. Done in Japanese acrylic paints, the realistic illustrations accurately portray the setting and capture the characters' various emotions." SLJ

Prevert, Jacques
★ **How** to paint the portrait of a bird; translated and illustrated by Mordicai Gerstein. Roaring Brook 2007 un il $14.95
Grades: K 1 2 3   E
1. Children's poetry 2. Birds -- Fiction
ISBN 1-59643-215-2; 978-1-59643-215-4
LC 2006-32183

"This petite, elegant picture book . . . delivers a mind-stretching allegory of artistic creation. First, a wordless sequence shows a mopheaded boy awakening to a bluebird's trill. Palette in hand, he follows a peculiar series of instructions for capturing its likeness: paint a cage; lure the bird into it; . . . erase the cage, replacing it with a forest; then see if the bird will sing. It's a delight to see how Gerstein's scribbly lines and loose washes cohere into playful, accessible images." Booklist

Priceman, Marjorie
★ **Hot** air; the (mostly) true story of the first hot-air balloon ride. Atheneum Books for Young Readers 2005 un il $16.95
Grades: K 1 2 3   E
1. Balloons
ISBN 0-689-82642-7
LC 2004-14743

A Caldecott Medal honor book, 2006
"With vibrant colors and varied use of panels, full-page illustrations, and spreads, Priceman paces the tale perfectly." SLJ

How to make a cherry pie and see the U.S.A. Alfred A. Knopf 2008 un il $16.99; lib bdg $19.99
Grades: PreK K 1 2   E
1. Baking -- Fiction 2. Voyages and travels -- Fiction 3. Manufactures -- Juvenile literature 4. Kitchen utensils -- Juvenile literature
ISBN 978-0-375-81255-2; 0-375-81255-5; 978-0-375-91255-9 lib bdg; 0-375-91255-X lib bdg
LC 2007-46064

Since the Cook Shop is closed, the reader is led around the United States to gather coal, cotton, granite, and other natural resources needed to make the utensils for preparing a cherry pie

"The trip is a madcap adventure. . . . The art brims with good cheer and excites with detail." Booklist

★ **How** to make an apple pie and see the world. Knopf 1994 un il $16; pa $6.99
Grades: PreK K 1 2   E
1. Baking -- Fiction 2. Voyages and travels -- Fiction
ISBN 0-679-83705-1; 0-679-88083-6 pa
LC 93-12341

Since the market is closed, the reader is led around the world to gather the ingredients for making an apple pie

"The perfect blend of whimsical illustrations and tongue-in-cheek humor makes this an irresistable offering. The recipe is included." Child Book Rev Serv

Prigger, Mary Skillings
Aunt Minnie McGranahan; illustrated by Betsy Lewin. Clarion Bks. 1999 31p il $15; pa $5.95
Grades: K 1 2 3   E
1. Aunts -- Fiction 2. Orphans -- Fiction 3. Orderliness -- Fiction
ISBN 0-395-82270-X; 0-618-60488-X pa
LC 98-33501

The townspeople in St. Clere, Kansas, are sure it will never work out when the neat and orderly spinster, Minnie McGranahan, takes her nine orphaned nieces and nephews into her home in 1920

"In a dexterous style, Prigger employs repetitive elements to establish and maintain a spry tempo in clipped, spruce sentences. . . . The black outlines of Lewin's . . . witty, loose watercolors punctuate the pages in a flurry of scribbles, suggesting the kind of bursting-at-the-seams activity." Publ Wkly

Another title about Aunt Minnie is:
Aunt Minnie and the twister (2002)

Primavera, Elise
Louise the big cheese and the Ooh-la-la Charm School; Elise Primavera; illustrated by Diane Goode. Simon & Schuster Books for Young Readers 2012 40 p.
Grades: PreK K 1 2   E
1. Etiquette -- Fiction 2. Popularity -- Fiction 3. Picture books for children 4. Female friendship -- Fiction 5. Friendship -- Fiction
ISBN 1442405996; 9781442405998
LC 2009047236

This picture book tells the story of "Louise, the little girl with big ideas about getting noticed. . . . A new kid, Claire Eclaire, takes Louise under her wing and shows her how life is lived in Paris. . . . When it becomes clear that Claire is from Paris, Maine, Louise not only knows she's been duped but regrets her treatment of best-friend Fern." (Booklist) ". . . Louise has high hopes of improving her status that don't quite work out as planned. . . . [T]here's also a villain of sorts who leads her astray: snooty Claire . . . [who] uses the promise of "charm school" lessons to coerce Louise into doing her chores and letting her win at games. In the process, Louise . . . embarrasses herself in front of family and friends as usual." (Kirkus)

Louise the big cheese and the back-to-school smarty-pants. Simon & Schuster 2011 il $16.99
Grades: PreK K 1 2   E
1. School stories
ISBN 978-1-4424-0600-1; 1-4424-0600-3

Louise the Big Cheese is determined to make the grade in school this year and that means straight As. But she's stuck with the toughest teacher ever.

"Watercolor and black-line illustrations energetically depict the irrepressible Louise and [a] host of supporting characters." SLJ

Louise the big cheese: divine diva; illustrated by Diane Goode. Simon & Schuster Books for Young Readers 2009 un il $16.99
Grades: PreK K 1 2   E
  1. Theater -- Fiction 2. Friendship -- Fiction
ISBN 978-1-4169-7180-1; 1-4169-7180-7
           LC 2008-23608
When she learns her class will be doing a play, little Louise Cheese has big dreams of being the star, but when her best friend is given the lead she learns that even the small roles count

"Primavera's breezy story . . . and Goode's distinctive artwork intermingle wonderfully. In both story and art, Louise makes a splash. . . . Goode is at her best here." Booklist

Other titles about Louise are:
  Louise the big cheese and the la-di-da shoes (2009)
  Louise the big cheese and the back-to-school smarty-pants (2011)

Prince, April Jones
  ★ **Twenty**-one elephants and still standing; written by April Jones Prince; illustrated by Francois Roca. Houghton Mifflin 2005 un il $16
Grades: K 1 2 3 4   E
  1. Circus executives 2. Elephants -- Fiction
ISBN 0-618-44887-X
           LC 2004-05229
Upon completion of the Brooklyn Bridge, P.T. Barnum and his twenty-one elephants parade across to prove to everyone that the bridge is safe.

A "well-researched, handsomely illustrated picture book. . . . The sparse, yet powerful text contains both alliteration and occasional rhyme, making it a pleasure for readers and listeners alike. Roca's masterful paintings capture both the spirit of the times and of the expansive bridge." SLJ

Pritchett, Dylan
  ★ The **first** music; as told by Dylan Pritchett; illustrated by Erin Bennett Banks. August House Little Folk 2006 un il $16.95
Grades: PreK K 1 2   E
  1. Music -- Fiction 2. Animals -- Fiction
ISBN 0-87483-776-6
A series of accidents in the jungle proves that everyone has something special to add when it comes to making music.

"Fresh and intriguing, this African cumulative tale of the origin of music unfolds in a vibrant storyteller's voice. . . . The message (everyone has something to add to the mix) is subtle, but clear enough for children to understand. However, it's the stylized, earth-toned illustrations, resembling carved wooden figures, that really rock and roll, evoking the synergy of the forest animals." Booklist

Prochovnic, Dawn Babb
  Hip hip hooray! it's Family Day! sign language for family. by Dawn Babb Prochovnic; illustrated by Stephanie Bauer. ABDO/Magic Wagon 2012 32 p. col. ill. $28.50
Grades: K 1 2   E
  1. Family 2. Counting 3. Sign language 4. Stories in rhyme 5. Sign Language 6. Families -- Fiction 7. Families -- Juvenile fiction 8. Parent and child -- Juvenile fiction 9. American Sign Language -- Juvenile

fiction
ISBN 1616418370; 9781616418373
           LC 2011027065
Author Dawn Babb Prochovnic "invites readers to chant along and learn American Sign Language signs for the members of a family including grandma, grandpa, cousins, siblings, and pets. . . . [The] literacy-based, finger-play [teaches signing for children]. . . . [Included are] illustrated handshapes for the alphabet, numbers 1-10, and signs from the stories." (Publisher's note)
  Includes bibliographical references (p. 32).

Proimos, James
  Patricia von Pleasantsquirrel. Dial Books for Young Readers 2009 un il $15.99
Grades: K 1 2   E
  1. Princesses -- Fiction
ISBN 978-0-8037-3066-3; 0-8037-3066-7
           LC 2008015776
After failing to convince her parents that she is a princess, Patricia von Pleasantsquirrel leaves her moatless house in search of a "princessdom."

"Proimos's story plays 'cheeky homage' to Sendak and Max, but the bold-lined, cartoon-style illustrations and Patricia's postmodern sassiness also owe a debt to James Marshall, calling to mind his bossy Goldilocks." SLJ

  Paulie Pastrami achieves world peace. Little Brown Books for Young Readers 2009 un il $15.99
Grades: K 1 2 3   E
  1. Peace -- Fiction 2. Kindness -- Fiction 3. Conduct of life -- Fiction
ISBN 978-0-316-03292-6; 0-316-03292-1
           LC 2008043800
Seven-year-old Paulie, an ordinary boy, brings peace to his home and school through small acts of kindness, but needs help to achieve his goal of world peace

"The peppy, colorful cartoon art incorporates witty, sometimes hyperbolic details. . . . The positive story conveys how small, individual actions can have a large, ripple effect." Booklist

  Swim! swim! [by Lerch; illustrations by James Proimos] Scholastic Inc. 2010 un il $16.99
Grades: PreK   E
  1. Fishes -- Fiction
ISBN 978-0-545-09419-1; 0-545-09419-4
"Lerch the goldfish wants a friend, which is difficult since he's the only fish in his tank. . . . Just when he thinks he's as lonely as a fish can be . . . a cat arrives outside the tank and talks to Lerch. But, uh-oh, he calls him Lunch. . . . Though Lerch gets the credit for this picture book, James Proimos is responsible for the art and story. He uses the comic-book format, with panels and word balloons, to great effect here. . . . The bright colors and clear art match the simple story." Booklist

  Todd's TV. Katherine Tegen Books 2010 un il $15.99
Grades: PreK K 1 2   E
  1. Parents -- Fiction 2. Television -- Fiction
ISBN 978-0-06-170985-2; 0-06-170985-9
           LC 2009-18507
When Todd's parents are too busy to take care of him, his television steps in to handle the parenting.

"With broad strokes and witty slapdashery, Proimos's light cartoon art and plotline carry some weighty themes. . . . Amusing cartoon drawings in shades of gray, black, and persimmony-red against a white background and a satiric twist at the story's end further enhance this funny-scary cautionary tale." SLJ

The **best** bike ride ever; James Proimos; [pictures by] Johanna Wright. Dial Books for Young Readers 2012 32 p. col. ill. (hardcover) $16.99

Grades: PreK K 1   E
1. Bicycles -- Fiction 2. Imagination -- Fiction 3. Humorous stories 4. Bicycles and bicycling -- Fiction
ISBN 0803738501; 9780803738508

LC 2011035449

In this children's picture book by James Proimos, "Bonnie O'Boy is so excited about her new pink polka-dotted bike that she hops on without asking how to use the brakes. As a result, she goes 'all willy-nilly. In fact, she had willy-nillied herself right down the hill.' From there, it's a long, strange trip, one that includes riding up to the top of the Statue of Liberty, down to the bottom of the Grand Canyon, and through a scene straight out of Jurassic Park." (Publishers Weekly)

Prokofiev, Sergey
   Peter and the wolf; translated by Maria Carlson; illustrated by Charles Mikolaycak. Viking 1982 un il hardcover o.p. pa $5.99

Grades: K 1 2 3 4   E
1. Fairy tales 2. Wolves -- Fiction
ISBN 0-14-050633-0 pa

LC 81-70402

This book retells the orchestral fairy tale of the boy who, ignoring his grandfather's warnings, proceeds to capture a wolf

"Prokofiev's classic, designed to teach children the instruments of an orchestra, has been published in picture book form before, but never better illustrated. The translation is smooth. . . . The paintings are rich in color, dramatic in details of costume or architecture, strong in composition, with distinctive individuality in the faces of people and of the wolf." Bull Cent Child Books

Prosek, James
   ★ **Bird,** butterfly, eel; story and paintings by James Prosek. Simon & Schuster Books for Young Readers 2009 un il map $16.99

Grades: K 1 2 3   E
1. Eels -- Fiction 2. Birds -- Fiction 3. Butterflies -- Fiction 4. Eels -- Juvenile literature 5. Birds -- Juvenile literature 6. Monarch butterfly -- Juvenile literature
ISBN 978-0-689-86829-0; 0-689-86829-4

LC 2007-15734

Follows a bird, a monarch butterfly, and an eel from summer on a farm until they make their respective fall voyages south, and then later begin to return north again when the weather warms.

"A well-designed and useful resource to pique curiosity about an amazing aspect of the lives of many animals." SLJ

   A **good** day's fishing. Simon & Schuster Bks. for Young Readers 2004 un il $15.95

Grades: 1 2 3 4   E
1. Fishing -- Fiction
ISBN 0-689-85327-0

LC 2003-7383

A child searches through the hooks, lures, bobbers, and other paraphernalia in his tacklebox for the one thing he needs to ensure a good day's fishing. Includes a detailed glossary

"A beautifully illustrated, simple story. . . . Young fishing enthusiasts will certainly learn more about which tackle works best to catch particular kinds of fish, while the wonderfully detailed, gentle watercolor illustrations of fish and gear offer a lovely introduction." Booklist

Protopopescu, Orel
   Thelonious Mouse; [by] Orel Protopopescu; pictures by Anne Wilsdorf. Farrar Straus Giroux 2011 un il $16.99

Grades: PreK K 1   E
1. Cats -- Fiction 2. Mice -- Fiction
ISBN 978-0-374-37447-1; 0-374-37447-3

Thelonious is a hipster mouse who cannot keep himself from taunting the cat of the house, but once Thelonious discovers a toy piano, he and the cat make some beautiful music together.

"Plenty of action and droll interior details to spy should capture kids' fancy, while grown-ups trying this as a read-aloud might need to pause to untangle their tongues. . . . Replete with scat-y, cat-and-mouse-y wordplay, this is giggle-worthy fun." Kirkus

Provensen, Alice
   ★ A **day** in the life of Murphy. Simon & Schuster Bks. for Young Readers 2003 un il $16.95; pa $6.99

Grades: PreK K 1 2 3   E
1. Dogs -- Fiction 2. Farm life -- Fiction 3. Terriers -- Juvenile fiction
ISBN 0-689-84884-6; 1-4169-1800-0 pa

LC 2002-4309

Murphy, a farm terrier, describes a day in his life as he gets fed in the kitchen, hunts mice, goes to the vet, returns to the house for dinner, investigates a noise outside, and retires to the barn for sleep

"With charming, lively illustrations and peppy, descriptive prose, Provensen portrays the smells, sounds, and activities of a delightful, active pup." Booklist

Pullen, Zachary
   ★ **Friday** my Radio Flyer flew; [by] Zachary Pullen. Simon & Schuster Books for Young Readers 2008 un il $16.99 E

1. Days -- Fiction 2. Flight -- Fiction 3. Imagination -- Fiction 4. Father-son relationship -- Fiction
ISBN 978-1-4169-3983-2; 1-4169-3983-0

LC 2007041852

A father and son find an old Radio Flyer wagon when cleaning out the attic and, through the course of a week, turn it back into a wonderful toy

"Subtle alliteration moves the story through the week. . . . Full-color spreads are oversize and beautifully done in oil paints. . . . The final spread . . . is take-your-breath-away wonderful. This is a strong first purchase, affirming the bond between boys and their fathers as well as the power of imagination." SLJ

Pulver, Robin

Christmas kitten; home at last. illustrated by Layne Johnson. Albert Whitman 2010 un il $16.99

Grades: PreK K 1 2   **E**

1. Cats -- Fiction 2. Christmas -- Fiction 3. Santa Claus -- Fiction

ISBN 978-0-8075-1157-2; 0-8075-1157-9

When Santa's allergies prevent him from keeping a homeless kitten, he and Mrs. Claus find it a perfect home.

"Johnson's oil paintings are rich with detail and expression, giving life to Cookie and all the North Pole denizens. The artist's careful attention to light and shadow, along with the use of bold primary colors, gives the book a perfect blend of warmth and exuberance. This is a sweet, fun read-aloud." SLJ

Happy endings; a story about suffixes. illustrated by Lynn Rowe Reed. Holiday House 2011 un il $16.95

Grades: 2 3 4   **E**

1. School stories 2. English language -- Fiction 3. English language -- Juvenile literature

ISBN 978-0-8234-2296-8; 0-8234-2296-8

LC 2010024066

When Mr. Wright makes his students study word endings on the last day of school, even the suffixes rebel.

"Reed's sunny acrylics keep the story light and humorous. . . . Grammar will be a lot less boring with a library of Ms. Pulver's books at hand." Horn Book

Never say boo! Holiday House 2009 un il $16.95

Grades: PreK K 1 2   **E**

1. Ghost stories 2. School stories

ISBN 978-0-8234-2110-7; 0-8234-2110-4

LC 2008022609

When Gordon, a ghost, moves to a new school, everyone is afraid of him until they learn that he is not as scary as they thought he was.

"In Lucke's creepy and comical gouache illustrations, Gordon's bulging eyes and pasty white skull stand out on the mostly black background and are in contrast to his orange-yellow striped shirt and human classmates. Add in Pulver's straightforward dialogue and you have an amusing read-aloud." SLJ

Nouns and verbs have a field day; illustrated by Lynn Rowe Reed. Holiday House 2006 un il $16.95; pa $6.95

Grades: 2 3 4   **E**

1. School stories 2. English language -- Fiction

ISBN 0-8234-1982-7; 0-8234-2097-3 pa; 978-0-8234-1982-1; 978-0-8234-2097-1 pa

LC 2005-46207

When the children in Mr. Wright's class have a field day, nouns and verbs in the classroom make their own fun. "Primary." (Horn Book)

"The nouns and verbs decide to have some fun of their own while the kids in Mr. Wright's class are away participating in a field day. The nouns pair up with other nouns and the verbs with other verbs, until they realize they must cooperate. . . . Reed's vividly colored cartoons capture the high-energy activity. . . . Although the emphasis is on silliness, Pulver makes her point about the parts of speech; even

the youngest listeners will realize that sentences need both nouns and verbs in order to make sense." Booklist

Punctuation takes a vacation; illustrated by Lynn Rowe Reed. Holiday House 2003 un il $16.95; pa $6.95

Grades: 2 3 4   **E**

1. School stories 2. Punctuation -- Fiction

ISBN 0-8234-1687-9; 0-8234-1820-0 pa

LC 2002-68915

When all the punctuation marks in Mr. Wright's class decide to take a vacation, the students discover just how difficult life can be without them

"Pulver's clever story moves along at a nice clip and makes its point without belaboring the matter. Reed's acrylics-on-canvas illustrations are rich in color and texture, and add to the amusement of the story." SLJ

Other titles in the author's series about Mr. Wright's class are:

Nouns and verbs have a field day (2006)

Silent letters loud and clear (2008)

Happy endings (2011)

Silent letters loud and clear; written by Robin Pulver; illustrated by Lynn Rowe Reed. Holiday House 2008 un il $16.95

Grades: 2 3 4   **E**

1. School stories 2. English language -- Fiction

ISBN 0-8234-2127-9; 978-0-8234-2127-5

LC 2007016057

When Mr. Wright's students express a dislike for silent letters, the offended letters decide to teach them a lesson by going on strike.

"Mr Wright's uncertain fate (happily resolved) adds a dose of drama to the absurd situation. The playful design points up the silent letters within the text, and the faux-naive mixed-media illustrations give both human and letter characters lots of personality." Horn Book

Thank you, Miss Doover; illustrated by Stephanie Roth Sisson. Holiday House 2010 un il $16.95

Grades: K 1 2 3   **E**

1. School stories 2. Letters -- Fiction 3. Teachers -- Fiction 4. Authorship -- Fiction

ISBN 978-0-8234-2046-9; 0-8234-2046-9

Jack learns the value of revision as he practices Miss Doover's lesson on how to write a proper thank-you note.

"Pulver's characterization of the elementary schoolers' thought processes and lack of tact is spot-on. Sisson's colored pencil-and-acrylic illustrations go hand-in-hand with the funny text." Kirkus

Purmell, Ann

Apple cider making days; illustrated by Joanne Friar. Millbrook Press 2002 un il lib bdg $21.90

Grades: K 1 2 3   **E**

1. Apples 2. Farm life 3. Apples -- Fiction 4. Apples -- Harvesting

ISBN 0-7613-2364-3

LC 2001-44920

Alex and Abigail join the whole family in processing and selling apples and apple cider at their grandfather's farm

"The comfortable, colorful art brings little ones up close to the process and gives them a good look at the conveyor belts and presses and other machinery involved. . . . A double-page spread, 'Cider Lore,' following the story, provides wonderful tidbits about the cider-making process. An excellent resource for autumn units or to use in preparation for a trip to the orchard." Booklist

Christmas tree farm; by Ann Purmell; illustrated by Jill Weber. Holiday House 2006 un il $16.95
Grades: K 1 2 3   E
1. Farm life -- Fiction 2. Family life -- Fiction 3. Grandfathers -- Fiction 4. Christmas tree growing -- Fiction
ISBN 978-0-8234-1886-2; 0-8234-1886-3
LC 2004-47502
A boy describes how he, his grandfather, and the rest of his family work on their tree farm throughout the year to prepare Christmas trees

"Purmell packs the friendly story with plenty of information. . . . The text makes the book interesting; the art gives it charm. The simply drawn, sometimes diminutive characters exude warmth and exemplify the work that goes into any kind of farming." Booklist

Maple syrup season; by Ann Purmell; illustrated by Jill Weber. Holiday House 2008 un il $16.95
Grades: K 1 2 3   E
1. Family life -- Fiction 2. Maple sugar -- Fiction 3. Grandfathers -- Fiction
ISBN 978-0-8234-1891-6; 0-8234-1891-X
LC 2006-03455
Grandpa leads the way as his family works together to tap maple trees, collect sap, and make syrup.

"This gentle story has a straightforward text and folksy, colorful gouache illustrations. . . . A glossary and two pages of maple syrup lore are appended. This book would be a great addition to units on seasons, farms, or plants and trees." SLJ

Puttock, Simon
Little lost cowboy; illustrated by Caroline Jayne Church. Egmont USA 2011 un il $16.99
Grades: PreK K 1 2   E
1. Coyotes -- Fiction
ISBN 978-1-60684-259-1; 1-60684-259-5
LC 2010050495
A kindly toad helps a "lonesome and lost" young coyote find his mother.

"The repetitive text is accessible and child-friendly, and the desert setting is skillfully evoked with warm, earth-toned illustrations created from beautifully textured handmade paper, finished with bold black lines." SLJ

Pym, Tasha
★ **Have** you ever seen a sneep? pictures by Joel Stewart. Farrar, Straus and Giroux 2009 un il $16.95
Grades: PreK K 1 2   E
1. Stories in rhyme 2. Monsters -- Fiction
ISBN 978-0-374-32868-9; 0-374-32868-4
LC 2008042985
"In rhyming text, a boy relates a woeful tale of trying to have fun but being plagued by monsters that ruin his every pleasure. Each encounter begins with the child asking readers if they've experienced a similar situation. . . . The pleasing and unexpected conclusion is sure to be met with a smile. The muted, almost fuzzy-looking illustrations feature

the small barefoot and straw-hatted boy. . . . The artwork alternates between full-color washes that cover the pages completely and spreads that isolate the boy against expanses of white space. Perfectly paced and quietly dramatic." SLJ

Qiong, Yu Li
★ A **New** Year's reunion. Candlewick Press 2011 un il $15.99
Grades: PreK K 1 2   E
1. Fathers -- Fiction 2. Family life -- Fiction 3. Chinese New Year -- Fiction
ISBN 978-0-7636-5881-6; 0-7636-5881-2
First published 2008 in Taipei
"Two things make this Chinese New Year story remarkable—Zhu's meticulously observed gouaches and the family's poignant backstory." Publ Wkly

Quackenbush, Robert M.
First grade jitters; written by Robert Quackenbush; illustrated by Yan Nascimbene. Harper 2010 un il $16.99
Grades: PreK K   E
1. School stories 2. Worry -- Fiction
ISBN 978-0-06-077632-9; 0-06-077632-3
LC 2009007290
A newly illustrated edition of the title first published 1982
Aidan is about to enter first grade and doesn't know quite what to expect. Will his friends be there? Will he have to know how to read and spell? What if he can't understand anything his teacher says?

"The text and pictures explore this common anxiety effectively and with a touch of humor." SLJ

Quattlebaum, Mary
Jo MacDonald saw a pond; by Mary Quattlebaum; illustrated by Laura J. Bryant. Dawn Publications 2011 il $16.95; pa $8.95
Grades: PreK K 1   E
1. Pond ecology -- Fiction 2. Folk songs -- United States
ISBN 978-1-58469-150-1; 1-58469-150-6; 978-1-58469-151-8 pa; 1-58469-151-4 pa
LC 2011011700
In this version of the classic song 'Old MacDonald Had a Farm,' the farmer's granddaughter discovers the creatures living at a pond. End notes present facts, outdoor activities, and games related to this lively ecosystem.

"The familiar tune starts on page one and never misses a beat, begging kids to participate. . . . Observant readers will notice the clever design of the illustrations that hides the last-mentioned animal and the next one within the spread. Bryant's softly colored watercolor creatures echo Jo's rosy-cheeked childhood innocence and have just a touch of expression in their faces." Kirkus
Includes bibliographical references

Pirate vs. pirate; the terrific tale of a big, blustery maritime match. written by Mary Quattlebaum; illustrated by Alexandra Boiger. Disney Hyperion Books 2011 un il $16.99
Grades: PreK K 1   E
1. Pirates -- Fiction
ISBN 978-1-4231-2201-2; 1-4231-2201-1

"Quattlebaum litters the pages with robust buccaneer lingo. . . . Boiger expertly blends droll humor with dramatic seascapes and detailed ship settings." SLJ

The **hungry** ghost of Rue Orleans; illustrated by Patricia Castelao. Random House 2011 un il $15.99; lib bdg $18.99

Grades: PreK K 1 2   **E**
1. Ghost stories 2. Restaurants -- Fiction
ISBN 978-0-375-86207-6; 0-375-86207-2; 978-0-375-96207-3 lib bdg; 0-375-96207-7 lib bdg
LC 2010037063

Fred the ghost is perfectly happy haunting his ramshackle New Orleans house until Pierre and his daughter Marie move in and turn the house into a restaurant.

"Castelao's illustrations have an ethereal, quirky quality that complements the story, and the details she includes help anchor its New Orleans setting." Kirkus

Quay, Emma

Good night, sleep tight; a book about bedtime. [illustrated by] Anna Walker. Board book ed.; Dial books for Young Readers 2011 un il (Hello friends!) bd bk $5.99

Grades: PreK   **E**
1. Board books for children 2. Owls -- Fiction 3. Sheep -- Fiction 4. Bedtime -- Fiction 5. Camping -- Fiction 6. Giant panda -- Fiction
ISBN 978-0-8037-3581-1; 0-8037-3581-2
LC 2010020620

First published 2010 in Australia

When Panda, Owl, and Sheep go camping, they find that only one has a comfortable sleeping bag.

Let's play house; a book about imagination. [illustrated by] Anna Walker. Board book ed.; Dial Books for Young Readers 2011 un il (Hello friends!) bd bk $5.99

Grades: PreK   **E**
1. Board books for children 2. Owls -- Fiction 3. Play -- Fiction 4. Sheep -- Fiction 5. Giant panda -- Fiction 6. Imagination -- Fiction
ISBN 978-0-8037-3569-9; 0-8037-3569-3
LC 2010020617

First published 2009 in Australia

When their playhouse turns out to be too small, Panda, Owl, and Sheep think of a different game to play.

Puddle jumping; a book about bravery. [illustrated by] Anna Walker. Board book ed.; Dial Books for Young Readers 2011 un il (Hello friends!) bd bk $5.99

Grades: PreK   **E**
1. Board books for children 2. Fear -- Fiction 3. Owls -- Fiction 4. Sheep -- Fiction 5. Courage -- Fiction 6. Giant panda -- Fiction
ISBN 978-0-8037-3570-5; 0-8037-3570-7
LC 2010020619

First published 2009 in Australia

Panda and Owl encourage Sheep to jump over a puddle, but Sheep is afraid she will fall and hurt herself.

Yummy ice cream; a book about sharing. [illustrated by] Anna Walker. Board book ed.; Dial books for Young Readers 2011 un il (Hello friends!) bd bk $5.99

Grades: PreK   **E**
1. Board books for children 2. Owls -- Fiction 3.

Sheep -- Fiction 4. Giant panda -- Fiction 5. Ice cream, ices, etc. -- Fiction
ISBN 978-0-8037-3568-2; 0-8037-3568-5
LC 2010020618

First published 2009 in Australia

Owl wishes he had some ice cream like his friends, and so Panda and Sheep find a way to share.

"Walker incorporates collaged fabric prints into creamy, sage backdrops, . . . providing a gentle contrast with the muted colors of the animals. Quay and Walker nicely convey both Owl's longing and joy when Panda and Sheep finally share. The well-trod message is delivered with panache and abundant sweetness." Publ Wkly

Other titles in this series are:
Let's play house (2011)
Puddle jumping (2011)
Good night, sleep tight (2011)

Raab, Brigitte

Where does pepper come from? illustrated by Manuela Olten; translated by J. Alison James. North-South 2006 un il $15.95

Grades: K 1 2 3   **E**
1. Questions and answers 2. Riddles, Juvenile 3. Children's questions and answers 4. Science -- Miscellanea -- Juvenile literature
ISBN 0-7358-2070-8

This is a "humorous cross between a science book and a riddle book. Each of seven questions is first given a funny answer. . . . Readers turn the page to see a child saying, 'No!' followed by a concise, factual answer. Topics range from the color of flamingos to the saltiness of the seas. The pattern works well. . . . The cartoon-style paintings use soft earth tones and subtle humor." SLJ

Raczka, Bob

Fall mixed up; illustrations by Chad Cameron. Carolrhoda Books 2011 un il lib bdg $17.95

Grades: PreK K 1 2   **E**
1. Stories in rhyme 2. Autumn -- Fiction
ISBN 978-0-7613-4606-7; 0-7613-4606-6
LC 2009038922

The delights of autumn are described in mixed-up verse and illustrations, and the reader is challenged to uncover the errors.

"Silly as the rhyming verses are, they need Cameron's zany illustrations to truly make them come alive. . . . Digital paintings with photo-collage elements draw readers' eye through the scenes. . . . A true celebration of fall certain to be a winner." Kirkus

Snowy, blowy winter; [by] Bob Raczka; illustrated by Judy Stead. Albert Whitman & Co. 2008 un il $16.99

Grades: PreK K 1 2   **E**
1. Stories in rhyme 2. Snow -- Fiction 3. Winter -- Fiction
ISBN 978-0-8075-7526-0; 0-8075-7526-7
LC 2007052608

Illustrations and simple rhyming text portray winter activities, from snowman-building, sledding, and sitting by a fire to feeding birds

"The text is simple and bouncy, and the cartoon illustrations are bright, clear, and inclusive. The book's quick pace and cheerful pictures make it a perfect choice for seasonal storytimes." SLJ

Spring things; by Bob Raczka; illustrated by Judy Stead. Albert Whitman 2007 un il $16.95
Grades: PreK K 1 2   E
  1. Spring -- Fiction
  ISBN 978-0-8075-7596-3
                LC 2006023403
Winter melts into spring with the sights and sounds of hopping and skipping, sowing and mowing, and blading and lemonading
"Stead's paintings add an entertaining element and useful clarification to the active text." SLJ

Summer wonders; illustrated by Judy Stead. Albert Whitman & Co. 2009 un il $16.99
Grades: PreK K 1 2   E
  1. Stories in rhyme 2. Summer -- Fiction
  ISBN 0-8075-7653-0; 978-0-8075-7653-3
                LC 2008031037
Illustrations and rhyming text celebrate the sights and sounds of summer, from days of diving and swimming to nights of stargazing and fireflies.
"Bright-hued acrylic illustrations bring the expressive verbal images to life. The paintings are festive and entertaining." SLJ

Who loves the fall? by Bob Raczka; illustrated by Judy Stead. Albert Whitman 2007 un il $16.95
Grades: PreK K 1 2   E
  1. Stories in rhyme 2. Autumn -- Fiction
  ISBN 978-0-8075-9037-9; 0-8075-9037-1
                LC 2007001506
Rhyming text and illustrations portray the sights and sounds of autumn, from "rakers, leapers, and corn crop reapers" to "trickers, treaters, and turkey eaters"
"The brightly colored, well-designed illustrations pulsate with energy, movement, and charm." SLJ

Radunsky, Vladimir
  What does peace feel like? by V. Radunsky and children just like you from around the world. Atheneum Books for Young Readers 2004 un il $14.95
Grades: K 1 2 3   E
  1. Peace
  ISBN 0-689-86676-3
                LC 2003-11506
Simple text and illustrations portray what peace looks, sounds, tastes, feels, and smells like to children around the world.
"As much a celebration of the five senses as an antiwar message, this bright picture book combines Radunsky's playful gouache double-page scenarios with quotes from grade-schoolers at an international school in Rome." Booklist

You? translated from Dog-ese to English by my learned dog, Tsetsa. Harcourt, Inc. 2009 un il $16
Grades: PreK K 1 2   E
  1. Dogs -- Fiction
  ISBN 978-0-15-205177-8; 0-15-205177-5
                LC 2008-3281
A lonely girl and a stray dog find one another in a park.

"Radunsky makes the most of his canvas. . . . Thin, energetic lines define the forms minimally on gouache blobs of color, all arrayed on a generous expanse of buff-colored handmade paper. . . . The heartfelt, plaintive dialogue will hold readers' interest, and the wait makes the inevitable discovery—'Woof! YOU!'—all the sweeter." Kirkus

The **mighty** asparagus. Silver Whistle/Harcourt 2004 un il $16
Grades: K 1 2 3   E
  1. Birds 2. Asparagus 3. Songbirds 4. Asparagus -- Fiction 5. Kings, queens, rulers, etc
  ISBN 0-15-216743-9
                LC 2003-12241
In Renaissance Italy, a large asparagus appears suddenly in the king's back yard, and he enlists the help of several people and animals, including a songbird, in order to get rid of it
"The lowbrow humor, the blind silliness, and the quirky exaggerations are childishness itself. For older children there is the appeal of random sarcasm and funky, distorted illustrations." SLJ

Rahaman, Vashanti
  Divali rose; [by] Vashanti Rahaman; illustrated by Jamel Akib. Boyds Mills Press 2008 un il $16.95
Grades: 2 3 4   E
  1. Divali -- Fiction 2. Prejudices -- Fiction 3. East Indians -- Fiction 4. Grandparents -- Fiction
  ISBN 978-1-59078-524-9; 1-59078-524-X
                LC 2007049686
As the festival of Divali approaches, Ricki wants to confess that he accidentally broke a rosebud off the bush he and his grandfather planted, but grandfather is busy blaming the neighbors who are newly arrived in Trinidad from India. Includes facts about Divali and the people and language of Trinidad
"This appealing, multilayered story will provoke discussion about resentments between different generations of immigrants. . . . Akib's impressionistic pastel paintings portray the tropical setting and Ricki's feelings of guilt." SLJ

Ramirez, Antonio
  Napi; story by Antonio Ramirez; pictures by Domi. Groundwood Books 2004 un il $15.95
Grades: K 1 2 3   E
  1. Dreams -- Fiction 2. Herons -- Fiction 3. Mazatec Indians -- Fiction 4. Native Americans -- Mexico -- Fiction
  ISBN 0-88899-610-1
Napi is a Mazatec Indian girl who loves to dream. One day, she dreams of becoming a heron and flying over the river.
"The clear, lyrical prose has a childlike charm that brilliantly recreates the joys of this child's experience. . . . Domi's primitive acrylic artwork enhances the sense of the story." SLJ
  Other titles about Napi are:
  Napi goes to the mountain (2006)
  Napi makes a village (2010)

Ramos, Jorge
  I'm just like my mom/I'm just like my dad; illustrated by Akemi Gutierrez. Rayo 2008 un il $16.99

Grades: PreK K   E

1. Bilingual books -- English-Spanish 2. Father-son relationship -- Fiction 3. Mother-daughter relationship -- Fiction

ISBN 978-0-06-123968-7; 0-06-123968-2

In two stories in English and Spanish, printed back to back, children reflect on how much they resemble their parents.

"This is a comforting celebration of family. . . . Spare illustrations is subtle colors completely fill each double-page spread and feature pleasant figures with enlarged oval heads, giving a happy, open, comfortable feel to the narratives." Booklist

Ramos, Mario

I am so strong; [translated by Jean Anderson] Gecko Press 2011 il

Grades: PreK K 1   E

1. Wolves -- Fiction

ISBN 0-9582-7877-6; 978-0-9582-7877-5

Original French edition, 2001

"This offering from Belgian author/illustrator Ramos is a single, drawn-out joke, but achieves keeper status with intelligent dialogue and Gallic sophistication. A megalomaniacal wolf strolls through the forest buttonholing fairy tale creatures and asking them to burnish his ego. . . . Ramos's thickly brushed paintings alternate between woodland scenes suggestive of stage scenery and closer shots of the wolf and other creatures against white backdrops, the better to appreciate the comic tension. . . . The wolf's comeuppance is deeply satisfying; the only disappointment is that the book is over so soon. Better read it again." Publ Wkly

Ramsey, Calvin Alexander

Belle, the last mule at Gee's Bend; [by] Calvin Alexander Ramsey and Bettye Stroud; illustrated by John Holyfield. Candlewick Press 2011 un il $15.99

Grades: PreK K 1 2   E

1. Clergy 2. Mules -- Fiction 3. Nonfiction writers 4. Civil rights activists 5. Nobel laureates for peace 6. African Americans -- Civil rights -- Fiction

ISBN 978-0-7636-4058-3; 0-7636-4058-1

LC 2010048132

In Gee's Bend, Alabama, Miz Pettway tells young Alex about the historic role her mule played in the struggle for civil rights led by Dr. Martin Luther King, Jr. Includes factual information about the community of Gee's Bend and Martin Luther King, Jr.

"Holyfield's intense acrylic paintings, in blues, yellows and browns, evoke the heat and the drama. . . . A solid choice for parents and teachers who are introducing the 1960s to young children. An intergenerational story filled with heart and soul." Kirkus

★ **Ruth** and the Green Book; [by] Calvin Alexander Ramsey, with Gwen Strauss; illustrations by Floyd Cooper. Carolrhoda Books 2010 un il

Grades: K 1 2 3   E

1. Segregation -- Fiction 2. Automobile travel -- Fiction 3. African Americans -- Segregation -- Fiction

ISBN 0761352554; 9780761352556

LC 2009034284

When Ruth and her parents take a motor trip from Chicago to Alabana to visit her grandmother, they rely on a pamphlet called "The Negro Motorist Green Book" to find places that will serve them. This title concludes with a historical note on the Green Book itself. "Ages five to nine." (Bull Cent Child Books)

This is a "powerful picture book. . . . Cooper's glowing, unframed, sepia-toned artwork delivers a strong sense of the period from a child's viewpoint. . . . This is a compelling addition to U.S. history offerings." Booklist

Rand, Ann

I know a lot of things; by Ann & Paul Rand. Chronicle Books 2009 un il $16.99

Grades: PreK K 1   E

1. Growth -- Fiction

ISBN 978-0-8118-6615-6

LC 2008020680

A reissue of the title first published 1956

Celebrates the many things young children know about their world, while looking forward to a time when they will know more

This is written "in poetic text. . . . Paul Rand's simply composed, ahead-of-their-time illustrations don't look the least bit dated and perfectly reflect the concepts in the text." Horn Book Guide

Sparkle and spin; a book about words. by Ann & Paul Rand. Chronicle Books 2006 un il $15.95

Grades: PreK K 1   E

1. Communication 2. English language

ISBN 978-0-8118-5003-2; 0-8118-5003-X

LC 2004-23260

A reissue of the title first published 1957 by Harcourt, Brace, and World

Lyrical text explores what words are and how they are used, highlighting such characteristics as that some words are spoken softly, some are shouted, some sound like their meaning, and some evoke certain feelings.

This "is a vibrantly eye-catching collection of visual puns and graphic double-entendres." NY Times Book Rev

Rand, Betseygail

Big Bunny; written by Betseygail Rand and Colleen Rand; illustrated by C. S. W. Rand. Tricycle Press 2011 un il $14.99; lib bdg $17.99

Grades: PreK K   E

1. Size -- Fiction 2. Easter -- Fiction 3. Rabbits -- Fiction

ISBN 978-1-58246-376-6; 1-58246-376-X; 978-1-58246-386-5 lib bdg; 1-58246-386-7 lib bdg

LC 2010018017

At first Big Bunny loves being big, taking the other little Easter bunnies for rides on her back throughout the countryside. When she accidentally breaks some of the Easter eggs she is helping decorate, she begins to feel clumsy and frustrated by her tremendous size. Happily, her little bunny friends show her how to help with their Easter tasks in a way only she can.

"This thoughtful, understated book with intriguing minimalist illustrations provides both an interesting Easter Bunny tale and a quiet message about helping someone who is different. . . . The unusual illustrations use simple, stylized shapes against whit backgrounds with bold colors and a minimum of detail." Kirkus

Randall, Alison L.

The **wheat** doll; [by] Alison L. Randall; illustrated by Bill Farnsworth. Peachtree Publishers 2008 30p il $16.95

Grades: K 1 2 3   E

1. Dolls -- Fiction 2. Storms -- Fiction 3. Frontier and pioneer life -- Fiction 4. Lost and found possessions -- Fiction

ISBN 978-1-56145-456-3; 1-56145-456-7

LC 2008-4562

On the nineteenth-century Utah frontier, Mary Ann is heartbroken when her doll Betty is lost during a fierce storm and her sadness lasts all winter long, until spring brings a wonderful surprise.

"This is a sweet story of loss and renewal told with empathy and feeling that is never heavy-handed. . . . Farnsworth's realistic oil paintings have a warm, soft quality that matches the tone of the text. . . . This picture book is a great addition." SLJ

Rania

The **sandwich** swap; by Her Majesty Queen Rania; with Kelly DiPucchio; illustrations by Tricia Tusa. Disney-Hyperion Books 2010 un il $16.99

Grades: PreK K 1 2   E

1. School stories 2. Food -- Fiction 3. Friendship -- Fiction 4. Toleration -- Fiction

ISBN 978-1-4231-2484-9; 1-4231-2484-7

LC 2009018673

"The day Lily stops eating her peanut butter and jelly sandwich to tell Salma her hummus and pita sandwich looks yucky—and vice versa—is the day they stop being friends. . . . When the two girls get caught in the middle of a food fight and called to the principal's office, they decide it's time to make some changes. . . . Soft watercolor cartoon illustrations portray a lively student body and a slightly forbidding principal. This engaging title reminds children that having the courage to try new things can result in positive experiences." SLJ

Rankin, Laura

Ruthie and the (not so) teeny tiny lie; [by] Laura Rankin. Bloomsbury Children's Books 2007 un il $15.95

Grades: PreK K 1 2   E

1. School stories 2. Foxes -- Fiction 3. Truthfulness and falsehood -- Fiction

ISBN 978-1-59990-010-0; 1-59990-010-6

LC 2006013192

Ruthie the fox loves tiny things and when she finds a tiny camera on the playground she is very happy, but after she lies and says the camera belongs to her, nothing seems to go right

"Emotionally authentic in text and art, this story gets its message across without preaching." SLJ

Ransom, Candice F.

The **old** blue pickup truck; written by Candice F. Ransom; illustrated by Jenny Mattheson. Walker & Co. 2009 un il $16.99; lib bdg $17.89

Grades: PreK K 1   E

1. Trucks -- Fiction 2. Father-daughter relationship -- Fiction

ISBN 978-0-8027-9591-5; 0-8027-9591-9; 978-0-8027-9592-2 lib bdg; 0-8027-9592-7 lib bdg

LC 2008-40316

As a girl and her father run errands in their old blue pickup, she discovers how many different ways they can use their truck.

"This enjoyable story is accompanied by oil on primed paper illustrations that have a bright and clean feel." SLJ

Ransome, James

Gunner, football hero; [by] James E. Ransome. Holiday House 2010 un il $16.95

Grades: PreK K 1   E

1. Football -- Fiction

ISBN 978-0-8234-2053-7; 0-8234-2053-1

LC 2008-48487

When short, round Gunner, the third-string quarterback, finally gets to play in a big game, everyone treats him like a hero.

"The simple, economical narrative supposes a fair amount of familiarity with football but certainly conveys the thrill of Gunner's short time on the field. . . . Ransome's watercolor-and-line drawings as well as page layouts are appropriately full of action, and the faces of the players and crowds engagingly expressive and humorous." Kirkus

New red bike! [by] James E. Ransome. Holiday House 2011 un il $16.95

Grades: PreK K 1   E

1. Cycling -- Fiction 2. Bicycles -- Fiction 3. Friendship -- Fiction

ISBN 978-0-8234-2226-5; 0-8234-2226-7

Tom enjoys the thrill of riding his brand new bicycle, and then shares it with a friend.

"Story takes a backseat to a bigger emotional truth: a bike is an awesome thing. Wearing a bright red helmet that matches the bike's frame, Tom is truly at one with his machine, and Ransome . . . provides Zenlike text to match. . . . Each moment of action . . . gets its own watercolor and pencil image and perspective. . . . Newbie bikers should find that this book gives full voice to the joys of having wheels of one's own." Publ Wkly

Rao, Sandhya

My mother's sari; illustrated by Nina Sabnani. North South Books 2006 un il $14.95; pa $6.95

Grades: PreK K 1 2   E

1. Clothing and dress -- Fiction 2. Mother-daughter relationship -- Fiction

ISBN 0-7358-2101-1; 0-7358-2233-6 pa

First published in India

A little girl is fascinated by her mother's sari and finds many uses for it.

"Subtle backgrounds, lightly decorated with objects from nature, provide a gentle showcase for the children and the saris. Rao [uses] . . . childlike drawings to represent the kids and photographs of the cloths, bringing the fabric designs, colors, and folds up close. A winsome look at a fresh subject." Booklist

Rappaport, Doreen

★ The **secret** seder; illustrated by Emily Arnold McCully. Hyperion Books for Children 2005 un il $16.99

Grades: 2 3 4   E

1. Jews -- Fiction 2. Passover -- Fiction 3. Holocaust,

1933-1945 -- Fiction
ISBN 0-7868-0777-6

LC 2003-57115

During the Nazi occupation of France, a boy and his father slip out of their village and into the mountains, where they join a group of fellow Jews at a humble seder table

"Rappaport interweaves themes and descriptive text to create a meaningful story in a distinctive setting. An excellent discussion starter." SLJ

Raschka, Chris

★ **Everyone** can learn to ride a bicycle; Chris Raschka. Schwartz & Wade Books 2013 32 p. (hardcover) $16.99
Grades: PreK K 1 2   E
1. Picture books for children 2. Bicycles -- Juvenile fiction 3. Father-daughter relationship -- Juvenile fiction 4. Fathers and daughters -- Fiction 5. Bicycles and bicycling -- Fiction
ISBN 0375870075; 9780375870071; 9780375970078

LC 2012009172

In this children's picture book, by Chris Raschka, "a father takes his daughter through all the steps in the process [of riding a bike]--from choosing the perfect bicycle to that triumphant first successful ride. . . . [The] picture book . . . not only shows kids how to learn to ride, but captures what it feels like to fall . . . get up . . . fall again . . . and finally . . . ride a bicycle!" (Publisher's note)

"Rendered in Raschka's signature style of fluid, kinetic brushstrokes, the ink-and-watercolor illustrations beautifully capture the action and emotion in each scene...Deceptively simple and perfectly paced for read-alouds, this latest from the two-time Caldecott medalist captures a child's everyday experience with gentle, joyful sensitivity." Booklist

Hip hop dog; words by Chris Raschka; pictures by Vladimir Radunsky. Harper 2010 un il $16.99; lib bdg $17.89
Grades: PreK K 1 2   E
1. Stories in rhyme 2. Dogs -- Fiction 3. Hip-hop -- Fiction 4. Rap music -- Fiction
ISBN 978-0-06-123963-2; 0-06-123963-1; 978-0-06-123964-9 lib bdg; 0-06-123964-X lib bdg

LC 2008031449

A neglected dog finds his purpose through rapping and rhyming.

"This is great for reading aloud. . . . The well-matched mixed-media illustrations show lively urban scenes. . . . Kids will chant along to the text, which slides and whirls across the pages." Booklist

Raschka, Christopher

Farmy farm; by Chris Raschka. Orchard Books 2011 il $8.99
Grades: PreK   E
1. Stories in rhyme 2. Sounds -- Fiction 3. Farm life -- Fiction 4. Domestic animals -- Fiction
ISBN 978-0-545-21981-5

LC 2010039061

Rhyming text and touch-and-feel illustrations introduce a variety of farm animals and the sounds they make.

"The book's repeated verse, buoyant palette, and soft texture should find an enthusiastic toddler-aged audience." Publ Wkly

Five for a little one; [by] Chris Raschka. Atheneum Books for Young Readers 2006 un il $16.95
Grades: PreK K   E
1. Counting 2. Stories in rhyme 3. Rabbits -- Fiction 4. Senses and sensation -- Fiction
ISBN 978-0-689-84599-4; 0-689-84599-5

LC 2005-08963

"A buoyant bunny, drawn in thick ink outline with a fuzzy body and delightfully mismatched ears (one downy and one plain), introduces readers to the senses, numbering them one through five. The rhyming verses and ebullient artwork convey a child's curiosity and enthusiasm for investigating the world in various ways." SLJ

John Coltrane's Giant steps; remixed by Chris Raschka. Atheneum Bks. for Young Readers 2002 33p il $17
Grades: K 1 2 3   E
1. Jazz music 2. Jazz
ISBN 0-689-84598-7

LC 2001-33755

John Coltrane's musical composition is performed by a box, a snowflake, some raindrops, and a kitten

"Like Coltrane, Raschka is creating something deeply personal here that we don't need to understand fully to appreciate. Instead, he asks us to trust our own understanding of raindrops, snowflakes, kittens, and music to experience the book. Anyone who's still intimidated by jazz after giving this book a chance is probably just trying too hard." Horn Book

★ **Little** black crow; [by] Chris Raschka. Atheneum Books for Young Readers 2010 un il $16.99
Grades: K 1 2 3   E
1. Stories in rhyme 2. Crows -- Fiction
ISBN 978-0-689-84601-4; 0-689-84601-0

LC 2009032110

A boy thinks about the life of a little black crow that he sees, wondering where it goes in the snow, where it sleeps, and whether or not it worries like he does.

"Impressionistic watercolor landscapes perfectly set the mood and style for these awe-filled inquiries of a curious child." SLJ

New York is English, Chattanooga is Creek; by Chris Raschka. Atheneum Books for Young Readers 2005 un il $16.95
Grades: K 1 2 3   E
1. Cities and towns -- Fiction 2. Geographic names -- Fiction
ISBN 0-689-84600-2

LC 2004-23188

New York City, though a bit boastful, decides to throw a party to make new friends of other unique cities like Chattanooga and Minneapolis

"This is both a fascinating exploration of the etymology and derivation of American city names and a characteristic Raschka farcical flight-of-fancy. . . . Raschka's illustrations rendered in ink and watercolor employ his loose, impressionistic, brushy style to perfect effect, giving the book its humor while artfully delivering his message and entertaining information." SLJ

★ **Peter** and the wolf; retold by Chris Raschka. Atheneum Books for Young Readers 2008 un il $17.99
Grades: PreK K 1 2   E
1. Fairy tales 2. Wolves -- Fiction
ISBN 978-0-689-85652-5; 0-689-85652-0
LC 2008-04472
Retells the orchestral fairy tale in which a boy ignores his grandfather's warnings and captures a wolf with the help of a bird, a duck, and a cat
"Raschka conveys the mounting suspense in lilting words, swerving zigzags and curves. . . . Raschka's pictures—of characters venturing close to the wolf's bear-trap jaws, of the cat's enormous face looming over a tiny Peter—gain extra energy from geometrically shaped color blocks on the same spreads. . . . One reading will not be enough to appreciate the artist's keen attention to detail." Publ Wkly

★ **Yo!** Yes? by Chris Raschka. Orchard Bks. 1993 un il $15.95
Grades: PreK K 1 2   E
1. Friendship -- Fiction 2. Race relations -- Fiction 3. African Americans -- Fiction
ISBN 0-531-05469-1
LC 92-25644
A Caldecott Medal honor book, 1994
Two lonely characters, one black and one white, meet on the street and become friends
"The design and drawing are bold, spare and expressive; the language has the strength and rhythm of a playground chant." Bull Cent Child Books
Another title about these characters is:
Ring! Yo? (2000)

★ A **ball** for Daisy; by Chris Raschka. Schwartz & Wade Books 2011 1 v. col. ill. $16.99; lib bdg $19.99
Grades: PreK K 1   E
1. Stories without words 2. Dogs -- Fiction 3. Play -- Fiction
ISBN 978-0-375-85861-1; 0-375-85861-X; 978-0-375-95861-8 lib bdg; 0-375-95861-4 lib bdg
LC 2010024132
Caldecott Medal (2012)
In this wordless picture book, Daisy the dog "loves playing with her ball . . . until the fateful moment that another dog bites too hard on the ball and deflates it. . . . Raschka uses fairly sophisticated comic-book arrangements . . . but masks them with soft watercolor edges instead of sharp corners. The result feels like something made of pure emotion, a pretty close approximation of what it's probably like to be a dog." Booklist

Rathmann, Peggy
★ **10** minutes till bedtime. Putnam 1998 un il $16.99; pa $6.99; bd bk $7.99
Grades: PreK K 1 2   E
1. Bedtime -- Fiction 2. Hamsters -- Fiction
ISBN 0-399-23103-X; 0-14-240024-6 pa; 0-399-23770-4 bd bk
LC 97-51295
A boy's hamster leads an increasingly large group of hamsters on a tour of the boy's house, while his father counts down the minutes to bedtime

"Children will pore over the comical details and follow closely the antics of the numbered hamsters, each one with a personality of its own." SLJ

★ **Good** night, Gorilla. Putnam 1994 un il
Grades: PreK K 1 2   E
1. Zoos -- Fiction 2. Animals -- Fiction
ISBN 0-399-22445-9; 0-399-23003-3 bd bk; 0-698-11649-6 pa
LC 92-29020
In this picture book, "a zookeeper makes his final rounds of the day, bidding his charges good night, while unbeknownst to him the gorilla, who has taken his keys, lets each animal out after the keeper has passed. . . . {They} follow the zookeeper home to his house and curl up for the night in his room, undiscovered until his wife says 'Good night, dear' and gets more responses than she had bargained for. Mrs. Zookeeper then trudges back to the zoo and returns the would-be guests, but the gorilla and his mouse sidekick sneak back again. . . . Ages two to five." (Bull Cent Child Books)
"In a book economical in text and simple in illustration, the many amusing, small details, as well as the tranquil tone of the story, make this an outstanding picture book." Horn Book Guide

★ **Officer** Buckle and Gloria. Putnam 1995 un il
Grades: PreK K 1 2   E
1. School stories 2. Dogs -- Fiction 3. Safety education -- Fiction
ISBN 0399226168
LC 93-43887
Awarded the Caldecott Medal, 1996
"When rotund, good-natured Officer Buckle visits school assemblies to read off his sensible safety tips, the children listen, bored and polite, dozing off one by one. But when the new police dog, Gloria, stands behind him, secretly miming the dire consequences of acting imprudently, the children suddenly become attentive, laughing uproariously and applauding loudly. The good policeman is first gratified with the response, then deflated to learn that Gloria was stealing the show. Finally, he realizes that he and Gloria make a great team, and they take their show on the road again, adding a new message, 'Always Stick With Your Buddy!'" (Booklist) "Kindergarten to grade three." (SLJ)
"When rotund, good-natured officer Buckle visits school assemblies to read off his sensible safety tips, the children listen, bored and polite, dozing off one by one. But when the new police dog, Gloria, stands behind him, secretly miming the dire consequences of acting imprudently, the children suddenly become attentive, laughing uproariously and applauding loudly. . . . The deadpan humor of the text and slapstick wit of the illustrations make a terrific combination. Large, expressive line drawings illustrate the characters with finesse, and the Kool-Aid-bright washes add energy and pizzazz." Booklist

★ The **day** the babies crawled away. Putnam 2003 un il $16.99
Grades: PreK K 1 2   E
1. Stories in rhyme 2. Infants -- Fiction
ISBN 0-399-23196-X
LC 2002-152002

A boy follows fives babies who crawl away from a picnic and saves the day by bringing them back

This is a "rollicking rhyming tale, illustrated in needle-sharp, atmospheric silhouettes against twilight skies." Publ Wkly

Rattigan, Jama Kim

Dumpling soup; illustrated by Lillian Hsu-Flanders. Little, Brown 1993 un il hardcover o.p. pa $6.99

Grades: K 1 2 3   E

1. New Year -- Fiction 2. Family life -- Fiction
ISBN 0-316-73445-4; 0-316-73047-5 pa

LC 91-42949

"Marisa, a seven-year-old Asian-American girl who lives in Hawaii, explains the traditions that exist in her family to celebrate the New Year. Her family . . . consists of people who are Japanese, Chinese, Korean, Hawaiian, and haole (Hawaiian for white person). . . . A glossary of English, Hawaiian, Japanese, and Korean words provides pronunciations and definitions for many of the possibly unfamiliar terms that weave in and out of the text. A thoroughly enjoyable celebration of family warmth and diverse traditions, illustrated with cheery watercolors." Horn Book

Rau, Dana Meachen, 1971-

Robot, Go Bot! by Dana Meachen Rau; illustrated by Wook Jin Jung. Random House Inc. 2013 32 p. col. ill. (paperback) $3.99; (library) $12.99

Grades: PreK K 1   E

1. Robots -- Juvenile fiction 2. Conduct of life -- Juvenile fiction 3. Robots -- Fiction 4. Cartoons and comics 5. Robots -- Cartoons and comics
ISBN 0375870830; 9780375870835; 9780375970832

LC 2012027691

In this book for beginning readers, "a girl assembles a robot and then treats it like a slave until it goes on strike. Having put the robot together from a jumble of loose parts, the budding engineer issues an increasingly peremptory series of rhymed orders--'Throw, Bot. / Row, Bot'--that turn from playful activities like chasing bubbles in the yard to tasks like hoeing the garden, mowing the lawn and towing her around in a wagon." (Kirkus Reviews)

Rausch, Molly

My cold went on vacation; [by] Molly Rausch and [illustrated by] Nora Krug. G.P. Putnam's Sons 2011 un il $16.99

Grades: PreK K   E

1. Sick -- Fiction 2. Cold (Disease) -- Fiction
ISBN 978-0-399-25474-1; 0-399-25474-9

A little boy is curious about all the places his cold might go after it leaves him.

"Bold, whimsical art neatly complements the text, adding fantastical details and additional humor. . . . A perfect choice for readers with the sniffles and those who enjoy their stories with a twist." SLJ

Raven, Margot

★ **Circle** unbroken; the story of a basket and its people. [by] Margot Theis Raven; pictures by E. B. Lewis. Farrar, Straus and Giroux 2004 un il $16; pa $7.99

Grades: K 1 2 3   E

1. Baskets -- Fiction 2. Gullahs -- Fiction 3. African

Americans -- Fiction
ISBN 0-374-31289-3; 0-312-37603-0 pa

LC 2002-24009

A grandmother tells the tale of Gullahs and their beautiful sweetgrass baskets that keep their African heritage alive

"Raven's text masterfully frames several hundred years of African-American history within the picture-book format. Lewis's double-page, watercolor images are poignant and perfectly matched to the text and mood." SLJ

★ **Night** boat to freedom; [by] Margot Theis Raven; pictures by E. B. Lewis. Farrar, Straus and Giroux 2006 un il $16; pa $6.99

Grades: 1 2 3 4   E

1. Quilts -- Fiction 2. Slavery -- Fiction 3. African Americans -- Fiction 4. Underground railroad -- Fiction
ISBN 978-0-374-31266-4; 0-374-31266-4; 978-0-312-55018-9 pa; 0-312-55018-9 pa

At the request of his fellow slave Granny Judith, Christmas John risks his life to take runaways across a river from Kentucky to Ohio.

"The older mentor is as tough as the young boy, and Lewis' beautiful, unframed double-page spreads depict the bond between them. . . . Words and pictures work perfectly together." Booklist

Ravishankar, Anushka

★ **Elephants** never forget; illustrated by Christiane Pieper. Houghton Mifflin Company 2008 un il $16

Grades: PreK K 1 2   E

1. Stories in rhyme 2. Elephants -- Fiction 3. Water buffalo -- Fiction
ISBN 978-0-618-99784-8; 0-618-99784-9

LC 2007-25745

A lonely elephant meets a herd of buffaloes and decides to stay with them, but when they meet up with some elephants, he must make an important decision

The "story is full of good read-aloud noises. . . . Pieper . . . produces digital woodcuts that . . . [eschew] cuteness in favor of strength and clarity. A two-color scheme—black and periwinkle on cream-colored paper—and bold, simple spreads focus attention on the ponderous forms of the elephant and buffalo. Varied compositions as well as printed letters that grow and shrink and dance across the pages match the dexterity of the text with a visual sprightliness." Publ Wkly

★ **Tiger** on a tree; [by] Anushka Ravishankar, Pulak Biswas. Farrar, Straus and Giroux 2004 un il $15

Grades: PreK K 1 2   E

1. Tigers 2. Stories in rhyme 3. Tigers -- Fiction
ISBN 0-374-37555-0

LC 2003-49050

First published 1997 in India

After trapping a tiger in a tree, a group of men must decide what to do with it

"This very simple chanting story is perfect for reading aloud with young preschoolers. . . . The thickly stroked illustrations, mostly black and white, have occasional splashes of orange." Booklist

Rawlinson, Julia

★ **Fletcher** and the falling leaves; pictures by Tiphanie Beeke. Greenwillow Books 2006 un il $16.99; pa $6.99

Grades: PreK K 1 2 **E**

1. Foxes -- Fiction 2. Trees -- Fiction 3. Autumn -- Fiction 4. Leaves -- Fiction

ISBN 978-0-06-113401-2; 0-06-113401-5; 978-0-06-157397-2 pa; 0-06-157397-3 pa

LC 2005-34348

When his favorite tree begins to lose its leaves, Fletcher the fox worries that it is sick, but instead a magical sight is in store for him.

"This potent synthesis of art and prose conveys a child's first awareness of the changing seasons with reverence and wonder. . . . Beeke's resplendent watercolors work beautifully with the book's tone, content, layout, and design." SLJ

Other titles about Fletcher the fox are:

Fletcher and the springtime blossoms (2009)
Fletcher and the snowflake Christmas (2010)

Fletcher and the snowflake Christmas; pictures by Tiphanie Beeke. Greenwillow Books 2010 un il $16.99

Grades: PreK K 1 2 **E**

1. Snow -- Fiction 2. Foxes -- Fiction 3. Winter -- Fiction 4. Rabbits -- Fiction 5. Christmas -- Fiction

ISBN 978-0-06-199033-5; 0-06-199033-7

At Christmastime, Fletcher the fox and the other forest animals lay a trail of sticks to help Santa find the rabbits' new burrow.

This offers "beautifully distinctive illustrations skillfully integrated with the text. . . . The gentle, simple story is deftly told with just the right amount of suspense and a nice balance of dialogue and exposition. Beeke's glowing pastel illustrations in her irresistible style captivate readers with their unusual hues and textures." Kirkus

Ray, Jane

Ahmed and the feather girl. Frances Lincoln Children's 2010 un il $17.95

Grades: K 1 2 3 **E**

1. Magic -- Fiction 2. Circus -- Fiction 3. Orphans -- Fiction

ISBN 978-1-84507-988-8; 1-84507-988-4

Ahmed is a poor orphan who lives with a travelling circus and works for cruel Madame Saleem. His life is changed forever when he finds a beautiful egg in the forest and brings it back to the circus. From the egg hatches a little girl called Aurelia, and as she grows she sprouts soft feathers that turn into wings.

"The moving story, layered with magical moments, is truly expressed in Ray's triumphant art. With her signature mix of patterning, collage, and golden flourishes, the spreads have much to look at." Booklist

★ The **apple** -pip princess. Candlewick Press 2008 un il $16.99

Grades: PreK K 1 2 **E**

1. Fairy tales 2. Seeds -- Fiction 3. Apples -- Fiction 4. Princesses -- Fiction

ISBN 978-0-7636-3747-7; 0-7636-3747-5

LC 2007-34239

In a land that has stood barren, parched by drought and ravaged by frosts since the Queen's death, the King sets his three daughters the task of making the kingdom bloom again, and discovers that sometimes the smallest things can make the biggest difference.

"Ray's rich language and sure pacing create a winning read-aloud, but it's the shining collage artwork that really stands out. Mixing color photos into her typically fine, elaborately decorated illustrations, Ray creates dramatic scenes." Booklist

The **dollhouse** fairy. Candlewick Press 2009 un il $16.99

Grades: PreK K 1 2 **E**

1. Sick -- Fiction 2. Fairies -- Fiction 3. Dollhouses -- Fiction 4. Father-daughter relationship -- Fiction

ISBN 978-0-7636-4411-6; 0-7636-4411-0

LC 2009-18405

Worried about her father's trip to the hospital, Rosy goes to play with the special dollhouse he built for her and finds Thistle, a very messy and mischievous fairy who needs a place to stay while her injured wing mends.

"The story unfolds with subtlety and sensitivity to the emotional issues at its heart. The book's large format gives plenty of space for the vibrant mixed-media artwork." Booklist

Ray, Mary Lyn

★ **Christmas** farm; illustrated by Barry Root. Harcourt 2008 un il $17

Grades: K 1 2 **E**

1. Trees -- Fiction 2. Gardening -- Fiction

ISBN 978-0-15-216290-0; 0-15-216290-9

LC 2007-15216

Wilma decides to plant Christmas trees with the help of her young neighbor, Parker.

"Root's appealing watercolor-and-gouache illustrations invite inspection. . . . [This is] a story that lovingly depicts the hard work, cooperation, and patience necessary to grow crops." Booklist

★ **Stars**. Beach Lane Books 2011 un il $16.99

Grades: PreK K 1 **E**

1. Stars -- Fiction

ISBN 978-1-4424-2249-0; 1-4424-2249-1

LC 2010033253

"A poetic paean to stars both real and metaphorical brings the heavenly down to readers without robbing it of mystery. . . . Frazee excels at illustrating textual details in fresh ways, keeping young children engaged and curious. . . . Her pictures ebb and flow with the text, alternating charming spots of self-possessed, spirited youngsters with ink-black or gloriously blue, starry heavens inviting dreamy meditation." Kirkus

Rayner, Catherine

★ **Ernest**, the moose who doesn't fit. Farrar, Straus and Giroux 2010 un il $16.99

Grades: PreK K 1 **E**

1. Size -- Fiction 2. Moose -- Fiction 3. Chipmunks -- Fiction

ISBN 978-0-374-32217-5; 0-374-32217-1

A rather large moose who cannot fit on the page teams up with his little chipmunk friend to find a solution. Final pages form a gatefold.

"The collage illustrations on a background of a softly hued green grid contrast the moose's grand dimensions with that of the tiny chipmunk in a gently humorous fashion. . . . The language is engaging and inventive." Kirkus

Solomon Crocodile. Farrar Straus & Giroux 2011 un il $15.99

Grades: PreK K 1   **E**

1. Play -- Fiction 2. Crocodiles -- Fiction 3. Friendship -- Fiction

ISBN 978-0-374-38064-9; 0-374-38064-3

LC 2010045855

Solomon Crocodile's rough play prevents him from making friends down by the river until a stranger comes stomping through the reeds!

"Rayner's lush illustrations reflect the tension between the puppyish croc and his staider neighbors. . . . Solomon practically vibrates energy. . . . The well-paced story has just enough tension to draw in little troublemakers who will cheer for Solomon's eventual triumph." Horn Book

★ The **bear** who shared. Dial Books for Young Readers 2011 un il $16.99

Grades: PreK K 1   **E**

1. Mice -- Fiction 2. Bears -- Fiction 3. Raccoons -- Fiction 4. Friendship -- Fiction

ISBN 978-0-8037-3576-7; 0-8037-3576-6

LC 2010012142

First published 2010 in the United Kingdom with title: Norris, the bear who shared

Norris the bear has been waiting patiently for the last ripe fruit to fall from the tree, and when it does he decides to share it with his two new friends, Tulip the raccoon and Violet the mouse.

"Rayner's quirky illustrations are the real star of the book; deceptively basic compositions with barely-there watercolor strokes that manage to look simultaneously haphazard and carefully applied. . . . The minimal text is accessible to the very youngest readers." Kirkus

Reasoner, Charles

One blue fish; a colorful counting book. Little Simon 2010 un il $9.99

Grades: PreK   **E**

1. Color 2. Counting

ISBN 978-1-4169-9672-9; 1-4169-9672-9

"Combining counting and color identification, this book introduces various pond-dwelling creatures. On the left side of the spread, a number from 1 to 10 is spelled out. On the right, the die-cut numeral is on a foldout flap. When the page is opened, a creature in the corresponding color and quantity is depicted with identifying text, such as '10 yellow ducks.' The layout successfully reinforces the simple concepts, and the bold digital illustrations are set against a solid background." SLJ

Recorvits, Helen

★ **My** name is Yoon; pictures by Gabi Swiatkowska. Frances Foster Bks. 2002 un il $16

Grades: PreK K 1 2   **E**

1. Immigrants -- Fiction 2. Korean Americans -- Fiction

ISBN 0-374-35114-7

LC 00-51395

Disliking her name as written in English, Korean-born Yoon, or "shining wisdom," refers to herself as "cat," "bird,"

and "cupcake," as a way to feel more comfortable in her new school and new country

"Swiatkowska's stunningly spare, almost surrealistic paintings enhance the story's message. . . . A powerful and inspiring picture book." SLJ

Other titles about Yoon are:

Yoon and the Christmas mitten (2006)

Yoon and the jade bracelet (2008)

Reed, Lynn Rowe

Basil's birds. Marshall Cavendish Children 2010 un il $17.99

Grades: K 1 2   **E**

1. Birds -- Fiction 2. Janitors -- Fiction

ISBN 978-0-7614-5627-8; 0-7614-5627-9

LC 2009007071

While Basil the school janitor is napping, birds build a nest atop his head and when the eggs hatch, he becomes a proud 'dad' to the chicks.

"Brightly painted clay birds and photographs of the nest and worms are scanned into Reed's gouache illustrations. Her childlike paintings are done in flat spring colors, often showing faces in profile and bodies so loose jointed that they hardly seem earthbound." SLJ

Color chaos! Holiday House 2010 un il $16.95

Grades: PreK K 1 2   **E**

1. School stories 2. Color -- Fiction 3. Illustrators -- Fiction

ISBN 978-0-8234-2257-9; 0-8234-2257-7

LC 2009029053

"The narrator, an aspiring illustrator who is itching to use his new box of 64 crayons, runs afoul of 'substitute principal' Mr. Greystone . . . who furiously confiscates all coloring tools and bans 'color of any kind.' With the school suddenly a sea of gray—not an ideal turn of events given that the day's guest is a famous illustrator, Maurice Coleur—can the discarded crayons, markers, and paints overcome their bickering . . . and stage a comeback? Reed's . . . terse, reportorial prose is the perfect counterfoil to the subtly controlled chaos of her collage and acrylic illustrations." Publ Wkly

Roscoe and the pelican rescue. Holiday House 2011 un il $14.95

Grades: PreK K 1   **E**

1. Pelicans -- Fiction 2. Vacations -- Fiction 3. Oil spills -- Fiction 4. Wildlife conservation -- Fiction 5. Gulf of Mexico oil spill, 2010 -- Fiction

ISBN 978-0-8234-2352-1; 0-8234-2352-2

LC 2010045005

The Gulf Coast oil spill turns Tony's summer vacation into an animal rescue mission.

"Reed's narrative is straightforward, ending happily. . . . Reed's illustrations are deliberately child-like. . . . This . . . should appeal to many young nature lovers." Booklist

Rees, Douglas

Jeannette Claus saves Christmas; illustrated by Olivier Latyk. Margaret K. McElderry Books 2010 un il $16.99

Grades: PreK K 1 2   **E**

1. Reindeer -- Fiction 2. Christmas -- Fiction 3. Santa Claus -- Fiction 4. Christmas stories -- Juvenile

literature
ISBN 978-1-4169-2686-3; 1-4169-2686-0

LC 2008023021

When Santa falls sick on Christmas Eve, his feisty daughter Jeannette takes his place in the sleigh and saves the day, despite rebellious reindeer.

"The Photoshop-rendered artwork has a retro cut-paper feel and is filled with implausibly pastel animals and romantic big-city backdrops. With its unlikely antagonists and plucky heroine, this has the potential to be a fan favorite." Booklist

Regan, Dian Curtis

The **Snow** Blew Inn; illustrated by Doug Cushman. Holiday House 2011 un il $16.95

Grades: PreK K 1   E

1. Snow -- Fiction 2. Animals -- Fiction 3. Cousins -- Fiction 4. Hotels and motels -- Fiction

ISBN 0-8234-2351-4; 978-0-8234-2351-4

Emma can't wait to have a sleepover with her cousin Abby! But snow is falling outside the Snow Blew Inn where Emma is waiting. Stranded travelers arrive seeking shelter, and soon the inn is packed. Emma even gives up her own room for the Fox family. When Abby finally arrives, she and Emma camp out on the parlor floor and have their sleepover at last!

"Regan and Cushman . . . pull readers into the story with strong atmospherics. With simple prose and crisp but warm watercolors, they conjure up the ever accumulating snow and guests—an array of anthropomorphized animals, dressed in vivid Victorian garb—and a palpable spirit of hospitality that turns a shelter into an arklike community brimming with Dickensian bonhomie and gratitude." Publ Wkly

Reibstein, Mark

★ **Wabi** Sabi; art by Ed Young. Little, Brown 2008 un il $16.99

Grades: 2 3 4   E

1. Cats -- Fiction 2. Animals -- Fiction 3. Aesthetics -- Fiction

ISBN 978-0-316-11825-5; 0-316-11825-7

LC 2007-50895

Wabi Sabi, a cat living in the city of Kyoto, learns about the Japanese concept of beauty through simplicity as she asks various animals she meets about the meaning of her name.

"Young's beautiful collages have an almost 3D effect and perfectly complement the spiritual, lyrical text." SLJ

Reich, Susanna

★ **Minette's** feast; the delicious story of Julia Child and her cat. by Susanna Reich; illustrated by Amy Bates. Abrams Books for Young Readers 2012 40 p.

Grades: K 1 2 3   E

1. Cats -- Fiction 2. French cooking -- Fiction 3. Paris (France) -- Fiction 4. Picture books for children 5. Food habits -- Fiction 6. Cooking, French -- Fiction

ISBN 1419701770; 9781419701771

LC 2011034275

This biographical picture book "introduces the iconic American chef Julia Child to a new audience of young readers through the story of her spirited cat, Minette, whom Julia adopted when living in Paris. While Julia is in the kitchen learning to master delicious French dishes, the only feast Minette is truly interested in is that of fresh mouse!" (Publisher's note)

Includes bibliographical references.

Reid, Alastair

Supposing; illustrated by Bob Gill. New York Review Books 2010 il (New York Review Children's Collection) $15.95

Grades: PreK K 1   E

1. Imagination -- Fiction

ISBN 978-1-59017-369-5; 1-59017-369-4

LC 2010016522

First published 1960 by Little, Brown

A child imagines many silly, impossible, and even naughty things and their possible consequences, from learning unusual languages to building a tiny boat and sailing around the world.

"The scenarios are (often surreal) springboards for readers' imaginations. . . . There's an understated but fitting whimsy in Gill's artwork." Publ Wkly

Reid, Barbara

★ **Perfect** snow. Albert Whitman & Company 2011 un il

Grades: K 1 2   E

1. School stories 2. Snow -- Fiction 3. Friendship -- Fiction

ISBN 0-8075-6492-3; 978-0-8075-6492-9

LC 2010045643

On the first snow of the season, Jim and Scott and their classmates build an enormous snowman fort.

"The boys' personality differences are marked throughout the book, but their rock-solid friendship is at the heart of the understated, but satisfying story. Reid's artwork takes two forms; large, colorful plasticine illustrations, and small ink drawings with sepia-toned, watercolor washes. In either medium, the figures of children are expressive and pleasing." Booklist

★ **Picture** a tree; Barbara Reid. Albert Whitman 2013 32 p. (hardcover) $16.99

Grades: PreK K 1   E

1. Trees -- Juvenile fiction 2. Picture books for children 3. Trees -- Fiction

ISBN 0807565261; 9780807565261

LC 2012019530

In this children's picture book, "viewers are invited to think about how trees can be pictured: as a drawing on the sky, a skeleton, a tunnel, an ocean, a pirate ship, and more. . . The book is not a guide to learning about trees but rather a lyrical request to explore them in our personal worlds." (School Library Journal)

"The book is not a guide to learning about trees but rather a lyrical request to explore them in our personal worlds... The vibrant pictures will draw in readers, while the text will encourage them to view the world in a different way." SLJ

The **Subway** mouse. Scholastic Press 2005 un il $15.95

Grades: PreK K 1 2   E

1. Mice -- Fiction 2. Subways -- Fiction

ISBN 0-439-72827-4

First published 2003 in Canada

Remembering childhood stories of a beautiful but dangerous place called Tunnel's End, a mouse named Nib leaves his dirty, crowded home under a busy subway station and sets out on a long journey, joined by Lola, a mouse he meets along the way.

"Reid creates a charming, lively adventure in short, smoothly paced sentences, but it's her marvelous collage illustrations that really bring the characters and richly imagined world to life. Working in found materials and expertly molded, brightly colored plasticine, she sculpts remarkably expressive characters and a vivid, subterranean world." Booklist

Reid, Rob

Comin' down to storytime; pictures by Nadine Bernard Westcott. Upstart Books 2009 32p il $17.95

Grades: PreK K 1   **E**

1. Songs 2. Farm life -- Fiction 3. Libraries -- Fiction 4. Storytelling -- Fiction

ISBN 978-1-60213-039-5; 1-60213-039-6

"Building on the familiar song 'She'll Be Coming 'Round the Mountain,' Reid's animal version begins, 'We'll be comin' down to storytime when we come, Yee ha!' as all the farm animals run excitedly to the barn. It ends with 'We will check out lots of books when we leave. Bye now!' . . . Illustrations fit the rollicking mood perfectly. Westcott imbues each scene with plenty of color and lively action." SLJ

Reidy, Jean

All through my town; by Jean Reidy; illustrated by Leo Timmers. Bloomsbury Childrens 2013 32 p. col. ill. (hardcover) $14.99; (library) $15.89

Grades: PreK   **E**

1. Stories in rhyme 2. Neighborhoods -- Fiction 3. City and town life -- Fiction

ISBN 9781599907857; 9781619630291

LC 2012023304

Light up the night; illustrations by Margaret Chodos-Irvine. Disney/Hyperion Books 2011 un il $16.99

Grades: PreK K 1 2   **E**

1. Stories in rhyme 2. Bedtime -- Fiction 3. Universe -- Fiction

ISBN 978-1-4231-2024-7; 1-4231-2024-8

LC 2011008523

In this cumulative, rhyming story, a young boy takes a nighttime ride from the distant stars in the Milky Way galaxy to his cozy bed, as his blanket becomes a rocket, a plane, and a skateboard.

"Soft assonant sounds soothe the cumulative rhyme that parallels nighttime routines through its repetition and structure. . . . Double-page spreads of bright but not overpowering collages depict [the boy's] journey, while the opening and closing actions (of going to bed and going to sleep) are shown in wordless panels, bringing the story full circle." Horn Book

Time (out) for monsters! by Jean Reidy; pictures by Robert Neubecker. Disney-Hyperion Books 2012 32 p.

Grades: K 1 2   **E**

1. Picture books for children 2. Monsters -- Juvenile fiction 3. Imagination -- Juvenile fiction 4. Behavior -- Fiction 5. Imagination -- Fiction

ISBN 1423131274; 9781423131274

LC 2011013049

In this children's book, by Jean Reidy, illustrated by Robert Neubecker, a young boy is dissatisfied with the decor of his "time-out corner. 'Mom says it's fine, but I know better. I spend a LOT of time there.' . . . So he conjures up a world of excitement that includes a killer view, a fire brigade, a dump truck full of ice cream, and some kingly accoutrements." (Publishers Weekly)

Too purpley! illustrated by Genevieve Leloup. Bloomsbury Children's Books 2010 un il $11.99; lib bdg $12.89

Grades: PreK K 1 2   **E**

1. Stories in rhyme 2. Clothing and dress -- Fiction

ISBN 978-1-59990-307-1; 1-59990-307-5; 978-1-59990-437-5 lib bdg; 1-59990-437-3 lib bdg

LC 2009004741

A young girl rejects many outfits before finding the perfect clothes to wear

"This fun book has lots of descriptive words that tickle the ear, great colors and patterns, and a charming protagonist." SLJ

Reiser, Lynn

My baby and me; concept and words by Lynn Reiser; photographs by Penny Gentieu. Alfred A. Knopf 2008 un il $16.99

Grades: PreK   **E**

1. Stories in rhyme 2. Infants -- Fiction 3. Siblings -- Fiction 4. Brothers and sisters -- Juvenile literature

ISBN 978-0-375-85205-3; 0-375-85205-0

LC 2007031949

Photographs and simple text portray interactions between babies and their toddler siblings.

"The photographs are just right for the very youngest, with each double-page spread foregrounding a pair of siblings and a few baby-friendly objects." Horn Book

★ **Tortillas** and lullabies. Tortillas y cancioncitas; pictures by Corazones Valientes; coordinated and translated by Rebecca Hart. Greenwillow Bks. 1998 40p il $16.99; pa $6.99

Grades: PreK K 1 2   **E**

1. Grandmothers -- Fiction 2. Mothers and daughters -- Fiction 3. Bilingual books -- English-Spanish 4. Mother-daughter relationship -- Fiction 5. Spanish language materials -- Bilingual

ISBN 0-688-14628-7; 0-06-089185-8 pa

LC 97-7096

In this "picture book, four everyday activities are depicted—making tortillas, gathering flowers, washing clothes, and singing a lullaby—as they are repeated by the women of a family over the last four generations. . . . Six Costa Rican women worked together to produce the striking acrylic folk-art paintings. With deeply saturated, glowing tones and a decidedly Central American style, the pictures enhance and extend the lyrical narrative, which is printed in English and in Spanish." SLJ

Rennert, Laura Joy

Buying, training & caring for your dinosaur; written by Laura Joy Rennert; pictures by Marc Brown. Alfred A. Knopf 2009 un il $16.99; lib bdg $19.99

Grades: PreK K 1 2   E

1. Pets -- Fiction 2. Dinosaurs -- Fiction

ISBN 978-0-375-83679-4; 0-375-83679-9; 978-0-375-93679-1 lib bdg; 0-375-93679-3 lib bdg

LC 2008-50680

Includes instructions for choosing and caring for a pet dinosaur

"This features funny, colorful illustrations. . . . Youngsters will quickly become absorbed in this enjoyable mix of facts, fantasy, and fossils." Booklist

Rex, Adam

Pssst! Harcourt 2007 un il $16

Grades: PreK K 1 2   E

1. Zoos -- Fiction 2. Animals -- Fiction

ISBN 978-0-15-205817-3; 0-15-205817-6

LC 2006-24551

"A zoo-going girl talks to the animals, but the novelty wears off when the pushy beasts send her on errands. . . . Rex packs increasingly crisp conversations into tight six-panel comics, relaxing into airy spreads as the girl meanders along zoo paths. . . . A very funny excursion." Publ Wkly

Rex, Michael

Goodnight goon; a petrifying parody. [by] Michael Rex. G.P. Putnam's Sons 2008 un il $14.99

Grades: K 1 2 3   E

1. Stories in rhyme 2. Bedtime -- Fiction 3. Monsters -- Fiction

ISBN 978-0-399-24534-3; 0-399-24534-0

LC 2007-16585

A young monster says goodnight to all of the other monsters in his bedroom.

"This book is a hilarious adaptation of the classic bedtime story, Goodnight Moon. . . . This is a delightfully funny and witty story containing adorable illustrations with tons of details. . . . Author and illustrator Michael Rex has created a wonderful page-by-page companion to the original." Libr Media Connect

Truck Duck; [by] Michael Rex. G.P. Putnam's Sons 2004 un il hardcover o.p. bd bk $7.99

Grades: PreK K 1 2   E

1. Animals 2. Vehicles 3. Stories in rhyme 4. Animals -- Fiction 5. Vehicles -- Fiction

ISBN 0-399-24009-8; 0-399-25092-1 bd bk

LC 2003-707

A variety of animals drive vehicles whose names rhyme with their own

"This is the stuff of toddlers' play, with vrooming action and small characters in charge. The sounds of the words add to the fun, and to little ones' vocabularies. The vehicles are big, bright, and clear." Booklist

A companion to this title is:

Dunk skunk (2005)

Rey, H. A.

★ **Curious** George. Houghton Mifflin 1941 un il $16; pa $6.95

Grades: PreK K 1   E

1. Monkeys -- Fiction

ISBN 0-395-15993-8; 0-395-15023-X pa

Colored picture book, with simple text, describing the adventures of a curious small monkey, and the difficulties

he had in getting used to city life, before he went to live in the zoo

"The bright lithographs in red, yellow, and blue, are gay and lighthearted, following the story closely with the same speed and animated humour." Ont Libr Rev

Other titles about Curious George are:

Curious George flies a kite (1958)

Curious George gets a medal (1957)

Curious George goes to the hospital (1966)

Curious George learns the alphabet (1963)

Curious George rides a bike (1952)

Curious George takes a job (1947)

Curious George: Cecily G. and the 9 monkeys; written and illustrated by H. A. Rey; afterword by Louise Borden. Houghton Mifflin Company 2007 un il $16; pa $6.99

Grades: PreK K 1   E

1. Monkeys -- Fiction 2. Giraffes -- Fiction

ISBN 978-0-618-80066-7; 0-618-80066-2; 978-0-618-99794-7 pa; 0-618-99794-6 pa

LC 2006-38698

First published 1942

A lonely giraffe teams up with the nine playful monkeys.

"This edition of the first story to feature Curious George includes a new afterword." Horn Book Guide

Rey, Margret

Whiteblack the penguin sees the world; [by] Margret & H. A. Rey. Houghton Mifflin 2000 un il $15; pa $5.95

Grades: PreK K 1   E

1. Animals 2. Penguins 3. Voyages and travels 4. Penguins -- Fiction

ISBN 0-618-07389-2; 0-618-07390-6 pa

LC 00-23196

In search of new stories for his radio program, Whiteblack the penguin sets out on a journey and has some interesting adventures

"The plot is very well crafted, and Whiteblack's adventures are appealingly silly, almost slapstick. H. A. Rey's watercolors make great use of the white paper, contrasting it with deep hues of yellow, red, and ultramarine blue and thick black outlines." Booklist

Reynolds, Aaron

★ **Back** of the bus; illustrated by Floyd Cooper. Philomel Books 2010 un il $16.99

Grades: K 1 2 3   E

1. Civil rights activists 2. Race relations -- Fiction 3. African Americans -- Fiction 4. African Americans -- Civil rights -- Fiction 5. African Americans -- Civil rights -- History -- Juvenile literature

ISBN 978-0-399-25091-0; 0-399-25091-3

LC 2008018109

From the back of the bus, an African American child watches the arrest of Rosa Parks.

Reynolds's "lyrical yet forceful text conveys the narrator's apprehension and Park's calm resolve. . . . Cooper's . . . filmy oil paintings are characterized by a fine mistlike texture, which results in warm, lifelike portraits that convincingly evoke the era, the intense emotional pitch of this incident, and the everyday heroism it embodied." Publ Wkly

★ **Creepy** carrots! words Aaron Reynolds; pictures Peter Brown. Simon & Schuster Books for Young Readers 2012 40 p. (hardcover: alk. paper) $16.99
Grades: PreK K 1 2   E
   1. Carrots -- Fiction 2. Rabbits -- Fiction 3. Picture books for children 4. Humorous stories
ISBN 1442402970; 9781442402973
                       LC 2010035099
Caldecott Honor Book (2013)
In this book, "Jasper Rabbit [didn't] think twice about plundering the carrots of Crackenhopper Field 'until they started following him.' Jasper glimpses three jack-o-lantern-jawed carrots behind him in the bathroom mirror (when he turns around it's just a washcloth, shampoo bottle, and rubber duck--or is it?), and he yells for his parents when a carrot shadow looms on his bedroom wall." (Publishers Weekly)

Metal man; illustrated by Paul Hoppe. Charlesbridge 2008 un il lib bdg $15.95; pa $7.95
Grades: PreK K 1 2   E
   1. Metalwork -- Fiction 2. Sculpture -- Fiction 3. African Americans -- Fiction
ISBN 978-1-58089-150-9 lib bdg; 1-58089-150-0 lib bdg; 978-1-58089-151-6 pa; 1-58089-151-9 pa
                       LC 2007-17187
One hot summer day, a man who makes sculpture out of junk helps a boy create what he sees in his mind's eye.
"Beautifully understated, the story is about the capacity of art to empower the artist and to affect how others see the world. The poetic text is visceral. . . . The cartoon illustrations, in rusty browns and shiny blues, depict the metal man as tall, strong, gentle, and wise, a larger-than-life hero. . . . A wonderful example of sensory writing and colloquial storytelling." SLJ

Snowbots; illustrated by David Barneda. Alfred A. Knopf 2010 un il $16.99; lib bdg $19.99
Grades: PreK K 1 2   E
   1. Stories in rhyme 2. Snow -- Fiction 3. Robots -- Fiction
ISBN 978-0-375-85873-4; 0-375-85873-3; 978-0-375-95873-1 lib bdg; 0-375-95873-8 lib bdg
Rhyming tale of a fun day young robots spend playing in new-fallen snow.
"The acrylic and colored pencil artwork features an array of mechanical kids and household props and plug-ins. The cool, blue-tinged snow scenes contrast with the warm yellows and browns of the house interiors. Libraries with robot fans won't want to pass on this snowy fun." SLJ

Superhero School; illustrated by Andy Rash. Bloomsbury Children's Books 2009 un il $16.99; lib bdg $17.89
Grades: K 1 2 3 4   E
   1. School stories 2. Mathematics -- Fiction 3. Superheroes -- Fiction
ISBN 978-1-59990-166-4; 1-59990-166-8; 978-1-59990-346-0 lib bdg; 1-59990-346-6 lib bdg
                    LC 2008031374
When Leonard starts attending Superhero School he is disappointed to find that all they learn is math, but when the ice zombies strike, Leonard and his classmates put their newly-acquired knowledge to good use

"Rash's illustrations in digital collage of gouache and Sharpies create his trademark cartoons that pulsate with energy and engage readers. Reynolds creatively blends the use of math skills in word-problem superhero settings that are playful, smart, and positive." SLJ

Reynolds, Peter
   ★ **I'm** here; [by] Peter H. Reynolds. Atheneum Books for Young Readers 2011 il $15.99
Grades: PreK K 1 2   E
   1. Parks -- Fiction 2. Friendship -- Fiction
ISBN 978-1-4169-9649-1; 1-4169-9649-4
                    LC 2010038962
In a crowded park, a boy makes an airplane out of a piece of paper carried to him by a gentle breeze, sends it on its way, and watches a new friend bring it back to him.
"Though back matter explains that the book was written 'to help us all reach out, embrace, and appreciate children in the autism spectrum,' the pared-down prose and artwork, painted in Reynolds's typical loose style, are open to multiple interpretations and may facilitate conversations about reaching out to others who are different—and alone—for many reasons." Publ Wkly

Ish; [by] Peter H. Reynolds. Candlewick Press 2004 un il $14
Grades: PreK K 1 2 3   E
   1. Drawing 2. Self-confidence 3. Drawing -- Fiction 4. Siblings -- Fiction 5. Brothers and sisters
ISBN 0-7636-2344-X
                    LC 2003-66196
Ramon loses confidence in his ability to draw, but his sister gives him a new perspective on things
"The overriding theme about creativity versus exactitude will resonate with many. The line-and-color artwork is simple, but it has great emotion and warmth." Booklist

Rose's garden; [by] Peter H. Reynolds. Candlewick Press 2009 un il $15.99
Grades: K 1 2 3   E
   1. Flowers -- Fiction 2. Gardens -- Fiction
ISBN 978-0-7636-4641-7; 0-7636-4641-5
                    LC 2009-24175
Rose finds a neglected patch of earth in the middle of a bustling city where she can plant the flower seeds collected from her travels in her magical teapot
"This inspiring fable will capture the hearts and imaginations of readers and show them that anything is possible. . . . Reynolds's outstanding illustrations done in watercolor and ink begin in shades of gray and then explode with color and joy as the garden evolves and people come to enjoy it." SLJ

The **dot**; [by] Peter H. Reynolds. Candlewick Press 2003 un il $14
Grades: PreK K 1 2   E
   1. School stories 2. Drawing -- Fiction
ISBN 0-7636-1961-2
                    LC 2002-041113
Vashti believes that she cannot draw, but her art teacher's encouragement leads her to change her mind
"In this engaging, inspiring tale, Reynolds . . . demonstrates the power of a little encouragement. . . . Rendered in watercolor, ink and tea, Reynolds's spare, wispy illustrations

exude a fresh, childlike quality pleasingly in sync with his hand-lettered text." Publ Wkly

Rice, Eve

Sam who never forgets. Greenwillow Bks. 1977 un il hardcover o.p. pa $5.99

Grades: PreK K E

1. Zoos -- Fiction 2. Animals -- Fiction
ISBN 0-688-07335-2 pa

LC 76-30370

"A simple, unpretentious story with child appeal that lies in the naive, straightforward telling and elemental emotional interactions of the characters. . . . Rice has forsaken her pen drawings for bright, unlined colored shapes. The figures are pleasantly stylized, the scenes evenly composed." Booklist

Richards, Beah

★ **Keep** climbing, girls; by Beah E. Richards; illustrated by R. Gregory Christie; introduction by LisaGay Hamilton. Simon & Schuster Books for Young Readers 2006 un il $15.95

Grades: PreK K 1 2 E

1. Children's poetry 2. Girls -- Poetry
ISBN 1-4169-0264-3

LC 2004-29153

"In this picture-book rendition of Richards's 1951 poem of the same name, girls are urged to 'keep climbing' no matter what obstacles get in the way. Bold gouache illustrations create a beguiling green-and-gold landscape with an irresistible tree and a determined little girl who climbs it higher and higher with every page turn." SLJ

Richards, Chuck

Critter sitter; [by] Chuck Richards. Walker & Company 2008 un il $16.99; lib bdg $17.89

Grades: 1 2 3 4 E

1. Pets -- Fiction
ISBN 978-0-8027-9595-3; 0-8027-9595-1; 978-0-8027-9596-0 lib bdg; 0-8027-9596-X lib bdg

LC 2008004314

When the Mahoney family hires Henry the Critter Sitter to watch their dog, cat, bird, fish, frog, and snake, he thinks he is up for the challenge since creature control is his game, but the pets have a different idea.

"The storytelling is well paced and amusing, but the artwork is the real grabber here. Created with colored-pencil and watercolor, the illustrations cleverly mix realism with humorous exaggeration." SLJ

Richards, Lucy

Ollie and the lost toy; a lift-the-flap story. Sterling Pub. 2011 un il $9.95

Grades: PreK K E

1. Fear -- Fiction 2. Toys -- Fiction 3. Lost and found possessions -- Fiction
ISBN 978-1-4027-7754-7; 1-4027-7754-X

LC 2010037979

First published 2006 in the United Kingdom

Ollie must face his fear of the dark to find Snaily, his favorite toy that has been missing all day.

"The soft, colorful illustrations will elicit an emotional response from children. . . . The book has many lift-the-flap elements." SLJ

Richardson, Justin

★ **And** Tango makes three; by Justin Richardson and Peter Parnell; illustrated by Henry Cole. Simon & Schuster Bks. for Young Readers 2005 un il $14.95

Grades: PreK K 1 2 E

1. Penguins -- Fiction 2. Homosexuality -- Fiction
ISBN 0-689-87845-1

At New York City's Central Park Zoo, two male penguins fall in love and start a family by taking turns sitting on an abandoned egg until it hatches

"Done in soft watercolors, the illustrations set the tone for this uplifting story, and readers will find it hard to resist the penguins' comical expressions. . . . This joyful story about the meaning of family is a must for any library." SLJ

Christian, the hugging lion; [by] Justin Richardson and Peter Parnell; illustrated by Amy Bates. Simon & Schuster Books for Young Readers 2010 un il $16.99

Grades: PreK K 1 2 E

1. Lions -- Fiction
ISBN 978-1-4169-8662-1; 1-4169-8662-6

LC 2009002297

When Ace and John find a lion cub for sale at Harrods department store, they buy him, name him Christian, and the three live happily for a year in a London apartment, but eventually Christian grows too big and they must let him go to live the life of a wild cat. Based on a true story; includes an author's note.

"Bates captures the friendship and love between Christian, Ace and John when they go visit him years later. Justin Richardson and Peter Parnell write this story like a fairy tale—whimsical and entertaining." Libr Media Connect

Richardson, Nan

The **pearl**; written by Nan Richardson; illustrations by Alexandra Young. Umbrage Editions, Inc. 2011 il $17

Grades: K 1 2 E

1. Actors 2. Opera -- Fiction 3. Singers -- Fiction
ISBN 978-1-884167-24-9; 1-884167-24-1

Tells the love story of Nicolas Cheremeteff, a wealthy courtier and Praskovia, a serf girl in eighteenth-century Russia.

"Richly illustrated in bold pen-and-ink and watercolor, the story is brought to life in sumptuous detail and precisely placed splashes of color. Readers will relish this unique, Russian Cinderella tale." SLJ

Ries, Lori

★ **Aggie** and Ben; three stories. illustrated by Frank W. Dormer. Charlesbridge 2006 48p il lib bdg $12.95; pa $5.95

Grades: K 1 2 E

1. Dogs -- Fiction
ISBN 978-1-57091-549-9 lib bdg; 1-57091-594-6 lib bdg; 978-1-57091-649-6 pa; 1-57091-649-7 pa

LC 2005-28702

After choosing a new dog, Ben describes what the pet Aggie can do and should not do around the house

"Funky but tender, Dormer's pen-and-ink cartoons with watercolor washes add depth to the simple story and provide that perfect illustration-to-text match that one seeks in successful easy readers." SLJ

Other titles about Aggie and Ben are:

Good dog, Aggie (2009)

Aggie the brave (2010)
Aggie gets lost (2011)

Aggie gets lost; illustrated by Frank Dormer. Charlesbridge 2011 il $12.95
Grades: K 1 2　　　　　　　　　　　　　　E
　　1. Dogs -- Fiction 2. Blind -- Fiction 3. Lost and found possessions -- Fiction
　　ISBN 978-1-570-91633-5; 1-570-91633-0
　　　　　　　　　　　　　　　　　LC 2010007533
Ben and Aggie are playing in the park when she chases a ball and does not return, but after looking for her and worrying about her, Ben speaks with his blind friend, Mr. Thomas, who suggests a different approach.
　　"Art in pen, ink and watercolor shows the characters and their emotions clearly in a faux childlike drawing style. . . . Anyone who has worried about the loss of a special friend will understand the feelings involved with great sympathy and empathy." Kirkus

Punk wig; illustrated by Erin Eitter-Kono. Boyds Mills Press 2008 un il $16.95
Grades: PreK K 1 2　　　　　　　　　　　　E
　　1. Wigs -- Fiction 2. Cancer -- Fiction 3. Mother-son relationship -- Fiction
　　ISBN 978-1-59078-486-0; 1-59078-486-3
　　　　　　　　　　　　　　　　　LC 2007-17688
A little boy does helpful things for his mother as she undergoes chemotherapy, and goes with her as she picks out a wig, which together they call her "punk wig."
　　"The story handles a tough subject with sensitivity, grace, and a sense of fun. It covers some of the issues facing families without giving too much information that might overwhelm a young child, and provides a good introduction to a hard subject. The watercolor pictures fit well with the text, portraying both the mother's treatment and her fun with the family." Libr Media Connect

Riggs, Shannon
　　★ **Not** in Room 204; illustrated by Jaime Zollars. Albert Whitman 2007 un il $15.95
Grades: K 1 2 3　　　　　　　　　　　　　E
　　1. School stories 2. Child sexual abuse -- Fiction
　　ISBN 978-0-8075-5764-8
　　　　　　　　　　　　　　　　　LC 2006023402
"Quiet Regina feels comfortable in her classroom, where Mrs. Salvador runs a tight ship and insists on hard work and fair play. When the teacher starts the annual Stranger Danger unit, she departs from the usual script by saying that most often an adult who touches a child inappropriately is not a stranger but someone known to the child. . . . The next morning, Regina arrives early at Room 204 to confide her secret, which involves her father. . . . This picture book's strength is in the forthrightness of its message and the sensitivity of its presentation. . . . The text and digitally enhanced artwork work together well to express the book's message smoothly. . . . This helpful picture book will raise children's awareness of sexual abuse without raising anxiety." Booklist

Riley, Linnea Asplind
　　Mouse mess; [by] Linnea Riley. Blue Sky Press (NY) 1997 un il $16.95
Grades: PreK K 1　　　　　　　　　　　　E
　　1. Stories in rhyme 2. Food -- Fiction 3. Mice --

Fiction
ISBN 0-590-10048-3
　　　　　　　　　　　　　　　　　LC 96-49499
A hungry mouse leaves a huge mess when it goes in search of a snack
　　"Cut-paper collages, set against black backgrounds, depict a chubby-cheeked mouse spilling, cutting, and eating a variety of colorful foods. . . . The rhyming text, filled with crunching and munching sounds, is rhythmic and fun to read aloud." SLJ

Rim, Sujean
　　Birdie's big-girl dress. Little, Brown 2011 il $16.99
Grades: PreK K　　　　　　　　　　　　　E
　　1. Parties -- Fiction 2. Birthdays -- Fiction 3. Clothing and dress -- Fiction
　　ISBN 978-0-316-13287-9; 0-316-13287-X
　　　　　　　　　　　　　　　　　LC 2010049435
Birdie's excitement over her approaching birthday party fades when she finds that her favorite party dress is too small, and nothing at her mother's favorite boutique is quite right.
　　"As Birdie shimmies into each potentially restrictive outfit, Rim's illustrations capture each halfhearted shrug and sucked-in breath. Collage and watercolor accents lend a sensory feel to chromatic, textured design . . . [and] canine companion Monster remains a supportive secondary choice, dressed to the nines in his top hat to rave reviews." Kirkus

　　Birdie's big-girl shoes. Little, Brown Books for Young Readers 2009 un il $15.99
Grades: PreK K　　　　　　　　　　　　　E
　　1. Play -- Fiction 2. Shoes -- Fiction 3. Mother-daughter relationship -- Fiction
　　ISBN 978-0-316-04470-7; 0-316-04470-9
　　　　　　　　　　　　　　　　　LC 2008-43799
Five-year-old Birdie loves her mother's shoes, but when she is finally granted permission to wear some for a little while, she discovers that her 'barefoot shoes' are best of all
　　"The bold, stylized watercolor and collage illustrations, paired with spare, simple text, are set against ample white space and burst with bright, attractive textile patterns. A light confection for the preschool dress-up set." SLJ
　　Another title about Birdie is:
　　Birdie's big-girl dress (2011)

Rinck, Maranke
　　I feel a foot! [by] Maranke Rinck & Martijn van der Linden. Lemniscaat 2008 un il $16.95
Grades: PreK K 1　　　　　　　　　　　　E
　　1. Animals -- Fiction 2. Imagination -- Fiction
　　ISBN 978-1-59078-638-3; 1-59078-638-6
　　　　　　　　　　　　　　　　　LC 2008000917
Five animal friends, awakened by a strange noise, discover a creature in the dark that seems to be a giant-sized version of each of them.
　　"With simple wording, Rinck injects personality into each animal and van der Linden's images interact well with the text. His stark black backgrounds spotlight expressively imagined animals that appear in psychedelic colors and patterns reminiscent of a kaleidoscope." SLJ

Ringgold, Faith
　　★ **Tar** Beach. Crown 1991 un il $18; lib bdg $18.99; pa $6.99

Grades: PreK K 1 2   E

1. Dreams -- Fiction 2. African Americans -- Fiction
ISBN 0-517-58030-6; 0-517-58031-4 lib bdg; 0-517-
88544-1 pa

LC 90-40410

A Caldecott Medal honor book, 1992

Eight-year-old Cassie dreams of flying above her Harlem home, claiming all she sees for herself and her family.
Based on the author's quilt painting of the same name

"Part autobiographical, part fictional, this allegorical tale
sparkles with symbolic and historical references central to
African-American culture. The spectacular artwork, a combination of primitive naive figures in a flattened perspective
against a boldly patterned cityscape, resonates with color
and texture." Horn Book

Another title about Cassie is:

Cassie's word quilt (2002)

Rinker, Sherri Duskey

★ **Goodnight**, goodnight, construction site; illustrated
by Tom Lichtenheld. Chronicle Books 2011 un il $16.99
Grades: PreK K 1   E

1. Stories in rhyme 2. Trucks -- Fiction 3. Bedtime
-- Fiction 4. Construction equipment -- Fiction
ISBN 0-8118-7782-5; 978-0-8118-7782-4

LC 2010025008

At sunset, when their work is done for the day, a crane
truck, a cement mixer, and other pieces of construction
equipment make their way to their resting places and go
to sleep.

"Lichtenheld's detailed and textured illustrations, rendered in wax oil pastels on vellum paper, perfectly complement the fun, rhyming text, cleverly personifying each truck
with expressive eyes and amusing details." SLJ

★ **Steam** train, dream train; by Sherri Duskey Rinker;
illustrated by Tom Lichtenheld. Chronicle Books 2013 40
p. ill. (hardcover) $16.99
Grades: PreK K 1   E

1. Animals -- Juvenile fiction 2. Bedtime -- Juvenile
fiction 3. Railroads -- Juvenile fiction 4. Stories in
rhyme 5. Animals -- Fiction 6. Railroad trains --
Fiction 7. Railroad trains -- Juvenile fiction
ISBN 1452109206; 9781452109206

LC 2012030942

In this children's story, by Sherri Duskey Rinker, illustrated by Tom Lichtenheld, "the dream train pulls into the
station, and one by one the train cars are loaded: polar bears
pack the reefer car with ice cream, elephants fill the tanker
cars with paints, tortoises stock the auto rack with race cars,
bouncy kangaroos stuff the hopper car with balls." (Publisher's note)

"The strength of this book is in the striking spreads in
wax oil pastel. ... The beginning and end of the book are
filled with expressive and enjoyable railroad sounds, yet the
rhyming text loses a bit of steam in the middle, describing
but not always enhancing the activity depicted in the illustrations. Still, this is a book that will...be embraced as a nighttime standard, particularly among train lovers everywhere."
SLJ

Riphagen, Loes

Animals home alone. Seven Footer Press 2011 il
$15.95

Grades: PreK K 1   E

1. Stories without words 2. Animals -- Fiction
ISBN 1-93473455-1; 978-193473455-1

This picture book introduces readers to fifteen animals
who begin to act in unusual ways when the humans are
away,. In wordless pages, each animal finds a unique activity
or bit of mischief to get into. At the book's conclusion, readers are asked questions about what the animals have done.

"This wordless picture book is a playful romp. . . . The
little dramas will have children (and adults) flipping back
and forth for more whimsical and hilarious details." SLJ

Ritchie, Alison

Duck says don't! Alison Ritchie; [illustrated by] Hannah George. Good Books 2012 26 p. col. ill. (hardcover:
alk. paper) $16.99
Grades: K 1 2   E

1. Picture books for children 2. Animals -- Juvenile
literature 3. Friendship -- Juvenile fiction 4. Ducks
-- Fiction 5. Geese -- Fiction 6. Ponds -- Fiction 7.
Bossiness -- Fiction 8. Pond animals -- Fiction
ISBN 9781561487455; 1561487457

LC 2011031770

Author Alison Ritchie presents a children's picture book.
"Goose leaves Duck in charge when she leaves her pond,
with unhappy results. Power goes immediately to Duck's
head. First, he stops the dragonflies from racing, although
they point out that flying is what they do . . . Soon he forbids
the kingfishers from fishing and the frogs from diving, and
. . . signs appear forbidding, well, everything. Then Duck
realizes all his friends have gone . . . and [he] welcomes
everyone back to do what they do." (Kirkus)

Ritz, Karen

Windows with birds; written and illustrated by Karen
Ritz. Boyds Mills Press 2010 un il $16.95
Grades: PreK K 1 2   E

1. Cats -- Fiction 2. Moving -- Fiction
ISBN 978-1-59078-656-7; 1-59078-656-4

LC 2009-19504

"This delicate and understated book tells a simple story
about a striped cat with green eyes that loves a boy and a
house. All of the feline's comforts are in that house, but one
day the boy takes it to live in an apartment. The cat sulks and
hides, while the boy tries to coax it out. . . . By morning, the
cat realizes that the things it loves best—hiding places, windows with birds, and the boy—are in the new environment
as well. . . . The realistic, closeup watercolors convey many
emotions. . . . This is a beautiful book for cat lovers and for
those who are uncomfortable with change." SLJ

Robbins, Jacqui

Two of a kind; [by] Jacqui Robbins and Matt Phelan.
Atheneum Books for Young Readers 2008 un il $16.99
Grades: K 1 2   E

1. School stories 2. Friendship -- Fiction
ISBN 978-1-4169-2437-1; 1-4169-2437-X

LC 2006033210

When Anna abandons her best friend, Julisa, to spend
time with Kayla and Melanie, whose friendship is considered very special, she soon learns that she has little in common with her new friends.

"Phelan's restrained watercolor-and-pencil illustrations
are particularly apt at capturing the emotions at play in the

story, while Kayla and Melanie's devilish expressions provide a gentle comic lift. A great introduction to early conversations are character, bullying, and peer pressure." Booklist

The **new** girl ... and me; story by Jacqui Robbins; with art by Matt Phelan. Atheneum 2006 un il $16.95

Grades: K 1 2   E

1. School stories 2. Iguanas -- Fiction 3. Friendship -- Fiction

ISBN 0-689-86468-X

LC 2004-09931

Two girls named Shakeeta and Mia become friends when Shakeeta boasts that she has a pet iguana and Mia learns how to help Shakeeta "feel at home" even when she is in school.

"The characters are realistically and sympathetically portrayed, and the conversations and actions of the children are natural. Phelan's cartoon-style watercolors depict a realistic-looking classroom with a mix of children from a variety of backgrounds." SLJ

Robert, Francois

★ **Find** a face; by Francois and Jean Robert, with Jane Gittings. Chronicle Books 2004 un il $15.95

Grades: PreK K 1 2   E

1. Face in art

ISBN 0-8118-4338-6

LC 2003-17593

Presents, with accompanying rhyming text, photographs of everyday objects depicting faces

This is "a fun book that demonstrates that faces can be found anywhere if you look hard enough. . . . The photographs are clear and bright, and set against boldly colored backgrounds. Youngsters will never again look at a light switch in the same way." SLJ

Robert, Na'ima bint

Ramadan moon; by Na'ima B. Robert; illustrated by Shirin Adl. Frances Lincoln Children's Books 2009 un il $17.99

Grades: K 1 2 3   E

1. Muslims -- Fiction 2. Ramadan -- Fiction

ISBN 978-1-84507-922-2; 1-84507-922-1

This "follows a Muslim family through its observance of the 'Month of Mercy.' . . . This book's poetic words and playful, patterned collage artwork capture both the solemnity and joy of religious practice and, in a series of scenes of worshippers of every type and hue, show the diversity of the Muslim community around the world." Booklist

Roberton, Fiona

Wanted: the perfect pet. G.P. Putnam's Sons 2010 un il $16.99

Grades: K 1 2   E

1. Dogs -- Fiction 2. Pets -- Fiction 3. Ducks -- Fiction

ISBN 978-0-399-25461-1; 0-399-25461-7

A boy who desperately wants a pet dog ends up with a duck instead.

"Roberton's line drawings have a palette of mostly of black and white, gray, and touches of green and yellow. They are very effective in conveying mood, action, and humor. The amusing text is placed in and among the illustrations for a seamless partnership between the two. An excellent tale about not getting what you thought you wanted but loving it anyway." SLJ

Roberts, Lynn

Little Red; a fizzingly good yarn. retold by Lynn Roberts; illustrated by David Roberts. Harry N. Abrams 2005 32p il $16.95

Grades: PreK K 1 2   E

1. Fairy tales 2. Wolves -- Fiction 3. Grandmothers -- Fiction

ISBN 0-8109-5783-3

LC 2004-29534

In this version of the Grimm fairy tale, Thomas—who is called Little Red—discovers a wolf in disguise at his grandmother's house and ingeniously uses ginger ale to save the day.

"The real strength of the book is David Roberts' stylish pen-and-ink and watercolor art, which creates a shadowy, detailed work that is deliciously creepy yet packed with humor." Bull Cent Child Books

Robinson, Fiona

What animals really like; a new song composed & conducted by Mr. Herbert Timerteeth. Abrams 2011 un il

Grades: 1 2   E

1. Animals -- Fiction

ISBN 0-8109-8976-X; 978-0-8109-8976-4

"This amusing story begins when readers open two foldouts to part a pair of red curtains. On stage is a large group of animals ready to give voice to the composer/conductor's new song. Unfortunately, his preconceived notions about the creatures are evident. . . . The pen, ink and marker-pens illustrations show a number of animals dressed in their finest. They become livelier and bolder as their performance goes on. Although Robinson keeps the focus and humor on the well-lit stage, she occasionally pans over to the audience where all readers see are the many colorful eyeballs peering out of the darkness. Sublime silliness." SLJ

Robinson, Michelle

What to do if an elephant stands on your foot; by Michelle Robinson; pictures by Peter H. Reynolds. Dial 2012 32 p. (hardback) $16.99

Grades: PreK K   E

1. Elephants -- Fiction 2. Jungle animals -- Fiction 3. Picture books for children 4. Humorous stories

ISBN 9780803733985

LC 2011035450

This children's picture book offers tongue-in-cheek information about "[s]afari etiquette . . . . From what to do if an elephant stands on your foot . . . to how to escape the attentions of a crocodile . . . , our . . . guide leads our unlucky hero on a jungle adventure, barely avoiding tigers, a rhino," and "snakes." (Amazon.com)

Robinson, Sharon

Jackie's gift; a true story of Christmas, Hanukkah, and Jackie Robinson. illustrated by E. B. Lewis. Viking 2010 un il $16.99

Grades: K 1 2 3   E

1. Baseball players 2. Army officers 3. Jews -- Fiction 4. Hanukkah -- Fiction 5. Christmas -- Fiction 6. Race relations -- Fiction

ISBN 978-0-670-01162-9; 0-670-01162-2

When young Steve, who is Jewish, tells his new neighbor, Jackie Robinson, that his family does not have a Christmas tree, Jackie brings one to his neighbors, not knowing that they celebrate Hanukkah instead of Christmas. Based on a true story.

"What could have been an awkward moment becomes a lesson in tolerance and friendship. Lewis's lovely paintings do a fine job of conveying the time and place in this heartwarming story." SLJ

Rocco, John

★ **Blackout**. Disney/Hyperion Books 2011 un il lib bdg $16.99

Grades: K 1 2 3 E

1. Night -- Fiction 2. Summer -- Fiction 3. Family life -- Fiction 4. City and town life -- Fiction 5. Electric power failures -- Fiction

ISBN 978-1-4231-2190-9 lib bdg; 1-4231-2190-2 lib bdg

"The plot line, conveyed with just a few sentences, is simple enough, but the dramatic illustrations illuminate the story. . . . Page composition effectively intermingles boxed pages and panels with double-page spreads, generating action. Brilliant designed, with comic bits." Kirkus

Moonpowder; story and pictures by John Rocco. Hyperion Books for Children 2008 un il $15.99

Grades: K 1 2 E

1. Dreams -- Fiction 2. Bedtime -- Fiction

ISBN 978-1-4231-0011-9; 1-4231-0011-5

LC 2007-042236

Even though Eli is the "Fixer of all things fixable," one thing he cannot fix is his bad dreams, until one night when Mr. Moon appears and asks him to come fix the Moonpowder factory, where sweet dreams are created.

"Steeped in dreamy sepia tones suffused with golden light and brightened by unexpected patches of electric blue, the illustrations are lush and painterly. Using spreads combined with comic-style panels, Rocco creates a hint of a graphic novel for the youngest readers." SLJ

Wolf! wolf! Hyperion Books for Children 2007 un il $15.99

Grades: K 1 2 3 E

1. Goats -- Fiction 2. Wolves -- Fiction

ISBN 1-4231-0012-3

LC 2007-04636

"This twisted treatment of Aesop's fable flips everything readers know about the boy who cried wolf on its head. . . . Ancient China unfolds as the stage and setting for this story. In this variant, children get a little insight into the wolf's point of view. . . . The purposeful use of frames, unusual setting, and visual humor makes this an excellent addition to any collection." SLJ

Rockliff, Mara

Me and Momma and Big John; text by Mara Rockliff; illustrations by William Low. Candlewick 2012 32 p. (hardback) $16.99

Grades: PreK K 1 2 E

1. Mothers -- Fiction 2. Cathedrals -- Fiction 3. Picture books for children 4. Building -- Fiction 5. Stonecutters -- Fiction 6. Mothers and sons -- Fiction 7. African Americans -- Fiction

ISBN 0763643599; 9780763643591

LC 2011046649

In this story, "our narrator . . . greets his mother . . . when she returns from work, tired and covered with gray dust. She has been hired to cut stone for the cathedral in the city called Big John." She spends many days on just one stone. "John expects to see his mother's name on the stone . . . . When the stone is finished, the whole" family goes to see it, and though "her name is not on it, Momma knows that many people will come and see it, high atop the cathedral." (Children's Literature)

My heart will not sit down; illustrations by Ann Tanksley. Alfred A. Knopf 2012 un il $17.99; lib bdg $20.99

Grades: K 1 2 3 E

1. School stories 2. Charity -- Fiction 3. Great Depression, 1929-1939 -- Fiction

ISBN 978-0-375-84569-7; 0-375-84569-0; 978-0-375-94569-4 lib bdg; 0-375-94569-5 lib bdg; 978-0-375-98728-1 ebook

LC 2011001117

In 1931 Cameroon, young Kedi is upset to learn that children in her American teacher's village of New York are going hungry because of the Great Depression, and she asks her mother, neighbors, and even the headman for money to help. Includes historical notes.

"Inspired by a true incident, [this] story demonstrates what real generosity looks like. . . . Rendered in watercolor, pen-and-ink, and oils, Tanksley's . . . pared-down, childlike pictures provide a sketch of Cameroon village life, their electric hues of orange, magenta, and scarlet jumping from the pages." Publ Wkly

The case of the July 4th jinx; by Lewis B. Montgomery; illustrated by Amy Wummer. Kane Press 2010 96p il (The Milo & Jazz mysteries) lib bdg $22.60; pa $6.95

Grades: 1 2 3 E

1. Mystery fiction

ISBN 978-1-57565-315-0 lib bdg; 1-57565-315-X lib bdg; 978-1-57565-308-2 pa; 1-57565-308-7 pa

LC 2009049886

With the help of ace detective Dash Marlowe, sleuths-in-training Mio and Jazz investigate a so-called jinx at the local Fourth of July fair

"The story is simple, and children will enjoy solving the mystery. Black-and-white spot art appears frequently throughout, creating a text that will not intimidate children just starting to read chapter books." SLJ

Rockwell, Anne F.

Apples and pumpkins; illustrated by Lizzy Rockwell. Simon & Schuster 2011 il $14.99

Grades: PreK E

1. Apples -- Fiction 2. Autumn -- Fiction 3. Pumpkin -- Fiction

ISBN 978-1-4424-0350-5; 1-4424-0350-0

A reissue of the title first published 1989

A little girl spends a glorious Fall day picking apples and searching for the perfect pumpkin.

This edition "has new cover art that punches up the fall colors, adds a chicken, and features apples and pumpkins in the foreground. The text's typeface has changed, but everything else is kept in its original perfection so that yet another generation of youngsters will celebrate autumn, from orchard visits to trick-or-treating." SLJ

Big wheels; by Anne Rockwell. Walker & Co. 2003 un il $14.95; bd bk $6.95

Grades: PreK K 1   **E**

1. Vehicles 2. Machinery 3. Motor vehicles 4. Machinery -- Juvenile literature 5. Motor vehicles -- Juvenile literature 6. Motor vehicles -- Wheels -- Juvenile literature

ISBN 0-8027-8882-3; 0-8027-8903-X bd bk

LC 2002-34348

A reissue of the title first published 1986 by Dutton Children's Bks.

Introduces a number of big-wheeled trucks, such as bulldozers, power shovels, and dump trucks, and explains what they do

"Although the author-artist has supplied a very brief text, she uses active, vivid verbs, such as dig, dump, and chop up, effectively conveying a sense of the machinery in the fewest words necessary. Likewise, her illustrations contain exactly the right amount of detail to satisfy but not confuse." Horn Book

★ **Father's** Day; by Anne Rockwell; pictures by Lizzy Rockwell. HarperCollins 2005 un il $14.99

Grades: PreK K 1   **E**

1. Fathers -- Fiction 2. Father's Day -- Fiction

ISBN 0-06-051377-2

LC 2004-6243

For Fathers' Day, the students in Mrs. Madoff's class write and illustrate books about their dads.

"The best part of the book is the way it reflects the differences in dads. . . . The artwork, with rounded shapes and smooth colors, has a simple, friendly look that puts the focus on the characters." Booklist

Other titles about Mrs. Madoff's class are:

100 school days (2002)

Career day (2000)

First day of school (2011)

Halloween day (1997)

Mother's Day (2004)

Presidents' Day (2007)

St. Patrick's Day (2010)

Thanksgiving Day (1999)

Valentine's Day (2001)

First day of school; pictures by Lizzy Rockwell. Harper 2011 un il $16.99

Grades: PreK K 1   **E**

1. School stories

ISBN 978-0-06-050191-4; 0-06-050191-X

LC 2010010167

Mrs. Madoff's students compare notes about getting ready for their first day of school after vacation.

"The uncluttered, brightly colored pictures capture the children's nervousness as they anticipate what's ahead, as well as their excitement as they prepare for their first day. . . . A cheerful, reassuring offering that nicely covers the range of first-day jitters." Booklist

★ **Four** seasons make a year; pictures by Megan Halsey. Walker & Co. 2004 un il $15.95; lib bdg $16.85

Grades: PreK K 1   **E**

1. Seasons 2. Seasons -- Juvenile literature

ISBN 0-8027-8883-1; 0-8027-8885-8 lib bdg

LC 2003-57171

Describes the passing of the seasons through the changes in plants and animals that occur on a farm

"The first-person text is simple and childlike, a tone reflected in the clearly delineated collages. Combining ink drawings with acrylic paintings on torn paper, these illustrations create eye-catching compositions." Booklist

My preschool; [by] Anne Rockwell. Holt 2008 un il $16.95

Grades: PreK   **E**

1. School stories

ISBN 978-0-8050-7955-5; 0-8050-7955-6

LC 2007002834

Follows a little boy during his day at preschool, from cheerful hellos in circle time, to painting colorful pictures and playing at the water table, to passing out paper cups for snack

In the illustrations Rockwell uses "colorful inks and traditional Japanese woodblock printing. . . . The detail and realistic depiction of the preschool experience will help to calm some newcomers' trepidations about attending school for the first time." SLJ

★ **The toolbox**; by Anne & Harlow Rockwell. Walker & Company 2004 un il hardcover o.p. bd bk $6.95

Grades: PreK K 1   **E**

1. Tools

ISBN 0-8027-8930-7; 0-8027-9609-5 bd bk

LC 2003-66562

A reissue of the title first published 1971 by Macmillan

An easy-to-read description of the basic tools found in a toolbox

"The brief text is printed in clear, handsome type. . . . [The illustrations] make ingenious use of watercolor to show textures and surfaces of wood and metal." Horn Book

Rockwell, Anne, 1934-

At the supermarket. Henry Holt 2010 un il $16.99

Grades: PreK   **E**

1. Shopping -- Fiction 2. Birthdays -- Fiction 3. Supermarkets -- Fiction

ISBN 0-8050-7662-X; 978-0-8050-7662-2

LC 2009009221

A revised and newly illustrated edition of The Supermarket, published 1979 by MacMillan

A boy and his mother fill a cart at the supermarket with everything from grapes to paper towels, finishing off with ingredients for a birthday cake.

"The well-written narration explains their trip from start to finish, including how the checkout line works. The brightly colored gouache illustrations on white backgrounds show the child helping to fill the cart and feature such items as produce and a container of ice cream alone on the page, making identification easy. This is a fun, educational read-aloud." SLJ

Rodman, Mary Ann

First grade stinks; written by Mary Ann Rodman; illustrated by Beth Spiegel. Peachtree 2006 un il $15.95; pa $8.95

Grades: K 1 2   E
  1. School stories
  ISBN 1-56145-377-3; 1-56145-462-1 pa
                   LC 2006-02711
First-grader Haley wishes she were back having fun in kindergarten with her old teacher, until she finds out that first-grade is special, too

"The scratchy, fluid, full-color watercolor-and-ink illustrations feature plenty of white space. Perfect as a read-aloud." SLJ

★ **My** best friend; illustrated by E.B. Lewis. Viking 2005 un il $14.99; pa $5.99
Grades: PreK K 1   E
  1. Friendship -- Fiction
  ISBN 0-670-05989-7; 0-14-240806-9 pa
                   LC 2004-22778
Six-year-old Lily has a best friend all picked out for play group day, but unfortunately the differences between first-graders and second-graders are sometimes very large

"Rodman's honest text captures the girl's heartbroken disappointment and makes it real for young readers, and Lewis's shining, sun-drenched illustrations convey both the harshness and warmth of the bright days at the pool." SLJ

★ **Surprise** soup; illustrated by G. Brian Karas. Viking 2009 un il $15.99
Grades: PreK K 1   E
  1. Bears -- Fiction 2. Soups -- Fiction 3. Cooking -- Fiction 4. Brothers -- Fiction 5. Family life -- Fiction
  ISBN 978-0-670-06274-4; 0-670-06274-X
                   LC 2008-22548
"Frequent, playful sound effects . . . will make read-alouds fun, and Rodman perfectly captures the rhythm and words of family dialogue. . . . Kara's collage artwork combines thickly lined, expressive figures with patterned details." Booklist

A **tree** for Emmy; written by Mary Ann Rodman; illustrated by Tatjana Mai-Wyss. Peachtree 2009 un il $15.95
Grades: K 1 2   E
  1. Trees -- Fiction 2. Birthdays -- Fiction
  ISBN 978-1-56145-475-4; 1-56145-475-3
                   LC 2008036745
Emmy loves the mimosa tree in her grandmother's yard and asks for one for her birthday, only to find that stores do not sell wild trees.

"The repetition of phrases, the cadence of the text, and the understanding of a child's emotions make this picture book a fine choice for reading aloud." Booklist

Rodriguez, Beatrice
  Fox and Hen together. Enchanted Lion 2011 un il $14.95
Grades: PreK K 1   E
  1. Stories without words 2. Eggs -- Fiction 3. Crabs -- Fiction 4. Foxes -- Fiction 5. Chickens -- Fiction
  ISBN 978-1-59270-109-4; 1-59270-109-4
This continues the story of The Chicken Thief, focusing on Fox and Hen's life together. As the illustrations quickly reveal, Crab has become a fast friend, Fox and Hen have an empty refrigerator, and Hen has laid an egg.

"It's a goofily harrowing but ultimately satisfying ride for most of the characters in this wordless story. Rodriguez

skillfully uses the format of wide, short pages to create dynamic scenes with a cinematic sense of movement. . . . Kids will love this funny and exciting story." SLJ

Rooster's revenge. Enchanted Lion 2011 il $14.95
Grades: PreK K 1   E
  1. Stories without words 2. Foxes -- Fiction 3. Chickens -- Fiction
  ISBN 978-1-59270-112-4; 1-59270-112-4
"This conclusion to the wordless trilogy that began with The Chicken Thief picks up where that book ended, with Rabbit, Bear, and Rooster departing the happy couple. At sea, a storm dumps them on a mysterious island, where Rooster discovers a glowing, green ball and runs off with it. In action-filled panoramas, Bear and Rabbit pursue Rooster through exceptionally surreal landscapes before returning to their cozy farm, where Rooster gets a big (and heartwarming) surprise after dropping his treasure. Rodriguez remains a master of body language and facial expressions, and the final scene leaves no doubt of a happily-ever-after for all involved." Publ Wkly

★ The **chicken** thief. Enchanted Lion Books 2010 un il $14.95
Grades: PreK K 1   E
  1. Stories without words 2. Foxes -- Fiction 3. Chickens -- Fiction
  ISBN 978-1-59270-092-9; 1-59270-092-6
"In Rodriguez's wordless debut, a bear and rabbit are enjoying a peaceful lunch in the garden outside their cottage when a fox makes off with one of their hens. The rooster wrings his wings melodramatically, and all three give chase. . . . Rodriguez succeeds in creating a distinctive personality for each of the characters, and her ability to capture the players' emotions via body language is masterful. . . . For readers who love a good chase—and who doesn't?—this one is a delight from beginning to end." Publ Wkly
  Other titles in this series are:
  Fox and Hen together (2011)
  Rooster's revenge (2011)

Rodriguez, Edel
  ★ **Sergio** makes a splash. Little, Brown 2008 un il $15.99
Grades: PreK K 1 2   E
  1. Penguins -- Fiction 2. Swimming -- Fiction
  ISBN 978-0-316-06616-7
Even though he loves water, Sergio the penguin is afraid to swim in the deep water until he learns how.

"The simple woodblock and digital art is stunningly rendered in bright orange, stark white, and cool aquamarine. Rodriquez uses bold graphics, lines, and angles to create a sense of play and space that draws in readers. The text is great fun for storytimes or for reading alone." SLJ
  Another title about Sergio is:
  Sergio saves the game! (2009)

Rogers, Gregory
  ★ **Midsummer** knight. Roaring Brook Press 2007 un il $16.95
Grades: K 1 2 3 4 5   E
  1. Stories without words 2. Bears -- Fiction 3. Fairies

-- Fiction 4. Heroes and heroines -- Fiction
ISBN 978-1-59643-183-6; 1-59643-183-0

LC 2006-51013

First published in Australia 2006

A bear is rescued by a fairy in an enchanted wood and agrees to return the favor by leading the battle against a usurper who has imprisoned the king and queen, along with their loyal subjects, in the dungeon of their castle

"This is another wordless adventure, depicted in colorful, comics-style panels that will delight young readers." Booklist

The **boy,** the bear, the baron, the bard. Roaring Brook 2004 un il $15.95; pa $7.95

Grades: K 1 2 3   E

1. Poets 2. Authors 3. Dramatists 4. Stories without words
ISBN 1-59643-009-5; 1-59643-267-5 pa

A boy playing among the warehouses of London kicks a soccer ball into an abandoned theater. There he finds an enchanted cape that transports him back in time right onto the stage of one of William Shakespeare's plays

"The plot in this wordless picture book unfolds straightforwardly. . . . The full watercolor-and-ink panels give kids . . . the chance to peek into another era while sympathizing with a contemporary young protagonist." Booklist

Another title about these characters is:
   Midsummer knight (2007)

The **hero** of Little Street; Gregory Rogers. Roaring Brook Press 2012 32 p.

Grades: PreK K 1 2 3   E

1. Stories without words 2. Picture books for children 3. Art museums -- Juvenile fiction 4. Dogs -- Fiction 5. Painting -- Fiction 6. Time travel -- Fiction
ISBN 1596437294; 9781596437296

LC 2010042371

This children's book by Gregory Rogers is the final entry in the "Boy, Bear" trilogy. "Narrowly escaping from a gang of bullies, a boy slips into a grand old gallery--the perfect hiding place, full of mystery and treasures. Suddenly, a painting comes to life and the boy finds himself on an adventure led by a mischievous dog that has leapt from the canvas. The two slip into a Vermeer painting and are transported to Little Street, Delft in seventeenth-century Holland, where the boy has to use every ounce of his ingenuity to rescue his new friend from an untimely fate." (Publisher's note)

Rogerson, Gillian

You can't eat a Princess! written by Gillian Rogerson; illustrated by Sarah McIntyre. Price Stern Sloan 2011 un il $9.99

Grades: PreK K 1 2   E

1. Chocolate -- Fiction 2. Princesses -- Fiction 3. Extraterrestrial beings -- Fiction
ISBN 978-0-8431-9881-2; 0-8431-9881-8

LC 2010008352

Princess Spaghetti blasts off into space to save her kidnapped father, King Cupcake, from hungry aliens, who are introduced to a wonderful new food: chocolate.

"Pastel hues, comical cartoon creatures, and zippy dialogue make this, on one level, a lighthearted story. But when young children beg to hear it again and again, it will undoubtedly be for the power conveyed by a shrewd little princess who can tame aliens and get them to eat chocolates out of her hand." SLJ

Rohmann, Eric

★ **Bone** dog. Roaring Brook Press 2011 un il $16.99

Grades: K 1 2   E

1. Dogs -- Fiction 2. Death -- Fiction 3. Skeleton -- Fiction 4. Halloween -- Fiction
ISBN 978-1-59643-150-8; 1-59643-150-4

LC 2010045142

Although devastated when his pet dog dies, a young boy goes trick-or-treating and receives a timely visit from an old friend during a scary encounter with graveyard skeletons.

"Rohmann's . . . friendly figures and soft, autumnal colors give this spooky story an overlay of tranquility. . . . It's an offbeat mixture of humor and sadness." Publ Wkly

★ **Clara** and Asha. Roaring Brook 2005 un il $16.95

Grades: PreK K 1 2   E

1. Fishes -- Fiction 2. Bedtime -- Fiction 3. Imaginary playmates -- Fiction
ISBN 1-59643-031-1

LC 2005-04677

Young Clara would rather play with her imaginary giant fish, Asha, than settle down to sleep.

"The oil paintings portray a natural world in all its glorious seasons, brimming with mystery and delight. . . . Children will revel in the opportunity to see their dreams and longings realized so enchantingly." SLJ

★ **My** friend Rabbit. Roaring Brook Press 2002 un il $15; pa $6.99

Grades: PreK K 1 2   E

1. Mice 2. Animals 3. Rabbits 4. Friendship 5. Mice -- Fiction 6. Rabbits -- Fiction 7. Friendship -- Fiction
ISBN 0-7613-1535-7; 0-312-36752-X pa

LC 2002-17764

Awarded the Caldecott Medal, 2003

Something always seems to go wrong when Rabbit is around, but Mouse lets him play with his toy plane anyway because he is his good friend

"The double-page, hand-colored relief prints with heavy black outlines are magnificent, and children will enjoy the comically expressive pictures of the animals." SLJ

Time flies. Crown 1994 un il $17; lib bdg $17.99; pa $6.99

Grades: PreK K 1 2   E

1. Stories without words 2. Birds -- Fiction 3. Dinosaurs -- Fiction
ISBN 0-517-59598-2; 0-517-59599-0 lib bdg; 0-517-88555-7 pa

LC 93-28200

A Caldecott Medal honor book, 1995

A wordless tale in which a bird flying around the dinosaur exhibit in a natural history museum has an unsettling experience when the dinosaur seems to come alive and view the bird as a potential meal

"The handsome, atmospheric paintings heighten the drama as they tell their simple, somewhat mysterious, and quite short story." Booklist

★ A **kitten** tale. Alfred A. Knopf 2008 un il $15.99; lib bdg $18.99

Grades: PreK E

1. Cats -- Fiction 2. Snow -- Fiction 3. Seasons -- Fiction

ISBN 978-0-517-70915-3; 978-0-517-70916-0 lib bdg

LC 2007-11093

As four kittens who have never seen winter watch the seasons pass, three of them declare the reasons they will dislike snow when it arrives, while the fourth cannot wait to experience it for himself

This is a "marvel of sly simplicity for the very young. . . . [Rohmann's] uncluttered, inventive scenes masterfully echo the repetitive rhythm in the words." Booklist

Roode, Daniel

Little Bea. Greenwillow Books 2011 un il $12.99

Grades: PreK E

1. Day -- Fiction 2. Bees -- Fiction 3. Animals -- Fiction 4. Friendship -- Fiction

ISBN 978-0-06-199392-3; 0-06-199392-1

LC 2009053681

From morning to night, Little Bea buzzes through her neighborhood helping friends and having fun.

"Roode's computer-generated images are highly stylized. . . . The text is full of sounds . . . internal rhymes, . . . and the simple pleasures of knock-knock jokes and games of 'duck, duck, goose' and 'peekaboo' . . . There's reassurance and contentment throughout. Friendly, fuzzy creatures abound; the lives of characters who live in a tightly knit community of friends they see and enjoy every day is a satisfying theme." Publ Wkly

Another title about Little Bea is:

Little Bea and the snowy day (2011)

Little Bea and the snowy day. Greenwillow Books 2011 32p il $12.99

Grades: PreK E

1. Bees -- Fiction 2. Snow -- Fiction 3. Animals -- Fiction

ISBN 978-0-06-199395-4; 0-06-199395-6

LC 2010032236

Little Bea and her friends enjoy a day of snow angels, skating, and even making a new snow friend.

"The simplistic text and singsong rhyme are best suited for two-year-olds. . . . Children will delight in the bright, animated digital art and large, two-dimensional perspective." SLJ

Roop, Peter

Down East in the ocean; a Maine counting book. written by Peter and Connie Roop; illustrated by Nicole Fazio. Down East 2011 il $16.95

Grades: PreK K 1 E

1. Counting 2. Stories in rhyme 3. Seashore -- Fiction 4. Marine animals -- Fiction

ISBN 978-0-89272-709-4; 0-89272-709-8

"This rhyming counting book features animals associated with the Maine seashore, but that can also be found on many other beaches. Each spread tells a mini story of parent and offspring while introducing the concept of counting. . . This is an engaging way to learn numbers and a great beach book. Music notations are included at the end to put the verses to song." SLJ

Roosa, Karen

Pippa at the parade; illustrated by Julie Fortenberry. Boyds Mills Press 2009 un il $16.95

Grades: PreK K E

1. Stories in rhyme 2. Parades -- Fiction

ISBN 978-1-59078-567-6; 1-59078-567-3

LC 2008028127

A young child has a fun-filled day with her parents at the big parade

"Bursting with movement, the spirited and free-flowing watercolors capture cartwheeling gymnasts and marching scout troops. . . . The brief rhyming verses . . . include a few onomatopoeic phrases that invite young listeners to join in." Booklist

Root, Phyllis

Big Momma makes the world; written by Phyllis Root; illustrated by Helen Oxenbury. Candlewick Press 2003 un il $16.99; pa $6.99

Grades: PreK K 1 2 E

1. Creation -- Fiction

ISBN 0-7636-1132-8; 0-7636-2600-7 pa

LC 2002-17498

Big Momma, with a baby on her hip and laundry piling up, makes the world and everything in it and, at the end of the sixth day, tells the people she has made that they must take care of her creation

"Root's text is strong and sassy, with a down-home cadence that has immediate appeal, and Oxenbury's Big Momma is the perfect embodiment of the story's earth mother." Booklist

Creak! said the bed; illustrated by Regan Dunnick. Candlewick Press 2010 un il $15.99

Grades: PreK K E

1. Beds -- Fiction 2. Noise -- Fiction

ISBN 978-0-7636-2004-2; 0-7636-2004-1

"The increasingly crowded bed . . . is by now a standard picture-book plotline. Fresh takes on the subject are hard to come by, but Root manages to make it feel new by punctuating the story with the sounds of impending disaster. . . . The economy of the story line is paralleled by gouache illustrations . . . that reinforce the bed-centered tale but also pull in and zoom out on its inhabitants for different perspectives. The lantern-jawed, snub-nosed family is cartoon cute, making for a perfect storytime read." Booklist

Flip, flap, fly! illustrated by David Walker. Candlewick 2009 un il $14.99

Grades: PreK E

1. Stories in rhyme 2. Animals -- Fiction 3. Animals -- Infancy -- Juvenile literature

ISBN 978-0-7636-3109-3; 0-7636-3109-4

An "assortment of baby animals flap, wiggle and splash their way through the forest, spotting each other in turn as they play with their mamas. Human babies and toddlers will love guessing which animal comes next as they follow clues from Root's contagious, rhyming text and Walker's bright and warm acrylic illustrations." Kirkus

Kiss the cow; illustrated by Will Hillenbrand. Candlewick Press 2000 un il hardcover o.p. pa $6.99

Grades: K 1 2 3   E
1. Cows 2. Milking 3. Cattle -- Fiction
ISBN 0-7636-0298-1; 0-7636-2003-3 pa

LC 00-20926

Annalisa, the most curious and stubborn of Mama May's children, disobeys her mother and upsets the family's magic cow by refusing to kiss her in return for the milk she gives

"Elements of folklore echo through the story that reads aloud rhythmically with a satisfying, folksy sound. . . . The well-conceived illustrations, warm in color and graceful in line, depict a variety of scenes with style and panache." Booklist

★ **Lucia** and the light; illustrated by Mary Grandpré. Candlewick Press 2006 un il $16.99
Grades: PreK K 1 2   E
1. Cats -- Fiction 2. Trolls -- Fiction 3. Winter -- Fiction
ISBN 978-0-7636-2296-1; 0-7636-2296-6

One winter in the Far North the sun disappears and Lucia, accompanied by her milk-white cat, braves the freezing cold and trolls who want to eat her, trying to find the sun and bring it back.

"Grandpré's evocative, dimly lit acrylics capture the eerie mystery and shivery suspense of the adventure. . . . Root's rich language and well-paced story are sure to capture a young crowd of eager listeners." Booklist

Paula Bunyan; illustrated by Kevin O'Malley. Farrar, Straus and Giroux 2009 un il $16.95
Grades: K 1 2 3   E
1. Tall tales 2. Size -- Fiction
ISBN 978-0-374-35759-7; 0-374-35759-5

LC 2007-43728

Recounts the exploits of Paul Bunyan's "little" sister, Paula, who lived in the North Woods, sang three-part harmony with the wolves, and used an angry bear for a foot warmer.

"O'Malley's white-framed, woodcutlike pictures, heavily outlined with intricate line shading, appear throughout this appropriately tall book. Sweeping panoramic views, Paula's thunderous voice depicted in large speech bubbles, bear-carrying mosquitoes, comical animal expressions, and energetic black-and-white drawings add to the fun. The timely environmental message is an added plus." SLJ

Scrawny cat; illustrated by Alison Friend. Candlewick Press 2011 un il $16.99
Grades: PreK K 1 2   E
1. Cats -- Fiction
ISBN 978-0-7636-4164-1; 0-7636-4164-2

LC 2010047671

A lost, lonely, and scrawny cat, hungry and afraid, unexpectedly meets someone who takes him in and loves him.

"Delicious language and a winsome feline ensure that this new iteration of an oft-told plot will find an appreciative audience. . . . Friend's gouache paintings, including vignettes, single pages and double page spreads, illuminate the straightforward action. . . . She captures the fluctuating reactions of the cat perfectly." Kirkus

Thirsty Thursday; illustrated by Helen Craig. Candlewick Press 2009 un il $9.99

Grades: PreK K   E
1. Rain -- Fiction 2. Flowers -- Fiction 3. Farm life -- Fiction
ISBN 978-0-7636-3628-9; 0-7636-3628-2

"It's Thursday on Bonnie Bumble's farm, and everyone is thirsty—especially the flowers. . . . Not a drop of rain is in sight, but luckily Bonnie has an idea. She puts the sheep on top of the cow and the pig on top of the sheep, and she climbs on top of the pig . . . and tickles the cloud with a feather. . . . Short, sweet and unabashedly darling, Root's text employs just the right amount of repetition to get toddlers chiming in by the second reading. Craig's ink, watercolor and pencil illustrations lend Bonnie, animals and flowers expressive personalities." Kirkus

Toot toot zoom! illustrated by Matthew Cordell. Candlewick Press 2009 un il $15.99
Grades: PreK K   E
1. Animals -- Fiction 2. Friendship -- Fiction 3. Automobiles -- Fiction
ISBN 978-0-7636-3452-0; 0-7636-3452-2

LC 2008-934781

"A simple storyline, great sound effects, a touch of humor, and big, bold illustrations make this a lively choice for storytime." Bull Cent Child Books

The **name** quilt; pictures by Margot Apple. Farrar, Straus & Giroux 2003 un il $16
Grades: K 1 2 3   E
1. Quilts 2. Grandmothers 3. Quilts -- Fiction 4. Grandmothers -- Fiction
ISBN 0-374-35484-7

LC 2002-69328

One of Sadie's favorite things to do when she visits her grandmother is to hear stories about the family members whose names are on a special quilt that Grandma had made, so Sadie is very sad when the quilt is blown away in a storm

"Root makes the most of the simple, intimate anecdotes that flow between generations, and the crayon-looking drawings bespeak a rustic informality." Publ Wkly

Rose, Deborah Lee

All the seasons of the year; illustrated by Kay Choaro. Abrams Books for Young Readers 2010 un il $16.95
Grades: PreK K 1   E
1. Stories in rhyme 2. Cats -- Fiction 3. Seasons -- Fiction 4. Mother-child relationship -- Fiction
ISBN 978-0-8109-8395-3; 0-8109-8395-8

"This rhyming story portrays a mother cat's love for her child. . . . With two spreads devoted to each season, the first-person narrative describes some of their favorite activities. Chorao's lush illustrations in gouache, colored pencils, and ink fill the pages with colorful pastel depictions of the momma and her kitten diving into a pile of autumn leaves, sledding down a winter slope, flying kites in the spring, watering summer blossoms, and celebrating the youngster's birthday in the fall." SLJ

Birthday zoo; written by Lee Rose; illustrated by Lynn Munsinger. Whitman, A. 2002 un il $15.95; pa $6.95
Grades: PreK K 1 2   E
1. Parties 2. Birthdays 3. Stories in rhyme 4. Zoo animals 5. Zoos -- Fiction 6. Animals -- Fiction 7.

Birthdays -- Fiction
ISBN 0-8075-0776-8; 0-8075-0777-6 pa

LC 2002-1726

Rhyming text describes the preparations made for a boy's birthday party by his hosts, the animals at the zoo

"While Rose's strong rhythm and rhymes will charm youngsters in a storytime, Munsinger's lively pen-and-ink and watercolor illustrations beg for closer inspection." SLJ

The **twelve** days of winter; a school counting book. illustrated by Carey Armstrong-Ellis. Abrams 2006 un il lib bdg $14.95

Grades: PreK K 1 2   E
1. Counting 2. Winter -- Fiction
ISBN 0-8109-5472-9

A cumulative counting verse in which a child lists items pertaining to winter given to him by his teacher, from twelve treats for tasting to one bird feeder in a snowy tree.

"While the book would work well as a read or singaloud, with so much to pore over and absorb in the art, it is best used for one-on-one sharing. A surefire choice to spice up the dreariest winter day." SLJ

Rose, Naomi C.
Tashi and the Tibetan flower cure. Lee & Low Books 2011 il $18.95

Grades: 1 2 3   E
1. Sick -- Fiction 2. Flowers -- Fiction 3. Grandfathers -- Fiction 4. Community life -- Fiction
ISBN 978-1-60060-425-6; 1-60060-425-0

LC 2011010556

"The softly brushed paintings have a naive, self-tutored look, but suit the text's homespun tone. The story, outwardly realistic, turns on two charming ideas: that of a child using ancient wisdom to restore the health of a relative, and that of a sterile American suburb becoming as close-knit as a Tibetan village." Publ Wkly

Rosen, Michael
Bear flies high; [illustrated by Adrian Reynolds] Bloomsbury 2009 un il $16.99; lib bdg $17.89

Grades: PreK K 1 2   E
1. Bears -- Fiction 2. Flight -- Fiction
ISBN 978-1-59990-386-6; 1-59990-386-5; 978-1-59990-387-3 lib bdg; 1-59990-387-3 lib bdg

LC 2008-55015

Bear usually spends his days on the beach, singing and watching birds, but when he leaves to visit a carnival, his dream of flying may just come true.

"The lyrical call-and-response and glowing illustrations give the book a cadence that's perfect for afternoon naps or lazy days." Publ Wkly

I'm number one; illustrated by Bob Graham. Candlewick Press 2009 un il $16.99

Grades: PreK K 1 2   E
1. Toys -- Fiction
ISBN 978-0-7636-4535-9; 0-7636-4535-4

LC 2009004246

A wind-up soldier bosses and berates the other toys, making them feel terrible, until they suddenly start to rebel.

"The pen-and-watercolor illustrations are filled with expressive characters and Graham's signature, whimsical details, such as the stuffed pig's snout ring. This simple, af-

fecting story will be welcome anywhere that more than two young kids are gathered together and where laughter, not mean words, is the lingua franca." Booklist

★ **Michael** Rosen's sad book; words by Michael Rosen; pictures by Quentin Blake. Candlewick Press 2005 un il $16.99; pa $6.99

Grades: K 1 2 3   E
1. Bereavement -- Fiction
ISBN 0-7636-2597-3; 0-7636-4104-9 pa

LC 2004-45787

A man tells about all the emotions that accompany his sadness over the death of his son, and how he tries to cope

"Blake's evocative watercolor-and-ink illustrations use shades of gray for the pictures where sadness has taken hold but brighten with color at the memory of happy times. This story is practical and universal and will be of comfort to those who are working through their bereavement. A brilliant and distinguished collaboration." SLJ

Red Ted and the lost things; illustrated by Joel Stewart. Candlewick Press 2009 40p il

Grades: PreK K 1 2   E
1. Toys -- Fiction 2. Teddy bears -- Fiction 3. Lost and found possessions -- Fiction
ISBN 0-7636-4537-0; 0-7636-4624-5 pa; 978-0-7636-4537-3; 978-0-7636-4624-0 pa

LC 2009-02992

When a teddy bear is accidentally left on the seat of a train, he uses his ingenuity—and some new friends—to search for the little girl who lost him. "Grades two to three." (Bull Cent Child Books)

"Rosen's quirky combination of characters is matched by Stewart's muted colors and deliberately hazy backgrounds, which nicely spotlight the stuffed animals. . . . The plucky and determined Red Ted deserves a place among the many lost-toys books on library shelves." SLJ

★ **Tiny** Little Fly; words by Michael Rosen; pictures by Kevin Waldron. Candlewick Press 2010 un il $15.99

Grades: PreK K   E
1. Stories in rhyme 2. Flies -- Fiction 3. Tigers -- Fiction 4. Elephants -- Fiction 5. Hippopotamus -- Fiction
ISBN 978-0-7636-4681-3; 0-7636-4681-4

LC 2010-07549

With a tramp and a roll and a swat, Great Big Elephant, Great Big Hippo, and Great Big Tiger try to capture Tiny Little Fly as he teases each one in turn.

"The consistently patterned, simple rhyming text is accompanied by rustic, large-scale, digitally enhanced pencil-and-gouache art. . . . The words and images create an easily absorbed, enjoyable adventure." Booklist

★ **Totally** wonderful Miss Plumberry; [by] Michael Rosen; illustrated by Chinlun Lee. Candlewick Press 2006 un il $15.99

Grades: PreK K 1 2   E
1. School stories 2. Teachers -- Fiction
ISBN 0-7636-2744-5

LC 2005045392

Molly's day turns from totally wonderful to totally horrible when her classmates are not interested in the special crystal she has brought to school, until Miss Plumberry steps in to help

"This gentle picture book captures the impact a sensitive teacher has on the lives of her students. . . . The soft watercolor-and-pencil illustrations reveal [Molly's] emotions and expose the fickle attention of children in engaging . . . spreads." SLJ

★ **We're** going on a bear hunt; anniversary edition of a modern classic. retold by Michael Rosen; illustrated by Helen Oxenbury. Margaret K. McElderry Books 2009 un il $18.99

Grades: PreK K 1 2   E
  1. Bears -- Fiction 2. Hunting -- Fiction
  ISBN 978-1-4169-8711-6; 1-4169-8711-8
                     LC 2008-53214
  First published 1989
Brave bear hunters go through grass, a river, mud, and other obstacles before the inevitable encounter with the bear forces a headlong retreat

"Glorious puddles of watercolor alternate with impish charcoal sketches in this refreshing interpretation of an old hand rhyme in which a man, four children, and a dog stalk the furry beast through mud and muck, high and low. A book with a genuine atmosphere of togetherness and boundless enthusiasm for the hunt." SLJ

Rosen, Michael J.
  ★ **Chanukah** lights; illustrations by Robert Sabuda. Candlewick Press 2011 un il $34.99
Grades: K 1 2   E
  1. Counting 2. Pop-up books 3. Jews -- Fiction 4. Hanukkah stories 5. Hanukkah -- Fiction
  ISBN 978-0-7636-5533-4; 0-7636-5533-3
                     LC 2011013664
Counts the candles of a menorah on each night of Hanukkah while recalling images of Jewish life in different places and times, such Herod's temple in Jerusalem, a shtetl in Russia, and a refugee ship bound for the New World.

"This is a gorgeous and fragile holiday book for adults and children to enjoy together." SLJ

  Night of the pumpkinheads; illustrations by Hugh McMahon. Dial Books for Young Readers 2011 il $16.99
Grades: K 1 2   E
  1. Pumpkin -- Fiction 2. Halloween -- Fiction 3. Vegetables -- Fiction
  ISBN 978-0-8037-3452-4; 0-8037-3452-2
                     LC 2010039314
Determined to make Halloween a frightening night of the pumpkinheads, the pumpkins transform themselves into a variety of scary monsters and then head for town hoping to terrify everyone they meet.

"Digitally assembled with photographs of McMahon's work and pencil drawings, the illustrations treat readers to spirited images of spunky pumpkins rising up to take an active part in trick-or-treating instead of remaining parked on porches. . . . A solid addition to the Halloween shelf, especially for those who have graduated from safer, sweeter stories." Kirkus

Rosenberg, Liz
  Nobody; illustrated by Julie Downing. Roaring Brook Press 2010 un il $16.99

Grades: PreK K   E
  1. Morning -- Fiction 2. Imaginary playmates -- Fiction 3. Parent-child relationship -- Fiction
  ISBN 978-1-59643-120-1; 1-59643-120-2
"Young George wakes up early one morning while his parents are asleep. His imaginary companion, Nobody, is there to keep him company and inspires plenty of mischief. . . . Color pops off the page with playful illustrations done in watercolor, colored pencil, pastels, and china marker. Downing cleverly contrasts Nobody in black and white. The visual impact is strong but simple and underscores the tightly written text, and the facial expressions are priceless. Perspective is creatively used, particularly in a spread where George and Nobody are exploring the contents of the refrigerator. Kids and their parents will love this one." SLJ

  Tyrannosuarus dad. Roaring Brook Press 2011 il $16.99
Grades: PreK K 1 2   E
  1. Fathers -- Fiction 2. Dinosaurs -- Fiction
  ISBN 9781596435315; 1596435313
Tobias's father is a lot like other fathers—he likes corny jokes, and doing magic tricks, and works really hard at the office. But there the resemblance ends. He has teeth as sharp as steak knives, is forty feet high, and weighs as much as a locomotive. He is, in fact, a tyrannosaurus.

"Rosenberg's well-paced dialogue and succinct descriptions result in a most engaging read. Myers' oil paintings truly amaze." Kirkus

Rosenberg, Madelyn
  Happy birthday, Tree; a Tu B'Shevat story. by Madelyn Rosenberg; illustrated by Jana Christy. Albert Whitman & Co. 2012 24 p. (hardcover) $15.99
Grades: PreK K 1 2   E
  1. Trees -- Juvenile fiction 2. Tu bi-Shevat -- Juvenile fiction 3. Jewish children -- Juvenile fiction 4. Jews -- Fiction 5. Trees -- Fiction 6. Tu bi-Shevat -- Fiction
  ISBN 0807531510; 9780807531518
                     LC 2011034187
In this children's picture book by Madelyn Rosenberg, illustrated by Jana Christy, "Joni strives to create a celebration befitting her old majestic tree . . . on the Jewish holiday of Tu B'Shevat, the birthday of the trees. . . . Determined to find the right gift for her leafy friend, Joni concludes that a new tree planted close by and a promise to continue to nurture her arboreal companions is the best way to observe the holiday." (Kirkus)

  The **Schmutzy** Family; by Madelyn Rosenberg; illustrated by Paul Meisel. Holiday House 2012 32 p. (hardcover) $16.95
Grades: PreK K 1   E
  1. Jews -- Fiction 2. Picture books for children 3. Sabbath -- Fiction 4. Cleanliness -- Fiction 5. Family life -- Fiction
  ISBN 0823423719; 9780823423712
                     LC 2011040341
In this children's picture book, "wading in Feldman Swamp, making mud pies, painting with tomato sauce, and other messy activities are a part of the Schmutzy family activities. Despite how grimy the playing gets, Mama Schmutzy does not mind one bit except on Friday when" they must prepare for the Sabbath. (Children's Literature)

Rosenberry, Vera

★ **Vera's** first day of school. Holt & Co. 1999 un il hardcover o.p. pa $6.95

Grades: PreK K 1 2   **E**

1. School stories 2. Schools -- Fiction 3. First day of school -- Fiction

ISBN 0-8050-5936-9; 0-8050-7269-1 pa

LC 98-43347

Vera cannot wait for the day when she starts school, but the first day does not go exactly as she has anticipated

"Rosenberry's playful, brightly colored gouache illustrations capture Vera's jubilation-turned-dismay." Horn Book Guide

Other titles about Vera are:

Vera goes to the dentist (2002)

Vera rides a bike (2004)

Vera runs away (2000)

Vera's baby sister (2005)

Vera's Halloween (2008)

Vera's new school (2006)

When Vera was sick (1998)

Rosenstock, Barbara

The **littlest** mountain; illustrated by Melanie Hall. Kar-Ben Pub. 2011 un il $17.95; pa $7.95

Grades: PreK K 1 2 3   **E**

1. Jewish legends 2. God -- Fiction 3. Mountains -- Fiction

ISBN 978-0-7613-4495-7; 0-7613-4495-0; 978-0-7613-4497-1 pa; 0-7613-4497-7 pa

LC 2010021249

"This pourquoi story about why God chose Mount Sinai as the location for giving the Ten Commandments has its roots in Jewish legend. Various mountains in the land of Israel list their best qualities and argue over which should be chosen. In the end, God picks humble, faithful Mount Sinai. . . . This is a lovely tale. . . . Kids will get a kick out of the folktale feeling and the talking mountains, caregivers will like the lesson on the value of being humble and faithful, and Jewish educators will be thrilled to have a great read-aloud for the holiday of Shavuot, which commemorates the receiving of the Ten Commandments." SLJ

Rosenthal, Amy Krouse

Al Pha's bet; illustrated by Delphine Durand. G. P. Putnam's Sons 2011 un il $16.99

Grades: PreK K   **E**

1. Alphabet -- Fiction

ISBN 978-0-399-24601-2; 0-399-24601-0

LC 2010028171

Al Pha makes a bet with himself that he can invent the perfect order for the twenty-six letters.

Durand's "loopy acrylic paintings carry the story through a long, long middle section about how Al comes to arrange each of the letters as he does . . . populating Al's world with a wacky assortment of proto-trees and flowers, as well as a cast of equally goofy-looking villagers and animals. Pages are well designed and visually lively throughout, the text peppered with spot illustrations. . . . Fans of dopey puns everywhere, rejoice!" Publ Wkly

Bedtime for Mommy; illustrated by LeUyen Pham. Bloomsbury 2010 un il $16.99; lib bdg $17.89

Grades: PreK K 1 2   **E**

1. Bedtime -- Fiction 2. Mother-daughter relationship -- Fiction

ISBN 978-1-59990-341-5; 1-59990-341-5; 978-1-59990-465-8 lib bdg; 1-59990-465-9 lib bdg

LC 2009-18205

In a reversal of the classic bedtime story, a child helps her mommy get ready for bed, enduring pleas for one more book, five more minutes of play time, and a glass of water before the lights go out.

"The facial expressions throughout are priceless, and the final illustration showing the parents peeking in at a sleeping daughter round out this tale. This very visual story will appeal to beginning readers as well as parents and librarians looking for a fun bedtime read-aloud." Libr Media Connect

Chopsticks; illustrated by Scott Magoon. Disney/Hyperion 2012 un il $16.99

Grades: PreK K 1 2   **E**

1. Chopsticks -- Fiction 2. Friendship -- Fiction

ISBN 978-1-4231-0796-5; 1-4231-0796-9

LC 2011010269

This book "outlines the . . . activities of a pair of chopsticks who are not only working partners but also BFFs. Then the tip of one chopstick is broken in an unfortunate encounter with an asparagus spear, and after getting medical attention (the glue bottle mends him and wraps the "wound" with a bandage) the injured chopstick must "stay off it until it sets." At first, the non-injured chopstick stays close by his friend's side, but the injured one finally tells him, "You need to get out . . . venture off on your own a bit." The chopsticks discover that time away from each other can also be a good thing." (Bulletin of the Center for Children's Books)

"The marriage of text, digital art, and design provide plentiful puns and laugh-out-laud humor." Publ Wkly

★ **Cookies**; bite-size life lessons. written by Amy Krouse Rosenthal; illustrated by Jane Dyer. HarperCollins Publishers 2006 un il $12.99; lib bdg $13.89

Grades: PreK K 1 2   **E**

1. Cookies 2. Conduct of life

ISBN 978-0-06-058081-0; 0-06-058081-X; 978-0-06-058082-7 lib bdg; 0-06-058082-8 lib bdg

LC 2005-15134

"Using the activity of making and eating cookies, the author defines some important concepts for young children, such as respect, trustworthiness, patience, politeness, loyalty, etc. . . . Lovely pastel watercolor illustrations show appealing children and anthropomorphic animals interacting with one another and the treats. . . . The utilization of the cookies to explain the concepts is a brilliant idea and works well on a child's level. The text is short and clear, and the book is delightful to look at and browse through." SLJ

Other titles in this series are:

Christmas cookies (2008)

Sugar cookies (2009)

One smart cookie (2010)

★ **Duck!** Rabbit! [illustrated by] Tom Lichtenheld. Chronicle Books 2009 un il $16.99

Grades: PreK K 1 2   E
  1. Ducks -- Fiction 2. Rabbits -- Fiction
  ISBN 978-0-8118-6865-5; 0-8118-6865-6

                  LC 2008-28102

Rosenthal and Lichtenheld play "with perspective and visual trickery, . . . using a classic image that looks like either a rabbit (with long ears) or a duck (with a long bill). . . . Two off-stage speakers, their words appearing on either side of the animal's head, argue their points of view. The snappy dialogue makes for [a] fine read-aloud." Publ Wkly

★ **Little** Hoot; illustrated by Jen Corace. Chronicle Books 2008 un il $12.99

Grades: PreK K   E
  1. Owls -- Fiction 2. Bedtime -- Fiction
  ISBN 978-0-8118-6023-9; 0-8118-6023-X

                  LC 2007-24960

Little Hoot wants to go to bed early, like all of his friends do, and he is hopping mad when Mama and Papa Owl insist that he stay up late and play.

The "owl family . . . feels recognizable. . . . This outing is not to be missed." Publ Wkly

Other titles in the series are:

Little oink (2009)

Little pea (2005)

The **OK** book; [by] Amy Krouse Rosenthal & Tom Lichtenheld. HarperCollins 2007 un il $12.99

Grades: PreK K 1 2   E
  1. Ability -- Fiction 2. Self-acceptance -- Fiction
  ISBN 978-0-06-115255-9; 0-06-115255-2

                  LC 2006030432

"The book's hero is a little stick figure whose head is the O of OK, and whose arms and legs are the K. . . . I like to try a lot of different things, the OK figure says. I'm not great at all of them, but I enjoy them all the same. . . . One day, I'll grow up to be really excellent at something, OK says, while lying in bed. . . . It can't hurt to remind kids that the pleasure we take in simple activities is what makes life worthwhile." Publ Wkly

★ **This** plus that; life's little equations. Amy + Krouse + Rosenthal = writer; Jen + Corace = artist. Harper 2011 un il $14.99

Grades: PreK K 1 2   E
  1. Mathematics -- Fiction 2. Conduct of life -- Fiction
  3. Addition -- Juvenile literature
  ISBN 978-0-06-172655-2; 0-06-172655-9

                  LC 2008-34357

"Two pigtailed girls squabble, then reason with each other. The outcome is a simple sum: 'yes + no = maybe.' The same two girls gossip through a tin-can telephone: 'laughter + keeping secrets + sharing = best friend.' Witty observations—'anything + sprinkles = better'—alternate with improving messages as well as nods to the seasons, arts, and kid-friendly activities. . . . Corace's stylized pen and ink vignettes show a world that's safe and secure; the same family members appear throughout. . . . It's the kind of math that children won't have any trouble comprehending." Publ Wkly

Yes Day! [by] Amy Krouse Rosenthal & [illustrated by] Tom Lichtenheld. HarperCollins 2009 un il $14.99; lib bdg $15.89

Grades: PreK K 1   E
  1. Day -- Fiction 2. Wishes -- Fiction
  ISBN 978-0-06-115259-7; 0-06-115259-5; 978-0-06-
  115260-3 lib bdg; 0-06-115260-9 lib bdg

                  LC 2008-20219

A little boy gets everything he asks for on Yes Day, a special day that only comes once a year.

"Lichtenheld's bright and funny cartoons bring the story to life, with character expressions that are right on the mark." SLJ

Rosenthal, Betsy R.

Which shoes would you choose? illustrated by Nancy Cote. G. P. Putnam's Sons 2010 un il $15.99

Grades: PreK   E
  1. Shoes -- Fiction
  ISBN 978-0-399-25013-2; 0-399-25013-1

"This picture book invites children to enjoy a shoe-themed guessing game as they follow a boy named Sherman through his day. The question-and-answer text alternates between two types of queries. The first asks Which shoes does he choose? A situation is described, followed by an answer and a reason for the choice. The second sort of question begins with the last shoes chosen and asks if they are worn in an amusingly inappropriate situation. . . . The questions are sure to garner responses from individual children or story hour crowds. . . . Almost cartoonlike in their simplicity, the pleasant gouache and watercolor-pencil drawings feature tousle-haired Sherman sporting an extraordinarily large wardrobe of footwear." Booklist

Rosenthal, Eileen

I must have Bobo! illustrated by Marc Rosenthal. Atheneum Books for Young Readers 2010 un il $14.99

Grades: PreK K 1   E
  1. Cats -- Fiction 2. Toys -- Fiction 3. Lost and found
  possessions -- Fiction
  ISBN 978-1-4424-0377-2; 1-4424-0377-2

                  LC 2010-04963

When Willy wakes up without his favorite toy, he looks everywhere until he finds it.

"Illustrator Marc Rosenthal's . . . ability to capture Earl's feline deviousness—the way Earl cranes his neck to see if Willy is coming, or hides under the covers with Bobo—is one of the book's chief charms. . . . Soft pencil drawings on cream-colored pages add to the generally calm, bedtime atmosphere." Publ Wkly

I'll save you Bobo! Eileen Rosenthal; illustrated by Marc Rosenthal. Atheneum Books for Young Readers 2012 40 p.

Grades: PreK K 1 2 3   E
  1. Cats -- Fiction 2. Toys -- Fiction 3. Drawing --
  Fiction 4. Picture books for children 5. Adventure
  fiction -- Juvenile fiction 6. Fear -- Fiction 7.
  Storytelling -- Fiction 8. Cats -- Juvenile fiction 9. Fear
  -- Juvenile fiction 10. Fear in children -- Fiction 11.
  Storytelling -- Juvenile fiction
  ISBN 1442403780; 9781442403789

                  LC 2011278288

This picture book tells the story of Willy, the young boy introduced in Eileen Rosenthal's previous book "'I Must Have Bobo!" and his companions, his favorite toy Bobo and Earl the cat. "Willy . . . here puts down the book he's reading in order to create a more exciting story himself, while his sock monkey Bobo serves as audience for his crayon drawings and narrative about a jungle adventure. . . . The cartoon illustrations create a kind of spotlight for the story: boy, drawing table and crayons, armchair, Bobo and cat." (Kirkus)

I will save you Bobo!

Rosenthal, Marc
Archie and the pirates. Joanna Cotler Books 2009 un il $16.99
Grades: K 1 2 3   E
  1. Islands -- Fiction 2. Monkeys -- Fiction 3. Pirates -- Fiction 4. Friendship -- Fiction
  ISBN 978-0-06-144164-6; 0-06-144164-3
                                          LC 2008-35251
When Archie the monkey finds himself on a strange island, he makes a multitude of new friends who help him defend their home from intruding pirates.

"Rosenthal relates the adventure in a simple, matter-of-fact way and pairs the narrative to neatly drawn . . . cartoons. . . . Loaded with child appeal." Booklist

Rosoff, Meg
  ★ **Jumpy** Jack and Googily; [by] Meg Rosoff; illustrated by Sophie Blackall. Henry Holt 2008 un il $16.95
Grades: PreK K 1   E
  1. Fear -- Fiction 2. Snails -- Fiction 3. Monsters -- Fiction 4. Friendship -- Fiction
  ISBN 978-0-8050-8066-7; 0-8050-8066-X
                                          LC 2007-07227
Jumpy Jack the snail is terrified that there are monsters around every corner despite the reassurances of his best friend, Googily.

"The interplay between the two creates a wonderfully safe space for children to explore their fears. . . . The text . . . employs a formal elevated tone that gently chides Jumpy Jack's childish fears, adding an element of dry humor. The illustrations are filled with whimsical details." SLJ

  ★ **Meet** wild boars; [written by] Meg Rosoff and [illustrated by] Sophie Blackall. Henry Holt & Co. 2005 un il $15.95; pa $6.99
Grades: PreK K 1 2   E
  1. Boars -- Fiction
  ISBN 0-8050-7488-0; 0-312-37963-3 pa
                                          LC 2004-8985
It is very hard to be friends with wild boars because they are dirty and smelly, bad-tempered, and rude

This is "bitingly funny and deeply satisfying. . . . Blackall's roll-on-the-ground-in-laughter illustrations are incisively rendered in ink and gouache." Booklist
  Another title about the wild boars is:
  Wild boars cook (2008)

Ross, Fiona
  Chilly Milly Moo. Candlewick Press 2011 il $15.99
Grades: PreK K   E
  1. Milk -- Fiction 2. Cattle -- Fiction 3. Weather --

Fiction
  ISBN 978-0-7636-5693-5; 0-7636-5693-3
                                          LC 2010051446
While the other cows are enjoying the sun and making plenty of milk, Milly Moo is too hot to make a drop but when the temperature falls, Milly Moo shows the farmer and the rest of the herd what she can do.

"This is a great addition to read-alouds centered on the theme of individuality (with a snack tie-in built right in). Delightfully different, just like Milly Moo." Kirkus

Ross, Michael Elsohn
  Mama's milk; by Michael Elsohn Ross; illustrated by Ashley Wolff. Tricycle Press 2007 un il $12.95
Grades: PreK K   E
  1. Stories in rhyme 2. Animals -- Fiction 3. Mammals -- Fiction 4. Breast feeding -- Fiction
  ISBN 978-1-58246-181-6; 1-58246-181-3
                                          LC 2006020873
"From humans to a variety of aquatic and land animals, Ross's rhyming text describes the different ways that mothers nurse their babies. . . . The pastel-infused watercolor illustrations tastefully depict the nursing pairs." SLJ

Ross, Pat
  Meet M & M; pictures by Marylin Hafner. Pantheon Bks. 1980 41p il hardcover o.p. pa $4.99
Grades: K 1 2   E
  1. Friendship -- Fiction
  ISBN 0-14-038731-5
                                          LC 79-190
"Beginning readers will have no difficulty with the humorously told, very real incidents. . . . The many black-and-white pencil drawings capture the girls' facial expressions especially well." Horn Book
  Other titles about M and M (Mandy and Mimi) are:
  M and M and the bad news babies (1983)
  M and M and the Halloween monster (1991)
  M and M and the haunted house game (1980)
  M and M and the mummy mess (1986)

Ross, Tony
  I want a party! written and illustrated by Tony Ross. Andersen Press 2011 un il $16.95
Grades: PreK K 1 2   E
  1. Parties -- Fiction 2. Princesses -- Fiction
  ISBN 978-0-7613-8089-4; 0-7613-8089-2
                                          LC 2011001597
Little Princess discovers that she can have a lovely party with just one guest.

"Ross's illustrations are produced in colorful ink and watercolors. The whimsy and simple story line will appeal to young children." SLJ

  I want my light on! Andersen Press USA 2010 un il $16.95
Grades: PreK K   E
  1. Fear -- Fiction 2. Princesses -- Fiction
  ISBN 978-0-7613-6443-6; 0-7613-6443-9
Everyone says there are no such things as ghosts that live under beds, but the Little Princess knows better.

"Clear, expressive watercolors add humor to the simple text, and the Little Princess formula still works well at cleverly addressing common early childhood issues." SLJ

Other titles about the Little Princess are:

I want a party! (2011)

I want to do it myself (2011)

I want to do it myself! Andersen Press 2011 un il $16.95

Grades: PreK K 1 2   **E**

1. Camping -- Fiction 2. Princesses -- Fiction

ISBN 978-0-7613-7412-1; 0-7613-7412-4

LC 2010032896

The Little Princess is determined to go on a camp-out without anyone's help.

"With gestural strokes, Ross's ink and watercolor illustrations play up the princess's impudence; readers should relate, while recognizing that a little assistance never hurts." Publ Wkly

I want two birthdays! Andersen Press 2010 un il $16.95

Grades: PreK K 1 2   **E**

1. Birthdays -- Fiction 2. Princesses -- Fiction

ISBN 978-0-76135-495-6; 0-76135-495-6

First published 2008 in the United Kingdom

A little princess decides that two birthdays would be better than one, and three better than two, until every day becomes her birthday, but she soon realizes that the more birthdays she has, the less special they are.

"Ross's bright, cheerful trademark watercolor illustrations add much humor to this already funny tale about having too much of a good thing." SLJ

Other titles about the little princess are:

I want my light on! (2010)

I want to do it myself! (2011)

Rossell, Judith

Oliver; written and illustrated by Judith Rossell. Harper 2012 32 p.

Grades: PreK K 1 2   **E**

1. Boys -- Fiction 2. Imagination -- Fiction 3. Picture books for children 4. Penguins -- Fiction 5. Mothers and sons -- Fiction

ISBN 0062022105; 9780062022103

LC 2011019368

This picture book tells the story of a curious young boy named Oliver, who wonders about where penguins go on vacation and especially about what lives in the drain. His mother won't let him feed a banana to whatever is down there making gurgling noises, "so Oliver builds a submarine and takes it for a ride to see just what the drain is harboring. Here Oliver turns into a kid's drawing . . . in watercolor and pencil, with a touch of collage elsewhere; maybe this is all in his head? And what's down the drain? Penguins, of course." (Kirkus)

Rostoker-Gruber, Karen

★ **Bandit**; illustrated by Vincent Nguyen. Marshall Cavendish Children's Books 2008 un il $15.99

Grades: PreK K 1 2   **E**

1. Cats -- Fiction 2. Moving -- Fiction

ISBN 978-0-7614-5382-6; 0-7614-5382-2

LC 2007011720

When Bandit's family moves to a new house, the cat runs away and returns to the only home he knows, but af-

ter he is brought back, he understands that the new house is now home

"By telling the story from the point of view of an extremely territorial pet, Rostoker-Gruber approaches the issue of moving in a fresh way. . . . Nguyen's mixed-media illustrations have an attractive Pop Art style. . . . A funny, stylish book." SLJ

Another title about Bandit is:

Bandit's surprise (2010)

★ **Ferret** fun; illustrated by Paul Ratz de Tagyos. Marshall Cavendish Children's 2011 un il

Grades: PreK K 1 2   **E**

1. Cats -- Fiction 2. Ferrets -- Fiction

ISBN 0-7614-5817-4; 978-0-7614-5817-3

LC 2010-21301

Two nervous pet ferrets named Fudge and Einstein try to convince a visiting cat that they are not rats. "Grades two to four." (Bull Cent Child Books)

"Rátz de Tagyos's magic-marker-and-ink graphic-novel-style illustrations are the real draw; the bouncy, fanged trio are a terrific balance between Saturday morning cartoon and real animals. Just enough lesson hidden in the fun." Kirkus

Tea time; [illustrated by] Viviana Garofoli. Marshall Cavendish 2010 un il (Board buddies) bd bk $7.99

Grades: PreK   **E**

1. Stories in rhyme 2. Board books for children 3. Tea -- Fiction 4. Parties -- Fiction

ISBN 978-0-7614-5638-4 bd bk; 0-7614-5638-4 bd bk

A young girl dresses up and prepares tea and cookies for her teddy bear and her mother.

"It's a just-right mix of text and illustration to coax the youngest readers into following a narrative; the familiarity of the activity serves to reinforce this. A sweet little beginning story." Kirkus

Roth, Carol

Will you still love me? illustrated by Daniel Howarth. Albert Whitman 2010 un il $15.99

Grades: PreK K   **E**

1. Love -- Fiction 2. Animals -- Fiction 3. Siblings -- Fiction 4. Parent-child relationship -- Fiction

ISBN 978-0-8075-9114-7; 0-8075-9114-9

Young animals and a little boy are reassured that their mothers will still love them after a new baby arrives.

"Howarth's sunny watercolor and ink illustrations match the upbeat tone of the bouncy, rhyming text." SLJ

The **little** school bus; illustrated by Pamela Paparone. North-South Bks. 2002 un il hardcover o.p. pa $6.95

Grades: PreK K   **E**

1. Animals 2. Stories in rhyme 3. School buses 4. Buses -- Fiction 5. Animals -- Fiction

ISBN 0-7358-1646-8; 0-7358-1905-X pa

LC 2002-71417

An assortment of animals, including a goat in a coat, a quick chick, and a hairy bear, ride the bus to and from school

"Paparone's bright, sprightly illustrations feature plenty of cheery mugging out the windows and other amusing side business. . . . This will take children on a verbal and visual ride that they'll want to repeat as often as possible." Booklist

Roth, Susan L.

Hard hat area; [by] Susan Roth. Bloomsbury Children's Books 2004 un il $17.95

Grades: PreK K 1 2   E

1. Building -- Fiction 2. Construction workers -- Fiction

ISBN 1-58234-946-0

LC 2003-65343

Construction workers ask Kristen, a young apprentice, to bring them snacks and supplies

"Stunning collages showcase the workers, their jobs, and their equipment in situ; clear explanatory notes describe the work and responsibilities for each person involved in the construction." Horn Book Guide

Rotner, Shelley

Senses at the seashore. Millbrook Press 2006 un il lib bdg $22.60

Grades: PreK K 1 2   E

1. Seashore 2. Senses and sensation

ISBN 978-0-7613-2897-1 lib bdg; 0-7613-2897-1 lib bdg

LC 2005-06151

"This picture book tells what children see, hear, smell, touch, and taste at the beach. . . . A few of the clear, colorful photos show adults (fishermen, a lifeguard) at work, but most of the illustrations are closeups of children at play. An inviting, kid-friendly introduction to the senses and the seashore." Booklist

Senses in the city; by Shelley Rotner. Millbrook Press 2008 un il (Shelley Rotner's early childhood library) lib bdg $23.93

Grades: PreK K 1   E

1. City and town life 2. Senses and sensation

ISBN 978-0-8225-7502-3 lib bdg; 0-8225-7502-7 lib bdg

"Both an exciting celebration of city life and a show-and-tell about the five senses, this photo-essay will draw even very young children. Clear, direct words and unframed pictures show children in the packed streets of an unnamed city, where they see the skyline and hear trains passing by, go inside tall buildings, and travel in a subway car." Booklist

Shades of people; by Shelley Rotner and Sheila M. Kelly; photographs by Shelley Rotner. Holiday House 2009 un il $16.95

Grades: PreK K 1   E

1. Race 2. Skin 3. Color

ISBN 978-0-8234-2191-6; 0-8234-2191-0

LC 2008022574

Explores the many different shades of human skin, and points out that skin is just a covering that does not reveal what someone is like inside.

"Filled with smiles and hugs, the pictures prove an upbeat confirmation of the book's central idea. . . . This will enrich and spark discussions of diversity." Booklist

Rubel, David

The carpenter's gift; a Christmas tale about the Rockefeller Center tree. illustrated by Jim LaMarche. Random House 2011 un il $17.99; lib bdg $20.99

Grades: K 1 2 3   E

1. Trees -- Fiction 2. Christmas stories 3. Kindness -- Fiction 4. Christmas -- Fiction

ISBN 978-0-375-86922-8; 0-375-86922-0; 978-0-375-96922-5 lib bdg; 0-375-96922-5 lib bdg; 978-0-375-98933-9 e-book

LC 2010033203

In Depression-era New York City, construction workers at the Rockefeller Center site help a family in need—a gift that is repaid years later in the donation of an enormous Christmas tree.

"Rubel's story . . . puts the now magnificent symbol in perspective. LaMarche conveys emotional resonance with gauzy, soft-hued paintings of the inspirational proceedings." Publ Wkly

Rubin, Adam

Those darn squirrels and the cat next door; illustrated by Daniel Salmieri. Clarion Books 2011 32p il $16.99

Grades: K 1 2 3   E

1. Cats -- Fiction 2. Birds -- Fiction 3. Squirrels -- Fiction

ISBN 978-0-547-42922-9; 0-547-42922-3

"Mr. Fookwire, his beloved backyard birds, and his relentlessly clever squirrel frenemies are united against a new neighbor and common enemy: a corpulent, take-no-prisoners cat named Muffins, whose idea of fun is giving the squirrels noogies, wet willies, and wedgies. . . . Rubin's sly ironies and Salmieri's spare but deeply goofy aesthetic is child-friendly urbanity at its best." Publ Wkly

Those darn squirrels! by Adam Rubin; illustrated by Daniel Salmieri. Clarion Books 2008 32p il $16

Grades: K 1 2 3   E

1. Birds -- Fiction 2. Old age -- Fiction 3. Squirrels -- Fiction

ISBN 978-0-547-00703-8; 0-547-00703-5

LC 2007040110

When grumpy Old Man Fookwire builds feeders to try to keep birds—the only creatures he likes—from leaving for the winter, he finds himself in a battle with clever, crafty squirrels who want a share of the abundant food

"This simple tale has a sneaky, edgy humor that erupts into hilarity. . . . [The] paintings [are] reminiscent of some of the best European children's book illustrations." SLJ

Another title about these characters is:

Those darn squirrels and the cat next door (2011)

Ruddell, Deborah

Who said coo? illustrated by Robin Luebs. Beach Lane Books 2010 un il $16.99

Grades: PreK K 1   E

1. Stories in rhyme 2. Pigs -- Fiction 3. Sounds -- Fiction 4. Animals -- Fiction 5. Bedtime -- Fiction

ISBN 978-1-4169-8510-5; 1-4169-8510-7

LC 2009000929

"Unbeknownst to Lulu the pig, Pigeon and Owl have shown up on her doorstep at bedtime. . . . Lulu's slumber is interrupted by a loud 'Cooooo' and then a 'Whooooo.' Lulu confronts the likely culprits, but Pigeon and Owl refuse to fess up. . . . Luebs's acrylic paintings feature a luminescent pastel palette, which makes the story's nighttime scenes glow. A few deft strokes convey Lulu's contentedness, exasperation, and anger." Publ Wkly

Ruddra, Anshumani

Dorje's stripes; illustrated by Gwangjo and Jung-a-Park. Kane Miller 2010 un il $15.99

Grades: 1 2 3 4   **E**

1. Monks -- Fiction 2. Tigers -- Fiction 3. Monasteries -- Fiction

ISBN 978-1-935279-98-3; 1-935279-98-X

Dorje is a beautiful Royal Bengal tiger but he has no stripes. In a small Buddhist monastery in Tibet, Master Wu explains the reasons behind Dorje's missing stripes, and offers hope for the future.

"This heartwarming story is enhanced by stunning watercolors that add to its peaceful tone and suggest a quiet beauty as well as depict the action and emotions of each character." SLJ

Rueda, Claudia

My little polar bear. Scholastic Press 2009 un il $16.99

Grades: PreK K 1 2   **E**

1. Polar bear -- Fiction 2. Mother-child relationship -- Fiction

ISBN 978-0-545-14600-5; 0-545-14600-3

LC 2008043079

When a cub asks if he is a polar bear, his mother describes what a polar bear is and does, reassuring him that she will teach him to hunt, walk securely on ice, and otherwise be true to his breed, and that she will always love him.

"The striking, minimalist style of illustration seem well suited to the Arctic scenes. Despite the cold setting, the story generates its own warmth." Booklist

★ **No**; translated by Elisa Amado. Groundwood Books/House of Anansi Press 2010 un il $18.95

Grades: PreK K   **E**

1. Snow -- Fiction 2. Bears -- Fiction 3. Winter -- Fiction 4. Hibernation -- Fiction 5. Mother-child relationship -- Fiction

ISBN 978-0-88899-991-7; 0-88899-991-7

Original Spanish edition 2009

"Mother suggests that it is time to hibernate for the winter, but little bear has other ideas. . . . But when a blinding snowstorm practically buries little bear, he realizes mother might have known best. . . . Flat figures in a minimal wintry palette nevertheless burst with personality, abetted by clever compositions." Kirkus

Ruelle, Karen Gray

★ The **Thanksgiving** beast feast. Holiday House 1999 32p il (Holiday House reader) $15.95

Grades: PreK K 1 2   **E**

1. Animals 2. Thanksgiving Day 3. Cats -- Fiction 4. Animals -- Fiction 5. Brothers and sisters 6. Thanksgiving Day -- Fiction

ISBN 0-8234-1511-2

LC 98-51339

Harry the cat and his sister Emily celebrate Thanksgiving by making a holiday feast for the animals in their yard

"Simple and child-centered, the story reads well and uses repetition in ways that sound natural, while reinforcing word recognition. Pleasantly childlike, the naive ink drawings are tinted with gentle washes." Booklist

Other titles about Harry and Emily are:

April fool (2002)

The crunchy, munchy Christmas tree (2003)

Dear Tooth Fairy (2006)

Easter egg disaster (2004)

Easy as apple pie (2002)

Great groundhogs! (2005)

Just in time for New Year's (2004)

The monster in Harry's backyard (1999)

Mother's Day mess (2003)

Snow valentines (2000)

Spookier than a ghost (2001)

Rumford, James

From the good mountain; how Gutenberg changed the world. James Rumford. 1st ed. Roaring Brook Press 2012 40 p. (reinforced: alk. paper) $17.99

Grades: 3 4 5   **E**

1. Riddles 2. Book industry 3. Printing -- History 4. Books -- History -- Juvenile literature 5. Printers -- Germany -- Biography -- Juvenile literature 6. Printing -- History -- Origin and antecedents -- Juvenile literature

ISBN 1596435429; 9781596435421

LC 2011033796

Author James Rumford presents a history on printmaking. "What was made of rags and bones, soot and seeds? What took a mountain to make? For the answer, travel back to the fifteenth century—to a time when books were made by hand and a man named Johannes Gutenberg invented a way to print books with movable type . . . [The book is w]ritten as a series of riddles . . . [with things] to learn about how the very thing you are holding in your hands came to be." (Publisher's note)

Includes bibliographical references and index.

★ **Rain** school; written and illustrated by James Rumford. Houghton Mifflin Books for Children 2010 un il $16.99

Grades: PreK K 1 2   **E**

1. School stories 2. Rain -- Fiction

ISBN 0-547-24307-3; 978-0-547-24307-8

LC 2009-49701

Thomas, who lives in Chad in Africa is ready for his first day of school, but "when he arrives at the schoolyard he finds that there is no school. . . . After Thomas and his schoolmates build the school from mud and grass, they're ready for their nine-month school year. . . . Ages five to eight." (Bull Cent Child Books)

"While serving as a Peace Corps volunteer, Rumford was a teacher in Chad, and the authentic details illuminate the spare text and beautiful artwork. . . . The colored-pencil, ink, and pastel images echo the words' elemental rhythms. . . . This moving offering will leave kids thinking about the daily lives of other young people around the world." Booklist

★ **Silent** music; a story of Baghdad. Roaring Brook Press 2008 un il $17.95

Grades: K 1 2 3   **E**

1. Calligraphy -- Fiction 2. Iraq War, 2003- -- Fiction

ISBN 978-1-59643-276-5; 1-59643-276-4

LC 2007-23600

As bombs and missiles fall on Baghdad in 2003, a young boy named Ali uses the art of calligraphy to distance himself from the horror of war.

"Art sings on the pages of this visual celebration of Arabic calligraphy as Rumford's . . . collages of floral and geometric designs and flowing lines deftly echo Arabic language and patterns. . . . Spreads incorporating stamps, money and postcards reinforce the Baghdad setting and complement representational scenes." Publ Wkly

Tiger and turtle. Roaring Brook 2010 un il $17.99
Grades: 1 2 3   E
1. Tigers -- Fiction 2. Turtles -- Fiction 3. Friendship -- Fiction
ISBN 978-1-59643-416-5; 1-59643-416-3
When a tiger and a turtle both want a flower that has fallen to the ground, they argue over it until a fight breaks out between them.
"The brief text is well paced, with repeated rising and falling action, and the resolution of the most suspenseful moments requires a page turn. Read this tale aloud . . . for a lively storyhour." SLJ

Runton, Andy
Owly and Wormy, friends all aflutter! Atheneum Books for Young Readers 2011 un il $15.99
Grades: PreK K 1 2   E
1. Stories without words 2. Owls -- Fiction 3. Worms -- Fiction 4. Butterflies -- Fiction
ISBN 978-1-4169-5774-4; 1-4169-5774-X
LC 2010-06123
Good friends Owly and Wormy are disappointed when their new plant attracts fat, green, bug-like things, instead of butterflies, until a metamorphosis occurs.
"Even very young children will be able to puzzle out the story's details from the expressions on the characters' faces, and Runton's unvarnished sentimentality creates an atmosphere of absolute security." Publ Wkly

Russell, Natalie
Moon rabbit. Viking Children's Books 2009 un il $16.99
Grades: PreK K 1   E
1. Rabbits -- Fiction 2. Friendship -- Fiction 3. City and town life -- Fiction
ISBN 978-0-670-01170-4; 0-670-01170-3
LC 2008022799
A city rabbit befriends a country rabbit, but soon she misses her home with its cafes and bright lights.
"The story's considerable appeal is amplified by Russell's exceptional artwork. Using her skills as a printmaker, she places her endearing characters on beautifully colored backgrounds so smooth they resemble suede." Booklist
Another title about these rabbits is:
Brown Rabbit in the city (2010)

Russo, Marisabina, 1950-
★ The **big** brown box. Greenwillow Bks. 2000 un il $16.99
Grades: PreK K 1 2   E
1. Play 2. Boxes 3. Brothers 4. Imagination 5. Sharing 6. Boxes -- Fiction 7. Brothers -- Fiction
ISBN 0-688-17096-X
LC 99-14871
As he plays in a very large box in his room and turns it into a house, then a cave, then a boat, Sam is reluctant to let his little brother Ben join him, but then he finds the perfect way for them to share.

"The well-paced, child-centered text is complemented by Russo's trademark two-dimensional gouache illustrations that realistically capture the creative play of children." SLJ

★ **I** will come back for you; a family in hiding during World War II. Schwartz & Wade 2011 un il $17.99; lib bdg $20.99
Grades: K 1 2 3   E
1. Bracelets -- Fiction 2. Grandmothers -- Fiction 3. Jews -- Italy -- Fiction 4. World War, 1939-1945 -- Italy -- Fiction
ISBN 978-0-375-86695-1; 0-375-86695-7; 978-0-375-96695-8 lib bdg; 0-375-96695-1 lib bdg
LC 2010044523
A grandmother tells her granddaughter the story of the charm bracelet that represent her own childhood experiences while she and her family tried to evade the Nazis in Italy during World War II.
"Russo bases this book on her own family history. Her writing is direct but always reassuring, and her naif [gouache] illustrations, rendered in saturated autumnal tones, feel very close to the actual family photographs that serve as the book's endpapers. Ingenuity and compassion are recurring themes in this eloquent portrayal of a family's struggle for freedom." Publ Wkly

Peter is just a baby; written and illustrated by Marisabina Russo. Eerdmans Books for Young Readers 2011 un il $16
Grades: PreK K 1   E
1. Infants -- Fiction 2. Siblings -- Fiction 3. French language -- Vocabulary
ISBN 978-0-8028-5384-4; 0-8028-5384-6
LC 2011022480
"The title is the favorite refrain of the narrator, an anthropomorphized six-year-old bear and Peter's big sister. . . . Delineating Peter's babyish ways . . . lets her cite all the ways she is more mature and sophisticated. . . . With help from her tutor, the narrator learns to say 'Bon appetit!' before eating and 'Quel dommage!' when disappointed. . . . This worldly-wise and ultimately accepting attitude, combined with the parallel story of learning French . . . gives an otherwise typical tale of sibling rivalry a stylish, refreshing twist. . . . [The book is illustrated with] cheery, naif gouache pictures." Publ Wkly

A **very** big bunny. Schwartz & Wade Books 2010 un il $17.99; lib bdg $20.99
Grades: PreK K 1 2   E
1. School stories 2. Size -- Fiction 3. Rabbits -- Fiction 4. Friendship -- Fiction
ISBN 978-0-375-84463-8; 0-375-84463-5; 978-0-375-94463-5 lib bdg; 0-375-94463-X lib bdg
LC 2008-39924
Amelia is so big that she is always last in line at school and none of the other students will play with her, but a special new classmate teaches her that size is not always the most important thing.
"Russo's tale about unlikely friends executes a familiar theme with abundant charm and humor. . . . Featuring a saturated palate, Russo's matte gouache illustrations amplify the snappy storytelling." Publ Wkly

Ruzzier, Sergio

Amandina. Roaring Brook Press 2008 un il $16.95
Grades: K 1 2 3   E
1. Dogs -- Fiction 2. Theater -- Fiction
ISBN 978-1-59643-236-9; 1-59643-236-5

LC 2007047914

Amandina decides to overcome her shyness and show the town what a talented little dog she is, but when no one shows up for her performance, she finds that she also has a lot of perseverance.

"The artwork combines delicate lines and faded colors to create a fanciful stage for this likable character." SLJ

Hey rabbit! Roaring Brook Press 2010 un il $16,99
Grades: K 1 2   E
1. Gifts -- Fiction 2. Magic -- Fiction 3. Animals -- Fiction 4. Rabbits -- Fiction
ISBN 978-1-59643-502-5; 1-59643-502-X

"Instead of a magician pulling a rabbit out of a hat, here we have a rabbit magically producing all sorts of things from a suitcase. An ode to gift giving, Ruzzier's latest picture book showcases his charming illustrations without letting a complicated plot get in the way. . . . Ruzzier's animals are a very appealing group . . . and each wish leads to a colorful and lively scene." Booklist

Ryan, Candace

Ribbit rabbit; illustrated by Mike Lowery. Walker Books for Young Readers 2011 un il
Grades: PreK K 1   E
1. Frogs -- Fiction 2. Rabbits -- Fiction 3. Friendship -- Fiction
ISBN 0-8027-2180-X; 0-8027-2181-8 lib bdg; 978-0-8027-2180-8; 978-0-8027-2181-5 lib bdg

LC 2010-08418

Frog and Bunny are the best of friends, even though they sometimes get into fights. "Ages three to five." (Bull Cent Child Books)

"The rhythmic, onomatopoetic text is a pretty music, the kind of song you'd sing in the dark to lift your spirits. Equally joyful and engaging—and that's a tall order—is Lowery's artwork. It has a childlike, elemental tone, with neat planes of color, but it is wonderfully, touchingly emotive." Kirkus

Ryan, Pam Muñoz

★ **Tony** Baloney; illustrated by Edwin Fotheringham. Scholastic Press 2011 un il $16.99
Grades: PreK K 1   E
1. Penguins -- Fiction 2. Siblings -- Fiction
ISBN 0-545-23135-3; 978-0-545-23135-0

LC 2009-51693

Tony, a macaroni penguin, is a middle child with very exasperating siblings, and although he never looks for trouble, it often finds him.

"Dominated by bold primary colors, Fotheringham's . . . hyperbolic digital illustrations counterbalance the slyly understated narrative, portraying Tony's (and Dandelion's) antics with humor." Publ Wkly

Ryder, Joanne

Dance by the light of the moon; written by Joanne Ryder; illustrated by Guy Francis. Hyperion Books for Children 2007 un il $15.99

Grades: PreK K 1 2   E
1. Dance -- Fiction 2. Animals -- Fiction
ISBN 0-7868-1820-4

"Buffalo Flo gets an invitation to 'come out tonight and dance by the light of the moon' and proceeds to collect her friends Goose, Cat, and Pig for the occasion. . . . The rhymes dance, and so do Francis's paintings. Detailed moonlit landscapes are filled with animal characters that seem to leap from the pages." SLJ

Each living thing; illustrations by Ashley Wolff. Harcourt 2000 un il $16
Grades: K 1 2 3   E
1. Stories in rhyme 2. Animals -- Fiction
ISBN 0-15-201898-0

LC 98-51832

Celebrates the creatures of the earth, from spiders dangling in their webs to owls hooting and hunting out of sight, and asks that we respect and care for them

"Wolff's intense gouache paintings, outlined in black, are as lyrical as the text, with just the right balance of simplicity and subtle detail." Booklist

My father's hands; illustrated by Mark Graham. Morrow Junior Bks. 1994 un il $16.99
Grades: PreK K 1 2   E
1. Gardening -- Fiction 2. Father-daughter relationship -- Fiction
ISBN 0-688-09189-X

LC 93-27116

"A little girl and her father share the wonders of nature as they examine several small creatures in the garden—a pink worm, a golden beetle, a sliding snail, and a praying mantis. Graham's lovely double-page, impressionistic oil paintings clearly focus on the man and his daughter, with closeups of faces and hands in nearly every illustration. The garden in the background, lush with flowers and vegetable plants, provides a picturesque setting for this simple, straightforward description of a special parent/child outing." SLJ

Rylant, Cynthia, 1954-

★ **All** in a day; illustrated by Nikki McClure. Abrams Books for Young Readers 2009 un il $17.95
Grades: PreK K 1 2   E
1. Stories in rhyme 2. Day -- Fiction
ISBN 978-0-8109-8321-2; 0-8109-8321-4

LC 2008030527

Illustrations and rhyming text pay homage to a new day, with promises for the future in its "perfect piece of time."

"Alternating backdrops of color, finch-yellow and a soft, muted blue, allow for a whole new outlook with every page turn. This uplifting picture book succeeds in introducing children to the perennial promise of tomorrow through lithe language and honed imagery." Kirkus

Alligator boy; [by] Cynthia Rylant & [illustrated by] Diane Goode. Harcourt 2007 un il $16
Grades: PreK K   E
1. Stories in rhyme 2. Alligators -- Fiction
ISBN 978-0-15-206092-3

LC 2006006049

A boy puts on an alligator head and tail and is transformed into an alligator boy.

"Goode's watercolor and gouache cartoon vignettes on white ground are reminiscent of the artist's other work in which she evokes a former time. . . . [A] charming story." SLJ

★ **Annie** and Snowball and the dress-up birthday; the first book of their adventures. illustrated by Suçie Stevenson. Simon & Schuster Books for Young Readers 2007 40p il (Ready-to-read) $15.95; pa $3.99

Grades: K 1 2　　　　　　　　　　　　　　　　　E
1. Parties -- Fiction 2. Rabbits -- Fiction 3. Birthdays -- Fiction
ISBN 978-1-4169-0938-5; 1-4169-0938-9; 978-1-4169-1459-4 pa; 1-4169-1459-5 pa
　　　　　　　　　　　　　　　　　　LC 2006-02516

Annie and her pet bunny, Snowball, love living next door to Annie's favorite cousin, Henry and his dog, Mudge. Whether it's playing Frisbee or watching old movies, there's no shortage of fun to be had when these four are together.

"Stevenson's lively pen-and-ink and watercolor illustrations depict lots of action in the story's four short chapters, and amplify the characters' warmth, affection, and laughter." SLJ

Other titles about Annie and Snowball are:
Annie and Snowball and the prettiest house (2007)
Annie and Snowball and the pink surprise (2008)
Annie and Snowball and the teacup club (2008)
Annie and Snowball and the cozy nest (2009)
Annie and Snowball and the shining star (2009)
Annie and Snowball and the magical house (2010)
Annie and Snowball and the wintry freeze (2010)
Annie and Snowball and the Book Bugs Club (2011)

Brownie & Pearl step out; pictures by Brian Biggs. Beach Lane Books 2010 un il $12.99

Grades: PreK K　　　　　　　　　　　　　　　　E
1. Cats -- Fiction 2. Parties -- Fiction 3. Birthdays -- Fiction
ISBN 978-1-4169-8632-4; 1-4169-8632-4
　　　　　　　　　　　　　　　　　　LC 2008032804

A little girl named Brownie arrives at a birthday party feeling shy while her cat Pearl confidently enters through the "kitty door."

"Rylant addresses the challenges and rewards of facing new social situations in short, conversational text perfectly suited to its young audience. Biggs' digitally rendered, cartoonlike illustrations . . . make this first title in the Brownie and Pearl series as delicious and appealing as a triple-layered birthday cake." Booklist

Other titles about Brownie & Pearl are:
Brownie & Pearl get dolled up (2010)
Brownie & Pearl see the sights (2010)
Brownie & Pearl take a dip (2011)
Brownie & Pearl grab a bite (2011)
Brownie & Pearl hit the hay (2011)

★ The **case** of the missing monkey; story by Cynthia Rylant; pictures by G. Brian Karas. Greenwillow Bks. 2000 48p il (High-rise private eyes) pa $3.99

Grades: K 1 2　　　　　　　　　　　　　　　　　E
1. Animals 2. Mystery fiction 3. Mystery and detective

stories
ISBN 0-06-444306-X
　　　　　　　　　　　　　　　　　　LC 99-16878

While having breakfast at their favorite diner, two detectives, Bunny and Jack, find a missing glass monkey

"The full-color illustrations, rendered in acrylic gouache, and pencil, capture the cartoonlike animals' animated expressions and poses. . . . Children will enjoy searching the pages for the reported clues." SLJ

Other titles in the High-rise private eyes series are:
The case of the baffled bear (2004)
The case of the climbing cate (2000)
The case of the desperate duck (2005)
The case of the fidgety fox (2003)
The case of the puzzling possum (2001)
The case of the sleepy sloth (2002)
The case of the troublesome turtle (2001)

★ **Henry** and Mudge; the first book of their adventures. story by Cynthia Rylant; pictures by Suçie Stevenson. Simon & Schuster Books for Young Readers 1996 39p il (Ready-to-read) $15.99; pa $3.99

Grades: K 1 2　　　　　　　　　　　　　　　　　E
1. Dogs -- Fiction
ISBN 0-689-81004-0; 0-689-81005-9 pa
First published 1987 by Bradbury Press

Henry, feeling lonely on a street without any other children, finds companionship and love in a big dog named Mudge.

"The stories are lighthearted and affectionate. Backed by line-and-wash cartoon drawings, they celebrate the familiar in a down-to-earth way that will please young readers." Booklist

Other titles about Henry and Mudge are:
Henry and Mudge and a very Merry Christmas (2004)
Henry and Mudge and Annie's good move (1998)
Henry and Mudge and Annie's perfect pet (2000)
Henry and Mudge and Mrs. Hopper's house (2003)
Henry and Mudge and the bedtime thumps (1991)
Henry and Mudge and the best day of all (1995)
Henry and Mudge and the big sleepover (2006)
Henry and Mudge and the careful cousin (1994)
Henry and Mudge and the forever sea (1989)
Henry and Mudge and the funny lunch (2004)
Henry and Mudge and the great grandpas (2005)
Henry and Mudge and the happy cat (1990)
Henry and Mudge and the long weekend (1992)
Henry and Mudge and the sneaky crackers (1998)
Henry and Mudge and the Snowman plan (1999)
Henry and Mudge and the starry night (1998)
Henry and Mudge and the tall tree house (1999)
Henry and Mudge and the tumbling trip (2005)
Henry and Mudge and the wild goose chase (2003)
Henry and Mudge and the wild wind (1993)
Henry and Mudge get the cold shivers (1989)
Henry and Mudge in puddle trouble (1987)
Henry and Mudge in the family trees (1997)
Henry and Mudge in the green time (1987)
Henry and Mudge in the sparkle days (1988)
Henry and Mudge take the big test (1991)
Henry and Mudge under the yellow moon (1987)

Moonlight: the Halloween cat; illustrated by Melissa Sweet. HarperCollins Pubs. 2003 un il $14.99; lib bdg $15.89; pa $6.99

Grades: PreK K 1 2   E
1. Cats -- Fiction 2. Halloween -- Fiction
ISBN 0-06-029711-5; 0-06-029712-3 lib bdg; 0-06-443814-7 pa

LC 2001-39511

Moonlight the cat loves everything about Halloween, from pumpkins to children to candy

"In simple, poetic prose, Rylant tracks the meandering cat's night journey. . . . Sweet's endearingly childlike, color-rich paintings convey an appreciation for the ever-deepening night. . . . A soothing, ghoul-free, utterly noncreepy Halloween picture book for the preschool set." Booklist

Mr. Putter & Tabby clear the decks. Houghton Mifflin Harcourt 2010 un il $15

Grades: K 1 2   E
1. Cats -- Fiction 2. Dogs -- Fiction 3. Boats and boating -- Fiction
ISBN 978-0-15-206715-1; 0-15-206715-9

"Rylant's adorable characters are bored, so Mr. [Putter's] neighbor Mrs. Teaberry suggests an adventure on a sightseeing boat. The Olden Days is the perfect vessel. Mrs. Teaberry's dog, Zeke, loves it so much that he doesn't want to leave and sinks his teeth into the mast, and the captain helps them out. Howard's delightful pictures created with pencil, watercolor, and gouache add humor and panache to the story." SLJ

★ **Mr.** Putter & Tabby pour the tea; illustrated by Arthur Howard. Harcourt Brace & Co. 1994 un il $14; pa $5.95

Grades: K 1 2   E
1. Cats -- Fiction 2. Old age -- Fiction
ISBN 0-15-256255-9; 0-15-200901-9 pa

LC 93-21470

"Rylant's charming story of two elderly characters is complemented and enhanced by Howard's delightful illustrations, done in pencil, watercolor, and gouache." SLJ

Other titles about Mr. Putter and Tabby are:
Mr. Putter & Tabby bake the cake (1994)
Mr. Putter & Tabby walk the dog (1994)
Mr. Putter & Tabby pick the pears (1995)
Mr. Putter & Tabby row the boat (1997)
Mr. Putter & Tabby fly the plane (1997)
Mr. Putter & Tabby take the train (1998)
Mr. Putter & Tabby toot the horn (1998)
Mr. Putter & Tabby paint the porch (2000)
Mr. Putter & Tabby feed the fish (2001)
Mr. Putter & Tabby catch the cold (2002)
Mr. Putter & Tabby stir the soup (2003)
Mr. Putter & Tabby write the book (2004)
Mr. Putter & Tabby make a wish (2005)
Mr. Putter & Tabby spin the yarn (2006)
Mr. Putter & Tabby see the stars (2007)
Mr. Putter & Tabby run the race (2008)
Mr. Putter & Tabby spill the beans (2009)
Mr. Putter & Tabby clear the decks (2010)
Mr. Putter & Tabby ring the bell (2011)

★ **Poppleton**; book one. illustrated by Mark Teague. Blue Sky Press (NY) 1997 48p il hardcover o.p. pa $3.99

Grades: K 1 2   E
1. Pigs -- Fiction 2. Friendship -- Fiction
ISBN 0-590-84783-X; 0-590-84782-1 pa

LC 96-3365

"City pig Poppleton adjusts to small-town life in this . . . chapter book. In 'Neighbors,' the polite Poppleton tries to think up a polite way to say 'no thanks' to Cherry Sue, a friendly llama who invites him to breakfast, lunch and dinner every single day. . . . The second vignette, 'The Library,' details Poppleton's reading ritual, which demands solitude. Finally, 'The Pill' introduces Fillmore, a sick goat who refuses to take his pill unless Poppleton hides it in a cake. . . . [Rylant's] concise sentences mimic the characters' good manners and wryly point up the failures of etiquette. Teague contributes fetching watercolor-and-pencil images of the pudgy pig, slender llama and dignified goat." Publ Wkly

Other titles about Poppleton are:
Poppleton and friends (1997)
Poppleton everyday (1998)
Poppleton forever (1998)
Poppleton has fun (2000)
Poppleton in Fall (1999)
Poppleton in Spring (1999)
Poppleton in Winter (2001)
Poppleton through and through (2000)

Puppies and piggies; illustrated by Ivan Bates. Harcourt 2008 32p il $16

Grades: PreK   E
1. Stories in rhyme 2. Animals -- Fiction
ISBN 978-0-15-202321-8; 0-15-202321-6

LC 2004-3136

Rhyming text describes what various animals do and what they love, as well as a baby who loves his bed and his mother.

"Told in reassuring rhyme, the simple upbeat text showcases happy animals doing what comes naturally while Bates's idyllic watercolor and crayon illustrations present a bucolic barnyard teeming with contented critters. . . . Comforting and carefree fare for tiny tots." Kirkus

★ The **relatives** came; story by Cynthia Rylant; illustrated by Stephen Gammell. rev format ed.; Atheneum Books for Young Readers 2001 un il $16.95; pa $6.99

Grades: PreK K 1 2   E
1. Family life -- Fiction
ISBN 0-689-84508-1; 0-689-71738-5 pa

A reformatted edition of the title first published 1985 by Bradbury Press

A Caldecott Medal honor book, 1986

"If there's anything more charming than the tone of voice in this story, it's the drawings that go with it. Stephen Gammell . . . fills the pages with bright, crayony pictures teeming with details that children should enjoy poring over for hours." NY Times Book Rev

★ **Snow**; illustrated by Lauren Stringer. Harcourt 2008 un il $17

Grades: PreK K 1 2   E
1. Snow -- Fiction
ISBN 978-0-15-205303-1; 0-15-205303-4

LC 2006-06171

Celebrates the beauty of a snowfall and its happy effects on children.

"Snow is not an uncommon subject in picture books, but few have both the grace and exuberance of this lovely collaboration featuring Rylant's evocative words and Stringer's entrancing paintings." Booklist

When I was young in the mountains; illustrated by Diane Goode. Dutton 1982 un il $15.99; pa $6.99
Grades: K 1 2 3   E
ISBN 0-525-42525-X; 0-525-44198-0 pa
LC 81-5359
A Caldecott Medal honor book, 1983
"The people in the story are poor in material things, but rich in family pleasures. The title becomes a pleasing refrain. . . . Illustrations and text are placed on a bed of white space, without borders, which makes them look uncrowded and imparts a great feeling of freedom." SLJ

Rymond, Lynda Gene
Oscar and the mooncats; by Lynda Gene Rymond; illustrated by Nicoletta Ceccoli. Houghton Mifflin Company 2007 un il $16
Grades: PreK K 1 2   E
1. Cats -- Fiction
ISBN 978-0-618-56316-6; 0-618-56316-4
LC 2006026079
Feeling more than a little wild, Oscar the cat leaps from one high spot to another until he lands on the Moon, where he plays with the mooncats until his boy begins to call and he must find a way back home or risk becoming a mooncat, himself.

"Mixed-media illustrations created with plasticine, acrylics, and computer graphics beautifully depict scenes. . . . The 3-D effect of the pictures and the unusual perspectives . . . are in perfect keeping with the surreal nature of the story." Booklist

Sabuda, Robert
Alice's adventures in Wonderland; a pop-up adaptation of Lewis Carroll's original tale. illustrated by Robert Sabuda. Little Simon 2003 un il $25.95
Grades: 1 2 3 4   E
1. Fantasy fiction 2. Pop-up books
ISBN 0-689-84743-2
A pop-up version of Lewis Carroll's classic tale of Alice who falls down the rabbit hole to find a new world.

"Sabuda brings Alice's world to life with breathtaking, three-dimensional images that are incredibly imaginative, intricately detailed, and perfectly executed. Carroll's text has been significantly abridged, and . . . the quickly paced narrative retains the flavor of the original." SLJ

The **Christmas** alphabet; deluxe anniversary edition; Orchard Books 2004 un il $22.95
Grades: K 1 2 3 4   E
1. Alphabet 2. Christmas 3. Pop-up books
ISBN 0-439-67256-2
First published 1994
"Four large flaps per spread—each representing a letter of the alphabet—open to reveal sophisticated 3D images, some with parts that move in uncommonly inventive ways. Many of the pop-ups are obvious Christmas symbols. . . .

Others have ambiguous—but resourceful—ties to the holiday. . . . A yuletide gem." Publ Wkly

The **Chronicles** of Narnia pop-up; based on the books by C. S. Lewis; pop-ups by Robert Sabuda. HarperCollinsPublishers 2007 un il $29.99
Grades: 3 4 5   E
1. Fantasy fiction 2. Pop-up books
ISBN 978-0-06-117612-8
"Sabuda works his pop-up magic once again, designing for each of the seven Narnia books a multilayered scene that unfolds and rears up dramatically as the spread is opened. Four spreads also contain a smaller pop-up behind a corner flap. The painted art is equal to the complex articulations, depicting Aslan and the rest of the cast as colorful, boldly drawn figures." SLJ

★ **Peter** Pan: a classic collectible pop-up. Simon & Schuster Children's Pub. 2008 un il $29.99
Grades: 2 3 4 5 6   E
1. Fairy tales 2. Pop-up books
ISBN 978-0-689-85364-7; 0-689-85364-5
"Sabuda enhances the already powerful enchantments of J. M. Barrie's classic 1902 tale with astonishing paper engineering. Illustrations suggest a hybrid of period styles, somewhere between arts and crafts, with their rich patterning, and art nouveau, with their Tiffany glass-like outlines and colorations. . . . Not to be missed." Publ Wkly

Sacre, Antonio
La Noche Buena; a Christmas story. illustrated by Angela Dominguez. Abrams Books for Young Readers 2010 un il $16.95
Grades: K 1 2 3   E
1. Christmas -- Fiction 2. Family life -- Fiction 3. Grandmothers -- Fiction 4. Cuban Americans -- Fiction 5. Christmas stories -- Juvenile literature
ISBN 978-0-8109-8967-2; 0-8109-8967-0
LC 2009052204
While spending Christmas with her Cuban American grandmother in Miami, Florida, young Nina misses her usual New England holiday but enjoys learning about the foods and other traditions her father knew as a child.

"Attractive paintings with simple lines and bright, solid colors help tell this warm, loving story in an understated way." Kirkus

A **mango** in the hand; a story told through proverbs. illustrated by Sebastia Serra. Abrams Books for Young Readers 2011 un il $16.95
Grades: K 1 2 3   E
1. Mangoes -- Fiction 2. Proverbs -- Fiction 3. Family life -- Fiction 4. Spanish language -- Vocabulary
ISBN 978-0-8109-9734-9; 0-8109-9734-7
LC 2010024423
Guided by proverbs from his father and other relatives, Francisco makes several attempts to bring ripe mangoes home for dessert on his saint day, and in the process learns lessons in love and generosity. Includes glossary of Spanish terms.

"Sacre's snappy storytelling avoids being overly moralistic, and Serra's digitally colored pencil-and-ink artwork creates a friendly, close-knit neighborhood for Francisco, the kind in which food, conversation—and proverbs—can be found in abundance." Publ Wkly

Safran, Sheri

Best friends; a pop-up book. illustrated by Mark Chambers. Tango 2011 un il $15.99
Grades: PreK K   E
1. Pop-up books 2. Friendship -- Fiction 3. Handicapped -- Fiction
ISBN 978-1-85707-711-7; 1-85707-711-3

"A cheerful cartoon girl in pigtails recounts the pretend games that she and her best friend, James—who is in a wheelchair—play together, their actions brought to life by pop-ups and other interactive elements. . . . To Safran's credit, her prose makes no mention of James's physical condition, letting his evident imagination, capability, and activity do the talking." Publ Wkly

Saint-Lot, Katia Novet

Amadi's snowman; illustrated by Dimitrea Tokunbo. Tilbury House 2008 un il $16.95
Grades: PreK K 1 2   E
1. Books and reading -- Fiction 2. Igbo (African people) -- Fiction
ISBN 978-0-88448-298-7; 0-88448-298-7
LC 2007043343

As a young Igbo man, Amadi does not understand why his mother insists he learn to read, since he already knows his numbers and will be a businessman one day, but an older boy teaches him the value of learning about the world through books

"Children will enjoy reading about Amadi's life in the village, depicted in the earth-toned, intimate scenes." Booklist

Sakai, Komako

Emily's balloon. Chronicle Books 2006 un il $14.95
Grades: PreK K 1   E
1. Balloons -- Fiction
ISBN 0-8118-5219-9
LC 2005-11283

A little girl's new friend is round, lighter than air, and looks like the moon at night.

"The yellow balloon and its blue string stand out in a simple color palette of white, gray, and tan with a few accents of red. The illustrations, rendered in watercolor and charcoal, are placed on tan pages and surrounded by unadorned thin, round-edged black frames. A tale of a common childhood experience, tenderly and sweetly told." SLJ

★ **Mad** at Mommy. Arthur A. Levine Books 2010 un il $16.99
Grades: PreK K 1   E
1. Anger -- Fiction 2. Rabbits -- Fiction 3. Mother-child relationship -- Fiction
ISBN 978-0-545-21209-0; 0-545-21209-X
Original Japanese edition, 2000

A little rabbit is very angry at his mother, and he tells her the reasons why.

"Sakai's paintings are simply composed and staged, allowing rabbit's expressive poses to shine. . . . A playful story that offers young readers—and their big feelings—a serious voice. Charming, classy and current." Kirkus

★ The **snow** day. Arthur A. Levine Books 2009 un il $16.99
Grades: PreK K   E
1. Snow -- Fiction 2. Rabbits -- Fiction
ISBN 978-0-545-01321-5; 0-545-01321-6
LC 2007-49949

Original Japanese edition 2005

A little rabbit enjoys having a day off from kindergarten and spending time with his mother during a snowstorm, but his father's flight home is cancelled until the snow stops falling.

Sakai's "subdued palette and minimalist text suggest the blanketed sound produced by a heavy snowfall. . . . The layers of paint are applied to a black ground with a combination of wet and dry brushes, producing a convincing depth and texture. . . . The sentences are appropriately concise, yet with lovely rhythms and interesting details." SLJ

Salerno, Steven

Harry hungry! written and illustrated by Steven Salerno. Harcourt 2009 un il $16
Grades: PreK K   E
1. Hunger -- Fiction 2. Infants -- Fiction
ISBN 978-0-15-206257-6; 0-15-206257-2
LC 2007-04375

Harry is a baby so hungry that he eats all the food in his house, then goes outside to find more.

"Done in his trademark retro style, Salerno's bright, sweeping illustrations and offbeat perspectives instantly capture this tiny tot's insatiable energy. . . . Children will delight in growling loudly along with Harry's tummy." Kirkus

Salley, Coleen

Epossumondas plays possum; written by Coleen Salley; illustrated by Janet Stevens. Harcourt Children's Books 2009 un il $16
Grades: K 1 2 3   E
1. Fear -- Fiction 2. Marshes -- Fiction 3. Opossums -- Fiction
ISBN 978-0-15-206420-4; 0-15-206420-6
LC 2009-7976

Forgetting his mother's warnings, Epossumondas goes into the swamp alone then must pretend to be dead time and again as he hears frightening sounds and fears they are being made by the dreaded loup garou.

"Rich with Southern flavor . . . it's an immersive piece of storytelling." Pub Wkly

Epossumondas saves the day; written by Coleen Salley; illustrated by Janet Stevens. Harcourt 2006 un il $16
Grades: K 1 2 3   E
1. Turtles -- Fiction 2. Opossums -- Fiction 3. Birthdays -- Fiction
ISBN 0-15-205701-3
LC 2005-27538

In this variation on the folktale, Sody Salyraytus, each of Epossumondas's birthday guests disappears until it is finally up to him to rescue them all and bring home the "sody" for his birthday biscuits.

"Salley's text is alive with the colorful expressions of the South . . . which make the story a delight to read aloud. Stevens's hilarious mixed-media illustrations are a perfect match for the narrative." SLJ

Saltzberg, Barney

Beautiful oops! Workman 2010 un il $11.95
Grades: PreK K 1 2   E
1. Errors -- Fiction 2. Creative ability -- Fiction
ISBN 978-0-7611-5728-1; 0-7611-5728-X

"A celebration of creative thinking, Saltzberg's small-format book encourages readers to view mistakes not as failures but opportunities. . . . Various spills and blobs are transformed into animals, a crumpled piece of paper becomes wool for a sheep, and . . . a panel with a hole in the center telescopes outward, accordian-style, to reveal a tiny creature way at the bottom. Inspirational without being saccharine." Publ Wkly

I want a dog! Random House Children's Books 2009 un il $11.99
Grades: PreK K   E
1. Pop-up books 2. Dogs -- Fiction
ISBN 978-0-375-85783-6; 0-375-85783-4

"The earnest speaker in this fun story, based on the author's song of the same title, pleads for a dog, promising that it 'will never, ever make a mess' (via a pull tab, she sweeps his 'mess' into a dustpan as she holds her nose). Other animals—a hippo, a pig—won't do (turning a wheel helps the girl feed an endless bucket of slop to a tubby swine). On a final pop-up spread, she embraces a dog, surrounded by blooming, red hearts. Effective interactive elements and simple humor will charm." Publ Wkly

Stanley and the class pet; [by] Barney Saltzberg. Candlewick Press 2008 un il $16.99
Grades: PreK K 1 2   E
1. School stories 2. Birds -- Fiction 3. Hamsters -- Fiction
ISBN 978-0-7636-3595-4; 0-7636-3595-2

LC 2007-40541

Stanley is excited about bringing the class pet, a bird, home for the weekend, but when his friend Larry urges him to open the cage and let Figgy out to fly, it is hard to know who is to blame for the ensuing disaster.

"With clearly lined acrylic paintings and a smoothly paced text that avoids a too-heavy message, Saltzberg deftly turns a common classroom scenario into a gentle story about peer pressure and responsibility." Booklist

Other titles about Stanley are:
Crazy hair day (2003)
Star of the week (2006)

Salzano, Tammi

One rainy day; illustrated by Hannah Wood. Tiger Tales 2011 un bd bk $8.95
Grades: PreK   E
1. Board books for children 2. Rain -- Fiction 3. Color -- Fiction 4. Ducks -- Fiction
ISBN 978-1-58925-860-0; 1-58925-860-6

"Beneath light showers of foil raindrops, a duckling sporting red boots and an orange umbrella happily encounters a green frog, pink worms, yellow flowers, and other color-linked items. The text in this padded-cover board book runs to just a short phrase per spread, and the fuzzy yellow duck's joie de vivre glows in each simply composed scene." Booklist

Samuels, Barbara

★ The **trucker**. Farrar, Straus and Giroux 2010 un il $16.99
Grades: PreK K 1   E
1. Cats -- Fiction 2. Toys -- Fiction 3. Trucks -- Fiction
ISBN 978-0-374-37804-2; 0-374-37804-5

LC 2007029266

A boy who loves trucks is disappointed when he receives a cat named Lola instead of a toy fire truck, but Lola proves to be a "trucker" after all.

"A winner for young children, this offers a real story along with all of the vehicle action. Kids will enjoy the combination of active play and cozy snuggling." Booklist

Sandall, Ellie

Birdsong. Egmont USA 2011 un il $16.99
Grades: PreK   E
1. Birds -- Fiction 2. Birdsongs -- Fiction
ISBN 978-1-60684-193-8; 1-60684-193-9

LC 2010017006

A crowd of birds lands in a tree, sharing their different songs, until one last winged creature proves to be too much.

"The book has rhythm, bird sounds that are great fun to hear and say, and illustrations that depict each cast member as a winged creature of distinction." Horn Book Guide

Sandburg, Carl

The **Huckabuck** family and how they raised popcorn in Nebraska and quit and came back; pictures by David Small. Farrar, Straus & Giroux 1999 un il $16; pa $6.95
Grades: 1 2 3 4   E
1. Humorous stories 2. Farm life -- Fiction
ISBN 0-374-33511-7; 0-374-43449-2 pa

LC 98-6676

After the popcorn the Huckabucks had raised explodes in a fire and Pony Pony Huckabuck finds a silver buckle inside a squash, the family decides it is time for a change

"Small's watercolors have a translucent, airy quality that suits the fantastical elements of Sandburg's story. . . . Sandburg's language is as bracing as a tonic, and the inherent humor and rhythms of his tale are as invigorating today as when it was first written." Bull Cent Child Books

Sandemose, Iben

Gracie & Grandma & the itsy, bitsy seed; translated from Norwegian by Tonje Vetleseter. MacKenzie Smiles 2009 un il $14.95
Grades: PreK K 1 2   E
1. Growth -- Fiction 2. Plants -- Fiction 3. Grandmothers -- Fiction
ISBN 978-0-9790347-5-6; 0-9790347-5-2

"Spunky and imaginative Gracie presents her equally exuberant grandmother with a surprise–an itsy, bitsy seed. But what will it grow into? As the plant gets larger and larger, Grandma incorrectly guesses that it is a banana, lemon, fried mackerel, balloon, jungle, cow, or ghost tree until she spots a large red dot growing at the top and shouts: 'A big tomato!' . . . The simple yet expressive text, in a large, bold typeface, perfectly complements the wacky, exaggerated, dazzlingly bright colored ink and marker cartoon illustrations." SLJ

Other titles in this series are:
Gracie & Grandma (2008)
Gracie & Grandma under water (2008)

Sanders-Wells, Linda

Maggie's monkeys; illustrated by Abby Carter. Candlewick Press 2009 un il $16.99

Grades: K 1 2   E

   1. Siblings -- Fiction 2. Family life -- Fiction 3. Imagination -- Fiction

ISBN 978-0-7636-3326-4; 0-7636-3326-7

                  LC 2008-28711

When Maggie reports that pink monkeys have moved into the refrigerator, her mother and father play along and accomodate the invisible visitors, much to the frustration of Maggie's older, reality-obsessed brother.

"Sanders-Wells wonderfully encapsulates the difficulties of being a middle child—simultaneously too old and too young. Carter's masterful facial expressions reflects this inner battle. Her gouache artwork is done in a bright, tropical palette that emphasizes the imaginative theme. . . . A humorous tale sure to make siblings smile, even as they inwardly groan." Kirkus

Sandin, Joan

At home in a new land. HarperCollinsPublishers 2007 64p il (I can read!) $15.99; lib bdg $16.89

Grades: 1 2 3   E

   1. Immigrants -- Fiction 2. Swedish Americans -- Fiction 3. Frontier and pioneer life -- Fiction

ISBN 978-0-06-058077-3; 0-06-058077-1; 978-0-06-058078-0 lib bdg; 0-06-058078-X lib bdg

                  LC 2006-36251

Carl Erik, a recent immigrant from Sweden, becomes the man of the house when his father and uncle go to work in a logging camp, and he learns many things about life in Minnesota while attending school, doing his chores, and trying to put meat on the table

"Watercolor and ink illustrations add realistic detail to a story that reveals Carl's lifestyle and warm bonds with his family and friends. . . . This book provides a solid introduction to historical fiction for early readers." SLJ

Santiago, Esmeralda

A doll for Navidades; illustrated by Enrique O. Sánchez. Scholastic Press 2005 un il $16.99

Grades: PreK K 1 2   E

   1. Gifts -- Fiction 2. Christmas -- Fiction

ISBN 0-439-55398-9

While preparing for Christmas in Puerto Rico, seven-year-old Esmeralda asks the Three Magi for a baby doll like her cousin's, but when they bring something else instead she gains a deeper understanding of the meaning of the holiday

"Santiago's autobiographical tale is both a universal story of holiday disappointment and a rich sensory portrait. . . . Sánchez's acrylic-on-canvas paintings add to the exotic flavor and the familiarity of the large family." SLJ

Santore, Charles

The Silk Princess. Random House Children's Books 2007 un il $17.99; lib bdg $20.99

Grades: 1 2 3   E

   1. Silk -- Fiction 2. Princesses -- Fiction

ISBN 978-0-375-83664-0; 978-0-375-93664-7 lib bdg

                  LC 2007-04764

After a cocoon falls into her tea cup and unravels to form a long, delicate thread, Hsi-Ling Chi, a princess in ancient China, meets a mysterious man who reveals how to transform the cocoons into silk.

The text "tells an exciting, vivid tale, but it's Santore's exquisitely detailed artwork, combining beautiful character close-ups with scenes resembling traditional Chinese landscapes, that is so extraordinary." Booklist

Sarcone-Roach, Julia

The secret plan. Alfred A. Knopf 2009 un il $16.99; lib bdg $19.99

Grades: PreK K 1 2   E

   1. Cats -- Fiction 2. Play -- Fiction 3. Bedtime -- Fiction 4. Elephants -- Fiction

ISBN 978-0-375-85858-1; 0-375-85858-X; 978-0-375-95858-8 lib bdg; 0-375-95858-4 lib bdg

                  LC 2008-39291

Continually thwarted in their efforts to escape bedtime and continue playing, Milo the elephant and three kittens named Henry, Hildy, and Harriet finally find a "perfect late night bedtime-free hideout."

"The age-old dilemma of wanting to stay up and play just a bit longer finds a gently humorous treatment in this tale, accompanied by swirly acrylic paintings that evoke dreamy nighttime fantasy." SLJ

   Subway story. Alfred A. Knopf 2011 un il $16.99; lib bdg $19.99

Grades: PreK K   E

   1. Subways -- Fiction

ISBN 978-0-375-85859-8; 0-375-85859-8; 978-0-375-95859-5 lib bdg; 0-375-95859-2 lib bdg

                  LC 2010045487

Jessie, a subway car 'born' in St. Louis, Missouri, enjoys many years as an important part of the New York City subway system, and after she is replaced by more modern cars she begins another important job.

"The author's acrylics gently anthropomorphize Jessie, giving her headlight-eyes and a winsome smile. Immensely readable and surprisingly touching, this large heft of metal totes a lot of charm." Kirkus

Includes bibliographical references

Sartell, Debra

Time for bed, baby Ted; illustrations by Kay Chorao. Holiday House 2010 un il $16.95

Grades: PreK   E

   1. Stories in rhyme 2. Bedtime -- Fiction

ISBN 978-0-8234-1968-5; 0-8234-1968-1

                  LC 2008-48652

At bedtime, Baby Ted finds many ways to avoid going to bed.

"The various animal sounds and action words in the short text, coupled with Chorao's pleasing illustrations, featuring a mop-topped Ted and his pretend menagerie, make this a fun read-aloud for parent and child and a natural for sharing with a young group of children." Booklist

Sasso, Sandy Eisenberg

The Shema in the mezuzah; listening to each other. Sandy Eisenberg Sasso; Illustrations by Joani Keller Rothenberg. Jewish Lights Pub. 2012 30 p. col. ill. $18.99

Grades: K 1 2 3   E

   1. Mezuzah -- Fiction 2. Listening -- Fiction 3. Judaism -- Customs and practices -- Juvenile fiction 4. Jews --

Fiction 5. Judaism -- Customs and practices -- Fiction
ISBN 1580235069; 9781580235068

LC 2012007709

National Jewish Book Awards: Illustrated Children's
Book (2012)

This Jewish children's story, by Rabbi Sandy Eisenberg
Sasso, is about "compromise and listening. The townspeople
have mezuzahs but cannot agree on how to put them up on
their doorways. . . . To end their arguing, they consult the
wise rabbi of the town, who advises them to carefully read
the Shema in the mezuzah to find the answer. This . . . tale
[is] based on a twelfth-century rabbinic debate." (Publisher's note)

Sattler, Jennifer

Chick 'n' Pug. Bloomsbury U.S.A. Children's Books
2010 un il $14.99; lib bdg $15.89

Grades: PreK K 1 2   E

1. Adventure fiction 2. Dogs -- Fiction 3. Roosters
-- Fiction

ISBN 978-1-59990-534-1; 1-59990-534-5; 978-1-
59990-535-8 lib bdg; 1-59990-535-3 lib bdg

LC 2010009330

Chick leaves the boring coop in order to find his hero,
Wonder Pug, and a little bit of excitement.

"Beautiful acrylic and color pencil drawings add depth
to this cute hero story. . . . With text that is appropriate for
the youngest listener and colorful pictures, this humorous
picture book will be great for reading aloud and ideal for
storytimes." Libr Media Connect

★ **Pig** kahuna. Bloomsbury Children's Books 2011 un
il $14.99; lib bdg $15.89

Grades: PreK K 1 2   E

1. Pigs -- Fiction 2. Surfing -- Fiction

ISBN 978-1-59990-635-5; 1-59990-635-X; 978-1-
59990-636-2 lib bdg; 1-59990-636-8 lib bdg

LC 2010035629

Fergus is afraid to go in the water, but he and his baby
brother Dink find a surfboard while collecting treasures
along the seashore.

"The briskly paced text . . . offers alliteration and deadpan humor. Together words and pictures create an utterly
engaging picture-book experience—eye-catching, thought-
provoking and just plain fun." Kirkus

Sylvie. Random House 2009 un il $15.99; lib bdg
$18.99

Grades: PreK K 1   E

1. Food -- Fiction 2. Color -- Fiction 3. Flamingos
-- Fiction

ISBN 978-0-375-85708-9; 0-375-85708-7; 978-0-375-
95708-6 lib bdg; 0-375-95708-1 lib bdg

LC 2008-11259

When Sylvie the pink flamingo learns her color comes
from the little pink shrimp she eats, she decides to expand
her choices, trying everything under the sun and, unfortunately, overdoing it.

"Sattler's art steals the show; the colors are eye-popping
and vibrant, right to the swirling bright endpapers. . . . This
title is sure to create storytime magic." SLJ

Uh-oh, dodo! Jennifer Sattler. Boyds Mills Press 2013
32 p. (reinforced) $15.95

Grades: PreK K   E

1. Dodo -- Juvenile fiction 2. Picture books for children
ISBN 9781590789292

LC 2012947460

In this children's story, written and illustrated by Jennifer Sattler, Dodo "loves an adventure. He is always willing to try new things. He enjoys making new friends. But
not everything turns out the way Dodo expects. Even a walk
with his Mama turns into a topsy-turvy day of discoveries,
challenges, and surprises. Good thing Dodo has a sense of
humor!" (Publisher's note)

Sauer, Tammi

Chicken dance; illustrated by Dan Santat. Sterling
2009 un il $14.95

Grades: PreK K 1   E

1. Chickens -- Fiction 2. Contests -- Fiction 3.
Domestic animals -- Fiction

ISBN 978-1-4027-5366-4; 1-4027-5366-7

LC 2008-50578

Determined to win tickets to an Elvis Poultry concert,
hens Marge and Lola enter the Barnyard Talent Show, then,
while the ducks who usually win the contest jeer, they test
out their abilities.

"The zippy narrative features punchy dialogue and witty
interactions. . . . Santat's rich ink-and-acrylic designs provide a humorous context through animated expressions. . . .
Fly the coop to enjoy this hilarious adventure." Kirkus

Mostly monsterly; illustrated by Scott Magoon. Simon
& Schuster Books for Young Readers 2010 un il $14.99

Grades: PreK K 1   E

1. School stories 2. Monsters -- Fiction

ISBN 978-1-4169-6110-9; 1-4169-6110-0

LC 2008-48676

On the outside, Bernadette is a lot like the other monsters
in her class but when she shows that she can be sweet, her
classmates reject her until she finds a way to fit in again.

"Sauer tells a well-paced story in simple, repetitive
phrases. The writing reveals just enough, allowing the artwork to fill in the rest of the story. . . . This artistic style
proves effective in conveying the look of monsters without
the frightening attributes. In fact, the art complements the
humorous tone of the story." SLJ

Nugget and Fang; friends forever--or snack time? Tammi Sauer; illustrated by Michael Slack. Harcourt Children's
Books 2013 40 p. (reinforced) $16.99

Grades: PreK K 1 2   E

1. Humorous stories 2. Fishes -- Fiction 3. Sharks --
Fiction 4. Minnows -- Fiction 5. Friendship -- Fiction
6. Peer pressure -- Fiction

ISBN 0547852851; 9780547852850

LC 2012025329

Saunders, Karen

Baby Badger's wonderful night; illustrated by Dubravka Kolanovic. Egmont USA 2011 un il $16.99

Grades: PreK K 1 2   E

1. Fear -- Fiction 2. Night -- Fiction 3. Badgers --
Fiction 4. Father-son relationship -- Fiction

ISBN 978-1-60684-172-3; 1-60684-172-6

LC 2010024427

Baby Badger is frightened as darkness falls, and so Papa Badger takes him on a walk, pointing out the beauty and wonder of the night.

"The conversations between Baby Badger and his dad are calming and conveyed in a patient, caring way. And by using light colors and rounded shapes, Kolanovic has created a world that looks welcoming and safe. . . . An ideal choice for bedtime." SLJ

Savadier, Elivia

Time to get dressed! Roaring Brook Press 2006 un il $14.95

Grades: PreK K   E

1. Clothing and dress -- Fiction 2. Father-son relationship -- Fiction

ISBN 978-1-59643-161-4; 1-59643-161-X

LC 2005-19923

"Savadier's skillfully rendered watercolors use thick, supple lines and soft colors set against lots of white space. With a rhythmic, lean text and charming pictures, this will be great for sharing, either in groups or one-on-one." SLJ

Will Sheila share? Roaring Brook Press 2008 un il $12.95

Grades: PreK   E

1. Grandmothers -- Fiction

ISBN 978-1-59643-289-5; 1-59643-289-6

LC 2007-10039

Nana helps teach her toddler granddaughter to share.

"Savadier's watercolor and ink pictures are particularly energetic. . . . The author shows a shrewd understanding of how an uncooperative child can unnerve everyone—including the kid in question. Her pithy text and expressive, economical pictures deliver a reassuring response along with solid comedy." Publ Wkly

Savage, Stephen

★ **Little** Tug; Stephen Savage. Roaring Book Press 2012 32 p. (alk. paper) $12.99

Grades: PreK K 1   E

1. Picture books for children 2. Tugboats -- Juvenile fiction

ISBN 1596436484; 9781596436480

LC 2011033799

This children's picture book "depicts Little Tug as beloved and helpful from the start. The story has the tempo of a waltz, as readers meet three other ships (a sailboat, a speedboat, and an ocean liner), each of which get into trouble of a sort, and are rescued in turn by Little Tug." (Publishers Weekly)

★ **Where's** Walrus? Scholastic Press 2011 un il

Grades: PreK K 1   E

1. Stories without words 2. Zoos -- Fiction 3. Walruses -- Fiction

ISBN 0-439-70049-3; 978-0-439-70049-8

LC 2010-922375

"With the zookeeper on his trail, an escaped walrus hides out in the city. . . . His trick is to blend in to each particular scene. However, he can't help but stand out in a diving competition where he wins a gold medal. . . . The collagelike illustrations in this wordless book were created in Adobe Illustrator. They are large, clear, and simple; the colors are bright, although flat. Young children will take delight in their ability to spot the wandering walrus." SLJ

Saxton, Jo

Snail trail; in search of a modern masterpiece. Frances Lincoln 2010 un il $17.95

Grades: PreK K 1 2   E

1. Art -- Fiction 2. Snails -- Fiction

ISBN 978-1-84780-021-3; 1-84780-021-1

"An affable snail tours fine-art masterpieces, inviting readers to discern which painting's based on him. . . . Each spread features one painting for comparison: Which is the snail's likeness? . . . Henri Mattise's collage-painting The Snail is the answer; in two rhyming couplets, Saxton neatly reveals how Matisse's abstract piece is really a portrait. . . . This [is a] playful, refeshingly clear introduction of 'how to look' at art." Kirkus

Say, Allen

★ **Allison**. Houghton Mifflin 1997 32p il $17; pa $6.95

Grades: PreK K 1 2   E

1. Adoption -- Fiction 2. Japanese Americans -- Fiction

ISBN 0-395-85895-X; 0-618-49537-1 pa

LC 97-7528

When Allison realizes that she looks more like her Japanese doll than like her parents, she comes to terms with this unwelcomed discovery through the help of a stray cat

"A subtle, sensitive probing of interracial adoption, this exquisitely illustrated story will encourage thoughtful adult-child dialogue on a potentially difficult issue." Publ Wkly

The **bicycle** man. Parnassus Press 1982 un il lib bdg $16; pa $5.95

Grades: K 1 2 3   E

1. Cycling -- Fiction

ISBN 0-395-32254-5 lib bdg; 0-395-50652-2 pa

LC 82-2980

The amazing tricks two American soldiers do on a borrowed bicycle are a fitting finale for the school sports day festivities in a small village in occupied Japan

"The kindly, openhearted story is beautifully pictured in a profusion of delicate pen-and-ink drawings washed in gentle colors." Horn Book

★ **Boy** in the garden; written and illustrated by Allen Say. Houghton Mifflin Harcourt 2010 un il $17.99

Grades: PreK K 1 2   E

1. Dreams -- Fiction 2. Cranes (Birds) -- Fiction

ISBN 978-0-547-21410-8; 0-547-21410-3

After Jiro encounters a life-like garden statue of a tall bird, he falls asleep and dreams of the story his mother once told him about a grateful crane.

"Say is a master of composition. . . . Positions and postures are eloquent. . . . A gently unsettling tale of the power of the imagination." Horn Book

★ **Erika**-san. Houghton Mifflin Books for Children 2009 un il $17

Grades: 2 3 4   E

1. Teachers -- Fiction

ISBN 978-0-618-88933-4; 0-618-88933-7

LC 2008-00601

After falling in love with Japan as a little girl, Erika becomes a teacher and fulfills her childhood dream by moving to a remote Japanese island.

"With luminous watercolors and economical text . . . Say . . . tells of an American girl whose ingenuous hopes of reaching 'old Japan' are finally realized." Publ Wkly

The **favorite** daughter; Allen Say. Arthur A. Levine Books 2013 32 p. (hardcover) $17.99
Grades: K 1 2 3   E
1. Picture books for children 2. Japanese Americans -- Juvenile fiction 3. Father-daughter relationship -- Juvenile fiction 4. Artists -- Fiction 5. Schools -- Fiction 6. Teasing -- Fiction 7. Japanese Americans -- Fiction 8. Fathers and daughters -- Fiction
ISBN 054517662X; 9780545176620
LC 2012026830
In this children's picture book, by Allen Say, "Yuriko hates her name when the children make fun of it. . . . The teasing makes her want to hide, to retreat even from the art projects she used to love. Fortunately she has a patient, kind father who finds gentle ways of drawing her out and reminding Yuriko of the traditions they share that have always brought her joy." (Publisher's note)

★ **Grandfather's** journey; written and illustrated by Allen Say. Houghton Mifflin 1993 32p il $16.95; pa $7.99
Grades: 1 2 3 4   E
1. Grandfathers -- Fiction 2. Japanese Americans -- Fiction 3. Voyages and travels -- Fiction
ISBN 0-395-57035-2; 0-547-07680-0 pa
LC 93-18836
Awarded the Caldecott Medal, 1994
A Japanese American man recounts his grandfather's journey to America which he later also undertakes, and the feelings of being torn by a love for two different countries
"The brief text is simple and unaffected, but the emotions expressed are deeply complex. The paintings are astonishingly still, like the captured moments found in a family photo album. Each translucent watercolor is suffused with light." SLJ

★ **Kamishibai** man; written and illustrated by Allen Say. Houghton Mifflin Co. 2005 32p il $17
Grades: PreK K 1 2 3   E
1. Entertainers -- Fiction
ISBN 0-618-47954-6
After many years of retirement, an old Kamishibai man—a Japanese street performer who tells stories and sells candies—decides to make his rounds once more even though such entertainment declined after the advent of television.
"The quietly dramatic, beautifully evocative tale contains a cliffhanger of its own, and its exquisite art, in the style of Kamishibai picture cards, will attract even the most jaded kid away from the TV to enjoy a good, good book." Booklist

The **lost** lake. Houghton Mifflin 1989 32p il $16; pa $6.95
Grades: K 1 2 3   E
1. Camping -- Fiction 2. Father-son relationship --

Fiction
ISBN 0-395-50933-5; 0-395-63036-3 pa
LC 89-11026
"Using colors as crisp and clean as the outdoors, Say effectively alternates between scenes where father and son are the focus and those where the landscape predominates. Both in story and art, a substantial piece." Booklist

★ **Tea** with milk. Houghton Mifflin 1999 32p il $17; pa $6.99
Grades: K 1 2 3 4   E
1. Homesickness -- Fiction 2. Japanese Americans -- Fiction
ISBN 0-395-90495-1; 0-547-23747-2 pa
LC 98-11667
After growing up near San Francisco, Masako (or May) returns with her parents to their native Japan, but she feels foreign and out of place until she finds a job in Osaka and marries a man with a similarly mixed background
"Say's masterfully executed watercolors tell as much of this story . . . as his eloquent prose." Publ Wkly

Tree of cranes; written and illustrated by Allen Say. Houghton Mifflin 1991 32p il $17.95; pa $7.99
Grades: K 1 2 3   E
1. Christmas -- Fiction 2. Mother-son relationship -- Fiction
ISBN 0-395-52024-X; 0-547-24830-X pa
LC 91-14107
A Japanese boy learns of Christmas when his mother decorates a pine tree with paper cranes
"The quiet, graciously told picture book is a perfect blend of text and art. Fine-lined and handsome, Say's watercolors not only capture fascinating details of the boy's far away home . . . but also depict, with simple grace, the rich and complex bond between mother and child that underlies the story." Booklist

Sayre, April Pulley
Dig, wait, listen; a desert toad's tale. pictures by Barbara Bash. Greenwillow Bks. 2001 un il $15.95
Grades: PreK K 1 2   E
1. Toads 2. Desert animals 3. Toads -- Fiction 4. Desert animals -- Fiction 5. Toads -- Juvenile fiction
ISBN 0-688-16614-8
LC 00-32111
A spadefoot toad waits under the sand for the rain, hears the sounds of other desert animals, and eventually mates and spawns other toads
"Created with pencil, pen and ink, and watercolor, Bash's pictures illustrate the desert scenes with pleasingly varied colors, perspectives, and layouts. Preschool and primary-grade children will find this well-crafted book a wholly satisfying introduction to the spadefoot toad in particular and desert animals and the idea of life cycles in general." Booklist

If you're hoppy; pictures by Jackie Urbanovic. Greenwillow Books 2011 un il $16.99
Grades: PreK K 1   E
1. Stories in rhyme 2. Animals -- Fiction
ISBN 978-0-06-156634-9; 0-06-156634-9
LC 2010-04103

In rhyming text reminiscent of the traditional song, "If you're happy and you know it," presents various animals that are hoppy, sloppy, growly, flappy, or slimy, scaly and mean.

"Urbanovic's sprightly watercolor-and-ink cartoons add humor and vivacious energy. . . . Sure to be a storytime staple, with many requests for repeat performances." SLJ

One is a snail, ten is a crab; a counting by feet book. [by] April Pulley Sayre and Jeff Sayre; illustrated by Randy Cecil. Candlewick Press 2003 un il hardcover o.p. pa $6.99
Grades: PreK K 1 2   E
    1. Foot 2. Animals 3. Counting
    ISBN 0-7636-1406-8; 0-7636-2631-7 pa
                   LC 2001-52494
A counting book featuring animals with different numbers of feet

"Very simple text in large type is appropriate for group use as well as beginning readers. Uncluttered, black-outlined, oil-on-paper pictures clearly illustrate the concepts, and Cecil's googly-eyed snails, sports-minded crabs, and other animals add a touch of humor." SLJ

Turtle, turtle, watch out! illustrated by Annie Patterson. Charlesbridge 2010 un il lib bdg $17.95; pa $7.95
Grades: K 1 2   E
    1. Sea turtles -- Fiction 2. Sea turtles -- Juvenile literature 3. Wildlife conservation -- Juvenile literature
    ISBN 978-1-58089-148-6 lib bdg; 1-58089-148-9 lib bdg; 978-1-58089-149-3 pa; 1-58089-149-7 pa
                   LC 2008025338
A newly illustrated edition of the title first published 2000 by Orchard Books

From before the time she hatches until she returns to the same beach to lay eggs of her own, a sea turtle is helped to escape from danger many times by different human hands.

"The simple, direct text reads aloud well, drawing readers into the turtles' story without anthropomorphism. Impressive pastel illustrations, including many dramatic double-page spreads, depict with power and beauty the turtles' world of sand and shore." Booklist

Scanlon, Liz Garton
    Noodle & Lou. Beach Lane Books 2011 un il $15.99
Grades: PreK K 1   E
    1. Birds -- Fiction 2. Worms -- Fiction 3. Friendship -- Fiction
    ISBN 978-1-4424-0288-1; 1-4424-0288-1
                   LC 2009-42950
Noodle and Lou are unlikely friends. One is a worm and one is a bird. When Noodle is having a bad day, Lou knows just what to say to cheer up his wormy friend and help him see what it means to be liked just the way you are.

"Howard's cartoon-style illustrations match the bouncy rhythm of Scanlon's couplets perfectly and keep the tone light. . . . Chirpy, instructive and fun." Kirkus

Schachner, Judith Byron
    The **Grannyman**. Dutton Children's Bks. 1999 un il $15.99; pa $6.99
Grades: PreK K 1 2   E
    1. Cats -- Fiction 2. Old age -- Fiction
    ISBN 0-525-46122-1; 0-14-250062-3 pa
                   LC 98-52964

Simon the cat is so old that most of his parts have stopped working, but just when he is ready to breathe his last breath, his family brings home a new kitten for him to raise

"Schachner's expressive watercolor-and-mixed-media artwork mirrors the affection, humor, and warmth of her finely crafted text." Booklist

    Skippyjon Jones class action; by Judy Schachner. Dutton Children's Books 2011 un il $16.99
Grades: PreK K 1   E
    1. School stories 2. Cats -- Fiction 3. Dogs -- Fiction
    ISBN 0-525-42228-5; 978-0-525-42228-0
                   LC 2009053293
Skippyjon Jones, a Siamese cat who would rather be his Chihuahua alter ego, is determined to attend dog obedience school.

"Schachner's style, the book has hilarious songs, wild antics, a smattering of Spanish words, and humor that everyone can appreciate. The zany illustrations add to its exuberant nature. Children will enjoy the amusing details on each page. As with the earlier books, this one makes for a wonderful read-aloud that will have young audiences laughing out loud." SLJ

Schade, Susan
    The **noisy** counting book; [by] Susan Schade and Jon Buller. Random House 2010 un il bd bk $7.99
Grades: PreK   E
    1. Counting 2. Board books for children 3. Sounds -- Fiction 4. Animals -- Fiction
    ISBN 978-0-375-85937-3; 0-375-85937-3
    First published 1987
A boy goes to the pond to fish but is interrupted by noisy animals that count their way from one to six with silly sounds.

Schaefer, Carole Lexa
    Big Little Monkey; illustrated by Pierre Pratt. Candlewick Press 2008 un il $16.99
Grades: PreK K 1 2   E
    1. Monkeys -- Fiction
    ISBN 978-0-7636-2006-6; 0-7636-2006-8
                   LC 2007052024
When Little Monkey decides to venture out into the jungle alone, beyond the gaze of his watchful Mama, he discovers that other animals are not as friendly and warm as his own family and that independence is not altogether a good thing

"Schaefer's text has the style and cadences of a folktale with the effective refrain 'bim-ba-lah, bim-ba-lah' appearing as the protagonist swings through the trees. . . . Pratt's stylized animals, done in sweeping, brightly colored acrylics . . . and the mostly full-bleed illustrations with their color-saturated backgrounds are eye-catching and will carry well in storytimes." SLJ

    Dragon dancing; illustrated by Pierr Morgan. Viking 2007 un il $16.99
Grades: PreK K 1   E
    1. School stories 2. Dragons -- Fiction 3. Birthdays -- Fiction 4. Imagination -- Fiction
    ISBN 0-670-06084-9
A group of children pretend that they are a dragon to celebrate their classmate's birthday.

"An excellent choice for storytime, the text features . . . many fun sounds. . . . The color of the gouache-and-marker illustrations increases in brightness as the students transition gradually from the classroom into their imaginative fantasy. . . . Pleasing to the eye and the ear." SLJ

Who's there? [illustrated by Pierr Morgan] Viking 2011 un il $15.99
Grades: PreK K 1   E
  1. Fear -- Fiction 2. Bedtime -- Fiction
  ISBN 978-0-670-01241-1; 0-670-01241-6
LC 2010-33334
A child, already tucked in for the night, is frightened by strange noises that grow ever closer.
"The combination of Morgan's vibrant, mock horrific evocation of the nighttime heebie-jeebies and Schaefer's read-aloud-savvy text (packed with repetition, rhetorical questions, and onomatopoeia) makes a return visit worthwhile." Publ Wkly

The **biggest** soap; pictures by Stacey Dressen-Mc-Queen. Farrar, Straus and Giroux 2004 un il
Grades: K 1 2 3   E
  1. Soap -- Fiction 2. Storytelling -- Fiction
  ISBN 0374306907
LC 2003-48512
When Kessy, who lives in the Truk Islands, is sent by his mother to buy laundry soap, he hurries back to listen to her storytelling, discovering that his own experience is a good story too
"Both the text and the pencil, oil pastel, and acrylic artwork, alive with the sun-drenched colors and patterns of the South Pacific, bubble with happiness. Refreshing, engaging, and thoroughly delightful." Booklist

Schaefer, Lola M.
  Frankie Stein; illustrated by Kevan J. Atteberry. Marshall Cavendish 2007 un il $14.99; pa $6.99
Grades: PreK K 1   E
  1. Monsters -- Fiction 2. Family life -- Fiction
  ISBN 978-0-7614-5358-1; 978-0-7614-5608-7 pa
LC 2007000256
"Frankie Stein is nothing like his monstrous, green-skinned parents. Instead, he is cute, with a pink face and golden hair. . . . In the end, little Frankie discovers his own way of being scary, which frightens even his parents. Purples and greens dominate the illustrations, emphasizing the cartoony creepiness of the Stein house." SLJ
  Another title about Frankie Stein is:
  Frankie Stein starts school (2010)

Happy Halloween, Mittens; story by Lola M. Schaefer; pictures by Susan Kathleen Hartung. Harper 2010 23p il (I can read!) $16.99; pa $3.99
Grades: PreK K 1   E
  1. Cats -- Fiction 2. Halloween -- Fiction
  ISBN 978-0-06-170222-8; 0-06-170222-6; 978-0-06-170221-1 pa; 0-06-170221-8 pa
LC 2008045065
While Nick prepares for Halloween, Mittens the kitten tries her best to help out.
"Mittens's exploits continue to be entertaining and satisfying for the very youngest readers." Horn Book Guide

★ **Loose** tooth; story by Lola M. Schaefer; pictures by Sylvie Wickstrom. HarperCollinsPublishers 2004 31p il (My first I can read book) hardcover o.p. pa $3.99
Grades: PreK K 1 2   E
  1. Teeth 2. Stories in rhyme 3. Teeth -- Fiction
  ISBN 0-06-052776-5; 0-06-052778-1 pa
LC 2003-6322
A young child experiences a loose tooth for the first time and eagerly waits for it to come out
"With a few words, lots of repetition, some rhyme, and good rhythm, this story is perfect for beginning readers. The cartoon illustrations add details to the plot and create interest." SLJ

Mittens; story by Lola M. Schaefer; pictures by Susan Kathleen Hartung. HarperCollinsPublishers 2006 25p il (I can read!) $16.99; lib bdg $15.89; pa $3.99
Grades: PreK K 1 2   E
  1. Cats -- Fiction
  ISBN 0-06-054659-X; 0-06-054660-3 lib bdg; 0-06-054661-1 pa
Nick helps Mittens the kitten adjust to life in a new home
"The controlled vocabulary in this gentle, unassuming story is made up primarily of one-syllable words, and the sentence structure is very basic. The soft pastel illustrations are simple and uncluttered and enhance the quiet tone of the text." SLJ
  Other titles about Mittens are:
  Follow me, Mittens (2007)
  What's that, Mittens (2008)
  Happy Halloween, Mittens (2010)
  Mittens, where is Max? (2011)

One special day; by Lola Schaefer; illustrated by Jessica Meserve. Disney/Hyperion Books 2012 40p.
Grades: PreK K 1 2   E
  1. Children's stories 2. Siblings -- Fiction 3. Picture books for children 4. Babies -- Fiction 5. Behavior -- Fiction 6. Brothers -- Fiction
  ISBN 1423137604; 9781423137603
LC 2011015977
In this book, "Spencer . . . [is] fast as a horse, tall as a giraffe, funny as a monkey and more. Yet when his parents come home with a new arrival, Spencer finds a new way to describe himself. He may be like animals in many respects, but now he's gentle, just as a big brother should be. . . .The text allows readers to guess what animal Spencer will come to resemble next, until finally there is only one thing left to be." (Kirkus Reviews)

This is the sunflower; pictures by Donald Crews. Greenwillow Bks. 2000 un il $15.99
Grades: PreK K 1 2   E
  1. Stories in rhyme 2. Sunflowers -- Fiction
  ISBN 0-688-16413-7
LC 98-46682
A cumulative verse describing how a sunflower in a garden blossoms and, with the help of the birds, spreads its seeds to create an entire patch of sunflowers
"A beautiful, noteworthy title. The velvety watercolors are clearly defined and saturated with color. . . . This is perfect for story hours; also recommend it to budding ornitholo-

gists, who will appreciate the illustrated key identifying the birds pictured in the text." Booklist

What's up, what's down? pictures by Barbara Bash. Greenwillow Bks. 2002 un il $15.99; lib bdg $17.89
Grades: PreK K 1 2   E
   1. Nature
   ISBN 0-06-029757-3; 0-06-029758-1 lib bdg

"On each page is the question 'What's up if you're ...?' from the viewpoint of various flora and fauna: a mole, a root, grass, a toad. . . . The highest thing 'up' is the moon, and then it's time to turn the book upside down and move down through sky and water to see 'what's down.' Children will have a chance to stretch their imaginations as they get a rudimentary idea of how the natural world works. The artwork, executed in chalks, has a muscular look that brings nature home." Booklist

Scheer, Julian
   Rain makes applesauce; by Julian Scheer & Marvin Bileck. Holiday House 1964 un il $16.95
Grades: PreK K 1 2   E
   ISBN 0-8234-0091-3

A Caldecott Medal honor book, 1965

"A book of original nonsense, illustrated with intricate drawings. Small children live the refrains, 'Rain makes applesauce' and 'You're just talking silly talk,' and enjoy the fantastic details in the pictures." Hodges. Books for Elem Sch Libr

Schertle, Alice
   1, 2, I love you; illustrated by Emily Arnold McCully. Chronicle Books 2004 un il $16.95
Grades: PreK K   E
   1. Play 2. Counting 3. Stories in rhyme 4. Parent and child 5. Elephants -- Fiction
   ISBN 0-8118-3518-9

                      LC 2003-21245

"A mother elephant addresses her little one as they engage in a variety of child-centered activities. . . . The numbers climb from 1 to 10 in the first half of the book, then descend until the end, when the little elephant goes to bed and to sleep. The rhythmic, rhyming verses are . . . engaging. . . . The colorful artwork features playful, large-scale paintings." Booklist

   Down the road; illustrated by E. B. Lewis. Browndeer Press 1995 un il $16; pa $6
Grades: PreK K 1 2   E
   1. Eggs -- Fiction 2. Country life -- Fiction
   ISBN 0-15-276622-7; 0-15-202471-9 pa

                      LC 94-9901

"The story is remarkable for its evocative imagery, and the loving interchange between the characters set a charming tone. The words are perfectly complemented by Lewis' dazzling, impressionistic watercolors." Booklist

   ★ **Little** Blue Truck; illustrated by Jill McElmurry. Harcourt Children's Books 2008 un il $16
Grades: PreK K 1 2   E
   1. Trucks -- Fiction 2. Animals -- Fiction 3. Friendship -- Fiction
   ISBN 0-15-205661-0; 978-0-15-205661-2

                      LC 2006-29445

A small blue truck finds his way out of a jam, with a little help from his friends. "Ages three to six." (Bull Cent Child Books)

"Schertle contrasts a huge dump truck, hurtling self-importantly down a country road, with a small pickup that greets each farm animal. . . . When the dump truck bogs down in a deep slough, its cries of distress go unanswered. When the pickup gets stuck while trying to help, the animals rush in to lend a hearty push. . . . McElmurry creates crisply drawn rural scenes. . . . Along with being a natural for storytime, this upbeat tale may spark a discussion about friendships and helping one another." Booklist

Another title about Little Blue Truck is:
   Little Blue Truck leads the way (2009)

Schimel, Lawrence
   Let's go see Papa! translated from Spanish by Elisa Amado; illustrated by Alba Marina Rivera. Groundwood Books 2011 un il $18.95
Grades: 1 2 3   E
   1. Immigrants -- Fiction 2. Father-daughter relationship -- Fiction
   ISBN 978-1-55498-106-9; 1-55498-106-9

"A young girl waits by the telephone every Sunday for a call from Papá. He left 'one year, eight months and twenty two days' ago to find work in the United States. . . . When Papá asks her and Mamá to join him, she is thrilled to be reunited, but also sad to leave her abuela and friends. Rivera's pencil, crayon, and watercolor illustrations capture the daily details of a loving extended family. . . . . The feelings of missing a loved one are realistically conveyed and will resonate with children." SLJ

Schmid, Paul
   Hugs from Pearl; story and pictures by Paul Schmid. Harper 2011 un il $14.99
Grades: PreK K   E
   1. School stories 2. Hugging -- Fiction 3. Porcupines -- Fiction
   ISBN 978-0-06-180434-2; 0-06-180434-7

                      LC 2010015906

A friendly porcupine figures out how to give hugs without hurting others with her sharp quills.

"With his simple pastel and charcoal illustrations set against pale green and blue pages, Schmid brings just the right touch of sweetness to this charming tale." SLJ

   Petunia goes wild; by Paul Schmid. HarperCollins 2012 40 p.
Grades: PreK K 1 2   E
   1. Temper tantrums 2. Tigers -- Fiction 3. Temper tantrums -- Fiction 4. Children's costumes -- Fiction 5. Parent-child relationship -- Fiction 6. Humorous stories 7. Behavior -- Fiction 8. Parent and child -- Fiction
   ISBN 9780061963346; 9780061963353

                      LC 2011001888

In this children's book, "Petunia . . . would much rather be an animal than a human girl, a preference that she expresses by wearing a tiger tail, roaring at passersby, and pleading with her parents for a cave in which to live. As a compromise, she offers to be their pet, an offer that provokes a page-long parental lecture: 'No, you may NOT! Where did you get such an idea? Of all the crazy things! That is NOT how nice little girls behave.' Feeling completely misunderstood, Petunia addresses a packing box to Africa and climbs in, only to have second thoughts when she overhears her mother singing in the kitchen ('Tigers did not sing, thought Petunia. Or tickle at bedtime, neither'), and she decides to stay." (Bulletin of the Center for Children's Books)

★ A **pet** for Petunia. Harper 2011 un il $12.99
Grades: PreK K 1   E
  1. Pets -- Fiction 2. Skunks -- Fiction 3. Parent-child relationship -- Fiction
ISBN 978-0-06-196331-5; 0-06-196331-3
Petunia so desperately wants a pet skunk that she refuses to believe her parents when they say skunks stink.
Schmid's "line drawings are simple, fluid, and convey lots of valuable information. . . . Enthusiastic and single-minded, Petunia makes delightful company; kids will recognize themselves and clamor for rereads." Publ Wkly

Schneider, Josh
The **meanest** birthday girl; by Josh Schneider. Clarion Books 2013 48 p. col. ill. (hardcover) $14.99
Grades: 1 2 3   E
  1. Birthdays -- Juvenile fiction 2. Elephants -- Juvenile fiction 3. Conduct of life -- Juvenile fiction 4. Gifts -- Fiction 5. Birthdays -- Fiction 6. Elephants -- Fiction
ISBN 054783814X; 9780547838144
                                                    LC 2011041587
In this children's story, by Josh Schneider, "it's Dana's birthday, so she can do what she likes. And what Dana likes to do is pinch. And call people names. And steal her classmates' desserts. You probably know a kid like Dana. What can stop her from being so mean? . . . Sometimes, it takes a little creativity (and possibly a very large pet) to change a mean kid's ways." (Publisher's note)

Schnur, Steven
Spring; an alphabet acrostic. illustrated by Leslie Evans. Clarion Bks. 1999 un il $15
Grades: K 1 2 3   E
  1. Spring 2. Alphabet 3. Acrostics
ISBN 0-395-82269-6
                                                      LC 98-22704
Describes spring, with its animals, green smells, and renewed outside activities. When read vertically, the first letters of the lines of text spell related words arranged alphabetically, from "April" to "zenith"
"The evocative free verse captures the season's promise, as do the colorful block-print illustrations." Horn Book Guide

Winter; an alphabet acrostic. illustrated by Leslie Evans. Clarion Bks. 2002 un il $15
Grades: K 1 2 3   E
  1. Winter 2. Alphabet 3. Acrostics 4. Winter -- Juvenile literature 5. Acrostics -- Juvenile literature
ISBN 0-618-02374-7
                                                    LC 2001-17358
"On each page, a winter-related word provides the basis for an acrostic that reads like a short poem. . . . A striking, hand-colored linoleum print illustrates each small, boxed acrostic." Booklist

Schnur, Susan
Tashlich at Turtle Rock; by Susan Schnur and Anna Schnur-Fishman; illustrated by Alex Steele-Morgan. Kar-Ben Pub. 2010 un il lib bdg $17.95; pa $7.95
Grades: K 1 2 3   E
  1. Jews -- Fiction 2. Rosh ha-Shanah -- Fiction
ISBN 978-0-7613-4509-1 lib bdg; 0-7613-4509-4 lib bdg; 978-0-7613-4510-7 pa; 0-7613-4510-8 pa
                                                    LC 2009001871
Annie leads her family on a Rosh Hashanah hike to observe tashlich, where each person will ask God's forgiveness for the things they regret doing the previous year. Includes facts about this Jewish custom.
"Throughout, the authors empahsize environmental awareness . . . and Steele-Morgan's boldly colored heavily textured illustrations highlight the rich colors of autumn. . . . Handled with a light touch, this is secular enough to make it useful for general as well as religious collections." Booklist

Schoenherr, Ian
Cat & mouse; [by] Ian Schoenherr. Greenwillow Books 2008 un il $16.95; lib bdg $17.89
Grades: PreK K 1 2   E
  1. Stories in rhyme 2. Cats -- Fiction 3. Mice -- Fiction 4. Play -- Fiction 5. Nursery rhymes -- Fiction
ISBN 978-0-06-136313-9; 0-06-136313-8; 978-0-06-136314-6 lib bdg; 0-06-136314-6 lib bdg
                                                    LC 2007036145
"Adapting and combining 'Hickory, Dickory, Dock,' 'Eeny Meeny Miney Mo,' and 'I Love Little Pussy,' Schoenherr crafts a wild romp featuring a paper-parasol-equipped mouse leading a cat on a merry chase. . . . The dynamic and realistic ink and acrylic illustrations feature a stop-action energy and changing perspectives that make the characters appear to actually move across the pages. This [is a] bright, funny book." SLJ

★ **Don't** spill the beans! Greenwillow Books 2010 un il $16.99; lib bdg $17.89
Grades: PreK   E
  1. Stories in rhyme 2. Bears -- Fiction 3. Animals -- Fiction 4. Birthdays -- Fiction
ISBN 978-0-06-172457-2; 0-06-172457-2; 978-0-06-172458-9 lib bdg; 0-06-172458-0 lib bdg
                                                    LC 2008042363
A bear tries hard to keep a birthday surprise a secret.
"The story is told in short rhyming sentences of large, colorful, hand-lettered text. The ink and acrylic paint illustrations depict cheerfully clothed animals with expressive faces." SLJ

★ **Read** it, don't eat it! Greenwillow Books 2009 un il $17.99; lib bdg $18.89
Grades: PreK K   E
  1. Stories in rhyme 2. Books and reading -- Fiction
ISBN 978-0-06-172455-8; 0-06-172455-6; 978-0-06-178034-9 lib bdg; 0-06-178034-0 lib bdg
                                                    LC 2008027716
Rhyming advice on how to take care of a library book
"One white, hand-lettered sentence per page is set against a bold color, and the ink and acrylic art features endearing animal library users on an expansive white space. The book is simple enough to use with preschool children and funny enough to be appreciated by early readers." SLJ

Schoettler, Joan

Good fortune in a wrapping cloth; illustrated by Jessica Lanan. Shen's Books 2011 il $17.95

Grades: 2 3 4   E

  1. Sewing -- Fiction 2. Clothing and dress -- Fiction 3. Mother-daughter relationship -- Fiction

  ISBN 978-1-885008-40-4; 1-885008-40-6

                   LC 2011001702

When Ji-su's mother is chosen by the emperor to be a seamstress in his court, Ji-su vows to learn to sew the beautiful Korean bojagi, or wrapping cloths, just as well so that she will also be summoned to the palace and be reunited with her mother.

"Descriptive language and stunning watercolor paintings show the seasons passing as Ji-su works toward her goal. With a masterful eye for color and skillful use of perspective, Lanan brings the text to life and adds depth to Ji-su's emotions." SLJ

Schoonmaker, Elizabeth

Square cat; written and illustrated by Elizabeth Schoonmaker. Aladdin 2011 un il $14.99

Grades: PreK K 1   E

  1. Cats -- Fiction 2. Shape -- Fiction 3. Individualism -- Fiction

  ISBN 978-1-4424-0619-3; 1-4424-0619-4

Eulah the cat is square and, while she longs to be round like other cats, her friends show her the benefits of the shape that she has.

"This title gently packs a powerful message about self-acceptance and friendship. . . . Ink and bright watercolor illustrations using basic shapes with simple and engaging facial expressions steal the show." SLJ

Schories, Pat

Jack wants a snack. Front Street 2008 un il $13.95

Grades: PreK K 1   E

  1. Stories without words 2. Dogs -- Fiction 3. Chipmunks -- Fiction

  ISBN 978-1-59078-546-1; 1-59078-546-0

                   LC 2007-52154

Jack the dog discovers that he is not the only uninvited guest at a tea party

"Schories does a masterful job of creating a clear plot that children will be able to follow despite the absence of text clues. The illustrations are warm, friendly, and full of movement." SLJ

Schotter, Roni

★ **Doo**-Wop Pop; by Roni Schotter; illustrated by Bryan Collier. Amistad/HarperCollins 2008 un il $16.99; lib bdg $17.89

Grades: K 1 2 3   E

  1. School stories 2. Stories in rhyme 3. Singing -- Fiction 4. Janitors -- Fiction

  ISBN 978-0-06-057968-5; 0-06-057968-4; 978-0-06-057974-6 lib bdg; 0-06-057974-9 lib bdg

                   LC 2008015212

A school janitor teaches children to sing and have confidence in themselves

"Schotter stacks the prose with rhymes, giving the first-person narrative an authentic, contemporary freestyle flow that begs to be read aloud. Collier's trademark collage paint-

ings, shaded with bursts of yellow and green, hum with the students' energy and pride." Booklist

★ **Mama,** I'll give you the world; by Roni Schotter; illustrated by S. Saelig Gallagher. Schwartz & Wade Books 2006 un il $16.95

Grades: K 1 2 3   E

  1. Birthdays -- Fiction 2. Beauty shops -- Fiction 3. Mother-daughter relationship -- Fiction

  ISBN 978-0-375-83612-1; 0-375-83612-8

At Walter's World of Beauty, Luisa's secret plans are underway to create a very special birthday celebration for her hardworking, single mother who is employed there as a stylist.

"Gallagher's bright-eyed, smiling, subtly modeled faces light up this loving mother-daughter tale." Booklist

★ **The boy** who loved words; pictures by Giselle Potter. Schwartz & Wade Books 2006 un il $16.95; lib bdg $18.99

Grades: K 1 2 3   E

  1. English language -- Fiction

  ISBN 0-375-83601-2; 0-375-93601-7 lib bdg

                   LC 2005-10850

Selig, who loves words and copies them on pieces of paper that he carries with him, goes on a trip to discover his purpose.

"Potter's signature naive-style art is light and comical, while Schotter's words are a lovely celebration of the power and the music of language." Booklist

Schroeder, Alan

★ **Satchmo's** blues; illustrated by Floyd Cooper. Doubleday Bks. for Young Readers 1996 un il hardcover o.p. pa $6.99

Grades: 1 2 3 4   E

  1. Singers 2. Jazz musicians 3. Band leaders 4. Trumpet players 5. African American musicians -- Fiction

  ISBN 0-385-32046-9; 0-440-41472-5 pa

                   LC 93-41082

A fictional recreation of the youth of trumpeter Louis Armstrong in New Orleans

"This book is full of gorgeous writing, accompanied by Cooper's atmospheric paintings." SLJ

Schubert, Ingrid

The **umbrella**; [by] Ingrid & Dieter Schubert. Lemniscaat 2011 il $16.95

Grades: PreK K 1 2   E

  1. Stories without words 2. Dogs -- Fiction 3. Voyages and travels -- Fiction 4. Umbrellas and parasols -- Fiction

  ISBN 978-1-9359-5400-2; 1-9359-5400-8

A little dog finds an umbrella in the garden on a windy day. The moment the dog picks up the umbrella, it catches the wind and pulls the dog skywards. The wind carries the umbrella and the dog all over the world, from the desert to the sea, from the jungle to the north pole.

"The illustrations easily tell the story; there's no need for words. The paintings excel at showing the different landscapes and depicting movement. What a great journey!" SLJ

Schubert, Leda

Feeding the sheep; pictures by Andrea U'Ren. Farrar Straus Giroux 2010 un il $16.99

Grades: PreK K 1 2   E

1. Stories in rhyme 2. Wool -- Fiction 3. Sheep -- Fiction 4. Weaving -- Fiction 5. Mother-daughter relationship -- Fiction

ISBN 978-0-374-32296-0; 0-374-32296-1

LC 2007-48843

In pictures and rhythmic text, a mother relates to her daughter all the steps involved in making her a snug, wooly sweater, starting at the very beginning with feeding the sheep

"The physicality of the words, . . . the fascinating facts, and the action-filled, brightly colored illustrations will capture kids' attention, as will the cozy family bond between parent and child." Booklist

★ The **Princess** of Borscht; illustrated by Bonnie Christensen. Roaring Brook Press 2011 un il $17.99

Grades: PreK K 1 2   E

1. Sick -- Fiction 2. Soups -- Fiction 3. Cooking -- Fiction 4. Grandmothers -- Fiction

ISBN 978-1-59643-515-5; 1-59643-515-1

LC 2010014520

Ruthie's grandmother, who is in the hospital with pneumonia, says she needs homemade borscht by five o'clock and young Ruthie, with the help of her neighbors, tries to make some even without the secret recipe.

"Of course, it's not just about borscht or even about cooking, though there's a great recipe included. Schubert has concocted a sweet mixture of traditions that bind and give comfort, along with love in many forms. . . . Christensen's heavily outlined, strongly colored illustrations emphasize equally strong personalities. The paintings are filled with details that add interest to the proceedings." Kirkus

Reading to Peanut; illustrated by Amanda Haley. Holiday House 2011 un il $16.95

Grades: PreK K 1 2   E

1. Dogs -- Fiction 2. Reading -- Fiction 3. Birthdays -- Fiction 4. Family life -- Fiction

ISBN 978-0-8234-2339-2; 0-8234-2339-5

LC 2010031412

Lucy works hard to learn to read and write before her dog's birthday.

"Colorful, energetic acrylics show Lucy and her ever-present pup Peanut in motion. . . . The appealing character, lively pictures and mild suspense make for a warm family story that shows the fun of having a pet and provides a strategy for learning to read that youngsters will eagerly embrace." Kirkus

Schuch, Steve

★ A **symphony** of whales; illustrated by Peter Sylvada. Harcourt Brace & Co. 1999 un il hardcover o.p. pa $7

Grades: 1 2 3 4   E

1. Music -- Fiction 2. Dreams -- Fiction 3. Whales -- Fiction 4. Wildlife rescue -- Fiction

ISBN 0-15-201670-8; 0-15-216548-7 pa

LC 98-17248

Young Glashka's dream of the singing of whales, accompanied by a special kind of music, leads to the rescue of thousands of whales stranded in a freezing Siberian bay

"This is a quiet, powerful story, beautifully extended by Sylvada's paintings of ghostly whale shapes and glowing, fin-shaped skies." Booklist

Schwartz, Amy

★ **Things** I learned in second grade. Katherine Tegen Books 2004 un il $15.99; lib bdg $16.89

Grades: K 1 2 3   E

1. Schools 2. School stories 3. Learning

ISBN 0-06-050936-8; 0-06-050937-6 lib bdg

LC 2002-155507

A young boy shares all of the things he learned and how he changed in second grade, what he still wonders about, and what he hopes to accomplish when he is in third grade.

"This sweet story is accompanied by precisely drawn, softly colored illustrations of the boy engaged in a variety of activities at home and in the classroom, and the optimistic and cheerful ending pulls it together to a satisfactory conclusion." SLJ

Tiny and Hercules. Roaring Brook Press 2009 un il $16.95

Grades: K 1 2 3   E

1. Mice -- Fiction 2. Elephants -- Fiction 3. Friendship -- Fiction

ISBN 978-1-59643-253-6; 1-59643-253-5

LC 2008-54268

Five short stories about the lives of two unusual friends: Tiny, an elephant with a fear of ice skating and a newfound love of knitting, and Hercules, a mouse with a heart of gold and a desire to learn to paint.

"Even the most sidesplitting moments in these stories . . . are secondary to the touching portrait of a devoted friendship." SLJ

★ **What** James likes best. Atheneum Bks. for Young Readers 2003 un il $16.95

Grades: PreK K 1 2   E

1. Transportation -- Fiction

ISBN 0-689-84059-4

LC 2001-22988

James goes with his parents on an express bus to visit twins, in a taxi to visit Grandma, and in a car to see the county fair, then walks next door with his mother for a play date

"Schwartz's pristine illustrations are streamlined and clean; the lucid, transparent colors make her gouache and pen-and-ink illustrations . . . seem almost weightless. This is a terrifically simple, successful way to get readers and listeners to interact with printed text." Bull Cent Child Books

A **beautiful** girl. Roaring Brook Press 2006 un il $16.95

Grades: PreK K   E

1. Animals -- Fiction 2. Human body -- Fiction

ISBN 978-1-59643-165-2; 1-59643-165-2

LC 2005-33022

On her way to the market, Jenna encounters an elephant, a robin, a fly, and a goldfish who discover some of the things that make little girls different from each of them.

"The short and snappy story line and dialogue will hold the attention of young audiences, as will the naive cartoon illustrations in bright, candy-colored watercolors on white backgrounds." SLJ

Schwartz, Amy, 1954-

Dee Dee and me; written and illustrated by Amy Schwartz. 1st ed. Holiday House 2013 32 p. ill. (reinforced) $16.95

Grades: PreK K 1 2   E
1. Picture books for children 2. Sisters -- Juvenile fiction 3. Sisters -- Fiction
ISBN 082342524X; 9780823425242

LC 2012016565

In this children's picture book, "Hannah is an easy target for Dee Dee. She's younger and shorter (Dee Dee says the brains are in the 5 1/2 inches of height Hannah's missing), and she longs for her sister's acceptance. But after one too many manipulations, Hannah learns to assert herself—and now she's sure her brains are growing!" (Kirkus Reviews)

Lucy can't sleep; Amy Schwartz. Roaring Brook Press 2012 32 p.

Grades: PreK K 1 2   E
1. Play 2. Sleep -- Juvenile fiction 3. Picture books for children
ISBN 1596435437; 9781596435438

LC 2011012743

This children's book by Amy Schwartz focuses on "[r]estless, sleepless Lucy, [who] decides to climb out of bed and wander through her hushed house. . . . Lucy drifts . . . into closets and the fridge, onto the porch, back upstairs and, finally, into bed. . . . Quiet solitary play (dressing-up, snacking, listening to far-off music outside, petting the family pup) suddenly seems exactly the way to find peace and slumber." (Kirkus Reviews)

Willie and Uncle Bill; Amy Schwartz. 1st ed. Holiday House 2012 40 p. col. ill. (hardcover) $16.95

Grades: K 1 2   E
1. Picture books for children 2. Uncles -- Juvenile fiction 3. Uncles -- Fiction 4. Babysitters -- Fiction
ISBN 0823422038; 9780823422036

LC 2011007274

In this picture book, "[e]ach of the three stories . . . begins 'The doorbell rang three times,' and in comes Uncle Bill to babysit. In the first story, as Uncle Bill . . . makes tacos and chocolate pudding for lunch. . . . The second story features a concoction they call 'Icky Stew.' . . . In the third story, the two of them go out at night and ride the subway to go listen to--and play along with--a garage band." (Horn Book Magazine)

Schwartz, Betty Ann

The **splendid** spotted snake. Workman 2011 un il $13.95

Grades: PreK K   E
1. Snakes -- Fiction
ISBN 978-0-7611-6360-2; 0-7611-6360-3

"A yellow snake, made from a ribbon that is woven through slots in the pages, is born with red spots, but as he gets longer, he gains additional spots of different colors. . . . Turning the pages pulls a new section of ribbon through, making the winding snake grow. Schwartz and Wilensky combine a satisfying tactile experience with a lighthearted lesson on size and color recognition, well-suited for preschoolers." Publ Wkly

Schwartz, Howard

Gathering sparks; illustrated by Kristina Swarner. Roaring Brook Press 2010 un il $16.99

Grades: K 1 2 3   E
1. Jews -- Fiction 2. Love -- Fiction 3. Stars -- Fiction 4. Kindness -- Fiction 5. Grandfathers -- Fiction 6. Conduct of life -- Fiction
ISBN 978-1-59643-280-2; 1-59643-280-2

Based on the Jewish concept of Tikkun olam, "the narration begins when 'you' ask 'your grandfather' about the origin of the stars. He responds that before people were created, God sent ships carrying light sailing across the sky. These fragile vessels broke apart, scattering their precious cargo across the Earth and sky. It is the job of the human race to gather the 'sparks of light' and restore them to their proper place by doing acts of kindness and love. . . . Schwartz's language is simple, personal, and poetic, and his use of the second person adds a sense of intimacy. . . . Swarner's stylized, painterly artwork is soft and gentle and complements the peaceful mood of the text. . . . This is a handsome book with a timeless message." SLJ

Schwartz, Joanne

★ **City** alphabet; words by Joanne Schwartz; photos by Matt Beam. Groundwood Books 2009 un il $18.95; pa $12.95

Grades: K 1 2 3 4   E
1. Alphabet 2. City and town life 3. Alphabet -- Juvenile literature
ISBN 978-0-88899-928-3; 0-88899-928-3; 978-0-88899-962-7 pa; 0-88899-962-3 pa

"Stark, metallic and urban, these images may encourage children to think about alternate ways of seeing their surroundings." Publ Wkly

City numbers; words by Joanne Schwartz; pictures by Matt Beam. Groundwood Books/House of Anansi Press 2011 un il $18.95

Grades: K 1 2 3 4   E
1. Counting 2. City and town life
ISBN 978-1-55498-081-9; 1-55498-081-X

"This team offers an impeccably designed yet playful twist on the traditional counting book, with photographs of numbers found in an urban landscape. While the numbers are chronological—from three rusty red zeros on a metal garbage bin to the number 20 on another garbage container—Schwartz and Beam also include decimals, percents, prices, a fraction, and an image of a multi-digit barcode where 21 might have been." Publ Wkly

★ **Our** corner grocery store; illustrated by Laura Beingessner. Tundra Books 2009 un il $19.95

Grades: K 1 2 3   E
1. Family life -- Fiction 2. Grandparents -- Fiction 3. Retail trade -- Fiction 4. Italian Americans -- Fiction
ISBN 978-0-88776-868-2; 0-88776-868-7

"This sweet story takes readers through young Anna Maria's Saturday as she helps her grandparents in their neighborhood store. The day is special for its simplicity; the book is special for its rich evocation of the delights of a little Italian market and the loving relationships between a girl and her grandparents. Beingessner's folksy illustrations and Schwartz's easy text fit well together and are filled with details." SLJ

Schwarz, Viviane

★ **There** are cats in this book. Candlewick Press 2008
un il $16.99
Grades: PreK   **E**
1. Cats -- Fiction 2. Play -- Fiction 3. Cats -- Juvenile
literature
ISBN 978-0-7636-3923-5; 0-7636-3923-0
LC 2007-52165
The reader is invited to lift the flaps and follow the cats
as they play with yarn, boxes, pillows, and fish.
"Interactive pages colored with ink, paint and photo collage invite readers to revel in what felines already know:
that the mere existence of cats is cause for festivity. . . . The
whirlwind of pure kinetic energy ensures that readers are
wholly part of the impenitent kitty world and will be reluctant to say goodbye." Publ Wkly

There are no cats in this book! Candlewick Press 2010
un il $16.99
Grades: PreK   **E**
1. Pop-up books 2. Cats -- Fiction 3. Books and
reading -- Fiction
ISBN 978-0-7636-4954-8; 0-7636-4954-6
LC 2009-51510
Filled with the spirit of adventure, three cats pack their
suitcases and try to escape from their book.
"This explores on the notion that the book—or at least
the cats in it—are looking back at the viewers and interacting with them, and the paper-engineering elements such as
foldouts and popups add playful entertainment. . . . The illustrations are uncomplicated yet fluid, with saturated watercolor pigments . . . against warm-toned pages, and elements of layered-paper collage adding dimension." Bull
Cent Child Books

Timothy and the strong pajamas; a superhero adventure. Arthur A. Levine Books 2008 un il $16.99
Grades: PreK K 1 2   **E**
1. Superheroes -- Fiction
ISBN 978-0-545-03329-9; 0-545-03329-2
LC 2007-06812
After his mother mends his favorite pajamas, Timothy
finds that he has super strength and decides to use it to help
others, but when the pajamas rip again, he loses his strength
just when he needs it most.
"The watercolor illustrations vary from small vignettes,
to vertical and horizontal paneled scenes, to full pages and
spreads. . . . Youngsters who long to be strong and powerful
will enter into this fantasy with gusto." SLJ

Scieszka, Jon
★ **Baloney** (Henry P.) received and decoded by Jon
Scieszka; visual recreation by Lane Smith. Viking 2001
un il $15.99
Grades: K 1 2 3   **E**
1. Schools 2. Life on other planets 3. Life on other
planets -- Fiction
ISBN 0-670-89248-3
LC 00-12041
A transmission received from outer space in a combina-
tion of different Earth languages tells of an alien schoolboy's
fantastic excuse for being late to school again
"Every Earth kid will immediately recognize a soul mate
in this extraterrestrial truth-stretcher and tall-tale teller. . . .

Illustrator Smith has been having equal fun stretching the
visual truth to create a vision of space that is not only artfully outer but also utterly outre. The result is wacky fun for
everyone." Booklist

Pete's party; written by Jon Scieszka; characters and
environments developed by the Design Garage: David Gordon, Loren Long, David Shannon. Aladdin 2008 un il
(Jon Scieszka's Trucktown: Ready-to-roll) lib bdg $13.89;
pa $3.99
Grades: PreK K 1   **E**
1. Trucks -- Fiction 2. Signs and signboards -- Fiction
ISBN 978-1-4169-4149-1 lib bdg; 1-4169-4149-5 lib
bdg; 978-1-4169-4138-5 pa; 1-4169-4138-X pa
LC 2007027154
The Trucktown trucks follow the road signs directing
them to Pete's party
This title "will draw beginning readers into the zany
world of anthropomorphic trucks, whose distinct personali-
ties and endearing facial expressions roll across the colorful
pages." SLJ
Other titles in this series are:
Dizzy Izzy (2010)
Kat's mystery (2009)
Melvin's valentine (2009)
Snow trucking! (2008)
Zoom! boom? bully (2008)
The spooky tire (2009)
Uh-oh Max (2009)

★ **Robot** Zot! illustrated by David Shannon. Simon
& Schuster Books for Young Readers 2009 un il $17.99
Grades: K 1 2   **E**
1. Robots -- Fiction
ISBN 978-1-4169-6394-3; 1-4169-6394-4
LC 2008-20031
On a mission to conquer planet Earth, tiny but fearless
Robot Zot and his mechanical sidekick leave a path of de-
struction as they battle kitchen appliances.
"Scieszka laces his action-filled narrative with rhymes
and repetitive robot phrases. . . . Shannon's acrylic artwork
offers bright colors and plenty of humor." Publ Wkly

★ **Science** verse; illustrated by Lane Smith. Viking
2004 un il $16.99
Grades: 2 3 4 5   **E**
1. Poetry -- Fiction 2. Science -- Fiction
ISBN 0-670-91057-0
LC 2004-1641
When the teacher tells his class that they can hear the poetry of science in everything, a student is struck with a curse
and begins hearing nothing but science verses that sound
very much like some well known poems.
"Children need not be familiar with the works upon
which the spoofs are based to enjoy the humor, but this is a
perfect opportunity to introduce the originals and to discuss
parody as a poetic form. The dynamic cartoons are an absolute delight." SLJ

Smash! crash! illustrated by David Shannon, Loren
Long, and David Gordon. Simon & Schuster 2008 un il
(Jon Scieszka's Trucktown) $16.99

Grades: PreK K   E
1. Trucks -- Fiction
ISBN 1-4169-4133-9

"Jack Truck, a red flatbed with chrome exhaust stacks, and best friend Dump Truck Dan, a blue guy with a yellow cab and mud flaps, adore the smash and crash of work in progress. . . . Scieszka . . . revs readers up with gear-grinding noise and rowdy antics. . . . Illustrators Shannon, Long and Gordon embed mechanical shapes in their punchy display type, and they contribute panoramic vistas." Publ Wkly

Other titles in this series are:
Melvin might? (2008)
Truckery rhymes (2009)

Scillian, Devin
Pappy's handkerchief; by Devin Scillian; illustrated by Chris Ellison. Sleeping Bear Press 2007 un il (Tales of young Americans) $17.95
Grades: 2 3 4   E
1. Family life -- Fiction 2. African Americans -- Fiction 3. Frontier and pioneer life -- Fiction
ISBN 978-1-58536-316-2
LC 2007006394

In 1889, young Moses and his family sell everything they own and leave their Baltimore, Maryland, home to join many other settlers—black and white—in a race to claim land in the newly-opened territory of Oklahoma.

"This history of a unique and interesting part of the settling of the West is illustrated in beautiful paintings of warm, soft browns, yellows, and blues that complement the narrative, together creating a fascinating look at the past." SLJ

Scott, Ann Herbert
Brave as a mountain lion; illustrated by Glo Coalson. Clarion Bks. 1996 31p il $16
Grades: K 1 2 3   E
1. School stories 2. Shoshoni Indians -- Fiction
ISBN 0-395-66760-7
LC 94-42906

Spider is afraid to get up on stage in front of everybody in the school spelling bee, but after listening to his father's advice, decides that he too will try to be as brave as his Shoshoni ancestors

"This story is well shaped and rhythmically told. Coalson's subdued watercolor and pastel illustrations depict the wintry landscapes and interiors with sensitivity and detail." SLJ

On Mother's lap; illustrated by Glo Coalson. Clarion Bks. 1992 32p il $16; pa $6.95; bd bk $5.95
Grades: PreK K   E
1. Inuit -- Fiction 2. Mother-child relationship -- Fiction
ISBN 0-395-58920-7; 0-395-62976-4 pa; 0-618-05159-7 bd bk
LC 91-17765

A newly illustrated edition of the title first published 1972 by McGraw-Hill

"Sitting on his mother's lap, a young Eskimo boy gathers his belongings until he, some toys, his puppy, and a blanket are all crowded together in the rocking chair. When his baby sister cries, the boy claims there is no room for her, but Mother proves him wrong, and the threesome settle comfortably in the chair. Soft illustrations depict a cozy scene and a loving family." Horn Book

Scotton, Rob
Russell the sheep; by Rob Scotton. HarperCollins 2005 un il $17.99; lib bdg $18.89
Grades: PreK K 1 2   E
1. Sheep -- Fiction 2. Bedtime -- Fiction
ISBN 0-06-059848-4; 0-06-059849-2 lib bdg
LC 2003-24274

Russell the sheep tries all different ways to get to sleep

"Scotton makes a captivating debut with this comical tale. He illustrates it with a witty, engaging, and fluffy character bathed in calming blue hues." SLJ

Other titles about Russell are:
Russell and the lost treasure (2006)
Russell's Christmas magic (2007)

Splat the cat. HarperCollins 2008 un il $16.99; lib bdg $17.89
Grades: K 1 2   E
1. School stories 2. Cats -- Fiction 3. Friendship -- Fiction
ISBN 978-0-06-083154-7; 0-06-083154-5; 978-0-06-083155-4 lib bdg; 0-06-083155-3 lib bdg
LC 2008-20218

"The fuzzy black feline is worried about his first day of school, and despite determined attempts to avoid the inevitable, he ends up there. . . . This lighthearted story, told with a generous helping of humor and goofy characterizations, will have broad appeal." SLJ

Other titles about Splat are:
Love, Splat (2008)
Merry Christmas, Splat (2009)
Scaredy-cat, Splat! (2010)
Splat the cat sings flat (2011)
Splish, splash, Splat! (2011)

Sebe, Masayuki
Let's count to 100! Kids Can Press 2011 il $16.95
Grades: PreK K 1 2   E
1. Counting
ISBN 978-1-55453-661-0; 1-55453-661-8

"Every spread in this high-energy counting book contains 100 cartoon people, objects, or animals, as Sebe provides enthusiastic prompts. . . . Conversations and interactions between the creatures add to the fun. . . . With much to discover, a wry sense of humor, and a clean aesthetic, it's a lively pick for readers ready for more adventurous counting challenges." Publ Wkly

Seder, Rufus Butler
Gallop! [by] Rufus Butler Seder. Workman Pub. 2007 un il $12.95
Grades: PreK K 1 2   E
1. Stories in rhyme 2. Animals -- Fiction 3. Animal locomotion -- Fiction
ISBN 978-0-7611-4763-3
LC 2007024247

"Readers will gasp with delight when they open this book." Publ Wkly

Swing! Workman Pub. 2008 un il $12.95
Grades: PreK K 1 2   E
1. Sports -- Fiction
ISBN 978-0-7611-5127-2; 0-7611-5127-3

"Open the die-cut cover and see a baseball player swing his bat at a ball, then watch as the ball zooms ever-larger to fit the acetate window showcasing all this action. . . . Colored fonts and multicolored borders offset the severity of the b&w pictures and generate reader participation. . . . On other spreads, child athletes perform soccer drills, run, cartwheel, twirl on ice skates, shoot hoops, swim and lead cheers—it's all jaw-dropping, even if the novelty technology has yet to find its most imaginative application." Publ Wkly

Waddle! Workman Pub. 2009 un il $12.95
Grades: PreK K 1 2   E
1. Animals -- Fiction 2. Animal locomotion -- Fiction
ISBN 978-0-7611-5112-8; 0-7611-5112-5
Text asks if the reader can move like a variety of animals. Striped acetate overlays on board pages give illustrations the illusion of movement.
"The level of detail . . . is striking . . . [and the] readers should find the animations mesmerizing." Publ Wkly

Sederman, Marty
Casey and Derek on the ice; illustrated by Zachary Pullen. Chronicle Books 2008 un il $15.99
Grades: PreK K 1 2   E
1. Stories in rhyme 2. Hockey -- Fiction
ISBN 978-0-8118-5132-9; 0-8118-5132-X
                                    LC 2007021063
A rhyming tale of an underdog hockey team's last minute attempt to win a big game.
"Hockey jargon abounds, but any sports enthusiast can enjoy this simple tale with basic brotherly concern. The oil-on-canvas illustrations show how the action intensifies as the illustrator uses varying angles and perspectives." SLJ

Sedgwick, Marcus
The **emperor's** new clothes; retold by Marcus Sedgwick; illustrated by Alison Jay. Chronicle Books 2004 un il $16.95
Grades: K 1 2 3 4   E
1. Animals 2. Authors 3. Novelists 4. Dramatists 5. Fairy tales 6. Stories in rhyme 7. Animals -- Fiction 8. Children's authors 9. Short story writers
ISBN 0-8118-4569-9
                                    LC 2004-2855
In this retelling of the Hans Christian Andersen story in which two rascals sell a vain emperor an invisible suit of clothes, all the characters are animals
"Sedgwick's . . . jaunty rhymed couplets and Jay's . . . signature stylized artwork ably accentuate the wry humor of this . . . tale." Publ Wkly
Includes bibliographical references

Seeger, Laura Vaccaro
★ **Black?** white! day? night! a book of opposites. Roaring Brook Press 2006 20p il $16.95
Grades: PreK K 1 2   E
1. Opposites 2. Vocabulary -- Juvenile literature 3. English language -- Synonyms and antonyms -- Juvenile literature
ISBN 978-1-59643-185-0; 1-59643-185-7
                                    LC 2005-32378
On the first page of this picture book "a large black flap with a cutout [reveals] a black bat set against a pure white background. The single word black? printed in white, stands

out clearly on the page. When kids lift the flap, they'll see the word white! (in white type) and discover that what appeared to be a bat is really the mouth of a ghost. Each of 18 opposites is similarly conveyed using only one word and the lift of a flap. . . . Each flap is a different bold color . . . and the scenes under the flaps are in keeping with the simple yet sophisticated graphic design of the book. Thick, shiny pages add to the sense of richness." Booklist

Bully; by Laura Vaccaro Seeger. 1st ed. Roaring Brook Press 2013 40 p. ill. (reinforced) $16.99
Grades: PreK K 1 2   E
1. Bullies -- Juvenile fiction 2. Invective -- Juvenile fiction 3. Bulls -- Fiction 4. Bullies -- Fiction
ISBN 1596436301; 9781596436305
                                    LC 2012012991
In this book, author Laura Vaccaro Seeger "uses . . . barnyard animals to tell her story about bullying, casting a bull in the title role. The trouble starts when the young bull is rejected by an older one: 'Go away!' it shouts. The young bull is shaken, but he's learned something--how to hurt others. . . .The more he abuses the others, the larger he grows, his angry bluster feeding his self-importance. At last a goat speaks truth to power: 'Bully!'" (Publishers Weekly)

★ **Dog** and Bear: two friends, three stories. Roaring Brook Press 2007 un il $12.95
Grades: PreK K   E
1. Dogs -- Fiction 2. Bears -- Fiction 3. Friendship -- Fiction
ISBN 978-1-59643-053-2; 1-59643-053-2
                                    LC 2006-11687
"Bear is a multicolored stuffed toy; Dog is a playful, rowdy dachshund. . . . In the first episode, Dog helps timid Bear down from a high stool. In the second, Dog wants to play, but Bear needs some quiet time alone. And in the final story, Dog suffers a small identity crisis, but Bear helps him recognize that he is just fine as he is. . . . Seeger's minimal text is perfectly paced for new readers, who will love the dose of humor at each story's close. In pictures as spare and charming as the text, Seeger captures preschoolers' expressions and body language." Booklist
Other titles about Dog and Bear are:
Dog and Bear: two's company (2008)
Dog and Bear: three to get ready (2009)

★ **First** the egg. Roaring Brook Press 2007 un il $14.95
Grades: PreK K   E
1. Growth 2. Developmental biology -- Juvenile literature
ISBN 978-1-59643-272-7; 1-59643-272-1
                                    LC 2006-32924
A Caldecott Medal honor book, 2008
"Pages are color-saturated and as minimalist as the text. . . . Cleverly conceived and executed cutouts reinforce the book's tactile appeal. . . . The best picture books creat a world in themselves, and this tour de force is one of them." Horn Book

★ **Green**; Laura Vaccaro Seeger. Roaring Brook Press 2012 40 p.

Grades: PreK K 1 2   E

1. Plants -- Color 2. Animals -- Color 3. Stories in rhyme 4. Picture books for children 5. Green -- Fiction
ISBN 9781596433977

LC 2011013495

Caldecott Honor Book (2013)

This picture book is an exploration of the color green. "In four simple quatrains, two-word lines each suggest a kind of green, introducing a scene that might show natural, domestic or built elements. . . . [Laura Vaccaro] Seeger's paintings vary in perspective; in their portrayal of animals such as fish, a tiger, and a lizard, trees and flowers, and children. The die-cuts reveal green-related words demonstrated by the vignettes within the paintings." (Kirkus Reviews)

The **hidden** alphabet. Roaring Brook Press 2010 un il $19.99

Grades: PreK K 1 2   E

1. Alphabet 2. Alphabet -- Juvenile literature
ISBN 978-1-59643-637-4; 1-59643-637-9

First published 2003

An alphabet book in which windows open to reveal the letters hidden within each picture.

"The concept of an object masquerading as a letter (or vice versa) is hardly new, but Seeger provides a novel twist by fashioning each object as negative space in the revealed letter. Once the viewer catches on to the pattern, most of the revelations will be predictable, but several are quite clever indeed. . . . Although this ABC romp could be used effectively to reinforce letter recognition, it's likelier to appeal to children with a knack for visualization and perhaps an urge to experiment with a DIY alphabet of their own." Bull Cent Child Books

★ **Lemons** are not red. Roaring Brook Press 2004 un il $14.95

Grades: PreK K 1 2   E

1. Color 2. Color -- Juvenile literature
ISBN 1-59643-008-7

"The first spread reads, 'Lemons are not/ RED.' The word 'RED' appears on a bright yellow page beneath the die-cut shape of a lemon with a red background showing through. When the page is turned, the die-cut shape falls on the correct yellow background, with the words 'Lemons are YELLOW' underneath. . . . This framework continues throughout the book. . . . Illustrated with richly colored yet simple oil paintings, this offering will delight preschoolers." SLJ

★ **One** boy. Roaring Brook Press 2008 un il $14.95

Grades: PreK K 1 2   E

1. Counting 2. Painting -- Fiction 3. Vocabulary -- Fiction 4. Counting -- Juvenile literature 5. Vocabulary -- Juvenile literature
ISBN 978-1-59643-274-1; 1-59643-274-8

LC 2007-45941

A Geisel Award honor book, 2009

A boy creates ten paintings in this counting book that also explores the relationship of words within words.

Seeger "crafts another nifty peek-a-boo book, counting to 10 and identifying new words by exposing or covering

letters with die-cuts. . . . Seeger uses pared-down digital art and flat saturated colors." Publ Wkly

★ **Walter** was worried. Roaring Book Press 2005 un il $15.95

Grades: PreK K 1 2   E

1. Storms -- Fiction 2. Emotions -- Fiction
ISBN 1-59643-066-8

LC 2004-024558

Children's faces, depicted with letters of the alphabet, react to the onset of a storm and its aftermath in this picture book, accompanied by simple alliterative text.

"The artwork uses bold colors with wide brush marks as backdrops and primary colors with almost graphic shapes to represent rain, snow flakes, leaves, and branches. With only one sentence per page, there is surprising depth in this wonderful collaboration of art and story." SLJ

★ **What** if? Roaring Brook Press 2010 un il $15.99

Grades: PreK K   E

1. Beaches -- Fiction 2. Seals (Animals) -- Fiction 3. Choice (Psychology) -- Juvenile literature
ISBN 978-1-59643-398-4; 1-59643-398-1

This book presents three different scenarios which show what happens when different choices are made. "Ages three to six." (Bull Cent Child Books)

"What if a boy found a beach ball and kicked it into the ocean? What if two seals found it and began to play? What if a third seal appeared on the beach looking for a friend? In this . . . book, Laura Vaccaro Seeger shows us the same story with three different outcomes, each highlighting the possibility in possibilities." Publisher's note

Seeger, Pete

The **deaf** musicians; by Pete Seeger and Paul DuBois Jacobs; illustrations by R. Gregory Christie. Putnam 2006 un il $16.99

Grades: K 1 2 3   E

1. Deaf -- Fiction 2. Musicians -- Fiction 3. Jazz music -- Fiction
ISBN 0-399-24316-X

LC 2005026901

Lee, a jazz pianist, has to leave his band when he begins losing his hearing, but he meets a deaf saxophone player in a sign language class and together they form a snazzy new band.

"Christie's snazzy style matches perfectly with the book's vivacity. The expressive faces and bold use of color make the story sing. . . . Both uplifting and inclusive, it is a celebration of music and resilience." SLJ

Segal, John

Alistair and Kip's great adventure; written and illustrated by John Segal. Margaret K. McElderry Books 2008 un il $15.99

Grades: PreK K 1 2   E

1. Cats -- Fiction 2. Dogs -- Fiction 3. Whales -- Fiction 4. Boats and boating -- Fiction
ISBN 978-1-4169-0280-5; 1-4169-0280-5

LC 2006019870

Alistair the cat and Kip the dog build a boat and soon find themselves sailing down the creek to the river to the bay and out to sea where a violent storm threatens to capsize them

"The quick-paced story is told through both dialogue and simple narrative. Beautifully rendered watercolors in bright hues comically depict the self-confident cat and his smaller canine pal." SLJ

Carrot soup; written and illustrated by John Segal. Margaret K. McElderry Books 2006 un il $12.95
Grades: PreK K 1 2   **E**
1. Carrots -- Fiction 2. Rabbits -- Fiction 3. Gardening -- Fiction
ISBN 0-689-87702-1

                   LC 2004-16963

After working hard on his garden all spring and summer, Rabbit looks forward to harvest time when he can make soup, but every carrot disappears and Rabbit must find out who has taken them. Includes a recipe for carrot soup

"The clues are in Segal's stylized pencil and watercolor pictures, and observant children won't have any trouble determining where the carrots went. The delicate springtime greens and browns used in the background contrast nicely with Rabbit's comically expressive face." Booklist

Far far away. Philomel Books 2009 un il $16.99
Grades: PreK K 1   **E**
1. Pigs -- Fiction 2. Runaway children -- Fiction 3. Mother-child relationship -- Fiction
ISBN 978-0-399-25007-1; 0-399-25007-7

                   LC 2008035855

When an unhappy young pig decides to run away, his mother helps him to see that everything he needs and wants is right there at home.

"Segal's art, executed in pencil and watercolors, features stylized pigs set against backgrounds that alternate between mottled colors and pure white. The pictures make good use of space and squeeze every bit of humor out of a familiar situation." Booklist

Pirates don't take baths. Philomel Books 2011 un il $16.99
Grades: PreK K   **E**
1. Pigs -- Fiction 2. Baths -- Fiction
ISBN 978-0-399-25425-3; 0-399-25425-0

                   LC 2010005390

A young pig tries to avoid taking a bath by claiming to be a variety of characters, from an astronaut to an Eskimo, as his mother tries to lure him into the tub.

"The flattened, geometric renderings and muted palette could have easily fallen flat. But Segal gives each spread a sly, silly magic, whether the piglet is having a sleepless night under the stars in the Old West, dodging a walrus and whale in the arctic circle, or trying to keep his cool in the middle of the desert." Publ Wkly

Segal, Lore Groszmann
Morris the artist; [by] Lore Segal; pictures by Boris Kulikov. Farrar, Straus & Giroux 2003 un il $16
Grades: PreK K 1 2   **E**
1. Birthdays -- Fiction
ISBN 0-374-35063-9

                   LC 2002-66295

Morris buys a set of paints as a birthday present for Benjamin, but he wants to keep them for himself

"This simple and realistic tale is made fantastical by Kulikov's bizarrely sophisticated paintings. . . . Youngsters

will enjoy the story, take the odd perspectives in stride, and maybe even learn a thing or two about friendship and generosity." SLJ

Seibold, J. Otto
★ **Olive** the other reindeer; by J. Otto Seibold and Vivian Walsh. Chronicle Bks. 1997 un il $15.99
Grades: PreK K 1 2   **E**
1. Dogs -- Fiction 2. Reindeer -- Fiction 3. Christmas -- Fiction 4. Santa Claus -- Fiction
ISBN 0-8118-1807-1

                   LC 97-9876

Thinking that "all of the other reindeer" she hears people singing about include her, Olive the dog reports to the North Pole to help Santa Claus on Christmas Eve

"Seibold has developed a signature style with computer digitized art, and his playful skewed lines and warm shades of ochre, pimento and olive green are user-friendly." Publ Wkly

Seki, Sunny
Yuko -chan and the Daruma doll; the adventures of a blind Japanese girl who saves her village. story and illustrations by Sunny Seki. Tuttle Pub. 2012 32 p.
Grades: 1 2 3   **E**
1. Fables 2. Blind -- Juvenile fiction 3. Dolls -- Juvenile fiction 4. Japan -- Juvenile fiction
ISBN 4805311878; 9784805311875

                   LC 2011031332

In this children's story, by Sunny Seki, "Yuko-chan, an adventurous blind orphan, . . . trips and tumbles down a snowy cliff. She discovers . . . her tea gourd, regardless of how she drops it, always lands right-side-up. . . . Inspired by this, she creates the famous Daruma doll toy, which rights itself when tipped--a true symbol of resilience. Thanks to Yuko-chan's invention, the villagers are able to earn a living and feed themselves by selling the dolls." (Publisher's note)

Selbert, Kathryn
War dogs; Churchill and Rufus. Kathryn Selbert. Charlesbridge 2013 48 p. ill. (reinforced) $17.95
Grades: 2 3 4   **E**
1. Dogs -- Juvenile literature 2. World War, 1939-1945 -- Great Britain -- Juvenile literature
ISBN 1580894143; 9781580894142

                   LC 2012000794

This children's book, by Kathryn Selbert, profiles Winston Churchill and his dog. "Churchill, often noted for his tenacious, bulldog-like personality, was one of the greatest wartime leaders of the modern era. But few people know that he was also a devoted poodle owner. The friendship between the British Bulldog and his faithful miniature poodle, Rufus, spans World War II and takes readers through the bombings of London, the invasion of Normandy, and postwar reconstruction." (Publisher's note)
Includes bibliographical references

Sendak, Maurice
★ **Alligators** all around; an alphabet. Harper & Row 1962 un il lib bdg $16.89; pa $5.95
Grades: PreK K 1 2   **E**
1. Alphabet
ISBN 0-06-025530-7 lib bdg; 0-06-443254-8 pa

Originally published in smaller format as volume one of the Nutshell library

An alphabet book of alligators doing dishes, juggling jelly beans, throwing tantrums and wearing wigs, all from A to Z

★ **Bumble**-Ardy. HarperCollins 2011 un il $17.95
Grades: PreK K 1 2   E
1. Counting 2. Stories in rhyme 3. Pigs -- Fiction 4. Parties -- Fiction 5. Birthdays -- Fiction
ISBN 978-0-06-205198-1; 0-06-205198-9
Bumble-Ardy is a mischievous pig who has reached the age of nine without ever having had a birthday party. But all that changes when Bumble throws a party for himself and invites all his friends, leading to a wild masquerade that quickly gets out of hand.

"Savvy readers will notice references to Sendak's previous books and an ebullient cameo; scholars will undoubtedly discover personal iconography in the densely populated watercolors. Familiar themes abound: the quest for home, the capacity children have for navigating their circumstances, the pleasure of cake, the presence of death.... Nobody does naughty quite like [Sendak] does." SLJ

★ **Chicken** soup with rice; a book of months. Harper & Row 1962 30p il lib bdg $16.89; pa $5.95
Grades: PreK K 1 2   E
1. Stories in rhyme 2. Seasons -- Fiction
ISBN 0-06-025535-8 lib bdg; 0-06-443253-X pa
Originally published in smaller format as volume two of the Nutshell library

Pictures and verse illustrate the delight of eating chicken soup with rice in every season of the year

★ **In** the night kitchen; 25th anniversary ed; HarperCollins Pubs. 1996 un il $17.95; lib bdg $18.89; pa $6.95
Grades: PreK K 1 2 3   E
1. Fantasy fiction
ISBN 0-06-026668-6; 0-06-026669-4 lib bdg; 0-06-443436-2 pa
First published 1970
A Caldecott Medal honor book, 1971
"A perfect midnight fantasy. The feelings, smells, sights, and comforting emotions which young children experience are here in lovely dream colors." Brooklyn. Art Books for Child

★ **Mommy?** [art by Maurice Sendak; scenario by Arthur Yorinks; paper engineering by Matthew Reinhart] Scholastic 2006 un il $24.95
Grades: PreK K 1 2   E
1. Pop-up books 2. Monsters -- Fiction
ISBN 0-439-88050-5
"This pop-up tour de force abounds with humor, vibrant artwork, and visual fireworks." SLJ

★ **One** was Johnny; a counting book. Harper & Row 1962 un il lib bdg $16.89; pa $5.95
Grades: PreK K 1 2   E
1. Counting
ISBN 0-06-025540-4 lib bdg; 0-06-443251-3 pa

Originally published in smaller format as volume three of the Nutshell library

Counting from one to ten and back again to one, Johnny, who starts off alone, acquires too many numbered visitors for his own comfort, until they disappear one by one

★ **Outside** over there. Harper & Row 1981 un il $22.95; pa $9.95
Grades: K 1 2 3   E
1. Fairy tales 2. Sisters -- Fiction
ISBN 0-06-025523-4; 0-06-443185-1 pa
LC 79-2682
A Caldecott Medal honor book, 1982
With Papa off to sea and Mama despondent, Ida must go outside over there to rescue her baby sister from goblins who steal her to be a goblin's bride

"A gentle yet powerful story in the romantic tradition. . . . Soft in tones, rich in the use of light and color . . . the pictures are particularly distinctive for the tenderness with which the children's faces are drawn, the classic handling of texture, the imaginative juxtaposition of infant faces and the baroque landscape details that might have come from Renaissance paintings." Bull Cent Child Books

★ **Pierre**; a cautionary tale in five chapters and a prologue. Harper & Row 1962 48p il lib bdg $16.89; pa $5.95
Grades: PreK K 1 2   E
1. Stories in rhyme
ISBN 0-06-025965-5 lib bdg; 0-06-443252-1 pa
Originally published in smaller format as volume four of the Nutshell library

A story in verse about a little boy called Pierre who insisted upon saying 'I don't care' until he said it once too often and learned a well needed lesson

★ **Where** the wild things are; story and pictures by Maurice Sendak. Harper & Row 1963 un il $17.95; lib bdg $18.89; pa $8.95
Grades: PreK K 1 2   E
1. Fantasy fiction
ISBN 0-06-025492-0; 0-06-025493-9 lib bdg; 0-06-443178-9 pa
Awarded the Caldecott Medal, 1964
"This vibrant picture book in luminous, understated full color has proved utterly engrossing to children with whom it has been shared. . . . A sincere, preceptive contribution which bears repeated examination." Horn Book

Senior, Olive
Birthday suit; by Olive Senior; paintings by Eugenie Fernandes. Annick Press 2012 32 p.
Grades: PreK K   E
1. Nudity 2. Picture books for children 3. Children's clothing -- Fiction
ISBN 1554513685; 9781554513680
This book tells the story of "Johnny, [who] likes to run around naked . . . . But now that he's 4, mom insists on clothes at all times. She buys him red trunks for playing in the water. As soon as her back is turned, however, he's out of them and back to the titular birthday suit. . . . It takes a man-to-man talk with dad for Johnny to realize that he really does want to be a big boy. He puts on his overalls and everybody

claps. Now he has fun with clothes, zipping and tying and snapping." (Kirkus Reviews)

Senir, Mirik

When I first held you; a lullaby from Israel. [by] Mirik Snir; [illustrated by] Eleyor Snir; translated from the Hebrew by Mary Jane Shubow. Kar-Ben 2009 un il $9.95
Grades: PreK K 1   E
   1. Lullabies 2. Stories in rhyme 3. Nature -- Fiction 4. Parent-child relationship -- Fiction
   ISBN 978-0-7613-5098-9; 0-7613-5098-5
                       LC 2008-53741
A parent describes, in rhyming text, the beauty of the world on the day a young child is born
   "The unassuming and calming melodious text, fluidly translated by Shubow, will certainly encourage serenity and comfort at the end of each day." Kirkus

Serfozo, Mary

Plumply, dumply pumpkin; written by Mary Serfozo; illustrated by Valeria Petrone. Margaret K. McElderry Bks. 2001 un il hardcover o.p. pa $6.99; bd bk $6.99
Grades: PreK K 1 2   E
   1. Pumpkin 2. Stories in rhyme 3. Jack-o-lanterns 4. Pumpkin -- Fiction 5. Halloween -- Fiction
   ISBN 0-689-83834-4; 0-689-87135-X pa; 0-689-86277-6 bd bk
                       LC 00-32421
Peter finds the perfect pumpkin so that he and his Dad can make a jack-o-lantern
   "Toddlers will relish the bouncy, rhyming stanzas and silly wordplay, which help make this a great, nonspooky Halloween storytime choice. The subtly textured computer-generated art has solid child appeal." Booklist

Whooo's there? by Mary Serfozo; illustrated by Jeffrey Scherer. Random House 2007 un il $9.99; lib bdg $12.99
Grades: PreK K 1   E
   1. Stories in rhyme 2. Owls -- Fiction 3. Animals -- Fiction
   ISBN 978-0-375-84050-0; 978-0-375-94050-7 lib bdg
                 LC 2006014438
An inquisitive owl keeps track of the comings and goings of woodland creatures all night long
   "The story is told in pleasing verse made up of quatrains. . . . Illustrations have thick lines of color that accentuate outlines, and the animals feature mostly friendly cartoonlike visages that are quite appealing." SLJ

Serrano, Francisco

La Malinche; the princess who helped Cortés conquer the Aztec Empire. Francisco Serrano. Groundwood Books/House of Anansi Press 2012 37 p. $18.95
Grades: 4 5 6   E
   1. Picture books for children 2. La Malinche, approximately 1505-1530
   ISBN 1554981115; 9781554981113
This is a "picture-book biography about the controversial Mexican figure 'La Malinche.' Malinali, a Nahuatl princess, was sold into slavery and eventually traded to Spanish explorer Hernán Cortés." (School Library Journal) "Presented here as an enigma La Malinche is viewed by some as the mother of a new culture and by others as a traitor who helped Cortes defeat an indigenous people of which she was a part.

What is agreed upon is that Cortes . . . may not have had success without her." (Children's Literature)

Seto, Loretta

Mooncakes; Loretta Seto, Renne Benoit. Orca Book Publishers 2013 32 p. (hardcover) $19.95
Grades: PreK K 1 2   E
   1. Moon -- Folklore 2. Festivals -- Juvenile fiction
   ISBN 1459801075; 9781459801073
                 LC 2012952944
This children's story, by Loretta Seto, illustrated by Renné Benoit, follows "a young girl who shares the special celebration of the Chinese Moon Festival with her parents. As they eat mooncakes, drink tea and watch the night sky together, Mama and Baba tell ancient tales of a magical tree that can never be cut down, the Jade Rabbit who came to live on the moon and one brave woman's journey to eternal life." (Publisher's note)

Seuss, Dr., 1904-1991

The **500** hats of Bartholomew Cubbins. Random House 1990 un il $14.95
Grades: PreK K 1 2 3   E
   1. Hats -- Fiction
   ISBN 0-394-84484-X
                  LC 88-38412
A reissue of the title first published 1938 by Vanguard Press
   "It is a lovely bit of tomfoolery which keeps up the suspense and surprise until the last page, and of the same ingenious and humorous imagination are the author's black and white illustrations in which a red cap and then an infinite number of red caps titillate the eye." N Y Times Book Rev

★ **And** to think that I saw it on Mulberry Street. Random House 1989 un il $14.95; lib bdg $15.99
Grades: PreK K 1 2   E
   1. Stories in rhyme
   ISBN 0-394-84494-7; 0-394-94494-1 lib bdg
                 LC 88-38411
A reissue of the title first published 1937 by Vanguard Press
   "A fresh, inspiring picture-story book in bright colors. . . . As convincing to a child as to the psychologist in quest of a book with an appeal to the child's imaginations." Horn Book

Bartholomew and the oobleck; written and illustrated by Dr. Seuss. Random House 1949 un il $14.95; lib bdg $15.99
Grades: PreK K 1 2   E
   ISBN 0-394-80075-3; 0-394-90075-8 lib bdg
   A Caldecott Medal honor book, 1950
   "Bored with the same old kinds of weather, the King of Didd commanded his magicians to stir up something new and different. What they produced was a gooey, gummy green stuff which might have wrecked the kingdom had it not been for Bartholomew Cubbins, the page boy." Booklist

★ The **Bippolo** Seed and other lost stories; by Dr. Seuss; introduction by Charles D. Cohen. Random House 2011 69p il $15

Grades: K 1 2   E
1. Short stories 2. Stories in rhyme
ISBN 978-0-375-86435-3; 0-375-86435-0

LC 2009052588

Presents seven Dr. Seuss stories first published in magazines between 1948 and 1959, with an introduction and commentary on each.

"The stories' rhymed couplets are pitch-perfect, the verse's rhythm as snappy as in any of Seuss's better-known works. . . . Fans old and young will deem these 'lost' stories a tremendous find." Publ Wkly

★ The **cat** in the hat; by Dr. Seuss. 50th anniversary ed.; Random House 2007 61p il $8.99 **E**
1. Stories in rhyme 2. Cats -- Fiction
ISBN 978-0-394-80001-1

A reissue of the title first published 1957

A nonsense story in verse illustrated by the author about an unusual cat and his tricks which he displayed for the children one rainy day

Another title about The cat in the hat is:
The cat in the hat comes back (1958)

★ **Green** eggs and ham. Beginner Bks. 1960 62p il $8.99; lib bdg $11.99; pa $9.95
Grades: PreK K 1 2   E
1. Stories in rhyme 2. Food -- Fiction
ISBN 0-394-80016-8; 0-394-90016-2 lib bdg; 0-394-89220-8 pa

"The happy theme of refusal-to-eat changing to relish will be doubly enjoyable to the child who finds many common edibles as nauseating as the title repast. The pacing throughout is magnificent, and the opening five pages, on which the focal character introduces himself with a placard: 'I am Sam,' are unsurpassed in the controlled-vocabulary literature." Saturday Rev

Hooray for Diffendoofer Day! [by] Dr. Seuss with some help from Jack Prelutsky & Lane Smith. Knopf 1998 un il $17; lib bdg $18.99
Grades: PreK K 1 2   E
1. School stories 2. Stories in rhyme 3. Schools -- Fiction 4. Teachers -- Fiction
ISBN 0-679-89008-4; 0-679-99008-9 lib bdg

LC 97-39725

The students of Diffendoofer School celebrate their unusual teachers and curriculum, including Miss Fribble who teaches laughing, Miss Bonkers who teaches frogs to dance, and Mr. Katz who builds robotic rats

"Given an unfinished manuscript (some sketches, snippets of verse, and jottings of names—but no plot) retrieved after Seuss's death, Prelutsky and Smith have brought this fragment to fruition in a style that does credit to all three artists." Horn Book Guide

★ **Horton** hatches the egg. Random House 1940 un il $14.95; lib bdg $15.99
Grades: PreK K 1 2   E
1. Stories in rhyme 2. Elephants -- Fiction
ISBN 0-394-80077-X; 0-394-90077-4 lib bdg

"Horton, the elephant, is faithful one hundred percent as he carries out his promise to watch a bird's egg while she takes a rest. Hilarious illustrations and a surprise ending." Adventuring with Books. 2d edition

★ **Horton** hears a Who! Random House 1954 un il $14.95; lib bdg $16.99
Grades: PreK K 1 2   E
1. Stories in rhyme 2. Elephants -- Fiction
ISBN 0-394-80078-8; 0-394-90078-2 lib bdg

"The verses are full of the usual lively, informal language and amazing rhymes that have delighted such a world-wide audience in the good 'doctor's' other books." N Y Her Trib Books

★ **How** the Grinch stole Christmas. Random House 1957 un il $15; lib bdg $18
Grades: PreK K 1 2   E
1. Stories in rhyme 2. Christmas -- Fiction
ISBN 0-394-80079-6; 0-394-90079-0 lib bdg

"The verse is as lively and the pages are as bright and colorful as anyone could wish." Saturday Rev

★ **If** I ran the circus. Random House 1956 un il $14.95; lib bdg $15.99
Grades: PreK K 1 2   E
1. Stories in rhyme 2. Circus -- Fiction
ISBN 0-394-80080-X; 0-394-90080-4 lib bdg

The author-illustrator "presents the fabulous Circus McGurkus with its highly imaginative young owner, Morris McGurk and its intrepid performer, Sneelock, behind whose store the circus is to be housed. There are the expected number of strange creatures with nonsensical names, but the real humor lies in the situations, and especially those involving Mr. Sneelock. There is fun for the entire family here." Bull Cent Child Books

★ **If** I ran the zoo. Random House 1950 un il $14.95; lib bdg $16.99
Grades: PreK K 1 2   E
1. Stories in rhyme 2. Zoos -- Fiction
ISBN 0-394-80081-8; 0-394-90081-2 lib bdg

A Caldecott Medal honor book, 1951

"As you turn the pages, the imaginings get wilder and funnier, the rhymes more hilarious. There will be no age limits for this book, because families will be forced to share rereading and quotation, for a long long time." NY Her Trib Books

McElligot's pool; written and illustrated by Dr. Seuss. Random House 1947 un il $14.95; lib bdg $16.99
Grades: PreK K 1 2   E
1. Stories in rhyme 2. Fishing -- Fiction
ISBN 0-394-80083-4; 0-394-90083-9 lib bdg

A Caldecott Medal honor book, 1948

"Fine color surrounding a host of strange creatures enlivens this amazing fish story for all ages." Horn Book

Yertle the turtle and other stories; A 50th anniversary retrospective. with 32 pages of rarely seen Seuss images and commentary by Charles D. Cohen. 50th anniversary ed.; Random House 2008 114p il $24.99; lib bdg $27.99

Grades: PreK K 1 2   E
1. Stories in rhyme 2. Turtles -- Fiction
ISBN 978-0-375-83850-7; 0-375-83850-3; 978-0-375-93850-4 lib bdg; 0-375-93850-8 lib bdg

LC 2007033486

A reissue of the title first published 1958
Includes three humorous stories in verse, Yertle the Turtle, Gertrude McFuzz, and The Big Brag, followed by commentary and end notes, reproductions of illustrations from other Dr. Seuss books, and two poems, 'The Ruckus' and 'The Kindly Snather'
Includes bibliographical references

Seven, John
The **ocean** story; written by John Seven; illustrated by Jana Christy. Picture Window Books 2011 un il
Grades: PreK K 1 2   E
1. Ocean -- Fiction 2. Water -- Fiction 3. Oil spills -- Fiction 4. Marine animals -- Fiction 5. Water pollution -- Fiction
ISBN 1-4048-6785-6; 978-1-4048-6785-7

LC 2011006480

Relates the story of the oceans that are home to so many creatures, that are part of the water cycle which produces rain, and that can become very messy if we do not take care of them.
"Endpapers filled with images of ocean life are the auspicious beginning of this beautiful eco-tale. . . . This splendid call to stewardship is gloriously illustrated with paintings, each a gift of color and texture that encourages lingering. . . . This book is a perfect blend of poetry, visual art, and science." SLJ

Seymour, Tres
Hunting the white cow; story by Tres Seymour; pictures by Wendy Anderson Halperin. Orchard Bks. 1993 un il $16.95
Grades: K 1 2 3   E
1. Cattle -- Fiction 2. Farm life -- Fiction
ISBN 0-531-05496-9

LC 92-43757

A child watches as more and more people join in the attempts to catch the family cow that has gotten loose, each remarking on how special the cow is
"Wendy Halperin's soft colored-pencil drawings of fields and woods that drift far back into the distant hills add to the mythic aura. A unique and imaginative book." Horn Book

Shahan, Sherry
Spicy hot colors: colores picantes; illustrated by Paula Barragan. August House 2004 un il $16.95
Grades: PreK K 1 2   E
1. Color 2. Bilingual books -- English-Spanish
ISBN 0-87483-741-3

This is an "introduction to the names of nine colors in Spanish. Snappy, image-filled verses bring to life some of the hues and traditions of Latino culture. . . . Vibrant paintings that have both ethnic and fine-art references are appealing and attention grabbing." SLJ

Shange, Ntozake
★ **Ellington** was not a street; written by Ntozake Shange; illustrations by Kadir Nelson. Simon & Schuster Bks. for Young Readers 2004 un il $15.95

Grades: K 1 2 3 4   E
1. Children's poetry 2. African Americans -- Poetry
ISBN 0-689-82884-5

LC 00-45060

"Nelson illustrates the noted poet's 'Mood Indigo,' from her collection entitled A Daughter's Geography. . . . In the poem, Shange recalls her childhood when her family entertained many of the . . . 'men/who changed the world,' including Paul Robeson, W.E.B. DuBois, Ray Barretto, Dizzy Gillespie, 'Sonny Til' Tilghman, Kwame Nkrumah, and Duke Ellington. Both the words and the rich, nostalgic illustrations are a tribute to these visionaries. . . . A biographical sketch of each man appears at the end, along with the poem reprinted on a single page." SLJ

Shannon, David, 1959-
★ **Alice** the fairy. Blue Sky Press 2004 un il $15.95
Grades: PreK K 1 2   E
1. Fairies -- Fiction 2. Imagination -- Fiction
ISBN 0-439-49025-1

LC 2003-23478

Alice, who claims to be a Temporary Fairy, still has a lot to learn, such as how to make her clothes put themselves away in the closet.
"Kids will find most of the humor right at their level, in terms of both wit and imagination. The pictures are richly colored, some almost effervescent in their playfulness." Booklist

★ **Duck** on a bike. Blue Sky Press (NY) 2002 un il $15.95
Grades: PreK K 1 2   E
1. Ducks 2. Domestic animals 3. Ducks -- Fiction 4. Cycling -- Fiction 5. Bicycles and bicycling 6. Domestic animals -- Fiction
ISBN 0-439-05023-5

LC 2001-35992

A duck decides to ride a bike and soon influences all the other animals on the farm to ride bikes too
"This delightful story will have youngsters chiming in on the repeated phrases and predicting, in no time, what will happen next, and the many animal sounds provide ample opportunities for role-playing. Shannon's brightly colored spreads are filled with humor." SLJ

★ **Good** boy, Fergus! Blue Sky Press 2006 un il $15.99
Grades: PreK K 1 2   E
1. Dogs -- Fiction
ISBN 0-439-49027-8

LC 2005-08541

Except for his bath, Fergus experiences the perfect doggy day, from chasing cats and motorcycles to being scratched on his favorite tickle spot.
"This book is all about the impressive, oversize visuals—pictures that show the adorable doggie in full canine-caper mode." Booklist

Shannon, David, 1959-
★ **No,** David! Blue Sky Press (NY) 1998 un il $16.99
Grades: PreK K 1 2   E
1. Behavior -- Fiction 2. Mother-son relationship --

Fiction
ISBN 0-590-93002-8

LC 97-35125

A Caldecott Medal honor book, 1999

A young boy is depicted doing a variety of naughty things for which he is repeatedly admonished, but finally he gets a hug. "Preschool to grade two." (SLJ)

"The vigorous and wacky full-color acrylic paintings portray a lively and imaginative boy whose stick-figure body conveys every nuance of anger, exuberance, defiance, and best of all, the reassurance of his mother's love." SLJ

Other titles about David are:

David goes to school (1999)

David gets in trouble (2002)

It's Christmas, David! (2010)

★ **Too** many toys. Blue Sky Press 2008 un il $16.99
Grades: PreK K 1 2   E

1. Toys -- Fiction

ISBN 0-439-49029-4; 978-0-439-49029-0

LC 2007-44753

Although he finally agrees that he has too many toys and needs to give them away, there is one toy that Spencer absolutely cannot part with. "Ages six to nine." (Bull Cent Child Books)

"A master at capturing the workings of a young mind, Shannon combines realistic dialogue with his boisterous illustrations to create another surefire hit." SLJ

★ The **rain** came down. Blue Sky Press (NY) 2000 un il lib bdg $15.95
Grades: PreK K 1 2   E

1. Quarreling 2. Rain -- Fiction 3. Rain and rainfall

ISBN 0-439-05021-9

LC 99-86363

An unexpected rain shower causes quarreling and confusion among the members of a small community. However, when the sun comes out, everyone feels better. "Ages five to eight." (Bull Cent Child Books)

"This deceptively simple story showcases Shannon's quirky humor and offbeat illustrations." SLJ

Shannon, George

Tippy -toe chick, go! pictures by Laura Dronzek. Greenwillow Bks. 2003 un il $15.99; lib bdg $16.89
Grades: PreK K 1 2   E

1. Dogs -- Fiction 2. Chickens -- Fiction

ISBN 0-06-029823-5; 0-06-029824-3 lib bdg

LC 2002-17509

When a mean dog blocks the path to the garden where a delicious breakfast awaits, Little Chick shows her family how brave and clever she is

"The narrative has a fresh, buoyant vitality that begs to be read aloud. . . . The bright, uncluttered acrylic illustrations neatly match the spare text." Booklist

★ **Tomorrow's** alphabet; pictures by Donald Crews. Greenwillow Bks. 1996 un il $17; pa $6.99
Grades: PreK K 1 2 3   E

1. Alphabet

ISBN 0-688-13504-8; 0-688-16424-2 pa

LC 94-19484

"In 26 double-page spreads, the letters of the alphabet are used to demonstrate where things come from. 'A is for seed'

is followed on the next page with 'tomorrow's APPLE.' 'D is for puppy—tomorrow's DOG.'. . . All of the combinations are clever, well chosen, and well within youngsters' experience. . . . Each two-page spread offers brightly colored, large and realistic depictions of the objects named." SLJ

★ **White** is for blueberry; pictures by Laura Dronzek. Greenwillow Books 2005 un il $17.99; lib bdg $17.89
Grades: PreK K 1 2 3   E

1. Color

ISBN 0-06-029275-X; 0-06-029276-8 lib bdg

LC 2004-10147

"The bold, uncluttered scenes, rendered in acrylics, have a sweetness and strength that is quite pleasing to the eye. Easy to read and fun to share, this paean to the wonder of cycles and the rewards of close observation is the perfect prelude to a thoughtful excursion." SLJ

Shannon, Margaret

The **red** wolf; written and illustrated by Margaret Shannon. Houghton Mifflin 2002 un il $15
Grades: K 1 2 3   E

1. Fairy tales 2. Princesses -- Fiction

ISBN 0-618-05544-4

LC 00-56742

Roselupin, a princess locked in a tower by her overprotective father, uses yarn to knit a red wolf suit to free herself

"Shannon's brightly colored illustrations and the creative design and layout enrich this original, delightful tale. A thoroughly enjoyable story of empowerment." SLJ

Shapiro, Zachary

★ **We're** all in the same boat; [by] Zachary Shapiro; illustrated by Jack E. Davis. G.P. Putnam's Sons 2008 un il $16.99
Grades: PreK K 1 2   E

1. Alphabet 2. Animals -- Fiction 3. Noah's ark -- Fiction

ISBN 978-0-399-24393-6; 0-399-24393-3

LC 2007041316

After being on the ark for months and months, the ants get antsy, the bees bored, and the llamas livid, and Noah must find a way to make everyone get along.

"Davis's hilarious illustrations of the facial expressions and actions of the various animals add to the liveliness and humor. Lots of interactions occur simultaneously, giving readers much to explore visually. . . . Shapiro has crafted a humorous alphabet story with an underlying message of cooperation—a winning combination." SLJ

Sharmat, Marjorie Weinman

Gila monsters meet you at the airport; pictures by Byron Barton. Macmillan 1980 un il hardcover o.p. pa $5.99
Grades: PreK K 1 2   E

1. Moving -- Fiction

ISBN 0-02-782450-0; 0-689-71383-5 pa

LC 80-12264

A New York City boy's preconceived ideas of life in the West make him very apprehensive about the family's move there

"The exaggeration is amusing, the style yeasty, with a nice final touch; the illustrations are comic and awkward, but add little that's not inherent in the story." Bull Cent Child Books

★ **Nate** the Great; illustrated by Marc Simont. Delacorte Press 2002 60p il $13.95; pa $4.50
Grades: K 1 2   **E**
1. Mystery fiction
ISBN 978-0-385-73017-4; 0-385-73017-9; 978-0-440-46126-5 pa; 0-440-46126-X pa

A reissue of the title first published 1972 by McCann & Geoghegan

Nate the Great, a junior detective who has found missing balloons, books, slippers, chickens and even a goldfish, is now in search of a painting of a dog by Annie, the girl down the street.

"The illustrations capture the exaggerated, tongue-in-cheek humor of the story." Booklist

Other titles about Nate the Great are:
Nate the Great and me: the case of the fleeing fang (1998)
Nate the Great and the big sniff (2001)
Nate the Great and the boring beach bag (1987)
Nate the Great and the crunchy Christmas (1996)
Nate the Great and the fishy prize (1985)
Nate the Great and the Halloween hunt (1989)
Nate the Great and the hungry book club (2009)
Nate the Great and the lost list (1975)
Nate the Great and the missing key (1981)
Nate the Great and the monster mess (1999)
Nate the Great and the mushy valentine (1994)
Nate the Great and the musical note (1990)
Nate the Great and the phony clue (1977)
Nate the Great and the pillowcase (1993)
Nate the Great and the snowy trail (1982)
Nate the Great and the sticky case (1978)
Nate the Great and the stolen base (1992)
Nate the Great and the tardy tortoise (1995)
Nate the Great goes down in the dumps (1989)
Nate the Great goes undercover (1974)
Nate the Great on the Owl Express (2003)
Nate the Great, San Francisco detective (2000)
Nate the Great saves the King of Sweden (1997)
Nate the Great stalks stupidweed (1986)
Nate the Great talks turkey (2006)

Sharmat, Mitchell
Gregory, the terrible eater; illustrated by Jose Aruego and Ariane Dewey. Four Winds Press 1985 un il $16.95
Grades: PreK K 1 2   **E**
1. Diet -- Fiction 2. Goats -- Fiction
ISBN 0-02-782250-8
LC 85-29290
A reissue of the title first published 1980

"Aruego and Dewey's illustrations are highly amusing, thanks to their goats' dot-eyed facial expressions. . . . There is energy in the pictures; they are beguiling and help to carry the humor." Booklist

Sharratt, Nick
What's in the witch's kitchen? Candlewick Press 2011 un il $12.99
Grades: PreK K   **E**
1. Stories in rhyme 2. Pop-up books 3. Witches --

Fiction 4. Halloween -- Fiction
ISBN 978-0-7636-5224-1; 0-7636-5224-5
LC 2010042323
The contents of the witch's kitchen are hidden by flaps that can be opened either to the left or right to reveal pop-up illustrations of either a delight or a nasty fright.

"Sharratt's digital illustrations are colorful and large. . . . Humorous contrasts, cheery colors, and smiling bats and ghosts make this book a perfect fit for storytimes about homes, rhymes, or surprises." SLJ

Shaskan, Stephen
A **dog** is a dog. Chronicle Books 2011 un il $14.99
Grades: PreK K 1   **E**
1. Stories in rhyme 2. Animals -- Fiction
ISBN 978-0-8118-7896-8; 0-8118-7896-1
LC 2010041949
Using various animals as examples, this rhyming picture book explores what makes them the same and what makes them different.

This "looks simple, but it's in fact a polished and controlled piece of work. . . . There's a chunky, woodcut feel to Shaskan's hip and cheery art, and he gives each of the animals abundant personality. Children attracted to Escher-like paradoxes will appreciate the endless loop of animal costumes and low-key surprises." Publ Wkly

Shaw, Charles
★ **It** looked like spilt milk. Harper & Row 1947 un il $16.99; lib bdg $18.89; pa $6.99; bd bk $6.99
Grades: PreK K 1   **E**
ISBN 0-06-025566-8; 0-06-025565-X lib bdg; 0-06-443159-2 pa; 0-694-00491-X bd bk

White silhouettes on a blue background with simple captions: "sometimes it looked like a tree," "Sometimes it looked like a bird," etc. lead to a surprise ending "sometimes it looked like split milk, but what it was was—"

"What one thing could look like all of these? On the last page you are told, and I could no more tell you now than I could spoil an adult mystery by a review that gives away its solution." N Y Her Trib Books

Shaw, Hannah
★ **School** for bandits. Alfred A. Knopf 2011 un il $16.99
Grades: K 1 2   **E**
1. Raccoons -- Fiction 2. Etiquette -- Fiction
ISBN 978-0-375-86768-2; 0-375-86768-6
LC 2010039516
Ralph Raccoon is too polite so his parents send him to Bandit School to learn to behave like a properly bad raccoon.

"This clever story is packed with childlike humor. The pen-and-ink drawings are in bold colors and are full of action and creative details." SLJ

★ **Sneaky** weasel. Alfred A. Knopf 2009 un il $15.99; lib bdg $18.99
Grades: K 1 2 3   **E**
1. Bullies -- Fiction 2. Parties -- Fiction 3. Weasels -- Fiction 4. Friendship -- Fiction
ISBN 978-0-375-85625-9; 0-375-85625-0; 978-0-375-95625-6 lib bdg; 0-375-95625-5 lib bdg
"Sneaky Weasel's schemes and scams have made him rich, but when nobody comes to his big party, Weasel de-

termines to discover why. . . . The descriptive, lively narrative offers an entertaining exploration of bullying. . . . The animated, colorful illustrations feature Weasel in intricately rendered scenes that are filled with clever details." Booklist

Shaw, Nancy

Raccoon tune; illustrated by Howard Fine. Holt & Co. 2003 un il $15.95

Grades: PreK K 1 2   E

1. Raccoons 2. Stories in rhyme 3. Raccoons -- Fiction

ISBN 0-8050-6544-X

LC 2002-5945

A family of raccoons prowls around a neighborhood making a ruckus until they find supper

"Playful illustrations expand the lighthearted mood of the story. Fine's use of blues, greens, and light makes nighttime scenes almost as bright as the white of the raccoons' markings, and such objects as the metal trash cans shine with reflected moonlight." SLJ

★ **Sheep** in a jeep; illustrated by Margot Apple. Houghton Mifflin 1986 32p il lib bdg $15; pa $5.95; bd bk $5.95

Grades: PreK K 1 2   E

1. Stories in rhyme 2. Sheep -- Fiction

ISBN 0-395-41105-X lib bdg; 0-395-47030-7 pa; 0-395-86786-X bd bk

LC 86-3101

"Shaw demonstrates a promising capacity for creating nonsense rhymes. . . . Veteran illustrator Apple's whimsical portraits of the sheep bring the story to life. Pleasing and lighthearted, this has much appeal for young readers." Publ Wkly

Other titles about the sheep are:

Sheep blast off! (2008)

Sheep in a shop (1991)

Sheep on a ship (1989)

Sheep out to eat (1992)

Sheep take a hike (1994)

Sheep trick or treat (1997)

Shea, Bob

★ **Big** plans; [illustrated by] Lane Smith. Hyperion 2008 42p il $17.99

Grades: 1 2 3 4   E

1. School stories 2. Imagination -- Fiction

ISBN 1-4231-1100-1; 978-1-4231-1100-9

LC 2008-00707

A little boy sits in the corner of his classroom dreaming about his big plans for his future.

"Smith is the perfect artist for this illogically logical scenario, with retro tones of gold and avocado predominating in his carefully disorganized oversized compositions. . . . An escapist adventure, a victory over important adults, and a new catch-phrase to triumphantly wield." Bull Cent Child Books

Cheetah can't lose; Bob Shea. Balzer + Bray 2013 40 p. (trade bdg.) $17.99

Grades: K 1 2   E

1. Racing -- Fiction 2. Animal babies -- Juvenile fiction 3. Humorous stories 4. Cheetah -- Fiction 5. Winning

and losing -- Fiction

ISBN 0061730831; 9780061730832

LC 2012008407

Author Bob Shea presents a children's story about a cheetah. "It's race day, and once and for all, it's time to determine the better feline: little cats or big cheetah. Cheetah might be bigger, taller, stronger, faster . . . but the little cats have some tricks up their sleeves, so don't count them out!" Shea presents a "story about the difference between brains and brawn." (Publisher's note)

★ **Dinosaur** vs. bedtime. Hyperion Books for Children 2008 un il $15.99

Grades: PreK   E

1. Bedtime -- Fiction 2. Dinosaurs -- Fiction

ISBN 978-1-4231-1335-5; 1-4231-1335-7

"Incorporating paper, paint, photo collage and quick strokes of crayon, Shea's freewheeling compositions convey both a beguiling spontaneity and a preschooler's sense of invincibility." Publ Wkly

Other titles about Dinosaur are:

Dinosaur vs. the potty (2010)

Dinosaur vs. the library (2011)

I'm a shark! Balzer + Bray 2011 un il $16.99

Grades: PreK K 1   E

1. Fear -- Fiction 2. Sharks -- Fiction 3. Courage -- Fiction 4. Sharks -- Juvenile literature

ISBN 978-0-06-199846-1; 0-06-199846-X

LC 2010-21850

A boastful shark is not afraid of anything, which impresses his underwater friends until they ask about spiders.

"Witty banter begs for audience participation. . . . Thick, dark crayon strokes convey both Shark's powerful physique and his endearing vulnerability. . . . Bold, uncluttered mixed-media spreads emphasize this predator's sharp-toothed, goofy grin." Kirkus

New socks; by Bob Shea. Little, Brown 2007 un il $12.99

Grades: PreK K 1 2   E

1. Chickens -- Fiction 2. Clothing and dress -- Fiction

ISBN 978-0-316-01357-4; 0-316-01357-9

LC 2006013741

A chicken is filled with excitement and self-confidence when he dons a new pair of orange socks

"The text, which presents a childlike blend of fervor and silliness, is wonderfully extended through the artwork. . . . The chick's body is a yellow lima-bean-shaped blob; black-dot eyes, a beak fashioned from two half-moons, and thick-rimmed glasses define his face and add expression." SLJ

★ **Oh,** Daddy! Balzer + Bray 2010 un il $16.99

Grades: PreK K   E

1. Hippopotamus -- Fiction 2. Father-child relationship -- Fiction

ISBN 978-0-06-173080-1; 0-06-173080-7

A young hippopotamus shows his father the right way to do things, such as getting dressed, watering the flowers, and especially giving big hugs.

"The concise text captures the child's voice perfectly. . . . The mixed-media illustrations incorporate collage elements into a spare, cartoonlike world. . . . The gentle humor . . . will keep kids entertained." SLJ

Race you to bed. Katherine Tegen Books 2010 un il $16.99
Grades: PreK K 1   E
1. Stories in rhyme 2. Bedtime -- Fiction 3. Rabbits -- Fiction
ISBN 978-0-06-170417-8; 0-06-170417-2
LC 2008044525

"A fuzzy white rabbit with an oversize head races readers to bed, but he finds many reasons to delay bedtime. Animals, toys, and other objects divert his attention. . . . The singsong rhyme flows as the rabbit cavorts through the flat colored pages. The backgrounds are all done in soothing pastel colors, with the exuberant youngster cavorting across the pages. Clever details in the art enhance the telling." SLJ

★ **Unicorn** thinks he's pretty great; by Bob Shea. Disney-Hyperion 2013 40 p. $15.99
Grades: PreK K 1 2   E
1. Picture books for children 2. Jealousy -- Juvenile fiction 3. Envy -- Fiction 4. Goats -- Fiction 5. Unicorns -- Fiction 6. Friendship -- Fiction
ISBN 1423159527; 9781423159520
LC 2012047987
In this children's book, a goat is jealous of a unicorn. "The goat bakes marsh-mallow squares. The unicorn can make it rain cupcakes! The goat tries a magic trick. The unicorn can turn things into gold! . . . It turns out that the unicorn actually has some goat envy," himself, and the two become friends. (Publishers Weekly)

"Rainbows, smiling cupcakes, and flying unicorns in one picture book can be a recipe for a cutesy-wootsy disaster, but not so in this hilarious friendship story... An ideal choice for fans of silliness." SLJ

Shea, Susan A.
★ **Do** you know which ones will grow? Blue Apple Books 2011 un il $16.99
Grades: PreK K 1   E
1. Life (Biology) 2. Stories in rhyme 3. Growth -- Fiction
ISBN 978-1-60905-062-7; 1-60905-062-2

"Shea's book debut is a clever, rhymed test of kids' notions of living and nonliving things that's great for both lap and group sharing. . . . [The book offers] a terrific interplay of rhyming questions and cunningly designed gatefold illustrations: 'If a calf grows and becomes a cow, / can a shovel grow and become . . . a plow?'. . . . Other rhymes include duck and truck, bear and chair, cat and hat . . . and kangaroo and you. . . . Slaughter's illustrations bring pop art to mind: vivid reds, blues, yellows and greens, few details, simple backgrounds and blocks of color." Kirkus

Shelby, Anne
★ The **man** who lived in a hollow tree; by Anne Shelby and Cor Hazelaar. Atheneum Books for Young Readers 2009 un il $17.99
Grades: K 1 2 3   E
1. Tall tales 2. Trees -- Fiction 3. Ecology -- Fiction

4. Carpentry -- Fiction
ISBN 978-0-689-86169-7; 0-689-86169-9
LC 2008-10369
Carpenter Harlan Burch, who builds everything from cradle to casket, plants two trees for every one he cuts down, and when he is very old his sap begins to rise, he grows young again, and starts a family that still lives all over the mountains.

"The storyteller's voice is vibrant, and the earth-toned acrylics on textured backgrounds of cardboard and linen have a quaint, collage-like feel." Booklist

Sheridan, Sara
I'm me! illustrated by Margaret Chamberlain. Chicken House 2011 un il $15.99
Grades: PreK K 1   E
1. Play -- Fiction 2. Aunts -- Fiction 3. Imagination -- Fiction
ISBN 978-0-545-28222-2; 0-545-28222-5
"Imogen's visits to her aunt's house are always an adventure. As the child rushes in, Auntie Sara asks her what she wants to play. 'Can we play pretend?' And the woman replies 'Yes, yes, yes, we can!' A turn of each page reveals a suggestion. . . . But to each inquiry, Imogen smilingly replies 'No! Today I want to be....' and she reveals she just wants to be herself. . . . The exuberant, candy-colored illustrations show the pair delighting in each other as they cavort across the spreads. There are few books starring an aunt and her niece, and this playful gem that explores pretending and being oneself will find a welcome place in libraries." SLJ

Sherman, Pat
Ben and the Emancipation Proclamation; written by Pat Sherman; illustrated by Floyd Cooper. Eerdmans Books for Young Readers 2010 un il $16.99
Grades: 3 4 5   E
1. Slaves 2. Teachers 3. Slavery -- Fiction 4. African Americans -- Fiction 5. Books and reading -- Fiction
ISBN 978-0-8028-5319-6; 0-8028-5319-6
"Based on the life of Benjamin Holmes, a slave who taught himself to read at a young age, this picture book is an inspiring account of overcoming oppression. Sherman's fictionalized telling is stirring, especially when Holmes revels in the discovery of new words. . . . Sherman's text has a stately simplicity. Cooper's paintings glow with a hopeful, golden warmth. . . . This is a powerful tale of a bright ray of light in a very dark period in America." SLJ

Includes bibliographical references

Sherry, Kevin
I'm the biggest thing in the ocean. Dial Books for Young Readers 2007 un il $16.99
Grades: PreK   E
1. Size -- Fiction 2. Squids -- Fiction 3. Marine animals -- Fiction
ISBN 978-0-8037-3192-9; 0-8037-3192-2
LC 2006-27815
A giant squid brags about being bigger than everything else in the ocean—almost.

"A lighthearted, clever story presented in an oversize, colorful package." SLJ

Another title about the giant squid is:
I'm the best artist in the ocean (2008)

Sheth, Kashmira

Monsoon afternoon; written by Kashmira Sheth; illustrated by Yoshiko Jaeggi. Peachtree 2008 un il $16.95
Grades: PreK K 1 2　　　　　　　　　　　　　**E**
　1. Rain -- Fiction　2. Monsoons -- Fiction　3. Grandfathers -- Fiction
　ISBN 978-1-56145-455-6; 1-56145-455-9

LC 2008004565

A young boy and his grandfather find much they can do together on a rainy day during monsoon season in India

"Jaeggi's atmospheric watercolors nicely translate the sensory details in the words. . . . The scenes give a strong sense of everyday life in the boy's Indian community, as well as the sweet bond between grandfather and grandson." Booklist

Slade, Suzanne

The **house** that George built; by Suzanne Slade; illustrated by Rebecca Bond. Charlesbridge 2011 48 p. il (reinforced for library use) $16.95
Grades: 1 2 3　　　　　　　　　　　　　　　**E**
　1. Presidents -- United States -- Homes　2. Presidents -- United States -- History -- Juvenile literature
　ISBN 1580892620; 9781580892629

LC 2011025781

This book by Suzanne Slade "describes how George Washington chose the design for what would become the White House and supervised its construction. Rhyming verses, interspersed with background paragraphs to fill out the narrative, describe how Washington found the site and held a contest to get design submissions. African American and white surveyors and laborers are included in the pictures." (School Library Journal)

My Dadima wears a sari; written by Kashmira Sheth; illustrated by Yoshiko Jaeggi. Peachtree 2007 un il $16.95
Grades: K 1 2 3　　　　　　　　　　　　　　**E**
　1. Grandmothers -- Fiction　2. Clothing and dress -- Fiction　3. East Indians -- United States -- Fiction
　ISBN 1-56145-392-7

LC 2006024334

Two young sisters raised in America learn about the beauty and art of wearing a sari from their wise Indian grandmother.

"Soft watercolor paintings capture the magnificent fabrics of Dadima's saris and accentuate the loving story." SLJ

★ **Tiger** in my soup; written by Kashmira Sheth; illustrated by Jeffrey Ebbeler. Peachtree Publishers 2013 32 p. (reinforced) $15.95
Grades: PreK K 1　　　　　　　　　　　　　**E**
　1. Siblings -- Juvenile fiction　2. Imagination -- Juvenile fiction　3. Books and reading -- Juvenile fiction　4. Babysitters -- Fiction　5. Books and reading -- Fiction　6. Brothers and sisters -- Fiction
　ISBN 1561456969; 9781561456963

LC 2012025539

In this book by Kashmira Sheth, "[a]n unnamed narrator is left in the care of his older sister. . . . Although he asks her to read him a book about a tiger, she would rather read her own book. He captures her attention long enough to get her to heat up some alphabet soup, but she . . . doesn't even notice when a tiger rises up out of the steaming bowl. The boy uses . . . handy utensils to fend off the raging beast

until his sister finally . . . agrees to read to him." (School Library Journal)

"Ebbeler truly knocks it out of the park, gleefully building on Sheth's prose with dynamic perspectives, a realistically detailed (and menacing) tiger, abundant visual hyperbole, and unexpected delights on nearly every page." Pub Wkly

Shields, Carol Diggory

Lucky pennies and hot chocolate; illustrated by Hiroe Nakata. Dutton Children's Bks. 2000 un il $13.99
Grades: PreK K 1 2　　　　　　　　　　　　**E**
　1. Grandfathers　2. Grandfathers -- Fiction
　ISBN 0-525-46450-6

LC 00-20967

A grandfather and his grandson enjoy sharing knock-knock jokes, playing games, hot chocolate, watching movies, reading books, playing baseball and just spending time together

"The illustrations are as warm, colorful, and winning as the story." Booklist

Wombat walkabout; illustrated by Sophie Blackall. Dutton Children's Books 2009 un il $16.99
Grades: PreK K　　　　　　　　　　　　　　**E**
　1. Counting　2. Stories in rhyme　3. Animals -- Fiction　4. Wombats -- Fiction
　ISBN 978-0-525-47865-2; 0-525-47865-5

LC 2008013885

Rhyming text follows six little wombats on walkabout and a hungry dingo following, envisioning them as his lunch until the wombats turn the tables on him.

"This picture book offers a nicely cadenced, rhyming story with a solid base in folklore and a distinctive locale. . . . The pleasing double-page paintings . . . use color sparingly but well." Booklist

Shields, Gillian

Library Lily; illustrated by Francesca Chessa. William B. Eerdmans 2011 un il $16
Grades: PreK K 1 2　　　　　　　　　　　　**E**
　1. Play -- Fiction　2. Libraries -- Fiction　3. Friendship -- Fiction　4. Books and reading -- Fiction
　ISBN 978-0-8028-5401-8; 0-8028-5401-X

LC 2010053737

From the day her mother introduces her to the library, Lily wants to spend all of her time reading until she meets Milly, who hates reading but loves adventure.

"The simple text includes some dialogue and quotes from the books that Lily is reading and is placed attractively around the illustrations. Bright, vibrant, cartoon artwork enhances the text and evokes a cheerful feeling." SLJ

When the world is ready for bed. Bloomsbury 2009 un il $14.99; lib bdg $15.89
Grades: PreK K　　　　　　　　　　　　　　**E**
　1. Stories in rhyme　2. Bedtime -- Fiction　3. Rabbits -- Fiction
　ISBN 978-1-59990-339-2; 1-59990-339-3; 978-1-59990-385-9 lib bdg; 1-59990-385-7 lib bdg

LC 2009002858

"This calming tale follows three brown bunnies as their day draws to a close. They have dinner, tidy up, tell dad about the fun they've had, brush their teeth, and listen to one last story. . . . The gentle singsong text makes for excellent bedtime reading, and the homey watercolors are equally pleasant. The bunnies wear distinctive outfits and have a variety of expressions." SLJ

Another title about this rabbit family is:

When the world was waiting for you (2011)

Shipton, Jonathan

★ **Baby** baby blah blah blah! illustrated by Francesca Chessa. Holiday House 2009 un il $16.95

Grades: PreK K 1 2   **E**

1. Twins -- Fiction 2. Infants -- Fiction 3. Siblings -- Fiction 4. Family life -- Fiction

ISBN 978-0-8234-2213-5; 0-8234-2213-5

LC 2008-34895

When her parents tell her that they are expecting a baby, Emily sets to work on a list of pros and cons.

"No matter how many new baby books you have on your shelves, you'll want to make room for this bright and bubbling treasure. . . . Chessa's colorfully messy, childlike illustrations perfectly match the breezy tone of the story." SLJ

Shireen, Nadia

Good little wolf. Alfred A. Knopf 2011 il

Grades: K 1 2   **E**

1. Wolves -- Fiction

ISBN 0-375-86904-2; 0-375-96904-7 lib bdg; 978-0-375-86904-4; 978-0-375-96904-1 lib bdg

LC 2011003517

Rolf is proud when his friend, Mrs. Boggins, calls him a good little wolf, but when the Big Bad Wolf teases him Rolf tries to prove himself by howling at the moon and blowing down Little Pig's house.

"Simple, strikingly colored illustrations, rendered in pencil, ink, and collage with digital enhancements, feature the characters against bare backgrounds, allowing them to pop off the pages. . . . These bold illustrations, as well as the short text, make this a good read-aloud for audiences old enough to understand the tongue-in-cheek humor." Booklist

Shirley, Debra

Best friend on wheels; by Debra Shirley; illustrated by Judy Stead. Albert Whitman & Co. 2008 un il $15.95

Grades: K 1 2 3   **E**

1. Stories in rhyme 2. Friendship -- Fiction 3. Physically handicapped children -- Fiction

ISBN 978-0-8075-8868-0; 0-8075-8868-7

LC 2007024252

A young girl relates all the ways she and her best friend, Sarah, are alike, in spite of the fact that Sarah uses a wheelchair.

"The colorful cartoon illustrations delightfully capture [the friends] in their favorite activities. . . . The rhyme moves quickly yet touches on many aspects of life for people in wheelchairs. . . . The artwork conveys the same positive fun as the text. The book's lesson is evident without being didactic." SLJ

Shulevitz, Uri

★ **How** I learned geography. Farrar, Straus & Giroux 2008 un il $16.95

Grades: PreK K 1 2   **E**

1. Maps -- Fiction 2. Refugees -- Fiction 3. Geography

-- Fiction 4. Imagination -- Fiction

ISBN 978-0-374-33499-4; 0-374-33499-4

LC 2007-11889

A Caldecott Medal honor book, 2009

As he spends hours studying his father's world map, a young boy escapes the hunger and misery of refugee life. Based on the author's childhood in Kazakhstan, where he lived as a Polish refugee during World War II.

The "text is clear and straightforward but vivid, and small memorable touches . . . add dimensionality. Watercolor illustrations avoid demonizing the boy's real-life: the town (Turkestan, according to Shulevitz' note) looks like an interesting place. . . . Chunky lines and sweeps of washy watercolor gain additional textures in the map worlds." Bull Cent Child Books

★ **Snow**. Farrar, Straus & Giroux 1998 un il $16; pa $6.99

Grades: PreK K 1 2   **E**

1. Snow -- Fiction

ISBN 0-374-37092-3; 0-374-46862-1 pa

LC 97-37257

A Caldecott Medal honor book, 1999

As snowflakes slowly come down, one by one, people in the city ignore them, and only a boy and his dog think that the snowfall will amount to anything

"Passersby are caricatured into humorous figures bent into impossible postures, their tall hats, parasols, and funny shoes giving them an almost circus-clown appearance. . . . The elegantly stark text suits the elegant architectural lines of the cityscape." Bull Cent Child Books

★ **So** sleepy story. Farrar Straus Giroux 2006 un il $16

Grades: PreK K 1 2   **E**

1. Night -- Fiction 2. Sleep -- Fiction

ISBN 0-374-37031-1

LC 2005-51146

"A sleepy sleepy boy is fast asleep in his sleepy sleepy bed along with everything else in his sleepy sleepy house until music comes drifting in, in ever louder tones. Then the child and his surroundings gradually come alive, dance, and shake to the beat, and drift back to sleep as the notes and instruments depart. The brief repetitive text takes a backseat to the whimsical watercolor-and-ink cartoon illustrations." SLJ

When I wore my sailor suit. Farrar, Straus & Giroux 2009 un il $16.95

Grades: K 1 2 3   **E**

1. Adventure fiction 2. Sailors -- Fiction 3. Imagination -- Fiction

ISBN 978-0-374-34749-9; 0-374-34749-2

LC 2008016187

A young child spends the day imagining himself to be a sailor on a grand adventure.

"Shulevitz combines child-size sentences with words that stretch and please. . . . The artist's mastery of the medium produces both warm, dappled interiors and Old Master severity, with convincing fades into the fantastic. . . . This is the work of a wise and wonderful storyteller." SLJ

Shulman, Lisa

★ The **moon** might be milk; [by] Lisa Shulman; illustrated by Will Hillenbrand. Dutton Children's Books 2007 un il $16.99

Grades: PreK K   E
1. Animals -- Fiction 2. Cookies -- Fiction 3. Grandmothers -- Fiction
ISBN 978-0-525-47647-4; 0-525-47647-4
        LC 2005032750

A young girl asks her animal friends what they think the moon is made of, and her grandmother proves that each theory is partly correct. Includes recipe

"The mixed-media artwork features Hillenbrand's strong, distinctive lines that define the characters, colors that range in intensity from brilliant to muted, and a rich array of patterned surfaces that make the settings varied and vivid. . . . The story reads aloud well." Booklist

Shulman, Mark

★ **Mom** and Dad are palindromes; a dilemma for words . . . and backwards. by Mark Shulman; illustrated by Adam McCauley. Chronicle Books 2006 un il $15.95

Grades: 1 2 3 4   E
1. Palindromes -- Fiction
ISBN 978-0-8118-4328-7; 0-8118-4328-9
        LC 2005023614

When Bob realizes that he is surrounded by palindromes, from his mom, dad, and sis Anna to his dog Otto, he discovers a way to deal with the palindrome puzzle

"In all, Shulman cleverly weaves over 101 palindromes into the text. . . . The mixed-media cartoon art amplifies the zany situation." SLJ

Siddals, Mary McKenna

Compost stew; an A to Z recipe for the earth. illustrated by Ashley Wolff. Tricycle Press 2010 un il $15.99; lib bdg $18.99

Grades: PreK K 1 2   E
1. Alphabet 2. Stories in rhyme 3. Compost -- Fiction
ISBN 978-1-58246-316-2; 1-58246-316-6; 978-1-58246-341-4 lib bdg; 1-58246-341-7 lib bdg
        LC 2009016300

"With bouncing, rhyming lines, this cheerful title uses the alphabet to introduce children to ingredients that make great compost, from apple cores to zinnias. . . . A short supplementary note about what compost is and why it is beneficial is included. . . . This title . . . provides a light-hearted introduction to an earth- and kid-friendly activity. The brightly patterned collage artwork featuring a cast of multicultural kids working together will easily draw a young audience." Booklist

I'll play with you; illustrated by David Wisniewski. Clarion Bks. 2000 28p il $14

Grades: PreK K 1 2   E
1. Play 2. Earth sciences 3. Play -- Fiction
ISBN 0-395-90373-4
        LC 99-57849

Children speak to the sun, wind, clouds, rain, stars, and moon, asking to play with them

"Despite the simplicity of the text, which is well suited for beginning readers, the words are poetic, mixing humor and glee into the reverence for nature. In his familiar cut-paper artwork, Wisniewski shows the children's profound satisfaction at play." Booklist

Sidman, Joyce

★ **Red** sings from treetops; a year in colors. illustrated by Pamela Zagarenski. Houghton Mifflin Harcourt 2009 un il $16

Grades: PreK K 1   E
1. Children's poetry 2. Color -- Juvenile literature 3. Seasons -- Juvenile literature
ISBN 978-0-547-01494-4; 0-547-01494-5
        LC 2008-35947

ALA ALSC Caldecott Medal Honor Book (2010)

Nature displays different colors to announce the seasons of the year.

"Fresh descriptions and inventive artistry are a charming inspiration to notice colors and correlate emotions. Details in the artwork will invite repeated readings and challenge kids to muse about other color icons." Kirkus

Siegel, Mark

★ **Moving** house. Roaring Brook Press 2011 il $16.99

Grades: PreK K 1   E
1. Home -- Fiction 2. Moving -- Fiction
ISBN 978-1-59643-635-0; 1-59643-635-2
        LC 2010036602

When Joey and Chloe and their family are getting ready to move, their house decides it wants to go too.

"Siegel's . . . background as an illustrator (and an editor) serve him well; his vignettes and spreads are drafted in clean ink lines, with watercolor washes of blue and red signaling the clean skies above Foggytown. He's crafted a strong story, too." Publ Wkly

Siegel, Randy

Grandma's smile; illustrated by Dyanne DiSalvo. Roaring Brook Press 2010 32p il $15.99

Grades: PreK K 1 2   E
1. Airports -- Fiction 2. Grandmothers -- Fiction
ISBN 978-1-59643-438-7; 1-59643-438-4

DiSalvo's "sketch-style watercolors achieve an authenticity and immediacy that should give even infrequent fliers a shudder of recognition. . . . This is a wry and contemporary reality check on the going-to-Grandma's genre." Publ Wkly

My snake Blake; Randy Siegel; illustrations by Serge Bloch. Roaring Brook Press 2012 32 p. $16.99

Grades: PreK K   E
1. Picture books for children 2. Snakes as pets -- Fiction 3. Human-animal relationships -- Fiction
ISBN 1596435844; 9781596435841
        LC 2011018402

This book "tell[s] the story of a 'super-long, bright green snake' who wows the young narrator by helping him with his homework, eating rejected Brussels sprouts, and fighting bullies. 'He's a perfectly polite, delightful snake,' the boy says." The illustrations show "Blake engaged in a series of charmingly unsnakelike activities: he cooks, finds lost keys, and enjoys cuddling on park benches." (Publishers Weekly)

Sierra, Judy

Ballyhoo Bay; illustrated by Derek Anderson. Simon & Schuster Books for Young Readers 2009 un il $16.99

Grades: K 1 2   E
    1. Stories in rhyme 2. Artists -- Fiction 3. Beaches -- Fiction 4. Social action -- Fiction 5. Environmental protection -- Fiction
    ISBN 978-1-4169-5888-8; 1-4169-5888-6
                       LC 2007-49720
    Mira Bella mobilizes her art students, from grandmothers to children, crabs to seagulls, to stop a dastardly plan for turning the beach at Ballyhoo Bay into an exclusive resort, and offers an alternative—leave the beach as it is
    "Lively, humorous acrylic cartoons have a buoyancy that captures the sparkle of the seaside setting and the exaggerated antics of the characters. This upbeat ecological message is delivered with plenty of panache. Told in rhyming couplets, the story reads aloud well." SLJ

    Born to read; story by Judy Sierra; pictures by Marc Brown. Alfred A. Knopf 2008 un il $16.99; lib bdg $19.99
Grades: PreK K 1 2   E
    1. Stories in rhyme 2. Reading -- Fiction
    ISBN 978-0-375-84687-8; 0-375-84687-5; 978-0-375-94687-5 lib bdg; 0-375-94687-X lib bdg
                       LC 2007-2306
    A little boy named Sam discovers the many unexpected ways in which a love of reading can come in handy, and sometimes even save the day
    This is written "in quick, quirky rhymed couplets.... Brown's gouache illustrations are cheery, and each page pours into the next through the use of subtly repeated background motifs.... This is an easy, obvious choice for events with literacy and early learning as their themes." SLJ

    Preschool to the rescue; illustrated by Will Hillenbrand. Harcourt 2001 un il $15
Grades: PreK   E
    1. Stories in rhyme 2. Mud 3. Helpfulness 4. Vehicles -- Fiction
    ISBN 0-15-202035-7
                       LC 99-6475
    When a mud puddle traps a pizza van, police car, tow truck, and other vehicles, a group of preschoolers comes along and saves the day
    "The repetition and rhyme carry the story along and the fun doesn't stop until the book is closed. The artwork is perfect." SLJ

    Sleepy little alphabet; a bedtime story from Alphabet Town. written by Judy Sierra; illustrated by Melissa Sweet. Alfred A. Knopf 2009 un il $16.99; lib bdg $19.99
Grades: PreK K 1   E
    1. Alphabet 2. Stories in rhyme 3. Children's poetry 4. Bedtime -- Fiction 5. Alphabet -- Juvenile literature
    ISBN 978-0-375-84002-9; 0-375-84002-8; 978-0-375-94002-6 lib bdg; 0-375-94002-2 lib bdg
                       LC 2008-24526
    Sleepy letters of the alphabet get ready for bed
    "The bounce of Sierra's meter, the time-for-bed theme and Sweet's offhand pencil and watercolor drawings make the story feel fresh. Throughout, Sierra inserts vocabulary items that incorporate the letters . . . while Sweet provides the laughs." Pub Wkly

    Tell the truth, B.B. Wolf; written by Judy Sierra; illustrated by J. Otto Seibold. Alfred A. Knopf 2010 un il $16.99; lib bdg $19.99
Grades: PreK K 1 2 3   E
    1. Wolves -- Fiction 2. Honesty -- Fiction
    ISBN 978-0-375-85620-4; 0-375-85620-X; 978-0-375-95620-1 lib bdg; 0-375-95620-4 lib bdg
                       LC 2009030778
    When Big Bad Wolf, who now lives at the Villain Villa Retirement Residence, is invited to tell his story at the library, he faces the truth about what he did to the three little pigs and decides to make amends.
    "This brilliant retelling deserves a place at the head of the fractured-fairy-tale pack. . . . Seibold's vivid computer illustrations, replete with comic touches, are a perfect match for Sierra's zany tale." SLJ
    Another title about B. B. Wolf is:
    Mind your manners, B. B. Wolf (2007)

    ★ **Thelonius** Monster's sky-high fly pie; illustrations by Edward Koren. Knopf 2006 un il $16.95; lib bdg $18.99
Grades: K 1 2 3   E
    1. Stories in rhyme 2. Pies -- Fiction 3. Flies -- Fiction 4. Monsters -- Fiction
    ISBN 0-375-83218-1; 0-375-93218-6 lib bdg
                       LC 2005-16773
    A good-natured monster thinks a pie made out of flies would be a good dessert, and invites all his friends and relatives over to try it.
    "An incomparable rhymester has teamed up with a master cartoonist to conjure up some haute cuisine on the fly.... The words are carefully chosen.... A lovable and entertaining work of art." SLJ

    We love our school! illustrated by Linda Davick. Alfred A. Knopf 2011 il $7.99; lib bdg $10.99
Grades: PreK K   E
    1. Riddles 2. School stories 3. Stories in rhyme 4. Animals -- Fiction
    ISBN 978-0-375-86728-6; 0-375-86728-7; 978-0-375-96728-3 lib bdg; 0-375-96728-1 lib bdg
    Rhyming text with rebuses follows a group of animals through their first day of school.
    "This is a simple but thoroughly charming little gem of a book. . . . For one thing, Sierra has told the tale in effortless rhyme. For another, the rebus format makes it a perfect lapsit choice with a parent or caregiver reading the words and a child 'reading' the easily decipherable pictures. The illustrations have a flat quality and appear to be digitally done, but they are bright and cheerful and should have considerable appeal for the new-to-school set." SLJ

    ★ **Wild** about books; by Judy Sierra; pictures by Marc Brown. Knopf 2004 un il $16.95
Grades: PreK K 1 2   E
    1. Stories in rhyme 2. Animals -- Fiction 3. Libraries -- Fiction 4. Books and reading -- Fiction
    ISBN 0-375-82538-X
    A librarian named Mavis McGrew introduces the animals in the zoo to the joy of reading when she drives her bookmobile to the zoo by mistake.

"Sierra's text has a wacky verve and enough clever asides and allusions to familiar characters to satisfy bibliophiles of all ages. . . . Brown's cheerful, full-color illustrations stretch his trademark art with ever-so-slightly stylized spreads that are rich in pattern, texture, and nuance." SLJ

Wild about you! Judy Sierra; pictures by Marc Brown. Alfred A. Knopf 2012 40 p. (library binding) $20.99
Grades: PreK K 1   E
1. Zoos -- Fiction 2. Picture books for children 3. Animal babies -- Juvenile fiction 4. Stories in rhyme 5. Zoo animals -- Fiction
ISBN 0375971076; 9780307931788; 9780375971075
LC 2011029010
This children's picture book looks at zoo animals. All the animals are "having babies, all except the tree kangaroo and the pandas. Even though some parents say that the babies are bothersome, none of them will give theirs up to the childless ones. When a van from Animal Rescue delivers an endangered egg, all of the birds refuse it, but the tree kangaroo offers her pouch." A baby penguin hatches, and all the animals pitch in to help the kangaroo feed it. (School Library Journal)

★ **ZooZical**; pictures by Marc Brown. Alfred A. Knopf 2011 un il $17.99; lib bdg $20.99
Grades: PreK K 1   E
1. Stories in rhyme 2. Zoos -- Fiction 3. Animals -- Fiction 4. Theater -- Fiction
ISBN 978-0-375-86847-4; 0-375-86847-X; 978-0-375-96847-1 lib bdg; 0-375-96847-4 lib bdg
LC 2010038565
When the winter doldrums arrive at the zoo, a very small hippo and a young kangaroo decide to stage a "ZooZical," a show to display their singing, dancing, acrobatic, and other talents to the people of Springfield.

"With humor and gusto, Brown's richly textured folk art-inspired pictures convey the characters' dramatic shift in moods and imbue them with abundant personality. Meanwhile, Sierra's riffs on familiar tunes guarantee that readings will be very musical affairs, with children enthusiastic participants." Publ Wkly

Silsbe, Brenda
The **bears** we know; [text by] Brenda Silsbe; [art by] Vlasta van Kampen. Annick Press 2009 un il $19.95; pa $7.95
Grades: PreK K 1 2   E
1. Bears -- Fiction
ISBN 978-1-55451-167-9; 1-55451-167-4; 978-1-55451-166-2 pa; 1-55451-166-6 pa
Nobody has seen the bears, but everybody knows where they live that their house is a mess, they eat bagfuls of chips, jump on the furniture, decorate with sawdust, and sing songs that make them cry.

"The warm, funny watercolors are a great match for the goofy creatures and their various antics. Their great brown bodies sprawl across the page (and the couches), and the simple text is clearly printed on a field of white." SLJ

Silverman, Erica
★ **Cowgirl** Kate and Cocoa; written by Erica Silverman; painted by Betsy Lewin. Harcourt 2005 un il $15

Grades: K 1 2   E
1. Horses -- Fiction 2. Cowhands -- Fiction
ISBN 0-15-202124-8
LC 2004-5739
Cowgirl Kate and her cowhorse Cocoa, who is always hungry, count cows, share a story, and help each other fall asleep.

"Children will . . . . recognize the friends' good-natured banter and lively dialogue. . . . Lewin's bold-lined illustrations extend the comedy and the affectionate friendship." Booklist
Other titles about Kate and Cocoa are:
Cowgirl Kate and Cocoa: partners (2006)
Cowgirl Kate and Cocoa: school days (2007)
Cowgirl Kate and Cocoa: rain or shine (2008)
Cowgirl Kate and Cocoa: horse in the house (2009)
Cowgirl Kate and Cocoa: spring babies (2010)

The **Hanukkah** hop; written by Erica Silverman; illustrated by Steven D'Amico. Simon & Schuster 2011 un il $12.99
Grades: PreK K 1   E
1. Hanukkah stories 2. Parties -- Fiction 3. Hanukkah -- Fiction 4. Jews -- United States -- Fiction
ISBN 978-1-4424-0604-9
Rhymed text and illustrations follow a family's activities as they prepare to celebrate Hanukkah.

"Like the enthusiastic revelers, Silverman's gleeful text has rhythm. D'Amico's angular illustrations, with their circa-1950s flair, keep up the pace. . . . Readers' toes are sure to be tapping throughout this unabashedly joyful Hanukkah romp." Horn Book

Silverstein, Shel
Who wants a cheap rhinoceros? Simon & Schuster 2009 un il $9.99
Grades: K 1 2 3   E
1. Rhinoceros -- Fiction
ISBN 978-1-4169-9613-2; 1-4169-9613-3
A revised and expanded edition of the title first published 1964
"Silverstein's economical black-line drawings illustrate the joys of owning a rhinoceros. . . . The deadpan text belies the goofiness of the pictures, with the rhinoceros jumping rope, playing pirates, and opening a soda can with his horn." Horn Book Guide

Siminovich, Lorena
★ **Alex** and Lulu: two of a kind. Templar Books 2009 un il $14.99
Grades: PreK K 1   E
1. Cats -- Fiction 2. Dogs -- Fiction 3. Friendship -- Fiction
ISBN 978-0-7636-4423-9; 0-7636-4423-4
"Alex, a white dog with a large black spot over one eye, is best friends with a white cat with black markings. One day, Lulu gets her pal thinking about the ways in which they are different. . . . He worries that their relationship is in jeopardy. To reassure him, Lulu offers several examples of true opposites . . . and reminds Alex that they share many interests in common. . . . Siminovich's spare scenes offer patterned backgrounds and an occasional charming detail.

... With their retro feel and lack of fuss, the artwork is delectable." SLJ

I like vegetables; a touch-and-feel board book. Templar Books 2011 un il (Petit collage) bd bk $6.99
Grades: PreK   E
1. Opposites 2. Vegetables 3. Board books for children
ISBN 978-0-7636-5283-8; 0-7636-5283-0
LC 2010039166
"Delightfully drawn with collage elements, including fabric places to pat, this sturdy book makes carrots, peas, corn, and pumpkins tantalizing. Comparisons are made by showing growth under- and aboveground or how a pumpkin can be big or little. . . . This board book is so attractive and useful that adults will enjoy sharing it with little ones." Booklist

Simmons, Jane
Together; [by] Jane Simmons. Alfred A. Knopf 2007 un il $15.95; lib bdg $18.99
Grades: PreK K 1   E
1. Dogs -- Fiction 2. Friendship -- Fiction
ISBN 978-0-375-84339-6; 978-0-375-94339-3 lib bdg
LC 2006022734
Two dogs, Mousse and Nut, learn that even though they may like different things, they can still be best friends
"Fat, rusty-colored Mousse and tiny Nut are utterly charming as they frolic across the well-designed pages. This is a book that is not only artistically pleasing but also offers something to talk about." Booklist

Simms, Laura
Rotten teeth; illustrated by David Catrow. Houghton Mifflin 1998 un il $16
Grades: K 1 2 3   E
1. School stories 2. Teeth -- Fiction 3. Schools -- Fiction 4. Show-and-tell presentations -- Fiction
ISBN 0-395-82850-3
LC 97-2528
When Melissa takes a big glass bottle of authentic pulled teeth from her father's dental office for a show-and-tell presentation, she becomes a first-grade celebrity
"Catrow's watercolors are a suitably twisted complement to Simms' somewhat warped sense of humor (actually, it's perfect for this audience)." Bull Cent Child Books

Simon, Norma
All kinds of friends; by Norma Simon; illustrated by Cherie Zamazing. Albert Whitman 2013 32 p. (hardcover) $16.99
Grades: PreK K 1 2   E
1. Friendship -- Juvenile literature
ISBN 9780807502839
LC 2012017376
"Simon . . . . offers an unassuming exploration of friendship. The text conveys information in a straightforward, simple way. . . . The illustrations also make the point that friendships can thrive across gender, age and ethnic boundaries, and children are sure to recognize themselves and others they know in the diverse array of characters that populate the pages." Kirkus

Simont, Marc
★ The **stray** dog; retold and illustrated by Marc Simont from a true story by Reiko Sassa. HarperCollins Pubs. 2001 un il $16.99; lib bdg $18.89
Grades: PreK K 1 2   E
1. Dogs
ISBN 0-06-028933-3; 0-06-028934-1 lib bdg
A Caldecott Medal honor book, 2002
"Simont's art and narrative play off each other strategically, together imparting the tale's humor and tenderness." Publ Wkly

Simpson, Lesley
Yuvi's candy tree; illustrated by Janice Lee Porter. KarBen Pub. 2011 un il lib bdg $17.95; pa $7.95
Grades: K 1 2 3   E
1. Trees -- Fiction 2. Jewish refugees -- Fiction 3. Jews -- Ethiopia -- Fiction
ISBN 978-0-7613-5651-6; 0-7613-5651-7; 978-0-7613-5652-3 pa; 0-7613-5652-5 pa
LC 2010003880
Fleeing famine in her native Ethiopia, five-year-old Yuvi is sure she will have a candy tree when she arrives in Jerusalem.
"Flowing illustrations in browns, blues, and oranges bring this story, based on one woman's experience with Operation Moses, to life." Horn Book Guide

Singer, Marilyn, 1948-
I'm your bus; pictures by Evan Polenghi. Scholastic Press 2009 un il $16.99
Grades: PreK   E
1. Buses -- Fiction
ISBN 978-0-545-08918-0; 0-545-08918-2
LC 2008017870
In rhyming text, a school bus describes its busy day transporting children to and from school.
"The digitally rendered pictures, composed of bold black outlines and bright colors, create a wholly endearing character. . . . Both energetic and reassuring." Booklist

Shoe bop! by Marilyn Singer; illustrated by Hiroe Nakata. Dutton Children's Books 2008 32p il $15.99
Grades: PreK K 1 2   E
1. Stories in rhyme 2. Shoes -- Fiction 3. Shopping -- Fiction
ISBN 978-0-525-47939-0; 0-525-47939-2
LC 2007028296
When her favorite purple tennis shoes fall apart, an almost-second-grader visits a shoe store, where she tries on footwear of all colors and styles before finding the pair that is right for her
Singer and Nakata "extol the joys of shoe shopping in a compendium of rhymed verses accompanied by a dizzying display of possibilities . . . in the watercolor spot illustrations. . . . The busy pages have the breathless feel of a shopping spree." Publ Wkly

Tallulah's tutu; illustrated by Alexandra Boiger. Clarion Books 2011 un il $16.99
Grades: PreK K 1 2   E
1. Ballet -- Fiction ISBN 978-0-547-17353-5; 0-547-17353-9
LC 2010-05441

Tallulah takes ballet lessons and eagerly awaits her coveted tutu, which, she learns, she must work hard to earn.

"Even children who don't share Tallulah's ballet dreams may long for such an idyllic world. . . . Boiger's expressive paintings emphasize Tallulah's enthusiasm, grace, and large-eyed innocence." Booklist

What is your dog doing? illustrated by Kathleen Habbley. Atheneum Books for Young Readers 2011 il $12.99
Grades: PreK K 1   E
1. Stories in rhyme 2. Dogs -- Fiction
ISBN 978-1-4169-7931-9; 1-4169-7931-X
LC 2010016351

Illustrations and simple, rhyming text reveal that dogs do much more than sit, stay, and roll over.

"This fun look at canine activities will be a hit with dog people, cat people, and all people at storytime or anytime." SLJ

Siomades, Lorianne
Katy did it! Boyds Mills Press 2009 un il $16.95
Grades: PreK K 1   E
1. Katydids -- Fiction
ISBN 978-1-59078-602-4; 1-59078-602-5
LC 2008028133

A katydid named Katy, who upsets other insects as she bounces through the garden, saves the day for a colony of ants

"Digitally created jewel-tone illustrations are airy and uncluttered against a pure white background. . . . Sound effects . . . mimic Katy's hops, ever advancing the story, and the insect's simplified face with round, googly eyes is especially expressive. This bright, bouncy story will be a favorite with youngsters." SLJ

Sis, Peter, 1949-
★ **Ballerina!** Greenwillow Bks. 2001 un il $14.95; bd bk $7.99
Grades: PreK K 1   E
1. Color 2. Imagination 3. Ballet dancing 4. Ballet -- Fiction
ISBN 0-688-17944-4; 0-06-075966-6 bd bk
LC 00-35401

A little girl puts on costumes of different colors and imagines herself dancing on stage

Sis "creates a beautifully realized spot-on view of creative kids at play." Booklist

★ **Dinosaur!** Greenwillow Bks. 2000 un il $15.99; bd bk $7.99
Grades: PreK K 1   E
1. Baths 2. Dinosaurs 3. Imagination 4. Stories without words
ISBN 0-688-17049-8; 0-06-075967-4 bd bk
LC 99-32923

While taking a bath, a young boy is joined by all sorts of dinosaurs

"A wordless picture book that takes readers on a wild adventure of the imagination. . . . This imaginative story with wonderful end-papers naming the creatures should appeal to all young dinosaur lovers. Sis's barely fleshed-out, cookie-cutter cartoons tell the story." SLJ

★ **Fire** truck. Greenwillow Bks. 1998 un il $15.99; bd bk $6.99
Grades: PreK K 1   E
1. Fire engines -- Fiction 2. Fire engines -- Pictorial works -- Juvenile fiction
ISBN 0-688-15878-1; 0-06-056259-5 bd bk
LC 97-29320

Matt, who loves fire trucks, wakes up one morning to find that he has become a fire truck, with one driver, two ladders, three hoses, and ten boots. Features a gate-fold illustration that opens into a three-page spread

"Sis blends simple text with bold pictures to give insight into one boy's vivid imagination." SLJ

Komodo! Greenwillow Bks. 1993 un il $17.99
Grades: K 1 2 3   E
1. Komodo dragon -- Fiction
ISBN 0-688-11583-7; 0-688-11584-5 lib bdg
LC 92-25811

"Mad about dragons, the boy who narrates this picture book is pleased when his doting parents decide to take him to Indonesia, home of the Komodo dragon (aka monitor lizard). When the family disembarks on the Island of Komodo, the parents join a throng of tourists waiting for the Dragon Show, but the shy lizard never ventures out of its leafy shelter. Their adventuresome son, however, takes the road less traveled through the jungle, where he encounters the dragon of his dreams." (Booklist) "Ages five to eight." (Bull Cent Child Books)

"The story, assisted by the art in its moodily surreal tone, is simply written buy implies worlds." Bull Cent Child Books

Madlenka. Farrar, Straus & Giroux 2000 un il $17
Grades: PreK K 1 2 3   E
1. Geography 2. Teeth -- Fiction
ISBN 0-374-39969-7
LC 99-57730

Madlenka, whose New York City neighbors include the French baker, the Indian news vendor, the Italian ice-cream man, the South American grocer, and the Chinese shopkeeper, goes around the block to show her friends her loose tooth and finds that it is like taking a trip around the world

"The real magic comes in the cleverly cut-away windows in each storefront through which children glimpse complex, global dreamscapes. Madlenka journeys through these mystical places, too, and it is these surreal, wordless stories-within-the-story that will excite a wide range of children, launching them in their own imagined departures." Booklist

Other titles about Madlenka are:
Madlenka's dog (2002)
Madlenka, soccer star (2010)

★ **Trucks,** trucks, trucks. Greenwillow Bks. 1999 un il $16.99; bd bk $7.99
Grades: PreK K   E
1. Trucks -- Fiction 2. Trucks -- Pictorial works -- Juvenile fiction
ISBN 0-688-16276-2; 0-06-056258-7 bd bk
LC 98-4482

A little boy cleans up his room using a variety of trucks and gives a one word description of their work such as hauling, plowing, and loading. Features a gate-fold illustration that opens into a three-page spread

"Sis creates a simple, bold look. . . . Gouache paints in yellow, black, and gray are set off by plenty of white space. The single verbs on each page are rendered in shades of blue, purple, green, and orange. This cheery romp is perfect for toddlers." SLJ

Sit, Danny

Tucker; little dog lost and found. Sterling 2011 un il $9.95

Grades: PreK K   E

1. Dogs -- Fiction 2. Beaches -- Fiction 3. Lost and found possessions -- Fiction

ISBN 978-1-4027-5999-4; 1-4027-5999-1

LC 2010031378

Tucker the Jack Russell terrier packs his bags and takes the train to the beach for an adventure, but after a fun day he discovers that he does not know how to get home.

"A strong narrative voice, charming photographs and an utterly appealing little dog protagonist coalesce to create a winning story about a Jack Russell terrier named Tucker. . . . Each page contains only a few sentences, making this a good choice for younger preschoolers and a possible selection for newly independent readers as well. Tucker's charming personality and the quality of the photographic illustrations help this stand out from the pack." Kirkus

Skeers, Linda

Tutus aren't my style; pictures by Anne Wilsdorf. Dial Books for Young Readers 2010 un il $16.99

Grades: K 1 2   E

1. Ballet -- Fiction

ISBN 978-0-8037-3212-4; 0-8037-3212-0

LC 2009009284

When she receives a ballerina costume from her uncle, Emma, who does not know how to be a ballerina, gets a lot of advice from friends and family.

"The simple but expressive illustrations are perfect for the story. The artwork, done in watercolor with images outlined in black ink, is very funny." SLJ

Sklansky, Amy E.

The duck who played the kazoo; illustrated by Tiphanie Beeke. Clarion Books 2008 un il $16.99

Grades: PreK K 1   E

1. Stories in rhyme 2. Ducks -- Fiction 3. Musicians -- Fiction 4. Friendship -- Fiction

ISBN 978-0-618-42854-0; 0-618-42854-2

LC 2006-29204

After a hurricane blows through and with only his kazoo for company, a lonely duck searches for friends but soon realizes there is no place like home.

"Told in rhyming couplets, the simple story is graced with sweet watercolor and mixed-media art. . . . The illustrations add a humorous touch. . . . This is a tender and charming tale of looking for and finding friendship." SLJ

Skofield, James

Detective Dinosaur undercover; illustrated by R. W. Alley. HarperCollins 2010 36p il (I can read) $16.99

Grades: K 1 2   E

1. Mystery fiction 2. Dinosaurs -- Fiction

ISBN 978-0-06-623878-4; 0-06-623878-1

In three brief mysteries, Detective Dinosaur learns about doing undercover work, gets chased by strange blobs, and finds rain on a sunny day.

"The dino's genial expressions projected in colorful pen-and-ink and watercolor cartoons follow the action. Conversation and onomatopoeia spice up the text, presented in large font. . . . His innocent confusion creates entertaining problems with simple solutions." SLJ

Other titles in this series are:

Detective Dinosaur (1996)

Detective Dinosaur: lost and found (1998)

Slack, Michael H.

Monkey Truck; [by] Michael Slack. Henry Holt & Co. 2011 un il $12.99

Grades: PreK K 1   E

1. Stories in rhyme 2. Trucks -- Fiction 3. Jungles -- Fiction 4. Monkeys -- Fiction

ISBN 978-0-8050-8878-6; 0-8050-8878-4

LC 2010011687

Monkey Truck comes racing to the rescue anytime there is trouble in the jungle.

"Slack produces a zippy jungle jaunt with enough action and rhythm for any preschooler in his first solo effort. The bright, blocky and, above all, goofy digitally painted illustrations will grab attention, and Monkey Truck's hooting mug (and tooting bottom) will keep the giggles flowing." Kirkus

Slate, Jenny

Marcel the Shell with shoes on; things about me. by Jenny Slate & Dean Fleischer-Camp; paintings by Amy Lind. Razorbill 2011 un il $18.99

Grades: K 1 2   E

1. Fantasy fiction 2. Shells -- Fiction

ISBN 978-1-59514-455-3; 1-59514-455-2

"Like the popular Internet video it's based on, this picture book stars a pink-shod, one-eyed snail shell who is happy to discuss his habits, preferences, and inner life, while revealing a life that's both miniature and writ large. . . . The artwork trades the jerky animation of the original for Lind's thick, luminous oil paintings, which provide a fittingly off-kilter realism." Publ Wkly

Slate, Joseph

★ I want to be free; illustrated by E. B. Lewis. G.P. Putnam's Sons 2009 un il $16.99

Grades: 2 3 4   E

1. Stories in rhyme 2. Slavery -- Fiction 3. African Americans -- Fiction

ISBN 978-0-399-24342-4; 0-399-24342-9

LC 2007-38356

Based on a sacred Buddhist tale as related in Rudyard Kipling's novel "Kim," tells of an escaped slave who rescues an abandoned baby from slave hunters.

"The spare words and pictures never sensationalize the drama or the universal themes of cruelty, courage, and kindness." Booklist

Miss Bindergarten celebrates the 100th day of kindergarten; illustrated by Ashley Wolff. Dutton Children's Bks. 1998 un il $16.99; pa $6.99

Grades: PreK K 1   E

  1. Stories in rhyme 2. Animals -- Fiction 3. Kindergarten -- Fiction 4. Hundred (The number) -- Fiction

  ISBN 0-525-46000-4; 0-14-250005-4 pa

LC 98-10486

To celebrate one hundred days in Miss Bindergarten's kindergarten class, all her students bring one hundred of something to school, including a one hundred-year-old relative, one hundred candy hearts, and one hundred polka dots

  "Wolff's sturdy, genially observed illustrations prove a perfect match for Slate's rhyming text." Publ Wkly

  Other titles about Miss Bindergarten are:

  Miss Bindergarten celebrates the last day of kindergarten (2006)

  Miss Bindergarten gets ready for kindergarten (1996)

  Miss Bindergarten has a wild day in kindergarten (2005)

  Miss Bindergarten stays home from kindergarten (2000)

  Miss Bindergarten takes a field trip with kindergarten (2001)

  Miss Bindergarten's craft center (1999)

Slater, Dashka

  Baby shoes; by Dashka Slater; pictures by Hiroe Nakata. Bloomsbury Children's Books 2006 un il $15.95

Grades: PreK   E

  1. Stories in rhyme 2. Color -- Fiction 3. Shoes -- Fiction

  ISBN 978-1-58234-684-7; 1-58234-684-4

LC 2005053581

After taking a walk with his mother, Baby's new white shoes with the blue stripe are covered with a variety of colors

  "In the text, loping lines of rhymed couplets are interspersed with staccato sections, followed by a refrain that reins in the pace. . . . The changing rhythm creates a pleasing pattern and gives listeners places to chime in. Setting a sunny tone for the excursion, Nakata's airy watercolor artwork sympathetically depicts an increasingly scruffy toddler and his tired but resilient mother." Booklist

  The **sea** serpent and me; by Dashka Slater; illustrated by Catia Chien. Houghton Mifflin Company 2008 un il $17

Grades: PreK K 1 2   E

  1. Growth -- Fiction 2. Sea monsters -- Fiction

  ISBN 978-0-618-72394-2; 0-618-72394-3

LC 2007015577

One day a small sea serpent falls from the faucet into the tub as a child is about to take a bath, and as the days go by and the serpent grows, they both realize that he needs to go back to the sea where he belongs.

  "The lovely watercolor illustrations are lush with vivid blues and greens, and the bathtub and underwater scenes are full of movement and life. . . . The text flows well and highlights the strong bond between the child and the serpent." SLJ

Slater, Kate

  Magpie's treasure. Andersen 2011 un il $16.99

Grades: PreK K   E

  1. Birds -- Fiction 2. Thieves -- Fiction

  ISBN 978-1-84939-008-8; 1-84939-008-8

  "Magnus Magpie, a bird with an eye for burglary, steals the shiniest, most dazzling things and stashes them secretly. . . . What he wants most of all, though, is the shining moon.

. . . With a sweet final twist, he find that home and a family of his own are what he wants most. . . . The energetic text is well paced for read-alouds, and kids will enjoy picking out the objects in Slater's vibrant, mixed-media collage illustrations." Booklist

Slater, Teddy

  Smooch your pooch; illustrations by Arthur Howard. Scholastic Inc. 2010 un il $14.99

Grades: PreK K   E

  1. Stories in rhyme 2. Dogs -- Fiction

  ISBN 978-0-545-16736-9; 0-545-16736-1

  "A winning cast of fun-loving children cavorts with an assortment of equally engaging dogs in this rhyming tale. Describing how to show love to a favorite four-legged friend, the short, punchy lines beg to be read aloud, engaging listeners and moving the action right along. . . . The cartoon illustrations, rendered in black line and watercolors, pair perfectly with the text in their movement and energy and are sure to prompt many giggles." SLJ

Slegers, Liesbet

  Bathing. Clavis 2011 un il bd bk $5.95

Grades: PreK   E

  1. Board books for children 2. Baths -- Fiction

  ISBN 978-1-60537-092-7; 1-60537-092-4

  "A smiling toddler makes bath time seem easy and fun in this warm board book. . . . He uses his orange washcloth, happily lets his mother shampoo his hair, and sails his red boat in the bathwater, finishing up with a cuddly towel. Slegers's characteristically bright, smudgy paintings convey a common experience with a light, appealing touch." Publ Wkly

  Katie goes to the doctor. Clavis Pub. 2011 un il $12.95

Grades: PreK   E

  1. Sick -- Fiction 2. Physicians -- Fiction

  ISBN 978-1-60537-076-7; 1-60537-076-2

Katie doesn't feel well—she has a cough, a runny nose, and she feels dizzy. Her mother explains that she has a fever and takes Katie to see the doctor.

  This "presents a common childhood experience through a friendly narrator who explains step-by-step what is happening. [It] will guide parents through a discussion of what to expect as they prepare and reassure their children. Large, colorful illustrations support the [text]." SLJ

  Kevin goes to the library. Clavis 2011 un il $12.95

Grades: PreK   E

  1. Libraries -- Fiction 2. Books and reading -- Fiction

  ISBN 978-1-60537-075-0; 1-60537-075-4

Explores the cyclical nature of borrowing library books and emphasizes the many joys of reading as Kevin, a young boy, describes his experiences at the library

  "Toddlers should be drawn to this straightforward depiction of a common experience." Publ Wkly

Sloat, Teri

  Berry magic; written by Teri Sloat and Betty Huffmon; illustrated by Teri Sloat. Alaska Northwest Books 2004 un il hardcover o.p. $15.95

Grades: K 1 2 3   E

1. Inuit -- Fiction 2. Berries -- Fiction

ISBN 0-88240-575-6; 0-88240-576-4 pa

LC 2003-70851

Long ago, the only berries on the tundra were hard, tasteless, little crowberries. When Anana sings, she turns four dolls into little girls who run and tumble over the tundra creating patches of fat, juicy berries: blueberries, cranberries, salmonberries, and raspberries

"Done in a palette of deep, earthy hues, ethereal blues, and bright highlights, Sloat's pictures are vibrant and engaging. . . . The rich language enlightens readers to different elements of the Eskimo culture." SLJ

I'm a duck! story and pictures by Teri Sloat. G.P. Putnam's Sons 2006 un il hardcover o.p. pa $6.99

Grades: PreK K 1 2   E

1. Stories in rhyme 2. Ducks -- Fiction

ISBN 0-399-24274-0; 0-14-241062-4 pa

LC 2004-20479

"From the moment he hatches, a duckling celebrates his duck-ness–his webbed feet, his perfect waddle, his strong quack, and his flapping wings. As he grows, he meets a mate, becomes a father, and continues his zestful take on life. Sloat's rhymed text captures the exuberance of this eternal optimist and gives a glimpse into the life cycle of a mallard. The full-color art is rendered in pastels and has bold lines and a variety of perspectives and page layouts." SLJ

There was an old man who painted the sky; illustrated by Stefano Vitale. Henry Holt 2009 32p il $16.95

Grades: PreK K 1 2   E

1. Songs 2. Prehistoric art -- Fiction 3. Cave drawings and paintings -- Fiction

ISBN 978-0-8050-6751-4; 0-8050-6751-5

LC 2008-18340

In this song based on 'The Old Woman Who Swallowed a Fly,' a prehistoric man, contemplating the creation of the world, paints images on the ceiling of a cave, that are later discovered by a young Spanish girl in 1879

"Vitale's vibrant illustrations, in mixed media on board, reference both cave drawings and folk art. Appropriate for a wide audience, this will find its ideal fit with families wishing to impart diverse beliefs about the Earth's beginnings to their children." Booklist

Slobodkina, Esphyr

★ **Caps** for sale; a tale of a peddler, some monkeys & their monkey business. told and illustrated by Esphyr Slobodkina. Addison Wesley Longman 1947 un il $17.99; pa $6.99

Grades: PreK K   E

1. Monkeys -- Fiction 2. Peddlers and peddling -- Fiction

ISBN 0-201-09147-X; 0-06-443143-6 pa

A picture book story which "provides hilarious confusion. A cap peddler takes a nap under a tree. When he wakes up, his caps have disappeared. He looks up in the tree and sees countless monkeys, each wearing a cap and grinning." Parent's Guide To Child Read

Small, David

Imogene's antlers; written and illustrated by David Small. Crown 2000 un il $16.99; pa $6.99

Grades: PreK K 1 2   E

1. Metamorphosis -- Juvenile fiction 2. Humorous fiction

ISBN 978-0-375-81048-0; 0-375-81048-X; 978-0-517-56242-0 pa; 0-517-56242-1 pa

First published 1985

One Thursday Imogene wakes up with a pair of antlers growing out of her head and causes a sensation wherever she goes

The author "maximizes the inherent humor of the absurd situation by allowing the imaginative possibilities of Imogene's predicament to run rampant. The brief text is supported by Small's expansive watercolors. They brim with humorous details." SLJ

Smallcomb, Pam

Earth to Clunk; pictures by Joe Berger. Dial Books for Young Readers 2011 un il $16.99

Grades: PreK K 1   E

1. Siblings -- Fiction 2. Extraterrestrial beings -- Fiction

ISBN 978-0-8037-3439-5; 0-8037-3439-5

LC 2010-20621

For a school assignment, a boy reluctantly writes a letter to Clunk of the planet Quazar, sending his older sister with it, but as more letters and packages are exchanged, he realizes that having an alien pen pal can be fun.

"The boy narrates in pitch-perfect deadpan style; the comedy lurks just below the surface, and the spare details leave boundless room for listeners' imaginations. . . . Berger's illustrations, composed in pencil, pen, and ink and colored digitally, are candy toned, with copious use of yellow, chartreuse, aqua, and bright orange." Bull Cent Child Books

★ **I'm** not; not drawn by Pam Smallcomb; not written by Robert Weinstock. Schwartz & Wade Books 2010 un il $15.99; lib bdg $18.99

Grades: PreK K 1   E

1. Friendship -- Fiction

ISBN 0-375-86115-7; 0-375-96115-1 lib bdg; 978-0-375-86115-4; 978-0-375-96115-1 lib bdg

LC 2009-46742

Our shy narrator lists all the things that her best friend, Evelyn, is good at—from jumping on the bed to roller skating really fast. Luckily, Evelyn points out what makes her so special: she's a one-of-a-kind true blue best friend.

"Weinstock captures the friends as rotund, squat reptiles who suggest trash-compacted dragons, and the scenes are confidently laced with absurdity. . . . This offers a nice reminder that good friendships always offer mutual benefits." Bull Cent Child Books

Smee, Nicola

Clip-clop. Boxer Books 2006 un il $12.95; bd bk $6.95

Grades: PreK K   E

1. Animals -- Fiction

ISBN 978-1-905417-09-4; 1-905417-09-8; 978-1-905417-60-5 bd bk; 1-905417-60-8 bd bk

When Mr. Horse gives a ride to his friends, Cat, Dog, Pig, and Duck, they urge him to go faster and faster

"With its simplicity of plot and design, lovable characters, repetitive sound effects, and captivating color illustrations, this laugh-out-loud picture book is first-rate." SLJ

Another title about Mr. Horse and his friends is

Jingle-jingle (2008)

What's the matter, Bunny Blue? Boxer Books 2010
un il $14.95
Grades: PreK   E
1. Animals -- Fiction 2. Rabbits -- Fiction 3.
Grandmothers -- Fiction
ISBN 978-1-906250-91-1; 1-906250-91-X

"A wide-eyed little blue bunny . . . calls, 'Granny! Granny! Where are you?' No sooner does he explain his dilemma
to Duck and Bee than the tears begin. A series of animals—
a tiger, alligator, bear, and fox—ask the despondent bunny
what Granny looks like. . . . All the animals join the ultimately successful search for Granny. The very real, small
details of twinkly eyes, a big smile, and soft furry arms are
just what matter to children when they experience separation anxiety. The uncluttered pages with lots of white space
and sympathetic, childlike animals are perfect for the toddler
set." Booklist

Smith, Alex T.
Foxy and Egg; a book by Alex T. Smith. Holiday
House 2011 un il $17.95
Grades: K 1 2   E
1. Eggs -- Fiction 2. Foxes -- Fiction 3. Alligators
-- Fiction
ISBN 978-0-8234-2330-9; 0-8234-2330-1
LC 2010026416
First published 2010 in the United Kingdom

"Foxy DuBois gives Egg shelter for the evening, but as
a chicken connoisseur, she plots to fatten up her guest and
make a tasty meal out of him. Her plans run afowl—sorry,
afoul—when Egg cracks open and reveals a sizable, mustachioed alligator named Alphonso hankering for a taste of
fox. Children will have fun poring over the spreads to find
silly touches like chicken wallpaper, fork and spoon finials
on the guest bed, and, in a neat little turn, the silhouettes of
a fox on Alphonso's teacup. Smith's art . . . [mixes] cartoonlike sketches with photographs of patterns and objects." SLJ

Smith, Brooke
Roger the rat is on the loose! written by Brooke Smith;
illustrated by Alli Arnold. Skyhorse Pub. 2012 83 p. (Mimi
and Maty to the rescue!) (hardcover: alk. paper) $14.95
Grades: 2 3 4   E
1. Dogs -- Juvenile fiction 2. Rats -- Juvenile fiction 3.
Animal rescue -- Juvenile fiction
ISBN 1620872528; 9781620872529
LC 2012013213

In this children's story, by Brooke Smith, illustrated by
Alli Arnold, "Mimi is an animal-loving girl and Maty is her
three-legged dog. . . . When their friend George calls and
needs to find a missing rat named Roger, Mimi and Maty
jump into action! Keeping track of all the clues in their trusty
rescue notebook, Mimi and Maty embark on an adventure
that involves their nasty friend Icky Vicky and her brother
Dicky, the Pom Pom Pie Place, and one smart dumbo rat!"
(Publisher's note)

Smith, Charles R., 1969-
Dance with me; [by] Charles R. Smith Jr.; illustrated by
Noah Z. Jones. Candlewick Press 2008 un il (Super sturdy
picture book) $8.99

Grades: PreK K 1 2   E
1. Stories in rhyme 2. Board books for children 3.
Dance -- Fiction
ISBN 978-0-7636-2246-6; 0-7636-2246-X
LC 2007-51886

Illustrations and simple, rhyming text encourage the
reader to wiggle, shake, and twirl to the beat.

"This features thick pages and large type aimed at emerging readers. The book's small trim size and abundant visual
details make it best suited for small groups of preschoolers,
who will find it hard to resist the story's encouragement to
move and groove." Booklist

Smith, Cynthia Leitich
★ **Holler** Loudly; illustrated by Barry Gott. Dutton
Children's Books 2010 un il $16.99
Grades: PreK K 1   E
1. Tall tales 2. Noise -- Fiction 3. Voice -- Fiction
ISBN 978-0-525-42256-3; 0-525-42256-0
LC 2009-53234

Unable to be quiet since he was born, Holler Loudly
only gets louder as he grows up which gets him in trouble at
school, the library, and the movie theater, but when a tornado
threatens the state fair, Holler's voice may save the day.

"This original Southwestern tall tale has an easy rhythm,
and repeated phrases and playful type make reading aloud a
pleasure. . . . A rambunctious, can't-lose read-aloud no one
will want to hush." Kirkus

Jingle dancer; illustrated by Cornelius Van Wright and
Ying-Hwa Hu. Morrow Junior Bks. 2000 un il $17.99;
lib bdg $18.89
Grades: K 1 2 3   E
1. Dance 2. Creek Indians 3. Indian dance 4. Creek
Indians -- Fiction 5. Native American dance -- Fiction
6. Creek Indians -- Juvenile fiction 7. Indians of North
America -- Oklahoma
ISBN 0-688-16241-X; 0-688-16242-8 lib bdg
LC 99-15503

Jenna, a member of the Muscogee, or Creek, Nation,
borrows jingles from the dresses of several friends and relatives so that she can perform the jingle dance at the powwow. Includes a note about the jingle dance tradition and
its regalia

"The colorful, well-executed watercolor illustrations
lend warmth to the story." Booklist

Smith, Danna
Pirate nap; a book of colors. illustrated by Valeria
Petrone. Clarion Books 2011 il $14.99
Grades: PreK K 1   E
1. Color 2. Stories in rhyme 3. Play -- Fiction 4.
Pirates -- Fiction 5. Brothers -- Fiction 6. Imagination
-- Fiction
ISBN 978-0-547-57531-5; 0-547-57531-9
LC 2010043253

Two brothers use their imaginations to turn their sur-
roundings--from a white bandana and yellow coins to a red
blanket and even their baby sister-- into a colorful pirate adventure before naptime.

"Clever rhyming text in 'pirate speak' and colorful, digital gouache illustrations in muted tones create a standout
concept book. . . . The eight basic colors are introduced in
the humorous text and in the imaginative pictures. . . . Chil-

dren will pore over the small and large details in the artwork. This title inspires creative play, and is likely to be a treasure for years to come." SLJ

Two at the zoo; illustrated by Valeria Petrone. Clarion 2009 32p il $16
Grades: PreK K   **E**
  1. Stories in rhyme 2. Zoos -- Fiction 3. Animals -- Fiction 4. Grandfathers -- Fiction
ISBN 978-0-547-04982-3; 0-547-04982-X
A grandfather and grandchild go to the zoo, where they count animals from one to ten.
"The digital gouache illustrations have vibrant colors, clean lines, and palpable texture. . . . An engaging read-aloud for storytime and one-on-one sharing." SLJ

Smith, Lane
  ★ **Abe** Lincoln's dream; written and illustrated by Lane Smith. 1st ed. Roaring Brook Press 2012 32 p. col. ill. (hardcover) $16.99
Grades: 1 2 3   **E**
  1. Ghost stories 2. United States -- Fiction 3. Ghosts -- Fiction
ISBN 1596436085; 9781596436084
        LC 2012020110
In this children's picture book by Lane Smith, "when a schoolgirl gets separated from her tour of the White House and finds herself in the Lincoln bedroom, she also discovers the ghost of the great man himself. Together they embark on a journey across the country to answer [Abraham] Lincoln's questions and quiet his concerns about the nation for which he gave his life." (Publisher's note)

The **big** elephant in the room. Hyperion Books for Children 2009 un il $16.99
Grades: K 1 2 3 4   **E**
  1. Donkeys -- Fiction 2. Communication -- Fiction
ISBN 978-1-4231-1667-7; 1-4231-1667-4
When one donkey tells his friend that they need to talk about 'the big elephant in the room,' his friend wonders what this embarrassing issue could possibly be.
"Done in muted tones, the droll artwork tells much of the story through lively layouts and funny details. With the roll of an eye or the flick of an ear, the animals convey a range of emotions. . . . Kids will get a kick out of this book (while also learning about idioms)." SLJ

★ **Grandpa** Green. Roaring Brook Press 2011 un il $16.99
Grades: K 1 2   **E**
  1. Gardens -- Fiction 2. Old age -- Fiction 3. Grandfathers -- Fiction
ISBN 978-1-59643-607-7; 1-59643-607-7
        LC 2010038729
"The idea of a garden as a lockbox of memories is not a new one, but rarely is it pulled off with this kind of panache. . . . Sketched with a finely lined fairy-tale wispiness and dominated by verdant green, the illustrations are not just creative but poignant. . . . The perfect book to help kids understand old age." Booklist

★ **It's** a book. Roaring Book Press 2010 un il $12.99
Grades: PreK K 1 2   **E**
  1. Animals -- Fiction 2. Electronic books -- Fiction 3.

Books and reading -- Fiction
ISBN 978-1-59643-606-0; 1-59643-606-9
"Smith jump-starts the action on the title page where readers meet the characters—a mouse, a jackass, and a monkey. . . . Slapstick humor ensues in an armchair face-off when one character, reared on a diet of Web 2.0 and gaming, cannot fathom what to do with a book and slings a barrage of annoying questions, 'Can you blog with it? How do you scroll down? Can you make the characters fight?' Readers know who is speaking by each animal's unique font type and color, achieving economy and elegance on each page. . . . A clever choice for readers, young and old, who love a good joke and admire the picture book's ability to embody in 32 stills the action of the cinema." SLJ

★ **John,** Paul, George & Ben. Hyperion Books for Children 2006 un il $16.99
Grades: 2 3 4   **E**
  1. Authors 2. Generals 3. Diplomats 4. Governors 5. Inventors 6. Statesmen 7. Architects 8. Presidents 9. Scientists 10. Vice-presidents 11. Artisans 12. Essayists 13. Metalworkers 14. Revolutionaries 15. Colonial leaders 16. Writers on science 17. Members of Congress
ISBN 0-7868-4893-6
        LC 2005-52735
This is a humorous look at George Washington, John Hancock, Paul Revere, Benjamin Franklin, and Thomas Jefferson. "Grades three to five." (Bull Cent Child Books)
"Describing each man in turn as either bold, noisy, honest, clever, or independent, and taking many liberties with the truth, Smith relates how the Founding Fathers of the title [John Hancock, Paul Revere, George Washington, Benjamin Franklin]—and [Thomas] Jefferson, too—played a part in securing America's freedom. . . . The pen-and-ink cartoon illustrations, richly textured with various techniques, add to the fun. . . . A true-and-false section in the back separates fact from fiction." SLJ

★ **Madam** President. Hyperion Books for Children 2008 un il lib bdg $16.99
Grades: K 1 2   **E**
  1. Sex role -- Fiction 2. Presidents -- Fiction
ISBN 1-4231-0846-9 lib bdg; 978-1-4231-0846-7 lib bdg
        LC 2008-04509
Katy imagines what her day would be like if she were President of the United States. "Ages six to ten." (Bull Cent Child Books)
This is a "sly, witty recitation of a president's responsibilities. . . . The list . . . does grow rather long. But the stretch can be forgiven because it provides more opportunity to enjoy Smith's amazing artwork. Madam President, with her boxy head and triangular body appears against a variety of backgrounds . . . with disparate uses of materials and images that often give the look of collage." Booklist

Smith, Linda
The **inside** tree; illustrated by David Parkins. HarperCollins 2010 un il $16.99; lib bdg $17.89

Grades: K 1 2 E

1. Dogs -- Fiction 2. Trees -- Fiction
ISBN 978-0-06-028241-7; 0-06-028241-X; 978-0-06-029818-0 lib bdg; 0-06-029818-9 lib bdg

LC 2005019699

When Mr. Potter decides to bring both his dog and a tree inside to share his cozy house, there are unexpected repercussions.

"Smith's text is perfectly complemented by the illustrations. . . . Parkins uses a mix of realistic details, excellent facial expressions, and varying perspectives to bring the story to life. This kindhearted tale is best read aloud with plenty of extra time for laughter and bemusement." SLJ

Smith, Maggie

Christmas with the Mousekins. Alfred A. Knopf 2010 un il $15.99; lib bdg $18.99
Grades: PreK K 1 E

1. Mice -- Fiction 2. Christmas -- Fiction 3. Family life -- Fiction 4. Christmas stories -- Juvenile literature
ISBN 978-0-375-83330-4; 0-375-83330-7; 978-0-375-93330-1 lib bdg; 0-375-93330-1 lib bdg

LC 2010003878

A mouse family tells stories, bakes cookies, makes crafts, and more as they prepare for Christmas. Includes directions for each of the crafts and recipes for cookies.

"The cheerful text and busy, colorful illustrations combine for a charmingly old-fashioned overall tone." Booklist

Snell, Gordon

The **King** of Quizzical Island; illustrated by David McKee. Candlewick Press 2009 un il
Grades: K 1 2 3 E

1. Stories in rhyme 2. Explorers -- Fiction 3. Kings and rulers -- Fiction 4. Voyages and travels -- Fiction
ISBN 0-7636-3857-9; 978-0-7636-3857-3

LC 2008-26510

When no one can answer his question about what is at the edge of the world, the King of Quizzical Island builds a boat and sets sail to find out for himself, despite the objections of his fearful people. "Ages six to nine." (Bull Cent Child Books)

"The text is a case study in clever rhyme, and the pen-and-ink and watercolor illustrations—in black-and-white except for the king—show readers that curiosity is like a light in the darkness." Horn Book Guide

Snicket, Lemony, 1970-

★ The **composer** is dead; written by Lemony Snicket; with music composed by Nathaniel Stookey and illustrations by Carson Ellis. HarperCollinsPublishers 2008 un il $17.99; lib bdg $18.89
Grades: K 1 2 3 E

1. Mystery fiction 2. Orchestra -- Fiction 3. Musical instruments -- Fiction
ISBN 978-0-06-123627-3; 0-06-123627-6; 978-0-06-123628-0 lib bdg; 0-06-123628-4 lib bdg

LC 2007-20834

An inspector seeks to solve a murder mystery at the symphony by questioning each of the musical instruments.

This offers "witty wordplay. . . . Ellis . . . brightens the heavily black stage scenes with coral, gold and sepia accents against expansive white backgrounds. . . . The accompanying CD features Snicket narrating and the San Francisco

Symphony Orchestra performing Stookey's original score." Publ Wkly

★ The **dark**; by Lemony Snicket; illustrated by Jon Klassen. Little, Brown and Co. 2013 40 p. (reinforced) $16.99
Grades: K 1 2 E

1. Fear -- Juvenile fiction 2. Picture books for children 3. Fear of the dark -- Fiction
ISBN 0316187488; 9780316187480

LC 2012026498

This children's picture book by Lemony Snicket offers a "suspenseful take on childhood fear. Laszlo, a solemn boy in blue pajamas, is scared of the dark, and it's easy to see why. He lives in a house with 'a creaky roof, smooth, cold windows, and several sets of stairs.' The floors are bare, the halls are empty, and the windows are uncurtained. And the dark in his house is not just any dark--it has a will of its own." (Publishers Weekly)

★ The **latke** who couldn't stop screaming; a Christmas story. by Lemony Snicket; illustrations by Lisa Brown. McSweeney's Books 2007 43p il $9.95
Grades: K 1 2 3 4 E

1. Hanukkah -- Fiction 2. Christmas -- Fiction
ISBN 978-1-932416-87-9

"The miraculous birth here is of a potato pancake, which . . . begins screaming the moment it gets cooked. Leaping out of the frying pan and into the great white spaces of Brown's retro-cool graphics, the latke screams even louder as it tries in vain to explain itself and its role at Hanukkah to flashing colored lights . . . and an equally Christmas-centric candy cane and tree. Embedding the satirical sting in his elegantly cadenced prose, the author . . . up-ends any number of conventions in what may be his funniest book yet." Publ Wkly

13 words; [illustrated by] Maira Kalman. HarperCollins 2010 un il
Grades: K 1 2 E

1. Vocabulary -- Fiction
ISBN 0061664650; 0061664669 lib bdg; 9780061664656; 9780061664663 lib bdg

LC 2009039671

A dog attempts to cheer up his friend, a despondent bird, in a tale that introduces a series of words from "baby" to "haberdashery."

"Snicket and Kalman are perfectly matched here, both revelers in life's delicious . . . details and things best left unexplained. . . . This charming chef-d'oeuvre sings like a mezzo-soprano." Kirkus

Snyder, Betsy E.

Sweet dreams lullaby. Random House Children's Books 2010 un il $15.99
Grades: PreK K E

1. Lullabies 2. Stories in rhyme 3. Dreams -- Fiction 4. Nature -- Fiction 5. Bedtime -- Fiction 6. Rabbits -- Fiction
ISBN 978-0-375-85852-9; 0-375-85852-0

LC 2008-52265

A young bunny goes to sleep and dreams of the soothing colors, shapes, sights, and sounds of nature.

Snyder, Laurel

Baxter, the pig who wanted to be kosher; illustrated by David Goldin. Tricycle Press 2010 un il $15.99; lib bdg $18.99

Grades: PreK K 1   E

1. Pigs -- Fiction 2. Sabbath -- Fiction 3. Jews -- United States -- Fiction

ISBN 978-1-58246-315-5; 1-58246-315-8; 978-1-58246-360-5 lib bdg; 1-58246-360-3 lib bdg

When Baxter the pig hears about the joys of Shabbat dinner he tries to become kosher so that he can participate.

"The delightfully expressive and comical pen-and-ink illustrations are digitally enhanced with photographs of storefronts, deli counters, pickle jars, and traditional Jewish foods. . . . The idea of a pig wanting to become kosher will entertain children and the adults reading to them, especially those familiar with Jewish traditions." SLJ

The **longest** night; a Passover story. Laurel Snyder; [illustrations by] Catia Chien. Schwartz & Wade Books 2013 40 p. col. ill. (hardcover) $17.99; (library) $20.99

Grades: K 1 2 3 4   E

1. Stories in rhyme 2. Picture books for children 3. Passover -- Juvenile fiction 4. Slavery -- Fiction 5. Jews -- History -- To 1200 B.C. -- Fiction

ISBN 0375869425; 037596942X; 9780375869426; 9780375969423

LC 2011011009

This children's picture book, by Laurel Snyder, illustrated by Catia Chien, offers a Passover story. "This . . . book in verse follows the actual story of the Exodus. Told through the eyes of a young slave girl, [the] author . . . and illustrator . . . skillfully and gently depict the story of Pharoah, Moses, the 10 plagues, and the parting of the Red Sea." (Publisher's note)

Soetoro-Ng, Maya

★ **Ladder** to the moon; illustrated by Yuyi Morales. Candlewick Press 2011 un il $16.99

Grades: K 1 2 3   E

1. Compassion -- Fiction 2. Grandmothers -- Fiction

ISBN 0-7636-4570-2; 978-0-7636-4570-0

LC 2010039183

Suhaila's wish to know her deceased grandmother is granted when a golden ladder appears at her window and Grandma Annie invites her on a journey to the moon, where they welcome people who are facing tragedy. Includes facts about the painting and woman who inspired the story.

This is "a lush, haunting story. . . . It's hard to imagine a more perfect illustrator for this text than Morales, whose rounded shapes, sunset colors, and softness and strength mirror the words." Booklist

Solheim, James

Born yesterday; the diary of a young journalist. illustrated by Simon James. Philomel Books 2010 un il lib bdg $15.99

Grades: PreK K   E

1. Diaries -- Fiction 2. Infants -- Fiction 3. Siblings -- Fiction

ISBN 978-0-399-25155-9 lib bdg; 0-399-25155-3 lib bdg

LC 2009006251

A baby who plans to grow up to be a writer records thoughts and events in a private journal.

"The watercolor and ink illustrations . . . faithfully follow the humorous text. . . . The book is a fresh and amusing slant on sibling adjustment." SLJ

Soltis, Sue

Nothing like a puffin; illustrated by Bob Kolar. Candlewick Press 2011 un il $15.99

Grades: PreK K 1 2   E

1. Puffins -- Fiction

ISBN 978-0-7636-3617-3; 0-7636-3617-7

LC 2010040796

A narrator sets out to prove that there is nothing like a puffin but discovers that many things, including a newspaper and a helicopter, are a little bit like one and that a penguin is very much like a puffin.

"Kolar's . . . bold, cheerful cartoons show the bird causing lighthearted havoc. . . . What's more, his restrained palette reinforces the similarities Soltis so effectively uncovers. . . . Delightful, thought-provoking fun." Publ Wkly

Soman, David

The **amazing** adventures of Bumblebee Boy; by David Soman & Jacky Davis. Dial Books for Young Readers 2011 il $16.99

Grades: PreK K 1   E

1. Play -- Fiction 2. Brothers -- Fiction 3. Imagination -- Fiction 4. Superheroes -- Fiction

ISBN 978-0-8037-3418-0; 0-8037-3418-2

LC 2011004567

As imaginary superhero Bumblebee Boy, Sam rejects his pesky little brother's help in defeating pirates, dragons, and saber-toothed lions, but when Sam comes up against some scary aliens, he discovers the advantage of having a sidekick.

"The contrast between Sam's brawny superhero exploits and the humble domestic scenes from which they derive . . . will charm readers, and so will the cute-as-a-button Owen in his blankie cape and aviator's hat with flaps." Publ Wkly

Souhami, Jessica

Foxy! written and illustrated by Jessica Souhami. Frances Lincoln Children's Books 2013 32 p. ill. (hardcover) $17.99

Grades: PreK K 1 2   E

1. Tricksters -- Folklore 2. Foxes -- Juvenile fiction 3. Picture books for children

ISBN 1847802184; 9781847802187

In this children's picture book, a trickster fox "catches a bee in the opening scene and places it in a sack." When he meets a woman with a fine rooster, he "asks the woman to watch after his sack, cautioning her not to look inside. Of course, the woman does just that, and after the rooster chases away the bee, Foxy claims the rooster as recompense. The pattern repeats, with Foxy trading up to gain a pig and then a small boy before he meets his match in a woman who turns the tables on him." (Publishers Weekly)

Spangler, Brie

Peg Leg Peke; [by] Brie Spangler. Alfred A. Knopf 2008 unp il $15.99; lib bdg $18.99

Grades: PreK K 1   E

1. Dogs -- Fiction 2. Pirates -- Fiction 3. Imagination

-- Fiction
ISBN 978-0-375-84888-9; 0-375-84888-6; 978-0-375-94888-6 lib bdg; 0-375-94888-0 lib bdg

LC 2007033241

When Peke, a pekingese puppy breaks his leg, he fantasizes that he is a pirate in search of buried treasure.

"Spangler keeps her pictures simple, with just enough details and splashes of colors to set a scene. Kids, empowered by their role as speaker, should find the drawings sweet and chummy." Publ Wkly

Spanyol, Jessica

★ **Little** neighbors on Sunnyside Street; [by] Jessica Spanyol. Candlewick Press 2007 un il $16.99
Grades: PreK K   E
1. Day -- Fiction 2. Animals -- Fiction
ISBN 978-0-7636-2986-1; 0-7636-2986-3

LC 2005053641

On Sunnyside Street "the animal and insect residents enjoy doing their own things. . . . [The] peek into their everyday activities is accompanied with boisterous word sounds [and] playful typefaces. . . . Pen-and-gouache illustrations are a melding of . . . simple shapes, flat dimension, and busy pages with plenty of preschool child appeal." SLJ

Sperring, Mark

The **sunflower** sword; illustrated by Miriam Latimer. Andersen 2011 un il $16.95
Grades: PreK K 1 2   E
1. Fairy tales 2. Dragons -- Fiction 3. Knights and knighthood -- Fiction
ISBN 0-7613-7486-8; 978-0-7613-7486-2

LC 2010032954

In a land marked by endless fighting between knights and dragons, a mother gives her eager little boy a sunflower rather than the sword he requests, and when he wields it against a real dragon, new understanding begins.

This is a "charming tale. . . . The cheerful patchwork illustrations painted in bright, springtime colors add touches of humor to the story." SLJ

Spiegelman, Art

Jack and the box; a toon book. Raw Junior 2008 32p il (Toon books) $12.95
Grades: K 1   E
1. Toys -- Fiction 2. Rabbits -- Fiction
ISBN 978-0-9799238-3-8; 0-9799238-3-2

"Spiegelman has produced a polished and fun story following a young bunny's struggle with his new jack-in-the-box, which proves to be hyperactive and rather argumentative. [This is filled] with plenty of word repetition and age-appropriate humor to keep pre- and early readers engaged and curious." Booklist

Spinelli, Eileen

Buzz; illustrated by Vincent Nguyen. Simon & Schuster Books for Young Readers 2010 un il $15.99
Grades: PreK K 1   E
1. Bees -- Fiction 2. Flight -- Fiction 3. Animals -- Fiction
ISBN 978-1-4169-4925-1; 1-4169-4925-9

LC 2008042191

After learning that a bee's body is too chunky for flight, Buzz the bumblebee defies the laws of aerodynamics to save a friend in need.

"Delightful mixed-media illustrations incorporate painted oils and Photoshop to show the pixie-faced Buzz and stage the uncluttered story line with gentle and luminous images." Booklist

Cold snap; by Eileen Spinelli; illustrated by Marjorie Priceman. Alfred A. Knopf 2012 40 p. $17.99
Grades: PreK K 1   E
1. Picture books for children 2. Winter -- Juvenile fiction 3. City and town life -- Fiction 4. Cold -- Fiction 5. Community life -- Fiction
ISBN 0375857001; 9780375857003; 9780375957000

LC 2011013290

In author Eileen Spinelli's book, "[t]he Toby Mills cold snap begins innocently enough on a Friday, with snow angels, sledding and an icicle on the nose of the statue of the town founder . . . By [next] Friday, the statue's icicle reaches the ground, along with everyone's patience. But the mayor's wife has just the solution—a warm winter surprise that brings out the best in everyone and makes them forget the cold." (Kirkus)

Do you have a cat? illustrated by Geraldo Valerio. Eerdmans Books for Young Readers 2010 un il $15.99
Grades: PreK K 1 2   E
1. Stories in rhyme 2. Cats -- Fiction 3. History -- Fiction 4. Biography -- Fiction
ISBN 978-0-8028-5351-6; 0-8028-5351-X

LC 2010001642

Simple, rhyming text introduces historical figures through the cats each owned. Includes facts about each person.

"Delightful, whimsical paintings contribute to this joyous portrait of pet ownership. The historical figures are as diverse as their feline companions. . . . Animal lovers are sure to enjoy this charming story." SLJ

Do you have a dog? illustrated by Geraldo Valerio. Eerdmans Books for Young Readers 2011 un il $16
Grades: PreK K 1 2   E
1. Stories in rhyme 2. Dogs -- Fiction
ISBN 978-0-8028-5387-5; 0-8028-5387-0

LC 2011005650

Rhyming text describes some famous historical figures, from Annie Oakley and Merriwether Lewis to Sigmund Freud and Billie Holiday, and their beloved dogs. Includes facts about the people cited in the book.

"Young readers itching for a furry friend will find only the benefits of dog ownership in Spinelli's buoyant verse and Valério's cheerful acrylics. Endpapers provide further details about the historical figures mentioned within." Publ Wkly

★ **Heat** wave; written by Eileen Spinelli; illustrated by Betsy Lewin. Harcourt 2007 un il $16
Grades: K 1 2 3   E
1. Heat -- Fiction 2. City and town life -- Fiction
ISBN 0-15-216779-X; 978-0-15-216779-0

LC 2005-18946

Abigail, Ralphie, and the other citizens of Lumberville struggle to endure a week-long heat wave in the days before air conditioning.

"While the story is simple and straightforward, the sun-drenched illustrations provide a spirited and evocative look back in time." SLJ

I know it's autumn; illustrated by Nancy Hayashi. HarperCollinsPublishers 2004 un il $15.99; lib bdg $16.89

Grades: PreK K 1 2   E

1. Autumn 2. Stories in rhyme 3. Autumn -- Fiction
ISBN 0-06-029422-1; 0-06-029423-X lib bdg

LC 2003-4099

A rhyming celebration of the sights, smells, and sounds of autumn, such as pumpkin muffins, turkey stickers on spelling papers, and piles of raked leaves

"Large enough for group sharing and as quiet and comfortable as the text, Hayashi's illustrations feature rounded lines, soft shading, and gentle colors." Booklist

Miss Fox's class goes green; illustrated by Anne Kennedy. Albert Whitman 2009 un il $16.99

Grades: K 1 2   E

1. School stories 2. Animals -- Fiction 3. Environmental protection -- Fiction
ISBN 978-0-8075-5166-0; 0-8075-5166-X

LC 2008055693

The students in Miss Fox's class lead their school in making choices to help keep the planet healthy, such as turning off lights when leaving a room, taking shorter showers, and using cloth bags instead of plastic ones

"The best part of this, besides Kennedy's exuberant watercolor pictures, is the way the kids consider their actions." Booklist

Other titles about Miss Fox's class are:
Peace Week in Miss Fox's class (2009)
Miss Fox's class earns a field trip (2010)
Miss Fox's class shapes up (2011)

Night shift daddy; illustrated by Melissa Iwai. Hyperion Bks. for Children 2000 un il $14.99

Grades: PreK K 1 2   E

1. Stories in rhyme 2. Bedtime -- Fiction 3. Fathers and daughters -- Fiction 4. Father-daughter relationship -- Fiction
ISBN 0-7868-0495-5

LC 98-52499

A father shares dinner and bedtime rituals with his daughter before going out to work the night shift

"The rhyming text manages to convey many feelings—love, loneliness, anticipation—in few words; the mood is reinforced beautifully by the rich, detailed illustrations, especially those depicting a child's room at night." Horn Book Guide

Nora's ark; written by Eileen Spinelli; illustrated by Nora Hilb. Zonderkidz 2013 32 p. (hardcover) $14.99

Grades: PreK K 1   E

1. Noah's Ark -- Juvenile fiction 2. Imagination -- Juvenile fiction
ISBN 0310720060; 9780310720065

LC 2011023551

In this children's book, by Eileen Spinelli, illustrated by Nora Hilb, "the weatherman predicted rain. So Nora built an ark. . . . Nora's passenger list includes two backyard spiders, a pair of battery-operated monkeys, and a couple of unimpressed cats. Nora also employs her little brother, some dusty wooden boxes, and a sizeable dose of contagious imagination in her distinctive re-creation of the timeless story." (Publisher's note)

Silly Tilly; by Eileen Spinelli; illustrated by David Slonim. Marshall Cavendish Children 2009 un il $16.99

Grades: PreK K 1 2   E

1. Stories in rhyme 2. Geese -- Fiction 3. Animals -- Fiction
ISBN 978-0-7614-5525-7; 0-7614-5525-6

LC 2008022880

"Tilly, a goose, bathes in apple juice, wears a pancake as a hat, and likes to tickle frogs. But her ways raise the ire of the other farm animals, who demand that she cease all silliness. . . . The acrylic, pencil, and ballpoint pen illustrations complement the rhyming text and do a nice job of conveying the animals' varying levels of frustration. Some pictures are laugh-out-loud funny." SLJ

★ **Sophie's** masterpiece; a spider's tale. illustrations by Jane Dyer. Simon & Schuster Bks. for Young Readers 2001 un il $16

Grades: PreK K 1 2   E

1. Spiders -- Fiction 2. Boardinghouses -- Fiction
ISBN 0-689-80112-2

LC 95-44063

Sophie the spider makes wondrous webs, but the residents of Beekman's Boarding House do not appreciate her until at last, old and tired, she weaves her final masterpiece

"The graceful telling glimmers with feeling and occasional humor, while the full-page watercolors and lacy spot art capture the delicate magic of Sophie's webs and enhance the tale's quiet mood." Horn Book Guide

★ **Three** pebbles and a song; pictures by S.D. Schindler. Dial Bks. for Young Readers 2003 un il $16.99

Grades: PreK K 1 2   E

1. Mice 2. Winter
ISBN 0-8037-2528-0

LC 2002-6822

As his mouse family endures a long, cold winter, Moses's contributions of a dance, a juggling act, and a little song prove more useful than he had supposed

"The plot is well developed, the text contains many descriptive words, and emergent readers will appreciate the repetitive and predictable language. Done in gouache, watercolors, inks, pastels, and chalk, Schindler's painterly artwork captures perfectly the chill of the coming winter and the warmth of a happy home." SLJ

Wanda's monster; written by Eileen Spinelli; illustrated by Nancy Hayashi. Whitman, A. 2002 un il $15.95; pa $6.95

Grades: PreK K 1 2   E

1. Monsters -- Fiction 2. Grandmothers -- Fiction
ISBN 0-8075-8656-0; 0-8075-8657-9 pa

LC 2002-1955

When Wanda fears that she has a monster in her closet, she takes her grandmother's advice and begins to look at things from the monster's point of view

"Hayashi's watercolor and colored-pencil illustrations do a great job of melding the real and the imaginary in Spinelli's story, staying true to the child's fearful fantasies and transforming them with warmth and affection." Booklist

When Papa comes home tonight; illustrated by David McPhail. Simon & Schuster Books for Young Readers 2009 un il $16.99
Grades: PreK E
1. Stories in rhyme 2. Bedtime -- Fiction 3. Father-child relationship -- Fiction
ISBN 978-1-4169-1028-2; 1-4169-1028-X
LC 2008008860
A father and child enjoy a range of activities together before bedtime.

"A sweet ode to family life, beautifully illustrated in pencil, pen-and-ink, and watercolor. . . . The rhyming phrases are gentle but not cloying." SLJ

When you are happy; illustrated by Geraldo Valério. Simon & Schuster Books for Young Readers 2006 un il $16.95
Grades: PreK K 1 E
1. Emotions -- Fiction 2. Family life -- Fiction
ISBN 0-689-86251-2
"Using a comforting refrain (When you are . . .) , each member of the young girl's family reassures her when she is cold, sick, lonely, tired, grumpy, lost, and happy. . . . Appealingly offbeat, whimsical illustrations characterize the girl's emotions." Booklist

The **best** story; [by] Eileen Spinelli; illustrations by Anne Wilsdorf. Dial Books for Young Readers 2008 un il $16.99
Grades: 1 2 3 E
1. Authorship -- Fiction
ISBN 978-0-8037-3055-7; 0-8037-3055-1
LC 2007028478
When a contest at the local library offers a prize for the best story, a girl tries to write one using her family's suggestions, but her story does not seem right until she listens to her heart.

"Lively energy and imagination permeate both the watercolor and ink illustrations and the warm text." Horn Book Guide

Spinelli, Jerry
I can be anything; illustrated by Jimmy Liao. Little, Brown 2010 un il $16.99
Grades: PreK K E
1. Stories in rhyme 2. Occupations -- Fiction
ISBN 0-316-16226-4; 978-0-316-16226-5
A little boy ponders the many possible jobs in his future, from paper-plane folder and puppy-dog holder to mixing-bowl licker and tin-can kicker.

"Aided by Liao's cleverly integrated full-bleed mixed-media illustrations, which radiate every hue of the rainbow, and dynamic typesetting with words that swoop and dive, the author's perspective on this adult-inspired question yields some refreshingly child-oriented answers. . . . An inspired take on a timeless question." Kirkus

Spinner, Stephanie
It's a miracle! a Hanukkah storybook. written by Stephanie Spinner; illustrated by Jill McElmurry. Atheneum Bks. for Young Readers 2003 un il $16.95
Grades: K 1 2 3 E
1. Hanukkah -- Fiction 2. Grandmothers -- Fiction
ISBN 0-689-84493-X
LC 2002-6137
"Owen Block, aged six and a half, has just been named O.C.L.-Official Candle Lighter. Each night, as he performs his duty, he listens to Grandma Karen's cozy stories of family life. . . . A brief retelling of the Hanukkah legend and blessings in Hebrew, English, and transliteration appear at the end of the book. McElmurry's gouache illustrations add a light, humorous touch. Adults will appreciate the lessons gracefully imparted, and children will enjoy the silliness of Grandma's fanciful, zany family stories." SLJ

The **Nutcracker**; retold by Stephanie Spinner; illustrated by Peter Malone; with a fully orchestrated CD of Peter Ilyich Tchaikovsky music. Alfred A. Knopf 2008 un il $16.99; lib bdg $19.99
Grades: K 1 2 3 4 E
1. Fairy tales 2. Christmas -- Fiction
ISBN 978-0-375-84464-5; 0-375-84464-3; 978-0-375-94464-2 lib bdg; 0-375-94464-8 lib bdg
LC 2007041524
In this retelling of the original 1816 German story, Godfather Drosselmeier gives young Marie a nutcracker for Christmas, and she finds herself in a magical realm where she saves the nutcracker and sees him change into a handsome prince

"Malone's richly colored, opaque watercolors embellish the dancers' magic. . . . This book, which comes with a CD, provides a good entry-point before attending a performance as well as a chance to relive the experience afterward." Horn Book

Spirin, Gennadii
Martha. Philomel Books 2005 un il $14.99
Grades: K 1 2 3 E
1. Crows
ISBN 0-399-23980-4
LC 2004-6735
The author relates how he and his Moscow family rescued Martha, a crow with a broken wing, and how she joined their household.

"The story will appeal to the picture book audience. . . . The lush art set in plentiful white space beautifully portrays a Moscow of a few decades ago." Horn Book Guide

A **apple** pie; art by Gennady Spirin. Philomel Books 2005 un il $16.99
Grades: PreK K 1 2 E
1. Alphabet 2. Nursery rhymes 3. Children's poetry 4. Alphabet rhymes
ISBN 0-399-23981-2
LC 2004030497
Introduces the letters A to Z while following the fortunes of an apple pie.

"Whimsically detailed watercolors revitalize an alphabet verse dating from the 1600s. . . . Delicately rendered vines and flowers are reminiscent of Victorian botanical prints. Busy details offer new discoveries with each reading. The letters, text, and paintings are unified in style and become a single work of art." SLJ

Spiro, Ruth

Lester Fizz, bubble-gum artist; illustrated by Thor Wickstrom. Dutton 2008 un il $16.99

Grades: 1 2 3   E

1. Art -- Fiction 2. Artists -- Fiction 3. Chewing gum -- Fiction

ISBN 978-0-525-47861-4; 0-525-47861-2

Everyone in the Fizz family is an artist. Everyone, that is, except Lester, whose paintings are pitiful and doodles are drab. He can't seem to find a way to fit in with the illustrious Fizzes, until one day a mouthful of gum becomes a work of art in Lester's talented lips.

"Spiro's droll text is infused with alliteration and punning that adds to the sense of fun, which is extended in colorful, whimsical illustrations. Wickstrom's playful images portray scenarios both realistic and fantastical and incorporate classic works by famous artists, including Joseph Cornell and Dorothea Lange." Booklist

Spohn, Kate

★ **Turtle** and Snake's day at the beach. Viking 2003 32p il (Viking easy-to-read) hardcover o.p. pa $3.99

Grades: K 1 2   E

1. Snakes 2. Animals 3. Beaches 4. Turtles 5. Contests 6. Sandcastles 7. Snakes -- Fiction 8. Beaches -- Fiction 9. Turtles -- Fiction

ISBN 0-670-03628-5; 0-14-240157-9 pa

LC 2002-153376

Turtle and Snake go to the beach, where they and some other animals participate in a sandcastle-making contest

"Brightly colored, simple drawings capture the pleasure of this fun-in-the-sun day at the beach. . . . It's difficult to find easy-to-read books that have charm and a real story, and this one does." SLJ

Other titles about Turtle and Snake are:

Turtle and Snake and the Christmas tree (2000)

Turtle and Snake at work (1999)

Turtle and Snake fix it (2002)

Turtle and Snake go camping (2000)

Turtle and Snake's spooky Halloween (2002)

Turtle and Snake's Valentine's Day (2003)

Springett, Martin

Kate and Pippin; Martin Springett; photos by Isobel Springett. Henry Holt 2012 32 p.

Grades: K 1 2 3   E

1. Deer 2. Dogs 3. Friendship 4. Animal babies 5. Picture books for children 6. Parental behavior in animals -- Fiction

ISBN 0805094873; 9780805094879

LC 2011033499

In this picture book, "[w]hen Pippin, a fawn abandoned by her mother, cries out for help, she is found by author Isobel Springett. After carrying the tiny fawn back to her home, Isobel places Pippin next to Kate, a Great Dane who has never had puppies of her own. What follows is a remarkable and unlikely friendship. Kate successfully raises Pippin to be an independent deer, and Pippin always returns from the forest to visit her best friend." (Publisher's note) "Pippin learns to negotiate a milk-bottle nipple and later a set of porch steps. . . . [T]he two plainly enjoy each other's company, and the

pictures underscore their closeness at rest or play. . . . [T]he narrative . . . notes that Pippin is a wild animal 'but she and Kate remain the best of friends.'" (Kirkus)

Srinivasan, Divya

★ **Little** Owl's night. Viking Childrens Books 2011 un il $16.99

Grades: PreK K 1   E

1. Owls -- Fiction 2. Night -- Fiction 3. Forest animals -- Fiction 4. Forests and forestry -- Fiction

ISBN 978-0-670-01295-4; 0-670-01295-5

LC 2010049513

Little Owl enjoys a lovely night in the forest visiting his friend the raccoon, listening to the frogs croak and the crickets chirp, and watching the fog that hovers overhead.

"The story's chief virtue is its graceful, balletic prose; the [artwork has] crisp edges and cold greens and blacks. . . . It's a provocative inversion of the classic bedtime story, and a solid first outing. Srinavasan's message is that night is a delightful place, and that's useful knowledge for small children." Publ Wkly

Octopus alone; by Divya Srinivasan. Viking 2013 40 p. (hardcover) $16.99

Grades: PreK K   E

1. Shyness -- Juvenile fiction 2. Octopuses -- Juvenile fiction

ISBN 0670785156; 9780670785155

LC 2012029678

This children's picture book, by Divya Srinivasan, is "about shy Octopus who lives on a lively reef, and what happens when she finds herself in a new place far from home, wonderfully, peacefully alone." In it the octopus is constantly interrupted by other sea creatures who live in the reef and she learns to appreciate her neighbors. (Publisher's note)

Staake, Bob

Bluebird; Bob Staake. 1st ed. Schwartz & Wade Books 2013 40 p. col. ill. (hardcover) $17.99; (library) $20.99

Grades: 2 3 4 5   E

1. Stories without words 2. Bluebirds -- Juvenile fiction 3. Human-animal relationship -- Juvenile fiction 4. Bluebirds -- Fiction 5. Friendship -- Fiction

ISBN 0375870377; 9780375870378; 9780375970382

LC 2012007043

This children's picture book, by Bob Staake, "explores . . . loneliness, bullying, and the importance of friendship. In this emotional picture book, readers will . . . follow the journey of a bluebird as he develops a friendship with a young boy and ultimately risks his life to save the boy from harm." (Publisher's note)

★ **Look!** A book! a zany seek-and-find adventure. Little, Brown 2011 un il $16.99

Grades: K 1 2   E

1. Picture puzzles 2. Stories in rhyme 3. Books and reading -- Fiction

ISBN 0-316-11862-1; 978-0-316-11862-0

LC 2010001540

Easy-to-read, rhyming text invites the reader to search for items on a different theme on each page, while celebrating the wonder of a picture book.

"With polished typography, minty-fresh layout, and crisp-edged figures, the book stays tidy despite the frenetic action, and the rhymed and metered text is carefully wrought." Publ Wkly

★ **Look!** Another book! Bob Staake. Little, Brown 2012 48 p. $16.99

Grades: PreK   E

1. Paper crafts 2. Picture books for children 3. Picture puzzles 4. Stories in rhyme 5. Books and reading -- Fiction

ISBN 0316204595; 9780316204590

LC 2011053200

This book is the sequel to Bob Staake's "Look! A Book!" The "solid-colored pages are graced with small die cuts that reveal little tidbits of the busy scenes hiding on the following spreads. Sometimes the page turns make the images blend seamlessly into the busy new scene . . . . The die cuts themselves also seem to disappear with the page turn, leading readers to touch the pages to find the circles and to prove that they are still there." (Kirkus)

The **donut** chef. Random House 2008 un il $14.99; lib bdg $17.99

Grades: PreK K 1 2   E

1. Stories in rhyme 2. Baking -- Fiction

ISBN 978-0-375-84403-4; 0-375-84403-1; 978-0-375-94716-2 lib bdg; 0-375-94716-7 lib bdg

A baker hangs out his shingle on a small street and soon the line for his donuts stretches down the block. But it's not long before the competition arrives and a battle of the bakers ensues.

"The entire book has a retro tone, from its lengthy rhyming text to its Art Deco-style illustrations, which are updated with more modern-looking graphic shapes and a multicolored palette. . . . The story's lively rhythmic text and colorful artwork should make it a good pick for storytime." SLJ

The **red** lemon. Golden Books 2006 un il $14.95; lib bdg $16.99

Grades: PreK K 1   E

1. Stories in rhyme 2. Lemons -- Fiction

ISBN 0-375-83593-8; 0-375-93593-2 lib bdg

LC 2005-09854

Farmer McPhee's yellow lemons are ready to be picked and made into lemonade, pies, and muffins, but when a red lemon is found in the crop and discarded, it eventually yields some surprises.

"Bold, enticing illustrations dominate the pages. Staake creates a fun, dynamic world . . . in its sweeping arcs, bright colors, multicolored cartoon people, and effortlessly rhyming text." SLJ

Stainton, Sue

I love cats; [written by] Sue Stainton; [illustrated by] Anne Mortimer. Katherine Tegen Books 2007 un il $15.99

Grades: PreK K   E

1. Cats -- Fiction

ISBN 978-0-06-085154-5; 0-06-085154-6; 978-0-06-085156-9 lib bdg; 0-06-085156-2 lib bdg

LC 2005018100

"The unseen narrator likes all kinds of cats, and there are plenty of cats to be seen: big cats, little cats, hairy cats, scaredy-cats. Using an almost photo-realistic technique, Mortimer offers more than two dozen cats to 'ooh' and 'ahh' over." Booklist

Stamp, Jorgen

Flying high. Enchanted Lion 2009 un il $16.95

Grades: K 1 2   E

1. Turtles -- Fiction 2. Giraffes -- Fiction 3. Air pilots -- Fiction

ISBN 978-1-59270-089-9; 1-59270-089-6

"Walter is a giraffe who wishes he could fly. He finds himself a book, and begins to build an airplane for himself. When Sonny the turtle meanders over and asks if he, too, can go flying, Walter tells his friend he's too slow and cowardly and hurts his feelings. . . . When his plane is hit by lightning and crashes into the lake, it is Sonny who swims out and saves him. . . . The colorful cartoon illustrations convey the fast pace of the tale and do a suitable job of moving things along to a satisfying conclusion." SLJ

Stanley, Diane

The **Giant** and the beanstalk; written and illustrated by Diane Stanley. HarperCollinsPublishers 2004 un il $17.99; lib bdg $17.89

Grades: K 1 2 3   E

1. Giants 2. Fairy tales 3. Characters from literature

ISBN 0-06-000010-4; 0-06-000011-2 lib bdg

LC 2003-1818

In this version of the traditional tale, a young giant chases Jack down the beanstalk to rescue his beloved hen and meets other Jacks from various nursery rhymes along the way

"Stanley injects her characteristic, understated humor into both text and art, and young ones will take pleasure in identifying the individual elements of the thoroughly mixed-up story." Booklist

Goldie and the three bears. HarperCollins Pubs. 2003 un il $15.99; lib bdg $17.89; pa $6.99

Grades: K 1 2 3   E

1. Bears -- Fiction 2. Friendship -- Fiction

ISBN 0-06-000008-2; 0-06-000009-0 lib bdg; 0-06-113611-5 pa

LC 2002-23843

In this story, loosely based on that of Goldilocks, Goldie, who has yet to find a friend to "love with all her heart," makes an unplanned visit to the house of some bears

"The writing is smooth, concise, and rhythmic. . . . The pictures are marvelous, with fine lines; soft, glowing colors; and winsome, telling details." SLJ

★ **Rumpelstiltskin's** daughter. Morrow Junior Bks. 1997 un il $17.99; lib bdg $16.89; pa $7.99

Grades: K 1 2 3   E

1. Fairy tales

ISBN 0-688-14327-X; 0-688-14328-8 lib bdg; 0-06-441095-1 pa

LC 96-14834

"Rumpelstiltskin's daughter relies on her cleverness instead of magic. When the king orders her to spin straw into gold, she tricks him out of his greedy ways and becomes prime minister of his kingdom. The illustrations provide splendid, detailed palace interiors and endow the characters, especially the king and his minions, with comically exaggerated features." Horn Book Guide

Saving Sweetness; illustrated by G. Brian Karas. Putnam 1996 un il $16.99; pa $5.99

Grades: K 1 2 3   **E**
1. Orphans -- Fiction
ISBN 0-399-22645-1; 0-698-11767-0 pa
LC 95-10621

The sheriff of a dusty western town rescues Sweetness, an unusually resourceful orphan, from nasty old Mrs. Sump and her terrible orphanage

"Telling the tale from the sheriff's point of view, Stanley packs this fast-paced adventure full of language that begs to be read aloud. . . . Combining gouache, acrylic, and pencil drawings with cyanotype photographs, Karas's illustrations evoke the arid landscape of the West yet remain wonderfully original." SLJ

Another title about Sweetness is:
Raising Sweetness (1999)

Thanksgiving on Plymouth Plantation; illustrations by Holly Berry. Joanna Cotler Books 2004 un il map (Time-traveling twins) $16.99
Grades: 2 3 4   **E**
1. Thanksgiving Day -- Fiction 2. Pilgrims (New England colonists) -- Fiction
ISBN 0-06-027069-1; 0-06-027076-4 lib bdg
LC 2002-20548

Twins Liz and Lenny, along with their time-traveling grandmother, visit Plymouth Plantation to see how the Pilgrims lived and to celebrate a big feast with the Pilgrims and Native Americans.

"In conjunction with her fast-paced and informative text, Stanley uses dialogue bubbles to give readers all sorts of interesting, comical, and possibly shocking tidbits. . . . Complementing the book's conversational flavor, Berry's cartoon illustrations are bright and appealing." SLJ

★ The **trouble** with wishes. HarperCollins Pubs. 2007 un il $16.99; lib bdg $17.89
Grades: 1 2 3 4   **E**
1. Wishes -- Fiction 2. Sculpture -- Fiction 3. Classical mythology -- Fiction
ISBN 0-06-055451-7; 0-06-055452-5 lib bdg

Jane wishes she were more like her friend Pyg the sculptor until Pyg's statue of a beautiful goddess comes to life and teaches them both to be careful what they wish for. Based on the Greek myth of Pygmalion

"Stanley's fresh artwork, which mixes the grandeur of old classical forms and the absurdity of the new, is in perfect balance with the parody." Booklist

Stanley, Malaika Rose
Baby Ruby bawled; with illustrations by Ken Wilson-Max. Transworld Publishers 2011 32p il pa $9.99
Grades: PreK   **E**
1. Infants -- Fiction 2. Siblings -- Fiction 3. Family life -- Fiction 4. Racially mixed people -- Fiction
ISBN 978-1-84-853017-1; 1-84-853017-X

"Theo's baby sister cries and cries whenever it is time to go to sleep. Dad tries soothing Ruby with a bath, Mum feeds her, Nana takes her for a ride in the car, Grandad carries her around in the baby backpack, and Uncle Clyde pushes her in the buggy. Nothing works until Theo sings her a lullaby. . . . Bright, bold painterly illustrations, sharply outlined in black, beautifully depict the love, and frustration, of this mixed-race family. Anyone who has ever struggled to get a fussy baby to sleep will relate to this British import, and the

ending will give older siblings a sense of pride and empowerment." SLJ

Stanton, Karen
Papi's gift; by Karen Stanton; illustrated by Rene King Moreno. Boyds Mills Press 2007 un il $16.95
Grades: K 1 2 3   **E**
1. Droughts -- Fiction 2. Birthdays -- Fiction 3. Father-daughter relationship -- Fiction
ISBN 978-1-59078-422-8; 1-59078-422-7
LC 2006011569

Graciela's Papi has been working in the United States for so long that she has almost forgotten his face, so when the box he promised for her seventh birthday does not arrive, she is very upset and nearly loses hope that he— and the rain—will someday return

"A few Spanish words and phrases add authenticity to the engaging text. Moreno uses pastels to render soothing, warm illustrations that have a Latin American flavor and elements of folk art." SLJ

Staub, Leslie
Everybody gets the blues; written by Leslie Staub; pictures by R.G. Roth. Houghton Mifflin Harcourt 2012 un il $16.99 **E**
1. Stories in rhyme 2. Emotions -- Fiction 3. Blues music -- Fiction
ISBN 978-0-15-206300-9; 0-15-206300-5
LC 2010043400

"Writing cheerfully about sadness sounds like an oxymoron, but Staub . . . performs this balancing act with casual grace. . . . Blues Guy, a sweet-faced, bulky gentleman dressed in tweed, sits with the boy, radiating sympathy and asking nothing. They sing together ('I've got the blues so bad,/ I want to cry, cry, cry'), and the strength of their song lifts them into the sky to bring comfort to 'everyone who's feeling low.' . . . Roth's . . . flat, cutout figures have a retro feel, but reflect the present-day world with figures of many ages, colors, and sizes. Staub's verses scan as neatly as an old radio hit." Publ Wkly

Stauffacher, Sue
★ **Bessie** Smith and the night riders; illustrated by John Holyfield. G. P. Putnam's Sons 2006 un il $16.99
Grades: K 1 2 3 4   **E**
1. Singers 2. Blues musicians 3. Songwriters 4. Blues music -- Fiction 5. African Americans -- Fiction
ISBN 0-399-24237-6
LC 2005010399

Black blues singer Bessie Smith singlehandedly scares off Ku Klux Klan members who are trying to disrupt her show one hot July night in Concord, North Carolina. Includes historical note

"Holyfield's brilliantly colored acrylic spreads aptly depict a larger-than-life individual. . . . The book is based on a true event. . . . This tale of courage would make a fine addition to units on the Civil Rights movement." SLJ

Includes bibliographical references

Stead, Philip C.
Bear has a story to tell; Philip C. Stead; illustrated by Erin E. Stead. 1st ed. Roaring Brook Press 2012 32 p. ill. (reinforced: alk. paper) $16.99

Grades: PreK K 1   **E**
1. Bears -- Fiction 2. Hibernation -- Fiction 3. Storytelling -- Fiction 4. Picture books for children 5. Animals -- Fiction
ISBN 1596437456; 9781596437456

LC 2011033795

In this children's picture book, "Bear wants to tell a story, but his friends Mouse, Duck, Frog, and Mole are busy preparing for winter. . . . Instead, Bear offers help to his friends." He "raises a great paw to check the wind for Duck and tucks Frog tenderly into his hole. When winter passes, the animals are reunited, but Bear has forgotten his story; now it's his friends' turn to help him." (Publishers Weekly)

Hello, my name is Ruby; Philip C. Stead. 1st ed. Henry Holt & Co 2013 40 p. (hardcover) $16.99
Grades: PreK K 1   **E**
1. Birds -- Juvenile fiction 2. Picture books for children 3. Birds -- Fiction 4. Friendship -- Fiction
ISBN 1596438096; 9781596438095

LC 2012046929

In this children's picture book, "Ruby is a diminutive, yellow bird whose frequent introductions are a touch formal: 'I am glad to meet you.' She fearlessly initiates conversation with much bigger birds and is the kind of friend who offers ideas and is willing to try the suggestions of others. In the process, much is gleaned about avian (and human) behavior." (Kirkus Reviews)

A **home** for Bird; Philip C. Stead. Roaring Brook Press 2012 32 p.
Grades: PreK K   **E**
1. Home -- Fiction 2. Birds -- Fiction 3. Toads -- Fiction 4. Picture books for children 5. Clocks and watches -- Fiction 6. Cuckoos -- Fiction
ISBN 1596437111; 9781596437111

LC 2011012742

In this picture book for children, "Vernon is both a toad and a forager for found objects. Ambling along with his latest haul, he chances upon a creature he seeks to know and then to help. . . . Vernon observes that 'Bird is shy . . . but also a very good listener,' when he introduces Bird to his friends. He and his pals conclude that Bird is lost and unhappy, so the thoughtful, resourceful amphibian readies a teacup boat for the journey to help this quiet stranger return home." (Kirkus Reviews)

★ A **sick** day for Amos McGee; written by Philip C. Stead; illustrated by Erin E. Stead. Roaring Brook Press 2010 un il $16.99
Grades: PreK K 1 2   **E**
1. Sick -- Fiction 2. Zoos -- Fiction 3. Animals -- Fiction
ISBN 978-1-59643-402-8; 1-59643-402-3
Awarded the Caldecott Medal, 2011

Amos McGee he spends a little bit of time each day with each of his friends at the zoo, running races with the tortoise, keeping the shy penguin company, and even reading bedtime stories to the owl. But when Amos is too sick to make it to the zoo, his animal friends decide it's time they returned the favor.

"The artwork in this quiet tale of good deeds rewarded uses woodblock-printing techniques, soft flat colors, and oc-

casional bits of red. Illustrations are positioned on the white space to move the tale along and underscore the bonds of friendship and loyalty. Whether read individually or shared, this gentle story will resonate with youngsters." SLJ

Stead, Philip Christian
Jonathan and the big blue boat; [by] Philip Christian Stead. Roaring Brook Press 2011 un il $16.99
Grades: K 1 2   **E**
1. Teddy bears -- Fiction 2. Boats and boating -- Fiction 3. Voyages and travels -- Fiction
ISBN 978-1-59643-562-9; 1-59643-562-3

LC 2010012952

When Jonathan's parents decide that he has gotten too old to have a stuffed animal, they trade his favorite bear, Frederick, for a toaster, so he sets off aboard a boat, looking for Frederick.

"Stead . . . uses squiggly ink lines and washes of warm color against a background of collaged newsprint, charts, and stamps that underscore the nautical theme and distance traveled. Frederick shows up at the end in the nicest possible way, and Jonathan's slow, reflective journey-filled with pitch-perfect details, sound effects, and vocabulary . . . offers a lovely, gentle adventure for younger readers." Publ Wkly

Steffensmeier, Alexander
★ **Millie** waits for the mail; [by] Alexander Steffensmeier. Walker & Co. 2007 un il $16.95; lib bdg $17.85
Grades: PreK K 1 2   **E**
1. Cattle -- Fiction 2. Letter carriers -- Fiction
ISBN 978-0-8027-9662-2; 0-8027-9662-1; 978-0-8027-9663-9 lib bdg; 0-8027-9663-X lib bdg

LC 2006035326

Millie the cow loves to scare the mailman and chase him off the farm, until the mailman comes up with a plan that ends up pleasing everyone.

"While the text is both lively and concise, most of the book's considerable charm emanates from the droll visual humor." Publ Wkly

Another title about Millie is:
Millie in the snow (2008)

Steggall, Susan
★ **Rattle** and rap; [illustrated by Susan Steggall] Frances Lincoln 2009 un il $15.95
Grades: PreK K 1   **E**
1. Railroads -- Fiction
ISBN 978-1-84507-703-7; 1-84507-703-2

Steggall's "virtuoso torn-paper collages follow a boy and his family on a train trip through the British countryside to the coast, where an unnamed (but grandmotherly) relative greets them with open arms. . . . The detail-rich, full-spread pictures . . . are stunning in their evocation of the real world." Publ Wkly

Steig, Jeanne
Fleas; illustrated by Britt Spencer. Philomel 2008 un il $16.99
Grades: PreK K 1 2   **E**
1. Barter -- Fiction 2. Circus -- Fiction
ISBN 978-0-399-24756-9; 0-399-24756-4

A cumulative tale in which Quantz, who is repaid in fleas for scratching a stray dog, makes a series of trades that turn one person's burden into the next one's joy and ultimately brings them all together for a circus performance.

Steig's "shaggy dog story, like the swapping stories found in folk or fairy tales, takes readers on a hilarious journey. . . . In Spencer's . . . capable hands, the intrepid hero looks like Ichabod Crane, and part of the joy is in seeing each new outlandish personage." Publ Wkly

Steig, William

★ The **amazing** bone. Farrar, Straus & Giroux 1976 un il $17.99; pa $7.99
Grades: PreK K 1 2 3   E
1. Pigs -- Fiction 2. Bones -- Fiction
ISBN 0-374-30248-0; 0-374-40358-9 pa
A Caldecott Medal honor book, 1977
On her way home from school, Pearl finds an unusual bone that has unexpected powers

"Steig's marvelously straightfaced telling comes with a panoply of ultra-spring landscapes for pink-dressed Pearl to tiptoe through. And there's no holding back the chortles at the wonderfully expressive faces the artist delights in. This is a tight mesh of witty storytelling and art bound to please any audience." Booklist

★ **Brave** Irene. Farrar, Straus & Giroux 1986 un il
Grades: PreK K 1 2 3   E
1. Courage -- Fiction 2. Blizzards -- Fiction
ISBN 0-374-30947-7; 0-374-40927-7 pa
LC 86-80957
Plucky Irene, a dressmaker's daughter, braves a fierce snowstorm to deliver a new gown to the duchess in time for the ball. "Ages five to nine." (N Y Times Book Rev)

"With sure writing and well-composed, riveting art, Steig keeps readers with Irene every step of the long way. The pictures . . . are done in winter blues, purples, and grays that gradually get darker as Irene trudges on." Booklist

Caleb & Kate. Farrar, Straus & Giroux 1977 un il hardcover o.p. pa $6.95
Grades: PreK K 1 2 3   E
1. Dogs -- Fiction 2. Witches -- Fiction
ISBN 0-374-41038-0 pa
LC 77-4947
"The well-cadenced storytelling has a certain old-fashioned elegance of language, and the humor is emphasized by an atmosphere of mock-pathos." Horn Book

★ **Doctor** De Soto. Farrar, Straus & Giroux 1982 un il $17; pa $7.99
Grades: PreK K 1 2   E
1. Mice -- Fiction 2. Animals -- Fiction 3. Dentists -- Fiction
ISBN 0-374-31803-4; 0-374-41810-1 pa
LC 82-15701
A Newbery Medal honor book, 1983
"The story achieves comic heights partly through the delightful irony of the situation. . . . Watercolor paintings, with the artist's firm line and luscious color, depict with aplomb the eminently dentistlike mouse as he goes about his business." Horn Book
Another title about Doctor De Soto is:
Doctor De Soto goes to Africa (1992)

★ **Pete's** a pizza. HarperCollins Pubs. 1998 un il $16.99; lib bdg $17.89
Grades: PreK K 1 2   E
1. Father-son relationship -- Fiction
ISBN 0-06-205157-1; 0-06-205158-X lib bdg
LC 97-78384
"The watercolor illustrations are executed in a clean palette with precise lines in tightly controlled compositions, the semi-formality of which only add to the hilarity. . . . This is a jolly, affectionate story." Bull Cent Child Books

Potch & Polly; with pictures by Jon Agee. Farrar, Straus & Giroux 2002 un il $16
Grades: K 1 2 3   E
1. Love -- Fiction
ISBN 0-374-36090-1
LC 00-29544
Lively Potch pursues the girl of his dreams, the darling Polly Pumpernickel
"This irresistible picture book has it all: a tongue-in-cheek text brimming with deliciously alliterative phrases, wry cartoons that mix visual gags with a comic-book punch, and a plot featuring two lovers who are taunted by twists of fate and turns of slapstick humor." SLJ

Shrek! twentieth anniversary edition; Farrar Straus Giroux 2010 un il $16.99
Grades: K 1 2 3 4   E
1. Monsters -- Fiction
ISBN 978-0-374-36879-1; 0-374-36879-1
A reissue of the title first published 1990
"The pictures are just as nutty as the story, blending with the text so thoroughly, sometimes echoing, sometimes expanding it, that it's hard to imagine one without the other. . . . The fast-forward movement of the story and the inventive challenging language, full of surprises, make this especially fun to read aloud." SLJ

★ **Sylvester** and the magic pebble. Simon & Schuster Books for Young Readers 2005 un il $16.95
Grades: PreK K 1 2 3   E
1. Donkeys -- Fiction
ISBN 1-4169-0206-6
LC 2004-15445
A reissue of the title first published 1969
Awarded the Caldecott Medal, 1970
In a moment of fright, Sylvester the donkey asks his magic pebble to turn him into a rock but then can not hold the pebble to wish himself back to normal again
"A remarkable atmosphere of childlike innocence pervades the book; beautiful pictures in full, natural color show daily and seasonal changes in the lush countryside and greatly extend the kindly humor and the warm, unselfconscious tenderness." Horn Book

When everybody wore a hat. Joanna Cotler Bks. 2003 un il $17.99; pa $8.99
Grades: PreK K 1 2 3   E
1. Artists 2. Authors 3. Cartoonists 4. Illustrators 5. Children's authors 6. Authors, American -- Homes and haunts -- New York (State) -- New York
ISBN 0-06-009700-0; 0-06-009702-7 pa
LC 2002-6512

"In 1916, Steig was eight years old. This autobiography describes that year of his life. . . . The childlike, watercolor artwork that accompanies the memories features flattened tables, nostrils on the sides of noses, and a sidewalk extending up into the air. Yet the illustrations' naiveté belies their underlying sophistication. With a few spare lines, the artist manages to convey body language, facial expression, and gesture." SLJ

Stein, David Ezra

Cowboy Ned and Andy; [by] David Ezra Stein. Simon & Schuster Books for Young Readers 2006 un il $14.95
Grades: PreK K 1 2   E
1. Horses -- Fiction 2. Cowhands -- Fiction 3. Birthdays -- Fiction
ISBN 978-1-4169-0041-2; 1-4169-0041-1
LC 2005006969
On a cattle drive in the desert on the night before Cowboy Ned's birthday, his horse Andy goes in search of a birthday cake, which he thinks will make Ned's birthday complete
"Stein's language is simple yet expressive. . . . Done in ink and watercolor, the cartoon illustrations make the most of the Western landscape." SLJ
Another title about Cowboy Ned and Andy is:
Ned's new friend (2007)

Dinosaur kisses; by David Ezra Stein. Candlewick Press 2013 32 p. ill. (reinforced) $15.99
Grades: PreK   E
1. Kissing -- Juvenile fiction 2. Dinosaurs -- Juvenile fiction
ISBN 076366104X; 9780763661045
LC 2012954335
In this book, written and illustrated by David Ezra Stein, "an energetic young dinosaur figures out her own way to give a kiss. For newly hatched dinosaur Dinah, the world is an exciting place. After a few disastrous attempts, can she figure out how to give someone a kiss without whomping, chomping, or stomping them first?" (Publsiher's note)

★ **Interrupting** chicken. Candlewick Press 2010 un il $16.99
Grades: PreK K 1 2   E
1. Bedtime -- Fiction 2. Chickens -- Fiction 3. Storytelling -- Fiction 4. Father-daughter relationship -- Fiction
ISBN 978-0-7636-4168-9; 0-7636-4168-5
LC 2009017523
A Caldecott Medal honor book, 2011
Little Red Chicken wants Papa to read her a bedtime story, but interrupts him almost as soon as he begins each tale.
"Stein's droll cartoons use watercolor, crayon, china marker, pen, and tea. The rich colors of the characters perfectly contrast with the sepia pages of the storybooks." SLJ

★ **Leaves.** Putnam 2007 un il $15.99
Grades: PreK K 1 2   E
1. Bears -- Fiction 2. Leaves -- Fiction 3. Seasons -- Fiction
ISBN 978-0-399-24636-4; 0-399-24636-3
LC 2006-24753
A curious bear observes how leaves change throughout the seasons.

"Bamboo pen and earth-toned watercolors are used to great effect. . . . The serene scenes and streamlined story line reflect perfectly the gentle passage of time." SLJ

★ **Love,** Mouserella. Nancy Paulsen Books un il $15.99
Grades: PreK K   E
1. Mice -- Fiction 2. Letters -- Fiction 3. Grandmothers -- Fiction
ISBN 978-0-399-25410-9; 0-399-25410-2
Mouserella misses her grandmouse, so she writes her a letter. At first she can't think of anything to say, but once she starts, the news begins to flow.
"Showing his customary gift for spot-on evocations of childlike voice and sensibility, . . . Stein . . . interweaves Mouserella's loosely connected comments with decorative crayon sketches, relatively more finished vignettes representing pictures in her imagination or scenes she is describing and painted 'photos' of a pet chrysalis, Dadmouse and other subjects. . . . Sometimes snail mail is just better. Here's proof." Kirkus

Monster hug! [by] David Ezra Stein. G.P. Putnam's Sons 2007 un il $15.99
Grades: PreK K 1 2   E
1. Play -- Fiction 2. Monsters -- Fiction
ISBN 978-0-399-24637-1
LC 2007008196
Two rambunctious young monsters have an action-packed day together
"Stein's rambunctious watercolors are as joyously messy as the characters they bring to life. His primary-color palette stands out boldly against the white backgrounds." SLJ

★ **Pouch!** G.P. Putnam's Sons 2009 un il $15.99
Grades: PreK K 1   E
1. Growth -- Fiction 2. Kangaroos -- Fiction 3. Mother-child relationship -- Fiction
ISBN 978-0-399-25051-4; 0-399-25051-4
LC 2008-53558
A baby kangaroo takes his first tentative hops outside of his mama's pouch, meeting other creatures and growing bolder each time.
"The short, pithy text tells a story young listeners will immediately understand. . . . Done in marker, watercolor, and crayon, the artwork has a fresh energetic quality that suits the story well." Booklist

Stein, Peter

Cars galore; illustrated by Bob Staake. Candlewick Press 2011 un il $15.99
Grades: PreK K 1 2   E
1. Stories in rhyme 2. Vehicles -- Fiction 3. Automobiles -- Fiction
ISBN 978-0-7636-4743-8; 0-7636-4743-8
LC 2010038923
"Rhythmic verse and lively illustrations showcase autos of every color, size, style, and speed. . . . The illustrator's familiar cartoon style easily matches the text. Crisp, clean lines and bright colors pop against the white background, while black traffic-filled roads crisscross and loop around the pages. Readers will eagerly search for and find every vehicle mentioned." SLJ

Stephens, Helen

★ **Fleabag**. Henry Holt and Company 2010 un il $16.99

Grades: PreK K 1　　　　　　　　　　　　　　E

1. Dogs -- Fiction 2. Moving -- Fiction
ISBN 978-0-8050-8975-2; 0-8050-8975-6

LC 2009009196

First published 2008 in the United Kingdom

A stray dog and a lonely boy become fast friends at a neighborhood park, but everything changes when the boy's family decides to move away.

"The illustrations are bright and happy, picturing an appealing little mutt. . . . An enjoyable story for groups or bedtime sharing." SLJ

The **big** adventure of the Smalls; Helen Stephens. Aladdin 2012 32 p. col. ill. $15.99

Grades: K 1 2　　　　　　　　　　　　　　E

1. Adventure fiction 2. Adventure stories 3. Children's stories
ISBN 1442450584; 9781442450585

LC 2011277645

In this children's book by Helen Stephens "it's the night of the Small Hall Ball, and everyone in the Small family is getting ready for one of the BIGGEST parties of the year. Everyone, that is, except for Paul and Sally Small, who are too young to join in the fun. But when Paul's tiny teddy bear goes missing, he and Sally have no choice but to sneak into the festivities, and nothing . . . will stop the smallest of the Smalls from finding Paul's furry little friend." (Publisher's note)

Stevens, April

★ **Edwin** speaks up; written by April Stevens; illustrated by Sophie Blackall. Schwartz & Wade Books 2011 un il $16.99; lib bdg $19.99

Grades: PreK K 1　　　　　　　　　　　　　　E

1. Ferrets -- Fiction 2. Infants -- Fiction 3. Shopping -- Fiction 4. Birthdays -- Fiction 5. Family life -- Fiction
ISBN 978-0-375-85337-1; 0-375-85337-5; 978-0-375-95633-1 lib bdg; 0-375-95633-6 lib bdg

LC 2009-28009

Before his family leaves the grocery store, Baby Edwin (a ferret) makes sure their grocery cart contains the last ingredient needed to make his birthday celebration complete.

"Stevens' spot-on story about every mother's nightmare, the group grocery-store shop, is matched by Blackall's delicious art. . . . This is a book that's clever in every sense of the word: skillful, original, and witty." Booklist

★ **Waking** up Wendell; written by April Stevens; illustrated by Tad Hills. Schwartz & Wade Books 2007 un il $15.99; lib bdg $18.99

Grades: PreK K 1 2　　　　　　　　　　　　　　E

1. Counting 2. Sounds -- Fiction
ISBN 978-0-375-83621-3; 0-375-83621-7; 978-0-375-83893-1 lib bdg; 0-375-93893-1 lib bdg

LC 2006030979

Early in the morning, a bird begins to sing at number One Fish Street, waking the man next door and his dog, and before long, as one noise leads to another, everyone on the street is awake.

"Hills's bright oil paint and colored pencil illustrations, done with simple lines and contrasting colors, enliven the

text and add extra humor. This picture book is both a clever and original counting book and a great read-aloud." SLJ

Stevens, Janet

★ **Cook**-a-doodle-doo! [by] Janet Stevens and Susan Stevens Crummel; illustrated by Janet Stevens. Harcourt Brace & Co. 1999 un il $17; pa $7

Grades: PreK K 1 2　　　　　　　　　　　　　　E

1. Animals -- Fiction 2. Cooking -- Fiction
ISBN 0-15-201924-3; 0-15-205658-0 pa

LC 98-8853

With the questionable help of his friends, Big Brown Rooster manages to bake a strawberry shortcake which would have pleased his great-grandmother, Little Red Hen

"With the main story and each hilarious, mouthwatering double-page picture of pandemonium, there is a quiet sidebar in small type that explains what recipes are, what ingredients are, what measuring and baking means, and how to make a strawberry shortcake, step by step. The luscious illustrations on hand-made paper are beautifully drawn and deliciously textured. . . . The full recipe is printed on the last page." Booklist

★ The **great** fuzz frenzy; written by Janet Stevens and Susan Stevens Crummel; illustrated by Janet Stevens. Harcourt 2005 un il $17

Grades: PreK K 1 2 3　　　　　　　　　　　　　　E

1. Prairie dogs -- Fiction
ISBN 0-15-204626-7

When a fuzzy tennis ball lands in a prairie-dog town, the prairie dogs discover that their newfound frenzy for fuzz creates no end of trouble.

"The marvelously rendered mixed-media illustrations, with vivid blues, earthy browns, and that luminescent green, capture the true fuzzy nature and greenish glow of the ball." SLJ

Help me, Mr. Mutt! expert answers for dogs with people problems. written by Janet Stevens and Susan Stevens Crummel; illustrated by Janet Stevens. Harcourt 2008 un il $17

Grades: 1 2 3　　　　　　　　　　　　　　E

1. Dogs -- Fiction
ISBN 978-0-15-204628-6; 0-15-204628-3

LC 2007020549

Dogs across the United States write to Mr. Mutt, a people expert, for help with their humans.

"Art and text work seemlessly, with plenty of visual and verbal jokes . . . to entice repeated readings." Booklist

Stevenson, James

★ **Flying** feet; a Mud Flat story. Greenwillow Books 2004 47p il $15.99; lib bdg $16.89

Grades: K 1 2　　　　　　　　　　　　　　E

1. Dance 2. Animals 3. Tap dancing 4. Animals -- Fiction 5. Tap dancing -- Fiction 6. Stanley and the the other animals of Mud Flat take dance lessons from some touring tap dancers and prepare for a big show
ISBN 0-06-051975-4; 0-06-051976-2 lib bdg

LC 2002-29785

Stanley and the the other animals of Mud Flat take dance lessons from some touring tap dancers and prepare for a big show

"Stevenson's trademark pen-and-watercolor illustrations lovingly depict exuberant characters and provide lots of special details. . . . Children will enjoy this zany story." SLJ

No laughing, no smiling, no giggling. Farrar, Straus and Giroux 2004 un il $16
Grades: PreK K 1 2   E
   1. Animals -- Fiction
   ISBN 0-374-31829-8

LC 2003-45508

The reader joins Freddy Fafnaffer the pig as he deals with Mr. Frimdimpny, a crocodile who never laughs and who decides on the rules for reading this book.

"Children will enjoy the humorous cartoons and delight in helping Freddy out of his predicament. The act of inviting readers to actively participate in the plot has great appeal." SLJ

Stevenson, Robert Louis
  Block city; illustrated by Daniel Kirk. Simon & Schuster Books for Young Readers 2005 un il $14.95
Grades: PreK K 1   E
   1. Play -- Fiction
   ISBN 0-689-86964-9

A child creates a world of his own which has mountains and sea, a city and ships, all from toy blocks.

"This colorfully illustrated version of Stevenson's poem is as relevant today as when it was written for A Child's Garden of Verses in 1883. . . . Done in colored pencils and gouache in rich, deep colors, the large, clear pictures have a retro feel." SLJ

  ★ The **moon**; [by] Robert Louis Stevenson; pictures by Tracey Campbell Pearson. Farrar, Straus and Giroux 2006 un il $16
Grades: PreK K 1 2   E
   ISBN 0-374-35046-9

LC 2005040067

"Stevenson's famous 12-line poem, which begins 'The moon has a face / like the clock in the hall,' becomes the text of a picture-book depiction of the nighttime outing of a contemporary father and his child. Leaving Mother and Baby behind, they climb into a truck with the dog, the cat, and some provisions; travel to the dock; and take their boat across a cove and back again while they watch the places and creatures illuminated by the moon. The pictured journey creates a vivid, visual counterpoint to the poetry, which flows as magically as an incantation. . . . The luminous ink-and-watercolor illustrations reflect Pearson's creative imagination and her sure sense of what is visually interesting to young children." Booklist

Stewart, Amber
  Bedtime for Button; [by] Amber Stewart & [illustrated by] Layn Marlow. Orchard Books 2009 un il lib bdg $12.99
Grades: PreK K   E
   1. Bears -- Fiction 2. Bedtime -- Fiction 3. Father-son relationship -- Fiction
   ISBN 978-0-545-12991-6 lib bdg; 0-545-12991-5 lib bdg

LC 2008-29859

First published 2008 in the United Kingdom with title: Just like tonight

When Button the bear remembers something frightening that happened during the day, he worries that he will have bad dreams until his father gives him something nice to think about—the day he was born.

"The soft colors and brushstrokes of Marlow's illustrations underscore the sweet, gentle nature of the tale." SLJ

  Little by little; [by] Amber Stewart; [illustrated by] Layn Marlow. Orchard Books 2008 un il $12.99
Grades: PreK K 1   E
   1. Otters -- Fiction 2. Siblings -- Fiction 3. Swimming -- Fiction
   ISBN 978-0-545-06163-6; 0-545-06163-6

LC 2007033288

Otto is a young otter who can do many things well, but swimming is not one of them until his older sister tells him to start small and, little by little, he is able to reach his goal, adding swimming to his 'I can do' list

"The message will resonate with children learning this skill and others 'little by little,' and Marlow's expressive watercolor and ink illustrations will capture their interest. The real star here, however, is the peppy text, which bounces along with all the energy of Otto rolling through the water." SLJ

  Puddle's new school; illustrated by Layn Marlow. Barron's 2011 un il pa $7.99
Grades: PreK K   E
   1. School stories 2. Ducks -- Fiction
   ISBN 978-0-7641-4683-1; 0-7641-4683-1

Puddle is a little duckling. He longs to go to school. But when his first day approaches he is suddenly not so sure.

"This is a reassuring tale for first time school-goers. Its universal theme, coupled with large naturalistic illustrations and large font size, makes it an excellent read-aloud for young children and for use in preschool/daycare and kindergarten settings." SLJ

Stewart, Joel
  Addis Berner Bear forgets; [by] Joel Stewart. Farrar, Straus and Giroux 2008 un il $16.95
Grades: K 1 2 3   E
   1. Bears -- Fiction 2. Memory -- Fiction 3. Musicians -- Fiction 4. City and town life -- Fiction
   ISBN 978-0-374-30036-4; 0-374-30036-4

LC 2007044778

A musical bear visits the city and finds the experience a bit overwhelming until he remembers the reason for his trip

"The delicate artwork fascinates, sometimes exacerbating, sometimes ameliorating the bleakest parts of the story. But there's happiness here as well in the vignettes and full-page art." Booklist

Stewart, Sarah
  ★ The **friend**; pictures by David Small. Farrar, Straus and Giroux 2004 un il $16
Grades: K 1 2 3   E
   1. Household employees -- Fiction
   ISBN 0-374-32463-8

LC 2003-64352

With Mom too busy and Dad away much of the time, Belle finds companionship with a household employee who after each day's work takes Belle "hand in hand" to the beach

"David Small's elegant, moving illustrations . . . . show the twosome touchingly small on the vast beach. . . . In both illustrations and text, Bea is not merely a playmate but her own person." NY Times Book Rev

★ The **gardener**; pictures by David Small. Farrar, Straus & Giroux 1997 un il $16; pa $6.95
Grades: K 1 2 3   E
1. Letters -- Fiction 2. Gardening -- Fiction 3. Great Depression, 1929-1939 -- Fiction
ISBN 0-374-32517-0; 0-374-42518-3 pa
LC 96-30894
A Caldecott Medal honor book, 1998
"Stewart's quiet story, relayed in the form of letters written by a little girl, focuses on a child who literally makes joy blossom. Small's illustrations . . . [offer] wonderfully expressive characters, ink-line details, and patches of pastel." Booklist

★ The **journey**; pictures by David Small. Farrar, Straus & Giroux 2001 un il $16; pa $6.95
Grades: K 1 2 3   E
1. Amish 2. Diaries 3. City and town life
ISBN 0-374-33905-8; 0-374-40010-5 pa
LC 99-31001
A young Amish girl tells her "silent friend," her diary, about all the wonderous experiences she has on her first trip to the city
"This title offers so much: a glimpse into Amish culture and Chicago treasures; a winsome main character and many sensitively depicted supporting personalities; a fresh, authentic voice; and a design perfectly melded to its subtle message." SLJ

The **quiet** place; Sarah Stewart; pictures by David Small. Margaret Ferguson Books 2012 44 p. $16.99
Grades: K 1 2 3   E
1. Home -- Juvenile fiction 2. Homesickness -- Juvenile fiction 3. Mexican Americans -- Juvenile fiction 4. Aunts -- Fiction 5. Letters -- Fiction 6. Immigrants -- Fiction 7. Homesickness -- Fiction 8. Mexican Americans -- Fiction
ISBN 0374325650; 9780374325657
LC 2011031768
This children's story, by Sarah Stewart, illustrated by David Small, is the winner of the "Kirkus Reviews" Best Children's Book award of 2012. "When Isabel and her family move to the United States, Isabel misses all the things she left behind in Mexico. . . . But she also experiences some wonderful new things. . . . Even better, Papa and her brother Chavo help her turn a big box into her own quiet place, where she keeps her books and toys and writes letters to Aunt Lupita." (Publisher's note)

Stiegemeyer, Julie
Gobble-gobble crash! by Julie Stiegemeyer; illustrated by Valeri Gorbachev. Dutton Childrens Books 2008 un il $16.99
Grades: PreK K 1   E
1. Counting 2. Stories in rhyme 3. Turkeys -- Fiction 4. Domestic animals -- Fiction
ISBN 978-0-525-47959-8; 0-525-47959-7
LC 2008003012

A flock of clumsy turkeys disrupts a quiet night on the farm, but when the farmer threatens them, all the barnyard animals help the noisy birds hide
"In rhythmic couplets, a numbers game unfolds. . . . Gorbachev's action-filled illustrations add to the fun. His animals cavort against moonlit teal backgrounds, with the text printed in white." SLJ

Seven little bunnies; pictures by Laura J. Bryant. Marshall Cavendish Children 2010 un il $15.99
Grades: PreK K   E
1. Counting 2. Stories in rhyme 3. Bedtime -- Fiction 4. Rabbits -- Fiction
ISBN 978-0-7614-5600-1; 0-7614-5600-7
LC 2009006337
Seven bunnies find many other things to do when it is time for them to go to bed.
"The sounds and action will appeal to young preschoolers in this lively bedtime rhyme that includes a counting exercise. . . . The words are lively . . . and as kids chant along, they'll also follow the subtraction and addition as seamless parts of the story." Booklist

Stier, Catherine
Bugs in my hair?! written by Catherine Stier; illustrated by Tammie Lyon. Albert Whitman & Co. 2008 un il $15.95
Grades: K 1 2 3   E
1. School stories 2. Lice -- Fiction
ISBN 0807509086; 9780807509081
LC 2007024250
When immaculately groomed Ellie gets head lice she is terribly upset, but once she learns some facts about the creatures, she calms down and figures out a way to help her classmates.
"Stier has taken a difficult topic and turned it into a charming story that demystifies the fears and false information surrounding lice infestation. The writing . . . comes across simply without sounding didactic. Cartoon illustrations capture Ellie's emotions." SLJ

Today on election day; Catherine Stier; illustrated by David Leonard. A. Whitman & Co. 2012 32 p. (hardcover) $16.99
Grades: 2 3 4   E
1. Picture books for children 2. Elections -- United States -- Juvenile literature
ISBN 0807580082; 9780807580080
LC 2011035248
This informational picture book about U.S. election day offers children a "salute to the first Tuesday after the first Monday in November." It presents "information . . . [on] political parties, campaigns, Congress, the history of the vote, Constitutional amendments, debates and voting." Author Catherine Stier "situates the activity around the children's school." (Kirkus Reviews)

Stileman, Kali
Roly-poly egg. Tiger Tales 2011 un il $12.95
Grades: PreK K 1   E
1. Eggs -- Fiction 2. Birds -- Fiction 3. Mother-child relationship -- Fiction
ISBN 978-1-58925-852-5; 1-58925-852-5

"Mother love leads to near tragedy in this tale of an egg. Rendered in smears of fiery red paint, Splotch the bird personifies her name. She learns the true testament of a mother's love after she lays a magnificent polka-dotted egg. . . . In her utter joy, she bounces her branch—and the egg falls off into the lush jungle habitat. Met with ambivalence by some and threat from others, the little one is tossed until it's gently returned to her grateful mom. . . . Paint streaks collide with textured papers, creating a bright array of rainbow hues. Spare, crisp sentences describe each action, leaving lots of room for expansion in the bold mixed-media spreads. Vibrant designs breathe life into this mama." Kirkus

Stimpson, Colin

Jack and the baked beanstalk; Colin Stimpson. Candlewick Press 2012 40 p. col. ill. (hardback) $15.99
Grades: K 1 2 3 4   E
1. Fairy tales 2. Restaurants -- Fiction 3. Picture books for children 4. Magic -- Fiction 5. Giants -- Fiction 6. Cooking -- Fiction 7. Characters in literature -- Fiction
ISBN 0763655635; 9780763655631
LC 2011047003

In this children's picture book, "Jack and his mother live and work in a broken-down burger truck parked at the edge of town. When a new overpass diverts traffic away from their location, business dries up. Jack is sent to the store with their last pennies for milk and coffee beans, but instead buys a can of magic baked beans from a mysterious stranger and is tossed out by his angry mother. After the purchase grows into a vine sprouting shiny cans of this delicious staple, the boy climbs up and meets a fearsome-looking giant, but soon discovers that this lonely individual would rather cook for him than eat him." (School Library Journal)

Stinson, Kathy

Big or little? Kathy Stinson [text]; Toni Goffe [illustrations] Annick Press 2009 un il $19.95; pa $6.95
Grades: PreK   E
1. Size -- Fiction 2. Growth -- Fiction
ISBN 978-1-55451-169-3; 1-55451-169-0; 978-1-55451-168-6 pa; 1-55451-168-2 pa

"Toby, a preschooler with flyaway hair, considers the benefits and responsibilities of being big, as well as the frustrations of being small. The mishaps of spilled milk or a wet bed, for instance, are balanced by the joys of helping to wash the car and remembering to return library books. Goffe's line drawings in a pastel palette depict a traditional family of five in a messy home. . . . Plenty of children will relate to [Toby]." SLJ

Stock, Catherine

★ **Gugu's** house. Clarion Bks. 2001 31p il $14
Grades: PreK K 1 2   E
1. Grandmothers 2. Rain and rainfall 3. Grandmothers -- Fiction
ISBN 0-618-00389-4
LC 00-43009

Kukamba loves helping her grandmother decorate her mud home in a dusty Zimbabwe village, but when the annual rains partially destroy all her art work, Kukamba learns to see the goodness of the rains

"Stock's watercolors capture not only the bright hues of landscape and traditional dress but also a clear sense of Gugu's deep serenity and the shared purpose that sends her

and Kukamba striding back from their walk to restore the house to its former glory." Booklist

A **porc** in New York; [by] Catherine Stock. Holiday House 2007 un il $16.95
Grades: PreK K 1 2   E
1. Animals -- Fiction 2. Vacations -- Fiction
ISBN 978-0-8234-1994-4; 0-8234-1994-0
LC 2006002015

Monsieur Monmouton and his dog Cabot fly from France to New York City in pursuit of his farm animals, who are taking a vacation to see such sights as Blooming Dells and MOOMA

"The story is fun, and the expansive, exuberant artwork shows Stock at the top of her game." Booklist

Stoeke, Janet Morgan

It's library day; [by] Janet Morgan Stoeke. Dutton Children's Books 2008 un il $12.99
Grades: K 1 2   E
1. School stories 2. Stories in rhyme 3. Libraries -- Fiction 4. Books and reading -- Fiction
ISBN 978-0-525-47944-4; 0-525-47944-9
LC 2007040589

"In short bursts of rhyme, this introduces kids who read . . . and captures the excitement they feel when it's library day at school. . . . The pure-colored illustrations, with an almost graphic edge, have tons of appeal." Booklist

★ The **Loopy** Coop hens. Dutton Children's Books 2011 un il $16.99
Grades: PreK K   E
1. Chickens -- Fiction 2. Roosters -- Fiction
ISBN 0-525-42190-4; 978-0-525-42190-0
LC 2010-13354

Chickens Pip, Midge, and Dot admire Rooster Sam and his ability to fly up to the barn roof, but when they spy on him to see how he does it, they get a big surprise. "Grades one to two." (Bull Cent Child Books)

"The simple text and sentences are ideal for new readers, but it is Stoeke's loose, unfussy artwork that emphasizes the slapstick humor and carries much of the character development. The fowls' body language is especially hilarious in scenes where they attempt to fly and find themselves flat on the ground, or when overconfident Rooster Sam strolls by." Publ Wkly

Minerva Louise and the red truck. Dutton Children's Bks. 2002 un il $14.99
Grades: PreK K 1 2   E
1. Trucks -- Fiction 2. Chickens -- Fiction
ISBN 0-525-46909-5

Minerva Louise the chicken "goes for a ride in the farmer's red truck. . . . She fits everything she sees into her own limited experience, so a backyard swimming pool becomes a beautiful lake, a church with a steeple is a 'silly barn wearing a hat,' and a construction site is a truck farm/playground. Kids who know just a little bit more about the world than Minerva Louise will delight in their superior knowledge. . . . The brief text and vibrant, well-composed illustrations are once again ideal for the intended audience." Horn Book

Waiting for May. Dutton Children's Bks. 2005 un il $16.99

Grades: PreK K 1 2   E

1. Adoption -- Fiction 2. Siblings -- Fiction
ISBN 0-525-47098-0

A young boy looks forward to the day when a new sister, who will be adopted from China, joins his family.

"The smoothly flowing text . . . imparts a surprising amount of information about requirements unique to international adoptions. . . . The colorful paintings enhance the narrative and capture the various emotions of the characters. . . . An excellent addition to all collections." SLJ

The **bus** stop; [by] Janet Morgan Stoeke. Dutton Children's Books 2007 un il $12.99

Grades: PreK K   E

1. School stories 2. Stories in rhyme 3. Buses -- Fiction
ISBN 978-0-525-47805-8

LC 2006024469

Kindergartners gather for their exciting first ride on the school bus.

"The cartoon artwork is colorful and inviting, showing characters with sweetly delineated features. The repetitive text invites participation while portraying this rite of passage in an upbeat manner." SLJ

★ A **hat** for Minerva Louise. Dutton Children's Bks. 1994 un il hardcover o.p. pa $5.99

Grades: PreK K 1 2   E

1. Hats -- Fiction 2. Chickens -- Fiction
ISBN 0-525-45328-8; 0-14-055666-4 pa

LC 94-2139

Minerva Louise, a snow-loving chicken, mistakes a pair of mittens for two hats to keep both ends warm

This "is a rare find: a picture book exactly on target for preschoolers that sacrifices none of the essential elements of plot, character, and humor. . . . The pictures, in large rectangles of bright primary colors, are easy for preschoolers to 'read' and contain most of the book's considerable humor." Horn Book

Other titles about Minerva Louise are:
A friend for Minerva Louise (1997)
Minerva Louise (1988)
Minerva Louise and the colorful eggs (2006)
Minerva Louise at school (1996)
Minerva Louise at the fair (2000)
Minerva Louise on Christmas Eve (2007)
Minerva Louise on Halloween (2009)

Stohner, Anu

Brave Charlotte; [illustrated by Henrike Wilson; translated from the German by Alyson Cole] Bloomsbury Children's Bks. 2005 un il $16.95

Grades: PreK K 1 2   E

1. Sheep -- Fiction
ISBN 1-58234-690-9

Charlotte, a headstrong sheep, rescues the flock when their shepherd is injured.

"There is a lot to like in 'Brave Charlotte': the gentle way the story unfolds, and the lovely way the illustrator . . . expresses an inviting, dingy fluffiness. . . . Each dreamlike image is suffused with colors that are rich yet subdued." NY Times Book Rev

Another title about Charlotte is:
Brave Charlotte and the wolves (2009)

Stojic, Manya

★ **Rain**; written and illustrated by Manya Stojic. Crown 2000 un il $15.95

Grades: PreK K 1 2   E

1. Senses and sensation 2. Rain -- Fiction 3. Rain and rainfall 4. Zoology -- Africa 5. Animals -- Fiction
ISBN 0-517-80085-3; 0-517-80086-1 lib bdg

LC 99-35298

The animals of the African savanna use their senses to predict and then enjoy the rain

"The brilliant double-page spreads, the play on the five senses, and a text that invites participation make this one trip to Africa you can't afford to miss!" SLJ

Stone, Kate

One spooky night; a Halloween adventure. Accord Publishing 2011 36p il pa $11.99

Grades: PreK K 1   E

1. Fear -- Fiction 2. Monsters -- Fiction 3. Halloween -- Fiction
ISBN 978-1-4494-0330-0; 1-4494-0330-1

"Cut pages and vellum layers combine to striking effect in this story about a little monster's nocturnal journey. The monster isn't afraid when an owl hoots, and he doesn't cower at grinning jacko'lanterns or ghosts. The transparent layers and stained glass-style cutouts with black, yellow, and purple accents create dramatic dimension. When the monster finally arrives at a haunted house, a bright foldout reveals that he is really a boy in costume." Publ Wkly

Stone, Tanya Lee

Who says women can't be doctors? the story of Elizabeth Blackwell. Tanya Lee Stone; illustrated by Marjorie Priceman. 1st ed. Christy Ottaviano Books/Henry Holt and Co. 2013 40 p. (reinforced) $16.99

Grades: K 1 2 3   E

1. Women -- History -- Juvenile literature 2. Women physicians -- United States -- Biography
ISBN 0805090487; 9780805090482

LC 2011043528

This children's book, by Tanya Lee Stone, illustrated by Marjorie Priceman, is a biographical story of Elizabeth Blackwell. "In the 1830s, . . . women were supposed to be wives and mothers. . . . Certainly no women were doctors. But Elizabeth refused to accept the common beliefs that women weren't smart enough to be doctors, or that they were too weak for such hard work. . . . Although she faced much opposition, she worked hard and finally . . . proved her detractors wrong." (Publisher's note)

Includes bibliographical references.

Stoop, Naoko

Red Knit Cap Girl; by Naoko Stoop. Little Brown & Co 2012 40 p.

Grades: PreK K 1   E

1. Moon -- Juvenile fiction 2. Picture books for children 3. Forest animals -- Juvenile fiction 4. Forest animals -- Fiction 5. Forests and forestry -- Fiction
ISBN 0316129461; 9780316129466

LC 2011025121

This children's picture book by Naoko Stoop, illustrated on wood grain, follows the character of "Red Knit Cap Girl [who] lives with her animal friends in an enchanted forest. There is so much to see and do, but more than anything Red

Knit Cap Girl wishes she could talk to the Moon. . . . Red Knit Cap Girl's curiosity, imagination, and joy" are the focus of the tale, "offer[ing] a . . . reminder to appreciate the beauty of the natural world around us." (Publisher's note)

Storad, Conrad J.
Rattlesnake rules; illustrated by Nathaniel P. Jensen. Five Star Publications 2009 40p il $16.95
Grades: PreK K 1   E
    1. Stories in rhyme 2. Rattlesnakes -- Fiction
    ISBN 978-1-58985-161-0; 1-58985-161-7
           LC 2009-27518
A mother rattlesnake who can locate food with her tongue and swallow prey in one gulp shares survival tips with her babies—and with humans.
"Nathaniel Jensen's illustrations are playfully rendered showcasing the love a mother rattlesnake has for her babies. The skillful combination of fiction and fact in this cleverly conceived story is sure to engage children and teachers alike." Libr Media Connect

Stott, Ann
Always; illustrated by Matt Phelan. Candlewick Press 2008 un il $15.99
Grades: PreK   E
    1. Love -- Fiction 2. Mother-son relationship -- Fiction
    ISBN 978-0-7636-3232-8; 0-7636-3232-5
           LC 2007052020
A child is reassured by his mother that she will love him even when he misbehaves.
"A sweet, understated story. . . . Phelan's illustrations bring this quiet text to exuberant life with pastel watercolors." SLJ

I'll be there; [illustration by Matt Phelan] Candlewick Press 2011 un il $14.99
Grades: PreK K 1 2   E
    1. Growth -- Fiction 2. Mother-son relationship -- Fiction
    ISBN 978-0-7636-4711-7; 0-7636-4711-X
           LC 2010039180
A young boy and his mother talk about what she did for him as a baby, what he can do for himself now, and that she will always be there when he needs her.
"Phelan's warm, sketchy watercolors in a restrained palette of blues, greens, and grays with orange accents reinforce the sweet sentiment. While the touching story, with its simple text and accessible images, is easily suitable for story hour, this will doubtless be a favorite for sharing at home, as well." Booklist

Straaten, Harmen van
Duck's tale; by Harmen van Straaten; translated by Marianne Martens. North-South Books 2007 un il $16.95
Grades: K 1 2   E
    1. Ducks -- Fiction 2. Toads -- Fiction 3. Reading -- Fiction 4. Authorship -- Fiction
    ISBN 978-0-7358-2133-0; 0-7358-2133-X
           LC 2006100310
When Toad finds some reading glasses and Duck finds a pen, they also acquire some skills they never knew they had
"The warm, softly colored illustrations suit the calm atmosphere of the story. Children will be drawn to these appealing creatures." SLJ

Another title about Duck and his friends is:
For me? (2008)

Strauss, Linda L.
Preschool day hooray! by Linda Leopold Strauss; illustrated by Hiroe Nakata. Cartwheel Books 2010 un il $8.99
Grades: PreK   E
    1. School stories 2. Stories in rhyme
    ISBN 978-0-545-17854-9; 0-545-17854-1
"Jaunty rhymes describe a child's typical day at preschool. . . . Strauss's economical text is age appropriate, and Nakata's colorful, blocky illustrations give kids lots to look at." Horn Book Guide

The princess gown; by Linda Leopold Strauss; illustrated by Malene Reynolds Laugesen. Houghton Mifflin Company 2008 un il $16
Grades: K 1 2 3   E
    1. Fairy tales 2. Embroidery -- Fiction 3. Princesses -- Fiction 4. Dressmaking -- Fiction 5. Clothing and dress -- Fiction
    ISBN 978-0-618-86259-7; 0-618-86259-5
           LC 2007012923
If the wedding dress young Hanna's family is making is not chosen for the princess, they will go to the poor house but thanks to Hanna's sharp eyes and artistic ability, her father stands a very good chance of becoming Embroiderer to the Princess.
Laugesen's "animation-style illustrations . . . are rendered in oil crayon and linseed oil on colored paper, creating a nearly tangible, saturated texture. . . . The pictures keep step with the well-paced tale." Publ Wkly

Stringer, Lauren
★ Winter is the warmest season; by Lauren Stringer. Harcourt 2006 un il $16
Grades: PreK K 1 2   E
    1. Winter -- Fiction
    ISBN 0-15-204967-3
           LC 2005005723
A child describes pleasant ways to stay warm during the winter, from sipping hot chocolate and eating grilled cheese sandwiches to wearing wooly sweaters and sitting near a glowing fireplace.
"It takes special art to accentuate the evocative words, and Stringer . . . provides distinctive pictures for herself. . . . The deeply hued acrylic artwork ranges from friendly to joyous. . . . A special book worthy of many readings, this radiates warmth." Booklist

Strom, Kellie
Sadie the air mail pilot. David Fickling Books 2007 un il $17.78
Grades: K 1 2 3   E
    1. Cats -- Fiction 2. Air pilots -- Fiction
    ISBN 978-0-385-60506-9; 0-385-60506-4
Although her day got off to a bad start, Sadie, a highflying cat, is confident that she can make the air mail run to Knuckle Peak Weather Station, even after the station reports that a storm is headed their way.
"Strom peppers the narrative with memorable rhymes. . . . Children will be fascinated by the courage of this determined pilot. They will pore over the antique-appearing

illustrations that glow in an orangish-red palette with rusty browns and golden yellows." SLJ

Stroud, Bettye

The **patchwork** path; a quilt map to freedom. illustrated by Erin Susanne Bennett. Candlewick Press 2005 32p il $15.99

Grades: K 1 2 3   E

1. Quilts -- Fiction 2. Slavery -- Fiction 3. African Americans -- Fiction 4. Underground railroad -- Fiction

ISBN 0-7636-2423-3

LC 2004-45786

While her father leads her toward Canada and away from the plantation where they have been slaves, a young girl thinks of the quilt her mother used to teach her a code that will help guide them to freedom.

"The exciting escape story makes the history immediate, and the fascinating quilt-code messages will have children revisiting the page that shows each symbol and its secret directions. Bennett's bright oil paintings make dramatic use of collage." Booklist

Stryer, Andrea Stenn

Kami and the yaks; [by] Andrea Stenn Stryer; illustrated by Bert Dodson. Bay Otter Press 2007 un il hardcover o.p. $15.95

Grades: K 1 2 3   E

1. Deaf -- Fiction 2. Yaks -- Fiction 3. Himalaya Mountains -- Fiction

ISBN 978-0-977896-10-3; 978-0-977896-11-0 pa

"Readers will be transported to the rugged Himalayas with this story of a deaf Sherpa boy in Nepal, who braves a storm in search of his family's yaks. . . . Although Kami's disability plays an important role in the story, the author focuses on his strength. . . . Dark, yet vivid watercolors extend the text." SLJ

Stuchner, Joan Betty

Can hens give milk? illustrated by Joe Weissmann. Orca Book Publishers 2011 un il $19.95

Grades: PreK K 1   E

1. Jews -- Folklore 2. Chickens -- Fiction

ISBN 978-1-55469-319-1; 1-55469-319-5

"On this visit to Chelm, which in Jewish folklore is the hotbed for all things silly, readers meet Shlomo and Rivka, a kindly couple who have 'five children, twelve scrawny hens, one rooster and not much money.' Yearning for a little milk and cheese and unable to afford a cow, Shlomo engages in some magical thinking of the animal husbandry kind. Since cows eat grass, he reasons, '...if we feed grass to our hens, they will still lay eggs, but they will also give us milk.'" Publ Wkly

Sturges, Philemon

★ **How** do you make a baby smile? by Philemon Sturges; illustrated by Bridget Strevens-Marzo. HarperCollinsPublishers 2007 un il $16.99

Grades: PreK   E

1. Stories in rhyme 2. Animals -- Fiction 3. Infants -- Fiction

ISBN 978-0-06-076072-4; 0-06-076072-9; 978-0-06-076073-1 lib bdg; 0-06-076073-7 lib bdg

LC 2007012488

Animal parents use their best tricks to make their babies smile, laugh, coo, and grin.

This is written "in catchy verse with large-scale, eye-catching artwork. . . . Broad black outlines and flat areas of bold colors clearly define the characters and settings with wit and style." Booklist

I love planes! illustrated by Shari Halpern. HarperCollins Pubs. 2003 un il $12.99; lib bdg $14.89

Grades: PreK K   E

1. Airplanes 2. Airplanes -- Fiction

ISBN 0-06-028898-1; 0-06-028899-X lib bdg

LC 2001-26483

A child celebrates his love of planes by naming his favorite kinds and their notable characteristics

"The simplicity of the child's words is well matched by the colorful, uncluttered images, outlined in black." Booklist

I love school! illustrated by Shari Halpern. HarperCollins Pubs. 2004 un il $12.99; lib bdg $14.89

Grades: PreK K   E

1. Schools 2. Kindergarten 3. School stories 4. Stories in rhyme 5. Brothers and sisters

ISBN 0-06-009284-X; 0-06-009285-8 lib bdg

LC 2002-68554

A brother and sister describe the things they love to do during their day at kindergarten

This book "is a good way to prepare nervous new preschoolers and kindergartners. . . . [It features] simple, rhymed text and big, clear color pictures outlined in thick black line." Booklist

I love trains! illustrated by Shari Halpern. HarperCollins Pubs. 2001 un il $12.95; lib bdg $13.89

Grades: PreK K   E

1. Stories in rhyme 2. Railroads -- Trains 3. Railroads -- Fiction

ISBN 0-06-028900-7; 0-06-028901-5 lib bdg

LC 99-86367

A boy expresses his love of trains, describing many kinds of train cars and their special jobs

This offers "clear, bright, double-page pictures with thick black lines and neon colors. . . . Toddlers will enjoy making the hoot, roar, and rumble sounds and identifying the various cars." Booklist

Stutson, Caroline

★ **By** the light of the Halloween moon; illustrated by Kevin Hawkes. Marshall Cavendish 2009 un il $16.99

Grades: PreK K 1 2   E

1. Stories in rhyme 2. Halloween -- Fiction

ISBN 978-0-7614-5553-0; 0-7614-5553-1

LC 2008022965

A reissue of the title first published 1993 by Lothrop, Lee, & Shepherd Books

In this cumulative tale, a host of Halloween spooks, including a cat, a witch, and a ghoul, are drawn to the tapping of a little girl's toe.

"Not only is the text rhythmically bouncy and appealing, but the illustrations are of the least fearful and most amusing of ghastly creatures, very effectively set against a black and gloomy background. A sure Halloween hit." Horn Book

Cats' night out; illustrated by J. Klassen. Simon & Schuster Books for Young Readers 2010 un il $15.99

Grades: K 1 2 3   E

   1. Stories in rhyme 2. Cats -- Fiction 3. Dance -- Fiction 4. City and town life -- Fiction

ISBN 978-1-4169-4005-0; 1-4169-4005-7

LC 2008-52268

Cats dance the night away out on the town, doing the tango, rumba, twist, fox trot, and more

"Klassen's eye-catching digitally rendered urban streetscapes resemble the sets of classic musical theater. . . . The finely detailed illustrations feature a subdued palette of brown, gray, and charcoal enlivened by splashes of color. The subtle charms of this lighter-than-air confection should delight young connoisseurs of dance and style." SLJ

Suen, Anastasia

   ★ **Red** light, green light; written by Anastasia Suen; illustrated by Ken Wilson-Max. Harcourt 2005 un il $16

Grades: PreK K 1   E

   1. Stories in rhyme 2. Transportation -- Fiction

ISBN 0-15-202582-0

A young boy creates an imaginary world filled with zooming cars, flashing traffic lights, and racing fire engines.

"The flowing text rhymes and has a good pace and rhythm, which makes it an ideal read-aloud for transportation fans. The illustrations are bright and full of detail." SLJ

Road work ahead; illustrated by Jannie Ho. Viking 2011 32p il $15.99

Grades: PreK K   E

   1. Stories in rhyme 2. Roads -- Fiction 3. Automobile travel -- Fiction 4. Construction equipment -- Fiction

ISBN 978-0-670-01288-6; 0-670-01288-2

When a family sets out on a trip to Grandma's, their journey proves to be more like a visit to a construction site. Sidewalks are being poured, streetlights repaired, roads resurfaced. The noise of jackhammers, whistles, and horns fills the air.

This is a "delightful story. . . . The cheerful illustrations enhance the smooth, rhyming text. They are full of detail and hum with activity." SLJ

Roadwork ahead; illustrated by Jannie Ho. Viking 2011 il $15.99

Grades: PreK K 1   E

   1. Stories in rhyme 2. Roads -- Fiction

ISBN 978-0-670-01288-6; 0-670-01288-2

LC 2011004545

On the drive to Grandma's house, a boy and his mother encounter work crews using machinery and tools to perform roadwork.

"Ho's brightly colored artwork is tailor-made for her audience. While her scenes are visually packed with people, vehicles and activity, all are rendered with basic shapes and colors and lack the distracting details that would overwhelm young children. Suen's sparse rhyming verse leads readers through the busy scenes and uses simple vocabulary that suits both the youngest listeners and those just beginning to read." Kirkus

   ★ **Subway**; written by Anastasia Suen; illustrated by Karen Katz. Viking 2004 un il $15.99

Grades: PreK K 1 2   E

   1. Subways 2. Stories in rhyme 3. Subways -- Fiction

ISBN 0-670-03622-6

LC 2003-14020

"In brief, rhyming verses, an African-American child describes her ride on the subway. . . . The rhythmic language captures the feel of her journey and a repeated refrain invites readers to participate in the telling of the story. The bright, bold artwork depicts each scene in a realistic manner from the child's point of view." SLJ

Sullivan, Mary

   Ball. Houghton Mifflin Harcourt 2013 40 p. $12.99

Grades: PreK K 1   E

   1. Dogs -- Juvenile fiction 2. Picture books for children

ISBN 0547759363; 9780547759364

This children's picture book is about a ball-obsessed dog. "The dog's curly headed owner is delighted to play with him, but after she leaves for school he's stuck with her meditating mother and a squalling baby. He tries listlessly to amuse himself, then dozes off. His dreams are a parade of mad, creative whimsy. A tiered cake dotted with balls, a monstrous baby, and an interstellar game of chase climax with a journey down the toilet and through a maze of pipes." (Publishers Weekly)

Sullivan, Sarah

   Once upon a baby brother; pictures by Tricia Tusa. Farrar Straus Giroux 2010 un il $16.99

Grades: PreK K 1 2   E

   1. Infants -- Fiction 2. Siblings -- Fiction 3. Authorship -- Fiction 4. Storytelling -- Fiction

ISBN 978-0-374-34635-5; 0-374-34635-6

LC 2008016791

Lizzie, who loves to tell and write stories, is surprised to discover that much of her storytelling inspiration comes from her messy baby brother.

"Sullivan has found an oblique way to write about the ups and downs of a school-age child adjusting to a much younger sibling, and she carries it out with skill. Bringing the story to life, Tusa's strong, quirky line-and-wash drawings define characters and settings, add bits of visual humor, amplify the book's emotional content, and give the jacket its winsome appeal." Booklist

   Passing the music down; illustrated by Barry Root. Candlewick Press 2010 un il $16.99

Grades: K 1 2 3   E

   1. Folk music -- Fiction 2. Violinists -- Fiction 3. Country life -- Fiction

ISBN 978-0-7636-3753-8; 0-7636-3753-X

LC 2008037104

A boy and his family befriend a country fiddler, who teaches the boy all about playing the old tunes, which the boy promises to help keep alive. Inspired by Melvin Wine and Jake Krack.

"Root's sweet illustrations in watercolor and gouache show the man and boy in an almost grandfather-grandson setting, making pancakes, hunting ginseng, and picking beans, and at the end of their hard day's work, they make music together. . . . Told in free verse, this picture book would be a good accompaniment to music-appreciation lessons focused on American roots music." SLJ

Surgal, Jon

Have you seen my dinosaur? illustrated by Joe Mathieu. Random House Children's Books 2010 un il $8.99

Grades: PreK K 1 2   E

1. Stories in rhyme 2. Dinosaurs -- Fiction 3. Lost and found possessions -- Fiction

ISBN 978-0-375-85639-6; 978-0-375-95639-3 lib bdg

LC 2007043166

A five-year-old boy searches high and low for his missing dinosaur, and the people he asks for help do not believe such a creature actually exists.

Sussman, Michael B.

Otto grows down; illustrated by Scott Magoon. Sterling Pub. Co. 2009 un il $14.95

Grades: PreK K 1   E

1. Growth -- Fiction 2. Wishes -- Fiction 3. Infants -- Fiction 4. Siblings -- Fiction

ISBN 978-1-4027-4703-8; 1-4027-4703-9

LC 2008028229

When time goes backwards, granting six-year-old Otto his wish that his attention-stealing baby sister was never born, it keeps going backwards, and Otto finds himself getting younger and younger.

"A refreshing take on the arrival of a new sibling and the rivalry that frequently follows. . . . Exaggerated cartoon art captures his predicament. With humor and poignancy, author and illustrator portray an age-old rite of passage." SLJ

Sutton, Jane

Don't call me Sidney; pictures by Renata Gallio. Dial Books for Young Readers 2010 un il $16.99

Grades: K 1 2 3   E

1. Pigs -- Fiction 2. Animals -- Fiction 3. Friendship -- Fiction 4. Personal names -- Fiction

ISBN 978-0-8037-2753-3; 0-8037-2753-4

LC 2008054962

Unable to find a rhyme for his name, Sidney the pig decides to become Joe, much to the dismay of his mother and friends.

"This amusing story about a poetic pig's search for his true identity is accompanied by humorous acrylic and pencil collage illustrations in which large figures of the characters dominate the subtly detailed scenes." SLJ

Sutton, Sally

Roadwork! [by] Sally Sutton; illustrated by Brian Lovelock. Candlewick Press 2008 32p il $15.99

Grades: PreK   E

1. Stories in rhyme 2. Trucks -- Fiction 3. Construction equipment -- Fiction

ISBN 978-0-7636-3912-9; 0-7636-3912-5

"Kids who love trucks and construction will find an ideal vehicle for their passions in this exuberant book from New Zealand, which uses full-bleed art and rhyming text to show how each of seven machines functions in the building of a road. Sutton's rhythms invite audience participation, as do the sound effects that end each verse . . . Using ink, acrylics and colored pencils, Lovelock conjures artful landscapes with visible brushwork, reserving a speckling effect not unlike concrete for the road." Publ Wkly

Suzuki, David T.

There's a barnyard in my bedroom; [by] David Suzuki; Eugenie Fernandes, illustrator. Greystone Books 2010 un il $12.95

Grades: K 1 2   E

1. Imagination -- Fiction 2. Natural history -- Fiction

ISBN 978-1-55365-532-9; 1-55365-532-X

With the help of their parents and their own imaginations, Jamie and Megan discover that natural magic is all around them, even in their own home. Sheets and pillows, fruits and furniture—they all come from nature. What's more, the air isn't just empty space—it's full of smells, sounds, water, and life-giving gases.

Suzuki "presents a whimsical and beautifully illustrated children's book that speaks to a child's imagination and creativity. . . . The illustrations are lively and boldly colored." Sci Books Films

Swaim, Jessica

The **hound** from the pound; illustrated by Jill McElmurry. Candlewick Press 2007 un il $15.99

Grades: K 1 2   E

1. Dogs -- Fiction

ISBN 978-0-7636-2330-2; 0-7636-2330-X

LC 2006051851

When lonely Miss Mary Lynn MacIntosh decides to adopt Blue, a basset hound from the pound, she gets far more companionship than she ever expected.

"Swaim's playful poetry, dog puns, and refreshingly sophisticated vocabulary . . . make for a lively and substantial read-aloud. McElmurry's gouache paintings project a retro sensibility yet feel modern and fresh. Her warm, color-washed scenes extend the humor." Booklist

Swain, Gwenyth

Riding to Washington; written by Gwenyth Swain; illustrated by David Geister. Sleeping Bear Press 2008 un il (Tales of young Americans) $17.95

Grades: 1 2 3 4   E

1. Clergy 2. Nonfiction writers 3. Civil rights activists 4. Nobel laureates for peace 5. Race relations -- Fiction 6. African Americans -- Fiction

ISBN 978-1-58536-324-7; 1-58536-324-3

"The illustrations provide a strong sense of the period. The soft earth tones and rounded forms create a mood of safety and stability. This heartfelt tale provides an unusual and compelling perspective on a historical event." SLJ

Swallow, Pamela Curtis

Groundhog gets a say; as told to Pamela Curtis Swallow; illustrated by Denise Brunkus. G.P. Putnam's Sons 2005 un il $15.99

Grades: PreK K 1 2   E

1. Crows -- Fiction 2. Marmots -- Fiction 3. Squirrels -- Fiction

ISBN 0-399-23876-X

A groundhog describes his various characteristics to a skeptical squirrel and crow. Text includes various facts about groundhogs

"The humorous text is completed by Brunkus's finely executed, animated, watercolor-and-colored-pencil drawings." SLJ

Swanson, Susan Marie

★ The **house** in the night; written by Susan Marie Swanson and illustrated by Beth Krommes. Houghton Mifflin Company 2008 un il $16

Grades: PreK K 1   E

1. Light -- Fiction 2. Night -- Fiction 3. Houses -- Fiction

ISBN 978-0-618-86244-3; 0-618-86244-7

LC 2007012921

Awarded the Caldecott Medal, 2009

Illustrations and easy-to-read text explore the light that makes a house in the night a home filled with light.

"Inspired by traditional cumulative poetry, Swanson weaves a soothing song that is as luminescent and soulful as the gorgeous illustrations that accompany her words. . . . Krommes's folk-style black-and-white etchings with touches of yellow-orange make the world of the poem an enchanted place." SLJ

To be like the sun; [by] Susan Marie Swanson; [illustrated by] Margaret Chodos-Irvine. Harcourt 2008 un il $16

Grades: K 1 2 3   E

1. Seeds -- Fiction 2. Sunflowers -- Fiction

ISBN 978-0-15-205796-1; 0-15-205796-X

LC 2006103262

A child reflects on how a small, striped gray seed eventually becomes a strong, beautiful sunflower

"The lyrical free verse is enhanced by Chodos-Irvine's colorful linocuts. The blocky yet realistic prints fit the mood perfectly and bring subtle layers of interpretation to the words." SLJ

The **first** thing my mama told me; illustrated by Christine Davenier. Harcourt 2002 un il $16

Grades: PreK K 1 2   E

1. Identity 2. Names, Personal 3. Growth -- Fiction 4. Personal names -- Fiction

ISBN 0-15-201075-0

LC 2001-986

"Davenier's delightful pictures are a great match for the text. Using a combination of pencil, ink, and pastel, she achieves a spunky, free-spirited look." Booklist

Swartz, Daniel J.

Bim and Bom; a Shabbat tale. illustrated by Melissa Iwai. rev ed.; Kar-Ben 2011 un il pa $8.95

Grades: PreK K 1 2   E

1. Jews -- Fiction 2. Sabbath -- Fiction

ISBN 978-0-7613-6717-8; 0-7613-6717-9

LC 2010028264

A revised and newly illustrated edition of the title first published 1996

Bim, a housebuilder, and Bom, a baker, work hard all week, and then spend every Friday doing good deeds, "mitzvot," and meet joyfully at sundown to celebrate Shabbat together.

"Great for sharing on Shabbat, this title concludes with the musical notation and lyrics to 'Shabbat Shalom.' Kids will appreciate the reversal of the traditional gender roles as well as the enduring message." Booklist

Sweet, Melissa

Carmine; a little more red. by Melissa Sweet. Houghton Mifflin 2005 un il $16

Grades: PreK K 1 2   E

1. Alphabet 2. Fairy tales 3. Dogs -- Fiction 4. Wolves -- Fiction

ISBN 0-618-38794-3

LC 2004-9212

While a little girl who loves red—and loves to dillydally—stops to paint a picture on the way to visit her grandmother, her dog Rufus meets a wolf and leads him directly to Granny's house.

"A fetching retelling of 'Little Red Riding Hood' that also works as an effective alphabet book. . . . The fresh and imaginative mixed-media art imitates the sketchbook of a child artist." SLJ

★ **Tupelo** rides the rails; written and illustrated by Melissa Sweet. Houghton Mifflin Company 2008 un il $17

Grades: K 1 2 3   E

1. Dogs -- Fiction 2. Stars -- Fiction 3. Tramps -- Fiction 4. Wishes -- Fiction 5. Railroads -- Fiction

ISBN 978-0-618-71714-9; 0-618-71714-5

LC 2007012924

After being left by the side of a road with nothing but her favorite sock toy, Tupelo meets a pack of dogs named the BONEHEADS (The Benevolent Order of Nature's Exalted Hounds Earnest And Doggedly Sublime), led by a hobo named Garbage Pail Tex. Tupelo joins them as they are wishing on Sirius, the Dog Star, for new homes, and as they catch a passing train.

"Sweet's beautifully detailed artwork, in watercolor and mixed-media, is packed with feeling and story." Booklist

Swift, Hildegarde Hoyt

★ The **little** red lighthouse and the great gray bridge; by Hildegarde H. Swift and [illustrated by] Lynd Ward. Harcourt 2002 un il $16

Grades: PreK K 1 2   E

1. Lighthouses 2. Lighthouses -- Fiction

ISBN 0-15-204571-6

LC 2001-7106

A reissue of the title first published 1942

"The story is written with imagination and a gift for bringing alive this little lighthouse and its troubles. . . . [Lynd Ward's] illustrations have some distinction and one in particular, the fog creeping over the river clutching at the river boats, has atmosphere, rhythm and good colour." Ont Libr Rev

Swinburne, Stephen R.

Whose shoes? a shoe for every job. Boyds Mills Press 2010 un il $16.95

Grades: PreK   E

1. Shoes

ISBN 978-1-59078-569-0; 1-59078-569-X

Swinburne "offers a guessing game in which a photo on the right-hand page shows a person below the knees and asks, Whose shoes? A turn of the page gives the answer and a full-length photo of a ballerina (or farmer, Army National Guard soldier, post office worker, clown . . .) on the left. The facing page repeats the question Whose Shoes? with a new photo. . . . The clear, colorful photos provide plenty of talking points, while the short text flows in a conversational way." Booklist

Swope, Sam

Gotta go! Gotta go! pictures by Sue Riddle. Farrar, Straus & Giroux 2000 un il hardcover o.p. pa $5.95
Grades: PreK K 1 2   E
1. Butterflies 2. Caterpillars 3. Monarch butterfly
ISBN 0-374-32757-2; 0-374-427867-0 pa
LC 99-28503

Although she does not know why or how, a caterpillar who becomes a monarch butterfly is certain that she must make her way to Mexico

"The rhythm and repetition are infectious; and the pen-and-ink and watercolor illustrations, set against expanses of white space, enlarge the book remarkably." Horn Book Guide

Sydor, Colleen

Timmerman was here; illustrated by Nicolas Debon. Tundra Books 2009 un il $19.95
Grades: K 1 2 3   E
1. Friendship -- Fiction
ISBN 978-0-88776-890-3; 0-88776-890-3

"A little girl is forced to contend with a boarder, Timmerman, when he temporarily occupies the bedroom of her Granddad, who has moved to a senior citizens' home. Despite her resentment, the little girl begins to appreciate the boarder's kindness, diligence, helpfulness and soft-spoken demeanor. But Timmerman's mysterious late-night walks, carrying a spade and burlap sack, raise everyone's suspicions. . . . Debon's deep, dark, Depression-era-style paintings rendered in gouache and colored and wax pencils show one man's work ethic opposite a child's intuitive yet waning confidence in a story filled with mystery, misperceptions, doubt and friendship. . . . Readers' and listeners' predictions will abound as will discussion of how one's actions should be interpreted and noted. Provocative." Kirkus

Sylvester, Kevin

Splinters; (this girl needs a miracle. . . .) Tundra Books 2010 un il $17.95
Grades: K 1 2 3   E
1. Fairy tales 2. Hockey -- Fiction
ISBN 978-0-88776-944-3; 0-88776-944-6

"Cindy is a destitute but excellent hockey player who can't catch a break. When she finally saves enough money to join a league, it's dominated by two evil sisters and their mother, the coach. They keep Cindy on the bench and nickname her 'Splinters.' When the acclaimed coach Charmaine Prince holds tryouts for the All-Star team, Cindy needs the help of her Fairy Goaltender to get to the rink on time on a new Zamboni. . . . The watercolor and pencil illustrations depict the actions and emotions of the characters perfectly. The facial expressions are spot-on." SLJ

Symes, Ruth

Harriet dancing; by Ruth Symes; illustrated by Caroline Jayne Church. Chicken House 2008 un il $16.99
Grades: PreK K 1   E
1. Dance -- Fiction 2. Hedgehogs -- Fiction 3. Butterflies -- Fiction
ISBN 978-0-545-03204-9; 0-545-03204-0
LC 2007015258

Harriet the hedgehog learns that dancing is for everyone, big and small

"Church's collage illustrations are charming and vibrant, and children will love the depictions of the protagonist as she progresses through the story." SLJ

Taback, Simms

★ I miss you every day; by Simms Taback. Viking Children's Books 2007 un il $16.99
Grades: PreK K 1 2   E
1. Stories in rhyme 2. Postal service -- Fiction
ISBN 978-0-670-06192-1
LC 2007008046

A little girl misses someone so much that she wraps herself up like a package and sends herself through the mail.

"Anyone who has ever yearned for an absent loved one will treasure this beautifully simple picture book. . . . Taback's trademark wavy outlines and simple shapes . . . add both whimsy and wide appeal." SLJ

Simms Taback's big book of words. Blue Apple Books 2004 un il $12.95
Grades: PreK K   E
1. Vocabulary 2. Reference books 3. Picture dictionaries
ISBN 1-59354-035-3

Illustrations and text present common toys, articles of clothing, foods and animals.

"A superb choice for emergent readers. The book's simple elegance is eye-catching. . . . The vibrant colors . . . draw children's attention to each picture." SLJ

Simms Taback's city animals. Blue Apple Books 2009 un il $12.99
Grades: PreK K 1   E
1. Animals -- Fiction 2. City and town life -- Fiction
ISBN 978-1-934706-52-7; 1-934706-52-3
LC 2008044713

The reader is invited to guess which animal is hiding beneath fold-outs that reveal a succession of clues

"Children will love this bright, bold foldout book. . . . The text is simple and direct, with a typeface that is easy to read." SLJ

Simms Taback's farm animals. Blue Apple Books 2011 un bd bk $12.99
Grades: PreK   E
1. Board books for children 2. Farm life -- Fiction 3. Domestic animals -- Fiction
ISBN 978-1-60905-078-8; 1-60905-078-9
LC 2011019081

The reader is invited to guess which farm animal is hiding beneath fold-outs that reveal a succession of clues.

"The simple, boldly outlined and brightly colored illustrations portray each animal standing against a monochromatic sky ranging in color from yellow to blue to purple. The pages are constructed of sturdy card stock, allowing small fingers to practice unfolding and re-folding the flaps. An amusing and instructive story." SLJ

★ Simms Taback's Safari animals. Blue Apple Books 2008 un il $12.95

Grades: PreK K   **E**
1. Animals -- Fiction
ISBN 978-1-934706-19-0; 1-934706-19-1

"This book is boldly illustrated and cheerful, with fold-out pages that contain guessing games. On the first verso, 'Who am I?' is written in a childlike, chunky font next to a pair of huge gray legs with pink-toed feet. The facing page is black, with the words 'I have big feet' in white letters. Open it upward and a larger view of the animal is unveiled. . . . The newly opened flap is a vivid blue and contains the words, 'I have a long nose.' The page folds out once again to reveal the whole animal: . . . 'I'm an ELEPHANT!' That's the formula for six creatures—but the formula doesn't begin to describe the wonder of opening up each page into a satis- fyingly enormous illustration in the master designer/illustra- tor's typically pleasing shapes with thick, black outlines and wildly contrasting colors." SLJ

Tafolla, Carmen

★ **Fiesta** babies; illustrated by Amy Cordova. Tricycle Press 2010 un il $12.99
Grades: PreK K   **E**
1. Stories in rhyme 2. Infants -- Fiction 3. Mexican Americans -- Fiction
ISBN 978-1-5824-6319-3; 1-5824-6319-0
             LC 2009016301
Pura Belpré Award honor book (Illustrator), 2011
"Short lines of bouncy, rhyming text describe how sev- eral adorable, chubby babies and toddlers participate in their local Hispanic celebration. . . . The length and rhythm of the text make this book an excellent choice for toddler and preschool storytimes. Córdova once again demonstrates how her award-winning style brilliantly brings an author's words to life. Her bold acrylic colors and brisk brushstrokes cap- ture the fiesta's energy and good cheer." SLJ

What can you do with a rebozo? by Carmen Tafolla; illustrations by Amy Cordova. Tricycle Press 2007 un il $14.95
Grades: PreK K 1   **E**
1. Stories in rhyme 2. Mexican Americans -- Fiction 3. Clothing and dress -- Fiction
ISBN 978-1-58246-220-2; 1-58246-220-8
             LC 2006-39624
A Pura Belpre Illustrator Award honor book, 2009
A spunky, young Mexican American girl explains the many uses of her mother's red rebozo, or long scarf.
"Bright, textured acrylic illustrations with a strong sense of line decorate this celebration of cultural heritage. An author's note gives more information about the rebozo as well as asking readers what they might do with one." Horn Book Guide

Tafuri, Nancy

All kinds of kisses. Little, Brown 2012 un il $16.99
Grades: PreK   **E**
1. Bedtime -- Fiction 2. Kissing -- Fiction 3. Domestic animals -- Fiction
ISBN 978-0-316-12235-1; 0-316-12235-1
             LC 2010049433
Each barnyard animal has its favorite kind of kiss, but the best of all is a mother's goodnight kiss.

"Using her distinctively recognizable artwork rendered in watercolor and colored pencil, Tafuri has created another loving book for toddlers." SLJ

The **big** storm; a very soggy counting book. Simon & Schuster Books for Young Readers 2009 un il $15.99
Grades: PreK K   **E**
1. Counting 2. Storms -- Fiction 3. Animals -- Fiction
ISBN 978-1-4169-6795-8; 1-4169-6795-8
             LC 2007047989
Ten animals find shelter in a hill hollow one by one, but when the storm is over, a rumbling tells them there is still danger afoot.
"This title accomplishes much with simplicity. Repeti- tive words . . . add tension to the plot. Dramatic poses picture the animals' wariness of the storm ahead. . . . An autumn- colored palette with orange-and-yellow leaves swirling across a spread is rendered in watercolor and watercolor pencils." SLJ

★ **Blue** Goose. Simon & Schuster Books for Young Readers 2008 un il $15.99
Grades: PreK K   **E**
1. Color -- Fiction 2. Animals -- Fiction 3. Farm life -- Fiction 4. Color -- Juvenile literature
ISBN 978-1-4169-2834-8; 1-4169-2834-0
             LC 2006-38368
When Farmer Gray goes away for the day, Blue Goose, Red Hen, Yellow Chick, and White Duck get together and paint their black and white farm.
"The scenes have the bold, graphic punch of murals. . . . [The] generously sized animals and pithy text extend a warm welcome to readers." Publ Wkly

★ **Five** little chicks. Simon & Schuster Books for Young Readers 2006 un il $14.95
Grades: PreK K   **E**
1. Chickens -- Fiction
ISBN 0-689-87342-5
Five chicks and their mother peck in the corn patch in search of breakfast.
"Created with brush pen, watercolor pencils, and ink, the gorgeous double-page spreads, in warm shades of red, yel- low, and brown, manage to be both clear and fuzzy, simple and rich." Booklist

★ **Have** you seen my duckling? Greenwillow Bks. 1984 un il $16.99; lib bdg $17.89; pa $6.99; bd bk $6.99
Grades: PreK K   **E**
1. Ducks -- Fiction
9 lib bdg; 0-688-10994-2 pa; 0-688-14899-9 bd bk
             LC 83-17196
A Caldecott Medal honor book, 1985
"Tafuri's artwork . . . features clean lines, generous fig- ures, and clear, cool colors. She also adds nice detail—feath- ers, for instance, that you can almost feel under your hands." Booklist

★ **This** is the farmer. Greenwillow Bks. 1994 un il $16.99

Grades: PreK K 1 2   E
1. Farm life -- Fiction
ISBN 0-688-09468-6

LC 92-30082

A farmer's kiss causes an amusing chain of events on
the farm

"The well-defined, watercolor-and-ink double-spread illustrations are . . . of the highest quality. The brief story is
rhythmic, predictable, and printed in extra-large type." SLJ

Whose chick are you? Greenwillow Books 2007 un il
$16.99; lib bdg $17.89
Grades: PreK K   E
1. Birds -- Fiction 2. Swans -- Fiction
ISBN 0-06-082514-6; 0-06-082515-4 lib bdg

Goose, Duck, Hen, Bird and the little chick, itself, cannot
tell to whom a new hatchling belongs, but its mother knows.

"The artwork's close-up perspective and the combination of large type, onomatopoeia, and the clues to Little
Chick's parents scattered through the pictures will draw
children into the scenes." Booklist

★ **You** are special, little one. Scholastic Press 2003 un
il $16.95; bd bk $7.99
Grades: PreK K   E
1. Animals -- Fiction
ISBN 0-439-39879-7; 0-439-68613-X bd bk

LC 2002-151459

A variety of baby animals ask the question, "How am
I special?" and receive loving answers from their mothers
and fathers

"Tafuri's colored-pencil-and-watercolor art fills the
oversize pages, depicting tranquil panoramas of various animal habitats as well as plenty of cozy close-ups of parents
and children snuggling. Young children will be comforted by
the text's rhythmic reassurances." Booklist

The **busy** little squirrel; [by] Nancy Tafuri. Simon
& Schuster Books for Young Readers 2007 un il $15.99
Grades: PreK K   E
1. Autumn -- Fiction 2. Animals -- Fiction 3. Squirrels
-- Fiction
ISBN 978-0-689-87341-6; 0-689-87341-7

LC 2005015520

Squirrel is too busy getting ready for winter to nibble a
pumpkin with Mouse, run in the field with Dog, or otherwise
play with any of the other animals

"The ink-and-watercolor pictures show squirrel's flurry
of activity. . . . . The basic words and large, clearly defined
pictures of familiar animals are perfectly suited for preschool read-alouds." Booklist

Tallec, Olivier
  Waterloo & trafalgar; Olivier Tallec. Enchanted Lion
Books 2012 64 p. (alk. paper) $17.95
Grades: 1 2 3 4 5   E
1. War stories 2. Soldiers -- Juvenile literature
ISBN 1592701272; 9781592701278

LC 2012937561

This children's picture book by Olivier Tallec "portrays two characters, separated only by narrow walls, who
watch each other ceaselessly through the seasons. Moving
between day and night . . . they fight their cold war, full
of suspicion, never daring to bridge the gap between them.

As time passes, a snail shows up, and then a bird, and one
day, to their utter surprise, they come face-to-face in a different way, and they discover that their differences don't make
them enemies."(Publisher's note)

Tankard, Jeremy
  Grumpy Bird. Scholastic Press 2007 un il $12.99
Grades: K 1 2 3   E
1. Birds -- Fiction 2. Emotions -- Fiction
ISBN 0-439-85147-5; 978-0-439-85147-3

LC 2006-03770

Feeling too grumpy to fly, Bird begins to walk and finds
that his mood changes as other animals join him.

"This straightforward story is enlivened by unusual
mixed-media illustrations. Each scene consists of sketches
of farmland or trees, layered over photographs of real farms
and trees. Cheerful flowers and stars are scribbled throughout. The animal characters are simplistic cartoons with thick
black outlines and comical facial expressions." SLJ
  Another title about Bird is:
  Boo hoo Bird (2009)

Me hungry! Candlewick Press 2008 un il $15.99
Grades: PreK K   E
1. Animals -- Fiction 2. Prehistoric peoples -- Fiction
ISBN 978-0-7636-3360-8; 0-7636-3360-7

LC 2007-35735

A little prehistoric boy decides to hunt for his own food,
and makes a new friend in the process.

"Tankard's bold, thick black lines, done in ink and digital media, outline the youngster and his many choices for a
snack, allowing the characters to jump off the monochromatic pages. Minimal but effective text perfectly complements the expressive prehistoric family. This energetic story
comes full circle with a humorous punch line that will make
all children with busy parents laugh out loud." SLJ

Tarlow, Ellen
  Pinwheel days; by Ellen Tarlow; art by Gretel Parker.
Star Bright Books 2007 56p il pa $6.95
Grades: K 1 2   E
1. Animals -- Fiction 2. Donkeys -- Fiction 3. Squirrels
-- Fiction 4. Friendship -- Fiction
ISBN 978-1-59572-059-7 pa; 1-59572-059-6 pa

In four separate stories, Pinwheel the donkey learns
about friendship when his loneliness ends after meeting his
"echo," a lovely picnic stems from a mistake, his rubbing on
a tree seems to break it, and his best dream ever comes true

"The four easy-to-read chapters feature abundant dialogue and humorous plots. Complementing the text, the
watercolor illustrations are characterized by round figures,
warm earth tones, and decorative elements such as multiple
patterns." SLJ

Tarpley, Natasha
  Bippity Bop barbershop; by Natasha Anastasia Tarpley;
illustrated by E.B. Lewis. Little, Brown 2002 un il $15.95
Grades: PreK K 1 2   E
1. African Americans 2. Barbershops 3. Haircutting
4. Fathers and sons 5. African Americans -- Fiction 6.
Barbers and barbershops -- Fiction
ISBN 0-316-52284-8

LC 00-30188

A story celebrating a young African-American boy's first trip to the barbershop

"Expressive watercolors showcase [the child's] curiosity, fear, and satisfaction, as well as a close father-son relationship." Horn Book Guide

Tarpley, Todd

How about a kiss for me? illustrated by Liza Woodruff. Dutton Chidren's Books 2010 un il $16.99
Grades: PreK E
1. Stories in rhyme 2. Animals -- Fiction 3. Kissing -- Fiction 4. Parent-child relationship -- Fiction
ISBN 978-0-525-42235-8; 0-525-42235-8

A baby tries to kiss things, from a dog and a frog to a mop and a jellyfish, before deciding that parents are the best recipients of kisses.

"The illustrations are sweet and humorous—readers can tell from the expression on the little boy's face whether or not he is inclined to kiss that animal. This book would be ideal as an individual lap-sit or storytime selection." SLJ

Tarshis, Lauren

I survived the Battle of Gettysburg, 1863; Lauren Tarshis. Scholastic 2013 89 p. (paperback) $4.99
Grades: 3 4 5 6 E
1. Fugitive slaves -- Juvenile fiction 2. Gettysburg (Pa.), Battle of, 1863 -- Juvenile fiction
ISBN 0545459362; 9780545459365

This children's book, by Lauren Tarshis, is book 7 in the "I Survived" series. "It's 1863, and Thomas and his little sister, Birdie, have fled the farm where they were born and raised as slaves. . . . They soon cross paths with a Union soldier . . . , marching with the army. But then orders come through: The men are called to battle in Pennsylvania. Thomas has made it so far . . . but does he have what it takes to survive Gettysburg?" (Publisher's note)

Tashiro, Chisato

Five nice mice; [by] Chisato Tashiro; translated from the Japanese by Sayako Uchida; adapted by Kate Westerlund. Penguin/Minedition 2007 un il $16.99
Grades: PreK K 1 2 E
1. Mice -- Fiction 2. Frogs -- Fiction 3. Music -- Fiction
ISBN 978-0-698-40058-0

"After five little mice sneak into the park to hear the frog chorus, they are enthralled; then they are thrown out of the frogs-only concert. Haunted by what they have heard, the mice decide to form their own orchestra. . . . When the mice perform to wild applause, frogs in the audience join in, and then they play music together. Filled with light and color, the double-page spreads, executed in watercolor and pastels, are crowded yet clear, and they extend the story of each individual. " Booklist

Tavares, Matt

Mudball; [by] Matt Tavares. Candlewick Press 2005 un il $15.99
Grades: K 1 2 3 E
1. Baseball -- Fiction
ISBN 0-7636-2387-3
LC 2004-40671

During a rainy Minneapolis Millers baseball game in 1903, Little Andy Oyler has the chance to become a hero by hitting the shortest and muddiest home run in history

"The large-scale, softly shaded pencil drawings have plenty of motion, just right for a sports story. . . . An attractive book for baseball fans who enjoy watching small heroes triumph and don't mind a bit of nostalgia." Booklist

Taxali, Gary

This is silly! Scholastic Press 2010 un il $17.99
Grades: PreK K E
1. Stories in rhyme
ISBN 978-0-439-71836-3; 0-439-71836-8

Billy, Willy, Dilly, and Lilly take turns being silly.

"The rhyming text is not plot-driven but revels in phonemic silliness, with lots of action and playful turns of phrase. . . . The combination of vibrant illustrations with rollicking rhymes will engage young readers and art buffs alike." SLJ

Taylor, Debbie A.

Sweet music in Harlem; illustrated by Frank Morrison. Lee & Low Books 2004 un il $16.95
Grades: K 1 2 3 E
1. Jazz musicians -- Fiction 2. African Americans -- Fiction
ISBN 1-58430-165-1
LC 2003-8994

C.J., who aspires to be as great a jazz musician as his uncle, searches for Uncle Click's hat in preparation for an important photograph and inadvertently gathers some of the greatest musicians of 1950s Harlem to join in on the picture

"This dazzling tale is filled with energy, rhythm, and style from its attention-grabbing cover to its satisfying ending. . . . The acrylic illustrations make the text come alive." SLJ

Taylor, Sean

Huck runs amuck! story by Sean Taylor; art by Peter H. Reynolds. Dial Books for Young Readers 2011 un il $16.99
Grades: PreK K 1 2 E
1. Goats -- Fiction
ISBN 0-8037-3261-9; 978-0-8037-3261-2

"Huck is a goat with an eclectic appetite. . . . His all-time favorite tasty treats are flowers. . . . Even flower patterns on clothing or table linens call to him. Huck tries, but each attempt to reach those elusive flowers leads to disaster. . . . Taylor employs simple, conversational language in a fast-paced, almost breathless, easy-breezy cadence that draws readers right into Huck's adventures. Double-page spreads of Reynolds' detailed, cartoon-like, watercolor, ink and tea illustrations on a bright, white background surround the large-print text. . . . [Huck's] expressions are wildly enthusiastic, goofy and totally demented. Hilarious, laugh-out-loud fun." Kirkus

The ring went zing! a story that ends with a kiss. pictures by Jill Barton. Dial Books for Young Readers 2010 un il $16.99
Grades: PreK K 1 2 E
1. Love -- Fiction 2. Frogs -- Fiction 3. Animals -- Fiction 4. Chickens -- Fiction
ISBN 978-0-8037-3311-4; 0-8037-3311-9
LC 2008001718

A frog, in love with a chicken, buys her a golden ring, but when the ring falls and skips away, they begin to chase after it, joined along the way by a jogging swan, a motorcycling sausage dog, and other helpful creatures.

"Taylor's rhyming prose mimics the bouncing ring with lots of delicious sound words thrown in. . . . A small surprise ending crowns the adventure. A love story that's long on charm and entirely free of mush." Publ Wkly

Robomop; by Sean Taylor; pictures by Edel Rodriguez. Dial Books for Young Readers 2013 32 p. (hardcover) $16.99

Grades: K 1 2   E

1. Robots -- Juvenile fiction 2. Humorous fiction -- Juvenile fiction 3. Humorous stories 4. Robots -- Fiction 5. Mops and mopsticks -- Fiction
ISBN 0803734115; 9780803734111
                                              LC 2012012901

This humorous children's story, by Sean Taylor, illustrated by Edel Rodriguez, follows "Robomop, a hardworking robot who's good at his job, which is cleaning . . . the public restroom. But it's not all mopping, slopping, rubbing, and scrubbing. Robomop also does a wicked honky-tonk dance to the window washer's radio, and he dreams of seeing the sun and sky. So when he's carried outside one day, Robomop believes his wish has come true at last." (Publisher's note)

When a monster is born; [illustrated by] Nick Sharratt. Roaring Brook Press 2007 un il $16.95

Grades: PreK K 1   E

1. Monsters -- Fiction
ISBN 978-1-59643-254-3; 1-59643-254-3
                                              LC 2006-20890

Explores the options available to a monster from the time it is born, such as becoming the scary monster under someone's bed or playing on the school basketball team.

"The words have the rhythm of a chant. . . . Sharratt's neon-toned artwork, which has the look of computer-generated collage, features a furry, round, lime-green monster, whose pink horns and buck teeth make an endearingly goofy star. Bright, funny, and interactive." Booklist

The **world** champion of staying awake; [illustrations by] Jimmy Liao. Candlewick Press 2011 il $15.99

Grades: PreK K 1   E

1. Toys -- Fiction 2. Bedtime -- Fiction
ISBN 978-0-7636-4957-9; 0-7636-4957-0
                                              LC 2009051511

At bedtime, Stella must find a way to make her toys fall asleep before she can go to sleep.

"In contrast to the spot illustrations of the main story, which are set against white backgrounds, the characters' imagined expeditions are rich, full-bleed watercolor scenes, accompanied by rhymed couplets that balance the rowdiness of the bedtime preparations with cozy imagery and soothing rhythms. It's just the thing for testing the mettle of those who would lay claim to the titular honorific." Publ Wkly

Taylor, Thomas
Little Mouse and the big cupcake; written by Thomas Taylor; illustrated by Jill Barton. Boxer Books 2010 un il $16.95

Grades: PreK K   E

1. Cake -- Fiction 2. Mice -- Fiction 3. Animals --

Fiction
ISBN 978-1-907152-47-4; 1-907152-47-4

When one small mouse finds one big cupcake he wonders how he will get it home. It's much too heavy for him to carry. So, one by one, Little Mouse asks his animal friends to help. They all say "yes" but only after taking a nibble of the yummy treat.

"Children will like the predictable rhythm, the rhyme on the last page, and the sound effects they are prompted to make throughout the book. Watercolor, pencil, and graphite ink illustrations and large brown text appear against a soft white background. The cheerfulness of this story extends to the jacket flap and endpapers. Sure to be a storytime favorite." SLJ

Teague, David
★ **Franklin's** big dreams; pictures by Boris Kulikov. Disney/Hyperion Books 2010 il $16.99

Grades: PreK K 1   E

1. Night -- Fiction 2. Dreams -- Fiction 3. Building -- Fiction
ISBN 978-1-4231-1919-7; 1-4231-1919-3
                                              LC 2010004520

"Teague imagines how dreams are made from the point of view of a young boy and his dog. Night after night, construction crews break into Franklin's bedroom to build train tracks, a runway, a canal; they're all deconstructed before the break of day. . . . It's the mystery that makes this so imaginative and fresh. Kulikov's dramatic paintings freature a chiaroscruo effect; Franklin's nighttime room is portrayed in navy blues and subdued colors, while warm yellow light pours from the towering forms of the train, jet, and boat." Booklist

Teague, Mark
Dear Mrs. LaRue; letters from obedience school. written and illustrated by Mark Teague. Scholastic Press 2002 un il $15.95

Grades: PreK K 1 2 3   E

1. Dogs 2. Pets 3. Letters 4. Dogs -- Fiction 5. Dogs -- Training 6. Humorous stories
ISBN 0-439-20663-4
                                              LC 2001-43479

Gertrude LaRue receives typewritten and paw-written letters from her dog Ike, entreating her to let him leave the Igor Brotweiler Canine Academy and come back home

"The humorous acrylic illustrations are, at times, a howl and the over-sized format is well-suited to storytelling." SLJ

Other titles about Mrs. LaRue and her dog Ike are:
Detective LaRue (2004)
LaRue for mayor (2008)
LaRue across America: postcards from the vacation (2011)

Firehouse! Orchard Books 2010 un il $16.99

Grades: PreK K   E

1. Dogs -- Fiction 2. Fire fighting -- Fiction
ISBN 978-0-439-91500-7; 0-439-91500-7
                                              LC 2009-12100

Edward and his cousin Judy come for a visit to the firehouse and learn how everything works with some unexpected results.

"The author's deadpan text is cleverly paired with silly, expansive antics depicted in the crisp oil artwork. . . . This perky blend of educational field trip and funny outing brings readers into the action with bold, often close-perspective scenes and a few entertaining details." Publ Wkly

Funny Farm. Orchard Books 2009 un il $16.99
Grades: PreK K E
   1. Dogs -- Fiction 2. Animals -- Fiction 3. Farm life -- Fiction
   ISBN 978-0-439-91499-4; 0-439-91499-X
LC 2008-02477

"When Edward, a city-slicker dog, arrives at his canine relatives' farm for a visit, Teague provides the perfect setup for this goofily sweet fish-out-of-water tale. . . . The narrative nature of the crisp oil illustrations reveals a much more entertaining version of the story than does the straightforward text. . . . Young readers will find plenty to revisit in the humorous bucolic scenes of barnyard creatures at work and play." Publ Wkly

Another title about Edward is:
Firehouse! (2010)

Pigsty. Scholastic 1994 un il hardcover o.p. pa $6.99
Grades: PreK K 1 2 3 E
   1. Pigs -- Fiction 2. Cleanliness -- Fiction
   ISBN 0-590-45915-5; 0-439-59843-5 pa
LC 93-21179

When Wendell doesn't clean up his room, a whole herd of pigs comes to live with him

"Much of the tale's fun resides in Teague's quirky acrylic art. . . . Whether Wendell and his friends are jumping on the bed or playing Monopoly on the rug, their antics are rendered in the bold palette of a gleefully inventive imagination. Highly recommended for neat-freaks and mess-makers alike." Publ Wkly

Teckentrup, Britta
   Big Smelly Bear; [by] Britta Teckentrup. Sterling Pub. 2007 un il $12.95
Grades: PreK K E
   1. Bears -- Fiction 2. Cleanliness -- Fiction
   ISBN 978-1-905417-37-7
LC 2006101350

Big Fluffy Bear insists that Big Smelly Bear visit the pond for a bath before she will scratch the itch he cannot reach

"This charming oversize book is accompanied by watercolor illustrations." SLJ

★ **Grumpy** cat; by Britta Teckentrup. Boxer 2008 un il $14.95
Grades: PreK K E
   1. Cats -- Fiction
   ISBN 978-1-905417-69-8; 1-905417-69-1

"The frowning, brown cat with black stripes sits alone, eats alone, and is considered grumpy by other cats. . . . One stormy night a tiny, orange kitten shows up, wet and soggy. . . . The characters are appealing, the story is short and linear, and the ending is warm and satisfactory. But the highpoint is the art: graphically inspired, textured, and large in scale." Booklist

Little wolf's song. Boxer Books 2010 un il $16.95

Grades: PreK K 1 E
   1. Wolves -- Fiction
   ISBN 978-1-907152-33-7; 1-907152-33-4

Even though Little Wolf's mom, dad, sister, and brothers all have their own special song, he can only manage a poor, pitiful squeak. But one snowy day, Little Wolf finds himself lost and alone in the woods and he discovers his own special, beautiful voice.

"This effective picture book touches on many issues that children experience. . . . Created using digital collage of hand-printed paper, the large-scale illustrations feature clean lines, simple forms, and restrained use of color." Booklist

Tegen, Katherine
   The **story** of the Jack O'Lantern; illustrated by Brandon Dorman. Harper 2010 un il $12.99; lib bdg $14.89
Grades: K 1 2 3 E
   1. Devil -- Fiction 2. Pumpkin -- Fiction 3. Halloween -- Fiction
   ISBN 978-0-06-143088-6; 0-06-143088-9; 978-0-06-143090-9 lib bdg; 0-06-143090-0 lib bdg
LC 2008046150

On Halloween night, Jack—a stingy and mean man—makes a deal with the devil for a free dinner, only to regret his choice many years later when the devil comes to collect.

"Lavish, carefully composed, full-page illustrations with the look of oil paintings clearly depict the actions of the despicable characters against pleasingly detailed backgrounds. . . . Well suited for use in a pumpkin-decorating program—or any Halloween program." Booklist

The **story** of the leprechaun; illustrated by Sally Anne Lambert. Harper 2011 un il $12.99; lib bdg $14.89
Grades: PreK K 1 2 E
   1. Magic -- Fiction 2. Wishes -- Fiction 3. Fairies -- Fiction 4. Leprechauns -- Fiction
   ISBN 978-0-06-143086-2; 0-06-143086-2; 978-0-06-143085-5 lib bdg; 0-06-143085-4 lib bdg
LC 2008034358

A clever leprechaun who has amassed a pot of gold by making beautiful shoes for people decides to hide his money at the end of a rainbow, knowing that no one will find it there.

"The descriptive, entertaining narrative is well paced and read-aloud-friendly, and enchanting color illustrations, with soft textures and patterns, portray characters, settings, and events in both small vignettes and page-filling spreads." Booklist

Tekavec, Heather
   Storm is coming! pictures by Margaret Spengler. Dial Bks. for Young Readers 2002 un il $14.99
Grades: PreK K 1 2 E
   1. Storms 2. Domestic animals 3. Storms -- Fiction 4. Domestic animals -- Fiction
   ISBN 0-8037-2626-0
LC 00-34622

The animals misunderstand the farmer's "Storm" warning and expect someone scary and mean

"Children will giggle over the animals' confusion and enjoy the well-paced buildup of suspense. Inviting pastel illustrations feature round, cartoonlike animals and dramatic use of perspective." Horn Book Guide

Tenzing Norbu

Secret of the snow leopard; [by] Tenzing Norbu, Lama with Stéphane Frattini. Douglas & McIntyre 2004 un il $16.95

Grades: 1 2 3 4   E

1. Himalaya Mountains -- Fiction

ISBN 0-88899-544-X

Tsering, a boy from a small Nepali village, and "his stepfather accompany the village healer, who is gravely ill, on a journey to the monastery where he will seek a cure. . . . On the way home, Tsering . . . asserts his independence by climbing the dangerous pass where his father . . . lost his life. . . . Handsome earth-tone paintings, stylized and carefully composed, portray the people and animals that belong to this stark landscape. . . . The quiet authority of the artwork and the drama of the story will engage children emotionally." SLJ

Another title about Tsering is:
Himalaya (2002)

Thayer, Jane

The **popcorn** dragon; written by Jane Thayer; illustrated by Lisa McCue. Morrow Junior Bks. 1989 un il $17.99

Grades: PreK K 1 2   E

1. Dragons -- Fiction

ISBN 0-688-08340-4

LC 88-39855

A newly illustrated edition of the title first published 1953

Though his hot breath is the envy of all the other animals, a young dragon learns that showing off does not make friends

"McCue's new full-color illustrations capture the whimsical mood of the fable. The animals, although too coy, have appealing humanlike expressions which convey their envy and contempt." SLJ

The **puppy** who wanted a boy; illustrated by Lisa McCue. HarperCollins Pubs. 2003 un il $14.99; lib bdg $15.89

Grades: PreK K 1 2   E

1. Dogs -- Fiction 2. Christmas -- Fiction

ISBN 0-06-052696-3; 0-06-052697-1 lib bdg

A reissue of the edition published 1986 by Morrow; story first published 1958 with different illustrations

When Petey the puppy decides that he wants a boy for Christmas, he discovers that he must go out and find one on his own

"It is the same, somewhat sentimental but certainly appealing tale that Thayer fashioned in 1958, when this was originally published; however, McCue's affectionately drawn, warmly colored illustrations go a long way toward perking up the story." Booklist

Thierry, Raphael

Green butterfly; a Superdog adventure. [by] Raphael Thierry. Handprint Books 2007 un il $7.95

Grades: 2 3 4   E

1. Dogs -- Fiction 2. Butterflies -- Fiction

ISBN 978-1-59354-198-9; 1-59354-198-8

Original French edition, 2000; first English language edition published 2005 in the United Kingdom

"Green Butterfly alights on Superdog's nose, notices that the white pup is tied to a post, and proceeds to flutter about, flaunting his own freedom. But wise Superdog is not to be bothered; he uses his imagination and a little optimism to find flexibility in his fetters. . . . Minimal text and a subdued, mostly mauve palette draw attention to Superdog's red choker and the white butterfly's wings in spring green. . . . Children . . . will innately understand that there is more to Superdog than meets the eye and delight in uncovering the meaning in this small gem." SLJ

Thiesing, Lisa

★ The **Aliens** are coming! Dutton Children's Books 2004 32p il $13.99

Grades: K 1 2   E

1. Musicians 2. Rock music 3. Pigs -- Fiction 4. Miscommunication 5. Rock musicians -- Fiction

ISBN 0-525-47277-0

LC 2003-19303

Peggy the pig becomes very worried when she hears that the Aliens are coming, but then she learns that they are a rock band.

"This clever tale will appeal to newly independent readers." SLJ

Other titles about Peggy are:
A dark and noisy night (2005)
The scarecrow's new clothes (2006)
The Viper (2002)

Thisdale, François, 1964-

Nini. Tundra Books 2011 un il $15.95

Grades: PreK K 1   E

1. Adoption -- Fiction

ISBN 978-1-77049-270-7; 1-77049-270-4

Original French edition published 2009 in Canada

Long before Nini was born, she was in a safe place where a familiar voice promised her a loving home. But once she was born, that soft voice was replaced by the words of care givers in an orphanage. Then, one day, a man and a woman on the other side of the world learned that their dreams were about to come true. They would finally have a baby to love.

This is a "heart-warming poetic story of adoption. . . . Thisdale's imaginative use of traditional drawing and painting, digitally manipulated, produces double pages that suggest rather than stipulate the images." SLJ

Thomas, Jan

Can you make a scary face? Beach Lane Books 2009 un il $12.99

Grades: PreK K 1   E

1. Frogs -- Fiction 2. Ladybugs -- Fiction 3. Imagination -- Fiction

ISBN 978-1-4169-8581-5; 1-4169-8581-6

LC 2008-38288

A ladybug invites the reader to play a game of "let's pretend."

"This book will have youngsters jumping, wiggling, dancing, pretending, and laughing. . . . The expressive ladybug is outlined in broad black lines and seems only inches away from readers. Adults will enjoy using this title to encourage lively activity and imaginative games. Children will love everything about it—especially the surprise ending." SLJ

Is everyone ready for fun? Beach Lane Books 2011 un il $12.99

Grades: PreK K 1   **E**

1. Cattle -- Fiction 2. Chickens -- Fiction
ISBN 978-1-4424-2364-0; 1-4424-2364-1

LC 2011005212

Chicken's cow visitors try to jump, dance, and wiggle on his couch, which is much too tiny for such exuberant activities.

"Thomas's illustrations energetically emphasize the cows' frenetic energy and the chicken's frustration, which are sure to draw giggles." Publ Wkly

★ **Rhyming** dust bunnies. Atheneum Books for Young Readers 2009 un il $12.99

Grades: K 1 2   **E**

1. Dust -- Fiction 2. Rhyme -- Fiction
ISBN 978-1-4169-7976-0; 1-4169-7976-X

LC 2008-28779

As three dust bunnies, Ed, Ned, and Ted, are demonstrating how much they love to rhyme, a fourth, Bob, is trying to warn them of approaching danger.

"The simple text and rhyming game-playing make this a natural as an early reader while also offering entertaining opportunities for readers-aloud. Digitally rendered art offers coloring-book strength and simplicity." Bull Cent Child Books

Another title about the dust bunnies is:
Here comes the big, mean dust bunny! (2009)

What will Fat Cat sit on? Harcourt 2007 un il $12.95

Grades: PreK K   **E**

1. Cats -- Fiction 2. Animals -- Fiction
ISBN 978-0-15-206051-0; 0-15-206051-0

LC 2006-24558

A group of animals is terrified at the prospect of being sat upon by the imposing Fat Cat, until the mouse comes up with a solution that satisfies everyone.

"Thomas . . . makes this book a laugh-out-loud pas de deux between Dick-and-Jane-get-stylish typography . . . and the supremely silly visual evocation of high anxiety. . . . She renders her barnyard characters in super-saturated colors and thick, bold outlines." Publ Wkly

The **doghouse**. Harcourt 2008 un il $12.95

Grades: PreK K   **E**

1. Dogs -- Fiction 2. Fear -- Fiction 3. Animals -- Fiction
ISBN 978-0-15-206533-1; 0-15-206533-4

LC 2007038355

Cow, Pig, Duck, and Mouse are afraid to retrieve their ball when it goes into the dog's house, but when they do go in they are pleasantly surprised.

"The simple cartoon characters, scenery, and dialogue balloons are outlined in thick, bold lines. Colors are smooth and flat, with backgrounds done in bright blues, purple, and lime green. The pictures are large and distinct, and will work well with a group." SLJ

Another title about Cow, Pig, Duck, and Mouse is:
A birthday for Cow! (2008)
Pumpkin trouble (2011)

Thomas, Patricia

Red sled; [by] Patricia Thomas; illustrated by Chris L. Demarest. Boyds Mills Press 2008 un il $16.95

Grades: PreK K 1   **E**

1. Stories in rhyme 2. Sledding -- Fiction 3. Father-son relationship -- Fiction
ISBN 978-1-59078-559-1; 1-59078-559-2

LC 2007-50838

A boy and his father lift one another's spirits by going sledding on a winter's night.

"The brief text consists of easy-to-read words in rhyming pairs. . . . Bright watercolor pictures capture perfectly the downcast faces of the characters when they are stuck inside during a snowstorm, . . . their expressions of happiness and excitement during their nocturnal adventure on the red sled." SLJ

Thomas, Shelley Moore

★ **Good** night, Good Knight; pictures by Jennifer Plecas. Dutton Children's Bks. 2000 47p il (Dutton easy reader) $13.99

Grades: PreK K 1 2   **E**

1. Bedtime 2. Dragons 3. Knights and knighthood
ISBN 0-525-46326-7

LC 99-28415

A Good Knight helps three little dragons who are having trouble getting to sleep.

"The short, simple, repetitive phrases are sure to capture the imaginations of young children. . . . With a palette dominated by the blues, grays, and purples of the nightime setting, Plecas's illustrations are a wonderful complement to this endearing tale." SLJ

Other titles about the Good Knight are:
A cold winter's Good Knight (2008)
Get well, Good Knight (2002)
Happy birthday, Good Knight (2006)
Take care Good Knight (2006)
A Good Knight's rest (2011)

Thomassie, Tynia

Feliciana Feyra LeRoux; a Cajun tall tale. illustrated by Cat Bowman Smith. Pelican 2005 un il $15.95

Grades: K 1 2 3   **E**

1. Cajuns -- Fiction 2. Alligators -- Fiction
ISBN 1-58980-286-1

A reissue of the title first published 1995 by Little, Brown

This "combines breezy watercolors and a swinging text that's perfect for reading aloud. A note on Cajun culture, a glossary, and a pronunciation guide are included." Booklist

Another title about Feliciana is:
Feliciana meets d'Loup Garou (1998)

Thompson, Carol

I like you the best. Holiday House 2011 un il

Grades: PreK K 1   **E**

1. Pigs -- Fiction 2. Rabbits -- Fiction 3. Friendship -- Fiction 4. Meditation -- Fiction
ISBN 0823423417; 9780823423415

LC 2010030747

Dolly the pig and Jack Rabbit are best friends, even after they have a fight. "Ages five to seven." (Bull Cent Child Books)

"Dolly and Jack overcome their feelings, thanks to some basic meditative skills. . . . Thompson's drawings, mostly spot images, are gems. Smudgy and rough-edged, they have a sketchbooklike immediacy and eloquently articulate two

personalities who like to turn the emotional dial up to 11."
Publ Wkly

Thompson, Emma, 1959-

The **Further** Tale of Peter Rabbit. Penguin Group USA
2012 72 p. $20.00

Grades: PreK K　　　　　　　　　　　　　　　　　E
　1. Rabbits -- Fiction 2. Scotland -- Fiction 3. Voyages
and travels -- Fiction
ISBN 0723269106; 9780723269106

This book is a "new adventure of the mischievous bunny
who first appeared 110 years ago in Beatrix Potter's original
tale. . . . Peter (again) wriggles under Mr. McGregor's gate,
this time into an 'interesting basket smelling of onions.' After eating the picnic lunch within, he nods off, awakened
later by the jostling of a horse-drawn cart he's been loaded
onto, which is en route to, of all places, Scotland," where
he meets his cousin and has an adventure in the Highland
Games. (Publishers Weekly)

Thompson, Lauren

The **Christmas** magic; illustrated by Jon J. Muth.
Scholastic Press 2009 un il $16.99

Grades: K 1 2 3　　　　　　　　　　　　　　　　E
　1. Magic -- Fiction 2. Christmas -- Fiction 3. Santa
Claus -- Fiction 4. Christmas stories -- Juvenile
literature
ISBN 978-0-439-77497-0; 0-439-77497-7

　　　　　　　　　　　　　　　　　　LC 2008-43308

As Santa prepares for the upcoming holiday season, it
is the Christmas magic that truly makes everything happen.

"Muth's haunting watercolor and pastel illustrations
bring the simple story to magical life. . . . This gentle and
lovely book is sheer enchantment." SLJ

How many cats? pictures by Robin Eley. Disney Hyperion Books 2009 un il $15.99

Grades: K 1 2　　　　　　　　　　　　　　　　　E
　1. Counting 2. Stories in rhyme 3. Cats -- Fiction
ISBN 978-1-4231-0801-6; 1-4231-0801-9

　　　　　　　　　　　　　　　　　　LC 2008-46540

From zero to twenty, a house becomes filled with frolicking cats, who then leave alone or in groups

"Eley paints exuberant bundles of fun that dance and
leap across the pages of Thompson's joyous and slyly math-
infused counting tale. . . . Sure to be a call-and-response
crowd-pleaser at any kitty-cat storytime." Kirkus

★ **Leap** back home to me; illustrated by Matthew
Cordell. Margaret K. McElderry Books 2011 un il $15.99

Grades: PreK K　　　　　　　　　　　　　　　　E
　1. Stories in rhyme 2. Frogs -- Fiction 3. Mother-child
relationship -- Fiction
ISBN 978-1-4169-0664-3; 1-4169-0664-9

　　　　　　　　　　　　　　　　　　LC 2009-53708

A little frog makes increasingly bold leaps out into
the world, and then comes back to his mother after
each excursion.

"Sweet and simple, lively and expressive, this picture
book provides a loving template for parents who want
to encourage their children to explore an ever-widening
world without losing their connection to home and family."
Publ Wkly

Little Quack; pictures by Derek Anderson. Simon &
Schuster Bks. for Young Readers 2003 un il $14.95

Grades: PreK K　　　　　　　　　　　　　　　　E
　1. Counting 2. Ducks -- Fiction
ISBN 0-689-84723-8

　　　　　　　　　　　　　　　　　　LC 2002-5567

One by one, four ducklings find the courage to jump
into the pond and paddle with Mama Duck, until only Little
Quack is left in the nest, trying to be brave

"Here's a familiar story kicked up a notch by a counting
element and irresistible art. The story is reassuring and utterly straightforward. . . . The charm is in Anderson's comical, eye-commanding acrylics." Booklist

Other titles about Little Quack are:
Little Quack's bedtime (2005)
Little Quack's hide and seek (2004)
Little Quack's new friend (2006)

★ **One** starry night; illustrated by Jonathan Bean.
Margaret K. McElderry Books 2011 un il $16.99

Grades: PreK K 1　　　　　　　　　　　　　　　E
　1. Stories in rhyme 2. Christmas stories 3. Animals
-- Fiction 4. Christmas -- Fiction
ISBN 978-0-689-82851-5; 0-689-82851-9

　　　　　　　　　　　　　　　　　　LC 2011008776

One starry night, as all sorts of animals watch over their
young, Mary and Joseph watch over their baby boy, Jesus,
in Bethlehem.

"This tender, poetic retelling of the age-old story takes
the form of a whispered prayer as it highlights the nurturing given to babies of many species. The art and the words
strike just the right tone of reverence and delight. A lovely
offering." SLJ

Polar bear morning; by Lauren Thompson; pictures by
Stephen Savage. Orchard Books 2013 32 p. (alk. paper)
$16.99

Grades: PreK K 1 2　　　　　　　　　　　　　　E
　1. Bears -- Fiction 2. Friendship -- Fiction 3. Polar
bear -- Fiction 4. Friendship -- Juvenile fiction 5. Polar
bear -- Juvenile fiction
ISBN 0439698855; 9780439698856

　　　　　　　　　　　　　　　　　　LC 2012024848

Polar bear night; illustrated by Stephen Savage. Scholastic Press 2004 un il $15.95

Grades: PreK K 1 2　　　　　　　　　　　　　　E
　1. Bears 2. Night 3. Polar bear 4. Night -- Fiction
ISBN 0-439-49524-5

　　　　　　　　　　　　　　　　　　LC 2003-27538

After wandering out at night to watch a magical star
shower, a polar bear cub returns home to snuggle with her
mother in their warm den.

"With comforting, carefully chosen words and soft pastels shading linocut prints, this book has all the elements to
make it a bedtime favorite." SLJ

Wee little bunny; illustrated by John Butler. Simon
& Schuster Books for Young Readers 2010 un il $14.99

Grades: PreK　　　　　　　　　　　　　　　　　E
　1. Animals -- Fiction 2. Rabbits -- Fiction
ISBN 978-1-4169-7937-1; 1-4169-7937-9

　　　　　　　　　　　　　　　　　　LC 2008044911

A young rabbit enjoys a 'busy, dizzy' day of playing in the meadow near his home

"This sweet follow-up to Little Chick and Little Lamb is ideal for kids who like adventures, but like coming home even more." Publ Wkly

Wee little chick; by Lauren Thompson; illustrated by John Butler. Simon & Schuster Books for Young Readers 2008 un il $14.99

Grades: PreK   E

1. Size -- Fiction 2. Animals -- Fiction 3. Chickens -- Fiction

ISBN 978-1-4169-3468-4; 1-4169-3468-5

LC 2007016411

When the other barnyard animals comment on how tiny the littlest chick is, the proud little one peeps louder, stands taller, and runs faster than any of them

"Thompson's simple, rhythmic text moves the action along at a brisk, even pace. Butler's bright acrylic and pencil illustrations artistically portray the story's springtime mood and warmhearted tone." SLJ

Wee little lamb; by Lauren Thompson; illustrated by John Butler. Simon & Schuster Books for Young Readers 2009 un il $14.99

Grades: PreK   E

1. Sheep -- Fiction 2. Animals -- Fiction

ISBN 978-1-4169-3469-1; 1-4169-3469-3

LC 2008004428

A little, newborn lamb, too shy to say hello to the rabbit or sing with the robin, is finally drawn out by a tiny fieldmouse

"This gentle, reassuring tale tells youngsters that they can explore their world at their own speed. The eye-catching spreads and simple language make this book a natural for toddler storytime." SLJ

★ The **apple** pie that Papa baked; illustrated by Jonathan Bean. Simon & Schuster Books for Young Readers 2007 un il $15.99

Grades: PreK K 1   E

1. Children's poetry 2. Pies -- Fiction 3. Trees -- Fiction 4. Apples -- Fiction

ISBN 1-4169-1240-1; 978-1-4169-1240-8

"A pigtailed girl introduces the apple pie 'warm and sweet that Papa baked.' Then moving backward, the girl runs . . . out to the tree 'crooked and strong,' where shiny red apples are waiting to be picked. The roots 'deep and fine,' feed the tree. . . . Rain waters the roots, clouds drop the rain, the sky carries the clouds, the sun lights the sky. . . . The text is dear, and it's well matched by delightful illustrations . . . The intricately detailed art is reminiscent of the time when picture books were rarely full color." Booklist

Thomson, Bill

★ **Chalk**. Marshall Cavendish Children 2010 un il $15.99

Grades: PreK K 1 2   E

1. Stories without words 2. Drawing -- Fiction

ISBN 978-0-7614-5526-4; 0-7614-5526-4

LC 2009014141

A wordless picture book about three children who go to a park on a rainy day, find some chalk, and draw pictures that come to life.

"With eye-catching, realistic illustrations, clever details, and some dramatic suspense, this wordless picture book offers a fresh take on the drawings-come-to-life theme. . . . . Vibrant acrylic and colored-pencil illustrations, rendered with intricate precision, nearly leap off the page." Booklist

Thomson, Sarah L.

Imagine a night; paintings by Rob Gonsalves; text by Sarah L. Thomson. Atheneum Books for Young Readers 2003 un il $16.95

Grades: 2 3 4 5 6   E

1. Night -- Fiction 2. Imagination -- Fiction

ISBN 0-689-85218-5

LC 2002-10718

Presents a night when imagination takes over and gravity does not work quite as expected.

"Magical realism permeates Gonsalves's large acrylic paintings, and they are essential to the lyrical text. . . . This is a fascinating foray into the imagination and a fine discussion starter for older children." SLJ

Other titles in this series are:

Imagine a day (2005)

Imagine a place (2008)

Pirates, ho! by Sarah L. Thomson; illustrated by Stephen Gilpin. Marshall Cavendish 2008 un il $14.99

Grades: K 1 2   E

1. Stories in rhyme 2. Pirates -- Fiction

ISBN 978-0-7614-5435-9; 0-7614-5435-7

LC 2007-29792

Pirates Peg-Leg Tom, Angus Black, Dreadful Nell, and One-Eyed Jack chase ships on the high seas, tell ghost stories, and fall asleep counting gold instead of sheep.

"Gilpin's wacky cartoons have a retro, take-no-prisoners abandon. . . . This funny, fabulously illustrated rhyme is certainly worth adding." SLJ

Thong, Roseanne

Fly free! illustrated by Eujin Kim Neilan. Boyds Mills Press 2010 un il $17.95

Grades: 3 4 5   E

1. Buddhism -- Fiction 2. Kindness -- Fiction 3. Conduct of life -- Fiction

ISBN 978-1-59078-550-8; 1-59078-550-9

LC 2009020248

When Mai feeds the caged birds at a Buddhist temple in Vietnam, her simple act of kindness starts a chain of thoughtful acts that ultimately comes back to her. Includes author's note explaining the Buddhist concepts of karma and samsara, or the wheel of life.

"The lesson of this simple story, that helping others is helpful to you, is universal. The muted and warm watercolor-on-board illustrations glow with gold, orange, red, and brown tones." SLJ

One is a drummer; written by Roseanne Thong; illustrated by Grace Lin. Chronicle Books 2004 un il $14.95; pa $6.99

Grades: PreK K 1 2   E

1. Counting 2. Stories in rhyme 3. Chinese Americans 4. Chinese Americans -- Fiction

ISBN 0-8118-3772-6; 0-8118-6482-4 pa

LC 2003-10810

A young girl numbers her discoveries in the world around her, from one dragon boat to four mahjong players to ten bamboo stalks

"The rhymes provide a pleasing framework for the book, and Lin's striking artwork gives it great visual appeal. . . . An appealing counting book, particularly for Chinese American children who want to learn a little about their heritage." Booklist

Red is a dragon; a book of colors. written by Roseanne Thong; illustrated by Grace Lin. Chronicle Bks. 2001 un il hardcover o.p. pa $6.99
Grades: PreK K 1 2   E
1. Color 2. Asian Americans 3. Stories in rhyme 4. Chinese Americans -- Fiction
ISBN 0-8118-3177-9; 0-8118-6481-2 pa
LC 2001-93
A Chinese American girl provides rhyming descriptions of the great variety of colors she sees around her, from the red of a dragon, firecrackers, and lychees to the brown of her teddy bear

"Lin's simply drawn gouache illustrations, outlined in black, fairly explode with color. . . . This is a must-have for libraries serving Chinese American populations, and it will be a welcome addition to preschool story hours for children of all backgrounds." Booklist

Round is a mooncake; a book of shapes. written by Roseanne Thong; illustrated by Grace Lin. Chronicle Books 2000 un il $15.99
Grades: PreK K 1 2   E
1. Shape 2. Stories in rhyme 3. Chinese Americans -- Fiction 4. Form perception -- Pictorial works -- Juvenile fiction 5. Geometrical constructions -- Pictorial works -- Juvenile fiction
ISBN 0-8118-2676-7
LC 99-50852
As a little girl discovers things round, square, and rectangular in her urban neighborhood, she is reminded of her Chinese American culture

"Lin's gouache paintings are bright and arresting, presenting scenes that have an interest beyond shape identification." Booklist

Thong, Roseanne Greenfield
★ **Round** is a tortilla; by Roseanne Greenfield Thong; illustrated by John Parra. Chronicle Books 2013 40 p. col. ill. (reinforced) $16.99
Grades: PreK K 1 2   E
1. Stories in rhyme 2. Shape -- Juvenile fiction 3. Hispanic Americans -- Fiction 4. Shape -- Fiction 5. Shapes -- Juvenile fiction 6. Form perception -- Juvenile fiction 7. Hispanic American children -- Juvenile fiction
ISBN 9781452106168
LC 2012013341
In this children's picture book, by Roseanne Greenfield Thong, illustrated by John Parra, "children discover a world of shapes all around them: rectangles are ice-cream carts and stone metates, triangles are slices of watermelon and quesadillas. Many of the featured objects are Latino in origin, and all are universal in appeal." (Publisher's note)

Thurber, James
★ **Many** moons; illustrated by Louis Slobodkin. Harcourt Brace Jovanovich 1943 un il $17; pa $7
Grades: 1 2 3 4   E
1. Fairy tales 2. Princesses -- Fiction
ISBN 0-15-251873-8; 0-15-656980-9 pa
Awarded the Caldecott Medal, 1944
"Louis Slobodkin's pictures float on the pages in four colors: black and white cannot represent them. They are the substance of dreams . . . the long thoughts little children, and some adults wise as they, have about life." N Y Her Trib Books

Thurlby, Paul
★ **Paul** Thurlby's alphabet. Candlewick Press 2011 un il $16.99
Grades: PreK K   E
1. Alphabet
ISBN 978-0-7636-5565-5; 0-7636-5565-1
LC 2010045400
"From a cover that features a boy's head and arms on a body shaped like the letter A to Z for zipper, the illustrator explains that he 'pursues the challenge of fusing the object of the word with the shape of the letter.' His approach succeeds in a fascinating way. The lower and uppercase letter is centered on the verso pages against textured, vividly colored papers, while the letter designs appear on the recto and have a posterlike quality. . . . The digital-media artwork has a distinctive look that will be best appreciated by young ones who already know the ABCs. Skillfully constructed and cleverly composed, it's an awesome alphabet book." Kirkus

Thurman, Kathryn K.
A **garden** for pig; written by Kathryn K. Thurman; illustrated by Lindsay Ward. Kane Miller 2010 un il $15.99
Grades: PreK K 1   E
1. Pigs -- Fiction 2. Apples -- Fiction 3. Gardens -- Fiction
ISBN 978-1-935279-24-2; 1-935279-24-6
"Pig, bored with the apples that farmer Mrs. Pippin provides, gobbles up the vegetable garden, then wishes he had vegetable seeds to plant. Luckily, when nature calls, 'Ploop! Out come the seeds!' Pig, with his patch of brown over one eye and farmer Mrs. Pippin, with her sticklike legs in wellies, make an endearing pair. Lots of organic gardening advice is appended." Horn Book Guide

Tibo, Gilles
My diary; the totally true story of me! illustrations by Josee Bisaillon. Magination Press 2011 un il pa $12.95
Grades: K 1 2   E
1. Diaries -- Fiction
ISBN 978-1-4338-095-83; 1-4338-0958-3
LC 2011007778
A young girl shares many things, including thoughts on becoming a big sister, freedom, joy, death, peace, and hope, through secrets, lists, poems, and inventions recorded in her diary.

"This well-crafted book would be useful as an example for a writing workshop. Others may find it equally as helpful as a means to begin discussions about emotions." SLJ

Tidholm, Anna-Clara

Knock! knock! adaptation by MaryChris Bradley. MacKenzie Smiles 2009 un il $9.95

Grades: PreK   E

1. Stories in rhyme 2. Color -- Fiction 3. Doors -- Fiction 4. Animals -- Fiction

ISBN 978-0-9815761-6-9; 0-9815761-6-8

"Young children are invited to knock on and then enter a succession of different colored doors. Behind the full-page panels are rooms filled with people or animals performing such simple daily actions as playing, eating, and, in the end, snoring. . . . Each color is introduced with a rhyming couplet. . . . Little hands will love turning the pages to see a cozy family of rabbits around a kitchen table, silly monkeys engaged in a pillow fight, and bears brushing their teeth. . . . The charming story offers an excellent rhythm and rhyme scheme, a review of colors, bright and playful cartoon illustrations, and an opportunity for listener participation." SLJ

Tierney, Fiona

Lion's lunch? illustrated by Margaret Chamberlain. Chicken House 2010 un il $17.99

Grades: K 1 2 3   E

1. Lions -- Fiction 2. Animals -- Fiction 3. Drawing -- Fiction

ISBN 978-0-545-17691-0; 0-545-17691-3

LC 2009-08267

When Lion comes upon Sarah walking in the jungle, he threatens to eat her unless she shows that she can do something none of the other animals can do.

"Vibrant, brightly colored illustrations of the lively animals and cheerful child fill every bit of space on the spreads and are sure to engage readers. This clever tale of courage and confidence teaches an important life lesson in a fun way." SLJ

Tillman, Nancy

On the night you were born. Feiwel & Friends 2006 un il $16.95

Grades: K 1 2   E

1. Stories in rhyme 2. Nature -- Fiction 3. Childbirth -- Fiction

ISBN 0-312-34606-9

First published 2005 by Darling Press

The moon, wind, rain, and a variety of animals celebrate the special occasion that is the birth of a child.

Tillman's "writing has the authenticity of whispered conversation. . . . The pictures subtly radiate golden glints of moonlight, and her almost sculptural rendering style gives her characters a hefty physicality that counterbalances the ethereal sentiments being expressed." Publ Wkly

The spirit of Christmas. Feiwel and Friends 2009 un il $16.99

Grades: PreK K 1 2   E

1. Stories in rhyme 2. Christmas -- Fiction

ISBN 978-0-312-54965-7; 0-312-54965-2

LC 2008-48139

Despite the arrival of the Spirit of Christmas, who brings all sorts of trimmings and reminders of seasonal joys, something is still lacking.

"Realism and fantasy are satisfyingly paired to bring the mixed-media illustrations of treasured holiday scenes to life. . . . A beautiful and timeless book." SLJ

Timberlake, Amy

The dirty cowboy; pictures by Adam Rex. Farrar, Straus & Giroux 2003 un il $16

Grades: K 1 2 3   E

1. Dogs -- Fiction 2. Cowhands -- Fiction

ISBN 0-374-31791-7

LC 2001-53224

Telling his faithful dog to make sure nobody touches his clothes but him, a cowboy jumps into a New Mexico river for a bath, not realizing just how much the scrubbing will change his scent

"Told in descriptive language that rolls off the tongue, this story makes the most of a humorous situation. . . . The paintings have a gritty, sinewy look that matches the earthy tone of the tale." SLJ

Timmers, Leo

Who is driving? [by] Leo Timmers. Bloomsbury Children's Books 2007 un il $12.95

Grades: PreK K   E

1. Animals -- Fiction 2. Vehicles -- Fiction

ISBN 978-1-59990-021-6; 1-59990-021-1

LC 2006009541

Easy-to-read text invites the reader to guess which animal is driving each of seven vehicles based on how they are dressed, then reveals their destinations and the vehicles' sounds

"The vivid acrylic illustrations in primary colors have a three-dimensional look and will delight toddlers." SLJ

Tinkham, Kelly

Hair for Mama; [by] Kelly A. Tinkham; illustrated by Amy June Bates. Dial Books for Young Readers 2007 un il $16.99

Grades: K 1 2 3   E

1. Hair -- Fiction 2. Cancer -- Fiction 3. African Americans -- Fiction 4. Mother-son relationship -- Fiction

ISBN 0-8037-2955-3; 978-0-8037-2955-1

LC 2005-10621

When Marcus's mother has chemotherapy for her cancer and loses her hair, he tries to find new hair for her to make her well again.

"This is a beautifully written story about an African-American family dealing with cancer. . . . The lovely watercolor illustrations fit the text well, using gold, brown, orange, and green tones to show a family going through tough times together." SLJ

Titcomb, Gordon

The last train; paintings by Wendall Minor. Roaring Brook Press 2010 un il $16.99

Grades: PreK K 1 2   E

1. Railroads -- Fiction

ISBN 978-1-59643-164-5; 1-59643-164-4

"Based on musician Titcomb's 2005 song, this stunning book both celebrates and eulogizes the golden era of railway travel. Minor's luminous, occasionally almost photographic, paintings portray the adult narrator as a boy, surrounded by a ghostly haze as he walks along the tracks." Publ Wkly

Titherington, Jeanne

Pumpkin, pumpkin. Greenwillow Bks. 1986 23p il $16.99; pa $6.99

Grades: PreK K 1 2   E

1. Pumpkin -- Fiction 2. Gardening -- Fiction
ISBN 0-688-05695-4; 0-688-09930-0 pa

LC 84-25334

Jamie "plants a seed, then grows and harvests a pumpkin from which he saves seeds for next year. The large, detailed drawings capture Jamie's anticipation and pleasure just right. . . . Nonreaders can easily follow the story in pictures alone. Very large, clear print on facing pages makes the simple narrative inviting for beginning readers, too." SLJ

Tobin, Jim

Sue MacDonald had a book; illustrated by Dave Coverly. Holt & Co. 2009 un il $16.95

Grades: K 1 2   E

1. Alphabet -- Fiction 2. Books and reading -- Fiction
ISBN 978-0-8050-8766-6; 0-8050-8766-4

"This lively grammar-related adventure is a sing-along to the tune of 'Old MacDonald Had a Farm' with the repeated refrain, 'AEIOU.' Sue MacDonald has a book called My Farm by O. MacDonald but can no longer read it after the vowels escape. . . . Done in vivid colors, the ink-and-watercolor illustrations feature high-energy cartoon figures. . . . This educational romp . . . is a strong choice for classroom and library collections." SLJ

Tolman, Marije

The **tree** house; [by] Marije Tolman & Ronald Tolman. Lemniscaat un il $17.95

Grades: PreK K 1   E

1. Stories without words 2. Animals -- Fiction
ISBN 978-1-59078-806-6; 1-59078-806-0
Original Dutch edition 2009

"A wordless picture book about an elaborate wooden structure in the tree. Three stories tall, it soaks up the water surrounding its base as animals inhabit its various nooks and crannies. Bears, peacocks, and owls, and a hippo all find different ways to amuse themselves while up so high. . . . Soft pastel spreads allow readers to see all the activity in and around the tree. . . . Children will gaze in wonder at this tree house. . . . This oversize picture book celebrates acceptance of others and the splendor of nature." SLJ

Tompert, Ann

Little Fox goes to the end of the world; illustrated by Laura J. Bryant. Marshall Cavendish 2010 un il $16.99

Grades: PreK K 1 2   E

1. Foxes -- Fiction 2. Mother-child relationship -- Fiction
ISBN 978-0-7614-5703-9; 0-7614-5703-8

A newly illustrated edition of the title first published 1976 by Crown

"Capturing a young child's yearning for independence, Tompert describes the story of Little Fox, who tells her mother, 'Some day . . . I'm going to travel to the end of the world.' Her mother's wise reply encourages Little Fox's imagination and conversation by asking appropriate questions such as, 'What will you see?' 'Won't you be scared?' Bryant's dramatic watercolor artwork frequently fills the spreads." SLJ

Tonatiuh, Duncan

★ **Dear** Primo; a letter to my cousin. Abrams 2010 un il $15.95

Grades: 1 2 3   E

1. Cousins -- Fiction 2. Country life -- Fiction 3. Mexican Americans -- Fiction 4. City and town life -- Fiction
ISBN 978-0-81093-872-4; 0-81093-872-3
Pura Belpré Award honor book (Illustrator), 2011

Two cousins, one in Mexico and one in New York City, write to each other and learn that even though their daily lives differ, at heart the boys are very similar.

"The digitally enhanced collage illustrations are based on traditional Mixtec art, and show the characters posed in profile in simply composed scenes. This useful method of comparing and contrasting can serve as a fine general introduction to contemporary rural life in Mexico, while it also demonstrates the fun of having a pen pal and reinforces the sense that kids around the world are more alike than different." Booklist

★ **Pancho** Rabbit and the coyote; a migrant's tale. by Duncan Tonatiuh. Abrams Books for Young Readers 2013 32 p. ill. (reinforced) $16.95

Grades: K 1 2   E

1. Allegories 2. Coyotes -- Juvenile fiction 3. Migrant labor -- Juvenile fiction 4. Coyote -- Fiction 5. Rabbits -- Fiction 6. Migrant labor -- Fiction 7. Voyages and travels -- Fiction
ISBN 1419705830; 9781419705830

LC 2012022573

"In this allegorical picture book, [by Duncan Tonatiuh,] a young rabbit named Pancho eagerly awaits his papa's return. Papa Rabbit traveled north two years ago to find work in the great carrot and lettuce fields. . . . When Papa does not return, Pancho sets out to find him. . . . He meets a coyote, who offers to help Pancho in exchange for some of Papa's food. They travel together until the food is gone and the coyote decides he is still hungry . . . for Pancho!" (Publisher's note)

Torrey, Rich

Almost. HarperCollinsPublishers 2009 un il $17.99; lib bdg $18.89

Grades: PreK K   E

1. Growth -- Fiction
ISBN 978-0-06-156166-5; 0-06-156166-5; 978-0-06-156167-2 lib bdg; 0-06-156167-3 lib bdg

LC 2008011724

Almost six-year-old Jack lists all the ways in which he is almost a grown-up.

"The large, cartoonlike spreads have plenty of pleasing color and detail, and expand on the simple text. . . . This simple story addresses both the desire of children to be older and sibling rivalry. It's sure to be a hit at storytime." SLJ

Other titles about Jack are:
Why? (2010)
Because (2011)

Because; [by] Richard Torrey. Harper 2011 un il $16.99

Grades: PreK K   E

1. Brothers -- Fiction 2. Family life -- Fiction
ISBN 978-0-06-156173-3; 0-06-156173-8

LC 2010010510

"Young Jack promises to show examples of why 'because' is a 'real answer.' Amusing drawings and the boy's single-sentence clarifications for questionable behavior justify why cereal is spread across the floor, why the dog is in timeout, and why boy and dog are covered in strawberry icing.... The story will allow youngsters to recall fondly their own 'because' moments." SLJ

Why? [by] Richard Torrey. Balzer & Bray 2010 un il $16.99

Grades: PreK K   E

1. Brothers -- Fiction

ISBN 978-0-06-156170-2; 0-06-156170-3

LC 2009-11749

Jack asks a lot of questions, including 'Why does everyone think I ask too many questions?'

"Torrey's affecting portrait of a small boy is made up almost entirely of questions, all of which begin with 'Why?' Torrey ... paints Jack's world with gentle colors and softly brushed forms.... Jack isn't just cute or just annoying; he's doing his best to understand the world, and Torrey's sensitivity brings Jack's feelings home to readers." Publ Wkly

Toscano, Charles

Papa's pastries; illustrated by Sonja Lamut. Zonderkidz 2010 un il $15.99

Grades: PreK K 1 2   E

1. Baking -- Fiction 2. Poverty -- Fiction 3. Kindness -- Fiction

ISBN 978-0-310-71602-0; 0-310-71602-0

Miguel sees the results of his father's faith and generosity when, although his own family is facing the oncoming winter with threadbare clothing, a leaky roof, and no firewood, Papa gives away the pastries he has baked.

"Effective use of repetition and a pleasing rhythm invigorate ... Toscano's predictable but touching tale.... The illustrations ... effectively convey communal warmth and industry against a backdrop of poverty and looming fear." Publ Wkly

Tougas, Chris

Art's supplies; by Chris Tougas. Orca Book Publishers 2008 un il $19.95

Grades: 1 2 3   E

1. Art -- Fiction

ISBN 978-1-55143-920-4; 1-55143-920-4

"Bright colors, heavy doses of humor, and puns to make readers groan fill the pages as a boy's art supplies prepare for a personality-plus party.... Art's endearing, off-centered features combine with google-eyed markers, crayons, boxes, brushes, tapes, scissors, and glue.... This lively title is sure to be a favorite of youngsters learning to appreciate both subtle humor and engaging cartoon art." SLJ

Townsend, Michael

Billy Tartle in Say Cheese! Alfred A. Knopf 2007 un il $15.99; lib bdg $18.99

Grades: K 1 2 3   E

1. School stories 2. Photography -- Fiction

ISBN 978-0-375-83932-0; 0-375-83932-1; 978-0-375-93932-7 lib bdg; 0-375-93932-6 lib bdg

LC 2006-24354

Billy is determined to find a way to make his school picture day less boring than usual.

The story "unfolds in comic-strip panels that effectively juggle their multitude of elements and palette of high-voltage colors with strategic design. Billy's ... adventurous take

on reality fits the comic-strip medium perfectly." Bull Cent Child Books

Monkey & Elephant's worst fight ever! Alfred A. Knopf 2011 un il $15.99; lib bdg $18.99

Grades: PreK K 1   E

1. Islands -- Fiction 2. Monkeys -- Fiction 3. Elephants -- Fiction 4. Friendship -- Fiction

ISBN 978-0-375-85717-1; 0-375-85717-6; 978-0-375-95717-8 lib bdg; 0-375-95717-0 lib bdg

LC 2010004135

The entire island is in an uproar when best friends Monkey and Elephant get into a fight.

"Young readers will relate to the injured feelings and unkind pranks in this comics-inspired book, presented in stylized, aptly silly doodles.... [Townsend's] goofy pen-and-ink illustrations, tinted with flat digital color, look jejune. Yet his sense of the 'all-out war' between ex-buddies rings true." Publ Wkly

Trachtenberg, Stanley

The **Elevator** Man; illustrated by Paul Cox. Eerdmans Books for Young Readers 2009 un il $18

Grades: PreK K 1   E

1. Elevators -- Fiction 2. Apartment houses -- Fiction

ISBN 978-0-8028-5315-8; 0-8028-5315-3

LC 2008-31737

When the elevator in a building in the 1950s is modernized, a young resident misses the operator

"Rich, appealing illustrations sketch the characters in broad, quick strokes of black filled in with warm golds, blues, greens, and maroons, against the backdrop of the building's ongoing activities." SLJ

Trapani, Iza

Haunted party. Charlesbridge 2009 un il lib bdg $15.95; pa $7.95

Grades: PreK K 1 2   E

1. Counting 2. Ghost stories 3. Stories in rhyme 4. Parties -- Fiction 5. Halloween -- Fiction 6. Supernatural -- Fiction

ISBN 978-1-58089-246-9 lib bdg; 1-58089-246-9 lib bdg; 978-1-58089-247-6 pa; 1-58089-247-7 pa

LC 2008025330

In this counting book that introduces the numbers from one to ten, a ghost and his supernatural friends have a party on Halloween night.

This is a "rollicking Halloween tale.... Rhyming stanzas build steadily then shrink to single lines, adding to the guests' speedy departure. Humor abounds ... in the watercolor, colored-pencil, and ink illustrations." Horn Book Guide

Tresselt, Alvin R.

Hide and seek fog; by Alvin Tresselt; illustrated by Roger Duvoisin. Lothrop, Lee & Shepard Bks. 1965 un il lib bdg $18.89; pa $6.99

Grades: PreK K 1   E

1. Fog

ISBN 0-688-51169-4 lib bdg; 0-688-07813-3 pa

A Caldecott Medal honor book, 1966

"This is ... a mood picture book ... describing a fog which rolls in from the sea to veil an Atlantic seacoast village for three days. The beautiful paintings ... and the brief, poetic text sensitively and effectively evoke the atmosphere of the 'worst fog in twenty years' and depict the reactions of children and grown-ups to it." Booklist

★ **White** snow, bright snow; by Alvin Tresselt; illustrated by Roger Duvoisin. Lothrop, Lee & Shepard Bks. 1988 un il $17.99; lib bdg $18.89; pa $6.99
Grades: PreK K 1   E
   1. Snow -- Fiction
   ISBN 0-688-41161-4; 0-688-51161-9 lib bdg; 0-688-08294-7 pa
                      LC 88-10018
   A reissue of the title first published 1947
   Awarded the Caldecott Medal, 1948
   When it begins to look, feel, and smell like snow, everyone prepares for a winter blizzard

Trewin, Trudie
   I lost my kisses; [by] Trudie Trewin; illustrations by Nick Bland. Scholastic 2008 32p il $14.99
Grades: PreK K   E
   1. Kissing -- Fiction 2. Lost and found possessions -- Fiction
   ISBN 0-545-05557-1; 978-0-545-05557-4
   Matilda Rose loves to kiss hello, goodbye, good morning, and goodnight, but on the day her father is to return from a trip, she cannot find her kisses anywhere, despite knowing how they feel, taste, and sound.
   "Bland's striking black-and-white pencil illustrations have splashes of watercolor highlighting the wide-eyed cow's polka-dotted tights as she searches high and low. . . . Matilda Rose has a whimsical charm." SLJ

Trottier, Maxine
   ★ **Migrant**; pictures by Isabelle Arsenault. Groundwood Books/House of Anansi Press 2011 un il $18.95
Grades: K 1 2 3   E
   1. Mennonites -- Fiction 2. Migrant agricultural laborers -- Fiction
   ISBN 978-0-88899-975-7; 0-88899-975-5
   "Each spring Anna leaves her home in Mexico and travels north with her family where they will work on farms harvesting fruits and vegetables. Sometimes she feels like a bird, flying north in the spring and south in the fall. Sometimes she feels like a jack rabbit living in an abandoned burrow, as her family moves into an empty house near the fields. But most of all she wonders what it would be like to stay in one place. The Low German-speaking Mennonites from Mexico are a unique group of migrants who moved from Canada to Mexico in the 1920s and became an important part of the farming community there. But it has become increasingly difficult for them to earn a livelihood, and so they come back to Canada each year as migrant workers in order to survive." (Publisher's note) "Ages four to seven." (Quill Quire)
   "Trottier frames the outlook of a child in a family of migrant workers within a series of metaphors and similes. Anna sees herself as part of a flock that travels its seasonal round from Mexico to Canada like migratory geese. . . . Arsenault's mixed-media images of doll-like figures in overalls and long print dresses, hats and headscarves effectively capture both Anna's sense of isolation and the close family ties that keep her immediate family and larger community together. [Anna] . . . belongs to a group of Low German-speaking Mennonite

farmers who emigrated to Mexico in the early 20th century but kept their Canadian citizenship and still travel northward each summer. . . . [This] is a moving, inventive and thoughtful look at a way of life many people share" Kirkus

   The **paint** box; [illustrations by] Stella East. Fitzhenry & Whiteside 2003 32p il $16.95; pa $8.95
Grades: 2 3 4   E
   1. Painters 2. Artists -- Fiction
   ISBN 1-55041-801-7; 1-55041-808-4 pa
                LC 2003-464840
   "'Long ago in Venice there was a girl named Marietta who loved to paint. She was the daughter of the great artist Tintoretto.' With her father's help, she disguises herself as a boy in order to explore the art world of Venice. . . . Marietta befriends an enslaved cabin boy and they spend their days sketching and exploring the city, and telling one another about their lives. When it is time for Piero's owner to leave the city, Marietta helps him escape and return to his family. This poignant tale has its roots in historical fact. . . . Trottier's fictional story about Marietta and her friend seems plausible, due in part to her descriptive and expressive writing style. East's painterly illustrations are magnificent. Each spread captures the feeling of Renaissance Venice and supports the accompanying text." SLJ

Tryon, Leslie
   Albert's birthday; written and illustrated by Leslie Tryon. Atheneum Bks. for Young Readers 1999 un il $16; pa $6.99
Grades: PreK K 1 2   E
   1. Animals -- Fiction 2. Parties -- Fiction 3. Birthdays -- Fiction
   ISBN 0-689-82296-0; 0-689-85251-7 pa
                LC 98-36621
   Patsy Pig plans a surprise birthday party for her friend Albert, giving careful instructions to all their friends, but she forgets to invite the guest of honor
   "The prose is personable and engaging, and colorful, exquisitely detailed illustrations portray the animal cast in such familiar human settings as a classroom and a town." Booklist
   Other titles about Albert are:
   Albert's alphabet (1991)
   Albert's ballgame (1996)
   Albert's Christmas (1997)
   Albert's field trip (1993)
   Albert's Halloween (1998)
   Albert's play (1992)
   Albert's Thanksgiving (1994)

Tseng, Kevin
   Ned's new home. Tricycle Press 2009 un il $14.99
Grades: PreK K 1   E
   1. Home -- Fiction 2. Fruit -- Fiction 3. Worms -- Fiction
   ISBN 978-1-58246-297-4; 1-58246-297-6
                LC 2008-42385
   A worm tries out a variety of new homes when the apple he has been living in starts to rot, but none—from a lemon to a watermelon—is satisfactory.
   "The cartoon illustrations are filled with warm colors and comic touches. Endpapers depict the life cycle of the apple from seed to fruit and back to seed. This reassuring

tale will be appreciated by the read-aloud crowd while also supplying a subtle lesson in ecology." SLJ

Tsiang, Sarah

A **flock** of shoes; story by Sarah Tsiang; art by Qin Leng. Annick Press 2010 un il lib bdg $19.95; pa $8.95

Grades: PreK K 1 2   E

1. Shoes -- Fiction 2. Seasons -- Fiction

ISBN 978-1-55451-249-2 lib bdg; 1-55451-249-2 lib bdg; 978-1-55451-248-5 pa; 1-55451-248-4 pa

"At the end of summer, Abby refuses to give up her sandals despite all her mother's reasons for letting them go. But while Abby's playing at the park . . . her flip-flops slip off her feet and fly away, joining other sandals headed southward in a V formation. At first, she grudgingly puts on boots and wears them all winter, though she imagines her sandals vacationing at the beach and sending her fond postcards. . . . Tsiang expresses childlike emotions and thoughts in a simple text that reads aloud well. Washed with cheerful colors, Leng's cartoon-style drawings interpret the story with originality and wit." Booklist

Tuck, Justin

Home-field advantage; illustrated by Leonardo Rodriguez. Simon & Schuster 2011 il $16.99

Grades: PreK K 1   E

1. Football players 2. Hair -- Fiction 3. Twins -- Fiction 4. Football -- Fiction 5. Siblings -- Fiction 6. Family life -- Fiction

ISBN 978-1-4424-0369-7; 1-4424-0369-1

LC 2010043733

New York Giants defensive end Justin Tuck observes that growing up with five sisters helped make him tough, and tells of when twins Christale and Tiffany gave him an unforgettable haircut.

"The plot is realistic and believable. Rodriguez's comical watercolor illustrations match well with the text." SLJ

Tucker, Kathy

The **seven** Chinese sisters; written by Kathy Tucker; illustrated by Grace Lin. Whitman, A. 2003 un il $15.95; pa $6.99

Grades: K 1 2 3   E

1. Dragons 2. Sisters 3. Dragons -- Fiction 4. Sisters -- Fiction

ISBN 0-8075-7309-4; 0-8075-7310-5 pa

LC 2002-11330

When a dragon snatches the youngest of seven talented Chinese sisters, the other six come to her rescue

Lin "expertly captures the drama and humor of the story with delightful paintings that reveal lovely Chinese landscapes and a quirky, not-too-scary dragon. A wonderful read-aloud." Booklist

Tucker, Lindy

Porkelia; a pig's tale. written and illustrated by Lindy Tucker. Mackinac Island Press, Inc. 2011 il $9.95

Grades: PreK K 1 2   E

1. Stories in rhyme 2. Pigs -- Fiction 3. Dancers -- Fiction

ISBN 978-1-934133-28-6; 1-934133-28-0

Porkelia has always wanted to be a dancer, but not just any dancer—a Rockette! But Porkelia is a pig. Everyone

laughs and makes fun of her, but she sets out on her own to be discovered and become famous.

"Tucker tells this appealing sty-to-Broadway fame story with an appealingly silly, rhyming text. . . . The spare pictures, rendered in clean black lines and pink accents, extend the fun." Booklist

Tudor, Tasha

1 is one. Simon & Schuster Bks. for Young Readers 2000 un il $16

Grades: PreK K 1 2   E

1. Counting 2. Stories in rhyme

ISBN 0-689-82843-8

LC 99-31290

A reissue of the title first published 1956 by Oxford University Press

A Caldecott Medal honor book, 1957

"The author-artist has with characteristic charming quaintness written and illustrated a counting book. Delicately tinted, decoratively bordered pictures and rhyming lines of text count from one to twenty." Booklist

Corgiville fair; by Tasha Tudor. Little, Brown & Company 1998 1v. (unpg) col. ill. $12.23; pa $6.95

Grades: PreK K 1 2   E

1. Fairs -- Fiction 2. Animals -- Fiction 3. Picture books for children 4. Cats -- Fiction 5. Dogs -- Fiction

ISBN 0-316-85312-7; 0-316-85329-1 pa; 9780316853125

LC 97029665

This picture book takes place in the "village of Corgiville, "west of New Hampshire and east of Vermont," the population of cats, rabbits, corgis ("enchanted" small dogs the color of foxes), and boggarts (toy-like "trolls") turn out for the annual country fair. The plan of young Caleb Brown, a corgi, to ride his goat Josephine in the Grand Race, is almost foiled by rival Edgar Tomcat who feeds Caleb a soporific hot dog and stuffs Josephine with mince pies and cigars. But Caleb's resourceful buddy Merton Boggart gets the groaning Josephine going by feeding her the rockets for his fireworks display. . . . Caleb wins the race, leads the grand parade, starts off the Virginia Reel with Miss Corgiville, . . . and applauds Merton's closing fireworks display." (Kirkus)

Tullet, Herve

The **book** with a hole. Abrams 2011 un il pa $14.50

Grades: PreK K 1 2   E

1. Imagination -- Fiction

ISBN 978-1-85437-946-7; 1-85437-946-1

"As the title suggests, this oversize book has a die-cut hole—a large semicircle is cut out of the book's spine, which becomes a full circle in the center of the book when opened, serving different interactive functions in a series of spare b&w scenes. . . . Tullet's simple innovation allows readers to become active participants in the experience of reading." Publ Wkly

The **game** of finger worms. Phaedon Press 2011 un il bd bk $8.95

Grades: PreK K   E

1. Games 2. Board books for children

ISBN 978-0-7148-6071-8; 0-7148-6071-9

LC 2011289051

Invites the reader to complete the illustrations by drawing eyes and a mouth on one's finger and inserting it through the die-cut hole in each page as a "finger worm."

The book has "whimsical art done in bold watercolors. The [book is] appropriate for hands-on learning in early education settings or one-on-one with an adult to help youngsters develop finger dexterity and fine motor skills." SLJ

The **game** of let's go! Phaedon Press 2011 un il bd bk $8.95

Grades: PreK K   E

1. Games 2. Board books for children
ISBN 978-0-7148-6075-6; 0-7148-6075-1
LC 2011289050

Invites the reader to close one's eyes and follow a felt line through the book with one's finger, around and through various die-cut holes, imagining where the journey leads.

The book has "whimsical art done in bold watercolors. The [book is] appropriate for hands-on learning in early education settings or one-on-one with an adult to help youngsters develop finger dexterity and fine motor skills." SLJ

The **game** of light. Phaidon 2011 un il bd bk $8.95
Grades: PreK K   E

1. Games 2. Board books for children
ISBN 978-0-7148-6189-0; 0-7148-6189-8

This board book "makes for a fun nighttime activity as simple cutout shapes on each page can be illuminated with a flashlight. . . .The [book has] whimsical art done in bold watercolors. The [book is] appropriate for hands-on learning in early education settings or one-on-one with an adult to help youngsters develop finger dexterity and fine motor skills." SLJ

The **game** of mix and match. Phaidon 2011 un il bd bk $8.95
Grades: PreK K   E

1. Games 2. Board books for children
ISBN 978-0-7148-6073-2; 0-7148-6073-5

In this board book, "each page contains four flaps that children can mix and match to create more than 50 pictures among familiar objects such as hearts, stars, and the sun. . . .The [book has] whimsical art done in bold watercolors. The [book is] appropriate for hands-on learning in early education settings or one-on-one with an adult to help youngsters develop finger dexterity and fine motor skills." SLJ

The **game** of mix-up art. Phaidon 2011 un il bd bk $8.95
Grades: PreK K   E

1. Games 2. Board books for children
ISBN 978-0-7148-6188-3; 0-7148-6188-X

This board book "contains colorful shapes and obscure patterns among zigzagged cut-page flaps that create new artwork and designs as different flaps are turned. . . . The [book has] whimsical art done in bold watercolors. The [book is] appropriate for hands-on learning in early education settings or one-on-one with an adult to help youngsters develop finger dexterity and fine motor skills." SLJ

The **game** of patterns. Phaidon 2011 un il bd bk $8.95

Grades: PreK K   E

1. Games 2. Board books for children
ISBN 978-0-7148-6187-6; 0-7148-6187-1

This board book "provides the opportunity to point out as many patterns and similarities children can find on each spread. They increase in difficulty as the book progresses. The [book has] whimsical art done in bold watercolors. The [book is] appropriate for hands-on learning in early education settings or one-on-one with an adult to help youngsters develop finger dexterity and fine motor skills." SLJ

Tullet, Hervé

★ **I** Am Blop! Hervé Tullet. Phaidon Inc Ltd 2013 110 p. col. ill. (hardcover) $19.95
Grades: PreK K   E

1. Color -- Juvenile literature 2. Shape -- Juvenile literature
ISBN 0714865338; 9780714865331
LC 2012285660

This children's story, by Hervé Tullet, explores "the world of Blop! A Blop is a simple shape, somewhere between a flower and a butterfly, a sponge and a drawing of a little man -- above all Blop is whatever you want it to be . . . explor[ing] many concepts encountered for the first time by young children, including up and down, single and plural, individual and family, city and countryside etc." (Publisher's note)

"The latest in a series of offbeat, imaginative creations by renowned French artist Tullet will intrigue children and encourage them to think outside the blop... Any child bored with standard activity-book fare will love using this openended, imaginative tool for creating their own universe...[T] aps directly into the heart of a child's natural creativity by avoiding the didactic explanatory tone of similar books." Kirkus

★ **Press** here; [translated by Christopher Franceschelli] Chronicle Books 2011 un il
Grades: PreK K 1 2   E

1. Toy and movable books 2. Imagination -- Fiction
ISBN 0-8118-7954-2; 978-0-8118-7954-5
LC 2010035579

Original French edition 2010

Instructs the reader on how to interact with the illustrations to create imaginative images.

"Tullet's brilliant creation proves that books need not lose out to electronic wizardry. . . . The fun continues as the dots proliferate, travel around the page, grow and shrink in response to commands to clap, shake, and tilt the book, etc." Publ Wkly

Turner, Ann Warren

★ **Dust** for dinner; story by Ann Turner; pictures by Robert Barrett. HarperCollins Pubs. 1995 64p il (I can read book) hardcover o.p. pa $3.99
Grades: K 1 2 3   E

1. Farm life -- Fiction 2. Family life -- Fiction 3. Great Depression, 1929-1939 -- Fiction
ISBN 0-06-023377-X lib bdg; 0-06-444225-X pa
LC 93-34634

Jake narrates the story of his family's life in the Oklahoma dust bowl and the journey from their ravaged farm to California during the Great Depression

"Turner takes a sad episode in history and fashions it into a story that has some depth as well as some drama. . . . Realistic, nicely executed illustrations decorate every page." Booklist

Turner-Denstaedt, Melanie
The **hat** that wore Clara B. pictures by Frank Morrison. Farrar, Straus & Giroux 2009 un il $16.95
Grades: K 1 2   E
   1. Hats -- Fiction
ISBN 978-0-374-32794-1; 0-374-32794-7
                        LC 2006-47606
   In church on Mothers' Sunday when all the older ladies dress in white and wear their most beautiful hats, Clara B., sitting in the pew behind her grandmother and admiring her every move, determines to find a way to wear her grandmother's hat.
   "Morrison's large and expressive paintings are suffused with warmth and reflect the text beautifully. This is a wonderful family story that celebrates the bond between generations." SLJ

Tusa, Tricia
  ★ **Follow** me; written and illustrated by Tricia Tusa. Harcourt Children's Books 2011 un il $16.99
Grades: PreK K 1 2   E
   1. Color -- Fiction 2. Imagination -- Fiction
ISBN 978-0-547-27201-6; 0-547-27201-4
                        LC 2010009061
A girl travels through an imaginative world of colors by way of a swing.
   "The beautiful etchings are rich in color and alive with vibrant line. . . . A glorious visual meditation on light, color and home for even the smallest child and artist." Kirkus

Twohy, Mike
  ★ **Poindexter** makes a friend. Simon & Schuster Books for Young Readers 2011 un il $15.99
Grades: K 1 2   E
   1. Pigs -- Fiction 2. Shyness -- Fiction 3. Turtles -- Fiction 4. Libraries -- Fiction 5. Friendship -- Fiction 6. Books and reading -- Fiction
ISBN 978-1-4424-0965-1; 1-4424-0965-7
                        LC 2010018489
Poindexter is a very shy pig who, while helping out at the library, meets a turtle who is also shy, and together they read a book about making a friend in four easy steps.
   "The watercolor illustrations in this gentle story are done in a cartoon style. Humorous details . . . will bring smiles. The pals' pleasure in sharing books with a dim-eyed mole and each other is palpable. . . . This reassuring story will envelop youngsters like a warm, cozy blanket." SLJ

U'Ren, Andrea
  Mary Smith. Farrar, Straus & Giroux 2003 un il $16
Grades: K 1 2 3   E
   1. City and town life -- Fiction
ISBN 0-374-34842-1
                        LC 2002-69775
   Early in the morning Mary Smith walks through the town, waking people up by shooting at their windows with her peashooter
   "Outlined in black, U'Ren's art has a clean, graphic appearance that perfectly complements the simplicity of the

story. . . . A historical note gives supplemental information about the real Mrs. Mary Smith and the role of the knocker-ups. A rollicking read." SLJ

Uchida, Yoshiko
  The **bracelet**; story by Yoshiko Uchida; illustrated by Joanna Yardley. Philomel Bks. 1993 un il $17.99; pa $6.99
Grades: K 1 2 3   E
   1. Friendship -- Fiction 2. World War, 1939-1945 -- Fiction 3. Japanese Americans -- Evacuation and relocation, 1942-1945 -- Fiction
ISBN 0-399-22503-X; 0-698-11390-X pa
                        LC 92-26196
   Emi, a Japanese American in the second grade, is sent with her family to an internment camp during World War II, but the loss of the bracelet her best friend has given her proves that she does not need a physical reminder of that friendship
   This "is a gentle, honest introduction to the treatment of the Japanese-Americans during the war, and Yardley's delicate pencil-and-watercolor paintings are cleanly drawn and richly colored." Bull Cent Child Books

Udry, Janice May
  The **moon** jumpers; Pictures by Maurice Sendak. Harper 1959 31 p. ill. (hardcover) $17.95
Grades: PreK K 1 2   E
   1. Night -- Fiction
ISBN 0060284609; 9780060284602
                        LC 58007757
   "A full moon on a summer night turns an ordinary landscape into a world of mystery and the uninhibited caperings of children into a joyous dance. There are black-and-white drawings and brief text in between double-page spreads in full ... color." (Horn Bk)

  ★ A **tree** is nice; pictures by Marc Simont. Harper & Row 1956 un il $17.99; lib bdg $18.89; pa $6.99
Grades: PreK K 1 2   E
   1. Trees -- Fiction
ISBN 0-06-026155-2; 0-06-026156-0 lib bdg; 0-06-443147-9 pa
Awarded the Caldecott Medal, 1957
   "In childlike terms and in enticing pictures, colored and black and white, author and artist set forth reasons why trees are nice to have around—trees fill up the sky, they make everything beautiful, cats get away from dogs in them, leaves come down and can be played in, and trees are nice to climb in, to hang a swing in, or to plant. A picture book sure to please young children." Booklist

Uegaki, Chieri
  Rosie and Buttercup; written by Chieri Uegaki; illustrated by Stéphane Jorisch. Kids Can Press 2008 un il $17.95
Grades: PreK K 1 2   E
   1. Sisters -- Fiction
ISBN 978-1-55337-997-3
   "At first Rosie's perfect life seems even more perfect when little sister Buttercup arrives. . . . In time, Rosie becomes disenchanted and gives Buttercup away—to her sitter, Oxford. . . . Predictably, she is soon sorry. . . . Uegaki's assured text assumes an intelligent reader. . . . Jorisch's

watercolor illustrations, uncluttered but dense with patterns, are crisp against generous fields of white space." Publ Wkly

Suki's kimono; written by Chieri Uegaki; illustrated by Stephane Jorisch. Kids Can Press 2003 un il hardcover o.p. pa $7.95
Grades: PreK K 1 2   E
1. Japanese -- Fiction
ISBN 1-55337-752-4 pa; 1-55337-084-8
LC 2003-495264
"On her first day of first grade [Suki] chooses to wear her beloved Japanese kimono to school, despite the objections of her older sisters and the initial laughter of other children on the playground. . . . Her day ends in triumph, with her teacher and classmates won over by her impromptu dance performance. . . . This is an appealing story of courage and independence. Delicate, playful watercolor-and-ink illustrations perfectly capture the child's neighborhood and the characters' facial expressions." SLJ

Uhlberg, Myron
Dad, Jackie, and me; illustrated by Colin Bootman. Peachtree Publishers 2005 un il $16.95
Grades: K 1 2 3   E
1. Baseball players 2. Army officers 3. Deaf -- Fiction 4. Baseball -- Fiction 5. Father-son relationship -- Fiction
ISBN 1-56145-329-3
LC 2004-16711
In Brooklyn, New York, in 1947, a boy learns about discrimination and tolerance as he and his deaf father share their enthusiasm over baseball and the Dodgers' first baseman, Jackie Robinson.
"Bootman's lovely watercolor paintings add detail and wistful nostalgia. . . . [Readers] will appreciate the story's insightful treatment of deafness as viewed through the eyes of a child." SLJ

★ A **storm** called Katrina; written by Myron Uhlberg; illustrated by Colin Bootman. Peachtree 2010 un il $17.95
Grades: 1 2 3 4   E
1. Floods -- Fiction 2. African Americans -- Fiction 3. Hurricane Katrina, 2005 -- Fiction
ISBN 978-1-56145-591-1; 1-56145-591-1
LC 2009024518
When flood waters submerge their New Orleans neighborhood in the aftermath of Hurricane Katrina, a young cornet player and his parents evacuate their home and struggle to survive and stay together.
"Bootman's dramatic oil paintings and the boy's first-person narration provide realistic immediacy. . . . Readers are in for a deeply personal and sometimes uncomfortable look at a disaster whose ramifications are still being felt." Publ Wkly

Ulmer, Wendy K.
A **isn't** for fox; an isn't alphabet. written by Wendy K. Ulmer; illustrated by Laura Knorr. Sleeping Bear Press 2008 un il $16.95
Grades: PreK K   E
1. Alphabet
ISBN 978-1-58536-319-3; 1-58536-319-7
LC 2007006436

"Though the entertaining non-examples show an appreciation for the audience's sense of the silly, Knorr's charming paintings of winking cats, smiling jellyfish, trumpeting lions, and pillow-fighting llamas are worth the purchase price alone." SLJ

Uman, Jennifer
Jemmy button; Jennifer Uman, Valerio Vidali. Candlewick Press 2013 48 p. (reinforced) $16.99
Grades: K 1 2 3   E
ISBN 9780763664879
LC 2012942662
"Exchanged for the single mother-of-pearl button that gave him his nickname, an indigenous Tierra del Fuegan boy named Orundellico spent many years in England in the early 1800s as part of a failed experiment in forced civilization. Less a biography than an attempt to represent this alienating experience from Jemmy's point of view, it is distinguished by lyrical prose-poetry...and intensely creative and beautifully conceived paintings." Publ Wkly

Underwood, Deborah
The **Christmas** quiet book; by Deborah Underwood; illustrated by Renata Liwska. Houghton Mifflin Books for Children 2012 32 p. $12.99
Grades: PreK K 1   E
1. Christmas 2. Quietude -- Fiction 3. Sound -- Juvenile fiction 4. Animals -- Fiction 5. Christmas -- Fiction
ISBN 0547558635; 9780547558639
LC 2011040920
In this children's book by Deborah Underwood, illustrated by Renata Liwska, "the holidays are filled with joyful noise. But Christmas is sometimes wrapped in quiet: 'Searching for presents quiet,' 'Getting caught quiet,' and 'Hoping for a snow day quiet.' . . . The book features "soft colored pencil illustrations of bunnies, bears, and more." (Publisher's note)

Granny Gomez & Jigsaw; illustrated by Scott Magoon. Disney Hyperion Books 2009 un il $16.99
Grades: PreK K 1 2   E
1. Pets -- Fiction 2. Pigs -- Fiction
ISBN 978-0-7868-5216-1; 0-7868-5216-X
LC 2008-46225
Granny Gomez's pet pig grows too big to live in the house, so she builds him his own barn but discovers that she is lonely without him.
"Colorful, cartoon-style illustrations ratchet up the laughs with comic details . . . but are equally endearing at other times. Jigsaw's floppy ears and lopsided grin are irresistible, as is Granny's spunk, in humorous contrast with her conventional, demure appearance (including a tidy gray bun)—further proof that friends can come in all kinds of packages." Publ Wkly

A **balloon** for Isabel; illustrations by Laura Rankin. Greenwillow Books 2010 un il $16.99
Grades: K 1 2   E
1. School stories 2. Candy -- Fiction 3. Balloons -- Fiction 4. Porcupines -- Fiction
ISBN 978-0-06-177987-9; 0-06-177987-3
LC 2009018759

As graduation day approaches, Isabel tries to convince her teacher that she and Walter, both porcupines, should receive balloons on the big day just like the other children.

"Illustrations full of color and personality add to the story's depth and appeal. Authentic dialogue, a touch of humor, and Isabel's ingenious invention make this title of desire and determination a keeper." SLJ

★ The **loud** book! illustrated by Renata Liwska. Houghton Mifflin Harcourt 2011 un il $12.99
Grades: PreK K   E
1. Day -- Fiction 2. Noise -- Fiction
ISBN 978-0-547-39008-6; 0-547-39008-4
LC 2010006784
From the blare of an alarm clock in the morning to snores and crickets in the evening, simple text explores the many loud noises one might hear during the course of a day.

"Fortified with the same charm and humor as the first book, this has enough activity and drama to elicit interesting observations and reactions from young audiences." Booklist

★ The **quiet** book; illustrated by Renata Liwska. Houghton Mifflin Books for Children 2010 un il $12.95
Grades: PreK K   E
1. Noise -- Fiction 2. Animals -- Fiction
ISBN 978-0-547-21567-9; 0-547-21567-3
From the quiet of being the first one awake in the morning to "sweet dreams quiet" when the last light is turned off, simple text explores the many kinds of quiet that can exist during the day.

"The soft, matte feel of the illustrations, created with pencil, are digitally enhanced, and are priceless. The animals' facial expressions and body language are endearing. . . . All of the scenarios are child-centric and realistic." SLJ

Ungerer, Tomi
Adelaide; the flying kangaroo. Phaidon Press 2011 un il $14.95
Grades: K 1 2   E
1. Flight -- Fiction 2. Kangaroos -- Fiction
ISBN 978-0-7148-6083-1; 0-7148-6083-2
First published 1959 by Harper
Adelaide is a little bit different to most kangaroos because most kangaroos don't have wings.

"Ungerer remains a master of suggestion: with marvelous skill, his agile pen embellishes the straightforward visual narrative, arrayed on spacious white, with a wealth of comical details of posture and countenance." Horn Book

★ **Crictor**. Harper & Row 1958 32p il $17.99; pa $6.99
Grades: PreK K 1 2   E
1. Snakes -- Fiction
ISBN 0-06-026180-3; 0-06-443044-8 pa
A story "about the boa constrictor that was sent to Madame Bodot, who lived and taught school in a little French town. . . . The boys used him for a slide and the girls for a jump-rope. When Crictor captured a burglar by coiling around him until the police came, he was awarded impressive tokens of esteem and affection of the townspeople. Engaging line drawings echo the restrained and elegant absurdities of the text." Bull Cent Child Books

★ **Otto**; the autobiography of a teddy bear. Phaidon Press 2010 un il $16.95
Grades: 1 2 3   E
1. Jews -- Fiction 2. Soldiers -- Fiction 3. Friendship -- Fiction 4. Teddy bears -- Fiction 5. Holocaust, 1933-1945 -- Fiction 6. World War, 1939-1945 -- Fiction
ISBN 978-0-7148-5766-4; 0-7148-5766-1
First published 1999 by Robert Rinehard
Otto the teddy bear belongs to David, a Jewish boy in Germany. When David and his parents are taken away by the Nazis, David gives Otto to his friend Oskar, whose father goes to war. After a bombing raid, Otto is found by an American soldier. Years later Oskar rediscovers Otto in antique store in the U.S. and David finds them too.

"Ungerer's illustrations—expressive, carefully worked paintings . . . —present some potentially scary images; parents and teachers should prepare for questions. But Otto's tranquil voice allows Ungerer to tell his story at a safe remove, and his unvarnished honesty makes this a vital account." Publ Wkly

Urban, Linda
Mouse was mad; illustrated by Henry Cole. Harcourt Children's Books 2009 un il $16
Grades: PreK K 1 2   E
1. Mice -- Fiction 2. Anger -- Fiction 3. Animals -- Fiction
ISBN 978-0-15-205337-6; 0-15-205337-9
LC 2007045081
Mouse struggles to find the right way to express his anger, modeling the behavior of Hare, Bear, Hedgehog, and Bobcat, only to discover that his own way may be the best way of all.

"Through playful language and expressive watercolors with colored pencil and ink, this story about anger management proves to be both entertaining and therapeutic." SLJ

Urbanovic, Jackie
Duck at the door. HarperCollins 2007 un il $16.99; lib bdg $17.89
Grades: PreK K 1 2   E
1. Ducks -- Fiction 2. Winter -- Fiction 3. Animals -- Fiction
ISBN 0-06-121438-8; 0-06-121439-6 lib bdg
When Max the duck decides to stay behind when his flock flies south, Irene invites him to stay with her for the winter.

"Urbanovic's animals, with their expressive, engaging facial features, take center stage in the open, cheery illustrations. . . . Great fun for storyhours." SLJ
Other titles about Max the duck are:
Duck soup (2008)
Duck and cover (2009)

Sitting duck. Harper 2010 un il $17.99; lib bdg $18.89
Grades: PreK K 1 2   E
1. Dogs -- Fiction 2. Ducks -- Fiction 3. Animals -- Fiction 4. Babysitters -- Fiction
ISBN 978-0-06-176583-4; 0-06-176583-X; 978-0-06-176584-1 lib bdg; 0-06-176584-8 lib bdg
LC 2009014565

Max the duck volunteers to babysit for puppy Anabel, unaware of all the mischief a puppy can get into.

"Young Max fans will enjoy the cartoon-style visual humor, which ramps up the energy was well as the chaos as the story unfolds." Booklist

Urdahl, Catherine

Polka -dot fixes kindergarten; illustrated by Mai S. Kemble. Charlesbridge 2011 un il $16.95; pa $7.95; e-book $6.99

Grades: PreK K   E

1. School stories 2. Kindergarten -- Fiction
ISBN 978-1-57091-737-0; 1-57091-737-X; 978-1-57091-738-7 pa; 1-57091-738-8 pa; 978-1-60734-312-7 e-book

On the first day of kindergarten, Polka-dot uses the fix-it kit her grandpa has prepared for her to help her make a friend.

"The colorful watercolor illustrations support the text well. Kemble does a particularly good job of rendering facial expressions to mirror the children's emotions: worry, anger, hopefulness, shame, discomfort, and ultimately, kindness. Character education is becoming increasingly important in schools, and this book will make a solid addition to the resource shelf." SLJ

Vail, Rachel

Jibberwillies at night; illustrated by Yumi Heo. Scholastic Press 2008 un il $16.99

Grades: PreK K 1 2   E

1. Fear -- Fiction 2. Bedtime -- Fiction
ISBN 978-0-439-42070-9; 0-439-42070-9

LC 2007-34087

Katie is almost always happy, but sometimes at night, when the Jibberwillies come and scare her, her mother must catch them in a bucket and throw them out the window before Katie can fall asleep

"Katie's personality leaps off the page via Vail's evocative language . . . and Heo's bright and kicky mixed-media compositions." Publ Wkly

Righty & Lefty; a tale of two feet. by Rachel Vail; illustrations by Matthew Cordell. Scholastic Press 2007 un il $16.99

Grades: PreK K   E

1. Foot -- Fiction
ISBN 978-0-439-63629-2; 0-439-63629-9

LC 2006-28840

Even though Lefty and Righty like different things, they find they must learn to get along together without tripping over each other.

"It's a wonderfully weird story, filled with hilarious detail and deadpan humor. . . . Cordell's easygoing line-and-watercolor illustrations . . . [keep] the feet so sustainedly in focus that they gain character through sheer persistance." Bull Cent Child Books

Sometimes I'm Bombaloo; illustrated by Yumi Heo. Scholastic Press 2001 un il $15.95

Grades: PreK K 1 2   E

1. Anger 2. Emotions
ISBN 0-439-08755-4

LC 99-58709

When Katie Honors feels angry and out of control, her mother helps her to be herself again

"Vail captures the intensity of emotion that children (and many adults) feel when they are angry, and then distills it with laughter. Heo uses lots of stripes and splotches of color to match Katie's emotions. . . . Kudos to Vail and Heo for making a scary subject manageable." Booklist

Vainio, Pirkko

Who hid the Easter eggs? NorthSouth Books 2011 un il $16.95

Grades: PreK K   E

1. Eggs -- Fiction 2. Birds -- Fiction 3. Easter -- Fiction 4. Squirrels -- Fiction 5. Grandmothers -- Fiction
ISBN 978-0-7358-2304-4; 0-7358-2304-9

"A loving grandmother . . . hides her beautiful, hand-painted Easter eggs for her five grandchildren to find. The story focuses on a charming squirrel named Harry who lives in the grandmother's backyard. He is horrified to discover that a jackdaw (a European bird like a crow) has stolen all the eggs and hidden them in his nest. . . . The simple story is predictable and sweet, but the large-format watercolor illustrations . . . elevate this effort beyond the usual Easter Bunny adventure. . . . The Easter eggs are painted in traditional Ukrainian style, with tiny geometric prints and patterns that add a special touch to this story." Kirkus

Valckx, Catharina

Lizette's green sock. Clarion Books 2005 un il $15

Grades: PreK K 1 2   E

1. Birds -- Fiction 2. Clothing and dress -- Fiction
ISBN 0-618-45298-2

LC 2004-12042

Original French edition, 2002

Lizette, a young bird, tries to figure out what to do with the one green sock that she finds while out walking one day

"Utterly simple and springtime fresh. . . . Valckx conveys an impressive range of mood and action through spare, swooping brushstrokes, and pale tones of lemon, mint, and sky blue allow the kelly green of the sock to draw the eye instantly." Booklist

Valdivia, Paloma

Up above and down below; Paloma Valdivia. Owlkids Books, Inc. 2012 32 p. col. ill., maps $15.95

Grades: PreK K   E

1. Earth 2. Geography 3. Picture books for children
ISBN 1926973399; 9781926973395

LC 2011943194

This children's picture book "highlights the notion that although different kinds of people live in different places around the world, we share many things in common. The title subtly references the Earth's northern and southern hemispheres, launching readers into a picture book with spreads characterized by a line bisecting each page into upper and lower halves." (Kirkus)

Vamos, Samantha R.

Before you were here, mi amor; illustrated by Santiago Cohen. Viking 2009 un il $15.99

Grades: PreK K 1   E

1. Infants -- Fiction 2. Family life -- Fiction 3. Spanish

language -- Vocabulary

ISBN 978-0-670-06301-7; 0-670-06301-0

LC 2008-21548

Family members lovingly prepare for arrival of a new baby. Spanish words are woven throughout the text.

"Cohen uses the texture of the paper and his watercolor paints to create depth and movement in the vividly colored illustrations. This lovely story may encourage discussions of individual birth preparations in readers' own families." SLJ

★ The **cazuela** that the farm maiden stirred. Charlesbridge 2011 un il lib bdg $17.95

Grades: PreK K 1 2   E

1. Cooking -- Fiction 2. Domestic animals -- Fiction 3. Spanish language -- Vocabulary

ISBN 978-1-58089-242-1; 1-58089-242-6

LC 2010007547

"Inspired by 'The House that Jack Built,' Vamos offers a fresh, new twist, playfully introducing Spanish into this cumulative tale.... Lopez's artwork, with its desert palette punctuated by brilliant primary colors and its graphic, hard edges, suggestive of folk art, is a perfect match. ... A wonderful read-aloud, filled with merriment and conviviality." Kirkus

Van Allsburg, Chris, 1949-

★ **Ben's** dream; story and pictures by Chris Van Allsburg. Houghton Mifflin 1982 31p il lib bdg $16.95

Grades: K 1 2 3 4   E

1. Dreams -- Fiction

ISBN 0-395-32084-4

LC 81-20029

"When rain spoils Ben's ball game with Margaret, he returns to an empty house, falls asleep in his father's chair, and embarks on a dream. In a marvelous series of double-page black-and-white pictures meticulously textured with hatching, one shares Ben's voyage past such sights as the Statue of Liberty, the Sphinx, and the Mount Rushmore presidents, all with flood waters lapping about their respective chins and waists. ... A visual tour de force." Horn Book

The **garden** of Abdul Gasazi; written and illustrated by Chris Van Allsburg. Houghton Mifflin 1979 un il lib bdg $18.95

Grades: 1 2 3 4   E

1. Dogs -- Fiction 2. Magic -- Fiction

ISBN 0-395-27804-X

A Caldecott Medal honor book, 1980

When the dog he is caring for runs away from Alan into the forbidden garden of a retired dog-hating magician, a spell seems to be cast over the contrary dog

The full page "lithographlike drawings are astonishing—eerie, monumental, surreal and witty all at once—and the effect of the whole is original and unforgettable." Books of the Times

★ **Jumanji**; written and illustrated by Chris Van Allsburg. Houghton Mifflin 1981 un il $18.95

Grades: K 1 2 3 4   E

1. Games -- Fiction

ISBN 0-395-30448-2

LC 80-29632

Awarded the Caldecott Medal, 1982

Left on their own for an afternoon, two bored and restless children find more excitement than they bargained for in a mysterious and mystical jungle adventure board game.

"Through the masterly use of light and shadow, the interplay of design elements, and audacious changes in perspective and composition, the artist conveys an impression of color without losing the dramatic contrast of black and white." Horn Book

Just a dream. Houghton Mifflin 1990 un il $18.95

Grades: K 1 2 3 4   E

1. Dreams -- Fiction 2. Pollution -- Fiction 3. Environmental protection -- Fiction

ISBN 0-395-53308-2

LC 90-41343

When he has a dream about a future Earth devastated by pollution, Walter begins to understand the importance of taking care of the environment.

"Van Allsburg demonstrates his unique artistic magic in combining foresight, wisdom and striking artwork to deliver an ecological message concerning conservation and renewal." Child Book Rev Serv

The **mysteries** of Harris Burdick. Houghton Mifflin 1984 un il lib bdg $18.95

Grades: 1 2 3 4   E

1. Imagination -- Fiction 2. Storytelling -- Fiction

ISBN 0-395-35393-9

LC 84-9006

Presents a series of loosely related drawings each accompanied by a title and a caption which the reader may use to make up his or her own story

Rendered in the author's "signature velvet black and white . . . the pictures are nothing short of spectacular. . . . While some may find this just an excuse for handsome artwork, others will see its great potential for stretching a child's imagination. Although the book could be used in countless ways, primarily it will make storytellers of children." Booklist

★ The **Polar** Express; written and illustrated by Chris Van Allsburg. Twentieth anniversary ed.; Houghton Mifflin 2005 un il $35

Grades: PreK K 1 2 3   E

1. Christmas -- Fiction 2. Santa Claus -- Fiction

ISBN 978-0-618-61169-0; 0-618-61169-X

LC 2005281613

A reissue of the title first published 1985

Awarded the Caldecott Medal, 1986

A magical train ride on Christmas Eve takes a boy to the North Pole to receive a special gift from Santa Claus.

This offers "stunning paintings in which Van Allsburg uses dark, rich colors and misty shapes in contrast with touches of bright white-gold light to create scenes, interior and exterior, that have a quality of mystery that imbues the strong composition to achieve a soft, evocative mood." Bull Cent Child Books

Zathura; a space adventure. written and illustrated by Chris Van Allsburg. Houghton Mifflin 2002 un il $18

Grades: 1 2 3 4   **E**

1. Games -- Fiction

ISBN 0-618-25396-3

LC 2002-1751

"Van Allsburg illustrates the surreal events in a grainy charcoal-black that seems to shimmer on a rough, cream-colored ground. His deathly quiet images . . . have a frozen stillness that leaves all color and activity to the imagination; with each new threat, the book seems to hold its breath. . . . Zathura, like Jumanji, is a satisfying enigma." Publ Wkly

The **stranger**. Houghton Mifflin 1986 un il lib bdg $18.95

Grades: 1 2 3 4   **E**

1. Seasons -- Fiction

ISBN 0-395-42331-7

LC 86-15235

The enigmatic origins of the stranger Farmer Bailey hits with his truck and brings home to recuperate seem to have a mysterious relation to the weather.

"The full-color illustrations, framed in white, evoke an old-fashioned New England landscape at the end of summer; some are remarkably peaceful in tone, others slightly spooky by virtue of brooding colors, unexpected perspectives, or the stranger's peculiar expressions." Bull Cent Child Books

The **sweetest** fig. Houghton Mifflin 1993 un il $18.95

Grades: 1 2 3 4   **E**

1. Dogs -- Fiction 2. Magic -- Fiction 3. Dreams -- Fiction

ISBN 0-395-67346-1

LC 93-12692

After being given two magical figs that make his dreams come true, Monsieur Bibot sees his plans for future wealth upset by his long-suffering dog

"The full-color, expressive illustrations are filled with nuance, detail and mystery. Once again, Van Allsburg weaves a spell with ultimate skill and creativity." Child Book Rev Serv

The **widow's** broom. Houghton Mifflin 1992 un il $18.95

Grades: 1 2 3 4   **E**

1. Magic -- Fiction 2. Witchcraft -- Fiction

ISBN 0-395-64051-2

LC 92-7110

A witch's worn-out broom serves a widow well, until her neighbors decide the thing is wicked and dangerous

"In addition to being a neatly understated piece of storytelling, this fuels Van Allsburg's best kind of illustration—darkly rounded, speckle-textured art with eerie effects." Bull Cent Child Books

The **wreck** of the Zephyr; written and illustrated by Chris Van Allsburg. Houghton Mifflin 1983 un il lib bdg $18.95

Grades: 1 2 3 4   **E**

1. Imagination -- Fiction 2. Boats and boating -- Fiction

ISBN 0-395-33075-0

LC 82-23371

A boy's ambition to be the greatest sailor in the world brings him to ruin when he misuses his new ability to sail his boat in the air.

This "displays recognizable hallmarks of the artist's work: beauty of composition, striking contrasts of light and shadow, and especially the fascinating ambiguity of illusion and reality." Horn Book

The **wretched** stone. Houghton Mifflin 1991 un il $18.95

Grades: 1 2 3 4   **E**

1. Sea stories

ISBN 0-395-53307-4

LC 91-11525

This book chronicles the "events that occur during the last voyage of the Rita Anne. . . . One month into the journey, an uncharted island is explored . . . {and} the captain brings aboard a strange, heavy object; one surface of the rock is flat and glassy and emits a 'glowing light that is quite beautiful and pleasing to look at.' . . . A trip into the hold, where the sailors have barricaded themselves with the stone, reveals . . . {that} the men have turned into grinning monkeys, and they are unable to understand their captain's words. After a lightning storm disables the stone, the captain discovers that when he reads to the sailors, they recover some of their alertness." (Horn Book) "Grades two to four." (SLJ)

"Although Van Allsburg clearly has a message to convey, he has added to the book an enjoyable and necessary dollop of humor. The story has a quiet, understated, yet suspenseful tone; most of the plot's considerable drama is conveyed in the impressive illustrations." Horn Book

Van Camp, Katie

Harry and Horsie; illustrated by Lincoln Agnew. Balzer & Bray 2009 un il $16.99

Grades: PreK K 1 2   **E**

1. Imagination -- Fiction

ISBN 978-0-06-175598-9; 0-06-175598-2

When a boy named Harry sneaks out of bed one night with his best friend, Horsie, to play with his Super Duper Bubble Blooper—an out-of-this-world adventure begins!

"Agnew's art uses an effectively limited color palette, faded dot patterns, and crisp lines to create a retro-cartoon feel. . . . With dashing visuals that capture Harry's deep-space adventure with verve to spare, and a comforting resolution, this has potential to be a bedtime favorite." Booklist

Another title about Harry and Horsie is:

Cookiebot! A Harry and Horsie adventure (2011)

Van Dusen, Chris

King Hugo's huge ego. Candlewick Press 2011 il

Grades: PreK K 1   **E**

1. Stories in rhyme 2. Kings and rulers -- Fiction

ISBN 0-7636-5004-8; 978-0-7636-5004-9

LC 2010040458

When haughty King Hugo tangles with a sorceress, she causes him to see himself in a more realistic light.

"A life lesson and true love tie up the loose ends, but not before readers are treated to a terrific mélange of satire, slapstick, and caricature, all served up with expert comic timing." Publ Wkly

Learning to ski with Mr. Magee. Chronicle Books 2010 un il $15.99

Grades: PreK K 1   **E**

1. Stories in rhyme 2. Dogs -- Fiction 3. Skiing --

Fiction

ISBN 978-0-8118-7495-3; 0-8118-7495-8

An encounter with a moose while they are learning to ski provides Mr. Magee and his dog with some unexpected excitement.

"The gouache illustrations are clean, crisp, and colorful. Various shades of blue, green, and purple nicely show the chill of the winter day. The rhyming text, with occasional bolded words, scans easily. Fans of Mr. Magee will feel at home with this one." SLJ

Other titles about Mr. Magee are:

A camping spree with Mr. Magee (2003)

Down to the sea with Mr. Magee (2000)

The **circus** ship. Candlewick Press 2009 un il $16.99

Grades: PreK K 1 2 3   E

1. Stories in rhyme 2. Circus -- Fiction 3. Animals -- Fiction 4. Shipwrecks -- Fiction

ISBN 978-0-7636-3090-4; 0-7636-3090-X

LC 2008938402

Van Dusen "uses an actual 1836 shipwreck as the seed for this charming and humorous picture book. . . . The rhyming text provides the structure for the story; however, the vividly colored, meticulously drawn illustrations articulate the story so well that they could practically stand on their own." Booklist

Van Fleet, Matthew

Heads. Simon & Schuster 2010 un il $17.99

Grades: PreK K   E

1. Pop-up books 2. Animals -- Fiction

ISBN 978-1-4424-0379-6; 1-4424-0379-9

"Children begin the safari that celebrates the traits of diverse animals by pulling a tab that allows a giraffe, elephant, rhino, tiger, and alligator to assemble jumbled letters to create the title. On each busy page, more tabs open a platypus egg, enlarge a frog's throat, and wiggle an elephant's ears. Watercolor cartoon critters rock the pages with greedy grins, loving licks, and astonished yelps. . . . This fun board book is designed to entertain toddlers time and again." SLJ

Moo; photos by Brian Stanton. Simon & Schuster 2011 il $16.99

Grades: PreK   E

1. Board books for children 2. Domestic animals -- Fiction

ISBN 978-1-4424-3503-2; 1-4424-3503-8

"Van Fleet's interactive board book identifies farm animals using simple, playful rhymes. . . . Textures—a woolly sheep, a duck's downy chest feathers—provide a touch-and-feel aspect, while flaps and pop-ups make this a playful excursion." Publ Wkly

Van Hout, Mies

Happy; Mies van Hout. Lemniscaat 2012 52 p.

Grades: PreK K 1 2 3   E

1. Fishes -- Fiction 2. Emotions -- Fiction 3. Vocabulary -- Fiction 4. Animals -- Pictorial works 5. Picture books for children

ISBN 1935954148; 9781935954149

In this picture book, "vibrant fish--although not ones found in nature--illustrate emotions in this art piece for children and for adults translated from the Dutch. Each double-page spread is constructed with an image of a fish on one side, in what looks like a chalk drawing on a blackboard. Opposite is a single hand-lettered word, also drawn in chalk or crown, on a jewel-toned, textured sheet. "Brave" is a very small pale fish with a tentative smile, isolated in the lower corner of the black page. . . . The "content" green fish aligns itself in the precise middle of the page; one can almost see it wriggling in its satisfaction. The "shocked" square-ish fish is shocking pink and purple and prickly, with open mouth and round eyes." (Kirkus)

Van Laan, Nancy

Nit-pickin' [by] Nancy Van Laan and [illustrated by] George Booth. Atheneum Books for Young Readers 2008 un il $15.99

Grades: PreK K 1   E

1. Stories in rhyme 2. Lice -- Fiction

ISBN 0-689-83898-0; 978-0-689-83898-9

LC 00-062077

Family members go to great lengths to rid their child of head lice.

"The lively text is complemented by the over-the-top antics observed in Booth's cartoon illustrations." SLJ

Teeny tiny tingly tales; illustrated by Victoria Chess. Atheneum Bks. for Young Readers 2001 un il $16

Grades: PreK K 1 2   E

1. Short stories 2. Horror fiction 3. Stories in rhyme

ISBN 0-689-81875-0

LC 97-37452

Three rhyming scary stories, including 'Old Doctor Wango Tango,' 'It,' and 'The Hairy Toe'

"Victoria Chess's squat figures, all teeth and beady eyes and unkempt hair, complement the zany, but a teeny-tiny bit scary, nature of these tales." Horn Book

When winter comes; illustrated by Susan Gaber. Atheneum Bks. for Young Readers 2000 un il $16

Grades: PreK K 1 2   E

1. Stories in rhyme 2. Winter -- Fiction 3. Animals -- Fiction

ISBN 0-689-81778-9

LC 97-32914

Rhyming text asks what happens to different animals and plants "when winter comes and the cold wind blows"

"The rhyming answers use simple and accessible language. Gaber's exuberant acrylic paintings show a child, mother, father, and dog taking a walk through the woods during a snowfall." SLJ

Van Leeuwen, Jean

★ **Amanda** Pig and the awful, scary monster; pictures by Ann Schweninger. Phyllis Fogelman Bks. 2003 48p il (PJF easy-to-read) hardcover o.p. pa $3.99

Grades: K 1 2   E

1. Fear 2. Pigs 3. Bedtime 4. Monsters

ISBN 0-8037-2766-6; 0-14-240203-6 pa

LC 2001-33519

Amanda pig sees monsters at night, but her parents and her brother find different ways to convince her that there are no monsters

"Van Leeuwen captures childhood emotions perfectly and includes just the right amount of humor. With bright illustrations done in carbon pencil, colored pencils, and watercolor washes on every page, this book will delight the piglet's many fans." SLJ

Other titles about Amanda Pig are:

Amanda Pig and her big brother Oliver (1982)

Tales of Amanda Pig (1983)

More tales of Amanda Pig (1985)

Oliver, Amanda, and Grandmother Pig (1987)

Oliver and Amanda's Christmas (1989)

Amanda Pig on her own (1991)

Oliver and Amanda's Halloween (1992)

Oliver and Amanda and the big snow (1995)

Amanda Pig, school girl (1997)

Amanda Pig and her best friend Lollipop (1998)

Amanda Pig and the really hot day (2005)

Amanda Pig, first grader (2007)

Amanda Pig and the wiggly tooth (2008)

Benny & beautiful baby Delilah; pictures by LeUyen Pham. Dial Books for Young Readers 2006 32p il $16.99
Grades: PreK K 1 2   E
1. Infants -- Fiction 2. Siblings -- Fiction
ISBN 0-8037-2891-3

LC 2004-19412

"Benny gets his very own little sister, but realizes pretty quickly that shes not much fun. . . . In the end, after a long session of crying, Benny takes charge and is able to get Delilah to smile. . . . While this well-paced story doesn't break any new ground thematically, it is realistic and heartwarming. What makes it truly shine is the art. . . . The characterizations, created with a heavy ink line, are expressive, jaunty, and lively." SLJ

Chicken soup; by Jean Van Leeuwen; illustrated by David Gavril. Abrams Books for Young Readers 2009 un il $16.95
Grades: PreK K 1   E
1. Chickens -- Fiction 2. Farm life -- Fiction
ISBN 978-0-8109-8326-7; 0-8109-8326-5

LC 2008030824

When they hear that Mrs. Farmer is making soup, all the frightenened chickens run for their lives, but Mr. Farmer finds Little Chickie, who has a bad cold, and he takes her to the kitchen for some nice hot vegetable soup.

"This simple, just-scary-enough story will appeal to preschoolers with its repetition and bright, childlike pen and watercolor illustrations." SLJ

★ **Oliver** the Mighty Pig; pictures by Ann Schweninger. Dial Bks. for Young Readers 2004 48p il (Dial easy-to-read) lib bdg $14.99
Grades: K 1 2   E
1. Pigs 2. Play 3. Imagination 4. Heroes 5. Pigs -- Fiction 6. Superheroes -- Fiction
ISBN 0-8037-2886-7

LC 2002-7310

Oliver feels like the superhero Mighty Pig when he wears his Mighty Pig cape, but he finds that being a superhero in the real world has some complications.

"Van Leeuwen's text is filled with lively dialogue and simple sentences that are just right for beginning readers. . . . The bright, uncluttered pictures on each page reinforce the meaning in the words and add layers of humor." Booklist

Other titles about Oliver Pig are:

Tales of Oliver Pig (1979)

More tales of Oliver Pig (1981)

Amanda Pig and her big brother Oliver (1982)

Oliver, Amanda, and Grandmother Pig (1987)

Oliver and Amanda's Christmas (1989)

Oliver Pig at school (1990)

Oliver and Amanda's Halloween (1992)

Oliver and Amanda and the big snow (1995)

Oliver and Albert, friends forever (2000)

Oliver Pig and the best fort ever (2006)

Papa and the pioneer quilt; [by] Jean Van Leeuwen; pictures by Rebecca Bond. Dial Books for Young Readers 2007 un il $16.99
Grades: K 1 2 3   E
1. Quilts -- Fiction 2. Frontier and pioneer life -- Fiction 3. Overland journeys to the Pacific -- Fiction
ISBN 0-8037-3028-4

LC 2005022983

As her family travels by wagon train to Oregon, a young girl gathers scraps of cloth so that she can make a quilt. Includes historical note.

"Bond's excellent illustrations, done in acrylics on watercolor paper, provide an ideal dreamy background for the story. The smooth first-person narrative, appealing dialogue, and sunny artwork vividly capture a child's experience in the early days of the United States." SLJ

Van Lieshout, Maria

Flight 1-2-3; by Maria van Lieshout. Chronicle Books 2013 40 p. (hardcover) $14.99
Grades: PreK K 1   E
1. Picture books for children 2. Airports -- Juvenile fiction 3. Air travel -- Juvenile fiction
ISBN 1452116628; 9781452116624

LC 2012033606

This children's counting story, by Maria van Lieshout, follows a boy on a airplane. "What can you see when you go on an airplane journey? 1 airplane, 2 luggage carts, 3 check-in counters, and so much more! Using familiar airport signs, this . . . book introduces little ones not only to numbers, but to the world around them." (Publisher's note)

Hopper and Wilson. Philomel Books 2011 un il $16.99
Grades: PreK K 1   E
1. Mice -- Fiction 2. Sailing -- Fiction 3. Elephants -- Fiction
ISBN 978-0-399-25184-9; 0-399-25184-7

LC 2010-19396

An elephant and a mouse embark on a journey to discover what it looks like at the end of the world.

Van Lieshout "plays up the suspense of the separation with lots of space in the spreads and long waits. . . . [The] story is filled with adventure, emotion, and imagery that supplies lots of effervescent warmth." Publ Wkly

Van Steenwyk, Elizabeth

Prairie Christmas; written by Elizabeth Van Steenwyk; illustrated by Ronald Himler. Eerdmans 2006 un il $17
Grades: 1 2 3 4   E
1. Midwives -- Fiction 2. Christmas -- Fiction 3. Mother-daughter relationship -- Fiction
ISBN 0-8028-5280-7

On the Nebraska prairie in 1880, eleven-year-old Emma finds a way to celebrate the spirit of Christmas while her mother, a midwife, delivers a baby on Christmas Eve.

"This memorable tale is beautifully told in clear and simple prose, which is complemented perfectly by the uncluttered, colored-pencil and watercolor drawings." SLJ

VanHecke, Susan

An **apple** pie for dinner; retold by Susan VanHecke; illustrated by Carol Baicker-McKee. Marshall Cavendish Children 2009 un il $17.99

Grades: K 1 2 3   E
   1. Apples -- Fiction 2. Baking -- Fiction 3. Barter -- Fiction

ISBN 978-0-7614-5452-6; 0-7614-5452-7

LC 2008003664

Wishing to bake an apple pie, Old Granny Smith sets out with a full basket, trading its contents for a series of objects until she gets the apples she needs.

"The bas-relief illustrations, made from baked clay and mixed-media of found objects, create a 3-D, Claymation effect. . . . The fascinating tactile details will have young and old poring over the pages. . . . Complete with a pie recipe and notes from both the author and illustrator that cite the origin of the tale (the English folktale 'An Apple Dumpling') and directions on how to make bas-reliefs, the book is a delicious treat to be shared anytime. " Booklist

Vander Zee, Ruth

Always with you; written by Ruth Vander Zee; illustrated by Ronald Himler. Eerdmans Books for Young Readers 2008 un il $17

Grades: 2 3 4   E
   1. Orphans -- Fiction 2. Mother-daughter relationship -- Fiction

ISBN 978-0-8028-5295-3

LC 2007009354

Orphaned at the age of four when her village in Vietnam is bombed, Kim is rescued by soldiers and raised in an orphanage, always finding comfort in her mother's last words "Don't be afraid. I will always be with you."

Mississippi morning; written by Ruth Vander Zee; illustrated by Floyd Cooper. Eerdmans Books for Young Readers 2004 un il $16

Grades: 1 2 3 4   E
   1. Race relations -- Fiction 2. Father-son relationship -- Fiction

ISBN 0-8028-5211-4

LC 2002-151212

Amidst the economic depression and the racial tension of the 1930s, a boy discovers a horrible secret of his father's involvement in the Ku Klux Klan

"Cooper's large, warm oil paintings create the perfect sense of time, place, and atmosphere. . . . A sad and poignant story." SLJ

Vanderwater, Amy Ludwig

Forest has a song; poems. by Amy Ludwig VanDerwater; illustrations by Robbin Gourley. Clarion Books 2013 40 p. col. ill. (reinforced) $16.99

Grades: 2 3 4   E
   1. Seasons -- Poetry 2. Picture books for children

ISBN 0618843493; 9780618843497

LC 2011052433

In this children's picture book, moving "through the seasons. newcomer [Amy Ludwig] VanDerwater shares a girl's experience of what the forest has to offer. On a chilly spring day, she 'stop[s] to read/ the Forest News! in mud or fallen snow./ Articles are printed/ by critters on the go.'" She encounters the forest in summer, autumn, and winter as well. (Publishers Weekly)

Varela, Barry

Gizmo; [by] Barry Varela; illustrations by Ed Briant. Roaring Brook Press 2007 un il $16.95

Grades: K 1 2 3   E
   1. Stories in rhyme 2. Machinery -- Fiction

ISBN 978-1-59643-115-7; 1-59643-115-6

LC 2006012007

When Professor Ludwig von Glink's contraption gets so out of hand that the City Buildings and Permits Inspector condemns his home, the City Contemporary Art Museum comes to the rescue

"The animation inherent in Briant's colorful line-and-wash artwork bolsters the humor, while Varela's playful sense of language leads to some inspired wordplay." Booklist

Varennes, Monique de

The **jewel** box ballerinas; [by] Monique de Varennes; pictures by Ana Juan. Schwartz & Wade Books 2007 un il $16.99; lib bdg $19.99

Grades: K 1 2 3   E
   1. Magic -- Fiction 2. Wealth -- Fiction 3. Friendship -- Fiction

ISBN 978-0-375-83605-3; 0-375-83605-5; 978-0-375-93605-0 lib bdg; 0-375-93605-X lib bdg

LC 2004-19622

Wealthy Bibi purchases a magic jewel box and sets out to make the two tiny ballerinas within it smile again

"The richly colored, jewel-toned art suits the surreal tale, gently spoofing Bibi and her possessions. . . . This story of transformation is made twice as nice by the pairing of equally witty text and illustrations." Horn Book

Varon, Sara

Chicken and Cat; by Sara Varon. Scholastic Press 2006 un il $16.99

Grades: PreK K 1 2   E
   1. Stories without words 2. Cats -- Fiction 3. Chickens -- Fiction 4. City and town life -- Fiction

ISBN 0-439-63406-7

LC 2003025297

When Cat feels sad about living in the hustle and bustle of the city, Chicken finds colorful ways to make Cat feel better

"In this wordless story, bold, full-bleed cartoon illustrations are amiably cluttered. . . . This book has a funny, big-eyed sweetness, and is packed with details that kids will relish discovering in successive readings." SLJ

Another title about Chicken and Cat is:
Chicken and Cat clean up (2009)

Velasquez, Eric

★ **Grandma's** gift. Walker 2010 un il $16.99; lib bdg $17.89

Grades: K 1 2 3   E

1. Gifts -- Fiction 2. Artists -- Fiction 3. Christmas -- Fiction 4. Grandmothers -- Fiction 5. Puerto Ricans -- Fiction 6. African Americans -- Fiction

ISBN 978-0-8027-2082-5; 0-8027-2082-X; 978-0-8027-2083-2 lib bdg; 0-8027-2083-8 lib bdg

LC 2010005326

Pura Belpré Award for illustration, 2011

The author describes Christmas at his grandmother's apartment in Spanish Harlem the year she introduced him to the Metropolitan Museum of Art and Diego Velazquez's portrait of Juan de Pareja, which has had a profound and lasting effect on him.

"The realistic oil paintings reveal a strong and stylish grandmother of great character and a polite child. . . . The sweetly understated story has Spanish words and sentences skillfully woven into the text throughout with translations provided in parenthesis." Kirkus

Veldkamp, Tjibbe

Tom the tamer; illustrated by Philip Hopman. Lemniscaat USA 2011 32p il

Grades: PreK K   E

1. Fear -- Fiction 2. Animals -- Fiction 3. Father-son relationship -- Fiction

ISBN 1-9359-5405-9; 978-1-9359-5405-7

"This tender, loopy, and unconventional work . . . stars a boy who wants to lure his phobic father away from his model railway and into the backyard so that the father can meet the animals he's frightened of face-to-face. . . . Tom purchases a polar bear from the local pet store and discovers that the bear can do an uncanny imitation of an armchair. . . . This success sets the stage for a full-scale animal-furniture renovation. . . . The episodes recall gentler moments from Roald Dahl or Russell Hoban. Similarly, Hopman's illustrations are first cousin to Quentin Blake's, full of fanciful color and a jumble of imagined detail."

Verburg, Bonnie

The **kiss** box; illustrated by Henry Cole. Orchard Books 2011 un il lib bdg $16.99

Grades: PreK   E

1. Love -- Fiction 2. Bears -- Fiction 3. Kissing -- Fiction 4. Mother-child relationship -- Fiction

ISBN 978-0-545-11284-0; 0-545-11284-2

LC 2009012102

As they prepare for a short separation, Mama Bear and Little Bear find a way to reassure each other while they are apart.

"Cole's charming and cheery watercolor and colored-pencil illustrations of Mama Bear and Little Bear enjoying the day before she leaves do much to make this title appealing." SLJ

Verde, Susan

The **museum**; written by Susan Verde; art by Peter H. Reynolds. Abrams Books for Young Readers 2013 32 p. (reinforced) $16.95

Grades: PreK K 1 2   E

1. Picture books for children 2. Art museums -- Juvenile

fiction 3. Stories in rhyme

ISBN 1419705946; 9781419705946

LC 2012022518

This children's picture book focuses on a girl's experience at an art museum. "A girl in pigtails embodies the emotions elicited by the paintings she sees, leaping, twirling, giggling, and—inspired by the famous Munch work—even shrieking, as she tours a museum gallery filled with European and American masterpieces." (Publishers Weekly)

Verdick, Elizabeth

Mealtime; illustrated by Marieka Heinlen. Free Spirit Pub. 2011 un il bd bk $7.95

Grades: PreK   E

1. Food 2. Etiquette 3. Nutrition 4. Board books for children

ISBN 978-1-57542-366-1; 1-57542-366-9

LC 2010045051

"Pretty much every main lesson adults try to impart about mealtime is covered here: washing hands, using utensils, displaying manners, trying new food, sitting still, and cleaning up. This . . . list of demands is relayed via a group of four beaming multicultural children wearing wild color and set before even more wildly colored backdrops." Booklist

Vere, Ed

Banana! Henry Holt & Co. 2010 un il $12.99

Grades: PreK K 1   E

1. Banana -- Fiction 2. Monkeys -- Fiction

ISBN 978-0-8050-9214-1; 0-8050-9214-5

LC 2009-936514

"Especially noteworthy are the bold graphic illustrations: the digitally scrawled figures are oversized, and in each spread they're set against a different field of solid color. . . . [The monkeys'] faces are remarkably expressive, showing a range of emotions from frustration to desperation to fury. . . . This would be a lively title to share in a toddler storytime, but its simplicity and illustratively conveyed plot make it an enjoyable work for youngsters to pore over solo." Bull Cent Child Books

Chick. Holt & Co. 2010 un il $9.99

Grades: PreK   E

1. Pop-up books 2. Chickens -- Fiction

ISBN 978-0-8050-9168-7; 0-8050-9168-8

First published 2009 in the United Kingdom

"A beak cracks through an orange pop-up egg—'crick crack crickety crack'—and out pops a yellow chick whose loud 'cheep!' brings its mother rushing to its side. She's a red chicken with a three-fingered crest, and together they eat and rest. . . . Humor, bold colors, and clever engineering make for a simple, memorable package." Publ Wkly

Vernick, Audrey

Is your buffalo ready for kindergarten? illustrated by Daniel Jennewein. Balzer + Bray 2010 un il $16.99

Grades: PreK K   E

1. School stories 2. Bison -- Fiction

ISBN 978-0-06-176275-8; 0-06-176275-X

LC 2009-11841

"This is a silly book about the first day of kindergarten with one's own buffalo. . . . The story prompts readers to remind the buffalo that finger painting is fun and it's okay to get messy; those hooves could create a masterpiece. Buffaloes (and children) learn how to get along without using their horns. . . . This wacky picture book, with its bold cartoon-like illustrations of a buffalo that snorts, dances, and makes faces, may help apprehensive youngsters to be more at ease about going to school." SLJ

Another title about the buffalo is:
Teach you buffalo to play drums (2011)

Teach your buffalo to play drums; written by Audrey Vernick; illustrated by Daniel Jennewein. Balzer + Bray 2011 un il $16.99
Grades: PreK K 1 2   E
1. Bison -- Fiction 2. Drums -- Fiction 3. Musicians -- Fiction
ISBN 978-0-06-176253-6; 0-06-176253-9
LC 2010007478
Encourages the reader, through practical advice, to support his or her buffalo's desire to play the drums, even if he has quickly lost interest in other activities in the past.

"Several small pictures appear on most pages . . . showing the huge animal trying to engage in human activities like skateboarding and showering, resulting in some very funny scenarios. His expressions are priceless." SLJ

Verplancke, Klaas
Applesauce; Klaas Verplancke, Helen Mixter. Groundwood Books/House of Anansi Press 2012 40 p. $18.95
Grades: PreK K 1   E
1. Anger -- Juvenile fiction 2. Picture books for children 3. Fathers -- Juvenile fiction 4. Father-son relationship -- Juvenile fiction
ISBN 1554981867; 9781554981861
This children's book by Klaas Verplancke is about a father-son relationship. "Johnny's daddy has smooth cheeks, an apple in his throat and sounds like a mom when he sings in the bath. . . . Other times his hands are cold and flash like lightning, and he becomes a thunder-daddy. When this happens Johnny wants to find a new daddy, but he eventually realizes that thunder-daddies don't last forever. And that there's nothing like the comfort that comes from those we love." (Publisher's note)

Vestergaard, Hope
Potty animals; what to know when you've gotta go! illustrated by Valeria Petrone. Sterling Pub. 2010 un il $14.95
Grades: PreK   E
1. Stories in rhyme 2. Animals -- Fiction 3. Toilet training -- Fiction
ISBN 978-1-4027-5996-3; 1-4027-5996-7
"Petrone's cheery digital characters and Vestergaard's decorous yet humorous rhymes invite readers to help civilize the bathroom habits of some uncouth preschool-age animals. . . . Petrone's wide-eyed cartoon animals capture a broad spectrum of toddler emotions." Publ Wkly

Vidal, Beatriz
Federico and the Magi's gift; a Latin American Christmas story. by Beatriz Vidal. Knopf 2004 un il $15.95; lib bdg $17.99

Grades: PreK K 1 2   E
1. Magi 2. Epiphany
ISBN 0-375-82518-5; 0-375-92518-X lib bdg
LC 2003-25880
Because he has misbehaved, four-year-old Federico is afraid the three kings will not bring him the toy horse he asked them for and, unable to sleep, he goes outside to await their arrival

"Decoratively patterned, the gouache-and-watercolor paintings employ naive forms and glowing colors. . . . With its quiet narrative and beautiful illustrations, this celebrates the end of the Christmas season in a distinctly Latin American way." Booklist

Vigil-Pinon, Evangelina
Marina's muumuu; illustrations by Pablo Torrecilla. Arte Público Press 2001 un il $14.95
Grades: PreK K 1 2   E
1. Clothing and dress -- Fiction 2. Bilingual books -- English-Spanish
ISBN 1-55885-350-2
LC 2001-21487
Marina has always dreamed of having a colorful muumuu, the traditional dress of the Hawaiian people, and finally goes to the bustling downtown with her grandmother to buy the fabric

"Gloriously bright tropical colors and patterns fill these gaily decorated pages." Booklist

Villeneuve, Anne
The **red** scarf. Tundra Books 2010 un il $17.95
Grades: PreK K 1   E
1. Circus -- Fiction 2. Animals -- Fiction 3. Taxicabs -- Fiction 4. Moles (Animals) -- Fiction 5. Lost and found possessions -- Fiction
ISBN 978-0-88776-989-4; 0-88776-989-6
"In this nearly wordless book, Turpin, a white mole, serves as taxi driver to a mysterious caped man who leaves behind a scarlet, fringed scarf. Determined to return the property, kind Turpin follows a trail leading to a circus. . . . Villeneuve's muted crayon palette gracefully swirls and smears scenes from city to center ring. The cartoons keep the action at forefront, with minimal backgrounds and energetic compositions. This gentle comedy with familiar adventures at the big top will please young audiences." SLJ

Villnave, Erica Pelton
Sophie's lovely locks. Marshall Cavendish 2011 un il $16.99
Grades: PreK K 1 2   E
1. Hair -- Fiction
ISBN 978-0-7614-5820-3; 0-7614-5820-4
LC 2010010055
Sophie loves her long hair, but when it becomes too hard to manage and she decides to get it cut, she finds something generous to do with it. Includes list of organizations that make wigs from donated hair.

"Soft lines in the watercolor illustrations show [the hair's] movement and [Sophie's] delight in it as she twirls and swirls. . . . The playful main character presents the obvious message in a joyous, engaging way." SLJ

Viorst, Judith

★ **Alexander** and the terrible, horrible, no good, very bad day; illustrated by Ray Cruz; with a new preface by Judith Viorst and Ray Cruz. Special limited ed.; Atheneum Books for Young Readers 2009 un il $17.99
Grades: PreK K 1 2   E
1. Day -- Fiction
ISBN 978-1-4169-8595-2; 1-4169-8595-6
                                        LC 2008049478
A reissue of the title first published 1972
On a day when everything goes wrong for him, Alexander is consoled by the thought that other people have bad days too.
"Small listeners can enjoy the litany of disaster, and perhaps be stimulated to discuss the possibility that one contributes by expectation. The illustrations capture the grumpy dolor of the story, ruefully funny." Sutherland. The Best In Child Books

Other titles about Alexander are:
Alexander, who is not (do you hear me?) going (I mean it) to move (1995)
Alexander, who used to be rich last Sunday (1978)

Earrings! illustrated by Nola Langner Malone. Atheneum Books for Young Readers 2010 un il $16.99
Grades: 1 2 3   E
1. Earrings -- Fiction
ISBN 978-1-4424-1281-1; 1-4424-1281-X
                                        LC 2010502964
A reissue of the title first published 1990
A young girl uses various arguments to convince her parents to let her have her ears pierced.
"Viorst homes in on minor childhood crises with the perfect blend of humor and insight, and Malone's expressive and comic figures are miniature character studies in themselves." Horn Book

Just in case; written by Judith Viorst; illustrated by Diana Cain Bluthenthal. Atheneum Books for Young Readers 2006 un il $15.95
Grades: PreK K 1 2   E
1. Worry -- Fiction
ISBN 0-689-87164-3
                                        LC 2003-26068
Charlie likes to be ready for anything, imagining that his house could be flooded or a mermaid might kidnap him, but he learns that it is sometimes good to be unprepared
"Blumenthal's colorful, mixed-media illustrations add some good cheer, sly wit, . . . and a companionable canine to the catalog of Charlie's hypothetical 'just in case' concerns." Booklist

Nobody here but me; [by] Judith Viorst; pictures by Christine Davenier. Farrar, Straus and Giroux 2008 un il $16.95
Grades: PreK K 1   E
1. Family life -- Fiction
ISBN 978-0-374-35540-1; 0-374-35540-1
                                        LC 2006-101606
With his mother on the phone, his father checking e-mail, and his sister playing with her friends, a little boy feels as if he is all alone in the house, and no matter how badly he behaves, no one comes to stop him

"Davenier's watercolor-and-ink illustrations place the boy in his pleasant house with his busy family. The muted colors reflect his mood. . . . This book addresses a universal childhood experience." SLJ

The **tenth** good thing about Barney; illustrated by Erik Blegvad. Atheneum Pubs. 1971 25p il $15.95; pa $5.99
Grades: PreK K 1 2   E
1. Cats -- Fiction 2. Death -- Fiction
ISBN 0-689-20688-7; 0-689-71203-0 pa
"The author succinctly and honestly handles both the emotions stemming from the loss of a beloved pet and the questions about the finality of death . . . An unusually good book that handles a difficult subject straightforwardly." Horn Book

Vischer, Frans
Fuddles; written and illustrated by Frans Vischer. Aladdin 2010 un il $15.99
Grades: PreK K 1   E
1. Cats -- Fiction
ISBN 1-4169-9155-7; 978-1-4169-9155-7
                                        LC 2010019049
When Fuddles the cat escapes from his house and goes to explore the great outdoors, his adventure is more taxing than he expected it to be.
Vischer "creates an appealing character in black-and-white Fuddles. The brief, repetitive sentences will read aloud well, but children will want to crowd around in close to catch all of the detail and expression in the digital illustrations, which are rendered in the style of traditional pencil drawings." Booklist

Viva, Frank
★ **Along** a long road. Little, Brown 2011 un il $16.99
Grades: PreK K 1 2   E
1. Cycling -- Fiction
ISBN 978-0-316-12925-1; 0-316-12925-9
                                        LC 2010019751
Illustrations and brief text evoke a bicycle ride, with its ups and downs, sweeping turns, and vivid views.
"Viva's artwork combines supple curves, big areas of soft black background, light blue for water and shading, and the occasional brick-red accent; it's simultaneously stylish and restrained. Simple, lilting text reproduces the smooth, rhythmic pace of cycling and the meditative state of mind it induces. . . . It's the kind of book that creates a mood rather than telling a story, evoking the freedom of traveling, the joy of movement, and the exhilaration of being outside." Publ Wkly

★ A **long** way away; Frank Viva. Little, Brown Books for Young Readers 2013 40 p. (hardback) $16.99
Grades: PreK K 1   E
1. Outer space -- Fiction 2. Voyages and travels -- Juvenile fiction 3. Ocean -- Fiction 4. Upside-down books
ISBN 0316221961; 9780316221962
                                        LC 2012028757
This children's picture book follows an alien family's journey. "Their alien child starts a downward slide along a yellow path past celestial bodies (and a shoe), through the Earth's atmosphere, past a whale and school of dapper fish, and into the blackest ocean depths. 'Deep asleep,' the final

page reads, as the alien lodges on an underwater cliff. The return trip shows the creature rising up through the ocean and back through deep space . . . before being reunited with his family." (Publishers Weekly)

Voake, Charlotte

Ginger and the mystery visitor. Candlewick Press 2010 un il $15.99

Grades: PreK K 1 2   E

1. Cats -- Fiction

ISBN 978-0-7636-4865-7; 0-7636-4865-5

LC 2009049505

Ginger and the small kitten are happy living with the little girl who looks after them but one day a large and hungry visitor appears in the kitchen and changes their comfortable routine.

"Voake's watercolor cats, energized by a loose, doodly ink line, are so expressive they almost talk. Charming, smug, hopeful, manipulative, indignant—she gets all the moods in this cat-centric narrative." Horn Book

Other titles about Ginger are:

The star of Ginger (1997)

Ginger Finds a Home (2003)

Hello, twins. Candlewick Press 2006 un il

Grades: PreK K   E

1. Twins -- Fiction 2. Siblings -- Fiction

ISBN 0-7636-3003-9

LC 2005-50185

Although twins Charlotte and Simon do everything differently and do not look alike, they still share a special bond. "Ages two to four." (Bull Cent Child Books)

"The lithesome watercolor-and-ink illustrations are amusing and consistently expand the simple text." SLJ

Vogel, Amos

★ **How** little Lori visited Times Square; pictures by Maurice Sendak. HarperCollins Pubs. 2001 un il $14.95

Grades: PreK K 1 2   E

ISBN 0-06-028462-5

A reissue of the title first published 1963

This "tells the story of Lori's many misadventures trying to get to Times Square on various modes of transportation, with a slow-moving turtle finally bearing him off." Horn Book Guide

Vries, Anke de

Raf; [illustrated by] Charlotte Dematons. Lemniscaat 2009 un il $16.95

Grades: PreK K   E

1. Toys -- Fiction 2. Voyages and travels -- Fiction

ISBN 978-1-59078-749-6

Original Dutch edition, 2008

This "follows a toy giraffe that spontaneously disappears from his child's room to travel through Africa. . . . In postcards sent to his owner/pal, Ben . . . Raf tells of encounters with camels, flamingos, elephants, monkeys, and giraffes. . . . Just in time for Ben's birthday, the toy arrives in the mail, dressed in kente cloth and colored beads. . . . In addition to being a great success with preschool fans of toy tales, this story could also be shared with primary-grade children in conjunction with units on biome study or continents." SLJ

Waber, Bernard

Evie & Margie. Houghton Mifflin 2003 32p il $15

Grades: PreK K 1 2   E

1. Theater -- Fiction 2. Friendship -- Fiction 3. Hippopotamus -- Fiction

ISBN 0-618-34124-2

LC 2003-533

Best friends hippopotamuses, Evie and Margie, are surprised to experience jealousy when they try out for the same part in the school play

"The book gets to the heart of what is important to children, and the color illustrations are vintage Waber with great facial expressions and humorous, child-friendly images." SLJ

★ **Ira** sleeps over. Houghton Mifflin 1972 48p il lib bdg $16; pa $6.95

Grades: PreK K 1 2   E

1. Friendship -- Fiction 2. Teddy bears -- Fiction

ISBN 0-395-13893-0 lib bdg; 0-395-20503-4 pa

Ira is excited at the prospect of spending the night at his friend's house but worries how he'll get along without his teddy bear

"An appealing picture book which depicts common childhood qualms with empathy and humor in brief text and colorful illustrations." Booklist

Another title about Ira is:

Ira says goodbye (1988)

★ **Lyle,** Lyle, crocodile. Houghton Mifflin 1965 48p il $16; pa $6.95

Grades: PreK K 1 2   E

1. Crocodiles -- Fiction

ISBN 0-395-16995-X; 0-395-13720-9 pa

"The illustrations are cartoon-like, lively, and colorful. . . . The situation is nicely exploited with a bland daffiness." Bull Cent Child Books Other titles about Lyle are:

Funny, funny Lyle (1987)

The house on East 88th Street (1962)

Lovable Lyle (1969)

Lyle and the birthday party (1966)

Lyle at Christmas (1998)

Lyle at the office (1994)

Lyle finds his mother (1974)

Lyle walks the dogs (2010)

The **house** on East 88th Street. Houghton Mifflin 1962 48p il lib bdg $16.95; pa $6.95

Grades: PreK K 1 2   E

1. Crocodiles -- Fiction

ISBN 0-395-18157-7; 0-395-19970-0 pa

LC 62-8144

"In an amusing fantasy, Mr. and Mrs. Joseph F. Primm and their young son Joshua move into a new home in New York City and discover a crocodile [named Lyle] in the bathtub. The illustrations detail the wrought iron railings, the graceful doorway with its fanlight, the sweeping staircase, elaborate fireplaces, and ornate chandeliers, characteristic of a comfortable old brownstone dwelling." Moorachian. What is a City?

The **mouse** that snored. Houghton Mifflin 2000 un il $15; pa $5.95

Grades: PreK K 1 2   E

1. Stories in rhyme 2. Mice -- Fiction 3. Noise -- Fiction 4. Snoring -- Fiction

ISBN 0-395-97518-2; 0-618-43954-4 pa

LC 98-47276

A loudly snoring mouse disturbs the residents of a quiet country house

"Using characteristically humorous pictures and a delightful, rhyming text, Waber creates a world-weary mouse with a snore that moves furniture." Booklist

Waddell, Martin

Can't you sleep, Little Bear? illustrated by Barbara Firth. special anniversary edition; Candlewick Press 2002 un il $15.99

Grades: PreK   E

1. Bears -- Fiction 2. Bedtime -- Fiction

ISBN 978-0-76361-929-9; 0-76361-929-9

First published 1988 in the United Kingdom

When bedtime comes Little Bear is afraid of the dark, until Big Bear brings him lights and love.

"Firth's brightly lit watercolor and soft pencil illustrations, framed in the dark blue of the night, capture the cozy, physical affection of the story, the playfulness of Little Bear, . . . the shadowy mystery of the moonlit landscape, and the huge comforting presence of a parent who is always there when you call." Booklist

Other titles about Little Bear are:

Good job, Little Bear! (1999)

Let's go home, Little Bear (1993)

Little Bear's baby book (2000)

Sleep tight Little Bear (2005)

Well done, Little Bear (1999)

You and me, Little Bear (1996)

★ **Captain** Small Pig; illustrated by Susan Varley. Peachtree Pubs. 2009 un il $15.95

Grades: PreK K   E

1. Pigs -- Fiction 2. Goats -- Fiction

ISBN 978-1-56145-519-5; 1-56145-519-9

Small Pig persuades Old Goat and Turkey to go out on Blue Lake in a row boat with him and fish for whales

"This book pleases at every level. The simplicity of its concept, the ease of its words, and the ink-and-watercolor art's subtle mix of wit and whimsy combine in a comfortable way." Booklist

★ **Farmer** duck; illustrated by Helen Oxenbury. Candlewick Press 1992 un il hardcover o.p. pa $5.99; bd bk $6.99

Grades: PreK K 1 2   E

1. Ducks -- Fiction 2. Farm life -- Fiction

ISBN 1-56402-009-6; 1-56402-596-9 pa; 0-7636-2167-6 bd bk

LC 91-71855

First published 1991 in the United Kingdom

When a kind and hardworking duck nearly collapses from overwork, while taking care of a farm because the owner is too lazy to do so, the rest of the animals get together and chase the farmer out of town

"Hilarious art masterfully captures the expressions of the put-upon duck, the supportive cast, and the slovenly ergophobic who reads the newspaper and chomps on bonbons in bed. . . . With its lilting, large-print text and satisfying

resolution, it's as perfect for beginning readers as it is for story hours." SLJ

It's quacking time! illustrated by Jill Barton. Candlewick Press 2005 un il $15.99

Grades: PreK K 1   E

1. Eggs -- Fiction 2. Ducks -- Fiction

ISBN 0-7636-2738-0

LC 2004-57039

A duckling and all his family happily await the hatching of his parents' new egg

"A warm tale. . . . Barton's expressive watercolor and pencil illustrations are appropriately full of life." Horn Book Guide

★ **Owl** babies; illustrated by Patrick Benson. Candlewick Press 1992 un il hardcover o.p. pa $6.99; bd bk $6.99

Grades: PreK K 1 2   E

1. Owls -- Fiction

ISBN 1-56402-101-7; 0-7636-1710-5 pa; 1-56402-965-4 bd bk

LC 91-58750

Three owl babies whose mother has gone out in the night try to stay calm while she is gone

"The illustrations, executed in black ink and watercolor, capture in every feather and expression the little owls' worry and watchfulness as well as their complete joy when Owl Mother returns." Horn Book

Snow bears; illustrated by Sarah Fox-Davies. Candlewick Press 2002 un il hardcover o.p. bd bk $6.99

Grades: PreK K 1 2   E

1. Snow -- Fiction 2. Bears -- Fiction

ISBN 0-7636-1906-X; 0-7636-2441-1 bd bk

LC 2001-58258

When three little bears play in the snow, they pretend to be "snow bears" and their mother goes along with the game

"Waddell's affectionate text offers an idyllic frosty gambol, and youngsters will appreciate the lulling repetition, the gentle trickery, and the smallest baby bear's struggles to keep up with her elder siblings." Bull Cent Child Books

The **super** hungry dinosaur; pictures by Leonie Lord. Dial Books for Young Readers 2009 un il $16.99

Grades: PreK K 1   E

1. Dinosaurs -- Fiction

ISBN 978-0-8037-3446-3; 0-8037-3446-8

LC 2008-51099

"When a Super Hungry Dinosaur charges into Hal's backyard, it's up to Hal to teach it some manners and keep himself, his parents, and even his dog from becoming lunch. The charming, naive illustrations look as though they are done in pencil and crayon. . . . Great fun." Booklist

★ **Tiny's** big adventure; illustrated by John Lawrence. Candlewick Press 2004 un il $15.99; pa $6.99

Grades: PreK K   E

1. Mice 2. Country life

ISBN 0-7636-2170-6; 0-7636-3819-6 pa

LC 2002-35004

Katy Mouse teaches her younger brother, Tiny, the names of some of the things they see, including a boot, a snail, and a pheasant, when they go to the cornfield to play games

"The rich mixture of vinyl engravings, watercolor washes, and printed wood textures gives a timeless flavor to the adventure, as do Waddell's sweet story line and clear sentences." Booklist

Wadham, Tim
  ★ The **Queen** of France; illustrated by Kady MacDonald Denton. Candlewick Press 2011 un il $16.99
Grades: PreK K 1   E
  1. Imagination -- Fiction 2. Kings and rulers -- Fiction
  3. Parent-child relationship -- Fiction
  ISBN 978-0-7636-4102-3; 0-7636-4102-2
                                            LC 2010039185
Rose wakes up one morning feeling royal and, donning jewels and a crown, she seeks her parents who behave as her royal subjects, causing Rose to wonder what they would think if the queen traded places with their daughter.

Wadham's "rhythmic prose and comic pacing feel elegant and effortless. . . . Denton . . . wonderfully conveys the story's impishness, emotional subtleties, and familial affections." Publ Wkly

Wadsworth, Olive A.
  ★ **Over** in the meadow; a counting rhyme. illustrated by Anna Vojtech. North-South Bks. 2002 un il $15.95
Grades: PreK K 1 2   E
  1. Counting 2. Nursery rhymes
  ISBN 0-7358-1596-8; 0-7358-1597-6 lib bdg
                                            LC 2001-51434
An old nursery poem introduces animals and their young and the number one through ten

"Although many versions of the verse, both traditional and nontraditional, are available, this is an accessible rendition that children will enjoy in storytime and on their own." SLJ

Waechter, Philip
  Bravo! illustrated by Moni Port; [translated from German by Sally-Ann Spencer] Gecko Press 2011 un il $17.95
Grades: PreK K 1   E
  1. Cats -- Fiction 2. Noise -- Fiction 3. Trumpet -- Fiction 4. Listening -- Fiction 5. Family life -- Fiction
  6. Father-daughter relationship -- Fiction
  ISBN 978-1-8774-6771-4; 1-8774-6771-5
"Helena, a trumpet-playing kitten who lives with her mother, father, and little brother, has almost a perfect life, except for one thing. Her father is a shouter who comes from a long line of shouters. She dislikes his yelling so much that she leaves home to find another person with whom to live. . . . The muted, full-color art is delicate and sketchy. The illustrations feature plenty of white space and large vistas that focus the action on the family. Children will respond to Helena." SLJ

Wahl, Jan
  The **art** collector; illustrated by Rosalinde Bonnet. Charlesbridge 2011 un il $15.95
Grades: K 1 2 3   E
  1. Art appreciation -- Fiction 2. Collectors and

collecting -- Fiction
  ISBN 978-1-58089-270-4; 1-58089-270-1
                                            LC 2010022760
Oscar is not pleased with his own artistic efforts but treasures his great-grandmother's drawing goes on to collect art throughout his life.

"Created with acrylic paint, pencil, and collage, the precisely drawn illustrations offer pleasing views of Oscar's world. An unusual, potentially eye-opening picture book." Booklist

  ★ **Candy** shop; illustrated by Nicole Wong. Charlesbridge 2004 un il lib bdg $15.95
Grades: K 1 2 3   E
  1. Toleration 2. African Americans 3. Taiwanese Americans 4. Neighborliness 5. Stores, Retail 6. Toleration -- Fiction 7. African Americans -- Fiction 8. Taiwanese Americans -- Fiction
  ISBN 1-57091-508-3
                                            LC 2003-3695
When a boy and his aunt find that a bigot has written hurtful words on the sidewalk just outside the candy shop owned by "Miz Chu," a new immigrant from Taiwan, they set out to comfort her

"The clean hues and supple lines of the pictures support Wahl's gentle message of comfort and tolerance." Booklist

The **golden** Christmas tree; illustrated by Leonard Weisgard. Golden Book 2010 un il $8.99; lib bdg $11.99
Grades: PreK K 1   E
  1. Trees -- Fiction 2. Animals -- Fiction 3. Christmas -- Fiction
  ISBN 978-0-375-82747-1; 0-375-82747-1; 978-0-375-92747-8 lib bdg; 0-375-92747-6 lib bdg
A reissue of the title first published 1988 by Western Pub.

"Animals gather to decorate a fir tree and celebrate Christmas together. Wahl's quiet, reverent text is extended by Weisgard's art in which the lines of the animals' fur connect them visually with the fir tree's needles, unifying the pages." Horn Book Guide

Wahman, Wendy
  A **cat** like that. Henry Holt 2011 il
Grades: PreK K 1   E
  1. Cats -- Fiction 2. Friendship -- Fiction
  ISBN 0-8050-8942-X; 978-0-8050-8942-4
                                            LC 2010026952
A cat presents the characteristics of a perfect human friend.

"Executed with the Photoshop lasso tool, the graphic elements here are standouts. . . . An attractive primer for kids who love cats—or may some day." Booklist

Waldron, Kevin
  Mr. Peek and the misunderstanding at the zoo. Candlewick Press 2010 il $15.99
Grades: PreK K 1 2   E
  1. Zoos -- Fiction 2. Worry -- Fiction 3. Animals -- Fiction
  ISBN 978-0-7636-4549-6; 0-7636-4549-4
                                            LC 2009015137
First published 2008 in the United Kingdom

"Poor Mr. Peek thinks he has suddenly gained a tremendous amount of weight when he puts on his zookeeper jacket and a button pops off. As he makes his morning rounds, he complains to himself about how fat and wrinkled he is. . . . He does not notice that the zoo animals are worried because they think he is talking to them. Luckily, he returns home to discover that he had inadvertently switched jackets with his son. . . . Waldron's digital-media illustrations humorously convey the alarmed expressions of the animals while the quirky font and creative text placement reinforce Mr. Peek's stream-of-consciousness muttering." SLJ

Walker, Anna

I love Christmas. Simon & Schuster Books for Young Readers 2009 un il $9.99
Grades: PreK K 1   E
1. Stories in rhyme 2. Dogs -- Fiction 3. Zebras -- Fiction 4. Christmas -- Fiction
ISBN 978-1-4169-8317-0; 1-4169-8317-1
"A zebra named Ollie runs down some of his favorite holiday activities. Sweet, soft watercolors show Ollie and his dog decorating the Christmas tree, baking holiday treats with Nanna, and waiting for Santa, creating a cozy, merry accompaniment to the simple rhyming text. This is a great choice for a lap-sit and also as a read-alone for beginning readers." SLJ
Other titles about Ollie are:
I love to dance (2009)
I love to sing (2009)
I love my dad (2010)
I love my mom (2010)
I love birthdays (2010)
I love vacations (2011)

Walker, Rob D.

★ Mama says; a book of love for mothers and sons. by Rob D. Walker; illustrations by Leo & Diane Dillon. The Blue Sky Press 2008 un il $16.99
Grades: K 1 2 3   E
1. Faith 2. Stories in rhyme 3. Conduct of life -- Fiction 4. Mother-son relationship -- Fiction
ISBN 978-0-439-93208-0; 0-439-93208-4
LC 2007029827
"This elegantly designed book pairs a series of poems with stunning illustrations to celebrate the bond between mothers and sons. . . . The poems appear in English as well as another language (among them Cherokee, Danish, Hebrew, and Inuktitut). . . . The illustrations . . . are well-researched and lavish, showing mothers in traditional dress lovingly engaged with their sons. . . . The Dillons' breathtaking paintings and the quiet dignity of the poems merit a wide audience." Publ Wkly

Walker, Sally M.

Druscilla's Halloween; illustrations by Lee White. Carolrhoda Books 2009 un il lib bdg $16.95
Grades: PreK K   E
1. Old age -- Fiction 2. Witches -- Fiction 3. Halloween -- Fiction
ISBN 978-0-8225-8941-9 lib bdg; 0-8225-8941-9 lib bdg
LC 2008-41163
In the time when witches tiptoe about to have their Halloween fun, ancient Druscilla knows her creaking knees will prevent her from being sneaky and sets out to find a silent conveyance for herself, her cat, and her jack-o-lantern

"Walker shows her lighter side in this witty picture book. White's expressive paintings, wonderfully varied in size and approach but unified by style, capture both the comedy and the pathos of Druscillas's predicament." Booklist

★ Freedom song; the story of Henry 'Box' Brown. illustrated by Sean Qualls. Harper 2012 il $17.99
Grades: 1 2 3   E
1. Slaves 2. Magicians 3. Abolitionists 4. Singing -- Fiction 5. Slavery -- Fiction 6. African Americans -- Fiction 7. Underground railroad -- Fiction
ISBN 978-0-06-058310-1; 0-06-058310-X
LC 2010024448
Henry Brown copes with slavery by singing, but after his wife and children are sold away he is left with only his freedom song, which gives him strength when friends put him in a box and mail him to a free state.
"A letter from the man who receives the box describes how Brown came out of it and sang a hymn, a fitting finale to Walker's rhythmic text. Qualls's primitive-style collage illustrations strongly convey the depth of Brown's emotions." SLJ

The Vowel family; a tale of lost letters. by Sally M. Walker; illustrated by Kevin Luthardt. Carolrhoda Books 2008 un il lib bdg $16.95
Grades: 1 2 3   E
1. English language -- Fiction
ISBN 978-0-8225-7982-3 lib bdg; 0-8225-7982-0 lib bdg
LC 2007-9952
The members of the Vowel family have a hard time talking until their children, Alan, Ellen, Iris, Otto, and Ursula, are born, and when one of them gets lost one day, it takes their Aunt Cyndy to fix the problem
"Luthardt's bright illustrations, featuring people with cartoonish balloon heads, ably echo the story's silliness. This clever approach to learning vowels will prove far more fun than just the basic recitation that's commonly taught." Booklist

Wallace, Carol

★ One nosy pup; illustrated by Steve Björkman. Holiday House 2005 40p il (Holiday House reader) $15.95
Grades: K 1 2   E
1. Dogs -- Fiction 2. Hamsters -- Fiction
ISBN 0-8234-1917-7
After moving to a new house, Poky the beagle befriends Charlie the hamster, who was accidentally left behind by the previous owners
"Wallace writes in short, simply constructed sentences and uses a brisk, basic vocabulary just right for new readers, and the expressive, color-washed art hums with activity and emotion." Booklist

The pumpkin mystery. Holiday House 2010 37p il (Holiday House reader) $15.95
Grades: 1 2 3 4   E
1. Mystery fiction 2. Cats -- Fiction 3. Dogs -- Fiction 4. Pumpkin -- Fiction 5. Rabbits -- Fiction 6. Halloween -- Fiction
ISBN 978-0-8234-2219-7; 0-8234-2219-4

Louie Rabbit helps Mocha the dog and Scruffy the cat solve the mystery of why the pumpkins don't grow in the human family's plot in time for Halloween.

The **Santa** secret; by Carol Wallace; illustrated by Steve Björkman. Holiday House 2007 40p il (Holiday House reader) $15.95
Grades: K 1 2   E
1. Dogs -- Fiction 2. Christmas -- Fiction 3. Family life -- Fiction 4. Santa Claus -- Fiction
ISBN 978-0-8234-2022-3; 0-8234-2022-1
With the help of the family bloodhound, a little girl's secret Christmas wish, known only to Santa, finally comes true
This is a "well-paced story. . . . The full-color, expressive cartoon drawings . . . play an integral part in helping youngsters decode and understand the text. This should be a popular choice for newly independent readers." SLJ

★ **Turkeys** together; illustrated by Jacqueline Rogers. Holiday House 2005 38p il (Holiday house reader) $15.95
Grades: K 1 2   E
1. Dogs -- Fiction 2. Eggs -- Fiction 3. Turkeys -- Fiction
ISBN 0-8234-1895-2
LC 2004-52392
A pointer dog puppy helps a mother turkey figure out how to protect her eggs from being stolen.
"A sweet tale about cooperation and friendship, with a satisfying conclusion. . . . Soft watercolor illustrations add meaning to the text and provide clues for some of the more difficult words. . . . The expressive animal faces are charming and realistic." SLJ

Wallace, Nancy Elizabeth
Pond walk; written and illustrated by Nancy Elizabeth Wallace. Marshall Cavendish Children's 2011 un il $17.99
Grades: PreK K 1 2   E
1. Ponds -- Fiction 2. Animals -- Fiction 3. Pond ecology -- Fiction
ISBN 978-0-7614-5816-6; 0-7614-5816-6
LC 2010025281
One summer day, Buddy Bear and his mother take a walk around a pond and observe the animals and insects that live there.
"Interspersed in the sequential text are Buddy's love of food and his sense of humor in the form of some nature jokes and puns. Wallace's familiar mixed-media collage illustrations (cut paper, photographs, and colored pencil) make this a visually appealing and informative look at limnology." SLJ

Pumpkin day! written and illustrated by Nancy Elizabeth Wallace. Marshall Cavendish 2002 un il $16.95
Grades: PreK K 1 2   E
1. Pumpkin -- Fiction 2. Rabbits -- Fiction
ISBN 0-7614-5128-5
LC 2002-834
A bunny family picks pumpkins at a local farm and learns pumpkin facts in the process
"Although there are many other books on the topic, this one stands apart because of its simple, yet dynamic collage artwork and the quality and quantity of information that is tucked into the text in all sorts of interesting ways." Booklist

Ready! Set! 100th day! written and illustrated by Nancy Elizabeth Wallace. Marshall Cavendish Children 2011 il $17.99
Grades: K 1   E
1. School stories 2. Rabbits -- Fiction 3. Set theory -- Fiction 4. Family life -- Fiction
ISBN 978-0-7614-5956-9; 0-7614-5956-1; 978-0-7614-6070-1 e-book
LC 2011001128
Minna's family pitches in to help her come up with the perfect project for the hundredth day of school, from twenty sets of five sticks to two sets of fifty pieces of pasta.
"This is definitely a book that will appeal to children. All of the characters are anthropomorphic brown rabbits done in large, colorful collages. The concepts are shown in a straightforward way that will be useful for introducing and reinforcing the number sets." SLJ

Recycle every day! written and illustrated by Nancy Elizabeth Wallace. Marshall Cavendish 2003 un il $16.95
Grades: PreK K 1 2   E
1. Rabbits -- Fiction 2. Recycling -- Fiction
ISBN 0-7614-5149-8
LC 2001-26050
When Minna has a school assignment to make a poster about recycling, her entire rabbit family spends the week practicing various kinds of recycling and suggesting ideas for her poster
"Using found materials to create the lovely art, the author/illustrator practices what she preaches and invites readers to search for the recycled materials. An activity and a game are appended. While the book's message is obvious, there is enough of a story to keep youngsters interested." SLJ
Other titles about Minna are:
The kindness quilt (2006)
Stars! Stars! Stars! (2009)

Seeds! Seeds! Seeds! written and illustrated by Nancy Elizabeth Wallace. Marshall Cavendish 2004 un il hardcover o.p. pa $5.99
Grades: PreK K 1 2   E
1. Bears 2. Seeds 3. Grandfathers 4. Bears -- Fiction 5. Seeds -- Fiction
ISBN 0-7614-5159-5; 0-7614-5366-0 pa
LC 2003-9318
Buddy Bear learns about different kinds of seeds and their uses when he opens a package sent by his grandfather
"The artwork consists of cut-paper collages with shadowing and life-sized photos of real seeds that look as though they can be picked right off the pages. The story is entertaining and educational." SLJ

Walsh, Barbara
★ **Sammy** in the sky; paintings by Jamie Wyeth. Candlewick Press 2011 un il $16.99
Grades: PreK K 1 2   E
1. Dogs -- Fiction 2. Death -- Fiction
ISBN 978-0-7636-4927-2; 0-7636-4927-9
LC 2010040744
A little girl tells about her special pet, Sammy, "the best hound dog in the whole world," and how, after he becomes sick and dies, she comes to know the truth of her mother's words, that Sammy's spirit is everywhere.

"This timeless story, told in straightforward prose, is brought to life in textured, soft-edged watercolor paintings in a predominant palette of blue, green, and gold. The feelings of the protagonist and the playful personality of the dog are palpably rendered in their facial expressions and body language." SLJ

Walsh, Ellen Stoll

Balancing act. Beach Lane 2010 un $16.99
Grades: PreK K   E
1. Mice -- Fiction 2. Animals -- Fiction 3. Balance -- Fiction
ISBN 978-1-4424-0757-2; 1-4424-0757-3
"This deceptively simple and creative book is loaded with fun. Two adorable mice create a teeter-totter using a stick balanced on a rock. A salamander joins one side, creating an imbalance, but then another one of equal weight joins the other mouse, and all is in order—until it happens again with a frog and a bird. . . . Observant children will want to converse about animal and color identification, as well as why the actions and reactions of the animals are creating balances/imbalances on the teeter-totter. The delightful illustrations were done using cut-paper collage and then splattered with acrylic paints. . . . This book is full of wonder and can be used at storytime or one-on-one." SLJ

For Pete's sake. Harcourt Brace & Co. 1998 un il $16
Grades: PreK K 1 2   E
1. Flamingos -- Fiction 2. Alligators -- Fiction 3. Individuality -- Fiction
ISBN 0-15-200324-X
LC 97-25677
Pete, an alligator who thinks that he is a flamingo, worries when he begins to notice the differences between him and his flamingo friends
"Walsh's precise paper-cut collages are just right. Subtly textured and with spacious, stark white backgrounds, they are pleasingly simple, giving the comedy and the message plenty of unencumbered opportunity to sink in." Booklist

★ **Mouse** shapes. Harcourt 2007 un il $16
Grades: PreK K   E
1. Mice -- Fiction 2. Shape -- Fiction
ISBN 978-0-15-206091-6
LC 2006-13695
Three mice make a variety of things out of different shapes as they hide from a scary cat
"The collage technique works well for distinguishing the brightly colored shapes, and the simple story is pitched perfectly for sharing with the youngest of listeners." SLJ
Other titles about the mice are:
Mouse paint (1989)
Mouse count (1991)

Walsh, Joanna

The **biggest** kiss; illustrated by Judi Abbot. Simon & Schuster Books for Young Readers 2011 il $12.99 E
1. Stories in rhyme 2. Kissing -- Fiction
ISBN 978-1-4424-2769-3; 1-4424-2769-8
LC 2011019442
A celebratioin of kisses from the sleepy goodnight kiss and the splishy splashy fish kiss to the sticky lipstick kiss and finally the best kiss of all.

"The engaging rhymes are perfectly complemented by the colorful, whimsical illustrations. A wonderful cuddle-up-and-read choice." SLJ

Walsh, Melanie

Living with mom and living with dad; Melanie Walsh. Candlewick Press 2012 40 p.
Grades: PreK K   E
1. Toy and movable books 2. Parent-child relationship -- Juvenile fiction 3. Children of divorced parents -- Juvenile fiction 4. Divorce -- Fiction
ISBN 0763658693; 9780763658694
LC 2011047029
This children's picture book follows a little girl whose parents are divorced. "Sometimes she lives with her mom, and sometimes with her dad. . . . [A] lift-the-flap design juxtaposes how things are in one home versus the other. On her birthday, the girl's mother makes a cake, and the flap lifts to show her dad taking her bowling. . . . Other pages show joint activities--both parents attend a school play, and both are included in a photo album that the girl can look at if she misses one of them." (Kirkus Reviews)

Walter, Mildred Pitts

Alec's primer; illustrated by Larry Johnson. Vermont Folklife Center 2004 un il (Vermont Folklife Center children's book series) $15.95
Grades: K 1 2 3   E
1. Reading 2. Slavery 3. African Americans 4. Reading -- Fiction 5. Slavery -- Fiction 6. African Americans -- Fiction
ISBN 0-916718-20-4
LC 2003-27716
A young slave's journey to freedom begins when a plantation owner's granddaughter teaches him how to read. Based on the childhood of Alec Turner (1845-1923) who escaped from slavery by joining the Union Army during the Civil War and later became a landowner in Vermont
"Walter's spare, dramatic words and Johnson's stirring double-page paintings present a glimpse of the history in a brutal world." Booklist

Walters, Virginia

Are we there yet, Daddy? illustrated by S.D. Schindler. Viking 1999 un il hardcover o.p, pa $6.99
Grades: PreK K 1 2   E
1. Maps 2. Stories in rhyme 3. Automobile travel 4. Maps -- Fiction 5. Fathers and sons 6. Automobile travel -- Fiction
ISBN 0-670-87402-7; 0-14-230013-6 pa
LC 97-18220
A young boy describes the trip he and his father make to Grandma's house, measuring how many miles are left at various points on the trip
"This unique picture book combines maps and counting skills with a bouncy refrain that invites kids to join in. . . . The flat, pastel pictures add enlivening details to the repetitive text." SLJ

Walton, Rick

Baby's first year; pictures by Caroline Jayne Church. G.P. Putnam's Sons 2011 un il $15.99

Grades: PreK   E
1. Stories in rhyme   2. Infants -- Fiction
ISBN 978-0-399-25025-5; 0-399-25025-5

LC 2008006564

In rhyming text, the milestones of Baby's first year are celebrated.

"Using ink and cut-paper collage, Church creates a series of endearing illustrations that reflect the playful tone of the text." Booklist

Wang Xiaohong
One year in Beijing; written by Xiaohong Wang; illustrated by Grace Lin. ChinaSprout 2006 un il map $16.95
Grades: PreK K 1 2   E
ISBN 0-97473-025-4; 978-0-97473-025-7

In this introduction to China and Chinese culture, an eight-year-old girl named "Ling Ling points out famous places as well as some of her favorite spots, describes foods eaten during special occasions, and explains traditions associated with particular celebrations throughout the year. . . . Grace Lin's bright, colorful illustrations and accompanying cartoonlike ink sketches accentuate the narrative's informality and make this engaging personal tour an excellent supplement to classroom textbooks." Booklist

Warburton, Tom
1000 times no; as told by Mr. Warburton. Laura Geringer Books 2009 un il $17.99
Grades: PreK K 1   E
1. Polyglot materials
ISBN 978-0-06-154263-3; 0-06-154263-6

LC 2007044270

When Noah's mother tells him that it is time to go, he finds more than a few ways to refuse.

"Gouache cartoon scenes visually reinforce Noah's multilingual vetoes, from a full-page sphinx and hieroglyphics to a small square panel with a text message. Endpapers provide identification of the languages, pronunciations, and cultures that the precocious youngster employs. Delightful fun in its theme and delivery, this story will be asked for again and again." SLJ

Ward, Helen
The rooster and the fox; retold & illustrated by Helen Ward. Millbrook Press 2003 un il $16.95; lib bdg $24.90
Grades: K 1 2 3   E
1. Poets 2. Fables 3. Authors 4. Roosters -- Fiction
ISBN 0-7613-1846-1; 0-7613-2920-X lib bdg
First published 2002 in the United Kingdom

"After being outsmarted by a cunning fox, a cocky rooster gathers his wits and turns the tables on his captor. Chaucer's Chanticleer is brought to life through a riveting retelling and magnificent, edge-of-your-seat artwork." SLJ

Ward, Helen, 1962-
★ The town mouse and the country mouse; an Aesop fable. Helen Ward. Candlewick Press 2012 48 p. $16.99
Grades: PreK K 1 2   E
1. Fables 2. Mice -- Juvenile fiction 3. City and town life -- Juvenile fiction
ISBN 0763660981; 9780763660987

LC 2012942271

This children's fable, retold by Helen Ward, is "set in a 1930s-era city at Christmastime. . . . Beguiled by his cousin's amazing tales, the country mouse visits the electric city. Unfortunately the town mouse forgot to mention that the city has a lot of noise, tall buildings . . . and dangerous dogs! . . . In the end the reader understands both why the town mouse loves his exciting life and why the country mouse is content with his peaceful home." (Publisher's note)

Ward, Jennifer
What will hatch? by Jennifer ward; illustrated by Susie Ghahremani. 1st ed. Walker & Company 2013 40 p. col. ill. (hardcover) $12.99; (library) $13.89
Grades: 1 2 3   E
1. Eggs -- Juvenile literature 2. Animal reproduction -- Juvenile literature 3. Eggs -- Incubation -- Juvenile literature
ISBN 080272311X; 9780802723116; 9780802723123

LC 2011046330

In this children's picture book, "[Jennifer] Ward introduces seven animals that hatch from eggs-sea turtle, penguin, tadpole, crocodile, robin, caterpillar, and platypus. The first spread includes a two to three word 'clue,' and the question, 'What Will Hatch?' On the second spread, the clue's rhyme is completed and the answer is provided in words and illustration (e.g., 'SANDY ball./WHAT will HATCH?/PADDLE and CRAWL-/SEA TURTLE.')." (School Library Journal)

The busy tree; illustrated by Lisa Falkenstern. Marshall Cavendish Children 2009 un il $17.99
Grades: PreK K 1 2   E
1. Stories in rhyme 2. Trees -- Fiction 3. Forest animals -- Fiction
ISBN 978-0-7614-5550-9; 0-7614-5550-7

LC 2008006005

"In rhyming couplets, an old oak introduces children to the wildlife that lives and feeds in and around it. . . . Handsome realistic oil paintings set on white pages show details of the tree and its denizens in daytime, at sunset, and at night, in fall and in summer. . . . Children will enjoy this brief glimpse at a familiar species that reinforces much that they have already observed." SLJ

Ward, Lindsay
Pelly and Mr. Harrison visit the moon. Kane Miller 2011 un il $15.99
Grades: PreK K 1 2   E
1. Space flight to the moon -- Fiction
ISBN 978-1-935279-77-8; 1-935279-77-7

Pelly and her dog Mr. Harrison, notice a rocket engine attached to the end of thee bath tub and use it to fly to the moon where they meet a friendly space alien.

"This is a wonderful book that will make going to bed an adventure for all readers. . . . The illustrations add to the adventure. Ward labels the illustrations to encourage readers to take a closer look at objects. This is a charming, easy to read picture book that will make a good addition to any library's read-aloud section." Libr Media Connect

Ward, Lynd Kendall
The biggest bear; by Lynd Ward. Houghton Mifflin 1988 84p il lib bdg $16; pa $6.95
Grades: PreK K 1 2   E
1. Bears -- Fiction
ISBN 0-395-14806-5 lib bdg; 0-395-15024-8 pa

LC 88-176366

A reissue of the title first published 1952

Awarded the Caldecott Medal, 1953

"Johnny Orchard never did acquire the bearskin for which he boldly went hunting. Instead, he brought home a cuddly bear cub, which grew in size and appetite to mammoth proportions and worried his family and neighbors half to death." Child Books Too Good to Miss

Wardlaw, Lee

Red, white, and boom! Lee Wardlaw; illustrated by Huy Voun Lee. Henry Holt 2012 32 p. col. ill. (hc: reinforced binding) $16.99

Grades: PreK K 1   E

1. Fourth of July -- Fiction 2. Holidays -- United States 3. Picture books for children 4. Stories in rhyme

ISBN 0805090657; 9780805090659

LC 2011018541

In this children's picture book from author Lee Wardlaw, "[i]t's the Fourth of July! [Readers can] [t]ravel across the country for a city parade, a beach picnic, and fireworks in the park in this . . . celebration of the many cultures and traditions that make America's birthday BOOM!" (Amazon. com)

★ **Won** Ton; a cat tale told in haiku. illustrated by Eugene Yelchin. Henry Holt and Company 2011 un il

Grades: PreK K 1   E

1. Haiku 2. Children's poetry 3. Cats -- Fiction 4. Animal shelters -- Fiction 5. Cats -- Juvenile literature 6. Haiku -- Juvenile literature

ISBN 0805089950; 9780805089950

A cat arrives at a shelter, arranges to go home with a good family, and settles in with them, all the while letting them know who is boss and, finally, sharing his real name.

"Wardlaw . . . has a fine understanding of the feline mind, and each 17-syllable poem packs a big impact—especially in the first section, which imagines the emotional life of a cat in a shelter. . . . The Japanese haiku theme . . . is carried through with elements and backgrounds lifted from old woodblock prints. The final page, a delicate painting of the boy nuzzling the cat, is a fitting reward for the boy's patience and Won Ton's resilience. A surprisingly powerful story in verse." Publ Wkly

Wargin, Kathy-Jo

Moose on the loose; written by Kathy-jo Wargin; illustrated by John Bendall-Brunello. Sleeping Bear Press 2009 un il $15.95

Grades: PreK K 1   E

1. Stories in rhyme 2. Moose -- Fiction

ISBN 978-1-58536-427-5; 1-58536-427-4

LC 2009004803

Rhyming text poses a series of questions about how the reader would deal with a moose that is on the loose, in the yard, in the house, or taking a bath

"Children will delight in the antics of both the moose and its young human companion. Bold, bright, cartoonlike illustrations capture the action in a humorous style." SLJ

Warhola, James

Uncle Andy's. Putnam 2003 un il $16.99

Grades: K 1 2 3   E

1. Artists 2. Artists -- United States 3. Motion picture

directors

ISBN 0-399-23869-7

LC 2002-7766

The author describes a trip to see his uncle, the soon-to-be-famous artist Andy Warhol, and the fun that he and his family had on the visit

"This catches the excitement that the creative process can engender, both for the established artist and for the dreamer." Booklist

Another title about Uncle Andy is:

Uncle Andy's cats (2009)

Waring, Geoffrey

Oscar and the bat; a book about sound. [by] Geoff Waring. Candlewick Press 2008 27p il (Start with science) $14.99

Grades: PreK K 1 2   E

1. Bats -- Fiction 2. Cats -- Fiction 3. Sound -- Fiction

ISBN 978-0-7636-4025-5; 0-7636-4025-5

LC 2007052195

First published 2006 in the United Kingdom

Bat teaches Oscar the kitten to hear and identify the sounds around him, whether they are made by animals and birds or by a passing thunderstorm

This is "clear and immediate. . . . Spacious digital color illustrations show Oscar the Cat in a meadow with his friend, Bat, who answers Oscar's questions with fascinating scientific detail." Booklist

Other titles about Oscar are:

Oscar and the bird (2009)

Oscar and the cricket (2008)

Oscar and the frog (2007)

Oscar and the moth (2007)

Oscar and the snail (2009)

Waring, Richard

★ **Hungry** hen; illustrated by Caroline Jayne Church. HarperCollins Pubs. 2001 un il $14.95

Grades: PreK K 1 2   E

1. Foxes 2. Chickens

ISBN 0-06-623880-3

LC 2001-24044

A greedy fox watches a hungry hen growing bigger every day, knowing that the longer he waits to eat her, the bigger she will be

"The story is simple and dramatic, with a perfect blend of words and pictures. . . . This is elemental storytelling, with tension rising until it's almost unbearable, and then the great surprise. The art is beautiful, with big, bright, clear shapes of the rosy hen and the sneaky fox on backgrounds of handmade paper." Booklist

Warnes, Tim

Chalk and Cheese. Simon & Schuster Books for Young Readers 2008 un il $16.99

Grades: K 1 2   E

1. Dogs -- Fiction 2. Mice -- Fiction 3. Friendship -- Fiction

ISBN 978-1-4169-1378-8; 1-4169-1378-5

LC 2007-18332

Cheese, an English country mouse, goes to visit his best friend, Chalk, a dog who lives in New York City, and even though the two of them are very different, they have a great time.

This is illustrated with "expansive, humor-laden art, some drawn in cartoon-strip style. . . . What's best is the sheer exuberance both feel about New York. . . . Kids . . . will enjoy both the travelogue and the unlikely friendship." Booklist

Daddy hug; by Tim Warnes; illustrated by Jane Chapman. HarperCollins 2008 un il $16.99; lib bdg $17.89
Grades: PreK K   E
1. Stories in rhyme 2. Animals -- Fiction 3. Fathers -- Fiction
ISBN 978-0-06-058950-9; 0-06-058950-7; 978-0-06-058951-6 lib bdg; 0-06-058951-5 lib bdg
LC 2005017867
"In a jolly, rhyming text, this book describes various animal fathers. . . . The vibrant, painterly illustrations, featuring fathers interacting with their offspring, are filled with action and color. . . . The simple text and warm-hued artwork create a feeling of security that will appeal to children." SLJ

Warwick, Dionne, 1940-
Little Man; by Dionne Warwick and David Freeman Wooley; illustrated by Fred Willingham. Charlesbridge 2011 un il $19.95
Grades: K 1 2   E
1. Drums -- Fiction 2. Musicians -- Fiction
ISBN 978-1-57091-731-8; 1-57091-731-0
Little Man is a drummer. With support from his father, Little Man practices every day. Soon he has enough confidence to play the drums at the local block party and is pleasantly surprised when his neighbors take up a collection for him. Now Little Man has money to buy a new bike to transport him to drum lessons!
"This success story, based on Wooley's city childhood, includes striking portraits in pastels and airbrush. . . . A CD of Warwick reading the book is included, her mellow tones adding to the pleasure of the tale. It also offers Wooley's demo of various drums and accessories, sure to pique the interest of young musicians." SLJ

Washington, Donna L.
★ **Li'l** Rabbit's Kwanzaa; illustrated by Shane W. Evans. Katherine Tegen Books 2010 un il $12.99
Grades: PreK K 1   E
1. Gifts -- Fiction 2. Kwanzaa -- Fiction 3. Rabbits -- Fiction 4. Grandmothers -- Fiction
ISBN 978-0-06-072816-8; 0-06-072816-7
L'il Rabbit searches for a gift for his grandmother when she is sick during Kwanzaa, and surprises her with the best gift of all. Includes 'The Nguzo Saba' The Seven Principles of Kwanzaa.
"The yellow undertones . . . add warmth to the cartoon artwork. Sweetly capturing the spirit of the season, the story comes in handy as a lovely supplement to resources that provide straightforward facts about Kwanzaa." SLJ

Watson, Jesse Joshua
Hope for Haiti. G.P. Putnam's Sons 2010 un il $16.99
Grades: K 1 2 3   E
1. Soccer -- Fiction 2. Earthquakes -- Fiction
ISBN 978-0-399-25547-2; 0-399-25547-8
LC 2010006835
A young boy finds hope when he is given an old soccer ball to play with in the wake of Haiti's devastating earthquake.

"In Watson's evocative, sunlit acrylic paintings, optimism radiates from the kids' faces." Publ Wkly

Watson, Renee
A **place** where hurricanes happen; illustrated by Shadra Strickland. Random House 2010 un il lib bdg $20.99
Grades: 1 2 3 4   E
1. Hurricane Katrina, 2005 -- Fiction
ISBN 978-0-375-85609-9; 0-375-85609-9; 978-0-375-95609-6 lib bdg; 0-375-95609-3 lib bdg
LC 2009017826
Told in alternating voices, four friends from the same New Orleans neighborhood describe what happens to them and their community when they are separated, then reunited, as a result of Hurricane Katrina.
"The text is lyrical and realistically portrays a child's point of view, deftly describing in a few words how the children are affected. . . . The evocative watercolor-and-ink illustrations in soft pastels and grays limn the devastation but also the good times of the neighborhood to great effect." SLJ

Watson, Wendy
★ **Bedtime** bunnies; story and pictures by Wendy Watson. Clarion Books 2010 un il $16
Grades: PreK K   E
1. Bedtime -- Fiction 2. Rabbits -- Fiction
ISBN 978-0-547-22312-4; 0-547-22312-9
Bunnies scamper, scurry, splash, zip, and snuggle as they get ready for bed.
"Rendered in pencil, watercolor, and acrylic paint, Watson's buoyant, gauzy pictures reveal several 'oops' moments: one bunny spills juice down the front of his overalls, and another drops a bar of soap while taking a bath. . . . At once soothing and spirited, this is a charmingly crafted bedtime tale for cold winter nights." Publ Wkly

Watt, Melanie
Have I got a book for you! Kids Can Press 2009 un il $16.95
Grades: PreK K 1 2   E
1. Selling -- Fiction 2. Books and reading -- Fiction
ISBN 978-1-55453-289-6; 1-55453-289-2
Mr. Al Foxword is one persistent salesman! He will do just about anything to sell you this book. Al tries every trick of the trade. But just when you're ready to close the book on him, he comes up with a clever tactic you simply can't refuse!
"Charcoal pencil illustrations are digitally assembled and feature bright orange, yellow, and green. Foxword's clever sales techniques make this book funny to the hilt." SLJ

Scaredy Squirrel has a birthday party. Kids Can Press 2011 un il $16.95
Grades: PreK K 1 2   E
1. Animals -- Fiction 2. Parties -- Fiction 3. Birthdays -- Fiction 4. Squirrels -- Fiction
ISBN 978-1-55453-468-5; 1-55453-468-2
Scaredy Squirrel would rather celebrate his birthday alone quietly in the safety of his nut tree and avoid any pesky party animals. When all his excessive plans are thrown up in the air like confetti, will Scaredy play dead and cancel, or will he face the music?

"The story unfolds with both humor and some useful etiquette tips. . . . Kids will find much to laugh at and think about. . . . Watt's wry digital illustrations make the most of the perceived mayhem, using a host of graphic conventions to tell her story." Kirkus

Watt, Mélanie, 1975-
Chester; written and illustrated by Melanie Watt. Kids Can Press 2007 un il $16.95
Grades: PreK K 1 2   E
1. Cats -- Fiction 2. Authorship -- Fiction
ISBN 1-55453-140-3; 978-1-55453-140-0
"Watt presents audiences with the story of a mouse—or she tries to, but her cat Chester has a red marker and his own idea about the subject of the story: himself. . . . Grades two to four." (Bull Cent Child Books)
"Watt presents audiences with the story of a mouse—or she tries to, but her cat Chester has a red marker and his own idea about the subject of the story: himself. . . . The notion is entertaining and its execution . . . is frequently hilarious. . . . This entertains both as a cat story and as an entry-level metatextual narrative." Bull Cent Child Books
Other titles about Chester are:
Chester's back! (2008)
Chester's masterpiece (2010)

Scaredy Squirrel. Kids Can Press 2006 un il $14.95
Grades: PreK K 1 2   E
1. Fear -- Fiction 2. Squirrels -- Fiction
ISBN 1-55337-959-4
Scaredy Squirrel never leaves his nut tree because he's afraid of the unknown "out there." But then, something unexpected happens that may just change his outlook.
"With his iconic nervous grin and over-the-top punctiliousness, Scaredy Squirrel is an endearing character. Thick-lined cartoons with bold patches of color, quirky charts and graphs, and clever asides provide humor that will appeal to children." SLJ
"Other titles about Scaredy Squirrel are:
Scaredy Squirrel makes a friend (2007) Scaredy Squirrel at the beach (2008) Scaredy Squirrel at night (2009) Scaredy Squirrel has a birthday party (2011)

Scaredy Squirrel Goes Camping; Melanie Watt. Kids Can Press 2013 32 p. (hardcover) $16.95
Grades: PreK K 1 2   E
1. Fear -- Juvenile fiction 2. Camping -- Juvenile fiction 3. Squirrels -- Juvenile fiction
ISBN 1894786866; 9781894786867
In this children's story, by Melanie Watt, "Scaredy Squirrel is not too comfortable with the idea of camping . . . unless it's on his couch! There will be no mosquitoes, skunks or zippers to worry about when he watches a show about the joys of camping on his brand-new TV. But first Scaredy must find an electrical outlet, and that means going into the woods!" (Publisher's note)

You're finally here! Disney/Hyperion Books 2011 un il $15.99
Grades: PreK K 1   E
1. Etiquette -- Fiction 2. Books and reading -- Fiction
ISBN 978-1-4231-3486-2; 1-4231-3486-9
"The title is the accusation/declaration hurled by a mercurial bunny who's peeved that he's been made to wait for

readers to show up. . . . Combining Watt's considerable gifts for metanarrative, social satire, outsize characters, and manic cartooning in one wonderfully silly tale, this is another keeper from a consistently funny talent." Publ Wkly

Watts, Bernadette
The Smallest Snowflake. North-South 2009 un il $16.95
Grades: PreK K 1 2   E
1. Snow -- Fiction 2. Spring -- Fiction 3. Winter -- Fiction
ISBN 978-0-7358-2258-0; 0-7358-2258-1
"Smallest Snowflake, longing for 'someplace special,' drifts along through the air until she lands in the window box of a little cottage. . . . Finally, green shoots push up through the dirt and snowdrop flowers open on the stalks. . . . Watts writes a tale as sturdy yet delicate as her artwork. . . . This quiet yet involving picture book is highly recommended for reading aloud as winter turns to spring." Booklist

The ugly duckling; by Hans Christian Andersen; adapted and illustrated by Bernadette Watts. North-South Bks. 2000 un il $15.95; lib bdg $16.95
Grades: K 1 2 3 4   E
1. Authors 2. Novelists 3. Dramatists 4. Fairy tales 5. Swans -- Fiction 6. Children's authors 7. Short story writers
ISBN 0-7358-1388-4; 0-7358-1389-2 lib bdg
LC 00-35125
An ugly duckling spends an unhappy year ostracized by the other animals before he grows into a beautiful swan
The "detailed double-paged spreads are beautiful. . . . Watts' active pastoral landscapes, filled with light and movement, capture the changing seasons and the sturdy, unwanted outsider's search for home." Booklist

Wax, Wendy
City witch, country switch; illustrated by Scott Gibala-Broxholm. Marshall Cavendish 2008 un il $16.99
Grades: K 1 2 3   E
1. Stories in rhyme 2. Cousins -- Fiction 3. Witches -- Fiction 4. Country life -- Fiction 5. City and town life -- Fiction
ISBN 978-0-7614-5429-8; 0-7614-5429-2
LC 2007-28355
While paying a surprise visit to her city-dwelling cousin, Muffletump misses her home in the country but when Mitzi leaves the city to see where Muffletump lives, she is just as uncomfortable until the two, together, conjure a solution.
"Told in rollicking, lyrical text accompanied by bright, colorful illustrations. . . . Children will want to check this book out again and again." Libr Media Connect

Wayland, April Halprin
New Year at the pier; a Rosh Hashanah story. illustrated by Stephane Jorisch. Dial Books for Young Readers 2009 un il $16.99
Grades: K 1 2 3   E
1. Jews -- Fiction 2. Rosh ha-Shanah -- Fiction
ISBN 978-0-8037-3279-7; 0-8037-3279-1
LC 2007039812
On Rosh Hashanah, Izzy and his family make lists of the wrongs they have committed over the past year, and after

they have apologized, they throw pieces of bread into the water to 'clean their hearts' in a ceremony called tashlich.

"The empathetic, low-key prose makes important points about personal responsibility without pummeling readers, while the stylish, keenly observed watercolors convey both Izzy's sheepish chagrin and the joys of communal tradition." Publ Wkly

Weatherby, Brenda

The **trucker**; written by Brenda Weatherby; illustrated by Mark Weatherby. Scholastic 2004 un il $15.95

Grades: PreK K 1 2   **E**

1. Trucks -- Fiction

ISBN 0-439-39877-0

LC 2002-70787

Wesley dreams his toy semi-flatbed rig grows big enough for him to have a trucking adventure but wakes to find he is in the back of his father's truck.

"The brief, simple text is filled with the lively sounds of the big machine on the road. . . . Using acrylic, sand, and, appropriately, road dirt, the pictures convey something of the story's blurry, dreamlike quality, while supplying plenty of realistic details of the trucker's life." Booklist

Weatherford, Carole Boston

Champions on the bench; the Cannon Street YMCA all-stars. by Carole Boston Weatherford; illustrations by Leonard Jenkins. Dial Books for Young Readers 2007 un il $16.99

Grades: 1 2 3 4   **E**

1. Baseball -- Fiction 2. Race relations -- Fiction 3. African Americans -- Fiction

ISBN 0-8037-2987-1; 978-0-8037-2987-2

LC 2003-19385

Story based on the discrimination faced by the 1955 Cannon Street YMCA Little League All-Stars when the white teams refused to play them in the series tournament.

"Done in pencil, acrylic, and spray paint, Jenkins's color-saturated illustrations imbue the text with warmth, passion, and nostalgia. This is a powerful story, well told." SLJ

★ **Freedom** on the menu; the Greensboro sit-ins. paintings by Jerome Lagarrigue. Dial Books for Young Readers 2005 un il $16.99

Grades: K 1 2 3   **E**

1. Race relations -- Fiction 2. African Americans -- Fiction 3. Civil rights demonstrations -- Fiction

ISBN 0-8037-2860-3

LC 2002-13226

The 1960 civil rights sit-ins at the Woolworth's lunch counter in Greensboro, North Carolina, are seen through the eyes of a young Southern black girl.

"Simple and straightforward, the first-person narrative relates events within the context of one close-knit family. . . . The well-composed, painterly illustrations show up well from a distance. A handsome book." Booklist

Weatherly, Lee

The **scariest** monster in the world; [by] Lee Weatherly & [illustrated by] Algy Craig Hall. Boxer Books 2009 un il $14.95

Grades: K 1 2   **E**

1. Monsters -- Fiction

ISBN 978-1-906250-40-9; 1-906250-40-5

"A scary, hairy monster with green teeth chases and frightens all of the woodland creatures. One day, he comes down with the hiccups. . . . When the other animals see him sitting on a rock and crying, they develop a novel idea for curing the problem. . . . The large illustrations, done in graphite stick and watercolor paints, are lively, fresh, and expressive, giving personality to the story." SLJ

Weaver, Tess

Cat jumped in! by Tess Weaver; illustrated by Emily Arnold McCully. Clarion Books 2007 32p il $16

Grades: PreK K 1 2   **E**

1. Cats -- Fiction

ISBN 978-0-618-61488-2

LC 2006039217

An inquisitive feline walks through the rooms of a house, jumping into one mess after another, before landing in the loving arms of its owner.

"Some 26 different verbs describe the cat's movements, infusing the story with plenty of action, and the bright watercolors seem quickly carefully rendered." Booklist

Frederick Finch, loudmouth; by Tess Weaver; illustrated by Debbie Tilley. Clarion Books 2008 un il $16

Grades: K 1 2   **E**

1. Fairs -- Fiction 2. Contests -- Fiction

ISBN 0-618-45239-7; 978-0-618-45239-2

LC 2007019114

After trying and trying to win a ribbon at the state fair, Frederick finally is rewarded for his true talent.

"This title uses humor to illustrate how even an unusual and often-considered-negative talent can be useful. . . . The watercolor-and-ink illustrations humorously depict the boy's trials without giving away the surprise ending." SLJ

Weber, Elka

One little chicken; illustrations by Elisa Kleven. Tricycle Press 2011 un il $16.99

Grades: K 1 2 3   **E**

1. Jews -- Fiction 2. Goats -- Fiction 3. Chickens -- Fiction 4. Conduct of life -- Fiction 5. Lost and found possessions -- Fiction

ISBN 1-58246-374-3; 978-1-58246-374-2

LC 2010008918

Retells a story in the Talmud about a family that cares for a lost chicken, turning its eggs into a profit which they later give to its owner.

"Kleven's engaging mixed-media folk-art collages brim with details like a border of cakes and pies, or a coy goat offering a bouquet to Leora. The colors are rich; the textures and patterns beg to be touched, and the ending is likely to leave readers pondering this story." SLJ

Webster, Sheryl

Noodle's knitting; [illustrated by] Caroline Pedler. Good Books 2010 un il $16.99

Grades: PreK K 1   **E**

1. Mice -- Fiction 2. Animals -- Fiction 3. Knitting -- Fiction

ISBN 978-1-56148-694-6; 1-56148-694-9

LC 2010004920

A mouse named Noodle finds a ball of wool and decides to knit a scarf, which grows so big that she is trapped inside her house.

"Webster's prose makes for a fluid read-aloud, and Pedler's full and double-page paintings are playful, warm, and cozy." SLJ

Weeks, Sarah

Drip, drop; story by Sarah Weeks; pictures by Jane Manning. HarperCollins Pubs. 2000 32p il (I can read book) hardcover o.p. pa $3.99

Grades: PreK K 1 2   E

1. Mice 2. Stories in rhyme 3. Mice -- Fiction 4. Rain -- Fiction 5. Rain and rainfall

ISBN 0-06-028523-0; 0-06-028524-9 lib bdg; 0-06-443597-0 pa

LC 00-21652

Pip Squeak the mouse is kept awake all night by the drips from his leaky roof

"Short, simple sentences keep the action moving along while a single problem focuses readers' attention. The snappy narrative is coupled with expressive, silly illustrations." SLJ

Another title about Pip Squeak is:
Pip Squeak (2007)

Ella, of course! written by Sarah Weeks; illustrated by Doug Cushman. Harcourt 2007 un il $16

Grades: PreK K   E

1. Pigs -- Fiction 2. Dance -- Fiction

ISBN 978-0-15-204943-0; 0-15-204943-6

LC 2005-25910

When Ella the pig is banned from bringing her umbrella to the dance recital, she comes up with an ingenious solution to the problem

"Weeks' short text includes lots of repetitive phrases and sound effects that will easily encourage participation. Cushman adds slapstick humor with double-page scenes." Booklist

Mac and Cheese; illustrated by Jane Manning. Laura Geringer Books 2010 32p il $16.99; pa $3.99

Grades: K 1 2   E

1. Stories in rhyme 2. Cats -- Fiction 3. Friendship -- Fiction

ISBN 978-0-06-117079-9; 0-06-117079-8; 978-0-06-117081-2 pa; 0-06-117081-X pa

LC 2008014199

Two cats that are as different as night and day are nevertheless best friends.

"The simple sentences with ample white space suit the brief snippets of rhyming dialogue between the two characters, and brightly colored watercolor illustrations of the feline alley friends reveal expressions ranging from Mac's sheer glee to Cheese's exasperated disgust. Simplicity of text, action illustrated to lead readers in turning the page, and a satisfying conclusion makes this easy reader a solid selection for all libraries." SLJ

Overboard! by Sarah Weeks; illustrated by Sam Williams. Harcourt, Inc. 2006 un il $14

Grades: PreK   E

1. Stories in rhyme 2. Play -- Fiction 3. Rabbits -- Fiction

ISBN 0-15-205046-9

From morning to night, a little bunny playfully grabs and throws items, including a bathtime rubber ducky and snacktime raisins.

"Bright and sunny as only a toddler's book on the subject could be, the rhyming, rhythmic text bounces merrily along, while the broad lines and bold colors of the artwork express the same carefree sense of exuberance." Booklist

Another title about this bunny is:
Bunny fun (2007)

★ **Sophie** Peterman tells the truth! illustrated by Robert Neubecker. Beach Lane Books 2009 un il $16.99

Grades: PreK K 1 2   E

1. Infants -- Fiction 2. Siblings -- Fiction

ISBN 978-1-4169-8686-7; 1-4169-8686-3

LC 2008-51058

A disgruntled big sister reveals unpleasant facts about babies.

This offers "thick-lined cartoon illustrations in bright colors and clear bold type that gets bigger and bigger. . . . The details of messy daily life and the honest, unsentimental expressions of rage and bonding are just right for young children to recognize and laugh about together." Booklist

Two eggs, please; written by Sarah Weeks; illustrated by Betsy Lewin. Atheneum Bks. for Young Readers 2003 un il $15.95

Grades: PreK K 1 2   E

1. Eggs -- Fiction 2. Animals -- Fiction 3. Restaurants -- Fiction

ISBN 0-689-83196-X

LC 2002-5291

"An all-night diner attracts a wide variety of customers in the middle of the night, including a rhino cab driver, two wolf police officers, and a crocodile street performer and his snake. One by one, they take stools at the counter and order the same thing, 'Two eggs, please,' but each order is different: soft-boiled, hard-boiled, poached, raw (for the snake). The premise is as basic as fried eggs, and handled with a light touch, but Lewin's inviting watercolor and ink illustrations add flavor and expand the story to involve young listeners and readers." Horn Book

★ **Woof;** a love story. illustrated by Holly Berry. Laura Geringer Books 2009 un il $16.99

Grades: PreK K 1 2   E

1. Stories in rhyme 2. Cats -- Fiction 3. Dogs -- Fiction 4. Love -- Fiction 5. Communication -- Fiction

ISBN 978-0-06-025007-2; 0-06-025007-0

LC 2006022295

Despite a language barrier, a dog and cat fall in love with the help of a buried trombone.

"This affectionate and funny story is told almost musically, in rhythmic . . . verse by expert storyteller Weeks. Berry's exuberant collage illustrations spill over the pages, gorgeously chaotic and filled with heart." SLJ

Weigel, Jeff

Atomic Ace; (he's just my dad) written and illustrated by Jeff Weigel. Albert Whitman & Co. 2004 un il $15.95

Grades: PreK K 1 2   E

1. Science fiction 2. Stories in rhyme 3. Fathers -- Fiction 4. Superheroes -- Fiction 5. Superheroes (Fictional characters) -- Fiction 6. Comic books, strips,

etc. -- Juvenile literature

ISBN 0-8075-3216-9

LC 2003-17523

In this rhyming story told in comic book format, a boy considers his family normal, though his superhero dad, Atomic Ace, does amazing feats, even battling the evil Insect King

"The juxtapositions between superheroics and regular-guy domesticity are clever, and Weigl's confident artwork . . . is guaranteed to satisfy children obsessed with caped crusaders." Booklist

Another title about Atomic Ace is:

Atomic Ace and the robot rampage (2006)

Weigelt, Udo

Super Guinea Pig to the rescue; [by] Udo Weigelt; illustrations by Nina Spranger. Walker & Co. 2007 un il $16.95

Grades: K 1 2 3   E

1. Pets -- Fiction   2. Guinea pigs -- Fiction   3. Superheroes -- Fiction

ISBN 0-8027-9705-9; 978-0-8027-9705-6

LC 2007-06668

A guinea pig gets upset when his fellow pets make fun of his favorite television superhero, and so he makes a costume and pretends to be Super Guinea Pig himself.

"Using lively language, Weigelt compassionately and humorously relates the guinea pig's earnest efforts, as expressive watercolor-and-acrylic illustrations show characters and events from a variety of perspectives." Booklist

Weinstein, Muriel Harris

When Louis Armstrong taught me scat; by Muriel Harris Weinstein; illustrated by R. Gregory Christie. Chronicle Books 2008 un il $16.99

Grades: PreK K 1 2   E

1. Singers   2. Jazz musicians   3. Band leaders   4. Trumpet players   5. Singing -- Fiction   6. Jazz music -- Fiction   7. African Americans -- Fiction

ISBN 978-0-8118-5131-2; 0-8118-5131-1

LC 2007044305

After dancing to music on the radio before she goes to bed, a young girl learns how to sing scat when Louis Armstrong comes to her in a dream. Includes facts about Louis Armstrong and scat singing.

"Decked out in bubble-gum pinks and soulful blues, scenes of the little girl and Satchmo cool-catting it across the pages will [get] kids moving, but it's the bop-happy nonsense words themselves that highlight the art." Booklist

Weis, Carol

When the cows got loose; [by] Carol Weis; [illustrated by] Ard Hoyt. Simon & Schuster Books for Young Readers 2006 un il $16.95

Grades: K 1 2 3   E

1. Cattle -- Fiction   2. Circus -- Fiction

ISBN 0-689-85166-9

"When a family of big-top performers' eccentric cow herd is on the loose, it's young Ida Mae's job to perform the roundup. . . . Ida Mae narrates in a droll, colloquial voice . . . and the tension between what her words leave out and what the pictures show makes most of the fun. . . . The expressive mixed-media images . . . will easily draw interest, giggles, and requests for repeated viewings." Booklist

Weiss, Ellen

Porky and Bess; by Ellen Weiss and Mel Friedman; illustrated by Marsha Winborn. Random House 2010 il $12.99

Grades: K 1 2 3   E

1. Cats -- Fiction   2. Pigs -- Fiction   3. Poetry -- Fiction   4. Friendship -- Fiction

ISBN 9780375854583; 9780375961137 lib bdg; 9780375861130 pa

LC 2009013384

Despite their differences, Porky the messy pig and Bess the fussy cat are best friends and support each other in all their endeavors, from poetry writing to cake baking.

The **taming** of Lola; a shrew story; a picture book in five acts. illustrated by Jerry Smath. Abrams Books for Young Readers 2010 un il $15.95

Grades: PreK K 1 2   E

1. Shrews -- Fiction   2. Cousins -- Fiction   3. Grandmothers -- Fiction

ISBN 978-0-8109-4066-6; 0-8109-4066-3

LC 2009-00617

Lola, a shrew, is famous all over West Meadow for her temper tantrums, but when her cousin Lester comes for a visit and gets special treatment just because he demands it, Lola begins to rethink her behavior.

"Screwball dialogue and banter, . . . asides from the narrator, and details about the shrew diet . . . combine to keep action and laughs coming. The pacing is even, the goody-goody peacemaking is leavened by the wisecracks, and there's even a surprise ending." Publ Wkly

Weitzman, Jacqueline Preiss

Superhero Joe; written by Jacqueline Preiss; drawn by Ron Barrett. Simon & Schuster Books for Young Readers 2011 un il $16.99

Grades: K 1 2   E

1. Fear -- Fiction   2. Imagination -- Fiction   3. Superheroes -- Fiction

ISBN 978-1-4169-9157-1; 1-4169-9157-3

LC 2009034390

Five-year-old Joey uses his super powers to help his parents out of a sticky situation.

"Barrett's line drawings are rendered in ink and colored digitally. The crisp text is hand lettered. The graphic-novel format and retro atmosphere mimic the comic books whose heroes Joe emulates. Weitzman acknowledges the boy's feelings and provides imaginative solutions followed by more practical ones. An upbeat, humorous selection." SLJ

★ **You** can't take a balloon into the Metropolitan Museum; story by Jacqueline Preiss Weitzman; pictures by Robin Preiss Glasser. Dial Bks. for Young Readers 1998 37p il hardcover o.p. pa $7.99

Grades: K 1 2 3   E

1. Stories without words   2. Museums -- Fiction

ISBN 0-8037-2301-6; 0-14-056816-6 pa

LC 97-31629

In this wordless story, a young girl and her grandmother view works inside the Metropolitan Museum of Art, while the balloon she has been forced to leave outside floats around New York City causing a series of mishaps that mirror scenes in the museum's artworks

"Lively, squiggly ink sketches with characters picked out in watercolor and gouache for accent, along with reproductions of art from the Met . . . tell a vivid, happy tale." Booklist

Other titles in this series are:

You can't take a balloon into the Museum of Fine Arts (2002)

You can't take a balloon into the National Gallery (2000)

Weller, Frances Ward

The **day** the animals came; a story of Saint Francis Day. illustrated by Loren Long. Philomel Bks. 2003 un il $16.99

Grades: K 1 2 3   E

1. Animals 2. Latinos (U.S.) 3. Neighbors 4. Animals -- Fiction 5. Hispanic Americans

ISBN 0-399-23630-9

LC 2002-6297

A young girl who misses her former home and her animal friends left behind in the West Indies makes new friends at the blessing of the animals at a cathedral in New York City on the Feast of St. Francis

"The acrylic paintings soar as Long looks at goings-on from many different perspectives. . . . Children will like seeing so many animals in such an unexpected place, and Ria's feeling of acceptance makes for a satisfying conclusion." Booklist

Wellington, Monica

Apple farmer Annie. Dutton Children's Bks. 2001 un il $14.99

Grades: PreK K 1 2   E

1. Apples 2. Apple growers 3. Farmers' markets 4. Apples -- Fiction

ISBN 0-525-46727-0

LC 00-46203

Annie the apple farmer saves her most beautiful apples to sell fresh at the farmers' market

"Charming and cheery, [this] story makes a great read-aloud. The illustrations seem to step right out of a coloring book with simple shapes, objects, and bright, crayon-box colors." SLJ

★ **Mr.** Cookie Baker; [by] Monica Wellington. rev ed.; Dutton Children's Books 2006 un il $15.99

Grades: PreK   E

1. Baking -- Fiction 2. Cookies -- Fiction

ISBN 0-525-47763-2

First published 1992

After a day of making and selling cookies, Mr. Baker gets to enjoy one himself. Includes cookie recipes.

"Done in gouache and colored pencil, the artwork features clean lines and flat colors that are as cheery as the cookies' sugar sprinkles." Booklist

Pizza at Sally's; [by] Monica Wellington. Dutton Children's Books 2006 un il $14.99

Grades: PreK K 1 2   E

1. Pizza -- Fiction 2. Cooking -- Fiction 3. Restaurants -- Fiction

ISBN 978-0-525-47715-0; 0-525-47715-2

LC 2005026498

With vegetables from her own garden and other fresh ingredients, Sally mixes and bakes hot and bubbly pizzas for her customers to take home or eat in her pizzeria

"Cheerful, precisely composed gouache paintings accented with photo collages of fresh ingredients add warmth and humor to the story." SLJ

Riki's birdhouse. Dutton Children's Books 2009 un il $15.99

Grades: PreK K 1 2   E

1. Birds -- Fiction 2. Birdhouses -- Fiction

ISBN 978-0-525-42079-8; 0-525-42079-7

LC 2008013890

Riki, who loves to watch, feed, and listen to the birds that come to his garden, decides to build a birdhouse

"Riki's passion for birds is evident, and likely to be contagious. . . . The bold colors, simple shapes and clean lines of the gouache illustrations are in sharp contrast to the details found in the photographic elements cut out and glued onto the artwork. . . . Backmatter includes instructions for building and installing a birdhouse, a recipe for bird-food cupcakes and information about birdbaths, feeders and bluebirds." Kirkus

Truck driver Tom; [by] Monica Wellington. Dutton Children's Books 2007 un il $15.99

Grades: PreK K   E

1. Trucks -- Fiction

ISBN 978-0-525-47831-7

LC 2006035911

The driver of a tractor-trailer picks up a load of fresh fruits and vegetables, then drives through the countryside, past small towns, and into the big city, passing farms, construction sites, and many other vehicles, then delivers the produce and relaxes with other drivers

"The simple text is printed in a large block font that is just right for beginning readers. . . . Clearly drawn gouache paintings are enhanced with meticulously cut photos to add texture and character to the scene." SLJ

Wells, Rosemary

★ **Emily's** first 100 days of school. Hyperion Bks. for Children 2000 un il hardcover o.p. pa $7.99

Grades: PreK K   E

1. Animals 2. Rabbits 3. Schools 4. Counting 5. School stories 6. Rabbits -- Fiction 7. First day of school

ISBN 0-7868-0507-2; 0-7868-1354-7 pa

LC 99-27021

Starting with number one for the first day of school, Emily the rabbit learns the numbers to one hundred in many different ways

"Wells manages to find fresh, engaging presentations for that many numbers. Alive with color and thematically relevant decoration, the oversized pages are sometimes divided into several panels, but never feel too busy." Horn Book Guide

Another title about Emily and her school is:

My kindergarten (2004)

Hands off, Harry! Katherine Tegen Books 2011 un il (Kindergators) $14.99

Grades: K 1 2   E

1. School stories 2. Alligators -- Fiction 3. Kindergarten

-- Fiction

ISBN 978-0-06-192112-4; 0-06-192112-2

LC 2010016046

Harry has trouble keeping his hands off his classmates until Tina thinks of the perfect piece of gym equipment to teach him about personal space.

Wells "builds a sense of drama while showing that she knows kindergarten inside and out. Kids will appreciate her faith in their inventiveness and sense of community—and they'll also enjoy the genial, neatly framed collaged images, which use textured materials to convey the alligators' bumpy skin and vibrant wardrobe." Publ Wkly

★ **Love** waves. Candlewick Press 2011 un il $15.99

Grades: PreK K E

1. Stories in rhyme 2. Love -- Fiction 3. Parent-child relationship -- Fiction

ISBN 978-0-7636-4989-0; 0-7636-4989-9

LC 2010040460

While they are at work a mother and father send powerful "love waves" to their child at home, offering reassurance and comfort in their absence.

"With cozy pastel scenes and gentle verse, Wells makes tangible the powerful emotional connection between parent and child, reminding children that longing and, more importantly, love are both two-way streets." Publ Wkly

Max & Ruby's treasure hunt; by Rosemary Wells. Viking 2012 32 p. (hardcover) $17.99

Grades: PreK K E

1. Treasure hunt (game) -- Juvenile fiction 2. Rabbits -- Fiction 3. Grandmothers -- Fiction 4. Brothers and sisters -- Fiction 5. Treasure hunt (Game) -- Fiction

ISBN 0670063177; 9780670063178

LC 2011048535

This children's book by Rosemary Wells presents a "return adventure for Max and Ruby. . . . When a thunderstorm ruins Ruby's tea party, Grandma suggests the four bunnies have a treasure hunt. . . . The final treasure box has five gold coins filled with chocolate -- but wait, there are only four bunnies! They decide to give the fifth to Lily's doll, Dagmar, but where is she? . . . [T]he bunnies retrace their steps and clues to find the doll." (Kirkus)

★ **McDuff** moves in; pictures by Susan Jeffers. Hyperion Books for Children 2005 un il $9.99

Grades: PreK K 1 2 E

1. Dogs -- Fiction

ISBN 0-7868-5677-7

A reissue of the title first published 1997

"This collaboration by Wells and Jeffers is as sweet, substantial, and comforting as that bowl of rice pudding and will suit the many children who like stories with simple words, clear story lines, and happily-ever-after endings." Booklist

Other titles about McDuff are:

McDuff and the baby (1997)

McDuff comes home (1997)

McDuff goes to school (2001)

McDuff saves the day (2001)

McDuff's Christmas (2005)

McDuff's favorite things (2004)

McDuff's new friend (1998)

McDuff's wild romp (2005)

★ **Morris's** disappearing bag. Viking 1999 un il hardcover o.p. pa $6.99

Grades: PreK K 1 2 E

1. Rabbits -- Fiction 2. Christmas -- Fiction

ISBN 0-670-88721-8; 0-14-230004-7 pa

LC 00-267633

First published 1975 by Dial Bks. for Young Readers

Morris is so disappointed with his Christmas present that he invents a disappearing bag, which gives him a chance to share his brother's and sister's gifts

In this version "Morris re-appears in a full-color, full-size edition of the Christmas day story." Horn Book Guide

★ **Noisy** Nora; with all new illustrations [by] Rosemary Wells. Dial Bks. for Young Readers 1997 un il $15.99; pa $6.99

Grades: PreK K 1 2 E

1. Stories in rhyme 2. Mice -- Fiction

ISBN 0-670-88722-6; 0-14-056728-3 pa

A newly illustrated edition of the title first published 1973

Little Nora, tired of being ignored, tries to gain her family's attention by being noisy. When this doesn't work Nora disappears but returns when she is sure she has been missed

"All new illustrations infuse this much-loved picture book . . . with energy. Vibrant colors and a larger format make the characters seem to jump out at readers." SLJ

Only you. Viking 2003 un il $14.99

Grades: PreK K E

1. Bears 2. Mother and child

ISBN 0-670-03634-X

LC 2002-15570

A little bear describes how much his mother means to him

"Wells's illustrations are right on target. Most of them feature parent and child as the central characters, cozily enclosed in a square and surrounded by a soft, pastel border. . . . Perfect for one-on-one sharing." SLJ

Otto runs for President. Scholastic Press 2008 un il $15.99

Grades: K 1 2 E

1. School stories 2. Dogs -- Fiction 3. Politics -- Fiction

ISBN 978-0-545-03722-8; 0-545-03722-0

LC 2007024816

While the popular Tiffany and athletic Charles make increasingly outrageous promises in their campaigns for President of Canine Country Day School, Otto quietly enters the race, vowing only to try to do what students really want.

"Wells' canine coterie . . . is satisfyingly personable and appealing, and kids will find the knowledge they accrue from the book very useful." Booklist

Read to your bunny. Scholastic 1998 un il $7.95; pa $3.99

Grades: PreK K E

1. Stories in rhyme 2. Rabbits -- Fiction 3. Books and reading -- Fiction

ISBN 0-590-30284-1; 0-439-08717-1 pa

LC 97-17704

Brief rhyming text and colorful illustrations tell what happens when parents and children share twenty minutes a day reading

"Each line of text gets one of Wells' delightful bordered pictures of parents and children at all sorts of activities, from bathing to skating, but always with a book in hand." Booklist

★ **Ruby's** beauty shop. Viking 2002 un il $16.99; pa $6.99

Grades: PreK K 1 2   E

1. Rabbits -- Fiction 2. Siblings -- Fiction 3. Beauty shops -- Fiction

ISBN 0-670-03553-X; 0-14-240194-3 pa

LC 2001-7730

Louise and Ruby use Louise's "Deluxe Beauty Kit" to give Max a make-over, but when Grandma calls to schedule her own make-over, she makes an appointment with Max

"Wells is in top form. . . . The author's affinity for kid-based glee is playfully evident." Bull Cent Child Books

Other titles about Max and Ruby are:

Bunny cakes (1997)

Bunny mail (2004)

Bunny money (1997)

Bunny party (2001)

Max and Ruby's bedtime book (2010)

Max and Ruby's first Greek myth: Pandora's box (1993)

Max and Ruby's Midas: another Greek myth (1995)

Max cleans up (2000)

Max counts his chickens (2007)

Max's ABC (2006)

Max's bath (1985)

Max's bedtime (1985)

Max's birthday (1985)

Max's breakfast (1985)

Max's bunny business (2008)

Max's chocolate chicken (1989)

Max's Christmas (1986)

Max's dragon shirt (1991)

Max's first word (1979)

Max's new suit (1979)

Max's ride (1979)

Max's toys (1979)

Shy Charles; [by] Rosemary Wells. Viking 2001 un il hardcover o.p. pa $5.99

Grades: PreK K 1 2   E

1. Stories in rhyme 2. Mice -- Fiction

ISBN 0-670-88729-3; 0-14-056843-3 pa

LC 2001-271649

A reissue of the title first published 1988 by Dial Books for Young Readers

"Wells' illustrations . . . show the plump, large-eared cast to be full of charm and cleverness. Facial expressions, posture, and background details substantially extend the humor of the story. The simple rhythm of the rhyming text is subtle and playful." SLJ

★ **Time**-out for Sophie; by Rosemary Wells. Viking Childrens books 2013 32 p. (hardcover) $15.99

Grades: PreK K 1   E

1. Mice -- Fiction 2. Picture books for children 3. Bad behavior -- Juvenile fiction 4. Behavior -- Fiction 5.

Family life -- Fiction

ISBN 0670785113; 9780670785117

LC 2012015263

In this children's book, "after getting sent to time-out for unnecessary roughness during dinner with Mama . . . and upsetting the laundry Daddy has folded . . . , Sophie comes up against a master: Granny. Instead of giving Sophie a time-out for repeated eyeglasses-snatching, Granny gives herself one, moving from the sofa to the rocking chair, where she sits implacably, arms folded." (Publishers Weekly)

Timothy's tales from Hilltop School. Viking 2002 64p il hardcover o.p. pa $7.99

Grades: K 1 2   E

1. School stories 2. Animals -- Fiction

ISBN 0-670-03554-8; 0-14-240156-0 pa

LC 2001-7360

A collection of six stories featuring the teachers and students of Hilltop School as they learn about taking turns, working together, and never giving up

"The language is evocative, the dilemmas are real, and the solutions are satisfying. Watercolor personality portraits and spot art throughout feature Wells' familiar and beloved animal characters." Bull Cent Child Books

★ **Yoko**. Hyperion Bks. for Children 1998 un il $14.95; pa $6.99

Grades: PreK K 1 2   E

1. Cats 2. Food 3. Sushi 4. Animals 5. Schools 6. School stories 7. Japanese Americans 8. Cats -- Fiction 9. Food -- Fiction 10. Japanese Americans -- Fiction

ISBN 0-7868-0395-9; 1-4231-1983-5 pa

LC 98-12342

When Yoko the cat brings sushi to school for lunch, her classmates make fun of what she eats—until one of them tries it for himself

"Wells sets the story in an active preschool classroom, and her clear ink-and-watercolor pictures have never been more expressive and tender, with a range of animal characters that are endearingly human in body language and expression." Booklist

Other titles about Yoko are:

Yoko writes her name (2008)

Yoko's paper cranes (2001)

Yoko's world of kindness (2005)

Yoko's show and tell (2010)

Yoko learns to read; Rosemary Wells. Disney-Hyperion Books 2012 32 p.

Grades: PreK K 1   E

1. Cats -- Juvenile fiction 2. Literacy -- Juvenile fiction 3. Japanese Americans -- Juvenile fiction 4. Mother-daughter relationship -- Juvenile fiction

ISBN 1423138236; 9781423138235

LC 2011010868

This children's story by Rosemary Wells tells of a cat learning how to read. "Like her classmates, Yoko yearns to see her name on the 'book tree' at school. . . . Her mother only reads Japanese, and, oddly, they own just the three books. A trip to the library solves at least one of these problems, and Yoko's determination carries her along as she sounds out words and uses pictures to predict plot. . . . The final picture shows Yoko beginning to teach her mother the English alphabet." (Kirkus)

The **miraculous** tale of the two Maries; illustrated by Petra Mathers. Viking 2006 un il $16.99
Grades: 1 2 3 4   E
1. Miracles -- Fiction
ISBN 0-670-05960-9
LC 2005017743

After perishing in a boating accident, two sixteen-year-old girls, both named Marie, ask God to allow them to return to the earth and intervene in the lives of villagers.

"Anchoring the story's ethereal themes are palpable south-of-France details, from the narrative's occasional French phrases to Mathers' alluring artwork, which captures the region's azure skies and sunbaked, salt-cured colors." Booklist

Wentworth, Marjory
Shackles; by Marjory Heath Wentworth; illustration by Leslie Darwin Pratt-Thomas. Legacy 2009 un il $16.99
Grades: 2 3 4 5   E
1. Slavery -- Fiction 2. African Americans -- Fiction
ISBN 978-0-93310-106-7; 0-93310-106-6
"Hunter, 11, watches his pesky little brothers dig for buried treasure in their backyard on Sullivan's Island, South Carolina. When they dig up 'an armful of mud and metal,' their neighbor . . . explains to them that what they have found are shackles used on slaves to prevent their escape. . . . Based on a true story, this compelling picture book speaks in clear, lyrical prose, true to Hunter's perspective, with beautiful oil paintings." Booklist

Weston, Carrie
If a chicken stayed for supper; by Carrie Weston; illustrated by Sophie Fatus. Holiday House 2007 un il $16.95
Grades: PreK K 1 2   E
1. Foxes -- Fiction 2. Night -- Fiction 3. Chickens -- Fiction
ISBN 978-0-8234-2067-4
LC 2006049511

First published 2006 in the United Kingdom
Even though they promise not to leave the den when their mother goes out hunting for a chicken for supper, five little foxes are unable to resist going outside to play in the dark.

"The language is engaging and precise, complemented by the vibrant and cheerful illustrations, rich with folk-art inspiration and a pleasing page layout." SLJ

Weston, Tamson
Hey, pancakes! words by Tamson Weston; pictures by Stephen Gammell. Harcourt 2003 un il $16
Grades: PreK K 1 2   E
1. Stories in rhyme 2. Breakfasts -- Fiction 3. Family life -- Fiction
ISBN 0-15-216502-9
LC 2001-6867

The day gets off to a rough start, but soon the smell of pancakes fills the air and a family gathers for a breakfast feast

"Weston's paean to pancakes has a bouncy breakfast beat that lends itself to reading aloud. . . . Gammell's pastel, pencil, and watercolor illustrations swirl around like food coloring in an enthusiastic blend." Bull Cent Child Books

Wewer, Iris
My wild sister and me. North-South 2011 un il $16.95
Grades: PreK K 1 2   E
1. Siblings -- Fiction
ISBN 978-0-7358-4003-4; 0-7358-4003-2
Having a wild big sister—who can be a giraffe one day, a giant bear the next, and a racing rabbit the day after that—is just about the very best thing that can happen to little brother.

"With great sensitivity and sweetness, German writer Wewer probes the never-quite-settled nature of sibling relationships. . . . Wewer doesn't promise an end to the hostilities, but her honesty will touch siblings on both sides of the age divide." Publ Wkly

Whatley, Bruce
Clinton Gregory's secret; [by] Bruce Whatley. Abrams Books for Young Readers 2008 un il $15.95
Grades: K 1 2   E
1. Dreams -- Fiction
ISBN 978-0-8109-9364-8; 0-8109-9364-3
LC 2007012760

Clinton Gregory has fantastic adventures every night, from fighting dragons to flying around the world with his friends, and he keeps each one a secret.

"Everything is big in Whatley's colorful and fantastical spreads, which include details sure to appeal to children. . . . An entertaining addition to help wind down the day." SLJ

Wait! No paint! written and illustrated by Bruce Whatley. HarperCollins Pubs. 2001 31p il hardcover o.p. pa $6.99
Grades: PreK K 1 2   E
1. Pigs 2. Wolves 3. Illustrators
ISBN 0-06-028270-3; 0-06-028271-1 lib bdg; 0-06-443546-6 pa
LC 00-61351

The three little pigs are in their usual trouble with the big bad wolf, until a mysterious Voice gets involved and mixes things up

"The 'Voice' is the careless illustrator of the story, and . . . he's run out of red paint! . . . A quirky retelling of a perennial favorite, this may appeal most to early-elementary-age children, who will delight in the picture's conceptual surprises." Booklist

Wheeler, Lisa
★ **Boogie** knights; words by Lisa Wheeler; pictures by Mark Siegel. Atheneum Books for Young Readers 2008 un il $16.99
Grades: PreK K 1   E
1. Stories in rhyme 2. Parties -- Fiction 3. Monsters -- Fiction 4. Knights and knighthood -- Fiction
ISBN 978-0-689-87639-4; 0-689-87639-4
LC 2007-24158

When the knights of the castle are awakened by the noise from the Madcap Monster Ball, they decide to join the party.

"Wheeler's rhythmic text is filled with taut rhymes, alliteration, and vivid images. . . . Done in charcoal, pencil, and Photoshop, Siegel's sophisticated, graphic-novel-style artwork . . . demands a second look. . . . Sepia tones, splashes of color, silhouettes, and outline sketches cleverly underscore the plot elements and keep the pages interesting." SLJ

Bubble gum, bubble gum; illustrated by Laura Huliska-Beith. Little, Brown and Co. 2004 un il $15.99

Grades: PreK K 1 2   **E**

1. Stories in rhyme 2. Animals -- Fiction

ISBN 0-316-98894-4

LC 2002-16268

After a variety of animals get stuck one by one in bubble gum melting in the road, they must survive encounters with a big blue truck and a burly black bear.

"A fast-paced, rhyming story with vibrant, bouncing illustrations." SLJ

Castaway cats; story by Lisa Wheeler; art by Ponder Goembel. Atheneum Books for Young Readers 2006 un il $16.95

Grades: PreK K 1 2   **E**

1. Stories in rhyme 2. Cats -- Fiction 3. Survival after airplane accidents, shipwrecks, etc. -- Fiction

ISBN 0-689-86232-6

LC 2004-541

Fifteen felines find themselves marooned on an island and are not sure what to do.

"This delightful book is told in verses that become smoother as the cats cooperate and find their groove. . . . Goembel's illustrations, done in acrylic and ink, are fantastic and provide wonderful insight into the side stories developing as the book progresses." SLJ

★ **Jazz** baby; illustrations by R. Gregory Christie. Harcourt 2007 un il $16

Grades: PreK K 1   **E**

1. Stories in rhyme 2. Infants -- Fiction 3. Jazz music -- Fiction 4. Family life -- Fiction

ISBN 978-0-15-202522-9; 0-15-202522-7

LC 2006-09236

Baby and his family make some jazzy music.

"The percussive text scans like a musical dream, a nearly flawless scat on music, dance, and the contagious joy of jazz. Christie's gouache illustrations—in a sixties palette of olive, gold, and brick—feature characters with fluid bodies and mobile faces that fill the images with movement and energy." Booklist

★ **Old** Cricket; illustrations by Ponder Goembel. Atheneum Bks. for Young Readers 2003 un il $16.95

Grades: PreK K 1 2   **E**

1. Crickets -- Fiction

ISBN 0-689-84510-3

LC 2002-2199

Old Cricket doesn't feel like helping his wife and neighbors to prepare for winter and so he pretends to have all sorts of ailments that require the doctor's care, but hungry Old Crow has other ideas

"Wheeler invests her delightful tale with all the characteristics of a good fable, and Goembel's sharp, highly detailed acrylic artwork gives a clever, humorous bug's-eye view of the world." Booklist

The **pet** project; cute and cuddly vicious verses. by Lisa Wheeler; illustrated by Zachariah OHora. Atheneum Books for Young Readers 2013 40 p. col. ill. (hardcover) $16.99

Grades: K 1 2 3 4 5   **E**

1. Stories in rhyme 2. Pets -- Juvenile fiction 3. Pets -- Fiction 4. Animals -- Fiction

ISBN 1416975950; 9781416975953

LC 2011029647

This children's book, by Lisa Wheeler, illustrated by Zachariah O'Hora, presents a series of poems focused on animals and pets. "If you think you'd like a cute and cuddly pet, you may need to do some research. . . . Join one budding young scientist as she catalogs the pros and pitfalls of potential pet ownership in this assortment of zany . . . poems that will change the way you look at cuddly animals--and give you the giggles." (Publisher's note)

Te amo, Bebe, little one; illustrated by Maribel Suárez. Little, Brown 2004 un il $15.95

Grades: PreK K 1   **E**

1. Stories in rhyme 2. Infants -- Fiction 3. Mother-child relationship -- Fiction

ISBN 0-316-61410-6

In this picture book "verses describe a baby's first year of life. As the seasons change, the infant and mother are shown engaging in a variety of activities including a trip to the beach, dancing to fiesta music at the country fair, and enjoying a winter's night. . . . Spanish words are smoothly incorporated into the text. The illustrations are done in bright, bold colors. . . . This is a good choice for intimate sharing with little ones." SLJ

Ugly Pie; illustrated by Heather Solomon. Harcourt 2010 un il $16

Grades: PreK K 1   **E**

1. Pies -- Fiction 2. Bears -- Fiction

ISBN 978-0-15-216754-7; 0-15-216754-4

LC 2008-4535

After baking a scrumptious Ugly Pie, made from ingredients donated by his neighbors, Ol' Bear invites everyone over for a slice. Includes pie recipe.

"Large, bright watercolors, acrylics, and collage trace the bear's search as he goes from house to house. . . . This humorous tale should appeal greatly to little cubs everywhere." SLJ

Whelan, Gloria

The **listeners**; written by Gloria Whelan; illustrated by Mike Benny. Sleeping Bear Press 2009 un il $17.95

Grades: 1 2 3   **E**

1. Slavery -- Fiction 2. African Americans -- Fiction

ISBN 978-1-58536-419-0; 1-58536-419-3

LC 2009005436

After a day of picking cotton in late 1860, Ella May, a young slave, joins her friends Bobby and Sue at their second job of listening outside the windows of their master's house for useful information

This is "a spare, lyrical narrative. . . . Benny's unframed, dusk-toned, double-page paintings emphasize the stark contrast between slave shacks and plantation mansion." Booklist

Waiting for the owl's call; [illustrated by] Pascal Milelli. Sleeping Bear Press 2009 un il (Tales of the world) $17.95

Grades: 2 3 4 5   **E**

1. Weaving -- Fiction 2. Child labor -- Fiction 3. Rugs

and carpets -- Fiction
ISBN 978-1-58536-418-3; 1-58536-418-5

LC 2009005437

For generations the women of Zulviya's family have earned their living by weaving rugs by hand. During one work day, Zulviya will tie thousands of knots. As she sits at her work, Zulviya weaves not one but two patterns. The pattern on the loom will become a fine rug. She weaves a second pattern in her mind.

"Impressionistic paintings in muted colors accompany Zulviya's lyrical description of her Afghan homeland and her yearning to escape 'the shadow of the loom.' An author's note provides details about illiegal child labor in the Afghani rug-making industry." Horn Book Guide

Yuki and the one thousand carriers; written by Gloria Whelan; illustrated by Yan Nascimbene. Sleeping Bear Press 2008 un il (Tales of the world) $17.95
Grades: 1 2 3   E
1. Haiku -- Fiction 2. Voyages and travels -- Fiction
ISBN 978-1-58536-352-0; 1-58536-352-9

LC 2007046318

In Japan, as a provincial governor, his wife, and daughter Yuki, followed by 1,000 attendants, travel the historic Tokaido Road to the Shogun's palace in Edo, Yuki keeps up with her lessons by writing poems describing the journey

"Nascimbene stays true to Yuki's childish perspective. . . . Accompanying the simple prose narrative, are haiku . . . that express intense feelings in clear, casual words." Booklist

Whitaker, Zai
Kali and the rat snake; story by Zai Whitaker; illustrations by Srividya Natarajan. Kane/Miller 2006 un il $15.95
Grades: 1 2 3   E
1. School stories 2. Snakes -- Fiction 3. Prejudices -- Fiction
ISBN 1-933605-10-3
First published 2000 in India

"Kali has always been proud of his father, who is the best snake catcher in their Indian village. But when he attends school, the children make fun of his Irula ways. . . . But one day the classroom is visited by a six-foot-long rat snake. . . . Kali grabs it and becomes the class hero. The text is smoothly written, with lots of cultural details. . . . Natarajan's stylized illustrations are a mixture of smaller pencil drawings and luscious larger paintings that seem to be done on silk." SLJ

White, Kathryn
When will it snow? [illustrations by] Alison Edgson. Good Books 2011 un il $16.99
Grades: PreK K 1   E
1. Snow -- Fiction 2. Bears -- Fiction 3. Squirrels -- Fiction 4. Friendship -- Fiction 5. Hibernation -- Fiction 6. Moles (Animals) -- Fiction
ISBN 9781561487295; 1561487295

LC 2011007763

When Little Bear's mother begins to prepare him for winter hibernation, he is sad because he will miss playing with his friends in the snow.

"This lament will strike an emotional chord with anyone who bemoans missing even a minute of fun. . . . Edgson's characters are the epitome of exuberance and joy." Kirkus

White, Linda
Too many turkeys; illustrated by Megan Lloyd. Holiday House 2010 un il $16.95
Grades: K 1 2 3   E
1. Turkeys -- Fiction 2. Farm life -- Fiction
ISBN 978-0-8234-2084-1; 0-8234-2084-1

LC 2008049210

Chaos ensues when Farmer Fred's wife fertilizes her beautiful garden with an secret ingredient that attracts turkeys from miles around.

"Bright watercolors wash over detailed illustrations. . . . Text moves readers forward with italicized first-person ruminations and the occasional 'but then . . .' encouragement to turn the page. An engaging story, . . . this book is a welcome addition for all libraries." SLJ

Whiting, Sue
The **firefighters**; [by] Sue Whiting; illustrated by Donna Rawlins. Candlewick Press 2008 un il $15.99
Grades: PreK K 1 2   E
1. School stories 2. Imagination -- Fiction 3. Fire fighters -- Fiction
ISBN 978-0-7636-4019-4; 0-7636-4019-0

LC 2007051895

After dressing up as fire fighters, building a fire truck out of a cardboard box, and extinguishing imaginary fires on the playground, Mrs. Iverson's students are surprised by the arrival of a real fire engine with real fire fighters on board

"Rawlins's acrylic illustrations feature bright, primary colors that stand out against the clean, white backgrounds. . . . A great choice for introducing not only fire safety, but also creative play." SLJ

Whitman, Candace
Lines that wiggle; illustrations by Steve Wilson. Blue Apple Books 2009 un il $14.99
Grades: K 1 2 3   E
1. Stories in rhyme 2. Monsters -- Fiction
ISBN 978-1-934706-54-1; 1-934706-54-X

LC 2008042383

A variety of monsters and other creatures demonstrate some of the different things that lines can do, from curve and curl to zig-zag

"Through bouncy verse and lively artwork, this creative collaboration explores the many different ways that lines are used. . . . Children will enjoy this book on many levels." SLJ

Whitman, Walt
When I heard the learn'd astronomer; words by Walt Whitman; pictures by Loren Long. Simon & Schuster Books for Young Readers 2004 un il $16.95
Grades: 1 2 3 4   E
1. Astronomy -- Poetry 2. Children's poetry, American 3. Astronomy -- Juvenile poetry 4. Outer space -- Juvenile poetry
ISBN 0-689-86397-7

LC 2004-7538

"A little boy obsessed with outer space has been dragged to an astronomy lecture. . . . The fidgety youngster takes his toy rocket ship outside, where he marvels at the 'perfect si-

lence of the stars, casting a decisive vote for creative speculation over chilly analysis.' The painterly artwork . . . gets its
own injection of childlike wonder through playful doodles
contributed by Long's two children." Booklist

Whybrow, Ian

Harry and the dinosaurs say Raahh! written by Ian
Whybrow; illustrated by Adrian Reynolds. Random House
2004 un il $14.95
Grades: PreK K 1   E
1. Toys 2. Dentists 3. Dinosaurs
ISBN 0-375-82542-8
           LC 2003-1480
First published 2001 in the United Kingdom
Harry takes his toy dinosaurs with him to help calm his
fears on his first visit to the dentist.
"All of the pictures are full-bleed spreads and are warm,
accessible, and realistic. The simple text flows easily and the
pacing is right on for younger listeners." SLJ

The **noisy** way to bed; illustrated by Tiphanie Beeke.
Arthur A. Levine Books 2004 un il $15.95
Grades: PreK K 1 2   E
1. Stories in rhyme 2. Animals -- Fiction 3. Bedtime
-- Fiction
ISBN 0-439-55689-9
           LC 2003-2785
As a sleepy boy decides it is bedtime and sets out across
the farm toward home, he meets several animals who, in
their noisy way, express the same idea
"This engaging bedtime story begs for participation from
children. . . . [Beeke's] full-page, mixed-media pictures are
captivating, providing an eye-pleasing blend of colors, textures, and facial expressions." SLJ

Wickberg, Susan

★ **Hey** Mr. Choo-Choo, where are you going? [by]
Susan Wickberg; illustrated by Yumi Heo. G.P. Putnam's
Sons 2008 un il $16.99
Grades: PreK K   E
1. Stories in rhyme 2. Railroads -- Fiction
ISBN 978-0-399-23993-9; 0-399-23993-6
           LC 2006034459
A train engine hauls his cars from the city to the sea,
answering questions about what he is pulling, seeing, and
hearing along the way.
"Heo's collages and oil paintings are chock-full of
friendly facets that will keep children coming back. Done in
a primitive style, the artwork sports a striped coal car, a robot
toy, a billboard of a fish, and a lamb rolling in the meadow. .
. . Readers will be anxious to climb back on Mr. Choo-Choo
for another energetic ride." SLJ

Wiesner, David

★ **Art** & Max. Clarion Books 2010 un il $17.99
Grades: K 1 2 3   E
1. Artists -- Fiction 2. Lizards -- Fiction 3. Painting
-- Fiction 4. Artists' materials -- Fiction
ISBN 978-0-618-75663-6; 0-618-75663-9
           LC 2010005205
Max the lizard wants to be an artist like Arthur, but
his first attempt at using a paintbrush sends the two
friends on a whirlwind trip through various media, with
unexpected consequences.

"This small-scale and surprisingly comedic story takes
place against a placid backdrop of pale desert colors, which
recedes to keep the focus squarely on the dynamic between
the two lizards and the wide range of emotions that Wiesner
masterfully evokes." Publ Wkly

★ **Flotsam**. Clarion Books 2006 un il $17
Grades: K 1 2 3 4   E
1. Stories without words 2. Beaches -- Fiction 3.
Cameras -- Fiction
ISBN 0-618-19457-6
Awarded the Caldecott Medal, 2007
"A wave deposits an old-fashioned contraption at the
feet of an inquisitive young beachcomber. It's a Melville
underwater camera, and the excited boy quickly develops
the film he finds inside. The photos are amazing. . . . This
wordless books vivid watercolor paintings have a crisp realism that anchors the elements of fantasy. . . . Filled with
inventive details and delightful twists, each snapshot is a tale
waiting to be told." SLJ

Free fall. Lothrop, Lee & Shepard Bks. 1988 un il lib
bdg $18.89; pa $6.99
Grades: K 1 2 3 4   E
1. Stories without words 2. Dreams -- Fiction
ISBN 0-688-05584-2 lib bdg; 0-688-10990-X pa
           LC 87-22834
A Caldecott Medal honor book, 1989
A young boy dreams of daring adventures in the company of imaginary creatures inspired by the things surrounding his bed
"Technical virtuosity is the trademark of the double-
page watercolor spreads. Especially notable is the solidity of
forms and architectural details." SLJ

Hurricane. Clarion Bks. 1990 un il $16; pa $6.95
Grades: K 1 2 3   E
1. Brothers -- Fiction 2. Hurricanes -- Fiction
ISBN 0-395-54382-7; 0-395-62974-8 pa
           LC 90-30070
"A family weathers a hurricane; the next day, in the post-
hurricane yard, the two boys in the family play on a great
fallen elm, imagining it to be a jungle, a pirate ship, and
a space ship. A handsome book, affording opportunities for
sharing fears and dreams of adventure." Horn Book Guide

June 29, 1999. Clarion Bks. 1992 un il $16; pa $5.95
Grades: K 1 2 3 4   E
1. Vegetables -- Fiction
ISBN 0-395-59762-5; 0-395-72767-7 pa
           LC 91-34854
"Here an understated, fairly straightforward text is a perfect foil for the outrageous scenes of vegetables run amok.
Realistic watercolors reveal red peppers that need to be
roped down, beans with bemused Arizona sheep clambering over them, and gargantuan peas floating down the Mississippi like logs to the sawmill. Fans of Wiesner's offbeat
sense of humor will be delighted." Horn Book

Mr. Wuffles! by David Wiesner. Clarion Books,
Houghton Mifflin Harcourt 2013 32 p ill. (hardcover)
$17.99

Grades: PreK K 1 2 3   E
  1. Cats -- Juvenile fiction 2. Picture books for children
ISBN 0618756612; 9780618756612

                 LC 2012046025

In this children's picture book, a housecat is battling some tiny aliens. The aliens' "initial celebration at landing turns to mayhem as their craft is buffeted by Mr. Wuffles. The aliens assess a smoldering engine part and disembark for help. . . . A ladybug and several ants assist them, and the repair's successfully made by harvesting cross sections of detritus: pencil eraser, M&M, marble and metal screw." (Kirkus Reviews)

★ **Sector** 7. Clarion Bks. 1999 un il $16
Grades: K 1 2 3 4   E
  1. Stories without words 2. Clouds -- Fiction
ISBN 0-395-74656-6

                 LC 96-40343

A Caldecott Medal honor book, 2000
While on a school trip to the Empire State Building, a boy is taken by a friendly cloud to visit Sector 7, where he discovers how clouds are shaped and channeled throughout the country
"Wiesner's lofty watercolors render words superfluous as he transforms the sky into magical scenes of marine life, reminding children of the innate power of their own imagination." Publ Wkly

★ **Tuesday**. Clarion Bks. 1991 un il $17; pa $6.95
Grades: K 1 2 3 4   E
  1. Frogs -- Fiction
ISBN 0-395-55113-7; 0-395-87082-8 pa

                 LC 90-39358

Awarded the Caldecott Medal, 1992
Frogs rise on their lily pads, float through the air, and explore the nearby houses while their inhabitants sleep
"Wiesner offers a fantasy watercolor journey accomplished with soft-edged realism. Studded with bits of humor, the narrative artwork tells a simple, pleasant story with a consistency and authenticity that makes the fantasy convincing." Booklist

★ The **three** pigs. Clarion Bks. 2001 un il $16
Grades: K 1 2 3 4   E
  1. Pigs 2. Pigs -- Fiction 3. Characters in literature
ISBN 0618007016

                 LC 00-57016

Awarded the Caldecott Medal, 2002
The three pigs escape the wolf by going into another world where they meet the cat and the fiddle, the cow that jumped over the moon, and a dragon. "Ages four to eight." (NY Times Book Rev)
"Wiesner's brilliant use of white space and perspective evokes a feeling that the characters can navigate endless possibilities—and that the range of story itself is limitless." Publ Wkly

Wilcoxen, Chuck
  Niccolini's song; illustrated by Mark Buehner. Dutton Children's Books 2004 un il $16.99
Grades: PreK K 1 2   E
  1. Bedtime -- Fiction 2. Lullabies -- Fiction 3. Railroads -- Fiction
ISBN 0-525-46805-6

A gentle night watchman at the railroad yard lulls anxious train engines to sleep by singing just the right song.
"The rhythmic pace of the text, short sentences, and alliterative phrases make this creative bedtime story ideal for reading aloud. Buehner's soft paintings are imbued with dusky, nighttime hues." SLJ

Wild, Margaret
  ★ **Harry** & Hopper. Feiwel & Friends 2011 un il $16.99
Grades: PreK K   E
  1. Dogs -- Fiction 2. Pets -- Fiction 3. Bereavement -- Fiction
ISBN 978-0-312-64261-7; 0-312-64261-X

"Redheaded Harry and his spotted dog, Hopper, are constant companions, accomplices . . . and bedmates. The dog's sudden death (an accident that happens while Harry is at school), leaves the boy devastated. . . . Wild's . . . understated, empathic prose offers both a voice for a child unable to articulate his grief and the reassurance that those we love never really disappear. Blackwood's . . . predominantly charcoal drawings are equally eloquent, particularly in her use of texture to capture the emotional essence of good and sad times." Publ Wkly

Itsy-bitsy babies; illustrated by Jan Ormerod. Little Hare Books 2010 un il $15.99
Grades: PreK   E
  1. Stories in rhyme 2. Infants -- Fiction
ISBN 978-1-9215413-6-0; 1-9215413-9-X

"This picture book introduces a multicultural cast of babies and toddlers engaged in everyday activities. . . . Short and precise, Wild's rhyming couplets offer plenty of chances for children to chime in with the end words. . . . Ormerod's clean, crayonlike drawings illustrate one or more babies with a few props . . . and create a sense of changing settings with flat, toned color above and below the horizon line in each picture." Booklist

Kiss kiss! [by] Margaret Wild & Bridget Strevens-Marzo. Simon & Schuster Books for Young Readers 2004 un il $12.95
Grades: PreK K   E
  1. Kissing 2. Hippopotamus 3. Mother and child 4. Hippopotamus -- Fiction 5. Mother-child relationship -- Fiction
ISBN 0-689-86279-2

                 LC 2002-154516

First published 2003 in Australia
Baby Hippo is in such a rush to play one morning he forgets to kiss his mama, but strangely all the jungle noises seem to remind him
"This is a story filled with movement and physical affection. The lap-sit audience will love the squishy, lumpy sounds and the repetition of the text as they point to the animals in the clear, bright pictures." Booklist

Midnight babies; illustrated by Ann James. Clarion Bks. 2001 un il $15
Grades: PreK K   E
  1. Infants -- Fiction
ISBN 0-618-10412-7

                 LC 00-58978

First published 1999 in Australia

Baby Brenda and her friends have fun at the Midnight Cafe, enjoying a "wibble wobble" dance, a "jiggly-joggly" treat, and a dip in the sprinklers before going home to bed

"The art is bold and delicious; the text captures the pure exuberance of the sweet, silly action." Booklist

★ **Our** granny; story by Margaret Wild; pictures by Julie Vivas. Ticknor & Fields 1994 un il $17; pa $6.95
Grades: PreK K 1 2   **E**
1. Grandmothers -- Fiction
ISBN 0-395-67023-3; 0-395-88395-4 pa
LC 93-11950
First published 1993 in Australia

"Two young children present a catalog of all the varying sizes, shapes, and types of grandmothers, interspersed with loving comments about their own granny, who has 'a wobbly bottom' and wears a funny bathing suit.... Vivas's lively illustrations capture the grandmothers in their most comic moments." Horn Book Guide

★ **Piglet** and Mama; illustrated by Stephen Michael King. Harry N. Abrams 2005 un il $14.95
Grades: PreK K   **E**
1. Pigs -- Fiction 2. Mothers -- Fiction 3. Farm life -- Fiction
ISBN 0-8109-5869-4
LC 2004-19497
When Piglet cannot find her mother, all of the barnyard animals try to make her feel better, but Piglet wants nothing but Mama.

"The text is reassuring and rhythmic. . . . The cheery watercolor cartoons depict farm life on a bright, sunny day, and the gentle pastel color scheme matches the tender tone of the text." SLJ

Other titles about Piglet are:
Piglet and Papa (2007)
Piglet and Granny (2009)

★ **Puffling**; illustrated by Julie Vivas. Feiwel and Friends 2009 un il $16.99
Grades: PreK K 1 2   **E**
1. Growth -- Fiction 2. Puffins -- Fiction 3. Parent-child relationship -- Fiction
ISBN 978-0-312-56570-1; 0-312-56570-4
LC 2008048137
As his affectionate parents nourish and protect him, a plucky young puffin impatiently waits—but not without some reservations—for the day when he is "strong enough and tall enough and brave enough" to leave his nest on the rocky cliff-face and waddle off to the sea

"The beautiful, spare illustrations, rendered in pastel and watercolor pencil on textured paper, show the tender bonds between family members while showcasing actual facts about puffin life." Booklist

Tom goes to kindergarten; [illustrated by] David Legge. Whitman, A. 2000 un il $15.95
Grades: PreK K   **E**
1. Schools 2. Kindergarten 3. School stories 4. Pandas 5. First day of school 6. Giant panda -- Fiction
ISBN 0-8075-8012-0
LC 99-50420

When Tom, a young panda, goes to his very first day of kindergarten, his whole family stays and plays and wishes they could be in kindergarten too

"Large, bright, whimsical watercolors make this a perfect book both for group storytelling and for one-on-one sharing." SLJ

The **little** crooked house; illustrated by Jonathan Bentley. Simply Read Books 2006 un il $16.95
Grades: PreK K 1 2 3   **E**
1. Houses -- Fiction 2. Moving -- Fiction
ISBN 1-894965-59-0

"Wild adds her own inimitable touch to this offering about a crooked man, his crooked cat, and their crooked mouse, all living in their crooked little house. The residents cannot remain in their home because of its unfortunate location at the side of the railroad tracks. Thus, one move leads to another, from a desert vicinity to riverside property. . . . Bentley's rollicking, rowdy watercolor illustrations beckon readers to come along on this topsy-turvy trip." SLJ

Wildsmith, Brian

Brian Wildsmith's ABC. Star Bright Bks. 1995 un bd bk $6.95
Grades: PreK K   **E**
1. Alphabet 2. Board books for children
ISBN 978-1-88773-402-8 bd bk; 1-88773-402-3 bd bk
LC 95-31730
First published 1962 in the United Kingdom; first U.S. edition 1963 by Watts

"From A/apple to Z/zebra, Wildsmith's 26 playful renderings of objects and animals are highlighted with an eye-catching, colorful design; kaleidoscopic animals constructed from bold circles, triangles and squares add an unexpected geometric element to the counting book." Publ Wkly

Brian Wildsmith's Amazing animal alphabet. Star Bright Books 2009 un $17.95; pa $7.95
Grades: PreK K   **E**
1. Animals 2. Alphabet
ISBN 978-1-59572-104-4; 1-59572-104-5; 978-1-59572-185-3 pa; 1-59572-185-1 pa
LC 2007033811
"Wildsmith's distinctive, detailed animals pop against brightly colored backgrounds as they illustrate each letter of the alphabet. Preschoolers will easily recognize most of the creatures, with a few refreshingly unusual exceptions (quetzel for Q, vole for V, xenops for X). Four pages of 'Amazing Animal Facts' conclude the animal parade." Horn Book Guide

Jungle party. Star Bright Books 2006 un il $16.95; pa $6.95
Grades: PreK K 1 2   **E**
1. Animals -- Fiction 2. Parties -- Fiction 3. Pythons -- Fiction
ISBN 978-1-59572-052-8; 1-59572-052-9; 978-1-59572-053-5 pa; 1-59572-053-7 pa
First published 1974 by Oxford University Press with title: Python's party
Although he is hungry, Python tries to prove his goodwill by throwing a party for all the jungle animals

"Wildsmith excels at bold, brightly colored illustrations of animals, and this cautionary tale is a visual delight." Horn Book Guide

Wiles, Deborah

Freedom Summer; illustrated by Jerome Lagarrigue. Atheneum Bks. for Young Readers 2001 un il $16
Grades: K 1 2 3   E
1. Friendship 2. Race relations 3. African Americans 4. Friendship -- Fiction 5. Race relations -- Fiction 6. African Americans -- Fiction 7. African Americans -- Juvenile fiction
ISBN 0-689-87829-X

LC 98-52805

In 1964, Joe is pleased that a new law will allow his best friend John Henry, who is colored, to share the town pool and other public places with him, but he is dismayed to find that prejudice still exists

"The text, though concise, is full of nuance, and the oil paintings shimmer with the heat of the South in summer." Horn Book Guide

Wilkes, Angela

★ **My** first word book. DK Pub. 1999 64p il hardcover o.p. bd bk $5.99
Grades: PreK   E
1. Vocabulary
ISBN 0-7894-3977-8; 0-7894-9905-3 bd bk

LC 99-206690

A slightly revised edition of the title first published 1991
"Common, familiar objects, animals, and activities—featured in clear, bright photos set against a white background or in small drawings—are grouped together on double-page spreads with such headings as 'On the farm' and 'Colors, shapes, and numbers.' Children will be drawn to the bright, cheerful pages of this first vocabulary lesson." Horn Book Guide

Willans, Tom

Wait! I want to tell you a story; written and illustrated by Tom Willans. Simon & Schuster Books for Young Readers 2005 un il $15.95
Grades: PreK K 1 2   E
1. Animals -- Fiction 2. Storytelling -- Fiction
ISBN 0-689-87166-X

First published 2004 in the United Kingdom
"To avoid being eaten by a tiger, a fast-talking muskrat spins a tale about a frog who's about to be eaten by a shark who tells a story about a lizard who's about to be eaten by a snake, and so on. This bouncy repetitive tale with a twist is made all the funnier by the zany ink and watercolor illustrations." Horn Book Guide

Willems, Mo

Big Frog can't fit in; a pop out book. paper engineering by Bruce Foster. Hyperion 2009 un il $19.99
Grades: PreK K 1   E
1. Pop-up books 2. Frogs -- Fiction
ISBN 978-1-4231-1436-9; 1-4231-1436-1

Big Frog really wants to fit in, but even this pop-up book can't hold her, so it takes a lot of work from some good friends to help her.

"A sunny tribute to the power of friendship to provide ingenuity, help and cheer." Publishers Weekly

★ **Cat** the Cat, who is that? Balzer & Bray 2010 un il $12.99; lib bdg $14.89
Grades: PreK K 1   E
1. Cats -- Fiction 2. Animals -- Fiction 3. Friendship -- Fiction
ISBN 978-0-06-172840-2; 0-06-172840-3; 978-0-06-172841-9 lib bdg; 0-06-172841-1 lib bdg

LC 2008-46187

An exuberant cat introduces readers to her friends.

"Willems provides just enough humor and surprise to entertain youngest audiences and . . . Cat could become another favorite; her personality sparkles in expansive gestures and gleeful interactions." Publ Wkly

Other titles about Cat the Cat and her friends are:
Let's say hi to friends who fly! (2010)
What's your sound, Hound the Hound ?(2010)
Time to sleep, Sheep the Sheep! (2010)

★ **City** Dog, Country Frog; words, Mo Willems; pictures, Jon J. Muth. Hyperion Books for Children 2010 un il
Grades: PreK K 1 2   E
1. Dogs -- Fiction 2. Frogs -- Fiction 3. Seasons -- Fiction 4. Friendship -- Fiction
ISBN 1423103009; 9781423103004

City Dog and Country Frog play together in the spring and summer and fall, but in winter Country Frog is gone. Then when spring comes again City Dog makes a new friend.

Willems "is gracefully spare here, making every word count. That leaves room for Muth's watercolors, richly seasonal, which fill every page. The pictures are imbued with hope and happiness, leaving and longing. This wonderful collaboration makes a significant impact with subtlety and wit." Booklist

★ **Don't** let the pigeon drive the bus! words and pictures by Mo Willems. Hyperion Bks. for Children 2003 un il $12.99
Grades: PreK K 1 2   E
1. Buses -- Fiction 2. Pigeons -- Fiction
ISBN 0-7868-1988-X

A Caldecott Medal honor book, 2004
"An unflinching and hilarious look at a child's potential for mischief. In a plain palette, with childishly elemental line drawings, Willems has captured the essence of unreasonableness in the very young." SLJ

Other titles about the pigeon are:
The pigeon finds a hot dog! (2004)
Don't let the pigeon stay up late (2006)
The pigeon wants a puppy (2008)

The **duckling** gets a cookie!? words and picture by Mo Willems. Hyperion Books for Children 2012 40 p.
Grades: PreK K 1 2   E
1. Ducks -- Fiction 2. Cookies -- Fiction 3. Pigeons -- Fiction 4. Etiquette -- Fiction 5. Temper tantrums -- Fiction 6. Humorous stories
ISBN 9781423151289

LC 2011012304

As this book "opens, the yellow Duckling requests a cookie, receives one immediately, and graciously thanks the unseen provider with a 'flappy flip flap!' The Pigeon, whom the Duckling cajoled into sharing a hot dog in the earlier book, soon arrives to express astonishment. Multipanel spreads and emphatic voice balloons reveal his outrage as The Pigeon throws a colossal tantrum ('I ask for things all the time!/ I ask to drive the bus! . . . I've asked for a walrus! . . . But do I get what I ask for? Noooooo!'). In an unexpected turn, the Duckling gives the Pigeon the entire cookie, shocking the bird." (Publishers Weekly)

Edwina, the dinosaur who didn't know she was extinct; words and pictures by Mo Willems. Hyperion 2006 un il $16.99

Grades: PreK K 1   E
1. Dinosaurs -- Fiction
ISBN 0-7868-3748-9

Everyone in town loves Edwina the dinosaur except Reginald, who is determined to prove to everyone, including Edwina, that dinosaurs are extinct.

"Set against plain, light-blue backdrops, the pictures, in Willem's familiar cartoon style, show Reginald up to his dastardly deeds. . . . Consider this an enjoyable visit to a happy community that has no room for curmudgeons." Booklist

★ **Goldilocks** and the three dinosaurs; as retold by Mo Willems. Balzer + Bray 2012 40 p. $17.99

Grades: PreK K 1 2 3   E
1. Dinosaurs -- Fiction 2. Fairy tales -- Fiction 3. Picture books for children
ISBN 0062104187; 9780062104182

In this book, Goldilocks "ventures into the home of three diabolical dinosaurs. Having cooked up three bowls of chocolate pudding and arranged their house 'just so,' the two olive-green T. rexes and smaller brown dino lick their lips. . . . Goldilocks doesn't hesitate to enter the dinos' house or stick her whole head in their food . . . and she wises up just in time to give herself, if not the dinosaurs, a happy ending." (Publishers Weekly)

★ **Hooray** for Amanda & her alligator! words and pictures by Mo Willems. Balzer + Bray 2011 68p $17.99

Grades: PreK K 1 2   E
1. Toys -- Fiction 2. Alligators -- Fiction 3. Friendship -- Fiction
ISBN 978-0-06-200400-0; 0-06-200400-X;
006200400X; 9780062004000

LC 2010009633

Amanda and her alligator have lots of fun together, but when Amanda's grandfather buys her a panda, Alligator must learn to make new friends.

"With the book's minimal backgrounds and roomy page design, the focus falls squarely on Willems' cleanly styled characters, whose facial expressions are carried in the simplest of just-so lines. Willems may not have the market cornered on best friends, but few do them better." Booklist

★ **Knuffle** Bunny; a cautionary tale. Hyperion Books for Children 2004 un il $15.99

Grades: PreK K 1 2   E
1. Lost and found possessions -- Fiction
ISBN 0-7868-1870-0

A Caldecott Medal honor book, 2005

After Trixie and daddy leave the laundromat, something very important turns up missing.

A "concise, deftly told narrative. . . . Printed on olive-green backdrops, the illustrations are a combination of muted, sepia-toned photographs upon which bright cartoon drawings of people have been superimposed. . . . A seamless and supremely satisfying presentation of art and text." SLJ

Other titles about Knuffle Bunny are:
Knuffle Bunny too (2007)
Knuffle Bunny free (2010)

★ **Leonardo,** the terrible monster. Hyperion 2005 un il $16.99

Grades: PreK K 1 2   E
1. Monsters -- Fiction
ISBN 0-7868-5294-1

Leonardo is a terrible monster he can't seem to frighten anyone. When he discovers the perfect nervous little boy, will he scare the lunch out of him? Or will he think of something better?

"Willems's familiar cartoon drawings work hand in glove with the brief text to tell this perfectly paced story." SLJ

★ **Naked** Mole Rat gets dressed; words and pictures by Mo Willems. Hyperion Books for Children 2009 un il $16.99

Grades: PreK K 1 2   E
1. Naked mole rat -- Fiction
ISBN 978-1-4231-1437-6; 1-4231-1437-X

LC 2008-48251

Willems "informs readers that 'for this story' they need only know three things about naked mole rats: '1. They are a little bit rat. 2. They are a little bit mole. 3. They are all naked.' The exception to point number three, however, is Wilbur, who revels in a wardrobe that ranges from a turtleneck and beret to an astronaut suit—infuriating his brethren. . . . [Willems'] legion of emotive, square-headed rodents . . . are paired successfully with droll prose." Publ Wkly

★ **That** Is Not a Good Idea! Mo Willems. Harpercollins Childrens Books 2013 48 p. ill. (hardcover) $17.99

Grades: PreK K 1 2   E
1. Geese -- Juvenile fiction 2. Motion pictures -- Juvenile fiction 3. Humorous fiction -- Juvenile fiction
ISBN 0062203096; 9780062203090

This children's story, by Mo Willems, "presents itself as a movie in book form, observed not only by readers, but by a gaggle of excitable goslings. The action begins when a dapper fox and a plump goose meet. . . . As the wide-eyed goose follows the fox from the city to his home in the woods. The goslings' antics grow progressively frantic . . . as their warnings increase in intensity. The climax proves that appearances can be deceiving." (Kirkus Reviews)

"This charmer is lovingly composed as an homage to silent movies and the concept of picture books as the "theater of the lap." Readers will become totally involved as they watch, along with several chicks, a drama unfolding, certain to end in tragedy... Children and adults will relish being taken for such a thrilling, suspenseful ride again and again." SLJ

★ **Today** I will fly! Hyperion Books for Children 2007 57p il $8.99

Grades: PreK K 1 2 **E**
  1. Pigs -- Fiction 2. Elephants -- Fiction 3. Friendship -- Fiction
  ISBN 978-14231-0295-3; 1-4231-0295-9
                LC 2006-49621

While Piggie is determined to fly, Elephant is skeptical, but when Piggie gets a little help from others, amazing things happen.

"Characters zip in and out of white space, proffer speech-bubble remarks, and express emotion through spot-on body language. . . . Accessible, appealing, and full of authentic emotions." Booklist

Other titles in this series are:
My friend is sad (2007)
I am invited to a party! (2007)
There is a bird on your head (2007)
I love my new toy! (2008)
I will surprise my friend! (2008)
Are you ready to play outside? (2008)
Elephants cannot dance! (2009)
Pigs make me sneeze! (2009)
Watch me throw the ball! (2009)
I am going! (2010)
Can I play too? (2010)
We are in a book! (2010)
I broke my trunk! (2011)
Should I share my ice cream? (2011)
Happy Pig Day! (2011)

★ A **big** guy took my ball! text and illustrations by Mo Willems. Hyperion Books for Children 2013 64 p. ill. (reinforced) $8.99
Grades: K 1 2 3 **E**
  1. Picture books for children 2. Bullies -- Juvenile fiction 3. Pigs -- Fiction 4. Play -- Fiction 5. Whales -- Fiction 6. Animals -- Fiction 7. Elephants -- Fiction 8. Friendship -- Fiction 9. Play -- Juvenile fiction 10. Swine -- Juvenile fiction 11. Whales -- Juvenile fiction 12. Elephants -- Juvenile fiction 13. Friendship -- Juvenile fiction
  ISBN 1423174917; 9781423174912

Willey, Margaret
  A **Clever** Beatrice Christmas; illustrated by Heather M. Solomon. Atheneum Books for Young Readers 2006 un il $16.95
Grades: K 1 2 3 **E**
  1. Christmas -- Fiction 2. Santa Claus -- Fiction
  ISBN 0-689-87017-5
                LC 2005-10281

As Christmas approaches, Clever Beatrice sets out to prove the existence of Père Noël to three questioning children

This is "a pleasing, seasonal picture book. Solomon's appealing artwork combines elements of acrylic and oil painting with fluid watercolors and collage elements that add unexpected textures to the illustrations." Booklist

Williams, Barbara
  Albert's impossible toothache; illustrated by Doug Cushman. Candlewick Press 2003 un il $15.99
Grades: PreK K 1 2 **E**
  1. Turtles -- Fiction
  ISBN 0-7636-1723-7
                LC 2002-67059

A newly illustrated edition of Albert's toothache, published 1974 by Dutton

When Albert the turtle complains of a toothache, no one in his family believes him, until his grandmother takes the time to really listen to him

"This title is a worthwhile addition to any picture-book collection." SLJ

Another title about Albert is:
Albert's gift for grandmother (2006)

Williams, Brenda
  Lin Yi's lantern; a Moon Festival tale. [text by] Brenda Williams; [illustrations by] Benjamin Lacombe. Barefoot Books 2009 un il $16.99
Grades: K 1 2 3 **E**
  1. Shopping -- Fiction 2. Festivals -- Fiction
  ISBN 978-1-84686-147-5; 1-84686-147-0
                LC 2008043900

When his mother sends him to the market to buy necessities for the upcoming festival, Lin Yi is certain his bargaining skills will get him the best prices and he will have money left over for his coveted red rabbit lantern

"Handsome, stylized gouache illustrations portray the Chinese characters and scenes from a variety of perspectives. . . . The length of the narrative and accompanying cultural information make this an excellent supplement for primary multicultural units." Booklist

Williams, C. K.
  A **not** scary story about big scary things; illustrated by Gabi Swiatkowska. Harcourt Children's Books 2010 un il $16.99
Grades: PreK K 1 2 **E**
  1. Fear -- Fiction 2. Monsters -- Fiction
  ISBN 978-0-15-205466-3; 0-15-205466-9

A little boy walking through an ordinary forest encounters an extraordinary monster.

"Sharing a surreal sense of logic and elegance, Williams and Swiatkowska convey a mood that's both dreamy and reassuringly matter-of-fact. Swiatkowska . . . is in particularly fine form, with wry drawings that range from florid to schematic, and clever collages that underscore the silliness of conventional wisdom." Publ Wkly

Williams, Karen Lynn
  Four feet, two sandals; written by Karen Lynn Williams and Khadra Mohammed; illustrated by Doug Chayka. Eerdmans Books for Young Readers 2007 un il $17
Grades: 2 3 4 **E**
  1. Shoes -- Fiction 2. Refugees -- Fiction 3. Friendship -- Fiction
  ISBN 978-0-8028-5296-0
                LC 2006002635

Two young Afghani girls living in a refugee camp in Pakistan share a precious pair of sandals brought by relief workers

"The thickly brushed, double-page paintings show the long lines of desperate refugees and then close-ups of the two Muslim girls. . . . This is a personal drama behind the daily news." Booklist

  Galimoto; illustrated by Catherine Stock. Lothrop, Lee & Shepard Bks. 1990 un il $16.95; pa $6.99

Grades: PreK K 1 2   E
1. Toys -- Fiction
ISBN 0-688-08789-2; 0-688-10991-8 pa

LC 89-2258

"In Malawi, Africa, according to the author's note, gali-moto are intricate and popular push toys crafted by children. Williams tells the story of seven-year-old Kondi's quest to find ample scrap material to fashion his own toy pickup truck. . . . Kondi's perseverance and the pleasure he takes in his accomplishment are just two of the delights of this appealing story. Stock's graceful watercolors portray life in a bustling village and include enough detail . . . to give readers the flavor of a day in this southern African nation." Horn Book

My name is Sangoel; written by Karen Lynn Williams and Khadra Mohammed; illustrated by Catherine Stock. Eerdmans Books for Young Readers 2009 un il $17
Grades: 1 2 3   E
1. Refugees -- Fiction 2. Immigrants -- Fiction 3. Personal names -- Fiction 4. Sudanese Americans -- Fiction
ISBN 978-0-8028-5307-3; 0-8028-5307-2

LC 2008-31735

As a refugee from Sudan to the United States, Sangoel is frustrated that no one can pronounce his name correctly until he finds a clever way to solve the problem.

"Stock's bright watercolor scenarios, accentuated with thick black lines, express the wrenching leave-taking and then the combination of exciting new things, . . . as well as disorienting ones. . . . [This is a] moving story." Booklist

Painted dreams; pictures by Catherine Stock. Lothrop, Lee & Shepard Bks. 1998 un il hardcover o.p. lib bdg $15.93
Grades: PreK K 1 2   E
1. Artists -- Fiction 2. Painting -- Juvenile fiction
ISBN 0-688-13901-9; 0-688-13902-7 lib bdg

LC 97-32920

Because her Haitian family is too poor to be able to buy paints for her, eight-year-old Ti Marie finds her own way to create pictures that make the heart sing

"Beautifully composed and full of life, Stock's watercolors suggest the personalities of the characters through their expressions and gestures." Booklist

★ A **beach** tail; illustrated by Floyd Cooper. Boyds Mills Press 2010 un il $17.95
Grades: PreK K 1 2   E
1. Beaches -- Fiction 2. African Americans -- Fiction 3. Father-son relationship -- Fiction
ISBN 978-1-59078-712-0; 1-59078-712-9

"At the beach with his father, Greg strays from his beach umbrella, but stays calm and remembers the two things Dad told him: 'Don't go in the water, and don't leave Sandy.' Sandy is a lion Greg has drawn in the sand, and because Greg hasn't lifted the stick with which he has drawn Sandy's long, long tail . . . he's able to retrace his steps to find his father. . . . Cooper . . . draws a startlingly real Greg in a series of tight closeups. . . . Grainy pastel and washed-out color evoke the seashore's bleached palette. . . . Williams's . . . even pacing and soothing text reassure children without losing momentum." Publ Wkly

Williams, Laura E.
The **Can** Man; illustrated by Craig Orback. Lee & Low 2010 un il $18.95
Grades: K 1 2 3   E
1. Homeless persons -- Fiction
ISBN 1-60060-266-5; 978-1-60060-266-5

"Tim wants a skateboard badly, but money is tight. Watching a homeless man every calls the Can Man . . . collect cans to redeem for cash, Tim decides to do the same to bankroll his skateboard. . . . Orback's . . . realistic oil paintings on canvas bring the tale's urban setting into clear focus in warmly lit scenes that illuminate the characters' feelings." Publ Wkly

Williams, Linda
★ The **little** old lady who was not afraid of anything; illustrated by Megan Lloyd. Crowell 1986 un il
Grades: PreK K 1 2   E
1. Fear -- Fiction
ISBN 0-06-443183-5 pa; 0-690-04584-0; 0-690-04586-7 lib bdg

LC 85-48250

Coming home late to her cabin by the woods, a fearless little old lady "sees two big shoes in her path. . . . She tells them to get out of the way, but they follow her, going 'CLOMP, CLOMP.' Shoes are followed by pants, 'WIGGLE, WIGGLE'; shirt, 'SHAKE, SHAKE'; gloves, 'CLAP, CLAP'; hat, 'NOD, NOD'; and, finally, a scary pumpkin, 'BOO, BOO.' Even the intrepid little old lady is a little shaken by this, and she runs home. She finally helps them all . . . by suggesting they become a scarecrow." (Horn Book) "Preschool to grade two." (SLJ)

"A delightful picture book, perfect for both independent reading pleasure and for telling aloud." SLJ

Williams, Sherley Anne
Working cotton; written by Sherley Anne Williams; illustrated by Carole Byard. Harcourt Brace Jovanovich 1992 un il hardcover o.p. pa $7
Grades: PreK K 1 2   E
1. Cotton -- Fiction 2. Migrant labor -- Fiction 3. African Americans -- Fiction
ISBN 0-15-299624-9; 0-15-201482-9 pa

LC 91-21586

A Caldecott Medal honor book, 1993

A young black girl relates the daily events of her family's migrant life in the cotton fields of central California

"Byard's acrylic paintings contribute weight and emotion to Williams's spare text. The fields and family members fill each full-page spread, drawing the reader very close to the action of the story. The mural-like paintings glow with blue and brown tones, recreating the textures and hues of the cotton fields. Williams's text, based on her poems, has a lyrical, rhythmic quality." Horn Book

Williams, Sue
Let's go visiting; written by Sue Williams; illustrated by Julie Vivas. Harcourt Brace & Co. 1998 un il hardcover o.p. pa $7; bd bk $6.95
Grades: PreK K   E
1. Counting 2. Stories in rhyme 3. Domestic animals

-- Fiction
ISBN 0-15-201823-9; 0-15-202410-7 pa; 0-15-204638-0 bd bk

LC 97-34398

A counting story in which a boy visits his farmyard friends, from one brown foal to six yellow puppies

"The bold illustrations, simple yet full of motion, combine with a lively text to make this perfect for toddler story hours." Booklist

Williams, Suzanne

Library Lil; illustrated by Steven Kellogg. Dial Bks. for Young Readers 1997 un il $16.99; pa $6.99

Grades: PreK K 1 2 3   E

1. Tall tales 2. Librarians -- Fiction 3. Books and reading -- Fiction
ISBN 0-8037-1698-2; 0-14-056837-9 pa

LC 95-23490

A formidable librarian makes readers not only out of the once resistant residents of her small town, but out of a tough-talking, television-watching motorcycle gang as well

"The silliness of both story and pictures are perfectly matched. Kellogg's distinctive toothy kids and laughing cats crowd the pages, fitting right in with the baby-faced biker banditos." SLJ

Williams, Treat

Air show! pictures by Robert Neubecker. Disney Hyperion 2010 un il $16.99

Grades: PreK K   E

1. Siblings -- Fiction 2. Airplanes -- Fiction
ISBN 978-1-4231-1185-6; 1-4231-1185-0

"Williams' story follows a sister and brother, Ellie and Gill, as their father flies them to the show, gives them a grand tour, and surprises Ellie with a trip in a stunt plane. . . . It's Neubecker's artwork that really shines here. . . . The large-scale, double page spreads pack in interest, and the foldout, which features almost two dozen aircraft, from a 1916 Spad to a 2009 Boeing 787, provides enough detail for aviation buffs to pore over for hours." Booklist

Williams, Vera B.

★ **Cherries** and cherry pits. Greenwillow Bks. 1986 un il hardcover o.p. $17.99; pa $6.99

Grades: PreK K 1 2 3   E

1. Drawing -- Fiction 2. African Americans -- Fiction
ISBN 0-688-05145-6; 0-688-05146-4 lib bdg; 0-688-10478-9 pa

LC 85-17156

"Williams' portraits of Bidemmi drawing are done in watercolor; the drawings Bidemmi makes are done with bright markers, some being simple sketches, others filling the page with color, looking like naive, but glorious icons. The interior stories are well integrated with each other, and the whole adds up to a study of child as artist that is fresh, vibrant, and exciting." Bull Cent Child Books

Lucky song. Greenwillow Bks. 1997 un il $16.99

Grades: PreK K 1   E

1. Day -- Fiction 2. Kites -- Fiction 3. Songs -- Fiction
ISBN 0-688-14459-4

LC 96-7151

"Evie flies the kite made by her grandfather until it's time to go home for supper all tired and ready for bed. This patterned story, showing a little girl surrounded by a loving family, ends by circling back to the beginning. It is illustrated using brilliantly colored watercolors." Child Book Rev Serv

★ **More** more more said the baby; 3 love stories. Greenwillow Bks. 1990 un il $17.99; lib bdg $18.89; pa $6.99; bd bk $7.99

Grades: PreK K 1   E

1. Infants -- Fiction 2. Family life -- Fiction
ISBN 0-688-09173-3; 0-688-09174-1 lib bdg; 0-688-814736-4 pa; 0-688-15634-7 bd bk

LC 89-2023

A Caldecott Medal honor book, 1991

Three babies are caught up in the air and given loving attention by a father, grandmother, and mother

"The pages reverberate with bright colors and vigorous forms, and the rhythmic language begs to be read aloud." Horn Book Guide

★ **Stringbean's** trip to the shining sea; greetings from Vera B. Williams, story and pictures; and Jennifer Williams, more pictures. Greenwillow Bks. 1987 un il hardcover o.p. $18.99; pa $7.99

Grades: K 1 2 3   E

1. Automobile travel -- Fiction
ISBN 0-688-07161-9; 0-688-07162-7 lib bdg; 0-688-16701-2 pa

LC 86-29502

"The use of mixed media—watercolors, Magic Markers, and colored pencils—is as aesthetically pleasing as it is skillful. Nothing has been forgotten; nothing more needs to be added. Not for the usual picture-book set, this travelogue storybook will appeal to slightly older audiences." Horn Book

Three days on a river in a red canoe. Greenwillow Bks. 1984 un il hardcover o.p. pa $6.99

Grades: K 1 2 3   E

1. Camping -- Fiction 2. Canoes and canoeing -- Fiction
ISBN 0-688-84307-7 lib bdg; 0-688-04072-1 pa

LC 80-23893

In this book, a "canoe trip for two children and two adults is recorded with all its interesting detail in a spontaneous first-person account and engaging full-color drawings on carefully designed pages. Driving to a river site, making camp, paddling the craft, negotiating a waterfall, swimming, fishing, dealing with a sudden storm, and even rescuing one overboard child are all described as important incidents in a summertime adventure." Horn Book

★ **A chair** for my mother. Greenwillow Bks. 1982 un il $15.99; lib bdg $16.89; pa $6.99

Grades: PreK K 1 2 3   E

1. Chairs -- Fiction 2. Family life -- Fiction 3. Saving and investment -- Fiction
ISBN 0-688-00914-X; 0-688-00915-8 lib bdg; 0-688-04074-8 pa

LC 81-7010

A Caldecott Medal honor book, 1983

Rosa, her waitress mother, and her grandmother save dimes to buy a comfortable armchair after all their furniture is lost in a fire

"The cheerful paintings take up the full left-hand page and face, in most cases, a small chunk of the text set against a modulated wash of a complementing color; a border containing a pertinent motif surrounds the two pages, further unifying the design. The result is a superbly conceived picture book expressing the joyful spirit of a loving family." Horn Book

Other titles about Rosa and her family are:

Music, music for everyone (1984)

Something special for me (1983)

A chair for always (2009)

Willis, Jeanne

★ **Cottonball** Colin; illustrated by Tony Ross. Eerdmans Books for Young Readers 2008 un il $16

Grades: PreK K 1 2   E

1. Mice -- Fiction 2. Size -- Fiction 3. Mother-son relationship -- Fiction

ISBN 978-0-8028-5331-8; 0-8028-5331-5

LC 2007009356

Afraid that her smallest child, Colin, will be hurt if he goes outside or plays, a mother mouse insists that he sit quietly indoors until his grandmother suggests wrapping him in cotton wool, which proves to be effective, but in a most unexpected way.

"Ross's elegant watercolor and ink drawings take Colin from domestic comedy to thrilling action-adventure without a hitch, and make his transformation from nebbish to cool dude totally believable." Publ Wkly

Gorilla! Gorilla! [by] Jeanne Willis and [illustrated by] Tony Ross. Simon & Schuster 2006 un il $15.95

Grades: PreK K 1 2   E

1. Mice -- Fiction 2. Gorillas -- Fiction

ISBN 978-1-4169-1490-7; 1-4169-1490-0

"While searching for her lost baby, a mouse is chased by a great, big, hairy, scary ape! . . . Young readers will guess what the mother mouse, in her terror, can't see—that the seemingly fierce gorilla is simply trying to return her baby to her. The brief, lively text and the melodramatic refrain make for a humorous and boisterous read-aloud. Ross's bright pastel illustrations capture the mouse's fear and the gorilla's determination with verve." SLJ

Mommy, do you love me? [by] Jeanne Willis; illustrated by Jan Fearnley. Candlewick Press 2008 un il $15.99

Grades: PreK   E

1. Love -- Fiction 2. Chickens -- Fiction 3. Mother-child relationship -- Fiction

ISBN 978-0-7636-3470-4; 0-7636-3470-0

"Through a series of tests—deliberate and not—a chick becomes almost totally convinced that his mother's affections are unshakable. Then, provoked by her son's almost manic cheeping, his mother momentarily loses it, and Little Chick is himself shaken. The mother hen repairs the breach with some unconditional reassurance. . . . Working in warm, translucent watercolors and velvety black outlines, Fearnley . . . gives her characters an endearing depth of expression and personality." Publ Wkly

★ **Susan** laughs; illustrated by Tony Ross. Holt & Co. 2000 un il $15

Grades: PreK K 1   E

1. Play 2. Emotions 3. Stories in rhyme 4. Play

-- Fiction 5. People with disabilities 6. Physically handicapped -- Fiction

ISBN 0-8050-6501-6

LC 99-59560

Rhyming couplets describe a wide range of common emotions and activities experienced by a little girl who uses a wheelchair

"Without being condescending or preachy, the words, pictures, and design of this very simple picture book show that a physically disabled child is 'just like me, just like you.' Only on the very last page do we discover that Susan uses a wheelchair." Booklist

★ The **bog** baby; written by Jeanne Willis; illustrated by Gwen Millward. Schwartz & Wade Books 2009 un il $16.99; lib bdg $19.99

Grades: K 1 2 3   E

1. Magic -- Fiction 2. Sisters -- Fiction

ISBN 978-0-375-86176-5; 0-375-86176-9; 978-0-375-96176-2 lib bdg; 0-375-96176-3 lib bdg

LC 2008-47635

First published 2008 in the United Kingdom

When two sisters go fishing in a magic pond, they find a winged blue bog baby and take it home with them.

"The glorious illustrations reveal a lush dreamscape of a backyard flush with tendrils, bluebells, Queen Anne's lace, birch trees, cherry trees, dragonflies, ladybugs, and more, all delicately and minutely drawn, and painted in watercolors. The child-voiced, economical narrative transports readers into the squelches and squeaks of tromping through the mud and spring plants." SLJ

Wilson, Karma

★ **Bear** snores on; illustrations by Jane Chapman. Margaret K. McElderry Bks. 2002 un il $16; bd bk $7.99

Grades: PreK K 1   E

1. Stories in rhyme 2. Bears -- Fiction 3. Animals -- Fiction 4. Parties -- Fiction

ISBN 0-689-83187-0; 1-4169-0272-4 bd bk

LC 00-28371

On a cold winter night many animals gather to party in the cave of a sleeping bear, who then awakes and protests that he has missed the food and the fun

"The characters are infused with warmth and humor. . . . The warm, soft tones of these acrylic illustrations perfectly capture the coziness of Bear's lair and capture the action." SLJ

Other titles in this series are:

Bear feels scared (2008)

Bear feels sick (2007)

Bear stays up for Christmas (2004)

Bear wants more (2003)

Bear's new friend (2006)

Bear's loose tooth; [illustrated by] Jane Chapman. Margaret K. McElderry Books 2011 il $16.99

Grades: K 1 2   E

1. Stories in rhyme 2. Bears -- Fiction 3. Teeth -- Fiction 4. Animals -- Fiction

ISBN 978-1-4169-5855-0; 1-4169-5855-X

LC 2009045690

When Bear discovers he has a loose tooth, his friends try to help make it fall out.

"With warm prose, comforting acrylics, and a healthy dose of physical comedy, the tale should amuse young readers." Publ Wkly

Hogwash; illustrated by Jim McMullan. Little, Brown 2011 un il $16.99

Grades: PreK K
E

1. Stories in rhyme 2. Pigs -- Fiction 3. Baths -- Fiction 4. Farmers -- Fiction 5. Cleanliness -- Fiction

ISBN 978-0-316-98840-7; 0-316-98840-5
LC 2010019754

When his stubborn pigs refuse a sudsy cleaning, a determined farmer learns that mud baths can be just as fun.

"Kids will be plenty entertained by the lanky, bespectacled Farmer's many disguises (and escalating frustration), but the crafty, confident, and expressive pigs hog the spotlight in every scene. It's a highly satisfying story." Publ Wkly

How to bake an American pie; illustrated by Raul Colón. Simon & Schuster 2007 un il $16.99

Grades: K 1 2 3
E

1. Stories in rhyme 2. Patriotism -- Fiction

ISBN 0-689-86506-6; 978-0-689-86506-0

Rhyming text and illustrations present a recipe for how to bake a pie from all the things that make America great.

"In these watercolor-and-ink paintings, the action rolls across the spreads in all sorts of fantastical ways. Purple mountain majesties grow out of teacups, and the cooks pull rainbows out of a sky studded with stars and stripes. . . . [This is a] wild, wonderful celebration." Booklist

Mama always comes home; illustrated by Brooke Dyer. HarperCollins 2005 un il $15.99; lib bdg $16.89

Grades: PreK K 1
E

1. Stories in rhyme 2. Animals -- Fiction 3. Mother-child relationship -- Fiction

ISBN 0-06-057505-0; 0-06-057506-9 lib bdg
LC 2003-26979

From Mama Bird to Mama Cat, mothers of all kinds come home to their children

"The consistently tender illustrations follow the text's well-crafted rhymes. . . . Presented with a delicate and loving touch, this book embodies the power of thoughtful text supported by insightful pictures." SLJ

Mama, why? illustrations by Simon Mendez. Margaret K. McElderry Books 2011 un il $16.99

Grades: PreK K 1
E

1. Stories in rhyme 2. Sky -- Fiction 3. Night -- Fiction 4. Bedtime -- Fiction 5. Polar bear -- Fiction 6. Mother-child relationship -- Fiction

ISBN 978-1-4169-4205-4; 1-4169-4205-X

A sleepy polar bear cub asks his mother questions about the night sky as he gets ready to go to sleep.

"Wilson's conversational style beautifully captures a homespun imagination and the feel of a mother's end-of-day murmurs to her 'dearest one.' There's genuine magic in Mendez's soft-focus arctic scenes, particularly the way his lighting conveys the warm glow of the moon, the glittering night, and the glacial air." Publ Wkly

Where is home, Little Pip? [by] Karma Wilson; illustrated by Jane Chapman. Margaret K. McElderry Books 2008 un il $16.99

Grades: PreK K 1
E

1. Animals -- Fiction 2. Penguins -- Fiction

ISBN 978-0-689-85983-0; 0-689-85983-X
LC 2006019094

After Little Pip the penguin gets lost she meets a whale, a kelp gull, and sled dogs who cannot help her, but with the aid of her family's song, home finds her

"Well-structured text, genuine emotions, and beautiful full-bleed illustrations in a palette that ranges from cool whites and blues to warm pinks, corals, and tans combine to produce a wonderful story of a loving family separated and then reunited." SLJ

Other titles about Little Pip are:
Don't be afraid, Little Pip (2009)
What's in the egg, Little Pip? (2010)

Whopper cake; [by] Karma Wilson; [illustrated by] Will Hillenbrand. Margaret K. McElderry Books 2007 un il $16.99

Grades: PreK K 1 2
E

1. Tall tales 2. Stories in rhyme 3. Cake -- Fiction 4. Birthdays -- Fiction

ISBN 0-689-83844-1
LC 00058742

Grandad bakes Grandma a whopper of a birthday cake. Includes recipe and directions for chocolate cake

"Rendered in ink and egg tempera, Hillenbrand's illustrations spill off the spreads." SLJ

The **cow** loves cookies; illustrated by Marcellus Hall. Margaret K. McElderry Books 2010 un il $16.99

Grades: PreK K 1 2
E

1. Stories in rhyme 2. Cattle -- Fiction 3. Cookies -- Fiction 4. Farmers -- Fiction 5. Domestic animals -- Fiction

ISBN 978-1-4169-4206-1; 1-4169-4206-8
LC 2009-00742

While all the other animals on the farm enjoy eating their regular food, the cow chooses to eat the one thing that she loves best.

"The big, clear watercolor pictures with thick ink lines leave lots of white space, and the simple rhyming lines, with descriptive words and messy action, will encourage preschoolers to join in." Booklist

A **frog** in the bog; [illustrated by] Joan Rankin. Margaret K. McElderry Bks. 2003 un il $16.95

Grades: PreK K 1
E

1. Frogs 2. Insects 3. Counting 4. Alligators 5. Stories in rhyme 6. Frogs -- Fiction 7. Insects -- Fiction

ISBN 0-689-84081-0
LC 2002-5903

A frog in the bog grows larger and larger as he eats more and more bugs, until he attracts the attention of an alligator who puts an end to his eating

"This gastronomic adventure is told in catchy rhyming verse, complemented by soft, dreamy watercolors that perfectly recreate the bog. The illustrations are enhanced by humorous details." SLJ

Wilson, Sarah

Friends and pals and brothers, too; illustrated by Leo Landry. Holt 2008 un il $16.95

Grades: PreK K 1 2   E

1. Stories in rhyme 2. Seasons -- Fiction 3. Brothers -- Fiction 4. Friendship -- Fiction

ISBN 978-0-8050-7643-1; 0-8050-7643-3

LC 2007002829

Two brothers who are best friends have fun together throughout the year

"Told in uncomplicated verse, one short line per page, this unassuming book captures the warmth and delight of being best friends. The rhyming is easy and predictable. . . . The childlike, unembellished watercolor and pencil illustrations fit the text perfectly, and the muted colors underscore the simplicity and joyful intimacy of the boys' relationship." SLJ

The day we danced in underpants; by Sarah Wilson; illustrations by Catherine Stock. Tricycle Press 2008 un il $14.95

Grades: PreK K 1   E

1. Stories in rhyme 2. Dance -- Fiction 3. Kings and rulers -- Fiction

ISBN 978-1-58246-205-9; 1-58246-205-4

LC 2007018172

When Papa's pants—worn thin from dancing on his visit to France—split as he sits down to picnic with the king, the embarrassing moment provides both cooling and comic relief for the guests, prompting them to take off their hot clothes and dance.

"Jaunty rhymed text and colorful pen-and-ink, watercolor, and collage illustrations evoke the joyous movement of dance." Horn Book Guide

Wimmer, Sonja

The word collector. Cuento de Luz 36 p. $15.95

Grades: 1 2 3   E

1. New words 2. Picture books for children

ISBN 8415241348; 9788415241348

This children's picture book tells of Luna, who lives in the sky and collects words. "But one day the words stop coming. Luna learns that the people have become too busy to remember the importance of words. With her collection, she travels across the land. Where Luna finds darkness and despair she plants words of compassion and love. When her words run out, people begin to create—and generously share—new words." (Kirkus)

Wing, Natasha

Go to bed, monster! written by Natasha Wing; illustrated by Sylvie Kantorovitz. Harcourt 2007 un il $16

Grades: PreK K 1   E

1. Bedtime -- Fiction 2. Monsters -- Fiction

ISBN 978-0-15-205775-6

LC 2006010849

Trying to avoid bedtime, Lucy uses her imagination and some crayons to draw a monster to play with.

"Kantorovitz's whimsical ink-and-watercolor pictures on open white backgrounds . . . are perfectly paired to Wing's engaging and breezy text and characters." SLJ

Winstanley, Nicola

Cinnamon baby; [text by] Nicola Winstanley; [illustrations by] Janice Nadeau. Kids Can Press 2011 un il $16.95

Grades: PreK K 1 2   E

1. Baking -- Fiction 2. Infants -- Fiction 3. Racially mixed people -- Fiction

ISBN 1-55337-821-0; 978-1-55337-821-1

Miriam the baker marries Sebastian and they have a baby who won't stop crying, until the smell of Miriam's cinnamon bread calms it.

"Both the words and pictures engage the senses in a heady, tangled mix. . . . Miriam is paper white, Sebastian is cocoa brown, and their cinammon-colored child gives the title a sly double meaning. A charming offering infused with warmth, romantic whimsy, and love." Booklist

Winter, Jeanette

Angelina's island. Farrar, Straus & Giroux 2007 un il $16

Grades: K 1 2 3   E

1. Immigrants -- Fiction

ISBN 978-0-374-30349-5; 0-374-30349-5

LC 2005052752

Every day, Angelina dreams of her home in Jamaica and imagines she is there, until her mother finds a wonderful way to convince her that New York is now their home

"Using simple, poetic text and small, framed, brilliantly colored pictures, Winter sets the child's two worlds on opposite sides of each double-page spread." Booklist

★ Biblioburro; a true story from Colombia. Beach Lane Books 2010 un il

Grades: PreK K 1 2   E

1. Libraries 2. Books and reading 3. Reading teachers 4. Elementary school teachers

ISBN 1416997784; 9781416997788

"After amassing piles of books, Luis, a voracious reader, dreams up a way to share his collection with 'faraway villages.' He starts with two burros—one for himself, one for books—and heads off. Tough terrain and menacing bandits challenge him along the way, but at last he reaches a remote town, where he holds a story hour and loans titles to eager kids before returning home to his wife and reading late into the night. Winter's captivating paintings evoke a South American feel in their brilliant palette and dense, green tropical scenes teeming with creatures, including large, orange-winged butterflies on every page. . . . Winter's text is spare and streamlined, as usual, and here it has a particularly engaging, repetitive rhythm that builds into a lulling bedtime beat." Booklist

★ Calavera abecedario; a Day of the Dead alphabet. Harcourt 2004 un il $16

Grades: PreK K 1 2   E

1. Alphabet 2. All Souls' Day -- Mexico 3. All Souls' Day -- Fiction 4. Spanish language -- Vocabulary

ISBN 0-15-205110-4

LC 2004-1554

Every year Don Pedro makes papier-mache skeletons, or calaveras, for Mexico's Day of the Dead fiesta. From Angel to Unicornio, each letter of the alphabet has its own special calavera. Spanish words illustrate each letter of the alphabet.

This "features jaunty illustrations inspired by Mexican folk art. . . . This is a lovely book that approaches the Day of the Dead from an unusual angle." SLJ

★ **Follow** the drinking gourd; story and pictures by Jeanette Winter. Alfred A. Knopf 2008 un il hardcover o.p. pa $7.99
Grades: K 1 2 3   E
1. Slavery -- Fiction 2. African Americans -- Fiction 3. Underground railroad -- Fiction
ISBN 978-0-394-89694-6; 978-0-679-81997-4 pa
A reissue of the title first published 1988

By following directions in a song, taught them by an old sailor, runaway slaves journey north along the Underground Railroad to freedom in Canada.

"Complementing the few lines of text per page are dark-hued illustrations horizontally framed with a fine black line and plenty of white space. . . . The art carries the weight of introducing children to a riveting piece of U.S. history, and the music included at the end of the book will fix it in their minds." Bull Cent Child Books

Kali's song; Jeanette Winter. Schwartz & Wade Books 2012 40 p.
Grades: PreK K 1 2   E
1. Music -- Fiction 2. Mammoths -- Fiction 3. Bow and arrow -- Fiction 4. Picture books for children 5. Prehistoric peoples -- Fiction 6. Hunting -- Fiction 7. Cave dwellers -- Fiction
ISBN 9780375870224; 9780375970221
LC 2011009357

In this illustrated children's book, "[w]hen young Kali . . . is given a bow to practice hunting, he discovers that if he puts it to his mouth and plucks the string he can make music. . . . [W]hen the big hunt occurs, Kali stuns everyone by playing his bow so musically that even the herd of mammoths is entranced. The people decide that Kali is a shaman . . . and he lives out his days healing and guiding his community." (Bulletin of the Center for Children's Books)

★ **Mama**; a true story in which a baby hippo loses his mama during a tsunami, but finds a new home, and a new mama. Harcourt 2006 un il $16
Grades: PreK K 1 2   E
1. Turtles 2. Hippopotamus 3. Indian Ocean earthquake and tsunami, 2004
ISBN 978-0-15-205495-3; 0-15-205495-2
LC 2005-20905

Set against the backdrop of the devastating 2004 tsunami, this book reveals the true story of a rescued baby hippo who adopts a new "mother" —a 130-year-old male tortoise

"This visually poetic book's subtitle is longer than its entire text. . . . Winter reassuringly portrays how friendship can ease a devastating loss." Publ Wkly

★ **September** roses. Farrar, Straus & Giroux 2004 un il $14
Grades: PreK K 1 2 3   E
1. Roses 2. September 11 terrorist attacks, 2001
ISBN 0-374-36736-1
LC 2003-54877

"Two sisters fly to New York from South Africa with thousands of roses meant for a flower show. The day they fly is September 11, 2001, and after the attack they are stranded at the airport with their flowers. They are offered shelter and offer their roses in return: at Union Square, they design two fallen towers made of roses. Winter . . . makes beautiful patterns with her figures and her roses using her signature thick black outlines. . . . This is understated and full of tenderness." Booklist

Winter, Jonah
★ **Here** comes the garbage barge! written by Jonah Winter; illustrated by Red Nose Studio. Schwartz & Wade Books 2010 un il $17.99; lib bdg $20.99
Grades: K 1 2   E
1. Voyages and travels -- Fiction 2. Refuse and refuse disposal -- Fiction 3. Refuse and refuse disposal -- Juvenile literature
ISBN 978-0-375-85218-3; 0-375-85218-2; 978-0-375-95218-0 lib bdg; 0-375-95218-7 lib bdg
LC 2008-40709

In the spring of 1987, the town of Islip, New York, with no place for its 3,168 tons of garbage, loads it on a barge that sets out on a 162-day journey along the east coast, around the Gulf of Mexico, down to Belize, and back again, in search of a place willing to accept and dispose of its very smelly cargo

"A fictionalized account of real events. . . . The illustrations are photographs of objects made from garbage. The people, full of personality and expression, were made from polymer clay, and wire, wood scraps, and leftover materials of all kinds were used for the tugboat and barge. The inside of the paper jacket explains how the art was done. This title should be a part of every elementary school ecology unit." SLJ

★ **Steel** Town; illustrated by Terry Widener. Atheneum Books for Young Readers 2008 un il $16.99
Grades: 2 3 4   E
1. Children's poetry 2. Factories -- Fiction 3. Steel industry -- Fiction 4. Cities and towns -- Fiction 5. Steel industry and trade -- Juvenile literature ISBN 978-1-4169-4081-4; 1-4169-4081-2
LC 2006-29284

In Steel Town, it's always raining, freight trains come and go, the big furnace roars, and the steel mill never sleeps.

"The acrylic artwork creates an atmosphere of gloom with fiery furnaces and gray skies. Against this backdrop is the rhythmic, repetitive language detailing a day in the life of Steel Town. . . . Both informative and visually stunning, . . . beautifully written and powerfully illustrated." SLJ

★ The **fabulous** feud of Gilbert & Sullivan; illustrated by Richard Egielski. Arthur A. Levine Books 2009 un il hardcover o.p. $16.99
Grades: K 1 2 3   E
1. Authors 2. Composers 3. Dramatists 4. Librettists 5. Authors -- Fiction 6. Operetta -- Fiction 7. Composers -- Fiction 8. Theatrical directors
ISBN 978-0-439-93050-5; 0-439-93050-2; 978-0-439-93051-2 pa; 0-439-93051-0 pa
LC 2008-27027

In the late nineteenth century, Mr. Gilbert and Mr. Sullivan, who write operas together for a theater called Topsy-Turvydom, have a falling-out when Mr. Sullivan refuses to write music for another ridiculous story that is like all the others.

"The clearly written story comes alive in a series of distinctive ink-and-watercolor illustrations that are full of intriguing details and show great skill in the use of color, shading, and composition." Booklist

Winters, Kay

My teacher for President; illustrated by Denise Brunkus. Dutton Children's Books 2004 un il $14.99

Grades: PreK K 1 2   E

1. Schools 2. Teachers

ISBN 0-525-47186-3

LC 2003-19222

A second-grader writes a television station with reasons why his teacher would make a good president, but only if she can continue teaching till the end of the year

"Brunkus' cheerful illustrations show a gray-haired woman in large, round glasses. . . . The humorous tone brings lofty ideals about desirable presidential qualities down to an everyday, accessible level." Booklist

This school year will be the best! illustrated by Renée Andriani. Dutton Children's Books 2010 un il $16.99

Grades: K 1 2   E

1. School stories

ISBN 978-0-525-42275-4; 0-525-42275-7

When a teacher asks her students on the first day of school what they wish for in the coming year, the answers range from having a good school picture to receiving a perfect report card.

"The short text leaves plenty of space for Andriani to work in, and she uses it imaginatively, creating upbeat and sometimes comical ink-and-wash illustrations. A good discussion starter for the beginning of the school year." Booklist

Whooo's that? Harcourt Children's Book 2009 un il $9.99

Grades: PreK   E

1. Halloween -- Fiction

ISBN 978-0-15-206480-8; 0-15-206480-X

LC 2007039823

"'Whooo's that prancing . . . in the park?/Whooo's that . . . prowling in the dark?' Why, it's trick-or-treaters, of course, as revealed on the book's final page. The volume is enhanced by its appealing trim size, the many engaging lift-the-flaps, and the softly spooky and expressive characters waiting to be uncovered from behind toothy jack-o-lanterns." Horn Book Guide

Winthrop, Elizabeth

Shoes; illustrated by William Joyce. Harper & Row 1986 19p il lib bdg $16.89; pa $6.99

Grades: PreK K   E

1. Stories in rhyme 2. Shoes -- Fiction

ISBN 0-06-026592-2 lib bdg; 0-06-443171-1 pa

LC 85-45841

"This lilting rhyme about shoes and feet easily pleases. . . . Backing the verses are full-color drawings of children busily involved with one kind of shoe or another. Joyce's pictures are animated, energetic, and warmly colored." Booklist

Squashed in the middle; illustrated by Pat Cummings. Holt 2005 un il $16.95

Grades: PreK K 1 2   E

1. Family life -- Fiction 2. African Americans -- Fiction

ISBN 0-8050-6497-4

When Daisy, a middle child, is invited to spend the night at her friend's house, her family finally pays attention to her.

"Cummings' recognizable robust style and intense palette are evident in the engaging design here, a bright amalgamation of bold full-page closeups that clearly reflect Daisy's feelings. . . . Homey and whimsical details . . . give Daisy and her African American family a thoroughly modern, familiar look." Booklist

The biggest parade; [by] Elizabeth Winthrop; illustrated by Mark Ulriksen. Henry Holt 2006 un il $16.95

Grades: K 1 2 3   E

1. Dogs -- Fiction 2. Parades -- Fiction

ISBN 978-0-8050-7685-1; 0-8050-7685-9

LC 2005019753

Harvey is so excited when the mayor appoints him Parade Chairman for a big celebration that he forgets something very important but, fortunately, his dog, Fred, remembers

"Winthrop's tale . . . is fun and quirky, with lots of humor. . . . The acrylic paintings almost resemble photographs in their detail, and Fred's expressions are priceless." SLJ

Wiseman, Bernard

Morris and Boris at the circus; by B. Wiseman. Harper & Row 1988 64p il (I can read book) hardcover o.p. pa $3.99

Grades: PreK K 1 2   E

1. Bears -- Fiction 2. Moose -- Fiction 3. Circus -- Fiction

ISBN 0-06-026478-0 lib bdg; 0-06-444143-1 pa

LC 87-45682

"The cartoon illustrations with bold colors provide ample context clues for beginning readers. This delightful combination of text and illustrations will entice children to read and re-read this book." SLJ

Wishinsky, Frieda

Maggie can't wait; illustrated by Dean Griffiths. Fitzhenry & Whiteside 2009 un il $17.95

Grades: PreK K 1   E

1. Cats -- Fiction 2. Infants -- Fiction 3. Sisters -- Fiction 4. Adoption -- Fiction

ISBN 978-1-55455-103-3; 1-55455-103-X

Maggie the cat "is excited about the arrival of her newly adopted baby sister. But when she takes a picture of Rose to school, a mean-spirited nemesis dubs the baby ugly. . . . The drama of a cruel comment is fully realized in a manner and tone that children will identify with; Maggie's mortification is as believable as her triumph." SLJ

Another title about Maggie is:

Give Maggie a chance (2002)

Please, Louise! [by] Frieda Wishinsky; illustrated by Marie-Louise Gay. Groundwood Books 2007 un il $17.95

Grades: PreK K 1 2   E

1. Dogs -- Fiction 2. Siblings -- Fiction

ISBN 0-88899-796-5; 978-0-88899-796-8

Jake is annoyed that his little sister Louise won't leave him alone. He wishes Louise were a dog. Suddenly Louise is gone and a little dog appears to be in her place. Jake is worried that his wish may have come true.

"Deft pencil drawings, brightened with watercolor washes and collage elements, capture every nuance of the characters' emotions. . . . [The] story . . . unfolds with surprise and wit." Booklist

You're mean, Lily Jean! illustrated by Kady MacDonald Denton. Albert Whitman 2011 un il $16.99
Grades: PreK K 1 2   **E**
1. Play -- Fiction 2. Sisters -- Fiction 3. Friendship -- Fiction
ISBN 0-8075-9476-8; 978-0-8075-9476-6
         LC 2010027028
Sisters Carly and Sandy have always played together, but when Lily moves in next door she only wants to play with Sandy, and insists that if Carly joins them she must be a baby, or a cow, or a dog.

"Wishinsky re-creates a common childhood experience through realistic dialogue and actions that convery every emotional shift. Just as engaging, Denton's watercolor illustrations capture the girls' attitudes with gestures and facial expressions that speak volumes. Well paced and fine for reading aloud." Booklist

Witte, Anna
★ **Lola's** fandango; written by Anna Witte; illustrated by Micha Archer. Barefoot Books 2010 un il $16.99
Grades: K 1 2 3   **E**
1. Dance -- Fiction 2. Flamenco -- Fiction 3. Hispanic Americans -- Fiction
ISBN 978-1-84686-174-1; 1-84686-174-8
         LC 2008028143
After learning how to dance a style of flamenco known as the fandango, Lola plans a surprise for her mother's birthday.

"Witte and Archer hit all the right notes here. The text dances across the pages, with 'tacs' and 'tocs' and 'ticas' beating out the rhythm. The action, both external and internal, is visualized in the charming collage-style artwork. . . . A CD is included, and a Spanish-language version is also available." Booklist

The **parrot** Tico Tango; written and illustrated by Anna Witte. Barefoot Books 2004 un il $15.99; pa $6.99
Grades: PreK K 1 2   **E**
1. Stories in rhyme 2. Parrots -- Fiction 3. Rain forest animals -- Fiction
ISBN 1-84148-243-9; 1-84148-890-9 pa
         LC 2004-17922
A cumulative rhyme in which a greedy parrot keeps taking fruit from the other creatures of the rainforest until he can hold no more.

"The rhymes are unusually taut and rhythmic, and the mixed-media art, which features fabric swatches, amounts to a feast of tropical colors." Horn Book Guide

Wiviott, Meg
★ **Benno** and the Night of Broken Glass; illustrated by Josee Bisaillon. Kar-Ben Pub. 2010 un il lib bdg $17.95; pa $7.95
Grades: 2 3 4 5   **E**
1. Cats -- Fiction 2. Jews -- Germany -- Fiction 3.

Kristallnacht, 1938 -- Fiction 4. Holocaust, 1933-1945 -- Fiction
ISBN 978-0-8225-9929-6 lib bdg; 0-8225-9929-5 lib bdg; 978-0-8225-9975-3 pa; 0-8225-9975-9 pa
         LC 2008033482
In 1938 Berlin, Germany, a cat sees Rosenstrasse change from a peaceful neighborhood of Jews and Gentiles to an unfriendly place where, one November night, men in brown shirts destroy Jewish-owned businesses and arrest or kill Jewish people. Includes facts about Kristallnacht and a list of related books and web resources.

"The straightforward text describes events without sentimentality. . . . But what truly distinguishes this book is the striking multimedia artwork composed of paper, fabric, and drawn images in hues of olive, brown, and red. Interesting angles, textures, and patterns add to the visual effect throughout. . . . The message of terror and sadness that marks the beginning of the Holocaust is transmitted in a way that is both meaningful and comprehensible." SLJ

Includes bibliographical references

Wojciechowski, Susan
The **Christmas** miracle of Jonathan Toomey; illustrated by P. J. Lynch. Candlewick Press 2004 un il $12.99
Grades: 1 2 3 4   **E**
1. Christmas -- Fiction 2. Friendship -- Fiction 3. Wood carving -- Fiction
ISBN 0-7636-2621-X
A reissue of the title first published 1995
The widow McDowell and her seven-year-old son Thomas ask the gruff Jonathan Toomey, the best woodcarver in the valley, to carve the figures for a Christmas creche

"The story verges on the sentimental, but it's told with feeling and lyricism. . . . Lynch's sweeping illustrations, in shades of wood grain, are both realistic and gloriously romantic, focusing on faces and hands at work before the fire and in the lamplight." Booklist

A **fine** St. Patrick's day; illustrated by Tom Curry. Random House 2004 un il hardcover o.p. pa $6.99
Grades: K 1 2 3   **E**
1. Leprechauns 2. Saint Patrick's Day 3. Competition (Psychology) 4. Saint Patrick's Day -- Fiction
ISBN 0-375-82386-7; 978-0-385-73640-4 pa; 0-385-73640-1 pa
         LC 2002-11684
Two towns, Tralee and Tralah, compete in an annual St. Patrick's Day decorating contest which Tralah boastfully always wins, but when their hearts are put to the test by a little man with pointed ears, Tralee wins with no effort at all

"Wojciechowski's charming tale is beautifully complemented by Curry's stylized depictions of green rolling hills and thatched-roof houses. Both text and art convey a sturdy feeling about community and charity, brushed with touch of whimsy." Booklist

Wolf, Sallie
Truck stuck; illustrated by Andy Robert Davies. Charlesbridge 2008 un il $14.95
Grades: PreK K 1   **E**
1. Stories in rhyme 2. Trucks -- Fiction 3. Vehicles -- Fiction
ISBN 978-1-58089-119-6; 1-58089-119-5

"A red 18-wheeler gets stuck under a viaduct and causes a huge traffic jam. Nearby, two children who have a lemonade stand observe the incident and try to keep everyone cool by selling their wares. . . . Eventually, a huge tow truck arrives and, after the air has been let out of the semi's tires, the road is cleared for traffic to resume just in time, because the children are out of lemonade. The bright, flat, cartoon art brings the minimal rhyming text to life and really tells the story." SLJ

Wolff, Ashley

Baby Bear sees blue; Ashley Wolff. Beach Lane Books 2012 40 p.
Grades: PreK K 1   E
1. Bears -- Fiction 2. Color -- Fiction 3. Nature -- Fiction 4. Picture books for children 5. Mother-child relationship -- Fiction
ISBN 1442413069; 9781442413061
LC 2010005992

This picture book about a "mother bear and cub . . . introduces colors and images from the natural world. Between awakening in the den and cuddling down for the night, Baby Bear's day is full of new experiences and prescient questions. "A glow creeps in. / 'Who is warming me, Mama?'/ asks Baby Bear. / 'That is the sun,' Mama says." Page turns . . . deliver the color lessons: Silhouetted against the golden light of dawn, "Baby Bear sees yellow." The cub sees green oak leaves waving, smells fragrant red strawberries, and hears the growl of thunder against a stormy gray sky. [Ashley] Wolff's . . . compositions feature inked linoleum block prints that render those bears a strikingly deep, matte black. . . . [W]atercolors illuminate the scenes--colors in the downpour's puddles reflect a rainbow." (Kirkus)

Me baby, you baby. Dutton Children's Books 2004 un il $14.99
Grades: PreK   E
1. Zoos 2. Stories in rhyme 3. Babies 4. Zoos -- Fiction 5. Infants -- Fiction
ISBN 0-525-46952-4
LC 2003-45219

Simple rhyming text describes a day in the life of two babies as they greet the day, go to the zoo with their mothers, and return home at night.

"With its rhythmic text and delicate gouache artwork, this is a delightful book to share with two and three-year-olds." SLJ

Wolff, Ferida

It is the wind; illustrated by James Ransome. Harper-Collins 2005 un il $14.99; lib bdg $15.89
Grades: PreK K 1 2   E
1. Sound -- Fiction 2. Bedtime -- Fiction
ISBN 0-06-028191-X; 0-06-028192-8 lib bdg
LC 00-63197

"In his room at night, a boy looks outside and tries to imagine what is making the noise he hears. . . . The mesmerizing effect of the verse makes this a good bedtime story. . . . Ransome makes the most of the simple story with graceful scenes of the African American boy and the rural night scenes he sees and imagines." Booklist

The **story** blanket; [written by Ferida Wolff and Harriet May Savitz; illustrated by Elena Odriozola] Peachtree 2008 un il $16.95
Grades: K 1 2 3   E
1. Gifts -- Fiction 2. Blankets -- Fiction 3. Storytelling -- Fiction
ISBN 978-1-56145-466-2; 1-56145-466-4
LC 2008-08627

With no wool to be found in the village, Babba Zarrah, the storyteller, starts unraveling her story blanket bit by bit, to secretly supply the needs of the community, and when the villagers realize what is happening they return the favor.

"Colorful illustrations accompany this story of generosity and ingenuity. Rosy-cheeked children and the bright folk art quilt suggest a timelessness to the story as well as the underlying message." Libr Media Connect

Wondriska, William

A **long** piece of string. Chronicle Books 2010 un il $15.99
Grades: PreK K 1   E
1. Alphabet 2. String figures -- Fiction
ISBN 978-0-8118-7493-9; 0-8118-7493-1
First published 1963 by Holt

Follows a piece of string through images that correspond to the letters of the alphabet.

"The string's journey is a page-turning visual narrative that subtly reveals the connections among the various objects throughout the book." Horn Book Guide

Wong, Janet S.

Apple pie 4th of July; pictures by Margaret Chodos-Irvine. Harcourt 2002 un il $16
Grades: PreK K 1 2   E
1. Fourth of July -- Fiction 2. Chinese Americans -- Fiction
ISBN 0-15-202543-X
LC 2001-1313

A Chinese American girl fears that the food her parents are preparing to sell on the Fourth of July will not be eaten

"An appealing story with believable characters and emotions, written in the girl's spare, lyrical voice. Chodos-Irvine . . . captures the story's uncluttered, elemental qualities in opaque prints that resemble paper cutouts." Booklist

Buzz; illustrated by Margaret Chodos-Irvine. Harcourt 2000 un il $15
Grades: PreK K 1 2   E
1. Bees -- Fiction 2. Morning -- Fiction
ISBN 0-15-201923-5
LC 99-6148

"Chodos-Irvine's use of various print-making techniques results in illustrations that are strongly geometric and graphically clean, in springtime colors that suit the cheerful tone of the text. The humor in both text and pictures contributes to the light-hearted atmosphere." Bull Cent Child Books

Hide & seek; pictures by Margaret Chodos-Irvine. Harcourt 2005 un il $16
Grades: PreK K   E
1. Counting
ISBN 0-15-204934-7
LC 2003-27737

In this counting book, a child and parent play hide-and-seek while they bake cookies

"The rhythmic words capture the breathless excitement of searching and hiding, and Chodos-Irvine's prints, in her signature style of simple, dynamic shapes and bright, saturated hues, match the vibrant energy and elemental sounds in the simple words." Booklist

Homegrown house; illustrated by E.B. Lewis. Margaret K. McElderry Books 2009 un il $16.99
Grades: K 1 2 3   E
1. Home -- Fiction 2. Moving -- Fiction 3. Grandmothers -- Fiction
ISBN 978-0-689-84718-9; 0-689-84718-1
LC 2006038599

A young girl describes her grandmother's comfortable, long-time home, and wishes that she and her parents could stay in the same house instead of moving so often.

"Wong's poignant poem nicely captures a child's sense of powerlessness and disorientation. With his usual mastery and sensitivity, Lewis creates a true story from the words in sensitive scenes." Booklist

This next New Year; pictures by Yangsook Choi. Foster Bks. 2000 un il $16
Grades: PreK K 1 2   E
1. Chinese New Year 2. Chinese New Year -- Fiction
ISBN 0-374-35503-7
LC 99-22377

"Choi's smooth, brightly colored paintings . . . ably illustrate the optimistic activity and the yearning in the accessible, rhythmic text." Booklist

Wood, Audrey
Blue sky; Audrey Wood. The Blue Sky Press 2012 32p
Grades: PreK K 1 2 3   E
1. Sky 2. Children's stories 3. Picture books for children 4. Sky -- Fiction 5. Nature -- Fiction
ISBN 9780545316101
LC 2011010374

In this children's picture book, "a child and his family experience the fun of a sunny-sky day at the beach, then the electricity of a thunder-storm sky, and finally the magical delight of a rainbow sky. . . . Using only two words per page -- 'Blue Sky,' 'Cloud Sky,' 'Storm Sky' . . . [the book] will encourage young readers to make up their own simple descriptions of the sky above." (Publisher's note) Other illustrations depict "Wish Sky/ Sleep Sky/ Dream Sky." The illustrations were created with "pastel paper in deep colors for the backgrounds . . . [and] gouache highlights and colored pencils." (Kirkus)

Elbert's bad word; illustrated by Audrey and Don Wood. Harcourt Brace Jovanovich 1988 un il hardcover o.p. pa $7
Grades: K 1 2 3 4   E
1. Parties -- Fiction
ISBN 0-15-225320-3; 0-15-201367-9 pa
LC 86-7557

"A bad word, spoken by a small boy at a fashionable garden party, creates havoc, and the child, Elbert, gets his mouth scrubbed out with soap. The bad word, in the shape of a long-tailed furry monster, will not go away until a wizard-gardener cooks up some really delicious, super-long words that everyone at the party applauds. This single-idea cautionary tale has lively, absurdist pictures of tiara-crowned, formally dressed adults recoiling in horror or cavorting with glee when Elbert, the only child at the party, speaks a word." SLJ

★ **Heckedy** Peg; illustrated by Don Wood. Harcourt Brace Jovanovich 1987 un il lib bdg $17; pa $7
Grades: K 1 2 3 4   E
1. Fairy tales 2. Witches -- Fiction
ISBN 0-15-233678-8 lib bdg; 0-15-233679-6 pa
LC 86-33639

"The poor mother of seven children, each named for a day of the week, goes off to market promising to return with individual gifts that each child has requested and admonishing them to lock the door to strangers and not to touch the fire. The gullible children are tricked into disobeying their mother by the witch, Heckedy Peg, who turns them all into various kinds of food. The mother can rescue her children only by guessing which child is the fish, the roast rib, the bread. . . . This story, deep and rich with folk wisdom, is stunningly illustrated with Don Wood's luminous paintings. . . . With variety of color and line he enhances every nuance of the text." SLJ

★ **King** Bidgood's in the bathtub; written by Audrey Wood; illustrated by Don Wood. Harcourt Brace Jovanovich 1985 un il lib bdg $17
Grades: K 1 2 3 4   E
1. Baths -- Fiction 2. Kings and rulers -- Fiction
ISBN 0-15-242730-9
LC 85-5472

A Caldecott Medal honor book, 1986
Despite pleas from his court, a fun-loving king refuses to get out of his bathtub to rule his kingdom

"The few simple words of text per large, well-designed page invite story-telling—but keep the group very small, so the children can be close enough to pore over the brilliant, robust illustrations." SLJ

Piggy Pie Po; 3 little stories. written by Audrey Wood; pictures drawn by Audrey Wood and painted by Don Wood. Harcourt Children's Books 2010 un il $16.99
Grades: PreK K   E
1. Stories in rhyme 2. Pigs -- Fiction
LC 2001-01312

"Three vignettes follow the antics of an active and curious piglet. In the first narrative, the lovable character displays some of his special clothes and what he likes to do while wearing them. . . . In the next, children hear about all the things the little piggy is good at. . . . In the last tale, Piggy Pie Po arrives at dinner before the other guests and helps himself to the delicious feast but regrets his final, unfortunate sampling of a red hot pepper. The jolly, alliterative rhyme dances merrily on the tongue, and the paintings of the endearing pig's adventures are surrounded by generous white space." SLJ

The **deep** blue sea; a book of colors. story by Audrey Wood; pictures of Bruce Wood. Blue Sky Press 2005 un il $15.99

Grades: PreK K   E
1. Color
ISBN 0-439-75382-1
Introduces various colors by presenting a colorful scene on a rock in the deep blue sea.

"Sharply focused, vividly hued artwork makes this concept book a standout. . . . The rhythmic text is enticing and reads aloud smoothly." SLJ

A **dog** needs a bone; story and pictures by Audrey Wood. Blue Sky Press 2007 un il $16.99
Grades: PreK K 1   E
1. Stories in rhyme 2. Dogs -- Fiction
ISBN 978-0-545-00005-5; 0-545-00005-X; 978-0-545-00006-2 pa; 0-545-00006-8 pa

LC 2006035625

In this rhyming tale, a dog makes extravagant promises to its mistress if only she will give it a bone.

"Jovial, cartoonlike illustrations, drawn using crayons on brown paper bags, create a comfortable, homelike atmosphere and perfectly capture the animal's antics and expressions. . . . Filled with child appeal, it's sure to be a winner." SLJ

Wood, Don
★ **Piggies**; written by Don and Audrey Wood; illustrated by Don Wood. Harcourt Brace Jovanovich 1991 un il $17; pa $8; bd bk $5.95
Grades: PreK K 1 2   E
1. Pigs -- Fiction 2. Bedtime -- Fiction
ISBN 0-15-256341-5; 0-15-200217-0 pa; 0-15-202638-X bd bk

LC 89-24598

Ten little piggies dance on a young child's fingers and toes before finally going to sleep

"A happy text and luxuriant, witty pictures make this a book to pore over again and again." Booklist

★ The **napping** house. Harcourt Children's Books 2009 un il $17.99
Grades: K 1 2 3   E
1. Sleep -- Fiction
ISBN 978-0-15-256708-8; 0-15-256708-9

A reissue, with new audio CD, of the title first published 1984

"The cool blues and greens are superseded by warm colors and bursts of action as each sleeper wakes, ending in an eruption of color and energy as naptime ends. A deft matching of text and pictures adds to the appeal of cumulation, and to the silliness of the mound of sleepers—just the right kind of humor for the lap audience." Bull Cent Child Books

Wood, Douglas
Miss Little's gift; illustrated by Jim Burke. Candlewick Press 2009 un il $16.99
Grades: 1 2 3   E
1. Reading 2. Teachers 3. Hyperactive children 4. Attention deficit disorder
ISBN 978-0-7636-1686-1; 0-7636-1686-9

LC 2008-17915

"This autobiographical picture book chronicles the author's struggles in second grade. Smaller than everyone else, new in town, and speaking with an unfamiliar Southern accent, Wood also found reading to be a chore. . . . . The story

works as a tribute to those unsung teacher heroes whose dedication to their craft and native intuition about children have changed lives. . . . Burke's large, realistic oils, with their rich greens and blues, complement the story nicely." SLJ

What dads can't do; pictures by Doug Cushman. Simon & Schuster Bks. for Young Readers 2000 un il $14
Grades: PreK K   E
1. Fathers -- Fiction
ISBN 0-689-82620-6

LC 98-41773

"This amusing picture book will tickle youngsters' funny bones and make every parent and child smile with recognition. . . . Cushman's large, delightful, pen-and-ink and watercolor cartoons . . . capture perfectly the father-and-son interactions." SLJ
Other titles in this series are:
What grandmas can't do (2005)
What moms can't do (2000)
What Santa can't do (2003)
What teachers can't do (2000)

When a dad says "I love you" Douglas Wood; illustrated by Jennifer A. Bell. 1st ed. Simon & Schuster Books for Young Readers 2013 32 p. col. ill. (hardcover) $16.99
Grades: PreK K   E
1. Love -- Juvenile fiction 2. Father-child relationship -- Juvenile fiction 3. Love -- Fiction 4. Fathers -- Fiction 5. Father and child -- Fiction
ISBN 0689875320; 9780689875328

LC 2012013268

This children's picture book, by Douglas Wood, illustrated by Jennifer A. Bell, shows how "dads know how to do everything. They can help with homework and carry you on their shoulders. They can make pancakes and teach you how to sing songs. These loving actions are just some of the ways dads show how much they care." (Publisher's note)

Where the sunrise begins; words by Douglas Wood; art by Wendy Popp. Simon & Schuster Books for Young Readers 2010 un il $16.99
Grades: PreK K 1   E
1. Nature -- Fiction
ISBN 978-0-689-86172-7; 0-689-86172-9
Reveals the part that each of us plays in the beginning of every day.

"Science is in full view as the author searches for the place where the sunrise begins. The beautiful watercolor drawings complement the simple but rich text. Not only are different cultures revealed, but geography is also put on display as the author, a naturalist, explores the world trying to find exactly where the sunrise begins. What the book unveils will amaze and delight the reader." Libr Media Connect

Wood, Nancy C.
Mr. and Mrs. God in the Creation Kitchen; illustrated by Timothy Basil Ering. Candlewick Press 2006 un il $16.99
Grades: K 1 2   E
1. Creation -- Fiction
ISBN 0-7636-1258-8

LC 2005-53187

"Mr. and Mrs. God putter in the Creation Kitchen, first roasting Sun and Earth in their enormous oven, then whipping up Earth's creatures in between marital tiffs, finishing off with two jut-jawed humans and speculations about 'how they'll turn out.' . . . . Ering's artwork captures the puckish spirit of Wood's telling. Spattered with dribbles and cluttered with gadgets, this chaotic kitchen reinforces the creators' portrayal as anything but perfect." Booklist

Woodruff, Elvira

Small beauties; the journey of Darcy Heart O'Hara. by Elvira Woodruff; pictures by Adam Rex. Alfred A. Knopf 2006 un il $15.95

Grades: 1 2 3 4   E

1. Immigrants -- Fiction 2. Family life -- Fiction

ISBN 0-375-82686-6

        LC 2005016038

Darcy Heart O'Hara, a young Irish girl who neglects her chores to observe the beauties of nature and everyday life, shares "family memories" with her homesick parents and siblings after the O'Haras are forced to emigrate to America in the 1840s

"Woodruff's simple, poetic storytelling combines with Rex's illustrations in charcoal, graphite pencils, and oil to present the drama through Darcy's eyes." Booklist

The **memory** coat; story by Elvira Woodruff; illustrations by Michael Dooling. Scholastic Press 1999 un il $17.99

Grades: K 1 2 3   E

1. Jews -- Fiction 2. Immigrants -- Fiction

ISBN 0-590-67717-9

        LC 95-30048

In the early 1900s, cousins Rachel and Grisha leave their Russian shtetl with the rest of their family to come to America, hopeful that they will all pass the dreaded inspection at Ellis Island

This offers "warm, realistic period paintings, some in color, some in sepia shades. . . . In a long, interesting author's note, Woodruff discusses the shtetl and immigrant history." Booklist

Woodson, Jacqueline

★ **Coming** on home soon; illustrated by E.B. Lewis. Putnam's 2004 un il $16.99

Grades: K 1 2 3   E

1. Grandmothers -- Fiction 2. African Americans -- Fiction 3. World War, 1939-1945 -- Fiction 4. Mother-child relationship -- Fiction

ISBN 0-399-23748-8

        LC 2003-21949

A Caldecott Medal honor book, 2005

After Mama takes a job in Chicago during World War II, Ada Ruth stays with Grandma but misses her mother who loves her more than rain and snow.

"Woodson and Lewis tell a moving historical story of longing and separation. . . . Lewis' beautiful watercolors establish the setting. . . . Period and place are wonderfully specific." Booklist

★ **Each** kindness; Jacqueline Woodson; illustrated by E.B. Lewis. Nancy Paulsen Books 2012 32 p. $16.99

Grades: 1 2 3 4   E

1. Bullies -- Juvenile fiction 2. Kindness -- Juvenile fiction 3. Schools -- Fiction 4. Kindness -- Fiction 5.

Friendship -- Fiction

ISBN 0399246525; 9780399246524

        LC 2011046800

Charlotte Zolotow Award (2012)

Coretta Scott King Author Honor Book (2013)

In this book, "Chloe, Kendra, and Sophie are a tight trio, and when new girl Maya arrives, with her shabby clothes and obvious desperation, they resist her overtures of friendship. . . . When their teacher leads an exercise about kindness and its effects, Chloe realizes she can't think of any kind act she's ever done, and when Maya leaves her classroom never to return, Chloe realizes that she'll never be able to rectify her rejection." (Bulletin of the Center for Children's Books)

★ **Pecan** pie baby; illustrated by Sophie Blackall. G.P. Putnam's Sons 2010 un il

Grades: PreK K 1   E

1. Infants -- Fiction 2. Siblings -- Fiction 3. Pregnancy -- Fiction 4. African Americans -- Fiction 5. Mother-daughter relationship -- Fiction

ISBN 0-399-23987-1; 978-0-399-23987-8

When Mama's pregnancy draws attention away from Gia, she worries that the special bond they share will disappear forever once the baby is born. "Preschool, primary." (Horn Book)

"Blackall's apt watercolor-and-ink pictures capture the grounded serenity of a multiracial family (and community) with its priorities on straight. . . . Fresh and wise." Kirkus

★ **Show** way; illustrated by Hudson Talbott. G. P. Putnam's Sons 2005 un il $16.99

Grades: K 1 2 3   E

1. Quilts -- Fiction 2. Slavery -- Fiction 3. African Americans -- Fiction

ISBN 0-399-23749-6

        LC 2004-28093

A Newbery Medal honor book, 2006

The making of "Show ways," or quilts which once served as secret maps for freedom-seeking slaves, is a tradition passed from mother to daughter in the author's family.

"The gorgeous, multimedia art includes chalk, watercolors, and muslin. An outstanding tribute, perfectly executed in terms of text, design, and illustration." SLJ

This is the rope; a story from the Great Migration. Jacqueline Woodson; illustrated by James Ransome. Nancy Paulsen Books, an imprint of Penguin Group (USA) Inc. 2013 32 p. ill. (reinforced) $16.99

Grades: PreK K 1 2   E

1. Rope -- Juvenile fiction 2. African Americans -- Migrations -- History -- 20th century -- Fiction 3. Rope -- Fiction 4. Families -- Fiction 5. African Americans -- History -- Fiction 6. African Americans -- Migrations -- Fiction 7. African Americans -- History -- Juvenile fiction 8. African Americans -- Migrations -- Juvenile fiction

ISBN 0399239863; 9780399239861

        LC 2012036569

This children's story, by Jacqueline Woodson, illustrated by James Ransome, follows "one family's journey north during the Great Migration. . . . A little girl in South Carolina . . . finds a rope under a tree one summer. . . . For three generations, that rope is passed down, used for everything from jump rope games to tying suitcases onto a car for the big move north to New York City, and even for a family reunion where that first little girl is now a grandmother." (Publisher's note)

Visiting day; illustrated by James E. Ransome. Scholastic Press 2002 un il $15.95

Grades: K 1 2 3   **E**

1. Fathers -- Fiction 2. Prisoners -- Fiction 3. African Americans -- Fiction

ISBN 0-590-40005-3

LC 00-35772

A young girl and her grandmother visit the girl's father in prison

"The text is spare, gentle, and reassuring. . . . Ransome's vibrant acrylic paintings fill each page at home with intense pinks, yellows, greens, and blues in contrast to the monotone hue of the prison walls. Both author and illustrator provide notes that relate this story to their own personal experiences." SLJ

We had a picnic this Sunday past; illustrated by Diane Greenseid. Hyperion Bks. for Children 1998 un il pa $5.99

Grades: K 1 2 3   **E**

1. Family life -- Fiction 2. African Americans -- Fiction

ISBN 0-7868-0242-1; 1-4231-0681-4 pa

LC 96-16312

Teeka describes her various relatives and the foods they bring to the annual family picnic

"If this is more character sketch than actual story, the solid acrylic paintings help bring all the people in this African American family to life." Booklist

★ The **other** side; illustrations by E. B. Lewis. Putnam 2001 un il $16.99

Grades: K 1 2 3   **E**

1. Summer 2. Friendship 3. Race relations 4. Friendship -- Fiction 5. Race relations -- Fiction 6. African Americans -- Fiction

ISBN 0-399-23116-1; 978-0-399-23116-2

LC 99-42055

Two girls, one white and one black, gradually get to know each other as they sit on the fence that divides their town. "Ages six to nine." (Bull Cent Child Books)

"Lewis' watercolors provide a telling backdrop to the action. . . . This is an emotionally intricate tale presented simply and intimately." Bull Cent Child Books

Wormell, Christopher

George and the dragon; [by] Chris Wormell. Knopf 2006 un il $16.95

Grades: PreK K 1 2   **E**

1. Mice -- Fiction 2. Dragons -- Fiction

ISBN 0-375-83315-3

First published in 2002 in the United Kingdom

A dragon terrorizes the kingdom until he is frightened by George the mouse.

Henry and the fox; [by] Chris Wormell. Random House 2008 un il hardcover o.p. pa $9.95

Grades: K 1 2   **E**

1. Foxes -- Fiction 2. Courage -- Fiction 3. Roosters

-- Fiction

ISBN 978-0-224-07044-7; 0-224-07044-4; 978-0-09-948383-0 pa; 0-09-948383-1 pa

First published 2006 in the United Kingdom

This "is gorgeously illustrated and delightfully written. . . . Wormell's lovely watercolors are reminiscent of the radiant work of Jerry Pinkney." SLJ

Teeth, tails, & tentacles; an animal counting book. Running Press 2004 64p il $18.95

Grades: PreK K 1 2   **E**

1. Animals 2. Counting

ISBN 0-7624-2100-2

The first portion of the work is a counting book covering the numbers one to twenty with block prints of animals. The second portion of the work has factual information concerning the animals.

"Within the art, limpid colors melt into single-hue light-to-dark continuums or flash in arresting contrast, while surprising shifts in perspective and shadow create an almost tangible visual texture and depth which invite repeated viewing." Bull Cent Child Books

Wortche, Allison

Rosie Sprout's time to shine; story by Allison Wortche; pictures by Patrice Barton. Alfred A. Knopf 2011 il $17.99; lib bdg $20.99

Grades: K 1 2 3   **E**

1. School stories 2. Plants -- Fiction

ISBN 978-0-375-86721-7; 978-0-375-96721-4 lib bdg; 978-0-375-98459-4 e-book

LC 2011004092

Rosie's rival, Violet, outdoes her in everything until the class plants seeds for a unit on gardening.

"Wortche possesses both a refreshing directness and a willingness to trust her readers. She also has the courage to conclude not with reconciliation, but with a bittersweet and profoundly wise acknowledgment that it takes all kinds. This impressive new author is well served by Barton . . . whose digital classroom sketches convey a tumult of emotion and have just the right amounts of energy and vulnerability." Publ Wkly

Wright, Betty Ren

The **blizzard**; illustrated by Ronald Himler. Holiday House 2003 un il $16.95

Grades: PreK K 1 2 3   **E**

1. Birthdays -- Fiction

ISBN 0-8234-1656-9

LC 2002-190764

Although a blizzard prevents his cousins from visiting for his birthday, a disappointed Billy ends up having a very special day when his teacher and classmates must stay overnight at his family's house to wait out the snowstorm

"This evocative story harkens back to an earlier, simpler time. . . . The feelings the events engender are tender and strong. Himler's artwork alternates between the white-gray of the blowing snow and the golden glow that comes from both inside the house and the hearts of those who live there." Booklist

Wright, Johanna

★ **Bandits**. Roaring Brook Press 2011 un il $16.99

Grades: PreK K 1 2   E
   1. Raccoons -- Fiction
   ISBN 978-1-59643-583-4; 1-59643-583-6
                  LC 2010027310

Raccoons wreak havoc on a town during the night, rummaging through garbage cans, stealing food, and then running off into the hills to enjoy their loot.

"The text reads like free verse, and it's clear that the words have been carefully chosen. . . . The true star of this book is the amazing artwork. The textural, expressive paintings are full of life, movement, and humor." SLJ

The **secret** circus. Roaring Brook Press 2009 un il $16.95
Grades: PreK K 1   E
   1. Mice -- Fiction 2. Circus -- Fiction
   ISBN 978-1-59643-403-5; 1-59643-403-1
                  LC 2008-54261

Mice carefully dress for an evening out, journey across Paris in a hot air balloon, and finally arrive at a secret place to see the circus.

This is written in "simple, rhythmic prose. . . . Rustic canvas paintings done in a subdued palette cast a mood of quiet mystery over the nocturnal activities of the mice. The artwork provides the clever details that the text never reveals." SLJ

Wright, Maureen
   ★ **Sleep,** Big Bear, sleep! illustrated by Will Hillenbrand. Marshall Cavendish Children 2009 un il $16.99
Grades: PreK K 1   E
   1. Stories in rhyme 2. Bears -- Fiction 3. Winter -- Fiction 4. Hibernation -- Fiction
   ISBN 978-0-7614-5560-8; 0-7614-5560-4
                  LC 2008029402

As winter comes and Big Bear prepares to hibernate, he keeps thinking he hears Old Man Winter giving him exhausting orders that prevent him from sleeping.

"The text moves at a steady clip, and the refrain will encourage child participation. . . . The story reads aloud well, and the limited text and oversize illustrations will be effective in storytime. The artwork is the real star here, though. Hillenbrand imbues his characters with motion and personality." SLJ
   Another title about Big Bear is:
   Sneeze, Big Bear, Sneeze (2011)

Sneeze, Big Bear, sneeze! illustrated by Will Hillenbrand. Marshall Cavendish Children 2011 un il $16.99
Grades: PreK K 1   E
   1. Stories in rhyme 2. Bears -- Fiction 3. Winds -- Fiction 4. Autumn -- Fiction 5. Sneezing -- Fiction
   ISBN 978-0-7614-59590; 0-7614-5959-6; 978-0-7614-6074-9 e-book
                  LC 2011001125

Big Bear thinks that his tremendous sneezes are causing the leaves and apples to fall off the trees and the geese to fly away, but when the wind finally convinces him otherwise, he knows what to do.

"Hillenbrand's sweeping mixed-media spreads should stir up anticipation for apple-picking season." Publ Wkly

Wright, Michael
   Jake goes peanuts. Feiwel and Friends 2010 un il $16.99
Grades: PreK K   E
   1. Stories in rhyme 2. Peanuts -- Fiction
   ISBN 978-0-312-54967-1; 0-312-54967-9

In an effort to get Jake to eat something other than peanut butter, his parents declare it "Peanut Butter Week" and create such dishes as peanut butter soup, peanut butter pot roast, and even peanut butter dog food for their pet.

"Wright's crisp rhymes and droll cartoons should make picky eaters smile, and perhaps consider a little diversity in their own diets." Publ Wkly
   Another title about Jake is:
   Jake starts school (2008)

Wright, Randall
   The **geezer** in the freezer; illustrated by Thor Wickstrom. Bloomsbury USA Children's Books 2009 un il $16.99; lib bdg $17.89
Grades: PreK K 1 2   E
   1. Stories in rhyme
   ISBN 978-1-59990-135-0; 1-59990-135-8; 978-1-59990-390-3 lib bdg; 1-59990-390-3 lib bdg
                  LC 2009004631

Stuck between a rump roast and a pie, the old man living in the freezer finally gets to tell his tale of woe.

"The horror-story premise is played beautifully for laughs, thanks to the expertly sustained country-flavored rhymes. Wickstrom's slathered-on oils capture the situation's absurdity—and tenderness, when the geezer is telling his tale of star-crossed love." Horn Book Guide

Wynne Pechter, Lesley
   Alligator, bear, crab; a baby's ABC. Orca Book Publishers 2011 un il bd bk $9.95
Grades: PreK   E
   1. Alphabet 2. Board books for children 3. Animals -- Fiction 4. Animals -- Juvenile literature 5. Alphabet -- Juvenile literature
   ISBN 978-1-55469-360-3; 1-55469-360-8
                  LC 2010-941967

"Endearing animals introduce the ABCs in an inviting board book. Pechter's organic paintings feature soft lines, kindly faces, and a soothing palette of creamy sunset colors and sky blues. . . . Uncommon additions like an urchin and a vole broaden the menagerie. . . . With care paid to each image, this is a charming, distinctive primer." Publ Wkly

Xinran
   ★ **Motherbridge** of love; text provided by Mother Bridge of Love; illustrated by Josee Masse. Barefoot 2007 un il $16.99
Grades: PreK K 1 2   E
   1. Mothers -- Fiction 2. Adoption -- Fiction
   ISBN 978-1-84686-047-8

Celebrates the bond between parent and child as the adoptive parent of a little Chinese girl speaks about her love for her adopted daughter.

"Simple, lyrical language and gorgeous art make this more than just another adoption story. . . . The sentiment is exactly right—loving, caring, and thoughtful—and the stylized acrylic illustrations, in thick brush strokes and swirl-

ing shapes, evoke the lyrical tone with grace and elegance."
Booklist

Yaccarino, Dan

★ **Doug** unplugged! Dan Yaccarino. Alfred A. Knopf
2013 40 p. (trade) $16.99

Grades: K 1 2 3 4   **E**

1. Robots -- Juvenile fiction 2. City and town life --
Juvenile fiction 3. Robots -- Fiction 4. City and town
life -- Fiction

ISBN 0375866434; 9780375866432; 9780375966439

LC 2011047496

This children's book, by Dan Yaccarino, follows a robot
named Doug. "His parents want him to be smart, so each
morning they plug him in and start the information download. After a morning spent learning facts about the city,
Doug suspects he could learn even more about the city by
going outside and exploring it. And so Doug . . . unplugs.
What follows is an exciting day of adventure and discovery."
(Publisher's note)

Every Friday. Henry Holt and Company 2007 32p
il $16.95

Grades: PreK K 1 2   **E**

1. Father-son relationship -- Fiction

ISBN 978-0-8050-7724-7; 0-8050-7724-3

LC 2005020253

A "boy describes the route that he and his dad walk
on their way to their weekly Friday breakfast at the corner
diner. . . . Yaccarino's clean lines, saturated colors, and very
simple words distill the story's emotions into clear, understated sweetness that's not too sugary." Booklist

Lawn to lawn. Alfred A. Knopf 2010 un il $17.99;
lib bdg $20.99

Grades: K 1 2 3   **E**

1. Adventure fiction 2. Gardens -- Fiction 3. Voyages
and travels -- Fiction

ISBN 978-0-375-85574-0; 0-375-85574-2; 978-0-375-
95574-7 lib bdg; 0-375-95574-7 lib bdg

LC 2009002303

When their family moves away and leaves them behind,
a group of lawn ornaments sets out on a dangerous trek
across the country to try to find them.

"Yaccarino's clean, bright illustrations have an appealing retro look, and the trek through suburbs, swamps, fields,
and city is a visual treat." Booklist

Yamasaki, Katie

Fish for Jimmy; based on one family's experience in
a Japanese American internment camp. Katie Yamasaki.
Holiday House 2013 40 p. (reinforced) $16.95

Grades: 1 2 3 4 5   **E**

1. Historical fiction 2. Picture books for children
3. Japanese Americans -- Evacuation and relocation,
1942-1945 -- Juvenile fiction 4. Brothers -- Fiction 5.
Japanese Americans -- Evacuation and relocation, 1942-
1945 -- Fiction

ISBN 0823423751; 9780823423750

LC 2012006584

In this children's picture book, "following the bombing
of Pearl Harbor, Taro's father is taken away for questioning
by the FBI, and Taro, his younger brother, and their mother
are transported to an internment camp. Jimmy refuses to eat

and becomes withdrawn and listless. Taro finds a way to
slip outside the camp fences to obtain fresh fish to entice his
brother to eat." (School Library Journal)

Yamashita, Haruo

Seven little mice go to school; illustrated by Kazuo
Iwamura. NorthSouth 2011 un il $16.95

Grades: PreK K 1 2   **E**

1. School stories 2. Mice -- Fiction

ISBN 978-0-7358-4012-6; 0-7358-4012-1

Original Japanese edition 1981

"Mama Mouse has seven little mice who are about to
start school. . . . The septuplets are reluctant to go. Clever
Mama gets an idea. . . . She takes two blue balls of yarn
and makes a path through the forest all the way to school.
The next morning she announces, 'All aboard! The train for
school is leaving now!.' . . . The children eagerly pick up on
the game and follow along. . . . The pen-and-ink and watercolor illustrations perfectly complement the story. The mice
are individualized with gently humorous details. . . . This
clever take on the afraid-to-go-to-school theme should have
broad appeal." SLJ

Another title about the seven little mice is:

Seven little mice have fun on the ice (2011)

Seven little mice have fun on the ice; illustrated by
Kazuo Iwamura. NorthSouth 2011 un il $16.95

Grades: PreK K 1 2   **E**

1. Mice -- Fiction 2. Ice fishing -- Fiction

ISBN 978-0-7358-4048-5; 0-7358-4048-2

"Following an afterschool ice-skating excursion, the
[seven little mice] are anxious to go ice fishing, just like
Little Weasel and his father. However, Father has to work,
and Mother is too afraid of slipping on the ice. . . . The softly
colored illustrations are extremely detailed, giving readers
much to peruse. . . . The mice are adorable and expressive."
Kirkus

Yang, Belle

Foo, the flying frog of Washtub Pond. Candlewick
2009 un il $16.99

Grades: PreK K 1 2   **E**

1. Size -- Fiction 2. Frogs -- Fiction 3. Ponds -- Fiction
4. Animals -- Fiction 5. Friendship -- Fiction

ISBN 978-0-7636-3615-9; 0-7636-3615-0

"Gouache illustrations made up of buoyant, spontaneous, and comedic strokes match the exaggeration of this
foolish frog." Booklist

Hannah is my name. Candlewick Press 2004 un il
$16.99

Grades: K 1 2 3   **E**

1. Immigrants -- Fiction 2. Chinese Americans --
Fiction

ISBN 0-7636-2223-0

LC 2003-69675

A young Chinese girl and her parents emigrate to the
United States and try their best to assimilate into their San
Francisco neighborhood while anxiously awaiting the ar-
rival of their green cards.

"The bright gouache pictures of San Francisco draw
strongly on Chinese and American traditions. . . . The struggle with documentation and the celebration when the green

cards finally arrive in the mail is a drama many immigrant families will recognize." Booklist

Yankovic, Al

When I grow up; illustrations by Wes Hargis. Harper 2011 un il $17.99
Grades: PreK K 1 2   E
   1. School stories 2. Stories in rhyme 3. Occupations -- Fiction
   ISBN 978-0-06-192691-4; 0-06-192691-4
                 LC 2010021966

An exuberant eight-year-old details for his teacher and classmates the astonishing variety of inventive careers he is thinking of pursuing when he grows up.

"As the boy's fantasies about his future get wilder and wilder, Hargis' hilarious, detailed illustrations in clear line and watercolor extend the uproarious nonsense. . . . Along with the imaginative play, the farce and parody make this a rare book with appeal to both kids and adults." Booklist

Yarrow, Peter

Puff the magic dragon pop-up book; [by] Peter Yarrow, Lenny Lipton; with paintings by Eric Puybaret and paper engineering by Bruce Foster. Sterling 2011 un il $26.95
Grades: PreK K 1 2   E
   1. Pop-up books 2. Dragons -- Fiction
   ISBN 978-1-4027-8711-9; 1-4027-8711-1

"Puybaret's capricious paintings combine elegantly with pop-up engineering by Bruce Foster in a condensed, interactive version of this bestselling 2007 picture book. The story unfolds in six graceful pop-up scenes, some of which have side panels that conceal additional pop-up effects. . . . Includes a four-song CD recording." Publ Wkly

Yates, Louise

★ **Dog** loves books. Alfred A. Knopf 2010 un il $16.99; lib bdg $19.99
Grades: PreK K 1 2   E
   1. Dogs -- Fiction 2. Books and reading -- Fiction
   ISBN 978-0-375-86449-0; 0-375-86449-0; 978-0-375-96449-7 lib bdg; 0-375-96449-5 lib bdg
                 LC 2009-11097

Dog loves books so much that he decides to open a book store.

"The simple story is accompanied by soft pastel pencil and watercolor drawings that give the book a whimsical, dreamy quality. Dog is surrounded by nonthreatening dinosaurs, space aliens, and other creatures when he is reading about them. Young children can enjoy the book by themselves by following the charming illustrations." SLJ

Dog loves drawing; Louise Yates. Alfred A. Knopf 2012 32 p. (trade) $16.99; $16.99
Grades: PreK K 1 2   E
   1. Dogs -- Fiction 2. Drawing -- Fiction 3. Picture books for children 4. Animals -- Fiction
   ISBN 9780307974495; 9780375870675; 9780375970672; 0375870679
                 LC 2011032353

In "this follow-up to the . . . 'Dog Loves Books' . . . the pup receives a blank book as a gift. He quickly realizes that it's a sketchbook, and though initially struck by artist's block, he soon uses his pencils and pens to draw himself some friends, a boat and a train to ride, and food for them

to feast on, all of which magically come to life on the page. When one of Dog's new friends draws a monster, though, Dog must quickly use his skills to contain it and create an escape route." (School Library Journal)

A **small** surprise. Alfred A. Knopf 2009 un il $16.99; lib bdg $19.99
Grades: PreK K 1   E
   1. Size -- Fiction 2. Circus -- Fiction 3. Rabbits -- Fiction
   ISBN 978-0-375-85698-3; 0-375-85698-6; 978-0-375-95698-0 lib bdg; 0-375-95698-0 lib bdg
                 LC 2008024535

A little rabbit, too small even to wipe his own nose, is just the right size to do one very special thing

"The illustrations are rendered in soft hues that are soothing yet colorful. The animals . . . have wonderfully expressive eyes and gestures. There are a few words in a large font on each page, making it easy for young children to follow along." SLJ

Yee, Wong Herbert

Detective Small in the amazing banana caper; written and illustrated by Wong Herbert Yee. Houghton Mifflin 2007 un il $15
Grades: PreK K 1 2   E
   1. Mystery fiction 2. Stories in rhyme 3. Animals -- Fiction
   ISBN 0-618-47285-1; 978-0-618-47285-7
                 LC 2006009821

When shop owners call on Detective Small to track down a banana thief, he follows the clues to a likely suspect, then learns that the real culprit is still on the loose

"The rhyming text creates an infectious, bouncing rhythm that will appeal to many young listeners. It's Yee's pencil-and-watercolor illustrations, though, that really extend the action and humor." Booklist

Mouse and Mole, a perfect Halloween. Houghton Mifflin Harcourt 2011 il $14.99
Grades: K 1 2 3   E
   1. Mice -- Fiction 2. Halloween -- Fiction 3. Friendship -- Fiction 4. Moles (Animals) -- Fiction
   ISBN 978-0-547-55152-4; 0-547-55152-5
                 LC 2010033432

As Halloween approaches, Mouse helps her friend Mole get over his fear and enjoy the holiday.

"Newly independent readers will find much humor and some challenging words, but Yee's small gouache-and-litho pencil illustrations cue perfectly. . . . This story within the story truly shows how sharing a good book with a friend can work wonders." Kirkus

Mouse and Mole, a winter wonderland. Houghton Mifflin Harcourt 2010 un $15
Grades: K 1 2 3   E
   1. Mice -- Fiction 2. Snow -- Fiction 3. Friendship -- Fiction 4. Moles (Animals) -- Fiction
   ISBN 978-0-547-34152-1; 0-547-34152-0
                 LC 2010000953

Best friends Mouse and Mole enjoy playing in the snow with Sno-Mouse and Sno-Mole, two more best friends.

"The bundled-up friends against the wintry background make an endearing complement to the quiet humor of the story. The vignettes are sprinkled throughout, breaking up the lines of text and giving young eyes a place to rest while they work. A tea-and-cookie retreat provides a cozy ending to a splendid beginning reader." Kirkus

Summer days and nights; Wong Herbert Yee. Henry Holt 2012 32 p. (hc) $14.99
Grades: PreK K 1 E
1. Stories in rhyme 2. Summer -- Juvenile fiction 3. Day -- Fiction 4. Night -- Fiction 5. Summer -- Fiction
ISBN 0805090789; 9780805090789
LC 2011028598
In this children's picture book by Wong Herbert Lee, "a little girl finds ways to entertain herself and stay cool. She catches a butterfly, sips lemonade, jumps in a pool, and goes on a picnic. At night, she sees an owl in a tree and a frog in a pond, and hears leaves rustling. Before long, she's fast asleep, dreaming about more summer days and summer nights." (Publisher's note)

Tracks in the snow. H. Holt 2003 un il $15.95
Grades: PreK K 1 2 E
1. Snow 2. Curiosity 3. Animal tracks 4. Stories in rhyme 5. Footprints 6. Snow -- Fiction 7. Animal tracks -- Fiction
ISBN 0-8050-6771-X
LC 2002-10854
A little girl investigates tracks in the snow, trying to determine what could have made them.
"The gentle, rhyming text makes an ideal read-aloud, and young listeners will chime in on the repeated phrases. The soft-focus, colored-pencil illustrations portray a small Asian girl exploring her safe world, but a world transformed by the fresh snowfall." SLJ

Upstairs Mouse, downstairs Mole. Houghton Mifflin Co. 2005 un il $15
Grades: K 1 2 3 E
1. Mice -- Fiction 2. Friendship -- Fiction 3. Moles (Animals) -- Fiction
ISBN 0-618-47313-0
LC 2004-5238
Mouse and her downstairs neighbor, Mole, discover that when they help each other, housecleaning and other daily tasks are much easier
"The expressive bamboo-pen and watercolor with colored-pencil illustrations capture the humor of the situations as well as the emotions of the characters. . . . A real winner." SLJ

Other titles about Mouse and Mole are:
Abracadabra! Magic with Mouse and Mole (2007)
A brand-new day with Mouse and Mole (2008)
Mouse and Mole: fine feathered friends (2009)
Mouse and Mole: a winter wonderland (2010)
Mouse and Mole: a perfect Halloween (2011)

Who likes rain? Holt & Co. 2007 un il $14.95
Grades: PreK K 1 E
1. Rain -- Fiction
ISBN 978-0-8050-7734-6; 0-8050-7734-0
LC 2006-03429

As a young girl splashes in the rain, she plays a guessing game with the reader about other living things that enjoy a cloudburst.
"The rhyming text tells the story as naturally as if the rhythm and rhyme just fell into place. . . . Fine strokes of color softly define the shapes of characters and settings." Booklist

Yeoman, John
The **wild** washerwomen; illustrated by Quentin Blake. Andersen 2009 un il lib bdg $16.95
Grades: K 1 2 3 E
1. Laundresses -- Fiction
ISBN 978-0-7613-5152-8; 0-7613-5152-3
LC 2008055432
A reissue of the title first published 1979 by Greenwillow Books
Seven washerwomen, sick of their work, go on an uncontrollable rampage, only to meet their match in seven very dirty woodcutters.
"The expressive illustrations—caricature line drawings washed with color—continuously echo and expand the preposterous, joyful text's often understated humor." Horn Book Guide

Yep, Laurence, 1948-
Auntie Tiger; pictures by Insu Lee. HarperCollinsPublishers 2009 un il $17.99; lib bdg $18.89
Grades: K 1 2 3 E
1. Fairy tales 2. Tigers -- Fiction 3. Sisters -- Fiction
ISBN 978-0-06-029551-6; 0-06-029551-1; 978-0-06-029552-3 lib bdg; 0-06-029552-X lib bdg
LC 2006-28649
In this version of Red Riding Hood set in China, Big Sister sets aside her differences with Little Sister to rescue her from a tiger in disguise.
"Bright, energetic illustrations done in jewel tones bring this story to life. The cunning tiger with his large head, bulging eyes, and small pointy teeth is scarcely contained in three of the spreads." SLJ

Yin
Brothers; by Yin; paintings by Chris Soentpiet. Philomel Books 2006 un il $16.99
Grades: 2 3 4 E
1. Friendship -- Fiction 2. Irish Americans -- Fiction 3. Chinese Americans -- Fiction
ISBN 0-399-23406-3
Having arrived in San Francisco from China to work in his brother's store, Ming is lonely until an Irish boy befriends him.
"Soentpiet's luminescent, photo-realistic paintings, which provide many vivid setting details, perfectly complement Yin's thoughtful text." Booklist
Includes bibliographical references

Coolies; illustrated by Chris K. Soentpiet. Philomel Bks. 2001 un il $16.99
Grades: 2 3 4 E
1. Brothers -- Fiction 2. Chinese Americans -- Fiction 3. Chinese Americans -- Juvenile fiction
ISBN 0-399-23227-3
LC 98-40403

A young boy hears the story of his great-great-great-grandfather and his brother who came to the United States to make a better life for themselves helping to build the transcontinental railroad

"Soentpiet's strong, realistic watercolor paintings, in shades of blue and gold, show the bond between the brothers. . . . The American history is powerful. Yin provides notes and a bibliography for readers who want to know more." Booklist

Yolen, Jane

★ **Baby** Bear's books; written by Jane Yolen; illustrated by Melissa Sweet. Harcourt 2006 un il $16
Grades: PreK K   E
    1. Stories in rhyme 2. Bears -- Fiction 3. Books and reading -- Fiction
    ISBN 0-15-205290-9
                    LC 2005019203
Throughout the day, Baby Bear finds a book to fit every special moment.

"Mixed-media and collage illustrations create a warm and comfortable world. . . . The charming double-page pictures are large enough to share with groups, and the rhymes will engage listeners." SLJ
    Other titles about Baby Bear are:
    Baby Bear's chairs (2005)
    Baby Bear's big dreams (2007)

Come to the fairies' ball; illustrated by Gary Lippincott. Wordsong 2009 un il $17.95
Grades: 1 2 3 4   E
    1. Stories in rhyme 2. Fairies -- Fiction
    ISBN 978-1-59078-464-8; 1-59078-464-2
                    LC 2009018247
All the fairies are excited to be invited to the King's ball, except for one young fairy whose only party dress is in tatters.

"An enchanting picture book full of whimsy and magic. . . . Lippincott's paintings take the forefront in this book, while Yolen's clever verse adds to the unfolding pictorial drama." SLJ

Commander Toad and the voyage home; pictures by Bruce Degen. Putnam 1998 64p il hardcover o.p. pa $5.99
Grades: 1 2 3 4   E
    1. Science fiction 2. Toads -- Fiction
    ISBN 0-399-23122-6; 0-698-11602-X pa
                    LC 96-21739
Commander Toad leads the lean green space machine "Star Warts" to find new worlds but runs into trouble when he sets course for home

"Yolen captures the high drama of space fiction in a delightful story that never loses sight of developing readers, who will be old enough to get the jokes but still young enough to relish the goofiness." Booklist
    Other titles about Commander Toad are:
    Commander Toad and the big black hole (1996)
    Commander Toad and the dis-asteroid (1996)
    Commander Toad and the intergalactic spy (1997)
    Commander Toad and the Planet of the Grapes (1996)
    Commander Toad and the space pirates (1997)
    Commander Toad in space (1996)

Creepy monsters, sleepy monsters; a lullaby. illustrated by Kelly Murphy. Candlewick Press 2011 32p il $14.99
Grades: PreK K 1   E
    1. Stories in rhyme 2. Bedtime -- Fiction 3. Monsters -- Fiction
    ISBN 978-0-7636-4201-3; 0-7636-4201-0
                    LC 2010040342
Two rambunctious monsters creep, gurgle, crawl, and tumble before falling asleep.

This is a "whimsical, warmhearted rhyme, which turns bumps in the night into the sweetest sounds of all. . . . Murphy's oil, acrylic, and gel illustrations instantly grab attention with their unusual points of view. . . . Bedtime fare you can count on." Booklist

★ The **day** Tiger Rose said goodbye; illustrations by Jim LaMarche. Random House 2011 un il
Grades: PreK K 1 2   E
    1. Cats -- Fiction 2. Death -- Fiction 3. Country life -- Fiction
    ISBN 0-375-86663-9; 0-375-96663-3 lib bdg; 978-0-375-86663-0; 978-0-375-96663-7 lib bdg
                    LC 2010013548
A cat whose kitten days are far behind her says goodbye to her human family, and the animals and places that have made her life special, before leaving this life behind.

"The calm tone of the text is just right: matter-of-fact but compassionate. Reflecting the delicate beauty of the writing, LaMarche's mixed-media illustrations show equal finesse in line, color, texture, and composition." Booklist

Dimity Duck; illustrated by Sebastien Braun. Philomel Books 2006 un il $15.99
Grades: PreK K   E
    1. Stories in rhyme 2. Ducks -- Fiction 3. Frogs -- Fiction 4. Friendship -- Fiction
    ISBN 0-399-24532-0
Dimity Duck and Frumity Frog have a fun day together in the pond, then go home when it gets dark outside.

"There's an appealing, old-fashioned sound to the verses that is reminiscent of nursery rhymes. . . . The pleasing artwork focuses on Dimity and Frumity as the main inhabitants of the simplified, sunlit world of the pond." Booklist

★ **Elsie's** bird; illustrated by David Small. Philomel Books 2010 un il $17.99
Grades: K 1 2 3   E
    1. Canaries -- Fiction 2. Frontier and pioneer life -- Fiction
    ISBN 978-0-399-25292-1; 0-399-25292-4
Young Elsie must find a way to adapt to her new home on the Nebraska prairie after she and her father leave their comfortable city life in Boston.

"Yolen's evocative story, full of wonder and warmth, rolls smoothly along on carefully worded phrases, capturing the child's emotions as well as the flavor of the time and setting in a simple yet heartfelt way. Small's delivery, completely in sync with the author's, brings Elsie deftly to life. The illustrations, rendered in brush and ink with watercolor and pastel, realize both the streets of Boston and the grasslands of Nebraska with equal ease and aplomb." SLJ

★ **How** do dinosaurs say goodnight? illustrated by Mark Teague. Blue Sky Press (NY) 2000 un il $15.95
Grades: PreK K 1 2 3   E
    1. Stories in rhyme 2. Bedtime -- Fiction 3. Dinosaurs -- Fiction
ISBN 0-590-31681-8
                          LC 98-56134

Mother and child ponder the different ways a dinosaur can say goodnight, from slamming his tail and pouting to giving a big hug and kiss

"The text is sweet and simple—just right for the wonderful pictures that really make this picture book special. . . . Endpapers introduce the critter cast in all their gorgeous glory: tyrannosaurus rex, dimetrodon, and more, in vivid, yet still earthbound colors." Booklist

Other titles in this series are:
How do dinosaurs eat their food? (2005)
How do dinosaurs get well soon? (2003)
How do dinosaurs go to school? (2007)
How do dinosaurs say happy birthday? (2011)
How do dinosaurs say I love you? (2009)

Hush, little horsie; written by Jane Yolen; illustrated by Ruth Sanderson. Random House 2010 un il $16.99; lib bdg $19.99
Grades: PreK K   E
    1. Stories in rhyme 2. Horses -- Fiction 3. Bedtime -- Fiction
ISBN 978-0-375-85853-6; 0-375-85853-9; 978-0-375-95853-3 lib bdg; 0-375-95853-3 lib bdg
                         LC 2008030184

"In this gentle picture book, a variety of mares stand guard as their foals and fillies play, run, leap, and finally sleep. . . . The horses are introduced in simple rhyme. In each case, readers are reassured that the mothers will always take care of their babies. . . . The book ends with a human mother and her daughter nestled beneath blankets at bedtime, reading stories and preparing for sleep. . . . Sanderson's lush and lovely paintings are an ideal match for the reflective text. With text and illustrations as tender as a lullaby, this picture book is ideal for bedtime sharing." SLJ

Mama's kiss; by Jane Yolen; illustrations by Daniel Baxter. Handprint Books 2008 un il $14.99
Grades: PreK K 1   E
    1. Stories in rhyme 2. Kissing -- Fiction
ISBN 978-0-8118-6683-5; 0-8118-6683-1
                         LC 2008021177

A kiss from Mama misses its intended target and instead embarks on a merry adventure as it slips, slides, and twists its way around the world.

"Yolen's jaunty rhymes are short and sweet; debut illustrator Baxter's droll, cartoonlike pictures practically jump from page to page." Publ Wkly

★ **My** Uncle Emily; illustrated by Nancy Carpenter. Philomel Books 2009 un il $17.99
Grades: K 1 2   E
    1. Poets 2. Authors 3. Poets -- Fiction
ISBN 978-0-399-24005-8; 0-399-24005-5
                         LC 2008-32614

In 1881 Amherst, Massachusetts, six-year-old Gilbert finds it both challenging and wonderful to spend time with his aunt, the reclusive poet Emily Dickinson, who lives next door.

"Yolen artfully incorporates elements from Dickinson's poetry and life to give readers an inside look at the enigmatic poet from her nephew's fresh and loving perspective. Carpenter's nostalgic, pastel-hued pen, ink and digital-media illustrations capture the atmosphere of late-19th-century Amherst as well as Gil's special relationship with his famous aunt in this poetic vignette." Kirkus

My father knows the names of things; illustrated by Stephane Jorisch. Simon & Schuster Books for Young Readers 2010 un il $15.99
Grades: PreK K 1   E
    1. Stories in rhyme 2. Father-child relationship -- Fiction
ISBN 978-1-4169-4895-7; 1-4169-4895-3
                         LC 2007-41840

Rhyming text depicts a father sharing with his child such things as seven words that all mean blue and the name of every kind of cloud.

"Yolen's easeful rhymes and Jorisch's warm illustrations craft a bighearted tribute to fathers' seemingly infinite capacities for information—and their willingness to share it." Publ Wkly

Naming Liberty; by Jane Yolen; illustrated by Jim Burke. Philomel Books 2008 un il $16.99
Grades: 1 2 3   E
    1. Artists 2. Sculptors 3. Jews -- Fiction 4. Immigrants -- Fiction
ISBN 978-0-399-24250-2; 0-399-24250-3

In parallel stories, a Ukrainian Jewish family prepares to emigrate to the United States in the late 1800s, and Frederic Auguste Bartholdi designs, raises funds for, and builds the Statue of Liberty in honor of the United States' centennial.

"Burke's luminous paintings, designed on burnt sienna oil-washed boards, convey the landscapes and details of nineteenth-century Europe and New York. . . . An ideal choice for introducing the concepts of immigration and liberty to young listeners." Booklist

Not all princesses dress in pink; [by] Jane Yolen and Heidi Stemple Yolen; illustrated by Anne-Sophie Lanquetin. Simon & Schuster Books for Young Readers 2010 un il $15.99
Grades: PreK K 1   E
    1. Stories in rhyme 2. Girls -- Fiction 3. Sex role -- Fiction 4. Princesses -- Fiction
ISBN 978-1-4169-8018-6; 1-4169-8018-0
                         LC 2008-38122

Rhyming text affirms that girls can pursue their many interests, from playing sports to planting flowers in the dirt, without giving up their tiaras.

"The snappy, upbeat illustrations and blithely confident characters are plenty of fun." Publ Wkly

Off we go! illustrated by Laurel Molk. Little, Brown 2000 un il lib bdg $12.95
Grades: PreK K   E
    1. Stories in rhyme 2. Animals -- Fiction 3.

Grandmothers -- Fiction 4. Animals -- Infancy -- Fiction
ISBN 0-316-90228-4

LC 98-6893

One by one, baby woodland creatures leave home and sing their way to visit grandma

"Rhyme, repetition, and the playful, onomatopoeic language make this especially appealing for read-alouds. Large watercolors in earthy tones of gray, green, and brown are soft and fluid." Horn Book Guide

★ Owl moon; illustrated by John Schoenherr. 20th anniversary edition; Philomel 2007 un il $16.99
Grades: PreK K 1 2   E
1. Owls -- Fiction 2. Father-daughter relationship -- Fiction
ISBN 978-0-399-24799-6; 0-399-24799-8
A reissue of the title first published 1987
Awarded the Caldecott Medal, 1988
On a winter's night under a full moon, a father and daughter trek into the woods to see the great horned owl
This book "conveys the scary majesty of winter woods at night in language that seldom overreaches either character or subject. . . . This book has a magic that is extremely rare in books for any age." NY Times Book Rev

Pretty princess pig; by Jane Yolen and Heidi E. Y. Stemple; illustrated by Sam Williams. Little Simon 2011 un il $9.99
Grades: PreK K 1   E
1. Stories in rhyme 2. Pigs -- Fiction 3. Parties -- Fiction
ISBN 978-1-4424-0833-3; 1-4424-0833-2
Follows Pretty Princess Pig as she gets ready to throw a party by painting the dining room, baking, and digging up flowers.

"With their pastel palette and nimble linework, Williams's watercolors match this princess's verve." Publ Wkly

Sleep, black bear, sleep; by Jane Yolen and Heidi E. Y. Stemple; illustrated by Brooke Dyer. HarperCollins 2007 un il $15.99; lib bdg $16.89
Grades: PreK K 1   E
1. Stories in rhyme 2. Winter -- Fiction 3. Animals -- Fiction 4. Bedtime -- Fiction 5. Hibernation -- Fiction
ISBN 978-0-06-081560-8; 0-06-081560-4; 978-0-06-081561-5 lib bdg; 0-06-081561-2 lib bdg

LC 2006000344

As winter's chill spreads, different animals settle into their cozy homes for a long sleep

"The rhyme scheme is as lilting as a lullaby, and Dyer's ineffably sweet watercolor illustrations enrich this bedtime story." Booklist

Yolleck, Joan
★ Paris in the spring with Picasso; illustrated by Marjorie Priceman. Schwartz & Wade Books 2010 un il $17.99; lib bdg $20.99
Grades: K 1 2 3   E
1. Poets 2. Artists 3. Authors 4. Painters 5. Novelists 6. Dramatists 7. Essayists 8. Memoirists 9. Art critics 10. Literary critics 11. Private secretaries
ISBN 978-0-375-83756-2; 0-375-83756-6; 978-0-375-93756-9 lib bdg; 0-375-93756-0 lib bdg

LC 2008-05867

Describes how some of Paris's famous artists and writers, such as Pablo Picasso, Max Jacob, and Guillaume Apollinaire, spend their day before preparing to attend a party at Gertrude Stein's apartment.

"Priceman's brightly colored illustrations exhibit energy, creativity, and general joie de vivre. . . . This whirlwind tour flows easily thanks to clear writing and carefully chosen details." SLJ

Yoo, Tae-Eun
★ The little red fish. Dial Books for Young Readers 2007 un il $15.99
Grades: PreK K 1 2   E
1. Magic -- Fiction 2. Fishes -- Fiction 3. Libraries -- Fiction
ISBN 978-0-8037-3145-5

LC 2006018427

A little boy named JeJe explores a magical library with his friend, a little red fish.

"Detailed hand-colored etchings match well with the quiet, mysterious story that unfolds. . . . The boy's fantastical experiences will resonate with readers." SLJ

Yoon, Salina
One, two, buckle my shoe; a counting nursery rhyme. Robin Corey Books 2011 un il bd bk $6.99
Grades: PreK   E
1. Counting 2. Board books for children 3. Circus -- Fiction
ISBN 978-0-375-86479-7; 0-375-86479-2
"Square die-cut windows offer clues about what comes next in this Big Top twist on the classic nursery rhyme. The opening spread places one purple square opposite a die-cut that frames two yellow circles. Turning the page reveals a polka-dotted clown's shoe, with the purple square becoming the buckle. . . . Watching abstract images turn into concrete shapes should please toddlers, and the inclusion of the words and numerals for each number cements the concept." Publ Wkly

Opposnakes; a lift-the-flap book about opposites. Little Simon 2009 un il $9.99
Grades: PreK K   E
1. Opposites 2. Snakes -- Fiction
ISBN 978-1-4169-7875-6; 1-4169-7875-5
"Yoon introduces opposites via friendly snakes. The spare text focuses on simple concepts: 'Cold snake/Hot snake,' 'Skinny snake/Plump snake,' 'One snake/Many snakes!' Brightly colored, cartoonlike reptiles stretch across the double-foldout spreads and are set against a white background. They are full of amusing details. . . . A book that entertains as it informs." SLJ

Penguin and Pinecone; a friendship story. Salina Yoon. Walker & Co. 2012 40 p. $12.99
Grades: PreK K 1 2   E
1. Penguins/Juvenile fiction 2. Trees -- Juvenile fiction 3. Friendship -- Juvenile fiction 4. Penguins -- Fiction 5. Friendship -- Fiction 6. Pine cones -- Fiction
ISBN 080272843X; 9780802728432; 9780802728449

LC 2011037221

In this children's book, by Salina Yoon, "when Penguin finds a lost pinecone one day, an unlikely friendship blooms. But Grandpa reminds Penguin that pinecones can't live in the snow--they belong in the warm forest far away. Though he will miss his friend, Penguin returns Pinecone to his home, dreaming of the day they can reunite. And when he finally returns to the forest to check on his friend, Penguin discovers that love only grows over time-and so do little pinecones!" (Publisher's note)

Super babies on the move; Mia on the move. G.P. Putnam's Sons 2009 un il $14.99
Grades: PreK E
 1. Infants -- Fiction
 ISBN 978-0-399-24755-2; 0-399-24755-6
      LC 2008000706
After following Baby Mia as she sneaks out during naptime to go to the playground, the reader may turn the book upside down to watch Baby Max skip bathtime to join in a backyard animal chase.
 "Toddlers will like these stories, both for the bright but simply styled visuals and the text." SLJ

Who do I see? Robin Corey Books 2011 un il bd bk $6.99
Grades: PreK E
 1. Color 2. Animals 3. Board books for children
 ISBN 978-0-375-87309-6; 0-375-87309-0
 "This guess-the-animal book contains circular die-cut windows that offer a peek at bright animal prints adorned with shimmery holographic foil. Prompts encourage readers to guess what animal appears on the next page. . . . Friendly-looking naïf animals and an eye-catching design make this a gentle introduction to colors and patterns." Publ Wkly

Yorinks, Arthur
Flappy and Scrappy; story by Arthur Yorinks; pictures by Aleksey and Olga Ivanov. HarperCollinsPublishers 2011 42p il (I can read!) $16.99
Grades: K 1 2 E
 1. Dogs -- Fiction 2. Play -- Fiction 3. Parties -- Fiction 4. Birthdays -- Fiction
 ISBN 978-0-06-205117-2; 0-06-205117-2
      LC 2008027467
After canine friends Scrappy and Flappy play an unusual game of catch, Scrappy complains that everyone has forgotten his birthday, but Flappy surprises him.
 "Emerging readers will enjoy the Ivanovs' cheerful, expressive illustrations, which are thoughtfully placed with the text in spot or full-spread layouts. Beginning readers in the city, suburbs, or country will enjoy these engaging animals and the very simple text." SLJ

★ **Happy** bees; by Arthur Yorinks; illustrated by Carey Armstrong-Ellis. Harry N. Abrams 2005 un il $15.95
Grades: PreK K 1 2 E
 1. Bees -- Fiction
 ISBN 0-8109-5866-X
      LC 2004-15454
Rhythmic text describes the carefree life of bees as they sting knees, munch on Swiss cheese, and laugh in the breeze.
 "The nonsensical text doubles as the lyrics of the first tune on the accompanying CD. . . . The happy-go-lucky insects have loads of personality. . . . Listeners will enjoy the romp, whether spoken or sung, and can discover more beguiling silliness in the other selections on the CD." SLJ

★ **Hey,** Al; story by Arthur Yorinks; pictures by Richard Egielski. Farrar, Straus & Giroux 1986 un il $17; pa $7.99
Grades: PreK K 1 2 3 E
 1. Fantasy fiction 2. Birds -- Fiction
 ISBN 0-374-33060-3; 0-374-42985-5 pa
      LC 86-80955
 Awarded the Caldecott Medal, 1987
 "Egielski's solid naturalism provides just the visual foil needed to establish the surreal character of this fantasy. . . . Text and pictures work together to challenge readers' concept of reality." SLJ

Homework; illustrations by Richard Egielski. Walker & Co. 2009 un il $16.99; lib bdg $17.89
Grades: K 1 2 E
 1. Homework -- Fiction 2. Writing -- Materials and instruments -- Fiction
 ISBN 978-0-8027-9585-4; 0-8027-9585-4; 978-0-8027-9586-1 lib bdg; 0-8027-9586-2 lib bdg
      LC 2008-28011
When Tony's pens, along with his pencil and eraser, come to life, the squabbling set of writing tools tries to complete Tony's neglected homework
 "Yorinks has devised a pleasing homage to the creative process and uses a light touch to show how inspiration can derive from the unlikeliest of places. . . . A simple but amusing winner." Booklist

★ The **invisible** man; illustrated by Doug Cushman. Harper 2011 un il $16.99
Grades: PreK K 1 2 E
 1. Fruit -- Fiction 2. Supernatural -- Fiction
 ISBN 978-0-06-156148-1; 0-06-156148-7
      LC 2009-1404
Sy Kravitz, a Brooklyn fruit seller, explains why becoming invisible should never happen to you.
 "Yorinks employs a narrative tone that's a cross between an old Jewish comedian and The Twilight Zone's Rod Serling, which adds to the deadpan humor, while Cushman's splendid watercolor art becomes ever more clever the closer you look. A fine bit of funnery." Booklist

The **witch's** child; by Arthur Yorinks; illustrated by Jos. A. Smith. Abrams Books for Young Readers 2007 un il $16.95
Grades: K 1 2 3 E
 1. Fairy tales 2. Witches -- Fiction
 ISBN 978-0-8109-9349-5
      LC 2006031980
Desiring a child of her own, Rosina the witch fashions one out of straw and scraps, but when she cannot bring the rag child to life she becomes enraged and turns the village children into shrubs, where they stay until a kind girl discovers the discarded doll and saves her.
 "Yorinks's flowing language is evocative, and the plot builds steadily to an exciting climax. Smith's detailed paintings depict Rosina with jet-black standing-on-end hair and exaggerated facial features that vividly—and frighteningly—express her emotions." SLJ

★ You read to me & I'll read to you; 20th-century stories to share. selected by Janet Schulman. Knopf 2001 250p il $34.95

    Grades: PreK K 1 2   E
    1. Short stories
    ISBN 0-375-81083-8

                 LC 2001-29211

This is a collection of 26 picture books and selections from early chapter books by such authors as Maurice Sendak, William Steig, Dr. Seuss, and Florence Parry Heide

"A great choice for family or classroom sharing." SLJ

Young, Amy

    Belinda, the ballerina. Viking 2002 un il $15.99
Grades: PreK K 1 2   E
    1. Foot 2. Size 3. Dance 4. Ballet dancing 5. Ballet -- Fiction
    ISBN 0-670-03549-1

                 LC 2001-8395

When Belinda auditions for the Spring Ballet Recital and the judges tell her she can not be a ballerina because her feet are too big, she tries to forget about dancing

This offers "spirited gouache paintings that capture the sadness, the humor and the triumph of Belinda's story. . . . The story puts physical defects into perspective and offers something to laugh about at the same time." Booklist

    Other titles about Belinda are:
    Belinda and the glass slipper (2006)
    Belinda begins ballet (2008)
    Belinda in Paris (2005)

Young, Cybèle

    ★ **Ten** birds. Kids Can Press 2011 un il $18.95
Grades: 1 2 3 4   E
    1. Counting 2. Birds -- Fiction 3. Problem solving -- Fiction
    ISBN 978-1-55453-568-2; 1-55453-568-9

"Ten birds are trying to figure out how to get to the other side of the river. The bird they call 'Brilliant' devises a pair of stilts. The bird they call 'Highly Satisfactory' engineers a raft. One by one, nine resourceful birds make the crossing until a single bird is left behind—the one they call 'Needs Improvement.' This bird's solution proves surprising—and absurdly simple." (Publisher's note) "Primary." (Horn Book)

"Ten small birds . . . need to get across a river and have only a deserted lot full of discarded odds and ends—and their own ingenuity—to help them. . . . The straightforward text provides structure and clarity, while the striking and intricate pen-and-ink illustrations perfectly capture the stillness of a night full of wintry snow, show the birds' innovative and slightly mystical solutions to the problem at hand and seamlessly depict the decreasing numbers that represent the birds who have yet to cross. . . . This quietly dazzling selection is a subtle celebration of individuality and creativity." Kirkus

    A **few** bites; by Cybele Young. Groundwood Books/ House of Anansi Press 2012 48 p. col. ill. (hardcover) $18.95
Grades: K 1 2   E
    1. Siblings -- Fiction 2. Vegetables -- Fiction 3. Imagination -- Fiction
    ISBN 1554982952; 9781554982950

Author Cybele Young tells a story of a sister who tries to entice her brother to eat his lunch by making up stories about the food. "Viola has made lunch for her little brother Ferdie: broccoli, carrot sticks, ravioli . . . Ferdie does not want this lunch . . . [so] Viola launches into a brilliant saga of dinosaurs [and] . . . aliens and their Orange Power Sticks." (Kirkus)

    ★ A **few** blocks. Groundwood Books 2011 un il $18.95
Grades: K 1 2   E
    1. Siblings -- Fiction 2. Imagination -- Fiction
    ISBN 978-0-88899-995-5; 0-88899-995-X

"It's time for school, but Viola's younger brother, Ferdie, isn't interested. . . . Resourceful and creative, Viola uses Ferdie's jacket, a leaf, and a piece of cardboard to turn their short walk into three heroic adventures, as they become superheroes, seek buried treasure, and prepare to battle a dragon. . . . Young's collages cast shadows on the white background below, with silhouettes of curling waves, sea creatures, and blobby monsters painted in pale blues, greens, and reds and filled in with crisp imagery of the duo's urban neighborhood. With empathy and respect for both characters' emotions, Young presents a loving story of sibling camaraderie." Publ Wkly

Young, Ed

    ★ **Hook**. Roaring Brook Press 2009 un il $17.95
Grades: PreK K 1   E
    1. Birds -- Fiction 2. Flight -- Fiction
    ISBN 978-1-59643-363-2; 1-59643-363-9

                 LC 2008-49331

A chick hatched by hens turns out to be an eagle who must get help from a boy in learning how to fly.

"Vibrant, minimal chalk drawings—hardly more than sketches, but glorious ones—utilize shifting perspectives to enhance the sky's imposing vastness. . . . Arresting and absorbing, this tale soars." Kirkus

    ★ **My** Mei Mei. Philomel Books 2006 un il $16.99
Grades: PreK K 1 2   E
    1. Sisters -- Fiction 2. Adoption -- Fiction 3. Chinese Americans -- Fiction
    ISBN 0-399-24339-9

Antonia gets her wish when her parents return to China to bring home a Mei Mei, or younger sister, for her.

"Young's vibrant collage illustrations joyously extend the spare, direct words." Booklist

Young, Judy Dockrey

    A **pet** for Miss Wright; written by Judy Young; illustrated by Andrea Wesson. Sleeping Bear Press 2011 un il $15.95
Grades: PreK K 1   E
    1. Pets -- Fiction 2. Authorship -- Fiction
    ISBN 978-1-58536-509-8; 1-58536-509-2

                 LC 2010034399

A lonely writer searches for the perfect pet to keep her company in her solitary work.

"Both the story and the illustrations have a light, charming flavor, with understated humor and a sophisticated air that assumes that intelligent children will enjoy this story." Kirkus

Yum, Hewon

★ **Last** night. Farrar, Straus & Giroux 2008 un il $15.95

Grades: K 1 2 3   E

1. Stories without words 2. Toys -- Fiction 3. Dreams -- Fiction

ISBN 978-0-374-34358-3; 0-374-34358-6

LC 2007030386

Sent to her room for refusing to eat her dinner, a little girl soon falls asleep and together with her bear friend begins a fantastic voyage deep into the forest where they dance and play all night

"Yum's evocative linocut illustrations offer ample context for a child to imagine what the little girl is feeling, and how her mood changes over the course of the night. White, pink, and yellow tones blend and contrast in her face to sometimes resemble a mask." SLJ

★ **Mom,** it's my first day of kindergarten! Hyewon Yum. Frances Foster Books 2012 40 p. col. ill. $16.99

Grades: PreK K   E

1. School stories 2. Picture books for children 3. Mother-son relationship -- Fiction 4. Worry -- Fiction 5. Schools -- Fiction 6. Kindergarten -- Fiction 7. Mothers and sons -- Fiction 8. First day of school -- Fiction

ISBN 0374350043; 9780374350048

LC 2011018294

This book "looks at the first day of school from two points of view—that of a little boy who is more than ready and a nervous mother not quite prepared to let him go. . . . [T]he 5-year-old shakes his mother awake on the first day of school." The text "enumerates her worries (that he won't have time to eat, she forgot some vital supply, he'll be late, he'll get lost, he won't have any friends)" but when "they reach his classroom door . . . [h]e quickly gets over itand has a great day at school." (Kirkus)

There are no scary wolves. Farrar, Straus and Giroux 2010 un il $16.99

Grades: PreK K   E

1. Fear -- Fiction 2. Wolves -- Fiction 3. Imagination -- Fiction 4. Mother-son relationship -- Fiction

ISBN 978-0-374-38060-1; 0-374-38060-0

LC 2009014144

A little boy is afraid of scary wolves without his mother, but when she is holding his hand he is much braver.

"Ephemera, photos, patterns, drawings and watercolors create crafty, engaging compositions. . . . This quirky, somewhat dark picture book cleverly projects the skewed perspective of a worrier." Kirkus

★ The **twins'** blanket. Farrar Straus Giroux 2011 un il $16.99

Grades: PreK K   E

1. Twins -- Fiction 2. Sisters -- Fiction 3. Blankets -- Fiction

ISBN 978-0-374-37972-8; 0-374-37972-6

Two twin girls, who have always shared everything, sleep in separate beds with their own blankets for the first time.

"It's an exquisitely designed book: lots of white space focuses attention on unexpected pleasures, like the feet of the twins as they stomp on the fabric in a wash basin. The book's inherent symmetry, with the twins mirroring each other on the left and right sides of the spreads, is a treat as well." Publ Wkly

Zalben, Jane Breskin

★ **Baby** shower. Roaring Brook Press 2010 un il $16.99

Grades: PreK K 1 2   E

1. Dogs -- Fiction 2. Pets -- Fiction 3. Aunts -- Fiction 4. Animals -- Fiction

ISBN 978-1-5964-3465-3; 1-5964-3465-1

"Zoe wants a pet. . . . To get her mind off dogs . . . and cats . . . Mama suggests that Zoe help with her aunt's baby shower. That night in bed Zoe . . . [dreams] about a baby shower—of puppies, kittens, and even piglets and ducklings. . . . Much of the charm comes from Zalben's sweet and funny ink-and-watercolor pictures, filled with delicious detail in both the homey scenes and windswept expanses of tumbling babies." Booklist

Mousterpiece; Jane Breskin Zalben. Roaring Brook Press 2012 30 p. $16.99

Grades: PreK K 1 2   E

1. Mice -- Fiction 2. Painting -- Fiction 3. Picture books for children 4. Artists -- Fiction 5. Museums -- Fiction 6. Art museums -- Fiction

ISBN 1596435496; 9781596435490

LC 2011021755

In this book, "Janson the mouse lives in an art museum . . . . When she happens upon the modern wing, she is mesmerized. Paintings by Picasso and Matisse, Munch and Pollack, Van Gogh and Warhol spark her creative talents and she emulates them all. When the wing is closed for renovation, Janson is bereft. . . . Rather than leave the space empty, she paints . . . until the room is once again filled with art. The museum director happens upon her work and mounts a show for her." (School Library Journal)

Zemach, Kaethe

★ **Just** enough and not too much. Levine Bks. 2003 un il $16.95

Grades: K 1 2 3   E

1. Musicians -- Fiction

ISBN 0-439-37724-2

LC 2003-399

Simon the fiddler decides he needs more—more chairs, more hats, more stuffed animals—until he discovers that his house is too full and must think of a way to get back to having just enough

"The rich watercolor-and-gouache illustrations, many emphasizing rounded forms, are full of movement and joy. . . . Perfect for storyhours or individual readings." SLJ

Ms. McCaw learns to draw; by Kaethe Zemach. Arthur A. Levine Books 2008 un il $16.99

Grades: 1 2 3   E

1. School stories 2. Drawing -- Fiction 3. Teachers -- Fiction 4. Learning disabilities -- Fiction

ISBN 978-0-439-82914-4; 0-439-82914-3

LC 2006016465

Dudley Ellington struggles to learn anything at school, but when his very patient teacher, Mrs. McGraw, is unable to draw a face on the board, he helps her figure out how to do it

"Because the text is simple and straightforward, the book is a good choice to read aloud. . . . The pen and watercolor illustrations are expressive and full of energy." SLJ

Zemach, Margot

Eating up Gladys; illustrated by Kaethe Zemach. Arthur A. Levine Books 2005 un il $16.99

Grades: PreK K 1 2   E

1. Sisters -- Fiction

ISBN 0-439-66490-X

When Hilda and Rose get fed up with their older sister's bossiness, they get revenge by threatening to have her for dinner

"The dialogue captures the essence of sibling interaction, and children will easily recognize themselves in these characters. The charming watercolor illustrations ensure the story remains lighthearted while clearly depicting the characters' many emotions." SLJ

Another title about Hilda and her sisters is:

To Hilda for helping (1977)

Zia, F.

Hot, hot roti for Dada-ji; art by Ken Min. Lee & Low Books 2011 il $17.95

Grades: K 1 2   E

1. Grandfathers -- Fiction 2. East Indian Americans -- Fiction

ISBN 978-1-60060-443-0; 1-60060-443-9

LC 2010034694

Aneel and his grandfather, Dada-ji, tell stories, use their imaginations, and make delicious roti, a traditional Indian flatbread.

"Min echoes the narrative's exuberance with bright, blocky acrylic scenes of an Indian family in Western surroundings, dressed in a mix of contemporary and traditional styles and headlined by the lad and his elder. . . . A natural for reading aloud, laced with great tastes, infectious sound effects and happy feelings." Kirkus

Includes glossary

Ziefert, Harriet

Bunny's lessons; paintings by Barroux. Blue Apple 2011 un il $16.99

Grades: PreK K 1 2   E

1. Toys -- Fiction 2. Rabbits -- Fiction

ISBN 978-1-60905-028-3; 1-60905-028-2

LC 2010046645

A stuffed rabbit learns much from Charlie, his constant companion, including the meaning of the words "loud," "ouch," and "messy," but also about saying you are sorry and knowing you are loved.

"With simple lines, Barroux creates emotions of surprise, anger, joy, and sadness in his childlike paintings. Thick paper and a matte finish give the book a sturdy, solid feel that complements the sturdy, solid message of friendship." Booklist

By the light of the harvest moon; illustrations by Mark Jones. Blue Apple Books 2009 un il $16.99

Grades: K 1 2   E

1. Autumn -- Fiction 2. Leaves -- Fiction

ISBN 978-1-934706-69-5; 1-934706-69-8

LC 2009-12658

As the fall harvest moon shines on the farm, leaf families gather to celebrate the autumnal equinox.

"This warm picture-book fantasy celebrates fall, especially the amazing movement, light, color, and sounds of autumn leaves. . . . The combination of fantasy and realism in the crisp autumn night will spark children's imagination about the leaf piles they find in their city, suburb, or country roads." Booklist

Home for Navidad; paintings by Santiago Cohen. Houghton Mifflin 2003 un il $15

Grades: K 1 2 3   E

1. Mothers -- Fiction 2. Christmas -- Fiction

ISBN 0-618-34976-6

LC 2002-156430

Ten-year-old Rosa hopes that her mother, whom she has not seen for three years, will leave her job in New York and come home to Santa Catarina, Mexico, for Christmas and maybe even longer. Includes a glossary of Spanish words used

"The combination of simple words and bold, vibrant art relays the wrenching family separation from the child's viewpoint." Booklist

Lucy rescued; Harriet Ziefert; paintings by Barroux. Blue Apple Books 2012 40 p. (hardback) $16.99

Grades: PreK K 1 2   E

1. Dogs -- Fiction 2. Toys -- Fiction 3. Picture books for children 4. Animals -- Infancy -- Fiction

ISBN 1609051874; 9781609051877

LC 2011039015

In this children's picture book, a family adopts a puppy named Lucy from the pound. "Out of nowhere that evening Lucy begins to howl a horrific howl. Morning, noon and night the howling went on and on. The little girl and her parents tried everything to stop it. . . . One night the little girl presented Lucy with a simple toy for her to snuggle with and the howling stopped. . . . But when one of Lucy's favorite toys comes up missing, the howling begins again." (Children's Literature)

Mighty Max; by Harriet Ziefert; illustrated by Elliot Kreloff. Blue Apple Books 2008 un il $15.95

Grades: PreK K 1 2   E

1. Play -- Fiction 2. Beaches -- Fiction 3. Imagination -- Fiction 4. Superheroes -- Fiction

ISBN 978-1-934706-36-7; 1-934706-36-1

LC 2008009662

As Max imagines himself as the super hero—Mighty Max—while at the beach, he saves a game, a castle, and his lunch from some hungry gulls

"Maxwell is a lively little boy with an active imagination. . . . The collage and crayon illustrations are colorful and exuberant." SLJ

My dog thinks I'm a genius; illustrated by Barroux. Blue Apple Books 2011 il $16.99

Grades: PreK K   E

1. Dogs -- Fiction 2. Painting -- Fiction

ISBN 978-1-60905-059-7; 1-60905-059-2

LC 2011018936

A budding artist goes to school after painting a picture with input from his dog Louie, and returns home to find that the dog has some talent, as well.

"Both the text and illustrations are true to the voice of an eight-year-old boy. . . . The colors in the illustrations are perfectly suited to the story. . . . Share this book as an introduction to art, or simply as a sweet dog story." SLJ

One smart skunk; [by] Harriet Ziefert; illustrated by Santiago Cohen. Blue Apple Books 2004 un il $15.95
Grades: PreK K 1 2   E
1. Skunks -- Fiction
ISBN 1-59354-064-7
     LC 2004-10533

Rebecca the skunk lives under a suburban family's deck, eluding the traps set to ensnare her, but the smell of moth balls and the noise of rap music finally convince her that the suburbs are no place to raise her family

"Cohen's illustrations are luminous, and the layout effectively varies text location and illustration size to create an appealing and modern background for this charming, informative text." SLJ

Snow party; illustrated by Mark Jones. Blue Apple Books 2008 un il $16.95
Grades: PreK K 1 2   E
1. Snow -- Fiction 2. Winter -- Fiction
ISBN 978-1-934706-28-2; 1-934706-28-0
     LC 2008005874

A newly illustrated edition of Snow magic, first published 1988 by Viking Kestrel

When the first snow of the year falls on the first day of winter, all the snow people have a snow party.

"Jones provides an emotional and fantasy counterpoint to the quiet intensity of Ziefert's . . . reportorial text. Jones takes full advantage of the book's horizontal format, varying his perspectives and infusing his pictures with a sense of bustle and plenty of detail. . . . He confers individuality upon the members of the snow people community—quite an accomplishment." Publ Wkly

The **big,** bigger, biggest book; illustrated by SAMi. Chronicle Books 2008 un il $14.95
Grades: PreK K   E
1. English language -- Grammar
ISBN 978-1-934706-39-8; 1-934706-39-6

"Using the most minimal text, this novelty book engagingly explores adjectives and adverbs in their absolute, comparative and superlative forms. Each spread incorporates a gatefold flap: at first, readers see only a single word, e.g., 'deep,' which accompanies a scuba diver in an underwater setting. This particular flap unfolds from the bottom of the page, once to show the diver swimming 'deeper' and again to show him 'deepest.'" Publ Wkly

A **bunny** is funny; and so is this book! [by] Harriet Ziefert and Fred Ehrlich; paintings by Todd McKie. Blue Apple Books 2008 un il $16.95
Grades: PreK K 1 2 3   E
1. Stories in rhyme 2. Animals -- Fiction
ISBN 978-1-934706-03-9; 1-934706-03-5
     LC 2007031196

Short rhymes point out traits that characterize different animals, such as an owl's keen eyesight or the beauty of a butterfly's wings

"Each witty rhyme is accompanied by a highly stylized and vibrantly colored illustration of the animal set against a solid-colored background. The charm of each poem is perfectly matched with the boldness of the art. The two pages that feature large flaps with die cuts increase the level of humor and appeal. This book is an excellent choice to share with a group of young children, as well as with an elementary class embarking on a creative-writing unit." SLJ

A **dozen** ducklings lost and found; illustrated by Donald Dreifuss. Houghton Mifflin 2003 un il $15
Grades: PreK K   E
1. Counting 2. Ducklings 3. Ducks -- Fiction
ISBN 0-618-14175-8
     LC 2002-9403

Between the pond and the farm house some of Mother Duck's new babies get lost

"Dreifuss' naive, impressionistic paintings have a simplicity of composition that makes them easy to for group viewing, with the fluffy yellow ducklings standing out against the verdant background." Bull Cent Child Books

Zimmerman, Andrea Griffing
★ **Dig!** [by] Andrea Zimmerman and David Clemesha; illustrated by Marc Rosenthal. Harcourt 2004 un il $16
Grades: PreK K   E
1. Dogs -- Fiction 2. Construction workers -- Fiction 3. Excavating machinery -- Fiction
ISBN 0-15-216785-4
     LC 2003-4373

Follows Mr. Rally and his dog, Lightning, as they travel the town on a big yellow digging machine, taking care of five important jobs

"Earth-tone illustrations are created with watercolor and Prismacolor pencil. . . . The pace, repetition, and word choices make the book appropriate for beginning readers. The uncluttered art, catchy refrain, and focus on heavy machinery make it a natural for storytimes." SLJ

★ **Digger** man; [by] Andrea Zimmerman & David Clemesha. Holt & Co. 2003 un il $15.95
Grades: PreK K   E
1. Brothers -- Fiction 2. Steam-shovels -- Fiction
ISBN 0-8050-6628-4
     LC 2002-10856

A young boy imagines how he will use his digger to make a park where he and his little brother can play

"The joyful acrylic illustrations and the sparse, confident text will delight other digger-wannabes." Booklist

Fire engine man; [by] Andrea Zimmerman & [illustrated by] David Clemesha. Henry Holt 2007 un il $15.95
Grades: PreK K   E
1. Brothers -- Fiction 2. Imagination -- Fiction 3. Fire fighters -- Fiction
ISBN 978-0-8050-7905-0
     LC 2006007909

A young boy imagines the work he will do and the safety gear he will wear when he becomes a fireman some day, as his younger brother first watches then joins him on the job

"The brothers from Digger Man (Holt, 2003) are back. . . . The same colorful acrylic illustrations greet readers, and have enough detail to interest yet not overwhelm them. The text moves at a brisk pace." SLJ

★ **Trashy** town; [by] Andrea Zimmerman and David Clemesha; illustrated by Dan Yaccarino. HarperCollins Pubs. 1999 un il $17.99

Grades: PreK K   E

1. Refuse and refuse disposal -- Fiction

ISBN 0-06-027139-6

LC 98-27495

Little by little, can by can, Mr. Gillie, the trash man, cleans up his town

"Short energetic sentences propel the tale. . . . Employing primary colors dominated by bold blues, Yaccarino's vibrant art has a retro look." Booklist

Zion, Gene

★ **Harry** the dirty dog; pictures by Margaret Bloy Graham. Harper & Row 1956 un il $17.99; lib bdg $17.89; pa $6.99; bd bk $7.99

Grades: PreK K   E

1. Dogs -- Fiction

ISBN 0-06-026865-4; 0-06-026866-2 lib bdg; 0-06-443009-X pa; 0-06-084244-X bd bk

"A runaway dog becomes so dirty his family almost doesn't recognize him. Harry's flight from scrubbing brush and bath water takes him on a tour of the city." Moorachian. What is a City?

Other titles about Harry are:

Harry and the lady next door (1960)

Harry by the sea (1965)

No roses for Harry! (1958)

Zolotow, Charlotte, 1915-2013

The **beautiful** Christmas tree; illustrated by Yan Nacimbene. Houghton Mifflin 1999 32p il $15

Grades: K 1 2 3   E

1. Pine -- Fiction 2. Trees -- Fiction 3. Christmas -- Fiction 4. City and town life -- Fiction

ISBN 0-395-91365-9

LC 98-50006

A newly illustrated edition of the title first published 1972 by Parnassus Press

Although his elegant neighbors do not appreciate his efforts, a kind old man transforms his rundown house and a small neglected pine tree into the best on the street

"In handsome depictions of the urban setting, Nascimbene's delicate watercolors convey the emotional warmth of Zolotow's testament to a simple man's faith and love." Horn Book Guide

A **father** like that; by Charlotte Zolotow; illustrated by LeUyen Pham. HarperCollinsPublishers 2007 un il $16.99; lib bdg $17.89

Grades: PreK K 1 2   E

1. Single parent family -- Fiction 2. Father-son relationship -- Fiction

ISBN 978-0-06-027864-9; 0-06-027864-1; 978-0-06-027865-6 lib bdg; 0-06-027865-X lib bdg

LC 2006000353

A newly illustrated edition of the title first published 1971

A young boy shares with his mother his daydreams about the father who left before he was born

"Zolotow's powerful story . . . has been updated with Pham's realistic, mixed-media illustrations featuring African-American characters. . . . The expressive artwork depicts the characters' emotions and the love they share." SLJ

If it weren't for you; by Charlotte Zolotow; pictures by G. Brian Karas. HarperCollins Pubs. 2006 un il $15.99; lib bdg $16.89

Grades: PreK K 1 2   E

1. Sisters -- Fiction

ISBN 0-06-027875-7; 0-06-027876-5 lib bdg

A newly illustrated edition of the title first published 1966

"Big sister is feeling sorry for herself as she imagines how good life would be without her younger sibling. . . . As she sulks, little sister gradually works her way into her sibling's heart with small acts of kindness. Finally big sister concedes that having a younger sister is not all bad. . . . The new illustrations not only change the gender of the main characters, but also give the story a fresh, contemporary look." SLJ

Mr. Rabbit and the lovely present; pictures by Maurice Sendak. Harper & Row 1962 un il $16.99; pa $5.99

Grades: PreK K 1 2   E

1. Color -- Fiction 2. Rabbits -- Fiction 3. Birthdays -- Fiction

ISBN 0-06-026945-6; 0-06-443020-0 pa

A Caldecott Medal honor book, 1963

"The quiet story, told in dialogue, is illustrated in richly colored pictures which exactly fit the fanciful mood." Hodges. Books for Elem Sch Libr

The **old** dog; paintings by James Ransome. rev and newly illustrated ed; HarperCollins Pubs. 1995 un il $16.99

Grades: K 1 2   E

1. Dogs -- Fiction 2. Death -- Fiction

ISBN 0-06-024409-7

LC 93-41081

A revised and newly illustrated edition of the title first published 1972 by Coward, McCann & Geoghegan under the author's pseudonym Sarah Abbott

When Ben finds his old dog dead one morning, he spends the rest of the day thinking about all the good times they had together

"Zolotow's elemental story . . . is newly illustrated here with rich oil paintings. . . . An unsentimental story about connection and loss and renewal." Booklist

The **seashore** book; paintings by Wendell Minor. HarperCollins Pubs. 1992 un il $16.99; pa $6.99

Grades: K 1 2   E

1. Seashore -- Fiction 2. Mother-son relationship -- Fiction

ISBN 0-06-020213-0; 0-06-443364-1 pa

LC 91-22783

A mother's words help a little boy imagine the sights and sounds of the seashore, even though he's never seen the ocean

"Minor's crisply detailed watercolors evoke place with imaginative accuracy and visual grace, and Zolotow's . . .

spare, poetic text provides a lyrical and nostalgic paean to the wonders of seaside life." Publ Wkly

When the wind stops; illustrated by Stefano Vitale. rev and newly illustrated ed; HarperCollins Pubs. 1995 un il hardcover o.p. pa $6.99

Grades: PreK K   E

1. Nature -- Fiction

ISBN 0-06-025425-4; 0-06-443472-9 pa

LC 94-14477

A revised and newly illustrated edition of the title first published 1962 by Abelard-Schuman

This is a revised edition of Zolotow's 1962 title, with a new illustrator. "A little boy feels sorry when the day is over, but his mother explains that day is beginning somewhere else, and that 'Nothing ends . . . It begins in another place or in a different way.'" (Bull Cent Child Books) "Ages four to eight." (Booklist)

"The full-color scenes, painted on wood, gloriously depict heaven and earth and give concrete meaning to abstract concepts. Not only wonderful for lap sharing, this beautiful book will also be a rich supplement for a science unit on the elements or the seasons." Booklist

★ **William's** doll; pictures by William Pène Du Bois. Harper & Row 1972 30p il $16.99; pa $6.99

Grades: PreK K 1 2   E

1. Dolls -- Fiction 2. Sex role -- Fiction

ISBN 0-06-027047-0; 0-06-027048-9 lib bdg; 0-06-443067-7 pa

When little William asks for a doll, the other boys scorn him and his father tries to interest him in conventional boys' playthings such as a basketball and a train. His sympathetic grandmother buys him the doll, explaining his need to have it to love and care for so that he can practice being a father

"Very, very special. The strong, yet delicate pictures . . . convey a gentleness of spirit and longing most effectively, as William pantomimes his craving." N Y Times Book Rev

Zuckerman, Andrew

★ **Creature** ABC. Chronicle Books 2009 un il $19.99

Grades: PreK K 1 2   E

1. Animals 2. Alphabet

ISBN 978-0-8118-6978-2; 0-8118-6978-4

LC 2009-04365

"This is a first choice for libraries." Bull Cent Child Books

Includes glossary

Zuffi, Stefano

Art 123; count from 1 to 12 with great works of art. Abrams Books for Young Readers 2011 32p $12.95

Grades: K 1 2   E

1. Counting 2. Art appreciation

ISBN 978-1-4197-0100-9; 1-4197-0100-2

LC 2011009728

"From Caravaggio to Lichtenstein, this enriching counting book features a different work of Western art for numbers one through 12, accompanied by a brief, descriptive rhyme. . . . In addition to introducing numbers and counting, the book works well as a basic primer on viewing (and thinking about) art." SLJ

Zullo, Germano

Little bird; Germano Zullo; illustrated by Albertine. Enchanted Lion Books 2012 72 p.

Grades: PreK K 1 2   E

1. Birds -- Fiction 2. Flight -- Fiction 3. Friendship -- Fiction 4. Picture books for children

ISBN 1592701183; 9781592701186

LC 2011052462

This picture book, a French Caldecott Medal winner, tells the story of a man who frees a group of birds from his truck so that they can fly away. When one small bird remains, he keeps it company and tries to show it how to fly. The little bird returns later with the entire flock, lifting up the man and flying with him. The story "suggests that little things can change lives--and perhaps even the world. Placing small, uncomplicated shapes against large fields of uniform color . . . [illustrator] Albertine provides a visual plot for [Germano] Zullo's meditative abstractions . . . the characters express fear, friendship, yearning and delight through glances, posture and other cues." (Kirkus)

Zuravicky, Oril

★ **C** is for city; an alphabet book. illustrated by Giuseppe Castellano. Little Simon 2011 il $7.99

Grades: PreK K   E

1. Alphabet 2. Stories in rhyme 3. Board books for children

ISBN 978-1-4424-2049-6; 1-4424-2049-9

"Mister Doodle may be a simple stick figure, but he lives in a vibrant photo-collage world. In this alphabet book, he and his dog, Sketch, share a new noun for every letter of the alphabet. . . . Mister Doodle's adventures unfold in bouncy, playful rhymes. . . . A great little introduction to the alphabet, this lively outing . . . should inspire kids to notice details." Publ Wkly

Fic FICTION

50 Cent (Musician), 1975-

Playground; with Aura Moser. Razorbill 2011 $17.99

Grades: 5 6 7 8   Fic

1. Bullies -- Fiction

ISBN 978-1-59514-434-8; 1-59514-434-X

Thirteen-year-old Butterball doesn't have much going for him. He's teased about his weight. He hates the Long Island suburb his mom moved them to so she could go to nursing school and start her life over. He wishes he still lived with his dad in New York City where there's always something happening, even if his dad doesn't have much time for him. Still, that's not why he beat up Maurice on the playground.

"Readers who were ever confused about having a gay parent, or being overweight, or going through a parental breakup, or just wanting to fit in and be accepted by their peers, will relate to Butterball. 50 Cents's debut young adult novel is a quick read that will be great for discussions on a variety of important and timely topics." Voice Youth Advocates

Abbott, Tony

Firegirl. Little, Brown 2006 145p $15.99; pa $5.99

Grades: 5 6 7 8   **Fic**
1. School stories 2. Burns and scalds -- Fiction
ISBN 978-0-316-01171-6; 0-316-01171-1; 978-0-316-01170-9 pa; 0-316-01170-3 pa

LC 2005-07964

A middle school boy's life is changed when Jessica, a girl disfigured by burns, starts attending his Catholic school while receiving treatment at a local hospital.

"Through realistic settings and dialogue, and believable characters, readers will be able to relate to the social dynamics of these adolescents who are trying to handle a difficult situation." SLJ

Kringle; illustrated by Greg Call. Scholastic Press 2005 324p il $14.99
Grades: 5 6 7 8   **Fic**
1. Fantasy fiction 2. Orphans -- Fiction 3. Santa Claus -- Fiction
ISBN 0-439-74942-5

LC 2005-12697

In the fifth century A.D., as order retreats from Britain with the departing Roman Army, orphaned, twelve-year-old Kringle determines to rescue his beloved guardian from the evil goblins who terrorize the countryside by kidnapping and enslaving humans and, in the process, with the help of elves and others along the way, discovers his true destiny.

"The enticing premise, appealing young hero, and non-stop action will appeal to many fantasy lovers." Booklist

The **postcard**. Little, Brown 2008 358p il $15.99; pa $5.99
Grades: 5 6 7 8   **Fic**
1. Mystery fiction 2. Grandmothers -- Fiction 3. Books and reading -- Fiction
ISBN 978-0-316-01172-3; 0-316-01172-X; 978-0-316-01173-0 pa; 0-316-01173-8 pa

LC 2007-31074

While in St. Petersburg, Florida, to help clean out his recently-deceased grandmother's house, thirteen-year-old Jason finds an old postcard which leads him on an adventure that blends figures from an old, unfinished detective story with his family's past.

"Mystery fans will appreciate the depth and intrigue of the dual level mysteries, and will also enjoy the wit and banter of the main characters." Libr Media Connect

Abdel-Fattah, Randa
★ **Where** the streets had a name; Randa Abdel-Fattah. Scholastic Press 2010 313p (reinforced binding) $17.99
Grades: 5 6 7 8   **Fic**
1. Jerusalem -- Fiction 2. Voyages and travels -- Fiction 3. Jewish-Arab relations -- Fiction 4. Muslims -- Fiction 5. Family life -- Fiction 6. Palestinian Arabs -- Fiction
ISBN 0545172926; 9780545172929; 978-0-545-17292-9; 0-545-17292-6

LC 2009043122

This book tells the story of 13-year-old Hayaat, who "lives behind the Israeli-built Separation Wall in the West Bank City of Bethlehem. When her beloved grandmother falls ill . . . [she] decides to make her way to Jerusalem to fill an empty hummus jar with soil from the land of her grandmother's ancestral home. She is certain that this will mend her heart. Unfortunately, although Jerusalem is merely minutes away, curfews, checkpoints, and an identity card that doesn't allow her to cross the border mean that Hayaat and her soccer-loving, troublemaker friend Samy face a perilous journey." (School Lib J) "At the many checkpoints, the friends encounter soldiers, both brutal and kind, and also an Israeli peacenik couple who helps the kids get past the towering barriers." (Booklist)

"Hayaat chronicles this life-altering journey in the first-person, present tense, giving readers an intimate glimpse into the life of her warm, eccentric Muslim family, who survive despite the volatile political environment. A refreshing and hopeful teen perspective on the Israeli-Palestinian dilemma." Kirkus

Abela, Deborah
The **ghosts** of Gribblesea Pier. Farrar Straus Giroux 2011 232p $16.99
Grades: 4 5 6   **Fic**
1. Ghost stories 2. Circus -- Fiction 3. Family life -- Fiction 4. Swindlers and swindling -- Fiction 5. Eccentrics and eccentricities -- Fiction
ISBN 978-0-374-36239-3; 0-374-36239-4

LC 2010022517

Aurelie Bonhoffen, who has grown up in the circus, discovers a remarkable family secret on her twelfth birthday that may help in dealing with a sinister man who wants to take over her family's pier.

This is a "charmer of a ghostly adventure tale. . . . This fast-paced, engaging, and charming story has echoes of Jeanne Birdsall's 'Penderwicks' . . . and some Dickensian elements, but in the end this is just a finely executed story of family and friendship and the ties that bind a community." SLJ

Abouet, Marguerite
Akissi; Feline Invasion. by Marguerite Abouet; illustrated by Mathiew Sapin. Flying Eye Books 2013 48 p. ill. (hardcover) $14.95
Grades: 2 3 4 5   **Fic**
1. Siblings -- Juvenile fiction 2. Conduct of life -- Juvenile fiction
ISBN 190926301X; 9781909263017

This book by Marguerite Abouet presents "African vignettes aimed at a younger audience. All seven episodes feature young Akissi and her brother Fofana or her friends getting into trouble for less-than-exemplary . . . behavior. In 'Good Mums,' . . . she borrows a neighbor's baby and tenderly feeds it a stew concocted from discarded scraps found in the market. 'Home Cinema' has her playing lookout while Fofana sells spots in front of the television set to neighborhood children." (Kirkus Reviews)

Abraham, Susan Gonzales
Cecilia's year; by Susan Gonzales Abraham & Denise Gonzales Abraham. Cinco Puntos Press 2004 210p il $16.95; pa $11.95
Grades: 4 5 6 7   **Fic**
1. Poverty -- Fiction 2. Sex role -- Fiction 3. Hispanic Americans -- Fiction
ISBN 978-0-938317-87-6; 0-938317-87-3; 978-1-933693-02-6 pa; 1-933693-02-9 pa

LC 2004-13374

Nearly fourteen and poor, Ceclia Gonzales wants desperately to go to high school and become a teacher until her mother's old-fashioned ideas about a woman's place threaten her dreams

"The cultural details are vivid and integrated into the story, providing a rich context and a snapshot of an entire community. . . . This fictionalized biography succeeds on several levels." SLJ

Another title about Cecilia is:
Surprising Cecilia (2005)

Acampora, Paul

Rachel Spinelli punched me in the face. Roaring Brook Press 2011 168p $15.99

Grades: 5 6 7 8   Fic
1. Moving -- Fiction 2. Trumpet -- Fiction 3. Musicians -- Fiction 4. Friendship -- Fiction 5. Family life -- Fiction 6. Single parent family -- Fiction
ISBN 978-1-59643-548-3; 1-59643-548-8
                                        LC 2010027436
When fourteen-year-old Zachary and his father move to Falls, Connecticut, he spends a summer falling in love, coming to terms with his mother's absence, and forming eclectic friendships.

"Realistic dialogue and poignantly amusing situations . . . all come together to gently flesh out a few months in the lives of people readers will savor getting to know. . . . An outstanding, humane coming-of-age tale of loss, yearning and forgiveness." Kirkus

Achebe, Chinua

How the leopard got his claws; [by] Chinua Achebe and John Iroaganachi; illustrated by Mary Grandpre. Candlewick Press 2011 il $16.99

Grades: 4 5 6   Fic
1. Allegories 2. Jungles -- Fiction 3. Leopards -- Fiction
ISBN 978-0-7636-4805-3; 0-7636-4805-1
                                        LC 2010040344
Recounts how the leopard got his claws and teeth and why he rules the forest with terror.

"First published in the 1970s, this political fable still makes provocative reading. Grand Pré's new Lion King-style illustrations both capture the tale's intensity and provide a needed contemporary look. . . . The stately prose will make a profound impression on readers, as will the large, dimly lit closeups of snarling jaws and strong animal bodies." Booklist

Ackerman, Karen

The night crossing; illustrated by Elizabeth Sayles. Knopf 1994 56p il hardcover o.p. pa $4.99

Grades: 3 4 5   Fic
1. Jews -- Fiction 2. Holocaust, 1933-1945 -- Fiction
ISBN 0-679-87040-7 pa
                                        LC 94-10805
In 1938, having begun to feel the persecution that all Jews are experiencing in their Austrian city, Clara and her family escape over the mountains into Switzerland

"Ackerman's writing is clear and direct; despite its simplicity, it is never banal. This is an excellent fictional introduction to the Holocaust." SLJ

Ada, Alma Flor, 1938-

Dancing home; [by] Alma Flor Ada and Gabriel M. Zubizarreta. Atheneum Books for Young Readers 2011 147p $14.99

Grades: 3 4 5 6   Fic
1. Cousins -- Fiction 2. Family life -- Fiction 3. Mexican Americans -- Fiction 4. Father-daughter relationship -- Fiction
ISBN 978-1-4169-0088-7; 1-4169-0088-8
                                        LC 2010013229
When Margie's cousin Lupe comes from Mexico to live in California with Margie's family, Lupe must adapt to America, while Margie, who thought it would be fun to have her cousin there, finds that she is embarrassed by her in school and jealous of her at home.

"This story will assist readers in embracing their own heritage and developing an appreciation for their classmates' backgrounds. It's an enjoyable offering (and a great read-aloud) that will capture readers' attention." SLJ

Adams, Richard

★ **Watership** Down; Scribner classics ed.; Scribner 1996 429p $30; pa $15

Grades: 6 7 8 9 10   Fic
1. Allegories 2. Rabbits -- Fiction
ISBN 0-684-83605-X; 0-7432-7770-8 pa
First published 1972 in the United Kingdom; first United States edition 1974 by Macmillan

"Faced with the annihilation of its warren, a small group of male rabbits sets out across the English downs in search of a new home. Internal struggles for power surface in this intricately woven, realistically told adult adventure when the protagonists must coordinate tactics in order to defeat an enemy rabbit fortress. It is clear that the author has done research on rabbit behavior, for this tale is truly authentic." Shapiro Fic for Youth. 3d edition

Adler, David A.

★ **Cam** Jansen and the mystery of the stolen diamonds; illustrated by Susanna Natti. Viking 1980 58p il hardcover o.p. $13.99

Grades: 2 3 4   Fic
1. Mystery fiction
ISBN 0-670-20039-5; 0-14-034670-8 pa
                                        LC 79-20695
Cam Jansen, a fifth-grader with a photographic memory, and her friend Eric help solve the mystery of the stolen diamonds

This is a "fast-action uncomplicated adventure . . . [with] a touch of humor, a breezy writing style, and some very enjoyable pen-and-ink drawings." Booklist

Other titles about Cam Jansen are:
Cam Jansen and the barking treasure mystery (1999)
Cam Jansen and the birthday mystery (2000)
Cam Jansen and the catnapping mystery (1998)
Cam Jansen and the chocolate fudge mystery (1993)
Cam Jansen and the first day of school mystery (2002)
Cam Jansen and the ghostly mystery (1996)
Cam Jansen and the mystery at the haunted house (1992)
Cam Jansen and the mystery at the monkey house (1985)
Cam Jansen and the mystery of Flight 54 (1989)
Cam Jansen and the mystery of the Babe Ruth baseball (1982)
Cam Jansen and the mystery of the carnival prize (1984)

Cam Jansen and the mystery of the circus clown (1983)

Cam Jansen and the mystery of the dinosaur bones (1981)

Cam Jansen and the mystery of the gold coins (1982)

Cam Jansen and the mystery of the monster movie (1984)

Cam Jansen and the mystery of the stolen corn popper (1986)

Cam Jansen and the mystery of the television dog (1981)

Cam Jansen and the mystery of the UFO (1980)

Cam Jansen and the scary snake mystery (1997)

Cam Jansen and the school play mystery (2001)

Cam Jansen and the Secret Service mystery (2006)

Cam Jansen and the snowy day mystery (2004)

Cam Jansen and the Sports Day mysteries (2009)

Cam Jansen and the summer camp mysteries (2007)

Cam Jansen and the tennis trophy mystery (2003)

Cam Jansen and the Triceratops Pops mystery (1995)

Cam Jansen and the Valentine baby mystery (2005)

Cam Jansen and the wedding cake mystery (2011)

Don't talk to me about the war. Viking 2008 216p $15.99; pa $6.99

Grades: 4 5 6 7   **Fic**

1. Friendship -- Fiction 2. Family life -- Fiction 3. World War, 1939-1945 -- Fiction

ISBN 978-0-670-06307-9; 0-670-06307-X; 978-0-14-241372-2 pa; 0-14-241372-0 pa

LC 2007-17889

In 1940, thirteen-year-old Tommy's routine of school, playing stickball in his Bronx, New York, neighborhood, talking with his friend Beth, and listening to Dodgers games on the radio changes as his mother's illness and his increasing awareness of the war in Europe transform his world.

"An engaging and very accessible historical novel." Booklist

Agell, Charlotte

The **accidental** adventures of India McAllister. Henry Holt 2010 151p il $16.99

Grades: 3 4 5   **Fic**

1. Divorce -- Fiction 2. Friendship -- Fiction 3. Homosexuality -- Fiction 4. Chinese Americans -- Fiction

ISBN 978-0-8050-8902-8; 0-8050-8902-0

LC 2009-18907

India, an unusual nine-and-a-half-year-old living in small-town Maine, has a series of adventures which bring her closer to her artist-mother, strengthen her friendship with a neighbor boy, and help her to accept the man for whom her father moved away.

Aguiar, Nadia

Secrets of Tamarind. Feiwel and Friends 2011 373p map (The Book of Tamarind) $16.99

Grades: 5 6 7 8   **Fic**

1. Adventure fiction 2. Magic -- Fiction 3. Islands -- Fiction 4. Siblings -- Fiction 5. Environmental degradation -- Fiction

ISBN 978-0-312-38030-4; 0-312-38030-5

LC 2010050898

Four years after leaving the lost island of Tamarind, Maya, Simon, and Penny Nelson return to stop the Red Cor-

al Project, a sinister group mining the magical mineral ophalla there and, in the process, ruining the magnificent island.

"Replete with ecological warnings applicable to real as well as fantasy worlds and glossed with lush descriptions of imaginary flora and fauna, the rapid-fire plot bristles with danger." Kirkus

The **lost** island of Tamarind; [by] Nadia Aguiar. Feiwel and Friends 2008 437p il map (The Book of Tamarind) $17.95

Grades: 5 6 7 8   **Fic**

1. War stories 2. Adventure fiction 3. Magic -- Fiction 4. Giants -- Fiction 5. Islands -- Fiction 6. Pirates -- Fiction 7. Siblings -- Fiction

ISBN 978-0-312-38029-8; 0-312-38029-1

LC 2008-5623

Thirteen-year-old Maya, who has spent her life at sea with her marine biologist parents, yearns for a normal life, but when a storm washes her parents overboard, life becomes anything but normal for Maya, her younger brother and baby sister, as they land at a mysterious, uncharted island filled with danger.

"Each detail of this fantasy is crafted with care; readers will be drawn into this dangerous, magical world where anything is possible and nothing can be fully explained." SLJ

Aiken, Joan

Black hearts in Battersea. Houghton Mifflin Co 1999 234p $7.99

Grades: 5 6 7 8   **Fic**

1. Orphans -- Fiction

ISBN 978-0-395-97128-4; 0-395-97128-4

A reissue of the title first published 1964 by Doubleday

Simon arrives in London to meet an old friend and pursue the study of painting, but he finds himself in the middle of a wicked crew's plan to overthrow good King James and the Duke and Duchess of Battersea.

Nightbirds on Nantucket. Houghton Mifflin 1999 218p (hardcover) $15.00; (paperback) $6.95

Grades: 5 6 7 8   **Fic**

ISBN 9780618153275; 9780395971246; 9780395971857

A reissue of the title first published 1966 by Doubleday

Having had enough of life on board the ship that saved her from a watery grave, Dido Twite wants nothing more than to sail home to England. Instead, Captain Casket's ship lands in Nantucket, where Dido and the captain's daughter, Dutiful Penitence, are left in the care of Dutiful's sinister Aunt Tribulation. In Tribulation's farmhouse, life is unbearable. When mysterious men lurk about in the evening fog, the resourceful Dido rallies against their shenanigans with help from Dutiful, a cabinboy named Nate, and a pink whale.

The **Witch** of Clatteringshaws. Delacorte Press 2005 131p pa $8.25

Grades: 5 6 7 8   **Fic**

1. Adventure fiction 2. Witches -- Fiction

ISBN 0-385-73226-0; 0-385-90252-2 lib bdg; 978-0-099-46406-8 pa

LC 2003027091

Dido travels to Scotland and, aided by Woodlouse and by Father Sam's cousin Malise, the Witch of Clatteringshaws, seeks another heir to the throne who can relieve her friend Simon of the burden of being king of England.

"Aiken somehow brings this story off with panache. Readers soon realize that her characters are just as amused by events as they are, swinging the story away from the ludicrous into a jolly romp of a fantasy." SLJ

★ The **wolves** of Willoughby Chase; illustrated by Pat Marriott. Delacorte Press 2000 181p il hardcover o.p. pa $6.99
Grades: 5 6 7 8   **Fic**
ISBN 0-385-32790-0; 0-440-49603-9 pa
First published 1962 in the United Kingdom; first United States edition 1963 by Doubleday
"Plot, characterization, and background blend perfectly into an amazing whole. . . . Highly recommended." SLJ
Other titles in this series are:
Black hearts in Battersea (1964)
Cold Shoulder Road (1996)
The cuckoo tree (1971)
Dangerous games (1999)
Is underground (1993)
Midwinter nightingale (2003)
Nightbirds on Nantucket (1966)
The stolen lake (1981)
The witch of Clatteringshaws (2005)

Albarn, Jessica
The **boy** in the oak; [text & illustrations by] Jessica Albarn. Simply Read Books 2010 un il $17.95
Grades: 4 5 6 7   **Fic**
1. Fantasy fiction 2. Magic -- Fiction 3. Trees -- Fiction 4. Fairies -- Fiction
ISBN 978-1-897476-52-9; 1-897476-52-3
"A spare, lightly haunting narrative tells a fairy-tale-like story of a lonely boy whose play in the woods was 'insensitive and cruel. He trampled the flowers. He tore limbs off trees and carved his initials into their trunks.' A group of fairies . . . trap him inside an ancient 'Druidic Oak,' where the boy watches the seasons pass until a young girl arrives. . . . Pages of prose alternate with wordless spreads featuring spindly artwork and semitranslucent sheets imprinted with close-up photos of nature textures. . . . The book draws the most lasting power from its harmonious layers of imagery and sophisticated bookmaking." Booklist

Alber, Merryl
And the tide comes in; exploring a Georgia salt marsh. by Merryl Alber; illustrated by Joyce Mihran Turley. Taylor Trade Pub. 2012 32 p. ill. (hardcover) $15.95
Grades: 1 2 3   **Fic**
1. Marshes 2. Picture books for children 3. Ecology -- Juvenile literature
ISBN 0981770053; 9780981770055
In this children's picture book, a "child in Georgia takes her Colorado cousin on daily visits to a nearby salt marsh. Ginger discovers the cyclical nature of this habitat as she observes and asks about this ecosystem. Alongside the description of the activities of the two girls is an explanation of an aspect of the marsh. Representational animals such as fiddler crabs, blue crabs, and shrimp and the importance of a marsh to their survival are described." (School Library Journal)

Alcott, Louisa May
Little women; illustrated by Scott McKowen. Sterling Pub. 2004 525p il $9.95
Grades: 5 6 7 8   **Fic**
1. Sisters -- Fiction 2. Family life -- Fiction
ISBN 978-1-4027-1458-0; 1-4027-1458-0
LC 2004-15669
First published 1868
Chronicles the joys and sorrows of the four March sisters as they grow into young women in mid-nineteenth-century New England.
Other titles about members of the March family are:
Eight cousins (1875)
Jo's boys (1886)
Little men (1871)
Rose in bloom (1876)

Alexander, Lloyd
The **Black** Cauldron; [by] Lloyd Alexander. rev. ed.; H. Holt 1999 182p (Chronicles of Prydain) $19.95
Grades: 5 6 7 8   **Fic**
1. Fantasy fiction
ISBN 0-8050-6131-2; 978-08050-6131-4
LC 98040896
First published 1965
Taran, Assistant Pig-Keeper of Prydain, faces even more dangers as he seeks the magical black cauldron, the chief implement of the evil powers of Arawn, lord of the Land of Death.

Taran Wanderer; [by] Lloyd Alexander. rev ed.; H. Holt 1999 222p (Chronicles of Prydain) $19.95
Grades: 5 6 7 8   **Fic**
1. Fantasy fiction
ISBN 0-8050-6134-7
LC 98040904
The fourth book of the Prydain cycle tells of the adventures that befell Taran when he went in search of his birthright and the truth about himself.

Westmark. Dutton 1981 184p hardcover o.p. pa $5.99
Grades: 5 6 7 8   **Fic**
1. Adventure fiction
ISBN 0-14-131068-5
A boy fleeing from criminal charges falls in with a charlatan, his dwarf attendant, and an urchin girl, travels with them about the kingdom of Westmark, and ultimately arrives at the palace where the king is grieving over the loss of his daughter
The author "peoples his tale with a marvelous cast of individuals, and weaves an intricate story of high adventure that climaxes in a superbly conceived conclusion, which, though predictable, is reached through carefully built tension and subtly added comic relief." Booklist
Other titles in this series are:
The Beggar Queen (1984)
The Kestrel (1982)

★ The **book** of three; rev ed.; Holt & Co. 1999 190p (Chronicles of Prydain) $19.95; pa $6.99

Grades: 5 6 7 8   **Fic**
1. Fantasy 2. Fantasy fiction
ISBN 978-0-8050-6132-1; 0-8050-6132-0; 978-0-8050-8048-3 pa; 0-8050-8048-1 pa

LC 98-40901

First published 1964
"Related in a simple, direct style, this fast-paced tale of high adventure has a well-balanced blend of fantasy, realism, and humor." SLJ
Other titles about the mythical land of Prydain are:
The black cauldron (1965)
The castle of Llyr (1966)
The foundling and other tales of Prydain (1999)
The high king (1968)
Taran Wanderer (1967)

The **castle** of Llyr; [by] Lloyd Alexander. rev.ed.; H. Holt 1999 172p (Chronicles of Prydain) $19.95
Grades: 5 6 7 8   **Fic**
1. Fantasy fiction
ISBN 0-8050-6133-9

LC 98040897

First published 1966
When Princess Eilonwy is sent to the Isle of Mona for training, she is bewitched by the evil enchantress Achren, so Taran and other friends must try to rescue her.

The **golden** dream of Carlo Chuchio. Henry Holt & Co. 2007 306p il $16.95
Grades: 5 6 7 8 9   **Fic**
1. Fantasy fiction 2. Buried treasure -- Fiction 3. Voyages and travels -- Fiction
ISBN 978-0-8050-8333-0; 0-8050-8333-2

LC 2006-49710

Naive and bumbling Carlo, his shady camel-puller Baksheesh, and Shira, a girl determined to return home, follow a treasure map through the deserts and cities of the infamous Golden Road, as mysterious strangers try in vain to point them toward real treasures
This "is an exuberant and compassionate tale of adventure." Publ Wkly

The **high** king; rev ed; Holt & Co. 1999 253p (Chronicles of Prydain) $19.95
Grades: 5 6 7 8   **Fic**
1. Fantasy 2. Fantasy fiction
ISBN 0-8050-6135-5

LC 98-40900

First published 1968
Awarded The Newbery Medal, 1969
"The fantasy has the depth and richness of a medieval tapestry, infinitely detailed and imaginative." Saturday Rev
The **iron** ring. Dutton Children's Bks. 1997 283p hardcover o.p. pa $5.99
Grades: 5 6 7 8   **Fic**
1. Adventure fiction
ISBN 0-14-130348-4 pa

LC 96-29730

"Young Tamar, ruler of a small Indian kingdom, wagers with a visiting king and loses his kingdom and his freedom. Traveling to the king's land to make good on his debt, he collects quite an entourage and eventually overcomes his enemies with his friends' help. This tale offers delightful

characters, a philosophical interest in the meaning of life, a thoughtful look at the caste system, and a clever use of Indian animal folktales." Horn Book Guide

The **remarkable** journey of Prince Jen. Dutton Children's Bks. 1991 273p hardcover o.p. pa $6.99
Grades: 5 6 7 8   **Fic**
1. Adventure fiction
ISBN 0-14-240225-7 pa

LC 91-13720

Bearing six unusual gifts, young Prince Jen in Tang Dynasty China embarks on a perilous quest and emerges triumphantly into manhood
"Alexander satisfies the taste for excitement, but his vivid characters and the food for thought he offers will nourish long after the last page is turned." SLJ

Allen, Crystal
How Lamar's bad prank won a Bubba-sized trophy. Balzer + Bray 2011 283p $16.99
Grades: 4 5 6   **Fic**
1. Bowling -- Fiction 2. Conduct of life -- Fiction 3. African Americans -- Fiction
ISBN 978-0-06-199272-8; 0-06-199272-0

LC 2010-08229

When thirteen-year-old, bowling-obsessed Lamar Washington finds out that his idol is coming to town, he finds himself involved in some unsavory activities as he tries to change his image to impress people.
"Under all the braggadocio is a boy with a big heart, and from the first sentence Lamar will have readers hooked." Publ Wkly

Allison, Jennifer
★ Gilda Joyce, psychic investigator. Sleuth/Dutton 2005 321p $13.99; pa $6.99
Grades: 5 6 7 8   **Fic**
1. Mystery fiction 2. Cousins -- Fiction
ISBN 978-0-525-47375-6; 0-525-47375-0; 978-0-14-240698-4 pa; 0-14-240698-8 pa

LC 2004-10834

During the summer before ninth grade, intrepid Gilda Joyce invites herself to the San Francisco mansion of distant cousin Lester Splinter and his thirteen-year-old daughter, where she uses her purported psychic abilities and detective skills to solve the mystery of the mansion's boarded-up tower.
"Allison pulls off something special here. She not only offers a credible mystery . . . but also . . . provides particularly strong characterizations." Booklist
Other titles about Gilda Joyce are:
Gilda Joyce: the Ladies of the Lake (2006)
Gilda Joyce: the ghost sonata (2007)
Gilda Joyce: the dead drop (2009)
Gilda Joyce: the bones of the holy (2011)

Almond, David
My dad's a birdman; illustrated by Polly Dunbar. Candlewick Press 2008 115p il $15.99
Grades: 4 5 6   **Fic**
1. Flight -- Fiction 2. Fathers -- Fiction
ISBN 978-0-7636-3667-8; 0-7636-3667-3

In a rainy town in the north of England, there are strange goings-on. Dad is building a pair of wings, eating flies, and feathering his nest. Lizzie is missing her Mom and looking after Dad by letting him follow his newfound whimsy. What's behind it all? It's the great human bird competition.

"Handsomely produced, the book is printed in varying size typefaces and enhanced by Dunbar's pencil, watercolor, and collage illustrations interspersed throughout the text. Casual yet evocative, they perfectly interpret Almond's broadly sketched characters. A fine read-aloud." SLJ

★ Skellig; 10th anniversary ed.; Delacorte Press 2009 182p $16.99; pa $6.99

Grades: 5 6 7 8 9 10   Fic
1. Fantasy fiction
ISBN 978-0-385-32653-7; 0-385-32653-X; 978-0-440-41602-9 pa; 0-440-41602-7 pa
First published 1998 in the United Kingdom; first United States edition 1999
Michael L. Printz Award honor book

Unhappy about his baby sister's illness and the chaos of moving into a dilapidated old house, Michael retreats to the garage and finds a mysterious stranger who is something like a bird and something like an angel.

"The plot is beautifully paced and the characters are drawn with a graceful, careful hand.... A lovingly done, thought-provoking novel." SLJ

Slog's dad; illustrated by Dave McKean. Candlewick Press 2011 52p il $15.99

Grades: 5 6 7 8   Fic
1. Death -- Fiction 2. Future life -- Fiction 3. Father-son relationship -- Fiction
ISBN 978-0-7636-4940-1; 0-7636-4940-6
    LC 2010-38700

When Slog's father died he promised to return for one last visit in the spring, but when Slog spots a scruffy man on a bench outside the butcher shop and identifies him as his father, his best friend Davie is skeptical.

"This grief-strafed wonder tale is brilliantly matched by some of McKean's most moving artwork yet. Text pages, featuring a voice steeped on Northern English flavor, are counterpoised against wordless illustration sequences that move readers from heaven to earth and back again, beginning with a celestial descent from the sky to a park bench by a man trailing clouds of watercolor glory." Bull Cent Child Books

The boy who climbed into the moon; illustrated by Polly Dunbar. Candlewick Press 2010 117p il $15.99

Grades: 3 4 5   Fic
1. Adventure fiction
ISBN 978-0-7636-4217-4; 0-7636-4217-7
    LC 2009-11158

Helped by a very long ladder, some unusual acquaintances, two rather worried parents, and a great deal of community spirit, a young English boy makes an astonishing discovery when he embarks on a mission to prove that the moon is nothing but a big hole in the sky

"Almond employs all manners of amusements ... while never losing sight of some refreshing realities: Paul's parents are a real presence, and the city feels appropriately dense. ... Dunbar's full-color illustrations ... nimbly dodge the prose." Booklist

Almond, David, 1951-
Heaven Eyes. Delacorte Press 2001 233p hardcover o.p. pa $5.50

Grades: 5 6 7 8   Fic
1. Orphans 2. Adventure fiction 3. Adventure and adventurers 4. Orphans -- Fiction
ISBN 0-385-32770-6; 0-440-22910-3 pa
    LC 00-31798
First published 2000 in the United Kingdom

Having escaped from their orphanage on a raft, Erin, January, and Mouse float down into another world of abandoned warehouses and factories, meeting a strange old man and an even stranger girl with webbed fingers and toes named Heaven Eyes. "Intermediate, middle school." (Horn Book)

"The ambiguous and surreal setting and the lyricism of the metaphor-laden prose make this a compelling and original novel." SLJ

Mouse bird snake wolf; David Almond, illustrated by David McKean. Candlewick Press 2013 80 p. (reinforced) $17.99

Grades: 4 5 6 7   Fic
1. Animals -- Juvenile fiction 2. Fantasy fiction -- Juvenile fiction
ISBN 0763659126; 9780763659127
    LC 2012950556

In this book, "Harry, Sue, and Little Ben live in a world whose lazy gods have made creatures like whales and camels but have given up their work, leaving blank spaces ... . The children discover that they can create animals themselves, using sticks, leaves, and clay; Little Ben makes a mouse; Sue, a bird; and Harry, a snake. But Harry and Sue aren't satisfied. They create a terrifying wolf that turns on them and eats them, and Little Ben must summon the courage to save them." (Publishers Weekly)

★ My name is Mina. Delacorte Press 2011 300p $15.99; lib bdg $18.99

Grades: 5 6 7 8   Fic
1. Authorship -- Fiction
ISBN 978-0-385-74073-9; 0-385-74073-5; 978-0-375-98964-3 lib bdg; 0-375-98964-1 lib bdg; 978-0-375-98965-0 e-book
    LC 2010040143

"This intimate prequel to Skellig is built around Mina McKee, the curious and brilliant home-schooled child who eventually befriends that book's protagonist, Michael. Mina, a budding writer, reveals her love of words in her journal; most of the book unfolds in a handwritten-looking font, with Mina's more emphatic entries exploding onto the pages in massive display type. Her lyrical, nonlinear prose records her reflections on her past, existential musings ... and self-directed writing exercises.... Almond gives readers a vivid picture of the joyfully freeform workings of Mina's mind and her mixed emotions about being an isolated child. Her gradual emergence from the protective shell of home is beautifully portrayed.... This novel will inspire children to let their imaginations soar." Publ Wkly

Alvarez, Julia
★ How Tia Lola came to visit/stay. Knopf 2001 147p $15.95; pa $5.50

Grades: 4 5 6 7   Fic
1. Aunts -- Fiction 2. Divorce -- Fiction 3. Dominican

Americans -- Fiction
ISBN 0-375-80215-0; 0-440-41870-4 pa

LC 00-62932

Although ten-year-old Miguel is at first embarrassed by his colorful aunt, Tia Lola, when she comes to Vermont from the Dominican Republic to stay with his mother, his sister, and him after his parents' divorce, he learns to love her.

"Readers will enjoy the funny situations, identify with the developing relationships and conflicting feelings of the characters, and will get a spicy taste of Caribbean culture in the bargain." SLJ

Other titles about Tia Lola are:

How Tia Lola learned to teach (2010)

How Tia Lola saved the summer (2011)

How Tia Lola ended up starting over (2011)

How Tia Lola ended up starting over. Alfred A. Knopf 2011 147p $15.99; lib bdg $18.99

Grades: 4 5 6 7 **Fic**

1. Aunts -- Fiction 2. Family life -- Fiction 3. Hotels and motels -- Fiction 4. Mexican Americans -- Fiction 5. Dominican Americans -- Fiction

ISBN 978-0-375-86914-3; 0-375-86914-X; 978-0-375-96914-0 lib bdg; 0-375-96914-4 lib bdg

LC 2011018153

Worried that Papa Espada cannot find a job, Tia Lola, Juanita, Miguel, and the 'Sword' sisters decide to start a bed and breakfast at Colonel Charlebois's Vermont house.

"Believable details about the individual children's lives bring further depth to the plot, while themes of xenophobia, blended families and acceptance make the novel relevant to Latino, immigrant and general audiences. The book's touching final chapter references the first three books in the series as well as the magic of libraries and reading. A fitting farewell to a memorable character." Kirkus

How Tia Lola learned to teach. Alfred A. Knopf 2010 134p $15.99; lib bdg $18.99

Grades: 4 5 6 7 **Fic**

1. School stories 2. Aunts -- Fiction 3. Divorce -- Fiction 4. Family life -- Fiction 5. Community life -- Fiction 6. Dominican Americans -- Fiction

ISBN 978-0-375-86460-5; 0-375-86460-1; 978-0-375-96460-2 lib bdg; 0-375-96460-6 lib bdg

LC 2010-04964

Juanita and Miguel's great aunt, Tia Lola, comes from the Dominican Republic to help take care of them after their parents divorce, and soon she is so involved in their small Vermont community that when her visa expires, the whole town turns out to support her.

"Fans of the previous story will definitely want to check this out, and those new to the series will have no trouble jumping in and catching up with everyone's favorite aunt." Bull Cent Child Books

How Tia Lola saved the summer. Alfred A. Knopf 2011 141p $15.99; lib bdg $18.99

Grades: 4 5 6 7 **Fic**

1. Aunts -- Fiction 2. Family life -- Fiction 3.

Dominican Americans -- Fiction
ISBN 978-0-375-86727-9; 0-375-86727-9; 978-0-375-96727-6 lib bdg; 0-375-96727-3 lib bdg; 978-0-375-89766-5 e-book

LC 2010024010

When three girls and their father visit for a week in the summer, it takes Tia Lola to make Miguel forget his unhappiness at the absence of any boys and embrace the adventures that ensue.

"Returning readers will rejoice in reconnecting with the effervescent Tia Lola and the rest of the gang, while even readers new to the tales will want to read more about Vermont's favorite Dominican aunt." Kirkus

★ **Return** to sender. Alfred A. Knopf 2009 325p $16.99; lib bdg $19.99

Grades: 4 5 6 7 **Fic**

1. Farm life -- Fiction 2. Friendship -- Fiction 3. Migrant labor -- Fiction 4. Illegal aliens -- Fiction

ISBN 978-0-375-85838-3; 0-375-85838-5; 978-0-375-95838-0 lib bdg; 0-375-95838-X lib bdg

LC 2008-23520

Awarded the Belpre Author Medal (2010)

After his family hires migrant Mexican workers to help save their Vermont farm from foreclosure, eleven-year-old Tyler befriends the oldest daughter, but when he discovers they may not be in the country legally, he realizes that real friendship knows no borders.

"Readers will be moved by small moments. . . . A tender, well-constructed book." Publ Wkly

Amato, Mary

Edgar Allan's official crime investigation notebook. Holiday House 2010 140p

Grades: 3 4 5 **Fic**

1. School stories 2. Mystery fiction 3. Poetry -- Fiction 4. Teachers -- Fiction 5. Lost and found possessions -- Fiction

ISBN 0-8234-2271-2; 978-0-8234-2271-5

LC 2010-11604

When someone takes a pet goldfish, then other items from Ms. Herschel's classroom, each time leaving a clue in the form of a poem, student Edgar Allan competes with a classmate to be the first to solve the mystery. "Grades three to five." (Bull Cent Child Books)

"While there is enough of a mystery plot here to satisfy genre fans, this is ulitmately a story about friendship, and Amato is particularly adept at developing strong characterizations of a diverse group of kids without delving into stereotypes." Bull Cent Child Books

Snarf attack, underfoodle, and the secret of life; the Riot brothers tell all. by Mary Amato; illustrated by Ethan Long. Holiday House 2004 151p il (The Riot Brothers) $16.95; pa $6.95

Grades: 2 3 4 **Fic**

1. School stories 2. Brothers -- Fiction

ISBN 0-8234-1750-6; 0-8234-2062-0 pa

Orville and Wilbur Riot have no shortage of daily adventures. Sometimes they are undercover detectives. Other times they challenge each other to see who can get the most underwear on his head in exactly thirty seconds.

"Young readers will appreciate the Riot brothers' attempts to make something exciting happen every day. Long's playful cartoon illustrations extend the fun." Booklist

Stinky and successful; the Riot brothers never stop. illustrated by Ethan Long. Holiday House 2007 152p il (The Riot Brothers) $16.95; pa $7.95
Grades: 2 3 4　　　　　　　　　　　　　　**Fic**
1. Brothers -- Fiction
ISBN 978-0-8234-2100-8; 0-8234-2100-7; 978-0-8234-2196-1 pa; 0-8234-2196-1 pa
　　　　　　　　　　　　　　LC 2007013366
Wilbur and Orville Riot "set out to rescue a damsel in distress, . . . trick their mother on April Fools' Day, and become mad scientists. . . . Plenty of wordplay; fast-paced, episodic chapters; and lively cartoon illustrations will keep readers engaged." SLJ

Other titles in this series are:
Snarf attack, underfoodle, and the secret of life (2004)
Drooling and dangerous (2006)
Take the mummy and run (2009)

Take the mummy and run; the Riot Brothers are on a roll. illustrated by Ethan Long. Holiday House 2009 226p il (The Riot brothers) $16.95
Grades: 2 3 4　　　　　　　　　　　　　　**Fic**
1. Brothers -- Fiction
ISBN 978-0-8234-2175-6; 0-8234-2175-9
　　　　　　　　　　　　　　LC 2008013299
The Riot brothers "are distressed upon hearing they'll be spending the first few days of their summer vacation with their cousin Amelia. All fears are put to rest, however, when they discover that she shares their wild sense of humor. When they're not cracking corny jokes, the youngsters devise boredom-busting games. . . . Divided into three mini-books with several short chapters that have large type and a generous number of zany cartoon drawings, this offering should be easy for newly independent readers to digest, while the nonstop humor will grab older children." SLJ

Anaya, Rudolfo A.
The **first** tortilla; a bilingual story. [by] Rudolfo Anaya; illustrated by Amy Cordova; translated into Spanish by Enrique R. Lamadrid. University of New Mexico 2007 un il $16.95
Grades: 2 3 4　　　　　　　　　　　　　　**Fic**
1. Bilingual books -- English-Spanish
ISBN 978-0-8263-4214-0
Guided by a blue hummingbird, Jade brings an offering to the Mountain Spirit who lives near her village in Mexico, and asks if he will send rain to end the drought that threatens the people.
"Anaya has retold a Mexican legend and made it his own with his spiritual prose. . . . Córdova's rich acrylic paintings lend a traditional feel to the setting while maintaining the tale's mystical elements. A beautifully written and illustrated title." SLJ

Andersen, Hans Christian
The **little** match girl; illustrated by Rachel Isadora. Putnam 1987 30p il $16.99
Grades: 3 4 5　　　　　　　　　　　　　　**Fic**
ISBN 0-399-21336-8
　　　　　　　　　　　　　　LC 85-30082

The wares of the poor little match girl illuminate her cold world, bringing some beauty to her brief, tragic life
"Isadora follows Andersen's lead, neither sensationalizing nor apologizing for the tale's potentially sentimental plot. . . . A moving, original picture-book interpretation of the classic tale." Booklist

The **princess** and the pea; illustrated by Dorothée Duntze. North-South Bks. 1985 un il $16.95; pa $7.95
Grades: K 1 2 3　　　　　　　　　　　　　　**Fic**
1. Fairy tales
ISBN 1-55858-034-4; 1-55858-381-5 pa
　　　　　　　　　　　　　　LC 85-7199
A young girl feels a pea through twenty mattresses and twenty featherbeds and proves she is a real princess
"This classic Andersen fairy tale is presented in simple text and with elaborate illustrations. . . . Duntze appears to set the story during the Renaissance, and her illustrations are precise, intricate and detailed." SLJ

Anderson, Janet, 1952-
The **last** treasure; [by] Janet S. Anderson. Dutton 2003 257p il hardcover o.p. pa $6.99
Grades: 5 6 7 8　　　　　　　　　　　　　　**Fic**
1. Family life -- Fiction 2. Buried treasure -- Fiction
ISBN 0-525-46919-2; 0-14-240217-6 pa
　　　　　　　　　　　　　　LC 2002-74143
Thirteen-year-old Ellsworth leaves his father to visit the relatives he has never met and eventually joins forces with Jess, his distant cousin, to uncover family secrets and search for their ancestor's hidden treasure
"Anderson has conjured up a fascinating read for puzzle lovers while sandwiching in an important message about intergenerational relationships." SLJ

Anderson, Jodi Lynn
May **Bird** among the stars; book two. [by] Jodi Lynn Anderson. 1st ed.; Atheneum Books for Young Readers 2006 260p $16.95
Grades: 5 6 7 8　　　　　　　　　　　　　　**Fic**
1. Fantasy fiction
ISBN 978-0-689-86924-2; 0-689-86924-X
　　　　　　　　　　　　　　LC 2005028832
Still trapped in The Ever After, ten-year-old May Bird struggles to decide whether to save the world of her ghostly friends from the evil Bo Cleevil or to return to her West Virginia home.
"Anderson has clearly had a great deal of fun creating a world not so different from our own where spirits go after death, and readers will love her humorous jabs at popular culture." SLJ

May **Bird**, warrior princess; book three. [by] Jodi Lynn Anderson. Atheneum Books for Young Readers 2007 244p $16.99
Grades: 5 6 7 8　　　　　　　　　　　　　　**Fic**
1. Fantasy fiction
ISBN 0-689-86925-8; 978-0-689-86925-9
　　　　　　　　　　　　　　LC 2007002944
Three years after her return from the Ever After, May Bird, now thirteen, draws her scattered friends—Pumpkin, Fabbio, Beatrice, and Lucius—out of hiding to take a final stand against Evil Bo Cleevil, as May herself makes ready to

live up to the prophecy that placed the fate of the Ever After, and her own world, in her hands.

"The novel . . . will not disappoint fans. A reading of the previous two titles is recommended." SLJ

Anderson, Laurie Halse

Fever, 1793. Simon & Schuster Bks. for Young Readers 2000 251p $17.99; pa $6.99

Grades: 5 6 7 8 9   Fic

1. Epidemics 2. Epidemics -- Fiction 3. Yellow fever -- Fiction 4. Yellow fever -- Pennsylvania -- Philadelphia
ISBN 978-0-689-83858-3; 0-689-83858-1; 978-0-689-84891-9 pa; 0-689-84891-9 pa

LC 00-32238

ALA YALSA Margaret A. Edwards Award (2009)

In 1793 Philadelphia, sixteen-year-old Matilda Cook, separated from her sick mother, learns about perseverance and self-reliance when she is forced to cope with the horrors of a yellow fever epidemic. "Age ten and up." (N Y Times Book Rev)

"A vivid work, rich with well-drawn and believable characters. Unexpected events pepper the top-flight novel that combines accurate historical detail with a spellbinding story line." Voice Youth Advocates

★ **Forge**. Atheneum Books for Young Readers 2010 297p (Seeds of America) $16.99

Grades: 6 7 8 9 10   Fic

1. Slavery -- Fiction 2. Soldiers -- Fiction 3. African Americans -- Fiction
ISBN 978-1-4169-6144-4; 1-4169-6144-5

LC 2010-15971

Separated from his friend Isabel after their daring escape from slavery, fifteen-year-old Curzon serves as a free man in the Continental Army at Valley Forge until he and Isabel are thrown together again, as slaves once more.

"Weaving a huge amount of historical detail seamlessly into the story, Anderson creates a vivid setting, believable characters both good and despicable and a clear portrayal of the moral ambiguity of the Revolutionary age. Not only can this sequel stand alone, for many readers it will be one of the best novels they have ever read." Kirkus

Anderson, Laurie Halse, 1961-

★ **Chains**; seeds of America. Simon & Schuster Books for Young Readers 2008 316p

Grades: 6 7 8 9 10   Fic

1. Spies -- Fiction 2. Slavery -- Fiction 3. African Americans -- Fiction
ISBN 1-4169-0585-5; 1-4169-0586-3 pa; 978-1-4169-0585-1; 978-1-4169-0586-8 pa

LC 2007-52139

After being sold to a cruel couple in New York City, a slave named Isabel spies for the rebels during the Revolutionary War. "Grades seven to ten." (Bull Cent Child Books)

"This gripping novel offers readers a startlingly provocative view of the Revolutionary War. . . . [Anderson's] solidly researched exploration of British and Patriot treatment of slaves during a war for freedom is nuanced and evenhanded, presented in service of a fast-moving, emotionally involving plot." Publ Wkly

Anderson, M. T.

Agent Q, or the smell of danger! illustrations by Kurt Cyrus. Beach Lane Books 2010 293p il (Pals in peril) $16.99

Grades: 4 5 6 7   Fic

1. Mystery fiction 2. Adventure fiction 3. Spies -- Fiction
ISBN 978-1-4169-8640-9; 1-4169-8640-5

LC 2009-51199

As Lily, Katie, and Jasper try to return home after their adventures in Delaware, they face a protoplasmic monster, sleeping gas, a runaway rice cart, sentient lobsters, and spies of the Awful and Adorable Autarch of Dagsboro.

"Among the energetic chase sequences, diverting authorial interjections, and appropriately quirky illustrations (including flip-book art) is a quiet message about the importance of home." Booklist

The **Game** of Sunken Places; [by] M. T. Anderson. Scholastic Press 2004 260p (The Norumbegan quartet) $16.95; pa $5.99

Grades: 5 6 7 8   Fic

1. Games 2. Games -- Fiction
ISBN 0-439-41660-4; 0-439-41661-2 pa

LC 2003-20055

When two boys stay with an eccentric relative at his mansion in rural Vermont, they discover an old-fashioned board game that draws them into a mysterious adventure.

"Deliciously scary, often funny, and crowned by a pair of deeply satisfying surprises, this tour de force leaves one marveling at Anderson's ability to slip between genres as fluidly as his middle-grade heroes straddle worlds." Booklist

Other titles in this series are:

The suburb beyond the stars (2010)
The empire of gut and bone (2011)

Jasper Dash and the flame-pits of Delaware; illustrations by Kurt Cyrus. Beach Lane Books 2009 423p il (Pals in peril) $16.99

Grades: 4 5 6 7   Fic

1. Mystery fiction 2. Adventure fiction 3. Young adult literature 4. Friendship -- Fiction
ISBN 978-1-4169-8639-3; 1-4169-8639-1

LC 2008044415

Boy Technonaut, Jasper Dash, and his friends Lily Gefelty and Katie Mulligan travel into the mist-shrouded heart of the forbidden mountainous realm of Delaware to try and unravel a terrible mystery.

"Extremely funny, it's for adults, who will get at least half the references, and for children, who will get the other half. Cyrus's illustrations are integral and pretty darn amusing, too." Kirkus

★ **Whales** on stilts; illustrations by Kurt Cyrus. Harcourt 2005 188p il (Pals in peril) $15; pa $5.95

Grades: 4 5 6 7   Fic

1. Science fiction
ISBN 0-15-205340-9; 0-15-205394-8 pa

LC 2004-17754

Racing against the clock, shy middle-school student Lily and her best friends, Katie and Jasper, must foil the plot of her father's conniving boss to conquer the world using an army of whales.

"A story written with the author's tongue shoved firmly into his cheek. . . . It's full of witty pokes at other series novels and Jasper's nutty inventions." SLJ

Other titles in this series are:

The clue of the linoleum lederhosen (2006)

Jasper Dash and the Flame-pits of Delaware (2009)

Agent Q., or the smell of danger! (2010)

Zombie mommy (2011)

The **empire** of gut and bone. Scholastic 2011 324p (The Norumbegan quartet) $17.99

Grades: 5 6 7 8 **Fic**

1. Games -- Fiction 2. Supernatural -- Fiction

ISBN 978-0-545-13884-0; 0-545-13884-1

"Bent on tracking down the elven Norumbegans in order to save Vermont from an invasion of dream-sucking Thusser, Brian, Gregory and the mechanical troll Kalgrash pass through an interdimensional curtain—to find themselves inside an organic alien body. . . . Returning fans will find the unapologetically intellectual looniness uncannily, happily familiar." Kirkus

The **suburb** beyond the stars. Scholastic Press 2010 223p (The Norumbegan quartet) $17.99

Grades: 5 6 7 8 **Fic**

1. Games -- Fiction 2. Supernatural -- Fiction

ISBN 978-0-545-13882-6; 0-545-13882-5

LC 2009051836

Friends Brian and Gregory have survived the Game of Sunken Places, but are once again drawn back to cousin Prudence's house in Vermont, where they discover that something has gone very wrong with time, people have disappeared, and danger is lurking everywhere.

"This is a fun and gripping read, with action, suspense, and creepy monsters." SLJ

Anderson, M. T., 1968-

The **chamber** in the sky. Scholastic Press 2012 282 p. (hardcover) $17.99

Grades: 5 6 7 8 **Fic**

1. American satire 2. Fantasy fiction 3. Human-alien encounters -- Fiction

ISBN 0545334934; 9780545334938

This novel, by National Book Award and Printz Honor winner M. T. Anderson, is book four of "The Norumbegan Quartet" series. "Brian and Gregory have . . . . gone to investigate intergalactic suburban sprawl that was infringing on the Vermont forests, and landed in the empire of New Norumbega inside the huge body of an alien. They've escaped certain death . . . and wreaked small amounts of havoc of their own. And finally, they're going to make sense of all their travels and adventures." (Publisher's note)

Angleberger, Tom

Fake mustache; or, how Jodie O'Rodeo and her wonder horse (and some nerdy guy) saved the U.S. Presidential election from a mad genius criminal mastermind. Tom Angleberger; illustrated by Jen Wang. Amulet Books 2012 196 p. ill. (hardback) $13.95

Grades: 2 3 4 5 6 **Fic**

1. Humorous stories 2. Disguise -- Fiction 3. Criminals -- Fiction 4. Hypnotism -- Fiction 5. Mustaches --

Fiction 6. Politics, Practical -- Fiction

ISBN 1419701940; 9781419701948

LC 2012000556

Edgar Award: Best Juvenile Shortlist (2013)

In this book, "[w]hen twelve-year-old Lenny . . . lends his best friend, Casper, ten dollars to purchase . . . [a] fake mustache at a local gag shop, he has no idea he's just become an accomplice in Casper's plot for world domination. In the days following, a mysterious man with some impressive facial hair . . . steamrolls his way into the governor's seat, takes over the . . . nation's leading manufacturer of voting booths and launches a presidential campaign." (Bulletin of the Center for Children's Books)

Darth Paper strikes back; an Origami Yoda book. Tom Angleberger. Amulet Books 2011 159p il $12.95

Grades: 4 5 6 7 **Fic**

1. School stories 2. Origami -- Fiction 3. Puppets and puppet plays -- Fiction 4. Eccentrics and eccentricities -- Fiction

ISBN 978-1-4197-0027-9; 1-4197-0027-8

LC 2011010388

Harvey, upset when his Darth Paper finger puppet brings humiliation, gets Dwight suspended, but Origami Yoda asks Tommy and Kellan, now in seventh grade, to make a new casefile to persuade the School Board to reinstate Dwight.

This is "a satisfying tale of friendship and just resistance to authority. Pitch-perfect middle-school milieu and enough Star Wars references (and laughs) to satisfy fans and win new ones." Kirkus

Horton Halfpott; or, The fiendish mystery of Smugwick Manor, or, The loosening of M'Lady Luggertuck's corset. Tom Angleberger with illustrations by the author. Amulet Books 2011 206p il $14.95

Grades: 4 5 6 7 **Fic**

1. Mystery fiction 2. Social classes -- Fiction 3. Household employees -- Fiction 4. Eccentrics and eccentricities -- Fiction

ISBN 978-0-8109-9715-8; 0-8109-9715-0

LC 2010-38096

Horton, an upstanding kitchen boy in a castle in nineteenth-century England, becomes embroiled in a mystery surrounding a series of thefts. "Grades four to six." (Bull Cent Child Books)

"Readers will enjoy Angleberger's . . . penchant for the absurd as well as his many droll asides. . . . The ending satisfies, and with Angleberger's many eclectic characters, his wild-and-witty storytelling, and a lighthearted but perplexing mystery . . . readers are in for a treat." Publ Wkly

The **strange** case of Origami Yoda; Tom Angleberger. Amulet Books 2010 141p il $12.95

Grades: 4 5 6 7 **Fic**

1. School stories 2. Origami -- Fiction 3. Puppets and puppet plays -- Fiction 5. Eccentrics and eccentricities -- Fiction

ISBN 978-0-8109-8425-7; 0-8109-8425-3

LC 2009-39748

Tommy and his friends describe their experiences with a paper puppet of Yoda, made by their sixth-grade classmate Dwight, as they try to decide whether or not the puppet can really predict the future. "Grades four to seven." (Bull Cent Child Books)

"The situations that Yoda has a hand in are pretty authentic, and the setting is broad enough to be any school. The plot is age-old but with the twist of being presented on crumpled pages with cartoon sketches, supposed hand printing, and varying typefaces. Kids should love it." SLJ

Angus, Jennifer

In search of Goliathus hercules; by Jennifer Angus. Albert Whitman 2012 350 p. (hardcover) $17.99

Grades: 3 4 5 6 7   **Fic**

1. Fantasy fiction 2. Insects -- Fiction 3. Human-animal communication -- Fiction 4. Metamorphosis -- Fiction

ISBN 0807529907; 9780807529904

LC 2011037135

In this novel, by Jennifer Angus, "Henri Bell, . . . in 1890 . . . strikes up a conversation with a friendly fly on the windowsill and discovers he possesses the astounding ability to speak with insects. Thus commences an epic journey for Henri as he manages a flea circus, commands an army of beetles, and ultimately sets out to British Malaya to find the mythical giant insect known as Goliathus Hercules." (Publisher's note)

Appelbaum, Susannah

The **Hollow** Bettle; illustrated by Jennifer Taylor. Alfred A. Knopf 2009 399p il (The Poisons of Caux) $16.99; lib bdg $19.99

Grades: 4 5 6 7   **Fic**

1. Fantasy fiction 2. Uncles -- Fiction 3. Poisons and poisoning -- Fiction

ISBN 978-0-375-85173-5; 0-375-85173-9; 978-0-375-95173-2 lib bdg; 0-375-95173-3 lib bdg

LC 2008-22626

Eleven-year-old Ivy Manx sets out with her new friend, a young "taster," to find her missing uncle, an outlawed healer, in the dangerous kingdom of Caux where magic, herbs, and poisons rule.

This "is a deeply satisfying, humor-laced quest with elements of wizardry and herbology, deeds of a dastardly nature, and, ultimately, redemption." Booklist

Other titles in this series are:
The Taster's Guild (2010)
The Shepherd of Weeds (2011)

The **Shepherd** of Weeds; illustrated by Andrea Offermann. Alfred A. Knopf 2011 447p il (The Poisons of Caux) $16.99; lib bdg $19.99

Grades: 4 5 6 7   **Fic**

1. Fantasy fiction 2. Uncles -- Fiction 3. Scarecrows -- Fiction 4. Poisons and poisoning -- Fiction

ISBN 978-0-375-85175-9; 0-375-85175-5; 978-0-375-95175-6 lib bdg; 0-375-95175-X lib bdg; 978-0-375-89897-6 e-book

LC 2010051351

With an army of scarecrows, a legion of birds, and her friends and uncle by her side, it is up to Ivy Manx to wage war against the evil Vidal Verjouce and the Tasters Guild, defeat her own father, and restore order to the plant world.

"In this third and final installment of the Poisons of Caux series, the fortunes of the multitude of characters encountered in the first two books come to a satisfactory conclu-sion. Caux is a well-designed fantasy world with enough appeal to satisfy younger readers." Voice Youth Advocates

The **Tasters** Guild; illustrated by Jennifer Taylor. Alfred A. Knopf 2010 366p il (The Poisons of Caux) $16.99

Grades: 4 5 6 7   **Fic**

1. Fantasy fiction 2. Poisons and poisoning -- Fiction

ISBN 978-0-375-85174-2; 0-375-85174-7

Eleven-year-old Ivy Manx sets out with her friends for the dangerous city of Rocamadour, where poison and the evil Tasters Guild rule, in the hopes of finding a door to the sister-land of Pimcaux and fulfilling a great and ancient prophecy

"This inventive story is full of strange and mysterious characters with peculiar names and viscerally descriptive locations. Kids are sure to love it." SLJ

Appelt, Kathi

★ **Keeper**; illustrations by August Hall. Atheneum Books for Young Readers 2010 399p il $16.99

Grades: 5 6 7 8   **Fic**

1. Ocean -- Fiction 2. Sailing -- Fiction 3. Mermaids and mermen -- Fiction 4. Mother-daughter relationship -- Fiction

ISBN 978-1-4169-5060-8; 1-4169-5060-5

LC 2010000795

On the night of the blue moon when mermaids are said to gather on a sandbar in the Gulf of Mexico, ten-year-old Keeper sets out in a small boat, with her dog BD and a seagull named Captain, determined to find her mother, a mermaid, as Keeper has always believed, who left long ago to return to the sea.

"Deftly spinning together mermaid lore, local legend and natural history, this stunning tale proves 'every landscape has its magical beings,' and the most unlikely ones can form a perfect family. Hall's black-and-white illustrations lend perspective and immediacy. Beautiful and evocative—an absolute 'keeper.'" Kirkus

★ The **true** blue scouts of Sugarman Swamp; by Kathi Appelt. 1st ed. Atheneum Books for Young Readers 2013 336 p. (hardcover) $16.99

Grades: 5 6 7 8   **Fic**

1. Swamps -- Fiction 2. Raccoons -- Fiction 3. Humorous stories 4. Swamp animals -- Fiction 5. Land developers -- Fiction 6. Scouting (Youth activity) -- Fiction

ISBN 1442421053; 9781442421059; 9781442481213

LC 2012023723

This book is "told from the perspectives of animals and humans. . . . The main concern of Bingo and Jeremiah, two raccoon Swamp Scouts, is the approaching brood of feral hogs, which could destroy the precious canebrake sugar used to make fried pies at the local Paradise Pies cafe. Meanwhile, 12-year-old Chap Brayburn, the cafe proprietor's son, is worried about rich, horrible Sonny Boy Beaucoup, who wants to turn the swamp into the 'Gator World Wrestling Arena and Theme Park.'" (Publishers Weekly)

★ The **underneath**; illustrated by David Small. Atheneum Books for Young Readers 2008 313p il $16.99; pa $7.99

Grades: 3 4 5 6 **Fic**
1. Cats -- Fiction 2. Dogs -- Fiction
ISBN 978-1-4169-5058-5; 1-4169-5058-3; 978-1-
4169-5059-2 pa; 1-4169-5059-1 pa
LC 2007031969
A Newbery Medal honor book, 2009
An abandoned "calico cat, about to have kittens, hears
the lonely howl of [Ranger], a chained-up hound deep in the
backwaters of the bayou. . . . Ranger urges the cat to hide
underneath the porch, to raise her kittens there because Gar-
Face, the man living inside the house, will surely use them
as alligator bait should he find them." (Publisher's note) "In-
temediate." (Horn Book)
"Well realized in Small's excellent full-page drawings,
this fine book is most of all distinguished by the originality of the story and the fresh beauty of its author's voice."
Horn Book

Applegate, Katherine
Home of the brave. Feiwel & Friends 2007 249p
$16.95
Grades: 5 6 7 8 **Fic**
1. Novels in verse 2. Cattle -- Fiction 3. Africans --
Fiction 4. Refugees -- Fiction 5. Immigrants -- Fiction
ISBN 0-312-36765-1; 978-0-312-36765-7
LC 2006-32053
Kek, an African refugee, is confronted by many strange
things at the Minneapolis home of his aunt and cousin, as
well as in his fifth grade classroom, and longs for his miss-
ing mother, but finds comfort in the company of a cow and
her owner.
"This beautiful story of hope and resilience is written in
free verse." Voice Youth Advocates

★ The **one** and only Ivan; illustrated by Patricia
Castelao. Harper 2012 il $16.99
Grades: 3 4 5 6 **Fic**
1. Gorillas -- Fiction 2. Elephants -- Fiction 3. Animal
welfare -- Fiction
ISBN 978-0-06-199225-4; 0-06-199225-9
LC 2011010034
John Newbery Medal (2013)
When Ivan, a gorilla who has lived for years in a down-
and-out circus-themed mall, meets Ruby, a baby elephant
that has been added to the mall, he decides that he must find
her a better life.
"Ivan narrates his tale in short, image-rich sentences
and acute, sometimes humorous, observations that are all
the more heartbreaking for their simple delivery. . . . Spot
art captures poignant moments throughout. Utterly believable, this bittersweet story, complete with an author's note
identifying the real Ivan, will inspire a new generation of
advocates." Kirkus

Arbuthnott, Gill
The **Keepers'** tattoo. Chicken House 2010 425p
$17.99
Grades: 6 7 8 9 **Fic**
1. Fantasy fiction 2. Dreams -- Fiction 3. Uncles --
Fiction 4. Tattooing -- Fiction 5. Identity (Psychology)
-- Fiction
ISBN 978-0-545-17166-3; 0-545-17166-0
LC 2009-26327

Months before her fifteenth birthday, Nyssa learns that
she is a special member of a legendary clan, the Keepers of
Knowledge, as she and her uncle try to escape from Alaric,
the White Wolf, who wants to use lines tattooed on her to
destroy the rest of her people.
Arbuthnott "writes with restraint and thoughtfulness,
never condescending to her readers. Nyssa is a convincing mixture of ignorance, courage, and resourcefulness."
Publ Wkly

Armstrong, Alan
Looking for Marco Polo; illustrated by Tim Jessell.
Random House 2009 286p $16.99
Grades: 4 5 6 7 **Fic**
1. Travelers 2. Travel writers 3. Missing persons --
Fiction
ISBN 978-0-375-83321-2; 0-375-83321-8
When they lose touch with his father's Gobi Desert expedition, eleven-year-old Mark accompanies his mother to
Venice, Italy, and there, while waiting for news of his father,
learns about the legendary Marco Polo and his adventures
in the Far East.
"Armstrong ably conjures up the atmosphere of damp,
foggy Venice in late December while blowing some dust
off of the accounts of Marco Polo's travels with his lively
storytelling. . . . Whether or not readers know the specifics
of Marco Polo's voyages, they will enjoy this entertaining
blend of contemporary and historical adventure." Booklist

Racing the moon; by Alan Armstrong; illustrated by
Tim Jessell. Random House 2012 214 p.
Grades: 5 6 7 8 **Fic**
1. Adventure fiction 2. Historical fiction 3. Siblings
-- Fiction 4. Aeronautics -- Fiction 5. Space flight
-- Fiction 6. Brothers and sisters -- Fiction 7. Rockets
(Aeronautics) -- Fiction 8. Adventure and adventurers
-- Fiction
ISBN 037585889X; 9780375858895;
9780375858901; 9780375893094
LC 2012016261
In this children's book by Alan Armstrong "Twelve-
year-old Alex hangs out with her reckless 17-year-old broth-
er Chuck, who's always getting them in trouble. . . . Alex
wants to be another Amelia Earhart [and][m]eeting her new
neighbor, Captain Ebbs, Alex finds a mentor. . . . She arranges for Alex to meet pioneer rocket scientist Wernher von
Braun, organizes a sailing trip to a Chesapeake Bay island
near a rocket launch and provides needed direction for the
risk-taking duo." (Kirkus)

Raleigh's page; illustrated by Tim Jessell. Random
House 2007 328p il $16.99; lib bdg $19.99
Grades: 4 5 6 7 **Fic**
1. Poets 2. Authors 3. Explorers 4. Historians 5.
Adventure fiction 6. Courtiers 7. Travel writers 8.
Native Americans -- Fiction
ISBN 978-0-375-83319-9; 978-0-375-93319-6 lib bdg
LC 2006-08434
In the late 16th century, fifteen-year-old Andrew leaves
school in England and must prove himself as a page to Sir
Walter Raleigh before embarking for Virginia, where he
helps to establish relations with the Indians.
Armstrong "weaves a richly detailed historical narrative.
. . . Historical figures such as Raleigh, Thomas Harriot, and

Manteo mix with fictional characters in an adventure that makes for compelling reading. Illustrated with expressive pencil drawings." Booklist

★ **Whittington**; illustrated by S. D. Schindler. Random House 2005 191p il $14.95; lib bdg $16.99; pa $6.50

Grades: 4 5 6   **Fic**

1. Cats -- Fiction 2. Domestic animals -- Fiction

ISBN 0-375-82864-8; 0-375-92864-2 lib bdg; 0-375-82865-6 pa

        LC 2004-05789

A Newbery Medal honor book, 2006

"A battered cat who calls himself Whittington takes up residence in a shabby barn already inhabited by a variety of scruffy livestock, owned by Bernie. . . . Bernie offers refuge not only to his animals but also to his parentless grandchildren, Abby and Ben, who carry burdens of their own. The children [can] communicate . . . with the animals, so Abby and Ben join the audience when Whittington the cat retells the story of Dick Whittington and his cat." (Bull Cent Child Books) "Intermediate, middle school." (Horn Book)

"The story works beautifully, both as historical fiction about medieval street life and commerce and as a witty, engaging tale of barnyard camaraderie and survival." Booklist

Armstrong, K. L.

Loki's wolves; by K.L. Armstrong and M.A. Marr. 1st ed. Little, Brown and Co. 2013 368 p. ill. (The Blackwell pages) (hardcover) $16.99

Grades: 4 5 6 7 8   **Fic**

1. Norse mythology -- Fiction 2. Adventure fiction -- Juvenile fiction 3. Gods -- Fiction 4. Monsters -- Fiction 5. Supernatural -- Fiction 6. Shapeshifting -- Fiction 7. Mythology, Norse -- Fiction 8. Adventure and adventurers -- Fiction

ISBN 031620496X; 9780316204965

        LC 2012029851

This juvenile fantasy novel, by K. L. Armstrong and M. A. Marr, is the first book in the "Blackwell Pages" series. "Matt hears the words, but he can't believe them. He's Thor's representative? Destined to fight trolls, monstrous wolves and giant serpents . . . or the world ends? He's only thirteen. . . . But now Ragnarok is coming, and it's up to the champions to fight in the place of the long-dead gods." (Publisher's note)

"It is so methodically constructed that readers will welcome the action Ragnarök will offer. . . . Norse mythology brought to life with engaging contemporary characters and future volumes that promise explosive action; ideal for Percy Jackson fans who want to branch out." Kirkus

Armstrong, William Howard

★ **Sounder**; [by] William H. Armstrong; illustrations by James Barkley. Harper & Row 1969 116p il $15.99; pa $5.99

Grades: 5 6 7 8   **Fic**

1. Dogs -- Fiction 2. Family life -- Fiction 3. African Americans -- Fiction

ISBN 0-06-020143-6; 0-06-440020-4 pa

Awarded the Newbery Medal, 1970

"Set in the South in the era of sharecropping and segregation, this succinctly told tale poignantly describes the courage of a father who steals a ham in order to feed his undernourished family; the determination of the eldest son, who searches for his father despite the apathy of prison authorities; and the devotion of a coon dog named Sounder." Shapiro. Fic for Youth. 3d edition

Arnosky, Jim

The **pirates** of Crocodile Swamp. G. P. Putnam's Sons 2009 230p il $15.99

Grades: 3 4 5 6   **Fic**

1. Adventure fiction 2. Brothers -- Fiction 3. Wetlands -- Fiction 4. Runaway children -- Fiction

ISBN 978-0-399-25068-2; 0-399-25068-9

Kidnapped by their father, two boys escape into the mangrove swamps of Key Largo, Florida, where they learn to live on their own among the wildlife.

This "is an exciting story, with plenty of Arnosky's trademark insight into the delights and dangers of the natural (and human) world. The prose is direct and gripping, the characterization strong, and the story includes just enough of the author's illustrations to enrich the fast-moving tale." SLJ

Arnston, Steven

★ The **Wikkeling**; illustrated by Daniela Jaglenka Terrazzini. Running Press Kids 2011 256p il $18

Grades: 4 5 6   **Fic**

1. Science fiction

ISBN 978-0-7624-3903-4; 0-7624-3903-3

"In Henrietta's world, every part of life is monitored and regulated by computers. House cats are considered wild and dangerous animals. Old houses and old books can make children sick. The girl's orderly and safe life is disrupted the day she discovers a secret attic above her bedroom. . . . Soon after this discovery, she starts seeing the Wikkeling, a menacing yellow creature that gives children headaches with the touch of a finger. . . . Arntson has created a detailed and fascinating dystopian world that seems eerily similar to our own, and Terrazzini's illustrations strike just the right note." SLJ

Aronson, Sarah

Beyond lucky. Dial Books for Young Readers 2011 250p $16.99

Grades: 4 5 6 7   **Fic**

1. Mystery fiction 2. Chance -- Fiction 3. Soccer -- Fiction 4. Brothers -- Fiction 5. Jews -- United States -- Fiction

ISBN 978-0-8037-3520-0; 0-8037-3520-0

        LC 2010-28800

Twelve-year-old Ari Fish is sure that the rare trading card he found has changed his luck and that of his soccer team, but after the card is stolen he comes to know that we make our own luck, and that heroes can be fallible.

"Aronson skillfully dodges the predictability of sports-themed books by creating multilayered characters and an intriguing whodunit. . . . Aronson . . . includes a lot of fun on-field action, but the off-field story is just as interesting. . . . Aronson's graceful storytelling will keep even nonsoccer buffs turning pages." Publ Wkly

Asch, Frank

Gravity buster; journal #2 of a cardboard genius. Kids Can Press 2007 143p il $14.95; pa $5.95

Grades: 3 4 5   **Fic**

1. Brothers -- Fiction 2. Inventors -- Fiction 3. Space

vehicles -- Fiction

ISBN 978-1-55453-068-7; 1-55453-068-7; 978-1-55453-069-4 pa; 1-55453-069-5 pa

"The young inventor featured in Star Jumper (Kids Can, 2006) returns in a second novel full of amazing contraptions and humorous escapades. This time, the self-proclaimed 'Boy Supergenius' perfects his spaceship and develops several other handy gadgets along the way. . . . Numerous black-and-white drawings contribute to the premise that the book is a scientist's journal and also match the text's whimsical tone. The combination of imaginative science and family humor should have strong appeal to children." SLJ

Star jumper; journal of a cardboard genius. Kids Can Press 2006 128p $14.95; pa $5.95

Grades: 3 4 5   Fic

1. Brothers -- Fiction 2. Inventors -- Fiction 3. Space vehicles -- Fiction

ISBN 978-1-55337-886-0; 1-55337-886-5; 978-1-55337-887-7 pa; 1-55337-887-3 pa

"Using his astounding scientific ability . . . Alex designs the Star Jumper. This advanced cardboard spacecraft will take him across the galaxy to a brother-free planet—if only he can keep the first grader out of the way until liftoff. The first-person narration is lively and realistic." SLJ

Other titles about Alex and his brother are:

Gravity buster (2007)

Time twister (2008)

Time twister; journal #3 of a cardboard genius. by Frank Asch. Kids Can Press 2008 144p il $14.95; pa $5.95

Grades: 3 4 5   Fic

1. Brothers -- Fiction 2. Inventors -- Fiction 3. Space flight -- Fiction 4. Space and time -- Fiction

ISBN 978-1-55453-230-8; 1-55453-230-2; 978-155453-231-5 pa; 1-55453-231-0 pa

Alex's "intergalactic spaceship, Star Jumper, is ready for deep space travel, but his copilot Zoe Breen finds a glitch: when Star Jumper returns from her voyage, more than fifty years will have passed on earth! It's time for Alex to invent a time machine." Publisher's note

Ashley, Bernard

Ronnie's war. Frances Lincoln Children's Books 2011 190p $16.95

Grades: 3 4 5   Fic

1. World War, 1939-1945 -- Fiction 2. Mother-son relationship -- Fiction

ISBN 978-1-84780-162-3; 1-84780-162-5

Eleven-year-old Ronnie and his mother struggle through hardships and joys caused by World War II in England.

"Ashley makes a clear, straightforward narrative that accommodates a surprising amount of information about England during the war, and he does it with a strong story lucid and true enough to engage younger readers. . . . A moving snapshot of a time that still resonates." Kirkus

Atinuke

★ **Anna** Hibiscus; illustrated by Lauren Tobia. Kane/Miller 2010 109p il

Grades: 1 2 3 4   Fic

1. Family life -- Fiction

ISBN 1-935279-73-4 pa; 978-1-935279-73-0 pa

"Linked short stories star Anna Hibiscus, who lives in a large house in a compound in 'amazing Africa' with baby brothers Double and Triple, parents and extended family. . . . The family goes on vacation, an auntie visits from America, Anna learns what it is to do hard work and she gets an invitation to visit her Canadian grandmother. . . . These stories celebrate the extended family and the combination of traditional ways with conveniences of the modern world; they contrast Anna's relatively privileged life with that of others in her country. . . . Tobia's sketches, pen-and-ink with a gray wash, will help early readers visualize the family, unfamiliar customs and clothing and Anna's community."

"Linked short stories star Anna Hibiscus, who lives in a large house in a compound in 'amazing Africa' with baby brothers Double and Triple, parents and extended family. . . . The family goes on vacation, an auntie visits from America, Anna learns what it is to do hard work and she gets an invitation to visit her Canadian grandmother. . . . These stories celebrate the extended family and the combination of traditional ways with conveniences of the modern world; they contrast Anna's relatively privileged life with that of others in her country. . . . Tobia's sketches, pen-and-ink with a gray wash, will help early readers visualize the family, unfamiliar customs and clothing and Anna's community." Kirkus

Other titles about Anna Hibiscus are:

Hooray for Anna Hibiscus! (2011)

Good luck, Anna Hibiscus! (2011)

Have fun, Anna Hibiscus! (2011)

Anna Hibiscus' song; [illustrated by] Lauren Tobia. Kane/Miller 2011 un il $15.99

Grades: PreK K   Fic

1. Happiness -- Fiction 2. Family life -- Fiction

ISBN 978-1-61067-040-1; 1-61067-040-X

"In amazing Africa, Anna Hibiscus discovers her own special way to show her happiness after trying out what other family members do. . . . Tobia illustrated the Anna Hibiscus chapter books with gray scale drawings, but here she presents Anna in full color. . . . Young readers and listeners will surely embrace her as enthusiastically as chapter-book readers already have." Kirkus Reviews

Good luck, Anna Hibiscus! illustrated by Lauren Tobia. Kane/Miller 2011 110p il pa $5.99

Grades: 1 2 3 4   Fic

1. Family life -- Fiction

ISBN 1-61067-007-8 pa; 978-1-61067-007-4 pa

Anna Hibiscus, who lives in Africa, is looking forward to visiting her grandmother in Canada, where she will see snow for the first time! But before she goes, she must find suitable clothes to keep her warm in the cold winter weather, and say goodbye to the family she loves.

"These gentle stories are illustrated on nearly every page with Tobia's gray-scale sketches. Accurate cultural details will appeal to readers curious about life in an unfamiliar world. . . . The third-person narration moves briskly, with plenty of dialogue." Kirkus

Have fun, Anna Hibiscus! illustrated by Lauren Tobia. Kane/Miller 2011 110p il pa $5.99

Grades: 1 2 3 4   Fic

1. Snow -- Fiction 2. Africans -- Fiction 3. Christmas

-- Fiction 4. Family life -- Fiction
ISBN 978-1-61067-008-1; 1-61067-008-6

Anna Hibiscus has never been away from her home in Africa, surrounded by her parents and baby brothers, as well as all of her aunts and uncles and cousins. But now she is going to Canada to visit her grandmother for Christmas. She has never met Granny Canada and she can't wait to see snow!

"The Nigerian-born author has drawn on her own childhood travel to make this experience real for young readers today. On every spread, Tobia's sketches, black and white with gray fill, add interest and appeal. A welcome addition to the sparse collection of stories for young readers about modern Africa." Kirkus

Hooray for Anna Hibiscus! illustrated by Lauren Tobia. Kane/Miller 2010 108p il pa $5.99

Grades: 1 2 3 4   **Fic**

1. Family life -- Fiction
ISBN 978-1-935279-74-7 pa; 1-935279-74-2 pa
First published 2008 in the United Kingdom

Anna Hibiscus lives in Africa with her family in a house in a beautiful garden in a big city. Anna sings for the president, gets in a terrible tangle with her hair and visits the other side of the city.

The **no.** 1 car spotter; illustrated by Warwick Johnson Cadwell. Kane/Miller 2011 il pa $5.99

Grades: 1 2 3   **Fic**

1. Travel -- Fiction 2. Automobiles -- Fiction
ISBN 978-1-61067-051-7; 1-61067-051-5

"Oluwalase Babatunde Benson, otherwise known as No. 1, is not only the best car-spotter in his African village, his electric ideas improve village life." Kirkus Reviews

Atkinson, E. J.

★ **I**, Emma Freke; [by] Elizabeth Atkinson. Carolrhoda Books 2010 234p $16.95

Grades: 4 5 6 7   **Fic**

1. Family life -- Fiction 2. Family reunions -- Fiction 3. Single parent family -- Fiction 4. Eccentrics and eccentricities -- Fiction
ISBN 978-0-7613-5604-2; 0-7613-5604-5

LC 2009-38923

Growing up near Boston with her free-spirited mother and old-world grandfather, twelve-year-old Emma has always felt out of place but when she attends the family reunion her father's family holds annually in Wisconsin, she is in for some surprises.

"This rich story of self-acceptance offers readers much to think about. . . . The first-person narrative moves along briskly, with believable dialogue and plenty of humor." Booklist

Atkinson, Elizabeth

From Alice to Zen and everyone in between; a novel. Carolrhoda Books 2008 247p $16.95

Grades: 5 6 7   **Fic**

1. School stories 2. Moving -- Fiction 3. Popularity -- Fiction 4. Family life -- Fiction 5. Eccentrics and eccentricities -- Fiction
ISBN 978-0-8225-7271-8; 0-8225-7271-0

LC 2007-9659

Upon moving from Boston to the suburbs, eleven-year-old tomboy Alice meets Zen, a very strange neighbor who is determined to help her become popular when they both begin middle school, although he himself is a loner.

"Atkinson describes Alice's ethical development credibly and engagingly." Booklist

Atwater, Richard Tupper

★ **Mr.** Popper's penguins; [by] Richard and Florence Atwater; illustrated by Robert Lawson. Little, Brown 1988 138p il $18.99; pa $6.99

Grades: 3 4 5   **Fic**

1. Penguins -- Fiction
ISBN 0-316-05842-4; 0-316-05843-2 pa
Reissue first published in 1938
A Newbery Medal honor book, 1939

When Mr. Popper, a mild little painter and decorator with a taste for books and movies on polar explorations, was presented with a penguin, he named it Captain Cook. From that moment on life was changed for the Popper family

"To the depiction of the penguins in all conceivable moods Robert Lawson [the] artist has brought not only his skill but his individual humor, and his portrayal of the wistful Mr. Popper is memorable." N Y Times Book Rev

Auch, Mary Jane

I was a third grade bodyguard; illustrated by Herm Auch. Holiday House 2003 73p il $16.95

Grades: 2 3 4   **Fic**

1. Dogs 2. Pets 3. Chickens 4. Christmas 5. Dogs -- Fiction 6. Chickens -- Fiction 7. Christmas -- Fiction
ISBN 0-8234-1775-1

LC 2002-68869

When Brian takes care of the third-grade class's pet chicken during Christmas vacation, Arful, his talking dog, has his paws full watching over it.

"The simple plot clips along with plenty of dialogue and minimal character development to a humorous resolution. Readers who have gone beyond beginning readers as well as younger listeners will welcome Auch's latest offering." SLJ

I was a third grade science project; illustrated by Herm Auch. Holiday House 1998 96p il $16.95; pa $5.50

Grades: 2 3 4   **Fic**

1. School stories 2. Cats -- Fiction 3. Dogs -- Fiction 4. Schools -- Fiction 5. Hypnotism -- Fiction 6. Science projects -- Fiction
ISBN 0-8234-1357-8; 0-440-41606-X

LC 97-41996

While trying to hypnotize his dog for the third grade science fair, Brian accidentally makes his best friend Josh think he's a cat

"Auch's wisecracking third-graders and superb comic timing will have readers rolling on the floor." Booklist

Other titles about Brian are:
I was a third grade bodyguard (2003)
I was a third grade spy (2001)

I was a third grade spy; illustrated by Herm Auch. Holiday House 2001 87p il hardcover o.p. pa $5.50

Grades: 2 3 4   **Fic**

1. Dogs 2. Schools 3. School stories 4. Talent shows

5. Dogs -- Fiction
ISBN 0-8234-1576-7; 0-440-41871-2 pa

LC 00-58060

When Brian's dog Arful suddenly begins talking, Brian and his two friends send the dog to find out what their classmates are planning for the school talent show

"Narrated in alternating chapters by Josh and Arful, this lively, intermediate chapter book is a good choice for introducing readers to the notion of multiple points of view." Booklist

Journey to nowhere. Holt & Co. 1997 202p hardcover o.p. pa $4.99
Grades: 4 5 6 7　　　　　　　　　　　　　　　　**Fic**
1. Frontier and pioneer life -- Fiction
ISBN 0-440-41491-1 pa

LC 96-42249

This is the first title in the Genesee trilogy. In 1815, while traveling by covered wagon to settle in the wilderness of western New York, eleven-year-old Mem experiences a flood and separation from her family

"A well-written, realistic, and thoroughly researched novel." Booklist

Other titles in the Genesee trilogy are
Frozen summer (1998)
The road to home (2000)

★ **One** -handed catch; [by] MJ Auch. Henry Holt and Co. 2006 248p $16.95; pa $6.99
Grades: 4 5 6　　　　　　　　　　　　　　　　**Fic**
1. Family life -- Fiction 2. Handicapped -- Fiction
ISBN 978-0-8050-7900-5; 0-8050-7900-9; 978-0-312-53575-9 pa; 0-312-53575-9 pa

LC 2006-00370

After losing his hand in an accident in his father's butcher shop in 1946, sixth-grader Norman uses hard work and humor to learn to live with his disability and to succeed at baseball, art, and other activities.

"Loosely based on childhood experiences of the author's husband, this story offers both inspiration and useful information, deftly wrapped in an engaging narrative." Booklist

Wing nut; [by] MJ Auch. Henry Holt & Co. 2005 231p $16.95
Grades: 4 5 6　　　　　　　　　　　　　　　　**Fic**
1. Birds -- Fiction 2. Moving -- Fiction 3. Old age -- Fiction
ISBN 0-8050-7531-3

LC 2004-54046

When twelve-year-old Grady and his mother relocate yet again, they find work taking care of an elderly man, who teaches Grady about cars, birds, and what it means to have a home

"Auch's story . . . . is engaging. . . . . What will attract readers . . . is the author's careful integration of bird lore and the unusual challenges of creating and maintaining a purple martin colony." Booklist

A **dog** on his own. Holiday House 2008 153p $16.95; pa $6.95

Grades: 3 4 5　　　　　　　　　　　　　　　　**Fic**
1. Dogs -- Fiction
ISBN 978-0-8234-2088-9; 0-8234-2088-4; 978-0-8234-2243-2 pa; 0-8234-2243-7 pa

LC 2008-15963

After a daring escape from the animal shelter, Pearl, Peppy, and K-10—so named because he is one step above all the other canines—explore the outside world while moving from one adventure to another.

"This is a compelling, affectionate story of opening not just one's home, but also one's heart." Booklist

Auxier, Jonathan
Peter Nimble and his fantastic eyes; a story. Amulet Books 2011 381p il $16.95
Grades: 4 5 6 7　　　　　　　　　　　　　　　　**Fic**
1. Eye -- Fiction 2. Blind -- Fiction 3. Magic -- Fiction 4. Orphans -- Fiction 5. Thieves -- Fiction
ISBN 978-1-4197-0025-5; 1-4197-0025-1

LC 2010048692

Raised to be a thief, blind orphan Peter Nimble, age ten, steals from a mysterious stranger three pairs of magical eyes, that lead him to a hidden island where he must decide to become a hero or resume his life of crime.

"The fast-paced, episodic story, accompanied by Auxier's occasional pen-and-ink drawings, is inventive, unpredictable, and—like its hero—nimble." Publ Wkly

Avi
Blue heron. Avon Bks. 1993 186p pa $6.99
Grades: 5 6 7 8　　　　　　　　　　　　　　　　**Fic**
1. Herons -- Fiction 2. Family life -- Fiction
ISBN 978-0-380-72043-9 pa; 0-380-72043-4 pa
First published 1992 by Bradbury Press

While spending the month of August on the Massachusetts shore with her father, stepmother, and their new baby, almost thirteen-year-old Maggie finds beauty in and draws strength from a great blue heron, even as the family around her unravels

"Maggie emerges as a sensitive heroine whose perceptions are genuine as well as compelling. Reflecting the complexity of people and their emotions, this novel explores rather than solves the conflicts introduced." Pub Wkly

The **Book** Without Words; a fable of medieval magic. Hyperion Books for Children 2005 203p hardcover o.p. pa $5.99
Grades: 5 6 7 8　　　　　　　　　　　　　　　　**Fic**
1. Magic -- Fiction 2. Middle Ages -- Fiction 3. Supernatural -- Fiction
ISBN 0-7868-0829-2; 0-7868-1659-7 pa

"At the dawning of the Middle Ages, Thorston, an old alchemist, works feverishly to create gold and to dose himself with a concoction that will enable him to live forever. The key to his success lies in a mysterious book with blank pages that can only be read by desperate, green-eyed people. . . . Avi's compelling language creates a dreary foreboding. . . . Clearly this is a story with a message, a true fable. Thoughtful readers will devour its absorbing plot and humorous elements, and learn a 'useful truth' along the way." SLJ

Crispin at the edge of the world. Hyperion Books for Children 2006 234p $16.99

Grades: 5 6 7 8 **Fic**
1. Orphans -- Fiction 2. Middle Ages -- Fiction
ISBN 0-7868-5152-X
LC 2006-41111

Branded as traitors by the king's authorities, Crispin and his guardian, Bear, flee to coastal towns in fourteenth-century England, where they perform a musical juggling act and bond as a family after befriending a disfigured girl.

"Along with plenty of action and adventure, this displays a solid emotional base." Booklist

★ **Crispin**: the cross of lead. Hyperion Bks. for Children 2002 $15.99; pa $6.99
Grades: 5 6 7 8 **Fic**
1. Orphans -- Fiction 2. Middle Ages -- Fiction
ISBN 0-7868-0828-4; 0-7868-1658-9 pa
LC 2001-51829

Awarded the Newbery Medal, 2001

Falsely accused of theft and murder, an orphaned peasant boy in fourteenth-century England flees his village and meets a larger-than-life juggler who holds a dangerous secret

This "book is a page-turner from beginning to end. . . . A meticulously crafted story, full of adventure, mystery, and action." SLJ

Other titles in this series are:
Crispin at the edge of the world (2006)
Crispin: the end of time (2010)

Crispin: the end of time. Balzer + Bray 2010 223p $16.99; lib bdg $17.89
Grades: 5 6 7 8 **Fic**
1. Orphans -- Fiction 2. Middle Ages -- Fiction
ISBN 978-0-06-174080-0; 0-06-174080-2; 978-0-06-174082-4 lib bdg; 0-06-174082-9 lib bdg

"Still grieving for the fatherly protector they called Bear, Crispin and his friend Troth wander northward through the fourteenth-century French countryside . . . hoping to journey to Iceland. They arrive at a convent where the nuns value Troth's skill with healing herbs, and she decides to stay. Alone and near starvation, Crispin joins a troupe of traveling musicians who prove to be a band of murderous thieves. . . . Even readers new to the series will find this a compelling, first-person narrative." Booklist

Ereth's birthday; illustrated by Brian Floca. HarperCollins Pubs. 2000 180p il (Dimwood Forest tales) pa $5.99
Grades: 3 4 5 **Fic**
1. Foxes 2. Animals 3. Porcupines 4. Foxes -- Fiction 5. Parent and child 6. Animals -- Fiction 7. Porcupines -- Fiction
ISBN 0-380-97734-6; 0-380-80490-5 pa
LC 99-46481

Feeling neglected on his birthday, Ereth, the cantankerous old porcupine, sets out looking for his favorite treat and instead finds himself acting as "mother" to three young fox kits.

"Avi delivers another crackling good read, one shot through with memorable descriptions . . . and crisp, credible dialogue." Publ Wkly

Iron thunder; the battle between the Monitor and the Merrimac, a civil war novel. Hyperion 2007 205p il $15.99; pa $5.99
Grades: 4 5 6 **Fic**
1. Ships -- Fiction
ISBN 978-1-4231-0446-9; 1-4231-0446-3; 978-1-4231-0518-3 pa; 1-4231-0518-4 pa

"This fascinating adventure taken from U.S. history begins in Brooklyn in 1862, when Tom Carroll, 13, is hired at the Iron Works in Greenpoint for a secret project, derisively known around the borough as Ericsson's Folly. John Ericsson, a Swedish inventor, is trying to build an ironclad ship that can battle the Merrimac, a Confederate ship being outfitted with metal plates in Virginia. . . . Illustrated with period engravings, this is gripping historical fiction from a keenly imagined perspective." Publ Wkly

Midnight magic. Scholastic Press 1999 249p hardcover o.p. pa $5.99
Grades: 5 6 7 8 **Fic**
1. Magicians -- Fiction 2. Renaissance -- Fiction
ISBN 0-590-36035-3; 0-439-24219-3 pa
LC 98-50192

In Italy in 1491, Mangus the magician and his apprentice are summoned to the castle of Duke Claudio to determine if his daughter is indeed being haunted by a ghost.

An "entertaining tale of mystery and intrigue." SLJ
Another title about Mangus and Fabrizio is:
Murder at midnight (2009)

Never mind! a twin novel. [by] Avi and Rachel Vail. HarperCollins 2004 200p hardcover o.p. lib bdg $16.89; pa $5.99
Grades: 5 6 7 8 **Fic**
1. Twins 2. Schools 3. Twins -- Fiction 4. Brothers and sisters
ISBN 0-06-054314-0; 0-06-054315-9 lib bdg; 0-06-054316-7 pa
LC 2003-21439

Twelve-year-old New York City twins Meg and Edward have nothing in common, so they are just as shocked as everyone else when Meg's hopes for popularity and Edward's mischievous schemes coincidentally collide in a hilarious showdown.

"The dialogue is great, especially the conversations that reveal how hard it is to listen and to say what you mean. . . . The wit and slapstick carry the story, which has moments of sadness that raise serious issues everyone will recognize. Best of all is the message: laugh at yourself." Booklist

★ **Poppy**; [by] Avi; illustrated by Brian Floca. Revised Harper Trophy ed.; HarperTrophy 2005 156p il pa $5.99
Grades: 3 4 5 **Fic**
1. Mice -- Fiction 2. Owls -- Fiction 3. Animals -- Fiction
ISBN 978-0-380-72769-8 pa; 0-380-72769-2 pa
LC 2005281589

First published 1995 by Orchard Books

Poppy the deer mouse urges her family to move next to a field of corn big enough to feed them all forever, but Mr. Ocax, a terrifying owl, has other ideas

"This exciting story is richly visual, subtly humorous, and skillfully laden with natural-history lessons. The anthropomorphism is believable and the characters are memorable." SLJ

Other titles in this series are:

Poppy and Rye (1998)

Ragweed (1999)

Ereth's birthday (2000)

Poppy's return (2005)

Poppy and Ereth (2009)

Poppy and Ereth; illustrated by Brian Floca. HarperCollinsPublishers 2009 208p il $15.99; $16.89

Grades: 3 4 5　　　　　　　　　　　　　　　　　　**Fic**

1. Bats -- Fiction 2. Mice -- Fiction 3. Friendship -- Fiction 4. Porcupines -- Fiction

ISBN 978-0-06-111969-9; 0-06-111969-5; 978-0-06-111970-5 lib bdg; 0-06-111970-9 lib bdg

LC 2008019662

After a long, hard winter in Dimwood forest, Poppy the deer mouse finds new adventure thrust upon her while rescuing Ereth the porcupine from the mud.

"Series fans will enjoy spending time with these endearing characters." Booklist

Poppy and Rye; illustrated by Brian Floca. Avon Bks. 1998 182p il $14

Grades: 3 4 5　　　　　　　　　　　　　　　　　　**Fic**

1. Animals -- Fiction

ISBN 0-380-97638-2

LC 97-31000

When their home next to a brook is destroyed by beavers, a large family of golden mice is aided by Poppy the deer mouse and her grumpy porcupine friend, who in the process forges a relationship with the son he had abandoned

"Accompanied once again by Brian Floca's witty yet pastoral pencil drawings, this is a sequel worthy of its predecessor." Horn Book

Poppy's return; illustrated by Brian Floca. HarperCollins Publishers 2005 223p il (Dimwood Forest tales) hardcover o.p. pa $5.99

Grades: 3 4 5　　　　　　　　　　　　　　　　　　**Fic**

1. Mice -- Fiction 2. Skunks -- Fiction 3. Animals -- Fiction 4. Porcupines -- Fiction

ISBN 0-06-000012-0; 0-06-000013-9 lib bdg; 0-06-000014-7 pa

LC 2004-30054

Poppy, accompanied by her troublesome son Junior, his skunk friend, and Uncle Ereth the porcupine, responds to a summons to return to her ancestral home, Gray House, to save the mice there from destruction by a bulldozer.

Prairie school; story by Avi; pictures by Bill Farnsworth. HarperCollins Pubs. 2001 47p il (I can read chapter book) hardcover o.p. pa $3.99

Grades: 2 3 4　　　　　　　　　　　　　　　　　　**Fic**

1. Aunts 2. Prairies 3. Wheelchairs 4. Books and reading 5. Aunts -- Fiction 6. People with disabilities 7. Books and reading -- Fiction 8. Physically handicapped -- Fiction 9. Frontier and pioneer life -- Fiction

ISBN 0-06-027664-9; 0-06-051318-7 pa

LC 00-38834

In 1880, Noah's aunt teaches the reluctant nine-year-old how to read as they explore the Colorado prairie together, Noah pushing Aunt Dora in her wheelchair

"Warm, soft-edged illustrations capture the intimacy of the loving family relationships and the vastness of the landscape. . . . This gentle story with a great message . . . would make a pleasant read-aloud as well as a good addition to easy chapter-book collections." SLJ

Ragweed; illustrated by Brian Floca. Avon Bks. 1999 178p il $17.99; pa $5.99

Grades: 3 4 5　　　　　　　　　　　　　　　　　　**Fic**

1. Mice -- Fiction

ISBN 0-380-97690-0; 0-380-80167-1 pa

LC 98-55160

Ragweed, a young country mouse, leaves his family and travels to the big city, where he finds excitement and danger and sees cats for the first time

"Consummate storyteller Avi outdoes himself . . . with a crackerjack tale that's pure delight from start to finish." Publ Wkly

S.O.R. losers. Avon Bks. 1986 90p pa $4.99

Grades: 5 6 7 8　　　　　　　　　　　　　　　　　**Fic**

1. School stories 2. Soccer -- Fiction

ISBN 978-0-380-69993-3 pa; 0-380-69993-1 pa

First published 1984 by Bradbury Press

Each member of the South Orange River seventh-grade soccer team has qualities of excellence, but not on the soccer field

"Short, pithy chapters highlighting key events maintain the pace necessary for successful comedy. . . . The style is vivid, believably articulate." Horn Book

Traitor's gate. Atheneum Books for Young Readers 2007 351p $17.99

Grades: 5 6 7 8　　　　　　　　　　　　　　　　　**Fic**

1. Spies -- Fiction 2. Poverty -- Fiction 3. Family life -- Fiction

ISBN 0-689-85335-1

When his father is arrested as a debtor in 1849 London, fourteen-year-old John Huffman must take on unexpected responsibilities, from asking a distant relative for help to determining why people are spying on him and his family.

"With plenty of period detail, this action-packed narrative of twists, turns, and treachery is another winner from a master craftsman." SLJ

The **barn**. Orchard Bks. 1994 106p hardcover o.p. pa $4.99

Grades: 4 5 6 7　　　　　　　　　　　　　　　　　**Fic**

1. Farm life -- Fiction 2. Father-son relationship -- Fiction 3. Frontier and pioneer life -- Fiction

ISBN 0-531-06861-7; 978-0-380-72562-5 pa

LC 94-6920

In an effort to fulfill their dying father's last request, nine-year-old Ben and his brother and sister construct a barn on their land in the Oregon Territory in the 1850s

"While focusing mainly on his characters, Avi presents a vivid picture of the time and place, including fairly involved details about how the barn is constructed. This novel . . .

is a thought-provoking and engaging piece of historical fiction." SLJ

A **beginning,** a muddle, and an end; the right way to write writing. with illustrations by Tricia Tusa. Harcourt 2008 164p il $14.95

Grades: 3 4 5   Fic
1. Ants -- Fiction 2. Snails -- Fiction 3. Animals -- Fiction 4. Authorship -- Fiction
ISBN 978-0-15-205555-4; 0-15-205555-X
                                                      LC 2007-16580

Avon the snail decides to become a writer with the help of his friend Edward the ant, which leads them into a series of adventures involving close encounters with an anteater, a crow, a tree frog, and a hungry fish.

"Clever prose provides thought-provoking scenes full of wit and charm, and well-placed sketches add insightful visuals into the mood of the characters." SLJ

The **end** of the beginning; being the adventures of a small snail (and an even smaller ant) with illustrations by Tricia Tusa. Harcourt 2004 143p il $14.95; pa $6.95

Grades: 3 4 5   Fic
1. Ants -- Fiction 2. Snails -- Fiction
ISBN 0-15-204968-1; 0-15-205532-0 pa
                                                      LC 2004-2696

Avon the snail and Edward, a take-charge ant, set off together on a journey to an undetermined destination in search of unspecified adventures.

"Whimsical pen-and-ink sketches add much to this wise little book. It's perfect for reading and discussing." SLJ

Another title about Avon the snail and Edward the ant is: A beginning, a muddle, and an end (2008)

The **fighting** ground. Lippincott 1984 157p hardcover o.p. lib bdg $16.89; pa $5.99; rpt $5.99

Grades: 5 6 7 8   Fic
ISBN 0-397-32073-6; 0-397-32074-4 lib bdg; 0-06-440185-5 pa; 9780064401852 rpt
                                                      LC 82-47719

"It's April 1776, and the fighting ground is both the farm country of Pennsylvania and the heart of a boy which is 'wonderful ripe for war.' Twenty-four hours transform Jonathan from a cocky 13-year-old, eager to take on the British, into a young man who now knows the horror, the pathos, the ambiguities of war." Voice Youth Advocates

The **good** dog. Atheneum Bks. for Young Readers 2001 243p $16; pa $5.99

Grades: 4 5 6   Fic
1. Dogs 2. Wolves 3. Dogs -- Fiction 4. Wolves -- Fiction 5. Dogs -- Juvenile fiction
ISBN 0-689-83824-7; 0-689-83825-5 pa
                                                      LC 00-53600

McKinley, a malamute, is torn between the domestic world of his human family and the wild world of Lupin, a wolf that is trying to recruit dogs to replenish the dwindling wolf pack

"Falling somewhere between a naturalistic account of animal life and a fantasy, the strongest parts of the book depict the communication gap between McKinley and the human family with whom he resides." Horn Book Guide

★ The **true** confessions of Charlotte Doyle; decorations by Ruth E. Murray. Orchard Bks. 1990 215p $16.95; pa $5.99; rpt $16.99

Grades: 5 6 7   Fic
1. Sea stories
ISBN 0-531-05893-X; 0-380-72885-0 pa; 9780545477116 rpt
                                                      LC 90-30624

A Newbery Medal honor book, 1991

"Charlotte Doyle, thirteen, returning from school in England to join her family in Rhode Island, is deposited on a seedy ship with a ruthless, mad captain and a mutinous crew. Refusing to heed warnings about Captain Jaggery's brutality, Charlotte seeks his guidance and approval only to become his victim. . . . Grades five to eight." (SLJ)

This is a "seafaring adventure, set in 1832. Charlotte Doyle, 13, returning from school in England to join her family in Rhode Island, is deposited on a seedy ship with a ruthless, mad captain and a mutinous crew. Refusing to heed warnings about Captain Jaggery's brutality, Charlotte seeks his guidance and approval only to become his victim, a pariah to the entire crew, and a convicted felon for the murder of the first mate." SLJ

Avi, 1937-
★ **City** of orphans; with illustrations by Greg Ruth. Atheneum Books for Young Readers 2011 350p il $16.99

Grades: 5 6 7 8   Fic
1. Mystery fiction 2. Gangs -- Fiction 3. Immigrants -- Fiction 4. Family life -- Fiction 5. Homeless persons -- Fiction
ISBN 978-1-4169-7102-3; 1-4169-7102-5
                                                      LC 2010049229

In 1893 New York, thirteen-year-old Maks, a newsboy, teams up with Willa, a homeless girl, to clear his older sister, Emma, from charges that she stole from the brand new Waldorf Hotel, where she works. Includes historical notes.

"Avi's vivid recreation of the sights and sounds of that time and place is spot on, masterfully weaving accurate historical details with Maks' experiences." Kirkus

Includes bibliographical references

★ **Sophia's** war; a tale of the Revolution. Avi. Beach Lane Books 2012 302 p. (hardcover) $16.99

Grades: 5 6 7 8   Fic
1. Traitors -- Fiction 2. Women spies -- Fiction 3. United States -- History -- 1775-1783, Revolution -- Fiction 4. Spies -- Fiction
ISBN 1442414413; 9781442414419; 9781442414426; 9781442414433
                                                      LC 2012007962

In this novel by Avi "Sophia Calderwood witnesses the execution of Nathan Hale in New York City, which is newly occupied by the British army . . . in 1776. . . . Recruited as a spy, . . . she becomes aware that someone in the American army might be switching sides, and she uncovers a plot that will grievously damage the Americans if it succeeds. But the identity of the would-be traitor is so shocking that no one believes her, and so Sophia decides to stop the treacherous plot herself." (Publisher's note)

Includes bibliographical references

Axelrod, Amy

Your friend in fashion, Abby Shapiro. Holiday House 2011 261p il $17.95

Grades: 4 5 6 **Fic**

1. Editors 2. Socialites 3. Letters -- Fiction 4. Spouses of presidents 5. Family life -- Fiction 6. Fashion designers -- Fiction 7. Jews -- United States -- Fiction
ISBN 978-0-8234-2340-8; 0-8234-2340-9

LC 2010-24185

Beginning in 1959, Abby, nearly eleven, writes a series of letters to Jackie Kennedy, each with sketches of outfits she has designed, as she faces family problems, concerns about neighbors, and her own desperate desire for both her first bra and a Barbie doll.

"Abby is an especially memorable protagonist, but all [Axelrod's] characters vibrate with life. . . . Funny, lively, sensitive—a real winner." Kirkus

Ayres, Katherine

Macaroni boy. Delacorte Press 2003 182p hardcover o.p. pa $5.99

Grades: 5 6 7 8 **Fic**

1. Schools 2. Food poisoning 3. School stories 4. Catholic schools 5. Depressions -- 1929 6. Family life -- Pennsylvania 7. Great Depression, 1929-1939 -- Fiction
ISBN 0-385-73016-0; 0-440-41884-4 pa

LC 2002-6768

In Pittsburgh in 1933, sixth-grader Mike Costa notices a connection between several strange occurrences, but the only way he can find out the truth about what's happening is to be nice to the class bully. Includes historical facts

"Actual places and events are interwoven with a heart-warming story of a close-knit family facing difficult times." Voice Youth Advocates

Babbitt, Natalie

★ **Jack** Plank tells tales. Scholastic 128p il $15.95

Grades: 3 4 5 6 **Fic**

1. Pirates -- Fiction 2. Storytelling -- Fiction
ISBN 978-0-5450-0496-1; 0-5450-0496-9

Jack Plank, a former pirate, tells stories at the boarding house where he lives explaining why he is not well suited to jobs such as farmer, baker, and fisherman.

"Written in a straightforward manner with touches of wry wit, Jack's stories unfold with the economy and assurance that readers expect of Babbitt." Booklist

Kneeknock Rise; story and pictures by Natalie Babbitt. Farrar, Straus & Giroux 1970 117p il hardcover o.p. pa $6.99

Grades: 4 5 6 **Fic**

1. Allegories 2. Superstition -- Fiction
ISBN 0-312-37009-1 pa

A Newbery Medal honor book, 1971

"An enchanting tale imbued with a folk flavor, enlivened with piquant imagery and satiric wit." Booklist

★ **Tuck** everlasting. Farrar, Straus & Giroux 1975 139p $16; pa $6.99

Grades: 5 6 7 8 **Fic**

1. Fantasy fiction
ISBN 0-374-37848-7; 0-312-36981-6 pa

The Tuck family is confronted with an agonizing situation when they discover that a ten-year-old girl and a malicious stranger now share their secret about a spring whose water prevents one from ever growing any older

"The story is macabre and moral, exciting and excellently written." N Y Times Book Rev

The **eyes** of the Amaryllis. Farrar, Straus & Giroux 1977 127p hardcover o.p. pa $6.99

Grades: 5 6 7 8 **Fic**

1. Sea stories 2. Grandmothers -- Fiction
ISBN 0-312-37008-3 pa

LC 77-11862

"The book succeeds as a well-wrought narrative in which a complex philosophic theme is developed through the balanced, subtle use of symbol and imagery. It is a rare story." Horn Book

The **moon** over High Street; Natalie Babbitt. Scholastic 2012 148 p.

Grades: 3 4 5 6 7 **Fic**

1. Family -- Juvenile fiction 2. Friendship -- Juvenile fiction 3. Decision making -- Juvenile fiction 4. Adopted children -- Juvenile fiction
ISBN 054537636X; 9780545376365

LC 2011926886

This children's novel by Natalie Babbitt "presents 12-year-old Joe. . . . Orphaned shortly after his birth, Joe, who loves the moon, has been raised by his Gran, but after she breaks a hip, he's sent to spend some of the summer with his father's cousin. . . . In nearly idyllic Midville, . . . he inadvertently comes to the attention of the very wealthy factory owner Mr. Boulderwall . . . who decides that he will adopt Joe and raise him to take over his company." (Kirkus)

The **search** for delicious. Farrar, Straus & Giroux 1969 167p il hardcover o.p. pa $6.99

Grades: 5 6 7 8 **Fic**

1. Fantasy fiction
ISBN 0-374-36534-2; 0-312-36982-4 pa

The Prime Minister is compiling a dictionary and when no one at court can agree on the meaning of delicious, the King sends his twelve-year-old messenger to poll the country

"The theme, foolish arguments can lead to great conflict, may not be clear to all children who will enjoy this fantasy." Best Sellers

Baccalario, Pierdomenico

City of wind; translated by Leah D. Janeczko. Random House 2011 290p (Century quartet) $16.99; lib bdg $19.99

Grades: 5 6 7 8 **Fic**

1. Mystery fiction 2. Adventure fiction 3. Good and evil -- Fiction
ISBN 978-0-375-85897-0; 0-375-85897-0; 978-0-375-95897-7 lib bdg; 0-375-95897-5 lib bdg

LC 2010029137

In their continuing quest to save the world from evil forces, Mistral, Elettra, Harvey, and Sheng meet again in Paris where they must search for the mysterious veil of Isis reportedly hidden in the heart of the city.

"Clever writing and a pell-mell plot will win over readers new to the series and satisfy its fans." Kirkus

Ring of fire; translated by Leah D. Janeczko; illustrations by Iacopo Bruno. Random House 2009 293p il (Century quartet) $16.99; lib bdg $19.99

Grades: 5 6 7 8   **Fic**

1. Good and evil -- Fiction

ISBN 978-0-375-85895-6; 0-375-85895-4; 978-0-375-95895-3 lib bdg; 0-375-95895-9 lib bdg

LC 2009-08204

Original Italian edition, 2006

Four seemingly unrelated children are brought together in a Rome hotel where they discover that they are destined to become involved in a deep and ancient mystery involving a briefcase full of artifacts that expose them to great danger

"There are some genuinely exciting moments and the premise is intriguing." Publ Wkly

Other titles in this series are:

Star of Stone (2010)

City of Wind (2011)

Star of Stone; translated by Leah D. Janeczko. Random House 2010 290p (Century quartet) $16.99; lib bdg $19.99

Grades: 5 6 7 8   **Fic**

1. Mystery fiction 2. Friendship -- Fiction 3. Good and evil -- Fiction

ISBN 978-0-375-85896-3; 0-375-85896-2; 978-0-375-95896-0 lib bdg; 0-375-95896-7 lib bdg

LC 2009030416

Original Italian edition, 2007

In their continuing adventures, Elettra, Sheng, and Minstral meet Harvey and Ermite in New York City and follow the clues to find the mysterious Star of Stone.

"Readers will be intrigued by the Manhattan setting, the clues and codes, and the sense of danger and urgency that follows the characters through their adventures." SLJ

The **door** to time; illustrations by Iacopo Bruno. Scholastic 2006 222p il (Ulysses Moore) $12.99

Grades: 4 5 6   **Fic**

1. Mystery fiction 2. Adventure fiction 3. Twins -- Fiction

ISBN 0-439-77438-1

Original Italian edition 2004

After moving from London to an old mansion on the English coast, eleven-year-old twins Jason and Julia discover that their new home has twisting tunnels, strange artifacts from around the world, and a mysterious, locked door

"The book offers a well-paced adventure story, attractive line drawings, and the promise of many time-travel fantasies to come in the series." Booklist

Another title in this series is:

The long-lost map (2006)

The **long**-lost map; [text by Pierdomenico Baccalario; original cover and illustrations by Iacopo Bruno; graphics by Iacopo Bruno and Laura Zuccotti; translation by Leah Janeczko] Scholastic 2006 261p il (Ulysses Moore) $12.99

Grades: 4 5 6   **Fic**

1. Mystery fiction 2. Adventure fiction 3. Twins -- Fiction

ISBN 0-439-77439-X

LC 2005032129

Eleven-year-old twins Jason and Julia, along with their friend Rick, find themselves in ancient Egypt in search of an important map after going through a magical door in their old English mansion.

"The characters are clearly delineated, but adventure is prime here. The illustrations (including handsome pencil drawings) at the beginnings of chapters have a three-dimensional quality in keeping with the book's pretense that readers are looking at the recovered manuscripts of the mysterious Ulysses Moore." Booklist

Baggott, Julianna

The **Prince** of Fenway Park. HarperCollinsPublishers 2009 322p $16.99; lib bdg $17.89

Grades: 4 5 6 7   **Fic**

1. Orphans -- Fiction 2. Baseball -- Fiction 3. Supernatural -- Fiction 4. Father-son relationship -- Fiction

ISBN 978-0-06-087242-7; 0-06-087242-X; 978-0-06-087243-4 lib bdg; 0-06-087243-8 lib bdg

LC 2008-19666

In the fall of 2004, twelve-year-old Oscar Egg is sent to live with his father in a strange netherworld under Boston's Fenway Park, where he joins the fairies, pooka, banshee, and other beings that are trapped there, waiting for someone to break the eighty-six-year-old curse that has prevented the Boston Red Sox from winning a World Series

"Both whimsical and provocative (the 'N' word crops up in some historical references), this story will engage readers who like clever tales, and also those who enjoy chewing over controversial themes." SLJ

Baker, Deirdre F.

Becca at sea. Groundwood 2007 165p $16.95

Grades: 4 5 6   **Fic**

1. Islands -- Fiction 2. Family life -- Fiction 3. Grandmothers -- Fiction

ISBN 978-0-88899-737-1

After Becca's mom becomes pregnant, Becca visits her grandmother at her rustic cabin by the sea alone, and although she dreads it at first, she finds adventures and friendship and returns to the island again and again.

"Each episode enriches the portrait of Becca's memorable extended family with delightfully preposterous, yet insightful detail.... This funny, endearing book should find a wide audience." Horn Book

Baker-Smith, Grahame

Farther; Grahame Baker-Smith. Templar Publishing 2010 32 p. (reinforced) $17.99

Grades: K 1 2   **Fic**

1. Flight -- Juvenile fiction 2. Picture books for children 3. Father-son relationship -- Juvenile fiction 4. Flight -- Pictorial works -- Juvenile fiction 5. Ambition -- Pictorial works -- Juvenile fiction 6. Fathers and sons -- Pictorial works -- Juvenile fiction

ISBN 0763663700; 9780763663704

LC 2011431018

In this Kate Greenaway Medal children's picture book, by Grahame Baker-Smith, "a boy lovingly remembers ... [how] his father worked ceaselessly to fashion a flying machine.... That dream is never to be realized, as the day comes when the father dons a uniform and leaves for a great war, never to return. Years later, the son, now grown, resumes work on the machine, succeeds and then shares the vision with his own son." (Kirkus Reviews)

Balliett, Blue

The **Calder** game; illustrated by Brett Helquist. Scholastic Press 2008 379p il $17.99

Grades: 5 6 7 8   **Fic**

1. Artists 2. Sculptors 3. Mystery fiction 4. Sculpture -- Fiction 5. Missing persons -- Fiction

ISBN 978-0-439-85207-4; 0-439-85207-2

LC 2007031385

When seventh-grader Calder Pillay disappears from a remote English village—along with an Alexander Calder sculpture to which he has felt strangely drawn—his friends Petra and Tommy fly from Chicago to help his father find him.

Balliett "outdoes herself with this ambitious novel. . . . The mystery is crafted more solidly than in either of Balliett's previous titles, and the setting . . . proves completely enticing. And once again Helquist encodes his b&w illustrations with puzzle pieces." Publ Wkly

★ **Chasing** Vermeer; illustrated by Brett Helquist. Scholastic Press 2004 254p il $16.95

Grades: 5 6 7 8   **Fic**

1. Art 2. Artists 3. Painters 4. Mystery fiction 5. Art -- Fiction

ISBN 0-439-37294-1

LC 2002-152106

When seemingly unrelated and strange events start to happen and a precious Vermeer painting disappears, eleven-year-olds Petra and Calder combine their talents to solve an international art scandal.

Balliett's purpose "seems to be to get children to think—about relationships, connections, coincidences, and the subtle language of artwork. . . . [This is] a book that offers children something new upon each reading. . . . Helquist . . . outdoes himself here, providing an interactive mystery in his pictures." Booklist

Other titles about Petra and Calder are:

The Wright 3 (2006)

The Calder game (2008)

★ The **Danger** Box. Scholastic Press 2010 306p $16.99

Grades: 5 6 7 8   **Fic**

1. Naturalists 2. Travel writers 3. Diaries -- Fiction 4. Writers on science 5. Antiques -- Fiction 6. Family life -- Fiction 7. Grandparents -- Fiction

ISBN 978-0-439-85209-8; 0-439-85209-9

LC 2010-16622

In small-town Michigan, twelve-year-old Zoomy and his new friend Lorrol investigate the journal found inside a mysterious box and find family secrets and a more valuable treasure, while a dangerous stranger watches and waits.

"This highly satisfying story will enlighten readers even as it inspires them to think about their own danger boxes." SLJ

★ **Hold** fast; by Blue Balliett. Scholastic Press 2013 288 p. (jacketed hardcover) $17.99

Grades: 3 4 5 6   **Fic**

1. Theft -- Juvenile fiction 2. Mystery fiction -- Juvenile fiction 3. Smuggling -- Fiction 4. Kidnapping -- Fiction

5. Missing persons -- Fiction 6. Homeless persons -- Fiction 7. Mystery and detective stories 8. Smuggling -- Juvenile fiction 9. Fathers and daughters -- Fiction 10. Missing persons -- Juvenile fiction 11. Homeless families -- Juvenile fiction 12. Kidnapping victims -- Juvenile fiction 13. Fathers and daughters -- Juvenile fiction 14. Family life -- Illinois -- Chicago -- Fiction

ISBN 0545299888; 9780545299886

LC 2012041035

This book focuses on "the Pearl family: Dash, Summer, 11-year-old Early, and the little Jubie. Do they have a lot? Well, yes, they have Dash's love of words, their devotion to each other, and their dream: to have a home. Trying to help that dream along, Dash, a page at the Chicago Public Library, makes extra money inventorying a private collection of old books. One . . . day, Dash disappears, and the family must move to a shelter after an odd robbery sees their . . . apartment destroyed." (Booklist)

The **Wright** 3; illustrated by Brett Helquist. Scholastic Press 2006 318p il $16.99

Grades: 5 6 7 8   **Fic**

1. Architects 2. School stories 3. Mystery fiction 4. Nonfiction writers

ISBN 0-439-69367-5

LC 2005-19608

In the midst of a series of unexplained accidents and mysterious coincidences, sixth-graders Calder, Petra, and Tommy lead their classmates in an attempt to keep Frank Lloyd Wright's famous Robie House from being demolished.

"The mystery itself and the perfectly realized setting make this an essential purchase." SLJ

Banerjee, Anjali

★ **Looking** for Bapu. Wendy Lamb Books 2006 162p hardcover o.p. pa $6.50

Grades: 4 5 6 7   **Fic**

1. Hindus -- Fiction 2. Bereavement -- Fiction 3. Grandfathers -- Fiction 4. East Indians -- United States -- Fiction

ISBN 978-0-385-74657-1; 0-385-90894-6; 978-0-553-49425-9 pa; 0-553-49425-2 pa

LC 2006-02021

When his beloved grandfather dies, eight-year-old Anu feels that his spirit is near and will stop at nothing to bring him back, including trying to become a Hindu holy man.

"With episodes that ring true to a boy's perspective, Banerjee's novel provides discussable issues and multicultural insights as well as humor and emotion. An excellent read aloud." Booklist

Seaglass summer. Wendy Lamb Books 2010 163p il $15.99; lib bdg $18.99

Grades: 4 5 6   **Fic**

1. Uncles -- Fiction 2. Veterinarians -- Fiction 3. East Indian Americans -- Fiction

ISBN 978-0-385-73567-4; 0-385-73567-7; 978-0-385-90555-8 lib bdg; 0-385-90555-6 lib bdg

LC 2009-25468

"Eleven-year-old Poppy wants to be a veterinarian like her uncle Sanjay. So while her parents are in India visiting relatives, she spends several weeks with him on Nisqually Island, Washington, helping out at his Furry Friends Animal Clinic. Episodic chapters focus on the people and animals

that Poppy meets, [and] her efforts to do a good job. . . .
There are many moving events here. . . . Sometimes amusing, sometimes gross, and always true to itself, this should
find a wide readership. Pencil illustrations enliven the chapter headings." Booklist

Banks, Kate

Dillon Dillon. Foster Bks. 2002 150p hardcover o.p.
pa $5.95

Grades: 4 5 6 7   **Fic**
1. Loons -- Fiction 2. Adoption -- Fiction 3. Family
life -- Fiction

ISBN 0-374-31786-0; 0-374-41715-6 pa
                                            LC 2001-33207

During the summer that he turns ten years old, Dillon
Dillon learns the surprising story behind his name and develops a relationship with three loons, living on the lake
near his family's New Hampshire cabin, that help him make
sense of his life

This "succeeds as an emotionally intricate, quietly well-
observed, symbolically charged novel." Horn Book

Banks, Lynne Reid

★ The Indian in the cupboard; illustrated by Brock
Cole. Doubleday 1980 181p il $16.95; pa $6.99

Grades: 5 6 7 8   **Fic**
1. Fantasy fiction

ISBN 0-385-17051-3; 0-375-84753-7 pa
                                              LC 79-6533

A nine-year-old boy receives a plastic Indian, a cupboard, and a little key for his birthday and finds himself involved in adventure when the Indian comes to life in the
cupboard and befriends him

Other titles in this series are:
The key to the Indian (1998)
The mystery of the cupboard (1993)
The return of the Indian (1986)
The secret of the Indian (1989)

Barden, Stephanie

★ Cinderella Smith; illustrations by Diane Goode.
Harper 2011 148p il

Grades: 3 4 5   **Fic**
1. School stories 2. Friendship -- Fiction 3. Family
life -- Fiction 4. Stepsisters -- Fiction 5. Tap dancing
-- Fiction 6. Seattle (Wash.) -- Fiction

ISBN 0-06-196423-9; 978-0-06-196423-7
                                            LC 2010015980

Cast off by her old friends, Cinderella agrees to help a
new student deal with the stepsisters she will soon have, and
meantime, a former friend tries to prevent Cinderella from
dancing the lead in their tap recital.

"Line illustrations by the gifted Goode enhance the
lightheartedness and fun of the story. . . . The awkwardness
Cinderella feels with her former friends is palpable yet not
overly serious, and her inclusive enjoyment of life is contagious. The resolution to the stepsister problem is especially
satisfying." Booklist

Barker, M. P.

A difficult boy. Holiday House 2008 298p $16.95;
pa $7.95

Grades: 5 6 7 8   **Fic**
1. Contract labor -- Fiction 2. Irish Americans -- Fiction

3. Swindlers and swindling -- Fiction
ISBN 978-0-8234-2086-5; 0-8234-2086-8; 978-0-
8234-2244-9 pa; 0-8234-2244-5 pa
                                            LC 2007-37059

In Farmington, Massachusetts, in 1839, nine-year-old
Ethan experiences hardships as an indentured servant of the
wealthy Lyman family alongside Daniel, a boy scorned simply for being Irish, and the boys bond as they try to right a
terrible wrong.

"A memorable tale of friendship and a fascinating
glimpse into mid-19th-century Massachusetts." SLJ

Barnett, Mac

★ The case of the case of mistaken identity; illustrations by Adam Rex. Simon & Schuster Books for Young
Readers 2009 179p il (The Brixton Brothers) $14.99

Grades: 4 5 6   **Fic**
1. Mystery fiction 2. Police -- Fiction 3. Quilts --
Fiction 4. Librarians -- Fiction

ISBN 978-1-4169-7815-2; 1-4169-7815-1
                                            LC 2008-43305

When twelve-year-old Steve Brixton, a fan of Bailey
Brothers detective novels, is mistaken for a real detective,
he must elude librarians, police, and the mysterious Mr. E
as he seeks a missing quilt containing coded information.

The book provides "action and adventure but adds a
level of humor that will sometimes have readers laughing
out loud. Similarly, Rex's illustrations have a mid-twentieth-
century look, and in an accomplished, deadpan manner, offer one of the book's funniest moments." Booklist

Other titles in this series are:
The ghostwriter secret (2010)
It happened on a train (2011)

Barnhill, Kelly Regan

★ The mostly true story of Jack; by Kelly Barnhill.
Little, Brown 2011 323p il $16.99

Grades: 5 6 7 8   **Fic**
1. Magic -- Fiction 2. Friendship -- Fiction 3. Family
life -- Fiction

ISBN 978-0-316-05670-0; 0-316-05670-7
                                            LC 2010044934

Jack is practically invisible at home, but when his parents send him to Hazelwood, Iowa, to spend a summer with
his odd aunt and uncle, he suddenly makes friends, is beaten
up by the town bully, and is plotted against by the richest
man in town.

"A truly splendid amalgamation of mystery, magic and
creeping horror will spellbind the middle-grade set. . . . The
mystery deepens with each chapter, revealing exactly the
right amount with each step. Answers are doled out so meticulously that readers will be continually intrigued rather
than frustrated. The result is the ultime page-turner." Kirkus

Barnholdt, Lauren

Girl meets ghost; by Lauren Barnholdt. Aladdin 2013
224 p. (alk. paper) $15.99

Grades: 4 5 6 7   **Fic**
1. Ghost stories -- Juvenile fiction 2. School stories
-- Juvenile fiction 3. Mystery fiction -- Juvenile fiction
4. Dead -- Fiction 5. Ghosts -- Fiction 6. Schools --
Fiction 7. Middle schools -- Fiction 8. Psychic ability

-- Fiction 9. Mystery and detective stories
ISBN 1442442468; 9781442442467

LC 2012032234

In this children's story, by Lauren Barnholt, "a tween girl becomes a reluctant medium. . . . There's an old saying that 'dead men tell no tales'--but that saying is definitely not true. Just ask twelve-year-old Kendall Williams, who can't get dead people to stop talking to her. . . . It's pretty frustrating being able to hear and see people that no one else can. . . . But Kendall is going to have to learn how to deal, because the only way to quiet the dead is to help them." (Publisher's note)

Hailey Twitch and the campground itch; pictures by Suzanne Beaky. Sourcebooks Jabberwocky 2011 130p il pa $6.99

Grades: 1 2   **Fic**

1. Camping -- Fiction 2. Family life -- Fiction
ISBN 978-1-4022-2446-1; 1-4022-2446-X

"Hailey Twitch's excitement turns sour when her teenage sister's demanding friend joins the family on a weekend getaway. . . . This series entry maintains a well-realized child-centered perspective through every humorous magical snafu. . . . The younger's energetic voice rings true." Kirkus

Hailey Twitch and the great teacher switch; illustrated by Suzanne Beaky. Sourcebooks Jabberwocky 2011 153p il pa $6.99

Grades: 1 2   **Fic**

1. Fairies -- Fiction 2. Theater -- Fiction
ISBN 978-1-4022-2445-4; 1-4022-2445-1

"The cantankerous Mr. Frisk doesn't stand a chance against precocious Hailey Twitch and her impish fairy Maybelle. Both aspire to befriend their elderly neighbor for personal gain; Hailey's efforts intensify as she enlists the seasoned actor as director in their school play. While the child's wacky attempts at friendship prove disastrous . . . her off-base efforts to apologize prove more appalling still. . . . Beaky's drawings make the most of the situational humor. Hailey's child-centered perceptions remain spot-on, combining laugh-out-loud moments with gentle insight." Kirkus

Hailey Twitch and the wedding glitch; pictures by Suzanne Beaky. Sourcebook Jackerwocky 2011 il pa $6.99

Grades: 1 2   **Fic**

1. Magic -- Fiction 2. Fairies -- Fiction 3. Weddings -- Fiction
ISBN 978-1-4022-2447-8; 1-4022-2447-8

This features a seven-year-old mastermind who tries really hard not to blame her invisible friend for getting her into heaps of trouble. Hailey's magic sprite, Maybelle, has finally gotten control of her magic. Does that mean that Maybelle no longer needs Hailey? As if that's not enough to worry Hailey, now she's got her hands full being a flower girl in her aunt's wedding.

Hailey Twitch is not a snitch; pictures by Suzanne Beaky. Sourcebooks Jabberwocky 2010 138p il pa $6.99

Grades: 1 2   **Fic**

1. School stories 2. Fairies -- Fiction 3. Family life -- Fiction
ISBN 978-1-4022-2444-7 pa; 1-4022-2444-3 pa

LC 2009-49937

Second-grader Hailey's frustration over a school project releases Maybelle, a sprite whose punishment for being a rulemonger will end when she grants Hailey's wish to have fun, but Maybelle's efforts only seem to cause trouble.

"Barnholt focuses on fledgling friendships and dreaded partner assignments to successfully capture elementary school's complex dynamics. The classmates' realistic dialogue supports the lighthearted tale. Hailey's engaging narration is developmentally egocentric and appropriately child-centered. . . . Beaky's animated illustrations extend the breezy narrative." Kirkus

Other titles about Hailey Twitch are:
Hailey Twitch and the great teacher switch (2011)
Hailey Twitch and the campground itch (2011)
Hailey Twitch and the wedding glitch (2011)

Barrett, Tracy
The **100**-year-old secret. Henry Holt and Co. 2008 157p (The Sherlock files) $15.95

Grades: 4 5 6 7   **Fic**

1. Mystery fiction 2. Siblings -- Fiction
ISBN 978-0-8050-8340-8; 0-8050-8340-5

LC 2007034004

Xena and Xander Holmes, an American brother and sister living in London for a year, discover that Sherlock Holmes was their great-great-great grandfather when they are inducted into the Society for the Preservation of Famous Detectives and given his unsolved casebook, from which they attempt to solve the case of a famous missing painting

"The main characters are observant, bright, and gifted with powers of deduction." SLJ

Other titles in this series are:
The beast of Blackslope (2009)
The case that time forgot (2010)
The missing heir (2011)

The **Beast** of Blackslope. Henry Holt 2009 174p $15.99

Grades: 4 5 6 7   **Fic**

1. Mystery fiction 2. Siblings -- Fiction
ISBN 978-0-8050-8341-5; 0-8050-8341-3

LC 2008036941

Xena and Xander Holmes, an American brother and sister spending a year in England, use clues in their ancestor Sherlock Holmes' casebook as they try to solve the mystery of a monster threatening a peaceful country village where a documentary film is being made.

"Xena's methodical and calm rationality balances with Xander's intuitive imaginativeness so that they complement one another." SLJ

Cold in summer. Holt & Co. 2003 203p $16.95

Grades: 5 6 7 8   **Fic**

1. Ghost stories
ISBN 0-8050-7052-4

LC 2002-67888

At the beginning of seventh grade, Ariadne moves to a Tennessee town near a former farming community submerged under a man-made lake and meets the ghost of a girl from the past

"This is a straightforward ghost tale with a doughty main character, a strong sense of history, and solid secondary players." Bull Cent Child Books

On Etruscan time. Henry Holt and Co. 2005 172p
$16.95
Grades: 5 6 7 8   **Fic**
1. Etruscans -- Fiction 2. Archeology -- Fiction
ISBN 0-8050-7569-0
LC 2004-52341
While spending the summer on an archaeological dig
near Florence, Italy, with his mother, eleven-year-old Hector
meets an Etruscan boy who needs help to foil his treacherous uncle's plan to make him a human sacrifice-1,000 years
in the past
"Barrett's accurate description of the archaeological dig
and the details of Etruscan daily life are well researched and
interesting. The plot holds excitement and suspense." SLJ

The **case** that time forgot. Henry Holt and Company
2010 158p (The Sherlock files) $15.99
Grades: 4 5 6 7   **Fic**
1. Mystery fiction 2. Siblings -- Fiction
ISBN 978-0-8050-8046-9; 0-8050-8046-5
"American kids living in London with their parents,
Xena and Xander are not just the descendants of Sherlock
Holmes. They have his notebook of unsolved cases, and
they're not afraid to use it. . . . After a classmate of Egyptian
descent asks for help finding an ancient amulet, the young
sleuths spring into action. . . . The third mystery in the Sherlock Files series will please fans intrigued by ancient Egypt,
codes, danger, and the tantalizing possibility of magic."
Booklist

The **missing** heir. Henry Holt and Co. 2011 172p
(The Sherlock files) $15.99
Grades: 4 5 6 7   **Fic**
1. Mystery fiction 2. Siblings -- Fiction 3. Princesses
-- Fiction 4. Missing persons -- Fiction
ISBN 978-0-8050-8047-6; 0-8050-8047-3
LC 2010041012
Xena and Xander Holmes, an American brother and sis-
ter living in London, use clues from their ancestor Sherlock
Holmes' casebook to help classmate Alice Banders, who
goes missing following the announcement that she will be
crowned queen of Borogovia after her thirteenth birthday.

Barrie, J. M.
Peter Pan; the complete and unabridged text. illus-
trated by Scott Gustafson. Viking 1991 184p il $24.99
Grades: 3 4 5 6   **Fic**
1. Fairy tales
ISBN 0-670-84180-3
LC 91-50392
First published 1911 by Scribner with title: Peter
and Wendy
The adventures of the three Darling children in Never-
land with Peter Pan, the boy who would not grow up.
"Gustafson's artwork opens doors to glimpses of old
friends and to new interpretations. Fifty oil paintings reveal
expressive, changing characters." SLJ

Peter Pan and Wendy; illustrated by Robert Ingpen;
foreword by David Barrie. Centenary edition; Sterling
2010 216p il $19.95
Grades: 3 4 5 6   **Fic**
1. Fairy tales
ISBN 978-1-4027-2868-6; 1-4027-2868-9

First published 1911 by Scribner with title: Peter
and Wendy; a reissue of the 2004 edition published by
Orchard Books
The adventures of the three Darling children in Neverland with Peter Pan, the boy who would not grow up.
This "edition is notable for its painterly illustrations,
which reflect touches of Sendak, Wyeth, the pre-Raphael-
ites, and others. The overall effect of the art is impressionistic, and the book itself is handsome." Horn Book Guide

Barron, T. A.
The **book** of magic; illustrated by August Hall.
Philomel Books 2011 il (Merlin) $17.99 **Fic**
1. Fantasy fiction 2. Magic -- Fiction 3. Merlin
(Legendary character) -- Fiction
ISBN 978-0-399-24741-5; 0-399-24741-6
LC 2011013552
A compendium of maps, character descriptions, magi-
cal terms, timelines, and other tidbits from the author's
Merlin saga.
"Guides to long-running series have two important jobs.
They should remind fans of all the things they particularly
love about the books, and they should whet the appetites of
newcomers, thus creating more fans. Barron's guide to his
12-book saga about Merlin succeeds in both objectives."
SLJ

The **fires** of Merlin. Philomel Bks. 1998 261p $20.99;
pa $5.99
Grades: 5 6 7 8   **Fic**
1. Fantasy 2. Fantasy fiction 3. Wizards -- Fiction
4. Merlin (Legendary character) -- Fiction 5. Merlin
(Legendary character) -- Juvenile fiction
ISBN 0-399-23020-3; 0-441-00957-3 pa
LC 97-49561
This is the third volume in the trilogy about Merlin's
youth. Having voyaged to the Otherworld in his quest to find
himself, the young wizard Merlin must face fire in many different forms and deal with the possibility of losing his own
magical power
This "saga just keeps getting richer in characterization,
ambience, and Celtic lore." Booklist

★ The **lost** years of Merlin. Philomel Bks. 1996 326p
$19.99; pa $7.99
Grades: 5 6 7 8   **Fic**
1. Fantasy fiction 2. Merlin (Legendary character) --
Fiction
ISBN 978-0-399-23018-1; 978-0-441-00668-7 pa
LC 96-33920
"A boy, hurled on the rocks by the sea, regains consciousness unable to remember anything—not his parents,
not his own name. He is sure that the secretive Branwen is
not his mother, despite her claims, and that Emrys is not his
real name. The two soon find themselves feared because of
Branwen's healing abilities and Emrys' growing powers. . .
. Barron has created not only a magical land populated by
remarkable beings but also a completely magical tale, filled
with ancient Celtic and Druidic lore, that will enchant readers." Booklist
Other titles in this series are:
The seven songs of Merlin (1997)
The fires of Merlin (1998)
The mirror of Merlin (1999)

The wings of Merlin (2000)
The book of magic (2011)

The **mirror** of Merlin. Philomel Bks. 1999 245p il $20.99; pa $7.99
Grades: 5 6 7 8 **Fic**
1. Fantasy 2. Fantasy fiction 3. Merlin (Legendary character) 4. Wizards 5. Merlin (Legendary character) -- Juvenile fiction
ISBN 0-399-23455-1; 0-441-00846-1 pa
LC 99-13043

This is the fourth volume in the author's series about Merlin's youth. Through adventures involving a haunted marsh, talking trees, and the creature called the ballymag, the young wizard Merlin continues to experience both his growing powers and his essential humanity

"With lots of surprises and some laugh-out-loud humor to leaven the palpable feeling of doom, this should be eagerly devoured by the saga's fans." Booklist

The **seven** songs of Merlin. Philomel Bks. 1997 306p $19.99; pa $7.99
Grades: 5 6 7 8 **Fic**
1. Fantasy fiction 2. Merlin (Legendary character) -- Fiction
ISBN 0-399-23019-X; 0-441-00701-5 pa
LC 97-9619

This is the second volume in the author's series about Merlin's youth. Having stumbled upon his hidden powers, the young wizard Merlin voyages to the Otherworld in his quest to find himself and the way to the realm of the spirit

"The tale is spellbinding (pun intended), and readers will relish not only the action and the well-crafted setting but also Merlin's growth from a callow youth to a wiser, more caring wizard-in-training." Booklist

The **wings** of Merlin. Philomel Books 2000 352p $21.99; pa $7.99
Grades: 5 6 7 8 **Fic**
1. Fantasy 2. Fantasy fiction 3. Merlin (Legendary character) 4. Wizards 5. Merlin (Legendary character) -- Fiction 6. Merlin (Legendary character) -- Juvenile fiction
ISBN 0-399-23456-X; 0-441-00988-3 pa
LC 00-27553

Merlin's fragile home on the isle of Fincayra is threatened by the attack of a mysterious warrior with swords for arms and by the escape of Stangmar from his imprisonment, as Merlin continues to move toward his ultimate destiny.

"Barron brings his Lost Years of Merlin saga to a resounding, satisfying close with this fifth volume." Booklist

Barrow, Randi G.
Saving Zasha; by Randi Barrow. Scholastic Press 2011 229p $16.99
Grades: 4 5 6 7 **Fic**
1. Dogs -- Fiction 2. Journalists -- Fiction 3. Single parent family -- Fiction 4. World War, 1939-1945 -- Fiction
ISBN 978-0-545-20632-7; 0-545-20632-4
LC 2010-16899

In 1945 Russia, those who own German shepherds are considered traitors, but thirteen-year-old Mikhail and his family are determined to keep the dog a dying man brought them, while his classmate Katia strives to learn his secret.

"Mikhail's sense of humor, concern for his family, and love of Zasha are all readily apparent in his narration, which smoothly incorporates background information for readers unfamiliar with 20th-century Russian life and history. . . . Barrow's novel is quick reading yet weighty, and captures the prejudices and aftereffects of war." Publ Wkly

Barrows, Annie
★ **Ivy** + Bean; written by Annie Barrows; illustrated by Sophie Blackall. Chronicle Books 2006 113p il $14.95; pa $5.99
Grades: 1 2 3 **Fic**
1. Friendship -- Fiction
ISBN 978-0-8118-4903-6; 0-8118-4903-1; 978-0-8118-4909-8 pa; 0-8118-4909-0 pa
LC 2005023944

When seven-year-old Bean plays a mean trick on her sister, she finds unexpected support for her antics from Ivy, the new neighbor, who is less boring than Bean first suspected.

"The deliciousness here is in the details, with both girls drawn distinctly and with flair. . . . Even with all the text's strong points, what takes the book to a higher level is Blackall's artwork, which captures the girls' spirit." Booklist

Other titles about Ivy and Bean are:
Ivy + Bean and the ghost that had to go (2006)
Ivy + Bean break the fossil record (2007)
Ivy + Bean take care of the babysitter (2008)
Ivy + Bean: bound to be bad (2009)
Ivy + Bean: doomed to dance (2009)
Ivy + Bean: what's the big idea? (2010)

Ivy + Bean and the ghost that had to go; written by Annie Barrows; illustrated by Sophie Blackall. Chronicle 2006 125p il $14.95
Grades: 1 2 3 **Fic**
1. Ghost stories 2. School stories 3. Friendship -- Fiction
ISBN 0-8118-4910-4

Second-graders Ivy and Bean set out to expel the ghost who is living in the girls' bathroom at their school.

"As before, the series' strong suits are humor and the spot-on take on relationships." Booklist

Ivy + Bean bound to be bad; [written by] Annie Barrows; [illustrated by] Sophie Blackall. Chronicle Books 2009 120p il $14.99
Grades: 1 2 3 **Fic**
1. Friendship -- Fiction 2. Family life -- Fiction
ISBN 978-0-8118-6265-3; 0-8118-6265-8
LC 2008005280

Best friends Ivy and Bean learn that being very good, or very bad, can be a real challenge when they set out to become like a man Ivy heard about who was so pure of heart that birds and animals followed him.

This is "plenty fun, especially for the duo's many fans. As always, Blackall's delightful illustrations add smiles and substance." Booklist

Ivy + Bean break the fossil record; written by Annie Barrows; illustrated by Sophie Blackall. Chronicle Books 2007 114p il $14.95

Grades: 1 2 3 **Fic**
1. Fossils -- Fiction 2. Friendship -- Fiction
ISBN 978-0-8118-5683-6; 0-8118-5683-6
LC 2007001471

Everyone in second grade seems set on breaking a world record and friends Ivy and Bean are no exception, deciding to become the youngest people ever to discover a dinosaur skeleton.

"Barrows' dynamic duo is as appealing here as in the first two books, and emergent readers will identify with their outrageous antics." Booklist

Ivy + Bean take care of the babysitter; by Annie Barrows; illustrated by Sophie Blackall. Chronicle Books 2008 122p il $14.99; pa $5.99
Grades: 1 2 3 **Fic**
1. Sisters -- Fiction 2. Babysitters -- Fiction
ISBN 978-0-8118-5685-0; 0-8118-5685-2; 978-0-8118-6584-5 pa; 0-8118-6584-3 pa
LC 2007028224

When Bean's parents leave her in the care of her older sister Nancy for the afternoon, she enlists her neighbor and best friend Ivy to come over and teach Nancy how to be a really good babysitter.

"The frequent black-and-white Chinese ink illustrations capture the mood and carefree attitude of the story well. Early chapter-book readers will enjoy this installment in this light-hearted series." SLJ

Ivy + Bean: doomed to dance; written by Annie Barrows; illustrated by Sophie Blackall. Chronicle Books 2009 129p il (Ivy + Bean) $14.99
Grades: 1 2 3 **Fic**
1. Ballet -- Fiction 2. Friendship -- Fiction
ISBN 978-0-8118-6266-0; 0-8118-6266-6
LC 2009004367

Second-grade best friends Ivy and Bean beg for ballet lessons, then, when they are cast as squids in their first recital, scheme to find a way out of what seems to be boring, hard, and potentially embarrassing.

"The story is solidly written, and the expressive black-and-white illustrations, some full page, add to the humor. Early chapter-book readers will appreciate and relate to the friends' dilemma." SLJ

Ivy + Bean: what's the big idea? written by Annie Barrows; illustrated by Sophie Blackall. Chronicle Books 2010 131p il (Ivy + Bean) $14.99
Grades: 1 2 3 **Fic**
1. School stories 2. Science projects -- Fiction
ISBN 978-0-8118-6692-7; 0-8118-6692-0
LC 2010008258

When all the second grade students must enter the science fair, which has global warming as its theme, best friends Ivy and Bean team up to create an unusual project.

"Barrows and Blackall deserve kudos for keeping this seventh book in the series original and fun." Horn Book

The **magic** half. Bloomsbury Children's Books 2008 211p il $15.95; pa $6.99

Grades: 3 4 5 **Fic**
1. Twins -- Fiction 2. Sisters -- Fiction
ISBN 978-1-59990-132-9; 1-59990-132-3; 978-1-59990-358-3 pa; 1-59990-358-X pa
LC 2007-23551

Eleven-year-old Miri Gill feels left out in her family, which has two sets of twins and her, until she travels back in time to 1935 and discovers Molly, her own lost twin, and brings her back to the present day.

"Readers will savor the author's lively observations . . . while the heroine's adaptability and independent thinking endow her with the appeal of a Ramona Quimby or a Clementine." Publ Wkly

Barry, Dave
Peter & the shadow thieves; by Dave Barry and Ridley Pearson; illustrations by Greg Call. Disney Editions/Hyperion Books for Children 2006 556p il $18.99
Grades: 5 6 7 **Fic**
1. Fairy tales 2. Adventure fiction
ISBN 0-7868-3787-X
LC 2005-56033

Realizing that Molly and the other Starcatchers are in danger when the sinister being Lord Ombra visits the island and seems to control people through their shadows, Peter and Tinker Bell travel to England to help save the stardust. "Age ten and up." (N Y Times Book Rev)

This "is filled with enough rollicking, death-defying adventure to satisfy anyone." SLJ

Peter and the Sword of Mercy; by Dave Barry and Ridley Pearson; illustrations by Greg Call. Disney/Hyperion Books 2009 515p il $18.99
Grades: 5 6 7 **Fic**
1. Fairy tales 2. Adventure fiction
ISBN 978-1-4231-2134-3; 1-4231-2134-1

James, one of Peter's original Lost Boys, is now working for Scotland Yard and suspects that the heir to England's throne, Prince Albert Edward, is under the influence of shadow creatures who are after starstuff hidden in an underground vault which has only one key: the Sword of Mercy.

"This adventure is fast and intense, and readers will feel compelled to find out what happens next." VOYA

Peter and the secret of Rundoon; by Dave Barry and Ridley Pearson; illustrations by Greg Call. Disney Editions/Hyperion Books for Children 2007 482p il $18.99
Grades: 5 6 7 **Fic**
1. Fairy tales 2. Adventure fiction
ISBN 0-7868-3788-8; 978-0-7868-3788-5
LC 2007006306

Fearing that the sinister Lord Ombra was not destroyed, Peter and Molly travel to the land of Rundoon, which is ruled by the evil King Zarboff.

"This is a fun, intense, and totally worthwhile adventure." SLJ

Peter and the starcatchers; by Dave Barry and Ridley Pearson; illustrations by Greg Call. Hyperion 2004 451p il $17.99; pa $7.99
Grades: 5 6 7 **Fic**
1. Fairy tales 2. Adventure fiction 3. Pirates -- Fiction
ISBN 0-7868-5445-6; 0-7868-4907-X pa
LC 2004-55275

Soon after Peter, an orphan, sets sail from England on the ship Never Land, he befriends Molly, a young Starcatcher, whose mission is to guard a trunk of magical stardust from a greedy pirate and the native inhabitants of a remote island. "Age ten and up." (N Y Times Book Rev)

"The authors plait multiple story lines together in short, fast-moving chapters. . . . Capitalizing on familiar material, this adventure is carefully crafted to set the stage for Peter's later exploits. This smoothly written page-turner just might send readers back to the original." SLJ

The **bridge** to Never Land; [by] Dave Barry and Ridley Pearson. Disney/Hyperion 2011 438p $18.99

Grades: 5 6 7   **Fic**

1. Fairy tales 2. Adventure fiction

ISBN 978-1-4231-3865-5; 1-4231-3865-1

"Bringing the Starcatchers series into the twenty-first century, this novel features Sarah and her brother, Aidan, who find a cryptic note in an antique desk and follow the clues to London, Princeton, and Orlando. Along the way, they clash with evil Lord Ombra, find an ally in Molly Darling's great-great-great nephew, and discover Einstein's part in the plan. The plot is a thrill ride of action and adventure, with plenty of chase scenes and (no surprise here) a trip to Never Land." Booklist

Barshaw, Ruth McNally

Ellie McDoodle: best friends fur-ever. Bloomsbury 2010 171p $12.99

Grades: 2 3 4 5   **Fic**

1. School stories 2. Pets -- Fiction 3. Drawing -- Fiction 4. Parrots -- Fiction 5. Family life -- Fiction

ISBN 978-1-59990-426-9; 1-59990-426-8

Ellie pet-sits for her neighbor's African grey parrot Alix, about whom she is writing a report, while her family argues over whether to get a cat or a dog, and her little brother accidentally lets Alix out of his cage, all of which is chronicled in Ellie's ever-present sketchbook.

"Interspersed in this story are instructions for games, yoga breathing, and crafts that add to the fun. . . . Exuberant black-and-white sketches and dialogue balloons enliven the pages." SLJ

Ellie McDoodle: have pen, will travel; written and illustrated by Ruth McNally Barshaw. Bloomsbury Children's Books 2007 170p il $11.95; pa $5.99

Grades: 2 3 4 5   **Fic**

1. Camping -- Fiction 2. Cousins -- Fiction

ISBN 978-1-58234-745-5; 1-58234-745-X; 978-1-59990-276-0 pa; 1-59990-276-1 pa

LC 2006-28424

Eleven-year-old Ellie McDoodle illustrates her sketchbook with chronicles of her adventures and mishaps while camping with her cousins, aunt, and uncle.

"The engaging text reflects a contemporary preadolescent sensibility and is chock-full of clean, distinguished line drawings on each spread." SLJ

Other titles about Ellie McDoodle are:

Ellie McDoodle: new kid in school (2008)

Ellie McDoodle: best friends fur-ever (2010)

Ellie McDoodle: new kid in school; written and illustrated by Ruth McNally Barshaw. Children's Books 2008 188p il $12.99

Grades: 2 3 4 5   **Fic**

1. School stories 2. Moving -- Fiction 3. Family life -- Fiction

ISBN 978-1-59990-238-8; 1-59990-238-9

LC 2007050833

Ellie writes and doodles in a journal of her family's move to a new home and her struggle to make friends, which gets a lot easier as she leads a nonviolent protest about long lunch lines at school.

This is "a humorous and realistic look at moving. . . . [Ellie's] story is told through a notebook, which is a combination of handwritten text and line drawings. The pictures, comic frames, and dialogue balloons serve to further the story. Reluctant and struggling readers and young fans of graphic novels are sure to find this title appealing." SLJ

Bartek, Mary

Funerals & fly fishing; [by] Mary Bartek. H. Holt 2004 148p $16.95; pa $6.99

Grades: 4 5 6 7   **Fic**

1. Family 2. Grandfathers 3. Undertakers and undertaking 4. Grandfathers -- Fiction 5. Funeral rites and ceremonies -- Fiction

ISBN 0-8050-7409-0; 0-312-56124-5 pa

LC 2003-57046

The summer after sixth grade, Brad Stanislawski travels to Pennsylvania by himself to visit the grandfather he has never met before, and overcomes some of the preconceived ideas he has gotten from his mother

"The characters are believable and well developed. . . . There is enough action to keep children's attention." SLJ

Bartoletti, Susan Campbell

★ The **boy** who dared. Scholastic Press 2008 202p $16.99

Grades: 5 6 7 8   **Fic**

1. Courage -- Fiction 2. Underground leaders 3. National socialism -- Fiction

ISBN 978-0-439-68013-4; 0-439-68013-1

LC 2007014166

In October, 1942, seventeen-year-old Helmuth Hübener, imprisoned for distributing anti-Nazi leaflets, recalls his past life and how he came to dedicate himself to bringing the truth about Hitler and the war to the German people.

Bartoletti "does and excellent job of conveying the political climate surrounding Hitler's ascent to power, seamlessly integrating a complex range of socioeconomic conditions into her absorbing drama." Publ Wkly

Base, Graeme

Enigma; a magical mystery. [by] Graeme Base. Abrams Books for Young Readers 2008 36p il $19.95

Grades: 3 4 5   **Fic**

1. Picture puzzles 2. Stories in rhyme 3. Badgers -- Fiction 4. Ciphers -- Fiction 5. Rabbits -- Fiction 6. Magicians -- Fiction 7. Grandfathers -- Fiction

ISBN 978-0-8109-7245-2; 0-8109-7245-X

LC 2007042397

When Bertie the badger visits his grandfather at a retirement home for magicians, he learns that his grandfather's rabbit, Enigma, has disappeared along with everyone's magical things, and the reader is invited to help break a code to find the items hidden throughout the book. Includes a built-in decoder.

"Readers could simply hunt for the missing objects, which Base conceals within elaborately detailed paintings, but then they would miss out on the tricky fun of mastering several codes also embedded in the book. . . . A set of bonus challenges will keep kids (and older siblings) poring closely over the pages for weeks, enthralled." Publ Wkly

Baskin, Nora Raleigh

★ **Anything** but typical. Simon & Schuster Books for Young Readers 2009 195p il $15.99

Grades: 4 5 6 7   **Fic**

1. School stories 2. Autism -- Fiction 3. Authorship -- Fiction 4. Family life -- Fiction

ISBN 978-1-4169-6378-3; 1-4169-6378-2

LC 2008-20994

ALA Schneider Family Book Award Honor Book (2010)

Jason, a twelve-year-old autistic boy who wants to become a writer, relates what his life is like as he tries to make sense of his world

"This is an enormously difficult subject, but Baskin, without dramatics or sentimentality, makes it universal." Booklist

The **truth** about my Bat Mitzvah. Simon & Schuster Books for Young Readers 2008 138p $15.99; pa $5.99

Grades: 5 6 7 8   **Fic**

1. Jews -- Fiction 2. Bat mitzvah -- Fiction 3. Grandmothers -- Fiction

ISBN 978-1-4169-3558-2; 1-4169-3558-4; 978-1-4169-7469-7 pa; 1-4169-7469-5 pa

LC 2007-01248

After her beloved grandmother, Nana, dies, non-religious twelve-year-old Caroline becomes curious about her mother's Jewish ancestry.

"Readers will identify with Caroline and her preoccupations. . . . This quick read will be a hit with preteens contemplating their own identities." Booklist

Bass, Guy

Dinkin Dings and the frightening things; illustrated by Pete Williamson. Grosset & Dunlap 2011 125p il $12.99; pa $4.99

Grades: 2 3 4   **Fic**

1. Fear -- Fiction 2. Zombies -- Fiction 3. Extraterrestrial beings -- Fiction

ISBN 978-0-448-45432-0; 0-448-45432-7; 978-0-448-45431-3 pa; 0-448-45431-9 pa

Young Dinkin Dings, who is afraid of literally everything, is certain that his new next-door neighbors are flesh-eating alien space zombies.

"This story has strong kid appeal and offbeat cartoon artwork that appears on nearly every page. The story line will definitely strike a chord with its target audience." Booklist

Bateman, Colin

Running with the Reservoir Pups; [by] Colin Bateman. Delacorte Press 2005 263p (Eddie & the gang with no name) hardcover o.p. lib bdg $17.99

Grades: 5 6 7 8   **Fic**

1. Gangs -- Fiction 2. Divorce -- Fiction

ISBN 0-385-73244-9; 0-385-90268-9 lib bdg

LC 2004-43912

First published 2003 in the United Kingdom

When his parents divorce and his mother moves with him to Belfast, Northern Ireland, twelve-year-old Eddie contends with the Reservoir Pups, a gang of children who rule his neighborhood.

This "author's hilarious, dark Northern Irish wit, penchant for action-packed mayhem, sense of irony, and snappy dialogue are all evident in this [book]." SLJ

Another title about Eddie is:
Bring me the head of Oliver Plunkett (2005)

Bateson, Catherine

Being Bee. Holiday House 2007 126p il $16.95; pa $7.95

Grades: 4 5 6   **Fic**

1. Family life -- Fiction 2. Guinea pigs -- Fiction 3. Father-daughter relationship -- Fiction

ISBN 978-0-8234-2104-6; 0-8234-2104-X; 978-0-8234-2208-1 pa; 0-8234-2208-9 pa

LC 2006-101561

Bee faces friction at home and at school when her widowed father begins seriously dating Jazzi, who seems to take over the house and their lives, but as shared secrets and common interests finally begin to draw them together, Jazzi accidentally makes a terrible mistake.

"Bee's emotions are perspectives are honest and clearly presented. . . . She is a likable, believable character." SLJ

Magenta McPhee. Holiday House 2010 170p $16.95

Grades: 4 5 6 7   **Fic**

1. Authorship -- Fiction 2. Single parent family -- Fiction 3. Dating (Social customs) -- Fiction 4. Father-daughter relationship -- Fiction

ISBN 978-0-8234-2253-1; 0-8234-2253-4

LC 2009-10854

First published 2009 in Australia

Thinking her father needs a new interest in his life after he is laid-off of work, teenaged Magenta, who envisions herself as a future fantasy author, decides to dabble in match-making which brings unexpected results.

"With a personality as colorful as her name, Bateson's . . . eponymous heroine has a narrative voice that is smart, wry, and down-to-earth. . . . This [is a] real and ultimately reassuring story." Publ Wkly

Stranded in Boringsville. Holiday House 2005 138p $16.95; pa $6.95

Grades: 5 6 7 8   **Fic**

1. Moving -- Fiction 2. Divorce -- Fiction 3. Friendship -- Fiction

ISBN 0-8234-1969-X; 0-8234-2113-9 pa

First published 2002 in Australia with title: Rain May and Captain Daniel

"Twelve year-old Rain's parents have separated. Her father has moved in with his trendy, younger girlfriend, and her mother has turned in her business suits for yoga and a simpler life in 'Boringsville,' tiny Clarkson, Central Victoria. . . . Her neighbor Daniel is almost 12, . . . and, as Rain learns, cruelly bullied at school. In alternating chapters, . . . Bateson deftly allows Rain and Daniel to chronicle their budding friendship. . . . Readers will ache for the kids, whose conflicted feelings seem all too real." Booklist

Baucom, Ian

Through the skylight; a Venice tale. Ian Baucom. 1st ed. Atheneum Books for Young Readers 2013 400 p. ill. (hardcover) $17.99

Grades: 5 6 7 8   **Fic**

1. Fantasy fiction 2. Time travel -- Fiction 3. Venice (Italy) -- Fiction 4. Magic -- Fiction 5. Americans -- Italy -- Fiction 6. Mystery and detective stories 7. Brothers and sisters -- Fiction

ISBN 1416917772; 9781416917779

LC 2012010642

In this juvenile novel, by Ian Baucom, illustrated by Justin Gerard, "when Jared, Shireen, and Miranda are each given one glittering gift from an old Venetian shopkeeper, they never fathom the powers they are now able to unleash. . . . For in another time, centuries earlier, another trio . . . have been kidnapped and, along with hundreds of other children, will be sold into child slavery. Unless, that is, they can find some way to save them all." (Publisher's note)

"Frequent black-and-white illustrations support the narrative. Baucom's familiarity with the setting and use of Italian words heighten the atmosphere. . . . The mix of protagonists' genders, historical details, and interesting magic creates a story with broad appeal and a message about the power of words. . ." SLJ

Bauer, A. C. E.

★ **Come** Fall. Random House 2010 231p $15.99; lib bdg $18.99

Grades: 4 5 6 7   **Fic**

1. School stories 2. Crows -- Fiction 3. Fairies -- Fiction 4. Friendship -- Fiction 5. Foster home care -- Fiction

ISBN 978-0-375-85825-3; 0-375-85825-3; 978-0-375-95855-7 lib bdg; 0-375-95855-X lib bdg

LC 2009-32419

Drawn together by a mentoring program and an unusual crow, middle school misfits Salman, Lu, and Blos form a strong friendship despite teasing by fellow students and the maneuverings of fairies Oberon, Titania, and Puck.

"Weaving in magic, dreams, doubles, contrasts, and other elements from the original play, Bauer spins an enticing variant." Booklist

No castles here. Random House 2007 270p $15.99; lib bdg $18.99

Grades: 4 5 6 7   **Fic**

1. Magic -- Fiction 2. Choirs (Music) -- Fiction 3. Books and reading -- Fiction 4. City and town life -- Fiction

ISBN 978-0-375-83921-4; 978-0-375-93921-1 lib bdg

LC 2006023601

Eleven-year-old Augie Boretski dreams of escaping his rundown Camden, New Jersey, neighborhood, but things start to turn around with help from a Big Brother, a music teacher, and a mysterious bookstore owner, so when his school is in trouble, he pulls the community together to save it

This is a "heartwarming novel." Booklist

Bauer, Joan

Almost home; by Joan Bauer. Viking 2012 264 p. (hardcover) $16.99

Grades: 5 6 7 8   **Fic**

1. Pets -- Fiction 2. Homeless persons -- Fiction 3. Mother-daughter relationship -- Fiction 4. Mothers and daughters -- Fiction

ISBN 0670012890; 9780670012893

LC 2011050483

In this book by Joan Bauer, "when twelve-year-old Sugar's grandfather dies and her gambling father takes off yet again, Sugar and her mother . . . head to Chicago for a fresh start, only to discover that fresh starts aren't so easy to come by for the homeless. . . . With the help of a rescue dog . . . a foster family . . . and her own grace and good humor, Sugar comes to understand that while she can't control the hand life deals her, she can control how she responds." (Publisher's note)

Close to famous. Viking 2011 250p

Grades: 5 6 7 8   **Fic**

1. Baking -- Fiction 2. Literacy -- Fiction 3. Country life -- Fiction 4. Single parent family -- Fiction

ISBN 0-670-01282-3; 978-0-670-01282-4

LC 2010030022

Twelve-year-old Foster McFee and her mother escape from her mother's abusive boyfriend and end up in the small town of Culpepper, West Virginia, where they use their strengths and challenge themselves to build a new life, with the help of the friends they make there.

"Bauer skillfully brings readers to the heart of Culpepper with rich depictions of contemporary small town and its residents and rhythms." Publ Wkly

Bauer, Marion Dane

★ **On** my honor. Clarion Bks. 1986 90p $15

Grades: 4 5 6 7   **Fic**

1. Accidents -- Fiction

ISBN 0-89919-439-7

LC 86-2679

A Newbery Medal honor book, 1987

When his best friend drowns while they are both swimming in a treacherous river that they had promised never to go near, Joel is devastated and terrified at having to tell both sets of parents the terrible consequences of their disobedience

"Bauer's association of Joel's guilt with the smell of the polluted river on his skin is particularly noteworthy. Its miasma almost rises off the pages. Descriptions are vivid, characterization and dialogue natural, and the style taut but unforced. A powerful, moving book." SLJ

Runt. Clarion Bks. 2002 138p $14

Grades: 4 5 6 7   **Fic**

1. Wolves -- Fiction 2. Wolves -- Juvenile fiction

ISBN 0-618-21261-2

LC 2002-3965

Runt, the smallest wolf cub in the litter, seeks to prove himself to his father King and the rest of the pack and to earn a new name

The author's "passion for the animals is evident throughout this compelling, poignant story." Booklist

A **bear** named Trouble. Clarion Books 2005 120p $15

Grades: 3 4 5 6   **Fic**

1. Zoos -- Fiction 2. Bears -- Fiction

ISBN 0-618-51738-3

LC 2004-21259

In Anchorage, Alaska, two lonely boys make a connection—a brown bear injured just after his mother sends him out on his own, and a human whose father is a new keeper at the Alaska Zoo and whose mother and sister are still in Minnesota.

"With a strong plot, well-developed characters, and an engaging writing format, this book is a great choice for young readers." SLJ

★ The **blue** ghost; illustrated by Suling Wang. Random House 2005 85p il $11.95; lib bdg $13.99; pa $3.99
Grades: 2 3 4   **Fic**
1. Ghost stories
ISBN 0-375-83179-7; 0-375-93179-1 lib bdg; 0-375-83339-0 pa

At her grandmother's log cabin, nine-year-old Liz is led to make contact with children she believes may be her ancestors.

"This gentle ghost story, written in simple prose, blends mild suspense with a look at how the past connects to and influences the present. Mystery fans will enjoy the spooky premise, and Wang's softly rendered black-and-white drawings increase the ghostly atmosphere." Booklist

Other titles in this series are:
The green ghost (2008)
The red ghost (2008)
The golden ghost (2011)

The **golden** ghost; illustrated by Peter Ferguson. Random House 2011 86p il $12.99; lib bdg $15.99
Grades: 2 3 4   **Fic**
1. Ghost stories 2. Dogs -- Fiction 3. Homeless persons -- Fiction
ISBN 978-0-375-86649-4; 0-375-86649-3; 978-0-375-96649-1 lib bdg; 0-375-96649-8 lib bdg; 978-0-375-89818-1 e-book
LC 2010-04116
On a bike outing to the abandoned houses by the old cement mill, Delsie and her friend Todd discover one of the houses is not empty—and a ghost dog haunts the area.

"Readers will be kept on the edge of their seats. Ferguson's charcoal illustrations bring an old-fashioned charm to this easy chapter book." Booklist

Bauer, Marion Dane, 1938-
Little dog, lost; Marion Dane Bauer; with illustrations by Jennifer Bell. Atheneum Books for Young Readers 2012 197 p. ill. (hardcover) $14.99
Grades: 4 5 6 7   **Fic**
1. Dogs -- Fiction 2. Picture books for children 3. Interpersonal relations -- Fiction 4. Novels in verse 5. Parks -- Fiction 6. Loneliness -- Fiction 7. City and town life -- Fiction
ISBN 1442434236; 9781442434233; 9781442434257
LC 2011034024
This book tells the tale of "three needy creatures." Buddy the dog is "re-homed with a clueless though kind woman" after her family moves; Mark "feels his life is empty without the dog he desperately needs but his mother won't permit"; and "Charles Larue, the aging caretaker of a nearby mansion . . . spends his lonely days waiting for something–anything– to bring meaning to his life." The story is written in "[l]ong, thin lines of free-verse text." Additionally, "black-and-white illustrations" are included. (Kirkus)

Bauer, Michael Gerard
Just a dog; Michael Gerard Bauer. Scholastic Press 2012 144 p. (hc) $15.99
Grades: 4 5 6   **Fic**
1. Dogs -- Juvenile fiction 2. Family life -- Juvenile fiction 3. Dogs -- Fiction 4. Dalmatians -- Fiction 5. Dalmatians -- Juvenile fiction
ISBN 0545374529; 9780545374521; 9780545374538
LC 2012014425
This children's book, by Michael Gerard Bauer, is about a family's pet dog. "Sometimes a dog isn't just a dog--sometimes he's the glue the holds a whole family together. Mr. Mosely is a special dog. . . . He's special because he seems to know exactly what everyone in Corey's family needs, even when they don't know themselves. This is the story of Mr. Mosely, from his puppyhood to the last time he curls up on the back porch." (Publisher's note)

Baum, L. Frank
The **Wizard** of Oz; illustrated by Charles Santore; with an introduction by Michael Patrick Hearn. Sterling 2009 96p il $16.95
Grades: 3 4 5   **Fic**
1. Fantasy fiction
ISBN 978-1-4027-6625-1; 1-4027-6625-4
LC 2008046862
A reissue of the edition first published 1991 by Random House
After a cyclone transports her to the land of Oz, Dorothy must seek out the great Wizard in order to return to Kansas

"This edition has been skillfully condensed for those not ready for the longer original work. Santore's many paintings, including spot art and full- and double-page spreads, add a successful dose of drama to the classic fantasy." Horn Book Guide

★ The **wonderful** Wizard of Oz; with pictures by W. W. Denslow. 100th anniversary ed.; HarperCollins Publishers 2000 267p $24.99
Grades: 3 4 5 6   **Fic**
1. Fantasy fiction
ISBN 0-06-029323-3
LC 2001-265945
First published 1900
After a cyclone transports her to the land of Oz, Dorothy must seek out the great wizard in order to return to Kansas.

"For those who want the look and feel of the 1900 publication, this fills the bill. It's a very handsome facsimile, printed on high-quality paper and containing all of W. W. Denslow's 24 original colorplates and 130 two-color drawings." Booklist

Bawden, Nina
Granny the Pag. Clarion Bks. 1996 184p $16
Grades: 4 5 6 7   **Fic**
1. Grandmothers -- Fiction 2. Parent-child relationship -- Fiction
ISBN 0-395-77604-X
LC 95-38191
First published 1995 in the United Kingdom
Originally abandoned by her actor parents who later attempt to gain custody, Cat wages a spirited campaign to decide her own fate and remain with her grandmother

"Bawden has created some enormously appealing characters in this funny and very touching novel." SLJ

Beard, Darleen Bailey

Annie Glover is not a tree lover; pictures by Heather Maione. Farrar Straus Giroux 2009 120p il $15.99

Grades: 3 4 5   **Fic**

1. Trees -- Fiction 2. Grandmothers -- Fiction 3. Environmental protection -- Fiction

ISBN 978-0-374-30351-8; 0-374-30351-7

LC 2008043418

When her grandmother chains herself to the tree across from the school to save it from being cut down, fourth-grader Annie wants to die of humiliation, but when she dicovers the town's history, her attitude changes.

"Light fun, with a save-the-planet message, Beard's fast-paced plot accompanied by Maione's comic illustrations will have plenty of fans, including reluctant readers." SLJ

Operation Clean Sweep; [by] Darleen Bailey Beard. Farrar Straus Giroux 2004 151p $16

Grades: 3 4 5 6   **Fic**

1. Elections 2. Women -- Suffrage 3. Elections -- Fiction 4. Women -- Suffrage -- Fiction

ISBN 0-374-38034-1

LC 2003-49430

In 1916, just four years after getting the right to vote, the women of Umatilla, Oregon band together to throw the mayor and other city officials out of office, replacing them with women

"Beard's story, based on real events, features believable characters, strong local color, and a plot that gently makes its point without offending anyone." Booklist

Bearn, Emily

★ **Tumtum** & Nutmeg: adventures beyond Nutmouse Hall. Little, Brown Books for Young Readers 2009 504p $16.99

Grades: 4 5 6   **Fic**

1. Mice -- Fiction 2. Siblings -- Fiction

ISBN 978-0-316-02703-8; 0-316-02703-0

LC 2008-45294

Wealthy, married mice Tumtum and Nutmeg find adventure when they secretly try to help two human siblings who live in a tumbledown cottage with their absent-minded inventor father.

"The stories are filled with descriptions of good food, cheering fires and warm beds. Price's black-and-white line drawings have a scratchy, comic air that brings a welcome edge to the gentle storytelling. . . . The sympathetic characters, enchanting setting and quickly paced plots will hold readers' interest." Publ Wkly

Another title in this series is:

Tumtum & Nutmeg: The Rose Cottage tales (2010)

Tumtum & Nutmeg: the Rose Cottage tales. Little, Brown 2010 398p $16.99

Grades: 4 5 6   **Fic**

1. Mice -- Fiction 2. Seashore -- Fiction 3. Siblings -- Fiction 4. Birthdays -- Fiction 5. Christmas -- Fiction

ISBN 0-316-08599-5; 978-0-316-08599-1

LC 2010032962

Wealthy, married mice Tumtum and Nutmeg have a series of adventures as they try to help the impoverished

human children, Arthur and Lucy Mildew, to have a good Christmas, enjoy a seaside holiday, and celebrate Arthur's birthday.

This book includes "three rousing adventures. . . . Even when [Tumtun & Nutmeg's] world gets exciting, though, it's still a cozy read." Kirkus

Beaty, Andrea

Attack of the fluffy bunnies; illustrated by Dan Santat. Amulet Books 2010 184p il $12.95

Grades: 3 4 5   **Fic**

1. Camps -- Fiction 2. Twins -- Fiction 3. Siblings -- Fiction 4. Extraterrestrial beings -- Fiction

ISBN 978-0-8109-8416-5; 0-8109-8416-4

At Camp Whatsitooya, twins Joules and Kevin and new friend Nelson face off against large, rabbitlike creatures from the Mallow Galaxy who thrive on sugar, but are not above hypnotizing and eating human campers.

"Beaty's tale of high silliness is sure to please, and it's dotted with Santat's mini-comics and spot illustrations, which move the story along. If at times the reach for a larff is a bit of a stretch, it's all in fun. The hint at a possible sequel will have humorous-adventure lovers asking." Kirkus

Cicada summer. Amulet Books 2008 167p $15.95

Grades: 4 5 6 7   **Fic**

1. Siblings -- Fiction 2. Bereavement -- Fiction

ISBN 978-0-8109-9472-0; 0-8109-9472-0

LC 2007-22266

Twelve-year-old Lily mourns her brother, and has not spoken since the accident she feels she could of prevented but the summer Tinny comes to town she is the only one who realizes Lily's secret.

"This is compelling fiction that will be a hit with young readers. . . . Rich and thought-provoking and yet . . . accessible." Horn Book

Dorko the magnificent; by Andrea Beaty. Amulet Books 2013 213 p. (hardcover) $16.95

Grades: 3 4 5 6   **Fic**

1. Magicians -- Fiction 2. Grandmothers -- Fiction 3. Humorous stories 4. Family life -- Fiction 5. Magic tricks -- Fiction

ISBN 1419706381; 9781419706387

LC 2012045674

In this book by Andrea Beaty "Robbie loves magic and he's good at it—sort of. When Grandma Melvyn moves in and takes over his room, Robbie discovers that she was once an internationally renowned magician and learns about the heartache that turned her into a bitter woman. Against all odds, Robbie and Grandma Melvyn form an uneasy alliance to show the world—or at least the kids of Hobson Elementary School—that he is a true magician." (Publisher's note)

Becker, Bonny

Holbrook; a lizard's tale. by Bonny Becker; illustrated by Abby Carter. Clarion Books 2006 150p il $15

Grades: 3 4 5   **Fic**

1. Artists -- Fiction 2. Lizards -- Fiction 3. City and town life -- Fiction

ISBN 978-0-618-71458-2; 0-618-71458-8

LC 2006-03962

Holbrook the lizard has an artist's soul, but when his paintings are ridiculed by the owls, geckoes, and other creatures in his desert town, he decides to seek his fortune in the big city, unaware of the dangers of urban life.

"The story moves along quickly, enlivened by dramatic situations, dry wit, and dynamic full-page illustrations. An enjoyable romp." Booklist

The **magical** Ms. Plum; illustrated by Amy Portnoy. Alfred A. Knopf 2009 104p il $12.99; lib bdg $15.99
Grades: 2 3 4   Fic
    1. School stories 2. Magic -- Fiction 3. Teachers -- Fiction
    ISBN 978-0-375-85637-2; 0-375-85637-4; 978-0-375-95637-9 lib bdg; 0-375-95637-9 lib bdg
                                                    LC 2008-42682
The students in Ms Plum's third grade class soon learn that there is something very special about their teacher and her classroom's mysterious supply closet.

"Readers will relate to the youngsters' problems and enjoy their magical resolutions. Illustrated with delightful black-and-white drawings and filled with clever and short vignettes, this fast-paced story is a good choice for struggling readers." SLJ

Behrens, Andy
    The **fast** and the furriest. Alfred A. Knopf 2010 247p $15.99; lib bdg $18.99
Grades: 4 5 6 7   Fic
    1. Dogs -- Fiction 2. Obesity -- Fiction 3. Football -- Fiction
    ISBN 978-0-375-85922-9; 0-375-85922-5; 978-0-375-95922-6 lib bdg; 0-375-95922-X lib bdg
                                                    LC 2009018365
The overweight and unathletic son of a famous former football star discovers that his equally fat and lazy dog is unexpectedly—and obsessively—interested in competing in dog agility contests.

"Behrens's engaging style will appeal to children. Students will relate to likable Kevin's self-deprecating humor, and Cromwell's perseverance gives anyone with an unrealized dream a glimmer of hope." SLJ

Beil, Michael
    The **Red** Blazer Girls: the mistaken masterpiece. Alfred A. Knopf 2011 309p $16.99; lib bdg $19.99
Grades: 5 6 7 8   Fic
    1. School stories 2. Mystery fiction 3. Puzzles -- Fiction 4. Art thefts -- Fiction
    ISBN 978-0-375-86740-8; 0-375-86740-6; 978-0-375-96740-5 lib bdg; 0-375-96740-0 lib bdg
                                                    LC 2010030006
Sophie and her friends, who call themselves The Red Blazer Girls, embark on solving a case involving mistaken identities, switched paintings, and some priceless family heirlooms.

"Sophie narrates with humor and self-effacing aplomb. Visual evidence inserted in the text invites reader participation." Kirkus

Beil, Michael D.
    The **Red** Blazer Girls: The vanishing violin. Alfred A. Knopf 2010 329p $16.99; lib bdg $19.99

Grades: 5 6 7 8   Fic
    1. Mystery fiction 2. Violins -- Fiction
    ISBN 978-0-375-86103-1; 0-375-86103-3; 978-0-375-96103-8 lib bdg; 0-375-96103-8 lib bdg
"Sophie, Margaret, Rebecca, and Leigh Ann . . . find themselves in the midst of several interlocking mysteries, mostly involving violins. . . . Beil has lost none of his edge when it comes to setting up sleuthing scenarios and offering kids codes and clues that will intrigue (or drive them crazy). Smartly plotted, smartly played." Booklist

★ The **Red** Blazer Girls: the ring of Rocamadour. Alfred A. Knopf 2009 299p $15.99; lib bdg $18.99
Grades: 5 6 7 8   Fic
    1. School stories 2. Mystery fiction 3. Puzzles -- Fiction 4. Friendship -- Fiction
    ISBN 978-0-375-84814-8; 0-375-84814-2; 978-0-375-94814-5 lib bdg; 0-375-94814-7 lib bdg
                                                    LC 2008-25254
Catholic-schooled seventh-graders Sophie, Margaret, Rebecca, and Leigh Ann help an elderly neighbor solve a puzzle her father left for her estranged daughter twenty years ago.

"The dialogue is fast and funny, the clues are often solvable." Booklist
    Other titles about the Red Blazer Girls are:
    The Red Blazer Girls: the vanishing violin (2010)
    The Red Blazer Girls: the mistaken masterpiece (2011)

Bell, Cathleen Davitt
    Little blog on the prairie. Bloomsbury 2010 276p $16.99
Grades: 6 7 8   Fic
    1. Camps -- Fiction 2. Weblogs -- Fiction 3. Frontier and pioneer life -- Fiction
    ISBN 978-1-59990-286-9; 1-59990-286-9
                                                    LC 2009-46897
Thirteen-year-old Genevieve's summer at a frontier family history camp in Laramie, Wyoming, with her parents and brother is filled with surprises, which she reports to friends back home on the cell phone she sneaked in, and which they turn into a blog.

This is a "lively journey with empathetic characters." Publ Wkly

Bell, Joanne
    Breaking trail. Groundwood Books/House of Anansi Press 2005 135p $15.95; pa $6.95
Grades: 5 6 7 8   Fic
    1. Sled dog racing -- Fiction 2. Depression (Psychology) -- Fiction
    ISBN 0-88899-630-6; 0-88899-662-4 pa
"Although there are no easy solutions to the difficulties that confront this family, their love and support for one another are touching and believable." SLJ

Bell, Krista
    If the shoe fits; [illustrated by] Craig Smith. Charlesbridge 2008 60p il $14.95; pa $5.95
Grades: 2 3 4   Fic
    1. Dance -- Fiction
    ISBN 978-1-58089-338-1; 1-58089-338-4; 978-1-58089-339-8 pa; 1-58089-339-2 pa
                                                    LC 2007027022

First published 2006 in Australia

Cassie wants to be a dancer when she grows up but is afraid to dance in front of anyone outside her family, until the day of her first jazz performance arrives and her mother and a new friend help her to gain confidence.

"The text tells a believable story in a straightforward way, and readers will empathize with the characters. Scribbly pencil drawings reflect Cassie's inner turmoil." Horn Book Guide

Bellairs, John

★ The **curse** of the blue figurine. Dial Bks. for Young Readers 1983 200p hardcover o.p. pa $5.99

Grades: 5 6 7 8   Fic

1. Mystery fiction

ISBN 0-8446-7138-4; 0-14-240258-3 pa

LC 82-73217

The author "intertwines real concerns with sorcery in a seamless fashion, bringing dimension to his characters and events with expert timing and sharply honed atmosphere." Booklist

Other titles about Johnny Dixon and Professor Childermass are:

The chessmen of doom (1989)

The eyes of the killer robot (1986)

The mummy, the will and the crypt (1983)

The revenge of the wizard's ghost (1985)

The secret of the underground room (1990)

The spell of the sorcerer's skull (1984)

The trolley to yesterday (1989)

★ The **house** with a clock in its walls; pictures by Edward Gorey. Dial Bks. for Young Readers 1973 179p il pa $5.99

Grades: 5 6 7 8   Fic

1. Witchcraft -- Fiction

ISBN 0-14-240257-5

In 1948, Lewis, a ten-year-old orphan, goes to New Zebedee, Michigan with his warlock Uncle Jonathan, who lives in a big mysterious house and practices white magic. Together with their neighbor, Mrs. Zimmerman, a witch, they search to find a clock that is programmed to end the world and has been hidden in the walls of the house by the evil Isaac Izard

"Bellairs's story and Edward Gorey's pictures are satisfyingly frightening." Publ Wkly

Other titles about Lewis are:

The doom of the haunted opera (1995)

The figure in the shadows (1975)

The ghost in the mirror (1993)

The letter, the witch, and the ring (1976)

The vengeance of the witch-finder (1993)

Bennett, Olivia

The **Allegra** Biscotti collection. Sourcebooks 2010 pa $8.99

Grades: 5 6 7 8   Fic

1. School stories 2. Fashion -- Fiction

ISBN 978-1-4022-4391-2; 1-4022-4391-X

By day, Emma Rose is a quiet, under-the-radar student who doesn't mix with the popular set. But when school's out, she becomes Queen of the Runway—whipping up cutting-edge designs.

"Credible characterizations and dialogue keep the novel real. . . . Bennett slips in detailed descriptions of the teens' outfits and Emma's designs, which appear in spot art." Publ Wkly

Who what wear; illustrated by Georgia Rucker. Sourcebooks Jabberwocky 2011 231p il (The Allegra Biscotti collection) pa $8.99

Grades: 5 6 7 8   Fic

1. Fashion designers -- Fiction

ISBN 978-1-4022-4392-9; 1-4022-4392-8

"Emma Rose, 14, is still trying to hide her identity as New York City's up-and-coming fashion designer, Allegra Biscotti, while juggling the pitfalls of friendship and middle school. . . . The novel . . . comes to a satisfying, if predictable, conclusion. Interspersed throughout are illustrations of Allegra's designs. . . . Who What Wear is a great recommendation for kids who dream of a career in fashion." SLJ

Berkeley, Jon

The **hidden** boy. Katherine Tegen Books 2010 262p (Bell Hoot fables) $16.99

Grades: 3 4 5 6   Fic

1. Adventure fiction 2. Siblings -- Fiction 3. Missing children -- Fiction

ISBN 978-0-06-168758-7; 0-06-168758-8; 978-0-06-168759-4 lib bdg; 0-06-168759-6 lib bdg

LC 2009-12272

When Bea and her family are transported aboard an underwater bus to a strange land, her younger brother Theo is lost during the voyage, and somehow it falls to Bea to find out what has become of him.

"Berkeley's arch writing and his characters' hilarious, pathos-inspiring temperments and abilities make this magical stew both compelling and delightful." Booklist

The **lightning** key. HarperCollins Pub. 2009 399p (The Wednesday tales) $16.99

Grades: 4 5 6 7   Fic

1. Adventure fiction 2. Angels -- Fiction 3. Orphans -- Fiction

ISBN 978-0-06-075513-3; 0-06-075513-X

Now that Miles Wednesday has discovered his link to a magical Tiger's Egg, he's suddenly at the wheel of a great voyage. Determined to recover the stolen stone and free the trapped soul within, Miles sets off with Little, a Song Angel, and the wisecracking blind explorer Baltinglass of Araby.

"Middle and junior high students will delight in this story, the most lyrical and sharply written of the series." Voice Youth Advocates

The **tiger's** egg; [by] Jon Berkeley; illustrated by Brandon Dorman. HarperCollinsPublishers 2007 400p il (The Wednesday tales) $16.99; lib bdg $17.89

Grades: 4 5 6 7   Fic

1. Adventure fiction 2. Angels -- Fiction 3. Circus -- Fiction 4. Tigers -- Fiction 5. Orphans -- Fiction

ISBN 978-0-06-075510-2; 0-06-075510-5; 978-0-06-075511-9 lib bdg; 0-06-075511-3 lib bdg

LC 2006039842

While working for the newly revamped circus, orphaned eleven-year-old Miles gains information about his past and sets off with his angel companion, Little, on a quest to find a mystical tiger's egg before it falls into the hands of their nemesis, Cortado.

"This novel is engaging from beginning to end. Fantasy lovers will enjoy a variety of plot twists that will surprise even the most perceptive reader." Voice Youth Advocates

Berlin, Eric

The **potato** chip puzzles; Eric Berlin; [drawings by Katrina Damkoehler] G.P. Putnam's Sons 2009 244p il $16.99; pa $7.99

Grades: 4 5 6 7 **Fic**

1. Mystery fiction 2. Puzzles -- Fiction 3. Contests -- Fiction

ISBN 978-0-399-25198-6; 0-399-25198-7; 978-0-14-241637-2 pa; 0-14-241637-1 pa

LC 2008-33698

Winston and his friends enter an all-day puzzle contest to win fifty-thousand dollars for their school, but they must also figure out who is trying to keep them from winning. Puzzles for the reader to solve are included throughout the text.

"The pace is suspenseful but allows for pauses for problem-solving. The joy for both contestants and readers of this brain-teasing mystery will be in the process." Kirkus

★ The **puzzling** world of Winston Breen; the secret in the box. Putnam 2007 215p il $16.99; pa $7.99

Grades: 4 5 6 7 **Fic**

1. Mystery fiction 2. Puzzles -- Fiction 3. Siblings -- Fiction

ISBN 978-0-399-24693-7; 0-399-24693-2; 978-0-14-241388-3 pa; 0-14-241388-7 pa

LC 2006-20531

Puzzle-crazy, twelve-year-old Winston and his ten-year-old sister Katie find themselves involved in a dangerous mystery involving a hidden ring. Puzzles for the reader to solve are included throughout the text

"A delightfully clever mystery. . . . There is plenty of suspense to engage readers." SLJ

Berner, Rotraut Susanne

Hound and hare; translated by Shelley Tanaka. Groundwood Books 2011 75p il $18.99

Grades: K 1 2 **Fic**

1. Dogs -- Fiction 2. Rabbits -- Fiction

ISBN 978-0-88899-987-0; 0-88899-987-9

"The illustrations are done in colored pencil and ink, each creature and picture frame defined by soft blue lines. Hounds and hares emerge as regular Hatfields and Mc-Coys and overtly harass each other with wickedly humorous, singsong taunts. Although classmates Harley Hare and Hugo Hound share interests, they've absorbed their families' prejudices and shun each other. . . . The happily-ever-after ending delivers a satisfying resolution to a story about tolerance that successfully uses humor and engaging artwork to avoid didacticism." Kirkus

Berry, Julie

The **colossal** fossil freakout; by Julie Gardner Berry and Sally Faye Gardner. Grosset & Dunlap 2011 190p il (Splurch Academy for Disruptive Boys) pa $6.99

Grades: 3 4 5 6 **Fic**

1. School stories 2. Monsters -- Fiction 3. Reformatories

-- Fiction

ISBN 978-0-448-45361-3; 0-448-45361-4

LC 2010034441

When Headmaster Farley's estranged sister takes over Splurch Academy, Cody and the other boys are pitted against their new classmates, the girls of Priscilla Prim Academy for Precious and Proper Young Ladies.

The **rat** brain fiasco; by Julie Gardner Berry; illustrated by Sally Faye Gardner. Grosset & Dunlap 2010 198p il (Splurch Academy for Disruptive Boys) pa $6.99

Grades: 3 4 5 6 **Fic**

1. School stories 2. Monsters -- Fiction 3. Reformatories -- Fiction

ISBN 978-0-448-45359-0 pa; 0-448-45359-2 pa

LC 2009053456

Cody Mack's misdeeds land him in a reformatory school, where he soon discovers that the principal and teachers are actual monsters with a sinister plan to alter the boys' brains

"This hybrid novel incorporates black-and-white illustrations in a comic-book format. The story contains harmless malevolence and revenge, which will keep readers coming back for more. The imaginative writing and goofy plot will attract reluctant readers. With a tongue-in-cheek style and hilarious cartoons, the laugh-out-loud story is sure to creep off the shelves." SLJ

Other titles in this series are:

Curse of the bizarro beetle (2010)

The colossal fossil freakout (2011)

Betancourt, Jeanne

Ava Tree and the wishes three. Feiwel and Friends 2009 130p il $14.99

Grades: 2 3 4 **Fic**

1. Wishes -- Fiction 2. Orphans -- Fiction 3. Parties -- Fiction 4. Siblings -- Fiction 5. Birthdays -- Fiction

ISBN 978-0-312-37760-1; 0-312-37760-6

LC 2008015265

"Waking up on her eighth birthday, Ava tears up thinking about her parents, who died in a car accident. . . . She now lives with her 22-year-old brother, Jack. . . . Struggling to clean her pet rabbit's litter box, Ava wishes it 'would use the toilet like a person' and when it suddenly does, Ava and Jack wonder if it could be a birthday gift from their mother, who had been a magician. Ava's 'wishing power' seems to continue, though some of her wishes—that her parents weren't dead—go unanswered. . . . Kids will embrace this bighearted novel and its thoughtful, resilient narrator." Publ Wkly

Bianco, Margery Williams

The **Velveteen** Rabbit; illustrated by Monique Felix. Creative Editions 2010 39p il $17.95

Grades: 2 3 4 **Fic**

1. Fairy tales 2. Toys -- Fiction 3. Rabbits -- Fiction

ISBN 978-1-56846-217-2; 1-56846-217-4

LC 2010004182

By the time the Velveteen Rabbit is dirty, worn out, and about to be burned, he has almost given up hope of ever finding the magic called Real.

"The complete text of the classic tale . . . is accompanied by . . . pastel pictures that are both ample and appealing. The handsomely designed book will please fans of the story." Horn Book Guide

★ The **velveteen** rabbit; or, How toys become real. by Margery Williams; with illustrations by William Nicholson. Doubleday 1991 33p il $13.95

Grades: 2 3 4   **Fic**

1. Fairy tales 2. Toys -- Fiction 3. Rabbits -- Fiction
ISBN 0-385-07725-4

LC 90-25339

First published 1922 by Doran

By the time the velveteen rabbit is dirty, worn out, and about to be burned, he has almost given up hope of ever finding the magic called Real.

"Quiet, graceful illustrations accentuate the classic tale's nostalgic tone." Publ Wkly

Billingsley, Franny

The **Folk** Keeper. Atheneum Bks. for Young Readers 1999 162p hardcover o.p. pa $4.99; pa $5.99

Grades: 5 6 7 8   **Fic**

1. Fantasy fiction 2. Fairies -- Fiction 3. Orphans -- Fiction 4. Selkies -- Fiction
ISBN 0-689-82876-4; 0-689-84461-1 pa; 9780689844614 pa

LC 98-48778

Boston Globe Horn Book Winner (2000)

Orphaned Corinna disguises herself as a boy to pose as a Folk Keeper, one who keeps the supernatural Folk underground at bay. She discovers her heritage as a seal maiden when she is summoned to become the Folk Keeper for a wealthy family in their manor by the sea. "Ages ten to fourteen." (N Y Times Book Rev)

"The intricate plot, vibrant characters, dangerous intrigue, and fantastical elements combine into a truly remarkable novel steeped in atmosphere." Horn Book

Binding, Tim

★ **Sylvie** and the songman; with illustrations by Angela Barrett. Random House 2009 339p il $15.99; lib bdg $18.99

Grades: 5 6 7 8   **Fic**

1. Fantasy fiction
ISBN 978-0-385-75157-5; 0-385-75159-1; 978-0-385-75159-9 lib bdg; 0-385-75159-1 lib bdg

"Sylvie's composer father . . . goes missing and that's the first odd thing that interrupts her happy routine. Next, the animals seem to have lost their voices. The third is the arrival of the eerie, malevolent Woodpecker Man. . . . The dense narrative is packed with surreal imagery. . . . It's a testament to Binding's assured writing that the abstractions become visceral thrills, like a dream you just can't shake. . . . An unforgettable tale." Booklist

Birdsall, Jeanne

★ The **Penderwicks**; a summer tale of four sisters, two rabbits, and a very interesting boy. Knopf 2005 262p (The Penderwicks) $15.95; lib bdg $17.77; pa $6.99

Grades: 3 4 5 6   **Fic**

1. Sisters -- Fiction 2. Single parent family -- Fiction
ISBN 0-375-83143-6; 0-375-93143-0 lib bdg; 0-440-42047-4 pa

LC 2004-20364

"Four sisters–Rosalind, Skye, Jane, and Batty–spend a few weeks with their father and dog at a cottage on the grounds of a stately home in the Berkshires, where they complicate the lives of a handsome gardener, a lonely boy, and the boy's officious mother. . . . Grades four to seven." (Bull Cent Child Books)

"This comforting family story . . . [offers] . . . four marvelously appealing sisters, true childhood behavior . . . , and a writing style that will draw readers close." Booklist

The **Penderwicks** at Point Mouette. Alfred A. Knopf 2011 295p (The Penderwicks) $16.99

Grades: 4 5 6 7   **Fic**

1. Summer -- Fiction 2. Vacations -- Fiction 3. Family life -- Fiction
ISBN 978-0-375-85851-2; 0-375-85851-2

This is the third book about the Penderwick family, who appeared previously in The Penderwicks (2005) and The Penderwicks on Gardam Street (2008). "When summer comes around, it's off to the beach for Rosalind . . . and off to Maine with Aunt Claire for the rest of the Penderwick girls, as well as their old friend, Jeffrey. That leaves Skye as OAP (oldest available Penderwick). . . . Things look good as they settle into their cozy cottage. . . . But can Skye hold it together long enough to figure out Rosalind's directions about not letting Batty explode? Will Jane's Love Survey come to a tragic conclusion after she meets the alluring Dominic? . . . And will Jeffrey be able to keep peace between the girls?"(Publisher's note) "Intermediate." (Horn Book)

"Balancing the novel's comedy is an affecting, neatly crafted subplot that builds up to the emotionally charged revelation involving Jeffrey. From start to finish, this is a summer holiday to savor." Publ Wkly

The **Penderwicks** on Gardam Street; [illustrations by David Frankland] Alfred A. Knopf 2008 307p il $15.99; lib bdg $18.99

Grades: 3 4 5 6 7   **Fic**

1. Sisters -- Fiction 2. Family life -- Fiction 3. Dating (Social customs) -- Fiction
ISBN 978-0-3758-4090-6; 978-0-375-94090-3 lib bdg

LC 2007-49232

The four Penderwick sisters are faced with the unimaginable prospect of their widowed father dating, and they hatch a plot to stop him.

"Laugh-out-loud moments abound and the humor comes naturally from the characters and situations. . . . This is a book to cherish." SLJ

Birdseye, Tom

Storm Mountain. Holiday House 2010 135p $16.95

Grades: 4 5 6 7   **Fic**

1. Adventure fiction 2. Cousins -- Fiction 3. Blizzards -- Fiction 4. Mountaineering -- Fiction 5. Wilderness survival -- Fiction
ISBN 978-0-8234-2130-5; 0-8234-2130-9

LC 2010005768

Two thirteen-year-old cousins Cat and Ty are trapped in a blizzard on the same treacherous mountain in the Cascades that claimed the lives of their world-famous, mountain-climber, twin fathers exactly two years earlier.

"Birdseye's prose, full of careening action, melodrama and overwrought similes, reflects Ty's bulldozing personality. Add believable characters, the author's mountain-climbing expertise and a tear-jerking conclusion, and there's plenty here for young adventure enthusiasts." Kirkus

A **tough** nut to crack. Holiday House 2006 113p $16.95

Grades: 5 6 7 8   **Fic**

1. Farm life -- Fiction 2. Family life -- Fiction
ISBN 978-0-8234-1967-8; 0-8234-1967-3

LC 2006-24887

Raised in Portland, Oregon, Cassie adapts quickly when an emergency brings her family to her grandfather's Kentucky farm, where she feels the spirits of her mother and grandmother as she tries to heal the rift between her father and grandfather.

"The novel's simplicity, humor, action, and warmth will appeal to a broad range of readers." SLJ

Birney, Betty G.
Adventure according to Humphrey; [by] Betty G. Birney. G.P. Putnam's Sons 2009 120p $14.99

Grades: 2 3 4   **Fic**

1. School stories 2. Hamsters -- Fiction
ISBN 978-0-399-24731-6; 0-399-24731-9

LC 2008002347

Humphrey the classroom hamster has adventures going to the library, learning about the ocean, and sailing across a pond on a sailboat.

Friendship according to Humphrey; [by] Betty G. Birney. G.P. Putnam's Sons 2005 150p $14.99; pa $5.99

Grades: 2 3 4   **Fic**

1. School stories 2. Frogs -- Fiction 3. Hamsters -- Fiction 4. Friendship -- Fiction
ISBN 0-399-24264-3; 978-0-399-24264-9; 0-14-240633-3 pa; 978-0-14-240633-5 pa

LC 2004009538

When Humphrey the hamster returns to Mrs. Brisbane's class after the winter break, a new class pet and some other surprises give him an opportunity to reflect on the meaning of friendship.

"The theme of friendship is as pervasive as the title implies, making this chapter book a charming read-aloud." SLJ

Summer according to Humphrey. G.P. Putnam's Sons 2010 167p $14.99

Grades: 2 3 4   **Fic**

1. Camps -- Fiction 2. Hamsters -- Fiction
ISBN 978-0-399-24732-3; 0-399-24732-7

LC 2009008532

When summer arrives, Humphrey, the pet hamster of Longfellow School's Room 26, is surprised and pleased to learn that he will be going to Camp Happy Hollow.

Surprises according to Humphrey; [by] Betty G. Birney. G. P. Putnam's Sons 2008 136p $14.99

Grades: 2 3 4   **Fic**

1. School stories 2. Hamsters -- Fiction
ISBN 978-0-399-24730-9; 0-399-24730-0

LC 2007007457

While continuing to help his classmates solve their problems, Humphrey, pet hamster of Longfellow School's Room 26, faces many surprises, like rolling in a hamster ball, a substitute janitor who might be an alien, and the possibility of Mrs. Brisbane retiring.

"Humphrey is a witty, fun, and lovable character with great kid appeal." SLJ

Trouble according to Humphrey; [by] Betty. G. Birney. Putnam 2007 167p $14.99; pa $5.99

Grades: 2 3 4   **Fic**

1. School stories 2. Hamsters -- Fiction
ISBN 978-0-399-24505-3; 0-399-24505-7; 978-0-14-241089-9 pa; 0-14-241089-6 pa

LC 2006003604

Humphrey, the pet hamster of Longfellow School's Room 26, relates the ups and downs experienced by his human classmates as they begin a project to create a model town complete with houses and community services.

"Humphrey's escapes . . . are related in a lively, first-person narrative, laced with humor, heart, and hamster facts." Booklist

The **seven** wonders of Sassafras Springs; written by Betty Birney; illustrated by Matt Phelan. Atheneum Books for Young Readers 2005 210p il $16.95; pa $6.99

Grades: 3 4 5 6   **Fic**

1. Family life -- Fiction 2. Country life -- Fiction
ISBN 0-689-87136-8; 1-4169-3489-8 pa

LC 2004-11399

Eben McAllister searches his small town to see if he can find anything comparable to the real Seven Wonders of the World

"Black-and-white sketches enhance the text and its folksy character. Perfect for reading aloud." SLJ

The **world** according to Humphrey. G. P. Putnam's Sons 2004 124p $14.99; pa $5.99

Grades: 2 3 4   **Fic**

1. School stories 2. Hamsters -- Fiction
ISBN 978-0-399-24198-7; 0-399-24198-1; 978-0-14-240352-5 pa; 0-14-240352-0 pa

LC 2003-5974

Humphrey, pet hamster at Longfellow School, learns that he has an important role to play in helping his classmates and teacher.

The "lively, first-person narrative, filled with witty commentary on human and hamster behavior, makes for an engaging, entertaining read." Booklist

Other titles about Humphrey are:
Friendship according to Humphrey (2005)
Trouble according to Humphrey (2007)
Surprises according to Humphrey (2008)
Adventure according to Humphrey (2009)
Summer according to Humphrey (2010)

Black, Holly, 1971-
★ **Doll** bones; Holly Black. 1st ed. Margaret K. McElderry Books 2013 256 p. (hardcover) $16.99

Grades: 5 6 7 8   **Fic**

1. Ghost stories 2. Dolls -- Fiction 3. Adventure fiction 4. Ghosts -- Fiction 5. Friendship -- Fiction 6. Family problems -- Fiction 7. Adventure and adventurers -- Fiction
ISBN 1416963987; 9781416963981; 9781442474871

LC 2012018299

In this book, by Holly Black, illustrated by Eliza Wheeler, "a doll that may be haunted leads three friends on a thrilling adventure. . . . Zach, Poppy, and Alice have been . . . playing one continuous, ever-changing game. . . . Ruling over all is the Great Queen, . . . cursing those who displease her. . . . Zach and Alice and Poppy set off on one last adventure to lay the Queen's ghost to rest. But nothing goes according to plan, and . . . creepy things begin to happen." (Publisher's note)

"Veteran Black packs both heft and depth into a deceptively simple (and convincingly uncanny) narrative. . . . A few rich metaphors . . . are woven throughout the story, as every encounter redraws the blurry lines between childishness and maturity, truth and lies, secrecy and honesty, magic and madness. Spooky, melancholy, elegiac and ultimately hopeful; a small gem." Kirkus

Blackwood, Gary L.
Second sight; [by] Gary Blackwood. Dutton 2005 279p hardcover o.p. pa $6.99
Grades: 5 6 7 8   **Fic**
1. Lawyers 2. Presidents 3. State legislators 4. Members of Congress 5. Clairvoyance -- Fiction
ISBN 0-525-47481-1; 0-14-240747-X pa

In Washington, D.C., during the last days of the Civil War, a teenage boy who performs in a mind reading act befriends a clairvoyant girl whose frightening visions foreshadow an assassination plot.

"This is a well-researched, engrossing story grounded in historical detail." SLJ

★ The **Shakespeare** stealer; [by] Gary Blackwood. Dutton Children's Bks. 1998 216p $15.99; pa $5.99
Grades: 5 6 7 8   **Fic**
1. Poets 2. Authors 3. Dramatists 4. Orphans -- Fiction 5. Theater -- Fiction 6. Actors and actresses -- Fiction 7. Great Britain -- History -- Elizabeth, 1558-1603 -- Fiction
ISBN 0-525-45863-8; 0-14-130595-9 pa
LC 97-42987

A young orphan boy is ordered by his master to infiltrate Shakespeare's acting troupe in order to steal the script of "Hamlet," but he discovers instead the meaning of friendship and loyalty

"Wry humor, cliffhanger chapter endings, and a plucky protagonist make this a fitting introduction to Shakespeare's world." Horn Book

Other titles in this series are:
Shakespeare's scribe (2000)
Shakespeare's spy (2003)

Shakespeare's scribe; [by] Gary Blackwood. Dutton Children's Bks. 2000 265p hardcover o.p. pa $6.99
Grades: 5 6 7 8   **Fic**
1. Poets 2. Authors 3. Orphans 4. Theater 5. Dramatists 6. Plague -- England 7. Orphans -- Fiction 8. Theater -- Fiction 9. Actors and actresses
ISBN 0-525-46444-1; 978-0-14-230066-4 pa; 0-14-230066-7 pa
LC 00-34603

In plague-ridden 1602 England, Widge, a fifteen-year-old orphan boy, who has become an apprentice actor, goes on the road with Shakespeare's troupe, and finds out more about his parents along the way

"The story is extremely well structured, with several interesting subplots. . . . The characters are well developed, with Widge being particularly memorable. The dialogue is realistic, and the humorous plays on words add another level of interest." SLJ

Shakespeare's spy; [by] Gary Blackwood. Dutton Children's Bks. 2003 281p $16.99; pa $6.99
Grades: 5 6 7 8   **Fic**
1. Orphans -- Fiction 2. Theater -- Fiction
ISBN 0-525-47145-6; 0-14-240311-3 pa
LC 2003-61659

The winter of 1602 brings many changes for Widge, a young apprentice at London's Globe Theatre, as he becomes infatuated with Shakespeare's daughter Judith, attempts to write a play, learns more about his past, endangers himself to help a friend, acquires a new identity, and finds a new purpose in life

"Blackwood's well-integrated plot and intriguing subplots ensure a fast-paced tale of Elizabethan England that fans of the earlier novels will love." SLJ

Blackwood, Sage
Jinx; Sage Blackwood. Harper 2013 368 p. (Jinx) (trade bdg.) $16.99
Grades: 4 5 6   **Fic**
1. Fantasy fiction 2. Magic -- Fiction 3. Voyages and travels -- Fiction 4. Fantasy
ISBN 0062129902; 9780062129901
LC 2012005249

This fantasy book is set "in the Urwald, an enormous, sentient forest where humans exist on sufferance . . . . After Jinx's brutal stepfather decides to abandon him in the forest, the boy is saved by a crusty, morally ambiguous wizard named Simon, who takes him in as a servant, eventually teaching him some magic. Years later, a 12-year-old Jinx and two new friends set off to find another wizard, the monstrous Bonemaster, in hopes he can help them overcome their respective magical troubles." (Publishers Weekly)

Block, Francesca Lia
★ **House** of dolls; illustrated by Barbara McClintock. Harper 2010 61p il $15.99
Grades: 3 4 5 6   **Fic**
1. Fantasy fiction 2. Dolls -- Fiction
ISBN 978-0-06-113094-6; 0-06-113094-X

"Young Madison is growing tired of her dollhouse and its residents. . . . Increasingly abandoned by her mother, Madison begins exercising a capacious cruelty [to the dolls]. . . . The reality/unreality of any of this is a tightrope Block toes with precision. . . . What at first seems to be about the perennial war between familial generations is expanded into a message about the global forces of pride and avarice that plunge innocents into devastation. This is powerful, haunting, and—just when you don't think it's possible—inspiring too." Booklist

Blom, Jen K.
Possum summer. Holiday House 2011 155p $17.95
Grades: 3 4 5   **Fic**
1. Dogs -- Fiction 2. Opossums -- Fiction 3. Ranch life -- Fiction 4. Father-daughter relationship -- Fiction
ISBN 978-0-8234-2331-6; 0-8234-2331-X
LC 2010023476

While her father is away at war, eleven-year-old Princess ignores his warning that pet ownership leads to pain when she raises an orphaned possum on their Oklahoma ranch, then tries to send it back to the wild.

"Animal-loving readers will sympathize with P throughout this well-paced coming-of-age story." Horn Book Guide

Blos, Joan W.

Letters from the corrugated castle; a novel of gold rush California, 1850-1852. Atheneum Books for Young Readers 2007 310p $17.99; pa $5.99

Grades: 5 6 7 8   **Fic**

1. Mexican Americans -- Fiction 2. Gold mines and mining -- Fiction 3. Frontier and pioneer life -- Fiction 4. Mother-daughter relationship -- Fiction

ISBN 978-0-689-87077-4; 0-689-87077-9; 978-0-689-87078-1 pa; 0-689-87078-7 pa

LC 2007-02673

A series of letters and newspaper articles reveals life in California in the 1850s, especially for thirteen-year-old Eldora, who was raised in Massachusetts as an orphan only to meet her influential mother in San Francisco, and Luke, who hopes to find a fortune in gold.

"It is Blos' sturdy characters, whose experiences reveal the complexity of human relationships and wisdom about 'the salt and the sweet of life,' who will make this last." Booklist

★ A **gathering** of days; a New England girl's journal, 1830-32; a novel. Scribner 1979 144p $16.95; pa $4.99

Grades: 6 7 8 9   **Fic**

ISBN 0-684-16340-3; 0-689-71419-X pa

LC 79-16898

Awarded the Newbery Medal, 1980

The journal of a 14-year-old girl, kept the last year she lived on the family farm, records daily events in her small New Hampshire town, her father's remarriage, and the death of her best friend

"The 'simple' life on the farm is not facilely idealized, the larger issues of the day are felt . . . but it is the small moments between parent and child, friend and friend that are at the fore, and the core, of this low-key, intense, and reflective book." SLJ

Blume, Judy

Are you there God?, it's me, Margaret; rev format ed.; Atheneum 2001 149p pbk. $8.99

Grades: 4 5 6 7   **Fic**

1. Religion -- Fiction

ISBN 9780385739863; 0-689-84158-2

A reissue of the title first published 1970 by Bradbury Press

A "story about the emotional, physical, and spiritual ups and downs experienced by 12-year-old Margaret, child of a Jewish-Protestant union." Natl Counc of Teach of Engl. Adventuring with Books. 2d edition

Cool zone with the Pain and the Great One; [illustrated by] James Stevenson. Delacorte Press 2008 109p il $12.99; lib bdg $19.99

Grades: 1 2 3   **Fic**

1. School stories 2. Siblings -- Fiction 3. Family life -- Fiction

ISBN 978-0-385-73306-9; 0-385-73306-2; 978-0-385-90325-7 lib bdg; 0-385-90325-1 lib bdg

LC 2007-17126

More adventures at school and at home with Jake, a first-grader, and his older sister Abigail, known to each other as the Pain and the Great One.

"Recently independent readers will find this just the book to push their skills forward. Stevenson's gray-washed line illustrations add to the fun." Booklist

Double Fudge. Dutton Children's Bks. 2002 213p $15.99; pa $5.99

Grades: 3 4 5 6   **Fic**

1. Brothers -- Fiction 2. Family life -- Fiction

ISBN 0-525-46926-5; 0-14-240878-6 pa

LC 2002-67774

His younger brother Fudge's obsession with money and the discovery of long-lost cousins Flora and Fauna provide many embarrassing moments for twelve-year-old Peter

"This is a snappy, humorous title that lends itself to being read aloud, and Fudge fans in need of a fix will find that it hits the spot." Bull Cent Child Books

Freckle juice; illustrated by Sonia O. Lisker. Four Winds Press 1971 40p il lib bdg $17.95

Grades: 2 3 4   **Fic**

ISBN 0-02-711690-5

"Spontaneous humor, sure to appeal to the youngest reader." Horn Book

Friend or fiend? with the Pain & the Great One; illustrations by James Stevenson. Delacorte Press 2009 108p il $12.99; lib bdg $16.99

Grades: 1 2 3   **Fic**

1. School stories 2. Siblings -- Fiction 3. Family life -- Fiction

ISBN 978-0-385-73308-3; 0-385-73308-9; 978-0-385-90327-1 lib bdg; 0-385-90327-8 lib bdg

LC 2008030780

First-grader Jake "The Pain" and his sister, third-grader Abigail "The Great One" have more adventures, including visiting their cousins in New York and celebrating their cat Fluzzy's birthday.

"Blume's singular ability to portray the minutiae of a child's everyday life with humor is perfectly complemented by Stevenson's occasional line drawings that extend the story's charm and fully shaped characters." Booklist

Fudge -a-mania. Dutton Children's Bks. 1990 147p hardcover o.p. pa $5.99

Grades: 3 4 5 6   **Fic**

1. Brothers -- Fiction 2. Vacations -- Fiction

ISBN 0-525-44672-9 lib bdg; 0-425-19382-9 pa

LC 90-39627

Pete describes the family vacation in Maine with the Tubmans, highlighted by the antics of his younger brother Fudge

"The story is filled with humor, and the upbeat mood is sustained at a hectic pace from first page to last." SLJ

Going, going, gone! with the Pain and the Great One; [by] Judy Blume; illustrations by James Stevenson. Delacorte Press 2008 109p il $12.99; lib bdg $16.99

Grades: 1 2 3   **Fic**

1. School stories 2. Siblings -- Fiction 3. Family life -- Fiction

ISBN 978-0-385-73307-6; 0-385-73307-0; 978-0-385-90326-4 lib bdg; 0-385-90326-X lib bdg

Further adventures of first-grader Jake "the Pain" and his sister, third-grader Abigail "the Great One," include a trip to the beach with Grandma, to a county fair with Aunt Diana, and to a mall with Dad.

The "stories beautifully capture the experiences of siblings who love one another but who don't always get along. . . . Stevenson's drawings perfectly complement the tales." SLJ

Otherwise known as Sheila the Great. Dutton Children's Books 2002 138p $16.99; pa $5.99

Grades: 4 5 6   **Fic**

1. Fear -- Fiction 2. Vacations -- Fiction
ISBN 978-0-525-46928-5; 0-525-46928-1; 978-0-14-240879-7 pa; 0-14-240879-4 pa

A reissue of the title first published 1972

A summer in Tarrytown, N.Y., is a lot of fun for ten-year-old Sheila even though her friends make her face up to some self-truths she doesn't want to admit.

"An unusual and merry treatment of the fears of a young girl. . . . This is a truly appealing book in which the author makes her points without a single preachy word." Publ Wkly

Soupy Saturdays with The Pain and The Great One; illustrations by James Stevenson. Delacorte Press 2007 108p il $12.99; lib bdg $16.99

Grades: 1 2 3   **Fic**

1. Siblings -- Fiction
ISBN 978-0-385-73305-2; 0-385-73305-4; 978-0-385-90324-0 lib bdg; 0-385-90324-3 lib bdg

LC 2006-26892

"Third-grader Abigail calls her little brother 'The Pain' because he causes so much trouble. Jake is in first grade and calls his older sister 'The Great One' because she thinks so highly of herself. The book . . . is a series of vignettes in which the children continually clash and then reconcile. . . . The stories are sweet and accurately depict the growing pains of childhood. Stevenson's black-and-white ink illustrations are entertaining." SLJ

Other titles about the The Pain and The Great One are:
Cool zone with The Pain and The Great One (2008)
Going, going, gone! with The Pain and The Great One (2008)
Friend or fiend? with The Pain and The Great One (2009)

Superfudge. Dutton Children's Books 2002 178p $15.99; pa $5.99

Grades: 3 4 5 6   **Fic**

1. Brothers -- Fiction 2. Family life -- Fiction
ISBN 0-525-46930-3; 0-14-240880-8 pa

LC 2004270849

A reissue of the title first published 1980

Peter describes the highs and lows of life with his younger brother, Fudge

"A genuinely funny story." NY Times Book Rev

★ **Tales** of a fourth grade nothing. Dutton Children's Books 2002 120p $15.99; pa $5.99

Grades: 3 4 5 6   **Fic**

1. Brothers -- Fiction 2. Family life -- Fiction
ISBN 0-525-46931-1; 0-14-240881-6 pa

A reissue of the title first published 1972

This story describes the trials and tribulations of nine-year-old Peter Hatcher who is saddled with a pesky two-year-old brother named Fudge who is constantly creating trouble, messing things up, and monopolizing their parents' attention. Things come to a climax when Fudge gets at Peter's pet turtle

"The episode structure makes the book a good choice for reading aloud." Saturday Rev

Other titles about Peter and Fudge are:
Double Fudge (2002)
Fudge-a-mania (1990)
Superfudge (1980)

Blume, Lesley M. M.

Cornelia and the audacious escapades of the Somerset sisters. Knopf 2006 264p $15.95; pa $5.99

Grades: 4 5 6   **Fic**

1. Sisters -- Fiction 2. Friendship -- Fiction 3. Storytelling -- Fiction
ISBN 0-375-83523-7; 0-440-42110-1 pa

LC 2005-18295

Cornelia, eleven-years-old and lonely, learns about language and life from an elderly new neighbor who has many stories to share about the fabulous adventures she and her sisters had while traveling around the world

This "is a fabulous read that will enchant its audience with the magic to be found in everyday life." SLJ

Tennyson. Alfred A. Knopf 2008 288p $15.99; lib bdg $18.99; pa $6.99

Grades: 6 7 8 9 10 11 12   **Fic**

1. Family life -- Fiction 2. Great Depression, 1929-1939 -- Fiction
ISBN 978-0-375-84703-5; 978-0-375-94703-2 lib bdg; 978-0-440-24061-7 pa

LC 2007-25983

After their mother abandons them during the Great Depression, eleven-year-old Tennyson Fontaine and her little sister Hattie are sent to live with their eccentric Aunt Henrietta in a decaying plantation house

"Many readers will respond to this novel's Southern gothic sensibility, especially Blume's beautiful, poetic writing about how the past resonates through the generations." Booklist

The **rising** star of Rusty Nail; [by] Lesley M.M. Blume. Alfred A. Knopf 2007 270p $15.99; lib bdg $18.99; pa $6.50

Grades: 4 5 6   **Fic**

1. Pianists -- Fiction 2. Musicians -- Fiction 3. Russian Americans -- Fiction
ISBN 978-0-375-83524-7; 978-0-375-93524-4 lib bdg; 978-0-440-42111-5 pa

LC 2006024252

In the small town of Rusty Nail, Minnesota, in the early 1950s, musically talented ten-year-old Franny wants to take advanced piano lessons from newcomer Olga Malenkov, a famous Russian musician suspected of being a communist spy by gossipy members of the community

"Blume has skillfully combined humor, history, and music to create an enjoyable novel that builds to a surprising crescendo." SLJ

Blundell, Judy

A **city** tossed and broken; the diary of Minnie Bonner. Judy Blundell. Scholastic Inc. 2013 224 p. (paper over board) $12.99

Grades: 4 5 6 7 **Fic**

1. Historical fiction -- Juvenile fiction 2. Household employees -- Juvenile fiction 3. San Francisco (Calif.) -- History -- Fiction 4. Diaries -- Fiction 5. Earthquakes -- Fiction 6. Diaries -- Juvenile fiction 7. Household employees -- Fiction 8. Family life -- California -- Fiction 9. San Francisco Earthquake and Fire, Calif., 1906 -- Fiction 10. San Francisco Earthquake and Fire, Calif., 1906 -- Juvenile fiction 11. Women household employees -- California -- San Francisco -- Juvenile fiction

ISBN 0545310229; 9780545310222

LC 2012014742

This novel, by Judy Blundell, presents the diary of the girl Minnie Bonner during the San Francisco, California earthquake of 1906 as part of the "Dear America" series. A "wealthy gentleman . . . offers Minnie a chance to work as a lady's maid. . . . But when a powerful earthquake strikes, Minnie finds herself the sole survivor among them. . . . Minnie has turned into an heiress overnight . . . and she is soon wrapped up in a deception that leads her down a dangerous path." (Publisher's note)

"The author deftly incorporates true events, circumstances and key historical figures into the rapidly unfolding fictional plot... Exciting, suspenseful, absorbing and informative." Kirkus

Bode, N. E.

The **Anybodies**. HarperCollins 2004 276p il $15.99; pa $6.99

Grades: 5 6 7 8 **Fic**

1. Magic -- Fiction

ISBN 0-06-055735-4; 0-06-055737-0 pa

After learning that she is not the biological daughter of boring Mr. and Mrs. Drudger, Fern embarks on magical adventures with her real father and finally finds "a place that feels like home."

"The writing is fluid, the characters are multifaceted, and the situations range from poignant to gloriously silly. Eye-catching, black-and-white sketches echo the story's nuances and add to the atmosphere. There's laugh-out-loud humor, fantasy, mystery, real-life family drama." SLJ

Other titles in this series are:

The nobodies (2005)

The somebodies (2006)

The **slippery** map; by N.E. Bode; illustrated by Brandon Dorman. HarperCollinsPublishers 2007 273p il $16.99; lib bdg $17.89

Grades: 4 5 6 **Fic**

1. Adventure fiction 2. Parents -- Fiction 3. Convents -- Fiction 4. Imagination -- Fiction

ISBN 978-0-06-079108-7; 0-06-079108-X; 978-0-06-079109-4 lib bdg; 0-06-079109-8 lib bdg

LC 2007010900

Oyster R. Motel, a lonely boy raised as a foundling in a Baltimore nunnery, travels through a portal to the imaginary world of his parents, where he heroically confronts the villainous Dark Mouth

The author "effortlessly renders an expansive, entertainingly quirky cast of creatures benign and malevolent. Her snappy prose makes the case for the story's explicit messages about the value of unbridled imagination." Publ Wkly

Boelts, Maribeth

Happy like soccer; illustrated by Lauren Castillo. 1st ed. Candlewick Press 2012 32 p. col. ill. (reinforced trade) $15.99

Grades: 2 3 4 **Fic**

1. Soccer teams 2. Soccer -- Fiction 3. Family life -- Fiction 4. Aunts -- Fiction 5. Social classes -- Fiction 6. Problem solving -- Fiction

ISBN 0763646164; 9780763646165

LC 2011018624

In this children's book by Maribeth Boelts, "Sierra struggles with conflicting emotions about her new soccer team. Traveling out of the city, Sierra now plays on . . . fields unlike the one near the apartment where she lives with her aunt, which is exciting. However, being on this new team has some drawbacks. . . . Sierra is sad to be the only player without family members to cheer for her during games. Yet, with a little ingenuity, Sierra discovers a solution to her dilemma." (Kirkus Reviews)

★ The **PS** brothers. Harcourt 2010 137p $15

Grades: 3 4 5 **Fic**

1. Dogs -- Fiction 2. Uncles -- Fiction 3. Bullies -- Fiction 4. Money-making projects for children -- Fiction

ISBN 978-0-547-34249-8; 0-547-34249-7

LC 2009-49975

Sixth-graders Russell and Shawn, poor and picked on, work together scooping dog droppings to earn money for a Rottweiler puppy to protect them from bullies, but when they learn the puppies' owner is running an illegal dog-fighting ring, they are torn about how to respond.

This is "a genuinely touching look at a boy who doesn't believe that there's anybody of consequence on his side. . . . There is humor in Russell and Shawn's business, but the kids are admirably industrious as well; the ethical quandary they encounter . . . is one that will hit kids right in their dog-loving and impoverished guts." Bull Cent Child Books

Boie, Kirsten

The **princess** plot; translated by David Henry Wilson. Scholastic 2009 378p $17.99

Grades: 5 6 7 8 **Fic**

1. Princesses -- Fiction 2. Conspiracies -- Fiction

ISBN 978-0-545-03220-9; 0-545-03220-2

LC 2008-24403

Original German edition, 2005

Believing that she is on a film set after auditioning and winning the role of a princess, fourteen-year-old Jenna becomes the unsuspecting pawn in a royal conspiracy

"This novel takes simple, straightforward writing and layers it with kidnappings, political intrigue, and an abundance of secret plots. Readers will enjoy leisurely uncovering the mystery of Jenna's heritage, right along with Jenna herself." Booklist

Another title about Jenna is:

The princess trap (2010)

The **princess** trap; translated by David Henry Wilson. Chicken House/Scholastic 2010 405p $17.99

Grades: 5 6 7 8 **Fic**

1. School stories 2. Princesses -- Fiction

ISBN 978-0-545-22261-7; 0-545-22261-3

LC 2010010072

Original German edition, 2007

Palace rules, boarding school, and paparazzi have Jenna, princess of the newly unified kingdom of Scandia, longing for her former anonymity, but when she runs away she finds herself in grave danger—and in a position to prevent the outbreak of civil war.

Bolden, Tonya

★ **Finding** family. Bloomsbury 2010 181p il $15.99

Grades: 4 5 6 7   **Fic**

1. Aunts -- Fiction 2. Family life -- Fiction 3. Grandfathers -- Fiction 4. African Americans -- Fiction

ISBN 978-1-59990-318-7; 1-59990-318-0

LC 2010-00535

Raised in Charleston, West Virginia, at the turn of the twentieth century by her grandfather and aunt on off-putting tales of family members she has never met, twelve-year-old Delana is shocked when, after Aunt Tilley dies, she learns the truth about her parents and some of her other relatives.

"This richly lyrical and historically persuasive coming-of-age story explores the ties that bind, break and renew an affuent African-American family. . . . Period photographic portraits from Bolden's personal collection illustrate the book. Each carefully posed subject is a fascinating enigma." Kirkus

Boles, Philana Marie

Little divas. Amistad 2006 164p $15.99; lib bdg $16.89; pa $5.99

Grades: 5 6 7 8   **Fic**

1. Cousins -- Fiction 2. Divorce -- Fiction 3. African Americans -- Fiction 4. Father-daughter relationship -- Fiction

ISBN 0-06-073299-7; 0-06-073300-4 lib bdg; 0-06-073301-2 pa

The summer before seventh grade, Cassidy Carter must come to terms with living with her father, practically a stranger, as well as her relationships with her cousins, all amidst the overall confusion of adolescence.

"Boles portrays this variable age well, and readers will feel for Cassidy's trials." SLJ

Boling, Katharine

January 1905. Harcourt 2004 170p $16; pa $5.95

Grades: 4 5 6 7   **Fic**

1. Twins -- Fiction 2. Sisters -- Fiction 3. Child labor -- Fiction

ISBN 0-15-205119-8; 0-15-205121-X pa

LC 2003-24470

In a 1905 mill town, eleven-year-old twin sisters, Pauline, who goes to work with the rest of the family, and Arlene, whose crippled foot keeps her home doing the cooking, cleaning, and washing, are convinced that the other sister has an easier life until a series of incidents helps them see each other in a new light.

"This vivid account will draw readers into the period." Horn Book Guide

Bond, Michael

★ **A bear** called Paddington; with drawings by Peggy Fortnum. Houghton Mifflin 1998 128p il $15; pa $4.95

Grades: 2 3 4 5   **Fic**

1. Bears -- Fiction

ISBN 0-395-92951-2; 0-618-15071-4 pa

First published 1958 in the United Kingdom; first United States edition 1960

"Mr. and Mrs. Brown first met Paddington on a railway platform in London. Noticing the sign on his neck reading 'Please look after this bear. Thank you,' they decided to do just that. From there on home was never the same though the Brown children were delighted." Publ Wkly

Other titles about Paddington Bear are:

More about Paddington

Paddington abroad

Paddington at large

Paddington at work

Paddington goes to town

Paddington here and now

Paddington helps out

Paddington marches on

Paddington on screen

Paddington on stage

Paddington on top

Paddington takes the air

Paddington takes the test

Paddington takes to TV

Paddington treasury

Bond, Nancy

A **string** in the harp. Atheneum Pubs. 1976 370p il $19.95; pa $6.99

Grades: 6 7 8 9   **Fic**

1. Fantasy fiction

ISBN 0-689-50036-X; 1-4169-2771-9 pa

LC 75-28181

A Newbery Medal honor book, 1977

"Present-day realism and the fantasy world of sixth-century Taliesin meet in an absorbing novel set in Wales. The story centers around the Morgans—Jen, Peter, Becky, and their father—their adjustment to another country, their mother's death, and especially, Peter's bitter despair, which threatens them all." LC. Child Books, 1976

Bond, Victoria

Zora and me; the song of Ivory. [by] Victoria Bond and T. R. Simon. Candlewick Press 2010 170p $16.99; pa $6.99

Grades: 4 5 6 7   **Fic**

1. Authors 2. Novelists 3. Dramatists 4. Memoirists 5. Folklorists 6. Short story writers 7. Race relations -- Fiction 8. African Americans -- Fiction

ISBN 978-0-7636-4300-3; 0-7636-4300-9; 978-0-7636-5814-4 pa; 0-7636-5814-6 pa

LC 2009-47410

Coretta Scott King/John Steptoe New Talent Award (Author), 2011

This is a fictionalized account of Zora Neale Hurston's childhood with her best friend Carrie, in Eatonville, Florida. Annotated bibliography. "Grades four to seven." (Bull Cent Child Books)

"The brilliance of this novel is its rendering of African-American child life during the Jim Crow era as a time of wonder and imagination, while also attending to its harsh realities. Absolutely outstanding." Kirkus

Bondoux, Anne-Laure

Vasco leader of the tribe; [by] Anne-Laure Bondoux; translated from the French by Y. Maudet. Delacorte Press 2007 336p $15.99; lib bdg $18.99; pa $6.99

Grades: 3 4 5 6   **Fic**

1. Rats -- Fiction 2. Voyages and travels -- Fiction

ISBN 978-0-385-73363-2; 978-0-385-90378-3 lib bdg; 978-0-440-42153-5 pa

Following his dreams of finding a safe haven in a new place, Vasco leads a motley group of rats out of the city, through a dangerous sea voyage, and finally to a forest where the rats, now a true tribe, can make a fresh start.

"Bondoux does an excellent job of setting the story firmly and believably in the rodent world while imbuing the characters with enough human qualities to allow young readers to relate to them." SLJ

★ A **time** of miracles. Delacorte Press 2010 180p map $17.99; lib bdg $20.99

Grades: 5 6 7 8   **Fic**

1. War stories 2. Refugees -- Fiction

ISBN 978-0-385-73922-1; 0-385-73922-2; 978-0-385-90777-4 lib bdg; 0-385-90777-X lib bdg

LC 2010008539

Mildred L. Batchelder Award, 2011

"Readers will find themselves mesmerized not only by the eloquent language but by a plot every bit as harrowing and surprising as Koumail's cherished bedtime story." Horn Book

Boniface, William

The **hero** revealed; [by] William Boniface; illustrations by Stephen Gilpin. HarperCollins Pub. 2006 294p il (The extraordinary adventures of Ordinary Boy) $15.99; lib bdg $16.89; pa $6.99

Grades: 4 5 6 7   **Fic**

1. Superheroes -- Fiction

ISBN 978-0-06-077464-6; 0-06-077464-9; 978-0-06-077465-3 lib bdg; 0-06-077465-7 lib bdg; 978-0-06-077466-0 pa; 0-06-077466-5 pa

LC 2005018676

Ordinary Boy, the only resident of Superopolis without a superpower, uncovers and foils a sinister plot to destroy the town

"This first book in a new series is great fun. . . . Boniface wields a cynical, but definitely kid-friendly, sense of humor, and Gilpin's illustrations are sharp and witty." SLJ

Other titles in this series are:

The return of Meteor Boy? (2007)

The great powers outage (2008)

Booraem, Ellen

★ **Small** persons with wings. Dial Books for Young Readers 2011 302p $16.99

Grades: 4 5 6 7   **Fic**

1. Fantasy fiction 2. Magic -- Fiction 3. Fairies -- Fiction 4. Grandfathers -- Fiction 5. Lost and found possessions -- Fiction

ISBN 978-0-8037-3471-5; 0-8037-3471-9

LC 2010008400

When Mellie Turpin's grandfather dies and leaves her family his run-down inn and bar, she learns that for generations her family members have been fairy guardians. "Grades five to eight." (Bull Cent Child Books)

"In a fairy story that's wistful, humorous, and clever, Booraem . . . suggests that the real world—with its disappointments and failings—is still better than living with illusions. . . . The theme of making progress, rather than ignoring problems, is a strong one, gently presented." Publ Wkly

Texting the underworld; by Ellen Booraem. Dial Books for Young Readers 2013 319 p. (hardcover) $16.99

Grades: 5 6 7 8   **Fic**

1. Banshees -- Juvenile fiction 2. School stories -- Juvenile fiction 3. Fantasy fiction -- Juvenile fiction 4. Death -- Fiction 5. Humorous stories 6. Schools -- Fiction 7. Banshees -- Fiction 8. Future life -- Fiction 9. Supernatural -- Fiction 10. Middle schools -- Fiction

ISBN 0803737041; 9780803737044

LC 2012032488

In this book by Ellen Booraem, "Conor O'Neill is a smart but timid seventh-grader. . . . When a banshee straight out of his Irish-born grandfather's stories appears in Conor's room, he's terrified that someone he loves is going to die soon. The banshee, Ashling, is new at her job, and . . . she's curious about the present day, [so] she masquerades as a new student at Conor's school." (Publishers Weekly)

Borden, Louise

Across the blue Pacific; a World War II story. illustrated by Robert Andrew Parker. Houghton Mifflin 2006 un il $17

Grades: 2 3 4 5   **Fic**

1. World War, 1939-1945 -- Fiction

ISBN 0-618-33922-1

LC 2004-9206

A woman reminisces about her neighbor's son who was the object of a letter writing campaign by some fourth-graders when he went away to war in 1943.

"Beautifully written in an understated tone, the story offers a believable picture of life during the war. . . . Restrained yet expressive, the artwork conveys moods and mindsets as well as a strong sense of the time and place." Booklist

The **greatest** skating race; a World War II story from the Netherlands. illustrated by Niki Daly. Margaret K. McElderry Books 2004 44p il $18.95

Grades: 2 3 4 5   **Fic**

1. Ice skating -- Fiction 2. World War, 1939-1945 -- Fiction

ISBN 0-689-84502-2

LC 2002-12040

During World War II in the Netherlands, a ten-year-old boy's dream of skating in a famous race allows him to help two children escape to Belgium by ice skating past German soldiers and other enemies.

"Told with immediacy and suspense. . . . The gorgeously detailed watercolor illustrations capture a sense of the time. The subdued, winter hues of brown and smoky gray are those often found in the oil paintings of Dutch and Flemish masters and match the quiet tone of the text." SLJ

The **last** day of school; written by Louise Borden; illustrated by Adam Gustavson. Margaret K. McElderry Books 2005 un il $15.95

Grades: 2 3 4   **Fic**
1. School stories 2. Gifts -- Fiction
ISBN 0-689-86869-3

LC 2003025124

Matthew Perez, the official timekeeper of Mrs. Mallory's third-grade class, has a special goodbye gift for her

"Varied sizes of colorful oil illustrations accompany the tale of Matts patient delivery of the perfect gift. True to a childs remembrance of final school days, each page recalls memorable moments for students and teachers." SLJ

The **lost** -and-found tooth; [by] Louise Borden; illustrated by Adam Gustavson. Margaret K. McElderry Books 2008 un il $16.99
Grades: K 1 2   **Fic**
1. School stories 2. Teeth -- Fiction 3. Lost and found possessions -- Fiction
ISBN 978-1-4169-1814-1; 1-4169-1814-0

LC 2006028761

A special calendar hangs in Mr. Reilly's second grade classroom, and Lucy Webb impatiently awaits the day when she can add her name for losing a tooth, but when her time arrives something unexpected happens

"The low-key story is nicely illustrated with watercolors and is well suited to either independent reading or classroom sharing." Booklist

Bosch, Pseudonymous
If you're reading this, it's too late; illustrations by Gilbert Ford. Little, Brown 2008 385p il $16.99
Grades: 4 5 6   **Fic**
1. Adventure fiction 2. Magic tricks -- Fiction
ISBN 978-0-316-11367-0; 0-316-11367-0

LC 2008012405

Cass and Max-Ernest discover the Museum of Magic, unscramble more coded messages, and solve new mysteries in their attempt to thwart the Terces Society's ambitions of discovering immortality.

This "combines mystery, adventure, and fantasy. . . . The numerous parenthetical comments and footnotes are often laugh-out-loud funny. . . . The dark illustrations, descending chapter numbers, and playful fonts will catch readers' attention." SLJ

This book is not good for you; chef de cuisine, Pseudonymous Bosch; illustrations by Gilbert Ford. Little, Brown 2009 394p $16.99
Grades: 4 5 6   **Fic**
1. Adventure fiction 2. Desserts -- Fiction 3. Immortality -- Fiction
ISBN 978-0-316-04086-0; 0-316-04086-X

As an evil dessert chef concocts a recipe for disaster in the form of a tempting chocolate bar, Cass and Max-Ernest attempt to stop an evil organization from carrying out its plot to gain immortality and wreak havoc on the world.

"Twists and turns in the ordering of the chapters give the author time for commentary and a choose-your-own-adventure for readers who will still be on the edges of their seats at the end for the Secret to be revealed." Voice Youth Advocates

This isn't what it looks like; illustrations by Gilbert Ford. Little, Brown 2010 423p il $16.99
Grades: 4 5 6   **Fic**
1. Adventure fiction 2. Magic -- Fiction 3. Chocolate

-- Fiction 4. Immortality -- Fiction 5. Time travel -- Fiction
ISBN 978-0-316-07625-8; 0-316-07625-2

LC 2010010519

Cass finds herself alone and disoriented in a dream-like world, while back at home she is in the hospital in a coma with Max-Ernest desperately searching for a way to awaken her.

"The book's blend of mystery, fantasy, puzzles, puns, and puckish, sometimes snarky sense of humor will keep readers engaged." Horn Book Guide

The **name** of this book is secret; by Pseudonymous Bosch; illustrations by Gilbert Ford. Little, Brown & Co. 2007 360p il $16.99; pa $5.99
Grades: 4 5 6   **Fic**
1. Adventure fiction 2. Immortality -- Fiction
ISBN 978-0-316-11366-3; 0-316-11366-2; 978-0-316-11369-4 pa; 0-316-11369-7 pa

LC 2007021909

Two eleven-year-old misfits try to solve the mystery of a dead magician and stop the evil Dr. L and Ms. Mauvais, who are searching for the secret of immortality

This "is equal parts supernatural whodunit, suspense-filled adventure and evocative coming-of-age tale." Publ Wkly

Other titles in this series are:
If you're reading this, it's too late (2008)
This book is not good for you (2009)
This isn't what it looks like (2010)

Boston, L. M.
The **children** of Green Knowe; illustrated by Peter Boston. Harcourt 2002 183p il hardcover o.p. pa $6
Grades: 4 5 6   **Fic**
1. Fantasy fiction
ISBN 0-15-202462-X; 0-15-202468-9 pa

LC 2001-51806

First published 1954 in the United Kingdom

Tolly comes to live with his great-grandmother at the ancient house of Green Knowe and becomes friends with three children who lived there in the seventeenth century.

"A special book for the imaginative child, in which mood predominates and fantasy and realism are skillfully blended." Booklist

Other titles about Green Knowe are:
An enemy of Green Knowe (c1976)
The river of Green Knowe (c1959)
A stranger of Green Knowe (c1961)
The treasure of Green Knowe (c1958)

Bouwman, H. M.
The **remarkable** and very true story of Lucy and Snowcap; [by] H.M. Bouwman. Marshall Cavendish 2008 270p $16.99
Grades: 5 6 7 8   **Fic**
1. Adventure fiction 2. Magic -- Fiction 3. Infants -- Fiction 4. Islands -- Fiction
ISBN 978-0-7614-5441-0; 0-7614-5441-1

LC 2008003180

In 1788, thirteen years after English convicts are shipwrecked on the magical islands of Tathenland, two twelve-year-old girls, one a native Colay, the other the child-governor of the English, set out on a journey to stop the treachery from which both peoples are suffering

"The page-turning adventure fronts for a subtle moral tale about loyalty, perseverance, and the power of finding one's own particular gifts. . . . The combination of historical and fantasy elements gives Lucy and Snowcap's quest folkloric as well as dramatic appeal." Bull Cent Child Books

Bowe, Julie

My best frenemy. Dial Books for Young Readers 2010 234p (Friends for keeps) $16.99

Grades: 2 3 4   **Fic**

1. School stories 2. Friendship -- Fiction

ISBN 978-0-8037-3501-9; 0-8037-3501-4

Ida May finally fits in at school after becoming best friends with Stacey Merriweather, who is universally liked by their classmates. But then Ida's frenemy, bossy Jenna Drews, brings in a game of truth or dare, and all the girls are suddenly daring one another to misbehave.

"Written in descriptive language . . . that sets the scene and gives readers insight into Ida's confusion and growth, the story is realistic and well told." SLJ

Bowen, Fred

Quarterback season; written by Fred Bowen. Peachtree 2011 132p pa $5.95

Grades: 4 5 6 7   **Fic**

1. Diaries -- Fiction 2. Football -- Fiction

ISBN 978-1-56145-594-2; 1-56145-594-6

LC 2011002673

As a school assignment, eighth-grader Matt Monroe keeps a journal about his team's football season.

This is "another absorbing sports tale from the prolific and dependable Bowen. . . . The author expertly balances the subplots and football action." Booklist

Touchdown trouble; written by Fred Bowen. Peachtree Publishers 2009 123p pa $5.95

Grades: 3 4 5   **Fic**

1. Football -- Fiction

ISBN 978-1-5614-5497-6; 1-5614-5497-4

LC 2008054867

Sam is proud that his touchdown in the final play of a game left his football team undefeated, but when a video-recording of the game reveals that the touchdown was scored illegally, he and the other Cowboys must decide whether to reveal the truth. Includes facts about a similar situation faced by Cornell University's team after a game with Dartmouth in 1940.

This book is "a great choice to hand off to reader's who'd rather be tossing pigskins that flipping pages." Booklist

Boyne, John

The **Terrible** Thing That Happened to Barnaby Brocket; John Boyne; illustrated by Oliver Jeffers. Knopf Books for Young Readers 2013 288 p. ill. $16.99

Grades: 2 3 4 5   **Fic**

1. Runaway children -- Juvenile fiction 2. Adventure fiction -- Juvenile fiction

ISBN 0307977625; 9780307977625; 9780307977632

LC 2012277133

In this novel, by John Boyne and illustrated by Oliver Jeffers, "Barnaby Brocket is an ordinary 8-year-old boy in most ways, but he was born different in one important way:

he floats. Unlike everyone else, Barnaby does not obey the law of gravity. . . . And when the unthinkable happens, Barnaby finds himself on a journey that takes him all over the world. From Brazil to New York, . . . and . . . meets all sorts of different people--and discovers who he really is along the way." (Publisher's note)

Bradford, Chris

Young samurai: the way of the sword. Disney-Hyperion Books 2010 422p $16.99

Grades: 4 5 6 7   **Fic**

1. Adventure fiction 2. Ninja -- Fiction 3. Orphans -- Fiction 4. Samurai -- Fiction 5. Martial arts -- Fiction

ISBN 978-1-4231-2025-4; 1-4231-2025-6

LC 2009008309

In 1611 Japan, English orphan Jack Fletcher continues his difficult training at Niten Ichi Ryu Samurai School, while also trying to get back the rutter, his father's navigational logbook, that an evil ninja wants to possess.

"With straightforward prose, [Bradford] has managed to pen lively and exciting fight sequences and is slowly beginning to develop a keen edge to his cast of characters, laying significant groundwork for future installments." Booklist

★ **Young** samurai: the way of the warrior. Hyperion Books for Children 2009 359p $16.99

Grades: 4 5 6 7   **Fic**

1. Adventure fiction 2. Samurai -- Fiction 3. Martial arts -- Fiction

ISBN 978-1-4231-1871-8; 1-4231-1871-5

LC 2008-46180

First published 2008 in the United Kingdom

Orphaned by a ninja pirate attack off the coast of Japan in 1611, twelve-year-old English lad Jack Fletcher is determined to prove himself, despite the bullying of fellow students, when the legendary sword master who rescued him begins training him as a samurai warrior.

"Jack's story alone makes for a page-turner, but coupling it with intriguing bits of Japanese history and culture, Bradford produces an adventure novel to rank among the genre's best." Publ Wkly

Includes bibliographical references

Bradley, Kimberly Brubaker

★ **Jefferson's** sons; a founding father's secret children. Dial Books for Young Readers 2011 368p $17.99

Grades: 5 6 7 8   **Fic**

1. Slaves 2. Architects 3. Presidents 4. Vice-presidents 5. Essayists 6. Mistresses 7. Slavery -- Fiction 8. African Americans -- Fiction

ISBN 978-0-8037-3499-9; 0-8037-3499-9

LC 2010049650

"The characters spring to life. . . . [This is a] fascinating story of an American family that represents so many of the contradictions of our history. The afterword is as fascinating as the novel." Kirkus

The **lacemaker** and the princess. Margaret K. McElderry Books 2007 199p $16.99; pa $6.99

Grades: 4 5 6 7 8   **Fic**

1. Queens 2. Friendship -- Fiction 3. Lace and lace making -- Fiction

ISBN 978-1-4169-1920-9; 1-4169-1920-1; 978-1-4169-8583-9 pa; 1-4169-8583-2 pa

In 1788, eleven-year-old Isabelle, living with her lace-maker grandmother and mother near the palace of Versailles, becomes close friends with Marie Antoinette's daughter, Princess Therese, and finds their relationship complicated not only by their different social class but by the growing political unrest and resentment of the French people.

"Skillfully integrated historical facts frame this engrossing, believable story." Booklist

Bragg, Georgia

Matisse on the loose. Delacorte Press 2009 149p $16.99; lib bdg $19.99

Grades: 4 5 6   **Fic**

1. Artists 2. Painters 3. Artists -- Fiction 4. Art museums -- Fiction 5. Family life -- Fiction
ISBN 978-0-385-73570-4; 0-385-73570-7; 978-0-385-90559-6 lib bdg; 0-385-90559-9 lib bdg

LC 2008019624

An aspiring artist's daily routine of being embarrassed by his eccentric family is interrupted when he finds himself in the middle of an art museum fiasco involving Matisse's 1909 portrait of his son Pierre.

"Bragg creates plenty of suspenseful, often comedic scenarios. . . . Readers will enjoy the diverse, memorable characters." Booklist

Brandeis, Gayle

My life with the Lincolns. Holt & Co. 2010 248p $16.99

Grades: 4 5 6 7   **Fic**

1. Family life -- Fiction 2. Race relations -- Fiction 3. African Americans -- Fiction
ISBN 978-0-8050-9013-0; 0-8050-9013-4

LC 2009-24151

"Twelve-year-old Mina Edelman is convinced that her family members are the Lincolns reincarnate, and she has many coincidences to back her up. . . . The strong theme of social justice creates a unifying thread in this informative, clear, personal, and passionate novel." Booklist

Branford, Anna

Violet Mackerel's brilliant plot; by Anna Branford; illustrated by Elanna Allen. Reprint Atheneum Books for Young Readers 2012 102 p. ill. (reinforced) $14.99; (paperback) $5.99

Grades: 1 2 3   **Fic**

1. Imagination -- Juvenile fiction 2. Flea markets -- Juvenile fiction 3. Individuality -- Juvenile fiction 4. Imagination -- Fiction 5. Individuality -- Fiction 6. Moneymaking projects -- Fiction
ISBN 1442435852; 9781442435858; 9781442435865

LC 2011022584

In this book by Anna Branford, "young Violet accompanies her older siblings and her mother to the flea market . . . . where Violet looks longingly at a blue china bird for sale in one of the stalls. She decides to hatch a plot to obtain the bird for her own, but her many efforts fail; a simple act of generosity on her part, though, gains the attention of Vincent, the stall owner, and he eventually gives Violet the very thing she wanted all along." (Bulletin of the Center for Children's Books)

Violet Mackerel's remarkable recovery; Anna Branford; illustrated by Elanna Allen. 1st ed. Atheneum Books

for Young Readers 2012 128 p. ill. (hardcover) $15.99; (paperback) $5.99

Grades: 1 2 3 4   **Fic**

1. Gifts -- Juvenile fiction 2. Tonsillectomy -- Juvenile fiction 3. Sick -- Fiction 4. Friendship -- Fiction 5. Tonsillectomy -- Fiction
ISBN 1442435887; 9781442435889; 9781442435896

LC 2011023703

In this children's story, by Anna Branford, "seven-year-old Violet Mackerel has a new theory: If someone has a problem and you give them something small, . . . that small thing might have a strange and special way of helping them. Violet gets the chance to put 'The Theory of Giving Small Things' to the test when a bad case of tonsillitis requires the removal of her tonsils, and she suspects that the purple lozenge from Doctor Singh may help her in quite an extraordinary way." (Publisher's note)

Branford, Henrietta

Fire, bed, & bone. Candlewick Press 1998 122p hardcover o.p. pa $5.99

Grades: 5 6 7 8   **Fic**

1. Dogs -- Fiction 2. Middle Ages -- Fiction 3. Tyler's Insurrection, 1381 -- Fiction 4. Tyler's Insurrection, 1381 -- Juvenile fiction
ISBN 0-7636-0338-4; 0-7636-2992-8 pa

LC 97-17491

In 1381 in England, a hunting dog recounts what happens to his beloved master Rufus and his family when they are arrested on suspicion of being part of the peasants' rebellion led by Wat Tyler and the preacher John Ball

"The dog's observant eye, sympathetic personality, and courageous acts hook the reader into what is both irresistible adventure and educational historical fiction." Booklist

Bransford, Nathan

Jacob Wonderbar and the cosmic space kapow. Dial Books for Young Readers 2011 281p il $14.99

Grades: 4 5 6   **Fic**

1. Adventure fiction 2. Fathers -- Fiction 3. Teachers -- Fiction 4. Interplanetary voyages -- Fiction
ISBN 978-0-8037-3537-8; 0-8037-3537-5

LC 2010-38152

When sixth-grade classroom terror Jacob Wonderbar and his friends Sarah and Dexter find a spaceship crashed in the woods near their suburban neighborhood, their discovery leads them to a series of adventures including space travel, substitute teachers, kidnapping, and more.

"Readers will appreciate Bransford's unique view of the universe. . . . Jacob's ongoing search for his father . . . promises to keep this series moving through at least two forthcoming sequels." Booklist

Jacob Wonderbar and the interstellar time warp; Nathan Bransford; illustrated by C.S. Jennings. Dial Books for Young Readers 2013 272 p. (hardback) $16.99

Grades: 4 5 6   **Fic**

1. Time travel -- Juvenile fiction 2. Science fiction -- Juvenile fiction 3. Interplanetary voyages -- Juvenile fiction 4. Science fiction 5. Space and time -- Fiction 6. Fathers and sons -- Fiction 7. Interplanetary voyages -- Fiction 8. Adventure and adventurers -- Fiction
ISBN 0803737033; 9780803737037

LC 2012020967

In this children's book, by Nathan Bransford, illustrated by C. S. Jennings, "Jacob Wonderbar must have hit a time warp on his way home after losing the election for President of the Universe, because fifty years have passed on Earth. What's worse, during that time the entire Astral society has come under threat of destruction, and it's up to Jacob to make things--including time itself--right." (Publisher's note)

Brauner, Barbara

The **glitter** trap; Barbara Brauner, James Iver Mattson. 1st ed. Disney-Hyperion Books 2013 240 p. (Oh my god-mother) (reinforced) $16.99

Grades: 4 5 6 7   **Fic**

1. Fairies -- Juvenile fiction 2. Middle schools -- Juvenile fiction 3. Humorous fiction -- Juvenile fiction

ISBN 1423163737; 9781423163732

LC 2013930976

In this children's novel, by Barbara Brauner, James Iver Mattson, and illustrated by Abigail Halpin, "middle school is far from a fairytale for adorkable misfit Lacey Unger-Ware. When Lacey ends up with popular girl Paige Harrington's smart-mouthed fairy godmother, Katarina, trapped in her hair, life gets more magical--just not in a 'prince charming' kind of way. Katarina's wings are too damaged to continue her fairy duties, and Lacey must take over as Paige's fairy godmother." (Publisher's note)

Breathed, Berke

Flawed dogs; the shocking raid on Westminster. written and illustrated by Berkeley Breathed. Philomel Books 2009 216p il $16.99

Grades: 4 5 6   **Fic**

1. Dogs -- Fiction

ISBN 978-0-399-25218-1; 0-399-25218-5

LC 2009-2638

After being framed by a jealous poodle, a dachshund is left for dead, but comes back with a group of mutts from the National Last Ditch Dog Depository to disrupt the prestigious Westminster Kennel Club dog show and exact revenge on Cassius the poodle.

"Dramatically lit and featuring comically exaggerated characters (human and canine alike), Berkeley's b&w artwork augments the story's drama and humor. A moving tale about the beauty of imperfections and the capacity for love." Publ Wkly

Bredsdorff, Bodil

The **Crow**-girl; translated from the Danish by Faith Ingwersen. Farrar Straus Giroux 2004 155p map (The children of Crow Cove) $16

Grades: 4 5 6   **Fic**

1. Orphans 2. Family life 3. Grandmothers 4. Conduct of life 5. Orphans -- Fiction 6. Grandmothers -- Fiction

ISBN 0-374-31247-8

LC 2003-49310

Original Danish editon, 1993

After the death of her grandmother, a young orphaned girl leaves her house by the cove and begins a journey which leads her to people and experiences that exemplify the wisdom her grandmother had shared with her

"Touching on universal themes, this quiet adventure story has the depth and flavor of a tale from long ago and far away." SLJ

Other titles in this series are:

Eidi (2009)

Tink (2011)

Breen, M. E.

Darkwood. Bloomsbury 2009 273p il $16.99

Grades: 5 6 7 8   **Fic**

1. Fantasy fiction 2. Adventure fiction 3. Wolves -- Fiction 4. Orphans -- Fiction 5. Sisters -- Fiction

ISBN 978-1-59990-259-3; 1-59990-259-1

LC 2008-44413

A clever and fearless orphan endures increasing danger while trying to escape from greedy, lawless men and elude the terrifying "kinderstalks"—animals who steal children—before discovering her true destiny.

"Breen's finely tuned storytelling—pithy description, quick and keen emotion, broad trust of readers' intelligence—offers equal gratification whether readers spot clues and connections early or late. Both grounded and wondrous." Kirkus

Brewster, Hugh

Carnation, Lily, Lily, Rose; the story of a painting. by Hugh Brewster; with paintings by John Singer Sargent. Kids Can Press 2007 48p il $17.95

Grades: 3 4 5   **Fic**

1. Artists 2. Painters

ISBN 978-1-55453-137-0; 1-55453-137-3

This volume "introduces a true episode from nineteenth-century art history, delivering facts about John Singer Sargent and his luminous masterwork, Carnation, Lily, Lily, Rose, through the imagined words of a child present during its creation. . . . Widely accessible are the profuse visuals, including some of Sargent's sketchbook doodles and real photos of the featured family." Booklist

Brezenoff, Steven

The **burglar** who bit the Big Apple; illustrated by C. B. Canga. Stone Arch Books 2009 81p il (Field trip mysteries) lib bdg $23.99; pa $5.95

Grades: 2 3 4   **Fic**

1. School stories 2. Mystery fiction

ISBN 978-1-4342-2139-1 lib bdg; 1-4342-2139-3 lib bdg; 978-1-4342-2771-3 pa; 1-4342-2771-5 pa

"Cat, Sam, Egg, and Gum are sixth-grade pals with a penchant for solving mysteries. . . . In [this book], they arrive in New York City just as a lunch box has been lifted from the Ralph Kramden statue in the Port Authority Bus Terminal. Later there is more vandalism at the Museum of Natural History and the Bronx Zoo, setting these kids on the trail of a suspicious girl who just happens to know their itinerary. . . . [This] compact chapter [book] offers leading characters of both genders, some full-page, full-color illustrations, a 'detective's dictionary' (aka glossary), a useful model of a school report on the featured city, and evidence-based discussion questions. [This title is an] excellent [introduction] to the mystery genre; the graphics and short chapters make [it] accessible to struggling or reluctant readers." SLJ

The **painting** that wasn't there; illustrated by C.B. Canga. Stone Arch Books 2010 $17.99

Grades: 3 4 5 6   **Fic**

1. School stories 2. Mystery fiction

ISBN 9781434216083

LC 2009002572

"This title...marries the always high-interest topic of an art heist with a breezy, straightforward story just right for reluctant readers." Booklist

The **zombie** who visited New Orleans; illustrated by C. B. Canga. Stone Arch Books 2010 80p il (Field trip mysteries) lib bdg $23.99; pa $5.95

Grades: 2 3 4　　　　　　　　　　　　　　　　Fic
1. School stories 2. Mystery fiction 3. Zombies -- Fiction
ISBN 978-1-4342-2141-4 lib bdg; 1-4342-2141-5 lib bdg; 978-1-4342-2773-7 pa; 1-4342-2773-1 pa
　　　　　　　　　　　　　　　　　LC 2010022580
"Cat, Sam, Egg, and Gum are sixth-grade pals with a penchant for solving mysteries. . . . In New Orleans, the friends witness acts of voodoo at every tourist attraction and wonder if certain people might be zombies in disguise. . . . [This] compact chapter [book] offers leading characters of both genders, some full-page, full-color illustrations, a 'detective's dictionary' (aka glossary), a useful model of a school report on the featured city, and evidence-based discussion questions. [This title is an] excellent [introduction] to the mystery genre; the graphics and short chapters make [it] accessible to struggling or reluctant readers." SLJ

Brink, Carol Ryrie
★ **Caddie** Woodlawn; illustrated by Trina Schart Hyman. Macmillan 1973 275p il $17.95; pa $6.99
Grades: 4 5 6　　　　　　　　　　　　　　　　Fic
1. Frontier and pioneer life -- Fiction
ISBN 0-02-713670-1; 1-4169-4028-6 pa
A newly illustrated edition of the title first published 1935
Awarded the Newbery Medal, 1936
Caddie Woodlawn was eleven in 1864. Because she was frail, she had been allowed to grow up a tomboy. Her capacity for adventure was practically limitless, and there was plenty of adventure on the Wisconsin frontier in those days. The story covers one year of life on the pioneer farm, closing with the news that Mr. Woodlawn had inherited an estate in England, and the unanimous decision of the family to stay in Wisconsin. Based upon the reminiscences of the author's grandmother
The typeface "is eminently clear and readable, and the illustrations in black and white . . . are attractive and expressive." Wis Libr Bull

Brittain, Bill
The **wish** giver; three tales of Coven Tree. drawings by Andrew Glass. Harper & Row 1983 181p il $16.89; pa $5.99
Grades: 5 6 7 8　　　　　　　　　　　　　　　Fic
1. Magic -- Fiction 2. Wishes -- Fiction
ISBN 0-06-020687-X; 0-06-440168-5 pa
　　　　　　　　　　　　　　　　　LC 82-48264
A Newbery Medal honor book, 1984
"Captivating, fresh, and infused with homespun humor." Horn Book
Other titles about Coven Tree are:
Dr. Dredd's wagon of wonders (1987)
Professor Popkin's prodigious polish (1990)

Broach, Elise
Masterpiece; illustrated by Kelly Murphy. Henry Holt & Co. 2008 292p il $16.95

Grades: 4 5 6 7　　　　　　　　　　　　　　　Fic
1. Mystery fiction 2. Artists -- Fiction 3. Beetles -- Fiction
ISBN 978-0-8050-8270-8; 0-8050-8270-0
After Marvin, a beetle, makes a miniature drawing as an eleventh birthday gift for James, a human with whom he shares a house, the two new friends work together to help recover a Durer drawing stolen from the Metropolitan Museum of Art.
Broach "packs this fast-moving story with perennially seductive themes: hidden lives and secret friendships, miniature worlds lost to disbelievers. . . . Loosely implying rather than imitating the Old Masters they reference, the finely hatched drawings depict the settings realistically and the characters, especially the beetles, with joyful comic license." Publ Wkly

★ **Missing** on Superstition Mountain; [illustrated by Antonio Javier Caparo] Henry Holt 2011 262p il $15.99
Grades: 3 4 5　　　　　　　　　　　　　　　　Fic
1. Mystery fiction 2. Brothers -- Fiction 3. Mountains -- Fiction
ISBN 978-0-8050-9047-5; 0-8050-9047-9
　　　　　　　　　　　　　　　　　LC 2010-49007
When brothers Simon, Henry, and Jack move with their parents to Arizona, they are irresistably drawn to explore the aptly named Superstition Mountain, in spite of warnings that it is not safe.
"Caparo's skillful grayscale illustrations add a spooky element: three skulls mark each new chapter, and images like a black cat sitting on a crooked gravestone inspire chills. Classic horror and thriller elements combine with modern touches in Broach's page-turner." Publ Wkly

Shakespeare's secret; [by] Elise Broach. Henry Holt 2005 250p il $16.95; pa $5.99
Grades: 5 6 7 8　　　　　　　　　　　　　　　Fic
1. Mystery fiction
ISBN 0-8050-7387-6; 0-312-37132-2 pa
　　　　　　　　　　　　　　　　　LC 2004-54020
Named after a character in a Shakespeare play, misfit sixth-grader Hero becomes interested in exploring this unusual connection because of a valuable diamond supposedly hidden in her new house, an intriguing neighbor, and the unexpected attention of the most popular boy in school.
"The mystery alone will engage readers. . . . The main characters are all well developed, and the dialogue is both realistic and well planned." SLJ

Treasure on Superstition Mountain; Elise Broach; illustrated by Antonio Javier Caparo. Henry Holt 2012 224 p. (hardcover) $15.99
Grades: 3 4 5　　　　　　　　　　　　　　　　Fic
1. Adventure fiction 2. Buried treasure -- Fiction 3. Brothers -- Fiction 4. Mountains -- Fiction 5. Mystery and detective stories 6. Gold mines and mining -- Fiction
ISBN 0805077634; 9780805077636; 9780805096408
　　　　　　　　　　　　　　　　　LC 2012006475
This is the second installment of Elise Broach's Superstition Mountain series. Here, "two weeks after the children's . . . escape from Arizona's Superstition Mountain, during which they unearthed a treasure map and a gold nugget,

the young adventurers—undeterred by Delilah's broken leg, their parents' admonishments, and anonymous warnings—are more determined than ever both to find a hidden gold mine and discover who is trying to stop them." (Publishers Weekly)

Brodien-Jones, Chris

The **Owl** Keeper; [illustrations by Maggie Kneen] Delacorte Press 2010 304p il $17.99

Grades: 5 6 7 8   **Fic**

1. Fantasy fiction 2. Owls -- Fiction 3. Magic -- Fiction

ISBN 978-0-385-73814-9; 0-385-73814-5; 978-0-385-90710-1 lib bdg; 0-385-90710-9 lib bdg

LC 2009-27321

Eleven-year-old Max partners with an unusual girl, Rose, who shares his appreciation of the silver owls that the High Echelon wants to destroy, and together they make a perilous journey seeking to fulfill a prophecy.

Bromley, Anne C.

The **lunch** thief; [by] Anne C. Bromley; illustrated by Robert Casilla. Tilbury House Publishers 2010 un il

Grades: 4 5 6   **Fic**

1. School stories 2. Theft -- Fiction 3. Homeless persons -- Fiction

ISBN 0-88448-311-8; 978-0-88448-311-3

LC 2008045822

Rafael is angry that a new student is stealing lunches, but he takes time to learn what the real problem is before acting.

"Full-color illustrations realistically portray the cast of characters and the boys' multicultural school. With a few well-placed remarks by Rafael's hardworking mother and no preachy overtones, this entirely credible story of how a thoughtful boy elects to 'light one candle' in response to the larger problem of homelessness and hunger would make an excellent touchstone for class discussion." SLJ

Brooks, Bruce

Everywhere. Harper & Row 1990 70p lib bdg $16.89

Grades: 4 5 6 7   **Fic**

1. Death -- Fiction 2. Grandfathers -- Fiction

ISBN 0-06-020729-9

LC 90-4073

Afraid that his beloved grandfather will die after suffering a heart attack, a nine-year-old boy agrees to join ten-year-old Dooley in performing a mysterious ritual called soul switching

"Echoes of the great Southern writers with their themes of loneliness and faith can be heard in this masterly novella. . . . Brooks's precise use of language is a tour de force." Horn Book

Brown, Susan Taylor

Hugging the rock; [by] Susan Taylor Brown; [cover illustration by Michael Morgenstern] Tricycle Press 2006 170p $14.95; pa $6.95

Grades: 5 6 7 8   **Fic**

1. Divorce -- Fiction 2. Father-daughter relationship -- Fiction 3. Mother-daughter relationship -- Fiction

ISBN 978-1-58246-180-9; 1-58246-180-5; 978-1-58246-236-3 pa; 1-58246-236-4 pa

LC 2006005738

Through a series of poems, Rachel expresses her feelings about her parents' divorce, living without her mother, and her changing attitude towards her father

"This is a poignant character study of a dysfunctional family. . . . Written in straightforward language, the text clearly reveals Rachel's emotions, describing moments both painful and reassuring." SLJ

Brown, Tami Lewis

The **map** of me. Farrar Straus Giroux 2011 152p $16.99

Grades: 4 5 6   **Fic**

1. Sisters -- Fiction 2. Family life -- Fiction 3. Automobile travel -- Fiction

ISBN 978-0-374-35655-2; 0-374-35655-6

LC 2010029261

Twelve-year-old Margie finds her sister, Peep, intolerable since the youngster skipped from third grade to sixth, but when their mother leaves home, Margie packs Peep into their father's car and starts driving across Kentucky to find her.

This novel "combines pathos and humor for an emotionally resonant story." Publ Wkly

Bruchac, Joseph

Bearwalker; [by] Joseph Bruchac; illustrations by Sally Wern Comport. HarperCollinsPublishers 2007 208p il $15.99; lib bdg $16.89; pa $5.99

Grades: 5 6 7 8   **Fic**

1. Bears -- Fiction 2. Camping -- Fiction 3. Mohawk Indians -- Fiction

ISBN 978-0-06-112309-2; 0-06-112309-9; 978-0-06-112311-5 lib bdg; 0-06-112311-0 lib bdg; 978-0-06-112315-3 pa; 0-06-112315-3 pa

LC 2006-30420

Although the littlest student in his class, thirteen-year-old Baron Braun calls upon the strength and wisdom of his Mohawk ancestors to face both man and beast when he tries to get help for his classmates, who are being terrorized during a school field trip in the Adirondacks.

"This exciting horror story, illustrated with b/w drawings, is based on Native American folklore." Kliatt

Children of the longhouse. Dial Bks. for Young Readers 1996 150p hardcover o.p. pa $5.99

Grades: 4 5 6 7   **Fic**

1. Twins -- Fiction 2. Siblings -- Fiction 3. Mohawk Indians -- Fiction

ISBN 0-8037-1793-8; 0-14-038504-5 pa

LC 95-11344

Eleven-year-old Ohkwa'ri and his twin sister Otsi:stia must make peace with a hostile gang of older boys in their Mohawk village during the late 1400s

"This is a fascinating story that will leave the middle-grade reader with an appreciation for Mohawk culture." Book Rep

Night wings; illustrations by Sally Wern Comport. HarperCollins 2009 194p $15.99; lib bdg $16.89

Grades: 5 6 7 8   **Fic**

1. Monsters -- Fiction 2. Abnaki Indians -- Fiction

ISBN 978-0-06-112318-4; 0-06-112318-8; 978-0-06-112319-1 lib bdg; 0-06-112319-6 lib bdg

LC 2008032096

After being taken captive by a band of treasure seekers, thirteen-year-old Paul and his Abenaki grandfather must face a legendary Native American monster at the top of Mount Washington.

"The intriguing Native lore, the realistic teen narrative, and cliffhanger sentences that build suspense at the end of each chapter are signature Bruchac and will captivate readers." SLJ

★ **Skeleton** man. HarperCollins Pubs. 2001 114p il $15.99; pa $4.99

Grades: 4 5 6 7   **Fic**

1. Kidnapping 2. Mohawk Indians 3. Psychopaths 4. Kidnapping -- Fiction 5. Mohawk Indians -- Fiction 6. Indians of North America -- New York (State)

ISBN 0-06-029075-7; 0-06-440888-4 pa

LC 00-54345

After her parents disappear and she is turned over to the care of a strange "great-uncle," Molly must rely on her dreams about an old Mohawk story for her safety and maybe even for her life

"The mix of traditional and contemporary cultural references adds to the story's haunting appeal, and the quick pace and suspense . . . will likely hold the interest of young readers." Publ Wkly

Another title about Skeleton man is:

The return of Skeleton man (2006)

The **arrow** over the door; pictures by James Watling. Dial Bks. for Young Readers 1998 89p il hardcover o.p. pa $4.99

Grades: 4 5 6   **Fic**

1. Quakers -- Fiction 2. Native Americans -- Fiction 3. Society of Friends -- Fiction 4. United States -- History -- 18th century -- Fiction 5. Indians of North America -- New York (State) -- Fiction 6. Indians of North America -- New York (State) -- Juvenile fiction

ISBN 0-8037-2078-5; 0-14-130571-1 pa

LC 96-36701

"Bruchac's elegant and powerful writing fills in much of the fascinating detail of this serendipitous wartime friendship. . . . Watling's rugged, textured pen-and-ink drawings provide an atmospheric backdrop." Publ Wkly

★ The **dark** pond; illustrations by Sally Wern Comport. HarperCollins 2004 142p il hardcover o.p. pa $6.99

Grades: 5 6 7 8   **Fic**

1. Ponds 2. Schools 3. Monsters 4. Shawnee Indians 5. Boarding schools 6. Ponds -- Fiction 7. Monsters -- Fiction 8. Indians of North America 9. Shawnee Indians -- Fiction

ISBN 0-06-052995-4; 0-06-052998-9 pa

LC 2003-22212

After he feels a mysterious pull drawing him toward a dark, shadowy pond in the woods, Armie looks to old Native American tales for guidance about the dangerous monster lurking in the water

"Effectively illustrated by Comport, this eerie story skillfully entwines Native American lore, suspense, and the realization that people and things are not always what they seem to be on the surface. . . . A perfect choice for reluctant readers." SLJ

The **winter** people. Dial Bks. 2002 168p $16.99; pa $5.99

Grades: 5 6 7 8   **Fic**

1. Abnaki Indians -- Fiction

ISBN 0-8037-2694-5; 0-14-240229-X pa

LC 2002-338

As the French and Indian War rages in October of 1759, Saxso, a fourteen-year-old Abenaki boy, pursues the English rangers who have attacked his village and taken his mother and sisters hostage

"The narrative itself is thrilling, its spiritual aspects enlightening." Booklist

Bruchac, Joseph, 1942-

Dragon castle. Dial Books for Young Readers 2011 346p $16.99

Grades: 4 5 6 7   **Fic**

1. Fairy tales 2. Dragons -- Fiction 3. Princes -- Fiction 4. Kings and rulers -- Fiction

ISBN 978-0-8037-3376-3; 0-8037-3376-3

LC 2010028798

Young prince Rashko, aided by wise old Georgi, must channel the power of his ancestor, Pavol the great, and harness a magical dragon to face the evil Baron Temny after the foolish King and Queen go missing.

Bruchac "spins a good-natured and humorous fairy tale. . . . With its subtle focus on peaceful resistance and use of classic folk-tale elements, this story exudes a gentle sense of fun." Publ Wkly

Squanto's journey; the story of the first Thanksgiving. Joseph Bruchac; illustrated by Greg Shed. Silver Whistle 2000 32 p. (paperback) $6.99; (prebind) $15.99; (reinforced) $17

Grades: 2 3 4 5   **Fic**

1. Wampanoag Indians 2. Pilgrims (New England colonists) -- Fiction 3. Wampanoag Indians -- Fiction 4. Wampanoag Indians -- Juvenile fiction 5. Pilgrims (New Plymouth Colony) -- Fiction 6. Indians of North America -- Massachusetts -- Fiction

ISBN 9780152060442; 9781442073890; 0152018174; 9780152018177

LC 99012012

This illustrated children's book, by Joseph Bruchac, illustrated by Greg Shed, tells the story of the 17th century Native American Squanto. "In 1620 an English ship called the Mayflower landed on the shores inhabited by the Pokanoket people, and it was Squanto who welcomed the newcomers and taught them how to survive in the rugged land they called Plymouth." (Publisher's note)

Bruel, Nick

A **Bad** Kitty Christmas. Roaring Brook Press 2011 un il $15.99

Grades: 2 3 4   **Fic**

1. Stories in rhyme 2. Cats -- Fiction 3. Christmas stories 4. Christmas -- Fiction

ISBN 978-1-59643-668-8; 1-59643-668-9

LC 2010037814

After destroying all of the gifts and decorations at home, Bad Kitty escapes from the car on Christmas Eve and finds a new friend, who helps her learn the true meaning of Christmas.

"Kitty's zany antics, three romps through the alphabet, and a warm reunion make this a gift indeed for Bad Kitty fans." Publ Wkly

Bad Kitty gets a bath. Roaring Brook Press 2008 125p il $12.95

Grades: 2 3 4   **Fic**

1. Cats -- Fiction 2. Baths -- Fiction
ISBN 978-1-59643-341-0; 1-59643-341-8

LC 2008-20296

Takes a humorous look at the normal way cats bathe, why it is inappropriate for humans to bathe that way, and the challenges of trying to give a cat a real bath with soap and water. Includes fun facts, glossary, and other information.

This "pairs Bruel's witty asides and spastic, tongue-in-cheek commentaries with more high-energy cartoon illustrations. . . . Young and reluctant readers will get plenty of laughs from this comic and informative chapter book." Booklist

Bad Kitty vs. Uncle Murray; the uproar at the front door. Roaring Brook Press 2010 157p il $13.99

Grades: 2 3 4   **Fic**

1. Cats -- Fiction
ISBN 978-1-59643-596-4; 1-59643-596-8

Uncle Murray "is here to 'pet sit' Bad Kitty and Poor Puppy. The feline is not happy with this arrangement and gives Uncle Murray a horrible time. . . . Different fonts and huge scrawling words appear throughout, and the black-and-white cartoons on every page often show Bad Kitty and Murray with exaggerated gestures. The style gives the book a fast pace and adds to the comedic atmosphere." SLJ

Bad kitty meets the baby. Roaring Brook Press 2011 143p il $13.99

Grades: 2 3 4   **Fic**

1. Cats -- Fiction 2. Infants -- Fiction 3. Adoption -- Fiction
ISBN 978-1-59643-597-1; 1-59643-597-6

LC 2010035699

Bad kitty is not pleased when a baby joins her family. Includes fun facts and tips for training a cat to perform tricks.

Bruel "offers his trademark spastic black-and-white illustrations in full-bleed and spots with plenty of baby and cat sounds in dialogue bubbles (translated into English where necessary). . . . Further proof that Bad Kitty can be good . . . especially in the eyes of her many fans." Kirkus

Happy birthday Bad Kitty. Roaring Brook Press 2009 159p il $13.99

Grades: 2 3 4   **Fic**

1. Cats -- Fiction 2. Birthdays -- Fiction
ISBN 978-1-59643-342-7; 1-59643-342-6

"Bad Kitty's day starts off with a special alphabetical "Birthday Breakfast" that includes Aardvark Bagels, Clam Doughnuts and Eel Fritters. Each chapter focuses on a different part of the day's festivities. . . . The story becomes a whodunit when Bad Kitty's presents vanish and the prime suspect ends up being the lovable slow-wit, Puppy. . . . Bruel has fun with the format, using footnotes, different font sizes, comedic/informative interludes about cat behavior. . . . As usual, it's Bad Kitty's unapologetic, curmudgeon nature that delivers the laugh-out-loud funny." SLJ

Buckingham, Royce

Demonkeeper. G. P. Putnam's Sons 2007 216p hardcover o.p. pa $7.99

Grades: 4 5 6 7   **Fic**

1. Horror fiction 2. Supernatural -- Fiction
ISBN 978-0-399-24649-4; 0-399-24649-5; 978-0-14-241166-7 pa; 0-14-241166-3 pa

LC 2006-26541

When Nat, the weirdest boy in Seattle, leaves for a date with the plainest girl in town, chaos breaks out in the houseful of demons of which he is the sole guardian.

"This is horror on the mild side. . . . The easygoing, breezy humor adds appeal to an already engaging premise." Bull Cent Child Books

Buckley, Michael

The **Everafter** War; pictures by Peter Ferguson. Amulet Books 2009 306p il (The Sisters Grimm) $14.95; pa $6.95

Grades: 4 5 6   **Fic**

1. War stories 2. Mystery fiction 3. Magic -- Fiction 4. Sisters -- Fiction
ISBN 978-0-8109-8355-7; 0-8109-8355-9; 978-0-8109-8429-5 pa; 0-8109-8429-6 pa

LC 2008045924

After their parents awake from a sleeping spell, Daphne and Sabrina become caught in the middle of a war between the Scarlet Hand and Prince Charming's Everafter army and learn a shocking secret about a deadly enemy.

Magic and other misdemeanors; pictures by Peter Ferguson. Amulet Books 2007 283p il (The Sisters Grimm) $14.95; pa $6.95

Grades: 4 5 6   **Fic**

1. Mystery fiction 2. Magic -- Fiction 3. Sisters -- Fiction 4. Grandmothers -- Fiction
ISBN 978-0-8109-9358-7; 0-8109-9358-9; 978-0-8109-7263-6 pa; 0-8109-7263-8 pa

LC 2007029429

Fairy-tale detectives Sabrina and Daphne Grimm face their first case without Granny Relda's help when the future gets mixed up with the past in Ferryport Landing, and because some of the future does not look bright, Puck helps them try to make some changes.

Once upon a crime; pictures by Peter Ferguson. Amulet Books 2007 271p (The Sisters Grimm) $14.95; pa $6.95

Grades: 4 5 6   **Fic**

1. Mystery fiction 2. Sisters -- Fiction 3. Grandmothers -- Fiction
ISBN 978-0-8109-1610-4; 0-8109-1610-X; 978-0-8109-9549-9 pa; 0-8109-9549-2 pa

LC 2006033516

When the fairy-tale detectives rush to New York City hoping to find an Everafter who can cure Puck, they trigger a chain of events that includes a murder mystery, and learn many new things about their mother who, along with their father, is still in an enchanted sleep.

Tales from the hood; pictures by Peter Ferguson. Amulet Books 2009 274p il (The Sisters Grimm) $14.95

Grades: 4 5 6   **Fic**

1. Mystery fiction 2. Magic -- Fiction 3. Trials --

Fiction 4. Sisters -- Fiction

ISBN 978-0-8109-9478-2; 0-8109-9478-X

LC 2008000962

When a kangaroo court of Everafters, led by Judge Mad Hatter, tries Mr. Canis for his past crimes as the Big Bad Wolf, the Grimms seek evidence to save their friend, although Sabrina questions whether he should be saved.

The **fairy** -tale detectives; pictures by Peter Ferguson. Amulet Books 2005 284p il (The sisters Grimm) $15.95

Grades: 4 5 6 **Fic**

1. Fairy tales 2. Orphans -- Fiction 3. Sisters -- Fiction 4. Monsters -- Fiction 5. Grandmothers -- Fiction

ISBN 0-8109-5925-9

LC 2005011784

"After the mysterious disappearance of their parents, Sabrina and Daphne Grimm spend a year and a half as victims of New York's foster care system until a woman claiming to be their long-dead grandmother comes to claim them. . . . Granny reveals to the girls that they are descendants of the Brothers Grimm, and the fairy tales that the brothers wrote are actually a history of the magical people known as 'Everafters.'. . . Sabrina and Daphne are intrepid heroines, and the modern interpretations of familiar fairy-tale characters are often truly hilarious." Voice Youth Advocates

Other titles in this series are:

The usual suspects (2005)

The problem child (2006)

Once upon a crime (2007)

Magic and other misdemeanors (2007)

Tales from the hood (2008)

The Everafter War (2009)

The inside story (2010)

The **inside** story; pictures by Peter Ferguson. Amulet Books 2010 il (The Sisters Grimm) $15.95

Grades: 4 5 6 **Fic**

1. Mystery fiction 2. Magic -- Fiction 3. Sisters -- Fiction

ISBN 978-0-8109-8430-1; 0-8109-8430-X

LC 2009052207

As the fairytale detectives race through the Book of Everafter searching for their baby brother, they encounter various characters including the Editor and his army of Revisers, who threaten the children with dire consequences if they continue to change the stories.

The **problem** child; pictures by Peter Ferguson. Abrams 2006 292p (The Sisters Grimm) $15.95; pa $6.95

Grades: 4 5 6 **Fic**

1. Mystery fiction 2. Orphans -- Fiction 3. Sisters -- Fiction 4. Grandmothers -- Fiction

ISBN 0-8109-4914-8; 0-8109-9359-7 pa

With the help of a long lost relative, and a little magic, Sabrina Grimm and her sister Daphne try to find out who has kidnapped their parents and rescue them.

"Recommend this to anyone who is craving a bit of dark humor rolled up with whimsy and adventure." SLJ

The **unusual** suspects; illustrated by Peter Ferguson. Amulet Books 2005 290p (The Sisters Grimm) $14.95; pa $6.95

Grades: 4 5 6 **Fic**

1. Mystery fiction 2. Orphans -- Fiction 3. Sisters -- Fiction 4. Monsters -- Fiction 5. Grandmothers -- Fiction

ISBN 978-0-8109-5926-2; 0-8109-5926-7; 978-0-8109-9323-5 pa; 0-8109-9323-6 pa

LC 2005024149

"In this second book in the series, Sabrina and Daphne continue their family's fairy-tale detective work in the Hudson River town of Ferryport Landing. . . . Here, the sisters start attending the local elementary school where the principal just happens to be the Pied Piper of Hamelin and Snow White is a most beloved teacher. Almost instantly, one of their teachers is found dead in his classroom. . . . The story is fast paced and the main characters are sympathetic and appealing." SLJ

Bunting, Eve

Blackwater. HarperCollins Pubs. 1999 146p hardcover o.p. pa $5.99

Grades: 5 6 7 8 **Fic**

1. Death -- Fiction 2. Guilt -- Fiction

ISBN 0-06-027843-9 lib bdg; 0-06-440890-6 pa

LC 99-24895

When a boy and girl are drowned in the Blackwater River, thirteen-year-old Brodie must decide whether to confess that he may have caused the accident

"Bunting's thought-provoking theme, solid characterization and skillful juggling of suspense and pathos make this a top-notch choice." Publ Wkly

Nasty, stinky sneakers. HarperCollins Pubs. 1994 105p hardcover o.p. lib bdg $15.89; pa $4.99

Grades: 4 5 6 **Fic**

ISBN 0-06-024236-1; 0-06-024237-X lib bdg; 0-06-440507-9 pa

LC 93-34641

Will ten-year-old Colin find his missing stinky sneakers in time to enter The Stinkiest Sneakers in the World contest?

"A fast-paced, funny book that should elicit some delighted groans." Horn Book Guide

Burch, Robert

Ida Early comes over the mountain. Viking 1980 145p hardcover o.p. pa $4.99

Grades: 4 5 6 7 **Fic**

1. Country life -- Fiction 2. Great Depression, 1929-1939 -- Fiction

ISBN 0-14-034534-5 pa

LC 79-20532

"The book works on two levels—the hilarious account of Ida Early's exotic housekeeping in which real cleverness and skill is as effective and amazing as any fantasy magic, and the gentle, touching story of an ungainly woman's longing for beauty and femininity. . . . [A] fine book." SLJ

Another title about Ida Early is:

Christmas with Ida Early (1983)

Queenie Peavy; illustrated by Jerry Lazare. Viking 1966 159p il hardcover o.p. pa $5.99

Grades: 5 6 7 8 **Fic**

ISBN 0-14-032305-8 pa

"Queenie is so real that the reader becomes deeply involved in everything that concerns her." Horn Book

Burnett, Frances Hodgson

A **little** princess; illustrated by Tasha Tudor. Harper-Collins 1999 245p il (Illustrated junior library) $17.99; pa $6.99

Grades: 4 5 6 **Fic**

1. School stories

ISBN 978-0-3973-0693-0; 0-3973-06938; 978-0-06-440187-6 pa; 0-06-440187-1 pa

First American edition published 1892 by Scribner in shorter form with title: Sara Crewe

The story of Sara Crewe, a girl who is sent from India to a boarding school in London, left in poverty by her father's death, and rescued by a mysterious benefactor

"The story is inevitably adorned with sentimental curlicues but the reader will hardly notice them since the story itself is such a satisfying one. Tasha Tudor's gentle, appropriate illustrations make this a lovely edition." Publ Wkly

The **secret** garden; illustrated by Inga Moore. Candlewick Press 2008 278p il $21.99

Grades: 3 4 5 6 **Fic**

1. Gardens -- Fiction 2. Orphans -- Fiction

ISBN 0-7636-3161-2; 978-0-7636-3161-1

LC 2006051838

First published 1911

A ten-year-old orphan comes to live in a lonely house on the Yorkshire moors where she discovers an invalid cousin and the mysteries of a locked garden.

"Burnett's tale . . . is presented in an elegant, oversize volume and handsomely illustrated with Moore's detailed ink and watercolor paintings. Cleanly laid-out text pages are balanced by artwork ranging from delicate spot images to full-page renderings." SLJ

Burns, Khephra

Mansa Musa; the lion of Mali. illustrated by Leo & Diane Dillon. Harcourt 2001 un il $18

Grades: 4 5 6 7 **Fic**

1. Kings

ISBN 0-15-200375-4

LC 97-50559

A fictional account of the nomadic wanderings of the boy who grew up to become Mali's great fourteenth-century leader, Mansa Musa

This is "part coming-of-age tale, part cautionary tale, and part fairy tale. . . . Burn's story moves in a languid magical atmosphere beautifully supported by the Dillons' jewel-like illustrations and stylized text ornaments, which, together with parchment-colored pages, give the impression of an illuminated manuscript." Horn Book

Butler, Dori Hillestad

The **case** of the fire alarm; pictures by Jeremy Tugeau. Albert Whitman & Co. 2010 132p il (The Buddy files) $14.99

Grades: 1 2 3 **Fic**

1. School stories 2. Mystery fiction 3. Dogs -- Fiction

ISBN 978-0-8075-0913-5; 0-8075-0913-2

LC 2010004326

When Buddy goes to school to become a therapy dog, he ends up helping figure out who pulled the fire alarm instead.

"Tugeau's sweet line drawings bring Buddy and friends to life, while Butler keeps the story entertaining and sometimes suspenseful." Kirkus

The **case** of the library monster; pictures by Jeremy Tugeau and Dan Crisp. Albert Whitman 2011 134p il (The Buddy files) $14.99

Grades: 1 2 3 **Fic**

1. School stories 2. Mystery fiction 3. Dogs -- Fiction 4. Libraries -- Fiction

ISBN 978-0-8075-0914-2; 0-8075-0914-0

LC 2010033301

Buddy the dog discovers a strange, blue-tongued creature in the school library, and investigates what it is and how it got there.

"The breezy text, friendly illustrations, and, above all, likable dog hero continue to make this series a solid choice for readers new to chapter books." Horn Book Guide

The **case** of the lost boy; pictures by Jeremy Tugeau. Albert Whitman 2010 123p il (The Buddy files) $14.99

Grades: 1 2 3 **Fic**

1. Mystery fiction 2. Dogs -- Fiction 3. Missing children -- Fiction

ISBN 978-0-8075-0910-4; 0-8075-0910-8

LC 2009-23763

While searching for his mysteriously lost human family, King the dog detective is adoped by another family, who names him Buddy.

"The type is large, the text is easy, and the occasional black-and-white illustrations complement the text well. The clues are unique and true to the fact that a dog is telling the story." SLJ

Other titles in this series are:

The case of the mixed up mutts (2010)

The case of the fire alarm (2010)

The case of the missing family (2010)

The case of the library monster (2011)

The **case** of the missing family; pictures by Jeremy Tugeau. Albert Whitman & Co. 2010 131p il (The Buddy files) $14.99

Grades: 1 2 3 **Fic**

1. Mystery fiction 2. Dogs -- Fiction 3. Missing persons -- Fiction

ISBN 978-0-8075-0912-8; 0-8075-0912-4

Buddy the dog risks everything when he leaves his new family to investigate what happened to his beloved Kayla and her father, his beloved former owners, by slipping into a van her uncle Marty is using to empty her house in the middle of the night.

"Effective twists and turns, humor, and the possibilities of becoming a school therapy dog and learning to read ease the bittersweet conclusion." SLJ

The **case** of the mixed-up mutts; pictures by Jeremy Tugeau. Albert Whitman 2010 128p il (The Buddy files) $14.99

Grades: 1 2 3 **Fic**

1. Mystery fiction 2. Dogs -- Fiction

ISBN 978-0-8075-0911-1; 0-8075-0911-6

While attending obedience class with his new humans, Buddy the dog helps solve a mystery involving two Pomeranians that were switched at the dog park.

The **truth** about Truman School; by Dori Hillestad Butler. Albert Whitman 2008 170p $15.95; pa $7.99

Grades: 5 6 7 8 **Fic**

1. School stories 2. Bullies -- Fiction 3. Journalism -- Fiction 4. Newspapers -- Fiction

ISBN 978-0-8075-8095-0; 0-8075-8095-3; 978-0-8075-8096-7 pa; 0-8075-8096-1 pa

LC 2007-29977

Tired of being told what to write by the school newspaper's advisor, Zibby and her friend Amr start an underground newspaper online where everyone is free to post anything, but things spiral out of control when a cyberbully starts using the site to harrass one popular girl.

"The story moves at a good pace and the timely subject of cyberbullying will be relevant to readers. The language is accessible and the students' voices ring true." SLJ

Butterworth, Oliver

★ The **enormous** egg; illustrated by Louis Darling. Little, Brown 1956 187p il hardcover o.p. pa $6.99

Grades: 4 5 6 7 **Fic**

1. Dinosaurs -- Fiction

ISBN 0-316-11920-2 pa

This story is "great fun. . . . And if you have any trouble visualizing a Triceratops moving placidly through the twentieth-century world you need only turn to Louis Darling's illustrations to believe." NY Times Book Rev

Buyea, Rob

★ **Because** of Mr. Terupt. Delacorte Press 2010 269p $16.99; lib bdg $19.99

Grades: 4 5 6 **Fic**

1. School stories 2. Teachers -- Fiction 3. Family life -- Fiction

ISBN 0-385-73882-X; 0-385-90749-4 lib bdg; 978-0-385-73882-8; 978-0-385-90749-1 lib bdg

LC 2010-03414

Seven fifth-graders at Snow Hill School in Connecticut relate how their lives are changed for the better by "rookie teacher" Mr. Terupt. "Grades four to six." (Bull Cent Child Books)

"Introducing characters and conflicts that will be familiar to any middle-school student, this powerful and emotional story is likely to spur discussion." Publ Wkly

Mr. Terupt falls again; Rob Buyea. Delacorte Press 2012 356 p. (hc) $16.99

Grades: 4 5 6 **Fic**

1. Love stories 2. School stories 3. Teacher-student relationship -- Fiction 4. Summer -- Fiction 5. Classrooms -- Fiction 6. Summer -- Juvenile fiction 7. Moving, Household -- Fiction 8. Classrooms -- Juvenile fiction 9. Moving, Household -- Juvenile fiction 10. Teacher-student relationships -- Fiction 11. Teacher-student relationships -- Juvenile fiction

ISBN 0385742053; 9780375989100; 9780375990380; 9780385742054

LC 2012010897

This book is a follow-up to Rob Buyea's "Because of Mr. Terupt." Here, "looping with his students into sixth grade, Mr. Terupt continues to surprise them with challenging projects and perfect reading suggestions." For the seven students who narrate the story, "family worries go along with lingering questions about the health of their teacher. Sixth-grade relationships and a grown-up romance" are also explored. (Kirkus)

Buzbee, Lewis

The **haunting** of Charles Dickens; [illustrated by] Greg Ruth. Feiwel and Friends 2009 357p il $17.99

Grades: 5 6 7 8 **Fic**

1. Authors 2. Novelists 3. Mystery fiction 4. Authors -- Fiction 5. Kidnapping -- Fiction 6. Family life -- Fiction 7. Missing persons -- Fiction

ISBN 978-0-312-38256-8; 0-312-38256-1

LC 2008028553

Twelve-year-old Meg travels the rooftops and streets of 1862 London, England, in search of her missing brother, Orion, accompanied by a family friend, the famed author Charles Dickens, whose quest is to find his next novel.

"Buzbee creates solid characters . . . and an authentic flavor of Dickensian London, enhanced by Ruth's striking and evocative b&w drawings . . . ., while addressing issues of feminism, the search for identity, and child abuse." Publ Wkly

Byars, Betsy Cromer

Little Horse; [by] Betsy Byars; illustrated by David McPhail. Holt & Co. 2001 45p il $15.95

Grades: 1 2 3 **Fic**

1. Horses 2. Horses -- Fiction

ISBN 0-8050-6413-3

LC 00-40983

Little Horse falls into the stream and is swept away into a dangerous adventure and a new life

"Byars deftly combines crisp action with a lyrically evoked setting. Language is simple, but not simplistic; uncommon terms are clearly defined in the text and the soft black-and-white art." Horn Book Guide

Another title about Little Horse is:

Little Horse on his own (2004)

The **SOS** file; [by] Betsy Byars, Betsy Duffey, Laurie Myers; illustrated by Arthur Howard. Henry Holt 2004 71p il $15.95

Grades: 3 4 5 **Fic**

1. Schools 2. Storytelling 3. School stories

ISBN 0-8050-6888-0

LC 2003-18240

The students in Mr. Magro's class submit stories for the SOS file about their biggest emergencies, and then they read them aloud for extra credit

"Some tales are poignant, others are humorous; all are as credible as the characters sketched. . . . Lighthearted sketches enhance characterization. . . . [An] engaging, plausible, and highly readable collection of anecdotes." SLJ

Tornado; by Betsy Byars; illustrations by Doron Ben-Ami. HarperCollins Pubs. 1996 49p il lib bdg $15.89; pa $4.99

Grades: 2 3 4 **Fic**

1. Dogs -- Fiction 2. Tornadoes -- Fiction

ISBN 0-06-026452-7 lib bdg; 0-06-442063-9 pa

LC 95-41584

As they wait out a tornado in their storm cellar, a family listens to their farmhand tell stories about the dog that was blown into his life by another tornado when he was a boy

"The handsome illustrations by Doron Ben-Ami give the volume a more distinguished, less juvenile look than the typical chapter book and convey the story's drama, warmth, and occasional humor. Parents and teachers will find this an excellent book to read aloud, and dog lovers of any age will find it irresistible." Booklist

★ The **dark** stairs; a Herculeah Jones mystery. by Betsy Byars. Viking 1994 130p hardcover o.p. pa $5.99
Grades: 4 5 6   **Fic**
  1. Mystery fiction
  ISBN 0-670-85487-5; 0-14-240592-2 pa
                 LC 94-14012

The intrepid Herculeah Jones helps her mother, a private investigator, solve a puzzling and frightening case

"There is plenty to laugh at in this book, including classic chapter headings guaranteed to cause shivers for the uninitiated; practiced mystery readers may feel that they are in on a bit of a joke and appreciate the hint of parody. This is a page-turner that is sure to entice the most reluctant readers." SLJ
Other titles about Herculeah Jones are:
Tarot says beware (1995)
Dead letter (1996)
Death's door (1997)
Disappearing acts (1998)
The black tower (2006)
King of murder (2006)

The **keeper** of the doves; by Betsy Byars. Viking 2002 121p $14.99; pa $5.99
Grades: 4 5 6 7   **Fic**
  1. Sisters -- Fiction 2. Family life -- Fiction
  ISBN 0-670-03576-9; 0-14-240063-7 pa
                 LC 2002-9283

In the late 1800s in Kentucky, Amie McBee and her four sisters both fear and torment the reclusive and seemingly sinister Mr. Tominski, but their father continues to provide for his needs

"This is Byars at her best—witty, appealing, thought-provoking." Horn Book

The **not** -just-anybody family; [by] Betsy Byars. Holiday House 2008 176p pa $6.95
Grades: 5 6 7 8   **Fic**
  1. Siblings -- Fiction 2. Family life -- Fiction
  ISBN 978-0-8234-2145-9 pa; 0-8234-2145-7 pa
                 LC 2007-42253

First published 1986 by Delacorte Press
With a young brother in the hospital, a grandfather in jail, and their mother traveling with a rodeo, Maggie and Vern try to settle family problems

"The story of the pathetically self-reliant, eccentric, but deeply loving family makes a book that is funny and sad, warm and wonderful." [review of 1986 edition] Horn Book
Other titles about the Blossom family are:
A Blossom promise (1987)
The Blossoms and the Green Phantom (1987)
The Blossoms meet the Vulture Lady (1986)

Wanted-Mud Blossom (1991)

★ The **pinballs**; [by] Betsy Byars. Harper & Row 1977 136p lib bdg $16.89; pa $5.99
Grades: 5 6 7 8   **Fic**
  1. Friendship -- Fiction 2. Foster home care -- Fiction
  ISBN 0-06-020918-6 lib bdg; 0-06-440198-7 pa

"A deceptively simple, eloquent story, its pain and acrimony constantly mitigated by the author's light, offhand style and by Carlie's wryly comic view of life." Horn Book

Cabot, Meg

Allie Finkle's rules for girls: book two; The new girl; [by] Meg Cabot. 1st ed.; Scholastic Press 2008 222p $15.99
Grades: 3 4 5   **Fic**
  1. School stories 2. Moving -- Fiction 3. Bullies -- Fiction 4. Friendship -- Fiction 5. Family life -- Fiction 6. Grandmothers -- Fiction
  ISBN 978-0-545-04049-5; 0-545-04049-3
                 LC 2007050719

Guided by her rules, nine-year-old Allie works to get past being just the new girl at school, eagerly awaits the arrival of her kitten, and faces turmoil when her grandmother visits while the family is still settling into their new home.

Best friends and drama queens. Scholastic Press 2009 202p (Allie Finkle's rules for girls) $15.99
Grades: 3 4 5   **Fic**
  1. School stories 2. Friendship -- Fiction
  ISBN 978-0-545-04043-3; 0-545-04043-4
                 LC 2008032678

Nine-year-old Allie Finkle's list of rules helps her navigate a tricky situation with a new girl at school.
This "sympathetically portrays the broad emotional range of fourth-graders." Booklist

Blast from the past. Scholastic Press 2010 224p (Allie Finkle's rules for girls) $15.99
Grades: 3 4 5   **Fic**
  1. School stories 2. Friendship -- Fiction
  ISBN 978-0-545-04048-8; 0-545-04048-5
                 LC 2010014160

Fourth-grader Allie establishes a new set of rules after she is forced to pair up with ex-best friend Mary Kay on a class trip to a historic one-room schoolhouse.
"Sometimes wryly amusing, this first-person chapter book . . . captures the day-to-day thoughts of this well-intentioned narrator." Booklist

Glitter girls and the great fake out. Scholastic Press 194p (Allie Finkle's rules for girls) $15.99
Grades: 3 4 5   **Fic**
  1. Friendship -- Fiction 2. Truthfulness and falsehood -- Fiction
  ISBN 978-0-545-04047-1; 0-545-04047-7

While trying to spare Erica's feelings so she could go to Brittany's birthday party, Allie disobeys one of her own rules and lies.
"Fine-tuned to the nuances of human relations and self-justification, Cabot creates another eminently readable, first-person narrative." Booklist

Moving day. Scholastic Press 2008 228p (Allie Finkle's rules for girls) $15.99; pa $5.99

Grades: 3 4 5   **Fic**

1. School stories 2. Moving -- Fiction 3. Friendship -- Fiction 4. Family life -- Fiction

ISBN 978-0-545-03947-5; 0-545-03947-9; 978-0-545-04041-9 pa; 0-545-04041-8 pa

               LC 2007-27836

Nine-year-old Allie Finkle has rules for everything and is even writing her own rule book, but her world is turned upside-down when she learns that her family is moving across town, which will mean a new house, school, best friend, and plenty of new rules.

Cabot's "trademark frank humor makes for compulsive reading—as always. . . . Allie is funny, believable and plucky . . . but most of all, and most interestingly, Allie is ambivalent." Publ Wkly

Other titles in this series are:

The new girl (2008)

Best friends and drama queens (2009)

Stage fright (2009)

Glitter girls and the great fake out (2010)

Blast from the past (2010)

Stage fright. Scholastic Press 2009 216p (Allie Finkle's rules for girls) $15.99

Grades: 3 4 5   **Fic**

1. School stories 2. Theater -- Fiction 3. Friendship -- Fiction 4. Family life -- Fiction

ISBN 978-0-545-04045-7; 0-545-04045-0

               LC 2009005422

Allie's theatrical hopes are crushed when, instead of being cast as the princess, she is given the role of the evil queen in the fourth-grade class play.

"Written in a convincingly childlike voice, Allie's appealing first-person narrative features wry observations of the foibles, actions, emotions, and relationships of both the children and the adults in her life." Booklist

Cadenhead, Mackenzie

Sally's bones; illustrated by T. S. Spookytooth. Sourcebook Jabberwocky 2011 il pa $6.99

Grades: 4 5 6   **Fic**

1. Mystery fiction 2. Dogs -- Fiction 3. Skeleton -- Fiction

ISBN 978-1-4022-5943-2; 1-4022-5943-3

2 Months, 28 Days, 9 Hours, and 12 minutes earlier Sally Simplesmith's life changed forever. She came face-to-face with death a delightful, dearly departed little dog she lovingly calls Bones. But when the cadaverous canine is accused of a crime he didn't commit, Sally decides to solve the case herself!

"Writing a novel that tackles tough issues like grief and loss while maintaining a measure of levity is no easy feat, but that is exactly what Cadenhead accomplishes here. . . . Spooky without being scary, dark without being morbid, this is a winning tale about loyalty in the face of loss." Booklist

Calkhoven, Laurie

Daniel at the Siege of Boston, 1776. Dutton Children's Books 2010 195p (Boys of wartime) $16.99

Grades: 4 5 6 7   **Fic**

1. Spies -- Fiction 2. Patriotism -- Fiction 3. Family

life -- Fiction

ISBN 978-0-525-42144-3; 0-525-42144-0

               LC 2009012125

In 1776 Boston, twelve-year-old Daniel Prescott enjoys assuming his father's role in taking care of his mother and sister, as well as his work as a spy and messenger for the American revolutionaries, but the pleasure ends when he witnesses the horrors of war firsthand, and learns that a trusted patriot is actually a British spy.

"This historical novel weaves actual people, places, and events of the Siege of Boston into an engaging fictional narrative." Booklist

Michael at the invasion of France, 1943; by Laurie Calkhoven. Dial Books for Young Readers 2012 231 p.

Grades: 4 5 6 7   **Fic**

1. Children and war -- Fiction 2. Nazi persecution -- Fiction 3. France -- History -- 1940-1945, German occupation -- Fiction 4. World War, 1939-1945 -- Underground movements -- France -- Fiction 5. World War, 1939-1945 -- Underground movements -- France -- Juvenile fiction

ISBN 0803737246; 9780803737242

               LC 2011021634

In this young adult novel, a "young Parisian joins the French Resistance in this Boys of Wartime series entry. . . . Michael joins a friend in distributing taunting leaflets. His involvement in Resistance activities soon escalates into helping captured British and American airmen make their way to Spain. At first he acts only as a courier of forged identity documents, but later he helps first to slip a Jewish neighbor's child out of the city, then hides an ailing American. . . . Meanwhile, he serves as a witness to . . . wartime life under the Nazis, while seeing friends, neighbors and his own older brother taken away and ultimately earning sufficient self-esteem to lose his dependence on his father's regard." (Kirkus)

Includes bibliographical references

Will at the Battle of Gettysburg, 1863. Dutton Children's Books 2011 230p (Boys of wartime) $16.99

Grades: 4 5 6 7   **Fic**

1. Gettysburg (Pa.), Battle of, 1863 -- Fiction

ISBN 978-0-525-42145-0; 0-525-42145-9

               LC 2010013307

In 1863, twelve-year-old Will, who longs to be a drummer in the Union army, is stuck in his sleepy hometown of Gettysburg, Pennsylvania, but when the Union and Confederate armies meet right there in his town, he and his family are caught up in the fight. Includes historical notes, glossary, and a timeline of events.

"This solid piece of fiction will appeal to history buffs and reluctant readers alike." SLJ

Includes glossary and bibliographical references

Cameron, Ann

Colibri. Farrar, Straus & Giroux 2003 227p $17; pa $5.99

Grades: 5 6 7 8   **Fic**

1. Mayas -- Fiction 2. Kidnapping -- Fiction

ISBN 0-374-31519-1; 0-440-42052-0 pa

               LC 2002-192542

Kidnapped when she was very young by an unscrupulous man who has forced her to lie and beg to get money, a twelve-year-old Mayan girl endures an abusive life, always wishing she could return to the parents she can hardly remember

"The taut, chilling suspense and search for riches will keep readers flying through the pages. But it's Cameron's beautiful language and Rosa's larger identity quest that make this novel extraordinary." Booklist

Gloria's way; pictures by Lis Toft. Farrar, Straus & Giroux 2000 96p il hardcover o.p. pa $4.99

Grades: 2 3 4   **Fic**
   1. Friendship 2. African Americans 3. Parent and child 4. Friendship -- Fiction 5. Family life -- Fiction 6. African Americans -- Fiction
   ISBN 0-374-32670-3; 0-14-230023-3 pa
                  LC 99-12104

This companion volume to the series featuring Julian and Huey centers on their friend Gloria. Gloria shares special times with her mother and father and with her friends

"Lis Toft's shaded pencil drawings portray these African American characters and their predicaments with warmth and humor." Booklist

Another title about Gloria is:
Gloria rising (2002)

★ **Spunky** tells all; pictures by Lauren Castillo. Farrar Straus Giroux 2011 105p il $15.99

Grades: 2 3 4   **Fic**
   1. Cats -- Fiction 2. Dogs -- Fiction
   ISBN 978-0-374-38000-7; 0-374-38000-7
                  LC 2010019815

Called a troublemaker by his human family, a reflective dog defends himself and then relates the family's adoption of an aristocratic but incompetent cat, who gives him a life purpose and and new way of looking at his world.

"Readers ready for chapter books will delight in seeing the world through Spunky's eyes and powerful nose." Kirkus

★ The **stories** Julian tells; illustrated by Ann Strugnell. Pantheon Bks. 1981 71p il hardcover o.p. pa $4.99

Grades: 2 3 4   **Fic**
   1. Family life -- Fiction 2. African Americans -- Fiction
   ISBN 0-394-82892-5 pa
                  LC 80-18023

"Strugnell's delightful drawings depict Julian, his little brother Huey and their parents as black, but they could be members of any family with a stern but loving and understanding father." Publ Wkly

Other titles about Julian and his family are:
Julian, dream doctor (1990)
Julian, secret agent (1988)
Julian's glorious summer (1987)
More stories Huey tells (1997)
More stories Julian tells (1986)
The stories Huey tells (1995)

Campbell, K. G.
   Lester's dreadful sweaters; Keith Campbell. Kids Can Press 2012 32 p. $16.95

Grades: PreK K 1 2   **Fic**
   1. Cousins -- Fiction 2. Picture books for children 3. Sweaters -- Juvenile fiction
   ISBN 1554537703; 9781554537709

In this book, "it's Cousin Clara who knits the dramatically awful, humiliating sweaters of the title. Lester's parents compel him to wear them. . . . One is a 'less-than-pleasant yellow' hoodie with a trailing sleeve and purple pom-poms . . .; another has knitted feathers and striped feet. . . . When a group of performing clowns fall in love with the sweaters . . ., Lester is able to offload his entire collection--and Cousin Clara." (Publishers Weekly)

Carbone, Elisa Lynn
   Blood on the river; James Town 1607. [by] Elisa Carbone. Viking 2006 237p $16.99; pa $6.99

Grades: 5 6 7 8   **Fic**
   1. Powhatan Indians -- Fiction
   ISBN 0-670-06060-7; 0-14-240932-4 pa
                  LC 2005023646

Traveling to the New World in 1606 as the page to Captain John Smith, twelve-year-old orphan Samuel Collier settles in the new colony of James Town, where he must quickly learn to distinguish between friend and foe.

"A strong, visceral story of the hardship and peril settlers faced, as well as the brutal realities of colonial conquest." Booklist

   Storm warriors; [by] Elisa Carbone. Knopf 2001 168p hardcover o.p. pa $6.50

Grades: 4 5 6 7   **Fic**
   1. African Americans -- Fiction
   ISBN 0-375-80664-4; 0-440-41879-8 pa
                  LC 00-59924

In 1895, after his mother's death, twelve-year-old Nathan moves with his father and grandfather to Pea Island off the coast of North Carolina, where he hopes to join the all-black crew at the nearby lifesaving station, despite his father's objections

"This thoughtfully crafted first-person narrative combines historical figures with created characters in the best traditions of the historical novel." Horn Book Guide

Carey, Benedict
   Poison most vial; a mystery. by Benedict Carey. Amulet Books 2012 215 p.

Grades: 5 6 7 8   **Fic**
   1. Mystery fiction 2. Forensic sciences -- Fiction 3. Murder -- Fiction 4. Neighbors -- Fiction 5. Mystery and detective stories 6. Fathers and daughters -- Fiction
   ISBN 1419700316; 9781419700316
                  LC 2011038222

In this novel by Benedict Carey "Ruby's janitor father becomes the prime suspect in a murder . . . [of] [f]orensics expert Dr. Ramachandran . . . [and] the eighth grader decides it's up to her to clear his name. . . . [She] enlists the aid of her large, Jamaican buddy, Rex, and reclusive, retired toxicologist Clara Whitmore, who lives in Ruby's building. What with hacking into computers, evading gangs and like spy-jinx, the mystery demands a lot of brain work." (Kirkus)

Carlson, Natalie Savage
   The **family** under the bridge; pictures by Garth Williams. Harper & Row 1958 99p il lib bdg $16.89; pa $5.99

Grades: 3 4 5   **Fic**
   1. Tramps -- Fiction 2. Christmas -- Fiction
   ISBN 0-06-020991-7 lib bdg; 0-06-440250-9 pa

A Newbery Medal honor book, 1959

"Garth Williams' illustrations are perfect for this thoroughly delightful story of humor and sentiment." Libr J

Carman, Patrick

Beyond the Valley of Thorns. Scholastic/Orchard 2005 221p (The land of Elyon) $12.95

Grades: 5 6 7 8   **Fic**

1. Fantasy fiction

ISBN 0-439-70094-9

When thirteen-year-old Alexa embarks on a mysterious quest, she finds her old friends Yipes the little man, Murphy the squirrel, Odessa the wolf, and Squire the hawk have been designated to help her.

The **Dark** Hills divide; [by] Patrick Carman. Orchard Books 2005 253p (The land of Elyon) $11.95

Grades: 4 5 6 7   **Fic**

1. Fantasy fiction

ISBN 0-439-70093-0

LC 2004-16312

When she finds the key to a secret passageway leading out of the walled city of Bridewell, twelve-year-old Alexa realizes her lifelong wish to explore the mysterious forests and mountains that lie beyond the wall

"Narrator Aasne Vigesaa clearly portrays Alexa's thoughtful, inquisitive nature and unsettled feelings. . . . Vigesaa's excellent use of pace, pitch, and tone help differentiate each character." SLJ

Other titles in this series are:

Beyond the Valley of Thorns (2005)

The tenth city (2006)

Into the mist (2007)

Stargazer (2008)

Floors. Scholastic Press 2011 261p $16.99

Grades: 3 4 5 6   **Fic**

1. Puzzles -- Fiction 2. Hotels and motels -- Fiction 3. Eccentrics and eccentricities -- Fiction

ISBN 978-0-545-25519-6; 0-545-25519-8

LC 2011032516

Ten-year-old Leo's future and the fate of the extraordinary Whippet Hotel, where his father is the maintenance man, are at stake when a series of cryptic boxes leads Leo to hidden floors, strange puzzles, and unexpected alliances.

"The author is a fine storyteller; he rides the mystery right up to the edge invests his characters with quirks that aren't merely cute but essential to the person's identity." Kirkus

Into the mist; by Patrick Carman. Orchard Books 2007 281p (The land of Elyon) $11.95; pa $5.99

Grades: 5 6 7 8   **Fic**

1. Fantasy fiction

ISBN 978-0-439-89952-9; 9780439899987 pa

LC 2006036628

Captain Roland Warvold tells Alexa and Yipes about the adventures he shared with his brother Thomas in Elyon, before the wall went up and divided the world in two.

"Narrator Ron McLarty's skillful, well-paced reading adds excitement, suspense, and thoughtful introspection when needed. He successfully conveys the personalities and emotions of the brothers. In addition to providing back-

ground information for fans of the trilogy, this book is also a fine stand-alone, action-packed fantasy." SLJ

Rivers of fire; [by] Patrick Carman. 1st ed.; Little, Brown & Co. 2008 303p il (Atherton) $16.99

Grades: 5 6 7 8   **Fic**

1. Science fiction 2. Monsters -- Fiction 3. Friendship -- Fiction 4. Social classes -- Fiction

ISBN 978-0-316-16672-0; 0-316-16672-3

LC 2007048366

After Atherton's three-tiered world collapses, ending the geographical division of the social classes, Edgar, Samuel, and Isabel try to restore the flow of water and uncover the world's mysterious origins in the process.

"There's plenty of surface excitement in the book's giant, electric eels; carniverous centipedes; and biblically rising floodwaters." Booklist

Stargazer; [by] Patrick Carman. 1st ed.; Scholastic Press 2008 276p (The land of Elyon) $11.99

Grades: 4 5 6 7   **Fic**

1. Fantasy fiction

ISBN 978-0-439-89951-2; 0-439-89951-6

LC 2007052348

Twelve-year-old Alexa and her companions unwittingly lead Abaddon, now in the form of an enormous, horrible sea monster, to the secret community known as the Five Stone Pillars when they go to bring the people living there home.

The **house** of power. Little, Brown & Co. 2007 330p il (Atherton) $16.99; $16.99; pa $5.99

Grades: 5 6 7 8   **Fic**

1. Science fiction 2. Orphans -- Fiction 3. Friendship -- Fiction 4. Earthquakes -- Fiction 5. Social classes -- Fiction

ISBN 978-0-316-16670-6; 0-316-16670-7; 978-0-316-16671-3 pa; 0-316-16671-5 pa

LC 2006025976

Edgar, an eleven-year-old orphan, finds a book that reveals significant secrets about Atherton, the strictly divided world on which he lives, even as geological changes threaten to shift the power structure that allows a select few to live off the labor of others.

This "is a fast-paced novel with a unique setting, fascinating plot, and cliffhanger ending. It shines because of the author's imagination and skill." SLJ

The **tenth** city; 1st ed.; Orchard Books 2006 186p (The land of Elyon) $11.99

Grades: 4 5 6 7   **Fic**

1. Fantasy fiction

ISBN 0-4397-0095-7

LC 2005008649

Alexa reveals the origin of the Land of Elyon while defending it against the evil Abaddon and his sinister forces, with not only the last Jocasta at stake but also the nature of the land itself.

Carmichael, Clay

★ **Wild** things; [written and illustrated by Clay Carmichael] Front Street 2009 248p il $18.95

Grades: 5 6 7 8   **Fic**

1. Cats -- Fiction 2. Uncles -- Fiction 3. Artists --

Fiction 4. Orphans -- Fiction 5. Family life -- Fiction
ISBN 978-1-59078-627-7; 1-59078-627-0

LC 2007-49911

Stubborn, self-reliant, eleven-year-old Zoe, recently orphaned, moves to the country to live with her prickly half-uncle, a famous doctor and sculptor, and together they learn about trust and the strength of family

"Carmichael gives a familiar plot a fresh new life in this touching story with a finely crafted sense of place." Booklist

Carris, Joan

★ **Welcome** to the Bed & Biscuit; [by] Joan Carris; illustrated by Noah Jones. Candlewick Press 2006 116p il $15.99; pa $5.99

Grades: 2 3 4 **Fic**

1. Animals -- Fiction 2. Veterinarians -- Fiction
ISBN 0-7636-2151-X; 0-7636-4621-0 pa

LC 2004062857

The family animals at the Bed & Biscuit begin to feel slighted when Dr. Bender returns from a fire with something that occupies the time usually reserved for them.

"This is a small, remarkably sweet beginning chapter book with more than its fair share of amusing illustrations and gentle humor." SLJ

Another title about the Bed & Biscuit is:
Wild times at the Bed & Biscuit (2009)

Carris, Joan Davenport

Wild times at the Bed & Biscuit; [by] Joan Carris; illustrated by Noah Z. Jones. Candlewick Press 2009 124p il $15.99; pa $5.99

Grades: 2 3 4 **Fic**

1. Animals -- Fiction 2. Veterinarians -- Fiction
ISBN 978-0-7636-3705-7; 0-7636-3705-X; 978-0-7636-5294-4 pa; 0-7636-5294-6 pa

LC 2008-938398

Ever since Grampa Bender opened his doors (and veterinary skills) to a despondent Canada goose, a cranky muskrat, and two tiny but rebellious fox kits, his animal boarding house has been turned upside down.

This "would make a great read-aloud for the primary grades and is sure to be a hit with competent easy-chapter-book readers." SLJ

Carroll, Lewis, 1832-1898

Alice's adventures in Wonderland; by Lewis Carroll; with forty-two illustrations by John Tenniel. Books of Wonder 1992 196p il $16.99

Grades: 4 5 6 7 **Fic**

1. Fantasy 2. Fantasy fiction
ISBN 0-688-11087-8

LC 91-31482

First published 1865

A little girl falls down a rabbit hole and discovers a world of nonsensical and amusing characters

Lewis Carroll's Alice in Wonderland; illustrated by Rodney Matthews. Candlewick Press 2009 95p il $24.99

Grades: 4 5 6 7 **Fic**

1. Fantasy fiction
ISBN 978-0-7636-4568-7; 0-7636-4568-0

On a hot summer day, a little girl sitting by her sister on the bank, having nothing to do, begins to let her imagination

grow. Her curiosity and hatred of logic cause her to dream of a nonsensical world filled with amusing characters

Matthews' illustrations "have an imagination-stretching, otherworldly veneer. . . . The cartoon artwork portrays Alice with a somewhat angular face and straight blond hair. The depictions of the other characters are fresh and creative. . . . The small-size type, which may demand more accomplished or patient readers, and the sophisticated visual tone make this volume appropriate for older Alice fans." SLJ

Carroll, Michael Owen, 1966-

Super human; Michael Carroll. Philomel Books 2010 325 p. ill. (hardcover) $16.99; (paperback) $8.99

Grades: 5 6 7 8 9 **Fic**

1. Superheroes -- Fiction 2. Good and evil -- Fiction
ISBN 9780399252976; 9780142419052; 0142419052; 0399252975

LC 2009-29965

A group of teenage superheroes tackle a powerful warrior who has been brought back from 4,000 years in the past to enslave the modern world. "Grades eight to ten." (Bull Cent Child Books)

The "exuberant prose is just right for setting, story, and characters alike-this is basically a novel-length superhero comic, sans illustrations, and should easily appeal to fans of the X-Men, Justice League, etc." Publ Wkly

"There is enough fighting in this book to appeal to middle school boys, and the telekinetic Roz, with a controlling superhero big brother, will appeal to girls. This title is a fast read with tension, suspense, and likeable characters." Libr Media Connect

Casanova, Mary

The **klipfish** code; by Mary Casanova. Houghton Mifflin Company 2007 227p map $16

Grades: 4 5 6 7 **Fic**

1. Family life -- Fiction 2. World War, 1939-1945 -- Norway -- Fiction 3. World War, 1939-1945 -- Underground movements -- Fiction
ISBN 978-0-618-88393-6; 0-618-88393-2

LC 2007012752

Sent with her younger brother to Godøy Island to live with her aunt and grandfather after Germans bomb Norway in 1940, ten-year-old Merit longs to join her parents in the Resistance and when her aunt, a teacher, is taken away two years later, she resents even more the Nazis' presence and her grandfather's refusal to oppose them.

"Casanova spins an adventure-filled and harrowing story." SLJ

Includes glossary and bibliographical references

Cassidy, Cathy

Dizzy; a novel. by Cathy Cassidy. Viking 2004 247p hardcover o.p. pa $6.99

Grades: 5 6 7 8 **Fic**

1. Mother-daughter relationship -- Fiction
ISBN 0-670-05936-6; 0-14-240474-8 pa

LC 2004-1642

After an eight-year absence, Dizzy's "New Age traveler" mother suddenly shows up on her twelfth birthday and whisks her away to a series of festivals throughout Scotland in her rattletrap van.

"The eclectic characters and their lifestyle are presented as captivating yet questionable in the girl's first-person narrative, and the well-developed plot fosters concern for Dizzy from the beginning. A unique, satisfying story." SLJ

Indigo Blue. Viking 2005 215p hardcover o.p. pa $6.99

Grades: 5 6 7 8 **Fic**

1. Moving -- Fiction 2. Abused women -- Fiction

ISBN 0-670-05927-7; 0-14-240703-8 pa

Eleven-year-old Indigo, her mother, and her toddler sister have to move out of their apartment because of troubles with Mum's boyfriend, while Indie is also having best friend problems at school, leaving her stressed, confused, and lonely.

"This British story of domestic abuse is firmly child-centered, and Indigo's confusion and fear . . . are sensitively portrayed. . . . The hopeful ending rings true." Booklist

Catalanotto, Peter

No more pumpkins; [by] Peter Catalanotto and Pamela Schembri. Henry Holt 2007 62p (2nd-grade friends) $15.95

Grades: 1 2 3 **Fic**

1. School stories 2. Pumpkin -- Fiction 3. Friendship -- Fiction

ISBN 978-0-8050-7839-8; 0-8050-7839-8

LC 2006035464

Second-grader Emily is tired of pumpkins being at the center of every lesson in school, but she is not prepared when a jealous friend damages the jacko-lantern portrait Emily made for Open House

"The black-and-white illustrations are well done and expressive. Fans of Barbara Park's 'Junie B. Jones' series and Patricia Reilly Giff's 'Polk Street School' books . . . will enjoy this beginning chapter book." SLJ

Other titles in this series are:

The secret lunch special (2006)

The Veteran's Day visitor (2008)

The **Veteran's** Day visitor; [by] Peter Catalanotto and Pamela Schembri. Henry Holt 2008 63p il (2nd-grade friends) $15.95

Grades: 1 2 3 **Fic**

1. Veterans -- Fiction 2. Narcolepsy -- Fiction 3. Grandfathers -- Fiction 4. Veterans Day -- Fiction

ISBN 978-0-8050-7840-4; 0-8050-7840-1

LC 2007-40938

"Frequent black-and-white illustrations keep the reader involved and move the story to its brisk resolution." Horn Book

The **secret** lunch special; [by] Peter Catalanotto and Pamela Schembri. Henry Holt and Company 2006 56p il (2nd-grade friends) $15.95

Grades: 1 2 3 **Fic**

1. School stories

ISBN 0-8050-7838-X; 978-0-8050-7838-1

LC 2006-02374

"The text provides a solid bridge from beginning readers to chapter books. Like the black-and-white illustrations, this gentle read is warm and smooth around the edges." SLJ

Catanese, P. W.

Dragon games. Aladdin 2010 373p il (The books of Umber)

Grades: 5 6 7 8 **Fic**

1. Fantasy fiction 2. Adventure fiction

ISBN 1-4169-7521-7; 978-1-4169-7521-2

LC 2009018743

This is a sequel to Happenstance Found (2009). Having learned more about his mysterious past, Happenstance accompanies Lord Umber on a journey that could affect the future of Kuraharen. "Grades seven to ten." (Bull Cent Child Books)

"The fast-paced and high-energy action of this video-game-like quest will please fantasy adventure fans." Kirkus

Happenstance found. Aladdin 2009 342p il (The books of Umber) $16.99

Grades: 5 6 7 8 **Fic**

1. Fantasy fiction 2. Adventure fiction 3. Magic -- Fiction

ISBN 978-1-4169-7519-9; 1-4169-7519-5

LC 2008-45966

A boy awakens, blindfolded, with no memory of even his name, but soon meets Lord Umber, an adventurer and inventor, who calls him Happenstance and tells him that he has a very important destiny—and a powerful enemy.

"Catanese packs a lot into the book: rich characterizations, . . . well-choreographed action sequences and genuinely surprising twists at the end." Publ Wkly

Catmull, Katherine

Summer and Bird; by Katherine Catmull. Dutton Children's Books 2012 344 p. (hardback) $16.99

Grades: 5 6 7 8 **Fic**

1. Fairy tales 2. Sisters -- Juvenile fiction 3. Fantasy fiction -- Juvenile fiction 4. Fantasy 5. Birds -- Fiction 6. Sisters -- Fiction 7. Puppeteers -- Fiction 8. Adventure and adventurers -- Fiction

ISBN 0525953469; 9780525953463

LC 2012015587

This children's book, by Katherine Catmull, is "an enchanting--and twisted--tale of two sisters' quest to find their parents. When their parents disappear in the middle of the night, young sisters Summer and Bird set off on a quest to find them. A cryptic picture message from their mother leads them to a familiar gate in the woods, but comfortable sights quickly give way to a new world entirely--Down--one inhabited by talking birds and the evil Puppeteer queen." (Publisher's note)

Cavanaugh, Nancy J.

★ **This** journal belongs to Ratchet; by Nancy J. Cavanaugh. Sourcebooks Jabberwocky 2013 320 p. (hardcover) $12.99

Grades: 4 5 6 7 **Fic**

1. Diaries -- Fiction 2. Home schooling -- Fiction 3. Father-daughter relationship -- Fiction 4. Self-acceptance -- Fiction 5. Fathers and daughters -- Fiction 6. Environmental protection -- Fiction

ISBN 1402281064; 9781402281068

LC 2012041339

This juvenile novel, by Nancy Cavanaugh, begins on "the first day of school for all the kids in the neighborhood. But not for me. I'm homeschooled. . . . The best I've got is this notebook. I'm supposed to use it for my writing assignments, but my dad never checks. Here's what I'm really going to use it for: Ratchet's Top Secret Plan . . . : turn my old, recycled, freakish, friendless, motherless life into something shiny and new." (Publisher's note)

"At first it seems artificial, with observations that are too on-the-nose. But as the novel's unexpectedly multifaceted plot comes together, it becomes increasingly compelling, suspenseful and moving. Triumphant enough to make readers cheer; touching enough to make them cry." Kirkus

Cervantes, Jennifer

Tortilla sun. Chronicle Books 2010 224p $16.99

Grades: 5 6 7 8   Fic

1. Grandmothers -- Fiction 2. Father-daughter relationship -- Fiction

ISBN 978-0-8118-7015-3; 0-8118-7015-4

While spending a summer in New Mexico with her grandmother, twelve-year-old Izzy makes new friends, learns to cook, and for the first time hears stories about her father, who died before she was born.

"Cervantes evokes the beauty of the setting and develops a memorable cast of characters, brought to life through Izzy's heartfelt narration. A beautiful and engaging debut novel." Kirkus

Chabon, Michael

Summerland. Hyperion Bks. for Children 2002 500p hardcover o.p. pa $8.95

Grades: 5 6 7 8   Fic

1. Fantasy fiction 2. Magic -- Fiction 3. Baseball -- Fiction

ISBN 0-7868-0877-2; 0-7868-1615-5 pa

LC 2002-27497

Ethan Feld, the worst baseball player in the history of the game, finds himself recruited by a 100-year-old scout to help a band of fairies triumph over an ancient enemy

"Much of the prose is beautifully descriptive as Chabon navigates vividly imagined other worlds and offers up some timeless themes." Horn Book

Chari, Sheela

Vanished. Disney/Hyperion Books 2011 240p $16.99

Grades: 5 6 7 8   Fic

1. Mystery fiction 2. East Indian Americans -- Fiction 3. Lost and found possessions -- Fiction

ISBN 978-1-4231-3163-2; 1-4231-3163-0

LC 2010019660

Eleven-year-old Neela must solve the mystery when her beautiful, but cursed, veena, a classical Indian musical instrument, goes missing.

"Well-paced and with moments of family humor . . . the novel offers a strong cast of characters and richly-described settings; both the legend and the contemporary come alive for readers. . . . Chari . . . strikes the right note with this engaging, intricate story that spans generations and two countries." Kirkus

Includes bibliographical references

Chatterton, Martin

The Brain finds a leg. Peachtree Publishers 2009 212p $16.95

Grades: 4 5 6   Fic

1. School stories 2. Mystery fiction 3. Animals --

Fiction 4. Intellect -- Fiction 5. Inventions -- Fiction

ISBN 978-1-56145-503-4; 1-56145-503-2

LC 2009-00304

First published 2007 in Australia

In Farrago Bay, Australia, thirteen-year-old Sheldon is recruited by a new student, Theo Brain, to help investigate a murder, which is tied not only to bizzare animal behavior but also to a diabolical plot to alter human intelligence.

"Several deaths in the story war against the comedy but the laughs win. Readers shouldn't expect anything remotely realistic and instead surrender themselves to the industrial-strength zaniness." Kirkus

Another title about The Brain is:

The Brain full of holes (2010)

The Brain full of holes. Peachtree 2010 250p $16.95

Grades: 4 5 6   Fic

1. Mystery fiction 2. Inventions -- Fiction

ISBN 978-1-56145-527-0; 1-56145-527-X

"Kid detective The Brain and his Watson are called in on a missing-person case. Their search takes them to Switzerland, home of the new super-particle accelerator, but their real adventure occurs in an alternate universe filled with zaniness. Chatterton explores speculations about physics throughout in amusing ways. . . . Those who like laughs along with a sf-influenced mystery will enjoy this." Booklist

Cheaney, J. B.

My friend, the enemy. Knopf 2005 266p hardcover o.p. pa $6.50

Grades: 5 6 7 8   Fic

1. Friendship -- Fiction 2. Japanese Americans -- Fiction 3. World War, 1939-1945 -- Fiction

ISBN 0-375-81432-9; 0-440-42102-0 pa

LC 2004-26927

During World War II, a twelve-year-old girl becomes friends with a young Japanese-American boy she discovers being sheltered and hidden by her neighbor.

"Written in first person, this novel offers quiet but finely tuned portrayal of the stresses that changed life on the home front and one child's attempts to cope with it all." Booklist

The middle of somewhere. Alfred A. Knopf 2007 218p $15.99; lib bdg $18.99; pa $6.50

Grades: 5 6 7 8   Fic

1. Siblings -- Fiction 2. Grandfathers -- Fiction 3. Automobile travel -- Fiction 4. Attention deficit disorder -- Fiction

ISBN 978-0-375-83790-6; 978-0-375-93790-3 lib bdg; 978-0-440-42165-8 pa

LC 2006-29202

Twelve-year-old Ronnie loves organization, especially because her brother has attention-deficit hyperactivity disorder, but traveling with their grandfather who is investigating wind power in Kansas brings some pleasant, if chaotic, surprises.

"The main characters are particularly well drawn and believable, and readers will root for both children as they attempt to overcome the obstacles placed in front of them." Booklist

Chen, Pauline

Peiling and the chicken-fried Christmas; [by] Pauline Chen. Bloomsbury Children's Books 2007 133p $15.95

Grades: 4 5 6   **Fic**
1. Christmas -- Fiction 2. Taiwanese Americans --
Fiction
ISBN 978-1-59990-122-0; 1-59990-122-6
LC 2006102095

Fifth-grader Peiling Wang wants to celebrate "a real
American Christmas," much to the displeasure of her traditional, Taiwanese-born father

"Peiling makes an appealingly levelheaded protagonist,
and . . . [Chen] doesn't miss much in this often-amusing picture of the Wang family working at fitting its new and old
cultures together." Booklist

Cheng, Andrea
Brushing Mom's hair; illustrations by Nicole Wong.
Wordsong 2009 59p il $17.95
Grades: 4 5 6 7 8   **Fic**
1. Novels in verse 2. Sick -- Fiction 3. Cancer --
Fiction 4. Mother-daughter relationship -- Fiction
ISBN 978-1-59078-599-7; 1-59078-599-1
LC 2009021965

A fourteen-year-old girl, whose mother's breast cancer
diagnosis and treatment have affected every aspect of their
lives, finds release in ballet and art classes.

"With one or two words on each line, the poems are a
fast read, but the chatty voice packs in emotion. . . . Wong's
small black-and-white pencil drawings on every page extend
the poetry through the characters' body language." Booklist

Honeysuckle house. Front Street 2004 136p $16.95;
pa $10.95
Grades: 3 4 5   **Fic**
1. Friendship -- Fiction 2. Immigrants -- Fiction 3.
Chinese Americans -- Fiction
ISBN 1-886910-99-5; 1-59078-632-7 pa

An all-American girl with Chinese ancestors and a new
immigrant from China find little in common when they meet
in their fourth grade classroom, but they are both missing
their best friends and soon discover other connections

"Told in first person in alternating chapters, the narratives balance well between large issues . . . and more intimate ones. . . . With a smoothly drawn and interesting plot,
strong characters, and graceful writing, the story has more
immediacy than much realistic contemporary fiction." SLJ

Only one year; illustrations by Nicole Wong. Lee &
Low Books 2010 97p il $16.95
Grades: 2 3 4   **Fic**
1. Siblings -- Fiction 2. Family life -- Fiction 3.
Chinese Americans -- Fiction
ISBN 978-1-60060-252-8; 1-60060-252-5
LC 201044

"Although she sometimes finds him troublesome, fourth-
grader Sharon can't bear the idea that her two-year-old
brother, Di Di, will spend a whole school year with relatives
in China while she and her first-grade sister, Mary, go to
school and her parents work. . . . Supportive black-and-white
illustrations and a glossary/pronunciation guide for the occasional Chinese words and phrases complete the appealing
package of this gentle family story." Booklist

Shanghai messenger; illustrated by Ed Young. Lee &
Low 2005 un il $18.95

Grades: 3 4 5 6   **Fic**
1. Novels in verse 2. Chinese Americans -- Fiction
ISBN 1-58430-238-0
LC 2004-4025934

A free-verse novel about eleven-year-old Xiao Mei's
visit with her extended family in China, where the Chinese-
American girl finds many differences but also the similarities that bind a family together.

"Cheng does an admirable job of capturing this experience from the perspective of a child, and each free-verse
chapter is brief but satisfying. . . . Young's illustrations delicately intertwine with the text, gently supporting each vignette. This is a superb book." SLJ

Where do you stay? Boyds Mills Press 2011 134p
$17.95
Grades: 4 5 6 7   **Fic**
1. Aunts -- Fiction 2. Cousins -- Fiction 3. Pianists --
Fiction 4. Bereavement -- Fiction 5. Homeless persons
-- Fiction
ISBN 1-59078-707-2; 978-1-59078-707-6

Jerome is staying with his Aunt Geneva and her family,
now that his mother has passed away. Aunt Geneva tries to
make Jerome feel welcome, but his cousins are not happy
about the new "member" of their family. Though Jerome has
a place to stay, he doesn't feel he has a home, until he meets
Mr. Willie, who lives in a ramshackle carriage house.

"In short chapters of lyrical prose, Cheng . . . provides
a moving tribute to a multigenerational community's ability to sustain and recreate itself in times of change through
resilience, hard work, and a commitment to beauty and kindness." Publ Wkly

Where the steps were. Front Street 2008 143p il
$16.95
Grades: 3 4 5 6   **Fic**
1. School stories 2. Novels in verse 3. Teachers --
Fiction 4. Friendship -- Fiction
ISBN 978-1-932425-88-8; 1-932425-88-8
LC 2007-18787

Verse from the perspectives of five students in Miss D.'s
third grade class details the children's last year together before their inner city school is to be torn down

This is "a spare, eloquent novel in verse illustrated in
[the author's] own bold block prints." Publ Wkly

The **lace** dowry. Front Street 2005 113p $16.95
Grades: 4 5 6 7   **Fic**
1. Sex role -- Fiction 2. Friendship -- Fiction
ISBN 1-932425-20-9
LC 2004-21186

In Hungary in 1933, a twelve-year-old from Budapest
befriends the Halas village family of lacemakers hired to
stitch her dowry.

"Cheng tells a familiar story of children discovering empathy across class and cultural divides, enriching the theme
with a vivid historical setting and Juli's strong narration,
which is written in spare language and a believable voice."
Booklist

Cheshire, Simon
★ The **curse** of the ancient mask and other case files;
pictures by R. W. Alley. Roaring Book Press 2009 169p il
(Saxby Smart, private detective) $13.95

Grades: 3 4 5 **Fic**
1. Mystery fiction 2. Lost and found possessions -- Fiction
ISBN 978-1-59643-474-5; 1-59643-474-0
First published 2007 in the United Kingdom

"Saxby Doyle Christie Chandler Ellin Allan Smart wants to be a detective as good as the greats. . . . In the first of three 'case files,' . . . Saxby . . . discovers that [an ancient] mask's real curse is a case of competitive sabotage. [In the] second case file . . . Saxby uncovers the secret behind the appearance of purple goo on his classmates' projects. In the third mystery, Saxby sets out to find the thief of a valuable coat clasp. . . . The stories are liberally illustrated with Alley's homey sketches plus representations of Saxby's notebooks. While each short mystery is involving, the distinguishing aspect of this series opener is Saxby's enthusiastic invitations to readers to participate in the sleuthing." Kirkus

Other titles in this series are:
The treasure of Dead Man's Lane and other case files (2010)
The pirate's blood and other case files (2011)

The **pirate's** blood and other case files; pictures by R. W. Alley. Roaring Brook Press 2011 224p il (Saxby Smart, private detective) $15.99
Grades: 3 4 5 **Fic**
1. School stories 2. Mystery fiction 3. Theft -- Fiction 4. Pirates -- Fiction
ISBN 978-1-59643-476-9; 1-59643-476-7
LC 2010029240

Saxby Smart, schoolboy private detective, invites the reader to follow the clues as he investigates three cases involving hidden treasure, a string of break-ins where nothing is stolen, and a rare comic book taken from an undamaged safe.

The **treasure** of Dead Man's Lane and other case files; pictures by R. W. Alley. Roaring Brook Press 2010 195p il (Saxby Smart, private detective) $15.99
Grades: 3 4 5 **Fic**
1. Mystery fiction
ISBN 978-1-59643-475-2; 1-59643-475-9

"In the first case, Saxby must find a rare comic book that's gone missing from a locked safe, and he uncovers lots of interesting comic-book trivia in the process of discovering the motive-old-fashioned greed—and the perp. The middle is the most engrossing of the three stories, involving an historic mansion with a dark past where Saxby's friend finds a scroll hidden in the wall. . . . Last, Saxby must unravel the enigma of six students who all have two things in common: home intruders and an anti-stress class. . . . Generously dappled with Alley's breezy line drawings, the cases are timely and twisting enough to keep the light bulb bright in the young sleuth's mind." Kirkus

Chick, Bryan
The **secret** zoo. Greenwillow Books 2010 295p $16.99
Grades: 4 5 6 **Fic**
1. Fantasy fiction 2. Mystery fiction 3. Zoos -- Fiction 4. Animals -- Fiction 5. Siblings -- Fiction
ISBN 978-0-06-198750-2; 0-06-198750-6
First published 2007 by Second Wish Press

Noah and his friends follow a trail of mysterious clues to uncover a secret behind the walls of the Clarksville City Zoo—a secret that must be protected at all costs.

"Chick debuts with an action-packed and breathless story about teamwork. . . . The story should appeal both to animal-lovers and a broader audience. While many threads are resolved, Chick lays the groundwork for later books." Publ Wkly

Other titles in this series are:
The secret zoo: secrets and shadows (2011)
The secret zoo: riddles and danger (2011)

The **secret** zoo: riddles and danger. Greenwillow Books 2011 284p $16.99
Grades: 4 5 6 **Fic**
1. Zoos -- Fiction 2. Magic -- Fiction 3. Friendship -- Fiction 4. Secret societies -- Fiction
ISBN 978-0-06-198927-8; 0-06-198927-4
LC 2011005930

Having discovered a magical society beneath the exhibits at the Clarksville City Zoo where animals and humans live harmoniously together as equals, Noah and his friends must protect the secret zoo at all costs.

The **secret** zoo: secrets and shadows. Greenwillow Books 2011 266p $16.99
Grades: 4 5 6 **Fic**
1. Mystery fiction 2. Zoos -- Fiction 3. Sasquatch -- Fiction 4. Friendship -- Fiction
ISBN 978-0-06-198925-4; 0-06-198925-8
LC 2010017221

Noah and his friends in the Secret Society join forces with four teens known as the Descenders to try to protect the Secret Zoo hidden below the Clarksville City Zoo from monstrous sasquatches and the evil Shadow Master.

"The four friends are well developed characters. . . . Descriptions are delightful. . . . Fans of fantasy, animal fiction, and adventure will enjoy this fast-moving story." SLJ

Child, Lauren
Clarice Bean spells trouble; [by] Lauren Child. Candlewick Press 2005 189p il $15.99; pa $5.99
Grades: 3 4 5 **Fic**
1. Authorship -- Fiction 2. Friendship -- Fiction
ISBN 0-7636-2813-1; 0-7636-2903-0 pa

Clarice Bean, aspiring actress and author, unsuccessfully tries to avoid getting into trouble as she attempts to help a friend in need by following the rules of the fictional spy, Ruby Redfort.

This is written "with fresh, childlike turns of phrase and a hyperawareness of words. . . . With a sprinkling of small, childlike line drawings, a few other illustrations, and some creative typography, this entertaining chapter book will please readers." Booklist

Other titles about Clarice Bean are:
Clarice Bean, don't look now (2007)
Utterly me, Clarice Bean (2003)

Clarice Bean, don't look now; [by] Lauren Child. Candlewick Press 2007 252p il $15.99
Grades: 3 4 5 **Fic**
1. School stories 2. Friendship -- Fiction 3. Family life -- Fiction
ISBN 978-0-7636-3536-7

"Clarice is codifying her fears into a list of worst worries when the kitchen ceiling comes crashing down after her older sister floods the bathroom. . . . Troubles continue at school when her best friend, Betty, annouces that she is moving to San Francisco, and a strange new student from Sweden arrives. . . . The story is told in Child's familiar stream-of-consciousness style and punctuated with creative vocabulary." SLJ

Utterly me, Clarice Bean. Candlewick Press 2003 190p il hardcover o.p. pa $5.99
Grades: 3 4 5 **Fic**
  1. Schools 2. School stories
  ISBN 0-7636-2186-2; 0-7636-2788-7 pa
                  LC 2002-41528
When someone steals the winner's trophy for the school book project, Clarice emulates her favorite book heroine, Ruby Redfort the detective

"Clarice is an exceptionally strong character, and her story, delivered in deadpan, forthright prose, perfectly captures a child's voice in a way that will elicit laughter even from the grumpy." Booklist

Choldenko, Gennifer
  Al Capone does my homework; by Gennifer Choldenko. Dial Books for Young Readers 2013 224 p. (Al Capone Trilogy) (hardcover) $17.99
Grades: 5 6 7 8 **Fic**
  1. Mystery fiction -- Juvenile fiction 2. Historical fiction -- Juvenile fiction 3. Fires -- Fiction 4. Autism -- Fiction 5. Brothers and sisters -- Fiction 6. Swindlers and swindling -- Fiction
  ISBN 0803734727; 9780803734722
                  LC 2012039138
This book, set on Alcatraz Island in the 1930s, is the third in Gennifer Choldenko's Al Capone trilogy. Moose lives with his parents and autistic sister on the island. "When Moose's dad gets promoted to Associate Warden, . . . it's a big deal. But the cons have a point system for targeting prison employees, and his dad is now in serious danger. After a fire starts in the Flanagan's apartment. Natalie is blamed, and Moose bands with the other kids to track down the possible arsonist." (Publisher's note)
Includes bibliographical references

  ★ **Al** Capone does my shirts. G.P. Putnam's Sons 2004 225p il $15.99; pa $6.99
Grades: 5 6 7 8 **Fic**
  1. Autism -- Fiction 2. Siblings -- Fiction 3. Alcatraz Island (Calif.) -- Fiction
  ISBN 0-399-23861-1; 0-14-240370-9 pa
                  LC 2002-31766
A Newbery Medal honor book, 2005
A twelve-year-old boy named Moose moves to Alcatraz Island in 1935 when guards' families were housed there, and has to contend with his extraordinary new environment in addition to life with his autistic sister.
"With its unique setting and well-developed characters, this warm, engaging coming-of-age story has plenty of appeal, and Choldenko offers some fascinating historical background on Alcatraz Island in an afterword." Booklist

  Al Capone shines my shoes. Dial Books for Young Readers 2009 274p $16.99

Grades: 5 6 7 8 **Fic**
  1. Autism -- Fiction 2. Siblings -- Fiction
  ISBN 978-0-8037-3460-9; 0-8037-3460-3
                  LC 2009-04157
Moose Flanagan, who lives on Alcatraz along with his family and the families of the other prison guards, is frightened when he discovers that noted gangster Al Capone, a prisoner there, wants a favor in return for the help that he secretly gave Moose.
"Effortless period dialogue, fully developed secondary characters and a perfectly paced plot combine to create a solid-gold sequel that will not disappoint." Kirkus
Includes bibliographical references

  If a tree falls at lunch period. Harcourt Children's Books 2007 216p $17; pa $6.99
Grades: 5 6 7 8 **Fic**
  1. School stories 2. Obesity -- Fiction 3. Race relations -- Fiction
  ISBN 978-0-15-205753-4; 0-15-205753-6; 978-0-15-206644-4 pa; 0-15-206644-6 pa
                  LC 2006-28664
Kirsten and Walk, seventh-graders at an elite private school, alternate telling how race, wealth, weight, and other issues shape their relationships as they and other misfits stand up to a mean but influential classmate, even as they are uncovering a long-kept secret about themselves.
"The sparkling characterization and touches of humor are real pluses." SLJ

  No passengers beyond this point. Dial Books for Young Readers 2011 244p $16.99
Grades: 5 6 7 8 **Fic**
  1. Fantasy fiction 2. Siblings -- Fiction 3. Space and time -- Fiction
  ISBN 978-0-8037-3534-7; 0-8037-3534-0
                  LC 2009-51661
With their house in foreclosure, sisters India and Mouse and brother Finn are sent to stay with an uncle in Colorado until their mother can join them, but when the plane lands, the children are welcomed by cheering crowds to a strange place where each of them has a perfect house and a clock that is ticking down the time.
"Choldenko keeps the plot moving rapidly and constantly shifts the point of view, with each chapter narrated by one of the three siblings, so that both readers and characters feel discombobulated—everything is both concrete yet dreamlike. . . . No one can write a hormonal teenage girl at war with her family like Choldenko, but in the end the family relationships and the determination each sibling has to protect the others is what saves them all." Horn Book

  Notes from a liar and her dog. Putnam 2001 216p hardcover o.p. pa $5.99
Grades: 5 6 7 8 **Fic**
  1. Dogs 2. Zoos 3. Honesty 4. Family life 5. Family life -- Fiction 6. Truthfulness and falsehood -- Fiction
  ISBN 0-399-23591-4; 0-14-250068-2 pa
                  LC 00-55354
Eleven-year-old Ant, stuck in a family that she does not like, copes by pretending that her "real" parents are coming to rescue her, by loving her dog Pistachio, by volunteering at the zoo, and by bending the truth and telling lies

"Choldenko's writing is snappy and tender, depicting both Ant's bravado and her isolation with sympathy." Bull Cent Child Books

Christopher, John

The **City** of gold and lead; 35th anniversary ed.; Simon & Schuster Books for Young Readers 2003 180p hardcover o.p. pa $5.99

Grades: 5 6 7 8   Fic

1. Science fiction

ISBN 0-689-85505-2; 0-689-85666-0 pa

LC 2002026670

A reissue of the title first published 1967

Three boys set out on a secret mission to penetrate the City of the Tripods and learn more about these strange beings that rule the earth.

When the Tripods came. Dutton 1988 151p hardcover o.p. pa $5.99

Grades: 5 6 7 8   Fic

1. Science fiction

ISBN 0-525-44397-5; 978-0-689-85762-1 pa; 0-689-85762-4 pa

LC 88-478

"A prequel to the author's well-known White Mountains trilogy . . . this relates how the Tripods came to Earth and imposed a new subservient order on its population. The protagonist is Laurie Corday, who, with his friend Andy, witnesses the first arrival of these towering metallic creatures. . . . The story's scenario exudes a chill; Laurie lives in the present, not some futuristic world, and the Tripods' insidious rise to power seems quite reasonable in the context of the story." Booklist

The **White** Mountains; 35th anniversary ed; Simon & Schuster Bks. for Young Readers 2003 164p hardcover o.p. pa $5.99

Grades: 5 6 7 8   Fic

1. Science fiction

ISBN 0-689-85504-4; 0-689-85672-5 pa

LC 2002-70808

A reissue of the title first published 1967 by Macmillan

Young Will Parker and his companions make a perilous journey toward an outpost of freedom where they hope to escape from the ruling Tripods, who capture mature human beings and make them docile, obedient servants

This "remarkable story . . . belongs to the school of science-fiction which puts philosophy before technology and is not afraid of telling an exciting story." Times Lit Suppl

Other titles about the Tripods are:

The city of gold and lead (2003 c1967)

The pool of fire (2003 c1968)

When the Tripods came (2003 c1988)

The **pool** of fire; 35th anniversary ed.; Simon & Schuster Books for Young Readers 2003 176p hardcover o.p. pa $5.99

Grades: 5 6 7 8   Fic

1. Science fiction

ISBN 0-689-85506-0; 0-689-85669-5 pa

LC 2002026883

A reissue of the title first published 1968

Will and a small group of free people plan to destroy the three great cities of the Tripods before the arrival of a space ship destined to doom humanity.

Christopher, Lucy

★ **Flyaway**; Lucy Christopher. Chicken House 2011 314p

Grades: 5 6 7 8   Fic

1. Sick -- Fiction 2. Swans -- Fiction 3. Hospitals -- Fiction 4. Wildlife conservation -- Fiction 5. Father-daughter relationship -- Juvenile fiction 6. Family life -- Fiction 7. Father-daughter relationship -- Fiction

ISBN 0545317711; 9780545317719

LC 2010051425

In this young adult novel, "when newly constructed power lines ruin the annual return of the whooping swans Isla and her father rise early to witness, the death of several of the wild creatures and her father's sudden and severe illness both confound Isla and emphasize her loneliness. At the hospital where her father awaits a heart operation, Harry, waiting there for a bone-marrow transplant, befriends Isla and points out the young swan he can see from his bed. . . . News broadcasts . . . about deadly outbreaks of bird flu contrast with the small unfolding of Isla's widowed grandfather's stiff grief as he helps her construct an art project--a harness and wings from an ancient stuffed swan--and innocent romance flutters between Isla and Harry even as the young swan regains flight and her father begins to recover." (Kirkus)

Christopher offers "readers a quiet but compelling story with several well-realized, idiosyncratic characters. She skillfully develops the novel's varied elements and weaves them into a unified narrative. . . . This sensitive novel will resonate with many readers." Booklist

Clark, Clara Gillow

Secrets of Greymoor. Candlewick Press 2009 166p $15.99

Grades: 4 5 6 7   Fic

1. School stories 2. Wealth -- Fiction 3. Grandmothers -- Fiction

ISBN 978-0-7636-3249-6; 0-7636-3249-X

LC 2008019063

As her grandmother's financial situation worsens, Hattie is forced to attend a "common school," in late nineteenth-century Kingston, New York, where she stands up to a show-off, shares embellished stories about life as a rich girl, and tries to recover her family's wealth.

"Even readers new to Hattie's story will cheer. . . . [This is an] accessible first-person narrative." Booklist

Clayton, Emma

The **Whisper**; Clayton, Emma. Chicken House/Scholastic 2012 309 p.

Grades: 5 6 7 8   Fic

1. Science fiction 2. Twins -- Fiction 3. Youth -- Fiction 4. Telepathy -- Fiction 5. Revolutions -- Fiction

ISBN 9780545433655; 0545433657; 054531772X; 9780545317726

LC 2011278492

In this book, "the story opens with the mutant Chosen Ones (Mika; his twin sister, Ellie; Audrey; and four other kids who remain entirely interchangeable) making their plans to stop Gorman (who has overdosed on Everlife-9 and is now a 13-year-old himself) and his equally scary counterpart, Raphael Mose, by taking control of . . . pretty much everything. Meanwhile Kobi (maybe the last free 13-year-old in London) and his father fall in with terrorists who will stop at nothing to blow up the towers where the rich people live. . . . Mika and company, with the help of Kobi, Grace (Raphael's mutant daughter), and a few functional adults actually do exactly what they set out to do—save the world." (School Libr J)

"Clayton writes for young people, and you can tell. The dialogue is authentic, and there is not a labored sentence or abrupt transition in sight." VOYA

The **roar**. Chicken House/Scholastic Inc. 2009 481p $17.99

Grades: 5 6 7 8   **Fic**
  1. Science fiction 2. Twins -- Fiction
  ISBN 978-0-439-92593-8; 0-439-92593-2

LC 2008-8311

"Mika and Ellie live in a future behind a wall: Solid concrete topped with high-voltage razor wire and guarded by a battalion of Ghengis Borgs, it was built to keep out the animals, because animals carry the plague. At least that's what Ellie, who was kidnapped as a child, has always been taught. But when she comes to suspect the truth behind her captivity, she's ready to risk exposure to the elements and answer the call of the wild." (Publisher's note) "Grades six to nine." (Bull Cent Child Books)

"This is an unusually gripping adventure that targets a younger audience than most young adult sci-fi." Bull Cent Child Books

Cleary, Beverly
  Beezus and Ramona; illustrated by Louis Darling. Avon Books 1990 159p il pa $5.99

Grades: 3 4 5   **Fic**
  1. Sisters -- Fiction
  ISBN 0-380-70918-X

A reissue of the title first published 1955

Beezus' biggest problem is her 4-year-old sister Ramona. Even though Beezus knows sisters are supposed to love each other, with a sister like Ramona, it seems impossible.

  Dear Mr. Henshaw; illustrated by Paul O. Zelinsky. Morrow 1983 133p il $15.99; lib bdg $16.89; pa $5.99

Grades: 4 5 6 7   **Fic**
  1. School stories 2. Divorce -- Fiction 3. Parent-child relationship -- Fiction
  ISBN 0-688-02405-X; 0-688-02406-8 lib bdg; 0-380-70958-9 pa

LC 83-5372

Awarded the Newbery Medal, 1984

"Leigh Botts lives with his recently divorced mother and writes to his favorite author, Boyd Henshaw. When Henshaw answers his letters and encourages him to keep a journal, he does so, and in the process solves the mystery of who is stealing food from his lunchbox, tries to write a novel, and in the end, writes a prize-winning short story about an experience with his father. . . . Grades four to seven." (SLJ)

"Leigh Botts started writing letters to his favorite author, Boyd Henshaw, in the second grade. Now, Leigh is in the sixth grade, in a new school, and his parents are recently divorced. This year he writes many letters to Mr. Henshaw, and also keeps a journal. Through these the reader learns how Leigh adjusts to new situations, and of his triumphs." Child Book Rev Serv

★ **Henry** Huggins; illustrated by Louis Darling. HarperCollins Pubs. 2000 155p il $15.99; pa $5.99

Grades: 3 4 5   **Fic**
  1. School stories 2. Family life -- Fiction
  ISBN 0-688-21385-5; 0-380-70912-0 pa

LC 00-27567

A reissue of the title first published 1950 by Morrow

"Henry Huggins is a typical small boy who, quite innocently, gets himself into all sorts of predicaments—often with the very apt thought, 'Won't Mom be surprised.' There is not a dull moment but some hilariously funny ones in the telling of Henry's adventures at home and at school." Booklist

Other titles about Henry Huggins are:
Henry and Beezus (1952)
Henry and Ribsy (1954)
Henry and the clubhouse (1962)
Henry and the paper route (1957)
Ribsy (1964)

  Henry and Beezus; illustrated by Louis Darling. Avon Books 2001 192p il pa $5.99

Grades: 3 4 5   **Fic**
  1. Bicycles -- Fiction 2. Friendship -- Fiction 3. Money-making projects for children -- Fiction
  ISBN 0-380-70914-7

LC 2001271522

A reissue of the title first published 1952

All Henry Huggins can think about is owning a bicycle, and he and his friend Beezus come up with various ideas to make money.

  Henry and Ribsy; illustrated by Louis Darling. Avon 1990 192p il pa $5.99

Grades: 3 4 5   **Fic**
  1. Dogs -- Fiction 2. Father-son relationship -- Fiction
  ISBN 0-380-70917-1

A reissue of the title first published 1954

Henry Huggins makes a deal with his father—if Henry can keep his dog Ribsy out of trouble for a month, he can go fishing with his father. Ribsy does his best to make Henry lose the deal.

"Genuinely funny." Booklist

★ **Muggie** Maggie; illustrated by Kay Life. Morrow Junior Bks. 1990 70p il $15.99; pa $5.99

Grades: 2 3 4   **Fic**
  1. School stories 2. Handwriting -- Fiction
  ISBN 0-688-08553-9; 0-380-71087-0 pa

LC 89-38959

Maggie resists learning cursive writing in the third grade, until she discovers that knowing how to read and write cursive promises to open up an entirely new world of knowledge for her

"This deceptively simple story is accessible to primary-grade readers able to read longhand, as some of the text is in script. . . . Everything in this book rings true, and Cleary has created a likable, funny heroine about whom readers will want to know more." SLJ

Ralph S. Mouse; illustrated by Paul O. Zelinsky. Harper Trophy 2000 160p il pa $5.99

Grades: 3 4 5   **Fic**

1. Mice -- Fiction

ISBN 0-380-70957-0

LC 2001278658

A reissue of the title first published 1982

Presents the further adventures of a motorcycle-riding mouse who goes to school and becomes the instigator of an investigation of rodents and the peacemaker for two lonely boys.

Ramona Quimby, age 8; illustrated by Alan Tiegreen. Morrow 1981 190p il $16.99; pa $5.99

Grades: 3 4 5   **Fic**

1. School stories 2. Family life -- Fiction

ISBN 0-688-00477-6; 0-380-70956-2 pa

LC 80028425

A Newbery Medal honor book, 1982

The further adventures of the Quimby family as Ramona enters the third grade.

Ramona and her father; illustrated by Alan Tiegreen. Morrow 1977 186p il lib bdg $16.99; pa $5.99

Grades: 3 4 5   **Fic**

1. Family life -- Fiction 2. Father-daughter relationship -- Fiction

ISBN 0-688-22114-9; 0-380-70916-3 pa

LC 77-1614

A Newbery Medal honor book, 1978

The family routine is upset during Ramona's year in second grade when her father unexpectedly loses his job.

Ramona and her mother; illustrated by Alan Tiegreen. HarperTrophy 2002 207p il pa $5.99

Grades: 3 4 5   **Fic**

1. Family life -- Fiction 2. Mother-daughter relationship -- Fiction

ISBN 0-380-70952-X

A reissue of the title first published 1979

Ramona at 7 1/2 sometimes feels discriminated against by being the youngest in the family.

Ramona forever; illustrated by Alan Tiegreen. Harper Trophy 2002 182p il pa $5.99

Grades: 3 4 5   **Fic**

1. School stories 2. Family life -- Fiction

ISBN 0-380-70960-0

A reissue of the title first published 1984

Ramona's year in third grade is highlighted by the arrival of Howie's rich uncle, a change in her afterschool situation, a surprise wedding, a death and a new arrival in the family, and her father's getting a job.

Ramona the brave; illustrated by Tracy Dockray. HarperTrophy 2006 176p il pa $5.99

Grades: 3 4 5   **Fic**

1. School stories 2. Family life -- Fiction

ISBN 978-0-380-70959-5; 0-380-70959-7

A reissue of the title first published 1975

Six-year-old Ramona tries to cope with an unsympathetic first-grade teacher.

★ **Ramona** the pest; illustrated by Louis Darling. Morrow 1968 192p il $16.99; pa $5.99

Grades: 3 4 5   **Fic**

1. School stories 2. Kindergarten -- Fiction

ISBN 0-688-21721-4; 0-380-70954-6 pa

"Ramona Quimby comes into her own. Beezus keeps telling her to stop acting like a pest, but Ramona is five now, and she is convinced that she is 'not' a pest; she feels very mature, having entered kindergarten, and she immediately becomes enamoured of her teacher. Ramona's insistence on having just the right kind of boots, her matter-of-fact interest in how Mike Mulligan got to a bathroom, her determination to kiss one of the boys in her class, and her refusal to go back to kindergarten because Miss Binney didn't love her any more—all of these incidents or situations are completely believable and are told in a light, humorous, zesty style." Bull Cent Child Books

Other titles about Ramona are:

Beezus and Ramona (1955)

Ramona and her father (1977)

Ramona and her mother (1979)

Ramona, forever (1984)

Ramona Quimby, age 8 (1981)

Ramona the brave (1975)

Ramona's world (1999)

Ramona's world; illustrated by Alan Tiegreen. Morrow Junior Bks. 1999 192p il $15; lib bdg $14.93; pa $5.99

Grades: 3 4 5   **Fic**

1. Schools 2. Family life 3. School stories 4. Family life -- Fiction

ISBN 0-688-16816-7; 0-688-16818-3 lib bdg; 0-380-73272-6 pa

LC 99-19038

Follows the adventures of nine-year-old Ramona at home with big sister Beezus and baby sister Roberta and at school in Mrs. Meacham's class

Runaway Ralph; illustrated by Louis Darling. Harper Trophy 2000 175p il pa $5.99

Grades: 3 4 5   **Fic**

1. Mice -- Fiction 2. Camps -- Fiction

ISBN 0-380-70953-8

LC 2001278668

A reissue of the title first published 1970

Ralph the mouse runs away looking for freedom but winds up a prisoner at a summer camp.

Socks; illustrated by Beatrice Darwin. Morrow 1973 156p il $16.99; pa $5.99

Grades: 3 4 5   **Fic**

1. Cats -- Fiction 2. Infants -- Fiction

ISBN 0-688-20067-2; 0-380-70926-0 pa

"Not being child-centered, this may have a smaller audience than earlier Cleary books, but it is written with the same easy grace, the same felicitous humor and sharply observant eye." Bull Cent Child Books

Strider; illustrated by Paul O. Zelinsky. Morrow Junior Bks. 1991 179p il hardcover o.p. lib bdg $16.89; pa $5.99

Grades: 4 5 6 7 **Fic**
1. Dogs -- Fiction 2. Divorce -- Fiction
ISBN 0-688-09900-9; 0-688-09901-7 lib bdg; 0-380-71236-9 pa

LC 90-6608

In a series of diary entries, Leigh tells how he comes to terms with his parents' divorce, acquires joint custody of an abandoned dog, and joins the track team at school

"The development of the narrative is vintage Beverly Cleary, an inimitable blend of comic and poignant moments." Horn Book

The **mouse** and the motorcycle; illustrated by Louis Darling. Morrow 1965 158p il $16; pa $5.99
Grades: 3 4 5 **Fic**
1. Mice -- Fiction
ISBN 0-688-21698-6; 0-380-70924-4 pa

"The author shows much insight into the thoughts of children. She carries the reader into an imaginative world that contains many realistic emotions." Wis Libr Bull

Other titles about Ralph are:
Ralph S. Mouse (1982)
Runaway Ralph (1970)

Cleaver, Vera
Where the lillies bloom; [by] Vera & Bill Cleaver; illustrated by Jim Spanfeller. Lippincott 1969 174p il hardcover o.p. pa $5.99
Grades: 5 6 7 8 **Fic**
1. Orphans -- Fiction 2. Siblings -- Fiction
ISBN 0-397-31111-7; 0-06-447005-9 pa

"The setting is fascinating, the characterization good, and the style of the first-person story distinctive." Bull Cent Child Books

Clements, Andrew
Extra credit; illustrations by Mark Elliott. Atheneum Books for Young Readers 2009 183p il $16.99
Grades: 4 5 6 **Fic**
1. Letters -- Fiction 2. Family life -- Fiction
ISBN 978-1-4169-4929-9; 1-4169-4929-1

LC 2008-42877

"Unless [Abby] wants to repeat the sixth grade, she'll have to meet some specific conditions, including taking on an extra-credit project: find a pen pal in a foreign country. Simple enough (even for a girl who hates homework). Abby's first letter arrives at a small school in Afghanistan, and Sadeed Bayat is chosen to be her pen pal.... Well, kind of. He is the best writer, but he is also a boy, and in his village it is not appropriate for a boy to correspond with a girl. So his younger sister dictates and signs the letter. Until Sadeed decides what his sister is telling Abby isn't what he'd like Abby to know." (Publisher's note) "Grades four to seven." (Bull Cent Child Books)

Clements "successfully bridges two cultures in this timely and insightful dual-perspective story." Publ Wkly

Fear itself; illustrated by Adam Stower. Atheneum Books for Young Readers 2010 204p il (Benjamin Pratt & the Keepers of the School) $14.99; pa $5.99
Grades: 4 5 6 **Fic**
1. School stories 2. Mystery fiction 3. Riddles --

Fiction
ISBN 978-1-4169-3887-3; 1-4169-3887-7; 978-1-4169-3908-5 pa; 1-4169-3908-3 pa

LC 2010015876

As the new Keepers of the School, sixth-graders Ben and Jill must decipher a handful of clues written as maritime riddles to save their school from demolition by a greedy company.

"Expressive pen-and-ink illustrations add detail and excitement to the adventure, including the clues and coins found. Solid writing, likable characters, danger, a seaside setting, and now treasure will make readers eager for the third installment." SLJ

★ **Frindle**; [by] Andrew Clements; pictures of Brian Selznick. Simon & Schuster Books for Young Readers 2006 105p il $15.95
Grades: 4 5 6 **Fic**
1. School stories
ISBN 978-0-689-80669-8; 0-689-80669-8
A reissue of the title first published 1996

When he decides to turn his fifth grade teacher's love of the dictionary around on her, clever Nick Allen invents a new word and begins a chain of events that quickly moves beyond his control.

"Sure to be popular with a wide range of readers, this will make a great read-aloud as well." Booklist

Lost and found; illustrations by Mark Elliott. Atheneum Books for Young Readers 2008 161p il $16.99
Grades: 4 5 6 **Fic**
1. School stories 2. Twins -- Fiction 3. Moving -- Fiction 4. Brothers -- Fiction
ISBN 978-1-4169-0985-9; 1-4169-0985-0

LC 2008-07018

Twelve-year-old identical twins Jay and Ray have long resented that everyone treats them as one person, and so they hatch a plot to take advantage of a clerical error at their new school and pretend they are just one

"This slim story has all the elements readers have come to expect from Clements . . . : a school setting, likable secondary characters, supportive adults and a challenge to the audience to see things from a different perspective." Publ Wkly

Lunch money; illustrations by Brian Selznick. Simon & Schuster Books for Young Readers 2005 222p il $15.95; pa $5.99
Grades: 4 5 6 **Fic**
1. School stories 2. Cartoons and comics -- Fiction 3. Money-making projects for children -- Fiction
ISBN 0-689-86683-6; 0-689-86685-2 pa

LC 2005-00061

Twelve-year-old Greg, who has always been good at moneymaking projects, is surprised to find himself teaming up with his lifelong rival, Maura, to create a series of comic books to sell at school.

"The characters are rich with interesting quirks and motivations. . . . Along with providing a fast-paced and humorous story line, the author examines concepts of true wealth, teamwork, community mindedness, and the value of creative expression. Selznick's pencil sketches add comic touches throughout." SLJ

★ **No** talking; illustrations by Mark Elliott. Simon & Schuster Books for Young Readers 2007 146p il $15.99; pa $5.99

Grades: 3 4 5 6   **Fic**

1. School stories

ISBN 978-1-4169-0983-5; 1-4169-0983-4; 978-1-4169-0984-2 pa; 1-4169-0984-2 pa

LC 2006-31883

The noisy fifth grade boys of Laketon Elementary School challenge the equally loud fifth grade girls to a "no talking" contest.

"This is an interesting and thought-provoking book. . . . The plot quickly draws readers in and keeps them turning pages. . . . The black-and-white pencil drawings add immediacy to the story." SLJ

Room one; a mystery or two. illustrations by Chris Blair. Simon & Schuster Books for Young Readers 2006 162p il $15.95; pa $5.99

Grades: 3 4 5   **Fic**

1. School stories 2. Mystery fiction 3. Homeless persons -- Fiction

ISBN 0-689-86686-9; 0-689-86687-9 pa

Ted Hammond, the only sixth grader in his small Nebraska town's one-room schoolhouse, searches for clues to the disappearance of a homeless family.

"There is a good balance of seriousness and humor with brisk, realistic dialogue and observations. Small black-and-white illustrations emphasize key points in the plot. Clements's usual excellent sense of character is evident." SLJ

We the children; illustrated by Adam Stower. Atheneum Books for Young Readers 2010 142p il (Benjamin Pratt and the Keepers of the School) $14.99

Grades: 4 5 6   **Fic**

1. School stories 2. Mystery fiction 3. Adventure fiction

ISBN 978-1-4169-3886-6; 1-4169-3886-9

LC 2009-36428

"Sixth-grader Ben Pratt is thrust into a mystery-adventure when his school's janitor shoves a gold coin in his hand, passing on the responsibility to save Oakes School from developers. Captain Oakes gave the school to the community back in 1783; its original building overlooks the Massachusetts town's harbor. But the land has been sold, and buildings will be razed to make way for a theme park. . . . Clements ably sets up his planned six-volume series with topical problems, convincing, likable characters and intriguing extra details." Kirkus

Another title in this series is Fear itself (2010)

Clements, Andrew, 1949-

About average; Andrew Clements; illustrations by Mark Elliott. Simon & Schuster 2012 120 p. (hardback) $16.99

Grades: 3 4 5 6   **Fic**

1. Natural disasters -- Fiction 2. Personal appearance -- Fiction 3. School stories -- Juvenile fiction 4. Heroes -- Fiction 5. Ability -- Fiction 6. Schools -- Fiction 7.

Tornadoes -- Fiction 8. Individuality -- Fiction

ISBN 1416997245; 9781416997245; 9781416997269

LC 2012015106

In author Andrew Clements's book, protagonist "Jordan Johnston is average. Not short, not tall. Not plump, not slim. Not blond, not brunette. Not gifted, not flunking out. Even her shoe size is average. She's ordinary for her school, for her town, for even the whole wide world, it seems. . . . Jordan feels doomed to a life of wallowing in the vast, soggy middle. So she makes a goal: By the end of the year, she will discover her great talent." (Publisher's note)

Troublemaker; Andrew Clements; illustrated by Mark Elliott. Atheneum Books for Young Readers 2011 p. cm. $16.99

Grades: 4 5 6 7   **Fic**

1. Schools -- Fiction 2. Behavior -- Fiction 3. Brothers -- Fiction

ISBN 978-1-4169-4930-5; 1-4169-4930-5; 1416949305; 9781416949305

LC 2010045018

When his older brother gets in serious trouble, sixth-grader Clay decides to change his own mischief-making ways, but he cannot seem to shake his reputation as a troublemaker.

"Clements here enters into provocative territory and pulls it off like the pro he is. Kids will easily relate to Clay, and the secondary characters come alive as well." Kirkus

The **report** card. Simon & Schuster Books for Young Readers 2004 173p

Grades: 4 5 6   **Fic**

1. School stories

ISBN 0689845154; 0689845243

LC 2003-7384

Fifth-grader Nora Rowley has always hidden the fact that she is a genius from everyone because all she wants is to be normal, but when she comes up with a plan to prove that grades are not important, things begin to get out of control. "Ages eight to twelve." (N Y Times Book Rev)

"Clements has . . . built a solid story around a controversial issue for which there is no easy answer, and to his credit, he never tries to offer one. . . . A novel sure to generate strong feelings and discussion." Booklist

Clifford, Eth

Help! I'm a prisoner in the library; illustrated by George Hughes. Houghton Mifflin 1979 105p il $16; pa $5.95

Grades: 3 4 5   **Fic**

1. Blizzards -- Fiction 2. Libraries -- Fiction

ISBN 0-395-28478-3; 0-618-49482-0 pa

LC 79-14447

"Caught in a blinding snowstorm with their car out of gas, Mary Rose and Jo-Beth are told to stay put while their father finds fuel for the stalled vehicle. Jo-Beth, however, develops 'an emergency' and Mary Rose takes her to a nearby library to find a restroom. . . . Without warning the girls find themselves locked in when the building closes early. As the storm worsens, the lights and telephone go out and a series of flying objects, creaking noises, and moaning sounds thoroughly frighten the girls. . . . Clifford uses a light touch while evoking a pleasingly scary atmosphere that children will enjoy. Spirited dialogue and swift pace are an additional plus." Booklist

Clifton, Lutricia

Freaky Fast Frankie Joe; Lutricia Clifton. Holiday House 2012 248 p. (hardcover) $16.95

Grades: 4 5 6 **Fic**

1. Boys -- Fiction 2. Family -- Fiction 3. Brothers -- Fiction 4. Stepfamilies -- Fiction 5. Mothers and sons -- Fiction 6. Delivery of goods -- Fiction 7. Family life -- Illinois -- Fiction 8. Community life -- Illinois -- Fiction

ISBN 0823423670; 9780823423675

LC 2011019976

This is the story of Frankie Joe. While "his mom is in jail, Frankie Joe tries to adjust to living with his newly surfaced father, FJ, his stepmother and "the four legitimate Huckaby sons." The brothers tease Frankie Joe because, academically, he is "freaky slow," which is at odds with how fast he is when he runs or bikes. . . . Frankie Joe . . . launches Frankie Joe's Freaky Fast Delivery Service. With his income, he plans his escape back home from Illinois to Texas. But with each day Frankie Joe becomes more integrated into—and essential to—the town and the family, starting with his friendship with another town oddball, elderly Miss Peachcott. She tells Frankie Joe his family history." (Kirkus)

Coatsworth, Elizabeth Jane

The **cat** who went to heaven; [by] Elizabeth Coatsworth; illustrated by Lynd Ward. Macmillan 1958 62p il $17.95; pa $4.99

Grades: 4 5 6 7 **Fic**

1. Cats -- Fiction

ISBN 0-02-719710-7; 1-4169-4973-9 pa

LC 58-10917

First published 1930. The 1958 edition is a reprint with new illustrations of the book which won the Newbery Medal award in 1931

"Into this lovely and imaginative story the author has put something of the serenity and beauty of the East and of the gentleness of a religion that has a place even for the humblest of living creatures." N Y Times Book Rev

Cody, Matthew

Powerless. Alfred A. Knopf 2009 279p $15.99; lib bdg $18.99

Grades: 5 6 7 8 **Fic**

1. School stories 2. Moving -- Fiction 3. Bullies -- Fiction 4. Family life -- Fiction 5. Superheroes -- Fiction 6. Supernatural -- Fiction

ISBN 978-0-375-85595-5; 0-375-85595-5; 978-0-375-95595-2 lib bdg; 0-375-95595-X lib bdg

LC 2008-40885

Soon after moving to Noble's Green, Pennsylvania, twelve-year-old Daniel learns that his new friends have super powers that they will lose when they turn thirteen, unless he can use his brain power to protect them.

"This first novel has an intriguing premise, appealing characters, and a straightforward narrative arc with plenty of action as well as some serious moments." Booklist

Super; Matthew Cody. Alfred A. Knopf 2012 298 p. (Sequel to Powerless) (trade) $16.99; (lib. bdg.) $19.99

Grades: 5 6 7 8 **Fic**

1. Superheroes -- Juvenile fiction 2. Supervillains -- Juvenile fiction 3. Adventure fiction -- Juvenile fiction 4. Superheroes -- Fiction 5. Supernatural -- Fiction 6.

Supervillains -- Fiction

ISBN 0375968946; 9780375868948; 9780375899799; 9780375968945

LC 2012008220

In this children's novel, by Matthew Cody, "Daniel Corrigan is as regular as can be, especially when compared to the Supers: kids in his new hometown with actual powers like flight and super strength. But . . . only he was able to stop the Shroud, a supervillian bent on stealing his newfound friends' powers. . . . Now Daniel himself is starting to display powers, while . . . his friends are losing theirs. . . . Daniel worries there may be something . . . sinister at work." (Publisher's note)

Cohagan, Carolyn

The **lost** children. Aladdin 2010 313p $16.99

Grades: 4 5 6 **Fic**

1. Friendship -- Fiction 2. Time travel -- Fiction 3. Voyages and travels -- Fiction

ISBN 978-1-4169-8616-4; 1-4169-8616-2

LC 2009-16608

When twelve-year-old Josephine falls through a wormhole in her garden shed into another time and place, she realizes the troubles she has at home are minor compared to what she has to tackle now in the world where she has landed.

"The main characters are well developed, particularly the spunky and plain-spoken Ida, the laconic but loyal Fargus, and Josephine." Booklist

Cohen, Barbara

Thank you, Jackie Robinson; drawings by Richard Cuffari. Lothrop, Lee & Shepard Bks. 1974 125p il hardcover o.p. pa $4.99

Grades: 4 5 6 **Fic**

1. Baseball -- Fiction 2. Friendship -- Fiction 3. African Americans -- Fiction

ISBN 0-688-15293-7 pa

"Cohen's characters have unusual depth and her story succeeds as a warm, understanding consideration of friendship and, finally, death." Booklist

Cohn, Rachel

The **Steps**. Simon & Schuster Bks. for Young Readers 2003 137p hardcover o.p. pa $4.99

Grades: 5 6 7 8 **Fic**

1. Family life -- Fiction 2. Stepfamilies -- Fiction

ISBN 978-0-689-84549-9; 0-689-84549-9; 978-0-689-87414-7 pa; 0-689-87414-6 pa

LC 2001-57566

Over Christmas vacation, Annabel goes from her home in Manhattan to visit her father, his new wife, and her half-and step-siblings in Sydney, Australia

"Packed with humorous incident, life lessons learned, Australian travel tidbits, and a litany of preteen-girl touchstones." Horn Book

Another title about this family is:

Two steps forward (2006)

Two steps forward. Simon & Schuster for Young Readers 2006 227p $15.95

Grades: 5 6 7 8 **Fic**

1. Family life -- Fiction 2. Stepfamilies -- Fiction

ISBN 0-689-86614-3

Fourteen-year-old Annabel's extended family gathers in Los Angeles for several weeks over the summer where she must contend with step and half sisters and brothers and her own mother's failing second marriage.

"With the four blended families converging, tensions and humor run high. Chapters are told from alternating viewpoints. . . . This blended narrative offers a lighthearted glimpse into weighty matters." SLJ

Cole, Henry

★ A **nest** for Celeste; a story about art, inspiration, and the meaning of home. [written and illustrated by] Henry Cole. Katherine Tegen Books 2010 342p il $16.99; lib bdg $17.89

Grades: 4 5 6   **Fic**

1. Artists 2. Painters 3. Illustrators 4. Ornithologists 5. Home -- Fiction 6. Mice -- Fiction 7. Artists -- Fiction 8. Writers on science

ISBN 978-0-06-170410-9; 0-06-170410-5; 978-0-06-170411-6 lib bdg; 0-06-170411-3 lib bdg

LC 2009-11813

Celeste, a mouse longing for a real home, becomes a source of inspiration to teenaged Joseph, assistant to the artist and naturalist John James Audubon, at a New Orleans, Louisiana, plantation in 1821

"Evocative illustrations, compelling characters, and thoughtful reflections on the nature of home combine to powerful effect." Publ Wkly

Cole, Stephen

Z. Raptor; [by] Steve Cole. Philomel Books 2011 265p (The hunting) $16.99

Grades: 5 6 7 8   **Fic**

1. Science fiction 2. Islands -- Fiction 3. Dinosaurs -- Fiction 4. Virtual reality -- Fiction 5. Father-son relationship -- Fiction

ISBN 978-0-399-25254-9; 0-399-25254-1

LC 2010041650

In New York City to spend Christmas with his father, thirteen-year-old Adam Adlar discovers that he and his father are still targets of sinister forces and, despite his father's objections, Adam finds himself drawn back into the struggle against hyper-evolved, deadly velociraptors determined to wreak havoc and spread terror.

"A non-stop ride from beginning to end, this installment is well constructed, larded with frequent and often violent action and reads even better than the first." Kirkus

Z. Rex; [by] Steve Cole. Philomel Books 2009 245p (The hunting) $16.99; pa $7.99

Grades: 5 6 7 8   **Fic**

1. Science fiction 2. Dinosaurs -- Fiction 3. Virtual reality -- Fiction 4. Father-son relationship -- Fiction

ISBN 978-0-399-25253-2; 0-399-25253-3; 978-0-14-241712-6 pa; 0-14-241712-2 pa

LC 2009-6637

From Santa Fe, New Mexico, to Edinburgh, Scotland, thirteen-year-old Adam Adlar must elude police while being hunted by a dinosaur come-to-life from a virtual reality game invented by his father, who has gone missing.

"Cole has created a likable character who manages to come out on top in an extraordinary situation. The science aspects offer an interesting perspective and dilemma for a discussion on genetic engineering. In addition, the adven-

ture, video gaming, and the perilous, sometimes bloody scenes will capture reluctant readers who may not normally devour their reading materials." SLJ

Colfer, Eoin

★ **Airman**; [by] Eoin Colfer. Hyperion Books for Children 2008 412p $17.99; pa $7.99

Grades: 5 6 7 8 9   **Fic**

1. Adventure fiction 2. Airplanes -- Fiction 3. Inventors -- Fiction 4. Prisoners -- Fiction

ISBN 978-1-4231-0750-7; 1-4231-0750-0; 978-1-4231-0751-4 pa; 1-4231-0751-9 pa

LC 2007-38415

In the late nineteenth century, when Conor Broekhart discovers a conspiracy to overthrow the king, he is branded a traitor, imprisoned, and forced to mine for diamonds under brutal conditions while he plans a daring escape from Little Saltee prison by way of a flying machine that he must design, build, and, hardest of all, trust to carry him to safety.

This is "polished, sophisticated storytelling. . . . A tour de force." Publ Wkly

★ **Artemis** Fowl. Hyperion Bks. for Children 2001 277p $16.95; pa $7.99

Grades: 5 6 7 8   **Fic**

1. Fantasy fiction 2. Fairies -- Fiction

ISBN 0-7868-0801-2; 1-4231-2452-9 pa

LC 2001-16632

When a twelve-year-old evil genius tries to restore his family fortune by capturing a fairy and demanding a ransom in gold, the fairies fight back with magic, technology, and a particularly nasty troll

"Colfer's antihero, techno fantasy is cleverly written and filled to the brim with action, suspense, and humor." SLJ

Other titles in this series are:

Artemis Fowl: the Arctic incident (2002)

Artemis Fowl: the Eternity code (2003)

Artemis Fowl: the Opal deception (2005)

Artemis Fowl: the lost colony (2006)

Artemis Fowl: the time paradox (2008)

Artemis Fowl: the Atlantis complex (2010)

Artemis Fowl: The Atlantis complex. Disney/Hyperion Books 2010 357p $17.99

Grades: 5 6 7 8   **Fic**

1. Fantasy fiction 2. Magic -- Fiction 3. Fairies -- Fiction 4. Space and time -- Fiction

ISBN 978-1-4231-2819-9; 1-4231-2819-2

LC 2010017154

Teenaged criminal mastermind Artemis Fowl must save the underwater fairy metropolis of Atlantis from danger, while battling a psychological affliction known as the Atlantis Complex.

"Colfer keeps the action moving with laughs and gadgetry." Booklist

Artemis Fowl: The opal deception. Miramax Books/Hyperion Books for Children 2005 342p $16.95; pa $7.99

Grades: 5 6 7 8   **Fic**

1. Fantasy fiction 2. Fairies -- Fiction

ISBN 0-7868-5289-5; 0-7868-5290-9 pa

LC 2006271670

After his last run-in with the fairies, Artemis Fowl's mind was wiped of memories of the world belowground and any goodness grudgingly learned is now gone with the young genius reverting to his criminal lifestyle.

Colfer "uses many different British accents and dialects to make both the human and the supernatural characters come alive, and his pacing is faultless throughout the dialogue and the narrative." SLJ

Artemis Fowl: the Arctic incident. Hyperion Books for Children 2002 277p $16.95
Grades: 5 6 7 8   Fic
1. Fantasy fiction 2. Fairies -- Fiction
ISBN 0-7868-0855-1

When Artemis learns that his father has been kidnapped by the Russian mob, he races to the Arctic Circle to make a daring rescue where he finds an old acquaintance, Captain Holly Short, who is investigating a plot of the goblin mob.

"Colfer's finger is firmly on the pulse of his target market, and along with extra helpings of sly humor." Publ Wkly

Artemis Fowl: the Eternity code. Miramax Books\Hyperion Books for Children 2003 309p $16.95; pa $5.99
Grades: 5 6 7 8   Fic
1. Fantasy fiction 2. Fairies -- Fiction
ISBN 0-7868-1914-6; 978-0-7868-5628-2 pa; 0-7868-5628-9 pa

LC 2003-46431

After Artemis uses stolen fairy technology to create a powerful microcomputer and it is snatched by a dangerous American businessman, Artemis, Juliet, Mulch, and the fairies join forces to try to retrieve it

This "features Colfer's trademark broad humor, engaging . . . characters, and high-speed action, not to mention the unlikely mix of magic and technology." Voice Youth Advocates

Artemis Fowl: the lost colony; [by] Eoin Colfer. Hyperion Books for Children 2006 385p $16.95
Grades: 5 6 7 8   Fic
1. Fantasy fiction 2. Fairies -- Fiction
ISBN 0-7868-4956-8

Once again, Artemis will have to pair up with his old comrade, Captain Holly Short, to track down the missing demon and rescue him before the time spell dissolves and the lost demon colony returns violently to Earth.

"Colfer delivers not only continuous action but also witty wordplay and dialogue, understated humor, and plenty of magical technology and gadgetry." Booklist

Artemis Fowl: the time paradox; [by] Eoin Colfer. Hyperion Books for Children 2008 391p $17.99
Grades: 4 5 6 7 8   Fic
1. Magic -- Fiction 2. Fairies -- Fiction 3. Space and time -- Fiction
ISBN 978-1-4231-0836-8; 1-4231-0836-1

Artemis's mother has contracted a deadly disease and the only cure lies in the brain fluid of African lemurs. Unfortunately, Artemis himself was responsible for making the lemurs extinct five years ago. Now he must enlist the aid of his fairy friends to travel back in time and save them. Not only that, but he must face his deadliest foe yet his younger self.

"The story flows with quick-witted humor and action-packed scenes, and Colfer's love of science shines through in the story's inventions and clever use of engineering. . . .

The author once again offers an exhilarating ride through the fantastical world of Artemis Fowl." SLJ

Benny and Babe. Miramax Books/Hyperion Books for Children 2007 282p $18.95
Grades: 5 6 7 8   Fic
1. Friendship -- Fiction 2. Hurling (Game) -- Fiction
ISBN 978-1-4231-0283-0; 1-4231-0283-5

LC 2006-100646

First published 1999 in Ireland

Thirteen-year-old Benny, a hurling fanatic, is convinced that he can take on the world—until he spends the summer living with his grandfather and meets resident tomboy and all-around tough-girl Babe Meara.

"Humor, sensitivity, and candor underscore this coming-of-age story that features incredibly well-drawn characters." SLJ

Another title about Benny is:
Benny and Omar (2007)

Colfer, Eoin, 1965-
Artemis Fowl; The last guardian. Eoin Colfer. 1st U.S. ed. Disney Hyperion Books 2012 328 p. (hardcover) $18.99
Grades: 4 5 6 7 8 9   Fic
1. Fantasy fiction 2. Magic -- Fiction 3. Fairies -- Fiction 4. Spirits -- Fiction 5. Genius -- Fiction 6. Space and time -- Fiction
ISBN 1423161610; 9781423161615

LC 2012009997

Odyssey Honor Audiobook (2013)

This book by Eoin Colfer is the eighth installment of the Artemis Fowl series. "This time his arch rival has reanimated dead fairy warriors who were buried in the grounds of Fowl Manor. . . . The warriors don't seem to realize that the battle they were fighting when they died is long over. Artemis has until sunrise to get the spirits to vacate his brothers and go back into the earth where they belong." (Publisher's note)

The **reluctant** assassin; Eoin Colfer. Hyperion Book CH 2013 352 p. (W.A.R.P.) (hardcover) $17.99
Grades: 5 6 7 8   Fic
1. Time travel -- Juvenile fiction 2. Alternative histories -- Juvenile fiction 3. Science fiction 4. Assassins -- Fiction 5. Time travel -- Fiction
ISBN 1423161629; 9781423161622

LC 2012048160

This is the first book in the time-travel W.A.R.R. series from Eoin Colfer. "After a bungled mission, [FBI agent] Chevie has been sent to London where she is 'baby-sitting a metal capsule,' which she learns is one end of a wormhole to the year 1898, when [young assassin] Riley (and a corpse) materialize, direct from the Victorian era." (Publishers Weekly)

Colin, Beatrice
My invisible sister; by Beatrice Colin and Sara Pinto, Bloomsbury 2010 119p il $15.99
Grades: 3 4 5   Fic
1. School stories 2. Science fiction 3. Moving -- Fiction 4. Siblings -- Fiction 5. Family life -- Fiction
ISBN 978-1-59990-488-7; 1-59990-488-8

LC 2009-32631

Ten-year-old Frank's thirteen-year-old sister Elizabeth, invisible since birth, continually causes trouble, forcing the family to move again and again, but Frank wants to stay put and decides to find a way to make her visible.

Collard, Sneed B.

Double eagle. Peachtree 2009 245p $15.95

Grades: 4 5 6 7 **Fic**

1. Coins -- Fiction 2. Hurricanes -- Fiction 3. Buried treasure -- Fiction

ISBN 978-1-56145-480-8; 1-56145-480-X

LC 2008036746

In 1973, Michael and Kyle's discovery of a rare Confederate coin near an old Civil War fort turns into a race against time as the boys try to find more coins before a hurricane hits Alabama's Gulf coast.

"Mike's narrative moves quickly with likable and believable characters. The story will have particular appeal to readers with an interest in historical places and artifacts." SLJ

Includes bibliographical references

Collier, James Lincoln

Jump ship to freedom; [by] James Lincoln Collier, Christopher Collier. Delacorte Press 1981 198p hardcover o.p. pa $5.99

Grades: 6 7 8 9 **Fic**

1. Slavery -- Fiction 2. African Americans -- Fiction

ISBN 0-440-44323-7 pa

LC 81-65492

In 1787 Dan Arabus, a fourteen-year-old slave, anxious to buy freedom for himself and his mother, escapes from his dishonest master and tries to find help in cashing the soldier's notes received by his father, Jack Arabus, for fighting in the Revolution

"The period seems well researched, and the speech has an authentic ring without trying to imitate a dialect." SLJ

Me and Billy; [by] James Lincoln Collier. Marshall Cavendish 2004 185p $15.95

Grades: 5 6 7 8 **Fic**

1. Orphans 2. Friendship 3. Conduct of life 4. Swindlers and swindling 5. Runaways 6. Best friends 7. Orphans -- Fiction 8. Friendship -- Fiction 9. Swindlers and swindling -- Fiction

ISBN 0-7614-5174-9

LC 2003-26865

After escaping the orphanage where they have spent their lives together, two boys become assistants to a con artist, and while Possum objects to the lying, stealing, and cheating, Billy only cares about making money and taking life easy

"A small gem. . . . The book's momentum is sustained by the author's wonderful use of vernacular and the friendship/tension between the boys." SLJ

★ My brother Sam is dead; by James Lincoln Collier and Christopher Collier. Four Winds Press 1985 216p $17.95

Grades: 6 7 8 9 **Fic**

1. United States -- History -- 1775-1783, Revolution -- Fiction

ISBN 0-02-722980-7

LC 84-28787

A reissue of the title first published 1974

A Newbery Medal honor book, 1975

"In 1775 the Meeker family lived in Redding, Connecticut, a Tory community. Sam, the eldest son, allied himself with the Patriots. The youngest son, Tim, watched a rift in the family grow because of his brother's decision. Before the war was over the Meeker family had suffered at the hands of both the British and the Patriots." Shapiro. Fic for Youth. 3d edition

War comes to Willy Freeman; [by] James Lincoln Collier, Christopher Collier. Delacorte Press 1983 178p hardcover o.p. pa $5.99

Grades: 6 7 8 9 **Fic**

1. Slavery -- Fiction 2. African Americans -- Fiction

ISBN 0-440-49504-0 pa

LC 82-70317

This deals with events prior to those in Jump ship to freedom, and involves members of the same family. "Willy is thirteen when she begins her story, which takes place during the last two years of the Revolutionary War; her father, a free man, has been killed fighting against the British, her mother has disappeared. Willy makes her danger-fraught way to Fraunces Tavern in New York, her uncle, Jack Arabus, having told her that Mr. Fraunces may be able to help her. She works at the tavern until the war is over, goes to the Arabus home to find her mother dying, and participates in the trial (historically accurate save for the fictional addition of Willy) in which her uncle sues for his freedom and wins." Bull Cent Child Books

Collins, Pat Lowery

Daughter of winter. Candlewick Press 2010 272p $16.99

Grades: 4 5 6 7 **Fic**

1. Winter -- Fiction 2. Wampanoag Indians -- Fiction 3. Wilderness survival -- Fiction

ISBN 978-0-7636-4500-7; 0-7636-4500-1

LC 2009049099

In the mid-nineteenth-century shipbuilding town of Essex, Massachusetts, twelve-year-old Addie learns a startling secret about her past when she escapes servitude by running away to live in the snowy woods and meets an elderly Wampanoag woman.

"Collins' sense of place, incorporation of cultural and historical details, and the richly evoked winter setting make for a vividly imagined novel. An engaging survival story intertwined with a search for identity." Booklist

Collins, Suzanne

Gregor and the Code of Claw. Scholastic Press 2007 412p (Underland chronicles) $17.99

Grades: 4 5 6 7 **Fic**

1. Fantasy fiction

ISBN 978-0-439-79143-4; 0-439-79143-X

LC 2006028839

When twelve-year-old Gregor finally learns the ancient prophecy, which foretells his death, he must gather his courage to defend Regalia from the army of rats, take his mother and sister home safely, and fight his own dark side.

Gregor and the curse of the warmbloods; by Suzanne Collins. 1st ed; Scholastic 2005 358p (Underland chronicles) $16.95

Grades: 4 5 6 7   **Fic**
1. Fantasy fiction
ISBN 0-439-65623-0

LC 2004-59010

Eleven-year-old Gregor and his younger sister, Boots,
return to the Underworld beneath New York City to find
the cure for a terrible plague that threatens the life of their
mother, as well as the lives of the people, bats, and rats who
populate the underworld.

This is a "fast-paced, suspenseful story." Booklist

Gregor and the marks of secret. Scholastic Press 2006
343p (Underland chronicles) $16.99
Grades: 4 5 6 7   **Fic**
1. Fantasy fiction
ISBN 0-439-79145-6

LC 2005-27969

Twelve-year-old Gregor returns to the world beneath
New York City, where he joins forces with Princess Lexa
and Ripred the rat to defend the Underlanders and the Nib-
blers from the army led by the adolescent rat king, the Bane.

Gregor and the prophecy of Bane. Scholastic Press
2004 312p (Underland chronicles) $16.95
Grades: 4 5 6 7   **Fic**
1. Fantasy fiction
ISBN 0-439-65075-5

In his second adventure, eleven-year-old Gregor returns
to the world beneath New York City to rescue his kidnapped
sister, Boots, and fulfill a prophecy that will restore peace to
the people, bats, rats, cockroaches, and spiders who populate
the underworld.

"Fans will not be disappointed with this exciting, action-
packed sequel, whose ending suggests more adventures to
come." Booklist

★ **Gregor** the Overlander. Scholastic Press 2003 311p
(Underland chronicles) $16.95; pa $5.99
Grades: 4 5 6 7   **Fic**
1. Fantasy fiction
ISBN 0-439-43536-6; 0-439-67813-7 pa

LC 2002-155865

When eleven-year-old Gregor and his two-year-old sister are pulled into a strange underground world, they trigger
an epic battle involving men, bats, rats, cockroaches, and
spiders while on a quest foretold by ancient prophecy

"Collins creates a fascinating, vivid, highly original
world and a superb story to go along with it." Booklist

Other titles in this series are:
Gregor and the prophecy of Bane (2004)
Gregor and the curse of the warmbloods (2005)
Gregor and the marks of secret (2006)
Gregor and the code of claw (2007)

Collins, Tim
Prince of Dorkness; more notes from a totally lame
vampire. by Tim Collins; illustrated by Andrew Pinder. 1st
Aladdin hardcover ed. Aladdin 2011 331 p. ill. (hardcover) $12.99
Grades: 6 7 8 9   **Fic**
1. Vampires -- Juvenile fiction 2. Occult fiction --
Juvenile fiction 3. School stories -- Juvenile fiction
4. Love -- Fiction 5. Diaries -- Fiction 6. Schools --

Fiction 7. Vampires -- Fiction 8. Werewolves -- Fiction
ISBN 1442433884; 9781442433885

LC 2011012349

In this book, "being a vampire and having a new girlfriend makes Nigel Mullet an instantly cool guy at school.
But his social success doesn't last long because a new, even
cooler, vampire comes into town and steal Nigel's thunder,
and his girlfriend! Nigel is back to being the dorkiest of the
dorks and tries his best to regain his social status." (Kids
World Magazine)

Collodi, Carlo
★ **Pinocchio**; illustrated by Quentin Greban; translated
by Claude Sartirano and Juanita Havill. North-South Books
2010 80p il $19.95
Grades: 3 4 5 6   **Fic**
1. Fantasy fiction 2. Puppets and puppet plays -- Fiction
ISBN 978-0-7358-2324-2; 0-7358-2324-3

A wooden puppet full of tricks and mischief, with a talent for getting into and out of trouble, wants more than anything else to become a real boy.

"This edition of the Italian classic Pinocchio strikes a
good balance between nineteenth-century writing conventions and modern readers' tastes. Translated and somewhat
abridged, the text offers a story that is true to the original in
spirit and detail. . . . Gréban . . . creates distinctive illustrations with notable clarity of line, drama of composition, and
subtlety of watercolor washes. Even libraries with several
editions of Pinocchio should consider adding this one, for
the clarity and grace of its writing as well as the luminous
beauty of its illustrations." Booklist

★ The **adventures** of Pinocchio; [by] Carlo Collodi;
illustrated by Roberto Innocenti; designed by Rita Marshall.
Creative Editions 2005 191p il $24.95
Grades: 3 4 5 6   **Fic**
1. Fairy tales 2. Puppets and puppet plays -- Fiction
ISBN 1-56846-190-9

LC 2003-62740

A wooden puppet full of tricks and mischief, with a talent for getting into and out of trouble, wants more than anything else to become a real boy

Innocenti's illustrations have a "19th-century European
setting, and the careful composition, use of perspective, and
dark earth tones are an apt visual expression of this complex
moral tale." SLJ

Columbus, Chris
House of secrets; Chris Columbus; Ned Vizzini. 1st ed.
Balzer + Bray 2013 496 p. (hardcover) $17.99
Grades: 5 6 7 8   **Fic**
1. Haunted houses -- Juvenile fiction 2. Fantasy fiction
-- Juvenile fiction 3. Adventure fiction -- Juvenile fiction
4. Fantasy 5. Dwellings -- Fiction 6. Supernatural --
Fiction 7. Books and reading -- Fiction 8. Brothers
and sisters -- Fiction 9. Adventure and adventurers --
Fiction
ISBN 0062192469; 9780062192462

LC 2012051815

In this juvenile fantasy story, by Chris Columbus and
Ned Vizzini, three siblings "relocate to an old Victorian
house that used to be the home of occult novelist Denver
Kristoff. . . . By the time the Walkers realize that one of their
neighbors has sinister plans for them, they're banished to a

primeval forest way off the grid. . . . Bloodthirsty medieval warriors patrol the woods around them, supernatural pirates roam the neighboring seas, and a power-hungry queen rules the land." (Publisher's note)

Coman, Carolyn

★ The **Memory** Bank; [by] Carolyn Coman & Rob Shepperson. Arthur A. Levine Books 2010 263p il $16.99

Grades: 3 4 5 6   **Fic**

1. Dreams -- Fiction 2. Memory -- Fiction 3. Sisters -- Fiction 4. Sabotage -- Fiction 5. Banks and banking -- Fiction

ISBN 978-0-545-21066-9; 0-545-21066-6

When Hope learns that, while her memory account is seriously low, she is a champion dreamer, she stays at the World Wide Memory Bank trying to locate her sister Honey, whom their parents abandoned and told Hope to forget.

"Energetic Quentin Blake-like pencil illustrations tell the tale of Hope's beloved Honey as she falls in with a rebel lot of lost children who threaten to overthrow the WWMB. Brilliantly crafted, thoroughly enjoyable and, though so very like Dahl, unique as a fascinating new way to ponder dreams and memories." Kirkus

Sneaking suspicions; [by] Carolyn Coman; drawings by Rob Shepperson. 1st ed.; Front Street 2007 245p il $16.95

Grades: 3 4 5 6   **Fic**

1. Siblings -- Fiction 2. Family life -- Fiction 3. Swindlers and swindling -- Fiction

ISBN 978-1-59078-491-4; 1-59078-491-X

LC 2006101610

Ivy and Ray accompany their parents on a trip to the Florida Everglades in order to find their only living relative, a distant cousin who, according to their great-grandfather's memoirs, absconded with a valuable, if unspecified, item.

"The children are believable characters. . . . Shepperson's black-and-white illustrations sprinkled liberally throughout masterfully capture the emotions of the Fitts family." SLJ

Comerford, Lynda B.

Rissa Bartholomew's declaration of independence. Scholastic Press 2009 250p $16.99

Grades: 4 5 6 7   **Fic**

1. School stories 2. Friendship -- Fiction

ISBN 978-0-545-05058-6; 0-545-05058-8

LC 2008-26618

Having told off all of her old friends at her eleventh birthday party, Rissa starts middle school determined to make new friends while being herself, not simply being part of a herd.

"Rissa's troubles are ones that many middle-schoolers will identify with: new schools, shifting allegiances, new feelings, and changing bodies. First-time novelist Comerford gives her readers an appealing heroine who, despite her flaws and quirks, finds herself along the way." Booklist

Compestine, Ying Chang

Crouching tiger; illustrated by Yan Nascimene. Candlewick Press 2011 il $16.99

Grades: 2 3 4   **Fic**

1. Grandfathers -- Fiction 2. Martial arts -- Fiction 3. Chinese Americans -- Fiction 4. Racially mixed people

-- Fiction 5. Chinese -- United States -- Fiction

ISBN 978-0-7636-4642-4; 0-7636-4642-3

LC 2010048133

When Ming Da's Chinese grandpa comes to visit, he overcomes his initial embarrassment at his grandfather's traditions and begins to appreciate him.

"Compestine creates a simple portrait of a familiar cultural bridge, conveying Vinson's awe, shyness and embarrassment about his serious grandfather. Nascimbene captures both the compact energy of the small boy and the graceful, composed grace of the adult. His contained, quiet style with warm colors nicely matches the low-key narrative. . . . A celebration of family and Chinese New Year along with a simple introduction to Wudang martial arts, especially tai chi-and to the idea that strength can be gentle." Kirkus

Revolution is not a dinner party; a novel. Henry Holt and Company 2007 256p map $16.95; pa $7.99

Grades: 5 6 7 8   **Fic**

1. Communism -- Fiction 2. Persecution -- Fiction

ISBN 978-0-8050-8207-4; 0-8050-8207-7; 978-0-312-58149-7 pa; 0-312-58149-1 pa

LC 2006035465

Starting in 1972 when she is nine years old, Ling, the daughter of two doctors, struggles to make sense of the communists' Cultural Revolution, which empties stores of food, homes of appliances deemed "bourgeois," and people of laughter.

"Readers should remain rapt by Compestine's storytelling throughout this gripping account of life during China's Cultural Revolution." Publ Wkly

Conford, Ellen

★ **Annabel** the actress starring in Gorilla my dreams; illustrated by Renée Williams-Andriani. Simon & Schuster Bks. for Young Readers 1999 64p il hardcover o.p. pa $3.99

Grades: 2 3 4   **Fic**

1. Humorous stories 2. Actors -- Fiction 3. Parties -- Fiction 4. Actors and actresses -- Fiction

ISBN 0-689-81404-6; 0-689-83883-2 pa

LC 97-39449

Though a little disappointed that her first acting part is to be a gorilla at a birthday party, Annabel determines to really get into the role

"The vocabulary is appropriate for those graduating from easy-readers, but the language is never stilted. Amusing pen-and-ink illustrations appear on almost every page." SLJ

Other titles about Annabel are:

Annabel the actress starring in Hound of the Barkervilles (2002)

Annabel the actress, starring in Camping it up (2004)

Annabel the actress, starring in Just a little extra (2000)

Jenny Archer, author; interior illustrations by Diane Palmisciano; cover illustration by Erik Brooks. Little, Brown 2006 61p il $12.99

Grades: 2 3 4   **Fic**

1. School stories 2. Authorship -- Fiction

ISBN 0-316-01487-7

LC 2006278952

A reissue of the title first published 1989

Stymied by an assignment to write her autobiography, Jenny decides to enhance her life story by using her considerable imagination.

This "is competent and entertaining. . . . Students will want their own teachers to read this to them and then to read it again on their own." SLJ

What's cooking, Jenny Archer? interior illustrations by Diane Palmisciano; cover illustration by Erik Brooks. Little, Brown 2006 69p il pa $10.99

Grades: 2 3 4   **Fic**
1. Cooking -- Fiction 2. Money-making projects for children -- Fiction
ISBN 0-316-01488-5
                                              LC 2006278885
A reissue of the title first published 1989
Follows the comic mishaps of Jenny Archer as she goes into business preparing lunches for friends at school.

★ A **case** for Jenny Archer; illustrated by Diane Palmisciano. Little, Brown 1988 61p il (Springboard books) hardcover o.p. pa $4.99

Grades: 2 3 4   **Fic**
1. Mystery fiction
ISBN 0-316-01486-9 pa
                                              LC 88-14169
After reading three mysteries in a row, Jenny becomes convinced that the neighbors across the street are up to no good and decides to investigate

"This lots-of-fun advanced easy reader contains eight chapters, all about three pages long, with large, clear print, and lots of white space. . . . The children here are lively, the adults funny, wise, and supportive." SLJ

Other titles about Jenny Archer are:
Can do, Jenny Archer (1991)
Get the picture, Jenny Archer (1994)
Jenny Archer, author (1989)
Jenny Archer to the rescue (1990)
A job for Jenny Archer (1988)
Nibble, nibble, Jenny Archer (1993)
What's cooking, Jenny Archer (1989)

Conkling, Winifred
Sylvia and Aki. Tricycle Press 2011 151p $16.99; lib bdg $19.99

Grades: 3 4 5 6   **Fic**
1. Farm life -- Fiction 2. Race relations -- Fiction 3. Mexican Americans -- Fiction 4. Segregation in education -- Fiction 5. Japanese Americans -- Evacuation and relocation, 1942-1945 -- Fiction
ISBN 978-1-58246-337-7; 1-58246-337-9; 978-1-58246-397-1 lib bdg; 1-58246-397-2 lib bdg
                                              LC 2010024182
At the start of World War II, Japanese-American third-grader Aki and her family are sent to an internment camp in Poston, Arizona, while Mexican-American third-grader Sylvia's family leases their Orange County, California, farm and begins a fight to stop school segregation.

"Told in alternating chapters from the girls' points of view, this story about institutional racism will enlighten readers to events in recent history. From the court case of Mendez v. Westminster to the conditions at Poston, readers will be moved by this novel based on true events." SLJ

Conly, Jane Leslie
Crazy lady! HarperCollins Pubs. 1993 180p lib bdg $18.89; pa $5.99

Grades: 5 6 7 8   **Fic**
1. Death -- Fiction 2. Alcoholism -- Fiction 3. Prejudices -- Fiction 4. Mentally handicapped -- Fiction
ISBN 0-06-021360-4 lib bdg; 0-06-440571-0 pa
                                              LC 92-18348
A Newbery Medal honor book, 1994

As he tries to come to terms with his mother's death, Vernon finds solace in his growing relationship with the neighborhood outcasts, an alcoholic and her retarded son

The narration "is fast and blunt, and the conversations are lively and true." Bull Cent Child Books

★ **Murder** afloat. Hyperion Books for Children 2010 164p $17.99

Grades: 5 6 7 8   **Fic**
1. Adventure fiction 2. Kidnapping -- Fiction 3. Seafaring life -- Fiction
ISBN 978-1-4231-0416-2; 1-4231-0416-1
Benjamin Franklin Orville is caught up in a scuffle, kidnapped with a group of immigrants and forced to work aboard the Ella Dawn—one of the most ill-reputed oystering vessels in Baltimore.

"With compelling characters and details of the little-known process of oystering woven throughout, Conly's tale touches on the hardships of many German immigrants to the U.S., whose desperate plights offer parallels to contemporary immigration issues. Short chapters and suspenseful plot twists will keep readers turning the pages in this engaging historical adventure." Booklist

Connor, Leslie
★ **Crunch**. Katherine Tegen Books 2010 330p $16.99; lib bdg $17.89

Grades: 5 6 7 8   **Fic**
1. Bicycles -- Fiction 2. Siblings -- Fiction 3. Family life -- Fiction 4. Energy conservation -- Fiction 5. Business enterprises -- Fiction
ISBN 978-0-06-169229-1; 0-06-169229-8; 978-0-06-169233-8 lib bdg; 0-06-169233-6 lib bdg
                                              LC 2009-24339
This novel concerns "the trials and tribulations of 14-year-old Dewey Mariss and his family. His parents are away from home, unable to return because of a gasoline shortage. Running their small family business, the Bike Barn, with his younger brother and helping older sister Lil look after the five-year-old twins keeps Dewey plenty busy. . . . Characters are colorful but believable, dialogue crisp and amusing. The New England setting is attractively realized, and the underlying energy crisis treated seriously but not sensationally." Kirkus

★ **Waiting** for normal. Katherine Tegen Books 2008 290p $16.99; lib bdg $17.89

Grades: 5 6 7 8   **Fic**
1. Mothers -- Fiction 2. Family life -- Fiction
ISBN 978-0-06-089088-9; 0-06-089088-6; 978-0-06-089089-6 lib bdg; 0-06-089089-4 lib bdg
                                              LC 2007-06881
Twelve-year-old Addie tries to cope with her mother's erratic behavior and being separated from her beloved stepfather and half-sisters when she and her mother go to live

in a small trailer by the railroad tracks on the outskirts of Schenectady, New York.

"Connor . . . . treats the subject of child neglect with honesty and grace in this poignant story. . . . Characters as persuasively optimistic as Addie are rare, and readers will gravitate to her." Publ Wkly

Conrad, Pam

★ **My** Daniel. Harper & Row 1989 137p pa $5.99

Grades: 5 6 7 8   **Fic**

ISBN 0-06-440309-2 pa

LC 88-19850

"Rendering scenes from both the past and the present with equal skill, Conrad is at the peak of her storytelling powers." Publ Wkly

Cook, Kacy

Nuts. Marshall Cavendish 2010 155p $16.99

Grades: 4 5 6   **Fic**

1. Pets -- Fiction 2. Squirrels -- Fiction 3. Family life -- Fiction

ISBN 978-0-7614-5652-0; 0-7614-5652-X

LC 2009-04354

When eleven-year-old Nell finds a tiny baby squirrel on the ground in her yard, she begs her parents to let her raise it as a pet, even after the research she does shows that this is not a good idea.

"Cook does a nice job of taking a seemingly innocent plot and almost sneaking in (a little like pureed vegetables) much weightier themes of love, honesty and death. . . . The straightforward, upbeat prose consistently engages readers, and her characters are dead on. There's more here than meets the eye." Kirkus

Coombs, Kate

The **runaway** dragon. Farrar, Straus and Giroux 2009 292p $16.99

Grades: 5 6 7 8   **Fic**

1. Fairy tales 2. Dragons -- Fiction 3. Princesses -- Fiction

ISBN 978-0-374-36361-1; 0-374-36361-7

LC 2008034362

When her beloved dragon Laddy runs away from the castle, Princess Meg and some of her friends embark on a quest to find him and bring him home.

"Funny, lighthearted. . . . Enchanted forests, rampant transmogrification, evil sorceresses and giants are all fine fodder for Coombs's inventive twists on traditional fairy tales." Kirkus

The **runaway** princess. Farrar, Straus and Giroux 2006 279p $17

Grades: 5 6 7 8   **Fic**

1. Fairy tales 2. Dragons -- Fiction 3. Princesses -- Fiction

ISBN 0-374-35546-0

LC 2005-51225

Fifteen-year-old Princess Meg uses magic and her wits to rescue a baby dragon and escape the unwanted attentions of princes hoping to gain her hand in marriage through a contest arranged by her father, the king.

"This witty, humorous tale will be popular with fantasy buffs who enjoy takeoffs on fairy tales." Booklist

Another title about Princess Meg is:

The runaway dragon (2009)

Cooper, Ilene

Absolutely Lucy; illustrated by Amanda Harvey. Golden Books 2000 76p il (Absolutely Lucy) pa $4.99

Grades: 2 3 4   **Fic**

1. Dogs 2. Dogs -- Fiction

ISBN 0-307-46502-0; 0-307-26502-1 pa

LC 99-36118

Bobby is a shy boy until he gets a beagle puppy named Lucy, who helps him to make new friends

"Children who are stretching their reading wings will enjoy [this] short chapter [book]." SLJ

Angel in my pocket. Feiwel and Friends 2011 278p $16.99

Grades: 4 5 6 7   **Fic**

1. School stories 2. Charms -- Fiction 3. Loss (Psychology) -- Fiction

ISBN 978-0-312-37014-5; 0-312-37014-8

LC 2010-34756

When seventh-grader Bette finds an angel coin she puts it in her pocket and forgets it but soon the mysterious and kind Gabby moves into her building and helps her face her major losses, and then the coin connects her with three classmates who all find new ways to believe in themselves.

"The characters and setting are lovingly crafted, and readers will be left contemplating the roles of luck, magic, and inner strength in the kids' transformed lives." Publ Wkly

Look at Lucy! illustrated by David Merrell. Random House 2009 102p il lib bdg $11.99; pa $4.99

Grades: 2 3 4   **Fic**

1. School stories 2. Dogs -- Fiction 3. Anxiety -- Fiction 4. Contests -- Fiction

ISBN 978-0-375-95558-7 lib bdg; 0-375-95558-5 lib bdg; 978-0-375-85558-0 pa; 0-375-85558-0 pa

LC 2008-36312

Entering his beagle, Lucy, in a contest to be "spokespet" for Pet-O-Rama helps shy, nine-year-old Bobby get over his anxiety about speaking in front of groups of people, from his third-grade classmates to the contest judges.

"This beginning chapter book has realistic characters that readers can identify with and root for. . . . The action and suspense will keep children engaged. The occasional drawings lend graphic support." SLJ

Other titles about Lucy and Bobby are:

Absolutely Lucy (2000)

Lucy on the loose (2007)

Lucy on the ball (2010)

Lucy on the ball; illustrated by David Merrell. Random House 2011 102p il (Absolutely Lucy) lib bdg $12.99; pa $4.99

Grades: 2 3 4   **Fic**

1. Dogs -- Fiction 2. Soccer -- Fiction

ISBN 978-0-375-95559-4 lib bdg; 0-375-95559-3 lib bdg; 978-0-375-85559-7 pa; 0-375-85559-9 pa; 978-0-375-89820-4 e-book

LC 2010005183

Lucy the beagle does not mind her humans very well until third-grader Bobby joins a soccer team, Lucy becomes the mascot, and the coach gives Lucy obedience training.

Lucy on the loose; illustrated by Amanda Harvey. Golden Books 2000 76p il (Absolutely Lucy) hardcover o.p. pa $4.99

Grades: 2 3 4   **Fic**

1. Cats -- Fiction 2. Dogs -- Fiction 3. Shyness -- Fiction 4. Lost and found possessions -- Fiction

ISBN 0-307-46508-X; 0-307-26508-0 pa

LC 00021432

When his beagle Lucy runs off chasing a big orange cat, Bobby must overcome his shyness in order to find them again.

Cooper, Susan

★ The **Boggart**. Margaret K. McElderry Bks. 1993 196p hardcover o.p. pa $5.99

Grades: 4 5 6 7   **Fic**

1. Supernatural -- Fiction

ISBN 0-689-50576-0; 0-689-86930-4 pa

LC 92-15527

After visiting the castle in Scotland which her family has inherited and returning home to Canada, twelve-year-old Emily finds that she has accidentally brought back with her a boggart, an invisible and mischievous spirit with a fondness for practical jokes

"Using both electronics and theater as metaphors for magic, Cooper has extended the world of high fantasy into contemporary children's lives through scenes superimposing the ordinary and the extraordinary." Bull Cent Child Books

Another title about the Boggart is:

The Boggart and the monster (1997)

The **Boggart** and the monster. Margaret K. McElderry Bks. 1997 185p $17.99; pa $5.99 **Fic**

1. Supernatural -- Fiction

ISBN 0-689-81330-9; 0-689-86931-2 pa

LC 96-42389

The Boggart, the invisible and mischievous spirit living in the Scottish Castle Keep, sets out to help save Nessie the Loch Ness Monster, one of its few remaining cousins

"Cooper adroitly incorporates ancient lore into a contemporary setting while producing an imaginative and compelling tale." Publ Wkly

★ **Ghost** Hawk; by Susan Cooper. 1st ed. Margaret K. McElderry Books 2013 328 p. map (hardcover) $16.99

Grades: 5 6 7 8   **Fic**

1. Friendship -- Juvenile fiction 2. Native Americans -- North America 3. Native Americans -- Relations with early settlers 4. Ghosts -- Fiction 5. Survival -- Fiction 6. Coming of age -- Fiction 7. Wampanoag Indians -- Fiction 8. Indians of North America -- Massachusetts -- Fiction

ISBN 1442481412; 9781442481411; 9781442481435

LC 2012039892

This novel by Susan Cooper is "a story of adventure and friendship between a young Native American and a colonial New England settler. Little Hawk is sent into the woods alone [and] if [he] survives three moons by himself, he will be a man. John Wakely is only ten when his father dies, but he has already experienced . . . friendship of the nearby tribes. John sees how quickly the relationships between settlers and natives are deteriorating. His friendship with Little Hawk will put both boys in grave danger." (Publisher's note)

Greenwitch. Simon Pulse 2007 147p pa $8.99

Grades: 4 5 6 7   **Fic**

1. Fantasy fiction 2. Good and evil -- Fiction

ISBN 978-1-416-94966-4; 1-416-94966-6

A reissue of the title first published 1974

Jane's invitation to witness the making of the Greenwitch begins a series of sinister events in which she and her two brothers help the Old Ones recover the grail stolen by the Dark.

★ **King** of shadows. Margaret K. McElderry Bks. 1999 186p $16; pa $4.99; pa $6.99

Grades: 5 6 7 8   **Fic**

1. Poets 2. Authors 3. Dramatists 4. Actors -- Fiction 5. Time travel -- Fiction 6. Actors and actresses -- Fiction

ISBN 0-689-82817-9; 0-689-84445-X pa; 9780689844454 pa

LC 98-51127

Boston Globe Horn Book Honor Book (2000)

"Nat Field is thrilled when theater director Richard Babbage chooses him to become a player in the Company of Boys, an American summer drama troupe that will appear in Shakespeare's A Midsummer Night's Dream at the new replica of the Globe Theater in London. Shortly after his arrival in England, though, Nat feels ill and falls into a troubled sleep. To the doctor's astonishment, he seems to be suffering from the effects of the bubonic plague. He awakens in 1599 as another Nat Field, a child actor from St. Paul's School who is about to go to the Globe to rehearse A Midsummer Night's Dream in the role of Puck." (Booklist) "Grades six to nine." (Bull Cent Child Books)

"Cleverly explicating old and new acting and performance techniques, Susan Cooper entertains her contemporary readers while giving them a first-rate theatrical education." N Y Times Book Rev

★ **Over** sea, under stone; illustrated by Margery Gill. Harcourt Brace Jovanovich 1966 252p il $19; pa $5.99

Grades: 5 6 7 8   **Fic**

1. Fantasy fiction 2. Good and evil -- Fiction

ISBN 0-15-259034-X; 0-689-84035-7 pa

First published 1965 in the United Kingdom

Three children on a holiday in Cornwall find an ancient manuscript which sends them on a dangerous quest for a grail that would reveal the true story of King Arthur and that entraps them in the eternal battle between the forces of the Light and the forces of the Dark.

"The air of mysticism and the allegorical quality of the continual contest between good and evil add much value to a fine plot, setting, and characterization." Horn Book

Other titles in this series are:

The dark is rising (1973)

Greenwitch (1974)

The grey king (1975)

Silver on the tree (1977)

Silver on the tree. Atheneum Pubs. 1977 ix, 269p $19.99; pa $8.99

Grades: 5 6 7 8   **Fic**

1. Fantasy fiction

ISBN 0-689-50088-2; 978-1-416-94968-8 pa

LC 77-5361

In this conclusion of the tale begun in "Over Sea, Under Stone," Will Stanton, the Welsh boy Bran, and the Drew children try to locate the crystal sword that alone can vanquish the strong forces of Dark

Victory. Margaret K. McElderry Books 2006 196p il $16.95; pa $6.99

Grades: 5 6 7 8 **Fic**

1. Admirals 2. Sea stories

ISBN 1-4169-1477-3; 1-4169-1478-1 pa

LC 2005-16747

Alternating chapters follow the mysterious connection between a homesick English girl living in present-day America and an eleven-year-old boy serving in the British Royal Navy in 1803, aboard the H.M.S. Victory, commanded by Admiral Horatio Nelson.

"Seamlessly weaving details of period seamanship into the narrative, Cooper offers a vivid historical tale within the framework of a compelling modern story." Booklist

The **dark** is rising. Simon Pulse 2007 244p il pa $8.99

Grades: 4 5 6 7 **Fic**

1. Fantasy fiction 2. Good and evil -- Fiction

ISBN 978-1-416-94965-7; 1-416-94965-8

A reissue of the title first published 1973

On his eleventh birthday, Will Stanton discovers that he is the last of the Old Ones, destined to seek the six magical Signs that will enable the Old Ones to triumph over the evil forces of the Dark.

★ The **grey** king; illustrated by Michael Heslop. Atheneum Pubs. 1975 208p il $19.99; pa $8.99

Grades: 5 6 7 8 **Fic**

1. Fantasy fiction 2. Good and evil -- Fiction

ISBN 0-689-50029-7; 1-4169-4967-4 pa

Awarded the Newbery Medal, 1976

"So well-crafted that it stands as an entity in itself, the novel . . . is nevertheless strengthened by its relationship to the preceding volumes—as the individual legends within the Arthurian cycles take on deeper significance in the context of the whole. A spellbinding tour de force." Horn Book

The **magician's** boy; illustrated by Serena Riglietti. Margaret K. McElderry Bks. 2005 100p il $15.95; pa $7.95

Grades: 2 3 4 **Fic**

1. Fairy tales 2. Magicians -- Fiction

ISBN 0-689-87622-X; 1-4169-1555-9 pa

A boy who works for a magician meets familiar fairy tale characters when he is transported to the Land of Story in search of a missing puppet

"Fanciful and mildly amusing, the dreamlike story flows along smoothly through a strange yet vaguely familiar wonderland. Riglietti contributes a series of expressive, stylized illustrations." Booklist

Corbett, Sue

Free baseball; [by] Sue Corbett. Dutton Children's Books 2006 152p $15.99; pa $5.99

Grades: 5 6 7 8 **Fic**

1. Baseball -- Fiction 2. Cuban Americans -- Fiction

ISBN 0-525-47120-0; 0-14-241080-2 pa

LC 2005004792

Angry with his mother for having too little time for him, eleven-year-old Felix takes advantage of an opportunity to become bat boy for a minor league baseball team, hoping to someday be like his father, a famous Cuban outfielder. Includes glossaries of baseball terms and Spanish words and phrases

"An engaging, well-written story with a satisfying ending." SLJ

The **last** newspaper boy in America. Dutton Childrens Books 2009 199p $16.99

Grades: 4 5 6 7 **Fic**

1. Mystery fiction 2. Newspaper carriers -- Fiction

ISBN 978-0-525-42205-1; 0-525-42205-6

When the newspaper company cancels his route, Wil David is prepared to fight to get his job back, but his focus changes when he stumbles upon a carnival mystery and a plot by a con man that could destroy the town.

"Corbett's graceful dialogue, lovingly drawn characters and clever plot form a timely and refreshing tale." Publ Wkly

Cornwell, Nicki

Christophe's story; [by] Nicki Cornwell; illustrated by Karin Littlewood. Frances Lincoln Children's 2007 74p il $14.95; pa $7.95

Grades: 2 3 4 **Fic**

1. School stories 2. Refugees -- Fiction 3. Immigrants -- Fiction

ISBN 978-1-84507-765-5; 1-84507-765-2; 978-1-84507-521-7 pa; 1-84507-521-8 pa

Coping with a new country, a new school and a new language, Christophe wants to tell everyone why he had to leave Rwanda.

"The book succeeds, giving insight into the refugee experience and a glimpse of the horrors in Rwanda that will not overwhelm young readers." Booklist

Correa, Shan

Gaff; written by Shan Correa. Peachtree 2010 212p $15.95

Grades: 4 5 6 7 **Fic**

1. Roosters -- Fiction 2. Animal welfare -- Fiction

ISBN 978-1-56145-526-3; 1-56145-526-1

In Hawaii, thirteen-year-old Paul Silva is determined to find a way to get his family out of the illegal cockfighting business.

"Correa's debut evokes the lush melange of sights, sounds and smells in 13-year-old Paulie's multicultural neighborhood in Hawaii. . . . Also woven into this ethical debate, rooted in economics and traditions, is Hawaiian pidgin English, which may challenge even experienced readers. . . . A fascinating look at the United States most mainlanders have never seen." Kirkus

Cotler, Steve

Cheesie Mack is cool in a duel; Steve Cotler; illustrated by Adam McCauley. Random House 2012 229 p. (hardcover library binding) $18.99

Grades: 4 5 6 **Fic**

1. Camps -- Fiction 2. Siblings -- Fiction 3. Interpersonal relations -- Fiction 4. Contests -- Fiction

ISBN 9780375864384; 9780375895715; 9780375964381

LC 2011016921

This book is the second in the Cheesie Mack series. "Ronald "Cheesie" Mack and his best friend Georgie secured the funds to go to summer camp on Bufflehead Lake in Maine. Days later, the duo climbs aboard a bus and head off to Camp Windward. Unfortunately Cheesie's older sister, June . . . will be none too far away at Camp Leeward. . . . T late registration results in both boys being stuck in a cabin with the older guys including Kevin, [June's] boyfriend. When Kevin gives Cheesie a hard time once too often, Cheesie suggests a Cool Duel. Each night the boys in the cabin will vote on who did the coolest thing; in a week, the loser will have to embarrass himself in front of the whole camp by bowing to the winner. Can Cheesie prevail and still have fun at the camp he worked so hard to attend?" (Kirkus Reviews)

Cheesie Mack is not a genius or anything; illustrated by Adam McCauley. Random House 2011 229p il $15.99; lib bdg $18.99

Grades: 4 5 6   **Fic**
1. Mystery fiction 2. Summer -- Fiction 3. Friendship -- Fiction
ISBN 978-0-375-86437-7; 0-375-86437-7; 978-0-375-96437-4 lib bdg; 0-375-96437-1 lib bdg; 978-0-375-89570-8 e-book

         LC 2009-33329

Ronald, aka Cheesie, Mack and his best friend Georgie find opportunies for summertime mischief "when Georgie finds a nearly century-old letter containing a worn penny and a locket, a mystery that eventually leads the pals to the Haunted Toad, a local rundown mansion. . . . Cheesie's . . . easygoing, accessible voice will certainly appeal to middle-grade readers. . . . The action . . . is all fun and games. . . . A light-hearted and fast-moving read for kids looking for middle-school shenanigans." Bull Cent Child Books

Cheesie Mack is running like crazy! by Steve Cotler; illustrated by Douglas Holgate. 1st ed. Random House Inc. 2013 256 p. ill. (hardcover) $15.99; (library) $18.99; (ebook) $47.97; (paperback) $6.99

Grades: 4 5 6   **Fic**
1. Elections -- Juvenile fiction 2. Friendship -- Juvenile fiction 3. Schools -- Fiction 4. Elections -- Fiction 5. Friendship -- Fiction 6. Best friends -- Fiction 7. Middle schools -- Fiction 8. Track and field -- Fiction 9. Brothers and sisters -- Fiction
ISBN 0307977145; 9780307977137; 9780307977144; 9780307977151; 9780307977168

         LC 2012017978

In this book by Steve Colter, "Cheesie and his best friend, Georgie, are off to the middle school, where there will be lots of new kids and new teachers. Cheesie has a terrific idea--what better way to meet all the new kids than to run for class president? Plus, if he wins, it'll drive his evil older sister nuts! Then Cheesie gets bad news. One of his friends from his old school is also running for president." (Publisher's note

Cottrell Boyce, Frank
★ **Cosmic**. Walden Pond Press 2010 311p $16.99; lib bdg $17.89

Grades: 4 5 6 7   **Fic**
1. Size -- Fiction 2. Outer space -- Exploration --

Fiction
ISBN 978-0-06-183683-1; 0-06-183683-4; 978-0-06-183686-2 lib bdg; 0-06-183686-9 lib bdg

         LC 2008277816

Boyce "knows how to tell a compellingly good story. But in his latest extravagantly imaginative and marvelously good-natured novel he has also written one that is bound to win readers' hearts." Booklist

Framed. HarperCollins 2006 306p $16.99; lib bdg $17.89; pa $6.99

Grades: 5 6 7 8   **Fic**
1. Art -- Fiction 2. Automobiles -- Fiction 3. Family life -- Fiction 4. Business enterprises -- Fiction
ISBN 0-06-073402-7; 0-06-073403-5 lib bdg; 0-06-073404-3 pa

         LC 2006-00557

Dylan and his sisters have some ideas about how to make Snowdonia Oasis Auto Marvel into a more profitable business, but it is not until some strange men arrive in their small town of Manod, Wales with valuable paintings, and their father disappears, that they consider turning to crime.

"The colorful characters steal the show—even the secondary players are cleverly drawn. But it is Dylan's narrative voice . . . that is truly a masterpiece." SLJ

Millions. HarperCollins 2004 247p hardcover o.p. pa $6.99

Grades: 5 6 7 8   **Fic**
1. Money -- Fiction
ISBN 0-06-073330-6; 0-06-073332-2 pa

After their mother dies, two brothers find a huge amount of money which they must spend quickly before England switches to the new European currency, but they disagree on what to do with it.

"The humor, the strong family story, and Damian's narrative voice make this satisfying novel succeed on several levels." SLJ

★ The **un**-forgotten coat. Candlewick Press 2011 92p il $15.99

Grades: 5 6 7 8 9   **Fic**
1. Refugees -- Fiction 2. Immigrants -- Fiction
ISBN 978-0-7636-5729-1; 0-7636-5729-8

         LC 2010048224

"Funny, sad, haunting and original, Cottrell Boyce's story leaves important elements unexpressed. . . . To complete the narrative, readers must actively participate. They'll find myriad paths to follow—immigration, demons, social networking, the mystery of cultural difference and the nature of enchantment. A tricky, magical delight." Kirkus

Cottrell Boyce, Frank, 1959-
Chitty Chitty Chitty Bang Bang flies again; Frank Cottrell Boyce; illustrated by Joe Berger. Candlewick Press 2012 192p.

Grades: 3 4 5 6   **Fic**
1. Family -- Fiction 2. Inventors -- Fiction 3. Vacations -- Fiction 4. Automobiles -- Fiction 5. Humorous stories 6. Family life --- Europe --- Fiction 7. Adventures & adventurers -- Fiction 8. Juvenile fiction -- Humorous stories 9. Juvenile fiction -- People & Places -- Europe

10. Juvenile fiction -- Transportation -- Cars & Trucks
ISBN 9780763659578

LC 2011046996

In this book, "to the distress of Lucy, Jem, and Little Harry Tooting, their father has been laid off from Very Small Parts for Very Big Machines. Hoping to keep the wacky inventor occupied, Mrs. Tooting provides him with a beat-up old camper to restore, and her husband pops in a super-charged engine that he finds at a scrap lot and declares the upgraded camper the perfect vehicle to take on a worldwide vacation. With its new engine, though, the camper has its own itinerary in mind, and the Tootings" trip takes a few detours as their automobile transforms from camper to airplane to submarine while narrowly escaping the clutches of foreign governments and unseemly bank robbers, all of whom are interested in the car's amazing abilities." (Bulletin of the Center for Children's Books)

The **unforgotten** coat; photographs by Carl Hunter and Clare Heney. Candlewick Press 2011 112p il $15.99
Grades: 3 4 5 6 **Fic**
1. Mongols -- Fiction 2. Brothers -- Fiction 3. Refugees -- Fiction 4. Friendship -- Fiction 5. Immigrants -- Fiction
ISBN 978-0-7636-5729-1; 0-7636-5729-8

LC 2010048224

This is "a tight, powerful story—brimming with humor, mystery, and pathos—about illegal immigration and the price it exacts on children." Publ Wkly

Couloumbis, Audrey
★ **Getting** near to baby. Putnam 1999 211p $17.99; pa $5.99
Grades: 5 6 7 8 **Fic**
1. Aunts -- Fiction 2. Death -- Fiction 3. Grief -- Fiction 4. Sisters -- Fiction
ISBN 0-399-23389-X; 0-698-11892-8 pa

LC 99-18191

A Newbery Medal honor book, 2000
Although thirteen-year-old Willa Jo and her Aunt Patty seem to be constantly at odds, staying with her and Uncle Hob helps Willa Jo and her younger sister come to terms with the death of their family's baby
"Couloumbis's writing is strong; she captures wonderfully the Southern voices of her characters and conveys with great depth powerful emotions. . . . A compelling novel." SLJ

Jake. Random House 2010 162p $15.99; lib bdg $18.99
Grades: 3 4 5 **Fic**
1. Accidents -- Fiction 2. Christmas -- Fiction 3. Hospitals -- Fiction 4. Grandfathers -- Fiction
ISBN 978-0-375-85630-3; 0-375-85630-7; 978-0-375-95630-0 lib bdg; 0-375-95630-1 lib bdg

LC 2009-29383

When ten-year-old Jake's widowed mother breaks her leg just before Christmas while her sister and best friend are both away, a grandfather Jake barely remembers must come to Baltimore, Maryland, to help a neighbor take care of him.
"Never message heavy, the drama about the meaning of family will touch readers." Booklist

★ **Lexie**; illustrated by Julia Denos. Random House 2011 199p il $15.99; lib bdg $18.99
Grades: 3 4 5 6 **Fic**
1. Beaches -- Fiction 2. Divorce -- Fiction 3. Vacations -- Fiction 4. Remarriage -- Fiction 5. Father-daughter relationship -- Fiction
ISBN 978-0-375-85632-7; 0-375-85632-3; 978-0-375-95632-4 lib bdg; 0-375-95632-8 lib bdg

LC 2010-20751

When ten-year-old Lexie goes with her father to the beach for a week, she is surprised to find that he has invited his girlfriend and her two sons to join them for the entire week.
"Couloumbis demonstrates her skill at writing with quiet understanding and unstudied polish for younger readers. Her ability to walk through complicated emotional dynamics in kid-accessible language . . . is impressive." Bull Cent Child Books

Love me tender. Random House 2008 209p $16.99; lib bdg $19.99; pa $6.50
Grades: 5 6 7 8 **Fic**
1. Pregnancy -- Fiction 2. Family life -- Fiction 3. Grandmothers -- Fiction
ISBN 978-0-375-83839-2; 0-375-83839-2; 978-0-375-93839-9 lib bdg; 0-375-93839-7 lib bdg; 978-0-375-83840-8 pa; 0-375-83840-6 pa

LC 2006033162

Thirteen-year-old Elvira worries about her future when, after a fight, her father heads to Las Vegas for an Elvis impersonator competition and her pregnant mother takes her and her younger sister to Memphis to visit a grandmother the girls have never met.
"Tart characterizations, lively dialogue and Elvira's frank narration keep this perceptive novel both credible and buoyant." Publ Wkly

Maude March on the run! or, Trouble is her middle name. Random House 2007 309p $15.99; lib bdg $17.99
Grades: 4 5 6 7 **Fic**
1. Adventure fiction 2. Orphans -- Fiction 3. Frontier and pioneer life -- Fiction
ISBN 978-0-375-83246-8; 978-0-375-93246-5 lib bdg; 978-0-375-83248-2 pa

LC 2005036133

Due to a misunderstanding over her involvement in a botched robbery, Maude, with younger sister Sallie, hides out at the home of an uncle, but when she is discovered and arrested, the orphaned sisters flee, trying to clear Maude's name.
"The excitement of the Wild West comes to life in this action-packed sequel to The Misadventures of Maude March." SLJ

★ **War** games; a novel based on a true story. [by] Audrey Couloumbis & Akila Couloumbis. Random House Children's Books 2009 232p $16.99; lib bdg $19.99
Grades: 5 6 7 8 **Fic**
1. Cousins -- Fiction 2. Brothers -- Fiction 3. World War, 1939-1945 -- Underground movements -- Fiction
ISBN 978-0-375-85628-0; 0-375-85628-5; 978-0-375-95628-7 lib bdg; 0-375-95628-X lib bdg

LC 2008-46784

"For 12-year-old Petros, World War II feels unreal and far away. . . . But when the Germans invade Greece, the war suddenly comes impossibly close. Overnight, neighbors become enemies. People begin to keep secrets (Petros's family most of all). And for the first time, Petros has the chance to show Zola that he's not just a little brother but that he can truly be counted on." (Publisher's note) "Grades six to nine."(Bull Cent Child Books)

"The climactic violence is believable, and the resolution—though it takes place offstage—is deeply satisfying. Memorable." SLJ

★ The **misadventures** of Maude March; or, Trouble rides a fast horse. [by] Audrey Couloumbis. Random House 2005 295p hardcover o.p. lib bdg $17.99; pa $7.50
Grades: 4 5 6 7   **Fic**
1. Adventure fiction 2. Orphans -- Fiction 3. Frontier and pioneer life -- Fiction
ISBN 0-375-83245-9; 0-375-93245-3 lib bdg; 0-375-83247-5 pa
     LC 2004-16464
After the death of the stern aunt who raised them since they were orphaned, eleven-year-old Sallie and her fifteen-year-old sister escape their self-serving guardians and begin an adventure resembling those in the dime novels Sallie loves to read. "Grades six to ten." (Bull Cent Child Books)

"Sallie's narration is delightful, with understatements that are laugh-out-loud hilarious. . . . Hard to put down, and a fun read-aloud." SLJ

Coville, Bruce
Amber Brown is tickled pink; written by Bruce Coville and Elizabeth Levy; illustrated by Tony Ross. G.P. Putnam's Sons 2013 154 p. (hardcover) $14.99
Grades: 2 3 4 5   **Fic**
1. Weddings -- Juvenile fiction 2. Remarriage -- Juvenile fiction 3. Children of divorced parents -- Juvenile fiction 4. Weddings -- Fiction 5. Remarriage -- Fiction
ISBN 0399256563; 9780399256561
     LC 2011039493
In this book by Bruce Coville and Elizabeth Levy, "Amber can't wait to be Best Child when her mom and Max get married, but planning a wedding comes with lots of headaches. Amber can't find the right dress, her dad keeps making mean cracks about Max, and Mom and Max have very different ideas about how much this wedding should cost. Her mother even suggests they go to city hall and skip the party altogether!" (Publisher's note)

★ **Jennifer** Murdley's toad; a magic shop book. illustrated by Gary A. Lippincott. Harcourt 2002 159p il $17; pa $5.95
Grades: 4 5 6   **Fic**
1. Magic 2. Toads 3. Fantasy fiction 4. Toads -- Fiction
ISBN 0-15-204613-5; 0-15-206246-7 pa
     LC 2002-24107
A reissue of the title first published 1992
When an ordinary-looking fifth grader purchases a talking toad, she embarks on a series of extraordinary adventures

"This light, fast-paced fantasy has touches of humor (at times low comedy), an implicit moral, and a hint that Jennifer may be in for more adventures." Booklist

★ **Jeremy** Thatcher, dragon hatcher; a magic shop book. illustrated by Gary A. Lippincott. Harcourt 2002 151p il $17; pa $5.95
Grades: 4 5 6   **Fic**
1. Pets 2. Size 3. Dragons 4. Drawing 5. Friendship 6. Fantasy fiction 7. Dragons -- Fiction
ISBN 0-15-204614-3; 0-15-206252-1 pa
     LC 2002-68714
A reissue of the title first published 1991
Small for his age but artistically talented, twelve-year-old Jeremy Thatcher unknowingly buys a dragon's egg
This is "right on target. Not only is the story involving but the reader can really get a feeling for Jeremy as a person. Coville's technique of combining the real world with a fantasy one works well in this story." Voice Youth Advocates

★ **Juliet** Dove, Queen of Love; a magic shop book. Harcourt 2003 190p $17; pa $5.95
Grades: 4 5 6   **Fic**
1. Magic 2. Bashfulness 3. Magic -- Fiction 4. Mythology, Greek 5. Classical mythology -- Fiction
ISBN 0-15-204561-9; 0-15-205217-8 pa
     LC 2003-11846
A shy twelve-year-old girl must solve a puzzle involving characters from Greek mythology to free herself from a spell which makes her irresistible to boys

"Although humorous, the story has surprising depth. . . . Coville capably interweaves mythological characters with realistic modern ones, keeping readers truly absorbed." SLJ

Thor's wedding day; by Thialfi, the goat boy. as told to and translated by Bruce Coville; illustrations by Matthew Cogswell. Harcourt 2005 137p il $15; pa $5.95
Grades: 4 5 6 7   **Fic**
1. Giants -- Fiction 2. Norse mythology -- Fiction
ISBN 0-15-201455-1; 0-15-205872-9 pa
     LC 2004-29580
Thialfi, the Norse thunder god's goat boy, tells how he inadvertently helped the giant Thrym to steal Thor's magic hammer, the lengths to which Thor must go to retrieve it, and his own assistance along the way.

"Coville takes a Norse poem called the Thrymskvitha and turns it into a delightful prose romp. . . . Throughout, he injects a modern sensibility while keeping the feel of the original myth." Booklist

★ The **skull** of truth; a magic shop book. illustrated by Gary A. Lippincott. Harcourt 2002 194p il $17
Grades: 4 5 6   **Fic**
1. Fantasy fiction 2. Honesty -- Fiction 3. Schools -- Fiction 4. Friendship -- Fiction 5. Family life -- Fiction 6. Truthfulness and falsehood -- Fiction
ISBN 0-15-204612-7
     LC 2002-24244
A reissue of the title first published 1997
Charlie, a sixth-grader with a compulsion to tell lies, acquires a mysterious skull that forces its owner to tell only the truth, causing some awkward moments before he understands its power

"Coville has structured the story very carefully, with a great deal of sensitivity to children's thought processes and emotions. The mood shifts from scary to funny to serious are fused with understandable language and sentence structures." SLJ

Cowing, Sue

You will call me Drog. Carolrhoda Books 2011 281p $16.95

Grades: 4 5 6 7   Fic

1. Aikido -- Fiction 2. Divorce -- Fiction 3. Supernatural -- Fiction 4. Puppets and puppet plays -- Fiction
ISBN 978-0-7613-6076-6; 0-7613-6076-X

LC 2010050891

Unless eleven-year-old Parker can find a way to remove the sinister puppet that refuses to leave his hand, he will wind up in military school or worse but first he must stand up for himself to his best friend Wren, his mother, and his nearly-absent father.

"There is nothing else out there quite like this, and Cowing shifts fluidly from sensitive drama to startling violence to high comedy. . . . A unique look at speaking your mind." Booklist

Cowley, Joy

Snake and Lizard; [written by] Joy Cowley; [illustrated by] Gavin Bishop. Kane Miller Pub. 2008 85p il $14.95

Grades: 2 3 4   Fic

1. Snakes -- Fiction 2. Lizards -- Fiction 3. Friendship -- Fiction
ISBN 978-1-933605-83-8; 1-933605-83-9

"Snake and Lizard were born to squabble. . . . Each argument begins in misunderstanding and ends in companionable accord; yet their disagreements spring so obviously from their natures, and their repartee is so comical—snappy, ludicrous yet logical—that the salutary message is absorbed with delight. . . . Bishop's art (apparently pen-and-ink, with cheery watercolor added) enlivens almost every spread of this attractive small volume, capturing each interaction with wit and affection." Horn Book

Cowley, Marjorie

The golden bull. Charlesbridge 2008 206p lib bdg $15.95

Grades: 5 6 7 8   Fic

1. Slavery -- Fiction 2. Goldwork -- Fiction 3. Siblings -- Fiction 4. Apprentices -- Fiction
ISBN 978-1-58089-181-3 lib bdg; 1-58089-181-0 lib bdg

LC 2007-42620

During a severe drought in Mesopotamia in 2600 B.C., when their parents can no longer support them, Jomar and his sister Zefa are sent to the city of Ur, where Jomar is apprenticed to a goldsmith and Zefa must try to find a way to keep from becoming a slave. Includes author's note on the history of the region.

"Pulsating action, suspenseful dilemmas, and well-chosen details of gold-smithing and Mesopotamian justice add up to a fine tale that entertains as it reveals the sophistication of society in the cradle of civilization." Booklist

Cox, Judy

Butterfly buddies; illustrated by Blanche Sims. Holiday House 2001 86p il $15.95

Grades: 2 3 4   Fic

1. Honesty 2. Schools 3. Friendship 4. Butterflies 5. School stories 6. Best friends 7. Friendship -- Fiction 8. Butterflies -- Fiction
ISBN 0-8234-1654-2

LC 2001-16720

Third grader Robin has a series of mishaps and learns the value of honesty as she tries to become best friends with Zoey, her partner for a class project on raising butterflies. Includes butterfly care tips

"Written in simple, highly descriptive language that brings settings and characters alive, and sprinkled with lively drawings, this warmhearted friendship story is a good choice for readers transitioning to chapter books." Booklist

Nora and the Texas terror; illustrated by Amanda Haley. Holiday House 2010 87p il $15.95

Grades: 2 3 4   Fic

1. School stories 2. Cousins -- Fiction 3. Family life -- Fiction
ISBN 978-0-8234-2283-8; 0-8234-2283-6

LC 2010-14329

When Nora's uncle loses his job and house in Texas, he and his family come to stay with Nora's family in Portland, Oregon, and Nora must try very hard to adjust to her cousin Ellie, who is loud, stubborn, and a tease.

"This is an entertaining and original early chapter book; the dynamic between Nora and Ellie is realistically portrayed, and the simple plot is well developed. . . . Monochromatic line-and-watercolor illustrations . . . add further entertainment value." Bull Cent Child Books

Puppy power; illustrated by Steve Björkman. Holiday House 2008 91p il $15.95; pa $6.95

Grades: 2 3 4   Fic

1. School stories 2. Dogs -- Fiction
ISBN 978-0-8234-2073-5; 0-8234-2073-6; 978-0-8234-2210-4 pa; 0-8234-2210-0 pa

LC 2007-28395

Boisterous third-grader Fran has trouble controlling herself, but learning how to train her gigantic Newfoundland puppy helps her gain enough self-control to win the part of princess in the class play. Includes instructions on puppy training.

This is an "entertaining novel full of believable kids with recognizable problems. . . . With a brisk plot, short chapters, and frequent pen-and-ink illustrations, this story is a choice selection." Booklist

The case of the purloined professor; with illustrations by Omar Rayyan. Marshall Cavendish 2009 245p il $16.99

Grades: 3 4 5   Fic

1. Mystery fiction 2. Adventure fiction 3. Rats -- Fiction 4. Kidnapping -- Fiction
ISBN 978-0-7614-5544-8; 0-7614-5544-2

LC 2008000293

Rat brothers Frederick and Ishbu again escape the comfort of their fifth-grade classroom to go on an adventure, this time to help their friend, Natasha, seek her missing father, who is a specialist in the biochemistry of domestic animals

"This fast-paced story has lovable characters, humor, and unique plot twists." SLJ

Another title about Frederick and Ishbu is:
The mystery of the Burmese bandicoot (2007)

Coy, John

Eyes on the goal. Feiwel and Friends 2010 164p (4 for 4) $16.99

Grades: 3 4 5 6   **Fic**

1. Soccer -- Fiction 2. Friendship -- Fiction

ISBN 978-0-312-37330-6; 0-312-37330-9

This "finds the quartet of Jackson, Gig, Isaac, and Diego readying for a trip to soccer camp, even though except for Diego, they're more taken by sports that don't bafflingly forbid the use of hands. Like before, Coy includes some issues for character depth, from Gig's father being sent to Afghanistan to Jackson maybe having to move in with his mom's new boyfriend, but these take a firm backseat to the action on the field, which Coy describes with straightforward, articulate prose. Light, enjoyable reading." Booklist

Love of the game. Feiwel and Friends 2011 182p $16.99

Grades: 4 5 6 7   **Fic**

1. School stories 2. Football -- Fiction 3. Family life -- Fiction

ISBN 978-0-312-37331-3; 0-312-37331-7

LC 2010050897

Sixth-grader Jackson has a rough start in middle school, with bullies on the bus, few classes with his friends, and changes at home but some good teachers, meeting a girl, joining a club, and playing football soon turn things around.

"Realistic characters, believable dialogue and a genuine feel for the rhythms and issues of middle-schoolers make this a satisfying addition to a solid middle-grade set." Kirkus

Top of the order. Feiwel and Friends 2009 182p $16.99

Grades: 3 4 5 6   **Fic**

1. School stories 2. Divorce -- Fiction 3. Baseball -- Fiction 4. Sex role -- Fiction 5. Friendship -- Fiction 6. Family life -- Fiction

ISBN 978-0-312-37329-0; 0-312-37329-5

LC 2008-28551

Ten-year-old Jackson lives for baseball, but becomes distracted by the approach of middle school, his mother's latest boyfriend, and the presence of a girl—his good friend's sister—on his team.

"Coy effortlessly captures the voices of boys on the verge of adolescence. Jackson and his friends are fully developed. . . . Gripping play-by-play and a fast-moving plot will appeal to sports enthusiasts and reluctant readers." SLJ

Another title about Jackson is:
Eyes on the goal (2010)

Creech, Sharon

★ **Absolutely** normal chaos. HarperCollins Pubs. 1995 230p $16.99; pa $5.99

Grades: 5 6 7 8   **Fic**

1. Family life -- Fiction

ISBN 0-06-026989-8; 0-06-440632-6 pa

LC 95-22448

First published 1990 in the United Kingdom

"Those in search of a light, humorous read will find it; those in search of something a little deeper will also be rewarded." SLJ

★ **Bloomability**. HarperCollins Pubs. 1998 273p hardcover o.p. pa $5.99

Grades: 5 6 7 8   **Fic**

1. School stories

ISBN 0-06-026993-6; 0-06-440823-X pa

LC 98-14601

When her aunt and uncle take her from New Mexico to Lugano, Switzerland, to attend an international school, thirteen-year-old Dinnie discovers her world expanding

"As if fresh, smart characters in a picturesque setting weren't engaging enough, Creech also poses an array of knotty questions, both personal and philosophical. . . . A story to stimulate both head and heart." Booklist

Chasing Redbird. HarperCollins Pubs. 1997 261p hardcover o.p. pa $5.99

Grades: 5 6 7 8   **Fic**

1. Family life -- Fiction

ISBN 0-06-026987-1; 0-06-440696-2 pa

LC 96-44128

Thirteen-year-old Zinnia Taylor uncovers family secrets and self truths while clearing a mysterious settler trail that begins on her family's farm in Kentucky

"With frequent flashbacks, the narrative makes clear the complexities of the story, while the unsolved puzzles lead the reader on to the end. The writing is laced with figurative language and folksy comments that intensify both atmosphere and emotion." Horn Book Guide

★ **Granny** Torrelli makes soup; drawings by Chris Raschka. HarperCollins Pubs. 2003 141p il $15.99; lib bdg $16.89; pa $5.99

Grades: 4 5 6   **Fic**

1. Grandmothers -- Fiction

ISBN 0-06-029290-3; 0-06-029291-1 lib bdg; 0-06-440960-0 pa

LC 2002-152662

With the help of her wise old grandmother, twelve-year-old Rosie manages to work out some problems in her relationship with her best friend, Bailey, the boy next door who is blind

"This gets high marks for its unique voice (make that voices) and for the way the subtleties that are woven into the story." Booklist

Hate that cat. Joanna Cotler Books 2008 153p $15.99; lib bdg $16.89

Grades: 4 5 6 7   **Fic**

1. School stories 2. Novels in verse 3. Poetry -- Fiction

ISBN 978-0-06-143092-3; 978-0-06-143093-0 lib bdg

LC 2007044182

Jack is studying poetry again in school, and he continues to write poems reflecting his understanding of famous poems and how they relate to his life.

"Creech employs sensitivity and spare verse to carve an indelible portrait of a boy who discovers the power of self-expression." Booklist

Love that dog. HarperCollins Pubs. 2001 86p $15.99; lib bdg $14.89; pa $5.99

Grades: 4 5 6 7   **Fic**

1. Poetry 2. School stories 3. Poetry -- Fiction
ISBN 0-06-029287-3; 0-06-029289-X lib bdg; 0-06-440959-7 pa

        LC 00-54233

"Creech has created a poignant, funny picture of a child's encounter with the power of poetry. . . . This book is a tiny treasure." SLJ

Another title about Jack is:
Hate that cat (2008)

★ **Ruby** Holler. HarperCollins Pubs. 2002 310p hardcover o.p. pa $5.99

Grades: 4 5 6 7   **Fic**

1. Twins -- Fiction 2. Orphans -- Fiction 3. Country life -- Fiction
ISBN 0-06-027732-7; 0-06-056015-0 pa

        LC 00-66371

Thirteen-year-old fraternal twins Dallas and Florida have grown up in a terrible orphanage but their lives change forever when an eccentric but sweet older couple invites them each on an adventure, beginning in an almost magical place called Ruby Holler

"This poignant story evokes a feeling as welcoming as fresh-baked bread. . . . The novel celebrates the healing effects of love and compassion." Publ Wkly

★ **Walk** two moons. HarperCollins Pubs. 1994 280p $16.99; lib bdg $17.89; pa $6.99

Grades: 6 7 8 9   **Fic**

1. Death -- Fiction 2. Friendship -- Fiction 3. Family life -- Fiction 4. Grandparents -- Fiction
ISBN 0-06-023334-6; 0-06-023337-0 lib bdg; 0-06-440517-6 pa

        LC 93-31277

Awarded the Newbery Medal, 1995

After her mother leaves home suddenly, thirteen-year-old Sal and her grandparents take a car trip retracing her mother's route. Along the way, Sal recounts the story of her friend Phoebe, whose mother also left

"An engaging story of love and loss, told with humor and suspense. . . . A richly layered novel about real and metaphorical journeys." SLJ

The **great** unexpected; Sharon Creech; edited by Alyson Day. HarperCollins 2012 240 p. (lib. bdg.) $17.89

Grades: 4 5 6 7   **Fic**

1. Ireland -- Fiction 2. Orphans -- Fiction 3. Friendship -- Fiction
ISBN 0061892335; 9780061892325; 9780061892332

        LC 2012942431

In this book by Sharon Creech, "best friends and orphans Naomi Deane and Lizzie Scatterding are surprised when a strange boy falls out of a tree in their little town of Blackbird Tree, USA. His name is Finn, and Naomi falls immediately under his spell. . . . Meanwhile, in Ireland, an old woman and her companion talk of murder and revenge." (Horn Book Magazine)

The **unfinished** angel. Joanna Cotler Books 2009 164p

Grades: 4 5 6   **Fic**

1. Angels -- Fiction 2. Orphans -- Fiction 3. Villages -- Fiction
ISBN 0-06-143095-1; 0-06-143096-X lib bdg; 0-06-143097-8 pa; 978-0-06-143095-4; 978-0-06-143096-1 lib bdg; 978-0-06-143097-8 pa

        LC 2009-02796

In a tiny village in the Swiss Alps, an angel meets an American girl named Zola who has come with her father to open a school, and together Zola and the angel rescue a group of homeless orphans. "Ages eight to twelve." (Publisher's note)

"Some books are absolute magic, and this is one of them. . . . Creech's protagonist is hugely likable. . . . Creech's offering deserves to be read out loud and more than once to truly enjoy the angel's hilarious malapropisms and outright invented words, and to appreciate the book's tender, comical celebration of the human spirit." SLJ

Cronin, Doreen

The **trouble** with chickens; a J. J. Tully mystery. illustrated by Kevin Cornell. Balzer + Bray 2011 119p il $14.99; lib bdg $15.89

Grades: 2 3 4   **Fic**

1. Mystery fiction 2. Dogs -- Fiction 3. Chickens -- Fiction
ISBN 978-0-06-121532-2; 0-06-121532-5; 978-0-06-121533-9 lib bdg; 0-06-121533-3 lib bdg

        LC 2009-31213

A hard-bitten former search-and-rescue dog helps solve a complicated missing chicken case.

"Fast-paced and funny, with interesting vocabulary and a well-constructed plot, this is terrific fare for readers who are ready to move beyond picture books, but are intimidated by longer works. Cornell's pencil drawings have a mix of energy and humor that adds to the fun." Publ Wkly

Crossan, Sarah

★ The **Weight** of Water; by Sarah Crossan. Bloomsbury USA 2013 224 p. $16.99

Grades: 5 6 7 8   **Fic**

1. Immigrants -- Juvenile fiction 2. School stories -- Juvenile fiction 3. Novels in verse -- Juvenile fiction 4. Novels in verse 5. Swimming -- Fiction 6. Race relations -- Fiction 7. Swimming -- Juvenile fiction 8. Immigrants -- England -- Fiction 9. Mothers and daughters -- Fiction 10. Mothers and daughters -- Juvenile fiction 11. Alienation (Social psychology) -- Juvenile fiction 12. Immigrants -- England -- Coventry -- Juvenile fiction
ISBN 1599909677; 9781599909677

        LC 2012038645

In this book, "12-year-old Kasienka moves with Mama from Gdansk, Poland, to Coventry, England, to find Tata, her father. The adjustment is difficult. At school, Kasienka is ostracized. At home, she questions why they are searching for a man who ran from them. When Kasienka complains, Mama questions her love. Kasienka feels powerful only when she swims at the pool—something Tata taught her to do. That is also where William, a schoolmate, first notices her." (Kirkus Reviews)

Crowley, James

Starfish; illustrations by Jim Madsen. Disney/Hyperion Books 2010 310p il $16.99

Grades: 4 5 6 7 **Fic**

1. Adventure fiction 2. Siblings -- Fiction 3. Siksika Indians -- Fiction 4. Runaway children -- Fiction

ISBN 978-1-4231-2588-4; 1-4231-2588-6

In the early part of the 1900s, Beatrice and Lionel, two Blackfeet Indian children, escape from the Chalk Bluff Indian Boarding School in Montana to find their grandfather, and must elude their pursuers and make a life for themselves in the wilderness.

"This is a fast-paced and interesting novel that will maintain reader interest. Readers will be drawn into the plight of Native Americans trying to survive brutal conditions." Libr Media Connect

Crum, Shutta

★ Thomas and the dragon queen; pictures by Lee Wildish. Alfred A. Knopf 2010 267p il $15.99; lib bdg $18.99

Grades: 3 4 5 **Fic**

1. Fairy tales 2. Dragons -- Fiction 3. Princesses -- Fiction 4. Knights and knighthood -- Fiction

ISBN 978-0-375-85703-4; 0-375-85703-6; 978-0-375-95703-1 lib bdg; 0-375-95703-0 lib bdg

LC 2009-53821

When the princess is kidnapped by a dragon queen, thirteen-year-old Thomas, a new—and very small—squire-in-training boldly sets out on a quest to rescue her.

"The many likable characters . . . serve the story well. . . . Black-and-white illustrations capture the tone of the storytelling. . . . This good-hearted chapter book delivers an adventure that many young readers will enjoy." Booklist

Cuevas, Michelle

The masterwork of a painting elephant; pictures by Ed Young. Frances Foster Books/Farrar Straus Giroux 2011 136p il $15.99

Grades: 3 4 5 6 **Fic**

1. Love -- Fiction 2. Artists -- Fiction 3. Orphans -- Fiction 4. Elephants -- Fiction 5. Voyages and travels -- Fiction

ISBN 978-0-374-34854-0; 0-374-34854-5

LC 2010033108

Pigeon Jones, abandoned as a baby, is found and raised by Birch, a white, former circus elephant who paints beautiful pictures, and through their travels and adventures they discover the meanings of love and family.

"Pigeon's first-person voice traces the story's meanderings with a natural poetry, while Young's spare ink drawings ground the procedings, conveying remarkable emotional weight in a few gestures. The unlikely combination of zany story arc, resonant illustrations, and graceful telling come together in a memorable and original offering." Booklist

Cuffe-Perez, Mary

Skylar; a story. illustrated by Renata Liwska. Philomel Books 2008 138p il $14.99

Grades: 3 4 5 **Fic**

1. Geese -- Fiction 2. Birds -- Migration -- Fiction

ISBN 978-0-399-24543-5; 0-399-24543-X

LC 2007-20437

Skylar, who claims he was once wild, leads four pond geese in their first attempt at migration when an injured heron asks their help in reaching Lost Pond, where the annual Before the Migration Convention is about to be held.

"Nature imagery and extensive information on the migratory habits of Canada geese infuse a text, punctuated by occasional soft, black-and-white full-page illustrations. . . . The pace quickens when the geese talk with each other, their near constant bickering adding a dose of humor." Booklist

Curry, Jane Louise

The Black Canary. Margaret K. McElderry Books 2005 279p $16.95

Grades: 5 6 7 8 **Fic**

1. Generals 2. Courtiers 3. Conspirators 4. Royal favorites 5. Singers -- Fiction 6. Racially mixed people -- Fiction

ISBN 0-689-86478-7

LC 2003-26150

As the child of two musicians, twelve-year-old James has no interest in music until he discovers a portal to seventeenth-century London in his uncle's basement, and finds himself in a situation where his beautiful voice and the fact that he is biracial might serve him well.

"A genuinely good story that conveys a sense of darkness and mystery in the textured backdrop of a storied time and place." Booklist

Curtis, Christopher Paul

Bucking the Sarge. Wendy Lamb Books 2004 259p $15.95; lib bdg $17.99; pa $6.99

Grades: 5 6 7 8 **Fic**

1. Fraud -- Fiction 2. Mothers -- Fiction 3. African Americans -- Fiction

ISBN 0-385-32307-7; 0-385-90159-3 lib bdg; 0-440-41331-1 pa

Deeply involved in his cold and manipulative mother's shady business dealings in Flint, Michigan, fourteen-year-old Luther keeps a sense of humor while running the Happy Neighbor Group Home For Men, all the while dreaming of going to college and becoming a philosopher.

This is a "hilarious, anguished novel. . . . There are some real surprises in plot and character. . . . The farce and the failure tell the truth in this gripping story." Booklist

★ Bud, not Buddy. Delacorte Press 1999 245p $16.95; pa $6.50

Grades: 4 5 6 7 **Fic**

1. Orphans -- Fiction 2. African Americans -- Fiction 3. Great Depression, 1929-1939 -- Fiction

ISBN 0-385-32306-9; 0-440-41328-1 pa

LC 99-10614

Awarded the Newbery Medal, 2000

Coretta Scott King Award for text

Ten-year-old Bud, a motherless boy living in Flint, Michigan, during the Great Depression, escapes a bad foster home and sets out in search of the man he believes to be his father—the renowned bandleader, H. E. Calloway of Grand Rapids

"Curtis says in a afterword that some of the characters are based on real people, including his own grandfathers, so it's not surprising that the rich blend of tall tale, slapstick, sorrow, and sweetness has the wry, teasing warmth of family folklore." Booklist

★ **Elijah** of Buxton. Scholastic 2007 341p $16.99; pa $7.99

Grades: 5 6 7 8   Fic

1. Slavery -- Fiction

ISBN 0-439-02344-0; 978-0-439-02344-3; 0-439-02345-9 pa; 978-0-439-02345-0 pa

LC 2007-05181

A Newbery Medal honor book, 2008

In 1859, eleven-year-old Elijah Freeman, the first free-born child in Buxton, Canada, which is a haven for slaves fleeing the American south, uses his wits and skills to try to bring to justice the lying preacher who has stolen money that was to be used to buy a family's freedom.

"Many readers drawn to the book by humor will find themselves at times on the edges of their seats in suspense and, at other moments, moved to tears." Booklist

★ The **Watsons** go to Birmingham--1963; a novel. Delacorte Press 1995 210p $16.95; pa $6.50

Grades: 4 5 6 7   Fic

1. Prejudices -- Fiction 2. Family life -- Fiction 3. African Americans -- Fiction

ISBN 0-385-32175-9; 0-440-41412-1 pa

LC 95-7091

A Newbery Medal honor book, 1996

The ordinary interactions and everyday routines of the Watsons, an African American family living in Flint, Michigan, are drastically changed after they go to visit Grandma in Alabama in the summer of 1963

"Curtis's ability to switch from fun and funky to pinpoint-accurate psychological imagery works unusually well. . . . Ribald humor, sly sibling digs, and a totally believable child's view of the world will make this book an instant hit." SLJ

The **mighty** Miss Malone; Christopher Paul Curtis. Wendy Lamb Books 2012 307 p.

Grades: 4 5 6   Fic

1. Girls -- Fiction 2. African Americans -- Fiction 3. Great Depression, 1929-1939 -- Fiction 4. Poverty -- Fiction 5. Family life -- Fiction 6. Depressions -- 1929 -- Fiction

ISBN 9780375897368; 9780385734912; 9780385904872; 9780440422143

LC 2011036317

This book tells the story of "Deza Malone, who shares dishwashing duties with Bud Caldwell during his brief stay at a Hooverville in Flint, Mich. . . . It's 1936 in Gary, Ind., and the Great Depression has put 12-year-old Deza's father out of work. After a near-death experience trying to catch fish for dinner, Roscoe Malone leaves for Flint, hoping he'll find work. But Deza's mother loses her job shortly after, putting all the Malones out on the street. . . . [Author Christopher Paul] Curtis threads . . . bits of African-American history throughout the narrative, using the Joe Louis-Max Schmeling fight to expose the racism prevalent even among people like the librarian who tells Deza that Louis is 'such a credit to your race.'" (Publishers Weekly)

Cushman, Karen

★ **Alchemy** and Meggy Swann. Clarion Books 2010 167p $16

Grades: 5 6 7 8   Fic

1. Alchemy -- Fiction 2. Poverty -- Fiction 3. Handicapped -- Fiction 4. Father-daughter relationship -- Fiction

ISBN 978-0-547-23184-6; 0-547-23184-9

LC 2009-16387

In 1573, the crippled, scorned, and destitute Meggy Swann goes to London, where she meets her father, an impoverished alchemist, and eventually discovers that although her legs are bent and weak, she has many other strengths.

"Writing with admirable economy and a lively ability to recreate the past believably, Cushman creates a memorable portrayal of a troubled, rather mulish girl who begins to use her strong will in positive ways." Booklist

★ **Catherine,** called Birdy. Clarion Bks. 1994 169p $16

Grades: 6 7 8 9   Fic

1. Middle Ages -- Fiction

ISBN 0-395-68186-3

LC 93-23333

A Newbery Medal honor book, 1995

The fourteen-year-old daughter of an English country knight keeps a journal in which she records the events of her life, particularly her longing for adventures beyond the usual role of women and her efforts to avoid being married off

"In the process of telling the routines of her young life, Birdy lays before readers a feast of details about medieval England. . . . Superb historical fiction." SLJ

Matilda Bone. Clarion Bks. 2000 167p $15; pa $5.99

Grades: 5 6 7 8   Fic

1. Physicians 2. Middle Ages 3. Medicine -- History 4. Physicians -- Fiction 5. Middle Ages -- Fiction

ISBN 0-395-88156-0; 0-440-41822-4 pa

LC 00-24032

Fourteen-year-old Matilda, an apprentice bonesetter and practitioner of medicine in a village in medieval England, tries to reconcile the various aspects of her life, both spiritual and practical

"A fascinating glimpse into the colorful life and times of the 14th century. . . . Cushman's character descriptions are spare, with each word carefully chosen to paint wonderful pictures." SLJ

Includes bibliographical references

★ **Rodzina**. Clarion Bks. 2003 215p $16; pa $6.50

Grades: 5 6 7 8   Fic

1. Orphans -- Fiction 2. Polish Americans -- Fiction 3. Polish Americans -- Juvenile fiction

ISBN 0-618-13351-8; 0-440-41993-X pa

LC 2002-15976

A twelve-year-old Polish American girl is boarded onto an orphan train in Chicago with fears about traveling to the West and a life of unpaid slavery

"The story features engaging characters, a vivid setting, and a prickly but endearing heroine. . . . Rodzina's musings and observations provide poignancy, humor, and a keen sense of the human and topographical landscape." SLJ

Includes bibliographical references

★ **Will** Sparrow's road; Karen Cushman. Clarion Books 2012 216 p. (hardback) $16.99

Grades: 5 6 7 8   **Fic**

1. Historical fiction 2. Runaway children -- Fiction 3. Swindlers and swindling -- Fiction 4. Freak shows -- Fiction 5. Conduct of life -- Fiction

ISBN 0547739621; 9780547739625

LC 2011045898

In this book by Karen Cushman, set in Elizabethan England, "Will Sparrow, liar and thief, becomes a runaway. On the road, he encounters a series of con artists . . . and learns that others are more adept than he at lying and thieving. Then he reluctantly joins a traveling troupe of 'oddities,' including a dwarf and a cat-faced girl. . . . . At last Will is forced to understand that appearances are misleading and that he has been his own worst deceiver." (Publisher's note)

Includes bibliographical references

The **ballad** of Lucy Whipple. Clarion Bks. 1996 195p $15; $16.00

Grades: 5 6 7 8   **Fic**

1. Family life -- Fiction 2. Frontier and pioneer life -- Fiction

ISBN 0-395-72806-1; 9780395728062

LC 95-45257

"Twelve-year-old Lucy is taken by her mother from their comfortable 19th-century home in Massachusetts to the rough-and-tumble California goldfields. Lucy's younger siblings don't object to this new life, but Lucy dislikes the dirt, hard work, and lack of civilization–especially reading material. When not helping Mama run Mr. Scatter's boarding house for miners, Lucy spends her time complaining or scheming a return to her beloved Massachusetts. Despite the losses she suffers in the makeshift town of Lucky Diggins, Lucy makes some surprising discoveries about herself and what she's gained in the West." (Christ Sci Monit) "Grades five to eight." (Booklist)

"Cushman's heroine is a delightful character, and the historical setting is authentically portrayed." SLJ

★ The **midwife's** apprentice. Clarion Bks. 1995 122p $12; pa $5.99

Grades: 6 7 8 9   **Fic**

1. Midwives -- Fiction 2. Middle Ages -- Fiction

ISBN 0-395-69229-6; 0-06-440630-X pa

LC 94-13792

Awarded the Newbery Medal, 1996

In medieval England, a nameless, homeless girl is taken in by a sharp-tempered midwife, and in spite of obstacles and hardship, eventually gains the three things she most wants: a full belly, a contented heart, and a place in this world

"Earthy humor, the foibles of humans both high and low, and a fascinating mix of superstition and genuinely helpful herbal remedies attached to childbirth make this a truly delightful introduction to a world seldom seen in children's literature." SLJ

Cutler, Jane

Leap, frog; pictures by Tracey Campbell Pearson. Farrar, Straus & Giroux 2002 197p il $16

Grades: 3 4 5   **Fic**

1. Frogs -- Fiction 2. Contests -- Fiction

ISBN 0-374-34362-4

LC 2001-54456

Edward and his new friend Charley prepare for the First Annual Mark Twain Memorial Jumping Frog Contest

There's "plenty for fans of the series to enjoy: humorous dialogue that doesn't strain too hard for laughs, eccentric secondary characters . . . and, in Edward, an appealing third-grade protagonist." Horn Book

Rats! pictures by Tracey Campbell Pearson. Farrar, Straus & Giroux 1996 114p il hardcover o.p. pa $5.95

Grades: 3 4 5   **Fic**

1. Brothers -- Fiction 2. Family life -- Fiction

ISBN 0-374-36181-9; 0-374-46203-8 pa

LC 95-22953

Fourth-grader Jason and his younger brother Edward shop for school clothes, get ready for Halloween, acquire a couple of pet rats, and deal with not-birthday presents from Aunt Bea

"The brothers, alternately squabbling and supporting each other, are convincing in this lighthearted episodic novel." Horn Book Guide

Other titles about Jason and Edward are:

'Gator aid (1999)

Leap, frog (2002)

No dogs allowed (1992)

D'Adamo, Francesco

Iqbal; a novel. written by Francesco D'Adamo; translated by Ann Leonori. Atheneum Bks. for Young Readers 2003 120p $15.95; pa $4.99

Grades: 5 6 7 8   **Fic**

1. Murder victims 2. Factory workers 3. Child labor -- Fiction 4. Children's rights advocates

ISBN 0-689-85445-5; 1-4169-0329-1 pa

LC 2002-153498

Original Italian edition, 2001

A fictionalized account of the Pakistani child who escaped from bondage in a carpet factory and went on to help liberate other children like him before being gunned down at the age of thirteen

"The situation and setting are made clear in this novel. Readers cannot help but be moved by the plight of these youngsters. . . . This readable book will certainly add breadth to most collections." SLJ

D'Lacey, Chris

Gauge; illustrated by Adam Stower. Orchard Books 105p il (The dragons of Wayward Crescent) $9.99

Grades: 2 3 4   **Fic**

1. Fantasy fiction 2. Dragons -- Fiction 3. Clocks and watches -- Fiction

ISBN 978-0-545-16831-1; 0-545-16831-7

When the town council decides to demolish the old library clock and replace it with a fancy modern one, Lucy and her mother try to save the historic timepiece—with the help of a dragon.

Gruffen; illustrated by Adam Stower. Orchard Books 2009 104p il (The dragons of Wayward Crescent) $9.99

Grades: 2 3 4   **Fic**

1. Fantasy fiction 2. Dragons -- Fiction

ISBN 978-0-545-16815-1; 0-545-16815-5

LC 2009011824

Lucy thinks there is a monster lurking outside her bedroom window, so her mother makes a dragon out of clay to protect her while she sleeps.

"This is a cozy and safe tale with bits of humor sprinkled throughout. Line drawings add visual interest; their cartoon style also enforces the light, upbeat mood." SLJ

Another title in this series is:

Gauge (2009)

Dahl, Michael

Guardian of Earth; written by Michael Dahl; illustrated by Dan Schoening. Stone Arch Books 2011 48p il (DC super heroes: Green Lantern) lib bdg $25.32; pa $5.95

Grades: 2 3 4   **Fic**

1. Superheroes -- Fiction 2. Extraterrestrial beings -- Fiction

ISBN 978-1-4342-2611-2 lib bdg; 1-4342-2611-5 lib bdg; 978-1-4342-3081-2 pa; 1-4342-3081-3 pa

LC 2010025600

Ace pilot Hal Jordan has a too-close-for-comfort encounter with a UFO. His jet takes a nosedive, but a gigantic green hand appears, grabs the aircraft, and prevents the crash. Hal's alien rescuer offers him an amazing green ring of untold power and announces that the human pilot is now the new Guardian of Earth.

This "chapter-book [adaptation] of [a] popular comic [superhero has] great, full-page illustrations and . . . onomatopoeia. . . . [The cover is a] 3-D [hologram] that will attract kids. . . . [This is] action-packed." SLJ

Includes glossary and bibliographical references

The **man** behind the mask; written by Michael Dahl; illustrated by Dan Schoening; Batman created by Bob Kane. Stone Arch Books 2010 48p il (DC super heroes. Batman) lib bdg $25.32; pa $5.95

Grades: 3 4 5   **Fic**

1. Batman (Fictional character) 2. Superheroes -- Fiction

ISBN 978-1-4342-1563-5 lib bdg; 1-4342-1563-6 lib bdg; 978-1-4342-1730-1 pa; 1-4342-1730-2 pa

LC 2009006303

This "full-color chapter [book is] fast moving and entertaining. . . . The story serves as a nice starting point for readers unfamiliar with the character. . . . The retro comic-book illustrations . . . appear every few pages, adding a vibrant visual element to the proceedings. Sound effects are displayed in large, expressive fonts and colors, capturing the feel of comics." SLJ

Dahl, Roald, 1916-1990

The **BFG**; pictures by Quentin Blake. Farrar, Straus & Giroux 1982 219p il $18

Grades: 4 5 6   **Fic**

1. Giants -- Fiction 2. Orphans -- Fiction

ISBN 0-374-30469-6

LC 82-15548

Kidsnatched from her orphanage by a BFG (Big Friendly Giant), who spends his life blowing happy dreams to children, Sophie concocts with him a plan to save the world from nine other man-gobbling cannybull giants

This "is a book not all adults will like, but most kids will. . . . Highly unusual, often hilarious, and occasionally vulgar, even grisly." Booklist

★ **Charlie** and the chocolate factory; illustrated by Quentin Blake. rev ed.; Knopf 2001 162p il $15.95; lib bdg $17.99

Grades: 4 5 6 7   **Fic**

1. Humorous stories 2. Behavior -- Fiction 3. Conduct of life -- Fiction

ISBN 0-375-81526-0; 0-375-91526-5 lib bdg

LC 2001-29461

A newly illustrated edition of the title first published 1964

Each of five children lucky enough to discover an entry ticket into Mr. Willy Wonka's mysterious chocolate factory takes advantage of the situation in his own way

"Blake's energetic black-and-white illustrations enliven and update Dahl's cautionary rags-to-riches story. . . . The slapdash effect of the whimsical drawings matches Wonka's hyperactive speech and the generally frenetic narrative." Horn Book Guide

★ **James** and the giant peach; a children's story. illustrated by Lane Smith. Knopf 1996 126p il $16; lib bdg $17.99

Grades: 4 5 6   **Fic**

1. Fantasy fiction

ISBN 0-679-88090-9; 0-679-98090-3 lib bdg

LC 91-33489

A newly illustrated edition of the title first published 1961

After the death of his parents, little James is forced to live with Aunt Sponge and Aunt Spike, two cruel old harpies. A magic potion causes the growing of a giant-sized peach on a puny peach tree. James sneaks inside the peach and finds a new world of insects. With his new family, James heads for many adventures

"A 'juicy' fantasy, 'dripping' with humor and imagination." Commonweal

Matilda; illustrations by Quentin Blake. Viking Kestrel 1988 240p il $16.99; pa $6.99

Grades: 4 5 6   **Fic**

1. School stories

ISBN 0-670-82439-9; 0-14-241037-3 pa

LC 88-40312

"Dahl has written another fun and funny book with a child's perspective on an adult world. As usual, Blake's comical sketches are the perfect complement to the satirical humor." SLJ

The **enormous** crocodile; illustrated by Quentin Blake. Knopf 2000 un il hardcover o.p. pa $7.99

Grades: 2 3 4   **Fic**

1. Animals -- Fiction 2. Crocodiles -- Fiction

ISBN 0-14-241453-0 pa

A reissue of the title first published 1978

"Mr. Dahl's gift for sonorous and inventive language carries the story along merrily . . . and Quentin Blake's squidgy jungle and scaly villain, colorful crowds and righteous elephant couldn't be improved upon." N Y Times Book Rev

The **magic** finger; illustrated by Quentin Blake. Viking 1995 62p il hardcover o.p. pa $5.99

Grades: 2 3 4   **Fic**
1. Magic -- Fiction 2. Hunting -- Fiction
ISBN 0-670-85252-X; 0-14-241385-2 pa
LC 92-31443
A newly illustrated edition of the title first published
1966 by Harper & Row
Angered by a neighboring family's sport hunting, an
eight-year-old girl turns her magic finger on them
This is an "original and intriguing fantasy." Booklist

Dakin, Glenn
The **Society** of Dread. Egmont USA 2010 318p (Candle Man) $15.99
Grades: 5 6 7 8   **Fic**
1. Adventure fiction 2. Superheroes -- Fiction
ISBN 978-1-60684-019-1; 1-60684-019-3
LC 2010023104
Now head of the Society of Good Works, teenaged Theo
must reluctantly use his mysterious ability to melt evil when
he ventures underground to face villains of old.
"This appealing contemporary fantasy has a fast-paced
plot and enough inventive monsters and villains to captivate
even the most reluctant readers." SLJ

The **Society** of Unrelenting Vigilance; [illustrations by
Greg Swearingen] Egmont 2009 300p il (Candle Man)
$15.99; lib bdg $18.99
Grades: 4 5 6 7   **Fic**
1. Adventure fiction 2. Superheroes -- Fiction
ISBN 978-1-60684-015-3; 1-60684-015-0; 978-1-
60684-047-4 lib bdg; 1-60684-047-9 lib bdg
LC 2009-14035
Thirteen-year-old Theo, who has lived in seclusion his
entire life, discovers he is the descendant of the Candle Man,
a Victorian vigilante with the ability to melt criminals with
a single touch.
This is a "lighthearted, action-driven adventure. . . .
With the help of a cast of appealing characters, the nonstop
action rolls to a satisfying conclusion." SLJ

Dale, Anna
Magical mischief. Bloomsbury Children's Books 2011
300p $16.99; pa $7.99
Grades: 4 5 6   **Fic**
1. Magic -- Fiction 2. Booksellers and bookselling --
Fiction
ISBN 1-59990-629-5; 1-59990-630-9 pa; 978-1-
59990-629-4; 978-1-59990-630-0 pa
LC 2010035627
Mr. Hardbattle, aided by his friends Miss Quint and resourceful thirteen-year-old Arthur, seeks a new place for all
of the magic that has gone out of control and taken over his
bookshop and home.
"Many charming details create their own sort of magic
in this unusual story. . . . This chapter book should appeal
to young readers who like their fantasy on the cozy side."
Booklist

Daley, Michael J.
Space station rat; by Michael J. Daley. Holiday House
2005 181p $15.95; pa $6.99
Grades: 4 5 6   **Fic**
1. Science fiction 2. Rats -- Fiction 3. Space stations

-- Fiction
ISBN 0-8234-1866-9; 0-8234-2151-1 pa
LC 2004-40534
A lavender rat that has escaped from a laboratory, and
Jeff, a lonely boy whose parents are scientists, meet on an or-
biting space station, communicate by email, and ultimately
find themselves in need of each other's help and friendship
"The point of view shifts between Jeff and Rat. . . . The
developing interspecies communication raises interesting
questions about the nature of intelligence and individuality.
A thoughtful and satisfying adventure." SLJ
Another title about Jeff and Rat is:
Rat trap (2008)

Daly, Niki
★ **Bettina** Valentino and the Picasso Club. Farrar,
Straus and Giroux 2009 103p il $16
Grades: 4 5 6   **Fic**
1. School stories 2. Art -- Fiction 3. Teachers -- Fiction
ISBN 978-0-374-30753-0; 0-374-30753-9
LC 2008-03827
A controversial new teacher at Bayside Preparatory
School introduces the exciting world of art to aspiring artist
Bettina Valentino and her fifth-grade classmates, encourag-
ing them to see everyday life in a different way.
"If the story's execution wasn't delightful enough (it is),
Daly provides wonderful ink-and-wash drawings . . . that up
the amusing ante. Not only are the cast's eccentricities on
display, but Daly sometimes draws on the styles of famous
artists." Booklist

Daneshvari, Gitty
Class is not dismissed! [illustrations by Carrie Gifford]
Little, Brown and Company 2010 307p il $16.99
Grades: 4 5 6   **Fic**
1. School stories 2. Phobias -- Fiction
ISBN 978-0-316-03328-2; 0-316-03328-6
LC 2010006889
Thirteen-year-olds Madeleine, Theo, and Lulu, fourteen-
year-old Garrison, and ten-year-old new "contestant" Hyacinth, must face their phobias and join forces to learn who is
stealing wigs and pageant trophies from the School of Fear.
"Filled with an eclectic, and often eccentric, cast of
characters, this sequel uses the wry humor and outrageous
situations that characterized the first book and makes for an
entertaining read." SLJ

School of Fear; illustrated by Carrie Gifford. Little,
Brown Books for Young Readers 2009 339p il $15.99
Grades: 4 5 6   **Fic**
1. School stories 2. Phobias -- Fiction
ISBN 978-0-316-03326-8; 0-316-03326-X
LC 2008051309
Twelve-year-olds Madeleine, Theo, and Lulu, and thir-
teen-year-old Garrison, are sent to a remote Massachusetts
school to overcome their phobias, but tragedy strikes and the
quartet must work together—with no adult assistance—to
face their fears.
This is "tautly paced, spine-tingling and quite funny."
Publ Wkly

Danneberg, Julie
Family reminders; illustrated by John Shelley. Charlesbridge 2009 105p il $14.95

Grades: 3 4 5   **Fic**

1. Family life -- Fiction 2. Frontier and pioneer life -- Fiction

ISBN 978-1-58089-320-6; 1-58089-320-1

In 1890s Cripple Creek, Colorado, when young Mary McHugh's father loses his leg in a mining accident, she tries to help, both by earning money and by encouraging her father to go back to carving wooden figurines and playing piano.

"Shelley's India ink and pen illustrations add to the historical feel of this gentle, yet gripping story. This is a heartwarming novel about overcoming hardship." SLJ

Danziger, Paula

★ **Amber** Brown is not a crayon; illustrated by Tony Ross. Putnam 1994 80p il $15.99; pa $4.99

Grades: 2 3 4   **Fic**

1. School stories 2. Moving -- Fiction 3. Friendship -- Fiction

ISBN 0-399-22509-9; 0-14-240619-8 pa

LC 92-34678

The year she is in the third grade is a sad time for Amber because her best friend Justin is getting ready to move to a distant state

"Ross's black-and-white sketches throughout add humor and keep the pages turning swiftly. Danziger reaches out to a younger audience in this funny, touching slice of third-grade life, told in the voice of a feisty, lovable heroine." SLJ

Other titles about Amber Brown are:

Amber Brown goes fourth (1995)

Amber Brown is feeling blue (1998)

Amber Brown is green with envy (2003)

Amber Brown sees red (1997)

Amber Brown wants extra credit (1996)

Forever Amber Brown (1996)

I, Amber Brown (1999)

You can't eat your chicken pox, Amber Brown (1995)

Davies, Jacqueline

The **lemonade** crime. Houghton Mifflin Harcourt 2011 152p $15.99

Grades: 3 4 5   **Fic**

1. School stories 2. Trials -- Fiction 3. Siblings -- Fiction

ISBN 978-0-547-27967-1; 0-547-27967-1

LC 2010015231

When money disappears from fourth-grader Evan's pocket and everyone thinks that his annoying classmate Scott stole it, Evan's younger sister stages a trial involving the entire class, trying to prove what happened.

"The realistic depiction of the children's emotions and ways of expressing them will resonate with readers. Great for discussion, this involving and, at times, riveting chapter book has something to say and a deceptively simple way of saying it." Booklist

The **lemonade** war. Houghton Mifflin Company 2007 173p $16; pa $6.99

Grades: 3 4 5   **Fic**

1. Siblings -- Fiction 2. Money-making projects for children -- Fiction

ISBN 978-0-618-75043-6; 0-618-75043-6; 978-0-547-23765-7 pa; 0-547-23765-0 pa

LC 2006026076

Evan and his younger sister, Jesse, react very differently to the news that they will be in the same class for fourth grade and as the end of summer approaches, they battle it out through lemonade stands, each trying to be the first to earn 100 dollars. Includes mathematical calculations and tips for running a successful lemonade stand.

The author "does a good job of showing the siblings' strengths, flaws, and points of view in this engaging chapter book." Booklist

Davies, Kate

The **great** hamster massacre; illustrated by Hannah Shaw. Beach Lane 2011 177p il (Great critter capers) $12.99

Grades: 2 3 4   **Fic**

1. Mystery fiction 2. Hamsters -- Fiction 3. Friendship -- Fiction

ISBN 978-1-4424-2062-5; 1-4424-2062-6

LC 2011-02046

Best friends and next-door neighbors Anna and Suzanne try to solve the mystery of the death of Anna's two pet hamsters.

"Inspired use of simple words, straightforward syntax and effective repetition make this a top pick for slow or reluctant readers. . . . Under the plot's frothy surface lie serious depths. . . . An auspicious debut." Kirkus

"Another title about Anna and Suzanne is:

The great rabbit rescue (2011)

The **great** rabbit rescue; illustrated by Hannah Shaw. Beach Lane Books 2012 il (Great critter capers) $12.99

Grades: 2 3 4   **Fic**

1. Sick -- Fiction 2. Rabbits -- Fiction 3. Friendship -- Fiction

ISBN 978-1-4424-2064-9; 1-4424-2064-2

LC 2011008326

When Joe goes to live with his father across town and must leave behind his beloved pet rabbit, his friends Anna and Suzanne try to take care of it for him, but when the rabbit becomes ill and then Joe follows suit, the girls are certain that both will die unless they are reunited.

This "showcases Davies' laconic style and deadpan humor, so well-matched to the chapter-book format. Neatly complementing the text, Shaw's sly, witty illustrations, pie charts and graphics are a treat." Kirkus

Davis, Aubrey

A **hen** for Izzy Pippik. Kids Can 2012 32 p.

Grades: K 1 2   **Fic**

1. Folklore 2. Poverty -- Fiction 3. Cooperation -- Fiction 4. Picture books for children 5. Chickens -- Juvenile fiction

ISBN 9781554532438

This picture book depicts the adventures of a girl named Shaina, who "discovers an unusual hen . . . and strives to find its rightful owner -- a man called Izzy Pippik. Despite Shaina's insistence that he take back the hen, Pippik allows the hen, Yevka, and her flock of chicks to remain in their poor town. . . . Author Aubrey Davis has drawn upon Talmudic and Islamic folklore." (Kirkus Reviews)

Davis, Tony

Roland Wright: brand-new page; illustrated by Gregory Rogers. Delacorte Press 2010 133p il $12.99

Grades: 2 3 4   **Fic**

1. Castles -- Fiction 2. Middle Ages -- Fiction 3. Knights and knighthood -- Fiction

ISBN 978-0-385-73802-6; 0-385-73802-1

First published 2008 in Australia

In 1409, aspiring knight Roland Wright joins the royal household at Twofold Castle as a new page, but his plan to impress King John and his knights quickly backfires.

"Goofy cartoon illustrations keep the mood light. . . . A solid choice for children who are ready to make the leap to chapter books." SLJ

Roland Wright: future knight. Delacorte Press 2009 129p il $12.99; lib bdg $15.99

Grades: 2 3 4   **Fic**

1. Middle Ages -- Fiction 2. Knights and knighthood -- Fiction

ISBN 978-0-385-73800-2; 0-385-73800-5; 978-0-385-90706-4 lib bdg; 0-385-90706-0 lib bdg

LC 2008053074

First published 2007 in the United Kingdom

In 1409, skinny, clumsy Roland, the ten-year-old son of a blacksmith, pursues his dream of becoming a knight.

"This engaging book, the first in a series, has accurate details about the Middle Ages and a feisty, persevering hero. . . . Rogers's charming pen-and-ink illustrations enhance the story and may also make it more appealing to reluctant readers." SLJ

Another title about Roland Wright is:
Roland Wright: brand-new page (2010)

Day, Karen

A **million** miles from Boston. Wendy Lamb Books 2011 215p $15.99; lib bdg $18.99

Grades: 4 5 6 7   **Fic**

1. Dogs -- Fiction 2. Summer -- Fiction 3. Vacations -- Fiction 4. Friendship -- Fiction 5. Family life -- Fiction 6. Single parent family -- Fiction

ISBN 978-0-385-73899-6; 0-385-73899-4; 978-0-385-90763-7 lib bdg; 0-385-90763-X lib bdg

LC 2010-16475

Rising seventh-grader Lucy plans on a perfect summer at the Maine lake where her family has owned a cottage for decades, but family of a classmate she dislikes has bought a home there and her widowed father is bringing a girlfriend to visit.

"Day delivers a well-paced, realistic 'summer of change' story. . . . Day persuasively renders Lucy's uneasiness with her complex shifting emotions and memories." Publ Wkly

De Angeli, Marguerite Lofft

Thee, Hannah! written and illustrated by Marguerite de Angeli. Herald Press 2000 99p il pa $15.99

Grades: 3 4 5   **Fic**

1. Society of Friends -- Fiction

ISBN 0-8361-9106-4

LC 99-52422

A reissue of the title first published 1940 by Doubleday

Nine-year-old Hannah, a Quaker living in Philadelphia just before the Civil War, longs to have some fashionable dresses like other girls but comes to appreciate her heritage

and its plain dressing when her family saves the life of a runaway slave

"Hannah and the other children are very real and, in addition to the [author's] lovely pictures that follow the story, the street cries of old Philadelphia are effectively introduced and illustrated at the beginning of each chapter." Libr J

The **door** in the wall; by Marguerite de Angeli. Doubleday 1989 120p il hardcover o.p. pa $4.99

Grades: 4 5 6   **Fic**

1. Middle Ages -- Fiction 2. Physically handicapped children -- Fiction

ISBN 0-385-07283-X; 0-440-22779-8 pa

First published 1949

Awarded the Newbery Medal, 1950

Robin, a crippled boy in fourteenth-century England, proves his courage and earns recognition from the King

"An enthralling and inspiring tale of triumph over handicap. Unusually beautiful illustrations, full of authentic detail, combine with the text to make life in England during the Middle Ages come alive." N Y Times Book Rev

De Guzman, Michael

Henrietta Hornbuckle's circus of life. Farrar, Straus and Giroux 2010 152p $16.99

Grades: 4 5 6   **Fic**

1. Death -- Fiction 2. Circus -- Fiction 3. Clowns -- Fiction 4. Bereavement -- Fiction 5. Family life -- Fiction

ISBN 978-0-374-33513-7; 0-374-33513-3

LC 2009-13602

Twelve-year-old Henrietta Hornbuckle and her parents perform as clowns in a tiny, ramshackle traveling circus until a family tragedy jeopardizes Henrietta's whole offbeat world

"The writing is worthy of a tall tale, but the details are all realistic. A simple and satisfying story with a likable, unusual star." Booklist

De Lint, Charles, 1951-

The **tangled** tale of a circle of cats; written by Charles de Lint; illustrated by Charles Vess. Little, Brown 2013 304 p. $17.99

Grades: 2 3 4 5   **Fic**

1. Cats -- Juvenile fiction 2. Trees -- Juvenile fiction 3. Fantasy fiction -- Juvenile fiction 4. Cats -- Fiction 5. Magic -- Fiction 6. Trees -- Fiction 7. Orphans -- Fiction 8. Snakebites -- Fiction

ISBN 0316053570; 9780316053570

LC 2011042982

In this children's story, by Charles de Lint, illustrated by Charles Vess, "Lillian Kindred spends her days exploring the Tanglewood Forest, a magical, rolling wilderness. . . . Until the day the cats of the forest save her life by transforming her into a kitten. Now Lillian must set out on a perilous adventure that will lead her through untamed lands of fabled creatures--from Old Mother Possum to the fearsome Bear People--to find a way to make things right." (Publisher's note)

De Quidt, Jeremy

★ The **toymaker**; with illustrations by Gary Blythe. David Fickling Books 2010 356p il $16.99; lib bdg $19.99

Grades: 5 6 7 8   **Fic**

1. Adventure fiction 2. Toys -- Fiction
ISBN 978-0-385-75180-3; 0-385-75180-X; 978-0-385-75181-0 lib bdg; 0-385-75181-8 lib bdg

"Mathias . . . upon the death of his conjurer grandfather, is spirited away from the decrepit carnival they called home. His unknown new guardian appears to be after the secret contained on an inherited piece of paper, which is now in Mathias' possession. . . . Moving briskly across an atmospheric Germanic setting, the characters are chased by howling wolves, a dangerous dwarf, and unforgiving cold in a bloody, mysterious, and darkly thrilling quest." Booklist

DeFelice, Cynthia C.

Bringing Ezra back. Farrar, Straus & Giroux 2006 147p $16

Grades: 4 5 6 7   **Fic**

1. Voyages and travels -- Fiction 2. Frontier and pioneer life -- Fiction
ISBN 0-374-39939-5

LC 2005-49763

In the mid-1800s, twelve-year-old Nathan journeys from his farm on the Ohio frontier to Western Pennsylvania to rescue a friend held captive by the owners of a freak show.

"Told in Nathan's voice, this adventure treats readers to a double-dip cliff-hanging plot and heart-searing maturation." SLJ

★ **Signal**. Farrar, Straus and Giroux 2009 151p $16.99

Grades: 5 6 7 8   **Fic**

1. Moving -- Fiction 2. Friendship -- Fiction 3. Loneliness -- Fiction 4. Child abuse -- Fiction 5. Country life -- Fiction
ISBN 978-0-374-39915-3; 0-374-39915-8

LC 2008-09278

After moving with his emotionally distant father to the Finger Lakes region of upstate New York, twelve-year-old Owen faces a lonely summer until he meets an abused girl who may be a space alien.

"Well-drawn secondary characters create a threatening backdrop to the developing mystery, while Owen's poignant relationship with his work-driven father elicits sympathy. The tension builds on several fronts to a gripping climax and satisfying conclusion. Owen's likable voice, the plot's quick pace and the science fiction overtones make this a winner." Publ Wkly

Weasel; [by] Cynthia DeFelice. Avon Books 1990 119p pa $4.99

Grades: 4 5 6 7   **Fic**

1. Frontier and pioneer life -- Fiction
ISBN 978-0-380-71358-5 pa; 0-380-71358-6 pa
First published 1990 by Macmillan

Alone in the frontier wilderness in the winter of 1839 while his father is recovering from an injury, eleven-year-old Nathan runs afoul of the renegade killer known as the weasel and makes a surprising discovery about the concept of revenge

"A masterfully told, riveting tale sure to inspire strong discussion about moral choices." SLJ

Wild life; by Cynthia DeFelice. Farrar, Straus and Giroux 2011 177p $16.99

Grades: 4 5 6   **Fic**

1. Dogs -- Fiction 2. Hunting -- Fiction 3. Grandparents -- Fiction 4. Runaway children -- Fiction 5. Wilderness survival -- Fiction
ISBN 978-0-374-38001-4; 0-374-38001-5

When twelve-year-old Eric's parents are deployed to Iraq, he goes to live with grandparents in small-town North Dakota, but his grandfather's hostility and the threat of losing the dog he has rescued are too much and Eric runs away.

"Themes of accepting change and learning to let go are woven into this winning tale of boy and dog." SLJ

The **ghost** and Mrs. Hobbs; [by] Cynthia DeFelice. Farrar, Straus & Giroux 2001 180p $16; pa $5.99

Grades: 4 5 6   **Fic**

1. Arson 2. Ghosts 3. Schools 4. Jealousy 5. Ghost stories 6. Mystery and detective stories
ISBN 0-374-38046-5; 0-06-001172-6 pa

LC 00-52827

Hindered by a fight with her friend Dub and a series of mysterious fires, eleven-year-old Allie investigates the fire seventeen years earlier which claimed the lives of the husband and infant son of a school cafeteria worker, as well as the handsome young man whose ghost asks Allie for help

"This is a diverting and suspenseful ghost story offering a likable protagonist and a thrilling romantic spark." Horn Book

The **ghost** of Cutler Creek; [by] Cynthia DeFelice. 1st ed; Farrar, Straus and Giroux 2004 181p $16; pa $5.95

Grades: 4 5 6   **Fic**

1. Dogs 2. Ghosts 3. Ghost stories 4. Mystery fiction 5. Dogs -- Fiction 6. Family problems 7. Mystery and detective stories
ISBN 0-374-38058-9; 0-374-40004-0 pa

LC 2003-49051

When Allie is contacted by the ghost of a dog, she and Dub investigate the surly new boy at school and his father, who may be running a puppy mill, to see if they are involved.

"DeFelice has created a suspenseful tale that will leave readers rapidly turning pages." SLJ

★ The **ghost** of Fossil Glen; by Cynthia DeFelice. Farrar, Straus & Giroux 1998 167p (Ghost Mysteries) $16; pa $7.99

Grades: 4 5 6   **Fic**

1. Ghost stories 2. Ghosts -- Fiction 3. Diaries -- Fiction 4. Imagination -- Fiction
ISBN 0-374-31787-9; 9780312602130 pa

LC 97-33230

"Strange events begin when a calm, unknown voice prevents Allie from panicking and falling from a dangerous cliff while fossil hunting. Then, an old journal mysteriously appears in her mailbox. Allie often feels a presence nearby and dreams of a girl falling from the cliff. She then discovers the grave marker of an 11-year-old girl who was missing and presumed dead in 1994. Because of her reputation for telling stories, Allie cannot convince anyone to believe her except her longtime friend and fellow fossil hunter, Dub. Driven to pursue the mystery, Allie finds an old diary that provides her with facts about the girl's death. Foolishly,

she reveals what she knows and endangers her own life. ... .
Grades four to six." (SLJ)

"Sixth-grader Allie Nichols encounters the ghost of
Lucy Stiles and becomes involved with Lucy's unsolved
death, eventually finding proof that Lucy was murdered."
Horn Book Guide

The **ghost** of Poplar Point; [by] Cynthia DeFelice. 1st
ed.; Farrar, Straus and Giroux 2007 183p $16
Grades: 4 5 6 7   **Fic**
1. Ghost stories 2. Seneca Indians -- Fiction
ISBN 0-374-32540-5; 978-0-374-32540-4
                                           LC 2006047329
Prompted by the ghost of a young Seneca Indian girl,
twelve-year-old Allie and her friend Dub are determined, despite the opposition of an unscrupulous property developer,
that the historical pageant celebrating the founding of their
town tells the truth about the fate of the Seneca people who
lived there during the Revolutionary War.
"This engaging book moves along quickly to a satisfying
conclusion." Booklist

The **missing** manatee; [by] Cynthia DeFelice. Farrar,
Straus and Giroux 2005 181p $16; pa $6.95
Grades: 5 6 7 8   **Fic**
1. Mystery fiction 2. Fishing -- Fiction
ISBN 0-374-31257-5; 0-374-40020-2 pa
                                           LC 2004-50633
While coping with his parents' separation, eleven-year-
old Skeet spends most of Spring Break in his skiff on a Florida river, where he finds a manatee shot to death and begins
looking for the killer
"DeFelice offers a realistic adventure story that is fast
paced and full of drama. . . . The characters are multifaceted
and well developed, and the story should prompt readers to
think about cause and effect." SLJ

DeGross, Monalisa
Donavan's double trouble; [by] Monalisa DeGross; illustrated by Amy Bates. Amistad 2008 180p il $15.99;
lib bdg $17.89
Grades: 2 3 4   **Fic**
1. School stories 2. Uncles -- Fiction 3. Amputees
-- Fiction 4. African Americans -- Fiction
ISBN 978-0-06-077293-2; 978-0-06-077294-9 lib bdg
                                           LC 2007011244
Fourth-grader Donavan is sensitive about the problems
he has understanding math, and then when his favorite uncle, a former high school basketball star, returns from Na-
tional Guard duty an amputee, Donavan's problems get even
worse as he struggles to accept this "new" Uncle Vic.
"The fast, funny dialogue between friends and the warm
family relationships will draw readers to the realistic story."
Booklist
Another title about Donavan is:
Donavan's word jar (1994)

DeJong, Meindert
The **wheel** on the school; pictures by Maurice Sendak.
Harper & Row 1954 298p il $18.95; pa $6.95
Grades: 4 5 6   **Fic**
1. School stories 2. Storks -- Fiction
ISBN 0-06-021585-2; 0-06-021586-0 lib bdg; 0-06-
440021-2 pa

Awarded the Newbery Medal, 1955
"This author goes deeply into the heart of childhood and
has written a moving story, filled with suspense and distinguished for the quality of its writing." Child Books Too
Good To Miss

DeKeyser, Stacy
The **Brixen** Witch; Stacy DeKeyser. Margaret K.
McElderry Books 2012 208 p. (hardcover) $15.99
Grades: 4 5 6 7 8   **Fic**
1. Horror fiction 2. Occult fiction 3. Witches -- Fiction
4. Rats -- Fiction 5. Magic -- Fiction 6. Witchcraft
-- Fiction 7. Community life -- Fiction
ISBN 9781442433281; 9781442433304
                                           LC 2011033680
In this book, "12-year-old Rudi Bauer thinks he's found
a treasure, [but] no good can come from taking something
that belongs to the Brixen Witch. His sleep is plagued by
nightmares, but when they stop there's no relief--the village
is infested with rats. . . . As his Oma points out, young Rudi,
the one child left behind after the children disappear and the
one who precipitated the crisis, is the one to make things
right." (Kirkus Reviews)

DeLaCroix, Alice
The **best** horse ever; illustrated by Ronald Himler.
Holiday House 2010 74p il $15.95
Grades: 3 4 5   **Fic**
1. Horses -- Fiction 2. Friendship -- Fiction
ISBN 978-0-8234-2254-8; 0-8234-2254-2
                                           LC 2009-25542
"Abby gets her heart's desire: her parents purchase Griffin, the gentle horse she has grown to love during her riding
lessons. But when her best friend, Devon, can't get past her
fear of the horse to share Abby's excitement, they quarrel. .
. . Although girls who love horses are the obvious audience,
other readers will also enjoy this appealing chapter book
with its simple plot and subtly drawn characters. . . . Himler
contributes shaded pencil drawings that capture the actions
and emotions of the characters." Booklist

DeMatteis, J. M.
Imaginalis. Katherine Tegen Books 2010 248p $16.99
Grades: 5 6 7 8   **Fic**
1. Fantasy fiction 2. Magic -- Fiction 3. Imagination
-- Fiction 4. Books and reading -- Fiction
ISBN 978-0-06-173286-7; 0-06-173286-9
Devastated that her favorite fantasy book series will not
be completed, twelve-year-old Mehera discovers that only
her belief, imagination, and courage will save the land of
Imaginalis and its inhabitants from being lost forever.
This is "a sure-footed fantasy. . . . The well-drawn
characters, abundant action and humor, and hopeful mes-
sage about the power of reading and belief keep it afloat."
Publ Wkly

Deedy, Carmen Agra
★ The **Cheshire** Cheese cat; a Dickens of a tale.
Peachtree Publishers 2011 228p il $16.95
Grades: 5 6 7 8   **Fic**
1. Cats -- Fiction 2. Mice -- Fiction
ISBN 978-1-56145-595-9; 1-56145-595-4
                                           LC 2010052275

"The vagaries of tavern life in 19th-century London come alive in this delightful tale. . . . The fast-moving plot is a masterwork of intricate detail that will keep readers enthralled, and the characters are well-rounded and believable. Language is a highlight of the novel; words both elegant and colorful fill the pages. . . . Combined with Moser's precise pencil sketches of personality-filled characters, the book is a success in every way." SLJ

The **yellow** star; the legend of King Christian X of Denmark. illustrated by Henri Sørensen. Peachtree Pubs. 2000 un il $16.95

Grades: 3 4 5   **Fic**
1. Kings 2. Holocaust, 1933-1945 -- Fiction 3. World War, 1939-1945 -- Fiction
ISBN 1-56145-208-4

LC 00-20602

Retells the story of King Christian X and the Danish resistance to the Nazis during World War II
"Deedy's language is simple and rhythmic. . . . This is an interesting and thought-provoking piece of work." SLJ

Delaney, Joseph

Attack of the Fiend; [by] Joseph Delaney; illustrations by Patrick Arrasmith. 1st ed.; Greenwillow Books 2008 532p il (The last apprentice) $16.99; lib bdg $17.89

Grades: 5 6 7 8   **Fic**
1. Devil -- Fiction 2. Witches -- Fiction 3. Apprentices -- Fiction 4. Supernatural -- Fiction
ISBN 978-0-06-089127-5; 978-0-06-089128-2 lib bdg; 978-0-06-089129-9 pa

LC 2007036739

First published 2007 in the United Kingdom with title: Spook's battle

When witches steal Tom's inheritance and kidnap his relatives, Tom, the Spook, and Alice set out for Pendle Hill, a particularly dangerous district, in hopes of preventing the three witch clans from uniting to raise the Fiend, the Devil himself, thus bringing about an age of darkness.

Clash of the demons; illustrations by Patrick Arrasmith. Greenwillow Books 2009 395p (The last apprentice) $17.99; lib bdg $18.89

Grades: 5 6 7 8   **Fic**
1. Apprentices -- Fiction 2. Supernatural -- Fiction
ISBN 978-0-06-134462-6; 0-06-134462-1; 978-0-06-134463-3 lib bdg; 0-06-134463-X lib bdg

LC 2009006188

Published in the United Kingdom with title: The Spook's sacrifice

Tom is reunited with his mother and must return to Greece to face a new and terrible threat from the dark forces, and a momentous decision must be made, causing a serious rift between Tom and the Spook that threatens to separate them forever.

"The writing is direct, and the plotting and characters, most not of the human variety, are smart and believable." Booklist

Curse of the bane; illustrations by Patrick Arrasmith. 1st American ed.; Greenwillow Books 2006 455p il (The last apprentice) $16.99; lib bdg $17.89

Grades: 5 6 7 8   **Fic**
1. Witches -- Fiction 2. Supernatural -- Fiction
ISBN 978-0-06-076621-4; 0-06-076621-2; 978-0-06-076622-1 lib bdg; 0-06-076622-0 lib bdg

LC 2005-46786

First published 2005 in the United Kingdom with title: Spook's curse

Now thirteen years old, Tom Ward continues his apprenticeship with the Spook as they confront a dangerous bane who can control people's thoughts.

"Despite the blood and gore, this tale is more than a well-crafted horror story. . . . Delaney also does an exceptional job of interweaving stories, with one plot point leading insistently to the next." Booklist

Night of the soul-stealer; illustrations by Patrick Arrasmith. Greenwillow Books 2007 489p il map (The last apprentice) $16.99; lib bdg $17.89

Grades: 5 6 7 8   **Fic**
1. Witches -- Fiction 2. Supernatural -- Fiction
ISBN 978-0-06-076624-5; 0-06-076624-7; 978-0-06-076625-2 lib bdg; 0-06-076625-5 lib bdg

LC 2006051423

First published 2006 in the United Kingdom with title: The Spook's secret

Tom is dismayed when his master the Spook decrees that they will be spending the winter on gloomy and forbidding Anglezarke Moor but soon discovers the reason for his master's decision, as they tangle with two dangerous witches and struggle to keep a dark mage from resurrecting an ancient evil.

"One of the best things about this well-written series is the uncompromising horror Delaney provides at every turn. . . . Better are the nuanced interpersonal relations." Booklist

Rage of the fallen; illustrations by Patrick Arrasmith. Greenwillow Books 2011 401p il (The last apprentice) $17.99; lib bdg $18.89

Grades: 5 6 7 8   **Fic**
1. Horror fiction 2. Witches -- Fiction 3. Apprentices -- Fiction 4. Supernatural -- Fiction
ISBN 978-0-06-202756-6; 0-06-202756-5; 978-0-06-202757-3 lib bdg; 0-06-202757-3 lib bdg

LC 2010034179

Apprentice Tom and the Spook for whom he works flee to Ireland, where a powerful witch has joined forces with the dark mages trying to call forth ancient powers to destroy Tom.

"Fans of the series will cheer the return of the witch assassin Grimalkin, possibly the books' most intriguing character, and having stuck with the series thus far, likely will be looking forward to the ninth installment." Voice Youth Advocates

★ **Revenge** of the witch; illustrations by Patrick Arrasmith. Greenwillow Bks. 2005 344p il (The last apprentice) $14.99; lib bdg $15.89; pa $7.99

Grades: 5 6 7 8   **Fic**
1. Witches -- Fiction 2. Supernatural -- Fiction
ISBN 0-06-076618-2; 0-06-076619-0 lib bdg; 0-06-076620-4 pa

LC 2004-54003

Young Tom, the seventh son of a seventh son, starts work as an apprentice for the village spook, whose job is to protect ordinary folk from "ghouls, boggarts, and all manner of wicked beasties"

"Delaney grabs readers by the throat and gives them a good shake in a smartly crafted story. . . . This is a gristly thriller. . . . Yet the twisted horror is amply buffered by an exquisitely normal young hero, matter-of-fact prose, and a workaday normalcy." Booklist

Other titles in this series are:

Curse of the bane (2006)

Night of the soul-stealer (2007)

Attack of the fiend (2008)

Wrath of the Bloodeye (2008)

Clash of the demons (2009)

Rise of the huntress (2010)

Rage of the fallen (2011)

Rise of the huntress; illustrations by Patrick Arrasmith. Greenwillow Books 2010 436p (The last apprentice) $17.99; pa $7.99

Grades: 5 6 7 8   Fic

1. Horror fiction 2. Witches -- Fiction 3. Apprentices -- Fiction 4. Supernatural -- Fiction

ISBN 978-0-06-171510-5; 0-06-171510-7; 978-0-06-171512-9 pa; 0-06-171512-3 pa

LC 2009044188

Returning from Greece, Tom and the Spook find that their home, including the Spook's precious library of knowledge, has been burned to the ground, and that their battle against the denizens of the dark must continue.

"Delaney once again combines chills with character development. . . . Arrasmith's black-and-white illustrations reinforce the idea that the supernatural creatures, even Tom's temporary cohorts, are worth a shudder." Horn Book Guide

The **Spook's** Bestiary; illustrated by Julek Heller. Greenwillow Books 2011 222p il (The last apprentice) $16.99

Grades: 5 6 7 8   Fic

1. Horror fiction 2. Apprentices -- Fiction 3. Supernatural -- Fiction

ISBN 978-0-06-208114-8; 0-06-208114-4

LC 2010049856

Ready to be presented to the last apprentice, Tom Ward, the spook's notebook contains instructions for vanquishing boggarts, witches, the unquiet dead, and other dark creatures and spirits.

"Heller's creepy drawings fill the pages and, like the whole book, they should delight fans of the series." SLJ

Wrath of the Bloodeye; [by] Joseph Delaney; illustrations by Patrick Arrasmith. 1st ed.; Greenwillow Books 2008 511p il (The last apprentice) $17.99; lib bdg $18.89; pa $7.99

Grades: 5 6 7 8   Fic

1. Witches -- Fiction 2. Apprentices -- Fiction 3. Supernatural -- Fiction

ISBN 978-0-06-134459-6; 0-06-134459-1; 978-0-06-134460-2 lib bdg; 0-06-134460-5 lib bdg; 978-0-06-134461-9 pa; 0-06-134461-3 pa

LC 2008017920

The continuing adventures of Tom, the seventh son of a seventh son and apprentice to the local Spook, who faces danger and death daily in his job protecting the region from evil.

Derby, Sally

Kyle's island. Charlesbridge 2010 191p $16.95

Grades: 5 6 7 8   Fic

1. Lakes -- Fiction 2. Islands -- Fiction 3. Siblings -- Fiction 4. Family life -- Fiction

ISBN 978-1-58089-316-9; 1-58089-316-3

LC 2009-17581

Kile, almost thirteen, spends much of the summer yearning to explore a nearby island, striving to be a good brother, fishing with an elderly neighbor, and fuming at his parents over their separation that is forcing his mother to sell the family's cabin on a Michigan lake.

"Derby writes a subtle coming-of-age novel that is engaging from start to finish. Kyle's character is so well developed that many readers will be able to understand the realistic emotions and situations taking place." Libr Media Connect

Deriso, Christine Hurley

The **Right** -Under Club; [by] Christine Hurley Deriso. Delacorte Press 2007 195p $15.99; lib bdg $18.99

Grades: 5 6 7 8   Fic

1. Friendship -- Fiction 2. Stepfamilies -- Fiction

ISBN 978-0-385-73334-2; 978-0-385-90351-6 lib bdg

LC 2006019768

Over the summer, five middle school girls form a club based on the fact that they all feel neglected and misunderstood by their blended families

"In this timely novel, Deriso introduces solid characters. . . . The changing voices are easy to navigate and lend charm to the narrative." SLJ

DiCamillo, Kate

★ **Because** of Winn-Dixie. Candlewick Press 2000 182p $15.99; pa $6.99

Grades: 4 5 6 7   Fic

1. Dogs 2. Dogs -- Fiction 3. City and town life -- Florida

ISBN 978-0-7636-0776-0; 0-7636-0776-2; 978-0-7636-4432-1 pa; 0-7636-4432-3 pa

LC 99-34260

A Newbery honor book, 2001

Ten-year-old India Opal Buloni describes her first summer in the town of Naomi, Florida, and all the good things that happen to her because of her big ugly dog Winn-Dixie

"This well-crafted, realistic, and heartwarming story will be read and reread as a new favorite deserving a long-term place on library shelves." SLJ

Mercy Watson fights crime; [by] Kate DiCamillo; illustrated by Chris Van Dusen. 1st ed.; Candlewick Press 2006 70p il $12.99

Grades: PreK K 1 2   Fic

1. Pigs -- Fiction

ISBN 0-7636-2590-6

LC 2005053639

Mercy the pig's love of buttered toast leads to the capture of a small thief who would rather be a cowboy.

"The shiny, retro pictures still amuse. Even beginning readers will wish for more." Booklist

Mercy Watson goes for a ride; [by] Kate DiCamillo; illustrated by Chris Van Dusen. 1st ed.; Candlewick Press 2006 72p il $12.99

Grades: K 1 2 3   **Fic**

1. Pigs -- Fiction

ISBN 0-7636-2332-6; 978-0-7636-2332-6

     LC 2004051832

After Mercy the pig snuggles to sleep with the Watsons, all three awaken with the bed teetering on the edge of a big hole in the floor.

"Van Dusen's larger-than-life characters and retro sensibility extend the dry humor of the situation, and his shiny, rainbow-bright gouache art shoots the energy . . . right off the page. Great for emergent readers." Booklist

Mercy Watson thinks like a pig; [by] Kate DiCamillo; illustrated by Chris Van Dusen. 1st ed.; Candlewick Press 2008 70p il $12.99

Grades: K 1 2 3   **Fic**

1. Pigs -- Fiction 2. Flowers -- Fiction

ISBN 978-0-7636-3265-6; 0-7636-3265-1

     LC 2007040623

After Mercy Watson follows the delightful scent and delicious taste of the pansies her thoughtful neighbors plant to beautify their yard, Animal Control Officer Francine Poulet is called out to handle the case, which brings unexpected results.

"As usual, Van Dusen's shiny, stylized artwork captures all the fun of Mercy's capers." Booklist

★ **Mercy** Watson to the rescue; illustrated by Chris Van Dusen. Candlewick Press 2005 68p il $12.99

Grades: K 1 2 3   **Fic**

1. Pigs -- Fiction

ISBN 0-7636-2270-2

     LC 2004-51896

After Mercy the pig snuggles to sleep with the Watsons, all three awaken with the bed teetering on the edge of a big hole in the floor.

"Appropriate as both a picture book and a beginning reader, this joyful story combines familiar elements . . . with a raucous telling that lets readers in on the joke. . . . The gouache illustrations are polished to a sheen and have plenty of heft." Booklist

Other titles about Mercy Watson are:

Mercy Watson fights crime (2006)

Mercy Watson goes for a ride (2006)

Mercy Watson: princess in disguise (2007)

Mercy Watson thinks like a pig (2008)

Mercy Watson: something wonky this way comes (2009)

Mercy Watson: princess in disguise; [by] Kate DiCamillo; illustrated by Chris Van Dusen. 1st ed.; Candlewick Press 2007 70p il $12.99

Grades: 1 2 3   **Fic**

1. Pigs -- Fiction 2. Halloween -- Fiction

ISBN 978-0-7636-3014-0; 0-7636-3014-4

     LC 2006051827

Persuaded by the word "treating" to dress up as a princess for Halloween, Mercy the pig's trick-or-treat outing has some very unexpected results.

"This installment has the same bright appeal as the previous books, and the pictures are priceless." Booklist

Mercy Watson: something wonky this way comes. Candlewick Press 2009 86p il $12.99

Grades: K 1 2 3   **Fic**

1. Pigs -- Fiction 2. Motion pictures -- Fiction

ISBN 978-0-7636-3644-9; 0-7636-3644-4

Mr. and Mrs. Watson take their pig, Mercy, to a drive-in movie.

"Illustrations are done in gouache using a bright, retro palette of glossy colors, bringing the text vibrantly to life. All of the elements of the earlier stories are here—jovial characters, good-humored mayhem, and effortless repetition that moves the story forward." SLJ

★ The **magician's** elephant; illustrated by Yoko Tanaka. Candlewick Press 2009 201p il $16.99

Grades: 4 5 6 7   **Fic**

1. Adventure fiction 2. Orphans -- Fiction 3. Siblings -- Fiction 4. Elephants -- Fiction 5. Missing children -- Fiction

ISBN 978-0-7636-4410-9; 0-7636-4410-2

     LC 2009-07359

When ten-year-old orphan Peter Augustus Duchene encounters a fortune teller in the marketplace one day and she tells him that his sister, who is presumed dead, is in fact alive, he embarks on a remarkable series of adventures as he desperately tries to find her.

"The profound and deeply affecting emotions at work in the story are buoyed up by the tale's succinct, lyrical text; gentle touches of humor; and uplifting message." Booklist

★ The **miraculous** journey of Edward Tulane; illustrated by Bagram Ibatoulline. Candlewick Press 2006 198p il $18.99; pa $6.99

Grades: 3 4 5 6   **Fic**

1. Toys -- Fiction 2. Rabbits -- Fiction

ISBN 0-7636-2589-2; 0-7636-4367-X pa

     LC 2004-56129

Edward Tulane, a coldhearted and proud toy rabbit, loves only himself until he is separated from the little girl who adores him and travels across the country, acquiring new owners and listening to their hopes, dreams, and histories.

"This achingly beautiful story shows a true master of writing at her very best. . . . Ibatoulline's lovely sepia-toned gouache illustrations and beautifully rendered color plates are exquisite." SLJ

★ The **tale** of Despereaux; being the story of a mouse, a princess, some soup, and a spool of thread. illustrated by Timothy Basil Ering. Candlewick Press 2003 267p il $17.99; pa $7.99

Grades: 3 4 5 6   **Fic**

1. Fairy tales 2. Mice -- Fiction

ISBN 0-7636-1722-9; 0-7636-2529-9 pa

     LC 2002-34760

Awarded the Newbery Medal, 2004

The adventures of Despereaux Tilling, a small mouse of unusual talents, the princess that he loves, the servant girl who longs to be a princess, and a devious rat determined to bring them all to ruin

"Forgiveness, light, love, and soup. These essential ingredients combine into a tale that is as soul stirring as it is delicious. . . . Ering's soft pencil illustrations reflect the story's charm." Booklist

DiSalvo, DyAnne

The **sloppy** copy slipup; [by] DyAnne DiSalvo. Holiday House 2006 103p il $16.95; pa $6.95

Grades: 2 3 4   **Fic**

1. School stories 2. Authorship -- Fiction

ISBN 0-8234-1947-9; 0-8234-2189-9 pa

Fourth-grader Brian Higman worries about how his teacher Miss Fromme—nicknamed The General—will react when he fails to hand in a writing assignment, but he ends up being able to tell his story, after all

"DiSalvo combines spot-on humor, vivid classroom scenes, and tension that builds from the first page, and Brian's story . . . will keep children eagerly engaged." Booklist

DiTerlizzi, Tony

Kenny & the dragon; [by] Tony DiTerlizzi. Simon & Schuster Books for Young Readers 2008 151p $15.99

Grades: 4 5 6 7   **Fic**

1. Dragons -- Fiction 2. Rabbits -- Fiction 3. Knights and knighthood -- Fiction

ISBN 978-1-4169-3977-1; 1-4169-3977-6

                         LC 2008-7309

Book-loving Kenny the rabbit has few friends in his farming community, so when one, bookstore owner George, is sent to kill another, gentle dragon Grahame, Kenny must find a way to prevent their battle while satisfying the dragon-crazed townspeople.

"DiTerlizzi's novel is lighthearted and his informal pencil sketches enhance the creative interpretation of what would otherwise be a simple animal story." Publ Wkly

A **hero** for WondLa; by Tony DiTerlizzi; with illustrations by the author. Simon & Schuster Books for Young Readers 2012 445 p. (hardcover) $17.99

Grades: 5 6 7 8   **Fic**

1. Science fiction 2. Rescue work -- Fiction 3. Life on other planets -- Fiction 4. Identity -- Fiction 5. Human-alien encounters -- Fiction

ISBN 1416983120; 9781416983125; 9781442450844

                        LC 2011037031

Author Tony DiTerlizzi tells a science fiction story. "Eva Nine had never seen another human, but after a human boy named Hailey rescues her along with her companions, she couldn't be happier. Eva thinks she has everything she's ever dreamed of, especially when Hailey brings her and her friends to the colony of New Attica, where humans of all shapes and sizes live in apparent peace and harmony. But all is not idyllic in New Attica, and Eva Nine soon realizes that something sinister is going on . . . [that] could mean the end of everything and everyone on planet Orbona." (Publisher's note)

★ The **search** for WondLa; with illustrations by the author. Simon & Schuster Books for Young Readers 2010 477p il $17.99

Grades: 5 6 7 8   **Fic**

1. Science fiction 2. Extraterrestrial beings -- Fiction

ISBN 978-1-4169-8310-1; 1-4169-8310-4

                        LC 2010-01326

Living in isolation with a robot on what appears to be an alien world populated with bizarre life forms, a twelve-year-old human girl called Eva Nine sets out on a journey to find others like her.

"The abundant illustrations, drawn in a flat, two-tone style, are lush and enhance readers' understanding of this unique universe. . . . DiTerlizzi is pushing the envelope in his latest work, nearly creating a new format that combines a traditional novel with a graphic novel and with the interactivity of the computer. Yet, beneath this impressive package lies a theme readers will easily relate to: the need to belong, to connect, to figure out one's place in the world. The novel's ending is a stunning shocker that will leave kids frantically awaiting the next installment." SLJ

Diamand, Emily

Flood and fire. Chicken House/Scholastic 2011 351p il (Raiders' ransom) $17.99

Grades: 4 5 6 7   **Fic**

1. Science fiction 2. Adventure fiction 3. Cats -- Fiction 4. Robots -- Fiction 5. Computers -- Fiction 6. Terrorism -- Fiction

ISBN 978-0-545-24268-4; 0-545-24268-1

                        LC 2010023544

In 22nd-century Cambridge, England, thirteen-year-old Lilly Melkun must try to stop the strange, uncontrollable robots that were activated when a sinister-looking chip in her hand-held computer triggered a false anti-terrorist alert.

"The rare combination of action at breakneck speed and significant, believable character development makes this just about impossible to put down." Kirkus

★ **Raiders'** ransom. Chicken House/Scholastic 2009 334p map $17.99

Grades: 4 5 6 7   **Fic**

1. Science fiction 2. Adventure fiction 3. Pirates -- Fiction 4. Kidnapping -- Fiction 5. Environmental degradation -- Fiction

ISBN 978-0-545-14297-7; 0-545-14297-0

                        LC 2008-43692

It's the 22nd century and, because of climate change, much of England is underwater. Poor Lilly is out fishing with her trusty sea-cat when greedy raiders pillage the town—and kidnap the prime minister's daughter. Her village blamed, Lilly decides to find the girl.

This is a "captivating story. . . . A well-drawn world, plot twists galore and spunky characters make this one a true page-turner." Kirkus

Dicamillo, Kate

★ **Bink** & Gollie; [by] Kate DiCamillo and Alison McGhee; illustrated by Tony Fucile. Candlewick Press 2010 81p il $15.99

Grades: 1 2 3   **Fic**

1. Friendship -- Fiction

ISBN 0-7636-3266-X; 978-0-7636-3266-3

                        LC 2009-49100

Two roller-skating best friends share adventures involving bright socks, a trek to the Andes, and an unlikely companion. "Ages six to eight." (N Y Times Book Rev)

"In the first tale, Bink's outrageous socks offend Gollie's sartorial eye, but the two compromise for friendship's sake. The second story sends Gollie on an imagined climb up the Andes, shutting Bink out of the house until she arrives at the door with a sandwich. . . . In the final episode, Gollie is jealous of Bink's new pet fish until Bink reassures her that no one can take her place. All three stories . . . offer delightful portrayals of two headstrong characters who, despite their differences and idiosyncratic quirks, know the importance of true friendship. The delightful digitalized cartoon illustrations . . . reinforce the humor of the text." SLJ

Another title about Bink & Gollie is:

Two for one (2012)

Dicamillo, Kate, 1964-
Bink and Gollie; best friends forever. Kate DiCamillo, Alison McGheeq, Tony Fucile. Candlewick Press 2013 96 p. (Bink and Gollie) (reinforced) $15.99

Grades: 1 2 3 4 **Fic**
1. Girls -- Juvenile fiction 2. Friendship -- Juvenile fiction
ISBN 0763634972; 9780763634971

LC 2012942669

In this children's story, by Kate DiCamillo and Alison McGhee, illustrated by Tony Fucile, "Gollie is quite sure she has royal blood in her veins, but can Bink survive her friend's queenly airs . . . ? Bink wonders what it would be like to be as tall as her friend, but how far will she stretch her luck to find out? And when Bink and Gollie long to get their picture into a book of record holders, where will they find the kudos they seek?" (Publisher's note)

★ **Flora** and Ulysses; The Illuminated Adventures. by Kate DiCamillo; illustrated by K. G. Campbell. Candlewick Press 2013 240 p. ill. (reinforced) $17.99

Grades: 5 6 7 8 **Fic**
1. Occult fiction -- Juvenile fiction 2. Children of divorced parents -- Juvenile fiction
ISBN 076366040X; 9780763660406

LC 2012947748

In this book by Newbury Medalist Kate DiCamillo, "bitter about her parents' divorce. Flora Buckman has withdrawn into her favorite comic book The Amazing Incandesto! and memorized the advisories in its ongoing bonus feature, Terrible Things Can Happen to You! She puts those life-saving tips into action when a squirrel is swallowed whole by a neighbor's new vacuum cleaner. . . . Flora resuscitates the squirrel," who now has superpowers. (Publishers Weekly)

Two for one; by Kate DiCamillo & Alison McGhee; illustrated by Tony Fucile. 1st ed. Candlewick Press 2012 75 p. ill. (some col.) (Bink & Gollie) (reinforced) $15.99; (prebind) $15.99; (paperback) $6.99

Grades: 2 3 4 **Fic**
1. Humorous fiction 2. Fairs -- Juvenile fiction 3. Friendship -- Juvenile fiction 4. Friendship -- Fiction
ISBN 0763633615; 9780763633615; 9781451740134; 9780763664459

LC 2011046625

This children's story by Kate DiCamillo and Alison McGhee, illustrated by Tony Fucile, continues the Theodor Seuss Geisel Award-winning "Bink and Gollie" series. "The state fair is in town, and now Bink and Gollie . . . must use teamwork and their gray matter while navigating its many

wonders. . . . As the undaunted duo steps into the mysterious tent of fortune-teller Madame Prunely, one prediction is crystal clear: this unlikely pair will always be the closest of pals." (Publisher's note)

Dickens, Charles, 1812-1870
★ A **Christmas** carol; [by] Charles Dickens; [illustrated by] Brett Helquist; [abridged by Josh Greenhut] HarperCollins 2009 un il $17.99; lib bdg $18.89

Grades: 3 4 5 6 **Fic**
1. Ghost stories 2. Christmas -- Fiction
ISBN 978-0-06-165099-4; 0-06-165099-4; 978-0-06-165100-7 lib bdg; 0-06-165100-1 lib bdg

LC 2008044031

A miser learns the true meaning of Christmas when three ghostly visitors review his past and foretell his future.

"Sacrificing none of Dickens's rich language, this retelling reads beautifully. The artist uses watercolor, pencil, and pastel to create cinematic artwork that contains amusing details; additionally, there are a number of pen-and-ink vignettes that help set the scenes. A winning combination of sparkling prose and exciting art." SLJ

Divakaruni, Chitra Banerjee
The **conch** bearer. Roaring Brook Press 2003 265p (Brotherhood of the conch) $16.95; lib bdg $23.90

Grades: 5 6 7 8 **Fic**
1. Magic -- Fiction
ISBN 978-0-7613-1935-1; 0-7613-1935-2; 978-0-7613-2793-6 lib bdg; 0-7613-2793-2 lib bdg

LC 2003-8578

In India, a healer invites twelve-year-old Anand to join him on a quest to return a magical conch to its safe and rightful home, high in the Himalayan mountains

"Divakaruni keeps her tale fresh and riveting." Publ Wkly

Other titles in this series are:
The mirror of fire and dreaming (2005)
Shadowland (2009)

Doder, Joshua
A **dog** called Grk. Delacorte Press 2007 249p hardcover o.p. pa $6.50

Grades: 5 6 7 **Fic**
1. Adventure fiction 2. Dogs -- Fiction
ISBN 978-0-385-73359-5; 0-385-73359-3; 978-0-440-42147-4 pa; 0-440-42147-0 pa

LC 2006-46258

A British schoolboy finds adventure when he travels to a dangerous foreign country to return a small dog to its rightful owner.

"This is fast-paced and entertaining." Booklist
Other titles about Grk are:
Grk and the Pelotti gang (2007)
Grk and the hot dog trail (2008)
Grk: Operation Tortoise (2009)
Grk smells a rat (2009)

Donovan, Gail
In loving memory of Gorfman T. Frog; [illustrated by Janet Pedersen] Dutton Children's Books 2009 180p il $15.99

Grades: 3 4 5 **Fic**
1. School stories 2. Frogs -- Fiction 3. Family life

-- Fiction

ISBN 978-0-525-42085-9; 0-525-42085-1

LC 2008-13897

When irrepressible fifth-grader Josh finds a five-legged frog in his backyard pond, it leads to him learning a lot about amphibians—and himself.

"Pedersen's full-page illustrations ramp up the comedy and action, and Donovan ably shows how the school world of kids is separate and little understood by adults." Booklist

Dorris, Michael

Morning Girl. Hyperion Bks. for Children 1992 74p hardcover o.p. pa $4.99

Grades: 4 5 6 7   Fic

1. Taino Indians -- Fiction

ISBN 0-7868-1358-X pa

LC 92-52989

Twelve year old Morning Girl, a Taino Indian who loves the day, and her younger brother Star Boy, who loves the night, take turns describing their life on a Bahamian island in 1492; in Morning Girl's last narrative, she witnesses the arrival of the first Europeans to her world

"The author uses a lyrical, yet easy-to-follow, style to place these compelling characters in historical context. . . . Dorris does a superb job of showing that family dynamics are complicated, regardless of time and place. . . . A touching glimpse into the humanity that connects us all." Horn Book

Sees Behind Trees. Hyperion Bks. for Children 1996 104p hardcover o.p. pa $4.99

Grades: 4 5 6 7   Fic

1. Native Americans -- Fiction 2. Vision disorders -- Fiction

ISBN 0-7868-1357-1 pa

LC 96-15859

"For the partially sighted Walnut, it is impossible to prove his right to a grown-up name by hitting a target with his bow and arrow. With his highly developed senses, however, he demonstrates that he can do something even better: he can see 'what cannot be seen' which earns him the name Sees Behind Trees. . . . Set in sixteenth-century America, this richly imagined and gorgeously written rite-of-passage story has the gravity of legend. Moreover, it has buoyant humor and the immediacy of a compelling story that is peopled with multidimensional characters." Booklist

Dowd, Siobhan

★ The **London** Eye mystery. David Fickling Books 2008 322p $15.99; lib bdg $18.99; pa $7.50

Grades: 5 6 7 8   Fic

1. Mystery fiction 2. Cousins -- Fiction 3. Siblings -- Fiction 4. Missing children -- Fiction 5. Asperger's syndrome -- Fiction

ISBN 978-0-375-84976-3; 0-375-84976-9; 978-0-375-94976-0 lib bdg; 0-375-84976-3 lib bdg; 978-0-385-75184-1 pa; 0-385-75184-2 pa

LC 2007-15119

First published 2007 in the United Kingdom

When Ted and Kat's cousin Salim disappears from the London Eye ferris wheel, the two siblings must work together—Ted with his brain that is "wired differently" and impatient Kat—to try to solve the mystery of what happened to Salim.

"Everything rings true here, the family relationships, the quirky connections of Ted's mental circuitry, and . . . . the mystery. . . . A page turner with heft." Booklist

Dowell, Frances O'Roark

★ **Chicken** boy. Atheneum Books for Young Readers 2005 201p $15.95; pa $5.99

Grades: 4 5 6 7   Fic

1. Chickens -- Fiction 2. Friendship -- Fiction 3. Family life -- Fiction

ISBN 0-689-85816-7; 1-4169-3482-0 pa

LC 2004-10928

Since the death of his mother, Tobin's family life and school life have been in disarray, but after he starts raising chickens with his seventh-grade classmate, Henry, everything starts to fall into place.

"There is no glib resolution, here. But the strong narration and the child's struggle with forgiveness make for poignant, aching drama." Booklist

★ **Dovey** Coe. Atheneum Bks. for Young Readers 2000 181p $16; pa $5.99

Grades: 5 6 7 8   Fic

1. Brothers and sisters 2. Mountain life -- Fiction 3. Mountain life -- North Carolina

ISBN 0-689-83174-9; 0-689-84667-3 pa

LC 99-46870

When accused of murder in her North Carolina mountain town in 1928, Dovey Coe, a stronged-willed twelve-year-old girl, comes to a new understanding of others, including her deaf brother

"Dowell has created a memorable character in Dovey, quick-witted and honest to a fault. . . . This is a delightful book, thoughtful and full of substance." Booklist

★ **Falling** in. Atheneum Books for Young Readers 2010 245p il $16.99

Grades: 4 5 6 7   Fic

1. Fantasy fiction

ISBN 978-1-4169-5032-5; 1-4169-5032-X

LC 2009-10412

Middle-schooler Isabelle Bean follows a mouse's squeak into a closet and falls into a parallel universe where the children believe she is the witch they have feared for years, finally come to devour them.

"This perfectly paced story has enough realistic elements to appeal even to nonfantasy readers." Booklist

The **kind** of friends we used to be. Atheneum Books for Young Readers 2009 234p $16.99

Grades: 5 6 7 8   Fic

1. School stories 2. Friendship -- Fiction

ISBN 978-1-4169-5031-8; 1-4169-5031-1

LC 2008-22245

Twelve-year-olds Kate and Marylin, friends since preschool, draw further apart as Marylin becomes involved in student government and cheerleading, while Kate wants to play guitar and write songs, and both develop unlikely friendships with other girls and boys.

"Dowell gets middle-school dynamics exactly right, and while her empathetic portraits of Kate and Marylin are genuine and heartfelt, even secondary characters are memorable.

A realistic and humorous look at the trials and tribulations of growing up and growing independent." SLJ

Phineas L. Macguire erupts! the first experiment. Atheneum Books for Young Readers 2006 167p il (From the highly scientific notebooks of Phineas L. MacGuire) $15.95; pa $4.99
Grades: 2 3 4 **Fic**
1. School stories 2. Science -- Experiments -- Fiction
ISBN 978-1-4169-0195-2; 1-4169-0195-7; 978-1-4169-4734-9 pa; 1-4169-4734-5 pa
LC 2005-12605
Fourth-grade science whiz Phineas MacGuire is forced to team up with the new boy in class on a science fair project, but the boy's quirky personality causes Phineas to wonder if they have any chance of winning.
"The type is large and well spaced, and black-and-white art playfully captures the characters. . . . Budding scientists will find instructions for their own experiments at the end of the book." Booklist
Other titles in this series are:
Phineas L. MacGuire . . . gets slimed! (2007)
Phineas L. MacGuire . . . blasts off! (2008)

★ The **second** life of Abigail Walker; Frances O'Roark Dowell. Atheneum Books for Young Readers 2012 228 p. (hardcover) $16.99
Grades: 4 5 6 7 **Fic**
1. Self-confidence -- Fiction 2. Friendship -- Juvenile fiction 3. Middle schools -- Juvenile fiction 4. Friendship -- Fiction 5. Overweight persons -- Fiction 6. Human-animal relationships -- Fiction
ISBN 1442405937; 9781442405936
LC 2012010646
This novel, by Frances O'Roark Dowell, follows a youth struggling with popularity. "Seventeen pounds. That's the difference between . . . chubby and slim, between teased and taunting. Abby is fine with her body, . . . so she speaks out against Kristen and her groupies--and becomes officially unpopular. Embracing her new status, Abby heads to an abandoned lot across the street and crosses an unfamiliar stream that leads her to a boy who's as different as they come." (Publisher's note)

The **secret** language of girls. Atheneum Books for Young Readers 2004 247p $15.95; pa $5.99
Grades: 5 6 7 8 **Fic**
1. School stories 2. Friendship -- Fiction
ISBN 0-689-84421-2; 978-1-4169-0717-6 pa
LC 2003-12026
Marylin and Kate have been friends since nursery school, but when Marylin becomes a middle school cheerleader and Kate begins to develop other interests, their relationship is put to the test.
"Excellent characterization, an accurate portrayal of the painful and often cruel machinations of preteens, and evocative dialogue will make this tale resonate with most readers." SLJ

★ **Shooting** the moon. Atheneum Books for Young Readers 2008 163p $16.99; pa $5.99
Grades: 4 5 6 7 **Fic**
1. Soldiers -- Fiction 2. Family life -- Fiction 3.

Vietnam War, 1961-1975 -- Fiction
ISBN 978-1-4169-2690-0; 1-4169-2690-9; 978-1-4169-7986-9 pa; 1-4169-7986-7 pa
LC 2006-100347
Boston Globe-Horn Book Award honor book: Fiction and Poetry (2008)
When her brother is sent to fight in Vietnam, twelve-year-old Jamie begins to reconsider the army world that she has grown up in.
"The clear, well-paced first-person prose is perfectly matched to this novel's spare setting and restrained plot. . . . This [is a] thoughtful and satisfying story. . . . Readers will find beauty in its resolution, and will leave this eloquent heroine reluctantly." SLJ

Downer, Ann
★ **Hatching** magic. Atheneum Bks. for Young Readers 2003 242p $16.95; pa $5.99
Grades: 4 5 6 7 **Fic**
1. Magic -- Fiction 2. Dragons -- Fiction
ISBN 0-689-83400-4; 0-689-87057-4 pa
LC 00-56570
When a thirteenth-century wizard confronts twenty-first century Boston while seeking his pet dragon, he is followed by a rival wizard and a very unhappy demon, but eleven-year-old Theodora Oglethorpe may hold the secret to setting everything right
"With likable characters, and laced with plenty of humor and adventure, Downer's fantasy will have solid appeal for young genre fans." Booklist
Another title about Theodora is:
The dragon of never-was (2006)

The **dragon** of Never-Was. Atheneum Books for Young Readers 2006 305p il hardcover o.p. pa $5.99
Grades: 4 5 6 7 **Fic**
1. Magic -- Fiction 2. Dragons -- Fiction
ISBN 978-0-689-85571-9; 0-689-85571-0; 978-1-4169-5453-8 pa; 1-4169-5453-8 pa
LC 2005017727
With the help of a bottle of blue fire and a magical brooch, Theodora searches for a dragon on an island off the coast of Scotland before it causes any harm.
"Smart, observant, and self-aware, Theodora makes a sympathetic character, convincing even in the most supernatural circumstances." Booklist

Drago, Ty
The **Undertakers**: rise of the Corpses. Sourcebooks Jabberwocky 2011 465p pa $10.99
Grades: 4 5 6 7 **Fic**
1. Horror fiction 2. Zombies -- Fiction
ISBN 978-1-4022-4785-9; 1-4022-4785-0
"Whatever you do, do not call them zombies! These are Corpses 'reanimated bodies that have been possessed,' and they are everywhere, although they are only visible to a select few, including 12-year-old Will Ritter. After realizing suddenly that he is able to see, Will is taken in by the Undertakers, a rogue group that rescues other, similarly targeted teens and fights to defeat the Corpses' evil plans to conquer Phildelphia and, ultimately, the world. . . . Calling into action a cast of distinctive characters with authentic voices and behaviors, . . . Will's breathless adventures . . . are thought-

ful and exciting, and the descriptions of decaying flesh will
likely both disgust and delight readers." Booklist

Drake, Salamanda

★ **Dragonsdale**; illustrations by Gilly Marklew.
Chicken House/Scholastic 2007 269p il (Dragonsdale)
$16.99

Grades: 3 4 5   **Fic**

1. Fantasy fiction 2. Dragons -- Fiction

ISBN 978-0-439-87173-0; 0-439-87173-5

LC 2006-32890

Cara yearns to ride her beloved Skydancer, a rare Gold-
enbrow dragon, but her father refuses to permit her to fly
and she must be content with mucking out stalls and helping raise young dragons at the famed stud and training farm
known as Dragonsdale.

"This will delight precisely the audience it's meant to—
young girls who find tame dragons captivating." Booklist

Draper, Sharon M. (Sharon Mills), 1948-

Little Sister is not my name. Scholastic Press 2009
102p (Sassy) $14.99

Grades: 3 4 5   **Fic**

1. Size -- Fiction 2. Family life -- Fiction 3. African
Americans -- Fiction

ISBN 978-0-545-07151-2; 0-545-07151-8

LC 2008-15634

Fashion-savy Sassy does not like being the smallest student in her fourth-grade class, until a family emergency calls
for a pint-sized hero.

"Draper hits her middle-grade target in this cheerful yet
reflective novel about feeling appreciated and finding one's
place. . . . Filled with energy and opinion, Sassy more than
lives up to her name." Publ Wkly

Other titles in this series are:

The birthday storm (2009)

The silver secret (2010)

The dazzle disaster dinner party (2010)

★ **Out** of my mind. Atheneum 2010 295p $16.99

Grades: 5 6 7 8   **Fic**

1. Cerebral palsy -- Fiction

ISBN 978-1-4169-7170-2; 1-4169-7170-X

LC 2009-18404

Josette Frank Award for Fiction, 2011

"Fifth-grader Melody has cerebral palsy, a condition that
affects her body but not her mind. Although she is unable to
walk, talk, or feed or care for herself, she can read, think,
and feel. A brilliant person is trapped inside her body, determined to make her mark in the world despite her physical
limitations. . . . Told in Melody's voice, this highly readable,
compelling novel quickly establishes her determination and
intelligence and the almost insurmountable challenges she
faces. . . . Uplifting and upsetting." Booklist

Du Bois, William Pene

The **twenty**-one balloons; written and illustrated by
William Pène Du Bois. Viking 1947 179p il $16.99; pa
$5.99

Grades: 5 6 7 8   **Fic**

1. Balloons -- Fiction

ISBN 0-670-73441-1; 0-14-032097-0 pa

Awarded the Newbery Medal, 1948

"Professor Sherman set off on a flight across the Pacific
in a giant balloon, but three weeks later the headlines read
'Professor Sherman in wrong ocean with too many balloons.' This book is concerned with the professor's explanation of this phenomenon. His account of his one stopover on
the island of Krakatoa which blew up with barely a minute
to spare to allow time for his escape, is the highlight of this
hilarious narrative." Ont Libr Rev

DuPrau, Jeanne

The **city** of Ember. Random House 2003 270p (Books
of Ember) $15.95; lib bdg $17.99; pa $6.99

Grades: 5 6 7 8   **Fic**

1. Science fiction

ISBN 0-375-82273-9; 0-375-92274-1 lib bdg; 0-385-
73628-2 pa

LC 2002-10239

"The writing and storytelling are agreeably spare and
remarkably suspenseful." Horn Book

Other titles in this series are:

The people of Sparks (2004)

The prophet of Yonwood (2006)

The diamond of Darkhold (2008)

The **diamond** of Darkhold. Random House 2008
285p (Books of Ember) $16.99; lib bdg $19.99

Grades: 5 6 7 8   **Fic**

1. Fantasy fiction

ISBN 978-0-375-85571-9; 0-375-85571-8; 978-0-375-
95571-6 lib bdg; 0-375-95571-2 lib bdg; 978-0-375-
85572-6 pa; 0-375-85572-6 pa

LC 2007-47929

When a roamer trades them an ancient book with only a
few pages remaining, Lina and Doon return to Ember to seek
the machine the book seems to describe in hopes that it will
get their new community, Sparks, through the winter.

"A solid and satisfying conclusion to the 'Ember Saga,'
set in a post-disaster future." SLJ

The **people** of Sparks. Random House 2004 338p
(Books of Ember) $15.95; lib bdg $17.99

Grades: 5 6 7 8   **Fic**

1. Fantasy 2. Science fiction

ISBN 0-375-82824-9; 0-375-92824-3 lib bdg

LC 2003-20760

"DuPrau continues the adventures of Lina and Doon,
who have led the 400 residents from the underground city of
Ember to the unfamiliar world above. The refugees are tentatively welcomed, housed, and fed by the people of Sparks,
located near the wasteland left by the long-ago Disaster that
destroyed most of civilization. Conflicts arise between the
two groups. . . . DuPrau clearly explores themes of nonviolence and when to stand up for oneself. The text smoothly
involves new readers and fans of the first story, creating a
range of three-dimensional characters." Booklist

The **prophet** of Yonwood. Random House 2006 289p
(Books of Ember) $15.95; lib bdg $17.99; pa $6.99

Grades: 5 6 7 8   **Fic**

1. Science fiction

ISBN 0-375-87526-3; 0-375-97526-8 lib bdg; 0-440-
42124-1 pa

LC 2005-22423

While visiting the small town of Yonwood, North Carolina, eleven-year-old Nickie makes some decisions about how to identify both good and evil when she witnesses the townspeople's reactions to the apocalyptic visions of one of their neighbors

"This novel has a great deal of immediacy in light of current world events. It sharply brings home the idea of people blindly following a belief without questioning it." SLJ

Dudley, David L.
The **bicycle** man. Clarion Books 2005 249p $16
Grades: 4 5 6   Fic
1. Country life -- Fiction 2. African Americans -- Fiction
ISBN 0-618-54233-7
LC 2005-06409

In poor, rural Georgia in 1927, twelve-year-old Carrisa and her suspicious mama take in an elderly drifter with a shiny bicycle, never expecting how profoundly his wise and patient ways will affect them.

Readers "will find complex characters and rich themes. . . . There is much here to digest and a wealth of material for book discussions." SLJ

Duey, Kathleen
Lara and the gray mare; by Kathleen Duey. Dutton Children's Books 2005 140p (Hoofbeats) hardcover o.p. pa $4.99
Grades: 4 5 6   Fic
1. Horses -- Fiction
ISBN 0-525-47332-7; 0-14-240230-3 pa
LC 2004-53521

While her father is away fighting the Normans and other Irish clans, nine-year-old Lara works hard to help harvest food and also cares for the pregnant gray mare that she loves

"Writing with a keen appreciation for everyday goings-on in thirteenth-century Ireland and an unusual ability to bring the past to life, Duey creates a convincing setting, a thoroughly likable heroine, and a strong narrative." Booklist

Other titles in the Hoofbeats series are:
Lara and the Moon-colored filly (book two) (2005)
Lara at Athnery Castle (book three) (2005)
Lara at the silent place (book four) (2005)
Silence and Lily (2007)

Silence and stone; illustrated by Sandara Tang. Aladdin 2010 109p il (The faeries' promise) $15.99; pa $4.99
Grades: 3 4 5   Fic
1. Magic -- Fiction 2. Fairies -- Fiction
ISBN 978-1-4169-8456-6; 1-4169-8456-9; 978-1-4169-8457-3 pa; 1-4169-8457-7 pa
LC 2009-42542

Kidnapped and confined to a room in a castle before she can develop her flying and magical skills, Alida the faerie patiently plans her escape—with the help of a human boy.

"With its magical tone, sturdy characters, and predictable yet satisfying plot, this simple fantasy will engage young readers and leave them eager to read the next book." SLJ

Other titles in this series are:
Following magic (2010)
The full moon (2011)
Wishes and wings (2011)

Dunrea, Olivier
Hanne's quest; [by] Olivier Dunrea. Philomel Books 2005 95p il $16.99
Grades: 3 4 5   Fic
1. Fairy tales 2. Chickens -- Fiction
ISBN 0-399-24216-3
LC 2004-9091

On an island off the coast of Scotland, a young hen must prove herself pure, wise, and brave in a quest to help her beloved owner, Mem Pocket, from losing her family's farm.

"Beautifully composed and often darkly atmospheric, the handsome full-page paintings rival . . . those in the best picture books. This handsome, well-written book will find a rapt audience among children who prefer sturdy, homespun fairy tales." Booklist

Durand, Hallie
Dessert first; illustrations by Christine Davenier. Atheneum Books for Young Readers 2009 153p il $14.99
Grades: 3 4 5   Fic
1. School stories 2. Family life -- Fiction 3. Restaurants -- Fiction
ISBN 978-1-4169-6385-1; 1-4169-6385-5
LC 2008-11390

Third-grader Dessert's love of treats leads to a change in her large family's dinner routine, then an awful mistake, and later a true sacrifice after her teacher, Mrs. Howdy Doody, urges students to march to the beat of their own drums

"Experiences are delightfully imagined through Dessert's realistic, child-centered perspective. Short chapters interspersed with Davenier's pen-and-ink washes add immediacy to the text." Kirkus

Other titles about Dessert are:
Just desserts (2010)
No room for Dessert (2011)

Just Desserts; illustrated by Christine Davenier. Atheneum Books for Young Readers 2010 190p il $15.99
Grades: 3 4 5   Fic
1. School stories 2. Clubs -- Fiction 3. Siblings -- Fiction 4. Family life -- Fiction 5. Restaurants -- Fiction
ISBN 978-1-4169-6387-5; 1-4169-6387-1
LC 2009018400

Third-grader Dessert, inspired by Mrs. Howdy Doody's lessons about the American Revolution, decides she and her friends should fight back against annoying siblings, but the club she starts only makes matters worse.

"The real-life application of taxation without representation is clever, providing an entertaining 'aha' as it develops. Pen-and-ink wash illustrations are scattered throughout." SLJ

No room for Dessert; illustrated by Christine Davenier. Atheneum Books for Young Readers 2011 177p il $14.99
Grades: 3 4 5   Fic
1. School stories 2. Siblings -- Fiction 3. Inventions -- Fiction 4. Family life -- Fiction 5. Restaurants -- Fiction
ISBN 978-1-4424-0360-4; 1-4424-0360-8
LC 2010022039

Eight-year-old Donahue 'Dessert' Schneider is feeling completely ignored and unloved at home, but she is certain that will change when her invention wins the Thomas Edison Contest at school.

"Davenier's sparkling line drawings help young readers visualize the action. Another romp full of zesty, true-life fun." Kirkus

Durango, Julia

The **walls** of Cartagena; by Julia Durango; illustrated by Tom Pohrt. Simon & Schuster Books for Young Readers 2008 152p il $15.99

Grades: 5 6 7 8   **Fic**

1. Leprosy -- Fiction 2. Slavery -- Fiction 3. Catholic Church -- Fiction

ISBN 978-1-4169-4102-6; 1-4169-4102-9

       LC 2007041861

Thirteen-year-old Calepino, an African slave in the seventeenth-century Caribbean city of Cartagena, works as a translator for a Jesuit priest who tends to newly-arrived slaves and, after working for a Jewish doctor in a leper colony and helping an Angolan boy and his mother escape, he realizes his true calling

"Illustrated with occasional small ink sketches, the ultimate rescue adventure is gripping, but more compelling is the authentic history of people desperate and brave." Booklist

Dutton, Sandra

Mary Mae and the gospel truth. Houghton Mifflin Books for Children 2010 134p $15

Grades: 4 5 6   **Fic**

1. School stories 2. Family -- Fiction 3. Creationism -- Fiction 4. Christian life -- Fiction 5. Mother-daughter relationship -- Fiction

ISBN 978-0-547-24966-7; 0-547-24966-7

       LC 2009-49706

Ten-year-old Mary Mae, living with her parents in fossil-rich southern Ohio, tries to reconcile, despite her mother's strong disapproval, her family's Creationist beliefs with the prehistoric fossils she studies in school.

"Very few books for this age group tackle religious subjects as this one does, in a way that shows respect for all sides. Dutton allows Mary Mae to retain both her questions and her faith; instead of a definitive answer, she shows evolutionists and creationists working to find a small, shared piece of middle ground. Mary Mae is a memorable character—spunky but not defiant—whose search for truth drives the narrative." Kirkus

Dyckman, Ame

Boy and Bot; by Ame Dyckman; illustrated by Dan Yaccarino. Alfred A. Knopf 2012 32 p.

Grades: PreK K   **Fic**

1. Boys -- Fiction 2. Robots -- Fiction 3. Friendship -- Fiction 4. Picture books for children

ISBN 9780375867569; 9780375987243

       LC 2011016682

This picture book tells the story of a friendship between a boy and a robot "that prevails over confusion." During the course of author Ame Dyckman's plot, Boy mistakes Bot for another child and later Bot thinks that Boy is also a robot, until an inventor steps in and explains the situation. Illustrator Dan Yaccarino's "stylized gouache paintings" include "final, nearly wordless spreads depicting the two wide-awake friends' happy, ongoing companionship." (Kirkus)

Dyer, Heather

Ibby's magic weekend; illustrated by Peter Bailey. Chicken House 2008 140p il $16.99

Grades: 2 3 4 5   **Fic**

1. Magic -- Fiction 2. Cousins -- Fiction 3. Magicians -- Fiction

ISBN 0-545-03209-1; 978-0-545-03209-4

While visiting her two troublemaking cousins, Ibby learns about a magic box the boys found in the attic in their country home. She soon stumbles upon the strange tale of Uncle Godfrey, a professional magician who mysteriously vanished many years ago.

"This action-filled story is just right for beginning chapter book readers, who will be fascinated with the magic as well as the personalities. Bailey's black-and-white line drawings help make the book accessible to reluctant readers." SLJ

Eager, Edward

★ **Half** magic; illustrated by N.M. Bodecker; introduction by Jack Gantos. 50th anniversary ed.; Harcourt 2004 217p il $18.95

Grades: 4 5 6   **Fic**

1. Fantasy fiction

ISBN 0-15-205302-6

A reissue with a new introduction of the title first published 1954

Faced with a dull summer in the city, Jane, Mark, Katharine, and Martha suddenly find themselves involved in a series of extraordinary adventures after Jane discovers an ordinary-looking coin that seems to grant wishes

"Entertaining and suspenseful fare for readers of make-believe." Booklist

Other titles in this series are:

Knight's castle (1956)

Magic by the lake (1957)

The time garden (1958)

Eames, Brian

The **dagger** Quick. Simon & Schuster Books for Young Readers 2011 320p $15.99

Grades: 4 5 6 7   **Fic**

1. Sea stories 2. Adventure fiction 3. Pirates -- Fiction 4. Handicapped -- Fiction

ISBN 978-1-4424-2311-4; 1-4424-2311-0

       LC 2011-04405

Twelve-year-old Christopher "Kitto" Wheale, a club-footed boy seemingly doomed to follow in the boring footsteps of his father as a cooper in seventeenth-century England, finds himself on a dangerous seafaring adventure with his newly discovered uncle, the infamous pirate William Quick.

"Thoroughly researched, fast-paced, and tense, this coming-of-age adventure doesn't sugarcoat the dangers of the era, even as it embraces the mythical glamour of a pirate's life." Publ Wkly

Easton, Kelly

The **outlandish** adventures of Liberty Aimes; illustrated by Greg Swearingen. Wendy Lamb Books 2009 214p il $15.99; lib bdg $18.99

Grades: 3 4 5 6   **Fic**

1. Adventure fiction 2. Inventors -- Fiction 3. Family

life -- Fiction 4. Runaway children -- Fiction
ISBN 978-0-375-83771-5; 0-375-83771-X; 978-0-
375-93771-2 lib bdg; 0-375-93771-4 lib bdg

LC 2008-22119

Ten-year-old Libby Aimes escapes her prison-like home by using a strange concoction of her father's, then tries to make her way to the boarding school of her dreams, aided by various people and animals.

"The understated humor and friendly, imperturbable tone of the narration bring to mind the fantasies of Eva Ibbotson. The charming illustrations sprinkled throughout add immense appeal to this warm, delightfully odd fantasy." SLJ

Eckert, Allan W.
Incident at Hawk's Hill; with illustrations by John Schoenherr. Little, Brown 1998 173p il hardcover o.p. pa $5.95
Grades: 6 7 8 9   Fic
1. Badgers -- Fiction 2. Wilderness survival -- Fiction
ISBN 0-316-21905-3; 0-316-20948-1 pa
First published 1971
A Newbery Medal honor book, 1972
This account of an actual incident in Saskatchewan at the turn of the century tells of six-year-old Ben Macdonald, more attuned to animals than to people, who gets lost on the prairie and is nurtured by a female badger for two months before being found. Although a strange bond continues between the boy and the badger, the parents' understanding of their son and his communication with them improve as a result of the bizarre experience

"A very deeply moving, well written book." Jr Bookshelf

Edgar, Elsbeth
The Visconti house. Candlewick Press 2011 287p $16.99
Grades: 4 5 6 7   Fic
1. Houses -- Fiction 2. Family life -- Fiction
ISBN 0-7636-5019-6; 978-0-7636-5019-3

LC 2010-39172

Laura Horton has always been an outsider, more interested in writing, drawing, or spending time with her free-spirited family than in her fellow teens, but she is drawn to Leon, a new student, as together they explore the mysteries of her eccentric old house.

"Convincing dialogue and well-drawn characters, both major and minor, bring energy to the story. . . . A fine, sensitive first novel." Booklist

Ehrlich, Amy
★ The Snow Queen; [by] Hans Christian Andersen; retold by Amy Ehrlich; [illustrated by] Susan Jeffers. Dutton Children's Books 2006 40p il $16.99
Grades: 2 3 4   Fic
1. Authors 2. Novelists 3. Dramatists 4. Fairy tales 5. Children's authors 6. Short story writers
ISBN 0-525-47694-6

LC 2006004415

A revised reissue of the edition published 1982 by Dial Books

The strength of a little girl's love enables her to overcome many obstacles and free a boy from the Snow Queen's spell

Elish, Dan
The School for the Insanely Gifted. Harper 2011 289p $15.99
Grades: 3 4 5 6   Fic
1. School stories 2. Genius -- Fiction 3. Missing persons -- Fiction 4. Voyages and travels -- Fiction
ISBN 978-0-06-113873-7; 0-06-113873-8

LC 2010-21962

Eleven-year-old musical genius Daphna Whispers embarks on a global journey to find her missing mother, only to uncover a shocking secret about the Blatt School for the Insanely Gifted where she is a student.

"Elish has created a school story with genius students and a likable main character. . . . This lively adventure parades enough gadgets to capture readers' imaginations" SLJ

The attack of the frozen woodchucks; by Dan Elish; illustrations by Greg Call. Laura Geringer Books 2008 247p il $16.99; lib bdg $17.89; pa $6.99
Grades: 4 5 6   Fic
1. Science fiction 2. Marmots -- Fiction 3. Extraterrestrial beings -- Fiction
ISBN 978-0-06-113870-6; 0-06-113870-3; 978-0-06-113871-3 lib bdg; 0-06-113871-1 lib bdg; 978-0-06-113872-0 pa; 0-06-113872-X pa

LC 2006-102962

When extraterrestrial woodchucks attack, ten-year-old Jimmy, his two-and-a-half-year-old sister, friend William, and an eccentric classmate who has built a flying saucer in her Manhattan brownstone, join forces to save the universe.

"This is ridiculous, over-the-top fun all the way. . . . Science fiction fans who welcome absurdity as much as planet-hopping in their reads will find this an ideal balance of both." Bull Cent Child Books

The family Hitchcock; story by Jennifer Flackett and Mark Levin; written by Dan Elish. HarperChildren's 2011 288p $16.99
Grades: 4 5 6   Fic
1. Adventure fiction 2. Family life -- Fiction
ISBN 978-0-06-189394-0; 0-06-189394-3

LC 2011016610

When they agree to a summertime house swap with an unknown family in Paris, the four members of the Hitchcock family inadvertently get mixed up in a ring of international espionage.

"The plot-driven story is preposterous fun with genuine touches of emotion about family dynamics." SLJ

Elliott, Laura
Give me liberty; [by] L. M. Elliott. Katherine Tegen Books 2006 376p $16.99; lib bdg $17.89; pa $7.99
Grades: 5 6 7 8   Fic
ISBN 0-06-074421-9; 0-06-074422-7 lib bdg; 0-06-074423-5 pa
Follows the life of thirteen-year-old Nathaniel Dunn, from May 1774 to December 1775, as he serves his indentureship with a music teacher in Williamsburg, Virginia, and witnesses the growing rift between patriots and loyalists, culminating in the American Revolution.

"Elliott packs a great deal of historical detail into a novel already filled with action, well-drawn characters, and a sympathetic understanding of many points of view." Booklist

Ellis, Deborah

I am a taxi. Groundwood Books/House of Anansi Press 2006 205p (The cocalero novels) $16.95; pa $9.95
Grades: 5 6 7 8   **Fic**
  1. Cocaine -- Fiction
ISBN 978-0-88899-735-7; 0-88899-735-3; 978-0-88899-736-4 pa; 0-88899-736-1 pa
"Diego, 12, lives in prison in the city of Cochabamba, Bolivia, stuck there with his parents, who have been falsely arrested for smuggling drugs. He attends school and works as a 'taxi,' running errands for the inmates in the great street market. Then his friend, Mando, persuades him to make big money, and the boys find themselves stomping coca leaves in cocaine pits in the jungle. . . . Readers will be caught up by the nonstop action in the prison, and also in the jungle survival adventure." Booklist

★ No ordinary day. Groundwood Books 2011 160p $16.95
Grades: 5 6 7   **Fic**
  1. Leprosy -- Fiction 2. Orphans -- Fiction 3. Poverty -- Fiction 4. Homeless persons -- Fiction
ISBN 978-1-55498-134-2; 1-55498-134-4
"Valli, about 10, lives in the poverty-stricken town of Jharia, India, where she is a coal picker. When she makes a shocking discovery about her family, she runs away and, after a series of harrowing events, reaches the bustling city of Kolkata. . . . While begging for change one day, she is befriended by a kind doctor who recognizes Valli's symptoms of leprosy. . . . With the help of the doctor and other leprosy patients, Valli gets treatment and education, learns tolerance for people different from herself, and simultaneously realizes her own self-worth. Although many important lessons are presented in this even-paced, clearly written story, it is never heavyhanded or didactic. Valli is a well-developed, realistic, and engaging narrator. . . . An important, inspiring tale." SLJ

Sacred leaf. Groundwood Books/House of Anansi Press 2007 206p (The cocalero novels) $16.95; pa $9.95
Grades: 5 6 7 8   **Fic**
  1. Cocaine -- Fiction
ISBN 978-0-88899-751-7; 978-0-88899-808-8 pa
Twelve year old Diego escapes from slavery at an illegal cocaine operation and is taken in by the Ricardos, coca farmers.
"An easy read that touches on issues seldom addressed for young teens." SLJ

Ellis, Sarah

The several lives of Orphan Jack; pictures by Bruno St-Aubin. Douglas & McIntyre 2003 84p il hardcover o.p. pa $7.95
Grades: 3 4 5 6   **Fic**
  1. Adventure fiction 2. Orphans -- Fiction
ISBN 0-88899-529-6; 0-88899-618-7 pa
When, at the age of twelve, he is sent out from the Opportunities School for Orphans and Foundlings to be a bookkeeper's apprentice, Jack finds his heretofore predictable life full of unusual adventures.
"Ellis has created a small gem here, with messages about following your heart tucked into the sentences, phrases, thoughts, and ideas that she seamlessly weaves together." Booklist

Emery, William

Kodoku; William Emery; illustrations by Hanae Rivera. Heyday 2012 32 p. col. ill. (hardcover: alk. paper) $16.95
Grades: 4 5 6   **Fic**
  1. Ocean travel -- Fiction 2. Voyages around the world -- Fiction 3. Voyages around the world -- Juvenile literature
ISBN 1597141739; 9781597141734
LC 2011032355
This children's picture book by William Emery presents a "recreation of the voyage of Kenichi Horie, the first (recorded) sailor to cross the Pacific solo. . . . Emery places the young mariner aboard a custom-built sailboat and sends him out for intense mid-ocean encounters with a typhoon, whales, sharks, jellyfish and a towering passenger ship before journey's end beneath the Golden Gate Bridge." (Kirkus Reviews)

Enderle, Dotti

Crosswire. Calkins Creek 2010 143p $17.95
Grades: 5 6 7 8   **Fic**
  1. Brothers -- Fiction 2. Droughts -- Fiction 3. Ranch life -- Fiction 4. Father-son relationship -- Fiction
ISBN 978-1-59078-751-9; 1-59078-751-X
LC 2010-07522
When an 1883 drought drives free-range cattlemen to shred Texas ranchers' barbed wire fences and steal water, thirteen-year-old Jesse works hard to help while dealing with his father and brother's falling-out and his own fear of guns.
"Enderle writes with restraint, her research neatly woven into the story, her characters carefully drawn. A small gem of a story." Kirkus
Includes bibliographical references

Engle, Margarita

The wild book; Margarita Engle. Harcourt Children's Books 2012 133p
Grades: 5 6 7 8   **Fic**
  1. Novels in verse 2. Children's stories 3. Dyslexia -- Fiction
ISBN 9780547581316
LC 2011027320
This book tells the story of "Josefa 'Fefa' de la Caridad Uría Peña. . . . Diagnosed with 'word blindness' (a misnomer for dyslexia), Fefa struggles at school. . . . Discounting a doctor's opinion . . . her mother gives her a blank diary: 'Let the words sprout / like seedlings, / then relax and watch / as your wild diary / grows.' . . . Her reading difficulties are heightened when bandits begin roving the countryside, kidnapping local children for ransom." (Kirkus Reviews)

English, Karen

Francie. Farrar, Straus & Giroux 1999 199p hardcover o.p. $17
Grades: 5 6 7 8   **Fic**
  1. Schools 2. Friendship 3. Race relations 4. African Americans 5. Race relations -- Fiction 6. African Americans -- Fiction 7. African Americans -- Juvenile fiction
ISBN 0-374-32456-5; 0-374-42459-4 pa
LC 98-53047
Coretta Scott King honor book for text, 2000

"The best student in her small, all-black school in pre-integration Alabama, 12-year-old Francie hopes for a better life. . . . When Jessie, an older school friend who is without family, is forced on the run by a racist employer, Francie leaves her mother's labeled canned food for him in the woods. Only when the sheriff begins searching their woods . . . does she realize the depth of the danger she may have brought to her family. Francie's smooth-flowing, well-paced narration is gently assisted by just the right touch of the vernacular. Characterization is evenhanded and believable, while place and time envelop readers." SLJ

Nikki & Deja; [illustrated by] Laura Freeman. Clarion Books 2007 80p il $15; pa $3.99

Grades: 2 3 4   **Fic**
1. School stories 2. Friendship -- Fiction 3. African Americans -- Fiction
ISBN 978-0-618-75238-6; 0-618-75238-2; 978-0-547-13362-1 pa; 0-547-13362-6 pa
           LC 2006-30974
When an arrogant new girl comes to school, third-graders and best friends Nikki and Deja decide to form a club that would exclude her but find the results not what they expected.

"More probing than many chapter books, this title delivers the satisfaction of a full-length novel." Publ Wkly

Other titles about Nikki and Deja are:
Nikki & Deja: birthday blues (2009)
Nikki & Deja: the newsy news newsletter (2010)
Nikki & Deja: election madness (2011)

Nikki & Deja: birthday blues; illustrated by Laura Freeman. Clarion Books 2009 92p il $15

Grades: 2 3 4   **Fic**
1. School stories 2. Aunts -- Fiction 3. Parties -- Fiction 4. Birthdays -- Fiction 5. Friendship -- Fiction 6. African Americans -- Fiction
ISBN 978-0-618-97787-1; 0-618-97787-2
           LC 2007-50189
As her eighth birthday approaches, Deja's biggest concern is whether her father will attend her party, until her aunt is called away on business and a classmate schedules a "just because party" on the same afternoon.

"Early chapter-book readers will relate to the protagonist's authentic emotions as English acknowledges the challenges and complexities of classroom life." SLJ

Companion volume to:
Nikki & Deja (2007)

Nikki & Deja: the newsy news newsletter. Clarion Books 2010 91p $15

Grades: 2 3 4   **Fic**
1. School stories 2. Friendship -- Fiction 3. Newspapers -- Fiction
ISBN 978-0-547-22247-9; 0-547-22247-5
           LC 2009015845
When Nikki and her best friend, Deja, start a newsletter about what is happening on their street and in their school, they focus more on writing exciting stories than on finding the truth.

"English writes with wit, feeling, and a spot-on voice that acknowledges the realistic friendship and problems of the protagonists. Freeman's cartoon illustrations enhance the story." SLJ

Nikki and Deja: election madness; illustrated by Laura Freeman. Clarion Books 2011 108p il $14.99

Grades: 2 3 4   **Fic**
1. School stories 2. Elections -- Fiction 3. Friendship -- Fiction 4. African Americans -- Fiction
ISBN 978-0-547-43558-9; 0-547-43558-4
           LC 2011008151
When Carver Elementary holds school-wide elections for the first time, third-grader Deja puts all her efforts into running for school president, ignoring her best friend Nikki's problems.

"Freeman's occasional black-and-white illustrations capture the dramatic tension between the girls." Kirkus

Enright, Elizabeth

Gone -Away Lake; illustrated by Beth and Joe Krush. Harcourt 2000 256p il hardcover o.p. pa $6

Grades: 4 5 6   **Fic**
1. Lakes 2. Cousins 3. Vacations
ISBN 0-15-202274-0; 0-15-202272-4 pa
           LC 99-55281
A reissue of the title first published 1957
A Newbery Medal honor book, 1958
Portia and her cousin Julian discover adventure in a hidden colony of forgotten summer houses on the shores of a swampy lake

"Excellent writing, clear in setting of scene and details of nature, and strong in appeal for children." Horn Book

Another title about Gone-Away Lake is:
Return to Gone-Away Lake (1961)

Epstein, Adam Jay

Secrets of the crown; [by] Adam Jay Epstein, Andrew Jacobson; art by Peter Chan & Kei Acedera. Harper 2011 374p il (The familiars) $16.99

Grades: 4 5 6   **Fic**
1. Fantasy fiction 2. Magic -- Fiction 3. Animals -- Fiction
ISBN 978-0-06-196111-3; 0-06-196111-6
           LC 2011002086
When human magic is destroyed, familiars Aldwyn the cat, Skylar the blue jay, and Gilbert the tree frog set out without their wizards to seek the Crown of the Snow Leopard, the only object that can save the kingdom of Vastia from the evil hare Paksahara.

"The familiars' adventures are exciting, and the revelations about Aldwyn's long-lost parents are touching. Fans of the first book will be pleased." SLJ

The **familiars**; [by] Adam Jay Epstein [and] Andrew Jacobson; art by Peter Chan & Kei Acedera. Harper 2010 360p il $16.99

Grades: 4 5 6   **Fic**
1. Adventure fiction 2. Cats -- Fiction 3. Magic -- Fiction
ISBN 978-0-06-196108-3; 0-06-196108-6
           LC 2010-13686
When a scrappy alley cat named Aldwyn passes himself off as a magical animal companion to Jack, a young wizard in training, Aldwyn and his fellow "familiars," a know-it-all

blue jay and bumbling tree frog, must save the kingdom after the evil queen of Vastia kidnaps Jack and two other wizards.

"The consistently suspenseful narrative moves quickly and is full of twists and turns. . . . This winning combination of action and humor will keep readers turning pages right up to the ending." SLJ

Erdrich, Louise

★ The **birchbark** house. Hyperion Bks. for Children 1999 244p il hardcover o.p. pa $6.99

Grades: 5 6 7 8   **Fic**

1. Ojibwa Indians -- Fiction

ISBN 0-7868-0300-2; 0-7868-1454-3 pa

LC 98-46366

Omakayas, a seven-year-old Native American girl of the Ojibwa tribe, lives through the joys of summer and the perils of winter on an island in Lake Superior in 1847.

"Erdrich crafts images of tender beauty while weaving Ojibwa words seamlessly into the text. Her gentle spot art throughout complements this first of several projected stories that will 'attempt to retrace [her] own family's history.'" Horn Book Guide

★ The **game** of silence; [by] Louise Erdrich. HarperCollins 2004 256p $15.99; lib bdg $16.89; pa $5.99

Grades: 5 6 7 8   **Fic**

1. Ojibwa Indians -- Fiction

ISBN 0-06-029789-1; 0-06-029790-5 lib bdg; 0-06-441029-3 pa

LC 2004-6018

Nine-year-old Omakayas, of the Ojibwa tribe, moves west with her family in 1849

"Erdrich's captivating tale of four seasons portrays a deep appreciation of our environment, our history, and our Native American sisters and brothers." SLJ

★ The **porcupine** year. HarperCollinsPublishers 2008 193p $15.99; lib bdg $16.89

Grades: 5 6 7 8   **Fic**

1. Family life -- Fiction 2. Ojibwa Indians -- Fiction 3. Voyages and travels -- Fiction

ISBN 978-0-06-029787-9; 0-06-029787-5; 978-0-06-029788-6 lib bdg; 0-06-029788-3 lib bdg

LC 2008000757

In 1852, forced by the United States government to leave their beloved Island of the Golden Breasted Woodpecker, fourteen-year-old Omokayas and her Ojibwe family travel in search of a new home.

"Based on Erdrich's own family history, this celebration of life will move readers with its mischief, its anger, and its sadness. What is left unspoken is as powerful as the story told." Booklist

Erdrich, Louise, 1954-

★ **Chickadee**; Louise Erdrich. Harper 2012 256p. (trade bdg.) $16.99

Grades: 5 6 7 8   **Fic**

1. Brothers -- Fiction 2. Ojibwe Indians -- Fiction 3. Voyages and travels -- Fiction 4. Kidnapping -- Fiction 5. Family life -- Fiction 6. Métis -- Fiction

ISBN 9780060577902; 9780060577919

LC 2012006565

Scott O'Dell Award for Historical Fiction (2013)

This book is the "fourth book of The Birchbark House Series. Omakayas is now a young mother with lively 8-year-old twins named Chickadee and Makoons." Makoons plays a trick on the tribe's bully, resulting in the bully's sons kidnapping Chickadee. He escapes, then "runs into his Uncle Quill driving an ox cart of furs to sell in St. Paul. Quill and Chickadee travel with fellow traders on the Red River ox cart trail, arriving in Pembina to find Makoons seriously ill." (Kirkus)

Erskine, Kathryn

★ **Mockingbird**. Philomel Books 2010 235p

Grades: 4 5 6   **Fic**

1. School stories 2. Siblings -- Fiction 3. Bereavement -- Fiction 4. Asperger's syndrome -- Fiction 5. Father-daughter relationship -- Fiction

ISBN 0-399-25264-9; 978-0-399-25264-8

LC 2009-06741

National Book Award, 2010

Ten-year-old Caitlin, who has Asperger's Syndrome, struggles to understand emotions, show empathy, and make friends at school, while at home she seeks closure by working on a project with her father. "Age ten and up." (Publisher's note)

"The sharp insights into Caitlyn's behavior enhance this fine addition to the recent group of books with narrators with autism and Asbergers." Booklist

The **absolute** value of Mike. Philomel Books 2011 247p $16.99

Grades: 5 6 7 8   **Fic**

1. Business enterprises -- Fiction 2. Father-son relationship -- Fiction 3. Eccentrics and eccentricities -- Fiction

ISBN 978-0-399-25505-2; 0-399-25505-2

LC 2010-13333

Fourteen-year-old Mike, whose father is a brilliant mathematician but who has no math aptitude himself, spends the summer in rural Pennsylvania with his elderly and eccentric relatives Moo and Poppy, helping the townspeople raise money to adopt a Romanian orphan.

"Erskine weaves together a large but entertaining cast of characters. . . . Despite many laugh-out-loud moments, the heart of the book is essentially serious." Horn Book

Estes, Eleanor

Ginger Pye; with illustrations by the author. Harcourt 2000 306p il $17; pa $6

Grades: 4 5 6   **Fic**

1. Dogs 2. Dogs -- Fiction 3. Brothers and sisters

ISBN 0-15-202499-9; 0-15-202505-7 pa

LC 00-26700

A reissue of the title first published 1951

Awarded the Newbery Medal, 1952

The disappearance of a new puppy named Ginger and the appearance of a mysterious man in a mustard yellow hat bring excitement into the lives of the Pye children

Estes' drawings are "vivid, amusing sketches that point up and confirm the atmosphere of the story. It is a book to read and reread." Saturday Rev

Another title about the Pye family is:

Pinky Pye (1958)

★ The **Moffats**; illustrated by Louis Slobodkin. Harcourt 2001 290p il $17; pa $6

Grades: 4 5 6   **Fic**

1. Brothers and sisters 2. Family life -- Fiction 3. Family life -- Connecticut

ISBN 0-15-202535-9; 0-15-202541-3 pa

LC 00-39726

A reissue of the title first published 1941

Relates the adventures and misadventures of the four Moffat children living with their widowed mother in a yellow house on New Dollar Street in the small town of Cranbury, Connecticut

"A captivating family story with highly individual characters. Each chapter is a separate episode, suitable for reading aloud." Hodges. Books for Elem Sch Libr

Other titles about the Moffats are:

The middle Moffat (1942)

The Moffat Museum (1983)

Rufus M. (1943)

The **hundred** dresses; illustrated by Louis Slobodkin. New ed; Harcourt 2004 80p il $16; pa $7

Grades: 4 5 6   **Fic**

1. Polish Americans -- Fiction 2. Friendship -- Fiction

ISBN 0-15-205170-8; 0-15-205260-7 pa

LC 2003-57037

A reissue of the title first published 1944

A Newbery honor book, 1945

"The 100 dresses are just dream dresses, pictures Wanda Petronski has drawn, but she describes them in self-defense as she appears daily in the same faded blue dress. Not until Wanda, snubbed and unhappy, moves away leaving her pictures at school for an art contest, do her classmates realize their cruelty." Books for Deaf Child

Etchemendy, Nancy

The **power** of Un. Front St./Cricket Bks. 2000 148p $16.95; pa $4.99

Grades: 4 5 6 7   **Fic**

1. Time travel 2. Fantasy fiction 3. Brothers and sisters

ISBN 0-8126-2850-0; 0-439-31331-7 pa

LC 99-58281

When he is given a device that will allow him to "undo" what has happened in the past, Gib Finney is not sure what event from the worst day in his life he should change in order to keep his sister from being hit by a truck

The author has a "knack for writing hilarious dialogue that perfectly paints the funny, poignant, and altogether unpredictable world of eleven and twelve year olds. . . . A unique, thought-provoking book." Voice Youth Advocates

Evans, Lissa

Horten's incredible illusions; magic, mystery & another very strange adventure. by Lissa Evans. Sterling Children's Books 2012 349 p. $14.95

Grades: 3 4 5 6 7   **Fic**

1. Adventure fiction 2. Magic -- Juvenile fiction 3. Magicians -- Juvenile literature

ISBN 1402798709; 9781402798702

In this sequel to "Horten's Miraculous Mechanisms" by Lissa Evans, "10-year-old Stuart Horten is catapulted on yet another adventure left to him by his Great-Uncle Tony. . . . It is up to Stuart to follow clues to locate the great magi-

cian's will. He and his friend April soon discover, however, that Tony's Tricks are truly magic: each one transports them to another time or place, where a puzzle must be solved." (School Library Journal)

Horten's miraculous mechanisms; magic, mystery & a very strange adventure. by Lissa Evans. Sterling 2012 270 p. $14.95

Grades: 3 4 5 6 7   **Fic**

1. Mystery fiction 2. Adventure fiction 3. Children's stories 4. Inventors -- Fiction 5. Magicians -- Fiction

ISBN 9781402798061

In this book, author Lissa "Evans borrows several classic tropes and themes—magic, riddles, a quest, and even a night at a museum—for the . . . story of 10-year-old Stuart Horten . . . who stumbles into a family mystery when he and his parents move to the small British town of Beeton. There, Stuart discovers that his Great-Uncle Tony Horten, who disappeared years ago without a trace, was both an inventor of mechanical devices and a magician. A chance phone call in a broken phone booth is the first step in a journey that leads Stuart around town, as he unearths his great-uncle's legacy and secrets. Stuart also draws the attention of April, May, and June (the journalistically inclined triplets next door), as well as Beeton residents with more sinister intentions." (Publishers Weekly)

Evans, Nate

Meet the beast; [by] Nate Evans and [illustrated by] Vince Evans. Soucebooks Jabberwocky 2010 111p il (Beast friends forever) pa $4.99

Grades: 2 3 4   **Fic**

1. Monsters -- Fiction 2. Siblings -- Fiction

ISBN 978-1-4022-4050-8 pa; 1-4022-4050-3 pa

"This well-plotted and fanciful opener promises a series that early chapter-book readers will appreciate. . . . Bouncy cartoon illustrations and a few passages in comic-strip format punctuate the brief chapters, but the narrative is seamless despite these multiple storytelling approaches." Booklist

Fagan, Cary

Banjo of destiny; pictures by Selçuk Demirel. Groundwood Books/House of Anansi Press 2011 127p il $14.95

Grades: 4 5 6   **Fic**

1. Banjos -- Fiction 2. Wealth -- Fiction

ISBN 978-1-55498-085-7; 1-55498-085-2; 978-1-55498-086-4 pa

"Jeremiah's nouveau riche parents want only the best for their gawky son—private school plus lessons in etiquette, dancing, art, and piano. When Jeremiah hears a banjo playing he becomes obsessed with following his true destiny. Fagan's straightforward, nondidactic narrative hints at the fact that individualism has its own rewards." Horn Book Guide

The **big** swim. Groundwood Books 2010 128p $14.95

Grades: 4 5 6   **Fic**

1. Camps -- Fiction 2. Summer -- Fiction 3. Friendship -- Fiction

ISBN 978-0-88899-969-6; 0-88899-969-0

"Ethan works hard to integrate himself into summer-camp routine. Much to his surprise, he makes friends easily and succeeds at not being the worst at any activity. Everything changes, though, when Zachary arrives, shrouded in a bad attitude and a mysterious past. . . . The setting is rich and the characters are interesting and fresh." SLJ

Fagan, Deva

Fortune's folly. Henry Holt 2009 260p $17.95

Grades: 5 6 7 8   **Fic**

1. Fairy tales 2. Adventure fiction 3. Prophecies -- Fiction

ISBN 978-0-8050-8742-0; 0-8050-8742-7

LC 2008-36780

Ever since her mother died and her father lost his shoe-making skills, Fortunata has survived by pretending to tell fortunes, but when she is tricked into telling the fortune of a prince, she is faced with the impossible task of fulfilling her wild prophecy to save her father's life.

"Fagan's language evokes images of fairy tales and legends, and the protagonist's first-person narrative sparkles with humor. In this book, words are powerful, impressive, mystical, and, sometimes, downright silly." SLJ

Fairlie, Emily

The lost treasure of Tuckernuck; Emily Fairlie. Katherine Tegen Books 2012 283 p. (hardback) $16.99

Grades: 4 5 6 7 8   **Fic**

1. Mystery fiction 2. Buried treasure -- Fiction 3. Historic buildings -- Fiction 4. Schools -- Fiction 5. Mystery and detective stories 6. Treasure hunt (Game) -- Fiction

ISBN 0062118900; 9780062118905

LC 2012025279

This book by Emily Fairlie "tells the story of Bud and Laurie's quest to find the infamous Tutweiler Treasure. They're hot (or at least lukewarm) on the trail of clues, but time is running out -- the school board wants to tear down Tuckernuck Hall. Can Bud and Laurie find the treasure before it's lost forever?" (Publisher's note)

Falls, Kat

Dark life. Scholastic Press 2010 297p $16.99; pa $6.99

Grades: 4 5 6 7   **Fic**

1. Science fiction 2. Ocean -- Fiction

ISBN 978-0-545-17814-3; 0-545-17814-2; 978-0-545-17815-0 pa; 0-545-17815-0 pa

LC 2009-24907

"Ty has lived subsea his entire life. His family members moved below the water to make a better life for themselves. In this future, the climate changes on Earth have been so drastic that hardly any solid ground exits anymore. . . . This book will appeal to middle grade readers, who will enjoy the novel's mystery and suspense. It is a definite must-read for SF fans." Voice Youth Advocates

Rip tide. Scholastic Press 2011 320p

Grades: 4 5 6 7   **Fic**

1. Science fiction 2. Ocean -- Fiction

ISBN 0-545-17843-6; 978-0-545-17843-3

"While preparing to sell the season's seaweed crop, Ty stumbles across an abandoned township, its doors chained shut and its residents murdered. Soon after, the colonists' deal with another township goes bad, and Ty's parents are kidnapped. As Ty and Gemma try to track down those responsible and save their loved ones, they're forced to join up with the notorious Seablite Gang, infiltrate the rough-

and-tumble town of Rip Tide, fight for their lives against sea monsters and human predators, and discover who's killing entire townships—and why. . . . There's no shortage of action, intrigue, or daring exploits in this aquatic thriller. Atmospheric and tense, built around an expertly used postapocalyptic meets Wild West setting, this story's a whole lot of fun." Publ Wkly

Farley, Walter

The Black Stallion; by Walter Farley; illustrated by Keith Ward. Random House 2008 275p il $15.99; lib bdg $18.99

Grades: 4 5 6 7   **Fic**

1. Horses -- Fiction

ISBN 978-0-375-85582-5; 0-375-85582-3; 978-0-375-95578-5 lib bdg; 0-375-95578-X lib bdg

A reissue of the title first published 1941

Young Alec Ramsay is shipwrecked on a desert island with a horse destined to play an important part in his life. Following their rescue their adventure continues in America.

Other titles in this series are:

The Black Stallion and Flame (1960)

The Black Stallion and the shape-shifter (2008) by Steven Farley

The Black Stallion returns (1945)

The Black Stallion's ghost (1969)

The Black Stallion's shadow (1996) by Steven Farley

The Black Stallion's steeplechaser (1997) by Steven Farley

Son of the Black Stallion (1947)

The young Black Stallion (1989)

Farmer, Nancy

★ The Ear, the Eye, and the Arm; a novel. Puffin Books 1995 311p pa $6.99

Grades: 6 7 8 9 10   **Fic**

1. Science fiction

ISBN 978-0-14-131109-8; 0-14-131109-6

LC 95019982

First published 1994 by Orchard Books

A Newbery Medal honor book, 1995

In 2194 in Zimbabwe, General Matsika's three children are kidnapped and put to work in a plastic mine while three mutant detectives use their special powers to search for them

"Throughout the story, it's the thrilling adventure that will grab readers, who will also like the comic, tender characterizations." Booklist

The Islands of the Blessed. Atheneum Books for Young Readers 2009 479p (Sea of Trolls) $18.99

Grades: 5 6 7 8 9   **Fic**

1. Fantasy fiction 2. Norse mythology -- Fiction 3. Druids and Druidism -- Fiction

ISBN 978-1-4169-0737-4; 1-4169-0737-8

LC 2008045415

Two years after their adventures in The Land of the Silver Apples, the apprentice bard Jack and his Viking companion Thorgil confront the malevolent spirit of a vengeful mermaid and begin a quest that casts them among the fin folk of Notland.

This is an "exciting story, which contains a cast of lively, multifaceted characters." Booklist

Includes bibliographical references

The **Land** of the Silver Apples. Atheneum Books for Young Readers 2007 496p il $18.99; pa $9.99

Grades: 5 6 7 8 9 **Fic**

1. Fantasy fiction 2. Vikings -- Fiction 3. Norse mythology -- Fiction 4. Druids and Druidism -- Fiction

ISBN 978-1-4169-0735-0; 1-4169-0735-1; 978-1-4169-0736-7 pa; 1-4169-0736-x pa

LC 2006-31433

After escaping from the Sea of Trolls, the apprentice bard Jack plunges into a new series of adventures, traveling underground to Elfland and uncovering the truth about his little sister Lucy.

"Farmer beautifully balances pell-mell action and quieter thematic points. . . . This hearty adventure, as personal as it is epic, will cradle readers in the 'hollow it its hand.'" Booklist

★ The **Sea** of Trolls. Atheneum Books for Young Readers 2004 459p $17.95; pa $9.99

Grades: 5 6 7 8 9 **Fic**

1. Saxons 2. Trolls 3. Vikings 4. Fantasy fiction 5. Mythology, Norse 6. Druids and Druidism 7. Bards and bardism 8. Vikings -- Fiction 9. Brothers and sisters 10. Norse mythology -- Fiction 11. Druids and Druidism -- Fiction

ISBN 0-689-86744-1; 0-689-86746-8 pa

LC 2003-19091

After Jack becomes apprenticed to a Druid bard, he and his little sister Lucy are captured by Viking Berserkers and taken to the home of King Ivar the Boneless and his half-troll queen, leading Jack to undertake a vital quest to Jotunheim, home of the trolls.

"This exciting and original fantasy will capture the hearts and imaginations of readers." SLJ

Includes bibliographical references

Other titles in this series are:

The Land of the Silver Apples (2007)

The Islands of the Blessed (2009)

★ A **girl** named Disaster. Orchard Bks. 1996 309p $19.95; pa $7.99

Grades: 6 7 8 9 **Fic**

1. Adventure fiction 2. Supernatural -- Fiction

ISBN 0-531-09539-8; 0-14-038635-1 pa

LC 96-15141

A Newbery Medal honor book, 1997

While journeying from Mozambique to Zimbabwe to escape an arranged marriage, eleven-year-old Nhamo struggles to escape drowning and starvation and in so doing comes close to the luminous world of the African spirits

"This story is humorous and heartwrenching, complex and multilayered." SLJ

Farrant, Natasha

After Iris; by Natasha Farrant. Dial Books for Young Readers 2013 272 p. (hardcover) $16.99

Grades: 5 6 7 8 **Fic**

1. Grief -- Fiction 2. Babysitters -- Fiction 3. Twins -- Fiction 4. Diaries -- Fiction 5. Au pairs -- Fiction 6. Brothers and sisters -- Fiction 7. Family life -- England -- London -- Fiction 8. Video recordings -- Production and direction -- Fiction

ISBN 0803739826; 9780803739826

LC 2012039136

In this book, 12-year-old "Bluebell Gadsby's family has been collapsing ever since Blue's twin sister, Iris, died three years ago. Blue's father is working on the other side of the country, and their mother is traveling overseas, which leaves new au pair Zoran in charge. Between Blue's older sister Flora's rebelliousness, her two younger siblings' antics, and the family's pet rats, which live in the garden of their London home, Zoran has his hands full." (Publishers Weekly)

Farrey, Brian

The **Vengekeep** prophecies; Brian Farrey; illustrated by Brett Helquist. Harper 2012 390 p. (hardback) $16.99

Grades: 4 5 6 7 **Fic**

1. Magic -- Fiction 2. Prophecies -- Fiction 3. Swindlers and swindling -- Fiction 4. Fantasy 5. Monsters -- Fiction

ISBN 0062049283; 9780062049285

LC 2012025282

In this book by Brian Farrey, "12-year-old Jaxter Grimjinx is anxious to prove himself at the family business: thievery. Jaxter's first attempt at burglary ends with . . . his family being jailed, but his parents have . . . replaced the prophetic tapestry that predicts the year ahead . . . with one that shows the Grimjinx family as heroes. The family quickly discovers, however, that the fake tapestry is actually enchanted, and every disaster it depicts is coming true." (Publishers Weekly)

Fawcett, Katie Pickard

To come and go like magic. Alfred A. Knopf 2010 263p $16.99; lib bdg $19.99

Grades: 5 6 7 8 **Fic**

1. Family life -- Fiction 2. Country life -- Fiction

ISBN 978-0-375-85846-8; 0-375-85846-6; 978-0-375-95846-5 lib bdg; 0-375-95846-0 lib bdg

LC 2008-52188

In the 1970s, twelve-year-old Chili Sue Mahoney longs to escape her tiny Kentucky home town and see the world, but she also learns to recognize beauty in the people and places around her.

"Chili's first-person narrative stretches from poetic thoughts . . . . to more down-to-earth observations. Her insights are absorbing and her setbacks heartbreaking, as she weighs the only home she's ever known against the possibilities that loom farther afield." Publ Wkly

Federle, Tim

Better Nate than ever; Tim Federle. Simon & Schuster Books for Young Readers 2013 288 p. (hardcover) $16.99

Grades: 5 6 7 8 **Fic**

1. Theater -- Fiction 2. Musicals -- Fiction 3. New York (N.Y.) -- Juvenile fiction 4. Auditions -- Fiction

ISBN 1442446897; 9781442446892; 9781442446908

LC 2011050388

In author Tim Federle's book, "Nate Foster has big dreams. His whole life, he's wanted to star in a Broadway show. (Heck, he'd settle for seeing a Broadway show.) But how is Nate supposed to make his dreams come true when he's stuck in Jankburg, Pennsylvania . . . . ? With Libby's help, Nate plans a daring overnight escape to New York. There's an open casting call for 'E.T.: The Musical,' and Nate knows this could be the difference between small-town blues and big-time stardom." (Publisher's note)

Feiffer, Kate

The **problem** with the Puddles; illustrated by Tricia Tusa. Simon & Schuster Books for Young Readers 2009 193p il $16.99

Grades: 3 4 5 **Fic**

1. Dogs -- Fiction 2. Family life -- Fiction 3. Lost and found possessions -- Fiction

ISBN 978-1-4169-4961-9; 1-4169-4961-5

LC 20080-51388

The Puddle parents cannot seem to agree about anything, but when their dogs go missing the whole family embarks on an unlikely quest that eventually answers many unasked questions.

"The kid-friendly humor . . . the full cast of eccentric characters and Tusa's . . . lively b&w spot art should readily win fans for the Puddle family." Publ Wkly

Fein, Eric

My frozen valentine; illustrated by Gregg Schigiel and Lee Loughridge; Batman created by Bob Kane. Stone Arch Books 2010 49p il (DC superheroes. Batman) lib bdg $25.32; pa $5.95

Grades: 3 4 5 **Fic**

1. Batman (Fictional character) 2. Superheroes -- Fiction 3. Valentine's Day -- Fiction

ISBN 978-1-4342-1564-2 lib bdg; 1-4342-1564-4 lib bdg; 978-1-4342-1731-8 pa; 1-4342-1731-0 pa

LC 2009006302

This " full-color chapter [book is] fast moving and entertaining. . . . The retro comic-book illustrations . . . appear every few pages, adding a vibrant visual element to the proceedings. Sound effects are displayed in large, expressive fonts and colors, capturing the feel of comics." SLJ

Fenner, Carol

Snowed in with Grandmother Silk; illustrated by Amanda Harvey. Dial Books for Young Readers 2003 75p il hardcover o.p. pa $6.99

Grades: 2 3 4 **Fic**

1. Snow -- Fiction 2. Grandmothers -- Fiction

ISBN 0-8037-2857-3; 0-14-240472-1 pa

LC 2002-152296

Ruddy is disappointed when his parents go on a cruise and he must stay with his fussy grandmother for a whole week, but an unexpected snowstorm reveals a surprising side of Grandmother Silk

"Harvey's pencil-and-watercolor artwork extends the warmth and gentle humor in this chapter book, which will be a good choice for beginning readers as well as for reading aloud." Booklist

Yolonda's genius. Margaret K. McElderry Bks. 1995 211p $18.95; pa $5.99

Grades: 4 5 6 **Fic**

1. Siblings -- Fiction 2. Musicians -- Fiction 3. African Americans -- Fiction

ISBN 0-689-80001-0; 0-689-81327-9 pa

LC 94-46962

A Newbery Medal honor book, 1996

After moving from Chicago to Grand River, Michigan, fifth grader Yolonda, big and strong for her age, determines to prove that her younger brother is not a slow learner but a true musical genius

"In this brisk and appealing narrative, readers are introduced to a close-knit, middle-class African-American family. . . . [This novel] is suffused with humor and spirit." Horn Book

Fergus, Maureen

Ortega. Kids Can Press 2010 224p $16.95

Grades: 5 6 7 8 **Fic**

1. Science fiction 2. Gorillas -- Fiction

ISBN 978-1-55453-474-6; 1-55453-474-7

Eleven years ago, an infant lowland gorilla was acquired by a privately funded laboratory. An elite surgical team undertook a series of radical procedures designed to make it physically possible for the infant gorilla to acquire speech.

"The story's excitement and suspense as well as the emotional drama will ensnare readers. This interesting, affecting novel will definitely find an audience." SLJ

Ferraiolo, Jack D.

The **big** splash; by Jack D. Ferraiolo. Amulet Books 2008 277p $15.95

Grades: 4 5 6 7 **Fic**

1. School stories 2. Mystery fiction

ISBN 978-0-8109-7067-0; 0-8109-7067-8

LC 2007-49978

Matt Stevens, an average middle schooler with a glib tongue and a knack for solving crimes, uncovers a mystery while working with "the organization," a mafia-like syndicate run by seventh-grader Vincent "Mr. Biggs" Biggio, specializing in forged hall passes, test-copying rings, black market candy selling, and taking out hits with water guns.

This "novel delivers plenty of laughs, especially in the opening chapters, and fans of private-eye spoofs will enjoy this entertaining read." Booklist

Ferrari, Michael

Born to fly. Delacorte Press 2009 212p $15.99; lib bdg $18.99

Grades: 4 5 6 **Fic**

1. Sex role -- Fiction 2. Air pilots -- Fiction 3. Friendship -- Fiction 4. Family life -- Fiction 5. World War, 1939-1945 -- Fiction

ISBN 978-0-385-73715-9; 0-385-73715-7; 978-0-385-90649-4 lib bdg; 0-385-90649-8 lib bdg

LC 2008035664

In 1942, an eleven-year-old girl who longs to be a pilot and her family try to manage their lives in Rhode Island when the father goes to fight in World War II.

"Ferrari's fast-paced plot and well-developed characters will keep readers engaged until the last page." Booklist

Ferris, Jean

Much ado about Grubstake. Harcourt 2006 265p $17

Grades: 5 6 7 8 **Fic**

1. Orphans -- Fiction 2. City and town life -- Fiction 3. Gold mines and mining -- Fiction

ISBN 0-15-205706-4

When two city folks arrive in the depressed mining town of Grubstake, Colorado in 1888, sixteen-year-old orphaned Arley tries to discover why they want to buy the supposedly worthless mines in the area

"Ferris combines adventure, love, and off-the-wall characters in a page-turning story full of good laughs and common sense messages." Voice Youth Advocates

Field, Rachel

Hitty: her first hundred years; [by] Rachel Field; with illustrations by Dorothy P. Lathrop. Macmillan 1929 207p il $19.99; pa $6.99

Grades: 4 5 6 7   **Fic**

1. Dolls -- Fiction

ISBN 0-02-734840-7; 0-689-82284-7 pa

Awarded the Newbery Medal, 1930

"Hitty, a doll of real character carved from a block of mountain ash, writes a story of her eventful life from the security of an antique-shop window which she shares with Theobold, a rather over-bearing cat. . . . The illustrations by Dorothy P. Lathrop are the happiest extension of the text." Cleveland Public Libr

Fine, Anne

Jamie and Angus together; illustrated by Penny Dale. Candlewick Press 2007 102p il $15.99

Grades: PreK K 1 2   **Fic**

1. Play -- Fiction 2. Toys -- Fiction 3. Friendship -- Fiction

ISBN 978-0-7636-3374-5; 0-7636-3374-7

LC 2007-25166

Best friends Jamie and his toy Highland bull Angus tackle a lively playmate, become muddled by a pretend game, and discover that playing is not fun unless they are doing it together.

"Fine renders another pitch-perfect transitional chapter book. . . . Spare yet vivid language captures Jamie's perspective while supplying humor for adult readers. . . . Soft pencil illustrations . . . capture Jamie's loving family and convey his deep friendship with Angus." Booklist

Another title about Jamie and Angus is:

The Jamie and Angus stories (2002)

The diary of a killer cat; [by] Anne Fine; pictures by Steve Cox. Farrar, Straus and Giroux 2006 58p il $15

Grades: 2 3 4   **Fic**

1. Cats -- Fiction

ISBN 0-374-31779-8

LC 2004-56212

First published 2001 in the United Kingdom

Tuffy the pet cat tries to defend himself against accusations of terrifying other animals and murdering the neighbor's rabbit

"The book is funny throughout. . . . The black-and-white sketches, some full page, bring movement and personality to the characters." SLJ

Another title about the killer cat is:

The return of the killer cat (2007)

Fireside, Bryna J.

Private Joel and the Sewell Mountain seder; by Bryna J. Fireside; illustrations by Shawn Costello. Kar-Ben Pub. 2008 47p il lib bdg $16.95; pa $6.95

Grades: 2 3 4   **Fic**

1. Passover -- Fiction 2. Jews -- United States -- Fiction

ISBN 978-0-8225-7240-4 lib bdg; 0-8225-7240-0 lib bdg; 978-0-8225-9050-7 pa; 0-8225-9050-6 pa

LC 2007005275

A group of Jewish soldiers, and three freed slaves, have a Passover seder in 1862 on the battlefields of the Civil War

The book is based "on a true story. . . . Costello's impressionistic artwork seems well suited to this nostalgic story.

Although respectful in tone, the illustrations also pick up on occasional humor." Booklist

Fitzgerald, Dawn

Soccer chick rules. Roaring Brook Press 2006 150p $16.95

Grades: 5 6 7 8   **Fic**

1. School stories 2. Soccer -- Fiction 3. Politics -- Fiction

ISBN 1-59643-137-7

While trying to focus on a winning soccer season, thirteen-year-old Tess becomes involved in local politics when she learns that all sports programs at her school will be stopped unless a tax levy is passed. "Grades five to eight." (Bull Cent Child Books)

This is "a fast-moving, true-to-life, amusing take on school life. The dialogue is especially spot-on." Booklist

Fitzgerald, John D.

★ The Great Brain; illustrated by Mercer Mayer. Dial Bks. for Young Readers 1967 175p il $17.99; pa $5.99

Grades: 4 5 6 7   **Fic**

ISBN 0-8037-2590-6; 0-14-240058-0 pa

"The Great Brain was Tom Dennis ('T.D.') Fitzgerald, age ten, of Adenville, Utah; the time, 1896. . . . This autobiographical yarn is spun by his brother John Dennis ('J.D.'), age seven . . . who can tell stories about himself and his family with enough tall-tale exaggeration to catch the imagination." Horn Book

Other titles about the Great Brain are:

The Great Brain at the academy (1972)

The Great Brain does it again (1975)

The Great Brain is back (1995)

The Great Brain reforms (1973)

Me and my little brain (1971)

More adventures of the Great Brain (1969)

The return of the Great Brain (1974)

The Great Brain is back; illustrated by Diane DeGroat. Dial Bks. for Young Readers 1995 121p il $16.99

Grades: 4 5 6 7   **Fic**

ISBN 0-8037-1346-0

LC 94-17433

"The year is 1899, and J.D. narrates this episodic novel. . . . It is J.D. on the defense as he describes his big brother Tom's conniving ways from the first chapter, in which Tom sells J.D. a wagonload of soap, through the last, in which J.D. claims that Tom is finally outswindled—by his own mother. DeGroat's full-page pencil drawings, one per chapter, capture the era well and portray the characters sympathetically, but the book's gentle humor finds expression mainly through the writing." Booklist

Fitzhugh, Louise

★ Harriet, the spy; written and illustrated by Louise Fitzhugh. Delacorte Press 2000 300p il $15.95

Grades: 4 5 6 7   **Fic**

1. School stories

ISBN 0-385-32783-8

LC 00712298

A reissue of the title first published 1964 by Harper & Row

Eleven-year-old Harriet keeps notes on her classmates and neighbors in a secret notebook, but when some of the students read the notebook, they seek revenge.

"A very, very funny and a very, very affective story; the characterizations are marvelously shrewd, the pictures of urban life and of the power structure of the sixth grade class are realistic." Bull Cent Child Books

Another title about Harriet is:
The long secret (1965)

Fitzmaurice, Kathryn

Destiny, rewritten; Kathryn Fitzmaurice; [edited by] Molly O'Neill. Katherine Tegen Books 2013 352 p. (hardcover) $16.99

Grades: 4 5 6 7   Fic
1. Father-daughter relationship -- Juvenile fiction
ISBN 0061625019; 9780061625015
LC 2012945971

In this novel, sixth-grader Emily, named for the poet Emily Dickinson, is pushed to become a poet by her mother "(she even commemorates the important moments of Emily's life in a first edition of Dickinson's poetry). Emily, however, thrives on predictability and order, and has no feel for poetry." She wants to find "her unknown father. . . . Just as Emily learns his name is hidden in the Dickinson book, it is accidentally taken and Emily sets out to find it." (Publishers Weekly)

A **diamond** in the desert; Kathryn Fitzmaurice. Viking 2012 258 p. (hardcover) $16.99

Grades: 5 6 7 8   Fic
1. Baseball -- Fiction 2. Father-son relationship -- Fiction 3. World War, 1939-1945 -- United States -- Fiction 4. Japanese Americans -- Evacuation and relocation, 1942-1945 -- Fiction 5. Guilt -- Fiction 6. Japanese Americans -- Evacuation and relocation, 1942-1945 -- Juvenile fiction
ISBN 0670012920; 9780670012923
LC 2011012041

In this book, "Tetsu is twelve when he and his mother and sister are relocated by World War II's infamous Executive Order 9066, which justified the internment of Japanese-Americans, to the camp at Gila River. His father, a leader in the Japanese-American community, is detained separately in another location, and Tetsu generally takes his responsibility as the oldest male in the immediate family very seriously. He's particularly solicitous of his younger sister, Kimi, who is . . . traumatized by the lack of privacy in the camp. . . . Kimi . . . wanders out into the desert, where she nearly dies. Guilt-stricken, Tetsu withdraws from baseball and from his friends, until his father arrives at Gila River and rekindles his son's interest in life." (Bulletin of the Center for Children's Books)

Includes bibliographical references (p. 255)

★ The **year** the swallows came early. Bowen Press 2009 277p $16.99; lib bdg $17.89

Grades: 4 5 6   Fic
1. Prisoners -- Fiction 2. Father-daughter relationship -- Fiction
ISBN 978-0-06-162497-1; 0-06-162497-7; 978-0-06-162499-5 lib bdg; 0-06-162499-3 lib bdg
LC 2008-20156

After her father is sent to jail, eleven-year-old Groovy Robinson must decide if she can forgive the failings of someone she loves.

This "novel is peopled with three-dimensional characters whose imperfections make them believable and interesting. . . . The well-structured plot is underscored by clear writing and authentic dialogue." SLJ

Fixmer, Elizabeth

★ **Saint** training. Zonderkidz 2010 239p $14.99

Grades: 5 6 7 8   Fic
1. School stories 2. Catholics -- Fiction 3. Family life -- Fiction 4. Christian life -- Fiction
ISBN 978-0-310-72018-8; 0-310-72018-4
LC 2010010831

During the turbulent 1960s, sixth-grader Mary Clare makes a deal with God: she will try to become a saint if He provides for her large, cash-strapped family.

"The politically fervent period of the late 1960s, with its dramatic upheavals in family, gender, social, and religious conventions, comes to life with pathos and humor in this powerful debut." Publ Wkly

Flake, Sharon G.

★ The **broken** bike boy and the Queen of 33rd Street. Jump at the Sun/Hyperion Books for Children 2007 132p il $15.99; pa $5.99

Grades: 4 5 6 7   Fic
1. School stories 2. Friendship -- Fiction 3. African Americans -- Fiction
ISBN 978-1-4231-0032-4; 1-4231-0032-8; 978-1-4231-0035-5 pa; 1-4231-0035-2 pa
LC 2006-35590

Ten-year-old Queen, a spoiled and conceited African American girl who is disliked by most of her classmates, learns a lesson about friendship from an unlikely "knight in shining armor."

"Complex intergenerational characters and a rich urban setting defy stereotyping. . . . Infrequent detailed pencil illustrations . . . add a welcome dimension." Horn Book

Flanagan, John

Erak's ransom. Philomel Books 2010 373p (Ranger's apprentice) $17.99

Grades: 5 6 7 8   Fic
1. War stories 2. Fantasy fiction 3. Deserts -- Fiction 4. Apprentices -- Fiction
ISBN 978-0-399-25205-1; 0-399-25205-3
LC 2009011665

First published 2007 in Australia

On a mission to pay the ransom of a new ally, apprentice Will and his friends find themselves in a desert wasteland awash with enemies.

"Bringing together many favorite characters for a grand adventure, this book delivers both excitement and quiet good times." Booklist

Halt's peril. Philomel Books 2010 386p (Ranger's apprentice) $17.99

Grades: 5 6 7 8   Fic
1. Fantasy fiction 2. Cults -- Fiction
ISBN 978-0-399-25207-5; 0-399-25207-X

Tennyson, the false prophet of the Outsider cult, has escaped and Halt is determined to stop him before he crosses the border into Araluen, but Genovesan assassins put Will and Halt's extraordinary archery skills to the test.

"Series fans will enjoy the dialogue and camaraderie as much as the action." Booklist

The **battle** for Skandia; [by] John Flanagan. 1st American ed.; Philomel Books 2008 294p (Ranger's apprentice) $16.99; pa $7.99

Grades: 5 6 7 8   **Fic**
1. Fantasy fiction
ISBN 978-0-399-24457-5; 0-399-24457-3; 978-0-14-241340-1 pa; 0-14-241340-2 pa
LC 2007023646

After Ranger's apprentice Will battles Temujai warriors to rescue Evanlyn, Will's kingdom of Skandia joins forces with rival kingdom Araluen to defeat a common enemy.

"Even readers drawn to the series for its deftly drawn characters and setting may find themselves caught up in the action." Booklist

The **burning** bridge. Philomel Books 2006 262p (Ranger's apprentice) $16.99

Grades: 5 6 7 8   **Fic**
1. Fantasy fiction
ISBN 0-399-24455-7

Will is forced to overcome his fear of Wargals, the foot soldiers of rebel warlord Morgarath, as Araluen's army prepares to battle Morgarath's forces.

"The pace is swift, and action is often at the forefront, but elements of humor and nuances of emotion are apparent as well." Booklist

The **emperor** of Nihon-Ja. Philomel Books 2011 438p (Ranger's apprentice) $17.99

Grades: 5 6 7 8   **Fic**
1. Fantasy fiction 2. Kings and rulers -- Fiction
ISBN 978-0-399-25500-7; 0-399-25500-1
LC 2010025784

In a faraway land, a young warrior must protect an emperor from an uprising and train an inexperienced army, with assistance from his Ranger friends.

The **hunters**; John Flanagan. Philomel 2012 403 p. (hardback) $18.99

Grades: 5 6 7 8   **Fic**
1. Pirates -- Juvenile fiction 2. Friendship -- Juvenile fiction 3. Adventure fiction -- Juvenile fiction 4. Fantasy 5. Courage -- Fiction 6. Pirates -- Fiction 7. Friendship -- Fiction 8. Seafaring life -- Fiction 9. Adventure and adventurers -- Fiction
ISBN 0399256210; 9780399256219
LC 2012020986

This book by John Flanagan is part of the Brotherband Chronicles series. "Hal and his brotherband crew are hot on the trail of the pirate Zavac and they have one thing only on their minds: Stopping the bloodthirsty thief before he can do more damage. Of course, they also know Zavac has the Andomal, the priceless Skandian artifact stolen when the brotherband let down their guard. The chase leads down mighty rivers, terrifying rapids, to the lawless fortress of Ragusa." (Publisher's note)

The **icebound** land; [by] John Flanagan. 1st American ed.; Philomel Books 2007 260p (Ranger's apprentice) $16.99

Grades: 5 6 7 8   **Fic**
1. Fantasy fiction
ISBN 978-0-399-24456-8
LC 2006034561

Chasing the Skandian slave-traders who kidnapped Will and Evanlyn, Ranger Halt and warrior student Horace find themselves in the frozen northern islands, where they battle a ruthless black-clad knight as they attempt to rescue their friends.

"Flanagan's deft character portrayals and well-paced story will engage readers." Booklist

The **invaders**; John Flanagan. Philomel Books 2012 429 p. (The Brotherband chronicles) (hardback) $18.99

Grades: 5 6 7 8   **Fic**
1. Pirates -- Juvenile fiction 2. Friendship -- Juvenile fiction 3. Adventure fiction -- Juvenile fiction 4. Fantasy 5. Courage -- Fiction 6. Pirates -- Fiction 7. Friendship -- Fiction 8. Seafaring life -- Fiction 9. Adventure and adventurers -- Fiction
ISBN 0399256202; 9780399256202
LC 2012000424

This book by John Flanagan is part of the Brotherband Chronicles series. "Hal and the Herons have done the impossible. This group of outsiders has beaten out the strongest, most skilled young warriors in all of Skandia to win the Brotherband competition. But their celebration comes to an abrupt end when the Skandians' most sacred artifact, the Andomal, is stolen--and the Herons are to blame." (Publisher's note)

The **kings** of Clonmel. Philomel Books 2010 358p (Ranger's apprentice) $17.99

Grades: 5 6 7 8   **Fic**
1. War stories 2. Fantasy fiction 3. Cults -- Fiction
ISBN 978-0-399-25206-8; 0-399-25206-1

Hair, Will, and Horace set out for Hiberia, where a quasi-religious group, the Outsiders, is sowing confusion and sedition, and they find that secrets from Halt's past may hold the key to restoring order before the last kingdom is undermined.

"There's wit as well as action here, and the revelation of Halt's backstory adds a new dimension to the saga." Booklist

★ The **outcasts**. Philomel Books 2011 434p (Brotherband chronicles) $18.99

Grades: 5 6 7 8   **Fic**
1. Fantasy fiction 2. Adventure fiction 3. Friendship -- Fiction
ISBN 978-0-399-25619-6; 0-399-25619-9

Hal, who does not fit into Skandian society, ends up in a brotherband, a group of boys learning the skills that they need to become warriors, with other outcasts, and they compete with other brotherbands in a series of challenges.

"This enjoyable, old-fashioned tale should have easy appeal for Flanagan's many fans, who are already invested in the world he's created." Publ Wkly

★ The **ruins** of Gorlan. Philomel Books 2005 249p (Ranger's apprentice) $15.99; pa $7.99

Grades: 5 6 7 8   **Fic**
1. Fantasy fiction
ISBN 0-399-24454-9; 0-14-240663-5 pa

When fifteen-year-old Will is rejected by battleschool, he becomes the reluctant apprentice to the mysterious Ranger Halt, and winds up protecting the kingdom from danger.

"Flanagan concentrates on character, offering readers a young protagonist they will care about and relationships that develop believably over time." Booklist

Other titles in this series are:
The burning bridge (2006)
The icebound land (2007)
The battle for Skandia (2008)
The sorcerer of the north (2008)
The siege of Macindaw (2009)
Erak's ransom (2010)
The kings of Clonmel (2010)
Halt's peril (2010)
The Emperor of Nihon-Ja (2011)

The **siege** of Macindaw. Philomel Books 2009 293p (Ranger's apprentice) $17.99; pa $7.99
Grades: 5 6 7 8   **Fic**
1. War stories 2. Fantasy fiction
ISBN 978-0-399-25033-0; 0-399-25033-6; 978-0-14-241524-5 pa; 0-14-241524-3 pa
LC 2008032630

Now a full-fledged Ranger, Will must rescue his friend Alyss from a rogue knight and uncover vital information needed to ward off a Scotti invasion.

"Series fans will relish the familiar details of warfare and comradeship as well as the surprising fireworks in both war and love." Booklist

The **sorcerer** of the north; [by] John Flanagan. Philomel Books 2008 288p (Ranger's apprentice) $16.99
Grades: 5 6 7 8   **Fic**
1. Fantasy fiction
ISBN 978-0-399-25032-3; 0-399-25032-8
LC 2008-16528

Now a full-fledged Ranger responsible for a sleepy fief, Will finds a new adventure seeking the traitors who poisoned the king, investigating rumors of sorcery, and trying to rescue his friend Alyss, who is taken hostage.

"Flanagan is to be complimented for creating a fantasy world that relies on character and action rather than magic." Voice Youth Advocates

Flavin, Teresa

The **Blackhope** enigma. Candlewick Press 2011 $15.99
Grades: 5 6 7 8   **Fic**
1. Adventure fiction 2. Magic -- Fiction 3. Painting -- Fiction 4. Space and time -- Fiction
ISBN 978-0-7636-5694-2; 0-7636-5694-1
LC 2010047654

Fourteen-year-old Sunni, her stepbrother Dean, and an art-student friend trace the footsteps of a labyrinth built in Blackhope Tower by a mysterious and brilliant sixteenth-century artist, and suddenly find themselves trapped inside his enchanted painting, trying desperately to get out.

"The settings are described in detail, and interesting facts about painting techniques are cleverly interwoven. . . .

. Readers . . . will be delighted with Flavin's fully-realized, action-packed debut." Kirkus

The **crimson** shard; Teresa Flavin. Candlewick 2012 275 p. (hardback) $15.99
Grades: 5 6 7 8   **Fic**
1. Fantasy fiction 2. Magic -- Fiction 3. Time travel -- Fiction 4. Painting -- Fiction 5. Space and time -- Fiction 6. Adventure and adventurers -- Fiction
ISBN 0763660930; 9780763660932
LC 2011048343

In this sequel to 'The Blackhope Enigma,' "a villain abducts Sunni and Blaise to discover the secrets they learned while inside magical artist Fausto Corvo's painting. Using an elixir to take them through a trompe l'oeil door, Throgmorton traps them in 1752 London. . . . With the help of two colorful thieves and a set of aristocrats seeking diversion, Sunni and Blaise escape and search for a magician who can help them travel back to the future." (Kirkus)

Fleischman, Paul

Bull Run; woodcuts by David Frampton. HarperCollins Pubs. 1993 104p il pa $4.99
Grades: 6 7 8 9   **Fic**
1. Bull Run, 1st Battle of, 1861 -- Fiction
ISBN 0-06-440588-5 pa
LC 92-14745

"Abandoning the conventions of narrative fiction, Fleischman tells a vivid, many-sided story in this original and moving book. An excellent choice for readers' theater in the classroom or on stage." Booklist

★ The **Half** -a-Moon Inn; illustrated by Kathy Jacobi. Harper & Row 1980 88p il hardcover o.p. pa $4.99
Grades: 4 5 6   **Fic**
1. Kidnapping -- Fiction 2. Hotels and motels -- Fiction 3. Physically handicapped children -- Fiction
ISBN 0-06-440364-5 pa
LC 79-2010

"Despite the grimness of Aaron's predicament, accentuated by dark scratch drawings of figures in grotesque proportion, the story's tone is hopeful and its style concrete and brisk. Elements of folklore exist in the story's characterization, structure, and narration." SLJ

★ The **dunderheads**; illustrated by David Roberts. Candlewick Press 2009 54p il
Grades: 2 3 4 5   **Fic**
1. School stories 2. Teachers -- Fiction
ISBN 0-7636-2498-5; 978-0-7636-2498-9; 978-0-7636-5239-5 pa

When Miss Breakbone confiscates Junkyard's crucial find, Wheels, Pencil, Spider, and the rest of the Dunderheads plot to teach her a lesson.

"Roberts's quirky watercolor and ink interpretations of Fleischman's deadpan humor and impeccable pacing produce hilarious results." SLJ

Fleischman, Sid

The **13th** floor; a ghost story. illustrations by Peter Sis. Greenwillow Bks. 1995 134p il $15.99; pa $5.99

Grades: 4 5 6   **Fic**

1. Fantasy fiction 2. Pirates -- Fiction
ISBN 0-688-14216-8; 0-06-134503-2 pa

LC 94-42806

When his older sister disappears, twelve-year-old Buddy Stebbins follows her back in time and finds himself aboard a seventeenth-century pirate ship captained by a distant relative

"Liberally laced with dry wit and thoroughly satisfying. . . . Readers could hardly ask for more." Publ Wkly

★ **By** the Great Horn Spoon! illustrated by Eric von Schmidt. Little, Brown 1963 193p il hardcover o.p. pa $6.99

Grades: 4 5 6   **Fic**

ISBN 0-316-28577-3; 0-316-28612-5 pa

"Jack and his aunt's butler, Praiseworthy, stow away on a ship bound for California. Here are their adventures aboard ship and in the Gold Rush of '49." Publ Wkly

★ **Here** comes McBroom! three more tall tales. illustrated by Quentin Blake. Greenwillow Bks. 1992 79p il hardcover o.p. pa $4.95

Grades: 3 4 5   **Fic**

1. Tall tales 2. Farm life -- Fiction
ISBN 0-688-16364-5 pa

LC 91-32689

The stories were originally published separately by Grosset and Dunlap

The tall tale adventures of a farm family

Fleischman's "humor is still as fresh as ever, and Quentin Blake's illustrations continue to delight." Booklist

Other titles about McBroom are:
McBroom tells a lie (1976)
McBroom tells the truth (1981)
McBroom's wonderful one-acre farm: three tall tales (1992)

McBroom's wonderful one-acre farm; three tall tales. illustrated by Quentin Blake. Greenwillow Bks. 1992 63p il hardcover o.p. pa $6.99

Grades: 3 4 5   **Fic**

1. Tall tales 2. Farms -- Fiction
ISBN 0-688-11159-9; 978-0-688-15595-7 pa

LC 91-31906

Three humorous tall tales on McBroom's wonderful one-acre prairie farm

★ The **dream** stealer; pictures by Peter Sís. Greenwillow Books 2009 89p il $16.99; lib bdg $17.89 **Fic**

1. Dreams -- Fiction 2. Mythical animals -- Fiction
ISBN 978-0-06-175563-7; 0-06-175563-X; 978-0-06-175564-4 lib bdg; 0-06-175564-8 lib bdg

LC 2008-47694

A plucky Mexican girl tries to recover her dream from the Dream Stealer who takes her to his castle where countless dreams and even more adventures await

"The range of imaginative inventions . . . will delight children, as will the narrator's expertly modulated storyteller's cadence." Booklist

★ The **whipping** boy; illustrations by Peter Sís. Greenwillow Bks. 1986 90p il $16.99; pa $5.99

Grades: 5 6 7 8   **Fic**

1. Adventure fiction 2. Thieves -- Fiction
ISBN 0-688-06216-4; 0-06-052122-8 pa

LC 85-17555

Awarded the Newbery Medal, 1987

"A round tale of adventure and humor, this follows the fortunes of Prince Roland (better known as Prince Brat) and his whipping boy, Jemmy, who has received all the hard knocks for the prince's mischief. . . . There's not a moment's lag in pace, and the stock characters, from Hold-Your-Nose Billy to Betsy's dancing bear Petunia, have enough inventive twists to project a lively air to it all." Bull Cent Child Books

★ The **white** elephant; [illustrated by] Robert McGuire. Greenwillow Books 2006 95p il $15.99; lib bdg $16.89

Grades: 3 4 5   **Fic**

1. Elephants -- Fiction
ISBN 978-0-06-113136-3; 0-06-113136-9; 978-0-06-113137-0 lib bdg; 0-06-113137-7 lib bdg

LC 2005-46793

In old Siam, young elephant trainer Run-Run and his old charge, Walking Mountain, must deal with the curse of a sacred white elephant.

"Fleischman successfully immerses readers in this ancient culture, creating clever and believable plot twists that bring the story to a satisfying but open-ended conclusion." SLJ

Fleming, Candace

Lowji discovers America. Atheneum Books for Young Readers 2005 152p $15.95; pa $5.99

Grades: 3 4 5   **Fic**

1. Moving -- Fiction 2. Immigrants -- Fiction 3. East Indians -- United States -- Fiction
ISBN 0-689-86299-7; 1-4169-5832-0 pa

LC 2004-6899

A nine-year-old East Indian boy tries to adjust to his new life in suburban America

"Fleming tells a gentle, effective story about the loneliness and bewilderment that come with moving, and her brisk, lively sentences make this a good choice for readers gaining confidence with chapter books." Booklist

The **fabled** fifth graders of Aesop Elementary School. Schwartz & Wade Books 2010 170p $15.99; lib bdg $18.99

Grades: 3 4 5   **Fic**

1. School stories
ISBN 978-0-375-86334-9; 0-375-86334-6; 978-0-375-96334-6 lib bdg; 0-375-96334-0 lib bdg

Throughout their fifth-grade year, a group of rambunctious students learns fable-like lessons from extraordinary activities, singing hamsters, and eccentric teachers, led by the inimitable Mr. Jupiter.

"A rare adventure—one that many teachers and students will take to heart." Horn Book

Fletcher, Charlie

Ironhand. Hyperion Books for Children 2008 400p (Stoneheart trilogy) lib bdg $16.99

Grades: 5 6 7 8   **Fic**

1. Fantasy fiction
ISBN 978-1-4231-0177-2 lib bdg; 1-4231-0177-4
lib bdg

LC 2007-42073

Having upset the balance between the warring statues
of London, twelve-year-old George is confronted with new
challenges as he tries to free his captured friends Edie and
The Gunner from the formidable Walker and deal with the
three strange veins of marble, bronze, and stone that have
begun to grow out of his hand.

"Cliff-hanger chapters . . . will leave readers breathless.
George's story is particularly vivid." Booklist

Silvertongue. Hyperion Books for Children 2009
(Stoneheart trilogy) $16.99
Grades: 5 6 7 8   **Fic**

1. Fantasy fiction
ISBN 978-1-4231-0179-6; 1-4231-0179-0
The battle between the statues and gargoyles of London
rages on-and 12-year-old George Chapman and his friend
Edie are caught in the middle. With the Walker intent on
forcing his evil designs on the city and the world, George
realizes that his destiny is inextricably tied to the Walker's destruction.

"George and Edie's action-packed experiences are told
in alternate chapters. . . . The book does not stand on its
own, but those familiar with the earlier titles will be satisfied." SLJ

Stoneheart. Hyperion Books for Children 2007 450p
(Stoneheart trilogy) $16.99; pa $7.99
Grades: 5 6 7 8   **Fic**

1. Fantasy fiction
ISBN 978-1-4231-0175-8; 1-4231-0175-8; 978-1-
4231-0176-5 pa; 1-4231-0176-6 pa

LC 2007-01138

When twelve-year-old George accidentally decapitates
a stone statue in London, England, he falls into a parallel
dimension where he must battle ancient "live" statues and
solve a dangerous riddle.

This "is an action-packed fantasy filled with battles,
chases, and an intriguing variety of characters." SLJ

Other titles in this series are:
Ironhand (2008)
Silvertongue (2009)

Fletcher, Ralph

★ **Flying** solo. Clarion Bks. 1998 138p $15; pa
$5.99
Grades: 5 6 7 8   **Fic**

1. School stories 2. Death -- Fiction 3. Schools --
Fiction 4. Teachers -- Fiction 5. Mutism, Elective --
Fiction
ISBN 0-395-87323-1; 0-547-07652-5 pa

LC 98-10775

Rachel, having chosen to be mute following the sudden
death of a classmate, shares responsibility with the other
sixth-graders who decide not to report that the substitute
teacher failed to show up

"Fletcher expertly balances a wide variety of emotions,
giving readers a story that is by turns sad, poignant, and
funny." Booklist

Fletcher, Susan

Shadow spinner. Atheneum Bks. for Young Readers
1998 219p hardcover o.p. pa $4.99
Grades: 6 7 8 9   **Fic**

1. Storytelling -- Fiction 2. Physically handicapped
-- Fiction
ISBN 0-689-81852-1; 0-689-83051-3 pa

LC 97-37346

When Marjan, a thirteen-year-old crippled girl, joins the
Sultan's harem in ancient Persia, she gathers for Shahrazad
the stories which will save the queen's life

"An elegantly written novel that will delight and entertain even as it teaches." SLJ

Flores-Gabis, Enrique

★ **90** miles to Havana. Roaring Brook Press 2010
292p $17.99
Grades: 5 6 7 8   **Fic**

1. Cuban refugees -- Fiction
ISBN 978-1-59643-168-3; 1-59643-168-7

"Drawing on his own experience as a child refugee from
Cuba, Flores-Galbis offers a gripping historical novel about
children who were evacuated from Cuba to the U.S. during
Operation Pedro Pan in 1961. Julian, a young Cuban boy,
experiences the violent revolution and watches mobs throw
out his family's furniture and move into their home. For his
safety, his parents send him to a refugee camp in Miami. . .
. This is a seldom-told refugee story that will move readers
with the first-person, present-tense rescue narrative, filled
with betrayal, kindness, and waiting for what may never
come." Booklist

Fogelin, Adrian

The **sorta** sisters; [by] Adrian Fogelin. Peachtree 2007
279p il $14.95
Grades: 5 6 7 8   **Fic**

1. Letters -- Fiction 2. Alcoholism -- Fiction 3.
Friendship -- Fiction 4. Foster home care -- Fiction 5.
Single parent family -- Fiction
ISBN 978-1-56145-424-2; 1-56145-424-9

LC 2007011735

In Florida, Anna Casey lives with what she hopes is
the last in a long line of foster mothers, and Mica Delano
lives with her father on their small boat, and when the two
of them begin corresponding, they discover they have a lot
in common.

This is written "with insight and compassion. . . . Lovely
sepia drawings by the author depict wildlife and the packages that the girls send to each other throughout the novel."
Booklist

Foley, Lizzie K.

Remarkable; a novel. by Lizzie K. Foley. Dial Books
for Young Readers 2012 325 p.
Grades: 3 4 5 6 7   **Fic**

1. Fantasy fiction 2. Humorous fiction 3. Ability --
Fiction 4. Young adult literature 5. Community life
-- Fiction 6. Humorous stories 7. Pirates -- Fiction
8. Secrets -- Fiction 9. Eccentrics and eccentricities
-- Fiction
ISBN 9780803737068

LC 2011021641

This book presents the story of an average girl named
Jane Doe who lives in "the town of Remarkable, so named

for its abundance of talented citizens, everyone lives up to its reputation. . . . Jane should be just as remarkable. Instead, this average 10-year-old girl is usually overlooked. . . . Mix in a rival town's dispute over jelly, hints of a Loch Ness Monster-like creature and a psychic pizzeria owner who sees the future in her reflective pizza pans. . . . With the help of her quiet Grandpa John, who's also forgotten most of the time, Jane learns to be true to herself and celebrate the ordinary in life." (Kirkus)

Fombelle, Timothee de

Toby alone; translated by Sarah Ardizzone; illustrated by François Place. Candlewick Press 2009 384p il $17.99; pa $8.99

Grades: 5 6 7 8   **Fic**

1. Fantasy fiction 2. Trees -- Fiction

ISBN 978-0-7636-4181-8; 0-7636-4181-2; 978-0-7636-4815-2 pa; 0-7636-4815-9 pa

Original French edition 2006

Toby is just one and a half millimeters tall, and he's the most wanted person in his world of the great oak Tree. When Toby's father discovers that the Tree is alive, he realizes that exploiting it could do damage to their world. Refusing to reveal the secret to an enraged community, Toby's parents have been imprisoned. Only Toby has managed to escape, but for how long?

"The impressive debut novel from French playwright de Fombelle deftly weaves mature political commentary, broad humor and some subtle satire into a thoroughly enjoyable adventure." Publ Wkly

Toby and the secrets of the tree; illustrated by François Place; translated by Sarah Ardizzone. Candlewick Press 2010 414p il $16.99

Grades: 5 6 7 8   **Fic**

1. Fantasy fiction 2. Trees -- Fiction

ISBN 978-0-7636-4655-4; 0-7636-4655-5

LC 2009014833

Thirteen-year-old Toby's tiny world is under greater threat than ever as Leo Blue holds Elisha prisoner while hunting the Grass People and anyone who stands in the way of his devastating plans for the oak Tree in which they all live, but this time Toby is not alone.

"Place's pen-and-ink illustrations are scattered generously throughout and enhance the overall quirkiness. . . . This interesting piece of eco-fantasy provides a satisfying conclusion for those who enjoyed the first book." SLJ

Forbes, Esther

Johnny Tremain; a novel for old & young. with illustrations by Lynd Ward. Houghton Mifflin Books for Children 1943 256p il $17; pa $6.99

Grades: 5 6 7 8   **Fic**

1. United States -- History -- 1775-1783, Revolution – Fiction

ISBN 978-0-395-06766-6; 0-395-06766-9; 978-0-440-44250-9 pa; 0-440-44250-8 pa

Awarded the Newbery Medal, 1944

"Johnny, an orphan, works as a favored apprentice to an aging silversmith until he burns his hand severely while working on an important project. During the Revolutionary War he serves as a dispatch rider for the Committee on Public Safety, meeting such men as Paul Revere and John Hancock. An outcast for a time, he finally learns on the battlefield of Lexington that his crippled hand can be put to use." Shapiro. Fic for Youth. 3d edition

Forester, Victoria

★ The **girl** who could fly. Feiwel and Friends 2008 329p $16.95

Grades: 4 5 6 7   **Fic**

1. School stories 2. Science fiction 3. Flight -- Fiction

ISBN 978-0-312-37462-4; 0-312-37462-3

LC 2008-06882

When homeschooled farm girl Piper McCloud reveals her ability to fly, she is quickly taken to a secret government facility to be trained with other exceptional children, but she soon realizes that something is very wrong and begins working with brilliant and wealthy Conrad to escape.

"The story soars, just like Piper, with enough loop-de-loops to keep kids uncertain about what will come next. . . . Best of all are the book's strong, lightly wrapped messages about friendship and authenticity and the difference between doing well and doing good." Booklist

Fox, Helen

★ **Eager**. Wendy Lamb Books 2004 280p hardcover o.p. pa $6.50

Grades: 5 6 7 8   **Fic**

1. Science fiction 2. Robots -- Fiction

ISBN 0-385-74672-5; 0-553-48795-7 pa

LC 2003-19489

Unlike Grumps, their old-fashioned robot, the Bell family's new robot, Eager, is programmed to not merely obey but to question, reason, and exercise free will.

"There is a lot of warmth and humor in this engaging . . . novel. . . . The characters are well developed and the action moves quickly. The author also raises thought-provoking questions about what it means to be human, the dangers of technology, and the concept of free will." SLJ Another title about Eager is:

Eager's nephew (2006)

Fox, Paula

★ The **slave** dancer. Atheneum 2001 176p $18.99; pa $6.99

Grades: 5 6 7 8   **Fic**

1. Sea stories 2. Slave trade -- Fiction

ISBN 978-0-689-84505-5; 0-689-84505-7; 978-1-4169-7139-9 pa; 1-4169-7139-4 pa

A reissue of the title first published 1973 by Bradbury Press

Awarded the Newbery Medal, 1974

"Thirteen-year-old Jessie Bollier is kidnapped from New Orleans and taken aboard a slave ship. Cruelly tyrannized by the ship's captain, Jessie is made to play his fife for the slaves during the exercise period into which they are forced in order to keep them fit for sale. When a hurricane destroys the ship, Jessie and Ras, a young slave, survive. They are helped by an old black man who finds them, spirits Ras north to freedom, and assists Jessie to return to his family." Shapiro. Fic for Youth. 3d edition

The **stone** -faced boy. Front Street 2005 83p pa $8.95

Grades: 4 5 6   **Fic**

1. Dogs -- Fiction 2. Siblings -- Fiction 3. Family life

-- Fiction

ISBN 978-1-932425-42-0 pa; 1-932425-42-X pa

LC 2005-12056

First published 1968 by Bradbury Press

Only his strange great-aunt seems to understand the thoughts behind a young boy's expressionless face as he returns on an eerie, snowy night from rescuing a dog that dislikes him

Fraustino, Lisa Rowe

The **Hole** in the Wall. Milkweed Editions 2010 214p $16.95

Grades: 4 5 6 **Fic**

1. Twins -- Fiction 2. Siblings -- Fiction 3. Family life -- Fiction 4. Supernatural -- Fiction 5. Coal mines and mining -- Fiction

ISBN 978-1-57131-696-7; 1-57131-696-5

LC 2010017732

An imaginative eleven-year-old named Sebby discovers that the strange things he has been seeing are real, and connected somehow with the strip-mining operation that has destroyed his town, but getting help from his bickering family seems unlikely.

"More than the science-fiction elements, it's the urgent details of conservation that will pull readers, and when the issues reach right to Sebby's home, the questions increase. . . . . This title will capture young environmentalists." Booklist

Frazier, Angie

The **mastermind** plot; by Angie Frazier. Scholastic Press 2012 231 p. (Suzanna Snow mysteries)

Grades: 4 5 6 7 **Fic**

1. Mystery fiction 2. Adventure fiction 3. Children's stories 4. Arson -- Fiction 5. Uncles -- Fiction 6. Schools -- Fiction 7. Grandmothers -- Fiction 8. Mystery and detective stories 9. Family life -- Massachusetts -- Boston -- Fiction

ISBN 0545208645; 9780545208642

LC 2011003770

This children's mystery by Angie Frazier continues the adventures of Suzanna Snow. "She's just arrived in Boston, the city she's wanted to visit for as long as she can remember. . . . Her grandmother and cousin, Will, welcome her warmly, but her famous detective uncle, Bruce Snow, seems anything but pleased. He doesn't want [her] meddling in his current case involving a string of mysterious warehouse fires along the harbor front. But Zanna can't help herself. Is someone setting the fires? Just when she thinks she's on to something, a strange man starts following her. Is he a threat? Zanna needs to solve the case before she has the chance to find out." (Publisher's note)

The **midnight** tunnel; a Suzanna Snow mystery. Scholastic Press 2011 283p $16.99

Grades: 4 5 6 7 **Fic**

1. Mystery fiction 2. Uncles -- Fiction 3. Missing children -- Fiction 4. Hotels and motels -- Fiction

ISBN 978-0-545-20862-8; 0-545-20862-9

LC 2010-26770

In 1905, Suzanna is in training to be a well-mannered hostess at a Loch Harbor, New Brunswick, hotel, but her dream of being a detective gets a boost when a seven-year-old guest goes missing and Suzanna's uncle, a famous detective, comes to solve the case.

"What Zanna lacks in grace and composure, she makes up for in pluck, persistence and cleverness, emerging a likely and likable Edwardian Nancy Drew." Kirkus

Frazier, Sundee Tucker

★ The **other** half of my heart; [by] Sundee T. Frazier. Delacorte Press 2010 296p $16.99

Grades: 5 6 7 8 **Fic**

1. Twins -- Fiction 2. Sisters -- Fiction 3. Prejudices -- Fiction 4. Grandmothers -- Fiction 5. Beauty contests -- Fiction 6. African Americans -- Fiction 7. Racially mixed people -- Fiction

ISBN 978-0-385-73440-0; 0-385-73440-9

LC 2009013209

Twin daughters of interracial parents, eleven-year-olds Keira and Minna have very different skin tones and personalities, but it is not until their African American grandmother enters them in the Miss Black Pearl Pre-Teen competition in North Carolina that red-haired and pale-skinned Minna realizes what life in their small town in the Pacific Northwest has been like for her more outgoing, darker-skinned sister.

"Frazier addresses issues faced by mixed-race children with a grace and humor that keep her from being pedantic. The story is enjoyable in its own right, and will also encourage readers to rethink racial boundries and what it means to be black or white in America." SLJ

Frederick, Heather Vogel

The **voyage** of Patience Goodspeed. Simon & Schuster Bks. for Young Readers 2002 219p hardcover o.p. pa $4.99

Grades: 5 6 7 8 **Fic**

1. Whaling -- Fiction 2. Navigation -- Fiction 3. Seafaring life -- Fiction

ISBN 0-689-84851-X; 0-689-84869-2 pa

LC 2001-49039

Following their mother's death in Nantucket, Captain Goodspeed brings twelve-year-old Patience and six-year-old Tad aboard his whaling ship, where a new crew member incites a mutiny and Patience puts her mathematical ability to good use

"This is an exciting voyage of peril and self-discovery." N Y Times Book Rev

Another title about Patience is:

The education of Patience Goodspeed (2004)

Freeman, Martha

Who is stealing the 12 days of Christmas? Holiday House 2003 200p (Chickadee Court mysteries) $16.95

Grades: 4 5 6 **Fic**

1. Mystery fiction 2. Christmas -- Fiction

ISBN 0-8234-1788-3

LC 2002-191920

When parts of outdoor Christmas displays go missing from neighborhood yards, nine-year-old Alex and his friend Yasmeen investigate.

Who stole Grandma's million-dollar pumpkin pie? Holiday House 2009 209p (The Chickadee Court mysteries) $16.95

Grades: 4 5 6 **Fic**

1. Mystery fiction 2. Pies -- Fiction 3. Thanksgiving

Day -- Fiction
ISBN 978-0-8234-2215-9; 0-8234-2215-1

LC 2008048486

When the recipe for his grandmother's famous pumpkin pie is suddenly missing just before Thanksgiving Day, Alex and his friend Yasmeen try to solve the mystery of its disappearance.

"Engaging text with a lot of humor. . . . Children who like fast-paced whodunits with a touch of humor will enjoy the story." SLJ

Who stole Halloween? Holiday House 2005 232p il (The Chickadee Court mysteries) $16.95; pa $7.95

Grades: 4 5 6 **Fic**

1. Mystery fiction 2. Cats -- Fiction 3. Halloween -- Fiction
ISBN 0-8234-1962-2; 0-8234-2170-8 pa

When nine-year-old Alex and his friend Yasmeen investigate the disappearance of cats in their neighborhood, they stumble onto a larger mystery involving a haunted house and a ghostly cat.

"The story unfolds to a satisfying resolution . . . Characters are well drawn, and the book will entice even reluctant readers with its action and humor." SLJ

Other titles about Alex and Yasmeen are:
Who is stealing the 12 days of Christmas (2003)
Who stole Uncle Sam? (2008)
Who stole Grandma's million-dollar pumpkin pie? (2009)

Who stole Uncle Sam? 1st ed.; Holiday House 2008 250p (Chickadee Court mysteries) $16.95

Grades: 4 5 6 **Fic**

1. Mystery fiction 2. Baseball -- Fiction 3. Family life -- Fiction 4. Memorial Day -- Fiction 5. Missing persons -- Fiction
ISBN 978-0-8234-2091-9; 0-8234-2091-4

LC 2007043054

When a local businessman and baseball coach disappears just before he is to portray Uncle Sam at the start of a Memorial Day race, ten-year-old Alex and his best friend Yasmeen investigate, despite their pact to stay away from mysteries.

"The plot depends mostly on humorous misunderstandings to draw readers into the story, but its most winning feature is Alex's narration, which always sums things up in a funny, kid-friendly way. This [is a] fast-paced read." SLJ

The **trouble** with babies; illustrated by Cat Bowman Smith. Holiday House 2002 121p il $15.95

Grades: 2 3 4 **Fic**

1. Moving -- Fiction
ISBN 0-8234-1698-4

LC 2001-51479

Nine-year-old Holly tries to adjust to a new home with a neighbor who has just invented a de-yukkification device

"Straightforward, intelligent prose is leavened by accessibly clever humor, and characterizations are pithy without being underwritten." Bull Cent Child Books

The **trouble** with cats; illustrated by Cat Bowman Smith. Holiday House 2000 77p il $15.95

Grades: 2 3 4 **Fic**

1. Cats 2. Schools 3. Stepfathers 4. School stories 5.

Cats -- Fiction 6. Stepfathers -- Fiction
ISBN 0-8234-1479-5

LC 99-29291

After a difficult first week of third grade, Holly begins to adjust to her new school and living in her new stepfather's tiny apartment with his four cats

"Bowman contributes pen-and-ink drawings with lines that quiver with energy. . . . Freeman has a knack for wholesome, undemanding fiction . . . with enough action and humor to carry the plot." Bull Cent Child Books

Other titles about Holly are:
The trouble with babies (2002)
The trouble with twins (2007)

The **trouble** with twins; illustrated by Cat Bowman Smith. Holiday House 2007 85p il $16.95

Grades: 2 3 4 **Fic**

1. Twins -- Fiction 2. Birthdays -- Fiction 3. Family life -- Fiction
ISBN 978-0-8234-2025-4; 0-8234-2025-6

LC 2006-41195

When teenaged Holly takes charge of a birthday celebration for her two-year-old twin brothers, she gets more than she bargains for in mayhem, madness, and mess.

The book offers "high energy action. . . . Smith's ink illustrations . . . will make readers smile." Booklist

Freymann-Weyr, Garret

★ **French** ducks in Venice; illustrated by Erin McGuire. Candlewick Press 2011 il $16.99

Grades: 2 3 4 **Fic**

1. Ducks -- Fiction 2. Canals -- Fiction
ISBN 978-0-7636-4173-3; 0-7636-4173-1

LC 2010047672

When Polina Panova's "prince" moves out of their Venice, California, house, two ducks that live on the canals but believe themselves to be French try to help Polina, a designer of magical dresses of thread, silk, velvet, grass, and pieces of night sky, by giving her something to make her stop being sad.

"Freymann-Weyr's mannered narrative voice keeps emotions firmly in check . . . and her storytelling gifts are unmistakable. . . . There's virtue in presenting a portrait of loss with a spoonful of sugar; readers learn how to talk about hurt . . . while McGuire's cinematically lit pictures recall classic Disney images of winsome animals consoling star-crossed heroines." Publ Wkly

Friedman, Laurie B.

Back to school, Mallory; by Laurie Friedman; illustrations by Tamara Schmitz. Lerner Pub. Group 2004 175p il lib bdg $15.95; pa $5.95

Grades: 2 3 4 **Fic**

1. School stories 2. Moving -- Fiction 3. Family life -- Fiction
ISBN 1-575-05658-5 lib bdg; 978-1-575-05658-6 lib bdg; 1-575-05865-0 pa; 978-1-575-05865-8 pa

LC 2003-18043

After moving, eight-year-old Mallory struggles with being new at school, especially because her mother is now the music teacher and director of the third grade play.

"A dynamic design, complete with handwritten notes and cartoon drawings, contributes to the chapter book's friendly feel." Horn Book Guide

Campfire Mallory; by Laurie Friedman; illustrations by Jennifer Kalis. Carolrhoda Books 2008 175p il lib bdg $15.95; pa $5.95
Grades: 2 3 4　　　　　　　　　　　　　　　　**Fic**
　1. Camps -- Fiction 2. Friendship -- Fiction
　ISBN 978-0-8225-7657-0 lib bdg; 0-8225-7657-0 lib bdg; 978-1-58013-841-3 pa; 1-58013-841-1 pa
　　　　　　　　　　　　　　　　LC 2007022218
Nine-and-a-half-year-old Mallory's trepidation about going to sleepaway camp is multiplied when she and her best friend are assigned to different cabins, and a new "friend" seems determined to get Mallory in trouble
"The plot is believable, and the language is well suited to the intended audience. Mallory's diary entries and black-and-white cartoons appear throughout. The action is well paced. . . . A lighthearted, enjoyable read." SLJ
　Other titles about Mallory are:
　Back to school Mallory (2004)
　Mallory on the move (2004)
　Mallory vs. Max (2005)
　Happy birthday, Mallory (2005)
　In business with Mallory (2006)
　Heart-to-heart with Mallory (2006)
　Mallory on board (2007)
　Honestly, Mallory (2007)
　Step fourth, Mallory (2008)
　Happy New Year, Mallory (2009)
　Red, white & true blue Mallory (2009)
　Mallory goes green (2010)
　Mallory in the spotlight (2010)
　Mallory's super sleepover (2011)
　Mallory's guide to boys, brothers, dads, and dogs (2011)

Happy New Year, Mallory! by Laurie Friedman; illustrations by Jennifer Kalis. Carolrhoda Books, Inc. 2009 $15.95
Grades: 2 3 4　　　　　　　　　　　　　　　　**Fic**
　1. Sick -- Fiction 2. New Year -- Fiction 3. Friendship -- Fiction 4. Family life -- Fiction
　ISBN 978-0-8225-8883-2; 0-8225-8883-8
　　　　　　　　　　　　　　　　LC 2008041164
When a bad stomachache sends Mallory to the hospital during a winter reunion with neighbor Mary Ann and their summer camp bunkmates, she is sad that her friends seem to be having great fun without her.
"This offers a very readable story and expressive black-and-white illustrations." Booklist

Happy birthday, Mallory! by Laurie Friedman; illustrations by Tamara Schmitz. Carolrhoda Books 2005 159p il lib bdg $15.95; pa $5.95
Grades: 2 3 4　　　　　　　　　　　　　　　　**Fic**
　1. Birthdays -- Fiction
　ISBN 1-575-05823-5 lib bdg; 978-1-575-05823-8 lib bdg; 0-8225-6502-1 pa; 978-0-8225-6502-4 pa
　　　　　　　　　　　　　　　　LC 2004031080
After a difficult year, Mallory plans a month-long celebration of her ninth birthday in hopes that her next year will be wonderful.

"Mallory's enthusiasm is infectious. . . . . Cartoonlike drawings and large print make the story accessible to early chapter-book readers." SLJ

Heart -to-heart with Mallory; by Laurie Friedman; illustrations by Barbara Pollak. Carolrhoda Books 2006 159p il lib bdg $15.95; pa $5.95
Grades: 2 3 4　　　　　　　　　　　　　　　　**Fic**
　1. Friendship -- Fiction 2. Remarriage -- Fiction 3. Valentine's Day -- Fiction
　ISBN 978-1-575-05932-7 lib bdg; 1-575-05932-0 lib bdg; 0-8225-7133-1 pa; 978-0-8225-7133-9
　　　　　　　　　　　　　　　　LC 2005034106
Nine-year-old Mallory turns to her diary to sort through her emotions when she finds out she has a secret admirer and her two best friends' parents may be getting engaged.
"Pencil cartoons and a font that resembles a child's handwriting lend appeal. Friedman finds a true voice for her likable . . . character." SLJ

Honestly, Mallory! by Laurie Friedman; illustrations by Barbara Pollak. Carolrhoda Books 2007 159p il lib bdg $15.95; pa $5.95
Grades: 2 3 4　　　　　　　　　　　　　　　　**Fic**
　1. School stories 2. Honesty -- Fiction
　ISBN 978-0-8225-6193-4 lib bdg; 0-8225-6193-X lib bdg; 978-1-580-13840-6 pa; 1-580-13840-3 pa
　　　　　　　　　　　　　　　　LC 2006101328
When Mallory cannot decide what to be on Career Day, it makes her feel like she is not good at anything and she ends up telling a lie that quickly gets out of control.
Mallory "faces the internal turmoil that comes with knowing you've done something wrong, and young readers will empathize with her. . . . Pollak's simple cartoon pictures appear throughout." SLJ

In business with Mallory; by Laurie Friedman; illustrations by Barbara Pollak. Carolrhoda Books 2006 159p il lib bdg $15.95; pa $5.95
Grades: 2 3 4　　　　　　　　　　　　　　　　**Fic**
　1. Money-making projects for children -- Fiction
　ISBN 978-1-575-05925-9 lib bdg; 1-575-05925-8 lib bdg; 978-0-8225-6561-1 pa; 0-8225-6561-7 pa
　　　　　　　　　　　　　　　　LC 2005020620
When Mallory's mother refuses to buy her a purse, Mallory tries a series of businesses in order to make money and buy it herself.
"The illustrations are dark and bold, and interesting to look at. From the characterizations to the visuals, this chapter book is a winner." SLJ

Mallory goes green; by Laurie Friedman; illustrations by Jennifer Kalis. Carolrhoda Books 2010 159p il $15.95
Grades: 2 3 4　　　　　　　　　　　　　　　　**Fic**
　1. School stories 2. Environmental protection -- Fiction
　ISBN 978-0-8225-8885-6; 0-8225-8885-4
　　　　　　　　　　　　　　　　LC 2009014503
When Mallory is appointed to the Fern Falls Elementary School Environmental Committee, which is deciding on class projects for the upcoming Green Fair, she rapidly succeeds in alienating her classmates, friends, and family by her overzealous efforts to save the planet.

"This features large type, widely spaced lines, and stylized illustrations. Good chapter-book fare." Booklist

Mallory in the spotlight; by Laurie Friedman; illustrations by Jennifer Kalis. Darby Creek 2010 158p il $14.99
Grades: 3 4 5   **Fic**
1. School stories 2. Theater -- Fiction 3. Friendship -- Fiction
ISBN 978-0-8225-8884-9; 0-8225-8884-6
     LC 2009045341
When Mallory gets the lead in the school play, she cannot understand why her best friend Mary Ann is not just as excited as she is, but eventually she finds out—and learns who her real friends are.
This "is a fast-moving chapter book. . . . Bold drawings add visual appeal." Booklist

Mallory on board; by Laurie Friedman; illustrations by Barbara Pollak. Carolrhoda Books 2007 175p il lib bdg $15.95; pa $5.95
Grades: 2 3 4   **Fic**
1. Friendship -- Fiction 2. Remarriage -- Fiction 3. Family life -- Fiction 4. Ocean travel -- Fiction
ISBN 978-0-8225-6194-1 lib bdg; 0-8225-6194-8 lib bdg; 978-0-8225-9023-1 pa; 0-8225-9023-9 pa
     LC 2006013841
Despite her fears of being a "third wheel," Mallory goes on a cruise for the wedding of the mother and father of her two best friends.

Mallory on the move; by Laurie B. Friedman; illustrations by Tamara Schmitz. Carolrhoda Books 2004 158p il lib bdg $15.95; pa $5.95
Grades: 2 3 4   **Fic**
1. Wishes 2. Friendship 3. Family life 4. Best friends 5. Moving -- Fiction 6. Moving, Household 7. Friendship -- Fiction 8. Family life -- Fiction
ISBN 1-575-05538-4 lib bdg; 978-1-575-05538-1 lib bdg; 1-575-05831-6 pa; 978-1-575-05831-3 pa
     LC 2003-8937
After moving to a new town, eight-year-old Mallory keeps throwing stones in the "Wishing Pond" but things will not go back to the way they were before, and she remains torn between old and new best friends.
"Black-and-white drawings and the lively text reveal some very contemporary kids." Horn Book Guide

Mallory vs. Max. Carolrhoda 159p il lib bdg $15.95; pa $5.95
Grades: 2 3 4   **Fic**
1. Dogs -- Fiction 2. Siblings -- Fiction 3. Family life -- Fiction
ISBN 1-57505-795-6 lib bdg; 978-1-57505-795-8 lib bdg; 1-575-05863-4 pa; 978-1-575-05863-4 pa
Eight-year-old Mallory feels left out when her older brother, Max, gets a dog that becomes the center of attention.
"Schmitz's expressive cartoon illustrations and the large typeface make the book appealing to beginning chapter-book readers." SLJ

Mallory's guide to boys, brothers, dads, and dogs; illustrations by Jennifer Kalis. Darby Creek 2011 159p il $15.95

Grades: 2 3 4   **Fic**
1. School stories 2. Dogs -- Fiction 3. Family life -- Fiction
ISBN 978-0-8225-8886-3; 0-8225-8886-2
     LC 2010022224
Ten-year-old Mallory's crush on J.T., a boy in her older brother's class, gets her in trouble with her teacher, her family, and her friends but no matter what she does, J.T. does not seem interested in her.
"The book's dynamic design, including numerous line drawings, emails, and journal entry style pages, help enliven the story." Horn Book Guide

Mallory's super sleepover; by Laurie Friedman; illustrations by Jennifer Kalis. Carolrhoda Books 2011 il $15.95
Grades: 2 3 4   **Fic**
1. Parties -- Fiction 2. Birthdays -- Fiction 3. Sleepovers -- Fiction
ISBN 978-0-8225-8887-0; 0-8225-8887-0
     LC 2010044418
When Mallory plans a sleepover to celebrate her tenth birthday, she has a hard time pleasing both her friends and her parents.

Red, white, and true blue Mallory; by Laurie Friedman; illustrations by Jennifer Kalis. Carolrhoda Books 2009 183p il $15.95
Grades: 2 3 4   **Fic**
1. School stories 2. Friendship -- Fiction
ISBN 978-0-8225-8882-5; 0-8225-8882-X
     LC 2008016035
Mallory's journal of her fourth-grade trip to Washington D.C. reveals how much fun she has, despite a loose tooth, being upset with her best friend Mary Ann and getting separated from her class in a museum.
"Pencil drawings, supposedly by Mallory, illustrate the journal effectively. . . . Fans of the Mallory series and young visitors to the nation's capital may enjoy her take on Washington D.C. sightseeing." Booklist

Step fourth, Mallory! by Laurie Friedman; illustrations by Jennifer Kalis. Carolrhoda Books 2008 175p il lib bdg $15.95
Grades: 2 3 4   **Fic**
1. School stories 2. Friendship -- Fiction
ISBN 978-0-8225-8881-8 lib bdg; 0-8225-8881-1 lib bdg
     LC 2007034771
Mallory enters fourth grade with high hopes for her best year ever, but instead she starts by breaking the teacher's rules and then feels left out when her best friend likes the same boy she does.
"Mallory's first-person narrative . . . convincingly portrays both her high hopes and her low spirits as she tries to find her way. Illustrated with fresh, childlike drawings." Booklist

Friend, Catherine
    Barn boot blues. Marshall Cavendish 2011 $16.99
Grades: 5 6 7 8   **Fic**
1. Moving -- Fiction 2. Farm life -- Fiction
ISBN 978-0-7614-5827-2; 0-7614-5827-1
     LC 2011001909

When her parents swap urban life in Minneapolis for rural life on a farm 100 miles away, twelve-year-old Taylor feels as if she is living on another planet.

"In this refreshingly compact novel, readers learn interesting, authentic details about everything from spinning wool to collecting eggs to in a kind-of-gross, kind-of-wonderful climax birthing lambs. In Taylor, Friend has created a plucky, lightly sarcastic protagonist whose frustration at her situation is palpable but who never comes off as unlikable or bratty." Horn Book

Friesen, Jonathan

★ The **last** Martin. Zonderkidz 2011 266p $14.99
Grades: 4 5 6 7   Fic
1. Family life -- Fiction
ISBN 978-0-310-72080-5; 0-310-72080-X

      LC 2010-48275
Thirteen-year-old Martin Boyle struggles to break a family curse after discovering that he has twelve weeks to live.

"Spiced with plenty of slapstick, the yarn speeds its protagonist through a succession of highs, lows and improbable triumphs on the way to a hilariously melodramatic finish." Kirkus

Frost, Helen

Spinning through the universe; a novel in poems from room 214. Farrar, Straus and Giroux 2004 93p $16
Grades: 4 5 6 7   Fic
1. Poetry 2. Schools 3. Family life 4. School stories 5. Interpersonal relations
ISBN 0-374-37159-8

      LC 2003-48056
A collection of poems written in the voices of Mrs. Williams of room 214, her students, and a custodian about their interactions with each other, their families, and the world around them. Includes notes on the poetic forms represented

"Interwoven dramatic stories and interesting poetic patterns give this book extra appeal. A boon for poetry classes." SLJ

Fry, Michael

The **Odd** Squad; Bully Bait. by Michael Fry. Disney Hyperion 2013 224 p. (hardcover) $12.99
Grades: 4 5 6 7   Fic
1. Bullies -- Juvenile fiction 2. Friendship -- Juvenile fiction 3. School stories -- Juvenile fiction 4. Bullies -- Fiction 5. Schools -- Fiction 6. Middle schools -- Fiction 7. Interpersonal relations -- Fiction
ISBN 1423169247; 9781423169246

      LC 2012014286
This children's story, by Michael Fry, is part of the "Odd Squad" series. "Nick is the shortest seventh-grader in the history of the world . . . , doesn't fit in . . . , and spends more time inside than outside his locker. . . . When a well-intentioned guidance counselor forces Nick to join the school's lamest club . . . , what starts off as a reluctant band of hopeless oddballs morphs into an effective and empowered team ready to face whatever middle school throws at them." (Publisher's note)

"Cartoonist Fry humorously mines the world of middle school as seen through the eyes of bullied Nick to answer the question: Can three oddballs team together to take down the school bully? ...Abundant cartoon-style illustrations en-

hance the book's silly yet sensitive portrayal of bullying and unlikely friendships." Kirkus

Fullick, Ann

Rebuilding the body; organ transplantation. Ann Fullick. Rev. and updated Heinemann Library 2002 64 p. col. ill. (library) $34.29; (library) $35
Grades: 5 6 7 8   Fic
1. Medicine 2. Medical ethics 3. Transplantation of organs, tissues, etc. 4. Transplantation of organs, tissues, etc 5. Transplantation of organs, tissues, etc. -- Juvenile literature
ISBN 9781588107008 out of print; 1432924524; 9781432924522

      LC 2001006082
This book is part of the Science at the Edge series and looks at organ transplantation. It "begins with a survey of the major human body organs. . . . This is followed by a description of the failure of major organs, infections that occur within them, and gradual damage and deterioration. This leads to a discussion about organ transplants . . . . The challenges of organ transplantation, pitfalls of rejection, and ethics of transplantation from the dead are all touched upon." (NSTA Recommends)

Includes bibliographical references (p. 63) and index.

Funke, Cornelia Caroline

★ **Dragon** rider; [by] Cornelia Funke; translated by Anthea Bell. Scholastic 2004 523p il $12.95
Grades: 5 6 7 8   Fic
1. Fantasy fiction 2. Dragons -- Fiction
ISBN 0-439-45695-9

      LC 2004-45419
Original German edition 1997
After learning that humans are headed toward his hidden home, Firedrake, a silver dragon, is joined by a brownie and an orphan boy in a quest to find the legendary valley known as the Rim of Heaven, encountering friendly and unfriendly creatures along the way, and struggling to evade the relentless pursuit of an old enemy.

"Funke proves she knows how to tickle the imaginations of younger readers. . . . This is a good, old-fashioned ensemble-cast quest." Booklist

Inkdeath; [by] Cornelia Funke; translated from the German by Anthea Bell. Scholastic 2008 683p il map $24.99
Grades: 5 6 7 8   Fic
1. Fantasy fiction 2. Kidnapping -- Fiction 3. Books and reading -- Fiction
ISBN 978-0-439-86628-6; 0-439-86628-6

      LC 2008-19922
As Bluejay—Mo's fictitious double—tries to keep the Book of Immortality from unraveling, Adderhead kidnaps all the children in the kingdom, asking for Bluejay's surrender or the children will be doomed to slavery in the silver mines.

"The assortment of villains is vivid and frightening. . . . The finale includes a thoroughly engrossing climax." SLJ

★ **Inkheart**; [by] Cornelia Funke; translated from the German by Anthea Bell. Scholastic 2003 534p $19.95; pa $9.99

Grades: 5 6 7 8   **Fic**

1. Fantasy fiction 2. Books and reading -- Fiction

ISBN 0-439-53164-0; 0-439-70910-5 pa

LC 2003-45844

Twelve-year-old Meggie learns that her father, who repairs and binds books for a living, can "read" fictional characters to life when one of those characters abducts them and tries to force him into service.

The author "proves the power of her imagination; readers will be captivated by the chilling and thrilling world she has created here." Publ Wkly

Other titles in this series are:

Inkspell (2005)

Inkdeath (2008)

Inkspell; [by] Cornelia Funke; translated from the German by Anthea Bell. Scholastic 2005 635p il $19.99

Grades: 5 6 7 8   **Fic**

1. Fantasy fiction 2. Books and reading -- Fiction

ISBN 0-439-55400-4

"This is an involving story that will draw readers smoothly to its conclusion and leave them waiting for the final volume in this projected trilogy." SLJ

Fusco, Kimberly Newton

★ The **wonder** of Charlie Anne. Alfred A. Knopf 2010 272p $16.99; lib bdg $19.99

Grades: 5 6 7 8   **Fic**

1. Farm life -- Fiction 2. Friendship -- Fiction 3. Race relations -- Fiction 4. African Americans -- Fiction 5. Great Depression, 1929-1939 -- Fiction

ISBN 978-0-375-86104-8; 0-375-86104-1; 978-0-375-96104-5 lib bdg; 0-375-96104-6 lib bdg

LC 2009-38831

In a 1930s Massachusetts farm town torn by the Depression, racial tension, and other hardships, Charlie Anne and her black next-door neighbor Phoebe form a friendship that begins to transform their community.

"Good humor, kindness and courage triumph in this warm, richly nuanced novel that cheers the heart like a song sweetly sung." Kirkus

Gaiman, Neil

Odd and the Frost Giants; illustrated by Brett Helquist. HarperCollinsPublishers 2009 117p il $14.99

Grades: 3 4 5 6   **Fic**

1. Norse mythology -- Fiction

ISBN 978-0-06-167173-9; 0-06-167173-8

LC 2009014574

An unlucky twelve-year-old Norwegian boy named Odd leads the Norse gods Loki, Thor, and Odin in an attempt to outwit evil Frost Giants who have taken over Asgard.

"Along with Gaiman's deft humor, lively prose, and agile imagination, a few unexpected themes—the double-edged allure of beauty, the value of family—sneak into this slim tale with particular appeal to kids drawn to Norse mythology, but suitable for any readers of light fantasy." Booklist

Gaiman, Neil, 1960-

★ **Coraline**; [by] Neil Gaiman; with illustrations by Dave McKean. HarperCollins Pubs. 2002 162p il

Grades: 5 6 7 8   **Fic**

1. Horror fiction 2. Supernatural -- Fiction

ISBN 0-380-80734-3 pa; 0-380-97778-8

LC 2002-18937

Looking for excitement, Coraline ventures through a mysterious door into a world that is similar, yet disturbingly different from her own, where she must challenge a gruesome entity in order to save herself, her parents, and the souls of three others

"Gaiman twines his taut tale with a menacing tone and crisp prose fraught with memorable imagery . . . yet keeps the narrative just this side of terrifying." Publ Wkly

★ The **graveyard** book; with illustrations by Dave McKean. HarperCollins 2008 312p il $17.99; lib bdg $18.89

Grades: 5 6 7 8 9 10   **Fic**

1. Death -- Fiction 2. Cemeteries -- Fiction 3. Supernatural -- Fiction

ISBN 0-06-053092-8; 0-06-053093-6 lib bdg; 978-0-06-053092-1; 978-0-06-053093-8 lib bdg

LC 2008-13860

Awarded the Newbery Medal (2009)

Nobody Owens, nicknamed Bod, is a normal boy, except that he has been raised by in a graveyard by ghosts. "Grades five to nine." (Bull Cent Child Books)

"Gaiman writes with charm and humor, and again he has a real winner." Voice Youth Advocates

Galante, Cecilia

Willowood. Simon & Schuster 2010 265p $16.99

Grades: 4 5 6 7   **Fic**

1. Geckos -- Fiction 2. Moving -- Fiction 3. Friendship -- Fiction 4. Single parent family -- Fiction

ISBN 978-1-4169-8022-3; 1-4169-8022-9

Eleven-year-old Lily has trouble leaving her best friend behind and moving to the city when her mother changes jobs, but she makes some very unlikely friends that soon become like family members.

"The characters . . . are fully realized individuals. . . . [This book has a] finely tuned plot and poetic language. . . . Children will enjoy the story of Lily's first few months in the big city." SLJ

Gale, Eric Kahn

The **Bully** Book; Eric Kahn Gale. Harpercollins Childrens Books 2012 240 p. $16.99

Grades: 4 5 6 7 8   **Fic**

1. School stories 2. Bullies -- Juvenile fiction

ISBN 0062125117; 9780062125118

This juvenile novel, by Eric Kahn Gale, is about school bullying. "When the author was eleven, he was bullied. This book is loosely based on incidents that happened to him in sixth grade. Eric Haskins, the new sixth-grade bully target, is searching for answers. And unlike many of us who experienced something awful growing up, he finds them. Though they may not be what he expected." (Publisher's note)

Gannett, Ruth Stiles

My father's dragon; story by Ruth Stiles Gannett; illustrations by Ruth Chrisman Gannett. 60th anniversary edition; Random House 2008 86p il $16.99; lib bdg $19.99

Grades: 1 2 3 4   **Fic**

1. Fantasy fiction 2. Animals -- Fiction 3. Dragons

-- Fiction

ISBN 978-0-375-85610-5; 0-375-85610-2; 978-0-375-95610-2 lib bdg; 0-375-95610-7 lib bdg

A reissue of the title first published 1948

A Newbery Medal honor book, 1949

This describes the adventures of a small boy, Elmer Elevator, who befriended an old alley cat and in return heard the story of the captive baby dragon on Wild Island. Right away Elmer decided to free the dragon. The tale of Elmer's voyage to Tangerina and his arrival on Wild Island, his encounters with various wild animals, and his subsequent rescue of the dragon follows

Other titles in this series are:

The dragons of Blueland (1951)

Elmer and the dragon (1950)

Gantos, Jack

★ **Dead** end in Norvelt; Jack Gantos. Farrar Straus Giroux 2011 341p $15.99

Grades: 4 5 6 7   Fic

1. Old age -- Fiction

ISBN 978-0-374-37993-3; 0-374-37993-9

                                    LC 2010054009

Newbery Medal (2012)

Scott O'Dell Historical Fiction Award (2012)

In the historic town of Norvelt, Pennsylvania, twelve-year-old Jack Gantos spends the summer of 1962 grounded for various offenses until he is assigned to help an elderly neighbor with a most unusual chore involving the newly dead, molten wax, twisted promises, Girl Scout cookies, underage driving, lessons from history, typewriting, and countless bloody noses.

This is a "wildly entertaining meld of truth and fiction... Memorable in every way." Publ Wkly

★ **Heads** or tails; stories from the sixth grade. Farrar, Straus Giroux 1994 151p il $16; pa $4.95

Grades: 5 6 7 8   Fic

1. School stories 2. Diaries -- Fiction 3. Family life -- Fiction

ISBN 0-374-32909-5; 0-374-42923-5 pa

                                    LC 93-43117

"Jack is trying to survive his sixth-grade year, and he narrates, through a series of short-stories-cum-chapters, his difficulties in dodging the obstacles life throws in his path... The writing is zingy and specific, with snappily authentic dialogue and a vivid sense of juvenile experience.... Jack and his family have a recognizably thorny relationship. This is a distinctive and lively sequence of everyday-life stories." Bull Cent Child Books

Other titles about Jack are:

Jack adrift (2003)

Jack on the tracks (1999)

Jack's black book (1997)

Jack's new power (1995)

I am not Joey Pigza. Farrar, Straus and Giroux 2007 215p $16

Grades: 5 6 7 8   Fic

1. Fathers -- Fiction 2. Restaurants -- Fiction 3. Attention deficit disorder -- Fiction

ISBN 978-0-374-39941-2; 0-374-39941-7

                                    LC 2006-38681

Joey's father returns, calling himself Charles Heinz and apologizing for his past bad behavior, and he swears that once Joey and his mother change their names and help him fix up the old diner he has bought, their lives will change for the better

"The plot doesn't move so much as careen from one over-the-top event to the next, the achievement being that every one of them feels entirely plausible." Publ Wkly

Jack Adrift; fourth grade without a clue. Farrar, Straus & Giroux 2003 197p $16.99; pa $7.99

Grades: 4 5 6 7   Fic

1. School stories 2. Family life -- Fiction

ISBN 0-374-39987-5; 0-374-43718-1 pa

                                    LC 2002-192880

When his father rejoins the Navy and moves the family to Cape Hatteras, North Carolina, ten-year-old Jack becomes confused by a crush on his teacher, contradictory advice from his parents, and a very strange neighbor

"Gantos' wonderful writing ... is witty, smart, and unafraid to tackle tough topics." Booklist

Jack on the tracks; four seasons of fifth grade. Farrar, Straus & Giroux 1999 182p il $16; pa $5.95

Grades: 5 6 7 8   Fic

1. School stories 2. Self-perception 3. Moving, Household 4. Brothers and sisters 5. Family life -- Fiction

ISBN 0-374-33665-2; 0-374-43717-3 pa

                                    LC 99-27897

Moving with his unbearable sister to Miami, Florida, Jack tries to break some of his bad habits but finds himself irresistibly drawn to things disgusting, gross, and weird

"Jack is a likable and appealing fifth grader. His first-person preadolescent musings and worries are poignant, funny, and real." SLJ

Other titles in this series are:

Heads or tails (1994)

Jack's black book (1997)

Jack's new power (1995)

Jack's black book. Farrar, Straus & Giroux 1997 165p hardcover o.p. pa $7.99

Grades: 5 6 7 8   Fic

1. Authorship -- Fiction

ISBN 0-374-33662-8; 0-374-43716-5 pa

                                    LC 96-53107

"Back in Florida, Jack decides that becoming a writer will allow him to turn his worst experiences, and he has many, into money. He flubs his IQ test, nearly flunks wood shop, almost gets a date with a beautiful girl, visits a fortune teller, digs up his dead dog not once but twice, and copes with members of an off-kilter family who constantly remind him of his stupidity.... The narrative sparkles with wit and, although exaggerated, rings with the authenticity of adolescent humor, embarrassment, and fascination with the absolutely gross." SLJ

Jack's new power; stories from a Caribbean year. Farrar, Straus & Giroux 1995 214p hardcover o.p. pa $8.99

Grades: 5 6 7 8   **Fic**
1. Family life -- Fiction
ISBN 0-374-33657-1; 978-0-374-43715-2 pa
         LC 94-44442

"Gantos achieves an intriguing balance of the bitter and the sweet in this account; young readers whose lives are similarly mixed will appreciate Jack's narrative." Bull Cent Child Books

Joey Pigza loses control. Farrar, Straus & Giroux 2000 195p $16
Grades: 5 6 7 8   **Fic**
1. Baseball 2. Alcoholism 3. Fathers and sons 4. Father-son relationship -- Fiction 5. Attention deficit disorder -- Fiction 6. Attention-deficit hyperactivity disorder
ISBN 0-374-39989-1
         LC 00-20098

A Newbery Medal honor book, 2001

Joey, who is still taking medication to keep him from getting too wired, goes to spend the summer with the hard-drinking father he has never known and tries to help the baseball team he coaches win the championship

"This high-voltage, honest novel mixes humor, pain, fear and courage with deceptive ease." Publ Wkly

★ **Joey** Pigza swallowed the key. Farrar, Straus & Giroux 1998 153p $16.99
Grades: 5 6 7 8   **Fic**
1. School stories 2. Schools -- Fiction 3. Single-parent families -- Fiction 4. Attention deficit disorder -- Fiction 5. Attention-deficit hyperactivity disorder -- Fiction
ISBN 0-374-33664-4
         LC 98-24264

To the constant disappointment of his mother and his teachers, Joey has trouble paying attention or controlling his mood swings when his prescription meds wear off and he starts getting worked up and acting wired

This "frenetic narrative pulls at heartstrings and tickles funny bones." SLJ

Other titles about Joey Pigza are:
Joey Pigza loses control (2000)
What would Joey do? (2002)
I am not Joey Pigza (2007)

What would Joey do? Farrar, Straus & Giroux 2002 229p $16.99; pa $5.99
Grades: 5 6 7 8   **Fic**
1. Grandmothers -- Fiction 2. Attention deficit disorder -- Fiction
ISBN 0-374-39986-7; 0-06-054403-1 pa
         LC 2002-22823

Joey tries to keep his life from degenerating into total chaos when his mother sends him to be home-schooled with a hostile blind girl, his divorced parents cannot stop fighting, and his grandmother is dying of emphysema

"The boy's first-person narration is as frenetically fun as it was in the first two books." SLJ

Garcia, Cristina
★ **I** wanna be your shoebox. Simon & Schuster Books for Children 2008 198p $16.99; pa $6.99
Grades: 4 5 6 7   **Fic**
1. Jews -- Fiction 2. Family life -- Fiction 3.

Grandfathers -- Fiction 4. Cuban Americans -- Fiction 5. Racially mixed people -- Fiction
ISBN 978-1-4169-3928-3; 1-4169-3928-8; 978-1-4169-7904-3 pa; 1-4169-7904-2 pa

Thirteen-year-old, clarinet-playing, Southern California surfer, Yumi Ruiz-Hirsch, comes from a complex family—her father is Jewish-Japanese, her mother is Cuban, and her parents are divorced—and when her grandfather Saul is diagnosed with terminal cancer, Yumi asks him to tell her his life story, which helps her to understand her own history and identity.

"García's . . . exceptional ability to channel a range of voices lights up her first children's novel. . . . The large personalities propel the story and bring tenderness and credibility to a classic message about change." Publ Wkly

Gardiner, John Reynolds
Stone Fox; illustrated by Marcia Sewall. Crowell 1980 81p il $15.99; lib bdg $16.89; pa $5.50
Grades: 2 3 4 5   **Fic**
1. Dogs -- Fiction 2. Sled dog racing -- Fiction
ISBN 0-690-03983-2; 0-690-03984-0 lib bdg; 0-06-440132-4 pa
         LC 79-7895

This story "is rooted in a Rocky Mountain legend, a locale faithfully represented in Sewall's wonderful drawings. . . . In Gardiner's bardic chronicle, the tension is teeth rattling, with the tale flying to a conclusion that is almost unbearably moving, one readers won't soon forget." Publ Wkly

Gardner, Lyn
★ **Into** the woods; pictures by Mini Grey. David Fickling Books 2007 427p il $16.99; lib bdg $19.99; pa $7.50
Grades: 4 5 6 7 8   **Fic**
1. Fantasy fiction 2. Sisters -- Fiction
ISBN 978-0-385-75115-5; 0-385-75115-X; 978-0-385-75116-2 lib bdg; 0-385-75116-8 lib bdg; 978-0-440-42223-5 pa; 0-440-42223-X pa
         LC 2006-24350

Pursued by the sinister Dr. DeWilde and his ravenous wolves, three sisters—Storm, the inheritor of a special musical pipe, the elder Aurora, and the baby Any—flee into the woods and begin a journey filled with danger as they try to find a way to defeat their pursuer and keep him from taking the pipe and control of the entire land. "Grades five to eight." (Bull Cent Child Books)

"Gardner's fast-paced fantasy-adventure cleverly borrows from well-known fairy tales, and astute readers will enjoy identifying the many folkloric references. . . . Grey's appealing black-and-white illustrations add humor and detail to the story." Booklist

Out of the woods; pictures by Mini Grey. David Fickling Books 2010 348p il $17.99; lib bdg $20.99
Grades: 4 5 6 7 8   **Fic**
1. Fantasy fiction 2. Sisters -- Fiction
ISBN 978-0-385-75154-4; 0-385-75154-0; 978-0-385-75156-8 lib bdg; 0-385-75156-7 lib bdg

This is a sequel to Into the Woods (2007). The Eden sisters "are being lured into a wicked witch's lair. . . . Belladonna wants Aurora's heart and Storm's all-powerful musical pipe, and she will stop at nothing to get them." (Publisher's note) "Grades five to eight." (Bull Cent Child Books)

"Aurora, Storm, and Any Eden thought their troubles were over when Storm tossed the Pied Piper's powerful, seductive pipe . . . into the sea and defeated the pipe's erstwhile owner, the villainous Dr. DeWilde. . . . But it seems their troubles have only begun. . . . A missing prince, a cowardly lion, a marauding dragon, seven dwarfs, and even the Grimm brothers all make appearances, and while the fractured fairy-tale stew is considerably more haphazard than that of the sisters' first outing, it's a well-conceived and entertaining mash-up nonetheless." Horn Book

Garlick, Nick

Aunt Severe and the dragons; illustrated by Nick Maland. Andersen 2010 120p il pa $7.99

Grades: 2 3 4　　　　　　　　　　　　　　　　**Fic**

1. Aunts -- Fiction 2. Dragons -- Fiction

ISBN 978-1-8493-9055-2; 1-8493-9055-X

　　　　　　　　　　　　　　　LC 2011290327

"Eight years old when his explorer parents disappear, Daniel goes to live with the relative he secretly names Aunt Severe. She packs away his books, feeds him cold spinach sandwiches, and forces him to help her collect rubbish from the gutters. Daniel's life brightens considerably when he befriends four young runaway dragons, who are hiding in his aunt's garden. . . . Garlick . . . infuses this appealing, eventful story with a childlike sense of imagination, humor, and justice. Well designed for readers new to chapter books, this attractive paperback features short chapters, a good-size type, and many engaging, crosshatched ink drawings." Booklist

Garretson, Dee

Wildfire run. Harper 2010 261p $16.99; pa $6.99

Grades: 5 6 7 8　　　　　　　　　　　　　　　**Fic**

1. Adventure fiction 2. Fires -- Fiction 3. Presidents -- Fiction 4. Earthquakes -- Fiction 5. Wilderness survival -- Fiction

ISBN 978-0-06-195347-7; 0-06-195347-4; 978-0-06-195350-7 pa; 0-06-195350-4 pa

　　　　　　　　　　　　　　　LC 2009049482

A relaxing retreat to Camp David turns deadly after a faraway earthquake sets off a chain of disastrous events that traps the president's twelve-year-old son, Luke, and his two friends within the compound.

"Along with a breathlessly paced plot, Garretson crafts a preteen protagonist who grows out of being a whiny, moody sort and, with his companions, displays generous measures of courage and ingenuity in rising to the occasion." Booklist

Garza, Xavier

★ **Lucha** libre: the Man in the Silver Mask; a bilingual cuento. written & illustrated by Xavier Garza. Cinco Puntos Press 2005 un il $17.95

Grades: 2 3 4 5　　　　　　　　　　　　　　　**Fic**

1. Uncles -- Fiction 2. Wrestling -- Fiction 3. Bilingual books -- English-Spanish

ISBN 0-938317-92-X

　　　　　　　　　　　　　　　LC 2004-29756

When Carlitos attends a wrestling match in Mexico City with his father, his favorite masked-wrestler has eyes that are strangely familiar.

"Smoothly integrated information in fluid colloquial English and Spanish combines with grainy graphic-novel-style illustrations executed in acrylic to create an oddly compelling and sophisticated package. An informative endnote,

in English only, presents a brief but engrossing history of lucha libre." SLJ

Maximilian and the mystery of the Guardian Angel; a bilingual lucha libre thriller. written and illustrated by Xavier Garza. 1st ed. Cinco Puntos Press 2011 207 p. ill. (paperback) $12.95

Grades: 3 4 5 6　　　　　　　　　　　　　　　**Fic**

1. Wrestling -- Juvenile fiction 2. Adventure fiction -- Juvenile fiction 3. Heroes -- Fiction 4. Uncles -- Fiction 5. Wrestling -- Fiction 6. Mexican Americans -- Fiction 7. Family life -- Texas -- Fiction 8. Spanish language materials -- Bilingual

ISBN 1933693983; 9781933693989

　　　　　　　　　　　　　　　LC 2010037400

In this book, "eleven-year-old Max is fascinated with the world of Lucha Libre and the great wrestler known as the Guardian Angel. . . . Max lives in Texas, where it has become tremendously popular. Much to his great joy, he is given the opportunity to attend a match . . . where his hero will be challenging the ruthless Red Devil. In all the emotion of attending the event, Max falls into the ring and thus into the Guardian Angel's path," discovering a familial connection with him. (School Library Journal)

Gassman, Julie

You can't spike your serves; illustrated by Jorge Santillan. Stone Arch Books 2011 49p il (Sports Illustrated kids) lib bdg $25.32; pa $5.95

Grades: 1 2 3 4　　　　　　　　　　　　　　　**Fic**

1. Volleyball -- Fiction

ISBN 978-1-4342-2231-2 lib bdg; 1-4342-2231-4 lib bdg; 978-1-4342-3080-5 pa; 1-4342-3080-5 pa

　　　　　　　　　　　　　　　LC 2010048182

"Alicia wants to help her pen pal, Jenny, earn money to purchase new pom-poms, and when an Olympic volleyball player comes to school to teach the fourth graders her sport, Alicia comes up with the idea of a tournament to raise the needed funds. . . . She discovers how hard serving is without being able to jump, but Reese suggests the perfect technique for her. Manga-style graphics give this book a cutting-edge look and enhance understanding of the text. Short chapters, colorful cartoon illustrations, and engaging subject matter make this title appropriate for those new to chapter books as well as older readers." SLJ

Includes glossary and bibliographical references

Gates, Doris

Blue willow; illustrated by Paul Lantz. Viking 1940 172p il hardcover o.p. pa $5.99

Grades: 4 5 6 7　　　　　　　　　　　　　　　**Fic**

1. Migrant labor -- Fiction

ISBN 0-14-030924-1 pa

"Having to move from one migrant camp to another intensifies Janey Larkin's desire for a permanent home, friends, and school. The only beautiful possession the family has is a blue willow plate handed down from generation to generation. It is a reminder of happier days in Texas and represents dreams and promises for a better future. Reading about this itinerant family's ways of life, often filled with despair and yet always hopeful, leaves little room for the reader's indifference." Read Ladders for Hum Relat. 6th edition

Gauch, Patricia Lee

★ **This** time, Tempe Wick? illustrated by Margot Tomes. Boyds Mills Press 2003 43p il hardcover o.p. $16.95

Grades: 3 4 5   **Fic**

ISBN 1-59078-179-1; 1-59078-185-6 pa

A reissue of the title first published 1974 by Coward, McCann & Geoghegan

Everyone knows Tempe Wick is a most surprising girl, but she exceeds even her own reputation when two mutinous Revolutionary soldiers try to steal her beloved horse.

"The writing is the perfect vehicle for the illustrations—in the artist's inimitable style—which capture the down-to-earth, unpretentious, and humorous quality of the storytelling." Horn Book

Geisert, Bonnie

Prairie winter. Houghton Mifflin Boos for Children 2009 220p $16

Grades: 4 5 6   **Fic**

1. Moving -- Fiction 2. Winter -- Fiction 3. Sisters -- Fiction 4. Farm life -- Fiction

ISBN 978-0-618-68588-2; 0-618-68588-X

"Like Prairie Summer (2001) and Lessons (2005), this third novel is based on Geisert's own childhood on a South Dakota farm in the 1950s. . . . After a giant snowstorm, [Rachel] is excited when she and her two sisters are moved into town so that they can continue to attend school. . . . The brutal winter is the drama here, and so it the honest view of leaving home." Booklist

George, Jean Craighead

Charlie's raven; written and illustrated by Jean Craighead George. Dutton Children's Books 2004 190p il hardcover o.p. pa $6.99

Grades: 5 6 7 8   **Fic**

1. Ravens -- Fiction 2. Naturalists -- Fiction 3. Grandfathers -- Fiction

ISBN 0-525-47219-3; 0-14-240547-7 pa

Charlie's friend, Singing Bird, a Teton Sioux, tells him that ravens have curing powers, so Charlie steals a baby bird from its nest, hoping to heal his ailing Granddad, a retired naturalist.

"The story is technically accurate and offers a vivid sense of place and a window into Native American beliefs through storytelling." SLJ

★ **My** side of the mountain trilogy; written and illustrated by Jean Craighead George. Dutton Children's Books 2000 177, 170, 258p il $24.99

Grades: 5 6 7 8   **Fic**

1. Falcons -- Fiction 2. Wilderness survival -- Fiction

ISBN 0-525-46269-4

LC 00-712305

Originally published as three separate volumes, 1959, 1990, and 1999 respectively

My side of the mountain was a Newbery honor book, 1960

In My Side of the Mountain Sam Gribley tells of his year in the wilderness of the Catskill Mountains. In On the Far Side of the Mountain Sam's peaceful existence in his wilderness home is disrupted when his sister runs away and his pet falcon is confiscated by a conservation officer. In Frightful's Mountain Sam's pet falcon must learn to live as a wild bird

There's an owl in the shower; illustrated by Christine Herman Merrill. HarperCollins Pubs. 1995 133p il hardcover o.p. pa $5.99

Grades: 3 4 5   **Fic**

1. Owls -- Fiction 2. Endangered species -- Fiction

ISBN 0-06-024891-2; 0-06-440682-2 pa

LC 94-38893

Because protecting spotted owls has cost Borden's father his job as a logger in the old growth forest of northern California, Borden intends to kill any spotted owl he sees, until he and his father find themselves taking care of a young owlet

"George's writing skill and knowledge of animal behavior turn what could have been nothing but a message into an absorbing story that shows both sides of the controversy. . . . Merrill's drawings perfectly capture the engaging bird and the family's affection for it." SLJ

The **cats** of Roxville Station; illustrated by Tom Pohrt. Dutton Children's Books 2009 163p il $16.99

Grades: 4 5 6   **Fic**

1. Cats -- Fiction

ISBN 978-0-525-42140-5; 0-525-42140-8

LC 2008034217

Thrown into a river by a cruel human, a young tiger-striped cat fights to survive amid feral cats and other creatures near Roxville train station, aided by Mike, an eleven-year-old foster boy who is not allowed to have a pet.

"George packs a lot of natural information on species from mosquitoes to owls in this slim volume. There is no anthropomorphization of the cats; when Ratchet and the other cats 'talk' it is with scent and body language. Pohrt's line drawings complement the text nicely." Kirkus

George, Jessica Day

Dragon flight; [by] Jessica Day George. 1st U.S. ed.; Bloomsbury Children's Books 2008 262p $16.95

Grades: 5 6 7 8   **Fic**

1. Fantasy fiction 2. Dragons -- Fiction

ISBN 978-1-59990-110-7; 1-59990-110-2

LC 2007050762

Young seamstress Creel finds herself strategizing with the dragon king Shardas once again when a renegade dragon in a distant country launches a war against their country, bringing an entire army of dragons into the mix.

"Fans of the first book will find the same strengths here: the imaginatively detailed scenes; the thrilling, spell-fueled action; the possibility of romance with a prince; and the appealing, brave heroine." Booklist

Tuesdays at the castle. Bloomsbury 2011 $16.99

Grades: 3 4 5 6   **Fic**

1. Fairy tales 2. Castles -- Fiction 3. Princesses -- Fiction 4. Kings and rulers -- Fiction

ISBN 978-1-59990-644-7; 1-59990-644-9

LC 2011016739

Eleven-year-old Princess Celie lives with her parents, the king and queen, and her brothers and sister at Castle Glower, which adds rooms or stairways or secret passageways most every Tuesday, and when the king and queen are ambushed while travelling, it is up to Celie—the castle's favorite—with her secret knowledge of its never-ending twists and turns, to protect their home and save their kingdom.

"Castle Glower is the true star of this charming story of court intrigue and magic. A satisfying mix of Hogwarts and Howl's Moving Castle, . . . Castle Glower helps its true citizens, but never at the expense of plot or character development." SLJ

Gephart, Donna

★ **How** to survive middle school. Delacorte Press 2010 247p $15.99; lib bdg $18.99

Grades: 5 6 7 8   **Fic**

1. School stories 2. Family life -- Fiction
ISBN 978-0-385-73793-7; 0-385-73793-9; 978-0-385-90701-9 lib bdg; 0-385-90701-X lib bdg

LC 2009-21809

When thirteen-year-old David Greenberg's best friend makes the start of middle school even worse than he feared it could be, David becomes friends with Penny, who shares his love of television shows and posts one of their skits on YouTube, making them wildly popular—online, at least.

"Gephart crafts for her likable protagonist an engaging, feel-good transition into adolescence that's well stocked with tears and laughter." Booklist

Olivia Bean, trivia queen; Donna Gephart. Delacorte Press 2012 278 p. $16.99

Grades: 3 4 5 6 7   **Fic**

1. Game shows -- Fiction 2. Children of divorced parents -- Fiction 3. Father-daughter relationship -- Fiction 4. Divorce -- Fiction 5. Fathers -- Fiction 6. Curiosities and wonders -- Fiction
ISBN 0385740522; 9780385740524

LC 2011006023

In this book, "Olivia Bean has watched 'Jeopardy!' every evening since she was a little girl, but the nightly tradition just hasn't been the same since her father . . . took off for California two years ago. When the show announces auditions for Kids Week, Olivia is intent on making the cut, not only to compete but, more importantly, to get a plane ticket out to the show's taping in L.A. with the hopes of meeting up with her estranged dad." (Bulletin of the Center for Children's Books).

Gewirtz, Adina Rishe

Zebra forest; Adina Rishe Gewirtz. Candlewick Press 2013 208 p. (reinforced) $15.99

Grades: 5 6 7 8   **Fic**

1. Hostages -- Fiction 2. Siblings -- Fiction
ISBN 0763660418; 9780763660413

LC 2012947251

In this novel, by Adina Rishe Gewirtz, "an escaped fugitive upends everything two siblings think they know about their family, their past, and themselves. . . . A rattling at the back door, an escapee from the prison holding them hostage in their own home, four lives that will never be the same. . . . [The book] portrays an unfolding standoff of truth against family secrets." (Publisher's note)

"Debut author Gewirtz successfully conveys the terror and tedium of being trapped. . . While the situation may frighten some readers, the matter-of-fact way [the protagonists] make the best of difficult circumstances . . . may be comforting to those whose families don't match the ideal.

An emotionally honest family story with an ending that's hopeful without being implausibly upbeat." Pub Wkly

Gibbs, Stuart

Belly up. Simon & Schuster Books for Young Readers 2010 294p $15.99; pa $6.99

Grades: 4 5 6 7   **Fic**

1. Mystery fiction 2. Zoos -- Fiction 3. Hippopotamus -- Fiction
ISBN 978-1-4169-8731-4; 1-4169-8731-2; 978-1-4169-8732-1 pa; 1-4169-8732-0 pa

LC 2009-34860

Twelve-year-old Teddy investigates when a popular Texas zoo's star attraction, Henry the hippopotamus, is murdered.

"The characters are well-developed and believable, making this book appealing to reluctant readers and those who enjoy animal stories and mysteries." Libr Media Connect

The **last** musketeer. Harper 2011 244p $16.99

Grades: 5 6 7 8   **Fic**

1. Cardinals 2. Statesmen 3. Adventure fiction 4. Time travel -- Fiction
ISBN 978-0-06-204838-7; 0-06-204838-4

LC 2011019376

In Paris with his parents to sell family heirlooms, fourteen-year-old Greg Rich suddenly finds himself four hundred years in the past, and is aided by boys who will one day be known as 'The Three Musketeers.'

"From the gripping first sentence . . . the excitement never flags in this newly imagined Musketeer adventure. . . . Using Alexandre Dumas' stories as a jumping-off point, Gibbs mixes fact, fantasy and thrills to create a galloping swashbuckler." Kirkus

Giblin, James

The **boy** who saved Cleveland; based on a true story. [by] James Cross Giblin; illustrated by Michael Dooling. Henry Holt and Company 2006 64p il $15.95

Grades: 3 4 5   **Fic**

1. Malaria -- Fiction 2. Epidemics -- Fiction 3. Frontier and pioneer life -- Fiction
ISBN 0-8050-7355-8; 978-0-8050-7355-3

LC 2005021695

During a malaria epidemic in late eighteenth-century Cleveland, Ohio, ten-year-old Seth Doan surprises his family, his neighbors, and himself by having the strength to carry and grind enough corn to feed everyone.

"Young readers will enjoy the clear writing and plot-driven pace. Dooling's full-page pencil-on-paper illustrations convey the time period as well as the emotional tone. A solid choice for those seeking pioneer fiction and strong characters." Booklist

Gidwitz, Adam

In a glass Grimmly; Adam Gidwitz. Dutton Juvenile 2012 314 p. (hardback) $16.99

Grades: 3 4 5 6   **Fic**

1. Horror fiction 2. Occult fiction 3. Fractured fairy tales 4. Fairy tales 5. Frogs -- Fiction 6. Humorous stories 7. Cousins -- Fiction 8. Characters in literature -- Fiction 9. Adventure and adventurers -- Fiction
ISBN 0525425810; 9780525425816

LC 2012015515

This book is Adam Gidwitz's second collection of re-imagined fairy tales. "The protagonists in this installment are Jack, Jill, and a talking frog, whose adventures begin separately in reworkings of 'The Frog Prince' and 'The Emperor's New Clothes,' before the three join forces in 'Jack and the Bean-stalk.'" (Publishers Weekly)

★ A **tale** dark & Grimm. Dutton 2010 256p il $16.99; $16.99

Grades: 5 6 7 8   **Fic**

1. Fairy tales 2. Siblings -- Fiction
ISBN 978-0-525-42334-8; 0-525-42334-6; 9780525425816

LC 2009-53289

This book follows Hansel and Gretel as they walk out of their own story and into eight more tales. "Age ten and up." (N Y Times Book Rev)

"An audacious debut that's wicked smart and wicked funny." Publ Wkly

Giff, Patricia Reilly

Big whopper; illustrated by Alasdair Bright. Wendy Lamb Books 2010 66p il (Zigzag kids) $12.99; lib bdg $15.99; pa $4.99

Grades: 2 3 4   **Fic**

1. School stories 2. Truthfulness and falsehood -- Fiction
ISBN 978-0-385-74688-5; 0-385-74688-1; 978-0-385-90926-6 lib bdg; 0-385-90926-8 lib bdg; 978-0-553-49469-3 pa; 0-553-49469-4 pa

LC 2009033020

The Zigzag School "Afternoon Center kids set out to list all of their discoveries. Everyone can think of at least something with the exception of Destiny, who, in desperation, makes up a 'discovery' about a famous ancestor. Soon, she is in over her head, trying to find her way out of her big whopper of a lie. . . . Readers new to chapter books will love [this] quick-paced, fun [story]. Spot illustrations and a generous font size add to [its] approachability." SLJ

Eleven. Wendy Lamb Books 2008 164p $15.99; lib bdg $18.99; pa $6.50

Grades: 4 5 6 7   **Fic**

1. Woodwork -- Fiction 2. Friendship -- Fiction 3. Kidnapping -- Fiction 4. Learning disabilities -- Fiction
ISBN 978-0-385-73069-3; 978-0-385-90098-0 lib bdg; 978-0-440-23802-7 pa

LC 2007-12638

When Sam, who can barely read, discovers an old newspaper clipping just before his eleventh birthday, it brings forth memories from his past, and, with the help of a new friend at school and the castle they are building for a school project, his questions are eventually answered.

This is an "exquisitely rendered story of self-discovery." Publ Wkly

Flying feet; illustrated by Alasdair Bright. Wendy Lamb Books 2011 71p il (Zigzag kids) $11.99; lib bdg $14.99; pa $4.99

Grades: 2 3 4   **Fic**

1. School stories 2. Inventors -- Fiction
ISBN 978-0-385-73887-3; 0-385-73887-0; 978-0-385-90754-5 lib bdg; 0-385-90754-0 lib bdg; 978-0-375-89637-8 e-book; 978-0-375-85911-3 pa; 0-375-85911-X pa

LC 2010022645

Charlie often thinks of inventions that seldom work, but his latest idea just might be able to help Jake the Sweeper get rid of a big pile of trash and save "Come as a Character" day, too.

"The cheerful drawings offer levity to the spare, straightforward prose laid out in one- or two-sentence paragraphs. The tension builds mildly, exploring the concept of individuality and the expanding pressures of growing up, demonstrating Giff's keen understanding of chapter-book readers." Kirkus

Lily's crossing. Delacorte Press 1997 180p $15.95; pa $6.50; $15.95

Grades: 4 5 6 7   **Fic**

1. Friendship -- Fiction 2. World War, 1939-1945 -- Fiction
ISBN 0-385-32142-2; 0-440-41453-9 pa; 9780385321426

LC 96-23021

A Newbery Medal honor book, 1998

"Set during World War II, this . . . story tells of the war's impact on two children, one an American and one a Hungarian refugee. Lily Mollahan, a spirited, sensitive youngster being raised by her grandmother and Poppy, her widower father, has a comfortable routine that includes the family's annual summer migration to Gram's beach house in Rockaway, NY. Lily looks forward to summer's freedom and fishing outings with Poppy. She meets Albert, a Hungarian boy who is staying at a neighbor's house. . . . Eventually the two become good friends. The war interferes directly with Lily's life when Poppy, an engineer, is sent to Europe to help with clean-up operations." (SLJ) "Grades five to eight." (Booklist)

"Gentle elements of danger and suspense . . . keep the plot moving forward, while the delicate balance of characters and setting gently coalesces into an emotional whole that is fully satisfying." Bull Cent Child Books

Maggie's door. Wendy Lamb Bks. 2003 158p pa $6.50

Grades: 5 6 7 8   **Fic**

1. Immigrants -- Fiction
ISBN 0-385-32658-0; 0-385-90095-3 lib bdg; 0-440-41581-0 pa

LC 2003-2415

In the mid-1800s, Nory and her neighbor and friend, Sean, set out separately on a dangerous journey from famine-plagued Ireland, hoping to reach a better life in America

"Giff uses vivid language and precisely detailed observation to convey both experience and emotion." Horn Book

Nory Ryan's song. Delacorte Press 2000 148p hardcover o.p. pa $5.99

Grades: 5 6 7 8   **Fic**

1. Survival 2. Famines -- Fiction 3. Famines -- Ireland 4. Brothers and sisters 5. Ireland -- History -- Famine,

1845-1852 -- Juvenile fiction
ISBN 0-385-32141-4; 0-440-41829-1 pa

LC 00-27690

When a terrible blight attacks Ireland's potato crop in 1845, twelve-year-old Nory Ryan's courage and ingenuity help her family and neighbors survive

"Giff brings the landscape and the cultural particulars of the era vividly to life and creates in Nory a heroine to cheer for. A beautiful, heart-wrenching novel that makes a devastating event understandable." Booklist

Another title about Nory is:

Maggie's door (2003)

Number one kid; illustrated by Alasdair Bright. Wendy Lamb Books 2010 67p il (Zigzag kids) $12.99; lib bdg $15.99; pa $4.99
Grades: 2 3 4   **Fic**
1. School stories 2. Siblings -- Fiction
ISBN 978-0-385-74687-8; 0-385-74687-3; 978-0-385-90925-9 lib bdg; 0-385-90925-X lib bdg; 978-0-553-49468-6 pa; 0-553-49468-6 pa

LC 2009033019

"This series kicks off with a spunky introduction to the students at Zelda A. Zigzag School. Mitchell and his sister, Angel, are the new kids. He's not too sure about some of his schoolmates or the Afternoon Center that they attend, but he's sure about one thing: he wants to win a medal on prize day. . . . Readers new to chapter books will love [this] quick-paced, fun [story]. Spot illustrations and a generous font size add to [its] approachability." SLJ

Other titles in this series are:

Big whopper (2010)

Flying feet (2011)

Star time (2011)

Pictures of Hollis Woods. Wendy Lamb Bks. 2002 166p $15.95; pa $6.50
Grades: 5 6 7 8   **Fic**
1. Artists -- Fiction 2. Old age -- Fiction 3. Foster home care -- Fiction
ISBN 0-385-32655-6; 0-440-41578-0 pa

LC 2002-426

A Newbery Medal honor book, 2003

"She was named for the place where she was found as an abandoned baby. Twelve-year-old Hollis Woods has been through many foster homes—and she runs away, every time. In her latest placement, with an artist named Josie, the tightly wound Hollis begins to relax ever so slightly. . . . But Josie is slowly slipping into dementia, and Hollis knows that she'll be taken away from her if Josie is found out. . . . Giff has a sure hand with language, and the narrative is taut and absorbing." Booklist

Star time; illustrated by Alasdair Bright. Wendy Lamb Books 2011 67p il (Zigzag kids) $11.99; lib bdg $14.99; pa $4.99; ebook $4.99
Grades: 2 3 4   **Fic**
1. School stories 2. Theater -- Fiction
ISBN 978-0-385-73888-0; 0-385-73888-9; 978-0-385-90755-2 lib bdg; 0-385-90755-9 lib bdg; 978-0-375-85912-0 pa; 0-375-85912-8 pa; 978-0-375-89638-5 ebook; 0-375-89638-4 ebook

LC 2010042517

Gina wants more than anything to be the star of the show that her class will perform, but everything seems to go wrong until she makes a generous choice.

"Amusingly drawn illustrations and Gina's accident-prone antics, usually involving something goopy, add giggly humor to the tale. Giff gives voice to a vulnerable yet tenacious youngster who believes in herself." Kirkus

Storyteller. Wendy Lamb Books 2010 166p $15.99; lib bdg $18.99
Grades: 5 6 7 8   **Fic**
1. Aunts -- Fiction 2. Family life -- Fiction 3. Father-daughter relationship -- Fiction
ISBN 978-0-375-83888-0; 0-375-83888-0; 978-0-375-93888-7 lib bdg; 0-375-93888-5 lib bdg

LC 2009-48130

Forced to spend months at an aunt's house, Elizabeth feel a connection to her ancestor Zee, whose picture hangs on the wall, and who reveals her story of hardships during the Revolutionary War as Elizabeth comes to terms with her own troubles

"As she brings these characters and history alive, Giff again demostrates her own gift for storytelling." Publ Wkly

Water Street. Wendy Lamb Books 2006 164p $15.95; lib bdg $17.99; pa $6.50
Grades: 5 6 7 8   **Fic**
1. Family life -- Fiction 2. Irish Americans -- Fiction
ISBN 978-0-385-90097-3; 0-385-73068-3; 978-0-385-90097-3 lib bdg; 0-385-90097-X lib bdg; 978-0-440-41921-1 pa; 0-440-41921-2 pa

LC 2006-02024

In the shadow of the construction of the Brooklyn Bridge, eighth-graders and new neighbors Bird Mallon and Thomas Neary make some decisions about what they want to do with their lives.

"Continuing the Irish American immigration story begun in Nory Ryan's Song (2000) and Maggie's Door (2003), [this] novel, set in 1875, is about the next generation. . . . A poignant immigration story of friendship, work, and the meaning of home." Booklist

Wild girl. Wendy Lamb Books 2009 147p $15.99; lib bdg $18.99
Grades: 3 4 5 6   **Fic**
1. Horses -- Fiction 2. Immigrants -- Fiction 3. Family life -- Fiction 4. Brazilian Americans -- Fiction
ISBN 978-0-375-83890-3; 0-375-83890-2; 978-0-375-93890-0 lib bdg; 0-375-93890-7 lib bdg

LC 2008-47733

When twelve-year-old Lydie leaves Brazil to join her father and brother on a horse ranch in New York, she has a hard time adjusting to her changed circumstances, as does a new horse that has come to the ranch.

"Readers who choose the book because of the horse on the jacket will find a satisfying girl-meets-horse story. Those looking for a convincing, sometimes moving immigrant story will find it here as well." Booklist

Giff, Patricia Reilly, 1935-

R my name is Rachel. Wendy Lamb Books 2011 166p $15.99; lib bdg $18.99; e-book $10.99
Grades: 4 5 6 7   **Fic**
1. Moving -- Fiction 2. Siblings -- Fiction 3. Farm

life -- Fiction 4. Great Depression, 1929-1939 -- Fiction
ISBN 978-0-375-83889-7; 0-375-83889-9; 978-0-375-
93889-4 lib bdg; 0-375-93889-3; 978-0-375-98389-4
e-book

LC 2011004303

Three city siblings, now living on a farm during the
Great Depression, must survive on their own when their father takes a construction job miles away.

"Rachel's searing, present-tense narrative exposes her
fears, determination, and hopefulness in the face of wrenching challenges. Recurring motifs—color, flowers, and drawings by a neighbor that Rachel discovers in unlikely places—
add lyricism to this story of family solidarity." Publ Wkly

Gifford, Peggy Elizabeth
★ **Moxy** Maxwell does not love Stuart Little. Schwartz
& Wade Books 2007 91p il $12.99; lib bdg $15.99; pa
$5.50
Grades: 2 3 4 **Fic**
1. Summer -- Fiction 2. Family life -- Fiction 3. Books
and reading -- Fiction
ISBN 0-375-83915-1; 978-0-375-83915-3; 0-375-
93915-6 lib bdg; 978-0-375-93915-0 lib bdg; 978-0-
440-42230-3 pa; 0-440-42230-2 pa

LC 2006-16869

With summer coming to an end, about-to-be-fourth-
grader Moxy Maxwell does a hundred different things to
avoid reading her assigned summer reading book.

"Moxy is funny. . . . A dryly observant narration, clever
chapter titles, and the spot-on illustrations provide added lift
to the story." SLJ

Other titles about Moxy Maxwell are:
Moxy Maxwell does not love writing thank-you notes
(2008)
Moxy Maxwell does not love practicing the piano (2009)

Moxy Maxwell does not love practicing the piano; photographs by Valorie Fisher. Schwartz & Wade Books 2009
176p il $12.99; lib bdg $15.99
Grades: 2 3 4 **Fic**
1. Twins -- Fiction 2. Concerts -- Fiction 3. Pianists
-- Fiction 4. Siblings -- Fiction
ISBN 978-0-375-84488-1; 0-375-84488-0; 978-0-375-
96688-0 lib bdg; 0-375-96688-9 lib bdg

LC 2008036639

On the day of her recital, ten-year-old Moxy prepares
in her usual flamboyant way, which creates chaos at home.

"This story offers a fresh, comical view of a child's outlook and experiences." Booklist

Moxy Maxwell does not love writing thank-you notes;
by Peggy Gifford; photographs by Valorie Fisher. Schwartz
& Wade Books 2008 159p il $12.99
Grades: 2 3 4 **Fic**
1. Twins -- Fiction 2. Siblings -- Fiction 3. Christmas
-- Fiction 4. Family life -- Fiction
ISBN 978-0-375-84270-2; 0-375-84270-5; 978-0-375-
94552-6 lib bdg; 0-375-94552-0 lib bdg

LC 2007-15686

Ten-year-old Moxy Maxwell has promised to write
twelve thank-you notes by the day after Christmas so that
she and her twin brother Mark can go to Hollywood to visit
their father, but all her brilliant ideas to help finish the task
more efficiently end up creating chaos in the house.

"This sequel continues in the same unusual format as the
first book: humorous chapter titles, some chapters with little
or no text, and photographs (purportedly taken by Mark).
The short chapters, which jump from topic to topic just like
Moxy's thoughts, help establish the frenetic mood." SLJ

Giles, Stephen M.
The **body** thief. Sourcebooks Jabberwocky 2010 221p
il (The death (and further adventures) of Silas Winterbot-
tom) $12.99
Grades: 3 4 5 6 **Fic**
1. Mystery fiction 2. Uncles -- Fiction 3. Cousins
-- Fiction 4. Immortality -- Fiction 5. Inheritance and
succession -- Fiction
ISBN 978-1-4022-4090-4; 1-4022-4090-2

LC 2010-14380

First published 2009 in Australia

Lured to their sick Uncle Silas's home under the pretense
of becoming heirs to his vast fortune, cousins Adele, Isabella, and Milo soon learn that the old man has a diabolical
plan to prevent his own death.

"Giles delivers even the macabre twists of the tale with
a light touch, giving readers plenty of incentive to stick with
the series." Publ Wkly

Gilman, Laura Anne
Grail quest: the Camelot spell; book one. HarperCollins 2006 291p $10.99; lib bdg $14.89
Grades: 5 6 7 8 **Fic**
1. Kings 2. Magic -- Fiction 3. Middle Ages -- Fiction
4. Knights and knighthood -- Fiction
ISBN 0-06-077279-4; 0-06-077280-8 lib bdg

Three teenagers living in Camelot are forced to undertake a dangerous mission when King Arthur's court falls
under a mysterious enchantment on the eve of the quest for
the Holy Grail.

"The believable dialogue, succint plot, and uncomplicated references to court life will appeal to middle graders
who are beginning to explore Aurthurian legend." Voice
Youth Advocates

Other titles in this series are:
Grail quest: Morgain's revenge (2006)
Grail quest: The shadow companion (2006)

Gilson, Jamie
Bug in a rug; illustrated by Diane deGroat. Clarion
Books 1998 69p il hardcover o.p. $15
Grades: 2 3 4 **Fic**
1. School stories 2. Uncles -- Fiction 3. Schools --
Fiction 4. Clothing and dress -- Fiction
ISBN 0-395-86616-2; 0-618-31670-1

LC 97-16437

Seven-year-old Richard is self-conscious when he receives a pair of purple pants from his aunt and uncle and has
to wear them to school, but he is even more worried when
his uncle shows up for a visit to his classroom

"Gilson captures the thoughts and fears of second graders
through authentic dialogue and solid characterization." SLJ

Other titles about Richard are:
Chess! I love it, I love it, I love it! (2008)
Gotcha! (2006)
It goes Eeeeeeeeeeee! (1994)
Itchy Richard (1991)

Chess! I love it, I love it, I love it! illustrated by Amy Wummer. Clarion Books 2008 82p il $15

Grades: 2 3 4   Fic

1. School stories 2. Chess -- Fiction

ISBN 978-0-6189-7790-1; 0-6189-7790-2

When second-grader Richard and three other members of the Sumac School Chess Club compete in their first tournament, they each learn something about luck, concentration, and teamwork.

"Gilson shows a sound knowlege of grade-school psychology in this entertaining chapter book." Booklist

Thirteen ways to sink a sub. Marshall Cavendish Children 2009 103p $15.99

Grades: 4 5 6   Fic

1. School stories 2. Teachers -- Fiction

ISBN 978-0-7614-5587-5; 0-7614-5587-6

LC 2008040559

A reissue of the title first published 1982 by Lothrop, Lee & Shepard

When a petite young substitute takes over Mr. Star's fourth grade class for a day, Hobie and his friends know how to test her to the limit.

This "has both child appeal and substance. . . . Gilson's narration is convincing and engaging." Horn Book Guide

Gipson, Frederick Benjamin

Old Yeller; [by] Fred Gipson; drawings by Carl Burger. Harper & Row 1956 158p il $23; pa $5.99

Grades: 6 7 8 9   Fic

1. Boys 2. Dogs 3. Dogs -- Fiction 4. Frontier and pioneer life -- Texas 5. Frontier and pioneer life -- Fiction

ISBN 0-06-011545-9; 0-06-440382-3 pa

LC 56-8780

A Newbery Medal honor book, 1957

"Travis at fourteen was the man of the family during the hard summer of 1860 when his father drove his herd of cattle from Texas to the Kansas market. It was the summer when an old yellow dog attached himself to the family and won Travis' reluctant friendship. Before the summer was over, Old Yeller proved more than a match for thieving raccoons, fighting bulls, grizzly bears, and mad wolves. This is a skillful tale of a boy's love for a dog as well as a description of a pioneer boyhood and it can't miss with any dog lover." Horn Book

Glaser, Linda

Bridge to America; based on a true story. Houghton Mifflin Co. 2005 200p $16

Grades: 4 5 6   Fic

1. Jews -- Fiction 2. Immigrants -- Fiction

ISBN 0-618-56301-6

Eight-year-old Fivel narrates the story of his family's Atlantic Ocean crossing to reunite with their father in the United States, from its desperate beginning in a shtetl in Poland in 1920 to his stirrings of identity as an American boy.

"Even reluctant readers will enjoy this riveting account and sensitive portrayal of what it means to be an immigrant." SLJ

Glass, Susan

The **great** eggscape; illustrations by Cornelius Van Wright. Star Bright Books 2011 un il $16.95

Grades: 2 3 4   Fic

1. Eggs -- Fiction 2. Food -- Fiction

ISBN 978-1-59572-261-4; 1-59572-261-0

LC 2009044870

Benedict and Aggie, two rotten eggs, wreak havoc on their neighbors, until Chip, a hapless cookie, becomes an unlikely hero.

"Action-packed panel illustrations and dialogue bubbles chock-full of eggy puns and other food-based wordplay will have readers giggling as these two bad eggs get their comeuppance." Horn Book Guide

Glatstein, Jacob

Emil and Karl; by Yankev Glatshteyn; translated by Jeffrey Shandler. Roaring Brook Press 2006 194p $17.95; pa $6.99

Grades: 5 6 7 8   Fic

1. Jews -- Fiction 2. Friendship -- Fiction 3. Holocaust, 1933-1945 -- Fiction

ISBN 1-59643-119-9; 0-312-37387-2 pa

LC 2005-26800

Original Yiddish edition 1940

A story about the dilemma faced by two young boys— one Jewish, the other not—when they suddenly find themselves without homes or families in Vienna on the eve of World War II.

"The fast-moving prose is stark and immediate. Glatshteyn was, of course, writing about what was happening to children in his time. . . . The translation, 65 years after the novel's original publication, is nothing short of haunting." Booklist

Glatt, Lisa

Abigail Iris: the one and only. Walker & Co. 2009 148p $14.99

Grades: 2 3 4   Fic

1. Siblings -- Fiction 2. Friendship -- Fiction 3. Family life -- Fiction 4. Children's literature -- Works -- Grades two through six

ISBN 978-0-8027-9782-7; 0-8027-9782-2

LC 2008007391

Abigail Iris thinks she would rather be an only child but after going on vacation with her best friend, who is an "Only," she realizes there are benefits of being one of many.

"Told in the first person from Abigail Iris' point of view, this chapter book comes to life through her ingenuous voice and reflections. Appealing black-and-white drawings show the characters' personalities, attitudes, and emotions." Booklist

Another title about Abigail Iris is:
Abigail Iris: the pet project (2010)

Abigail Iris: the pet project; [by] Lisa Glatt and Suzanne Greenberg; illustrated by Joy Allen. Walker 2010 164p il $14.99; pa $6.99

Grades: 2 3 4   Fic

1. Cats -- Fiction 2. Family life -- Fiction

ISBN 978-0-8027-8657-9; 0-8027-8657-X; 978-0-8027-2235-5 pa; 0-8027-2235-0 pa

When Abigail Iris finally gets the new kitten she has been wanting, she learns about the responsibilities that come with pet ownership, as well as the impact a kitten can have on a large family like hers.

"Fast-paced conversation, coupled with realistic events, creates a fun read while full-page black-and-white illustrations add interest." SLJ

Glickman, Susan

Bernadette in the doghouse. Second Story Press 2011 pa $8.95

Grades: 2 3 4   **Fic**

1. Friendship -- Fiction

ISBN 978-1-897187-92-0; 1-897187-92-0

"When her former best friend Jasmine comes to visit during winter break, third-grader Bernadette ignores her current friends, hurting their feelings and coming close to breaking up the Lunch Bunch. . . . Glickman again portrays elementary-school life realistically. . . . The relatively long, mostly unillustrated chapters are best suited for the most able chapter-book readers, who will appreciate the challenge and are less often served by material appropriate to their lives and experiences. A satisfying sequel leaving room for more." Kirkus

Gliori, Debi

Witch Baby and me. Corgi 2010 246p il pa $7.99

Grades: 4 5 6   **Fic**

1. Magic -- Fiction 2. Infants -- Fiction 3. Sisters -- Fiction 4. Witches -- Fiction

ISBN 978-0-552-55676-7; 0-552-55676-9

"Three witches from Ben Screeeiiighe, a wildly remote area of Scotland, are searching for a baby. Their plan, at first, is to cast a spell on an infant, allow the human parents to raise her, then take over her witchy education when she becomes older. . . . But the witches do not foresee that Baby Daisy MacRae's sister [Lily] . . . can see their magic, and knows that her sister is a witch even if no one believes her. . . . Readers will laugh at Lily's imagination and her attempts to keep people from finding out that her sister is really a spell-casting witch-in-training. Entertaining line drawings complement the [text]." SLJ

Other titles in this series are:

Witch Baby and me after dark (2010)

Witch Baby and me at school (2009)

Witch Baby and me on stage (2011)

Witch Baby and me after dark. IPG 2010 291p il pa $7.99

Grades: 4 5 6   **Fic**

1. Sisters -- Fiction 2. Witches -- Fiction

ISBN 978-0-552-55678-1; 0-552-55678-5

Nine-year-old Lily has her hands full trying to protect baby sister Daisy from being exposed as a witch.

"Readers will laugh at Lily's imagination and her attempts to keep people from finding out that her sister is really a spell-casting witch-in-training. Entertaining line drawings complement the [text]." SLJ

Witch Baby and me on stage. Corgi 2011 il pa $7.99

Grades: 4 5 6   **Fic**

1. Magic -- Fiction 2. Sisters -- Fiction 3. Witches -- Fiction

ISBN 978-0-552-55679-8; 0-552-55679-3

This "finds Lily preparing to play the bagpipes for a school concert, toddler-sibling Daisy (aka Witch Baby) continuing to experiment with spells and nocturnal neighborhood flights, and the Sisters of Hiss (Nose, Chin, and Toad)

unexpectedly yearning for motherhood. . . . Gliori's upbeat style, comical black-line drawings, footnoted asides, and much diaper humor are sure to please series fans." Booklist

Godden, Rumer

The **doll's** house; illustrated by Tasha Tudor. Viking 1962 136p il hardcover o.p. pa $5.99

Grades: 2 3 4   **Fic**

1. Dolls -- Fiction 2. Dollhouses -- Fiction

ISBN 0-14-030942-X pa

First published 1947 in the United Kingdom; first United States edition illustrated by Dana Saintsbury published 1948

Adventures of a brave little hundred-year-old Dutch farthing doll, her family, their Victorian dollhouse home and the two little English girls to whom they all belonged. Tottie's great adventure was when she went to the exhibition, Dolls through the ages, and was singled out for notice by the Queen who opened the exhibition

"Each doll has a firmly drawn, recognizably true character; the children think and behave convincingly. . . . The story is enthralling, and complete in every detail." Spectator

Going, K. L.

The **garden** of Eve. Harcourt 2007 234p $17; pa $6.99

Grades: 4 5 6 7   **Fic**

1. Death -- Fiction 2. Magic -- Fiction 3. Bereavement -- Fiction 4. Children's literature -- Works -- Grades two through six

ISBN 978-0-15-205986-6; 0-15-205986-5; 978-0-15-206614-7 pa; 0-15-206614-4 pa

LC 2007-05074

Eve gave up her belief in stories and magic after her mother's death, but a mysterious seed given to her as an eleventh-birthday gift by someone she has never met takes her and a boy who claims to be a ghost on a strange journey, to where their supposedly cursed town of Beaumont, New York, flourishes.

"Believably and with delicacy, Going paints a suspenseful story suffused with the poignant questions of what it means to be alive, and what might await on the other side." Horn Book

Gordon, Domenica More

Archie; by Domenica More Gordon. Bloomsbury Childrens Books 2012 48 p. (hardcover) $17.99

Grades: PreK K 1   **Fic**

1. Sewing -- Fiction 2. Success -- Fiction 3. Clothing and dress -- Juvenile literature 4. Dogs -- Fiction 5. Humorous stories 6. Stories without words 7. Fashion design -- Fiction

ISBN 1599909367; 9781599909363

LC 2012009329

Author Domenica More Gordon's character "Archie, a well-dressed dog, receives a sewing machine as a gift. He takes to it immediately, creating smart outfits for his own pet dog, his friends' dogs, and his friends. His phone is ringing off the hook by book's end--the final call comes from a canine monarch with a crown, handbag, and pet corgi . . . Even without the success Archie finds, his life as a clothing designer living alone with his dog is a winning premise." (Publishers Weekly)

Goscinny

Nicholas; [by] Rene Goscinny & [illustrated by] Jean-Jacques Sempe; translated by Anthea Bell. Phaidon 2005 126p il $19.95

Grades: 4 5 6   **Fic**

1. School stories

ISBN 0-7148-4529-9

"This classic book about a mischievous schoolboy and his friends, originally published in French in 1959, is now available in English. The expertly translated text is enlivened by artwork by a New Yorker cartoonist to create the unforgettable milieu of Nicholas and his rowdy friends. A collection of 19 escapades, the stories introduce the protagonist and his cohorts as they wreak havoc out of simple, everyday situations at school, on the playground, and at home." SLJ

Other titles about Nicholas are:

Nicholas again (2006)

Nicholas on vacation (2007)

Nicholas on vacation; [by] René Goscinny; [illustrated by] Jean-Jacques Sempe; translated by Anthea Bell. Phaidon 2006 126p il $19.95

Grades: 4 5 6   **Fic**

1. Vacations -- Fiction

ISBN 978-0-7148-4678-1

This "features a number of vignettes spanning a couple of summers. Each chapter opens with a few sentences from Nicholas or excerpts from correspondence between the boy and his parents. Nicholas's forthright voice is full of childlike repetition and exclamations. . . . Sempé's charming cartoon illustrations appear throughout and reinforce the tone." SLJ

Gosselink, John

The **defense** of Thaddeus A. Ledbetter; a novel. drawings by Jason Rosenstock. Amulet Books 2010 231p il $14.95

Grades: 4 5 6 7   **Fic**

1. School stories

ISBN 978-0-8109-8977-1; 0-8109-8977-8

LC 2009052209

Twelve-year-old Thaddeus A. Ledbetter, who considers it a duty to share his knowledge and talent with others, refutes each of the charges which have sent him to "In-School Suspension" for the remainder of seventh grade.

"This original and entertaining book, with its smarty-pants narrator and case-file format, will draw comparisons to the Wimpy Kid series." Booklist

Grabenstein, Chris

Escape from Mr. Lemoncello's library; Chris Grabenstein. 1st ed. Random House Inc. 2013 304 p. (hardcover) $16.99; (library) $19.99

Grades: 5 6 7   **Fic**

1. Contests -- Juvenile fiction 2. Libraries -- Juvenile fiction 3. Games -- Fiction 4. Libraries -- Fiction 5. Books and reading -- Fiction

ISBN 037587089X; 9780375870897; 9780375970894

LC 2012048122

In this book, twelve "seventh-graders win a chance to spend an overnight lock-in previewing their town's new public library," which was "conceived by Luigi Lemoncello, the . . . founder of Mr. Lemoncello's Imagination Factory, which is a source for every kind of game imaginable. Dur-

ing the lock-in the winners . . . are offered a further challenge: 'Find your way out of the library using only what's in the library.' The winner will become spokesperson for the Imagination Factory." (Publishers Weekly)

The **Hanging** Hill. Random House 2009 322p (Haunted places mystery) $16.99; lib bdg $19.99

Grades: 5 6 7 8   **Fic**

1. Ghost stories 2. Theater -- Fiction 3. Criminals -- Fiction 4. Stepmothers -- Fiction

ISBN 978-0-375-84699-1; 0-375-84699-9; 978-0-375-94699-8 lib bdg; 978-0-375-84700-4 pa

LC 2008027274

While working at a summer stock theater, eleven-year-old Zack and his stepmother encounter the ghost of one of Connecticut's most notorious criminals.

"The story line is hauntingly delicious as the fully fleshed-out creepiness comes tempered with humor." SLJ

The **black** heart crypt; a haunted mystery. Random House 2011 328p (Haunted places mystery) $16.99; lib bdg $19.99; e-book $16.99

Grades: 5 6 7 8   **Fic**

1. Ghost stories 2. Mystery fiction 3. Demonology -- Fiction

ISBN 978-0-375-86900-6; 0-375-86900-X; 978-0-375-96900-3 lib bdg; 0-375-96900-4 lib bdg; 978-0-375-89987-4 e-book

LC 2011001939

A 200-year-old ghost inhabits a living ancestor in order to take revenge on eleven-year-old Zack and his family.

"The pace never flags. Through flurries of ultrashort chapters, events spiral to a suspenseful climax, and the mix of corpses and comedy add up to a faintly macabre tone that isn't dispelled even by the end's just deserts and happy outcomes." Kirkus

The **crossroads**. Random House 2008 325p (Haunted places mystery) $16.99; lib bdg $19.99; pa $6.99

Grades: 5 6 7 8   **Fic**

1. Ghost stories 2. Stepmothers -- Fiction

ISBN 978-0-375-84697-7; 0-375-84697-2; 978-0-375-94697-4 lib bdg; 0-375-94697-7 lib bdg; 978-0-375-84698-4 pa; 0-375-84698-0 pa

LC 2007024803

When eleven-year-old Zack Jennings moves to Connecticut with his father and new stepmother, they must deal with the ghosts left behind by a terrible accident, as well as another kind of ghost from Zack's past

"An absorbing psychological thriller . . . as well as a rip-roaring ghost story, this switches points of view among humans, trees, and ghosts with astonishing élan." Booklist

Other titles in this series are:

The Hanging Hill (2009)

The smoky corridor (2010)

The Black Heart Crypt (2011)

The **smoky** corridor. Random House 2010 326p (Haunted places mystery) $16.99; lib bdg $19.99

Grades: 5 6 7 8   **Fic**

1. Ghost stories 2. School stories 3. Zombies -- Fiction 4. Family life -- Fiction 5. Stepmothers -- Fiction 6. Buried treasure -- Fiction 7. Young adult literature --

Works 8. Children's literature -- Works -- Grades two through six

ISBN 978-0-375-86511-4; 0-375-86511-X; 978-0-375-96511-1 lib bdg; 0-375-96511-4 lib bdg

LC 2009-50694

With the help of his stepmother, his dog Zipper, and new friend Malik, Zack Jennings faces ghosts and zombies at his new middle school, which is said to house a lost Confederate treasure.

"Grabenstein is a riveting storyteller most kids won't be able to put this book down. Its appeal will be wide, as it is a mystery, a thriller, a ghost story, a school story, an action adventure, and a humorous book." SLJ

Grabien, Deborah

Dark's tale. Egmont USA 2010 300p $15.99

Grades: 4 5 6   **Fic**

1. Cats -- Fiction 2. Parks -- Fiction 3. Animals -- Fiction

ISBN 978-1-60684-037-5; 1-60684-037-1

"Dark, a house cat abandoned in San Francisco's Golden Gate Park, must learn to survive in her new habitat. Befriended by a raccoon, she learns to recognize park inhabitants she must fear, like the 'crazybad' people, and those she can trust, including a wise owl named Memorie and a magical woman in rags who calls herself Streetwise Sal. . . . Written in first person from Dark's point of view, the novel creates a believable natural world, where predators hunt smaller animals and a cat must rely on her senses, her skills, and her friends for survival." Booklist

Graff, Lisa

Sophie Simon solves them all; pictures by Jason Beene. Farrar, Straus & Giroux 2010 103p il $14.99

Grades: 2 3 4   **Fic**

1. School stories 2. Friendship -- Fiction

ISBN 978-0-374-37125-8; 0-374-37125-3

Sophie Simon, a third-grade genius, wants a graphing calculator so she can continue to study calculus while she rides the bus to school, but her parents are more concerned that she does not have any friends.

"Sometimes exaggerated for comic effect and occasionally poignant, the black-and-white illustrations capture the story's sense of humor as well as its sense of style. A fresh, funny chapter book for young readers." Booklist

A **tangle** of knots; Lisa Graff. Philomel Books 2013 240 p. $16.99

Grades: 3 4 5 6   **Fic**

1. Baking -- Fiction 2. Orphans -- Juvenile fiction 3. Ability -- Fiction 4. Orphans -- Fiction 5. Identity -- Fiction 6. Family life -- New York -- Fiction

ISBN 0399255176; 9780399255175

LC 2012009573

This juvenile novel, by Lisa Graff, is set "in a slightly magical world where everyone has a Talent. . . . Eleven-year-old Cady is an orphan with a phenomenal Talent for cake baking. . . . And her destiny leads her to a mysterious address that houses a lost luggage emporium, an old recipe, a family of children searching for their own Talents, and a Talent Thief who will alter her life forever. However, these encounters hold the key to Cady's past and how she became an orphan." (Publisher's note)

The **thing** about Georgie; a novel. by Lisa Graff. Laura Geringer Books 2006 220p $15.99; lib bdg $16.89; pa $5.99

Grades: 3 4 5 6   **Fic**

1. School stories 2. Dwarfism -- Fiction 3. Friendship -- Fiction 4. Family life -- Fiction

ISBN 978-0-06-087589-3; 0-06-087589-5; 978-0-06-087590-9 lib bdg; 0-06-087590-9 lib bdg; 978-0-06-087591-6 pa; 0-06-087591-7 pa

LC 2006000393

Georgie's dwarfism causes problems, but he could always rely on his parents, his best friend, and classmate Jeanie the Meanie's teasing, until a surprising announcement, a new boy in school, and a class project shake things up

"An upbeat and sensitive look at what it's like to be different, this novel will spark discussion." Booklist

Umbrella summer. Laura Geringer Books 2009 235p $15.99

Grades: 4 5 6   **Fic**

1. Death -- Fiction 2. Worry -- Fiction 3. Bereavement -- Fiction

ISBN 978-0-06-143187-6; 0-06-143187-7

LC 2008-26015

After her brother Jared dies, ten-year-old Annie worries about the hidden dangers of everything, from bug bites to bicycle riding, until she is befriended by a new neighbor who is grieving her own loss.

"Annie's story deals with death with sensitivity, love, and understanding." SLJ

Grahame, Kenneth

★ The **wind** in the willows; by Kenneth Grahame; illustrated in color and black and white by Ernest H. Shepard. 75th anniversary ed.; Scribner 1983 244p il $15.96

Grades: 3 4 5 6   **Fic**

1. Animals -- Fiction

ISBN 0-684-17957-1

First published 1908

In this fantasy "the characters are Mole, Water Rat, Mr. Toad, and other small animals, who live and talk like humans but have charming individual animal characters. The book is a tender portrait of the English countryside." Reader's Ency

Grant, Katy

Hide and seek. Peachtree 2010 230p $15.95

Grades: 5 6 7 8   **Fic**

1. Divorce -- Fiction 2. Kidnapping -- Fiction 3. Family life -- Fiction 4. Wilderness survival -- Fiction

ISBN 978-1-56145-542-3; 1-56145-542-3

LC 2009040519

In the remote mountains of Arizona where he lives with his mother, stepfather, and two sisters, fourteen-year-old Chase discovers two kidnapped boys and gets caught up in a dangerous adventure when he comes up with a plan to get them to safety.

"Mystery and adventure propel this readable survival story that will hit the spot with Gary Paulsen's fans and may also entice reluctant readers." SLJ

Grant, Michael, 1954-

★ The **call**; Michael Grant. 1st ed. Katherine Tegen Books 2010 243 p. ill. (hardcover) $16.99

Grades: 4 5 6 **Fic**
1. Fantasy fiction 2. Adventure fiction 3. Fantasy 4. Humorous stories 5. Good and evil -- Fiction 6. Young adult literature -- Works 7. Adventure and adventurers -- Fiction
ISBN 0061833665; 9780061833663

LC 2009044815

A seemingly average twelve-year-old learns that he is destined to gather a team of similarly gifted children to try to save the world from a nameless evil, which is threatening to reappear after an absence of three thousand years. "Age ten and up." (Publisher's note)

"The author keeps the story moving at a brisk pace with suspenseful action and laugh-out-loud humor." Kirkus

The **trap**. Katherine Tegen Books 2011 294p (The Magnificent 12)
Grades: 4 5 6 **Fic**
1. Fantasy fiction 2. Adventure fiction 3. Good and evil -- Fiction
ISBN 0-06-183368-1; 978-0-06-183368-7

LC 2010040580

Mack MacAvoy, an average-seeming twelve-year-old boy who happens to have special powers, travels to China in an effort to assemble an elite team of his peers to help him thwart the evil Pale Queen.

Gratz, Alan
★ The **Brooklyn** nine; a novel in nine innings. Dial Books 2009 299p $16.99
Grades: 5 6 7 8 9 **Fic**
1. Baseball -- Fiction 2. Family life -- Fiction 3. German Americans -- Fiction 4. Young adult literature -- Works
ISBN 978-0-8037-3224-7; 0-8037-3224-4

LC 2008-21263

This novel follows the fortunes of a German immigrant family through nine generations, beginning in 1845, as they experience American life and play baseball. "Grades five to nine." (Bull Cent Child Books)

Gratz "builds this novel upon a clever . . . conceit . . . and executes it with polish and precision." Booklist

Graves, Keith
The **orphan** of Awkward Falls. Chronicle Books 2011 337p $16.99
Grades: 4 5 6 7 **Fic**
1. Mystery fiction 2. Orphans -- Fiction 3. Homicide -- Fiction 4. Inventors -- Fiction 5. Mentally ill -- Fiction 6. Science -- Experiments -- Fiction
ISBN 978-0-8118-7814-2; 0-8118-7814-7

LC 2011008008

Josephine Cravitz, the new girl in Awkward Falls, and her neighbor Thaddeus Hibble, a reclusive and orphaned boy inventor, become the targets of a mad cannibal from the local asylum for the criminally insane.

"Graves crafts a quick-moving plot composed of macabre twists. . . . Wordless opening and closing sequences, plus a handful of interior illustrations, both fill in background detail and intensify the overall macabre atmosphere." Kirkus

Green, Tim, 1963-
Baseball great. HarperCollinsPublishers 2009 250p $16.99; lib bdg $17.89

Grades: 5 6 7 8 **Fic**
1. School stories 2. Baseball -- Fiction 3. Father-son relationship -- Fiction
ISBN 978-0-06-162686-9; 0-06-162686-4; 978-0-06-162687-6 lib bdg; 0-06-162687-2 lib bdg

LC 2008051778

All twelve-year-old Josh wants to do is play baseball but when his father, a minor league pitcher, signs him up for a youth championship team, Josh finds himself embroiled in a situation with potentially illegal consequences.

"Issues of peer and family pressure are well handled, and the short, punchy chapters and crisp dialogue are likely to hold the attention of young baseball fans." SLJ

Other titles in this series are:
Rivals (2010)
Best of the best (2011)

Football genius. HarperCollinsPublishers 2007 244p $16.99; lib bdg $17.89; pa $6.99
Grades: 5 6 7 8 **Fic**
1. Football -- Fiction 2. Young adult literature -- Works
ISBN 978-0-06-112270-5; 0-06-112270-X; 978-0-06-112272-9 lib bdg; 0-06-112272-6 lib bdg; 978-0-06-112273-6 pa; 0-06-112273-4 pa

LC 2006-29470

Troy, a sixth-grader with an unusual gift for predicting football plays before they occur, attempts to use his ability to help his favorite team, the Atlanta Falcons, but he must first prove himself to the coach and players.

The author "imparts many insider details that football fans will love. Green makes Troy a winning hero, and he ties everything together with a fast-moving plot." Booklist

Other titles in this series are:
Football champ (2009)
The big time (2010)
Deep zone (2011)

Force out; Tim Green. 1st ed. Harper 2013 288 p. (hardcover) $16.99
Grades: 4 5 6 **Fic**
1. Baseball -- Juvenile fiction 2. Friendship -- Juvenile fiction 3. Baseball -- Fiction 4. Friendship -- Fiction 5. Best friends -- Fiction 6. Conduct of life -- Fiction 7. Competition (Psychology) -- Fiction
ISBN 0062089595; 9780062089595

LC 2012026752

In this juvenile novel, by Tim Green, "Joey and Zach have always been best friends. They're also two of the best baseball players in their league, and shoo-ins for the all-star team at the end of the season. Their dream is to play together on the Center State select team, and they will do anything to help each other get there. . . . Then the unthinkable happens: The boys learn there's only one open spot on the select team." (Publisher's note)

"Though Green is no stylist, he does a better job of avoiding the sports fantasy and sticking to real life than usual. There's plenty of play-by-play for those who want the sports to be the focus, but the interactions off the field are never shortchanged. . . . A slice of life for middle school readers who know that their sport is a microcosm of the larger world." Kirkus

Greene, Bette

★ **Philip** Hall likes me, I reckon maybe; pictures by Charles Lilly. Dial Bks. for Young Readers 1974 135p il hardcover o.p. pa $5.99

Grades: 4 5 6   **Fic**

1. Friendship -- Fiction 2. African Americans -- Fiction

ISBN 0-14-130312-3 pa

A Newbery Medal honor book, 1975

Eleven-year-old Beth, an African American girl from Arkansas, thinks that Philip Hall likes her, but their on-again, off-again relationship sometimes makes her wonder

"The action is sustained; . . . the illustrations are excellent black-and-white pencil sketches." Read Teach

Other titles about Beth and Philip Hall are:

Get out of here, Philip Hall (1981)

I've already forgotten your name, Philip Hall (2004)

Greene, Jacqueline Dembar

★ The **secret** shofar of Barcelona; illustrated by Doug Chayka. Kar-Ben 2009 un il lib bdg $17.95

Grades: 2 3 4 5   **Fic**

1. Musicians -- Fiction 2. Jews -- Spain -- Fiction 3. Rosh ha-Shanah -- Fiction

ISBN 978-0-8225-9915-9 lib bdg; 0-8225-9915-5 lib bdg

LC 2008031197

In the late 1500s, while the conductor of the Royal Orchestra of Barcelona prepares for a concert to celebrate Spain's colonies in the New World, his son secretly practices playing the Shofar to help Jews, who must hide their faith from the Inquisition, to celebrate Rosh Hashanah. Includes historical facts and glossary

"Based on a legend, this intriguing slice of converso life offers a thoughtful hero and a suspenseful plot. The warm opaque paintings are expressive and create a strong sense of place." SLJ

Greene, Stephanie

Happy birthday, Sophie Hartley. Clarion Books 2010 127p $16

Grades: 3 4 5   **Fic**

1. Siblings -- Fiction 2. Birthdays -- Fiction 3. Family life -- Fiction 4. Children's literature -- Works -- Grades two through six 5. Children's literature -- Works -- Preschool through grade two

ISBN 978-0-547-25128-8; 0-547-25128-9

A girl in a large family is looking forward to her first "double digit" birthday, but soon discovers that growing up brings some unwanted changes.

"All the plot strands merge in a satisfying denouement that's tidy but not in the least predictable. Greene explores her themes of identity, ambivalence about growing up, and friendship with an unusual naturalness and depth, yet the themes never trump story or character." Horn Book

Moose's big idea; illustrated by Joe Mathieu. Marshall Cavendish 2005 51p il (Moose and Hildy) $14.95

Grades: 1 2 3   **Fic**

1. Pigs -- Fiction 2. Moose -- Fiction

ISBN 0-7614-5212-5

LC 2004-22536

"Moose is sad upon losing his very large antlers, but cheers up a bit when his pig friend, Hildy, is now able to observe his pretty eyes and muscular legs. . . . In the next chapter, he stays inside during hunting season. . . . When cabin fever ensues, Moose gets the idea to sell doughnuts, coffee, and original artwork to hunters. . . . making a sale to a naive hunter. In another chapter, this same man finds Moose's old antlers but won't give them back. Finally, Moose's new antlers begin to grow. . . . Readers stepping up to chapter books will laughingly turn these pages and clamor for more. Mathieu's frequent black-and-white illustrations expand on the fun." SLJ

Other titles about Moose and Hildy are:

Moose crossing (2005)

Pig pickin' (2006)

The show-off (2007)

Princess Posey and the first grade parade; illustrated by Stephanie Roth Sisson. G.P. Putnam's Sons 2010 83p il $12.99

Grades: K 1 2   **Fic**

1. School stories 2. Fear -- Fiction

ISBN 978-0-399-25167-2; 0-399-25167-7

LC 2009-12471

Posey's fear of starting first grade is alleviated when her teacher invites the students to wear their most comfortable clothes to school on the first day.

"Emergent readers can be anxious as they make the transition from easy readers to early chapter books and, like Posey, can be overwhelmed by new challenges. Short sentences, a generous font, ample white space and Sisson's charming, expressive black-and-white illustrations make this sweet story just right for them." Kirkus

Other titles about Princess Posey are:

Princess Posey and the perfect present (2011)

Princess Posey and the next-door dog (2011)

Sophie Hartley, on strike. Clarion Books 2006 152p $15

Grades: 3 4 5   **Fic**

1. Family life -- Fiction 2. Children's literature -- Works -- Grades two through six

ISBN 978-0-618-71960-0; 0-618-71960-1

LC 2006-08375

After their mother sets up a new list of household chores for them to do, Sophie and her siblings argue about housekeeping and finally go on strike

"Readers will empathize with this spunky youngster and her true-to-life problems." SLJ

The **show-off**; by Stephanie Greene; illustrated by Joe Mathieu. 1st ed.; Marshall Cavendish 2007 50p il $14.99

Grades: 1 2 3   **Fic**

1. Pigs -- Fiction 2. Moose -- Fiction 3. Friendship -- Fiction

ISBN 978-0-7614-5374-1

LC 2007000253

Hildy looks forward to a visit from her cousin, Winston, but when he arrives he bores her and annoys all of her friends by declaring his superior intelligence and expertise on every subject, until Moose convinces him to try something different.

"This beginning chapter book is full of gentle humor. The pencil-and-gray-wash illustrations work well with the story." SLJ

Greenfield, Eloise

Sister; drawings by Moneta Barnett. Crowell 1974
83p il hardcover o.p. pa $4.99

Grades: 4 5 6 7   **Fic**

1. Sisters -- Fiction 2. African Americans -- Fiction 3.
Single parent family -- Fiction

ISBN 0-690-00497-4; 0-06-440199-5 pa

A 13-year-old black girl whose father is dead watches
her 16-year-old sister drifting away from her and her mother
and fears she may fall into the same self-destructive behavior herself. While waiting for her sister's return home, she
leafs through her diary, reliving both happy and unhappy experiences while gradually recognizing her own individuality

"The book is strong . . . strong in perception, in its sensitivity, in its realism." Bull Cent Child Books

★ The **friendly** four; illustrations by Jan Spivey Gilchrist. HarperCollins/Amistad 2006 47p il $16.99; lib
bdg $17.89

Grades: 2 3 4   **Fic**

1. Summer -- Fiction 2. Friendship -- Fiction 3.
African Americans -- Fiction 4. Children's literature
-- Works -- Grades two through six

ISBN 978-0-06-000759-1; 0-06-000759-1; 978-0-06-
000760-7 lib bdg; 0-06-000760-5 lib bdg

LC 2005-18588

"Free-verse poems tell the story of a group of children
who find each other during one otherwise lonely summer. . .
. The African-American friends all bond, play, and build and
paint an elaborate cardboard town they call Goodsummer.
The simple watercolors work well at setting scenes of tidy
streets lined with homes and lots of backyards and parks.
Gilchrist's talent shows in her use of color, splashed with
light. . . . For a younger audience than most novels-in-verse,
this accessible and well-written book has a nostalgic tone."
SLJ

Greenwald, Lisa

My life in pink and green. Amulet Books 2010 288 p.

Grades: 4 5 6 7   **Fic**

1. Cosmetics -- Fiction 2. Environmental protection --
Fiction 3. Mother-daughter relationship -- Fiction

ISBN 0810983524; 0810989840 pa; 9780810983526;
9780810989849

LC 2008025577

When the family's drugstore is failing, seventh-grader
Lucy uses her problem solving talents to come up with solution that might resuscitate the business, along with helping
the environment.

"Greenwald deftly blends eco-facts and makeup tips,
friendship dynamics, and spot-on middle-school politics
into a warm, uplifting story." Booklist

Greenwald, Sheila

Rosy Cole's memoir explosion; a heartbreaking story
about losing friends, annoying family, and ruining romance.
Farrar, Straus and Giroux 2006 103p il $16

Grades: 3 4 5   **Fic**

1. School stories 2. Authorship -- Fiction 3. Children's
literature -- Works -- Preschool through grade two

ISBN 0-374-36347-1

LC 2004053260

When Rosy writes a memoir about herself and her
friends for a school assignment, she is surprised when they
are not thrilled with the result.

"Crisp line drawings record the nuances of the characters' emotions with economy and style. Written in first-
person, Greenwald's account of Rosy's hubris, downfall, despair, humility, and amends will please longtime series fans
as well as those meeting Rosy for the first time." Booklist

Watch out world, Rosy Cole is going green! Rosy
Cole's bright, though not exactly popular, ideas about gar-
bage, worms, dirt, and other gifts of nature. Farrar, Straus
Giroux 2010 102p il $15.99

Grades: 3 4 5   **Fic**

1. School stories 2. Fairs -- Fiction 3. Environmental
protection -- Fiction

ISBN 978-0-374-36280-5; 0-374-36280-7

LC 2008055563

Rosy's team comes up with some creative ideas for
the Read School Fall Fair, whose mission is to sell "green-
themed" products.

"The story's comedy and spirited line-drawings make
this an enjoyable addition to the Rosy Cole series." Booklist

Greenwald, Tommy

★ **Charlie** Joe Jackson's guide to not reading. Roaring
Brook Press 2011 220p il $14.99

Grades: 4 5 6 7   **Fic**

1. School stories 2. Books and reading -- Fiction 3.
Young adult literature -- Works

ISBN 978-1-59643-691-6; 1-59643-691-3

LC 2010-24079

Middle schooler Charlie Joe is proud of his success at
avoiding reading, but eventually his schemes go too far.

"With its subversive humor and contemporary details
drawn straight from kids' worlds, this clever title should attract a wide following." Booklist

Charlie Joe Jackson's guide to summer vacation; by
Tommy Greenwald; illustrated by J. P. Coovert. 1st ed.
Roaring Brook Press 2013 231 p. ill. (hardcover) $14.99

Grades: 4 5 6 7   **Fic**

1. Camps -- Juvenile fiction 2. Reading -- Juvenile
fiction 3. Vacations -- Juvenile fiction 4. Camps --
Fiction 5. Humorous stories 6. Interpersonal relations
-- Fiction

ISBN 159643757X; 9781596437579; 9781596438804

LC 2012034249

In this graphic novel by Tommy Greenwald "Charlie
Joe Jackson finds himself in a terrible dream he can't wake
up from: Camp Rituhbukkee . . . a place filled with grammar workshops, Read-a-Ramas, and kids who actually like
reading. But Charlie Joe is determined to convince the entire camp to hate reading and writing—one genius at a time.
Tommy Greenwald's 'Charlie Joe Jackson's Guide to Summer Vacation' is another . . . installment in the life of a reluctant reader." (Publisher's note)

Griffin, Peni R.

The **ghost** sitter. Dutton Children's Bks. 2001 131p
$14.99; pa $5.99

Grades: 4 5 6 7 **Fic**
1. Ghosts 2. Ghost stories 3. Brothers and sisters
ISBN 0-525-46676-2; 0-14-230216-3 pa
LC 00-65859

When she realizes that her new house is haunted by the ghost of a ten-year-old girl who used to live there, Charlotte tries to help her find peace

"Griffin's book has several strong appeals: new best friends solving a mystery together, a just-scary-enough ghost girl, and a deathless bond between sisters that provides the book with its resoundingly satisfying conclusion and bang-up last sentence." Horn Book

Grimes, Nikki

Make way for Dyamonde Daniel; illustrated by R. Gregory Christie. G.P. Putnam's Sons 2009 74p il $10.99
Grades: 2 3 4 **Fic**
1. Moving -- Fiction 2. Friendship -- Fiction 3. African Americans -- Fiction 4. Children's literature -- Works -- Grades two through six
ISBN 978-0-399-25175-7; 0-399-25175-8
LC 2008-26788

Spunky third-grader Dyamonde Daniel misses her old neighborhood, but when she befriends a boy named Free, another new student at school, she finally starts to feel at home.

"Dyamonde . . . is a memorable main character. . . . Her actions and feelings ring true. Christie's illustrations flesh out the characters, and along with patterned page borders, contribute child appeal." SLJ

Other titles about Dyamonde Daniel are:
Rich (2009)
Almost zero (2010)

★ **Planet** Middle School. Bloomsbury Childrens 2011 154p $15.99
Grades: 4 5 6 7 **Fic**
1. School stories 2. Novels in verse 3. Basketball -- Fiction 4. Friendship -- Fiction 5. Family life -- Fiction
ISBN 978-1-59990-284-5; 1-59990-284-2
LC 2010050744

A series of poems describes all the baffling changes at home and at school in twelve-year-old Joylin's transition from tomboy basketball player to not-quite-girly girl.

"In freeflowing free-verse poems, multi–awardwinning author and poet Grimes . . . explores the riot of hormones and expected gender roles that can make negotiating the preteen years such a challenge. . . . A work that should help adolescent readers find the courage and humor to grow into the individuals they already are." Kirkus

The **road** to Paris. G. P. Putnam's Sons 2006 153p $15.99; pa $6.99
Grades: 4 5 6 7 **Fic**
1. Siblings -- Fiction 2. Foster home care -- Fiction 3. Racially mixed people -- Fiction 4. Children's literature -- Works -- Grades two through six
ISBN 0-399-24537-5; 978-0-399-24537-4; 978-0-14-241082-0 pa; 0-14-241082-9 pa
LC 2005-28920

Inconsolable at being separated from her older brother, eight-year-old Paris is apprehensive about her new foster family but just as she learns to trust them, she faces a life-changing decision.

"In clear, short chapters, Grimes tells a beautiful story of family, friendship, and faith from the viewpoint of a child in search of home in a harsh world." Booklist

Grindley, Sally

Dear Max; by D. J. Lucas a.k.a. Sally Gindley; [illustrated by Tony Ross] Margaret K. McElderry Books 2006 140p il $14.95; pa $4.99
Grades: 2 3 4 **Fic**
1. Letters -- Fiction 2. Authorship -- Fiction 3. Friendship -- Fiction
ISBN 978-1-4169-0392-5; 1-4169-0392-5; 978-1-4169-3443-1 pa; 1-4169-3443-X pa
First published 2004 in the United Kingdom

As Max—who is almost ten—and his favorite author, D.J. Lucas, exchange letters, the two writers help each other with their new books and develop a special friendship

This "is a charming story full of likable, multidimensional characters that will inspire young writers and satisfy readers. . . . Ross' line drawings add to the fun." Booklist
Another title about Max is:
Bravo, Max! (2007)

Grisham, John, 1955-

Theodore Boone: kid lawyer. Dutton Children's Books 2010 263p
Grades: 4 5 6 7 **Fic**
1. Mystery fiction 2. Lawyers -- Fiction 3. Young adult literature -- Works
ISBN 0-525-42384-2; 978-0-525-42384-3

With two attorneys for parents, thirteen-year-old Theodore Boone knows more about the law than most lawyers do. But when a high profile murder trial comes to his small town and Theo gets pulled into it, it's up to this amateur attorney to save the day.

"Grisham serves up a dandy legal adventure that moves along quickly. Without intruding on the story's trajectory, he gives plenty of background about the legal process and explores various ethical questions." Horn Book Guide
Another title about Theodore Boone is:
Theodore Boone: the abduction (2011)

Gunderson, JessicaStranger on the silk road; a story of
ancient China. by Jessica Gunderson; illustrated by Caroline Hu. Picture Window Books 2009 64p il (Read-it! chapter books: historical tales) lib bdg $21.26
Grades: 2 3 4 **Fic**
1. Silk -- Fiction
ISBN 978-1-4048-4736-1 lib bdg; 1-4048-4736-7 lib bdg
LC 2008006308

Song Sun likes to talk but never listens. After talking too much to a stranger, Song Sun accidentally gives away the Chinese secret of silk making

"Sassy, graphic-novel-style illustrations give [this] great little first chapter [book] extra appeal. . . . [This is a] wonderful [introduction] to historical fiction." SLJ

Guo Yue

★ **Little** Leap Forward; a boy in Beijing. by Guo Yue and Clare Farrow; illustrated by Helen Cann. Barefoot Books 2008 126p il $16.99
Grades: 3 4 5 6 **Fic**
1. Communism -- Fiction 2. Friendship -- Fiction 3.

Family life -- Fiction 4. Young adult literature -- Works
5. Children's literature -- Works -- Grades two through
six
ISBN 978-1-84686-114-7; 1-84686-114-4

LC 2007-42676

In Communist China in 1966, eight-year-old Leap Forward learns about freedom while flying kites with his best
friend, by trying to get a caged wild bird to sing, and through
the music he is learning to play on a bamboo flute. Includes
author's notes on his childhood in Beijing, life under Mao
Zedong, and the Cultural Revolution.

"The simple prose is quiet and physical. . . . The beautifully detailed, clear illustrations in ink and brilliant watercolors combine realistic group scenes with spare, individual
portraits." Booklist

Gutman, Dan

The **Christmas** genie; illustrated by Dan Santat. Si-
mon & Schuster Books for Young Readers 2009 150p il
$15.99
Grades: 3 4 5   **Fic**
1. School stories 2. Wishes -- Fiction 3. Christmas
-- Fiction 4. Meteorites -- Fiction
ISBN 978-1-4169-9001-7; 1-4169-9001-1

LC 2009017765

When a meteorite crashes into a fifth-grade classroom at
Lincoln School in Oak Park, Illinois, the genie inside agrees
to grant the class a Christmas wish—if they can agree on one
within an hour.

This is "lively, thought-provoking, and hilarious. . . .
Gutman packs plenty of history, science, and ethics lessons
in this fun, well-paced fantasy." SLJ

Mission unstoppable. Harper 2011 293p (The genius
files) $16.99; lib bdg $17.89
Grades: 5 6 7 8   **Fic**
1. Adventure fiction 2. Twins -- Fiction 3. Genius --
Fiction 4. Siblings -- Fiction 5. Family life -- Fiction
6. Young adult literature -- Works
ISBN 0-06-182764-9; 0-06-182765-7 lib bdg; 978-0-
06-182764-8; 978-0-06-182765-5 lib bdg

LC 2010-09390

On a cross-country vacation with their parents, twins
Coke and Pepsi, soon to be thirteen, fend off strange assassins as they try to come to terms with their being part
of a top-secret government organization known as The
Genius Files.

"Gutman's novel offers a quirky look at Americana that
will engage curious minds. . . . Those looking for a fun and
suspenseful read . . . will not be disappointed." Booklist

Another title in this series is:
Never say genius (2012)

Never say genius. Harper 2012 (Genius files) $16.99;
lib bdg $17.89
Grades: 5 6 7 8   **Fic**
1. Adventure fiction 2. Twins -- Fiction 3. Genius --
Fiction 4. Siblings -- Fiction 5. Family life -- Fiction
ISBN 978-0-06-182767-9; 0-0-6182767-3; 978-0-06-
182768-6 lib bdg; 0-06-182768-1 lib bdg

LC 2011019363

As their cross-country journey with their parents continues through the midwest, twins Coke and Pepsi, now thir-

teen, again face strange assassins at such places as the first
McDonald's restaurant and Cedar Point amusement park.

"The author brings his confused but resourceful youngsters to an explosive climax and a shocking revelation that
guarantees further adventures on the road back to the left
coast." Kirkus

Shoeless Joe & me; a baseball card adventure. Harper-
Collins Pubs. 2002 163p (Baseball card adventures) hardcover o.p. lib bdg $17.89; pa $5.99
Grades: 4 5 6 7   **Fic**
1. Baseball players 2. Baseball -- Fiction
ISBN 0-06-029253-9; 0-06-029254-7 lib bdg; 0-06-
447259-0 pa

LC 2001-24638

Joe Stoshack travels back to 1919, where he meets Shoeless Joe Jackson and tries to prevent the fixing of the World
Series in which Jackson was wrongly implicated

"Shoeless Joe is compelling, and Joe's adventures are
exciting." Voice Youth Advocates

Other titles in the Baseball card adventures series are:
Abner & me (2005)
Babe & me (2000)
Honus & me (1997)
Jackie & me (1999)
Jim & me (2008)
Mickey & me (2003)
Ray & me (2009)
Roberto & me (2010)
Satch & me (2006)

The **homework** machine. Simon & Schuster Books for
Young Readers 2006 146p $15.95; pa $5.99
Grades: 4 5 6   **Fic**
1. School stories
ISBN 0-689-87678-5; 0-689-87679-3 pa

LC 2005-19785

Four fifth-grade students—a geek, a class clown, a teacher's pet, and a slacker—as well as their teacher and mothers,
each relate events surrounding a computer programmed to
complete homework assignments.

"This fast-paced, entertaining book has something for
everyone: convincing characters deftly portrayed . . .; points
of discussion on ethics and student computer use; and every
child's dream machine." Booklist

The **return** of the homework machine. Simon &
Schuster Books for Young Readers 2009 162p $15.99
Grades: 4 5 6   **Fic**
1. School stories
ISBN 978-1-4169-5416-3; 1-4169-5416-3

LC 2008029543

After discarding their infamous homework machine,
four friends, now in sixth grade, find themselves once again
at the police station, this time giving testimony about an incident involving a powerful computer chip, a Grand Canyon
treasure, and a dead body.

Gwaltney, Doris

Homefront. Simon & Schuster Books for Young Readers 2006 310p $16.99; pa $6.99
Grades: 5 6 7 8   **Fic**
1. Family life -- Fiction 2. World War, 1939-1945 --

Fiction 3. Young adult literature -- Works
ISBN 0-689-86842-1; 1-4169-9572-2 pa

LC 2006-283492

"As Margaret Ann Motley looks forward to seventh grade, the only changes she sees on the horizon are her sister's leaving for college and, immediately afterwards, moving . . . into her sister's old room. With the U.S. on the brink of World War II, though, greater changes are in store. . . . Gwaltney provides vivid character portrayals. . . . Well grounded in the Tidewater area of Virginia, the novel's social context is made real." Booklist

Haddix, Margaret Peterson, 1964-

Caught; Book 5 Margaret Peterson Haddix. Simon & Schuster Books for Young Readers 2012 343 p. (The Missing) (hardcover: alk. paper) $16.99

Grades: 5 6 7 8   **Fic**

1. Science fiction 2. Time travel -- Fiction 3. Einstein, Albert, 1879-1955 -- Fiction 4. Space and time -- Fiction
ISBN 141698982X; 9781416989820; 9781442422889

LC 2011018654

In this fifth installment of Margaret Peterson Haddix's "Missing" series, "Jonah and Katherine are accustomed to traveling through time, but when learn they next have to return Albert Einstein's daughter to history, they think it's a joke -- they've only heard of his sons. But it turns out that Albert Einstein really did have a daughter, Lieserl, whose 1902 birth and subsequent disappearance was shrouded in mystery." (Publisher's note)

★ **Found**. Simon & Schuster Books for Young Readers 2008 314p (The missing) $15.99; pa $6.99

Grades: 5 6 7 8 9   **Fic**

1. Science fiction 2. Adoption -- Fiction 3. Young adult literature -- Works
ISBN 978-1-4169-5417-0; 1-4169-5417-1; 978-1-4169-5421-7 pa; 1-4169-5421-X pa

LC 2007-23614

When thirteen-year-olds Jonah and Chip, who are both adopted, learn they were discovered on a plane that appeared out of nowhere, full of babies with no adults on board, they realize that they have uncovered a mystery involving time travel and two opposing forces, each trying to repair the fabric of time.

This is "a tantalizing opener to a new series. . . . Readers will be hard-pressed to wait for the next installment." Publ Wkly

Other titles in this series are:

Sent (2009)
Sabotaged (2010)
Torn (2011)

Haddon, Mark

Boom! (or 70,000 light years) David Fickling Books 2010 194p $15.99; lib bdg $18.99

Grades: 4 5 6 7   **Fic**

1. Science fiction 2. Interplanetary voyages -- Fiction 3. Extraterrestrial beings -- Fiction
ISBN 978-0-385-75187-2; 0-385-75187-7; 978-0-385-75188-9 lib bdg; 0-385-75188-5 lib bdg

First published 1992 in the United Kingdom with title: Gridzbi spudvetch

When Jim and Charlie overhear two of their teachers talking in a secret language and the two friends set out to solve the mystery, they do not expect the dire consequences of their actions.

"Adventure and quirky humor keep the pages turning, and readers will connect to Jimbo with little difficulty. If they can overcome some of the cultural differences, they will appreciate the simple and engaging tale." SLJ

Hahn, Mary Downing

All the lovely bad ones; a ghost story. Clarion Books 2008 182p $16; pa $5.99

Grades: 4 5 6 7   **Fic**

1. Ghost stories 2. Siblings -- Fiction 3. Hotels and motels -- Fiction 4. Young adult literature -- Works
ISBN 978-0-618-85467-7; 978-0-547-24878-3 pa

LC 2007-37932

While spending the summer at their grandmother's Vermont inn, two prankster siblings awaken young ghosts from the inn's distant past who refuse to "rest in peace."

"In addition to crafting some genuinely spine-chilling moments, the author takes a unique approach to a well-traversed genre." Publ Wkly

Deep and dark and dangerous; a ghost story. Clarion Books 2007 187p $16; pa $5.99

Grades: 5 6 7 8   **Fic**

1. Ghost stories 2. Cousins -- Fiction 3. Mother-daughter relationship -- Fiction
ISBN 978-0-618-66545-7; 0-618-66545-5; 978-0-547-07645-4 pa; 0-547-07645-2 pa

LC 2006-25652

When thirteen-year-old Ali spends the summer with her aunt and cousin at the family's vacation home, she stumbles upon a secret that her mother and aunt have been hiding for over thirty years

"Hahn weaves into the story some classic mystery elements such as a torn photograph, a waterlogged doll, dense fog, and an empty grave, all of which add to the suspense and keep the well-plotted story moving along to a satisfying conclusion." SLJ

★ **Hear** the wind blow. Clarion Bks. 2003 212p $15

Grades: 5 6 7 8   **Fic**

1. Siblings -- Fiction
ISBN 0-618-18190-3

LC 2002-15977

With their mother dead and their home burned, a thirteen-year-old boy and his little sister set out across Virginia in search of relatives during the final days of the Civil War

The author "gives readers an entertaining and thought-provoking combination: a strong adventure inextricably bound to a specific time and place, but one that resonates with universal themes." Horn Book

Stepping on the cracks. Clarion Bks. 1991 216p $16; pa $6.99

Grades: 5 6 7 8   **Fic**

1. World War, 1939-1945 -- Fiction 2. Young adult literature -- Works
ISBN 0-395-58507-4; 0-547-07660-6 pa

LC 91-7706

In 1944, while her brother is overseas fighting in World War II, eleven-year-old Margaret gets a new view of the school bully Gordy when she finds him hiding his own brother, an army deserter, and decides to help him

"Well-drawn characters and a satisfying plot. . . . There is plenty of action and page-turning suspense to please those who want a quick read, but there is much to ponder and reflect on as well." SLJ

Time for Andrew; a ghost story. Clarion Bks. 1994 165p hardcover o.p. pa $5.95

Grades: 5 6 7 8   Fic

1. Ghost stories 2. Space and time -- Fiction 3. Young adult literature -- Works 4. Children's literature -- Works -- Grades two through six

ISBN 0-395-66556-6; 0-618-87316-3 pa

LC 93-2877

When he goes to spend the summer with his great-aunt in the family's old house, eleven-year-old Drew is drawn eighty years into the past to trade places with his great-great-uncle who is dying of diphtheria

"There's plenty to enjoy in this delightful time-slip fantasy: a fascinating premise, a dastardly cousin, some good suspense, and a roundup of characters to care about." Booklist

★ **Wait** till Helen comes; a ghost story. Clarion Bks. 1986 184p $15; pa $5.95; pa $6.99

Grades: 4 5 6   Fic

1. Ghost stories 2. Stepchildren -- Fiction 3. Young adult literature -- Works

ISBN 0-89919-453-2; 0-547-02864-4 pa; 9780380704422 pa

LC 86-2648

"Molly, the 12-year-old narrator, and her brother Michael dislike their bratty 5-year-old stepsister Heather and resent the family move to an isolated converted church in the country. The adjourning graveyard frightens Molly, but Heather seems drawn to it. Molly discovers that the ghost of a child (Helen) who died in a fire a century ago wants to lure Heather to her doom. Molly determines to save her stepsister. In so doing, she learns that Heather's strange behavior stems from her feelings of guilt at having accidentally caused her mother's death by playing near a stove and starting a fire. Eventually, Molly wrests Heather from Helen's arms as the ghost attempts to drown them. The girls discover the skeletons of Helen's parents, and their burial finally puts to rest Helen's spirit. . . . Grades four to seven." (SLJ)

"Intertwined with the ghost story is the question of Molly's moral imperative to save a child she truly dislikes. Though the emotional turnaround may be a bit quick for some, this still scores as a first-rate thriller." Booklist

★ **Witch** catcher. Clarion Books 2006 236p $16

Grades: 3 4 5 6   Fic

1. Fairies -- Fiction 2. Witches -- Fiction 3. Father-daughter relationship -- Fiction

ISBN 0-618-50457-5

LC 2005-24795

Having just moved into the West Virginia home they inherited from a distant relative, twelve-year-old Jen is surprised that her father is already dating a local antiques dealer, but more surprised by what the spooky woman really wants.

"A fast-paced, suspenseful fantasy in which an appealing heroine stands against forces seemingly beyond her control." Booklist

★ The **ghost** of Crutchfield Hall. Clarion Books 2010 153p $17

Grades: 5 6 7 8   Fic

1. Ghost stories 2. Cousins -- Fiction 3. Orphans -- Fiction 4. Young adult literature -- Works

ISBN 978-0-547-38560-0; 0-547-38560-9

In the nineteenth century, ten-year-old Florence Crutchfield leaves a London orphanage to live with her great-uncle, great-aunt, and sickly cousin James, but she soon realizes the home has another resident, who means to do her and James harm.

"A deliciously spine-tingling tale that even the most reluctant readers will enjoy." SLJ

Hale, Bruce

From Russia with lunch. Harcourt 2009 112p il (Chet Gecko mystery) $15; pa $4.99

Grades: 3 4 5   Fic

1. School stories 2. Mystery fiction 3. Geckos -- Fiction 4. Animals -- Fiction 5. Inventions -- Fiction

ISBN 978-0-15-205488-5; 0-15-205488-X; 978-0-547-32882-9 pa; 0-547-32882-6 pa

LC 2008004261

Detectives Chet Gecko and his partner Natalie Attired try to solve the mystery of why Emerson Hicky Elementary school students have suddenly started acting strangely.

"Chet's nonstop wisecracks and sidekick Natalie's jokes are . . . giggle- (and groan-) inducing. Black-and-white illustrations display the animal cast's antics." Horn Book Guide

Other titles in this series are:

The chameleon wore chartreuse (2000)

The mystery of Mr. Nice (2000)

Farewell my lunchbag (2001)

The big nap (2001)

The hamster of the Baskervilles (2002)

This gum for hire (2002)

Trouble is my beeswax (2003)

The malted falcon (2003)

Give my regrets to Broadway (2004)

Murder my tweet (2004)

Key Lardo (2006)

The possum always rings twice (2006)

Hiss me deadly (2007)

Dial M for mongoose (2009)

Hale, Marian

The **truth** about sparrows. Henry Holt & Co. 2004 260p $16.95; pa $6.99

Grades: 5 6 7 8   Fic

1. Moving -- Fiction 2. Friendship -- Fiction 3. Young adult literature -- Works 4. Great Depression, 1929-1939 -- Fiction 5. Children's literature -- Works -- Grades two through six

ISBN 0-8050-7584-4; 0-312-37133-0 pa

LC 2003-56981

Twelve-year-old Sadie promises that she will always be Wilma's best friend when their families leave drought-stricken Missouri in 1933, but once in Texas, Sadie learns that she must try to make a new home—and new friends, too

"Rich with social history, this first novel is informative, enjoyable, and evocative." SLJ

Hall, Teri

Away. Dial Books 2011 234 p. $16.99

Grades: 5 6 7 8   **Fic**
1. Science fiction 2. Resistance to government -- Fiction
ISBN 9780803735026; 0803735022

LC 2011001163

After helping heal Malgam, Rachel learns that her father is still living in the devastated territory of Away, captured by members of another clan who are planning to use him to make a deal with the government on the other side of the Line, and she joins the rescue party that must risk much to save him.

"This worthy sequel . . . continues to build a dystopian world rich with suspense and moral choices." Kirkus

The **Line**. Dial Books 2010 219p $16.99
Grades: 5 6 7 8   **Fic**
1. Science fiction 2. Young adult literature -- Works
ISBN 978-0-8037-3466-1; 0-8037-3466-2

LC 2009-12301

Rachel thinks that she and her mother are safe working for Ms. Moore at her estate close to The Line, an invisible border of the Unified States, but when Rachel has an opportunity to Cross into the forbidden zone, she is both frightened and intrigued

This "sets readers up for a series about another world that might have come from situations too close to our own." Libr Media Connect

Halpern, Jake

Dormia; written by Jake Halpern & Peter Kujawinski. Houghton Mifflin Harcourt 2009 506p il $17
Grades: 4 5 6   **Fic**
1. Fantasy fiction 2. Sleep -- Fiction 3. Young adult literature -- Works
ISBN 978-0-547-07665-2; 0-547-07665-7

LC 2008-36108

After learning of his ancestral ties to Dormia, a hidden kingdom in the Ural Mountains whose inhabitants possess the ancient power of 'wakeful sleeping,' twelve-year-old Alfonso sets out on a mission to save the kingdom from destruction, discovering secrets that lurk in his own sleep.

This "is old-fashioned storytelling, ably done, where action supports story development rather than substituting for it. This fantasy is a wonderful intergenerational read-along and is a strong choice for readers still mourning the end of the Harry Potter books." Booklist

World's End; written by Jake Halpern and Peter Kujawinski. Houghton Mifflin 2011 487p $18
Grades: 4 5 6   **Fic**
1. Fantasy fiction 2. Sleep -- Fiction
ISBN 978-0-547-48037-4; 0-547-48037-7

LC 2010008129

After learning that his presumed-dead father may still be alive, Alfonso Perplexon, now fifteen years old, takes on the dangerous task of returning to the land of Dormia to search for him.

"Fans of the first book will enjoy this complex, well-paced installment." Horn Book Guide

Hamilton, Virginia

Drylongso; illustrated by Jerry Pinkney. Harcourt Brace Jovanovich 1992 54p il hardcover o.p. pa $10

Grades: 3 4 5   **Fic**
1. Droughts -- Fiction 2. Farm life -- Fiction 3. African Americans -- Fiction
ISBN 0-15-201587-6 pa

LC 91-25575

As a great wall of dust moves across their drought-stricken farm, a family's distress is relieved by a young man called Drylongso, who literally blows into their lives with the storm

"In an understand story of drought and hard times and longing for rain, a great writer and a great artists have pared down their rich, exuberant styles to something quieter but no less intense." Booklist

★ **M.C.** Higgins, the great; 25th anniversary ed; Simon & Schuster 1999 232p $18; pa $5.99
Grades: 5 6 7 8   **Fic**
1. Family life -- Fiction 2. African Americans -- Fiction
ISBN 0-689-83074-2; 1-4169-1407-2 pa

LC 99014288

Awarded the Newbery Medal, 1975

As a slag heap, the result of strip mining, creeps closer to his house in the Ohio hills, fifteen-year-old M.C. is torn between trying to get his family away and fighting for the home they love

"This is a deeply involving story possessing a folklorish quality." Child Book Rev Serv

Zeely. Macmillan 1967 122p il hardcover o.p. pa $5.99
Grades: 4 5 6 7   **Fic**
1. African Americans -- Fiction
ISBN 0-02-742470-7; 1-4169-1413-7 pa

"Imaginative eleven-year-old Geeder is stirred when she sees Zeely Tayber, who is dignified, stately, and six-and-a-half feet tall. Geeder thinks Zeely looks like the magazine picture of the Watusi queen. Through meeting Zeely personally and getting to know her, Geeder finally returns to reality." Read Ladders for Hum Relat. 5th edition

★ The **house** of Dies Drear; illustrated by Eros Keith. Macmillan 1968 246p il hardcover o.p. pa $5.99
Grades: 5 6 7 8   **Fic**
1. Mystery fiction 2. African Americans -- Fiction
ISBN 0-02-742500-2; 1-4169-1405-6 pa

"The answer to the mystery comes in a startling dramatic dénouement that is pure theater. This is gifted writing; the characterization is unforgettable, the plot imbued with mounting tension." Saturday Rev

The **planet** of Junior Brown. Macmillan 1971 210p hardcover o.p. pa $5.99
Grades: 6 7 8 9   **Fic**
1. Friendship -- Fiction 2. African Americans -- Fiction
ISBN 0-689-71721-0; 1-4169-1410-2 pa

A Newbery Medal honor book, 1972

"This is the story of a crucial week in the lives of two black, eighth-grade dropouts who have been spending their time with the school janitor. Each boy is presented as a distinct individual. Jr. is a three-hundred pound musical prodigy as neurotic as his overprotective mother. Buddy has learned to live by his wits in a world of homeless children. Buddy becomes Jr. Brown's protector and says to the other boys, 'We are together because we have to learn to live for each other.'" Read Ladders for Hum Relat. 6th edition

Han, Jenny

★ **Clara** Lee and the apple pie dream; with pictures by Julia Kuo. Little, Brown and Company 2011 149p il $14.99

Grades: 2 3 4 **Fic**

1. School stories 2. Family life -- Fiction 3. Korean Americans -- Fiction

ISBN 978-0-316-07038-6; 0-316-07038-6

LC 2010-06900

Korean American fourth-grader Clara Lee longs to be Little Miss Apple Pie, and when her luck seems suddenly to change for the better, she overcomes her fear of public speaking and enters the competition.

Han "captures an 8-year-old's perspective perfectly. . . . The message shines through but doesn't overwhelm this engaging chapter book that will be welcomed by middle-grade fans of Clementine." Kirkus

Hannigan, Katherine

★ **Emmaline** and the bunny. Greenwillow Books 2009 94p il $14.99

Grades: 1 2 3 **Fic**

1. Rabbits -- Fiction 2. Loneliness -- Fiction 3. Cleanliness -- Fiction 4. Children's literature -- Works -- Grades two through six 5. Children's literature -- Works -- Preschool through grade two

ISBN 978-0-06-162654-8; 0-06-162654-6

LC 2008012639

Everyone and everything in the town of Neatasapin is tidy, except Emmaline who likes to dig dirt and jump in puddles, and wants to adopt an untidy bunny.

"Told in very short chapters and using language in unusual ways, this is a small delight, cunningly illustrated by Hannigan's own sweet watercolors." Booklist

Ida B; --and her plans to maximize fun, avoid disaster, and (possibly) save the world. Greenwillow Books 2004 246p $15.99; pa $6.99

Grades: 4 5 6 **Fic**

1. School stories 2. Cancer -- Fiction 3. Family life -- Fiction 4. Children's literature -- Works -- Grades two through six

ISBN 0-06-073024-2; 0-06-073026-9 pa

LC 2003-25625

In Wisconsin, fourth-grader Ida B spends happy hours being home-schooled and playing in her family's apple orchard, until her mother begins treatment for breast cancer and her parents must sell part of the orchard and send her to public school

"Through a masterful use of voice, Hannigan's first-person narration captures an unforgettable heroine with intelligence, spirit, and a unique imagination." SLJ

True (. . . sort of) Greenwillow Books 2011 360p $16.99; lib bdg $17.89

Grades: 4 5 6 **Fic**

1. School stories 2. Siblings -- Fiction 3. Friendship -- Fiction 4. Family life -- Fiction 5. Young adult literature -- Works

ISBN 978-0-06-196873-0; 0-06-196873-0; 978-0-06-196874-7 lib bdg; 0-06-196874-9 lib bdg

For most of her eleven years, Delly has been in trouble without knowing why, until her little brother, R. B., and a strange, silent new friend, Ferris, help her find a way to be good—and happy—again.

"Told in carefully crafted language that begs to be read aloud, the story runs the gamut from laugh-out-loud funny to emotionally wrenching." SLJ

Hansen, Joyce

Home is with our family; [illustrated by] E. B. Lewis. Hyperion 2010 272p il (Black pioneers) $16.99

Grades: 4 5 6 7 **Fic**

1. Abolitionists -- Fiction 2. African Americans -- Fiction

ISBN 978-0-7868-5217-8; 0-7868-5217-8

Maria Peterson is looking forward to turning 13. She envisions new adult prestige and responsibility, like attending abolitionist meetings and listening to inspiring speakers like Sojourner Truth. However, she doesn't bank on all the unexpected changes that her 13th year brings.

"The plot flows quickly and has enough action to hold a reader's attention. Teachers can use this book to provide their students with a deeper understanding of the Fugitive Slave Act." Libr Media Connect

Hanson, Mary Elizabeth

How to save your tail; if you are a rat nabbed by cats who really like stories about magic spoons, wolves with snout-warts, big hairy chimney trolls . . . and cookies too. illustrated by John Hendrix. Schwartz & Wade Books 2007 93p il $15.99; lib bdg $18.99; pa $5.50

Grades: 2 3 4 5 **Fic**

1. Fairy tales 2. Cats -- Fiction 3. Rats -- Fiction 4. Storytelling -- Fiction

ISBN 978-0-375-83755-5; 0-375-83755-8; 978-0-375-93755-2 lib bdg; 0-375-93755-2 lib bdg; 978-0-440-42228-0 pa; 0-440-42228-0 pa

LC 2006-03833

When he is captured by two of the queen's cats, Bob the rat prolongs his life by sharing fresh-baked cookies and stories of his ancestors, whose escapades are remarkably similar to those of well-known fairy tale heroes

"Clever wordplay and large doses of humor make this a most enjoyable selection that has great potential as a read-aloud. The black-and-white cartoon-style illustrations add to the fun." SLJ

Haptie, Charlotte

Otto and the flying twins; the first book of the Karmidee. [by] Charlotte Haptie. Holiday House 2004 304p il $17.95

Grades: 4 5 6 7 **Fic**

1. Magic 2. Prejudices 3. Fantasy fiction 4. Magic -- Fiction

ISBN 0-8234-1826-X

LC 2003-57135

First published 2002 in the United Kingdom

Young Otto comes to the rescue when he discovers that his family and city are the last remnants of an ancient magical world now under threat from the Normal Police

"The amazing oddities and quirks of this world and its residents are described with delicious nonchalance. . . . The characters are equally surprising and unpredictable. . . . The writing is as fresh and invigorating as the setting." SLJ

Another title about Otto is:

Otto and the bird charmers (2005)

Hardinge, Frances

★ **Fly** by night. HarperCollinsPublishers 2006 487p hardcover o.p. lib bdg $17.89; pa $7.99

Grades: 5 6 7 8   **Fic**

1. Fantasy fiction 2. Young adult literature -- Works
ISBN 978-0-06-087627-2; 0-06-087627-1; 978-0-06-087629-6 lib bdg; 0-06-087629-8 lib bdg; 978-0-06-087630-2 pa; 0-06-087630-1 pa

LC 2005-20598

Mosca Mye and her homicidal goose, Saracen, travel to the city of Mandelion on the heels of smooth-talking con-man, Eponymous Clent.

"Through rich, colorful language and a sure sense of plot and pacing, Hardinge has created a distinctly imaginative world full of engaging characters, robust humor, and true suspense." SLJ

Fly trap. Harper 2011 584p $16.99

Grades: 5 6 7 8   **Fic**

1. Fantasy fiction 2. Young adult literature -- Works
ISBN 978-0-06-088044-6; 0-06-088044-9

LC 2010027755

Adventurous orphan Mosca Mye, her savage goose, Saracen, and their sometimes-loyal companion, Eponymous Clent, become embroiled in the intrigues of Toll, a town that changes entirely as day turns to night.

Crammed with eccentric, Dickensian characters, unexpected plot turns, and numerous very niche gods and goddesses . . ., Hardinge's world is rich enough to fuel two or three fantasy novels. It's a beautifully written tale, by turns humorous and heartbreaking and a sheer pleasure to read. Publ Wkly

Hardy, Janice

Blue fire. Balzer + Bray 2010 373p (The Healing Wars) $16.99

Grades: 5 6 7 8   **Fic**

1. War stories 2. Fantasy fiction 3. Orphans -- Fiction
4. Sisters -- Fiction 5. Young adult literature -- Works
ISBN 978-0-06-174741-0; 0-06-174741-6

LC 2009053446

While trying to lead the Takers out of Geveg, fifteen-year-old Nya is captured by bounty-hunters and taken to Baseer, where she escapes and soon finds herself helping the Baseeri.

"The climax . . . yields much narrative tension but doesn't resolve the driving issues of the story. For that, readers will have to wait for book three in this thrilling, complex saga." Horn Book

Darkfall. Balzer + Bray 2011 418p (The healing wars) $16.99

Grades: 5 6 7 8   **Fic**

1. Fantasy fiction 2. Orphans -- Fiction 3. Sisters -- Fiction
ISBN 978-0-06-174750-2; 0-06-174750-5

LC 2011001946

With the rebellion in full swing, fifteen year-old Nya's loyaltie are put to the ultimate test,and she is forced to choose between leading an army against the Duke or abandoning her people to save her sister.

"The finale offers suspense, resolution of prior wrongs, the sweetness of first love and a battle-tested heroine who fights with her head and heart." Kirkus

The **shifter**. Balzer + Bray 2009 370p (The Healing Wars) $16.99; pa $7.99

Grades: 5 6 7 8   **Fic**

1. War stories 2. Fantasy fiction 3. Orphans -- Fiction
4. Sisters -- Fiction 5. Young adult literature -- Works
ISBN 978-0-06-174704-5; 0-06-174704-1; 978-0-06-174708-3 pa; 0-06-174708-4 pa

LC 2008-47673

Nya is an orphan struggling for survival in a city crippled by war. She is also a Taker—with her touch, she can heal injuries, pulling pain from another person into her own body. But unlike her sister, Tali, and the other Takers who become Healers' League apprentices, Nya's skill is flawed: She can't push that pain into pynvium, the enchanted metal used to store it. All she can do is shift it into another person

"The ethical dilemmas raised . . . provide thoughtful discussion material and also make the story accessible to more than just fantasy readers." Booklist

Other titles in this series are:

Blue fire (2010)

Darkfall (2011)

Harkrader, Lisa

The **adventures** of Beanboy; written and illustrated by Lisa Harkrader. Houghton Mifflin Harcourt 2012 234p. ill.

Grades: 4 5 6 7 8   **Fic**

1. Family -- Fiction 2. Domestic relations 3. Superhero comic books, strips, etc. 4. Comic books, strips, etc. -- Fiction 5. Schools -- Fiction 6. Contests -- Fiction 7. Middle schools -- Fiction 8. Family problems -- Fiction
ISBN 9780547550787

LC 2011012161

In this book, "Tucker MacBean is a collector and aspiring creator of comic books, a preoccupation that he realizes doesn't rank high 'on the sliding scale of middle-school coolness.' He enters a contest to create a sidekick for his favorite superhero, convinced that a win will jump-start his popularity; he plans to give the prize--a college scholarship--to his overextended single mother, who's juggling classes and work. Tucker joins the art club to prepare his entry, and Sam (a classmate who Tucker sees as 'arch nemesis to the world') is hired to babysit his special-needs brother after school. . . . Tucker displays his own heroism when he reaches out to Sam after discovering why she is so belligerent and defensive." (Publishers Weekly)

Harlow, Joan Hiatt

Star in the storm. Margaret K. McElderry Bks. 2000 150p $16; pa $4.99 **Fic**

1. Dogs 2. Dogs -- Fiction 3. Newfoundland dog 4. Newfoundland and Labrador
ISBN 0-689-82905-1; 0-689-84621-5 pa

LC 99-20416

In 1912, fearing for the safety of her beloved Newfoundland dog Sirius because of a new law outlawing non-sheep-herding dogs in her Newfoundland village, twelve-year-old Maggie tries to save him by keeping him hidden

"Containing many authentic details of life in a remote region in days gone by, this story is educational as well as exciting." Booklist

Harper, Charise Mericle

Just Grace. Houghton Mifflin 2007 138p il $15; pa $4.99

Grades: 2 3 4 **Fic**

1. School stories

ISBN 978-0-618-64642-5; 0-618-64642-6; 978-0-547-01440-1 pa; 0-547-01440-6 pa

LC 2006-17062

Misnamed by her teacher, seven-year-old Just Grace prides herself on being empathetic, but when she tries to help a neighbor feel better, her good intentions backfire.

"Grace is a funny, mischievous protagonist who should easily find a place in the pantheon of precocious third graders." SLJ

Other titles about Just Grace are:

Still Just Grace (2007)

Just Grace walks the dog (2008)

Just Grace goes green (2009)

Just Grace and the snack attack (2009)

Just Grace and the Terrible Tutu (2011)

Just Grace and the double surprise (2011)

Just Grace and the trouble with cupcakes; written and illustrated by Charise Mericle Harper. Houghton Mifflin Books for Children, Houghton Mifflin Harcourt 2013 208 p. (hardcover) $15.99

Grades: 2 3 4 **Fic**

1. School stories -- Juvenile fiction 2. Female friendship -- Juvenile fiction 3. Fairs -- Fiction 4. Schools -- Fiction 5. Cupcakes -- Fiction

ISBN 0547877447; 9780547877440

LC 2012033824

This is the tenth installment of Charise Mericle Harper's Just Grace series. Here, "Just Grace is still in third grade, her best friend, Mimi, lives next door, and she loves to romp with her dog, Mr. Scruffers. . . . The plot centers on a visit from Grace's grandmother, her excellent cupcake recipe . . . and the annual school fair. When Grace accidentally suggests cupcakes for the fair theme, she breaks a pinky-swear promise with Mimi: to support Mimi's idea that candy should be the theme." (Kirkus)

Harper, Jessica

★ Uh-oh, Cleo; illustrated by Jon Berkeley. G. P. Putnam's Sons 2008 58p il $14.99

Grades: K 1 2 3 **Fic**

1. Twins -- Fiction 2. Siblings -- Fiction 3. Family life -- Fiction 4. Medical care -- Fiction 5. Wounds and injuries -- Fiction

ISBN 978-0-399-24671-5; 0-399-24671-1

LC 2007027507

What starts out as a perfectly ordinary day in the Small house turns into Stiches Saturday when Cleo gets a cut on the head after her twin brother, Jack, accidentally pulls down their "Toy House."

This is an "engaging early chapter book. . . . The story is studded with observations, incidents, and conversations that reflect true-to-life sibling relationships and realistic individual foibles. . . . Large type, spacious design, and appealing drawings add to the accessiblity." Booklist

Other titles about Cleo re:

Underpants on my head (2009)

I barfed on Mrs. Kenly (2010)

Underpants on my head; illustrated by Jon Berkeley. G.P. Putnam's Sons 2009 60p il (Uh-oh Cleo) $14.99

Grades: K 1 2 3 **Fic**

1. Hiking -- Fiction 2. Vacations -- Fiction 3. Family life -- Fiction

ISBN 978-0-399-24672-2; 0-399-24672-X

LC 2007-39268

When Cleo and her family go on vacation, they experience a freak August snow storm while hiking on Mt. Baldy.

"Cleo's chatty narration and Berkeley's warm black-and-white illustrations will appeal to early chapter-book readers." SLJ

Harper, Suzanne

A **gaggle** of goblins. Greenwillow Books 2011 300p (The unseen world of Poppy Malone) $16.99

Grades: 4 5 6 **Fic**

1. Goblins -- Fiction 2. Family life -- Fiction

ISBN 0-06-199607-6; 978-0-06-199607-8

LC 2010025558

Eleven-year-old Poppy's parents are paranormal investigators who have never actually found anything, but that may change when they move to Austin, Texas, and Poppy meets a goblin in the attic of their new house.

"The book shines through the consistently amusing dynamics and dialogue among the Malones; Harper has abundant fun with the Malone parents' eccentricities, and kids will too. Readers will want more from this family." Publ Wkly

Harrington, Karen

Sure signs of crazy; by Karen Harrington. 1st ed. Little Brown & Co 2013 288 p. (hardcover) $17

Grades: 4 5 6 7 8 **Fic**

1. Adolescence -- Juvenile fiction 2. Parent-child relationship -- Juvenile fiction 3. Coming of age -- Fiction 4. Mental illness -- Fiction 5. Family problems -- Fiction

ISBN 0316210587; 9780316210584

LC 2012030683

In this book, "worried that she will grow up to be crazy like her mother or alcoholic like her father, rising seventh-grader Sarah Nelson takes courage from Harper Lee's 'To Kill a Mockingbird,' writing letters to Atticus Finch and discovering her own strengths. . . . She describes the events of the summer she turns 12, gets her period, develops a crush on a neighbor and fellow word lover, and comes to terms with her parents' failings." (Kirkus Reviews)

Harris, Lewis

A **taste** for red. Clarion Books 2009 169p $16

Grades: 4 5 6 **Fic**

1. Vampires -- Fiction 2. Friendship -- Fiction 3. Missing children -- Fiction 4. Young adult literature -- Works

ISBN 978-0-547-14462-7; 0-547-14462-8

LC 2008-25318

When some of her classmates disappear, sixth-grader Svetlana, along with her new friends go in search of the missing students using her newfound ability as an Olfactive, one who has heightened smell, hearing, and the ability to detect vampires.

"Svetlana comes across as a strong character. . . . Her first-person narrative is fast-paced and witty, and her mild scorn for everything she encounters at school will appeal to angst-ridden tweens. Sure to be a crowd-pleaser." SLJ

Harrison, Michelle

13 curses. Little, Brown 2011 486p (13 Treasures Trilogy) $15.99; pa $6.99

Grades: 5 6 7 8 **Fic**

1. Magic -- Fiction 2. Fairies -- Fiction 3. Orphans -- Fiction 4. Kidnapping -- Fiction

ISBN 978-0-316-04150-8; 0-316-04150-5; 978-0316041492 pa

When fairies steal her brother, thirteen-year-old Rowan Fox promises that in exchange for his return she will find the thirteen charms that the fairies have enchanted and hidden in the human world.

"The sure-handed storytelling creates a completely credible setting—by turns violent and tender, sinister and poignant. . . . Contrasts between human emotion and commitment and the cold, often cruel magic and mischief of the fairy realm create terrific tension and afford opportunities for heroism for the young protagonists." Kirkus

★ 13 treasures. Little, Brown Books for Young Readers 2010 355p il $15.99

Grades: 5 6 7 8 **Fic**

1. Mystery fiction 2. Fairies -- Fiction 3. Grandmothers -- Fiction 4. Young adult literature -- Works

ISBN 978-0-316-04148-5; 0-316-04148-3

LC 2008-45511

Bedeviled by evil fairies that only she can see, thirteen-year-old Tanya is sent to stay with her cold and distant grandmother at Elvesden Manor, where she and the caretaker's son solve a disturbing mystery that leads them to the discovery that Tanya's life is in danger.

"Harrison writes with great assuredness, creating a seductive setting and memorable, fully developed characters. . . . It's an excellent choice for fans of the Spiderwick Chronicles and other modern-day fairy tales." Publ Wkly

Harrison, Troon

Red River stallion; by Troon Harrison. Bloomsbury 2013 352 p. (hardback: alk. paper) $16.99

Grades: 3 4 5 **Fic**

1. Horses -- Fiction 2. Historical fiction 3. Canada -- History -- Fiction 4. Fathers -- Fiction 5. Voyages and travels -- Fiction 6. Racially mixed people -- Fiction 7. Cree Indians -- Canada -- Fiction 8. Indians of North America -- Fiction

ISBN 159990845X; 9781599908458

LC 2012014147

This novel, by Troon Harrison, is set in 19th-century Canada. "When her mother dies, Rose is left feeling completely alone in the world, but the promise of a new friendship arrives on an English ship. Fireway, a red stallion, has made the long trip to North America and Rose falls in love with his beauty instantly. The horse is headed on a westward expedition to the Red River Valley-the same place where Rose's father is rumored to be. Together, Rose and Fireaway make the journey." (Publisher's note)

"...The language is beautiful and accomplished, making this novel of discovery and survival an enjoyable and authentic read." SLJ

The **horse** road; by Troon Harrison. Bloomsbury 2012 320 p. (alk. paper) $16.99

Grades: 4 5 6 7 **Fic**

1. Horses -- Fiction 2. Historical fiction 3. Horsemanship -- Fiction

ISBN 1599908468; 9781599908465

LC 2012014010

This book is "the first of a projected trio of horse-centered historical novels. . . . Kalli, shy and stammering everywhere but on a horse, begins to prove herself when she and her friend Batu catch a glimpse over a mountainside of thousands of Middle Kingdom warriors preparing to attack their town. . . . When her own mare, Swan, is stolen, she dons armor and weapons and rides to the rescue. In the end, she wins Swan not in battle, but through shrewd bargaining." (Kirkus Reviews)

"Densely descriptive prose, rife with historical and equine detail for horse-fiction fans, vividly portrays aspects of daily life and culture." Booklist

Hartnett, Sonya

The **Midnight** zoo; illustrated by Andrea Offermann. Candlewick Press 2011 217p il $16.99

Grades: 4 5 6 7 **Fic**

1. Zoos -- Fiction 2. Animals -- Fiction 3. Freedom -- Fiction 4. Gypsies -- Fiction 5. Refugees -- Fiction 6. Siblings -- Fiction 7. World War, 1939-1945 -- Fiction

ISBN 978-0-7636-5339-2; 0-7636-5339-X

LC 2010042794

Twelve-year-old Andrej, nine-year-old Tomas, and their baby sister Wilma flee their Romany encampment when it is attacked by Germans during World War II, and in an abandoned town they find a zoo where the animals tell their stories, helping the children understand what has become of their lives and what it means to be free.

"Written in lyrical, spare prose, the plot encompasses a single night in which doomed animals and brave boys cling to hope in a world that makes no sense. Black-and-white spot art highlights animals and key scenes." Kirkus

Sadie and Ratz; Sonya Hartnett; illustrated by Ann James. 1st U.S. ed. Candlewick Press 2012 59 p. ill. (reinforced) $14.99

Grades: K 1 2 3 **Fic**

1. Hand -- Fiction 2. Imagination -- Fiction 3. Sibling rivalry -- Fiction

ISBN 0763653152; 9780763653156

LC 2011045899

In this children's picture book by Sonya Hartnett, "Sadie and Ratz are the names of Hannah's hands. . . . They're always after four-year-old Baby Boy (whom Sadie wishes were a dog). . . . Baby Boy knows how to turn the tables, though, and when he spills milk on the carpet, he tells Grandma that Sadie and Ratz pushed him. But when Baby Boy goes too far, Hannah may have to send Sadie and Ratz on vacation to prove their innocence." (Publisher's note)

★ The **silver** donkey; illustrated by Don T. Powers. Candlewick Press 2006 266p il $15.99; pa $7.99

Grades: 5 6 7 8 **Fic**

1. Soldiers -- Fiction 2. World War, 1914-1918 --

Fiction 3. Young adult literature -- Works
ISBN 978-0-7636-2937-3; 0-7636-2937-5; 978-0-
7636-3681-4 pa; 0-7636-3681-9 pa

LC 2006-42582

First published 2004 in Australia

In France during World War I, four French children learn
about honesty, loyalty, and courage from an English army
deserter who tells them a series of stories related to his small,
silver donkey charm

"Occasional full-page black-and-white art deftly suggests setting and mood without intruding on readers'
imaginations. Provocative, timely, and elegantly honed."
Horn Book

Hartry, Nancy

Watching Jimmy. Tundra Books 2009 152p $16.95
Grades: 5 6 7 8   **Fic**
1. Child abuse -- Fiction 2. Brain -- Wounds and
injuries -- Fiction
ISBN 0-88776-871-7; 978-0-88776-871-2

This story takes place in Canadia in 1958. Eleven-year-
old Carolyn walks an emotional tightrope knowing what really happened to her best friend, Jimmy, the day his Uncle
Ted chose to teach him a lesson that left Jimmy brain-dam-
aged. But when Uncle Ted threatens his beleaguered family
with even more abuse and the loss of their home, Carolyn
must find the courage to match wits with him and to speak
out, using the truth as her only weapon. "Age nine and up."
(Quill Quire)

"Like a steady beat that pulses louder and louder, the story unfolds against a backdrop of postwar social and political
concerns and Remembrance Day. Carolyn is a passionate
and feisty character, delineated with love and precision, and
readers will be drawn to her. A compelling and satisfying
novel." SLJ

Harvey, Jacqueline

Alice-Miranda at school. Delacorte Press 2011 257p il
$14.99; lib bdg $17.99
Grades: 2 3 4   **Fic**
1. School stories 2. Mystery fiction
ISBN 978-0-385-73993-1; 0-385-73993-1; 978-0-385-
90811-5 lib bdg; 0-385-90811-3 lib bdg; 978-0-375-
89858-7 e-book

LC 2010-23723

Soon after arriving at the Winchesterfield-Downsford-
vale Academy for Proper Young Ladies, resourceful sev-
en-and-one-quarter-year-old Alice-Miranda finds her new
boarding school to be a very curious establishment with no
flowers in the gardens, a headmistress that has not been seen
for years, and a mysterious stranger that seems to be hiding
out on the premises.

"The ultimate extreme in cute, rich, kind, and genius, she
is a good role model with her ability always to see the best
in everyone. . . . This would make an excellent classroom
read-aloud. A fun mystery, with fantastical, over-the-top elements." SLJ

Harvey, Matthea

Cecil the pet glacier; Matthea Harvey; illustrated by
Giselle Potter. Schwartz & Wade Books 2012 40 p. $17.99
Grades: PreK K 1 2   **Fic**
1. Pets -- Fiction 2. Glaciers -- Fiction 3. Picture books

for children 4. Eccentrics and eccentricities -- Fiction
ISBN 9780375867736; 9780375967733

LC 2011018657

This book is "[Matthea] Harvey's . . . tale of a misunderstood child and her equally misunderstood glacier. Lonely
Ruby has flamboyantly eccentric parents who run a topiary
and tiara business. . . . A family trip to Norway nets Ruby a
pet, a pint-size glacier named Cecil who follows her everywhere; Ruby--who wanted a dog--scorns him." It isn't until
"Cecil . . . performs a daring rescue. . . that Ruby realizes
how wrong she's been." (Publishers Weekly)

Haskell, Merrie

The **princess** curse. Harper 2011 325p $16.99
Grades: 4 5 6 7   **Fic**
1. Fairy tales 2. Magic -- Fiction 3. Princesses --
Fiction
ISBN 978-0-06-200813-8; 0-06-200813-7

LC 2010040424

"Author Haskell has her way with the story of 'The
Twelve Dancing Princesses,' incorporating references to
other myths and legends and adding many twists of her own,
not least of which is making the royals' attempted rescuer
a strong-willed, 13-year-old apprentice herbalist, Reveka. .
. . When Vasile offers the hand of any of his daughters in
marriage to anyone who banishes the curse (or a 'fabulous
dowry' if the curse-breaker is female), Reveka is determined
to win the reward. . . . With a good sense of humor, an able
and empowered protagonist, and a highly original take
on this tale, Haskell's story gives readers much to enjoy."
Publ Wkly

Hathaway, Barbara

Missy Violet & me. Houghton 2004 100p $15
Grades: 4 5 6   **Fic**
1. Midwives -- Fiction 2. Childbirth -- Fiction 3.
African Americans -- Fiction
ISBN 978-0-618-37163-1; 0-618-37163-X

During the early 1900s, eleven-year-old Viney spends
her summer working for the local midwife and learns firsthand about birth, death, and "catchin' babies."

"Unspooled as leisurely as a summer afternoon spent on
the front porch, this appealingly nostalgic tale conveys the
tenor of the time as well as the affable narrator's growth during one momentous summer." Publ Wkly

Hawkins, Aaron R.

The **year** money grew on trees; written and illustrated
by Aaron R. Hawkins. Houghton Mifflin 2010 293p il $16
Grades: 5 6 7 8   **Fic**
1. Apples -- Fiction 2. Cousins -- Fiction 3. Siblings
-- Fiction 4. Farm life -- Fiction 5. Money-making
projects for children -- Fiction
ISBN 978-0-547-27977-0; 0-547-27977-9

In early 1980s New Mexico, thirteen-year-old Jackson
Jones recruits his cousins and sisters to help tend an elderly
neighbor's neglected apple orchard for the chance to make
big money and, perhaps, to own the orchard.

"Hawkins's children's book debut is rich with details that
feel drawn from memory, . . . and Jackson's narration sparkles. His hard work, setbacks, and motivations make this a
highly relatable adventure in entrepreneurship." Publ Wkly

Haworth, Danette

Me & Jack. Walker 2011 232p $16.99

Grades: 3 4 5 6   **Fic**

1. School stories 2. Dogs -- Fiction 3. Bullies --
Fiction 4. Country life -- Fiction

ISBN 978-0-8027-9453-6; 0-8027-9453-X

      LC 2010034338

During the Vietnam War, when twelve-year-old Josh
and his Air Force recruiter father move to a small town in
the mountains of Pennsylvania and get a dog from the local
shelter, Josh is forced to stop hanging back and takes on the
unfriendly town residents, a mountain, and the meanest boy
in school.

"Joshua is vividly depicted through his first-person narration and amusing interior monologues, and the conflicts he
deals with are effectively realized. In all, it's an entertaining boy-and-dog adventure set against a not-often-depicted
era of political strife that's notably similar to the present."
Kirkus

Haydon, Elizabeth

The **Floating** Island; the lost journals of Ven Polypheme. illustrated by Brett Helquist. Starscape 2006 368p
il $17.95; pa $5.99

Grades: 5 6 7 8   **Fic**

1. Fantasy fiction

ISBN 0-7653-0867-3; 0-7653-4772-5 pa

      LC 2006005768

Ven, the youngest son of a long line of famous ship-
wrights, dreams of sailing to far-off lands where magic
thrives. He gets his chance when he is chosen to direct the
Inspection of his family's latest ship and sets sail on the journey of a lifetime

The author's "world building is as successful as her characters, with Helquist's occasional loose sketches providing
some visual distraction and additional atmosphere. A delightful epic fantasy." Booklist

The **Thief** Queen's daughter; 1st hardcover ed.; Tom
Doherty Associates 2007 319p (Lost journals of Ven Polypheme) $17.95; pa $6.99

Grades: 5 6 7 8   **Fic**

1. Fantasy fiction

ISBN 978-0-7653-0868-9; 0-7653-0868-1; 978-0-
7653-4773-2 pa; 0-7653-4773-3 pa

      LC 2007007933

Young Ven Polypheme is sent on a secret mission within
the walls of the Gated City, a former penal colony in the land
of Serendair, where he and his friends face kidnapping and
even worse dangers from the ruthless Thief Queen, who is
trying to reclaim her runaway daughter.

"Haydon uses snippets of Ven's diary entries, fast-paced
action, and plenty of humorous touches to keep readers engaged." SLJ

Hayles, Marsha

Breathing room; Marsha Hayles. Henry Holt and Co.
2012 244 p. (hc) $17.99

Grades: 5 6 7 8   **Fic**

1. Bildungsromans 2. Historical fiction 3. Teenagers
-- Fiction 4. Tuberculosis -- Fiction 5. Sick -- Fiction
6. Hospitals -- Fiction 7. Coming of age -- Fiction

ISBN 0805089616; 9780805089615

      LC 2011034055

Author Marsha Hayles' book is "set in 1940 at a sanitarium in Loon Lake, Minn. . . . Thirteen-year-old Evvy Hoff-
meister has tuberculosis and feels abandoned by her family
when she's sent to the sanitarium to be cured. The cold nurses, strict rules, mind-numbing routines, and endless bed rest
are dispiriting for Evvy and her roommates: kind Beverly,
glamorous Pearl, and defensive Dena. . . . Nonetheless, the
girls find strength in each other and discover creative ways
to bring cheer." (Publishers Weekly)

Hazen, Lynn E.

Cinder Rabbit; [by] Lynn E. Hazen; illustrated by Ely-
se Pastel. Henry Holt & Co. 2008 64p il $15.95

Grades: K 1 2   **Fic**

1. School stories 2. Rabbits -- Fiction 3. Theater --
Fiction

ISBN 978-0-8050-8194-7; 0-8050-8194-1

      LC 2007027318

Zoe is chosen for the role of Cinder Rabbit in her school
play and is also supposed to lead the class in the Bunny Hop
at the end, but ever since wicked Winifred laughed at her
for landing in a mud puddle, Zoe has forgotten how to hop

"This simple, sweet beginning chapter book contains the
right amount of story for children just starting to read longer
books; and the charming black-and-white illustrations, decorating every page, will engage kids." Booklist

The **amazing** trail of Seymour Snail; illustrated by
Doug Cushman. Henry Holt and Co. 2009 64p il $16.95

Grades: 1 2 3   **Fic**

1. Snails -- Fiction 2. Artists -- Fiction

ISBN 978-0-8050-8698-0; 0-8050-8698-6

      LC 2008036939

Hoping to become a famous artist one day, Seymour
Snail takes a job in a New York City art gallery, where everyone is buzzing about a "magnificent mystery artist."

"With only a few sentences and at least one illustration
per page, this title is perfect for students transitioning to
chapter books. . . . Cushman's black-and-white cartoons delineate the characters and add humor and perspective." SLJ

Healy, Christopher

The **hero's** guide to saving your kingdom; written by
Christopher Healy; with drawings by Todd Harris. Walden
Pond Press 2012 438 p. ill., map $16.99

Grades: 4 5 6 7   **Fic**

1. Princes -- Fiction 2. Fairy tales -- Fiction 3. Heroes
and heroines -- Fiction 4. Fairy tales 5. Humorous
stories 6. Witches -- Fiction

ISBN 0062117432; 9780062117434

      LC 2011053347

In this book, "four Princes . . . must team up on a . . . quest
to save their kingdoms. . . . Cinderella wants adventure more
than sheltered Prince Frederic does. Prince Gustav's pride is
still badly damaged from having needed Rapunzel's teary-
eyed rescue. Through Sleeping Beauty, Prince Liam learns
kissing someone out of enchanted sleep doesn't guarantee
compatibility. . . . Although she loves wacky Prince Duncan,
Snow White needs some solitude." (Kirkus Reviews)

The **hero's** guide to storming the castle; by Christopher
Healy; with drawings by Todd Harris. Walden Pond Press,
an imprint of HarperCollinsPublishers 2013 496 p. (Hero's
Guide) (hardcover) $16.99

Grades: 4 5 6 7 **Fic**

1. Fractured fairy tales 2. Humorous fiction -- Juvenile fiction 3. Fairy tales 4. Humorous stories 5. Heroes -- Fiction 6. Princes -- Fiction 7. Characters in literature -- Fiction

ISBN 0062118455; 9780062118455

LC 2012050668

In this humorous, middle-grade fantasy story, by Christopher Healy, illustrated by Todd Harris, "the charming princes from the fairy tales of Cinderella, Rapunzel, Snow White, and Briar Rose, saved the countryside from an evil witch in 'The Hero's Guide to Saving Your Kingdom.' And now, they have to save the day again, by keeping a magical object from falling into the hands of power-mad warlords who would use it for evil." (Publisher's note)

Heide, Florence Parry

Dillweed's revenge; a deadly dose of magic. [by] Florence Parry Heide, with Roxanne Heide Pierce, David Fisher Parry, and Jeanne McReynolds Parry; illustrated by Carson Ellis. Harcourt Children's Books 2010 un il $16.99

Grades: 2 3 4 5 **Fic**

1. Monsters -- Fiction

ISBN 978-0-15-206394-8; 0-15-206394-3

LC 2009-27599

An adventure-deprived young boy's neglectful parents and abusive servants receive their just desserts.

"Terse sentences and repeated refrains inject humor while leaving room for the playful ink and gouache illustrations, which recall Edward Gorey's work, to fill in the details. . . . The mixture of humor and gruesomeness may offend some, but for fans of Roald Dahl, Lemony Snicket, or Hilaire Belloc, it's right on target." SLJ

The **shrinking** of Treehorn; drawings by Edward Gorey. Holiday House 1971 un il lib bdg $16.95; pa $6.95

Grades: 2 3 4 5 **Fic**

ISBN 0-8234-0189-8 lib bdg; 0-8234-0975-9 pa

Treehorn spends an unhappy day and night shrinking. Yet when he tells his mother, father, teacher and principal of his problem they're all too busy to do anything about it. To Treehorn's great relief he finally discovers a magical game that restores him to his natural size, but then he starts turning green!

This "is an imaginative little whimsy, whose sly humor and macabre touches are perfectly matched in Edward Gorey's illustrations." Book World

Heldring, Thatcher

Roy Morelli steps up to the plate. Delacorte Press 2010 229p $15.99; lib bdg $18.99

Grades: 5 6 7 8 **Fic**

1. School stories 2. Divorce -- Fiction 3. Baseball -- Fiction

ISBN 978-0-385-73391-5; 0-385-73391-7; 978-0-385-90406-3 lib bdg; 0-385-90406-1 lib bdg

LC 2009033845

When eighth-grader Roy Morelli's divorced parents find out he is failing history, they ban him from playing on his beloved all-star baseball team, and, even worse, he winds up being tutored by his father's new girlfriend.

"The novel features good characterization and some sizzling dialogue. . . . The game action is fast paced and exciting, the depiction of middle school dynamics rings true, and

the main character shows genuine emotional growth over the course of the novel." SLJ

Helgerson, Joseph

Crows & cards; a novel. written with diligence by Mr. Joseph Helgerson; to which are added fine illustrations by Mr. Peter Desève; also included is Dictionarium Americannicum; being the words herein most arcane and alien and their definitions. Houghton Mifflin Harcourt 2009 344p il $16; pa $5.99

Grades: 4 5 6 7 **Fic**

1. Slavery -- Fiction 2. Gambling -- Fiction 3. Apprentices -- Fiction 4. Native Americans -- Fiction 5. Young adult literature -- Works

ISBN 978-0-618-88395-0; 0-618-88395-9; 978-0-547-33909-2 pa; 0-547-33909-7 pa

LC 2008013308

In 1849, Zeb's parents ship him off to St. Louis to become an apprentice tanner, but the naive twelve-year-old rebels, casting his lot with a cheating riverboat gambler, while a slave and an Indian medicine man try to get Zeb back on the right path. Includes historical notes, glossary, and bibliographical references

"Helgerson surrounds Zeb with a lively cast. . . . A solid choice for fans of high-spun yarns and not-too-tall tales." Booklist

★ **Horns** & wrinkles. Houghton Mifflin 2006 357p il $16; pa $4.95

Grades: 4 5 6 7 **Fic**

1. Magic -- Fiction 2. Trolls -- Fiction 3. Bullies -- Fiction

ISBN 0-618-61679-9; 0-618-98178-0 pa

LC 2005025448

Along a magic-saturated stretch of the Mississippi River near Blue Wing, Minnesota, twelve-year-old Claire and her bullying cousin Duke are drawn into an adventure involving Bodacious Deepthink the Great Rock Troll, a helpful fairy, and a group of trolls searching for their fathers.

"Tongue-in-cheek humor brings a delightful zing to the playfully inventive storytelling and fast-paced plot. Enchanting sketches foreshadow each chapter, adding to the wonder." SLJ

Hemingway, Edith Morris

Road to Tater Hill; [by] Edith M. Hemingway. Delacorte Press 2009 213p map $16.99; lib bdg $19.99

Grades: 5 6 7 8 **Fic**

1. Friendship -- Fiction 2. Bereavement -- Fiction 3. Grandparents -- Fiction 4. Mountain life -- Fiction 5. Young adult literature -- Works 6. Depression (Psychology) -- Fiction

ISBN 978-0-385-73677-0; 0-385-73677-0; 978-0-385-90627-2 lib bdg; 0-385-90627-7 lib bdg

LC 2008-24906

At her grandparents' North Carolina mountain home during the summer of 1963, eleven-year-old Annie Winters, grief-stricken by the death of her newborn sister and isolated by her mother's deepening depression, finds comfort in holding an oblong stone 'rock baby' and in the friendship of a neighbor boy and a reclusive mountain woman with a devastating secret

"Drawing on the author's childhood roots, the heart of this first novel is the sense of place, described in simple lyrical words. . . . True to Annie's viewpoint, the particulars tell a universal drama of childhood grief, complete in all its sadness, anger, loneliness, and healing." Booklist

Hemphill, Helen

The **adventurous** deeds of Deadwood Jones. Front Street 2008 228p $16.95

Grades: 5 6 7 8   **Fic**

1. Cousins -- Fiction 2. Cowhands -- Fiction 3. Race relations -- Fiction 4. African Americans -- Fiction 5. Young adult literature -- Works

ISBN 978-1-59078-637-6; 1-59078-637-8

LC 2008005422

Thirteen-year-old Prometheus Jones and his eleven-year-old cousin Omer flee Tennessee and join a cattle drive that will eventually take them to Texas, where Prometheus hopes his father lives, and they find adventure and face challenges as African Americans in a land still recovering from the Civil War.

"Prometheus is an always sympathetic and engaging character, and the dangers and misadventures he encounters . . . make for compelling reading." Booklist

Hemphill, Michael

Stonewall Hinkleman and the Battle of Bull Run; [by] Michael Hemphill and Sam Riddleburger. Dial Books for Young Readers 2009 168p $16.99

Grades: 4 5 6   **Fic**

1. Time travel -- Fiction 2. Young adult literature -- Works 3. Bull Run, 1st Battle of, 1861 -- Fiction 4. Children's literature -- Works -- Grades two through six

ISBN 978-0-8037-3179-0; 0-8037-3179-5

LC 2008-15795

While participating in a reenactment of the Battle of Bull Run, twelve-year-old Stonewall Hinkleman is transported back to the actual Civil War battle by means of a magic bugle.

This is a "well-paced time-travel novel. . . . Stonewall is a likable character whose attitude changes for the better in the story. . . . A good choice for historical fiction fans." SLJ

Henham, R. D.

The **red** dragon codex. Mirrorstone 2008 244p il map (Dragon condices) pa $9.95

Grades: 4 5 6   **Fic**

1. Fantasy fiction 2. Dragons -- Fiction

ISBN 978-0-7869-4925-0 pa; 0-7869-4925-2 pa

LC 2007014679

Mudd must seek a silver dragon's help to rescue Shemnara, an old woman who is practically his mother, when she is kidnapped by a red dragon.

"Inventive details, dimensional characterizations, and fast-paced action make this a good introduction to the fantasy genre." Booklist

Henkes, Kevin

★ **Bird** Lake moon. Greenwillow Books 2008 179p $15.99; lib bdg $16.89; pa $5.99

Grades: 4 5 6 7   **Fic**

1. Lakes -- Fiction 2. Divorce -- Fiction 3. Friendship -- Fiction 4. Bereavement -- Fiction 5. Family life --

Fiction 6. Young adult literature -- Works

ISBN 978-0-06-147076-9; 0-06-147076-7; 978-0-06-147078-3 lib bdg; 0-06-147078-3 lib bdg; 978-0-06-147079-0 pa; 0-06-147079-1 pa

LC 2007-36564

Twelve-year-old Mitch and his mother are spending the summer with his grandparents at Bird Lake after his parents separate, and ten-year-old Spencer and his family have returned to the lake where Spencer's little brother drowned long ago, and as the boys become friends and spend time together, each of them begins to heal

"Characters are gently and believably developed as the story weaves in and around the beautiful Wisconsin setting. The superbly crafted plot moves smoothly and unhurriedly, mirroring a slow summer pace." SLJ

★ **Olive's** ocean. Greenwillow Bks. 2003 217p $15.99; pa $6.99

Grades: 5 6 7 8   **Fic**

1. Family life -- Fiction 2. Grandmothers -- Fiction

ISBN 0-06-053543-1; 0-06-053545-8 pa

LC 2002-29782

A Newbery Medal honor book, 2004

On a summer visit to her grandmother's cottage by the ocean, twelve-year-old Martha gains perspective on the death of a classmate, on her relationship with her grandmother, on her feelings for an older boy, and on her plans to be a writer.

"Rich characterizations move this compelling novel to its satisfying and emotionally authentic conclusion." SLJ

★ **Protecting** Marie. Greenwillow Bks. 1995 195p $18.99; pa $5.99

Grades: 5 6 7 8   **Fic**

1. Dogs -- Fiction 2. Young adult literature -- Works 3. Father-daughter relationship -- Fiction 4. Children's literature -- Works -- Grades two through six

ISBN 0-688-13958-2; 0-06-053545-8 pa

LC 94-16387

Relates twelve-year-old Fanny's love-hate relationship with her father, a temperamental artist, who has given Fanny a new dog

"The characters ring heartbreakingly true in this quiet, wise story; they are complex and difficult—like all of us—and worthy of our attention." Horn Book

★ **Sun** & Spoon. Greenwillow Bks. 1997 135p $15.99; pa $5.99

Grades: 4 5 6 7   **Fic**

1. Death -- Fiction 2. Grandmothers -- Fiction

ISBN 0-688-15232-5; 0-06-128875-6 pa

LC 96-46259

"Sensitively placed metaphors enrich the narrative, embuing its perceptive depictions of grief with a powerful message of affirmation." Publ Wkly

Words of stone. Greenwillow Bks. 1992 152p $18.99; pa $6.99

Grades: 5 6 7 8   **Fic**

1. Friendship -- Fiction 2. Young adult literature -- Works

ISBN 0-688-11356-7; 0-06-078230-7 pa

LC 91-28543

Busy trying to deal with his many fears and his troubled feelings for his dead mother, ten-year-old Blaze has his life changed when he meets the boisterous and irresistible Joselle

"A story rich in characterization, dramatic subplots, and some very creepy moments." SLJ

★ The **birthday** room. Greenwillow Bks. 1999 152p $15.99; pa $5.99

Grades: 5 6 7 8   **Fic**

1. Uncles 2. Artists 3. Family life 4. Self-acceptance 5. Uncles -- Fiction 6. Family life -- Fiction

ISBN 0-688-16733-0; 0-06-443828-7 pa

LC 98-39887

"Told in spare, unobtrusive prose, a story that helps us see our own chances for benefiting from mutual tolerance, creative conflict resolution, and other forms of good will." Horn Book

The **year** of Billy Miller; by Kevin Henkes. 1st ed. Harpercollins Childrens Books 2013 240 p. (hardcover) $16.99; (library) $17.89

Grades: 2 3 4 5   **Fic**

1. Siblings -- Juvenile fiction 2. School stories -- Juvenile fiction 3. Parent-child relationship -- Juvenile fiction 4. Humorous stories 5. Schools -- Fiction 6. Family life -- Wisconsin -- Fiction

ISBN 0062268120; 9780062268129; 9780062268136

LC 2012050373

This book follows second-grader Billy Miller. It's the "year of several dilemmas for the boy, including the fear he might 'start forgetting things' due to bumping his head while on vacation over the summer. Then there's the habitat diorama that Billy is assigned—the bat cave he creates doesn't turn out quite like he'd hoped." His relationships with his teacher, father, mother, and sister are examined. (Publishers Weekly)

Henry, Marguerite

Brighty of the Grand Canyon; illustrated by Wesley Dennis. Macmillan 1991 222p il hardcover o.p. pa $3.95

Grades: 4 5 6 7   **Fic**

1. Donkeys -- Fiction

ISBN 0-02-743664-0; 0-689-71485-8 pa

LC 90-28636

First published 1953 by Rand McNally

"Only those who are unfamiliar with the West would say it is too packed with drama to be true. And the author's understanding warmth for all of God's creatures still shines through her superb ability as a story teller making this a vivid tale." Christ Sci Monit

★ **King** of the wind; illustrated by Wesley Dennis. Macmillan 1991 172p il $18.95; pa $5.99

Grades: 4 5 6 7   **Fic**

1. Horses -- Fiction

ISBN 0-02-743629-2; 0-689-71486-6 pa

LC 91-13474

A reissue of the title first published 1948 by Rand McNally

Awarded the Newbery Medal, 1949

"A beautiful, sympathetic story of the famous [ancestor of a line of great thoroughbred horses] . . . and the little mute Arabian stable boy who accompanies him on his journey across the seas to France and England [in the eighteenth

century]. The lad's fierce devotion to his horse and his great faith and loyalty are skillfully woven into an enthralling tale which children will long remember. The moving quality of the writing is reflected in the handsome illustrations." Wis Libr Bull

★ **Misty** of Chincoteague; illustrated by Wesley Dennis. Macmillan 1991 173p il hardcover o.p. pa $5.99

Grades: 4 5 6 7   **Fic**

1. Horses -- Fiction

ISBN 0-02-743622-5; 1-4169-2783-2 pa

LC 90-27237

First published 1947 by Rand McNally

A Newbery Medal honor book, 1948

"The beauty and pride of the wild horses is the highpoint in the story, and skillful drawings of them reveal their grace and swiftness." Ont Libr Rev

Other titles about the ponies of Chincoteague Island are:

Sea star, orphan of Chincoteague (1949)

Stormy, Misty's foal (1963)

Herlong, M.H.

Buddy; by M. H. Herlong. Viking Childrens Books 2012 p. cm.

Grades: 4 5 6   **Fic**

1. Dogs -- Juvenile fiction 2. Pets -- Juvenile fiction 3. Hurricane Katrina, 2005 -- Fiction 4. Dogs -- Fiction 5. African Americans -- Fiction 6. Family life -- Louisiana -- Fiction 7. Lost and found possessions -- Fiction

ISBN 9780670014033

LC 2011042854

This book tells the story of Li'l T Roberts, who "meets Buddy when his family's car accidentally hits the stray dog. . . . Buddy turns out to be the dog Li'l T's always wished for--until Hurricane Katrina comes to New Orleans and he must leave Buddy behind. . . . But Li'l T refuses to give up his quest to find his best friend." (Publisher's Note)

Hermes, Patricia

Emma Dilemma and the new nanny. Marshall Cavendish 2006 106p il $15.95

Grades: 2 3 4   **Fic**

1. Family life -- Fiction

ISBN 0-7614-5286-9; 978-0-7614-5286-7

LC 2005024668

Emma tries to help her parents understand that, although their beloved new nanny has made a few mistakes, no one can behave perfectly responsibly all the time

"The tumult in a family with five preteen children, several pets, and two working parents provides a lively setting, and the author lightly but effectively conveys the ideas that adults aren't perfect and that admitting mistakes is often the first step toward solutions that leave everyone pleased." Booklist

Other titles about Emma are:

Emma Dilemma and the two nannies (2007)

Emma Dilemma and the soccer nanny (2008)

Emma Dilemma and the camping nanny (2009)

Emma Dilemma, the nanny, and the secret ferret (2010)

Emma Dilemma, the nanny, and the best horse ever (2011)

Herrick, Steven

Naked bunyip dancing; pictures by Beth Norling. Front Street 2008 201p il $16.95

Grades: 3 4 5 6　　　　　　　　　　　　Fic

1. School stories 2. Novels in verse 3. Teachers -- Fiction

ISBN 978-1-59078-499-0

LC 2007-18353

First published 2005 in Australia

This novel in verse follows the school year of Australian students in classroom 6C, as their unconventional teacher encourages them to discover their own strengths and talents and perform in a memorable concert. "The novel captures the humor and unpredictability of 11 and 12-year-olds. . . . The terse free verse, in short clear lines, is easily accessible. Funny, with some touches of poignancy. . . . The childlike, black-and-white illustrations are reminiscent of the drawings of Shel Silverstein and complement the narrative." SLJ

Hesse, Karen

★ **Brooklyn** Bridge; a novel. Feiwel and Friends 2008 229p il map $17.95

Grades: 5 6 7 8 9 10　　　　　　　　　Fic

1. Immigrants -- Fiction 2. Family life -- Fiction 3. Social classes -- Fiction 4. Homeless persons -- Fiction 5. Russian Americans -- Fiction 6. Young adult literature -- Works

ISBN 978-0-312-37886-8; 0-312-37886-6

LC 2008-05624

In 1903 Brooklyn, fourteen-year-old Joseph Michtom's life changes for the worse when his parents, Russian immigrants, invent the teddy bear and turn their apartment into a factory, while nearby the glitter of Coney Island contrasts with the dismal lives of children dwelling under the Brooklyn Bridge.

Hesse "applies her gift for narrative voice to this memorable story. . . . The novel explodes with dark drama before its eerie but moving resolution." Publ Wkly

★ **Letters** from Rifka. Holt & Co. 1992 148p $16.95; pa $6.99

Grades: 5 6 7 8　　　　　　　　　　　　Fic

1. Jews -- Fiction 2. Letters -- Fiction 3. Immigrants -- Fiction 4. Young adult literature -- Works

ISBN 0-8050-1964-2; 0-312-53561-9 pa

LC 91-48007

In letters to her cousin, Rifka, a young Jewish girl, chronicles her family's flight from Russia in 1919 and her own experiences when she must be left in Belgium for a while when the others emigrate to America

"Based on the true story of the author's great-aunt, the moving account of a brave young girl's story brings to life the day-to-day trials and horrors experienced by many immigrants as well as the resourcefulness and strength they found within themselves." Horn Book

★ **Out** of the dust. Scholastic 1997 227p $16.95; pa $6.99

Grades: 5 6 7 8　　　　　　　　　　　　Fic

1. Novels in verse 2. Farm life -- Fiction 3. Dust storms -- Fiction 4. Young adult literature -- Works 5. Great Depression, 1929-1939 -- Fiction

ISBN 0-590-36080-9; 0-590-37125-8 pa

LC 96-40344

Awarded the Newbery Medal, 1998

"Hesse's writing transcends the gloom and transforms it into a powerfully compelling tale of a girl with enormous strength, courage, and love. The entire novel is written in very readable blank verse." Booklist

Stowaway; with drawings by Robert Andrew Parker. Margaret K. McElderry Bks. 2000 319p il $17.95; pa $6.99

Grades: 5 6 7 8　　　　　　　　　　　　Fic

1. Diaries 2. Explorers 3. Sea stories 4. Voyages around the world 5. Naval officers 6. Travel writers 7. Voyages around the world -- Fiction

ISBN 0-689-83987-1; 0-689-83989-8 pa

LC 00-56976

A fictional journal relates the experiences of Nicholas, a young stowaway, from 1768 to 1771 aboard the Endeavor which sailed around the world under Captain James Cook

"Hesse is a master storyteller who gives Nicholas an authentic voice. . . . The author's subtle yet thorough attention to detail creates a memorable tale that is a virtual encyclopedia of life in the days when England ruled the seas." SLJ

★ **Witness**. Scholastic Press 2001 161p $16.95; pa $5.99

Grades: 6 7 8 9　　　　　　　　　　　　Fic

1. Prejudices 2. Novels in verse 3. Ku Klux Klan 4. Prejudices -- Fiction

ISBN 0-439-27199-1; 0-439-27200-9 pa

LC 00-54139

A series of poems express the views of eleven people in a small Vermont town, including a young black girl and a young Jewish girl, during the early 1920s when the Ku Klux Klan is trying to infiltrate the town

"The story is divided into five acts, and would lend itself beautifully to performance. The plot unfolds smoothly, and the author creates multidimensional characters." SLJ

Hest, Amy

★ **Remembering** Mrs. Rossi; [illustrated by] Heather Maione. Candlewick Press 2007 184p il $14.99; pa $6.99

Grades: 3 4 5　　　　　　　　　　　　Fic

1. Death -- Fiction 2. Mothers -- Fiction 3. Teachers -- Fiction 4. Father-daughter relationship -- Fiction

ISBN 978-0-7636-2163-6; 0-7636-2163-3; 978-0-7636-4089-7 pa

LC 2006-41649

Although she loves her father, their home in New York City, and third-grade teacher Miss Meadows, Annie misses her mother who died recently

"Hest imbues her characters with warmth, humor, and realistic imperfections. . . . Maione's ink sketches highlight the tender affections." Booklist

Hiaasen, Carl

★ **Flush**. Knopf 2005 263p $16.95; lib bdg $18.99; pa $8.99

Grades: 5 6 7 8　　　　　　　　　　　　Fic

1. Boats and boating -- Fiction 2. Young adult literature -- Works 3. Environmental protection -- Fiction

ISBN 0-375-82182-1; 0-375-92182-6 lib bdg; 0-375-84185-7 pa

LC 2005-05259

With their father jailed for sinking a river boat, Noah Underwood and his younger sister, Abbey, must gather evidence that the owner of this floating casino is emptying his bilge tanks into the protected waters around their Florida Keys home

"This quick-reading, fun, family adventure harkens back to the Hardy Boys in its simplicity and quirky characters." SLJ

★ **Hoot**. Knopf 2002 292p $15.95; pa $8.95

Grades: 5 6 7 8   Fic
1. Owls -- Fiction 2. Environmental protection -- Fiction
ISBN 0-375-82181-3; 0-375-82916-4 pa
                                        LC 2002-25478
A Newbery Medal honor book, 2003
Roy, who is new to his small Florida community, becomes involved in another boy's attempt to save a colony of burrowing owls from a proposed construction site

"The story is full of offbeat humor, buffoonish yet charming supporting characters, and genuinely touching scenes of children enjoying the wildness of nature." Booklist

★ **Scat**. Knopf 2009 371p $16.99; lib bdg $19.99; pa $8.99

Grades: 5 6 7 8   Fic
1. Teachers -- Fiction 2. Missing persons -- Fiction 3. Young adult literature -- Works 4. Wildlife conservation -- Fiction
ISBN 978-0-375-83486-8; 0-375-83486-9; 978-0-375-93486-5 lib bdg; 0-375-93486-3 lib bdg; 978-0-375-83487-5 pa; 0-375-83487-7 pa
                                        LC 2008-28266
Nick and his friend Marta decide to investigate when a mysterious fire starts near a Florida wildlife preserve and an unpopular teacher goes missing.

"Once again, Hiaasen has written an edge-of-the-seat eco-thriller. . . . From the first sentence, readers will be hooked. . . . This well-written and smoothly plotted story, with fully realized characters, will certainly appeal to mystery lovers." SLJ

Hicks, Betty
    Basketball Bats; illustrated by Adam McCauley. Roaring Brook Press 2008 55p il (Gym shorts) $15.95
Grades: 2 3 4   Fic
1. Basketball -- Fiction
ISBN 978-1-59643-243-7; 1-59643-243-8
                                        LC 2007-019501
Henry and his basketball teammates, the Bats, take on the Tigers, and Henry learns a lesson about working as a team.

"Hicks finds just the right balance between story line, play-by-play action, and wry humor. . . . Nearly every double-page spread includes a droll illustration by McCauley, the illustrator of Scieszka's Time Warp Trio series." Booklist
Other titles in this series are:
Goof-off goalie (2008)
Swimming with sharks (2008)
Scaredy-cat catcher (2009)
Track attack (2009)
Doubles troubles (2010)

Doubles troubles; illustrated by Simon Gane. Roaring Brook Press 55p il (Gym shorts) $15.99
Grades: 2 3 4   Fic
1. Tennis -- Fiction 2. Friendship -- Fiction
ISBN 978-1-5964-3489-9; 1-5964-3489-9
"This offers useful life lessons within a story in which . . . friends share a love of sports and a bond of friendship that weathers some realistic trials. Attractive line drawings enhance the appeal of this beginning chapter book." Booklist

Goof -off goalie; [by] Betty Hicks; illustrated by Adam McCauley. 1st ed.; Roaring Brook Press 2008 54p il (Gym shorts) $15.95
Grades: 2 3 4   Fic
1. Soccer -- Fiction 2. Friendship -- Fiction
ISBN 978-1-59643-244-4; 1-59643-244-6
                                        LC 2007015223
Ten-year-old Goose is best at goofing off, but when he decides to become the goalie for their soccer team, his friend Henry sets up a practice schedule and enlists their other friends to help Goose improve his skills.

"McCauley's illustrations have a childlike quality. . . . [This is] ideal for easy chapter-book readers." SLJ

★ **Out** of order. Roaring Brook Press 2005 169p $15.95; pa $6.99
Grades: 4 5 6   Fic
1. Stepfamilies -- Fiction 2. Young adult literature -- Works 3. Children's literature -- Works -- Grades two through six
ISBN 1-59643-061-3; 0-312-37355-4 pa
                                        LC 2004-30107
Four youngsters, ages nine to fifteen, narrate one side of the story of their newly blended family's adjustment, interwoven with grief and loss.

"Hicks provides readers with a fresh look at blended families, offering much food for thought and several multi-layered characters." SLJ

Scaredy -cat catcher; illustrated by Adam McCauley. Roaring Brook Press 2009 55p il (Gym shorts) $16.95
Grades: 2 3 4   Fic
1. Fear -- Fiction 2. Baseball -- Fiction
ISBN 978-1-59643-246-8; 1-59643-246-2
When Rocky, a talented catcher who was injured during the previous baseball season by an out-of-control runner, develops a reflex that keeps him from tagging the runner out, Rocky's friends—and his dog Chops—help him overcome his fear.

"The fast-moving plot, straightforward writing style, and illustrations on every spread make this selection ideal for students new to chapter books and for reluctant readers, as well as fans of the previous titles in the series." SLJ

Swimming with Sharks; illustrated by Adam McCauley. Roaring Brook Press 2008 55p il (Gym shorts) $15.95
Grades: 2 3 4   Fic
1. Swimming -- Fiction 2. Friendship -- Fiction 3. Children's literature -- Works -- Grades two through six
ISBN 978-1-59643-245-1; 1-59643-245-4
                                        LC 2008-11126
Rita tries to improve her times and flip turns as she struggles to decide whether to remain the best swimmer on the

Dolphins team or the worst on the Sharks team, where she could be with her friends.

"Lively black-and-white illustrations . . . add humor and provide ample visual cues on each spread, helping the new reader gain confidence with chapter books." Horn Book

Other titles in this series are:

Goof-off goalie (2008)

Scaredy-cat catcher (2009)

Track attack. Roaring Brook Press 2009 55p il (Gym shorts) $15.99

Grades: 2 3 4   **Fic**

1. Track athletics -- Fiction   2. Father-daughter relationship -- Fiction

ISBN 978-1-59643-488-2; 1-59643-488-0

Jazz loves running sprints on her track team. Her dad loves that she's on the team too, but his enthusiasm is taking all the fun out of running.

"Many expressive black-and-white pictures illustrate this solid addition to the Gym Shorts series." Booklist

The **worm** whisperer; Betty Hicks; illustrated by Ben Hatke. Roaring Brook Press 2012 192 p. (hardcover) $16.99

Grades: 4 5 6   **Fic**

1. Picture books for children 2. Caterpillars -- Juvenile fiction 3. Human-animal communication -- Juvenile fiction 4. Worms -- Fiction 5. Racing -- Fiction 6. Insects -- Fiction 7. Human-animal communication -- Fiction

ISBN 1596434902; 9781596434905; 9781596438460

LC 2012013790

In this children's book by Betty Hicks, illustrated by Ben Hatke, "Ellis Coffey loves animals. He spends so much time outdoors that sometimes he thinks he can talk with them. When he discovers a caterpillar that seems to follow his directions, he knows he has a chance to win the annual Woolly Worm race. The prize money is $1,000—exactly the amount of the deductible for his dad's back surgery." (Publisher's note)

Higgins, F. E.

★ The **Black** Book of Secrets. Feiwel and Friends 2007 273p $14.95

Grades: 4 5 6 7   **Fic**

1. Apprentices -- Fiction 2. Pawnbrokers -- Fiction 3. Young adult literature -- Works

ISBN 978-0-312-36844-9; 0-312-36844-5

LC 2007-32559

When Ludlow Fitch runs away from his thieving parents in the City, he meets up with the mysterious Joe Zabbidou, who calls himself a secret pawnbroker, and who takes Ludlow as an apprentice to record the confessions of the townspeople of Pagus Parvus, where resentments are many and trust is scarce.

This is "an intriguing blend of adventure and historical fiction spiced with a light touch of the fantastic." Voice Youth Advocates

The **bone** magician. Feiwel and Friends 2008 272p $14.95

Grades: 4 5 6 7   **Fic**

1. Mystery fiction 2. Magicians -- Fiction 3. Young adult literature -- Works 4. Undertakers and undertaking -- Fiction

ISBN 978-0-312-36845-6; 0-312-36845-3

LC 2008-6777

With his father, a fugitive, falsely accused of multiple murders and the real serial killer stalking the wretched streets of Urbs Umida, Pin Carpue, a young undertaker's assistant, investigates and soon discovers that all of the victims may have attended the performance of a stage magician who claims to be able to raise corpses and make the dead speak.

This offers "no end of picaresque charms, creepy turns, and beguiling cast members." Booklist

Higgins, Simon

Moonshadow; rise of the ninja. Little Brown & Co. 2010 325p il $15.99

Grades: 4 5 6 7   **Fic**

1. Ninja -- Fiction 2. Spies -- Fiction 3. Secret societies -- Fiction

ISBN 978-0-316-05531-4; 0-316-05531-X

First published 2008 in Australia with title: Moonshadow: eye of the beast

It's the dawn of an age of peace in medieval Japan. But a power-hungry warlord is plotting to plunge the national into a deadly civil war. Enter Moonshadow, the newest agent for the Grey Light Order, a secret brotherhood of ninja spy warriors. Can Moonshadow defeat the evil warlord or will his first mission be his last?

"The swordplay is fast and furious, and Japanese terms and places are integrated in a manner that reluctant readers will find accessible. This adventure is part spy novel, part magic, and all fun." SLJ

The **nightmare** ninja. Little, Brown 2011 368p (Moonshadow) $15.99

Grades: 4 5 6 7   **Fic**

1. Ninja -- Fiction 2. Orphans -- Fiction 3. Supernatural -- Fiction

ISBN 978-0-316-05533-8; 0-316-05533-6

LC 2010043177

Battling a power-hungry warlord in medieval Japan, teenaged Moonshadow, an orphaned ninja in the shogun's secret service with the ability to see through the eyes of animals, encounters a weaponless assassin who enters the mind of his victims during their sleep.

"Higgins effectively uses this work to set the stage for a compelling third installment." Kirkus

Hill, Kirkpatrick

Bo at Ballard Creek; Kirkpatrick Hill; illustrated by LeUyen Pham. Henry Holt and Co. 2013 288 p. (hardcover) $15.99

Grades: 2 3 4   **Fic**

1. Historical fiction 2. Adopted children -- Fiction 3. Eskimos -- Fiction 4. Fathers -- Fiction 5. Adoption -- Fiction

ISBN 0805093516; 9780805093513

LC 2012046055

In this historical novel, "Bo, a 5-year-old girl, was adopted as a newborn by two gruff but tenderhearted blacksmiths who've toiled in the mining camps of the Yukon for years. These unlikely fathers smoke a bit and swear a bit, but they love Bo with all their hearts. Theirs is an extraordinarily generous, solicitous, close-knit community, comprised of

indigenous neighbors and workers from around the world."
(Kirkus)

The **year** of Miss Agnes. Margaret K. McElderry Bks.
2000 115p $16; pa $5.99

Grades: 3 4 5   **Fic**
1. Schools 2. Teachers 3. School stories 4. Athapascan
Indians 5. Teachers -- Fiction 6. Athapascan Indians
-- Fiction 7. Indians of North America -- Alaska
ISBN 0-689-82933-7; 0-689-85124-3 pa

LC 99-46912

Ten-year-old Fred (short for Frederika) narrates the story
of school and village life among the Athapascans in Alaska
during 1948 when Miss Agnes arrived as the new teacher

"Hill has created more than just an appealing cast of
characters; she introduces readers to a whole community
and makes a long-ago and faraway place seem real and very
much alive. This is an inspirational story." SLJ

Hilmo, Tess
★ **With** a name like Love. Margaret Ferguson Books/
Farrar Straus Giroux 2011 249p $16.99

Grades: 5 6 7 8   **Fic**
1. Mystery fiction 2. Country life -- Fiction 3. Christian
life -- Fiction 4. Conduct of life -- Fiction
ISBN 978-0-374-38465-4; 0-374-38465-7

LC 2010036314

Thirteen-year-old Olivene Love gets tangled up in a
murder mystery when her itinerant preaching family arrives
in the small town of Binder, Arkansas in 1957.

"Hilmo creates a family, town and a mystery that readers
won't soon forget." Kirkus

Hines-Stephens, Sarah
Midway monkey madness; illustrated by Art Baltazar;
Superman created by Jerry Siegel and Joe Shuster. Picture
Window Books 2011 48p il (DC super-pets!) lib bdg
$22.65; pa $4.95

Grades: 1 2 3   **Fic**
1. Monkeys -- Fiction 2. Gorillas -- Fiction 3.
Chimpanzees -- Fiction 4. Superheroes -- Fiction
ISBN 978-1-4048-6305-7 lib bdg; 1-4048-6305-2 lib
bdg; 978-1-4048-6619-5 pa; 1-4048-6619-1 pa

LC 2010036775

"Beppo the Super-Monkey battles Gorilla Grodd when
Bazooka's Carnival comes to Metropolis. A day of fun turns
into a nightmare when the evil ape starts opening cages,
freeing wild beasts and terrorizing humans. Beppo saves the
day, aided by the Wonder Twins, Jayna and Zan, and Gleek,
their space chimp. [The book is] full of action, including
colorful graphics within the text, reminiscent of the old live-
action Batman TV show. [The] title has a colorful spread
in the heat of the action. [A] solid [introduction] to comic-
book-style writing." SLJ

Hirahara, Naomi
1001 cranes. Delacorte Press 2008 230p $15.99; lib
bdg $18.99; pa $6.50

Grades: 5 6 7 8   **Fic**
1. Family life -- Fiction 2. Grandparents -- Fiction 3.
Japanese Americans -- Fiction 4. Young adult literature

-- Works
ISBN 978-0-385-73556-8; 0-385-73556-1; 978-0-385-
90541-1 lib bdg; 0-385-90541-6 lib bdg; 978-0-440-
42234-1 pa; 0-440-42234-5 pa

LC 2007-27655

With her parents on the verge of separating, Angela, a
twelve-year-old Japanese American girl, spends the summer in Los Angeles with her grandparents, where she folds
paper cranes into wedding displays, becomes involved with
a young skateboarder, and learns how complicated relationships can be.

Angela's "colorful, bold voice captures the excitement
of her first love as well as the anxiety of not understanding
the many secrets of the adults around her. By experiencing
her family's support, by learning about her Japanese heritage, and by acknowledging the various ways that love is expressed, Angela emerges into a strong, caring person." SLJ

Hiranandani, Veera
★ The **whole** story of half a girl. Delacorte Press 2012
$16.99; lib bdg $19.99

Grades: 4 5 6 7   **Fic**
1. School stories 2. East Indian Americans -- Fiction
3. Racially mixed people -- Fiction 4. Depression
(Psychology) -- Fiction
ISBN 978-0-385-74128-6; 0-385-74128-6; 978-0-375-
98995-7 lib bdg; 0-375-98995-1 lib bdg; 978-0-375-
98441-9 ebook

LC 2011026178

In this book, "[w]hen Sonia's father loses his job at the
end of her fifth-grade year, it means she can't return to her
beloved private school and instead must navigate the rocky
waters of public school for the first time. Up until this point,
eleven-year-old Sonia has never thought that much about her
identity as the daughter of an Indian father and a Jewish-
American mother, but she is suddenly faced with questions
that she can't always answer about her race, her ethnicity,
and her core values. She . . . begins two friendships: with
Kate, a very perky, popular girl who encourages Sonia to
try out for cheerleading but seems very keen on transforming her into something she isn't, and with Alisha, who, like
Sonia, aspires to be a writer." (Bulletin of the Center for
Children's Books).

"Sonia's struggles are painfully realistic. . . True to life,
her problems do not wrap up neatly, but Sonia's growth is
deeply rewarding in this thoughtful and beautifully wrought
novel." Publ Wkly

Hirsch, Odo
Darius Bell and the glitter pool. Kane/Miller 2010
214p $15.99

Grades: 4 5 6 7   **Fic**
1. Gifts -- Fiction 2. Poverty -- Fiction
ISBN 978-1-935279-65-5; 1-935279-65-3
First published 2009 in Australia

The Bell family's ancestors were showered with hon-
ours, gifts and grants of land. In exchange, they have bestowed a Gift, once every 25 years, on the town. Now it's
Darius's father's turn and there is no money for an impressive gift. When an earthquake reveals a glorious cave, with
the most beautiful minerals lining the walls, he thinks he's
found the answer.

"With an inventive cast of characters and a surprise twist at the end, this gentle, appealing story would make a terrific read-aloud for a young audience." Booklist

Hitchcock, Shannon

The **ballad** of Jessie Pearl; Shannon Hitchcock. 1st ed. Namelos llc 2012 131 p. ill. (hardcover) $18.95

Grades: 5 6 7 8   **Fic**

1. Love stories 2. Historical fiction 3. Tuberculosis -- Fiction

ISBN 160898141X; 9781608981410; 9781608981427

LC 2012936706

In this novel, by Shannon Hitchcock, "it's 1922, and Jessie has big plans for her future, but that's before tuberculosis strikes. Though she has no talent for cooking, cleaning, or nursing, Jessie puts her dreams on hold to help her family. She falls in love for the first time ever, and suddenly what she wants is not so simple anymore." (Publisher's note)

Hobbs, Valerie

Defiance. Farrar, Straus and Giroux 2005 116p $16; pa $7.99

Grades: 5 6 7 8   **Fic**

1. Death -- Fiction 2. Cancer -- Fiction 3. Country life -- Fiction 4. Young adult literature -- Works 5. Children's literature -- Works -- Grades two through six

ISBN 0-374-30847-0; 0-312-53581-3 pa

LC 2004-61524

While vacationing in the country, eleven-year-old Toby, a cancer patient, learns some important lessons about living and dying from an elderly poet and her cow.

"Spare, graceful writing, with just enough detail to bring the characters and setting to life, skillfully paces the action and keeps the focus on Toby's conflicted feelings. . . . A quiet, yet resonant story." SLJ

Maggie and Oliver, or, A bone of one's own; art by Jennifer Thermes. Henry Holt and Company 2011 181p il $15.99

Grades: 4 5 6   **Fic**

1. Dogs -- Fiction 2. Orphans -- Fiction 3. Poverty -- Fiction 4. Homeless persons -- Fiction

ISBN 978-0-8050-9294-3; 0-8050-9294-3

LC 2011005791

A dog whose beloved owner has died and an orphaned ten-year-old girl find each other while enduring poverty and homelessness in early-twentieth-century Boston.

"Thermes' black-and-white illustrations quietly match both tone and period. A touching and emotionally satisfying foundling tale." Kirkus

★ The **last** best days of summer. Frances Foster Books 2010 197p $16.99

Grades: 5 6 7 8   **Fic**

1. Artists -- Fiction 2. Old age -- Fiction 3. Popularity -- Fiction 4. Grandmothers -- Fiction 5. Down syndrome -- Fiction 6. Young adult literature -- Works 7. Children's literature -- Works -- Grades two through six

ISBN 978-0-374-34670-6; 0-374-34670-4

LC 2008-47145

During a summer visit, twelve-year-old Lucy must come to terms with both her grandmother's failing memory and how her mentally-challenged neighbor will impact her popularity when both enter the same middle school in the fall.

"The story's finely tuned realism is refreshing, particularly in Lucy's yearning for social acceptance and in the fully drawn and wholly memorable characters." Booklist

Hobbs, Will

Crossing the wire. HarperCollins 2006 216p $15.99; lib bdg $16.89; pa $5.99

Grades: 5 6 7 8   **Fic**

1. Mexicans -- Fiction 2. Illegal aliens -- Fiction 3. Young adult literature -- Works

ISBN 978-0-06-074138-9; 0-06-074138-4; 978-0-06-074139-6 lib bdg; 0-06-074139-2 lib bdg; 978-0-06-074140-2 pa; 0-06-074140-6 pa

LC 2005-19697

Fifteen-year-old Victor Flores journeys north in a desperate attempt to cross the Arizona border and find work in the United States to support his family in central Mexico.

This is "an exciting story in a vital contemporary setting." Voice Youth Advocates

★ **Jason's** gold. Morrow Junior Bks. 1999 221p $16.99; pa $5.99

Grades: 5 6 7 8   **Fic**

1. Orphans -- Fiction 2. Voyages and travels -- Fiction 3. Klondike River Valley (Yukon) -- Gold discoveries -- Fiction 4. Klondike River Valley (Yukon) -- Gold discoveries -- Juvenile fiction

ISBN 0-688-15093-4; 0-380-72914-8 pa

LC 99-17973

When news of the discovery of gold in Canada's Yukon Territory in 1897 reaches fifteen-year-old Jason, he embarks on a 10,000-mile journey to strike it rich

"The successful presentation of a fascinating era, coupled with plenty of action, makes this a good historical fiction choice." SLJ

Never say die; by Will Hobbs. HarperCollins Children's Books 2012 224 p. (trade bdg.) $16.99

Grades: 4 5 6 7   **Fic**

1. Canada -- Fiction 2. Wilderness survival -- Fiction 3. Adventure fiction -- Juvenile fiction 4. Bears -- Fiction 5. Caribou -- Fiction 6. Eskimos -- Fiction 7. Brothers -- Fiction 8. Inuit -- Canada -- Fiction 9. Photojournalism -- Fiction 10. Climatic changes -- Fiction 11. Adventure and adventurers -- Fiction

ISBN 006170878X; 9780061708787; 9780061708794

LC 2011053289

This juvenile adventure novel, by Will Hobbs, is set "in Canada's Arctic, [where] Nick Thrasher is an accomplished Inuit hunter at fifteen. . . . Ryan Powers . . . invites Nick to come along and help him find the caribou. Barely down the river, disaster strikes. . . . With nothing but the clothes on his back and the knife on his hip, Nick is up against it in a world of wolves, caribou, and grizzlies. All the while, the monstrous grolar bear stalks the land." (Publisher's note)

Take me to the river. HarperCollins 2011 184p $15.99; lib bdg $16.89

Grades: 5 6 7 8   **Fic**

1. Cousins -- Fiction 2. Canoes and canoeing -- Fiction

3. Young adult literature -- Works

ISBN 978-0-06-074144-0; 0-06-074144-9; 978-0-06-074145-7 lib bdg; 0-06-074145-7 lib bdg

LC 2010003147

When North Carolina fourteen-year-old Dylan Sands joins his fifteen-year-old cousin Rio in running the Rio Grande River, they face a tropical storm and a fugitive kidnapper.

"The story unfolds in a disarming manner. The pace is quick, and the challenges are relentless, but the writing is so grounded in physical details and emotional realism that every turn of events seems convincing within the context of the story." Booklist

Hoberman, Mary Ann

★ **Strawberry** Hill; illustrated by Wendy Anderson Halperin. Little, Brown Books for Young Readers 2009 230p il $15.99

Grades: 3 4 5   Fic

1. Moving -- Fiction 2. Friendship -- Fiction 3. Country life -- Fiction 4. Jews -- United States -- Fiction 5. Great Depression, 1929-1939 -- Fiction

ISBN 978-0-316-04136-2; 0-316-04136-X

LC 2008045300

Ten-year-old Allie's family moves from urban New Haven to rural Stamford, Connecticut, in the midst of the Great Depression.

This "is a small yet highly evocative story. . . . [This offers] story lines that are simple but never simplistic and perfectly drafted chapters in which the ordinary has the opportunity to become special." Booklist

Hof, Marjolijn

Against the odds; translated by Johanna H. Prins and Johanna W. Prins. Groundwood Books/House of Anansi Press 2009 125p $17.95

Grades: 3 4 5   Fic

1. War stories 2. Worry -- Fiction 3. Fathers -- Fiction 4. Physicians -- Fiction

ISBN 978-0-88899-935-1; 0-88899-935-6; 978-0-88899-950-4 pa

"Kiki's father is traveling to a war zone as a doctor, and the child and her mother worry that he won't return. As soon as he leaves, Kiki starts planning to increase the odds that he will be safe. . . . The language and writing style are a bit old-fashioned, yet comforting. The story is engaging and gives readers a chance to develop empathy." SLJ

Mother number zero. Groundwood Books 2011 179p $16.95

Grades: 4 5 6 7   Fic

1. Adoption -- Fiction 2. Siblings -- Fiction 3. Family life -- Fiction 4. Children's literature -- Works -- Grades two through six

ISBN 978-1-55498-078-9; 1-55498-078-X

Fay "and his older sister An Bing Wa were both adopted; she was an abandoned baby in China, and he was born to a mother traumatized in the Bosnian conflict. A new girl in the neighborhood, Maud, takes a keen interest in Fay's story and urges him to find his birth mother. . . . Hof . . . writes Fay's narration with a calm, matter-of-fact voice that possesses a literalness and simplicity in keeping with his youth. . . . The story nonetheless treats the characters with quiet percipience. . . . Younger fans of domestic novels who like a tale

with more gravitas if not reading difficulty will appreciate this thoughtful family story." Bull Cent Child Books

Hoffman, Mary

Bravo Grace! illustrations by June Allan. Frances Lincoln Children's Books 2005 112p il $14.95

Grades: 3 4 5   Fic

1. School stories 2. Friendship -- Fiction 3. Stepfamilies -- Fiction 4. African Americans -- Fiction

ISBN 978-1-84507-057-1; 1-84507-057-7

Grace is older now, and she finds lots of changes at home and at school. Mom remarries, and Grace must get used to her new stepdad and to Mom's having a baby. At school, boys and girls spend less time together as friends, though some connect as couples. And Grace deals with a bully and analyzes why her friend is anorexic. As usual Grace turns to her Nana for advice.

"Those familiar with Grace will embrace this continuing story of her life, and new readers will be enchanted with this creative and compassionate African-American girl with quite an entertaining imagination. Hoffman does a fine job with this story about life, love, friendships, and real problems that many children face." SLJ

★ **Starring** Grace; pictures by Caroline Binch. Fogelman Pub. 2000 95p il hardcover o.p. pa $4.99

Grades: 3 4 5   Fic

1. Grandmothers -- Fiction 2. African Americans -- Fiction

ISBN 0-8037-2559-0; 0-14-230022-5 pa

Grace and her friends have all sorts of adventures during their summer vacation—going to the circus, taking an imaginary safari, making friends with an elderly neighbor, pretending to be astronauts, and calling the paramedics when her grandmother has an accident

"Hoffman's text reads easily and is filled with humor and the wide-eyed innocence of young children at play." SLJ

Other chapter-book titles about Grace are:

Bravo Grace! (2005)

Encore Grace! (2003)

Hoffmann, E. T. A.

Nutcracker; pictures by Maurice Sendak; translated by Ralph Manheim. Crown 1984 102p il $40

Grades: 4 5 6 7   Fic

1. Fairy tales 2. Christmas -- Fiction

ISBN 0-609-61049-X

LC 83-25266

"The smooth, elegant, new translation re-creates the flavor of the period and does justice to the story. . . . The occasional quirkiness of the pictures . . . eerily reflect the mysterious story. Altogether a magnificent, splendid combination of talents." Horn Book

Holling, Holling C.

Paddle-to-the-sea; written and illustrated by Holling Clancy Holling. Houghton Mifflin 1941 un il lib bdg $20; pa $11.95

Grades: 4 5 6   Fic

ISBN 0-395-15082-5 lib bdg; 0-395-29203-4 pa

A Caldecott Medal honor book, 1942

A toy canoe with a seated Indian figure is launched in Lake Nipigon by the Indian boy who carved it and in four years travels through all the Great Lakes and the St. Lawrence River to the Atlantic. An interesting picture of the shore life of the lakes and the river with striking full page pictures in bright colors and marginal pencil drawings

"The canoe's journey is used to show the flow of currents and of traffic, and each occurrence is made to seem plausible. . . . There are also diagrams of a sawmill, a freighter, the canal locks at the Soo, and Niagara Falls." Libr J

Holm, Jennifer L.

Game on! by Jennifer and Matthew Holm. 1st ed. Random House 2013 96 p. (Squish) (paperback) $6.99; (library) $12.99

Grades: 2 3 4 5   **Fic**

1. Amoeba -- Fiction 2. Video games -- Graphic novels 3. Graphic novels 4. Superheroes -- Fiction 5. Video games -- Fiction 6. Cartoons and comics -- Fiction

ISBN 0307982998; 9780307982995; 9780307983008

LC 2012016421

In this graphic novel, by Jennifer L. Holm and Matt Holm, "Squish can't get enough of his awesome new video game Mitosis! . . . In fact, he may even be obsessed! He plays at home . . . at school. . . even in his sleep! Are video games taking over Squish's life?! And can Squish's favorite comic book hero, Super Amoeba, stop the Creeping Black Mold that's taking over Small Pond?" (Publisher's note)

★ **Middle** school is worse than meatloaf; a year told through stuff. by Jennifer L. Holm; pictures by Elicia Castaldi. Atheneum Books for Young Readers 2007 un il $12.99

Grades: 5 6 7 8   **Fic**

1. School stories 2. Family life -- Fiction

ISBN 0-689-85281-9

"Ginny Davis begins seventh grade with a list of items to accomplish. This list, along with lots of other 'stuff'—including diary entries, refrigerator notes, cards from Grandpa, and IM screen messages—convey a year full of ups and downs. Digitally rendered collage illustrations realistically depict the various means of communication, and the story flows easily from one colorful page to the next. . . . The story combines honesty and humor to create a believable and appealing voice." SLJ

★ **Our** only May Amelia. HarperCollins Pubs. 1999 253p il hardcover o.p. pa $5.99

Grades: 5 6 7 8   **Fic**

1. Sex role -- Fiction 2. Family life -- Fiction 3. Finnish Americans -- Fiction 4. Brothers and sisters -- Fiction 5. Frontier and pioneer life -- Fiction 6. Frontier and pioneer life -- Washington (State) -- Fiction

ISBN 0-06-027822-6; 0-06-440856-6 pa

LC 98-47504

A Newbery Medal honor book, 2000

As the only girl in a Finnish American family of seven brothers, May Amelia Jackson resents being expected to act like a lady while growing up in Washington State in 1899

"The voice of the colloquial first-person narrative rings true and provides a vivid picture of frontier and pioneer life. . . . An afterword discusses Holm's research into her own family's history and that of other Finnish immigrants." Horn Book Guide

★ **Penny** from heaven. Random House 2006 274p il $15.95; lib bdg $17.99; pa $6.99

Grades: 5 6 7 8   **Fic**

1. Family life -- Fiction 2. Italian Americans -- Fiction 3. Young adult literature -- Works

ISBN 0-375-83687-X; 0-375-93687-4 lib bdg; 0-375-83689-6 pa

LC 2005-13896

A Newbery Medal honor book, 2007

As she turns twelve during the summer of 1953, Penny gains new insights into herself and her family while also learning a secret about her father's death.

"Holm impressively wraps pathos with comedy in this coming-of-age story, populated by a cast of vivid characters." Booklist

★ **Turtle** in paradise. Random House 2010 191p $16.99; lib bdg $19.99

Grades: 3 4 5   **Fic**

1. Adventure fiction 2. Cousins -- Fiction 3. Family life -- Fiction 4. Young adult literature -- Works 5. Great Depression, 1929-1939 -- Fiction

ISBN 978-0-375-83688-6; 0-375-83688-8; 978-0-375-93688-3 lib bdg; 0-375-93688-2 lib bdg

LC 2009-19077

A Newbery Medal honor book, 2011

In 1935, when her mother gets a job housekeeping for a woman who does not like children, eleven-year-old Turtle is sent to stay with relatives she has never met in far away Key West, Florida.

"Holm's voice for Turtle is winning and authentic—that of a practical, clear-eyed observer—and her nimble way with dialogue creates laugh-out-loud moments. Sweet, funny and superb." Kirkus

The **trouble** with May Amelia; illustrated by Adam Gustavson. Atheneum Books for Young Readers 2011 204p il

Grades: 5 6 7 8   **Fic**

1. Sex role -- Fiction 2. Siblings -- Fiction 3. Finnish Americans -- Fiction 4. Frontier and pioneer life -- Fiction

ISBN 1-4169-1373-4; 978-1-4169-1373-3

LC 2010042092

Living with seven brothers and her father, who thinks girls are useless, a thirteen-year-old Finnish American farm girl is determined to prove her worth when a enterprising gentleman tries to purchase their cash-strapped family settlement in Washington State in 1900.

"Holm gets her heroine just right. Narrating events in dryly witty, plainspoken first-person, this indomitable teen draws readers in with her account, through which her world comes alive." Kirkus

Holmes, Sara Lewis

★ **Operation** Yes. Arthur A. Levine Books 2009 234p $16.99

Grades: 5 6 7 8   **Fic**

1. School stories 2. Acting -- Fiction 3. Cousins -- Fiction 4. Teachers -- Fiction 5. Military bases -- Fiction 6. Young adult literature -- Works

ISBN 978-0-545-10795-2; 0-545-10795-4; 978-0-545-10796-9 pa; 0-545-10796-2 pa

LC 2008053732

In her first ever teaching job, Miss Loupe uses improvisational acting exercises with her sixth-grade students at an Air Force base school, and when she experiences a family tragedy, her previously skeptical class members use what they have learned to help her, her brother, and other wounded soldiers

"Quick, funny, sad, full of heart, and irresistibly absorbing." Booklist

Holt, Kimberly Willis

★ **Dancing** in Cadillac light. Putnam 2001 167p hardcover o.p. pa $5.99

Grades: 5 6 7 8   **Fic**

1. Old age 2. Grandfathers 3. Old age -- Fiction 4. Family life -- Texas 5. Grandfathers -- Fiction 6. City and town life -- Texas

ISBN 0-399-23402-0; 0-698-11970-3 pa

LC 00-40267

In 1968, eleven-year-old Jaynell's life in the town of Moon, Texas, is enlivened when her eccentric Grandpap comes to live with her family

"This nostalgic parable about loss and redemption is at once gritty and poetic, stark and sentimental, howlingly funny and depressingly sad, but it is a solid page-turner." SLJ

Piper Reed, Navy brat. Henry Holt 2007 146p il $14.95; pa $6.99

Grades: 3 4 5   **Fic**

1. Moving -- Fiction 2. Family life -- Fiction 3. Children's literature -- Works -- Grades two through six

ISBN 978-0-8050-8197-8; 0-8050-8197-6; 978-0-312-38020-5 pa; 0-312-38020-8 pa

LC 2006-35467

Piper is sad about leaving her home and friends behind when her father, a Navy aircraft mechanic, is transferred yet again, but with help from her often-annoying sisters and a surprise from their parents, she finds happiness in their new home in Pensacola, Florida.

"Holt tells a lively family story. . . . Davenier's occasional black-and-white pictures capture the daily family dramas." Booklist

Other titles about Piper Reed are:

Piper Reed, the great gypsy (2008)

Piper Reed gets a job (2009)

Piper Reed, campfire girl (2011)

★ **When** Zachary Beaver came to town. Holt & Co. 1999 227p $17.99

Grades: 5 6 7 8   **Fic**

1. Obesity 2. Friendship 3. Best friends 4. Obesity -- Fiction 5. Friendship -- Fiction 6. City and town life -- Texas

ISBN 0-8050-6116-9

LC 99-27998

During the summer of 1971 in a small Texas town, thirteen-year-old Toby and his best friend Cal meet the star of a sideshow act, 600-pound Zachary, the fattest boy in the world

"Holt writes with a subtle sense of humor and sensitivity, and reading her work is a delightful experience." Voice Youth Advocates

Holub, Joan

Bed, bats, and beyond; by Joan Holub; illustrated by Mernie Gallagher-Cole. Darby Creek Pub. 2008 64p il $14.95

Grades: 1 2 3   **Fic**

1. Bats -- Fiction 2. Bedtime -- Fiction 3. Storytelling -- Fiction

ISBN 978-1-58196-077-8; 1-58196-077-8

It's dawn and time for bats to go to bed, but Fang's brother Fink can't sleep. Soon the whole family tries different bedtime stories to lull Fink to sleep

"The narrative as a whole feels satisfying. . . . Gallagher-Cole's illustrations add humorous details. . . . With no more than 15 lines per page and illustrations on every spread, the story is ideal for students who have just graduated to chapter books. Charming and full of humor." SLJ

Holyoke, Polly

The **Neptune** Project; Polly Holyoke. 1st ed. Disney-Hyperion Books 2013 352 p. (reinforced) $16.99

Grades: 4 5 6 7   **Fic**

1. Science fiction 2. Ocean -- Fiction 3. Genetic engineering -- Fiction 4. Survival -- Fiction 5. Undersea colonies -- Fiction 6. Environmental degradation -- Fiction

ISBN 1423157567; 9781423157564

LC 2013000353

In this novel, by Polly Holyoke, "Nere . . . is one of a group of kids who . . . have been genetically altered to survive in the ocean. . . . In order to reach the safe haven of the Neptune colony, Nere and her fellow mutates must swim through hundreds of miles of dangerous waters, relying only on their wits, dolphins, and each other to evade terrifying undersea creatures and a government that will stop at nothing to capture the Neptune kids." (Publisher's note)

Hopkins, Karen Leigh

Labracadabra; [by Jessie Nelson & Karen Leigh Hopkins; illustrated by Deborah Melmon] Viking 2011 36p il $14.99

Grades: 1 2 3   **Fic**

1. Dogs -- Fiction 2. Magic -- Fiction 3. Children's literature -- Works -- Grades two through six

ISBN 978-0-670-01251-0; 0-670-01251-3

LC 2010-25109

Zach always wanted a dog but Larry, the full-grown mongrel his parents choose, is not it, however, he soon discovers that there is something very special—even magical—about Larry's tail.

"This early chapter book is a beaut of brevity and pacing. . . . With plenty of illustrations and white space, this five-chapter romp flies along. . . . Transitioning independent readers will enjoy getting to know the unnamed narrator and watching his attitude progress as Larry changes from a 'used dog' to 'my dog.'" Kirkus

Hopkinson, Deborah

Birdie's lighthouse; written by Deborah Hopkinson; illustrated by Kimberly Bulcken Root. Atheneum Bks. for Young Readers 1997 un il hardcover o.p. pa $6.99

Grades: 1 2 3   **Fic**

1. Lighthouses -- Fiction

ISBN 0-689-81052-0; 0-689-83529-9 pa

LC 94-24097

"With an exemplary assemblage of genre paintings perfectly attuned to the flow of the text, the whole is restrained yet charged with emotion." Horn Book

A **boy** called Dickens; Deborah Hopkinson; illustrations by John Hendrix. 1st ed. Schwartz & Wade Books 2012 40 p. col. ill. (hardcover) $17.99; (lib. bdg.) $20.99; (ebook) $17.99

Grades: 4 5 6 **Fic**

1. Authors 2. Child labor 3. Novelists 4. Authors -- Fiction

ISBN 037596732X; 9780375867323; 9780375967320; 9780375987403

LC 2010048531

This book presents an "account of Charles Dickens' boyhood, specifically his tenure wrapping and labeling bottles of boot blacking while his father and family languish in debtors' prison. Here young Charles passes the ten-hour days by regaling a fellow worker with made-up stories, elements of which would later appear in his best-known novels. . . . A closing note comments more fully on autobiographic references in Dicken's work." (Bulletin of the Center for Children's Books)

Into the firestorm; a novel of San Francisco, 1906. Alfred A. Knopf 2006 200p hardcover o.p. pa $5.99

Grades: 5 6 7 8 **Fic**

1. Orphans -- Fiction 2. Earthquakes -- Fiction 3. Children's literature -- Works -- Grades two through six

ISBN 0-375-83652-7; 0-440-42129-2 pa

LC 2005-37189

Days after arriving in San Francisco from Texas, eleven-year-old orphan Nicholas Dray tries to help his new neighbors survive the 1906 San Francisco earthquake and the subsequent fires.

"The terror of the 1906 disaster is brought powerfully alive in this fast-paced tale. . . . Nick is a thoroughly developed protagonist, as are the supporting characters." SLJ

Includes bibliographical references

Horowitz, Anthony

★ **Public** enemy number two; a Diamond brothers mystery. Philomel Books 2004 190p $16.99; pa $5.99

Grades: 5 6 7 8 **Fic**

1. Mystery fiction

ISBN 0-399-24154-X; 0-14-240218-4 pa

LC 2004-10418

When thirteen-year-old Nick is framed for a jewel robbery, he and his brother, the bumbling detective Tim Diamond, attempt to clear his name by capturing the master criminal known as the Fence.

"Horowitz has a knack for puns and humor, and he successfully combines it with a nonstop action mystery that has everything from hydraulically controlled buses to secret caverns. A readable and exciting adventure." SLJ

Other titles in the Diamond Brothers Mystery series are:

The falcon's Maltester (2004)
South by southeast (2005)
Three of Diamonds (2005)
The Greek who stole Christmas (2008)

★ **Stormbreaker**. Philomel Books 2001 192p (An Alex Rider adventure) $17.99; pa $7.99

Grades: 5 6 7 8 **Fic**

1. Spies 2. Orphans 3. Terrorism 4. Adventure fiction 5. Spies -- Fiction 6. Orphans -- Fiction 7. Terrorism -- Fiction

ISBN 0-399-23620-1; 0-14-240611-2 pa

LC 00-63683

First published 2000 in the United Kingdom

After the death of the uncle who had been his guardian, fourteen-year-old Alex Rider is coerced to continue his uncle's dangerous work for Britain's intelligence agency, MI6

"Horowitz thoughtfully balances Alex's super-spy finesse with typical teen insecurities to create a likable hero living a fantasy come true. An entertaining, nicely layered novel." Booklist

Other titles about Alex Rider are:

Point blank (2002)
Skeleton key (2003)
Eagle strike (2004)
Scorpia (2005)
Alex Rider, the gadgets (2006)
Ark angel (2006)
Snakehead (2007)
Crocodile tears (2009)
Scorpia rising (2011)

Three of diamonds; three Diamonds Brothers mysteries. [by] Anthony Horowitz. Philomel Books 2005 214p $16.99

Grades: 5 6 7 8 **Fic**

1. Mystery fiction

ISBN 0-399-24157-4

LC 2005276176

A collection of three Diamond Brothers mysteries in which Tim and Nick bungle their way through a search for a missing philanthropist, find themselves in a Parisian prison, and are stranded on a Scottish island with a murderer.

"Nick is a realistic character with a voice that is sarcastic and fresh, while Tim's lack of intelligence makes even the most dangerous situations laughable. Plenty of plays on words add to the humor." SLJ

The **switch**; [by] Anthony Horowitz. Philomel Books 2009 162p $16.99

Grades: 5 6 7 8 **Fic**

1. Wealth -- Fiction 2. Criminals -- Fiction 3. Supernatural -- Fiction

ISBN 978-0-399-25062-0; 0-399-25062-X

LC 2008-32380

When wealthy, spoiled, thirteen-year-old Tad Spencer wishes he were someone else, he awakens as Bob Snarby, the uncouth, impoverished son of carnival workers, and as he is drawn into a life of crime he begins to discover truths about himself and his family.

"A fun, tongue-in-cheek read that will captivate children who like adventure and mystery." SLJ

Horvath, Polly

Everything on a waffle. Farrar, Straus & Giroux 2001 149p hardcover o.p. $16

Grades: 4 5 6 7 **Fic**

1. Uncles 2. Self-reliance 3. Foster home care 4. Interpersonal relations 5. Parent and child 6. Uncles -- Fiction

ISBN 0-374-32236-8; 0-374-42208-7 pa

LC 00-35399

A Newbery Medal honor book, 2002

Eleven-year-old Primrose living in a small fishing village in British Columbia recounts her experiences and all that she learns about human nature and the unpredictability of life in the months after her parents are lost at sea

"The story is full of subtle humor and wisdom, presented through the eyes of a uniquely appealing young protagonist." SLJ

★ **My** one hundred adventures. Schwartz & Wade Books 2008 260p $16.99; lib bdg $19.99; pa $7.99
Grades: 4 5 6 7   **Fic**
1. Summer -- Fiction 2. Beaches -- Fiction 3. Siblings -- Fiction 4. Babysitters -- Fiction 5. Single parent family -- Fiction 6. Young adult literature -- Works
ISBN 978-0-375-84582-6; 0-375-84582-8; 978-0-375-95582-2 lib bdg; 0-375-95582-8 lib bdg; 978-0-375-85526-9 pa; 0-375-85526-2 pa
LC 2008-02243
Twelve-year-old Jane, who lives at the beach in a run-down old house with her mother, two brothers, and sister, has an eventful summer accompanying her pastor on bible deliveries, meeting former boyfriends of her mother's, and being coerced into babysitting for a family of ill-mannered children.

With writing as foamy as waves, as gritty as sand, or as deep as the sea, this book may startle readers with the freedom given the heroine. . . . Unconventionality is Horvath's stock and trade, but here the high quirkiness quotient rests easily against Jane's inner story with its honest, childlike core. Booklist

Northward to the moon. Schwartz & Wade Books 2010 244p $17.99; lib bdg $20.99
Grades: 4 5 6 7   **Fic**
1. Ranch life -- Fiction 2. Family life -- Fiction 3. Grandmothers -- Fiction 4. Automobile travel -- Fiction 5. Young adult literature -- Works
ISBN 978-0-375-86110-9; 0-375-86110-6; 978-0-375-96110-6 lib bdg; 0-375-96110-0 lib bdg
LC 2009-10133
When her stepfather loses his job in Saskatchewan, Jane and the rest of the family set off on a car trip, ending up in Nevada after improbably being given a bag full of possibly stolen money.

"Many characters here are distinct, wonderfully idiosyncratic individuals, and Horvath's fine-tuned observations are conveyed with subtlety and precision." Booklist

The **Pepins** and their problems; pictures by Marylin Hafner. Farrar Straus Giroux 2004 179p il $16; pa $6.99
Grades: 3 4 5 6   **Fic**
1. Family life -- Fiction 2. Children's literature -- Works -- Grades two through six
ISBN 0-374-35817-6; 0-312-37751-7 pa
LC 2003-60196
The reader is invited to help solve the Pepin family's unusual problems, which include having a cow who creates lemonade rather than milk and having to cope with a competitive neighbor

"Horvath spins a delightful yarn. . . . Absurd characters and situations and witty repartee are Horvath's strengths, and . . . the wordplay is a great argument for reading this aloud." Booklist

House, Silas
★ **Eli** the Good. Candlewick Press 2009 295p $16.99
Grades: 5 6 7 8   **Fic**
1. Aunts -- Fiction 2. Veterans -- Fiction 3. Friendship -- Fiction 4. Family life -- Fiction 5. Post-traumatic stress disorder -- Fiction
ISBN 978-0-7636-4341-6; 0-7636-4341-6
LC 2009004589
In the summer of 1976, ten-year-old Eli Book's excitement over Bicentennial celebrations is tempered by his father's flashbacks to the Vietnam War and other family problems, as well as concern about his tough but troubled best friend, Edie.

"House writes beautifully, with a gentle tone. He lays out Eli's world in exquisite detail. . . . The story flows along as steadily as a stream. . . . Eli is good company and children will enjoy accompanying him on his journey." SLJ

Howard, Ellen
The **crimson** cap. Holiday House 2009 177p $16.95
Grades: 5 6 7 8   **Fic**
1. Explorers 2. Explorers -- Fiction 3. Native Americans -- Fiction
ISBN 978-0-8234-2152-7; 0-8234-2152-X
LC 2009-25551
In 1684, wearing his father's faded cap, eleven-year-old Pierre Talon joins explorer Rene-Robert Cavelier on an ill-fated expedition to seek the Mississippi River, but after the expedition falls apart Pierre, deathly ill, is taken in by Hasinai Indians. Includes historical facts.

"A riveting adventure that will prove to be hard to put down. Howard's fast-paced writing brings the story to life. This solid coming-of-age story is based on real events and historical figures." SLJ

The **gate** in the wall. Atheneum Bks. for Young Readers 1999 148p il hardcover o.p. pa $9.95
Grades: 5 6 7 8   **Fic**
1. Canals -- Fiction 2. Orphans -- Fiction 3. Child labor -- Fiction
ISBN 0-689-82295-2; 1-4169-6796-6 pa
LC 98-22250
In nineteenth-century England, ten-year-old Emma, accustomed to long working hours at the silk mill and the poverty and hunger of her sister's house, finds her life completely changed when she inadvertently gets a job on a canal boat carrying cargoes between several northern towns

"Howard has given her story a highly interesting venue and has created a cast of characters who are fully dimensional and engaging." Horn Book Guide

Howe, Deborah
★ **Bunnicula**; a rabbit-tale of mystery. by Deborah and James Howe; illustrated by Alan Daniel. 25th anniversary edition; Atheneum Books for Young Readers 2004 92p il $16.95
Grades: 4 5 6   **Fic**
1. Mystery fiction 2. Animals -- Fiction
ISBN 0-689-86775-1
A reissue of the title first published 1979
Though scoffed at by Harold the dog, Chester the cat tries to warn his human family that their foundling baby bunny must be a vampire

This book is "blithe, sophisticated, and distinguished for the wit and humor of the dialogue." Bull Cent Child Books

Howe, James, 1946-

★ **Addie** on the inside. Atheneum Books for Young Readers 2011 206p

Grades: 5 6 7 8   **Fic**

1. School stories 2. Novels in verse 3. Grandmothers -- Fiction 4. Self-acceptance -- Fiction

ISBN 141691384X; 9781416913849

LC 2010024497

Outspoken thirteen-year-old Addie Carle learns about love, loss, and staying true to herself as she navigates seventh grade, enjoys a visit from her grandmother, fights with her boyfriend, and endures gossip and meanness from her former best friend.

"Howe's artfully crafted lines show Addie's intelligence and wit, and his imagery evokes the aura of sadness surrounding 'this purgatory of/ the middle school years/ when so many things/ that never mattered before/ and will never matter again/ matter.' Readers will empathize with Addie's anguish and admire her courage to keep fighting." Publ Wkly

★ **Dew** drop dead; a Sebastian Barth mystery. Atheneum Pubs. 1990 156p hardcover o.p. pa $4.99

Grades: 4 5 6   **Fic**

1. Mystery fiction 2. Homeless persons -- Fiction

ISBN 0-689-31425-6; 0-689-80760-0 pa

LC 89-34697

"The story is well crafted and has substance beyond escapist fare as a result of Howe's inclusion of secondary storylines involving the homeless and Sebastian's own worries about his father's pending job loss." Booklist

Other titles about Sebastian Barth are:

Eat your poison, dear (1986)

Stage fright (1986)

What Eric knew (1985)

Howe, Peter

Waggit again; drawings by Omar Rayyan. HarperCollinsPublishers 2009 292p il $16.99; lib bdg $17.89

Grades: 5 6 7   **Fic**

1. Dogs -- Fiction

ISBN 978-0-06-124264-9; 0-06-124264-0; 978-0-06-124265-6 lib bdg; 0-06-124265-9 lib bdg

LC 2008020213

After being left in the country by his owner, Waggit sets out on the long journey to New York City and meets some unexpected friends along the way.

Felicia's "relationship with the dogs is made wonderfully plausible. Waggit's growth in self-understanding is also fully developed and well handled, and the ending will satisfy readers deeply." Kirkus

Waggit's tale; drawings by Omar Rayyan. HarperCollinsPublishers 2008 288p il $16.99; lib bdg $17.89; pa $6.99

Grades: 5 6 7   **Fic**

1. Dogs -- Fiction

ISBN 978-0-06-124261-8; 0-06-124261-6; 978-0-06-124262-5 lib bdg; 0-06-124262-4 lib bdg; 978-0-06-124263-2 pa; 0-06-124263-2 pa

LC 2007020878

When Waggit is abandoned by his owner as a puppy, he meets a pack of wild dogs who become his friends and teach him to survive in the city park, but when he has a chance to go home with a kind woman who wants to adopt him, he takes it

"The novel celebrates the wild freedom of the feral dog pack, while also emphasizing the many hazards of urban life for homeless companion animals." Voice Youth Advocates

Warriors of the black shroud. Harper 2012 $16.99

Grades: 3 4 5   **Fic**

1. Fantasy fiction

ISBN 978-0-06-172987-4; 0-06-172987-6

LC 2011026147

A shy, bookish boy is pulled into an underground land called Nebula and asked to lead a kingdom in its fight against darkness.

This is a "fast-paced fantasy novel. . . . The climax and resolution have just enough surprise to satisfy readers. This attractive world (warriors ride unicorns!) and likable characters—boy heroes with a strong girl sidekick—will give fledgling readers of fantasy a treat." Kirkus

Howell, Troy

The **dragon** of Cripple Creek; a novel. Amulet Books 2011 385p $19.95

Grades: 5 6 7 8   **Fic**

1. Fantasy fiction 2. Adventure fiction 3. Gold -- Fiction 4. Dragons -- Fiction 5. Young adult literature -- Works

ISBN 978-0-8109-9713-4; 0-8109-9713-4

LC 2010-34362

When Kat, her father, and brother visit an old gold mine that has been turned into an amusement park, she falls down a shaft and meets an ancient dragon, the last of his kind, and inadvertently triggers a twenty-first century gold rush.

"Writing in Kat's first person narrative, which is wry and funny, clipped and eloquent, Howell, best known as an illustrator, mixes fantasy adventure with a moving conservation story in a debut that blends sadness, secrecy, and pure fantasy." Booklist

Hughes, Mark Peter

A **crack** in the sky. Delacorte Press 2010 405p il $16.99; lib bdg $19.99

Grades: 5 6 7 8   **Fic**

1. Science fiction 2. Young adult literature -- Works 3. Children's literature -- Works -- Grades two through six

ISBN 978-0-385-73708-1; 0-385-73708-4; 978-0-385-90645-6 lib bdg; 0-385-90645-5 lib bdg

LC 2009-43532

In a post-apocalyptic world, thirteen-year-old Eli, part of the most powerful family in the world, keeps noticing problems with the operations of his domed city but his family denies them, while in the surrounding desert, the Outsiders struggle to survive while awaiting a prophesied savior.

"Hughes keeps his protagonist an individual, and in fact an amiable, scrappy one with whom readers will identify." Bull Cent Child Books

Hughes, Shirley, 1927-

★ **Hero** on a bicycle; Shirley Hughes. Candlewick Press 2013 224 p. $15.99

Grades: 5 6 7   **Fic**

1. Historical fiction 2. World War, 1939-1945 -- Fiction
ISBN 076366037X; 9780763660376

LC 2012943650

This book is set in Italy during World War II. "The narrative focuses on a city under German occupation, events being perceived principally through the eyes of three members of the Crivelli family: teenager Paolo, his older sister Constanza and Rosemary, their English-born mother. . . . When an opportunity arises for Paolo, Constanza and Rosemary to lend their practical support to the Partisan cause Paolo, in particular, seizes it enthusiastically." (School Librarian)

Hughes, Ted, 1930-1998

★ The **iron** giant; a story in five nights. illustrated by Andrew Davidson. Knopf 1999 79p il hardcover o.p. pa $4.99
Grades: 4 5 6   **Fic**

1. Science fiction
ISBN 0-375-80153-7 pa

LC 98-41368

A newly illustrated edition of the title first published 1968 by Harper & Row; published in the United Kingdom with title: The iron man

This is the story of an Iron Giant "who appears from nowhere and stalks the earth, devouring tractors and barbed wire for his supper. . . . But in the end he has to save the world from a creature from Outer Space." NY Times Book Rev

Hulme, John

★ The **glitch** in sleep; [by] John Hulme and Michael Wexler; illustrations by Gideon Kendall. Bloomsbury Children's Books 2007 277p il (The Seems) $16.95; pa $7.99
Grades: 4 5 6 7   **Fic**

1. Science fiction 2. Sleep -- Fiction
ISBN 978-1-59990-129-9; 1-59990-129-3; 978-1-59990-298-2 pa; 1-59990-298-2 pa

LC 2007-2598

When twelve-year-old Becker Drane is recruited by The Seems, a parallel universe that runs everything in The World, he must fix a disastrous glitch in the Department of Sleep that threatens everyone's ability to ever fall asleep again

"The story is upbeat and full of humor. . . . Dynamic full-page illustrations appear throughout." SLJ

Another title in this series is:
The split second (2008)

The **split** second; by John Hulme and Michael Wexler; illustrations by Gideon Kendall. 1st U.S. ed.; Bloomsbury Children's Books 2008 301p il (The Seems) $16.99
Grades: 5 6 7 8   **Fic**

1. Science fiction 2. Terrorism -- Fiction
ISBN 978-1-599-90130-5; 1-599-90130-7

LC 2008012241

Now thirteen-years-old and still a Fixer in the parallel universe called the Seems, Becker Drane is called upon to repair the damage caused by an enormous bomb planted in the Department of Time, an act of terrorism perpetrated by the evil members of the Tide, a group that is trying to destroy the World.

"This sequel continues to develop a truly ingenious setting while proving every bit as much as a nail-biter as the first." Booklist

Hunt, Irene

Across five Aprils. Berkley Jam Books 2002 212p pa $5.99
Grades: 5 6 7 8   **Fic**

1. Farm life -- Fiction
ISBN 978-0-425-18278-9; 0-425-18278-9
First published 1964 by Follett
A Newbery Medal honor book, 1965

Young Jethro Creighton grows from a boy to a man when he is left to take care of the family farm in Illinois during the difficult years of the Civil War.

"Authentic background, a feeling for the people of that time, and a story that never loses the reader's interest." Wilson Libr Bull

Hunt, Lynda Mullaly

One for the Murphys; Lynda Mullaly Hunt. Nancy Paulsen Books 2012 224 p.
Grades: 5 6 7 8   **Fic**

1. Girls -- Juvenile fiction 2. Family -- Juvenile fiction 3. Foster children -- Juvenile fiction 4. Stepfathers -- Fiction 5. Family problems -- Fiction 6. Foster home care -- Fiction 7. Mothers and daughters -- Fiction
ISBN 0399256156; 9780399256158

LC 2011046708

This book by Lynda Mullaly Hunt follows "eighth-grader Carley Connors [as she] learns about a different kind of family life, first resisting and then resisting having to leave the loving, loyal Murphys. . . . She's torn between her love for her mother and her memory of the fight that sent her to the hospital, when her mother caught and held her for her stepfather. Slowly won over at home . . . Carley also finds a friend at school in the prickly, Wicked-obsessed Toni." (Kirkus Reviews)

Hurd, Thacher

Bongo fishing. Henry Holt 2011 233p il $16.99
Grades: 3 4 5   **Fic**

1. Science fiction 2. Family life -- Fiction 3. Space flight -- Fiction 4. Extraterrestrial beings -- Fiction
ISBN 978-0-8050-9100-7; 0-8050-9100-9

LC 2010-11696

Berkeley, California, middle-schooler Jason Jameson has a close encounter of the fun kind when Sam, a bluish alien from the Pleiades, arrives in a 1960 Dodge Dart spaceship and invites Jason to go fishing.

"The funniest moments come through twists of Earth conventions. . . . Intriguing gadgets and amusing descriptions of alien technology add to the fun, as do the lively illustrations. . . . Sam and his wife are delightfully atypical aliens . . . and the moments of humor are consistently strong throughout." SLJ

Hurst, Carol Otis

You come to Yokum; with illustrations by Kay Life. Houghton Mifflin Co. 2005 137p il $15
Grades: 3 4 5   **Fic**

1. Feminism -- Fiction 2. Family life -- Fiction 3. Women -- Suffrage -- Fiction
ISBN 0-618-55122-0

Twelve-year-old Frank witnesses his mother's struggles to muster support for women's right to vote even as the family's life is transformed by a year running a lodge in western Massachusetts in the early 1920s.

"With mostly short chapters and charming black-and-white illustrations, this is a satisfying read." SLJ

Hurwitz, Johanna

Amazing Monty; illustrated by Anik McGrory. Candlewick Press 2010 106p il $15.99

Grades: K 1 2   **Fic**

1. School stories 2. Pets -- Fiction 3. Infants -- Fiction 4. Family life -- Fiction

ISBN 978-0-7636-4154-2; 0-7636-4154-5

LC 2008045982

First-grader Montgomery Gerald Morris enjoys an exciting year as his class acquires a pair of parakeets as pets, he loses his first tooth, and he becomes a big brother.

"Monty's quiet but amusing adventures, shown in unfussy black-and-white watercolor illustrations, ring true to first-grade life." Horn Book Guide

★ **Baseball** fever; illustrated by Ray Cruz. Morrow 1981 128p il hardcover o.p. pa $4.99

Grades: 3 4 5   **Fic**

1. Baseball -- Fiction 2. Father-son relationship -- Fiction

ISBN 0-380-73255-6 pa

LC 81-5633

"A brisk, breezy story about a believable family is told with warmth and humor." Bull Cent Child Books

Fourth-grade fuss; illustrated by Andy Hammond. HarperCollins 2004 132p $15.99; lib bdg $16.89

Grades: 2 3 4   **Fic**

1. School stories

ISBN 0-06-052343-3; 0-06-052344-1 lib bdg

LC 2003-22216

A yard sale, ice skating, class pictures, and a surprise party are a few of the things that make fourth grade fun for Julio and his friends, but they must get serious about studying as the statewide end-of-year test approaches.

"Fans of this series as well as young test takers everywhere are sure to appreciate the humorous, reassuring story." Booklist

Mighty Monty; illustrated by Anik McGrory. Candlewick Press 2008 106p il $15.99

Grades: 1 2 3   **Fic**

1. School stories 2. Asthma -- Fiction 3. Children's literature -- Works -- Grades two through six

ISBN 978-0-7636-2977-9; 0-7636-2977-4

Monty, a quiet first-grader continues to come into his own—playing the part of a tree in a comically miscued school play, sharing his enthusiasm for ants at an outdoor birthday party, and even signing up for karate class despite his asthma.

"Even readers who do not have to deal with asthma or an overprotective parent will see something of themselves in Monty." Booklist

Mostly Monty. Candlewick Press 2007 86p il $15.99; pa $5.99

Grades: 1 2 3   **Fic**

1. Asthma -- Fiction 2. Friendship -- Fiction

ISBN 978-0-7636-2831-4; 0-7636-2831-X; 978-0-7636-4062-0 pa; 0-7636-4062-X pa

LC 2006-49024

Because he suffers from asthma, six-year-old Monty is nervous about starting first grade but he soon learns to cope with his illness and use his special talents to make friends.

"Watercolor illustrations . . . appear every few pages, breaking up the text with pictures of cheerful button-nose children. More reserved children . . . will appreciate seeing themselves reflected in this gently funny story about learning to like oneself." Booklist

Other titles about Monty are:

Mighty Monty (2008)

Magical Monty (2012)

★ The **adventures** of Ali Baba Bernstein; illustrated by Gail Owens. Morrow 1985 82p il hardcover o.p. pa $5.99

Grades: 2 3 4   **Fic**

1. Personal names -- Fiction

ISBN 0-688-04161-2; 0-380-72349-2 pa

LC 84-27387

"Hurwitz' characters, as always, are believable, the situations realistic and the plot well developed." SLJ

Another title about Ali Baba Bernstein is:

Hurray for Ali Baba Bernstein (1989)

Hurwitz, Michele Weber

Calli be gold. Wendy Lamb Books 2011 198p $15.99; lib bdg $18.99

Grades: 4 5 6   **Fic**

1. School stories 2. Family life -- Fiction 3. Young adult literature -- Works

ISBN 978-0-385-73970-2; 0-385-73970-2; 978-0-385-90802-3 lib bdg; 0-385-90802-4 lib bdg

LC 2010-13157

Eleven-year-old Calli, the third child in a family of busy high-achievers, likes to take her time and observe rather than rush around, and when she meets an awkward, insecure second-grader named Noah and is paired with him in the Peer Helper Program, she finds satisfaction and strength in working with him.

"Callie's often-insightful first-person narration provides a thoughtful, child-eyed view look at how adults too often try to find success through their children's achievements. The sometimes over-the-top depiction of stage parents pokes gentle but oh-so-true fun at them, adding to the appeal of this amusing debut." Kirkus

Hyde, Natalie

I owe you one. Orca 2011 125p (Orca young readers) pa $7.95

Grades: 3 4 5   **Fic**

1. Friendship -- Fiction

ISBN 978-1-55469-414-3; 1-55469-414-0

"After old Mrs. Minton saves him from drowning, Wes strikes up an unexpected friendship with her. His friend says that he owes Mrs. Minton a 'life debt,' and Wes worries how he could ever repay it. His chance comes when the town's aspiring pyrotechnic blows up the television tower. . . . The plot moves quickly from one humorous situation to another. Quirky but believable characters populate the small Canadian town. . . . With its slim length, fast pace, and humor, this title will appeal to a wide range of readers." Booklist

★ **Saving** ARM PIT. Fitzhenry & Whiteside 2011

Grades: 3 4 5 6   **Fic**
   1. Letters -- Fiction 2. Baseball -- Fiction 3. Postal service -- Fiction
   ISBN 1-55455-151-X; 978-1-55455-151-4

The Harmony Point baseball team hasn't won a game in two seasons, and vandals have deleted letters on the the town sign so that it says "arm Pit." A new postmaster becomes the new ball coach, but it takes a letter-writing campaign to save the coach's job and the baseball team.

"This book would be a terrific read-aloud for students to learn about citizenship, community service, and collaboration. Sportsmanship and hard work, respect for coaches are also valuable lessons within the story." SLJ

Ibbotson, Eva
   Dial-a-ghost. Dutton Children's Bks. 2001 195p hardcover o.p. pa $5.99
Grades: 4 5 6   **Fic**
   1. Ghosts 2. Orphans 3. Ghost stories 4. Orphans -- Fiction
   ISBN 0-525-46693-2; 0-14-250018-6 pa

LC 00-52287
A family of nice ghosts protects a British orphan from the diabolical plans of his evil guardians

"The book is filled with a large and delightful cast of characters. . . . The black-and-white illustrations have an eerie charm." SLJ

Another title about the nice ghosts is:
The great ghost rescue (2002)

   ★ The **Ogre** of Oglefort; [illustrations by Lisa K. Weber] Dutton Children's Books 2011 246p il $16.99
Grades: 4 5 6   **Fic**
   1. Fairy tales 2. Magic -- Fiction 3. Orphans -- Fiction 4. Princesses -- Fiction 5. Children's literature -- Works -- Grades two through six
   ISBN 978-0-525-42382-9; 0-525-42382-6

LC 2010038137
When the Hag of Dribble, an orphan boy, and a troll called Ulf are sent to rescue a princess from an ogre, it turns out to be far from the routine magical mission they expect.

"Magical creatures abound in this effervescent fairy tale that effectively merges classic tropes with modern sensibilities." Bull Cent Child Books

   One dog and his boy; by Eva Ibbotson. Scholastic Press 2012 271 p.
Grades: 3 4 5 6   **Fic**
   1. Children's stories 2. Dogs -- Juvenile fiction 3. Pets -- Juvenile fiction 4. Dogs -- Fiction 5. Wealth -- Fiction 6. Voyages and travels -- Fiction 7. Human-animal relationships -- Fiction 8. Family life -- England -- London -- Fiction
   ISBN 0545351960; 9780545351966

LC 2011003773
In this book, by Eva Ibbotson, "[all] Hal has ever wanted is a dog. His busy parents, hoping that he'll tire of the idea, rent a dog from Easy Pets, run by the heartless Mr. and Mrs. Carker. Hal and Fleck, the dog he chooses, bond immediately, and they are both heartbroken when Hal's mother, realizing that Hal's interest isn't waning, sneaks the dog back to Easy Pets. Hal decides to get Fleck back and run away to his grandparents." (Bulletin of the Center for Children's Books)

The **beasts** of Clawstone Castle; illustrated by Kevin Hawkes. Dutton Children's Books 2006 243p il hardcover o.p.
Grades: 4 5 6   **Fic**
   1. Ghost stories 2. Cattle -- Fiction 3. Castles -- Fiction 4. Young adult literature -- Works
   ISBN 0-14-240931-6 pa; 0-525-47719-5

LC 2005-29188
While spending the summer with elderly relatives at Clawstone Castle in northern England, Madlyn and her brother Rollo, with the help of several ghosts, attempt to save the rare cattle that live on the castle grounds. "Grades four to seven." (Bull Cent Child Books)

"Ibbotson's charismatic ghosts are great. . . .—as human as they are horrific—and there's plenty of quirky humor in this energetic, diverting read, loaded with charm." Booklist

   ★ The **dragonfly** pool; illustrated by Kevin Hawkes. Dutton Children's Books 2008 377p il $17.99; pa $7.99
Grades: 5 6 7 8   **Fic**
   1. School stories 2. World War, 1939-1945 -- Fiction 3. Young adult literature -- Works
   ISBN 978-0-525-42064-4; 0-525-42064-9; 978-0-14-241486-6 pa; 0-14-241486-7 pa

"Ibbotson's trademark eccentric characters and strongly contrasted principles of right and wrong brighten and broaden this uplifting tale." Booklist

   ★ The **secret** of platform 13; illustrated by Sue Porter. Dutton Children's Bks. 1998 231p il hardcover o.p. pa $5.99
Grades: 5 6 7 8   **Fic**
   1. Fairy tales 2. Fantasy fiction
   ISBN 0-525-45929-4; 0-14-130286-0 pa

LC 97-44601
First published 1994 in the United Kingdom
Odge Gribble, a young hag, accompanies an old wizard, a gentle fey, and a giant ogre on their mission through a magical tunnel from their island in London to rescue their King and Queen's son who had been stolen as an infant

"Lively, funny fantasy with a case of mistaken identity and a cast of eccentric characters." SLJ

   ★ The **star** of Kazan; illustrated by Kevin Hawkes. Dutton 2004 405p il $16.99; pa $7.99
Grades: 5 6 7 8   **Fic**
   1. Mystery fiction
   ISBN 0-525-47347-5; 0-14-240582-5 pa

LC 2004-45455
After twelve-year-old Annika, a foundling living in late nineteenth-century Vienna, inherits a trunk of costume jewelry, a woman claiming to be her aristocratic mother arrives and takes her to live in a strangely decrepit mansion in Germany

"This is a rich saga . . . full of stalwart friends, sly villains, a brave heroine, and good triumphing over evil. . . . An intensely satisfying read." SLJ

Iggulden, Conn
   ★ **Tollins**; explosive tales for children. illustrated by Lizzy Duncan. Harper 2009 172p il $16.99
Grades: 3 4 5 6   **Fic**
   1. Fantasy fiction
   ISBN 978-0-06-173098-6; 0-06-173098-X

"Tollins are tiny, nectar-eating woodland creatures with elf ears and wings but bigger than the fairies they casually use as handkerchiefs. They enjoy an idyllic existence until a fireworks factory is built in the village of Chorleywood. . . . The men of the village hunt the Tollins down to use as fodder for their fireworks. . . . Duncan's full-color illustrations and maps bring the world to witty life. A note at the end likens the Tollin's fate to child labor during the Industrial Revolution. There is much to think about and love in this beautifully realized world." Booklist

Ignatow, Amy

Words of (questionable) wisdom from Lydia Goldblatt & Julie Graham-Chang. Amulet Books 2011 204p (The popularity papers) $15.95

Grades: 3 4 5 6   Fic

1. School stories 2. Friendship -- Fiction 3. Popularity -- Fiction 4. Scrapbooks -- Fiction

ISBN 978-1-4197-0063-7; 1-4197-0063-4

LC 2011285303

Twelve-year-old best friends Julie and Lydia are reunited after six months apart, but the news that their friend Sukie's mother has died after a long illness causes them to reevaluate their goals and focus on being supportive of the friends they already have.

The **long** -distance dispatch between Lydia Goldblatt and Julie Graham-Chang. Amulet Books 2011 205p il (The popularity papers) $15.95

Grades: 3 4 5 6   Fic

1. School stories 2. Friendship -- Fiction 3. Popularity -- Fiction

ISBN 978-0-8109-9724-0; 0-8109-9724-X

After spending all of fifth grade studying popularity together, Julie and Lydia are finally ready to put their hard-earned lessons to use in junior high. But before they can, tragedy strikes: Lydia's mom gets a job in London for six whole months! Meanwhile Julie's stuck navigating the cliques of American junior high on her own, where she is adopted by a group of troublemaking eighth graders known as the Bichons.

"The girls' feelings are authentic, and their fun is contagious." Booklist

★ The **popularity** papers; research for the social improvement and general betterment of Lydia Goldblatt & Julie Graham-Chang. Amulet Books 204p il $15.95

Grades: 3 4 5 6   Fic

1. School stories 2. Popularity -- Fiction

ISBN 978-0-8109-8421-9; 0-8109-8421-0

LC 2009-39741

"Before they leave elementary school behind, two fifth-grade best friends are determined to uncover the secrets of popularity by observing, recording, discussing, and replicating the behaviors of the cool girls. . . . In a notebook format, this heavily illustrated title shows their research in dramatic, alternating, handwritten entries and colorful, hilarious drawings. . . . Ignatow offers a quick, fun, well-developed story that invites repeated readings." Booklist

Other titles about Lydia and Julie are:

The long distance dispatch between Lydia Goldblatt and Julie Graham-Chang (2011)

Words of (questionable) wisdom from Lydia Goldblatt & Julie Graham-Chang (2011)

Irving, Washington

The **Legend** of Sleepy Hollow; illustrated by Gris Grimly. Atheneum Books for Young Readers 2007 un il $16.99

Grades: 4 5 6   Fic

1. Ghost stories 2. Ghost stories -- Juvenile literature

ISBN 1-4169-0625-8; 978-1-4169-0625-4

LC 2005-27502

A superstitious schoolmaster, in love with a wealthy farmer's daughter, has a terrifying encounter with a headless horseman.

"The tale, . . . slightly condensed but with language and ambiguities intact, is reimagined here with humor, vigor, [and] clarity. . . . Irving's language is challenging . . . but Grimly's numerous Halloween-hued panel and spot illustrations . . . parse it into comprehensible tidbits. The comically amplified emotions and warm yellow and orange tones balance the horror aspects of the text." Horn Book

Washington Irving's Rip van Winkle; illustrated by Arthur Rackham. Dover Publications 2005 19p pa $12.95

Grades: 5 6 7 8   Fic

ISBN 0-486-44242-X

LC 2004063543

A reissue of the edition first published 1905 by Doubleday

Rip Van Winkle "is based on a folk tale. Henpecked Rip and his dog Wolf wander into the Catskill mountains before the Revolutionary War. There they meet a dwarf, whom Rip helps to carry a keg. They join a group of dwarfs playing ninepins. When Rip drinks from the keg, he falls asleep and wakes 20 years later, an old man. Returning to his town, he discovers his termagant wife dead, his daughter married, and the portrait of King George replaced by one of George Washington. Irving uses the folk tale to present the contrast between the new and old societies." Reader's Ency. 3d edition

Jackson, Alison

★ **Eggs** over Evie; illustrated by Tuesday Mourning. Henry Holt 2010 215p il $16.99

Grades: 4 5 6   Fic

1. Pets -- Fiction 2. Cooking -- Fiction 3. Divorce -- Fiction 4. Stepfamilies -- Fiction 5. Young adult literature -- Works 6. Children's literature -- Works -- Grades two through six

ISBN 978-0-8050-8294-4; 0-8050-8294-8

LC 2009-50762

Evie feels unsettled and sad after her parents divorce, her father remarries and takes the family dog, and his new wife becomes pregnant, but a cooking class and helping the elderly lady next door with her cat give Evie a way to cope with the changes in her life. Includes recipes.

"Evie tells her story with a pinch of humor and a dash of vulnerability, sifting together the people in her life and blending them into a surprising new family. . . . Sweet and savory." Kirkus

Includes bibliographical references

Rainmaker. Boyds Mills Press 2005 192p $16.95

Grades: 5 6 7 8   Fic

1. Droughts -- Fiction 2. Great Depression, 1929-1939 -- Fiction

ISBN 1-59078-309-3

"For 13-year-old Pidge Martin, the summer of 1939 brings changes and challenges. Her town, Frostfree, Florida, faces its longest drought in 40 years, and if it doesn't rain soon, area families . . . may lose their farms. A miracle is in order, and Pidge's father hopes a rainmaker can provide one. . . . Pidge is a well-characterized, sympathetic protagonist that readers will connect with." Booklist

Jacobson, Jennifer Richard, 1958

Andy Shane and the very bossy Dolores Starbuckle; [by] Jennifer Richard Jacobson; illustrated by Abby Carter. Candlewick Press 2005 56p il $13.99; pa $4.99
Grades: 1 2 3   Fic
1. School stories 2. Grandmothers -- Fiction
ISBN 0-7636-1940-X; 0-7636-3044-6 pa
LC 2004-57040

Andy Shane hates school, mainly because of a tattletale know-it-all named Dolores Starbuckle, but Granny Webb, who has taken care of him all his life, joins him in class one day and helps him solve the problem

"The characters are complex and realistic. . . . The narrative voice is fresh and whimsical. . . . The pen-and-ink illustrations effectively depict Andy's frustration, Dolores's temper, and Granny's zany self-assuredness." SLJ

Other titles about Andy Shane are:
Andy Shane and the pumpkin trick (2006)
Andy Shane and the Queen of Egypt (2008)
Andy Shane is NOT in love (2008)
Andy Shane and the barn sale mystery (2009)
Andy Shane, hero at last (2010)

★ **Small** as an elephant; [by] Jennifer Richard Jacobson. Candlewick Press 2011 275p $15.99
Grades: 5 6 7 8   Fic
1. Adventure fiction 2. Abandoned children -- Fiction 3. Young adult literature -- Works 4. Mother-son relationship -- Fiction
ISBN 0-7636-4155-3; 978-0-7636-4155-9
LC 2010039175

When his mother disappears from an Acadia National Park campground, Jack tries to make his way back home to Boston, with only a small toy elephant for company. "Intermediate, middle school." (Horn Book)

"Jacobson masterfully puts readers into Jack's mind—he loves and understands his mother, but sometimes his judgments are not always good, and readers understand. . . . Jack's journey to a new kind of family is inspiring and never sappy." Kirkus

Jacques, Brian

Rakkety Tam; illustrated by David Elliot. Philomel Books 2004 372p il pa $7.99
Grades: 5 6 7 8 9   Fic
1. Animals 2. Fantasy 3. Squirrels 4. Wolverines 5. Fantasy fiction 6. Animals -- Fiction
ISBN 0-399-23725-9; 0-441-01318-X pa
LC 2003-66449

Two warrior squirrels lead the battle against Gulo, a bloodthirsty wolverine who will stop at nothing to recover the Walking Stone that will give him the authority to rule the lands of ice beyond the Great Sea.

"The colorful writing style, the strong cast of characters, and twisting plot will continue to delight fans of the series." SLJ

★ **Redwall**; illustrated by Gary Chalk. 20th anniversary ed.; Philomel 2007 351p il $23.99; pa $7.99
Grades: 5 6 7 8 9   Fic
1. Fantasy fiction 2. Mice -- Fiction 3. Animals -- Fiction
ISBN 978-0-399-24794-1; 0-399-24794-7; 978-0-441-00548-2 pa; 0-441-00548-9 pa
First published 1986

"Thoroughly engrossing, this novel captivates despite its length. . . . The theme will linger long after the story is finished." Booklist

Other titles in this series are:
The Bellmaker (1995)
Doomwyte (2008)
Eulalia! (2007)
High Rhulain (2005)
The legend of Luke (2000)
Loamhedge (2003)
The long patrol (1998)
Lord Brocktree (2000)
Mariel of Redwall (1992)
Marlfox (1998)
Martin the Warrior (1994)
Mattimeo (1990)
Mossflower (1998)
The outcast of Redwall (1996)
Pearls of Lutra (1997)
Rakkety Tam (2004)
The Rogue Crew (2011)
Sable Quean (2009)
Salamandastron (1993)
Taggerung (2001)
Triss (2002)

James, Helen Foster

Paper son; Lee's journey to America. written by Helen Foster James and Virginia Shin-Mui Loh; illustrated by Wilson Ong. Sleeping Bear Press 2013 32 p. ill. (reinforced) $16.99
Grades: 5 6 7 8   Fic
1. Chinese Americans -- Juvenile fiction 2. Historical fiction -- Juvenile fiction 3. Immigrants -- United States -- Juvenile fiction 4. Orphans -- Fiction 5. Immigrants -- Fiction 6. Chinese Americans -- Fiction 7. Emigration and immigration -- Fiction
ISBN 1585368334; 9781585368334
LC 2012033691

This historical novel, by Helen Foster James, Virginia Shin-Mui Loh, and illustrated by Wilson Ong, is part of the "Tales of Young Americans" series. "In 1926, 12-year-old Fu Lee['s] . . . parents . . . spent all of their money buying a 'paper son slot' for Lee to go to America. Being a 'paper son' means pretending to be the son of a family already in America. . . . But first he must pass the test at Angel Island Immigration Station in San Francisco." (Publisher's note)

Janisch, Heinz

Fantastic adventures of Baron Munchausen; traditional and newly discovered tales of Karl Friedrich Hieronymus von Munchausen. with illustrations by Aljoscha Blau; translated by Belinda Cooper. Enchanted Lion Books 2010 30p il $17.95

Grades: 1 2 3 **Fic**

1. Soldiers 2. Tall tales 3. Voyages and travels -- Fiction

ISBN 978-1-59270-091-2; 1-59270-091-8

LC 2010001115

Retells Baron Munchausen's boastful account of some of his incredible adventures around the world, including riding a cannonball during a spy mission and entering a whale's mouth to hear a musical concert.

"In his retellings of the Baron's tall tales, Janisch . . . combines the bravura of Paul Bunyan with the elegance of Voltaire's Candide. Each story appears on the left, accompanied by a painting on the right of the beak-nosed Baron. . . . Children with a romantic streak will be taken both with the Baron and his courtly fictions and by Blau's misty, stately portraits." Publ Wkly

Jaramillo, Ann

La linea. Roaring Brook Press 2006 131p $16.95; pa $7.99

Grades: 5 6 7 8 **Fic**

1. Mexicans -- Fiction 2. Siblings -- Fiction 3. Immigrants -- Fiction 4. Young adult literature -- Works

ISBN 1-59643-154-7; 0-312-37354-6 pa

LC 2005-20133

When fifteen-year-old Miguel's time finally comes to leave his poor Mexican village, cross the border illegally, and join his parents in California, his younger sister's determination to join him soon imperils them both.

"A gripping contemporary survival adventure, this spare first novel is also a heart-wrenching family story of courage, betrayal, and love." Booklist

Jarrell, Randall

★ The **animal** family; decorations by Maurice Sendak. HarperCollins Pubs. 1996 179p il $16.99; pa $8.95

Grades: 4 5 6 7 **Fic**

1. Fantasy fiction 2. Animals -- Fiction

ISBN 0-06-205088-5; 0-06-205904-1 pa

LC 94-76270

A reissue of the title first published 1965 by Pantheon Bks.

A lonely hunter living in the wilderness beside the sea gains a family made up of a mermaid, a bear, a lynx, and a boy

This story is "sensitively related with touches of humor and wisdom. A delight for the imaginative reader." Booklist

The **bat**-poet; pictures by Maurice Sendak. HarperCollins Pubs. 1996 42p il $15.95; pa $7.95

Grades: 2 3 4 **Fic**

1. Bats -- Fiction 2. Poetry -- Fiction

ISBN 0-06-205084-2; 0-06-205905-X pa

LC 94-76271

A reissue of the title first published 1964 by MacMillan

A bat who can't sleep days makes up poems about the woodland creatures he now perceives for the first time

"A lovely book, perfectly illustrated—one well worth a child's attention and affection." Publ Wkly

Jeffrey, Mark

Max Quick: the pocket and the pendant. Harper 2011 294p $15.99

Grades: 4 5 6 7 **Fic**

1. Science fiction 2. Time -- Fiction 3. Voyages and travels -- Fiction 4. Young adult literature -- Works 5. Identity (Psychology) -- Fiction

ISBN 978-0-06-198892-9; 0-06-198892-8

LC 2010-42663

First released 2005 as a podcast audiobook

Young Max, a troubled boy with a mysterious past, joins two other youths unaffected when the rest of the world was frozen in time on a journey across America—and time itself—seeking the source of the "Time-stop."

"This fast-paced adventure . . . will keep readers turning pages." SLJ

Jenkins, Emily

Invisible Inkling; illustrations by Harry Bliss. Balzer + Bray 2011 154p il

Grades: 3 4 5 **Fic**

1. Bullies -- Fiction 2. Imaginary playmates -- Fiction

ISBN 0-06-180220-4; 978-0-06-180220-1

LC 2010-46238

When Hank Wolowitz runs into trouble in the form a of lunch-stealing bully, he finds an unlikely ally in an invisible refugee pumpkin-loving bandapat named Inkling.

"Jenkins' possible series starter . . . is a gently humorous and nicely realistic . . . tale about coping with the loss of a lifelong best friend. . . . Anyone who has ever had an imaginary friend will appreciate sassy Inkling (who's invisible—not imaginary)." Kirkus

★ **Toys** go out; being the adventures of a knowledgeable Stingray, a toughy little Buffalo, and someone called Plastic. illustrated by Paul O. Zelinsky. Schwartz & Wade Bks. 2006 116p il $16.95; lib bdg $18.99; pa $5.99

Grades: 1 2 3 **Fic**

1. Toys -- Fiction 2. Friendship -- Fiction

ISBN 0-375-83604-7; 0-375-93604-1 lib bdg; 0-385-73661-4 pa

"For beginning chapter-book readers, this . . . relates the experiences of three engaging toy best friends: Lumphy the buffalo, plush StingRay, and Plastic. . . . The simple prose is clever and often hilarious, incorporating dialogue and musings that ring kid-perspective true, and Zelinsky's charming black-and-white illustrations, wonderfully detailed and textured, expressively portray character situations and feelings." Booklist

Other titles about Lumphy, StingRay, and Plastic are:
Toy dance party (2008)
Toys come home (2011)

Jennings, Patrick

Guinea dog. Egmont USA 2010 135p $15.99; lib bdg $18.99

Grades: 3 4 5 **Fic**

1. School stories 2. Family life -- Fiction 3. Guinea pigs -- Fiction

ISBN 1-60684-053-3; 1-60684-069-X lib bdg; 978-1-60684-053-5; 978-1-60684-069-6 lib bdg

LC 2009-25117

When his mother brings home a guinea pig instead of the dog he has always wanted, fifth-grader Rufus is not happy—until the rodent starts acting exactly like a dog. "Grades three to five." (Bull Cent Child Books)

"Children will have no problem accepting the absurdity of the situation. Early chapter-book readers will enjoy this humorous tale." SLJ

Out standing in my field. Scholastic Press 2005 165p hardcover o.p. pa $5.99

Grades: 4 5 6   **Fic**

1. Baseball -- Fiction 2. Father-son relationship -- Fiction

ISBN 0-439-46581-8; 0-439-48749-8 pa

     LC 2004-41619

Although fifth-grader Ty Cutter is named after base-ball great Ty Cobb, he is the worst player on the Brewer's team—which happens to be coached by his overly-competitive father

"The book is funny, poignant, and deeper than one might think at first glance." SLJ

We can't all be rattlesnakes. HarperCollins Pubs. 2009 121p $15.99

Grades: 3 4 5 6   **Fic**

1. Pets -- Fiction 2. Snakes -- Fiction

ISBN 978-0-06-082114-2; 0-06-082114-0

     LC 2008-07118

When Crusher the snake is captured, her only thought is to escape but as time goes by and she befriends the other inmates of the "zoo," she realizes that freedom also means leaving companions behind

"Crusher is a compelling narrator, her voice dripping with sarcasm. . . . [Kids will enjoy] Crusher's commentary on human habits and absorbing the facts about snakes that are seamlessly integrated into the narrative." SLJ

Jennings, Richard W.

★ **Orwell's** luck; [by] Richard Jennings. Houghton Mifflin 2000 146p $15; pa $6.95

Grades: 5 6 7 8   **Fic**

1. Rabbits 2. Horoscopes

ISBN 0-618-03628-8; 0-618-69335-1 pa

     LC 99-33501

While caring for an injured rabbit which becomes her confidant, horoscope writer, and source of good luck, a thoughtful seventh grade girl learns to see things in more than one way

"This absolutely captivating tale is about everyday magic . . . filled with quiet humor and seamless invention. The characters . . . are the sort that readers fall in love with." Booklist

Jobling, Curtis

The **rise** of the wolf. Viking Childrens Books 2011 (Wereworld) $16.99

Grades: 4 5 6 7   **Fic**

1. Fantasy fiction 2. Adventure fiction 3. Werewolves -- Fiction

ISBN 978-0-670-01330-2; 0-670-01330-7

     LC 2010049517

When a vicious beast invades his father's farm and six-teen-year-old Drew suddenly transforms into a werewolf, he runs away from his family, seeking refuge in the most out of the way parts of Lyssia, only to be captured by Lord Bergan's men and forced to battle numerous werecreatures while trying to prove that he is not the enemy.

"Jobling's characterizations are solid, his world-building is complex and fascinating, and the combat scenes are suit-ably exciting. The book's themes are familiar—lost prince in exile, voyage of self-discovery, young heroes rebelling against injustice and evil—but Jobling uses them to tell a thoroughly enjoyable adventure that makes particularly in-ventive use of its shapeshifter elements and mythology." Publ Wkly

Jocelyn, Marthe

★ **Mable** Riley; a reliable record of humdrum, peril, and romance. Candlewick Press 2004 279p $15.99; pa $6.99

Grades: 5 6 7 8   **Fic**

1. Teachers -- Fiction 2. Women's rights -- Fiction

ISBN 0-7636-2120-X; 0-7636-3287-2 pa

     LC 2003-55322

In 1901, fourteen-year-old Mable Riley dreams of being a writer and having adventures while stuck in Perth County, Ontario, assisting her sister in teaching school and secretly becoming friends with a neighbor who holds scandalous opinions on women's rights.

"This book is a funny and inspiring tale of a young girl finding her voice and the courage to make it heard." Voice Youth Advocates

Johnson, Angela

Bird. Dial Books 2004 133p $15.99; pa $5.99

Grades: 5 6 7 8   **Fic**

1. Stepfathers -- Fiction 2. African Americans -- Fiction 3. Runaway teenagers -- Fiction

ISBN 0-8037-2847-6; 0-14-240544-2 pa

     LC 2003-22793

Devastated by the loss of a second father, thirteen-year-old Bird follows her stepfather from Cleveland to Alabama in hopes of convincing him to come home, and along the way helps two boys cope with their difficulties

"Johnson writes with a poet's knowledge of rhythm and knows how to use the space between words. . . . Johnson also creates a visceral sense of each character's search for love and connection." Booklist

★ A **cool** moonlight. Dial Bks. 2003 133p hardcover o.p. pa $6.99

Grades: 4 5 6   **Fic**

1. Sisters 2. Skin -- Diseases 3. Imaginary friends 4. Skin -- Diseases -- Fiction

ISBN 0-8037-2846-8; 0-14-240284-2 pa

     LC 2002-31521

Nine-year-old Lila, born with xeroderma pigmentosum, a skin disease that make her sensitive to sunlight, makes se-cret plans to feel the sun's rays on her tenth birthday

"The book's real magic resides in the spell cast by John-son's spare, lucid, lyrical prose. Using simple words and viv-id sensory images, she creates Lila's inner world as a place of quiet intensity." Booklist

Johnson, Peter

The **amazing** adventures of John Smith, Jr., aka Houdi-ni; by Peter Johnson. HarperCollins Children's Books 2012 168p.

Grades: 4 5 6   **Fic**

1. Domestic relations 2. Teenagers -- Fiction 3. Child authors -- Fiction 4. Authorship -- Fiction 5.

Neighborliness -- Fiction 6. Moneymaking projects -- Fiction 7. Interpersonal relations -- Fiction 8. Family life -- Rhode Island -- Fiction
ISBN 9780061988905

LC 2011019387

In this book, "thirteen-year-old John Smith, Jr., also known as Houdini, meets the author of a children's book . . . [and] decides to try . . . writing a novel. . . . [Peter] Johnson offers this title as Houdini's own work, wherein he shares stories about . . . his rough and tumble neighborhood in Providence, Rhode Island; his older brother who is fighting in Iraq; Angel Dimitri, the local bully; and Jackson, the neighborhood crazy/Vietnam vet." (Bulletin of the Center for Children's Books)

Includes bibliographical references

Johnson-Shelton, Nils

The **Invisible** Tower. HarperCollins 2011 (Otherworld chronicles) $16.99

Grades: 4 5 6 7   Fic

1. Adventure fiction 2. Kings
ISBN 978-0-06-207086-9; 0-06-207086-X

LC 2011022928

A twelve-year-old boy learns that he is actually King Arthur brought back to life in the twenty-first century—and that the fate of the universe rests in his hands.

"This new take on the Arthurian legends, told in third-person, pits wisecracking contemporary teens with their contemporary banter. . . . against all manner of obstacles. . . . It's always high-spirited and fun. Gives new life to Arthurian legends and may just send readers back to more traditional tellings." Kirkus

The **seven** swords; Nils Johnson-Shelton. HarperCollins 2013 368 p. (Otherworld chronicles) (hardback) $16.99

Grades: 4 5 6 7   Fic

1. Arthurian romances -- Adaptations 2. Fantasy fiction -- Juvenile fiction 3. Adventure fiction -- Juvenile fiction
ISBN 0062070940; 9780062070944

LC 2012019088

This juvenile adventure fantasy, by Nils Johnson-Shelton, second in the "Otherworld Chronicles," follows "Artie Kingfisher, the new King Arthur. On a quest to recover seven magical swords of the Dark Ages, Artie and Kay gather 'New Knights of the Round Table' and try to unite two worlds. Standing in their way is Lordess Morgaine. . . . Artie and his band travel from Ohio via crossover points between worlds in search of swords in Sweden, France and Japan." (Kirkus Reviews)

Johnston, Julie

A **very** fine line. Tundra Books 2006 198p $18.95; pa $10.95

Grades: 5 6 7 8   Fic

1. Clairvoyance -- Fiction
ISBN 978-0-88776-746-3; 0-88776-746-X; 978-0-88776-829-3 pa; 0-88776-829-6 pa

Then thirteen-year-old Rosalind's "aunt informs her that as the seventh daughter of a seventh daughter, she can . . . see glimpses of the future, she balks. . . . The story begins in Kepston, Ontario, in 1941. . . . Readers who come to the book intrigued by the idea of clairvoyance will fine much

more: several vivid characters, a well-realized setting, and a sensitively nuanced resolution." Booklist

Johnston, Tony

Any small goodness; a novel of the barrio. illustrations by Raúl Colón. Blue Sky Press (NY) 2001 128p il $16.95; pa $4.99

Grades: 4 5 6 7   Fic

1. Mexican Americans -- Fiction
ISBN 0-439-18936-5; 0-439-23384-4 pa

LC 99-59877

Arturo and his family and friends share all kinds of experiences living in the barrio of East Los Angeles—reclaiming their names, playing basketball, championing the school librarian, and even starting their own gang

"The characters are likable and warm. . . . The message is positive and the episodes, while occasionally serious, are more often humorous and gratifying." SLJ

Jonell, Lynne

★ **Emmy** and the incredible shrinking rat. Henry Holt 2007 346p il $16.95; pa $6.99

Grades: 3 4 5 6   Fic

1. Rats -- Fiction
ISBN 978-0-8050-8150-3; 0-8050-8150-X; 978-0-312-38460-9 pa; 0-312-38460-2 pa

LC 2006-35461

When Emmy discovers that she and her formerly loving parents are being drugged by their evil nanny with rodent potions that can change people in frightening ways, she and some new friends must try everything possible to return things to normal.

"This tale turns smoothly on its fanciful premise and fabulous characters." Booklist

Other titles about Emmy are:
Emmy and the Home for Troubled Girls (2008)
Emmy and the rats in the Belfry (2011)

★ The **secret** of zoom. Henry Holt 2009 291p $16.99

Grades: 4 5 6   Fic

1. Adventure fiction 2. Orphans -- Fiction 3. Energy resources -- Fiction
ISBN 978-0-8050-8856-4; 0-8050-8856-3

LC 2008-50276

Ten-year-old Christina lives a sheltered life until she discovers a secret tunnel, an evil plot to enslave orphans, and a mysterious source of energy known as zoom.

"This exciting tale, with just a touch of fantasy and humor, is a winner. . . . Complete with a cast of clearly drawn characters, the adventure proceeds at a breakneck pace until all is resolved and a happy ending completes the picture." SLJ

Jones, Allan Frewin

Fair wind to widdershins; illustrated by Gary Chalk. Greenwillow Books 2011 162p il (The six crowns) $15.99

Grades: 4 5 6   Fic

1. Adventure fiction 2. Aunts -- Fiction 3. Animals -- Fiction 4. Badgers -- Fiction 5. Hedgehogs -- Fiction 6. Prophecies -- Fiction
ISBN 978-0-06-200626-4; 0-06-200626-6

LC 2010049000

First published 2010 in the United Kingdom

Hedgehogs Trundle and Esmeralda, along with their new friend Jack Nimble, sail out into the Sundered Lands to find Esmeralda's aunt, who they hope will help them unravel the clues to find the next of the six crowns.

"Jones' plot is peppy and his prose funny, sporting excellent names—'Pounceman Donk'—and word strings—'the meanest, bloodthirstiest, wickedest pirate ever to sail the skies' . . . A fast and jolly gambol, with four more promised." Kirkus

Trundle's quest; [by] Allan Jones; [illustrated by] Gary Chalk. Greenwillow Books 2011 151p il (The six crowns) $15.99

Grades: 4 5 6　　　　　　　　　　　　**Fic**
1. Fantasy fiction 2. Animals -- Fiction 3. Badgers -- Fiction 4. Hedgehogs -- Fiction 5. Prophecies -- Fiction
ISBN 978-0-06-200623-3; 0-06-200623-1
　　　　　　　　　　　　LC 2010-10341

Trundle Boldoak's simple life as the town lamplighter is turned upside-down the night he meets Esmeralda, a Roamany hedgehog, who whisks him away on a quest to find six fabled crowns and fulfill his role in an ancient prophecy.

"Jones has woven a tale with protagonists that readers will root for. Chalk's detailed illustrations look almost life-like and add character to each animal, the airships, and the pirates." SLJ

Another title about Trundle and Esmeralda is:
Fair wind to Widdershins (2011)

Jones, Diana Wynne
★ **Castle** in the air. Greenwillow Bks. 1991 199p hardcover o.p. pa $6.99

Grades: 6 7 8 9　　　　　　　　　　　　**Fic**
1. Fantasy fiction
ISBN 0-688-09686-7; 0-06-447345-7 pa
　　　　　　　　　　　　LC 90-30266

In this "follow-up to Howl'sMoving Castle . . . the protagonist is a young carpet merchant called Abdullah, who spends much of his time creating a richly developed daydream in which he is the long-lost son of a great prince, kidnapped as a child by a villainous bandit. . . . Feisty Sophie and the Wizard Howl (from Howl's Moving Castle do not become apparent till late in the story, but their fortunes do link up with those of Abdullah and his love. Jones maintains both suspense and wit throughout, demonstrating once again that frequently nothing is what it seems to be." Booklist

House of many ways. Greenwillow Books 2008 404p $17.99; lib bdg $18.89; pa $8.99

Grades: 5 6 7 8　　　　　　　　　　　　**Fic**
1. Fantasy fiction 2. Magic -- Fiction 3. Houses -- Fiction 4. Uncles -- Fiction
ISBN 978-0-06-147795-9; 0-06-147795-8; 978-0-06-147796-6 lib bdg; 0-06-147796-6 lib bdg; 978-0-06-147797-3 pa; 0-06-147797-4 pa
　　　　　　　　　　　　LC 2007036147

When Charmain is asked to housesit for Great Uncle William, the Royal Wizard of Norland, she is ecstatic to get away from her parents, but finds that his house is much more than it seems.

This is "a buoyantly entertaining read. . . . [Jones'] comic pacing and wit are amply evident." Horn Book

Jones, Diana Wynne, 1934-2011
Earwig and the witch; illustrator, Paul O. Zelinsky. Greenwillow Books 2012 140p il

Grades: 2 3 4　　　　　　　　　　　　**Fic**
1. Orphans -- Fiction 2. Witches -- Fiction
ISBN 0-06-207511-X; 978-0-06-207511-6
　　　　　　　　　　　　LC 2010048999

This book tells the story of Earwig, who "rules the roost at St. Morwald's Home for Children until she is adopted by a witchy woman named Bella Yaga with "one brown eye and one blue one, and a raggety, ribby look to her face." Earwig hopes to learn magic from Bella Yaga, but is trapped in the woman's decrepit house, sharing it with the Mandrake, an impossibly tall and grouchy being. Powerful and evil, Bella Yaga uses Earwig as a second pair of hands for grinding up disgusting things in bowls ("The only thing wrong with magic is that it smells so awful," Earwig quips)." (Publishers Weekly)

"Earwig, illustrated with marvelous vitality by Zelinsky, is not to be trifled with. There's just the right level of grotesquerie and scariness . . . in this utterly charming chapter book." Kirkus

★ **Howl's** moving castle. Greenwillow Books 1986 212p hardcover o.p. pa $6.99

Grades: 5 6 7 8　　　　　　　　　　　　**Fic**
1. Fantasy fiction
ISBN 0-06-147878-4 pa; 0-688-06233-4; 978-0-06-147878-9 pa
　　　　　　　　　　　　LC 85-21981

Sophie "resigns herself to making a living as a hatter and helping her younger sisters prepare to make their fortunes. But adventure seeks her out in the shop where she sits alone dreaming over her hats. The wicked Witch of the Waste, angered by 'competition' in the area, turns her into an old woman, so she seeks refuge inside the strange moving castle of the wizard Howl. Howl, advertised by his apprentice as an eater of souls, lives a mad, frantic life trying to escape the curse the witch has placed on him, find the perfect girl of his dreams and end the contract he and his fire demon have entered. Sophie, against her best instincts and at first unaware of her own powers, falls in love. . . . Grade six and up." (SLJ)

"Satisfyingly, Sophie meets a fate far exceeding her dreary expectations. This novel is an exciting, multi-faceted puzzle, peopled with vibrant, captivating characters. A generous sprinkling of humor adds potency to this skillful author's spell." Voice Youth Advocates

Jones, Kimberly K.
Sand dollar summer. Margaret K. McElderry Books 2006 206p $15.95; pa $5.99

Grades: 5 6 7 8　　　　　　　　　　　　**Fic**
1. Islands -- Fiction 2. Family life -- Fiction
ISBN 978-1-4169-0362-8; 1-4169-0362-3; 978-1-4169-5834-5 pa; 1-4169-5834-7 pa
　　　　　　　　　　　　LC 2005012740

When twelve-year-old Lise spends the summer on an island in Maine with her self-reliant mother and bright—but oddly mute—younger brother, her formerly safe world is complicated by an aged Indian neighbor, her mother's childhood friend, and a hurricane.

"The drama in [the] smart, tough, first-person narrative is understated; the spaces between the words are as eloquent

as what is said. . . . The family story . . . is exquisitely told."
Booklist

Jones, Traci L.

★ **Silhouetted** by the blue. Farrar, Straus & Giroux 2011 200p $16.99

Grades: 5 6 7 8   **Fic**

1. School stories 2. Theater -- Fiction 3. Bereavement -- Fiction 4. African Americans -- Fiction 5. Depression (Psychology) -- Fiction

ISBN 978-0-374-36914-9; 0-374-36914-3

LC 2010008419

After the death of her mother in an automobile accident, seventh-grader Serena, who has gotten the lead in her middle school play, is left to handle the day-to-day challenges of caring for herself and her younger brother when their father cannot pull himself out of his depression.

"Jones has written another winner with this beautiful, haunting tale rich in story and characterization." Booklist

Jordan, Rosa

Lost Goat Lane. Peachtree Publisher 2004 197p $14.95

Grades: 5 6 7 8   **Fic**

1. Goats -- Fiction 2. Race relations -- Fiction 3. African Americans -- Fiction

ISBN 1-56145-325-0

LC 2004-5343

Two families—one white, one black—living near one another in rural Florida overcome their suspicions of each other and find ways to work together, with the help of their children and a few goats

"The fully realized characters and the warmth of the story make up for the small sermons. A tender, satisfying offering." SLJ

Other titles in this series are:

The goatnappers (2007)
The last wild place (2008)

Joseph, Lynn

The **color** of my words. HarperCollins Pubs. 2000 138p hardcover o.p. pa $5.99

Grades: 5 6 7 8   **Fic**

1. Siblings -- Fiction 2. Family life -- Fiction 3. Family -- Dominican Republic

ISBN 0-06-028232-0; 0-06-447204-3 pa

LC 00-22440

When life gets difficult for Ana Rosa, a twelve-year-old would-be writer living in a small village in the Dominican Republic, she can depend on her older brother to make her feel better—until the life-changing events on her thirteenth birthday

"A finely crafted novel, lovely and lyrical." SLJ

Jung, Mike

Geeks, girls, and secret identities; by Mike Jung; with illustrations by Mike Maihack. Arthur A. Levine Books 2012 307 p. (hardcover: alk. paper) $16.99

Grades: 3 4 5 6 7   **Fic**

1. Boys' clubs 2. Secrecy -- Fiction 3. Friendship -- Juvenile fiction 4. Science fiction 5. Clubs -- Fiction 6. Humorous stories 7. Robots -- Fiction 8. Schools -- Fiction 9. Superheroes -- Fiction 10. Middle schools

-- Fiction

ISBN 0545335485; 9780545335485; 9780545335492; 9780545392518

LC 2011042548

In author Mike Jung's book, "Vincent Wu is Captain Stupendous's No. 1 Fan, but even he has to admit that Captain Stupendous has been a little off lately. During Professor Mayhem's latest attack, Captain Stupendous barely made it out alive, although he did manage to save Vincent from a giant monster robot. It's Vincent's dream come true . . . until he finds out Captain Stupendous's secret identity: It's Polly Winnicott-Lee, the girl Vincent happens to have a crush on." (Publisher's note)

Juster, Norton

★ The **phantom** tollbooth; illustrated by Jules Feiffer. Random House 1961 255p il $19.95; pa $6.50

Grades: 5 6 7 8   **Fic**

1. Fantasy fiction

ISBN 0-394-81500-9; 0-394-82037-1 pa

"It's all very clever. The author plays most ingeniously on words and phrases . . . and on concepts of averages and infinity and such . . . while the pictures are even more diverting than the text, for they add interesting details." N Y Her Trib Books

Kadohata, Cynthia

★ **Cracker!** the best dog in Vietnam. Atheneum Books for Young Readers 2007 312p $16.99; pa $7.99

Grades: 5 6 7 8   **Fic**

1. Dogs -- Fiction 2. Vietnam War, 1961-1975 -- Fiction

ISBN 978-1-4169-0637-7; 1-4169-0637-1; 978-1-4169-0638-4 pa; 1-4169-0638-X pa

LC 2006-22022

The author "tells a stirring, realistic story of America's war in Vietnam, using the alternating viewpoints of an army dog named Cracker and her 17-year-old handler, Rick Hanski. . . . The heartfelt tale explores the close bond of the scout-dog team." Booklist

★ **Kira**-Kira. Atheneum Bks. for Young Readers 2004 244p $15.95; pa $6.99

Grades: 5 6 7 8   **Fic**

1. Death -- Fiction 2. Sisters -- Fiction 3. Japanese Americans -- Fiction 4. Young adult literature -- Works

ISBN 0-689-85639-3; 0-689-85640-7 pa

Awarded the Newbery Medal, 2005

Chronicles the close friendship between two Japanese-American sisters growing up in rural Georgia during the late 1950s and early 1960s, and the despair when one sister becomes terminally ill.

"This beautifully written story tells of a girl struggling to find her own way in a family torn by illness and horrendous work conditions. . . . All of the characters are believable and well developed." SLJ

★ A **million** shades of gray. Atheneum Books for Young Readers 2010 216p $16.99

Grades: 5 6 7 8   **Fic**

1. Elephants -- Fiction 2. Wilderness survival -- Fiction 3. Young adult literature -- Works

ISBN 978-1-4169-1883-7; 1-4169-1883-3

LC 2009-33307

In 1975 after American troops pull out of Vietnam, a thirteen-year-old boy and his beloved elephant escape into the jungle when the Viet Cong attack his village.

"Kadohata delves deep into the soul of her protagonist while making a faraway place and stark consequences of war seem very near." Publ Wkly

Outside beauty. Atheneum Books for Young Readers 2008 265p $16.99; pa $8.99
Grades: 5 6 7 8   Fic
1. Sisters -- Fiction 2. Japanese Americans -- Fiction 3. Father-daughter relationship -- Fiction 4. Mother-daughter relationship -- Fiction
ISBN 978-0-689-86575-6; 0-689-86575-9; 978-1-4169-9818-1 pa; 1-4169-9818-7 pa
LC 2007-39711
Thirteen-year-old Shelby and her three sisters must go to live with their respective fathers while their mother, who has trained them to rely on their looks, recovers from a car accident that scarred her face

Kadohata's "gifts for creating and containing drama and for careful definition of character prove as powerful as ever in this wise, tender and compelling novel." Publ Wkly

★ The **thing** about luck; Cynthia Kadohata; illustrated by Julia Kuo. 1st ed. Atheneum Books for Young Readers 2013 288 p. (hardcover) $16.99
Grades: 5 6 7 8   Fic
1. Luck -- Fiction 2. Japanese Americans -- Fiction 3. Brothers and sisters -- Fiction 4. Grandparents -- Fiction 5. Farm life -- Kansas -- Fiction
ISBN 1416918825; 9781416918820; 9781442474673
LC 2012021287
National Book Award Finalist (2013)

In this novel, by Newbery Medalist Cynthia Kadohata, "Summer knows that kouun means 'good luck' in Japanese, and this year her family has none of it. Just when she thinks nothing else can possibly go wrong, an emergency whisks her parents away to Japan--right before harvest season. Summer and her little brother, Jaz, are left in the care of their grandparents, who come out of retirement in order to harvest wheat and help pay the bills." (Publisher's note)

"Kadohata expertly captures the uncertainties of the tween years as Summer navigates the balance of childlike concerns with the onset of increasingly grown-up responsibilities." (SLJ)

★ **Weedflower**. Atheneum Books for Young Readers 2006 260p $16.95; pa $5.99
Grades: 5 6 7 8   Fic
1. World War, 1939-1945 -- Fiction 2. Young adult literature -- Works 3. Japanese Americans -- Evacuation and relocation, 1942-1945 -- Fiction
ISBN 0-689-86574-0; 1-4169-7566-7 pa
LC 2004-24912
After twelve-year-old Sumiko and her Japanese-American family are relocated from their flower farm in southern California to an internment camp on a Mojave Indian reservation in Arizona, she helps her family and neighbors, becomes friends with a local Indian boy, and tries to hold on to her dream of owning a flower shop.

Sumiko "is a sympathetic heroine, surrounded by well-crafted, fascinating people. The concise yet lyrical prose conveys her story in a compelling narrative." SLJ

Kang, Hildi
Chengli and the Silk Road caravan. Tanglewood 2011 $14.95
Grades: 5 6 7 8   Fic
1. Fathers -- Fiction 2. Princesses -- Fiction 3. Trade routes -- Fiction
ISBN 978-1-933718-54-5; 1-933718-54-4
LC 2010047359
Called to follow the wind and search for information about his father who disappeared many years ago, thirteen-year-old Chengli, carrying a piece of jade with strange writing that had belonged to his father, joins a caravan charged with giving safe passage to the Emperor's daughter as it navigates the constant dangers of the Silk Road in 630 A.D.

"This fast-paced adventure is filled with friendship, historical detail, changing scenery, and action. It will appeal to a wide range of readers." SLJ

Karr, Kathleen
Fortune's fool. Alfred A. Knopf 2008 201p $15.99; lib bdg $18.99; pa $6.50
Grades: 5 6 7 8   Fic
1. Middle Ages -- Fiction 2. Fools and jesters -- Fiction
ISBN 978-0-375-84816-2; 0-375-84816-9; 978-0-375-94816-9 lib bdg; 0-375-84816-3 lib bdg; 978-0-375-84307-5 pa; 0-375-84307-8 pa
LC 2007-49034
In medieval Germany, fifteen-year-old Conrad, a court jester, and his beloved Christa, a servant girl, escape from a cruel master and journey through the countryside on a quest to find a kind lord who will give them sanctuary.

"Karr does an splendid job of recreating the medieval milieu, especially the life of a professional entertainer with all of its challenges and hardships." Booklist

Kehret, Peg
Abduction! Dutton Children's Books 2004 215p $16.99; pa $6.99
Grades: 5 6 7 8   Fic
1. Kidnapping 2. Fathers and sons 3. Brothers and sisters 4. Kidnapping -- Fiction
ISBN 0-525-47294-0; 0-14-240617-1 pa
LC 2003-63531
Thirteen-year-old Bonnie has a feeling of foreboding on the very day that her six-year-old brother Matt and their dog Pookie are abducted, and she becomes involved in a major search effort as well as a frightening adventure

"This novel has enough suspense to keep children interested, and it will also appeal to reluctant readers." SLJ

Ghost dog secrets. Dutton Children's Books 2010 184p $16.99
Grades: 4 5 6   Fic
1. Ghost stories 2. Dogs -- Fiction
ISBN 978-0-525-42178-8; 0-525-42178-5
LC 2009053256
"Sixth-grader Rusty comes across a German shepherd chained outside with no food, water, or shelter, and knows he has to do something about it. He begins by sneaking food to the dog, but when a ghostly apparition of a collie appears to

Rusty, and he realizes that the dog has been hurt, he decides he has to do something more. . . . Dog lovers and fans of thorny moral dilemmas will appreciate this fast-paced story. And three cheers for the author for depicting adults who are loving, involved, and competent." SLJ

The **ghost's** grave. Dutton Children's Books 2005 210p $16.99; pa $5.99

Grades: 5 6 7 8   **Fic**

1. Ghost stories 2. Coal miners -- Fiction
ISBN 0-525-46162-0; 0-14-240819-0 pa
LC 2004022064

Apprehensive about spending the summer in Washington State with his Aunt Ethel when his parents get an overseas job, twelve-year-old Josh soon finds adventure when he meets the ghost of a coal miner.

"This fast-paced and engaging book should be a hit with fans of ghost stories. Josh is a rich character to whom readers can relate." SLJ

Keith, Harold

Rifles for Watie. Crowell 1957 332p lib bdg $16.89; pa $5.99

Grades: 6 7 8 9   **Fic**

1. Generals 2. Indian leaders
ISBN 0-690-04907-2 lib bdg; 0-06-447030-X pa
Awarded the Newbery Medal, 1958

"Young Jeff Bussey longs for the life of a Union soldier during the Civil War, but before long he realizes the cruelty and savagery of some men in the army situation. The war loses its glamor as he sees his very young friends die. When he is made a scout, his duties take him into the ranks of Stand Watie, leader of the rebel troops of the Cherokee Indian Nation, as a spy." Stensland. Lit By & About the Am Indian

Kelley, Jane

The **girl** behind the glass; [by] Jane Kelley. Random House 2011 183p $16.99; lib bdg $19.99; e-book $16.99

Grades: 4 5 6 7   **Fic**

1. Ghost stories 2. Twins -- Fiction 3. Moving -- Fiction 4. Sisters -- Fiction 5. Family life -- Fiction
ISBN 978-0-375-86220-5; 0-375-86220-X; 978-0-375-96220-2 lib bdg; 0-375-96220-4 lib bdg; 978-0-375-88996-7 e-book
LC 2010-43568

Moving from Brooklyn to a rental house in the country strains the relationship between eleven-year-old identical twins Hannah and Anna Zimmer, a situation made worse by the ghost of a girl who is trapped in the house because of problems with her own sister eighty years before.

"Both chilling and lyrical. . . . The tensions within the Zimmer family are especially well-observed, and Kelley . . . conveys an impressive amount of emotion with few words. The ethereal tone and steady parceling out of warning, clues, and bits of information . . . maintain the novel's intrigue and will keep readers invested in the unfolding mystery." Publ Wkly

Kelly, David A.

The **Fenway** foul-up; illustrated by Mark Meyers. Random House 2011 101p il (Ballpark mysteries) lib bdg $12.99; pa $4.99

Grades: 2 3 4   **Fic**

1. Mystery fiction 2. Cousins -- Fiction 3. Baseball

-- Fiction
ISBN 978-0-375-96703-0 lib bdg; 0-375-96703-6 lib bdg; 978-0-375-86703-3 pa; 0-375-86703-1 pa; 978-0-375-89816-7 e-book
LC 2010-08521

"Two nine-year-old sleuths bring sharp powers of observation and deduction into play when a Red Sox slugger's favorite bat disappears. Cousins Mike and Kate are thrilled when Kate's sports-reporter mom brings them to a game, and they are up to the challenge when star player Big D's bat goes missing after batting practice. Folding information about Fenway Park and its colorful history into the tale, Kelly also artfully slips in simple red herrings along with real clues to the thief's identity and the bat's whereabouts. . . . This book should draw baseball fans as well as budding whodunit aficionados." Booklist

Other titles in this series are:
The pinstripe ghost (2011)
The L.A. Dodger (2011)

Kelly, Jacqueline

★ The **evolution** of Calpurnia Tate. Henry Holt and Co. 2009 340p $16.99

Grades: 4 5 6 7   **Fic**

1. Nature -- Fiction 2. Family life -- Fiction 3. Naturalists -- Fiction 4. Grandfathers -- Fiction
ISBN 978-0-8050-8841-0; 0-8050-8841-5
LC 2008-40595

A Newbery Medal honor book (2010)

In central Texas in 1899, eleven-year-old Callie Vee Tate is instructed to be a lady by her mother, learns about love from the older three of her six brothers, and studies the natural world with her grandfather, the latter of which leads to an important discovery.

"Callie is a charming, inquisitive protagonist; a joyous, bright, and thoughtful creation. . . . Several scenes . . . mix gentle humor and pathos to great effect." SLJ

Kelly, Katy

Lucy Rose, here's the thing about me; illustrated by Adam Rex. Delacorte Press 2004 137p il hardcover o.p. pa $5.99

Grades: 2 3 4   **Fic**

1. School stories 2. Moving -- Fiction 3. Family life -- Fiction
ISBN 0-385-73203-1; 0-440-42026-1 pa
LC 2003-20754

Eight-year-old Lucy Rose keeps a diary of her first year in Washington, D.C., her home since her parents separation, where she spends time with her grandparents, makes new friends, and longs to convince her teacher to let her take care of the class pet during a holiday

"There's something especially endearing about Lucy Rose, and her interactions with her parents, grandparents, teacher, and friends seem believable and comfortable." Booklist

Other titles about Lucy Rose are:
Lucy Rose, big on plans (2005)
Lucy Rose, busy like you can't believe (2006)
Lucy Rose, working myself to pieces and bits (2007)

Melonhead; illustrated by Gillian Johnson. Delacorte Press 2009 209p il $12.99; lib bdg $15.99

Grades: 3 4 5   **Fic**
1. Inventors -- Fiction
ISBN 978-0-385-73409-7; 0-385-73409-3; 978-0-385-90426-1 lib bdg; 0-385-90426-6 lib bdg
LC 2007-46076

In the Washington, D.C. neighborhood of Capitol Hill, Lucy Rose's friend Adam "Melonhead" Melon, a budding inventor with a knack for getting into trouble, enters a science contest that challenges students to recycle an older invention into a new invention.

This is "laugh-out-loud funny. . . . The capital setting and a unique cast of characters round out this strong chapter-book offering." SLJ

Other titles about Melonhead are:
Melonhead and the big stink (2010)
Melonhead and the undercover operation (2011)

Kelly, Lynne
Chained; Lynne Kelly. Farrar Straus Giroux 2012 248 p. (hardcover) $16.99
Grades: 4 5 6   **Fic**
1. Debt 2. Circus performers -- Fiction 3. Human-animal relationship -- Fiction 4. Circus -- Fiction 5. Elephants -- Fiction 6. Child labor -- Fiction 7. Conduct of life -- Fiction 8. Animals -- Treatment -- Fiction
ISBN 0374312370; 9780374312374; 9780374312503
LC 2011031767

In author Lynne Kelly's book, "after ten-year-old Hastin's family borrows money to pay for his sister's hospital bill, he leaves his village in northern India to take a job as an elephant keeper and work off the debt. . . . The crowds that come to the circus see a lively animal . . . but Hastin sees Nandita, a sweet elephant and his best friend, who is chained when she's not performing and hurt with a hook until she learns tricks perfectly. Hastin protects Nandita as best as he can, knowing that the only way they will both survive is if he can find a way for them to escape." (Publisher's note)

Kelsey, Marybeth
A **recipe** 4 robbery. Greenwillow Books 2009 282p $16.99; lib bdg $17.89
Grades: 4 5 6   **Fic**
1. Mystery fiction
ISBN 978-0-06-128843-2; 0-06-128843-8; 978-0-06-128845-6 lib bdg; 0-06-128845-4 lib bdg
LC 2008-29145

An unsupervised goose, missing family heirlooms, and some suspicious characters turn the annual cucumber festival into a robbery investigation for three sixth-grade friends.

"The novel is full of likable characters and fun twists and turns. The plot moves quickly, and Kelsey writes with wit and verve." SLJ

Kendall, Carol
The **Gammage** Cup; a novel of the Minnipins. illustrated by Erik Blegvad. Harcourt 2000 283p il hardcover o.p. pa $6
Grades: 5 6 7 8   **Fic**
1. Fantasy 2. Fantasy fiction
ISBN 0-15-202487-5; 0-15-202493-X pa
LC 99-55279

A reissue of the title first published 1959
A Newbery Medal honor book, 1960

A handful of Minnipins, a sober and sedate people, rise up against the Periods, the leading family of an isolated mountain valley, and are exiled to a mountain where they discover that the ancient enemies of their people are preparing to attack

"An original and wholly delightful tale." Booklist
Another title about the Minnipins is:
The whisper of Glocken (1965)

Kennedy, Emma
Wilma Tenderfoot: the case of the frozen hearts. Dial Books for Young Readers 2011 335p $16.99
Grades: 4 5 6   **Fic**
1. Mystery fiction 2. Orphans -- Fiction
ISBN 978-0-8037-3540-8; 0-8037-3540-5
LC 2009040050

Wilma Tenderfoot, a ten-year-old orphan who lives at Cooper Island's Lowside Institute for Woeful Children, dreams of escape and of becoming the apprentice of the world-famous detective Theodore P. Goodman, whose every case she follows devotedly in the newspaper.

"Wilma is an appealing character, ever-hopeful that Goodman will take her on as an apprentice and help her find out more about her origins. The fast-paced plot twists and turns, but the conflict between good and evil is clear." Kirkus
Another title in this series is:
Wilma Tenderfoot: the case if the putrid poison (2011)

Kennedy, Marlane
Me and the pumpkin queen. Greenwillow Books 2007 181p $15.99; lib bdg $16.89; pa $5.99
Grades: 3 4 5   **Fic**
1. Aunts -- Fiction 2. Pumpkin -- Fiction 3. Gardening -- Fiction 4. Bereavement -- Fiction
ISBN 978-0-06-114022-8; 0-06-114022-8; 978-0-06-114023-5 lib bdg; 0-06-114023-6 lib bdg; 978-0-06-114024-2 pa; 0-06-114024-4 pa
LC 2006-20019

Although Aunt Arlene tries to interest her in clothing and growing up, ten-year-old Mildred is entirely focused on growing a pumpkin big enough to win the annual Circleville, Ohio, contest, as her mother dreamed of doing before she died.

"The author combines the art and science of horticulture with a gentle family story, a feel for a child in mourning, and just the right amount of humor and tension to keep the plot moving along." SLJ

The **dog** days of Charlotte Hayes. Greenwillow Books 2009 233p $15.99; lib bdg $16.89
Grades: 4 5 6   **Fic**
1. Dogs -- Fiction 2. Old age -- Fiction 3. Family life -- Fiction
ISBN 978-0-06-145241-3; 0-06-145241-6; 978-0-06-145242-0 lib bdg; 0-06-145242-4 lib bdg
LC 2008-07507

Eleven-year-old Charlotte is not a dog person but does not like that the rest of her family neglects their Saint Bernard puppy, and so with a lot of determination and a little sneakiness, she works on finding a good home for the gentle giant.

This is a "gentle, appealing story. . . . The familiar family and friendship issues and satisfying resolution make this an agreeable read." Booklist

Kent, Rose

Kimchi & calamari. HarperCollinsPublishers 2007 220p $15.99; lib bdg $16.89

Grades: 4 5 6 7   **Fic**

1. Adoption -- Fiction 2. Korean Americans -- Fiction 3. Italian Americans -- Fiction

ISBN 978-0-06-083769-3; 0-06-083769-1; 978-0-06-083770-9 lib bdg; 0-06-083770-5 lib bdg

LC 2006-20041

"Fourteen-year-old Korean adoptee Joseph Calderaro is stumped when his social studies teacher assigns an ancestry essay. . . . Kent's debut novel humorously captures the feelings of a young teen who thoroughly enjoys his Italian-American family but still wonders about his birth parents." Booklist

Kerley, Barbara

Greetings from planet Earth. Scholastic Press 2007 246p $16.99

Grades: 5 6 7 8   **Fic**

1. Family life -- Fiction 2. Vietnam War, 1961-1975 -- Fiction 3. Father-son relationship -- Fiction

ISBN 0-439-80203-2; 978-0-439-80203-1

LC 2006-11300

In 1977, as twelve-year-old Theo struggles with a science class project on space exploration, questions emerge about why his father never returned from Vietnam and why Theo's mother has been keeping secrets for many years.

"The novel convincingly portrays a family overshadowed by secrets." Booklist

Kerrin, Jessica Scott

★ Martin Bridge: ready for takeoff! written by Jessica Scott Kerrin; illustrated by Joseph Kelly. Kids Can Press 2005 120p il $14.95; pa $4.95

Grades: 2 3 4   **Fic**

ISBN 1-55337-688-9; 1-55337-772-9 pa

"Martin Bridge usually has a scheme or project under way. In the three school and home stories presented in this beginning chapter book, he sees how a happy surprise intended for one person makes a positive difference for another, figures out what to say to a little girl whose hamster has died, and suffers the consequences of jealousy. . . . [Martin's] responses are on target for a third grader. Kerrin relates the episodes in a straightforward way that incorporates rich language. Kelly's full-page illustrations and spot art follow the narrative closely enough to support the newly independent readers for whom this book is written." SLJ

Other titles about Martin Bridge are:

Martin Bridge on the lookout! (2005)
Martin Bridge blazing ahead! (2006)
Martin Bridge out of orbit! (2007)
Martin Bridge sound the alarm (2007)
Martin Bridge in high gear! (2008)
Martin Bridge: the sky's the limit (2008)
Martin Bridge: onwards and upwards! (2009)

Kerz, Anna

Better than weird. Orca Book Publishers 2011 218p pa $9.95

Grades: 4 5 6 7   **Fic**

1. School stories 2. Autism -- Fiction 3. Bullies -- Fiction 4. Father-son relationship -- Fiction

ISBN 978-1-55469-362-7 pa; 1-55469-362-4 pa

When Aaron's long-absent father returns, Aaron must cope with bullying at school, his grandmother's illness and his father's pregnant new wife.

"Yet another in a long line of recent books about kids with autism, Kerz's effort nevertheless shines. . . . A heartwarming read for fans of realistic fiction." Booklist

The gnome's eye. Orca Book Publishers 2010 210p pa $12.95

Grades: 4 5 6 7   **Fic**

1. Fear -- Fiction 2. Immigrants -- Fiction

ISBN 978-1-55469-195-1 pa; 1-55469-195-8 pa

When Theresa and her family immigrate to Canada after World War II, she confronts her many fears with the help of a talisman given to her by a friend in Austria.

"Both laughter and genuine concern will be evident through Theresa's imaginative storytelling and descriptive narrative." SLJ

Ketchum, Liza

Where the great hawk flies. Clarion Books 2005 264p $16

Grades: 5 6 7 8   **Fic**

1. Prejudices -- Fiction 2. Pequot Indians -- Fiction

ISBN 0-618-40085-0

LC 2004-29832

Years after a violent New England raid by the Redcoats and their Revolutionary War Indian allies, two families, one that suffered during that raid and one with an Indian mother and Patriot father, become neighbors and must deal with past trauma and prejudices before they can help each other in the present. Based on the author's family history. Includes historical notes and notes on the Pequot Indians.

The author writes "in prose as sturdy and well crafted as a cedar-frame wigwam or hand-pegged pine barn." Booklist

Key, Watt

Alabama moon. Farrar, Straus & Giroux 2006 294p $16; pa $6.99

Grades: 5 6 7 8   **Fic**

1. Orphans -- Fiction 2. Wilderness survival -- Fiction

ISBN 0-374-30184-0; 0-312-38428-9 pa

LC 2005-40165

After the death of his father, ten-year-old Moon leaves their forest shelter home and is sent to an Alabama institution, becoming entangled in the outside world he has never known and making good friends, a relentless enemy, and finally a new life

"The book is well written with a flowing style, plenty of dialogue, and lots of action. The characters are well drawn and three-dimensional." SLJ

Kilworth, Garry

Attica. Little, Brown 2009 334p pa $11.95

Grades: 5 6 7 8   **Fic**

1. Fantasy fiction 2. Stepfamilies -- Fiction

ISBN 978-1-904233-56-5 pa; 1-904233-56-2 pa

"The children have distinct personalities and react to Attica in realistic ways, finding their own strengths in this exhilarating, unpredictable environment. This book is a rare find." Booklist

CHILDREN'S CORE COLLECTION

Kimmel, Elizabeth Cody

School spirit. Little, Brown and Co. 2008 316p (Suddenly supernatural) $15.99

Grades: 5 6 7 8 **Fic**

1. Ghost stories 2. School stories 3. Popularity -- Fiction 4. Clairvoyance -- Fiction 5. Mother-daughter relationship -- Fiction

ISBN 978-0-316-06683-9; 0-316-06683-4

LC 2007-031542

Like her mother, a professional medium, Kat has been able to see dead people since turning thirteen, and although they would prefer to be normal, Kat and her best friend come to terms with their own talents while helping free the spirit of a girl trapped at their middle school.

"This delightfully fun and well-written story is a fast, clean read. . . . Its nice blend of supernatural and reality will attract fantasy and non-fantasy readers alike." Voice Youth Advocates

Other titles in this series are:

Scaredy Kat (2009)

Unhappy medium (2009)

★ The **reinvention** of Moxie Roosevelt. Dial Books for Young Readers 2010 256p $16.99

Grades: 4 5 6 7 **Fic**

1. School stories

ISBN 978-0-8037-3303-9; 0-8037-3303-8

LC 2009-37939

On her first day of boarding school, a thirteen-year-old girl who feels boring and invisible decides to change her personality to match her unusual name.

"Kimmel's sharply observed novel reflects a keen understanding of the agony of self-definition that is adolescence. Readers will cheer for Moxie as she charts her path toward self-acceptance." Kirkus

King, Caro

Seven sorcerers. Aladdin 2011 324p $15.99

Grades: 5 6 7 8 **Fic**

1. Fantasy fiction 2. Adventure fiction 3. Siblings -- Fiction 4. Missing children -- Fiction

ISBN 978-1-4424-2042-7; 1-4424-2042-1

LC 2011001432

First published 2009 in the United Kingdom

When eleven-year-old Nin Redfern wakes up one rainy Wednesday morning to discover that her younger brother has ceased to exist, she must venture into a magical land called the Drift where she grapples with bogeymen, tombfolk, mudmen, and the spirits of sorcerers to try and rescue him.

"King has written a complex, intelligent fantasy that is at turns funny and terrifying." Booklist

King, Thomas

A **Coyote** solstice tale; pictures by Gary Clement. Groundwood Books 2009 un il $14.95

Grades: 1 2 3 4 **Fic**

1. Stories in rhyme 2. Christmas stories 3. Animals -- Fiction 4. Coyotes -- Fiction 5. Shopping -- Fiction 6. Winter solstice -- Fiction

ISBN 978-0-88899-929-0; 0-88899-929-1

ALA America Indian Library Association American Indian Youth Literature Award (2010)

"Coyote is expecting Beaver, Bear, Otter, and Moose for a solstice dinner at his small house in the woods but a little girl in a reindeer costume shows up first. When the friends follow her tracks to discover where she came from, they discover a huge and frenzied mall just beyond the woods, where Coyote goes wild shopping until he discovers that he has to pay for the stuff. The humor is dry and affectionate, the rhyming text delights with sly turns of phrase, the watercolor cartoons are whimsical, and the small size of the book (a bit bigger than a DVD case) adds to the charm." SLJ

King-Smith, Dick

★ **Babe**; the gallant pig. illustrated by Maggie Kneen. Twentieth anniversary edition; Knopf 2005 130p il $16.95

Grades: 3 4 5 **Fic**

1. Pigs -- Fiction

ISBN 0-375-82970-9

LC 2004-5832

First published 1983 in the United Kingdom with title: The sheep-pig; first United States edition 1985 by Crown

A piglet destined for eventual butchering arrives at the farmyard, is adopted by an old sheep dog, and discovers a special secret to success

"Mary Rayner's engaging black-and-white drawings capture the essence of Babe and the skittishness of sheep and enhance this splendid book-which should once and for all establish the intelligence and nobility of pigs." Horn Book

Clever duck; illustrated by Nick Bruel. Roaring Brook Press 2008 85p il $15.95

Grades: 1 2 3 **Fic**

1. Pigs -- Fiction 2. Ducks -- Fiction 3. Farm life -- Fiction

ISBN 978-1-59643-327-4; 1-59643-327-2

LC 2008-11138

First published 1996 in the United Kingdom

When the pigs start picking on all the other farm animals, Damaris, who is a very clever duck, and her best friend, Rory the sheepdog, find a way to exact revenge, only to find their plot backfiring.

"Engaging characters fill this wonderfully wacky farm. Humorous black-and-white illustrations add even more personality to the already exuberant animals." Horn Book Guide

Dinosaur trouble; [by] Dick King-Smith; illustrated by Nick Bruel. Roaring Brook Press 2008 118p il $14.95

Grades: 2 3 4 **Fic**

1. Dinosaurs -- Fiction

ISBN 978-1-59643-324-3; 1-59643-324-8

Young dinosaurs Nosy, a pterodactyl, and Banty, an apatosaurus, become friends, despite their parents' prejudices

"Much of the book's humor relies on wordplay and the juxtaposition of the clever mothers next to their dim-witted husbands. Frequent black-and-white cartoon illustrations . . . enliven the text and add a light comic touch." Booklist

Funny Frank; illustrated by John Eastwood. Knopf 2002 108p il hardcover o.p. pa $5.50

Grades: 3 4 5 **Fic**

1. Ducks -- Fiction 2. Chickens -- Fiction

ISBN 0-375-81460-4; 0-440-41880-1 pa

LC 2001-29539

First published 2001 in the United Kingdom

Gertie the hen is appalled when her son Frank wants to swim with the ducks, but Jemima and her mother, the farmer's wife, make him a special outfit so that his dream can come true

"Illustrated with comic line drawings, the short chapter book is entertaining and easy to read." Horn Book Guide

The **golden** goose; illustrated by Ann Kronheimer. Knopf 2005 113p il hardcover o.p. pa $5.50

Grades: 2 3 4   **Fic**

1. Geese -- Fiction 2. Farm life -- Fiction
ISBN 0-375-82984-9; 0-440-4203-0X pa

LC 2004-40842

First published 2003 in the United Kingdom

Farmer Skint and his family on Woebegone Farm have fallen on hard times, but their luck changes with the arrival of a special golden goose

"The novel's breezy premise, Kronheimer's simple and appealing halftone illustrations, the text's relatively large typeface and brief chapters make this perhaps best suited to those just embarking on chapter books, but reluctant readers will also take a fancy to it. And all will be tickled by the up-lifting conclusion that caps this engaging story." Publ Wkly

Lady Lollipop; illustrated by Jill Barton. Candlewick Press 2001 120p il $14.99; pa $6.99

Grades: 3 4 5   **Fic**

1. Pigs 2. Princesses 3. Behavior 4. Pigs -- Fiction 5. Princesses -- Fiction
ISBN 0-7636-1269-3; 0-7636-2181-1 pa

LC 00-58498

A quick-witted swineherd and a pig named Lollipop are royally rewarded after they reform a spoiled princess

"The short chapters and the book's open, lively design and engaging pencil illustrations add to this amusing book's appeal." Horn Book Guide

Another title about Lollipop is:

Clever Lollipop (2003)

The **mouse** family Robinson; [by] Dick King-Smith; illustrated by Nick Bruel. Roaring Brook Press 2008 71p il $15.95

Grades: 3 4 5   **Fic**

1. Mice -- Fiction 2. Family life -- Fiction
ISBN 978-1-59643-326-7; 1-59643-326-4

LC 2008011139

After a close call with the cat who stalks the hallways, a family of wild mice, including adventurous, young Beaumont and elderly Uncle Brown, emigrates to a more mouse-friendly house down the block

"The lively, often droll narrative, divided into short chapters, and the many captivating illustrations . . . provide an accessible, engaging read filled with everyday details of imagined mouse life and appealing characters." Booklist

Kingfisher, Rupert

Madame Pamplemousse and her incredible edibles; [by] Rupert Kingfisher; illustrated by Sue Hellard. Blooms-bury Children's Books 2008 138p il $15.99

Grades: 2 3 4   **Fic**

1. Food -- Fiction 2. Restaurants -- Fiction
ISBN 978-1-59990-306-4; 1-59990-306-7

LC 2008-10409

Forced to work in her unpleasant uncle's horrible restaurant, a Parisian girl finds comfort and companionship in

a shop nearby that sells otherworldly foods prepared by a mysterious cook and her cat

"Kingfisher writes in whimsical, humorous prose, creating vivid scenarios and intriguing characters. . . . This droll title is sprinkled with fanciful line drawings and topped with a moral about the magical power and rewards of following one's heart." Booklist

Kinney, Jeff

★ **Diary** of a wimpy kid: Greg Heffley's journal. Amulet Books 2007 217p pa $14.95

Grades: 5 6 7 8   **Fic**

1. School stories 2. Friendship -- Fiction
ISBN 978-0-8109-9313-6 pa; 0-8109-9313-9 pa

LC 2006-31847

Greg records his sixth grade experiences in a middle school where he and his best friend, Rowley, undersized weaklings amid boys who need to shave twice daily, hope just to survive, but when Rowley grows more popular, Greg must take drastic measures to save their friendship

"Kinney's background as a cartoonist is apparent in this hybrid book that falls somewhere between traditional prose and graphic novel. . . . The pace moves quickly. The first of three installments, it is an excellent choice for reluctant readers, but more experienced readers will also find much to enjoy and relate to." SLJ

Other titles about Greg are:

Diary of a wimpy kid: Rodrick rules (2008)
Diary of a wimpy kid: the last straw (2009)
Diary of a wimpy kid: dog days (2009)

The **third** wheel; Jeff Kinney. Amulet Books 2012 217 p. (Diary of a wimpy kid) $13.95; $13.95

Grades: 5 6 7 8   **Fic**

1. Dance -- Juvenile fiction 2. School stories -- Juvenile fiction 3. Humorous fiction -- Juvenile fiction
ISBN 1419705849; 9781419705847

This children's story, by Jeff Kinney, is book 7 in the "Diary of a Wimpy Kid" series. "A dance at Greg's middle school has everyone scrambling to find a partner, and Greg is determined not to be left by the wayside. So he concocts a desperate plan to find someone . . . to go with on the big night. But Greg's schemes go hilariously awry, and his only option is to attend the dance with his best friend, Rowley Jefferson, and a female classmate as a 'group of friends.'" (Publisher's note)

Kinsey-Warnock, Natalie

True colors; by Natalie Kinsey-Warnock. Alfred A. Knopf Books for Young Readers 2012 242 p. (hard cover) $15.99

Grades: 4 5 6 7   **Fic**

1. Absent mothers -- Fiction 2. Orphans -- Juvenile fiction 3. Abandoned children -- Fiction 4. Identity (Psychology) -- Juvenile fiction 5. Identity -- Fiction 6. Foundlings -- Fiction 7. Farm life -- Vermont -- Fiction 8. People with mental disabilities -- Fiction
ISBN 0375860991; 9780375854538; 9780375860997; 9780375897061; 9780375960994

LC 2011037863

This book by Natalie Kinsey-Warnock "tells the story of one girl's journey to find the mother she never had, set against the period backdrop of a small farming town in 1950s Vermont. For her entire life, 10-year-old Blue has never known her mother. . . . Over the course of one summer, she resolves to finally find out who she is. . . . Her search leads her down a road of self-discovery that will change her life forever." (Publisher's note)

Kirby, Matthew J.
★ The **clockwork** three. Scholastic Press 2010 391p $17.99

Grades: 5 6 7 8 **Fic**
1. Fantasy fiction 2. Friendship -- Fiction 3. Clocks and watches -- Fiction 4. Young adult literature -- Works
ISBN 978-0-545-20337-1; 0-545-20337-6

LC 2009-37879
As mysterious circumstances bring Giuseppe, Frederick, and Hannah together, their lives soon interlock like the turning gears in a clock and they realize that each one holds a key to solving the others' mysteries

This is a "riveting historical fantasy. . . . Kirby has assembled all the ingredients for a rousing adventure, which he delivers with rich, transporting prose." Publ Wkly

Icefall. Scholastic Press 2011 325p $17.99

Grades: 5 6 7 8 **Fic**
1. Fantasy fiction 2. Ice -- Fiction 3. Winter -- Fiction 4. Storytelling -- Fiction
ISBN 978-0-545-27424-1; 0-545-27424-9

LC 2011000890
"Kirby turns in a claustrophobic, thought-provoking coming-of-age adventure that shows a young woman growing into her own, while demonstrating the power of myth and legend. Kirby's attention to detail and stark descriptions make this an effective mood piece." Publ Wkly

Klages, Ellen
White sands, red menace. Viking 2008 337p $16.99

Grades: 5 6 7 8 **Fic**
1. Cold war -- Fiction 2. Scientists -- Fiction 3. Atomic bomb -- Fiction
ISBN 978-0-670-06235-5; 0-670-06235-9
"The groundbreaking science is part of daily life for the smart techno-teens, and the adult characters are as compelling as the kids. . . . Along with . . . global issues, Klages' compelling story explores personal relationships and what it means to be a family." Booklist

★ The **green** glass sea. Viking 2006 321p $16.99; pa $7.99

Grades: 5 6 7 8 **Fic**
1. Scientists -- Fiction 2. Atomic bomb -- Fiction 3. World War, 1939-1945 -- Fiction 4. Young adult literature -- Works
ISBN 0-670-06134-4; 0-14-241149-3 pa
It is 1943, and 11-year-old Dewey Kerrigan is traveling west on a train to live with her scientist father—but no one will tell her exactly where he is. When she reaches Los Alamos, New Mexico, she learns why: he's working on a top secret government program.

"Many readers will know as little about the true nature of the project as the girls do, so the gradual revelation of facts is especially effective, while those who already know about Los Alamos's historical significance will experience the story in a different, but equally powerful, way." SLJ

Klass, David
★ **Stuck** on Earth. Farrar Straus & Giroux 2010 227p $16.99

Grades: 4 5 6 7 **Fic**
1. Science fiction 2. Bullies -- Fiction 3. Extraterrestrial beings -- Fiction
ISBN 978-0-374-39951-1; 0-374-39951-4

LC 2008--48133
On a secret mission to evaluate whether the human race should be annihilated, a space alien inhabits the body of a bullied fourteen-year-old boy.

"Klass's . . . thoughtful, often wrenching book offers plenty to think about, from what's really going on in Tom's head to questions about human responsibility to the planet and each other. It takes 'alienation' to a whole new level." Publ Wkly

Klimo, Kate
The **dragon** in the sock drawer; with illustrations by John Schroades. Random House Childrens Books 2008 159p il (Dragon keepers) $14.99; lib bdg $17.99

Grades: 3 4 5 **Fic**
1. Eggs -- Fiction 2. Cousins -- Fiction 3. Dragons -- Fiction
ISBN 978-0-375-85587-0; 0-375-85587-4; 978-0-375-95587-7 lib bdg; 0-375-95587-9 lib bdg

LC 2007-42306
Cousins Jesse and Daisy always knew they would have a magical adventure, but they are not prepared when the "thunder egg" Jesse has found turns out to be a dragon egg that is about to hatch

"Illustrated with small black-and-white drawings to introduce each of the 11 chapters, this novel, with its unique and modern twists, is a great addition to the dragon genre for younger readers." SLJ

Other titles in this series are:
The dragon in the driveway (2009)
The dragon in the library (2010)
The dragon in the volcano (2011)

Kline, Suzy
★ **Horrible** Harry in room 2B; pictures by Frank Remkiewicz. Viking Kestrel 1988 56p il hardcover o.p. pa $3.99

Grades: 2 3 4 **Fic**
1. School stories
ISBN 0-14-038552-5 pa

LC 88-14204
Harry "is the devilish second grader who plays pranks and gets into mischief but can still end up a good friend. In a series of brief scenes, children meet Harry as he shows a garter snake to Song Lee and later ends up being a snake himself for Halloween. His trick to make scary people out of pencil stubs backfires when no one is scared, and his budding romance with Song Lee goes nowhere on the trip to the aquarium. . . . This story should prove to be popular with those just starting chapter books." SLJ

Other titles about Horrible Harry and Song Lee are:
Horrible Harry and the ant invasion (1989)
Horrible Harry and the Christmas surprise (1991)
Horrible Harry and the dragon war (2002)
Horrible Harry and the Drop of Doom (1998)
Horrible Harry and the dungeon (1996)
Horrible Harry and the goog (2005)

Horrible Harry and the green slime (1989)
Horrible Harry and the holidaze (2003)
Horrible Harry and the kickball wedding (1992)
Horrible Harry and the locked closet (2004)
Horrible Harry and the mud gremlins (2003)
Horrible Harry and the purple people (1997)
Horrible Harry and the secret treasure (2011)
Horrible Harry and the triple revenge (2006)
Horrible Harry at Halloween (2000)
Horrible Harry bugs the three bears (2008)
Horrible Harry goes to the moon (2000)
Horrible Harry moves up to third grade (1998)
Horrible Harry takes the cake (2006)
Horrible Harry's secret (1990)
Song Lee and Leech Man (1995)
Song Lee and the hamster hunt (1994)
Song Lee and the I hate you notes (1999)
Song Lee in room 2B (1993)

Klise, Kate

Dying to meet you; illustrated by M. Sarah Klise. Harcourt 2009 147p il (43 Old Cemetery Road) $15
Grades: 3 4 5 6   **Fic**
1. Ghost stories 2. Authors -- Fiction 3. Letters -- Fiction
ISBN 978-0-15-205727-5; 0-15-205727-7

LC 2007-28534

In this story told mostly through letters, children's book author, I. B. Grumply, gets more than he bargained for when he rents a quiet place to write for the summer.

"This first title in a new series will appeal to readers, especially reluctant ones, as it moves quickly and leaves its audience eager for book two, which is announced in this ghastly and fun tale." SLJ

Other titles in this series are:
Over my dead body (2009)
Till death do us bark (2011)

★ **Grounded**. Feiwel and Friends 2010 196p $16.99
Grades: 4 5 6 7   **Fic**
1. Death -- Fiction 2. Bereavement -- Fiction 3. Swindlers and swindling -- Fiction
ISBN 978-0-312-57039-2; 0-312-57039-2

LC 2010013008

After her father, brother, and sister are killed in a plane crash, twelve-year-old Daralynn's life in tiny Digginsville, Missouri, proceeds as her mother turns angry and embittered, her grandmother becomes senile, and her flamboyant aunt continues to run the Summer Sunset Retirement Home for Distinguished Gentlemen, while being courted by the owner of the town's new crematorium.

"Dark humor melds with genuine pathos in Klise's moving novel. . . . This quiet story illuminates and celebrates the human need for connection beyond the grave." Booklist

Homesick; Kate Klise. 1st ed. Feiwel and Friends 2012 192 p. (hardcover) $16.99
Grades: 4 5 6 7 8   **Fic**
1. Divorce -- Fiction 2. Family life -- Fiction
ISBN 1250008425; 9781250008428

In this book by Kate Klise, "Benny's parents are splitting up. . . . Benny's dad has always liked clutter, but now, he begins hoarding everything. . . . As his house grows more cluttered and his father grows more distant, Benny tries to

sort out whether he can change anything at all. Meanwhile, a local teacher enters their quiet Missouri town in America's Most Charming Small Town contest, and the pressure is on to clean up the area, especially Benny's ramshackle of a house." (Publisher's note)

Regarding the sink; where, oh where, did Waters go? illustrated by M. Sarah Klise. Harcourt 2004 127p il $15
Grades: 4 5 6 7   **Fic**
1. School stories
ISBN 0-15-205019-1

LC 2003-26560

A series of letters reveals the selection of the famous fountain designer, Florence Waters, to design a new sink for the Geyser Creek Middle School cafeteria, her subsequent disappearance, and the efforts of a class of sixth-graders to find her

"Piecing the story and clues together is satisfying. Introduce this book to savvy readers who are ready for the jump to a clever, unconventional reading experience." SLJ

Other titles in this series are:
Regarding the bathrooms (2006)
Regarding the bees (2007)
Regarding the fountain (1998)
Regarding the trees (2005)

Kluger, Jeffrey

★ **Freedom** stone. Philomel Books 2011 316p $16.99
Grades: 4 5 6   **Fic**
1. Magic -- Fiction 2. Slavery -- Fiction 3. African Americans -- Fiction
ISBN 978-0-399-25214-3; 0-399-25214-2

LC 2010-06028

With the help of a magical stone from Africa, a thirteen-year-old slave travels to the battle of Vicksburg to clear her father's name and free her family from bondage.

Kluger "adeptly mixes drama, fantasy, romance, and history, while creating characters so determined to survive that readers can't help being drawn into their plights. In a climax that breaks with reality but that will keep readers hungry to learn the outcome, Kluger proves his storytelling prowess." Publ Wkly

Knight, Joan

Charlotte in Giverny; by Joan MacPhail Knight; watercolor illustrations by Melissa Sweet. Chronicle Bks. 2000 un il $16.95; pa $6.95
Grades: 3 4 5   **Fic**
1. Artists -- Fiction 2. Painting, French -- Juvenile fiction 3. Impressionism (Art) -- Juvenile fiction
ISBN 0-8118-2383-0; 0-8118-5803-0 pa

LC 99-6878

While living in France in 1892, Charlotte, a young American girl, writes a journal of her experiences including those among the Impressionist painters at the artist colony of Giverny. Includes profiles of artists who appear in the journal and a glossary of French words

"The profuse illustrations, a mix of 1890s postcards and other memorabilia, reproductions of (mostly) impressionistic paintings by the mentioned artists, and Melissa Sweet's delicately drawn vignettes of vegetables and other items, lay an air of sunny, well-bred tranquility over the scene." Booklist

Other titles in this series are:

Charlotte in New York (2006)

Charlotte in Paris (2003)

Charlotte in London (2009)

Knudsen, Michelle

The **dragon** of Trelian. Candlewick Press 2009 407p
$16.99

Grades: 4 5 6 7   **Fic**

1. Fantasy fiction 2. Magic -- Fiction 3. Dragons --
Fiction 4. Princesses -- Fiction

ISBN 978-0-7636-3455-1; 0-7636-3455-7

LC 2008025378

A mage's apprentice, a princess, and a dragon combine
their strength and magic to bring down a traitor and restore
peace to the kingdom of Trelian.

"Knudsen does a fantastic job of creating sympathetic
and realistic characters that really drive the story. The tale is
adventurous and exciting with many twists and turns along
the way." SLJ

The **princess** of Trelian; Michelle Knudsen. Candlewick Press 2012 437 p.

Grades: 4 5 6 7   **Fic**

1. Magic -- Juvenile fiction 2. Dragons -- Juvenile
fiction 3. Princesses -- Juvenile fiction 4. Fantasy
fiction -- Juvenile fiction 5. Fantasy 6. Magic -- Fiction
7. Dragons -- Fiction 8. Princesses -- Fiction

ISBN 0763650625; 9780763650629

LC 2011047174

In this juvenile fantasy novel, by Michelle Knudsen, a
"sequel to 'The Dragon of Trelian,' . . . Princess Meg is now
heir to the throne, but her subjects are uneasy about her . . .
dragon, and it only becomes worse when a neighboring king
accuses the dragon of ravaging the countryside. . . . Meanwhile, Meg's best friend Calen has earned his mage's mark,
but a mysterious, magical attack occurs. . . . [T]he deposed
villain from the previous book is behind all the mischief."
(Horn Book Magazine)

Knudson, Mike

Raymond and Graham rule the school; by Mike Knudson and Steve Wilkinson; illustrated by Stacy Curtis. Viking
Childrens Books 2008 136p il $14.99; pa $6.99

Grades: 2 3 4   **Fic**

1. School stories 2. Theater -- Fiction 3. Friendship
-- Fiction

ISBN 978-0-670-01101-8; 0-670-01101-0; 978-0-14-
241426-2 pa; 0-14-241426-3 pa

LC 2007033350

Best friends Raymond and Graham have looked forward
to being the "oldest, coolest, toughest" boys at East Mill-
creek Elementary School, but from the start of fourth grade
everything goes wrong, from getting the scary teacher to not
getting the lead in the school play

"This story is filled with nonstop action and kid-friendly
humor. Done in an exaggerated cartoon style, Curtis's occasional black-and-white illustrations perfectly suit the tone
of the text." SLJ

Other titles about Raymond and Graham are:

Raymond and Graham, dancing dudes (2008)

Raymond and Graham: bases loaded (2010)

Raymond and Graham: cool campers (2010)

Konigsburg, E. L.

★ **From** the mixed-up files of Mrs. Basil E. Frankweiler. Atheneum Pubs. 1967 162p il $16; pa $9.99

Grades: 4 5 6   **Fic**

ISBN 0-689-20586-4; 1-4169-4975-5 pa

Awarded the Newbery Medal, 1968

"Claudia, feeling misunderstood at home, takes her
younger brother and runs away to New York where she sets
up housekeeping in the Metropolitan Museum of Art, making ingenious arrangements for sleeping, bathing, and laun-
dering. She and James also look for clues to the authenticity
of an alleged Michelangelo statue, the true story of which
is locked in the files of Mrs. Frankweiler, its former owner.
Claudia's progress toward maturity is also a unique introduction to the Metropolitan Museum." Moorachian. What
is a City?

Jennifer, Hecate, Macbeth, William McKinley, and me,
Elizabeth. Atheneum Pubs. 1967 117p il $16; pa $5.99

Grades: 4 5 6   **Fic**

1. Friendship -- Fiction 2. Witchcraft -- Fiction 3.
African Americans -- Fiction

ISBN 0-689-30007-7; 1-4169-3396-4 pa

A Newbery Medal honor book, 1968

"Two fifth grade girls, one of whom is the first black
child in a middle-income suburb, play at being apprentice
witches in this amusing and perceptive story." NY Public
Libr. Black Exper in Child Books

Up from Jericho Tel. Atheneum Pubs. 1986 178p
hardcover o.p. pa $4.99

Grades: 5 6 7 8   **Fic**

1. Mystery fiction 2. Actors -- Fiction

ISBN 0-689-31194-X; 0-689-82332-0 pa

LC 85-20061

"Konigsburg always provides fresh ideas, tart wit and
humor, and memorable characters. As for style, she is a natural and gifted storyteller. . . . This is a lively, clever, and very
funny book." Bull Cent Child Books

The **mysterious** edge of the heroic world. Atheneum
Books for Young Readers 2007 244p $16.99; pa $5.99

Grades: 5 6 7 8   **Fic**

1. Friendship -- Fiction 2. Art museums -- Fiction 3.
Young adult literature -- Works

ISBN 978-1-4169-4972-5; 1-4169-4972-0; 978-1-
4169-5353-1 pa; 1-4169-5353-1 pa

"This humorous, poignant, tragic, and mysterious story
has intertwining plots that peel away like the layers of an
onion." SLJ

A **proud** taste for scarlet and miniver. Atheneum Pubs.
1973 201p il $18.95; pa $5.99

Grades: 5 6 7 8   **Fic**

1. Queens

ISBN 0-689-30111-1; 0-689-84624-X pa

This is an historical novel about the 12th century queen,
Eleanor of Aquitaine, wife of kings of France and England
and mother of King Richard the Lion Hearted and King
John. Impatiently awaiting the arrival of her second husband, King Henry II, in heaven, she recalls her life with the
aid of some contemporaries

The author "has succeeded in making history amusing as well as interesting. . . . The characterization is superb. . . . The black-and-white drawings are skillfully as well as appropriately modeled upon medieval manuscript illuminations and add their share of joy to the book." Horn Book

★ The **view** from Saturday. Atheneum Bks. for Young Readers 1996 163p $16.95; pa $5.99

Grades: 4 5 6 7   **Fic**
1. School stories 2. Friendship -- Fiction 3. Physically handicapped -- Fiction
ISBN 0-689-80993-X; 0-689-81721-5 pa

             LC 95-52624

Awarded the Newbery Medal, 1997

Four students, with their own individual stories, develop a special bond and attract the attention of their teacher, a paraplegic, who choses them to represent their sixth-grade class in the Academic Bowl competition

"Glowing with humor and dusted with magic. . . . Wrought with deep compassion and a keen sense of balance." Publ Wkly

Koppe, Susanne

The **Nutcracker**; [by] E. T. A. Hoffmann; illustrated by Lisbeth Zwerger; retold by Susanne Koppe; translated from the German by Anthea Bell; North-South Books 2004 un il $15.95; lib bdg $16.50

Grades: 3 4 5   **Fic**
1. Fairy tales 2. Christmas -- Fiction
ISBN 0-7358-1733-2; 0-7358-1734-0 lib bdg

In this retelling of the original 1816 German story, Godfather Drosselmeier gives young Marie a nutcracker for Christmas, and she finds herself in a magical realm where she saves a boy from an evil curse

"This version features somewhat surreal, almost theatrically presented tableaux, delicately and darkly rendered in pen and ink and watercolor. . . . Koppe's retelling is . . . accessible and detailed." SLJ

Korman, Gordon

Framed. Scholastic Press 2011 234p $16.99

Grades: 3 4 5 6   **Fic**
1. School stories 2. Adventure fiction 3. Theft -- Fiction 4. Friendship -- Fiction
ISBN 978-0-545-17849-5; 0-545-17849-5

            LC 2010002583

Griffin Bing is in big trouble when a Super Bowl ring disappears from his middle school's display case, replaced by Griffin's retainer, and the more he and his friends investigate, the worse his situation becomes.

"This mystery will draw readers in with its quickly developing plot that combines unconventional characters and situations with believable dialogue and plot twists." SLJ

No more dead dogs. Hyperion Bks. for Children 2000 180p $15.99; pa $5.99

Grades: 5 6 7 8   **Fic**
1. Schools 2. Theater 3. Football 4. School stories 5. Humorous stories 6. Theater -- Fiction
ISBN 0-7868-0531-5; 0-7868-1601-5 pa

            LC 00-24313

"Humor abounds here, but underlying is the true angst of the middle school student." Voice Youth Advocates

The **sixth** grade nickname game. Hyperion Bks. for Children 1998 154p hardcover o.p. pa $5.99

Grades: 4 5 6 7   **Fic**
1. School stories 2. Humorous stories 3. Schools -- Fiction 4. Nicknames -- Fiction
ISBN 0-7868-0432-7; 0-7868-5190-2 pa

            LC 98-12343

Eleven-year-old best friends Jeff and Wiley, who like to give nicknames to their classmates, try to find the right one for the new girl Cassandra, while adjusting to the football coach who has become their new teacher

"This is a funny, fast-paced grade-school romp." Bull Cent Child Books

Swindle. Scholastic Press 2008 252p (Swindle)

Grades: 4 5 6   **Fic**
1. Baseball cards -- Fiction 2. Swindlers and swindling -- Fiction
ISBN 0-439-90344-0; 0-439-90345-9 pa; 978-0-439-90344-8; 978-0-439-90345-5 pa

            LC 2007-17225

After unscrupulous collector S. Wendell Palomino cons him out of a valuable baseball card, sixth-grader Griffin Bing puts together a band of misfits to break into Palomino's store and steal the card back, planning to use the money to finance his father's failing invention, the SmartPick fruit picker. "Grades four to six." (Bull Cent Child Books)

"The plot is the main attraction, and its clever intricacies—silly, deceptively predictable, and seasoned with the occasional unexpected twist—do not disappoint." Booklist

Zoobreak. Scholastic Press 2009 230p $16.99; pa $6.99

Grades: 3 4 5 6   **Fic**
1. Adventure fiction 2. Zoos -- Fiction 3. Theft -- Fiction 4. Lost and found possessions -- Fiction
ISBN 978-0-545-12499-7; 0-545-12499-9; 978-0-545-12500-0 pa; 0-545-12500-6 pa

            LC 2009015456

After a class trip to a floating zoo where animals are mistreated and Savannah's missing pet monkey is found in a cage, Long Island sixth-grader Griffin Bing and his band of misfits plan a rescue.

"Both children and adults will find the story fast moving and enjoyable. The often-unpredictable plot is interesting, full of humor, and good fun." Voice Youth Advocates

Kornblatt, Marc

Izzy's place. Margaret K. McElderry Bks. 2003 118p $16.95

Grades: 4 5 6   **Fic**
1. Death 2. Grandparents 3. Family problems 4. Death -- Fiction
ISBN 0-689-84639-8

            LC 2002-6185

While spending the summer at his grandmother's Indiana home, ten-year-old Henry Stone gets help from a new friend in coping with the recent death of his grandfather and the possibility of his parents getting divorced

"In straightforward language, Kornblatt writes a realistic, affecting account of the challenges of coming to terms with grief and family difficulties and the process of acceptance and healing." Booklist

Koss, Amy Goldman

The **girls**. Dial Bks. for Young Readers 2000 121p
$16.99; pa $5.99

Grades: 5 6 7 8   **Fic**

1. Friendship 2. Interpersonal relations 3. Behavior 4.
Friendship -- Fiction

ISBN 0-8037-2494-2; 0-14-230033-0 pa

LC 99-19318

"This provocative page-turner will be passed from one
girl to the next." SLJ

Krensky, Stephen

Dangerous crossing; the revolutionary voyage of John
Quincy Adams. by Stephen Krensky; illustrated by Greg
Harlin. Dutton Children's Books 2005 un il $16.99

Grades: 2 3 4   **Fic**

1. Presidents 2. Vice-presidents 3. Senators 4.
Members of Congress 5. Secretaries of state 6. Voyages
and travels -- Fiction

ISBN 0-525-46966-4

LC 2003-40852

In 1778, ten-year-old Johnny Adams and his father make
a dangerous midwinter voyage from Massachusetts to Paris in hopes of gaining support for the colonies during the
American Revolution

"Harlin's richly atmospheric paintings dramatize scene
after scene with subtle hues and lighting effects. . . . The
story offers a stirring account of life aboard ship, spiced with
details from the voyage. An appended author's note comments on the story's source and the illustrious careers of the
two Adamses." Booklist

Krieg, Jim

★ **Griff** Carver, hallway patrol. Razorbill 2010 224p
$15.99

Grades: 4 5 6 7   **Fic**

1. School stories 2. Counterfeits and counterfeiting --
Fiction

ISBN 978-1-59514-276-4; 1-59514-276-2

LC 2009-32553

Legendary Griff Carver joins the Rampart Middle
School Hallway Patrol and, with the help of his friend Tommy, Griff solves the case of counterfeit hall passes.

"With comically over-the-top cop lingo . . . Griff and
Tommy tell their stories through incident reports and interviews, adding drama and humor to the most mundane aspects
of school. . . . Krieg will keep readers chuckling through the
hilarious but action-packed showdown." Publ Wkly

Krishnaswami, Uma

The **Girl** of the Wish Garden; A Thumbelina Story.
Pgw 2013 32 p. (hardcover) $17.95

Grades: K 1 2   **Fic**

1. Fairy tales 2. Picture books for children

ISBN 155498324X; 9781554983247

In this picture book, the "thumb-size Lina begins her
journey when she is captured by a giant frog and then the
story loosely follows the path of the original [Hans Christian Andersen] tale. She is swept along at the mercy of the
winds and follows the tunes of the birds, and each new encounter is foreshadowed by her sung cries for help." (School
Library Journal)

★ The **grand** plan to fix everything; [illustrations by
Abigail Halpin] Atheneum Books for Young Readers 2011
224p il $16.99

Grades: 4 5 6 7   **Fic**

1. Actors -- Fiction 2. Moving -- Fiction 3. Friendship
-- Fiction 4. East Indian Americans -- Fiction

ISBN 978-1-4169-9589-0; 1-4169-9589-7

LC 2010035145

Eleven-year-old Dini loves movies, and so when she
learns that her family is moving to India for two years,
her devastation over leaving her best friend in Maryland is
tempered by the possibility of meeting her favorite actress,
Dolly Singh.

"An out-of-the-ordinary setting, a distinctive middle-
grade character with an unusual passion, and the pace of
a lively Bollywood 'fillum' make this novel a delight."
Publ Wkly

Krull, Kathleen

Fartiste; [by] Kathleen Krull and Paul Brewer; illustrated by Boris Kulikov. Simon & Schuster Books for Young
Readers 2008 un il $16.99

Grades: 3 4 5   **Fic**

1. Entertainers 2. Stories in rhyme 3. Entertainers
-- Fiction

ISBN 978-1-4169-2828-7; 1-4169-2828-6

LC 2007-37526

In nineteenth-century France, Joseph Pujol, a little boy
who can control his farts, grows up to become Le Petomaine,
making audiences laugh at the Moulin Rouge in Paris with
his animal noises, songs, and other sounds. Includes facts
about Joseph Pujol and life in turn-of-the-century Paris.

"Written in well-rhymed couplets, this gleefully tasteless
tale reads easily. Kulikov's illustrations allude to the age of
vaudevillian stage performance, painted playbills, and fire-
hazard footlights that bronzed everything nearest them in
golden warmth." SLJ

Krumgold, Joseph

Onion John; illustrated by Symeon Shimin. Crowell
1959 248p il lib bdg $15.89; pa $5.95

Grades: 5 6 7 8   **Fic**

1. Friendship -- Fiction

ISBN 0-690-04698-7 lib bdg; 0-06-440144-8 pa

Awarded the Newbery Medal, 1960

"The writing has dignity and strength. There is conflict,
drama, and excellent character portrayal." SLJ

Kuhlman, Evan

The **last** invisible boy; written by Evan Kuhlman; illustrated by J. P. Coovert. Atheneum Books for Young Readers
2008 233p il $16.99; pa $5.99

Grades: 4 5 6 7   **Fic**

1. School stories 2. Bereavement -- Fiction 3. Family
life -- Fiction 4. Father-son relationship -- Fiction

ISBN 978-1-4169-5797-3; 1-4169-5797-9; 978-1-
4169-6089-8 pa; 1-4169-6089-9 pa

LC 2007-40258

In the wake of his father's sudden death, twelve-year-
old Finn feels he is becoming invisible as his hair and skin
become whiter by the day, and so he writes and illustrates a
book to try to understand what is happening and to hold on
to himself and his father

"Vivid details . . . add depth to the characterizations and grow in meaning as the story progresses. . . . Finn's distinct narrative voice, and the sweet precision with which the story unfolds, give this title a touching resonance." Booklist

Kuijer, Guus
The **book** of everything; a novel. translated by John Nieuwenhuizen. Arthur A. Levine Books 2006 101p hardcover o.p. $16.99
Grades: 5 6 7 8   **Fic**
  1. Family life -- Fiction 2. Christian life -- Fiction
  ISBN 0-439-74918-2; 0-439-74919-0 pa
                                    LC 2005-18717
Nine-year-old Thomas receives encouragement from many sources, including candid talks with Jesus, to help him tolerate the strict family life dictated by his deeply-religious father.
"Set in Amsterdam in 1951, this slender Dutch novel is filled with quirky characters, frightening family confrontations, and laugh-out-loud moments. Dark humor and a wry, ironic tone . . . give the story a sharp edge." Booklist

Kurtz, Chris
The **adventures** of a South Pole pig; a novel of snow and courage. Chris Kurtz; illustrations by Jennifer Black Reinhardt. Harcourt Children's Books, Houghton Mifflin Harcourt 2013 288 p. $16.99
Grades: 4 5 6 7   **Fic**
  1. Pigs -- Juvenile fiction 2. Antarctica -- Juvenile fiction
  3. Sled dog racing -- Juvenile fiction 4. Adventure fiction -- Juvenile fiction 5. Dogs -- Fiction 6. Pigs -- Fiction 7. Sled dogs -- Fiction 8. Dogsledding -- Fiction 9. Adventure and adventurers -- Fiction
  ISBN 0547634552; 9780547634555
                                    LC 2012027226
In this children's story, by Chris Kurtz, illustrated by Jennifer Black Reinhardt, "the day Flora spots a team of sled dogs is the day she sets her heart on becoming a sled pig. Before she knows it, she's on board a ship to Antarctica for the most exhilarating--and dangerous--adventure of her life." (Publisher's note)

The **pup** who cried wolf; illustrations by Guy Francis. Bloomsbury 2010 132p il (Animal tales) $15.99; pa $5.99
Grades: 2 3 4   **Fic**
  1. Dogs -- Fiction 2. Wolves -- Fiction
  ISBN 978-1-59990-497-9; 1-59990-497-7; 978-1-59990-492-4 pa; 1-59990-492-6 pa
Lobo, a Chihuahua from New York City who feels he is truly a wolf in an undersized body, goes to Yellowstone National Park with his mistress and dreams of running wild with his wolf brothers.
"Children will love this humorous story and empathize with feisty, misguided Lobo. . . . A few black-and-white illustrations, some full page, are scattered throughout. This story will appeal to beginning chapter book and reluctant readers alike." SLJ

Kurtz, Jane
The **storyteller's** beads. Harcourt Brace & Co. 1998 154p $15
Grades: 5 6 7 8   **Fic**
  1. Blind -- Fiction 2. Friendship -- Fiction 3. Prejudices

-- Fiction
  ISBN 0-15-201074-2
                                    LC 97-42312
During the political strife and famine of the 1980's, two Ethiopian girls, one Christian and the other Jewish and blind, struggle to overcome many difficulties, including their prejudices about each other, as they make the dangerous journey out of Ethiopia
"The novel presents an involving portrait of Ethiopian culture through the eyes of two well-defined characters." Horn Book Guide

Kushner, Ellen
The **golden** dreydl; [by] Ellen Kushner; illustrations by Ilene Winn-Lederer. Charlesbridge 2007 126p il $15.95
Grades: 3 4 5   **Fic**
  1. Jews -- Fiction 2. Magic -- Fiction 3. Hanukkah -- Fiction
  ISBN 978-1-58089-135-6
                                    LC 2006021257
After receiving a magic dreydl at Aunt Leah's Chanukah party, Sara is catapulted into an alternate world of demons, fools, sorcerers, and sages
"The chatty storytelling is fast, furious, and sometimes funny, . . . and scattered throughout are delicate black-and-white illustrations that capture the magical realism." Booklist

L'Engle, Madeleine
Meet the Austins. Farrar, Straus & Giroux 1997 216p hardcover o.p. pa $6.99
Grades: 5 6 7 8   **Fic**
  1. Orphans -- Fiction 2. Family life -- Fiction
  ISBN 0-374-34929-0; 0-312-37931-5 pa
                                    LC 96-27655
A revised edition of the title first published 1960 by Vanguard Press
ALA YALSA Margaret A. Edwards Award (1998)
A "story of the family of a country doctor, told by the twelve-year-old daughter, during a year in which a spoiled young orphan, Maggy, comes to live with them. . . . [This is an] account of the family's adjustment to Maggy and hers to them." Horn Book
Other titles about the Austins are:
  The moon by night (1963)
  A ring of endless light (1980)
  Troubling a star (1994)

The **twenty**-four days before Christmas; an Austin family story. illustrated by Jill Weber. Farrar, Straus & Giroux 2010 45p il $12.99
Grades: 3 4 5   **Fic**
  1. Christmas -- Fiction 2. Family life -- Fiction 3. Christmas stories -- Juvenile literature
  ISBN 978-0-374-38005-2; 0-374-38005-8
A new edition of the title first published 1984
"Vicky Austin, teenage star of L'Engle's Austin Family Chronicles, narrates this story set in her childhood. It's a busy time for the family: while seven-year-old Vicky nervously rehearses for the Christmas pageant, the entire clan prepares for the arrival of a new baby. This edition includes unobtrusive spot illustrations done in an inviting folk-art style." Horn Book Guide

★ **A wrinkle** in time. Farrar, Straus & Giroux 1962
211p $17; pa $7.99

Grades: 5 6 7 8 9 10   **Fic**

1. Fantasy fiction

ISBN 0-374-38613-7; 0-312-36754-6 pa

ALA YALSA Margaret A. Edwards Award (1998)

Awarded The Newbery Medal, 1963

This book "makes unusual demands on the imagination
and consequently gives great rewards." Horn Book

Other titles in this series are:

A swiftly tilting planet (1978)

A wind in the door (1973)

La Fevers, R. L.

Flight of the phoenix; illustrated by Kelly Murphy.
Houghton Mifflin Books for Children 2009 137p il (Nathaniel Fludd, Beastologist) $16

Grades: 3 4 5   **Fic**

1. Adventure fiction 2. Cousins -- Fiction 3. Orphans
-- Fiction 4. Bedouins -- Fiction 5. Mythical animals
-- Fiction 6. Phoenix (Mythical bird) -- Fiction

ISBN 978-0-547-23865-4; 0-547-23865-7

LC 2009-28799

In 1928, when timid ten-year-old Nate learns that his
parents have been lost at sea, he joins his father's cousin
on a flight to Arabia where they must oversee the death
and rebirth of the phoenix, thus beginning his training as a
"beastologist."

"This is a solid start to a new series. . . . The story is
packed with adventure and mythological creatures. Children
who love fantasy, myth, exotic settings, and even a little
dose of history will relate to Nate." SLJ

Other title in this series are:

The basilisk's lair (2010)

The unicorn's tale (2011)

Theodosia and the Serpents of Chaos; illustrated by
Yoko Tanaka. Houghton Mifflin 2007 343p il $16; pa
$6.99

Grades: 4 5 6 7   **Fic**

1. Adventure fiction 2. Magic -- Fiction 3. Museums
-- Fiction

ISBN 978-0-618-75638-4; 0-618-75638-8; 978-0-618-
99976-7 pa; 0-618-99976-0 pa

LC 2006-34284

Set in 1906 London and Cairo, this mystery adventure
introduces an intrepid heroine—Theodosia Throckmorton,
who is thrust into the heart of a mystery when she learns
an ancient Egyptian amulet carries a curse that threatens to
crumble the British Empire

"It's the delicious, precise, and atmospheric details
(nicely extended in Tanaka's few, stylized illustrations) that
will capture and hold readers." Booklist

Other titles about Theodosia are:

Theodosia and the Staff of Osiris (2008)

Theodosia and the Eyes of Horus (2010)

Theodosia and the last Pharoah (2011)

La Valley, Josanne

The **Vine** basket; by Josanne La Valley. Clarion Books
2013 252 p. (hardcover) $16.99

Grades: 4 5 6 7 8   **Fic**

1. China -- Fiction 2. Farm life -- Fiction 3. Basket

making -- Fiction 4. Ethnic relations -- Fiction 5.
Farm life -- China -- Fiction 6. Fathers and daughters
-- Fiction 7. Uighur (Turkic people) -- Fiction

ISBN 0547848013; 9780547848013

LC 2012021007

In this novel, by Josanne La Valley, "things aren't looking good for fourteen-year-old Mehrigul. She yearns to be
in school, but she's needed on the family farm. . . . Her only
hope is an American woman who buys one of her decorative
vine baskets for a staggering sum and says she will return in
three weeks for more. Mehrigul must brave terrible storms,
torn-up hands from working the fields, and her father's scorn
to get the baskets done." (Publisher's note)

"The vivid and authentic sense of place, custom, and
politics serves as an effective vehicle for the skillfully characterized, emotionally charged story. . . . The realistic and
satisfying resolution will resonate with readers . . . An absorbing read and an excellent choice for expanding global
understanding." SLJ

LaFaye, A.

Water steps. Milkweed Editions 2009 175p $16.95;
pa $6.95

Grades: 4 5 6 7   **Fic**

1. Water -- Fiction 2. Phobias -- Fiction 3. Irish
Americans -- Fiction

ISBN 978-1-57131-687-5; 1-57131-687-6; 978-1-
57131-686-8 pa; 1-57131-686-8 pa

LC 2008011684

Eleven-year-old Kyna, terrified of water since her family
drowned in a storm that nearly took her life as well, works
to overcome her phobia when her adoptive parents, Irish immigrants with a mysterious past, rent a cabin on Lake Champlain for the summer.

"The language is almost poetic with its use of sensory
detail, alliteration, and precise word choices. A satisfying
story of overcoming one's fears and discovering secrets."
SLJ

Worth. Simon & Schuster Books for Young Readers
2004 144p $15.95; pa $5.99

Grades: 5 6 7 8   **Fic**

1. Orphans -- Fiction 2. Frontier and pioneer life --
Fiction

ISBN 0-689-85730-6; 1-4169-1624-5 pa

LC 2003-8101

After breaking his leg, eleven-year-old Nate feels useless
because he cannot work on the family farm in nineteenth-
century Nebraska, so when his father brings home an orphan
boy to help with the chores, Nate feels even worse.

"This short tale has a quietly epic sweep." Horn
Book Guide

LaFleur, Suzanne

Eight keys; by Suzanne LaFleur. Wendy Lamb Books
2011 216p $16.99; lib bdg $19.99

Grades: 3 4 5 6   **Fic**

1. School stories 2. Orphans -- Fiction 3. Friendship
-- Fiction 4. Family life -- Fiction

ISBN 978-0-385-74030-2; 0-385-74030-1; 978-0-385-
90833-7 lib bdg; 978-0-375-89905-8 e-book

LC 2010040137

When twelve-year-old Elise, orphaned since age nine,
becomes disheartened by middle school, with its bullies,

changing relationships, and higher expectations, keys to long-locked rooms and messages from her late father help her cope.

LaFleur "writes with uncommon sensitivity to the fraught period between childhood and the teenage years, when friendships balance on a razor's edge and nothing feels certain. The heart of the story lies in the layered relationships and characters that give the novel its powerful sense of realism." Publ Wkly

★ **Love,** Aubrey. Wendy Lamb Books 2009 262p $15.99; lib bdg $18.99

Grades: 5 6 7 8   **Fic**
1. School stories 2. Letters -- Fiction 3. Friendship -- Fiction 4. Bereavement -- Fiction 5. Grandmothers -- Fiction 6. Abandoned children -- Fiction 7. Depression (Psychology) -- Fiction

ISBN 978-0-385-73774-6; 0-385-73774-2; 978-0-385-90686-9 lib bdg; 0-385-90686-2 lib bdg

LC 2008-31742

While living with her Gram in Vermont, eleven-year-old Aubrey writes letters as a way of dealing with losing her father and sister in a car accident, and then being abandoned by her grief-stricken mother.

Aubrey's "detailed progression from denial to acceptance makes her both brave and credible in this honest and realistic portrayal of grief." Kirkus

Lacey, Josh
Island of Thieves; Josh Lacey. Houghton Mifflin 2012 228 p.

Grades: 4 5 6 7 8   **Fic**
1. Peru -- Fiction 2. Adventure fiction 3. Uncles -- Fiction 4. Pirates -- Fiction 5. Buried treasure -- Fiction 6. Islands -- Fiction 7. Mystery and detective stories 8. Adventure and adventurers -- Fiction

ISBN 0547763271; 9780547763279

LC 2011033893

In this children's novel, a boy takes part in "swashbuckling adventures in faraway places, freed from the strictures of parents, school, siblings and caregivers. . . . Tom nearly ruins his parents' vacation by accidentally burning down the shed in his backyard. . . . Harvey welcomes Tom . . . but as soon as Tom's parents leave, he starts packing for Peru. . . . When he tells Tom it's because he has an opportunity to hunt for pirate treasure, Tom blackmails his uncle into taking him along." (Kirkus)

Lai, Thanhha
★ **Inside** out and back again. Harper 2011 262p $15.99

Grades: 4 5 6 7   **Fic**
1. Novels in verse 2. Immigrants -- Fiction 3. Vietnamese Americans -- Fiction

ISBN 978-0-06-196278-3; 0-06-196278-3

LC 2010007855

"Based on Lai's personal experience, this first novel captures a child-refugee's struggle with rare honesty. Written in accessible, short free-verse poems." Booklist

Lairamore, Dawn
Ivy and the meanstalk. Holiday House 2011 227p $16.95

Grades: 4 5 6 7   **Fic**
1. Fairy tales 2. Giants -- Fiction 3. Dragons -- Fiction

4. Princesses -- Fiction
ISBN 978-0-8234-2392-7; 0-8234-2392-1

LC 2010048627

Fourteen-year-old Princess Ivy wants nothing more than to have a little fun in the company of her dragon friend, Elridge, but unless she can recover the magical harp snatched by a thieving youth named Jack long ago, her entire kingdom will suffer an unspeakable fate.

This is "delightful and humorous. . . . Lairamore's well-developed characters are excellent riffs on fairy-tale traditions. . . . Various settings are depicted in rich detail while never detracting from the narrative. The plot is filled with action-packed scenes." SLJ

★ **Ivy's** ever after. Holiday House 2010 311p $16.95

Grades: 4 5 6 7   **Fic**
1. Fairy tales 2. Dragons -- Fiction 3. Princesses -- Fiction

ISBN 978-0-8234-2261-6; 0-8234-2261-5

LC 2009-43288

Fourteen-year-old Ivy, a most unroyal princess, befriends Elridge, the dragon sent to keep her in a tower, and together they set out on a perilous quest to find Ivy's fairy godmother, who may be able to save both from their dire fates.

"Ivy is an engaging alternative to the standard damsel-in-distress figure, and with a lushly vivid setting, witty dialogue, and lots of adventure, this well-plotted first novel will appeal to fans of Vivian Vande Velde's A Hidden Magic (1985) and A Well-Timed Enchantment (1990)." Booklist

Landy, Derek
★ **Skulduggery** Pleasant. HarperCollinsPublishers 2007 392p $17.99; lib bdg $18.89; pa $7.99

Grades: 4 5 6 7   **Fic**
1. Fantasy fiction 2. Magic -- Fiction

ISBN 978-0-06-123115-5; 0-06-123115-0; 978-0-06-123116-2 lib bdg; 0-06-123116-9 lib bdg; 978-0-06-123117-9 pa; 0-06-123117-7 pa

LC 2006-29403

When twelve-year-old Stephanie inherits her weird uncle's estate, she must join forces with Skulduggery Pleasant, a skeleton mage, to save the world from the Faceless Ones

This "is a rich fantasy that is as engaging in its creative protagonists and villains as it is in the lightning-paced plot and sharp humor." Bulletin Cent Child Books

Other titles in this series are:
Playing with fire (2008)
The faceless ones (2009)

Lane, Andrew
Black ice; Andrew Lane. Farrar Straus Giroux 2013 288 p. (Sherlock Holmes. The legend begins) (hardcover) $17.99

Grades: 5 6 7 8   **Fic**
1. Mystery fiction 2. Holmes, Sherlock (Fictional character) -- Fiction 3. Murder -- Fiction 4. Mystery and detective stories

ISBN 0374387699; 9780374387693

LC 2012004996

This novel, by Andrew Lane, is the third book of the "Sherlock Holmes: The Legend Begins" series. "When Sherlock and Amyus Crowe, his American tutor, visit Sherlock's brother, Mycroft, in London, all they are expecting is lunch and some polite conversation. What they find shocks both of them to the core: a locked room, a dead body, and Mycroft holding a knife. . . . Threatened with the gallows, Mycroft needs Sherlock to save him." (Publisher's note)

Rebel fire; Andrew Lane. Farrar Straus Giroux 2012 343 p. (Sherlock Holmes. The legend begins) $16.99
Grades: 5 6 7 8   Fic
1. Mystery fiction 2. Holmes, Sherlock (Fictional character) -- Fiction 3. Mystery and detective stories
ISBN 0374387680; 9780374387686
                                        LC 2011000124
This novel, by Andrew Lane, is part of the "Sherlock Holmes: The Legend Begins" series. "Fourteen-year-old Sherlock Holmes knows that Amyus Crowe, his mysterious American tutor, has some dark secrets. But he didn't expect to find John Wilkes Booth, the notorious assassin, apparently alive and well in England--and Crowe somehow mixed up in it. . . . And so begins an adventure that will take Sherlock across the Atlantic, to the center of a deadly web." (Publisher's note)
Includes bibliographical references

Langton, Jane
The **fledgling**. Harper & Row 1980 182p il lib bdg $15.89; pa $5.95
Grades: 5 6 7 8   Fic
1. Fantasy fiction 2. Geese -- Fiction
ISBN 0-06-023679-5 lib bdg; 0-06-440121-9 pa
                                         LC 79-2008
A Newbery Medal honor book, 1981
"The writing is alternately solemn and funny, elevated and colloquial. It is mythic, almost sacred, in passages involving Georgie and the goose; it is satiric, almost irreverent, when it relates to Mr. Preek and Miss Prawn." Horn Book

Larson, Kirby
The **friendship** doll. Delacorte Press 2011 201p $15.99; lib bdg $18.99
Grades: 4 5 6   Fic
1. Dolls -- Fiction
ISBN 978-0-385-73745-6; 0-385-73745-9; 978-0-385-90667-8 lib bdg; 0-385-90667-6 lib bdg
                                        LC 2010-20615
Throughout the twentieth century, Miss Kanagawa, one of fifty-eight dolls made to serve as ambassadors from Japan to the United States, travels the country learning to love while changing the lives of those who need her.
"Larson brings her talent for historical fiction to this story. . . . Heavy topics such as death, grief, and aging are addressed in a straightforward yet remarkably affecting manner. The book's background is meticulously researched . . . and authentic Japanese cultural details are thoughtfully described. . . . This [is a] lovely tribute to a little-known piece of history." SLJ

Lasky, Kathryn
Felix takes the stage; illustrated by Stephen Gilpin. Scholastic Press 2010 142p il (The Deadlies) $15.99
Grades: 3 4 5   Fic
1. Moving -- Fiction 2. Spiders -- Fiction
ISBN 978-0-545-11681-7; 0-545-11681-3
Having been discovered, a family of poisonous but friendly brown recluse spiders must flee their cozy home in a symphony hall and go searching for a new place to live.

"Humor and action seamlessly blend as these arachnids struggle for survival against the scary E-Men who threaten them with extermination. Vivid characters, from the theatrical godspider Fat Cat to the pompous orb weaver Oliphant Uxbridge, make up the clever supporting cast. Genuinely funny dialogue helps move the brief chapters along, and Gilpin's lively black-and-white drawings provide an animated accompaniment." Kirkus

Hawksmaid; the untold story of Robin Hood and Maid Marian. Harper 2010 292p $16.99
Grades: 5 6 7 8   Fic
1. Falconry -- Fiction 2. Robin Hood (Legendary character) -- Fiction 3. Maid Marian (Legendary character) -- Fiction
ISBN 978-0-06-000071-4; 0-06-000071-6
In twelfth-century England, Matty grows up to be a master falconer, able to communicate with the devoted birds who later help her and Fynn, also known as Robin Hood, to foil Prince John's plot to steal the crown.
"Lasky nicely weaves details of 12th-century life into this suspenseful adventure whose fantasy ending may surprise but will certainly please readers." SLJ

Lone wolf. Scholastic Press 2010 219p il map (Wolves of the Beyond) $16.99
Grades: 5 6 7 8   Fic
1. Fantasy fiction 2. Wolves -- Fiction
ISBN 978-0-545-09310-1; 0-545-09310-4
                                        LC 2009-17007
Abandoned by his pack, a baby wolf with a mysterious mark on his deformed paw survives and embarks on a journey that will change the world of the wolves of the Beyond.
"Lasky merges anthropomorphic fantasy with realistic details about wolves and bears to produce an almost plausible emotional narrative, complete with dialogue and personalities. . . . The author builds a captivating world of forest, snow and volcanoes populated by intelligent animals and weaves a compelling story sure to bring readers back for the second installment." Kirkus
Other titles in this series are:
Shadow wolf (2010)
Watch wolf (2011)
Frost wolf (2011)

Spiders on the case; illustrated by Stephen Gilpin. Scholastic Press 2011 171p il (The Deadlies) $15.99
Grades: 3 4 5   Fic
1. Mystery fiction 2. Spiders -- Fiction 3. Libraries -- Fiction 4. Books and reading -- Fiction
ISBN 978-0-545-11682-4; 0-545-11682-1
                                        LC 2010047587
Buster, a walnut orb weaving spider, enlists the help of Jo Beth, one of a family of poisonous but friendly brown recluse spiders, to help stop humans who are stealing from the rare books room of the Boston Public Library, where the spiders live.
"Young readers will relate to the family drama and rivalry between Jo Bell and her siblings. There are moments of good humor. The spiders in the illustrations are full of expression, and the drawings help move the story along." SLJ

Latham, Irene

Leaving Gee's Bend. G.P. Putnam's Sons 2010 230p $16.99

Grades: 5 6 7 8   **Fic**

1. Quilts -- Fiction 2. African Americans -- Fiction

ISBN 978-0-399-25179-5; 0-399-25179-0

LC 2009-08732

Ludelphia Bennett, a determined, ten-year-old African American girl in 1932 Gee's Bend, Alabama, leaves home in an effort to find medical help for her sick mother, and she recounts her ensuing adventures in a quilt she is making.

"Ludelphia's voice is authentic and memorable, and Latham captures the tension of her dangerous journey and the racism she encounters." Booklist

Law, Ingrid

★ **Savvy**. Dial Books for Young Readers 2008 342p $16.99

Grades: 4 5 6 7   **Fic**

1. Magic -- Fiction 2. Family life -- Fiction 3. Voyages and travels -- Fiction

ISBN 978-0-8037-3306-0; 0-8037-3306-2

LC 2007-39814

A Newbery Medal honor book, 2009 Boston Globe-Horn Book Award honor book: Fiction and Poetry (2008)

Recounts the adventures of Mississippi (Mibs) Beaumont, whose thirteenth birthday has revealed her "savvy"—a magical power unique to each member of her family—just as her father is injured in a terrible accident

"Short chapters and cliffhangers keep the pace quick, while the mix of traditional language and vernacular helps the story feel both fresh and timeless. . . . [This is] a vibrant and cinematic novel that readers are going to love." Publ Wkly

★ **Scumble**. Dial Books for Young Readers 2010 400p il $16.99

Grades: 4 5 6 7   **Fic**

1. Magic -- Fiction 2. Ranch life -- Fiction

ISBN 978-0-8037-3307-7; 0-8037-3307-0

LC 2010-02444

Mibs's cousin Ledge is disappointed to discover that his "savvy"—the magical power unique to each member of their family—is to make things fall apart, which endangers his uncle Autry's ranch and reveals the family secret to future reporter Sarah.

This provides a "satisfying plot, delightful characters, alliterative language, and rich imagery." Booklist

Lawlor, Laurie

He will go fearless; [by] Laurie Lawlor. Simon & Schuster Books for Young Readers 2006 210p $15.95

Grades: 5 6 7 8   **Fic**

1. Father-son relationship -- Fiction 2. Overland journeys to the Pacific -- Fiction

ISBN 0-689-86579-1

LC 2005-06129

With the Civil War ended and Reconstruction begun, fifteen-year-old Billy resolves to make the dangerous and challenging journey West in search of real fortune – his true father.

"Danger, adventure, and survival combine to make this a richly detailed story." SLJ

The **school** at Crooked Creek; illustrated by Ronald Himler. Holiday House 2004 83p il map $15.95

Grades: 3 4 5   **Fic**

1. School stories 2. Frontier and pioneer life -- Fiction

ISBN 0-8234-1812-X

LC 2003-56759

Living on the nineteenth-century Indiana frontier with his parents and irritable older sister Louise, six-year-old Beansie dreads his first day of school, but his resilience surprises even his sister.

"The book is rich with colloquial language, superstitions, and information about the lifestyle of this pioneer family. Nicely done shaded, pencil drawings help set the tone." SLJ

Lawrence, Caroline

★ **P.K.** Pinkerton and the petrified man; Caroline Lawrence. G.P. Putnam's Sons 2013 320 p. (hardcover) $16.99

Grades: 4 5 6   **Fic**

1. Mystery fiction 2. Western stories 3. Orphans -- Fiction 4. Disguise -- Fiction 5. Mystery and detective stories 6. Racially mixed people -- Fiction

ISBN 0399256342; 9780399256349

LC 2012026737

This western mystery adventure novel, by Caroline Lawrence, is "starring Master-of-Disguise, P.K. Pinkerton. After vanquishing three notorious Desperados, twelve-year-old P.K. Pinkerton opens a private-eye business in Virginia City. P.K.'s skills are quickly put to the test: When a maid named Martha witnesses a murder, she hires the young detective to track the killer before he finds her too." (Publisher's note)

Lawrence, Iain

Lord of the nutcracker men. Delacorte Press 2001 212p map hardcover o.p. pa $5.99

Grades: 5 6 7 8   **Fic**

1. War 2. Fathers and sons 3. World War, 1914-1918 -- France 4. World War, 1914-1918 -- England

ISBN 0-385-72924-3; 0-440-41812-7 pa

LC 2001-17254

Johnny, a ten year old English boy, comes to believe that the battles he enacts with his toy soldiers control the war his father is fighting on the front in World War I

"There's realism in the grief of the village people and also in Dad's poignant letters. . . . This will be a fine introduction to World War I, both for personal interest and for curriculum use." Booklist

★ The **giant**-slayer. Delacorte Press 2009 292p $16.99

Grades: 5 6 7 8   **Fic**

1. Imagination -- Fiction 2. Medical care -- Fiction 3. Storytelling -- Fiction 4. Poliomyelitis -- Fiction 5. Father-daughter relationship -- Fiction

ISBN 978-0-385-73376-2; 0-385-73376-3

LC 2008-35409

When her eight-year-old neighbor is stricken with polio in 1955, eleven-year-old Laurie discovers that there is power in her imagination as she weaves a story during her visits with him and other patients confined to iron lung machines.

This is "compelling. . . . This effectively shows how children face life-changing challenges with incredible determination." Booklist

The **smugglers**. Delacorte Press 1999 183p $15.95;
pa $6.50

Grades: 5 6 7 8　　　　　　　　　　　　　　　**Fic**

1. Ships -- Fiction 2. Smuggling -- Fiction 3. Adventure
and adventurers -- Fiction

ISBN 0-385-32663-7; 0-440-41596-9 pa

　　　　　　　　　　　　　　　　　　LC 98-41582

As the nineteenth century begins, sixteen-year-old John
Spencer sets out to sail his father's schooner, The Dragon,
from Kent to London and becomes involved in smuggling
and danger

"The book's nonstop action, fast-paced plot, and picturesque characters make for a real page-turner." SLJ

★ The **wreckers**. Delacorte Press 1998 196p hardcover o.p. pa $5.99

Grades: 5 6 7 8　　　　　　　　　　　　　　　**Fic**

1. Adventure fiction 2. Survival -- Fiction 3.
Shipwrecks -- Fiction

ISBN 0-385-32535-5; 0-440-41545-4 pa

　　　　　　　　　　　　　　　　　　LC 97-31625

"In 1799 fourteen-year-old John Spencer survives a
shipwreck on the coast of Cornwall. To his horror, he soon
learns that the villagers are not rescuers, but pirates who lure
ships ashore in order to plunder their cargoes. . . . Lawrence
creates an edge-of-the-chair survival/mystery story. Fast-
moving, mesmerizing." Horn Book Guide

Other titles in this series are:

The smugglers (1999)

The buccaneers (2001)

Lawson, Robert

Ben and me; a new and astonishing life of Benjamin
Franklin, as written by his good mouse Amos. lately discovered, edited and illustrated by Robert Lawson. Little, Brown
1939 113p il hardcover o.p. pa $5.95

Grades: 5 6 7 8　　　　　　　　　　　　　　　**Fic**

1. Authors 2. Diplomats 3. Inventors 4. Statesmen 5.
Scientists 6. Mice -- Fiction 7. Writers on science 8.
Members of Congress

ISBN 0-316-51732-1; 0-316-51730-5 pa

"The sophisticated and clever story is illustrated by even
more sophisticated and clever line drawings." Roundabout
of Books

Mr. Revere and I; set down and embellished with numerous drawings by Robert Lawson. Little, Brown 1953
152p il hardcover o.p. pa $5.95

Grades: 5 6 7 8　　　　　　　　　　　　　　　**Fic**

1. Artisans 2. Metalworkers 3. Revolutionaries 4.
Horses -- Fiction

ISBN 0-316-51729-1 pa

"A delightful tale which is perfect for reading aloud to
the whole family. The make-up is excellent, illustrations are
wonderful, and the reader will get a very interesting picture
of the American Revolution." Libr J

Rabbit Hill. Viking 1944 127p il lib bdg $16.99;
pa $5.99

Grades: 3 4 5 6　　　　　　　　　　　　　　　**Fic**

1. Animals -- Fiction 2. Rabbits -- Fiction

ISBN 0-670-58675-7 lib bdg; 0-14-240796-8 pa

Awarded the Newbery Medal, 1945

"Robert Lawson, because he loves the Connecticut country and the little animals of field and wood and looks at them
with the eye of an artist, a poet and a child, has created for
the boy and girl, indeed for the sensitive reader of any age, a
whole, fresh, lively, amusing world." N Y Times Book Rev

Le Guin, Ursula K.

Gifts. Harcourt 2004 274p $17; $17; pa $7.95

Grades: 7 8 9 10　　　　　　　　　　　　　　**Fic**

1. Fantasy fiction

ISBN 9780152051235; 0-15-205123-6; 0-15-205124-
4 pa

　　　　　　　　　　　　　　　　　　LC 2003-21449

"Brantors, or chiefs, of the various clans of the Uplands
have powers passed down through generations, powers to
call animals to the hunt, start fires, cast a wasting disease, or
undo the very essence of a life or thing. The clans live isolated from the inhabitants of the Lowland cities in an uneasy
truce, where each people's ambitions are kept at bay by fear
of the other's vengeance. Two Upland teenagers, Gry and
Orrec, have grown from childhood friendship into romance
and also into a repudiation of their hereditary powers. . . .
Rejecting traditions that bind them to roles unwanted and
undesired, Gry and Orrec decide to leave their homes and
seek a freer if less privileged life in the Lowlands. . . . Grades
seven to twelve." (Bull Cent Child Books)

"Although intriguing as a coming-of-age allegory, Orrec's story is also rich in . . . earthy magic and intelligent
plot twists." Booklist

Leach, Sara

Count me in. Orca Book Publishers 2011 pa $9.95

Grades: 4 5 6 7　　　　　　　　　　　　　　　**Fic**

1. Hiking -- Fiction 2. Cousins -- Fiction

ISBN 978-1-55469-404-4; 1-55469-404-3

"The characters and their motivations are well developed. The plot is simple, but entertaining, and the survival
aspects of the story are realistic and suspenseful. Chapter
transitions are smooth and easy to follow." SLJ

Jake Reynolds: chicken or eagle? Orca Book Publishers 2009 101p (Orca young readers) pa $7.95

Grades: 3 4 5　　　　　　　　　　　　　　　**Fic**

1. Fear -- Fiction 2. Wolves -- Fiction 3. Courage --
Fiction 4. Islands -- Fiction

ISBN 978-1-55469-145-6 pa; 1-55469-145-1 pa

Jake dreams of being a superhero, but he's not exactly
brave, especially when it comes to wolves living on the island where he and his family are staying

"The theme of confronting fear is made vivid in this
chapter book. . . . [The book offers] a heart-pounding climax
and a very satisfying resolution." Booklist

Leal, Ann Haywood

A **finders**-keepers place. Henry Holt 2010 259p
$16.99

Grades: 5 6 7　　　　　　　　　　　　　　　**Fic**

1. School stories 2. Sisters -- Fiction 3. Mental illness
-- Fiction 4. Missing persons -- Fiction 5. Single parent
family -- Fiction 6. Manic-depressive illness -- Fiction

ISBN 978-0-8050-8882-3; 0-8050-8882-2

　　　　　　　　　　　　　　　　　　LC 2009-50771

As their mother's manic-depression grows worse, eleven-year-old Esther and her sister Ruth visit various churches

hoping to find their father, a preacher named Ezekiel who left them seven years before in 1966.

"Leal excels in pithy characterization, mainly through spot-on dialogue, yielding sympathetic characters, a gripping plot, and no shortage of heartbreaking moments." Publ Wkly

Lean, Sarah

★ A **dog** called Homeless; Sarah Lean. Katherine Tegen Books 2012 202 p. (trade bdg) $16.99

Grades: 3 4 5 6 7   **Fic**

1. Dogs -- Juvenile fiction 2. Grief -- Juvenile fiction 3. Handicapped -- Juvenile fiction 4. Dogs -- Fiction 5. Blind -- Fiction 6. Grief -- Fiction 7. Hearing impaired -- Fiction 8. Selective mutism -- Fiction 9. Single-parent families -- Fiction 10. People with disabilities -- Fiction

ISBN 0062122207; 9780062122209

LC 2011044628

Schneider Family Book Award (2013)

In this book by Sarah Lean, "a girl grieving for her dead mother gives up talking when she becomes convinced that what she says doesn't matter. . . . Cally begins to see her mother . . . dressed in a red raincoat and sometimes accompanied by a very large dog. . . . Cally also meets Mrs. Cooper, a neighbor in their new apartment building who lovingly cares for her blind, nearly deaf 11-year-old son, Sam." (Kirkus Reviews)

Leck, James

★ The **adventures** of Jack Lime; written by James Leck. Kids Can Press 2010 126p $16.95; pa $8.95

Grades: 5 6 7 8   **Fic**

1. Mystery fiction 2. Narcolepsy -- Fiction

ISBN 978-1-55453-364-0; 1-55453-364-3; 978-1-55453-365-7 pa; 1-55453-365-1 pa

"Jack Lime is the guy you come to if you've got a problem. . . . He'll find out what needs finding out. . . . This slim volume contains three cases. In the first, Jack susses out the whereabouts of a missing bike. In the second, he shakes down a hamster-napping and blackmail scheme. And in the final, he recounts his first case on the job. . . . All the touchstones that make for great noir are translated for kids. . . . The lingo that makes hard-boiled reading so much fun is here, but never schticky, and Leck knows that a great hero needs a debilitating flaw: for Jack, it's his narcolepsy." Booklist

Lee, Milly

Landed; [by] Milly Lee; pictures by Yangsook Choi. Farrar, Straus & Giroux 2006 un il $16 **Fic**

1. Immigrants -- Fiction 2. Chinese Americans -- Fiction

ISBN 0-374-34314-4

LC 2004-47216

After leaving his village in southeastern China, twelve-year-old Sun is held at Angel Island, San Francisco, before being released to join his father, a merchant living in the area. Includes historical notes

"The story is told with quiet restraint. . . . Choi's beautiful, full-page oil paintings, in sepia tones and shades of green, are quiet and packed with feeling." Booklist

Leeds, Constance

The **unfortunate** son; by Constance Leeds. Viking Childrens Books 2012 302 p. (hardcover) $16.99

Grades: 4 5 6 7   **Fic**

1. Bildungsromans 2. Historical fiction 3. Pirates -- Fiction 4. Kidnapping -- Fiction 5. Luck -- Fiction 6. Fishing -- Fiction 7. Slavery -- Fiction 8. Identity -- Fiction 9. Abnormalities, Human -- Fiction

ISBN 0670013986; 9780670013982

LC 2011027530

This book is the story of Luc, whose "father hates him, seemingly without reason, so" the boy runs away "to apprentice with a local fisherman. . . . Living with the fisherman's family he grows close to their ward, the beautiful Beatrice, and things seem to be looking up . . . until he's kidnapped by pirates and sold to a Tunisian in North Africa. While Luc receives an education from his learned master, Beatrice" attempts to unravel Luc's past. (Kirkus Reviews)

Lendroth, Susan

Calico Dorsey; mail dog of the mining camps. illustrations by Adam Gustavson. Tricycle Press 2010 un il $16.99; lib bdg $19.99

Grades: 2 3 4 5   **Fic**

1. Dogs -- Fiction 2. Postal service -- Fiction 3. Silver mines and mining -- Fiction

ISBN 978-1-58246-318-6; 1-58246-318-2; 978-1-58246-367-4 lib bdg; 1-58246-367-0 lib bdg

A Border Collie named Dorsey works with Al to deliver the mail and carry supplies to the miners living in Calico, California, during the nineteenth century, but on the morning that Al decides to postpone his duties Dorsey has other plans.

"Gustavson's paintings are intergrated into the text, flowing from page through the centerfold to page, making this obscure story larger than life. The vitality of the characters is enhanced by the artist's accurate, yet expressive details that add humor and sweetness to the faces of both the people and Dorsey." SLJ

Lerangis, Peter

The **colossus** rises; Peter Lerangis. Harper 2013 368 p. (Seven wonders) (hardback) $13.99

Grades: 3 4 5   **Fic**

1. Fantasy fiction -- Juvenile fiction 2. Adventure fiction -- Juvenile fiction 3. Atlantis (Legendary place) -- Juvenile fiction 4. Science fiction 5. Ability -- Fiction 6. Friendship -- Fiction 7. Adventure and adventurers -- Fiction 8. Atlantis (Legendary place) -- Fiction

ISBN 0062070401; 9780062070401

LC 2012025334

This children's fantasy story, by Peter Lerangis, illustrated by Torstein Norstrand and Mike Reagan, is the first of the "Seven Wonders" series. "13-year-old Jack McKinley will die unless he can locate the magic Loculi containing the ancient powers of Atlantis. . . . The problem is that . . . Atlantis was . . . divided into seven containers and hidden in the Seven Wonders of the Ancient World. Finding the powers will not only save Jack's life, but also give him superpowers." (Kirkus Reviews)

Lester, Julius

★ The **old** African; illustrated by Jerry Pinkney. Dial Bks. 2005 79p il $19.99

Grades: 3 4 5 6 **Fic**
1. Slavery -- Fiction 2. African Americans -- Fiction 3.
Extrasensory perception -- Fiction
ISBN 0-8037-2564-7

LC 2003-15671

An elderly slave uses the power of his mind to ease the
suffering of his fellow slaves and eventually lead them back
to Africa.

"The stirring illustrations, glowing with color and swirling with action, beautifully depict the dramatic escape fantasy (which is based on legend), but they never deny the
horror." Booklist

Levine, Gail Carson, 1947-
Ella enchanted. HarperCollins Pubs. 1997 232p
$16.99; lib bdg $17.89; pa $6.50
Grades: 5 6 7 8 **Fic**
1. Fairy tales 2. Fantasy fiction
ISBN 0-06-027510-3; 0-06-027511-1 lib bdg; 0-06-
440705-5 pa

LC 96-30734

A Newbery Medal honor book, 1998

"Ella is blessed by a fairy at birth with the gift of obedience. But the blessing is a horror for Ella, who must literally do what everyone tells her, from sweeping the floor to
giving up a beloved heirloom necklace. After her mother
dies, and her covetous, caustic father leaves on a trading trip,
Ella's world is turned upside down. She battles both ogres
and wicked stepsisters, makes friends and loses them, and
must deny her love for her prince, Charmont, to save his life
and his realm. In making this ultimate sacrifice, she breaks
the curse." (Booklist) "Grades five to eight." (Bull Cent
Child Books)

"As finely designed as a tapestry, Ella's story both neatly
incorporates elements of the original tale and mightily expands them." Booklist

★ **Ever.** HarperCollinsPublishers 2008 256p $16.99;
lib bdg $17.89; pa $6.99
Grades: 5 6 7 8 **Fic**
1. Winds -- Fiction 2. Immortality -- Fiction 3. Fate
and fatalism -- Fiction 4. Gods and goddesses -- Fiction
ISBN 978-0-06-122962-6; 0-06-122962-8; 978-0-06-
122963-3 lib bdg; 0-06-122963-6 lib bdg; 978-0-06-
122964-0 pa; 0-06-122964-4 pa

LC 2007-32289

Fourteen-year-old Kezi and Olus, Akkan god of the
winds, fall in love and together try to change her fate—to
be sacrificed to a Hyte god because of a rash promise her
father made—through a series of quests that might make
her immortal.

"Levine conducts a riveting journey, offering passion
and profound pondering along the way." Publ Wkly

★ A **tale** of Two Castles. Harper 2011 328p $16.99;
lib bdg $17.89
Grades: 4 5 6 **Fic**
1. Fantasy fiction 2. Mystery fiction 3. Dragons --
Fiction 4. Apprentices -- Fiction 5. Kings and rulers
-- Fiction
ISBN 978-0-06-122965-7; 0-06-122965-2; 978-0-06-
122966-4 lib bdg; 0-06-122966-0 lib bdg

LC 2010027756

"Hoping to apprentice as an actor, Elodie travels from
her rural home to the city of Two Castles. . . . When she's
robbed and then rejected as an actor, she apprentices herself to crafty dragon Meenore as a detective. Shape-shifting
Count Jonty Um, a kindly ogre, is their first client. . . . But
who is to be trusted and who isn't? . . . Intermediate, middle
school." (Horn Book)

"Readers are certain to be pulled, like Elodie herself,
right into the midst of the rich and swirling life of Two
Castles." SLJ

The **two** princesses of Bamarre. HarperCollins Pubs.
2001 241p $15.99; pa $5.99
Grades: 5 6 7 8 **Fic**
1. Magic 2. Sisters 3. Princesses 4. Fantasy fiction
5. Self-confidence 6. Wizards 7. Sisters -- Fiction 8.
Princesses -- Fiction
ISBN 0-06-029315-2; 0-06-440966-X pa

LC 00-47953

With her adventurous sister, Meryl, suffering from the
Gray Death, meek and timid Princess Addie sets out to find
a cure

"A lively tale with vivid characters and an exciting plot."
Book Rep

Levine, Kristin
★ The **best** bad luck I ever had. Putnam 2009 266p
$16.99
Grades: 5 6 7 8 **Fic**
1. Friendship -- Fiction 2. Prejudices -- Fiction 3.
Family life -- Fiction 4. Country life -- Fiction 5. Race
relations -- Fiction
ISBN 978-0-399-25090-3; 0-399-25090-5

LC 2008-11570

In Moundville, Alabama, in 1917, twelve-year-old Dit
hopes the new postmaster will have a son his age, but instead
he meets Emma, who is black, and their friendship challenges accepted ways of thinking and leads them to save the life
of a condemned man.

"Tension builds just below the surface of this energetic,
seamlessly narrated . . . novel. . . . Levine handles the setting
with grace and nuance." Publ Wkly

★ The **lions** of Little Rock; Kristin Levine. G. P.
Putnam's Sons 2012 298p.
Grades: 5 6 7 8 **Fic**
1. School stories 2. African Americans -- Fiction 3.
School integration -- Fiction 4. Schools -- Fiction
5. Friendship -- Fiction 6. Bashfulness -- Fiction 7.
Middle schools -- Fiction 8. Race relations -- Fiction 9.
Family life -- Arkansas -- Fiction
ISBN 9780399256448

LC 2011031835

This book presents a "portrait of 1958 Little Rock, Ark.,
the tumultuous year when the governor refused integration
by closing local high schools. The story is told through the
. . . voice of painfully quiet 12-year-old Marlee Nisbett,
who makes a rare friend in Liz, a new student at her middle
school. Liz instills some much-needed confidence in Marlee, but when it's revealed that Liz is 'passing' as a white
student, Liz must leave school abruptly, putting their friendship to the test. The girls meet in secret, and Marlee joins an
antisegregationist organization, both actions inviting serious
risk amid escalating racist threats." (Publishers Weekly)

Levitin, Sonia

    Journey to America; illustrated by Charles Robinson. Atheneum Pubs. 1993 150p il hardcover o.p. pa $4.99

Grades: 4 5 6 7   **Fic**

    1. Family life -- Fiction 2. Jewish refugees -- Fiction 3. World War, 1939-1945 -- Fiction

    ISBN 0-689-71130-1 pa

            LC 93-163980

    A reissue of the title first published 1970

    "In a strong immigration story, Lisa Platt, the middle daughter, tells how her family is forced to leave Nazi Germany and make a new life in the United States. First their father leaves, then the others escape to Switzerland, where they endure harsh conditions. After months of separation, the family is reunited in New York." Rochman. Against borders

Levy, Elizabeth

    My life as a fifth-grade comedian. HarperCollins Pubs. 1997 184p hardcover o.p. pa $4.95

Grades: 4 5 6   **Fic**

    1. School stories

    ISBN 0-06-026602-3; 0-06-440723-3 pa

            LC 97-3842

    "Levy incorporates a cornucopia of jokes and a wealth of subtle advice on becoming a comic. There is great pleasure in seeing Bobby and his father's earlier sarcasm and angry dialogue transformed by a turn of attitude into universal, and really funny comedy." SLJ

Lewis, C.S. (Clive Staples), 1898-1963

    ★ The **lion**, the witch, and the wardrobe; illustrated by Pauline Baynes. HarperCollins Pubs. 1994 189p il (The chronicles of Narnia) $17.99; lib bdg $18.89; pa $7.99

Grades: 4 5 6 7   **Fic**

    1. Fantasy fiction

    ISBN 0-06-023481-4; 0-06-023482-2 lib bdg; 0-06-440499-4 pa

            LC 93-8889

    A reissue of the title first published 1950 by Macmillan

    Four English schoolchildren find their way through the back of a wardrobe into the magic land of Narnia and assist Aslan, the golden lion, to triumph over the White Witch, who has cursed the land with eternal winter

    This begins "the 'Narnia' stories, outstanding modern fairy tales with an underlying theme of good overcoming evil." Child Books Too Good to Miss

    Other titles in this series are:

    Prince Caspian (1951)

    The voyage of the Dawn Treader (1952)

    The silver chair (1953)

    The horse and his boy (1954)

    The magician's nephew (1956)

    The last battle (1956)

Lewis, Elizabeth Foreman

    Young Fu of the upper Yangtze; [by] Elizabeth Foreman Lewis; illustrations by William Low. 75th anniversary ed.; Henry Holt 2007 302p il $17.95; pa $7.99

Grades: 4 5 6   **Fic**

    1. City and town life -- Fiction

    ISBN 978-0-8050-8113-8; 0-8050-8113-5; 978-0-312-38007-6 pa; 0-312-38007-0 pa

            LC 2006049633

    A newly illustrated edition of the title first published 1932 by The John C. Winston Company

    Awarded the Newbery Medal, 1933

    In the 1920's, a Chinese youth from the country comes to Chungking with his mother where the bustling city offers adventure and his apprenticeship to a coppersmith brings good fortune

    This edition "features a foreword by Katherine Paterson, extensive end-notes comparing China then and now, and new, atmospheric black-and-white illustrations." Horn Book Guide

Lewis, Gill

    ★ **Wild** wings; illustrated by Yuta Onoda. Atheneum Books for Young Readers 2011 287p il $15.99

Grades: 4 5 6 7   **Fic**

    1. Ospreys -- Fiction 2. Farm life -- Fiction 3. Friendship -- Fiction

    ISBN 1-4424-1445-6; 978-1-4424-1445-7

            LC 2010-49228

    Callum becomes friends with Iona, a practically feral classmate who has discovered an osprey, thought to be gone from Scotland, on Callum's family farm, and they eventually share the secret with others, including Jeneba who encounters the same bird at her home in Gambia.

    This is a "rich, moving tale. . . . The suspenseful story line is surrounded with precise details. . . . Short chapters, some with cliffhanging endings, will read-aloud well. . . . A powerfully memorable story." Kirkus

Lewis, J. Patrick

    ★ **And** the soldiers sang; [written by] J. Patrick Lewis & [illustrations by] Gary Kelley. Creative Editions 2011 31p il $17.99

Grades: 2 3 4 5 6   **Fic**

    1. Soldiers -- Fiction 2. Christmas -- Fiction 3. World War, 1914-1918 -- Fiction

    ISBN 978-1-5684-6220-2; 1-5684-6220-4

            LC 2010028644

    A young Welsh soldier fights along the Western Front during World War I, experiencing the horrors of trench warfare before participating in the famed Christmas Truce of 1914.

    This offers "a terse yet lyrical text and stark, dramatic illustrations. . . . Kelley's compelling artwork features mostly dark shades and strong, angular compositions. . . . Grim, upsetting and utterly beautiful, this is both a strong antiwar statement and a fascinating glimpse of a little-known historical event." Kirkus

Lewis, Maggie

    ★ **Morgy** makes his move; illustrated by Michael Chesworth. Houghton Mifflin 1999 74p il $15; pa $4.95

Grades: 2 3 4   **Fic**

    1. School stories 2. Moving -- Fiction 3. Schools -- Fiction 4. Moving, Household -- Fiction

    ISBN 0-395-92284-4; 0-618-19680-3 pa

            LC 98-43245

    When third-grader Morgy MacDougal-MacDuff moves from California to Massachusetts with his parents, he has a lot of new things to get used to before he feels comfortable

    "Heavy issues are handled lightly; language is simple and straightforward; Michael Chesworth's illustrations are funny and exaggerated." Booklist

Other titles about Morgy are:
Morgy coast to coast (2005)
Morgy's musical summer (2008)

Lin, Grace

★ **Starry** River of the Sky; by Grace Lin. Little, Brown 2012 288 p. col. ill.
Grades: 3 4 5 6 **Fic**
1. Fairy tales 2. Moon -- Fiction 3. Villages -- Fiction 4. Storytelling -- Fiction
ISBN 0316125954; 9780316125956

LC 2012012651

In this novel by Grace Lin, "the moon is missing from the remote Village of Clear Sky, but only a young boy named Rendi seems to notice! Rendi has run away from home and is now working as a chore boy at the village inn. He can't help but notice the village's peculiar inhabitants and their problems . . . but one day, a mysterious lady arrives at the Inn with the gift of storytelling, and slowly transforms the villagers and Rendi himself." (Publisher's note)

Includes bibliographical references.

★ **Where** the mountain meets the moon. Little, Brown and Co. 2009 278p il $16.99
Grades: 4 5 6 7 **Fic**
1. Fairy tales 2. Dragons -- Fiction
ISBN 978-0-316-11427-1; 0-316-11427-8

LC 2008-32818

A Newbery Medal honor book, 2010

Minli, an adventurous girl from a poor village, buys a magical goldfish, and then joins a dragon who cannot fly on a quest to find the Old Man of the Moon in hopes of bringing life to Fruitless Mountain and freshness to Jade River

"With beautiful language, Lin creates a strong, memorable heroine and a mystical land. . . . Children will embrace this accessible, timeless story about the evil of greed and the joy of gratitude." Booklist

★ The **Year** of the Dog; a novel. Little, Brown 2006 134p il $14.99; pa $5.99
Grades: 3 4 5 **Fic**
1. Chinese New Year -- Fiction 2. Taiwanese Americans -- Fiction
ISBN 0-316-06000-3; 0-316-06002-X pa

LC 2005-02586

Frustrated at her seeming lack of talent for anything, Pacy, a young Taiwanese American girl, sets out to apply the lessons of the Chinese Year of the Dog, those of making best friends and finding oneself, to her own life.

"The story . . . is entertaining and often illuminating. Appealing, childlike decorative drawings add a delightful flavor to a gentle tale full of humor." Horn Book

Other titles about Pacy are:
The Year of the Rat (2008)
Dumpling days (2011)

Lindgren, Astrid

★ **Pippi** Longstocking; [by] Astrid Lindgren; translated by Tiina Nunnally; illustrated by Lauren Child. Viking Children's Books 2007 207p il $25
Grades: 3 4 5 6 **Fic**
ISBN 978-0-670-06276-8

Original Swedish edition, 1945; first English language edition 1950

Escapades of a lucky little girl who lives with a horse and a monkey—but without any parents—at the edge of a Swedish village

"This oversize edition of the classic story has much to offer a new generation of readers. It has full-color illustrations . . . and a new translation. . . . Nunnally's language flows naturally and gives a fresh, modern feel to the line drawings, filled with color and pattern." SLJ

Other titles about Pippi Longstocking are:
Pippi goes on board (1957)
Pippi in the South Seas (1959)

Lindo, Elvira

Manolito Four-Eyes; illustrated by Emilio Urberuaga; translated by Joanne Moriarity. Marshall Cavendish Children 2008 144p il (Manolito Four-Eyes) $15.99
Grades: 4 5 6 **Fic**
1. School stories 2. Family life -- Fiction 3. Grandfathers -- Fiction
ISBN 978-0-7614-5303-1; 0-7614-5303-2

Original Spanish edition 2003

Recounts the exploits of the irrepressible Manolito as he navigates the world of his small Madrid neighborhood, along with his grandpa, his little brother, and his school friends.

"The protagonist is a wild, spunky, dramatic, comical sort of character sure to be popular with children, who will probably find him, in Manolito's own inimitable words, a 'whole lotta cool.' Lively cartoon illustrations are scattered throughout." SLJ

Other titles about Manolito are:
Manolito Four-Eyes: the 2nd volume of the great encyclopedia of my life (2009)
Manolito Four-Eyes: the 3rd volume of the great encyclopedia of my life (2010)

Lipsyte, Robert

The **twinning** project; by Robert Lipsyte. Clarion Books 2012 269 p. (hardback) $16.99
Grades: 4 5 6 7 **Fic**
1. Science fiction 2. Twins -- Fiction 3. Parallel universes -- Fiction 4. Schools -- Fiction 5. Middle schools -- Fiction 6. Space and time -- Fiction
ISBN 0547645716; 9780547645711

LC 2011050252

This book by Robert Lipsyte follows protagonist Tom, who has been "expelled from school after school for fighting bullies. . . . The boy's only comfort comes from talking through his problems with his imaginary twin, Eddie, a jock who lives on a version of Earth 50 years behind Tom's. . . . When the boys' 'grandfather' on both Earths reveals that the twin planets were created by alien scientists, the boys switch places to fight for the survival of both Earths." (Publishers Weekly)

Lisle, Holly

The **Ruby** Key. Orchard Books 2008 361p (Moon & sun) $16.99; pa $7.99
Grades: 5 6 7 8 **Fic**
1. Fantasy fiction 2. Siblings -- Fiction
ISBN 978-0-545-00012-3; 0-545-00012-2; 978-0-545-00013-0 pa; 0-545-00013-0 pa

LC 2007-30217

In a world where an uneasy peace binds Humans and Nightlings, fourteen-year-old Genna and her twelve-year-old brother Dan learn of their uncle's plot to gain immortality in exchange for human lives, and the two strike their own bargain with the Nightling lord, which sets them on a dangerous journey along the Moonroads in search of a key.

"Lisle's fertile imagination provides the nightworlds with monsters . . . but it is her clever plotting in this . . . fantasy, leading up to a thrilling finish . . . That will bewitch her audience." Horn Book

The **silver** door. Orchard Books 2009 366p (Moon & sun) $17.99
Grades: 5 6 7 8   Fic
1. War stories 2. Fantasy fiction
ISBN 978-0-545-00014-7; 0-545-00014-9
                                        LC 2008-40153
When Genna is chosen as the Sunrider of prophecy, her destiny is to unite the magic of the sun and the moon for the good of both Nightlings and humans.

"This second book of the Moon & Sun series has jarring stop-start feel, but the complexities of the interlaced human and nightling societies continue to unfold in fascinating way, creating a multi-hued, fully realized world for readers to explore." Horn Book

Lisle, Janet Taylor
Afternoon of the elves. Orchard Bks. 1989 122p hardcover o.p. pa $6.99
Grades: 4 5 6   Fic
1. Friendship -- Fiction 2. Mentally ill -- Fiction
ISBN 0-531-05837-9; 0-698-11806-5 pa
                                        LC 88-35099
A Newbery Medal honor book, 1990
"'Afternoon of the elves' is a distinctive portrayal of the way children figure out ways to inhabit the world when there aren't any adults around." N Y Times Book Rev

★ The **art** of keeping cool. Atheneum Bks. for Young Readers 2000 207p hardcover o.p.
Grades: 5 6 7 8   Fic
1. Artists 2. Cousins 3. Grandparents 4. Family problems 5. World War, 1939-1945 -- Fiction 6. World War, 1939-1945 -- United States 7. World War, 1939-1945 -- Rhode Island -- Juvenile fiction
ISBN 0689837879; 0689837887
                                        LC 00-32778
In 1942, Robert and his cousin Elliot uncover long-hidden family secrets while staying in their grandparents' Rhode Island town. They also become involved with a German artist who is suspected of being a spy. "Ages ten to fourteen." (N Y Times Book Rev)
"Lisle develops an unforgettable cast of characters placed against a fully realized setting. Engrossing, challenging, and well paced." Horn Book

Little, Kimberley Griffiths
★ **Circle** of secrets. Scholastic Press 2011 326p $17.99
Grades: 5 6 7 8   Fic
1. Ghost stories 2. Guilt -- Fiction 3. Mother-daughter relationship -- Fiction
ISBN 978-0-545-16561-7; 0-545-16561-X
                                        LC 2011000889

A year after her mother has deserted the family, eleven-year-old Shelby goes to stay with her, deep in the Louisiana bayou, where they both confront old hurts and regrets.

"The gently spooky ghost angle is handled nicely with some religious overtones. A very dramatic climax leads to a sweet, satisfying ending with some surprising twists and with reconciliation occurring for several characters." Kirkus

The **healing** spell. Scholastic Press 2010 354p $17.99
Grades: 5 6 7 8   Fic
1. Coma -- Fiction 2. Guilt -- Fiction 3. Mother-daughter relationship -- Fiction
ISBN 978-0-545-16559-4; 0-545-16559-8
                                        LC 2009-28016
Twelve-year-old Livie is living with a secret and it's crushing her. She knows she is responsible for her mother's coma, but she can't tell anyone. It's up to her to find a way to wake her momma up.

"Little explores the extremes of childhood guilt and its consequences in this harsh yet well-crafted story about fully drawn people. The bayou, with its rich culture, is an atmospheric character that overlays the story with mystery and dread." Booklist

Llewellyn, Sam
Darksolstice. Orchard Books 2010 365p map (Lyonesse) $17.99
Grades: 5 6 7 8   Fic
1. Fantasy fiction 2. Kings
ISBN 978-0-439-93471-8; 0-439-93471-0
                                        LC 2009006283
While Idris Limpet, Rightful King of the Land of Lyonesse, is making the treacherous journey to the distant land of Aegypt to rescue his dear friend and sister, Morgan, he meets a company of friends who shall become his Knights of the Round Table and lead armies to battle the evil regent, Fisheagle.

The **well** between the worlds. Orchard Books 2009 339p (Lyonesse) $17.99
Grades: 5 6 7 8   Fic
1. Fantasy fiction 2. Kings
ISBN 978-0-439-93469-5; 0-439-93469-9
                                        LC 2008-20075
Eleven-year-old Idris Limpet, living with his family in the once noble but now evil and corrupt island country of Lyonesse, finds his life taking a dramatic turn when, after a near-drowning incident, he is accused of being allied to the feared sea monsters and is rescued from a death sentence by a mysterious and fearsome stranger.

"Seldom does one find a new fantasy that is so richly textured, so original in concept, and with such a wonderfully interesting story. . . . Fantasy lovers will be impatient to find out where their paths take them." Voice Youth Advocates

Lloyd, Alison
Year of the tiger. Holiday House 2010 194p $16.95
Grades: 5 6 7 8   Fic
1. Adventure fiction 2. Archery -- Fiction 3. Social classes -- Fiction
ISBN 978-0-8234-2277-7; 0-8234-2277-1
                                        LC 2009033651
First published 2008 in Australia

In ancient China, Hu and Ren forge an unlikely alliance in an effort to become expert archers and, ultimately, to save their city from invading barbarians.

"Brimming with details of daily life in the Han Dynasty, this fast-paced story alternates in the third person between Hu and Ren." Kirkus

Lobel, Arnold

★ **Fables**; written and illustrated by Arnold Lobel. Harper & Row 1980 40p il $16.99; lib bdg $18.89; pa $6.99

Grades: 3 4 5   Fic

1. Animals -- Fiction

ISBN 0-06-023973-5; 0-06-023974-3 lib bdg; 0-06-443046-4 pa

LC 79-2004

Awarded the Caldecott Medal, 1981

"Short, original fables, complete with moral, poke subtle fun at human foibles through the antics of 20 memorable animal characters. . . . Despite the large picture-book format, the best audience will be older readers who can understand the innuendos and underlying messages. Children of all ages, however, will appreciate and be intrigued by the artist's fine, full-color illustrations. Tones are deftly blended to luminescent shadings, and the pictorial simplicity of ideas, droll expressions, and caricature of behavior work in many instances as complete and humorous stories in themselves." Booklist

Lofting, Hugh

The **voyages** of Doctor Dolittle; told by Hugh Lofting; illustrated by Michael Hague; edited with a foreword by Patricia C. McKissack and Fredrick L. McKissack; afterword by Peter Glassman. HarperCollins Pubs. 2001 355p il $22.95

Grades: 4 5 6 7   Fic

1. Animals 2. Fantasy 3. Fantasy fiction 4. Animals -- Fiction

ISBN 0-688-14002-5

A newly illustrated and revised edition of the title first published 1922 by Stokes

Awarded the Newbery Medal, 1923

When his colleague Long Arrow disappears, Dr. Dolittle sets off with his assistant, Tommy Stubbins, his dog, Jip, and Polynesia the parrot on an adventurous voyage over tropical seas to floating Spidermonkey Island

Loizeaux, William

Clarence Cochran, a human boy; pictures by Anne Wilsdorf. Farrar, Straus and Giroux 2009 152p il $16

Grades: 4 5 6   Fic

1. Toleration -- Fiction 2. Cockroaches -- Fiction 3. Environmental protection -- Fiction

ISBN 978-0-374-31323-4; 0-374-31323-7

LC 2007-35358

With the threat of extermination looming, a cockroach who has been transformed into a tiny human learns to communicate with his human hosts, leading to an agreement both sides can live with, and a friendship between Clarence and ten-year-old Mimi, a human environmentalist.

"There's a serious message here about environmentalism and the power of words, and the action and suspense make this a good read-aloud or classroom-discussion choice." SLJ

Lombard, Jenny

★ **Drita,** my homegirl. G. P. Putnam's Sons 2006 135p $15.99; pa $5.99

Grades: 3 4 5   Fic

1. Refugees -- Fiction 2. Albanians -- Fiction 3. Friendship -- Fiction 4. African Americans -- Fiction

ISBN 0-399-24380-1; 0-14-240905-7 pa

LC 2005-13501

When ten-year-old Drita and her family, refugees from Kosovo, move to New York, Drita is teased about not speaking English well, but after a popular student named Maxine is forced to learn about Kosovo as a punishment for teasing Drita, the two girls soon bond.

"Maxie's attempts to help Drita understand American ways are touching, and Drita's understanding of her friend's loss is a testament to the emotional intelligence of children." SLJ

London, C. Alexander

We are not eaten by yaks; with art by Jonny Duddle. Philomel Books 2011 355p il (An accidental adventure) $12.99

Grades: 3 4 5 6   Fic

1. Adventure fiction 2. Twins -- Fiction 3. Parents -- Fiction 4. Siblings -- Fiction 5. Explorers -- Fiction 6. Television -- Fiction

ISBN 978-0-399-25487-1; 0-399-25487-0

LC 2010-06020

As the children of two world-famous explorers, eleven-year-old twins Celia and Oliver prefer television-watching to adventure-seeking until their father takes them to Tibet to help search for their long-lost mother.

"This text will appeal to reluctant readers who appreciate magic, humor, and predicatble parental behaviors that will cause any tween to roll their eyes. The improbable connection between ubiquitous television shows, poison witches, talking yaks, and reluctant heroes works to make this a light yet intriguing read." Libr Media Connect

Another title in this series is:

We dine with cannibals (2011)

Look, Lenore

Alvin Ho; allergic to babies, burglars, and other bumps in the night. by Lenore Look; pictures by LeUyen Pham. 1st ed. Schwartz & Wade Books 2013 192 p. (hardcover) $15.99; (library) $18.99; (ebook) $47.97

Grades: 2 3 4 5   Fic

1. Siblings -- Juvenile fiction 2. Pregnancy -- Juvenile fiction 3. Fear -- Fiction 4. Schools -- Fiction 5. Pregnancy -- Fiction 6. Chinese Americans -- Fiction 7. Interpersonal relations -- Fiction

ISBN 0375870334; 9780375870330; 9780375970337; 9780375988899

LC 2012011455

This is the fifth installment in Lenore Look's Alvin Ho series. Here, "though his mom assures a dubious Alvin that she told him months ago about her pregnancy, his new sibling's imminent arrival introduces a whole new set of worries for nerve-wracked Alvin. Paramount among them is his misunderstanding that the 'simply pathetic' (read: sympathetic) pregnancy his mother suggests he's experiencing will result in him actually giving birth." (Kirkus)

★ **Alvin** Ho: allergic to girls, school, and other scary things; pictures by LeUyen Pham. Schwartz & Wade Books 2008 170p il $15.99; lib bdg $18.99

Grades: 2 3 4 5   Fic

1. Fear -- Fiction 2. Chinese Americans -- Fiction
ISBN 978-0-375-83914-6; 0-375-83914-3; 978-0-375-93914-3 lib bdg; 0-375-93914-8 lib bdg

LC 2007-029456

Alvin Ho, a young boy in Concord, Massachusetts, who loves superheroes and comes from a long line of brave Chinese farmer-warriors, wants to make friends, but first he must overcome his fear of everything.

Look's "intuitive grasp of children's emotions is rivaled only by her flair for comic exaggeration." Publ Wkly

Other titles about Alvin Ho are:

Alvin Ho: allergic to camping, hiking, and other natural disasters (2009)

Alvin Ho: allergic to birthday parties, science projects, and other man-made catastrophies (2010)

Alvin Ho
allergic to dead bodies, funerals, and other fatal circumstances (2011)

★ **Ruby** Lu, brave and true; illustrated by Anne Wilsdorf. Atheneum Books for Young Readers 2004 105p il $15.95; pa $3.99

Grades: 1 2 3   Fic

1. Chinese Americans -- Fiction
ISBN 0-689-84907-9; 1-4169-1389-0 pa

LC 2003-3605

"Almost-eight-year-old" Ruby Lu spends time with her baby brother, goes to Chinese school, performs magic tricks and learns to drive, and has adventures with both old and new friends.

This is a "funny and charming chapter book. . . . [It offers] generous font, ample white space, and animated and active illustrations rendered in India ink." SLJ

Other titles about Ruby Lu are:

Ruby Lu, empress of everything (2006)

Ruby Lu, star of the show (2011)

Lopez, Diana

Ask my mood ring how I feel; by Diana Lopez. 1st ed. Little, Brown and Co. 2013 324 p. (hardcover) $17

Grades: 4 5 6 7   Fic

1. Breast cancer -- Juvenile fiction 2. Children of cancer patients -- Juvenile fiction 3. Cancer -- Fiction 4. Promises -- Fiction 5. Friendship -- Fiction 6. Fundraising -- Fiction 7. Christian life -- Fiction 8. Hispanic Americans -- Fiction 9. Family life -- Texas -- Fiction
ISBN 0316209961; 9780316209960

LC 2012029856

In this book, Chia's "mother is diagnosed with breast cancer, which spurs . . . changes throughout their family. . . . After visiting the Basilica of Our Lady of San Juan del Valle in southern Texas, Chia dedicates herself to a promesa, vowing to secure 500 sponsors for a Walk for the Cure in exchange (she hopes) for her mother's recovery." (Publishers Weekly)

Confetti girl. Little, Brown and Company 2009 198p $15.99

Grades: 4 5 6 7   Fic

1. School stories 2. Friendship -- Fiction 3. Bereavement -- Fiction 4. Mexican Americans -- Fiction 5. Father-daughter relationship -- Fiction
ISBN 978-0-316-02955-1; 0-316-02955-6

LC 2008032819

After the death of her mother, Texas sixth-grader Lina's grades and mood drop as she watches her father lose himself more and more in books, while her best friend uses Lina as an excuse to secretly meet her boyfriend.

"Lopez effectively portrays the Texas setting and the characters' Latino heritage. . . . This . . . novel puts at its center a likable girl facing realistic problems on her own terms." Booklist

Lord, Bette Bao

In the Year of the Boar and Jackie Robinson; illustrations by Marc Simont. Harper & Row 1984 169p il lib bdg $15.89; pa $4.95

Grades: 4 5 6   Fic

1. School stories 2. Chinese Americans -- Fiction
ISBN 0-06-024004-0 lib bdg; 0-06-440175-8 pa

LC 83-48440

"Warm-hearted, fresh, and dappled with humor, the episodic book, which successfully encompasses both Chinese dragons and the Brooklyn Dodgers, stands out in the bevy of contemporary problem novels. And the unusual flavor of the text infiltrates the striking illustrations picturing the pert, pigtailed heroine making her way in 'Mei Guo'—her new 'Beautiful Country.'" Horn Book

Lord, Cynthia

★ **Rules**; [by] Cynthia Lord. Scholastic Press 2006 200p $15.99; pa $6.99

Grades: 4 5 6 7   Fic

1. Autism -- Fiction 2. Siblings -- Fiction 3. Handicapped -- Fiction
ISBN 0-439-44382-2; 0-439-44383-0 pa

LC 2005017519

A Newbery Medal honor book, 2007

Frustrated at life with an autistic brother, twelve-year-old Catherine longs for a normal existence but her world is further complicated by a friendship with an young paraplegic

"The details of autistic behavior are handled well, as are depictions of relationships. . . . . A heartwarming first novel." Booklist

★ **Touch** blue. Scholastic Press 2010 186p $16.99

Grades: 4 5 6 7   Fic

1. Islands -- Fiction 2. Foster home care -- Fiction
ISBN 978-0-545-03531-6; 0-545-03531-7

LC 2009042306

When the state of Maine threatens to shut down their island's one-room schoolhouse because of dwindling enrollment, eleven-year-old Tess, a strong believer in luck, and her family take in a trumpet-playing foster child named Aaron to increase the school's population.

"Aaron's relationship with his foster family . . . develops believably. The tight-knit community and lobster-catching details make for a warm, colorful environment. This is a feel-good story." Booklist

Lottridge, Celia Barker

The **listening** tree. Fitzhenry & Whiteside 2011 172p $11.95

Grades: 4 5 6 7   **Fic**

1. Courage -- Fiction 2. Great Depression, 1929-1939 -- Fiction

ISBN 978-1-55455-052-4; 1-55455-052-1

It's 1935, and Ellen and her mother must leave their dried-up Saskatchewan farm to board with Aunt Gladys in Toronto. Intimidated by her new surroundings, Ellen chooses to hide in the branches of the large leafy tree outside her window and watch the neighbourhood children playing, rather than joining in their games. But when Ellen overhears a plan to evict the family-next-door from their home, she must overcome her fears and help her neighbours.

"Lottridge provides a wealth of well-developed, believable characters, especially Ellen. The story is a deftly-written, heartbreaking, and heartwarming tale of friendship and the perseverance to withstand hardships. This is a great book to introduce young readers to the impact of the Great Depression." Voice Youth Advocates

Love, D. Anne

Semiprecious. Margaret K. McElderry Books 2006 293p $16.95; pa $6.99

Grades: 5 6 7 8   **Fic**

1. Family life -- Fiction

ISBN 978-0-689-85638-9; 0-689-85638-5; 978-0-689-87389-8 pa; 0-689-87389-1 pa

LC 2005-14906

Uprooted and living with an aunt in 1960s Oklahoma, thirteen-year-old Garnet and her older sister Opal brave their mother's desertion and their father's recovery from an accident, learning that "the best home of all is the one you make inside yourself"

"An involving novel of hurt, healing, and adjustment." Booklist

Lovelace, Maud Hart, 1892-1980

Betsy-Tacy; illustrated by Lois Lenski. HarperCollins Pubs. 1994 112p il hardcover o.p. pa $5.99

Grades: 2 3 4   **Fic**

1. Friendship -- Fiction

ISBN 0-06-024415-1; 0-06-440096-4 pa

A reissue of the title first published 1940 by Crowell

Betsy and Tacy (short for Anastacia) were two little five-year-olds, such inseparable friends that they were regarded almost as one person. This is the story of their friendship in a little Minnesota town in the early 1900's

The author "has written a story of real literary merit as well as one with good story interest." Libr J

Other titles about Betsy through adolescence and young womanhood with reading levels to grade 5 and up are:

Betsy and Joe (1948)

Betsy and Tacy go downtown (1943)

Betsy and Tacy go over the big hill (1942)

Betsy and the great world (1952)

Betsy in spite of herself (1946)

Betsy, Tacy and Tib (1941)

Betsy was a junior (1947)

Betsy's wedding (1955)

Heavens to Betsy (1945)

Lowry, Lois, 1937-

★ **Anastasia** Krupnik. Houghton Mifflin 1979 113p $17; pa $5.99

Grades: 4 5 6   **Fic**

1. Family life -- Fiction

ISBN 0-395-28629-8; 0-440-40852-0 pa

Anastasia's 10th year has some good things like falling in love and really getting to know her grandmother and some bad things like finding out about an impending baby brother

"Anastasia's father and mother—an English professor and an artist—are among the most humorous, sensible, and understanding parents to be found in . . . children's fiction, and Anastasia herself is an amusing and engaging heroine." Horn Book

Other titles about Anastasia Krupnik are:

Anastasia again! (1981)

Anastasia at your service (1982)

Anastasia, ask your analyst (1984)

Anastasia on her own (1985)

Anastasia has the answers (1986)

Anastasia's chosen career (1987)

Anastasia at this address (1991)

Anastasia, absolutely (1995)

★ **Autumn** Street. Houghton Mifflin 1980 188p $17; $16

Grades: 4 5 6 7   **Fic**

1. Friendship -- Fiction 2. World War, 1939-1945 -- Fiction

ISBN 9780395278123; 0-395-27812-0

LC 80-376

"Elizabeth, the teller of the story, feels danger around her when her father goes to fight in World War II. She, her older sister, and her pregnant mother go to live with her grandparents on Autumn Street. Tatie, the black cook-housekeeper, and her street-wise grandson Charley love Elizabeth and reassure her during this difficult time." Child Book Rev Serv

★ The **birthday** ball; illustrations by Jules Feiffer. Houghton Mifflin Harcourt 2010 186p il $16

Grades: 3 4 5   **Fic**

1. School stories 2. Birthdays -- Fiction 3. Princesses -- Fiction

ISBN 978-0-547-23869-2; 0-547-23869-X

LC 2009-32966

Princess Patricia Priscilla is bored with life as a royal life and the preparations for her 16th birthday ball. "Disguised as a peasant, she attends the village school . . . and attracts friends and the attention of the handsome school master. . . . What began as a cure for boredom, becomes a chance for [the princess] to break the rules and marry the man she loves." (Publisher's note) "Intermediate." (Horn Book)

"Lowry uses her knack for cleverly turning familiar stories on their heads . . . in this tale about a princess who's utterly bored with privileged palace life. . . . Feiffer's wiry ink illustrations paint the characters in offhand caricatures, adding to the merriment. Employing elements from the 'Prince and the Pauper' as well as ample doses of humor and slapstick, Lowry sets the stage for a rowdy denouement." Publ Wkly

Bless this mouse; illustrated by Eric Rohmann. Houghton Mifflin Books for Children 2011 151p il $15.99

Grades: 4 5 6   **Fic**
1. Mice -- Fiction
ISBN 978-0-547-39009-3; 0-547-39009-2
         LC 2010-07331

Mouse Mistress Hildegarde musters all her ingenuity to keep a large colony of church mice safe from the exterminator and to see that they make it through the dangerous Blessing of the Animals. "Grades three to five." (Bull Cent Child Books)

"The book is an impeccably constructed, good-humored adventure filled with master plans, near disasters, and brave rescues, all gently frightening for readers even younger than the target audience. . . . Fun and lighthearted." Publ Wkly

★ The **giver**. Houghton Mifflin 1993 180p $17; pa $8.95
Grades: 6 7 8 9 10   **Fic**
1. Science fiction
ISBN 0-395-64566-2; 0-385-73255-4 pa
         LC 92-15034

Awarded the Newbery Medal, 1994

Given his lifetime assignment at the Ceremony of Twelve, Jonas becomes the receiver of memories shared by only one other in his community and discovers the terrible truth about the society in which he lives.

"A riveting, chilling story that inspires a new appreciation for diversity, love, and even pain. Truly memorable." SLJ

Gooney Bird Greene; illustrated by Middy Thomas. Houghton Mifflin 2002 88p il $15
Grades: 2 3 4   **Fic**
1. School stories 2. Storytelling -- Fiction
ISBN 0-618-23848-4
         LC 2002-1478

A most unusual new student who loves to be the center of attention entertains her teacher and fellow second graders by telling absolutely true stories about herself, including how she got her name

"Lowry's masterful writing style reaches directly into her audience, managing both to appeal to young listeners and to engage older readers." Bull Cent Child Books

Other titles about Gooney Bird are:
Gooney Bird and the room mother (2005)
Gooney Bird is so absurd (2009)
Gooney Bird on the map (2011)
Gooney the fabulous (2007)

★ **Number** the stars. Houghton Mifflin 1989 137p $16
Grades: 4 5 6 7   **Fic**
1. Jews -- Fiction 2. Friendship -- Fiction 3. World War, 1939-1945 -- Fiction
ISBN 0-395-51060-0
         LC 88-37134

Awarded the Newbery Medal, 1990

In 1943, during the German occupation of Denmark, ten-year-old Annemarie learns how to be brave and courageous when she helps shelter her Jewish friend from the Nazis

"The appended details the historical incidents upon which Lowry bases her plot. . . . The whole work is seamless, compelling, and memorable." Horn Book

Son; by Lois Lowry. Houghton Mifflin 2012 393 p. $17.99
Grades: 6 7 8 9 10 11 12   **Fic**
1. Science fiction 2. Dystopian fiction 3. Amnesia -- Fiction 4. Mothers -- Fiction 5. Secrecy -- Fiction 6. Identity -- Fiction 7. Mother-child relationship -- Fiction 8. Mother and child -- Fiction 9. Separation (Psychology) -- Fiction
ISBN 0547887205; 9780547887203
         LC 2012014034

Author Lois Lowry tells the story of "14-year-old Claire, [who] has no contact with her baby Gabe until she surreptitiously bonds with him in the community Nurturing Center. . . . After living for years with Alys, a childless healer, Claire's memory returns. Intent on finding Gabe, she . . . encounters the sinister Trademaster and exchanges her youth for his help in finding her child, now living in the same village as middle-aged Jonas and his wife Kira. Elderly and failing, Claire reveals her identity to Gabe, who must use his unique talent to save the village." (Kirkus Reviews)

Stay! Keeper's story. Houghton Mifflin 1997 127p il $15
Grades: 5 6 7 8   **Fic**
1. Dogs -- Fiction
ISBN 0-395-87048-8
         LC 97-1569

"The author proves she is as well versed in animal behavior as in human sensibilities. Her warm sense of humor and vivid imagination . . . accentuate Keeper's unorthodox perceptions of the world." Publ Wkly

A **summer** to die; illustrated by Jenni Oliver. Houghton Mifflin 1977 154p il $16
Grades: 5 6 7 8   **Fic**
1. Death -- Fiction 2. Sisters -- Fiction
ISBN 0-395-25338-1
         LC 77-83

"As told by Meg, the chronicle of this experience is a sensitive exploration of the complex emotions underlying the adolescent's first confrontation with human mortality; the author suggests nuances of contemporary conversation and situations without sacrificing the finesse with which she limns her characters." Horn Book

Lunn, Janet Louise Swoboda
Laura Secord: a story of courage; [by] Janet Lunn; illustrated by Maxwell Newhouse. Tundra Bks. 2001 un il maps $16.95
Grades: 3 4 5   **Fic**
1. Pioneers 2. War of 1812 -- Fiction
ISBN 0-88776-538-6

"The folkloric rhythm of the tale is underscored in the dramatically colored, naively rendered illustrations." Horn Book Guide

Luper, Eric
Jeremy Bender vs. the Cupcake Cadets. Balzer + Bray 2011 235p $15.99
Grades: 4 5 6   **Fic**
1. Contests -- Fiction 2. Sex role -- Fiction 3. Boats and boating -- Fiction 4. Money-making projects for

children -- Fiction
ISBN 978-0-06-201512-9; 0-06-201512-5

                            LC 2010-40808

When sixth-grader Jeremy Bender damages his father's prized boat and needs to come up with a lot of money to get it repaired, he and his best friend dress up as girls and infiltrate the Cupcake Cadet troop in an attempt to win the Windjammer Whirl model sailboat contest, and the prize money that comes with it.

"A not-so-lightweight tale rises above drag jokes to reveal surprising profundity." Kirkus

Lupica, Mike

Heat. Philomel Books 2006 220p $16.99

Grades: 5 6 7 8   **Fic**

1. Cubans -- Fiction 2. Orphans -- Fiction 3. Baseball -- Fiction 4. Illegal aliens -- Fiction

ISBN 0-14-240757-7 pa; 0-399-24301-1

                            LC 2005013521

Pitching prodigy Michael Arroyo is on the run from social services after being banned from playing Little League baseball because rival coaches doubt he is only twelve years old and he has no parents to offer them proof. "Grades five to eight." (Bull Cent Child Books)

"The dialogue crackles, and the rich cast of supporting characters' . . . nearly steals the show. Topnotch entertainment." Booklist

Hot hand; [by] Mike Lupica. Philomel Books 2007 165p (Comeback kids) $9.99; pa $6.99

Grades: 3 4 5   **Fic**

1. Bullies -- Fiction 2. Basketball -- Fiction 3. Father-son relationship -- Fiction

ISBN 978-0-399-24714-9; 978-0-14-241441-5 pa

                            LC 2006034562

In the wake of his parents' separation, ten-year-old Billy seems to have continual conflicts with his father, who is also his basketball coach, but his quiet, younger brother Ben, a piano prodigy, is having even more trouble adjusting, and only Billy seems to notice.

"The characters . . . are always sympathetic . . . and the adults have complexity and depth. . . . The strongest point . . . is the quality of the sports play-by-play; Lupica portrays the action clearly and vividly." SLJ

Other titles in this series are:

Two-minute drill (2007)
Safe at home (2008)
Long shot (2008)
Shoot-out (2010)

Play Makers; Mike Lupica. Scholastic 2013 224 p. (hardcover) $16.99

Grades: 3 4 5 6 7   **Fic**

1. School stories 2. Basketball -- Fiction 3. Competition (Psychology) -- Fiction

ISBN 0545381835; 9780545381833

This novel, by Mike Lupica, is the book 2 of the "Game Changers" series. "Ben McBain and his crew must now prepare for basketball season. . . . But there is a new kid in town, Chase Braggs, a point guard like Ben who seems to be better, stronger, and faster. . . . Ben's rivalry with Chase seems to take the fun out of playing ball with his best friends. Will

Ben be able to pull it together for his team and for himself?" (Publisher's note)

The **batboy.** Philomel Books 2010 247p $17.99

Grades: 5 6 7 8   **Fic**

1. Baseball -- Fiction 2. Mother-son relationship -- Fiction

ISBN 978-0-399-25000-2; 0-399-25000-X

                            LC 2009015067

Even though his mother feels baseball ruined her marriage to his father, she allows fourteen-year-old Brian to become a bat boy for the Detroit Tigers, who have just drafted his favorite player back onto the team.

Lupica gives "his readers a behind-the-scenes look at major league sports. In this novel, he adds genuine insights into family dynamics and the emotional state of his hero." Booklist

Lyga, Barry

Archvillain. Scholastic Press 2010 180p $16.99

Grades: 4 5 6 7   **Fic**

1. Science fiction 2. Superheroes -- Fiction 3. Good and evil -- Fiction 4. Extraterrestrial beings -- Fiction

ISBN 978-0-545-19649-9; 0-545-19649-3

                            LC 2010-05291

Twelve-year-old Kyle Camden develops greater mental agility and superpowers during a plasma storm that also brings Mighty Mike, an alien, to the town of Bouring, but while each does what he thinks is best, Kyle is labeled a villain and Mike a hero.

"Comic book fans in particular will appreciate this clever origin story, first in a new series. . . . Lyga . . . laces his story with ample humor. . . . Readers will find plenty to ponder." Publ Wkly

Lyons, Mary E.

★ **Letters** from a slave girl; the story of Harriet Jacobs. Scribner 1992 146p il hardcover o.p. pa $5.99; pa $5.99

Grades: 6 7 8 9   **Fic**

1. Slaves 2. Authors 3. Domestics 4. Memoirists 5. Letters -- Fiction 6. Slavery -- Fiction 7. African Americans -- Fiction

ISBN 0-684-19446-5; 1-4169-3637-8 pa; 9781416936374 pa

                            LC 91-45778

This is a fictionalized version of the life of Harriet Jacobs, told in the form of letters that she might have written during her slavery in North Carolina and as she prepared to escape to the North in 1842. Glossary. Bibliography. "Age twelve and up." (Horn Book)

This "is historical fiction at its best. . . . Mary Lyons has remained faithful to Jacobs's actual autobiography throughout her readable, compelling novel. . . . Her observations of the horrors of slavery are concise and lucid. The letters are written in dialect, based on Jacobs's own writing and on other slave narrations of the period." Horn Book

MacDonald, Alan

Trolls go home! [by] Alan MacDonald; illustrations by Mark Beech. Bloomsbury Children's Books 2007 124p il $14.95; pa $5.95

Grades: 2 3 4 5 **Fic**

1. Trolls -- Fiction
ISBN 978-1-59990-077-3; 1-59990-077-7; 978-1-59990-078-0 pa; 1-59990-078-5 pa

LC 2006-49887

When the Trolls move next door to the Priddles, both families find the other strange, which causes many misunderstandings.

"MacDonald includes deliciously silly vocabulary; . . . inventive details about the Troll lifestyle; and fractured-fairy-tale references to the Billy Goats Gruff. Beech's scribbly line drawings turn up the humor." Booklist

MacDonald, Amy

Too much flapdoodle! [illustrations by Cat Bowman Smith] Farrar Straus Giroux 2008 182p il $16.95

Grades: 3 4 5 6 **Fic**

1. Aunts -- Fiction 2. Uncles -- Fiction 3. Farm life -- Fiction 4. Country life -- Fiction
ISBN 978-0-374-37671-0; 0-374-37671-9

LC 2007033273

Twelve-year-old Parker reluctantly goes to spend the summer with his eccentric great-aunt and great-uncle on their dilapidated farm, where he discovers that there is more to life than the latest game system and the coolest cell phone

"Hilarious antics ensue as the boy matures and realizes that there is more to life than the latest video game. Black-and-white line drawings enhance the lighthearted text." SLJ

Other titles about these characters are:
No more nice (1996)
No more nasty (2001)

MacDonald, Bailey

Wicked Will. Aladdin 2009 201p $16.99

Grades: 5 6 7 **Fic**

1. Poets 2. Authors 3. Dramatists 4. Mystery fiction 5. Orphans -- Fiction 6. Theater -- Fiction
ISBN 1-4169-8660-X; 978-1-4169-8660-7

LC 2008-50818

Performing in the English town of Stratford-on-Avon in 1576, Viola, a young actress (disguised as a boy) and a local lad named Will Shakespeare uncover a murder mystery.

"The chapters themselves logically reveal the twists and turns of the plot in concise, readable prose. The realistic details put flesh on the bones of not only the primary characters, but also of the secondary personages as well." SLJ

The secret of the sealed room; a mystery of young Benjamin Franklin. Aladdin 2010 208p $16.99

Grades: 4 5 6 7 **Fic**

1. Authors 2. Diplomats 3. Inventors 4. Statesmen 5. Scientists 6. Mystery fiction 7. Writers on science 8. Members of Congress
ISBN 978-1-4169-9760-3; 1-4169-9760-1

When she runs away after her master dies, indentured servant Patience Martin is accused of stealing and needs the help of a young Benjamin Franklin to prove her innocence.

"MacDonald creates a series of events that could very well be factual and leaves the reader curious to know more. Replete with historical facts without being blatant, the well-developed plot will keep mystery lovers guessing until the very last chapter." Booklist

MacDonald, Betty

Nancy and Plum; illustrated by Mary Grandpre; with an introduction by Jeanne Birdsall. Alfred A. Knopf 2010 222p il $15.99; lib bdg $18.99

Grades: 3 4 5 **Fic**

1. Orphans -- Fiction 2. Sisters -- Fiction
ISBN 978-0-375-86685-2; 0-375-86685-X; 978-0-375-96685-9 lib bdg; 0-375-96685-4 lib bdg

A reissue of the title first published 1952

"Orphans Nancy and Plum lead deprived lives at cruel Mrs. Monday's boarding school. . . . The sisters manage to escape her clutches, find wonderful new guardians, redeem their neglectful uncle, and even improve the lot of the other orphans. . . . Their dialogue is full of humorous teasing, and they pull no punches with their feelings about the villainous Mrs. Monday and her dreadful niece. . . . GrandPré's pencil and wash illustrations strike just the right note: old-fashioned yet cheeky." Horn Book

MacDonald, George

The light princess; with pictures by Maurice Sendak. Farrar, Straus & Giroux 1969 110p il hardcover o.p. pa $5.95

Grades: 3 4 5 6 **Fic**

1. Fairy tales
ISBN 0-374-44458-7 pa

This fairy story originally appeared 1864 in the author's novel Adela Cathcart and was reprinted in his 1867 story collection Dealings with the fairies

"The problems of the princess who had been deprived, as an infant, of her gravity and whose life hung in the balance when she grew up are amusing as ever and the sweet capitulation to love that brings her (literally) to her feet, just as touching. All of the best of Macdonald is reflected in the Sendak illustrations: the humor and wit, the sweetness and tenderness, and the sophistication—and they are beautiful." Sutherland. The Best in Child Books

MacHale, D. J.

SYLO; by D.J. MacHale. Penguin Group USA 2013 416 p. (hardcover) $17.99

Grades: 5 6 7 8 9 **Fic**

1. Dystopian juvenile fiction 2. Adventure fiction -- Juvenile fiction
ISBN 1595146652; 9781595146656

This is the first book in a proposed trilogy from D.J. MacHale. Here, Tucker Pierce has a small but satisfying life on a small island. But when the island is quarantined by the U.S. Navy, things start to fall apart. . . . People start dying. The girl he wants to get to know a whole lot better, Tori, is captured along with Tucker and imprisoned behind barbed wire." They must escape to the mainland and try to figure out what this SYLO organization that is imprisoning them is. (Kirkus Reviews)

MacLachlan, Patricia, 1938-

The facts and fictions of Minna Pratt. Harper & Row 1988 136p pa $4.95

Grades: 4 5 6 7 **Fic**

1. Musicians -- Fiction
ISBN 0-06-440265-7

LC 85-45388

"Ms. MacLachlan's skillful handling of her subject, and above all her vivid characterization . . . place her story in the ranks of outstanding middle-grade fiction." N Y Times Book Rev

Kindred souls; Patricia MacLachlan. HarperCollins 2012 119 p.

Grades: 4 5 6   **Fic**

1. Bereavement -- Fiction 2. Family life -- Fiction 3. Family farms -- Fiction 4. Grandfathers -- Fiction 5. Houses -- Remodeling -- Fiction 6. Dogs -- Fiction 7. Old age -- Fiction 8. Prairies -- Fiction 9. Farm life -- Fiction 10. Sod houses -- Fiction

ISBN 9780060522971; 9780060522988

LC 2011016617

This book follows narrator Jake and his 88-year-old grandfather Billy, the eponymous kindred souls of the story's title. The pair "live on a farm that their family has owned for generations; in fact, Billy was born in a sod house he remembers fondly, the ruins of which still exist on the property." To comfort their dying grandfather, "Jake and his siblings undertake a remarkably ambitious project: They rebuild the sod house; Billy moves into it, and he eventually passes away there." The "first-person account of a boy coping with his grandfather's death . . . portrays . . . the opportunity to grieve for a loved one even while he is still alive." (Kirkus)

★ **Sarah,** plain and tall. Harper & Row 58p $14.99; lib bdg $15.89; pa $4.99

Grades: 3 4 5   **Fic**

1. Stepmothers -- Fiction 2. Frontier and pioneer life -- Fiction

ISBN 0-06-024101-2; 0-06-024102-0 lib bdg; 0-06-440205-3 pa

LC 83-49481

Awarded the Newbery Medal, 1986

When their father invites a mail-order bride to come live with them in their prairie home, Caleb and Anna are captivated by their new mother and hope that she will stay

"It is the simplest of love stories expressed in the simplest of prose. Embedded in these unadorned declarative sentences about ordinary people, actions, animals, facts, objects and colors are evocations of the deepest feelings of loss and fear, love and hope." N Y Times Book Rev

Other titles in this series are:

Caleb's story (2001)

Grandfather's dance (2006)

More perfect than the moon (2004)

Skylark (1994)

Seven kisses in a row; pictures by Maria Pia Marrella. Harper & Row 1983 56p il pa $4.95

Grades: 2 3 4   **Fic**

1. Aunts -- Fiction 2. Uncles -- Fiction 3. Family life -- Fiction

ISBN 0-06-440231-2

LC 82-47718

"The brief understated story makes few demands on the reader, but it is full of humor and the warmth of family caring and mutual affection. Informal, offhand pen-and-ink drawings reflect the tone of both story and style." Horn Book

The **true** gift; a Christmas story. illustrated by Brian Floca. Atheneum Books for Young Readers 2009 81p il $12.99

Grades: 2 3 4   **Fic**

1. Cattle -- Fiction 2. Siblings -- Fiction 3. Christmas -- Fiction 4. Farm life -- Fiction 5. Grandparents -- Fiction 6. Books and reading -- Fiction 7. Christmas stories -- Juvenile literature

ISBN 978-1-4169-9081-9; 1-4169-9081-X

LC 2009-375

While spending Christmas at their grandparents' farm, Lily becomes convinced that her younger brother Liam is right about White Cow being lonely and helps him seek a companion for her, leaving little time for Christmas preparations or reading.

"With MacLachlan's well-drawn characters and Floca's simple pencil and graphite drawings, it's a poignant story with a a classic feel." Publ Wkly

★ **Waiting** for the magic; illustrated by Amy June Bates. Atheneum Books for Young Readers 2011 143p il $15.99

Grades: 3 4 5 6   **Fic**

1. Cats -- Fiction 2. Dogs -- Fiction 3. Family life -- Fiction

ISBN 978-1-4169-2745-7; 1-4169-2745-X

LC 2010019668

When Papa goes away for a little while, his family tries to cope with the separation by adopting four dogs and a cat.

"MacLachlan tackles the familiar yet always heart-wrenching subject of parental separation in her venerable spare and moving style. . . . The characters are individualistic, believable, and likable." Publ Wkly

White fur flying; Patricia MacLachlan. 1st ed. Margaret K. McElderry Books 2013 128 p. (hardcover) $15.99

Grades: 2 3 4 5   **Fic**

1. Dogs -- Juvenile fiction 2. Human-animal relationship -- Juvenile fiction 3. Dogs -- Fiction 4. Rescue dogs -- Fiction 5. Family problems -- Fiction 6. Human-animal relationships -- Fiction

ISBN 1442421711; 9781442421714

LC 2011046125

In this children's book, by Newbery Medalist Patricia MacLachlan, "A young boy tries to find his voice with the help of some four-legged friends. . . . Zoe's family rescues dogs in need. . . . But the house across the street is always silent these days. A new family has moved in and Phillip, the boy, has stopped speaking. He doesn't even want to try. Zoe knows that saving dogs and saving boys are different jobs, but she learns that some parts are the same." (Publisher's note)

★ **Word** after word after word. HarperCollins 2010 128p $14.99; lib bdg $15.89

Grades: 2 3 4 5   **Fic**

1. School stories 2. Cancer -- Fiction 3. Poetry -- Fiction 4. Authorship -- Fiction 5. Mother-daughter relationship -- Fiction

ISBN 978-0-06-027971-4; 0-06-027971-0; 978-0-06-027972-1 lib bdg; 0-06-027972-9 lib bdg

"Mrs. Mirabel, a visiting poet, works with a fourth-grade class over several weeks as they first discuss why people write poetry and then attempt to express themselves in verse. . . . Narrator Lucy, whose mother is recovering from cancer treatments, often meets her friends to talk about their hopes, their fears, their families, and their charismatic mentor. . . ."

Showing great respect for both her readers and her craft, . . . MacLachlan makes every word count in Lucy's smooth-flowing economical narrative." Booklis

MacLean, Christine Kole

Mary Margaret meets her match. Dutton 2007 148p $15.99

Grades: 3 4 5 **Fic**

1. Horses -- Fiction

ISBN 978-0-525-47775-4; 0-525-47775-6

Mary Margaret is excited to be going to a dude ranch, but then finds herself stuck with an uncooperative horse.

"There are some laugh-out-loud moments. MacLean writes with a sense of humor and tenderness." SLJ

Mack, Tracy

The **fall** of the Amazing Zalindas; casebook no. 1. by Tracy Mack and Michael Citrin; illustrations by Greg Ruth. Orchard Books 2006 259p il (Sherlock Holmes and the Baker Street irregulars) $16.99; pa $6.99

Grades: 4 5 6 7 **Fic**

1. Mystery fiction 2. Circus -- Fiction

ISBN 0-439-82836-8; 0-545-06939-4 pa

LC 2005-34000

The ragamuffin boys known as the Baker Street Irregulars help Sherlock Holmes solve the mysterious deaths of a family of circus tightrope walkers.

"Colorful, well-defined characters . . . and plenty of historical detail, Cockney slang . . . and Sherlockian references bring Victorian England to life. Vintage-style design elements and evocative black-and-white illustrations further the effect." Booklist

The **mystery** of the conjured man; [by] Tracy Mack & Michael Citrin; [illustrations by Greg Ruth] Orchard Books 2009 il (Sherlock Holmes and the Baker Street Irregulars) hardcover o.p.

Grades: 4 5 6 **Fic**

1. Mystery fiction 2. Spiritualism -- Fiction 3. Swindlers and swindling -- Fiction

ISBN 978-0-439-83667-8 pa

LC 2006035701

The ragtag group of orphan boys known as the Baker Street Irregulars faces shady characters and seemingly real ghosts when they assist the famous detective, Sherlock Holmes, in investigating the mysterious death of Greta Berlinger during a seance.

"A great addition to an entertaining series." SLJ

Mack, Winnie

After all, you're Callie Boone. Feiwel & Friends 2010 179p il $16.99

Grades: 4 5 6 **Fic**

1. Summer -- Fiction 2. Friendship -- Fiction 3. Family life -- Fiction

ISBN 978-0-312-56331-8; 0-312-56331-0

"Eleven-year-old Callie's summer has gotten off to a bad start. Her large extended family, . . . embarrasses her in full view of the neighbors and her ex-best friend, Amy. . . . Callie loves to swim but a humiliating belly flop finds her banned from the community pool. She yearns for a friend who still prefers riding bikes to mooning over boys. Then Hoot moves in next door and becomes an unexpected pal. . . . Callie is a well-limned child with recognizable flaws and a rueful inner

voice. . . . Mack's well-drawn personalities and lighthearted touch keep the narrative lively and engaging." SLJ

Maclear, Kyo

Virginia Wolf; Kyo Maclear; [illustrated by] Isabelle Arsenault. Kids Can Press 2012 32 p.

Grades: K 1 2 **Fic**

1. Wolves -- Fiction 2. Painting -- Fiction 3. Picture books for children 4. Depression (Psychology) -- Fiction

ISBN 9781554536498; 1554536499

This picture book tells the story of a girl named Virginia whose bad mood turns her into a wolf. Her sister Vanessa, the narrator, tries to help by painting pictures for her. "The wolf--previously a black near-silhouette with snout and tail, wearing a dress--morphs back into a girl. Wolf ears, silhouetted from behind, become a hair bow. Ink, pencil and paint . . . divide color from black-and-white as emotional symbolism." Kyo Maclear combines the real-life story of writer Virginia Woolf and her sister, painter Vanessa Bell, with "a bad-day/bad-mood or animal-transformation tale" that presents "literal and metaphorical glimpses of real depression." (Kirkus)

Madden, Kerry

Gentle's Holler. Viking 2005 237p $16.99; pa $6.99

Grades: 5 6 7 8 **Fic**

1. Poverty -- Fiction 2. Family life -- Fiction

ISBN 0-670-05998-6; 0-14-240751-8 pa

LC 2004-18424

In the early 1960s, twelve-year-old songwriter Livy Two Weems dreams of seeing the world beyond the Maggie Valley, North Carolina, holler where she lives in poverty with her parents and eight brothers and sisters, but understands that she must put family first.

"Livy's narration rings true and is wonderfully voiced, and Madden's message about the importance of forgiveness will be well received." SLJ

Other titles in this series are:

Louisiana's song (2007)

Jessie's mountain (2008)

Madison, Alan

100 days and 99 nights; illustrated by Julia Denos. Little, Brown 2008 137p il $14.99; pa $5.99

Grades: 3 4 5 **Fic**

1. Toys -- Fiction 2. Soldiers -- Fiction 3. Imagination -- Fiction 4. Father-daughter relationship -- Fiction

ISBN 978-0-316-11354-0; 0-316-11354-9; 978-0-316-11798-2 pa; 0-316-11798-6 pa

As Esme introduces her stuffed animal collection that is alphabetically arranged from Alvin the aardvark to Zelda the zebra she also relates her family's military life and her father's deployment

"In this moving debut novel, wordplay is part of every chapter. . . . This is a mix of hilarious language and one child's terror that there could be bad news." Booklist

Magnin, Joyce

Carrying Mason; [by] Joyce Magnin. Zonderkidz 2011 153p $14.99

Grades: 5 6 7 8 **Fic**

1. Family life -- Fiction 2. Country life -- Fiction 3.

Mentally handicapped -- Fiction

ISBN 978-0-310-72681-4; 0-310-72681-6

LC 2011014462

In rural Pennsylvania in 1958, when thirteen-year-old Luna's best friend Mason dies, she decides to move in with his mentally disabled mother and care for her as Mason did.

"Gently, deliberately paced, Luna's first-person tale provides a fresh look at mental disabilities and the additional burden of negative attitudes. While Ruby's disability is apparent, this effort also celebrates her capabilities. Although the primary focus is Luna, her quirky father, supportive mother and boy-crazy older sister are also sufficiently developed to provide additional depth. A quiet coming-of-age tale with heart offers a fresh look at mentally disabled adults." Kirkus

Magoon, Kekla

Camo girl. Aladdin 2010 218p $16.99

Grades: 5 6 7 8   Fic

1. Friendship -- Fiction 2. Prejudices -- Fiction 3. Racially mixed people -- Fiction

ISBN 978-1-4169-7804-6; 1-4169-7804-6

A novel about a biracial girl living in the suburbs of Las Vegas examines the friendships that grow out of, and despite, her race.

"Magoon . . . offers a sensitive and articulate portrayal of a pair of middle-school outsiders. . . . This poetic and nuanced story addresses the courage it takes to truly know and support someone, as well as the difficult choices that come with growing up." Publ Wkly

Mahy, Margaret. 1936-2012

Maddigan's Fantasia. Margaret K. McElderry Books 2007 499p $15.99

Grades: 4 5 6 7   Fic

1. Fantasy fiction 2. Magic -- Fiction 3. Circus -- Fiction

ISBN 1-4169-1812-4; 978-1-4169-1817-7

LC 2006-15512

In a world made uncertain by "the Chaos," two time-traveling boys, fifteen-year-old Timon and eleven-year-old Eden, seek to protect a magic talisman, aided by twelve-year-old Garland, a member of a traveling circus known as Maddigan's Fantasia.

"A well-drawn character, Garland resembles other Mahy protagonists—cranky, assertive and filled with self-doubt—and her adventures are invariably exciting." Publ Wkly

Mister Whistler; Margaret Mahy. Lerner Pub Group 2013 32 p. $17.95

Grades: PreK K   Fic

1. Dance -- Juvenile fiction 2. Humorous fiction -- Juvenile fiction 3. Lost and found possessions -- Juvenile fiction

ISBN 187746791X; 9781877467912

In this humorous picture book for children, by Margaret Mahy, illustrated by Gavin Bishop, "Mister Whistler always has a song in his head and a dance in his legs. But when he has to catch the train, he is so distracted he loses his ticket--and has to dance his way out of his clothes to find it!" (Publisher's note)

Malaghan, Michael

Greek ransom. Andersen Press 2010 264p pa $9.99

Grades: 5 6 7 8   Fic

1. Adventure fiction 2. Siblings -- Fiction 3. Kidnapping -- Fiction

ISBN 978-184270-786-9; 1-84270-786-8

"Nick and Callie Latham are on the Greek island of Theta with their archaeologist parents for a working vacation. Then the children discover that Mum and Dad have lost the family's money in a reckless bid to locate the lost treasure of King Akanon. A shifty businessman kidnaps the couple in order to acquire it for himself. After Nick and Callie barely escape capture themselves, it's up to them to find a way to free their parents. . . . Readers will be on the edge of their seats throughout to see what happens next. . . . The relationship between Nick and Callie is spot-on, and kids will enjoy this high-spirited tale." SLJ

Malaspina, Ann

Yasmin's hammer; illustrated by Doug Chayka. Lee & Low Books 2010 un il $18.95

Grades: 2 3 4 5   Fic

1. Child labor -- Fiction

ISBN 978-1-60060-359-4; 1-60060-359-9

"Swinging a hammer all day as she and her little sister break bricks in the city heat of Dhaka, Bangladesh, Yasmin dreams of going to school. In a moving voice true to her viewpoint, Yasmin speaks in smooth free verse about her longing. . . . Stirring oil paintings bring the setting to a close with images of the sisters in the brickyard and their father pedaling a rickshaw through the crowded streets. The back matter includes a clear map, a glossary, and a bibliography with online sites about how to help children like Yasmin." Booklist

Includes glossary and bibliographical references

Malchow, Alex

The **Sword** of Darrow; [by] Alex and Hal Malchow. BenBella 2011 531p map $17.99

Grades: 5 6 7 8   Fic

1. Fantasy fiction 2. Magic -- Fiction 3. Fairies -- Fiction 4. Princesses -- Fiction

ISBN 978-1-9356-1846-1; 1-9356-1846-6

LC 2011012233

"For 10 years the people of Sonnencrest endured the cruel and tyrannical rule of the Goblins. Then Princess Babette, the only surviving member of the royal family, and Darrow, a crippled boy, become the unlikely forces in the fight against the oppressors. The authors paint convincing portraits of the characters. . . . Readers will be drawn to this fledgling rebellion and follow it to its spectacular success. Magic, monsters, and wizards add to the excitement." SLJ

Manivong, Laura

Escaping the tiger. Harper 2010 216p il $15.99

Grades: 6 7 8 9   Fic

1. Refugees -- Fiction 2. Family life -- Fiction

ISBN 978-0-06-166177-8; 0-06-166177-5

LC 2009-24095

In 1982, twelve-year-old Vonlai, his parents, and sister, Dalah, escape from Laos to a Thai refugee camp, where they spend four long years struggling to survive in hopes on one day reaching America.

"This compelling novel offers significant historical background. This is certainly a book to prompt purposeful discussion to increase historical and multicultural awareness." SLJ

Manley, Candace

Skeeter's dream; a novel. La Frontera Pub. 2010 183p pa $14.95

Grades: 4 5 6 **Fic**

1. Adventure fiction 2. Family life -- Fiction 3. Stepfamilies -- Fiction 4. Runaway children -- Fiction 5. Frontier and pioneer life -- Fiction

ISBN 978-0-9785634-8-6; 0-9785634-8-4

LC 2010027719

When thirteen-year-old Robert "Skeeter" Tates, fed up with his Yankee stepfather and stepbrothers, leaves his Arkansas home for Texas in 1867, he meets up with unexpected traveling companions as well as outlaws and the lawmen tracking them.

"This is a well-written story with believable characters and an intriguing plot. The dialog is authentic and the action is fast-paced. Give this book to fans of historical fiction or to boys looking for a thrilling adventure story." Libr Media Connect

Margolis, Leslie

Everybody bugs out. Bloomsbury Children's Books 2011 195p $15.99

Grades: 4 5 6 **Fic**

1. School stories 2. Friendship -- Fiction 3. Family life -- Fiction

ISBN 1-59990-526-4; 978-1-59990-526-6

LC 2010035628

Sixth-grader Annabelle realizes that she has a crush on Oliver, with whom she is doing a science fair project, just before the Valentine's Day dance—and just before her friend Claire announces her crush on him.

"Margolis' breezy tone nicely conveys the peaks and valleys of middle-school life." Kirkus

Girl's best friend. Bloomsbury USA Childrens Books 2010 261p $14.99

Grades: 4 5 6 7 **Fic**

1. School stories 2. Mystery fiction 3. Dogs -- Fiction 4. Twins -- Fiction 5. Siblings -- Fiction 6. Family life -- Fiction

ISBN 978-1-59990-525-9; 1-59990-525-6

LC 2010000562

In Brooklyn, New York, twelve-year-old dog-walker Maggie, aided by her twin brother Finn and best friend Lucy, investigates someone she believes is stealing pets.

"Characters are well-developed, typical preteens. Readers will easily identify with these seventh graders, and they will love the eccentric landlady who adds a bit of humor. Mystery fans will enjoy this lighthearted whodunit." SLJ

Girls acting catty. Bloomsbury 2009 179p $15.99

Grades: 4 5 6 **Fic**

1. School stories 2. Remarriage -- Fiction 3. Family life -- Fiction

ISBN 978-1-59990-237-1; 1-59990-237-0

LC 2009002144

Sixth-grader Annabelle spends autumn coping with competing groups of friends at school, her mother's prewedding stress, learning to get along with a cute stepbrother-

to-be, and such momentous events as wearing her first bra and learning to shave her legs.

"Margolis handles Annabelle's minor crises with sensitivity and humor." SLJ

Marino, Nan

★ **Neil** Armstrong is my uncle; & other lies Muscle Man McGinty told me. Roaring Brook Press 2009 154p $16.95

Grades: 3 4 5 6 **Fic**

1. Bullies -- Fiction 2. Friendship -- Fiction 3. Foster home care -- Fiction

ISBN 978-1-59643-499-8; 1-59643-499-6

"It's the summer of 1969, when astronauts land on the moon, and Tamara Ann Simpson is not having a good time. Foster child and best friend Kebsie has suddenly moved away and now Douglas McGinty is in her spot with Mrs. Kutchner. Tammy dubs him 'Muscle Man' after one outrageous lie. . . . Fierce and plaintive, Tammy's voice crackles with originality and yet is completely childlike. The '60s setting comes to life with sharply honed details. . . . The authenticity of the time and the voice combine with a poignant plot to reveal a depth unusual in such a straightforward first-person narrative." Kirkus

Marsden, Carolyn, 1950-

The **Buddha's** diamonds; [by] Carolyn Marsden and Thay Phap Niem. Candlewick Press 2008 97p $14.99

Grades: 4 5 6 **Fic**

1. Fishing -- Fiction 2. Buddhism -- Fiction

ISBN 978-0-7636-3380-6; 0-7636-3380-1

LC 2007023025

As a storm sweeps in, Tinh's father tells him to tie up their fishing boat but the storm scares him and he runs away, but when the damage to the boat is discovered, Tinh realizes what he must do.

"Buddhist concepts are gently introduced and explained in the context of the story, but, more importantly, they are reflected in the tone and style. . . . Cultural references are beautifully integrated into this lovely coming-of-age story." SLJ

★ The **gold**-threaded dress. Candlewick Press 2002 73p hardcover o.p. pa $5.99

Grades: 3 4 5 **Fic**

1. Friendship 2. Prejudices 3. School stories 4. Thai Americans 5. Identity 6. Moving, Household 7. Prejudices -- Fiction 8. Thai Americans -- Fiction

ISBN 0-7636-1569-2; 0-7636-2993-6 pa

LC 2001-25132

When Oy and her Thai American family move to a new neighborhood, her third-grade classmates tease and exclude her because she is different

"Marsden writes with keen observation and finesse about the social dynamics of the classroom and with simplicity reveals the layers of emotion experienced by Oy." Booklist

Another title about Oy is:

The Quail Club (2006)

Moon runner; [by] Carolyn Marsden. Candlewick Press 2005 97p hardcover o.p. pa $5.99

Grades: 3 4 5 **Fic**

1. Running -- Fiction 2. Friendship -- Fiction

ISBN 0-7636-2117-X; 0-7636-3304-6 pa

LC 2004-58143

When Mina discovers that she can run faster than her athlete friend, Ruth, she thinks she must choose between running and friendship

"A quiet, lyrical story that sensitively explores issues of friendship and being true to oneself. . . . The lucid prose is full of haunting metaphors. " SLJ

★ **Silk** umbrellas; [by] Carolyn Marsden. Candlewick Press 2004 134p $15.99; pa $5.99

Grades: 3 4 5 6   **Fic**

1. Artists 2. Artists -- Fiction 3. Family life -- Fiction 4. Family life -- Thailand 5. Self-actualization (Psychology)

ISBN 0-7636-2257-5; 0-7636-3376-3 pa

     LC 2003-55323

Eleven-year-old Noi worries that she will have to stop painting the silk umbrellas her family sells at the market near their Thai village and be forced to join her older sister in difficult work at a local factory instead.

"In simple, lucid prose, Marsden tells a story that is foreign in detail and texture but universal in appeal. . . . This gracefully told story will resonate with many young readers." Booklist

★ **Take** me with you. Candlewick Press 2010 160p $14.99

Grades: 4 5 6 7   **Fic**

1. Orphans -- Fiction 2. Friendship -- Fiction 3. Racially mixed people -- Fiction

ISBN 978-0-7636-3739-2; 0-7636-3739-4

     LC 2009-38053

This story is set in "Italy after World War II. Pina and Susanna have lived at their Naples orphanage since they were babies. . . . Pina, pretty and blonde, . . . is sure the nuns tell prospective parents she is bad. Susanna is the daughter of an Italian woman and a black American solider. . . ; no one looks like her. Then two very different parents come into the girls' lives. . . . Both satisfy the girls' dreams in unexpected ways. Marsden often puts crafts like sewing or crocheting into her stories, and in many ways she is like a master craftsman, using words instead of stitches for her deceptively simple design." Booklist

When heaven fell. Candlewick Press 2007 183p $15.99; pa $8.99

Grades: 4 5 6   **Fic**

1. Aunts -- Fiction 2. Family life -- Fiction

ISBN 978-0-7636-3175-8; 0-7636-3175-2; 978-0-7636-4381-2 pa; 0-7636-4381-5 pa

     LC 2006-51712

When her grandmother reveals that the daughter that she had given up for adoption is coming from America to visit her Vietnamese family, nine-year-old Binh is convinced that her newly-discovered aunt is wealthy and will take care of all the family's needs.

"Marsden sensitively portrays expectations and disappointments on both sides. . . . An unusually accessible introduction to the culture of modern Vietnam." Booklist

Martin, Ann M., 1955-

★ **Belle** Teal. Scholastic Press 2001 214p hardcover o.p. pa $5.99

Grades: 4 5 6 7   **Fic**

1. School stories 2. Race relations -- Fiction

ISBN 0-439-09823-8; 0-439-09824-6 pa

     LC 00-136292

Belle Teal Harper is from a poor family in the country, and beginning fifth-grade is a challenge as her grandmother's memory is slipping away, her brother and father are fighting again, and she becomes involved with the two new African American children in her class.

"This is a solid piece of work with an absorbing plot." SLJ

Better to wish; Ann M. Martin. 1st ed. Scholastic 2013 240 p. (Family tree) (hardcover) $16.99

Grades: 3 4 5 6 7   **Fic**

1. Discrimination -- Juvenile fiction 2. Historical fiction -- Juvenile fiction 3. Depressions -- 1929 -- Fiction 4. Family life -- Maine -- Fiction 5. Families -- Maine -- Juvenile fiction 6. Depressions -- 1929 -- Juvenile fiction

ISBN 0545359422; 9780545359429

     LC 2012047940

This is the first book in Ann M. Martin's Family Tree series. "Growing up in Maine, eight-year-old Abby Nichols is the oldest daughter of an ambitious carpenter eager to realize the American Dream. But his prejudices are strong, too: he won't let Abby associate with her Irish Catholic neighbor, Orrin. . . . As Abby's father gains success, she enjoys more privileges, . . . but the family's newfound prosperity doesn't ease her outrage over her father's mistreatment of the less fortunate." (Publishers Weekly)

★ **A corner** of the universe. Scholastic Press 2002 189p $15.95; pa $5.99

Grades: 5 6 7 8   **Fic**

1. Uncles -- Fiction 2. Friendship -- Fiction 3. Mentally handicapped -- Fiction

ISBN 0-439-38880-5; 0-439-38881-3 pa

     LC 2001-57611

A Newbery Medal honor book, 2003

The summer that Hattie turns twelve, she meets the childlike uncle she never knew and becomes friends with a girl who works at the carnival that comes to Hattie's small town

"Martin delivers wonderfully real characters and an engrossing plot through the viewpoint of a girl who tries so earnestly to connect with those around her." SLJ

The **doll** people; by Ann M. Martin and Laura Godwin; with pictures by Brian Selznick. Hyperion Bks. for Children 2000 256p il $15.99; pa $6.99

Grades: 3 4 5   **Fic**

1. Dolls -- Fiction

ISBN 0-7868-0361-4; 0-7868-1240-0 pa

     LC 98-12344

A family of porcelain dolls that has lived in the same house for one hundred years is taken aback when a new family of plastic dolls arrives and doesn't follow The Doll Code of Honor

"Superbly nuanced drawings echo the action that breathes life into these extraordinary playthings." SLJ

Other titles about the doll family are:

The meanest doll in the world (2003)

The runaway dolls (2008)

The **summer** before. Scholastic Press 2010 215p
(The Babysitters Club) $16.99

Grades: 4 5 6 **Fic**

1. Moving -- Fiction 2. Friendship -- Fiction 3. Dating
(Social customs) -- Fiction

ISBN 978-0-545-16093-3; 0-545-16093-6

During the summer before their seventh-grade year,
Kristy, Mary Anne, Claudia, and Stacey tackle difficulties,
including family problems, crushes, moving, and making
new friends.

"Martin credibly and affectingly blends the friends' stories and resolves their issues, while deftly foreshadowing
what lies ahead." Publ Wkly

★ **Ten** rules for living with my sister. Feiwel & Friends
2011 228p $16.99

Grades: 3 4 5 6 **Fic**

1. Sisters -- Fiction 2. Family life -- Fiction 3.
Grandfathers -- Fiction 4. Apartment houses -- Fiction

ISBN 978-0-312-36766-4; 0-312-36766-X

LC 2011009166

Nine-year-old Pearl and her popular, thirteen-year-old
sister, Lexie, do not get along very well, but when their
grandfather moves in and the girls have to share a room,
they must find common ground.

"Credible characterizations, on-the-nail humor, and
well-observed family dynamics add up to another hit from
. . . author Martin." Publ Wkly

Martin, Patricia

Lulu Atlantis and the quest for true blue love; [by]
Patricia Martin. Schwartz & Wade Books 2008 228p il
$15.99; lib bdg $18.99

Grades: 3 4 5 **Fic**

1. Spiders -- Fiction 2. Siblings -- Fiction 3. Imaginary
playmates -- Fiction

ISBN 978-0-375-84016-6; 0-375-84016-8; 978-0-375-
94016-3 lib bdg; 0-375-94016-2 lib bdg

LC 2007002082

Lulu Atlantis is peeved when her mother brings home
little brother Sam, and she turns to her imaginary friend,
Harry the daddy longlegs spider, for comfort, companionship, help, and advice as she is getting used to the addition
to the family

"The scenarios are whimsical; the emotions run true."
Publ Wkly

Martinez, Arturo O.

Pedrito's world. Texas Tech University Press 2007
131p il pa $16.95

Grades: 4 5 6 **Fic**

1. Farm life -- Fiction 2. Mexican Americans -- Fiction

ISBN 978-0-89672-600-0 pa; 0-89672-600-2 pa

LC 2006-21628

In southern Texas in 1941, six-year-old Pedrito holds
onto his hope for a better future as he helps to grow watermelons on his parents' farm and sell them in San Antonio,
and attends school five miles from home.

"Readers will be moved . . . through clean writing and
well-chosen details that breathe life into the characters and
give heft to the setting." Booklist

Mason, Simon

Moon pie. David Fickling Books 2011 327p $16.99

Grades: 3 4 5 6 **Fic**

1. Fathers -- Fiction 2. Alcoholism -- Fiction

ISBN 978-0-385-75235-0; 0-385-75235-0

LC 2010051354

Eleven-year-old Martha tries to keep her fam-
ily together after her mother's death as her father struggles
with alcoholism.

"Mason has conjured a rarity indeed—a tremendously
charming, unflinching account of a parent's downward spiral. . . . While the dialogue is realistic and rat-a-tat-tat quick,
lyrical prose wends its way throughout. . . . Love conquers
all in this bighearted and heartbreaking story." Kirkus

Mason, Timothy

The **last** synapsid. Delacorte Press 2009 311p il
$16.99; lib bdg $19.99

Grades: 5 6 7 8 **Fic**

1. Time travel -- Fiction 2. Space and time -- Fiction 3.
Prehistoric animals -- Fiction

ISBN 978-0-385-73581-0; 0-385-73581-2; 978-0-385-
90567-1 lib bdg; 0-385-90567-X lib bdg

LC 2008-35678

On a mountain near their tiny town of Faith, Colorado,
best friends Rob and Phoebe discover a squat, drooly creature from thirty million years before the dinosaurs, that
needs their help in tracking down a violent carnivore that
must be returned to its proper place in time, or humans will
never evolve.

"Mason has written a highly engaging fantasy that includes something for all readers. . . . Readers will find it
difficult to put this book down until they have reached the
last page." Libr Media Connect

Mass, Wendy

11 birthdays. Scholastic Press 2009 267p $16.99;
pa $6.99

Grades: 4 5 6 **Fic**

1. Time -- Fiction 2. Birthdays -- Fiction 3. Friendship
-- Fiction

ISBN 978-0-545-05239-9; 0-545-05239-4; 978-0-545-
05240-5 pa; 0-545-05240-8 pa

LC 2008-09784

After celebrating their first nine same-day birthdays together, Amanda and Leo, having fallen out on their tenth and
not speaking to each other for the last year, prepare to celebrate their eleventh birthday separately but peculiar things
begin to happen as the day of their birthday begins to repeat
itself over and over again.

"From the double-entendre title to the solid character
portrayals to the clarity and wit of the writing, this novel
offers a fresh twist on the familiar themes of middle-grade
family and school dynamics." Booklist

Other titles in this series are:

Finally (2010)

13 gifts (2011)

★ **Every** soul a star; a novel. Little, Brown and Co.
2008 322p $15.99; pa $6.99

Grades: 5 6 7 8 **Fic**

1. Friendship -- Fiction 2. Solar eclipses -- Fiction
ISBN 978-0-316-00256-1; 0-316-00256-9; 978-0-316-
00257-8 pa; 0-316-00257-7 pa

LC 2008009259

Ally, Bree, and Jack meet at the one place the Great
Eclipse can be seen in totality, each carrying the burden
of different personal problems, which become dim when
compared to the task they embark upon and the friendship
they find.

Mass "combines astronomy and storytelling for a well-
balanced look at friendships and the role they play in shaping identity.... Information about solar eclipses and astronomy is carefully woven into the plot to build drama and will
almost certainly intrigue readers." Publ Wkly

Includes bibliographical references

Jeremy Fink and the meaning of life. Little, Brown
2006 289p $15.99; pa $6.99

Grades: 5 6 7 8 **Fic**

1. Conduct of life -- Fiction 2. Father-son relationship
-- Fiction
ISBN 978-0-316-05829-2; 0-316-05829-7; 978-0-316-
05849-0 pa; 0-316-05849-1 pa

LC 2005037291

Just before his thirteenth birthday, Jeremy Fink receives
a keyless locked box—set aside by his father before his
death five years earlier—that purportedly contains the meaning of life.

"Mass fashions an adventure in which both journey and
destination are worth the trip." Horn Book

Pi in the sky; Wendy Mass. 1st ed. Little, Brown and
Co. 2013 256 p. (hardcover) $17

Grades: 3 4 5 6 7 **Fic**

1. Creation -- Fiction 2. Science fiction -- Juvenile
fiction 3. Science fiction
ISBN 0316089168; 9780316089166

LC 2012030638

In this humorous children's novel, by Wendy Mass,
"Joss is the seventh son of the Supreme Overlord of the Universe, and all he gets to do is deliver pies.... But when Earth
suddenly disappears, Joss is tasked with the not-so-simple
job of bringing it back. With the help of an outspoken girl
from Earth named Annika, Joss embarks on the adventure
of a lifetime and learns that the universe is an even stranger
place than he'd imagined." (Publisher's note)

The **candymakers**. Little, Brown 2010 453p $16.99

Grades: 3 4 5 6 **Fic**

1. Candy -- Fiction 2. Contests -- Fiction 3. Friendship
-- Fiction
ISBN 978-0-316-00258-5; 0-316-00258-5

LC 2010008621

When four twelve-year-olds, including Logan, who has
grown up never leaving his parents' Life Is Sweet candy
factory, compete in the Confectionary Association's annual
contest, they unexpectedly become friends and uncover secrets about themselves during the process.

"Mass has crafted a solid mystery dipped in sweet can-
dymaking details. Character development moves a lengthy
story forward in smooth increments. As each child's story
emerges, the mystery becomes one bit clearer, making this a

real page-turner. The characters are intricate, flawed heroes
with whom readers will identify." SLJ

Mathews, Ellie

The **linden** tree; [by] Ellie Mathews. Milkweed Editions 2007 195p hardcover o.p. pa $6.95

Grades: 3 4 5 6 **Fic**

1. Aunts -- Fiction 2. Farm life -- Fiction 3.
Bereavement -- Fiction 4. Family life -- Fiction
ISBN 978-1-57131-673-8; 1-57131-673-6; 978-1-
57131-674-5 pa; 1-57131-674-4 pa

LC 2006-38831

In 1948, nine-year-old Katy Sue's mother dies suddenly,
and she and her family spend the next year trying to recover
from their loss, assisted by her Aunt Katherine, who quits
her teaching job to help out on their Iowa farm

Matthews "tells a timeless, heartfelt story of family, loss,
and love." Booklist

Matthews, Tom L.

Danger in the dark; a Houdini & Nate mystery. [by]
Tom Lalicki; pictures by Carlyn Cerniglia. Farrar, Straus
and Giroux 2006 186p il $14.95

Grades: 4 5 6 7 **Fic**

1. Magicians 2. Mystery fiction 3. Nonfiction writers
4. Magicians -- Fiction 5. Spiritualism -- Fiction
ISBN 0-374-31680-5

LC 2005052111

Thirteen-year-old Nathaniel, aided by the famous magician Harry Houdini, plots to unmask a phony spirit advisor
attempting to relieve the boy's great-aunt of her fortune.

"The action is nonstop, and even a flurry of enormous
coincidences won't spoil enthusiasm for this entertaining
story." Booklist

Other titles in this series are:
Shots at sea (2007)
Frame-up on the Bowery (2009)

Frame-up on the Bowery; a Houdini & Nate mystery.
[by] Tom Lalicki; pictures by Carlyn Beccia. Farrar, Straus
and Giroux 2009 203p il $15.99

Grades: 5 6 7 8 **Fic**

1. Magicians 2. Mystery fiction 3. Cousins -- Fiction
4. Nonfiction writers 5. Magicians -- Fiction
ISBN 978-0-374-39930-6; 0-374-39930-1

LC 2008045607

Thirteen-year-old Nate, aided by his newly-discovered
cousin and the famous magician Harry Houdini, catches the
Fifth Avenue Slasher, solves a string of burglaries, and stops
a notorious gang leader.

This "delivers action, appealing characters, and contemporary issues within an engaging historical context." Voice
Youth Advocates

Matti, Truus

★ **Departure** time; translated from the Dutch by Nancy Forest-Flier. Namelos 2010 214p $18.95; pa $9.95

Grades: 5 6 7 8 **Fic**

1. Memory -- Fiction 2. Father-daughter relationship
-- Fiction
ISBN 978-1-60898-087-1; 1-60898-087-1; 978-1-
60898-009-3 pa; 1-60898-009-X pa
Original Dutch edition 2009

"A 10-year-old girl is lost in a surrealistic landscape—a red-earth desert threatened by an approaching storm. Nothing looks familiar. She can't remember how she got to this place. Alternating with this classic bad-dream setting, which is narrated in the third person, is a first-person, furious tirade by a girl who feels abandoned by her father and neglected by her mother. Readers will be intrigued by the way Matti interweaves these stories and tantalizes with the possible connections between them. . . . Remarkable and arresting and wholly original, this novel lingers in the mind long after the last page has been read." SLJ

Mister Orange; Truus Matti; translated from the Dutch by Laura Watkinson. Enchanged Lion Books 2013 156 p. (hardcover) $16.95

Grades: 5 6 7 8   **Fic**

1. Friendship -- Juvenile fiction 2. Historical fiction -- Juvenile fiction 3. Child-adult relationship -- Juvenile fiction 4. Artists -- Fiction 5. Friendship -- Fiction 6. World War, 1939-1945 -- Fiction

ISBN 159270123X; 9781592701230

LC 2012051313

This children's story, by Truus Matti, translated by Laura Watkinson, is set in Manhattan in "1943. . . . Linus Muller works at the family grocery store in the east 70s. . . . One of his customers . . . arranges to have a crate of oranges delivered every other week. Over the course of these deliveries, an intimacy develops between Linus and . . . Mister Orange. In the peacefulness of Mister Orange's spare kitchen, they discuss the war, the future, freedom and imagination." (Publisher's note)

Mayer, Mercer

What a good kitty; Mercer Mayer; edited by Mary-Kate Gaudet. HarperCollins 2012 32 p. (trade bdg.) $3.99

Grades: K 1 2 3   **Fic**

1. Cats -- Juvenile fiction 2. Pets -- Juvenile fiction

ISBN 0060835656; 9780060835651; 9780060835668

LC 2011941958

In this children's book by Mercer Mayer, "Little Critter loves his kitty, despite the cat's multiple naughty deeds. Wreaking havoc with Dad's newspaper, Mom's knitting, and Little Sister's dolls . . . the cat even disturbs the family dog and pet fish. She is exiled to the yard, and the fire department must come when she and Dad get stuck in a tree. But . . . when a mean dog scares Little Sister, Kitty successfully chases him away." (School Library Journal)

Mazer, Norma Fox

Ten ways to make my sister disappear. Arthur A. Levine Books 2007 148p $16.99

Grades: 3 4 5 6   **Fic**

1. Sisters -- Fiction 2. Friendship -- Fiction 3. Family life -- Fiction

ISBN 0-439-83983-1; 978-0-439-83983-9

LC 2007-09784

Ten-year-old Sprig no longer gets along with her twelve-year-old sister, Dakota, but the two pull together during their father's extended business trip to Afghanistan, sharing concerns about his safety, an elderly neighbor's health, fights with their best friends, and boys.

"The author excels at depicting the complexity of pre-teens' emotions and relationships, especially sibling rela-tionships; many readers will recognize their own feelings here." Publ Wkly

McCall Smith, Alexander, 1948-

The **great** cake mystery; Precious Ramotswe's very first case. Alexander McCall Smith; illustrations by Iain McIntosh. Anchor Books 2012 73 p.

Grades: 2 3 4 5   **Fic**

1. School stories 2. Mystery fiction 3. Children's stories 4. Blacks -- Botswana -- Fiction 5. Mystery and detective stories

ISBN 0307743896; 9780307743893

LC 2011026494

This children's book by Alexander McCall Smith is part of the "Number 1 Ladies' Detective Agency" series and tells the story of an eight-year-old African school girl in Botswana who wants to become a detective. "Her name is Precious. When a piece of cake goes missing from her classroom . . . Precious . . . sets out to find the real thief. Along the way she learns that your first guess isn't always right. She also learns how to be a detective." (Publisher's note)

McCaughrean, Geraldine

Peter Pan in scarlet; by Geraldine McCaughrean; illustrations by Scott M. Fischer. Margaret K. McElderry Books 2006 309p il $17.99; pa $6.99

Grades: 4 5 6 7   **Fic**

1. Fairy tales

ISBN 978-1-4169-1808-0; 1-4169-1808-6; 978-1-4169-1809-7 pa; 1-4169-1809-4 pa

In the 1930s, all is not well. Nightmares are leaking out of Neverland. Fearing for Peter Pan's life, Wendy and the Lost Boys go back to Neverland with the help of the fairy Fireflyer only to discover their worst nightmares coming true!

"McCaughrean's story, with its picaresque descriptions, faithfully rekindled characters and an ending that leaves room for sequels, will keep the pages turning." Publ Wkly

★ The **death**-defying Pepper Roux. Harper 2010 328p $16.99; lib bdg $17.89

Grades: 5 6 7 8   **Fic**

1. Adventure fiction 2. Fate and fatalism -- Fiction

ISBN 978-0-06-183665-7; 0-06-183665-6; 978-0-06-183666-4 lib bdg; 0-06-183666-4 lib bdg

LC 2009-39665

Having been raised believing he will die before he reaches the age of fourteen, Pepper Roux runs away on his fourteenth birthday in an attempt to elude his fate, assumes another identity, and continues to try to outrun death, no matter the consequences.

"McCaughrean's exuberant prose and whirling humor animate an unforgettable cast of characters." Booklist

★ The **glorious** adventures of the Sunshine Queen. Harper 2011 325p $16.99

Grades: 5 6 7 8   **Fic**

1. Adventure fiction 2. Theater -- Fiction

ISBN 978-0-06-200806-0; 0-06-200806-4

LC 2010021958

When a diphtheria outbreak forces twelve-year-old Cissy to leave her Oklahoma hometown in the 1890s, she and her two classmates embark on a wild adventure down the

Missouri River with a team of traveling actors who are living on a dilapidated paddle steamer.

"McCaughrean invests her characters with humanity and shows a farcical sense for dialogue, while her arch narrative voice, includes the theatrical and clever turns of phrase." Booklist

The **kite** rider; a novel. HarperCollins Pubs. 2002 272p maps hardcover o.p. pa $6.99

Grades: 5 6 7 8   **Fic**

1. Kites 2. Circus 3. Family 4. Mongols 5. Kings 6. Kites -- Fiction 7. China -- History -- Yüan dynasty, 1260-1368 -- Juvenile fiction

ISBN 0-06-623874-9; 0-06-441091-9 pa

LC 2001-39522

In thirteenth-century China, after trying to save his widowed mother from a horrendous second marriage, twelve-year-old Haoyou has life-changing adventures when he takes to the sky as a circus kite rider and ends up meeting the great Mongol ruler Kublai Khan

"The story is a genuine page-turner. . . . McCaughrean fully immerses her memorable characters in the culture and lore of the ancient Chinese and Mongols, which make this not only a solid adventure story but also a window to a fascinating time and place." Booklist

McCloskey, Robert, 1914-2003

★ **Homer** Price. Viking 1943 149p il $16.99; pa $5.99

Grades: 4 5 6   **Fic**

ISBN 0-670-37729-5; 0-14-240415-2 pa

"Text and pictures are pure Americana, hilarious and convincing in their portrayal of midwestern small-town life." Child Books Too Good to Miss

Another title about Homer Price is:
Centerburg tales (1951)

McCrite, K. D.

In front of God and everybody. Thomas Nelson 2011 298p (Confessions of April Grace) pa $9.99

Grades: 4 5 6 7   **Fic**

1. Farm life -- Fiction 2. Christian life -- Fiction 3. Swindlers and swindling -- Fiction

ISBN 978-1-4003-1722-6; 1-4003-1722-3

LC 2011005583

In the summer of 1986, eleven-year-old April Grace, who lives on a rural Arkansas farm with her family, across a field from her grandmother, has her sense of Christian charity tested when a snooty couple from San Francisco moves into a dilapidated house down the road and her grandmother takes up with a loud, obnoxious, and suspicious-acting Texan.

"With keen eyes and good humor, April Grace notes the quirks, presumptions, and motivations of family and neighbors; she has plenty of fodder—the characters' personalities are dialed up to 11." Publ Wkly

McCulloch, Michael

The **other** Felix. Roaring Brook Press 2011 $16.99

Grades: 3 4 5 6   **Fic**

1. School stories 2. Fear -- Fiction 3. Dreams -- Fiction 4. Bullies -- Fiction

ISBN 978-1-5964-3655-8; 1-5964-3655-7

LC 2010050605

Worrying about his father losing his job and the bully at school, fourth-grader Felix has terrifying dreams of the same monster-filled place every night until he meets someone there who looks and sounds strangely familiar.

"The story has a beautifully crafted innocence. . . . This is a satisfying tale in and of itself, as well as a helpful and sensitive guide for those children who are just learning to confront life's sticky challenges. The ending is exquisite." SLJ

McDonald, Megan, 1959-

Cloudy with a chance of boys. Candlewick Press 2011 260p il (The Sisters Club) $15.99; pa $5.99

Grades: 3 4 5 6   **Fic**

1. Clubs -- Fiction 2. Acting -- Fiction 3. Sisters -- Fiction 4. Family life -- Fiction 5. Dating (Social customs) -- Fiction

ISBN 978-0-7636-4615-8; 0-7636-4615-6; 978-0-7636-5577-8 pa

LC 2010-39179

While older sister Alex is trying to orchestrate a perfect first kiss with her heartthrob and younger sister Joey prefers frogs to boys, Stevie Reel wonders if she is ready for a boyfriend while being pursued by a new boy in her class.

"The sisters are solidly developed, each with a distinctive narrative style made clear by formatting. . . . Breezy and light-hearted, this makes a nice recommendation for young readers looking for girl power." Bull Cent Child Books

Other titles in this series are:
The Sisters Club (2003)
Rule of three (2009)

★ **Judy** Moody; illustrated by Peter Reynolds. Candlewick Press 2000 160p il $15.99; pa $5.99

Grades: 2 3 4   **Fic**

1. School stories

ISBN 0-7636-0685-5; 0-7636-1231-6 pa

LC 99-13464

Third grader Judy Moody is in a first day of school bad mood until she gets an assignment to create a collage all about herself and begins creating her masterpiece, the Me collage.

"This beginning chapter book features large type; simple, expressive prose and dialogue; and plenty of child-appealing humor." Booklist

Other titles about Judy Moody are:
Judy Moody & Stink: the holly joliday (2007)
Judy Moody: around the world in 8 1/2 days (2006)
Judy Moody declares independence (2005)
Judy Moody gets famous (2001)
Judy Moody, girl detective (2010)
Judy Moody goes to college (2008)
Judy Moody M.D., the doctor is in (2004)
Judy Moody predicts the future (2003)
Judy Moody saves the world (2002)

★ **Stink**: the incredible shrinking kid; illustrated by Peter H. Reynolds. Candlewick Press 2005 102p il $12.99

Grades: 2 3 4   **Fic**

1. School stories

ISBN 0-7636-2025-4

LC 2003-65246

The shortest kid in the second grade, James Moody, also known as Stink, learns all about the shortest president of the

United States, James Madison, when they celebrate Presidents' Day at school

"Delightful full-page and spot-art cartoons and playful language in large type bring the child's adventures to life." SLJ

Other titles about Stink are:

Judy Moody & Stink: the holly joliday (2007)

Stink and the great Guinea Pig Express (2008)

Stink and the incredible super-galactic jawbreaker (2006)

Stink and the world's worst super-stinky sneakers (2007)

Stink: solar system superhero (2010)

Stink and the ultimate thumb-wrestling smackdown (2011)

The **doll** shop downstairs; illustrated by Heather Maione. Viking 2009 118p il $14.99

Grades: 2 3 4 5   **Fic**

1. Dolls -- Fiction 2. Immigrants -- Fiction 3. Family life -- Fiction 4. World War, 1914-1918 -- Fiction 5. Jews -- United States -- Fiction

ISBN 978-0-670-01091-2; 0-670-01091-X

LC 2009-01934

When World War I breaks out, nine-year-old Anna thinks of a way to save her family's beloved New York City doll repair shop. Includes brief author's note about the history of the Madame Alexander doll, a glossary, and timeline.

"Anna's first person narrative creates convincing portrayals of her sisters and parents as well as her personal ups and downs. . . . Pleasant black-and-white pictures illustrate the action while helping children to visualize the period setting." Booklist

Another title about Anna and the doll shop is:

The cats in the doll shop (2011)

★ The **doll** with the yellow star; illustrated by Kimberly Bulcken Root. Henry Holt and Co. 2005 90p il $16.95

Grades: 3 4 5   **Fic**

1. Jews -- Fiction 2. Dolls -- Fiction 3. Holocaust, 1933-1945 -- Fiction

ISBN 0-8050-6337-4

LC 2002-27554

When France falls to Germany at the start of World War II, nine-year-old Claudine must leave her beloved parents and friends to stay with relatives in America, accompanied by her doll, Violette

"This fiction book is informative, enjoyable, and passionately written." Libr Media Connect

McDowell, Marilyn Taylor

★ **Carolina** Harmony. Delacorte 2009 288p $16.99; lib bdg $19.99

Grades: 4 5 6 7   **Fic**

1. Orphans -- Fiction 2. Farm life -- Fiction

ISBN 978-0-385-73590-2; 0-385-73590-1; 978-0-385-90575-6 lib bdg; 0-385-90575-0 lib bdg

"After Carolina's beloved Auntie Shen suffers a stroke, Carolina escapes from an unpleasant foster placement. The orphaned 10-year-old finds love at Harmony Farm, but the web of lies she spins almost leads to losing that home too. . . . This third-person narrative unwinds leisurely, with plenty of backtracking to fill in details of Carolina's life and the glories of her world in the Blue Ridge Mountains. . . . McDowell reveals her love for this part of the world, savoring

the language, the environment, and the traditions of mountain culture." Booklist

McElligott, Matthew

Benjamin Franklinstein lives! [by] Matthew McElligott & Larry Tuxbury; illustrated by Matthew McElligott. G. P. Putnam's Sons 2010 121p il $12.99

Grades: 4 5 6 7   **Fic**

1. Authors 2. Diplomats 3. Inventors 4. Statesmen 5. Scientists 6. Science fiction 7. Writers on science 8. Zombies -- Fiction 9. Members of Congress

ISBN 978-0-399-25229-7; 0-399-25229-0

While working on a science fair project, a Philadelphia school boy discovers both a secret laboratory in his basement and Benjamin Franklin, who comes to life after receiving a jolt of electricity.

"It's a light fun read, and McElligott's many diagrams, graphs, and drawings are a nice addition." Booklist

Benjamin Franklinstein meets the Fright brothers; by Matthew McElligott and Larry Tuxbury; [illustrated by Matthew McElligott] G. P. Putnam's Sons 2011 147p il $16.99

Grades: 4 5 6 7   **Fic**

1. Authors 2. Diplomats 3. Inventors 4. Statesmen 5. Scientists 6. Writers on science 7. Members of Congress 8. Scientists -- Fiction 9. Secret societies -- Fiction

ISBN 978-0-399-25480-2; 0-399-25480-3

LC 2010040431

Victor and his friends, aided by Benjamin Franklin, uncover an evil scheme involving giant bats and two mysterious brothers, and learn more about the secretive Modern Order of Prometheus.

"Enhanced by frequent charts, diagrams, lists and other visual aids, a spirit of rational (if often reckless) scientific inquiry pervades the tale, as Ben and his allies translate coded messages, analyze evidence, get a lesson in meteorology and conduct experiments using both real and science-fictional gear on the way to a literally electrifying climax. . . . The authors have way too much fun taking the opener's premise and evil conspiracy to the next level. Readers will too." Kirkus

McGhee, Alison

★ **Julia** Gillian (and the art of knowing) pictures by Drazen Kozjan. Scholastic Press 2008 280p il $15.99

Grades: 3 4 5   **Fic**

1. Dogs -- Fiction 2. Fear -- Fiction 3. Family life -- Fiction

ISBN 978-0-545-03348-0; 0-545-03348-9

LC 2007024898

Nine-year-old Julia Gillian learns a lot about facing fear as she and her St. Bernard, Bigfoot, take long walks through their Minneapolis neighborhood one hot summer, and she seeks the courage to finish a book that could have an unhappy ending.

"Julia Gillian's fears and their ultimate resolution are very relatable. The book is well paced, laced with line drawings that capture Julia Gillian's slightly whimsical personality." Publ Wkly

Other titles in this series are:

Julia Gillian (and the quest for joy) (2009)

Julia Gillian (and the dream of the dog) (2010)

Snap; a novel. Candlewick Press 2004 129p $15.99
Grades: 5 6 7 8　　　　　　　　　　　　　　**Fic**
1. Grief 2. Change 3. Friendship 4. Grandmothers 5.
Best friends 6. Death -- Fiction 7. Friendship -- Fiction
8. Grandmothers -- Fiction
ISBN 0-7636-2002-5
　　　　　　　　　　　　　　　　LC 2002-34998
Eleven-year-old Edwina confronts old and new challenges when her longtime best friend Sally faces the inevitable death of the grandmother who raised her.
　This "features memorable characters and a tolerance for
eccentricity, emotional subtlety and complexity, themes of
acceptance of death and love, and a spare and poetic text that
begs to be reread and savored." SLJ

McGraw, Eloise Jarvis
　The **moorchild**; [by] Eloise McGraw. Margaret K.
McElderry Bks. 1996 241p $17; pa $5.99
Grades: 4 5 6 7　　　　　　　　　　　　　　**Fic**
1. Fantasy fiction 2. Fairies -- Fiction
ISBN 0-689-80654-X; 1-4169-2768-9 pa
　　　　　　　　　　　　　　　　LC 95-34107
A Newbery Medal honor book, 1997
　"Incorporating some classic fantasy motifs and icons,
McGraw . . . conjures up an appreciably familiar world that,
as evidence of her storytelling power, still strikes an original
chord." Publ Wkly

　Dog Friday. Margaret K. McElderry Bks. 1995 135p
hardcover o.p. pa $4.99
Grades: 4 5 6　　　　　　　　　　　　　　**Fic**
1. Dogs -- Fiction
ISBN 0-689-80383-4; 0-689-81765-7 pa
　　　　　　　　　　　　　　　　LC 95-4446
First published 1994 in the United Kingdom
　Ten-year-old Robin Brogan is determined to keep the
dog he finds abandoned on the beach from being impounded
by the police
　"The sharply realized characters, fast-paced story, and
witty dialogue make this English novel both distinctive and
refreshing." Booklist
　Other titles about the Brogan family and their friends
are:
　The amber cat (1997)
　Dolphin luck (1999)

　★ **Saffy's** angel. Margaret K. McElderry Bks. 2002
152p $16; pa $4.99
Grades: 5 6 7 8　　　　　　　　　　　　　　**Fic**
1. Artists 2. Adoption 3. Family life 4. Adoption --
Fiction 5. Brothers and sisters 6. Family life -- Fiction
ISBN 0-689-84933-8; 0-689-84934-6 pa
　　　　　　　　　　　　　　　　LC 2001-44110
First published 2001 in the United Kingdom
　After learning that she was adopted, thirteen-year-old
Saffron's relationship with her eccentric, artistic family
changes, until they help her go back to Italy where she was
born to find a special momento of her past
　"Like the Casson household itself, the plot is a chaotic
whirl that careens off in several directions simultaneously.
But McKay always skillfully draws each clearly defined
character back into the story with witty, well-edited details;
rapid dialogue; and fine pacing." Booklist
　Other titles in this series are:

　Indigo's star (2004)
　Permanent Rose (2005)
　Caddy ever after (2006)
　Forever Rose (2008)

　Wishing for tomorrow; the sequel to A little princess.
illustrated by Nick Maland. Margaret K. McElderry Books
2010 273p il $16.99
Grades: 4 5 6　　　　　　　　　　　　　　**Fic**
1. School stories 2. Friendship -- Fiction
ISBN 978-1-4424-0169-3; 1-4424-0169-9
　　　　　　　　　　　　　　　　LC 2009-24868
Relates what becomes of Ermengarde and the other
girls left behind at Miss Minchin's School after Sara Crewe
leaves to live with her guardian, the Indian gentleman.
　"Enhanced by Maland's period illustrations, the novel
convincingly evokes the Victorian era, even as McKay interjects a contemporary sensibility. A surprising, dramatic
denouement caps this droll and heartwarming tale, a very
worthy follow-up to a well-loved classic." Publ Wkly

McKay, Hilary, 1959-
　Lulu and the dog from the sea; by Hilary McKay; il-
lustrated by Priscilla Lamont. Albert Whitman 2013 112 p.
(reinforced) $13.99
Grades: 2 3 4　　　　　　　　　　　　　　**Fic**
1. Dogs -- Juvenile fiction 2. Vacations -- Juvenile
fiction 3. Dogs -- Fiction 4. Beaches -- Fiction 5.
Vacations -- Fiction
ISBN 0807548200; 9780807548202
　　　　　　　　　　　　　　　　LC 2012013697
This children's story, by Hilary McKay, illustrated by
Priscilla Lamont, is the second volume in the "Lulu" series.
"Lulu loves animals. When Lulu goes on vacation, she finds
there's a stray dog living on the beach. Everyone in the town
thinks the dog is trouble. But Lulu is sure he just needs a
friend. And that he's been waiting for someone just like her."
(Publisher's note)

　Lulu and the duck in the park; by Hilary McKay; illustrated by Priscilla Lamont. Albert Whitman 2012 104
p. $13.99
Grades: 2 3 4 5　　　　　　　　　　　　　　**Fic**
1. School stories 2. Pets -- Fiction 3. Ducks -- Fiction
4. Humorous stories 5. Animals -- Fiction 6. Schools
-- Fiction
ISBN 0807548081; 9780807548080
　　　　　　　　　　　　　　　　LC 2012008229
This book introduces Lulu, a "girl with a penchant
acquiring pets. . . . The crux of the novel is Lulu's rescue
of a duck egg she finds after dogs storm the park during a class outing. She sneaks the egg into school and, in
one" scene "quacks to the egg so 'it doesn't get lonely.'"
(Publishers Weekly)
　"McKay shows a rare ability to capture a younger audi-
ence in this involving chapter book for transitional readers."
Booklist

McKinlay, Meg
　Below; Meg McKinlay. Candlewick Press 2013 224
p. (reinforced) $15.99

Grades: 4 5 6 7   **Fic**
   1. Reservoirs -- Fiction 2. Extinct cities -- Fiction
ISBN 0763661260; 9780763661267
                  LC 2012943652

In this book by Meg McKinlay, "Cassie was . . . the first baby born in the Australian town of New Lower Grange, which was established after the intentional flooding of the previous town to accommodate a dam. . . . [S]he feels the pull of the forbidden lake above Old Lower Grange. There, she is joined by Liam, a classmate whose life was altered in a tragic accident, and together they search for the truth about the town's past as its centenary celebration approaches." (Publishers Weekly)

"Although the author does a masterful job of making sure all the pieces fit at the end, the central mystery is hard to buy. This is mitigated by a reasonably suspenseful climax, an earned family solidarity message and the lesson: that to find the truth, one must delve below the surface. A quietly intriguing meditation on history and truth." Kirkus

   Duck for a day; illustrated by Leila Rudge. Candlewick Press 2012 89 p. $12.99
Grades: 1 2 3   **Fic**
   1. Children and animals 2. Pets -- Juvenile fiction 3. Friendship -- Juvenile fiction 4. School stories 5. Ducks -- Fiction 6. Lost and found possessions -- Fiction
ISBN 0763657840; 9780763657840
                  LC 2011018608

In author Meg McKinlay's book, "class pet is a duck named Max, and pet-deprived Abby longs to earn the privilege of taking him home overnight. Active and involving right from the first, . . . the plot unfolds . . . to include a contest to build Max the ideal 'aquatic environment,' a well-deserved visit to Abby's house, and an exciting chase to find Max after he escapes from her backyard." (Horn Book Magazine)

McKinnon, Hannah Roberts
   ★ **Franny** Parker. Farrar Straus Giroux 2009 149p $16
Grades: 5 6 7 8   **Fic**
   1. Droughts -- Fiction 2. Violence -- Fiction 3. Family life -- Fiction
ISBN 978-0-374-32469-8; 0-374-32469-7
                  LC 2008-01702

Through a hot, dry Oklahoma summer, twelve-year-old Franny tends wild animals brought by her neighbors, hears gossip during a weekly quilting bee, befriends a new neighbor who has some big secrets, and learns to hope.

"Franny is a relatable and consistent narrator, the homey rural setting is throughtfully rendered and the easy prose should appeal to reluctant readers." Publ Wkly

   The **properties** of water. Farrar, Straus, and Giroux 2010 166p $16.99
Grades: 5 6 7 8   **Fic**
   1. Sisters -- Fiction 2. Accidents -- Fiction
ISBN 978-0-374-36145-7; 0-374-36145-2

When her older sister, Marni, is paralyzed jumping off the cliffs into the lake near their house, twelve-year-old Lace feels responsible for the accident and struggles to find a way to help heal her family.

McKinnon "has created a cast of believably imperfect characters, and Lace's emotions ring true." Publ Wkly

McKissack, Pat, 1944-
   Abby takes a stand; illustrated [by] Gordon C. James. Viking 2005 104p il (Scraps of time) $14.99; pa $4.99
Grades: 2 3 4   **Fic**
   1. African Americans -- Fiction 2. Civil rights demonstrations -- Fiction
ISBN 0-670-06011-9; 0-14-240687-2 pa
                  LC 2004-21641

Gee recalls for her grandchildren what happened in 1960 in Nashville, Tennessee, when she, aged ten, passed out flyers while her cousin and other adults held sit-ins at restaurants and lunch counters to protest segregation.

"Although short and simply told, the book gives readers a kid's-eye view of important happenings and reminds them that history is something that is always in the making. Fine black-and-white art adds to the ambience of the time." Booklist

   Other titles in this series are:
   Away west (2006)
   A song for Harlem (2007)
   The homerun king (2008)

   Cyborg; a Clone codes novel. [by] Patricia C. McKissack, Fredrick L. McKissack, John P. McKissack. Scholastic Press 2011 107p $16.99
Grades: 4 5 6 7   **Fic**
   1. Science fiction 2. Civil rights -- Fiction 3. Artificial intelligence -- Fiction
ISBN 978-0-439-92985-1; 0-439-92985-7
                  LC 2010016075

Seventeen-year-old Houston, a cyborg since the age of seven, and a fugitive living on the Moon, joins with other cyborgs all over the world in non-violent protest marches to challenge the Cyborg Act 2130 and hopefully secure increased civil liberties.

"The McKissacks continue to successfully draw parallels between a futuristic world that tries to control those considered different and historic racial struggles. . . . The worldbuilding is intriguing, there is plenty of action and ethnic diversity in a science-fiction tale is welcome." Kirkus

   The **clone** codes; [by] Patricia C. McKissack, Fredrick L. McKissack [and] John McKissack. Scholastic 2010 173p $16.99
Grades: 4 5 6 7   **Fic**
   1. Science fiction 2. Cloning -- Fiction 3. Segregation -- Fiction 4. Identity (Psychology) -- Fiction
ISBN 978-0-439-92983-7; 0-439-92983-0
                  LC 2009-24076

On the run from a bounty hunter who arrested her mother for being part of a secret society devoted to freeing clones, thirteen-year-old Leanna learns amazing truths about herself and her family as she is forced to consider the value of freedom and what it really means to be human in 2170 America.

"The story is tight and fast-paced, yet makes room for historical parallels that are vivid without being preachy. An intriguing start to a planned trilogy." Publ Wkly

   ★ **Let** my people go; Bible stories told by a freeman of color to his daughter, Charlotte, in Charleston, South Carolina, 1806-16. by Patricia and Fredrick McKissack; illustrated by James Ransome. Atheneum Bks. for Young Readers 1998 134p il $20

Grades: 4 5 6 7   **Fic**
1. Bible stories 2. Slavery -- Fiction 3. African
Americans -- Fiction
ISBN 0-689-80856-9

                 LC 97-19983

Charlotte, the daughter of a free black man who
worked as a blacksmith in Charleston, South Carolina, in
the early 1800s recalls the stories from the Bible that her
father shared with her, relating them to the experiences of
African Americans

"The poignant juxtaposition of the Biblical characters
and Charlotte's personal narrative is authentic and moving.
. . . The occasional illustrations are powerful oil paintings in
rich colors, emotional and evocative." SLJ

Includes bibliographical references

★ **Never** forgotten. Schwartz & Wade Books 2011 un il
$18.99; lib bdg $21.99

Grades: 3 4 5 6   **Fic**
1. Novels in verse 2. Slavery -- Fiction 3. African
Americans -- Fiction
ISBN 978-0-375-84384-6; 0-375-84384-1; 978-0-375-
94453-6 lib bdg; 0-375-94453-2 lib bdg

                 LC 2010024789

McKissack's "story about a Malian boy abducted and
sold into slavery has frightening moments, but carries dignity and even triumph away from them. . . . The willingness
to turn the dark history of the past into literature takes not
just talent but courage. McKissack has both." Publ Wkly

Stitchin' and pullin' a Gee's Bend quilt. illustrated by
Cozbi A. Cabrera. Random House 2008 un il $17.99; lib
bdg $20.99

Grades: 2 3 4 5   **Fic**
1. Novels in verse 2. Quilts -- Fiction 3. Family life
-- Fiction 4. African Americans -- Fiction 5. Quilting
-- Juvenile literature
ISBN 978-0-375-83163-8; 0-375-83163-0; 978-0-375-
93163-5 lib bdg; 0-375-93163-5 lib bdg

                 LC 2007011066

As a young African American girl pieces her first quilt
together, the history of her family, community, and the struggle for justice and freedom in Gee's Bend, Alabama unfolds.

"Rich naïf-style paintings in a warm, deep palette bring
the poems to life and reflect their tone and spirit. . . . It's
marvelously clear that McKissack understands the creative
pulse of the quilter and artist." Horn Book

★ **Tippy** Lemmey; illustrated by Susan Keeter. Simon
& Schuster 2003 59p il (Ready-for-chapters) pa $3.99

Grades: 2 3 4   **Fic**
1. Dogs -- Fiction 2. African Americans -- Fiction
ISBN 0-689-85019-0

"In 1951, in Templeton, TN, Leanne Martin and her
friends Paul and Jeannie are at war with Tippy Lemmey, a
dog that frightens them. . . . The kids learn that Tippy is simply a puppy who wants to play, and that his owner is fighting
in Korea. Leanne remains unconvinced about the dog's good
intentions, but when the friends see thieves stealing him and
other neighborhood dogs to sell across state, they rescue the
animals and are rewarded when Tippy gets them out of a
dangerous situation. . . . This charming and humorous story

moves along at a fast pace, making it perfect for readers just
venturing into chapter-book territory." SLJ

McMullan, Kate
  School! adventures at the Harvey N. Trouble Elementary School. written by Kate McMullan; inspired and illustrated by George Booth. Feiwel and Friends 2010 149p
il $12.99

Grades: 1 2 3 4   **Fic**
1. School stories
ISBN 978-0-312-37592-8; 0-312-37592-1

                 LC 2008-15263

"The story takes readers into Ron's week, from Hotsy-
Totsy Monday to Hunky-Dory Thursday, at his outlandish
school, where, through extreme silliness, little life lessons
are learned. . . . The characters all have giggle-worthy names
that relate to their personalities or attributes. . . . Booth's
great cartoon illustrations add whimsy and pure fun to every
page, a quality that, when paired with McMullan's simple,
quirky story, may well draw in reluctant readers." SLJ

McMullan, Margaret
  How I found the Strong; a Civil War story. Houghton
Mifflin 2004 136p $15

Grades: 5 6 7 8   **Fic**
1. Slavery -- Fiction
ISBN 0-618-35008-X

                 LC 2003-12294

Frank Russell, known as Shanks, wishes he could have
gone with his father and brother to fight for Mississippi and
the Confederacy, but his experiences with the war and his
changing relationship with the family slave, Buck, change
his thinking.

"The crisply written narrative is full of regional speech
and detail, creating a vivid portrait." Voice Youth Advocates

  When I crossed No-Bob. Houghton Mifflin Company
2007 209p $16

Grades: 5 6 7 8   **Fic**
1. Farm life -- Fiction 2. Race relations -- Fiction 3.
Abandoned children -- Fiction 4. Reconstruction (1865-
1876) -- Fiction
ISBN 978-0-618-71715-6; 0-618-71715-3

                 LC 2007-12753

Ten years after the Civil War's end, twelve-year-old
Addy, abandoned by her parents, is taken from the horrid
town of No-Bob by schoolteacher Frank Russell and his
bride, but when her father returns to claim her she must find
another way to leave her O'Donnell past behind.

"The simple prose can be pure poetry. . . . Readers will
be drawn by the history close-up and by the elemental moral
choice." Booklist

McNamee, Eoin
  The **Ring** of Five. Wendy Lamb Books 2010 345p
$16.99; lib bdg $19.99

Grades: 5 6 7 8   **Fic**
1. School stories 2. Fantasy fiction 3. Spies -- Fiction
ISBN 978-0-385-73731-9; 0-385-73731-9; 978-0-385-
90658-6 lib bdg; 0-385-90658-7 lib bdg

                 LC 2009-33345

Kidnapped on his way to boarding school, Danny Caul-
field, who has one blue eye and one brown eye, ends up at
a mysterious academy of spies, where he is to be trained in

the art of espionage in an effort to keep the Upper and Lower worlds from colliding.

McSwigan, Marie

★ **Snow** treasure; [by] Marie McSwigan; illustrated by Mary Reardon. Dutton's Children's Books 2005 196p il $10.99; pa $5.99

Grades: 3 4 5 6   Fic

1. World War, 1939-1945 -- Fiction

ISBN 0-525-47626-1; 0-14-240224-9 pa

LC 2005042108

A reissue of the title first published 1942

In 1940, when the Nazi invasion of Norway reaches their village in the far north, twelve-year-old Peter and his friends use their sleds to transport nine million dollars worth of gold bullion past the German soldiers to the secret harbor where Peter's uncle keeps his ship ready to take the gold for safe-keeping in the United States.

"A dramatic reconstruction of an actual happening. . . . Well written." Booklist

Mead, Alice

★ **Junebug**. Farrar, Straus & Giroux 1995 101p hard-cover o.p. pa $6.99

Grades: 3 4 5   Fic

1. Sailing -- Fiction 2. African Americans -- Fiction

ISBN 0-374-33964-3; 0-312-56126-1 pa

LC 95-5421

"Junebug approaches his tenth birthday with fear because he knows he'll be forced by the older boys in his housing project to join a gang. On his birthday, with luck and persistence, Junebug realizes his secret dream of one day sailing a boat. The novel contains vivid descriptions of the grim realities of inner-city life but also demonstrates that strong convictions and warm hearts can bring about change." Horn Book Guide

Other titles about Junebug are:

Junebug and the Reverend (1998)

Junebug in trouble (2003)

Meddaugh, Susan

Lulu's hat. Houghton Mifflin 2002 74p il $15; pa $6.95

Grades: 3 4 5   Fic

1. Magicians 2. Magicians -- Fiction

ISBN 0-618-15277-6; 0-618-77127-1 pa

LC 2001-16787

"With plot twists, cliff-hanger chapter endings, a large dose of originality, sparkling humor, and even an epilogue, this witty chapter book will hold readers' attention." SLJ

Meloy, Colin

Under Wildwood; Colin Meloy; illustrated by Carson Ellis. Balzer + Bray 2012 559 p. (hardback) $17.99

Grades: 5 6 7 8   Fic

1. Fantasy fiction 2. Adventure fiction 3. Fantasy 4. Animals -- Fiction

ISBN 006202471X; 9780062024718

LC 2012019040

This children's picture book is a sequel to "Wildwood." Here, bookish "Prue and bandit-in-training Curtis team up once again to fight a nefarious governess and evil science teacher in this fast-paced fantasy set in Oregon. . . . In this strange land, it can be difficult to tell friend from foe, mak-

ing for deliciously suspenseful adventures with a rat named Septimus and a circus bear with hooks instead of paws." (Children's Literature)

★ **Wildwood**; illustrations by Carson Ellis. Balzer + Bray 2011 541p il $16.99

Grades: 5 6 7 8   Fic

1. Fantasy fiction 2. Animals -- Fiction 3. Siblings -- Fiction 4. Missing persons -- Fiction

ISBN 978-0-06-202468-8; 0-06-202468-X

LC 2011010072

When her baby brother is kidnapped by crows, seventh-grader Prue McKeel ventures into the forbidden Impassable Wilderness—a dangerous and magical forest in the middle of Portland, Oregon—and soon finds herself involved in a war among the various inhabitants.

"Illustrations by Ellis . . . bring forest and inhabitants to gently whimsical life. A satisfying blend of fantasy, adventure story, eco-fable and political satire with broad appeal." Kirkus

Merrill, Jean

★ The **pushcart** war; by Jean Merrill; with illustrations by Ronni Solbert. Bantam Doubleday Dell Books for Young Readers 1987 222p il pa $6.50

Grades: 5 6 7 8   Fic

1. Trucks -- Fiction

ISBN 0-440-47147-8

A reissue of the title first published 1964 by W. R. Scott

The outbreak of a war between truck drivers and push-cart peddlers brings the mounting problems of traffic to the attention of both the city of New York and the world.

"A book that is both humorous and downright funny. . . . Such a lively book will need little introducing." Horn Book

The **toothpaste** millionaire; by Jean Merrill; prepared by the Bank Street College of Education. 35th anniversary ed.; Houghton Mifflin 2006 129p il $16; pa $5.95

Grades: 4 5 6   Fic

1. Mathematics -- Fiction 2. Business enterprises -- Fiction

ISBN 978-0-618-75924-8; 0-618-75924-7; 978-0-618-75925-5 pa; 0-618-75925-5 pa

A reissue of the title first published 1972

A young girl describes how her school friend made over a million dollars by creating and marketing a cheaper and better toothpaste

"The illustrations are engaging, the style is light, the project interesting (with more than a few swipes taken at advertising and business practices in our society) and Rufus a believable genius." Bull Cent Child Books

Messer, Stephen

★ **Windblowne**. Random House 2010 304p $16.99

Grades: 4 5 6 7   Fic

1. Fantasy fiction 2. Kites -- Fiction 3. Uncles -- Fiction 4. Space and time -- Fiction

ISBN 978-0-375-86195-6; 0-375-86195-5

LC 2008-43777

Hapless Oliver, who lives in the trees in the town of Windblowne, seeks his eccentric great-uncle Gilbert's help in creating a kite for the all-important kite festival, but when Gilbert suddenly disappears, Oliver is guided by one of Gilbert's kites in a quest through different worlds to find him.

"Messer constructs a tale that moves along at a powerful, steady pace to a climactic faceoff, and Oliver's realization that the gateway to worlds is open for those who can truly listen to the wind's voices sparks a memorable sea change in his self-image." Kirkus

The **death** of Yorik Mortwell; illustrated by Gris Grimly. Random House Children's Books 2011 173p il $15.99; lib bdg $18.99; e-book $15.95
Grades: 5 6 7 8 **Fic**
1. Ghost stories 2. Fantasy fiction 3. Magic -- Fiction 4. Siblings -- Fiction 5. Demonology -- Fiction 6. Good and evil -- Fiction 7. Social classes -- Fiction
ISBN 978-0-375-86858-0; 978-0-375-96858-7 lib bdg; 978-0-375-89928-7 e-book
LC 2010014255
Following his death at the hands of fellow twelve-year-old, Lord Thomas, Yorik returns as a ghost to protect his sister from a similar fate but soon learns of ancient magical beings, both good and evil, who are vying for power at the Estate.
"Full-page, macabre illustrations appear throughout. Lemony Snicket, Harry Potter, and Neil Gaiman enthusiasts will appreciate this engaging, eccentric adventure." SLJ

Messner, Kate
Marty McGuire; illustrated by Brian Floca. Scholastic Press 2011 129p il $15.99; pa $5.99
Grades: 2 3 4 **Fic**
1. School stories 2. Theater -- Fiction Grades two
ISBN 978-0-545-14244-1; 0-545-14244-X; 978-0-545-14246-5 pa; 0-545-14246-6 pa
LC 2010-31291
When tomboy Marty is cast as the princess in the third-grade play, she learns about improvisation, which helps her become more adaptable.
"Messner gets all the details of third grade right. . . . Floca's black-and-white sketches are filled with movement and emotion and are frequent enough to help new chapter-book readers keep up with this longer text. [The book features] believable and endearing characters in a realistic elementary-school setting." Kirkus

Marty McGuire digs worms! by Kate Messner; illustrated by Brian Floca. Scholastic Press 2012 161 p.
Grades: K 1 2 3 **Fic**
1. Worms -- Fiction 2. Compost -- Fiction 3. Recycling -- Fiction 4. School children -- Fiction 5. Environmental protection -- Fiction 6. Schools -- Fiction 7. Grandmothers -- Fiction 8. Recycling (Waste) -- Fiction
ISBN 0545142458; 9780545142458; 9780545142472
LC 2011016291
In this book, "Marty McGuire's third-grade class has a special assignment: Save the Earth! Even more exciting, the best project wins a special award. Marty's pretty sure her classmates' ideas won't stand a chance against her plan to turn the garbage from the school cafeteria into fertilizer. All she needs is a little help from her teammate and best friend, Annie—and the worms in her grandma's garden. . . . [W]hen the critters escape, the whole class starts grumbling. Can Marty save the Earth without losing her friends?" (Publisher's note)

Sugar and ice. Walker & Co. 2010 275p $16.99
Grades: 4 5 6 7 **Fic**
1. Ice skating -- Fiction
ISBN 978-0-8027-2081-8; 0-8027-2081-1
LC 2009-54217
When Russian skating coach Andrei Grosheva offers farm girl Claire a scholarship to train with the elite in Lake Placid, she encounters a world of mean girls on ice, where competition is everything
"The dialogue between classmates and siblings is realistic, and the intergenerational or extended family relationships are interesting. The author shows the intensity of the world of competitive skating without dwelling on its rough edges, making it accessible not only to tween readers, but also to those who might have Olympic aspirations." SLJ

Meyer, Susan
Black radishes; [by] Susan Lynn Meyer. Delacorte Press 2010 228p map $16.99; lib bdg $19.99
Grades: 5 6 7 8 **Fic**
1. Jews -- France -- Fiction 2. Holocaust, 1933-1945 -- Fiction
ISBN 978-0-385-73881-1; 0-385-73881-1; 978-0-385-90748-4 lib bdg; 0-385-90748-6 lib bdg
LC 2009-47613
"Set in France during World War II, this historical novel follows eleven-year-old Gustave as his family escapes Paris for safer quarters in the small, provincial town of Saint-Georges. . . . Not long after Gustave's family arrives in Saint-Georges, the Nazis invade and occupy Paris and establish a demarcation line between occupied northern France and unoccupied Vichy France in the south. . . . The episodic narrative offers abundant detail, and the wartime dangers, especially Gustave's father's illicit travel between occupied and unoccupied zones, adds considerable suspense. Gustave's growth over the course of the novel is both realistic and relatable, making this an appealing topical entry for the upper elementary/middle school set." Bull Cent Child Books

Miles, Miska
Annie and the Old One; illustrated by Peter Parnall. Little, Brown 1971 44p il lib bdg $16.95; pa $7.95
Grades: 1 2 3 4 **Fic**
1. Death -- Fiction 2. Navajo Indians -- Fiction
ISBN 0-316-57117-2 lib bdg; 0-316-57120-2 pa
A Newbery Medal honor book, 1972
This is "a poignant, understated, rather brave story of a very real child, set against a background of Navajo traditions and contemporary Indian life. Fine expressive drawings match the simplicity of the story." Horn Book

Milford, Kate
★ The **Boneshaker**; [illustrations by Andrea Offermann] Clarion Books 2010 372p il $17
Grades: 5 6 7 8 9 **Fic**
1. Bicycles -- Fiction 2. Demonology -- Fiction 3. Supernatural -- Fiction
ISBN 978-0-547-24187-6; 0-547-24187-9
LC 2009-45350
When Jake Limberleg brings his traveling medicine show to a small Missouri town in 1913, thirteen-year-old Natalie senses that something is wrong and, after investigating, learns that her love of automata and other machines make her the only one who can set things right.

"Natalie is a well-drawn protagonist with sturdy support-ing characters around her. The tension built into the solidly constructed plot is complemented by themes that explore the literal and metaphorical role of crossroads and that thin line between good and evil." Kirkus

The **Broken** Lands; by Kate Milford; with illustrations by Andrea Offermann. Clarion Books 2012 455 p. ill. (hardback) $16.99

Grades: 5 6 7 8 9 10   **Fic**
    1. Bridges -- Fiction 2. Supernatural -- Fiction 3. New York (N.Y.) -- Fiction 4. Orphans -- Fiction 5. Demonology -- Fiction 6. Good and evil -- Fiction
    ISBN 0547739664; 9780547739663
                                        LC 2011049466
This book, a prequel to "Kate Milford's 'The Bone-shaker,' [is] set in . . . nineteenth-century Coney Island and New York City. Few crossroads compare to the one being formed by the Brooklyn Bridge and the East River, and as the bridge's construction progresses, forces of unimaginable evil seek to bend that power to their advantage. . . . Can the teenagers Sam, a card sharp, and Jin, a fireworks expert, stop them before it's too late?" (Publisher's note)

Millard, Glenda
    Layla, Queen of hearts; illustrated by Patrice Barton. Farrar Straus Giroux 2010 119p il $16.99

Grades: 3 4 5   **Fic**
    1. Old age -- Fiction 2. Friendship -- Fiction 3. Family life -- Fiction
    ISBN 0-374-34360-8; 978-0-374-34360-6
                                        LC 2008-38748
First published 2006 in Australia
Even though she loves the family of her best friend, Grif-fin Silk, especially grandmother Nell, Layla Elliott, who no longer has a grandmother, determines, despite many difficul-ties, to find an old person of her own to bring to the school's Senior Citizens' Day.
    "Barton's illustrations gently convey the bonds of af-fection among the author's eccentric, engaging characters." Kirkus

The **naming** of Tishkin Silk; illustrated by Patrice Bar-ton. Farrar, Straus and Giroux 2009 101p il $15.99

Grades: 3 4 5   **Fic**
    1. Death -- Fiction 2. Friendship -- Fiction 3. Family life -- Fiction 4. Personal names -- Fiction
    ISBN 978-0-374-35481-7; 0-374-35481-2
                                        LC 2008-16796
First published 2003 in Australia
Griffin Silk feels responsible for the absence of his mother and baby sister, but he and his new friend Layla find the perfect way to make everyone feel a little bit better.
    "Illustrated with softly rendered black-and-white draw-ings, the gentle, descriptive narrative [is] touched with droll humor . . . and features a likable protagonist and other ap-pealing, diverse characters." Booklist

Miller, Kirsten
    Kiki Strike; the darkness dwellers. by Kirsten Miller. Bloomsbury 2013 416 p. (hardback) $17.99

Grades: 5 6 7 8   **Fic**
    1. Girls -- Fiction 2. Adventure fiction 3. Teenagers -- Fiction 4. Crime -- Fiction 5. Identity -- Fiction 6.

New York (N.Y.) -- Fiction
    ISBN 1599907364; 9781599907369
                                        LC 2012023303
This teen adventure novel, by Kirsten Miller, is part of the "Kiki Strike" series. "First they ventured deep under New York to save the city itself. Then things got personal as the Irregulars ventured into a haunted mansion in Chinatown to uncover an evil twin. Now, . . . this . . . group of delinquent geniuses jump feet first into a[n] . . . international pursuit, going underground in Paris to pursue a pair of treacherous royals who have killed Kiki's parents." (Publisher's note)

Kiki Strike: inside the shadow city; [by] Kirsten Miller. Bloomsbury Children's Books 2006 387p $16.95

Grades: 5 6 7 8   **Fic**
    1. Mystery fiction
    ISBN 978-1-58234-960-2; 1-58234-960-6
                                        LC 2005030945
Life becomes more interesting for Ananka Fishbein when, at the age of twelve, she discovers an underground room in the park across from her New York City apartment and meets a mysterious girl called Kiki Strike who claims that she, too, wants to explore the subterranean world
    "If a 12-year-old can be a hardboiled detective, Ananka Fishbein is one. Her narration is fresh and funny, and the author's unadorned, economical, yet descriptive style carries her character through with verve." SLJ
    Another title about Kiki Strike is:
    Kiki Strike: The empress's tomb (2007)

Kiki Strike: the Empress's tomb. Bloomsbury Chil-dren's Books 2007 369p $16.95

Grades: 5 6 7 8   **Fic**
    1. Mystery fiction
    ISBN 978-1-59990-047-6; 1-59990-047-5
                                        LC 2007012000
Fourteen-year-olds Ananka Fishbein, Kiki Strike, and the other Irregulars encounter a Chinese mummy, a ghost, trained squirrels, and old enemies as they try to stop an art forgery ring and safeguard the secret streets hidden beneath New York City.
    "A must-have for libraries where the first book is popular and a recommended purchase for collections that could use a good ghost/spy/action/mystery/story." SLJ

Millet, Lydia
    The **fires** beneath the sea. Big Mouth House 2011 256p (The dissenters) $16.95

Grades: 4 5 6 7   **Fic**
    1. Otters -- Fiction 2. Mothers -- Fiction 3. Supernatural -- Fiction
    ISBN 978-1-931520-71-3; 1-931520-71-2
    "Mom vanished two months ago, and summer's ending. While swimming in the ocean, Cara spots a sea otter—but sea otters don't belong on Atlantic beaches. Cara reaches out her fingertips, and the otter streams words into Cara's mind. . . . Millet's prose is lyrically evocative. . . . A lush and intel-ligent opener for a topical eco-fantasy series." Kirkus

Mills, Claudia, 1954-
    ★ 7 x 9; pictures by G. Brian Karas. Farrar, Straus & Giroux 2002 103p il $15; pa $6.95

Grades: 2 3 4   **Fic**
    1. Schools 2. Brothers 3. School stories 4. Mathematics

-- Fiction 5. Multiplication -- Tables
ISBN 0-374-36746-9; 0-374-46452-9 pa

LC 2001-16028

Third-grader Wilson struggles with his times-tables in order to beat the class deadline

"Mills' sympathetic and detailed treatment of Wilson's travails makes this both a suspenseful and satisfying beginning chapter book." Bull Cent Child Books

Being Teddy Roosevelt; pictures by R.W. Alley. Farrar, Straus and Giroux 2007 89p il $16
Grades: 2 3 4   Fic
  1. School stories
  ISBN 978-0-374-30657-1; 0-374-30657-51

LC 2006-48978

When he is assigned Teddy Roosevelt as his biography project in school, fourth-grader Riley finds himself inspired by Roosevelt's tenacity and perseverance and resolves to find a way to get what he most wants—a saxophone and music lessons

"Lots of funny lines and comical situations enliven the simple story, which is also enriched by its portrait of grade-school friendships and goofy classroom happenings, depicted in Alley's appealing spot drawings." Booklist

Fractions; [pictures by G. Brian Karas] Farrar Straus Giroux 2011 113p il $15.99
Grades: 2 3 4   Fic
  1. School stories 2. Fractions -- Fiction 3. Science projects -- Fiction
  ISBN 978-0-374-36716-9; 0-374-36716-7

LC 2010-08395

While trying to decide on a science fair project, third-grader Wilson struggles with with fractions and, much to his embarrassment, his parents sign him up to work with a math tutor.

"Familiar school concerns, nicely resolved, make this another excellent selection for early chapter-book readers." Kirkus

★ **How** Oliver Olson changed the world; pictures by Heather Maione. Farrar, Straus and Giroux 2009 103p il $15.95
Grades: 2 3 4   Fic
  1. School stories 2. Science projects -- Fiction
  ISBN 0-374-33487-0; 978-0-374-33487-1

LC 2007-48846

Afraid he will always be an outsider like ex-planet Pluto, nine-year-old Oliver finally shows his extremely overprotective parents that he is capable of doing great things without their help while his class is studying the solar system.

"An engaging and thought-provoking chapter book." Booklist

One square inch. Farrar, Straus and Giroux 2010 168p $16.99
Grades: 4 5 6 7   Fic
  1. Mothers -- Fiction 2. Siblings -- Fiction 3. Imagination -- Fiction 4. Manic-depressive illness -- Fiction
  ISBN 978-0-374-35652-1; 0-374-35652-1

When their mother's behavior changes and she starts to neglect her children, seventh-grader Cooper and his little

sister take refuge in Inchland, an imaginary country inspired by deeds to one square inch of land that their grandfather gave them.

Mills "delivers a compassionate story about life with a bipolar parent. . . . The twist of [Cooper's] emotions and depth of his concern for his mother and sister are believable and deeply moving." Publ Wkly

Pet disasters. Alfred A. Knopf 2011 154p (Mason Dixon) $12.99; lib bdg $15.99
Grades: 3 4 5   Fic
  1. Dogs -- Fiction 2. Pets -- Fiction 3. Friendship -- Fiction
  ISBN 978-0-375-86873-3; 0-375-86873-9; 978-0-375-96873-0 lib bdg; 0-375-96873-3 lib bdg

LC 2010029724

Nine-year-old Mason's parents keep trying to get him a pet, but until he and his best friend Brody adopt a three-legged dog, he's not interested.

"Mills's account of this quirky kid and his trials and tribulations is both funny and touching. . . . An enjoyable read with cartoon-style pen-and-ink illustrations scattered throughout." SLJ

Other titles about Mason Dixon are:
Fourth grade disasters (2011)
Basketball disasters (2012)

The **totally** made-up Civil War diary of Amanda MacLeish. Farrar, Straus and Giroux 2008 197p $16
Grades: 3 4 5   Fic
  1. School stories 2. Family life -- Fiction
  ISBN 978-0-374-37696-3; 0-374-37696-4

LC 2007-09162

While dealing with her parents' separation and her best friend's distance, Amanda is able to work out some of her anxiety through her fifth-grade project—writing a diary from the point of view of a ten-year-old girl whose brothers fight on opposite sides in the Civil War.

"Mills handles the MacLeish family's separation realistically. . . . Subplots provide the novel's lighter moments. . . . This makes a good choice for Mills' many fans, as well as for children in search of a satisfying family story." Booklist

Mills, Rob
  Charlie's key. Orca Book Publishers 2011 254p pa $9.99
Grades: 5 6 7 8 9   Fic
  1. Mystery fiction 2. Orphans -- Fiction
  ISBN 978-1-55469-872-1; 1-55469-872-3

A young orphan struggles to unlock the significance of an old key left by his dying father.

"A fast-paced, often riveting mystery with a plausible, thrilling climax." Kirkus

Milne, A. A. (Alan Alexander), 1882-1956

★ The **House** at Pooh Corner; with decorations by Ernest H. Shepard. Dutton 1985 180p il $9.95; pa $4.99
Grades: 1 2 3 4   Fic
  1. Toys -- Fiction 2. Bears -- Fiction 3. Animals -- Fiction
  ISBN 0-525-32302-3; 0-14-036122-7 pa
  First published 1928

"It is hard to tell what Pooh Bear and his friends would have been without the able assistance of Ernest H. Shepard to see them and picture them so cleverly. . . . They are, and should be, classics." N Y Times Book Rev

★ **Winnie**-the-Pooh; illustrated by Ernest H. Shepard, colored by Hilda Scott. Dutton 1974 161p il $10.99; pa $4.99

Grades: 1 2 3 4 **Fic**
1. Toys -- Fiction 2. Bears -- Fiction 3. Animals -- Fiction
ISBN 0-525-44443-2; 0-14-036121-9 pa
First published 1926

"The kindly, lovable Pooh is one of an imaginative cast of animal characters which includes Eeyore, the wistfully gloomy donkey, Tigger, Piglet, Kanga, and Roo, all living in a fantasy world presided over by Milne's young son, Christopher Robin. Many of the animals are drawn from figures in Milne's life, though each emerges as a universally recognizable type." Reader's Ency

Milway, Katie Smith

The **good** garden; how one family went from hunger to having enough. written by Katie Smith Milway; illustrated by Sylvie Daigneault. Kids Can Press 2010 30p il (CitizenKid) $18.95

Grades: 3 4 5 **Fic**
1. Vegetable gardening -- Fiction 2. Sustainable agriculture -- Fiction
ISBN 978-1-55453-488-3; 1-55453-488-7

"When María Luz's Papa makes the tough decision to leave their hillside home in Honduras to seek employment elsewhere, he puts the girl in charge of planting and tending their winter garden. . . . A new teacher has arrived at her school with fresh ideas for how to feed and restore the soil. . . . [Maria] also learns that they need not rely on the unscrupulous 'coyotes' who have historically acted as loan sharks and middlemen. . . . Taken at a literal level, this is a story of how sustainable farming practices can nourish families and the earth simultaneously. On a deeper level, it is about social justice and self-sustaining economies. . . . The stylized colored-pencil artwork is appropriately lush and idealized." SLJ

Mimi's Village; And How Basic Health Care Transformed It. Katie Smith Milway. Kids Can Press 2012 32 p. $18.95

Grades: 1 2 3 4 **Fic**
1. Public health 2. Kenya -- Fiction 3. Malaria -- Fiction
ISBN 1554537223; 9781554537228

Author Katie Smith Milway presents a story on public health care in Kenya. "Mimi Malaho and her family help bring basic health care to their community. By making small changes like sleeping under mosquito nets and big ones like building a clinic with outside help, the Malahos and their neighbors transform their Kenyan village from one afraid of illness to a thriving community." (Publisher's note)

Mitchell, Stephen

The **nightingale**; [by] Hans Christian Andersen; retold by Stephen Mitchell; illustrated by Bagram Ibatoulline. Candlewick Press 2002 un il hardcover o.p. pa $6.95

Grades: 2 3 4 **Fic**
1. Authors 2. Novelists 3. Dramatists 4. Fairy tales 5. Children's authors 6. Short story writers 7. Nightingales -- Fiction
ISBN 0-7636-1521-8; 0-7636-2406-3 pa
LC 2001-25144

Though the emperor banishes the nightingale in preference of a jeweled mechanical imitation, the little bird remains faithful and returns years later when the emperor is near death and no one else can help him

"This is an elegant piece of bookmaking. Mixed-media illustrations (ink, gouache, watercolor) based on Chinese art and costume are rendered in a ceremonial, fairy-tale style." Bull Cent Child Books

The **tinderbox**; [by] Hans Christian Andersen; retold by Stephen Mitchell; illustrated by Bagram Ibatoulline. Candlewick Press 2007 un il $17.99

Grades: 2 3 4 5 **Fic**
1. Authors 2. Novelists 3. Dramatists 4. Fairy tales 5. Children's authors 6. Short story writers
ISBN 978-0-7636-2078-3; 0-7636-2078-5
LC 2006-47554

With the help of a magic tinderbox, a soldier finds a fortune and pursues a princess imprisoned in a castle.

"The soldier may be handsome and the princess lovely, but the old witch and the three giant dogs along with the beautifully developed settings really create the superb fairy-tale ambience of this robust telling of Andersen's tale. Ibatoulline's finely hatched pen drawings, washed in muted tones, resemble lithographs." SLJ

Mobley, Jeannie

★ **Katerina's** wish; Jeannie Mobley. Margaret K. McElderry Books 2012 256 p. (hardcover) $15.99

Grades: 4 5 6 7 **Fic**
1. Wishes -- Fiction 2. Historical fiction 3. Immigrants -- Fiction 4. Czech Americans -- Fiction 5. Coal mines and mining -- Fiction 6. Family life -- Colorado -- Fiction
ISBN 1442433434; 9781442433434; 9781442433458
LC 2011044392

In this young adult novel, Katerina and her family have immigrated from Bohemia and "settled in a coal mining camp, [where] they are still buried in work and trapped by debt. Then Trina sees a fish that reminds her of a fairy tale about a magic carp; soon after, her two younger sisters' frivolous wishes are granted. Initially skeptical, Trina eventually makes her wish: for a farm that will make her family happy." (Publishers Weekly)

Mohr, Nicholasa

Felita; pictures by Ray Cruz. Dial Bks. 1979 112p il hardcover o.p. pa $5.99

Grades: 3 4 5 **Fic**
1. Puerto Ricans -- Fiction 2. City and town life -- Fiction
ISBN 0-8037-3143-4; 0-8037-3144-2 lib bdg; 0-14-130643-2 pa
LC 79-50151

The everyday experiences of eight-year-old Felita, a Puerto Rican girl growing up in a close-knit, urban community

Going home. Dial Bks. for Young Readers 1986 192p hardcover o.p. pa $4.95

Grades: 4 5 6 **Fic**

1. Puerto Ricans -- New York (N.Y.) -- Fiction

ISBN 0-14-130644-0 pa

LC 85-20621

Feeling like an outsider when she visits her relatives in Puerto Rico for the first time, eleven-year-old Felita tries to come to terms with the heritage she always took for granted

"This is a convincing story that captures the universality of preteen relationships." Rochman. Against borders

Another title about Felita is:

Felita (1979)

Moloney, James

The **Book** of Lies. HarperCollinsPublishers 2007 360p $16.99; lib bdg $17.89

Grades: 5 6 7 8 **Fic**

1. Fantasy fiction 2. Magic -- Fiction 3. Orphans -- Fiction

ISBN 978-0-06-057842-8; 0-06-057842-4; 978-0-06-057843-5 lib bdg; 0-06-057843-2 lib bdg

LC 2006-29874

On the night he was brought to an orphanage, Marcel's memories were taken by a sorceror and replaced with new ones by his Book of Lies, but Bea, a girl with the ability to make herself invisible, was watching and is determined to help him discover his true identity.

"Readers who enjoy the mixture of mystery, riddles, action, and camaraderie will be pleased that the open-ended conclusion leads to a planned sequel." Booklist

Mone, Gregory

Fish. Scholastic Press 2010 241p $16.99

Grades: 4 5 6 7 **Fic**

1. Adventure fiction 2. Ciphers -- Fiction 3. Pirates -- Fiction 4. Buried treasure -- Fiction

ISBN 978-0-545-11632-9; 0-545-11632-5

Eleven-year-old Fish, seeking a way to help his family financially, becomes a reluctant cabin boy on a pirate ship, where he soon makes friends—and enemies—and is asked to help decipher clues that might lead to a legendary treasure.

"Mone seamlessly integrates factual information into his tale of friendship, loyalty, and exploration. . . . Fish makes a splashing good addition to adventure fiction." SLJ

Montgomery, Lewis B.

The **case** of the stinky socks; by Lewis B. Montgomery; illustrated by Amy Wummer. Kane Press 2009 94p il (Milo & Jazz mysteries) pa $6.95; $22.60

Grades: 1 2 3 4 **Fic**

1. Mystery fiction 2. Baseball -- Fiction 3. Clothing and dress -- Fiction

ISBN 1-57565-285-4 pa; 1-57565-288-9; 978-1-57565-285-6 pa; 978-1-57565-288-7

LC 2008027536

Detectives-in-training Milo and Jazz join forces to tackle their first big case—finding out who stole the lucky socks from the high school baseball team's star pitcher.

This book "gets it just right: a fun, easy-to-solve mystery, readily identifiable young detectives, and some extras readers will enjoy. . . . The short chapters, written in a large typeface, are punctuated by pen-and-ink illustrations of better quality than those often seen in series books." Booklist

Other titles in this series are:

The case of the poisoned pig (2009)

The case of the haunted haunted house (2009)

The case of the Amazing Zelda (2009)

The case of the July 4th jinx (2010)

The case of the missing moose (2011)

Moodie, Craig

Into the trap. Roaring Brook Press 2011 199p $15.99

Grades: 5 6 7 8 **Fic**

1. Adventure fiction 2. Islands -- Fiction 3. Thieves -- Fiction 4. Lobsters -- Fiction

ISBN 978-1-59643-585-8; 1-59643-585-2

LC 2010029238

Twelve-year-old Eddie Atwell accidentally learns who has been stealing lobsters from Fog Island lobstermen and enlists thirteen-year-old Briggs Fairfield, a summer visitor, to help foil their plans.

"Set over a single, tense day, the novel's chapter titles track the hours and give the book an immediate, real-time pace. An exciting drama." Booklist

Morey, Walt

Gentle Ben; illustrated by John Schoenherr. Dutton 1965 191p il hardcover o.p. pa $6.99

Grades: 5 6 7 8 **Fic**

1. Bears -- Fiction

ISBN 0-14-240551-5 pa

Set in Alaska before statehood, this is the story of 13-year-old Mark Anderson who befriends a huge brown bear which has been chained in a shed since it was a cub. Finally Mark's father buys the bear, but Orca City's inhabitants eventually insist that the animal, named Ben, be shipped to an uninhabited island. However, the friendship of Mark and Ben endures

The author "has written a vivid chronicle of Alaska, its people and places, challenges and beauties. Told with a simplicity and dignity which befits its characters, human and animal, [it] is a memorable reading experience." SLJ

Morgan, Clay

The **boy** who returned from the sea; [by] Clay Morgan. 1st ed.; Dutton Children's Books 2007 245p $16.99

Grades: 3 4 5 **Fic**

1. Adventure fiction 2. Dogs -- Fiction 3. Orphans -- Fiction

ISBN 978-0-5254-7401-2; 0-5254-7401-3

LC 2006036819

Jack is reunited with his beloved sheepdog Moxie on the island where they first met, but the dangerous Blackburn Jukes is there too, searching for valuable amber that is hidden in the island's bogs.

"Morgan's evocation of Moxie's inner life is thorough and engaging." Booklist

Morgenstern, Susie Hoch

★ A **book** of coupons; by Susie Morgenstern; illustrated by Serge Bloch; translated by Gill Rosner. Viking 2001 62p il $12.99

Grades: 3 4 5 **Fic**

1. Schools 2. Teachers 3. School stories 4. Humorous stories 5. Teachers -- Fiction

ISBN 0-670-89970-4

LC 00-11940

Original French edition, 1999

Elderly Monsieur Noel, the very unconventional new teacher, gives coupon books for such things as dancing in class and sleeping late, which are bound to get him in trouble with the military discipline of Principal Incarnation Perez

"Morgenstern's witty and poignant tribute to great teachers everywhere proclaims what education should be about. Her message may be pointed, but no reader will be unmoved." Horn Book Guide

Moriarty, Chris

The **inquisitor's** apprentice; illustrations by Mark Edward Geyer. Harcourt Children's Books 2011 345p il $16.99

Grades: 4 5 6 7   **Fic**

1. Inventors 2. Gangs -- Fiction 3. Magic -- Fiction 4. Witches -- Fiction 5. Apprentices -- Fiction 6. Jews -- United States -- Fiction

ISBN 978-0-547-58135-4; 0-547-58135-1

In early twentieth-century New York, Sacha Kessler's ability to see witches earns him an apprenticeship to the police department's star Inquisitor, Maximillian Wolf, to help stop magical crime and, with fellow apprentice Lily Astral, Sacha investigates who is trying to kill Thomas Edison, whose mechanical witch detector that could unleash the worst witch-hunt in American history.

"Sacha, Lily and Inspector Wolf are all fully developed and multilayered characters, as are the many other distinctive personalities that appear in the tale. The author employs rich language and syntax that please the ear and touch the senses, making it all come alive." Kirkus

The **watcher** in the shadows; Chris Moriarty; [illustrated by] Mark Edward Geyer. Harcourt Children's Books 2013 336 p. (hardcover) $16.99

Grades: 4 5 6 7   **Fic**

1. Fantasy fiction 2. Jews -- Fiction 3. Mystery fiction

ISBN 0547466323; 9780547466323

LC 2013003919

This juvenile novel, by Chris Moriarty, is part of the "Inquisitor's Apprentice" series. "New York's Bowery District becomes the scene of a terrible murder when the Klezmer King gets fried to a crisp by his Electric Tuxedo--on stage! The Inquisitor's apprentice, thirteen-year-old Sacha Kessler, tries to help find the killer, but the closer he gets to solving the crime, the more it sounds as if the creature that haunted him in his first adventure is back." (Publisher's note)

"Rich language, colorful syntax, vivid description and a brilliant cast of characters beckon readers right into both the adventure and the heartfelt emotional landscape. Exciting, action-packed and absolutely marvelous." Kirkus

Morpurgo, Michael

★ **Kensuke's** kingdom. Scholastic Press 2003 164p hardcover o.p. pa $5.99

Grades: 4 5 6 7   **Fic**

1. Islands 2. Japanese 3. Survival 4. Castaways 5. Survival after airplane accidents, shipwrecks, etc. -- Fiction

ISBN 0-439-38202-5; 0-439-59181-3 pa

LC 2002-9078

First published 1999 in the United Kingdom

When Michael is swept off his family's yacht, he washes up on a desert island, where he struggles to survive—until he finds he is not alone

This is "highly readable. . . . The end is bittersweet but believable, and the epilogue is a sad commentary on the long-lasting effects of war." Booklist

★ **On** angel wings; illustrated by Quentin Blake. Candlewick Press 2007 un il $8.99

Grades: 3 4 5   **Fic**

1. Angels -- Fiction 2. Shepherds -- Fiction

ISBN 978-0-7636-3466-7; 0-7636-3466-2

"Morpurgo's tone blends reverence with wit, a combination matched in Blake's pen-and-ink and watercolor cartoons." Publ Wkly

Waiting for Anya. Viking 1991 172p hardcover o.p. pa $4.99

Grades: 5 6 7 8   **Fic**

1. Jews -- Fiction 2. World War, 1939-1945 -- Fiction

ISBN 0-670-83735-0; 0-14-038431-6 pa

LC 90-50560

First published 1990 in the United Kingdom

"A World War II adventure story set in Vichy, France, this centers on a young shepherd, Jo, who becomes involved in smuggling Jewish children across the border from his mountain village to Spain. Morpurgo has injected the basic conventions of heroism and villainy with some complexities of character. . . . Independent readers will appreciate the simple, clear style and fast-paced plot of the book, which will also hold up well in group read-alouds, commanding attention to ethics as well as action." Bull Cent Child Books

War horse; by Michael Morpurgo. Scholastic 2007 165p $16.99

Grades: 5 6 7 8   **Fic**

1. Horses -- Fiction 2. World War, 1914-1918 -- Fiction

ISBN 978-0-439-79663-7; 0-439-79663-6

LC 2006044368

First published 1982 in the United Kingdom

Joey the horse recalls his experiences growing up on an English farm, his struggle for survival as a cavalry horse during World War I, and his reunion with his beloved master

"At times deeply affecting, the story balances the horror with moments of respite and care." Horn Book Guide

Morris, Gerald

The **adventures** of Sir Lancelot the Great; illustrated by Aaron Renier. Houghton Mifflin Company 2008 92p il (The knights' tales) $15; pa $4.99

Grades: 3 4 5 6   **Fic**

1. Kings 2. Knights and knighthood -- Fiction 3. Lancelot (Legendary character) -- Fiction 4. Lancelot (Legendary character) -- Juvenile literature

ISBN 978-0-618-77714-3; 0-618-77714-8; 978-0-547-23756-5 pa; 0-547-23756-1 pa

LC 2007-41167

This novel relates the story of Sir Lancelot, the bravest knight in King Arthur's court.

"This trim novel, with simple vocabulary and brief, witty chapters, is an ideal fit for early readers. . . . Fans of the legendary characters may find particular delight in this irreverent and unabashedly silly exploration of Arthur's court and his most influential knight. . . . Frequent black-and-white illustrations supplement the text, highlighting (and in most cases, exaggerating) elements from humorous passages." Bull Cent Child Books

Other titles in this series are:

The adventures of Sir Givret the Short (2008)

The adventures of Sir Gawain the True (2011)

Morris, Jackie

East of the Sun, West of the Moon; Jackie Morris. Pgw 2013 176 p. (hardcover) $14.99

Grades: 6 7 8 9   Fic

1. Bears -- Juvenile Fiction 2. Girls -- Juvenile fiction 3. Fantasy fiction -- Juvenile fiction

ISBN 184780294X; 9781847802941

This book, by Jackie Morris, describes a friendship between a girl and a bear. The girl goes "first to the bear's secret palace in faraway mountains, where she is treated so courteously, but where she experiences the bear's unfathomable sadness, and a deep mystery. . . As the bear's secret unravels, another journey unfolds . . . that takes the girl to the homes of the four Winds and beyond, to the castle east of the sun, west of the moon." (Publisher's note)

Morrison, P. R.

Wave traveller; by P.R. Morrison. 1st U.S. ed.; Bloomsbury Children's Books 2007 317p $16.95

Grades: 4 5 6   Fic

1. Adventure fiction 2. Uncles -- Fiction 3. Supernatural -- Fiction

ISBN 978-1-59990-123-7; 1-59990-123-4

LC 2007002608

Archie Stringweed must team up with his uncle to fight another curse which brings strange and dangerous sea creatures to life.

Wind tamer. Bloomsbury Children's Books 2006 335p $16.95

Grades: 4 5 6   Fic

1. Winds -- Fiction 2. Courage -- Fiction 3. Hurricanes -- Fiction

ISBN 1-58234-781-6

Archie learns on his tenth birthday that he is about to inherit the family curse of cowardice unless he fights the powerful hurricane that will take his bravery.

"The fantasy atmosphere is well defined, with intriguing characters and imaginative magical elements." SLJ

Morse, Scott

Magic Pickle and the garden of evil. Graphix 2009 136p il pa $5.99

Grades: 2 3 4 5   Fic

1. Vegetables -- Fiction 2. Superheroes -- Fiction

ISBN 978-0-545-13580-1; 0-545-13580-X

LC 2008037614

Magic Pickle, a fearless, dill superhero, comes to the rescue when Jo Jo's class garden yields a monstrous lettuce plant bent on world domination.

"One of a series of illustrated chapter books coming on the heels of Morse's graphic novel. . . . The spot illustrations are lively, with crackling energy dots and a constant sense of action and movement. . . . The comic segments, typography sound effects, and the like are cues wtih which struggling readers can propel themselves along." SLJ

Moses, Shelia P.

★ **Sallie** Gal and the Wall-a-kee man; illustrated by Niki Daly. Scholastic 2007 152p il $15.99

Grades: 3 4 5   Fic

1. Family life -- Fiction 2. African Americans -- Fiction

ISBN 978-0-439-90890-0; 0-439-90890-6

LC 2006033171

More than anything, Sallie Gal wants pretty ribbons to wear in her hair, but she knows that they cannot afford them and Momma has too much dignity to accept charity.

"Appealing black-and-white illustrations in various sizes embellish the text. Moses takes a fond look at strong family ties and the values of honesty and hard work. Short paragraphs and peppy dialogue make this easy chapter book a candidate for reading aloud." SLJ

Moss, Jenny

Winnie's war. Walker & Co. 2009 178p $16.99

Grades: 5 6 7 8   Fic

1. Epidemics -- Fiction 2. Influenza -- Fiction 3. Family life -- Fiction

ISBN 978-0-8027-9819-0; 0-8027-9819-5

LC 2008-23233

Living in the shadow of a Texas cemetery, twelve-year-old Winnie Grace struggles to keep the Spanish influenza of 1918 from touching her family—her coffin-building father, her troubled mother, and her two baby sisters.

"The small town of Coward Creek comes to life in Moss's writing. . . . Winnie and the others populate a solid plot, but it is the setting and the characters that will make this book last as a popular favorite with a space on shelves well into the future." Voice Youth Advocates

Moss, Marissa

Alien Eraser to the rescue. Candlewick Press 2009 52p il (Max Disaster) $16.99; pa $6.99

Grades: 3 4 5   Fic

1. Extraterrestrial beings -- Fiction

ISBN 978-0-7636-3577-0; 0-7636-3577-4; 978-0-7636-4407-9 pa; 0-7636-4407-2 pa

Welcome to Max's book of inventions, experiments, comic strips, and random thoughts about school, pimply older brothers, mutant marshmallows, erasers and good parents who get into bad fights.

"Moss is a master at verbalizing kids' anxieties and channeling their astute observations of family life—both as it breaks apart and begins to mend." Publ Wkly

Other titles in the Max Disaster series are:

Alien Eraser unravels the mystery of the pyramids (2009)

Alien Eraser reveals the secrets of evolution (2009)

★ **Amelia's** 6th-grade notebook. Simon & Schuster Books for Young Readers 2005 un il $9.95

Grades: 3 4 5 6   Fic

1. School stories

ISBN 0-689-87040-X

LC 2004-45309

Problems arise for Amelia when she starts sixth grade at the same middle school where her older sister Cleo is an eighth-grader, and she gets the school's meanest teacher for three of her classes

"Both insightful and entertaining, Amelia's first-person narrative rings true. . . . [This] features a handwritten format;

colorful, cartoonlike illustrations; and charming doodles with descriptive asides." Booklist

Other titles about Amelia are:

The all-new Amelia (1999)

Amelia lends a hand (2002)

Amelia works it out (2000)

Amelia writes again (1996)

Amelia's are-we-there-yet longest ever car trip (1997)

Amelia's BFF (2011)

Amelia's book of notes & note passing (2006)

Amelia's boredom survival guide (1999)

Amelia's bully survival guide (1998)

Amelia's family ties (2000)

Amelia's 5th-grade notebook (2003)

Amelia's guide to gossip (2006)

Amelia's itchy-twitchy, lovey-dovey summer at Camp Mosquito (2008)

Amelia's longest, biggest, most-fights-ever family reunion (2006)

Amelia's most unforgettable embarrassing moments (2005)

Amelia's must-keep resolutions for the best year ever! (2007)

Amelia's notebook (1995)

Amelia's school survival guide (2002)

Amelia's science fair disaster (2009)

Luv, Amelia luv, Nadia (1999)

Oh boy, Amelia! (2001)

Vote 4 Amelia (2007)

Amelia's notebook. Simon & Schuster Books for Young Readers 2006 un il $9.95

Grades: 3 4 5 **Fic**

1. School stories 2. Moving -- Fiction 3. Diaries -- Fiction 4. Sisters -- Fiction 5. Friendship -- Fiction

ISBN 978-1-416-90905-7; 1-416-90905-2

LC 2005047750

A reissue of the title first published 1995 by Tricycle Press

The hand-lettered contents of a nine-year-old girl's notebook, in which she records her thoughts and feelings about moving, starting school, and dealing with her older sister, as well as keeping her old best friend and making a new one.

"Both the language and the art style are on target for the age group-Amelia is droll and funny and not too sophisticated for her years; she's also poignant and real." Booklist

Mira's Diary; Lost in Paris. Marissa Moss. Sourcebooks Inc 2012 224 p. $12.99

Grades: 4 5 6 **Fic**

1. Time travel -- Juvenile fiction 2. Missing persons -- Juvenile fiction

ISBN 1402266065; 9781402266065

In this children's story, by Marissa Moss, "when Mira receives a cryptic postcard from her missing mother, she sets off with her father and brother to find her in Paris. . . . With an innocent touch to a gargoyle sculpture on the roof of Notre Dame, Mira is whisked into the past. There she learns her mother isn't just avoiding the family, she's in serious trouble. Following her mother's clues, Mira travels through time to help change history and bring her mother home." (Publisher's note)

Mould, Chris

★ The **wooden** mile. Roaring Brook Press 2008 176p il (Something wickedly weird) $9.95

Grades: 3 4 5 6 **Fic**

1. Pirates -- Fiction 2. Werewolves -- Fiction 3. Supernatural -- Fiction

ISBN 978-1-59643-383-0; 1-59643-383-3

LC 2008011258

First published 2007 in the United Kingdom

Eleven-year-old Stanley Buggle, happily anticipating a long summer vacation in the house he inherits from his great-uncle, discovers, soon after arriving in the seemingly peaceful village of Crampton Rock, that along with the house he has also inherited some sinister neighbors, a talking stuffed fish, and a host of mysteries surrounding his great-uncle's death.

"With its fairly easy text, many black-and-white illustrations, and a dramatic scene silhouetted on the cover, this chapter book will appeal to young readers who like their fiction fast-paced and a bit scary. Mould's richly atmospheric ink drawings capture the rather macabre tone of the story." Booklist

Other titles in this series are:

The icy hand (2008)

The darkling curse (2009)

Smugglers' mine (2010)

Moulton, Erin E.

Flutter; the story of four sisters and an incredible journey. Philomel Books 2011

Grades: 4 5 6 **Fic**

1. Adventure fiction 2. Nature -- Fiction 3. Sisters -- Fiction 4. Poaching -- Fiction 5. Family life -- Fiction

ISBN 0-399-25515-X; 978-0-399-25515-1

LC 2010014507

Nine-and-a-half-year-old Maple and her older sister, Dawn, must work together to face treacherous terrain, wild animals, and poachers as they trek through Vermont's Green Mountains seeking a miracle for their prematurely-born sister.

"Moulton describes the girls' journey—and their motivation—in vivid, heart-wrenching prose." Horn Book Guide

Mourlevat, Jean-Claude

★ The **pull** of the ocean; [by] Jean-Claude Mourlevat; translated from the French by Y. Maudet. Delacorte Press 2006 190p hardcover o.p. lib bdg $17.99; pa $6.50

Grades: 5 6 7 **Fic**

1. Size -- Fiction 2. Twins -- Fiction 3. Brothers -- Fiction

ISBN 978-0-385-73348-9; 0-385-73348-8; 978-0-385-90364-6 lib bdg; 0-385-90364-2 lib bdg; 978-0-385-73666-4 pa; 0-385-73666-5 pa

LC 2006001802

Loosely based on Charles Perrault's "Tom Thumb," seven brothers in modern-day France flee their poor parents' farm, led by the youngest who, although mute and unusually small, is exceptionally wise.

This "is a memorable novel that readers will find engaging and intellectually satisfying." SLJ

Mull, Brandon

★ A **world** without heroes. Aladdin 2011 454p (Beyonders) $19.99

Grades: 4 5 6 7 **Fic**

1. Fantasy fiction 2. Magic -- Fiction 3. Space and time -- Fiction 4. Heroes and heroines -- Fiction
ISBN 978-1-4169-9792-4; 1-4169-9792-X

LC 2010-23437

Fourteen-year-old Jason Walker is transported to a strange world called Lyrian, where he joins Rachel, who was also drawn there from our world, and a few rebels, to piece together the Word that can destroy the malicious wizard emperor, Surroth.

"Mull moves his story at a brisk pace, preventing the tragedies from overwhelming the adventure, while offering ample action and feisty dialogue to keep fantasy lovers entertained." Publ Wkly

Murphy, Jill

Dear hound. Walker Books for Young Readers 2010 175p

Grades: 2 3 4 **Fic**

1. Dogs -- Fiction 2. Foxes -- Fiction
ISBN 0-8027-2190-7; 978-0-8027-2190-7

LC 2010006833

When Alfie, a timid deerhound puppy, gets lost in the woods, he will do almost anything—including befriending a pair of foxes—to find his way home to his beloved boy, Charlie, who refuses to believe Alfie is gone for good.

"Murphy deftly conveys the dog's angst with occasional all-caps dialogue. Her charming black-and-white line illustrations appear on every spread, extending the simple text and making this an excellent choice for readers recently transitioned to chapter books." Kirkus

Murphy, Jim

Desperate journey. Scholastic Press 2006 278p il map $16.99

Grades: 5 6 7 8 **Fic**

1. Family life -- Fiction
ISBN 0-439-07806-7

LC 2006-02526

In the mid-1800s, with both her father and her uncle in jail on an assault charge, Maggie, her brother, and her ailing mother rush their barge along the Erie Canal to deliver their heavy cargo or lose everything.

This is a "gripping novel." Booklist

Murphy, Rita

Bird. Delacorte Press 2008 151p $15.99; lib bdg $18.99

Grades: 5 6 7 8 **Fic**

1. Kites -- Fiction 2. Flight -- Fiction 3. Houses -- Fiction 4. Supernatural -- Fiction
ISBN 978-0-385-73018-1; 0-385-73018-7; 978-0-385-90557-2 lib bdg; 0-385-90557-2 lib bdg

LC 2008-04690

Miranda, a small, delicate girl easily carried off by the wind, lands at Bourne Manor on the coast of Lake Champlain and is raised by the dour Wysteria Barrows, but she begins to believe rumors that the Manor is cursed and, aided by a new friend and kites secreted in an attic, seeks to escape.

"This enchanting novel is well written with lyrical text and beautiful descriptions. . . . Good for middle school students, this book will make a nice addition to school and public libraries alike." Libr Media Connect

Murphy, Sally

★ **Pearl** verses the world; [illustrations by Heather Potter] Candlewick Press 2011 73p il $14.99

Grades: 3 4 5 **Fic**

1. School stories 2. Novels in verse 3. Death -- Fiction 4. Poetry -- Fiction 5. Loneliness -- Fiction 6. Bereavement -- Fiction 7. Family life -- Fiction 8. Grandmothers -- Fiction
ISBN 978-0-7636-4821-3; 0-7636-4821-3

LC 2010040149

Pearl feels like an island in school, isolated and alone, but at home she feels loved and secure until her grandmother's illness changes the way Pearl views her world.

This is a "poignantly illustrated novella in free verse. . . . Potter's evocative pencil-and-wash drawings, with their excellent renderings of facial expressions and mood, wonderfully complement Murphy's thoughtful narrative." Kirkus

Musgrove, Marianne

Lucy the good; illustrated by Cheryl Orsini. Henry Holt 2010 137p il $16.99

Grades: 2 3 4 **Fic**

1. School stories 2. Family life -- Fiction
ISBN 978-0-8050-9051-2; 0-8050-9051-7

LC 2009050766

When Lucy's great-aunt Bep comes from Holland to Adelaide, Australia, to visit, she is shocked by some of Lucy's behavior, and Lucy begins to wonder about herself. Includes a glossary of Dutch words and a recipe.

"The dichotomy between what Lucy says and thinks adds ample humor to this heartfelt novel. . . . With humor of their own, Orsini's b&w spot illustrations portray Lucy's behavior." Publ Wkly

Myers, Christopher

H.O.R.S.E. a game of basketball and imagination. Christopher Myers. Egmont USA 2012 1 p. (hardback) $18.99

Grades: 1 2 3 **Fic**

1. Games -- Fiction 2. Sports -- Juvenile fiction 3. Friendship -- Juvenile fiction 4. Basketball -- Fiction
ISBN 1606842188; 9781606842188

LC 2012003793

Coretta Scott King Illustrator Honor Book (2013)

Author Christopher Myers' book presents a children's story. "One day at the basketball court, two kids, a familiar challenge--H.O.R.S.E.? But this isn't your grandmother's game of hoops. Not when a layup from the other side of the court standing on one foot with your eyes closed is just the warm-up. Around the neighborhood, around the world, off Saturn's rings, the pair goes back and forth. The game is as much about skill as it is about imagination." (Publisher's note)

Myers, Laurie

Escape by night; a Civil War adventure. illustrated by Amy June Bates. Henry Holt 2011 120p il $14.99

Grades: 3 4 5 **Fic**

1. Christian life -- Fiction
ISBN 978-0-8050-8825-0; 0-8050-8825-3

LC 2010-30117

Tommy, the son of a Presbyterian minister in Augusta, Georgia, during the Civil War, must search his conscience to decide whether he should help a Yankee soldier escape and return home. Inspired by the early life of Woodrow Wilson.

"Sporadic full-page, black-and-white illustrations by Bates bring the characters . . . to life. This quick and exciting chapter book isn't shy about advancing a moral message but does so with a light touch." Booklist

★ **Lewis** and Clark and me; a dog's tale. illustrations by Michael Dooling. Holt & Co. 2002 64p il $16.95

Grades: 3 4 5 6   **Fic**

1. Explorers 2. Dogs -- Fiction 3. Territorial governors 4. Seaman (Dog) -- Juvenile fiction

ISBN 0-8050-6368-4

LC 00-47298

Seaman, Meriwether Lewis's Newfoundland dog, describes Lewis and Clark's expedition, which he accompanied from St. Louis to the Pacific Ocean

"Myers is a dog lover, and that respect comes through in the dignified portrayal of Seaman. Attractive, realistic paintings illustrate the book, giving a feel for the period and, most importantly, a visual personality to Seaman." SLJ

Includes bibliographical references

Myers, Walter Dean, 1937-

Three swords for Granada; illustrated by John Speirs. Holiday House 2002 154p il $15.95

Grades: 3 4 5 6   **Fic**

1. Cats 2. Dogs 3. Friendship 4. Fantasy fiction 5. Cats -- Fiction 6. Dogs -- Fiction 7. Spain -- History

ISBN 0-8234-1676-3

LC 2001-59357

In 1420 Spain, three young cat friends join the warrior cats as they struggle to save their beloved Granada from the vicious dogs of the Fidorean Guard

"The snappy dialogue, flashing swords, and daring action, as well as the charming ink-and-wash drawings, will appeal to readers who enjoy high adventure laced with a touch of whimsy." SLJ

Myklusch, Matt

Jack Blank and the Imagine Nation. Aladdin 2010 480p $16.99

Grades: 4 5 6 7   **Fic**

1. Fantasy fiction 2. Science fiction 3. Orphans -- Fiction 4. Superheroes -- Fiction

ISBN 978-1-4169-9561-6; 1-4169-9561-7

Twelve-year-old Jack, freed from a dismal orphanage, makes his way to the elusive and impossible Imagine Nation, where a mentor saves him from dissection and trains him to use his superpower, despite the virus he carries that makes him a threat.

This creates "a richly imagined world with strong appeal to fans of comics. The island is populated by a fun cast of heroes and villains. . . . Brisk narration captures the superhero world with a mixture of fast-paced action, wry humor, and occasional heartfelt speeches about courage and friendship." SLJ

The **secret** war. Aladdin 2011 529p $16.99

Grades: 4 5 6 7   **Fic**

1. Fantasy fiction 2. Orphans -- Fiction 3. Viruses -- Fiction 4. Superheroes -- Fiction

ISBN 978-1-4169-9564-7; 1-4169-9564-1

LC 2010041779

Twelve-year-old Jack may be the Imagine Nation's only hope of fending off a new Rustov attack, with the help of his fellow superheroes-in-training, but the virus he carries, and Jonas's suspicions, provide new complications.

Myracle, Lauren

Eleven. Dutton Children's Books 2004 201p (The Winnie years) $16.99; pa $6.99

Grades: 4 5 6 7   **Fic**

1. Schools 2. Friendship 3. Family life 4. Best friends 5. Friendship -- Fiction 6. Family life -- Fiction

ISBN 0-525-47165-0; 0-14-240346-6 pa

LC 2003-49076

The year between turning eleven and turning twelve bring many changes for Winnie and her friends

"The inclusion of details about the everyday lives of these girls . . . will make this novel enjoyable, even for reluctant readers. However, it's the book's occasional revelation of harder truths that lifts it out of the ordinary." SLJ

Other titles in this series are:

Twelve (2007)
Thirteen (2008)
Thirteen plus one (2010)
Ten (2011)

★ **Luv** ya bunches. Amulet Books 2009 335p $15.95

Grades: 4 5 6   **Fic**

1. School stories 2. Friendship -- Fiction

ISBN 978-0-8109-4211-0; 0-8109-4211-9

LC 2009012585

Four friends—each named after a flower—navigate the ups and downs of fifth grade. Told through text messages, blog posts, screenplay, and straight narrative

Myracle "displays a shining awareness of and sensitivity to the highly textured society of tween girls. . . . This is a fun, challenging, and gently edifying story." Booklist

Another title about these characters is:

Violet in bloom (2010)

Violet in bloom; a flower power book. Amulet Books 2010 366p $15.95

Grades: 4 5 6   **Fic**

1. School stories 2. Food -- Fiction 3. Friendship -- Fiction

ISBN 978-0-8109-8983-2; 0-8109-8983-2

LC 2010-24319

Fifth-graders Katie-Rose, Violet, Milla, and Yasaman seem to have little in common except their flower-related names, but they nurture their new friendship through a social-networking site and a campaign to have healthier snacks served at school.

This is "a realistic, easy-to-relate-to riot of pre-adolescent exuberance. A triumph." Kirkus

Naftali, Joel

The **rendering**; [by] Joel Naftali. Egmont USA 2011 275p $15.99

Grades: 5 6 7 8   **Fic**

1. Science fiction 2. Adventure fiction 3. Weblogs -- Fiction

ISBN 978-1-60684-118-1; 1-60684-118-1

LC 2010-36640

Thirteen-year-old Doug relates in a series of blog posts the story of how he saved the world but was falsely branded a terrorist and murderer, forced to fight the evil Dr. Roach and his armored biodroid army with an electronics-destroying superpower of his own.

"Naftali balances tragedy and absurd humor with aplomb, not an easy task when dealing with horrific explosions and giant wisecracking skunks. Readers seeking a fast-paced, action-packed adventure will find this eminently suitable." Bull Cent Child Books

Nagda, Ann Whitehead

Tarantula power! by Ann Whitehead Nagda; illustrated by Stephanie Roth. Holiday House 2007 93p il $15.95
Grades: 2 3 4　　　　　**Fic**
　　1. School stories　2. Bullies -- Fiction　3. Tarantulas -- Fiction
　　ISBN 978-0-8234-1991-3; 0-8234-1991-6

Forced to work with the class bully on a project to design a new breakfast cereal, Richard also tries to stop him from picking on second-graders by using tarantula power.

"The convincing dialogue is crammed with interesting facts. . . . The characters and plot develop at a quick and mostly believable pace. Black-and-white wash illustrations match the action." SLJ

The **perfect** cat-sitter; illustrated by Stephanie Roth. Holiday House 2007 104p il $15.95
Grades: 2 3 4　　　　　**Fic**
　　1. School stories　2. Cats -- Fiction
　　ISBN 978-0-8234-2112-1; 0-8234-2112-0
　　　　　　　　　　　　LC 2007-18301

When her friend Rana goes to India, Susan volunteers to take care of her cat and her sister's fish, but the job turns out to be much more difficult than she expected.

"Humor infuses the story. . . . Classroom dynamics and school friendships are well rendered, as are all sides of Susan's perfectionism. . . . Soft black-and-white illustrations capture Susan's emotions throughout her escapades." Booklist

Naidoo, Beverley

★ **Journey** to Jo'burg; a South African story. illustrations by Eric Velasquez. Lippincott 1986 80p il hardcover o.p. pa $4.99
Grades: 5 6 7 8　　　　　**Fic**
　　ISBN 0-06-440237-1 pa
　　　　　　　　　　　　LC 85-45508

"This touching novel graphically depicts the plight of Africans living in the horror of South Africa. Thirteen-year-old Maledi and her 9-year-old brother leave their small village, take the perilous journey to the city, and encounter, firsthand, the painful struggle for justice, freedom, and dignity in the 'City of Gold.' A provocative story with a message readers will long remember." Soc Educ

Napoli, Donna Jo, 1948-

Lights on the Nile. HarperCollins 2011 278p $16.99; lib bdg $17.89
Grades: 4 5 6 7　　　　　**Fic**
　　1. Baboons -- Fiction　2. Fairies -- Fiction　3. Kidnapping -- Fiction
　　ISBN 978-0-06-166793-0; 0-06-166793-5; 978-0-06-166794-7 lib bdg; 0-06-166794-3 lib bdg
　　　　　　　　　　　　LC 2011010179

Ten-year-old Kepi, a young girl in ancient Egypt, embarks on a journey to save her family when she is unexpectedly taken captive, along with the baby baboon she has rescued from a crocodile.

Napoli "crafts a mystical coming-of-age tale and a love letter of sorts to Egypt, saturated with proverbs, intriguing details of everyday life at the time, and rich descriptions of the places Kepi visits. . . . Kepi's survival skills and perspective are challenged in this absorbing adventure." Publ Wkly

The **prince** of the pond; otherwise known as De Fawg Pin. illustrated by Judy Schachner. Dutton Children's Bks. 1992 151p il hardcover o.p. pa $4.99
Grades: 4 5 6　　　　　**Fic**
　　1. Frogs -- Fiction
　　ISBN 0-525-44976-0; 0-14-037151-6 pa
　　　　　　　　　　　　LC 91-40340

"An animal fantasy that fairy tale readers will relish. . . . Schachner's numerous ink-and-wash drawings go far in supporting the characterization." Bull Cent Child Books

Sly the Sleuth and the pet mysteries; by Donna Jo Napoli and Robert Furrow; illustrated by Heather Maione. Dial Books for Young Readers 2005 96p il $15.99
Grades: 2 3 4　　　　　**Fic**
　　1. Mystery fiction　2. Pets -- Fiction
　　ISBN 0-8037-2993-6
　　　　　　　　　　　　LC 2003-24090

Sly the Sleuth, also known as Sylvia, solves three mysteries for her friends and neighbors, all involving pets, through her detective agency, Sleuth for Hire.

"The stories are easy to read and engaging, the pen-and-ink illustrations convey the light tone of the adventures, and Sly's first-person narration is convincing." Horn Book Guide
Other titles about Sly the Sleuth are:
Sly the Sleuth and the sports mysteries (2006)
Sly the Sleuth and the food mysteries (2007)
Sly the Sleuth and the code mysteries (2009)

Stones in water. Dutton Children's Bks. 1997 209p hardcover o.p. pa $5.99
Grades: 5 6 7 8　　　　　**Fic**
　　1. World War, 1939-1945 -- Fiction
　　ISBN 0-525-45842-5; 0-14-130600-9 pa
　　　　　　　　　　　　LC 97-14253

After being taken by German soldiers from a local movie theater along with other Italian boys including his Jewish friend, Roberto is forced to work in Germany, escapes into the Ukrainian winter, before desperately trying to make his way back home to Venice

This is a "gripping, meticulously researched story (loosely based on the life of an actual survivor)." Publ Wkly

Naylor, Phyllis Reynolds

Alice in rapture, sort of. Atheneum Pubs. 1989 166p hardcover o.p. pa $5.99
Grades: 5 6 7 8　　　　　**Fic**
　　1. Family life -- Fiction
　　ISBN 0-689-31466-3; 1-442-42362-5 pa
　　　　　　　　　　　　LC 88-8174

The summer before she enters the seventh grade becomes the summer of Alice's first boyfriend, and she discovers that love is about the most mixed-up thing that can possibly happen to you, especially since she has no mother to go to for advice

"A book that is wise, perceptive, and hilarious." SLJ

Alice in-between. Atheneum Pubs. 1994 144p pa $5.99

Grades: 4 5 6 7   Fic

1. Family life -- Fiction

ISBN 0-689-31890-1; 1-416-96770-2 pa

LC 93-8167

When motherless Alice turns thirteen she feels in-between, no longer a child but not yet a woman, and discovers that growing up can be both frustrating and wonderful

"This is bound to reassure the many adolescent fans who can identify with the 'in-between blues.'" SLJ

Alice the brave. Atheneum Bks. for Young Readers 1995 130p pa $7.99

Grades: 5 6 7 8   Fic

1. Fear -- Fiction 2. Family life -- Fiction

ISBN 0-689-80095-9; 1-416-97542-X pa

LC 94-32340

The summer before eighth grade, Alice tries to confront her fears, not the least of which is a fear of deep water.

"Alice's wry, funny, vulnerable voice expresses every girl's fears about what is 'normal' in an imperfect world." Booklist

All but Alice. Atheneum Pubs. 1992 151p hardcover o.p. pa $5.99

Grades: 5 6 7 8   Fic

1. School stories 2. Clubs -- Fiction

ISBN 0-689-31773-5; 1-442-42756-6 pa

LC 91-28722

Seventh grader Alice decides that the only way to stave off personal and social disasters is to be part of the crowd, especially the "in" crowd, no matter how boring and, potentially, difficult

"Naylor's light, but deft touch with important thematic concerns is most appealing." SLJ

★ **Emily's** fortune; illustrated by Ross Collins. Delacorte Press 2010 147p il $14.99

Grades: 3 4 5 6   Fic

1. Uncles -- Fiction 2. Orphans -- Fiction 3. Voyages and travels -- Fiction 4. Inheritance and succession -- Fiction

ISBN 978-0-385-73616-9; 0-385-73616-9

LC 2009013096

While traveling to her aunt's home in Redbud by train and stagecoach, quiet young Emily and her turtle, Rufus, team up with Jackson, fellow orphan and troublemaker extraordinaire, to outsmart mean Uncle Victor, who is after Emily's inheritance.

"The local vernacular is lively and fun and the characters are well developed. Cliff-hangers between chapters are written in large boldface to keep readers hooked. . . . Simple, black-and-white illustrations complement the unfolding story. A rip-roaring good time." SLJ

Faith, hope, and Ivy June. Delacorte Press 2009 280p $16.99; lib bdg $19.99

Grades: 5 6 7 8   Fic

1. School stories

ISBN 978-0-385-73615-2; 0-385-73615-0; 978-0-385-90588-6 lib bdg; 0-385-90588-2 lib bdg

LC 2008-19625

During a student exchange program, seventh-graders Ivy June and Catherine share their lives, homes, and communities, and find that although their lifestyles are total opposites they have a lot in common.

"This finely crafted novel . . . depicts a deep friendship growing slowly through understanding. As both girls wait out tragedies at the book's end, they cling to hope—and each other—in a thoroughly real and unaffected way. Naylor depicts Appalachia with sympathetic realism." Kirkus

Outrageously Alice. Atheneum Bks. for Young Readers 1997 133p $16.99; pa $5.99

Grades: 5 6 7 8   Fic

1. School stories 2. Family life -- Fiction

ISBN 0-689-80354-0; 0-689-80596-9 pa

LC 96-7744

"Alice is, as always, likable, humorous, and true to life." SLJ

★ **Roxie** and the Hooligans; with illustrations by Alexandra Boiger. Atheneum Books for Young Readers 2006 115p il $15.95; pa $4.99

Grades: 3 4 5   Fic

1. Adventure fiction

ISBN 1-4169-0243-0; 1-4169-0244-9 pa

LC 2004-24645

Roxie Warbler, the niece of a famous explorer, follows Uncle Dangerfoot's advice on how to survive any crisis when she becomes stranded on an island with a gang of school bullies and a pair of murderous bank robbers.

This "mixes fantasy, absurdity, and reality in a way that never diminishes or overwhelms the story's heart. Boiger's black-and-white illustrations catch the energy of Naylor's over-the-top yet sympathetically portrayed characters." Booklist

★ **Shiloh**. Atheneum Pubs. 1991 144p $16.95; pa $6.99

Grades: 4 5 6   Fic

1. Dogs -- Fiction

ISBN 0-689-31614-3; 0-689-83582-5 pa

LC 90-603

Awarded the Newbery Medal, 1992

When he finds a lost beagle in the hills behind his West Virginia home, Marty tries to hide it from his family and the dog's real owner, a mean-spirited man known to shoot deer out of season and to mistreat his dogs

"A credible plot and characters, a well-drawn setting, and nicely paced narration combine in a story that leaves the reader feeling good." Horn Book

Other titles about Shiloh are:

Shiloh season (1996)

Saving Shiloh (1997)

★ **Starting** with Alice. Atheneum Bks. for Young Readers 2002 181p hardcover o.p. pa $4.99

Grades: 3 4 5 6   Fic

1. School stories 2. Friendship -- Fiction 3. Family

life -- Fiction
ISBN 0-689-84395-X; 0-689-84396-8 pa
LC 2001-53610

This, the first of three prequels to the series about Alice, is written for younger readers. After she, her older brother, and their father move from Chicago to Maryland, Alice has trouble fitting into her new third grade class, but with the help of some new friends and her own unique outlook, she survives

"New characters and realistic third-grade situations are explored, but young Alice's humor and earnestness are refreshingly the same." Horn Book

Other prequels to the Alice series are:
Alice in Blunderland (2003)
Lovingly Alice (2004)

Nelson, Nina

Bringing the boy home; by N.A. Nelson. HarperCollinsPublishers 2008 211p $15.99; lib bdg $16.89
Grades: 5 6 7 8 **Fic**
1. Rain forests -- Fiction 2. Senses and sensation -- Fiction 3. Extrasensory perception -- Fiction
ISBN 978-0-06-088698-1; 0-06-088698-6; 978-0-06-088699-8 lib bdg; 0-06-088699-4 lib bdg
LC 2007-31702

As two Takunami youths approach their thirteenth birthdays, Luka reaches the culmination of his mother's training for the tribe's manhood test while Tirio, raised in Miami, Florida, by his adoptive mother, feels called to begin preparations to prove himself during his upcoming visit to the Amazon rain forest where he was born.

"The vivid setting, imagined cultural particulars . . . and magical realism will captivate readers." Booklist

Neri, G.

Ghetto cowboy; [by] G. Neri; illustrated by Jesse Joshua Watson. Candlewick Press 2011 218p il $15.99
Grades: 4 5 6 7 **Fic**
1. Horses -- Fiction 2. Moving -- Fiction 3. African Americans -- Fiction 4. City and town life -- Fiction 5. Father-son relationship -- Fiction
ISBN 978-0-7636-4922-7; 0-7636-4922-8
LC 2010007565

Twelve-year-old Cole's behavior causes his mother to drive him from Detroit to Philadelphia to live with a father he has never known, but who soon has Cole involved with a group of African-American "cowboys" who rescue horses and use them to steer youths away from drugs and gangs.

"This well-written book is based on a true story of urban cowboys in Philadelphia and New York. Cole's spot-on emotional insight is conveyed through believable dialogue. . . . Watson's illustrations punctuate the intriguing aspects of the story and make the novel more appealing." SLJ

Neri, Greg

Chess rumble; by G. Neri; art by Jesse Joshua Watson. Lee & Low Books 2007 64p il $18.95
Grades: 5 6 7 8 **Fic**
1. Chess -- Fiction 2. African Americans -- Fiction
ISBN 978-1-58430-279-7
LC 2007010772

Branded a troublemaker due to his anger over everything from being bullied to his sister's death a year before, Marcus begins to control himself and cope with his problems at home and at his inner-city school when an unlikely mentor teaches him to play chess

"Neri expertly captures Marcus's voice and delicately teases out his alternating vulnerability and rage. The cadence and emotion of the verse are masterfully echoed through Watson's expressive acrylic illustrations." SLJ

Nesbit, E.

★ **Five** children and it; illustrated by H.R. Millar; with an introduction by Laurel Snyder. Random House 2010 255p il (Looking Glass library) $9.99; lib bdg $12.99
Grades: 4 5 6 **Fic**
1. Wishes -- Fiction 2. Fairies -- Fiction 3. Siblings -- Fiction
ISBN 978-0-375-86336-3; 0-375-86336-2; 978-0-375-96336-0 lib bdg; 0-375-96336-7 lib bdg
LC 2008-54569

First published 1902 in the United Kingdom; first United States edition 1905 by Dodd, Mead & Co.

When four brothers and sisters discover a Psammead, or sand-fairy, in the gravel pit near the country house where they are staying, they have no way of knowing all the adventures its wish-granting will bring them

Other titles in this series are:
The Phoenix and the carpet (1904)
The story of the amulet (1907)

★ **The enchanted** castle; illustrated by Paul O. Zelinsky; afterword by Peter Glassman. Morrow Junior Bks. 1992 292p il lib bdg $22.95
Grades: 4 5 6 **Fic**
1. Fantasy fiction
ISBN 0-688-05435-8
LC 91-46267

First published 1907 in the United Kingdom; first United States edition 1908 by Harper & Brothers

Four English children find a wonderful world of magic through an enchanted wishing ring

"With fine, cross-hatched lines tinted in luminous colors, Zelinsky's artwork is as lively as the story and very much of the period." Booklist

Nesbo, Jo, 1960-

Doctor Proctor's fart powder; illustrated by Mike Lowery. Aladdin 2010 265p il $14.99
Grades: 4 5 6 **Fic**
1. Bullies -- Fiction 2. Inventors -- Fiction 3. Friendship -- Fiction
ISBN 978-1-4169-7972-2; 1-4169-7972-7
LC 2009-27204

New friends Nilly and Lisa help eccentric professor Doctor Proctor to develop his latest invention, a powder that makes one fart, making them very popular at school, but someone is planning to steal the industrial-strength formula for evil purposes.

"Nesbo tells his fantastical story in a matter-of-fact, deadpan style, and Lowery's simple illustrations match the dry, comedic tone well." Booklist

Neumeier, Rachel

The **Floating** Islands. Alfred A. Knopf 2011 388p map $16.99; lib bdg $19.99
Grades: 5 6 7 **Fic**
1. Fantasy fiction 2. Magic -- Fiction 3. Flight --

Fiction 4. Cousins -- Fiction

ISBN 0-375-84705-7; 0-375-94705-1 lib bdg; 978-0-375-84705-9; 978-0-375-94705-6 lib bdg

LC 2010-12772

The adventures of two teenaged cousins who live in a place called The Floating Islands, one of whom is studying to become a mage and the other one of the legendary island flyers.

"The author delineates complex characters, geographies and societies alike with a dab hand, deftly weaves them all— along with dragons of several sorts, mouthwatering kitchen talk, flashes of humor and a late-blooming romance—into a suspenseful plot and delivers and outstanding tale that is self-contained but full of promise for sequels." Kirkus

Neville, Emily Cheney

It's like this, Cat; [by] Emily Neville; illustrated by Emil Weiss. Harper & Row 1963 180p il $16.99; lib bdg $17.89; pa $5.99

Grades: 5 6 7 8　　　　　　　　　　　　　　　　Fic

1. Cats -- Fiction

ISBN 0-06-024390-2; 0-06-024391-0 lib bdg; 0-06-440073-5 pa

Awarded the Newbery Medal, 1964

"A story told with a great amount of insight into human relationships. . . . This all provides a wonderfully real picture of a city boy's outlets and of one likable adolescent's inner feelings. An exceedingly fresh, honest, and well-rounded piece of writing." Horn Book

Newbery, Linda

At the firefly gate. David Fickling Books 2007 152p hardcover o.p. pa $6.50

Grades: 5 6 7 8　　　　　　　　　　　　　　　　Fic

1. Supernatural -- Fiction 2. World War, 1939-1945 -- Fiction

ISBN 978-0-385-75113-1; 978-0-440-42188-7 pa

LC 2006-01796

After moving with his parents from London to Suffolk near a former World War II airfield , Henry sees the shadowy image of a man by the orchard gate and feels an unusual affinity with an eldery woman who lives next door

"This is a well-written book, with an old-fashioned tone, that emphasizes character and feelings over plot. It's for thoughtful readers who appreciate a book that lingers in their minds." SLJ

Lost boy. David Fickling Books 2008 194p $15.99; lib bdg $18.99

Grades: 4 5 6 7　　　　　　　　　　　　　　　　Fic

1. Ghost stories 2. Mystery fiction 3. Traffic accidents -- Fiction

ISBN 978-0-375-84574-1; 978-0-375-93617-3 lib bdg

LC 2007-15041

First published 2005 in the United Kingdom

After Matt moves to Hay-on-Wye in Wales, a boy his age who bears the same initials and was killed in a car accident many years earlier, appears to Matt.

"With its imaginative melding of present-day concerns, good storytelling, lush descriptions of the landscape and even a faithful dog, this novel will ensnare readers." Publ Wkly

Lucy and the green man; illustrated by Pam Smy. David Fickling Books 2010 217p il $16.99; lib bdg $19.99

Grades: 3 4 5　　　　　　　　　　　　　　　　Fic

1. Gardening -- Fiction 2. Bereavement -- Fiction 3. Grandfathers -- Fiction

ISBN 978-0-385-75204-6; 0-385-75204-0; 978-0-385-75207-7 lib bdg; 0-385-75207-5 lib bdg

LC 2010-13653

Lucy and her grandfather are special because only they can see Lob, the magical 'green man' who helps in the garden, but then something terrible happens and Lucy fears she will never see Lob again

"Black-and-white line spot art and occasional spreads capture the flavor of the story. . . . This gentle fantasy has an old-fashioned quality that will appeal to families and young sensitive readers." SLJ

Newbound, Andrew

Ghoul strike! Chicken House 2010 309p $16.99

Grades: 4 5 6 7　　　　　　　　　　　　　　　　Fic

1. Angels -- Fiction 2. Monsters -- Fiction 3. Supernatural -- Fiction

ISBN 978-0-545-22938-8; 0-545-22938-3

LC 2010013580

When twelve-year-old, psychic ghost hunter Alannah Malarra faces demons from another dimension, rather than the treasure-hoarding ghosts she is used to, she needs the help of protectors from the Attack-ready Network of Global Evanescent Law-enforcers (A.N.G.E.L.) police force to help her quell the dangerous uprising

"Alannah is a great female hero. . . . The other main characters are also multidimensional, and descriptions of the various creatures are detailed and entertaining. Readers will enjoy the fast-paced plot and the friendship between Alannah and Wortley." SLJ

Newman, John

Mimi. Candlewick Press 2011 186p $15.99

Grades: 2 3 4 5　　　　　　　　　　　　　　　　Fic

1. Bereavement -- Fiction 2. Family life -- Fiction

ISBN 978-0-7636-5415-3; 0-7636-5415-9

LC 2010040147

Mimi is determined not to give up on anyone or anything, but since Mammy died, her father never smiles, her sister Sally is in a bad mood, brother Conor keeps to himself, and even Sparkler the dog does not want to go for walks.

Newman "will win readers' hearts through the conversational tone and openhearted observations of . . . narrator Mimi. . . . Newman ably conveys a family hanging together by a thread; that Mimi, who is Chinese, is adopted is nearly incidental to the plot—until a climactic scene in which she stands up to a school bully." Publ Wkly

Newman, Leslea

★ Hachiko waits; illustrated by Machiyo Kodaira. Henry Holt and Co. 2004 96p il $15.95; pa $6.99

Grades: 3 4 5　　　　　　　　　　　　　　　　Fic

1. Dogs 2. Akita dog 3. Dogs -- Fiction

ISBN 0-8050-7336-1; 0-312-55806-6 pa

LC 2003-68589

Professor Ueno's loyal Akita, Hachiko, waits for him at the train station every afternoon, and even after the professor has a fatal heart attack while at work, Hachiko faithfully continues to await his return until the day the dog dies. Based on a true story

"Yasuo brings a childhood focus to the poignant story . . . and Kodaira's soft, black-and-white sketches help to break up the chapters for younger readers and add interest to the story." Booklist

Nicholls, Sally

★ **Season** of secrets. Arthur A. Levine Books 2011 225p $16.99

Grades: 4 5 6   **Fic**

1. Sisters -- Fiction 2. Bereavement -- Fiction 3. Family life -- Fiction

ISBN 978-0-545-21825-2; 0-545-21825-X

LC 2010017070

Sent by their father to live in the country with their grandparents after the sudden death of their mother, Molly's older sister Hannah expresses her grief in a raging rebellion while imaginative Molly finds herself increasingly distracted by visions, that seemingly only she can see, of a strange hunt in the nearby forest.

"Written in gently flowing prose, the plot appropriately transitions from autumn into summer as Molly emerges from grief to acceptance and hope. A poignant story of healing tinged with mystery." Kirkus

★ **Ways** to live forever; [by] Sally Nicholls. Arthur A. Levine Books 2008 212p il $16.99

Grades: 4 5 6 7   **Fic**

1. Death -- Fiction 2. Leukemia -- Fiction 3. Authorship -- Fiction 4. Family life -- Fiction

ISBN 978-0-545-06948-9; 0-545-06948-3

LC 2007047341

Eleven-year-old Sam McQueen, who has leukemia, writes a book during the last three months of his life, in which he tells about what he would like to accomplish, how he feels, and things that have happened to him.

This "skirts easy sentiment to confront the hard questions head-on, intelligently and realistically and with an enormous range of feeling." Publ Wkly

Nielsen, Jennifer A.

Elliot and the goblin war; illustrated by Gideon Kendall. Sourcebooks Jabberwocky 2010 181p il (Underworld chronicles) $14.99

Grades: 4 5 6 7   **Fic**

1. Fantasy fiction 2. Boys -- Fiction 3. Goblins -- Fiction

ISBN 978-1-4022-4019-5; 1-4022-4019-8

This "begins Halloween night, when unsuspecting reluctant hero Elliot happens to save a real Brownie named Patches from a trio of real Goblins. Elliot's good deed results in his acclamation as King of the Brownies, and these spunky but weak creatures truly need a king to help them end a three-year-long war with the evil Goblins. Nielsen ably draws readers into a tale chock-full of light adventure and humor, as each chapter details the somewhat over-the-top yet entertaining dilemmas Patches and Elliot face. . . . Recommended for those who avoid dark and serious fantasies, as it's sure to evoke more giggles than gasps, despite the introductory admonitions." Kirkus

Other titles in this series are:

Elliot and the pixie plot (2011)

Elliot and the Yeti threat (2011)

Nielsen, Susin

Dear George Clooney; please marry my mom. Tundra Books 2010 229p $15.95

Grades: 5 6 7 8   **Fic**

1. Divorce -- Fiction 2. Letters -- Fiction

ISBN 978-0-88776-977-1; 0-88776-977-2

"Smarting from her parent's divorce—her director father left her mother to marry an actress—Violet is fed up with all the 'losers' her mother has since dated. . . . She pens a letter to George Clooney . . . explaining that she's trying to find a suitable suitor for her parent. . . . Nielsen skillfully balances her story's keen humor . . . with poignancy." Publ Wkly

★ **Word** nerd. Tundra Books 2008 248p $18.95; pa $12.95

Grades: 5 6 7 8   **Fic**

1. Friendship -- Fiction 2. Scrabble (Game) -- Fiction 3. Mother-son relationship -- Fiction

ISBN 978-0-88776-875-0; 0-88776-875-X; 978-0-88776-990-0 pa; 0-88776-990-X pa

"Twelve-year-old Ambrose Bukowski and his widowed, overprotective mother . . . move frequently. When he almost dies after he bites into a peanut that bullies put in his sandwich, just to see if he is really allergic, Irene . . . decides to homeschool him. . . . Ambrose gets to know 25-year-old-Cosmo, recently released from jail and the son of the Bukowskis' . . . landlords. . . . Ambrose . . . talks Cosmo into taking him to a Scrabble Club. . . . This is a tender, often funny story with some really interesting characters. It will appeal to word nerds, but even more to anyone who has ever longed for acceptance or had to fight unreasonable parental restrictions." SLJ

Nigg, Joe

How to raise and keep a dragon; by John Topsell; executive editor, Joseph Nigg; illustrations, Dan Malone. Barron's 2006 128p il $18.99

Grades: 5 6 7 8   **Fic**

1. Dragons -- Fiction

ISBN 0-7641-5920-8

"Posing as dragon-breeder John Topsell . . . Nigg instructs readers in selecting and caring for a breed of dragon suited for them. . . . While not intended as a serious book on mythology, Nigg does share many bits of real dragon lore while spinning out details of what it might be like to live in a world where people breed, register, and show these creatures. Malone's full-color illustrations on every page offer fans many cool pictures to copy or sketch. With its tongue firmly in cheek, this book is a lot of lighthearted fun." SLJ

Nimmo, Jenny

The **Chestnut** Soldier. Orchard Books 2007 203p (The magician trilogy) pa $5.99; $9.99

Grades: 4 5 6 7   **Fic**

1. Magic -- Fiction

ISBN 0-439-84677-3; 978-0-545-07127-7 pa; 0-545-07127-5 pa; 978-0-439-84677-6

LC 2006-19123

First published 1989 in the United Kingdom; first U.S. edition 1991 by Dutton

To purge the anger from an ancient Welsh demonic god that he had helped release, and to soothe a moody, troubled soldier, Gwyn Griffiths draws on the strength of his namesake and ancestor in Welsh magic, Gwydion Gwyn.

"Nimmo has skillfully woven the ancient story into the modern one, making it accessible to those who do not know the legend. This satisfying fantasy introduces young readers to the genre." SLJ

Midnight for Charlie Bone. Orchard Bks. 2003 401p (Children of the Red King) $12.99

Grades: 5 6 7 8   Fic

1. School stories 2. Magic -- Fiction
ISBN 978-0-439-47429-0; 0-439-47429-9

                    LC 2002-30738

First published 2002 in the United Kingdom

Charlie Bone's life with his widowed mother and two grandmothers undergoes a dramatic change when he discovers that he can hear people in photographs talking.

"This marvelous fantasy is able to stand on its own despite inevitable comparisons to the students of Hogwarts." Voice Youth Advocates

Other titles in this series are:

Charlie Bone and the time twister (2003)

Charlie Bone and the invisible boy (2004)

Charlie Bone and the castle of mirrors (2005)

Charlie Bone and the hidden king (2006)

Charlie Bone and the beast (2007)

Charlie Bone and the shadow (2008)

Charlie Bone and the Red Knight (2010)

The **secret** kingdom. Scholastic Press 2011 207p (Chronicles of the red king) $16.99

Grades: 4 5 6   Fic

1. Magic -- Fiction 2. Camels -- Fiction 3. Siblings -- Fiction 4. Voyages and travels -- Fiction
ISBN 978-0-439-84673-8; 0-439-84673-0

                  LC 2010035710

Timoken and his sister, Zobayda, under the protection of a forest jinni but pursued by evil virideed, straddle the world of men and the world of enchantments, seeking a home while remaining young by drinking a potion called Alixir.

"The narrative voice is direct and matter-of-fact, conveying the fantastic as well as the mundane facts of Timoken's incredible life accessibly; new readers will have no difficulty making this an introduction to Nimmo's work. . . . Timoken is a highly appealing young hero, and his panoply of human and magical friends provide just the right amount of help without stealing the show." Publ Wkly

★ The **snow** spider; [by] Jenny Nimmo. Orchard Books 2006 146p (Magician trilogy) $9.99

Grades: 4 5 6 7   Fic

1. Magic -- Fiction 2. Father-son relationship -- Fiction
ISBN 978-0-439-84675-2; 0-439-84675-7

                  LC 2006009445

A reissue of the title first published 1987 by Dutton

Gifts from Gwyn's grandmother on his ninth birthday open up a whole new world to him, as he discovers he has magical powers that help him heal the breach with his father that has existed ever since his sister's mysterious disappearance four years before

"The narration is paced well and builds in excitement along with the tale." SLJ

Other titles in this series are:

Emlyn's moon (2007)

Chestnut solider (2007)

Nix, Garth, 1963-

Troubletwisters; [by] Garth Nix and Sean Williams. Scholastic Press 2011 293p $16.99

Grades: 5 6 7 8   Fic

1. Fantasy fiction 2. Magic -- Fiction 3. Twins -- Fiction 4. Siblings -- Fiction 5. Grandmothers -- Fiction
ISBN 978-0-545-25897-5; 0-545-25897-9

              LC 2011015765

When their house mysteriously explodes and they are sent to live with an unknown relative named Grandma X, twelve-year-old twins Jaide and Jack Shield learn that they are troubletwisters, young Wardens just coming into their powers, who must protect humanity from The Evil trying to break into Earth's dimension.

"Full of adventure and the unexpected, . . . [this] is delightfully twisted. The pacing is perfect, the setting is eerily dark, the faceless Evil rings true, and the resolution is satisfying." Booklist

Nixon, Joan Lowery

Laugh till you cry. Delacorte Press 2004 99p hardcover o.p. lib bdg $17.99

Grades: 5 6 7 8   Fic

1. School stories 2. Moving -- Fiction 3. Family life -- Fiction
ISBN 0-385-73027-6; 0-385-90186-0 lib bdg

             LC 2004-9557

Thirteen years old and a budding comedian, Cody has little to laugh about after he and his mother move from California to Texas to help his sick grandmother and he finds himself framed by his jealous cousin for calling in bomb threats to their school.

"The pacing of the story, Cody's humorous side, and the book's length make this mystery ideal for reluctant readers." SLJ

Noe, Katherine Schlick

Something to hold. Clarion 2011 $16.99

Grades: 4 5 6   Fic

1. School stories 2. Prejudices -- Fiction 3. Native Americans -- Fiction
ISBN 978-0-547-55813-4; 0-547-55813-9

This book follows "Kitty," [who] is so used to moving with each of her father's job reassignments that making friends in each new location is usually not much of an issue. The Warm Springs Reservation in central Oregon is, however, a new experience, since she and her brothers are among the handful of white students in their new school. The brothers easily bond with Wasco, Warm Springs, and Paiute boys through common enthusiasm for baseball, but Kitty is intimidated by a pair of her classmates—dour, bullying Raymond and his snappish, aloof sister, Jewel. . . . Raymond and Jewel are often at the mercy of their abusive white stepfather, and . . . the reservation police and their municipal police are so gridlocked by jurisdictional mandates and prejudice that the children feel they have no legal recourse. . . Kitty's gradual involvement with Raymond and Jewel forms the backbone of the novel" (Bulletin of the Center for Children's Books).

"Kitty Schlick is apprehensive about starting sixth grade on Oregon's Warm Springs Indian Reservation, home to

Paiute, Warm Springs and Wasco people, where her father's job has taken the family in 1962. . . . One of the school's few white students, she feels isolated until she's befriended by Pinky, a Wasco classmate whose mother, like Kitty's dad, staffs a fire lookout. As Kitty finds her footing, she's troubled by the preferential treatment teachers give white students and the casual racism of the white girls attending her church. . . . Noe . . . resists didacticism. Kitty's discoveries and ethical dilemmas are age and era-appropriate, the characters affectionately portrayed, rounded individuals." Kirkus

Noel, Alyson
    Radiance. Square Fish 2010 183p pa $7.99
Grades: 5 6 7 8   Fic
    1. Ghost stories 2. Dead -- Fiction 3. Future life -- Fiction
    ISBN 978-0-312-62917-5; 0-312-62917-6
                                                    LC 2010015840
    After crossing the bridge into the afterlife, a place called Here where the time is always Now, Riley's existence continues in much the same way as when she was alive until she is given the job of Soul Catcher and, together with her teacher Bodhi, returns to earth for her first assignment, a ghost called the Radiant Boy who has been haunting an English castle for centuries and resisted all previous attempts to get him across the bridge.
    "Narrating in a contemporary voice with an honest and comfortable cadence, Riley is imperfect, but always likable. . . . In the midst of this wildly fanciful setting, Noël is able to capture with nail-on-the-head accuracy common worries and concerns of today's tweens." SLJ
    Other titles in this series are:
    Dreamland (2011)
    Shimmer (2011)

Nolan, Lucy A.
    ★ **On** the road; by Lucy Nolan; illustrated by Mike Reed. Marshall Cavendish 2005 54p il (Down Girl and Sit) $14.95
Grades: 1 2 3   Fic
    1. Dogs -- Fiction
    ISBN 0-7614-5234-6; 978-0-7614-5234-8
                                                    LC 2004-27511
    A dog who thinks her name is Down Girl goes on a car ride to the beach, goes camping in the woods, and reluctantly pays a visit to the vet with her master, Rruff.
    "Narrated from a dog's point of view, this easy chapter book covers the hilarious antics of two canine friends. . . . A small black-and-white illustration appears on almost every page, supporting the text's humor." SLJ
    Other titles in this series are:
    Smarter than squirrels (2005)
    Bad to the bone (2008)
    Home on the range (2010)

    Smarter than squirrels; illustrations by Mike Reed. Marshall Cavendish 2004 64p il (Down Girl and Sit) $14.95
Grades: 1 2 3   Fic
    1. Dogs -- Fiction
    ISBN 0-7614-5184-6
                                                    LC 2004-1400

Recounts the adventures of a rambunctious dog who thinks her name is Down Girl and her next door neighbor, Sit, as they try to keep the world safe from dangerous squirrels, the paper boy, and a frightening creature named Here Kitty Kitty.
    "Reed's humorous black-and-white illustrations add to the charm of this transitional chapter book." SLJ

Nolen, Jerdine
    Eliza's freedom road; an Underground Railroad diary. Simon & Schuster Books for Young Readers 2011 139p il map $14.99
Grades: 4 5 6 7   Fic
    1. Diaries -- Fiction 2. Slavery -- Fiction 3. African Americans -- Fiction 4. Underground railroad -- Fiction
    ISBN 1-4169-5814-2; 978-1-4169-5814-7
                                                    LC 2010-20931
    A twelve-year-old slave girl begins writing in a journal where she documents her journey via the Underground Railroad from Alexandria, Virginia, to freedom in St. Catharines, Canada.
    "Nolen reveals some of the traumas and tragedies of slavery but keeps her focus on those things that allow Eliza the power to escape: literacy, her mother's legacy, a bit of luck and a great deal of courage." Kirkus
    Includes bibliographical references

Norcliffe, James
    The **boy** who could fly. Egmont USA 2010 312p $15.99
Grades: 5 6 7 8   Fic
    1. Fantasy fiction 2. Flight -- Fiction 3. Siblings -- Fiction 4. Abandoned children -- Fiction
    ISBN 978-1-60684-084-9; 1-60684-084-3
                                                    LC 2009-41167
    First published 2009 in New Zealand with title: The loblolly boy
    Having grown up in a miserable home for abandoned children, a young boy jumps at the chance to exchange places with the mysterious, flying "loblolly boy," but once he takes on this new identity, he discovers what a harsh price he must pay.
    "Norcliffe has written an imaginative and richly atmospheric fantasy with sympathetic characters. . . . This is . . . a haunting tale that will capture most readers' imaginations." Booklist

Northrop, Michael
    Plunked; Michael Northrop. Scholastic Press 2012 247p.
Grades: 4 5 6 7 8   Fic
    1. Fear -- Juvenile fiction 2. Ethics -- Juvenile fiction 3. Baseball -- Juvenile fiction 4. Little League Baseball -- Juvenile fiction 5. Fear -- Fiction 6. Schools -- Fiction 7. Baseball -- Fiction 8. Perseverance (Ethics) -- Fiction
    ISBN 0545297141; 9780545297141
                                                    LC 2011032737
    This children's story by Michael Northrop centers on "Sixth grader Jack Mogens [who] has it all figured out: He's got his batting routine down, and his outfielding earns him a starting spot alongside his best friend Andy on their Little League team, the Tall Pines Braves. He even manages to have a not-totally-embarrassing conversation with Katie, the team's killer shortstop. But in the first game of the season,

a powerful stray pitch brings everything Jack's worked so hard for crashing down around his ears. . . ." Jack then has to face his fears and anxieties and return to the game. (Publisher's note)

Norton, Mary

Bed-knob and broomstick; illustrated by Erik Blegvad. Harcourt 2000 227p il hardcover o.p. pa $6

Grades: 3 4 5 6   Fic
1. Magic 2. Witches 3. Space and time 4. Fantasy fiction 5. Witchcraft -- Fiction
ISBN 0-15-202450-6; 0-15-202456-5 pa

LC 99-89153

A combined edition of The magic bed-knob (1943) and Bonfires and broomsticks (1947); present title is a reissue of the 1957 edition

With the powers they acquire from a spinster who is studying to be a witch, three English children have a series of exciting and perilous adventures traveling on a flying bed that takes them to a London police station, a tropical island, and back in time to the seventeenth century

Noyce, Pendred

Lost in Lexicon; an adventure in words and numbers. by Pendred Noyce; illustrations by Joan Charles. Scarletta Press 2011 il

Grades: 5 6 7 8   Fic
1. Fantasy fiction 2. Cousins -- Fiction 3. Mathematics -- Fiction 4. English language -- Fiction
ISBN 9780983021926 pa; 0983021929 pa; 9780983021933 e-book; 0983021937 e-book

LC 2011013583

When Aunt Adelaide sends thirteen-year-old cousins Ivan and Daphne on a treasure hunt in the rain, they never expect to stumble into a whole new world where words and numbers run wild.

Nylund, Eric S.

The Resisters; [by] Eric Nylund. Random House 2011 210p $16.99; lib bdg $19.99

Grades: 5 6 7 8   Fic
1. Science fiction 2. Brainwashing -- Fiction 3. Extraterrestrial beings -- Fiction
ISBN 978-0-375-86856-6; 0-375-86856-9; 978-0-375-96856-3 lib bdg; 0-375-96856-3 lib bdg

LC 2010-19230

When twelve-year-olds Madison and Felix kidnap him, Ethan learns that the Earth has been taken over by aliens and that all the adults in the world are under mind control.

"Ethan, Felix, and Madison are multidimensional characters with authentic emotions and realistic attitudes and motives. This book mixes considerable background exposition with fast-moving action. While the immediate plot issues are resolved, there are plenty of threads left dangling. Middle school boys will enjoy the high-tech battle action and will look forward to the next installment." SLJ

O'Brien, Annemarie   •

Lara's gift; by Annemarie O'Brien. Alfred A. Knopf 2013 176 p. (hardcover) $16.99; (ebook) $50.97; (library binding) 19.99

Grades: 5 6 7 8 9   Fic
1. Historical fiction -- Juvenile fiction 2. Dogs -- Breeding -- Juvenile literature 3. Dogs -- Fiction 4.

Borzoi -- Fiction 5. Visions -- Fiction 6. Sex role -- Fiction 7. Family life -- Russia -- Fiction 8. Fathers and daughters -- Fiction
ISBN 0307931749; 9780307931740; 9780307975485; 9780375971051

LC 2012034070

In this book, on "a remote estate in 1910s Russia, Lara must prove herself capable of following in her father's footsteps as the head of a prestigious borzoi breeding kennel. There are so many things between her and the realization of her dream. That she is female is the biggest obstacle, but she must also hide the fact that she has visions of future occurrences that involve the dogs and the dangerous wolves that populate the estate." (Kirkus Reviews)

O'Brien, Robert C.

★ Mrs. Frisby and the rats of NIMH; [by] Robert C. O'Brien; illustrated by Zena Bernstein. Atheneum Books for Young Readers 2006 233p il $18; pa $6.99

Grades: 4 5 6 7   Fic
1. Mice -- Fiction 2. Rats -- Fiction
ISBN 978-0-689-20651-1; 0-689-20651-8; 978-0-689-71068-1 pa; 0-689-71068-2 pa

A reissue of the title first published 1971

Awarded the Newbery Medal, 1972

Having no one to help her with her problems, a widowed mouse visits the rats whose former imprisonment in a laboratory made them wise and long lived.

"The story is fresh and ingenious, the style witty, and the plot both hilarious and convincing." Saturday Rev

O'Connell, Rebecca

Penina Levine is a hard-boiled egg; [by] Rebecca O'Connell; illustrated by Majella Lue Sue. Roaring Brook Press 2007 163p il $16.95; pa $6.99

Grades: 4 5 6   Fic
1. School stories 2. Jews -- Fiction 3. Easter -- Fiction 4. Passover -- Fiction
ISBN 978-1-59643-140-9; 1-59643-140-7; 978-0-312-55026-4 pa; 0-312-55026-X pa

LC 2006016677

"Penina Levine's new teacher has given an assignment to send cards as the Easter Bunny to kindergartners at a neighboring school, and the sixth grader is uncomfortable with it because she is Jewish. . . . The story moves along at an entertaining pace. . . . Penina is a feisty and thoroughly enjoyable heroine. . . . O'Connell's artful weaving of Jewish traditions and history throughout the novel makes it all the richer, and the occasional illustrations complement the dynamic humor." SLJ

Another title about Penina Levine is:

Penina Levine is a potato pancake (2008)

O'Connor, Barbara

★ Fame and glory in Freedom, Georgia. Farrar, Straus & Giroux 2003 104p $16; pa $6.95

Grades: 4 5 6 7   Fic
1. School stories 2. Contests -- Fiction
ISBN 0-374-32258-9; 0-374-40018-0 pa

LC 2002-190212

Unpopular sixth-grader Burdette Bird Weaver persuades the new boy at school, whom everyone thinks is mean and dumb, to be her partner for a spelling bee that might win her everything she's ever wanted

"An idiosyncratic group of characters play out this touching and well-paced story about friendship, family, and connection." Horn Books

★ The **fantastic** secret of Owen Jester. Farrar Straus Giroux 2010 168p $15.99

Grades: 3 4 5   **Fic**

1. Adventure fiction 2. Frogs -- Fiction 3. Family life -- Fiction 4. Submersibles -- Fiction

ISBN 978-0-374-36850-0; 0-374-36850-3

After Owen captures an enormous bullfrog, names it Tooley Graham, then has to release it, he and two friends try to use a small submarine that fell from a passing train to search for Tooley in the Carter, Georgia, pond it came from, while avoiding nosy neighbor Viola.

"O'Connor has spun a lovely read that perfectly captures the schemes and plans of school-age kids in the long days of summer." Kirkus

★ **How** to steal a dog; a novel. Farrar, Straus & Giroux 2007 170p pa $6.99; $16

Grades: 4 5 6   **Fic**

1. Dogs -- Fiction 2. Siblings -- Fiction 3. Homeless persons -- Fiction

ISBN 0-312-56112-1 pa; 0-374-33497-8; 978-0-312-56112-3 pa; 978-0-374-33497-0

LC 2005-40166

Living in the family car in their small North Carolina town, Georgina persuades her younger brother to help her in an elaborate scheme to get money by stealing a dog and then claiming the reward that the owners are bound to offer

This is told "in stripped-down, unsentimental prose. . . . The myriad effects of homelessness and the realistic picture of a moral quandary will surely generate discussion." Booklist

On the road to Mr. Mineo's; Barbara O'Connor. Frances Foster Books 2012 181 p. (hardcover) $16.99

Grades: 5 6   **Fic**

1. Pigeons -- Fiction 2. Homing pigeons -- Fiction

ISBN 0374380023; 9780374380021

LC 2011049679

In this novel by Barbara O'Connor, "Sherman the one-legged pigeon flies into . . . Meadville, South Carolina . . . and causes a ruckus. First Stella, who's been begging for a dog, spots him on top of a garage roof and decides she wants him for a pet. Then there's Ethel and Amos, an old couple who sees the pigeon in their barn keeping company with a little brown dog that barks all night. Meanwhile, across town, Mr. Mineo has one less homing pigeon than he used to." (Publisher's note)

★ The **small** adventure of Popeye and Elvis. Frances Foster Books 2009 149p $16.99

Grades: 3 4 5 6   **Fic**

1. Adventure fiction 2. Dogs -- Fiction 3. Friendship -- Fiction 4. Grandmothers -- Fiction

ISBN 978-0-374-37055-8; 0-374-37055-9

LC 2008-24145

In Fayette, South Carolina, the highlight of Popeye's summer is learning vocabulary words with his grandmother until a motor home gets stuck nearby and Elvis, the old-

est boy living inside, joins Popeye in finding the source of strange boats floating down the creek.

"Elvis and Popeye's journey reminds readers to look for and enjoy the small treasures in their lives. Save a spot on your shelves for this small adventure with a grand heart." SLJ

O'Connor, Sheila

★ **Sparrow** Road. G. P. Putnam's Sons 2011 247p $16.99

Grades: 5 6 7 8   **Fic**

1. Artists -- Fiction

ISBN 978-0-399-25458-1; 0-399-25458-7

LC 2010-28290

Twelve-year-old Raine spends the summer at a mysterious artists colony and discovers a secret about her past.

This is a "beautifully written novel. . . . Readers finding themselves in this quiet world will find plenty of space to imagine and dream for themselves." Kirkus

O'Dell, Kathleen

Agnes Parker . . . girl in progress. Dial Bks. 2003 156p hardcover o.p. pa $6.99

Grades: 4 5 6 7   **Fic**

1. Bullies 2. Friendship 3. School stories 4. Conduct of life 5. Best friends

ISBN 0-8037-2648-1; 0-14-240228-1 pa

LC 2001-58256

As she starts in the sixth grade, Agnes faces challenges with her old best friend, a longtime bully, a wonderful new classmate and neighbor, and herself

"This is a thoughtful, gently humorous, and resonant cusp-of-coming-of-age novel." Horn Book Guide

Other titles about Agnes Parker are:

Agnes Parker . . . Happy camper? (2005)

Agnes Parker . . . Keeping cool in middle school (2007)

The **aviary**. Alfred A. Knopf 2011 339p $15.99; lib bdg $18.99

Grades: 3 4 5   **Fic**

1. Birds -- Fiction 2. Magic -- Fiction 3. Friendship -- Fiction 4. Family life -- Fiction 5. Inheritance and succession -- Fiction

ISBN 978-0-375-85605-1; 0-375-85605-6; 978-0-375-95605-8 lib bdg; 0-375-95605-0 lib bdg

LC 2010045778

In late nineteenth-century Maine, isolated, eleven-year-old Clara Dooley gains a friend and uncovers a magical secret that changes her life when she learns to care for the once-feared birds in the aviary attached to the Glendoveer mansion where she lives.

"The honeycreeper's encouragement leads to discovery after discovery in a well-paced, high-tension mystery that draws not only on Burnett, but also C.S. Lewis, Zilpha Keatley Snyder, and Neil Gaiman, joining a rich heritage of stories about children with a secret 'room of their own.'" Publ Wkly

O'Dell, Scott

★ **Island** of the Blue Dolphins; illustrated by Ted Lewin. 50th anniversary ed.; Houghton Mifflin Books for Children 2010 177p il $22

Grades: 5 6 7 8   **Fic**

1. Native Americans -- Fiction 2. Wilderness survival

-- Fiction

ISBN 978-0-547-42483-5; 0-547-42483-3

A reissue of the newly illustrated edition published 1990; first published 1960

Awarded the Newbery Medal, 1961

Left alone on a beautiful but isolated island off the coast of California, a young Indian girl spends eighteen years, not only merely surviving through her enormous courage and self-reliance, but also finding a measure of happiness in her solitary life.

The edition illustrated by Ted Lewin "features twelve full-page, full-color watercolors in purple and blue hues that are appropriate to the island setting. This handsome gift-edition version includes a new introduction by Lois Lowry to commemorate the book's fiftieth anniversary." Horn Book Guide

Sing down the moon. Houghton Mifflin 1970 137p hardcover o.p. pa $6.99

Grades: 5 6 7 8   **Fic**

1. Navajo Indians -- Fiction

ISBN 0-395-10919-1; 978-0-547-40632-9 pa; 0-547-40632-0 pa

A Newbery Medal honor book, 1971

"There is a poetic sonority of style, a sense of identification, and a note of indomitable courage and stoicism that is touching and impressive." Saturday Rev

Streams to the river, river to the sea; a novel of Sacagawea. Houghton Mifflin 1986 191p hardcover o.p. pa $6.99

Grades: 5 6 7 8   **Fic**

1. Interpreters 2. Guides (Persons) 3. Native Americans -- Fiction

ISBN 0-395-40430-4; 0-618-96642-0 pa

LC 86-936

"An informative and involving choice for American history students and pioneer-adventure readers." Bull Cent Child Books

Zia. Houghton Mifflin 1976 179p hardcover o.p. pa $6.95

Grades: 5 6 7 8   **Fic**

1. Native Americans -- Fiction 2. Christian missions -- Fiction

ISBN 0-395-24393-9; 978-0-547-40633-6 pa; 0-547-40633-9 pa

LC 75-44156

"Zia is an excellent story in its own right, written in a clear, quiet, and reflective style which is in harmony with the plot and characterization." SLJ

Obed, Ellen Bryan, 1944-

★ **Twelve** kinds of ice; by Ellen Bryan Obed; illustrated by Barbara McClintock. Houghton Mifflin Books for Children 2012 p. cm.

Grades: 1 2 3 4   **Fic**

1. Ice -- Fiction 2. Winter -- Fiction 3. Family life -- Fiction 4. Ice skating -- Fiction

ISBN 9780618891290

LC 2011046417

This book presents a "memoir of [Ellen Bryan] Obed's dreamy childhood in Maine, built around the 12 kinds of ice that served as successive signposts of the advancing

season." (New York Times Book Review) "This homage to rural winter celebrates the gradual freezing of barn buckets and fields, the happy heights of ice-skating season, and the inevitable spring thaw." (Publishers Weekly)

Odyssey, Shawn Thomas

The **Wizard** of Dark Street; an Oona Crate mystery. Egmont USA 2011 352p $16.99

Grades: 5 6 7   **Fic**

1. Mystery fiction 2. Magic -- Fiction 3. Uncles -- Fiction 4. Orphans -- Fiction 5. Witchcraft -- Fiction 6. Apprentices -- Fiction

ISBN 978-1-60684-143-3; 1-60684-143-2

LC 2011-02496

In 1877, in an enchantment shop on the last of the Faerie roads linking New York City to the Land of the Fey, just after twelve-year-old Oona opts to relinquish her apprenticeship to her uncle, the Wizard, and become a detective, her uncle is stabbed, testing her skills.

"Upbeat in tone, this delight is an excellent blend of fantasy and mystery with a variety of suspicious characters and enough red herrings to keep the reader guessing all the way to the end." Booklist

Oertel, Andreas

The **Archaeolojesters**. Lobster Press 2010 192p pa $10.95

Grades: 4 5 6   **Fic**

1. Antiquities -- Fiction

ISBN 978-1-897550-83-0 pa

"A group of kids make history, literally, after they carve Egyptian-seeming hieroglyphics into clay and allow the ancient artifact to be discovered in the river near their small town in Manitoba, Canada." Booklist

Okimoto, Jean Davies

Maya and the cotton candy boy. Endicott and Hugh 2011 $16.99; pa $9.99

Grades: 4 5 6 7   **Fic**

1. School stories 2. Siblings -- Fiction 3. Immigrants -- Fiction

ISBN 978-0-9823167-4-0; 0-9823167-4-7; 978-0-9823167-5-7 pa; 0-9823167-5-5 pa

Newly arrived from Kazakhstan, twelve-year-old Maya Alazova resents the way her mother babies her brother, but when she leaves her English Language Learner program for mainstream classes and has to deal with a boy, a bully, and conflict at home, she finds her brother can help with their new culture in ways their parents can't.

"Maya tells her story well, and observant readers will come away with a better understanding of the sacrifices made by similar families." SLJ

Oliver, Lauren

★ **Liesl** & Po; illustrated by Kei Acedera. Harper 2011 307p il $16.99

Grades: 4 5 6 7   **Fic**

1. Ghost stories 2. Fantasy fiction 3. Magic -- Fiction 4. Bereavement -- Fiction

ISBN 978-0-06-201451-1; 0-06-201451-X

Liesl lives in a tiny attic bedroom, locked away by her cruel stepmother. Her only friends are the shadows and the mice—until one night a ghost appears from the darkness. It is Po, who comes from the Other Side. That same night, an alchemist's apprentice, Will, accidentally bungles an important delivery. He switches a box containing the most powerful magic in the world with one containing something decidedly less remarkable.

This is a "charming, insightful fantasy. . . . This original fairy tale, told by a wise and humorous omniscient narrator and peopled with broadly drawn but instantly recognizable characters, avoids sentimentality to show the magic of accepting loss without letting go and finding joy in the lives left behind." Booklist

★ The **spindlers**; Lauren Oliver; illustrated by Iacopo Bruno. 1st ed. Harper 2012 246 p. ill. (hardcover) $16.99
Grades: 4 5 6   **Fic**
1. Monsters -- Juvenile fiction 2. Fantasy fiction -- Juvenile fiction 3. Brothers and sisters -- Juvenile fiction 4. Fantasy 5. Soul -- Fiction 6. Brothers and sisters -- Fiction
ISBN 0061978086; 9780061978081
LC 2012009698

This children's fantasy novel, by Lauren Oliver, is about a young girl who travels to a fantasy realm to rescue her younger brother from monsters. "When Liza's brother, Patrick, changes overnight, Liza knows exactly what has happened: The spindlers have gotten to him and stolen his soul. . . . To rescue Patrick, Liza must go Below, armed with little more than her wits and a broom. There, she uncovers a vast world populated with . . . terrible dangers." (Publisher's note)

Oppel, Kenneth
Silverwing. Simon & Schuster Bks. for Young Readers 1997 217p hardcover o.p. pa $6.99
Grades: 5 6 7 8   **Fic**
1. Bats -- Fiction
ISBN 0-689-81529-8; 1-4169-4998-4 pa
LC 97-10977

When a newborn bat named Shade but sometimes called "Runt" becomes separated from his colony during migration, he grows in ways that prepare him for even greater journeys

"Oppel's bats are fully developed characters who, if not quite cuddly, will certainly earn readers' sympathy and respect. In Silverwing the author has created an intriguing microcosm of rival species, factions, and religions." Horn Book
Other titles in this series are:
Sunwing (2000)
Firewing (2003)
Darkwing (2007)

Orlev, Uri
The **man** from the other side; translated from the Hebrew by Hillel Halkin. Puffin Books 1995 186p pa $6.99
Grades: 5 6 7 8   **Fic**
1. Jews -- Poland -- Fiction 2. Holocaust, 1933-1945 -- Fiction 3. World War, 1939-1945 -- Fiction
ISBN 0-14-037088-9; 978-0-14-037088-1
LC 94-30189

Living on the outskirts of the Warsaw Ghetto during World War II, fourteen-year-old Marek and his grandparents shelter a Jewish man in the days before the Jewish uprising

"This is a story of individual bravery and national shame that highlights just how hopeless was the fate of the Warsaw Jews as they fought alone and heroically against the Nazi war machine." SLJ

★ The **song** of the whales; translated by Hillel Halkin. Houghton Mifflin Books for Children 2010 108p $16
Grades: 5 6 7 8   **Fic**
1. Jews -- Fiction 2. Dreams -- Fiction 3. Old age -- Fiction 4. Family life -- Fiction 5. Grandfathers -- Fiction
ISBN 978-0-547-25752-5; 0-547-25752-X
LC 2009-49720

At age eight, Mikha'el knows he is different from other boys, but over the course of three years as he helps his parents care for his elderly grandfather in Jerusalem, Grandpa teaches Mikha'el to use the gift they share of making other people's dreams sweeter.

This is "the sort of story that operates on many different levels. . . . With a clean sense that less is more, Orlev has crafted a sweetly mysterious and quietly moving read." Booklist

Orr, Wendy
Lost! A dog called Bear; illustrations by Susan Boase. Henry Holt 2011 103p il (Rainbow Street Shelter) $15.99
Grades: 2 3 4   **Fic**
1. Dogs -- Fiction 2. Moving -- Fiction 3. Divorce -- Fiction 4. Lost and found possessions -- Fiction
ISBN 978-0-8050-8931-8; 0-8050-8931-4
LC 2010029886

When Logan's dog runs away as he and his mother are moving to a new home after his parents separate, a girl named Hannah, who longs for a dog of her own, finds him.

"The book is well designed for readers moving up to chapter books, with its short sentences, well-spaced lines of type, and attractive illustrations. Expressing emotions through subtle physical cues, Boase's shaded pencil drawings depict both people and dogs with grace and sensitivity." Booklist

Missing! A cat called Buster; illustrations by Susan Boase. Henry Holt and Company 2011 116p il (Rainbow Street Shelter) $15.99; pa $5.99
Grades: 2 3 4   **Fic**
1. Cats -- Fiction 2. Pets -- Fiction 3. Loss (Psychology) -- Fiction 4. Lost and found possessions -- Fiction
ISBN 978-0-8050-8932-5; 0-8050-8932-2; 978-0-8050-9382-7 pa; 0-8050-9382-6 pa
LC 2010044786

After his pet rabbit dies, Josh feels sad and does not want to own another pet until an elderly neighbor's cat goes missing.

"This effort sympathetically, if briefly, deals with some complex issues, including the responsibilities of pet ownership, death and aging, but always within the framework of an optimistic, childlike perspective appropriate for the target audience. . . . Attractive black-and-white full and half-page sketches, one or two per chapter, offer some visual interest as well. This early chapter book with plenty of heart and a bit of suspense will appeal to young pet lovers." Kirkus

Mokie & Bik; [by] Wendy Orr; illustrations by Jonathan Bean. Henry Holt 2007 72p il $15.95
Grades: 2 3 4   **Fic**
1. Twins -- Fiction 2. Siblings -- Fiction 3. Boats and

boating -- Fiction
ISBN 978-0-8050-7979-1; 0-8050-7979-3
LC 2006011150

For two rambunctious twins, living on a boat means always being underfoot or overboard

"Orr's colorful use of language brings energy to the story. The many crosshatch drawings . . . are often graceful and always appealing." Booklist

Another title about Mokie & Bik is:
Mokie & Bik go to sea (2008)

Mokie & Bik go to sea; illustrations by Jonathan Bean. Henry Holt and Company 2010 75p il $16.95
Grades: 2 3 4   **Fic**
1. Twins -- Fiction 2. Siblings -- Fiction 3. Boats and boating -- Fiction
ISBN 978-0-8050-8174-9; 0-8050-8174-7
LC 2007027590

With their father home from the sea, the rambunctious twins Mokie and Bik make the Bullfrog shipshape for a voyage out to sea, where they make friends with a scaredy-seal, save a runaway boat, and keep track of Waggles.

"Written in a whimsical style that borders on poetry. . . . Frequent black-and-white illustrations add to the zaniness of the fast-paced story." SLJ

Oswald, Nancy
Nothing here but stones; a Jewish pioneer story. [by] Nancy Oswald. Henry Holt 2004 215p $16.95
Grades: 5 6 7 8   **Fic**
1. Jews -- Fiction 2. Immigrants -- Fiction 3. Jews -- United States 4. Frontier and pioneer life -- Fiction 5. Jews -- Colorado -- Juvenile fiction 6. Frontier and pioneer life -- Colorado
ISBN 0-8050-7465-1
LC 2003-56969

In 1882, ten-year-old Emma and her family, along with other Russian Jewish immigrants, arrive in Cotopaxi, Colorado, where they face inhospitable conditions as they attempt to start an agricultural colony, and lonely Emma is comforted by the horse whose life she saved

"This well-paced, vivid account should capture readers' attention." SLJ

Oz, Amos
★ **Suddenly** in the depths of the forest; translated from the Hebrew by Sondra Silverston. Harcourt 2011 134p $15.99
Grades: 4 5 6 7   **Fic**
1. Fables 2. Animals -- Fiction
ISBN 978-0-547-55153-1; 0-547-55153-3
LC 2011-08664

In a gray and gloomy village, all of the animals—from dogs and cats to fish and snails—disappeared years before. No one talks about it and no one knows why, though everyone agrees that the village has been cursed. But when two children see a fish—a tiny one and just for a second—they become determined to unravel the mystery of where the animals have gone.

"In this swiftly moving fable . . . Oz creates palpable tension with a repetitive, almost hypnotic rhythm and lyrical language that twists a discussion-provoking morality tale into something much more enchanting." Booklist

Palacio, R. J.
★ **Wonder**; by R.J. Palacio. Alfred A. Knopf 2012 315 p.
Grades: 3 4 5 6   **Fic**
1. Middle schools 2. Interpersonal relations 3. Birth defects -- Fiction 4. Schools -- Fiction 5. Self-acceptance -- Fiction
ISBN 9780375869020; 9780375899881; 9780375969027
LC 2011027133

In this book, "[a]fter being homeschooled for years, Auggie Pullman is about to start fifth grade, but he's worried: How will he fit into middle-school life when he looks so different from everyone else? Auggie has had 27 surgeries to correct facial anomalies he was born with, but he still has a face that has earned him such cruel nicknames as Freak, Freddy Krueger, Gross-out and Lizard face. . . . Palacio divides the novel into eight parts, interspersing Auggie's first-person narrative with the voices of family members and classmates, . . . expanding the story beyond Auggie's viewpoint and demonstrating that Auggie's arrival at school doesn't test only him, it affects everyone in the community." (Kirkus)

Palatini, Margie
Geek Chic; the Zoey zone. Katherine Tegen Books 2008 184p $10.99; lib bdg $14.89
Grades: 3 4 5   **Fic**
1. School stories
ISBN 978-0-06-113898-0; 0-06-113898-3; 978-0-06-113899-7 lib bdg; 0-06-113899-1 lib bdg

A contemporary Cinderella story about Zoey, 10, who desperately needs a fairy godmother to give her a makeover and teach her about style if she is ever going to make it into the cool crowd in the lunchroom.

"This amalgamation of graphic novel and chapter book cleverly integrates wrinkled-looking notes, varied typefaces, wacky line drawings, and movie countdowns with straightforward prose to tell the funny if farfetched tale." SLJ

Paley, Jane
Hooper finds a family; a Hurricane Katrina dog's survival tale. Harper 2011 137p il $15.99
Grades: 4 5 6   **Fic**
1. Dogs -- Fiction 2. Hurricane Katrina, 2005 -- Fiction
ISBN 978-0-06-201103-9; 0-06-201103-0
LC 2011002088

Jimmy, a yellow Labrador puppy, is separated from his Lake Charles, Louisiana, family and survives the horrors of Hurricane Katrina on his own before being rescued and taken to New York City, where he tries to fit in with a new family and the many neighborhood dogs, and accept his new name.

"A harsh but ultimately heartwarming story about moving forward after trauma and loss by making space for new loves ones and new possibilities." Kirkus

Papademetriou, Lisa
Chasing normal; [by] Lisa Papademetriou. Hyperion Books for Children 2008 193p $15.99; pa $5.99
Grades: 3 4 5 6   **Fic**
1. Cousins -- Fiction 2. Family life -- Fiction 3.

Grandmothers -- Fiction
ISBN 978-1-4231-0340-0; 1-4231-0340-8; 978-1-4231-0341-7 pa; 1-4231-0341-6 pa

LC 2007022418

When her mean, grouchy grandmother in Texas has a heart attack and she and father go to help, twelve-year-old Mieka meets her cousins' family and wishes for their "normal" type of life.

This "is solid fare for readers looking for a family-centered story and a protagonist who is smart, funny, and instantly recognizable." Booklist

Paratore, Coleen

Sunny Holiday; [by] Coleen Murtagh Paratore. Scholastic Press 2009 160p $15.99; pa $5.99
Grades: 2 3 4   Fic
1. African Americans -- Fiction 2. Mother-daughter relationship -- Fiction
ISBN 978-0-545-07579-4; 0-545-07579-3; 978-0-545-07588-6 pa; 0-545-07588-2 pa

LC 2008009786

Spunky third-grader Sunny Holiday tries to make the best out of every situation, and even though her father is in prison, she and her mother count their blessings and manage to find joy in every day

"Difficult situations are handled gently, but realistically. . . . The text is not difficult and includes some fun images for abstract ideas." SLJ

Sweet and sunny; by Coleen Murtagh Paratore. Scholastic Press 2010 178p $16.99
Grades: 2 3 4   Fic
1. School stories 2. Holidays -- Fiction 3. Valentine's Day -- Fiction 4. African Americans -- Fiction 5. Mother-daughter relationship -- Fiction
ISBN 978-0-545-07582-4; 0-545-07582-3

LC 2009-7162

Despite facing a host of problems, old and new, optimistic third-grader Sunny continues her quest to create a national Kid's Day and improve other holidays, especially the upcoming Valentine's Day, while bringing joy to those around her.

"A satisfying if predictable finale lives up to the book's title." Publ Wkly

Park, Barbara

Junie B. Jones and her big fat mouth; illustrated by Denise Brunkus. Random House 1993 69p il lib bdg $11.99; pa $4.99
Grades: 1 2 3   Fic
1. School stories
ISBN 0-679-94407-9 lib bdg; 0-679-84407-4 pa

LC 92-50957

When her kindergarten class has Job Day, Junie B. goes through much confusion and excitement before deciding on the "bestest" job of all

"Brunkus' energetic drawings pick up the slapstick action and the spunky comic hero." Booklist

Other titles about Junie B. Jones are:
Junie B., first grader: Aloha-ha-ha (2006)
Junie B., first grader (at last!) (2001)
Junie B., first grader: boo . . . and I mean it! (2003)
Junie B., first grader: boss of lunch (2002)
Junie B., first grader: cheater pants (2003)

Junie B., first grader: dumb bunny (2007)
Junie B., first grader: jingle bells, Batman smells! (p.s. so does May) (2005)
Junie B., first grader: one-man band (2003)
Junie B., first grader: shipwrecked (2003)
Junie B., first grader: toothless wonder (2002)
Junie B. Jones and a little monkey business (1993)
Junie B. Jones and some sneaky peeky spying (1994)
Junie B. Jones and that meanie Jim's birthday (1996)
Junie B. Jones and the mushy gushy valentine (1999)
Junie B. Jones and the stupid smelly bus (1992)
Junie B. Jones and the yucky blucky fruitcake (1995)
Junie B. Jones has a monster under her bed (1997)
Junie B. Jones has a peep in her pocket (2000)
Junie B. Jones is a beauty shop guy (1998)
Junie B. Jones is a graduation girl (2001)
Junie B. Jones is a party animal (1997)
Junie B. Jones is (almost) a flower girl (1999)
Junie B. Jones is Captain Field Day (2000)
Junie B. Jones is not a crook (1997)
Junie B. Jones loves handsome Warren (1996)
Junie B. Jones smells something fishy (1998)

Mick Harte was here. Apple Soup Bks. 1995 89p hardcover o.p. pa $4.99
Grades: 4 5 6   Fic
1. Death -- Fiction 2. Siblings -- Fiction
ISBN 0-679-87088-1; 0-679-88203-0 pa

LC 94-27272

Thirteen-year-old Phoebe recalls her younger brother Mick and his death in a bicycle accident

"The author is adept at portraying the stages of grief and the effects of this sudden tragedy on the family. The book's tone of sadness is mitigated by humor, reassurance, and hope." SLJ

Park, Linda Sue, 1960-

Project Mulberry; a novel. Clarion 2005 225p $16; pa $6.99
Grades: 5 6 7 8   Fic
1. Korean Americans -- Fiction
ISBN 0-618-47786-1; 0-440-42163-2 pa

LC 2004-18159

While working on a project for an afterschool club, Julia, a Korean American girl, and her friend Patrick learn not just about silkworms, but also about tolerance, prejudice, friendship, patience, and more. Between the chapters are short dialogues between the author and main character about the writing of the book

"The unforgettable family and friendship story, the quiet, almost unspoken racism, and the excitement of the science make this a great cross-curriculum title." Booklist

★ A **single** shard. Clarion Bks. 2001 152p $15; pa $6.99
Grades: 5 6 7 8   Fic
1. Pottery 2. Pottery -- Fiction
ISBN 0-395-97827-0; 0-440-41851-8 pa

LC 00-43102

Awarded the Newbery Medal, 2002

Tree-ear, a thirteen-year-old orphan in medieval Korea, lives under a bridge in a potters' village, and longs to learn how to throw the delicate celadon ceramics himself

"This quiet, but involving, story draws readers into a very different time and place.... A well-crafted novel with an unusual setting." Booklist

Storm warning. Scholastic 2010 190p (The 39 clues) $12.99
Grades: 4 5 6 7   **Fic**
  1. Ciphers -- Fiction
ISBN 978-0-545-06049-3; 0-545-06049-4

Amy and Dan hit the high seas as they follow the trail of some infamous ancestors to track down a long lost treasure. However, the real prize isn't hidden in a chest. It's the discovery of the Madrigals' most dangerous secret and, even more shockingly, the true identity of the mysterious man in black.

Trust no one; Linda Sue Park. 1st ed. Scholastic Press 2013 190 p. (reinforced) $12.99
Grades: 4 5 6 7   **Fic**
  1. Spy stories -- Juvenile fiction 2. Mystery fiction -- Juvenile fiction
ISBN 0545298431; 9780545298438
                   LC 2012939109

This is the fifth installment of Linda Sue Park's Cahills vs. Vespers series. Here, "Amy and Dan discover that one of their friends is a spy for the Vespers, a group of evil agents who kidnapped seven of their family members. But which friend is it? The shocking secrets continue when the Cahill siblings finally figure out the Vespers' real plan, and it's much worse than they originally thought." (Owl Magazine)

★ **When** my name was Keoko. Clarion Bks. 2002 199p $16; pa $6.99
Grades: 5 6 7 8   **Fic**
  1. Courage 2. Patriotism 3. Military occupation 4. Family life -- Korea 5. World War, 1939-1945 -- Fiction 6. World War, 1939-1945 -- Underground movements -- Korea 7. Korea -- History -- Japanese occupation, 1910-1945 -- Juvenile fiction
ISBN 0-618-13335-6; 0-440-41944-1 pa
                   LC 2001-32487

With national pride and occasional fear, a brother and sister face the increasingly oppressive occupation of Korea by Japan during World War II, which threatens to suppress Korean culture entirely

"Park is a masterful prose stylist, and her characters are developed beautifully. She excels at making traditional Korean culture accessible to Western readers." Voice Youth Advocates

Includes bibliographical references

Parker, Marjorie Hodgson
  David and the Mighty Eighth; a British boy and a Texas airman in World War II. by Marjorie Hodgson Parker; illustrated by Mark Postlethwaite. Bright Sky Press 2007 176p il $17.95
Grades: 4 5 6 7   **Fic**
  1. World War, 1939-1945 -- Fiction
ISBN 978-1-931721-93-6; 1-931721-93-9
                   LC 2007025999

When, during the London Blitz, he and his older sister are evacuated to go live on their grandparents' East Anglia farm, a young English boy finds it difficult to adjust to his new life until the arrival of the pilots and crews of the U.S.

Eight Air Force at nearby airfields brings excitement, friendship, and hope for the future.

This is an "exciting novel, based on a true story.... The story is framed by extensive historical notes.... Spacious type, thick paper, and an occasional black-and-white drawings make this an appealing package all around." Booklist

Parkinson, Siobhan
  Blue like Friday. Roaring Brook Press 2008 160p $16.95
Grades: 4 5 6 7   **Fic**
  1. Family life -- Fiction 2. Synesthesia -- Fiction 3. Missing persons -- Fiction
ISBN 978-1-59643-340-3; 1-59643-340-X

When Olivia helps her quirky friend Hal, whose synesthesia causes him to experience everything in colors, with a prank intended to get rid of Hal's potential stepfather, there are unexpected consequences, including the disappearance of Hal's mother.

"Parkinson creates a warm, moving story of real families facing real problems.... The economy of her prose is admirable; all the characters are well drawn." Booklist

Parnell, Robyn
  The **mighty** Quinn; by Robyn Parnell; illustrated by Aaron and Katie DeYoe. 1st ed. Scarletta Press 2013 263 p. ill. (paperback) $10.95
Grades: 4 5 6 7   **Fic**
  1. Bullies -- Juvenile fiction 2. Friendship -- Juvenile fiction 3. School stories -- Juvenile fiction 4. Bullies -- Fiction 5. Schools -- Fiction 6. Friendship -- Fiction
ISBN 1938063104; 9781938063107
                   LC 2012031518

In this story, by Robyn Parnell, "Quinn Andrews-Lee ... faces a dismal school year. His little sister outshines him ... , he yearns for a service award his peers disdain, and charismatic bigot Matt Barker's goal in life is to torment Quinn. . . . When Quinn reports an act of vandalism, he is accused of injuring Matt. . . . A free-spirited new kid in Quinn's class, helps Quinn deduce who hurt Matt, but Matt would probably die . . . before admitting the truth." (Publisher's note)

Paros, Jennifer
  Violet Bing and the Grand House. Viking Childrens Books 2007 105p il $14.99
Grades: 1 2 3 4   **Fic**
  1. Aunts -- Fiction 2. Houses -- Fiction 3. Friendship -- Fiction
ISBN 978-0-670-06151-8; 0-670-06151-4
                   LC 2006-10199

Very definite in her likes and dislikes, seven (nearly eight) year-old Violet Bing goes to stay with her unusual Great-aunt Astrid in the Grand House

"The writing is exquisitely understated.... The author's pen-and-ink illustrations complement this fine, subtle early chapter book perfectly." SLJ

Parry, Rosanne
  ★ **Heart** of a shepherd; [by] Rosanne Parry. Random House Children's Books 2009 161p lib bdg $18.99; $15.99
Grades: 4 5 6 7   **Fic**
  1. Ranch life -- Fiction 2. Family life -- Fiction 3.

Christian life -- Fiction 4. Iraq War, 2003- -- Fiction
ISBN 0-375-84802-9; 978-0-375-94802-2 lib bdg;
0-375-94802-3 lib bdg; 978-0-375-84802-5

         LC 2007-48094

Ignatius 'Brother' Alderman, nearly twelve, promises to
help his grandparents keep the family's Oregon ranch the
same while his brothers are away and his father is deployed
to Iraq, but as he comes to accept the inevitability of change,
he also sees the man he is meant to be

There is "more action than introspection afoot, with sibling tensions, a wildfire, and the grandfather's death along
the journey. It's refreshing . . . to find a protagonist with his
eyes and heart open to positive adult examples . . . and who
matches his mettle to theirs." Bull Cent Child Books

Partridge, Elizabeth

   ★ **Dogtag** summer. Bloomsbury Books for Young
Readers 2011 226p $16.99

Grades: 4 5 6 7   Fic

   1. Hippies -- Fiction 2. Adoption -- Fiction 3. Family
life -- Fiction 4. Vietnamese Americans -- Fiction 5.
Racially mixed people -- Fiction 6. Vietnam War, 1961-
1975 -- Fiction

   ISBN 978-1-59990-183-1; 1-59990-183-8

         LC 2010-25515

In the summer of 1980 before she starts junior high
school in Santa Rosa, California, Tracy, who was adopted
from Vietnam when she was six years old, finds an old
ammo box with a dog tag and picture that bring up painful
memories for both her Vietnam-veteran father and her.

"This gripping yet tender coming-of-age story reveals
multiple nuanced perspectives of the Vietnam War and its
aftermath. . . . Powerful historical fiction." Publ Wkly

Pastis, Stephan

   Timmy failure; mistakes were made. Stephan Pastis.
Candlewick Press 2013 304 p. (reinforced) $14.99

Grades: 4 5 6 7   Fic

   1. Mystery graphic novels 2. Picture books for children

   ISBN 0763660507; 9780763660505

         LC 2012942409

This children's graphic novel focuses on Timmy and his
detective agency Total Failure Inc. Questions abound: "Who
stole the Halloween candy of Timmy's classmate Gabe?
Who is the mysterious girl Timmy refuses to discuss? Why
is no one fazed that Timmy has a pet polar bear named Total?" (Publishers Weekly)

Paterson, John

   ★ The **Flint** Heart; a fairy story. freely abriged from
Eden Phillpott's 1910 fantasy; by Katherine and John Paterson; illustrated by John Rocco. Candlewick Press 2011
288p il $19.99

Grades: 3 4 5 6   Fic

   1. Fairy tales

   ISBN 978-0-7636-4712-4; 0-7636-4712-8

         LC 2010048225

An ambitious Stone Age man demands a talisman that
will harden his heart, allowing him to take control of his
tribe. Against his better judgment, the tribe's magic man
creates the Flint Heart, but the cruelty of it causes the destruction of the tribe. Thousands of years later, the talisman
reemerges to corrupt a kindly farmer, an innocent fairy creature, and a familial badger.

"The tale will make an excellent read-aloud. . . . The
Patersons have done a lovely job updating and abridging this
tale for today's readers. . . . Rocco's fantastic illustrations
alone make this edition worth purchasing." SLJ

Paterson, Katherine

   ★ **Bread** and roses, too. Clarion Books 2006 275p
$16; pa $6.99

Grades: 5 6 7 8   Fic

   1. Strikes -- Fiction 2. Immigrants -- Fiction

   ISBN 978-0-618-65479-6; 0-618-65479-8; 978-0-547-
07651-5 pa; 0-547-07651-7 pa

         LC 2005-31702

Jake and Rosa, two children, form an unlikely friendship
as they try to survive and understand the 1912 Bread and
Roses strike of mill workers in Lawrence, Massachusetts.

"Paterson has skillfully woven true events and real historical figures into the fictional story and created vivid settings, clearly drawn characters, and a strong sense of the
hardship and injustice faced by the mostly immigrant mill
workers." SLJ

   ★ **Bridge** to Terabithia; illustrated by Donna Diamond.
Crowell 1977 128p il $15.99; lib bdg $16.89; pa $5.99

Grades: 4 5 6 7   Fic

   1. Death -- Fiction 2. Friendship -- Fiction

   ISBN 0-690-01359-0; 0-690-04635-9 lib bdg; 0-06-
440184-7 pa

         LC 77-2221

Awarded the Newbery Medal, 1978

The life of Jess, a ten-year-old boy in rural Virginia
expands when he becomes friends with a newcomer who
subsequently meets an untimely death trying to reach their
hideaway, Terabithia, during a storm

"Jess and his family are magnificently characterized; the
book abounds in descriptive vignettes, humorous sidelights
on the clash of cultures, and realistic depictions of rural
school life." Horn Book

   Come sing, Jimmy Jo. Lodestar Bks. 1985 193p hardcover o.p. pa $5.99

Grades: 5 6 7 8   Fic

   1. Family life -- Fiction 2. Country music -- Fiction

   ISBN 0-525-67167-6; 0-14-037397-7 pa

         LC 84-21123

When his family becomes a successful country music
group and makes him a featured singer, eleven-year-old
James has to deal with big changes in all aspects of his life,
even his name

"What Katherine Paterson does so well is catch the cadence of the locale without sounding fake. There isn't a false
note in her diction. She has created a West Virginian world
that is entirely believable: homely, honest, goodhearted. .
. . This book is James's personal inward journey, and it is
deeply felt." Christ Sci Monit

   ★ The **great** Gilly Hopkins. Crowell 1978 148p
$15.99; lib bdg $16.89; pa $5.99

Grades: 5 6 7 8   Fic

   1. Foster home care -- Fiction

   ISBN 0-690-03837-2; 0-690-03838-0 lib bdg; 0-06-
440201-0 pa

         LC 77-27075

A Newbery Medal honor book, 1979

"A well-structured story, [this] has vitality of writing style, natural dialogue, deep insight in characterization, and a keen sense of the fluid dynamics in human relationships." Bull Cent Child Books

Jip; his story. Lodestar Bks. 1996 181p hardcover o.p. pa $6.99

Grades: 5 6 7 8   Fic

1. Slavery -- Fiction 2. African Americans -- Fiction 3. Racially mixed people -- Fiction

ISBN 0-525-67543-4; 0-14-240411-X pa

LC 96-2680

While living on a Vermont poor farm during 1855 and 1856, Jip learns that his mother was a runaway slave, and that his father, the plantation owner, plans to reclaim him as property

"This historically accurate story is full of revelations and surprises, one of which is the return appearance of the heroine of Lyddie.... The taut, extremely readable narrative and its tender depictions of friendship and loyalty provide first-rate entertainment." Publ Wkly

★ **Lyddie**. Lodestar Bks. 1991 182p $17.99; pa $6.99

Grades: 5 6 7 8 9   Fic

1. Factories -- Fiction

ISBN 0-525-67338-5; 0-14-240254-0 pa

LC 90-42944

Impoverished Vermont farm girl Lyddie Worthen is determined to gain her independence by becoming a factory worker in Lowell, Massachusetts, in the 1840s

"Not only does the book contain a riveting plot, engaging characters, and a splendid setting, but the language—graceful, evocative, and rhythmic—incorporates the rural speech patterns of Lyddie's folk, the simple Quaker expressions of the farm neighbors, and the lilt of fellow mill girl Bridget's Irish brogue.... A superb story of grit, determination, and personal growth." Horn Book

★ **Park's** quest. Lodestar Bks. 1988 148p hardcover o.p. pa $5.99

Grades: 5 6 7 8   Fic

1. Farm life -- Fiction 2. Vietnamese Americans -- Fiction

ISBN 0-14-034262-1 pa

LC 87-32422

Eleven-year-old Park makes some startling discoveries when he travels to his grandfather's farm in Virginia to learn about his father who died in the Vietnam War and meets a Vietnamese-American girl named Thanh

The author "confronts the complexity, the ambiguity, of the war and the emotions of those it involved with an honesty that young readers are sure to recognize and appreciate." N Y Times Book Rev

The **same** stuff as stars. Clarion Bks. 2002 242p $15

Grades: 5 6 7 8   Fic

ISBN 0-618-24744-0

LC 2002-3967

When Angel's self-absorbed mother leaves her and her younger brother with their poor great-grandmother, the eleven-year-old girl worries not only about her mother and brother, her imprisoned father, the frail old woman, but also about a mysterious man who begins sharing with her the wonder of the stars

"Paterson's deft hand at characterization, her insight into the human soul, and her glorious prose make this book one to rejoice over." Voice Youth Advocates

Patneaude, David

A **piece** of the sky; [by] David Patneaude; [cover illustration by Layne Johnson] Albert Whitman 2007 178p il $15.95

Grades: 5 6 7 8   Fic

1. Meteorites -- Fiction 2. Mountaineering -- Fiction

ISBN 978-0-8075-6536-0

LC 2006023529

Fourteen-year-old Russell, his friend Phoebe, and her brother Isaac must find a legendary meteor in the Oregon mountains before it is exploited

"This old-fashioned adventure story has contemporary appeal." Booklist

Patron, Susan

Behind the masks; the diary of Angeline Reddy. Susan Patron. Scholastic 2012 293 p. ill., map

Grades: 5 6 7 8 9   Fic

1. Mystery fiction 2. Diaries -- Fiction 3. Thieves -- Fiction 4. Gold mines and mining -- Fiction 5. Frontier and pioneer life -- California -- Fiction 6. Lawyers -- Fiction 7. Mystery and detective stories 8. Robbers and outlaws -- Fiction

ISBN 9780545304375

LC 2011023826

"[T]his Dear America series title [is] set in Bodie, California, in 1880. Fourteen-year-old diarist and would-be dramatist Angeline Reddy does not believe her father, criminal lawyer Patrick Reddy, has been murdered. Convinced his disappearance is purposeful, Angie investigates his 'demise' and tries to bring him back to their rough-and-tumble mining community. Assisted by friends, a dashing young Wells Fargo clerk, and the members of a local theater troupe, . . . Angie offers a revealing look at frontier life "especially preoccupations with thespian entertainments, racial and social prejudices, and vigilante justice."(Booklist)

★ The **higher** power of Lucky; with illustrations by Matt Phelan. Atheneum Books for Young Readers 2006 134p il $16.95; pa $6.99

Grades: 4 5 6   Fic

1. Runaway children -- Fiction

ISBN 978-1-4169-0194-5; 1-4169-0194-9; 978-1-4169-7557-1 pa; 1-4169-7557-8 pa

LC 2005-21767

Awarded the Newbery Medal, 2007

Fearing that her legal guardian plans to abandon her to return to France, ten-year-old aspiring scientist Lucky Trimble determines to run away while also continuing to seek the Higher Power that will bring stability to her life

"Patron's plotting is as tight as her characters are endearing. Lucky is a true heroine." Booklist

Other books about Lucky are:

Lucky breaks (2009)

Lucky for good (2011)

Maybe yes, maybe no, maybe maybe; illustrated by Abigail Halpin. Aladdin Paperbacks 2009 107p il pa $5.99

Grades: 3 4 5   **Fic**

1. Moving -- Fiction 2. Sisters -- Fiction
ISBN 978-1-4169-6176-5 pa; 1-4169-6176-3 pa
First published 1993 by Orchard Books

When her hardworking mother decides to move, eight-year-old PK uses her imagination and storytelling to help her older and younger sisters adjust

Patt, Beverly

★ **Best** friends forever; a World War II scrapbook. with illustrations by Shula Klinger. Marshall Cavendish 2010 92p il $17.99

Grades: 5 6 7 8   **Fic**

1. Friendship -- Fiction 2. World War, 1939-1945 -- Fiction 3. Japanese Americans -- Evacuation and relocation, 1942-1945 -- Fiction
ISBN 978-0-7614-5577-6; 0-7614-5577-9
                                        LC 2008-20875

Fourteen-year-old Louise keeps a scrapbook detailing the events in her life after her best friend, Dottie, a Japanese-American girl, and her family are sent to a relocation camp during World War II.

"If the drama of the girls separation isn't enough, a romantic subplot and the antics of Dottie's goofy dog (living with Louise in her absence) will surely keep young readers interested. This heartwarming tale of steadfast friendship makes a wonderful access point for learning more about World War II and Japanese internment." SLJ

Includes bibliographical references

Patten, E. J.

Return to Exile; illustrated by John Rocco. Simon & Schuster 2011 512p (The Hunter chronicles) $16.99

Grades: 5 6 7 8   **Fic**

1. Fantasy fiction 2. Uncles -- Fiction 3. Monsters -- Fiction
ISBN 978-1-4424-2032-8; 1-4424-2032-4; 978-1-4169-8259-3 e-book
                                        LC 2010053480

"Sky's twelfth birthday is a mix. His mother's delicious homemade goulash cannot overshadow the disappearance of his beloved uncle, Phineas, or the family's return to the small town of Exile. Sky has grown up reading about the Hunters of Legend, but he never dreamed that they were real until monsters appear in Exile and make Sky their target. . . . Patten's first novel excels at world building and pacing; the monsters . . . are fully formed and vividly drawn. . . . Interspersed with humor to keep an otherwise dark story from becoming overbearing, the balance is just right." Booklist

Patterson, James

★ **Middle** school, the worst years of my life. Little, Brown 2011 281p il $15.99

Grades: 4 5 6 7   **Fic**

1. School stories 2. Bereavement -- Fiction 3. Family life -- Fiction
ISBN 978-0-316-10187-5; 0-316-10187-7
                                        LC 2010022852

"The book's ultrashort chapters, dynamic artwork, and message that 'normal is boring' should go a long way toward

assuring kids who don't fit the mold that there's a place for them, too." Publ Wkly

Patterson, Nancy Ruth

Ellie ever; pictures by Patty Weise. Farrar, Straus & Giroux 2010 117p il $15.99

Grades: 3 4 5   **Fic**

1. School stories 2. Horses -- Fiction 3. Moving -- Fiction 4. Bereavement -- Fiction
ISBN 978-0-374-32108-6; 0-374-32108-6
                                        LC 2009013604

After losing her father and all their possessions in a hurricane, nine-year-old Ellie and her mother move to a small apartment on a horse farm in Virginia, where her new classmates think that she lives in a mansion and is a princess.

"Horses and animals . . . will initially attract readers, but it's the straightforward story of the little family, rebounding from terrible tragedy with bravery, honesty, and character, that is the heart of this book's appeal." Horn Book

The **winner's** walk; pictures by Thomas F. Yezerski. Farrar, Straus and Giroux 2006 114p il $16

Grades: 3 4 5   **Fic**

1. Dogs -- Fiction 2. Family life -- Fiction
ISBN 978-0-374-38445-6; 0-374-38445-2
                                        LC 2005-49461

Surrounded by a multitalented family, nine-year-old Case Callahan feels driven to succeed, but his failed attempts at various competitions discourage him until he finds a stray dog with a surprising past

"With short, action-packed chapters, frequent full-page pencil illustrations, and interesting information about service dogs, this solid book will appeal to young animal lovers." Horn Book

Paulsen, Gary

The **amazing** life of birds; the twenty-day puberty journal of Duane Homer. Wendy Lamb Books 2006 84p $13.95; pa $6.50

Grades: 5 6 7 8   **Fic**

1. Boys -- Fiction 2. Birds -- Fiction 3. Puberty -- Fiction
ISBN 0-385-74660-1; 0-553-49428-7 pa; 0385746601; 0553494287 pa

As twelve-year-old Duane endures the confusing and humiliating aspects of puberty, he watches a newborn bird in a nest on his windowsill begin to grow and become more independent, all of which he records in his journal.

The author "has captured a very uncomfortable time of life amazingly well. . . . Paulsen's writing is beautiful." Voice Youth Advocates

Crush; the theory, practice, and destructive properties of love. Gary Paulsen. Wendy Lamb Books 2012 136 p.

Grades: 5 6 7 8   **Fic**

1. Love -- Fiction 2. Humorous fiction 3. Crushes -- Fiction 4. High school students -- Fiction 5. Dating (Social customs) -- Fiction 6. Humorous stories 7. Interpersonal relations -- Fiction
ISBN 0385742304; 9780307974532; 9780375990540; 9780385742306; 9780385742313
                                        LC 2011028915

In this book, "Tina, aka the most beautiful girl he's ever seen, has stolen Kevin's heart, although she's blissfully oblivious to the effect she has on him. .... Rather than reveal his ardor outright, Kevin decides it's safer to first make a scientific study of just how love works by setting up romantic opportunities for his victims (otherwise known as study subjects). He starts by trying to create a candlelit dinner for his parents, although he accidentally causes a fire." (Kirkus Reviews)

Flat broke. Wendy Lamb Books 2011 118p $12.99; lib bdg $15.99
Grades: 4 5 6   **Fic**
1. Friendship -- Fiction 2. Family life -- Fiction 3. Business enterprises -- Fiction 4. Money-making projects for children -- Fiction
ISBN 978-0-385-74002-9; 0-385-74002-6; 978-0-385-90818-4 lib bdg; 0-385-90818-0 lib bdg
LC 2010049415
Fourteen-year-old Kevin is a hard worker, so when his income is cut off he begins a series of businesses, from poker games to selling snacks, earning money to take a girl to a dance, but his partners soon tire of his methods.
"A jocular, fast-paced voyage into the sometimes simple but never quiet mind of an ambitious eighth grader." Kirkus

★ **Lawn** Boy. Wendy Lamb Books 2007 88p $12.99; lib bdg $15.99; pa $6.50
Grades: 4 5 6 7   **Fic**
1. Summer employment -- Fiction 2. Business enterprises -- Fiction
ISBN 978-0-385-74686-1; 978-0-385-90923-5 lib bdg; 978-0-553-49465-5 pa
LC 2006-39731
Things get out of hand for a twelve-year-old boy when a neighbor convinces him to expand his summer lawn mowing business
"This rags-to-riches success story has colorful characters, a villain, and enough tongue-in-cheek humor to make it an enjoyable selection for the whole family." SLJ

Lawn Boy returns. Wendy Lamb Books 2010 101p $12.99; lib bdg $15.99
Grades: 4 5 6 7   **Fic**
1. Business enterprises -- Fiction ISBN 978-0-385-74662-5; 0-385-74662-8; 978-0-385-90899-3 lib bdg; 0-385-90899-7 lib bdg
LC 2009054046
Having expanded his summer lawn mowing job into an ever-growing business conglomerate, a twelve-year-old boy gets involved in high finance thanks to his hippie stockbroker, takes on sponsorship of a boxer, and becomes a media sensation.
"This is an extremely fast and funny story, good for struggling and reluctant readers." SLJ

★ The **legend** of Bass Reeves; being the true and fictional account of the most valiant marshal in the West. Wendy Lamb Books 2006 137p $15.95; pa $6.50
Grades: 5 6 7 8   **Fic**
1. Sheriffs 2. Slavery -- Fiction 3. African Americans -- Fiction
ISBN 0-385-74661-X; 0-553-49429-5 pa
LC 2006-11492

"This engrossingly told tale fills in the unrecorded youth of an unjustly obscure historical figure who was born a slave, became a successful rancher, then later in his long life went on to play an integral role in taming the rough-hewn Oklahoma Territory. .... A stirring tale of adventure." Booklist

Liar, liar; the theory, practice, and destructive properties of deception. Wendy Lamb Books 2011 120p $12.99; lib bdg $15.99
Grades: 4 5 6   **Fic**
1. School stories 2. Family life -- Fiction 3. Truthfulness and falsehood -- Fiction
ISBN 0-385-74001-8; 0-385-90817-2 lib bdg; 978-0-385-74001-2; 978-0-385-90817-7 lib bdg
LC 2010-28356
Fourteen-year-old Kevin is very good at lying and doing so makes life easier, until he finds himself in big trouble with his friends, family, and teachers. "Ages eight to twelve." (Publisher's note)
"Kevin's grappling with family troubles adds . . . emotional dimension to Paulsen's novel." Publ Wkly

Masters of disaster. Wendy Lamb Books 2010 102p $12.95; lib bdg $15.99
Grades: 3 4 5 6   **Fic**
1. Friendship -- Fiction
ISBN 978-0-385-73997-9; 0-385-73997-4; 978-0-385-90816-0 lib bdg; 0-385-90816-4 lib bdg
LC 2010013180
"Henry convinces his best friends, Riley and Reed, that the three 12-year-olds should prove their manhood by undertaking a series a daring exploits. . . . Readers willing to suspend disbelief and follow the boys' over-the-top exploits will enjoy plenty of laughs along the way." Booklist

Mr. Tucket. Delacorte Press 1994 166p hardcover o.p. pa $6.99
Grades: 4 5 6 7   **Fic**
1. Frontier and pioneer life -- Fiction
ISBN 0-385-31169-9; 0-440-41133-5 pa
LC 93-31180
In 1848, while on a wagon train headed for Oregon, fourteen-year-old Francis Tucket is kidnapped by Pawnee Indians and then falls in with a one-armed trapper who teaches him how to live in the wild
"Superb characterizations, splendidly evoked setting and thrill-a-minute plot make this book a joy to gallop through." Publ Wkly
Other titles in this series are:
Call me Francis Tucket (1995)
Tucket's ride (1997)
Tucket's gold (1999)
Tucket's home (2000)

Mudshark. Wendy Lamb Books 2009 83p
Grades: 3 4 5 6   **Fic**
1. School stories 2. Lost and found possessions -- Fiction
ISBN 0-385-74685-7; 0-385-90922-5 lib bdg; 978-0-385-74685-4; 978-0-385-90922-8 lib bdg
LC 2008033271
Principal Wagner confidently deals with a faculty washroom crisis, a psychic parrot, and a terrorizing gerbil, but

when sixty-five erasers go missing, he enlists the help of the school's best problem solver and locator of lost items, twelve-year-old Lyle Williams, aka Mudshark.

"Diversions . . . keep this compact story quick and light. Yet . . . Paulsen . . . delves deeper, shaping Mudshark as a credible and compassionate protagonist." Publ Wkly

Notes from the dog. Wendy Lamb Books 2009 133p $15.99; lib bdg $18.99

Grades: 5 6 7 8   Fic
1. Cancer -- Fiction 2. Gardening -- Fiction
ISBN 0-385-73845-5; 0-385-90730-3 lib bdg; 978-0-385-73845-3; 978-0-385-90730-9 lib bdg
LC 2009-13300

When Johanna shows up at the beginning of summer to house-sit next door to Finn, he has no idea of the profound effect she will have on his life by the time summer vacation is over.

"The plot is straightforward, but Paulsen's thoughtful characters are compelling and their interactions realistic. This emotional, coming-of-age journey about taking responsibilty for one's own happiness and making personal connections will not disappoint." Publ Wkly

Vote; the theory, practice, and destructive properties of politics. Gary Paulsen. 1st ed. Wendy Lamb Books 2013 144 p. (hardcover) $12.99; (ebook) $38.97; (hardcover) $12.99

Grades: 5 6 7 8   Fic
1. School stories 2. Humorous fiction 3. Elections -- Fiction 4. Humorous stories 5. Schools -- Fiction 6. Middle schools -- Fiction 7. Politics, Practical -- Fiction 8. Interpersonal relations -- Fiction
ISBN 0385742282; 9780307974525; 9780375990533; 9780385742283 trade; 9780385742290
LC 2012023059

In this humorous children's novel, by Gary Paulsen, the author's lead character from previous stories is reprised when he runs for school office. "Kevin Spencer . . . has a knack for tackling big ideas and goofing up, so what's next? Politics, of course! He's running for office, and his campaign is truly unique." (Publisher's note)

"Those who started this four-book series at the beginning may sense that our protagonist is maturing a wee bit, but not so much as to dampen the humor for fans or newcomers. . . . Fast-paced action and Kevin's penchant for getting into ridiculous situations make this the perfect book bait for not-so-eager readers." BookList

★ The **winter** room. Orchard Bks. 1989 103p $16.95; pa $5.99

Grades: 5 6 7 8   Fic
1. Farm life -- Fiction
ISBN 0-531-05839-5; 0-545-08534-9 pa
LC 89-42541

A Newbery Medal honor book, 1990

A young boy growing up on a northern Minnesota farm describes the scenes around him and recounts his old Norwegian uncle's tales of an almost mythological logging past

"While this seems at first to be a collection of anecdotes organized around the progression of the farm calendar, Paulsen subtly builds a conflict that becomes apparent in the last brief chapters, forceful and well-prepared. . . . Lyrical

and only occasionally sentimental, the prose is clean, clear, and deceptively simple." Bull Cent Child Books

Paver, Michelle
Wolf brother. HarperCollins 2005 295p (Chronicles of ancient darkness) $16.99; lib bdg $17.89; pa $6.99

Grades: 5 6 7 8   Fic
1. Bears -- Fiction 2. Wolves -- Fiction 3. Demoniac possession -- Fiction 4. Prehistoric peoples -- Fiction
ISBN 0-06-072825-6; 0-06-072826-4 lib bdg; 0-06-072827-2 pa
LC 2004-8857

First published 2004 in the United Kingdom

6,000 years in the past, twelve-year-old Tarak and his guide, a wolf cub, set out on a dangerous journey to fulfill an oath the boy made to his dying father—to travel to the Mountain of the World Spirit seeking a way to destroy a demon-possessed bear that threatens all the clans

"Paver's depth of research into the spiritual world of primitive peoples makes this impressive British import, slated to be the first in a six-book series, intriguing and believable." SLJ

Other titles in this series are:
Spirit walker (2006)
Soul eater (2007)
Outcast (2008)
Oath breaker (2009)
Ghost hunter (2010)

Payne, C. C.
Something to sing about; written by C. C. Payne. Eerdmans Books for Young Readers 2008 167p pa $8.50

Grades: 4 5 6   Fic
1. Bees -- Fiction 2. Fear -- Fiction 3. Singing -- Fiction 4. Family life -- Fiction 5. Choirs (Music) -- Fiction 6. Christian life -- Fiction
ISBN 978-0-8028-5344-8 pa; 0-8028-5344-7 pa
LC 2008006100

Ten-year-old Jamie Jo's fear of bees keeps her inside most of the time, but a series of events that begins when her mother is excluded from the church choir brings about many changes, including new friendships and greater trust in God

"The word wholesome sometimes gets a bad rap, but here it's leavened by gentle humor and considerable insight, and it fits this book just fine." Booklist

Peacock, Carol Antoinette
Red thread sisters; by Carol Antoinette Peacock. Viking 2012 236 p. (hardcover) $15.99

Grades: 4 5 6 7 8   Fic
1. Adoptees -- Fiction 2. Friendship -- Fiction 3. Chinese Americans -- Fiction 4. Adoption -- Fiction 5. Family life -- Fiction 6. Interracial adoption -- Fiction 7. Intercountry adoption -- Fiction
ISBN 0670013862; 9780670013869
LC 2012019511

This novel, by Carol Antoinette Peacock, offers a "story of friendship, family, and love. Wen has spent the first eleven years of her life at an orphanage in rural China . . . [with] her best friend, Shu Ling. When Wen is adopted by an American couple, she struggles . . . knowing that Shu Ling remains back at the orphanage, alone. Wen knows that her best friend deserves a family and a future, too. But finding a home for Shu Ling isn't easy, and time is running out." (Publisher's note)

Pearce, Emily Smith

 Isabel and the miracle baby; [by] Emily Smith Pearce. Front Street 2007 125p $15.95

Grades: 2 3 4 5 **Fic**

 1. Cancer -- Fiction 2. Infants -- Fiction 3. Family life -- Fiction 4. Mother-daughter relationship -- Fiction
 ISBN 978-1-932425-44-4

LC 2006101750

Eight-year-old Isabel feels her mother no longer cares about her because she has no time or energy even to listen when Isa tries to share her sadness about being unpopular, her jealousy over her new baby sister, and, most importantly, her fear that her mother's cancer will come back

 "Pearce gets into the mind and soul of a child. . . . [The child's] struggle is what sets this book apart from the dozens of others with the new-sibling theme." SLJ

Pearce, Philippa

 ★ **Tom's** midnight garden; illustrated by Susan Einzig. Lippincott 1959 229p il hardcover o.p. pa $5.95

Grades: 4 5 6 7 **Fic**

 1. Fantasy fiction 2. Space and time -- Fiction
 ISBN 0-397-30477-3; 0-06-440445-5 pa

First published 1958 in the United Kingdom

 "Daytime life for Tom at his aunt's home in England is dull, but each night he participates through fantasy in the lives of the former inhabitants of the interesting old house in which he is spending an enforced vacation. The book is British in setting and atmosphere. The element of mystery is well sustained, and the reader is left to make his own interpretation of the reality of the story." Adventuring with Books

 A **finder's** magic; illustrated by Helen Craig. Candlewick Press 2009 119p il $15.99

Grades: 3 4 5 **Fic**

 1. Magic -- Fiction 2. Lost and found possessions -- Fiction
 ISBN 978-0-7636-4072-9; 0-7636-4072-7

After a mysterious stranger offers to help Till find his dog, they embark on a magical quest, interviewing various witnesses including a heron, a mole, a riddling cat, and Miss Mousey, whose sketch of a peaceful riverbank offers a vital clue.

 "The posthumous publication by classic author Pearce envinces her usual gift for blending reality and fantasy in plain and approachable style. . . . Younger readers who crave gentle shivers without terrors will appreciate this cozy fantasy quest to find a lost pet." Bull Cent Child Books

Pearsall, Shelley

 All of the above; a novel. illustrations by Javaka Steptoe. Little, Brown 2006 234p il hardcover o.p. pa $5.99

Grades: 5 6 7 8 **Fic**

 1. School stories 2. City and town life -- Fiction
 ISBN 0-316-11524-X; 978-0-316-11524-7; 978-0-316-11526-1 pa; 0-316-11526-6 pa

LC 2005-33109

Five urban middle school students, their teacher, and other community members relate how a school project to build the world's largest tetrahedron affects the lives of everyone involved.

 "Pearsall's novel, based on a real event in 2002—is a delightful story about the power of a vision and the importance of a goal. The authentic voices of the students and the well-intentioned, supportive adults surrounding them illustrate all that is good about schools, family, friendship, and community." Booklist

Peck, Richard

 Fair weather; a novel. Dial Bks. 2001 130p il $16.99; pa $5.99

Grades: 5 6 7 8 **Fic**

 1. Actors 2. Singers 3. Family life 4. Scouts 5. Hunters 6. Circus executives 7. Circus performers 8. Family life -- Fiction
 ISBN 0-8037-2516-7; 0-14-250034-8 pa

LC 00-55561

In 1893, thirteen-year-old Rosie and members of her family travel from their Illinois farm to Chicago to visit Aunt Euterpe and attend the World's Columbian Exposition which, along with an encounter with Buffalo Bill and Lillian Russell, turns out to be a life-changing experience for everyone

 "Peck's unforgettable characters, cunning dialogue and fast-paced action will keep readers in stitches." Publ Wkly

 Here lies the librarian. Dial Books 2006 145p $16.99; pa $6.99

Grades: 4 5 6 **Fic**

 1. Librarians -- Fiction 2. Automobiles -- Fiction 3. Country life -- Fiction
 ISBN 0-8037-3080-2; 0-14-240908-1 pa

LC 2005-20279

Fourteen-year-old Eleanor "Peewee" McGrath, a tomboy and automobile enthusiast, discovers new possibilities for her future after the 1914 arrival in her small Indiana town of four young librarians.

 "Another gem from Peck, with his signature combination of quirky characters, poignancy, and outrageous farce." SLJ

 ★ **On** the wings of heroes. Dial Books 2007 148p $16.99; pa $6.99

Grades: 4 5 6 7 **Fic**

 1. World War, 1939-1945 -- Fiction
 ISBN 0-8037-3081-0; 0-14-241204-X pa

LC 2006011906

A boy in Illinois remembers the homefront years of World War II, especially his two heroes, his brother in the Air Force and his father, who fought in the previous war.

 "Peck's masterful, detail-rich prose describes wartime in the United States. . . . Peck's characters are memorable. . . . This book is an absolute delight." SLJ

 ★ **A season** of gifts. Dial Books for Young Readers 2009 156p $16.99

Grades: 5 6 7 8 **Fic**

 1. Moving -- Fiction
 ISBN 978-0-8037-3082-3; 0-8037-3082-9

LC 2008-48050

Relates the surprising gifts bestowed on twelve-year-old Bob Barnhart and his family, who have recently moved to a small Illinois town in 1958, by their larger-than-life neighbor, Mrs. Dowdel.

"The type of down-home humor and vibrant character-izations Peck fans have come to adore re-emerge in full as Peck resurrects Mrs. Dowdel, the irrepressible, self-sufficient grandmother featured in A Year Down Yonder and A Long Way from Chicago." Publ Wkly

★ The **teacher's** funeral; a comedy in three parts. Dial Books 2004 190p $16.99; pa $6.99

Grades: 5 6 7 8   **Fic**
1. Teachers -- Fiction 2. Country life -- Fiction
ISBN 0-8037-2736-4; 0-14-240507-8 pa
LC 2004-4361

In rural Indiana in 1904, fifteen-year-old Russell's dream of quitting school and joining a wheat threshing crew is disrupted when his older sister takes over the teaching at his one-room schoolhouse after mean, old Myrt Arbuckle "hauls off and dies."

"The dry wit and unpretentious tone make the story's events comical, its characters memorable, and its conclusion unexpectedly moving." Booklist

★ A **year** down yonder. Dial Bks. for Young Readers 2000 130p $16.99; pa $5.99

Grades: 5 6 7 8   **Fic**
1. Grandmothers 2. Depressions -- 1929 3. Grandmothers -- Fiction 4. Country life -- Illinois 5. Great Depression, 1929-1939 -- Fiction
ISBN 0-8037-2518-3; 0-14-230070-5 pa
LC 99-43159

Awarded the Newbery Medal, 2001
"Peck has created a delightful, insightful tale that resounds with a storyteller's wit, humor, and vivid description." SLJ

Peck, Richard, 1934-
★ **Secrets** at sea; illustrations by Kelly Murphy. Dial Books for Young Readers 2011 238p il $16.99

Grades: 3 4 5 6   **Fic**
1. Adventure fiction 2. Mice -- Fiction 3. Siblings -- Fiction 4. Ocean travel -- Fiction 5. Social classes -- Fiction
ISBN 978-0-8037-3455-5; 0-8037-3455-7
LC 2011001162

In 1887, the social-climbing Cranstons voyage from New York to London, where they hope to find a husband for their awkward older daughter, secretly accompanied by Helena and her mouse siblings, for whom the journey is both terrifying and wondrous as they meet an array of titled humans despite their best efforts at remaining hidden.

This is a "rollicking comedy of manners that begs to be read aloud. . . . Peck's droll take on human and mouse society is exquisite. . . . Helena's meticulous observations . . . . [are] enhanced by hilariously upended clichés . . . and by Murphy's dandy and detailed pencil illustrations that add just the right air of royalty." Horn Book

★ A **long** way from Chicago; a novel in stories. Dial Bks. for Young Readers 1998 148p pa $5.99; $15.99

Grades: 5 6 7 8   **Fic**
1. Grandmothers -- Fiction 2. Depressions -- 1929 -- Fiction 3. Country life -- Illinois -- Fiction 4. Great Depression, 1929-1939 -- Fiction
ISBN 0-14-240110-2 pa; 0-8037-2290-7
LC 98-10953

A Newbery Medal honor book, 1999
Joe recounts his annual summer trips to rural Illinois with his sister during the Great Depression to visit their larger-than-life grandmother

"The novel reveals a strong sense of place, a depth of characterization, and a rich sense of humor." Horn Book

The **mouse** with the question mark tail; a novel. by Richard Peck; illustrated by Kelly Murphy. Dial Books for Young Readers 2013 240 p. ill. (hardcover) $16.99

Grades: 3 4 5 6   **Fic**
1. Mice -- Juvenile fiction 2. Adventure fiction -- Juvenile fiction 3. Mice -- Fiction 4. Identity -- Fiction 5. Social classes -- Fiction 6. Adventure and adventurers -- Fiction 7. Kings, queens, rulers, etc. -- Fiction
ISBN 0803738382; 9780803738386
LC 2012027992

In this children's story, by Richard Peck, illustrated by Kelly Murphy, "the smallest mouse in London's Royal Mews is such a little mystery that he hasn't even a name. . . . His Aunt Marigold, Head Needlemouse, sews him a uniform and sends him off to be educated at the Royal Mews Mouse Academy. . . . Soon he's running for his life, looking high and low through the grand precincts of Buckingham Palace to find out who he is and who he might become." (Publisher's note)

Peet, Mal
★ **Cloud** Tea monkeys; by Mal Peet & Elspeth Graham; illustrated by Juan Wijngaard. Candlewick Press 2010 un il lib bdg $15.99

Grades: 1 2 3 4   **Fic**
1. Tea -- Fiction 2. Monkeys -- Fiction 3. Mother-daughter relationship -- Fiction
ISBN 978-0-7636-4453-6 lib bdg; 0-7636-4453-6 lib bdg
LC 2009-11868

When her mother becomes too ill to harvest tea on the nearby plantation, Shenaz is too small to fill in, but when she tells the monkeys she has befriended why she is sad, they bring her a basket filled with rare and valuable wild tea.

"The tale has the feel of a time-honed fable—simple, elegant, and moving—which is especially well complemented by Wijngaard's sumptuous illustrations." Booklist

Peirce, Lincoln
★ **Big** Nate; in a class by himself. Harper 2010 214p $12.99

Grades: 3 4 5   **Fic**
1. School stories
ISBN 978-0-06-194434-5; 0-06-194434-3; 978-0-06-194435-2 lib bdg; 0-06-194435-1 lib bdg
LC 2009-39668

The author "uses a mix of prose and cartoons to tell a quick story about a day in the life of an extroverted, impish kid. . . . Nate, has been the star of a long-running daily comic strip. . . . He wakes up feeling fine, sweats a bit about an upcoming test, then opens a fortune cookie at school that reads, 'Today you will surpass all others.' . . . The cartoons provide plenty of gags at the expense of various adults and classmates, and Nate's persistent good cheer and moxie make him a likable new proxy for young misfits." Booklist
Other titles in this series are:

Big Nate strikes again (2010)

Big Nate on a roll (2011)

Pennypacker, Sara, 1951-

★ **Clementine**; [illustrated by] Marla Frazee. Hyperion Books for Children 2006 144p il $14.99; pa $4.99

Grades: 2 3 4 **Fic**

1. School stories 2. Friendship -- Fiction 3. Family life -- Fiction

ISBN 0-7868-3882-5; 0-7868-3883-3 pa

LC 2005-50458

While sorting through difficulties in her friendship with her neighbor Margaret, eight-year-old Clementine gains several unique hairstyles while also helping her father in his efforts to banish pigeons from the front of their apartment building.

"Humorous scenarios tumble together, blending picturesque dialogue with a fresh perspective. . . . Frazee's engaging pen-and-ink drawings capture the energy and fresh-faced expressions of the irrepressible heroine." SLJ

Other titles about Clementine are:

The talented Clementine (2007)

Clementine's letter (2008)

Clementine, Friend of the Week (2010)

Clementine and the family meeting (2011)

★ The **summer** of the gypsy moths; Sara Pennypacker. Balzer + Bray 2012 275 p.

Grades: 4 5 6 **Fic**

1. Siblings -- Juvenile fiction 2. Family life -- Juvenile fiction 3. Foster children -- Juvenile fiction 4. Loss (Psychology) -- Juvenile fiction 5. Death -- Fiction 6. Secrets -- Fiction 7. Great aunts -- Fiction 8. Loss (Psychology) -- Fiction

ISBN 0061964204; 9780061964206

LC 2011026095

This middle reader story by Sara Pennypacker follows "Stella[, who] loves living with Great-aunt Louise in her big old house near the water on Cape Cod . . . since her mom is . . . unreliable. So while Mom 'finds herself,' Stella fantasizes that someday she'll come back to the Cape and settle down. The only obstacle to her plan? Angel, the foster kid Louise has taken in. . . . [T]he girls hardly speak to each other. But when tragedy unexpectedly strikes, Stella and Angel are forced to rely on each other to survive." (Publisher's note)

Perkins, Lynne Rae

All alone in the universe. Greenwillow Bks. 1999 140p il hardcover o.p. pa $5.99

Grades: 5 6 7 8 **Fic**

1. Friendship -- Fiction 2. Best friends -- Fiction

ISBN 0-688-16881-7; 0-380-73302-1 pa

LC 98-50093

Debbie is dismayed when her best friend Maureen starts spending time with ordinary, boring Glenna

"A poignant story written with sensitivity and tenderness." SLJ

★ **Criss** cross. Greenwillow Books 2005 337p $16.99; lib bdg $17.89; pa $6.99

Grades: 6 7 8 9 **Fic**

1. Nineteen sixties -- Fiction 2. Identity (Psychology) --Juvenile fiction

ISBN 0-06-009272-6; 0-06-009273-4 lib bdg; 0-06-

009274-2 pa

LC 2004-54023

Awarded the Newbery Medal, 2006

Teenagers in a small town in the 1960s experience new thoughts and feelings, question their identities, connect, and disconnect as they search for the meaning of life and love.

"Debbie . . . and Hector . . . narrate most of the novel. Both are 14 years old. Hector is a fabulous character with a wry humor and an appealing sense of self-awareness. . . . The descriptive, measured writing includes poems, prose, haiku, and question-and-answer formats. There is a great deal of humor in this gentle story." SLJ

Perkins, Mitali

★ **Bamboo** people. Charlesbridge 2010 272p $16.95

Grades: 5 6 7 8 **Fic**

1. Wilderness survival -- Fiction

ISBN 978-1-58089-328-2; 1-58089-328-7

LC 2009005495

Two Burmese boys, one a Karenni refugee and the other the son of an imprisoned Burmese doctor, meet in the jungle and in order to survive they must learn to trust each other.

"Perkins seamlessly blends cultural, political, religious, and philosophical context into her story, which is distinguished by humor, astute insights into human nature, and memorable characters." Publ Wkly

★ **Rickshaw** girl; illustrated by Jamie Hogan. Charlesbridge 2007 91p il lib bdg $13.95

Grades: 3 4 5 **Fic**

1. Painting -- Fiction 2. Sex role -- Fiction

ISBN 978-1-58089-308-4

LC 2006-09031

In her Bangladesh village, ten-year-old Naimi excels at painting designs called alpanas, but to help her impoverished family financially she would have to be a boy—or disguise herself as one

"This short chapter book tells a realistic story with surprises that continue until the end. Hogan's bold black-and-white sketches show the brave girl, the beautiful traditional alpana painting and rickshaw art, and the contemporary changes in the girl's rural home." Booklist

Perl, Erica S.

When life gives you O.J. Alfred A. Knopf 2011 198p $15.99; lib bdg $18.99

Grades: 3 4 5 **Fic**

1. Dogs -- Fiction 2. Family life -- Fiction 3. Grandfathers -- Fiction 4. Jews -- United States -- Fiction

ISBN 978-0-375-85924-3; 0-375-85924-1; 978-0-375-95924-0 lib bdg; 0-375-95924-6 lib bdg

LC 2010023844

Zelly Fried wants a dog more than anything, so at the urging of her grandfather, during the summer before sixth grade she takes care of a "practice dog" made out of an orange juice jug to show her parents that she is ready for the responsibility, even though she is sometimes not entirely sure about the idea.

"Zelly is a sympathetic, believably flawed character. . . . [This is a] funny, often wise novel." Booklist

Perro, Bryan

The **key** of Braha; Bryan Perro; translated from the French by Y. Maudet. Delacorte Press 2012 184 p.

Grades: 4 5 6 7   **Fic**

1. Fantasy fiction 2. Adventure fiction 3. Dead -- Juvenile fiction 4. Mythology -- Juvenile fiction 5. Fantasy 6. Dead -- Fiction 7. Good and evil -- Fiction 8. Adventure and adventurers -- Fiction

ISBN 0385907672; 9780375896941; 9780385739047; 9780385907675

LC 2011026173

This book is the second in Bryan Perro's "Amos Daragon" young adult fantasy series, translated from French, in which a 12-year-old sorcerer named Amos, "unwittingly takes on a hazardous mission: He's killed so he can pass into and fix a netherworld crowded with dead souls who aren't being permitted to pass on to their appointed fates. . . . Once there Amos receives aid against numerous enemies from a varied cast of . . . characters, many of whom are figures from mythology (explained in a lexicon)." (Kirkus)

The **mask** wearer; translated from the French by Y. Maudet. Delacorte Press 2011 167p (Amos Paragon) $16.99; lib bdg $19.99

Grades: 4 5 6 7   **Fic**

1. Fantasy fiction 2. Adventure fiction 3. Good and evil -- Fiction

ISBN 0-385-73903-6; 0-385-90766-4 lib bdg; 978-0-385-73903-0; 978-0-385-90766-8 lib bdg

LC 2010023725

To defeat the forces of evil which threaten his world, young Amos Daragon, aided by mythical animal friends, sets out on a journey to find four masks that harness the forces of nature and sixteen powerful stones that give the masks their magic.

"Amos's journey of self-discovery and his quick thinking are sure to keep readers turning the pages to discover the truth behind the never-ending chaos." SLJ

Petersen, P. J.

Wild river. Delacorte Press 2009 120p $14.99; lib bdg $17.99

Grades: 4 5 6 7   **Fic**

1. Brothers -- Fiction 2. Kayaks and kayaking -- Fiction 3. Wilderness survival -- Fiction

ISBN 978-0-385-73724-1; 0-385-73724-6; 978-0-385-90656-2 lib bdg; 0-385-90656-0 lib bdg

LC 2008-24921

Considered lazy and unathletic, twelve-year-old Ryan discovers a heroic side of himself when a kayak trip with his older brother goes horribly awry.

"The compelling first-person narration sets this apart from other adventure stories. . . . With sharp pacing, short sentences, and an unintimidating length, this is a strong, accessible choice for younger readers." Booklist

Peterson, Lois J.

The **ballad** of Knuckles McGraw; written by Lois Peterson. Orca Book Publishers 2010 105p (Orca young readers) pa $7.95

Grades: 3 4 5   **Fic**

1. Grandparents -- Fiction 2. Foster home care -- Fiction 3. Abandoned children -- Fiction

ISBN 978-1-55469-203-3 pa; 1-55469-203-2 pa

After Kevin's mother abandons him, he takes refuge in his fantasy of becoming a cowboy, but his reality is a foster home and grandparents he doesn't know.

"The author understands how kids think, a fact that will allow kids in your library to thoroughly enjoy this book." Libr Media Connect

Phelan, Matt

Bluffton; my summers with Buster Keaton. written and illustrated by Matt Phelan. Candlewick Press 2013 240 p. ill. (reinforced) $22.99

Grades: 3 4 5 6   **Fic**

1. Vaudeville -- Fiction

ISBN 076365079X; 9780763650797

LC 2012947260

In this graphic novel by Matt Phelan, set "in the summer of 1908, in Muskegon, Michigan, a visiting troupe of vaudeville performers is about the most exciting thing since baseball. Henry has a few months to ogle . . . a slapstick actor his own age named Buster Keaton. Henry longs to learn to take a fall like Buster . . . but Buster just wants to play ball with Henry and his friends." (Publisher's note)

Philbrick, W. R.

★ The **mostly** true adventures of Homer P. Figg; [by] Rodman Philbrick. Blue Sky Press 2009 224p $16.99

Grades: 5 6 7 8   **Fic**

1. Adventure fiction 2. Orphans -- Fiction 3. Brothers -- Fiction

ISBN 978-0-439-66818-7; 0-439-66818-2

LC 2008-16925

A Newbery Medal honor book, 2010

Twelve-year-old Homer, a poor but clever orphan, has extraordinary adventures after running away from his evil uncle to rescue his brother, who has been sold into service in the Civil War

"The book wouldn't be nearly as much fun without Homer's tall tales, but there are serious moments, too, and the horror of war and injustice of slavery ring clearly above the din of playful exaggerations." Publ Wkly

★ The **young** man and the sea; [by] Rodman Philbrick. Blue Sky Press 2004 192p $16.95; pa $4.99

Grades: 5 6 7 8   **Fic**

1. Fishing -- Fiction

ISBN 0-439-36829-4; 0-439-36830-8 pa

LC 2003-050233

After his mother's death, twelve-year-old Skiff Beaman decides that it is up to him to earn money to take care of himself and his father, so he undertakes a dangerous trip alone out on the ocean off the coast of Maine to try to catch a hugh bluefin tuna

"This excellent maritime bildungsroman has all of the makings of a juvenile classic: wide-open adventure, heart-pounding suspense, and just the right amount of tear-jerking pathos, all neatly wrapped up in an ending that . . . is purely triumphant." SLJ

Pierce, Tamora

Magic steps; book one of the Circle opens quartet. Scholastic Press 2000 264p (Circle opens quartet) hardcover o.p. pa $5.99

Grades: 5 6 7 8   **Fic**

1. Magic 2. Fantasy 3. Fantasy fiction 4. Magic

-- Fiction
ISBN 0-590-39588-2; 0-590-39605-6 pa

LC 99-31943

"Using descriptive, personable prose, Pierce combines dimensional characters, intricate details, plot twists, and alternating story lines for a gripping read. . . . There is some vivid violence." Booklist

Other titles in this series are:
Street magic (2001)
Cold fire (2002)
Shatterglass (2003)

Pinkney, Andrea Davis

★ **Bird** in a box; illustrations by Sean Qualls. Little, Brown Books for Young Readers 2011 278p il $16.99
Grades: 4 5 6 7   **Fic**
1. Boxing -- Fiction 2. African Americans -- Fiction
3. Radio broadcasting -- Fiction 4. Great Depression, 1929-1939 -- Fiction
ISBN 978-0-316-07403-2; 0-316-07403-9

LC 2010-22851

In 1936, three children meet at the Mercy Home for Negro Orphans in New York State, and while not all three are orphans, they are all dealing with grief and loss which together, along with the help of a sympathetic staff member and the boxing matches of Joe Louis, they manage to overcome.

"Pinkney weaves quite a bit of 1930s history into her story and succeeds admirably in showing how Louis came to represent so much more than his sport. Her detailed notes make this an accessible and inspiring piece of historical fiction that belongs in most collections." SLJ

With the might of angels; the diary of Dawnie Rae Johnson. Scholastic 2011 324p il map (Dear America)
Grades: 5 6 7 8   **Fic**
1. School stories 2. Diaries -- Fiction 3. Family life -- Fiction 4. Race relations -- Fiction 5. African Americans -- Fiction 6. School integration -- Fiction
ISBN 0-545-29705-2; 978-0-545-29705-9

LC 2011001363

In 1955 Hadley, Virginia, twelve-year-old Dawnie Rae Johnson, a tomboy who excels at baseball and at her studies, becomes the first African American student to attend the all-white Prettyman Coburn school, turning her world upside down. Includes historical notes about the period.

"Dawnie's journal is realistic, encompassing thoughts and emotions one would expect of someone so stressed. . . . The author seamlessly incorporates historical events into the child's journal. The end matter contains age-appropriate photographs, a time line, and brief biographical sketches of the people mentioned. A first purchase." SLJ

Pinkwater, Daniel Manus

Adventures of a cat-whiskered girl; illustrations by Calef Brown. Houghton Mifflin Books for Children 2010 268p il $16
Grades: 4 5 6   **Fic**
1. Science fiction 2. Cats -- Fiction 3. Extraterrestrial beings -- Fiction
ISBN 978-0-547-22324-7; 0-547-22324-2

Big Audrey, who has catlike whiskers, and her telepathic friend Molly set out on a journey to find out why flying saucers are landing behind the old stone barn in Poughkeep-

sie, New York, and, more importantly, to determine whether another cat-whiskered girl really exists.

"Mixing the absurd with the profound, Pinkwater's odd narration will have even the most serious readers laughing at the chaos." Booklist

The **Hoboken** chicken emergency; by Daniel Pinkwater; illustrated by Tony Auth. Atheneum Books for Young Readers 2007 101p il $16.99; pa $4.99
Grades: 3 4 5 6   **Fic**
1. Chickens -- Fiction
ISBN 978-1-4169-2809-6; 1-4169-2809-X; 978-1-4169-2810-2 pa; 1-4169-2810-3 pa

LC 2006101544

First published 1977 by Simon & Schuster

Arthur goes to pick up the turkey for Thanksgiving dinner but comes back with a 266-pound chicken.

"A contemporary tall tale that will stretch middle graders' imagination, sense of humor, and enthusiasm for reading." Booklist

Other titles about Henrietta the chicken are:
The Artsy Smartsy Club (2005)
Looking for Bobowicz (2004)

Lizard music; written and illustrated by Daniel Pinkwater. New York Review of Books 2011 157p il $15.95
Grades: 4 5 6   **Fic**
1. Science fiction 2. Lizards -- Fiction 3. Extraterrestrial beings -- Fiction
ISBN 978-1-59017-387-9; 1-59017-387-2

LC 2010026945

A reissue of the title first published 1976 by Dodd, Mead

When left to take care of himself, a young boy becomes involved with a community of intelligent lizards who tell him of a little known invasion from outer space.

"The book—part satire, part sci-fi/fantasy—is amusing the original. Occasional Escher-esque drawings reflect the story's peculiarities." Horn Book Guide

The **Neddiad**; how Neddie took the train, went to Hollywood, and saved civilization. by Daniel Pinkwater; illustrations by Calef Brown. Houghton Mifflin 2007 307p il $16
Grades: 5 6 7 8   **Fic**
1. Turtles -- Fiction
ISBN 978-0-618-59444-3; 0-618-59444-2

LC 2006033944

When shoelace heir Neddie Wentworthstein and his family take the train from Chicago to Los Angeles in the 1940s, he winds up in possession of a valuable Indian turtle artifact whose owner is supposed to be able to prevent the impending destruction of the world, but he is not sure exactly how.

"A bright and breezy adventure with a smart and funny narrator. . . . [This is a] goofy and lovingly nostalgic historical fantasy." SLJ

The **Yggyssey**; how Iggy wondered what happened to all the ghosts, found out where they went, and went there. illustrations by Calef Brown. Houghton Mifflin Co. 2009 245p il $16

Grades: 4 5 6   **Fic**
1. Ghost stories 2. Hotels and motels -- Fiction
ISBN 978-0-618-59445-0; 0-618-59445-0

LC 2008-01874

In the mid-1950s, Yggdrasil Birnbaum and her friends, Seamus and Neddie, journey to Old New Hackensack, which is on another plane, to try to learn why ghosts are disappearing from the Birnbaum's hotel and other Hollywood, California, locations.

"Once again, Pinkwater combines a goofy plot, myth and fairy tale references, and an obvious affection for yesteryear Los Angeles in a supernaturally funny read." Booklist

Pinter, Jason
    Zeke Bartholomew, superspy. Sourcebooks Jabberwocky 2011 256p pa $7.99
Grades: 4 5 6 7   **Fic**
1. Adventure fiction 2. Spies -- Fiction
ISBN 978-1-4022-5755-1; 1-4022-5755-4

Zeke Bartholomew has always dreamed of being a spy. But when a case of mistaken identity goes horribly wrong, he's thrust into a world of real-life espionage beyond his wildest dreams. Soon this 7th grade nobody finds himself hunted by the lava-powered behemoth Ragnarok, aided by a mysterious butt-kicking girl who goes only by the codename 'Sparrow.'

"Zeke's first-person narration and ample one-liners provide plenty of laughs in a novel that combines espionage, wild sci-fi, and a satiric take on the ever-growing kids-save-the-world subgenre." Booklist

Pitchford, Dean
    Captain Nobody. G.P. Putnam's Sons 2009 195p $16.99; pa $6.99
Grades: 3 4 5 6   **Fic**
1. Costume -- Fiction 2. Brothers -- Fiction 3. Halloween -- Fiction
ISBN 978-0-399-25034-7; 0-399-25034-4; 978-0-14-241667-9 pa; 0-14-241667-3 pa

LC 2008-27733

When ten-year-old Newton dresses up as an unusual superhero for Halloween, he decides to keep wearing the costume after the holiday to help save townspeople and eventually his injured brother.

The author "builds suspense adeptly. . . . The young narrator's earnest voice—and his raw sense of helplessness—are real and affecting." Publ Wkly

Place, Francois
    The **old** man mad about drawing; a tale of Hokusai. translated from the French by William Rodarmor. David R. Godine 2004 105p il $19.95
Grades: 3 4 5 6   **Fic**
1. Artists 2. Artists -- Fiction
ISBN 1-56792-260-0

LC 2003-13521

Tojiro, a young seller of rice cakes in the Japanese capital of Edo, later known as Tokyo, is amazed to discover that the grumpy and shabby old man who buys his cakes is a famous artist renowned for his sketches, prints, and paintings of flowers, animals, and landscapes.

This book "features fine reproductions of Hokusai's work, as well as . . . elegant detailed sketches of the quiet studio and crowded streets." Booklist

Platt, Chris
    Astra. Peachtree 2010 144p $15.95
Grades: 5 6 7 8   **Fic**
1. Horses -- Fiction 2. Father-daughter relationship -- Fiction
ISBN 978-1-56145-541-6; 1-56145-541-5

LC 2010001654

Forbidden to ride after her mother's death in a riding accident, thirteen-year-old Lily nurses her mother's beloved horse, Astra, back to health, hoping that someday Astra will win the Tevis Cup endurance race

"Filled with information about endurance racing as well as a cast of interesting supporting characters, including the dishy new boy in town, this novel is a quick and enjoyable read." SLJ

Platt, Randall Beth
    Hellie Jondoe; [by] Randall Platt. Texas Tech University Press 2009 216p pa $16.95
Grades: 5 6 7 8   **Fic**
1. Orphans -- Fiction
ISBN 978-0-89672-663-5 pa; 0-89672-663-0 pa

LC 2009-21514

In 1918, as the Great War ends and the Spanish influenza pandemic begins, thirteen-year-old Hellie Jondoe survives on the streets of New York as a beggar and pickpocket until she boards the orphan train to Oregon, where she learns about loyalty, honesty, and the meaning of family

"This is solid historical fiction with a scrappy heroine who is genuinely tough and a true survivor. Irrepressible and irreverent." Kirkus

Poblocki, Dan
    The **stone** child. Random House 2009 274p $15.99; lib bdg $18.99
Grades: 5 6 7 8   **Fic**
1. Authors -- Fiction 2. Monsters -- Fiction 3. Supernatural -- Fiction 4. Books and reading -- Fiction
ISBN 978-0-375-84254-2; 0-375-84254-3; 978-0-375-94254-9 lib bdg; 0-375-94254-8 lib bdg

LC 2008-21722

When friends Eddie, Harris, and Maggie discover that the scary adventures in their favorite author's fictional books come true, they must find a way to close the portal that allows evil creatures and witches to enter their hometown of Gatesweed.

"The creep factor is high but not graphic, and the kids act and react like real kids. . . . This briskly paced novel is sure to be popular with fans of scary stuff." SLJ

Pogue, David
    Abby Carnelia's one and only magical power. Roaring Brook Press 2010 277p $15.99
Grades: 3 4 5   **Fic**
1. Camps -- Fiction 2. Magic -- Fiction
ISBN 978-1-59643-384-7; 1-59643-384-1

LC 2009-46619

After eleven-year-old Abby discovers that she has a completely useless magical power, she finds herself at a magic camp where her hope of finding others like herself is realized, but when a select group is taken to a different camp, a sinister plot comes to light.

"This book is a whimsical feast for children. The characters are well developed; the story is magical and reminiscent of Eva Ibbotsen's wonderful books. The chapters are short and move the plot along quickly. It is an adventure from beginning to end and a plain good story." Libr Media Connect

Polacco, Patricia

★ **January's** sparrow. Philomel Books 2009 94p il $21.99

Grades: 4 5 6   **Fic**
     1. Slavery -- Fiction 2. Family life -- Fiction 3. African Americans -- Fiction 4. Underground railroad -- Fiction
     ISBN 978-0-399-25077-4; 0-399-25077-8

                          LC 2008-52726

After a fellow slave is beaten to death, Sadie and her family flee the plantation for freedom through the Underground Railroad.

"The illustrations, which include scenes of a bloody whipping and a heavily scarred back, have an urgent, unsettled look that fully captures the sharply felt danger and terror of Sadie's experiences. . . . This moving account effectively highlights a significant instance of nonviolent community resistance to injustice." SLJ

Just in time, Abraham Lincoln. G. P. Putnam's Sons 2011 un il $17.99

Grades: 2 3 4 5   **Fic**
     1. Lawyers 2. Presidents 3. State legislators 4. Brothers -- Fiction 5. Members of Congress 6. Time travel -- Fiction 7. Grandmothers -- Fiction 8. Antietam (Md.), Battle of, 1862 -- Fiction
     ISBN 0-399-25471-4; 978-0-399-25471-0

                          LC 2010-23200

When two brothers visit a museum in Harper's Ferry, West Virginia, with their grandmother, they find themselves in a very realistic Civil War setting where they see the Antietam battlefield and meet historical figures from the aftermath of that momentous battle. Includes author's note on the Battle of Antietam.

"Climaxed by two wordless spreads of fields covered with twisted, bloodstained victims, the illustrations convey the boys' emotional shifts from boredom to astonishment, excitement to horror. . . . Rounded off with an afterword noting where some historical details have been telescoped, the episode will take a strong grip on readers' hearts and minds both." Kirkus

The junkyard wonders. Philomel 2010 un il $17.99

Grades: 2 3 4 5   **Fic**
     1. School stories 2. Teachers -- Fiction 3. Special education -- Fiction 4. Airplanes -- Models -- Fiction
     ISBN 978-0-399-25078-1; 0-399-25078-6

"Looking forward to a fresh start at a new school, Trisha is crestfallen when she is assigned to a special class with children who are different. Their teacher, Mrs. Peterson, proudly calls them the junkyard and takes them to an actual junkyard, which she describes as a place of wondrous possibilities. . . . Reclaiming and rebuilding an old model plane they intend to send to the moon, Trisha's tribe manages a triumphant launch. Illustrations, rendered in pencil and marker, portray children in saddle oxfords and poodle skirts brimming with energy and excitement, guided by a model teacher. Based on her own childhood, Polacco's inspiring story will touch children and teachers alike." Booklist

Polikoff, Barbara Garland

Why does the coqui sing? Holiday House 2004 213p $16.95

Grades: 5 6 7 8   **Fic**
     1. Puerto Ricans 2. Moving -- Fiction 3. Moving, Household 4. Puerto Ricans -- Fiction 5. Family life -- Puerto Rico 6. Puerto Ricans -- Juvenile fiction
     ISBN 0-8234-1817-0

                          LC 2003-56776

When thirteen-year-old Luz and her family move from Chicago to her stepfather's native home of Puerto Rico, she and her brother Rome struggle to adjust and to decide where it is they really belong

"Luz, an aspiring poet, beautifully describes the pain of leaving and resettling in a sensitive, sometimes lyrical voice that's always true to her age." Booklist

Porter, Tracey

★ **Billy** Creekmore. Joanna Cotler Books 2007 305p $16.99; lib bdg $17.89; pa $6.99

Grades: 5 6 7 8   **Fic**
     1. Circus -- Fiction 2. Orphanages -- Fiction 3. Coal mines and mining -- Fiction
     ISBN 978-0-06-077570-4; 0-06-0-77570-X; 978-0-06-077571-1 lib bdg; 0-06-077571-8 lib bdg; 978-0-06-077572-8 pa; 0-06-077572-6 pa

                          LC 2007-00001

In 1905, ten-year-old Billy is taken from an orphanage to live with an aunt and uncle he never knew he had, and he enjoys his first taste of family life until his work in a coal mine and involvement with a union brings trouble, then he joins a circus in hopes of finding his father.

"Porter's writing is strong, and the story, told in Billy's steadfast yet child-true voice, makes the shocking history about the lives of children at the turn of the last century come alive for today's readers." Booklist

Potter, Ellen

The **humming** room; Ellen Potter. 1st ed. Feiwel & Friends 2012 184 p. $16.99

Grades: 4 5 6 7   **Fic**
     1. Children's stories 2. Family -- Juvenile fiction 3. Haunted houses -- Juvenile fiction 4. Foster children -- Juvenile fiction 5. Gardens -- Fiction 6. Islands -- Fiction 7. Orphans -- Fiction
     ISBN 0312644388; 9780312644383

                          LC 2011033583

In this book by Ellen Potter, "[h]idden under the family trailer, Roo hears . . . the murder of her drug-dealing father. . . . [S]he is sent to live with her . . . reclusive uncle on Cough Rock, a spooky old house named for its former use as a sanitarium. . . . [The cast of characters includes a] personal assistant, a cheerful local servant, a mysterious wild boy, and a secluded boy cousin with a fearful temper who is not expected to live." (Bulletin of the Center for Children's Books)

★ The **Kneebone** boy. Feiwel and Friends 2010 282p $16.99

Grades: 3 4 5 6   **Fic**
     1. Adventure fiction 2. Mothers -- Fiction 3. Siblings -- Fiction 4. Eccentrics and eccentricities -- Fiction
     ISBN 978-0-312-37772-4; 0-312-37772-X

                          LC 2010012572

Otto, Lucia, and Max Hardscrabble, whose mother has been missing for many years, have unexpected and illuminating adventures in the village of Snoring-by-the-Sea after their father, who paints portraits of deposed monarchs, goes away on a business trip.

"With a dark, witty absurdity . . . Potter . . . draws readers into this compelling mystery-adventure. . . . Potter's voice is distinguished by sharp, humorous, and poignant observations. . . . Often laugh-out-loud funny." Publ Wkly

★ **Olivia** Kidney; illustrated by Peter Reynolds. Philomel Bks. 2003 155p il $15.99; pa $5.99
Grades: 3 4 5 6 **Fic**
1. Apartment houses -- Fiction
ISBN 0-399-23850-6; 0-14-240234-6 pa
LC 2002-3660

Twelve-year-old Olivia explores her new apartment building and finds a psychic, talking lizards, a shrunken ex-pirate, an exiled princess, ghosts, and other unusual characters

"Potter has written a first-rate novel to be enjoyed on many levels. Its plot is so tightly woven that it's difficult to separate the mystical from the fantastical. Occasional full-page illustrations add another dimension to this narrative, which is wonderful medicine for the lonely." SLJ

Other titles about Olivia Kidney are:
Olivia Kidney and the Exit Academy (2005)
Olivia Kidney and the secret beneath the city (2007)

Slob. Philomel Books 2009 199p $16.99
Grades: 5 6 7 8 **Fic**
1. Obesity -- Fiction 2. Orphans -- Fiction 3. Siblings -- Fiction 4. Inventions -- Fiction 5. Bereavement -- Fiction
ISBN 978-0-399-24705-7; 0-399-24705-X
LC 2008-40476

Picked on, overweight genius Owen tries to invent a television that can see the past to find out what happened the day his parents were killed.

"An intriguingly offbeat mystery, . . . at turns humorous, suspenseful and poignant." Kirkus

Poulsen, David A.
Old Man; David A. Poulsen. Dundurn Group Ltd 2013 224 p. $12.99
Grades: 6 7 8 **Fic**
1. Automobile travel -- Fiction 2. Father-son relationship -- Fiction 3. Vietnam War, 1961-1975 -- Veterans
ISBN 1459705475; 9781459705470

In this novel, by David A. Poulsen, "Nate Huffman's plans are unexpectedly shelved for the most unlikely of reasons: the reappearance of his estranged father. . . . Nate finds himself in a pickup with a man he can't stand. His father wants to reconnect, and he wants Nate to really understand him. Larry Huffman has chosen to make this happen by taking his son into his own past, which has the Vietnam War as its centrepiece." (Publisher's note)

Pratchett, Terry
★ **Only** you can save mankind. HarperCollins 2005 207p hardcover o.p. lib bdg $16.89; pa $6.99

Grades: 5 6 7 8 **Fic**
1. War stories 2. Computer games -- Fiction
ISBN 0-06-054185-7; 0-06-054186-5 lib bdg; 0-06-054187-3 pa

First published 1992 in the United Kingdom

Twelve-year-old Johnny endures tensions between his parents, watches television coverage of the Gulf War, and plays a computer game called Only You Can Save Mankind, in which he is increasingly drawn into the reality of the alien ScreeWee

This is "a wild ride, full of Pratchett's trademark humor; digs at primitive, low-resolution games . . . ; and some not-so-subtle philosophy about war and peace." Booklist

Other titles in this trilogy are:
Johnny and the dead (2006)
Johnny and the bomb (2006)

Preller, James
Justin Fisher declares war! Scholastic Press 2010 135p $15.99
Grades: 3 4 5 **Fic**
1. School stories 2. Teachers -- Fiction 3. Popularity -- Fiction
ISBN 978-0-545-03301-5; 0-545-03301-2
LC 2009053641

When Justin Fisher, longtime class clown, realizes that his classmates are growing tired of his misdeeds, he declares war on their fifth-grade teacher, Mr. Tripp, in hopes of regaining his popularity.

"This quiet, universal story . . . will make a good classroom read. Preller handles sensitive issues with dignity, and kids will identify with Justin's eagerness to be liked and his snarky jokes." SLJ

★ **Six** innings; a game in the life. Feiwel and Friends 2008 147p $16.95
Grades: 4 5 6 7 **Fic**
1. Cancer -- Fiction 2. Baseball -- Fiction
ISBN 978-0-312-36763-3; 0-312-36763-5
LC 2007-32846

Earl Grubb's Pool Supplies plays Northeast Gas & Electric in the Little League championship game, while Sam, who has cancer and is in a wheelchair, has to call the play-by-play instead of participating in the game.

"The outcome is predictable but the journey is nailbitingly tense. Kids will be nodding in agreement at the truths laid bare." Publ Wkly

Prevost, Guillaume
The **book** of time; [by] Guillaume Prévost; translated by William Rodarmor. Arthur A. Levine Books 2007 213p $16.99; pa $6.99
Grades: 5 6 7 8 **Fic**
1. Science fiction 2. Missing persons -- Fiction
ISBN 978-0-439-88375-7; 0-439-88375-X; 978-0-439-88379-5 pa; 0-439-88379-2 pa
LC 2006-38446

Original French edition 2006

Sam Faulkner travels back in time to medieval Ireland, ancient Egypt and Renaissance Bruges in search of his missing father

"The appeal of the novel . . . comes from both well-drawn characters and a swiftly moving story." Booklist

Other titles in this series are:

The gate of days (2008)

The circle of gold (2009)

Priestley, Chris

Tales of terror from the Black Ship; by Chris Priestley; illustrated by David Roberts. Bloomsbury Children's Books 2008 243p il $12.99

Grades: 5 6 7 8   **Fic**

1. Sea stories 2. Horror fiction 3. Siblings -- Fiction 4. Storytelling -- Fiction

ISBN 978-1-59990-290-6; 1-59990-290-7

LC 2008-10408

One stormy night, in their family's otherwise deserted Cornwall inn, twelve-year-old Ethan and his sister Cathy shelter a mysterious guest who indulges their love of the macabre by telling horror stories of the sea

"Priestley and Roberts, whose Gorey-esque line illustrations can distill spirits from a nightmare, understand full well what kids want to read under the covers by flashlight." Bull Cent Child Books

Primavera, Elise

Libby of High Hopes; story and pictures by Elise Primavera. Simon & Schuster Books for Young Readers 2012 185 p. (alk. paper) $14.99

Grades: 2 3 4   **Fic**

1. Horses -- Fiction 2. Sisters -- Fiction 3. Horseback riding -- Fiction 4. Horsemanship -- Fiction

ISBN 1416955429; 9781416955429

LC 2011043908

In this children's novel, Libby wants to take horseback riding lessons. "Libby's parents do indeed fork out for lessons--for Libby's older sister, Laurel. Libby does at least get the privilege of riding an old pony during Laurel's class, and she hangs around the barn and learns as much as she can, taking a special interest in a retired jumper, Princess, and getting involved in the human drama of the stable's owners." (Bulletin of the Center for Children's Books)

Prineas, Sarah

★ The magic thief; illustrations by Antonio Javier Caparo. HarperCollins Pubs. 2008 419p il map

Grades: 4 5 6 7   **Fic**

1. Fantasy fiction 2. Magic -- Fiction 3. Thieves -- Fiction 4. Apprentices -- Fiction

ISBN 0-06-137587-X; 0-06-137588-8 lib bdg; 0-06-137590-X pa; 978-0-06-137587-3; 978-0-06-137588-0 lib bdg; 978-0-06-137590-3 pa

LC 2007031704

Conn is a young thief who is drawn into a life of adventure after picking the pocket of the wizard Nevery Flinglas. Finglas has returned from exile to try to reverse the decline of magic in Wellmet City. "Grades five to nine." (Bull Cent Child Books)

"Conn is a thief but, through desire and inevitability, becomes a wizard . . . This evolution begins when Conn picks the pocket of the wizard Nevery. . . . What works wonderfully well here is the boy's irresistable voice." Booklist

Other titles in this series are:

Lost (2009)

Found (2010)

Pryor, Bonnie

Simon's escape; a story of the Holocaust. Enslow Publishers 2010 160p (Historical fiction adventures) lib bdg $27.93; pa $14.95

Grades: 4 5 6   **Fic**

1. Jews -- Poland -- Fiction 2. Holocaust, 1933-1945 -- Fiction 3. World War, 1939-1945 -- Fiction

ISBN 978-0-7660-3388-7 lib bdg; 0-7660-3388-0 lib bdg; 978-1-59845-216-7 pa; 1-59845-216-9 pa

LC 2009029322

Simon, a young Polish Jew, and his family are forced by Nazis to leave their home for the filth and hunger of the Warsaw ghetto then, when his family is all taken away, he escapes to fight for survival in the countryside. Includes facts about the Holocaust

This "is a compelling, informative introduction to Holocaust history." Booklist

The iron dragon; the courageous story of Lee Chin. Enslow Publishers 2010 160p (Historical fiction adventures) lib bdg $27.93; pa $14.95

Grades: 4 5 6   **Fic**

1. Railroads -- Fiction 2. Immigrants -- Fiction 3. Chinese Americans -- Fiction

ISBN 978-0-7660-3389-4 lib bdg; 0-7660-3389-9 lib bdg; 978-1-59845-215-0 pa; 1-59845-215-0 pa

LC 2009017930

In the mid-nineteenth century, teenager Lee Chin and his father leave China for California to work on the transcontinental railroad, where Lee defies his father's wishes and saves money to free his younger sister from slavery in China, then brings her to join him in beginning a new life in America. Includes historical note about the Chinese who helped build the transcontinental railroad

"Lee Chin's tale is compellingly told. . . . Historical information is accurate and honest about the period depicted." SLJ

Pullman, Philip, 1946-

★ Clockwork; or, All wound up. with illustrations by Leonid Gore. Levine Bks. 1998 112p il hardcover o.p. pa $4.99

Grades: 4 5 6 7   **Fic**

1. Supernatural -- Fiction

ISBN 0-590-12999-6; 0-590-12998-8 pa

LC 97-27458

First published 1996 in the United Kingdom

Long ago in Germany, a storyteller's story and an apprentice clockwork-maker's nightmare meet in a menacing, lifelike figure created by the strange Dr. Kalmenius

"Pullman laces his tale with subtle humor while maintaining the suspense until the end. Misty, moody, and atmospheric black-and-white drawings by Leonid Gore make a perfect fit for this gothic gem." Voice Youth Advocates

★ I was a rat! illustrated by Kevin Hawkes. Knopf 2000 164p il $15.95; pa $4.99

Grades: 4 5 6 7   **Fic**

1. Fantasy fiction 2. Humorous stories

ISBN 0-375-80176-6; 0-440-41661-2 pa

LC 99-31806

First published 1999 in the United Kingdom with illustrations by Peter Bailey

"Pullman tells what happens to Cinderella's rat-turned-pageboy, who, busily sliding down banisters at the palace, misses the pumpkin-coach ride home and gets trapped in boy form. Young readers will find the story completely entertaining, whether or not they appreciate the playful spoofing of sensational news stories, mob mentality, and the royal family." Horn Book Guide

Two crafty criminals! and how they were captured by the daring detectives of the New Cut Gang; including Thunderbolt's Waxwork & the gas-fitters' ball. Philip Pullman. Alfred A. Knopf 2012 281 p.

Grades: 5 6 7 8   **Fic**

1. Mystery fiction 2. Crime -- Fiction 3. Gangs -- Fiction 4. Humorous fiction 5. Children's stories 6. Humorous stories 7. Mystery and detective stories 8. Adventure and adventurers -- Fiction
ISBN 9780375870293; 9780375970290; 9780375988684

           LC 2011042391

This children's book by Philip Pullman was published in 1994 as two novellas: "Thunderbolt's Waxwork" and "The Gas-Fitters' Ball," which are set in "1894 London . . . [and] star . . . the intrepid boy and girl detectives of the New Cut Gang. . . . Thunderbolt Dobney sees his own father hauled off to jail for what he thinks must be 'coining.' . . . [H]e and the New Cut Gang expose the real criminal. . . . In 'The Gas-Fitters' Ball,' . . . the Gas-Fitters' Hall is burgled." (Kirkus Reviews)

Pyron, Bobbie

★ A **dog's** way home. Katherine Tegen Books 2011 321p lib bdg $17.89; $16.99

Grades: 4 5 6 7   **Fic**

1. Dogs -- Fiction 2. Traffic accidents -- Fiction
ISBN 0-06-198673-9 lib bdg; 0-06-198674-7; 978-0-06-198673-4 lib bdg; 978-0-06-198674-1

           LC 2010006960

After a car accident strands them at opposite ends of the Blue Ridge Parkway, eleven-year-old Abby and her beloved sheltie Tam overcome months filled with physical and emotional challenges to find their way back to each other.

"A heartwarming, suspenseful tale. . . . With vibrant, sympathetic characterizations, Pyron creates an inspiring portrayal of devotion and survival against all odds." Publ Wkly

The **dogs** of winter; by Bobbie Pyron. Arthur A. Levine Books 2012 312 p. (hardcover: alk. paper) $16.99

Grades: 5 6 7 8   **Fic**

1. Wild dogs -- Fiction 2. Dogs -- Juvenile fiction 3. Abandoned children -- Fiction 4. Wilderness survival -- Fiction 5. Dogs -- Fiction 6. Gangs -- Fiction 7. Street children -- Fiction 8. Homeless persons -- Fiction 9. Human-animal relationships -- Fiction
ISBN 0545399300; 9780545399302; 9780545399319; 9780545469852

           LC 2011051519

In this book by Bobbie Pyron "Ivan's mother disappears, [and] he's abandoned on the streets of Moscow, with little chance to make it through the harsh winter. But help comes in an unexpected form: Ivan is adopted by a pack of dogs, and the dogs quickly become more than just his street companions: They become his family. Soon Ivan, who used

to love reading fairytales, is practically living in one." But "when help is finally offered to him, will he be able to accept it?" (Publisher's note)

Quattlebaum, Mary

Jackson Jones and Mission Greentop. Delacorte Press 2004 101p hardcover o.p. pa $5.50

Grades: 3 4 5   **Fic**

1. Gardens -- Fiction 2. African Americans -- Fiction
ISBN 0-385-73114-0; 0-440-41957-3 pa

           LC 2003-11823

His plot in a community garden brings 10-year-old Jackson Jones more zucchini than he cares to see and the unwanted attention of a bully, but when a company plans to destroy the garden, Jackson turns his attention to trying to save it.

"Quattlebaum's talent for depicting a lively, diverse neighborhood and funny interchanges between kids remains strong, as does her gift for simple conversational writing." Horn Book Guide

Other titles about Jackson Jones are:
Jackson Jones and the curse of the outlaw rose (2006)
Jackson Jones and the puddle of thorns (1995)

Jackson Jones and the curse of the outlaw rose; [by] Mary Quattlebaum. Delacorte Press 2006 100p $14.95; lib bdg $16.99

Grades: 3 4 5   **Fic**

1. Gardens -- Fiction 2. African Americans -- Fiction
ISBN 978-0-385-73349-6; 978-0-385-90365-3 lib bdg

           LC 2006001804

When Jackson and Reuben take a rose cutting from a graveyard for Mr. Kerring, events make them believe it is cursed and will continue to threaten anyone in its vicinity until it is returned.

"A well-written, fast-paced adventure for early chapter book readers." SLJ

Quirk, Katie

A **girl** called Problem; by Katie Quirk. Eerdmans Books for Young Readers 2013 191 p. $8

Grades: 4 5 6   **Fic**

1. Historical fiction 2. Tanzania -- Fiction 3. Healers -- Fiction 4. Villages -- Fiction 5. Moving, Household -- Fiction 6. Blessing and cursing -- Fiction 7. Farm life -- Tanzania -- Fiction 8. Mothers and daughters -- Fiction 9. Sukuma (African people) -- Fiction
ISBN 0802854044; 9780802854049

           LC 2012025468

In this novel, Shida looks forward to an education when "President Nyerere asks Shida's village to become a model of ujamaa (familyhood) for the country by moving to Njia Panda and farming communally. . . . After the move, however, the cotton crop mysteriously fails overnight, the villagers' prize possessions, their cattle, escape from their pens, and Furaha dies of fever. With the help of Shida and her cousin Grace, Babu, their grandfather and the village elder, unearths the truth." (Kirkus)

Railsback, Lisa

Noonie's masterpiece; art by Sarajo Frieden. Chronicle Books 2010 208p il $18.99

Grades: 4 5 6 7   **Fic**

1. School stories 2. Artists -- Fiction 3. Family life -- Fiction 4. Father-daughter relationship -- Fiction 5.

Eccentrics and eccentricities -- Fiction
ISBN 978-0-8118-6654-5; 0-8118-6654-8

LC 2008-26831

Upon learning that her deceased mother, an artist, went through a "Purple Period," ten-year-old Noonie decides to do the same, hoping that this will bring her archaeologist father home to see her win a school art contest and that the aunt, uncle, and cousin she lives with will come to understand her just a little.

"Noonie may be an unreliable and even unlikable narrator at times, but her pain and vulnerability are as evident as her belief in herself as an artist, and by the end of the story, she'll have readers in her corner. The ink-and-watercolor illustrations, appearing throughout the book, have a 1960s-retro look." Booklist

Ramthun, Bonnie
The **White** Gates; by Bonnie Ramthun. Random House 2008 242p $16.99; lib bdg $19.99; pa $7.99
Grades: 4 5 6 7   **Fic**
1. Mystery fiction 2. Physicians -- Fiction 3. Ute Indians -- Fiction 4. Snowboarding -- Fiction 5. Mother-son relationship -- Fiction
ISBN 978-0-375-84554-3; 0-375-84554-2; 978-0-375-94554-0 lib bdg; 0-375-94554-7 lib bdg; 978-0-375-84555-0 pa; 0-375-84555-0 pa

LC 2007-12800

When his mother becomes the doctor in Snow Park, Colorado, twelve-year-old Tor learns of a curse placed on the town's doctors many years before by an eccentric Ute woman, but suspects that a modern-day villain is hiding behind that curse.

"Solutions to puzzles come as swiftly and dramatically as an avalanche that nearly takes Tor's life, but the distinctive location and thrilling snowboard scenes overcome improbabilities in the denouement." Publ Wkly

Ransom, Candice
Rebel McKenzie; Candice Ransom. Disney Hyperion 2012 270 p.
Grades: 4 5 6 7   **Fic**
1. Country life -- Fiction 2. Beauty contests -- Fiction 3. Money-making projects for children -- Fiction 4. Nephews -- Fiction 5. Trailer camps -- Fiction 6. Loss (Psychology) -- Fiction 7. Country life -- Virginia -- Fiction
ISBN 1423145399; 9781423145394

LC 2011032729

In this novel by Candice Ransom "Rebel McKenzie wants to spend her summer attending . . . a camp where kids discover prehistoric bones, right alongside real paleontologists. But digs cost money, and Rebel is broker than four o'clock. When she finds out her annoying neighbor Bambi Lovering won five hundred dollars by playing a ukulele behind her head in a beauty contest, Rebel decides to win the Frog Level Volunteer Fire Department's beauty pageant." (Publisher's note)

Ransom, Candice F.
Finding Day's Bottom. Carolrhoda Books 2006 176p lib bdg $15.95
Grades: 4 5 6   **Fic**
1. Bereavement -- Fiction 2. Country life -- Fiction 3.

Grandfathers -- Fiction
ISBN 1-57505-933-9

After her father dies, eleven-year-old Jane-Ery slowly finds healing through her relationship with her grandfather and their rural Virginia home.

"This affecting first-person novel is an involving story of loss, pain, healing, and family love." Booklist

Rappaport, Doreen
Freedom ship. Hyperion Books for Children 2006 un il $15.99
Grades: 3 4 5 6   **Fic**
1. Slaves 2. State legislators 3. Slavery -- Fiction 4. Members of Congress 5. African Americans -- Fiction
ISBN 0-7868-0645-1

"In 1862, Robert Smalls, 23, a black wheelman on the Confederate steamship Planter, and other members of the ship's slave crew, seized the ship and delivered it to the Union Army. Five black women and three children escaped to freedom with the crew, and Rappaport uses the fictionalized viewpoint of one of the children to tell her story. . . . Though personal narrative gives the story immediacy, and the handsome illustrations show the strong child and his proud, smiling family standing tall, Rappaport's lengthy note about Smalls is even more exciting than the fiction." Booklist

Raschka, Chris
Seriously, Norman! [by] Chris Raschka. Scholastic/di Capua 2011 342p il $17.95
Grades: 3 4 5   **Fic**
1. Teachers -- Fiction 2. Friendship -- Fiction 3. Family life -- Fiction
ISBN 978-0-545-29877-3; 0-545-29877-6

Why are grownups so insane? That's the question Leonard, Norman, Anna and Emma (the twins) try to answer with the help of Norman's new tutor, Balthazar Birdsong (who is also fairly nuts).

"Don't expect a linear plot here but rather an ode to ten-year-old humor . . . and improbable characters and situations. . . . Emellished with Raschka's spot art, this rousing tale contains strong wordplay, a little vocabulary instruction . . . and a lot of humor." Horn Book

Raskin, Ellen
Figgs & phantoms. Dutton 2011 152p $16.99; pa $6.99
Grades: 4 5 6   **Fic**
1. Family life -- Fiction
ISBN 978-0-525-42367-6; 0-525-42367-2; 978-0-14-241169-8 pa; 0-14-241169-8 pa
A reissue of the title first published 1974

Chronicles the adventures of the unusual Figg family after they left show business and settled in the town of Pineapple.

This speaks "to both head and heart . . . a most poignant exploration of grief." Horn Book Guide

★ The **Westing** game. Dutton Children's Books 2003 182p $16.99; pa $5.99
Grades: 5 6 7 8   **Fic**
1. Mystery fiction
ISBN 0-525-47137-5; 0-14-240120-X pa

LC 2004-268658

First published 1978

Awarded the Newbery Medal, 1979

"The rules of the game make eight pairs of the players; each oddly matched couple is given a ten thousand dollar check and a set of clues. The result is a fascinating medley of word games, disguises, multiple aliases and subterfuges—in a demanding but rewarding book." Horn Book

The **mysterious** disappearance of Leon (I mean Noel) Dutton 2011 149p $16.99; pa $6.99

Grades: 4 5 6 **Fic**

1. Mystery fiction

ISBN 978-0-525-42369-0; 0-525-42369-9; 978-0-14-241700-3 pa; 0-14-241700-9 pa

A reissue of the title first published 1971

The disappearance of her husband is only the first of the mysteries Mrs. Carillon must solve.

Raskin welcomes "readers in as participants in solving the story's mystery. . . . [The book speaks] to both the head and heart." Horn Book Guide

The **tattooed** potato and other clues. Dutton 2011 170p $16.99; pa $6.99

Grades: 4 5 6 **Fic**

1. Mystery fiction

ISBN 978-0-525-42368-3; 0-525-42368-0; 978-0-14-241699-0 pa; 0-14-241699-1 pa

A reissue of the title first published 1975

A Greenwich Village detective posing as an artist hires a student to act as his apprentice, spy, and eyewitness to murder.

Raskin welcomes "readers in as participants in solving the story's mystery. . . . [It speaks] to both head and heart." Horn Book Guide

Rawlings, Marjorie Kinnan

★ The **secret** river; illustrated by Leo and Diane Dillon. Atheneum Books for Young Readers 2011 un il $19.99

Grades: K 1 2 3 **Fic**

1. Dogs -- Fiction 2. Hunger -- Fiction 3. Fishing -- Fiction 4. Forest animals -- Fiction 5. Forests and forestry -- Fiction

ISBN 978-1-4169-1179-1; 1-4169-1179-0

LC 2007-33292

A newly illustrated edition of the title first published 1955 by Scribner

Young Calpurnia takes her dog, Buggy-horse, and follows her nose to a secret river in a Florida forest, where she catches enough fresh fish to feed her hungry neighbors, even after giving some to the forest creatures she meets on the way home.

"Mesmerizing patterns and colors distinguish the Dillons' spreads, which balance large, captivating panels with smaller vignettes clustered around the text. Their acrylics are a foray into magical realism . . . and their portraits are always true to Rawlings's imaginings. Not to be missed." Publ Wkly

The **yearling**; with pictures by N. C. Wyeth. Scribner 1985 400p il hardcover o.p. pa $5.95

Grades: 5 6 7 8 **Fic**

1. Deer -- Fiction

ISBN 0-684-18461-3; 0-02-044931-3 pa

LC 85-40301

Reissue of the title first published 1938; awarded Pulitzer Prize, 1939

"With its excellent descriptions of Florida scrub landscapes, its skillful use of native vernacular, its tender relation between Jody and his pet fawn, The Yearling is a simply written, picturesque story of boyhood." Time

Rawls, Wilson

★ **Where** the red fern grows; the story of two dogs and a boy. Bantam Bks. 1996 212p $16.95; pa $5.99

Grades: 4 5 6 7 **Fic**

1. Dogs -- Fiction

ISBN 0-385-32330-1; 0-440-41267-6 pa

First published 1961 by Doubleday

"Looking back more than 50 years to his boyhood in the Ozarks, the narrator, recalls how he achieved his heart's desire in the ownership of two redbone hounds, how he taught them all the tricks of hunting, and how they won the championship coon hunt before Old Dan was killed by a mountain lion and Little Ann died of grief. Although some readers may find this novel hackneyed and entirely too sentimental, others will enjoy the fine coonhunting episodes and appreciate the author's feelings for nature." Booklist

Ray, Delia

Ghost girl; a Blue Ridge Mountain story. Clarion Bks. 2003 216p il $15

Grades: 5 6 7 8 **Fic**

1. Presidents 2. School stories 3. Philanthropists 4. Teachers -- Fiction 5. Spouses of presidents 6. Secretaries of commerce

ISBN 0-618-33377-0

LC 2003-4115

Eleven-year-old April is delighted when President and Mrs. Hoover build a school near her Madison County, Virginia, home but her family's poverty, grief over the accidental death of her brother, and other problems may mean that April can never learn to read from the wonderful teacher, Miss Vest

"This excellent portrayal of four important years in a girl's life rises to the top. Based on a real school and teacher, this novel seamlessly incorporates historical facts into the narrative." SLJ

Here lies Linc. Alfred A. Knopf 2011 308p $16.99; lib bdg $19.99

Grades: 5 6 7 8 **Fic**

1. School stories 2. Death -- Fiction 3. Cemeteries -- Fiction 4. Family life -- Fiction

ISBN 978-0-375-86757-6; 0-375-86757-0; 978-0-375-96756-6 lib bdg; 0-375-96756-7 lib bdg

LC 2010030004

While researching a rumored-to-be-haunted grave for a local history project, twelve-year-old Lincoln Crenshaw unearths some startling truths about his own family.

"Ray's tale, which centers around a real legend, strikes the perfect balance of humor, realistic chills and near-teen angst." Kirkus

Singing hands. Clarion Books 2006 248p il $16

Grades: 4 5 6 7 **Fic**
1. Deaf -- Fiction 2. Clergy -- Fiction 3. Family life
-- Fiction
ISBN 0-618-65762-2

LC 2005-22972

In the late 1940s, twelve-year-old Gussie, a minister's
daughter, learns the definition of integrity while helping
with a celebration at the Alabama School for the Deaf—
her punishment for misdeeds against her deaf parents and
their boarders.

"While the portrayal of a signing household is natural and convincing, the focus is on Gussie's rebellion and
growth, the real heart of the story." Horn Book Guide

Reeder, Carolyn
Across the lines. Atheneum Bks. for Young Readers
1997 220p hardcover o.p. pa $5.99
Grades: 5 6 7 8 **Fic**
1. Race relations -- Fiction 2. African Americans --
Fiction
ISBN 0-689-81133-0; 0-380-73073-1 pa

LC 96-31068

Edward, the son of a white plantation owner, and his
black house servant and friend Simon witness the siege of
Petersburg during the Civil War

"Told in the alternating voices of Edward and Simon,
this thoughtful Civil War story resonates with authenticity."
Horn Book Guide

Reedy, Trent
Words in the dust. Arthur A. Levine Books 2011 266p
Grades: 5 6 7 8 **Fic**
1. Literacy -- Fiction 2. Sex role -- Fiction 3. Birth
defects -- Fiction
ISBN 0-545-26125-2; 978-0-545-26125-8

LC 2010-26160

Zulaikha, a thirteen-year-old girl in Afghanistan, faces a
series of frightening but exhilarating changes in her life as
she defies her father and secretly meets with an old woman
who teaches her to read, her older sister gets married, and
American troops offer her surgery to fix her disfiguring
cleft lip.

"The evolution of key relationships presents a nuanced
look at family dynamics and Afghan culture. Though unsentimental and fraught with tragedy, Reedy's narrative offers
hope and will go a long way toward helping readers understand the people behind the headlines." Publ Wkly

Rees, Douglas
Uncle Pirate; illustrated by Tony Auth. Margaret K.
McElderry Books 2008 100p il $15.99
Grades: 2 3 4 **Fic**
1. School stories 2. Uncles -- Fiction 3. Pirates --
Fiction 4. Penguins -- Fiction
ISBN 978-1-4169-4762-2; 1-4169-4762-0

LC 2006-39003

Wilson is one of the most bullied fourth-graders at the
chaotic Very Elementary School until his long-lost uncle,
Desperate Evil Wicked Boba pirate—and his talking penguin arrive and begin making everything shipshape, one
classroom at a time

"The story's goofy humor will entertain pirate fans.
Lively black-and-white pen-and-ink and watercolor spot art
illustrates most pages." Horn Book Guide

Another title about Uncle Pirate is:
Uncle Pirate to the rescue (2010)

Uncle Pirate to the rescue; illustrated by Tony Auth.
Margaret K. McElderry Books 2010 il pa $5.99
Grades: 2 3 4 **Fic**
1. School stories 2. Uncles -- Fiction 3. Pirates --
Fiction 4. Penguins -- Fiction
ISBN 978-1-4169-7505-2; 1-4169-7505-5

LC 2009009130

When Captain Desperate Evil Wicked Bob receives a
plea from his former crew, he heads out to rescue them and
is soon followed by his nephew Wilson, Commodore Pur-
vis, Captain Jack, and others who fear that he needs to be
rescued, as well.

"Auth's illustrations lend depth to the comedic elements
and pirate analogies throughout the story. Avid and reluctant
readers alike will be enchanted and hoping to find their own
mutinous crew to rescue." SLJ

Reeve, Philip
Larklight; or, The revenge of the white spiders!, or To
Saturn's rings and back!: a rousing tale of dauntless pluck in
the farthest reaches of space. as chronicl'd by Art Mumby,
with the aid of Philip Reeve; and decorated throughout by
David Wyatt. Bloomsbury 2006 399p il $16.95; pa $7.95
Grades: 5 6 7 8 **Fic**
1. Science fiction
ISBN 1-59990-020-3; 1-59990-145-5 pa

In an alternate Victorian England, young Arthur and his
sister Myrtle, residents of Larklight, a floating house in one
of Her Majesty's outer space territories, uncover a spidery
plot to destroy the solar system

"This wildly imaginative sci-fi pirate adventure has
tongue-in-cheek humor and social commentary on accepting
those who are different, among other things." SLJ

Other titles about the Mumby family are:
Starcross (2007)
Mothstorm (2008)

Mothstorm; or the horror from beyond Georgium Si-
dus!; or a tale of two shapers. as told by Art Mumby to Philip
Reeve; decorated throughout by David Wyatt. Bloomsbury
U.S.A. Children's Books 2008 390p il $16.99; pa $7.99
Grades: 5 6 7 8 **Fic**
1. Science fiction 2. Adventure fiction 3. Siblings
-- Fiction
ISBN 978-1-59990-303-3; 1-59990-303-2; 978-1-
59990-382-8 pa; 1-59990-382-2 pa

LC 2008008192

Reports of a strange phenomenon at the fringe of the
galaxy and its connection to one of Father's old friends send
the entire Mumby family, accompanied by Jack and other
friends, to a far-off planet where they must find a way to
prevent a new invasion of the solar system by giant moths.

This "is a clever blending of genres including science
fiction, historical fiction, fantasy, and adventure with a liberal dash of British humor and style." SLJ

No such thing as dragons. Scholastic Press 2010 186p
$16.99
Grades: 4 5 6 7 **Fic**
1. Fantasy fiction 2. Dragons -- Fiction
ISBN 978-0-545-22224-2; 0-545-22224-9

A young, mute boy who is apprenticed to a dragon-slayer suspects that the winged beasts do not exist, until he—and his master—learn the truth.

"This is certainly different from anything that Reeve has done previously, but is still shot through with his trademark imagination and feel for action. It will be eagerly devoured by young readers." SLJ

Starcross; or The coming of the moobs!, or, Our adventures in the fourth dimension: a stirring adventure of spies, time travel and curious hats. as narrated by Art Mumby, (& Miss Myrtle Mumby) to their amanuensis, Philip Reeve & illustrated throughout by David Wyatt. Bloomsbury U.S.A. Children's Books 2007 368p il $16.95; pa $7.99

Grades: 5 6 7 8   **Fic**

   1. Science fiction

   ISBN 978-1-59990-121-3; 1-59990-121-8; 978-1-59990-296-8 pa; 1-59990-296-6 pa

                     LC 2007-12002

Young Arthur Mumby, his sister Myrtle, and their mother accept an invitation to take a holiday at an up-and-coming resort in the asteroid belt, where they become involved in a dastardly plot involving spies, time travel, and mind-altering clothing

"It's all very tongue-in-cheek with plenty of jokes and puns in the best traditions of British humor." Booklist

Reh, Rusalka

Pizzicato; the abduction of the magic violin. translated by David Henry Wilson. AmazonCrossing 2011 124p pa $9.95

Grades: 4 5 6 7   **Fic**

   1. Magic -- Fiction 2. Orphans -- Fiction 3. Violins -- Fiction

   ISBN 978-1-6110-9004-8; 1-6110-9004-0

Darius is none too pleased to be paired with Archibald Archinola, a master violinmaker, for a school project, especially when he thinks about his rival—fellow orphan and constant nemesis Max—being surrounded by Porsches at Auto Frederick for the same assignment. But when Darius discovers an old violin in a glass case and strikes the chords, a cut on his hand magically disappears, and suddenly studying with the violinmaker proves to be anything but dull.

This story "has an Old World European charm, from the cast of eccentric, lovable characters to the scenes of café life. Readers will delight in watching the buffoonish villains get their comeuppance, but it's Darius' wish-fulfillment . . . that will satisfy readers most." Booklist

Reiche, Dietlof

Freddy in peril; book two in the Golden Hamster saga. translated from the German by John Brownjohn; illustrated by Joe Cepeda. Scholastic Press 2004 202p il $16.95

Grades: 3 4 5   **Fic**

   1. Pets 2. Hamsters 3. Scientists 4. Golden hamster 5. Hamsters -- Fiction

   ISBN 0-439-53155-1

                     LC 2003-10779

A cat, two guinea pigs, and a colony of brave sewer rats band together in order to save Freddy, a golden hamster, from an evil scientist who's discovered that Freddy can read and write, and plans to hamster-nap him in order to dissect his brain.

"Witty prose, snappy dialogue, endearing characters, and a liberal scattering of stylized, black-and-white illustrations add to the book's appeal." Booklist

Freddy to the rescue; book three in the golden hamster saga. by Dietlof Reiche; translated from the German by John Brownjohn; illustrated by Joe Cepeda. 1st American ed; Scholastic 2005 il $16.95; pa $4.99

Grades: 3 4 5   **Fic**

   ISBN 0-439-53157-8; 0-439-53158-6 pa

                     LC 2004-10001

Freddy, a golden hamster who can read and write, joins his animal and human friends to save a colony of endangered field hamsters from being killed when an automobile plant is constructed on their land.

"Kids will find this to be a genuinely funny tale." SLJ

Freddy's final quest; book five in the golden hamster saga. by Dietlof Reiche; translated from the German by John Brownjohn; illustrated by Joe Cepeda. 1st American ed.; Scholastic Press 2007 295p il $16.99

Grades: 3 4 5   **Fic**

   1. Hamsters -- Fiction

   ISBN 0-439-87414-9; 978-0-439-87414-4

                     LC 2006004616

Original German edition, 2003

Freddy the golden hamster and his animal cohorts, along with a computerized, robotic golden hamster, travel back in time to Assyria, where some of them are captured by crusaders and Freddy gets a taste of undomesticated living.

★ **I,** Freddy; book one in the golden hamster saga. translated from the German by John Brownjohn; illustrated by Joe Cepeda. Scholastic Press 2003 201p il hardcover o.p. pa $4.99

Grades: 3 4 5   **Fic**

   1. Hamsters -- Fiction

   ISBN 0-439-28356-6; 0-439-28357-4 pa

                     LC 2002-6981

Freddy, a remarkably intelligent golden hamster, learns how to read and how to write on a computer and escapes captivity to become an independent and civilized creature

"Illustrated with amusing black-ink sketches, this engaging story will appeal to fans of animal fantasies." SLJ

Other titles about Freddy are:

Freddy in peril (2004)

Freddy to the rescue (2005)

The haunting of Freddy (2006)

Freddy's final quest (2007)

The **haunting** of Freddy; book four in the golden hamster saga. by Dietlof Reiche; translated from the German by John Brownjohn; illustrated by Joe Cepeda. 1st American ed.; Scholastic Press 2006 311p il $16.99; pa $5.99

Grades: 3 4 5   **Fic**

   1. Hamsters -- Fiction

   ISBN 0-439-53159-4; 0-439-53160-8 pa

                     LC 2005008757

In this novel about Freddy the intelligent hamster, an evil fifteenth-century poacher and his ferrets, mysteriously come to life, endangering Freddy and his friends and drawing them to an English castle near where the poacher once lived.

This is "an entertaining blend of suspense and fantasy. . . . Reiche's high-energy sketches . . . add plenty of punch to the scenes and characters." Booklist

Reinhardt, Dana

Odessa again; Dana Reinhardt. 1st ed. Wendy Lamb Books 2013 208 p. (ebook) $47.97; (hardcover) $15.99; (library) $18.99

Grades: 4 5 6 7 **Fic**

1. Remarriage -- Juvenile fiction 2. Time travel -- Juvenile fiction 3. Remarriage -- Fiction 4. Time travel -- Fiction

ISBN 0385739567; 9780375897887; 9780385739566; 9780385907934

LC 2012008231

In this children's novel, by Dana Reinhardt, "fourth grader Odessa Green-Light lives with her mom and her toad of a little brother, Oliver. Her dad is getting remarried. . . . Meanwhile, Odessa moves into the attic room of their new house. One day [it] . . . turns out that Odessa has gone back in time a whole day! With this new power she can fix all sorts of things--embarrassing moments, big mistakes, and even help Oliver be less of a toad. Her biggest goal: reunite Mom and Dad." (Publisher's note)

"Realistically drawn, Odessa is a believable, likable kid on the brink of growing up, struggling with family changes. . . . With humor as well as depth, this is an endearing story of a spunky girl who realizes that life gets more, not less, confusing as she grows up." Kirkus

The **summer** I learned to fly. Wendy Lamb Books 2011 216p $15.99; lib bdg $18.99; e-book $15.99

Grades: 5 6 7 8 **Fic**

1. Rats -- Fiction 2. Family life -- Fiction 3. Retail trade -- Fiction 4. Single parent family -- Fiction

ISBN 978-0-385-73954-2; 0-385-73954-0; 978-0-385-90792-7 lib bdg; 0-385-90792-3 lib bdg; 978-0-375-89787-0 e-book; 0-375-89787-9 e-book

LC 2010029412

Thirteen-year-old Drew starts the summer of 1986 helping in her mother's cheese shop and dreaming about co-worker Nick, but when her widowed mother begins dating, Drew's father's book of lists, her pet rat, and Emmett, a boy on a quest, help her cope.

"This quiet novel invites readers to share in its heroine's deepest yearnings, changing moods, and difficult realizations." Publ Wkly

Remkiewicz, Frank

Song Lee in Room 2B; pictures by Frank Remkiewicz. Viking 1993 56p il hardcover o.p. pa $3.99

Grades: 2 3 4 **Fic**

1. School stories 2. Korean Americans -- Fiction

ISBN 0-670-84772-0; 0-14-130408-1 pa

LC 92-41523

Spring becomes a memorable time for Miss Mackle's second-grade classroom because of the antics of Horrible Harry and the special insights of shy Song Lee

"The school setting has great appeal, and the familiar 2B kids deliver lots of funny moments." Booklist

Repka, Janice

The **clueless** girl's guide to being a genius. Dutton Children's Books 2011 218p $16.99

Grades: 4 5 6 **Fic**

1. School stories 2. Genius -- Fiction 3. Teachers -- Fiction 4. Friendship -- Fiction 5. Mathematics -- Fiction 6. Baton twirling -- Fiction

ISBN 978-0-525-42333-1; 0-525-42333-8

LC 2010038139

When Aphrodite Wigglesmith, a thirteen-year-old, Harvard-educated mathematics genius, returns home to teach remedial math to middle school students, both she and her students end up getting unexpected lessons.

"A lighthearted, funny and often bizarre saga of middle-school mayhem. . . . Equal parts silly and endearing." Kirkus

Resau, Laura

★ **Star** in the forest. Delacorte Press 2010 149p il $14.99; lib bdg $17.99

Grades: 4 5 6 **Fic**

1. Dogs -- Fiction 2. Fathers -- Fiction 3. Friendship -- Fiction 4. Illegal aliens -- Fiction 5. Mexican Americans -- Fiction

ISBN 978-0-385-73792-0; 0-385-73792-0; 978-0-385-90700-2 lib bdg; 0-385-90700-1 lib bdg

LC 2009-03898

After eleven-year-old Zitlally's father is deported to Mexico, she takes refuge in her trailer park's forest of rusted car parts, where she befriends a spunky neighbor and finds a stray dog that she nurses back to health and believes she must keep safe so that her father will return.

"Resau has woven details of immigrant life into a compelling story. . . . This is a well-told and deeply satisfying read." SLJ

★ **What** the moon saw; a novel. Delacorte Press 2006 258p $15.95; pa $5.99

Grades: 5 6 7 8 **Fic**

1. Country life -- Fiction 2. Grandparents -- Fiction

ISBN 0-385-73343-7; 0-440-23957-5 pa

LC 2006-04571

Fourteen-year-old Clara Luna spends the summer with her grandparents in the tiny, remote village of Yucuyoo, Mexico, learning about her grandmother's life as a healer, her father's decision to leave home for the United States, and her own place in the world.

This is an "exquisitely crafted narrative. . . . The characters are well developed. . . . Resau does an exceptional job of portraying the agricultural society sympathetically and realistically." SLJ

Rex, Adam

★ **Cold** cereal. Balzer + Bray 2012 il $16.99

Grades: 4 5 6 7 **Fic**

1. Adventure fiction 2. Food -- Fiction 3. Magic -- Fiction 4. Twins -- Fiction 5. Siblings -- Fiction

ISBN 978-0-06-206002-0; 0-06-206002-3

LC 2011019538

A boy who may be part changeling, twins involved in a bizarre secret experiment, and a clurichaun in a red tracksuit try to save the world from an evil cereal company whose ultimate goal is world domination.

"The author tucks in portrait illustrations and hilariously odd TV-commercial storyboards, along with a hooded Secret Society, figures from Arthurian legend, magical spells and potions, a certain amount of violence, many wonderful throwaway lines. . . . All in all, it's a mad scramble that culminates in the revelation of a dastardly plot that will require sequels to foil." Kirkus

Unlucky charms; Adam Rex. Balzer + Bray 2013 400 p. (The cold cereal saga) (hardback) $16.99
Grades: 4 5 6 7   Fic
1. Fantasy fiction -- Juvenile fiction 2. Humorous fiction -- Juvenile fiction 3. Prepared cereals -- Juvenile fiction 4. Magic -- Fiction 5. Twins -- Fiction 6. Cereals, Prepared -- Fiction 7. Brothers and sisters -- Fiction 8. JUVENILE FICTION -- Fantasy & Magic 9. Adventure and adventurers -- Fiction 10. JUVENILE FICTION -- Humorous Stories 11. JUVENILE FICTION -- Legends, Myths, Fables -- Arthurian
ISBN 0062060058; 9780062060051
LC 2012026714
This humorous juvenile fantasy book, by Adam Rex, is part of the "Cold Cereal Saga." "In this hectic middle volume, [Adam] Rex's notably diverse crew of human, part-human and nonhuman allies splits up in hopes of scotching the schemes of the sorceress Nimue, who is out to create a worldwide army of mind-controlled 'sugar zombies' through magically enhanced breakfast cereal." (Kirkus Reviews)

★ The **true** meaning of Smekday. Hyperion Books for Children 2007 423p il $16.99; pa $6.99
Grades: 5 6 7 8   Fic
1. Science fiction 2. End of the world -- Fiction 3. Extraterrestrial beings -- Fiction
ISBN 0-7868-4900-2; 978-0-7868-4900-0; 0-7868-4901-0 pa; 978-0-7868-4901-7 pa
When her mother is abducted by aliens on Christmas Eve (or "Smekday" Eve since the Boov invasion), 11 year-old Tip hops in the family car and heads south to find her and meets an alien Boov mechanic who agrees to help her and save the planet from disaster.
"Incorporating dozens of his weird and wonderful illustrations and fruitfully manipulating the narrative structure, Rex skewers any number of subjects." Publ Wkly

Reynolds, Peter H.
★ **Sky** color; Peter H. Reynolds. Candlewick 2012 32 p. (hardback) $14.00
Grades: PreK K 1 2   Fic
1. Sky -- Fiction 2. Picture books for children 3. Mural painting and decoration -- Juvenile literature 4. Color -- Fiction 5. Paint -- Fiction 6. Artists -- Fiction 7. Schools -- Fiction 8. JUVENILE FICTION -- Art & Architecture 9. JUVENILE FICTION -- Concepts -- Colors
ISBN 0763623458; 9780763623456
LC 2011048374
In this children's picture book, "Marisol is an artist, famous at school for her art . . . . When their teacher tells her class that they are going to paint a mural in the library, . . . Marisol volunteers to paint the sky. But to her dismay, in the box of paint there is no blue." She agonizes until she realizes that the sky isn't always blue and comes up with a solution. "On a wordless double page, her classmates admire the 'sky color' she has created." (Children's Literature)

Rhodes, Jewell Parker
★ **Ninth** Ward. Little, Brown 2010 217p $15.99

Grades: 5 6 7 8   Fic
1. Extrasensory perception -- Fiction 2. Hurricane Katrina, 2005 -- Fiction
ISBN 978-0-316-04307-6; 0-316-04307-9
LC 2009-34423
Coretta Scott King Author Award honor book, 2011
In New Orleans' Ninth Ward, twelve-year-old Lanesha, who can see spirits, and her adopted grandmother have no choice but to stay and weather the storm as Hurricane Katrina bears down upon them.
"The dynamics of the diverse community enrich the survival story, and the contemporary struggle of one brave child humanizes the historic tragedy." Booklist

Sugar; Jewell Parker Rhodes. 1st ed. Little, Brown and Co. 2013 288 p. (hardcover) $16.99
Grades: 3 4 5 6 7 8   Fic
1. Race relations -- Juvenile fiction 2. Plantation life -- Juvenile fiction 3. Historical fiction -- Juvenile fiction 4. Race relations -- Fiction 5. African Americans -- Fiction 6. Chinese Americans -- Fiction 7. Plantation life -- Louisiana -- Fiction 8. Reconstruction (U.S. history, 1865-1877) -- Fiction
ISBN 0316043052; 9780316043052
LC 2012026218
In this historical novel, by Jewell Parker Rhodes, "ten-year-old Sugar lives on the River Road sugar plantation along the banks of the Mississippi. Slavery is over, but laboring in the fields all day doesn't make her feel very free. . . . Here's another tale of a strong, spirited young girl who rises beyond her circumstances and inspires others to work toward a brighter future." (Publisher's note)
"Sugar's clipped narration is personable and engaging, strongly evoking the novel's historical setting and myriad racial tensions, making them accessible and meaningful to beginning readers." Pub Wkly

Richards, Jasmine
The **book** of wonders. HarperCollins 2012 $14.99
Grades: 4 5 6 7   Fic
1. Fantasy fiction 2. Adventure fiction 3. Friendship -- Fiction
ISBN 978-0-06-201007-0; 0-06-201007-7
LC 2011009153
In a tale loosely based on the Arabian nights, thirteen-year-old Zardi and her best friend, Ridhan, join forces with Captain Sinbad to defeat an evil sultan and restore magic to the world of Arribitha.
"This buoyant debut offers a fresh plot, brisk pacing and engaging characters. . . . Richards deftly borrows from lesser-known tales of the 1001 Arabian Nights to enrich her complex storyline while keeping style and syntax simple and direct." Kirkus

Richards, Justin
Thunder Raker; illustrated by Jim Hansen. IPG/HarperCollins 2010 139p il (Agent Alfie) pa $6.99
Grades: 3 4 5   Fic
1. School stories 2. Spies -- Fiction
ISBN 978-0-00-727357-7; 0-00-727357-6
"After Alfie moves to a new town, he is enrolled by mistake at Thunder Raker Manor, a top-secret school that trains children to be future British spies. At his new school, Alfie encounters a host of eccentric teachers and swashbuckling

students. Although at first Alfie seems in over his head, his good sense and practical ideas help him get the best grades in the class on his first homework assignment, and by the end of the novel, he manages to thwart agents from the evil organization SPUD. . . . The bright concept, short length, and humorous, action-packed drawings that fill each chapter should keep this in demand and leave readers eager for the series' next installment." Booklist

Richter, Jutta

Beyond the station lies the sea; translated from the German by Anna Brailovsky. Milkweed Editions 2009 81p $14

Grades: 4 5 6 7   **Fic**

1. Angels -- Fiction 2. Homeless persons -- Fiction
ISBN 978-1-57131-690-5; 1-57131-690-6

        LC 2009018135

Trying to get to the beach where it is warm, two homeless boys enlist the aid of a rich woman who gives them money in exchange for a guardian angel.

"Richter presents a darkly poetic, masterfully crafted view of life on the streets." Publ Wkly

Riddell, Chris

★ **Ottoline** and the yellow cat. HarperCollinsPublishers 2008 171p il $10.99; lib bdg $14.89; pa $6.99

Grades: 2 3 4 5   **Fic**

1. Mystery fiction 2. Cats -- Fiction 3. Dogs -- Fiction
ISBN 978-0-06-144879-9; 0-06-144879-6; 978-0-06-144880-5 lib bdg; 0-06-144880-X lib bdg; 978-0-06-144881-2 pa; 0-06-144881-8 pa

"While her parents are off traveling the world collecting 'interesting things,' Ottoline Brown lives in an elaborate apartment in Big City with her best friend, guardian, and accomplice in forming clever plans. He is called Mr. Monroe and is a silent creature from Norway. . . . Ottoline solves a mystery involving a cat burglar, who is actually a cat, and the missing lapdogs of well-to-do women. The story is told through the text and the detailed line drawings that appear on each page. Done in black and white with red highlighting a quirky detail or two, the illustrations add humor, depth, and momentum to the narrative. The quickly moving plot is grounded in real emotion." SLJ

Another title about Ottoline is:
Ottoline goes to school (2009)

Riel, Jorn

The **raiders**; written by Jørn Riel; illustrated by Helen Cann; translated by John Mason. Barefoot Books 2012 127 p. (alk. paper) $12.99

Grades: 4 5 6   **Fic**

1. Historical fiction 2. Vikings -- Juvenile fiction 3. Greenland -- History -- To 1500 -- Juvenile fiction 4. Inuit -- Greenland -- Fiction 5. Eskimos -- Greenland -- Fiction
ISBN 1846867444; 9781846867446

        LC 2011044383

This book by Jorn Riel, part of the Inuk Quartet series, "continues the exciting adventures of Leiv, Apuluk and Narua established in 'The Shipwreck.' The story begins with our trio settled peacefully on Thor Gunnarrsson's farmstead in Greenland. When Viking raiders arrive at the farmstead, their quiet world is disturbed forever. Leiv, Apuluk and Na-

rua must rely on their wits, their courage, and their friendship to protect their new home." (Publisher's note)

The **shipwreck**; translated from Danish by John Mason; illustrated by Helen Cann. Barefoot Books 2011 il (The Inuk quartet) pa $12.99

Grades: 4 5 6   **Fic**

1. Adventure fiction 2. Inuit -- Fiction 3. Vikings -- Fiction
ISBN 978-1-84686-335-6; 1-84686-335-X

"This beautifully illustrated epic adventure, set circa 1000 CE, begins with the shocking, retaliatory beheading of young Viking Leiv's father by Thorstein Gunnarsson. The playful boy becomes withdrawn and vows to take revenge. When Thorstein casts off from Iceland for Greenland to serve out his sentence of exile, Leiv stows away onboard but is swept into the sea during a storm. An Inuit brother and sister, Apuluk, 12, and Narua, 11, find him and care for him in secret. . . . The narrative is straightforward and well paced, with several engaging dramatic episodes. Riel skillfully interweaves information about the Inuit culture, language, and environment without being didactic. . . . Vocabulary may pose a challenge for less-advanced readers, and mention of beheadings and amputations may be unsuitable for others. But Cann's ethereal watercolor, graphite, and collage illustrations in cool blue tones and browns have a calmer mood that will enchant readers with the beauty of the Arctic landscape." SLJ

The **snowstorm**; written by Jørn Riel; illustrated by Helen Cann; translation by John Mason. Barefoot Books 2012 126 p. (alk. paper) $12.99

Grades: 4 5 6   **Fic**

1. Greenland -- Fiction 2. Inuit -- Juvenile fiction 3. Adventure fiction -- Juvenile fiction 4. Voyages and travels -- Juvenile fiction 5. Inuit -- Fiction 6. Eskimos -- Fiction 7. Voyages and travels -- Fiction
ISBN 1846867975; 9781846867972

        LC 2012009599

This book by Jørn Riel, "the third in a four-part Viking-era adventure, pits four young Greenlanders against both a howling gale and a crew of brutal pirates. . . . Leiv, his Inuit brother-and-sister companions Apuluk and Narua, and rescued serf Sølvi sled northward in search of the vanished chieftain Thorstein. . . . The explorers weather a journey highlighted by a violent . . . storm . . . [and a] battle aboard an iced-in British longship." (Kirkus Reviews)

Riley, James

Half upon a time. Aladdin 2010 385p $15.99

Grades: 5 6 7 8   **Fic**

1. Fairy tales 2. Adventure fiction
ISBN 978-1-4169-9593-7; 1-4169-9593-5

        LC 2010012714

In the village of Giant's Hand Jack's grandfather has been pushing him to find a princess and get married, so when a young lady falls out of the sky wearing a shirt that says "Punk Princess," and she tells Jack that her grandmother, who looks suspiciously like the long-missing Snow White, has been kidnapped, Jack decides to help her.

"Riley does a wonderful job of combining the 21st century with the world in which fairies are alive, as well as creating characters that middle school students will relate to." Libr Media Connect

Riordan, Rick

The **Sea** of Monsters. Miramax Books/Hyperion Books for Children 2006 279p (Percy Jackson & the Olympians) $17.95; pa $7.99

Grades: 5 6 7 8 9   **Fic**

1. Classical mythology -- Fiction

ISBN 978-0-7868-5686-2; 0-7868-5686-6; 978-1-4231-0334-9 pa; 1-4231-0334-3 pa

LC 2006280771

Demigod Percy Jackson and his friends must journey into the Sea of Monsters to save their camp. But first Percy will discover a secret that makes him wonder whether being claimed as Poseidon's son is an honor or a cruel joke

"Adventure follows chaotic adventure at a rapid pace, and readers with even a passing acquaintance with the Odyssey will enjoy this fresh use of familiar stories." SLJ

The **Serpent's** Shadow; Rick Riordan. Disney/Hyperion Books 2012 viii, 406 p.p (hardcover) $19.99

Grades: 4 5 6 7   **Fic**

1. Adventure fiction 2. Supernatural -- Fiction 3. Mythology -- Juvenile fiction 4. Magic -- Fiction 5. Mythology, Egyptian -- Fiction 6. Voyages and travels -- Fiction 7. Brothers and sisters -- Fiction 8. Adventure and adventurers -- Fiction

ISBN 1423140575; 9781423140573

LC 2012454979

This book by Rick Riordan is the third installment of the Kane Chronicles series. "Despite their best efforts, Carter and Sadie Kane can't seem to keep Apophis, the chaos snake, down. Now Apophis is threatening to plunge the world into eternal darkness, and the Kanes are faced with the impossible task of having to destroy him once and for all." (Publisher's note)

The **Titan's** curse. Miramax Books/Hyperion Books for Children 2007 312p (Percy Jackson & the Olympians) $17.95; pa $7.99

Grades: 5 6 7 8 9   **Fic**

1. Classical mythology -- Fiction

ISBN 978-1-4231-0145-1; 1-4231-0145-6; 978-1-4231-0145-1 pa; 1-4231-0148-0 pa

LC 2006-35731

When the goddess Artemis disappears while hunting a rare, ancient monster, a group of her followers joins Percy and his friends in an attempt to find and rescue her before the winter solstice, when her influence is needed to sway the Olympian Council regarding the war with the Titans.

"Intricate prophecies and relationships are neatly braided into the adventurous plot." SLJ

Vespers rising; [by] Rick Riordan, Peter Lerangis, Gordon Korman, Jude Watson. Scholastic 2011 238p (The 39 clues) $12.99

Grades: 4 5 6 7   **Fic**

1. Ciphers -- Fiction

ISBN 978-0-545-29059-3; 0-545-32606-0

Fourteen-year-old Amy Cahill and her younger brother Dan thought they could return to their regular lives when they found the 39 clues. But the Vespers, powerful enemies, will stop at nothing to get the clues. And with the Vespers rising, the world is in jeopardy.

The **battle** of the Labyrinth. Hyperion Books for Children 2008 361p (Percy Jackson & the Olympians) lib bdg $17.99; pa $7.99

Grades: 5 6 7 8 9   **Fic**

1. Classical mythology -- Fiction

ISBN 978-1-4231-0146-8 lib bdg; 1-4231-0146-4 lib bdg; 978-1-4231-0149-9 pa; 1-4231-0149-9 pa

LC 2007-42957

When demonic cheerleaders invade his high school, Percy Jackson hurries to Camp Half Blood, from whence he and his demigod friends set out on a quest through the Labyrinth, while the war between the Olympians and the evil Titan lord Kronos draws near.

"The wit, rousing swordplay and breakneck pace will once again keep kids hooked." Publ Wkly

The **last** Olympian. Hyperion Books for Children 2009 381p map (Percy Jackson & the Olympians) $17.99

Grades: 5 6 7 8 9   **Fic**

1. Classical mythology -- Fiction

ISBN 978-1-4231-0147-5; 1-4231-0147-5

All year the half-bloods have been preparing for battle against the Titans. Now it's up to Percy Jackson and an army of young demi-gods to stop the Lord of Time.

"Riordan masterfully orchestrates the huge cast of characters and manages a coherent, powerful tale at once exciting, philosophical and tear-jerking." Kirkus

★ The **lightning** thief. Miramax Books/Hyperion Books for Children 2005 377p (Percy Jackson & the Olympians)

Grades: 5 6 7 8 9   **Fic**

1. Classical mythology -- Fiction

ISBN 0-7868-5629-7; 1-4231-3494-X pa; 978-0-6417-2344-5; 978-1-4231-3494-7 pa

LC 2005-299400

Twelve-year-old Percy Jackson learns he is a demigod, the son of a mortal woman and Poseidon, god of the sea. His mother sends him to a summer camp for demigods where he and his new friends set out on a quest to prevent a war between the gods.

"Riordan's fast-paced adventure is fresh, dangerous, and funny." Booklist

Other titles in this series are:

The Sea of Monsters (2006)

The Titan's curse (2007)

The battle of the Labyrinth (2008)

The last Olympian (2009)

The **lost** hero. Disney/Hyperion Books 2010 553p $18.99

Grades: 5 6 7 8   **Fic**

1. Camps -- Fiction 2. Monsters -- Fiction 3. Classical mythology -- Fiction

ISBN 978-1-4231-1339-3; 1-4231-1339-X

LC 2010015469

"Completely in control of pacing and tone, . . . [Riordan] . . . balances a faultless comic banter against deeper notes that reveal the characters' vulnerabilities." Horn Book

★ The **maze** of bones. Scholastic 2008 220p il (The 39 clues) $12.99

Grades: 4 5 6 7 **Fic**
1. Family -- Fiction 2. Ciphers -- Fiction
ISBN 978-0-545-06039-4; 0-545-06039-7
At the reading of their grandmother's will, Dan and Amy Cahill are given the choice of receiving a million dollars or uncovering the 39 clues hidden around the world that will lead to the source of the family's power, but by taking on the clues, they end up in a dangerous race against their own family members.

"Adeptly incorporating a genuine kids' perspective, the narrative unfolds like a boulder rolling downhill and keeps readers glued to the pages. . . . The book dazzles with suspense, plot twists, and snappy humor." SLJ

Other titles in this series are:
One false note by Gordon Korman (2008)
The sword thief by Peter Lerangis (2009)
The black circle by Patrick Carman (2009)
Beyond the grave by Jude Watson (2009)
In too deep by Jude Watson (2010)
The viper's nest by Peter Lerangis (2010)
The emperor's code by Gordon Korman (2010)
Storm warning by Linda Sue Park (2010)
Into the gauntlet by Margaret Peterson Haddix (2010)

The **son** of Neptune. Disney/Hyperion Books 2011 521p (The heroes of Olympus) $19.99
Grades: 5 6 7 8 **Fic**
1. Camps -- Fiction 2. Monsters -- Fiction 3. Prophecies -- Fiction 4. Classical mythology -- Fiction
ISBN 978-1-4231-4059-7; 1-4231-4059-1
LC 2011017658
Demigod Percy Jackson, still with no memory, and his new friends from Camp Jupiter, Hazel and Frank, go on a quest to free Death, but their bigger task is to unite the Greek and Roman camps so that the Prophecy of Seven can be fulfilled.

The **throne** of fire; Rick Riordan. Disney/Hyperion Books 2011 (Kane chronicles) $18.99
Grades: 4 5 6 7 **Fic**
ISBN 978-1-4231-4056-6; 1-4231-4056-7;
1423140567; 9781423140566
Carter and Sadie, offspring of the brilliant Egyptologist Dr. Julius Kane, embark on a worldwide search for the Book of Ra, but the House of Life and the gods of chaos are determined to stop them.

"Lit by flashes of humor, this fantasy adventure is an engaging addition to the Kane Chronicles series." Booklist

Rising, Janet
The **word** on the yard. Sourcebooks 2010 189p (The pony whisperer) pa $6.99
Grades: 4 5 6 **Fic**
1. Horses -- Fiction
ISBN 978-1-4022-3952-6 pa; 1-4022-3952-1 pa
First published 2009 in the United Kingdom
Pia finally starts to feel like she belongs in her new town after people begin to hear that she can communicate with horses, but her popularity is not the only thing she has to worry about when things start to go wrong.

"This combination of magic and a quick-moving, contemporary plot woven around horse and human conflicts and friendships is a light and enjoyable read for fans of this genre." SLJ

Riskind, Mary
Apple is my sign. Houghton Mifflin 1981 146p hardcover o.p. pa $5.95
Grades: 5 6 7 8 **Fic**
1. Deaf -- Fiction
ISBN 0-395-30852-6; 0-395-65747-4 pa
"In a lengthy note the author explains that she had deaf parents and learned sign language before she learned to speak. She also explores some characteristics of sign language, which has been translated into print via sentence syntax and spelling. A warm, unpretentious story." Booklist

Roberts, Ken
Thumb and the bad guys; illustrated by Leanne Franson. Groundwood Books/House of Anansi Press 2009 119p il $17.95
Grades: 3 4 5 **Fic**
1. Mystery fiction
ISBN 978-0-88899-916-0; 0-88899-916-X
"Entertaining for children who've moved beyond early readers and want some thrills but who are not ready for too much complexity or fright." Kirkus

Thumb on a diamond; illustrated by Leanne Franson. Groundwood Books/House of Anansi Press 2006 128p il $15.95; pa $6.95
Grades: 3 4 5 **Fic**
1. Baseball -- Fiction
ISBN 0-88899-629-2; 0-88899-705-1 pa
The kids from New Auckland are dying to see something outside of their little villiage. Then, Thumb comes up with a plan to form a baseball team so the kids can go to the big tournament in Vancouver, but there are a few problems with their plan. There is no grass in New Auckland, no baseball diamond and no place large enough to put one. Also, none of the kids have ever played baseball before.

"The characters are appealing and the plot unfolds naturally to create a satisfying and plausible story." SLJ

Others titles about Thumb and his friends are:
Thumb in the box (2001)
Thumb and the bad guys (2009)

The **thumb** in the box; illustrated by Leanne Franson. Groundwood Books 2001 95p hardcover o.p. pa $5.95
Grades: 3 4 5 **Fic**
ISBN 978-0-88899-421-9; 0-88899-421-4; 978-0-88899-422-6 pa; 0-88899-422-2 pa
When Little Charlie returns to the island town of New Auckland in British Columbia to build a fire station for the soon-to-arrive fire engine, he astounds everyone, particularly young Leon Mazzei, by being able to remove his thumb.

"The story's humor and insight will appeal even to the most reluctant readers." Booklist

Roberts, Laura Peyton
Green. Delacorte Press 2010 261p $16.99; lib bdg $19.99
Grades: 5 6 7 8 **Fic**
1. Fantasy fiction 2. Leprechauns -- Fiction 3. Grandmothers -- Fiction
ISBN 978-0-385-73558-2; 0-385-73558-8; 978-0-385-90543-5 lib bdg; 0-385-90543-2 lib bdg
LC 2008-54241

Abducted by leprechauns on her thirteenth birthday, Lilybet Green learns that there is more to her family tree—and to her bond with her late grandmother—than she ever imagined.

"A fun, fresh take on leprechaun lore that pushes well past typical depictions to embrace banking transactions, lepro-human relations, and some creative problem-solving. Lily is a credible hero, by turns scared and confident, and definitely one young readers will enjoy following." Booklist

Roberts, Marion

Sunny side up. Wendy Lamb Books 2009 244p il $15.99; lib bdg $18.99

Grades: 4 5 6 7 **Fic**

1. Friendship -- Fiction 2. Family life -- Fiction

ISBN 978-0-385-73672-5; 0-385-73672-X; 978-0-385-90624-1 lib bdg; 0-385-90624-2 lib bdg

LC 2008-08633

First published 2008 in Australia

As the hot Australian summer draws to an end, eleven-year-old Sunny, content to be an only child with amicably divorced parents, finds her life getting much too complicated when her mother's boyfriend moves in with his two children, her best friend begins to develop an interest in boys, and she is contacted by her long-estranged grandmother.

"Character development is strong, as the girl is quick to observe and comment on the people in her life, and the setting forms an interesting backdrop. Small black-and-white photos are liberally scattered throughout." SLJ

Roberts, Willo Davis

The **kidnappers**. Atheneum Bks. for Young Readers 1998 137p hardcover o.p. pa $4.99

Grades: 4 5 6 7 **Fic**

1. Wealth -- Fiction 2. Bullies -- Fiction 3. Kidnapping -- Fiction

ISBN 0-689-81394-5; 0-689-81393-7 pa

LC 96-53677

No one believes eleven-year-old Joey, who has a reputation for telling tall tales, when he claims to have witnessed the kidnapping of the class bully outside their expensive New York City private school

"The combination of a witty narrative and a suspenseful plot makes this a good page-turner that will leave even the most reluctant readers glued to their seats." Booklist

The **one** left behind; [by] Willo Davis Roberts. Atheneum Books for Young Readers 2006 139p $16.95; pa $5.99

Grades: 5 6 7 8 **Fic**

1. Twins -- Fiction 2. Sisters -- Fiction 3. Kidnapping -- Fiction 4. Bereavement -- Fiction

ISBN 978-0-689-85075-2; 0-689-85075-1; 978-0-689-85083-7 pa; 0-689-85083-2 pa

LC 2005018196

"Since losing her vivacious twin sister, Angel, nearly a year ago, . . . 11-year-old [Mandy] drifts through the days, aching for her dead sister's company. But when someone breaks into the house and steals food, Mandy snaps into action and investigates what might be going on. . . . The suspense mounts to a desperate climax before all is resolved safely. An introspective page-turner." Booklist

★ The **view** from the cherry tree. Atheneum Pubs. 1975 181p hardcover o.p. pa $5.99

Grades: 5 6 7 8 **Fic**

1. Mystery fiction

ISBN 0-689-30483-8; 0-689-71784-9 pa

"Although written in a direct and unpretentious style, this is essentially a sophisticated story, solidly constructed, imbued with suspense, evenly paced, and effective in conveying the atmosphere of a household coping with the last-minute problems and pressures of a family wedding." Bull Cent Child Books

Robertson, Keith

★ **Henry** Reed, Inc. illustrated by Robert McCloskey. Viking 1958 239p il hardcover o.p. pa $4.99

Grades: 4 5 6 **Fic**

ISBN 0-14-034144-7 pa

"Henry Reed, on vacation from the American School in Naples, keeps a record of his research into the American free-enterprise system, to be used as a school report on his return. With a neighbor, Midge Glass, he starts a business in pure and applied research, which results in some very free and widely enterprising experiences, all recorded deadpan in his journal. Very funny and original escapades." Hodges. Books for Elem Sch Libr

Another title about Henry Reed is:

Henry Reed's babysitting service (1966)

Robertson, M. P.

Frank n stan; M. P. Robertson. Pgw 2012 32 p. $17.99

Grades: K 1 2 3 **Fic**

1. Robots -- Juvenile fiction 2. Siblings -- Juvenile fiction 3. Friendship -- Juvenile fiction

ISBN 1847801307; 9781847801302

In author M. P. Robertson's book, "young Franklin P. Shelley often asks his mother for a younger sibling . . . Industrious Frank decides to take matters into his own hands and sets out to build one . . . [named Stan.] Frank charges up the battery, and the light in Stan's chest begins to glow . . . One day, Mum surprises Frank with a cute baby girl, and the boy begins to spend more time with his sister, Mary, and less with Stan. One snowy evening, Stan leaves. It doesn't take long for him to freeze or for the family to miss him. A big hug convinces the big mechanical lug to return." (Kirkus Reviews)

Robinet, Harriette Gillem

★ **Forty** acres and maybe a mule. Atheneum Bks. for Young Readers 1998 132p hardcover o.p. pa $4.99

Grades: 4 5 6 7 **Fic**

1. African Americans -- Fiction 2. Reconstruction (1865-1876) -- Fiction

ISBN 0-689-82078-X; 0-689-83317-2 pa

LC 97-39169

Born with a withered leg and hand, Pascal, who is about twelve years old, joins other former slaves in a search for a farm and the freedom which it promises

"Robinet skillfully balances her in-depth historical knowledge with the feelings of her characters, creating a story that moves along rapidly and comes to a bittersweet conclusion." Booklist

Walking to the bus-rider blues. Atheneum Bks. for Young Readers 2000 146p hardcover o.p. pa $4.99
Grades: 5 6 7 8 **Fic**
1. Race relations -- Fiction 2. African Americans -- Fiction
ISBN 0-689-83191-9; 0-689-83886-7 pa
LC 99-29054

Twelve-year-old Alfa Merryfield, his older sister, and their grandmother struggle for rent money, food, and their dignity as they participate in the Montgomery, Alabama bus boycott in the summer of 1956

"Ingredients of mystery, suspense, and humor enhance and personalize this well-constructed story that offers insight into a troubled era." SLJ

Robinson, Barbara
★ The **best** Christmas pageant ever; pictures by Judith Gwyn Brown. Harper & Row 1972 80p il $15.99; lib bdg $16.89; pa $5.99
Grades: 4 5 6 **Fic**
1. Pageants -- Fiction 2. Christmas -- Fiction
ISBN 0-06-025043-7; 0-06-025044-5 lib bdg; 0-06-440275-4 pa

In this story the six Herdmans, "absolutely the worst kids in the history of the world," discover the meaning of Christmas when they bully their way into the leading roles of the local church nativity play

The story "romps through the festive preparations with comic relish, and if the Herdmans are so gauche as to seem exaggerated, they are still enjoyable, as are the not-so-subtle pokes at pageant-planning in general." Bull Cent Child Books

Other titles about the Herdmans are:
The best Halloween ever (2004)
The best school year ever (1994)

Robinson, Mabel L.
Bright Island; Mabel L. Robinson; with decorations by Lynd Ward. 75th anniversary ed. Random House Books for Young Readers 2012 276 p. ill. (hardback) $16.99
Grades: 3 4 5 **Fic**
1. Bildungsromans 2. School stories 3. Maine -- Fiction 4. Schools -- Fiction 5. Coming of age -- Fiction 6. Boarding schools -- Fiction 7. Islands -- Maine -- Fiction
ISBN 0394809866; 9780394809861
LC 2012009178

Newbery Honor Book (1938)
This book by Mabel L. Robinson follows "Thankful Curtis, [who] is more like her sea captain grandfather than any of her older brothers are. Nothing suits her better than sailing and helping her father with the farm. But when her dreaded sisters-in-law suggest that Thankful get some proper schooling on the mainland . . . Thankful finds the uncharted waters of school difficult to navigate." (Publisher's note)

Robinson, Sharon
Safe at home. Scholastic Press 2006 151p $16.99; pa $5.99
Grades: 4 5 6 **Fic**
1. Baseball -- Fiction 2. African Americans -- Fiction
ISBN 0-439-67197-3; 0-439-67198-1 pa
LC 2005-50250

After the death of his father, Elijah Breeze, a ten-year-old African American boy, moves back to New York City with his mother and attends a summer baseball camp as he tries to make new friends and adapt to urban ways.

The author "has created two intriguing protagonists and a group of equally colorful secondary characters. . . . Regardless of their interest in baseball, readers will identify with these youngsters and appreciate the simple story." SLJ

Another title about Elijah Breeze is:
Slam dunk! (2007)

Slam dunk! by Sharon Robinson. 1st ed.; Scholastic Press 2007 151p $16.99
Grades: 4 5 6 **Fic**
1. Basketball -- Fiction 2. Friendship -- Fiction 3. Family life -- Fiction 4. African Americans -- Fiction
ISBN 978-0-439-67199-6; 0-439-67199-X
LC 2006102462

At Harlem's Langston Hughes Middle School, eleven-year-old Elijah "Jumper" Breeze and his friends complete against Nia and her girlfriends on the basketball court, in a video dance tournament, and for a Student Council seat, and, meanwhile, several of the students face issues with their fathers.

"While serious issues broached in the earlier book . . . are given renewed attention, this is really an amiable story about friends who stay that way, a theme that translates well in any community." Booklist

Rockliff, Mara
The **case** of the Amazing Zelda; illustrated by Amy Wummer. Kane Press 2009 96p il (Jazz & Milo mysteries) $22.60; pa $6.95
Grades: 1 2 3 4 **Fic**
1. Mystery fiction 2. Pets -- Fiction 3. Spiritualism -- Fiction
ISBN 978-1-57565-298-6; 1-57565-298-6; 978-1-57565-296-2 pa; 1-57565-296-X pa
LC 2008050212

Detectives-in-training Milo and Jazz investigate whether their town's new pet psychic is a fraud.

This "will appeal to young independent readers with short chapters, easy-to-read typeface, and good quality illustrations. The [mystery is] also [an] excellent [choice] for a classroom or library read-alouds." Libr Media Connect

The **case** of the haunted haunted house; illustrated by Amy Wummer. Kane Press 2009 96p il (Milo & Jazz mysteries) lib bdg $22.60; pa $6.95
Grades: 1 2 3 4 **Fic**
1. Ghost stories 2. School stories 3. Mystery fiction
ISBN 978-1-57565-297-9 lib bdg; 1-57565-297-8 lib bdg; 978-1-57565-295-5 pa; 1-57565-295-1 pa
LC 2008049804

Amateur detectives Milo and Jazz try to figure out if the haunted house they are building for the school fair has a real ghost.

This "will appeal to young independent readers with short chapters, easy-to-read typeface, and good quality illustrations. The [mystery is] also [an] excellent [choice] for a classroom or library read-alouds." Libr Media Connect

The **case** of the missing moose; by Lewis B. Montgomery; illustrated by Amy Wummer. Kane Press 2011 96p il (Milo & Jazz mysteries) lib bdg $22.60; pa $6.95

Grades: 1 2 3 4   **Fic**

1. Mystery fiction 2. Camps -- Fiction 3. Lost and found possessions -- Fiction

ISBN 978-1-57565-331-0 lib bdg; 1-57565-331-1 lib bdg; 978-1-57565-322-8 pa; 1-57565-322-2 pa

LC 2010023478

While Milo and Jazz, detectives-in-training, are at summer camps on the same lake, the mascot built by Milo's team for the color wars disappears.

"The short, easy chapters are accompanied by playful pen-and-ink illustrations that enhance the story. This early chapter book mystery is engaging." Booklist

The **case** of the poisoned pig; Ilustrated by Amy Wummer. Kane Press 2009 96p il (Milo & Jazz mysteries) $22.60; pa $6.95

Grades: 1 2 3 4 5   **Fic**

1. Mystery fiction 2. Pigs -- Fiction

ISBN 978-1-57565-289-4; 1-57565-289-7; 978-1-57565-286-3 pa; 1-57565-286-2 pa

LC 2008027537

When Jazz's pet piglet gets sick and the veterinarian suspects it was poisoned, she and Milo use their detective skills to try to figure out who did it.

The "volume ends with additional 'brain stretchers' and mini-cases. . . . The [story is] quick and satisfying, and challenges at the back of the [book contributes] to the enjoyment. Wummer's pencil and ink illustrations add a humorous touch and are perfect for the [story]." SLJ

Rocklin, Joanne

★ **One** day and one amazing morning on Orange Street. Amulet Books 2011 207p $16.95

Grades: 3 4 5   **Fic**

1. Trees -- Fiction 2. Oranges -- Fiction 3. Friendship -- Fiction 4. Family life -- Fiction

ISBN 0-8109-9719-3; 978-0-8109-9719-6

LC 2010-23452

The last remaining orange tree on a Southern California street brings together neighbors of all ages as they face their problems and anxieties, including the possibility that a mysterious stranger is a threat to their tree. "Grades four to six." (Bull Cent Child Books)

"Fully realized characters and setting definitely make this one morning on Orange Street amazing." Kirkus

The **five** lives of our cat Zook; by Joanne Rocklin. Amulet Books 2012 218 p.

Grades: 3 4 5 6   **Fic**

1. Cats -- Juvenile fiction 2. Siblings -- Juvenile fiction 3. Family life -- Juvenile fiction 4. Cats -- Fiction 5. Brothers and sisters -- Fiction

ISBN 1419701924; 9781419701924

LC 2011041088

"In this . . . middle-grade novel, Oona and her brother, Fred, love their cat Zook (short for Zucchini), but Zook is sick. As they conspire to break him out of the vet's office, convinced he can only get better at home with them, Oona tells Fred the story of Zook's previous lives, ranging in style from fairy tale to grand epic to slice of life. Each of Zook's lives has echoes in Oona's own family life, which is going

through a transition she's not yet ready to face." (Publisher's note)

Rockwell, Thomas

★ **How** to eat fried worms; pictures by Emily McCully. Watts 1973 115p il lib bdg $29; pa $5.99

Grades: 3 4 5 6   **Fic**

1. Worms -- Fiction

ISBN 0-531-02631-0 lib bdg; 0-440-44545-0 pa

"A hilarious story that will revolt and delight bumptious, unreachable, intermediate-grade boys and any other less particular mortals that read or listen to it." Booklist

Rodda, Emily

★ **The key** to Rondo. Scholastic Press 2008 342p $16.99; pa $6.99

Grades: 5 6 7 8   **Fic**

1. Fantasy fiction 2. Magic -- Fiction 3. Cousins -- Fiction

ISBN 0-545-03535-X; 978-0-545-03535-4; 0-545-03536-8 pa; 978-0-545-03536-1 pa

LC 2007-16873

Through an heirloom music box, Leo, a serious, responsible boy, and his badly-behaved cousin Mimi enter the magical world of Rondo to rescue Mimi's dog from a sorceress, who wishes to exchange him for the key that allows free travel between worlds.

"Rodda fills the cousins' quest with image-rich prose and compelling action." Bull Cent Child Books

Another title about Rondo is:

The Wizard of Rondo (2009)

Rowan and the Travelers. Greenwillow Bks. 2001 170p pa $5.99

Grades: 4 5 6   **Fic**

1. Fantasy 2. Riddles 3. Fantasy fiction 4. Heroes

ISBN 0-06-029775-1; 0-06-029774-3 lib bdg; 0-06-056072-X pa

LC 00-50333

When an ancient evil threatens to devastate Rin, overcoming its people with a fatal sleeping sickness, young Rowan, with help from a tribe called the Travelers, must decipher a rhyming riddle in order to save the land and its inhabitants.

"Rodda's likable characters, fast-paced action, tantalizing mystery, and unpredictable story line make for an exciting read." SLJ

Rowan and the Zebak. Greenwillow Bks. 2002 198p hardcover o.p. pa $5.99

Grades: 4 5 6   **Fic**

1. Fantasy 2. Riddles 3. Fantasy fiction 4. Heroes

ISBN 0-06-029778-6; 0-06-029779-4 lib bdg; 0-06-056074-6 pa

LC 00-52796

After a flying lizard carries off his little sister, Rowan of Rin and three companions are guided by a rhyming riddle on a journey to the land of their old enemy, the Zebak, in order to rescue her.

"Rodda's alien landscapes and imaginative creatures will intrigue young audiences, but it's the characters, who seem fully human, that are the strength of the book." Booklist

Rowan of Rin. Greenwillow Books 2001 151p il hardcover o.p. pa $6.99

Grades: 4 5 6   **Fic**

1. Fantasy 2. Fantasy fiction 3. Heroes

ISBN 0-06-029707-7; 0-06-056071-1 pa

LC 00-63619

First published 1993 in Australia

Because only he can read the magical map, young, weak and timid Rowan joins six other villagers to climb a mountain and try to restore their water supply, as fears of a dragon and other horrors threaten to drive them back

The author has created "a fully conceived fantasy world complete with its own flora and fauna, a well-developed back story, and fascinating characters." Booklist

Other titles about Rowan are:

Rowan and the travelers (2001)

Rowan and the Keeper of the Crystal (2002)

Rowan and the Zebak (2002)

Rowan and the Ice creepers (2003)

Rodgers, Mary

Freaky Friday. Harper & Row 1972 145p hardcover o.p. pa $5.99

Grades: 4 5 6 7   **Fic**

1. Mother-daughter relationship -- Fiction

ISBN 0-06-025048-8; 0-06-025049-6 lib bdg; 0-06-057010-5 pa

"A fresh, imaginative, and entertaining story." Bull Cent Child Books

Rodman, Mary Ann

★ **Jimmy's** stars. Farrar, Straus & Giroux 2008 257p $16.95

Grades: 5 6 7 8   **Fic**

1. Siblings -- Fiction 2. Soldiers -- Fiction 3. Family life -- Fiction 4. World War, 1939-1945 -- Fiction

ISBN 978-0-374-33703-2; 0-374-33703-9

LC 2007-05091

In 1943, eleven-year-old Ellie is her brother Jimmy's "best girl," and when he leaves Pittsburgh just before Thanksgiving to fight in World War II, he promises he will return, asks her to leave the Christmas tree up until he does, and reminds her to "let the joy out."

Rodman "finds beauty in every emotional nuance. . . . The lively spirit of working-class Pittsburgh . . . extends Ellie's person story with a broader sense of home-front life." Booklist

Yankee girl. Farrar, Straus and Giroux 2004 219p $17; pa $7.99

Grades: 4 5 6 7   **Fic**

1. Schools 2. Friendship 3. Race relations 4. School stories 5. African Americans 6. School integration 7. Civil rights workers 8. Race relations -- Fiction

ISBN 0-374-38661-7; 0-312-53576-7 pa

LC 2003-49048

When her FBI-agent father is transferred to Jackson, Mississippi, in 1964, eleven-year-old Alice wants to be popular but also wants to reach out to the one black girl in her class in a newly-integrated school.

"Rodman shows characters grappling with hard choices, sometimes courageously, sometimes willfully, sometimes inconsistently, but invariably believably." Publ Wkly

Rodowsky, Colby F.

The **next**-door dogs; [by] Colby Rodowsky; pictures by Amy June Bates. Farrar, Straus & Giroux 2005 103p il $15

Grades: 2 3 4   **Fic**

1. Dogs -- Fiction 2. Fear -- Fiction

ISBN 0-374-36410-9

LC 2004-43333

Although terrified of dogs, nine-year-old Sara forces herself to face a labrador retriever and a dalmatian when she must help her next-door neighbor, who has fallen and broken her leg

"Rodowsky makes Sara's fear palpable and her eventual recovery believable. Plentiful pencil illustrations add to the book's accessibility." Horn Book Guide

Rogan, S. Jones

The **Curse** of the Romany wolves; by S. Jones Rogan; pictures by Christian Slade. Alfred A. Knopf 2009 il $16.99; lib bdg $19.99

Grades: 4 5 6   **Fic**

1. Adventure fiction 2. Foxes -- Fiction 3. Wolves -- Fiction 4. Animals -- Fiction

ISBN 978-0-375-85602-0; 0-375-85602-1; 978-0-375-95602-7 lib bdg; 0-375-95602-6 lib bdg

LC 2008040882

When wolf cubs Donald and Dora, then other villagers, succumb to a strange fever, the brave fox Penhaligon Brush sets out to find a cure, which includes an ingredient found only on the deserted Howling Island.

"Short chapters and frequent pencil illustrations of the costumed animals add appeal." Booklist

The **daring** adventures of Penhaligon Brush; pictures by Christian Slade. Alfred A. Knopf 2007 230p il $15.99; pa $6.50

Grades: 4 5 6   **Fic**

1. Adventure fiction 2. Foxes -- Fiction 3. Animals -- Fiction

ISBN 978-0-375-84344-0; 0-375-84344-2; 978-0-440-42208-2 pa; 0-440-42208-6 pa

LC 2006-35566

When Penhaligon Brush the fox is summoned by his stepbrother to the seaside town of Porthleven, he finds immediately upon arrival that his brother is incarcerated in the dungeon at Ferball Manor

This is a "swift-paced, large-scale adventure. . . . Slade's halftone art . . . [represents] these robust characters in theatrical costume and with plenty of personality." Publ Wkly

Another title about Penhaligon Brush is:

The curse of the Romany wolves (2009)

Rollins, James

Jake Ransom and the Skull King's shadow. HarperCollins 2009 399p il map $16.99; lib bdg $17.89; pa $7.99

Grades: 5 6 7 8   **Fic**

1. Adventure fiction 2. Mayas -- Fiction 3. Siblings -- Fiction 4. Archeology -- Fiction

ISBN 978-0-06-147379-1; 0-06-147379-0; 978-0-06-147380-7 lib bdg; 0-06-147380-4 lib bdg; 978-0-06-147381-4 pa; 0-06-147381-2 pa

LC 2009-14570

Connecticut middle-schooler Jake and his older sister Kady are transported by a Mayan artifact to a strange world inhabited by a mix of people from long-lost civilizations who are threatened by prehistoric creatures and an evil alchemist, the Skull King.

This is an "exciting time-travel adventure. . . . Rollins . . . presents a wide range of interesting historical information while telling a rollicking good story that should please a wide range of readers." Publ Wkly

Another title about Jake Ransom is:

Jake Ransom and the howling sphinx (2011)

Root, Phyllis

Lilly and the pirates; pictures by Rob Shepperson. Boyds Mills Press 2010 116p il $16.95

Grades: 3 4 5 6   Fic

1. Adventure fiction 2. Pirates -- Fiction

ISBN 978-1-59078-583-6; 1-59078-583-5

LC 2009030494

Ten-year-old Lilly, a worrier who greatly fears the sea, leaves the home of her librarian great-uncle and sets out with an old woman pirate to rescue her parents, who were shipwrecked while seeking the elusive frangipani fruit fly on an uncharted island.

"Many children will relate to this rather cozy adventure story and its lovably flawed heroine. Like the story, Shepperson's many full-page illustrations are lively, engaging, and occasionally humorous." Booklist

Rose, Caroline Starr

★ **May** B. a novel-in-verse. Schwartz & Wade Books 2012 $15.99; lib bdg $18.99

Grades: 4 5 6 7   Fic

1. Novels in verse 2. Frontier and pioneer life -- Fiction

ISBN 978-1-58246-393-3; 1-58246-393-X; 978-1-58246-412-1 lib bdg; 1-58246-412-X lib bdg

LC 2010033222

When a failed wheat crop nearly bankrupts the Betterly family, Pa pulls twelve-year-old May from school and hires her out to a couple new to the Kansas frontier.

"If May is a brave, stubborn fighter, the short, free-verse lines are one-two punches in this Laura Ingalls Wilder-inspired ode to the human spirit." Kirkus

Rosen, Michael J.

Running with trains; a novel in poetry and two voices. Michael J. Rosen. Boyds Mills 2012 102 p. (reinforced) $15.95

Grades: 5 6 7   Fic

1. Locomotives 2. Novels in verse 3. Farm life -- Fiction

ISBN 159078863X; 9781590788639

Author Michael Rosen's "story begins as 13-year-old Perry makes the train trip from his grandmother's for his weekly visit with his mother. . . . He is waiting for his father, missing in action in Vietnam, to return . . . [and] for his mother to finish nursing school so they can resume the life they knew prior to his father's going to war. Watching that same train, whose tracks bisect his family's farm, is 9-year-old Steve, who feels trapped by the constancy of his doting parents and farm chores and wishes he could ride that train to exotic locales." (Kirkus Reviews)

Sailing the unknown; around the world with Captain Cook. written by Michael J. Rosen; illustrated by Maria Cristina Pritelli. Creative Editions 2012 37 p. $17.99

Grades: 3 4 5 6 7   Fic

1. Sea stories 2. Explorers -- Fiction 3. Voyages around the world -- Fiction 4. Diaries -- Fiction

ISBN 1568462166; 9781568462165

LC 2011040840

This children's book, by Michael J. Rosen, illustrated by Maria Cristina Pritelli, tells the story of "an 11-year-old sailor named Nicholas, . . . [who in 1768] took to the seas with British explorer James Cook on a 3-year expedition of discovery, venturing into an uncharted world filled with strange lands, mysterious peoples, and peculiar creatures." (Publisher's note)

Ross, Gary

Bartholomew Biddle and the very big wind; Gary Ross, Matthew Meyers. Candlewick Press 2012 96 p. $17.99

Grades: 1 2 3 4 5 6   Fic

1. Novels in verse 2. Adventure fiction 3. Voyages and travels -- Juvenile fiction

ISBN 0763649201; 9780763649203

LC 2012942303

Author Gary Ross presents an adventure story. "Bartholomew Biddle's life has always been pretty ordinary, but when a huge wind blows past his window one night, he feels the call of adventure -- and he can't resist the urge to grab his bedsheet and catch a ride. Soon he's soaring far above his little town, heading wherever the wind takes him! . . . Bart finds himself in a mysterious cove where the wind doesn't blow. Stuck, Bart is forced to face the fact that his flying days might be over. Will he ever get home again?" (Publisher's note)

Rowling, J. K., 1965-

★ **Harry** Potter and the Sorcerer's Stone; illustrations by Mary Grandpré. Arthur A. Levine Bks. 1998 309p il $22.99; pa $8.99

Grades: 4 5 6 7 8 9 10   Fic

1. Fantasy fiction 2. Witches -- Fiction

ISBN 0-590-35340-3; 0-590-35342-X pa

LC 97-39059

First published 1997 in the United Kingdom with title: Harry Potter and the Philosopher's Stone

Rescued from the outrageous neglect of his aunt and uncle, a young boy with a great destiny proves his worth while attending Hogwarts School for Witchcraft and Wizardry.

This "is a brilliantly imagined and beautifully written fantasy." Booklist

Other titles in this series are:

Harry Potter and the Chamber of Secrets (1999)

Harry Potter and the Deathly Hallows (2007)

Harry Potter and Goblet of Fire (2000)

Harry Potter and the Half-Blood Prince (2005)

Harry Potter and the Order of the Phoenix (2003)

Harry Potter and the prisoner of Azkaban (1999)

Roy, James

Max Quigley; technically not a bully. written and illustrated by James Roy. Houghton Mifflin Harcourt 2009 202p il $12.95

Grades: 4 5 6   Fic

1. Bullies -- Fiction 2. Friendship -- Fiction

ISBN 978-0-547-15263-9; 0-547-15263-9

LC 2008-36110

First published 2007 in Australia

After playing a prank on one of his "geeky" classmates, sixth-grader Max Quigley's punishment is to be tutored by him.

"Straightforward chronology, believable dialogue, self-contained chapters, and plenty of humor make this accessible to reluctant readers and particularly appealing to boys who may see a bit of themselves in this realistic school story." Booklist

Roy, Jennifer Rozines

Yellow star; by Jennifer Roy. Marshall Cavendish 2006 227p $16.95

Grades: 5 6 7 8   **Fic**

1. Jews -- Fiction 2. Holocaust, 1933-1945 -- Fiction

ISBN 0-7614-5277-X; 978-0-7614-5277-5

LC 2005-50788

From 1939, when Syvia is four and a half years old, to 1945 when she has just turned ten, a Jewish girl and her family struggle to survive in Poland's Lodz ghetto during the Nazi occupation.

"In a thoughtful, vividly descriptive, almost poetic prose, Roy retells the true story of her Aunt Syvia's experiences. . . . This book is a standout in the genre of Holocaust literature." SLJ

Ruby, Laura

The **Wall** and the Wing; [by] Laura Ruby. Eos 2006 327p $16.99; pa $6.99

Grades: 5 6 7 8   **Fic**

1. Fantasy fiction 2. Orphans -- Fiction

ISBN 978-0-06-075255-2; 0-06-075255-6; 978-0-06-075257-6 pa; 0-06-075257-2 pa

LC 2005-23170

In a future New York where most people can fly and cats are a rarity, a nondescript resident of Hope House for the Homeless and Hopeless discovers that although she is shunned as a "leadfoot," she has the surprising ability to become invisible

"This poor-little-rich-girl story is packed with wildly eccentric characters. . . . All of this fast-paced wackiness is told with humor, often black, that will have young readers giggling." SLJ

The **chaos** king. Eos 2007 325p $16.99; lib bdg $17.89

Grades: 5 6 7 8   **Fic**

1. Fantasy fiction 2. Orphans -- Fiction

ISBN 978-0-06-075258-3; 0-06-075258-0; 978-0-06-075259-0 lib bdg; 0-06-075259-9 lib bdg

LC 2007-08621

Thirteen-year-old Georgie and Bug, a year older, have been pulled apart by the demands of their newfound fame and fortune, but join forces again when a punk, vampires, a giant sloth, and other creatures come after them on the streets of a New York City of the future.

This "is a wonderful story about how being different can be infinitely preferable to being ordinarily beautiful or talented, and Ruby's off-the-wall writing style and infinite imagination make the lesson fun to learn." Kliatt

Runholt, Susan

The **mystery** of the third Lucretia. Viking Childrens Books 2008 288p $16.99; pa $6.99

Grades: 5 6 7 8   **Fic**

1. Mystery fiction 2. Art -- Fiction 3. Friendship -- Fiction

ISBN 978-0-670-06252-2; 0-670-06252-9; 978-0-14-241338-8 pa; 0-14-241338-0 pa

LC 2007-24009

While traveling in London, Paris, and Amsterdam, fourteen-year-old best friends Kari and Lucas solve an international art forgery mystery.

"There are enough artistic details for fans of art mysteries and enough spying and fleeing for fans of detective adventure." Bull Cent Child Books

Other titles about Kari and Lucas are:

Rescuing Seneca Crane (2009)

The adventure at Simba Hill (2011)

Rupp, Rebecca

After Eli; Rebecca Rupp. 1st ed. Candlewick 2012 245 p. (hardcover) $15.99; (ebook) $15.99

Grades: 4 5 6 7 8   **Fic**

1. Bildungsromans 2. Family -- Fiction 3. Brothers -- Fiction 4. Bereavement -- Fiction 5. Death -- Fiction 6. Books and reading -- Fiction 7. Interpersonal relations -- Fiction

ISBN 0763658103; 9780763658106; 9780763661946

LC 2011048344

In this book, "Daniel, a wry and thoughtful narrator, looks back on the summer when he was 14, three years after his older brother, Eli, died in Iraq at age 22." Daniel's "memories of larger-than-life Eli and his lingering anger about his death" are interwoven with "Daniel's day-to-day challenges, including his dysfunctional family . . .; his frustrations with his . . . friends; his attraction to Isabelle, a . . . newcomer to town; and his nascent friendship with school outcast Walter." (Publishers Weekly)

★ **Octavia** Boone's big questions about life, the universe, and everything. Candlewick Press 2010 185p $15.99

Grades: 5 6 7 8   **Fic**

1. School stories 2. Religion -- Fiction 3. Family life -- Fiction 4. Christian life -- Fiction

ISBN 978-0-7636-4491-8; 0-7636-4491-9

LC 2009-47408

Seventh-grader Octavia puzzles over life's biggest questions when her mother seems to find the answers in a conservative Christian church, while her artist father believes the writings of Henry David Thoreau hold the key.

"This hopeful novel highlights the resilience of children and the courage of those who seek truth in a complicated world." Publ Wkly

★ **Sarah** Simpson's Rules for Living. Candlewick Press 2008 84p $13.99

Grades: 4 5 6   **Fic**

1. School stories 2. Remarriage -- Fiction 3. Family life -- Fiction

ISBN 978-0-7636-3220-5

LC 2007-34214

In a journal, twelve-year old Sarah Simpson records important lists and the daily events of her life at home and in school, beginning one year after her father moved from Vermont to California to divorce her mother and marry someone else.

"Although Sarah's tone ranges widely, from resentful to full-out funny, . . . her vulnerable yet take-charge personality comes through." Publ Wkly

Ruskin, John

The **king** of the Golden River; [by] John Ruskin; illustrated by Iassen Ghiuselev. Simply Read Books 2005 65p il $19.95

Grades: 3 4 5   **Fic**

1. Fairy tales

ISBN 978-1-894965-15-6; 1-894965-15-9

Written 1841

After Gluck's cruel and greedy older brothers refuse hospitality to a mysterious visitor, their prosperous farm fails and one by one each brother makes the perilous journey to find treasure in the nearby Golden River

"Exquisite drawings by Bulgarian artist Ghiuselev illustrate this . . . edition of Ruskin's classic fairy tale. . . . A well-designed and very handsome edition of the timeless tale." Booklist

Russell, Ching Yeung

★ **Tofu** quilt. Lee & Low Books 2009 125p il $16.95

Grades: 4 5 6   **Fic**

1. Novels in verse 2. Sex role -- Fiction 3. Authorship -- Fiction

ISBN 978-1-60060-423-2; 1-60060-423-4

LC 2009-16903

Growing up in 1960s Hong Kong, a young girl dreams of becoming a writer in spite of conventional limits placed on her by society and family.

"The story is revealed through Russell's tender poems that beautifully describe Yeung Ying's surroundings, her home life, her family, and her inner thoughts. The poems are simple, yet filled with images and language that create an atmosphere that brings the child's early years to light." SLJ

Russell, Christopher

Dogboy. Greenwillow Books 2006 259p $15.99; $15.99; lib bdg $16.89

Grades: 5 6 7 8   **Fic**

1. Dogs -- Fiction 2. Orphans -- Fiction 3. Middle Ages -- Fiction 4. Knights and knighthood -- Fiction 5. Hundred Years' War, 1339-1453 -- Fiction

ISBN 978-0-06-084116-4; 0-06-084116-8; 978-0-06-084117-1 lib bdg; 0-06-084117-6 lib bdg

LC 2005-08525

First published 2005 in the United Kingdom

In 1346, twelve-year-old Brind, an orphaned kennel boy raised with hunting dogs at an English manor, accompanies his master, along with half of the manor's prized mastiffs, to France, where he must fend for himself when both his master and the dogs are lost at the decisive battle of Crécy

"The action is fast-paced with narrow escapes at every turn and elements of dry humor at the most unlikely times." SLJ

Hunted; [by] Christopher Russell. Greenwillow Books 2007 254p hardcover o.p. lib bdg $16.89

Grades: 5 6 7 8   **Fic**

1. Dogs -- Fiction 2. Plague -- Fiction 3. Middle Ages

-- Fiction

ISBN 978-0-06-084119-5; 0-06-084119-2; 978-0-06-084120-1 lib bdg; 0-06-084120-6 lib bdg

LC 2006000946

First published 2006 in the United Kingdom with title: Brind: the plague sorcerer

When the landlord's wife dies of the Plague, he banishes his foster daughter, Aurélie, along dogboy Brind, from the manor. The pair take along two dogs in search of a safe haven, only to discover that sickness and death are everywhere

"The story is action driven, enhanced by the well-characterized dog companions. . . . An entertaining romp through the Middle Ages." SLJ

Russell, Krista

Chasing the Nightbird. Peachtree 2011 200p

Grades: 5 6 7 8   **Fic**

1. Sailors -- Fiction 2. Slavery -- Fiction 3. Abolitionists -- Fiction

ISBN 1561455970; 9781561455973

LC 2011002665

In 1851 New Bedford, Massachusetts, fourteen-year-old Cape Verdean sailor Lucky Valera is kidnapped by his estranged half-brother and forced to work in a mill, but while Lucky is plotting his escape he meets a former slave and a young Quaker girl who influence his plans.

"Without slowing the story's pace, Russell gives readers plenty to think about regarding the turbulent racial dynamics of the period—Lucky, who is dark-skinned yet free, initially sees little connection between his life and the plight of slaves. Strong-willed and goodhearted, Lucky is an especially vibrant hero in this multifaceted and suspenseful historical adventure." Publ Wkly

Rutkoski, Marie

★ The **Cabinet** of Wonders; [by] Marie Rutkoski. Farrar Straus Giroux 2008 258p (The Kronos Chronicles) $16.95; pa $6.99

Grades: 5 6 7 8   **Fic**

1. Fantasy fiction 2. Magic -- Fiction 3. Gypsies -- Fiction 4. Princes -- Fiction

ISBN 978-0-374-31026-4; 0-374-31026-2; 978-0-312-60239-0 pa; 0-312-60239-1 pa

LC 2007037702

Twelve-year-old Petra, accompanied by her magical tin spider, goes to Prague hoping to retrieve the enchanted eyes the Prince of Bohemia took from her father, and is aided in her quest by a Roma boy and his sister.

"Add this heady mix of history and enchantment to the season's list of astonishingly accomplished first novels. . . . Infusions of folklore (and Rutkowski's embellishments of them) don't slow the fast plot but more deeply entrance readers." Publ Wkly

Other titles in this series are:

The Celestial Globe (2009)

The Jewel of the Kalderash (2011)

Ryan, Pam Muñoz

★ **Becoming** Naomi Leon; [by] Pam Muñoz Ryan. Scholastic Press 2004 246p $16.95; pa $6.99

Grades: 5 6 7 8   **Fic**

1. Mexican Americans 2. Family problems 3. Great-grandmothers 4. Brothers and sisters 5. Family life

-- Fiction 6. Mexican Americans -- Fiction
ISBN 0-439-26969-5; 0-439-26997-0 pa

LC 2004-346

When Naomi's absent mother resurfaces to claim her, Naomi runs away to Mexico with her great-grandmother and younger brother in search of her father

"Ryan has written a moving book about family dynamics. . . . All of the characters are well drawn." SLJ

★ The **dreamer**; drawings by Peter Sís. Scholastic Press 2010 372p il $17.99

Grades: 4 5 6 7   **Fic**

1. Authors 2. Diplomats 3. Novelists 4. Novelist 5. Nobel laureates for peace 6. Nobel laureates for literature 7. Father-son relationship -- Fiction 8. Biography, Individual -- Juvenile literature
ISBN 978-0-439-26970-4; 0-439-26970-9

Boston Globe-Horn Book Award honor book: Fiction (2010)

Neftali finds beauty and wonder everywhere. He loves to collect treasures, daydream, and write—pastimes his authoritarian father thinks are for fools. Against all odds, Neftali prevails against his father's cruelty and his own crippling shyness to become one of the most widely read poets in the world, Pablo Neruda.

"Ryan loads the narrative with vivid sensory details. And although it isn't poetry, it eloquently evokes the sensation of experiencing the world as someone who savors the rhythms of words and gets lost in the intricate surprises of nature. The neat squares of Sis' meticulously stippled illustrations, richly symbolic in their own right, complement and deepen the lyrical quality of the book." Booklist

★ **Esperanza** rising. Scholastic Press 2000 262p $15.95; pa $4.99

Grades: 5 6 7 8   **Fic**

1. Agricultural laborers 2. Mexican Americans -- Fiction 3. Mexican Americans -- California 4. Agricultural laborers -- Fiction 5. Mexican Americans -- California -- Juvenile fiction
ISBN 0-439-12041-1; 0-439-12042-X pa

LC 00-24186

Esperanza and her mother are forced to leave their life of wealth and privilege in Mexico to go work in the labor camps of Southern California, where they must adapt to the harsh circumstances facing Mexican farm workers on the eve of the Great Depression

"Ryan writes movingly in clear, poetic language that children will sink into, and the [book] offers excellent opportunities for discussion and curriculum support." Booklist

Rylander, Chris

The **fourth** stall. Walden Pond Press 2011 314p $15.99

Grades: 4 5 6 7   **Fic**

1. School stories 2. Bullies -- Fiction 3. Friendship -- Fiction 4. Business enterprises -- Fiction
ISBN 978-0-06-199496-8; 0-06-199496-0

LC 2010016280

Sixth-graders Mac and Vince operate a business charging schoolmates for protection from bullies and for help to negotiate conflicts peacefully, with amazing challenges and results.

"Rylander mines a substantial amount of humor and heart from this combination hardboiled crime novel and middle-grade character piece. . . . A light and enjoyable caper." Publ Wkly

Rylant, Cynthia, 1954-

A **blue**-eyed daisy. Bradbury Press 1985 99p hardcover o.p. pa $6.99

Grades: 5 6 7 8   **Fic**

1. Family life -- Fiction
ISBN 0-02-777960-2; 0-689-84495-6 pa

LC 84-21554

"Episodic in nature, the story captures, as if in a frozen frame, the brief moments between childhood and adolescence." Horn Book

★ A **fine** white dust. Simon & Schuster 2000 106p $25; pa $4.99

Grades: 5 6 7 8   **Fic**

1. Religion -- Fiction 2. Friendship -- Fiction 3. Family life -- Fiction
ISBN 978-0-689-84087-6; 0-689-84087-X; 978-1-4169-2769-3 pa; 1-4169-2769-7 pa

A reissue of the title first published 1986 by Bradbury Press

A Newbery Medal honor book, 1987

The visit of the traveling Preacher Man to his small North Carolina town gives new impetus to thirteen-year-old Peter's struggle to reconcile his own deeply felt religious belief with the beliefs and non-beliefs of his family and friends

"Blending humor and intense emotion with a poetic use of language, Cynthia Rylant has created a taut, finely drawn portrait of a boy's growth from seeking for belief, through seduction and betrayal, to a spiritual acceptance and a readiness 'for something whole.'" Horn Book

★ **Missing** May. Orchard Bks. 1992 89p hardcover o.p. pa $5.99

Grades: 5 6 7 8   **Fic**

1. Death -- Fiction
ISBN 0-531-05996-0; 0-439-61383-3 pa

LC 91-23303

Awarded the Newbery Medal, 1993

After the death of the beloved aunt who has raised her, twelve-year-old Summer and her uncle Ob leave their West Virginia trailer in search of the strength to go on living

"There is much to ponder here, from the meaning of life and death to the power of love. That it all succeeds is a tribute to a fine writer who brings to the task a natural grace of language, an earthly sense of humor, and a well-grounded sense of the spiritual." SLJ

Sachar, Louis

★ **Holes**; [by] Louis Sachar. 10th anniversary ed.; Farrar, Straus and Giroux 2008 265p $18

Grades: 5 6 7 8   **Fic**

1. Friendship -- Fiction 2. Buried treasure -- Fiction 3. Homeless persons -- Fiction 4. Juvenile delinquency -- Fiction
ISBN 978-0-374-33266-2; 0-374-33266-5

LC 2007045430

A reissue of the title first published 1998. Includes additional information about the author and his Newbery acceptance speech

Awarded the Newbery Medal, 1999

As further evidence of his family's bad fortune which they attribute to a curse on a distant relative, Stanley Yelnats is sent to a hellish correctional camp in the Texas desert where he finds his first real friend, a treasure, and a new sense of himself

"This delightfully clever story is well-crafted and thought-provoking, with a bit of a folklore thrown in for good measure." Voice Youth Advocates

Marvin Redpost, kidnapped at birth? illustrated by Neal Hughes. Random House 1992 68p il $11.99; pa $3.99

Grades: 1 2 3   **Fic**

1. Family life -- Fiction
ISBN 0-679-91946-5; 0-679-81946-0 pa

LC 91-51105

Red-haired Marvin is convinced that the reason he looks different from the rest of his family is that he is really the lost prince of Shampoon

"Written almost completely in dialogue, the story is fast paced, easy to read, and full of humor." SLJ

Other titles about Marvin Redpost are:
Marvin Redpost, a flying birthday cake (1999)
Marvin Redpost, a magic crystal (2000)
Marvin Redpost, alone in his teacher's house (1994)
Marvin Redpost, class president (1999)
Marvin Redpost, is he a girl? (1993)
Marvin Redpost, super fast, out of control (2000)
Marvin Redpost, why pick on me? (1993)

Wayside School gets a little stranger; illustrated by Joel Schick. Morrow Junior Bks. 1995 168p il $15.99; pa $4.95

Grades: 3 4 5 6   **Fic**

1. School stories
ISBN 0-688-13694-X; 0-380-72381-6 pa

LC 94-25448

"Sachar's offering contains hilarity, malevolence, romance, relentless punning, goofiness, inspiration, revenge, and poignancy." SLJ

Other titles about Wayside School are:
Sideways stories from Wayside School (1978)
Wayside School is falling down (1989)

Sage, Angie

★ **Magyk**; Septimus Heap, book one. illustrations by Mark Zug. Katherine Tegen Books 2005 576p il $16.99; lib bdg $17.89; pa $7.99

Grades: 5 6 7 8   **Fic**

1. Fantasy fiction 2. Magic -- Fiction
ISBN 0-06-057731-2; 0-06-057732-0 lib bdg; 0-06-057733-9 pa

LC 2003-28185

After learning that she is the Princess, Jenna is whisked from her home and carried toward safety by the Extraordinary Wizard, those she always believed were her father and brother, and a young guard known only as Boy 412, pursued by agents of those who killed her mother ten years earlier.

"Youngsters will lose themselves happily in Sage's fluent, charismatic storytelling, which enfolds supportive allies

and horrific enemies, abundant quirky details, and poignant moments of self-discovery." Booklist

Other titles in this series are:
Flyte (2006)
Physik (2007)
Queste (2008)
Syren (2009)
Darke (2011)

The **Magykal** papers; illustrations by Mark Zug. Katherine Tegen Books 2009 167p il (Septimus Heap)

Grades: 5 6 7 8   **Fic**

1. Fantasy fiction 2. Magic -- Fiction 3. Princesses -- Fiction
ISBN 0-06-170416-4; 978-0-06-170416-1

LC 2008027110

Purports to be a compilation of pamphlets, journals, restaurant reviews, maps, historical information, and other never-before-published papers from the world of the apprentice alchemist, Septimus Heap.

"Fans of Sage's saga will rejoice in the little pieces if 'magyk' collected here. Beautifully rendered in full color." SLJ

My haunted house; as told to Angie Sage; illustrated by Jimmy Pickering. Katherine Tegen Books 2006 132p il (Araminta Spookie) $8.99; lib bdg $14.89; pa $4.99

Grades: 3 4 5   **Fic**

1. Ghost stories
ISBN 978-0-06-077481-3; 0-06-077481-9; 978-0-06-077482-0 lib bdg; 0-06-077482-7 lib bdg; 978-0-06-077483-7 pa; 0-06-077483-5 pa

LC 2005-23815

Araminta enlists the help of several ghosts in an attempt to stop her Aunt Tabby from selling Spook House.

This is a "humorous, fast-paced . . . caper. . . . Pickering's quirky art adds to the kooky—and in spots somewhat spooky—fun." Publ Wkly

Other titles in this series are:
The sword in the grotto (2006)
Frognapped (2007)
Vampire brat (2007)
Ghostsitters (2008)

Physik; Septimus Heap, book three. [by] Angie Sage; illustrations by Mark Zug. Katherine Tegen Books 2007 544p il $17.99; lib bdg $18.89; pa $7.99

Grades: 5 6 7 8   **Fic**

1. Fantasy fiction 2. Magic -- Fiction
ISBN 978-0-06-057737-7; 0-06-057737-1; 978-0-06-057738-4 lib bdg; 0-06-057738-X lib bdg; 978-0-06-057739-1 pa; 0-06-057739-8 pa

LC 2006019858

Pulled through a glass that brings him back in time, Septimus Heap becomes the apprentice of an alchemist

"Few fans of the . . . Septimus Heap series will be disappointed by this excellent third adventure." Booklist

Queste; Septimus Heap, book four. illustrated by Mark Zug. Katherine Tegen Books 2008 596p il $17.99; lib bdg $18.89; pa $7.99

Grades: 5 6 7 8   **Fic**

1. Fantasy fiction 2. Magic -- Fiction 3. Apprentices

-- Fiction
ISBN 978-0-06-088207-5; 0-06-088207-7; 978-0-06-088208-2 lib bdg; 0-06-088208-5 lib bdg; 978-0-06-08820-9 pa; 0-06-088209-3 pa
LC 2007049661

Nicki and Snorri are trapped in Time, and Septimus Heap goes on a quest to find the House of Foryx, a place where all Time meets.

This offers "vibrant storytelling and inventive flourishes." Booklist

Syren; Septimus Heap, book five. illustrations by Mark Zug. Katherine Tegen Books 2009 628p il
Grades: 5 6 7 8 **Fic**
1. Fantasy fiction 2. Magic -- Fiction
ISBN 0-06-088210-7; 0-06-088211-5 lib bdg; 0-06-088212-3 pa; 978-0-06-088210-5; 978-0-06-088211-2 lib bdg; 978-0-06-088212-9 pa
LC 2009009514

Wolf Boy is sent on a Task by Aunt Zelda, while Septimus and the dragon, Spit Fyre, fly off to bring their friends home, but they all wind up on an island whose secrets are as dangerous as its inhabitants.

This is "full of fun, adventure, humor, irony, friendship, loyalty, and nonstop action." SLJ

Vampire brat; as told to Angie Sage; illustrated by Jimmy Pickering. 1st ed.; Katherine Tegen Books 2007 194p il (Araminta Spookie) $8.99; lib bdg $14.89
Grades: 3 4 5 **Fic**
1. Ghost stories 2. Cousins -- Fiction 3. Vampires -- Fiction
ISBN 978-0-06-077490-5; 0-06-077490-8; 978-0-06-077491-2 lib bdg; 0-06-077491-6 lib bdg
LC 2006036099

Things get even spookier at Spookie House when Uncle Drac's nephew Max comes to stay for a week and Araminta goes on a combined werewolf and vampire hunting expedition.

The sword in the grotto; illustrated by Jimmy Pickering. Katherine Tegen Books 2006 146p il (Araminta Spookie) pa $4.99
Grades: 3 4 5 **Fic**
1. Ghost stories
ISBN 978-0-06-077484-4; 978-0-06-077485-1 lib bdg; 978-0-06-077486-8 pa
LC 2005023816

With the help of the ghost Edmund, Araminta and Wanda survive a trip through a secret tunnel to bring back a present for Sir Horace's birthday.

Saint-Exupery, Antoine de
★ The **little** prince; written and illustrated by Antoine de Saint-Exupery; translated from the French by Richard Howard. Harcourt 2000 83p il $18; pa $12
Grades: 4 5 6 7 8 9 10 11 12 Adult **Fic**
1. Princes 2. Air pilots 3. Allegories 4. Fairy tales 5. Fantasy fiction 6. Extraterrestrial beings 7. Fantasies 8. Princes -- Fiction 9. Philosophical novels 10. Air pilots -- Fiction 11. Interplanetary visitors 12. Extraterrestrial beings -- Fiction
ISBN 0-15-202398-4; 0-15-601219-7 pa
LC 99-50439

A new translation of the title first published 1943 by Reynal & Hitchcock

"This many-dimensional fable of an airplane pilot who has crashed in the desert is for readers of all ages. The pilot comes upon the little prince soon after the crash. The prince tells of his adventures on different planets and on Earth as he attempts to learn about the universe in order to live peacefully on his own small planet. A spiritual quality enhances the seemingly simple observations of the little prince." Shapiro. Fic for Youth. 3d edition

The **little** prince: deluxe pop-up book; unabridged text. translated from the French by Richard Howard. Houghton Mifflin Harcourt 2009 60p il $35
Grades: 4 5 6 **Fic**
1. Fantasy fiction 2. Pop-up books 3. Princes -- Fiction 4. Air pilots -- Fiction 5. Extraterrestrial beings -- Fiction
ISBN 978-0-547-26069-3; 0-547-26069-5

An aviator whose plane is forced down in the Sahara Desert encounters a little prince from a small planet who relates his adventures in seeking the secret of what is important in life

This "volume is a beautiful piece of bookmaking that actually extends the classic story. In 3-D form, the original artwork feels new, and inventive design elements . . . add whimsy while focusing even more attention on the images." Booklist

Salisbury, Graham
Calvin Coconut: trouble magnet; illustrated by Jacqueline Rogers. Wendy Lamb Books 2009 152p il $12.99; lib bdg $15.99; pa $6.99
Grades: 3 4 5 **Fic**
1. School stories 2. Bullies -- Fiction 3. Family life -- Fiction
ISBN 978-0-385-73701-2; 0-385-73701-7; 978-0-385-90639-5 lib bdg; 0-385-90639-0 lib bdg; 978-0-375-84600-7 pa; 0-375-84600-X pa
LC 2008-1415

Nine-year-old Calvin catches the attention of the school bully on the day before he starts fourth grade, while at home, the unfriendly, fifteen-year-old daughter of his mother's best friend has taken over his room

"The familial relationships among Calvin and his sister, their mom and her boyfriend are touching, realistically tempered with moments of frustration. Rogers's lively ink-and-wash drawings augment the story and evoke a playful feel." Kirkus

Other titles about Calvin are:
Calvin Coconut: the zippy fix (2009)
Calvin Coconut: dog heaven (2010)
Calvin Coconut: zoo breath (2010)
Calvin Coconut: hero of Hawaii (2011)
Calvin Coconut: kung fooey (2011)

Lord of the deep. Delacorte Press 2001 182p hardcover o.p. pa $7.99
Grades: 5 6 7 8 **Fic**
1. Fishing 2. Stepfathers 3. Fishing -- Fiction 4. Stepfathers -- Fiction
ISBN 0-385-72918-9; 0-440-22911-1 pa
LC 00-60280

Working for Bill, his stepfather, on a charter fishing boat in Hawaii teaches thirteen-year-old Mikey about fishing, and about taking risks, making sacrifices, and facing some of life's difficult choices

"With its vivid Hawaiian setting, this fine novel is a natural for book-discussion groups that enjoy pondering moral ambiguity. Its action-packed scenes will also lure in reluctant readers." SLJ

★ **Night** of the howling dogs; a novel. Wendy Lamb Books 2007 191p $16.99; lib bdg $19.99; pa $6.50
Grades: 5 6 7 8 **Fic**
1. Camping -- Fiction 2. Tsunamis -- Fiction 3. Earthquakes -- Fiction 5. Survival after airplane accidents, shipwrecks, etc. -- Fiction
ISBN 978-0-385-73122-5; 978-0-385-90146-8 lib bdg; 978-0-440-23839-3 pa

LC 2007-07054

In 1975, eleven Boy Scouts, their leaders, and some new friends camping at Halape, Hawaii, find their survival skills put to the test when a massive earthquake strikes, followed by a tsunami.

This is a "vivid adventure. . . . Salisbury weaves Hawaiian legend into the modern-day narrative to create a haunting, unusual novel." Booklist

Saller, Carol Fisher
Eddie's war; [by] Carol Fisher Saller. Namelos 2011 ix, 194p
Grades: 5 6 7 8 **Fic**
1. Novels in verse 2. Brothers -- Fiction 3. Farm life -- Fiction 4. World War, 1939-1945 -- Fiction
ISBN 1-60898-108-8; 1-60898-109-6 pa; 978-1-60898-108-3; 978-1-60898-109-0 pa

"When we meet him in 1934, Eddie is five, Tom ten. In the next ten years the brothers develop friendships, discover family secrets, . . . and ponder the causes of European conflict . . . as well as the virulent prejudice rife in their own farming community. Tom's enlisting in 1943 unveils the real nature of war that has inspired the boys' games. Narrated by Eddie, these seventy-six vignettes are beautifully phrased and vividly revealing of character." Horn Book

Salten, Felix
Bambi; a life in the woods. [by] Felix Salten; illustrated by Barbara Cooney. Pocket Books 1988 190p il pa $5.99
Grades: 4 5 6 **Fic**
1. Deer -- Fiction
ISBN 978-0-671-66607-1 pa; 0-671-66607-X pa
Original German edition 1923; first United States edition published 1928 by Simon & Schuster
Describes the life of a deer in the forest as he grows into a beautiful stag

Sanchez, Anita
The **invasion** of Sandy Bay; [by] Anita Sanchez. Calkins Creek 2008 147p $16.95
Grades: 5 6 7 8 **Fic**
1. Adventure fiction 2. War of 1812 -- Fiction
ISBN 978-1-59078-560-7; 1-59078-560-6

LC 2007051224

In 1814, as the War of 1812 rages, twelve-year-old Lemuel Brooks tries to save the sleepy fishing village of Sandy Bay, Massachussetts, where he, himself, is an outsider, from bumbling British invaders. Includes historical notes

"Clearly Sanchez has researched the period well, but the history never overwhelms the narrative. . . . History buffs will enjoy reading a war story that is so well grounded in actual events." Booklist

Includes bibliographical references

Sanderson, Brandon
★ **Alcatraz** versus the evil Librarians. Scholastic Press 2007 308p $16.99; pa $6.99
Grades: 4 5 6 7 **Fic**
1. Fantasy fiction 2. Librarians -- Fiction 3. Grandfathers -- Fiction
ISBN 0-439-92550-9; 978-0-439-92550-1; 0-439-92552-5 pa; 978-0-439-92552-5 pa

LC 2006-38378

On his thirteenth birthday, foster child Alcatraz Smedry receives a bag of sand which is immediately stolen by the evil Librarians who are trying to take over the world. Soon, Alcatraz is introduced to his grandfather and his own special talent, and told that he must use it to save civilization.

"Readers whose sense of humor runs toward the subversive will be instantly captivated. . . . This nutty novel isn't for everyone, but it's also sure to win passionate fans." Publ Wkly

Other titles about Alcatraz are:
Alcatraz versus the scrivener's bones (2008)
Alcatraz versus the Knights of Crystallia (2009)
Alcatraz versus the shattered lens (2010)

Santopolo, Jill
The **Nina**, the Pinta, and the vanishing treasure; illustrations by C.B. Canga. Orchard Books 2008 183p il (Alec Flint, super sleuth) $15.99; pa $5.99
Grades: 3 4 5 **Fic**
1. Mystery fiction 2. Theft -- Fiction 3. Museums -- Fiction 4. Missing persons -- Fiction
ISBN 978-0-439-90352-3; 0-439-90352-1; 978-0-439-90353-0 pa; 0-439-90353-X pa

LC 2007-30218

When the entire Christopher Columbus exhibit disappears from the local museum, fourth-grade sleuth-in-training Alec Flint investigates, aided by his new classmate and potential partner, Gina, who wants his help looking into the disappearance of a teacher.

"Smartly combining a crime drama with some American history, this book succeeds in being both entertaining and informative." Horn Book Guide

Another title in this series is:
The ransom note blues (2009)

The **ransom** note blues; illustrations by Nathan Hale. Orchard Books 164p il (Alec Flint, super sleuth) pa $5.99
Grades: 3 4 5 **Fic**
1. Mystery fiction
ISBN 978-0-439-91255-6; 0-439-91255-5
When the newspaper announces that something belonging to the whole town has been stolen, fourth-grade sleuth Alec Flint investigates, aided by his partner, Gina.

"Readers of Donald Sobol's 'Encyclopedia Brown', . . . David Adler's 'Cam Jansen', . . . and Ron Roy's 'A to Z Mysteries' . . . will have something to cheer about with this series." SLJ

Saunders, Kate

★ **Beswitched**. Delacorte Press 2011 $16.99

Grades: 4 5 6 7   **Fic**

1. School stories 2. Magic -- Fiction 3. Time travel -- Fiction

ISBN 978-0-385-74075-3

LC 2011000747

First published 2010 in the United Kingdom

On her way, reluctantly, to a boarding school in present-day England, Flora suddenly finds herself in 1935, the new girl at St. Winifred's, having been summoned via a magic spell by her new dormitory mates.

"This absorbing novel . . . features a dimensional, delightful protagonist, whose personality and growth ring true. . . . Along with the entertaining magical elements, the universal themes of self-discovery and looking beyond appearances combine into a wholly engaging and enjoyable read." Booklist

The **Whizz** Pop Chocolate Shop; Kate Saunders. 1st ed. Delacorte Press 2013 293 p. (hardcover) $16.99

Grades: 5 6 7 8   **Fic**

1. Chocolate -- Fiction 2. Fantasy fiction -- Juvenile fiction 3. Brothers and sisters -- Juvenile fiction 4. Cats -- Fiction 5. Magic -- Fiction 6. Twins -- Fiction 7. Immortality -- Fiction 8. Brothers and sisters -- Fiction 9. Adventure and adventurers -- Fiction

ISBN 0385743017; 9780385743013

LC 2011053081

In this children's story, by Kate Saunders, "the family of eleven-year-old twins Oz and Lily have inherited [a house], together with the mysterious shop downstairs. Long ago, the shop's famous chocolate-makers . . . were clever sorcerers. Now evil villains are hunting for the secret of their greatest recipe. . . . This magic chocolate [has] the ability to destroy the world. . . . It's up to them to stop the villains and keep the magical chocolate recipe out of harm's way." (Publisher's note)

Sawyer, Ruth

★ **Roller** skates; written by Ruth Sawyer and illustrated by Valenti Angelo. Viking 1995 186p il hardcover o.p. pa $5.99

Grades: 4 5 6   **Fic**

ISBN 0-670-60310-4; 0-14-030358-8 pa

LC 85-43418

A reissue of the title first published 1936

Awarded the Newbery Medal, 1937

"For one never-to-be forgotten year Lucinda Wyman (ten years old) was free to explore New York on roller skates. She made friends with Patrick Gilligan and his hansom cab, with Policeman M'Gonegal, with the fruit vendor, Vittore Coppicco and his son Tony, and with many others. All Lucinda's adventures are true and happened to the author herself as is borne out by the occasional pages of Lucinda's diary which are a part of the story." Horn Book

Sazaklis, John

Royal rodent rescue; illustrated by Art Baltazar; Superman created by Jerry Siegel and Joe Shuster. Picture Window Books 2011 48p il (DC super-pets!) lib bdg $22.65; pa $4.95

Grades: 1 2 3   **Fic**

1. Cats -- Fiction 2. Superheroes -- Fiction

ISBN 978-1-4048-6307-1 lib bdg; 1-4048-6307-9 lib bdg; 978-1-4048-6622-5 pa; 1-4048-6622-1 pa

LC 2010036376

"Streaky the Super-Cat saves Queen Markela of Kardamyla's pet hamster, Prince Zouli, from the clutches of the evil cat, Rozz. . . . [The book is] full of action, including colorful graphics within the text, reminiscent of the old live-action Batman TV show. [The] title has a colorful spread in the heat of the action. [A] solid [introduction] to comic-book-style writing." SLJ

Scaletta, Kurtis

Mamba Point. Alfred A. Knopf 2010 268p il $16.99; lib bdg $19.99

Grades: 5 6 7 8   **Fic**

1. Fear -- Fiction 2. Snakes -- Fiction

ISBN 978-0-375-86180-2; 0-375-86180-7; 978-0-375-96180-9 lib bdg; 0-375-96180-1 lib bdg

LC 2009-22084

After moving with his family to Liberia, twelve-year-old Linus discovers that he has a mystical connection with the black mamba, one of the deadliest snakes in Africa, which he is told will give him some of the snake's characteristics. Includes facts about the author's experiences as a thirteen-year-old American living in Liberia in 1982

Scaletta "has created an appealing, well-written protagonist whose everyday and extraordinary experiences . . . change his life in unexpected, positive ways. . . . The engaging first-person narrative and array of diversely drawn characters further enliven the novel." Booklist

Scattergood, Augusta

★ **Glory** be; by Augusta Scattergood. 1st ed. Scholastic Press 2012 202 p. (hardcover) $16.99; (ebook) $16.99

Grades: 4 5 6   **Fic**

1. Racism -- History 2. Blacks -- Civil rights 3. African Americans -- Southern States 4. Sisters -- Fiction 5. Segregation -- Fiction 6. Race relations -- Fiction

ISBN 9780545331807; 9780545331814; 9780545452328

LC 2011028308

Author Augusta Scattergood tells a story of "a girl trying to make sense of the tumultuous era of the Civil Rights Movement. It's the summer of 1964 in a small Mississippi town, and [it's Glory's 12th birthday] . . . Her sister Jesslyn is entering high school and no longer has any time, and things have suddenly gotten awkward with Glory's best friend, Frankie. Plus, a new girl from the North has arrived, and everyone is riled up about what to do about the town's segregated pool. Whether she wants to or not, Glory has to make some big decisions." (Publisher's note)

Schirripa, Steven R.

Nicky Deuce: home for the holidays; [by] Steven R. Schirripa and Charles Fleming. Delacorte Press 2007 193p $15.95; lib bdg $17.99

Grades: 4 5 6   **Fic**

1. Family life -- Fiction 2. Italian Americans -- Fiction

ISBN 0-385-73258-9; 0-385-90276-X lib bdg

LC 2006004584

Life in New Jersey seems boring to Nicky after spending the summer in Brooklyn with his Italian-American family, so when his father invites the relatives and Nicky's friend Tommy to their lavish home for a New Year's Eve party, Nicky is sure that adventures will follow

"Readers will be hooked on personable Nicky and his relatives." SLJ

Schlitz, Laura Amy

★ **Splendors** and glooms; Laura Amy Schlitz. Candlewick 2012 384 p.

Grades: 4 5 6 7   **Fic**
1. Mystery fiction 2. Orphans -- Fiction 3. Kidnapping -- Fiction 4. Puppets and puppet plays -- Fiction 5. Puppets -- Fiction 6. Witches -- Fiction 7. Blessing and cursing -- Fiction
ISBN 0763653802; 9780763653804
                                            LC 2011048366

John Newbery Honor Book (2013)
In this book by Laura Amy Schlitz "Clara Wintermute . . . invites . . . the master puppeteer, Gaspare Grisini, . . . to entertain at her birthday party. . . . When Clara vanishes that night, suspicion of kidnapping falls upon the puppeteer and, by association, Lizzie Rose and Parsefall. As they seek to puzzle out Clara's whereabouts, Lizzie and Parse uncover Grisini's criminal past." (Publisher's note)

★ A **drowned** maiden's hair; a melodrama. Candlewick Press 2006 389p $15.99

Grades: 5 6 7 8   **Fic**
1. Orphans -- Fiction 2. Spiritualism -- Fiction
ISBN 978-0-7636-2930-4; 0-7636-2930-8
                                            LC 2006-49056

At the Barbary Asylum for Female Orphans, eleven-year-old Maud is adopted by three spinster sisters moonlighting as mediums who take her home and reveal to her the role she will play in their seances.

"Filled with heavy atmosphere and suspense, this story recreates life in early-20th-century New England. . . . Maud is a charismatic, three-dimensional character." SLJ

★ The **night** fairy; illustrated by Angela Barrett. Candlewick Press 2010 117p il lib bdg $16.99; pa $6.99

Grades: 4 5 6   **Fic**
1. Adventure fiction 2. Magic -- Fiction 3. Fairies -- Fiction 4. Friendship -- Fiction
ISBN 978-0-7636-3674-6 lib bdg; 0-7636-3674-6 lib bdg; 978-07636-5295-1 pa; 0-7636-5295-4 pa
                                            LC 2008-27659

When Flory the night fairy's wings are accidentally broken and she cannot fly, she has to learn to do everything differently.

"Schlitz writes with strength of vision and delicate precision of word choice. . . . Beautifully composed, the artwork combines subtle use of color with a keen observation of nature. . . . This finely crafted and unusually dynamic fairy story is a natural for reading aloud." Booklist

Schmatz, Pat

★ **Bluefish.** Candlewick Press 2011 226p $15.99

Grades: 5 6 7 8   **Fic**
1. School stories 2. Literacy -- Fiction 3. Teachers -- Fiction
ISBN 978-0-7636-5334-7; 0-7636-5334-9
                                            LC 2010044815

"A cast of richly developed characters peoples this work of contemporary fiction, told in the third person from Travis' point of view, with first-person vignettes from Velveeta's perspective peppered throughout. . . . A story rife with unusual honesty and hope." Kirkus

Schmidt, Gary D.

★ **Okay** for now. Clarion Books 2011 360p il $16.99

Grades: 4 5 6 7   **Fic**
1. Moving -- Fiction 2. City and town life -- Fiction
ISBN 978-0-547-15260-8; 0-547-15260-4
                                            LC 2010942981

"It's 1968. The Vietnam War and Apollo 11 are in the background, and . . . Doug Swieteck starts a new life in tiny Marysville, N.Y. . . . He may have moved away, but his cruel father and abusive brothers are still with him. . . . This is Schmidt's best novel yet—darker than The Wednesday Wars and written with more restraint, but with the same expert attention to voice, character and big ideas." Kirkus

★ The **Wednesday** wars. Clarion Books 2007 264p pa $6.99; $16

Grades: 5 6 7 8   **Fic**
1. Poets 2. Authors 3. Dramatists 4. School stories
ISBN 054723760X; 0618724834; 9780547237602; 9780618724833
                                            LC 2006-23660

A Newbery Medal honor book, 2008
During the 1967 school year, on Wednesday afternoons when all his classmates go to either Catechism or Hebrew school, seventh-grader Holling Hoodhound stays in Mrs. Baker's classroom where they read the plays of William Shakespeare and Holling learns something of value about the world he lives in. "Grades five to seven." (Bull Cent Child Books)

"The serious issues are leavened with ample humor, and the supporting cast . . . is fully dimensional. Best of all is the hero." Publ Wkly

Schneider, Josh

Tales for very picky eaters. Clarion Books 2011 47p il $14.99

Grades: K 1 2 3   **Fic**
1. Food -- Fiction 2. Father-son relationship -- Fiction
ISBN 978-0-547-14956-1; 0-547-14956-5
                                            LC 2010-24767

"The comical illustrations are done in watercolor, ink, and colored pencil and are surrounded by plenty of white space. A perfect segue into chapter books, this easy reader is sure to be a crowd pleaser." SLJ

Schneider, Robyn

Knightley Academy; by Violet Haberdasher. Aladdin 2010 469p $15.99

Grades: 5 6 7 8   **Fic**
1. School stories 2. Orphans -- Fiction 3. Knights and knighthood -- Fiction
ISBN 978-1-4169-9143-4; 1-4169-9143-3
                                            LC 2009-23443

In an alternate Victorian England, fourteen-year-old orphan Henry Grim, a maltreated servant at an exclusive school for the "sons of Gentry and Quality," begins a new life when he unexpectedly becomes the first commoner to be accepted at Knightley Academy, a prestigious boarding school for knights.

"Robyn Schneider . . . writing as the pseudonymous Haberdasher, delivers a cute novel that balances its simple plot with a solid lead character, witty dialogue, and a jaunty narrative voice. . . . The nebulous historical setting and focus on military training and chivalry are a welcome change of pace from fictional academies that revolve around magic." Publ Wkly

The **secret** prince; [by] Violet Haberdasher. Aladdin 2011 503p $16.99

Grades: 5 6 7 8   **Fic**

1. School stories 2. Orphans -- Fiction 3. Secret societies -- Fiction 4. Knights and knighthood -- Fiction
ISBN 978-1-4169-9145-8; 1-4169-9145-X

LC 2010038855

Fourteen-year-old orphan Henry Grim's schooling at the prestigious Knightley Academy continues, as he and some friends discover an old classroom filled with forgotten weapons which lead them into a dangerous adventure.

"Though some of the past events can be gleaned from this book, it's more enjoyable for those who have read Knightley Academy. . . . The fast-moving plotline in this installment is wrapped up nicely, but enough is left hanging and the characters are interesting enough to make readers eagerly anticipate the next in the series." SLJ

Schoenberg, Jane

Stuey Lewis against all odds; stories from the third grade. Jane Schoenberg; pictures by Cambria Evans. Farrar Straus Giroux 2012 136 p.

Grades: 2 3   **Fic**

1. Boys -- Juvenile fiction 2. Field trips -- Juvenile fiction 3. School stories -- Juvenile fiction 4. Schools -- Fiction 5. Family life -- Fiction
ISBN 0374399018; 9780374399016

LC 2011008224

This book, by Jane Schoenberg, part of the Stuey Lewis series, "takes up just where the first left off, with Stuey and his friends comforted that their second-grade teacher, Ginger Curtis, is moving on to third grade with them. . . . With the school year as the frame, these four loosely joined stories show our hero facing new challenges while growing into a more independent, less worried young man." (Kirkus Reviews)

The **one** and only Stuey Lewis; stories from the second grade. pictures by Cambria Evans. Farrar Straus Giroux 2011 115p il $16.99

Grades: 1 2 3   **Fic**

1. School stories 2. Teachers -- Fiction 3. Family life -- Fiction
ISBN 978-0-374-37292-7; 0-374-37292-6

LC 2010-22312

Stuey Lewis makes his way through second grade facing reading problems, pulling off a great Halloween caper, joining a soccer team, and more with the help of family, friends, and a special teacher.

This is a "hilarious early chapter book. . . . Evans' trim-lined, stylized cartoonish illustrations play up the comedy in the text while offering occasional independent chuckles." Bull Cent Child Books

Schroder, Monika

Saraswati's way. Farrar Straus Giroux 2010 233p $15.99

Grades: 5 6 7 8   **Fic**

1. Education -- Fiction 2. Mathematics -- Fiction
ISBN 978-0-374-36411-3; 0-374-36411-7

LC 2009-37286

Leaving his village in rural India to find a better education, mathematically gifted, twelve-year-old Akash ends up at the New Delhi train station, where he relies on Saraswati, the Hindu goddess of knowledge, to guide him as he negotiates life on the street, resists the temptations of easy money, and learns whom he can trust.

"With skillfully integrated cultural details . . . and a fully realized child's story, Schröder presents a view, sobering and inspiring, of remarkably resilient young people surviving poverty without losing themselves." Booklist

Schroeder, Lisa

It's Raining Cupcakes. Aladdin 2010 193p $15.99

Grades: 4 5 6 7   **Fic**

1. Baking -- Fiction 2. Contests -- Fiction 3. Family life -- Fiction 4. Mother-daughter relationship -- Fiction
ISBN 978-1-4169-9084-0; 1-4169-9084-4

LC 2009-14812

Twelve-year-old Isabel dreams of seeing the world but has never left Oregon, and so when her best friend, Sophie, tells her of a baking contest whose winners travel to New York City, she eagerly enters despite concerns about her mother, who is opening a cupcake bakery. Includes recipes.

Schulman, Janet

★ The **nutcracker**; [by] E.T.A. Hoffmann; adapted by Janet Schulman; illustrated by Renée Graef; audio CD narrated by Claire Bloom with music by Peter Ilyich Tchaikovsky. HarperCollins Pubs. 1999 34p il $19.95

Grades: 4 5 6 7   **Fic**

1. Fairy tales 2. Christmas -- Fiction
ISBN 0-06-027814-5

LC 97-22346

This adaptation of the Nutcracker with illustrations by Kay Chorao was published 1979 by Dutton

One Christmas after hearing how the toy nutcracker made by her godfather got his ugly face, a little girl helps break the spell and watches him change into a handsome prince

"Graef's illustrations are floridly old-fashioned, with careful attention to period detail." Booklist

Schur, Maxine

Gullible Gus; by Maxine Rose Schur; illustrated by Andrew Glass. Clarion Books 2009 45p il $16

Grades: 2 3 4 5   **Fic**

1. Tall tales 2. Cowhands -- Fiction
ISBN 978-0-618-92710-4; 0-618-92710-7

LC 2008-10477

Tired of the teasing he gets for being the most gullible man in Texas, Cowboy Gus goes to Fibrock to find the biggest liar there in hopes of hearing a tall tale that is impossible for anyone—even him—to believe.

"The stories are filled with exaggeration and alliteration. A Western twang is used to create mood. Readers will laugh out loud and share passages with friends. . . . Glass's bright oil crayon cartoons fit the exaggerated storytelling style to a tee." SLJ

Schwabach, Karen

The **storm** before Atlanta. Random House 2010 307p $16.99; lib bdg $19.99

Grades: 5 6 7 8   **Fic**

1. Freedom -- Fiction 2. Slavery -- Fiction 3. Soldiers -- Fiction 4. Runaway children -- Fiction

ISBN 978-0-375-85866-6; 0-375-85866-0; 978-0-375-95866-3 lib bdg; 0-375-95866-5 lib bdg

LC 2010014514

In 1863 northwestern Georgia, an unlikely alliance forms between ten-year-old New York drummer boy Jeremy, fourteen-year-old Confederate Charlie, and runaway slave Dulcie as they learn truths about the Civil War, slavery, and freedom.

"Richly detailed and well paced, the story provides both well-developed characters and plenty of suspense and gore. For those who like to know the facts behind historical fiction, the author provides historical notes and selected sources. An appealing Civil War title for readers with strong stomachs." Kirkus

Schwartz, Ellen

★ **Stealing** home. Tundra Books 2006 217p pa $8.95

Grades: 5 6 7 8   **Fic**

1. Jews -- Fiction 2. Orphans -- Fiction 3. Family life -- Fiction 4. Racially mixed people -- Fiction

ISBN 978-0-88776-765-4 pa; 0-88776-765-6 pa

"Joey, an orphaned, mixed-race 10-year-old isn't the only one who has to make adjustments after he's taken in by Jewish relatives he never knew he had. Wondering why his mother never told him about her side of the family, Joey moves to Brooklyn—to find a warm welcome from Aunt Frieda, an instant ally in baseball-loving cousin Bobbie, and a decidedly cold shoulder from his grandfather. . . . Keenly felt internal conflicts, lightened by some sparky banter, put this more than a cut above the average." Booklist

Schwarz, Viviane

The **Sleepwalkers**; Viviane Schwarz. Candlewick Press 2013 96 p. (paperback) $9.99

Grades: 2 3 4 5   **Fic**

1. Nightmares -- Juvenile fiction 2. Fantasy fiction -- Juvenile fiction

ISBN 0763662305; 9780763662301

LC 2012947253

This book by Viviane Schwarz offers a "tale of a band of intrepid dream warriors who rescue defenseless sleeping children from nightmares. Bonno (short for Bonifacius), a blanket transformed into a timid bear; Amali, an exuberant sock monkey; and Sophia, a crow made from a writing quill who communicates by writing, are the Sleepwalkers' newest recruits, learning the ropes from a trio of seasoned sheep." (Publishers Weekly)

Scieszka, Jon, 1954-

★ **Knights** of the kitchen table; illustrated by Lane Smith. Viking 1991 55p il (Time Warp Trio) $15.99; pa $4.99

Grades: 3 4 5   **Fic**

1. Fantasy fiction 2. Middle Ages -- Fiction 3. Time travel -- Fiction 4. Knights and knighthood -- Fiction

ISBN 0-670-83622-2; 0-14-240043-2 pa

LC 90-51009

"Transported to the Middle Ages, three friends save themselves from a dragon and a giant through quick thinking. The tongue-in-cheek narrative makes for laugh-out-loud enjoyment, and the easy-to-read sentences and zany dialogue perfectly suit the breathless pace." SLJ

Other titles about The Time Warp Trio are:

2095 (1995)

Da wild, da crazy, da Vinci (2004)

The good, the bad, and the goofy (1992)

Hey kid, want to buy a bridge? (2002)

It's all Greek to me (1999)

Marco? Polo! (2006)

Me oh Maya! (2003)

The not-so-jolly Roger (1991)

Oh say I can't see (2005)

Sam Samurai (2001)

See you later, gladiator (2000)

Summer reading is killing me! (1998)

Tut, tut (1996)

Viking it & liking it (2002)

Your mother was a Neanderthal (1993)

Seen Art? [by] Jon Scieszka and Lane Smith. Viking 2005 un il $16.99

Grades: 4 5 6 7   **Fic**

1. Art appreciation -- Fiction

ISBN 0-670-05986-2

While looking for his friend Art, a boy wanders through the Museum of Modern Art and is amazed by what he discovers there.

"The unusually long and narrow shape of the book and the stylized characters echo the modern-art theme while the muted background tones are an effective foil for the well-reproduced if sometimes diminutive artwork. . . . For anyone planning a trip to MoMA with a youngster, this is a provocative read." SLJ

★ **Spaceheadz**; [by] Jon Scieszka with Francesco Sedita; illustrated by Shane Prigmore. Simon & Schuster Books for Young Readers 2010 163p il (SPHDZ) $14.99

Grades: 3 4 5   **Fic**

1. School stories 2. Spies -- Fiction 3. Moving -- Fiction 4. Family life -- Fiction 5. Extraterrestrial beings -- Fiction

ISBN 978-1-4169-7951-7; 1-4169-7951-4

LC 2010001983

On his first day at Brooklyn's P.S. 858, fifth-grader Michael K. is teamed with two very strange students, and while he gradually comes to believe they are aliens who need his help, he has trouble convincing anyone else of the truth

This is "fun enough to become the next big word-of-mouth, multiplatform attention suck." Booklist

Spaceheadz, book 2; illustrated by Shane Prigmore; sugar-free goodness by Casey Scieszka; high-fiber extras by Steven Weinberg. Simon & Schuster 2010 230p il (SPHDZ) $14.99

Grades: 3 4 5   **Fic**

1. School stories 2. Extraterrestrial beings -- Fiction

ISBN 978-1-4169-7953-1; 1-4169-7953-0

This "continues the adventures of fifth-grader Michael K. and the influx of aliens . . . who pose as students. The joke-filled, intentionally disjointed, post-modern narration eventually involves the Spaceheadz in a kindergarten play. . . . Lots of humor leads this multiplatform effort with links to websites that are sure to expand the series' fan base." Booklist

Spaceheadz, book 3; illustrated by Shane Prigmore. Simon & Schuster 2011 213p il (SPHDZ) $15.99
Grades: 3 4 5   **Fic**
1. School stories 2. Extraterrestrial beings -- Fiction
ISBN 978-1-4169-7955-5; 1-4169-7955-7

"An imperiled world once more relies on rescue from Brooklyn fifth-graders Michael K. and his friends, along with aliens who are disguised as fifth-graders. . . . Meanwhile, Agent Umber of the AAA (Anti Alien Agency) is on a nonstop campaign to thwart the Spaceheadz. Finally, a tough-talking military-type Santa recruits Michael K. into a search for a stolen brain wave. . . . With plenty of twists, lots of well-timed comic noises . . . this is sure to delight fans, while recruiting new ones." Booklist

Scott, Elaine
Secrets of the Cirque Medrano. Charlesbridge 2008 216p lib bdg $15.95
Grades: 4 5 6 7   **Fic**
1. Artists 2. Painters 3. Circus -- Fiction 4. Orphans -- Fiction 5. Restaurants -- Fiction
ISBN 978-1-57091-712-7 lib bdg; 1-57091-712-4 lib bdg
LC 2007-2329

In the Paris village of Montmartre in 1904, fourteen-year-old Brigitte works long hours in her aunt's cafe, where she serves such regular customers as the young artist Pablo Picasso, encounters Russian revolutionaries, and longs to attend the exciting circus nearby. Includes author's note on the Picasso painting "Family of Saltimbanques"

This "places an interesting historical moment within the grasp of middle-schoolers." Kirkus

Scotto, Michael
Postcards from Pismo; Michael Scotto; [edited by] Ashley Mortimer. Midlandia Press 2012 180 p.
Grades: 4 5 6   **Fic**
1. Afghan War, 2001- -- Fiction 2. Filipino Americans -- Fiction 3. Military personnel -- United States -- Correspondence -- Fiction
ISBN 0983724369; 9780983724360
LC 2011943050

In this book, a "class assignment blossoms into friendship as a fourth-grade (later fifth-) Californian showers a young soldier stationed in Afghanistan with letters, e-mail messages and postcards. [Michael] Scotto supplies only chatty Felix's side of the continuing correspondence. . . . Felix queries his pen pal about what soldiers do while detailing his own interests, teachers, town, hard-working Filipino American parents (and their reactions when his restless big brother enlists)." (Kirkus)

Seabrooke, Brenda
Wolf pie; illustrated by Liz Callen. Clarion Books 2010 46p il $16
Grades: 1 2 3   **Fic**
1. Pigs -- Fiction 2. Wolves -- Fiction 3. Friendship

-- Fiction
ISBN 978-0-547-04403-3; 0-547-04403-8
LC 2009-15820

When Wilfong the wolf fails to blow down the house of the Pygg brothers, he stays outside their door all winter learning their games and listening to their jokes and stories, but although he claims to be reformed, the pigs are reluctant to offer friendship.

"Callen's humorous, vibrant multimedia art deftly matches the tone of Seabrooke's amusing tale, resulting in a winning collaboration for independent readers ready to move on to meatier texts." Kirkus

Sebestyen, Ouida
★ **Words** by heart. Little, Brown 1979 162p pa $5.50
Grades: 5 6 7 8   **Fic**
1. Family life -- Fiction 2. Race relations -- Fiction 3. African Americans -- Fiction
ISBN 0-440-22688-0
LC 78-27847

"It is 1910, and Lena's family is the only black family in her small Southwestern town. When Lena wins a scripture reciting contest that a white boy is supposed to win, her family is threatened. Lena's father tries to make her understand that by hating the people who did this, the problems that cause their behavior are not solved. Only more hatred and violence cause Lena and the village to understand the words of her father." ALAN

Seegert, Scott
How to grow up and rule the world; illustrated by John Martin. Egmont USA 2010 191p il (Vordak the Incomprehensible) $13.99
Grades: 3 4 5 6   **Fic**
1. Science fiction 2. Superheroes -- Fiction
ISBN 978-1-60684-013-9; 1-60684-013-4

"Evil mastermind Vordak the Incomprehensible shares his 'evilosity' with aspiring supervillains in this hilarious spoof on superheroes. . . . Comical black-and-white cartoons on nearly every page extend the humor. . . . Vordak's distinctive voice, peppered with alliteration typical of the genre, remains fresh and funny throughout." SLJ

Seidler, Tor
★ **Gully's** travels; pictures by Brock Cole. Michael di Capua Books 2008 173p il $16.95
Grades: 4 5 6   **Fic**
1. Dogs -- Fiction 2. Voyages and travels -- Fiction
ISBN 978-0-545-02506-5; 0-545-02506-0

Gulliver leads a life of luxury with his master. But when his master falls in love with a woman who is allergic to dogs, Gulliver is sent to a new home. He finds himself with a family of raucous human beings and three mutts. But just as Gulliver begins to make a grudging peace with his new reality, he gets swept up in a harrowing new adventure.

"Gulliver is a character readers won't forget. . . . Seidler vividly evokes each setting. . . . Cole's expressive, scribbled sketches of interesting characters appear on almost every page." Booklist

The **Wainscott** weasel; illustrated by Fred Marcellino. HarperCollins Pubs. 1993 193p il pa $11.95

Grades: 4 5 6   **Fic**
1. Animals -- Fiction 2. Weasels -- Fiction
ISBN 0-06-205911-4 pa

LC 92-54526

"Seidler's pacing is superb; he builds a solid structure within each chapter. A dry wit inspires his characterizations. . . . Marcellino enhances and even extends the beguiling ambiance with his exceptionally expressive art." Publ Wkly

The **dulcimer** boy; illustrations by Brian Selznick. Laura Geringer Bks. 2003 153p il hardcover o.p. pa $6.99
Grades: 4 5 6 7   **Fic**
1. Twins -- Fiction 2. Brothers -- Fiction 3. Dulcimers -- Fiction
ISBN 0-06-623609-6; 0-06-441048-X pa

LC 2001-23875

A newly illustrated edition of the title first published 1979 by Viking Press

"Tracing the footsteps of musically gifted William Carbuncle from his arrival on his uncaring uncle's doorstep in a box containing him, his brother, and a silver-stringed dulcimer, the story follows William's escape and journey south. . . . Seidler's simple yet eloquent prose likens William's plight to a caged songbird. . . . Selznick's detailed sense of light and shadow shines as his soft-textured acrylic paintings not only echo the novel's overall poetic melancholy, but also serve as integral pieces of the plot itself." SLJ

Selden, George

★ The **cricket** in Times Square; illustrated by Garth Williams. Farrar, Straus & Giroux 1960 151p il $16; pa $6.99
Grades: 3 4 5 6   **Fic**
1. Cats -- Fiction 2. Mice -- Fiction 3. Crickets -- Fiction
ISBN 0-374-31650-3; 0-312-38003-8 pa

A Newbery Medal honor book, 1961

"A touch of magic comes to Times Square subway station with Chester, a cricket from rural Connecticut. He is introduced to the distinctive character of city life by three friends: Mario Bellini, whose parents operate a newsstand; Tucker, a glib Broadway mouse; and Harry, a sagacious cat. Chester saves the Bellinis' business by giving concerts from the newsstand, bringing to rushing commuters moments of beauty and repose. This modern fantasy shows that, in New York, anything can happen." Moorachian. What is a City?

Other titles about Chester and his friends are:
Chester Cricket's new home (1983)
Chester Cricket's pigeon ride (1981)
Harry Cat's pet puppy (1974)
Harry Kitten and Tucker Mouse (1986)
The old meadow (1987)
Tucker's countryside (1969)

Selfors, Suzanne

Fortune's magic farm; illustrated by Catia Chien. Little, Brown 2009 264p il $14.99; pa $5.99
Grades: 4 5 6   **Fic**
1. Farms -- Fiction 2. Magic -- Fiction 3. Orphans -- Fiction
ISBN 978-0-316-01818-0; 0-316-01818-X; 978-0-316-01819-7 pa; 0-316-01819-8 pa

LC 2008-12493

Rescued from a rainy, boggy town where she works in a dismal factory, ten-year-old orphan Isabelle learns that she is the last surviving member of a family that tends the world's only remaining magic-producing farm.

"Readers will cozy up to the tale's quirky characters and enjoy the many twists and turns of this magical adventure." Kirkus

Smells like dog. Little, Brown 2010 360p $15.99
Grades: 4 5 6 7   **Fic**
1. Dogs -- Fiction 2. Uncles -- Fiction 3. Buried treasure -- Fiction
ISBN 978-0-316-04398-4; 0-316-04398-2

When farm boy Homer Pudding's explorer-uncle dies and leaves him a droopy dog with a mysterious coin hidden on its collar, it leads him to The City, where they meet Madame La Directeur, the conniving head of the Natural History Museum, who is trying to steal the coin and take Homer's place in a secret society of adventurers.

"Full of fantasy, fun, and humorous dialogue, this will attract dog lovers, mystery enthusiasts, adventure addicts, and reluctant readers. A thoroughly enjoyable read." Voice Youth Advocates

Another title about Homer Pudding is:
Smells like treasure (2011)

To catch a mermaid; illustrated by Catia Chien. Little, Brown 2007 245p il hardcover o.p. pa $5.99
Grades: 4 5 6   **Fic**
1. Siblings -- Fiction 2. Mermaids and mermen -- Fiction
ISBN 978-0-316-01816-6; 0-316-01816-3; 978-0-316-01817-3 pa; 0-316-01817-1 pa

LC 2007-22700

When twelve-year-old Boomerang Broom discovers a wish-granting baby mermaid, he takes her home and his little sister begs to keep her, with unexpected consequences.

"This amusing story has lots of kid appeal. Selfors has conjured up great characters and settings, and her narrative voice never falters." SLJ

Selzer, Adam

I put a spell on you; from the files of Chrissie Woodward, spelling bee detective. Delacorte Press 2008 247p $15.99; lib bdg $18.99
Grades: 4 5 6 7   **Fic**
1. School stories 2. Mystery fiction 3. Spelling bees -- Fiction
ISBN 978-0-385-73504-9; 0-385-73504-9; 978-0-385-90498-8 lib bdg; 0-385-90498-3 lib bdg

LC 2008035673

When Gordon Liddy Community School's resident tattletale-detective, Chrissie Woodward, realizes that the adults are out to fix the big spelling bee, she transfers her loyalty to her fellow students and starts collecting evidence. Told through in-class letters, administrative memos, file notes from Chrissie's investigation, and testimony from spelling bee contestants

"The wit in this school story is directed almost entirely against the grownups in a scathingly funny indictment of a shady principal and insanely competitive parents." Horn Book

Selznick, Brian

The **Houdini** box. Atheneum Books for Young Readers 2008 un il $17.99; pa $6.99

Grades: 3 4 5   **Fic**

1. Magicians 2. Nonfiction writers 3. Magicians -- Fiction

ISBN 978-1-4169-6878-8; 1-4169-6878-4; 978-0-689-84451-5 pa; 0-689-84451-4 pa

LC 2008024693

A reissue of the title first published 1991 by Knopf

A chance encounter with Harry Houdini leaves a small boy in possession of a mysterious box—one that might hold the secrets to the greatest magic tricks ever performed.

"In this new edition, Selznick follows his intriguing tale with bonus material: a biographical note on Houdini, an illustrated magic trick, research notes on the writing of the book, and early sketches for the artwork. . . . It is sure to intrigue youngsters, particularly those interested in magic." SLJ

★ **Wonderstruck**; a novel in words and pictures. Scholastic Press 2011 637p il $29.99

Grades: 4 5 6 7   **Fic**

1. Deaf -- Fiction 2. Museums -- Fiction 3. Runaway children -- Fiction

ISBN 978-0-545-02789-2; 0-545-02789-6

LC 2011009113

"Readers know that the two stories will converge, but Selznick keeps them guessing, cutting back and forth with expert precision. . . . Both stories are equally immersive and impeccably paced. . . . Visually stunning, completely compelling." Kirkus

★ The **invention** of Hugo Cabret; a novel in words and pictures. Scholastic Press 2007 533p il $22.95

Grades: 4 5 6 7   **Fic**

1. Robots -- Fiction 2. Orphans -- Fiction 3. Motion picture directors 4. Motion pictures -- Fiction

ISBN 0-439-81378-6

LC 2006-07119

Awarded the Caldecott Medal, 2008

When twelve-year-old Hugo, an orphan living and repairing clocks within the walls of a Paris train station in 1931, meets a mysterious toyseller and his goddaughter, his undercover life and his biggest secret are jeopardized.

"With characteristic intelligence, exquisite images, and a breathtaking design, Selznick shatters conventions related to the art of bookmaking." SLJ

Sendak, Maurice

★ **Higglety** pigglety pop! or, There must be more to life. story and pictures by Maurice Sendak. HarperCollins Pubs. 1979 69p il $14.95; pa $8.95

Grades: 2 3 4   **Fic**

1. Dogs -- Fiction

ISBN 0-06-028479-X; 0-06-443021-9 pa

"The story has elements of tenderness and humor; it also has . . . typically macabre Sendak touches. . . . The illustrations are beautiful, amusing, and distinctive." Sutherland. The Best in Child Books

Sensel, Joni

The **Farwalker's** quest. Bloomsbury U.S.A Children's Books 2009 372p $16.99

Grades: 5 6 7 8   **Fic**

1. Fantasy fiction

ISBN 978-1-59990-272-2; 1-59990-272-9

LC 2008-30523

When twelve-year-old Ariel and her friend Zeke find a mysterious artifact the like of which has not been seen in a long time, it proves to be the beginning of a long and arduous journey that will untimately reveal to them their true identities.

"This is a solid and well-paced fantasy in which the journey is more important than the conclusion." SLJ

The **timekeeper's** moon; [drawings by Yelena Safronova] Bloomsbury 2010 339p il $16.99

Grades: 5 6 7 8   **Fic**

1. Fantasy fiction

ISBN 978-1-59990-457-3; 1-59990-457-8

LC 2009-16690

Summoned by the moon to embark on a dangerous journey, thirteen-year-old Ariel Farwalker, knowing she must obey or risk destruction, sets out with her guardian, Scarl, to follow a mysterious map to an unknown entity called "Timekeeper"

"Vivid world building and tight pacing mark this sequel . . . further distinguished by rich characters with believable relationships." Booklist

Seredy, Kate

The **Good** Master; written and illustrated by Kate Seredy. Viking 1935 210p il hardcover o.p. pa $4.99

Grades: 4 5 6   **Fic**

1. Farm life -- Fiction

ISBN 0-14-030133-X

A Newbery Medal honor book, 1936

Into this story of Jancsi, a ten-year-old Hungarian farm boy and his little hoyden of a cousin Kate from Budapest, is woven a description of Hungarian farm life, fairs, festivals, and folk tales. Under the tutelage of Jancsi's kind father, called by the neighbors The Good Master, Kate calms down and becomes a more docile young person

"The steady warm understanding of the wise father, the Good Master, is a shining quality throughout." Horn Book

The **white** stag; written and illustrated by Kate Seredy. Viking 1937 94p il hardcover o.p. pa $4.99

Grades: 4 5 6   **Fic**

ISBN 0-14-031258-7 pa

Awarded the Newbery Medal, 1938

"Striking illustrations interpret this hero tale of the legendary founding of Hungary, when a white stag and a red eagle led the people to their promised land." Hodges. Books for Elem Sch Libr

Service, Pamela F.

Escape from planet Yastol; illustrated by Mike Gorman. Darby Creek 2011 102p il $15.95; pa $5.95

Grades: 4 5 6   **Fic**

1. Science fiction 2. Siblings -- Fiction 3. Authorship -- Fiction 4. Kidnapping -- Fiction 5. Books and reading -- Fiction 6. Extraterrestrial beings -- Fiction

ISBN 978-0-7613-7918-8; 0-7613-7918-5; 978-0-7613-7921-8 pa; 0-7613-7921-5 pa

LC 2010049235

Eleven-year-old Joshua Higgins' prize-winning science fiction novel draws the attention of sinister blue aliens who capture Josh and his sister Maggie and take them to the planet Yastol, the setting of his novel.

"Readers ready for longer chapter books will enjoy having some science fiction to choose from and welcome further adventures." Kirkus

Seuling, Barbara

Robert and the happy endings; illustrated by Paul Brewer. Cricket Books 2007 148p il $16.95

Grades: 2 3 4   Fic

1. School stories 2. Pirates -- Fiction

ISBN 978-0-8126-2748-0; 0-8126-2748-2

LC 2006100051

Pirate problems plague Robert as the class rehearses a pirate play, his bike is pirated away, and bossy Susanne Lee invites only half the class to a pirate party.

"Writing with a fine-tuned perception of children's concerns, Seuling underscores the idea that even a seemingly unlikely person can become a friend." Booklist

Robert and the practical jokes; by Barbara Seuling; illustrated by Paul Brewer. Cricket Books 2006 133p il $16.95

Grades: 2 3 4   Fic

1. School stories 2. Sex role -- Fiction

ISBN 0-8126-2741-5

LC 2005025411

As a boys-versus-girls war of practical jokes escalates in his third-grade classroom, Robert finds it difficult to ask a girl's help in learning to dance in time for a family wedding reception.

"Seuling captures Robert's feelings and the middle-grade milieu with sympathy and a tinge of humor, reflected in Brewer's expressive black-and-white illustrations." Booklist

Robert goes to camp; by Barbara Seuling; illustrated by Paul Brewer. 1st hardcover ed.; Cricket Books 2007 111p il $16.95

Grades: 2 3 4   Fic

1. Camps -- Fiction 2. Friendship -- Fiction

ISBN 978-0-8126-2753-4; 0-8126-2753-9

LC 2007014443

Eight-year-old Robert learns a lot about friendship at Camp Chicopee day camp when he decides to avoid his classmate Lester by spending time with a new friend, Zach, who soon reveals himself to be a troublemaker.

"Brewer's quirky pen-and-ink cartoon illustrations keep the tone light and humorous. This installment in the series is as engaging as its predecessors." SLJ

Robert takes a stand; illustrated by Paul Brewer. Cricket Books 2004 168p il hardcover o.p. $15.95

Grades: 2 3 4   Fic

1. School stories 2. Endangered species -- Fiction

ISBN 0-8126-2712-1

LC 2003-18499

Political experience gained in a class election comes in handy when Robert and his friend Paul act on behalf of endangered animals.

"The simple text, short chapters, and quirky black-and-white charcoal drawings all contribute to making this a great choice for beginning independent readers. Equally impor-

tant, most primary-grade children will relate to earnest, charming Robert, his world, his concerns, and his everyday adventures." Booklist

Sewell, Anna, 1820-1878

★ **Black** Beauty; the autobiography of a horse. by Anna Sewell; text illustrated by Fritz Eichenberg. Grosset & Dunlap 1995 301p il $17.99

Grades: 4 5 6   Fic

1. Horses -- Fiction

ISBN 0-448-40942-9

LC 94040990

First published 1877 in the United Kingdom; first United States edition, 1891

A horse in nineteenth-century England recounts his experiences with both good and bad masters.

Shahan, Sherry

Ice island. Delacorte Press 2012 $10.99; lib bdg $18.99; ebook $10.99

Grades: 4 5 6 7   Fic

1. Dogs -- Fiction 2. Sled dog racing -- Fiction 3. Wilderness survival -- Fiction 4. Iditarod Trail Sled Dog Race, Alaska -- Fiction

ISBN 978-0-385-74154-5; 0-385-74154-5; 978-0-375-99009-0 lib bdg; 0-375-99009-7 lib bdg; 978-0-375-98575-1 ebook

LC 2011003838

Thirteen-year-old Tatum's dream of competing in the grueling 1,049-mile Iditerod Trail Sled Dog Race may be at an end when she becomes lost in a freak snowstorm during a training run on Alaska's remote Santa Ysabel Island.

"Riveting and atmospheric. . . . This survival adventure creates an almost otherworldly experience within a treacherous and bracingly beautiful landscape." Kirkus

Shang, Wendy Wan-Long

The **great** wall of Lucy Wu; [by] Wendy Wan-Long Shang. Scholastic Press 2011 312p $17.99

Grades: 4 5 6   Fic

1. School stories 2. Family life -- Fiction 3. Chinese Americans -- Fiction

ISBN 0-545-16215-7; 978-0-545-16215-9

LC 2010-13536

Eleven-year-old aspiring basketball star and interior designer Lucy Wu is excited about finally having her own bedroom, until she learns that her great-aunt is coming to visit and Lucy will have to share a room with her for several months, shattering her plans for a perfect sixth-grade year. "Grades four to six." (Bull Cent Child Books)

"Bolstered by frequent use of Chinese language and proverbs, this is a realistic and amusing portrait of family dynamics, heritage, and the challenge of feeling like an outsider—even in one's own family." Publ Wkly

Sharmat, Marjorie Weinman

Nate the Great and the hungry book club; by Marjorie Weinman Sharmat and Mitchell Sharmat; illustrated by Jody Wheeler. Delacorte Press 2009 62p il $12.99; lib bdg $15.99

Grades: K 1 2 **Fic**
1. Mystery fiction 2. Books and reading -- Fiction
ISBN 978-0-385-73695-4; 0-385-73695-9; 978-0-385-90637-1 lib bdg; 0-385-90637-4 lib bdg
LC 2009030319
Nate and his dog Sludge help Rosamond discover who has been tearing pages out of her books.

Shaw, Susan
Tunnel vision. Margaret K. McElderry Books 2011 272p $16.99
Grades: 5 6 7 8 **Fic**
1. Crime -- Fiction 2. Homicide -- Fiction 3. Witnesses -- Fiction 4. Organized crime -- Fiction
ISBN 978-1-4424-0839-5; 1-4424-0839-1
LC 2010036306
After witnessing her mother's murder, sixteen-year-old high school student Liza Wellington and her father go into the witness protection program.
"The author creates a completely believable character in Liza, who often reverts to childlike emotions only to learn the hard way that cold reality takes precedence over even dearly held wishes. Kudos for the unexpected double ending, both illusory and realistic, giving readers a choice." Kirkus

Shefelman, Janice Jordan
Anna Maria's gift; by Janice Shefelman; illustrated by Robert Papp. Random House 2010 104p il $12.99; lib bdg $15.99
Grades: 2 3 4 **Fic**
1. Composers 2. Violinists 3. School stories 4. Orphans -- Fiction 5. Violinists -- Fiction
ISBN 978-0-375-85881-9; 0-375-85881-4; 978-0-375-95881-6 lib bdg; 0-375-95881-9 lib bdg
LC 2009004553
In 1715 Italy, eight-year-old Anna Maria Lombardini arrives at a Venice orphanage with little but the special violin her father made for her, but when her teacher, Antonio Vivaldi, favors her over a fellow student, the beloved instrument winds up in a canal
"Strong emotions . . . lie at the heart of the story. . . . [This is a] short, appealing historical novel." Booklist
Includes glossary

Sheinmel, Courtney
All the things you are. Simon & Schuster Books for Young Readers 2011 244p $15.99
Grades: 5 6 7 8 **Fic**
1. Theft -- Fiction 2. Friendship -- Fiction 3. Family life -- Fiction 4. Stepfamilies -- Fiction
ISBN 978-1-4169-9717-7; 1-4169-9717-2
LC 2010010090
When Carly Wheeler's mother is arrested for embezzling, Carly's perfect life begins to fall apart as friends at her prestigious private school stop talking to her, her beloved stepfather starts worrying about finances, and her image of herself and her family changes.
"Sheinmel persuasively and sensitively conveys Carly's conflicting emotions and her attempts to make sense of what's been thrust upon her." Publ Wkly

Sherlock, Patti
Letters from Wolfie. Viking 2004 232p $16.99; pa $6.99
Grades: 5 6 7 8 **Fic**
1. Dogs -- Fiction 2. Vietnam War, 1961-1975 -- Fiction
ISBN 0-670-03694-3; 0-14-240358-X pa
LC 2003-24316
Certain that he is doing the right thing by donating his dog, Wolfie, to the Army's scout program in Vietnam, thirteen-year-old Mark begins to have second thoughts when the Army refuses to say when and if Wolfie will ever return.
"In this topnotch novel, Sherlock weaves together numerous threads of emotion, information, and plot so seamlessly that readers will be surprised by how much they've learned by the time they finish this deceptively simple story." SLJ

Sherman, Deborah
The **BEDMAS** conspiracy. Fitzhenry & Whiteside 2011 pa $9.95
Grades: 4 5 6 7 **Fic**
1. School stories 2. Bands (Music) -- Fiction
ISBN 978-1-55455-181-1; 1-55455-181-1
Adam's band, Sick on a Snow Day, is challenged by more than just an unusual name: Adam is mistakenly accused of cheating on a test and must maintain a clean record and B-average if he wants to stay in the band. Then his lead singer, Daniela, gets stage fright.
"Adam's academic difficulties and Daniela's stage fright are only two of the challenges thrown their way, but both are handled imaginatively and with humor. . . . A genial read." SLJ

Sherman, Delia
Changeling. Viking 2006 292p $16.99; pa $8.99
Grades: 5 6 7 8 **Fic**
1. Fantasy fiction
ISBN 0-670-05967-6; 0-14-241188-4 pa
"Neef is a changeling, a human baby stolen by fairies. She lives in 'New York Between,' an invisible parallel city, and she was raised under the protection of her godmother (a white rat) and the Green Lady of Central Park. . . . After breaking Fairy Law, Neef is expelled, and she must complete a heroic quest . . . in order to regain entry to her community. . . . Silly, profound, and lightning paced all at once, this novel will please adventure fans and fantasy readers alike." Bull Cent Child Books Another title about Neef is:
The Magic Mirror of the Mermaid Queen (2009)

Sherrard, Valerie
★ **Tumbleweed** skies. Fitzhenry & Whiteside 2010 153p pa $11.95
Grades: 3 4 5 6 **Fic**
1. Grandmothers -- Fiction
ISBN 978-1-55455-113-2; 1-55455-113-7
"In the summer of 1954, Ellie's grandma reluctantly agrees to look after 10-year-old Ellie in Saskatchewan so that her dad can take a job as a traveling salesman. Ellie's mother died on the day that Ellie was born, and Grandma blames Ellie for her death. . . . Many kids will recognize the sorrow and difficulty of living with a hostile, bitter relative. . . . The girl next door, a spoiled, bossy brat, offers some levity, but true to Ellie's viewpoint, the spare first-person

narrative tells a heartbreaking family story with no mushy reconciliation." Booklist

The **glory** wind. Fitzhenry & Whiteside 2011 222p pa $12.95
Grades: 5 6 7 8   **Fic**
1. Prejudices -- Fiction 2. Country life -- Fiction
ISBN 978-1-55455-170-5; 1-55455-170-6

Eleven-year-old Luke must come to terms with the moral prejudices of his small town in rural 1950s Ontario when he befriends Gracie, the daughter of a young widow who moves in next door.

"Luke's first person narration is fresh and emotionally true. . . . The haunting depiction of small-mindedness will leave readers wondering, as Luke comes to, about Gracie's true nature: heavenly child—or angel?" Kirkus

Sherry, Maureen

Walls within walls; illustrated by Adam Stower. Katherine Tegen Books 2010 349p il $16.99
Grades: 4 5 6 7   **Fic**
1. Mystery fiction 2. Siblings -- Fiction
ISBN 978-0-06-176700-5; 0-06-176700-X
             LC 2010-09494

When the Smithfork family moves into a lavish Manhattan apartment building, they discover clues to a decades-old mystery hidden behind the walls of their new home.

This "packs all sorts of interesting information about topics like history and architecture into a mystery that kids can (almost) solve. . . . Readers will get a real feel for the uniqueness that is New York City." Booklist

Sheth, Kashmira

Blue jasmine; [by] Kashmira Sheth. Hyperion Books for Children 2004 186p $15.99; pa $5.99
Grades: 5 6 7 8   **Fic**
1. Immigrants 2. East Indian Americans 3. Interpersonal relations 4. Family life -- India 5. Immigrants -- Fiction 6. East Indians -- Fiction
ISBN 0-7868-1855-7; 0-7868-5565-7 pa
             LC 2003-50818

When twelve-year-old Seema moves to Iowa City with her parents and younger sister, she leaves friends and family behind in her native India but gradually begins to feel at home in her new country

"Seema's story, which articulates the ache for distant home and family, will resonate with fellow immigrants and enlighten their classmates." Booklist

Boys without names. Balzer & Bray 2010 316p $15.99
Grades: 4 5 6 7   **Fic**
1. Slavery -- Fiction 2. Child labor -- Fiction 3. Missing persons -- Fiction
ISBN 978-0-06-185760-7; 0-06-185760-2
             LC 2009-11747

Eleven-year-old Gopal and his family leave their rural Indian village for life with his uncle in Mumbai, but when they arrive his father goes missing and Gopal ends up locked in a sweatshop from which there is no escape.

"Readers quickly come to care for this clever, perceptive boy who tries hard to do the right thing. . . . The author includes more about child labor at the end of this well-told survival story with a social conscience." SLJ

Shimko, Bonnie

★ The **private** thoughts of Amelia E. Rye. Farrar, Straus Giroux 2010 234p $16.99
Grades: 5 6 7 8   **Fic**
1. Friendship -- Fiction 2. Mother-daughter relationship -- Fiction
ISBN 978-0-374-36131-0; 0-374-36131-2
             LC 2008048092

Growing up in a small town in upstate New York during the 1960s, 13-year-old Amelia E. Ryel, unwanted by her mother, searches for love and acceptance.

"The book is peopled with believable, multilayered characters. . . . Shimko's . . . story is original, and Amelia's distinctive voice and likable nature will have readers rooting for her in times of trouble and cheering her ultimate good fortune." Publ Wkly

Shreve, Susan Richards

★ The **flunking** of Joshua T. Bates; [by] Susan Shreve; illustrated by Diane de Groat. Knopf 1984 82p il hardcover o.p. pa $4.99
Grades: 3 4 5   **Fic**
1. School stories 2. Teachers -- Fiction 3. Family life -- Fiction
ISBN 0-679-84187-3 pa
             LC 83-19636

Driving home from the beach on Labor Day, Joshua receives some shocking news from his mother: he must repeat third grade.

"In addition to the warm depiction of a teacher-pupil relationship, the story has other relationships, astutely drawn: Joshua's parents, the former classmate who teases Joshua, the best friend who stoutly defends him. The dialogue is particularly good, often contributing to characterization, just as often crisply humorous." Bull Cent Child Books

Other titles about Joshua are:
Joshua T. Bates in trouble again (1997)
Joshua T. Bates takes charge (1993)

Shulman, Polly

★ The **Grimm** Legacy. G. P. Putnam's Sons 2010 325p $16.99
Grades: 5 6 7 8   **Fic**
1. Fantasy fiction 2. Magic -- Fiction 3. Libraries -- Fiction
ISBN 0-399-25096-4; 978-0-399-25096-5
             LC 2009028919

New York high school student Elizabeth gets an afterschool job as a page at the "New-York Circulating Material Repository," and when she gains coveted access to its Grimm Collection of magical objects, she and the other pages are drawn into a series of frightening adventures involving mythical creatures and stolen goods.

"This modern fantasy has intrigue, adventure, and romance, and the magical aspects of the tale are both clever and intricately woven. . . . Shulman's prose is fast paced, filled with humor, and peopled with characters who are either true to life or delightfully bizarre." SLJ

The **Wells** Bequest; by Polly Shulman. Nancy Paulsen Books, an imprint of Penguin Group (USA) Inc. 2013 272 p. (hardcover) $16.99
Grades: 5 6 7 8   **Fic**
1. Time travel -- Juvenile fiction 2. Fantasy fiction

-- Juvenile fiction 3. Science fiction 4. Time travel
-- Fiction

ISBN 0399256466; 9780399256462

LC 2012036571

This book is a companion to Polly Shulman's "The Grimm Legacy." Here, New York Circulating Material Repository page "Leo notices an object materializing on the floor. The glittering, football-sized machine has 'gears and rods and knobs and a little saddle'—and two miniscule humans, one of whom is himself." He discovers that he and his fellow page Jaya must travel in time to prevent another page from misusing Nikola Tesla's death ray. (Kirkus Reviews)

Shurtliff, Liesl

Rump; the true story of Rumpelstiltskin. Liesl Shurtliff. 1st ed. Alfred A. Knopf 2013 272 p. (hardcover) $16.99

Grades: 3 4 5 6 7 **Fic**
1. Fractured fairy tales 2. Magic -- Juvenile fiction 3. Fairy tales 4. Gold -- Fiction 5. Humorous stories 6. Magic -- Fiction 7. Names, Personal -- Fiction

ISBN 0307977935; 9780307977939 trade; 9780307977946; 9780307977953; 9780307977960

LC 2012005093

In this fractured fairy tale, by Liesl Shurtliff, "12-year-old [Rumpelstiltskin] . . . finds an old spinning wheel, . . . [and] discovers he has a gift for spinning straw into gold. His best friend, Red Riding Hood, warns him that magic is dangerous, and she's right. With each thread he spins, he weaves himself deeper into a curse. To break the spell, Rump must go on a perilous quest, fighting off pixies, trolls, poison apples, and a wickedly foolish queen." (Publisher's note)

"Debut author Shurtliff upends the traditional characterization of this fairy tale's antihero, recasting Rumpelstiltskin as a sympathetic and tragically doomed protagonist. . . . [T] he picaresque-style narrative gives the maligned character a refreshingly plainspoken voice, while honoring the original story's hauntingly strange events." Pub Wkly

Silberberg, Alan

★ **Milo**; sticky notes and brain freeze. written and illustrated by Alan Silberberg. Aladdin 2010 275p il $15.99

Grades: 5 6 7 8 **Fic**
1. Death -- Fiction 2. Mothers -- Fiction 3. Friendship -- Fiction 4. Bereavement -- Fiction

ISBN 978-1-4169-9430-5; 1-4169-9430-0

LC 2010012708

"This is more than just another funny story about a middle school misfit who is the new kid in the neighborhood. While Milo does struggle with all the normal tween anxieties and self-consciousness about his family, there is more. Silberberg details the daily events with Wimpy Kid-like drawings and quick-witted humor that will keep the pages turning. Milo's new friendships with classmates Marshall and Hillary and elderly neighbor Sylvia Poole allow readers to glimpse at the deeper truth–Milo's mother's death–as it emerges between laugh lines. Silberberg takes on a tough topic and always stays true to the age of the character through dialogue and artwork while maintaining that wisecracking, 12-year-old humor." SLJ

Simmons, Jane

Beryl; a pig's tale. Little, Brown Books for Young Readers 2010 216p $14.99

Grades: 2 3 4 5 **Fic**
1. Adventure fiction 2. Pigs -- Fiction 3. Family -- Fiction 4. Toleration -- Fiction

ISBN 978-0-316-04410-3; 0-316-04410-5

LC 2009-3800

Tired of being mistreated and cooped up, Beryl the piglet escapes her farm and meets a group of wild pigs, whose settlement splits up over the decision of whether to let her stay, and with her new "family" she sets out to find a new home

"Simmons interjects humorous episodes through her colorful cast of animal characters, providing a rich contrast to the serious topics she explores. Before the hopeful ending is neatly resolved, Beryl and her cohorts face cruelty and despair. Vivid black-and-white drawings convey a range of emotion by varying shade and light. Expressive faces highlight a wealth of feeling." SLJ

Simon, Francesca

Horrid Henry; illustrated by Tony Ross. Sourcebooks 2009 90p il pa $4.99

Grades: 2 3 4 **Fic**
ISBN 978-1-4022-1775-3; 1-4022-1775-7

First published 1994 in the United Kingdom

"Four short chapters follow Henry as he tries to have a perfect day (and upstages his brother, Perfect Peter), disrupts a dance recital with his imitation of a pterodactyl, meets his piratical match in neighbor Moody Margaret, and sabotages a family camping vacation. . . . Short, easy-to-read chapters will appeal to early readers, who will laugh at Henry's exaggerated antics and relate to his rambunctious personality. . . . Ross's comical illustrations perfectly complement the [text]." SLJ

Other titles in this series are:
Horrid Henry and the mega-mean time machine (2009)
Horrid Henry and the scary sitter (2009)
Horrid Henry tricks the tooth fairy (2009)
Horrid Henry's Christmas (2009)
Horrid Henry's stinkbomb (2009)
Horrid Henry rocks (2011)
Horrid Henry wakes the dead (2011)

Singh, Vandana

★ **Younguncle** comes to town; illustrated by B. M. Kamath. Viking 2006 153p il $14.99

Grades: 3 4 5 **Fic**
1. Uncles -- Fiction

ISBN 978-0-670-06051-1; 0-670-06051-8

LC 2005-14146

First published 2004 in India

In a small town in northern India, three siblings await their father's youngest brother, Younguncle, who is said to be somewhat eccentric

"Singh's prose is humorous and delightfully understated." SLJ

Skelton, Matthew

★ **Endymion** Spring. Delacorte Press 2006 392p il $17.95; lib bdg $19.99; pa $9.99

Grades: 5 6 7 8 **Fic**
1. Inventors 2. Printers 3. Magic -- Fiction 4. Books and reading -- Fiction

ISBN 0-385-73380-1; 0-385-90397-9 lib bdg; 0-385-73456-5 pa

LC 2006-46259

Having reluctantly accompanied his academic mother and pesky younger sister to Oxford, twelve-year-old Blake Winters is at loose ends until he stumbles across an ancient and magical book, secretly brought to England in 1453 by Gutenberg's mute apprentice to save it from evil forces, and which now draws Blake into a dangerous and life-threatening quest

"This book is certain to reach an audience looking for a page-turner, and it just might motivate readers to explore the . . . facts behind the fiction." SLJ

★ The **story** of Cirrus Flux. Delacorte Press 2010 288p il $17.99; lib bdg $20.99
Grades: 4 5 6 7   **Fic**
1. Adventure fiction 2. Orphans -- Fiction 3. Supernatural -- Fiction
ISBN 978-0-385-73381-6; 0-385-73381-X; 978-0-385-90398-1 lib bdg; 0-385-90398-7 lib bdg
LC 2009-18987

In 1783 London, the destiny of an orphaned boy and girl becomes intertwined as the boy, Cirrus Flux, is pursued by a sinister woman mesmerist, a tiny man with an all-seeing eye, and a skull-collecting scoundrel, all of whom believe that he possesses an orb containing a divine power.

Skelton "neatly weaves touches of fantasy into a late-eighteenth century London setting. . . . His literary sensibility and grubby atmospherics are strong enough to carry the tale." Booklist

Skye, Obert
Wonkenstein: the creature from my closet. Henry Holt and Co. 2011 224p $13.99
Grades: 4 5 6   **Fic**
1. School stories 2. Monsters -- Fiction 3. Family life -- Fiction 4. Books and reading -- Fiction
ISBN 978-0-8050-9268-4; 0-8050-9268-4
LC 2011004870

Twelve-year-old Rob has stuffed his closet with old laboratory experiments, unread books, and more, and when a creature emerges from that chaos causing a great deal of trouble, Rob has to do such horrible things as visit a library and speak at a school assembly to set things right again.

"The writing is quite funny and has a lot of laugh-out-loud moments." SLJ

Slade, Arthur G.
Jolted; Newton Starker's rules for survival. [by] Arthur Slade. Wendy Lamb Books 2009 227p $15.99; lib bdg $18.99
Grades: 5 6 7 8   **Fic**
1. School stories 2. Lightning -- Fiction
ISBN 978-0-385-74700-4; 0-385-74700-4; 978-0-385-90944-0 lib bdg; 0-385-90944-6 lib bdg
LC 2008-8632

First published 2008 in Canada
Many of Newton Starker's ancestors, including his mother, have been killed by lightning strikes, so when he enrolls at the eccentric Jerry Potts Academy of Higher Learning and Survival in Moose Jaw, Saskatchewan, he tries to be a model student so that he can avoid the same fate.

"The premise will snag readers immediately [and] . . . Slade's portrayal of Newton's sweep of emotions as he deals with his perceived fate–fear, fury, dogged determination–is especially convincing." Publ Wkly

Sleator, William
Interstellar pig. Dutton 1984 197p hardcover o.p. pa $6.99
Grades: 5 6 7 8   **Fic**
1. Science fiction
ISBN 0-14-037595-3 pa
LC 84-4132

Barney's boring seaside vacation suddenly becomes more interesting when the cottage next door is occupied by three exotic neighbors who are addicted to a game they call "Interstellar Pig."

The author "draws the reader in with intimations of danger and horror, but the climactic battle is more slapstick than horrific, and the victor's prize could scarcely be more ironic. Problematic as straight science fiction but great fun as a spoof on human-alien contact." Booklist

Another title about Barney is:
Parasite Pig (2002)

The **boxes**. Dutton Children's Bks. 1998 196p hardcover o.p. pa $4.99
Grades: 6 7 8 9   **Fic**
1. Science fiction
ISBN 0-525-46012-8; 0-14-130810-9 pa
LC 98-9285

When she opens two strange boxes left in her care by her mysterious uncle, fifteen-year-old Annie discovers a swarm of telepathic creatures and unleashes a power capable of slowing down time

"Sleator has written a page-turner. . . . His writing is crisp and clean, letting the story speak for itself." Voice Youth Advocates

Slote, Alfred
★ **Finding** Buck McHenry. HarperCollins Pubs. 1991 250p pa $4.95
Grades: 4 5 6   **Fic**
1. Baseball -- Fiction 2. African Americans -- Fiction
ISBN 0-06-440469-2 pa
LC 90-39190

Eleven-year-old Jason, believing the school custodian Mack Henry to be Buck McHenry, a famous pitcher from the old Negro League, tries to enlist him as a coach for his Little League team by revealing his identity to the world

"Slote skillfully blends comedy, suspense and baseball in a highly entertaining tale." Publ Wkly

Smiley, Jane
★ The **Georges** and the Jewels; with illustrations by Elaine Clayton. Alfred A. Knopf 2009 232p il $16.99; lib bdg $19.99
Grades: 4 5 6 7   **Fic**
1. Horses -- Fiction 2. Ranch life -- Fiction 3. Christian life -- Fiction
ISBN 978-0-375-86227-4; 0-375-86227-7; 978-0-375-96227-1 lib bdg; 0-375-96227-1 lib bdg
LC 2009-06241

Seventh-grader Abby Lovitt grows up on her family's California horse ranch in the 1960s, learning to train the horses her father sells and trying to reconcile her strict religious upbringing with her own ideas about life.

"As might be expected from the skilled hands of Smiley . . . there are synchronous storylines . . . [and] many will find it difficult to say goodbye to Abby, Jack and especially to Ornery George." Publ Wkly

Other titles in this series are:
A good horse (2010)
True blue (2011)

Smith, Clete Barrett

Aliens on vacation; illustrated by Christian Slade. Hyperion 2011 251p il (The intergalactic bed & breakfast) $16.99

Grades: 4 5 6   Fic
1. Vacations -- Fiction 2. Hotels and motels -- Fiction 3. Extraterrestrial beings -- Fiction
ISBN 1-4231-3363-3; 978-1-4231-3363-6

Unhappy at being sent to stay with his grandmother at the inn she operates, The Intergalactic Bed & Breakfast, Scrub discovers that each room is actually a portal to space and the inn's visitors are aliens who are vacationing on Earth.

Smith "delivers a first novel about being a stranger in a strange land that many middle-schoolers will find funny and relatable. Slade adds a few goofy touches in the black-and-white spot art." Booklist

Smith, Cynthia Leitich

Indian shoes; illustrated by Jim Madsen. HarperCollins Pubs. 2002 66p il $15.95

Grades: 3 4 5   Fic
1. Grandfathers 2. Grandfathers -- Fiction 3. Indians of North America 4. Native Americans -- Fiction
ISBN 0-06-029531-7

LC 2001-39510

Together with Grampa, Ray Halfmoon, a Seminole-Cherokee boy, finds creative and amusing solutions to life's challenges

"The writing is warm and lively; the situations are sometimes humorous, sometimes poignant; and Ray and Grampa's loving relationship is depicted believably and without sentimentality." Horn Book Guide

Smith, Doris Buchanan

★ A **taste** of blackberries; illustrated by Charles Robinson. Crowell 1973 58p il lib bdg $14.89; pa $4.95

Grades: 4 5 6   Fic
1. Death -- Fiction 2. Friendship -- Fiction
ISBN 0-690-80512-8 lib bdg; 0-06-440238-4 pa

"A difficult and sensitive subject, treated with taste and honesty, is woven into a moving story about a believable little boy. The black-and-white illustrations are honest, affective, and sensitive." Horn Book

Smith, Hope Anita

★ **Keeping** the night watch; with illustrations by E.B. Lewis. Henry Holt 2008 73p il $18.95

Grades: 4 5 6 7   Fic
1. Novels in verse 2. Fathers -- Fiction 3. Family life -- Fiction 4. African Americans -- Fiction
ISBN 978-0-8050-7202-0; 0-8050-7202-0

LC 2007-12372

Coretta Scott King honor book for text, 2009

A thirteen-year-old African American boy chronicles what happens to his family when his father, who temporarily left, returns home and they all must deal with their feelings of anger, hope, abandonment, and fear.

"The words are simple . . . and the beautiful watercolor pictures of the African American family have the same quiet intensity as pictures in the first book. . . . Although mainly in free verse, there's also a sonnet." Booklist

The **way** a door closes; [by] Hope Anita Smith; with illustrations by Shane W. Evans. Holt & Co. 2003 52p il $18.95

Grades: 4 5 6 7   Fic
1. Novels in verse 2. Fathers -- Fiction 3. Family life -- Fiction 4. African Americans -- Fiction
ISBN 0-8050-6477-X

LC 2002-67884

In this novel in verse "readers are drawn into the thoughts and feelings of a 13-year-old African American as he tries to understand and cope with a parent's departure from the family. . . . In carefully chosen, straightforward language, Smith conveys the boy's roller-coaster emotions with pinpoint accuracy. The results are poems that are heartbreaking, angry, and tender. Done in warm shades of mostly brown, blue, and gold, Evans's color spot and full-page paintings have a realistic, slightly sculptural appearance and are a perfect complement to the poems." SLJ

Smith, Icy

Half spoon of rice; a survival story of the Cambodian genocide. written by Icy Smith; illustrated by Sopaul Nhem. East West Discovery Press 2010 42p il

Grades: 5 6 7 8   Fic
1. Genocide -- Fiction
ISBN 0-9821675-8-X; 978-0-9821675-8-8

LC 2009002973

Nine-year-old Nat and his family are forced from their home on April 17, 1975, marched for many days, separated from each other, and forced to work in the rice fields, where Nat concentrates on survival. Includes historical notes and photographs documenting the Cambodian genocide

"Bold, impressionistic oil paintings, mainly full page but some full spreads, speak volumes, and archival photographs are appended. This powerful child's eye view of war is harsh and realistic—like its subject—though accessible and thought-provoking." SLJ

Smith, Robert Kimmel

★ **Chocolate** fever; illustrated by Gioia Fiammenghi. Putnam 1989 93p il $14.99; pa $4.99

Grades: 4 5 6   Fic
1. Chocolate -- Fiction
ISBN 978-0-399-24355-4; 0-399-24355-0; 978-0-14-240595-6 pa; 0-14-240595-7 pa

LC 88-23508

A reissue of the title first published 1972 by Coward-McCann

"It's all quite preposterous and lots of laughs, and so are the cartoon illustrations." Publ Wkly

Smith, Roland

Cryptid hunters. Hyperion Books for Children 2005 348p $15.99; pa $5.99

Grades: 5 6 7 8   Fic
1. Adventure fiction 2. Twins -- Fiction
ISBN 0-7868-5161-9; 0-7868-5162-7 pa

Twins, Grace and Marty, along with a mysterious uncle, are dropped into the middle of the Congolese jungle in search of their missing photojournalist parents.

"The action is nonstop in this well-paced jungle adventure, and Smith adds a deeper layer in scenes of Marty and Grace discovering truths about their complicated family relationships." Booklist

Eruption; Roland Smith. Scholastic Press 2012 156 p. (Storm runners.)
Grades: 5 6 7 8   **Fic**
1. Circus -- Fiction 2. Rescue work -- Fiction 3. Volcanoes -- Mexico -- Fiction 4. Earthquakes -- Mexico -- Fiction 5. Father-son relationship -- Fiction 6. Survival -- Fiction 7. Volcanoes -- Fiction 8. Earthquakes -- Fiction 9. Storm chasers -- Fiction 10. Circus animals -- Fiction 11. Fathers and sons -- Fiction 12. Survival -- Juvenile fiction 13. Volcanoes -- Juvenile fiction 14. Earthquakes -- Juvenile fiction 15. Storm chasers -- Juvenile fiction 16. Circus animals -- Juvenile fiction 17. Fathers and sons -- Juvenile fiction
ISBN 0545081742; 9780545081740
LC 2011042743
In the third "installment in the Storm Runners series, Chase and his father are off to Mexico to find the missing Rossi Family Circus. . . . [T]hey end up near a rumbling volcano. [Roland] Smith . . . gives the survival story an extra dose of octane with some escaped wild animals—in this case, a tiger that nearly devours Chase." (Booklist)

". . . [A]ll contact has been lost with the Rossi Brothers' Circus, on tour near Mexico City, in the wake of a major earthquake. This sends a crew headed by catastrophe experts Chase and his father John to the rescue. . . . [They find themselves on] Popocatepetl's shaking, landslide ridden slopes amid clouds of ash to discover human corpses, dead elephants and big cats, desperados, trapped refugees, dozens of badly injured villagers and . . . an escaped tiger." (Kirkus)

I, Q.: book one, Independence Hall. Sleeping Bear Press 2008 302p pa $8.95
Grades: 5 6 7 8   **Fic**
1. Adventure fiction 2. Spies -- Fiction 3. Terrorism -- Fiction
ISBN 978-1-58536-325-4 pa; 1-58536-325-1 pa
In Philadelphia, Angela realizes she's being followed, and Q soon learns the secret about Angela's real mother, a former Secret Service agent

"Adventure, suspense, humor, fascinating characters, and plot twists galore will draw middle-graders to this series starter." Booklist

I. Q.: book two, The White House. Sleeping Bear Press 2010 pa $8.95
Grades: 5 6 7 8   **Fic**
1. Spies -- Fiction 2. Siblings -- Fiction 3. Terrorism -- Fiction 4. Remarriage -- Fiction
ISBN 978-1-58536-456-5; 1-58536-456-8
LC 2011378292
Q (Quest) and Angela make it to the White House in Washington, D.C. to find that it is even harder to determine who are the 'good' and 'bad' guys than ever before.

"This spellbinding James Bond genre espionage novel for the middle school set will leave readers breathlessly waiting for the next installment." Voice Youth Advocates

Storm runners. Scholastic Press 2011 143p $16.99
Grades: 5 6 7 8   **Fic**
1. Hurricanes -- Fiction 2. Father-son relationship -- Fiction
ISBN 978-0-545-08175-7; 0-545-08175-0
LC 2010-32720
Twelve-year-old Chase Masters travels the country with his father, a "storm runner," but he is tested in ways he never could have imagined when he and a new friend are caught in a hurricane near St. Petersburg, Florida.

"This is an exciting, quick read. . . . Readers will feel engaged with Chase and his friends in their struggles to survive." SLJ

Tentacles. Scholastic Press 2009 318p $16.99
Grades: 5 6 7 8   **Fic**
1. Mystery fiction 2. Adventure fiction 3. Squids -- Fiction
ISBN 978-0-545-16688-1; 0-545-16688-8
LC 2009011125
After the mysterious disappearance of their parents, Marty and Grace go to live with their scientist uncle and accompany him on, what soon becomes, an increasingly dangerous expedition to New Zealand to track a giant squid.

The **surge**. Scholastic Press 2011 133p il (Storm runners) $16.99
Grades: 5 6 7 8   **Fic**
1. Circus -- Fiction 2. Storms -- Fiction 3. Hurricanes -- Fiction
ISBN 978-0-545-08179-5; 0-545-08179-3
LC 2011017358
After barely surviving a terrifying hurricane, Chase and his friends Nicole and Rashawn have made it to the safety of Nicole's family farm, which is also the winter home of the Rossi Brothers Circus, where flood waters are rising and dangerous circus animals are on the loose.

"A high-velocity page-turner." Kirkus

Sneve, Virginia Driving Hawk
Lana's Lakota moons. University of Nebraska Press 2007 116p pa $12.95
Grades: 3 4 5   **Fic**
1. Death -- Fiction 2. Cancer -- Fiction 3. Cousins -- Fiction 4. Teton Indians -- Fiction 5. Hmong (Asian people) -- Fiction
ISBN 978-0-8032-6028-3 pa; 0-8032-6028-8 pa
LC 2007-05469
Cousins Lori and Lana, Lakota Indians who have a close but competitive relationship, learn about their heritage and culture throughout the year, and when a Laotian-Hmong girl comes to their school, they make friends with her and "adopt" her as one of their own

This is an "unassuming yet potent chronicle. . . . This novel repays readers with its portraits of the sisters and their living heritage." Publ Wkly

Snicket, Lemony, 1970-

The **bad** beginning; illustrations by Brett Helquist. HarperCollins Pubs. 1999 162p il (A series of unfortunate events) $11.99; pa $6.99

Grades: 4 5 6   **Fic**

1. Orphans -- Fiction

ISBN 0-06-440766-7; 0-06-114630-7 pa

LC 99-14750

After the sudden death of their parents, the three Baudelaire children must depend on each other and their wits when it turns out that the distant relative who is appointed their guardian is determined to use any means necessary to get their fortune

"While the misfortunes hover on the edge of being ridiculous, Snicket's energetic blend of humor, dramatic irony, and literary flair makes it all perfectly believable. . . . Excellent for reading aloud." SLJ

Other titles in this series are:

The reptile room (1999)

The wide window (2000)

The miserable mill (2000)

The austere academy (2000)

The ersatz elevator (2000)

The vile village (2001)

The hostile hospital (2001)

The carnivorous carnival (2003)

The slippery slope (2003)

The grim grotto (2004)

The penultimate peril (2005)

The end (2006)

Lemony Snicket: the unauthorized autobiography. HarperCollins Pubs. 2002 212p il $11.99; pa $6.99

Grades: 4 5 6 7   **Fic**

ISBN 0-06-000719-2; 0-06-056225-0 pa

LC 2001-51745

"The story of the fictitious Lemony Snicket and how he has dedicated his life to the case of the orphaned Baudelaire children. . . . Snicket tells you what he cannot tell you and then tells you, but what he tells you makes no sense. . . . [A] hilarious and clever book. . . . Lemony Snicket fans will love it, and new readers will laugh so much that they will want to read the series." Voice Youth Advocates

★ **Who** could that be at this hour? by Lemony Snicket; art by Seth. Little, Brown 2012 272 p.

Grades: 3 4 5 6 7   **Fic**

1. Bildungsromans 2. Mystery fiction -- Juvenile fiction 3. Humorous fiction -- Juvenile fiction 4. Humorous stories 5. Statues -- Fiction 6. Stealing -- Fiction 7. Apprentices -- Fiction 8. Mystery and detective stories

ISBN 0316123080; 9780316123082

LC 2012012657

This children's adventure mystery, by Lemony Snicket, begins in "Stain'd-by-the-Sea, the mostly deserted town where 12-year-old Lemony Snicket takes his first case as apprentice to chaperone S. Theodora Markson. They have been hired by Mrs. Murphy Sallis to retrieve a vastly valuable statue of the local legend, the Bombinating Beast. . . . With the help and/or hindrance of girls Moxie and Ellington, can Snicket keep his promises and come close to solving a mystery?" (Kirkus Reviews)

Sniegoski, Tom

Billy Hooten, Owlboy; by Thomas E. Sniegoski; illustrated by Eric Powell. Yearling 2007 242p il lib bdg $11.99; pa $5.99

Grades: 3 4 5 6   **Fic**

1. Superheroes -- Fiction 2. Cartoons and comics -- Fiction

ISBN 978-0-385-90402-5 lib bdg; 978-0-440-42180-1 pa

LC 2007001552

Unassuming twelve-year-old Billy Hooten, who loves reading superhero comic books, suddenly learns that he has been chosen to become the next Owlboy, whose destiny it is to save the inhabitants of Monstros, a city underneath the cemetery next to Billy's house

"This lively tale should be a hit, especially with reluctant readers. A few black-and-white sketches appear throughout." SLJ

Others title about Owlboy are:

Billy Hooten, Owlboy: the girl with the destructo touch (2007)

Billy Hooten, Owlboy: the flock of fury (2008)

Billy Hooten, Owlboy: tremble at the terror of Zisboom-bah (2008)

Quest for the Spark; Book 2 written by Tom Sniegoski; illustrated by Jeff Smith; color by Steve Hamaker. Graphix 2012 234 p.

Grades: 4 5 6 7   **Fic**

1. Fantasy fiction 2. Magic -- Fiction 3. Adventure fiction 4. Dreams -- Fiction 5. Dragons -- Fiction 6. Fantasy 7. Humorous stories 8. Heroes -- Fiction 9. Adventure and adventurers -- Fiction

ISBN 9780545141031; 9780545141048

LC 2011020281

This book is set in the world of illustrator Jeff Smith's "Bone" graphic novels. Here, author Tom Sniegoski tells the story of "Tom, a Valley turnip farmer" who "receives a vision that the peaceful otherworld of the Dreaming is under attack. The evil Nacht, a renegade Dragon, seeks to control the dreamland, and through it, the Waking World as well. A mysterious forest woman tells Tom that he has been chosen to lead a quest to find the scattered pieces of the Spark--the light of creation that can drive back the dark power. When his family falls under the Nacht's corrupted sleep spell, Tom realizes that he has no choice and sets out with his best friend, a talking raccoon." (School Libr J)

Quest for the spark; book one. written by Tom Sniegoski; illustrated by Jeff Smith; color by Steve Hamaker. Graphix 2011 218p il (Bone) $22.99; pa $10.99

Grades: 4 5 6 7   **Fic**

1. Fantasy fiction 2. Adventure fiction 3. Magic -- Fiction 4. Dreams -- Fiction 5. Heroes and heroines -- Fiction

ISBN 978-0-545-14101-7; 0-545-14101-X; 978-0-545-14102-4 pa; 0-545-14102-8 pa

LC 2010017002

Twelve-year-old Tom Elm, his raccoon friend Roderick, Percival, Abbey, and Barclay Bone, warrior-priest Randolf, and forest-woman Lorimar join in a quest to find the pieces of the Spark that can save Dreaming—and the Waking World—from a Darkness created by the Nacht.

"At long last . . . we return to the Valley that was the setting for Smith's comics-landscape-changing Bone, though this adventure takes place in prose rather than panels. . . . As long as fans are not expecting a repeat of the old magic and not too disappointed that there isn't nearly enough of Smith's always excellent full-color, full-page artwork helping out, it looks as if they're in for a cheery jaunt back through a beloved world." Booklist

Snow, Alan

Here be monsters! an adventure involving magic, trolls, and other creatures. written and illustrated by Alan Snow. Atheneum Books for Young Readers 2006 529p il (The Ratbridge chronicles) $17.95; pa $8.99

Grades: 4 5 6 7   **Fic**

1. Fantasy fiction 2. Monsters -- Fiction
ISBN 978-0-689-87047-7; 0-689-87047-7; 978-0-689-87048-4 pa; 0-689-87048-5 pa

LC 2005-24438

While gathering food to bring to his grandfather, young Arthur becomes trapped in the city of Ratbridge, where he and some new friends try to stop a plot to shrink the monsters of Arthur's home, the Underworld, for a nefarious purpose

"Helpful in creating the settings and bringing the more fantastic characters to life, the illustrations, which are often amusing, also make the book accessible to younger children who like lengthy books. Snow's inventive fantasy . . . combines stout hearts, terrible troubles, and inspired lunacy." Booklist

Snow, Maya

Sisters of the sword. HarperCollins 2008 275p (Sisters of the sword) $16.99; lib bdg $17.89; pa $6.99

Grades: 5 6 7 8   **Fic**

1. Samurai -- Fiction 2. Sisters -- Fiction 3. Sex role -- Fiction
ISBN 978-0-06-124387-5; 0-06-124387-6; 978-0-06-124388-2 lib bdg; 0-06-124388-4 lib bdg; 978-0-06-124389-9 pa; 0-06-124389-2 pa

LC 2007-029610

Two aristocratic sisters in ancient Japan disguise themselves as samurai warriors to take revenge on the uncle who betrayed their family.

"This rousing new series . . . starts off with a bang, or more accurately, the silent thrust of a sword." Booklist

Other titles in this series are:
Chasing the secret (2009)
Journey through fire (2009)

Snyder, Laurel

Any which wall; drawings by LeUyen Pham. Random House 2009 242p il $16.99; lib bdg $19.99

Grades: 4 5 6 7   **Fic**

1. Magic -- Fiction 2. Wishes -- Fiction 3. Siblings -- Fiction 4. Space and time -- Fiction
ISBN 978-0-375-85560-3; 0-375-85560-2; 978-0-375-95560-0 lib bdg; 0-375-95560-7 lib bdg

LC 2008-22605

In the middle of an Iowa cornfield, four children find a magic wall that enables them to travel through time and space.

"Snyder's fresh, down-to-earth voice is complemented by Pham's energetic illustrations, which seem at once retro

and modern. Fantasy fans will enjoy this novel, but so will readers who like stories about ordinary kids." SLJ

Bigger than a bread box. Random House 2011 226p $16.99

Grades: 4 5 6   **Fic**

1. Magic -- Fiction 2. Family life -- Fiction
ISBN 978-0-375-86916-7; 0-375-86916-6

Twelve-year-old Rebecca is struggling with her parents' separation, as well as a sudden move to her Gran's house in another state. For a while, a magic bread box, discovered in the attic, makes life away from home a little easier. Then suddenly it starts to make things much, much more difficult, and Rebecca is forced to decide not just where, but who she really wants to be.

"Introspective and rich with delicate imagery. . . . The insightful, memorable, and complex characters that Snyder creates result in a story with the same qualities." Publ Wkly

★ **Penny** Dreadful; drawings by Abigail Halpin. Random House 2010 304p il $16.99; lib bdg $19.99

Grades: 3 4 5   **Fic**

1. Family life -- Fiction 2. Country life -- Fiction
ISBN 978-0-375-86199-4; 0-375-86199-8; 978-0-375-96199-1 lib bdg; 0-375-96199-2 lib bdg

LC 2009-32104

When her father suddenly quits his job, the almost-ten-year-old, friendless Penny and her neglectful parents leave.

"Snyder's characters are well-developed and endearing, and the author strikes an excellent balance between the reality of the Greys' financial straits and the quiet magic that everyday life has to offer." Publ Wkly

Snyder, Zilpha Keatley

★ The **Egypt** game; drawings by Alton Raible. Atheneum Books for Young Readers 2007 215p il $16.99; pa $6.99

Grades: 5 6 7 8   **Fic**

1. Games -- Fiction 2. Imagination -- Fiction
ISBN 978-1-4169-6065-2; 1-4169-6065-1; 978-1-4169-9051-2 pa; 1-4169-9051-8 pa
First published 1967
A Newbery Medal honor book, 1968

A group of children, entranced with the study of Egypt, play their own Egypt game, are visited by a secret oracle, become involved in a murder, and befriend the Professor before they move on to new interests, such as Gypsies.

William S. and the great escape. Atheneum Books for Young Readers 2009 214p $16.99

Grades: 5 6 7 8   **Fic**

1. Acting -- Fiction 2. Siblings -- Fiction
ISBN 978-1-4169-6763-7; 1-4169-6763-X

LC 2008-10377

In 1938, twelve-year-old William has already decided to leave home when his younger sister informs him that she and their brother and sister are going too, and right away, but complications arise when an acquaintance decides to "help" them.

"Wit and pluck are rewarded in this quick-paced, high-drama adventure, which may also whet young appetites for Shakespeare." Publ Wkly

William's midsummer dreams. Atheneum Books for Young Readers 2011 209p

Grades: 5 6 7 8   **Fic**

1. Aunts -- Fiction 2. Acting -- Fiction 3. Theater -- Fiction 4. Adoption -- Fiction 5. Siblings -- Fiction
ISBN 978-1-4424-1997-1; 9781442419995 e-book

LC 2010036958

Now permanently settled with Aunt Fiona, who has adopted him and his siblings, thirteen-year-old William gets the chance to play Puck in a professional production of A Midsummer Night's Dream.

"An adventure story with a lot to say about identity, ambition and character." Kirkus

The **bronze pen.** Atheneum Books for Young Readers 2008 200p $16.99; pa $5.99

Grades: 4 5 6   **Fic**

1. Magic -- Fiction 2. Authorship -- Fiction 3. Family life -- Fiction
ISBN 978-1-4169-4201-6; 1-4169-4201-7; 978-1-4169-4208-5 pa; 1-4169-4208-4 pa

LC 2006-102314

With her father's failing health and the family's shaky finances, twelve-year-old Audrey's dreams of becoming a writer seem very impractical until she is given a peculiar bronze pen that appears to have unusual powers.

"Snyder knows just how to allow magical elements to swell gradually from whispers to shouts, and how to open her characters' minds to uncanny possibilities." Booklist

★ The **headless cupid;** illustrated by Alton Raible. Atheneum Books for Young Readers 2009 219p il $16.99; pa $6.99

Grades: 5 6 7 8   **Fic**

1. Occultism -- Fiction
ISBN 978-1-4169-9532-6; 1-4169-9532-3; 978-1-4169-9052-9 pa; 1-4169-9052-6 pa

A reissue of the title first published 1971

A Newbery Medal honor book, 1972

Life is never quite the same again for eleven-year-old David after the arrival of his new stepsister, a student of the occult.

"The author portrays children with acute understanding, evident both in her delineation of Amanda and David and of the distinctively different younger children. Good style, good characterization, good dialogue, good story." Sutherland. The Best in Child Books

The **witches** of Worm; illustrated by Alton Raible. Atheneum Books for Young Readers 2009 183p il $16.99; pa $6.99

Grades: 5 6 7 8   **Fic**

1. Cats -- Fiction 2. Witchcraft -- Fiction
ISBN 978-1-4169-9531-9; 1-4169-9531-5; 978-1-4169-9053-6 pa; 1-4169-9053-4 pa

A reissue of the title first published 1972

A Newbery Medal honor book, 1973

Lonely, twelve-year-old Jessica is convinced that the cat she finds is possessed by a witch and is responsible for her own strange behavior.

"This is a haunting story of the power of mind and ritual, as well as of misunderstanding, anger, loneliness and friendship. It is written with humor, pace, a sure feeling for conversation and a warm understanding of human nature." Commonwealth

Sobol, Donald J.

Encyclopedia Brown, boy detective; illustrated by Leonard Shortall. Dutton Children's Bks. 1963 88p il hardcover o.p. pa $4.99

Grades: 3 4 5   **Fic**

1. Mystery fiction
ISBN 978-0-14-240888-9; 0-14-240888-3

First published by Thomas Nelson

"The answers are logical; some are tricky, but there are no trick questions, and readers who like puzzles should enjoy the . . . challenge. The episodes are lightly humorous, brief, and simply written." Bull Cent Child Books

Other titles about Encyclopedia Brown are:

Encyclopedia Brown and the case of the carnival crime (2011)

Encyclopedia Brown and the case of the dead eagles (1975)

Encyclopedia Brown and the case of the disgusting sneakers (1990)

Encyclopedia Brown and the case of the jumping frogs (2003)

Encyclopedia Brown and the case of the midnight visitor (1977)

Encyclopedia Brown and the case of the mysterious handprints (1985)

Encyclopedia Brown and the case of Pablo's nose (1996)

Encyclopedia Brown and the case of the secret pitch (1965)

Encyclopedia Brown and the case of the secret UFO (2010)

Encyclopedia Brown and the case of the sleeping dog (1998)

Encyclopedia Brown and the case of the slippery salamander (1999)

Encyclopedia Brown and the case of the treasure hunt (1988)

Encyclopedia Brown and the case of the two spies (1994)

Encyclopedia Brown cracks the case (2007)

Encyclopedia Brown finds the clues (1966)

Encyclopedia Brown gets his man (1967)

Encyclopedia Brown keeps the peace (1969)

Encyclopedia Brown lends a hand (1974)

Encyclopedia Brown saves the day (1970)

Encyclopedia Brown sets the pace (1982)

Encyclopedia Brown shows the way (1972)

Encyclopedia Brown solves them all (1968)

Encyclopedia Brown: super sleuth (2009)

Encyclopedia Brown takes the cake! (1983)

Encyclopedia Brown takes the case (1973)

Encyclopedia Brown tracks them down (1971)

Sonneborn, Scott

Shell shocker; written by Scott Sonneborn; illustrated by Dan Schoening, Mike DeCarlo, and Lee Loughridge. Stone Arch Books 2011 48p il (DC super heroes: The Flash) lib bdg $25.32; pa $5.95

Grades: 2 3 4   **Fic**

1. Superheroes -- Fiction
ISBN 978-1-4342-2615-0 lib bdg; 1-4342-2615-8 lib bdg; 978-1-4342-3092-8 pa; 1-4342-3092-9 pa

LC 2010025350

While deactivating an explosive for the bomb squad, the police scientist receives a call, tipping him off about a robbery across town. Luckily, Barry is secretly the fastest man alive, the Flash!

This "chapter-book [adaptation] of [a] popular comic [superhero has] great, full-page illustrations and . . . onomatopoeia. . . . [The cover is a] 3D [hologram] that will attract kids. . . . [This is] action-packed." SLJ

Includes glossary and bibliographical references

Sonnenblick, Jordan

★ **After** ever after. Scholastic Press 2010 260p $16.99

Grades: 5 6 7 8   **Fic**

1. School stories 2. Cancer -- Fiction 3. Friendship -- Fiction 4. Family life -- Fiction

ISBN 978-0-439-83706-4; 0-439-83706-5

Jeffery's cancer is in remission but the chemotherapy and radiation treatments have left him with concentration problems, and he worries about school work, his friends, his family, and a girl who likes him

"Sonnenblick imbues Jeffrey with a smooth, likable, and unaffected voice. . . . As hilarious as it is tragic, and as honest as it is hopeful . . . [this book is] irresistable reading." Booklist

Zen and the art of faking it. Scholastic Press 2007 264p $16.99; pa $7.99

Grades: 5 6 7 8   **Fic**

1. School stories 2. Zen Buddhism -- Fiction 3. Asian Americans -- Fiction

ISBN 978-0-439-83707-1; 0-439-83707-3; 978-0-439-83709-5 pa; 0-439-83709-X pa

LC 2006-28841

When thirteen-year-old San Lee moves to a new town and school for the umpteenth time, he is looking for a way to stand out when his knowledge of Zen Buddhism, gained in his previous school, provides the answer—and the need to quickly become a convincing Zen master.

The author gives readers "plenty to laugh at. . . . Mixed with more serious scenes, . . . lighter moments take a basic message about the importance of honesty and forgiveness and treat it with panache." Publ Wkly

Soto, Gary

The **skirt**; illustrated by Eric Velasquez. Delacorte Press 2008 74p il $14.99; lib bdg $17.99; pa $5.99

Grades: 1 2 3   **Fic**

1. Mexican Americans -- Fiction 2. Clothing and dress -- Fiction 3. Lost and found possessions -- Fiction

ISBN 978-0-385-30665-2; 0-385-30665-2; 978-0-385-90534-3 lib bdg; 0-385-90534-3 lib bdg; 978-0-440-40924-3 pa; 0-440-40924-1 pa

A reissue of the title first published 1992

When Miata leaves on the school bus the skirt that she is to wear in a dance performance, she needs all her wits to get it back without her parents' finding out that she has lost something yet again.

"This is a light, engaging narrative that successfully combines information on Hispanic culture with familiar and recognizable childhood themes. . . . A fine read-aloud and discussion starter, this story blends cultural differences with human similarities to create both interest and understanding." SLJ

★ **Taking** sides. Harcourt Brace Jovanovich 1991 138p hardcover o.p. pa $5.95

Grades: 5 6 7 8   **Fic**

1. Basketball -- Fiction 2. Hispanic Americans -- Fiction

ISBN 0-15-284076-1; 0-15-204694-1 pa

LC 91-11082

Fourteen-year-old Lincoln Mendoza, an aspiring basketball player, must come to terms with his divided loyalties when he moves from the Hispanic inner city to a white suburban neighborhood

This is a "light but appealing story. . . . Because of its subject matter and its clear, straightforward prose, it will be especially good for reluctant readers." SLJ

Includes glossary

Soup, Cuthbert

Another whole nother story; illustrations by Jeffrey Stewart Timmons. Bloomsbury Books for Young Readers 2010 290p il $16.99

Grades: 3 4 5 6   **Fic**

1. Inventions -- Fiction 2. Family life -- Fiction 3. Time travel -- Fiction

ISBN 978-1-59990-436-8; 1-59990-436-5

LC 2010025634

Ethan Cheeseman takes his children, ages eight, twelve, and fourteen, and Captain Jibby and crew, to the year 1668 to end an ancient family curse and save the children's mother, but damage to the time machine and the arrival of Mr. 5 complicate their return.

"The laugh-out-loud moments are many, and the puns are clever and sarcastic." SLJ

A **whole** nother story; illustrations by Jeffrey Stewart Timmins. Bloomsbury 2010 264p il $16.99

Grades: 3 4 5 6   **Fic**

1. Spies -- Fiction 2. Moving -- Fiction 3. Inventions -- Fiction 4. Family life -- Fiction 5. Automobile travel -- Fiction

ISBN 978-1-59990-435-1; 1-59990-435-7

LC 2009-21998

Ethan Cheeseman and his children, ages eight, twelve, and fourteen, hope to settle in a nice small town, at least long enough to complete work on a time machine, but spies and government agents have been pursuing them for two years and are about to catch up

"The storytelling, which merges deadpan narration with an absurdist sense of humor, is the real star of this fast-paced adventure." Publ Wkly

Speare, Elizabeth George

The **bronze bow**. Houghton Mifflin 1961 255p $16; pa $6.95

Grades: 6 7 8 9   **Fic**

1. Christianity -- Fiction

ISBN 0-395-07113-5; 0-395-13719-5 pa

Awarded the Newbery Medal, 1962

"Daniel had sworn vengence against the Romans who had killed his parents, and he had become one of a band of outlaws. . . . Each time he saw the Rabbi Jesus, the youth was drawn to his cause; at last he resolved his own conflict by giving up his hatred and, as a follower of the Master, accepting his enemies. The story has drama and pace, fine characterization, and colorful background detail." Bull Cent Child Books

The **sign** of the beaver. Houghton Mifflin 1983 135p $16

Grades: 5 6 7 8   **Fic**

1. Friendship -- Fiction 2. Native Americans -- Fiction 3. Frontier and pioneer life -- Fiction

ISBN 0-395-33890-5

LC 83-118

A Newbery Medal honor book, 1984

Left alone to guard the family's wilderness home in eighteenth-century Maine, Matt is hard-pressed to survive until local Indians teach him their skills

Matt "begins to understand the Indians' ingenuity and respect for nature and the devastating impact of the encroachment of the white man. In a quiet but not unsuspenseful story . . . the author articulates historical facts along with the adventures and the thoughts, emotions, and developing insights of a young adolescent." Horn Book

★ The **witch** of Blackbird Pond. Houghton Mifflin 1958 249p $17

Grades: 6 7 8 9   **Fic**

1. Puritans -- Fiction 2. Witchcraft -- Fiction

ISBN 0-395-07114-3

LC 58-11063

Awarded the Newbery Medal, 1959

"Headstrong and undisciplined, Barbados-bred Kit Tyler is an embarrassment to her Puritan relatives, and her sincere attempts to aid a reputed witch soon bring her to trial as a suspect." Child Books Too Good to Miss

Speck, Katie

Maybelle goes to tea; [by] Katie Speck; illustrations by Paul Ratz de Tagyos. 1st ed.; Henry Holt 2008 60p il $15.95

Grades: 2 3 4   **Fic**

1. Insects -- Fiction 2. Cockroaches -- Fiction

ISBN 978-0-8050-8093-3; 0-8050-8093-7

LC 2007040937

Maybelle the cockroach follows the advice of her new fly friend Maurice and tumbles into a terrifying but tasty adventure during Mrs. Peabody's Ladies' Spring Tea.

"Easy-reader graduates will delight in Maybelle's antics and enjoy her housefly pal, Maurice. . . . With humorous illustrations on nearly every spread, this is a sweet offering." SLJ

Sperry, Armstrong

Call it courage. Simon & Schuster Books for Young Readers 1968 95p il $17.99; pa $5.99

Grades: 5 6 7 8   **Fic**

1. Courage -- Fiction 2. Wilderness survival -- Fiction

ISBN 978-0-02-786030-6; 0-02-786030-2; 978-1-4169-5368-5 pa; 1-4169-5368-X pa

First published 1940 by Macmillan

Awarded the Newbery Medal, 1941

"Because he fears the ocean, a Polynesian boy is scorned by his people and must redeem himself by an act of courage. His lone journey to a sacred island and the dangers he faces there earn him the name Mafatu, 'Stout Heart.' Dramatic il-

lustrations add atmosphere and mystery." Hodges. Books for Elem Sch Libr

Spinelli, Eileen

The **Dancing** Pancake; illustrated by Joanne Lew-Vriethoff. Alfred A. Knopf 2010 248p il $12.99; lib bdg $15.99

Grades: 3 4 5   **Fic**

1. Novels in verse 2. Divorce -- Fiction 3. Restaurants -- Fiction

ISBN 978-0-375-85870-3; 0-375-85870-9; 978-0-375-95870-0 lib bdg; 0-375-95870-3 lib bdg

LC 2009-22645

"Bindi's life is pretty normal. She loves to read and has good friends and a loving extended family. This normalcy ends when her parents announce that they are separating and that her father is moving to another city to look for a job. Told entirely in verse, the story relates the sixth grader's experiences, her feelings, and snippets of her daily life. . . . The poetic structure of this novel succeeds in capturing the child's voice and deepest feelings. The verse also provides sound development of secondary characters. Lew-Vriethoff's lively pen-and-ink illustrations add texture to the story and offer touches of humor." SLJ

★ **Where** I live; illustrated by Matt Phelan. Dial Books 2007 un il $16.99

Grades: 1 2 3 4   **Fic**

1. Novels in verse 2. Moving -- Fiction 3. Family life -- Fiction

ISBN 978-0-8037-3122-6; 0-8037-3122-1

LC 2006-30971

In a series of poems, Diana writes about her life, both before and after her father loses his job and she and her family move far away to live with Grandpa Joe.

"Spinelli crafts a reassuring and engaging story in verse. . . . Phelan's charming pencil drawings are a perfect complement to this heartfelt tale." SLJ

Spinelli, Jerry, 1941-

Crash. Knopf 1996 162p hardcover o.p. pa $6.99; lib bdg $17.99

Grades: 5 6 7 8   **Fic**

1. Football -- Fiction 2. Friendship -- Fiction 3. Grandfathers -- Fiction

ISBN 0440238579; 0679879579; 0679979573

LC 95030942

"Crash is a star football player. He torments Penn, a classmate who is everything Crash is not—friendly, small, and a pacifist. When his beloved grandfather comes to live with his family and suffers a debilitating stroke, Crash begins to see value in many of the things he has scorned." Horn Book Guide

Hokey Pokey; by Jerry Spinelli. Alfred A. Knopf Books for Young Readers 2013 304 p. (hard cover) $15.99

Grades: 5 6 7 8   **Fic**

1. Bildungsromans 2. Fantasy fiction 3. Imaginary places 4. Play -- Fiction 5. Growth -- Fiction

ISBN 0375831983; 9780307975706; 9780375831980; 9780375832017; 9780375931987

LC 2012004177

In this book, Jerry Spinelli "creates a surreal landscape." There are no adults in "Hokey Pokey, where boys and girls dine on flavored ice and spend their days watching cartoons, playing cowboy games, and using their bicycles as trusty steeds. Jack's bike, Scramjet, is . . . stolen by his archenemy, Jubilee. This marks the first of a series of unsettling events that give Jack, a boy on the brink of adolescence, the eerie impression that 'things have shifted.'" (Publishers Weekly)

Jake and Lily; Jerry Spinelli. 1st ed. Balzer + Bray 2012 335 p. (hardback) $15.99

Grades: 3 4 5 6 7   **Fic**

1. Twins -- Fiction 2. Bullies -- Fiction 3. Children's stories 4. Friendship -- Fiction 5. Individuality -- Fiction 6. Brothers and sisters -- Fiction

ISBN 9780060281359; 9780060281366

LC 2011053362

This book offers a "story about a pair of twins growing apart. For almost as long as they can remember, Jake and Lily have shared a 'special sense,' which they call 'goom-bla.' . . . Lily tries to find out who she is without her brother, but it's hard work, and most of her attempts are unsuccessful. . . . Though the twins eventually rediscover their 'goombla,' . . . [author Jerry] Spinelli doesn't suggest that the two will go back to being the people they once were." (Publishers Weekly)

Loser. HarperCollins Pubs. 2002 218p $15.99; lib bdg $16.89; pa $5.99

Grades: 4 5 6 7   **Fic**

1. Schools 2. Family life 3. School stories

ISBN 0-06-000193-3; 0-06-000483-5 lib bdg; 0-06-054074-5 pa

LC 2001-47484

Even though his classmates from first grade on have considered him strange and a loser, Daniel Zinkoff's optimism and exuberance and the support of his loving family do not allow him to feel that way about himself

"This novel is an offbeat, affectionate, colorful, and melancholy work." Voice Youth Advocates

★ **Maniac** Magee; a novel. Little, Brown 1990 184p $16.99; pa $6.99

Grades: 5 6 7 8   **Fic**

1. Orphans -- Fiction 2. Race relations -- Fiction 3. Homeless persons -- Fiction

ISBN 0-316-80722-2; 0-316-80906-3 pa

LC 89-27144

Awarded the Newbery Medal, 1991

"Orphaned at three, Jeffery Lionel Magee, after eight unhappy years with relatives, one day takes off running. A year later, he ends up 200 miles away in Two Mills, a highly segregated community. Part tall tale and part contemporary realistic fiction, this unusual novel magically weaves timely issues of homelessness, racial prejudice, and illiteracy into an energetic story that bursts with creativity, enthusiasm, and hope for the future. In short, it's a celebration of life." Booklist

There's a girl in my hammerlock. Simon & Schuster Bks. for Young Readers 1991 199p hardcover o.p. pa $5.99

Grades: 5 6 7 8   **Fic**

1. School stories 2. Sex role -- Fiction 3. Wrestling -- Fiction

ISBN 1-4169-3937-7 pa

LC 91-8765

Thirteen-year-old Maisie joins her school's formerly all-male wrestling team and tries to last through the season, despite opposition from other students, her best friend, and her own teammates

The author "tackles a meaty subject—traditional gender roles—with his usual humor and finesse. The result, written in a breezy, first-person style, is a rattling good sports story that is clever, witty and tightly written." Publ Wkly

Wringer. HarperCollins Pubs. 1997 228p $16.99; lib bdg $16.89; pa $6.50

Grades: 4 5 6 7   **Fic**

1. Courage -- Fiction 2. Pigeons -- Fiction 3. Violence -- Fiction

ISBN 0-06-024913-7; 0-06-024914-5 lib bdg; 0-06-440578-8 pa

LC 96-37897

A Newbery Medal honor book, 1998

"During the annual pigeon shoot, it is a town tradition for 10-year-old boys to break the necks of wounded birds. In this riveting story told with verve and suspense, Palmer rebels." SLJ

Spratt, R. A.

★ The **adventures** of Nanny Piggins; illustrated by Dan Santat. Little, Brown 2010 239p il $15.99

Grades: 3 4 5 6   **Fic**

1. Pigs -- Fiction 2. Nannies -- Fiction 3. Siblings -- Fiction

ISBN 978-0-316-06819-2; 0-316-06819-5

LC 2009045047

When Mr. Green, a stingy widower with three children he cannot be bothered with, decides to find a nanny for his children, he winds up hiring a glamorous ex-circus pig who knows nothing about children but a lot about chocolate.

"This is smart, sly, funny, and marvelously illustrated with drawings that capture Nanny's sheer pigginess." Booklist

Springer, Nancy

★ **Rowan** Hood, outlaw girl of Sherwood Forest. Philomel Bks. 2001 170p hardcover o.p. pa $5.99

Grades: 4 5 6 7   **Fic**

1. Elves 2. Gender role 3. Middle Ages 4. Adventure fiction 5. Adventure and adventurers 6. Robin Hood (Legendary character) 7. Sex role 8. Fathers and daughters 9. Middle Ages -- Fiction

ISBN 0-399-23368-7; 0-698-11972-X pa

LC 00-63694

In her quest to connect with Robin Hood, the father she has never met, thirteen-year-old Rosemary disguises herself as a boy, befriends a half-wolf, half-dog, a runaway princess, and an overgrown boy whose singing is hypnotic, and makes peace with her elfin heritage

"This tale is a charmer, filled with exciting action, plenty of humor, engaging characters, and a nice fantasy twist." Booklist

Other titles about Rowan Hood are:

Lionclaw (2002)
Outlaw princess of Sherwood (2003)
Wild boy (2004)

Rowan Hood returns (2005)

★ The **case** of the missing marquess; an Enola Holmes mystery. Philomel Books 2006 216p pa $6.99; $10.99
Grades: 5 6 7 8   Fic
   1. Mystery fiction 2. Missing persons -- Fiction
   ISBN 0-14-240933-2 pa; 0-399-24304-6
Enola Holmes, much younger sister of detective Sherlock Holmes, must travel to London in disguise to unravel the disappearance of her missing mother. "Grades four to eight." (Bull Cent Child Books)
   "Enola's loneliness, intelligence, sense of humor, and sheer pluck make her an extremely appealing heroine." SLJ
   Other titles about Enola Holmes are:
   The case of the left-handed lady (2007)
   The case of the bizarre bouquets (2008)
   The case of the peculiar pink fan (2008)
   The case of the cryptic crinoline (2009)
   The case of the gypsy good-bye (2010)

Springstubb, Tricia
   Mo Wren, lost and found. Balzer + Bray 2011 248p $15.99
Grades: 3 4 5 6   Fic
   1. Moving -- Fiction 2. Family life -- Fiction 3. Restaurants -- Fiction
   ISBN 978-0-06-199039-7; 0-06-199039-6
               LC 2011001896
When eleven-year-old Mo's mother dies in an accident and Mo's devastated father deals with the loss by moving the family to a new town and starting a new life as the owner of a sports bar, Mo must leave her much loved neighborhood on Fox Street to live in an apartment above the 'cursed' Corky's Tavern.
   "Readers will feel both inspired and comforted by these indefatigable sisters, whose humanity brings out the very same qualities in others." Booklist

★ **What** happened on Fox Street. Balzer + Bray 2010 218p $15.99
Grades: 3 4 5 6   Fic
   1. Friendship -- Fiction 2. Family life -- Fiction 3. Father-daughter relationship -- Fiction
   ISBN 978-0-06-198635-2; 0-06-198635-6
               LC 2009053563
Fox Street means everything to Mo Wren, who is nearly eleven, and so she is very upset when a land developer offers to buy her father's house, especially since she has not yet found the fox she is sure lives in the nearby ravine.
   "Springstubb creates a richly human and believable story of the conflicts of growing up and a well-paced, interesting plot with plenty of surprises that readers should find pleasurable and satisfying." SLJ

Spyri, Johanna
   ★ **Heidi**; by Johanna Spyri; illustrated by Jessie Willcox Smith. Morrow/Books of Wonder 1996 383p il $24.99
Grades: 4 5 6   Fic
   1. Orphans -- Fiction
   ISBN 0-688-14519-1
   First published 1880
A Swiss orphan is heartbroken when she must leave her beloved grandfather and their happy home in the mountains to go to school and to care for an invalid girl in the city.

St. John, Lauren
   The **white** giraffe; illustrated by David Dean. Dial Books for Young Readers 2007 180p il $16.99; pa $6.99
Grades: 4 5 6 7   Fic
   1. Orphans -- Fiction 2. Giraffes -- Fiction 3. Mythical animals -- Fiction
   ISBN 978-0-8037-3211-7; 0-8037-3211-2; 978-0-14-241152-0 pa; 0-14-241152-3 pa
               LC 2006-21323
After a fire kills her parents, eleven-year-old Martine must leave England to live with her grandmother on a wildlife game reserve in South Africa, where she befriends a mythical white giraffe
   "The story is captivating and well spun." SLJ
   Other titles in this series are:
   Dolphin song (2008)
   Last leopard (2009)
   The elephant's tale (2010)

StJohn, Amanda, 1982-
   Bridget and Bo build a blog; by Amanda St John; illustrated by Katie McDee. Norwood House Press 2012 32 p.
Grades: K 1 2 3   Fic
   1. Weblogs -- Fiction 2. Internet and children 3. Child authors -- Fiction 4. Online authorship 5. Language arts (Elementary) 6. Online authorship -- Juvenile literature
   ISBN 1599535076; 9781599535074
               LC 2011039361
This children's book presents "introductions to a number of tasks young writers will eventually tackle. . . . This volume introduces nine-year-old Bo, whose recent experience blogging from a family stay in England gives him the expertise to show his friend, Bridget, how it's done. . . . Bridget's concerns are understandable: 'Well, does my blog have to be as long as yours?' Bo's answers are a little my-way-or-the-highway, but nonetheless bring up good things to consider: a design template, the intended audience, and using correct terminology such as posting. They read other blogs for inspiration, which is where they learn never to gossip or use full names or personal info. The wisecracks never intrude upon the learning, and the advice can easily extend to other kinds of writing." (Booklist)
   Includes bibliographical references (p. 32)

Stadler, Alexander
   ★ **Julian** Rodriguez: episode one, Trash crisis on earth. Scholastic Press 2008 123p $15.99; pa $5.99
Grades: 2 3 4   Fic
   1. Science fiction 2. Extraterrestrial beings -- Fiction
   ISBN 978-0-439-91966-1; 0-439-91966-5; 978-0-439-91970-8 pa; 0-439-91970-3 pa
   "This hybrid of fiction and graphic novel dusts off a favorite conceit with a slick swipe of edgy visuals and tart commentary. . . . It's impossible to read this without laughing." Publ Wkly
   Another title in this series is:
   Julian Rodriguez: episode two, Invasion of the relatives (2009)

   Julian Rodriguez: episode two, Invasion of the relatives. Scholastic Press 131p $16.99

Grades: 2 3 4　　　　　　　　　　　　　　　**Fic**

1. Science fiction 2. Extraterrestrial beings -- Fiction
ISBN 978-0-439-91967-8; 0-439-91967-3

First Officer Julian Rodriguez, imaginary space warrior, must endure the odious and unhygienic festivities of genetically linked minibrains when members of his extended family visit over the holidays.

"This entry in the Julian Rodriguez series is even sharper and funnier than the first." Booklist

Staib, Walter

A **feast** of freedom; tasty tidbits from the City Tavern. by Walter Staib and Jennifer Fox; illustrated by Fernando Juarez. RP Kids 2010 un il map $15.95

Grades: 3 4 5 6　　　　　　　　　　　　　**Fic**

1. Mice -- Fiction
ISBN 978-0-7624-3598-2; 0-7624-3598-4

"The City Tavern, a pedigreed Philadelphia institution, bore witness to much of the behind-the-scenes wrangling and politicking of a country on the verge of independence. . . . This book's initial, chronological spreads cover the building's conception, the basic floor plans, the importance of its location to both trade and politics, and how people ate, partied, did business, and kept up with the news in the late 1700s. Later spreads describe the building's historical connections. . . . Closing pages include a recipe for corn bread, a time line, and an update on the City Tavern as it now stands. A Disneyesque mouse in a tricornered hat leads readers through the pages, adding a touch of humor with brief quips in speech bubbles. . . . Add this title for a fresh look at a requisite time in U.S. history." SLJ

Standiford, Natalie

The **secret** tree; Natalie Standiford. Scholastic Press 2012 245 p.

Grades: 4 5 6 7　　　　　　　　　　　　**Fic**

1. Bildungsromans 2. Mystery fiction 3. Children's stories 4. Friendship -- Juvenile fiction
ISBN 0545334799; 9780545334792

This coming of age story combines "[m]iddle-school dynamics, pesky sibling relations, a rumored haunted house, . . . and a mystery. . . . When 10-year-old Minty discovers a hollow tree in the woods . . . [and] find[s] a secret written on a scrap of paper stashed inside, it sets the stage for a . . . mystery. . . . [W]hile Minty tries to figure out what's going on, she . . . befriend[s] an apparently parentless kid, Raymond, who seems to live in an abandoned spec house." (Kirkus)

Staniszewski, Anna

My very unfairy tale life. Sourcebooks Jabberwocky 2011 198p pa $6.99

Grades: 4 5 6 7　　　　　　　　　　　　**Fic**

1. Fairy tales 2. Magic -- Fiction
ISBN 978-1-4022-5946-3; 1-4022-5946-8

Jenny, a professional adventurer, would prefer spending time with her friends over helping magical kingdoms around the universe, but soon she is given the choice to return to her normal life or go into a battle she doesn't think she can win.

"An eye for imaginative detail mixes with these likable characters and a theme of empathy for others to keep the story appropriate to a younger audience, who easily will identify with Jenny. Charming." Kirkus

Stanley, Diane

★ **Bella** at midnight; illustrated by Bagram Ibatoulline. HarperCollins Pubs. 2006 278p il $15.99; lib bdg $16.89; pa $6.99

Grades: 5 6 7 8　　　　　　　　　　　　**Fic**

1. Fairy tales 2. Knights and knighthood -- Fiction
ISBN 978-0-06-077573-5; 0-06-077573-4; 978-0-06-077574-2 lib bdg; 0-06-077574-2 lib bdg; 978-0-06-077575-9 pa; 0-06-077575-0 pa

LC 2005-05906

Raised by peasants, Bella discovers that she is actually the daughter of a knight and finds herself caught up in a terrible plot that will change her life and the kingdom forever

"What raises this above other recreated fairy tales is the quality of the writing, dotted with jeweled description and anchored by the strong values—loyalty, truth, honor." Booklist

Roughing it on the Oregon Trail; illustrated by Holly Berry. HarperCollins Pubs. 2000 un il (Time-traveling twins) hardcover o.p. pa $7.99

Grades: 2 3 4　　　　　　　　　　　　　**Fic**

1. Oregon Trail -- Fiction 2. Frontier and pioneer life -- Fiction 3. Overland journeys to the Pacific -- Fiction
ISBN 0-06-027065-9; 0-06-449006-8 pa

LC 98-41711

Twins Liz and Lenny, along with their time-traveling grandmother, join a group of pioneers journeying west on the Oregon Trail in 1843

"An engaging trip and a painless history lesson." SLJ
Other titles in this series are:
Joining the Boston Tea Party (2001)
Thanksgiving on Plymouth Plantation (2004)

★ **Saving** Sky. Harper 2010 199p $15.99

Grades: 5 6 7 8　　　　　　　　　　　　**Fic**

1. Terrorism -- Fiction 2. Immigrants -- Fiction 3. Prejudices -- Fiction 4. Ranch life -- Fiction 5. Family life -- Fiction
ISBN 978-0-06-123905-2; 0-06-123905-4

LC 2010-09393

In an America that has suffered continual terrorist attacks since 9/11, seventh-grader Sky stands up for what is right and helps a classmate of Middle Eastern descent, although doing so places her and her family at great risk.

"Readers will have much to discuss after finishing this beautifully written, disturbing book." Booklist

The **cup** and the crown; Diane Stanley. Harper 2012 344 p. (hardback) $16.99

Grades: 5 6 7 8　　　　　　　　　　　　**Fic**

1. Fantasy fiction 2. Magic -- Fiction 3. Fantasy 4. Identity -- Fiction 5. Clairvoyance -- Fiction 6. Drinking cups -- Fiction
ISBN 0061963216; 9780061963216

LC 2012025280

In this fantasy novel by Diane Stanley "Molly has visions of a beautiful goblet: one of her grandfather's loving cups, which he filled with magic that bound people together. So it hardly surprises Molly when handsome King Alaric asks her to find a loving cup to help him win the heart of the beautiful Princess of Cortova. As Molly and her friends Winifred and Tobias journey far beyond the safe borders of

Westria, a mysterious raven appears to guide their quest."
(Publisher's note)

The **mysterious** case of the Allbright Academy. HarperCollinsPublishers 2008 258p $16.99; lib bdg $17.89

Grades: 4 5 6 7   **Fic**

1. School stories 2. Mystery fiction

ISBN 978-0-06-085817-9; 0-06-085817-6; 978-0-06-085818-6 lib bdg; 0-06-085818-4 lib bdg

LC 2007-10910

Eighth-grader Franny and her friends investigate why most of the students at their exclusive boarding school are brilliant, beautiful, and perfectly behaved.

"Stanley delivers another humorous and thoroughly enjoyable mystery." Publ Wkly

The **mysterious** matter of I.M. Fine. HarperCollins Pubs. 2001 201p hardcover o.p. pa $5.99

Grades: 4 5 6 7   **Fic**

1. Magic 2. Mystery fiction 3. Books and reading 4. Magic -- Fiction 5. Books and reading -- Fiction 6. Mystery and detective stories

ISBN 0-688-17546-5; 0-380-73327-7 pa

LC 00-54040

Noticing that a popular series of horror novels is having a bizarre effect on the behavior of its readers, Franny and Beamer set out to find the mysterious author

"The solidly constructed mystery, well-rounded characters, and playful jab at wildly successful horror writers go down a treat." Horn Book Guide

Another title about Franny and her friends is:

The mysterious case of the Allbright Academy (2008)

★ The **silver** bowl. Harper 2011 307p $16.99

Grades: 5 6 7 8   **Fic**

1. Fantasy fiction 2. Clairvoyance -- Fiction

ISBN 978-0-06-157543-3; 0-06-157543-7

"Molly is a young scullery maid in the castle of King Edmund, and like her mother before her, she sees visions and hears voices that offer glimpses of the future. But is this a blessing or a curse?. . . . The girl's choice of silence . . . is challenged when she learns that a rumored curse on the royal family is true and only by sharing her visions might they be saved. Combining carefully chosen details of setting with a richly realized fantasy premise, Stanley succeeds in creating a believable world large enough to accommodate not only menace and evil but also loyalty, enduring friendship, and love." Booklist

Staples, Suzanne Fisher

The **green** dog; a mostly true story. Farrar, Straus & Giroux 2003 119p $16

Grades: 4 5 6   **Fic**

1. Dogs -- Fiction 2. Summer -- Fiction

ISBN 0-374-32779-3

LC 2002-26575

During the summer before fifth grade, Suzanne, a daydreaming loner who likes to fish and walk through the woods, acquires a canine companion. Based on the author's childhood in northeastern Pennsylvania

The author's "writing is rich and descriptive, yet clear and simple." SLJ

Starke, Ruth

Noodle pie. Kane Miller 2010 il $15.99

Grades: 4 5 6 7   **Fic**

1. Vietnamese -- Fiction

ISBN 978-1-935279-25-9; 1-935279-25-4

"Eleven-year-old Andy's first trip to Vietnam with his father, a 'Viet Kieu' (someone born in Vietnam who now lives overseas), exposes him to internalized prejudices about his heritage. . . . Andy distinguishes himself from his pushy relatives by emphasizing his Australian citizenship and criticizing customs that seem unfair. . . . This humorous, touching novel is a delicious cross-cultural treat, and includes an appendix of Vietnamese recipes." Publ Wkly

Starmer, Aaron

The **only** ones. Delacorte Press 2011 321p $17.99; lib bdg $20.99; e-book $17.99

Grades: 4 5 6 7   **Fic**

1. Supernatural -- Fiction

ISBN 978-0-385-74043-2; 0-385-74043-3; 978-0-385-90839-9 lib bdg; 0-385-90839-3 lib bdg; 978-0-375-89919-5 e-book

LC 2010040383

After setting off from the island where he has been leading a solitary existence, thirteen-year-old Martin discovers a village with other children who have been living similarly without any adults, since the grown-ups have all been spirited away.

"Both literary and engaging, this is the kind of book readers will want to return to for new discoveries." Kirkus

Stauffacher, Sue

★ **Gator** on the loose! illustrated by Priscilla Lamont. Alfred A. Knopf 2010 149p il (Animal rescue team) $12.99; lib bdg $15.99

Grades: 4 5 6   **Fic**

1. Alligators -- Fiction 2. Family life -- Fiction 3. Racially mixed people -- Fiction

ISBN 978-0-375-85847-5; 0-375-85847-4; 978-0-375-95847-2 lib bdg; 0-375-95847-9 lib bdg

LC 2009018340

Chaos ensues when Keisha's father brings an escaped alligator home to Carter's Urban Rescue, but it gets out of the bathroom while Grandma is guarding it.

"Situational comedy, appealing spot art, and a personable protagonist will give this series broad appeal." Booklist

Other titles about Keisha and the Carter family are:

Hide and seek (2010)

Show time (2011)

Special delivery (2010)

★ **Harry** Sue. Knopf 2005 288p hardcover o.p. lib bdg $17.99; pa $6.50

Grades: 5 6 7 8   **Fic**

1. Prisoners -- Fiction 2. Handicapped -- Fiction 3. Mother-daughter relationship -- Fiction

ISBN 0-375-83274-2; 0-375-93274-7 lib bdg; 0-440-42064-4 pa

LC 2004-16945

Although tough-talking Harry Sue would like to start a life of crime in order to be "sent up" and find her incarcerated mother, she must first protect the children at her neglectful grandmother's home day care center and befriend a paralyzed boy.

"This is a riveting story, dramatically and well told, with characters whom readers won't soon forget." SLJ

Hide and seek; illustrated by Priscilla Lamont. Alfred A. Knopf 2010 143p il (Animal rescue team) $12.99; lib bdg $15.99

Grades: 4 5 6   Fic

1. Deer -- Fiction 2. Dogs -- Fiction 3. Halloween -- Fiction 4. Family life -- Fiction 5. Racially mixed people -- Fiction

ISBN 978-0-375-85849-9; 0-375-85849-0; 978-0-375-95849-6 lib bdg; 0-375-95849-5 lib bdg

LC 2009040073

The Carter family's Halloween preparations are complicated by a deer with a pumpkin stuck on its head and a puppy that is part dog, part coyote.

"Lamont's light and lively cartoon art is the perfect complement to the storytelling. An entertaining, feel-good read." SLJ

Show time; illustrated by Priscilla Lamont. Alfred A. Knopf 2011 147p il (Animal rescue team) $12.99; lib bdg $15.99

Grades: 4 5 6   Fic

1. Squirrels -- Fiction 2. Family life -- Fiction 3. Rope skipping -- Fiction 4. Racially mixed people -- Fiction 5. Wildlife conservation -- Fiction

ISBN 978-0-375-85850-5; 0-375-85850-4; 978-0-375-95850-2 lib bdg; 0-375-95850-9 lib bdg

LC 2010004759

Keisha's family's animal rescue center is asked to help at a nearby college that is being overrun with squirrels, while Keisha is trying to deal with her nervousness as she prepares for the regional jump-rope competition.

Special delivery! illustrated by Priscilla Lamont. Alfred A. Knopf 2010 164p il (Animal rescue team) $12.99

Grades: 4 5 6   Fic

1. Crows -- Fiction 2. Skunks -- Fiction 3. Family life -- Fiction 4. Racially mixed people -- Fiction

ISBN 978-0-375-85848-2; 0-375-85848-2

Ten-year-old Keisha and her family's animal rescue center face more challenges involving a baby crow in a mailbox and a skunk found in the nearby community garden.

"Cheerful cartoon illustrations highlight the overall snug and secure feeling. . . . [This book] will find an audience with animal lovers and those who enjoy mellow realistic fiction." SLJ

Stead, Rebecca

First light. Wendy Lamb Books 2007 328p $15.99; lib bdg $18.99; pa $6.99

Grades: 5 6 7 8   Fic

1. Supernatural -- Fiction 2. Greenhouse effect -- Fiction

ISBN 978-0-375-84017-3; 0-375-84017-6; 987-0-375-094017-0 lib bdg; 0-375-94017-0 lib bdg; 978-0-440-42222-8 pa; 0-440-42222-1 pa

LC 2006-39733

This "novel is an exciting, engaging mix of science fiction, mystery, and adventure. . . . Peter and Thea are fully developed main characters." SLJ

Liar & spy; by Rebecca Stead. Wendy Lamb Books 2012 180 p. (hardback) $15.99

Grades: 4 5 6 7 8   Fic

1. Spy stories 2. Boys -- Fiction 3. Neighbors -- Fiction 4. Friendship -- Fiction 5. Spies -- Fiction 6. Schools -- Fiction 7. Middle schools -- Fiction 8. Apartment houses -- Fiction 9. Family life -- New York (State) -- New York -- Fiction

ISBN 0385737432; 9780375899539; 9780385737432; 9780385906654

LC 2011042674

In this book, protagonist "Georges has a lot going on. Dad was laid off so Mom has started working extra shifts at the hospital, and they had to sell their house in Brooklyn and move into an apartment. One good thing about the new building is Safer, an unusual boy who lives on the top floor. He's determined to teach Georges how to be a spy. Their main case: spy on the mysterious Mr. X in the apartment above Georges. As Georges and Safer go deeper into their Mr. X plan, the line between games, lies, and reality begin to blur." (Barnes and Noble)

★ **When** you reach me. Wendy Lamb Books 2009 199p $15.99; lib bdg $18.99

Grades: 5 6 7 8   Fic

1. Space and time -- Fiction

ISBN 978-0-385-73742-5; 0-385-73742-4; 978-0-385-90664-7 lib bdg; 0-385-90664-1 lib bdg

LC 2008-24998

Awarded the Newbery Medal, 2010

Boston Globe-Horn Book Award: Fiction (2010)

As her mother prepares to be a contestant on the 1970s television game show, "The $20,000 Pyramid," a twelve-year-old New York City girl tries to make sense of a series of mysterious notes received from an anonymous source that seems to defy the laws of time and space

"The '70s New York setting is an honest reverberation of the era; the mental gymnastics required of readers are invigorating; and the characters . . . are honest bits of humanity." Booklist

Steele, William Owen

The **perilous** road; [by] William O. Steele; with an introduction by Jean Fritz. Harcourt 2004 156p $17; pa $5.95

Grades: 5 6 7 8   Fic

ISBN 0-15-205203-8; 0-15-205204-6 pa

A reissue of the title first published 1958

A Newbery Medal honor book, 1959

Fourteen-year-old Chris, bitterly hating the Yankees for invading his Tennessee mountain home, learns a difficult lesson about the waste of war and the meaning of tolerance and courage when he reports the approach of a Yankee supply troop to the Confederates, only to learn that his brother is probably part of that troop.

"Mr. Steele makes the tensions and excitements of the Brother's War very real, and customs of the mountain people, the speech and setting are well integrated into the narrative." NY Times Book Rev

Steer, Dugald

The **dragon** diary; [by] Dugald A. Steer; illustrated by Douglas Carrel. Candlewick Press 2009 248p il (Dragonology chronicles) $16.99

Grades: 5 6 7 8   Fic
1. Fantasy fiction 2. Dragons -- Fiction 3. Siblings
-- Fiction
ISBN 978-0-7636-3425-4; 0-7636-3425-5
LC 2009005795

Apprentice dragonologists Daniel and Beatrice Cook's
mentor is called away at a crucial time, leaving the brother
and sister alone to search for an ancient diary that could cure
some gravely ill dragons

"This fast-paced fantasy features sibling rivalry, multi-
tudes of dragons, and mid-air heroics." Horn Book Guide

Steig, William

★ **Abel's** island. Farrar, Straus & Giroux 1976 117p
il $15; pa $5.99
Grades: 3 4 5   Fic
1. Mice -- Fiction 2. Survival after airplane accidents,
shipwrecks, etc. -- Fiction
ISBN 0-374-30010-0; 0-312-37143-8 pa
A Newbery Medal honor book, 1977

Castaway on an uninhabited island, Abel, a very civilized mouse, finds his resourcefulness and endurance tested
to the limit as he struggles to survive and return to his home.

"The line drawings washed with gray faithfully and delightfully record not only the rigors of Abel's experiences
but the refinement of his domestic existence." Horn Book

Dominic; story and pictures by William Steig. Farrar,
Straus & Giroux 1972 145p il hardcover o.p. pa $5.99
Grades: 3 4 5   Fic
1. Dogs -- Fiction
ISBN 0-312-37144-6 pa

Dominic, a gregarious dog, sets out on the high road
one day, going no place in particular, but moving along to
find whatever he can. And that turns out to be plenty, including an invalid pig who leaves Dominic his fortune; a
variety of friends and adventures; and even—in the end—his
life's companion

"A singular blend of naiveté and sophistication, comic
commentary and philosophizing, the narrative handles situation clichés with humor and flair—perhaps because of the
author's felicitous turn of phrase, his verbal cartooning, and
his integration of text and illustrations. A chivalrous and optimistic tribute to gallantry and romance." Horn Book

★ The **real** thief; story and pictures by William Steig.
Farrar, Straus & Giroux 1973 58p il hardcover o.p. pa
$5.99
Grades: 3 4 5   Fic
1. Animals -- Fiction 2. Thieves -- Fiction
ISBN 0-312-37145-4 pa

"Steig's gray line-and-wash drawings provide a charming accompaniment to a wholly winning story." SLJ

Steinhofel, Andreas

An **elk** dropped in; [by] Andreas Steinhofel; pictures
by Kerstin Meyer; translated by Alissa Jaffa. Front Street
2006 78p il $16.95
Grades: 2 3 4   Fic
1. Elk -- Fiction 2. Christmas stories 3. Christmas
-- Fiction 4. Santa Claus -- Fiction
ISBN 1-932425-80-2; 978-1-932425-80-2
LC 2006-00804

While on a pre-Christmas trial run for the famous man
in red, an elk named Mr. Moose crashes through the roof of
a house and, while recuperating from a sprain, regales Billy
Wagner and his family with stories.

"Winsome watercolor illustrations, droll details, and a
young narrator who relates both wild and everyday details in
the same matter-of-fact tone combine to create a charming,
if offbeat, Christmas fantasy." SLJ

Stellings, Caroline

The **contest**. Seventh Generation 2009 123p pa $9.95
Grades: 4 5 6 7   Fic
1. Poverty -- Fiction 2. Contests -- Fiction 3. Friendship
-- Fiction 4. Books and reading -- Fiction 5. Racially
mixed people -- Fiction
ISBN 978-0-9779183-5-5 pa; 0-9779183-5-1 pa
LC 2009-20294

Rosy, a poor, eleven-year-old, half-Mohawk girl from
Hamilton, Ontario, Canada enters an Anne of Green Ga-
bles look-alike contest in hopes of winning a set of Anne
books, and gains a new friend and deeper understanding of
Anne's character

"Readers will enjoy Rosy and her spunky attitude. . . .
Some readers will finish this book and go seeking the Anne
series to read, and those already familiar with the Anne
books will enjoy the connection." Libr Media Connect

Stemple, Adam

B.U.G. (Big Ugly Guy) by Jane Yolen and Adam Stemple. Dutton Children's Books 2013 344 p.
Grades: 4 5 6 7 8   Fic
1. Golem -- Juvenile fiction 2. Bullies -- Juvenile
fiction 3. School stories -- Juvenile fiction 4. Golem
-- Fiction 5. Magic -- Fiction 6. Bullies -- Fiction
7. Friendship -- Fiction 8. Bands (Music) -- Fiction
9. Klezmer music -- Fiction 10. Jews -- United States
-- Fiction
ISBN 9780525422389
LC 2012018217

A constant target for bullies, Sammy Greenburg is glad
to make friends with a boy named Skink, who even agrees
to "start up a Klezmer fusion garage band after Sammy introduces Skink to the unique combination of jazz and Jewish
folk music. When the bullies beat up Skink, however, Sammy decides enough is enough, and, using a formula he finds
in his rabbi's study, he creates a golem to take vengeance on
his enemies—and fill the missing drummer spot in his new
band." (Bulletin of the Center for Children's Books)

Stephens, John

★ The **emerald** atlas. Alfred A. Knopf 2011 417p
(The books of beginning) $17.99; lib bdg $20.99
Grades: 4 5 6   Fic
1. Magic -- Fiction 2. Monsters -- Fiction 3. Siblings
-- Fiction 4. Prophecies -- Fiction 5. Space and time
-- Fiction 6. Books and reading -- Fiction
ISBN 978-0-375-86870-2; 0-375-86870-4; 978-0-375-
96870-9 lib bdg; 0-375-96870-9 lib bdg
LC 2010029100

Kate, Michael, and Emma have passed from one orphanage to another in the ten years since their parents disappeared to protect them, but now they learn that they have
special powers, a prophesied quest to find a magical book,
and a fearsome enemy.

"This fast-paced, fully imagined fantasy is by turns frightening and funny, and the siblings are well-crafted and empathetic heroes. Highly enjoyable, it should find many readers." Publ Wkly

★ The fire chronicle; John Stephens. Alfred A. Knopf 2012 437 p. (hardback) $17.99

Grades: 4 5 6   Fic
1. Fantasy fiction 2. Adventure fiction 3. Time travel -- Juvenile fiction 4. Magic -- Fiction 5. Identity -- Fiction 6. Monsters -- Fiction 7. Prophecies -- Fiction 8. Space and time -- Fiction 9. Books and reading -- Fiction 10. Brothers and sisters -- Fiction
ISBN 0375868712; 9780375868719; 9780375899560; 9780375968716

LC 2012016139

In this novel by John Stephens, part of the Books of Beginning series, "Kate, Michael, and Emma long to continue the hunt for their missing parents. . . . A frantic chase sends Kate a hundred years into the past, to a perilous, enchanted New York City. . . . Meanwhile, Michael and Emma have set off to find the second of the Books of Beginning. A series of clues leads them into a hidden world where they must brave harsh polar storms, track down an ancient order of warriors, and confront terrible monsters." (Publisher's note)

Sternberg, Julie

Like pickle juice on a cookie; illustrations by Matthew Cordell. Amulet Books 2011 122p il $14.95

Grades: 3 4 5   Fic
1. Novels in verse 2. Babysitters -- Fiction 3. Loss (Psychology) -- Fiction
ISBN 0-8109-8424-5; 978-0-8109-8424-0

LC 2009-15975

When nine-year-old Eleanor's beloved babysitter Bibi moves away to take care of her ailing father, Eleanor must spend the summer adjusting to a new babysitter while mourning the loss of her old one. "Grades two to three." (Bull Cent Child Books)

"Eleanor's gradual warming to her new sitter is affectingly narrated, and Cordell's halftone cartoons convey the story's pathos and humor, as well as Eleanor's changeable moods." Publ Wkly

Stevenson, Robert Louis, 1850-1894

Treasure Island; by Robert Louis Stevenson; illustrated by N.C. Wyeth. Scribner 1981 xvi, 273 p., [13] leaves of platesp col. ill. (paperback) $6.99; (reinforced) $29.99

Grades: 5 6 7 8 9 10 11 12 Adult   Fic
1. Adventure fiction 2. Pirates -- Fiction 3. Buried treasure -- Fiction
ISBN 0689832125; 9780689832123; 9780684171609; 0684171600

LC 81008788

Originally published: 1911.

Young Jim Hawkins discovers a treasure map in the chest of an old sailor who dies under mysterious circumstances at his mother's inn. He shows it to Dr. Livesey and Squire Trelawney who agree to outfit a ship and sail to Treasure Island. Among the crew is the pirate Long John Silver and his followers who are in pursuit of the treasure

Stevenson, Steve

The curse of the pharaoh; by Sir Steve Stevenson; illustrated by Stefano Turconi; translated by Siobhan Kelly; translation adapted by Maya Gold. Grosset & Dunlap, an imprint of Penguin Group (USA) Inc. 2013 144 p. (Agatha Mistery) (pbk: alk. paper) $5.99

Grades: 3 4 5   Fic
1. Mystery fiction -- Juvenile fiction 2. Adventure fiction -- Juvenile fiction 3. Eccentrics and eccentricities -- Juvenile fiction 4. Memory -- Fiction 5. Mystery and detective stories 6. Adventure and adventurers -- Fiction 7. Eccentrics and eccentricities -- Fiction
ISBN 0448462176; 9780448462172

LC 2012031484

This children's novel, by Steve Stevenson, illustrated by Stefano Turconi, is first in the "Agatha: Girl of Mystery" series. It features "a headstrong girl detective who jets off on exotic . . . adventures with the help of her hulking bodyguard and loyal cat named . . . Watson. . . . Rumors of a mysterious tablet unearthed in the Valley of the Kings may be just the clue that Agatha needs to unlock the secret curse of an ancient Pharaoh." (Publisher's note)

"A well-plotted mystery full of quirky details... and carefully constructed clues." Booklist

Stevermer, Caroline

Magic below stairs. Dial Books for Young Readers 2010 199p $16.99

Grades: 4 5 6 7   Fic
1. Magic -- Fiction 2. Orphans -- Fiction 3. Household employees -- Fiction
ISBN 978-0-8037-3467-8; 0-8037-3467-0

LC 2009-25100

Ten-year-old Frederick, who is surreptitiously watched over by a household elf, is plucked from a London orphanage to be a servant to a wealthy wizard, and eventually his uncanny abilities lead him to become the wizard's apprentice.

"A well-developed fictional world and the many concrete details of belowstairs life make the magical events in this engaging chapter book more believable." Booklist

Stewart, Paul

★ Beyond the Deepwoods; [by] Paul Stewart, Chris Riddell. David Fickling Bks. 2004 276p il (Edge chronicles) $12.95; lib bdg $14.99; pa $6.99

Grades: 4 5 6   Fic
1. Fantasy fiction
ISBN 0-385-75068-4; 0-385-75069-2 lib bdg; 0-440-42087-3 pa

First published 1998 in the United Kingdom

Thirteen-year-old Twig, having always looked and felt different from his woodtroll family, learns that he is adopted and travels out of his Deepwoods home to find the place where he belongs

"Those with hearty appetites for adventure (and strong stomachs) will find this a tremendously exciting fantasy. Riddell's wonderfully detailed ink drawings, on nearly every page, create a strong sense of the believable, well-imagined otherworld and bring its strange creatures to life." Booklist

Other titles in The Edge Chronicles series are:
Stormchaser (2004)
Midnight over Sanctaphrax (2004)
The curse of the Gloamglozer (2005)
The last of the sky pirates (2005)

Vox (2005)
Freeglader (2006)
The winter knights (2007)
Clash of the sky galleons (2007)
Immortals (2010)

The **curse** of the night wolf; [by] Paul Stewart and Chris Riddell; illustrated by Chris Riddell. David Fickling Books 2008 204p il (Barnaby Grimes) $15.99; lib bdg $18.99

Grades: 4 5 6 7   **Fic**
1. Mystery fiction 2. Physicians -- Fiction 3. Werewolves -- Fiction
ISBN 978-0-385-75125-4; 0-385-75125-7; 978-0-385-75126-1 lib bdg; 0-385-75126-5 lib bdg
LC 2008-01697

Soon after Victorian messenger Barnaby Grimes is attacked by a huge beast while crossing London's rooftops, he becomes entangled in a mystery involving patent medicine, impoverished patients, and very expensive furs.

"Moody, highly detailed pen-and-ink drawings provide ornamentation throughout, lending a classic Victorian feel to help punctuate the drama. . . . Possessing an easy confidence and quick wit . . . Barnaby is an appealing character." Booklist

Other titles in this series are:
Return of the emerald skull (2009)
Legion of the Dead (2010)

★ **Fergus** Crane; [by] Paul Stewart & Chris Riddell. David Fickling Books 2006 214p (Far-flung adventures) $14.95

Grades: 3 4 5   **Fic**
1. Adventure fiction
ISBN 0-385-75088-9
LC 2005018478

Nine-year-old Fergus Crane's life is filled with classes on the school ship Betty Jeanne, interesting neighbors, and helping with his mother's work until a mysterious box flies into his window and leads him toward adventure

"With a simple plot, a few hints of mystery, and many intriguing details, this story will quickly hook readers. Riddell's expressive ink drawings make the fantastic elements more believable and add enormously to the book's appeal." Booklist

Other titles in this series are:
Corby Flood (2006)
Hugo Pepper (2007)

The **immortals**; [by] Paul Stewart & Chris Riddell. David Fickling Books 2010 668p il (Edge chronicles) $19.99; lib bdg $22.99

Grades: 4 5 6   **Fic**
1. Fantasy fiction
ISBN 978-0-375-83743-2; 0-375-83743-4; 978-0-375-93743-9 lib bdg; 0-375-93743-9 lib bdg
LC 2010013658

Nate Quarter, a lowly lamplighter in the phraxmines of the Eastern Woods, must flee for his life when the mine sargeant wants him killed, while elsewhere, a storm unlike any ever seen is building.

"The extensive saga of the Edge Chronicles concludes in this exciting yet weighty tome that ties past plots to the pres-

ent and still leaves the door ajar for future outings. Multiple story lines eventually join, enriched (again) by Riddell's line drawings; species and character names remain feats of linguistic acrobatics; and the never-ending action will satisfy returning fans and adventurous new readers." Booklist

Midnight over Sanctaphrax; [by] Paul Stewart & Chris Riddell. David Fickling Books 2004 361p il (Edge chronicles) $12.95; pa $7.99

Grades: 4 5 6   **Fic**
1. Fantasy fiction
ISBN 0-385-75072-2; 0-385-75073-0 lib bdg; 978-0-440-42098-9 pa; 0-440-42098-9 pa
LC 2003-26539

Twig, a young sky pirate captain, is the only one who can save the floating city of Sanctaphrax from the Mother Storm.

"The action-oriented plot and fantastic world of this third volume in Chronicles of Edge will delight fans and entice new readers. Riddell again contributes skillful ink drawings." Booklist

Phantom of Blood Alley; [by] Paul Stewart & Chris Riddell; illustrated by Chris Riddell. David Fickling Books 2010 201p il (Barnaby Grimes) $16.99

Grades: 4 5 6 7   **Fic**
1. Mystery fiction 2. Photography -- Fiction 3. Supernatural -- Fiction
ISBN 978-0-385-75134-6; 0-385-75134-6
First published 2009 in the United Kingdom

Barnaby finds himself in the fiercely competitive world of early photography, where the rewards are immense but so are the risks. After an experiment goes disastrously wrong, Barnaby is on the trail of a mad chemist with a talent for disappearing into thin air.

The **Winter** Knights; [by] Paul Stewart & Chris Riddell. David Fickling Books 2007 381p il (Edge chronicles) $12.99; lib bdg $14.99; pa $7.99

Grades: 4 5 6   **Fic**
1. Fantasy fiction
ISBN 978-0-375-83741-8; 978-0-375-93741-5 lib bdg; 978-0-385-73612-1 pa
LC 2006012404

First published 2005 in the United Kingdom

Quint finally begins his training at the Knights Academy, Maris adjusts to life in Undertown, and Sanctaphrax shivers in anticipation of a legendary storm, while a storm of a different kind brews between sky-scholars and earth-scholars.

"This legend and its accompanying drawings are . . . successful in maintaining a high level of suspense and action, still finding time for both droll humor and drama." Voice Youth Advocates

Stewart, Trenton Lee
The **extraordinary** education of Nicholas Benedict; by Trenton Lee Stewart; illustrated by Diana Sudyka. Little, Brown 2012 470 p.

Grades: 4 5 6 7 8   **Fic**
1. Bullies -- Fiction 2. Orphans -- Fiction 3. Friendship -- Fiction 4. Narcolepsy -- Fiction 5. Orphanages -- Fiction 6. Genius -- Fiction 7. Mystery and detective stories 8. Adventure and adventurers -- Fiction
ISBN 9780316176194
LC 2011031690

This book tells the story of Nicholas Benedict who "is just 9 years. . . . Small in physical stature but intellectually gifted, he has an 'unfortunate' nose . . . and a medical condition that prompts 'unpredictable sleeping episodes' that drop 'him from consciousness like a trapdoor into a black dungeon' at the least opportune of times. . . . What has long made him a nuisance to less intelligent adults and target practice for bullies also makes him a curiosity for a slightly older boy who befriends him at his new home — the ominously named Rothschild's End. The orphanage is housed in a two-story mansion. . . . [The book] revolves around . . . the . . . themes . . . [of] orphans, friendship and the sorts of surrogate families that form as a result." (LA Times)

★ The **mysterious** Benedict Society; illustrated by Carson Ellis. Little, Brown 2007 485p il $16.99; pa $6.99

Grades: 5 6 7 8　　　　　Fic
1. Science fiction 2. Adventure fiction
ISBN 978-0-316-05777-6; 0-316-05777-0; 978-0-316-00395-7 pa; 0-316-00395-6 pa
　　　　　　　　　　　LC 2006-09925
After passing a series of mind-bending tests, four children are selected for a secret mission that requires them to go undercover at the Learning Institute for the Very Enlightened, where the only rule is that there are no rules
"Stewart's unusual characters, threatening villains, and dramatic plot twists will grab and hold readers' attention." SLJ
Other titles about the Benedict Society are:
The mysterious Benedict Society and the perilous journey (2008)
The mysterious Benedict Society and the prisoner's dilemma (2009)

The **mysterious** Benedict Society and the perilous journey; by Trenton Lee Stewart; illustrated by Carson Ellis. Little, Brown and Co. 2008 440p il $16.99

Grades: 5 6 7 8　　　　　Fic
1. Science fiction 2. Adventure fiction
ISBN 978-0-316-05780-6; 0-316-05780-0
　　　　　　　　　　　LC 2007031540
Reynie, Kate, Sticky, and Constance, all graduates of the Learning Institute for the Very Enlightened and members of the Benedict Society, embark on a scavenger hunt that turns into a desperate search for the missing Mr. Benedict.
"This is pure adventure—lots of racing, scheming, fighting." Booklist

The **mysterious** Benedict Society and the prisoner's dilemma; written by Trenton Lee Stewart; illustrations by Diana Sudyka. Little, Brown and Company 2009 391p il $16.99

Grades: 5 6 7 8　　　　　Fic
1. School stories 2. Science fiction 3. Adventure fiction 4. Friendship -- Fiction
ISBN 978-0-316-04552-0; 0-316-04552-7
　　　　　　　　　　　LC 2009-25459
When an unexplained blackout engulfs Stonetown, Benedict Society members Reynie, Kate, Sticky, and Constance follow clues on an adventure that threatens to separate them from their families, friends, and even one another.

"The children's well-delineated characters are believable as those of young prodigies, the narrative puzzles mesh with thumping good action scenes, and the good-versus-evil plot balances the warmth of family connections with the excitement of deathly peril." Horn Book

Stier, Catherine
The **terrible** secrets of the Tell-All Club. Albert Whitman & Co. 2009 125p $14.99
Grades: 4 5 6　　　　　Fic
1. School stories 2. Clubs -- Fiction 3. Friendship -- Fiction
ISBN 978-0-8075-7798-1; 0-8075-7798-7
　　　　　　　　　　　LC 2008055704
When four fifth-grade friends complete a "tell-all" survey, tensions arise and come to a head during an overnight class trip
"Told in the four voices of the club members, the story shows the characters' insecurities and the family issues they face. Reluctant readers will find it fast paced, easy to follow, and populated with likable personalities." SLJ

Stine, R. L., 1943-
★ It's the first day of school--forever! Feiwel and Friends 2011 183p $15.99
Grades: 3 4 5　　　　　Fic
1. Horror fiction 2. School stories 3. Monsters -- Fiction
ISBN 978-0-312-64954-8; 0-312-64954-1
　　　　　　　　　　　LC 2010050896
Everything goes wrong for eleven-year-old Artie on his first day at Ardmore Middle School, from the moment his alarm goes off until the next morning, when everything is repeated exactly the same way.
"Stine delivers the hilarity and horror that readers love, and his mastery of sustaining mood will not disappoint." SLJ

Stockton, Frank
The bee-man of Orn; [by] Frank R. Stockton; illustrated by P.J. Lynch. Candlewick Press 2003 un il $17.99
Grades: 2 3 4　　　　　Fic
1. Fairy tales
ISBN 0-7636-2239-7
　　　　　　　　　　　LC 2003-48454
Story first published in St. Nicholas magazine 1883
When a Sorcerer tells him that he has been transformed from another sort of being, the Beeman sets out to discover what he was in his earlier incarnation. Story is accompanied by a DVD which provides a behind-the-scenes look at the illustrator at work.
"Lynch's spirited artwork, richly detailed and darkly atmospheric, provides a series of imaginative settings and creates a romantic and broadly appealing vision of this original fairy tale. . . . This edition is a read-aloud treasure for good listeners." Booklist

Stone, Phoebe
Deep down popular; a novel. by Phoebe Stone. Arthur A. Levine Books 2008 280p $16.99; pa $4.99
Grades: 4 5 6 7　　　　　Fic
1. School stories 2. Friendship -- Fiction 3. Family life

-- Fiction 4. Country life -- Fiction
ISBN 978-0-439-80245-1; 0-439-80245-8; 978-0-439-80244-4 pa; 0-439-80244-X pa

LC 2007017198

In a small Virginia town, sixth-grader Jessie Lou Ferguson has a crush on the hugely popular Conrad Parker Smith, and when he suddenly develops a medical problem and the teacher asks Jessie Lou to help him, they become friends, to her surprise

"Jessie Lou tells her tale with the strong, rough-edged purity of a young poet, which she is; equally strong are the story's underpinnings, longing and laughter, and a willingness to believe in something despite the facts." Booklist

★ The **Romeo** and Juliet code. Arthur A. Levine Books 2011 300p $16.99

Grades: 4 5 6 7   **Fic**

1. Ciphers -- Fiction 2. Family life -- Fiction 3. World War, 1939-1945 -- United States -- Fiction 4. World War, 1939-1945 -- Evacuation of civilians -- Fiction
ISBN 978-0-545-21511-4; 0-545-21511-0

LC 2010-30005

During World War II, eleven-year-old Felicity is sent from London to Bottlebay, Maine, to live with her grandmother, aunt, uncle, and a reclusive boy who helps her decode mysterious letters that contain the truth about her missing parents.

Felicity "is endearingly portrayed, and the back story, so gradually revealed, provides a peek into the depths of the souls of some of the adults. The pacing is deliberately slow, yet Felicity's growing awareness of how she can help heal the troubled adults makes this an eminently satisfying read." Kirkus

Romeo blue; by Phoebe Stone. 1st ed. Arthur A. Levine Books 2013 352 p. (hardcover) $16.99

Grades: 4 5 6 7   **Fic**

1. Espionage -- Fiction 2. World War, 1939-1945 -- Children -- Fiction 3. World War, 1939-1945 -- Evacuation of civilians -- Fiction 4. Identity -- Fiction 5. Foster children -- Fiction 6. Families -- Juvenile fiction 7. Family life -- Maine -- Fiction 8. World War, 1939-1945 -- Maine -- Fiction 9. Foster children -- Maine -- Juvenile fiction 10. World War, 1939-1945 -- Maine -- Juvenile fiction 11. World War, 1939-1945 -- Evacuation of civilians -- Great Britain -- Fiction 12. World War, 1939-1945 -- Evacuation of civilians -- Great Britain -- Juvenile fiction
ISBN 0545443601; 9780545443609

LC 2012038060

"In this sequel to the WWII historical mystery 'The Romeo and Juliet Code,' . . . twelve-year old . . . Flissy now knows her Uncle Gideon is actually her biological father. . . . And she knows her whole family are some kind of spies, but she does not know . . . if they are still alive. And she has no idea why the creepy neighbor, Mr. Fitzwilliam, has invited her and adopted cousin Derek for tea, how he seems to know about her parents' secret activities." (Children's Literature)

The **boy** on Cinnamon Street; by Phoebe Stone. Arthur A. Levine Books 2012 234 p.

Grades: 3 4 5 6 7 8   **Fic**

1. Girls -- Psychology 2. Friendship -- Fiction 3.

Memory -- Juvenile fiction 4. Grandparent-grandchild relationship 5. Memory -- Fiction 6. Schools -- Fiction 7. Best friends -- Fiction 8. Grandparents -- Fiction
ISBN 0545215129; 9780545215121

LC 2011017862

This book tells the story of "seventh-grader [Louise who] lives with her grandparents in their condo and she's quit [gymnastics], . . . instead spending her time with friends Reni and her brother Henderson Elliot, whose warm and embracing family she adores. When a cute ninth-grader turns up on her doorstep delivering pizza, and she then finds a note under the mat confessing interest in Louise, she's transported into her first serious crush." (Bulletin of the Center for Children's Books)

Stout, Shawn K.

Fiona Finkelstein meets her match!! illustrated by Angela Martini. Aladdin 2010 146p il $14.99; pa $4.99

Grades: 2 3 4   **Fic**

1. School stories 2. Clubs -- Fiction 3. Family life -- Fiction
ISBN 978-1-4169-7928-9; 1-4169-7928-X; 978-1-4169-7110-8 pa; 1-4169-7110-6 pa

LC 2010026829

Fiona Finkelstein does not get along with Milo, a new student in her Ordinary, Maryland, fourth-grade class, and when he starts a meteorology club she responds by trying to start a matchmaking club.

"Stout continues to develop her protagonist in this entertaining installment." Horn Book Guide

Fiona Finkelstein, big-time ballerina! illustrated by Angela Martini. Aladdin 2009 166p il $14.99; pa $4.99

Grades: 2 3 4   **Fic**

1. Worry -- Fiction 2. Ballet -- Fiction 3. Family life -- Fiction 4. Weather forecasting -- Fiction
ISBN 978-1-4169-7927-2; 1-4169-7927-1; 978-1-4169-7109-2 pa; 1-4169-7109-2 pa

LC 2009022593

Nine-year-old Marylander Fiona Finkelstein tries to deal with stage-fright, missing her mother who is an actress in California, and hoping that her father, a television meteorologist, does not get in trouble when she antagonizes the anchorman.

"This novel is light and fun, with just enough wit and sass to keep young readers entertained. . . . The story maintains a fast pace throughout, and the illustrations give Fiona and company a sweet look that is simple and charming." SLJ

Another title about Fiona Finkelstein is:
Fiona Finkelstein meets her match (2010)

Strickland, Brad

John Bellairs's Lewis Barnavelt in The whistle, the grave, and the ghost. Dial Bks. for Young Readers 2003 152p $16.99

Grades: 4 5 6 7   **Fic**

1. Witchcraft -- Fiction
ISBN 0-8037-2622-8

LC 2002-10817

In the woods near his home in Michigan, thirteen-year-old Lewis Barnavelt stumbles upon an ancient grave and silver whistle that draw him, his best friend Rose Rita Pottinger, his uncle Jonathan, and their friend Mrs. Zimmermann into a battle with an ancient evil

"Strickland excels at heart-in-your-throat suspense that he maintains until the final paragraphs." Booklist

The **house** where nobody lived; a John Bellairs mystery featuring Lewis Barnavelt. [by] Brad Strickland. Sleuth 2006 173p $16.99
Grades: 4 5 6 7   **Fic**
1. Witchcraft -- Fiction
ISBN 0-8037-3148-5
                    LC 2006001673

Twelve-year-old Lewis and his best friend Rose Rita investigate a strange old house in their home town and discover that they may be dealing with powerful ancient Hawaiian spirits.

"Filled with likable, kooky characters, this mystery is fast paced and funny." SLJ

The **sign** of the sinister sorcerer; [by] Brad Strickland. Dial Books for Young Readers 2008 168p $16.99
Grades: 4 5 6 7   **Fic**
1. Mystery fiction 2. Magic -- Fiction 3. Uncles -- Fiction 4. Orphans -- Fiction 5. Witches -- Fiction 6. Supernatural -- Fiction
ISBN 978-0-8037-3151-6; 0-8037-3151-5
                    LC 2008007698

In Michigan in the mid-1950s, Lewis Barnavelt is convinced that the series of accidents he and his uncle are experiencing are the result of a curse by a mysterious, hooded figure that may be part of his uncle's past.

"For readers who enjoy trying to solve the mystery as they read, there are abundant clues including an anagram. A quick, exciting read." SLJ

Other titles about Lewis Barnavelt by Brad Strickland are:

The beast under the wizard's bridge (2000)
The house where nobody lived (2006)
The spector from the magician's museum (1998)
The tower at the end of the world (2001)
The whistle, the grave, and the ghost (2003)

Stringer, Helen
★ **Spellbinder**. Feiwel and Friends 2009 372p $17.99
Grades: 5 6 7 8   **Fic**
1. Ghost stories 2. Dead -- Fiction
ISBN 978-0-312-38763-1; 0-312-38763-6
                    LC 2008-28552

Twelve-year-old Belladonna Johnson, who lives with the ghosts of her parents in the north of England, teams up with an always-in-trouble classmate to investigate why all of the ghosts in the world have suddenly disappeared.

"Magical creatures, amulets, and verses are all a part of this delightful tale.... Stringer maintains the humor and logic of preteens who are awkwardly coming into their magical destinies." SLJ

The **midnight** gate. Feiwel and Friends 2011 376p
Grades: 5 6 7 8   **Fic**
1. Ghost stories 2. School stories 3. Orphans -- Fiction 4. Supernatural -- Fiction
ISBN 0-312-38764-4; 978-0-312-38764-8
                    LC 2010036476

Twelve-year-old Belladonna Johnson, who lives with the ghosts of her parents, once again teams up with her classmate Steve, whose mother has suddenly disappeared, when

they are given a dangerous assignment by a ghostly monk involving a return to the Dark Times.

"Stringer's vivid descriptions and irreverent nods to all sorts of mythology, along with well-paced cliff-hangers throughout, are just right for fantasy and adventure buffs." Booklist

Stuchner, Joan Betty
Honey cake; illustrated by Cynthia Nugent. Random House 2008 101p il $11.99; lib bdg $14.99; pa $4.99
Grades: 3 4 5   **Fic**
1. Jews -- Fiction 2. Holocaust, 1933-1945 -- Fiction
ISBN 978-0-375-85189-6; 0-375-85189-5; 978-0-375-95189-3 lib bdg; 0-375-95189-X lib bdg; 978-0-375-85190-2 pa; 0-375-85190-9 pa
                    LC 2007-11501

First published 2007 in the United Kingdom and Canada

David and his family live in Denmark during the Nazi occupation, until September 1943 when their neighbors help smuggle them to Sweden to escape Hitler's orders to send the Danish Jews to concentration camps. Includes a recipe for honey cake, typically made to celebrate the Jewish New Year.

"The simply told story and black-and-white illustrations convey tension, fear, and hope." Horn Book Guide

Sullivan, Laura L.
Guardian of the Green Hill; [illustrations by David Wyatt] Henry Holt and Company 2011 293p il $16.99
Grades: 5 6 7 8   **Fic**
1. Fantasy fiction 2. Fairies -- Fiction 3. Siblings -- Fiction 4. Supernatural -- Fiction
ISBN 978-0-8050-8985-1; 0-8050-8985-3
                    LC 2010029231

After the Midsummer War ends, Meg Morgan faces a madman in the battle for control of the last bastion of fairies in England, aided by her siblings Rowan, Silly, and James, and American neighbors Dickie Rhys, and Finn Fachan.

"Sullivan's writing has a timelessness that contrasts nicely with Meg's distinctly modern ideas and weaves a compelling story that will pull readers along." SLJ

Under the green hill. Henry Holt and Company 2010 308p $16.99
Grades: 5 6 7 8   **Fic**
1. Fantasy fiction 2. Fairies -- Fiction 3. Siblings -- Fiction 4. Supernatural -- Fiction
ISBN 978-0-8050-8984-4; 0-8050-8984-5
                    LC 2009-50772

While staying with distant relatives in England, Americans Rowan, Meg, Silly, and James Morgan, with their neighbors Dickie Rhys and Finn Fachan, learn that one of them must fight to the death in the Midsummer War required by the local fairies

"Sullivan draws heavily on her knowledge of Middle English folklore and creates a story rich with memorable characters and evocative language." SLJ

Summers, Susan
The **greatest** gift; the story of the other Wise Man. retold by Susan Summers; illustrated by Jackie Morris. Barefoot Books 2011 il $16.99
Grades: K 1 2 3   **Fic**
1. Magi -- Fiction 2. Christmas stories 3. Voyages and

travels -- Fiction
ISBN 978-1-84686-578-7; 1-84686-578-6

LC 2011015507

Artaban, a fourth Wise Man, delays journeying with the other Magi to see the newborn Jesus, but after thirty-three years of helping others he has an unusual opportunity to meet his Savior.

"This intriguing story unfolds in flowing prose with the feeling of a folktale, conveying a subtle message in Artaban's kindness toward the needy of any religion. Morris provides handsome watercolor illustrations in a smoky palette of earth tones, with a soft focus that complements the ancient setting." Kirkus

Swinburne, Stephen R.
Wiff and Dirty George: the Z.E.B.R.A. Incident. Boyds Mills Press 2010 167p il $17.95
Grades: 4 5 6 7   Fic
1. Great Britain -- Fiction 2. Nineteen sixties -- Fiction
ISBN 978-1-59078-755-7; 1-59078-755-2

"London in 1969 was a trippy place, no doubt, but it's made even more psychodelic with the adventures of Wiff and Dirty George, two twelve-year-olds who follow their noses into a world of trouble. While on a morning train, the boys are slightly horrified when everyone's pants fall down, but instead of worrying overmuch about their own embarrassment, they take off after the large white rabbit who seems to be the instigator of the mass humiliation. . . . The humor is more situational than verbal; the characters are all comedic straight men in a twisted, absurd world. . . . Delightfully daft 'clues' precede each chapter, and a glossary of Britishisms will help young Yanks navigate the dialect." Bull Cent Child Books

Taback, Simms
Postcards from camp. Nancy Paulsen Books 2011 un il $17.99
Grades: 1 2 3   Fic
1. Camps -- Fiction 2. Letters -- Fiction
ISBN 978-0-399-23973-1; 0-399-23973-1

"Taback's signature illustrative style is perfect for this brief tale. Michael's scrawl and his father's cursive share space with collaged stamps and photographs as well as illustrations that suit the correspondents' ages." Kirkus

Tacang, Brian
Bully-be-gone; [by] Brian Tacang. HarperCollins 2006 216p (Misadventures of Millicent Madding) $15.99
Grades: 3 4 5 6   Fic
1. Bullies -- Fiction 2. Friendship -- Fiction 3. Inventions -- Fiction
ISBN 0-06-073911-8

LC 2005-07777

Budding-inventor Millicent Madding launches her latest invention to disastrous results, and she has only days to create an antidote before the local bullies wreak havoc and her dearest friendships are destroyed forever

"The book has zippy dialogue and brilliant use of alliteration. . . . The eccentric characters are fun, and the silly but substantive plot will surely appeal to children." SLJ

Tak, Bibi Dumon
Soldier bear; written by Bibi Dumon Tak; illustrated by Philip Hopman; translated by Laura Watkinson. Eerdmans Books for Young Readers 2011 145p il $13
Grades: 4 5 6 7   Fic
1. Bears -- Fiction 2. Soldiers -- Fiction 3. World War, 1939-1945 -- Fiction
ISBN 978-0-8028-5375-2; 0-8028-5375-7

LC 2011013963

An orphaned Syrian brown bear cub is adopted by Polish soldiers during World War II and serves for five years as their mischievous mascot in Iran and Italy. Based on a true story.

"This is smoothly translated and engagingly illustrated with sketches and helpful maps. Funny, fresh and heartwarming." Kirkus

Tanner, Lian
City of lies. Delacorte Press 2011 278 p. (The Keeper's trilogy) lib bdg $20.99; $17.99
Grades: 5 6 7 8   Fic
1. Fantasy fiction 2. Adventure fiction 3. Thieves -- Fiction 4. Kidnapping -- Fiction
ISBN 0385739060; 0385907699 lib bdg; 9780385907699 lib bdg; 9780385739061

LC 2010048579

Twelve-year-old Goldie, impulsive and bold, relies on her skills as a liar and a thief to try to rescue her captured friends from the child-stealers running rampant in the City of Spoke.

Museum of thieves. Delacorte Press 2010 312p (The Keepers Trilogy) $16.99; lib bdg $19.99
Grades: 5 6 7 8   Fic
1. Fantasy fiction 2. Adventure fiction 3. Museums -- Fiction 4. Thieves -- Fiction
ISBN 978-0-385-73905-4; 0-385-73905-2; 978-0-385-90768-2 lib bdg; 0-385-90768-0 lib bdg

LC 2009053655

Goldie, an impulsive and bold twelve-year-old, escapes the oppressive city of Jewel, where children are required to wear guardchains for their protection, and finds refuge in the extraordinary Museum of Dunt, an ever-shifting world where she discovers a useful talent for thievery and mysterious secrets that threaten her city and everyone she loves.

"Readers will be quickly caught up in the highly dramatic chases, the intriguing museum that shifts layout at will, and the nifty otherworld elements. There's depth beneath that, though. . . . [The book] may set young readers thinking about their own world's choices." Bull Cent Child Books

Tarshis, Lauren
Emma-Jean Lazarus fell in love. Dial Books for Young Readers 2009 169p $16.99; pa $6.99
Grades: 5 6 7   Fic
1. School stories 2. Friendship -- Fiction
ISBN 978-0-8037-3321-3; 0-8037-3321-6; 978-0-14-241568-9 pa; 0-14-241568-5 pa

Seventh-grader Emma-Jean Lazarus uses her logical, scientific mind to navigate the mysteries of the upcoming Spring Fling, her friend Colleen's secret admirer, and other love-related dilemmas

"Tarshis deftly weaves in important details from the previous book . . . providing those new to Emma-Jean some necessary back story. . . . Fans will appreciate the continuity and relish the reappearance of familiar characters, especially Ms Wright, the lovable school janitor, and the rest of Emma Jean's true blue friends. The story ends on a happy note with the possibility of more adventures to come." Kirkus

★ **Emma**-Jean Lazarus fell out of a tree. Dial Books for Young Readers 2007 199p $16.99

Grades: 5 6 7 **Fic**

1. School stories 2. Friendship -- Fiction

ISBN 978-0-8037-3164-6; 0-8037-3164-7

LC 2006-18428

A quirky and utterly logical seventh-grade girl named Emma-Jean Lazarus discovers some interesting results when she gets involved in the messy everyday problems of her peers.

"Readers will be fascinated by Emma-Jean's emotionless observations and her adult-level vocabulary. Tarshis pulls off a balancing act, showing the child's detachment yet making her a sympathetic character. Exceptionally fleshed-out secondary characters add warmth to the story." SLJ

I survived Hurricane Katrina, 2005; illustrated by Scott Dawson. Scholastic 2011 95p il (I survived) $16.99; pa $4.99

Grades: 3 4 5 6 **Fic**

1. Hurricane Katrina, 2005 -- Fiction

ISBN 978-0-545-20689-1; 0-545-20689-8; 978-0-545-20696-9 pa; 0-545-20696-0 pa

Barry's family tries to evacuate before Hurricane Katrina hits their home in New Orleans. But when Barry's little sister gets terribly sick, they're forced to stay home and wait out the storm.

"Expressive illustrations capture the drama of the storm and its aftermath, but the book's real power comes from its exploration of what it means to be a hero." Booklist

I survived the bombing of Pearl Harbor, 1941; illustrated by Scott Dawson. Scholastic Inc. 2011 86p il (I survived) pa $4.99

Grades: 3 4 5 6 **Fic**

1. World War, 1939-1945 -- Fiction 2. Pearl Harbor (Oahu, Hawaii), Attack on, 1941 -- Fiction

ISBN 978-0-545-20698-3; 0-545-20698-7

Eleven-year-old Danny Crane is alone on his favorite beach in Hawaii when the world is torn apart and World War II officially hits the United States. Does he have what it takes to find his way home in the midst of the bombs, the smoke, and the destruction of the day that will live in infamy?

I survived the shark attacks of 1916; illustrated by Scott Dawson. Scholastic 2010 87p il (I survived) $16.99; pa $4.99

Grades: 3 4 5 6 **Fic**

1. Sharks -- Fiction

ISBN 978-0-545-20688-4; 0-545-20688-4; 978-0-545-20695-2 pa; 0-545-20695-2 pa

In the summer of 1916, ten year-old Chet Roscow is captivated by the local news: A great white shark has been attacking and killing people up and down the Atlantic coast, not far from Chet's hometown of Springfield, New Jersey.

"An absorbing story. . . . Black-and-white illustrations that resemble old photographs enhance the events of the

story. Tarshis incorporates information about the real attacks and fictionalizes it, then follows the story with facts about the attacks and sharks. This is a gripping story that will hold the interest of reluctant readers." SLJ

Other titles in this series are:

I survived the sinking of the Titanic, 1912 (2010)

I survived Hurricane Katrina, 2005 (2011)

I survived the bombing of Pearl Harbor, 1941 (2011)

I survived the sinking of the Titanic, 1912; illustrated by Scott Dawson. Scholastic 2010 96p il (I survived) $16.99; pa $4.99

Grades: 3 4 5 6 **Fic**

1. Shipwrecks -- Fiction 2. Ocean travel -- Fiction

ISBN 978-0-545-20687-7; 0-545-20687-1; 978-0-545-20694-5 pa; 0-545-20694-4 pa

Excited to board the Titanic with his aunt and little sister, ten-year-old George begins to explore the ill-fated ship's first-class storage cabin when the ship is rocked by a collision with an iceberg and begins to sink.

"The fast pace and intrinsically fascinating disaster story will keep readers turning the pages." Kirkus

Tashjian, Janet

★ **My** life as a book; with cartoons by Jake Tashjian. Henry Holt 2010 211p il $16.99; pa $6.99

Grades: 4 5 6 7 **Fic**

1. Summer -- Fiction 2. Animals -- Fiction 3. Family life -- Fiction 4. Books and reading -- Fiction

ISBN 978-0-8050-8903-5; 0-8050-8903-9; 978-0-312-67289-8 pa; 0-312-67289-6 pa

LC 2009-18909

Dubbed a "reluctant reader" by his teacher, twelve-year-old Derek spends summer vacation learning important lessons even though he does not complete his summer reading list.

"The protagonist is by turns likable and irritating, but always interesting. He is sure to engage fans of Jeff Kinney's 'Diary of a Wimpy Kid' books . . . as well as those looking for a spunky, contemporary boy with a mystery to solve. Reluctant readers will appreciate the book's large print and quick-paced story." SLJ

"Another title about Derek is:

My life as a stuntboy (2011)

My life as a stuntboy; with cartoons by Jake Tashjian. Henry Holt and Company 2011 256p il $13.99

Grades: 4 5 6 7 **Fic**

1. School stories 2. Monkeys -- Fiction 3. Stunt flying -- Fiction 4. Motion pictures -- Fiction

ISBN 978-0-8050-8904-2; 0-8050-8904-7

LC 2010029884

Twelve-year-old Derek Fallon has the opportunity of a lifetime--to perform stunts in a movie featuring a popular twelve-year-old star—but complications arise involving his best friend, a capuchin monkey, and Derek's chronic inability to concentrate on schoolwork.

"The generous margins are filled with Derek's often quite clever stick-figure cartoons illustrating vocabulary words such as 'flabbergasted' and 'camouflage'—all rendered by the author's teenage son. Another fun, emotionally resonant read for the Wimpy Kid set and beyond." Kirkus

Tate, Eleanora E.

Celeste's Harlem Renaissance. Little, Brown 2007 279p $15.99; pa $5.99

Grades: 4 5 6 7   **Fic**

1. Aunts -- Fiction 2. African Americans -- Fiction 3. Harlem Renaissance -- Fiction

ISBN 978-0-316-52394-3; 978-0-316-11362-5 pa

In 1921, thirteen-year-old Celeste leaves North Carolina to stay with her glamorous Aunt Valentina in Harlem, New York, where she discovers the vibrant Harlem Renaissance in full swing, even though her aunt's life is not exactly what she was led to believe.

"Both sobering and inspiring, Tate's novel is a moving portrait of growing up black and female in 1920s America." Booklist

Tate, Lindsey

Kate Larkin, bone expert; [by] Lindsey Tate; illustrated by Diane Palmisciano. Henry Holt 2008 72p il $16.95

Grades: 1 2 3 4   **Fic**

1. Bones -- Fiction 2. Family life -- Fiction

ISBN 978-0-8050-7901-2; 0-8050-7901-7

LC 2007027588

When Kate breaks her arm, she learns all about bones, from how x-rays work to how bones heal, and by the time she gets her cast removed at the end of the summer, she is an expert. Includes related activities and glossary

"The format is appealing: large type, short chapters, and black-and-white illustrations generously dispersed throughout. . . . This is a solid choice for newly independent readers or for science-minded children looking for some fiction." SLJ

Taylor, Mildred D.

★ The **friendship**; pictures by Max Ginsburg. Dial Bks. for Young Readers 1987 53p il $15.99; pa $4.99

Grades: 4 5 6 7   **Fic**

1. Race relations -- Fiction 2. African Americans -- Fiction

ISBN 0-8037-0417-8; 0-14-038964-4 pa

LC 86-29309

Coretta Scott King Award for text

This "story about race relations in rural Mississippi during the Depression focuses on an incident between an old Black man, Mr. Tom Bee, and a white storekeeper, Mr. John Wallace. Indebted to Tom for saving his life as a young man, John had promised they would always be friends. But now, years later, John insists that Tom call him 'Mister' and shoots the old man for defiantly—and publicly—calling him by his first name. Narrator Cassie Logan and her brothers . . . are verbally abused by Wallace's villainous sons before witnessing the encounter." Bull Cent Child Books

★ The **gold** Cadillac; pictures by Michael Hays. Dial Bks. for Young Readers 1987 43p il $16.99; pa $4.99

Grades: 4 5 6 7   **Fic**

1. Prejudices -- Fiction 2. Race relations -- Fiction 3. African Americans -- Fiction

ISBN 0-8037-0342-2; 0-14-038963-6 pa

LC 86-11526

"Full-page sepia paintings effectively portray the characters, setting, and mood of the story events as Hays ably demonstrates his understanding of the social and emotional environments which existed for blacks during this period." SLJ

★ Let the circle be unbroken. Dial Bks. for Young Readers 1981 394p $17.99; pa $7.99

Grades: 4 5 6 7   **Fic**

1. African Americans -- Fiction 2. Great Depression, 1929-1939 -- Fiction

ISBN 0-8037-4748-9; 0-14-034892-1 pa

LC 81-65854

The author "provides her readers with a literal sense of witnessing important American history. . . . Moreover, [she] never neglects the details of her volatile 9-year-old heroine's interior life. The daydreams, the jealousy, the incredible ardor of that age come alive." N Y Times Book Rev

★ **Mississippi** bridge; by Mildred Taylor; pictures by Max Ginsburg. Dial Bks. for Young Readers 1990 62p il hardcover o.p. pa $4.99

Grades: 4 5 6 7   **Fic**

1. Prejudices -- Fiction 2. Race relations -- Fiction 3. African Americans -- Fiction

ISBN 0-14-130817-6 pa

LC 89-27898

"Taylor has shaped this episode into a haunting meditation that will leave readers vividly informed about segregation practices and the unequal rights that prevailed in that era. . . . The incident and its context constitute a telling piece of social history." Booklist

★ The **road** to Memphis; by Mildred Taylor. Dial Bks. 1989 290p $18.99; pa $6.99

Grades: 4 5 6 7   **Fic**

1. Race relations -- Fiction 2. African Americans -- Fiction

ISBN 0-8037-0340-6; 0-14-036077-8 pa

LC 88-33654

Coretta Scott King Award for text

Sadistically teased by two white boys in 1940's rural Mississippi, Cassie Logan's friend, Moe, severely injures one of the boys with a tire iron and enlists Cassie's help in trying to flee the state

"Taylor's continued smooth, easy language provides readability for all ages, with a focus on universal human pride, worthy values, and individual responsibility. This action-packed drama is highly recommended." Voice Youth Advocates

★ **Roll** of thunder, hear my cry; 25th anniversary ed; Phyllis Fogelman Books 2001 276p $17.99; pa $7.99

Grades: 4 5 6 7 8 9   **Fic**

1. African Americans -- Fiction

ISBN 0-8037-2647-3; 0-14-240112-9 pa

LC 00-39378

First published 1976 by Dial Press

Awarded the Newbery Medal, 1977

"The time is 1933. The place is Spokane, Mississippi where the Logans, the only black family who own their own land, wage a courageous struggle to remain independent, displeasing a white plantation owner bent on taking their land. But this suspenseful tale is also about the story's young narrator, Cassie, and her three brothers who decide to wage their own personal battles to maintain the self-dignity and pride with which they were raised. . . . Ms. Taylor's richly textured novel shows a strong, proud black family . . . resisting rather than succumbing to oppression." Child Book Rev Serv

Song of the trees; pictures by Jerry Pinkney. Dial Bks. for Young Readers 1975 48p il hardcover o.p. pa $5.99
Grades: 4 5 6 7   **Fic**
1. African Americans -- Fiction 2. Great Depression, 1929-1939 -- Fiction
ISBN 0-8037-5452-3; 0-14-250075-5 pa
Eight-year-old Cassie Logan tells how her family "leaving Mississippi during the Depression was cheated into selling for practically nothing valuable and beautiful giant old pines and hickories, beeches and walnuts in the forest surrounding their house." Adventuring with Books

★ The **well**; David's story. Dial Bks. for Young Readers 1995 92p hardcover o.p. pa $5.99
Grades: 4 5 6 7   **Fic**
1. Race relations -- Fiction 2. African Americans -- Fiction
ISBN 0-8037-1802-0; 0-14-038642-4 pa
                                    LC 94-25360
This story "delivers an emotional wallop in a concentrated span of time and action. . . . This story reverberates in the heart long after the final paragraph is read." Horn Book

Taylor, S. S.
The **Expeditioners** and the Treasure of Drowned Man's Canyon; and the Treasure of Drowned Man's Canyon. by S. S. Taylor; illustrated by Katherine Roy. Pgw 2012 320 p. $22
Grades: 5 6 7 8   **Fic**
1. Adventure fiction 2. Maps -- Juvenile fiction 3. Exploration -- Juvenile fiction
ISBN 1938073061; 9781938073069
In this book by S. S. Taylor, illustrated by Katherine Roy, "computers have failed, electricity is extinct, and the race to discover new lands is underway! Brilliant explorer Alexander West has just died under mysterious circumstances, but not before smuggling half of a strange map to his intrepid children--Kit the brain, M.K. the tinkerer, and Zander the brave. Why are so many government agents trying to steal the half-map? (And where is the other half?)" (Publisher's note)

Taylor, Sydney
★ **All**-of-a-kind family; illustrations by Helen John. Delacorte Press 2005 188p il hardcover o.p. pa $5.99
Grades: 4 5 6   **Fic**
1. Jews -- Fiction
ISBN 0-385-73295-3; 0-440-40059-7 pa
First published 1951 by Follett
"A genuine and delightful picture of a Jewish family . . . with an understanding mother and father, rich in kindness and fun though poor in money. The important part the public library played in the lives of these children is happily evident; and the Jewish holiday celebrations are particularly well described." Horn Book
Other titles about this family are:
All-of-a-kind family downtown (1957)
All-of-a-kind family uptown (1957)
Ella of all-of-a-kind family (1978)

More all-of-a-kind family (1954)

Taylor, Theodore
Ice drift; [by] Theodore Taylor. Harcourt 2005 224p $16; pa $5.95
Grades: 4 5 6 7   **Fic**
1. Inuit -- Fiction 2. Brothers -- Fiction
ISBN 0-15-205081-7; 0-15-205550-9 pa
                                    LC 2003-27783
Two Inuit brothers must fend for themselves while stranded on an ice floe that is adrift in the Greenland Strait.
This is "a masterful and detailed look into a culture unfamiliar to most Americans, a gripping adventure, and a moving depiction of brotherly love." SLJ

★ **Teetoncey**. Harcourt 2004 208p hardcover o.p. pa $5.95
Grades: 5 6 7 8   **Fic**
1. Amnesia -- Fiction
ISBN 0-15-205298-4; 0-15-205294-1 pa
                                    LC 2003-67745
A reissue of the title first published 1974 by Doubleday
In this first novel of the Cape Hatteras trilogy, eleven-year-old Ben rescues an English girl from a shipwreck off the Outer Banks of North Carolina; and, though she becomes part of his family, she never speaks.
"The novel is rich with details of of local geography, history, and folklore." Horn Book
Other titles in the Cape Hatteras trilogy are:
The odyssey of Ben O'Neal (2004 c1977)
Teetoncey and Ben O'Neal (2004 c1975)

Timothy of the cay. Harcourt Brace & Co. 1993 161p hardcover o.p. pa $5.95
Grades: 5 6 7 8   **Fic**
1. Blind -- Fiction 2. Race relations -- Fiction 3. Survival after airplane accidents, shipwrecks, etc. -- Fiction
ISBN 0-15-288358-4; 0-15-206320-X pa
                                    LC 93-7898
Having survived being blinded and shipwrecked on a tiny Caribbean island with the old black man Timothy, twelve-year-old white Phillip is rescued and hopes to regain his sight with an operation. Alternate chapters follow the life of Timothy from his days as a young cabin boy
"Somewhat more thoughtful than its well-loved antecedent, this boldly drawn novel is no less commanding." Publ Wkly

★ The **cay**. Delacorte Press 1987 137p $16.95; pa $5.50
Grades: 5 6 7 8   **Fic**
1. Blind -- Fiction 2. Race relations -- Fiction 3. Survival after airplane accidents, shipwrecks, etc. -- Fiction
ISBN 0-385-07906-0; 0-440-22912-X pa
A reissue of the title first published 1969
When the freighter on which they are traveling is torpedoed by a German submarine during World War II, Phillip, an adolescent white boy blinded by a blow on the head, and Timothy, an old black man, are stranded on a tiny Caribbean island where the boy acquires a new kind of vision, courage, and love from his old companion

"Starkly dramatic, believable and compelling." Saturday Rev

The **trouble** with Tuck. Doubleday 1981 110p hardcover o.p. pa $4.50

Grades: 5 6 7 8   **Fic**
1. Dogs -- Fiction 2. Blind -- Fiction
ISBN 0-385-17774-7; 0-440-41696-5 pa
      LC 81-43139

Helen trains her blind dog Tuck to follow and trust a seeing-eye companion dog

This is "a touching dog story, written with good flow, pace, and structure." Bull Cent Child Books

Another title about Helen and Tuck is:

Tuck triumphant (1991)

Teague, Mark
★ The **doom** machine; a novel. Blue Sky Press 2009 376p $17.99

Grades: 4 5 6 7   **Fic**
1. Science fiction 2. Space and time -- Fiction 3. Extraterrestrial beings -- Fiction
ISBN 978-0-545-15142-9; 0-545-15142-2
      LC 2009-14262

When a spaceship lands in the small town of Vern Hollow in 1956, juvenile delinquent Jack Creedle and prim, studious Isadora Shumway form an unexpected alliance as they try to keep a group of extraterrestrials from stealing eccentric Uncle Bud's space travel machine.

"This book is filled with humor and dramatic figurative language that makes the setting completely approachable. It is a great fit for science fiction, humor, and adventure genre fans." Voice Youth Advocates

Tellegen, Toon
Letters to anyone and everyone; stories by Toon Tellegen; illustrated by Jessica Ahlberg; translated by Martin Cleaver. Boxer Books 2010 154p il lib bdg $12.95

Grades: 2 3 4 5   **Fic**
1. Animals -- Fiction 2. Letters -- Fiction
ISBN 978-1-906250-95-9 lib bdg; 1-906250-95-2 lib bdg

"In this novel, snails, elephants, bears, and ants write letters to one another, to the Sun, and to other letter writers. . . . Every brief missive is written in a distinct voice, and the complete collection reveals Tellegen's richly imagined world in which the creatures reside. The book was originally published in Holland, and Cleaver's smooth English translation retains humor and charm." SLJ

TenNapel, Doug
Cardboard; Doug TenNapel. Graphix / Scholastic 2012 288 p.

Grades: 5 6 7 8   **Fic**
1. Boxes -- Fiction 2. Gifts -- Graphic novels 3. Magic -- Graphic novels 4. Bullies -- Graphic novels 5. Father-son relationship -- Graphic novels
ISBN 0545418720; 9780545418720; 9780545418737
      LC 2011934533

In this graphic novel, "Cam Howerton's out-of-work father is so broke, the best he can do for Cam's birthday is an empty cardboard box purchased from a toy seller with two mysterious rules: return every unused scrap of cardboard and don't ask for any more. . . . [T]he box becomes a project.

What should father and son make out of the box? 'A boxer,' Cam suggests. . . . 'Boxer Bill,' created from inanimate material, comes alive. Unfortunately, Marcus, the neighborhood bully . . . steals the scrap materials, and begins turning out a whole evil empire of cardboard monsters. . . . [A]fter losing control of them he must unite with Cam and his father to defeat the massive cardboard army. . . . [Q]uestions are raised about what it means to be a man, what makes a good man, and what forms people's character." (Horn Book)

Teplin, Scott
The **clock** without a face; a Gus Twintig mystery. [by Scott Teplin, Mac Barnett & Eli Horowitz; plus faces by Adam Rex & numbers by Anna Sheffield] McSweeney's 2010 un il $19.95

Grades: 4 5 6 7   **Fic**
1. Mystery fiction 2. Picture puzzles 3. Theft -- Fiction 4. Apartment houses -- Fiction 5. Clocks and watches -- Fiction
ISBN 978-1-934781-71-5; 1-934781-71-1

Narrator Gus Twintig and Roy Dodge "are summoned to a 13-story apartment building to investigate a string of robberies: the emerald-encrusted numbers have been stolen from a clock belonging to owner Bevel Ternky, and his 12 tenants have also been burgled. . . . The right side of each spread is an overhead cutaway view of each apartment, ostensibly drawn by Twintig. Given the potential of discovering clues to where the actual bejeweled numbers . . . have been hidden, kids should be plenty motivated to pore over each scene." Publ Wkly

Testa, Maria
Almost forever. Candlewick Press 2003 69p $14.99; pa $5.99

Grades: 3 4 5   **Fic**
1. Vietnam War, 1961-1975 -- Fiction
ISBN 0-7636-1996-5; 0-7636-3366-6 pa
      LC 2002-34757

In free verse, a young girl describes what she, her brother, and their mother do during the year that her doctor father is serving in the Army in Vietnam

This is "sensitive and moving. . . . Testa's poems give her young speaker a believable, sympathetic voice." Publ Wkly

Thomason, Mark
Moonrunner. Kane/Miller 2009 217p $15.95

Grades: 4 5 6 7   **Fic**
1. Horses -- Fiction
ISBN 978-1-935279-03-7; 1-935279-03-3

First published 2008 in Australia

"In the 1890s, Casey and his parents immigrate to Australia, to a homestead that they inherited from his grandfather. The 12-year-old finds the change difficult. He is bullied at school, and he misses his baseball team in Montana and his horse. Then he happens upon a magnificent wild stallion, and he is determined to befriend the brumby, whom he names Moonrunner. . . . This well-paced story effectively portrays the family's struggles. Casey is a strong, engaging protagonist whose interactions with the other characters are believable and interesting." SLJ

Thompson, Colin

Good neighbors; by Colin Thompson; illustrated by Crab Scrambly. HarperCollinsPublishers 2008 214p il (The Floods) lib bdg $16.89; pa $5.99

Grades: 3 4 5 6   **Fic**

1. Magic -- Fiction 2. Witches -- Fiction
ISBN 978-0-06-113199-8 lib bdg; 0-06-113196-2 lib bdg; 978-0-06-113197-4 pa; 0-06-113197-0 pa

A family of wizards and witches living in an ordinary neighborhood in an ordinary town decides that they have had enough of the noisy family living next-door and makes them disappear.

The author "careens wildly from one extreme scenario to the next, letting the Floods get away with everything—despite their appearances, they're the good guys. Kids can enjoy the prankishness; adults can rest easy given the conventional underpinnings." Publ Wkly

Another title in this series is:
School plot (2008)

Thompson, Kate

Highway robbery; illustrated by Jonny Duddle and Robert Dress. Greenwillow Books 2009 118p il $15.99

Grades: 3 4 5 6   **Fic**

1. Thieves 2. Adventure fiction 3. Horses -- Fiction 4. Thieves -- Fiction
ISBN 978-0-06-173034-4; 0-06-173034-3

LC 2008-27720

On a cold day in eighteenth-century England, a poor young boy agrees to watch a stranger's fine horse for a golden guinea but soon finds himself in a difficult situation when the king's guard appears and wants to use him as bait in their pursuit of a notorious highwayman

"It's a suspenseful and tautly written story as is, and Thompson's sly twist makes it all the richer." Publ Wkly

Most wanted; illustrated by Jonny Duddle. Greenwillow Books 2010 136p il $15.99

Grades: 3 4 5   **Fic**

1. Emperors 2. Horses -- Fiction 3. Slavery -- Fiction
ISBN 978-0-06-173037-5; 0-06-173037-8; 978-0-06-173038-2 lib bdg; 0-06-173038-6 lib bdg

In first century Rome, in the turmoil after a rumor circulates that mad Emperor "Littleboots" is dead, young Marcus brings home a horse that the emperor had proclaimed a consul and his family decides they must treat it as an honored guest.

"This brief chapter book is nicely suited for reading aloud or for those independent readers who enjoy their adventure and history touched with humor. Marcus's voice is engaging and credible.... A cleverly told tale of an odd and interesting piece of history that will intrigue young readers." Publ Wkly

Thompson, Paul B.

The **devil's** door; a Salem witchcraft story. Enslow Publishers 2010 160p (Historical fiction adventures) lib bdg $27.93; pa $14.95

Grades: 4 5 6   **Fic**

1. Trials -- Fiction 2. Witchcraft -- Fiction
ISBN 978-0-7660-3387-0 lib bdg; 0-7660-3387-2 lib bdg; 978-1-59845-214-3 pa; 1-59845-214-2 pa

Sarah Wright and her father Ephraim move to Salem Village, Massachusetts, in 1692, where they witness the Salem witchcraft hysteria, during which Ephraim is arrested and Sarah must try to help him escape from jail.

"Factual material is incorporated into the narrative, creating a fast-paced, fascinating read." SLJ

Thomson, Melissa

Keena Ford and the second-grade mixup; pictures by Frank Morrison. Dial Books for Young Readers 2008 102p il $14.99; pa $5.99

Grades: 1 2 3   **Fic**

1. School stories 2. Diaries -- Fiction 3. African Americans -- Fiction
ISBN 978-0-8037-3263-6; 0-8037-3263-5; 978-0-14-241396-8 pa; 0-14-241396-8 pa

LC 2007-43749

Keena Ford chronicles her many mishaps as she begins second grade

"Thomson, a former teacher, skillfully zeroes in on an eight-year-old's anxieties and creates a vivid sense of Keena's world, both at school and at home.... Morrison's full-page pencil sketches extend both the comedy and the emotions, particularly Keena's sense that she is accepted and loved, even as she clears up mistakes with family and friends." Booklist

Other titles about Keena Ford are:
Keena Ford and the field trip mix-up (2009)
Keena Ford and the secret journal mix-up (2010)

Keena Ford and the secret journal mix-up; illustrated by Frank Morrison. Dial Books for Children 2010 118p il $15.99

Grades: 1 2 3   **Fic**

1. School stories 2. Diaries -- Fiction 3. Friendship -- Fiction
ISBN 978-0-8037-3465-4; 0-8037-3465-4

"Second-grader Keena Ford keeps a journal full of her thoughts about her friends and her family. When it falls into the hands of the resident mean girl, she risks having her secrets spill out unless she does whatever Tiffany commands.... The story is written in journal style, with Keena describing daily events. Young readers will relate to her friendship dilemma and appreciate her vibrant personality. Morrison's occasional full-page drawings capture the interactions of the children and are great at depicting their facial expressions." SLJ

Thomson, Sarah L.

Dragon's egg; by Sarah L. Thomson. Greenwillow Books 2007 267p $16.99; lib bdg $17.89

Grades: 3 4 5 6   **Fic**

1. Fantasy fiction 2. Dragons -- Fiction
ISBN 978-0-06-128848-7; 978-0-06-128847-0 lib bdg

LC 2007009145

Mella, a young girl trained as a dragon keeper, learns that the legends of old are true when she is entrusted with carrying a dragon's egg to the fabled Hatching Grounds, a dangerous journey on which she is assisted by a knight's squire

This is a "lively adventure.... Thomson's richly descriptive writing creates a fantasy world readers will want to revisit." Booklist

Thor, Annika

★ A **faraway** island; translated from the Swedish by Linda Schenck. Delacorte Press 2009 247p map $16.99; lib bdg $19.99

Grades: 4 5 6 7 **Fic**

1. Jews -- Fiction 2. Islands -- Fiction 3. Sisters -- Fiction 4. Refugees -- Fiction 5. World War, 1939-1945 -- Fiction

ISBN 978-0-385-73617-6; 0-385-73617-7; 978-0-385-90590-9 lib bdg; 0-385-90590-4 lib bdg

LC 2009-15420

ALA ALSC Batchelder Award (2010)

In 1939 Sweden, two Jewish sisters wait for their parents to flee the Nazis in Austria, but while eight-year-old Nellie settles in quickly, twelve-year-old Stephie feels stranded at the end of the world, with a foster mother who is as cold and unforgiving as the island on which they live.

"Children will readily empathize with Stephie's courage. Both sisters are well-drawn, likable characters. This is the first of four books Thor has written about the two girls." SLJ

The **lily** pond. Delacorte Press 2011 217p $16.99; lib bdg $19.99

Grades: 4 5 6 7 **Fic**

1. School stories 2. Refugees -- Fiction 3. Friendship -- Fiction 4. Jews -- Sweden -- Fiction 5. World War, 1939-1945 -- Fiction

ISBN 978-0-385-74039-5; 0-385-74039-5; 978-0-385-90838-2 lib bdg; 0-385-90838-5 lib bdg; 978-0-375-89914-0 e-book

LC 2010053548

Timberlake, Amy

★ **One** came home; Amy Timberlake. Alfred A. Knopf 2012 272 p. (hard cover) $16.99

Grades: 4 5 6 **Fic**

1. Missing persons -- Juvenile fiction 2. Historical fiction -- Juvenile fiction 3. Frontier and pioneer life -- Wisconsin -- Juvenile fiction 4. Sharpshooters -- Fiction 5. Missing persons -- Fiction 6. Counterfeits and counterfeiting -- Fiction 7. Frontier and pioneer life -- Wisconsin -- Fiction

ISBN 0375869255; 9780375869259; 9780375969256; 9780375989346

LC 2011037095

This novel, by Amy Timberlake, is set "in the town of Placid, Wisconsin, in 1871, . . .when Georgie blurts out something she shouldn't, her older sister Agatha flees. . . . And when the sheriff returns to town with an unidentifiable body--wearing Agatha's blue-green ball gown--everyone assumes the worst. Except Georgie. Refusing to believe the facts that are laid down (and coffined) before her, Georgie sets out on a journey to find her sister." (Publisher's note)

That girl Lucy Moon. Hyperion 2006 294p $15.99; pa $5.99

Grades: 5 6 7 8 **Fic**

1. School stories 2. Sledding -- Fiction 3. Social action -- Fiction

ISBN 0-7868-5298-4; 0-7868-5299-2 pa

LC 2005-55105

"Life has changed for injustice-fighting Lucy Moon. Not only is junior high less accepting than elementary school of her activism . . . but there are also those annoying boys. .

. . To top it off, the town's richest citizen, Miss Wiggins, has fenced off her beloved sledding hill. True to form, Lucy organizes a Free Wiggins Hill campaign. . . . Timberlake develops her feisty character through believable dialogue. . . . The carefully crafted plot moves through most of the school year." SLJ

Tingle, Tim

★ **Crossing** Bok Chitto; a Choctaw tale of friendship & freedom. illustrated by Jeanne Rorex Bridges. Cinco Puntos Press 2006 un il $17.95; pa $8.95

Grades: 2 3 4 5 **Fic**

1. Slavery -- Fiction 2. Friendship -- Fiction 3. Choctaw Indians -- Fiction 4. African Americans -- Fiction

ISBN 978-0-938317-77-7; 0-938317-77-6; 978-1-933693-20-0 pa; 1-933693-20-7 pa

LC 2005-23612

In the 1800s, a Choctaw girl becomes friends with a slave boy from a plantation across the great river, and when she learns that his family is in trouble, she helps them cross to freedom

The "text has the rhythm and grace of . . . oral tradition. It will be easily and effectively read aloud. The paintings are dark and solemn, and the artist has done a wonderful job of depicting all of the characters as individuals." Booklist

Tocher, Timothy

Bill Pennant, Babe Ruth, and me. Cricket Books 2009 178p $16.95

Grades: 5 6 7 8 **Fic**

1. Baseball players 2. Baseball managers 3. Baseball -- Fiction

ISBN 978-0-8126-2755-8; 0-8126-2755-5

LC 2008026829

In 1920, sixteen-year-old Hank finds his loyalties divided when he is assigned to care for the Giants' mascot, a wildcat named Bill Pennant, as well as keep an eye on Babe Ruth in Ruth's first season with the New York Yankees.

The author "seamlessly blends fact and fiction. He recreates the era with scrupulous attention to its syntax and slang, as well as details of daily life. Ruth, McGraw and the other historical figures come alive for readers, and the fictional Hank is a sympathetic, fully developed character." Kirkus

Toft, Di

Wolven. Scholastic 2010 322p $16.99; pa $7.99

Grades: 5 6 7 8 **Fic**

1. Werewolves -- Fiction 2. Supernatural -- Fiction

ISBN 978-0-545-17109-0; 0-545-17109-1; 978-0-545-17110-6 pa; 0-545-17110-5 pa

Twelve-year-old Nat, with help from his friends, and his "pet" Woody, a wolf that turns into a boy, must face werewolves that have been altered as part of a dastardly plan.

"Toft spins an incredible tale full of action, mystery, and suspense. This hair-raising adventure with its fresh perspective on werewolf lore is perfect for audiences not ready for some of the edgier material out there. A satisfying read with a fly-off-the-shelves cover." SLJ

Another title in this series is:
The twilight circus (2011)

Toksvig, Sandi

★ **Hitler's** canary. Roaring Brook Press 2007 191p $16.95

Grades: 5 6 7 8   **Fic**
1. Jews -- Fiction 2. World War, 1939-1945 -- Fiction
ISBN 978-1-59643-247-5; 1-59643-247-0
LC 2006-16607
Ten-year-old Bamse and his Jewish friend Anton partici-
pate in the Danish Resistance during World War II.

"Though . . . suspenseful episodes will thrill readers, it is
Bamse's growing courage and deepening understanding that
drive the story." Booklist

Tolan, Stephanie S.
Listen! HarperCollins Publishers 2006 197p $15.99;
lib bdg $16.89; pa $5.99
Grades: 4 5 6 7   **Fic**
1. Dogs -- Fiction 2. Bereavement -- Fiction 3. Wounds
and injuries -- Fiction
ISBN 978-0-06-057935-7; 0-06-057935-8; 978-0-06-
057936-4 lib bdg; 0-06-057936-6 lib bdg; 978-0-06-
057937-1 pa; 0-06-057937-4 pa
LC 2005-17792
During her solitary convalescence from a crippling accident, twelve-year-old Charley finds a wild dog, and the arduous process of training him leads her to explore her feelings
about her mother's death two years earlier.

"This is a sweet, gentle story of healing and the strong
bond that can develop between humans and animals. The
lovely imagery and involving plot should appeal to more
than just animal lovers." SLJ

Surviving the Applewhites. HarperCollins Pubs. 2002
216p $15.99; lib bdg $17.89; pa $5.99
Grades: 5 6 7 8   **Fic**
1. Theater -- Fiction 2. Family life -- Fiction 3.
Eccentrics and eccentricities -- Fiction
ISBN 0-06-623602-9; 0-06-623603-7 lib bdg; 0-06-
441044-7 pa
LC 2002-1474
A Newbery Medal honor book, 2003
Jake, a budding juvenile delinquent, is sent for home
schooling to the arty and eccentric Applewhite family's Creative Academy, where he discovers talents and interests he
never knew he had

This is a "thoroughly enjoyable book with humor, well-
drawn characters, and a super cover." Voice Youth Advocates

Wishworks, Inc. illustrated by Amy June Bates. Arthur
A. Levine Books 2009 146p il $15.99
Grades: 3 4 5   **Fic**
1. Dogs -- Fiction 2. Moving -- Fiction 3. Wishes --
Fiction 4. Divorce -- Fiction 5. Friendship -- Fiction
6. Imagination -- Fiction
ISBN 978-0-545-03154-7; 0-545-03154-0
LC 2008-42694
When he is granted his wish for a dog from Wishworks,
Inc., third-grader Max is disappointed to find that his new
pet is nothing like the dog of his imagination.

"Tolan's vivid, clean writing is deceptively uncomplicated and the many issues touched upon are handled well." SLJ

Tolkien, J. R. R. (John Ronald Reuel), 1892-1973
The **hobbit**; or, There and back again. illustrated by
Michael Hague. Houghton Mifflin 1984 290p il $29.95
Grades: 5 6 7 8 9 10 11 12 Adult   **Fic**
1. Magic 2. Satire 3. Allegories 4. Fantasy fiction 5.

Fantasies 6. Imaginary kingdoms
ISBN 0-395-36290-3
LC 84-9023
First published 1937 in the United Kingdom; first United
States edition 1938
Bilbo Baggins, a respectable, well-to-do hobbit, lives
comfortably in his hobbit-hole until the day the wandering
wizard Gandalf chooses him to share in an adventure from
which he may never return. "Grades four to eight." (Bull
Cent Child Books)

"It must be understood that this is a children's book only
in the sense that the first of many readings can be undertaken
in the nursery. . . . [The hobbit] will be funniest to its youngest readers, and only years later, at a tenth or twentieth reading, will they begin to realize what deft scholarship and profound reflection have gone to make everything in it so ripe,
so friendly, and in its own way so true." Times Lit Suppl

Tooke, Wes
King of the mound; my summer with Satchel Paige.
Simon & Schuster Books for Young Readers 2012 $15.99
Grades: 4 5 6   **Fic**
1. Baseball players 2. Baseball -- Fiction 3.
Handicapped -- Fiction 4. Poliomyelitis -- Fiction 5.
African Americans -- Fiction 6. Father-son relationship
-- Fiction
ISBN 978-1-4424-3346-5; 1-4424-3346-9
LC 2011012740
Twelve-year-old Nick loves baseball so after a year in
the hospital fighting polio and with a brace on one leg, Nick
takes a job with the minor league team for which his father is
catcher and gets to see the great pitcher, Satchel Paige, play
during the 1935 season. Includes historical notes.

"Tooke sticks closely to historical records, with the addition of a few extra Paige exploits and aphorisms, and . . . the
fictional overlay offers a comfortably predictable 'hard work
brings just rewards' arc. Nourishing fare for Matt Christopher graduates." Kirkus

Towell, Ann
Grease town. Tundra Books 2010 232p $19.99
Grades: 5 6 7 8   **Fic**
1. Race relations -- Fiction
ISBN 978-0-88776-983-2; 0-88776-983-7
"In 1863, oil has recently been discovered in Oil Springs,
Ontario, and a variety of people, black and white, and from
many different walks of life, are settling there. Orphans Lem
and Titus Sullivan live in their aunt's stuffy and regimented house. When 19-year-old Lem sets out for Oil Springs,
13-year-old Titus stows away in his brother's wagon. . . .
Towell skillfully creates the setting of this mucky little town
and its colorful inhabitants. Titus, who narrates, has a voice
that is believable and uncontrived. . . . Supporting characters
are equally strong and well developed. . . . Towell has created a strong narrator and a compelling plot." SLJ

Towell, Katy
Skary childrin and the carousel of sorrow. Alfred A.
Knopf 2011 265p $16.99; lib bdg $19.99; ebook $16.99
Grades: 4 5 6 7   **Fic**
1. Ghost stories 2. School stories 3. Supernatural

-- Fiction

ISBN 978-0-375-86859-7; 0-375-86859-3; 978-0-375-96860-0 lib bdg; 0-375-96860-1 lib bdg; 978-0-375-89931-7 e-book; 0-375-89931-6 e-book

LC 2010-38830

In Widowsbury, an isolated village where people believe "known is good, new is bad," three outcasts from the girls' school join forces with a home-schooled boy to uncover and combat the evil that is making people disappear.

"Towell tucks violent tempests, maggoty slime, hideous transformations, nightmares, sudden terrors and like atmosphere-building elements into a rousingly melodramatic literary debut." Kirkus

Townley, Rod

The **blue** shoe; a tale of thievery, villainy, sorcery, and shoes. by Roderick Townley; illustrated by Mary GrandPré. Alfred A. Knopf 2009 254p il $16.99; lib bdg $19.99

Grades: 4 5 6 7 **Fic**

1. Fables 2. Fairy tales

ISBN 978-0-375-85600-6; 0-375-85600-5; 978-0-375-95600-3 lib bdg; 0-375-95600-X lib bdg

LC 2008-43851

A mysterious stranger commissions a single, valuable shoe from a humble cobbler, changing the cobbler's life and the life of his young apprentice forever.

This is a "fun, whimsical fairy tale.... The good-versus-evil plotline, dynamic cast of characters, ... light romance between Hap and Sophia, and copious amounts of magic and intrigue will be a hit with a wide range of readers." Booklist

Townley, Roderick

The **door** in the forest; [by] Roderick Townley. Alfred A. Knopf 2011 245p $16.99; lib bdg $19.99

Grades: 4 5 6 **Fic**

1. Magic -- Fiction 2. Honesty -- Fiction 3. Soldiers -- Fiction 4. Space and time -- Fiction

ISBN 0-375-85601-3; 0-375-95601-8 lib bdg; 978-0-375-85601-3; 978-0-375-95601-0 lib bdg

LC 2010034710

While trying to outwit the soldiers who are occupying their small town, fourteen-year-old Daniel, who cannot lie, and Emily, who discovers she has magical powers, are inexplicably drawn to a mysterious island in the heart of the forest where townsfolk have been warned never to go. "Intermediate." (Horn Book)

"Townley's fanciful story swings like a pendulum from Wild West tall tale to a vague mysticism that is enlivened by colorful imagery.... At its considerable best, it is quirky and engaging; sentences hurry purposefully along, deepening atmosphere, theme, and plot." Horn Book

Townsend, Wendy

★ The **sundown** rule. Namelos 2011 128p $18.95

Grades: 5 6 7 8 **Fic**

1. Aunts -- Fiction 2. Uncles -- Fiction 3. Wildlife conservation -- Fiction 4. Father-daughter relationship -- Fiction

ISBN 1-60898-099-5; 978-1-60898-099-4

Louise and her dad live an idyllic life surrounded by nature. When he gets an assignment to go to Brazil to write an article for a magazine, Louise has to go live in a suburb with her aunt and uncle, leaving her cat, Cash, behind, since Aunt Kay is allergic to animals. Her dad says that it will be for only six weeks, and that everything will be okay. But it isn't, especially when Cash gets hit by a car and dies. And when a new friend's dad shoots a crow for no reason. And when her own dad gets sick, really sick, and might not be coming home.

"Townsend builds a rich, moving story that is refreshing for its subject matter and lyrical realism." Publ Wkly

Tracy, Kristen

Bessica Lefter bites back; by Kristen Tracy. Delacorte Press 2012 263 p.

Grades: 4 5 6 7 **Fic**

1. Gifts -- Fiction 2. Mascots -- Fiction 3. Middle schools -- Fiction 4. School children -- Fiction 5. Friendship -- Juvenile fiction 6. Schools -- Fiction

ISBN 9780385740692; 0385740697

LC 2011045677

In this children's book, "[s]ixth-grader Bessica's new middle-school persona meets a host of problems, including mending a friendship damaged by mean text messages, facing a bully in her first outing as team mascot and coming to terms with her grandmother's boyfriend.... Rumor has it the opposing mascot in the first game will facebomb her. Neither Bessica nor readers learn what facebombing actually is in this context until after the disastrous event." (Kirkus Reviews)

★ **Camille** McPhee fell under the bus. Delacorte Press 2009 293p $16.99; lib bdg $19.99

Grades: 3 4 5 **Fic**

1. School stories 2. Friendship -- Fiction 3. Family life -- Fiction

ISBN 978-0-385-73687-9; 0-385-73687-8; 978-0-385-90633-3 lib bdg; 0-385-90633-1 lib bdg

LC 2008-24903

Ten-year-old Camille McPhee relates the ups and downs of her fourth-grade year at her Idaho elementary school as she tries to adjust to the absence of her best friend, maintain control of her low-blood sugar, cope with the intensifying conflict between her parents, and understand the importance of honesty and fairness.

"The lively, first-person narrative moves readers through possibly banal or overly traumatic episodes with a gentleness and humor that has them rooting for Camille." SLJ

The **reinvention** of Bessica Lefter. Delacorte Press 2011 305p $15.99

Grades: 4 5 6 7 **Fic**

1. School stories 2. Friendship -- Fiction

ISBN 978-0-385-90634-0; 0-385-90634-X

LC 2010-04844

Eleven-year-old Bessica's plans to begin North Teton Middle School as a new person begin to fall apart even before school begins.

Tracy "offers a positive and comforting message about learning to make adjustments, ending the book on a happy note, with Bessica finding her niche as school mascot." Publ Wkly

Trafton, Jennifer

★ The **rise** and fall of Mount Majestic; illustrations by Brett Helquist. Dial Books for Young Readers 2010 338p il $16.99

Grades: 4 5 6 7   **Fic**
1. Fairy tales 2. Adventure fiction 3. Giants -- Fiction
ISBN 978-0-8037-3375-6; 0-8037-3375-5
                                         LC 2009-51659
Ten-year-old Persimmony Smudge, who longs for heroic adventures, overhears a secret that thrusts her into the
middle of a dangerous mission that could destroy the island
on which she lives.
"Trafton imbues her tale with a delightful sense of fun
and fascinating, well-rounded characters-playful word-
smithing and flowing dialogue make this an excellent choice
for bedtime read-aloud." Publ Wkly

Travers, P. L. (Pamela L.), 1899-1996
★ **Mary** Poppins; illustrated by Mary Shepard. rev ed;
Harcourt Brace & Co. 1997 202p il $12.95; pa $6
Grades: 4 5 6   **Fic**
1. Fantasy fiction
ISBN 0-15-205810-9; 0-15-201717-8 pa
                                         LC 97-223987
First published 1934; this is a reissue of the 1981
revised edition
An extraordinary English nanny blows in on the East
Wind with her parrot-headed umbrella and magic carpet-
bag and introduces her charges, Jane and Michael Banks, to
some delightful people and experiences
"The chapter 'Bad Tuesday,' in which Mary and the
Banks children travel to the four corners of the earth and
meet the inhabitants, has been criticized for portraying mi-
norities in an unfavorable light. . . . [In] the revised edition . .
. the entourage meet up with a polar bear, macaw, panda, and
dolphin instead of Eskimos, Africans, Chinese, and American Indians." Booklist
Other titles about Mary Poppins are:
Mary Poppins comes back (1935)
Mary Poppins in the kitchen (1975)
Mary Poppins in the park (1952)
Mary Poppins opens the door (1943)

Trevino, Elizabeth Borton de
I, Juan de Pareja. Farrar, Straus & Giroux 1965 180p
$17; pa $6.99
Grades: 6 7 8 9   **Fic**
1. Slaves 2. Artists 3. Painters 4. Artists -- Fiction 5.
Slavery -- Fiction
ISBN 0-374-33531-1; 0-312-38005-4 pa
                                         LC 65-19330
Awarded the Newbery Medal, 1966
The black slave boy, Juan de Pareja, "began a new life
when he was taken into the household of the Spanish painter,
Velázquez. As he worked beside the great artist learning how
to grind and mix colors and prepare canvases, there grew
between them a warm friendship based on mutual respect
and love of art. Created from meager but authentic facts,
the story, told by Juan, depicts the life and character of Velázquez and the loyalty of the talented seventeenth-century
slave who eventually won his freedom and the right to be an
artist." Booklist

Tripp, Jenny
Pete & Fremont; [by] Jenny Tripp; with illustrations
by John Manders. Harcourt 2007 180p il $16; pa $5.95
Grades: 2 3 4   **Fic**
1. Dogs -- Fiction 2. Bears -- Fiction 3. Circus --

Fiction
ISBN 978-0-15-205629-2; 0-15-205629-7; 978-0-15-
206238-5 pa; 0-15-206238-6 pa
                                         LC 2006008757
When circus owner Mike decides Pete the poodle has
grown too old to continue as the starring act, Pete forms an
unlikely alliance with a young grizzly bear, who only wants
to go home to the woods
"Manders's busy, freewheeling illustrations add an appropriate and enticing touch to this entertaining chapter
book." SLJ
Another title about Pete is:
Pete's disappearing act (2009)

Trivas, Tracy
The **wish** stealers. Aladdin 2010 283p $16.99
Grades: 4 5 6 7   **Fic**
1. Wishes -- Fiction
ISBN 978-1-4169-8725-3; 1-4169-8725-8
                                         LC 2009-42742
"Wish-obsessed sixth-grader Griffin Penshine's life
changes dramatically following a chance encounter with an
evil old woman, who curses her with a gift of 11 Indian Head
pennies. Each penny represents a wish stolen from a wishing fountain, and the curse says that the person holding the
stolen wishes will never have a good wish come true (bad
ones will, though)." Publ Wkly

Trueit, Trudi Strain
Mom, there's a dinosaur in Beeson's Lake; illustrated
by Jim Paillot. Aladdin Paperbacks 2009 145p il (Secrets
of a lab rat) $14.99
Grades: 2 3 4   **Fic**
1. Dogs -- Fiction 2. Fear -- Fiction 3. Twins -- Fiction
4. Siblings -- Fiction 5. Swimming -- Fiction
ISBN 978-1-4169-7593-9; 1-4169-7593-4
                                         LC 2008022330
When ten-year-old "Scab" McNally takes swimming
lessons, he is afraid he will be forced to reveal his secret fear
of deep water.
This is a "laugh-out-loud volume. With high energy and
ingenious ideas, the 10-year-old skates (just barely!) through
one sticky situation after another." SLJ

No girls allowed (dogs okay) [illustrated by Jim Pail-
lot] Aladdin Paperbacks 2009 128p il (Secrets of a lab rat)
$14.99; pa $4.99
Grades: 2 3 4   **Fic**
1. School stories 2. Twins -- Fiction 3. Siblings --
Fiction
ISBN 978-1-4169-7592-2; 1-4169-7592-6; 978-1-
4169-6111-6 pa; 1-4169-6111-9 pa
                                         LC 2008-22329
Fearless nine-year-old 'Scab' McNally tries to get his
twin sister's help in convincing their parents to let them get
a dog, but when he embarrasses her in school with a particularly obnoxious invention, it looks like he has lost her
cooperation forever.
"Scab is a likable, freethinking boy who is full of charm
and humor. . . . His many tips, diagrams, and facts scattered
throughout are entertaining, as are the numerous comical
black-and-white illustrations." SLJ
Other titles in this series are:
Mom, there's a dinosaur in Beeson's Lake (2010)

Scab for president? (2011)

Scab for treasurer? illustrated by Jim Paillot. Aladdin 2011 142p il (Secrets of a lab rat) $14.99

Grades: 2 3 4   **Fic**

1. Dogs -- Fiction 2. Friendship -- Fiction

ISBN 978-1-4169-7594-6; 1-4169-7594-2

When teacher's pet Never Missy Malone who never misses her multiplication tables runs for class president, Scrab dares to go up against her.

"Scab is always getting into hilarious jams with his friends, but he never seems malicious. Paillot's zany illustrations appear throughout. This book, with its amusing sidebar secrets and lists, is simple and funny enough to pull in reluctant readers, and youngsters will jump right in and enjoy the humor, fast-paced action, and gross-out moments." SLJ

Trueman, Terry

Hurricane; a novel. HarperCollins 2008 137p $15.99; lib bdg $16.89

Grades: 5 6 7   **Fic**

1. Hurricanes -- Fiction 3. Survival after airplane accidents, shipwrecks, etc. -- Fiction

ISBN 978-0-06-000018-9; 0-06-000018-X; 978-0-06-000019-6 lib bdg; 0-06-000019-8 lib bdg

LC 2007-02990

A revised edition of Swallowing the sun, published 2004 in the United Kingdom

"Thirteen-year-old Jose lives with his family in Honduras. A hurricane hits, causing the recently clear-cut hillside adjacent to his village to become a mudslide that smothers and kills most of its fifty inhabitants. . . . Jose quickly takes charge and becomes a resourceful member of his ailing community. This survival tale is concise but engaging. Trueman's descriptions of the village buried in mud and of the difficulties it creates for the survivors are vivid." Voice Youth Advocates

Tuck, Pamela M.

As fast as words could fly; by Pamela M. Tuck; illustrations by Eric Velasquez. Lee & Low Books 2013 40 p. (hardcover) $18.95

Grades: K 1 2 3   **Fic**

1. Picture books for children 2. Segregation in education -- Juvenile fiction 3. Racism -- Fiction 4. Typewriting -- Fiction 5. African Americans -- Fiction 6. School integration -- Fiction 7. Civil rights movements -- Fiction 8. Family life -- North Carolina -- Fiction

ISBN 1600603483; 9781600603488

LC 2012030983

This book by Pamela M. Tuck, which won Lee & Low's New Voices award in 2007, is based on Tuck's "father's personal experiences with school segregation in 1960s North Carolina. . . . Mason Steele helps his father's civil rights efforts by writing letters for him; when the Steeles get a manual typewriter, Mason shows a gift for typing quickly and accurately. . . . Mason's typing skills earn him the chance to represent the school at a typing competition, but his record-setting victory there is tinged by prejudice." (Publishers Weekly)

Tunis, John R.

The **kid** from Tomkinsville; with an introduction by Bruce Brooks. Odyssey Classic/Harcourt 2006 278p pa $5.95

Grades: 4 5 6 7   **Fic**

1. Baseball -- Fiction

ISBN 0-15-205641-6

LC 2006277855

A reissue of the title first published 1940

As the newest addition to the Brooklyn Dodgers, young Roy Tucker's pitching helps pull the team out of a slump; but, when a freak accident ends his career as a pitcher, he must try to find another place for himself on the team.

Other titles about Roy Tucker and the Brooklyn Dodgers are:

World series (1941)
Keystone kids (1943)
Rookie of the year (1944)
The kid comes back (1946)

Turnage, Sheila

★ **Three** times lucky; by Sheila Turnage. Dial Books for Young Readers 2012 256 p. (hardcover) $16.99

Grades: 5 6 7 8   **Fic**

1. Absent mothers -- Fiction 2. Adopted children -- Fiction 3. Abandoned children -- Fiction 4. Murder -- Fiction 5. Identity -- Fiction 6. Foundlings -- Fiction 7. Restaurants -- Fiction 8. Mystery and detective stories 9. Community life -- North Carolina -- Fiction

ISBN 0803736703; 9780803736702

LC 2011035027

John Newbery Honor Book (2013)

This is the story of Mo LoBeau, who washed downstream as an infant 11 years ago and who has since been in the care of the Colonel, "a stranger who can't remember anything about his own past," and "Miss Lana, owner of the Tupelo Cafe. Mo . . . loves the Colonel and Lana, but" wonders about her origins. She "send[s] messages in bottles to her 'Upstream Mother.'" Also featured are "an out-of-town detective, a dead body . . . , a long-forgotten bank robbery, and a kidnapping." (Publishers Weekly)

Turner, Ann Warren

Grasshopper summer. Macmillan 1989 166p hardcover o.p. pa $4.99

Grades: 4 5 6   **Fic**

1. Frontier and pioneer life -- Fiction

ISBN 0-689-83522-1 pa

LC 88-13847

In 1874 eleven-year-old Sam and his family move from Kentucky to the southern Dakota Territory, where harsh conditions and a plague of hungry grasshoppers threaten their chances for survival

"Carefully selected details, skillfully woven into the story line, evoke a sense of place and time. . . . Both a family story and an account of pioneer living, the book is accessible as well as informative." Horn Book

Twain, Mark, 1835-1910

★ The **adventures** of Tom Sawyer; illustrated by Barry Moser; afterward by Peter Glassman. Books of Wonder 1989 261p il $24.99

Grades: 5 6 7 8   **Fic**

ISBN 0-688-07510-X

First published 1876

The adventures and pranks of a mischievous boy growing up in a Mississippi River town on the early nineteenth century.

Uchida, Yoshiko

★ **Journey** to Topaz; a story of the Japanese-American evacuation. illustrated by Donald Carrick. Heyday Books 2005 149p il pa $9.95

Grades: 5 6 7 8   **Fic**

1. World War, 1939-1945 -- Fiction 2. Japanese Americans -- Evacuation and relocation, 1942-1945 -- Fiction

ISBN 978-1-890771-91-1 pa; 1-890771-91-0 pa

LC 2004-16537

First published 1971 by Scribner

After the Pearl Harbor attack an eleven-year-old Japanese-American girl and her family are forced to go to an aliens camp in Utah

The **best** bad thing. Atheneum Pubs. 1983 120p hardcover o.p. pa $5.99

Grades: 5 6 7 8   **Fic**

1. Poverty -- Fiction 2. Family life -- Fiction 3. Japanese Americans -- Fiction

ISBN 0-689-50290-7; 0-689-71745-8 pa

LC 83-2833

At first dismayed at having to spend the last month of her summer vacation helping out in the household of recently widowed Mrs. Hata, Rinko discovers there are pleasant surprises for her, but then bad things start to happen.

★ A **jar** of dreams. Atheneum Pubs. 1981 131p hardcover o.p. pa $4.99

Grades: 5 6 7 8   **Fic**

1. Prejudices -- Fiction 2. Family life -- Fiction 3. Japanese Americans -- Fiction

ISBN 0-689-50210-9; 0-689-71672-9 pa

LC 81-3480

"Rinko in her guilelessness is genuine and refreshing, and her worries and concerns seem wholly natural, honest, and convincing." Horn Book

Other titles about Rinko Tsujimura and her family are:
The best bad thing (1983)
The happiest ending (1985)

Umansky, Kaye

Clover Twig and the magical cottage; illustrated by Johanna Wright. Roaring Brook 2009 297p il $16.99

Grades: 4 5 6   **Fic**

1. Magic -- Fiction 2. Witches -- Fiction

ISBN 978-1-59643-507-0; 1-59643-507-0

"British author Umansky's giggle-worthy characterizations and dialogue make this winsome read-aloud stand out from the pack." Kirkus

Solomon Snow and the stolen jewel. Candlewick Press 2007 245p $12.99

Grades: 5 6 7 8   **Fic**

1. Orphans -- Fiction

ISBN 978-0-7636-2793-5; 0-7636-2793-3

LC 2006-47331

While trying to rescue Prudence's father from prison, Solomon, Prudence, the Infant Prodigy, and Mr. Skippy the

rabbit find themselves caught up in the mad plans of the villainous Dr. Calimari to steal a fabulous and cursed ruby.

"Fans of Lemony Snicket will enjoy this fast-paced read. . . . Reluctant readers might find the short chapters, silly comedy, and simple characters attractive." SLJ

Updale, Eleanor

Johnny Swanson. David Fickling Books 2011 383p $16.99; lib bdg $19.99

Grades: 4 5 6   **Fic**

1. Mystery fiction 2. Fraud -- Fiction 3. Honesty -- Fiction 4. Homicide -- Fiction 5. Single parent family -- Fiction 6. Mother-son relationship -- Fiction

ISBN 0-385-75198-2; 0-385-75199-0 lib bdg; 978-0-385-75198-8; 978-0-385-75199-5 lib bdg

LC 2010-11762

In 1929 England, eleven-year-old Johnny Swanson helps his widowed mother by starting a newspaper advertising scam, which leads him to a real-life murder mystery. "Grades five to eight." (Bull Cent Child Books)

This is "a compelling tale. . . . Updale spins an enjoyable tale, seamlessly mixing the humor of Johnny's fraudulent ads . . . with the seriousness of medical fraud and murder, as well as painting a fascinating picture of an England that is just starting to forget the sacrifices made by WWI soldiers." Publ Wkly

Upjohn, Rebecca

The **secret** of the village fool; by Rebecca Upjohn; illustrated by Renne Benoit. Second Story Press 2012 32 p. $18.95

Grades: 5 6 7 8   **Fic**

1. World War, 1939-1945 -- Jews -- Juvenile fiction 2. World War, 1939-1945 -- Poland -- Juvenile fiction 3. World War, 1939-1945 -- Children -- Juvenile fiction

ISBN 1926920759; 9781926920757

In this children's book by Rebecca Upjohn, illustrated by Renne Benoit, "Milek and his brother Munio live in a sleepy village in Poland. . . . They reluctantly do as their mother asks when she asks them to visit their neighbor Anton, knowing that the rest of the village laughs at him because of his strange habits of speaking to animals and only eating vegetables. Things change quickly when war comes to their town in the form of Nazi soldiers searching for Jewish families like that of Milek and Munio." (Publisher's note)

Urban, Linda

★ **Hound** dog true. Harcourt 2011 152p $15.99

Grades: 3 4 5   **Fic**

1. School stories 2. Moving -- Fiction 3. Shyness -- Fiction 4. Janitors -- Fiction 5. Friendship -- Fiction 6. Family life -- Fiction

ISBN 978-0-547-55869-1; 0-547-55869-4

LC 2011009599

Mattie, a shy fifth-grader, wants to hide out at her new school by acting as apprentice to her Uncle Potluck, the custodian, but her plan falls apart when she summons the courage to speak about what matters most and finds a true friend.

"Combining Mattie's poignant writing and interior monologue, exquisite character development and a slow, deliberate pace, Urban spins a story that rings true." Kirkus

★ The **center** of everything; by Linda Urban. Houghton Mifflin Harcourt 2013 208 p. $15.99

Grades: 4 5 6 7   **Fic**

1. Wishes -- Juvenile fiction 2. Bereavement -- Juvenile fiction

ISBN 0547763484; 9780547763484

LC 2012954515

In this book, "months after her grandmother's death, 12-year-old Ruby Pepperdine composes a winning essay honoring her New Hampshire town's namesake" and will get to read it to the community. But she's more concerned that "she didn't listen to her grandmother's final words before she died. Ruby thinks that maybe if she wishes hard enough, 'everything will be back to how it is supposed to be,' but making a wish the right way is a tricky business." (Publishers Weekly)

★ **A crooked** kind of perfect. Harcourt 2007 213p $16; pa $5.95

Grades: 4 5 6   **Fic**

1. School stories 2. Musicians -- Fiction 3. Family life -- Fiction 4. Organ (Musical instrument) -- Fiction

ISBN 978-0-15-206007-7; 0-15-206007-3; 978-0-15-206608-6 pa; 0-15-206608-X pa

LC 2006-100622

Ten-year-old Zoe Elias, who longs to play the piano but must resign herself to learning the organ, instead, finds that her musicianship has a positive impact on her workaholic mother, her jittery father, and her school social life.

"An impressive and poignant debut novel. . . . The refreshing writing is full of pearls of wisdom, and readers will relate to this fully developed character. The sensitive story is filled with hope and humor." SLJ

Ursu, Anne

★ **Breadcrumbs**; drawings by Erin McGuire. Walden Pond Press 2011 313p il $16.99

Grades: 4 5 6 7   **Fic**

1. Fairy tales 2. Magic -- Fiction 3. Friendship -- Fiction

ISBN 978-0-06-201505-1; 0-06-201505-2

LC 2010045666

"Fifth-grader Hazel embarks on a memorable journey into the Minnesota woods to find her best friend Jack, who vanishes after a shard of glass pierces his eye. . . . Hazel enters the woods to find 'an entirely different place,' populated by creatures from the pages of Hans Christian Andersen. . . . [This is a] multi-layered, artfully crafted, transforming testament to the power of friendship." Kirkus

The **Real** Boy. Harpercollins Childrens Books 2013 288 p. (hardcover) $16.99

Grades: 3 4 5 6 7   **Fic**

1. Occult fiction -- Juvenile fiction 2. Fantasy fiction -- Juvenile fiction

ISBN 0062015079; 9780062015075

LC 2013021861

In this book, "an isolated, insecure orphan living in magical Aletheia becomes a 'real boy' when his ordered world crumbles and he must rely on himself." Oscar works for the magician Caleb. "When urgent business takes Caleb away, his apprentice is murdered, and Oscar must run Caleb's shop. Lacking social skills, Oscar longs to fold 'up, like an envelope,' but he manages the shop with help from a kindhearted girl who befriends him." More things go wrong, and Oscar must help. (Kirkus Reviews)

Usher, Mark David

The **golden** ass of Lucius Apuleius; adapted from the Latin original by M.D. Usher; illustrations by T. Motley. David R. Godine 2011 il $17.95

Grades: 4 5 6 7   **Fic**

1. Magic -- Fiction 2. Social classes -- Fiction 3. Classical mythology -- Fiction

ISBN 978-1-56792-418-3; 1-56792-418-2

LC 2010032978

Lucius Apuleius, a young nobleman fascinated by magic, accidentally turns himself into an ass and then sets out on a journey that reveals to him the conditions of peasants and slaves in and around Thessaly and leads him to find redemption as a follower of Isis and Osiris.

"A faithful (if relatively clean) version of the world's oldest surviving complete novel. . . . Though all of the sex and most of the dissolute behavior has been excised, the lad's first transformation is milked throughout for double entendres . . . and there are plenty of silly incidents and names . . . to lighten the overall tone. Motley's elaborate illustrated initials and pen-and-ink drawings add satiric bite. . . . An entertaining romp." Kirkus

Vail, Rachel

★ **Justin** Case; school, drool, and other daily disasters. illustrated by Matthew Cordell. Feiwel and Friends 2010 245p il $16.99

Grades: 3 4 5   **Fic**

1. School stories 2. Family life -- Fiction

ISBN 978-0-312-53290-1; 0-312-53290-3

"Honest and full of heart, Justin Case is a story for an oft-ignored segment of kids: the sensitive, introverted, and observant." SLJ

Valente, Catherynne M.

★ The **girl** who circumnavigated Fairyland in a ship of her own making. Feiwel and Friends 2011 247p il $16.99

Grades: 4 5 6 7   **Fic**

1. Fantasy fiction

ISBN 978-0-312-64961-6; 0-312-64961-4

LC 2010050895

"The book's appeal is crystal clear from the outset; this is a kind of The Wonderful Wizard of Oz by way of Alice's Adventures in Wonderland, made vivid by Juan's Tenniel-inflected illustrations. . . . Those who thrill to lovingly wrought tales of fantasy and adventure . . . will be enchanted." Publ Wkly

The **girl** who fell beneath Fairyland and led the revels there; by Catherynne M. Valente; with illustrations by Ana Juan. Feiwel and Friends 2012 258 p. $16.99

Grades: 4 5 6 7   **Fic**

1. Fantasy fiction 2. Magic -- Juvenile fiction 3. Fairies -- Juvenile fiction

ISBN 0312649622; 9780312649623

In this book by Catherynne M. Valente, illustrated by Ana Juan, "September has longed to return to Fairyland after her first adventure there. And when she finally does, she learns that its inhabitants have been losing their shadows--and their magic--to the world of Fairyland Below. This underworld has a new ruler: Halloween, the Hollow Queen, who is September's shadow. And Halloween does not want to give Fairyland's shadows back." (Publisher's note)

Van Cleve, Kathleen
★ **Drizzle**. Dial Books for Young Readers 2010 358p
il $16.99
Grades: 4 5 6   **Fic**
1. Rain -- Fiction 2. Farms -- Fiction 3. Magic --
Fiction 4. Droughts -- Fiction
ISBN 978-0-8037-3362-6; 0-8037-3362-3
LC 2009-23819
When a drought threatens her family's magical rhubarb
farm, eleven-year-old Polly tries to find a way to make it
rain again
"Van Cleve's debut is emotionally subtle and action
packed with a highly memorable setting." Publ Wkly

Van Draanen, Wendelin, 1965-
Flipped. Knopf 2001 212p $14.95
Grades: 6 7 8 9   **Fic**
1. Family life 2. Conduct of life 3. Self-perception 4.
Interpersonal relations
ISBN 9780375811746; 0-375-81174-5; 0-375-82544-
4 pa
LC 2001-29238
In alternating chapters, two teenagers describe how their
feelings about themselves, each other, and their families
have changed over the years. "Grades six to nine." (Bull
Cent Child Books)
"There's lots of laugh-out-loud egg puns and humor in
this novel. There's also, however, a substantial amount of
serious social commentary woven in, as well as an exploration of the importance of perspective in relationships." SLJ

★ **Sammy** Keyes and the hotel thief. Knopf 1998
163p il hardcover o.p. pa $6.50
Grades: 4 5 6 7   **Fic**
1. Mystery fiction 2. Grandmothers -- Fiction 3.
Mystery and detective stories 4. Robbers and outlaws
-- Fiction
ISBN 978-0-679-88839-0; 0-679-89264-8 pa
LC 97-40776
Thirteen-year-old Sammy's penchant for speaking her
mind gets her in trouble when she involves herself in the
investigation of a robbery at the "seedy" hotel across the
street from the seniors' building where she is living with
her grandmother
"This is a breezy novel with vivid characters." Bull Cent
Child Books
Other titles about Sammy Keyes are:
Sammy Keyes and the art of deception (2003)
Sammy Keyes and the cold hard cash (2008)
Sammy Keyes and the curse of Moustache Mary (2000)
Sammy Keyes and the dead giveaway (2005)
Sammy Keyes and the Hollywood mummy (2001)
Sammy Keyes and the night of skulls (2011)
Sammy Keyes and the psycho Kitty Queen (2004)
Sammy Keyes and the runaway elf (1999)
Sammy Keyes and the search for snake eyes (2002)
Sammy Keyes and the Sisters of Mercy (1999)
Sammy Keyes and the skeleton man (1998)
Sammy Keyes and the wedding crasher (2010)
Sammy Keyes and the wild things (2007)

Van Eekhout, Greg
The boy at the end of the world. Bloomsbury Children's Books 2011 212p $16.99

Grades: 4 5 6 7   **Fic**
1. Science fiction 2. Robots -- Fiction
ISBN 978-1-59990-524-2; 1-59990-524-8
LC 2010035741
Born half-grown in a world that is being destroyed, Fisher has instinctive knowledge of many things, including that
he must avoid the robot that knows his name.
"A pleaser for readers who prefer their sf livened up with
unpredictable elements and emotional complexity." Booklist

Van Leeuwen, Jean
★ **Bound** for Oregon; pictures by James Watling. Dial
Bks. for Young Readers 1994 167p il map hardcover o.p.
pa $5.99
Grades: 4 5 6   **Fic**
1. Oregon Trail -- Fiction 2. Overland journeys to the
Pacific -- Fiction
ISBN 0-14-038319-0 pa
LC 93-26709
A fictionalized account of the journey made by nine-
year-old Mary Ellen Todd and her family from their home in
Arkansas westward over the Oregon Trail in 1852
"The appealing narrator, the forthright telling, and the
concrete details of life along the Oregon Trail will draw
readers into the story." Booklist

Cabin on Trouble Creek. Dial Books for Young Read-
ers 2004 119p $16.99; pa $6.99
Grades: 4 5 6 7   **Fic**
1. Brothers 2. Self-reliance 3. Brothers -- Fiction 4.
Frontier and pioneer life -- Ohio 5. Frontier and pioneer
life -- Fiction
ISBN 0-8037-2548-5; 0-14-241164-7 pa
LC 2003-14151
In 1803 in Ohio, two young brothers are left to finish the
log cabin and guard the land while their father goes back
to Pennsylvania to fetch their mother and younger siblings.
"Excellent pacing is what makes this novel work so well.
. . . The suspense builds consistently. The boys' struggle is
portrayed realistically, without sugarcoating nature's harsh-
ness." SLJ

Van Leeuwen, Joke
Eep! Joke van Leeuwen; translated by Bill Nagelkerke.
Gecko Press 2012 149 p. ill.
Grades: 3 4 5   **Fic**
1. Fantasy fiction 2. Birds -- Fiction 3. Girls -- Fiction
4. Friendship -- Juvenile fiction
ISBN 1877579076; 9781877579073
In this children's book by Dutch children's author Joke
van Leeuwen, "avid bird watcher Warren finds a strange
creature under a bush. 'This was a bird in the shape of a little
girl. Or a little girl in the shape of a bird.' . . . He takes the
bird-girl home to his reclusive wife, Tina. . . . When Beedy
flies away one day without a good-bye, Warren and Tina . . .
begin to search for their bird-girl. On their quest, they meet a
host of equally downtrodden individuals." (Kirkus Reviews)
"This original and creative work is compelling from the
opening drawing right to the end of the book." SLJ

Vande Velde, Vivian
8 class pets + one squirrel one dog; illustrated by Steve
Björkman. Holiday House 2011 68p il $15.95

Grades: 2 3 4 **Fic**

1. School stories 2. Animals -- Fiction
ISBN 978-0-8234-2364-4; 0-8234-2364-6

LC 2010048153

A dog chases a squirrel into an elementary school one night, creating monumental chaos.

This is a "fast-paced romp. . . . The action is predictably frenetic, but the changes in voice from chapter to chapter provide a refreshing and humorous diversion from most chapter-book fare. . . . Occasional pen-and-ink spot illustrations add energy to an already high-octane story." Kirkus

Smart dog. Harcourt Brace & Co. 1998 145p hardcover o.p. pa $5.95

Grades: 4 5 6 **Fic**

1. Dogs -- Fiction 2. Human-animal communication -- Fiction
ISBN 0-15-201847-6; 0-15-206172-X pa

LC 98-4771

Fifth grader Amy finds her life growing complicated when she meets and tries to hide an intelligent, talking dog who has escaped from a university lab

"The accessible vocabulary, quick-moving plot, and humor make the novel appealing for reluctant readers as well as a good choice for reading aloud." Horn Book

Three good deeds. Harcourt 2005 147p $16; pa $5.95

Grades: 3 4 5 **Fic**

1. Geese -- Fiction 2. Witches -- Fiction
ISBN 0-15-205382-4; 0-15-205455-3 pa

LC 2004-29578

Caught stealing some goose eggs from a witch, Howard is cursed for his heartlessness and turned into a goose himself, and he can only become human again by performing three good deeds.

"With well-spaced print, plenty of dialogue, a strong dose of humor, and more invention than many books written at this level, this goose tale is a nicely accomplished, entertaining read." Booklist

Wizard at work; a novel in stories. Harcourt 2003 134p $16; pa $5.95

Grades: 3 4 5 6 **Fic**

1. Magic -- Fiction 2. Princesses -- Fiction
ISBN 0-15-204559-7; 0-15-205309-3 pa

LC 2002-68665

A young wizard, who runs a school to teach wizards, looks forward to a quiet summer off but is drawn into adventures with princesses, unicorns, and ghosts instead

"A lot of fairy-tale conventions are turned on their heads. . . . The language sparkles with sunny good humor. . . . Light-hearted and sly." Booklist

Vanderpool, Clare

★ **Moon** over Manifest. Delacorte Press 2010 351p $16.99; lib bdg $19.99

Grades: 5 6 7 8 **Fic**

1. Fathers -- Fiction 2. Great Depression, 1929-1939 -- Fiction
ISBN 978-0-385-73883-5; 0-385-73883-8; 978-0-385-90750-7 lib bdg; 0-385-90750-8 lib bdg

LC 2009-40042

Awarded the Newbery Medal, 2011

Twelve-year-old Abilene Tucker is the daughter of a drifter who, in the summer of 1936, sends her to stay with an old friend in Manifest, Kansas, where he grew up, and where she hopes to find out some things about his past.

"The absolute necessity of story as a way to redemption and healing past wounds is at the heart of this beautiful debut, and readers will cherish every word up to the heartbreaking yet hopeful and deeply gratifying ending." Kirkus

Navigating Early; Clare Vanderpool. Delacorte Press 2013 320 p. $16.99

Grades: 5 6 7 8 **Fic**

1. Adventure fiction -- Juvenile fiction 2. Appalachian Trail -- Juvenile fiction 3. Eccentrics and eccentricities -- Juvenile fiction 4. Schools -- Fiction 5. Boarding schools -- Fiction 6. Adventure and adventurers -- Fiction 7. Eccentrics and eccentricities -- Fiction
ISBN 0385742096; 9780307974129; 9780375990403; 9780385742092

LC 2012014973

In this children's novel, by Clare Vanderpool, "Jack Baker, . . . after his mother's death, . . . [is] placed in a boy's boarding school in Maine. There, Jack encounters Early Auden. . . . Newcomer Jack feels lost yet can't help being drawn to Early. . . . When the boys find themselves unexpectedly alone at school, they embark on a quest on the Appalachian Trail in search of the great black bear. But what they are searching for is sometimes different from what they find." (Publisher's note)

Vaupel, Robin

The **rules** of the universe by Austin W. Hale. Holiday House 2007 265p $16.95

Grades: 4 5 6 7 **Fic**

1. Science fiction 2. Death -- Fiction 3. Grandfathers -- Fiction
ISBN 978-0-8234-1811-4; 0-8234-1811-1

LC 2003-56751

Thirteen-year-old Austin Hale, an aspiring scientist and disciple of his grandfather, a Nobel Prize-winning molecular physicist, finds himself in control of a powerful energy force that can turn back time and turn his orbit upside down

"The captivating blend of scientific research and magic is effectively balanced against the stark realism of a boy facing his first significant losses; the overall tone is one of cautious optimism." Bull Cent Child Books

Vawter, Vince

Paperboy; Vince Vawter. 1st ed. Delacorte Press 2013 240 p. (library) $19.99; (hardcover) $16.99

Grades: 5 6 7 8 **Fic**

1. Stuttering -- Fiction 2. Race relations -- Fiction 3. Newspaper carriers -- Fiction 4. Self-esteem -- Fiction 5. Interpersonal relations -- Fiction 6. Family life -- Tennessee -- Fiction
ISBN 0385742444; 9780307975058; 9780375990588; 9780385742443

LC 2012030546

In this book by Vince Vawter, "[a]fter an overthrown baseball busts his best friend's lip, 11-year-old Victor Vollmer takes over the boy's paper route. This is a particularly daunting task for the able-armed Victor, as he has a prominent stutter that embarrasses him. . . .Through the paper route he meets a number of people, gains a much-needed sense of self and community, and has a life-threatening showdown with a local cart man." (School Library Journal)

"Carefully crafted language, authenticity of setting and quirky characters that ring fully true all combine to make this a worthwhile read. Although Little Man's stutter holds up dialogue, that annoyance also powerfully reflects its stultifying impact on his life. An engaging and heartfelt presentation that never whitewashes the difficult time and situation as Little Man comes of age." Kirkus

Venkatraman, Padma

★ **Island's** end. G.P. Putnam's Sons 2011 240p $16.99

Grades: 5 6 7 8 9   **Fic**

1. Islands -- Fiction 2. Apprentices -- Fiction

ISBN 978-0-399-25099-6; 0-399-25099-9

LC 2010036298

"Uido's clear, intelligent, present-tense voice consistently engrosses as she pushes through doubt and loss to find the right path. The beach, jungle and cliff settings are palpable. . . . There is very little information known about Andaman Islanders, making it hard to gauge the authenticity of this portrayal; the author's note indicates a respectful and diligent approach to her subject. . . . Refreshingly hopeful and beautifully written." Kirkus

Venuti, Kristin Clark

Leaving the Bellweathers. Egmont USA 2009 242p $15.99; lib bdg $18.99

Grades: 4 5 6   **Fic**

1. Authorship -- Fiction 2. Family life -- Fiction 3. Lighthouses -- Fiction 4. Household employees -- Fiction 5. Eccentrics and eccentricities -- Fiction

ISBN 978-1-60684-006-1; 1-60684-006-1; 978-1-60684-050-4 lib bdg; 1-60684-050-9 lib bdg

LC 2009016244

In Eel-Smack-by-the-Bay, put-upon butler Tristan Benway writes a memoir of his years spent working for the chaotic and eccentric Bellweather family in their lighthouse, as he prepares for his long-awaited departure from indentured servitude

"Venuti's entertaining and humorous debut features an eccentric cast, absurdities, and droll details. . . . Readers will find much amusement in the quirky characters and scenarios touched with heart." Booklist

Another title about the Bellweathers is:

The butler gets a break (2010)

The **butler** gets a break; a Bellweather tale. Egmont USA 2010 225p $15.99

Grades: 4 5 6   **Fic**

1. Family life -- Fiction 2. Household employees -- Fiction 3. Eccentrics and eccentricities -- Fiction

ISBN 978-1-60684-087-0; 1-60684-087-8

"Benway the butler, after breaking his leg in an unfortunate accident precipitated by over-the-top ten-year-old triplets Sassy, Brick and Spike, is confined to the hospital, while Spider, 15, tries to round up the violent, endangered squirrels he inadvertently set loose on Eel-by-the-Bay, do-gooder Ninda, 14, works to aid a large group of displaced immigrants and the Bellweather parents relentlessly pursue their own interests (wall painting and inventing)." Kirkus

Verne, Jules

★ **20,000** leagues under the sea; illustrated by the Dillons; translated by Anthony Bonner. Books of Wonder 2000 394p il $21.95

Grades: 5 6 7 8 9 10 11 12 Adult   **Fic**

1. Sea stories 2. Science fiction 3. Submarines (Ships) 4. Submarines -- Fiction

ISBN 0-688-10535-1

LC 00-24336

Original French edition, 1870

Retells the adventures of a French professor and his two companions as they sail above and below the world's oceans as prisoners on the fabulous electric submarine of the deranged Captain Nemo

Vernick, Audrey

★ **Water** balloon. Clarion Books 2011 312p $16.99

Grades: 4 5 6 7   **Fic**

1. Dogs -- Fiction 2. Divorce -- Fiction 3. Friendship -- Fiction 4. Babysitters -- Fiction 5. Father-daughter relationship -- Fiction

ISBN 978-0-547-59554-2; 0-547-59554-9

LC 2011009847

With her best friends pulling away from her, her newly-separated parents deciding she should spend the summer at her father's new home, and a babysitting job she does not want, Marley's life is already as precarious as an overfull water balloon when a cute boy enters the picture.

"The book moves along at a pace that will keep tweens interested, and the dialogue among the characters feels real. Marley's relationships with her friends and family are complex, and even the most reluctant readers will relate to her and the choices that she makes." SLJ

Vernick, Shirley Reva

The **blood** lie; a novel. Cinco Puntos Press 2011 141p $15.95

Grades: 5 6 7 8   **Fic**

1. Love -- Fiction 2. Prejudices -- Fiction 3. Antisemitism -- Fiction 4. Jews -- United States -- Fiction

ISBN 978-1-933693-84-2; 1-933693-84-3

LC 2011011429

"Based on an actual incident in Massena in 1928, the slim novel effectively mines layers of ignorance, fear, intolerance and manipulation, and it connects the incident to Henry Ford's anti-Semitic writing and to the lynching of Jewish businessman Leo Frank in 1915." Kirkus

Vernon, Ursula

★ **Dragonbreath**: attack of the ninja frogs. Dial Books for Young Readers 2010 203p il $16

Grades: 3 4 5   **Fic**

1. Ninja -- Fiction 2. Dragons -- Fiction 3. Reptiles -- Fiction 4. Amphibians -- Fiction 5. Friendship -- Fiction

ISBN 978-0-8037-3365-7; 0-8037-3365-8

LC 2009012273

When Suki the salamander—the new foreign exchange student—is being stalked by ninja frogs, Danny, Wendell the iguana, and Suki travel to Great-grandfather Dragonbreath's home in mythical Japan to find a solution for the problem.

"The spirited illustrations, done in green and black with touches of red, capture the humor of the characters' adventures. This delightful easy chapter book could tempt reluctant readers into turning another page." SLJ

Other titles in this series are:

Dragonbreath (2009)

Dragonbreath: curse of the were-wiener (2010)

Dragonbreath: lair of the bat monster (2011)

Dragonbreath: no such thing as ghosts (2011)

Vigilante, Danette

Trouble with half a moon. G. P. Putnam's Sons 2011 181p $16.99

Grades: 5 6 7 8   **Fic**

1. Faith -- Fiction   2. Friendship -- Fiction   3. Bereavement -- Fiction   4. Child abuse -- Fiction   5. Puerto Ricans -- Fiction   6. City and town life -- Fiction   7. Jamaican Americans -- Fiction

ISBN 978-0-399-25159-7; 0-399-25159-6

LC 2010-07377

Overwhelmed by grief and guilt over her brother's death and its impact on her mother, and at odds with her best friend, thirteen-year-old Dellie reaches out to a neglected boy in her building in the projects and learns from a new neighbor to have faith in herself and others.

"The story is told with considerable appeal and accessibility, and kids won't have to lead the same life as Dellie to recognize her travails." Bull Cent Child Books

Vining, Elizabeth Gray

Adam of the road; illustrated by Robert Lawson. Viking 1942 317p il $19.99; pa $6.99

Grades: 5 6 7 8   **Fic**

1. Minstrels -- Fiction 2. Middle Ages -- Fiction

ISBN 0-670-10435-3; 0-14-240659-7 pa

Awarded the Newbery Medal, 1943

Tale of a minstrel and his son Adam, who wandered through southeastern England in the thirteenth century. Adam's adventures in search of his lost dog and his beloved father led him from St. Alban's Abbey to London, and thence to Winchester, back to London, and then to Oxford where the three were at last reunited

Viorst, Judith

Lulu and the brontosaurus; illustrated by Lane Smith. Atheneum Books for Young Readers 2010 113p il $15.99

Grades: 2 3 4 5   **Fic**

1. Birthdays -- Fiction 2. Dinosaurs -- Fiction

ISBN 978-1-4169-9961-4; 1-4169-9961-2

Lulu's parents refuse to give in when she demands a brontosaurus for her birthday and so she sets out to find her own, but while the brontosaurus she finally meets approves of pets, he does not intend to be Lulu's.

"Plenty of child-friendly humor. . . . This inventive, lighthearted fantasy should be a solid hit with young readers looking for a lively first chapter book." SLJ

Lulu walks the dogs; Judith Viorst; illustrated by Lane Smith. Atheneum Books for Young Readers 2012 144 p.

Grades: 1 2 3 4 5   **Fic**

1. Dogs -- Juvenile fiction 2. Dog walking -- Juvenile fiction

ISBN 1442435798; 9781442435797

LC 2011023841

This children's book by Judith Viorst tells the story of "Lulu, [who] has decided it's time to buckle down and earn

some cash. . . . After some failed attempts at lucrative gigs (baking cookies, spying, reading to old people), dog walking seems like a sensible choice. But Brutus, Pookie, and Cordelia are not interested in making the job easy, and the infuriatingly helpful neighborhood goody-goody, Fleischman, has Lulu at the end of her rope." (Publisher's note)

Voake, Steve

Daisy Dawson is on her way! illustrated by Jessica Meserve. Candlewick Press 2008 98p il $14.99; pa $5.99

Grades: 2 3 4   **Fic**

1. Dogs -- Fiction 2. Animals -- Fiction

ISBN 978-0-7636-3740-8; 0-7636-3740-8; 978-0-7636-4294-5 pa; 0-7636-4294-0 pa

LC 2007-23150

One day when Daisy is late for school, an encounter with a butterfly leaves her suddenly able to communicate with animals, and when Boom, a stray dog, is caught by the pound, she enlists the help of a host of other animals to rescue him.

"Sprightly illustrations in a variety of shapes appear throughout. First in a series, this charmer, long on whimsy and adventure, is sure to appeal to newly independent and reluctant readers." SLJ

Other titles about Daisy Dawson are:

Daisy Dawson and the secret pond (2009)

Daisy Dawson and the big freeze (2010)

Daisy Dawson at the beach (2011)

Daisy Dawson on the farm (2012)

Voelkel, J&P

The river of no return; J&P Voelkel. Egmont USA 2012 348 p. ill., maps (hardcover) $16.99; (ebook) $16.99

Grades: 5 6 7 8   **Fic**

1. Mayas -- Fiction 2. Fantasy fiction -- Juvenile fiction 3. Supernatural -- Fiction 4. Adventure and adventurers -- Fiction 5. Indians of Central America -- Fiction

ISBN 1606840738; 9781606840733; 9781606842706

LC 2012007093

This is the third book in the Jaguar Stones series from J. and P. Voelkel. Here, "after spending the previous two books evading the disgusting and power-hungry machinations of the Death Lords of the Mayan Underworld, Max and Lola are back together again, trying to stop the same bad guys from taking over the world yet again." (School Library Journal)

Voelkel, J.

Middleworld; [by] J & P Voelkel [i.e., Jon Voelkel, Pamela Craik Voelkel] Smith and Kraus Publishers 2007 397p il (The Jaguar stones) $17.95; pa $8.99

Grades: 4 5 6 7   **Fic**

1. Adventure fiction 2. Mayas -- Fiction

ISBN 978-1-57525-561-3; 1-57525-561-8; 978-1-60684-071-9 pa; 1-60684-071-1 pa

"Suspense and intrigue, human sacrifice, smuggling, and secret doors and escape routes through pyramids ensure that the novel, the first in a projected trilogy, is likely to win legions of fans." SLJ

The end of the world club; [by] J&P Voelkel. Egmont USA 2011 384p (The Jaguar stones) $16.99

Grades: 4 5 6 7   **Fic**

1. Adventure fiction 2. Mayas -- Fiction 3. Supernatural

-- Fiction
ISBN 978-1-60684-072-6; 1-60684-072-X
LC 2010036641

With the end of the Mayan calendar fast approaching, fourteen-year-old Max Murphy and his friend Lola, the Maya girl who saved his life in the perilous jungle, race against time to outwit the twelve villainous Lords of Death, following the trail of the conquistadors into a forgotten land steeped in legend and superstition.

"The authors use Maya mythology and terms and add interesting facts about Spain and Spanish culture. This is a fast-paced book, and the action starts right away." SLJ

Voigt, Cynthia

Dicey's song. Atheneum Pubs. 1982 196p $17.95; pa $6.99

Grades: 5 6 7 8   **Fic**

1. Siblings -- Fiction 2. Grandmothers -- Fiction
ISBN 0-689-30944-9; 0-689-86362-4 pa
LC 82-3882

Awarded the Newbery Medal, 1983

"The vividness of Dicey is striking; Voigt has plumbed and probed her character inside out to fashion a memorable protagonist." Booklist

Mister Max; the book of lost things. by Cynthia Voigt; illustrated by Iacopo Bruno. Alfred A. Knopf 2013 384 p. (hardcover) $16.99; (library) $19.99

Grades: 5 6 7 8   **Fic**

1. Abandoned children -- Juvenile fiction 2. Historical fiction -- Juvenile fiction 3. Self-reliance -- Fiction 4. Problem solving -- Fiction
ISBN 0307976815; 9780307976819; 9780307976826; 9780375971235
LC 2012033823

In this book, Max "is left at the dock when he misses a boat to India, where his [actor] parents supposedly have been invited by a maharajah to start a theater. . . . Although his wise yet bossy librarian grandmother lives next door, 12-year-old Max wants to earn his keep and be independent. Cleverly donning the costumes and different roles performed by his missing parents, Max discovers an aptitude for finding lost things. . . . He is a 'solutioneer,' solving people's problems." (Kirkus Reviews)

★ **Young** Fredle. Alfred A. Knopf 2011 227p il $16.99; lib bdg $19.99

Grades: 3 4 5 6   **Fic**

1. Adventure fiction 2. Cats -- Fiction 3. Dogs -- Fiction 4. Mice -- Fiction 5. Freedom -- Fiction
ISBN 978-0-375-86457-5; 0-375-86457-1; 978-0-375-96457-2 lib bdg; 0-375-96457-6 lib bdg
LC 2010-11430

"Readers will identify with the universal conflict at the heart of Fredle's journey—even as he longs for home, he enjoys the newfound freedom and experiences that contrast with the restrictive regulations of his clan. Yates's expressive cartoon spot art counters the book's darker, sadder moments with cheeriness." Publ Wkly

Wagner, Hilary

Nightshade City; [illustrations by Omar Rayyan] Holiday House 2010 262p il $17.95

Grades: 5 6 7 8   **Fic**

1. Fantasy fiction 2. Rats -- Fiction
ISBN 978-0-8234-2285-2; 0-8234-2285-2
LC 2010-02474

Eleven years after the cruel Killdeer took over the Catacombs far beneath the human's Trillium City, Juniper Belancourt, assisted by Vincent and Victor Nightshade, leads a maverick band of rats to escape and establish their own city.

"The themes of love, loss and loyalty resonate through the novel, and the moments of darkness and violence are ultimately overpowered by hope and redemption. A good story well-told." Kirkus

The **white** assassin. Holiday House 2011 il (The Nightshade chronicles)

Grades: 5 6 7 8   **Fic**

1. Fantasy fiction 2. Rats -- Fiction
ISBN 978-0-8234-2333-0
LC 2011009579

Snakes, bats, and rats join forces to save Nightshade from Billycan and his horde of brutal swamp rats, aided by an antidote to the drug that made Billycan the way he is, but the revelation of secrets proves an even more powerful weapon in the fight for peace.

Waite, Michael P.

The **witches** of Dredmoore Hollow; by Riford McKenzie; with illustrations by Peter Ferguson. Marshall Cavendish Children 2008 264p il $16.99

Grades: 4 5 6 7   **Fic**

1. Aunts -- Fiction 2. Witches -- Fiction
ISBN 978-0-7614-5458-8; 0-7614-5458-6
LC 2007-29781

Strange things begin happening at Elijah's New England home just before his twelfth birthday in 1927, especially after two aunts he had never met whisk him away to Moaning Marsh, where he realizes that they are witches who need something from him in order to remove a curse.

"The book has continuous action and piles of demonic atmosphere." SLJ

Walden, Mark

H.I.V.E; The Higher Institute of Villainous Education. Simon & Schuster Books for Young Readers 2007 309p $15.99; pa $6.99

Grades: 5 6 7 8   **Fic**

1. Criminals -- Fiction
ISBN 1-4169-3571-1; 978-1-4169-3571-1; 978-1-4169-3572-8 pa; 1-4169-3572-X pa
LC 2007-16205

"H.I.V.E. is operated on a volcanic island in a distant ocean by G.L.O.V.E., a shadowy organization of worldwide wickedness. And, as 13-year-old master of mischief Otto Malpense soon discovers, here the slickest of young tricksters, thieves, and hackers have been brought against their will to be trained as the next generation of supervillains. . . . [This] novel is a real page-turner; those who love superhero stories will eat it up." SLJ

Another title about H.I.V.E. is:

H.I.V.E.: The Overlord protocol (2008)
H.I.V.E.: Escape velocity (2011)
H.I.V.E.: Dreadnought (2011)

Walker, Kate

I hate books! [by] Kate Walker; illustrated by David Cox. Cricket Books 2007 78p il $16.95

Grades: 2 3 4 5   **Fic**

1. School stories 2. Brothers -- Fiction 3. Books and reading -- Fiction

ISBN 978-0-8126-2745-9; 0-8126-2745-8

LC 2006-36492

Although he is a great storyteller and good at art, Hamish cannot read, even with remedial classes, but his brother Nathan finally comes up with a way to teach him

"This is a warm and fast-paced story. . . . Witty black-and-white line drawings enhance the narrative." SLJ

Wallace, Bill

★ **Skinny**-dipping at Monster Lake. Simon & Schuster Bks. for Young Readers 2003 212p hardcover o.p. pa $5.99

Grades: 4 5 6 7   **Fic**

ISBN 0-689-85150-2; 0-689-85151-0 pa

LC 2002-152820

When twelve-year-old Kent helps his father in a daring underwater rescue, he wins the respect he has always craved.

"This old-fashioned adventure has wide appeal, and the youngsters' games and camaraderie will hook even reluctant readers." SLJ

The **legend** of thunderfoot. Simon & Schuster Books for Young Readers 2006 150p $15.95; pa $5.99

Grades: 3 4 5 6   **Fic**

1. Roadrunners -- Fiction

ISBN 978-1-4169-0691-9; 1-4169-0691-6; 978-1-4169-0692-6 pa; 1-4169-0692-4 pa

"After a young roadrunner is bitten by a rattlesnake, his feet swell to an enormous size. At first this seems to be a handicap. . . . After taking the advice of a wise old tortoise, though, the roadrunner, now called Thunderfoot, undergoes an exercise program. . . . The newly pumped-up Thunderfoot . . . winds up his days as a legendary figure in the animal world. Wallace creates a lively fantasy, with a cliff-hanging closing for nearly every chapter." Booklist

Wallace, Rich

Sports camp. Alfred A. Knopf 2010 149p $15.99; lib bdg $18.99

Grades: 4 5 6   **Fic**

1. Camps -- Fiction 2. Sports -- Fiction

ISBN 978-0-375-84059-3; 0-375-84059-1; 978-0-375-94059-0 lib bdg; 0-375-94059-6 lib bdg

LC 2009-04278

Eleven-year-old Riley Liston tries to fit in at Camp Olympia, a summer sports camp where he is one of the youngest boys.

The **ball** hogs; illustrated by Jimmy Holder. Alfred A. Knopf 2010 119p il (Kickers) $12.99

Grades: 2 3 4   **Fic**

1. Soccer -- Fiction

ISBN 978-0-375-85754-6; 0-375-85754-0

Nine-year-old Ben, a natural athlete and member of the Bobcats coed soccer team, wants to overcome his inexperience and prove himself on the field, but his obnoxious teammate, Mark, keeps hogging the ball.

"A good sports story for younger readers, this beginning chapter book balances bits of information about playing the game with realistic scenes on the field, at home, and at school. . . . Lively black-and-white drawings illustrate the story." Booklist

Other titles in this series are:

Fake out (2010)

Benched (2010)

Game-day jitters (2011)

Wallace, Sandra Neil

Little Joe; illustrated by Mark Elliott. Alfred A. Knopf 2010 192p il $15.99; lib bdg $18.99

Grades: 3 4 5 6   **Fic**

1. Bulls -- Fiction 2. Farm life -- Fiction 3. Family life -- Fiction 4. Grandfathers -- Fiction 5. Father-son relationship -- Fiction

ISBN 978-0-375-86097-3; 0-375-86097-5; 978-0-375-96097-0 lib bdg; 0-375-96097-X lib bdg

"This is a sweet book about the relationships among three generations of farmers—Eli Stegner, his father, and his grandfather. It is also about Eli's connection to the first calf he gets to call his own. Little Joe is destined to be a winner at the county fair cattle show, but that blue ribbon will pretty much insure that he goes to the highest bidder and then to the butcher. . . . This thoughtful, tender book will appeal to those readers who are familiar with the Stegners' world, and many more will be able to identify with the highs and lows of familial love." SLJ

Walliams, David

★ **Mr.** Stink; illustrated by Quentin Blake. Razorbill 2010 265p il pa $9.99

Grades: 4 5 6   **Fic**

1. School stories 2. Family life -- Fiction 3. Homeless persons -- Fiction

ISBN 978-1-59514-332-7 pa; 1-59514-332-7 pa

Walliams "has a gift for crafting memorable scenes and, in the person of Mr. Stink, has created a delightfully offbeat character. . . . Readers of all ages will be thrilled with the in-a-word perfect illustrations of the great Quentin Blake." Booklist

★ The **boy** in the dress; illustrated by Quentin Blake. Razorbill 2009 231p il $15.99

Grades: 4 5 6 7   **Fic**

1. School stories 2. Soccer -- Fiction 3. Transvestites -- Fiction

ISBN 978-1-59514-299-3; 1-59514-299-1

"Dennis is a bit surprised—but not terribly nonplussed—to discover that he enjoys wearing dresses. The 12-year-old does, however, realize this is not the kind of revelation he wants to share with his truck-driving dad, his older brother, or his mates on the school football team, where he is the star player. . . . Walliams . . . has written a witty, high-spirited, and, well, sensible story about cross-dressing and other real-life issues." Booklist

Walsh, Pat

★ The **Crowfield** curse. Chicken House 2010 326p il

Grades: 5 6 7 8   **Fic**

1. Magic -- Fiction 2. Orphans -- Fiction 3. Monasteries

-- Fiction
ISBN 0-545-22922-7; 978-0-545-22922-7
LC 2009-51483

In 1347, when fourteen-year-old orphan William Paynel, an impoverished servant at Crowfield Abbey, goes into the forest to gather wood and finds a magical creature caught in a trap, he discovers he has the ability to see fays and becomes embroiled in a strange mystery involving Old Magic, a bitter feud, and ancient secrets.

"This suspenseful and spooky story will thrill readers. . . . With fascinating attention to detail and an edgy battle between evil and good, Walsh sweeps readers almost effortlessly into another time and place." SLJ

The **Crowfield** demon; Pat Walsh. Scholastic 2012 360 p.

Grades: 5 6 7 8   **Fic**

1. Fantasy fiction 2. Adventure fiction 3. Children's stories 4. Demonology -- Fiction 5. Magic -- Fiction 6. Orphans -- Fiction 7. Identity -- Fiction 8. Monasteries -- Fiction 9. Blessing and cursing -- Fiction
ISBN 054531769X; 9780545317696; 9780545373500
LC 2011029246

This juvenile historical fantasy novel by Pat Walsh is the sequel to his earlier story "The Crowfield Curse." "In 'The Crowfield Curse,' young monks' apprentice Will learned he was gifted with the Sight: able to see beyond this mortal coil into the spirit realms of Old Magic. Protected by the warrior fay Shadlok -- and befriended by the wry, wary hobgoblin called Brother Walter -- the boy is just coming into his strange powers. But now, from its very foundations, Crowfield Abbey has begun to crumble. As Will slaves to salvage the chapel, he discovers something truly terrifying. A heathen creature from a pagan past is creeping up through the rubble -- avowed to unleash havoc on holy ground!" (Publisher's note)

Walter, Mildred Pitts

★ **Justin** and the best biscuits in the world; with illustrations by Catherine Stock. Lothrop, Lee & Shepard Bks. 1986 122p il $16; pa $7.99

Grades: 3 4 5 6   **Fic**

1. Sex role -- Fiction 2. Family life -- Fiction 3. Grandfathers -- Fiction 4. African Americans -- Fiction
ISBN 0-688-06645-3; 0-06-195891-3 pa
LC 86-7148

Coretta Scott King Award for text

"The strong, well-developed characters and humorous situations in this warm family story will appeal to intermediate readers; the large print will draw slow or reluctant readers." SLJ

Walters, Eric

Catboy. Orca Book Publishers 2011 229p pa $9.95

Grades: 4 5 6 7   **Fic**

1. Boys -- Fiction 2. Cats -- Fiction
ISBN 978-1-55469-953-7 pa; 1-55469-953-3 pa

The wild cat colony Taylor has been caring for is at risk of being destroyed, and in order to save it, Taylor will need the help of all his friends.

"Walters' story . . . moves fast and is plenty appealing. . . . Solid writing, strong kid characters, caring adults, and cute animals could make this a popular choice." Booklist

The **money** pit mystery. Fitzhenry & Whiteside 2011 pa $9.95

Grades: 4 5 6 7   **Fic**

1. Mystery fiction 2. Islands -- Fiction 3. Family life -- Fiction 4. Buried treasure -- Fiction
ISBN 978-1-55455-123-1; 1-55455-123-4

"Sam's grandfather and mother had a fight years ago, and now Sam, his sister, and their mother are visiting him for the first time in years. When they arrive on tiny Oak Island, they are shocked to discover how rundown the man's once-immaculate house has become. To make matters worse, he isn't even there. When Sam, Beth, and their friend, Buzz, do some exploring, they are surprised by some security guards at the town's 'money pit.' Some folks believe that Captain Kidd buried treasure here. . . . This is a well-thought-out mystery with lots of suspense and a fully realized picture of a struggling family." SLJ

Ward, David

Between two ends. Amulet Books 2011 288p $16.95

Grades: 4 5 6   **Fic**

1. Fantasy fiction 2. Adventure fiction 3. Pirates -- Fiction 4. Books and reading -- Fiction
ISBN 978-0-8109-9714-1; 0-8109-9714-2
LC 2010-23696

Trying to help his father deal with his long-standing depression, Yeats and his parents visit his grandmother's old and eerie house, where he discovers a pair of pirate bookends that unlock a thirty-year-old secret that Yeats must try to resolve by entering the exotic world of The Arabian Nights.

"Quickly sketching credible characters in both worlds, Ward plunges Yeats into a series of adventures. . . . Unexpected moments of humor lighten the gloomy prospect of failure and offer hope that the ending will resolve the family crisis so vividly portrayed in the opening chapters. A satisfying chapter-book fantasy." Booklist

Warner, Penny

The **secret** of the skeleton key. Egmont USA 2011 209p (The Code Busters Club) $15.99; e-book $15.99

Grades: 3 4 5 6   **Fic**

1. Mystery fiction 2. Ciphers -- Fiction 3. Cousins -- Fiction
ISBN 978-1-60684-162-4; 1-60684-162-9; 978-1-6068-4281-2 e-book
LC 2011003240

"Cody and Quinn notice their neighbor Mr. Skelton signaling from his window; later his house burns and cousins Jasper and Jezabel appear, searching for Mr. Skelton's will. By solving Mr. Skelton's coded clues, the club members manage to unearth the authentic document before his cousins can force him to sign a new one. . . . This well-crafted mystery reads smoothly; characters are well developed, clues . . . skillfully dropped, and the solution feels plausible." Booklist

Warner, Sally

Best friend Emma; [by] Sally Warner; illustrated by Jamie Harper. Viking 2007 102p il $14.99

Grades: 2 3 4   **Fic**

1. Friendship -- Fiction
ISBN 978-0-670-06173-0
LC 2006027629

When a new girl joins her third-grade class just before Thanksgiving, Emma thinks only about gaining her friendship before the popular Cynthia can, and hurts her best friend Annie Pat's feelings in the process.

"Harper's whimsical drawings add humor and warmth to the story." SLJ

EllRay Jakes is not a chicken! illustrated by Jamie Harper. Viking Children's Books 2011 108p il $14.99
Grades: 1 2 3   **Fic**
1. School stories 2. Bullies -- Fiction 3. Family life -- Fiction
ISBN 978-0-670-06243-0; 0-670-06243-X
                                                        LC 2010-25106
Eight-year-old EllRay's father has promised a family trip to Disneyland if EllRay can stay out of trouble for a week, but not defending himself against Jared, the class bully, proves to be a real challenge.

"Warner's clever plotting brings an unexpected and rewarding ending. EllRay's ingenuous narration and the well-observed classroom dynamics are the main draw, and Harper's cartoons, incorporated throughout, further enliven the story." Publ Wkly
Another title about EllRay is:
EllRay Jakes is a rock star! (2011)

It's only temporary; written and illustrated by Sally Warner. Viking Childrens Books 2008 182p il $15.99
Grades: 4 5 6 7   **Fic**
1. Bullies -- Fiction 2. Siblings -- Fiction 3. Grandmothers -- Fiction 4. Brain -- Wounds and injuries -- Fiction
ISBN 978-0-670-06111-2; 0-670-06111-5
                                                        LC 2007-038220
When Skye's older brother comes home after a devastating accident, she moves from Albuquerque, New Mexico, to California to live with her grandmother and attend middle school, where she somewhat reluctantly makes new friends, learns to stand up for herself and those she cares about, and begins to craft a new relationship with her changed brother.

"Warner deftly handles Skye's anger toward her brain-injured brother, also infusing her with a convincingly developed sense of compassion. Witty line art decorates some pages." Horn Book Guide

Only Emma; illustrated by Jamie Harper. Viking 2004 115p il $14.99; pa $5.99
Grades: 2 3 4   **Fic**
ISBN 0-670-05979-X; 0-14-240711-9 pa
                                                        LC 2004-12478
Third-grader Emma's peaceful life as an only child is disrupted when she has to temporarily share her tidy bedroom with four-year-old Anthony Scarpetto.

"The black-and-white illustrations are charming, and thumbnail sidebars present fun scientific facts about animals mentioned in the story. . . . Emma is a likable character whose feelings and behaviors are common to many children." SLJ
Other titles about Emma are:
Not-so-weird Emma (2005)
Super Emma (2006)
Best friend Emma (2007)
Excellent Emma (2009)

Happily ever Emma (2010)

This isn't about the money. Viking 2002 209p $15.99
Grades: 5 6 7 8   **Fic**
1. Death -- Fiction 2. Orphans -- Fiction
ISBN 0-670-03574-2
                                                        LC 2001-56797
Twelve-year-old Janey tries to adjust in the aftermath of an automobile accident that kills her parents, severely injures her face, and forces her and her younger sister to move from Arizona to California to live with their grandfather and great-aunt

"Warner's dialog and characterization are rich and real." Booklist

Waters, Zack C.
Blood moon rider; [by] Zack C. Waters. Pineapple Press 2006 126p $13.95
Grades: 5 6 7 8   **Fic**
1. Ranch life -- Fiction 2. Grandfathers -- Fiction 3. World War, 1939-1945 -- Fiction
ISBN 978-1-56164-350-9; 1-56164-350-5
                                                        LC 2005030749
After his father's death in World War II, fourteen-year-old Harley Wallace tries to join the Marines but is, instead, sent to live with his grandfather in Peru Landing, Florida, where he soon joins a covert effort to stop Nazis from destroying a secret airbase on Tampa Bay

This is "an adventure filled with unexpected kindnesses and the irrepressibility of family ties, as well as a brush with espionage and a couple of suspenseful shoot'em-up scenes. A colorful cast of characters and a nod to teenage romance help make this a good choice for middle school boys." SLJ

Watkins, Yoko Kawashima
My brother, my sister, and I. Bradbury Press 1994 275p hardcover o.p. pa $5.99
Grades: 6 7 8 9   **Fic**
1. World War, 1939-1945 -- Fiction
ISBN 0-02-792526-9; 0-689-80656-6 pa
                                                        LC 93-23535
"Watkins's first-person narrative is beautifully direct and emotionally honest." Publ Wkly

★ **So** far from the bamboo grove. Lothrop, Lee & Shepard Bks. 1986 183p map hardcover o.p. pa $5.99
Grades: 6 7 8 9   **Fic**
1. World War, 1939-1945 -- Fiction
ISBN 0-688-13115-8 pa
                                                        LC 85-15939
A fictionalized autobiography in which eight-year-old Yoko escapes from Korea to Japan with her mother and sister at the end of World War II

"An admirably told and absorbing novel." Horn Book

Watson, Geoff
Edison's gold. Egmont USA 2010 312p $15.99; lib bdg $18.99
Grades: 4 5 6 7   **Fic**
1. Inventors 2. Mystery fiction 3. Adventure fiction 4. Electrical engineers 5. Inventors -- Fiction 6. Secret

societies -- Fiction

ISBN 978-1-60684-094-8; 1-60684-094-0; 978-1-60684-095-5 lib bdg; 1-60684-095-9 lib bdg

LC 2010-11312

Tom Edison and his friends become embroiled in a mystery involving his 'double-great' grandfather's inventions, a secret society, and a vendetta being carried out by a descendant of inventor Nikola Tesla.

This "is a fast-paced adventure filled mystery that middle schoolers will like." SLJ

Watson, Jude

Beyond the grave. Scholastic 2009 190p (The 39 clues) $12.99

Grades: 4 5 6 7 **Fic**

1. Ciphers -- Fiction 2. Orphans -- Fiction 3. Siblings -- Fiction

ISBN 978-0-545-06044-8; 0-545-06044-3

A clue sends Amy and Dan jetting off to find out just what's behind the fierce rivalry between the Tomas and Ekaterina branches of the Cahill family. Was a Clue stolen from the Tomas branch? Where is it now? And most important, can Amy and Dan get their hands on it before their rivals do?

"Like the previous books, historical information is woven into the fast-paced adventure." SLJ

In too deep. Scholastic 2009 206p (The 39 clues) $12.99

Grades: 4 5 6 7 **Fic**

1. Adventure fiction 2. Ciphers -- Fiction 3. Orphans -- Fiction 4. Siblings -- Fiction

ISBN 978-0-545-09064-3; 0-545-09064-4

"Amy and Dan fly to Australia. Attemping to trace their late parents' journey eight years earlier, they link Amelia Earhart's last flight to their own family quest. . . . The spy-versus-spy mentality will keep readers guessing. . . . The series' fans will devour the breathless action scenes in this fast-paced adventure." Booklist

Watson, Renee

What Momma left me. Bloomsbury 2010 224p $15.99

Grades: 5 6 7 8 **Fic**

1. Orphans -- Fiction 2. Bereavement -- Fiction 3. Family life -- Fiction 4. Grandparents -- Fiction 5. Christian life -- Fiction 6. African Americans -- Fiction

ISBN 978-1-59990-446-7; 1-59990-446-2

LC 2009-18263

After the death of their mother, thirteen-year-old Serenity Evans and her younger brother go to live with their grandparents, who try to keep them safe from bad influences and help them come to terms with what has happened to their family.

"Serenity's struggles and insights, as she wrestles with her parents' legacy and an uncertain future, are inspiring, authentic, and told in a straighforward yet poetic style. The first-person narration is consistent, and the mystery of the painful circumstances of her mother's death—as well as additional tragedies—propels the story." Publ Wkly

Watson, Stephanie Elaine

Elvis & Olive; by Stephanie Watson. Scholastic Press 2008 230p $15.99

Grades: 3 4 5 **Fic**

1. Friendship -- Fiction

ISBN 978-0-545-03183-7; 0-545-03183-4

LC 2007023924

In spite of their differences, Natalie Wallis and Annie Beckett become friends and decide to spend their summer spying on their neighbors

This is an "accomplished first novel." Publ Wkly

Another title about Elvis & Olive is:

Elvis & Olive: super detectives (2010)

Watts, Frances

Extraordinary Ernie and Marvelous Maud; illustrated by Judy Watson. Eerdmans Books for Young Readers 2010 66p il (Ernie & Maude) pa $5.99

Grades: 2 3 4 **Fic**

1. Sheep -- Fiction 2. Superheroes -- Fiction

ISBN 978-0-8028-5363-9; 0-8028-5363-3

Ten-year-old Ernie is thrilled when he wins a contest to be trained as a superhero, and although he is disappointed that his sidekick is a talking sheep, just looking at his costume makes him feel heroic

"The action is tame . . . but the slapstick premise and banter between superhero and sidekick save the day. The brevity, spry pace, and humorous line art make Watts's . . . story a good choice for kids." Publ Wkly

Other titles about Ernie and Maud are:

The middle sheep (2010)

The greatest sheep in history (2011)

Weatherford, Carole Boston

Dear Mr. Rosenwald; by Carole Boston Weatherford; illustrated by Gregory Christie. Scholastic Press 2006 un il $16.99

Grades: 2 3 4 **Fic**

1. School stories 2. Philanthropists 3. Retail executives 4. African Americans -- Fiction 5. Segregation in education -- Fiction

ISBN 0-439-49522-9

LC 2005-27971

Young Ovella rejoices as her community comes together to raise money and build a much-needed school in the 1920s, with matching funds from Julius Rosenwald, the president of Sears, Roebuck, and Company

"Christie's gouache and colored-pencil illustrations have the variegated look and stylized layout of collage art—a good complement to the child's rough-around-the-edges narration. An afterword explains Rosenwald's impact on thousands of poor black communities. An uplifting and inspiring story." SLJ

Webb, Philip

Six days. Chicken House 2011 336p $17.99

Grades: 5 6 7 8 **Fic**

1. Science fiction 2. Siblings -- Fiction 3. Space and time -- Fiction

ISBN 978-0-545-31767-2; 0-545-31767-3

LC 2010054233

Cass and her brother Wilbur scavenge in the ruins of a future London seeking an artifact for their Russian masters, but the search takes on a new urgency after the arrival of Erin and Peyto, strangers from afar who claim to hold the key to locating the mysterious object.

Webb "has created a complex and intriguing dystopia filled with devastation, clever devices . . . and lots of local color. . . . The novel's rapid pacing will hook readers and keep them turning pages." Booklist

Weber, Elka

★ The **Yankee** at the seder; illustrated by Adam Gustavson. Tricycle Press 2009 un il $16.99
Grades: 2 3 4 5   **Fic**
1. Jews -- Fiction 2. Passover -- Fiction 3. Soldiers -- Fiction
ISBN 978-1-58246-256-1; 1-58246-256-9
LC 2008-11229

As a Confederate family prepares for Passover the day after the Civil War has ended, a Yankee arrives on their Virginia doorstep and is invited to share their meal, to the dismay of ten-year-old Jacob. Includes historical notes about Corporal Myer Levy, on whom the story is based, and his prominent Philadelphia family.

"With a cinematic flair and rich, realist oils, Gustavson . . . depicts how a détente between North and South is forged—albeit tenuously—by the timeless values of faith, civility and chicken soup. Basing her writing on a historical incident, Weber makes an impressive debut. . . . Sensitively written and beautifully illustrated." Publ Wkly

Wedekind, Annie

Wild Blue; the story of a mustang Appaloosa. Feiwel and Friends 2009 124p (Breyer horse collection) $16.99; pa $5.99
Grades: 3 4 5   **Fic**
1. Horses -- Fiction
ISBN 978-0-312-38424-1; 0-312-38424-6; 978-0-312-59917-1 pa; 0-312-59917-X pa
LC 2008-34742

After being captured by men, Blue the Appaloosa grabs a chance at freedom and tries to find her way home.

"A modern-day adventure that reads like an exuberant nature journal, this novel will grip readers from start to finish." SLJ

A **horse** of her own; by Annie Wedekind. Feiwel and Friends 2008 275p $16.95; pa $7.99
Grades: 5 6 7 8   **Fic**
1. Camps -- Fiction 2. Horses -- Fiction 3. Horsemanship -- Fiction
ISBN 978-0-312-36927-9; 0-312-36927-1; 978-0-312-58146-6 pa; 0-312-58146-7 pa
LC 2007032769

At summer camp Jane feels like an outsider among the cliquish rich girls who board their horses at Sunny Acres farm, and when the horse she has been riding is sold to another camper, she feels even worse until her teacher asks her to help train a beautiful but skittish new horse, and the experience brings out the best in her.

"Tenacious and thoughtful, Jane is an appealing protagonist who gradually recognizes that being accepted no longer matters to her. The plot . . . has enough twists, including a hint of romance, to sustain readers' interest." SLJ

Weeks, Sarah

As simple as it seems. Laura Geringer Books 2010 181p $15.99; lib bdg $16.89

Grades: 4 5 6   **Fic**
1. Ghost stories 2. Adoption -- Fiction 3. Friendship -- Fiction
ISBN 978-0-06-084663-3; 0-06-084663-1; 978-0-06-084664-0 lib bdg; 0-06-084664-X lib bdg

Eleven-year-old Verbena Polter gets through a difficult summer of turbulent emotions and the revelation of a disturbing family secret with an odd new friend who believes she is the ghost of a girl who drowned many years before.

"Weeks's characters are well rounded and her story line is engaging." Horn Book Guide

Guy wire. HarperCollins Pubs. 2002 138p $16.99
Grades: 4 5 6   **Fic**
1. Friendship 2. Best friends 3. Mothers and sons 4. Friendship -- Fiction 5. Mother-son relationship -- Fiction
ISBN 0-06-029492-2; 0-06-029493-0 lib bdg
LC 2001-40997

When his best friend is seriously injured in a bike accident, Guy recounts their first meeting and how the friendship grew despite the weird antics of Guy's eccentric mother

"There are touching moments in this lightweight and funny novel." SLJ

Jumping the scratch; a novel. Laura Geringer Books 2006 167p il $15.99; pa $5.99
Grades: 5 6 7 8   **Fic**
1. Aunts -- Fiction 2. Memory -- Fiction 3. Child sexual abuse -- Fiction
ISBN 978-0-06-054109-5; 0-06-054109-1; 978-0-06-054110-1 pa; 0-06-054111-3 pa
LC 2005-17776

After moving with his mother to a trailer park to care for an injured aunt, eleven-year-old Jamie Reardon struggles to cope with a deeply buried secret

"Weeks alludes to sexual abuse, but with a broad brush and no graphic details. . . . Weeks perfectly captures not only the guilt, shame, and pain of the abused boy but also the tenor of a fifth-grade classroom from the point of view of a new student who is friendless, targeted, and belittled by an insensitive teacher. Touches of humor ameliorate the pain and poignancy." SLJ

Oggie Cooder. Levithan/Scholastic Press 2008 172p il $16.99; pa $5.99
Grades: 3 4 5   **Fic**
1. School stories 2. Friendship -- Fiction 3. Eccentrics and eccentricities -- Fiction
ISBN 978-0-439-92791-8; 0-439-92791-9; 978-0-439-92794-9 pa; 0-439-92794-3 pa
LC 2007-18645

Quirky fourth-grader Oggie Cooder goes from being shunned to everyone's best friend when his uncanny ability to chew slices of cheese into the shapes of states wins him a slot on a popular television talent show, but he soon learns the perils of being a celebrity—and having a neighbor girl as his manager.

The author "delivers a funny, fast-paced story, with the likable Oggie at its center." Booklist

Oggie Cooder, party animal; illustrations by Doug Holgate. Scholastic Press 2009 165p il $16.99

Grades: 3 4 5   **Fic**

1. School stories 2. Parties -- Fiction 3. Birthdays -- Fiction 4. Friendship -- Fiction 5. Eccentrics and eccentricities -- Fiction

ISBN 978-0-439-92792-5; 0-439-92792-7

LC 2009024909

Neither a long list of rules, nor the inability to find the perfect gift—Cheddar Jam—nor being locked in a bathroom with a juggling bear will keep quirky fourth-grader Oggie Cooder from attending neighbor Donnica Perfecto's birthday pool party.

"A fast-paced chapter book with cheerful cartoon illustrations provided by Holgate, this can easily be read on its own and will certainly win Oggie new fans." Kirkus

★ **Pie**. Scholastic Press 2011 183p $16.99

Grades: 4 5 6 7   **Fic**

1. Cats -- Fiction 2. Pies -- Fiction 3. Aunts -- Fiction

ISBN 978-0-545-27011-3; 0-545-27011-1

In the 1950s in the small town of Ipswitch, PA, Polly Portman dies and leaves the recipe for her prize-winning piecrust to her cat Lardo, in the care of her niece Alice, but then the cat is kidnapped and the bakery is trashed.

"Weeks deftly leavens moments of hilarity with the process of grieving in this sweet coming-of-age story in which Alice learns from Aunt Polly to follow her heart and to open it as well. Readers will close the book with a satisfied sigh and may seek out an adult to help them bake a pie. Recipes included." SLJ

Regular Guy. HarperCollins Pubs. 1999 120p hardcover o.p. pa $4.99

Grades: 4 5 6   **Fic**

1. Identity -- Fiction 2. Parent and child -- Fiction 3. Parent-child relationship -- Fiction

ISBN 0-06-028367-X; 0-06-440782-9 pa

LC 99-12118

Because he is so different from his eccentric parents, twelve-year-old Guy is convinced he has been switched at birth with a classmate whose parents seem more normal

"Weeks treats the situation with wild exaggeration, a farcical plot, and just a touch of tenderness. . . . Many middlegraders will enjoy the gross humor (lots of snot and clatter and fishy smells) as much as the view of embarrassing adults who love you even though they drive you nuts." Booklist

Other titles about Guy are:

Guy time (2000)

My Guy (2001)

Guy wire (2002)

★ **So** B. it; a novel. Laura Geringer Books 2004 245p $15.99; pa $6.99

Grades: 5 6 7 8   **Fic**

1. Mental illness -- Fiction 2. Mentally handicapped -- Fiction

ISBN 0-06-623622-3; 0-06-441047-1 pa

LC 2003-15643

After spending her life with her mentally retarded mother and agoraphobic neighbor, twelve-year-old Heidi sets out from Reno, Nevada, to New York to find out who she is.

"This is lovely writing—real, touching, and pared cleanly down to the essentials." Booklist

Weissman, Elissa Brent

Nerd camp. Atheneum Books for Young Readers 2011 261p $15.99

Grades: 4 5 6   **Fic**

1. Camps -- Fiction

ISBN 1-4424-1703-X; 978-1-4424-1703-8

LC 2010-42913

For ten-year-old Gabe, the Summer Center for Gifted Enrichment is all that he dreamed it would be, but he must work hard to write about the fun in letters to Zach, his cool future stepbrother, without revealing that it is a camp for "nerds."

This "novel features an appealing 10-year-old. . . . Weissman depicts a camp whose academic classes sound almost as fun as kayaking and color war." Booklist

The **short** seller; Elissa Brent Weissman. 1st ed. Atheneum Books for Young Readers 2013 256 p. (hardcover) $15.99

Grades: 3 4 5 6   **Fic**

1. Girls -- Fiction 2. Stocks -- Fiction 3. Friendship -- Fiction 4. Best friends -- Fiction 5. Mononucleosis -- Fiction 6. Electronic trading of securities -- Fiction

ISBN 1442452552; 9781442452558

LC 2012018632

In this middle-grade novel, by Elissa Brent Weissman, "a twelve-year-old takes on the stock market. . . . It all starts when seventh grader Lindy Sachs is granted $100 and access to her father's online trading account. . . . With trading talent and access to her parents' savings, the opportunity to make some real dough is too tempting to pass up. In fact, given how well Lindy's stocks are doing, it would be a disservice to not invest it all. . . . Right?" (Publisher's note)

The **trouble** with Mark Hopper. Dutton Children's Books 2009 227p $16.99

Grades: 5 6 7 8   **Fic**

1. School stories 2. Contests -- Fiction 3. Identity (Psychology) -- Fiction

ISBN 978-0-525-42067-5; 0-525-42067-3

LC 2008-34211

When two eleven-year-olds with the same name, similar looks, and very different personalities go to the same Maryland middle school, confusion and bad feelings ensue, but things improve after a teacher insists that they become study partners.

"Realistic school interactions give Weissman's novel a lot of kid appeal with substance." Horn Book Guide

Welch, Sheila Kelly

Waiting to forget. Namelos 2011 170p $18.95

Grades: 5 6 7 8   **Fic**

1. Siblings -- Fiction 2. Foster home care -- Fiction

ISBN 978-1-60898-114-4; 1-60898-114-2

T.J. and his sister, Angela, learn how to move forward and be happy while in foster care.

"T.J.'s authentic voice and the multilayered presentation of his memories, shifting between the waiting room and his past, make for a poignant, realistic tale of child-survivors." Kirkus

Wells, Ken

Rascal; a dog and his boy. illustrations by Christian Slade. Alfred A. Knopf 2010 201p il $16.99; lib bdg $19.99

Grades: 4 5 6 7   **Fic**

1. Dogs -- Fiction

ISBN 978-0-375-86652-4; 0-375-86652-3; 978-0-375-96652-1 lib bdg; 0-375-96652-8 lib bdg

LC 2009-37606

Rascal may be the happiest beagle ever to live. He used to live on Voclain's Farm, but now he lives with his very own boy, Meely. Together they explore the Louisiana bayou. But when Meely gets stuck on a rotting bridge deep in the bayou, it's up to Rascal to save his boy from danger.

"This is a cracking good animal story of classic pedigree. . . . Characterizations of both humans and animals are sharp and distinct. . . . [The] narration sings with the same lively Cajun-flavored spice as the dialogue, and it's an easy dialect to get the hang of." Bull Cent Child Books

Wells, Kitty

Paw power; illustrated by Joanna Harrison. David Fickling Books 2011 199p il (Pocket cats) $13.99; lib bdg $16.99

Grades: 2 3 4   **Fic**

1. School stories 2. Cats -- Fiction 3. Magic -- Fiction 4. Bullies -- Fiction

ISBN 978-0-385-75201-5; 0-385-75201-6; 978-0-385-75202-2 lib bdg; 0-385-75202-4 lib bdg

LC 2010011892

"Nine-year-old Maddy Lloyd is desperate for a kitten, but younger brother Jack is allergic, so she settles for three small ceramic cats purchased at a flea market. Later, Maddy is surprised when one of the figurines, Greykin, comes to life, explaining that he has been sent to help her do a job—eventually revealed to be dealing with school-bully Sherry. . . . Newly independent readers will identify with Maddy's concerns about friendship and self-assertiveness (as well as her desire for a cat), and the inclusion of large type and frequent illustrations . . . will support those readers through the book's lengthy chapters." Booklist

Shadow magic; [illustrations by Joanna Harrison] David Fickling Books 2011 201p il (Pocket cats) $13.99

Grades: 2 3 4   **Fic**

1. School stories 2. Cats -- Fiction 3. Magic -- Fiction 4. Moving -- Fiction 5. Cousins -- Fiction

ISBN 978-0-385-75200-8; 0-385-75200-8

LC 2010029508

A small ceramic cat comes to life to help Maddy's cousin Chloe, who is staying with her and is having trouble adjusting to a new school.

Wells, Rosemary

★ Ivy takes care; Rosemary Wells, illustrated by Jim LaMarche. Candlewick Press 2013 208 p. $15.99

Grades: 2 3 4   **Fic**

1. Pets -- Juvenile fiction 2. Historical fiction -- Juvenile fiction

ISBN 0763653527; 9780763653521

LC 2012942383

This book is "set in 1949 on a ranch near Reno, Nev., where almost-sixth-grader Ivy's parents work. Ivy's deep compassion for animals spurs her to offer herself as care-

taker for pets and farm animals while their owners are away; her experiences inspire her aspirations to become a veterinarian." (Publishers Weekly)

Lincoln and his boys; illustrated by P.J. Lynch. Candlewick Press 2009 96p il $16.99

Grades: 3 4 5 6   **Fic**

1. Lawyers 2. Presidents 3. State legislators 4. Members of Congress 5. Presidents -- Fiction 6. Children of presidents 7. Father-son relationship -- Fiction

ISBN 978-0-7636-3723-1; 0-7636-3723-8

LC 2008-21418

"Inspired by a 200-word essay by Willie Lincoln, Wells offers a fictional account of Lincoln and his boys. Written first from Willie's point of view, then Tad's after Willie dies, it's a touching account of Lincoln as a patient and loving father. . . . Lynch captures the people and the warmth of their interactions in carefully researched oil paintings that reflect his mastery with light, perspective, and portraiture." SLJ

My Havana; [by] Rosemary Wells with Secundino Fernandez; illustrated by Peter Ferguson. Candlewick Press 2010 65p il $17.99

Grades: 4 5 6 7   **Fic**

1. Architects 2. Dictators -- Fiction 3. Family life -- Fiction

ISBN 978-0-7636-4305-8; 0-7636-4305-X

LC 2009-12053

Relates events in the childhood of architect Secundino Fernandez, who left his beloved Havana, Cuba, with his parents, first to spend a year in Spain, and later to move to New York City.

"Wells has chosen anecdotes wisely, and Ferguson's illustrations are atmospheric, capturing Dino's childlike enthusiasm and longing." Kirkus

★ On the Blue Comet; illustrated by Bagram Ibatoulline. Candlewick Press 2010 329p il $16.99

Grades: 5 6 7 8   **Fic**

1. Adventure fiction 2. Railroads -- Fiction 3. Space and time -- Fiction

ISBN 978-0-7636-3722-4; 0-7636-3722-X

LC 2009051358

During the Great Depression, Oscar's dad must sell their home and head west in search of work. Oscar meets a mysterious drifter and witnesses a crime so stunning it catapults Oscar on a train journey from coast to coast, from one decade to another.

"Ibatoulline's full-color, atmospheric Norman Rockwell-like vignettes enhance the nostalgic feel of this warm, cleverly crafted adventure." Kirkus

Welsh, M. L.

Heart of stone; a Verity Gallant tale. M.L. Welsh. David Fickling Books 2012 409 p. (hard cover) $16.99

Grades: 5 6 7 8   **Fic**

1. Love stories 2. Occult fiction 3. Witches -- Fiction 4. Fantasy 5. Sailing -- Fiction 6. Betrayal -- Fiction 7. Friendship -- Fiction 8. Family life -- Fiction 9. Books and reading -- Fiction

ISBN 0385752431; 9780375899164; 9780385752428; 9780385752435

LC 2011023878

This book is a "companion novel to 'Mistress Of The Storm' . . . tell[ing] the story of heroine Verity Gallant's fight against an evil force determined to put an end to all happily-ever-after stories. . . . The evil force appears to be trying to destroy Verity's cliffside hometown of Wellow, which is rapidly being eroded by white sand gathering as if it had a single motive—to erase all the 'Original Stories' with happy endings." (Voice of Youth Advocates)

★ **Mistress** of the Storm; a Verity Gallant tale. David Fickling Books 2011 318p $16.99; lib bdg $19.99
Grades: 5 6 7 8 Fic
1. Fantasy fiction 2. Sailing -- Fiction 3. Witches -- Fiction 4. Friendship -- Fiction 5. Family life -- Fiction 6. Books and reading -- Fiction
ISBN 978-0-385-75244-2; 0-385-75244-X; 978-0-385-75245-9 lib bdg; 0-385-75245-8 lib bdg
LC 2010018721
First published in the United Kingdom
After a stranger gives an ancient book to unpopular, twelve-year-old Verity Gallant, she and her new-found friends, Henry and Martha, uncover secrets stirring in the harbor town of Wellow and use them to face a powerful, vengeful witch.
"Welsh's prose is lovely, her characters are well-drawn, and the atmosphere of the town is palpable. In creating a place in the world where a story read aloud can become true, Welsh offers a benediction of sorts to readers, that 'every child who is alone or out of place will find the friends they need, and the love they deserve.'" Publ Wkly

West, Jacqueline
Spellbound; illustrated by Poly Bernatene. Dial Books for Young Readers 2011 il (The books of elsewhere) $16.99
Grades: 4 5 6 Fic
1. Cats -- Fiction 2. Magic -- Fiction 3. Space and time -- Fiction 4. Books and reading -- Fiction
ISBN 978-0-8037-3441-8; 0-8037-3441-7
LC 2010041865
Eleven-year-old Olive finds herself drawn to the grimoire of the witches who built her house and tries to use its spells to uncover the house's magic and control the cats themselves, but the book is more wicked than it seems.
"This is a suspenseful read that leaves plenty of room for the next title in the series. While it stands on its own, it will be enjoyed most by readers familiar with the first book. Occasional full-page, black-and-white drawings are appropriately dark and mysterious." SLJ

The **shadows**; illustrated by Poly Bernatene. Dial Books for Young Readers 2010 241p il (The books of elsewhere) $16.99
Grades: 4 5 6 Fic
1. Cats -- Fiction 2. Magic -- Fiction 3. Painting -- Fiction 4. Space and time -- Fiction
ISBN 978-0-8037-3440-1; 0-8037-3440-9
LC 2009-13128
When eleven-year-old Olive and her distracted parents move into an old Victorian mansion, Olive finds herself ensnared in a dark plan involving some mysterious paintings, a trapped and angry nine-year-old boy, and three talking cats.

"The expressive black-and-white illustrations contribute to the overall spooky mood of the story. The plot moves quickly as Olive pieces together clues." SLJ

Westera, Marleen
★ **Sheep** and Goat; by Marleen Westera; illustrations by Sylvia van Ommen; translation by Nancy Forest-Flier. Front Street 2006 99p il $16.95
Grades: 1 2 3 Fic
1. Goats -- Fiction 2. Sheep -- Fiction 3. Friendship -- Fiction
ISBN 978-1-932425-81-9
LC 2006000793
Follows the daily activities of Sheep and Goat who, despite often being grouchy or grumpy, are always there for one another when it counts
"Told with a subtle and consistent undercurrent of wit, these 18 short stories are pleasant bedtime reading. . . . The occasional pen-and-ink drawings are pitch perfect and more than a little extraordinary. They convey the low-key humor exquisitely." SLJ

Weston, Carol
The **diary** of Melanie Martin; or, How I survived Matt the Brat, Michelangelo, and the Leaning Tower of Pizza. Knopf 2000 144p hardcover o.p. pa $5.50
Grades: 3 4 5 6 Fic
1. Family life -- Fiction 2. Voyages and travels -- Fiction
ISBN 0-375-80509-5; 0-440-41667-1 pa
LC 99-53384
Fourth-grader Melanie Martin writes in her diary, describing her family's trip to Italy and all that she learned
"Sections of the book are laugh-out-loud funny and Weston's descriptions will have readers wanting to see the country for themselves. An enjoyable read." SLJ
Other titles about Melanie Martin are:
Melanie in Manhattan (2005)
Melanie Martin goes Dutch (2002)
With love from Spain, Melanie Martin (2005)

Weston, Robert Paul
Prince Puggly of Spud and the Kingdom of Spiff; Robert Paul Weston. Penguin Group USA 2013 256 p. $15.99
Grades: 2 3 4 5 Fic
1. Fashion -- Juvenille fiction 2. Humorous fiction -- Juvenile fiction
ISBN 1595145672; 9781595145673
In this "middle-grade rhyming novel . . . [by Robert Paul Weston] Prince Puggly of the . . . Kingdom of Spud . . . receives an invitation to a lavish ball in the far more chic Kingdom of Spiff. Puggly is sure that the Spiffs will take one look at him and laugh him out of their kingdom. . . . But then Puggly meets Francesca, the bookish Princess of Spiff, and together the two set out to teach Francesca's Spiffian countrymen an absurd lesson in style." (Publisher's note)
"Plot, theme, and writing style make this a terrific read-aloud." SLJ

★ **Zorgamazoo**. Razorbill 2008 281p il $15.99
Grades: 4 5 6 7 Fic
1. Novels in verse 2. Adventure fiction 3. Imagination

-- Fiction
ISBN 978-1-59514-199-6; 1-59514-199-5

LC 2007-51682

Imaginative and adventurous Katrina eludes her mania-cal guardian to help Morty, a member of a vanishing breed of zorgles, with his quest to uncover the fate of the fabled zorgles of Zorgmazoo as well as of other creatures that seem to have disappeared from the earth.

"This book is a natural descendant to the works of Dr. Seuss and Roald Dahl." Booklist

Wharton, Thomas

The **shadow** of Malabron. Candlewick Press 2009 382p (The perilous realm) $16.99

Grades: 5 6 7 8   **Fic**

1. Fantasy fiction
ISBN 978-0-7636-3911-2; 0-7636-3911-7

LC 2009-7768

When Will, a rebellious teen, stumbles from the present into the realm where stories come from, he learns he has a mission concerning the evil Malabron and, aided by some of the story folk, he faces a host of perils while seeking the gateless gate that will take him home.

"Lush descriptive prose, cleverly sustained suspense, a sprinkling of humor and an exciting climax will keep readers riveted to the story, while those who know their folklore will be delighted by Wharton's twisting of the tropes and tales of myth and legend." Kirkus

Whelan, Gloria

★ **Homeless** bird. HarperCollins Pubs. 2000 216p hardcover o.p. pa $5.99

Grades: 6 7 8 9 10   **Fic**

1. Courage 2. Women -- India -- Fiction
ISBN 0-06-028454-4; 0-06-440819-1 pa

LC 99-33241

When thirteen-year-old Koly enters into an ill-fated ar-ranged marriage, she must either suffer a destiny dictated by India's tradition or find the courage to oppose it.

"This beautifully told, inspiring story takes readers on a fascinating journey through modern India and the universal intricacies of a young woman's heart." Booklist

★ **Listening** for lions. HarperCollins 2005 194p $15.99; lib bdg $16.89; pa $5.99

Grades: 5 6 7 8   **Fic**

1. Orphans -- Fiction 2. Physicians -- Fiction
ISBN 0-06-058174-3; 0-06-058175-1 lib bdg; 0-06-058176-X pa

Left an orphan after the influenza epidemic in British East Africa in 1918, thirteen-year-old Rachel is tricked into assuming a deceased neighbor's identity to travel to Eng-land, where her only dream is to return to Africa and rebuild her parents' mission hospital.

"In a straightforward, sympathetic voice, Rachel tells an involving, episodic story." Booklist

★ The **locked** garden. HarperCollins Children's Books 2009 168p $15.99

Grades: 4 5 6 7   **Fic**

1. Family life -- Fiction 2. Mental illness -- Fiction 3. Psychiatric hospitals -- Fiction
ISBN 978-0-06-079094-3; 0-06-079094-6

LC 2008-24637

After their mother dies of typhoid, Verna and her young-er sister Carlie move with their father, a psychiatrist, and stern Aunt Maude to an asylum for the mentally ill in early-twentieth-century Michigan, where new ideas in the treat-ment of mental illness are being proposed, but old prejudices still hold sway.

"Whelan establishes a strong sense of time, unusual set-ting and characters. . . . This convincing melodrama portrays an atypical attitude toward treating mental illness." Kirkus

White, E. B.

★ **Charlotte's** web; pictures by Garth Williams. Harp-er & Row 1952 184p il $16.95; lib bdg $16.89; pa $5.95

Grades: 3 4 5 6   **Fic**

1. Pigs -- Fiction 2. Spiders -- Fiction
ISBN 0-06-026385-7; 0-06-026386-5 lib bdg; 0-06-440055-7 pa

A Newbery Medal honor book, 1953

The story of a little girl who could talk to animals, but especially the story of the pig, Wilbur, and his friendship with Charlotte, the spider, who could not only talk but write as well

"Illustrated with amusing sketches . . . [this] story is a fa-ble for adults as well as children and can be recommended to older children and parents as an amusing story and a gentle essay on friendship." Libr J

★ **Stuart** Little; pictures by Garth Williams. Harper & Row 1945 131p il $16.95; lib bdg $16.89; pa $5.95

Grades: 3 4 5 6   **Fic**

1. Mice -- Fiction
ISBN 0-06-026395-4; 0-06-026396-2 lib bdg; 0-06-440056-5 pa

This is "the story of a 'Tom Thumb'-like child born to a New York couple who is to all intents and purposes a mouse. . . . The first part of the book explores, with dead-pan humour, the advantages and disadvantages of having a mouse in one's family circle. Then Stuart sets out on a quest in search of his inamorata, a bird named Margalo, and the story ends in mid-air. The book is outstandingly funny and sometimes touching." Oxford Companion to Child Lit

★ The **trumpet** of the swan; illustrated by Fred Mar-cellino. HarperCollins Pubs. 2000 251p il $16.95; pa $5.95

Grades: 3 4 5 6   **Fic**

1. Swans -- Fiction
ISBN 0-06-028935-X; 0-06-440867-1 pa

LC 99-44250

A newly illustrated edition of the title first published 1970

Louis, a voiceless Trumpeter swan, finds himself far from his wilderness home when he determines to communi-cate by learning to play a stolen trumpet

The author "deftly blends true birdlore with fanciful ad-ventures in a witty, captivating fantasy." Booklist

White, Ruth

★ **Belle** Prater's boy. Farrar, Straus & Giroux 1996 196p $17

Grades: 5 6 7 8   **Fic**

1. Cousins -- Fiction
ISBN 0-374-30668-0

LC 94-43625

A Newbery Medal honor book, 1997

"Gypsy and her cousin Woodrow become close friends after Woodrow's mother disappears. Both sixth-graders feel deserted by their parents—Gypsy discovers that her father committed suicide—and need to define themselves apart from these tragedies. White's prose evokes the coal mining region of Virginia and the emotional quality of her characters' transformations." Horn Book Guide

Another title about Belle Prater is:
The search for Belle Prater (2005)

★ **Little** Audrey. Farrar, Straus & Giroux 2008 145p $16

Grades: 5 6 7 8 **Fic**
1. Death -- Fiction 2. Coal miners -- Fiction 3. Country life -- Fiction
ISBN 978-0-374-34580-8; 0-374-34580-5
LC 2007-29310

In 1948, eleven-year-old Audrey lives with her father, mother, and three younger sisters in Jewell Valley, a coal mining camp in Southwest Virginia, where her mother still mourns the death of a baby, her father goes on drinking binges on paydays, and Audrey tries to recover from the scarlet fever that has left her skinny and needing to wear glasses.

"The setting is perfectly portrayed and the characterizations ring true." Voice Youth Advocates

★ **Way** Down Deep. Farrar, Straus and Giroux 2007 197p $16

Grades: 5 6 7 8 **Fic**
1. Orphans -- Fiction
ISBN 0-374-38251-4; 978-0-374-38251-3
LC 2006-46324

In the West Virginia town of Way Down Deep in the 1950s, a foundling called Ruby June is happily living with Miss Arbutus at the local boarding house when suddenly, after the arrival of a family of outsiders, the mystery of Ruby's past begins to unravel.

This is "a story as tender as a breeze and as sharp as a tack. . . . At the heart of the story are profound questions that readers will enjoy puzzling out." Booklist

You'll like it here (everybody does) Delacorte Press 2011 272p $16.99; lib bdg $19.99

Grades: 4 5 6 7 **Fic**
1. Science fiction 2. Family life -- Fiction 3. Interplanetary voyages -- Fiction 4. Extraterrestrial beings -- Fiction
ISBN 978-0-385-73998-6; 0-385-73998-2; 978-0-385-90813-9 lib bdg; 0-385-90813-X lib bdg
LC 2010-32153

Although Meggie Blue seems to be an average sixth-grader she is abnormally frightened when residents of her small, North Carolina town become fixated on aliens, and soon she and her family are forced to flee, making it clear that all is not as it seems.

White's "considerable writing skills elevate a story with many familiar elements, including the importance of individuality, the pitfalls of conformity, and the tyranny of a dictatorship. Kids will like this, but it's also a fun jumping off point for serious discussion." Booklist

White, T. H.

★ The **sword** in the stone; with illustrations by Dennis Nolan. Putnam 1993 256p il $24.99

Grades: 4 5 6 7 **Fic**
1. Kings 2. Merlin (Legendary character) -- Fiction
ISBN 0-399-22502-1
LC 92-24808

A newly illustrated edition of the title first published 1938 in the United Kingdom; first United States edition 1939 by G.P Putnam's Sons

"In White's classic story about the boyhood of King Arthur, Wart—unaware of his true identity—is tutored by Merlyn, who occasionally transform the young boy into various animals as part of his schooling. Contemporary children will still enjoy the text, which is both fantastical and down-to-earth." Horn Book Guide

Whittemore, Jo

Odd girl in. Simon & Schuster 2011 234p pa $6.99

Grades: 4 5 6 **Fic**
1. School stories 2. Siblings -- Fiction
ISBN 978-1-4424-1284-2; 1-4424-1284-4

"Spunky 12-year-old Alex doesn't really want friends or a social life. . . . She hates girly giggling parties and doesn't see any other girls in her middle school that she'd want to have as a friend, so she just concentrates on following in the footsteps of her prankster older twin brothers. . . . Alex's absent mother provides an element of drama in this otherwise witty, laugh-out-loud romp. Whittemore handles not only the comedy but deftly portrays Alex's and her brothers' advancement into a more mature state of mind. It should keep middle-schoolers laughing from start to finish." Kirkus

Whittenberg, Allison

Hollywood & Maine. Delacorte Press 2009 166p $15.99; lib bdg $18.99

Grades: 5 6 7 8 **Fic**
1. School stories 2. Family life -- Fiction 3. African Americans -- Fiction
ISBN 978-0-385-73671-8; 0-385-73671-1; 978-0-385-90623-4 lib bdg; 0-385-90623-4 lib bdg
LC 2008-35679

In 1976 Pennsylvania, middle-schooler Charmaine Upshaw contemplates a career as a model or actress while coping with boyfriend problems and the return of her uncle, a fugitive who cost her family $1,000 in bail money a year earlier.

"The family's personal trials, triumphs, individual growth, and many personalities are the book's focus and its heart. Zinger dialogue and clever narration promise laughs and an enjoyable read." SLJ

Sweet Thang. Delacorte Press 2006 149p $15.95

Grades: 5 6 7 8 **Fic**
1. School stories 2. Family life -- Fiction 3. African Americans -- Fiction
ISBN 0-385-73292-9
LC 2005-03809

In 1975, life is not fair for fourteen-year-old Charmaine Upshaw, who shares a room with her brother, tries to impress a handsome classmate, and acts as caretaker for a rambunctious six-year-old cousin who has taken over the family.

"Whittenberg has created a refreshing cast and a good read." SLJ

Another title about the Upshaw family is:
Hollywood & Maine (2009)

Wildavsky, Rachel

The **secret** of Rover. Amulet Books 2011 351p $16.95

Grades: 5 6 7 8 **Fic**

1. Twins -- Fiction 2. Uncles -- Fiction 3. Siblings -- Fiction 4. Inventions -- Fiction 5. Kidnapping -- Fiction 6. Voyages and travels -- Fiction

ISBN 0-8109-9710-X; 978-0-8109-9710-3

LC 2010-23450

Twelve-year-old twins Katie and David Bowen evade foreign militants and make their way from Washington, D.C. to their uncle's Vermont home, hoping he can help rescue their parents, who were kidnapped because of their secret invention, Rover.

"Kids making the transition from series mysteries to more sophisticated thrillers will do well by this suspenseful and age-appropriate drama." Bull Cent Child Books

Wilder, Laura Ingalls, 1867-1957

★ **Little** house in the big woods; illustrated by Garth Williams. newly illustrated, uniform ed; Harper & Row 1953 237p il (Little house) $16.95; lib bdg $16.89; pa $6.99

Grades: 4 5 6 **Fic**

1. Family life -- Fiction 2. Frontier and pioneer life -- Fiction

ISBN 0-06-026430-6; 0-06-026431-4 lib bdg; 0-06-440001-8 pa

First published 1932

A year in the life of two young girls growing up on the Wisconsin frontier, as they help their mother with the daily chores, enjoy their father's stories and singing, and share special occasions when they get together with relatives or neighbors.

Other titles in the Little House series are:

Farmer boy (1933)

Little house on the prairie (1935)

On the banks of Plum Creek (1937)

By the shores of Silver Lake (1939)

The long winter (1940)

Little town on the prairie (1941)

These happy golden years (1943)

The first four years (1971)

Wiles, Deborah

★ The **Aurora** County All-Stars. Harcourt 2007 242p il $16; pa $5.99

Grades: 4 5 6 **Fic**

1. Death -- Fiction 2. Baseball -- Fiction 3. Race relations -- Fiction

ISBN 978-0-15-206068-8; 0-15-206068-5; 978-0-15-206626-0 pa; 0-15-206626-8 pa

LC 2006-102551

In a small Mississippi town, after the death of the old man to whom twelve-year-old star pitcher House Jackson has been secretly reading for a year, House uncovers secrets about the man and the history of baseball in Aurora County.

"Quotations from Walt Whitman's poetry, baseball players and Aurora County news dispatches pepper the story and add color. . . . A home run for Wiles." Publ Wkly

★ **Countdown**. Scholastic 2010 377p il (The sixties trilogy) $17.99

Grades: 4 5 6 7 **Fic**

1. Cold war -- Fiction 2. Family life -- Fiction 3.

Cuban Missile Crisis, 1962 -- Fiction

ISBN 978-0-545-10605-4; 0-545-10605-2

It's 1962, and it seems everyone is living in fear. Twelve-year-old Franny Chapman lives with her family in Washington, DC, during the days surrounding the Cuban Missile Crisis. Amidst the pervasive threat of nuclear war, Franny must face the tension between herself and her younger brother, figure out where she fits in with her family, and look beyond outward appearances.

"Wiles skillfully keeps many balls in the air, giving readers a story that appeals across the decades as well as offering enticing paths into the history." Booklist

Love, Ruby Lavender. Harcourt 2001 188p il $16; pa $5.95

Grades: 4 5 6 **Fic**

1. Death 2. Chickens 3. Grandparents 4. Self-reliance 5. Grandparents -- Fiction

ISBN 0-15-202314-3; 0-15-205478-2 pa

LC 00-11159

When her quirky grandmother goes to Hawaii for the summer, nine-year-old Ruby learns to survive on her own in Mississippi by writing letters, befriending chickens as well as the new girl in town, and finally coping with her grandfather's death

"The engaging narrative . . . is witty and fast paced and the quirky, diverse cast of human and poultry characters is colorful and spirited, if not totally realistic." SLJ

Williams, Alex

The **talent** thief; an extraordinary tale of an ordinary boy. Philomel Books 2010 300p $16.99

Grades: 5 6 7 8 **Fic**

1. Adventure fiction 2. Orphans -- Fiction

ISBN 978-0-399-25278-5; 0-399-25278-9

Orphaned Cressida, a magnificent singer, and her twelve-year-old brother Adam attend the by-invitation-only Festival of Youthful Genius, where they join forces with a former race car driver to try to stop a bizarre creature from stealing the talents of the young prodigies.

"This is a story that fantasy and adventure fans will enjoy, and the well-paced action will propel them to the end." SLJ

Williams, Laura E.

Slant; [by] Laura E. Williams. Milkweed Editions 2008 149p $16.95; pa $6.95

Grades: 5 6 7 8 9 **Fic**

1. Mothers -- Fiction 2. Adoption -- Fiction 3. Friendship -- Fiction 4. Prejudices -- Fiction 5. Plastic surgery -- Fiction 6. Korean Americans -- Fiction

ISBN 978-1-57131-681-3; 1-57131-681-7; 978-1-57131-682-0 pa; 1-57131-682-5 pa

LC 2008007093

Thirteen-year-old Lauren, a Korean-American adoptee, is tired of being called "slant" and "gook," and longs to have plastic surgery on her eyes, but when her father finds out about her wish—and a long-kept secret about her mother's death is revealed—Lauren starts to question some of her own assumptions

"The characters are exceptionally well drawn, and the friendship between Julie and Lauren is not only believable, featuring humor, conflict, and true wit, but also captures both girls' gains in maturity." SLJ

Williams, Maiya

The **Fizzy** Whiz kid. Amulet Books 2010 273p $16.95

Grades: 5 6 7 8   **Fic**

1. Moving -- Fiction 2. Advertising -- Fiction

ISBN 978-0-8109-8347-2; 0-8109-8347-8

Moving to Hollywood with his academic parents, eleven-year-old Mitch feels like an outsider in his school where everyone has connections to the powerful and famous in the entertainment industry, until he is cast in a soda commercial that launches a popular catchphrase.

"Williams' breezy tale is as addictive and bubbly as a Fizzy Whiz itself, and her experience in the entertainment industry packs real value into her descriptions of auditions, movie sets, and agent negotiations. . . . Mitchell's realization that he is a product being assembled is both goofy and poignant." Booklist

Williams, Marcia

Archie's war; my scrapbook of the First World War, 1914-1918. Candlewick Press 2007 45p il $17.99

Grades: 3 4 5 6   **Fic**

1. World War, 1914-1918 -- Fiction

ISBN 978-0-7636-3532-9; 0-7636-3532-4

LC 2007-23012

When Archie is given a scrapbook for his tenth birthday in 1914, he chronicles the next four years of his life using documents, artifacts, and comic strips

"The large-format pages, jam-packed with tiny colored-pencil drawings with extensive captions, detailed sidebars, and pasted-in letters and postcards, flesh out the story and characters. . . . This imaginative presentation of historical fiction puts them in context and provides a highly visual experience that readers will pore over again and again." SLJ

My secret war diary, by Flossie Albright; my history of the Second World War, 1939-1945. Candlewick Press 2008 141p il lib bdg $21.99

Grades: 3 4 5 6   **Fic**

1. Diaries -- Fiction 2. World War, 1939-1945 -- Fiction

ISBN 978-0-7636-4111-5 lib bdg; 0-7636-4111-1 lib bdg

Marcia Williams uses her own childhood momentos to create a diary of a nine-year-old girl in Britain during World War II

"Children will quickly come to enjoy Flossie's energetic delivery and endless doodling. They will love poring over the extras-asides, sidebars, and letters found under flaps and in envelopes, that Williams has compiled to give the book the feel that one has stumbled into a real girl's private keepsake. . . . Children who enjoy history will be fascinated by Flossie and will undoubtedly be inspired to learn more about the events she describes." SLJ

Williams, Mary

Brothers in hope; the story of the Lost Boys of Sudan. illustrated by R. Gregory Christie. Lee & Low Books 2005 un il $17.95

Grades: 3 4 5   **Fic**

1. War stories 2. Refugees -- Fiction

ISBN 1-58430-232-1

LC 2004-20965

Eight-year-old Garang, orphaned by a civil war in Sudan, finds the inner strength to help lead other boys as they trek hundreds of miles seeking safety in Ethiopia, then Kenya, and finally in the United States.

"Christie's distinctive acrylic illustrations, done in broad strokes of predominantly green, yellow, and burnt orange, are arresting in their combination of realism and the abstract. . . . This important profile in courage is one that belongs in most collections." SLJ

Williams, Michael

★ **Now** is the time for running. Little, Brown 2011 233p $17.99

Grades: 6 7 8 9 10   **Fic**

1. Soccer -- Fiction 2. Brothers -- Fiction 3. Refugees -- Fiction 4. Homeless persons -- Fiction 5. Mentally handicapped -- Fiction

ISBN 978-0-316-07790-3; 0-316-07790-9

LC 2010043460

"There is plenty of material to captivate readers: fast-paced soccer matches every bit as tough as the players; the determination of Deo and his fellow refugees to survive unthinkably harsh conditions; and raw depictions of violence. . . . But it's the tender relationship between Deo and Innocent, along with some heartbreaking twists of fate, that will endure in readers' minds." Publ Wkly

Williams, Tad

The **dragons** of Ordinary Farm; by Tad Williams and Deborah Beale; pictures by Greg Swearingen. Harper 2009 412p il $16.99

Grades: 4 5 6 7   **Fic**

1. Farms -- Fiction 2. Uncles -- Fiction 3. Siblings -- Fiction 4. Supernatural -- Fiction 5. Mythical animals -- Fiction

ISBN 978-0-06-154345-6; 0-06-154345-4

LC 2008035298

When their great-uncle Gideon invites Tyler and Lucinda to his farm for the summer, they discover his animals are extremely unusual.

"Williams and Beale have created a gripping fantasy with realistic but appealing characters as well as scientific magic that explains the appearance of legendary creatures." SLJ

Williams-Garcia, Rita

★ **One** crazy summer. Amistad 2010 218p $15.99; lib bdg $16.89

Grades: 4 5 6 7   **Fic**

1. Poets -- Fiction 2. Mothers -- Fiction 3. Sisters -- Fiction 4. African Americans -- Civil rights -- Fiction

ISBN 978-0-06-076088-5; 0-06-076088-5; 978-0-06-076089-2 lib bdg; 0-06-076089-3 lib bdg

LC 2009-09293

A Newbery Medal honor book, 2011

In the summer of 1968, after travelling from Brooklyn to Oakland, California, to spend a month with the mother they barely know, eleven-year-old Delphine and her two younger sisters arrive to a cold welcome as they discover that their mother, a dedicated poet and printer, is resentful of the intrusion of their visit and wants them to attend a nearby Black Panther summer camp.

"Delphine's growing awareness of injustice on a personal and universal level is smoothly woven into the story

in poetic language that will stimulate and move readers."
Publ Wkly

★ **P.S.** Be Eleven; Rita Williams-Garcia. Harpercollins Childrens Books 2013 288 p. $16.99

Grades: 4 5 6 7 8   Fic

1. Historical fiction -- Juvenile fiction 2. African American children -- Juvenile fiction

ISBN 0061938629; 9780061938627

This book is a follow-up to Rita Williams-Garcia's Newbery Honor-winning "One Crazy Summer." Here, "Delphine and her sisters return to Brooklyn from visiting their estranged mother, Cecile, a poet .... Change and conflict have the Gaither household in upheaval: Pa has a new girlfriend, Uncle Darnell returns from Vietnam a damaged young man, and the sixth-grade teacher Delphine hoped to get has been replaced by a man from Zambia." (Publishers Weekly)

"...Soars as a finely drawn portrait of a family in flux and as a memorable slice of a specific time in our nation's history." Booklist

Willingham, Bill

★ **Down** the Mysterly River; illustrations by Mark Buckingham. Tor/Starscape 2011 333p il $15.99

Grades: 4 5 6 7   Fic

1. Fantasy fiction 2. Memory -- Fiction 3. Animals -- Fiction 4. Forests and forestry -- Fiction

ISBN 978-0-7653-2792-5; 0-7653-2792-9

LC 2011018958

Top notch Boy Scout Max "the Wolf" cannot remember how he came to be in a strange forest, but soon he and three talking animals are on the run from the Blue Cutters, hunters who will alter the foursome's very essence if they can catch them.

"Willingham roles out his themes slowly, only fully spelling them out in the final scene, but they don't interfere with the rollicking story, nasty (but fully realized) villains, and heroic camaraderie.... [This] is a stellar example of a novel working both as an adventure tale and as metafiction." Publ Wkly

Willner-Pardo, Gina

Figuring out Frances. Clarion Bks. 1999 134p $14

Grades: 4 5 6   Fic

1. Schools -- Fiction 2. Friendship -- Fiction 3. Best friends -- Fiction 4. Grandmothers -- Fiction 5. Alzheimer's disease -- Fiction

ISBN 0-395-91510-4

LC 98-50082

Ten-year-old Abigail's neighbor Travis, her best friend although he is at a different school, upsets her when he transfers to her school, ignores her, and laughs at her grandmother's Alzheimer's along with his new friends

"The writing is witty, sincere, and insightful. This is a gem of a book." SLJ

The **hard** kind of promise. Clarion Books/Houghton Mifflin Harcourt 2010 200p $16

Grades: 4 5 6 7   Fic

1. School stories 2. Friendship -- Fiction 3. Popularity -- Fiction

ISBN 978-0-547-24395-5; 0-547-24395-2

California seventh-graders Sarah and Marjorie made a promise in kindergarten to always be friends, but Marjorie

is weird and Sarah, wanting to be at least somewhat popular, makes friends with a fellow choir member.

"Willner-Pardo's avoidance of overblown crises and dramatic climaxes creates a steadily paced, authentic story" Publ Wkly

Willocks, Tim

Doglands. Random House 2011 308p $16.99; lib bdg $19.99; ebook $16.99

Grades: 5 6 7 8   Fic

1. Adventure fiction 2. Dogs -- Fiction 3. Supernatural -- Fiction 4. Animal welfare -- Fiction

ISBN 978-0-375-86571-8; 0-375-86571-3; 978-0-375-96571-5 lib bdg; 0-375-96571-8 lib bdg; 978-0-375-89604-0 ebook; 0-375-89604-X ebook

LC 2009033328

Furgal, a half-greyhound puppy, escapes a cruel dog-track owner and sets out in the hope of finding his father and the fabled Doglands, later returning to try to free his mother, sisters, and the other abused dogs.

"The dogs each have distinct personalities, and the mystic lore of the Doglands adds a secondary fantasy layer to the narrative. Humans are only sketched in, which is fitting, since the tale is told from the dog point of view. A riveting dog tale with a healthy serving of savagery, not all on the part of the four-legged characters." Kirkus

Wilson, Daniel H.

A **boy** and his bot. Bloomsbury 2011 180p $16.99

Grades: 4 5 6 7   Fic

1. Science fiction 2. Robots -- Fiction

ISBN 978-1-59990-280-7; 1-59990-280-X

LC 2010-10635

When timid young Code falls down a hole into Mekhos, where everything is made of metal and circuitry, he must obtain the legendary Robonomicon from evil Immortalis in order to save the robots of this subterranean world and return home.

"Wilson ably balances Code's grief about his grandfather's fate with his astonishment and excitement about the quest upon which he embarks; both sets of emotions feel authentic.... Readers who are curious about the ways robots work or about electronics in general will find the level of detail throughout particularly interesting." Bull Cent Child Books

Wilson, Jacqueline

Best friends. Roaring Brook Press 2008 229p $15.95; pa $7.99

Grades: 4 5 6 7   Fic

1. School stories 2. Friendship -- Fiction

ISBN 978-1-59643-278-9; 1-59643-278-0; 978-0-312-58144-2 pa; 0-312-58144-0 pa

LC 2006-39716

Rambunctious and irrepressible Gemma has been best friends with Alice ever since they were born on the same day, so when Alice moves miles away to Scotland, Gemma is distraught over the idea that Alice might find a new best friend.

"Believable, sympathetic characters; recognizable home and school situations; and plenty of humor .... will ensure that this becomes ... a popular read for middle-grade girls." Booklist

Candyfloss; [illustrated by] Nick Sharratt. Roaring Brook Press 2007 339p il $14.95; pa $6.99
Grades: 4 5 6 **Fic**
1. Divorce -- Fiction 2. Friendship -- Fiction 3. Father-daughter relationship -- Fiction
ISBN 978-1-59643-241-3; 1-59643-241-1; 978-0-312-38418-0 pa; 0-312-38418-1 pa
LC 2006-19923
When her mother plans to move to Australia with her new husband and baby, Floss must decide whether her loyalties lie with her mother or her father, while at the same time, her best friend begins to make fun of her and reject her.
This is "a novel that contains many compelling, sometimes gritty, elements." Publ Wkly

Cookie; illustrated by Nick Sharratt. Roaring Brook Press 2009 320p il $16.99
Grades: 4 5 6 7 **Fic**
1. Friendship -- Fiction 2. Father-daughter relationship -- Fiction
ISBN 978-1-59643-534-6; 1-59643-534-8
Cookie is plain and shy, not the confident, popular girl her father wanted when he named her Beauty Cookson. Her mother helps her cook up a clever scheme to change her image—but, as usual, Dad doesn't approve, and this time his anger reaches frightening new heights
"Wilson's talent shows again in this novel with strong, compelling characters and a plot that makes the book hard to put down." SLJ

The **illustrated** Mum; [by] Jacqueline Wilson. Delacorte Press 2005 282p hardcover o.p. pa $5.50
Grades: 5 6 7 8 **Fic**
1. Sisters -- Fiction 2. Tattooing -- Fiction 3. Manic-depressive illness -- Fiction 4. Mother-daughter relationship -- Fiction
ISBN 0-385-73237-6; 0-440-42043-1 pa
LC 2003-70123
First published 1999 in the United Kingdom
Ten-year-old Dolphin is determined to stay with her family, no matter what, but when her sister goes to live with her newly-discovered father, sending their mother further into manic-depression, Dolphin's life takes a turn for the better.
"Dolphin is a sympathetic character and the relationship between the sisters is realistically portrayed, as is Marigold's mental illness." SLJ

Wilson, N. D.
★ The **dragon's** tooth; [by] N. D. Wilson. Random House 2011 485p (Ashtown burials) $16.99; lib bdg $19.99; e-book $16.99
Grades: 5 6 7 8 **Fic**
1. Fantasy fiction 2. Magic -- Fiction 3. Siblings -- Fiction 4. Secret societies -- Fiction
ISBN 978-0-375-86439-1; 0-375-86439-3; 978-0-375-96439-8 lib bdg; 0-375-96439-8 lib bdg; 978-0-375-89572-2 e-book
LC 2009038651
"This fast-paced fantasy quickly draws readers in to its alternate reality. . . . Allusions to mythology and complex character development . . . make Wilson's first in a proposed series a gem." Booklist

The **drowned** vault; N.D. Wilson. Random House 2012 449 p. (Ashtown burials) (lib. bdg.) $19.99
Grades: 5 6 7 8 **Fic**
1. Occult fiction 2. Fantasy fiction 3. Magic -- Fiction 4. Apprentices -- Fiction 5. Supernatural -- Fiction 6. Secret societies -- Fiction
ISBN 0375964401; 9780375864407; 9780375895739; 9780375964404
LC 2011051618
This book is N.D. Wilson's sequel to "The Dragon's Tooth." "Thanks to Cyrus and Antigone Smith, Dr. Phoenix now possesses the Dragon's Tooth—and he's been using it to hunt and kill immortals worldwide. Phoenix has a dark agenda, but an evil alliance of immortals, Ordo Draconis, also seeks the tooth's power. Worse, the Ordos have a centuries-old vendetta against the Smith family." (School Library Journal)

Wilson, Nancy Hope
Mountain pose. Farrar, Straus & Giroux 2001 233p $17
Grades: 5 6 7 8 **Fic**
1. Wills 2. Diaries 3. Grandmothers 4. Diaries -- Fiction 5. Grandmothers -- Fiction
ISBN 0-374-35078-7
LC 00-57269
When twelve-year-old Ellie inherits an old Vermont farm from her cruel and heartless grandmother Aurelia, she reads a set of diaries written by an ancestor and discovers secrets from the past
"Beautifully written and suspenseful, this novel explores the many emotions associated with the tragedy of spousal and child abuse." Voice Youth Advocates

Wilson, Nathan D.
100 cupboards; [by] N. D. Wilson. Random House 2007 289p $16.99; lib bdg $19.99; pa $6.99
Grades: 5 6 7 8 **Fic**
1. Magic -- Fiction 2. Cousins -- Fiction
ISBN 978-0-375-83881-1; 978-0-375-93881-8 lib bdg; 978-0-375-83882-8 pa
LC 2007-00164
After his parents are kidnapped, timid twelve-year-old Henry York leaves his sheltered Boston life and moves to small-town Kansas, where he and his cousin Henrietta discover and explore hidden doors in his attic room that seem to open onto other worlds
"There's an appealing blend of genuine creepiness and kindly domesticity here." Bull Cent Child Books
Other titles in this series are:
Dandelion Fire (2008)
The Chestnut King (2010)

The **Chestnut** King; book 3 of the 100 cupboards. [by] N.D. Wilson. Random House 2010 183p $17.99; lib bdg $20.99
Grades: 5 6 7 8 **Fic**
1. Magic -- Fiction 2. Cousins -- Fiction 3. Fairies -- Fiction 4. Family life -- Fiction 5. Space and time -- Fiction
ISBN 978-0-375-83885-9; 0-375-83885-6; 978-0-375-93885-6 lib bdg; 0-375-93885-0 lib bdg; 978-0-375-83886-6 pa; 0-375-83886-4 pa
LC 2008032748

Twelve-year-old Henry York, finally reunited with his family, works with them and the Chestnut King, the long-deposed and mythic leader of the faeren people, to destroy Nimiane and her forces of evil.

"Undeniably the most visceral of the 100 Cupboards series, this title takes some time to find its feet yet ends with an entirely satisfying finish." Kirkus

Dandelion fire; [by] N.D. Wilson. Random House 2008 466p $16.99; lib bdg $19.99

Grades: 5 6 7 8 **Fic**

1. Magic -- Fiction 2. Cousins -- Fiction
ISBN 978-0-375-83883-5; 0-375-83883-X; 978-0-375-93883-2 lib bdg; 0-375-93883-4 lib bdg

LC 2008003037

Presents the continuing adventures of Henry York, who has been living in Kansas with his cousins, where he discovers doorways leading to other worlds and becomes involved in a multi-world struggle between good and evil.

This is a "dense and worthy sequel to 100 Cupboards. . . . A quiet and quirky humor warms up the proceedings . . . leavening even the most intense scenes." SLJ

★ **Leepike** Ridge; [by] N. D. Wilson. Random House 2007 224p $15.99; lib bdg $18.99; pa $6.99

Grades: 4 5 6 7 **Fic**

1. Adventure fiction 2. Caves -- Fiction 3. Missing persons -- Fiction 4. Mother-son relationship -- Fiction
ISBN 978-0-375-83873-6; 0-375-83873-2; 978-0-375-93873-3 lib bdg; 0-375-93873-7 lib bdg; 978-0-375-83874-3 pa; 0-375-83874-0 pa

LC 2006-13352

While his widowed mother continues to search for him, eleven-year-old Tom, presumed dead after drifting away down a river, finds himself trapped in a series of underground caves with another survivor and a dog, and pursued by murderous treasure-hunters

"While Leepike Ridge is primarily an adventure story involving murder, treachery, and betrayal, Wilson's rich imagination and his quirky characters are a true delight." SLJ

Winerip, Michael

Adam Canfield of the Slash. Candlewick Press 2005 326p $15.99; pa $6.99

Grades: 5 6 7 8 **Fic**

1. School stories 2. Journalism -- Fiction
ISBN 0-7636-2340-7; 0-7636-2794-1 pa

While serving as co-editors of their school newspaper, middle-schoolers Adam and Jennifer uncover fraud and corruption in their school and in the city's government.

"This is a deceptively fun read that somehow manages to present kids with some of the most subtle social and ethical questions currently shaping their futures." SLJ

Other titles about Adam Canfield are:
Adam Canfield, watch you back! (2007)
Adam Canfield, the last reporter (2009)

Winston, Sherri

President of the whole fifth grade. Little, Brown 2010 273p $15.99

Grades: 3 4 5 **Fic**

1. School stories 2. Baking -- Fiction 3. Elections --

Fiction 4. Friendship -- Fiction
ISBN 0-316-11432-4; 978-0-316-11432-5

LC 2010-06366

To gain leadership skills needed to run a cupcake-baking empire when she grows up, Brianna runs for president of the fifth grade—expecting little competition—until a new girl enters the race.

"The story will resonate with preteens navigating the ups, downs, and drama that come with the territory of many young girls' friendships." SLJ

Winters, Ben H.

The **secret** life of Ms. Finkleman. Harper 2010 247p $16.99

Grades: 4 5 6 7 **Fic**

1. School stories 2. Teachers -- Fiction 3. Musicians -- Fiction 4. Rock music -- Fiction
ISBN 978-0-06-196541-8; 0-06-196541-3

LC 2010-04601

Spurred by a special project from her social studies teacher, seventh-grader Bethesda Fielding uncovers the secret identity of her music teacher, which leads to a most unusual concert performance and a tutoring assignment.

"Liberally laced with humor and featuring an upbeat heroine, unexpected friendship and rock-music trivia, this witty middle-school drama offers a lighthearted lesson in the importance of getting the facts straight." Kirkus

Another title about Bethesda Fielding is:
The mystery of missing everything (2011)

Winterson, Jeanette

Tanglewreck. Bloomsbury Children's Books 2006 414p $16.95; pa $6.95

Grades: 5 6 7 8 **Fic**

1. Science fiction 2. Space and time -- Fiction 3. Clocks and watches -- Fiction
ISBN 978-1-58234-919-0; 1-58234-919-3; 978-1-59990-081-0 pa; 1-59990-081-5 pa

LC 2005-30630

Eleven-year-old Silver sets out to find the Timekeeper—a clock that controls time—and to protect it from falling into the hands of two people who want to use the device for their own nefarious ends

"Winterson seamlessly combines rousing adventure with time warps, quantum physics, and a few wonderfully hapless flunkies." Booklist

Winthrop, Elizabeth

Counting on Grace. Wendy Lamb Books 2006 232p $15.95; lib bdg $17.99; pa $6.99

Grades: 5 6 7 8 **Fic**

1. Photographers 2. Factories -- Fiction 3. Child labor -- Fiction 4. Photographers -- Fiction
ISBN 0-385-74644-X; 0-385-90878-4 lib bdg; 0-553-48783-3 pa

It's 1910 in Pownal, Vermont. At 12 Grace and her best friend Arthur must go to work in the mill, helping their mothers work the looms. Together Grace and Arthur write a secret letter to the Child Labor Board about underage children working in the mill. A few weeks later, Lewis Hine, a famous reformer, arrives undercover to gather evidence. Grace meets him and appears in some of his photographs, changing her life forever.

"Much information on early photography and the workings of the textile mills is conveyed, and history and fiction are woven seamlessly together in this beautifully written novel." SLJ

Wise, William

Christopher Mouse; the tale of a small traveler. illustrations by Patrick Benson. Bloomsbury Children's Books 2004 152p il $15.95; pa $5.95

Grades: 3 4 5   **Fic**

1. Mice -- Fiction

ISBN 1-58234-878-2; 1-58234-708-5 pa

LC 2003-56393

After being sold to an unscrupulous pet store owner, a young mouse lives with several owners and has many adventures, before ending up with an appreciative family.

"The writing is nicely mannered but very accessible, making the book not only a winner for reading aloud but also a delightful offering for children moving past beginning readers. The ink illustrations and the enticing cover will help them along." Booklist

Wiseman, David

Jeremy Visick. Houghton Mifflin 1981 170p hardcover o.p. pa $5.95

Grades: 5 6 7 8   **Fic**

1. Miners -- Fiction 2. Supernatural -- Fiction 3. Space and time -- Fiction

ISBN 0-618-34514-0 pa

LC 80-28116

Twelve-year-old Matthew is drawn almost against his will to help a boy his own age who was lost in a mining disaster a century before.

"This story blends the mystery and awe of the supernatural with the real terror and peril of descending the shaft of an 1850 Cornish copper mine." SLJ

Wissinger, Tamera Will

Gone fishing; a novel. by Tamera Will Wissinger. Houghton Mifflin Books for Children 2013 128 p. (hardcover) $15.99

Grades: 1 2 3 4   **Fic**

1. Novels in verse 2. Fishing -- Poetry 3. Fishing -- Fiction 4. Brothers and sisters -- Fiction

ISBN 0547820119; 9780547820118

LC 2012032796

This book from Tamera Will Wissinger "offers a collection of more than 40 poems, which join to form a novel in verse about a family's fishing trip. Sam is initially distraught when his sister, Lucy, worms her way into his fishing trip with his father; as the day progresses, though, sibling rivalry turns to appreciation, especially after Sam catches a giant catfish." (Publishers Weekly)

Wittlinger, Ellen

This means war! Simon & Schuster Books for Young Readers 2010 224p $16.99

Grades: 5 6 7 8   **Fic**

1. Fear -- Fiction 2. Contests -- Fiction 3. Friendship -- Fiction

ISBN 978-1-4169-97101-6; 1-4169-7101-7

LC 2008-32586

In 1962, when her best friend Lowell begins to hang around new friends who think girls are losers, Juliet, a fearful fifth-grader, teams up with bold, brave Patsy who challenges the boys to a series of increasingly dangerous contests

"Wittlinger latches on to a poignant metaphor for war in the lively and readable tale set against the backdrop of the 1962 Cuban missile crisis." Booklist

Woelfle, Gretchen

All the world's a stage; a novel in five acts. illustrated by Thomas Cox. Holiday House 2011 163p il $16.95

Grades: 4 5 6 7   **Fic**

1. Actors -- Fiction 2. Orphans -- Fiction 3. Theater -- Fiction 4. Apprentices -- Fiction

ISBN 978-0-8234-2281-4; 0-8234-2281-X

LC 2010023474

Twelve-year-old orphan Christopher "Kit" Buckles becomes a stage boy in a London theater in 1598, tries his hand at acting, and later helps build the Globe Theater for playwright William Shakespeare and the Chamberlain's Men acting troupe.

"The most compelling drama is Kit's universal search for his calling and his shifting friendships. . . . Frequent charming drawings enhance the sense of time and place." Booklist

Includes glossary and bibliographical references

Wojciechowska, Maia

Shadow of a bull; drawings by Alvin Smith. Atheneum Pubs. 1964 165p il $16; pa $5.99

Grades: 6 7 8 9   **Fic**

1. Bullfights -- Fiction

ISBN 0-689-30042-5; 1-4169-3395-6 pa

Awarded the Newbery Medal, 1965

"In spare, economical prose [the author] makes one feel, see, smell the heat, endure the hot Andalusian sun and shows one the sand and glare of the bullring. Above all, she lifts the veil and gives glimpses of the terrible loneliness in the soul of a boy. . . . Superbly illustrated." N Y Times Book Rev

Wolf, Joan M.

★ **Someone** named Eva. Clarion Books 2007 200p $16; pa $6.99

Grades: 5 6 7 8   **Fic**

1. School stories 2. National socialism -- Fiction 3. World War, 1939-1945 -- Fiction

ISBN 0-618-53579-9; 0-547-23766-9 pa

LC 2006-26070

From her home in Lidice, Czechoslovakia, in 1942, eleven-year-old Milada is taken with other blond, blue-eyed children to a school in Poland to be trained as "proper Germans" for adoption by German families, but all the while she remembers her true name and history.

"This amazing, eye-opening story, masterfully written, is an essential part of World War II literature and belongs on the shelves of every library." SLJ

Wolf-Morgenlander, Karl

Ragtag. Clarion Books 2009 225p il $16

Grades: 3 4 5 6   **Fic**

1. War stories 2. Fantasy fiction 3. Birds -- Fiction

ISBN 978-0-547-07424-5; 0-547-07424-7

LC 2008025319

A young swallow leads a band of birds against an empire of raptors that has invaded Boston

"This novel opens up the world of these lively feathered creatures and their way of life. The story line moves quickly." SLJ

Wolfson, Jill

Home, and other big, fat lies. Henry Holt 2006 281p $16.95

Grades: 5 6 7 8   **Fic**

1. Nature -- Fiction 2. Foster home care -- Fiction 3. Environmental protection -- Fiction

ISBN 978-0-8050-7670-7; 0-8050-7670-0

LC 200035843

Eleven-year-old Termite, a foster child with an eye for the beauty of nature and a talent for getting into trouble, takes on the loggers in her new home town when she tries to save the biggest tree in the forest.

"Written with humor and sensitivity." Voice Youth Advocates

What I call life. Holt & Co. 2005 270p $16.95; pa $6.99

Grades: 5 6 7 8   **Fic**

1. Foster home care -- Fiction

ISBN 0-8050-7669-7; 0-312-37752-5 pa

Placed in a group foster home, eleven-year-old Cal Lavender learns how to cope with life from the four other girls who live there and from their storytelling guardian, the Knitting Lady.

"Wolfson paints her characters with delightful authenticity. Her debut novel is a treasure of quiet good humor and skillful storytelling that conveys subtle messages about kindness, compassion, and the gift of family regardless of its configuration." Booklist

Wolitzer, Meg

The fingertips of Duncan Dorfman. Dutton Childrens Books 2011 294p $16.99

Grades: 4 5 6 7   **Fic**

1. Contests -- Fiction 2. Individualism -- Fiction 3. Scrabble (Game) -- Fiction

ISBN 978-0-525-42304-1; 0-525-42304-4

LC 2011005228

"The novel is shot through with Scrabble words and rules in a way that is reminiscent of Louis Sachar's The Cardturner (2010). Readers will identify with and root for the characters as their tales intertwine to a satisfying if slightly too cheery close. Word wizards aren't the only ones who will enjoy this readable rumination on ethics, competition and identity." Kirkus

Wong, Janet S.

Me and Rolly Maloo; illustrated by Elizabeth Buttler. Charlesbridge 2010 121p il $15.95

Grades: 3 4 5   **Fic**

1. School stories 2. Honesty -- Fiction 3. Popularity -- Fiction 4. Mathematics -- Fiction

ISBN 978-1-58089-158-5; 1-58089-158-6

"The characterizations are spot-on, and Buttler's frequent graphic-novel-style artwork and dialogue balloons emphsize reactions and emotions . . . The story is one worth telling." SLJ

Minn and Jake; [by] Janet Wong; pictures by Geneviève Côté. Farrar, Straus & Giroux 2003 146p il $16; pa $6.95

Grades: 3 4 5   **Fic**

1. School stories 2. Novels in verse 3. Friendship -- Fiction

ISBN 0-374-34987-8; 978-0-374-34987-5; 978-0-374-40021-7 pa; 0-374-40021-0 pa

LC 2002-35421

Fifth-grader Minn, the tallest girl in school, begins a rocky friendship with Jake, a new student who is not only very short, but is also afraid of the worms and lizards that Minn likes to collect

"This breezy free-verse novel introduces memorable characters in recognizable situations. . . . [Côté's] b&w illustrations achieve unusual dimension. Incorporating what seem to be collage elements, her strikingly graphic compositions mirror the deceptive ease of the verse narration." Publ Wkly

Another title about Minn and Jake is:
Minn and Jake's almost terrible summer (2008)

Minn and Jake's almost terrible summer; [by] Janet S. Wong; pictures by Geneviève Côté. Farrar, Straus and Giroux 2008 98p il $15

Grades: 3 4 5   **Fic**

1. Summer -- Fiction 2. Friendship -- Fiction 3. Family life -- Fiction

ISBN 978-0-374-34977-6; 0-374-34977-0

LC 2007-34416

Ten-year-old Jake's summer starts off badly, goes downhill when his family visits Los Angeles, California, and his old friends are too busy for him, then gets even worse after he disagrees with Minn when her family joins his for a trip to Disneyland.

"Minn and Jake are back in this new free-verse installment. . . . Whimsical ink sketches enhance the storytelling in this creative early chapter book that features smart, endearing characters and humorous antics." SLJ

Wood, Maryrose

The hidden gallery; illustrated by Jon Klassen. Balzer + Bray 2011 313p il (Incorrigible children of Ashton Place) $15.99

Grades: 4 5 6   **Fic**

1. Orphans -- Fiction 2. Wild children -- Fiction

ISBN 978-0-06-179112-3; 0-06-179112-1

LC 2010-32737

Fifteen-year-old Miss Penelope Lumley, a governess trained at the Swanburne Academy for Poor Bright Females, takes the three Incorrigible Children of Ashton Place to London, England, and learns they are under a curse.

"Humorous antics and a climactic cliffhanger ending will keep children turning pages and clamoring for the next volume, while more sophisticated readers will take away much more. Frequent plate-sized illustrations add wit and period flair." SLJ

★ The mysterious howling; illustrated by Jon Klassen. Balzer & Bray 2010 267p il (The incorrigible children of Ashton Place) $15.99

Grades: 4 5 6   **Fic**

1. Orphans -- Fiction 2. Christmas -- Fiction 3. Wild

children -- Fiction

ISBN 978-0-06-179105-5; 0-06-179105-9

Fifteen-year-old Miss Penelope Lumley, a recent graduate of the Swanburne Academy for Poor Bright Females, is
hired as governess to three young children who have been
raised by wolves and must teach them to behave in a civilized manner quickly, in preparation for a Christmas ball.

"Smartly written with a middle-grade audience in mind,
this is both fun and funny and sprinkled with dollops of wisdom." Booklist

Another title in this series is:

The hidden gallery (2011)

The **unseen** guest; by Maryrose Wood; illustrated by
Jon Klassen. Balzer + Bray 2012 340 p. (hardback) $15.99
Grades: 4 5 6   **Fic**
1. Mystery fiction 2. Wolves -- Fiction 3. Nannies
-- Fiction 4. Wild children -- Fiction 5. Great Britain --
History -- 19th century -- Fiction 6. Orphans -- Fiction
7. Secrets -- Fiction 8. Governesses -- Fiction 9. Feral
children -- Fiction

ISBN 9780061791185

LC 2011053315

This young adult novel offers a "Victorian mystery [sto-
ry about] teenage governess Penelope Lumley [who] takes
on threats to her wolfish young charges that include a hustler
after the Ashton fortune. . . . Once he meets the three feral
children Penelope is charged with training up to be human,
Faucet's scheme to finance the introduction of ostrich racing
to the British Isles by marrying the Dowager Lady Ashton is
transformed to visions of wolf racing and sideshow exhibitions. . . . Along with . . . pitching her plucky protagonist into
one crisis after another . . . the author slips in a few more
seemingly significant Clues to the Ashtons' curious history
and Penelope's apparent involvement in it." (Kirkus)

Woodruff, Elvira

Fearless. Scholastic Press 2008 224p il $16.99; pa
$6.99
Grades: 5 6 7 8   **Fic**
1. Artists 2. Engravers 3. Inventors 4. Architects 5.
Adventure fiction 6. Orphans -- Fiction 7. Lighthouses
-- Fiction

ISBN 978-0-439-67703-5; 0-439-67703-3; 978-0-439-
67704-2 pa; 0-439-67704-1 pa

LC 2006-10137

In late seventeenth-century England, eleven-year-old
Digory, forced to leave his hometown after his father is lost
at sea, becomes an apprentice to the architect Henry Winstanley, who built a lighthouse on the treacherous Eddystone
Reef—the very rocks that sank Digory's grandfather's ship
years before.

"This fascinating, well-written story is closely based on
the life of the real Henry Winstanley. . . . The characters are
finely drawn and the action is nonstop." SLJ

George Washington's spy; a time travel adventure.
Scholastic Press 2010 229p $16.99
Grades: 4 5 6   **Fic**
1. Authors 2. Diplomats 3. Inventors 4. Statesmen
5. Scientists 6. Writers on science 7. Members of
Congress 8. Time travel -- Fiction

ISBN 978-0-545-10487-6; 0-545-10487-4

LC 2009032700

Ten-year-old Matt and six other children travel to 1776
Boston, living out American history as they meet Benjamin
Franklin, learn about colonial medicine, and become part of
a rebel spy ring

"Woodruff does an excellent job of conveying the complexities of war. . . . This is a great introduction to the Revolutionary period. . . . The story is fast paced, exciting, and
informative." SLJ

The **Ravenmaster's** secret. Scholastic Press 2003
225p $15.95; pa $5.99
Grades: 5 6 7 8   **Fic**
1. Ravens -- Fiction

ISBN 0-439-28133-4; 0-439-28134-2 pa

LC 2002-15963

The eleven-year-old son of the Ravenmaster at the
Tower of London befriends a Jacobite rebel being held
prisoner there.

"An absorbing historical adventure with a unique and
colorful setting. . . . The novel can be read for its exciting
plot and sympathetic characters, but readers will also sense
its underlying theme of courage." Booklist

Woods, Brenda

My name is Sally Little Song. G.P. Putnam's Sons
2006 182p $15.99; pa $5.99
Grades: 4 5 6 7   **Fic**
1. Slavery -- Fiction 2. Seminole Indians -- Fiction 3.
African Americans -- Fiction

ISBN 0-399-24312-7; 0-14-240943-X pa

LC 2005-32651

When their owner plans to sell one of them in 1802,
twelve-year-old Sally and her family run away from their
Georgia plantation to look for both freedom from slavery
and a home in Florida with the Seminole Indians.

"Based on historical accounts, this novel provides readers with an alternative view of the realities of slavery—an
escape to the South rather than North. . . . This accessible
tale will prove a rich resource for study and discussion." SLJ

★ **Saint** Louis Armstrong Beach. Nancy Paulsen
Books 2011 137p $16.99
Grades: 4 5 6   **Fic**
1. Dogs -- Fiction 2. Musicians -- Fiction 3. Hurricane
Katrina, 2005 -- Fiction

ISBN 978-0-399-25507-6; 0-399-25507-9

Saint Louis Armstrong Beach is enjoying life in New
Orleans, playing clarinet for the tourists in his spare time,
accompanied by Shadow, a local stray dog. When Hurricane
Katrina approaches, Saint faces unexpected challenges in
trying to rescue Shadow.

This is a "gripping addition to the growing body of fiction portraying Katrina's profound effect on children and
families. . . . Woods' marvelous characterizations of Saint
and Miz Moran more than stand up to the vivid backdrop of
the flooded, chaotic city. Shadow's credulity-straining heroics will please kids." Kirkus

The **red** rose box. Putnam 2002 136p $16.99; pa
$5.99
Grades: 5 6 7 8   **Fic**
1. Sisters 2. Segregation 3. African Americans 4.

African Americans -- Fiction
ISBN 0-399-23702-X; 0-14-250151-4 pa
LC 2001-18354

In 1953, Leah Hopper dreams of leaving the poverty and segregation of her home in Sulphur, Louisiana, and when Aunt Olivia sends train tickets to Los Angeles as part of her tenth birthday present, Leah gets a first taste of freedom

"In language made musical with southern phrases, this . . . novel shapes the era and characters with both well-chosen particulars and universal emotions." Booklist

Woodson, Jacqueline

★ **Feathers**. G.P. Putnam's Sons 2007 118p $15.99; pa $6.99

Grades: 4 5 6 7   **Fic**

1. Religion -- Fiction 2. Race relations -- Fiction 3. African Americans -- Fiction
ISBN 978-0-399-23989-2; 0-399-23989-8; 978-0-14-241198-8 pa; 0-14-241198-1 pa
LC 2006-24713

A Newbery Medal honor book, 2008

When a new, white student nicknamed "The Jesus Boy" joins her sixth grade class in the winter of 1971, Frannie's growing friendship with him makes her start to see some things in a new light.

"Woodson creates in Frannie a strong protagonist who thinks for herself and recognizes the value and meaning of family. The story ends with hope and thoughtfulness while speaking to those adolescents who struggle with race, faith, and prejudice." SLJ

★ **Locomotion**. Putnam 2003 100p $17.99; pa $5.99

Grades: 4 5 6 7   **Fic**

1. Orphans 2. Novels in verse 3. African Americans -- Poetry 4. Foster home care -- Fiction 5. African Americans -- Fiction
ISBN 978-0-399-23115-5; 0-399-23115-3; 978-0-14-241552-8 pa; 0-14-241552-9 pa
LC 2002-69779

In a series of poems, eleven-year-old Lonnie writes about his life, after the death of his parents, separated from his younger sister, living in a foster home, and finding his poetic voice at school

"In a masterful use of voice, Woodson allows Lonnie's poems to tell a complex story of loss and grief and to create a gritty, urban environment. Despite the spare text, Lonnie's foster mother and the other minor characters are three-dimensional, making the boy's world a convincingly real one." SLJ

★ **Peace**, Locomotion. G.P. Putnam's Sons 2009 134p $15.99; pa $7.99

Grades: 4 5 6 7   **Fic**

1. Letters -- Fiction 2. Orphans -- Fiction 3. Siblings -- Fiction 4. Foster home care -- Fiction 5. African Americans -- Fiction
ISBN 978-0-399-24655-5; 0-399-24655-X; 978-0-14-241512-2 pa; 0-14-241512-X pa
LC 2008-18583

Through letters to his little sister, who is living in a different foster home, sixth-grader Lonnie, also known as "Locomotion," keeps a record of their lives while they are apart, describing his own foster family, including his foster brother who returns home after losing a leg in the Iraq War

"Woodson creates a full-bodied character in kind, sensitive Lonnie. Readers will understand his quest for peace, and appreciate the hard work he does to find it." Publ Wkly

Worley, Rob M.

Scratch 9; created and written by Rob M. Worley; illustrated by Jason T. Kruse. Ape Entertainment 2011 100p. 1

Grades: 3 4 5   **Fic**

1. Cats -- Fiction 2. Pets -- Fiction 3. Comic books, strips, etc.
ISBN 9781936340538

In this collection of comics, named one of the Best Comics for Kids 2010 by School Library Journal, "mad science gives an ordinary cat named Scratch the ability to summon any of his nine lives. He must use his powers to save his pet friends from the CRUEL corporation." (Publisher's note) The protagonist "can summon any of his previous or future lives and fight side-by-side with them, a handy skill when you were a saber-toothed tiger, a ninja, and a minor Egyptian deity in your previous lives!" (School Libr J)

Wrede, Patricia C.

Calling on dragons. Harcourt Brace 1993 244p (The Enchanted Forest Chronicles) hardcover o.p. pa $6.99

Grades: 5 6 7 8   **Fic**

1. Fairy tales 2. Magic -- Fiction 3. Dragons -- Fiction
ISBN 0-15-200950-7; 0-15-204692-5 pa
LC 92-35469

Queen Cimorene turns to her friends Morwen, Telemain, and Kazul for help when troublesome wizards make their way back into the Enchanted Forest and begin to soak up its magic

"Wrede's strengths are numerous: sparkling dialogue, amusingly fractured fairy-tale conventions, solid characterization, plenty of action, and truly terrific chapter headings." SLJ

Dealing with dragons. Harcourt Brace Jovanovich 1990 212p (The Enchanted Forest Chronicles) hardcover o.p. pa $6.99

Grades: 5 6 7 8   **Fic**

1. Fairy tales 2. Magic -- Fiction 3. Dragons -- Fiction
ISBN 0-15-222900-0; 0-15-204566-X pa
LC 89-24599

Bored with traditional palace life, a princess goes off to live with a group of dragons and soon becomes involved with fighting against some disreputable wizards who want to steal away the dragons' kingdom

"A decidedly diverting novel with plenty of action and many slightly skewed fairy-tale conventions that add to the laugh-out-loud reading pleasure and give the story a wide appeal." Booklist

Other titles in this series are:
Searching for dragons (1991)
Calling on dragons (1993)
Talking to dragons (1993)

Wright, Barbara

★ **Crow**. Random House 2012 $16.99; lib bdg $19.99; ebook $10.99

Grades: 4 5 6   **Fic**

1. Friendship -- Fiction 2. Family life -- Fiction 3.

Race relations -- Fiction 4. African Americans -- Fiction
ISBN 978-0-375-86928-0; 0-375-86928-X; 978-0-
375-96928-7 lib bdg; 0-375-96928-4; 978-0-375-
98270-5 ebook

LC 2011014892

In 1898, Moses Thomas's summer vacation does not go
exactly as planned as he contends with family problems and
the ever-changing alliances among his friends at the same
time as he is exposed to the escalating tension between the
African-American and white communities of Wilmington,
North Carolina.

"An intensely moving, first-person narrative of a disturbing historical footnote told from the perspective of a very
likable, credible young hero." Kirkus

Wright, Betty Ren

Princess for a week; illustrated by Jacqueline Rogers.
Holiday House 2006 105p il $16.95; pa $6.95
Grades: 2 3 4   **Fic**
1. Ghost stories 2. Mystery fiction
ISBN 0-8234-1945-2; 0-8234-2111-2 pa

LC 2005-50288

When a confident girl named Princess arrives to spend
a week at Roddy's house, she encourages him to help her
investigate the suspicious activities happening at a supposedly haunted house.

"The story moves quickly and is excellently paced. .
. . The full-page illustrations add realism and depth to the
story." SLJ

The **dollhouse** murders. Holiday House 1983 149p
$17.95; pa $7.95
Grades: 4 5 6 7   **Fic**
1. Mystery fiction
ISBN 0-8234-0497-8; 0-8234-2172-4 pa

LC 83-6147

A dollhouse filled with a ghostly light in the middle of
the night and dolls that have moved from where she last left
them lead Amy and her retarded sister to unravel the mystery
surrounding grisly murders that took place years ago

"More than just a mystery, this offers keen insight into
the relationship between handicapped and nonhandicapped
siblings and glimpses into the darker adult emotions of guilt
and anger. A successful, full-bodied work." Booklist

Wynne-Jones, Tim

★ **Rex** Zero and the end of the world. Farrar, Straus &
Giroux 2007 86p $16
Grades: 4 5 6   **Fic**
1. Moving -- Fiction 2. Cold war -- Fiction 3. Family
life -- Fiction
ISBN 0-374-33467-6; 978-0-374-33467-3

LC 2006-45172

In the summer of 1962 with everyone nervous about a
possible nuclear war, ten-nearly-eleven-year-old Rex, having just moved to Ottawa from Vancouver with his parents
and five siblings, faces his own personal challenges as he
discovers new friends and a new understanding of the world
around him.

"Despite the weighty themes, Wynne-Jones writes with a
light, often humorous touch and maintains a perspective true
to an 11-year-old's perspective." Publ Wkly

Other titles about Rex Zero are:
Rex Zero, king of nothing (2008)

Rex Zero, the great pretender (2010)

Wyss, Johann David

The **Swiss** family Robinson; by Johann Wyss; edited
by William H. G. Kingston; illustrated by Lynd Ward. Grosset & Dunlap 1999 388p il $18.99
Grades: 5 6 7 8   **Fic**
1. Survival after airplane accidents, shipwrecks, etc. --
Fiction
ISBN 0-448-06022-1

Originally published 1812-1813 in Switzerland

When a Swiss couple and their four sons are shipwrecked on an isolated island, they adapt to their "New
Switzerland" using many imaginative methods of farming
and animal taming.

Wyss, Thelma Hatch

Bear dancer; the story of a Ute girl. Margaret K.
McElderry Books 2005 181p il $15.95
Grades: 5 6 7 8   **Fic**
1. Ute Indians -- Fiction
ISBN 1-4169-0285-6

LC 2005-40620

In late nineteenth-century Colorado, Elk Girl, sister of
Ute chief Ouray, is captured by Cheyenne and Arapaho warriors, rescued by the white "enemy," and finally returned to
her home. Includes historical notes.

"This fascinating story is based on a real person. . . . An
excellent addition to historical-fiction collections." SLJ

A **tale** of gold; [by] Thelma Hatch Wyss. Margaret K.
McElderry Books 2007 152p $15.99
Grades: 4 5 6   **Fic**
1. Orphans -- Fiction 2. Friendship -- Fiction 3. Gold
mines and mining -- Fiction
ISBN 978-1-4169-4212-2; 1-4169-4212-2

LC 2006037545

Orphaned fourteen-year-old James decides to join the
"stampeders" heading to the Yukon gold rush, and along the
way joins up with two unusual partners who share a common
bond of wanting to strike it rich

"Filled with interesting characters and fast-paced action,
the book is well worth reading on a number of levels." SLJ

Yee, Lisa

Aloha, Kanani; illustrations by Sarah Davis. American
Girl 2011 116p il (American girl) $12.95; pa $6.95
Grades: 3 4 5   **Fic**
1. Cousins -- Fiction 2. Racially mixed people -- Fiction
ISBN 978-1-59369-840-9; 1-59369-840-2; 978-1-
59369-839-3 pa; 1-59369-839-9 pa

LC 2010046870

When the tropical paradise of Kauai, Hawaii, fails to impress her cousin from New York City, ten-year-old Kanani
wonders why nothing seems to make her happy.

"In this story with an animal-rescue sub-plot, beautiful
full-color illustrations and a Hawaiian glossary are included,
along with several ending pages about real-life girls who
have helped animals." Booklist

Another title about Kanani is:
Good job, Kanani (2011)

Bobby vs. girls (accidentally) illustrated by Dan Santat. Arthur A. Levine Books 2009 170p il $15.99; pa $5.99

Grades: 3 4 5   **Fic**

1. School stories 2. Friendship -- Fiction

ISBN 978-0-545-05592-5; 0-545-05592-X; 978-0-545-05593-2 pa; 0-545-05593-8 pa

When Bobby inadvertently gets into a fight with his best friend Holly, their disagreement develops into a boys versus girls war involving their whole fourth-grade class.

"Yee really understands children's thought processes and presents them with tact and good humor. . . . Santat's drawings manage the fine line between cartoon and realism and add dimension to the events. Readers will recognize themselves and learn some gentle lessons about relationships while they are laughing at the antics." Kirkus

Another title about Bobby is:

Bobby the brave (sometimes) (2010)

Millicent Min, girl genius. Arthur A. Levine Books 2003 248p $16.95; pa $4.99

Grades: 5 6 7   **Fic**

1. School stories 2. Gifted children -- Fiction 3. Chinese Americans -- Fiction

ISBN 0-439-42519-0; 0-439-42520-4 pa

LC 2003-3747

"At the tender age of eleven, Millicent Min has completed her junior year of high school. Summer school is Millie's idea of fun, so she is excited that her parents are allowing her to take a college poetry course. . . . The tension between Millie's formal, overly intellectual way of expressing herself and her emotional immaturity makes her a very funny narrator. . . . Readers considerably older than Millicent's eleven years will enjoy this strong debut novel." Voice Youth Advocates

Other titles about Millicent Min and her friends are:

Stanford Wong flunks big-time (2005)

So totally Emily Ebers (2007)

So totally Emily Ebers. Arthur A. Levine Books 2007 280p $16.99

Grades: 5 6 7   **Fic**

1. Moving -- Fiction 2. Divorce -- Fiction 3. Friendship -- Fiction

ISBN 978-0-439-83847-4; 0-439-83847-9; 978-0-439-83848-1; 0-439-83848-7

LC 2006-22738

In a series of letters to her absent father, twelve-year-old Emily Ebers deals with moving cross-country, her parents' divorce, a new friendship, and her first serious crush.

"There aren't many authors who can bring energy to the same basic story three times running, but Yee manages to do it in this companion to Millicent Min, Girl Genius (2003) and Stanford Wong Flunks Big-Time (2005). . . . Fans of the first two books will enjoy seeing how this telling expands its predecessors' take on the same events." Booklist

Warp speed. Arthur A. Levine Books 2011 310p $16.99

Grades: 5 6 7 8   **Fic**

1. School stories 2. Bullies -- Fiction 3. Popularity -- Fiction 4. Family life -- Fiction

ISBN 978-0-545-12276-4; 0-545-12276-7

LC 2010-24228

"Yee's combination of humor and sympathy works a charm here, giving Marley a life of his own and a chance at success in this solid addition to her prismatic look at middle school." Kirkus

Yelchin, Eugene

★ **Breaking** Stalin's nose; written and illustrated by Eugene Yelchin. Henry Holt and Company 2011 140p il

Grades: 4 5 6 7   **Fic**

1. Communism -- Fiction 2. Father-son relationship -- Fiction

ISBN 0-8050-9216-1; 978-0-8050-9216-5

LC 2011005792

In the Stalinist era of the Soviet Union, ten-year-old Sasha idolizes his father, a devoted Communist, but when police take his father away and leave Sasha homeless, he is forced to examine his own perceptions, values, and beliefs.

"Readers will quickly pick up on the dichotomy between Sasha's ardent beliefs and the reality of life under Stalinism, and be glad for his ultimate disillusion, even as they worry for his future. An author's note concisely presents the chilling historical background and personal connection that underlie the story." Publ Wkly

Yep, Laurence, 1948-

City of fire. Tom Doherty Associates 2009 320p $15.99

Grades: 5 6 7 8   **Fic**

1. Fantasy fiction 2. Magic -- Fiction 3. Dragons -- Fiction

ISBN 978-0-7653-1924-1; 0-7653-1924-1

LC 2009016737

Twelve-year-old Scirye and her companions travel to Houlani, a new Hawaiian island created by magic, where they enlist the help of volcano goddess Pele in an attempt to stop an evil dragon and a mysterious man from altering the universe.

"Readers will be on tenterhooks awaiting the next episode of this exhilarating chase." Booklist

City of ice. Tor 2011 383p $17.99

Grades: 5 6 7 8   **Fic**

1. Fantasy fiction 2. Magic -- Fiction 3. Dragons -- Fiction

ISBN 978-0-7653-1925-8; 0-7653-1925-X

LC 2011007411

From the islands of Hawaii, Scirye and her loyal companions pursue the villainous Mr. Roland and evil dragon Badik all the way to the city of Nova Hafnia in the icy Arctic Circle, to prevent Roland from obtaining the power to alter the universe.

"Readers who enjoy inner conflicts, barbed dialogue, casts replete with supernatural creatures and fantasy epics that don't take themselves too seriously will find it a treat." Kirkus

Mia; by Laurence Yep. American Girl Pub. 2008 130p il pa $6.95

Grades: 2 3 4 5   **Fic**

1. Ice skating -- Fiction

ISBN 978-1-59369-409-8 pa; 1-59369-409-1 pa

Mia has grown up playing ice hockey with her three older brothers and has the skills she needs to become a star hockey player. But she's tired of skating in her brothers' shadows and has decided to pursue her passion for figure skating instead. With the help of a new coach, Mia finds out whether she has what it takes to grow and compete as a figure skater.

"Readers . . . get a closer look into the world of competitive figure skating. Illustrations . . . look like digitized photos and are mostly of Mia with her family or free skating. . . . Well written and fun." SLJ

Another title about Mia is:

Bravo, Mia! (2008)

When the circus came to town; drawings by Suling Wang. HarperCollins Pubs. 2002 113p il hardcover o.p. pa $5.99

Grades: 3 4 5   Fic

1. Circus 2. Smallpox 3. Self-esteem 4. Chinese New Year 5. Chinese Americans 6. Circus -- Fiction 7. Chinese New Year -- Fiction 8. Chinese Americans -- Fiction 9. Frontier and pioneer life -- Fiction 10. Frontier and pioneer life -- Montana

ISBN 0-06-029325-X; 0-06-440965-1 pa

LC 2001-39290

An Asian cook and a Chinese New Year celebration help ten-year-old Ursula at a Montana stage coach station to regain her confidence after smallpox scars her face

"Yep has based his novel on a true story, and his writing is, by turns, direct, humorous, and poignant." Booklist

★ The **dragon's** child; a story of Angel Island. [by] Laurence Yep, with Kathleen S. Yep. HarperCollinsPublishers 2008 133p $15.99; lib bdg $16.89

Grades: 3 4 5 6   Fic

1. Immigrants -- Fiction 2. Chinese Americans -- Fiction

ISBN 978-0-06-027692-8; 0-06-027692-4; 978-0-06-027693-5 lib bdg; 0-06-027693-2 lib bdg

LC 2007-18373

"In a dramatic blend of fact and fiction, Laurence Yep and his niece draw on family stories, immigration records, and memories of Laurence's own conversations to tell his dad's story of coming to America at age 10 with his Chinese American dad. . . . With family photos, a historical note, and a long bibliography, this stirring narrative will spark readers' own search for roots." Booklist

The **magic** paintbrush; drawings by Suling Wang. HarperCollins Pubs. 2000 89p il hardcover o.p. pa $5.99

Grades: 3 4 5   Fic

1. Magic 2. Wishes 3. Old age 4. Orphans 5. Grandfathers 6. Chinese Americans 7. Magic -- Fiction 8. Chinese Americans -- Fiction 9. Chinese Americans -- Juvenile fiction

ISBN 0-06-028199-5; 0-06-440852-3 pa

LC 99-34959

A magic paintbrush transports Steve and his elderly caretakers from their drab apartment in Chinatown to a world of adventures

"Yep's crisp style keeps the pages turning, and he leavens his story with snappy dialogue, realistic characters and plenty of wise humor." Publ Wkly

★ The **star** maker. Harper 2010 100p $15.99; lib bdg $16.89

Grades: 5 6 7 8   Fic

1. Uncles -- Fiction 2. Family life -- Fiction 3. Chinese New Year -- Fiction 4. Chinese Americans -- Fiction

ISBN 978-0-06-025315-8; 0-06-025315-0; 978-0-06-025316-5 lib bdg; 0-06-025316-9 lib bdg

LC 2010-07856

With the help of his popular Uncle Chester, a young Chinese American boy tries hard to fulfill a promise to have firecrackers for everyone on the Chinese New Year in 1954. Includes an afterword with information about the Chinese customs portrayed in the story.

"Yep skillfully portrays the significance and emotional nature of common childhood dramas, from fears of going back on one's word to worries of losing a favorite uncle to a new girlfriend. . . . Yep has crafted other memorable characters, including Chinatown itself, which sparkle with energy and camaraderie." Publ Wkly

Includes bibliographical references

★ The **traitor**; Golden Mountain chronicles, 1885. HarperCollins Pubs. 2003 310p hardcover o.p. pa $6.99

Grades: 5 6 7 8   Fic

1. Friendship 2. Prejudices 3. Chinese Americans 4. Coal mines and mining 5. Friendship -- Fiction 6. Illegitimate children 7. Prejudices -- Fiction 8. Chinese Americans -- Fiction 9. Rock Springs Massacre, Rock Springs, Wyo., 1885

ISBN 0-06-027522-7; 0-06-000831-8 pa

LC 2002-22534

In 1885, a lonely illegitimate American boy and a lonely Chinese American boy develop an unlikely friendship in the midst of prejudices and racial tension in their coal mining town of Rock Springs, Wyoming

"The short chapters read quickly, and readers will become involved through the first-person voices that capture each boy's feelings of being an outsider and a traitor." Booklist

Ylvisaker, Anne

Little Klein. Candlewick Press 2007 186p $15.99; pa $6.99

Grades: 3 4 5 6   Fic

1. Dogs -- Fiction 2. Size -- Fiction 3. Brothers -- Fiction 4. Family life -- Fiction

ISBN 978-0-7636-3359-2; 0-7636-3359-3; 978-0-7636-4338-6 pa; 0-7636-4338-6 pa

LC 2007-24189

Harold "Little" Klein is so much smaller than his three older brothers, a boisterous gang held together by bighearted Mother Klein, that he often feels small and left out but when disaster strikes, it is up to Harold and LeRoy, the stray dog he has adopted, to save the day.

"Ylvisaker's pleasing text is rich with wit and flows seamlessly; her knack for capturing a character's essence is remarkable." Voice Youth Advocates

The **luck** of the Buttons. Candlewick Press 2011 224p $15.99

Grades: 4 5 6   Fic

1. Mystery fiction 2. Chance -- Fiction 3. Friendship -- Fiction 4. Family life -- Fiction 5. Photography -- Fiction 6. Great Depression, 1929-1939 -- Fiction

ISBN 978-0-7636-5066-7; 0-7636-5066-8

LC 2010039169

In Iowa circa 1929, spunky twelve-year-old Tugs vows to turn her family's luck around, with the help of a Brownie camera and a small-town mystery that only she can solve.

"The tale has a whiff of nostalgia, . . . but the good old days are balanced by the strongly realized, immediate characters and the delicacy and originality of the writing." Horn Book

Yohalem, Eve
★ **Escape** under the forever sky; a novel. Chronicle Books 2009 220p $16.99

Grades: 4 5 6 7 **Fic**
1. Kidnapping -- Fiction 2. Wilderness survival -- Fiction 3. Mother-daughter relationship -- Fiction
ISBN 978-0-8118-6653-8; 0-8118-6653-X
LC 2008-19565

As a future conservation zoologist whose mother is the United States Ambassador to Ethiopia, thirteen-year-old Lucy uses her knowledge for survival when she is kidnapped and subsequently escapes.

"Lucy's past and present are gracefully woven together, through well-integrated flashbacks, into a powerful picture of the life of a foreigner in Ethiopia. The story should appeal to all with a sense of adventure." Publ Wkly

Yolen, Jane
Snow in Summer. Philomel Books 2011

Grades: 4 5 6 7 **Fic**
1. Fairy tales 2. Magic -- Fiction 3. Stepmothers -- Fiction
ISBN 0-399-25663-6; 978-0-399-25663-9
LC 2010044242

Recasts the tale of Snow White, setting it in West Virginia in the 1940s with a stepmother who is a snake-handler.

"This story is beautifully written and deliciously scary, with just enough differences from familiar versions to keep readers guessing." Publ Wkly

Yoo, David
The **detention** club. Balzer + Bray 2011 299p $16.99

Grades: 5 6 7 8 **Fic**
1. School stories 2. Siblings -- Fiction 3. Popularity -- Fiction 4. Korean Americans -- Fiction
ISBN 978-0-06-178378-4; 0-06-178378-1
LC 2010-46211

Sixth-grader Peter Lee, in a desperate attempt to regain the popularity he had in elementary school, discovers that serving detention can win him important friends, much to the dismay of his over-achieving eighth-grade sister, Sunny.

"Even readers who guess the thief's identity early on will be entertained by the boys' hijinks and empathize with their desire to fit in." Publ Wkly

Young, Judy
A **book** for black-eyed Susan; written by Judy Young; illustrated by Doris Ettlinger. Sleeping Bear Press 2011 un il $16.95

Grades: 2 3 4 **Fic**
1. Sewing -- Fiction 2. Sisters -- Fiction 3. Books and reading -- Fiction 4. Frontier and pioneer life -- Fiction 5. Overland journeys to the Pacific -- Fiction
ISBN 978-1-58536-463-3; 1-58536-463-0
LC 2010028422

While traveling along the Oregon Trail, ten-year-old Cora and her newborn baby sister suffer the loss of their mother and are separated, but Cora stitches a book to tell the dark-eyed baby of their journey and family.

"The surprise ending, however unlikely, will warm readers' hearts. Realistic watercolor images reveal the intricacies of pioneer life and the emotional turmoil of the characters. An engaging introduction to life during the Westward expansion." SLJ

Minnow and Rose; an Oregon trail story. written by Judy Young; illustrated by Bill Farnsworth. Sleeping Bear Press 2009 un il (Tales of young Americans) $17.95

Grades: 3 4 5 **Fic**
1. Friendship -- Fiction 2. Native Americans -- Fiction 3. Frontier and pioneer life -- Fiction
ISBN 978-1-58536-421-3; 1-58536-421-5
LC 2008024768

Traveling west with her pioneer family in a wagon train, Rose meets Minnow, who lives in a native American village along the banks of a river.

"Beautiful oil paintings . . . lend additional action and understanding to the story." SLJ

Young, Karen Romano
Doodlebug; a novel in doodles. Feiwel and Friends 2010 un il $14.99

Grades: 4 5 6 7 **Fic**
1. School stories 2. Moving -- Fiction 3. Family life -- Fiction 4. Racially mixed people -- Fiction
ISBN 978-0-312-56156-7; 0-312-56156-3

Doreen Bussey, aka Dodo, takes the nickname Doodlebug when her family moves from Los Angeles to San Francisco and she records her experiences in a notebook with words, scribbles, and drawings.

This offers "an engaging, originial heroine, a satisfying story and lots of great pictures. . . . Some details, like the fact that the family is interracial, are shown but not stated, rewarding careful examination of the artwork. . . . Charming and thoughtful." Kirkus

Zahler, Diane
The **thirteenth** princess. Harper 2009 243p

Grades: 4 5 6 7 **Fic**
1. Fairy tales 2. Magic -- Fiction 3. Sisters -- Fiction 4. Princesses -- Fiction 5. Household employees -- Fiction 6. Father-daughter relationship -- Fiction 7. Folklore -- Germany -- Juvenile literature
ISBN 0-06-182498-4; 0-06-182499-2 lib bdg; 978-0-06-182498-2; 978-0-06-182499-9 lib bdg
LC 2009-14575

Zita, cast aside by her father and raised as a kitchen maid, learns when she is nearly twelve that she is a princess and that her twelve sisters love her, and so when she discovers they are victims of an evil enchantment, she desperately tries to save them. Inspired by the Grimm fairy tale, "The twelve dancing princesses."

Zahler "deftly and thoughtfully embellishes the tale's classic elements. . . . Zahler takes a light story and gives it gratifying depth, rounding out the characters and their motivations without betraying the source material and wrapping it all together in a graceful and cohesive romantic drama." Publ Wkly

A **true** princess. Harper 2011 182p $15.99
Grades: 4 5 6   **Fic**
  1. Fairy tales 2. Friendship -- Fiction 3. Princesses
-- Fiction 4. Voyages and travels -- Fiction
ISBN 978-0-06-182501-9; 0-06-182501-8
                     LC 2010017846
Twelve-year-old Lilia goes north to seek the family she
has never known, accompanied by her friends Kai and Kar-
ina and their dog Ove, on an adventure fraught with peril,
especially when they become lost in Bitra Forest, the Elf
King's domain. Inspired by the Hans Christian Andersen
tale, The princess and the pea.
  "Readers who enjoyed . . . Zahler's The Thirteenth Princess . . . will also relish this tale." SLJ

Zalben, Jane Breskin
  Brenda Berman, wedding expert; illustrated by Victo-
ria Chess. Clarion Books 2009 48p il lib bdg $16
Grades: 2 3 4   **Fic**
  1. Uncles -- Fiction 2. Weddings -- Fiction 3.
Friendship -- Fiction
ISBN 978-0-618-31321-1 lib bdg; 0-618-31321-4
lib bdg
                    LC 2006-34851
When Brenda's favorite uncle decides to marry, Brenda
sees visions of a gold lame flower-girl's outfit, until Uncle
Harry and his bride-to-be show up with her niece. Includes
cake recipe.
  "Brenda's robust personality drives the narrative as well
as the art, as Chess's folksy watercolors capture the girl's
expressions, which vacillate wildly between outrage and exhilaration." Publ Wkly

Zimmer, Tracie Vaughn
  42 miles; illustrated by Elaine Clayton. Clarion Books
2008 73p il $16
Grades: 4 5 6   **Fic**
  1. In verse 2. Divorce -- Fiction 3. Farm life -- Fiction
4. Family life -- Fiction 5. City and town life -- Fiction
ISBN 978-0-618-61867-5; 0-618-61867-8
                    LC 2007-31032
As her thirteenth birthday approaches, JoEllen decides to
bring together her two separate lives—one as Joey, who enjoys weekends with her father and other relatives on a farm,
and another as Ellen, who lives with her mother in an apartment near her school and friends.
  "Using free verse, Zimmer shows the richness in both
places, while black-and-white composit illustrations bright
the bits and pieces together." Booklist

  Sketches from a spy tree; poems by Tracie Vaughn
Zimmer; illustrated by Andrew Glass. Clarion Books 2005
63p il $16
Grades: 3 4 5 6   **Fic**
  1. Twins -- Fiction 2. Divorce -- Fiction 3. Sisters
-- Fiction 4. Stepfamilies -- Fiction
ISBN 0-618-23479-9
                    LC 2003-27768
In a series of poems, narrator Anne Marie paints pictures
of family life from grief to hope after her father abandons
his "four girls" Anne Marie and her mother and twin and
baby sister.

  "The writing is lyrical yet fresh. . . . Glass's remarkable
watercolors, sketches, photographs, and collages bring Anne
Marie's experiences to life." SLJ

  The **floating** circus; by Tracie Vaughn Zimmer.
Bloomsbury Children's Books 2008 198p $15.99
Grades: 4 5 6   **Fic**
  1. Circus -- Fiction 2. Boats and boating -- Fiction 3.
Abandoned children -- Fiction
ISBN 978-1-59990-185-5; 1-59990-185-4
                    LC 2007038998
In 1850s Pittsburgh, thirteen-year-old Owen leaves his
younger brother and sneaks aboard a circus housed in a riverboat, where he befriends a freed slave, learns to work with
elephants, and finally comes to terms with the choices he has
made in his difficult life
  This is a "lively historical novel. Readers will be hooked
from the start by the voice of the narrator. . . . Bittersweet
and satisfying." Publ Wkly

Zoehfeld, Kathleen Weidner
  ★ **Secrets** of the garden; food chains and the food web
in our backyard. illustrated by Priscilla Lamont. Alfred A.
Knopf 2012 il $16.99; lib bdg $19.99
Grades: K 1 2 3   **Fic**
  1. Gardens -- Fiction 2. Gardening -- Fiction 3. Food
chains (Ecology) -- Fiction
ISBN 978-0-517-70990-0; 0-517-70990-2; 978-0-517-
70991-7 lib bdg; 0-517-70991-0 lib bdg; 978-0-375-
98730-4 ebook
                    LC 2011032059
This "is a wonderfully informative and enjoyable journey through one family's backyard garden, from spring
planting to fall harvest. Covering a dazzling array of topics,
the author still manages to hold onto a story line that will
draw readers in and allow them to experience both the good
and the bad right along with narrator Alice. . . . The text
comes alive through Lamont's pen-and-watercolor illustrations, which reinforce the learning while entertaining at the
same time." Kirkus

Zucker, Naomi Flink
  ★ **Callie's** rules; by Naomi Zucker. Egmont USA
2009 240p $15.99; lib bdg $18.99
Grades: 4 5 6 7   **Fic**
  1. School stories 2. Halloween -- Fiction 3. Family
life -- Fiction
ISBN 978-1-60684-027-6; 1-60684-027-4; 978-1-
60684-052-8 lib bdg; 1-60684-052-5 lib bdg
                    LC 2009-15419
Eleven-year-old Callie Jones tries to keep track of all
the rules for fitting in that other middle schoolers seem to
know, but when the town decides to replace Halloween
with an Autumn Festival, Callie leads her large family in an
unusual protest.
  "Callie herself is both funny and resourceful. Worthwhile and entertaining." Kirkus

  Write on, Callie Jones; by Naomi Zucker. Egmont
USA 2010 188p $15.99
Grades: 4 5 6 7   **Fic**
  1. School stories 2. Authorship -- Fiction 3.

Newspapers -- Fiction
ISBN 978-1-60684-028-3; 1-60684-028-2

LC 2010-23134

As she continues to establish rules for navigating middle school, aspiring author Callie writes for the school newspaper until the principal cancels her article and Callie's quest to have her voice heard leads to a series of unexpected consequences.

"Playful, entertaining writing peppers this novel. . . . A quick, easy read for fans of the first book." SLJ

S C   STORY COLLECTIONS

Aiken, Joan

Shadows and moonshine; stories. illustrations by Pamela Johnson. Godine 2001 171p il hardcover o.p. pa $10.95

Grades: 4 5 6 7   S C
1. Short stories 2. Fantasy fiction
ISBN 1-56792-167-1; 1-56792-346-1 pa

LC 2001-23830

This is a collection of 13 stories about such things as witches, enchanted pigs, mermaids, and dragons, selected from the author's earlier anthologies

"Whether scary, satiric, or poetic, Aiken's tales have strong settings, memorable characters, insight, and humor." SLJ

Alexander, Lloyd

★ The **foundling** and other tales of Prydain; rev & expanded ed; Holt & Co. 1999 98p hardcover o.p. pa $5.99

Grades: 5 6 7 8   S C
1. Fantasy 2. Short stories 3. Fantasy fiction 4. Children's stories, American
ISBN 0-8050-6130-4; 0-8050-8053-8 pa

LC 98-42807

First published 1973; this revised and expanded edition includes two additional stories Coll and his white pig and The truthful harp, first published separately 1965 and 1967 respectively

Eight short stories dealing with events that preceded the birth of Taran, the Assistant Pig-Keeper and key figure in the author's five works on the Kingdom of Prydain which began with The book of three

"The stories are written with vivid grace and humor." Chicago. Children's Book Center [review of 1973 edition]

Andersen, Hans Christian, 1805-1875

★ **Hans** Christian Andersen's Fairy Tales; selected and illustrated by Lisbeth Zwerger; translated by Anthea Bell. Minedition 2006 104p il $19.99

Grades: 4 5 6 7   S C
1. Fairy tales 2. Short stories
ISBN 0-698-40035-6

A reissue of the edition first published 1991

"This collection of . . . tales includes relatively unknown stories, such as 'The Rose Tree Regiment,' along with such familiar favorites as 'The Princess & the Pea.' Bell's finesse in writing is well matched by Zwerger's delicate, understated approach in the illustrations, which are introspective rather than dramatic. Sophisticated in design, the book fea-

tures fluid watercolors and wide-bordered text on tall, white pages." Booklist

Arato, Rona

On a medieval day; story voyages around the world. illustrated by Peter Ferguson. Maple Tree Press 2010 96p il $24.95; pa $15.95

Grades: 4 5 6   S C
1. Short stories 2. Middle Ages -- Fiction 3. Middle Ages -- Juvenile literature
ISBN 978-1-897349-94-6; 1-897349-94-7; 978-1-897349-95-3 pa; 1-897349-95-5 pa

"Alternating between male and female narrators, this book presents stories about nine fictional youth of the medieval period. From the Mayan Civilization in 720 to the Kingdom of Castile in 1395, with stops in Vinland in 1002, Japan in 1205, and other places and years, their tales provide readers with a worldview of the era. Each chapter follows one child or teen through a day in which a conflict or crisis for the protagonist brings in some cultural and social context of the period. . . . The fast-paced stories make for entertaining reading. Each chapter ends with a brief history of the period and includes a simple map. . . . The book is a wonderful attempt to expand the usual concept of the medieval world beyond Europe." SLJ

Avi

Strange happenings; five tales of transformation. Harcourt 2006 147p $15; pa $5.95

Grades: 5 6 7 8   S C
1. Short stories 2. Supernatural -- Fiction
ISBN 0-15-205790-0; 0-15-206461-3 pa

LC 2004-29579

"In this short story collection, Avi offers five fantastical tales, set in both contemporary and fairy-tale lands, that explore the notion of transformation. . . . The pieces are vividly imagined and shot through with a captivating, edgy spookiness, which, along with their brevity and some droll, crackling dialogue, makes them great choices for sharing aloud in class or as inspiration in creative-writing units." Booklist

What do fish have to do with anything? and other stories; illustrated by Tracy Mitchell. Candlewick Press 1997 202p il hardcover o.p. pa $6.99

Grades: 4 5 6 7   S C
1. Short stories
ISBN 0-7636-0329-5; 0-7636-2319-9 pa

LC 97-1354

"While Avi's endings are not tidy, they are effective: each story brings its protagonist beyond childhood self-absorption to the realization that one is an integral part of a bigger picture." Horn Book

★ **Baseball** crazy: ten short stories that cover all the bases; edited by Nancy E. Mercado. Dial Books for Young Readers 2008 191p $16.99; pa $6.99

Grades: 4 5 6 7   S C
1. Short stories 2. Baseball -- Fiction 3. Baseball -- Juvenile literature 4. Short stories -- Collections -- Juvenile literature
ISBN 978-0-8037-3162-2; 0-8037-3162-0; 978-0-14-241371-5 pa; 0-14-241371-2 pa

LC 2007-26649

"There's no shortage of great writing in this collection of 10 stories. Baseball unifies the entries, but there the similarities end. . . . Readers will be drawn in by the masterful storytelling." Publ Wkly

Babbitt, Natalie

The **Devil's** storybook; stories and pictures by Natalie Babbitt. Farrar, Straus & Giroux 1974 101p il hardcover o.p. pa $3.95

Grades: 4 5 6   S C

1. Short stories 2. Devil -- Fiction

ISBN 0-374-41708-3 pa

"Twists of plot within traditional themes and a briskly witty style distinguish this book, illustrated amusingly with black-and-white line drawings." Booklist

★ **Best** shorts; favorite short stories for sharing. selected by Avi; assisted by Carolyn Shute; afterword by Katherine Paterson; [illustrations by Chris Raschka] Houghton Mifflin 2006 342p $16.95

Grades: 5 6 7 8   S C

1. Short stories

ISBN 978-0-618-47603-9; 0-618-47603-2

LC 2006011535

"There is no integrating theme in the 24 short stories included here—just fine writing, cultural diversity, and timeless creativity. With such strong writers as Richard Peck, Natalie Babbitt, Lloyd Alexander, and Rafe Martin, one would expect nothing less." SLJ

The **big** book of pirates; text abridged and adapted by Alissa Heyman; illustrated by Xose Tomas; [original Spanish text by by Joan and Albert Vinyoli] Sterling Pub. Co. 2011 103p il $12.95

Grades: 3 4 5 6   S C

1. Short stories 2. Adventure fiction 3. Pirates -- Fiction

ISBN 978-1-4027-8056-1; 1-4027-8056-7

LC 2010015049

This "is a treasure trove of abridged yarns by the likes of Sir Arthur Conan Doyle, Joseph Conrad, Daniel Defoe, and others. Of course the stories deal with pillaging, treachery, and all-around bad behavior on the open seas. The artwork is a dark, graphic-novel-like spin on N.C. Wyeth's illustrations for classics such as Treasure Island and Robinson Crusoe. Tomás uses a bold color palette and has given many of his characters angular faces and staring eyes, all to an appropriately menacing effect. This entertaining package will not make port on the shelves for long." SLJ

Byars, Betsy Cromer

Cat diaries; secret writings of the MEOW Society. [by] Betsy Byars, Betsy Duffey, Laurie Myers; illustrated by Erik Brooks. Henry Holt and Company 2010 80p il $15.99

Grades: 2 3 4   S C

1. Short stories 2. Cats -- Fiction

ISBN 978-0-8050-8717-8; 0-8050-8717-6

LC 2009-18877

On one night every year, cats in the MEOW Society, which stands for "Memories Expressed In Our Writing," gather to read from their diaries, hearing stories of a gypsy cat, a Caribbean pirate cat, a library cat, and many others.

"This is a solid collection of stories that young readers will enjoy." Libr Media Connect

Dog diaries; secret writings of the WOOF Society. [by] Betsy Byars, Betsy Duffey, Laurie Myers; illustrated by Erik Brooks. Henry Holt 2007 72p il $15.95

Grades: 2 3 4   S C

1. Short stories 2. Dogs -- Fiction 3. Storytelling -- Fiction

ISBN 978-0-8050-7957-9; 0-8050-7957-2

LC 2006011634

At the first annual meeting of WOOF—Words of Our Friends—assorted dogs preserve their heritage by sharing tales of canines throughout history, including Abu, who ruled all of Egypt except for one pesky cat, and Zippy, who simply must find the squeaky toy

"This collection of short stories combines the bedrocks of mass appeal: dogs, humor, and short chapters brimming with illustrations. . . . Expressive, energetic pencil illustrations adorn nearly every page." Booklist

★ The **Chronicles** of Harris Burdick; 14 amazing authors tell the tales. Houghton Mifflin Harcourt 2011 un il $24.99

Grades: 5 6 7 8 9   S C

1. Short stories

ISBN 978-0-547-54810-4; 0-547-54810-9; 0547548109; 9780547548104

LC 2011006564

"Van Allsburg's The Mysteries of Harris Burdick, published in 1984, paired foreboding sentences with cryptic, highly detailed charcoal-pencil illustrations. With mostly stimulating, sometimes conventional results, seasoned authors (and Van Allsburg himself) play the game children have for decades, incorporating the sentences and visual cues into new stories . . . that expand on the original's enigmas. The liveliest entries pick up on Van Allsburg's haunting ambiguity: Jon Scieszka ends with a cliffhanger, Gregory Maguire weaves a complex tale of magic, and M.T. Anderson concocts a chilling Halloween offering. For a lakeside picture of two children, Sherman Alexie writes a sinister narrative about exasperating twins who pretend to have a third sibling, until their creepy prank backfires. . . . This star-studded exercise in creative writing tests the wits of favorite authors and shows readers how even the big shots hone their craft." Publ Wkly

Conrad, Pam

★ **Our** house; pictures by Brian Selznick. 10th anniversary ed; Scholastic Press 2005 130p il $16.99

Grades: 4 5 6 7   S C

1. Short stories

ISBN 0-439-74508-X

LC 2004065082

A reissue of the title first published 1995. Includes a new artist's note by Brian Selznick

Six stories, one from each decade from the 1940s to the 1990s, about children growing up in Levittown, New York

"Vivid descriptions and poignant observations leave indelible impressions. . . . Conrad's fresh, imaginative approach to the concept of 'home' makes this an ideal starting point for discussion, creative writing, and other class activities." Booklist

Del Negro, Janice

★ **Passion** and poison; tales of shape-shifters, ghosts, and spirited women. Marshall Cavendish 2007 64p il $16.99

Grades: 5 6 7 8   S C
1. Ghost stories 2. Short stories 3. Supernatural -- Fiction 4. Short stories -- By individual authors -- Juvenile literature

ISBN 978-0-7614-5361-1; 0-7614-5361-X
LC 2007-07237

"Including both original tales and retellings, this collection of seven stories . . . features diverse female protagonists facing challenges and perils—from human bullies to ghosts. More eerie than scary, the tales of bravery, revenge, grief, and redemption share a gothic sensibility. . . . The black-and-white illustrations . . . evoke bygone times." Booklist

Delacre, Lulu

★ **Salsa** stories; stories and linocuts by Lulu Delacre. Scholastic Press 2000 105p il hardcover o.p. $16.99

Grades: 4 5 6   S C
1. Short stories 2. Family life -- Fiction

ISBN 0-590-63118-7; 0-590-63121-7 pa
LC 99-25534

A collection of stories within the story of a family celebration where the guests relate their memories of growing up in various Latin American countries. Also contains recipes

"Kids will respond to both the warmth and the anxiety of the family life described in the vivid writing, and in Delacre's nicely composed linocuts." Booklist

Delaney, Joseph

The **Spook's** tale and other horrors; illustrations by Patrick Arrasmith. Greenwillow Books 2009 166p il (The last apprentice) $10.95; lib bdg $14.89

Grades: 5 6 7 8   S C
1. Short stories 2. Witches -- Fiction 3. Supernatural -- Fiction

ISBN 978-0-06-173028-3; 0-06-173028-9; 978-0-06-173030-6 lib bdg; 0-06-173030-0 lib bdg
LC 2008042235

As sixty-year-old John Gregory reflects on the past, he reveals how the world of ghosts, ghasts, witches, and boggarts was exposed to him and he later became the Spook, even though his first intention had been to join the priesthood.

"These short stories are narrated by secondary characters from the popular series, giving insight into some of Tom Ward's well-known companions. A 'Gallery of Villains' section identifies additional characters and gives a citation to the novels. . . . This book would be perfect for pulling reluctant readers into the series. The occasional black-and-white illustrations add a creepy, atmospheric touch." SLJ

Explorer; the mystery boxes. edited by Kazu Kibuishi. Amulet Books 2012 126 p.

Grades: 4 5 6 7 8   SC
1. Short stories 2. Graphic novels 3. Boxes -- Fiction 4. Mystery graphic novels 5. Boxes -- Juvenile fiction 6. Children's stories, American

ISBN 9781419700095; 9781419700101
LC 2011025343

This collection of short stories offers "[s]even . . . stories [which] answer one simple question: what's in the box? . . .

[E]ach of these . . . illustrated short graphic works revolves around a central theme: a mysterious box and the marvels-or mayhem--inside. Artists include . . . Kazu Kibuishi, Raina Telgemeier ('Smile'), and Dave Roman ('Astronaut Academy'), as well as Jason Caffoe, Stuart Livingston, Johane Matte, Rad Sechrist (all contributors to the . . . comics anthology series 'Flight'), and . . . artist Emily Carroll." (Publisher's note)

Flanagan, John, 1944-

The **lost** stories. Philomel 2011 422p (Ranger's apprentice) $17.99 S C
1. Short stories 2. Fantasy fiction

ISBN 978-0-399-25618-9; 0-399-25618-0

This is "a collection of nine stories showing events not recorded in the books [of the Ranger's Apprentice series] and following the familiar characters during certain unrecorded times. In the framework story, set in 1896, an archaeologist discovers the fabled lost stories of the medieval Kingdom of Araluen. . . . Inspired by questions from readers, these short stories retain the adventure and the camaraderis of the novels." Booklist

Fleischman, Paul

Friends; stories about new friends, old friends, and unexpectedly true friends. edited by Ann M. Martin and David Levithan. Scholastic Press 2005 185p $16.95

Grades: 5 6 7 8   S C
1. Short stories 2. Friendship -- Fiction 3. Short stories -- Collections -- Juvenile literature

ISBN 0-439-72991-2
LC 2004-27758

"This collection of stories by well-known authors spans a broad definition of the term 'friend,' and also approaches the topic from a wide variety of viewpoints. . . . The selections by Ann M. Martin, Pam Muñoz Ryan, Rachel Cohn, David Levithan, and Patricia McCormick are among the more outstanding entries. . . . It is also likely that every reader will find at least one that hits home." SLJ

Girl meets boy; edited by Kelly Milner Halls. Chronicle Books 2012 v. cm.
SC
1. Short stories 2. Teenagers -- Fiction 3. Interpersonal relations -- Fiction 4. Short stories, American 5. Perspective (Philosophy) -- Fiction 6. Interpersonal relations -- Juvenile fiction 7. Perspective (Philosophy) -- Juvenile fiction

ISBN 9781452102641
LC 2011025405

In this book "[t]welve writers answer [editor Kelly Milner] Halls's question: 'What if a group of authors took on the challenge of perception—boys versus girls?' Together, they create a thoughtful collection of paired short stories (and one joint offering) that give two distinct perspectives on the same events. While romantically themed, the stories do not all end in love connections. In James Howe and Ellen Wittlinger's stories, a gay teen learns the person he has been chatting with online is actually a girl; meanwhile, in Sarah Ryan and Randy Powell's joint story, 'Launchpad to Neptune,' a teen reunites with his first crush, only to find Stephanie has transitioned to Stephen." (Publishers Weekly)

Give me shelter; stories about children who seek asylum. edited by Tony Bradman. Frances Lincoln 2007 220p $16.95

Grades: 5 6 7 8　　　　　　　　　　　　**S C**

1. Short stories 2. Refugees -- Fiction

ISBN 978-1-84507-522-4; 1-84507-522-6

This is a "moving collection of 11 powerful narratives, quite different in their particulars but astonishingly similar in their sense of loss and loneliness. . . . While most of the stories focus on current asylum-seekers in Britain, one looks back to a Vietnamese child's trip to Australia, and another is set in an unnamed Eastern European country." SLJ

Graven images; three stories. by Paul Fleischman; illustrations by Bagram Ibatoulline. Candlewick Press 2006 116p il $16.99; pa $5.99

Grades: 5 6 7 8　　　　　　　　　　　　**S C**

1. Short stories 2. Supernatural -- Fiction

ISBN 0-7636-2775-5; 0-7636-2984-7 pa

LC 2005054283

A newly illustrated edition with a new afterword of the title first published 1982 by Harper & Row

A Newbery Medal honor book, 1983

A collection of three stories about a child who reads the lips of those who whisper secrets into a statue's ear; a daydreaming shoemaker's apprentice who must find ways to make the girl he loves notice him; and a stone carver who creates a statue of a ghost.

"Readers will be delighted with the return to print of [this title] with haunting new acrylic gouache illustrations . . . evoking the spinetingling aspects of this trio of tales. . . . Via a new afterword, the author explains the stories' inspiration and describes this book's significance early in his career." Publ Wkly

★ **Guys** read: funny business; edited and with an introduction by Jon Scieszka; stories by Mac Barnett [et al.]; with illustrations by Adam Rex. Walden Pond Press 2010 268p il $16.99; pa $5.99

Grades: 4 5 6 7　　　　　　　　　　　　**S C**

1. Short stories 2. Humorous fiction 3. Boys -- Fiction 4. Short stories -- Collections -- Juvenile literature

ISBN 978-0-06-196374-2; 0-06-196374-7; 978-0-06-196373-5 pa; 0-06-196373-9 pa

LC 2010-08122

A collection of humorous stories featuring a teenaged mummy, a homicidal turkey, and the world's largest pool of chocolate milk.

"A must-have collection for the boys in your library—and while you're at it, get a copy for the girls too!" Booklist

★ **Guys** read: thriller. Walden Pond Press 2011 viii, 272p $16.99; pa $6.99

Grades: 5 6 7 8　　　　　　　　　　　　**S C**

1. Short stories 2. Adventure fiction

ISBN 978-0-06-196376-6; 0-06-196376-3; 978-0-06-196375-9 pa; 0-06-196375-5 pa

"Scieszka has gathered 10 thrilling stories from stellar writers. There are ghost stories, a deeply touching tale of a wish-granting machine and one about monsters that live in storm drains. . . . This anthology is brimming with choice stuff for guys who appreciate the uncanny, the uncouth and the unput-down-able." Kirkus

★ **Half**-minute horrors; edited by Susan Rich. HarperCollinsPublishers 2009 141p il $12.99

Grades: 5 6 7 8　　　　　　　　　　　　**S C**

1. Short stories 2. Horror fiction 3. Short stories -- Collections -- Juvenile literature

ISBN 978-0-06-183379-3; 0-06-183379-7

LC 2009-18293

An anthology of very short, scary stories by an assortment of authors and illustrators including Chris Raschka, Joyce Carol Oates, Neil Gaiman, Jack Gantos, and Lane Smith.

"This collection of more than 70 chilling snippets is ideal for campfires and car trips. The stories—some a couple sentences, some a few pages—range from darkly humorous . . . to outright creepy. . . . These are inherently quick reads, but with enough plot and detail to encourage further imagining." Publ Wkly

Hawes, Louise

Black pearls; a faerie strand. by Louise Hawes; illustrations by Rebecca Guay. Houghton Mifflin Company 2008 211p il $16

Grades: 5 6 7 8 9 10 11 12　　　　　　　**S C**

1. Fairy tales 2. Short stories 3. Short stories -- By individual authors -- Juvenile literature

ISBN 978-0-618-74797-9; 0-618-74797-4

LC 2007-41166

"Seven gems based on traditional fairy tales make up this collection of unique short stories. . . . Each contains enough clues to guide teens back to the familiar and sometimes innuendo-laden classic fairy tales of their childhoods, and Guay's fantastical pencil drawings . . . enhance the sense of character and magic. Twisted, clever, and artfully written." Booklist

Hearne, Betsy Gould

The **canine** connection: stories about dogs and people; [by] Betsy Hearne. Margaret K. McElderry Bks. 2003 113p hardcover o.p. pa $8.95

Grades: 5 6 7 8　　　　　　　　　　　　**S C**

1. Dogs 2. Short stories 3. Dogs -- Fiction 4. Dogs -- Juvenile fiction 5. Human-animal relationships 6. Children's stories, American

ISBN 0-689-85258-4; 1-4169-6817-2 pa

LC 2001-58991

Twelve short stories that reflect the varied ways that dogs and humans relate

"The emotions and dialogue are pitch perfect. . . . A rewarding collection that will stay with readers." Booklist

Horse tales; collected by June Crebbin; illustrated by Inga Moore. Candlewick Press 2005 148p il $18.99

Grades: 4 5 6 7　　　　　　　　　　　　**S C**

1. Short stories 2. Horses -- Fiction

ISBN 0-7636-2657-0

LC 2004-51897

In these "short stories, the remarkable nature of the horse is revealed. . . . The offerings excerpted from novels work well as short stories here and may inspire readers to look for the full-length books. . . . This is an excellently conceived and executed collection with wonderful art." SLJ

I fooled you; ten stories of tricks, jokes, and switcheroos. collected and edited by Johanna Hurwitz. Candlewick Press 2010 174p il $16.99; pa $6.99

Grades: 4 5 6

S C

1. Short stories 2. Short stories -- Collections -- Juvenile literature

ISBN 978-0-7636-3789-7; 0-7636-3789-0; 978-0-7636-4877-0 pa; 0-7636-4877-9 pa

LC 2009-26017

"Hurwitz asked 10 authors to write a piece with the tagline of the title. . . . Megan McDonald uses her familiar characters, Judy Moody and Stink. . . . Douglas Florian's poem is distinctively in his style, but contains unexpected elements, nonetheless. . . . Michelle Knudsen's 'The Bridge to Highlandsville' is absolutely logical yet lacks the ending most would expect. Matthew Holm's almost wordless 'Sam and Pam' . . . adds a nice graphic-novel-style component to the package. Most readers will likely find something that they appreciate and something that they don't—which may be the best indication of the range of depth and complexity in this collection." SLJ

Ionesco, Eugène, 1912-1994

Stories 1,2,3,4; Eugene Ionesco; illustrated by Etienne Delessert. Pgw 2012 112 p. $19.95

Grades: K 1 2 3

S C

1. Children's stories 2. Picture books for children

ISBN 1936365510; 9781936365517

In this collection of stories by Eugene Ionesco, illustrated by Etienne Delessert, provides "snippets of playful conversation between Papa, Mama, their daughter Josette, and Jacqueline the maid. . . . In Story 3, the father tells Josette about an airplane journey they'll take together . . . over the Paris rooftops, and on to the moon. . . . Visual quotes (including plenty of Ionesco rhinoceri) pop up everywhere." (Publishers Weekly)

Juster, Norton

Alberic the Wise and other journeys; illustrated by Domenico Gnoli. 2010 88p il pa $5.99

Grades: 3 4 5 6

S C

1. Short stories

ISBN 978-0-375-86699-9; 0-375-86699-X

A reissue of the title first published 1965 by Pantheon

"Three stories leave readers wondering: What happened next? The first tells of Alberic, who spent his life searching without knowing what for. In the second a modern boy steps into a Renaissance painting. The third tells of two kings who briefly exchange kingdoms. Juster's smooth storytelling weaves together action and characterization. Gnoli's striking illustrations have a medieval feeling and are in perfect harmony." Horn Book Guide

Kipling, Rudyard, 1865-1936

★ A **collection** of Rudyard Kipling's Just so stories. Candlewick Press 2004 127p il $22.99

Grades: 3 4 5 6

S C

1. Short stories 2. Animals -- Fiction

ISBN 0-7636-2629-5

LC 2004-45858

"This colorful collection of eight tales distinguishes itself with its range of artwork. Well-known children's book artists, including Peter Sis, Jane Ray, and Satoshi Kitamura, contributed the art, each one illustrating a different story.

The vibrant mix of styles and materials adds new dimension to favorite stories. . . . A lively, accessible edition." Booklist

The **jungle** book: Mowgli's story; [illustrated by] Nicola Bayley. Candlewick Press 2005 151p il $19.99

Grades: 4 5 6 7

S C

1. Short stories 2. Animals -- Fiction

ISBN 0-7636-2317-2

"Three stories–'Mowgli's Brothers,' 'Kaa's Hunting,' and 'Tiger! Tiger!'–and six of the poetic songs from Kipling's classic work are accompanied by painterly illustrations. . . . A combination of detailed miniature drawings and small framed paintings is strategically placed throughout the text. . . . The masterful use of light, detail, rich color, and texture creates striking and evocative visual effects." SLJ

Just so stories; illustrated by Barry Moser; afterword by Peter Glassman. Morrow 1996 148p il $24.99

Grades: 3 4 5 6

S C

1. Short stories 2. Animals -- Fiction

ISBN 0-688-13957-4

LC 95-13714

First published 1902

A set of tales that "give far-fetched humorous explanations of the chief physical characteristics of certain animals." Oxford Companion to Child Lit

Marcantonio, Patricia Santos

Red ridin' in the hood; and other cuentos. pictures by Renato Alarcão. Farrar, Straus & Giroux 2005 181p il $16

Grades: 3 4 5

S C

1. Fairy tales 2. Short stories 3. Hispanic Americans -- Fiction

ISBN 0-374-36241-6

"The fractured fairy tale gets cool Latino flavor in this lively collection of 11 fresh retellings, with witty reversals of class and gender roles and powerful, full-page pictures that set the drama in venues ranging from the desert and the barrio to a skyscraper." Booklist

Marshall, James, 1942-1992

Rats on the roof, and other stories. Dial Bks. for Young Readers 1991 79p il hardcover o.p. pa $4.99

Grades: 2 3 4

S C

1. Short stories 2. Animals -- Fiction

ISBN 0-8037-0835-1; 0-14-038646-7 pa

LC 90-44084

An illustrated collection of seven stories about various animals, including a frog with magnificent legs, a hungry brontosaurus, and a mouse who gets married

"Marshall's fertile imagination gets lots of exercise here as does his sardonic wit, and he's included plenty of expressive illustrations, all done in his signature style." Booklist

McKissack, Pat, 1946-

★ **Porch** lies; tales of slicksters, tricksters, and other wily characters. [by] Patricia C. McKissack; illustrated by André Carrilho. Schwartz & Wade Books 2006 146p il $18.95; lib bdg $22.99

Grades: 4 5 6 7

S C

1. Short stories 2. African Americans -- Fiction

ISBN 0-375-83619-5; 0-375-93619-X lib bdg

LC 2005-22048

The "original tales in this uproarious collection draw on African American oral tradition and blend history and legend with sly humor, creepy horror, villainous characters, and wild farce. McKissack based the stories on those she heard as a child while sitting on her grandparents' porch. . . . Carrilho's full-page illustrations—part cartoon, part portrait in silhouette—combine realistic characters with scary monsters." Booklist

★ The **dark**-thirty; Southern tales of the supernatural. illustrated by Brian Pinkney. Knopf 1992 122p il $18.95; lib bdg $20.99; pa $6.50

Grades: 4 5 6 7   S C

1. Ghost stories 2. Short stories 3. African Americans -- Fiction

ISBN 0-679-81863-4; 0-679-91853-9 lib bdg; 0-679-89006-8 pa

LC 92-3021

Coretta Scott King Award for text, 1993; A Newbery honor book, 1993

A collection of ghost stories with African American themes, designed to be told during the Dark Thirty—the half hour before sunset—when ghosts seem all too believable

"Strong characterizations are superbly drawn in a few words. The atmosphere of each selection is skillfully developed and sustained to the very end. Pinkney's stark scratchboard illustrations evoke an eerie mood, which heightens the suspense of each tale." SLJ

Naidoo, Beverley

Out of bounds: seven stories of conflict and hope. HarperCollins Pubs. 2003 175p $16.99; pa $5.99

Grades: 5 6 7 8   S C

1. Short stories 2. Apartheid -- Juvenile fiction 3. Children's stories, South African (English)

ISBN 0-06-050799-3; 0-06-050801-9 pa

LC 2002-68901

First published 2001 in the United Kingdom

Seven stories, spanning the time period from 1948 to 2000, chronicle the experiences of young people from different races and ethnic groups as they try to cope with the restrictions placed on their lives by South Africa's apartheid laws

"Naidoo's book reveals our humanity and inhumanity with starkness and precision. . . . She honors her country's past, present, and future with these brave tales." Horn Book

Nix, Garth

One beastly beast; (two aliens, three inventors, four fantastic tales) illustrated by Brian Biggs. HarperCollinsPublishers 2007 158p il $15.99; lib bdg $16.89

Grades: 3 4 5   S C

1. Short stories 2. Fantasy fiction 3. Short stories -- By individual authors -- Juvenile literature

ISBN 0-06-084319-5; 0-06-084320-9 lib bdg

LC 2006-27916

A collection of four fantasy tales in which a boy joins a strange navy in pursuit of video pirates, a neglected princess seeks adventure, an orphaned inventor seeks the perfect parents, and a genius girl faces a sea serpent.

"Black-and-white cartoon illustrations complement the lighthearted tone. The positive message and amusing stories make this a good choice for younger fantasy fans." SLJ

Paulsen, Gary

Paintings from the cave; three novellas. Wendy Lamb Books 2011 161p $15.99; lib bdg $18.99

Grades: 4 5 6 7   S C

1. Short stories 2. Art -- Fiction 3. Dogs -- Fiction 4. Violence -- Fiction 5. Homeless persons -- Fiction

ISBN 978-0-385-74684-7; 978-0-385-90921-1 lib bdg; 978-0-375-89743-6 e-book

LC 2011016287

"These novellas portray an unflinching look at children who have endured neglectful and abusive homes and are surviving on their own. The atmospheric first tale, 'Man of the Iron Heads,' is narrated by Jake, a boy of about 11, who hides from the local gang until he finds the courage to outsmart its violent leader. 'Jo-Jo the Dog-Faced Girl' presents a lonely girl with three adopted dogs who finds acceptance in befriending a girl with leukemia. Finally, 'Erik's Rules' celebrates the power of art and is told by Jamie, the younger of two homeless brothers, whose unstable existence changes after a chance encounter with a friendly volunteer at the animal shelter. By incorporating the solace found in dogs, art, libraries, and new friends into these tales of heartache and redemption, Paulsen provides his readers with hope of a better life." SLJ

Priestley, Chris

Uncle Montague's tales of terror; [by] Chris Priestley; illustrations by David Roberts. Bloomsbury Children's Books 2007 238p il $12.95

Grades: 5 6 7 8 9   S C

1. Short stories 2. Horror fiction 3. Uncles -- Fiction 4. Storytelling -- Fiction

ISBN 978-1-59990-118-3; 1-59990-118-8

"Ghosts, demons, jinns, and deadly trees populate these 10 chilly short stories set in the late 19th century, with the language and black-and-white illustrations capturing the feel of Victorian times. Young Edgar hears these tales while visiting his eccentric Uncle Montague, and each one is connected to a strange object in his uncle's study. . . . An enjoyable collection with enough creepy atmosphere (and some gruesome action) to hold readers' attention." SLJ

The **Random** House book of bedtime stories; illustrated by Jane Dyer. Random House 2007 137p il $21.99

Grades: K 1 2 3 4   S C

1. Folklore 2. Short stories

ISBN 978-0-679-80832-9

A reissue of the title first published 1994

"The 21 lyrically told stories include many European folktales and fairy tales . . . as well as childhood classics. . . . Dyer's brightly colored, precisely detailed illustrations are warm and gentle, with an old-fashioned, affectionate character. . . . A fine collection to read at bedtime or any time, these are stories every child should know." Booklist

Reichenstetter, Friederun

Andersen's fairy tales; retold by Friederun Reichenstetter; illustrated by Silke Leffler. North-South 2007 92p il $19.95

Grades: 4 5 6   S C

1. Authors 2. Novelists 3. Dramatists 4. Fairy tales 5. Children's authors 6. Short story writers

ISBN 0-7358-2141-0

"Thirteen tales . . . are adapted from excellent translations by Anthea Bell and H. P. Paul. . . . Leffler's often-humorous painted folk-art illustrations show cute little people with chubby line-drawn faces dressed in clothing of 18th-century style. . . . The volume . . . is quite handsome." SLJ

Root, Phyllis
Aunt Nancy and the bothersome visitors; illustrated by David Parkins. Candlewick Press 2007 57p il $16.99
Grades: 1 2 3 4   S C
1. Aunts -- Fiction 2. Cousins -- Fiction
ISBN 978-0-7636-3074-4; 0-7636-3074-8
                                             LC 2007-60856
Includes two stories previously published separately in picture book format: Aunt Nancy and Old Man Trouble (1996) and Aunt Nancy and Cousin Lazybones (1998)
Clever Aunt Nancy manages to foil all those who try to get the better of her.
"Root's folksy style shines in every sentence. . . . Parkins provides full-color paintings to introduce each story, but his wit really shows itself in the droll silhouettes that milk body language for all it's worth." Horn Book

Rowling, J. K., 1965-
The **tales** of Beedle the Bard; translated from the ancient runes by Hermione Granger; commentary by Albus Dumbledore; introduction, notes, and illustrations by J.K. Rowling. Arthur A. Levine 2008 111p il $12.99
Grades: 5 6 7 8 9 10 11 12   S C
1. Fairy tales 2. Short stories 3. Magic -- Fiction 4. Short stories -- By individual authors -- Juvenile literature
ISBN 978-0-545-12828-5; 0-545-12828-5
A collection of tales from the world of Harry Potter.
"The introduction is captivating . . . [and] the tales themselves are entertaining. . . . Rowling is at the top of her game as a superb storyteller, providing her legions of fans with an enchanting collection of wizard folklore." Voice Youth Advocates

San Souci, Robert
★ **Dare** to be scared; thirteen stories to chill and thrill. illustrations by David Ouimet. Cricket Bks. 2003 159p il $15.95
Grades: 4 5 6 7   S C
1. Short stories 2. Horror fiction
ISBN 0-8126-2688-5
                                             LC 2002-152827
"With crisp, straightforward delivery and some intriguing endings, these 13 tales are great fun for young readers who like to be spooked." Booklist

Dare to be scared 4; thirteen more tales of terror. [by] Robert D. San Souci; illustrations by David Ouimet. Cricket Books 2009 275p il $17.95
Grades: 4 5 6 7   S C
1. Short stories 2. Horror fiction
ISBN 978-0-8126-2754-1; 0-8126-2754-7
                                             LC 2009018490
"These deliciously shivery tales are perfect for campfire spookiness or as Halloween read-alouds. As in the previous books in the series, San Souci relies heavily on folklore and urban legends, giving the stories an even more chilling impact. . . . Strong themes such as death and murder are

prevalent throughout. Ouimet's dark illustrations are paired perfectly with this creepy collection." SLJ

Double-dare to be scared: another thirteen chilling tales; [by] Robert D. San Souci; illustrated by David Ouimet. Cricket Books 2004 170p il $15.95
Grades: 4 5 6 7   S C
1. Short stories 2. Horror fiction 3. Horror stories 4. Horror tales, American 5. Children's stories, American
ISBN 0-8126-2716-4
                                             LC 2003-26610
"San Souci uses elements of urban legend and folklore to weave powerful and suspenseful yet age-appropriate stories that youngsters will revisit, finding new meaning with each reading." SLJ

Haunted houses; [by] Robert D. San Souci; illustrated by Kelly Murphy and Antoine Revoy. Henry Holt 2010 276p il (Are you scared yet?) $16.99
Grades: 4 5 6 7   S C
1. Ghost stories 2. Short stories 3. Horror fiction 4. Short stories -- By individual authors -- Juvenile literature
ISBN 978-0-8050-8750-5; 0-8050-8750-8
                                             LC 2009-50763
"These 10 spooky stories include a classic Halloween scare: visitors get their admission fee of $25 back if they make it to the top floor of a haunted house—but can they? In another, the primary occupant of a dollhouse is a ghost of a child who needs help moving from one consciousness to another. . . . The stories are well paced and satisfyingly startling. . . . This book won't stay on the shelves for long. Murphy and Revoy's black-and-white illustrations heighten the fright factor, making San Souci's collection even more riveting." SLJ

Triple-dare to be scared; thirteen further freaky tales. [by] Robert D. San Souci; illustrations by David Ouimet. Cricket Books 2007 229p il $16.95
Grades: 4 5 6 7   S C
1. Short stories 2. Horror fiction
ISBN 978-0-8126-2749-7; 0-8126-2749-0
                                             LC 2006025899
"San Souci serves up 13 more spooky tales, and Ouimet's macabre black-and-white illustrations are a perfect complement to each one. The selections are short enough for read-alouds or for independent readers to complete in one sitting." SLJ

Sandburg, Carl
★ **Rootabaga** stories; illustrated by Maud and Miska Petersham. Harcourt 2003 176p il hardcover o.p. pa $5.95 S C
1. Fairy tales 2. Short stories 3. Children's stories, American 4. Fairy tales -- United States
ISBN 0-15-204709-3; 0-15-204714-X pa
                                             LC 2002-191949
First published 1922; previously published as: Rootabaga stories, part one
A selection of tales from Rootabaga Country peopled with such characters as the Potato Face Blind Man, the Blue Wind Boy, and many others

★ **Shelf** life: stories by the book; edited by Gary Paulsen. Simon & Schuster Bks. for Young Readers 2003 173p $16.95

Grades: 5 6 7 8   S C

1. Short stories 2. Books and reading 3. Books and reading -- Fiction 4. Children's stories, American 5. Books and reading -- Juvenile fiction

ISBN 0-689-84180-9

LC 2002-66901

Ten short stories in which the lives of young people in different circumstances are changed by their encounters with books

"Covering almost every genre of fiction, including mystery, SF, fantasy and realism, these well-crafted stories by familiar authors offer sharply drawn characterizations and intriguing premises." Publ Wkly

Shusterman, Neal

Darkness creeping; twenty twisted tales. Puffin Books 2007 291p pa $7.99

Grades: 5 6 7 8   S C

1. Short stories 2. Horror fiction 3. Short stories -- By individual authors -- Juvenile literature

ISBN 0-14-240721-6

"The author takes a walk on the dark side in this collection of spooky stories, some old, some new, all delightfully creepy. He knows his audience, providing enough horrific touches to appeal to the most challenging readers—those hard-to-reach middle school boys. Each story is introduced with a brief statement describing where he got the idea." Voice Youth Advocates

Singer, Isaac Bashevis

Stories for children. Farrar, Straus & Giroux 1984 337p hardcover o.p. pa $14

Grades: 4 5 6 7   S C

1. Short stories 2. Jews -- Fiction

ISBN 0-374-37266-7; 0-374-46489-8 pa

LC 84-13612

This collection of thirty-six stories includes "parables, beast fables, allegories and reminiscences. Some stories are silly and charming, while others are wildly fantastic, dealing with savagery and miracles in mythical, medieval Poland. Frequently they are about scary situations, but all tend to end happily, with an edifying idea. Most appealing is the Nobel Prize winner's sheer story-telling power. In this respect, he has no equal among contemporaries." N Y Times Book Rev

Smith, Charles R., 1969-

Winning words; sports stories and photographs. [by] Charles R. Smith. Candlewick Press 2008 70p il $17.99

Grades: 5 6 7 8   S C

1. Short stories 2. Sports -- Fiction

ISBN 978-0-7636-1445-4; 0-7636-1445-9

In this collection of short stories and photographs, Charles R. Smith Jr. shows young athletes overcoming their fears and challenging themselves to do their best.

"This outstanding collection consists of six readable and engaging stories. . . . Smith does a fine job of evoking the action and character of the games, in words and in close-up photos." SLJ

Soto, Gary

★ **Baseball** in April, and other stories; 10th anniversary ed; Harcourt Brace Jovanovich 2000 111p $16; pa $6

Grades: 5 6 7 8   S C

1. Short stories 2. Mexican Americans -- Fiction 3. Short stories -- By individual authors -- Juvenile literature

ISBN 0-15-202573-1; 0-15-202567-7 pa

A reissue of the title first published 1990

A collection of eleven short stories focusing on the everyday adventures of Hispanic young people growing up in Fresno, California

Each story "gets at the heart of some aspect of growing up. The insecurities, the embarrassments, the triumphs, the inequities of it all are chronicled with wit and charm. Soto's characters ring true and his knowledge of, and affection for, their shared Mexican-American heritage is obvious and infectious." Voice Youth Advocates

Facts of life; stories. Harcourt 2008 176p $16

Grades: 5 6 7 8   S C

1. Short stories 2. Mexican Americans -- Fiction 3. Short stories -- By individual authors -- Juvenile literature

ISBN 978-0-15-206181-4; 0-15-206181-9

LC 2007-35765

"Pivitol moments in the lives of California Latino teens and tweens provide the starting points for Soto's collection of 10 . . . stories. For Letty, it's the realization that her boyfriend loves her money more than he does her; for Hector, it's the announcement of his parents' plan to divorce. . . . Soto's affection and concern for his characters is evident throughout." Booklist

Local news. Harcourt Brace Jovanovich 1993 148p hardcover o.p. pa $5.95

Grades: 5 6 7 8   S C

1. Short stories 2. Mexican Americans -- Fiction 3. Short stories -- By individual authors -- Juvenile literature

ISBN 0-15-248117-6; 0-15-204695-X pa

LC 92-37905

A collection of thirteen short stories about the everyday lives of Mexican American young people in California's Central Valley

"These stories resonate with integrity, verve, and compassion." Horn Book

Petty crimes. Harcourt Brace & Co. 1998 157p $16; pa $6.99

Grades: 5 6 7 8   S C

1. Short stories 2. Children's stories, American 3. Mexican Americans -- Fiction 4. Mexican Americans -- California -- Fiction 5. Mexican Americans -- California -- Juvenile fiction

ISBN 0-15-201658-9; 0-15-205437-5 pa

LC 97-37114

A collection of short stories about Mexican American youth growing up in California's Central Valley

"A sense of family strength relieves the under-current of sadness in these raw stories." Horn Book Guide

Spinelli, Jerry, 1941-

The **library** card. Scholastic 1997 148p pa $4.99

Grades: 4 5 6 7   **S C**
1. Short stories 2. Books and reading -- Fiction 3. Short stories -- By individual authors -- Juvenile literature
ISBN 0-590-38633-6
LC 96-18412

"A library card is the magical object common to each of these four stories in which a budding street thug, a television addict, a homeless orphan, and a lonely girl are all transformed by the power and the possibilities that await them within the walls of the public library. Spinelli's characters . . . are unusual and memorable; his writing both humorous and convincing." Horn Book Guide

Sports shorts. Darby Creek Pub. 2005 127p il $15.99; pa $4.99
     Grades: 5 6 7 8   **S C**
1. Short stories 2. Sports -- Fiction
ISBN 9780761385363; 1-58196-040-9; 1-58196-058-1 pa

A collection of eight semi-autobiographical stories about the authors' experiences with sports while growing up.
"Some of the vignettes are laugh-out-loud funny. . . . The book's smaller-than-standard trim size and inviting page design will help attract readers to this rewarding collection." Booklist

Stine, R. L., 1943-
The **haunting** hour. HarperCollins Pubs. 2001 153p il $11.95; pa $5.99
Grades: 4 5 6 7   **S C**
1. Short stories 2. Horror fiction 3. Occult 4. Horror stories 5. Horror tales, American 6. Children's stories, American
ISBN 0-06-623604-5; 0-06-441045-5 pa
LC 2001-39142

A collection of ten short horror stories featuring a ghoulish Halloween party, a long, mysterious car trip, and a very dangerous imaginary friend. Each story includes drawings by a different illustrator
"The predictability of the stories and the unsophisticated storytelling won't keep Stine fans old and new from swallowing this down in one big gulp." Bull Cent Child Books

Tan, Shaun
★ **Lost** & found; 3 by Shaun Tan. Arthur A. Levine Books 2011 un il $21.99
Grades: 5 6 7 8   **S C**
1. Short stories 2. Short stories -- By individual authors -- Juvenile literature
ISBN 978-0-545-22924-1; 0-545-22924-3
LC 2010030936

This book comprises three previously published stories by the Australian author-illustrator "In 'The Red Tree,' a young girl moves listlessly through her day with a sense of dreadful ennui that escalates with each page turn . . . until finally finding some hope at the end. In 'The Lost Thing,' a young boy discovers a most peculiar object and dutifully tries to find a proper home for it. . . . Finally, 'The Rabbits' (with a text by John Marsden) is a colonization fable, as rabbits invade and populate a new land, overwhelming the native animal population and severely altering the landscape. . . . Intermediate, middle school." (Horn Book)

"'The Red Tree' follows a solitary girl through a single, not very good day, exploring her feelings as they shift from disappointment and confusion to alienation and despair. The spare, lyrical text provides an anchor for Tan's large, moody, beautiful paintings. 'The Lost Thing' is a more upbeat tale of a boy who discovers an unusual object and then must decide what to do with it. Freedom and imagination are the themes in this story, and here the art includes fascinating and sometimes humorous bits of technical drawings. The prose of John Marsden's 'The Rabbits,' an allegory about imperialism, is so simple and melodic that it verges on poetry. The artist emphasizes the invasive foreignness of the rabbits by dressing them in baroque uniforms, drawing mystifying, gigantic machines and buildings for them to build and deploy in their inexorable drive to dominate." SLJ

★ **Troll's** eye view; a book of villainous tales. Viking 2009 200p $16.99; pa $7.99
     Grades: 5 6 7 8   **S C**
1. Fairy tales 2. Short stories
ISBN 978-0-670-06141-9; 0-670-06141-7; 978-0-14-241673-0 pa; 0-14-241673-8 pa

Everyone thinks they know the real story behind the villains in fairy tales—evil, no two ways about it. But the villains themselves beg to differ. In this anthology for younger readers, you'll hear from the Giant's wife (from Jack and the Beanstalk), Rumpelstiltskin, the oldest of the Twelve Dancing Princesses, and more.
"A mixed bag of funny, quirky, and downright creepy entries. . . . The collection is largely accessible and very enjoyable." Booklist

Under my hat; tales from the cauldron. edited by Jonathan Strahan. Random House 2012 415 p. (trade) $16.99
     Grades: 5 6 7 8   **S C**
1. Short stories 2. Witches -- Fiction 3. Children's stories 4. Witches -- Juvenile fiction
ISBN 0375868305; 9780375868047; 9780375868306; 9780375898815; 9780375968303
LC 2011031253

This book presents "eighteen short tales about witches. . . . Garth Nix's 'A Handful of Ashes' features a library and librarian. Delia Sherman's 'The Witch in the Woods' . . . [features] deer and bear shape-shifters and no small darkness. . . . Jane Yolen makes Hans Christian Andersen's life a tale itself." (Kirkus Reviews)

Under the weather; stories about climate change. edited by Tony Bradman. Frances Lincoln Children's 2009 215p pbk. $8.99; $16.95
     Grades: 5 6 7 8   **S C**
1. Short stories 2. Greenhouse effect -- Fiction
ISBN 9781845079444; 1-84507-930-2; 978-1-84507-930-7

"Eight stories by a variety of authors attempt to make the facts about climate change and its global ramifications relevant to today's children. The majority of the selections are about youngsters enacting change and working toward solutions in tangible ways. For example, 'How to Build the Perfect Sandcastle' is about a Philippino boy who works to rebuild the coral reefs, which are dying due to the rise in ocean temperature. . . . Overall . . . this is a worthwhile effort that will appeal to children wanting to make a difference in their world as well as to teachers trying to make the scientific reality of climate change real to their students." SLJ

Lay-ups and long shots; an anthology of short stories. by Joseph Bruchac . . . [et al.] Darby Creek Pub. 2008
112p il $15.95

Grades: 4 5 6   **S C**

1. Short stories 2. Sports -- Fiction

ISBN 978-1-58196-078-5; 1-58196-078-6

"These nine new short stories feature tweens or teens who, despite lack of skill or other obstacles, engage in athletic pursuits. Some . . . have autobiographical elements. . . . Consistently readable and engaging, the collection should have as much appeal for geeks as it does for jocks." Booklist

AUTHOR, TITLE, AND SUBJECT INDEX

This index to the books in the Classified Collection includes author, title, and subject entries; added entries for publishers' series, illustrators, joint authors, and editors of works entered under title; and name and subject cross-references; all arranged in one alphabet.

The number or symbol in bold face type at the end of each entry refers to the Dewey Decimal Classification or to the Fiction (Fic) or Story Collection (S C), or Easy Books (E) section where the main entry for the book will be found. Works classed in 92 will be found under the headings for the biographies' subject.

Abe Lincoln goes to Washington, 1837-1865. Harness, C.   **92**
Abe Lincoln remembers. Turner, A. W.   **973.7**
Abe Lincoln's dream. Smith, L.   **E**
Abe's fish. Bryant, J.   **E**
Abe's honest words. Rappaport, D.   **92**
Abel (Biblical figure)
About
   Sasso, S. E. Cain & Abel   **222**
Abel's island. Steig, W.   **Fic**
Abela, Deborah
   The ghosts of Gribblesea Pier   **Fic**
Abernathy, Alexia
About
   Thimmesh, C. Girls think of everything   **920**
Abigail Adams. Wallner, A.   **973.4**
Abigail Iris: the one and only. Glatt, L.   **Fic**
Abigail Iris: the pet project. Glatt, L.   **Fic**
Abigail spells. Alter, A.   **E**
ABILITY -- FICTION
   Foley, L. K. Remarkable   **Fic**
ABILITY -- TESTING
   See also Educational tests and measurements; Intelligence tests; Psychological tests
Abiyoyo. Seeger, P.   **398.2**
Ablow, Gail
   A horse in the house, and other strange but true animal stories   **590**
ABNAKI INDIANS -- FICTION
   Bruchac, J. Night wings   **Fic**
   Bruchac, J. The winter people   **Fic**
ABNAKI INDIANS -- FOLKLORE
   Bruchac, J. Raccoon's last race   **398.2**
Abner & me. Gutman, D.   **Fic**
ABNORMAL PSYCHOLOGY
   See also Mind and body; Nervous system
ABNORMALITIES, HUMAN -- FICTION
   Leeds, C. The unfortunate son   **Fic**
   Palacio, R. J. Wonder   **Fic**
Aboff, Marcie
   Pigs, cows, and probability   **519.2**
Abolafia, Yossi
   (il) Prelutsky, J. It's snowing! it's snowing!   **811**
   (il) Prelutsky, J. It's Valentine's Day   **811**
ABOLITION OF SLAVERY *See* Abolitionists; Slavery; Slaves -- Emancipation
ABOLITIONISTS
   Adler, D. A. A picture book of Harriet Beecher Stowe   **92**
   Adler, D. A. A picture book of Harriet Tubman   **305.5**
   Adler, D. A. A picture book of Sojourner Truth   **305.5**
   Armand, G. Love twelve miles long   **E**
   Clinton, C. When Harriet met Sojourner   **92**
   Evans, S. W. Underground   **973.7**
   Figley, M. R. Prisoner for liberty   **92**
   Fritz, J. Harriet Beecher Stowe and the Beecher preachers   **813**
   Haskins, J. Get on board: the story of the Underground Railroad   **326**
   Hendrix, J. John Brown   **92**
   Huey, L. M. American archaeology uncovers the Underground Railroad   **973.7**
   Jurmain, S. The forbidden schoolhouse   **92**
   Krull, K. Lives of extraordinary women   **920**
   Landau, E. Fleeing to freedom on the Underground Railroad   **973.7**
   Lawrence, J. Harriet and the Promised Land   **811**
   Levine, E. Henry's freedom box   **E**
   McKissack, P. C. Black hands, white sails   **639.2**
   Morrow, B. O. A good night for freedom   **E**

   Murphy, C. R. Marching with Aunt Susan   **E**
   Pinkney, A. D. Let it shine   **920**
   Pinkney, A. D. Sojourner Truth's step-stomp stride   **92**
   Rockwell, A. F. Only passing through: the story of Sojourner Truth   **92**
   Rosenberg, A. The Civil War   **920**
   Rossi, A. Freedom struggle   **973.7**
   Schroeder, A. Minty: a story of young Harriet Tubman   **305.5**
   Turner, G. T. An apple for Harriet Tubman   **92**
   Walker, S. M. Freedom song   **E**
   Weatherford, C. B. Moses   **92**
ABOLITIONISTS
   See also Reformers
ABOLITIONISTS -- FICTION
   Hansen, J. Home is with our family   **Fic**
   Russell, K. Chasing the Nightbird   **Fic**
ABOLITIONISTS -- UNITED STATES
   Freedman, R. Abraham Lincoln and Frederick Douglass   **973.709**
ABOLITIONISTS -- UNITED STATES -- BIOGRAPHY -- JUVENILE LITERATURE
   Horn, G. M. Sojourner Truth   **305.5**
ABORIGINAL AUSTRALIAN ART
   See also Art
ABORIGINAL AUSTRALIANS
   Arnold, C. Uluru, Australia's Aboriginal heart   **994**
   Connolly, S. The Americas and the Pacific   **970.004**
ABORIGINAL AUSTRALIANS -- FICTION
   Morgan, S. Sam's bush journey   **E**
ABORIGINAL AUSTRALIANS -- FOLKLORE
   Marshall, J. V. Stories from the Billabong   **398.2**
ABORIGINES, AUSTRALIAN *See* Aboriginal Australians
ABORTION -- ETHICAL ASPECTS
   See also Ethics
ABORTION -- LAW AND LEGISLATION
   See also Law; Legislation
Abouet, Marguerite
   Akissi   **Fic**
Abouraya, Karen Leggett
   Hands around the library   **962.055**
About average. Clements, A.   **Fic**
About crustaceans. Sill, C. P.   **595.3**
About habitats [series]
   Sill, C. P. Grasslands   **577.4**
   Sill, C. P. Wetlands   **577.6**
About hummingbirds. Sill, C.   **598**
About marsupials. Sill, C. P.   **599.2**
About raptors. Sill, C. P.   **598**
About rodents. Sill, C. P.   **599.35**
About time. Koscielniak, B.   **529**
The **abracadabra** kid. Fleischman, S.   **813**
Abraham (Biblical figure)
About
   Gerstein, M. The white ram   **E**
   Jules, J. Abraham's search for God   **222**
   Jules, J. Sarah laughs   **222**
Abraham (Biblical figure) -- Fiction
About
   Gerstein, M. The white ram   **E**
Abraham Lincoln. Gilpin, C. C.   **973.709**
Abraham Lincoln and Frederick Douglass. Freedman, R.   **973.709**
Abraham Lincoln comes home. Burleigh, R.   **92**
Abraham Lincoln for kids. Herbert, J.   **92**
Abraham's search for God. Jules, J.   **222**
Abraham, Denise Gonzales
   Abraham, S. G. Cecilia's year   **Fic**
Abraham, Susan Gonzales

AFRICAN AMERICAN SOLDIERS

Blair, M. W. Liberty or death	973.3
Clinton, C. Hold the flag high	973.7
Stone, T. L. Courage has no color, the true story of the Triple Nickles	940.54

AFRICAN AMERICAN SOLDIERS -- FICTION

Garland, S. The buffalo soldier	E
Hopkinson, D. From slave to soldier	E
Myers, W. D. Patrol	E
Polacco, P. Pink and Say	E

AFRICAN AMERICAN SOLDIERS -- JUVENILE LITERATURE

Blair, M. W. Liberty or death	973.3

AFRICAN AMERICAN SONGS *See* African American music

The **African** American story. Masoff, J.	305.8

AFRICAN AMERICAN WOMEN

Adler, D. A. A picture book of Harriet Tubman	305.5
Adler, D. A. A picture book of Sojourner Truth	305.5
Angelou, M. Maya Angelou	811
Bolden, T. Maritcha	92
Freedman, R. The voice that challenged a nation	92
Jemison, M. C. Find where the wind goes	92
Lasky, K. Vision of beauty: the story of Sarah Breedlove Walker	B
Lowery, L. Aunt Clara Brown	978.8
McKissack, F. Mary McLeod Bethune	370.92
Miller, N. Stompin' at the Savoy	92
Parks, R. Rosa Parks: my story	976.1
Pinkney, A. D. Ella Fitzgerald	92
Pinkney, A. D. Let it shine	920
Rockwell, A. F. Only passing through: the story of Sojourner Truth	92
Rosa	92
Ryan, P. M. When Marian sang: the true recital of Marian Anderson, the voice of a century	92
Turner, G. T. An apple for Harriet Tubman	92
Washburn, K. Heart of a champion	796.440
Weatherford, C. B. Moses	92

AFRICAN AMERICAN WOMEN

See also Black women; Women

AFRICAN AMERICAN WOMEN -- BIOGRAPHY

Adler, D. A. A picture book of Harriet Tubman	305.5
Adler, D. A. A picture book of Sojourner Truth	305.5
Amoroso, C. Rosa Parks	92
Bolden, T. Maritcha	92
Brophy, D. Michelle Obama	92
Clinton, C. When Harriet met Sojourner	92
Colbert, D. Michelle Obama	92
Dray, P. Yours for justice, Ida B. Wells	92
Freedman, R. The voice that challenged a nation	92
Hopkinson, D. Michelle	92
Jemison, M. C. Find where the wind goes	92
Jones, L. Mrs. Lincoln's dressmaker: the unlikely friendship of Elizabeth Keckley and Mary Todd Lincoln	92
Kesselring, S. Michelle Obama	92
Lasky, K. Vision of beauty: the story of Sarah Breedlove Walker	B
Lowery, L. Aunt Clara Brown	978.8
Malaspina, A. Phillis sings out freedom	92
Miller, N. Stompin' at the Savoy	92
Myers, W. D. Ida B. Wells	92
Odetta, the queen of folk	92
Orgill, R. Skit-scat raggedy cat: Ella Fitzgerald	92
Parks, R. Rosa Parks: my story	976.1
Pinkney, A. D. Ella Fitzgerald	92
Pinkney, A. D. Let it shine	920
Pinkney, A. D. Sojourner Truth's step-stomp stride	92

Raatma, L. Shirley Chisholm	92
Rockwell, A. F. Only passing through: the story of Sojourner Truth	92
Rosa	92
Ryan, P. M. When Marian sang: the true recital of Marian Anderson, the voice of a century	92
Shange, N. Coretta Scott	92
She loved baseball: the Effa Manley story	92
Turner, G. T. An apple for Harriet Tubman	92
Weatherford, C. B. Moses	92
Weatherford, C. B. Oprah	92
Winter, J. Jazz age Josephine	92

AFRICAN AMERICAN WOMEN -- BIOGRAPHY -- JUVENILE LITERATURE

Adler, D. A. Harriet Tubman and the Underground Railroad	973.7
Fradin, D. B. Zora!	813
Horn, G. M. Sojourner Truth	305.5

AFRICAN AMERICAN WOMEN ASTRONAUTS -- BIOGRAPHY -- JUVENILE LITERATURE

Jemison, M. C. Find where the wind goes	92

AFRICAN AMERICAN WOMEN ATHLETES -- UNITED STATES -- JUVENILE LITERATURE

Malaspina, A. Touch the sky	796.42

AFRICAN AMERICAN WOMEN CIVIL RIGHTS WORKERS -- BIOGRAPHY

Pinkney, A. D. Let it shine	920

AFRICAN AMERICAN WOMEN EDUCATORS -- BIOGRAPHY -- JUVENILE LITERATURE

McKissack, F. Mary McLeod Bethune	370.92

AFRICAN AMERICAN WOMEN EXECUTIVES

Lasky, K. Vision of beauty: the story of Sarah Breedlove Walker	B

AFRICAN AMERICAN WOMEN PIONEERS -- COLORADO -- BIOGRAPHY -- JUVENILE LITERATURE

Lowery, L. Aunt Clara Brown	978.8

AFRICAN AMERICAN WOMEN SOCIAL REFORMERS -- BIOGRAPHY -- JUVENILE LITERATURE

McKissack, F. Mary McLeod Bethune	370.92

AFRICAN AMERICAN YOUTH

See also Youth

AFRICAN AMERICANS

Barbour, K. Mr. Williams	92
Bolden, T. Tell all the children our story	305.8
Cameron, A. Gloria's way	Fic
Cooke, T. Full, full, full of love	E
Coy, J. Strong to the hoop	E
Curtis, G. The bat boy & his violin	E
Dillon, L. Rap a tap tap	792.7
English, K. Francie	Fic
Green, M. Y. A strong right arm: the story of Mamie Peanut Johnson	92
Gutman, D. Jackie & me	Fic
Hartfield, C. Me and Uncle Romie	E
Hesse, K. Come on, rain!	E
Howard, E. F. Virgie goes to school with us boys	E
Hudson, W. Powerful words	081
In the hollow of your hand	782.42
Keats, E. J. Hi, cat!	E
Keedle, J. West African Americans	305.8
Lester, J. Black cowboy, wild horses	E
Lindsey, K. Sweet potato pie	E
Macceca, S. George Washington Carver	630
McKissack, P. C. Black hands, white sails	639.2
Mead, A. Junebug in trouble	Fic
Pinkney, S. L. Shades of black	305.23
Rodman, M. A. Yankee girl	Fic
San Souci, R. The secret of the stones	398.2

Alexander, Jessica
  Shore, D. Z. This is the dream | 811
Alexander, Kwame
  Acoustic Rooster and his barnyard band | E
Alexander, Lloyd
  The Black Cauldron | Fic
  The book of three | Fic
  The castle of Llyr | Fic
  The fortune-tellers | E
  The foundling and other tales of Prydain | S
  The golden dream of Carlo Chuchio | Fic
  The high king | Fic
  The iron ring | Fic
  The remarkable journey of Prince Jen | Fic
  Taran Wanderer | Fic
  Westmark | Fic
Alexander, Martha G.
  Max and the dumb flower picture | E
Alexander, Robert Joseph
  Alexander, S. H. She touched the world: Laura Bridgman, deaf-blind pioneer | 92
Alexander, Sally Hobart
  She touched the world: Laura Bridgman, deaf-blind pioneer | 92
Alexander, the Great, 356-323 B.C.
  About
  Adams, S. Alexander | 92
  Demi Alexander the Great | 92
Alfie and the big boys. Hughes, S. | E
Alfie runs away. Cadow, K. M. | E
ALGAE
  Arato, R. Protists | 579
  Twist, C. A little book of slime | 590
ALGAE
  See also Marine plants
ALGAE -- JUVENILE LITERATURE
  Arato, R. Protists | 579
ALGEBRA
  Adler, D. A. Mystery math | 512
  Green, D. Algebra & geometry | 516.2
ALGEBRA
  See also Mathematical analysis; Mathematics
Algebra & geometry. Green, D. | 516.2
ALGEBRA -- JUVENILE LITERATURE
  Adler, D. A. Mystery math | 512
Algeria. Kagda, F. | 965
Ali Baba and the forty thieves. Manning, M. K. | 741.5
Ali, Muhammad, 1942-
  About
  Bolden, T. The champ! | 92
  Myers, W. D. Muhammad Ali | 92
  Smith, C. R. Twelve rounds to glory: the story of Muhammad Ali | 92
  Winter, J. Muhammad Ali | 92
Ali, Rubina
  Slumgirl dreaming | 92
Ali, Rubina
  About
  Ali, R. Slumgirl dreaming | 92
Ali, Sharifah Enayat
  Afghanistan | 958.1
Ali-Walsh, Rasheda
  I'll hold your hand so you won't fall | 616.8
Alicavusoglu, Leyla
  Hawker, F. Islam in Turkey | 297
Alice in Blunderland. Naylor, P. R. | Fic
Alice in rapture, sort of. Naylor, P. R. | Fic
Alice in-between. Naylor, P. R. | Fic

Alice the brave. Naylor, P. R. | Fic
Alice the fairy. Shannon, D. | E
Alice's adventures in Wonderland. Carroll, L. | Fic
Alice's adventures in Wonderland. Sabuda, R. | E
Alice's adventures in Wonderland. Carroll, L. | Fic
Alice-Miranda at school. Harvey, J. | Fic
Alicia Alonso. Bernier-Grand, C. T. | 92
Alien abductions. Erickson, J. | 001.9
Alien deep. Hague, B. | 551.2
Alien Eraser reveals the secrets of evolution. Moss, M. | Fic
Alien Eraser to the rescue. Moss, M. | Fic
Alien Hunter's Handbook. Brake, M. | 576.8
Alien invaders. Drake, J. | 578.6
Alien invasion. Jackson, C. | 578.6
Alien snow. Dahl, M. | 741.5
ALIENATION (SOCIAL PSYCHOLOGY) -- JUVENILE FICTION
  Crossan, S. The Weight of Water | Fic
Aliens are coming! McCarthy, M. | 791.44
The Aliens are coming! Thiesing, L. | E
Aliens from Earth. Batten, M. | 578.6
ALIENS FROM OUTER SPACE *See* Extraterrestrial beings
Aliens on vacation. | Fic
Aliki
  Ah, music! | 780
  All by myself! | E
  Corn is maize | 633.1
  Feelings | 152.4
  Fossils tell of long ago | 560
  The gods and goddesses of Olympus | 292
  Manners | 395
  A medieval feast | 940.1
  Milk from cow to carton | 637
  My feet | 612
  My five senses | 612.8
  My hands | 612
  My visit to the aquarium | 639.34
  Painted words: Marianthe's story one | E
  A play's the thing | E
  Push button | E
  Quiet in the garden | E
  The two of them | E
  We are best friends | E
  Wild and woolly mammoths | 569
  William Shakespeare & the Globe | 792.09
ALIMONY
  See also Divorce
Alire, Camila
  Serving Latino communities | 027.6
Alison's zinnia. Lobel, A. | 411
Alistair and Kip's great adventure. Segal, J. | E
Alko, Selina
  Every-day dress-up | E
All aboard! Zimmermann, K. R. | 385
All aboard! Demarest, C. L. | E
All aboard!: Elijah McCoy's steam engine. Kulling, M. | 92
All about America [series]
  Isaacs, S. S. Colonists and independence | 973
  Staton, H. Cowboys and the wild West | 978
  Todras, E. H. Wagon trains and settlers | 973.8
  Walker, P. R. Gold rush and riches | 979.4
All about Braille. Jeffrey, L. S. | 411
All about drawing [series]
  Farrell, R. All about drawing horses & pets | 743
  Farrell, R. All about drawing sea creatures & animals | 743
  Fisher, D. All about drawing dinosaurs & reptiles | 743
All about drawing dinosaurs & reptiles. Fisher, D. | 743
All about drawing horses & pets. Farrell, R. | 743

Lendroth, S. Ocean wide, ocean deep   **E**

Allen, Rick

(il) Dark Emperor and other poems of the night   **811**

Allen, Thomas

About

Bildner, P. The Hallelujah Flight   **E**

Allen, Thomas -- Fiction

About

Bildner, P. The Hallelujah Flight   **E**

Allen, Thomas B.

Remember Pearl Harbor   **940.54**

Remember Valley Forge   **973.3**

(il) Bulla, C. R. The chalk box kid   **E**

Allergies. Royston, A.   **616.97**

ALLERGIES *See* Allergy

ALLERGIES, FOOD *See* Food allergy

ALLERGY

Robbins, L. How to deal with allergies   **616.97**

Royston, A. Allergies   **616.97**

Siy, A. Sneeze!   **612.2**

Thomas, P. I think I am going to sneeze   **616.97**

ALLERGY -- FICTION

Koster, G. The Peanut-Free Cafe   **E**

ALLERGY, FOOD *See* Food allergy

Alley, R. W.

(il) Alley, Z. B. There's a princess in the palace   **398.2**

(il) Alley, Z. B. There's a wolf at the door   **398.2**

(il) Bradley, K. B. Ballerino Nate   **E**

(il) Cheshire, S. The curse of the ancient mask and other case files   **Fic**

(il) Cheshire, S. The pirate's blood and other case files   **Fic**

(il) Cheshire, S. The treasure of Dead Man's Lane and other case files   **Fic**

(il) Demas, C. Halloween surprise   **E**

(il) Demas, C. Valentine surprise   **E**

(il) Fore, S. J. Read to Tiger   **E**

(il) Grandits, J. The travel game   **E**

(il) Hamilton, K. R. Police officers on patrol   **E**

(il) McMullan, K. Pearl and Wagner: four eyes   **E**

(il) McMullan, K. Pearl and Wagner: one funny day   **E**

(il) Mills, C. Being Teddy Roosevelt   **Fic**

(il) Skofield, J. Detective Dinosaur   **E**

(il) Skofield, J. Detective Dinosaur undercover   **E**

(il) Skofield, J. Detective Dinosaur: lost and found   **E**

Alley, Zoe B.

There's a princess in the palace   **398.2**

There's a wolf at the door   **398.2**

Allgor, Marie

Endangered desert animals   **591.68**

Allie Finkle's rules for girls [series]

Cabot, M. Best friends and drama queens   **Fic**

Cabot, M. Blast from the past   **Fic**

Cabot, M. Glitter girls and the great fake out   **Fic**

Cabot, M. Moving day   **Fic**

Cabot, M. The New Girl   **Fic**

Cabot, M. Stage fright   **Fic**

Alligator boy. Rylant, C.   **E**

Alligator or crocodile? Stewart, M.   **597.98**

Alligator, bear, crab. Wynne Pechter, L.   **E**

Alligators. Gish, M.   **597.98**

Alligators. Riggs, K.   **597.98**

ALLIGATORS

Feigenbaum, A. American alligators   **597.98**

Gibbons, G. Alligators and crocodiles   **597.98**

Gish, M. Alligators   **597.98**

Otfinoski, S. Alligators   **597.98**

Pringle, L. P. Alligators and crocodiles!   **597.98**

Rockwell, A. F. Who lives in an alligator hole?   **597.98**

Simon, S. Crocodiles & alligators   **597.98**

Stewart, M. Alligator or crocodile?   **597.98**

Wilson, K. A frog in the bog   **E**

ALLIGATORS

See also Reptiles

Alligators. Otfinoski, S.   **597.98**

ALLIGATORS -- FICTION

Baker, K. Meet Mr. and Mrs. Green   **E**

Bergman, M. Snip snap!   **E**

Gravett, E. The odd egg   **E**

Hurd, T. Mama don't allow   **E**

Lewin, B. You can do it!   **E**

Minarik, E. H. No fighting, no biting!   **E**

Mozelle, S. Zack's alligator and the first snow   **E**

Rylant, C. Alligator boy   **E**

Smith, A. T. Foxy and Egg   **E**

Stauffacher, S. Gator on the loose!   **Fic**

Thomassie, T. Feliciana Feyra LeRoux   **E**

Walsh, E. S. For Pete's sake   **E**

Wells, R. Hands off, Harry!   **E**

Willems, M. Hooray for Amanda & her alligator!   **E**

ALLIGATORS -- FOLKLORE

Riggs, K. Alligators   **597.98**

ALLIGATORS -- JUVENILE LITERATURE

Riggs, K. Alligators   **597.98**

Alligators all around. Sendak, M.   **E**

Alligators and crocodiles. Gibbons, G.   **597.98**

Alligators and crocodiles! Pringle, L. P.   **597.98**

Allison. Say, A.   **E**

Allison, Jennifer

Gilda Joyce, psychic investigator   **Fic**

Gilda Joyce, psychic investigator: the bones of the holy   **Fic**

Gilda Joyce: the dead drop   **Fic**

Gilda Joyce: the ghost sonata   **Fic**

Gilda Joyce: the Ladies of the Lake   **Fic**

Allman, Toney

Are extraterrestrials a threat to mankind?   **001.9**

Allman, Toney

Are extraterrestrials a threat to mankind?   **001.9**

Drugs   **616.86**

The Jaws of Life   **628.9**

The Nexi robot   **629.8**

Obesity   **616.3**

Recycled tires   **678**

ALLOCATION OF TIME *See* Time management

ALLOSAURUS

See also Dinosaurs

ALLOYS

See also Industrial chemistry; Metals

Allred, Scott

(il) How to get rich in the California Gold Rush   **979.4**

(il) Olson, T. How to get rich on a Texas cattle drive   **978**

(il) Olson, T. How to get rich on the Oregon Trail   **978**

Allsopp, Sophie

(il) Kroll, V. L. Everybody has a teddy   **E**

Allwright, Deborah

(il) Green, A. The fox in the dark   **E**

(il) Lewis, J. Don't read this book!   **E**

Allyn, Pam

What to read when   **028.5**

Alma Flor Ada. Parker-Rock, M.   **92**

ALMANACS

Hopkins, L. B. Days to celebrate   **051**

The World almanac for kids   **031.02**

ALMANACS, CHILDREN'S

Hopkins, L. B. Days to celebrate   **051**

Almond, David, 1951-

The boy who climbed into the moon   **Fic**

Spirin, G. A apple pie .... E
Stewig, J. W. The animals watched 222
Sweet, M. Carmine .... E
Thurlby, P. Paul Thurlby's alphabet .... E
Ulmer, W. K. A isn't for fox .... E
Van Allsburg, C. The Z was zapped 411
Werner, S. Alphabeasties and other amazing types ... 411
When royals wore ruffles 391
Wilbur, R. The disappearing alphabet 811
Wildsmith, B. Brian Wildsmith's ABC ...... E
Wildsmith, B. Brian Wildsmith's Amazing animal alphabet E
Winter, J. Calavera abecedario .... E
Wondriska, W. A long piece of string .... E
Wynne Pechter, L. Alligator, bear, crab .... E
Ziefert, H. ABC dentist 617.6
Zuckerman, A. Creature ABC .... E
Zuravicky, O. C is for city .... E

ALPHABET
    See also Writing

ALPHABET -- FICTION
Bingham, K. Z is for Moose .... E
Brown, S. G. Bang! Boom! Roar! .... E

ALPHABET -- HISTORY
Donoughue, C. The story of writing 411
Robb, D. Ox, house, stick 411

ALPHABET -- JUVENILE FICTION
Boldt, M. 123 versus ABC .... E
Horowitz, D. Twenty-six pirates .... E

ALPHABET -- JUVENILE LITERATURE
ABC's of baseball .... E
Ada, A. F. Gathering the sun 811
Ashley Bryan's ABC of African-American poetry ... 811
Ashman, L. M is for mischief .... E
Baker, K. LMNO peas .... E
Bataille, M. ABC3D .... E
Bayer, J. A my name is Alice 411
Demarest, C. L. All aboard! .... E
Ehlert, L. Eating the alphabet 411
Floca, B. The racecar alphabet 411
Forss, S. Alphasaurs and other prehistoric types ... 567.9
Gaiman, N. The dangerous alphabet .... E
Geisert, A. Country road ABC .... E
Hoban, T. 26 letters and 99 cents 411
Horowitz, D. Twenty-six princesses .... E
Johnson, S. Alphabet city 411
Kontis, A. AlphaOops!: H is for Halloween .. E
Lawlor, L. Muddy as a duck puddle and other American similes ... 425
Lobel, A. Alison's zinnia 411
Macdonald, S. Alphabatics 411
Marsalis, W. Jazz A-B-Z 781.65
Pelletier, D. The graphic alphabet 411
Schwartz, D. M. Q is for quark 500
Schwartz, J. City alphabet .... E
Seeger, L. V. The hidden alphabet .... E
Sierra, J. Sleepy little alphabet .... E
Stewig, J. W. The animals watched 222
Van Allsburg, C. The Z was zapped 411
Wynne Pechter, L. Alligator, bear, crab ..... E

ALPHABET -- POETRY
Wilbur, R. The disappearing alphabet 811
Alphabet animals. Macdonald, S. .... E
ALPHABET BOOKS *See* Alphabet
Alphabet city. Johnson, S. 411
Alphabet explosion! Nickle, J. 793.73
The **alphabet** from A to Y with bonus letter, Z! Martin, S. E
ALPHABET RHYMES
Spirin, G. A apple pie .... E

Alphabet under construction. Fleming, D. 411
ALPHABETS
    See also Alphabet; Sign painting
AlphaOops!: H is for Halloween. Kontis, A. .... E
Alphasaurs and other prehistoric types. Forss, S. ... 567.9
ALPINE ANIMALS *See* Mountain animals
ALPINE FAUNA *See* Mountain animals
Alsdurf, Phyllis
It's milking time .... E
Alsop, Marin
Helsby, G. Those amazing musical instruments ... 784.19
Alter, Anna
Abigail spells .... E
Disappearing Desmond .... E
A photo for Greta .... E
What can you do with an old red shoe? 745.5
(il) Broyles, A. Priscilla and the hollyhocks ... E
Alter, Judy
John Barclay Armstrong 92
ALTERNATE ENERGY RESOURCES *See* Renewable energy resources
Alternative cars. Wheeler, J. C. 629.222
Alternative energy beyond fossil fuels. Rau, D. M. ... 333.79
ALTERNATIVE ENERGY RESOURCES *See* Renewable energy resources
ALTERNATIVE FUEL VEHICLES
Wheeler, J. C. Alternative cars 629.222
ALTERNATIVE FUEL VEHICLES
    See also Motor vehicles
ALTERNATIVE HISTORIES
    See also Fantasy fiction
ALTERNATIVE HISTORIES -- JUVENILE FICTION
Colfer, E. The reluctant assassin .... Fic
ALTERNATIVE LIFESTYLES
    See also Lifestyles
ALTERNATIVE MEDICINE
    See also Medicine
Altes, Marta
My grandpa .... E
ALTITUDES -- FICTION
Long, E. Up, tall and high .... E
ALTITUDES -- MEASUREMENT -- EXPERIMENTS
Gardner, R. Far-out science projects with height and depth ... 530.8
ALTITUDES -- MEASUREMENT -- EXPERIMENTS -- JUVENILE LITERATURE
Gardner, R. Far-out science projects with height and depth ... 530.8
Altman, Linda Jacobs
Arkansas 976.7
Big dogs 636.7
Colorado 978.8
Parrots 636.6
Texas 976.4
ALTRUISM
    See also Conduct of life
ALTRUISTS *See* Philanthropists
Aluminum. Farndon, J. 546
ALUMINUM
    See also Metals
ALUMINUM
Farndon, J. Aluminum 546
ALUMINUM -- RECYCLING
    See also Recycling
ALUMINUM FOIL
    See also Aluminum; Packaging
Alvarez, Julia
A gift of gracias .... E

Kalz, J. An A-MAZE-ing amusement park adventure **793.73**

AMUSEMENT PARKS -- FICTION

Steinke, A. N. The Super Duper Dog Park   **741.5**

AMUSEMENTS -- FICTION

Moss, M. Amelia's boredom survival guide   **Fic**

AMUSEMENTS -- JUVENILE LITERATURE

Glenn, J. Unbored   **790**

Amy's light. Nutt, R.   **E**

ANABOLIC STEROIDS *See* Steroids

Anaconda. Ganeri, A.   **597.96**

ANACONDAS

Ganeri, A. Anaconda   **597.96**

ANALOGY

Berkes, M. C. Animalogy   **590**

ANALYTIC GEOMETRY

See also Geometry

ANALYTICAL CHEMISTRY

See also Chemistry

Analyze this! Glass, S.   **507**

Ananse and the lizard. Cummings, P.   **398.2**

Ananse's feast. Mollel, T. M.   **398.209**

ANANSI (LEGENDARY CHARACTER)

Aardema, V. Anansi does the impossible!   **398.209**

Anansi the spider-man Anansi and the talking melon **398.24**

Anansi the spider-man Anansi goes fishing   **398.24**

Badoe, A. The pot of wisdom: Ananse stories   **398.2**

Haley, G. E. A story, a story   **398.2**

Kimmel, E. A. Anansi and the moss-covered rock   **398.2**

Kimmel, E. A. Anansi's party time   **398.2**

Krensky, S. Anansi and the box of stories   **398.2**

McDermott, G. Anansi the spider   **398.2**

Mollel, T. M. Ananse's feast   **398.209**

Paye The talking vegetables   **398.2**

ANANSI (LEGENDARY CHARACTER)

See also Legendary characters

Anansi and the box of stories. Krensky, S.   **398.2**

Anansi and the magic stick. Kimmel, E. A.   **398.24**

Anansi and the moss-covered rock. Kimmel, E. A.   **398.2**

Anansi and the talking melon. Anansi the spider-man   **398.24**

Anansi does the impossible! Aardema, V.   **398.209**

Anansi goes fishing. Anansi the spider-man   **398.24**

Anansi the spider. McDermott, G.   **398.2**

Anansi the spider-man

Anansi and the talking melon   **398.24**

Anansi goes fishing   **398.24**

Anansi's party time. Kimmel, E. A.   **398.2**

ANARCHISM AND ANARCHISTS

See also Freedom; Political crimes and offenses; Political science

Anastasia Krupnik. Lowry, L.   **Fic**

ANATOMY

Green, J. Inside animals   **571**

ANATOMY

See also Biology; Medicine

ANATOMY OF ANIMALS *See* Animals -- Anatomy

Anaya, Rudolfo A.

The first tortilla   **Fic**

ANCESTOR WORSHIP

See also Religion

ANCESTRY *See* Genealogy; Heredity

Ancient Africa. Bowden, R.   **960**

Ancient Africa. Sherrow, V.   **939**

Ancient and medieval people [series]

Park, L. The Japanese samurai   **355**

Park, L. The medieval knights   **940.1**

Park, L. The Pharaohs' armies   **355**

Park, L. The Roman gladiators   **937**

Park, L. The Scandinavian Vikings   **948**

Park, L. The Spartan hoplites   **938**

ANCIENT ARCHITECTURE

See also Archeology; Architecture

ANCIENT ART

See also Art

Ancient Aztec. Cooke, T.   **972**

Ancient Celts. Green, J.   **936**

Ancient China. Shuter, J.   **931**

Ancient China. Ball, J. A.   **931**

ANCIENT CIVILIZATION

Adams, S. Alexander   **92**

Adams, S. The Kingfisher atlas of the ancient world   **930**

Chrisp, P. Atlas of ancient worlds   **911**

Compoint, S. Buried treasures   **930.1**

Croy, A. Exploring the past   **930.1**

The Library of Alexandria   **027**

Matthews, R. Ancient mysteries   **930.1**

Panchyk, R. Archaeology for kids   **930.1**

ANCIENT CIVILIZATION -- JUVENILE LITERATURE

Ancient treasures   **930.1**

Ancient civilizations [series]

Ancient Egypt   **932**

Ancient Greece   **938**

Ancient Rome   **937**

The **ancient** cliff dwellers of Mesa Verde. Arnold, C. **970.004**

Ancient Egypt. Rubalcaba, J.   **932**

Ancient Egypt. Smith, M.   **932**

Ancient Egypt.   **932**

Ancient Egypt. Williams, M.   **299**

Ancient Egyptian warfare. Jestice, P. G.   **932**

The **ancient** formula. Thielbar, M.   **741.5**

ANCIENT GEOGRAPHY

See also Ancient history; Historical geography

ANCIENT GEOGRAPHY -- JUVENILE LITERATURE

The librarian who measured the earth   **520**

Ancient Greece   **938**

Ancient Greece. Langley, A.   **709.3**

Ancient Greece. McGee, M.   **938**

Ancient Greece. Steele, P.   **938**

Ancient Greece!   **745**

Ancient Greek warfare. Rice, R. S.   **938**

ANCIENT HISTORY

See also World history

The **ancient** Inca. Calvert, P.   **985**

Ancient Inca. Gruber, B.   **985**

Ancient Iraq. Gruber, B.   **935**

Ancient Maya. Harris, N.   **972**

Ancient Mexico. Campbell-Hinshaw, K.   **709.3**

Ancient mysteries. Matthews, R.   **930.1**

Ancient Persian warfare. Jestice, P. G.   **935**

ANCIENT PHILOSOPHY

See also Philosophy

Ancient Pueblo. Croy, A.   **978**

Ancient Roman warfare. Rice, R. S.   **937**

The **ancient** Romans. Lassieur, A.   **937**

Ancient Rome. Deckker, Z.   **937**

Ancient Rome.   **937**

Ancient Rome. James, S.   **937**

Ancient treasures.   **930.1**

Ancient warfare [series]

Jestice, P. G. Ancient Egyptian warfare   **932**

Jestice, P. G. Ancient Persian warfare   **935**

Rice, R. S. Ancient Greek warfare   **938**

Rice, R. S. Ancient Roman warfare   **937**

Ancients in their own words [series]

Kerrigan, M. Egyptians   **932**

Kerrigan, M. Greeks   **938**

Kerrigan, M. Mesopotamians   **935**

Landau, E. Big cats   **599.75**

Animals alive.   **590**

Animals and me. Greenwood, M..   **612**

ANIMALS AND THE HANDICAPPED

Bozzo, L. Service dog heroes   **362.4**

Goldish, M. Prison puppies   **362.4**

Hoffman, M. A. Helping dogs   **362.4**

Kent, D. Animal helpers for the disabled   **636.088**

Martin, C. Helpers   **362.4**

Patent, D. H. The right dog for the job   **362.4**

Animals and their families. Nascimbeni, B.   **E**

Animals animals [series]

Bailer, D. Geese   **598**

Mara, W. Coyotes   **599.77**

Mara, W. Deer   **599.65**

Mara, W. Ducks   **598**

Otfinoski, S. Alligators   **597.98**

Otfinoski, S. Skunks   **599.7**

ANIMALS AS AIDS FOR PEOPLE WITH DISABILITIES -- JUVENILE LITERATURE

Kent, D. Animal helpers for the disabled   **636.088**

ANIMALS AS CARRIERS OF DISEASE

Plagues, pox, and pestilence   **614.4**

Animals at work [series]

Barnes, J. Camels and llamas at work   **636.2**

Barnes, J. Elephants at work   **636.9**

Barnes, J. Horses at work   **636.1**

Animals Charles Darwin saw. Markle, S.   **92**

Animals Christopher Columbus saw. Markle, S.   **970.01**

Animals don't, so I won't! Derrick, D. G.   **E**

Animals home alone. Riphagen, L.   **E**

ANIMALS IN ART

Ames, L. J. Draw 50 animal 'toons   **741.5**

Ames, L. J. Draw 50 baby animals   **743**

Ames, L. J. Draw 50 endangered animals   **743**

Bergin, M. How to draw pets   **743**

Cuxart, B. Modeling clay animals   **738.1**

Farrell, R. All about drawing horses & pets   **743**

Harbo, C. L. Easy animal origami   **736**

Hart, C. The cartoonist's big book of drawing animals   **741.5**

Hill, I. Urban animals   **729**

ANIMALS IN ENTERTAINMENT

Grayson, R. Performers   **791.8**

Laidlaw, R. On parade   **791.8**

Animals in fall. Rustad, M. E. H.   **578.4**

ANIMALS IN LITERATURE

Lewis, J. P. Last laughs   **818**

ANIMALS IN MOTION PICTURES

Helfer, R. World's greatest lion   **E**

ANIMALS IN MOTION PICTURES

See also Motion pictures

ANIMALS IN MOTION PICTURES -- CALIFORNIA -- LOS ANGELES -- BIOGRAPHY -- JUVENILE LITERATURE

Helfer, R. World's greatest lion   **E**

Animals in order [series]

Miller, S. S. Woodpeckers, toucans, and their kin   **598**

ANIMALS IN POLICE WORK

Bozzo, L. Police dog heroes   **363.2**

Mezzanotte, J. Police   **363.2**

ANIMALS IN POLICE WORK

See also Police; Working animals

ANIMALS IN THE BIBLE -- JUVENILE LITERATURE

Animals of the Bible   **220.8**

Animals in the house. Keenan, S.   **636**

Animals in winter. Bancroft, H.   **591.56**

Animals Marco Polo saw. Markle, S.   **92**

Animals of the Bible.   **220.8**

Animals of the snow and ice [series]

Landau, E. Beluga whales   **599.5**

Landau, E. Emperor penguins   **598**

Animals on the edge. Pobst, S.   **578.68**

Animals on the edge [series]

Allen, K. Sea turtles' race to the sea   **597.92**

Animals on the trail with Lewis and Clark. Patent, D. H.   **917**

Animals Robert Scott saw. Markle, S.   **998**

Animals that changed the world. Thomas, K.   **590**

Animals under our feet. McKay, S.   **590**

Animals up close. Siwanowicz, I.   **590**

The **animals** watched. Stewig, J. W.   **222**

Animals welcome. Kehret, P.   **636.08**

Animals with armor. Racanelli, M.   **591.47**

Animals with awesome armor. Mitchell, S. K.   **591.47**

Animals with crafty camouflage. Mitchell, S. K.   **591.47**

Animals with pockets. Racanelli, M.   **599.2**

Animals with super powers [series]

Lunis, N. Electric animals   **591.4**

Lunis, N. Glow-in-the-dark animals   **572**

Lunis, N. See-through animals   **591.47**

Yaw, V. Color-changing animals   **591.47**

Animals with wicked weapons. Mitchell, S. K.   **591.47**

ANIMALS' RIGHTS *See* Animal rights

Animals, animals [series]

Bailer, D. Donkeys   **636.1**

Bailer, D. Prairie dogs   **599.3**

Dornfeld, M. Bats   **599.4**

Estigarribia, D. Cheetahs   **599.75**

Jango-Cohen, J. Armadillos   **599.3**

Jango-Cohen, J. Bees   **595.7**

Jango-Cohen, J. Hippopotamuses   **599.63**

King, D. C. Jellyfish   **593.5**

Noble-Goodman, K. Zebras   **599.66**

Nobleman, M. T. Foxes   **599.77**

Otfinoski, S. Scorpions   **595.4**

Otfinoski, S. Squirrels   **599.3**

Perry, P. J. Buffalo   **599.64**

Rebman, R. C. Cats   **636.8**

Rebman, R. C. Vultures   **598**

Rebman, R. C. Walruses   **599.79**

ANIMALS, FOSSIL -- JUVENILE LITERATURE

Bonner, H. When fish got feet, sharks got teeth, and bugs began to swarm   **560**

ANIMALS, MYTHICAL *See* Mythical animals

ANIMALS, MYTHICAL -- FICTION

Kraegel, K. King Arthur's very great grandson   **E**

Larios, J. H. Imaginary menagerie   **811**

ANIMALS, PREHISTORIC *See* Prehistoric animals

ANIMATED CARTOONS *See* Animated films

ANIMATED FILMS

Bliss, J. Art that moves   **791.43**

Buckley, A. M. Pixar   **338.7**

Cech, J. Imagination and innovation   **791.43**

ANIMATED FILMS

See also Cartoons and caricatures; Motion pictures

ANIMATED TELEVISION PROGRAMS

See also Television programs

ANIMATION (CINEMATOGRAPHY)

Cohn, J. Animator   **791.43**

Animator. Cohn, J.   **791.43**

ANIMATORS

Sis, P. The wall   **92**

ANIME

Brenner, R. E. Understanding manga and anime   **025.2**

ANIME

See also Animated films; Animated television programs

ANIMISM

Anton can do magic. Konnecke, O.   E

Anton, Mauricio
    Turner, A. National Geographic prehistoric mammals   569

Antonini, Gabriele
    (il) Blackford, A. The hungry little monkey   E

ANTONYMS See Opposites

Ants. Trueit, T. S.   595.7

Ants. Lockwood, S.   595.7

ANTS
    Aronin, M. The ant's nest   595.7
    Cannon, J. Crickwing   E
    Dorros, A. Ant cities   595.7
    Lockwood, S. Ants   595.7
    Micucci, C. The life and times of the ant   595.79
    Nirgiotis, N. Killer ants   595.7
    Rissman, R. Ants   595.79
    Rodriguez, A. M. Secret of the plant-killing ants and more!   595.7
    Rustad, M. E. H. Ants and aphids work together   595.7
    Stewart, M. Ants   595.7
    Trueit, T. S. Ants   595.7

Ants. Rissman, R.   595.79

ANTS
    See also Insects

Ants. Stewart, M.   595.7

ANTS -- FICTION
    Ant and Grasshopper   E
    The ant and the grasshopper   E
    Avi A beginning, a muddle, and an end   Fic
    Avi The end of the beginning   Fic
    Baker, K. Just how long can a long string be!?   E
    Barner, B. Bug safari   E
    Cannon, J. Crickwing   E
    Farooqi, M. The cobbler's holiday, or, why ants don't have shoes   E
    Giovanni, N. The grasshopper's song   E
    Holub, J. Spring is here!   E
    McDonald, M. Ant and Honey Bee   E
    McElligott, M. The lion's share   E

ANTS -- JUVENILE LITERATURE
    Aronin, M. The ant's nest   595.7
    Micucci, C. The life and times of the ant   595.79
    Nirgiotis, N. Killer ants   595.7
    Rissman, R. Ants   595.79

Ants and aphids work together. Rustad, M. E. H.   595.7

Ants in your pants, worms in your plants! De Groat, D.   E

Anwar, Merry
    Cornell, K. A. Cooking the Indonesian way   641.5

ANXIETIES See Anxiety

ANXIETY
    Hamlisch, M. Marvin makes music   E

ANXIETY
    See also Emotions; Neuroses; Stress (Psychology)

ANXIETY -- FICTION
    Justin Case   Fic

ANXIOUSNESS See Anxiety

Any small goodness. Johnston, T.   Fic

Any which wall. Snyder, L.   Fic

The Anybodies. Bode, N. E.   Fic

Anything but typical. Baskin, N. R.   Fic

Anzovin, Steven
    Kane, J. N. Famous first facts   031.02

Aoyagi, Nora
    (il) Cassino, M. The story of snow   551.57

Apache. Kissock, H.   970.004

APACHE INDIANS
    Ehrlich, A. Wounded Knee: an Indian history of the American West   970.004

Kissock, H. Apache   970.004

APARTHEID
    See also Segregation; South Africa -- Race relations

APARTHEID -- JUVENILE FICTION
    Naidoo, B. Out of bounds: seven stories of conflict and hope   S

APARTMENT HOUSES
    See also Buildings; Domestic architecture; Houses; Housing

APARTMENT HOUSES -- FICTION
    Cole, B. The money we'll save   E
    Keats, E. J. Apt. 3   E
    Martin, A. M. Ten rules for living with my sister   Fic
    Potter, E. Olivia Kidney   Fic
    Stead, R. Liar & spy   Fic
    Teplin, S. The clock without a face   Fic
    Trachtenberg, S. The Elevator Man   E

Ape. Jenkins, M.   599.8

Ape in a cape. Eichenberg, F.   E

APES
    Barker, D. Top 50 reasons to care about great apes   599.8
    Bustos, E. Going ape!   599.8
    Jenkins, M. Ape   599.8

APES
    See also Primates

APHIDS
    Rustad, M. E. H. Ants and aphids work together   595.7

APHRODITE (GREEK DEITY)
    See also Gods and goddesses

APICULTURE See Beekeeping

APOCALYPTIC FICTION
    The city of Ember   Fic

APOCALYPTIC FILMS
    See also Motion pictures

Apodaca, Blanca
    Behind the canvas   700.23

Apollinaire, Guillaume, 1880-1918
    Yolleck, J. Paris in the spring with Picasso   E

APOLLO (GREEK DEITY)
    See also Gods and goddesses

APOLLO 13 (SPACECRAFT) -- JUVENILE LITERATURE
    Holden, H. M. Danger in space   629.45

Apollo moonwalks. Vogt, G.   629.45

APOLLO PROJECT
    Burleigh, R. One giant leap   629.45
    Holden, H. M. Danger in space   629.45

APOLLO PROJECT
    See also Life support systems (Space environment); Orbital rendezvous (Space flight); Space flight to the moon

APOLLO PROJECT -- GRAPHIC NOVELS
    Ottaviani, J. T-Minus: the race to the moon   629.45

APOLLO PROJECT -- JUVENILE LITERATURE
    Bodden, V. To the moon   629.45

APOLOGIZING -- JUVENILE POETRY.
    Sidman, J. This is just to say   811

APOSTLES
    See also Christian saints; Church history -- 30-600, Early church

APOSTROPHE -- JUVENILE LITERATURE
    Truss, L. The girl's like spaghetti   428

The apothecary. Petersen, C.   615

Appalachia. Rylant, C.   974

APPALACHIAN TRAIL -- JUVENILE FICTION
    Vanderpool, C. Navigating Early   Fic

APPARATUS, ELECTRIC See Electric apparatus and appliances

See also Mathematics

ASTRONOMY -- MISCELLANEA -- JUVENILE LITERA-TURE

Ward, D. J. Seven wonders of space phenomena **520**

ASTRONOMY -- POETRY

Florian, D. Comets, stars, the Moon, and Mars **811**

Whitman, W. When I heard the learn'd astronomer **E**

ASTRONOMY -- RESEARCH -- JUVENILE LITERA-TURE

Cole, M. D. Eye on the universe **522**

ASTROPHYSICISTS

Turner, P. S. Life on earth--and beyond **576.8**

Wittenstein, V. O. Planet hunter **523.2**

ASTROPHYSICS

See also Astronomy; Physics

At Gleason's gym. Lewin, T. **796.8**

At home in a new land. Sandin, J. **E**

At home in your body. Simons, R. **613**

At Jerusalem's gate. Grimes, N. **811**

At night. Bean, J. **E**

AT RISK STUDENTS

See also Students

At the beach. Lee, H. V. **495.1**

At the firefly gate. Newbery, L. **Fic**

At the sea floor cafe. Bulion, L. **811**

At the supermarket. **E**

At this very moment. Arnosky, J. **E**

Atha, Antony

Fitness for young people **613.7**

Athans, Pete, 1957-

About

Athans, S. K. Tales from the top of the world **796.522**

Athans, Sandra K.

Tales from the top of the world **796.522**

ATHAPASCAN INDIANS

Hill, K. The year of Miss Agnes **Fic**

ATHAPASCAN INDIANS -- FICTION

Hill, K. The year of Miss Agnes **Fic**

ATHEISM

See also Religion; Secularism; Theology

Athena. O'Connor, G. **741.5**

ATHENA (GREEK DEITY)

O'Connor, G. Athena **741.5**

ATHENA (GREEK DEITY)

See also Gods and goddesses

ATHENS (GREECE) -- BUILDINGS, STRUCTURES, ETC -- JUVENILE LITERATURE

Curlee, L. Parthenon **726**

Atherton [series]

Carman, P. The house of power **Fic**

Carman, P. Rivers of fire **Fic**

ATHLETES

Becoming a ballerina **792.8**

Krull, K. Lives of the athletes **796**

Pele For the love of soccer! **92**

Torsiello, D. P. Michael Phelps **92**

Whitfield, S. Simon says gold: Simon Whitfield's pursuit of athletic excellence **92**

ATHLETES -- BIOGRAPHY -- JUVENILE LITERATURE

Krull, K. Lives of the athletes **796**

ATHLETES -- DRUG USE

Schaefer, A. Steroids **362.29**

ATHLETES -- UNITED STATES -- BIOGRAPHY -- JUVE-NILE LITERATURE

Freedman, R. Babe Didrikson Zaharias **796.352**

ATHLETES IN ART

Ames, L. J. Draw 50 athletes **743**

ATHLETES, BLACK See Black athletes

ATHLETICS

Kaner, E. And the Winner Is ... **612.7**

Atinuke

Anna Hibiscus **Fic**

Anna Hibiscus' song **Fic**

Good luck, Anna Hibiscus! **Fic**

Have fun, Anna Hibiscus! **Fic**

Hooray for Anna Hibiscus! **Fic**

The no. 1 car spotter **Fic**

Atkins, Jeannine

Anne Hutchinson's way **92**

Atkinson, E. J.

I, Emma Freke **Fic**

Atkinson, Elizabeth

From Alice to Zen and everyone in between **Fic**

ATLANTIC COD

Kurlansky, M. The cod's tale **639.2**

ATLANTIC COD -- JUVENILE LITERATURE

Kurlansky, M. The cod's tale **639.2**

ATLANTIC OCEAN

See also Ocean

ATLANTIC PUFFIN -- INFANCY -- ICELAND -- HEI-MAEY (WESTMAN ISLANDS)

Lewin, B. Puffling patrol **E**

Atlantis. Michels, T. **001.9**

ATLANTIS

Michels, T. Atlantis **001.9**

ATLANTIS (LEGENDARY PLACE) -- FICTION

Lerangis, P. The colossus rises **Fic**

ATLANTIS (LEGENDARY PLACE) -- JUVENILE FIC-TION

Lerangis, P. The colossus rises **Fic**

Atlas. Rafter, D. **741.5**

Atlas of ancient worlds. Chrisp, P. **911**

Atlas of Australia. Foster, K. **994**

Atlas of Europe. Foster, K. **940**

Atlas of North America. Foster, K. **970**

Atlas of South America. Foster, K. **980**

Atlas of Southwest and Central Asia. Law, F. **950**

Atlas of the Far East and Southeast Asia. Law, F. **950**

Atlas of the Poles and Oceans. Foster, K. **998**

Atlas of the universe. Garlick, M. A. **520**

ATLASES

Beginner's United States atlas **912**

Boyer, C. National Geographic kids ultimate U.S. road trip atlas **912**

Crane, N. Barefoot Books world atlas **912**

National Geographic atlas of the world **912**

National Geographic Kids beginner's world atlas **912**

National Geographic United States atlas for young explorers **912**

National Geographic world atlas for young explorers **912**

Student atlas **912**

Wojtanik, A. The National Geographic Bee ultimate fact book **910**

ATLASES

See also Geography; Maps

Atmosphere. Gallant, R. A. **551.51**

ATMOSPHERE

See also Air; Earth

ATMOSPHERE

Cosgrove, B. Weather **551.5**

Gallant, R. A. Atmosphere **551.51**

ATMOSPHERE -- JUVENILE LITERATURE

Cosgrove, B. Weather **551.5**

Gallant, R. A. Atmosphere **551.51**

ATMOSPHERE -- POLLUTION See Air pollution

ATMOSPHERIC DUST See Dust

ATMOSPHERIC GREENHOUSE EFFECT *See* Global warming

ATMOSPHERIC HUMIDITY *See* Humidity

ATOLLS *See* Coral reefs and islands

The **atom.** Cregan, E. R.   **539.7**

Atomic Ace. Weigel, J.   **E**

ATOMIC BOMB
Lawton, C. Hiroshima   **940.54**

ATOMIC BOMB
     See also Bombs; Nuclear weapons

ATOMIC BOMB -- FICTION
Klages, E. The green glass sea   **Fic**
Klages, E. White sands, red menace   **Fic**

ATOMIC BOMB -- GERMANY -- HISTORY
Sheinkin, S. Bomb   **623.4**

ATOMIC BOMB -- HISTORY
Sheinkin, S. Bomb   **623.4**

ATOMIC BOMB -- JUVENILE LITERATURE
Lawton, C. Hiroshima   **940.54**

ATOMIC BOMB -- PHYSIOLOGICAL EFFECT
Coerr, E. Sadako   **92**
Coerr, E. Sadako and the thousand paper cranes   **92**

ATOMIC ENERGY *See* Nuclear energy

ATOMIC NUCLEI *See* Nuclear physics

ATOMIC POWER *See* Nuclear energy

ATOMIC POWER PLANTS *See* Nuclear power plants

ATOMIC STRUCTURE -- JUVENILE LITERATURE
Campbell, M. C. Discovering atoms   **539.7**
Claybourne, A. Who split the atom?   **539**

ATOMIC THEORY
Cregan, E. R. The atom   **539.7**
McLean, A. What is atomic theory?   **539.7**

ATOMIC THEORY -- HISTORY -- JUVENILE LITERATURE
Campbell, M. C. Discovering atoms   **539.7**

Atomic universe. Jerome, K. B.   **539.7**

ATOMIC WARFARE *See* Nuclear warfare

ATOMIC WEAPONS *See* Nuclear weapons

ATOMS
Baxter, R. The particle model of matter   **530**
Claybourne, A. Who split the atom?   **539**
Cregan, E. R. The atom   **539.7**
Lepora, N. Atoms and molecules   **539.7**
Older than the stars   **523.1**

ATOMS -- JUVENILE LITERATURE
Campbell, M. C. Discovering atoms   **539.7**

Atoms and molecules. Lepora, N.   **539.7**

ATONEMENT -- CHRISTIANITY
     See also Christianity; Sacrifice; Salvation

ATONEMENT -- JUDAISM
     See also Judaism

ATONEMENT, DAY OF *See* Yom Kippur

ATROCITIES
     See also Crime; Cruelty

Attack of the Fiend. Delaney, J.   **Fic**

Attack of the fluffy bunnies. Beaty, A.   **Fic**

The **attack** of the frozen woodchucks. Elish, D.   **Fic**

Attacked by a crocodile. Hamilton, S. L.   **597.98**

ATTACKS BY ANIMALS *See* Animal attacks

Atteberry, Kevan
   (il) Schaefer, L. M. Frankie Stein   **E**
   (il) Schaefer, L. M. Frankie Stein starts school   **E**

ATTENTION
     See also Apperception; Educational psychology; Memory; Psychology; Thought and thinking

ATTENTION DEFICIT DISORDER
Capaccio, G. ADD and ADHD   **616.85**
Chilman-Blair, K. Medikidz explain ADHD   **616.85**

Kraus, J. Annie's plan   **371.3**

Quinn, P. O. Attention, girls!   **616.85**

Robbins, L. How to deal with ADHD   **616.85**

Silverstein, A. The ADHD update   **616.85**

Taylor, J. F. The survival guide for kids with ADD or ADHD   **616.85**

Wood, D. Miss Little's gift   **E**

ATTENTION DEFICIT DISORDER -- FICTION
Cheaney, J. B. The middle of somewhere   **Fic**
Gantos, J. I am not Joey Pigza   **Fic**
Gantos, J. Joey Pigza loses control   **Fic**
Gantos, J. Joey Pigza swallowed the key   **Fic**
Gantos, J. What would Joey do?   **Fic**

ATTENTION DEFICIT DISORDER IN ADOLESCENCE *See* Attention deficit disorder

ATTENTION DEFICIT DISORDER IN ADULTS *See* Attention deficit disorder

Attention, girls! Quinn, P. O.   **616.85**

ATTENTION-DEFICIT HYPERACTIVITY DISORDER
Gantos, J. Joey Pigza loses control   **Fic**

ATTENTION-DEFICIT HYPERACTIVITY DISORDER *See* Attention deficit disorder

ATTENTION-DEFICIT HYPERACTIVITY DISORDER -- FICTION
Gantos, J. Joey Pigza swallowed the key   **Fic**

ATTENTION-DEFICIT HYPERACTIVITY DISORDER -- JUVENILE LITERATURE
Silverstein, A. The ADHD update   **616.85**

Attica. Kilworth, G.   **Fic**

ATTITUDE (PSYCHOLOGY)
     See also Emotions; Psychology

Attoe, Steve
   (il) Becker, H. What's the big idea?   **609**

ATTORNEYS *See* Lawyers

ATTORNEYS GENERAL
Krull, K. The brothers Kennedy   **920**

ATTRACTING WILDLIFE *See* Wildlife attracting

Atwater, Florence Carroll
Atwater, R. T. Mr. Popper's penguins   **Fic**

Atwater, Richard Tupper
Mr. Popper's penguins   **Fic**

Atwell, Debby
   (il) Miss Moore thought otherwise   **020.92**

AU PAIRS -- FICTION
Farrant, N. After Iris   **Fic**

Auch, Alison
All about temperature   **536**

Auch, Herm
Auch, M. J. Beauty and the beaks   **E**
   (il) Auch, M. J. I was a third grade bodyguard   **Fic**
   (il) Auch, M. J. I was a third grade science project   **Fic**
   (il) Auch, M. J. I was a third grade spy   **Fic**
Auch, M. J. The plot chickens   **E**

Auch, Mary Jane
Beauty and the beaks   **E**
A dog on his own   **Fic**
I was a third grade bodyguard   **Fic**
I was a third grade science project   **Fic**
I was a third grade spy   **Fic**
Journey to nowhere   **Fic**
One-handed catch   **Fic**
The plot chickens   **E**
Wing nut   **Fic**

AUCTIONS
Gitlin, M. eBay   **338.7**

Auden, Scott
Medical mysteries   **610**
New Hampshire, 1603-1776   **974.2**

Latvia **947.96**
Uganda **967.61**
The **barn.** Avi **Fic**
Barn boot blues. Friend, C. **Fic**
Barn dance! Martin, B. **E**
Barn storm. Ghigna, C. **E**
Barnaby Grimes [series]
Stewart, P. The curse of the night wolf **Fic**
Stewart, P. Legion of the Dead **Fic**
Stewart, P. Phantom of Blood Alley **Fic**
Stewart, P. Return of the emerald skull **Fic**
Barnard, Alan
(il) Brewster, H. Dinosaurs in your backyard **567.9**
(il) Tanaka, S. New dinos **567.9**
Barnard, Bryn
The genius of Islam **297**
(il) Discovery in the cave **944**
Barnard, Bryn
The genius of Islam **297**
Outbreak **614.4**
(il) Redmond Tentacles! **594**
Barneda, David
(il) Reynolds, A. Snowbots **E**
Barner, Bob
Animal baths **591.5**
Barner, Bob
Animal baths **591.5**
Bears! bears! bears! **599.78**
Bug safari **E**
Dem bones **612.7**
Dinosaurs roar, butterflies soar! **560**
Penguins, penguins, everywhere! **598**
(il) Lewis, J. P. Big is big (and little, little) **E**
Barnes, Julia
Camels and llamas at work **636.2**
Elephants at work **636.9**
Horses at work **636.1**
Pet cats **636.8**
Pet dogs **636.7**
Pet guinea pigs **636.9**
Pet rabbits **636.9**
Barnes, Trevor
The Kingfisher children's illustrated Bible **220.9**
Barnett, Mac
Oh no! Not again! **E**
Barnett, Mac
Billy Twitters and his big blue whale problem **E**
The case of the case of mistaken identity **Fic**
Extra yarn **E**
The ghostwriter secret **Fic**
Guess again! **E**
It happened on a train **Fic**
Oh no!, or, How my science project destroyed the world **E**
Mustache! **E**
Teplin, S. The clock without a face **Fic**
Barnett, Moneta
(il) Greenfield, E. Sister **Fic**
Barnham, Kay
Recycle **363.7**
Barnhart, Norm
Amazing magic tricks: a beginner level **793.8**
Amazing magic tricks: apprentice level **793.8**
Amazing magic tricks: expert level **793.8**
Amazing magic tricks: master level **793.8**
Barnhill, Kelly Regan
The mostly true story of Jack **Fic**
Barnhill, Kelly Regan
Monsters of the deep **591.7**

The mostly true story of Jack **Fic**
Barnholdt, Lauren
Girl meets ghost **Fic**
Barnholdt, Lauren
Hailey Twitch and the campground itch **Fic**
Hailey Twitch and the great teacher switch **Fic**
Hailey Twitch and the wedding glitch **Fic**
Hailey Twitch is not a snitch **Fic**
Barnum's bones. Fern, T. **560.9**
Barnum, P. T. (Phineas Taylor), 1810-1891
About
Prince, A. J. Twenty-one elephants and still standing **E**
Barnum, P. T. (Phineas Taylor), 1810-1891
About
Fleming, C. The great and only Barnum **92**
Barnum, P. T. (Phineas Taylor), 1810-1891 -- Fiction
About
Prince, A. J. Twenty-one elephants and still standing **E**
Barnyard banter. Fleming, D. **813**
BAROQUE ARCHITECTURE
See also Architecture
BAROQUE ART
See also Art
Barr, Catherine
Thomas, R. L. Popular series fiction for K-6 readers **016**
Barracca, Debra
The adventures of Taxi Dog **813**
Barracca, Sal
Barracca, D. The adventures of Taxi Dog **813**
Barraclough, Sue
Fair play **175**
Honesty **179**
Leadership **303.3**
Reusing things **363.7**
Sharing **177**
Barragan, Paula
Shahan, S. Spicy hot colors: colores picantes **E**
Barrager, Brigette
The twelve dancing princesses **398.2**
Barrett, Amanda
African cats **599.75**
Barrett, Angela
(il) Binding, T. Sylvie and the songman **Fic**
(il) Eilenberg, M. Beauty and the beast **398.2**
(il) Schlitz, L. A. The night fairy **Fic**
Barrett, Judi
Santa from Cincinnati **E**
Barrett, Judi
Cloudy with a chance of meatballs **E**
Never take a shark to the dentist and other things not to do **E**
Barrett, Mary Brigid
Shoebox Sam **E**
Barrett, Robert
(il) Turner, A. W. Dust for dinner **E**
(il) Weatherford, C. B. Obama **92**
Barrett, Ron
(il) Barrett, J. Cloudy with a chance of meatballs **E**
(il) Weitzman, J. P. Superhero Joe **E**
Barrett, Tracy
The 100-year-old secret **Fic**
The Beast of Blackslope **Fic**
The case that time forgot **Fic**
Cold in summer **Fic**
Kentucky **976.9**
The missing heir **Fic**
On Etruscan time **Fic**
Tennessee **976.8**
Barretta, Gene

Riggs, K. Bats | 599.4
Rodriguez, C. Bats | 599.4
Stewart, M. How do bats fly in the dark? | 599.4
Vogel, J. Bats | 599.4
Bats. Vogel, J. | 599.4
Bats. Bekkering, A. | 599.4
Bats. Gibbons, G. | 599.4
Bats. Riggs, K. | 599.4
Bats. Rodriguez, C. | 599.4
Bats. Carney, E. | 599.4

BATS -- FICTION

Appelt, K. Bats around the clock | E
Avi Poppy and Ereth | Fic
Buhler, C. v. But who will bell the cats? | E
Cannon, J. Stellaluna | E
Dyer, S. Batty | E
Holub, J. Bed, bats, and beyond | Fic
Jarrell, R. The bat-poet | Fic
Lies, B. Bats at the beach | E
Oppel, K. Silverwing | Fic
Waring, G. Oscar and the bat | E

BATS -- FOLKLORE

Riggs, K. Bats | 599.4

BATS -- JUVENILE FICTION

Oppel, K. Firewing | Fic
Oppel, K. Sunwing | Fic

BATS -- JUVENILE LITERATURE

Carson, M. K. The bat scientists | 599.4
Gibbons, G. Bats | 599.4
Lunde, D. P. Hello, bumblebee bat | 599.4
A place for bats | 599.4
Riggs, K. Bats | 599.4

Bats around the clock. Appelt, K. | E
Bats at the beach. Lies, B. | E
Bats in the dark. Gonzales, D. | 599.4

Batten, John D.

(il) Jacobs, J. English fairy tales | 398.2

Batten, Mary

Aliens from Earth | 578.6
Please don't wake the animals | 591.5

Batter. Glaser, J. | 796.357

Battersby, Katherine

Squish Rabbit | E

The **battle** for Skandia. Flanagan, J. | Fic
The **battle** of Iwo Jima. Hama, L. | 940.54
Battle of the dinosaur bones. Johnson, R. L. | 560.973
The **battle** of the Labyrinth. Riordan, R. | Fic

BATTLES

See also Military art and science; Military history; War
Battles & weapons: exploring history through art. Chapman, C. | 355

Battut, Eric

The fox and the hen | E
Little Mouse's big secret | E

Batty. Dyer, S. | E

Baucom, Ian

Through the skylight | Fic

Bauer, A. C. E.

Come Fall | Fic
No castles here | Fic

Bauer, Caroline Feller

Caroline Feller Bauer's new handbook for storytellers | 372.6
Leading kids to books through crafts | 027.62
Leading kids to books through magic | 027.62
Leading kids to books through puppets | 027.62

Bauer, Helen

Beethoven for kids | 92

Bauer, Joan

Almost home | Fic
Close to famous | Fic

Bauer, Marion Dane

Bauer, M. D. In like a lion, out like a lamb | E
A bear named Trouble | Fic
The blue ghost | Fic
The golden ghost | Fic
The longest night | E
On my honor | Fic
One brown bunny | E
Runt | Fic
Thank you for me! | E
Wind | 551.51

Bauer, Marion Dane, 1938-

In like a lion, out like a lamb | E
Little dog, lost | Fic

Bauer, Michael Gerard

Just a dog | Fic

Bauer, Stephanie

(il) Hip hip hooray! it's Family Day! | E

Bauer, Stephanie

(il) Blackstone, S. Octopus opposites | E

Baum, L. Frank, 1856-1919

Cavallaro, M. L. Frank Baum's The Wizard of Oz | 741.5
Krull, K. The road to Oz | 92
The Wizard of Oz | Fic
The wonderful Wizard of Oz | Fic

Baum, L. Frank, 1856-1919 -- Adaptations

Cavallaro, M. L. Frank Baum's The Wizard of Oz | 741.5

Baum, Maxie

I have a little dreidel | 782.42

Baumbach, Donna

Less is more | 025.2

Bausum, Ann

Dragon bones and dinosaur eggs: a photobiography of Roy Chapman Andrews | 92
Freedom Riders | 323.1
Our country's first ladies | 920
Our Country's Presidents | 973.09

Baviera, Rocco

(il) Bruchac, J. A boy called Slow: the true story of Sitting Bull | 92

Bawden, Nina

Granny the Pag | Fic

Baxter, Daniel

(il) Yolen, J. Mama's kiss | E

Baxter, Katherine

(il) Adams, S. The Kingfisher atlas of the ancient world | 930

Baxter, Kathleen A.

From cover to cover | 028.1
Gotcha again for guys! | 028.5
Gotcha good! | 028.5

Baxter, Roberta

Chemical reaction | 540
The particle model of matter | 530

Baxter, the pig who wanted to be kosher. Snyder, L. | E

Bayer, Jane

A my name is Alice | 411

Bayley, Nicola

(il) The big snuggle-up | E

Bayley, Nicola

(il) The big snuggle-up | E
(il) Kipling, R. The jungle book: Mowgli's story | S

Baylor, Byrd

When clay sings | 970.004

Baynes, Pauline

Questionable creatures | 398.2
Koralek, J. The coat of many colors | 222

Bearn, Emily
Tumtum & Nutmeg: adventures beyond Nutmouse Hall   **Fic**
Tumtum & Nutmeg: the Rose Cottage tales   **Fic**
Bears. Schwabacher, M.   **599.78**
BEARS
   See also Mammals
BEARS
Agee, J. Milo's hat trick   **E**
Baines, R. A den is a bed for a bear   **599.78**
Bekoff, M. Jasper's story   **599.78**
Berman, R. Let's look at brown bears   **599.78**
Bunting, E. Little Bear's little boat   **E**
Carlstrom, N. W. Climb the family tree, Jesse Bear!   **E**
De Vries, M. Fraser bear   **599.78**
Dewey, A. Splash!   **E**
Dunrea, O. Bear Noel   **E**
Guiberson, B. Z. Moon bear   **599.78**
Hamilton, S. L. Mauled by a bear   **599.78**
Hest, A. Kiss good night   **E**
Hirschi, R. Our three bears   **599.78**
Johnson, D. B. Henry hikes to Fitchburg   **E**
Kvatum, L. Saving Yasha   **599.78**
McAllister, I. Salmon bears   **599.78**
Montgomery, S. Search for the golden moon bear   **599.78**
Schwabacher, M. Bears   **599.78**
Searching for grizzlies   **599.78**
Swinburne, S. R. Black bear   **599.78**
Thompson, L. Polar bear night   **E**
Wallace, N. E. Seeds! Seeds! Seeds!   **E**
Wells, R. Only you   **E**
Bears. Krauss, R.   **E**
BEARS -- FICTION
Bear has a story to tell   **E**
Bear in love   **E**
Hillenbrand, W. Kite day   **E**
Wolff, A. Baby Bear sees blue   **E**
BEARS -- GRAPHIC NOVELS
Coudray, P. Benjamin Bear in Fuzzy thinking   **741.5**
BEARS -- JUVENILE FICTION
Banks, K. The bear in the book   **E**
Bunting, E. Big Bear's big boat   **E**
Doremus, G. Bear despair   **E**
Dunrea, O. Little Cub   **E**
East of the Sun, West of the Moon   **Fic**
BEARS -- JUVENILE LITERATURE
Baines, R. A den is a bed for a bear   **599.78**
McAllister, I. Salmon bears   **599.78**
Montgomery, S. Search for the golden moon bear   **599.78**
Bears on chairs. Parenteau, S.   **E**
The **bears** we know. Silsbe, B.   **E**
Bears! bears! bears! Barner, B.   **599.78**
The **Bearskinner.** Schlitz, L. A.   **398.2**
Bearwalker. Bruchac, J.   **Fic**
Beast Friends Forever. Forbes, R. L.   **811**
Beast friends forever [series]
Evans, N. Meet the beast   **Fic**
The **Beast** of Blackslope. Barrett, T.   **Fic**
BEASTS *See* Animals
The **beasts** of Clawstone Castle.   **Fic**
A **beasty** story. Martin, B.   **E**
BEAT GENERATION
   See also American literature; Bohemianism
The **beatitudes.** Weatherford, C. B.   **323.1**
The **Beatles** were fab (and they were funny) Brewer, P. **782.421**
Beaton, Clare
(il) Gannij, J. Hidden hippo   **590**
Beatrice doesn't want to. Numeroff, L. J.   **E**
Beatrice spells some lulus and learns to write a letter. Best,

C.   **E**
Beatrice's dream. Williams, K. L.   **967.62**
Beatrice, Chris
(il) Moerbeek, K. Aesop's fables: a pop-up book of classic
  tales   **398.2**
Beatty, Richard
Boron   **546**
Copper   **546**
The lanthanides   **546**
Manganese   **546**
Phosphorus   **546**
Sulfur   **546**
(ed) Exploring the world of mammals   **599**
Beaty, Andrea
Artist Ted   **E**
Attack of the fluffy bunnies   **Fic**
Cicada summer   **Fic**
Doctor Ted   **E**
Dorko the magnificent   **Fic**
Firefighter Ted   **E**
When giants come to play   **E**
Beaudoin, Marie-Nathalie
Responding to the culture of bullying and disrespect   **371.5**
BEAUFORT SCALE -- JUVENILE LITERATURE
Malone, P. Close to the wind   **551.51**
Beaufort, Francis Sir, 1774-1857
      About
Malone, P. Close to the wind   **551.51**
Beaumont, Karen
Baby danced the polka   **E**
Doggone dogs!   **E**
Duck, duck, goose!   **E**
I ain't gonna paint no more!   **E**
Move over, Rover   **E**
No sleep for the sheep!   **E**
Shoe-la-la!   **E**
Where's my t-r-u-c-k?   **E**
Who ate all the cookie dough?   **E**
Beautiful ballerina. Nelson, M.   **792.8**
Beautiful beads. Ross, K.   **745.58**
Beautiful blackbird. Bryan, A.   **398.2**
The **beautiful** Christmas tree. Zolotow, C.   **E**
A **beautiful** girl. Schwartz, A.   **E**
Beautiful oops! Saltzberg, B.   **E**
The **beautiful** stories of life. Rylant, C.   **292**
Beautiful warrior. McCully, E. A.   **E**
Beautiful Yetta. Pinkwater, D. M.   **E**
Beauty & the beast. Sabuda, R.   **398.2**
Beauty and the beaks. Auch, M. J.   **E**
Beauty and the beast.   **398.2**
Beauty and the beast. Eilenberg, M.   **398.2**
Beauty and the beast
Beauty and the beast   **398.2**
BEAUTY CONTESTS
   See also Contests
BEAUTY CONTESTS -- FICTION
Ransom, C. Rebel McKenzie   **Fic**
The **Beauty** of the beast.   **811**
BEAUTY SHOPS
   See also Business enterprises
BEAUTY SHOPS -- FICTION
Choung Minji's salon   **E**
Daly, N. A song for Jamela   **E**
Schotter, R. Mama, I'll give you the world   **E**
Wells, R. Ruby's beauty shop   **E**
BEAUTY, PERSONAL *See* Personal appearance; Personal
  grooming
Beaver is lost. Cooper, E.   **E**

Benioff, Carol

(il) A big night for salamanders   E

Benjamin (Biblical figure)
About

Jules, J. Benjamin and the silver goblet   222

Benjamin and Bumper to the rescue. Coxe, M.   E

Benjamin and the silver goblet. Jules, J.   222

Benjamin Banneker. Maupin, M.   92

Benjamin Bear in "Bright ideas!"   741.5

Benjamin Bear in Fuzzy thinking. Coudray, P.   741.5

Benjamin Franklin, American genius. Miller, B. M.   92

Benjamin Franklinstein lives! McElligott, M.   Fic

Benjamin Franklinstein meets the Fright brothers.   Fic

Benjamin Pratt & the Keepers of the School [series]

Clements, A. Fear itself   Fic

Clements, A. We the children   Fic

Benjamin, Daniel

Prius   629.222

Bennett, Clayton

Montana   978.6

Bennett, Erin Susanne

(il) Stroud, B. The patchwork path   E

Bennett, Howard J.

Max Archer, kid detective: the case of the wet bed   616.85

Bennett, Jamie

(il) Weird zone   796.1

Bennett, Kelly

Dad and Pop   E

Your daddy was just like you   E

Your mommy was just like you   E

Bennett, Michelle

Missouri   977.8

Bennett, Nneka

Lasky, K. Vision of beauty: the story of Sarah Breedlove Walker   B

Bennett, Olivia

The Allegra Biscotti collection   Fic

Who what wear   Fic

Bennett, Richard

(il) Farshtey, G. Bionicle #1: rise of the Toa Nuva   741.5

Benno and the Night of Broken Glass. Wiviott, M.   E

Benny & beautiful baby Delilah. Van Leeuwen, J.   E

Benny and Babe. Colfer, E.   Fic

Benny and Penny in just pretend. Hayes, G.   741.5

Benny, Mike

(il) Grimes, N. Oh, brother!   E

(il) Whelan, G. The listeners   E

Benoit, Peter

The BP oil spill   363.7

The Haitian earthquake of 2010   972.94

The Hindenburg disaster   363.1

Hurricane Katrina   976.3

The Krakatau eruption   551.2

The nuclear age   355.02

Nuclear meltdowns   363.1

September 11 we will never forget   973.931

The space race   629.4

The surrender at Appomattox   973.7

The Titanic disaster   910.4

Cunningham, K. The Cheyenne   970.004

Cunningham, K. The Comanche   970.004

Cunningham, K. The Inuit   970.004

Cunningham, K. The Navajo   970.004

Cunningham, K. The Pueblo   970.004

Cunningham, K. The Sioux   970.004

Cunningham, K. The Zuni   970.004

Dolbear, E. J. The Iroquois   970.004

Benoit, Renné

(il) Barclay, J. Proud as a peacock, brave as a lion   E

(il) Seto, L. Mooncakes   E

(il) Upjohn, R. The secret of the village fool   Fic

De Vries, M. Fraser bear   599.78

Benson, Kathleen

Haskins, J. John Lewis in the lead   92

Haskins, J. The rise of Jim Crow   305.8

Benson, Patrick

(il) Waddell, M. Owl babies   E

(il) Wise, W. Christopher Mouse   Fic

Bentley, Jonathan

(il) Holmes, J. A. Have you seen Duck?   E

(il) Wild, M. The little crooked house   E

Bentley, Wilson Alwyn, 1865-1931
About

Martin, J. B. Snowflake Bentley   551.57

Bently, Peter

King Jack and the dragon   E

Benton, Gail

Ready-to-go storytimes   027.62

Benton, Mike

The Kingfisher dinosaur encyclopedia   567.9

Beowulf. Rumford, J.   398.2

Beowulf. Storrie, P. D.   741.5

Beowulf. Morpurgo, M.   398.2

BEQUESTS *See* Gifts; Inheritance and succession; Wills

Bereal, JaeMe

(il) Schroeder, A. In her hands   92

BEREAVEMENT

Brown, L. K. When dinosaurs die   155.9

Huneck, S. Even bad dogs go to heaven   636.7

Krementz, J. How it feels when a parent dies   155.9

Murphy, P. J. Death   155.9

Thornhill, J. I found a dead bird   306.9

BEREAVEMENT

See also Emotions

BEREAVEMENT -- FICTION

MacLachlan, P. Kindred souls   Fic

Rupp, R. After Eli   Fic

BEREAVEMENT -- JUVENILE FICTION

Missing mommy   E

Urban, L. The center of everything   Fic

BEREAVEMENT -- JUVENILE LITERATURE

Brown, L. K. When dinosaurs die   155.9

BEREAVEMENT -- POETRY

Smith, H. A. Mother poems   811

Berendt, John

My baby blue jays   598

Berenzy, Alix

(il) Guiberson, B. Z. Into the sea   597.92

Berg, Elizabeth

Senegal   966.3

Berg, Michelle

(il) Sidman, J. Meow ruff   811

Bergen, David

Life-size dinosaurs   567.9

BERGEN-BELSEN (GERMANY: CONCENTRATION CAMP)

See also Concentration camps

Berger, Barbara

All the way to Lhasa   398.2

Berger, Carin

(il) Stardines swim high across the sky and other poems   811

Berger, Carin

Forever friends   E

The little yellow leaf   E

OK go   E

(il) Prelutsky, J. Behold the bold umbrellaphant   811

Better than weird. Kerz, A. — **Fic**
Better than you. Ludwig, T. — **E**
Better to wish. Martin, A. M. — **Fic**
Bettina Valentino and the Picasso Club. Daly, N. — **Fic**
Bettoli, Delana
    (il) Cotten, C. This is the stable — **E**
Betty Bunny didn't do it. — **E**
Betty Bunny loves chocolate cake. — **E**
Between earth & sky. Bruchac, J. — **398.2**
Between heaven and earth. Norman, H. — **398.2**
Between two ends. Ward, D. — **Fic**
BEVERAGE INDUSTRY
    See also Food industry
BEVERAGES
    LaPenta, M. Way cool drinks — **641.5**
BEVERAGES
    See also Diet; Food
Bevis, Mary Elizabeth
    Wolf song — **E**
Beware, take care. Moore, L. — **811**
Beyl, Charles
    (il) Kraus, J. Annie's plan — **371.3**
Beyond lucky. Aronson, S. — **Fic**
Beyond Old MacDonald. Hoce, C. — **811**
Beyond Pluto. Landau, E. — **523.4**
Beyond the Deepwoods. Stewart, P. — **Fic**
Beyond the dinosaurs. Brown, C. L. — **560**
Beyond the grave. Watson, J. — **Fic**
Beyond the great mountains. Young, E. — **811**
Beyond the ridge. Goble, P. — **E**
Beyond the solar system. Carson, M. K. — **520.9**
Beyond the station lies the sea. Richter, J. — **Fic**
Beyond the Valley of Thorns. Carman, P. — **Fic**
Beyonders [series]
    Mull, B. A world without heroes — **Fic**
The **BFG.** Dahl, R. — **Fic**
Bhargava, Neirah
    (il) Jani, M. What you will see inside a Hindu temple — **294.5**
Bhatia, Mohini Kaur
    Hawker, F. Sikhism in India — **294.6**
Bhushan, Rahul
    (il) Arnold, C. Taj Mahal — **954**
Bhutto, Benazir
    About
    Naden, C. J. Benazir Bhutto — **92**
BI-RACIAL PEOPLE *See* Racially mixed people
Bial, Raymond
    Amish home — **289.7**
    Ellis Island — **325**
    A handful of dirt — **577.5**
    Nauvoo — **289.3**
    Rescuing Rover — **636.7**
    The super soybean — **633.3**
    Tenement — **974.7**
    The Underground Railroad — **326**
BIAS (PSYCHOLOGY) *See* Prejudices
BIAS ATTACKS *See* Hate crimes
BIAS CRIMES *See* Hate crimes
Bias in the media. Marcovitz, H. — **302.23**
Bible
    The Bible: Authorized King James Version — **220.5**
    The Holy Bible — **220.5**
BIBLE -- ANTIQUITIES
    See also Antiquities; Archeology
BIBLE -- ASTRONOMY
    See also Astronomy
BIBLE -- BIOGRAPHY
    See also Biography

BIBLE -- DICTIONARIES
    See also Encyclopedias and dictionaries
BIBLE -- GEOGRAPHY
    See also Atlases; Geography
BIBLE -- NATURAL HISTORY
    See also Natural history
BIBLE -- PSYCHOLOGY
    See also Psychology
BIBLE -- READING
    See also Books and reading
BIBLE -- WOMEN *See* Women in the Bible
BIBLE (AS SUBJECT)
    Brown, A. The Bible and Christianity — **220**
    Feiler, B. S. Walking the Bible — **222**
The **Bible** and Christianity. Brown, A. — **220**
BIBLE AND SCIENCE
    See also Religion and science; Science
BIBLE FILMS
    See also Motion pictures
The **Bible** for children from Good Books. Watts, M. — **220.9**
The **Bible** for young children. Delval — **220.9**
BIBLE GAMES AND PUZZLES
    See also Games; Puzzles
BIBLE IN LITERATURE
    See also Literature
BIBLE STORIES
    Barnes, T. The Kingfisher children's illustrated Bible — **220.9**
    Brown, L. The Children's illustrated Jewish Bible — **220.9**
    Chaikin, M. Angels sweep the desert floor — **296.1**
    De Paola, T. Tomie dePaola's book of Bible stories — **220.9**
    Delval The Bible for young children — **220.9**
    Fischer, C. In the beginning: the art of Genesis — **222**
    Graham, L. B. How God fix Jonah — **220.9**
    Hanft, J. E. Miracles of the Bible — **221.9**
    Hodges, M. Moses — **222**
    Jules, J. Benjamin and the silver goblet — **222**
    Jules, J. Miriam in the desert — **222**
    Jules, J. Sarah laughs — **222**
    Kimmel, E. A. The story of Esther — **222**
    Koralek, J. The coat of many colors — **222**
    Koralek, J. The story of Queen Esther — **222**
    Lepp, R. David: Shepard's song, vol. 1 — **741.5**
    Lottridge, C. B. Stories from Adam and Eve to Ezekiel — **220.9**
    Lottridge, C. B. Stories from the life of Jesus — **232.9**
    Manushkin, F. Miriam's cup — **222**
    McKissack, P. C. Let my people go — **Fic**
    Osborne, M. P. The Random House book of Bible stories — **220.9**
    Paterson, K. The angel and the donkey — **222**
    Pinsker, M. In the days of sand and stars — **296.1**
    Pirotta, S. Children's stories from the Bible — **220.9**
    Ray, J. Adam and Eve and the Garden of Eden — **222**
    Sasso, S. E. But God remembered — **221.9**
    Sasso, S. E. Cain & Abel — **222**
    Skevington, A. The story of Jesus — **232.9**
    Spier, P. Noah's ark — **222**
    Ward, E. M. Old Testament women — **221.9**
    Watts, M. The Bible for children from Good Books — **220.9**
BIBLE STORIES -- GRAPHIC NOVELS
    Lepp, R. David: Shepard's song, vol. 1 — **741.5**
BIBLE STORIES -- JUVENILE LITERATURE
    De Paola, T. Tomie dePaola's book of Bible stories — **220.9**
    Hodges, M. Moses — **222**
    Paterson, K. The angel and the donkey — **222**
    Ray, J. Adam and Eve and the Garden of Eden — **222**
Bible/English/Authorized
    Jesus — **232.9**
Bible/N.T.

The **black** book of colors. Cottin, M.   E
The **Black** Book of Secrets. Higgins, F. E.   Fic
BLACK BUSINESSPEOPLE
    See also Businesspeople
The **Black** Canary. Curry, J. L.   Fic
Black cat. Myers, C.   E
The **Black** Cauldron. Alexander, L.   Fic
BLACK CHILDREN
    See also Children
Black cowboy, wild horses. Lester, J.   E
The **Black** Death. Ollhoff, J.   616.9
BLACK DEATH *See* Plague
Black dog. Pinfold, L.   E
Black Elk's vision. Nelson, S. D.   92
Black Elk, 1863-1950
    About
    Nelson, S. D. Black Elk's vision   92
Black hands, white sails. McKissack, P. C.   639.2
The **black** heart crypt. Grabenstein, C.   Fic
Black hearts in Battersea. Aiken, J.   Fic
Black history in the pages of children's literature. Casement,
  R.   028.5
A **black** hole is not a hole.   523.8
Black holes. Rau, D. M.   523.8
BLACK HOLES (ASTRONOMY)
    Jackson, E. B. The mysterious universe   523.8
    Rau, D. M. Black holes   523.8
    Venezia, M. Stephen Hawking   92
    Waxman, L. H. Exploring black holes   523.8
BLACK HOLES (ASTRONOMY)
    See also Astronomy; Astrophysics; Stars
**BLACK HOLES (ASTRONOMY) -- JUVENILE LITERA-
  TURE**
    A black hole is not a hole   523.8
BLACK HUMOR (LITERATURE)
    See also Fiction; Literature; Wit and humor
Black ice. Lane, A.   Fic
Black is brown is tan. Adoff, A.   E
Black Jack: the ballad of Jack Johnson. Smith, C. R.   92
BLACK LIBRARIANS
    See also Librarians
Black magic. Johnson, D.   E
BLACK MAGIC (WITCHCRAFT) *See* Magic; Witchcraft
BLACK MARKET
    See also Commerce
BLACK MUSIC
    See also Music
BLACK MUSICIANS
    See also Musicians
BLACK MUSLIM LEADERS
    Gunderson, J. X: the biography of Malcolm X   92
    Malcolm X   92
BLACK MUSLIMS
    Gunderson, J. X: the biography of Malcolm X   92
**BLACK MUSLIMS -- BIOGRAPHY -- JUVENILE LIT-
  ERATURE**
    Malcolm X   92
Black on white. Hoban, T.   E
Black pearls. Hawes, L.   S
Black pioneers [series]
    Hansen, J. Home is with our family   Fic
The **Black** rabbit.   E
Black radishes. Meyer, S.   Fic
Black spiny-tailed iguana. Lunis, N.   597.95
The **Black** Stallion. Farley, W.   Fic
Black widows. Markle, S.   595.4
BLACK WOMEN
    See also Women

Black, Angela
  Sheehan, S. Jamaica   972.92
Black, Ann N.
  Readers theatre for middle school boys   812
Black, Holly, 1971-
  Doll bones   Fic
Black, Jake
  Snider, J. Toy Story   741.5
Black, Jess
  A year in the life of Bindi   333.720
Black, Michael Ian
  Chicken cheeks   E
  A pig parade is a terrible idea   E
  The purple kangaroo   E
Black? white! day? night! Seeger, L. V.   E
Blackaby, Susan
  Brownie Groundhog and the February fox   E
  Cleopatra   92
  Nest, nook & cranny   811
Blackall, Sophie
  Are you awake?   E
  (il) Manners mash-up: a goofy guide to good behavior   395
  (il) The mighty Lalouche   E
  (il) Pecan pie baby   E
  (il) Barrows, A. Ivy + Bean   Fic
  (il) Barrows, A. Ivy + Bean and the ghost that had to go Fic
  (il) Barrows, A. Ivy + Bean bound to be bad   Fic
  (il) Barrows, A. Ivy + Bean break the fossil record   Fic
  (il) Barrows, A. Ivy + Bean: doomed to dance   Fic
  (il) Barrows, A. Ivy + Bean take care of the babysitter   Fic
  (il) Barrows, A. Ivy + Bean: what's the big idea?   Fic
  (il) Best, C. What's so bad about being an only child?   E
  (il) Bridges, S. Y. Ruby's wish   E
  (il) Edwin speaks up   E
  (il) Khan, R. Big red lollipop   E
  (il) Noyes, D. Red butterfly   E
  (il) Pecan pie baby   E
  (il) Rosoff, M. Jumpy Jack and Googily   E
  (il) Rosoff, M. Meet wild boars   E
  (il) Shields, C. D. Wombat walkabout   E
  Spinster Goose   811
Blackbeard, 1680?-1718 -- Poetry
  Lewis, J. P. Blackbeard, the pirate king   811
Blackburn, Lena, 1886-1968 -- Juvenile literature
    About
  Miracle mud   B
The **blacker** the berry. Thomas, J. C.   811
Blackford, Andy
  Bill's bike   E
  The hungry little monkey   E
The **Blackhope** enigma. Flavin, T.   Fic
Blackout. Rocco, J.   E
BLACKS -- BIOGRAPHY
  Washburn, K. Heart of a champion   796.440
BLACKS -- BIOGRAPHY
    See also Biography
BLACKS -- BOTSWANA -- FICTION
  McCall Smith, A. The great cake mystery   Fic
BLACKS -- CANADA
  Warner, J. Viola Desmond won't be budged!   92
BLACKS -- CIVIL RIGHTS
  Scattergood, A. Glory be   Fic
BLACKS -- CIVIL RIGHTS
    See also Blacks -- Political activity; Civil rights
BLACKS -- ECONOMIC CONDITIONS
    See also Economic conditions
BLACKS -- FICTION
  Medearis, A. S. Seven spools of thread   E

Clifford, E. Help! I'm a prisoner in the library   **Fic**
Crummel, S. S. Ten-Gallon Bart beats the heat   **E**
Hurst, C. O. Terrible storm   **E**
Steig, W. Brave Irene   **E**
Wilder, L. I. The long winter   **Fic**

BLIZZARDS -- GRAPHIC NOVELS
Wetterer, M. K. The snowshoeing adventure of Milton Daub, blizzard trekker   **741.5**
Blizzards and winter storms. Stewart, M.   **551.55**

Blobaum, Cindy
Awesome snake science   **597.960**
Geology rocks!   **551**
Insectigation!   **595.7**
(il) I dare you not to yawn   **E**
(il) My snake Blake   **E**

Bloch, Serge
Butterflies in my stomach and other school hazards   **E**
Snowed under and other Christmas confusions   **E**
(il) Cali, D. The enemy   **E**
(il) Lewis, J. P. The underwear salesman   **811**
(il) Morgenstern, S. H. A book of coupons   **Fic**

Block city. Stevenson, R. L.   **E**
Block, Francesca Lia
House of dolls   **Fic**
Block, Ira
(il) Lange, K. E. 1607   **975.5**
Blockhead. D'Agnese, J.   **92**
BLOGS *See* Weblogs
Blogs, wikis, podcasts, and other powerful Web tools for classrooms. Richardson, W.   **371.3**
Blom, Jen K.
Possum summer   **Fic**
Blomgren, Jennifer
Where do I sleep?   **E**

BLOOD
Newquist, H. The book of blood   **612.1**
Showers, P. A drop of blood   **612.1**
Venezia, M. Charles Drew   **92**
BLOOD
See also Physiology
BLOOD -- CIRCULATION
Corcoran, M. K. The circulatory story   **612.1**
Yount, L. William Harvey   **92**
BLOOD -- CIRCULATION -- JUVENILE LITERATURE
Jakab, C. The circulatory system
BLOOD -- DISEASES
See also Diseases
BLOOD -- JUVENILE LITERATURE
Kyi, T. L. Seeing red   **612.1**
BLOOD GROUPS
See also Blood
The **blood** lie. Vernick, S. R.   **Fic**
Blood moon rider. Waters, Z. C.   **Fic**
Blood on the river. Carbone, E. L.   **Fic**
BLOOD PRESSURE
See also Blood
BLOODSUCKING ANIMALS
Knapp, R. Bloodsucking creatures   **591.5**
Bloodsucking creatures. Knapp, R.   **591.5**
Bloom! Lieshout, M. v.   **E**
Bloom, Suzanne
Feeding friendsies   **E**
A mighty fine time machine   **E**
A splendid friend, indeed   **E**
(il) Bunting, E. Girls A to Z   **E**
(il) Bunting, E. My special day at Third Street School   **E**
Bloom, Tom
(il) While You Were Sleeping   **031.02**

Bloomability. Creech, S.   **Fic**
Bloomfield, Alan
Jennings, M. Baseball step-by-step   **796.357**
Bloomfield, Jill
Jewish holidays cookbook   **641.5**
Blos, Joan W.
A gathering of days: a New England girl's journal, 1830-32   **Fic**
Letters from the corrugated castle   **Fic**
Blough, Paula
Dixon, T. The sound of storytime   **027.62**
Blount, Marcellus
(ed) African American Poetry   **811.008**
Blue 2. Carter, D. A.   **E**
The **blue** book on information age inquiry, instruction and literacy. Callison, D.   **028.7**
Blue chameleon. Gravett, E.   **E**
Blue chicken. Freedman, D.   **E**
BLUE COLLAR WORKERS *See* Labor; Working class
The **Blue** fairy book.   **398.2**
Blue fire. Hardy, J.   **Fic**
The **blue** ghost. Bauer, M. D.   **Fic**
Blue Goose. Tafuri, N.   **E**
Blue heron. Avi   **Fic**
The **blue** house dog. Blumenthal, D.   **E**
Blue jasmine. Sheth, K.   **Fic**
BLUE JAYS
Berendt, J. My baby blue jays   **598**
Blue like Friday. Parkinson, S.   **Fic**
Blue lipstick. Grandits, J.   **811**
Blue Moo. Boynton, S.   **782.42**
Blue potatoes, orange tomatoes. Creasy, R.   **635**
The **blue** shoe. Townley, R.   **Fic**
Blue sky. Wood, A.   **E**
Blue whales up close. Rake, J. S.   **599.5**
Blue willow. Gates, D.   **Fic**
Blue, Rose
Ron's big mission   **E**
Naden, C. J. James Monroe   **92**
A **blue-eyed** daisy. Rylant, C.   **Fic**
Blue-ribbon dad. Glass, B. R.   **E**
Blueberries for Sal. McCloskey, R.   **E**
Bluebird. Staake, B.   **E**
BLUEBIRDS
Kirby, P. F. What bluebirds do   **598**
BLUEBIRDS -- FICTION
Staake, B. Bluebird   **E**
BLUEBIRDS -- JUVENILE FICTION
Staake, B. Bluebird   **E**
BLUEBIRDS -- JUVENILE LITERATURE
Kirby, P. F. What bluebirds do   **598**
Bluefish. Schmatz, P.   **Fic**
BLUEGRASS MUSIC
See also Music
Bluemel Oldfield, Dawn
Leaping ground frogs   **597.8**
Bluemle, Elizabeth
Dogs on the bed   **E**
How do you wokka-wokka?   **E**
Blues. Handyside, C.   **781.643**
BLUES (MUSIC)
Myers, W. D. The blues of Flats Brown   **E**
BLUES (MUSIC) -- HISTORY AND CRITICISM -- JUVENILE LITERATURE
Adoff, A. Roots and blues   **811**
Blues journey. Myers, W. D.   **811**
BLUES MUSIC
Handyside, C. Blues   **781.643**

BLUES MUSIC

See also African American music; Folk music -- United States; Popular music

BLUES MUSIC -- FICTION

Crow, K. The middle-child blues	E
Harvey, J. My hands sing the blues	E
Myers, W. D. The blues of Flats Brown	E
Staub, L. Everybody gets the blues	E
Stauffacher, S. Bessie Smith and the night riders	E

BLUES MUSIC -- POETRY

Adoff, A. Roots and blues	811
Myers, W. D. Blues journey	811

BLUES MUSICIANS

Boynton, S. Sandra Boynton's One shoe blues	782.42
Stauffacher, S. Bessie Smith and the night riders	E

The **blues** of Flats Brown. Myers, W. D.   E

BLUES SONGS *See* Blues music

Bluffton. Phelan, M.	Fic

Bluhm, Joe

  (il) The fantastic flying books of Mr. Morris Lessmore   E

Blumberg, Rhoda

Commodore Perry in the land of the Shogun	952
Shipwrecked!: the true adventures of a Japanese boy	92

Blume, Judy

Are you there God?, it's me, Margaret	Fic
Cool zone with the Pain and the Great One	Fic
Double Fudge	Fic
Freckle juice	Fic
Friend or fiend? with the Pain & the Great One	Fic
Fudge-a-mania	Fic
Going, going, gone! with the Pain and the Great One	Fic
Otherwise known as Sheila the Great	Fic
The Pain and the Great One	E
Soupy Saturdays with The Pain and The Great One	Fic
Superfudge	Fic
Tales of a fourth grade nothing	Fic

Blume, Lesley M. M.

Cornelia and the audacious escapades of the Somerset sisters	Fic
The rising star of Rusty Nail	Fic
Tennyson	Fic

Blumenthal, Deborah

The blue house dog	E

Blumenthal, Karen

Let me play	796
Mr. Sam	92

Blundell, Judy

A city tossed and broken	Fic

Bluthenthal, Diana Cain

(il) Edwards, P. D. The neat line	E
(il) Viorst, J. Just in case	E

Bly, Nellie, 1864-1922

About

Macy, S. Bylines: a photobiography of Nellie Bly	92

Blythe, Gary

(il) Davies, N. Ice bear	599.78
(il) De Quidt, J. The toymaker	Fic
(il) Ehrlich, A. A treasury of princess stories	398.2

Bo at Ballard Creek. Hill, K.   Fic

Boake, Kathy

(il) Swanson, D. You are weird	612

BOARD BOOKS

Klausmeier, J. Open this little book	E
Light, S. Trains go	E

BOARD BOOKS FOR CHILDREN

Balouch, K. Feelings	E
Bancroft, B. W is for wombat	E
Basher, S. Go! go! Bobo: colors	E

Boynton, S. Happy Hippo, angry Duck	E
Brown, H. The robot book	E
Caterpillar Inc. My big book of trucks & diggers	621.8
Dahl, M. Nap time for Kitty	E
Doodler, T. H. What color is Bear's underwear?	E
Dowdy, L. C. All kinds of kisses	E
DwellStudio (Firm) Good morning, toucan	E
DwellStudio (Firm) Goodnight, owl	E
Emberley, E. Where's my sweetie pie?	E
Endle, K. Bunny Rabbit in the sunlight	E
Franceschelli, C. (oliver)	E
Gershator, P. Who's in the forest?	E
Global Fund for Children (Organization) American babies	E
Global Fund for Children (Organization) Global babies	E
Henkes, K. A good day	E
Hoban, T. Black on white	E
Hoban, T. White on black	E
Horacek, P. Choo choo	E
Hubbell, P. Firefighters! speeding! spraying! saving!	E
Isol It's useful to have a duck	E
Janovitz, M. Baby baby baby!	E
Katz, S. ABC, baby me!	E
Kim, S. How does a seed grow?	581.4
Klinting, L. What do you want?	E
Kubler, A. Humpty Dumpty	E
Laval, T. Colors	E
Lester, J. D. Daddy calls me doodlebug	E
Lester, J. D. Grandma calls me gigglepie	E
Lester, J. D. Mommy calls me monkeypants	E
Light, S. Trains go	E
Macdonald, S. Alphabet animals	E
Martin, D. Christmas tree	E
Martin, D. Hanukkah lights	E
McBratney, S. When I'm big	E
Moore, C. C. The night before Christmas	811
Mother Goose Hop a little, jump a little!	398.8
Newman, L. Daddy, papa, and me	E
Newman, L. Mommy, mama, and me	E
O'Connell, R. The baby goes beep	E
Pat-a-cake	398.8
Patricelli, L. Potty	E
Patricelli, L. Tubby	E
Penn, A. A bedtime kiss for Chester Raccoon	E
Perrin, M. Look who's there!	E
Perrin, M. What do you see?	E
Quay, E. Good night, sleep tight	E
Quay, E. Let's play house	E
Quay, E. Puddle jumping	E
Quay, E. Yummy ice cream	E
Rostoker-Gruber, K. Tea time	E
Salzano, T. One rainy day	E
Schade, S. The noisy counting book	E
Schindel, J. Busy gorillas	599.8
Sellier, M. Renoir's colors	759.05
Siminovich, L. I like vegetables	E
Slegers, L. Bathing	E
Smith, C. R. Dance with me	E
Taback, S. Simms Taback's farm animals	E
Tullet, H. The game of finger worms	E
Tullet, H. The game of let's go!	E
Tullet, H. The game of light	E
Tullet, H. The game of mix and match	E
Tullet, H. The game of mix-up art	E
Tullet, H. The game of patterns	E
Van Fleet, M. Moo	E
Verdick, E. Mealtime	E
Wildsmith, B. Brian Wildsmith's ABC	E
Wynne Pechter, L. Alligator, bear, crab	E

Yolen, J. How do dinosaurs say happy birthday? **E**
Yoon, S. One, two, buckle my shoe **E**
Yoon, S. Who do I see? **E**
Zuravicky, O. C is for city **E**

BOARD BOOKS FOR CHILDREN
See also Picture books for children

Board buddies [series]
Rostoker-Gruber, K. Tea time **E**

BOARD GAMES
Mayer, B. Libraries got game **025.2**

BOARD GAMES
See also Games

BOARDING HOUSES See Hotels and motels

BOARDING SCHOOLS
Bruchac, J. The dark pond **Fic**

BOARDING SCHOOLS See Private schools

BOARDING SCHOOLS -- FICTION
Robinson, M. L. Bright Island **Fic**
Vanderpool, C. Navigating Early **Fic**

BOARDINGHOUSES -- FICTION
Spinelli, E. Sophie's masterpiece **E**

BOARS -- FICTION
Rosoff, M. Meet wild boars **E**

Boase, Susan
(il) Orr, W. Lost! A dog called Bear **Fic**
(il) Orr, W. Missing! A cat called Buster **Fic**

BOAT RACING
See also Boats and boating; Racing

BOATING See Boats and boating

Boats. Barton, B. **387.2**
Boats. Hubbell, P. **E**

BOATS AND BOATING
Barton, B. Boats **387.2**
Bunting, E. Little Bear's little boat **E**
Paulsen, G. Caught by the sea **818**

BOATS AND BOATING
See also Water sports

BOATS AND BOATING -- FICTION
Bunting, E. Big Bear's big boat **E**
De Seve, R. The toy boat **E**
Docherty, T. Little boat **E**
Hiaasen, C. Flush **Fic**
Hubbell, P. Boats **E**
Lamb, A. The abandoned lighthouse **E**
Logan, B. The Sea of Bath **E**
Luper, E. Jeremy Bender vs. the Cupcake Cadets **Fic**
Orr, W. Mokie & Bik **Fic**
Orr, W. Mokie & Bik go to sea **Fic**
Rylant, C. Mr. Putter & Tabby clear the decks **E**
Segal, J. Alistair and Kip's great adventure **E**
Stead, P. C. Jonathan and the big blue boat **E**
Van Allsburg, C. The wreck of the Zephyr **E**
Waddell, M. Captain Small Pig **E**
Zimmer, T. V. The floating circus **Fic**

BOATS AND BOATING -- JUVENILE FICTION
Bunting, E. Big Bear's big boat **E**

BOATS AND BOATING -- JUVENILE LITERATURE
Hubbell, P. Boats **E**
Paulsen, G. Caught by the sea **818**

BOATS AND BOATING -- JUVENILE LITERATURE.
Clark, W. Boats on the move **623.82**

BOATS AND BOATING -- POETRY
Sturges, P. Down to the sea in ships **811**

Boats on the move. Clark, W. **623.82**
Bob. Pearson, T. C. **E**
Bob and Otto. Bruel, R. O. **E**
Bob the Alien discovers the Dewey decimal system. Donovan, S. **025.4**

Bob's best ever friend. Bartram, S. **E**
The **bobbin** girl. McCully, E. A. **E**
Bobby vs. girls (accidentally) Yee, L. **Fic**
Bobcats. Marks, J. L. **599.75**

BOBCATS
Marks, J. L. Bobcats **599.75**

Bobrick, Benson
A passion for victory: the story of the Olympics in ancient and early modern times **796.4**
Fight for freedom **973.3**

Bochner, Arthur Berg
The new totally awesome business book for kids (and their parents) **658**
Bochner, R. The new totally awesome money book for kids (and their parents) **332.024**

Bochner, Rose
Bochner, A. B. The new totally awesome business book for kids (and their parents) **658**
The new totally awesome money book for kids (and their parents) **332.024**

Bockenhauer, Mark H.
Our fifty states **973**

Bodach, Vijaya
Bar graphs **510**
Pictographs **510**
Pie graphs **510**
Tally charts **510**

Bodden, Valerie
Cockroaches **595.7**
Columbus reaches the New World **970.01**
Concrete poetry **809.1**
Crocodiles **597.98**
Frank Gehry **92**
Haiku **809.1**
Jaguars **599.75**
Komodo dragons **597.95**
Levers **621.8**
Limericks **809.1**
Lions **599.75**
Man walks on the Moon **629.45**
Monkeys **599.8**
Nursery rhymes **398.8**
Owls **598.9**
Parrots **598**
Penguins **598**
Polar bears **599.78**
Pulleys **621.8**
Screws **621.8**
Sharks **597**
Slugs **594**
Snakes **597.96**
Termites **595.7**
Through the American West **917.804**
Ticks **595.4**
To the heart of Africa **916.704**
To the moon **629.45**
To the ocean deep **551.46**
To the top of Mount Everest **796.522**
Vincent van Gogh **92**
Wheels and axles **621.8**

Bode, N. E.
The Anybodies **Fic**
The slippery map **Fic**

Bodecker, N. M.
(il) Eager, E. Half magic **Fic**

Bodeen, S. A.
Elizabeti's doll **E**
Elizabeti's school **E**

relations

Bourgeois, Paulette
The dirt on dirt   631.4

Bourguignon, Laurence
Heart in the pocket   E

Bourseiller, Philippe
(il) Volcans racontes aux enfants/English Volcanoes   551.2

Boursin, Didier
Folding for fun   736
Origami for everyone   736

Boutavant, Marc
(il) What happens next?   E
(il) Who lives here?   E

Boutignon, Beatrice
Not all animals are blue   E

Bouwman, H. M.
The remarkable and very true story of Lucy and Snowcap   Fic

BOW AND ARROW
Adamson, T. K. Bowhunting   799.2

BOW AND ARROW
See also Weapons

BOW AND ARROW -- FICTION
Winter, J. Kali's song   E

Bow, James
Baseball science   796.357
Cycling science   796.6
Earth's secrets   550

Bow, Patricia
Chimpanzee rescue   599.8
Tennis science   796.342

Bow-Wow bugs a bug. Newgarden, M.   E
Bow-wow wiggle waggle. DePalma, M. N.   E

Bowden, Rob, 1973-
African culture   960
Ancient Africa   960
Changing Africa   960
Jerusalem   956.94
Modern Africa   960

Bowe, Julie
My best frenemy   Fic

BOWED INSTRUMENTS *See* Stringed instruments

Bowen, Anne
I know an old teacher   E

Bowen, Betsy
(il) Lunge-Larsen, L. The troll with no heart in his body and other tales of trolls from Norway   398.2
(il) Root, P. Big belching bog   577.6
(il) Van Laan, N. Shingebiss   398.2

Bowen, Fred
No easy way   92
Quarterback season   Fic
Touchdown trouble   Fic

Bowers, Nathan
4-H guide to training horses   636.1

Bowers, Sharon
Ghoulish goodies   641.5

Bowers, Tim
(il) Alexander, K. Acoustic Rooster and his barnyard band   E
(il) Dogku   811
(il) Heiligman, D. Cool dog, school dog   E
(il) Palatini, M. Gorgonzola   E

Bowers, Vivien
Hey Canada!   971

BOWHEAD WHALE -- JUVENILE LITERATURE
Lourie, P. Whaling season   599.5
Bowhunting. Adamson, T. K.   799.2

BOWHUNTING
See also Hunting

Bowler, Ann Martin
All about Korea   951.9

BOWLING
See also Ball games

BOWLING -- FICTION
Allen, C. How Lamar's bad prank won a Bubba-sized trophy   Fic
A **box** full of tales. MacMillan, K.   027.6
Box Turtle at Long Pond. George, W. T.   E

BOXERS (PERSONS)
Adler, D. A. Joe Louis   92
Bolden, T. The champ!   92
De la Pena, M. A nation's hope   92
Myers, W. D. Muhammad Ali   92
Smith, C. R. Black Jack: the ballad of Jack Johnson   92
Smith, C. R. Twelve rounds to glory: the story of Muhammad Ali   92
Winter, J. Muhammad Ali   92
The **boxes.** Sleator, W.   Fic

BOXES
Russo, M. The big brown box   E
Walsh, D. The cardboard box book   745.54

BOXES -- COLLECTORS AND COLLECTING
See also Collectors and collecting

BOXES -- FICTION
Explorer   Fic
TenNapel, D. Cardboard   Fic

BOXES -- JUVENILE FICTION
Explorer   Fic
Boxes for Katje. Fleming, C.   E
Boxing. Mason, P.   796.8

BOXING
See also Athletics; Self-defense

BOXING
Lewin, T. At Gleason's gym   796.8
Mason, P. Boxing   796.8

BOXING -- BIOGRAPHY
Adler, D. A. Joe Louis   92
Bolden, T. The champ!   92
De la Pena, M. A nation's hope   92
Myers, W. D. Muhammad Ali   92
Smith, C. R. Black Jack: the ballad of Jack Johnson   92
Smith, C. R. Twelve rounds to glory: the story of Muhammad Ali   92
Winter, J. Muhammad Ali   92

BOXING -- FICTION
Jimmy the greatest!   E

BOXING -- JUVENILE FICTION
The mighty Lalouche   E

BOXING -- JUVENILE LITERATURE
De la Pena, M. A nation's hope   92
Lewin, T. At Gleason's gym   796.8
Smith, C. R. Black Jack: the ballad of Jack Johnson   92
Boy and Bot.   FIC
A **boy** and his bot. Wilson, D. H.   Fic
The **boy** at the end of the world. Van Eekhout, G.   Fic
A **boy** called Dickens.   Fic
A **boy** called Slow: the true story of Sitting Bull. Bruchac, J. 92
Boy dumplings. Compestine, Y. C.   E
The **boy** from the dragon palace. MacDonald, M. R.   398.2
A **boy** had a mother who bought him a hat. Kuskin, K.   E
The **boy** in the dress. Walliams, D.   Fic
Boy in the garden. Say, A.   E
The **boy** in the oak. Albarn, J.   Fic
A **boy** named Beckoning: the true story of Dr. Carlos Montezuma, Native American hero. Capaldi, J.   92
A **boy** named FDR. Krull, K.   92
The **boy** of the three-year nap. Snyder, D.   398.2

The **boy** on Cinnamon Street. Stone, P.   **FIC**
The **boy** on Fairfield Street: how Ted Geisel grew up to become Dr. Seuss.   **92**
Boy on the lion throne. Kimmel, E. C.   **92**
BOY SCOUTS
    See also Boys' clubs; Scouts and scouting
Boy talk.   **612.6**
Boy were we wrong about the solar system! Kudlinski, K. V.   **523.2**
The **boy** who bit Picasso. Penrose, A.   **92**
The **boy** who climbed into the moon. Almond, D.   **Fic**
The **boy** who could fly. Norcliffe, J.   **Fic**
The **boy** who cried ninja. Latimer, A.   **E**
The **boy** who cried wolf. Hennessy, B. G.   **398.2**
The **boy** who dared. Bartoletti, S. C.   **Fic**
The **boy** who drew birds: a story of John James Audubon. Davies, J.   **92**
The **boy** who invented TV: the story of Philo Farnsworth. Krull, K.   **92**
The **boy** who loved math. Heiligman, D.   **510.92**
The **boy** who loved to draw: Benjamin West. Brenner, B.   **92**
The **boy** who loved words. Schotter, R.   **E**
The **boy** who painted dragons. Demi   **E**
The **boy** who returned from the sea. Morgan, C.   **Fic**
The **boy** who saved Cleveland. Giblin, J.   **Fic**
The **boy** who wouldn't swim. Lucke, D.   **E**
Boy wonders. Brown, C.   **E**
A **boy**, a dog, and a frog. Mayer, M.   **E**
Boy, Bird, and Dog. McPhail, D. M.   **E**
The **boy**, the bear, the baron, the bard. Rogers, G.   **E**
Boy, were we wrong about dinosaurs! Kudlinski, K. V.   **567.9**
Boyce, Natalie Pope
   Osborne, M. P. The Random House book of Bible stories   **220.9**
Boycott blues. Pinkney, A. D.   **E**
BOYCOTTS
    See also Commerce; Consumers; Passive resistance
BOYCOTTS -- JUVENILE LITERATURE
   Freedman, R. Freedom walkers   **323.1**
   Pinkney, A. D. Boycott blues   **E**
Boyer, Cecile
   Woof, meow, tweet-tweet   **E**
Boyer, Crispin
   National Geographic kids ultimate U.S. road trip atlas   **912**
Boyer, Crispin
   Everything castles   **940.1**
Boyl, Brian
   Castella, K. Discovering nature's alphabet   **E**
Boyle, Bob
   Hugo and the really, really, really long string   **E**
Boyne, John
   Noah   Barleywater   runs   away
   The Terrible Thing That Happened to Barnaby Brocket   **Fic**
Boynton, Sandra
   Amazing cows   **636.2**
   Blue Moo   **782.42**
   Dog train   **782.42**
   Happy Hippo, angry Duck   **E**
   Philadelphia chickens   **782.42**
   Sandra Boynton's One shoe blues   **782.42**
The **boys**. Newman, J.   **E**
BOYS
   Aronson, M. For boys only   **031.02**
   Boy talk   **612.6**
   Dude!   **810**
   Gipson, F. B. Old Yeller   **Fic**
   Iggulden, C. The dangerous book for boys   **031.02**
   Mar, J. The body book for boys   **612.6**

BOYS
    See also Children
BOYS -- BOOKS AND READING
   Fletcher, R. Guy-write   **808.06**
BOYS -- FICTION
   Boy and Bot   **Fic**
   Clifton, L. Freaky Fast Frankie Joe   **Fic**
   Justin Case   **Fic**
   Neubecker, R. What little boys are made of   **E**
   Oliver   **E**
   Stead, R. Liar & spy   **Fic**
BOYS -- HEALTH AND HYGIENE
   Will puberty last my whole life?   **613**
BOYS -- JUVENILE FICTION
   Stuey Lewis against all odds   **Fic**
BOYS -- JUVENILE LITERATURE
   Aronson, M. For boys only   **031.02**
   Baxter, K. A. Gotcha again for guys!   **028.5**
   Sullivan, M. Serving boys through readers' advisory   **028.5**
   Zbaracki, M. D. Best books for boys   **028.5**
BOYS -- POETRY
   Raczka, B. Guyku   **811**
BOYS -- SOCIETIES *See* Boys' clubs
Boys and literacy. Knowles, E.   **028.5**
Boys of Steel.   **741.5**
Boys of steel. Nobleman, M. T.   **92**
Boys of wartime [series]
   Calkhoven, L. Daniel at the Siege of Boston, 1776   **Fic**
   Calkhoven, L. Will at the Battle of Gettysburg, 1863   **Fic**
Boys without names. Sheth, K.   **Fic**
BOYS' CLUBS
   Jung, M. Geeks, girls, and secret identities   **Fic**
BOYS' CLUBS
    See also Clubs; Societies
The **boys'** war. Murphy, J.   **973.7**
Bozzo, Linda
   Fire dog heroes   **636.7**
   Guide dog heroes   **362.4**
   My first bird   **636.6**
   My first cat   **636.8**
   My first dog   **636.7**
   My first fish   **639.34**
   My first guinea pig and other small pets   **636.9**
   My first horse   **636.1**
   Police dog heroes   **363.2**
   Search and rescue dog heroes   **636.7**
   Service dog heroes   **362.4**
   Therapy dog heroes   **615.8**
The **BP** oil spill. Benoit, P.   **363.7**
Braasch, Gary
   Cherry, L. How we know what we know about our changing climate   **363.7**
The **bracelet**. Uchida, Y.   **E**
BRACELETS
   Rau, D. M. Get connected   **745.594**
BRACELETS -- FICTION
   Russo, M. I will come back for you   **E**
BRACHIOSAURUS
    See also Dinosaurs
Bradberry, Sarah
   Kids knit!   **746.43**
Bradby, Marie
   Momma, where are you from?   **E**
   More than anything else   **E**
Bradford, Chris
   Young samurai: the way of the sword   **Fic**
   Young samurai: the way of the warrior   **Fic**
Bradford, June

The **broken** bike boy and the Queen of 33rd Street. Flake, S. G. **Fic**

Broken bones. Landau, E. **617.1**

The **Broken** Lands. Milford, K. **Fic**

Bromann, Jennifer
  More storytime action! **027.62**

Bromine. West, K. **546**

BROMINE
  West, K. Bromine **546**

Bromley, Anne C.
  The lunch thief **Fic**

BRONCHIAL ASTHMA *See* Asthma

Bronte, Charlotte
  About
  Lives of the writers **809**

Bronte, Emily
  About
  Lives of the writers **809**

Brontorina. Howe, J. **E**

The **bronze** bow. Speare, E. G. **Fic**

The **bronze** pen. Snyder, Z. K. **Fic**

BRONZES
  Fritz, J. Leonardo's horse **730.92**

BRONZES
  See also Archeology; Art; Art metalwork; Decoration and ornament; Metalwork; Sculpture

BRONZES, AMERICAN -- 20TH CENTURY -- JUVENILE LITERATURE
  Fritz, J. Leonardo's horse **730.92**

Bronzeville boys and girls. Brooks, G. **811**

The **brook** book. Arnosky, J. **577.6**

Brooker, Kyrsten
  (il) Davies, J. The night is singing **E**
  (il) Dodds, D. A. The prince won't go to bed **E**
  (il) The Honeybee Man **E**
  (il) Lazo, C. E. Someday when my cat can talk **E**
  (il) McKissack, P. C. Precious and the Boo Hag **E**

Brooklyn Bridge. Hesse, K. **Fic**

BROOKLYN BRIDGE (NEW YORK, N.Y.) -- JUVENILE LITERATURE
  Curlee, L. Brooklyn Bridge **624.2**
  Prince, A. J. Twenty-one elephants and still standing **E**

The **Brooklyn** nine. Gratz, A. **Fic**

Brooks, Bruce
  Everywhere **Fic**

Brooks, Erik
  Polar opposites **E**
  Byars, B. C. Boo's surprise **E**
  (il) Byars, B. C. Cat diaries **S**
  (il) Byars, B. C. Dog diaries **S**
  (il) Climo, S. Monkey business **398.2**
  (il) Who has these feet? **591.4**

Brooks, Gwendolyn
  Bronzeville boys and girls **811**

Brooks, Jeremy
  Let there be peace **242**
  My first prayers **242**
  A world of prayers **242**

Brooks, Susie
  Get into Art! **E**

Brooks, Wanda M.
  Embracing, evaluating, and examining African American children's and young adult literature **028.5**
  (ed) Embracing, evaluating, and examining African American children's and young adult literature **028.5**

Brooks-Young, Susan
  Teaching with the tools kids really use **372**

Broom, zoom! Cohen, C. L. **E**

BROOMS -- FICTION
  Lyons, K. S. Ellen's broom **E**

BROOMS AND BRUSHES -- FICTION
  Grey, M. Traction Man and the beach odyssey **E**
  Lyons, K. S. Ellen's broom **E**

Brophy, David
  Michelle Obama **92**

Brosnan, Rosemary
  (ed) Chu's day **E**

Brother Juniper. Gibfried, D. **E**

Brother Sun, Sister Moon. **E**

Brother William's year. Pancheri, J. **E**

Brotherband chronicles [series]
  Flanagan, J. The outcasts **Fic**

The **Brotherband chronicles** [series]
  Flanagan, J. The invaders **Fic**

Brotherhood of the conch [series]
  Divakaruni, C. B. The conch bearer **Fic**

Brothers. Yin **E**

BROTHERS
  Bunting, E. Jin Woo **E**
  Fisher, V. My big brother **E**
  Giblin, J. Good brother, bad brother **92**
  Horowitz, A. The Falcon's Malteser **Fic**
  Krull, K. The brothers Kennedy **920**
  Medearis, A. S. Seven spools of thread **E**
  Mills, C. 7 x 9 **Fic**
  Russo, M. The big brown box **E**
  Van Leeuwen, J. Cabin on Trouble Creek **Fic**
  Vernick, A. Brothers at bat **796.357**

BROTHERS
  See also Men; Siblings

Brothers & sisters. Greenfield, E. **811**

BROTHERS -- FICTION
  Clifton, L. Freaky Fast Frankie Joe **Fic**
  Erdrich, L. Chickadee **Fic**
  Rupp, R. After Eli **Fic**

BROTHERS -- FOLKLORE
  Smith, C. One city, two brothers **398.2**

BROTHERS -- GRAPHIC NOVELS
  Conway, G. Crawling with zombies **741.5**

BROTHERS -- JUVENILE FICTION
  Max & Milo go to sleep! **E**

BROTHERS -- NEW JERSEY -- BIOGRAPHY -- JUVENILE LITERATURE
  Vernick, A. Brothers at bat **796.357**

BROTHERS -- UNITED STATES -- BIOGRAPHY -- JUVENILE LITERATURE
  Vernick, A. Brothers at bat **796.357**

BROTHERS AND SISTERS
  Avi Never mind! **Fic**
  Brown, M. T. D.W.'s library card **E**
  De Paola, T. Meet the Barkers **E**
  Dowell, F. O. Dovey Coe **Fic**
  Estes, E. Ginger Pye **Fic**
  Estes, E. The Moffats **Fic**
  Etchemendy, N. The power of Un **Fic**
  Farmer, N. The Sea of Trolls **Fic**
  Gantos, J. Jack on the tracks **Fic**
  Giff, P. R. Nory Ryan's song **Fic**
  Griffin, P. R. The ghost sitter **Fic**
  Kehret, P. Abduction! **Fic**
  McDonald, M. Judy Moody gets famous **Fic**
  McKay, H. Saffy's angel **Fic**
  Numeroff, L. J. Beatrice doesn't want to **E**
  Reynolds, P. Ish **E**
  Ruelle, K. G. The Thanksgiving beast feast **E**
  Ryan, P. M. Becoming Naomi Leon **Fic**

The winter people | **Fic**
Caduto, M. J. Keepers of the night | **398.2**

Bruchac, Joseph, 1942-
Buffalo song | **92**
Dragon castle | **Fic**
Squanto's journey | **Fic**

About
Parker-Rock, M. Joseph Bruchac | **92**

Bruchac, Margaret M.
Grace, C. O. 1621 | **394.264**

Bruel, Nick
Bad Kitty | **E**
A Bad Kitty Christmas | **Fic**
Bad Kitty gets a bath | **Fic**
Bad kitty meets the baby | **Fic**
Bad Kitty vs. Uncle Murray | **Fic**
Happy birthday Bad Kitty | **Fic**
Little red bird | **E**
(il) Bruel, R. O. Bob and Otto | **E**
(il) King-Smith, D. Clever duck | **Fic**
(il) King-Smith, D. Dinosaur trouble | **Fic**
(il) King-Smith, D. The mouse family Robinson | **Fic**

Bruel, Robert O.
Bob and Otto | **E**

Bruh Rabbit and the tar baby girl. Hamilton, V. | **398.2**

Bruhn, Aron
Inside the human body | **612**

Bruins, David
The call of the cowboy | **E**
The legend of Ninja Cowboy Bear | **E**
The way of the Ninja | **E**

Brun-Cosme, Nadine
Big Wolf & Little Wolf | **E**
Big Wolf & Little Wolf, such a beautiful orange! | **E**
Big Wolf & Little Wolf, the little leaf that wouldn't fall | **E**

Brunelle, Lynn
Shannon, G. Chicken scratches | **811**

Brunelleschi, Filippo, 1377-1446
About
Fern, T. E. Pippo the Fool | **E**

Brunelleschi, Filippo, 1377-1446 -- Fiction
About
Fern, T. E. Pippo the Fool | **E**

Brunhoff, Jean de
The story of Babar, the little elephant | **E**

Brunhoff, Laurent de
Babar's Celesteville games | **E**

Brunkus, Denise
(il) Keane, D. Sloppy Joe | **E**
(il) Park, B. Junie B. Jones and her big fat mouth | **Fic**
(il) Swallow, P. C. Groundhog gets a say | **E**
(il) Winters, K. My teacher for President | **E**

Bruno Munari's zoo. Munari, B. | **E**

Bruno, Elsa Knight
A punctuation celebration! | **428**

Bruno, Iacopo
(il) Mister Max | **Fic**
(il) The spindlers | **Fic**

Bruno, Iacopo
(il) Baccalario, P. The door to time | **Fic**
(il) Baccalario, P. The long-lost map | **Fic**
(il) Baccalario, P. Ring of fire | **Fic**

Brush of the gods. Look, L. | **E**
Brushing Mom's hair. Cheng, A. | **Fic**

Bruss, Deborah
Book! book! book! | **E**

Bryan, Ashley, 1923-
(il) Alexander, C. F. All things bright and beautiful | **264**

(comp) All night, all day | **782.25**
(il) Ashley Bryan's ABC of African-American poetry | **811**
Ashley Bryan | **92**
Ashley Bryan's African tales, uh-huh | **398.2**
Beautiful blackbird | **398.2**
Sing to the sun | **811**
(il) Gilchrist, J. S. My America | **E**
(il) Giovanni, N. The sun is so quiet | **811**
(il) Graham, L. B. How God fix Jonah | **220.9**
(il) Let it shine | **782.25**
(comp) The Night has ears | **398.9**

Bryan, Ashley, 1923-
About
Bryan, A. Ashley Bryan | **92**

Bryant, Jen
A splash of red | **759.13**

Bryant, Jennifer
Abe's fish | **E**
Georgia's bones | **92**
A river of words: the story of William Carlos Williams | **92**

BRYANT, KOBE, 1978- -- JUVENILE LITERATURE
Thornley, S. Kobe Bryant | **796.323**

Bryant, Kobe, 1978- -- Juvenile literature
About
Thornley, S. Kobe Bryant | **796.323**

Bryant, Laura J.
(il) Bergren, L. T. God found us you | **E**
(il) Martin, B. Kitty cat, kitty cat, are you going to sleep? | **E**
(il) Martin, B. Kitty Cat, Kitty Cat, are you waking up? | **E**
(il) Morales, M. Jam & honey | **E**
(il) Quattlebaum, M. Jo MacDonald saw a pond | **E**
(il) Stiegemeyer, J. Seven little bunnies | **E**
(il) Tompert, A. Little Fox goes to the end of the world | **E**

Bryant, Megan E.
Oh my gods! | **292**
She's all that! | **292**

Bryner, John
Lanning, S. Essential reference services for today's school media specialists | **025.5**

Bryson, Bill
A really short history of nearly everything | **500**

BUBBLE GUM
McCarthy, M. Pop! | **664**

Bubble gum, bubble gum. Wheeler, L. | **E**
Bubble homes and fish farts. Bayrock, F. | **590**
Bubble trouble. Mahy, M. | **E**

BUBBLES
Bayrock, F. Bubble homes and fish farts | **590**
Bradley, K. B. Pop! | **530.4**
Shores, L. How to make bubbles | **530.4**
Weakland, M. Bubbles float, bubbles pop | **530.4**
Wheeler-Toppen, J. Science experiments that fizz and bubble | **507.8**

BUBBLES
See also Air; Gases

BUBBLES -- FICTION
Mahy, M. Bubble trouble | **E**

BUBBLES -- JUVENILE LITERATURE
Bayrock, F. Bubble homes and fish farts | **590**
Bubbles float, bubbles pop. Weakland, M. | **530.4**
Bubonic plague. Person, S. | **614.5**

BUBONIC PLAGUE *See* Plague

The **buccaneers.** Lawrence, I.
BUCCANEERS *See* Pirates

Buchanan, Andrea J.
The daring book for girls | **646.700**

Buchanan, Andrea J.
The daring book for girls | **031.02**

Busy-busy Little Chick. Harrington, J. N.   E

But and for, yet and nor. Cleary, B. P.   425

But God remembered. Sasso, S. E.   221.9

But I wanted a baby brother! Feiffer, K.   E

But who will bell the cats? Buhler, C. v.   E

But why can't I? Graves, S.   152.4

But, excuse me, that is my book. Child, L.   E

The butler gets a break. Venuti, K. C.   Fic

Butler, Dori Hillestad

The case of the fire alarm   Fic

The case of the library monster   Fic

The case of the lost boy   Fic

The case of the missing family   Fic

The case of the mixed-up mutts   Fic

My grandpa had a stroke   E

My mom's having a baby!   612.6

The truth about Truman School   Fic

F is for firefighting   628.9

Butler, John

Bedtime in the jungle   E

(il) Thompson, L. Wee little bunny   E

(il) Thompson, L. Wee little chick   E

(il) Thompson, L. Wee little lamb   E

(il) When Anju loved being an elephant   E

Butler, M. Christina

The smiley snowman   E

Butler, Rebecca P.

Copyright for teachers & librarians in the 21st century   346

Butschler, Margaret

(il) Harley, A. Sea stars   811

The butter man. Alalou, A.   E

Butterfield, Moira

Events   796.48

History   796.48

Scandals   796.48

Butterflies. Simon, S.   595.7

Butterflies. Marsh, L.   595.7

BUTTERFLIES

     See also Insects

BUTTERFLIES

Aston, D. A butterfly is patient   595.78

Barner, B. Dinosaurs roar, butterflies soar!   560

Bishop, N. Butterflies   595.7

Bishop, N. Nic Bishop butterflies and moths   595.7

Collard, S. B. Butterfly count   E

Cox, J. Butterfly buddies   Fic

Dickmann, N. A butterfly's life   595.7

Ehlert, L. Waiting for wings   595.78

Engle, M. Summer birds: the butterflies of Maria Merian   92

Gibbons, G. Monarch butterfly   595.78

Heiligman, D. From caterpillar to butterfly   595.78

Johnson, J. Butterfly   595.7

Knudsen, S. From egg to butterfly   595.7

Koontz, R. M. What's the difference between a butterfly and a moth?   595.7

Malam, J. Grow your own butterfly farm   638

Marsh, L. Butterflies   595.7

Marsh, L. Caterpillar to butterfly   595.78

Murawski, D. Face to face with butterflies   595.7

Simon, S. Butterflies   595.7

Stewart, M. Butterfly or moth?   595.7

Swope, S. Gotta go! Gotta go!   E

Whalley, P. E. S. Butterfly & moth   595.7

Winnick, N. Butterflies   595.7

Butterflies. Winnick, N.   595.7

Butterflies. Bishop, N.   595.7

BUTTERFLIES -- FICTION

Markle, S. Butterfly tree   E

BUTTERFLIES -- JUVENILE LITERATURE

Whalley, P. Butterfly & moth   595.78

BUTTERFLIES -- LIFE CYCLES

Knudsen, S. From egg to butterfly   595.7

BUTTERFLIES -- METAMORPHOSIS -- JUVENILE LITERATURE

Engle, M. Summer birds: the butterflies of Maria Merian   92

BUTTERFLIES -- MIGRATION

Catt, T. Migrating with the monarch butterfly   595.7

BUTTERFLIES -- POETRY

Harley, A. The monarch's progress   811

Butterflies in my stomach and other school hazards. Bloch, S.   E

The butterfly. Polacco, P.   E

Butterfly. Johnson, J.   595.7

Butterfly & moth. Whalley, P. E. S.   595.78

Butterfly buddies. Cox, J.   Fic

Butterfly count. Collard, S. B.   E

Butterfly eyes and other secrets of the meadow. Sidman, J.   811

BUTTERFLY GARDENS

Ehlert, L. Waiting for wings   595.78

Harkins, S. S. Design your own butterfly garden   638

Butterfly house. Bunting, E.   E

A butterfly is patient. Aston, D.   595.78

Butterfly or moth? Stewart, M.   595.7

Butterfly tree. Markle, S.   E

BUTTERFLY WATCHING

Collard, S. B. Butterfly count   E

A butterfly's life. Dickmann, N.   595.7

Butterworth, Chris

How Did That Get in My Lunchbox?   641.3

Butterworth, Christine

Butterworth, C. How Did That Get in My Lunchbox?   641.3

Sea horse   597

Butterworth, Oliver

The enormous egg   Fic

Buttler, Elizabeth

(il) Wong, J. S. Me and Rolly Maloo   Fic

Button up! Schertle, A.   811

Button, Lana

Willow's whispers   E

Buttons. Cole, B.   E

BUTTONS

     See also Clothing and dress

Butts, Ed

Bodyguards!   363.28

Butts, Edward

Shipwrecks, monsters, and mysteries of the Great Lakes   917

Buxton, Jane

The littlest llama   E

Buyea, Rob

Because of Mr. Terupt   Fic

Mr. Terupt falls again   Fic

Buying, training & caring for your dinosaur. Rennert, L. J.   E

Buzbee, Lewis

The haunting of Charles Dickens   Fic

Buzz. Spinelli, E.   E

Buzz. Wong, J. S.   E

The buzz on bees. Rotner, S.   595.7

Buzzeo, Toni

Adventure Annie goes to kindergarten   E

Adventure Annie goes to work   E

Collaborating to meet standards: teacher/librarian partnerships for K-6   027.8

The collaboration handbook   027.8

Inside the books   E

One cool friend   E

Penelope Popper, book doctor   E

Ready or not, Dawdle Duckling
Grandpre, M. The sea chest   E
By air. Parker, S.   387.7
By the Great Horn Spoon! Fleischman, S.   Fic
By the light of the Halloween moon. Stutson, C.   E
By the light of the harvest moon. Ziefert, H.   E

Byam, Michele
    Arms & armor   355.8

Byard, Carole
    (il) Greenfield, E. Africa dream   E
    (il) Williams, S. A. Working cotton   E

Byars, Betsy Cromer
    Boo's surprise   E
    Cat diaries   S
    The dark stairs   Fic
    Dog diaries   S
    The Golly sisters go West   E
    The keeper of the doves   Fic
    Little Horse   Fic
    The not-just-anybody family   Fic
    The pinballs   Fic
    The SOS file   Fic
    Tornado   Fic
Bye-bye baby brother!   E
Bye-bye, baby! Morris, R. T.   E
Bye-bye, crib. McGhee, A.   E

Byers, Ann
    Jobs as green builders and planners   690
    West Virginia   975.4
    Wyoming   978.7
Bylines: a photobiography of Nellie Bly. Macy, S.   92

Bynum, Eboni
    Jamari's drum   E

Bynum, Janie
    Kiki's blankie   E

Byrd, Robert
    Electric Ben   973.309

Byrd, Robert
    The hero and the minotaur   398.2
    (il) Kroll, S. Barbarians!   940.1
    (il) Krull, K. Kubla Khan   92
    (il) Schlitz, L. A. Good masters! Sweet ladies!   940.1
    Schlitz, L. A. The hero Schliemann   92

Byrd, Samuel
    (il) Adler, D. A. A picture book of Harriet Tubman   305.5

Byrne, John
    Donald & Benoit   E

Byrne, Mike
    (il) Hooks, G. Pet costume party   E

BYZANTINE ARCHITECTURE
    See also Ancient architecture; Architecture; Medieval architecture

BYZANTINE ART
    See also Ancient art; Art; Medieval art
The **Byzantine** Empire. Vanvoorst, J. F.   949.5

BYZANTINE EMPIRE -- CIVILIZATION -- JUVENILE LITERATURE
    Vanvoorst, J. F. The Byzantine Empire   949.5

C

C D B. Steig, W.   793.73
C D C? Steig, W.   793.73
C is for city. Zuravicky, O.   E

Cézanne, Paul, 1839-1906
    Fiction
    Anholt, L. Cezanne and the apple boy   E

CABALA
    See also Hebrew literature; Jewish literature; Judaism; Mysticism; Occultism

Cabban, Vanessa
    (il) Emmett, J. The best gift of all   E
    (il) Freedman, C. Gooseberry Goose   E

CABIN BOYS -- GERMANY -- BIOGRAPHY -- JUVENILE LITERATURE
    Surviving the Hindenburg   363.12
Cabin on Trouble Creek. Van Leeuwen, J.   Fic

CABINET MEMBERS
    Blashfield, J. F. Golda Meir   92
    Franklin and Winston   940.53
    Krull, K. Lives of extraordinary women   920
The **Cabinet** of Wonders. Rutkoski, M.   Fic

CABINETWORK
    See also Carpentry

CABLE RAILROADS
    See also Railroads

Cabot, John, 1450-1498
         About
    Fritz, J. Around the world in a hundred years   910.92

Cabot, Meg
    Allie Finkle's rules for girls: book two; The new girl   Fic
    Best friends and drama queens   Fic
    Blast from the past   Fic
    Glitter girls and the great fake out   Fic
    Moving day   Fic
    Stage fright   Fic

Cabral, Olga
    The seven sneezes   E

Cabral, Pedro Alvares, 1460?-1526?
         About
    Fritz, J. Around the world in a hundred years   910.92

Cabrera, Cozbi A.
    (il) Cook, M. Our children can soar   920
    (il) Grimes, N. Thanks a million   811
    (il) Hegamin, T. Most loved in all the world   E
    (il) McKissack, P. C. Stitchin' and pullin'   Fic

Cabrera, Jane
    Here we go round the mulberry bush   E
    If you're happy and you know it   E
    Kitty's cuddles   E
    Mommy, carry me please!   E
    Old MacDonald had a farm   782.42
    Old Mother Hubbard   398.8
    One, two, buckle my shoe   E
    Twinkle, twinkle, little star   E
    The wheels on the bus   782.42

Caceres, Ana Palmero
    Nazoa, A. A small Nativity   E
A **cache** of jewels and other collective nouns. Heller, R.   428

CACTUS
    Bash, B. Desert giant   583
    Gould, M. Prickly plants   581.4
    Guiberson, B. Z. Cactus hotel   583

CACTUS
    See also Desert plants

CACTUS -- JUVENILE LITERATURE
    Guiberson, B. Z. Cactus hotel   583
Cactus hotel. Guiberson, B. Z.   583
Cada nino/Every child. Hinojosa, T.   782.42
Caddie Woodlawn. Brink, C. R.   Fic
Caddo. Kissock, H.   970.004

CADDO INDIANS
    Kissock, H. Caddo   970.004
Caddy ever after. McKay, H.   Fic

Cadena, Beth

McDonald, M. Stink and the incredible super-galactic jaw-breaker **Fic**

Underwood, D. A balloon for Isabel **E**

Candy bomber. Tunnell, M. **92**

Candy shop. Wahl, J. **E**

Candyfloss. Wilson, J. **Fic**

The **candymakers.** Mass, W. **Fic**

Cane toad. Somervill, B. A. **597.8**

Caney, Steven
Steven Caney's ultimate building book **624**

Canga, C. B.
(il) Bateman, T. Paul Bunyan vs. Hals Halson **E**

Canga, C. B.
(il) Brezenoff, S. The painting that wasn't there **Fic**

Canga, Chris
Bateman, T. Paul Bunyan vs. Hals Halson **E**
(il) Brezenoff, S. The burglar who bit the Big Apple **Fic**
(il) Brezenoff, S. The zombie who visited New Orleans **Fic**
(il) Santopolo, J. The Nina, the Pinta, and the vanishing treasure **Fic**

The **canine** connection: stories about dogs and people. Hearne, B. G. **S**

Cann, Helen
(il) The raiders **Fic**
(il) The shipwreck **Fic**
(il) The snowstorm **Fic**
(il) Guo Yue Little Leap Forward **Fic**
(il) Matthews, C. Fireside stories **398.2**
(il) Milligan, B. Brigid's cloak **398.2**
(il) Watts, M. The Bible for children from Good Books **220.9**
(il) Yolen, J. The Barefoot book of dance stories **398.2**

CANNABIS See Marijuana

Cannarella, Deborah
Kansas **978.1**

Cannavale, Matthew C.
Florida, 1513-1821 **975.9**
North Carolina, 1524-1776 **975.6**

Cannell, Jon
(il) Holmes, M. T. A giraffe goes to Paris **E**
(il) Holmes, M. T. My travels with Clara **599.66**
(il) McCutcheon, M. The kid who named Pluto **509**

CANNIBALISM
See also Ethnology; Human behavior

CANNING AND PRESERVING
See also Cooking; Food -- Preservation; Industrial chemistry

Cannon, A. E.
Sophie's fish **E**

Cannon, Annie
(il) Crenson, V. Horseshoe crabs and shorebirds **577.7**

Cannon, Annie Jump, 1863-1941
About
Gerber, C. Annie Jump Cannon, astronomer **92**

Cannon, Janell
Crickwing **E**
Stellaluna **E**

Cannon, Kevin
(il) Ottaviani, J. T-Minus: the race to the moon **629.45**

Cannon, Zander
(il) Ottaviani, J. T-Minus: the race to the moon **629.45**

Canoeing and kayaking. Thorpe, Y. **797.1**

CANOES AND CANOEING
Thorpe, Y. Canoeing and kayaking **797.1**

CANOES AND CANOEING
See also Boats and boating; Water sports

CANOES AND CANOEING -- FICTION
Hobbs, W. Take me to the river **Fic**
Williams, V. B. Three days on a river in a red canoe **E**

CANONIZATION
See also Christian saints; Rites and ceremonies

Cans. Blaxland, W. **671**

CANS
Blaxland, W. Cans **671**

Canterbury tales. Cohen, B. **821**

Canto familiar. Soto, G. **811**

Cantone, Anna-Laura
(il) French, V. The Daddy Goose treasury **E**
(il) Goodhart, P. Three little ghosties **E**

Cantrell, Charlie
A friend for Einstein **E**

Cantrell, Katie
(il) Dunston, M. The magic of giving **E**

Canwell, Diane
Sutherland, J. Aircraft carriers **623.82**
Sutherland, J. Container ships and oil tankers **623.82**
Sutherland, J. Cruise ships **623.82**
Sutherland, J. Submarines **623.82**

Canyon, Jeanette
(il) Berkes, M. C. Over in the jungle **E**

Capaccio, George
ADD and ADHD **616.85**
Jupiter **523.4**
Mars **523.4**
The sun **523.7**

Capaldi, Gina
A boy named Beckoning: the true story of Dr. Carlos Montezuma, Native American hero **92**
(il) Red Bird sings: the story of Zitkala-Sa **92**

Caparo, Antonio Javier
Broach, E. Missing on Superstition Mountain **Fic**
(il) Broach, E. Treasure on Superstition Mountain **Fic**
(il) The magic thief **Fic**
(il) Prineas, S. Found **Fic**
(il) Prineas, S. Lost **Fic**

CAPE HATTERAS NATIONAL SEASHORE (N.C.)
Reed, J. Cape Hatteras National Seashore **975.6**

Caper, William
American bison **599.64**

CAPITAL ACCUMULATION See Saving and investment

CAPITAL FORMATION See Saving and investment

CAPITALISTS AND FINANCIERS
See also Businesspeople

CAPITALS (CITIES)
See also Cities and towns

Caple, Kathy
Duck & Company **E**
Duck & Company Christmas **E**
The friendship tree **E**

Caple, Laurie A.
(il) Arnold, C. Giant sea reptiles of the dinosaur age **567.9**
(il) Arnold, C. Giant shark: megalodon, prehistoric super predator **567**
(il) Arnold, C. Global warming and the dinosaurs **567.9**
(il) Arnold, C. Pterosaurs **567.9**
(il) Arnold, C. When mammoths walked the earth **569**

Capoeira. Haney, J. **793.3**

Capoeira. Ancona, G. **793.3**

CAPOEIRA (DANCE)
Ancona, G. Capoeira **793.3**
Haney, J. Capoeira **793.3**

Cappon, Manuela
(il) Platt, R. London **942**
(il) Platt, R. New York City **974.7**

Caps for sale. Slobodkina, E. **E**

Captain Invincible and the space shapes. Murphy, S. J. **516**

CAPTAIN MARVEL (FICTIONAL CHARACTER)

(il) Sanders-Wells, L. Maggie's monkeys   E
Carter, David A.
  Hide and Seek   E
Carter, David A.
  600 black spots   E
  Blue 2   E
  Lots of bots   E
  One red dot   E
  White noise   E
  Yellow square   E
Carter, Noelle
  Carter, D. A. Lots of bots   E
Cartlidge, Cherese
  Home windmills   **621.4**
  Water from air   **628.1**
CARTOGRAPHERS
  Morrison, T. The coast mappers   **623.89**
CARTOGRAPHY See Map drawing; Maps
CARTOGRAPHY -- JUVENILE LITERATURE
  Morrison, T. The coast mappers   **623.89**
Cartooning. Roche, A.   **741.5**
CARTOONING
  See also Cartoons and caricatures; Wit and humor
CARTOONING -- TECHNIQUE
  Ames, L. J. Draw 50 animal 'toons   **741.5**
  Artell, M. Funny cartooning for kids   **741.5**
  Caldwell, B. Fantasy! cartooning   **741.5**
  Roche, A. Cartooning   **741.5**
CARTOONING -- TECHNIQUE -- JUVENILE LITERA-
TURE
  Sturm, J. Adventures in cartooning   **741.5**
The **cartoonist's** big book of drawing animals. Hart, C. **741.5**
CARTOONISTS
  Amoroso, C. Charles Schulz   **92**
  Gherman, B. Sparky: the life and art of Charles Schulz **92**
  Nobleman, M. T. Boys of steel   **92**
  Stamaty, M. A. Shake, rattle & turn that noise down! **781.66**
  Steig, J. Cats, dogs, men, women, ninnies, & clowns **741.5**
  Steig, W. When everybody wore a hat   **E**
CARTOONS AND CARICATURES
  Barks, C. Walt Disney's Donald Duck: lost in the Andes **741.5**
  Dawson, W. Lila & Ecco's do-it-yourself comics club **741.5**
  Giarrano, V. Comics crash course   **741.5**
  Hart, C. The cartoonist's big book of drawing animals **741.5**
  Hart, C. Drawing the new adventure cartoons   **741.5**
  Hart, C. Kids draw Manga Shoujo   **741.5**
  Hart, C. You can draw cartoon animals   **741.5**
  Stephens, J. Heroes!   **741.5**
  Stephens, J. Monsters!   **741.5**
  Stephens, J. Robots!   **741.5**
CARTOONS AND CARICATURES
  See also Pictures; Portraits
CARTOONS AND COMICS
  Caldwell, B. Fantasy! cartooning   **741.5**
  Giarrano, V. Comics crash course   **741.5**
  Hart, C. Kids draw Manga Shoujo   **741.5**
  Hergé The secret of the unicorn   **741.5**
  Roche, A. Cartooning   **741.5**
CARTOONS AND COMICS -- FICTION
  Clements, A. Lunch money   Fic
  Holm, J. L. Game on!   Fic
  Sniegoski, T. Billy Hooten, Owlboy   Fic
CARTOONS, ANIMATED See Animated films
Carver, George Washington, 1864?-1943
About
  Bolden, T. George Washington Carver   **92**
Carver, George Washington, 1864?-1943
About

Harness, C. The groundbreaking, chance-taking life of George
  Washington Carver and science & invention in America **92**
Carver, George Washington, 1864?-1943
About
  Grigsby, S. In the garden with Dr. Carver   E
Carver, George Washington, 1864?-1943 -- Fiction
About
  Grigsby, S. In the garden with Dr. Carver   E
Carver, George Washington, 1864?-1943 -- Juvenile litera-
ture
About
  Macceca, S. George Washington Carver   **630**
CARVING (DECORATIVE ARTS)
  See also Decorative arts
CARVING (MEAT, ETC.)
  See also Dining; Entertaining; Meat
Casanova, Mary
  The day Dirk Yeller came to town   E
Casanova, Mary
  The day Dirk Yeller came to town   E
  The hunter   **398.209**
  The klipfish code   Fic
  Some dog!   E
  Utterly otterly day   E
  Utterly otterly night   E
Casarosa, Enrico
  La Luna   E
A **case** for Jenny Archer. Conford, E.   Fic
The **case** of the Amazing Zelda. Rockliff, M.   Fic
The **case** of the case of mistaken identity. Barnett, M.   Fic
The **case** of the fire alarm. Butler, D. H.   Fic
The **case** of the flesh-eating bacteria. Faulk, M.   **616.5**
The **case** of the haunted haunted house. Rockliff, M.   Fic
The **case** of the hungry stranger. Bonsall, C. N.   E
The **case** of the July 4th jinx. Rockliff, M.   E
The **case** of the lost boy. Butler, D. H.   Fic
The **case** of the missing family. Butler, D. H.   Fic
The **case** of the missing marquess. Springer, N.   Fic
The **case** of the missing monkey. Rylant, C.   E
The **case** of the missing moose. Rockliff, M.   Fic
The **case** of the mixed-up mutts. Butler, D. H.   Fic
The **case** of the poisoned pig. Rockliff, M.   Fic
The **case** of the purloined professor. Cox, J.   Fic
The **case** of the scaredy cats. Bonsall, C. N.   E
The **case** of the stinky socks. Montgomery, L. B.   Fic
The **case** of the vanishing golden frogs. Markle, S.   **597.8**
The **case** that time forgot. Barrett, T.   Fic
Case, Chris
  Sophie and the next-door monsters   E
Caseley, Judith
  On the town   E
Casement, Rose
  Black history in the pages of children's literature   **028.5**
Casey and Derek on the ice. Sederman, M.   E
Casey at the bat. Thayer, E. L.   **811**
Casey back at bat. Gutman, D.   **811**
Casey, Dawn
  The Barefoot book of Earth tales   **398.2**
  The great race   **398.2**
Cash, Megan Montague
  Newgarden, M. Bow-Wow bugs a bug   E
Cash-Walsh, Tina
  (il) D'Amico, J. The science chef   **641.3**
  (il) The math chef   **510**
Casil, Amy Sterling
  Mississippi   **976.2**
Casilla, Robert
  (il) Adler, D. A. A picture book of Jackie Robinson **796.357**

Bjorklund, R. Kansas **978.1**
Bjorklund, R. Nebraska **978.2**
Brill, M. T. Michigan **977.4**
Dornfeld, M. Maine **974.1**
Elish, D. Washington, D.C. **975.3**
Hart, J. Florida **975.9**
Hoffman, N. South Carolina **975.7**
Hoffman, N. West Virginia **975.4**
Klein, T. Rhode Island **974.5**
LeVert, S. Massachusetts **974.4**
McDaniel, M. Arizona **979.1**
McDaniel, M. New Mexico **972**
McDaniel, M. North Dakota **978.4**
Moragne, W. New Jersey **974.9**
Morrice, P. A. Iowa **977.7**
Otfinoski, S. Georgia **975.8**
Otfinoski, S. New Hampshire **974.2**
Peters, S. Pennsylvania **974.8**
Pietrzyk, L. Maryland **975.2**
Schomp, V. New York **974.7**
Schuman, M. Delaware **975.1**
Schwabacher, M. Minnesota **977.6**
Schwabacher, M. Puerto Rico **972.95**
Sherrow, V. Ohio **977.1**
Shirley, D. Alabama **976.1**
Shirley, D. Mississippi **976.2**
Shirley, D. North Carolina **975.6**
Stefoff, R. Idaho **979.6**
Stefoff, R. Nevada **979.3**
Stefoff, R. Utah **979.2**
Stefoff, R. Washington **979.7**
Celebrate the USA. Kuntz, L. **973**
Celebrate Valentine's Day. Otto, C. **394.26**
Celebrate with books. Blass, R. J. **028.1**
Celebrating a Quinceanera. Hoyt-Goldsmith, D. **395.2**
Celebrating culture in your library [series]
Pavon 25 Latino craft projects **027.62**
Celebrating Hanukkah. Hoyt-Goldsmith, D. **296.4**
Celebrating Passover. Hoyt-Goldsmith, D. **296.4**
Celebrating Ramadan. Hoyt-Goldsmith, D. **297.3**
CELEBRITIES
Alcorn, S. A gift of days **808.88**
Reusser, K. Celebrities giving back **361.7**
CELEBRITIES -- DEATH -- JUVENILE LITERATURE
Bragg, G. How they croaked **920**
CELEBRITIES -- FICTION
Daly, N. A song for Jamela **E**
Celebrities giving back. Reusser, K. **361.7**
Celebritrees. Preus, M. **582.16**
CELEBRITY See Fame
Celenza, Anna Harwell
Duke Ellington's Nutcracker suite **E**
Gershwin's Rhapsody in Blue **E**
CELERY
See also Vegetables
Celeste's Harlem Renaissance. Tate, E. E. **Fic**
The **Celestial** Globe. Rutkoski, M. **Fic**
Celestine, drama queen. Ives, P. **E**
CELIBACY
See also Clergy; Religious life
CELL PHONES See Cellular telephones
Cell systems. McManus, L. **570**
CELLO
See also Stringed instruments
Cells. Lee, K. F. **571.6**
CELLS
See also Biology; Physiology; Reproduction
CELLS

Cohen, M. What is cell theory? **571.6**
Green, J. Inside animals **571**
Johnson, R. L. Mighty animal cells **571.6**
Lee, K. F. Cells **571.6**
McManus, L. Cell systems **570**
Rand, C. DNA and heredity **572.8**
Somervill, B. A. Cells and disease **571.9**
Cells and disease. Somervill, B. A. **571.9**
CELLULAR PHONES See Cellular telephones
CELLULAR TELEPHONES
Spilsbury, R. The telephone **621.385**
Wilkinson, C. Mobile platforms **004**
CELLULAR TELEPHONES
See also Telephone
CELTIC ART
See also Art
CELTIC CIVILIZATION
Green, J. Ancient Celts **936**
CELTIC LEGENDS
See also Legends
CELTIC MYTHOLOGY
See also Mythology
CELTS
Green, J. Ancient Celts **936**
CELTS -- FOLKLORE
Muller, R. The nightwood **398.2**
CEMENT
See also Adhesives; Building materials; Ceramics;
Masonry; Plaster and plastering
CEMETERIES
See also Burial; Public health; Sanitation
CEMETERIES -- FICTION
Gaiman, N. The graveyard book **Fic**
Ray, D. Here lies Linc **Fic**
Cendrars, Blaise
Shadow **841**
Cendrillon. San Souci, R. **398.2**
CENSORSHIP
Adams, H. R. Ensuring intellectual freedom and access to
information in the school library media program **027.8**
CENSORSHIP
See also Intellectual freedom
CENSUS
See also Population; Statistics; Vital statistics
CENSUS -- FICTION
Davies, J. Tricking the Tallyman **E**
CENTENARIANS
Bartoletti, S. C. Kids on strike! **331.892**
Brown, D. Far beyond the garden gate: Alexandra David-
Neel's journey to Lhasa **92**
Freedman, R. Indian chiefs **970.004**
Warren, A. Pioneer girl **92**
Whitehead, K. Art from her heart: folk artist Clementine
Hunter **92**
The **Center** for Cartoon Studies presents Annie Sullivan and
the trials of Helen Keller. **362.4**
The **center** of everything. Urban, L. **Fic**
Centerburg tales. McCloskey, R. **Fic**
Centipede. Povey, K. D. **595.6**
CENTIPEDES
Elkin, M. 20 fun facts about centipedes **595.6**
Povey, K. D. Centipede **595.6**
CENTIPEDES -- JUVENILE LITERATURE
Povey, K. D. Centipede **595.6**
**CENTIPEDES -- MISCELLANEA -- JUVENILE LITERA-
TURE**
Elkin, M. 20 fun facts about centipedes **595.6**
CENTRAL AMERICAN AMERICANS

See also Charities; Public welfare; Social work

A **child's** book of prayers. | 242
A **child's** calendar. Updike, J. | 811
A **child's** Christmas in Wales. Thomas, D. | 828
A **child's** Christmas in Wales. Thomas, D. | 828
A **child's** day. Pearle, I. | E
A **child's** first book of prayers. Rock, L. | 242
A **child's** garden of verses. Stevenson, R. L. | 821
A **child's** garden of verses. Stevenson, R. L. | 821
A **child's** garden of verses. Stevenson, R. L. | 821
A **child's** good morning book. Brown, M. W. | E
A **child's** introduction to poetry. Driscoll, M. | 808.81

Child's World (Firm)

Buckley, J. The Child's World encyclopedia of the NFL | 796.332
The Child's World encyclopedia of baseball | 796.357
The **Child's** World encyclopedia of baseball. | 796.357
The **Child's** World encyclopedia of the NFL. Buckley, J. | 796.332

Child, Julia

About

Hartland, J. Bon appetit! | 641.509

Child, Julia -- Fiction

About

Minette's feast | E

Child, Julia -- Juvenile literature

About

Hartland, J. Bon appetit! | 641.509

Child, Lauren

But, excuse me, that is my book | E
Clarice Bean spells trouble | Fic
Clarice Bean, don't look now | Fic
I am not sleepy and I will not go to bed | E
I am too absolutely small for school | E
I will never not ever eat a tomato | E
Say cheese! | E
Snow is my favorite and my best | E
Utterly me, Clarice Bean | Fic
Who wants to be a poodle I don't | E
(il) Lindgren, A. Pippi Longstocking | Fic

Child, Lydia Maria Francis

Over the river and through the wood | 811

CHILD-ADULT RELATIONSHIP

See also Children

CHILD-ADULT RELATIONSHIP -- JUVENILE FICTION

Matti, T. Mister Orange | Fic

CHILDBIRTH

Butler, D. H. My mom's having a baby! | 612.6
Cole, J. How you were born | 612.6
Cole, J. When you were inside Mommy | 612.6
Frasier, D. On the day you were born | E
Harris, R. H. It's not the stork! | 612.6
Harris, R. H. It's so amazing! | 612.6
Pringle, L. P. Everybody has a bellybutton | 612.6
Sears, W. Baby on the way | 612.6

CHILDBIRTH -- FICTION

English, K. The baby on the way | E
Hathaway, B. Missy Violet & me | Fic
Tillman, N. On the night you were born | E

CHILDLESSNESS

See also Children; Family size

Children. Micklethwait, L. | 750

CHILDREN

Ali, R. Slumgirl dreaming | 92
Asael, A. Children of the world | 305.23
Coerr, E. Sadako | 92
Coerr, E. Sadako and the thousand paper cranes | 92
Frank, A. The diary of a young girl: the definitive edi-

tion | 940.53
Heidbreder, R. Noisy poems for a busy day | 811
Hoose, P. M. We were there, too! | 973
Hurwitz, J. Anne Frank: life in hiding | 940.53
Metselaar, M. Anne Frank: her life in words and pictures | 92
Rol, R. v. d. Anne Frank, beyond the diary | 940.53
Rubin, S. G. The Anne Frank Case: Simon Wiesenthal's search for the truth | 92
Shoveller, H. Ryan and Jimmy | 361.7
This child, every child | 305.23
UNICEF A Life like mine | 305.23
UNICEF A school like mine | 371.82

CHILDREN

See also Age; Family

CHILDREN -- ABUSE See Child abuse

CHILDREN -- ADOPTION See Adoption

CHILDREN -- AFGHANISTAN

O'Brien, T. Afghan dreams | 958.1

CHILDREN -- AFGHANISTAN -- JUVENILE LITERATURE

O'Brien, T. Afghan dreams | 958.1

CHILDREN -- BIOGRAPHY -- JUVENILE LITERATURE

Cotter, C. Kids who rule | 920

CHILDREN -- BOOKS AND READING

Keane, N. J. 101 great, ready-to-use book lists for children | 028.5
Ollhoff, J. Middle Eastern Mythology | 398.209

CHILDREN -- BOOKS AND READING

See also Books and reading

CHILDREN -- BOOKS AND READING -- HISTORY

Neuburger, E. K. Minders of make-believe | 070.5

CHILDREN -- BOOKS AND READING -- UNITED STATES

Hearne, B. G. Choosing books for children | 011.62
Keane, N. J. 101 great, ready-to-use book lists for children | 028.5
Larson, J. C. Bringing mysteries alive for children and young adults | 028.5

CHILDREN -- CHINA

Chen, J. H. Mao and me | 951.05

CHILDREN -- CIVIL RIGHTS

I have the right to be a child | 323.3

CHILDREN -- CIVIL RIGHTS

See also Civil rights

CHILDREN -- CONDUCT OF LIFE

See also Conduct of life

CHILDREN -- CROSS-CULTURAL STUDIES -- JUVENILE LITERATURE

UNICEF A Life like mine | 305.23

CHILDREN -- DEATH

See also Death

CHILDREN -- DISEASES

See also Diseases

CHILDREN -- EDUCATION See Elementary education; Preschool education

CHILDREN -- EMPLOYMENT See Child labor

CHILDREN -- EMPLOYMENT -- JUVENILE LITERATURE

Freedman, R. Kids at work | 331.3

CHILDREN -- EMPLOYMENT -- UNITED STATES -- JUVENILE LITERATURE

Bartoletti, S. C. Growing up in coal country | 331.3

CHILDREN -- ETIQUETTE See Etiquette for children and teenagers

CHILDREN -- FOOD See Children -- Nutrition

CHILDREN -- GROWTH -- PICTORIAL WORKS -- JUVENILE FICTION

Brown, M. W. Another important book | E

S.   E

CHRISTMAS MUSIC

Coots, J. F. Santa Claus is comin' to town   **782.42**

The **Christmas** quiet book.   E

Christmas remembered. De Paola, T.   **92**

CHRISTMAS STORIES

Brett, J. Home for Christmas   E

Bruel, N. A Bad Kitty Christmas   Fic

Buck, N. A Christmas goodnight   E

The carpenter's gift   E

The Christmas coat   **92**

Cole, B. The money we'll save   E

Cole, H. The littlest evergreen   E

Cushman, D. Christmas Eve good night   E

De Paola, T. The legend of the poinsettia   **398.24**

dePaola, T. Strega Nona's gift   E

Dunrea, O. A Christmas tree for Pyn   E

Godden, R. The story of Holly & Ivy   E

The greatest gift   Fic

Hodges, M. The wee Christmas cabin   E

Jennings, S. A Chanukah Noel   E

Jingle bells   E

King, T. A Coyote solstice tale   Fic

Listen to the silent night   E

Menotti, G. C. Amahl and the night visitors   **232.9**

One starry night   E

Palatini, M. Three French hens   E

Rosen, M. J. Elijah's angel   **813**

Soto, G. Too many tamales   **813**

Steinhofel, A. An elk dropped in   Fic

CHRISTMAS STORIES *See* Christmas -- Fiction

CHRISTMAS STORIES -- JUVENILE LITERATURE

Banks, K. What's coming for Christmas?   E

Dewdney, A. Llama Llama holiday drama   E

Egielski, R. Captain Sky Blue   E

Fackelmayer, R. The gifts   E

Hale, N. The twelve bots of Christmas   E

Horacek, P. Suzy Goose and the Christmas star   E

Hughes, S. The Christmas Eve ghost   E

Kimmel, E. A. The spider's gift   **398.2**

L'Engle, M. The twenty-four days before Christmas   Fic

Lester, H. Tacky's Christmas   E

Light, S. The Christmas giant   E

MacLachlan, P. The true gift   Fic

McCourt, F. Angela and the baby Jesus   E

McGinley, P. A year without a Santa Claus   E

McKissack, P. C. The all-I'll-ever-want Christmas doll   E

Milgrim, D. Santa Duck and his merry helpers   E

Rees, D. Jeannette Claus saves Christmas   E

Sacre, A. La Noche Buena   E

Shannon, D. It's Christmas, David   E

Smith, M. Christmas with the Mousekins   E

Thompson, L. The Christmas magic   E

Willey, M. A Clever Beatrice Christmas   E

Christmas tree. Martin, D.   E

Christmas tree farm. Purmell, A.   E

A **Christmas** tree for Pyn. Dunrea, O.   E

CHRISTMAS TREE GROWING

See also Forests and forestry

CHRISTMAS TREE GROWING -- FICTION

Purmell, A. Christmas tree farm   E

CHRISTMAS TREES

Farmer, J. O Christmas tree   **394.26**

CHRISTMAS TREES

See also Christmas decorations; Trees

CHRISTMAS TREES -- FICTION

Cole, H. The littlest evergreen   E

CHRISTMAS TREES -- JUVENILE LTERATURE

Farmer, J. O Christmas tree   **394.26**

Obed, E. B. Who would like a Christmas tree?   E

CHRISTMAS TRUCE, 1914 -- JUVENILE LITERATURE

Murphy, J. Truce   **940.4**

Christmas with the Mousekins. Smith, M.   E

Christmas wombat. French, J.   E

Christophe's story. Cornwell, N.   Fic

Christopher counting. Gorbachev, V.   E

Christopher Mouse. Wise, W.   Fic

Christopher Paul Curtis. Parker-Rock, M.   **92**

Christopher, John

The City of gold and lead   Fic

The pool of fire   Fic

When the Tripods came   Fic

The White Mountains   Fic

Christopher, Lucy

Flyaway   Fic

Christopherson, Sara Cohen

Top 50 reasons to care about marine turtles   **597.92**

Top 50 reasons to care about whales and dolphins   **599.5**

Christy, Jana

(il) Happy birthday, Tree   E

(il) The ocean story   E

Christy, Jana

(il) Aigner-Clark, J. You are the best medicine   E

(il) Buzzeo, T. Penelope Popper, book doctor   E

(il) The ocean story   E

Chromium. Lepora, N.   **546**

CHROMIUM

Lepora, N. Chromium   **546**

CHROMIUM -- JUVENILE LITERATURE

Lepora, N. Chromium   **546**

CHROMOSOMES

See also Genetics; Heredity

CHRONIC DISEASES

See also Diseases

CHRONIC FATIGUE SYNDROME

See also Diseases

CHRONIC PAIN

See also Chronic diseases; Pain

Chronicles of ancient darkness [series]

Paver, M. Wolf brother   Fic

The **chronicles** of Harris Burdick.   S

The chronicles of Narnia [series]

Lewis, C. S. The horse and his boy   Fic

Lewis, C. S. The last battle   Fic

Lewis, C. S. The lion, the witch, and the wardrobe   Fic

Lewis, C. S. The magician's nephew   Fic

Lewis, C. S. Prince Caspian   Fic

Lewis, C. S. The silver chair   Fic

Lewis, C. S. The voyage of the Dawn Treader   Fic

The **Chronicles** of Narnia pop-up. Sabuda, R.   E

Chronicles of Prydain [series]

Alexander, L. The Black Cauldron   Fic

Alexander, L. The book of three   Fic

Alexander, L. The castle of Llyr   Fic

Alexander, L. The high king   Fic

Alexander, L. Taran Wanderer   Fic

Chronicles of the red king [series]

Nimmo, J. The secret kingdom   Fic

CHRONOLOGY

See also Astronomy; History; Time

CHRONOMETERS

Galat, J. M. The discovery of longitude   **526**

CHRONOMETERS -- HISTORY

Galat, J. M. The discovery of longitude   **526**

CHRONOMETERS -- HISTORY -- JUVENILE LITERA-TURE

Craats, R. Columbus Day **394.26**

Columbus reaches the New World. Bodden, V. **970.01**

Columbus, Chris

House of secrets **Fic**

Columbus, Christopher, 1451-1506

About

Where do you think you're going, Christopher Columbus? **92**

Bodden, V. Columbus reaches the New World **970.01**

Craats, R. Columbus Day **394.26**

Fritz, J. Around the world in a hundred years **910.92**

Markle, S. Animals Christopher Columbus saw **970.01**

COLUMBUS, CHRISTOPHER, 1451-1506 -- JUVENILE LITERATURE

Demi Columbus **970.01**

COLUMNISTS

Cooney, B. Eleanor **973.917**

Fleming, C. Our Eleanor **92**

Freedman, R. Eleanor Roosevelt **973.917**

Krull, K. Lives of extraordinary women **920**

Rappaport, D. Eleanor, quiet no more **92**

COLUMNISTS See Journalists

Colvin, Claudette

About

Freedman, R. Freedom walkers **323.1**

COMA -- FICTION

Little, K. G. The healing spell **Fic**

Coman, Carolyn

The Memory Bank **Fic**

Sneaking suspicions **Fic**

The **Comanche**. De Capua, S. **970.004**

Comanche. Kissock, H. **970.004**

The **Comanche**. Cunningham, K. **970.004**

COMANCHE INDIANS

Cunningham, K. The Comanche **970.004**

De Capua, S. The Comanche **970.004**

Freedman, R. Indian chiefs **970.004**

Kissock, H. Comanche **970.004**

Combat sports [series]

Mason, P. Boxing **796.8**

COMBUSTION

See also Chemistry

Comden, Betty

What's new at the zoo? **E**

Come and eat. Ancona, G. **394.1**

Come and play. **305.23**

Come back, cat. Lexau, J. M. **E**

Come back, salmon. Cone, M. **639.3**

Come Fall. Bauer, A. C. E. **Fic**

Come fly with me. Ichikawa, S. **E**

Come look with me: Asian art. Lane, K. **709**

Come look with me: discovering African American art for children. Rolling, J. H. **704**

Come look with me: discovering women artists for children. Coyne, J. T. **704**

Come look with me: Latin American art. Lane, K. **709**

Come on, rain! Hesse, K. **E**

Come see the Earth turn: the story of Leon Foucault. **92**

Come sing, Jimmy Jo. Paterson, K. **Fic**

Come to the castle! Ashman, L. **940.1**

Come to the fairies' ball. Yolen, J. **E**

Come to the ocean's edge. Pringle, L. P. **577.7**

Come with me. Nye, N. S. **811**

Comeback kids [series]

Lupica, M. Hot hand **Fic**

Lupica, M. Long shot **Fic**

Lupica, M. Safe at home **Fic**

Lupica, M. Shoot-out **Fic**

Lupica, M. Two-minute drill **Fic**

COMEDIANS

Fleischman, S. Sir Charlie **92**

COMEDIANS

See also Actors; Entertainers

COMEDIANS -- FICTION

Landry, L. Grin and bear it **E**

O'Malley, K. Animal crackers fly the coop **E**

COMEDIES

See also Drama; Wit and humor

COMEDY

See also Drama; Wit and humor

COMEDY FILMS

See also Comedies; Motion pictures

COMEDY TELEVISION PROGRAMS

See also Comedies; Television programs

Comerford, Lynda B.

Rissa Bartholomew's declaration of independence **Fic**

COMETS

Carson, M. K. Far-out guide to asteroids and comets **523.4**

Poynter, M. Doomsday rocks from space **523.4**

Sherman, J. Asteroids, meteors, and comets **523.4**

Silverman, B. Exploring dangers in space **551.3**

Simon, S. Comets, meteors, and asteroids **523.6**

COMETS

See also Astronomy; Solar system

COMETS -- JUVENILE LITERATURE

Simon, S. Comets, meteors, and asteroids **523.6**

Comets, meteors, and asteroids. Simon, S. **523.6**

Comets, stars, the Moon, and Mars. Florian, D. **811**

Comic book collections for libraries. Fagan, B. D. **025.2**

COMIC BOOK NOVELS See Graphic novels

COMIC BOOK WRITERS

Nobleman, M. T. Boys of steel **92**

Siegel, S. C. To dance **741.5**

COMIC BOOKS, STRIPS, ETC.

Fagan, B. D. Comic book collections for libraries **025.2**

Graphic novels and comic books **741.5**

The TOON treasury of classic children's comics **741.5**

Worley, R. M. Scratch 9 **Fic**

COMIC BOOKS, STRIPS, ETC.

See also Wit and humor

COMIC BOOKS, STRIPS, ETC. -- AUTHORSHIP

Sturm, J. Adventures in cartooning **741.5**

COMIC BOOKS, STRIPS, ETC. -- BIBLIOGRAPHY

Fagan, B. D. Comic book collections for libraries **025.2**

COMIC BOOKS, STRIPS, ETC. -- FICTION

Harkrader, L. The adventures of Beanboy **Fic**

COMIC BOOKS, STRIPS, ETC. -- HISTORY AND CRITICISM

Fagan, B. D. Comic book collections for libraries **025.2**

Graphic novels and comic books **741.5**

Graphic novels beyond the basics **025.2**

Rosinsky, N. M. Graphic content! **741.5**

COMIC BOOKS, STRIPS, ETC. -- JUVENILE LITERATURE

Sturm, J. Adventures in cartooning **741.5**

Weigel, J. Atomic Ace **E**

COMIC LITERATURE See Burlesque (Literature); Comedy; Parody; Satire

COMIC NOVELS See Humorous fiction

COMIC OPERA See Opera; Operetta

COMIC STRIPS See Comic books, strips, etc.

COMIC VERSE See Humorous poetry

Comics crash course. Giarrano, V. **741.5**

Comin' down to storytime. Reid, R. **E**

Coming home. Cooper, F. **818**

COMING OF AGE -- FICTION

Cooper, S. Ghost Hawk **Fic**

The woman who outshone the sun 398.21
Cruz, Ray
 (il) Hurwitz, J. Baseball fever **Fic**
 (il) Mohr, N. Felita **Fic**
 (il) Viorst, J. Alexander and the terrible, horrible, no good, very bad day **E**
Cryobiology. Winner, C. 571.4
CRYOBIOLOGY
 Winner, C. Cryobiology 571.4
CRYOBIOLOGY
 See also Biology; Cold; Low temperatures
CRYOSURGERY
 See also Cold -- Therapeutic use; Surgery
Cryptid hunters. Smith, R. **Fic**
CRYPTOGRAPHY
 Bell-Rehwoldt, S. Speaking secret codes 652
 Blackwood, G. L. Mysterious messages 652
 Gilbert, A. Codes and ciphers 652
 Gregory, J. Breaking secret codes 652
 Gregory, J. Making secret codes 652
 Mitchell, S. K. Spy codes and ciphers 652
CRYPTOGRAPHY
 See also Signs and symbols; Writing
CRYPTOGRAPHY -- JUVENILE LITERATURE
 Blackwood, G. L. Mysterious messages 652
CRYSTAL METH (DRUG)
 See also Designer drugs; Methamphetamine
CRYSTALLIZATION *See* Crystals
CRYSTALLOGRAPHY *See* Crystals
Crystals. Spilsbury, R. 549
CRYSTALS
 Spilsbury, R. Crystals 549
 Stangl, J. Crystals and crystal gardens you can grow 548
CRYSTALS
 See also Physical chemistry; Solids
CRYSTALS -- JUVENILE LITERATURE
 Stangl, J. Crystals and crystal gardens you can grow 548
Crystals and crystal gardens you can grow. Stangl, J. 548
Cuba. Sheehan, S. 972.91
CUBA
 See also Islands
Cuba. Green, J. 972.91
**CUBA -- INTELLECTUAL LIFE -- JUVENILE LITERA-
 TURE**
 Ada, A. F. Under the royal palms 813
CUBA -- SOCIAL LIFE AND CUSTOMS
 Ada, A. F. Under the royal palms 813
 Sheen, B. Foods of Cuba 641.5
**CUBA -- SOCIAL LIFE AND CUSTOMS -- JUVENILE
 LITERATURE**
 Ada, A. F. Under the royal palms 813
CUBAN AMERICANS
 Parker-Rock, M. Alma Flor Ada 92
CUBAN AMERICANS -- FICTION
 Colon, E. Good-bye, Havana! Hola, New York! **E**
 Corbett, S. Free baseball **Fic**
 Garcia, C. I wanna be your shoebox **Fic**
 Sacre, A. La Noche Buena **E**
CUBAN COOKING
 Sheen, B. Foods of Cuba 641.5
Cuban Missile Crisis. Stein, R. C. 972.91
CUBAN MISSILE CRISIS, 1962
 Stein, R. C. Cuban Missile Crisis 972.91
CUBAN MISSILE CRISIS, 1962 -- FICTION
 Wiles, D. Countdown **Fic**
CUBAN REFUGEES -- FICTION
 Flores-Gabis, E. 90 miles to Havana **Fic**
CUBANS

Bernier-Grand, C. T. Alicia Alonso 92
CUBANS -- FICTION
 Lupica, M. Heat **Fic**
CUBE ROOT
 See also Arithmetic
Cubes. Olson, N. 516
CUBES
 Olson, N. Cubes 516
CUBIC EQUATIONS
 See also Equations
CUBIC MEASUREMENT *See* Volume (Cubic content)
CUBISM
 See also Art
CUCHULAIN (LEGENDARY CHARACTER)
 See also Legendary characters
The **cuckoo's** haiku. Rosen, M. J. 811
Cuckoo. Cucu. Ehlert, L. 398.2
CUCKOOS -- FICTION
 Stead, P. C. A home for Bird **E**
Cuddle up, goodnight. Cleminson, K. **E**
Cuevas, Michelle
 The masterwork of a painting elephant **Fic**
Cuffari, Richard
 (il) Cohen, B. Thank you, Jackie Robinson **Fic**
Cuffe-Perez, Mary
 Skylar **Fic**
Cullum, Carolyn N.
 The storytime sourcebook II 027.62
CULTIVATED PLANTS
 See also Agriculture; Gardening; Plants
CULTS
 See also Religions
CULTS -- FICTION
 Flanagan, J. Halt's peril **Fic**
 Flanagan, J. The kings of Clonmel **Fic**
Cultural atlas for young people [series]
 Corbishley, M. The Middle Ages 940.1
 Murray, J. Africa 960
A cultural history of women in America [series]
 Bingham, J. The Great Depression 973.91
 Bingham, J. Women at war 305.4
 Coster, P. A new deal for women 305.4
 Gorman, J. L. The modern feminist movement 305.4
 Stearman, K. Women of today 305.4
Cultural Journeys. Gates, P. 372
**CULTURAL PLURALISM -- UNITED STATES -- HISTO-
 RY -- JUVENILE LITERATURE**
 Stefoff, R. A different mirror for young people 305.8
CULTURAL POLICY
 See also Culture; Intellectual life
**CULTURAL PROPERTY -- PROTECTION -- JUVENILE
 LITERATURE**
 Abouraya, K. L. Hands around the library 962.055
CULTURAL RELATIONS
 See also Intellectual cooperation; International coop-
 eration; International relations
CULTURAL TOURISM
 See also Tourist trade
CULTURE
 Banting, E. England 942
CULTURE -- JUVENILE LITERATURE
 Foo Yuk Yee Malaysia 959.5
 Kent, D. Mexico 972
 Sheehan, S. Malta 945.8
CULTURE CONFLICT
 See also Ethnic relations; Ethnopsychology; Race re-
 lations
Culture in action [series]

D

D is for drums. Chorao, K.   **975.5**

D'Adamo, Anthony
Ames, L. J. Draw 50 birds   **743**

D'Adamo, Francesco
Iqbal   **Fic**

D'Agnese, Joseph
Blockhead   **92**

D'Agnese, Joseph
Blockhead   **92**
Kiernan, D. Signing our lives away   **920**

D'Aluisio, Faith
Menzel, P. What the world eats   **641.3**

D'Amico, Carmela
Ella sets sail   **E**
Ella sets the stage   **E**
Ella takes the cake   **E**
Ella the Elegant Elephant   **E**
Suki, the very loud bunny   **E**

D'Amico, Joan
The coming to America cookbook   **641.5**
The science chef   **641.3**
The math chef   **510**

D'Amico, Steven
(il) The Hanukkah hop   **E**

D'Amico, Steven
D'Amico, C. Ella sets sail   **E**
D'Amico, C. Ella sets the stage   **E**
D'Amico, C. Ella takes the cake   **E**
D'Amico, C. Ella the Elegant Elephant   **E**
D'Amico, C. Suki, the very loud bunny   **E**
(il) The Hanukkah hop   **E**

D'Anda, Carlos
(il) Farshtey, G. Bionicle #1: rise of the Toa Nuva   **741.5**

D'Antona, Robin
Kevorkian, M. 101 facts about bullying   **302.3**

D'Argo, Laura
(il) Carson, M. K. The Wright Brothers for kids   **629.13**

D'Aulaire, Edgar Parin
D'Aulaire, I. Foxie   **E**
D'Aulaire, I. The terrible troll-bird   **398.2**
D'Aulaire, I. The two cars   **E**

D'Aulaire, Ingri
Foxie   **E**
The terrible troll-bird   **398.2**
The two cars   **E**

D'Cruz, Anna-Marie
Make your own books   **686**
Make your own masks   **646.4**
Make your own musical instruments   **784.19**
Make your own puppets   **791.5**
Make your own purses and bags   **646.4**
Make your own slippers and shoes   **685**

D'Harcourt, Claire
Masterpieces up close   **750**

D'Lacey, Chris
Gauge   **Fic**
Gruffen   **Fic**

D.W. all wet. Brown, M. T.   **E**
D.W.'s library card. Brown, M. T.   **E**

Da Costa, Deborah
Hanukkah moon   **E**

Da wild, da crazy, da Vinci. Scieszka, J.   **Fic**

Dabcovich, Lydia
The polar bear son   **398.2**

Dabek, Lisa
     About

Montgomery, S. Quest for the tree kangaroo   **599.2**

Dabrowski, Kristen
My first monologue book   **812**
My second monologue book   **812**
My third monologue book   **812**

Dacey, Bob
(il) Firestone, M. What's the difference between a frog and a toad?   **597.8**
(il) Koontz, R. M. What's the difference between a butterfly and a moth?   **595.7**
(il) Manushkin, F. Miriam's cup   **222**

The dachshund. Schweitzer, K.   **636.7**

DaCosta, Barbara
Nighttime Ninja   **E**

Dad and Pop. Bennett, K.   **E**
Dad, Jackie, and me. Uhlberg, M.   **E**

DADAISM -- FICTION
Jackson, S. Mimi's Dada Catifesto   **E**

Dadblamed Union Army cow. Fletcher, S.   **E**

Daddo, Andrew
Goodnight, me   **E**

Daddy Adventure Day. Keane, D.   **E**
Daddy calls me doodlebug. Lester, J. D.   **E**
The Daddy Goose treasury. French, V.   **E**
Daddy hug. Warnes, T.   **E**
Daddy makes the best spaghetti. Hines, A. G.   **E**
Daddy, papa, and me. Newman, L.   **E**
Daffodil, crocodile. Jenkins, E.   **E**
The dagger Quick. Eames, B.   **Fic**

Dahl, Michael
Alien snow   **741.5**
Guardian of Earth   **Fic**
The man behind the mask   **Fic**
Nap time for Kitty   **E**

Dahl, Roald, 1916-1990
The BFG   **Fic**
Charlie and the chocolate factory   **Fic**
The enormous crocodile   **Fic**
James and the giant peach   **Fic**
The magic finger   **Fic**
Matilda   **Fic**
The missing golden ticket and other splendiferous secrets   **92**
More about Boy   **92**
Vile verses   **821**
     About
Dahl, R. More about Boy   **92**
Dahl, R. The missing golden ticket and other splendiferous secrets   **92**

Dahlia. McClintock, B.   **E**

Daigle, Stephan
Charles, V. M. The birdman   **E**

Daigneault, Sylvie
(il) Milway, K. S. The good garden   **Fic**

The Daily Comet. Asch, F.   **E**
Daily life in a Plains Indian village, 1868. Terry, M. B. H.   **970.004**

DAIRIES See Dairying
DAIRY CATTLE
     See also Cattle; Dairying
DAIRY CATTLE -- JUVENILE LITERATURE
Gibbons, G. The milk makers   **637**
DAIRY FARMING See Dairying
DAIRY INDUSTRY See Dairying
DAIRY PROCESSING -- JUVENILE LITERATURE
Malam, J. Journey of a glass of milk   **637**
DAIRY-FREE COOKING
     See also Cooking
DAIRYING

Hopgood, T. Wow! said the owl	E
Lamb, A. Tell me the day backwards	E
Levine, A. A. Monday is one day	E
The loud book!	E
Martin, R. Moon dreams	E
Melvin, A. Counting birds	E
Milgrim, D. Time to get up, time to go	E
Ormerod, J. Miss Mouse's day	E
Roode, D. Little Bea	E
Rosenthal, A. K. Yes Day!	E
Rylant, C. All in a day	E
Spanyol, J. Little neighbors on Sunnyside Street	E
Viorst, J. Alexander and the terrible, horrible, no good, very bad day	E
Williams, V. B. Lucky song	E
Yee, W. H. Summer days and nights	E

DAY -- JUVENILE LITERATURE

Bailey, J. Sun up, sun down	525
Day and night. Rau, D. M.	508
A **day** at the New Amsterdam Theatre. Amendola, D.	792.6
Day by day. Gal, S.	E
The **day** Dirk Yeller came to town. Casanova, M.	E

DAY DREAMS *See* Fantasy

The **day** I had to play with my sister. Bonsall, C. N.	E
A **day** in the life of Murphy. Provensen, A.	E

A day in the life. Rain forest animals [series]

Ganeri, A. Anaconda	597.96
Ganeri, A. Capybara	599.35
Ganeri, A. Howler monkey	599.8
Ganeri, A. Jaguar	599.75
Ganeri, A. Lemur	599.8
Ganeri, A. Macaw	598
Ganeri, A. Orangutan	599.8
Ganeri, A. Piranha	597
Ganeri, A. Poison dart frog	597.8
Ganeri, A. Tarantula	595.4

A day in the life. sea animals [series]

Spilsbury, L. Jellyfish	593.5
Spilsbury, L. Octopus	594
Spilsbury, L. Sea turtle	597.92
Spilsbury, L. Seal	599.79

A day in the life: desert animals [series]

Ganeri, A. Arabian oryx	599.64
Ganeri, A. Fennec fox	599.77
Ganeri, A. Meerkat	599.74
Ganeri, A. Scorpion	595.4

A day in the life: sea animals [series]

Spilsbury, L. Dolphin	599.5
A **day** in the office of Doctor Bugspit. Gravel, E.	741.5
The **day** Jimmy's boa ate the wash. Noble, T. H.	E
The **day** Leo said I hate you. Harris, R. H.	E
Day light, night light. Branley, F. M.	535
The **day** of Ahmed's secret. Heide, F. P.	E

DAY OF ATONEMENT *See* Yom Kippur

Day of the Dead. Johnston, T.	394.2

DAY OF THE DEAD

See also Holidays

The **day** Ray got away. Johnson, A.	E
The **day** the animals came. Weller, F. W.	E
The **day** the babies crawled away. Rathmann, P.	E
The **day** the cow sneezed. Flora, J.	E
The **day** the dinosaurs died. Brown, C. L.	567.9
The **day** Tiger Rose said goodbye.	E
The **day** we danced in underpants. Wilson, S.	E
A **day** with Dad. Holmberg, B. R.	E
A **day** with paramedics. Shepherd, J.	362.18
A **day** with Wilbur Robinson. Joyce, W.	E

Day, Alexandra

Carl and the puppies	E
Carl's sleepy afternoon	E
Frank and Ernest	E
Frank and Ernest play ball	E
Good dog, Carl	E

Day, Alyson

(ed) Creech, S. The great unexpected	Fic

Day, Betsy

(il) Press, J. Around-the-world art & activities	372.5

Day, Jeff

Don't touch that!	615.9

Day, Karen

A million miles from Boston	Fic

Day, Larry

(il) Crowley, N. Nanook & Pryce	E
(il) Fradin, D. B. Duel!	973.4
(il) Fradin, D. B. Let it begin here!	973.3
(il) Jurmain, S. The worst of friends	973.4
(il) Morris, R. T. Bye-bye, baby!	E
(il) Winters, K. Colonial voices	973.3

Day, Nancy Raines

On a windy night	E
The **Day-Glo** brothers. Barton, C.	535.6

Dayrell, Elphinstone

Why the Sun and the Moon live in the sky	398.2

DAYS

See also Calendars

DAYS -- FICTION

Himmelman, J. Chickens to the rescue	E
Lobel, A. One lighthouse, one moon	E
Pullen, Z. Friday my Radio Flyer flew	E

Days of change [series]

Bodden, V. Columbus reaches the New World	970.01
Bodden, V. Man walks on the Moon	629.45
Riggs, K. The French Revolution	944.04
Days of the ducklings. McMillan, B.	598.4
Days to celebrate. Hopkins, L. B.	051
The **Daytona** 500. Pimm, N. R.	796.72
The **dazzle** disaster dinner party. Draper, S. M.	Fic
A **dazzling** display of dogs.	811
Dazzling dragonflies. Glaser, L.	595.7
Dazzling science projects with light and color. Gardner, R.	535

DC super heroes. Batman [series]

Dahl, M. The man behind the mask	Fic

DC super heroes: Green Lantern [series]

Dahl, M. Guardian of Earth	Fic

DC super heroes: The Flash [series]

Sonneborn, S. Shell shocker	Fic
DC super heroes: The ultimate pop-up book. Reinhart, M.	741.5

DC super-pets! [series]

Hines-Stephens, S. Midway monkey madness	Fic
Sazaklis, J. Royal rodent rescue	Fic

DC superheroes. Batman [series]

Fein, E. My frozen valentine	Fic

De Angeli, Marguerite Lofft

The door in the wall	Fic
Thee, Hannah!	Fic

De Campi, Alex

Kat & Mouse: Teacher torture	741.5

De Capua, Sarah

The Cheyenne	970.004
The Choctaw	970.004
Colombia	986.1
The Comanche	970.004
The Menominee	970.004
The Shawnee	970.004
The Shoshone	970.004
The Tuskegee airmen	940.54

Roly Poly pangolin   E

DEWEY DECIMAL CLASSIFICATION

Donovan, S. Bob the Alien discovers the Dewey decimal system   **025.4**

DEWEY DECIMAL CLASSIFICATION

    See also Library classification

Dewey the library cat. Myron, V.   **636.8**

Dewey, Ariane

Aruego, J. The last laugh   E

Aruego, J. Weird friends   **577.8**

(il) Beaumont, K. Duck, duck, goose!   E

(il) Bruchac, J. How Chipmunk got his stripes   **398.2**

(il) Bruchac, J. Raccoon's last race   **398.2**

(il) Bruchac, J. Turtle's race with Beaver   **398.2**

Splash!   E

(il) Five little ducks   **782.42**

(il) Ginsburg, M. The chick and the duckling   E

(il) Sharmat, M. Gregory, the terrible eater   E

Dewey, Jennifer

Once I knew a spider   E

DeYoe, Aaron

(il) The mighty Quinn   **Fic**

DeYoe, Katie

(il) The mighty Quinn   **Fic**

Dheenshaw, Cleve

Whitfield, S. Simon says gold: Simon Whitfield's pursuit of athletic excellence   **92**

Dhilawala, Sakina

Bassis, V. Ukraine   **947.7**

Armenia   **947.5**

Sheehan, P. Luxembourg   **949.35**

Dhom, Christel

The Advent Craft and Activity Book   **745**

Di Capua, Michael

(ed) My brother's book   **808**

Di Domenico, Kelly

Women scientists who changed the world   **509.2**

Di Giacomo, Kris

(il) Rabbit and the Not-So-Big-Bad Wolf   E

Di Salle, Rachel

Junk drawer jewelry   **745.594**

Dia's story cloth. Cha, D.   **305.8**

DIABETES

Glaser, J. Juvenile diabetes   **616.4**

Loughrey, A. Explaining diabetes   **616.4**

Pirner, C. W. Even little kids get diabetes   **616.4**

Robbins, L. How to deal with diabetes   **616.4**

DIABETES

    See also Diseases

DIAGNOSIS

    See also Medicine

Diakite, Penda

I lost my tooth in Africa   E

Dial easy-to-read [series]

Hall, K. Creepy riddles   **793.73**

Hall, K. Dino riddles   **793.73**

Hall, K. Ribbit riddles   **793.73**

Hall, K. Snakey riddles   **793.73**

Hall, K. Turkey riddles   **793.73**

Holub, J. Why do birds sing?   **598**

Holub, J. Why do cats meow?   **636.8**

Holub, J. Why do dogs bark?   **636.7**

Holub, J. Why do horses neigh?   **636.1**

Holub, J. Why do rabbits hop?   **636.9**

Holub, J. Why do snakes hiss?   **597.96**

Marshall, E. Fox and his friends   E

Marshall, E. Three by the sea   E

McMullan, K. Pearl and Wagner: four eyes   E

McMullan, K. Pearl and Wagner: one funny day   E

Van Leeuwen, J. Oliver the Mighty Pig   E

Dial M for mongoose. Hale, B.   **Fic**

Dial-a-ghost. Ibbotson, E.   **Fic**

Diamand, Emily

Flood and fire   **Fic**

Raiders' ransom   **Fic**

Diamant-Cohen, Betsy

(ed) Children's services   **027.62**

Booktalking bonanza   **028.5**

Crash course in library services to preschool children   **027.62**

Early literacy programming en Espanol   **027.6**

A **diamond** in the desert. Fitzmaurice, K.   **Fic**

Diamond Jim Dandy and the sheriff. Burell, S.   E

Diamond life. Smith, C. R.   **796.357**

The **diamond** of Darkhold. DuPrau, J.   **Fic**

Diamond, Donna

(il) Paterson, K. Bridge to Terabithia   **Fic**

DIAMONDS

Moore, H. The story behind diamonds   **553.8**

DIAMONDS

    See also Carbon; Precious stones

DIARIES

Hesse, K. Stowaway   **Fic**

Mack, J. Journals and blogging   **808**

Stewart, S. The journey   E

Webb, S. Looking for seabirds   **598**

Wilson, N. H. Mountain pose   **Fic**

DIARIES

    See also Literature

DIARIES -- FICTION

Cavanaugh, N. J. This journal belongs to Ratchet   **Fic**

Patron, S. Behind the masks   **Fic**

DIARIES -- JUVENILE FICTION

Fleischman, P. The Matchbox diary   E

DIARISTS

Frank, A. The diary of a young girl: the definitive edition   **940.53**

Halilbegovich, N. My childhood under fire   **949.7**

Hurwitz, J. Anne Frank: life in hiding   **940.53**

Metselaar, M. Anne Frank: her life in words and pictures   **92**

Rol, R. v. d. Anne Frank, beyond the diary   **940.53**

Rubin, S. G. The Anne Frank Case: Simon Wiesenthal's search for the truth   **92**

Diary of a baby wombat. French, J.   E

Diary of a fly. Cronin, D.   E

The **diary** of a killer cat. Fine, A.   **Fic**

Diary of a spider. Cronin, D.   E

Diary of a wimpy kid [series]

Kinney, J. The third wheel   **Fic**

Diary of a wimpy kid: dog days. Kinney, J.   **Fic**

Diary of a wimpy kid: Greg Heffley's journal. Kinney, J.   **Fic**

Diary of a wimpy kid: Rodrick rules. Kinney, J.   **Fic**

Diary of a wimpy kid: the last straw. Kinney, J.   **Fic**

Diary of a wombat. French, J.   E

Diary of a worm.   E

The **diary** of a young girl: the definitive edition. Frank, A.   **940.53**

The **diary** of Melanie Martin; or, How I survived Matt the Brat, Michelangelo, and the Leaning Tower of Pizza. Weston, C.   **Fic**

Dias, Bartholomeu, 1450?-1500

About

Fritz, J. Around the world in a hundred years   **910.92**

Diaz, David

(il) Andrews-Goebel, N. The pot that Juan built   **738**

(il) Bernier-Grand, C. T. Cesar   **811**

(il) Bernier-Grand, C. T. Pablo Picasso   **709.2**

Dubuc, Marianne
　Animal masquerade　　　　　　　　　　　E
　In front of my house　　　　　　　　　　E

DuBurke, Randy
　(il) Omololu, C. J.　When it's six o'clock in San Francisco　E
The **Duchess** of Whimsy.　De Seve, R.　　　E
Duck.　Savage, S.　　　　　　　　　　　598
Duck.　Johnson, J.　　　　　　　　　　598
Duck.　Cecil, R.　　　　　　　　　　　E
Duck & Company.　Caple, K.　　　　　　E
Duck & Company Christmas.　Caple, K.　E
Duck & Goose.　Hills, T.　　　　　　　E
Duck at the door.　Urbanovic, J.　　　　E
Duck for a day.　McKinlay, M.　　　　　Fic
Duck for President.　Cronin, D.　　　　　E
Duck for Turkey Day.　Jules, J.　　　　　E
Duck hunting.　Adamson, T. K.　　　　　799.2
Duck in the truck.　Alborough, J.　　　　E
Duck on a bike.　Shannon, D.　　　　　　E
Duck says don't!　　　　　　　　　　　E
Duck skates.　Berry, L.　　　　　　　　E
Duck sock hop.　Kohuth, J.　　　　　　　E
The **duck** who played the kazoo.　Sklansky, A. E.　E
Duck! Rabbit!　Rosenthal, A. K.　　　　　E
Duck's tale.　Straaten, H. v.　　　　　　E
Duck, duck, goose!　Beaumont, K.　　　　E
Duckie's ducklings.　Barry, F.　　　　　E
The **duckling** gets a cookie!?　　　　　　E

DUCKLINGS
　Ziefert, H.　A dozen ducklings lost and found　E
Ducks.　Mara, W.　　　　　　　　　　　598
Ducks.　Minden, C.　　　　　　　　　　636.5

DUCKS
　Adamson, T. K.　Duck hunting　　　　　　799.2
　Cronin, D.　Duck for President　　　　　　E
　Cronin, D.　Giggle, giggle, quack　　　　　E
　Goldin, A. R.　Ducks don't get wet　　　　598
　Johnson, J.　Duck　　　　　　　　　　　598
　Luthardt, K.　Peep!　　　　　　　　　　E
　Mara, W.　Ducks　　　　　　　　　　　598
　McMillan, B.　Days of the ducklings　　　　598.4
　Minden, C.　Ducks　　　　　　　　　　　636.5
　Savage, S.　Duck　　　　　　　　　　　598
　Shannon, D.　Duck on a bike　　　　　　　E

DUCKS
　See also Birds; Poultry

DUCKS -- FICTION
　The duckling gets a cookie!?　　　　　　E
　Kohuth, J.　Duck sock hop　　　　　　　E
　Lucky Ducklings　　　　　　　　　　　E
　Lulu and the duck in the park　　　　　　Fic

DUCKS -- FOLKLORE
　Paterson, K.　The tale of the mandarin ducks　398.24
　Van Laan, N.　Shingebiss　　　　　　　　398.2

DUCKS -- JUVENILE FICTION
　Bunting, E.　Have you seen my new blue socks?　E

DUCKS -- JUVENILE LITERATURE
　Goldin, A. R.　Ducks don't get wet　　　　598

DUCKS -- PICTORIAL WORKS -- JUVENILE FICTION
　Peters, L. W.　Cold little duck, duck, duck　E

DUCKS -- POETRY
　Lear, E.　Edward Lear's The duck & the kangaroo　821

DUCKS -- SONGS
　Bates, I.　Five little ducks　　　　　　　782.42
　Five little ducks　　　　　　　　　　　782.42
Ducks don't get wet.　Goldin, A. R.　　　598
Ducks don't wear socks.　Nedwidek, J.　　E
Ducks go vroom.　Kohuth, J.　　　　　　E

Duddle, Jonny
　(il) London, C. A.　We are not eaten by yaks　Fic
　(il) Thompson, K.　Highway robbery　　　Fic
　(il) Thompson, K.　Most wanted　　　　　Fic
Dude!　　　　　　　　　　　　　　　810

Dudley, David L.
　The bicycle man　　　　　　　　　　　Fic

DUE PROCESS OF LAW
　See also Administration of justice;　Civil rights
Duel!　Fradin, D. B.　　　　　　　　　973.4

DUELING
　See also Manners and customs;　Martial arts

Duey, Kathleen
　Following magic　　　　　　　　　　　Fic
　The full moon　　　　　　　　　　　　Fic
　Lara and the gray mare　　　　　　　　　Fic
　Silence and stone　　　　　　　　　　　Fic
　Wishes and wings　　　　　　　　　　　Fic

Duffey, Betsy
　Byars, B. C.　Cat diaries　　　　　　　　S
　Byars, B. C.　Dog diaries　　　　　　　S
　Byars, B. C.　The SOS file　　　　　　　Fic

Duffy, Carol Ann
　The gift　　　　　　　　　　　　　　E

Duffy, Chris
　Nursery rhyme comics　　　　　　　　　741.5

Duffy, Daniel M.
　(il) Cohen, B.　Molly's pilgrim　　　　　E

Dugan, Karen
　(il) Lankford, M. D.　Christmas around the world　394.26
　(il) Lankford, M. D.　Mazes around the world　793.73
　(il) Wadsworth, G.　Camping with the president　92

Dugar, Divya
　Ali, R.　Slumgirl dreaming　　　　　　　92

Duggleby, John
　Story painter: the life of Jacob Lawrence　759.13

Duivenvoorden, Yvonne
　(il) What's for lunch?　　　　　　　　　371.7
Duke Ellington.　Pinkney, A. D.　　　　781.65
Duke Ellington.　Stein, S.　　　　　　　92
Duke Ellington's Nutcracker suite.　Celenza, A. H.　E

Duke, Kate
　Ready for pumpkins　　　　　　　　　　E

Duke, Kate
　(il) Baker, B.　One Saturday evening　　　E

Duke, Shirley Smith
　Infections, infestations, and disease　　　616.9
　You can't wear these genes　　　　　　　576.5
The **dulcimer** boy.　　　　　　　　　　Fic

DULCIMERS -- FICTION
　The dulcimer boy　　　　　　　　　　　Fic
Dull Knife, Cheyenne Chief, d. 1883
　　　　　　　　　　About
　Ehrlich, A.　Wounded Knee: an Indian history of the American West　970.004

Dumbleton, Mike
　Cat　　　　　　　　　　　　　　　　E

Dumm, Brian Caleb
　(il) Kenney, K. L.　Firefighters at work　628.9
　(il) Kenney, K. L.　Librarians at work　　020
　(il) Kenney, K. L.　Mail carriers at work　383
　(il) Kenney, K. L.　Nurses at work　　　610.73
　(il) Kenney, K. L.　Police officers at work　363.2
　(il) Kenney, K. L.　Teachers at work　　　371.1

Dumont, Jean-François
　The chickens build a wall　　　　　　　E
Dumpling days.　Lin, G.　　　　　　　　Fic
Dumpling soup.　Rattigan, J. K.　　　　　E

Dutch colonies in America. Englar, M.   **974.7**
DUTIES *See* Tariff; Taxation
Dutton easy reader [series]
    Thomas, S. M. A Good Knight's rest   **E**
    Thomas, S. M. Good night, Good Knight   **E**
Dutton, Mike
    (il) Newman, L. Donovan's big day   **E**
Dutton, Sandra
    Mary Mae and the gospel truth   **Fic**
DUTY
       See also Ethics; Human behavior
Duval, Kathy
    The Three Bears' Halloween   **E**
Duvoisin, Roger
    Petunia   **E**
    (il) Tresselt, A. R. Hide and seek fog   **E**
    (il) Tresselt, A. R. White snow, bright snow   **E**
Duwel, Lucretia I.
    Simpson, M. S. Bringing classes into the public library **027.62**
DWARF TREES
       See also Trees
DWARFISM -- FICTION
    Graff, L. The thing about Georgie   **Fic**
DWELLINGS
    Ashman, L. Castles, caves, and honeycombs   **E**
    DiSalvo, D. A castle on Viola Street   **E**
DWELLINGS *See* Domestic architecture; Houses; Housing
DWELLINGS -- DESIGN AND CONSTRUCTION -- FIC-
TION
    Bean, J. Building our house   **E**
DWELLINGS -- FICTION
    Columbus, C. House of secrets   **Fic**
DWELLINGS -- JUVENILE LITERATURE
    Newhouse, M. The house that Max built   **690**
DwellStudio (Firm)
    Good morning, toucan   **E**
    Goodnight, owl   **E**
Dwight Eisenhower. Mara, W.   **92**
Dwyer, Helen
    Earthquakes!   **551.2**
    Floods!   **551.48**
    Tsunamis!   **551.46**
Dyer, Alan
    Mission to the moon   **629.45**
Dyer, Brooke
    (il) Wilson, K. Mama always comes home   **E**
    (il) Yolen, J. Sleep, black bear, sleep   **E**
Dyer, Heather
    Ibby's magic weekend   **Fic**
Dyer, Jane
    (il) Appelt, K. Oh my baby, little one   **E**
    (il) Babies on the go   **E**
    (il) Beaumont, K. Move over, Rover   **E**
    (il) Krull, K. A woman for president   **92**
    (il) Lewis, R. A. Every year on your birthday   **E**
    (il) Lewis, R. A. I love you like crazy cakes   **E**
    (il) Melmed, L. K. Hurry! Hurry! Have you heard?   **E**
    (il) The Random House book of bedtime stories   **S**
    (il) Rosenthal, A. K. Cookies   **E**
    (il) Spinelli, E. Sophie's masterpiece   **E**
Dyer, Sarah
    Monster day at work   **E**
Dyer, Sarah
    Batty   **E**
    Monster day at work   **E**
DYES AND DYEING
       See also Color; Pigments; Textile chemistry; Textile
    industry

DYING PATIENTS *See* Terminally ill
Dying to meet you. Klise, K.   **Fic**
Dylan, Bob
    Man gave names to all the animals   **782.42**
Dylan, Bob, 1941-
          About
    When Bob met Woody   **92**
Dylan, Bob, 1941- -- Juvenile literature
          About
    When Bob met Woody   **92**
Dynamic drag racers. Sandler, M.   **629.228**
DYNAMICS
       See also Mathematics; Mechanics
DYSLEXIA -- FICTION
    Engle, M. The wild book   **Fic**
Dyson, Marianne J.
    Home on the moon   **629.45**
DYSTOPIAN FICTION
    Lowry, L. Son   **Fic**
DYSTOPIAN FICTION
       See also Fantasy fiction; Science fiction
DYSTOPIAN JUVENILE FICTION
    MacHale, D. J. SYLO   **Fic**
DYSTOPIAS
       See also Political science
DYSTOPIAS -- FICTION *See* Dystopian fiction

E

E-mergency. Lichtenheld, T.   **E**
Each kindness.   **E**
Each living thing. Ryder, J.   **E**
Each orange had 8 slices. Giganti, P.   **513.5**
Eagen, Rachel
    NASCAR   **796.72**
Eager. Fox, H.   **Fic**
Eager, Edward
    Half magic   **Fic**
Eagle Strike. Horowitz, A.   **Fic**
Eagles. Gish, M.   **598**
EAGLES
    Bardhan-Quallen, S. Flying eagle   **598**
    Gish, M. Eagles   **598**
    Markle, S. Eagles   **598**
    Read, T. C. Exploring the world of eagles   **598**
    Wilcox, C. Bald eagles   **598**
Eagles. Riggs, K.   **598.9**
EAGLES
       See also Birds; Birds of prey
Eagles. Markle, S.   **598**
EAGLES -- FICTION
    Brett, J. The 3 little dassies   **E**
EAGLES -- FOLKLORE
    Gregorowski, C. Fly, eagle, fly!   **398.2**
EAGLES -- JUVENILE LITERATURE
    Bardhan-Quallen, S. Flying eagle   **598**
    Gish, M. Eagles   **598**
    Riggs, K. Eagles   **598.9**
Eamer, Claire
    Before the World Was Ready   **509**
    Lizards in the sky   **591.4**
    Super crocs & monster wings   **591.3**
    The world in your lunch box   **641.3**
Eames, Brian
    The dagger Quick   **Fic**
EAR
    Larsen, C. S. Crust and spray   **612.8**

EPIDEMICS

    See also Diseases; Public health

Epidemics & plagues. Walker, R.   **614.4**

EPIDEMICS -- FICTION

  Anderson, L. H. Fever, 1793   **Fic**

  Giblin, J. The boy who saved Cleveland   **Fic**

  Moss, J. Winnie's war   **Fic**

EPIDEMICS -- HISTORY

  Plagues, pox, and pestilence   **614.4**

EPIGRAMS

    See also Wit and humor

Epilepsy. Bjorklund, R.   **616.8**

EPILEPSY

  Bender, L. Explaining epilepsy   **616.8**

  Bjorklund, R. Epilepsy   **616.8**

EPIPHANY

  Hoyt-Goldsmith, D. Three Kings Day   **394.26**

  Vidal, B. Federico and the Magi's gift   **E**

EPIPHANY -- FICTION

  Vidal, B. Federico and the Magi's gift   **E**

EPISTOLARY POETRY

    See also Poetry

EPITAPHS

    See also Biography; Cemeteries; Inscriptions; Tombs

EPITHETS *See* Names; Nicknames

EPIZOA *See* Parasites

Epossumondas. Salley, C.   **398.21**

Epossumondas plays possum. Salley, C.   **E**

Epossumondas saves the day. Salley, C.   **E**

Epstein, Adam Jay

  The familiars   **Fic**

  Secrets of the crown   **Fic**

Epstein, Joyce Levy

  Hutchins, D. J. Family reading night   **372.4**

Epstein, Lori

  (il) Delano, M. F. Master George's people   **973.4**

EQUAL RIGHTS AMENDMENTS

    See also Constitutions; Sex discrimination

EQUALITY

  King, M. L. J. I have a dream   **323.092**

EQUALITY

    See also Political science; Sociology

EQUATIONS

  Murphy, S. J. Safari Park   **512.9**

EQUATIONS

    See also Mathematics

EQUATIONS -- NUMERICAL SOLUTIONS -- JUVENILE LITERATURE

  Murphy, S. J. Safari Park   **512.9**

EQUESTRIANISM *See* Horsemanship

ER vets. Jackson, D. M.   **636.089**

Erak's ransom. Flanagan, J.   **Fic**

Erandi's braids. Madrigal, A. H.   **E**

Erased by a tornado! Rudolph, J.   **551.55**

The eraserheads. Banks, K.   **E**

Eratosthenes, 3rd cent. B.C.

    About

  The librarian who measured the earth   **520**

Ercolini, David

  (il) Lewis, K. Not inside this house!   **E**

Erdős, Paul, 1913-1996 -- Juvenile literature

    About

  Heiligman, D. The boy who loved math   **510.92**

Erdrich, Louise, 1954-

  The birchbark house   **Fic**

  Chickadee   **Fic**

  The game of silence   **Fic**

  The porcupine year   **Fic**

Ereth's birthday. Avi   **Fic**

Eric Carle's animals, animals.   **808.81**

Eric Carle's dragons dragons and other creatures that never were.   **808.81**

Erickson, Justin

  Alien abductions   **001.9**

Ericsson, Jennifer A.

  A piece of chalk   **E**

  Whoo goes there?   **E**

The Erie Canal. Kendall, M. E.   **386**

ERIE CANAL (N.Y.) -- JUVENILE LITERATURE

  Harness, C. The amazing impossible Erie Canal   **386**

Erika-san. Say, A.   **E**

Erikson, Rolf

  Designing a school library media center for the future   **027.8**

Eriksson, Eva

  (il) Holmberg, B. R. A day with Dad   **E**

  (il) Lindgren, B. Julia wants a pet   **E**

Ering, Timothy Basil

  (il) DiCamillo, K. The tale of Despereaux   **Fic**

  (il) Elliott, D. Finn throws a fit   **E**

  (il) Nelson, M. Snook alone   **E**

  (il) Wood, N. C. Mr. and Mrs. God in the Creation Kitchen   **E**

Eritrea. NgCheong-Lum, R.   **963.5**

Ernest L. Thayer's Casey at the bat. Thayer, E. L.   **811**

Ernest, the moose who doesn't fit. Rayner, C.   **E**

Ernie & Maud [series]

  Watts, F. Extraordinary Ernie and Marvelous Maud   **Fic**

  Watts, F. The greatest sheep in history   **Fic**

  Watts, F. The middle sheep   **Fic**

Ernst, Linda L.

  Baby rhyming time   **027.62**

Ernst, Lisa Campbell, 1957-

  The Gingerbread Girl   **E**

  The Gingerbread Girl goes animal crackers   **E**

  How things work in the house   **640**

  How things work in the yard   **578.7**

  Little Red Riding Hood: a newfangled prairie tale   **398.2**

  Round like a ball!   **E**

  Sam Johnson and the blue ribbon quilt   **E**

  Snow surprise   **E**

  Sylvia Jean, scout supreme   **E**

  The turn-around upside-down alphabet book   **E**

  Zinnia and Dot   **E**

EROS (GREEK DEITY)

  Craft, M. Cupid and Psyche   **292.1**

EROSION

  Stewart, M. How does sand become glass?   **666**

EROSION

    See also Geology

EROTIC ART

    See also Art; Erotica

EROTIC FILMS

    See also Motion pictures

EROTIC LITERATURE

    See also Erotica; Literature

EROTIC POETRY

    See also Erotic literature; Poetry

ERRORS -- FICTION

  Saltzberg, B. Beautiful oops!   **E**

ERRORS, SCIENTIFIC -- JUVENILE LITERATURE

  Kudlinski, K. V. Boy were we wrong about the solar system!   **523.2**

  YES mag (Periodical) Hoaxed!   **500**

Erskine, Kathryn

  The absolute value of Mike   **Fic**

  Mockingbird   **Fic**

Eruption. Smith, R.   **Fic**

Eruption! Rusch, E.   **363.34**

Esbaum, Jill

Apples for everyone   **634**

Everything spring   **508.2**

Seed, sprout, pumpkin, pie   **635**

Stanza   **E**

To the big top   **E**

Tom's tweet   **E**

Esbensen, Barbara Juster

Baby whales drink milk   **599.5**

Swing around the sun   **811**

Escape by night   **Fic**

Escape from Mr. Lemoncello's library. Grabenstein, C.   **Fic**

Escape from planet Yastol. Service, P. F.   **Fic**

Escape under the forever sky. Yohalem, E.   **Fic**

Escape velocity. Walden, M.   **Fic**

Escape! Fleischman, S.   **92**

ESCAPES

Spradlin, M. P. Daniel Boone's great escape   **92**

ESCAPES

See also Adventure and adventurers; Prisons

ESCAPES -- FICTION

Grifalconi, A. The village that vanished   **E**

ESCAPES -- IRELAND -- HISTORY -- 19TH CENTURY -- JUVENILE LITERATURE

Fradin, D. B. The Irish potato famine   **941.508**

Escaping the tiger. Manivong, L.   **Fic**

Escoffier, Michael

Rabbit and the Not-So-Big-Bad Wolf   **E**

Escriva, Vivi

Pio peep!   **398.8**

ESKIMOS *See* Inuit

ESKIMOS -- FICTION

George, J. C. Nutik, the wolf pup   **E**

Hill, K. Bo at Ballard Creek   **Fic**

Hobbs, W. Never say die   **Fic**

Riel, J. The snowstorm   **Fic**

ESKIMOS -- GREENLAND -- FICTION

The raiders   **Fic**

ESKIMOS -- JUVENILE FICTION

George, J. C. Nutik, the wolf pup   **E**

Espeland, Pamela

(ed) Fox, J. S. Get organized without losing it   **371.3**

Esperanza rising. Ryan, P. M.   **Fic**

Espinosa, Rod

The courageous princess   **741.5**

ESPIONAGE

Earnest, P. The real spy's guide to becoming a spy   **327.12**

Gilbert, A. Codes and ciphers   **652**

Gilbert, A. Spy school   **327.12**

Gilbert, A. Top technology   **621.389**

Janeczko, P. B. The dark game   **327.12**

Mitchell, S. K. Spies and lies   **327.12**

Mitchell, S. K. Spies, double agents, and traitors   **327.12**

Mitchell, S. K. Spy codes and ciphers   **652**

Mitchell, S. K. Spy gizmos and gadgets   **327.12**

Spyology   **327.12**

ESPIONAGE

See also Intelligence service; Secret service; Subversive activities

ESPIONAGE -- FICTION

Stone, P. Romeo blue   **Fic**

ESPIONAGE -- HISTORY -- 20TH CENTURY -- JUVENILE LITERATURE

Samuels, C. Spying and security   **940.54**

ESPIONAGE -- JUVENILE LITERATURE

Earnest, P. The real spy's guide to becoming a spy   **327.12**

ESPIONAGE STORIES *See* Spy stories

ESQUIMAUX *See* Inuit

Essakalli, Julie Klear

(il) Alalou, A. The butter man   **E**

ESSAY

See also Literature

ESSAYISTS

Abrams, D. Gary Soto   **92**

Adler, D. A. A picture book of Thomas Jefferson   **973.4**

The adventures of Mark Twain by Huckleberry Finn   **92**

Bradley, K. B. Jefferson's sons   **Fic**

Brown, D. American boy: the adventures of Mark Twain   **818**

Bryant, J. A river of words: the story of William Carlos Williams   **92**

Demi Gandhi   **954.03**

Dray, P. Yours for justice, Ida B. Wells   **92**

Ellis, S. From reader to writer   **028**

Fleischman, S. The trouble begins at 8   **92**

Fleming, C. The hatmaker's sign   **E**

Grant, A. Robert Louis Stevenson's Strange case of Dr. Jekyll and Mr. Hyde   **741.5**

Harness, C. The literary adventures of Washington Irving   **92**

Johnson, D. B. Henry hikes to Fitchburg   **E**

Jurmain, S. The worst of friends   **973.4**

Kerley, B. The extraordinary Mark Twain (according to Susy)   **92**

Kerley, B. Those rebels, John and Tom   **973.4**

Kerley, B. Walt Whitman   **92**

Macdonald, F. Kidnapped   **741.5**

McCurdy, M. Walden then & now   **818**

Miller, B. M. Thomas Jefferson for kids   **92**

Miller, W. Richard Wright and the library card   **92**

Mora, P. Tomas and the library lady   **E**

Murphy, J. Across America on an emigrant train   **385**

Myers, W. D. Ida B. Wells   **92**

Pinkney, A. D. Let it shine   **920**

Red Bird sings: the story of Zitkala-Sa   **92**

Rubin, S. G. The Anne Frank Case: Simon Wiesenthal's search for the truth   **92**

Sfar, J. The little prince   **741.5**

Smith, L. John, Paul, George & Ben   **E**

Whiting, J. W.E.B. Du Bois   **92**

Wilkinson, P. Gandhi   **92**

Winter, J. Gertrude is Gertrude is Gertrude is Gertrude   **92**

Yolen, J. Lost boy   **92**

Yolleck, J. Paris in the spring with Picasso   **E**

ESSENCES AND ESSENTIAL OILS

See also Distillation; Oils and fats

ESSENES

See also Jews

Essential documents for school libraries. MacDonell, C. **025.1**

Essential lives [series]

Gitlin, M. Sonia Sotomayor   **92**

Peterson-Hilleque, V. J.K. Rowling, extraordinary author   **92**

Essential reference services for today's school media specialists. Lanning, S.   **025.5**

Essex, Robert Devereux, 2nd Earl of, 1566-1601

About

Curry, J. L. The Black Canary   **Fic**

Essex, Robert Devereux, 2nd Earl of, 1566-1601 -- Fiction

About

Curry, J. L. The Black Canary   **Fic**

ESTATE PLANNING

See also Personal finance; Planning

Estela's swap. O'Neill, A.   **E**

Estes, Eleanor

Ginger Pye   **Fic**

The hundred dresses   **Fic**

The Moffats   **Fic**

Docalavich, H. Denmark   **948.9**
Docalavich, H. Poland   **943.8**
Docalavich, H. Sweden   **948.5**
Etingoff, K. Greece   **949.5**
Etingoff, K. Portugal   **946.9**
Hanks, R. R. Spain   **946**
Indovino, S. C. Spain   **946**
EUTHANASIA
  See also Homicide; Medical ethics
Eva Peron. Favor, L. J.   **92**
EVACUATION OF CIVILIANS
  See also Civil defense; Disaster relief
EVACUATION OF CIVILIANS -- VIETNAM
Skrypuch, M. F. Last airlift   **959.704**
EVALUATION OF LITERATURE *See* Best books; Books
  and reading; Criticism; Literature -- History and criticism
Evans, Arthur John Sir, 1851-1941
About
Scarre, C. The Palace of Minos at Knossos   **728.8**
Evans, Bill
It's raining fish and spiders   **551.6**
Evans, Cambria
Bone soup   **E**
  (il) The one and only Stuey Lewis   **Fic**
  (il) Stuey Lewis against all odds   **Fic**
Evans, Dilys
Show & tell   **741.6**
Evans, Freddi Williams
Hush harbor   **E**
Evans, Kristina
What's special about me, Mama?   **E**
Evans, Leslie
  (il) Bulion, L. At the sea floor cafe   **811**
  (il) Bulion, L. Hey there, stink bug!   **595.7**
  (il) Gerber, C. Leaf jumpers   **E**
  (il) Gerber, C. Winter trees   **582.16**
  (il) Schnur, S. Autumn   **793.73**
  (il) Schnur, S. Spring   **E**
  (il) Schnur, S. Summer   **793.73**
  (il) Schnur, S. Winter   **E**
Evans, Lezlie
Can you greet the whole wide world?   **413**
Who loves the little lamb?   **E**
Evans, Lissa
Horten's incredible illusions   **Fic**
Horten's miraculous mechanisms   **Fic**
Evans, Michael
The adventures of Medical Man   **616**
Poggle and the treasure   **E**
Evans, Nate
  (jt. auth) Brown, S. G. Bang! Boom! Roar!   **E**
  (jt. auth) Meet the beast   **Fic**
  (jt. auth) Numeroff, L. J. The Jellybeans and the big camp
    kickoff   **E**
  (jt. auth) Numeroff, L. J. Ponyella   **E**
Evans, Shane
  (il) Clinton, C. Hold the flag high   **973.7**
  (il) Clinton, C. When Harriet met Sojourner   **92**
Diggs, T. Chocolate me!   **E**
  (il) Grimes, N. When Gorilla goes walking   **811**
My brother Charlie   **E**
  (il) Rappaport, D. Free at last!   **305.8**
  (il) Rappaport, D. Nobody gonna turn me 'round   **323.1**
  (il) Smith, C. R. Black Jack: the ballad of Jack Johnson   **92**
  (il) Smith, H. A. The way a door closes   **Fic**
  (il) Washington, D. L. Li'l Rabbit's Kwanzaa   **E**
  (il) Whitehead, K. Art from her heart: folk artist Clementine
    Hunter   **92**

Underground   **973.7**
We march   **E**
Evans, Vince
  (il) Evans, N. Meet the beast   **Fic**
Eve (Biblical figure)
About
Ray, J. Adam and Eve and the Garden of Eden   **222**
Even an ostrich needs a nest. Kelly, I.   **598**
Even bad dogs go to heaven. Huneck, S.   **636.7**
Even higher! Kimmel, E. A.   **398.2**
Even little kids get diabetes. Pirner, C. W.   **616.4**
Even monsters need haircuts. McElligott, M.   **E**
Even or odd? Mattern, J.   **513**
EVENING AND CONTINUATION SCHOOLS
  See also Compulsory education; Continuing education;
  Education; Public schools; Schools; Secondary educa-
  tion; Technical education
Events. Butterfield, M.   **796.48**
Ever. Levine, G. C.   **Fic**
The **Everafter** War. Buckley, M.   **Fic**
EVEREST, MOUNT (CHINA AND NEPAL)
  Athans, S. K. Tales from the top of the world   **796.522**
  Jenkins, S. The top of the world   **796.52**
EVEREST, MOUNT (CHINA AND NEPAL) *See* Mount
  Everest (China and Nepal)
Everett, J. H.
  Haunted histories   **133.1**
Everglades. George, J. C.   **975.9**
The **Everglades.** Lynch, W.   **508**
EVERGLADES (FLA.) -- JUVENILE LITERATURE
  Larsen, L. One night in the Everglades   **577.097**
Everglades forever. Marx, T.   **577.6**
Everglades National Park. Jankowski, S.   **975.9**
EVERGLADES NATIONAL PARK (FLA.)
  Jankowski, S. Everglades National Park   **975.9**
**EVERGLADES NATIONAL PARK (FLA.) -- JUVENILE
  LITERATURE**
  George, J. C. Everglades   **975.9**
EVERGREENS
  See also Landscape gardening; Shrubs; Trees
Everitt, Betsy
Mean soup   **E**
Eversole, Robyn Harbert
East Dragon, West Dragon   **E**
Evert, Laura
Birds of prey   **598**
Every book is a social studies book. Libresco, A. S.   **372**
Every cowgirl needs a horse. Janni, R.   **E**
Every cowgirl needs dancing boots. Janni, R.   **E**
Every Friday. Yaccarino, D.   **E**
Every human has rights. National Geographic Society
  (U.S.)   **323**
Every planet has a place. Baines, R.   **523.2**
Every season. Rotner, S.   **508.2**
Every second something happens. San Jose, C.   **811**
Every soul a star. Mass, W.   **Fic**
Every thing on it. Silverstein, S.   **811**
Every year on your birthday. Lewis, R. A.   **E**
Every-day dress-up. Alko, S.   **E**
Everybody bonjours! Kimmelman, L.   **E**
Everybody bugs out. Margolis, L.   **Fic**
Everybody gets the blues. Staub, L.   **E**
Everybody has a bellybutton. Pringle, L. P.   **612.6**
Everybody has a teddy. Kroll, V. L.   **E**
Everybody was a baby once, and other poems. Ahlberg, A.   **811**
Everybody's revolution. Fleming, T. J.   **973.3**
Everyday economics [series]
  Morrison, J. Investing   **332.6**

Eyewitness disaster [series]

Dwyer, H. Earthquakes!	**551.2**
Dwyer, H. Tsunamis!	**551.46**
Royston, A. Hurricanes!	**551.55**
Royston, A. Storms!	**551.55**

Eyewitness Disaster [series]

Dwyer, H. Floods!	**551.48**

F

F is for fiesta. Elya, S. M.	**E**
F is for firefighting.	**628.9**
The **fabled** fifth graders of Aesop Elementary School. Fleming, C.	**Fic**
Fables. Lobel, A.	**Fic**

FABLES

See also Fiction; Literature

FABLES

Anansi the spider-man Anansi and the talking melon	**398.24**
Anansi the spider-man Anansi goes fishing	**398.24**
The ant and the grasshopper	**E**
Bannerman, H. The story of Little Babaji	**823**
Bolt, R. The hare and the tortoise and other fables of La Fontaine	**398.2**
Brown, M. Once a mouse	**398.2**
Burkert, R. Mouse & Lion	**E**
Cooney, B. Chanticleer and the fox	**E**
Country mouse and the city mouse Town mouse, country mouse	**398.24**
D'Aulaire, I. The two cars	**E**
De Paola, T. Tomie dePaola's Favorite nursery tales	**398.2**
Demi Buddha stories	**294.3**
Downard, B. The race of the century	**398.2**
Forest, H. The contest between the Sun and the Wind	**398.2**
Gregorowski, C. Fly, eagle, fly!	**398.2**
Hartman, B. The Lion storyteller book of animal tales	**398.2**
Hartman, B. Mr. Aesop's story shop	**398.2**
Hoberman, M. A. Very short fables to read together	**398.2**
Johnston, T. The tale of Rabbit and Coyote	**398.24**
Lester, J. The tales of Uncle Remus	**398.2**
MacDonald, M. R. Bat's big game	**398.2**
McDermott, G. Zomo the Rabbit	**398.24**
Moerbeek, K. Aesop's fables: a pop-up book of classic tales	**398.2**
Monkey and the crocodile The monkey and the crocodile	**398.2**
Morpurgo, M. The McElderry book of Aesop's fables	**398.2**
Naidoo, B. Aesop's fables	**398.2**
O'Malley, K. The great race	**398.2**
Oz, A. Suddenly in the depths of the forest	**Fic**
Palatini, M. Lousy rotten stinkin' grapes	**398.2**
Pinkney, J. The lion & the mouse	**E**
Shannon, G. Rabbit's gift	**398.2**
Stevens, J. Coyote steals the blanket	**398.2**
Three little pigs The three little pigs	**398.2**
Townley, R. The blue shoe	**Fic**
Trivizas, E. The three little wolves and the big bad pig	**398.24**
Valeri, M. E. The hare and the tortoise	**398.2**
Ward, H. The town mouse and the country mouse	**E**
Ward, H. The hare and the tortoise	**398.24**
Ward, H. The rooster and the fox	**E**
Ward, H. Unwitting wisdom	**398.2**
Waters, F. Aesop's fables	**398.2**
Wormell, C. Mice, morals, & monkey business	**398.2**
Young, E. Seven blind mice	**398.24**
Yuko-chan and the Daruma doll	**E**

FABLES -- JUVENILE LITERATURE

Bolt, R. The hare and the tortoise and other fables of La Fontaine	**398.2**
Buhler, C. v. But who will bell the cats?	**E**
Burkert, R. Mouse & Lion	**E**
Hoberman, M. A. Very short fables to read together	**398.2**
O'Malley, K. The great race	**398.2**
Pinkney, J. The lion & the mouse	**E**
Ward, H. Unwitting wisdom	**398.2**

FABRICS

Morris, N. Textiles	**677**

FABRICS

See also Decorative arts

FABRICS -- JUVENILE LITERATURE

Roessel, M. Songs from the loom	**746.1**
The **fabulous** bouncing Chowder. Brown, P.	**E**
Fabulous bridges. Graham, I.	**624.2**
A **fabulous** fair alphabet. Frasier, D.	**E**
The **fabulous** feud of Gilbert & Sullivan. Winter, J.	**E**
Fabulous fishes. Stockdale, S.	**597**
The **fabulous** flying machines of Alberto Santos-Dumont. Griffith, V.	**92**
Fabulous fractions. Long, L.	**513.2**
Fabulous! Christensen, B.	**92**

FACE

Alda, A. Here a face, there a face	**E**

FACE

See also Head

Face bug. Lewis, J. P.	**E**

FACE IN ART

Close, C. Chuck Close	**759.13**
Dawes, K. S. N. I saw your face	**811**
Emberley, E. Ed Emberley's drawing book of faces	**743**
Kesselring, S. 5 steps to drawing faces	**746**
Robert, F. Find a face	**E**
Face painting. Silver, P.	**745.5**

FACE PAINTING

Silver, P. Face painting	**745.5**

Face to face [series]

Brandenburg, J. Face to face with wolves	**599.77**
Doubilet, D. Face to face with sharks	**597**
Johns, C. Face to face with cheetahs	**599.75**
Joubert, B. Face to face with elephants	**599.67**
Joubert, B. Face to face with leopards	**599.75**
Joubert, B. Face to face with lions	**599.75**
Laman, T. Face to face with orangutans	**599.8**
Moffett, M. W. Face to face with frogs	**597.8**
Momatiuk, Y. Face to face with penguins	**598**
Momatiuk, Y. Face to face with wild horses	**599.66**
Murawski, D. Face to face with butterflies	**595.7**
Murawski, D. Face to face with caterpillars	**595.7**
Nichols, M. Face to face with gorillas	**599.8**
Nicklin, F. Face to face with dolphins	**599.5**
Nicklin, F. Face to face with whales	**599.5**
Rosing, N. Face to face with polar bears	**599.78**
Sartore, J. Face to face with grizzlies	**599.78**
Skerry, B. Face to face with manatees	**599.5**
Face to face with butterflies. Murawski, D.	**595.7**
Face to face with caterpillars. Murawski, D.	**595.7**
Face to face with cheetahs. Johns, C.	**599.75**
Face to face with dolphins. Nicklin, F.	**599.5**
Face to face with elephants. Joubert, B.	**599.67**
Face to face with frogs. Moffett, M. W.	**597.8**
Face to face with gorillas. Nichols, M.	**599.8**
Face to face with grizzlies. Sartore, J.	**599.78**
Face to face with leopards. Joubert, B.	**599.75**
Face to face with lions. Joubert, B.	**599.75**
Face to face with manatees. Skerry, B.	**599.5**
Face to face with orangutans. Laman, T.	**599.8**

(il) Johnson, R. L. Mighty animal cells **571.6**
FAIRNESS
    See also Conduct of life
FAIRS -- FICTION
    Tudor, T. Corgiville fair **E**
FAIRS -- JUVENILE FICTION
    Dicamillo, K. Two for one **Fic**
FAIRS -- POETRY
    Fitch, S. Night Sky Wheel Ride **811**
The **Fairy** Ring, or, Elsie and Frances Fool the World. Losure, M. **398**
Fairy tale feasts. Yolen, J. **641.5**
FAIRY TALE WRITERS
    Bolt, R. The hare and the tortoise and other fables of La Fontaine **398.2**
    Mann, E. Statue of Liberty **974.7**
Fairy tales. Doherty, B. **398.2**
FAIRY TALES
    See also Children's literature; Fiction
FAIRY TALES -- FICTION
    Healy, C. The hero's guide to saving your kingdom **Fic**
    Willems, M. Goldilocks and the three dinosaurs **E**
FAIRY TALES -- GRAPHIC NOVELS
    Aguirre, J. Giants beware! **741.5**
FAIRY TALES -- PARODIES, IMITATIONS, ETC. *See* Fractured fairy tales
FAIRY TALES -- POETRY
    Follow follow **811**
FAIRY TALES -- UNITED STATES
    Sandburg, C. Rootabaga stories **S**
Fairy tales of the Brothers Grimm. Grimm, J. **398.2**
Fairy trails. Elya, S. M. **E**
The **fairy-tale** detectives. Buckley, M. **Fic**
Faith. Ajmera, M. **200**
FAITH
    Walker, R. D. Mama says **E**
FAITH
    See also Religion; Salvation; Spiritual life; Theology; Virtue
FAITH -- FICTION
    Vigilante, D. Trouble with half a moon **Fic**
A **faith** like mine. Buller, L. **200**
Faith Ringgold. Venezia, M. **92**
Faith, hope, and Ivy June. Naylor, P. R. **Fic**
The **faithful** friend. San Souci, R. **398.21**
Fake foods. Johanson, P. **613.2**
Fake mustache. Angleberger, T. **Fic**
Falcon. Jessell, T. **E**
The **Falcon's** Malteser. Horowitz, A. **Fic**
Falconer, Ian
    Olivia **E**
    Olivia and the fairy princesses **E**
    (il) Olivia goes to Venice **E**
FALCONRY
    See also Game and game birds; Hunting
FALCONRY -- FICTION
    Lasky, K. Hawksmaid **Fic**
FALCONS
    Jessell, T. Falcon **E**
    Lunis, N. Peregrine falcon **598**
FALCONS -- FICTION
    George, J. C. My side of the mountain trilogy **Fic**
    Jessell, T. Falcon **E**
Falken, Linda C.
    Can you find it? America **759.13**
Falkenstern, Lisa
    A dragon moves in **E**
Falkenstern, Lisa

A dragon moves in **E**
    (il) Ward, J. The busy tree **E**
Fall. Smith, S. **508.2**
FALL *See* Autumn
Fall apples. Rustad, M. E. H. **634**
Fall harvests. Rustad, M. E. H. **631.5**
Fall leaves. Rustad, M. E. H. **581.4**
Fall mixed up. **E**
The **fall** of the Amazing Zalindas. Mack, T. **Fic**
Fall pumpkins. Rustad, M. E. H. **635**
Fall weather. Rustad, M. E. H. **508.2**
Fall's here [series]
    Rustad, M. E. H. Fall pumpkins **635**
Fall's here! [series]
    Rustad, M. E. H. Animals in fall **578.4**
    Rustad, M. E. H. Fall apples **634**
    Rustad, M. E. H. Fall harvests **631.5**
    Rustad, M. E. H. Fall leaves **581.4**
    Rustad, M. E. H. Fall weather **508.2**
Faller, Regis
    The adventures of Polo **E**
Falling down the page. **811**
Falling in. Dowell, F. O. **Fic**
FALLING STARS *See* Meteors
Falling up. Silverstein, S. **811**
Falls, Kat
    Rip tide **Fic**
Falls, Kat
    Dark life **Fic**
    Rip tide **Fic**
FALSE MEMORY SYNDROME
    See also Memory
Falvey, David
    Letters to a soldier **956.7**
Falvey, David -- Correspondence
    Falvey, D. Letters to a soldier **956.7**
Falwell, Cathryn
    David's drawings **E**
    Gobble, gobble **E**
    Pond babies **E**
    Scoot! **E**
    Shape capers **E**
    Turtle splash! **E**
FAME
    McDonald, M. Judy Moody gets famous **Fic**
FAME -- FICTION
    Phillipps, J. C. Wink: the ninja who wanted to nap **E**
Fame and glory in Freedom, Georgia. O'Connor, B. **Fic**
The **familiars.** Epstein, A. J. **Fic**
The **familiars** [series]
    Secrets of the crown **Fic**
FAMILIES -- FICTION
    Elliott, R. Zoo girl **E**
    Harris, R. H. Who's in my family? **E**
    Hip hip hooray! it's Family Day! **E**
    This is the rope **E**
FAMILIES -- JUVENILE FICTION
    Elliott, R. Zoo girl **E**
    Hip hip hooray! it's Family Day! **E**
    Stone, P. Romeo blue **Fic**
FAMILIES -- JUVENILE LITERATURE
    This is my family a first look at same sex parents **306.874**
FAMILIES -- MAINE -- JUVENILE FICTION
    Martin, A. M. Better to wish **Fic**
Families and their faiths [series]
    Hawker, F. Buddhism in Thailand **294.3**
    Hawker, F. Christianity in Mexico **282**
    Hawker, F. Hinduism in Bali **294.5**

Monte, R. The dragon of Krakow and other Polish stories **398.2**

Monte, R. The mermaid of Warsaw **398.2**

FOLKLORE -- PUERTO RICO
Montes, M. Juan Bobo goes to work **398.2**

FOLKLORE -- ROMANIA
Rascol, S. I. The impudent rooster **398.2**

FOLKLORE -- RUSSIA
Babouschka Baboushka and the three kings **398.2**

De las Casas, D. The gigantic sweet potato **398.2**

Ginsburg, M. Clay boy **398.2**

McCaughrean, G. Grandma Chickenlegs **398.209**

Pirotta, S. Firebird **398.2**

Polacco, P. Luba and the wren **398.2**

Shepard, A. The sea king's daughter **398.2**

Spirin, G. The tale of the Firebird **398.2**

Vasilisa the beauty Baba Yaga and Vasilisa the brave **398.21**

FOLKLORE -- RUSSIA -- JUVENILE LITERATURE
Ginsburg, M. Clay boy **398.2**

Mother Goose Babushka's Mother Goose **398.8**

Shepard, A. The sea king's daughter **398.2**

Spirin, G. The tale of the Firebird **398.2**

Vasilisa the beauty Baba Yaga and Vasilisa the brave **398.21**

FOLKLORE -- SCOTLAND
MacDonald, M. R. Too many fairies **398.2**

Pirican Pic and Pirican Mor **398.2**

FOLKLORE -- SOUTH AFRICA
Seeger, P. Abiyoyo **398.2**

FOLKLORE -- SOUTH AMERICA
Bateman, T. The Frog with the Big Mouth **398.2**

FOLKLORE -- SOUTHERN STATES
Chase, R. The Jack tales **398.2**

Curry, J. L. Hold up the sky; and other Native American tales from Texas and the Southern Plains **398.2**

Grandfather tales **398.2**

Salley, C. Epossumondas **398.21**

San Souci, R. Little Gold Star **398.2**

San Souci, R. Sister tricksters **398.2**

San Souci, R. The talking eggs **398.2**

Thomas, J. C. The three witches **398.2**

Thomas, J. C. What's the hurry, Fox? **398.2**

Wooldridge, C. N. Wicked Jack **398.21**

Yonder mountain **398.2**

FOLKLORE -- SPAIN
Kimmel, E. A. Medio Pollito **398.2**

FOLKLORE -- SPAIN -- JUVENILE LITERATURE
Campoy, F. I. Tales our abuelitas told **398.2**

FOLKLORE -- TIBET
Berger, B. All the way to Lhasa **398.2**

FOLKLORE -- TIBET (CHINA)
Berger, B. All the way to Lhasa **398.2**

FOLKLORE -- TURKEY
Demi The hungry coat **398.2**

A donkey reads **398.2**

Goha the wise fool **398.2**

Singh, R. Nearly nonsense **398.2**

FOLKLORE -- UKRAINE
Aylesworth, J. The mitten **398.2**

Brett, J. The mitten **398.2**

Kimmel, E. A. The spider's gift **398.2**

FOLKLORE -- UKRAINE -- JUVENILE LITERATURE
Kimmel, E. A. The spider's gift **398.2**

FOLKLORE -- UNITED STATES
Keats, E. J. John Henry **398.2**

Krensky, S. John Henry **398.2**

Krensky, S. Paul Bunyan **398.2**

Krensky, S. Pecos Bill **398.2**

Lester, J. John Henry **398.2**

Lyons, M. E. Roy makes a car **398.2**

McGill, A. Way up and over everything **398.2**

Miller, B. Davy Crockett gets hitched **398.2**

Miller, B. One fine trade **398.2**

Osborne, M. P. American tall tales **398.2**

San Souci, R. Cut from the same cloth **398.2**

San Souci, R. The secret of the stones **398.2**

Sanfield, S. The adventures of High John the Conqueror **398.2**

Schwartz, A. More scary stories to tell in the dark **398.2**

Schwartz, A. Scary stories 3 **398.2**

Schwartz, A. Scary stories to tell in the dark **398.25**

Stockings of buttermilk: American folktales **398.209**

Taily-po The tailypo **398.2**

Thomas, J. C. The six fools **398.2**

Thomas, J. C. What's the hurry, Fox? **398.2**

Willey, M. Clever Beatrice **398.2**

FOLKLORE -- UNITED STATES -- JUVENILE LITERATURE
Kellogg, S. Mike Fink **398.22**

Kellogg, S. Pecos Bill **398.2**

San Souci, R. Cut from the same cloth **398.2**

San Souci, R. The talking eggs **398.2**

Wooldridge, C. N. Wicked Jack **398.21**

FOLKLORE -- VIETNAM
Garland, S. Children of the dragon **398.209**

FOLKLORE -- VIRGINIA
Quattlebaum, M. Sparks fly high **398.2**

FOLKLORE -- VIRGINIA -- JUVENILE LITERATURE
Quattlebaum, M. Sparks fly high **398.2**

FOLKLORE -- WEST AFRICA
Aardema, V. Anansi does the impossible! **398.209**

Aardema, V. Why mosquitoes buzz in people's ears **398.2**

Badoe, A. The pot of wisdom: Ananse stories **398.2**

Graham, L. B. How God fix Jonah **220.9**

Kimmel, E. A. Anansi and the moss-covered rock **398.2**

Kimmel, E. A. Anansi's party time **398.2**

Krensky, S. Anansi and the box of stories **398.2**

Paye The talking vegetables **398.2**

Souhami, J. The sticky doll trap **398.2**

Wague Diakite, B. The hatseller and the monkeys **398.2**

Wague Diakite, B. The hunterman and the crocodile **398.209**

FOLKLORE -- WEST AFRICA -- JUVENILE LITERATURE
Aardema, V. Anansi does the impossible! **398.209**

Wague Diakite, B. The hunterman and the crocodile **398.209**

FOLKLORE -- WEST INDIES
Hamilton, V. The girl who spun gold **398.2**

Hamilton, V. A ring of tricksters **398.2**

FOLKLORE -- WEST INDIES -- JUVENILE LITERATURE
Hamilton, V. A ring of tricksters **398.2**

FOLKLORE -- ZAMBIA
Bryan, A. Beautiful blackbird **398.2**

FOLKLORE -- ZANZIBAR
Aardema, V. Rabbit makes a monkey of lion **398.2**

FOLKLORE AND CHILDREN
Yolen, J. Touch magic **028.5**

FOLKLORISTS
Berner, R. S. Definitely not for little ones **398.2**

Bond, V. Zora and me **Fic**

Hettinga, D. R. The Brothers Grimm **430**

Hopkinson, D. Home on the range **92**

McKissack, P. C. A song for Harlem **Fic**

Myers, C. Lies and other tall tales **398.2**

Pirotta, S. The McElderry book of Grimms' fairy tales **398.2**

Thomas, J. C. The six fools **398.2**

Thomas, J. C. The skull talks back and other haunting tales **398.2**

(il) Fleischman, P. Big talk   **811**
Giant African snail. Gray, S. H.   **594**
The **giant** and how he humbugged America. Murphy, J. **974.7**
The **Giant** and the beanstalk. Stanley, D.   **E**
A **giant** crush. Choldenko, G.   **E**
The **giant** hug. Horning, S.   **E**
The **giant** jam sandwich. Lord, J. V.   **E**
The **giant** of Seville. Andreasen, D.   **E**
GIANT PANDA
   Bortolotti, D. Panda rescue   **599.78**
   Firestone, M. Top 50 reasons to care about giant pandas   **599.78**
   Gish, M. Pandas   **599.78**
   Markle, S. How many baby pandas?   **599.78**
   Nagda, A. W. Panda math   **513**
   Ryder, J. Little panda   **599.74**
   Schreiber, A. Pandas   **599.78**
   Sirota, L. A. Giant pandas   **599.78**
GIANT PANDA -- FICTION
   Baek, M. J. Panda and polar bear   **E**
   Dowson, N. Tracks of a panda   **E**
   Liwska, R. Little panda   **E**
   Muth, J. J. Zen ghosts   **E**
   Muth, J. J. Zen shorts   **E**
   Quay, E. Good night, sleep tight   **E**
   Quay, E. Let's play house   **E**
   Quay, E. Puddle jumping   **E**
   Quay, E. Yummy ice cream   **E**
   Wild, M. Tom goes to kindergarten   **E**
GIANT PANDA -- JUVENILE LITERATURE
   Markle, S. How many baby pandas?   **599.78**
Giant pandas. Sirota, L. A.   **599.78**
Giant plants. Gould, M.   **580**
Giant sea reptiles of the dinosaur age. Arnold, C.   **567.9**
Giant shark: megalodon, prehistoric super predator. Arnold, C.   **567**
Giant snakes. Simon, S.   **597.96**
Giant squid. Cerullo, M. M.   **594**
GIANT SQUIDS
   Redmond Tentacles!   **594**
GIANT SQUIDS -- JUVENILE LITERATURE
   Cerullo, M. M. Giant squid   **594**
Giant steps to change the world. Lee, S.   **E**
Giant vs. giant. Bacchin, M.   **567.9**
The **giant-slayer**. Lawrence, I.   **Fic**
Giants. Malam, J.   **398.2**
GIANTS
   See also Folklore; Monsters
GIANTS
   Andreasen, D. The giant of Seville   **E**
   Klise, K. Stand straight, Ella Kate   **E**
   Osborne, M. P. Kate and the beanstalk   **398.2**
   Stanley, D. The Giant and the beanstalk   **E**
GIANTS -- FICTION
   Aguiar, N. The lost island of Tamarind   **Fic**
   Beaty, A. When giants come to play   **E**
   Coville, B. Thor's wedding day   **Fic**
   Dahl, R. The BFG   **Fic**
   Friedman, C. How do you feed a hungry giant?   **E**
   Gerstein, M. Carolinda clatter!   **E**
   King-Smith, D. The twin giants   **E**
   Klise, K. Stand straight, Ella Kate   **E**
   Lairamore, D. Ivy and the meanstalk   **Fic**
   Light, S. The Christmas giant   **E**
   Mora, P. Dona Flor   **E**
   Nolen, J. Hewitt Anderson's great big life   **E**
   Stimpson, C. Jack and the baked beanstalk   **E**
   Trafton, J. The rise and fall of Mount Majestic   **Fic**

GIANTS -- FOLKLORE
   Bunting, E. Finn McCool and the great fish   **398.2**
   Cech, J. Jack and the beanstalk   **398.2**
   Crews, N. Jack and the beanstalk   **398.2**
   Jack and the bean-stalk   **398.21**
   Johnson, P. B. Jack outwits the giants   **398.2**
   Malam, J. Giants   **398.2**
   Nesbit, E. Jack and the beanstalk   **398.2**
   Osborne, M. P. Kate and the beanstalk   **398.2**
   Seeger, P. Abiyoyo   **398.2**
   Souhami, J. Mrs. McCool and the giant Cuhullin   **398.2**
   Willey, M. Clever Beatrice   **398.2**
GIANTS -- GRAPHIC NOVELS
   Aguirre, J. Giants beware!   **741.5**
Giants beware! Aguirre, J.   **741.5**
Giants of science [series]
   Krull, K. Albert Einstein   **92**
   Krull, K. Charles Darwin   **92**
   Krull, K. Isaac Newton   **92**
   Krull, K. Leonardo da Vinci   **92**
   Krull, K. Marie Curie   **92**
Giarrano, Vince
   Comics crash course   **741.5**
Giarrusso, Chris
   G-Man, volume 1: learning to fly   **741.5**
Gibala-Broxholm, Scott
   (il) Wax, W. City witch, country switch   **E**
Gibb, Sarah
   (il) Sage, A. Rapunzel   **398.2**
Gibbon, Rebecca
   (il) Players in pigtails   **E**
   (il) Preus, M. Celebritrees   **582.16**
   (il) Stone, T. L. Elizabeth leads the way: Elizabeth Cady Stanton and the right to vote   **92**
Gibbons, Gail
   Alligators and crocodiles   **597.98**
   Apples   **634**
   Bats   **599.4**
   The berry book   **634**
   Bicycle book   **629.227**
   Cats   **636.8**
   Chicks & chickens   **636.5**
   Coral reefs   **577.7**
   Corn   **633.1**
   Dinosaurs!   **567.9**
   Dogs   **636.7**
   Easter   **394.26**
   Elephants of Africa   **599.67**
   Exploring the deep, dark sea   **551.46**
   Frogs   **597.8**
   Galaxies, galaxies!   **523.1**
   Gorillas   **599.8**
   Groundhog day!   **394.26**
   Gulls--gulls--gulls   **598.3**
   Halloween is--   **394.26**
   Horses!   **636.1**
   How a house is built   **690**
   Hurricanes!   **551.55**
   Ice cream   **641.8**
   It's snowing!   **551.57**
   Knights in shining armor   **394**
   Ladybugs   **595.76**
   Marshes & swamps   **577.68**
   The milk makers   **637**
   Monarch butterfly   **595.78**
   The moon book   **523.3**
   My baseball book   **796.357**
   My basketball book   **796.323**

GLASSWARE
    See also Decorative arts; Tableware
Glatstein, Jacob
    Emil and Karl   **Fic**
Glatt, Lisa
    Abigail Iris: the one and only   **Fic**
    Abigail Iris: the pet project   **Fic**
Glazer, Tom
    Johnson, P. B. On top of spaghetti   **E**
GLAZES
    See also Ceramics; Pottery
Gleason, Carrie
    Feasting bedbugs, mites, and ticks   **614.4**
Gleason, Derek M.
    (ed) Junior worldmark encyclopedia of the nations   **910.3**
Gleeson, Libby
    Clancy & Millie, and the very fine house   **E**
    The great bear   **E**
    Half a world away   **E**
Gleick, Beth
    Time is when   **529**
Glenn, John W.
    Aronson, M. The world made new   **910.4**
Glenn, John, 1921-
        About
    Bredeson, C. John Glenn returns to orbit   **629.4**
Glenn, John, 1921-
        About
    Mitchell, D. Liftoff   **92**
Glenn, Joshua
    Unbored   **790**
Glenn, Sharlee Mullins
    Just what Mama needs   **E**
Glick, Sharon
    (il) Guy, G. F. Perros! Perros! Dogs! Dogs!   **E**
Glickman, Susan
    Bernadette in the doghouse   **Fic**
GLIDERS (AERONAUTICS)
    See also Aeronautics; Airplanes
GLIDING AND SOARING
    See also Aeronautics
Gliori, Debi
    What's the time, Mr. Wolf?   **E**
Gliori, Debi
    No matter what   **E**
    Stormy weather   **E**
    The trouble with dragons   **E**
    Witch Baby and me   **Fic**
    Witch Baby and me after dark   **Fic**
    Witch Baby and me on stage   **Fic**
Glister and the haunted teapot. Watson, A.   **741.5**
The **glitch** in sleep. Hulme, J.   **Fic**
Glitter girls and the great fake out. Cabot, M.   **Fic**
The **glitter** trap. Brauner, B.   **Fic**
Global babies. Global Fund for Children (Organization)   **E**
Global Fund for Children (Organization)
    American babies   **E**
    Global babies   **E**
GLOBAL POSITIONING SYSTEM
    See also Navigation
Global warming. Royston, A.   **363.7**
GLOBAL WARMING
    See also Climate; Solar radiation
GLOBAL WARMING
    Arnold, C. A warmer world   **363.738**
    Meyer, S. Adapting to flooding and rising sea levels   **363.34**
Global warming. Simon, S.   **363.7**
Global warming. Morris, N.   **363.7**

GLOBAL WARMING -- JUVENILE LITERATURE
    Markle, S. Waiting for ice   **599.786**
Global warming and the dinosaurs. Arnold, C.   **567.9**
GLOBES
    See also Maps
Gloria's way. Cameron, A.   **Fic**
The **glorious** adventures of the Sunshine Queen. McCaughrean, G.   **Fic**
The **glorious** flight: across the Channel with Louis Bleriot, July 25, 1909. Provensen, A.   **92**
Glory be. Scattergood, A.   **Fic**
The **glory** wind. Sherrard, V.   **Fic**
GLOSSARIES *See* Encyclopedias and dictionaries
Glow-in-the-dark animals. Lunis, N.   **572**
GLOW-IN-THE-DARK BOOKS
    See also Picture books for children; Toy and movable books
Glucksman, Jodi
    (jt. auth) Aronica-Buck, B. Over the moon   **811**
Gnash, gnaw, dinosaur! Mitton, T.   **811**
Gnojewski, Carol
    Cinco de Mayo crafts   **745.594**
Gnoli, Domenico
    (il) Juster, N. Alberic the Wise and other journeys   **S**
The **gnome's** eye. Kerz, A.   **Fic**
GNOMES
    See also Folklore
GNOSTICISM
    See also Church history -- 30-600, Early church; Philosophy; Religions
GNUS
    Catt, T. Migrating with the wildebeest   **599.64**
    Meinking, M. Crocodile vs. wildebeest   **597.98**
    Walden, K. Wildebeests   **599.64**
Go away, big green monster! Emberley, E.   **E**
Go easy on energy. Bullard, L.   **333.79**
Go figure! Ball, J.   **793.74**
Go fly a bike! Haduch, B.   **629.227**
Go green [series]
    Lanz, H. Shopping choices   **381**
Go out and play! Rose, J.   **796**
Go straight to the source. Fontichiaro, K.   **020**
Go to bed, monster! Wing, N.   **E**
Go to sleep, Gecko! MacDonald, M. R.   **398.2**
Go to sleep, Groundhog! Cox, J.   **E**
Go west, Amelia Bedelia! Parish, H.   **E**
Go! go! Bobo: colors. Basher, S.   **E**
Go! go! go! Munro, R.   **E**
Go, go America. Yaccarino, D.   **973**
Go, go, grapes! Sayre, A. P.   **641.3**
Go-go gorillas. Durango, J.   **E**
Goal!   **E**
Goal! Woods, M.   **796.334**
Goal! science projects with soccer. Goodstein, M.   **507.8**
Goal!: the fire and fury of soccer's greatest moment. Stewart, M.   **796.334**
The **goat-faced** girl.   **398.2**
The **goatnappers.** Jordan, R.   **Fic**
GOATS
    Polacco, P. G is for goat   **E**
GOATS -- FICTION
    Berry, L. What floats in a moat?   **E**
    Cole, H. Trudy   **E**
    Fox, M. Let's count goats!   **E**
    Gorbachev, V. That's what friends are for   **E**
    Huck runs amuck!   **E**
    Jordan, R. The goatnappers   **Fic**
    Jordan, R. Lost Goat Lane   **Fic**

Google. Hamen, S. E.   338.7
GOOGLE
> *See also* Web search engines; Web sites
Gooney Bird Greene. Lowry, L.   Fic
GOOSE *See* Geese
Goose and Duck. George, J. C.   E
The **goose** man. Greenstein, E.   92
Goose's story. Best, C.   E
Gooseberry Goose. Freedman, C.   E
Goossens, Philippe
> (il) Friester, P. Owl howl   E
Goran's great escape. Lindgren, A.   E
Gorbachev, Valeri
> Christopher counting   E
> Dragon is coming!   E
> The missing chick   E
> Molly who flew away   E
> Ms. Turtle the babysitter   E
> Shhh!   E
> That's what friends are for   E
> Turtle's penguin day   E
> Two little chicks   E
> What's the big idea, Molly?   E
> (il) Horning, S. The giant hug   E
> (il) Moser, L. Squirrel's world   E
> (il) Stiegemeyer, J. Gobble-gobble crash!   E
Gordon, Cambria
> David, L. The down-to-earth guide to global warming   363.7
Gordon, David
> (il) Esbaum, J. To the big top   E
> Scieszka, J. Dizzy Izzy   E
> Scieszka, J. Kat's mystery gift   E
> Scieszka, J. Melvin's valentine   E
> Scieszka, J. Pete's party   E
> (il) Scieszka, J. Smash! crash!   E
> Scieszka, J. The spooky tire   E
> Scieszka, J. Truckery rhymes   811
> Scieszka, J. Uh-oh Max   E
Gordon, Domenica More
> Archie   Fic
Gordon, Mike
> (il) Heneghan, J. Once there was a seed   581.4
Gordon, Stephanie Jacob
> Enderle, J. R. Smile, Principessa!   E
Gordon-Harris, Tory
> (jt. auth) Arlon, P. Emergency vehicles   629.04
Gore, Al
> An inconvenient truth   363.7
Gore, Leonid
> (il) Anderson, J. L. May Bird and The Ever After
> The wonderful book   E
> Worms for lunch?   E
Gore, Leonid
> (il) Anderson, J. L. May Bird and The Ever After
> Danny's first snow   E
> Mommy, where are you?   E
> When I grow up   E
> The wonderful book   E
> Worms for lunch?   E
> (il) Pullman, P. Clockwork   Fic
> (il) Quattlebaum, M. Sparks fly high   398.2
> (il) Shepard, A. The princess mouse   398.2
Gorey, Edward
> (il) Bellairs, J. The house with a clock in its walls   Fic
> (il) Ciardi, J. You read to me, I'll read to you   811
> (il) Heide, F. P. The shrinking of Treehorn   Fic
GORGE-PURGE SYNDROME *See* Bulimia
Gorgonzola. Palatini, M.   E

Gorilla. Eszterhas, S.   599.884
GORILLA -- FICTION
> Browne, A. Voices in the park   E
> O'Hora, Z. No fits, Nilson!   E
GORILLA -- JUVENILE LITERATURE
> Hatkoff, C. Looking for Miza   599.8
> Riggs, K. Gorillas   599.884
Gorilla! Gorilla! Willis, J.   E
Gorillas. Gish, M.   599.8
Gorillas. Riggs, K.   599.884
GORILLAS
> *See also* Apes
GORILLAS
> Bustos, E. Going ape!   599.8
> Eszterhas, S. Gorilla   599.884
> Gibbons, G. Gorillas   599.8
> Gish, M. Gorillas   599.8
> Hatkoff, C. Looking for Miza   599.8
> Kushner, J. M. Who on earth is Dian Fossey?   92
> Nichols, M. Face to face with gorillas   599.8
> Riggs, K. Gorillas   599.884
> Schindel, J. Busy gorillas   599.8
Gorillas. Gibbons, G.   599.8
GORILLAS -- FICTION
> Adams, S. Gary and Ray   E
> Applegate, K. The one and only Ivan   Fic
> Browne, A. Little Beauty   E
> Browne, A. Voices in the park   E
> Durango, J. Go-go gorillas   E
> Fergus, M. Ortega   Fic
> Hines-Stephens, S. Midway monkey madness   Fic
> Willis, J. Gorilla! Gorilla!   E
Gorman, Jacqueline Laks
> The modern feminist movement   305.4
Gorman, Mike
> (il) Service, P. F. Escape from planet Yastol   Fic
Gormley, Greg
> Dog in boots   E
Gorrell, Gena K.
> Heart and soul: the story of Florence Nightingale   92
> In the land of the jaguar   980
> Working like a dog   636.7
Gorski, Jason
> (il) Murphy, P. Exploratopia   507.8
Gorton, Julia
> (il) Cobb, V. I fall down   531
Gorton, Julia
> (il) Cobb, V. I fall down   531
> (il) Cobb, V. I face the wind   551.51
> (il) Cobb, V. I get wet   532
> (il) Cobb, V. I see myself   535
Gorton, Steve
> (il) Stott, C. Space exploration   629.4
Goscinny
> Nicholas   Fic
> Nicholas on vacation   Fic
GOSPEL MUSIC
> Igus, T. I see the rhythm of gospel   782.25
GOSPEL MUSIC
> *See also* African American music; Church music; Popular music
GOSPEL MUSIC -- FICTION
> Freedom song   E
GOSPEL MUSIC -- JUVENILE LITERATURE
> Igus, T. I see the rhythm of gospel   782.25
Goss, Gary
> Rotner, S. Where does food come from?   664
Gosselink, John

Grandma's gloves.   **E**
Grandma's smile. Siegel, R.   **E**
Grandmama's pride. Birtha, B.   **E**
Grandmother Bryant's pocket. Martin, J. B.   **E**

GRANDMOTHERS
Bredsdorff, B. The Crow-girl   **Fic**
Cooke, T. Full, full, full of love   **E**
LaMarche, J. The raft   **E**
McGhee, A. Snap   **Fic**
The name quilt   **E**
Peck, R. A year down yonder   **Fic**
Saltypie   **92**
Stock, C. Gugu's house   **E**
Wilson, N. H. Mountain pose   **Fic**

GRANDMOTHERS
See also Grandparents

GRANDMOTHERS -- FICTION
Beaty, A. Dorko the magnificent   **Fic**
Chapman, J. I'm not sleepy!   **E**
Klise, K. Grammy Lamby and the secret handshake   **E**
Grandpa Green. Smith, L.   **E**
Grandpa Jack's tattoo tales. Foreman, M.   **E**
Grandpa's face. Greenfield, E.   **E**
Grandpa's tractor. Garland, M.   **E**
Grandpappy snippy snappies. Plourde, L.   **E**

GRANDPARENT AND CHILD *See* Grandparent-grandchild relationship

GRANDPARENT-GRANDCHILD RELATIONSHIP
Stone, P. The boy on Cinnamon Street   **Fic**

GRANDPARENT-GRANDCHILD RELATIONSHIP
See also Family; Grandparents

GRANDPARENT-GRANDCHILD RELATIONSHIP -- JUVENILE FICTION
Best, C. Beatrice spells some lulus and learns to write a letter   **E**
Cooper, F. Max and the tag-along moon   **E**

GRANDPARENTING
See also Grandparents; Parenting

GRANDPARENTS
Ajmera, M. Our grandparents   **306.8**
Bateman, T. April foolishness   **E**
Hamanaka, S. Grandparents song   **E**
Konrad, M. S. Grand   **306.8**
Kornblatt, M. Izzy's place   **Fic**
Lisle, J. T. The art of keeping cool   **Fic**
McCully, E. A. First snow   **E**
Wiles, D. Love, Ruby Lavender   **Fic**

GRANDPARENTS
See also Family

GRANDPARENTS -- FICTION
Balliett, B. The Danger Box   **Fic**
Cazet, D. The shrunken head   **E**
Cazet, D. A snout for chocolate   **E**
Creech, S. Walk two moons   **Fic**
DeFelice, C. C. Wild life   **Fic**
Frazee, M. A couple of boys have the best week ever   **E**
Hamanaka, S. Grandparents song   **E**
Hemingway, E. M. Road to Tater Hill   **Fic**
Hirahara, N. 1001 cranes   **Fic**
Horrocks, A. Silas' seven grandparents   **E**
Jones, S. L. The ultimate guide to grandmas and grandpas   **E**
Juster, N. The hello, goodbye window   **E**
Kadohata, C. The thing about luck   **Fic**
Kinsey-Warnock, N. Nora's ark   **E**
MacLachlan, P. The true gift   **Fic**
Parish, H. Amelia Bedelia's first apple pie   **E**
Peterson, L. J. The ballad of Knuckles McGraw   **Fic**
Rahaman, V. Divali rose   **E**

Resau, L. What the moon saw   **Fic**
Schwartz, J. Our corner grocery store   **E**
Stone, P. The boy on Cinnamon Street   **Fic**
Watson, R. What Momma left me   **Fic**
Wiles, D. Love, Ruby Lavender   **Fic**

GRANDPARENTS AS PARENTS
See also Grandparents; Parenting
Grandparents song. Hamanaka, S.   **E**

Grandpre, Mary, 1954-
(il) Achebe, C. How the leopard got his claws   **Fic**
(il) Buzzeo, T. The sea chest   **E**
(il) MacDonald, B. Nancy and Plum   **Fic**
(il) Prelutsky, J. The carnival of the animals   **811**
(il) Root, P. Lucia and the light   **E**
(il) Rowling, J. K. Harry Potter and the Chamber of Secrets   **Fic**
(il) Rowling, J. K. Harry Potter and the deathly hallows   **Fic**
(il) Rowling, J. K. Harry Potter and the Goblet of Fire   **Fic**
(il) Rowling, J. K. Harry Potter and the Half-blood Prince   **Fic**
(il) Rowling, J. K. Harry Potter and the Order of the Phoenix   **Fic**
(il) Rowling, J. K. Harry Potter and the prisoner of Azkaban   **Fic**
(il) Rowling, J. K. Harry Potter and the Sorcerer's Stone   **Fic**
(il) Townley, R. The blue shoe   **Fic**

Granfield, Linda
Out of slavery   **264**

Grange, Red, 1903-1991
About
Krull, K. Lives of the athletes   **796**

GRANITE
See also Rocks; Stone
Granite baby. Bertrand, L.   **E**
Granny Gomez & Jigsaw. Underwood, D.   **E**
Granny the Pag. Bawden, N.   **Fic**
Granny Torrelli makes soup.   **Fic**
Granny's clan. Hodson, S.   **E**
The **Grannyman.** Schachner, J. B.   **E**

Granstrom, Brita
Baby knows best   **E**
Nature adventures   **508**
Hindley, J. Baby talk   **E**
Lewis, P. No more yawning!   **E**
Manning, M. Charles Dickens   **92**
Manning, M. Snap!   **E**
Manning, M. Tail-end Charlie   **940.54**
Manning, M. Under your skin   **612**
Manning, M. Woolly mammoth   **569**

Grant, Alan
Robert Louis Stevenson's Strange case of Dr. Jekyll and Mr. Hyde   **741.5**

Grant, Judyann
Chicken said, Cluck!   **E**

Grant, Karima
Sofie and the city   **E**

Grant, Katy
Hide and seek   **Fic**

Grant, Michael, 1954-
The call   **Fic**
The trap   **Fic**

Grant, Shauntay
Up home   **811**

Grant, Ulysses S. (Ulysses Simpson), 1822-1885
About
Stark, K. Marching to Appomattox   **973.7**
Juvenile Literature
Benoit, P. The surrender at Appomattox   **973.7**

GRANTS *See* Grants-in-aid; Subsidies

Hamaker, Steve	
(il) Quest for the Spark	Fic
Hamanaka, Sheila	
All the colors of the earth	813
Grandparents song	E
Hambleton, Vicki	
(jt. auth) Greenwood, C. So, you wanna be a writer?	808
Hamen, Susan E.	
Google	338.7

Hamer, Fannie Lou Townsend, 1917-1977
About

Pinkney, A. D. Let it shine — 920

Hamilton, Alexander, 1757-1804
About

Fradin, D. B. Duel! — 973.4

Hamilton, Alexander, 1757-1804
About

Fritz, J. Alexander Hamilton — 92

Hamilton, Alexander, 1757-1804 -- Juvenile literature
About

Fritz, J. Alexander Hamilton — 92

Hamilton, Emma Walton

(ed) Julie Andrews' treasury for all seasons — 808.81

Hamilton, Emma Walton

Andrews, J. The very fairy princess — E
Andrews, J. The very fairy princess takes the stage — E
(ed) Julie Andrews' collection of poems, songs, and lullabies — 808.8

Hamilton, John

How a bill becomes a law — 328
Tsunamis — 551.46

Hamilton, K. R.

Police officers on patrol — E
Red Truck — E

Hamilton, Libby

Horse: the essential guide for young equestrians — 636.1

Hamilton, Lynn

Ferret — 636.9
Presidents' Day — 394.26
Turtle — 639.3

Hamilton, Martha

The ghost catcher — 398.2

Hamilton, Meredith

(il) Driscoll, M. A child's introduction to poetry — 808.81

Hamilton, Sue L.

Ambushed by a cougar — 599.75
Attacked by a crocodile — 597.98
Bitten by a rattlesnake — 597.96
Eaten by a shark — 597
Mauled by a bear — 599.78
Swarmed by bees — 595.7

Hamilton, Virginia

Bruh Rabbit and the tar baby girl — 398.2
Drylongso — Fic
The girl who spun gold — 398.2
The house of Dies Drear — Fic
In the beginning; creation stories from around the world — 201
M.C. Higgins, the great — Fic
Many thousand gone — 326
The people could fly: American Black folktales — 398.2
The people could fly: the picture book — 398.2
The planet of Junior Brown — Fic
A ring of tricksters — 398.2
Virginia Hamilton: speeches, essays, and conversations — 813
Wee Winnie Witch's Skinny — E
Zeely — Fic

Hamilton, Virginia, 1936-2002
About

Ellis, S. From reader to writer — 028

Hamlin, Janet

(il) Stewart, M. Germ wars! — 571.9
(il) Stewart, M. Give me a hand — 591.4
(il) Stewart, M. Here we grow — 612.7
(il) Stewart, M. Moving and grooving — 612.7
(il) Stewart, M. The skin you're in — 591.47
(il) Stewart, M. You've got nerve! — 612.8

Hamlisch, Marvin -- Childhood and youth -- Fiction
About

Hamlisch, M. Marvin makes music — E

Hamlisch, Marvin -- Childhood and youth -- Juvenile fiction
About

Hamlisch, M. Marvin makes music — E

Hamlisch, Marvin, 1944-2012

Marvin makes music — E

Hamm, Mia

Winners never quit! — E

Hammered by a heat wave! DeLallo, L. — 551.5

HAMMERHEAD SHARKS

Mallory, K. Swimming with hammerhead sharks — 597.3

HAMMERHEAD SHARKS -- RESEARCH -- JUVENILE LITERATURE

Mallory, K. Swimming with hammerhead sharks — 597.3

Hammerin' Hank Greenberg. Sommer, S. — 92

Hammill, Matt

Sir Reginald's logbook — E

Hammond family
About

VanHecke, S. Raggin', jazzin', rockin' — 784.19

Hammond, Andy

(il) Hurwitz, J. Fourth-grade fuss — Fic

Hammond, Richard

Super science lab — 507.8

Hammond, Ted

(il) Littlefield, H. The rooftop adventure of Minnie and Tessa, factory fire survivors — 741.5

Hampire! Bardhan-Quallen, S. — E

Hamster and cheese. Venable, C. A. — 741.5

Hamster champs. Murphy, S. J. — 516

The **hamster** of the Baskervilles. Hale, B. — Fic

HAMSTERS

Bozzo, L. My first guinea pig and other small pets — 636.9
Ellis, C. Hamsters and gerbils — 636.9
Holub, J. Why do rabbits hop? — 636.9
Jeffrey, L. S. Hamsters, gerbils, guinea pigs, rabbits, ferrets, mice, and rats — 636.9
Johnson, J. Hamsters and gerbils — 636.9
Newcomb, R. Is my hamster wild? — 636.9
Reiche, D. Freddy in peril — Fic
Richardson, A. Caring for your hamster — 636.9
Ripley, C. How? — 031.02

HAMSTERS -- FICTION

Deacon, A. A place to call home — E

HAMSTERS -- GRAPHIC NOVELS

Venable, C. A. Hamster and cheese — 741.5

Hamsters and gerbils. Ellis, C. — 636.9
Hamsters and gerbils. Johnson, J. — 636.9

HAMSTERS AS PETS -- MISCELLANEA -- JUVENILE LITERATURE

Holub, J. Why do rabbits hop? — 636.9

Hamsters, gerbils, guinea pigs, rabbits, ferrets, mice, and rats. Jeffrey, L. S. — 636.9

Hamsters, shells, and spelling bees. — 811

Hamzat's journey. Robinson, A. — 947

Han, Jenny

Clara Lee and the apple pie dream — Fic

Han, Kan, ca. 715-ca. 781

Wall paintings	751.7

Harris, Pamela K.
Welcome to Switzerland — **949.4**

Harris, Robie H.
The day Leo said I hate you — **E**
Goodbye, Mousie — **E**
I am not going to school today — **E**
It's not the stork! — **612.6**
It's perfectly normal — **613.9**
It's so amazing! — **612.6**
Mail Harry to the moon! — **E**
Maybe a bear ate it! — **E**
Who has what? — **612.6**
Who's in my family? — **E**

Harris, Teresa E.
Summer Jackson: grown up — **E**

Harris, Tim
(ed) Reptiles and amphibians — **333.95**

Harris, Todd
(il) The hero's guide to storming the castle — **Fic**

Harris, Trudy
The clock struck one — **E**
Say something, Perico — **E**
Tally cat keeps track — **E**

Harrison, David L. (David Lee)
(ed) Dude! — **810**
Glaciers — **551.3**
Mammoth bones and broken stones — **970.01**
A monster is coming! — **E**
Vacation — **811**
Volcanoes: nature's incredible fireworks — **551.2**

Juvenile humor
Brewer, P. The Beatles were fab (and they were funny) — **782.421**

Harrison, Joanna
Grizzly dad — **E**
(il) Wells, K. Paw power — **Fic**
(il) Wells, K. Shadow magic — **Fic**

Harrison, John, 1693-1776
About
The man who made time travel — **526**
Borden, L. Sea clocks — **526**
Galat, J. M. The discovery of longitude — **526**

Harrison, Michael
(ed) The Oxford book of story poems — **808.81**

Harrison, Michelle
13 curses — **Fic**
13 treasures — **Fic**

Harrison, Ted
(il) Service, R. W. The cremation of Sam McGee — **811**

Harrison, Troon
The horse road — **Fic**
Red River stallion — **Fic**

Harry & Hopper. Wild, M. — **E**
Harry and Horsie. Van Camp, K. — **E**
Harry and the dinosaurs say Raahh! Whybrow, I. — **E**
Harry Cat and Tucker Mouse: Harry to the rescue! Feldman, T. — **E**
Harry Cat and Tucker Mouse: starring Harry. Feldman, T. — **E**
Harry Cat and Tucker Mouse: Tucker's beetle band. Feldman, T. — **E**
Harry Houdini. Weaver, J. — **92**
Harry Houdini for kids. Carlson, L. M. — **92**
Harry hungry! Salerno, S. — **E**
Harry on the rocks. Meddaugh, S. — **E**
Harry Potter and the Chamber of Secrets. Rowling, J. K. — **Fic**
Harry Potter and the deathly hallows. — **Fic**
Harry Potter and the Goblet of Fire. Rowling, J. K. — **Fic**

Harry Potter and the Half-blood Prince. Rowling, J. K. — **Fic**
Harry Potter and the Order of the Phoenix. Rowling, J. K. — **Fic**
Harry Potter and the prisoner of Azkaban. Rowling, J. K. — **Fic**
Harry Potter and the Sorcerer's Stone. Rowling, J. K. — **Fic**
Harry Sue. Stauffacher, S. — **Fic**
Harry the dirty dog. Zion, G. — **E**

Harshman, Marc
Only one neighborhood — **E**

Hart, Avery
Ancient Greece! — **745**

Hart, Christopher
The cartoonist's big book of drawing animals — **741.5**
Drawing the new adventure cartoons — **741.5**
Kids draw Manga Shoujo — **741.5**
You can draw cartoon animals — **741.5**

Hart, Joyce
Baldwin, G. Oklahoma — **976.6**
Baldwin, G. Wyoming — **978.7**
Bennett, M. Missouri — **977.8**
Dornfeld, M. Maine — **974.1**
Big dogs — **636.7**
Cats — **636.8**
Florida — **975.9**
Pennsylvania — **974.8**
Small dogs — **636.7**
Snakes — **639.3**
Hoffman, N. South Carolina — **975.7**
Hoffman, N. West Virginia — **975.4**
Morrice, P. A. Iowa — **977.7**
Peters, S. Pennsylvania — **974.8**
Shirley, D. Alabama — **976.1**
Shirley, D. North Carolina — **975.6**

Hart, Rebecca
Reiser, L. Tortillas and lullabies. Tortillas y cancioncitas — **E**

Harter, Debbie
(il) Blackstone, S. Bear's birthday — **E**

Hartfield, Claire
Me and Uncle Romie — **E**

Hartland, Jessie
Bon appetit! — **641.509**

Hartland, Jessie
(il) Franco, B. Messing around on the monkey bars — **811**
How the dinosaur got to the museum — **567.9**
How the sphinx got to the museum — **932**
Night shift — **E**
O'Connor, J. The perfect puppy for me — **E**

Hartlove, Chris
(il) Swett, S. Kids weaving — **746.41**

Hartman, Bob
Mr. Aesop's story shop — **398.2**

Hartman, Bob
The Lion storyteller book of animal tales — **398.2**
Mr. Aesop's story shop — **398.2**

Hartman, Carrie
(il) Harris, T. The clock struck one — **E**

Hartman, Cassie
(il) Patent, D. H. When the wolves returned — **599.77**

Hartman, Dan
(il) Patent, D. H. When the wolves returned — **599.77**

Hartman, Eve
Changing life on Earth — **576.8**
Climate change — **551.6**
Fossil fuels — **333.8**
Light and sound — **530**
Mission to Mars — **629.45**
Science ethics and controversies — **174**

Hartnett, Sonya
Hartnett, S. The Midnight zoo — **Fic**

See also Biology; Breeding

HERESY

    See also Religion

Hereville: how Mirka got her sword. Deutsch, B.   741.5

Herge

    The adventures of Tintin, vol. 1   741.5

    The secret of the unicorn   741.5

Herlong, M.H.

    Buddy   Fic

Herman, Charlotte

    First rain   E

Herman, Emily

    Hubknuckles   E

Hermes, Patricia

    Emma Dilemma and the camping nanny   Fic

    Emma Dilemma and the new nanny   Fic

    Emma Dilemma and the soccer nanny   Fic

    Emma Dilemma and the two nannies   Fic

    Emma Dilemma, the nanny, and the best horse ever   Fic

    Emma Dilemma, the nanny, and the secret ferret   Fic

The **hermit** crab. Goodrich, C.   E

HERMITS -- JUVENILE FICTION

    Arnosky, J. Crinkleroot's guide to giving back to nature   333.95

Hernandez de la Cruz, Maria

    Endredy, J. The journey of Tunuri and the Blue Deer   398.2

Hernandez, Leeza

    Dog gone!   E

Hernandez, Leeza

    (il) Donovan, S. Bored Bella learns about fiction and nonfiction   025.4

    (il) McCallum, A. Eat your math homework   641.5

Hernandez, Roger E.

    1898 to World War II   305.8

    The Civil War, 1840s-1890s   973.7

    Early explorations: the 1500s   970.01

    New Spain: 1600-1760s   973.1

Hernandez-Divers, Sonia

    Geckos   639.3

The **hero** and the minotaur. Byrd, R.   398.2

Hero dad. Hardin, M.   E

A **hero** for WondLa. DiTerlizzi, T.   Fic

The **hero** of Little Street. Rogers, G.   E

Hero of the high seas. Cooper, M. L.   92

Hero on a bicycle. Hughes, S.   Fic

The **hero** revealed. Boniface, W.   Fic

The **hero** Schliemann. Schlitz, L. A.   92

Hero's Guide [series]

    The hero's guide to storming the castle   Fic

The **hero's** guide to saving your kingdom. Healy, C.   Fic

The **hero's** guide to storming the castle.   Fic

Heroes. Mochizuki, K.   E

HEROES

    Rodda, E. Rowan and the Travelers   Fic

    Rodda, E. Rowan and the Zebak   Fic

    Rodda, E. Rowan of Rin   Fic

    Van Leeuwen, J. Oliver the Mighty Pig   E

Heroes [series]

    McCaughrean, G. Hercules   292

    McCaughrean, G. Odysseus   292

    McCaughrean, G. Perseus   292

HEROES -- FICTION

    Clements, A. About average   Fic

    Garza, X. Maximilian and the mystery of the Guardian Angel   Fic

    The hero's guide to storming the castle   Fic

    Quest for the Spark   Fic

HEROES AND HEROINES

Haven, K. F. Reluctant heroes   920

Of thee I sing   179

Roop, P. Tales of famous heroes   920

Winter, J. Peaceful heroes   920

HEROES AND HEROINES

    See also Adventure and adventurers

HEROES AND HEROINES -- FICTION

    Healy, C. The hero's guide to saving your kingdom   Fic

HEROES AND HEROINES -- POETRY

    Corcoran, J. Dare to dream--change the world   811.6

Heroes for civil rights. Adler, D. A.   920

Heroes of baseball. Lipsyte, R.   796.357

The heroes of Olympus [series]

    Riordan, R. The son of Neptune   Fic

Heroes of the environment. Rohmer, H.   333.72

Heroes of the surf. Carbone, E.   E

Heroes! Stephens, J.   741.5

HEROINES *See* Heroes and heroines

HEROISM *See* Courage; Heroes and heroines

Herold, Maggie Rugg

    A very important day   E

HERONS -- FICTION

    Avi Blue heron   Fic

    Ramirez, A. Napi   E

HERONS -- POETRY

    Yolen, J. An egret's day   811

HEROS -- BIOGRAPHY -- JUVENILE LITERATURE

    McCann, M. R. Girls who rocked the world   920.72

Herrera, Juan Felipe, 1948-

    Laughing out loud, I fly   811

        About

    Herrera, J. F. The upside down boy   92

Herrick, Steven

    Naked bunyip dancing   Fic

Herrod, Mike

    Doggie dreams   741.5

Herschel, William Sir, 1738-1822

        About

    Sherman, J. Uranus   523.4

Hershel and the Hanukkah goblins. Kimmel, E. A.   398.2

Hershenhorn, Esther

    S is for story   808.3

Herweck, Don

    Robert Fulton   92

Herxheimer, Sophie

    (il) Clayton, S. P. Amazons!   398.2

    (il) Clayton, S. P. Tales told in tents   398.2

Heschel, Abraham Joshua, 1907-1972

        About

    Michelson, R. As good as anybody: Martin Luther King Jr. and Abraham Joshua Heschel's amazing march toward freedom   92

Heslop, Michael

    (il) Cooper, S. The grey king   Fic

Hess, Debra

    Florida   975.9

Hess, Nina

    (jt. auth) Greenberg, D. Whales   599.5

Hess, Paul

    (il) Maddern, E. The cow on the roof   398.2

    (il) Maddern, E. Nail soup   398.2

    (il) Monte, R. The dragon of Krakow and other Polish stories   398.2

    (il) Monte, R. The mermaid of Warsaw   398.2

Hesse, Karen

    Brooklyn Bridge   Fic

    The cats in Krasinski Square   E

    Come on, rain!   E

Louie!   **E**
Mother Goose picture puzzles   **398.8**
Spring is here!   **E**
(il) Livingston, M. C. Calendar   **E**
(il) Miller, B. One fine trade   **398.2**
(il) Root, P. Kiss the cow   **E**
(il) Shulman, L. The moon might be milk   **E**
(il) Sierra, J. Preschool to the rescue   **E**
(il) St. George, J. The journey of the one and only Declaration of Independence   **973.3**
(il) This little piggy   **398.8**
(il) Wilson, K. Whopper cake   **E**
(il) Wooldridge, C. N. Wicked Jack   **398.21**
(il) Wright, M. Sleep, Big Bear, sleep!   **E**
(il) Wright, M. Sneeze, Big Bear, sneeze!   **E**
Hilliard, Richard
(il) Harrison, D. L. Mammoth bones and broken stones **970.01**
Hillman, Ben
How big is it?   **153.7**
How fast is it?   **531**
How strong is it?   **620.1**
How weird is it   **500**
Hills, Tad
Duck & Goose   **E**
How Rocket learned to read   **E**
Rocket writes a story   **E**
(il) Stevens, A. Waking up Wendell   **E**
Hilmo, Tess
With a name like Love   **Fic**
HIMALAYA MOUNTAINS -- FICTION
Cossi, O. Pemba Sherpa   **E**
Himler, Ronald
(il) Always with you   **E**
Himler, Ronald
(il) Adler, D. A. A picture book of Dolley and James Madison   **92**
(il) Adler, D. A. A picture book of John and Abigail Adams   **92**
(il) Adler, D. A. A picture book of John Hancock   **92**
(il) Always with you   **E**
(il) Bunting, E. Fly away home   **E**
(il) Bunting, E. Someday a tree   **E**
(il) Bunting, E. The Wall   **E**
(il) Coerr, E. Sadako and the thousand paper cranes   **92**
(il) Cohen, M. First grade takes a test   **E**
(il) Cohen, M. My big brother   **E**
(il) Cohen, M. Will I have a friend?   **E**
(il) DeLaCroix, A. The best horse ever   **Fic**
(il) Fritz, J. Why not, Lafayette?   **973.3**
(il) Garland, S. The buffalo soldier   **E**
(il) Lawlor, L. The school at Crooked Creek   **Fic**
(il) Newman, L. The best cat in the world   **E**
(il) Van Steenwyk, E. Prairie Christmas   **E**
(il) Wright, B. R. The blizzard   **E**
Himmelman, John
Noisy bug sing-along   **595.715**
Himmelman, John
10 little hot dogs   **E**
Chickens to the rescue   **E**
Cows to the rescue   **E**
Frog in a bog   **E**
Katie loves the kittens   **E**
Who's at the seashore?   **591.7**
HINDENBURG (AIRSHIP) -- JUVENILE LITERATURE
Surviving the Hindenburg   **363.12**
The **Hindenburg** disaster. Benoit, P.   **363.1**
Hindley, Judy
Baby talk   **E**

Hinds, Gareth
(il) Gifts from the gods   **401**
HINDU HOLIDAYS
MacMillan, D. M. Diwali--Hindu festival of lights **394.26**
HINDU HOLIDAYS
See also Religious holidays
HINDU MYTHOLOGY
Gavin, J. Tales from India   **398.2**
HINDU MYTHOLOGY -- GRAPHIC NOVELS
Arni, S. Sita's Ramayana   **741.5**
HINDU PHILOSOPHY
See also Philosophy
Hinduism. Rasamandala Das   **294.5**
HINDUISM
Ganeri, A. The Ramayana and Hinduism   **294.5**
George, C. What makes me a Hindu?   **294.5**
Hawker, F. Hinduism in Bali   **294.5**
Jani, M. What you will see inside a Hindu temple   **294.5**
Ollhoff, J. Indian mythology   **294**
Osborne, M. P. One world, many religions   **200**
Rasamandala Das Hinduism   **294.5**
HINDUISM
See also Religions
HINDUISM -- JUVENILE LITERATURE
George, C. What makes me a Hindu?   **294.5**
Hinduism in Bali. Hawker, F.   **294.5**
HINDUS -- FICTION
Banerjee, A. Looking for Bapu   **Fic**
Hine, Lewis Wickes, 1874-1940
About
Freedman, R. Kids at work   **331.3**
Hine, Lewis Wickes, 1874-1940
Fiction
Winthrop, E. Counting on Grace   **Fic**
Hines, Anna Grossnickle
1, 2, buckle my shoe   **E**
Daddy makes the best spaghetti   **E**
I am a backhoe   **E**
I am a Tyrannosaurus   **E**
Peaceful pieces   **811**
Pieces   **811**
Winter lights   **811**
Hines, Gary
Midnight forests   **92**
Hines-Stephens, Sarah
Midway monkey madness   **Fic**
Show off   **790.1**
Hinman, Bonnie
We visit Pakistan   **954.91**
Hinojosa, Tish
Cada nino/Every child   **782.42**
Hintz, Martin
The Bahamas   **972.96**
Hip & Hop, don't stop. Czekaj, J.   **E**
Hip hip hooray! it's Family Day!   **E**
Hip hop dog.   **E**
Hip hop speaks to children.   **811**
HIP-HOP
Garofoli, W. Hip-hop dancing   **793.3**
Harris, A. R. Tupac Shakur   **92**
HIP-HOP -- FICTION
Hip hop dog   **E**
Hip-hop dancing. Garofoli, W.   **793.3**
Hip-pocket papa. Markle, S.   **597.8**
HIPPIES -- FICTION
Lindbergh, R. My hippie grandmother   **E**
Mr. and Mrs. Bunny-- detectives extraordinaire!   **Fic**
Partridge, E. Dogtag summer   **Fic**

Gerdner, L. Grandfather's story cloth   E
Sneve, V. D. H. Lana's Lakota moons   Fic
HMONG (ASIAN PEOPLE) -- FOLKLORE
Blia Xiong Nine-in-one, Grr! Grr!   **398.2**
HMONG (ASIAN PEOPLE) -- JUVENILE LITERATURE
Cha, D. Dia's story cloth   **305.8**
Ho, Jannie
   (il) Suen, A. Road work ahead   E
   (il) Suen, A. Roadwork ahead   E
Ho, Minfong
   Hush!   **782.4**
Hoaxed! YES mag (Periodical)   **500**
HOAXES See Impostors and imposture
Hoban, Lillian
   Arthur's Christmas cookies   E
   Silly Tilly's Thanksgiving dinner   E
Hoban, Russell
   Bedtime for Frances   E
   Rosie's magic horse   E
Hoban, Tana
   26 letters and 99 cents   **411**
   Black on white   E
   Colors everywhere   **535.6**
   Construction zone   **621.8**
   Exactly the opposite   **428**
   Is it larger? Is it smaller?   **516**
   Is it red? Is it yellow? Is it blue?   E
   Let's count   **513.2**
   Of colors and things   **535.6**
   Over, under & through, and other spatial concepts   E
   Shadows and reflections   **779**
   Shapes, shapes, shapes   **516**
   So many circles, so many squares   **516**
   White on black   E
Hobbie, Holly
   Gem   E
Hobbie, Holly
   Everything but the horse   E
   Toot & Puddle   E
   Toot & Puddle: let it snow   E
   Toot & Puddle: the new friend   E
   Toot & Puddle: wish you were here   E
   Toot and Puddle: you are my sunshine   E
HOBBIES
   See also Amusements; Leisure; Recreation
The **hobbit**, or, There and back again. Tolkien, J. R. R.   Fic
Hobbs, Valerie
   Maggie and Oliver, or, A bone of one's own   Fic
Hobbs, Valerie
   Defiance   Fic
   The last best days of summer   Fic
   Maggie and Oliver, or, A bone of one's own   Fic
Hobbs, Will
   Crossing the wire   Fic
   Jason's gold   Fic
   Never say die   Fic
   Take me to the river   Fic
Hoberman, Mary Ann
   (ed) Forget-me-nots   **811**
   I like old clothes   E
   You read to me, I'll read to you   **811**
Hoblin, Paul
   Swimming & diving   **797.2**
The **Hoboken** chicken emergency. Pinkwater, D. M.   Fic
Hoce, Charley
   Beyond Old MacDonald   **811**
Hockey. Johnstone, R.   **796.962**
Hockey. McClellan, R.   **796.962**

HOCKEY
   See also Winter sports
HOCKEY
   Adams, C. Queens of the ice   **796.962**
   Johnstone, R. Hockey   **796.962**
   McClellan, R. Hockey   **796.962**
   McKinley, M. Ice time   **796.962**
   McMahon, D. Hockey   **796.962**
   Sharp, A. W. Ice hockey   **796.962**
   Stewart, M. Score!   **796.962**
   Wiseman, B. Stanley Cup   **796.96**
Hockey. McMahon, D.   **796.962**
HOCKEY -- CANADA -- JUVENILE LITERATURE
   McKinley, M. Ice time   **796.962**
HOCKEY -- FICTION
   Sederman, M. Casey and Derek on the ice   E
   Sylvester, K. Splinters   E
HOCKEY PLAYERS
   Krull, K. Lives of the athletes   **796**
Hocus Pocus. Desrosiers, S.   E
Hodge, Deborah
   Desert animals   **591.7**
   Forest animals   **591.7**
   Polar animals   **591.7**
   Rain forest animals   **591.7**
   Rescuing the children   **940.53**
   Savanna animals   **591.7**
   Up we grow!   **630**
   Watch me grow!   **630**
   Wetland animals   **591.7**
Hodges, Gary
   Chapman, G. Coffee   **641.3**
Hodges, Margaret
   Dick Whittington and his cat   **398.2**
   The kitchen knight   **398.22**
   Merlin and the making of the king   **398.2**
   Moses   **222**
   Saint George and the dragon   **398.2**
   The wee Christmas cabin   E
Hodgkins, Fran
   Amazing eggs   **591.4**
Hodgkins, Fran
   Amazing eggs   **591.4**
   Champions of the ocean   **920**
   How people learned to fly   **629.13**
   The whale scientists   **599.5**
   Who's been here?   E
Hodgkinson, Jo
   The talent show   E
Hodgkinson, Leigh
   Limelight Larry   E
   Smile!   E
Hodgman, Ann
   The house of a million pets   **92**
   How to die of embarrassment every day   **92**
Hodgman, Ann
       About
   Hodgman, A. The house of a million pets   **92**
Hodgman, Ann
       About
   Hodgman, A. How to die of embarrassment every day   **92**
Hodson, Sally
   Granny's clan   E
Hoena, B. A.
   Jack and the beanstalk: the graphic novel   **741.5**
Hof, Marjolijn
   Against the odds   Fic
   Mother number zero   Fic

Thomas, J. C. The skull talks back and other haunting tales   **398.2**

HORROR STORIES *See* Horror fiction

HORROR TALES

Thomas, J. C. The skull talks back and other haunting tales   **398.2**

HORROR TALES *See* Horror fiction

HORROR TALES -- AUTHORSHIP -- JUVENILE LITERATURE

Litwin, L. B. Write horror fiction in 5 simple steps   **808.3**

HORROR TALES -- TECHNIQUE -- JUVENILE LITERATURE

Litwin, L. B. Write horror fiction in 5 simple steps   **808.3**

HORROR TALES, AMERICAN

San Souci, R. Double-dare to be scared: another thirteen chilling tales   **S**

Stine, R. L. The haunting hour   **S**

HORROR TELEVISION PROGRAMS

See also Television programs

Horse. Lomberg, M.   **636.1**

Horse & pony breeds. Ransford, S.   **636.1**

Horse & pony care. Ransford, S.   **636.1**

The **horse** and his boy. Lewis, C. S.   **Fic**

The **horse** and the Plains indians.   **978**

Horse crafts. Hendry, L.   **745.5**

Horse hooves and chicken feet: Mexican folktales.   **398.2**

A **horse** in the house, and other strange but true animal stories. Ablow, G.   **590**

A **horse** of her own. Wedekind, A.   **Fic**

HORSE RACING

Lewin, B. Horse song   **951**

McCarthy, M. Seabiscuit   **798.4**

Scanlan, L. The big red horse   **798.4**

Tate, N. Behind the scenes: the racehorse   **798.4**

Wiseman, B. Kentucky Derby   **798.4**

HORSE RACING

See also Racing

HORSE RACING -- JUVENILE LITERATURE

Lewin, B. Horse song   **951**

McCarthy, M. Seabiscuit   **798.4**

Tate, N. Behind the scenes: the racehorse   **798.4**

HORSE RIDING *See* Horsemanship

The **horse** road. Harrison, T.   **Fic**

Horse song. Lewin, B.   **951**

Horse tales.   **S**

Horse, Harry

Little Rabbit lost   **E**

Horse: the essential guide for young equestrians. Hamilton, L.   **636.1**

HORSEBACK RIDING *See* Horsemanship

HORSEBACK RIDING -- FICTION

Primavera, E. Libby of High Hopes   **Fic**

HORSEMANSHIP

Draper, J. My first horse and pony book   **636.1**

Draper, J. My first horse and pony care book   **636.1**

Gibbons, G. Horses!   **636.1**

Ransford, S. The Kingfisher illustrated horse & pony encyclopedia   **636.1**

HORSEMANSHIP -- FICTION

Harrison, T. The horse road   **Fic**

HORSEMANSHIP -- JUVENILE LITERATURE

Jeffrey, L. S. Horses   **636.1**

Horsepower.   **636.1**

Horses. Jeffrey, L. S.   **636.1**

Horses. Mack, G.   **636.1**

Horses. Simon, S.   **636.1**

HORSES

See also Mammals

HORSES

Barnes, J. Horses at work   **636.1**

Bozzo, L. My first horse   **636.1**

Byars, B. C. Little Horse   **Fic**

Classic horse stories   **808.8**

Collard III, S. B. The world famous Miles City Bucking Horse Sale   **791.8**

Crosby, J. Harness horses, bucking broncos & pit ponies   **636.1**

Draper, J. My first horse and pony book   **636.1**

Draper, J. My first horse and pony care book   **636.1**

Friddell, C. Goliath   **975.2**

Gibbons, G. Horses!   **636.1**

Hamilton, L. Horse: the essential guide for young equestrians   **636.1**

Hendry, L. Horse crafts   **745.5**

The horse and the Plains Indians   **978**

Horsepower   **636.1**

Jeffrey, L. S. Horses   **636.1**

Lester, J. Black cowboy, wild horses   **E**

Lewin, T. Stable   **636.1**

Lomberg, M. Horse   **636.1**

Lunis, N. Miniature horses   **636.1**

Mack, G. Horses   **636.1**

MacLeod, E. Why do horses have manes?   **636.1**

Momatiuk, Y. Face to face with wild horses   **599.66**

Niven, F. L. Learning to care for a horse   **636.1**

Ransford, S. Horse & pony breeds   **636.1**

Ransford, S. Horse & pony care   **636.1**

Ransford, S. The Kingfisher illustrated horse & pony encyclopedia   **636.1**

Rockwood, L. Horses are smart!   **636.1**

Simon, S. Horses   **636.1**

Wilsdon, C. For horse-crazy girls only   **636.1**

Horses. Hubbell, P.   **E**

HORSES -- DISEASES

See also Animals -- Diseases

HORSES -- FICTION

Harrison, T. The horse road   **Fic**

Harrison, T. Red River stallion   **Fic**

Primavera, E. Libby of High Hopes   **Fic**

HORSES -- FOLKLORE

Chen, J. H. The magic horse of Han Gan   **398.2**

Cohen, C. L. The mud pony   **398.2**

Goble, P. The girl who loved wild horses   **398.2**

Hausman, G. Horses of myth   **398.2**

Otsuka, Y. Suho's white horse   **398.2**

HORSES -- GRAPHIC NOVELS

Ransom, C. F. The lifesaving adventure of Sam Deal, shipwreck rescuer   **741.5**

HORSES -- GREAT PLAINS -- HISTORY -- JUVENILE LITERATURE

The horse and the Plains Indians   **978**

HORSES -- JUVENILE FICTION

Lester, A. Noni the pony   **E**

HORSES -- JUVENILE LITERATURE

Gibbons, G. Horses!   **636.1**

Jeffrey, L. S. Horses   **636.1**

McCully, E. A. Wonder horse   **E**

HORSES -- MISCELLANEA -- JUVENILE LITERATURE

Holub, J. Why do horses neigh?   **636.1**

HORSES -- TRAINING

Bowers, N. 4-H guide to training horses   **636.1**

HORSES -- TRAINING

See also Horsemanship

Horses are smart! Rockwood, L.   **636.1**

Horses at work. Barnes, J.   **636.1**

HORSES IN ART

Hanukkah lights	**811**
Hazen, B. S. Digby	**E**
Hoban, L. Arthur's Christmas cookies	**E**
Hoban, L. Silly Tilly's Thanksgiving dinner	**E**
Hoff, S. Danny and the dinosaur	**E**
Hoff, S. Oliver	**E**
Hoff, S. Sammy the seal	**E**
Hurd, E. T. Johnny Lion's book	**E**
Kenah, K. The best seat in second grade	**E**
Kessler, L. P. Here comes the strikeout	**E**
Kessler, L. P. Kick, pass, and run	**E**
Kessler, L. P. Last one in is a rotten egg	**E**
Little, J. Emma's yucky brother	**E**
Lobel, A. Frog and Toad are friends	**E**
Lobel, A. Grasshopper on the road	**E**
Lobel, A. Mouse soup	**E**
Lobel, A. Mouse tales	**E**
Lobel, A. Owl at home	**E**
Lobel, A. Small pig	**E**
Lobel, A. Uncle Elephant	**E**
Maestro, M. What do you hear when cows sing?	**793.73**
McCully, E. A. The grandma mix-up	**E**
Minarik, E. H. Little Bear	**E**
Minarik, E. H. No fighting, no biting!	**E**
Monjo, F. N. The drinking gourd	**E**
Parish, P. Amelia Bedelia	**E**
Prelutsky, J. It's snowing! it's snowing!	**811**
Schwartz, A. All of our noses are here, and other noodle tales	**398.2**
Schwartz, A. Ghosts!	**398.2**
Schwartz, A. I saw you in the bathtub, and other folk rhymes	**398.2**
Schwartz, A. In a dark, dark room, and other scary stories	**398.2**
Schwartz, A. There is a carrot in my ear, and other noodle tales	**398.2**
Skofield, J. Detective Dinosaur	**E**
Skofield, J. Detective Dinosaur: lost and found	**E**
Thomson, S. L. Amazing whales!	**599.5**
Turner, A. W. Dust for dinner	**E**
Weeks, S. Drip, drop	**E**
Wiseman, B. Morris and Boris at the circus	**E**
Wyler, R. Magic secrets	**793.8**
An I can read book [series]	
Parish, H. Amelia Bedelia bakes off	**E**
I can read chapter book [series]	
Avi Finding Providence: the story of Roger Williams	**92**
Avi Prairie school	**Fic**
I can read mystery [series]	
Bonsall, C. N. The case of the scaredy cats	**E**
I can read mystery book [series]	
Benchley, N. A ghost named Fred	**E**
I can read! [series]	
Bottner, B. Pish and Posh wish for fairy wings	**E**
Brown, C. L. After the dinosaurs	**569**
Brown, C. L. Beyond the dinosaurs	**560**
Capucilli, A. Biscuit and the lost teddy bear	**E**
Capucilli, A. Pedro's burro	**E**
Cazet, D. Minnie and Moo and the haunted sweater	**E**
Cazet, D. The octopus	**E**
Cazet, D. The shrunken head	**E**
Cazet, D. A snout for chocolate	**E**
Cushman, D. Dirk Bones and the mystery of the missing books	**E**
De Groat, D. Gilbert, the surfer dude	**E**
Dizzy dinosaurs	**811**
George, J. C. Goose and Duck	**E**
Gilman, G. Dixie	**E**

Hamsters, shells, and spelling bees	**811**
Hill, S. Ruby's perfect day	**E**
Hoff, S. The littlest leaguer	**E**
Mozelle, S. Zack's alligator and the first snow	**E**
Prelutsky, J. It's Christmas!	**811**
Prelutsky, J. It's Thanksgiving!	**811**
Sandin, J. At home in a new land	**E**
Schaefer, L. M. Happy Halloween, Mittens	**E**
Schaefer, L. M. Mittens	**E**
Scotton, R. Splat the cat sings flat	**E**
Yorinks, A. Flappy and Scrappy	**E**
I can say a prayer. Piper, S.	**242**
I could be, you could be. Owen, K.	**E**
I could do that! White, L.	**92**
I dare you not to yawn.	**E**
I didn't do it. MacLachlan, P.	**811**
I don't want a cool cat! Dodd, E.	**E**
I don't want a posh dog! Dodd, E.	**E**
I don't want to go to school! Blake, S.	**E**
I dream of trains.	**E**
I dreamed of flying like a bird. Haas, R. B.	**779**
I eat when I'm sad. Simons, R.	**616.85**
I face the wind. Cobb, V.	**551.51**
I fall down. Cobb, V.	**531**
I feel a foot! Rinck, M.	**E**
I feel better with a frog in my throat: history's strangest cures. Beccia, C.	**615.8**
I fooled you.	**S**
I found a dead bird. Thornhill, J.	**306.9**
I get wet. Cobb, V.	**532**
I had a favorite dress. Ashburn, B.	**E**
I haiku you. Snyder, B.	**811**
I hate books! Walker, K.	**Fic**
I have a dream. King, M. L.	**305.896**
I have a dream. King, M. L. J.	**323.092**
I have a little dreidel. Baum, M.	**782.42**
I have asthma. Moore-Mallinos, J.	**616.2**
I have the right to be a child.	**323.3**
I have two homes. De Smet, M.	**E**
I hear America singing!	**782.42**
I heard it from Alice Zucchini. Havill, J.	**811**
I imagine. Rivett, R.	**242**
I kissed the baby. Murphy, M.	**E**
I know a lot of things. Rand, A.	**E**
I know a wee piggy.	**E**
I know an old teacher. Bowen, A.	**E**
I know here. Croza, L.	**E**
I know it's autumn. Spinelli, E.	**E**
I like me! Carlson, N. L.	**E**
I like old clothes.	**E**
I like plants! [series]	
Wade, M. D. Flowers bloom!	**582.13**
Wade, M. D. People need plants!	**581.6**
Wade, M. D. Plants grow!	**571.8**
Wade, M. D. Plants live everywhere!	**581**
Wade, M. D. Seeds sprout!	**581.4**
Wade, M. D. Trees, weeds, and vegetables--so many kinds of plants!	**580**
I like space! [series]	
Bredeson, C. What do astronauts do	**629.45**
Bredeson, C. What is the solar system?	**523.2**
I like to play. Konrad, M. S.	**305.23**
I like to read [series]	
Bjorkman, S. Dinosaurs don't, dinosaurs do	**E**
Emberley, E. Mice on ice	**E**
Lewin, B. You can do it!	**E**
Meisel, P. See me dig	**E**
I like to read picture book [series]	

Emberley, R. The lion and the mice   E
McPhail, D. M. Boy, Bird, and Dog   E
I like vegetables. Siminovich, L.   E
I like you the best. Thompson, C.   E
I live in Tokyo. Takabayashi, M.   952
I lost my kisses. Trewin, T.   E
I lost my tooth in Africa. Diakite, P.   E
I love birthdays. Walker, A.   E
I love bugs. Dodd, E.   E
I love cats.   E
I love chocolate. Cali, D.   E
I love Christmas. Walker, A.   E
I love my mommy. Andreae, G.   E
I love my pirate papa. Leuck, L.   E
I love our Earth. Martin, B.   525
I love planes! Sturges, P.   E
I love school! Sturges, P.   E
I love to draw horses! Lipsey, J.   743
I love to finger paint! Lipsey, J.   751.4
I love to paint! Lipsey, J.   751.4
I love trains! Sturges, P.   E
I love vacations. Walker, A.   E
I love you like crazy cakes. Lewis, R. A.   E
I love you, Little Monkey. Durant, A.   E
I miss you every day. Taback, S.   E
I miss you Mouse. Foley, G.   E
I must go down to the beach again. Shapiro, K. J.   811
I must have Bobo! Rosenthal, E.   E
--I never saw another butterfly-- Volavkova, H.   741.9
I owe you one. Hyde, N.   Fic
I put a spell on you. Selzer, A.   Fic
I remember Miss Perry. Brisson, P.   E
I said no! Burstein, J.   158
I saw Esau.   398.8
I saw you in the bathtub, and other folk rhymes. Schwartz, A.   398.2
I saw your face. Dawes, K. S. N.   811
I see a kookaburra! Jenkins, S.   591.7
I see I learn [series]
    Murphy, S. J. Emma's friendwich   E
    Murphy, S. J. Freda is found   E
I see myself. Cobb, V.   535
I see the rhythm. Igus, T.   780.89
I see the rhythm of gospel. Igus, T.   782.25
I see the sun in Afghanistan. King, D.   E
I spy. Wick, W.   793.73
I spy a Christmas tree. Marzollo, J.   793.73
I spy an egg in a nest. Marzollo, J.   793.73
I spy extreme challenger! Wick, W.   793.73
I spy fantasy. Wick, W.   793.73
I spy gold challenger! Wick, W.   793.73
I spy school days. Marzollo, J.   793.73
I spy spooky night. Wick, W.   793.73
I spy super challenger! Wick, W.   793.73
I spy treasure hunt. Wick, W.   793.73
I spy ultimate challenger! Wick, W.   793.73
I spy with my little eye. Gibbs, E.   590
I spy: an alphabet in art. Micklethwait, L.   E
I stink! McMullan, K.   E
I survived [series]
    Tarshis, L. I survived Hurricane Katrina, 2005   Fic
    Tarshis, L. I survived the bombing of Pearl Harbor, 1941   Fic
    Tarshis, L. I survived the shark attacks of 1916   Fic
    Tarshis, L. I survived the sinking of the Titanic, 1912   Fic
I survived Hurricane Katrina, 2005. Tarshis, L.   Fic
I survived the Battle of Gettysburg, 1863. Tarshis, L.   E
I survived the bombing of Pearl Harbor, 1941. Tarshis, L.   Fic
I survived the shark attacks of 1916. Tarshis, L.   Fic

I survived the sinking of the Titanic, 1912. Tarshis, L.   Fic
I think I am going to sneeze. Thomas, P.   616.97
I took a walk. Cole, H.   508
I wanna be your shoebox. Garcia, C.   Fic
I wanna iguana. Orloff, K. K.   E
I wanna new room. Orloff, K. K.   E
I want a dog! Bansch, H.   E
I want a dog! Saltzberg, B.   E
I want a party! Ross, T.   E
I want my hat back. Klassen, J.   E
I want my light on! Ross, T.   E
I want to be free. Slate, J.   E
I want to do it myself! Ross, T.   E
I want two birthdays! Ross, T.   E
I was a rat! Pullman, P.   Fic
I was a third grade bodyguard. Auch, M. J.   Fic
I was a third grade science project. Auch, M. J.   Fic
I was a third grade spy. Auch, M. J.   Fic
I was dreaming to come to America.   304.8
I will come back for you. Russo, M.   E
I will never not ever eat a tomato. Child, L.   E
I will not read this book. Meng, C.   E
I would tuck you in. Asper-Smith, S.   E
I'll be there. Stott, A.   E
I'll hold your hand so you won't fall. Ali-Walsh, R.   616.8
I'll play with you. Siddals, M. M.   E
I'll save you Bobo! Rosenthal, E.   E
I'm 3! look what I can do. Carluccio, M.   E
I'm a duck! Sloat, T.   E
I'm a scientist [series]
    Burke, L. Backyard   507.8
    Burke, L. Kitchen   507.8
I'm a shark! Shea, B.   E
I'm a truck driver. London, J.   E
I'm a turkey! Arnosky, J.   E
I'm adopted! Rotner, S.   362.7
I'm bad. McMullan, K.   E
I'm big! McMullan, K.   E
I'm dirty! McMullan, K.   E
I'm getting a checkup. Singer, M.   610
I'm gonna like me. Curtis, J. L.   E
I'm here. Reynolds, P.   E
I'm just like my mom/I'm just like my dad. Ramos, J.   E
I'm me! Sheridan, S.   E
I'm mighty! McMullan, K.   E
I'm not. Smallcomb, P.   E
I'm not happy. Graves, S.   152.4
I'm not Santa! Allen, J.   E
I'm not scared! Allen, J.   E
I'm not sleepy! Chapman, J.   E
I'm number one. Rosen, M.   E
I'm still scared. De Paola, T.   92
I'm the best. Cousins, L.   E
I'm the biggest thing in the ocean. Sherry, K.   E
I'm your bus. Singer, M.   E
I've lost my hippopotamus. Prelutsky, J.   811
I've seen the promised land. Myers, W. D.   92
I, crocodile. Marcellino, F.   E
I, Emma Freke. Atkinson, E. J.   Fic
I, Freddy. Reiche, D.   Fic
I, Galileo. Christensen, B.   520.92
I, Juan de Pareja. Trevino, E. B. d.   Fic
I, Q.: book one, Independence Hall. Smith, R.   Fic
I, too, am America.   811
I, too, sing America.   811
I, Vivaldi. Shefelman, J. J.   92
I. Q.: book two, The White House. Smith, R.   Fic
Ibatoulline, Bagram

See also Art

IMPRESSIONISM (ART) -- FICTION
Knight, J. Charlotte in Paris   **Fic**

IMPRESSIONISM (ART) -- JUVENILE FICTION
Knight, J. Charlotte in Giverny   **Fic**

IMPRESSIONISM (ART) -- JUVENILE LITERATURE
Danneberg, J. Monet paints a day   **E**

IMPRESSIONISM (ART) -- TECHNIQUE -- JUVENILE LITERATURE
Raimondo, J. Picture this!   **759.05**

IMPRESSIONIST ARTISTS -- FRANCE -- BIOGRAPHY -- JUVENILE LITERATURE
Sabbeth, C. Monet and the impressionists for kids   759.05

Improving endurance. Mason, P.   **613.7**
Improving flexibility. Mason, P.   **613.7**
Improving speed. Mason, P.   **613.7**
Improving strength & power. Mason, P.   **613.7**
The **impudent** rooster. Rascol, S. I.   **398.2**
In a blue room. Averbeck, J.   **E**
In a dark, dark room, and other scary stories. Schwartz, A.   **398.2**
In a glass Grimmly. Gidwitz, A.   **Fic**
In a word. Baker, R. F.   **422**
In an emergency. Champion, N.   **613.6**
In Aunt Giraffe's green garden. Prelutsky, J.   **811**
In daddy's arms I am tall.   **811**
In front of God and everybody. McCrite, K. D.   **Fic**
In front of my house. Dubuc, M.   **E**
In God's hands. Kushner, L.   **E**
In her hands. Schroeder, A.   **92**
In like a lion, out like a lamb. Bauer, M. D.   **E**
In loving memory of Gorfman T. Frog.   **Fic**
In our mothers' house. Polacco, P.   **E**
In search of Goliathus hercules. Angus, J.   **Fic**
In search of Sasquatch. Halls, K. M.   **001.9**
In temperate zones. Baker, S.   **551.6**
In the Antarctic. Baker, S.   **508**
In the Arctic. Baker, S.   **971**
In the bag! Kulling, M.   **E**
In the beginning: the art of Genesis. Fischer, C.   **222**
In the beginning; creation stories from around the world. Hamilton, V.   **201**
In the belly of an ox: the unexpected photographic adventures of Richard and Cherry Kearton. Bond, R.   **92**
In the days of sand and stars. Pinsker, M.   **296.1**
In the days of the Salem witchcraft trials. Roach, M. K.   **133.4**
In the days of the vaqueros. Freedman, R.   **636.2**
In the deep sea. Collard, S. B.   **572**
In the doghouse. Kimmelman, L.   **E**
In the garden with Dr. Carver. Grigsby, S.   **E**
In the hollow of your hand.   **782.42**
In the land of the jaguar. Gorrell, G. K.   **980**
In the library [series]
Donovan, S. Bob the Alien discovers the Dewey decimal system   **025.4**
Donovan, S. Bored Bella learns about fiction and nonfiction   **025.4**
Donovan, S. Pingpong Perry experiences how a book is made   **070.5**
In the meadow. Kato, Y.   **E**
In the night kitchen. Sendak, M.   **E**
In the picture. Micklethwait, L.   **750**
In the rain forest canopy. Collard, S. B.   **578**
In the sea. Elliott, D.   **811**
In the small, small pond. Fleming, D.   **813**
In the tall, tall grass. Fleming, D.   **813**
In the town all year 'round. Berner, R. S.   **E**
In the trees, honeybees! Mortensen, L.   **595.7**

In the tropics. Baker, S.   **508**
In the wild. Elliott, D.   **811**
In the woods: who's been here? George, L. B.   **591**
In the Year of the Boar and Jackie Robinson. Lord, B. B.   **Fic**
In the zone [series]
Johnstone, R. Hockey   **796.962**
In too deep. Watson, J.   **Fic**
In touch with basic science [series]
Spilsbury, L. What is light?   **535**
Spilsbury, R. What are forces and motion?   **531**
Spilsbury, R. What are solids, liquids, and gases?   **530.4**
Spilsbury, R. What is electricity and magnetism?   **537**
Spilsbury, R. What is energy?   **621**
Spilsbury, R. What is sound?   **534**
The **Inca** empire. Newman, S.   **985**

INCANDESCENT LAMPS *See* Electric lamps

INCAS
Calvert, P. The ancient Inca   **985**
Gruber, B. Ancient Inca   **985**
Newman, S. The Inca empire   **985**

Inch by inch. Mallett, D.   **782.42**
Inch by inch. Lionni, L.   **E**
Incident at Hawk's Hill. Eckert, A. W.   **Fic**

INCINERATION *See* Cremation; Refuse and refuse disposal
Inclined planes. Howse, J.   **621.8**

INCLINED PLANES
See also Simple machines

INCLINED PLANES
Howse, J. Inclined planes   **621.8**
Thales, S. Inclined planes to the rescue   **621.8**
Walker, S. M. Put inclined planes to the test   **621.8**
Inclined planes to the rescue. Thales, S.   **621.8**

INCOME TAX
See also Internal revenue; Taxation
An **inconvenient** truth. Gore, A.   **363.7**
Incorrigible children of Ashton Place [series]
Wood, M. The hidden gallery   **Fic**
The **incorrigible children of Ashton Place** [series]
Wood, M. The mysterious howling   **Fic**
The **incredible** book eating boy. Jeffers, O.   **E**
Incredible deep-sea adventures [series]
Matsen, B. The incredible record-setting deep-sea dive of the bathysphere   **551.46**
Incredible inventions.   **811**
The **incredible** life of Balto. McCarthy, M.   **636.7**
The **incredible** record-setting deep-sea dive of the bathysphere. Matsen, B.   **551.46**
Incredible skyscrapers. Barker, G. P.   **720**
The **incredible** voyage of Ulysses. Landmann, B.   **883**
The **Incredibles**: secrets & lies. Walker, L. Q.   **741.5**
Incredibly disgusting food [series]
Furgang, A. Carbonated beverages   **613.2**
Furgang, A. Salty and sugary snacks   **613.2**
Johanson, P. Fake foods   **613.2**
Watson, S. Mystery meat   **613.2**

INCUNABULA
See also Books

INDEBTEDNESS *See* Debt

INDEPENDENCE DAY (UNITED STATES) *See* Fourth of July

Independence Hall. Staton, H.   **974.8**
Independent dames. Anderson, L. H.   **973.3**

INDEPENDENT FILMS
See also Motion pictures
Independent school libraries.   **025.1**

INDEPENDENT SCHOOLS *See* Private schools

INDEPENDENT STUDY
See also Study skills; Tutors and tutoring

Sullivan, G. Helen Keller   **92**

INSTALLMENT PLAN

    See also Business; Consumer credit; Credit; Purchasing

INSTINCT

    See also Animal behavior; Psychology

INSTITUTIONAL CARE

    See also Charities; Medical charities; Public welfare

INSTITUTIONS, CHARITABLE AND PHILANTHROPIC

  See Charities

INSTRUCTION *See* Education; Teaching

INSTRUCTIONAL GAMES *See* Educational games

INSTRUCTIONAL MATERIALS CENTERS

  Bishop, K. Connecting libraries with classrooms   **375**

  Farmer, L. S. J. Collaborating with administrators and educational support staff   **027.8**

  Farmer, L. S. J. Neal-Schuman technology management handbook for school library media centers   **025.1**

  Gaines, A. Master the library and media center   **020**

  Harada, V. H. Assessing for learning   **027.8**

  Martin, B. S. Fundamentals of school library media management   **025.1**

  Morris, B. J. Administering the school library media center   **027.8**

  Safford, B. R. Guide to reference materials for school library media centers   **011.6**

  Stephens, C. G. Library 101   **027.8**

INSTRUCTIONAL MATERIALS CENTERS

    See also Libraries

INSTRUCTIONAL MATERIALS CENTERS -- DESIGN AND CONSTRUCTION

  Erikson, R. Designing a school library media center for the future   **027.8**

Instructions. Gaiman, N.   **E**

INSTRUCTIVE GAMES *See* Educational games

INSTRUMENTAL MUSIC

    See also Music

INSTRUMENTALISTS

    See also Musicians

INSTRUMENTATION AND ORCHESTRATION

    See also Bands (Music); Composition (Music); Music; Orchestra

INSTRUMENTS, MEASURING *See* Measuring instruments

INSTRUMENTS, MUSICAL *See* Musical instruments

INSTRUMENTS, SCIENTIFIC *See* Scientific apparatus and instruments

INSURANCE

    See also Estate planning; Finance; Personal finance

INSURANCE, HEALTH *See* Health insurance

INTEGRATED CURRICULUM *See* Interdisciplinary approach in education

INTEGRATED SCHOOLS *See* School integration

INTEGRATION IN EDUCATION *See* School integration; Segregation in education

INTEGRATION, RACIAL *See* Race relations

INTELLECT

    See also Psychology

INTELLECT -- FICTION

  Chatterton, M. The Brain finds a leg   **Fic**

INTELLECTUAL COOPERATION

    See also International cooperation

INTELLECTUAL FREEDOM

  Scales, P. R. Protecting intellectual freedom in your school library   **025.2**

INTELLECTUAL FREEDOM

    See also Freedom

INTELLECTUAL FREEDOM -- UNITED STATES -- HANDBOOKS, MANUALS, ETC.

Intellectual freedom manual   **025.2**

Intellectual freedom front lines [series]

  Scales, P. R. Protecting intellectual freedom in your school library   **025.2**

Intellectual freedom manual.   **025.2**

INTELLECTUAL LIFE

    See also Culture

INTELLIGENCE AGENTS *See* Spies

INTELLIGENCE OF ANIMALS *See* Animal intelligence

INTELLIGENCE SERVICE

  Earnest, P. The real spy's guide to becoming a spy   **327.12**

INTELLIGENCE SERVICE

    See also Public administration; Research

INTELLIGENCE SERVICE -- JUVENILE LITERATURE

  Earnest, P. The real spy's guide to becoming a spy   **327.12**

INTELLIGENCE TESTS

    See also Child psychology; Educational psychology

INTEMPERANCE *See* Alcoholism; Temperance

INTERACTIVE MEDIA *See* Multimedia

INTERACTIVE MULTIMEDIA *See* Multimedia

INTERBEHAVIORIAL PSYCHOLOGY *See* Behaviorism

INTERCOMMUNICATION SYSTEMS

    See also Electronic apparatus and appliances; Telecommunication

INTERCOUNTRY ADOPTION

  Lewis, R. A. I love you like crazy cakes   **E**

INTERCOUNTRY ADOPTION *See* International adoption

INTERCOUNTRY ADOPTION -- FICTION

  Goyangi means cat   **E**

  Peacock, C. A. Red thread sisters   **Fic**

INTERCULTURAL EDUCATION *See* Multicultural education

INTERDISCIPLINARITY IN EDUCATION *See* Interdisciplinary approach in education

INTERDISCIPLINARY APPROACH IN EDUCATION

  Larson, J. C. Bringing mysteries alive for children and young adults   **028.5**

INTERDISCIPLINARY STUDIES *See* Interdisciplinary approach in education

INTEREST GROUPS *See* Lobbying; Political action committees

The intergalactic bed & breakfast [series]

  Aliens on vacation   **Fic**

INTERGENERATIONAL RELATIONS -- FICTION

  Casarosa, E. La Luna   **E**

INTERGOVERNMENTAL TAX RELATIONS

    See also Taxation

INTERIOR DECORATION *See* Interior design

INTERIOR DESIGN

  Torres, L. Rock your room   **746**

  Weaver, J. It's your room   **747**

INTERIOR DESIGN

    See also Art; Decoration and ornament; Design; Home economics

Interjections.   **428**

INTERLIBRARY LOANS

    See also Library circulation; Library cooperation

INTERMEDIATE SCHOOLS *See* Middle schools

INTERNAL COMBUSTION ENGINES

    See also Engines

INTERNAL MIGRATION

    See also Colonization; Population

INTERNAL REVENUE

    See also Taxation

INTERNAL REVENUE LAW

    See also Law

INTERNATIONAL ADOPTION

  Skrypuch, M. F. Last airlift   **959.704**

J

Jeong, Kyoung-Sim

  (il) Kim Korean children's favorite stories   **398.2**

Jepson, J. Beth

  (il) Corcoran, J. Dare to dream--change the world   **811.6**

Jeram, Anita

  (il) Hest, A. Kiss good night   **E**

  (il) Hest, A. Little Chick   **E**

  (il) King-Smith, D. All pigs are beautiful   **636.4**

  (il) McBratney, S. Guess how much I love you   **E**

  (il) McBratney, S. When I'm big   **E**

Jeremy Bender vs. the Cupcake Cadets. Luper, E.   **Fic**

Jeremy draws a monster. McCarty, P.   **E**

Jeremy Fink and the meaning of life. Mass, W.   **Fic**

Jeremy Thatcher, dragon hatcher. Coville, B.   **Fic**

Jeremy Visick. Wiseman, D.   **Fic**

Jermyn, Leslie

  Cheong-Lum, R. N. Haiti   **972.94**

  Foley, E. Dominican Republic   **972.93**

  Foley, E. Ecuador   **986.6**

  Belize   **972.82**

  Cuba   **972.91**

  Guyana   **988.1**

  Paraguay   **989.2**

  Uruguay   **989.5**

Jerome, Kate Boehm

  Atomic universe   **539.7**

Jerusalem. Bowden, R.   **956.94**

JERUSALEM -- FICTION

  Abdel-Fattah, R. Where the streets had a name   **Fic**

Jerusalem sky. Podwal, M. H.   **811**

Jesse Bear, what will you wear? Carlstrom, N. W.   **E**

Jessell, Tim

  (il) Armstrong, A. Racing the moon   **Fic**

  Falcon   **E**

Jessell, Tim

  (il) Armstrong, A. Looking for Marco Polo   **Fic**

  (il) Armstrong, A. Raleigh's page   **Fic**

Jesset, Aurore

  Loopy   **E**

Jessica. Henkes, K.   **E**

Jestice, Phyllis G.

  Ancient Egyptian warfare   **932**

  Ancient Persian warfare   **935**

Jesus. Wildsmith, B.   **232.9**

Jesus. Bible/N.T.   **232.9**

Jesus Christ

        About

  The third gift   **E**

  Billingsley, M. The life of Jesus   **242**

  Crossley-Holland, K. How many miles to Bethlehem?   **232.9**

  Grimes, N. At Jerusalem's gate   **811**

  Hillenbrand, W. Cock-a-doodle Christmas!   **E**

  Jones, S. L. Little one, we knew you'd come   **232.9**

  Lottridge, C. B. Stories from the life of Jesus   **232.9**

  Melmed, L. K. Hurry! Hurry! Have you heard?   **E**

  Paterson, K. The light of the world   **232.9**

  Skevington, A. The story of Jesus   **232.9**

  Wildsmith, B. Jesus   **232.9**

Jesus Christ -- Fiction

        About

  Menotti, G. C. Amahl and the night visitors   **232.9**

  Speare, E. G. The bronze bow   **Fic**

Jesus Christ -- Nativity

        About

  Bible/N.T./Luke Christmas is here   **232.9**

  Bible/N.T. The story of Christmas   **232.9**

  The greatest gift   **Fic**

  Listen to the silent night   **E**

  One starry night   **E**

  Song of the stars   **E**

  The third gift   **E**

  Buck, N. A Christmas goodnight   **E**

  Cotten, C. This is the stable   **E**

  Hillenbrand, W. Cock-a-doodle Christmas!   **E**

  Jones, S. L. Little one, we knew you'd come   **232.9**

  Crossley-Holland, K. How many miles to Bethlehem?   **232.9**

  Milligan, B. Brigid's cloak   **398.2**

  Morpurgo, M. On angel wings   **Fic**

  Nazoa, A. A small Nativity   **E**

  Slegers, L. The child in the manger   **232.9**

  Williams, S. The first Christmas   **232.9**

Jesus Christ -- Nativity/Fiction

        About

  Melmed, L. K. Hurry! Hurry! Have you heard?   **E**

Jesus Christ -- Poetry

        About

  Grimes, N. At Jerusalem's gate   **811**

Jesus Christ -- Resurrection

        About

  The story of Easter   **263**

JET AIRPLANES *See* Jet planes

Jet plane. Keenan, S.   **629.133**

JET PLANES

  Keenan, S. Jet plane   **629.133**

JET PLANES

    See also Airplanes

JET PROPULSION

  Sandler, M. Jet-powered speed   **629.228**

Jet-powered speed. Sandler, M.   **629.228**

Jeter, Derek, 1974- -- Juvenile literature

        About

  Rappoport, K. Derek Jeter   **796.357**

JETS (AIRPLANES) *See* Jet planes

Jeunesse, Gallimard

  Inside the body   **611**

The **jewel** box ballerinas. Varennes, M. d.   **E**

The **Jewel** Fish of Karnak. Base, G.   **E**

The **Jewel** of the Kalderash. Rutkoski, M.   **Fic**

JEWELRY

  Di Salle, R. Junk drawer jewelry   **745.594**

  Haab, S. Dangles and bangles   **745.5**

  Jazzy jewelry   **745.594**

  Kenney, K. L. Super simple jewelry   **739.27**

  Sadler, J. A. Hemp jewelry   **746.42**

  Scheunemann, P. Cool beaded jewelry   **745.58**

JEWELRY

    See also Clothing and dress; Costume; Decorative arts

JEWELRY MAKING -- JUVENILE LITERATURE

  Sadler, J. A. Hemp jewelry   **746.42**

  Warwick, E. Everywear   **745.5**

JEWELS *See* Gems; Jewelry; Precious stones

JEWISH ART AND SYMBOLISM

  Chaikin, M. Menorahs, mezuzas, and other Jewish symbols   **296.4**

JEWISH CHILDREN -- JUVENILE FICTION

  Happy birthday, Tree   **E**

JEWISH CHILDREN IN THE HOLOCAUST

  Hodge, D. Rescuing the children   **940.53**

JEWISH CHILDREN IN THE HOLOCAUST

    See also Holocaust, 1939-1945

JEWISH CHILDREN IN THE HOLOCAUST -- BIOGRAPHY -- JUVENILE LITERATURE

  Warren, A. Surviving Hitler   **940.53**

JEWISH CHILDREN IN THE HOLOCAUST -- CZECH REPUBLIC -- NOVÃ‰ MÌŒESTO NAD METUJI -- BIOGRAPHY -- JUVENILE LITERATURE

See also Martial arts; Self-defense

JUDO

Ellis, C. Judo and jujitsu   **796.8**

Mason, P. Judo   **796.815**

Judo and jujitsu. Ellis, C.   **796.8**

Judy Moody. McDonald, M.   **Fic**

Judy Moody & Stink: the holly joliday. McDonald, M.   **Fic**

Judy Moody & Stink: the mad, mad, mad, mad treasure hunt. McDonald, M.   **Fic**

Judy Moody declares independence. McDonald, M.   **Fic**

Judy Moody gets famous. McDonald, M.   **Fic**

Judy Moody goes to college. McDonald, M.   **Fic**

Judy Moody goes to Hollywood. McDonald, M.   **791.43**

Judy Moody predicts the future. McDonald, M.   **Fic**

Judy Moody saves the world! McDonald, M.   **Fic**

Judy Moody, girl detective. McDonald, M.   **Fic**

Judy Moody, M.D. McDonald, M.   **Fic**

Judy Moody: around the world in 8 1/2 days. McDonald, M.   **Fic**

Juettner, Bonnie

Hybrid cars   **629.222**

Molecules   **540**

The seed vault   **631.5**

JUGGLING

See also Amusements; Tricks

JUJITSU *See* Jiu-jitsu

Jukes, Mavis

Growing up: it's a girl thing   **612.6**

Jules, Jacqueline

Abraham's search for God   **222**

Benjamin and the silver goblet   **222**

Duck for Turkey Day   **E**

Miriam in the desert   **222**

Sarah laughs   **222**

Unite or die   **973.3**

Julia Gillian (and the art of knowing) McGhee, A.   **Fic**

Julia Morgan built a castle. Mannis, C. D.   **92**

Julia wants a pet. Lindgren, B.   **E**

Julian Rodriguez: episode one, Trash crisis on earth. Stadler, A.   **Fic**

Julian Rodriguez: episode two, Invasion of the relatives. Stadler, A.   **Fic**

Julie Andrews' collection of poems, songs, and lullabies. **808.8**

Julie Andrews' treasury for all seasons.   **808.81**

JULIET (FICTITIOUS CHARACTER) -- JUVENILE FICTION

Coville, B. William Shakespeare's Romeo and Juliet   **822.3**

Juliet Dove, Queen of Love. Coville, B.   **Fic**

Julio's magic. Dorros, A.   **E**

Julius Caesar. Galford, E.   **92**

Julius, the baby of the world. Henkes, K.   **E**

JULY FOURTH *See* Fourth of July

Jumanji. Van Allsburg, C.   **E**

The **jumbo** book of art. Luxbacher, I.   **702.8**

The **jumbo** book of needlecrafts. Sadler, J. A.   **746.4**

The **jumbo** book of outdoor art. Luxbacher, I.   **704.9**

Jump into science [series]

Tomecek, S. Moon   **523.3**

Tomecek, S. Rocks & minerals   **552**

JUMP ROPE RHYMES

Anna Banana: 101 jump-rope rhymes   **398.8**

Dotlich, R. K. Over in the pink house   **811**

Sierra, J. Schoolyard rhymes   **398.8**

Jump ship to freedom. Collier, J. L.   **Fic**

Jump! Cooper, F.   **92**

Jump! Fischer, S. M.   **E**

Jump, frog, jump! Kalan, R.   **E**

Jump, kangaroo, jump! Murphy, S. J.   **513**

Jumper, Betty Mae, 1923-

About

Annino, J. G. She sang promise: the story of Betty Mae Jumper, Seminole tribal leader   **92**

JUMPING -- UNITED STATES -- JUVENILE LITERATURE

Malaspina, A. Touch the sky   **796.42**

Jumping spiders. Markle, S.   **595.4**

JUMPING SPIDERS -- JUVENILE LITERATURE

Markle, S. Jumping spiders   **595.4**

Jumping the scratch. Weeks, S.   **Fic**

Jumpy Jack and Googily. Rosoff, M.   **E**

Jun Lim

Socrates   **183**

June 29, 1999. Wiesner, D.   **E**

Junebug. Mead, A.   **Fic**

Juneteenth. Nelson, V. M.   **394.26**

JUNETEENTH

Nelson, V. M. Juneteenth   **394.26**

JUNETEENTH -- JUVENILE LITERATURE

Nelson, V. M. Juneteenth   **394.26**

Jung, Mike

Geeks, girls, and secret identities   **Fic**

Jungle. Greenaway, T.   **577.3**

JUNGLE ANIMALS

See also Animals; Forest animals

JUNGLE ANIMALS -- FICTION

Fleming, C. Oh, no!   **E**

What to do if an elephant stands on your foot   **E**

The **jungle** book: Mowgli's story. Kipling, R.   **S**

JUNGLE ECOLOGY

See also Ecology; Forest ecology

The **jungle** grapevine. Beard, A.   **E**

Jungle party. Wildsmith, B.   **E**

JUNGLES

See also Forests and forestry

JUNGLES -- FICTION

Achebe, C. How the leopard got his claws   **Fic**

Broach, E. Gumption!   **E**

Slack, M. H. Monkey Truck   **E**

Junie B. Jones and her big fat mouth. Park, B.   **Fic**

Junior authors & illustrators series

Rockman, C. C. Tenth book of junior authors and illustrators   **920.003**

JUNIOR HIGH SCHOOLS

See also High schools; Public schools; Schools

Junior Worldmark encyclopedia of the Canadian provinces.   **971**

Junior Worldmark encyclopedia of the Mexican states.   **972**

Junior worldmark encyclopedia of the nations.   **910.3**

Junior Worldmark encyclopedia of the states.   **973**

Junk drawer jewelry. Di Salle, R.   **745.594**

Junk food. Cobb, V.   **664**

Junk food. Currie, S.   **613.2**

JUNK IN SPACE *See* Space debris

Junkyard science. Young, K. R.   **507.8**

The **junkyard** wonders. Polacco, P.   **Fic**

Junor, Betty

Fun & funky knits   **746.43**

Jupiter. Capaccio, G.   **523.4**

Jupiter. Landau, E.   **523.4**

JUPITER (PLANET)

See also Planets

JUPITER (PLANET) -- JUVENILE LITERATURE

Mist, R. Jupiter and Saturn   **523.45**

Jupiter and Saturn. Mist, R.   **523.45**

Jurassic poop. Berkowitz, J.   **567.9**

JURISPRUDENCE *See* Law

JURISTS *See* Lawyers

Jurmain, Suzanne
　The forbidden schoolhouse　　92
　The worst of friends　　973.4

Just a dog. Bauer, M. G.　　Fic
Just a dream. Van Allsburg, C.　　E
Just a minute. Morales, Y.　　398.2
Just a second. Jenkins, S.　　529
Just add water.　　546
Just because. Elliott, R.　　E
Just behave, Pablo Picasso!　　709.2
Just being Audrey. Cardillo, M.　　92
Just Desserts. Durand, H.　　Fic
Just enough and not too much. Zemach, K.　　E
Just enough carrots. Murphy, S. J.　　513.2
Just fine the way they are.　　388
Just for elephants. Buckley, C.　　639.9
Just for kids! [series]
　Hart, C. You can draw cartoon animals　　741.5
Just Grace. Harper, C. M.　　Fic
Just Grace and the double surprise.　　Fic
Just Grace and the snack attack. Harper, C. M.　　Fic
Just Grace and the Terrible Tutu. Harper, C. M.　　Fic
Just Grace and the trouble with cupcakes.　　Fic
Just Grace goes green. Harper, C. M.　　Fic
Just Grace walks the dog. Harper, C. M.　　Fic
Just how long can a long string be!? Baker, K.　　E
Just in case. Morales, Y.　　E
Just in case. Viorst, J.　　E
Just in time, Abraham Lincoln. Polacco, P.　　Fic
Just like a baby. Havill, J.　　E
Just like Josh Gibson. Johnson, A.　　E
Just like you. Dodd, E.　　E
Just one bite. Schaefer, L. M.　　591.4
Just so stories. Kipling, R.　　S
Just the basics [series]
　Franklin, P. School library collection development　　025.2
Just the right size. Davies, N.　　591.4
Just what Mama needs. Glenn, S. M.　　E
Juster, Norton
　Neville　　E
Juster, Norton
　Alberic the Wise and other journeys　　S
　The annotated Phantom tollbooth　　813
　The hello, goodbye window　　E
　Neville　　E
　The odious Ogre　　E
　The phantom tollbooth　　Fic
Juster, Norton, 1929-
　　　　About
　Juster, N. The annotated Phantom tollbooth　　813
Juster, Norton, 1929- -- Work -- Phantom tollbooth
　　　　About
　Juster, N. The annotated Phantom tollbooth　　813
JUSTICE
　See also Ethics; Law; Virtue
JUSTICE LEAGUE (FICTIONAL CHARACTERS)
　See also Fictional characters; Superheroes
JUSTICES OF THE PEACE
　White, L. I could do that!　　92
Justin and the best biscuits in the world. Walter, M. P.　　Fic
Justin Bieber. Yasuda, A.　　92
Justin Bieber: first step 2 forever. Bieber, J.　　92
Justin Case. Vail, R.　　Fic
Justin Fisher declares war! Preller, J.　　Fic
Jutte, Jan
　(il) Joosse, B. M. Roawr!　　E
　(il) Joosse, B. M. Sleepover at gramma's house　　E

JUVENILE DELINQUENCY
　Mead, A. Junebug in trouble　　Fic
JUVENILE DELINQUENCY
　See also Crime; Social problems
JUVENILE DELINQUENCY -- FICTION
　Mead, A. Junebug in trouble　　Fic
　Sachar, L. Holes　　Fic
JUVENILE DELINQUENTS *See* Juvenile delinquency
Juvenile diabetes. Glaser, J.　　616.4
JUVENILE FICTION -- ACTION & ADVENTURE --
　GENERAL
　Bransford, N. Jacob Wonderbar and the interstellar time
　　warp　　Fic
　Catmull, K. Summer and Bird　　Fic
　Flavin, T. The crimson shard　　Fic
　Gal, S. Day by day　　E
　Obed, E. B. Twelve kinds of ice　　Fic
JUVENILE PROSTITUTION
　See also Juvenile delinquency; Prostitution
Jyotirmayee Mohapatra. Woog, A.　　92

K

K is for Korea. Cheung, H.　　951.9
Kaboom! Richardson, G.　　500
Kacer, Kathy
　Hiding Edith　　940.53
Kaddish for Grandpa in Jesus' name, amen. Howe, J.　　E
Kadohata, Cynthia
　Cracker!　　Fic
　Kira-Kira　　Fic
　A million shades of gray　　Fic
　Outside beauty　　Fic
　The thing about luck　　Fic
　Weedflower　　Fic
Kagda, Falaq
　Algeria　　965
　Hong Kong　　951.25
Kagda, Sakina
　Lithuania　　947.93
Kahanamoku, Duke, 1890-1968
　　　　About
　Krull, K. Lives of the athletes　　796
Kahanamoku, Duke, 1890-1968
　　　　About
　Crowe, E. Surfer of the century　　92
Kahlo, Frida, 1907-1954
　　　　About
　Winter, J. Frida　　759.9
　Frith, M. Frida Kahlo　　92
　　　　Fiction
　Me, Frida　　E
Kahumbu, Paula
　Hatkoff, C. Looking for Miza　　599.8
　Hatkoff, I. Owen & Mzee　　599.63
　Hatkoff, I. Owen & Mzee: the language of friendship　　599.63
Kai-Mook. Genechten, G. v.　　E
Kain, Karen
　The Nutcracker　　E
Kajikawa, Kimiko
　Close to you　　591.3
　Tsunami!　　398.2
KAKAPO -- JUVENILE LITERATURE
　Montgomery, S. Kakapo rescue　　639.9
Kakapo rescue. Montgomery, S.　　639.9
Kakeda, Aya
　(il) Budnitz, P. The hole in the middle　　E

Kalan, Robert
  Jump, frog, jump!   E
Kaleidopops [series]
  Martin, R. Bugs   595.7
Kaleidoscope [series]
  Gallant, R. A. Fossils   560
  Gallant, R. A. Water   551.48
Kali and the rat snake. Whitaker, Z.   E
Kali's song. Winter, J.   E
Kalis, Jennifer
  (il) Friedman, L. B. Campfire Mallory   Fic
KALISPEL INDIANS
  Bruchac, J. Buffalo song   92
Kallen, Stuart A.
  Crop circles   001.9
  The sphinx   398
  Werewolves   398
Kalman, Bobbie
  Baby carnivores   599.713
  Baby mammals   591.3
  Baby primates   599.813
  Baby rodents   599.351
  The life cycle of a beaver   599.3
  The life cycle of an emperor penguin   598
  What are opposites in nature?   508
  What is symmetry in nature?   570
Kalman, Maira
  (il) 13 words   E
  Looking at Lincoln   973.709
Kalz, Jill
  An A-MAZE-ing amusement park adventure   793.73
Kamath, B. M.
  (il) Singh, V. Younguncle comes to town   Fic
Kami and the yaks. Stryer, A. S.   E
Kamishibai man. Say, A.   E
Kan, Katharine
  (ed) Graphic novels and comic books   741.5
Kane chronicles [series]
  Collar, O. The Red Pyramid   741.5
  Riordan, R. The throne of fire   Fic
Kane, Joseph Nathan
  Famous first facts   031.02
Kaner, Etta
  And the Winner Is ...   612.7
  Earth-friendly buildings, bridges, and more   720.47
Kaner, Etta
  Have you ever seen a hippo with sunscreen?   591.4
  Who likes the rain?   551.57
  Who likes the snow?   551.57
  Who likes the wind?   551.51
Kanevsky, Polly
  Sleepy boy   E
Kang, Hildi
  Chengli and the Silk Road caravan   Fic
Kangaroo and crocodile.   E
Kangaroos. Riggs, K.   599.2
KANGAROOS
  Bredeson, C. Kangaroos up close   599.2
  Doudna, K. It's a baby kangaroo!   599.2
  Gish, M. Kangaroos   599.2
  Riggs, K. Kangaroos   599.2
Kangaroos. Gish, M.   599.2
KANGAROOS -- FICTION
  Bourguignon, L. Heart in the pocket   E
  Payne, E. Katy No-Pocket   E
  Stein, D. E. Pouch!   E
  Ungerer, T. Adelaide   E
KANGAROOS -- JUVENILE LITERATURE

Riggs, K. Kangaroos   599.2
KANGAROOS -- POETRY
  Lear, E. Edward Lear's The duck & the kangaroo   821
Kangaroos up close. Bredeson, C.   599.2
Kangas, Juli
  (comp) A child's book of prayers   242
Kanninen, Barbara J.
  A story with pictures   E
Kansas. Bjorklund, R.   978.1
Kansas. Cannarella, D.   978.1
Kansas. Bailey, D.   978.1
KANSAS -- GRAPHIC NOVELS
  Phelan, M. The storm in the barn   741.5
Kantorovitz, Sylvie
  (il) Hays, A. J. Smarty Sara   E
  (il) Murphy, S. J. Room for Ripley   530.8
  (il) Schaefer, L. M. Loose tooth   E
  (il) Wing, N. Go to bed, monster!   E
Kaplan, Bruce Eric
  Monsters eat whiny children   E
Kaplan, Elizabeth
  Brill, M. T. Minnesota   977.6
  Price-Groff, C. Illinois   977.3
Kaplan, Michael B.
  Betty Bunny didn't do it   E
  Betty Bunny loves chocolate cake   E
Kaplowitz, Joan R.
  (jt. auth) Grassian, E. S. Information literacy instruction   025.5
Kaposy, Jeremy
  (il) O'Meara, S. J. Are you afraid yet? the science behind scary stuff   500
Karas, G. Brian
  (il) Fleming, C. Clever Jack takes the cake   E
  (il) Fractions   Fic
  (il) Jenkins, E. Lemonade in winter   E
  (il) Juster, N. Neville   E
  (il) Switching on the moon   811
Karas, G. Brian
  (il) Beeler, S. B. Throw your tooth on the roof   398
  (il) Billingsley, F. Big Bad Bunny   E
  (il) Elya, S. M. F is for fiesta   E
  (il) Elya, S. M. Oh no, gotta go!   E
  (il) Fleming, C. Clever Jack takes the cake   E
  (il) Fleming, C. Muncha! Muncha! Muncha!   E
  (il) Fractions   Fic
  (il) Hort, L. The seals on the bus   782.421
  (il) Juster, N. Neville   E
  On Earth   525
  The Village Garage   E
  Young Zeus   292
  (il) Kobayashi, I. Today and today   895.6
  (il) McDonald, M. Ant and Honey Bee   E
  (il) McNamara, M. How many seeds in a pumpkin?   E
  (il) Mills, C. 7 x 9   Fic
  (il) Murphy, S. J. Elevator magic   513
  (il) Rodman, M. A. Surprise soup   E
  (il) Rylant, C. The case of the missing monkey   E
  (il) Stanley, D. Saving Sweetness   E
  (il) Switching on the moon   811
  (il) Zolotow, C. If it weren't for you   E
Karas, Roma
  (il) Moore, L. Mural on Second Avenue, and other city poems   811
Karate. Hicks, T. A.   796.8
KARATE
  See also Judo; Martial arts; Self-defense
KARATE

A friend's tale — E
Library mouse — E
Kirk, Daniel
  (il) Edwards, P. D. While the world is sleeping — E
  Honk honk! Beep beep! — E
  Keisha Ann can! — E
  Library mouse — E
  (il) Stevenson, R. L. Block city — E
Kirk, David, 1955-
  Oh So Tiny Bunny — E
Kirk, Katie
  Eli, no! — E
Kirk, Shoshanna
  T is for tugboat — 623.82
Kirk, Steve
  (il) Camper, C. Bugs before time — 560
Kirker, Christine
  Multicultural storytime magic — 027.62
Kirker, Christine
  MacMillan, K. Storytime magic — 027.62
Kirkland, Katherine
  (il) Andrews, B. Why are you so scared? — 616.85
Kirkpatrick, John Simpson, 1892-1915
      About
  Greenwood, M. The donkey of Gallipoli — 940.4
Kirkpatrick, Katherine A.
  Snow baby — 92
Kirsch, Vincent X.
  (il) Ferris, J. C. Noah Webster and his words — 423
Kirsch, Vincent X.
  Forsythia & me — E
  Natalie & Naughtily — E
  Two little boys from Toolittle Toys — E
Kirwan, Wednesday
  Minerva the monster — E
Kishka for Koppel. Davis, A. — E
The **kiss** box. — E
Kiss good night. Hest, A. — E
Kiss kiss! Wild, M. — E
A **Kiss** like this. Murphy, M. — E
Kiss me! (I'm a prince!) — E
Kiss the cow. Root, P. — E
Kissel, Richard
  Kelly, E. Evolving planet — 551
Kisseloff, Jeff
  Who is baseball's greatest pitcher? — 796.357
Kisses on the wind. Moser, L. — E
KISSING
  Loupy, C. Hugs and kisses — E
  Wild, M. Kiss kiss! — E
KISSING -- FICTION
  Dowdy, L. C. All kinds of kisses — E
  The kiss box — E
  Monari, M. Zero kisses for me! — E
  Paul, A. W. If animals kissed good night-- — E
  Tafuri, N. All kinds of kisses — E
  Tarpley, T. How about a kiss for me? — E
  Trewin, T. I lost my kisses — E
  Walsh, J. The biggest kiss — E
  Yolen, J. Mama's kiss — E
KISSING -- JUVENILE FICTION
  Murphy, M. A Kiss like this — E
  Stein, D. E. Dinosaur kisses — E
Kissock, Heather
  Apache — 970.004
  Caddo — 970.004
  Cherokee — 970.004
  Comanche — 970.004

Tigua — 970.004
Kit Feeny: on the move. Townsend, M. — 741.5
Kit Feeny: the ugly necklace. Townsend, M. — 741.5
Kitain, Sandra
  Shelf-esteem — 028.5
Kitamura, Satoshi
  (il) Carnival of the animals — 811
  Stone Age boy — E
  (il) McNaughton, C. Once upon an ordinary school day — E
Kitchel, JoAnn E.
  (il) Gershwin's Rhapsody in Blue — E
Kitchen. Burke, L. — 507.8
Kitchen dance. Manning, M. — E
KITCHEN GARDENS *See* Vegetable gardening
KITCHEN GARDENS -- JUVENILE LITERATURE
  What's in the garden? — 635
  The **kitchen** knight. Hodges, M. — 398.22
  Kitchen science experiments. Bardhan-Quallen, S. — 579
KITCHEN UTENSILS
  Ernst, L. C. How things work in the house — 640
KITCHEN UTENSILS
  See also Household equipment and supplies
KITCHEN UTENSILS -- JUVENILE LITERATURE
  Priceman, M. How to make a cherry pie and see the U.S.A. — E
Kitchen, Bert
  (il) Whoo goes there? — E
KITCHENS
  See also Houses; Rooms
KITCHENS -- JUVENILE LITERATURE
  Burke, L. Kitchen — 507.8
KITCHENWARE *See* Kitchen utensils
Kite day. Hillenbrand, W. — E
Kite flying. Lin, G. — E
The **kite** rider. McCaughrean, G. — Fic
KITES
  Hosking, W. Asian kites — 629.133
  Ichikawa, S. My pig Amarillo — E
  Lin, G. Kite flying — E
  McCaughrean, G. The kite rider — Fic
  Murphy, S. J. Let's fly a kite — 516
KITES
  See also Aeronautics
KITES -- FICTION
  Hillenbrand, W. Kite day — E
KITES -- JUVENILE LITERATURE
  Lin, G. Kite flying — E
Kites sail high: a book about verbs. Heller, R. — 428
A **kitten** tale. Rohmann, E. — E
Kitten's autumn. Eugenie — E
Kitten's first full moon. Henkes, K. — E
Kitten's spring. Eugenie — E
Kitten's summer. Eugenie — E
Kitten's winter. Eugenie — E
KITTENS *See* Cats
Kittens! Kittens! Kittens! Meyers, S. — E
Kittinger, Jo S.
  Rosa's bus — 323.1
Kitty cat, kitty cat, are you going to sleep? Martin, B. — E
Kitty Cat, Kitty Cat, are you waking up? Martin, B. — E
Kitty's cuddles. Cabrera, J. — E
Kladstrup, Kristin
  The gingerbread pirates — E
Klaffke, Ben
  (il) Landau, E. Smokejumpers — 628.9
Klages, Ellen
  The green glass sea — Fic
  White sands, red menace — Fic
Klass, David

Face to face with orangutans   **599.8**

Lamanna, Paolo

   (il) Colfer, E. Artemis Fowl: the graphic novel   **741.5**

LaMarca, Luke

   (il) Johnson, A. The day Ray got away   **E**

LaMarche, Jim

   (il) The carpenter's gift   **E**

   (il) The day Tiger Rose said goodbye   **E**

   (il) Ivy takes care   **Fic**

   (il) Hanson, W. The Sea of Sleep   **E**

   (il) Napoli, D. J. Albert   **E**

   Lost and found   **E**

   The raft   **E**

   Up   **E**

Lamb, Albert

   The abandoned lighthouse   **E**

Lamb, Albert

   The abandoned lighthouse   **E**

   Tell me the day backwards   **E**

Lamb, Susan Condie

   (il) Houston, G. Miss Dorothy and her bookmobile   **E**

   (il) Houston, G. My great-aunt Arizona   **371.1**

Lambert, Sally Anne

   (il) Tegen, K. The story of the leprechaun   **E**

LAMBS *See* Sheep

Laminack, Lester L.

   Three hens and a peacock   **E**

Lamont, Priscilla

   (il) Dowdy, L. C. All kinds of kisses   **E**

   (il) George, J. C. Goose and Duck   **E**

   (il) Lulu and the dog from the sea   **Fic**

   (il) Lulu and the duck in the park   **Fic**

   (il) Stauffacher, S. Gator on the loose!   **Fic**

   (il) Stauffacher, S. Hide and seek   **Fic**

   (il) Stauffacher, S. Show time   **Fic**

   (il) Stauffacher, S. Special delivery!   **Fic**

   (il) Zoehfeld, K. W. Secrets of the garden   **Fic**

Lamorisse, Albert

   The red balloon   **E**

Lamour, Sandrine

   (il) My Little Handbook of Experiments   **E**

The **lamp**, the ice, and the boat called Fish. Martin, J. B.   **919**

Lamstein, Sarah Marwil

   A big night for salamanders   **E**

Lamut, Sonja

   (il) Toscano, C. Papa's pastries   **E**

Lana's Lakota moons. Sneve, V. D. H.   **Fic**

Lanan, Jessica

   (il) Schoettler, J. Good fortune in a wrapping cloth   **E**

LANCELOT (LEGENDARY CHARACTER)

   See also Legendary characters

LANCELOT (LEGENDARY CHARACTER) -- FICTION

   Morris, G. The adventures of Sir Lancelot the Great   **Fic**

LANCELOT (LEGENDARY CHARACTER) -- JUVENILE LITERATURE

   Morris, G. The adventures of Sir Lancelot the Great   **Fic**

LAND DEVELOPERS -- FICTION

   Appelt, K. The true blue scouts of Sugarman Swamp   **Fic**

The land is our storybook [series]

   Andre We feel good out here   **970.004**

   Enzoe, P. The caribou feed our soul   **970.004**

   McLeod, T. The Delta is my home   **970.004**

   Zoe, T. Living stories   **970.004**

A **land** of big dreamers. Waldman, N.   **920**

The land of Elyon [series]

   Carman, P. Beyond the Valley of Thorns   **Fic**

   Carman, P. The Dark Hills divide   **Fic**

   Carman, P. Into the mist   **Fic**

Carman, P. Stargazer   **Fic**

Carman, P. The tenth city   **Fic**

The **land** of the dragon king and other Korean stories. McClure, G.   **398.2**

The **Land** of the Silver Apples. Farmer, N.   **Fic**

Land roamers. Parker, S.   **560**

LAND SURVEYING *See* Surveying

LAND SURVEYS *See* Surveying

Landau, Elaine

   Apples   **634**

   Are the drums for you?   **786.9**

   Asthma   **616.2**

   Bananas   **634**

   Beluga whales   **599.5**

   Beyond Pluto   **523.4**

   Big cats   **599.75**

   Bites and stings   **617.1**

   Broken bones   **617.1**

   Bumps, bruises, and scrapes   **617.1**

   Burns   **617.1**

   Cavities and toothaches   **617.6**

   Chickenpox   **616.9**

   The common cold   **616.2**

   Corn   **633.1**

   Earaches   **617.8**

   Earth   **525**

   Emperor penguins   **598**

   Fleeing to freedom on the Underground Railroad   **973.7**

   Food allergies   **616.97**

   The history of everyday life   **609**

   Is singing for you?   **783**

   Is the flute for you?   **788**

   Is the guitar for you?   **787.87**

   Is the trumpet for you?   **788**

   Is the violin for you?   **787.2**

   Jupiter   **523.4**

   Mars   **523.4**

   Mercury   **523.4**

   The moon   **523.3**

   Neptune   **523.4**

   Oil spill!   **363.7**

   Pluto   **523.4**

   Popcorn   **641.3**

   Saturn   **523.4**

   Smokejumpers   **628.9**

   Sprains and strains   **617.1**

   Strep throat   **616.9**

   The sun   **523.7**

   Uranus   **523.4**

   Venus   **523.4**

   Warts   **616.5**

   Wheat   **633.1**

Landed. Lee, M.   **Fic**

LANDFILLS -- FICTION

   Kooser, T. Bag in the wind   **E**

LANDFORMS

   See also Earth -- Surface; Geology

Landforms [series]

   Sepehri, S. Glaciers   **551.3**

   Sepehri, S. Rivers   **551.48**

   Sheehan, T. F. Islands   **551.4**

   Sheehan, T. F. Mountains   **551.4**

Landman, Tanya

   Mary's penny   **E**

Landmann, Bimba

   The fate of Achilles   **883**

   The incredible voyage of Ulysses   **883**

The **last** battle. Lewis, C. S.   **Fic**
The **last** best days of summer. Hobbs, V.   **Fic**
The **last** brother. Noble, T. H.   **E**
The **last** day of kindergarten. Loewen, N.   **E**
The **last** day of school. Borden, L.   **Fic**
The **last** invisible boy. Kuhlman, E.   **Fic**
The **last** laugh. Aruego, J.   **E**
Last laughs. Lewis, J. P.   **818**
The **last** Martin. Friesen, J.   **Fic**
The **last** musketeer. Gibbs, S.   **Fic**
The **last** newspaper boy in America. Corbett, S.   **Fic**
Last night. Yum, H.   **E**
The **last** of the sky pirates. Stewart, P.   **Fic**
The **last** Olympian. Riordan, R.   **Fic**
Last one in is a rotten egg. Kessler, L. P.   **E**
Last one in is a rotten egg! De Groat, D.   **E**
The **last** river. Waldman, S.   **978**
Last song. Guthrie, J.   **E**
The **last** synapsid. Mason, T.   **Fic**
The **last** train. Titcomb, G.   **E**
The **last** treasure. Anderson, J.   **Fic**
Last-minute science fair projects. Bardhan-Quallen, S.   **507.8**
Late for school. Martin, S.   **782.42**
Late for school! Calmenson, S.   **E**
Latham, Donna
   Amazing biome projects you can build yourself   **577**
   Backyard Biology   **570.78**
   Ecology   **577**
Latham, Irene
   Leaving Gee's Bend   **Fic**
Lathrop, Dorothy P.
   (il) Animals of the Bible   **220.8**
   (il) Field, R. Hitty: her first hundred years   **Fic**
Latif, Zawiah Abdul
   Gish, S. Ethiopia   **963**
   Hassig, S. M. Somalia   **967.73**
   Heale, J. Madagascar   **969.1**
   Kagda, F. Algeria   **965**
   Kagda, S. Lithuania   **947.93**
   Levy, P. Sudan   **962.4**
   Sheehan, S. Lebanon   **956.92**
Latimer, Alex
   The boy who cried ninja   **E**
Latimer, Jonathan P.
   Caterpillars   **595.7**
Latimer, Miriam
   (il) Harvey, M. Shopping with Dad   **E**
   (il) The sunflower sword   **E**
LATIN AMERICA -- POLITICS AND GOVERNMENT
   See also Politics
Latin America and the Caribbean. Solway, A.   **780.9**
LATIN AMERICAN ART
   Lane, K. Come look with me: Latin American art   **709**
LATIN AMERICAN ART
   See also Art
LATIN AMERICAN FOLK SONGS -- JUVENILE LITERATURE
   De colores and other Latin-American folk songs for children   **781.62**
LATIN AMERICAN LITERATURE
   See also Literature
LATIN AMERICAN LITERATURE -- BIBLIOGRAPHY
   Schon, I. Recommended books in Spanish for children and young adults, 2004-2008   **011.6**
LATIN AMERICANS -- POETRY
   Under the mambo moon   **811**
LATIN LITERATURE
   See also Literature

LATINOS (U.S.)
   Hernandez, R. E. The Civil War, 1840s-1890s   **973.7**
   Otfinoski, S. The new republic: 1760-1840s   **973.3**
   Wachale! poetry and prose on growing up Latino in America   **810**
   Weller, F. W. The day the animals came   **E**
LATITUDE
   See also Earth; Geodesy; Nautical astronomy
The **latke** who couldn't stop screaming. Snicket, L.   **E**
Latkes, latkes, good to eat. Howland, N.   **E**
Latno, Mark
   The paper boomerang book   **745.54**
Latrobe, Kathy Howard
   The children's literature dictionary   **028.5**
Latta, Sara L.
   The good, the bad, the slimy   **579**
LATTER-DAY SAINTS *See* Church of Jesus Christ of Latter-day Saints
Latvia. Barlas, R.   **947.96**
Latyk, Olivier
   (il) Martin, R. Moon dreams   **E**
   (il) Rees, D. Jeannette Claus saves Christmas   **E**
Lau, Ruth
   Berg, E. Senegal   **966.3**
Lauber, Patricia
   Be a friend to trees   **582.16**
   What you never knew about beds, bedrooms, and pajamas **392**
   What you never knew about fingers, forks, & chopsticks **394.1**
   Who eats what?   **577**
   You're aboard Spaceship Earth   **550**
Laugesen, Malene
   (il) Strauss, L. L. The princess gown   **E**
Laugh & learn [series]
   Crist, J. J. Siblings   **306.8**
   Fox, J. S. Get organized without losing it   **371.3**
   Verdick, E. Don't behave like you live in a cave   **395**
Laugh till you cry. Nixon, J. L.   **Fic**
Laugh-eteria. Florian, D.   **811**
Laughing out loud, I fly. Herrera, J. F.   **811**
LAUGHTER
   See also Emotions
LAUNDRESSES -- FICTION
   Yeoman, J. The wild washerwomen   **E**
LAUNDRY -- FICTION
   Hughes, S. The Christmas Eve ghost   **E**
Laundry day. Manning, M. J.   **E**
Laura Ingalls Wilder. Berne, E. C.   **92**
Laura Secord: a story of courage. Lunn, J. L. S.   **Fic**
Laure, Jason
   Altman, L. J. Arkansas   **976.7**
   Blauer, E. Mali   **966.2**
   Blauer, E. Mauritania   **966.1**
   McDaniel, M. New Mexico   **972**
Laurell, RoseAleta
      About
   King, M. G. Librarian on the roof!   **027.4**
Lauren, Jill
   That's like me!   **371.9**
Laurent, Richard
   (il) Bauer, C. F. Leading kids to books through magic **027.62**
   (il) Bauer, C. F. Leading kids to books through puppets   **027.62**
Lauw, Darlene
   Light   **535**
   Water   **553.7**
   Weather   **551.5**
Laval, Thierry
   Colors   **E**

Durango, J. The walls of Cartagena   **Fic**
Ellis, D. No ordinary day   **Fic**
Lerangis, Peter
  The colossus rises   **Fic**
Lerangis, Peter
  Riordan, R. Vespers rising   **Fic**
Lerer, Seth
  Children's literature   **028.5**
Lerman, Josh
  How to raise Mom and Dad   **E**
LESBIAN MOTHERS
  Garden, N. Molly's family   **E**
**LESBIAN MOTHERS -- FAMILY RELATIONSHIPS -- JU-
  VENILE LITERATURE**
  This is my family a first look at same sex parents   **306.874**
LESBIANS
    See also Women
LESBIANS -- FICTION
  Garden, N. Molly's family   **E**
  Newman, L. Donovan's big day   **E**
  Newman, L. Mommy, mama, and me   **E**
  Polacco, P. In our mothers' house   **E**
LESBIANS' WRITINGS
    See also Literature
Leshem, Yossi
  Vogel, C. G. The man who flies with birds   **598**
Less is more. Baumbach, D.   **025.2**
Less than zero. Murphy, S. J.   **513**
Lessac, Frané, 1954-
  Greenwood, M. The donkey of Gallipoli   **940.4**
  (il) Greenwood, M. Drummer boy of John John   **786.9**
  Melmed, L. K. Heart of Texas   **976.4**
  Melmed, L. K. New York, New York   **974.7**
  Pomerantz, C. The chalk doll   **E**
  Rockwell, A. F. Clouds   **551.57**
Lessem, Don
  The fastest dinosaurs   **567.9**
  Feathered dinosaurs   **567.9**
  Flying giants of dinosaur time   **567.9**
  Sea giants of dinosaur time   **567.9**
  The smartest dinosaurs   **567.9**
  The ultimate dinopedia   **567.9**
Lesser, Rika
  Hansel and Gretel   **398.2**
Lester Fizz, bubble-gum artist. Spiro, R.   **E**
Lester's dreadful sweaters. Campbell, K. G.   **Fic**
Lester, Alison
  Noni the pony   **E**
  Running with the horses   **E**
Lester, Helen, 1936-
  Author   **813**
  Happy birdday, Tacky!   **E**
  Hooway for Wodney Wat   **E**
  The sheep in wolf's clothing   **E**
  Tacky's Christmas   **E**
  Three cheers for Tacky   **E**
  Wodney Wat's wobot   **E**
        About
  Lester, H. Author   **813**
Lester, J. D.
  Daddy calls me doodlebug   **E**
  Grandma calls me gigglepie   **E**
  Mommy calls me monkeypants   **E**
Lester, Julius
  Black cowboy, wild horses   **E**
  From slave ship to freedom road   **306.3**
  John Henry   **398.2**
  Let's talk about race   **305.8**

  The old African   **Fic**
  Sam and the tigers   **E**
  The tales of Uncle Remus   **398.2**
  To be a slave   **326**
  Uncle Remus, the complete tales   **398.2**
Lester, Mike
  (il) Crow, K. Cool Daddy Rat   **E**
  (il) Marcus, K. Scritch-scratch a perfect match   **E**
Lesynski, Loris
  Crazy about soccer   **811**
Let it begin here! Fradin, D. B.   **973.3**
Let it begin here! Brown, D.   **973.3**
Let it blow! Learn about air. Vogel, J.   **551.5**
Let it shine. Pinkney, A. D.   **920**
Let it shine.   **782.25**
Let me play. Blumenthal, K.   **796**
Let my people go. McKissack, P. C.   **Fic**
Let the circle be unbroken. Taylor, M. D.   **Fic**
Let the whole earth sing praise. De Paola, T.   **231.7**
Let there be peace. Brooks, J.   **242**
Let there be peace on earth. Jackson, J.   **782.42**
Let's build a playground.   **790.06**
Let's count. Hoban, T.   **513.2**
Let's count goats! Fox, M.   **E**
Let's count to 100! Sebe, M.   **E**
Let's do nothing! Fucile, T.   **E**
Let's explore science [series]
  Duke, S. S. Infections, infestations, and disease   **616.9**
  Duke, S. S. You can't wear these genes   **576.5**
  Farrell, C. Build it green   **720**
  Farrell, C. Plants out of place   **581.6**
  Tourville, A. D. Animal invaders   **591.6**
  Tourville, A. D. Exploring the solar system   **523.2**
Let's fly a kite. Murphy, S. J.   **516**
Let's get a pup, said Kate. Graham, B.   **E**
Let's get cooking! [series]
  Lee, F. Fun with Chinese cooking   **641.5**
Let's go rock collecting. Gans, R.   **552**
Let's go see Papa! Schimel, L.   **E**
Let's go visiting. Williams, S.   **E**
Let's go! Flatt, L.   **388**
Let's go, Hugo! Dominguez, A.   **E**
Let's hear it for Almigal. Kupfer, W.   **E**
Let's look at bats. Berman, R.   **599.4**
Let's look at brown bears. Berman, R.   **599.78**
Let's look at dinosaurs. Barry, F.   **567.9**
Let's look at fall. Schuette, S. L.   **508.2**
Let's look at iguanas. Jango-Cohen, J.   **597.95**
Let's look at pigeons. Piehl, J.   **598**
Let's look at prairie dogs. Zuchora-Walske, C.   **599.3**
Let's look at snails. Waxman, L. H.   **594**
Let's look at spring. Schuette, S. L.   **508.2**
Let's look at summer. Schuette, S. L.   **508.2**
Let's look at the rainforest close up. Allaire, C.   **591.7**
Let's look at winter. Schuette, S. L.   **508.2**
Let's play house. Quay, E.   **E**
Let's play in the forest while the wolf is not around. Rueda, C.   **782.42**
Let's rock [series]
  Spilsbury, R. Crystals   **549**
  Spilsbury, R. Fossils   **560**
  Spilsbury, R. Minerals   **549**
  Spilsbury, R. Soil   **631.4**
Let's save the animals. Barry, F.   **591.68**
Let's sign! Ault, K.   **419**
Let's sing together.   **782.42**
Let's start! science [series]
  Hewitt, S. Hear this!   **612.8**

Grossberg, B. Asperger's rules! **618.92**

LIFE SKILLS GUIDES *See* Life skills

LIFE SKILLS GUIDES -- JUVENILE LITERATURE

Katz, A. Girl in the know **612.6**

LIFE SPAN PROLONGATION *See* Longevity

Life story. Burton, V. L. **560**

LIFE STYLES *See* Lifestyles

LIFE SUPPORT SYSTEMS (MEDICAL ENVIRONMENT)

See also Hospitals; Terminal care

Life under ice. Cerullo, M. M. **578.7**

Life under occupation. Samuels, C. **940.53**

Life, Kay

(il) Cleary, B. Muggie Maggie **Fic**

(il) Hurst, C. O. You come to Yokum **Fic**

Life-size aquarium. Komiya, T. **591.7**

Life-size dinosaurs. Bergen, D. **567.9**

Life-size reptiles. Wilson, H. **597.9**

Life-size zoo. Komiya, T. **590**

LIFESAVING

See also Rescue work

The **lifesaving** adventure of Sam Deal, shipwreck rescuer. Ransom, C. F. **741.5**

LIFESTYLES

Simons, R. Does television make you fat? **613**

LIFESTYLES

See also Human behavior; Manners and customs

Lift every voice and sing. Johnson, J. W. **782.42**

LIFT-THE-FLAP BOOKS -- SPECIMENS

Low, W. Machines go to work in the city **E**

Liftoff. Mitchell, D. **92**

LIFTS *See* Elevators; Hoisting machinery

Light. Lauw, D. **535**

LIGHT

See also Electromagnetic waves; Physics

LIGHT

Branley, F. M. Day light, night light **535**

Burnie, D. Light **535**

Claybourne, A. Light and dark **535**

Cobb, V. I see myself **535**

Farndon, J. Light and optics **535**

Gardner, R. Dazzling science projects with light and color **535**

Hartman, E. Light and sound **530**

Lauw, D. Light **535**

Meiani, A. Light **535**

Riley, P. D. Light **535**

Sitarski, A. Cold light **572**

Spilsbury, L. What is light? **535**

Light. Meiani, A. **535**

Light. Riley, P. D. **535**

Light. Burnie, D. **535**

LIGHT -- EXPERIMENTS

Farndon, J. Light and optics **535**

Lauw, D. Light **535**

LIGHT -- EXPERIMENTS -- JUVENILE LITERATURE

Lauw, D. Light **535**

LIGHT -- FICTION

Blechman, N. Night light **E**

Gal, S. Night lights **E**

Swanson, S. M. The house in the night **E**

LIGHT -- JUVENILE FICTION

Blechman, N. Night light **E**

LIGHT -- JUVENILE LITERATURE

Branley, F. M. Day light, night light **535**

Farndon, J. Light and optics **535**

Gardner, R. Dazzling science projects with light and color **535**

Riley, P. D. Light **535**

LIGHT -- JUVENILE POETRY

Flicker flash **811**

LIGHT -- POETRY

Flicker flash **811**

LIGHT -- SPEED -- JUVENILE LITERATURE

Caes, C. J. Discovering the speed of light **535**

LIGHT -- SPEED -- MEASUREMENT -- JUVENILE LITERATURE

Caes, C. J. Discovering the speed of light **535**

LIGHT -- STUDY AND TEACHING -- HISTORY

Caes, C. J. Discovering the speed of light **535**

Light and dark. Claybourne, A. **535**

Light and optics. Farndon, J. **535**

LIGHT AND SHADE *See* Shades and shadows

Light and sound. Hartman, E. **530**

A **light** in the attic. Silverstein, S. **811**

Light in the darkness. Cline-Ransome, L. **E**

The **light** of the world. Paterson, K. **232.9**

The **light** princess. MacDonald, G. **Fic**

LIGHT PRODUCTION IN ANIMALS *See* Bioluminescence

LIGHT SHIPS *See* Lightships

Light up the night. **E**

LIGHT VERSE *See* Humorous poetry

Light your way. Mooney, C. **745.593**

Light, Steve

Trains go **E**

Zephyr takes flight **E**

Light, Steven

The Christmas giant **E**

Puss in boots **398.2**

Lightburn, Ron

(il) Becker, H. Juba this, juba that **E**

Lightfoot, Gordon

Canadian railroad trilogy **782.42**

LIGHTHOUSE KEEPERS

Moss, M. The bravest woman in America **92**

Roop, P. The stormy adventure of Abbie Burgess, lighthouse keeper **741.5**

LIGHTHOUSES

Grandpre, M. The sea chest **E**

House, K. L. Lighthouses for kids **387.1**

Moss, M. The bravest woman in America **92**

Swift, H. H. The little red lighthouse and the great gray bridge **E**

LIGHTHOUSES

See also Navigation

LIGHTHOUSES -- FICTION

Brown, R. Gracie the lighthouse cat **E**

Gauch, S. Voyage to the Pharos **E**

Grandpre, M. The sea chest **E**

Haas, R. d. Peter and the winter sleepers **E**

Hopkinson, D. Birdie's lighthouse **Fic**

Krensky, S. Sisters of Scituate Light **E**

Lamb, A. The abandoned lighthouse **E**

Swift, H. H. The little red lighthouse and the great gray bridge **E**

Venuti, K. C. Leaving the Bellwethers **Fic**

Woodruff, E. Fearless **Fic**

LIGHTHOUSES -- GRAPHIC NOVELS

Roop, P. The stormy adventure of Abbie Burgess, lighthouse keeper **741.5**

Lighthouses for kids. House, K. L. **387.1**

LIGHTING

See also Interior design; Light

Lightning. Simon, S. **551.56**

LIGHTNING

See also Electricity; Meteorology; Thunderstorms

LIGHTNING

Little newts. Goldish, M.   **597.8**
Little Night. Morales, Y.   **E**
The little old lady who was not afraid of anything.   **E**
Little One Step. James, S.   **E**
Little one, we knew you'd come. Jones, S. L.   **232.9**
Little owl lost. Haughton, C.   **E**
Little Owl's night. Srinivasan, D.   **E**
Little panda. Ryder, J.   **599.74**
Little panda. Liwska, R.   **E**
A little peace. Kerley, B.   **327.1**
Little people and a lost world. Goldenberg, L.   **599.93**
The little piano girl. Ingalls, A.   **E**
The little prince. Saint-Exupery, A. d.   **Fic**
The little prince. Sfar, J.   **741.5**
The little prince: deluxe pop-up book. Saint-Exupery, A. d. **Fic**
A little princess. Burnett, F. H.   **Fic**
Little Quack. Thompson, L.   **E**
Little Quack's bedtime. Thompson, L.   **E**
Little Rabbit lost. Horse, H.   **E**
The little rabbit who liked to say moo. Allen, J.   **E**
Little Rat makes music. Bang-Campbell, M.   **E**
Little Rat rides. Bang-Campbell, M.   **E**
Little Red. Little Red Riding Hood./English   **E**
Little red bird. Bruel, N.   **E**
Little Red Cap. Grimm, J.   **398.2**
The little red elf. McGrath, B. B.   **E**
The little red fish. Yoo   **E**
The little red hen. Pinkney, J.   **398.2**
The little red hen. Galdone, P.   **398.2**
The little red hen. Little red hen   **398.2**
The little red hen. Little red hen   **398.2**
The little red hen. Forest, H.   **398.2**
The little red hen. Little red hen   **398.2**
The Little Red Hen (makes a pizza) Sturges, P.   **398.2**
The Little Red Hen and the Passover matzah. Kimmelman, L.   **398.2**
The little red lighthouse and the great gray bridge. Swift, H. H.   **E**
The Little Red Pen. Crummel, S. S.   **E**
Little Red Riding Hood. Wisnewski, A.   **398.2**
Little Red Riding Hood. Ziefert, H.   **398.2**
Little Red Riding Hood. Little Red Riding Hood   **398.2**
Little Red Riding Hood. Little Red Riding Hood   **398.2**
Little Red Riding Hood. Spirin, G.   **398.2**
Little Red Riding Hood. Grimm, J.   **398.2**
Little Red Riding Hood.   **E**
Little Red Riding Hood./English
   Little Red   **E**
Little Red Riding Hood: a newfangled prairie tale. Ernst, L. C.   **398.2**
Little Rooster's diamond button. MacDonald, M. R.   **398.2**
The little scarecrow boy. Brown, M. W.   **E**
The little school bus. Roth, C.   **E**
Little shark. Rockwell, A. F.   **597**
The little ships.   **813**
Little sister and the month brothers. De Regniers, B. S. **398.2**
Little Sister is not my name. Draper, S. M.   **Fic**
LITTLE THEATER MOVEMENT
   See also Theater
Little Toot. Gramatky, H.   **E**
Little treasures. Ogburn, J. K.   **413**
Little trucks with big jobs. Maass, R.   **629.224**
Little Tug. Savage, S.   **E**
Little Vampire.   **741.5**
Little White Duck. Liu, N.   **741.5**
The little white owl. Corderoy, T.   **E**
Little white rabbit. Henkes, K.   **E**
Little wolf's song. Teckentrup, B.   **E**

Little women. Alcott, L. M.   **Fic**
Little world math concepts [series]
   Mattern, J. Even or odd?   **513**
Little world social studies [series]
   Hord, C. My safe community   **331.7**
   Hord, C. Need it or want it?   **332.024**
The little yellow leaf. Berger, C.   **E**
Little yoga. Whitford, R.   **613.7**
Little, Jean
   Emma's yucky brother   **E**
Little, Jean, 1932-
         About
   Ellis, S. From reader to writer   **028**
Little, Kimberley Griffiths
   Circle of secrets   **Fic**
   The healing spell   **Fic**
The little, little house. Souhami, J.   **398.2**
Littlefield, Holly
   The rooftop adventure of Minnie and Tessa, factory fire survivors   **741.5**
The littlest dinosaur's big adventure. Foreman, M.   **E**
The littlest evergreen. Cole, H.   **E**
The littlest leaguer. Hoff, S.   **E**
The littlest llama. Buxton, J.   **E**
The littlest mountain. Rosenstock, B.   **E**
Littlewood, Karin
   (il) Conway, D. The most important gift of all   **E**
   (il) Cornwell, N. Christophe's story   **Fic**
   (il) Hoffman, M. The color of home   **E**
   Immi's gift   **E**
   (il) Lobel, G. Moonshadow's journey   **E**
   (il) Moore, G. Catherine's story   **E**
LITURGIES
   See also Public worship; Rites and ceremonies
Litwin, Eric
   Pete the cat: I love my white shoes   **E**
Litwin, Laura Baskes
   Write horror fiction in 5 simple steps   **808.3**
Litzinger, Rosanne
   (il) Greene, E. The little golden lamb   **398.2**
   (il) Kimmel, E. A. The frog princess   **398.2**
   (il) Nishizuka, K. The beckoning cat   **398.2**
   (il) Paul, A. W. Snail's good night   **E**
   (il) Stewig, J. W. The animals watched   **222**
Liu, Jae Soo
   Yellow umbrella   **E**
Liu, Na
   Little White Duck   **741.5**
Lively Elizabeth! what happens when you push. Bergman, M.   **E**
Lively plant science projects. Benbow, A.   **580.7**
Lives cut short [series]
   Anderson, J. J. John Lennon   **92**
   Harris, A. R. Tupac Shakur   **92**
   Watson, S. Heath Ledger   **92**
Lives of extraordinary women. Krull, K.   **920**
The lives of stars. Croswell, K.   **523.8**
Lives of the artists. Krull, K.   **709.2**
Lives of the athletes. Krull, K.   **796**
Lives of the great artists. Ayres, C.   **709**
Lives of the musicians. Krull, K.   **780.92**
Lives of the presidents. Krull, K.   **920**
Lives of the writers.   **809**
Lives: poems about famous Americans.   **811**
LIVESTOCK *See* Domestic animals; Livestock industry
LIVESTOCK -- HANDLING -- UNITED STATES -- JUVENILE LITERATURE
   Montgomery, S. Temple Grandin   **636**

Corey, S. Here come the Girl Scouts!   **369.463**

Low, Mordecai-Mark Mac

Abramson, A. S. Inside stars   **523.8**

Low, William

(il) Barron, T. A. Ghost hands   **E**

Machines go to work in the city   **E**

(il) Me and Momma and Big John   **E**

Low, William

(il) Barron, T. A. Ghost hands   **E**

(il) Hall, B. E. Henry and the kite dragon   **E**

(il) Lewis, E. F. Young Fu of the upper Yangtze   **Fic**

Machines go to work   **621.8**

Old Penn Station   **725**

LOW-CALORIE DIET

See also Diet

LOW-CARBOHYDRATE DIET

See also Diet

LOW-CHOLESTEROL DIET

See also Diet

LOW-FAT DIET

See also Diet

Lowdown on earthworms. Dixon, N.   **592**

Lowe, Ayana

(ed) Come and play   **305.23**

Lowe, Joy L.

Puppet magic   **027.62**

Matthew, K. I. Neal-Schuman guide to recommended children's books and media for use with every elementary subject   **011.6**

Lowe, Wes

(il) Galat, J. M. The discovery of longitude   **526**

Lowell, Susan

The elephant quilt   **E**

Lowen, Cynthia

(ed) Bully   **371.58**

Lowenstein, Felicia

All about sign language   **419**

Lowery, Linda

Aunt Clara Brown   **978.8**

The tale of La Llorona   **398.2**

Lowery, Mike

(il) The gingerbread man loose in the school   **E**

(il) Ribbit rabbit   **E**

Lowery, Mike

(il) The gingerbread man loose in the school   **E**

(il) Nesbo, J. Doctor Proctor's fart powder   **Fic**

(il) Ribbit rabbit   **E**

Lowji discovers America. Fleming, C.   **Fic**

Lowman, Margaret

About

Lasky, K. The most beautiful roof in the world   **577.3**

Lowry, Lois, 1937-

Anastasia Krupnik   **Fic**

Autumn Street   **Fic**

The birthday ball   **Fic**

Bless this mouse   **Fic**

Crow call   **E**

The giver   **Fic**

Gooney Bird Greene   **Fic**

Gooney Bird on the map   **Fic**

Looking back   **813**

Number the stars   **Fic**

Stay!   **Fic**

A summer to die   **Fic**

Loy, Jessica

When I grow up   **331.702**

Loy, Roy Chan Yoon

(il) Lauw, D. Light   **535**

LOYALTY

See also Ethics; Virtue

Luba and the wren. Polacco, P.   **398.2**

LUBRICATION AND LUBRICANTS

See also Machinery

Lucas, Cedric

(il) Miller, W. Night golf   **E**

Lucas, David

The Skeleton pirate   **E**

Lucas, David

The robot and the bluebird   **E**

Something to do   **E**

Lucha libre: the Man in the Silver Mask. Garza, X.   **Fic**

Lucia and the light. Root, P.   **E**

Luciani, Brigitte

A hubbub   **741.5**

The meeting   **741.5**

Luck. George, J. C.   **E**

LUCK -- FICTION

Kadohata, C. The thing about luck   **Fic**

The **luck** of the Buttons. Ylvisaker, A.   **Fic**

The **luck** of the Loch Ness monster. Flaherty, A.   **E**

Lucke, Deb

The boy who wouldn't swim   **E**

Sneezenesia   **E**

(il) Pulver, R. Never say boo!   **E**

Lucky beans. Birtha, B.   **E**

Lucky breaks. Patron, S.   **Fic**

Lucky Ducklings.   **E**

Lucky for good.   **Fic**

Lucky Jake. Addy, S.   **E**

Lucky leaf. O'Malley, K.   **E**

Lucky pennies and hot chocolate. Shields, C. D.   **E**

Lucky song. Williams, V. B.   **E**

Lucy and the bully. Alexander, C.   **E**

Lucy and the green man. Newbery, L.   **Fic**

Lucy can't sleep. Schwartz, A.   **E**

Lucy long ago. Thimmesh, C.   **599.93**

Lucy on the ball. Cooper, I.   **Fic**

Lucy on the loose. Cooper, I.   **Fic**

Lucy rescued.   **E**

Lucy Rose, big on plans. Kelly, K.   **Fic**

Lucy Rose, busy like you can't believe. Kelly, K.   **Fic**

Lucy Rose, here's the thing about me. Kelly, K.   **Fic**

Lucy Rose, working myself to pieces and bits. Kelly, K.   **Fic**

Lucy the good. Musgrove, M.   **Fic**

Ludwig, Trudy

Better than you   **E**

Ludwig, William F., 1879-1973

About

VanHecke, S. Raggin', jazzin', rockin'   **784.19**

Ludwig, William F., 1916-2008

About

VanHecke, S. Raggin', jazzin', rockin'   **784.19**

Lue Sue, Majella

(il) O'Connell, R. Penina Levine is a hard-boiled egg   **Fic**

(il) O'Connell, R. Penina Levine is a potato pancake   **Fic**

Luebs, Robin

Please pick me up, Mama!   **E**

(il) Ruddell, D. Who said coo?   **E**

Lugalbanda. Henderson, K.   **398.2**

Luis Alvarez. Venezia, M.   **92**

Lujan, Jorge

Colors! Colores!   **861**

Doggy slippers   **811**

Luka's quilt. Guback, G.   **E**

Luke on the loose. Bliss, H.   **741.5**

Lukenbill, W. Bernard

See also Machine design; Models and modelmaking

MACHINES *See* Machinery

Machines at work. Barton, B.   690

Machines at work [series]
  Bingham, C. Fire truck   628.9

Machines go to work. Low, W.   621.8

Machines go to work in the city. Low, W.   E

Machines of the future [series]
  McMahon, P. Ultimate trains   385

MACHINES, SIMPLE *See* Simple machines

Macintosh, Tessa
  (il) Andre We feel good out here   970.004
  (jt. auth) Enzoe, P. The caribou feed our soul   970.004
  (il) McLeod, T. The Delta is my home   970.004
  (il) Proud to be Inuvialuit   970.004
  (il) Zoe, T. Living stories   970.004

Mack made movies. Brown, D.   791.43

Mack, Gail
  Horses   636.1
  Kickboxing   796.8
  The stars   523.8

Mack, James
  Journals and blogging   808

Mack, Jeff
  (il) Boo, bunny!   E
  (il) Bunting, E. Hurry! hurry!   E
  Good news, bad news   E
  Hippo and Rabbit in 3 more tales: brave like me   E
  Hippo and Rabbit in three short tales   741.5
  Hush little polar bear   E
  (il) McDonnell, C. Dog wants to play   E

Mack, Scott
  (il) Graber, J. Muktar and the camels   E

Mack, Steve
  (il) Cleary, B. P. Six sheep sip thick shakes   398.8

Mack, Steve
  (il) Berkowitz, J. Jurassic poop   567.9
  (il) Cleary, B. P. Six sheep sip thick shakes   398.8

Mack, Tracy
  The fall of the Amazing Zalindas   Fic
  The mystery of the conjured man   Fic

Mack, Winnie
  After all, you're Callie Boone   Fic

Mackall, Dandi Daley
  Listen to the silent night   E
  First day   E

MacKall, Dandi Daley, 1949-
  Listen to the silent night   E

Macken, JoAnn Early
  Baby says moo!   E
  The dinosaur museum   567.9
  Flip, float, fly   581.4
  Waiting out the storm   E

Mackenzie, Robert
  (il) Burleigh, R. Fly, Cher Ami, fly!   940.4
  (il) Cech, J. Jack and the beanstalk   398.2

Mackey, Bonnie
  A librarian's guide to cultivating an elementary school garden   372

Mackintosh, David
  Marshall Armstrong is new to our school   E

MacLachlan, Patricia, 1938-
  All the places to love   E
  Before you came   E
  Bittle   E
  The facts and fictions of Minna Pratt   Fic
  I didn't do it   811
  Kindred souls   Fic

  Lala salama   E
  Once I ate a pie   811
  Painting the wind   E
  Sarah, plain and tall   Fic
  Seven kisses in a row   Fic
  Waiting for the magic   Fic
  White fur flying   Fic
  Word after word after word   Fic
  Your moon, my moon   E

MacLean, Christine Kole
  Mary Margaret meets her match   Fic

Maclear, Kyo
  Spork   E
  Virginia Wolf   Fic

MacLennan, Cathy
  Chicky chicky chook chook   E

MacLeod, Doug
  Heather Fell in the Water   E

MacLeod, Elizabeth
  Bake and make amazing cakes   641.8
  Bake and make amazing cookies   641.8
  Bones Never Lie   363.25
  Chock full of chocolate   641.6
  Monster fliers   567.9
  Samuel de Champlain   92
  Why do cats have whiskers?   636.8
  Why do horses have manes?   636.1
  Skreslet, L. To the top of Everest   796.52

Macmillan dictionary for children.   423

MacMillan, Dianne M.
  Diwali--Hindu festival of lights   394.26
  Ramadan and Id al-Fitr   297.3

MacMillan, Kathy
  (jt. auth) Kirker, C. Multicultural storytime magic   027.62
  A box full of tales   027.6
  Storytime magic   027.62

Macnaughton, Tina
  (il) Butler, M. C. The smiley snowman   E

Macquitty, Miranda
  Shark   597.3

MACRAME
  Sadler, J. A. Hemp jewelry   746.42

Macy, Sue
  Basketball belles   796.323
  Bylines: a photobiography of Nellie Bly   92
  Freeze frame   796.98
  Swifter, higher, stronger   796.48
  Wheels of change   796.6

Mad as a wet hen! and other funny idioms. Terban, M.   423

Mad at Mommy. Sakai, K.   E

Mad science [series]
  Bardhan-Quallen, S. Kitchen science experiments   579
  Bardhan-Quallen, S. Nature science experiments   508

Madagascar. Heale, J.   969.1

Madam President. Smith, L.   E

Madame Pamplemousse and her incredible edibles. Kingfisher, R.   Fic

Madaras, Area
  Madaras, L. The what's happening to my body? book for boys   612.6
  Madaras, L. The what's happening to my body? book for girls   612.6

Madaras, Lynda
  On your mark, get set, grow!   612.6
  Ready, set, grow!   612.6
  The what's happening to my body? book for boys   612.6
  The what's happening to my body? book for girls   612.6

Madden, Kerry

Making graphs [series]

  Bodach, V. Bar graphs   **510**

  Bodach, V. Pictographs   **510**

  Bodach, V. Pie graphs   **510**

  Bodach, V. Tally charts   **510**

Making magic windows. Garza, C. L.   **745.54**

Making masks. Schwarz, R.   **646.4**

Making mischief. Maguire, G.   **741.6**

Making music. Wiseman, A. S.   **784.19**

The **making** of America. Johnston, R. D.   **973**

Making secret codes. Gregory, J.   **652**

Making shelter. Champion, N.   **613.6**

Making sounds. Guillain, C.   **534**

Making the moose out of life. Oldland, N.   **E**

Mal and Chad. McCranie, S.   **741.5**

Malaghan, Michael

  Greek ransom   **Fic**

Malam, John

  Journey of a glass of milk   **637**

Malam, John

  Dragons   **398.2**

  The Egyptians   **932**

  Fairies   **398.2**

  Giants   **398.2**

  The Greeks   **938**

  Grow your own butterfly farm   **638**

  Grow your own cat toy   **636.8**

  Grow your own sandwich   **635**

  Grow your own smoothie   **634**

  Grow your own snack   **641.3**

  Grow your own soup   **635**

  Monsters   **398.2**

  Pinnipeds   **599.79**

  The Romans   **937**

  The Vikings   **948**

Maland, Nick

  (il) Bergman, M. Snip snap!   **E**

  (il) Bergman, M. Yum yum! What fun!   **E**

  (il) Davies, N. Big blue whale   **599.5**

  (il) Garlick, N. Aunt Severe and the dragons   **Fic**

  (il) McKay, H. Wishing for tomorrow   **Fic**

Malaria. Person, S.   **614.5**

Malaria. Ollhoff, J.   **616.9**

MALARIA

  See also Diseases

MALARIA

  Ollhoff, J. Malaria   **616.9**

  Person, S. Malaria   **614.5**

MALARIA -- FICTION

  Mimi's Village   **Fic**

Malaspina, Ann

  Heart on fire   **E**

  Touch the sky   **796.42**

Malaspina, Ann

  Phillis sings out freedom   **92**

  Yasmin's hammer   **Fic**

Malaysia. Foo Yuk Yee   **959.5**

MALAYSIA -- JUVENILE LITERATURE

  Foo Yuk Yee Malaysia   **959.5**

Malchow, Alex

  The Sword of Darrow   **Fic**

Malchow, Hal

  Malchow, A. The Sword of Darrow   **Fic**

Malcolm X.   **92**

Malcolm X, 1925-1965

About

  Malcolm X   **92**

Malcolm X, 1925-1965

About

  Gunderson, J. X: the biography of Malcolm X   **92**

Maldives. NgCheong-Lum, R.   **954.9**

MALE ACTORS

  See also Actors

MALE IMPERSONATORS

  Kay, V. Rough, tough Charley   **92**

MALE IMPERSONATORS

  See also Impostors and imposture

MALE ROLE *See* Gender role

Malepart, Celine

  Ross, K. Earth-friendly crafts   **745.5**

Maley, Adrienne Houk

  20 fun facts about praying mantises   **595.7**

Malhotra, Sonali

  Iraq   **956.7**

Mali. Blauer, E.   **966.2**

Mali under the night sky. Youme   **92**

MALIGNANT TUMORS *See* Cancer

Mall mania. Murphy, S. J.   **513**

Mallett, David

  Inch by inch   **782.42**

Mallory, Kenneth

  Adventure beneath the sea   **551.46**

  Diving to a deep-sea volcano   **551.46**

  Swimming with hammerhead sharks   **597.3**

Malnor, Bruce

  Champions of the wilderness   **920**

  Malnor, C. Champions of wild animals   **920**

Malnor, Carol

  Malnor, B. Champions of the wilderness   **920**

  Champions of wild animals   **920**

MALNUTRITION

  See also Nutrition

Malone, Dan

  (il) Nigg, J. How to raise and keep a dragon   **Fic**

Malone, Nola Langner

  (il) Viorst, J. Earrings!   **E**

Malone, Peter

  (il) Crompton, S. W. The Boston Tea Party   **973.3**

Malone, Peter

  (il) Crossley-Holland, K. How many miles to Bethlehem?   **232.9**

  (il) Krull, K. Big wig   **391**

  Close to the wind   **551.51**

  (il) Spinner, S. The Nutcracker   **E**

Maloney, Peter

  One foot two feet   **E**

Malory, Thomas

  Hodges, M. Merlin and the making of the king   **398.2**

Malta. Sheehan, S.   **945.8**

MALTA -- JUVENILE LITERATURE

  Sheehan, S. Malta   **945.8**

Maltbie, P. I.

  Claude Monet   **92**

The **malted** falcon. Hale, B.   **Fic**

The **Maltese** mummy. Robbins, T.   **741.5**

Mama. Winter, J.   **E**

Mama & Papa have a store. Carling, A. L.   **E**

Mama always comes home. Wilson, K.   **E**

Mama and me. Dorros, A.   **E**

Mama cat has three kittens. Fleming, D.   **E**

Mama don't allow. Hurd, T.   **E**

Mama Elizabeti. Bodeen, S. A.   **E**

Mama Miti: Wangari Maathai and the trees of Kenya. Napoli, D. J.   **92**

Mama says. Walker, R. D.   **E**

Mama's day. Ashman, L.   **E**

Bear in the air E

Kittens! Kittens! Kittens! E

MEZUZAH -- FICTION

The Shema in the mezuzah E

Mezzanotte, Jim

Police 363.2

Mhlophe, Gcina

African tales 398.2

Mia. Yep, L. Fic

Mia and the too big tutu. Farley, R. E

Mia's story. Foreman, M. E

Micawber. Lithgow, J. E

Mice. Fyleman, R. E

MICE

> *See also* Mammals

MICE

Bozzo, L. My first guinea pig and other small pets 636.9

Emberley, E. Thanks, Mom! E

George, L. B. Inside mouse, outside mouse E

Harris, R. H. Goodbye, Mousie E

Henkes, K. Wemberly worried E

Jeffrey, L. S. Hamsters, gerbils, guinea pigs, rabbits, ferrets, mice, and rats 636.9

Johnson, J. Rats and mice 636.9

MacDonald, M. R. Fat cat 398.209

Markle, S. Outside and inside rats and mice 599.35

McCully, E. A. First snow E

Ormerod, J. Miss Mouse's day E

Rohmann, E. My friend Rabbit E

Savage, S. Mouse 599.35

Spinelli, E. Three pebbles and a song E

Tait, L. Mice 599.35

Waddell, M. Tiny's big adventure E

Weeks, S. Drip, drop E

Mice. Tait, L. 599.35

MICE -- ANATOMY -- JUVENILE LITERATURE

Markle, S. Outside and inside rats and mice 599.35

MICE -- FICTION

Hayes, G. Benny and Penny in Lights out! E

Henkes, K. Penny and her doll E

Henkes, K. Penny and her song E

Kirk, D. A friend's tale E

Wells, R. Time-out for Sophie E

Zalben, J. B. Mousterpiece E

MICE -- FOLKLORE

Country mouse and the city mouse Town mouse, country mouse 398.24

MacDonald, M. R. Fat cat 398.209

MacDonald, M. R. Mabela the clever 398.209

Shepard, A. The princess mouse 398.2

Steptoe, J. The story of Jumping Mouse 398.2

Young, E. Seven blind mice 398.24

MICE -- GRAPHIC NOVELS

Freedom! 741.5

MICE -- JUVENILE FICTION

Beiser, T. Miss Mousie's blind date E

Emberley, E. Mice on ice E

Fyleman, R. Mice E

Henkes, K. Penny and her marble E

The mouse with the question mark tail Fic

Ward, H. The town mouse and the country mouse E

MICE -- JUVENILE LITERATURE

Markle, S. Outside and inside rats and mice 599.35

MICE -- SONGS

Langstaff, J. M. Frog went a-courtin' 782.42

Mice on ice. Emberley, E. E

Mice, morals, & monkey business. Wormell, C. 398.2

Michael at the invasion of France, 1943. Calkhoven, L. Fic

Michael Phelps. Torsiello, D. P. 92

Michael Rosen's sad book. Rosen, M. E

Michael Townsend's amazing Greek myths of wonder and blunders. Townsend, M. 292

Michael, Pamela

(ed) River of words 808.81

Michael, Ted

So you wanna be a superstar? 792.602

Michalak, Jamie

Joe and Sparky, superstars! E

Michelangelo. Stanley, D. 92

Michelangelo Buonarroti, 1475-1564

About

Stanley, D. Michelangelo 92

Michelin, Linda

Zuzu's wishing cake E

Michelle. Hopkinson, D. 92

Michelle Obama. Brophy, D. 92

Michelle Obama. Colbert, D. 92

Michelle Obama. Kesselring, S. 92

Michels, Troy

Atlantis 001.9

Michelson, Richard

Lipman Pike 92

Twice as good 796.352

Michelson, Richard

Across the alley E

As good as anybody: Martin Luther King Jr. and Abraham Joshua Heschel's amazing march toward freedom 92

Busing Brewster E

Lipman Pike 92

Tuttle's Red Barn 630

Michigan. Brill, M. T. 977.4

Michigan. Levy, J. 977.4

Michigan. Raatma, L. 977.4

Mick Harte was here. Park, B. Fic

Mickey & me. Gutman, D. Fic

MICKEY MOUSE (CARTOON CHARACTER)

Casty Walt Disney's Mickey Mouse and the world to come 741.5

Petrucha, S. Mickey Mouse: 300 Mickeys 741.5

Mickey Mouse: 300 Mickeys. Petrucha, S. 741.5

Micklethwait, Lucy

Children 750

I spy: an alphabet in art

In the picture 750

Micklos, John

The brave women and children of the American Revolution 973.3

Micro mania. Brown, J. 579

Micro monsters 579

MICROBES *See* Bacteria; Germ theory of disease; Microorganisms; Viruses

MICROBIAL ENERGY CONVERSION *See* Biomass energy

MICROBIOLOGISTS

Hyde, N. What is germ theory? 615

Jackson, D. M. Extreme scientists 509

Ollhoff, J. The germ detectives 616.9

Zamosky, L. Louis Pasteur 92

MICROBIOLOGISTS -- FRANCE -- BIOGRAPHY -- JUVENILE LITERATURE

Miles, L. Louis Pasteur 509.2

MICROBIOLOGY

Bardhan-Quallen, S. Kitchen science experiments 579

Kornberg, A. Germ stories 616.9

Ollhoff, J. The germ detectives 616.9

Owen, R. Icky house invaders 578.6

Mongolia. Pang   951.7
MONGOLS
  Demi Genghis Khan   92
  Kroll, S. Barbarians!   940.1
  Krull, K. Kubla Khan   92
  McCaughrean, G. The kite rider   **Fic**
MONGOLS -- FICTION
  Cottrell Boyce, F. The unforgotten coat   **Fic**
MONGOLS -- HISTORY -- JUVENILE LITERATURE
  Krull, K. Kubla Khan   92
MONGOLS -- JUVENILE LITERATURE
  Kroll, S. Barbarians!   940.1
MONGOOSES
  Somervill, B. A. Small Indian Mongoose   599.74
MONGOOSES -- FICTION
  Pinkney, J. Rikki-tikki-tavi   E
Monitor lizard. Somervill, B. A.   597.95
Monjo, F. N.
  The drinking gourd   E
Monkey. McDermott, G.   398.2
Monkey & Elephant's worst fight ever! Townsend, M.   E
Monkey and me. Gravett, E.   E
The **monkey** and the crocodile. Monkey and the croco-
  dile   398.2
Monkey and the crocodile
  The monkey and the crocodile   398.2
Monkey business. Climo, S.   398.2
Monkey colors. Lunde, D.   E
Monkey reader [series]
  Banks, K. Monkeys and the universe   E
Monkey see monkey draw. Beard, A.   E
Monkey Truck. Slack, M. H.   E
Monkey with a tool belt. Monroe, C.   E
Monkey with a tool belt and the seaside shenanigans. Monroe,
  C.   E
Monkeys. Bodden, V.   599.8
MONKEYS
  Bodden, V. Monkeys   599.8
  Bustos, E. Going ape!   599.8
  Ganeri, A. Howler monkey   599.8
  Jiang The magical Monkey King   398.209
  Lunde, D. Monkey colors   E
  Sayre, A. P. Meet the howlers   599.8
MONKEYS
    See also Primates
MONKEYS -- BEHAVIOR
    See also Animal behavior
MONKEYS -- COLOR -- JUVENILE LITERATURE
  Lunde, D. Monkey colors   E
MONKEYS -- FICTION
  Banks, K. Monkeys and the universe   E
  Beard, A. Monkey see monkey draw   E
  Blackford, A. The hungry little monkey   E
  Bynum, J. Kiki's blankie   E
  Christelow, E. Five little monkeys jumping on the bed   E
  Donaldson, J. Where's my mom?   E
  Durant, A. I love you, Little Monkey   E
  Franco, B. Double play!   E
  Heide, F. P. The one and only Marigold   E
  Hines-Stephens, S. Midway monkey madness   Fic
  McGrory, A. Quick, slow, mango!   E
  Monroe, C. Monkey with a tool belt   E
  Monroe, C. Monkey with a tool belt and the seaside shenani-
    gans   E
  Myers, W. D. Looking for the easy life   E
  Patricelli, L. Be quiet, Mike!   E
  Peet, M. Cloud Tea monkeys   Fic
  Rey, H. A. Curious George   E

  Rey, H. A. Curious George: Cecily G. and the 9 monkeys   E
  Rosenthal, M. Archie and the pirates   E
  Schaefer, C. L. Big Little Monkey   E
  Slack, M. H. Monkey Truck   E
  Slobodkina, E. Caps for sale   E
  Tashjian, J. My life as a stuntboy   Fic
  Townsend, M. Monkey & Elephant's worst fight ever!   E
  Two little monkeys   E
  Vere, E. Banana!   E
  Water hole waiting   E
MONKEYS -- FOLKLORE
  Climo, S. Monkey business   398.2
  Jiang The magical Monkey King   398.209
  McDermott, G. Monkey   398.2
  Monkey and the crocodile   The monkey and the croco-
    dile   398.2
  Wague Diakite, B. The hatseller and the monkeys   398.2
MONKEYS -- JUVENILE FICTION
  Two little monkeys   E
Monkeys and dog days. Banks, K.   E
Monkeys and the universe. Banks, K.   E
MONKS
  Fritz, J. Brendan the Navigator   398.2
  Norris, K. The holy twins: Benedict and Scholastica   271
MONKS -- FICTION
  Millen, C. M. The ink garden of brother Theophane   E
  Nelson, M. Snook alone   E
  Pancheri, J. Brother William's year   E
  Ruddra, A. Dorje's stripes   E
Monks, Lydia
  (il) Donaldson, J. What the ladybug heard   E
MONMOUTH, BATTLE OF, FREEHOLD, N.J., 1778 -- JU-
  VENILE LITERATURE
  Rockwell, A. F. They called her Molly Pitcher   973.3
MONOLOGUES
  Dabrowski, K. My first monologue book   812
  Dabrowski, K. My second monologue book   812
  Dabrowski, K. My third monologue book   812
  Schlitz, L. A. Good masters! Sweet ladies!   940.1
MONONUCLEOSIS -- FICTION
  Weissman, E. B. The short seller   Fic
MONOPOLIES
    See also Commerce; Economics
MONORAIL RAILROADS
    See also Railroads
MONOTHEISM
    See also Religion; Theism
Monroe, Chris
  (il) Kling, K. Big little brother   E
  Monkey with a tool belt   E
  Monkey with a tool belt and the seaside shenanigans   E
  Sneaky sheep   E
Monroe, James, 1758-1831
    About
  Naden, C. J. James Monroe   92
Monroe, Mary Alice
  Turtle summer   597.92
Monroy, Manuel
  (il) Amado, E. What are you doing?   E
Monroy, Manuel
  (il) Amado, E. What are you doing?   E
  Delano, P. When I was a boy Neruda called me Policarpo 92
Monsieur Marceau.   792.309
Monsoon. Krishnaswami, U.   E
Monsoon afternoon. Sheth, K.   E
MONSOONS
    See also Meteorology
MONSOONS -- FICTION

Moore, Ella Sheppard, 1851-1914
    About
  Hopkinson, D. A band of angels   **E**
Moore, Ella Sheppard, 1851-1914 -- Fiction
    About
  Hopkinson, D. A band of angels   **E**
Moore, Eva
  Lucky Ducklings   **E**
Moore, Genevieve
  Catherine's story   **E**
Moore, Gustav
  (il) Ross, M. E. Earth cycles   **525**
Moore, Heidi
  The story behind cotton   **633.5**
  The story behind diamonds   **553.8**
  The story behind salt   **553.6**
Moore, Inga
  A house in the woods   **E**
Moore, Inga
  Burnett, F. H. The secret garden   **Fic**
  (il) Grahame, K. The wind in the willows   **Fic**
  (il) Horse tales   **S**
  A house in the woods   **E**
Moore, Jodi
  When a dragon moves in   **E**
Moore, Lilian
  Beware, take care   **811**
  Mural on Second Avenue, and other city poems   **811**
Moore, Margie
  (il) Glass, B. R. Blue-ribbon dad   **E**
Moore, Margie
  (il) Carlstrom, N. W. It's your first day of school, Annie
  Claire   **E**
  (il) Glass, B. R. Blue-ribbon dad   **E**
  (il) Hill, S. Ruby's perfect day   **E**
Moore, Patrick
  The mighty street sweeper   **E**
Moore, Willamarie
  All about Japan   **952**
Moore-Mallinos, Jennifer
  I have asthma   **616.2**
MOORS *See* Muslims
Moose. Riggs, K.   **599.65**
Moose. Gish, M.   **599.65**
MOOSE
  Arnold, C. A moose's world   **599.65**
  Gish, M. Moose   **599.65**
  Riggs, K. Moose   **599.65**
MOOSE -- FICTION
  Bingham, K. Z is for Moose   **E**
MOOSE -- JUVENILE FICTION
  Jeffers, O. This moose belongs to me   **E**
MOOSE -- JUVENILE LITERATURE
  Riggs, K. Moose   **599.65**
Moose and Hildy [series]
  Greene, S. Moose's big idea   **Fic**
MOOSE AS PETS -- FICTION
  Jeffers, O. This moose belongs to me   **E**
Moose on the loose. Wargin   **E**
Moose's big idea. Greene, S.   **Fic**
A **moose's** world. Arnold, C.   **599.65**
Mooshka. Paschkis, J.   **E**
MOPS AND MOPSTICKS -- FICTION
  Robomop   **E**
Mora, Andy
  (il) McMahon, P. Ultimate trains   **385**
Mora, Francisco X.
  (il) Climo, S. Tuko and the birds   **398.2**

Mora, Pat
  Gracias   **E**
Mora, Pat
  Gracias   **E**
  Abuelos   **E**
  Book fiesta!   **E**
  Dona Flor   **E**
  Here, kitty, kitty   **E**
  Tomas and the library lady   **E**
  Uno, dos, tres: one, two, three   **E**
  Wiggling pockets   **E**
  Yum! mmmm! que rico!   **811**
Moragne, Wendy
  New Jersey   **974.9**
MORAL AND PHILOSOPHIC STORIES *See* Didactic fiction; Fables; Parables
MORAL DEVELOPMENT
    See also Child psychology; Moral education
MORAL EDUCATION
  Barker, D. Maybe right, maybe wrong   **370.1**
MORAL EDUCATION
    See also Education; Ethics
MORAL PHILOSOPHY *See* Ethics
MORALE
    See also Courage
Morales, Magaly
  (il) Brown, M. Chavela and the Magic Bubble   **E**
Morales, Melita
  Jam & honey   **E**
Morales, Yuyi
  (il) Georgia in Hawaii   **E**
  (il) Ladder to the moon   **E**
  Niño wrestles the world   **E**
Morales, Yuyi
  (il) Johnston, T. My abuelita   **E**
  (il) Krull, K. Harvesting hope   **92**
  (il) Lacamara, L. Floating on Mama's song   **E**
  (il) Ladder to the moon   **E**
  (il) Montes, M. Los gatos black on Halloween   **E**
  Just a minute   **398.2**
  Just in case   **E**
  Little Night   **E**
MORALITY *See* Ethics
MORALITY PLAYS
    See also Drama; English drama; Religious drama; Theater
MORALS *See* Conduct of life; Ethics; Human behavior; Moral conditions
Moran, Thomas, 1837-1926
    About
  Judge, L. Yellowstone Moran   **92**
Moray eels and cleaner shrimp work together. Rustad, M. E. H.   **597**
Mordan, C. B.
  Dendy, L. A. Guinea pig scientists   **616**
  (il) Marrin, A. Oh, rats!   **599.35**
  (il) Silent movie   **E**
Morden, Daniel
  Lupton, H. The adventures of Odysseus   **292**
Mordhorst, Heidi
  Pumpkin butterfly   **811**
More about Boy. Dahl, R.   **92**
More bears! Nesbitt, K.   **E**
More bones. Olson, A. N.   **398.2**
More bullies in more books. Bott, C. J.   **371.5**
More family storytimes. Reid, R.   **027.62**
More life-size zoo. Komiya, T.   **590**
More more more said the baby. Williams, V. B.   **E**

More or less. Murphy, S. J. **513**

More perfect than the moon. MacLachlan, P. **Fic**

A **more** perfect union. Maestro, B. **342**

More pocket poems. **811**

More scary stories to tell in the dark. Schwartz, A. **398.2**

More simple science fair projects, grades 3-5. Tocci, S. **507.8**

More stories to solve. Shannon, G. **398.2**

More storytime action! Bromann, J. **027.62**

More than anything else. Bradby, M. **E**

More than meets the eye. Raczka, B. **750**

Moreau, Helene
   (il) What a party! **E**

Moreillon, Judi
   Collaborative strategies for teaching reading comprehension **372.4**

Moreno, Rene King
   (il) Goldman, J. Uncle monarch and the Day of the Dead **E**
   (il) Guy, G. F. Fiesta! **E**
   (il) Stanton, K. Papi's gift **E**

Morey, Walt
   Gentle Ben **Fic**

MORGAN LE FAY (LEGENDARY CHARACTER)
   See also Legendary characters

Morgan, Clay
   The boy who returned from the sea **Fic**

Morgan, Jody
   Elephant rescue **599.67**

Morgan, Julia
About
   Mannis, C. D. Julia Morgan built a castle **92**

Morgan, Pierr
   (il) Schaefer, C. L. Dragon dancing **E**
   (il) Who's there? **E**

Morgan, Sally
   Animal rescue **333.95**
   Me and my dad **E**
   Pollution **363.7**
   Sam's bush journey **E**
   Waste and recycling **363.7**

Morgenstern, Susie Hoch
   A book of coupons **Fic**

Morgy makes his move. Lewis, M. **Fic**

Moriarty, Chris
   The watcher in the shadows **Fic**

Moriarty, Chris
   The inquisitor's apprentice **Fic**

Morin, Paul
   (il) Mollel, T. M. The orphan boy **398.21**

Moriuchi, Mique
   (il) Fisher, A. L. The story goes on **E**
   (il) My village **808.81**
   (il) Piper, S. Prayers for a better world **242**
   (il) Rivett, R. I imagine **242**

Morley, Agnes, 1874-1958
About
   Basketball belles **796.323**

Morley, Agnes, 1874-1958 -- Juvenile literature
About
   Basketball belles **796.323**

Morley, Christine
   Freaky facts about spiders **595.4**

Morley, Taia
   (il) Tang, G. Math fables too **513**

Morlock, Lisa
   Track that scat! **591.47**

MORMON CHURCH *See* Church of Jesus Christ of Latter-day Saints

MORMONS

Bial, R. Nauvoo **289.3**

George, C. What makes me a Mormon? **289.3**

Hailstone, R. The white ox **92**

Morn, September B.
   The pug **636.7**

MORNING -- FICTION
   Brown, M. W. A child's good morning book **E**
   DwellStudio (Firm) Good morning, toucan **E**
   Krauss, R. The backward day **E**
   Lobel, A. Hello, day! **E**
   Rosenberg, L. Nobody **E**
   Wong, J. S. Buzz **E**

Morning Girl. Dorris, M. **Fic**

Morning, noon, and night. George, J. C. **E**

Morocco. Seward, P. **964**

Morpurgo, Michael
   Beowulf **398.2**
   Hansel and Gretel **398.2**
   Kensuke's kingdom **Fic**
   The McElderry book of Aesop's fables **398.2**
   Mirror **E**
   On angel wings **Fic**
   The Pied Piper of Hamelin **398.2**
   Sir Gawain and the Green Knight **398.2**
   Waiting for Anya **Fic**
   War horse **Fic**
   Wave **E**

Morrice, Polly Alison
   Iowa **977.7**

Morris and Boris at the circus. Wiseman, B. **E**

Morris the artist. Segal, L. G. **E**

Morris's disappearing bag. Wells, R. **E**

Morris, Ann
   Bread, bread, bread **641.8**
   Hats, hats, hats **391**
   Shoes, shoes, shoes **391**
   Tsunami **959.3**

Morris, Betty J.
   Administering the school library media center **027.8**

Morris, Christopher G.
   (ed) Macmillan dictionary for children **423**

Morris, Esther Hobart, 1814-1902
About
   White, L. I could do that! **92**

Morris, Gerald
   The adventures of Sir Gawain the True **Fic**
   The adventures of Sir Givret the Short **Fic**
   The adventures of Sir Lancelot the Great **Fic**

Morris, Jackie
   (il) East of the Sun, West of the Moon **Fic**
   (il) The greatest gift **Fic**
   (il) I am cat **E**
   The cat and the fiddle **398.8**

Morris, Jackie
   (il) The greatest gift **Fic**
   (il) Jones, S. L. Little one, we knew you'd come **232.9**
   The cat and the fiddle **398.8**

Morris, Karyn
   The Kids Can Press jumbo book of gardening **635**

Morris, Neil
   Glass **620.1**
   Global warming **363.7**
   Metals **620.1**
   Paper **676**
   Plastics **668.4**
   Textiles **677**
   Wood **634.9**

Morris, Richard T.

See also Biography

MOTION PICTURES -- CENSORSHIP

    See also Censorship

MOTION PICTURES -- ETHICAL ASPECTS

    See also Ethics

MOTION PICTURES -- FICTION

DiCamillo, K. Mercy Watson: something wonky this way comes   **Fic**

Mass, W. Finally   **Fic**

Selznick, B. The invention of Hugo Cabret   **Fic**

Tashjian, J. My life as a stuntboy   **Fic**

MOTION PICTURES -- HISTORY AND CRITICISM

Roza, G. Drawing Dracula   743

Roza, G. Drawing Frankenstein   743

Roza, G. Drawing Godzilla   743

Roza, G. Drawing King Kong   743

MOTION PICTURES -- JUVENILE FICTION

Willems, M. That Is Not a Good Idea!   **E**

MOTION PICTURES -- PRODUCTION AND DIREC-TION

Green, J. Shooting video to make learning fun   778.5

Kinney, J. The wimpy kid movie diary   791.43

McDonald, M. Judy Moody goes to Hollywood   791.43

O'Brien, L. Lights, camera, action!   791.43

MOTION PICTURES -- PRODUCTION AND DIREC-TION -- FICTION

Milgrim, D. Amelia makes a movie   **E**

MOTION PICTURES AND CHILDREN

    See also Children; Motion pictures

MOTION PICTURES IN EDUCATION

    See also Audiovisual education; Motion pictures; Teaching -- Aids and devices

Motion, magnets and more. Mason, A.   530

MOTIVATION (PSYCHOLOGY)

    See also Psychology

Motley, Tom

  (il) Usher, M. D. The golden ass of Lucius Apuleius   **Fic**

MOTOR BUSES See Buses

MOTOR CARS See Automobiles

MOTOR CYCLES See Motorcycles

MOTOR TRUCKS See Trucks

MOTOR VEHICLE INDUSTRY See Automobile industry

MOTOR VEHICLES

Rockwell, A. F. Big wheels   **E**

MOTOR VEHICLES -- JUVENILE LITERATURE

Rockwell, A. F. Big wheels   **E**

MOTOR VEHICLES -- WHEELS -- JUVENILE LITERA-TURE

Rockwell, A. F. Big wheels   **E**

MOTORBOATS

    See also Boats and boating

MOTORBOATS -- MODELS

    See also Models and modelmaking

MOTORCYCLES

Clark, W. Motorcycles on the move   629.227

Smedman, L. From boneshakers to choppers   629.227

Woods, B. Hottest motorcycles   629.227

MOTORCYCLES

    See also Bicycles

MOTORCYCLES -- HISTORY -- JUVENILE LITERA-TURE

Smedman, L. From boneshakers to choppers   629.227

Motorcycles on the move. Clark, W.   629.227

MOTORCYCLING

    See also Cycling

MOTORING See Automobile travel

MOTORS See Electric motors; Engines

Mould, Chris

The darkling curse   **Fic**

The icy hand   **Fic**

Smugglers' mine   **Fic**

The wooden mile   **Fic**

Moulton, Erin E.

Flutter   **Fic**

Moulton, Mark Kimball

The very best pumpkin   **E**

Mouly, Francoise

Big fat Little Lit   741.5

The TOON treasury of classic children's comics   741.5

Mound, L. A.

Insect   595.7

Moundlic, Charlotte

The scar   **E**

MOUNDS AND MOUND BUILDERS

    See also Archeology; Burial; Tombs

MOUNT EVEREST (CHINA AND NEPAL)

Athans, S. K. Tales from the top of the world   796.522

Jenkins, S. The top of the world   796.52

MOUNT EVEREST (CHINA AND NEPAL)

    See also Mountains

MOUNT EVEREST (CHINA AND NEPAL) -- JUVENILE LITERATURE

Bodden, V. To the top of Mount Everest   796.522

MOUNT RAINIER (WASH.)

    See also Mountains

Mount Rushmore. Thomas, W.   978.3

Mount Rushmore. Kenney, K. L.   978.3

MOUNT VERNON (VA. : ESTATE)

Delano, M. F. Master George's people   973.4

MOUNTAIN ANIMALS

Bredeson, C. Baby animals of the mountains   591.7

Lynette, R. Who lives on a towering mountain?   591.7

MOUNTAIN ANIMALS

    See also Animals

MOUNTAIN BIKES

    See also All terrain vehicles; Bicycles

Mountain biking. Schoenherr, A.   796.6

MOUNTAIN BIKING

Schoenherr, A. Mountain biking   796.6

MOUNTAIN BIKING

    See also Cycling

MOUNTAIN CLIMBING See Mountaineering

MOUNTAIN ECOLOGY

Levy, J. Discovering mountains   577.5

This is the mountain   577.5

MOUNTAIN ECOLOGY

    See also Ecology

MOUNTAIN FAUNA See Mountain animals

MOUNTAIN LIFE

    See also Country life

MOUNTAIN LIFE -- FICTION

Dowell, F. O. Dovey Coe   **Fic**

Hemingway, E. M. Road to Tater Hill   **Fic**

MOUNTAIN LIFE -- NORTH CAROLINA

Dowell, F. O. Dovey Coe   **Fic**

Mountain lions. Shores, E. L.   599.75

A **mountain** of mittens. Plourde, L.   **E**

MOUNTAIN PLANTS

    See also Plant ecology; Plants

Mountain pose. Wilson, N. H.   **Fic**

MOUNTAINEERING

Athans, S. K. Tales from the top of the world   796.522

Burleigh, R. Tiger of the snows   92

Cleare, J. Epic climbs   796.52

Coburn, B. Triumph on Everest: a photobiography of Sir Edmund Hillary   92

Barnholdt, L. Girl meets ghost **Fic**
Baucom, I. Through the skylight **Fic**
Broach, E. Treasure on Superstition Mountain **Fic**
Carey, B. Poison most vial **Fic**
The curse of the pharaoh **Fic**
Cushman, D. Inspector Hopper **E**
Cushman, D. Mystery at the Club Sandwich **E**
DeFelice, C. C. The ghost and Mrs. Hobbs **Fic**
DeFelice, C. C. The ghost of Cutler Creek **Fic**
Draanen, W. v. Sammy Keyes and the hotel thief **Fic**
Draanen, W. v. Sammy Keyes and the search for Snake Eyes **Fic**
Fairlie, E. The lost treasure of Tuckernuck **Fic**
Frazier, A. The mastermind plot **Fic**
Hale, B. The big nap **Fic**
Hale, B. Farewell, my lunchbag **Fic**
Hale, B. Give my regrets to Broadway **Fic**
Hale, B. Trouble is my beeswax **Fic**
Lacey, J. Island of Thieves **Fic**
Lane, A. Black ice **Fic**
Lane, A. Rebel fire **Fic**
Lawrence, C. P.K. Pinkerton and the petrified man **Fic**
McCall Smith, A. The great cake mystery **Fic**
Mr. and Mrs. Bunny-- detectives extraordinaire! **Fic**
Pullman, P. Two crafty criminals! **Fic**
Rylant, C. The case of the missing monkey **E**
Stanley, D. The mysterious matter of I.M. Fine **Fic**
Stewart, T. L. The extraordinary education of Nicholas Benedict **Fic**
Turnage, S. Three times lucky **Fic**
Van Draanen, W. Sammy Keyes and the showdown in Sin City **Fic**
Who could that be at this hour? **Fic**

MYSTERY AND DETECTIVE STORIES *See* Mystery fiction

Mystery at the Club Sandwich. Cushman, D. **E**

MYSTERY COMIC BOOKS, STRIPS, ETC.
See also Comic books, strips, etc.

MYSTERY FICTION
Abbott, T. The postcard **Fic**
Adler, D. A. Young Cam Jansen and the dinosaur game **E**
Allison, J. Gilda Joyce, psychic investigator **Fic**
Allison, J. Gilda Joyce, psychic investigator: the bones of the holy **Fic**
Allison, J. Gilda Joyce: the dead drop **Fic**
Allison, J. Gilda Joyce: the ghost sonata **Fic**
Allison, J. Gilda Joyce: the Ladies of the Lake **Fic**
Amato, M. Edgar Allan's official crime investigation notebook **Fic**
Anderson, M. T. Agent Q, or the smell of danger! **Fic**
Anderson, M. T. Jasper Dash and the flame-pits of Delaware **Fic**
Angleberger, T. Horton Halfpott **Fic**
Aronson, S. Beyond lucky **Fic**
Avi City of orphans **Fic**
Baccalario, P. City of wind **Fic**
Baccalario, P. The door to time **Fic**
Baccalario, P. The long-lost map **Fic**
Baccalario, P. Star of Stone **Fic**
Balliett, B. The Calder game **Fic**
Balliett, B. Chasing Vermeer **Fic**
Balliett, B. The Wright 3 **Fic**
Barnett, M. The case of the case of mistaken identity **Fic**
Barnett, M. The ghostwriter secret **Fic**
Barnett, M. It happened on a train **Fic**
Barrett, T. The 100-year-old secret **Fic**
Barrett, T. The Beast of Blackslope **Fic**
Barrett, T. The case that time forgot **Fic**

Barrett, T. The missing heir **Fic**
Beil, M. D. The Red Blazer Girls: the ring of Rocamadour **Fic**
Beil, M. D. The Red Blazer Girls: The vanishing violin **Fic**
Beil, M. The Red Blazer Girls: the mistaken masterpiece **Fic**
Bellairs, J. The curse of the blue figurine **Fic**
Berlin, E. The potato chip puzzles **Fic**
Berlin, E. The puzzling world of Winston Breen **Fic**
Biedrzycki, D. Ace Lacewing, bug detective: the big swat **E**
The big flush **741.5**
Bonsall, C. N. The case of the hungry stranger **E**
Bonsall, C. N. The case of the scaredy cats **E**
Brezenoff, S. The burglar who bit the Big Apple **Fic**
Brezenoff, S. The painting that wasn't there **Fic**
Brezenoff, S. The zombie who visited New Orleans **Fic**
Broach, E. Masterpiece **Fic**
Broach, E. Missing on Superstition Mountain **Fic**
Broach, E. Shakespeare's secret **Fic**
Buckley, M. The Everafter War **Fic**
Buckley, M. The inside story **Fic**
Buckley, M. Magic and other misdemeanors **Fic**
Buckley, M. Once upon a crime **Fic**
Buckley, M. The problem child **Fic**
Buckley, M. Tales from the hood **Fic**
Buckley, M. The unusual suspects **Fic**
Butler, D. H. The case of the fire alarm **Fic**
Butler, D. H. The case of the library monster **Fic**
Butler, D. H. The case of the lost boy **Fic**
Butler, D. H. The case of the missing family **Fic**
Butler, D. H. The case of the mixed-up mutts **Fic**
Buzbee, L. The haunting of Charles Dickens **Fic**
Byars, B. C. The dark stairs **Fic**
Cadenhead, M. Sally's bones **Fic**
Carey, B. Poison most vial **Fic**
Chari, S. Vanished **Fic**
Chatterton, M. The Brain finds a leg **Fic**
Chatterton, M. The Brain full of holes **Fic**
Cheshire, S. The curse of the ancient mask and other case files **Fic**
Cheshire, S. The pirate's blood and other case files **Fic**
Cheshire, S. The treasure of Dead Man's Lane and other case files **Fic**
Chick, B. The secret zoo **Fic**
Chick, B. The secret zoo: secrets and shadows **Fic**
Chu's day **E**
Clements, A. Fear itself **Fic**
Clements, A. Room one **Fic**
Clements, A. We the children **Fic**
Conford, E. A case for Jenny Archer **Fic**
Corbett, S. The last newspaper boy in America **Fic**
Cotler, S. Cheesie Mack is not a genius or anything **Fic**
Cox, J. The case of the purloined professor **Fic**
Cushman, D. Dirk Bones and the mystery of the haunted house **E**
Cushman, D. Dirk Bones and the mystery of the missing books **E**
Cushman, D. Inspector Hopper **E**
Cushman, D. Mystery at the Club Sandwich **E**
Davies, K. The great hamster massacre **Fic**
De Campi, A. Kat & Mouse: Teacher torture **741.5**
DeFelice, C. C. The ghost of Cutler Creek **Fic**
DeFelice, C. C. The missing manatee **Fic**
Detective Blue **E**
Dowd, S. The London Eye mystery **Fic**
Draanen, W. v. Sammy Keyes and the hotel thief **Fic**
Evans, L. Horten's miraculous mechanisms **Fic**
Fairlie, E. The lost treasure of Tuckernuck **Fic**
Ferraiolo, J. D. The big splash **Fic**
Frazier, A. The mastermind plot **Fic**

NATIVE AMERICAN MEDICINE
    See also Medicine
NATIVE AMERICAN MUSIC
    See also Music
NATIVE AMERICAN NAMES
    See also Names
NATIVE AMERICAN SIGN LANGUAGE
    See also Sign language
NATIVE AMERICAN SILVERWORK
    See also Silverwork
NATIVE AMERICAN WOMEN
    Nelson, M. The life of Sacagawea   978
    Ray, D. K. Paiute princess   979.004
    Tallchief, M. Tallchief   92
NATIVE AMERICAN WOMEN
    See also Women
NATIVE AMERICANS
    A Braid of lives   970.004
    Dennis, Y. W. Children of native America today   970.004
    Goble, P. All our relatives   970.004
    January, B. Native American art & culture   704
    King, D. C. First people   970.004
    McNeese, T. The fascinating history of American Indians   970.004
    Molin, P. F. American Indian stereotypes in the world of children   970.004
    Murdoch, D. H. North American Indian   970.004
    Perritano, J. Spanish missions   266
    Swamp, J. Giving thanks   299.7
    Weber, E. N. R. Rattlesnake Mesa   92
NATIVE AMERICANS -- AGRICULTURE
    See also Agriculture
NATIVE AMERICANS -- ANTIQUITIES
    Quigley, M. Mesa Verde   978.8
NATIVE AMERICANS -- ANTIQUITIES
    See also Antiquities
NATIVE AMERICANS -- BIOGRAPHY
    Nelson, M. The life of Sacagawea   978
NATIVE AMERICANS -- CANADA
    Andre We feel good out here   970.004
    Fatty legs   92
    Jordan-Fenton, C. A stranger at home   92
    McLeod, T. The Delta is my home   970.004
    Zoe, T. Living stories   970.004
NATIVE AMERICANS -- CAPTIVITIES
    See also Frontier and pioneer life
NATIVE AMERICANS -- ECONOMIC CONDITIONS
    See also Economic conditions
NATIVE AMERICANS -- FICTION
    Armstrong, A. Raleigh's page   Fic
    Barron, T. A. Ghost hands   E
    Broyles, A. Priscilla and the hollyhocks   E
    Bruchac, J. The arrow over the door   Fic
    Campbell, N. I. Shi-shi-etko   E
    The crossing   E
    Dorris, M. Sees Behind Trees   Fic
    Goble, P. Beyond the ridge   E
    Helgerson, J. Crows & cards   Fic
    Howard, E. The crimson cap   Fic
    Martin, B. Knots on a counting rope   E
    Noe, K. S. Something to hold   Fic
    O'Dell, S. Island of the Blue Dolphins   Fic
    O'Dell, S. Streams to the river, river to the sea   Fic
    O'Dell, S. Zia   Fic
    Smith, C. L. Indian shoes   Fic
    Speare, E. G. The sign of the beaver   Fic
    Young, J. Minnow and Rose   Fic
NATIVE AMERICANS -- FOLKLORE

Bruchac, J. The girl who helped thunder and other Native American folktales   398.2
Bruchac, J. Between earth & sky   398.2
Bruchac, J. How Chipmunk got his stripes   398.2
Bruchac, J. Thirteen moons on a turtle's back   398.2
Caduto, M. J. Keepers of the night   398.2
Curry, J. L. Hold up the sky: and other Native American tales from Texas and the Southern Plains   398.2
De Paola, T. The legend of the Indian paintbrush   398.2
Delacre, L. Golden tales   398.209
Goble, P. Buffalo woman   398.2
Goble, P. The girl who loved wild horses   398.2
Goble, P. The legend of the White Buffalo Woman   398.2
Goble, P. The woman who lived with wolves, & other stories from the tipi   398.2
James, E. The woman who married a bear   398.2
Larson, J. C. Hummingbirds   598
Longfellow, H. W. Hiawatha   811
McDermott, G. Coyote: a trickster tale from the American Southwest   398.2
McDermott, G. Jabuti the tortoise   398.2
McDermott, G. Raven   398.2
Steptoe, J. The story of Jumping Mouse   398.2
Taylor, C. J. Spirits, fairies, and merpeople   398.2
Trickster: Native American tales   398.2
Van Laan, N. The magic bean tree   398.2
Zoe, T. Living stories   970.004
NATIVE AMERICANS -- FOLKLORE
    See also Folklore
NATIVE AMERICANS -- FOLKLORE -- MEXICO
    Endredy, J. The journey of Tunuri and the Blue Deer   398.2
NATIVE AMERICANS -- GREAT PLAINS
    The horse and the Plains indians   978
NATIVE AMERICANS -- HISTORY
    Connolly, S. The Americas and the Pacific   970.004
    Dennis, Y. W. A kid's guide to native American history   970.004
    Mann, C. C. Before Columbus   970.01
NATIVE AMERICANS -- HUNTING
    See also Hunting
NATIVE AMERICANS -- MEDICAL CARE
    See also Medical care
NATIVE AMERICANS -- MEXICO -- FICTION
    Ramirez, A. Napi   E
NATIVE AMERICANS -- NORTH AMERICA
    Cooper, S. Ghost Hawk   Fic
NATIVE AMERICANS -- NORTHWEST COAST OF NORTH AMERICA
    Proud to be Inuvialuit   970.004
NATIVE AMERICANS -- ORIGIN
    Mann, C. C. Before Columbus   970.01
NATIVE AMERICANS -- PERU
    Krebs, L. Up and down the Andes   985
NATIVE AMERICANS -- POETRY
    Bruchac, J. Thirteen moons on a turtle's back   398.2
    Dancing teepees: poems of American Indian youth   897
    Longfellow, H. W. Hiawatha   811
NATIVE AMERICANS -- POLITICS AND GOVERNMENT
    See also Politics
NATIVE AMERICANS -- RELATIONS WITH EARLY SETTLERS
    Cooper, S. Ghost Hawk   Fic
NATIVE AMERICANS -- RELIGION
    See also Religion
NATIVE AMERICANS -- RELOCATION
    Bjornlund, L. D. The Trail of Tears   970.004
    Bruchac, J. The Trail of Tears   970.004

Nelson, Kadir
  (il) Allen, D. Dancing in the wings   E
  (il) De la Pena, M. A nation's hope   92
  (il) Grifalconi, A. The village that vanished   E
  (il) Jordan, D. Salt in his shoes   E
  (il) Levine, E. Henry's freedom box   E
  (il) Napoli, D. J. Mama Miti: Wangari Maathai and the trees
    of Kenya   92
  Heart and soul   305.8
  He's got the whole world in his hands   782.25
  We are the ship   796.357
  (il) Nolen, J. Big Jabe   E
  (il) Nolen, J. Hewitt Anderson's great big life   E
  (il) Nolen, J. Thunder Rose   E
  (il) Obama, B. Change has come   328
  (il) Rappaport, D. Abe's honest words   92
  (il) Robinson, S. Testing the ice: a true story about Jackie
    Robinson   92
  (il) Shange, N. Coretta Scott   92
  (il) Shange, N. Ellington was not a street   E
  (il) Staines, B. All God's critters   782.42
  (il) Weatherford, C. B. Moses   92
Nelson, Kristin L.
  Monster trucks on the move   796.7
Nelson, Maria
  20 fun facts about dragonflies   595.7
  The life of Sacagawea   978
Nelson, Marilyn
  Beautiful ballerina   792.8
  Snook alone   E
  Sweethearts of rhythm   811
Nelson, Nina
  Bringing the boy home   Fic
Nelson, S. D.
  Bruchac, J. Crazy Horse's vision   E
  Black Elk's vision   92
Nelson, Sara Kirsten
  Stay safe!   613.6
Nelson, Scott Reynolds
  Ain't nothing but a man   92
Nelson, Vaunda Micheaux
  Bad news for outlaws   92
  Juneteenth   394.26
  Who will I be, Lord?   E
Nelson-Schmidt, Michelle
  Cats, cats!   E
  Dogs, Dogs!   E
Neo Leo. Barretta, G.   609
NEO-IMPRESSIONISM (ART) *See* Impressionism (Art)
NEON GENESIS EVANGELION (FICTIONAL ROBOT)
  See also Fictional robots; Manga; Mecha
NEOPAGANISM
  See also Religions
NEPHEWS -- FICTION
  Ransom, C. Rebel McKenzie   Fic
NEPHILA MACULATA -- JUVENILE LITERATURE
  Stronger Than Steel   595.4
Neptune. Sherman, J.   523.4
Neptune. Landau, E.   523.4
NEPTUNE (PLANET)
  See also Planets
The **Neptune** Project. Holyoke, P.   Fic
Nerd camp. Weissman, E. B.   Fic
Neri, G.
  Ghetto cowboy   Fic
Neri, Greg
  Neri, G. Ghetto cowboy   Fic
  Chess rumble   Fic

Neruda, Pablo, 1904-1973
  Brown, M. Pablo Neruda   92
  Delano, P. When I was a boy Neruda called me Policarpo   92
Neruda, Pablo, 1904-1973 -- Fiction
  Ryan, P. M. The dreamer   Fic
Neruda, Pablo, 1904-1973 -- Juvenile literature
  Brown, M. Pablo Neruda   92
  Ryan, P. M. The dreamer   Fic
NERVES
  See also Nervous system
Nervous system. Tieck, S.   612.8
NERVOUS SYSTEM
  See also Anatomy; Physiology
NERVOUS SYSTEM
  Berger, M. Why I sneeze, shiver, hiccup, and yawn   612.7
  Rotner, S. Body actions   612
  Simon, S. The brain   612.8
  Stewart, M. You've got nerve!   612.8
  Tieck, S. Nervous system   612.8
NERVOUS SYSTEM -- DISEASES
  See also Diseases
NERVOUS SYSTEM -- JUVENILE LITERATURE
  Gold, M. V. Learning about the nervous system   612.8
Nesbit, E.
  The enchanted castle   Fic
  Five children and it   Fic
  Jack and the beanstalk   398.2
Nesbitt, Kenn
  More bears!   E
  My hippo has the hiccups   811
Nesbo, Jo, 1960-
  Doctor Proctor's fart powder   Fic
Nespeca, Sue McCleaf
  Picture books plus   028.5
Nesquens, Daniel
  My tattooed dad   E
Ness, Evaline
  Sam, Bangs & Moonshine   E
NEST BUILDING
  See also Animal behavior; Animals -- Habitations
A **nest** for Celeste. Cole, H.   Fic
Nest, nook & cranny. Blackaby, S.   811
The **Netherlands.** Docalavich, H.   949.2
NETHERLANDS -- JUVENILE LITERATURE
  Docalavich, H. The Netherlands   949.2
Nethery, Mary
  Dennis, B. Nubs   636.7
  Larson, K. Two Bobbies   636.08
Nettleton, Pamela Hill
  William Shakespeare   822.3
Networked. Rainie, L.   006.7
Neubecker, Robert
  (il) Florian, D. Shiver me timbers   E
  What little boys are made of   E
  Wow! Ocean!   E
  (il) Time (out) for monsters!   E
Neubecker, Robert
  (il) Bagert, B. School fever   811
  (il) Braeuner, S. The great dog wash   E
  (il) Cuyler, M. Tick tock clock   E
  (il) Kimmel, E. C. The top job   E
  (il) Lund, D. Monsters on machines   E
  Wow! America!   E
  Wow! city!   E
  Wow! Ocean!   E
  Wow! school!   E
  (il) Weeks, S. Sophie Peterman tells the truth!   E
  (il) Williams, T. Air show!   E

Neuburger, Emily K.

Juster, N. The annotated Phantom tollbooth	**813**
A Caldecott celebration	**741.6**
Golden legacy	**070.5**
Minders of make-believe	**070.5**
Side by side	**070.5**

Neumeier, Rachel

The Floating Islands	**Fic**

NEUROLOGY *See* Nervous system

NEUROSCIENCES

> *See also* Medicine

NEUTRON WEAPONS

> *See also* Nuclear weapons

NEUTRONS

> *See also* Atoms; Particles (Nuclear physics)

Nevada. Stefoff, R.	**979.3**
Nevada. Roza, G.	**979.3**
Nevada. Heinrichs, A.	**979.3**
Never forgotten.	**Fic**
Never mind! Avi	**Fic**
Never say boo! Pulver, R.	**E**
Never say die. Hobbs, W.	**Fic**
Never say genius. Gutman, D.	**Fic**
Never smile at a monkey. Jenkins, S.	**591.6**
Never take a shark to the dentist and other things not to do. Barrett, J.	**E**
Never to forget: the Jews of the Holocaust. Meltzer, M.	**940.53**
Neville. Juster, N.	**E**

Neville, Emily Cheney

It's like this, Cat	**Fic**

Nevius, Carol

Baseball hour	**796.357**
Building with Dad	**E**
Karate hour	**E**
Soccer hour	**E**
The **new** Americans. Maestro, B.	**970.02**

New Americans [series]

Keedle, J. Americans from the Caribbean and Central America	**305.8**
Keedle, J. Mexican Americans	**305.8**
Keedle, J. West African Americans	**305.8**
Park, K. Americans from India and other South Asian countries	**305.8**
Thomas, W. D. Korean Americans	**305.8**
Wachtel, A. Southeast Asian Americans	**305.8**
Weiss, G. G. Americans from Russia and Eastern Europe	**305.8**
The **new** baby at your house. Cole, J.	**306.875**
A **new** beginning. Pfeffer, W.	**394.26**

Newbery Medal titles

Applegate, K. The one and only Ivan	**Fic**
Armstrong, W. H. Sounder	**Fic**
Avi. Crispin: the cross of lead	**Fic**
Blos, J. W. A gathering of days: a New England girl's journal, 1830-32	**Fic**
Brink, C. R. Caddie Woodlawn	**Fic**
Byars, B. C. The summer of the swans	**Fic**
Cleary, B. Dear Mr. Henshaw	**Fic**
Coatsworth, E. J. The cat who went to heaven	**Fic**
Cooper, S. The grey king	**Fic**
Creech, S. Walk two moons	**Fic**
Curtis, C. P. Bud, not Buddy	**Fic**
Cushman, K. The midwife's apprentice	**Fic**
De Angeli, M. L. The door in the wall	**Fic**
DeJong, M. The wheel on the school	**Fic**
DiCamillo, K. The tale of Despereaux	**Fic**
Du Bois, W. P. The twenty-one balloons	**Fic**
Estes, E. Ginger Pye	**Fic**

Field, R. Hitty: her first hundred years	**Fic**
Fleischman, P. Joyful noise: poems for two voices	**811**
Fleischman, S. The whipping boy	**Fic**
Freedman, R. Lincoln: a photobiography	**92**
Gaiman, N. The graveyard book	**Fic**
Gantos, J. Dead end in Norvelt	**Fic**
George, J. C. Julie of the wolves	**Fic**
Hamilton, V. M.C. Higgins, the great	**Fic**
Henry, M. King of the wind	**Fic**
Hesse, K. Out of the dust	**Fic**
Kadohata, C. Kira-Kira	**Fic**
Keith, H. Rifles for Watie	**Fic**
Konigsburg, E. L. From the mixed-up files of Mrs. Basil E. Frankweiler	**Fic**
Konigsburg, E. L. The view from Saturday	**Fic**
Krumgold, J. Onion John	**Fic**
Lawson, R. Rabbit Hill	**Fic**
L'Engle, M. A wrinkle in time	**Fic**
Lowry, L. The giver	**Fic**
Lowry, L. Number the stars	**Fic**
MacLachlan, P. Sarah, plain and tall	**Fic**
Naylor, P. R. Shiloh	**Fic**
Neville, E. C. It's like this, Cat	**Fic**
O'Brien, R. C. Mrs. Frisby and the rats of NIMH	**Fic**
O'Dell, S. Island of the Blue Dolphins	**Fic**
Park, L. S. A single shard	**Fic**
Paterson, K. Bridge to Terabithia	**Fic**
Patron, S. The higher power of Lucky	**Fic**
Peck, R. A year down yonder	**Fic**
Perkins, L. R. Criss cross	**Fic**
Raskin, E. The Westing game	**Fic**
Rylant, C. Missing May	**Fic**
Sachar, L. Holes	**Fic**
Sawyer, R. Roller skates	**Fic**
Schlitz, L. A. Good masters! Sweet ladies!	**940.1**
Seredy, K. The white stag	**Fic**
Speare, E. G. The bronze bow	**Fic**
Speare, E. G. The witch of Blackbird Pond	**Fic**
Sperry, A. Call it courage	**Fic**
Spinelli, J. Maniac Magee	**Fic**
Stead, R. When you reach me	**Fic**
Taylor, M. D. Roll of thunder, hear my cry	**Fic**
Treviño, E. B. d. I, Juan de Pareja	**Fic**
Vanderpool, C. Moon over Manifest	**Fic**
Vining, E. G. Adam of the road	**Fic**
Voigt, C. Dicey's song	**Fic**
Willard, N. A visit to William Blake's inn	**811**
Wojciechowska, M. Shadow of a bull	**Fic**
Yates, E. Amos Fortune, free man	**92**
A **new** brother or sister. Guillain, C.	**306.8**

NEW BUSINESS ENTERPRISES

> *See also* Business enterprises

New clothes for New Year's Day. Bae	**E**
A **new** deal for women. Coster, P.	**305.4**
New dinos. Tanaka, S.	**567.9**

NEW ENGLAND -- FICTION

Alcott, L. M. Little women	**Fic**
Connor, L. Crunch	**Fic**
The dulcimer boy	**Fic**
Hall, D. Ox-cart man	**E**
Isaacs, A. Pancakes for supper!	**E**
Jacobson, J. R. Small as an elephant	**Fic**
Lendroth, S. Ocean wide, ocean deep	**E**
MacLachlan, P. Your moon, my moon	**E**
Waite, M. P. The witches of Dredmoore Hollow	**Fic**
New France, 1534-1763. Worth, R.	**971.01**

NORTHERN DANCER (RACE HORSE) -- JUVENILE LITERATURE
Joyce, G. Northern Dancer   **798.400**
Northern lights books for children [series]
Bastedo, J. Free as the wind   **E**
NORTHMEN *See* Vikings
Northrop, Michael
Plunked   **Fic**
Northward to the moon. Horvath, P.   **Fic**
The **Norton** anthology of children's literature.   **808.8**
Norton, Mary
Bed-knob and broomstick   **Fic**
The **Norumbegan quartet** [series]
Anderson, M. T. The empire of gut and bone   **Fic**
Anderson, M. T. The Game of Sunken Places   **Fic**
Anderson, M. T. The suburb beyond the stars   **Fic**
NORWEGIAN LITERATURE
   See also Literature; Scandinavian literature
Norwich, Grace
I am Harriet Tubman   **973.7**
I am Sacagawea   **978.004**
Norwich, Grace
Mar, J. The body book for boys   **612.6**
Norworth, Jack
Take me out to the ball game   **782.42**
Nory Ryan's song. Giff, P. R.   **Fic**
NOSE
Korb, R. My nose   **612.2**
Larsen, C. S. Crust and spray   **612.8**
Miller, S. S. All kinds of noses   **591.4**
NOSE
   See also Face; Head
NOSE -- FICTION
Brown, M. T. Arthur's nose   **E**
Nostradamus. Doft, T.   **133.3**
Nostradamus, 1503-1566
         About
Doft, T. Nostradamus   **133.3**
Nosy Rosie. Keller, H.   **E**
Not a box. Portis, A.   **E**
Not a buzz to be found. Glaser, L.   **595.7**
Not a drop to drink. Burgan, M.   **363.6**
Not a stick. Portis, A.   **E**
Not all animals are blue. Boutignon, B.   **E**
Not all princesses dress in pink. Yolen, J.   **E**
Not fair, won't share. Graves, S.   **152.4**
Not in Room 204. Riggs, S.   **E**
Not inside this house! Lewis, K.   **E**
Not last night but the night before. McNaughton, C.   **E**
Not me! Killen, N.   **E**
Not one damsel in distress. Yolen, J.   **398.22**
A **not** scary story about big scary things. Williams, C. K.   **E**
Not yet, Rose. Hill, S. L.   **E**
Not your parents' money book. Chatzky, J.   **332.024**
Not your typical book about the environment. Kelsey, E.   **333.72**
The **not-just-anybody** family. Byars, B. C.   **Fic**
Not-quite-so-easy origami. Meinking, M.   **736**
The **not-so-scary** Snorklum. Bright, P.   **E**
Not-so-weird Emma. Warner, S.   **Fic**
NOTE-TAKING
Green, J. Write it down   **371.3**
Notes from a liar and her dog. Choldenko, G.   **Fic**
Notes from the dog. Paulsen, G.   **Fic**
Nothing. Agee, J.   **E**
Nothing but a dog. Katz, B.   **E**
Nothing but trouble. Stauffacher, S.   **92**
Nothing here but stones. Oswald, N.   **Fic**
Nothing like a puffin. Soltis, S.   **E**

Noullet, Georgette
Bed hog   **E**
Nouns. Heinrichs, A.   **428**
Nouns and verbs have a field day. Pulver, R.   **E**
Novak, Matt
A wish for you   **E**
NOVÁ‰ MÌŒESTO NAD METUJI (CZECH REPUBLIC) -- BIOGRAPHY -- JUVENILE LITERATURE
Levine, K. Hana's suitcase   **940.53**
NOVELIST
Ryan, P. M. The dreamer   **Fic**
NOVELISTS
Abrams, D. Gary Soto   **92**
Adler, D. A. A picture book of Harriet Beecher Stowe   **92**
The adventures of Mark Twain by Huckleberry Finn   **92**
Alderson, B. Thumbelina   **E**
Andersen, H. C. The nightingale   **E**
Anderson, W. T. Pioneer girl: the story of Laura Ingalls Wilder   **92**
Berne, E. C. Laura Ingalls Wilder   **92**
Bledsoe, L. J. How to survive in Antarctica   **998**
Bond, V. Zora and me   **Fic**
Braun, S. The ugly duckling   **E**
Brown, D. American boy: the adventures of Mark Twain   **818**
Brown, M. Pablo Neruda   **92**
Buzbee, L. The haunting of Charles Dickens   **Fic**
Cech, J. The princess and the pea   **E**
The Christmas coat   **92**
Colbert, D. The magical worlds of Harry Potter   **823**
Cooper, F. Coming home   **818**
Delano, P. When I was a boy Neruda called me Policarpo   **92**
Demi The emperor's new clothes   **E**
Dickens   **92**
Ehrlich, A. The Snow Queen   **Fic**
Ehrlich, A. Thumbelina   **E**
Ellis, S. From reader to writer   **028**
The Emperor's cool clothes   **E**
Fleischman, S. The trouble begins at 8   **92**
Fritz, J. Harriet Beecher Stowe and the Beecher preachers   **813**
Glaser, L. Emma's poem   **974.7**
Grant, A. Robert Louis Stevenson's Strange case of Dr. Jekyll and Mr. Hyde   **741.5**
Huget, J. L. Thanks a LOT, Emily Post!   **E**
Isadora, R. The ugly duckling   **E**
Kerley, B. The extraordinary Mark Twain (according to Susy)   **92**
Liberty's voice: the story of Emma Lazarus   **92**
The Little House cookbook   **641.5**
Lives of the writers   **809**
Long, S. Sylvia Long's Thumbelina   **E**
Lowry, L. Looking back   **813**
Macdonald, F. Journey to the Center of the Earth   **741.5**
Macdonald, F. Kidnapped   **741.5**
Manning, M. Charles Dickens   **92**
McDonough, Y. Z. Louisa   **92**
McKissack, P. C. A song for Harlem   **Fic**
Miller, W. Richard Wright and the library card   **92**
Mitchell, S. The nightingale   **Fic**
Mitchell, S. The tinderbox   **Fic**
Mitchell, S. The ugly duckling   **E**
Mora, P. Tomas and the library lady   **E**
Moss, M. Sky high: the true story of Maggie Gee   **92**
Murphy, J. Across America on an emigrant train   **385**
Myers, C. Lies and other tall tales   **398.2**
Peterson-Hilleque, V. J.K. Rowling, extraordinary author   **92**
Pinkney, J. The little match girl   **E**
Pinkney, J. Rikki-tikki-tavi   **E**

Simon, S. Now you see it, now you don't **152.14**

OPTICAL INSTRUMENTS
> *See also* Scientific apparatus and instruments

OPTICS
Cobb, V. I see myself **535**
Farndon, J. Light and optics **535**
Lauw, D. Light **535**
Mooney, C. Becoming invisible **623**
Spilsbury, L. What is light? **535**

OPTICS
> *See also* Physics

OPTICS -- EXPERIMENTS
Farndon, J. Light and optics **535**
Lauw, D. Light **535**

OPTICS -- JUVENILE LITERATURE
Farndon, J. Light and optics **535**

OPTIMISM -- FICTION
Mack, J. Good news, bad news **E**
An **orange** in January. Aston, D. H. **E**
Orange pear apple bear. Gravett, E. **E**

ORANGES -- FICTION
Alvarez, J. A gift of gracias **E**
Aston, D. H. An orange in January **E**
Rocklin, J. One day and one amazing morning on Orange Street **Fic**
Oranges on Golden Mountain. Partridge, E. **E**
Orangutan. Ganeri, A. **599.8**

ORANGUTAN
Bredeson, C. Orangutans up close **599.8**
Ganeri, A. Orangutan **599.8**
Laman, T. Face to face with orangutans **599.8**
Mattern, J. Orangutans **599.8**

ORANGUTAN -- FICTION
Antle, B. Suryia swims!: the true story of how an orangutan learned to swim **E**
Daddo, A. Goodnight, me **E**

ORANGUTAN -- JUVENILE FICTION
Antle, B. Suryia swims!: the true story of how an orangutan learned to swim **E**

ORANGUTAN -- JUVENILE LITERATURE
Antle, B. Suryia swims! : the true story of how an orangutan learned to swim **E**
Orangutan tongs. Agee, J. **811**
Orangutans. Mattern, J. **599.8**
Orangutans are ticklish. Grubman, S. **590**
Orangutans up close. Bredeson, C. **599.8**
Orani. Nivola, C. A. **945**

ORATIONS *See* Speeches
ORATORY *See* Public speaking
Orb weavers. Markle, S. **595.4**

ORB WEAVERS -- JUVENILE FICTION
Dewey, J. Once I knew a spider **E**

Orback, Craig
(il) The Can Man **E**
(il) The Can Man **E**
(il) Figley, M. R. John Greenwood's journey to Bunker Hill **973.3**
(il) Figley, M. R. Prisoner for liberty **92**
(il) Krensky, S. Paul Bunyan **398.2**
(il) Mortensen, L. Paul Revere's ride **92**
(il) Thomas, P. Nature's paintbox **811**

ORBITAL LABORATORIES *See* Space stations
ORBITAL RENDEZVOUS (SPACE FLIGHT)
> *See also* Space flight; Space stations; Space vehicles

ORBITING VEHICLES *See* Artificial satellites; Space stations
Orca young readers [series]
Hyde, N. I owe you one **Fic**

Leach, S. Jake Reynolds: chicken or eagle? **Fic**
Peterson, L. J. The ballad of Knuckles McGraw **Fic**

ORCHESTRA
Ganeri, A. The young person's guide to the orchestra **784.2**
Koscielniak, B. The story of the incredible orchestra **784.2**

ORCHESTRA -- FICTION
Cummings, P. Boom bah! **E**
Snicket, L. The composer is dead **E**

ORCHESTRA -- JUVENILE LITERATURE
Ganeri, A. The young person's guide to the orchestra **784.2**
Koscielniak, B. The story of the incredible orchestra **784.2**

ORCHESTRAL MUSIC
> *See also* Instrumental music; Music; Orchestra

ORDERLINESS
Murphy, S. J. Mighty Maddie **389**

ORDERLINESS -- FICTION
Prigger, M. S. Aunt Minnie McGranahan **E**

ORDERLINESS -- GRAPHIC NOVELS
Wight, E. Frankie Pickle and the closet of doom **741.5**

ORDINATION
> *See also* Rites and ceremonies; Sacraments

ORDNANCE
> *See also* Military art and science

ORE DEPOSITS
> *See also* Geology

Oregon. Roza, G. **979.5**
Oregon. Kent, D. **979.5**
The **Oregon** Trail. Friedman, M. **978**

OREGON TRAIL
Friedman, M. The Oregon Trail **978**
Olson, T. How to get rich on the Oregon Trail **978**

OREGON TRAIL
> *See also* Overland journeys to the Pacific; United States

OREGON TRAIL -- FICTION
Stanley, D. Roughing it on the Oregon Trail **Fic**
Van Leeuwen, J. Bound for Oregon **Fic**

ORES
> *See also* Minerals

ORGAN (MUSICAL INSTRUMENT) -- FICTION
Urban, L. A crooked kind of perfect **Fic**

ORGAN MUSIC
> *See also* Church music; Instrumental music; Music

ORGAN TRANSPLANTS *See* Transplantation of organs, tissues, etc.
ORGANIC AGRICULTURE *See* Organic farming
ORGANIC CHEMISTRY
> *See also* Chemistry

Organic crafts. Monaghan, K. **745.5**

ORGANIC FARMING
Hodge, D. Up we grow! **630**

ORGANIC FARMING
> *See also* Agriculture

ORGANIC GARDENING
> *See also* Gardening; Horticulture

ORGANIC WASTE AS FUEL *See* Waste products as fuel
ORGANICALLY GROWN FOODS *See* Natural foods
ORGANICULTURE *See* Organic farming; Organic gardening
ORGANIZATION OFFICIALS
Pinkney, A. D. Let it shine **920**

ORGANIZED CRIME
> *See also* Crime

ORGANIZED CRIME -- FICTION
Shaw, S. Tunnel vision **Fic**

ORGANIZED LABOR *See* Labor unions
ORGANS (ANATOMY) -- JUVENILE LITERATURE
Parker, N. W. Organs! **612**

ORGANS (MUSICAL INSTRUMENTS)

OUTER PLANETS -- JUVENILE LITERATURE
Miller, R. Seven wonders of the gas giants and their
   moons   **523.4**
OUTER SPACE
Universe   **523.1**
OUTER SPACE
    See also Astronautics; Astronomy; Space sciences
OUTER SPACE -- EXPLORATION
Cole, M. D. Eye on the universe   **522**
McReynolds, L. Eight days gone   **629.45**
Zoom, rocket, zoom!   **E**
OUTER SPACE -- EXPLORATION
    See also Exploration; Interplanetary voyages; Space
    flight
OUTER SPACE -- EXPLORATION -- FICTION
Cottrell Boyce, F. Cosmic   **Fic**
Greenberg, D. Enchanted lions   **E**
The three little aliens and the big bad robot   **E**
Zoom, rocket, zoom!   **E**
**OUTER SPACE -- EXPLORATION -- JUVENILE LIT-
   ERATURE**
Aldrin, B. Look to the stars   **629.4**
Berkowitz, J. Out of this world   **576.8**
Bortz, A. B. Seven wonders of space technology   **629.4**
Jedicke, P. Great moments in space exploration   **629.4**
Scott, E. Space, stars, and the beginning of time   **522**
OUTER SPACE -- FICTION
Viva, F. A long way away   **E**
OUTER SPACE -- JUVENILE LITERATURE
Green, C. R. Spacewalk   **629.45**
Out of this world   **811**
OUTER SPACE -- JUVENILE POETRY
Out of this world   **811**
Whitman, W. When I heard the learn'd astronomer   **E**
OUTER SPACE -- POETRY
Out of this world   **811**
Outfielders. Glaser, J.   **796.357**
The **outlandish** adventures of Liberty Aimes. Easton, K. **Fic**
OUTLAWS *See* Criminals; Thieves
Outrageous women of the Middle Ages. León, V.   **920.72**
Outrageously Alice. Naylor, P. R.   **Fic**
Outside and inside dinosaurs. Markle, S.   **567.9**
Outside and inside mummies. Markle, S.   **393**
Outside and inside rats and mice. Markle, S.   **599.35**
Outside and inside woolly mammoths. Markle, S.   **569**
Outside beauty. Kadohata, C.   **Fic**
Outside over there. Sendak, M.   **E**
Outside your window. Davies, N.   **E**
OUTSIDER ART
The fantastic jungles of Henri Rousseau   **759**
OUTSIDER ART
    See also Art
Outstanding library service to children. Cerny, R.   **027.62**
Over and under the snow. Messner, K.   **591.4**
Over at the castle. Ashburn, B.   **E**
Over in Australia. Berkes, M. C.   **782.42**
Over in the forest. Berkes, M.   **E**
Over in the hollow. Dickinson, R.   **E**
Over in the jungle. Berkes, M. C.   **E**
Over in the meadow. Keats, E. J.   **E**
Over in the meadow. Wadsworth, O. A.   **E**
Over in the meadow. Langstaff, J. M.   **782.42**
Over in the pink house. Dotlich, R. K.   **811**
Over my dead body. Klise, K.   **Fic**
Over sea, under stone. Cooper, S.   **Fic**
Over the moon. Aronica-Buck, B.   **811**
Over the rainbow. Harburg, E. Y.   **782.42**
Over the river and through the wood. Child, L. M. F.   **811**

Over under. Jocelyn, M.   **E**
Over, under & through, and other spatial concepts. Hoban, T. **E**
Overboard! Weeks, S.   **E**
OVERLAND JOURNEY TO THE PACIFIC -- FICTION
Kay, V. Covered wagons, bumpy trails   **E**
OVERLAND JOURNEYS TO THE PACIFIC
Calabro, M. The perilous journey of the Donner Party **979.4**
Friedman, M. The Oregon Trail   **978**
Harness, C. The tragic tale of Narcissa Whitman and a faithful
   history of the Oregon Trail   **92**
Olson, T. How to get rich on the Oregon Trail   **978**
Todras, E. H. Wagon trains and settlers   **973.8**
OVERLAND JOURNEYS TO THE PACIFIC
    See also Frontier and pioneer life; Voyages and travels
OVERLAND JOURNEYS TO THE PACIFIC -- FICTION
Applegate, K. The buffalo storm   **E**
Coerr, E. The Josefina story quilt   **E**
The crossing   **E**
Hopkinson, D. Apples to Oregon   **E**
Kay, V. Covered wagons, bumpy trails   **E**
Lawlor, L. He will go fearless   **Fic**
Lowell, S. The elephant quilt   **E**
Stanley, D. Roughing it on the Oregon Trail   **Fic**
Van Leeuwen, J. Bound for Oregon   **Fic**
Van Leeuwen, J. Papa and the pioneer quilt   **E**
Wagons ho!   **E**
Young, J. A book for black-eyed Susan   **Fic**
**OVERLAND JOURNEYS TO THE PACIFIC -- JUVE-
   NILE LITERATURE**
Harness, C. The tragic tale of Narcissa Whitman and a faithful
   history of the Oregon Trail   **92**
Olson, T. How to get rich on the Oregon Trail   **978**
OVERPOPULATION
    See also Population
OVERWEIGHT *See* Obesity
OVERWEIGHT PERSONS -- FICTION
Dowell, F. O. The second life of Abigail Walker   **Fic**
Owen. Henkes, K.   **E**
Owen & Mzee. Hatkoff, I.   **599.63**
Owen & Mzee: the language of friendship. Hatkoff, I. **599.63**
Owen Foote, frontiersman. Greene, S.   **Fic**
Owen Foote, mighty scientist. Greene, S.   **Fic**
Owen Foote, money man. Greene, S.   **Fic**
Owen Foote, super spy. Greene, S.   **Fic**
Owen, Cheryl
Gifts for kids to make   **745.5**
Owen, Karen
I could be, you could be   **E**
Owen, Ruth
Gross body invaders   **578.6**
Valentine's Day origami   **736**
Owen, Ruth
Creepy backyard invaders   **578.7**
Disgusting food invaders   **615.9**
Gross body invaders   **578.6**
Icky house invaders   **578.6**
Woods, M. Ace!   **796.342**
Woods, M. Goal!   **796.334**
Woods, M. Slam dunk!   **796.323**
Woods, M. Xtreme! Extreme sports facts and stats   **796**
Owens, Gail
  (il) Hurwitz, J. The adventures of Ali Baba Bernstein **Fic**
Owens, Jesse, 1913-1980
       About
Adler, D. A. A picture book of Jesse Owens   **796.42**
Krull, K. Lives of the athletes   **796**
Owens, L. L.
The life cycle of a snail   **594**

Burleigh, R. Pandora   **398.2**
Pang Guek-Cheng
  (jt. auth) Layton, L. Singapore   **959.57**
Pang, Guek-Cheng, 1950-
  Grenada   **972.98**
  Kazakhstan   **958.4**
  Mongolia   **951.7**
PANGOLINS -- FICTION
  Dewdney, A. Roly Poly pangolin   **E**
PANICS (FINANCE) *See* Financial crises
Panke, Jan
  (il) Food and faith   **204**
Panorama. Marceau, F.   **E**
PANTHEISM
    See also Philosophy; Religion
PANTHERS -- FICTION
  Orr, W. The princess and her panther   **E**
Pantoja, Tintin
  (il) Thielbar, M. The ancient formula   **741.5**
PANTOMIMES
    See also Acting; Amateur theater; Drama; Theater
Panzieri, Lucia
  The kindhearted crocodile   **E**
Paolilli, Paul
  Silver seeds   **811**
Papa and me. Dorros, A.   **E**
Papa and the pioneer quilt. Van Leeuwen, J.   **E**
Papa's latkes. Edwards, M.   **E**
Papa's mechanical fish. Fleming, C.   **E**
Papa's pastries. Toscano, C.   **E**
Papa, do you love me? Joosse, B. M.   **E**
Papa, please get the moon for me. Carle, E.   **E**
Papademetriou, Lisa
  Chasing normal   **Fic**
Papagayo. McDermott, G.   **E**
PAPAL VISITS
    See also Voyages and travels
Paparone, Pamela
  (il) Love, D. A. Of numbers and stars   **92**
  (il) Macken, J. E. Flip, float, fly   **581.4**
  (il) Roth, C. The little school bus   **E**
  (il) Where do chicks come from?   **636.5**
Paper. Morris, N.   **676**
PAPER
  Langley, A. Paper products   **676**
  Morris, N. Paper   **676**
The **paper** airplane book.   **629**
PAPER AIRPLANES
  Mercer, B. The flying machine book   **745.592**
PAPER AIRPLANES *See* Airplanes -- Models
Paper airplanes: Captain, level 4. Harbo, C. L.   **745.592**
Paper airplanes: Copilot, level 2. Harbo, C. L.   **745.592**
Paper airplanes: Flight school, level 1. Harbo, C. L.   **745.592**
Paper airplanes: Pilot, level 3. Harbo, C. L.   **745.592**
The **paper** boomerang book. Latno, M.   **745.54**
Paper craft fun for holidays [series]
  McGee, R. Paper crafts for Chinese New Year   **745.594**
  McGee, R. Paper crafts for Christmas   **745.594**
  McGee, R. Paper crafts for Day of the Dead   **745.594**
  McGee, R. Paper crafts for Halloween   **745.594**
  McGee, R. Paper crafts for Kwanzaa   **745.594**
  McGee, R. Paper crafts for Valentine's Day   **745.594**
PAPER CRAFTS
  Ancona, G. The pinata maker: El pinatero   **745.594**
  Carter, D. A. Hide and Seek   **E**
  Castleforte, B. Papertoy monsters   **745.592**
  Dobson, C. Wind power   **333.9**
  Fritsch, P. Pennsylvania Dutch Halloween scheren-

  schnitte   **745.594**
  Garza, C. L. Making magic windows   **745.54**
  Harbo, C. L. The kids' guide to paper airplanes   **745.592**
  Harbo, C. L. Paper airplanes: Captain, level 4   **745.592**
  Harbo, C. L. Paper airplanes: Copilot, level 2   **745.592**
  Harbo, C. L. Paper airplanes: Flight school, level 1   **745.592**
  Harbo, C. L. Paper airplanes: Pilot, level 3   **745.592**
  Henry, S. Paper folding   **736**
  Latno, M. The paper boomerang book   **745.54**
  Llimos, A. Easy paper crafts in 5 steps   **745.54**
  McGee, R. Paper crafts for Chinese New Year   **745.594**
  McGee, R. Paper crafts for Christmas   **745.594**
  McGee, R. Paper crafts for Day of the Dead   **745.594**
  McGee, R. Paper crafts for Halloween   **745.594**
  McGee, R. Paper crafts for Kwanzaa   **745.594**
  McGee, R. Paper crafts for Valentine's Day   **745.594**
The paper airplane book   **629**
  Staake, B. Look! Another book!   **E**
  Torres, L. Rock your party   **745.54**
  Tremaine, J. Paper tricks   **793.8**
PAPER CRAFTS
    See also Handicraft
Paper crafts for Chinese New Year. McGee, R.   **745.594**
Paper crafts for Christmas. McGee, R.   **745.594**
Paper crafts for Day of the Dead. McGee, R.   **745.594**
Paper crafts for Halloween. McGee, R.   **745.594**
Paper crafts for Kwanzaa. McGee, R.   **745.594**
Paper crafts for Valentine's Day. McGee, R.   **745.594**
The **paper** crane. Bang, M.   **E**
Paper folding. Henry, S.   **736**
PAPER FOLDING *See* Origami; Paper crafts
PAPER MAKING *See* Papermaking
PAPER MANUFACTURE *See* Papermaking
PAPER MONEY
  Forest, C. The dollar bill in translation   **332.4**
PAPER MONEY
    See also Money
Paper products. Langley, A.   **676**
PAPER SCULPTURE *See* Paper crafts
Paper son. James, H. F.   **Fic**
Paper tricks. Tremaine, J.   **793.8**
PAPER WORK
  Garza, C. L. Making magic windows   **745.54**
PAPER WORK *See* Paper crafts
PAPER WORK -- JUVENILE LITERATURE
  Garza, C. L. Making magic windows   **745.54**
PAPERBACK BOOKS
    See also Books; Editions
The **paperboy.** Pilkey, D.   **E**
Paperboy. Vawter, V.   **Fic**
PAPERHANGING
    See also Interior design
PAPERMAKING
  Langley, A. Paper products   **676**
PAPERMAKING
    See also Manufactures; Paper
Papertoy monsters. Castleforte, B.   **745.592**
Papi's gift. Stanton, K.   **E**
PAPIER-MÂCHÉ *See* Paper crafts
Papp, Robert
  (il) Noble, T. H. The last brother   **E**
  (il) Shefelman, J. J. Anna Maria's gift   **Fic**
Pappy's handkerchief. Scillian, D.   **E**
Paprocki, Greg
  (il) Math-terpieces   **510**
Papua New Guinea. Gascoigne, I.   **995.3**
PARACHUTE TROOPS
  Stone, T. L. Courage has no color, the true story of the Triple

Nickles   **940.54**

PARACHUTE TROOPS
> *See also* Military aeronautics; Parachutes

PARACHUTES
> *See also* Aeronautics

Parade. Crews, D.   **E**

PARADE FLOATS *See* Parades

PARADES
Crews, D. Parade   **E**
Sweet, M. Balloons over Broadway   **92**

PARADES
> *See also* Festivals; Pageants

PARADES -- FICTION
Andy Shane, hero at last   **Fic**
Black, M. I. A pig parade is a terrible idea   **E**
Boswell, A. K. The rain stomper   **E**
Johnson, A. The day Ray got away   **E**
Kerrin, J. S. Martin Bridge out of orbit!   **Fic**
Roosa, K. Pippa at the parade   **E**
Winthrop, E. The biggest parade   **E**

PARADES -- JUVENILE LITERATURE
Count me in   **513.2**

Paraguay. Jermyn, L.   **989.2**

PARALLEL UNIVERSES -- FICTION
Lipsyte, R. The twinning project   **Fic**

PARALYSIS, CEREBRAL *See* Cerebral palsy

PARAMEDICAL PERSONNEL *See* Allied health personnel;
Emergency medical technicians

PARAMEDICS, EMERGENCY *See* Emergency medical
technicians

PARANORMAL PHENOMENA *See* Parapsychology

PARAPROFESSIONALS
> *See also* Occupations; Professions

PARAPSYCHOLOGY
Allen, J. Unexplained   **001.9**
Gudgeon, C. Ghost trackers   **133.1**
Matthews, R. Disappearances   **001.9**

PARAPSYCHOLOGY
> *See also* Psychology; Research; Supernatural

PARASAUROLOPHUS
> *See also* Dinosaurs

PARASITES
Davies, N. What's eating you?   **591.6**
Graham, I. Microscopic scary creatures   **591.6**
Owen, R. Disgusting food invaders   **615.9**
Owen, R. Gross body invaders   **578.6**

Parasites [series]
Jarrow, G. Chiggers   **616.9**

PARASITES -- JUVENILE LITERATURE
Johnson, R. L. Zombie makers   **578.6**

Paratore, Coleen
Sunny Holiday   **Fic**
Sweet and sunny   **Fic**

PARATROOPS *See* Parachute troops

PARCEL POST *See* Postal service

PARENT AND CHILD
Alborough, J. Some dogs do   **E**
Avi Ereth's birthday   **Fic**
Cameron, A. Gloria's way   **Fic**
Ehlert, L. Hands   **E**
Horvath, P. Everything on a waffle   **Fic**
Schertle, A. 1, 2, I love you   **E**

PARENT AND CHILD *See* Parent-child relationship

PARENT AND CHILD -- FICTION
Hatsue Nakawaki Wait! wait!   **E**
How Martha saved her parents from green beans   **E**
Schmid, P. Petunia goes wild   **E**
Weeks, S. Regular Guy   **Fic**

PARENT AND CHILD -- JUVENILE FICTION
Hip hip hooray! it's Family Day!   **E**

PARENT AND CHILD -- JUVENILE LITERATURE
Joosse, B. M. Mama, do you love me?   **306.874**
Kerley, B. You and me together   **E**

PARENT-CHILD RELATIONSHIP
Kerley, B. You and me together   **E**

PARENT-CHILD RELATIONSHIP
> *See also* Child-adult relationship; Children; Family;
> Parents

PARENT-CHILD RELATIONSHIP -- FICTION
Schmid, P. Petunia goes wild   **E**

**PARENT-CHILD RELATIONSHIP -- JUVENILE FIC-
TION**
Harrington, K. Sure signs of crazy   **Fic**
Hatsue Nakawaki Wait! wait!   **E**
Henkes, K. The year of Billy Miller   **Fic**
Murphy, M. A Kiss like this   **E**
Walsh, M. Living with mom and living with dad   **E**

PARENTAL BEHAVIOR *See* Parenting

PARENTAL BEHAVIOR IN ANIMALS
Babies on the go   **E**
Fraser, M. A. How animal babies stay safe   **591.56**
Tatham, B. Penguin chick   **598.47**
Zoehfeld, K. W. Dinosaur parents, dinosaur young   **567.9**

PARENTAL BEHAVIOR IN ANIMALS -- FICTION
Kate and Pippin   **E**

**PARENTAL BEHAVIOR IN ANIMALS -- JUVENILE LIT-
ERATURE**
Babies on the go   **E**
Fraser, M. A. How animal babies stay safe   **591.56**
Guiberson, B. Z. The emperor lays an egg   **598.47**
Zoehfeld, K. W. Dinosaur parents, dinosaur young   **567.9**

Parenteau, Shirley
Bears on chairs   **E**

PARENTHOOD
> *See also* Family

PARENTING
Wells, R. My shining star   **649**

PARENTING
> *See also* Parent-child relationship

PARENTS
> *See also* Family; Parents

PARENTS -- FICTION
Bode, N. E. The slippery map   **Fic**
Lerman, J. How to raise Mom and Dad   **E**
London, C. A. We are not eaten by yaks   **Fic**
Numeroff, L. J. Would I trade my parents?   **E**
Proimos, J. Todd's TV   **E**

PARENTS OF AUTISTIC CHILDREN
The survival guide for kids with autism spectrum disorders
(and their parents)   **618.92**

**PARENTS OF AUTISTIC CHILDREN -- JUVENILE LIT-
ERATURE**
The survival guide for kids with autism spectrum disorders
(and their parents)   **618.92**

PARENTS OF PRESIDENTS
Adler, D. A. A picture book of John and Abigail Adams   **92**
Wallner, A. Abigail Adams   **973.4**

Pares, Roberta
(il) Dahl, M. Alien snow   **741.5**

Parfitt, Rachael
(il) Love your world   **333.72**

PARIS (FRANCE) -- FICTION
Minette's feast   **E**

Paris in the spring with Picasso. Yolleck, J.   **E**

Parish, Herman
Amelia Bedelia bakes off   **E**

(il) Look, L. Alvin Ho: allergic to girls, school, and other scary things **Fic**
All the things I love about you **E**
(il) Rosenthal, A. K. Bedtime for Mommy **E**
Singer, M. A stick is an excellent thing **811**
(il) Snyder, L. Any which wall **Fic**
(il) Tutu, D. God's dream **231.7**
(il) Van Leeuwen, J. Benny & beautiful baby Delilah **E**
(il) Zolotow, C. A father like that **E**
Phantom of Blood Alley. Stewart, P. **Fic**
The **phantom** tollbooth. Juster, N. **Fic**
PHANTOMS *See* Apparitions; Ghosts
Pharaoh. Kennett, D. **932**
Pharaoh's boat. Weitzman, D. L. **932**
PHARAOHS -- JUVENILE LITERATURE
Kennett, D. Pharaoh **932**
The **Pharaohs'** armies. Park, L. **355**
PHARMACEUTICAL CHEMISTRY
See also Chemistry
PHARMACOLOGY
See also Medicine
PHARMACY
Petersen, C. The apothecary **615**
PHARMACY
See also Chemistry; Medicine
PHEASANTS
See also Birds; Game and game birds
Pheidippides, fl. 490 B.C.
About
Reynolds, S. The first marathon: the legend of Pheidippides **938**
Phelan, Glen
Invisible force **531**
Phelan, Matt
Bluffton **Fic**
Phelan, Matt
(il) Birdsall, J. Flora's very windy day **E**
(il) Birney, B. G. The seven wonders of Sassafras Springs **Fic**
(il) Mazer, A. Spilling ink **808.3**
(il) Patron, S. The higher power of Lucky **Fic**
(il) Patron, S. Lucky breaks **Fic**
Around the world **741.5**
The storm in the barn **741.5**
(il) Robbins, J. The new girl . . . and me **E**
(il) Robbins, J. Two of a kind **E**
(il) Rockwell, A. F. Big George: how a shy boy became President Washington **92**
(il) Spinelli, E. Where I live **Fic**
(il) Stott, A. Always **E**
(il) Stott, A. I'll be there **E**
Phelps, Michael, 1985-
About
Torsiello, D. P. Michael Phelps **92**
PHILADELPHIA (PA.) -- HISTORY
Murphy, J. An American plague **614.5**
Philadelphia chickens. Boynton, S. **782.42**
PHILANTHROPISTS
Alexander, S. H. She touched the world: Laura Bridgman, deaf-blind pioneer **92**
Figley, M. R. Prisoner for liberty **92**
Glaser, L. Emma's poem **974.7**
Kulling, M. It's a snap! **92**
Lasky, K. Vision of beauty: the story of Sarah Breedlove Walker **B**
Liberty's voice: the story of Emma Lazarus **92**
Mitchell, D. Driven **92**
Pinkney, A. D. Let it shine **920**
Ray, D. Ghost girl **Fic**

Reusser, K. Celebrities giving back **361.7**
Wadsworth, G. First Girl Scout **369.463**
Weatherford, C. B. Dear Mr. Rosenwald **Fic**
Weatherford, C. B. Oprah **92**
PHILANTHROPISTS -- TEXAS -- BIOGRAPHY -- JUVENILE LITERATURE
Henrietta King, la patrona **976.4**
PHILATELISTS
Franklin and Winston **940.53**
Freedman, R. Franklin Delano Roosevelt **973.917**
Krull, K. A boy named FDR **92**
Panchyk, R. Franklin Delano Roosevelt for kids **92**
St. George, J. Make your mark, Franklin Roosevelt **92**
Philbrick, W. R.
The mostly true adventures of Homer P. Figg **Fic**
The young man and the sea **Fic**
Philip Hall likes me, I reckon maybe. Greene, B. **Fic**
Philip, Neil
(ed) A Braid of lives **970.004**
Horse hooves and chicken feet: Mexican folktales **398.2**
The pirate princess and other fairy tales **398.2**
(ed) Stockings of buttermilk: American folktales **398.209**
(ed) War and the pity of war **808.81**
(ed) Weave little stars into my sleep **782.42**
Phillipps, Julie C.
Wink: the ninja who wanted to be noticed **E**
Wink: the ninja who wanted to nap **E**
Phillips, Chad
(il) Marzollo, J. Help me learn numbers 0-20 **E**
(il) Marzollo, J. Help me learn subtraction **513.2**
Phillips, Charles
Japan **952**
Sweden **948.5**
Phillips, Craig
(il) Holub, J. Zeus and the thunderbolt of doom **E**
Phillips, Gary R.
(il) Blessing, C. New old shoes **E**
Phillips, John
Leonardo da Vinci **92**
Phillips, L. D. (Lodner Darvontis), 1825-1869 -- Fiction
About
Fleming, C. Papa's mechanical fish **E**
Phillips, Lily Renee
About
Robbins, T. Lily Renee, escape artist **940.53**
Phillips, Louise
(il) Silver, P. Face painting **745.5**
Phillips, Susan P.
Great displays for your library step by step **021.7**
Phillips-Duke, Barbara J.
(il) Hazen, B. S. Digby **E**
Phillis sings out freedom. Malaspina, A. **92**
Phillis's big test. Clinton, C. **92**
PHILOLOGISTS
Berner, R. S. Definitely not for little ones **398.2**
Ellis, S. From reader to writer **028**
Hettinga, D. R. The Brothers Grimm **430**
Pirotta, S. The McElderry book of Grimms' fairy tales **398.2**
PHILOLOGISTS -- GERMANY -- BIOGRAPHY
Hettinga, D. R. The Brothers Grimm **430**
PHILOSOPHERS
Demi Buddha **294.3**
Demi The legend of Lao Tzu and the Tao te ching **299.5**
Love, D. A. Of numbers and stars **92**
PHILOSOPHERS -- JUVENILE LITERATURE
Jun Lim Socrates **183**
PHILOSOPHICAL NOVELS
Saint-Exupery, A. d. The little prince **Fic**

Ball, J. Why pi 530.8

Pi in the sky. Mass, W. Fic

PIANISTS

Celenza, A. H. Duke Ellington's Nutcracker suite E

Hopkinson, D. A band of angels E

Ingalls, A. The little piano girl E

Krull, K. Lives of the musicians 780.92

LeBlanc, A. The red piano 92

Parker, R. A. Piano starts here: the young Art Tatum 92

Raven, M. Happy birthday to you! 782.42

Reich, S. Clara Schumann 786.2

PIANISTS -- FICTION

Allison, J. Gilda Joyce: the ghost sonata Fic

Blume, L. M. M. The rising star of Rusty Nail Fic

Cheng, A. Where do you stay? Fic

Gifford, P. E. Moxy Maxwell does not love practicing the piano Fic

Hamlisch, M. Marvin makes music E

Ingalls, A. The little piano girl E

McGhee, A. Song of middle C E

PIANISTS -- GERMANY -- BIOGRAPHY -- JUVENILE LITERATURE

Reich, S. Clara Schumann 786.2

PIANO MUSIC

See also Instrumental music; Music

Piano starts here: the young Art Tatum. Parker, R. A. 92

PIANOS

See also Percussion instruments

PIANOS -- FICTION

Perkins, L. R. The cardboard piano E

Pianos and Keyboards. Ganeri, A. 786

PICARESQUE LITERATURE

See also Fiction; Literature

Picasso, Pablo, 1881-1973

About

Jacobson, R. Picasso 92

Niepold, M. Oooh! Picasso 730.9

Penrose, A. The boy who bit Picasso 92

Scott, E. Secrets of the Cirque Medrano Fic

Serres, A. And Picasso painted Guernica 759

Yolleck, J. Paris in the spring with Picasso E

Picasso, Pablo, 1881-1973 Juvenile literature

Just behave, Pablo Picasso! 709.2

Bernier-Grand, C. T. Pablo Picasso 709.2

Fiction

Scott, E. Secrets of the Cirque Medrano Fic

Yolleck, J. Paris in the spring with Picasso E

Picasso, Pablo, 1881-1973 -- Work -- Guernica

About

Serres, A. And Picasso painted Guernica 759

Piccard, Jacques -- Juvenile literature

About

Bodden, V. To the ocean deep 551.46

PICCOLO -- FICTION

Draper, S. M. The silver secret Fic

Pichon, Liz

Penguins E

The three horrid little pigs E

PICIFORMES -- JUVENILE LITERATURE

Miller, S. S. Woodpeckers, toucans, and their kin 598

Pick a pup. Chall, M. W. E

Pick, pull, snap! Schaefer, L. M. 582

Pickering, Jimmy

(il) Prelutsky, J. The swamps of Sleethe 811

(il) Sage, A. Frognapped Fic

(il) Sage, A. Ghostsitters Fic

(il) Sage, A. My haunted house Fic

(il) Sage, A. Vampire brat Fic

PICKETING *See* Strikes

Pickett, Bill, ca. 1860-1932

About

Bill Pickett, rodeo-ridin' cowboy 636.2

PICKLES -- FICTION

The great lollipop caper E

Pickup trucks on the move. Zuehlke, J. 629.224

The picky little witch. Brokamp, E. E

PICNICS -- FICTION

Mack, J. Good news, bad news E

Pictographs. Bodach, V. 510

Picture a tree. Reid, B. E

A picture book of Amelia Earhart. 629.13

A picture book of Cesar Chavez. Adler, D. A. 92

A picture book of Dolley and James Madison. Adler, D. A. 92

A picture book of Harriet Beecher Stowe. Adler, D. A. 92

A picture book of Harriet Tubman. Adler, D. A. 305.5

A picture book of Jackie Robinson. Adler, D. A. 796.357

A picture book of Jesse Owens. Adler, D. A. 796.42

A picture book of John and Abigail Adams. Adler, D. A. 92

A picture book of John F. Kennedy. Adler, D. A. 973.922

A picture book of John Hancock. Adler, D. A. 92

A picture book of Louis Braille. Adler, D. A. 686.2

A picture book of Sacagawea. Adler, D. A. 978

A picture book of Sojourner Truth. Adler, D. A. 305.5

A picture book of Thomas Jefferson. Adler, D. A. 973.4

A picture book of Thurgood Marshall. Adler, D. A. 347

PICTURE BOOKS

Bromann, J. More storytime action! 027.62

Neuburger, E. K. Side by side 070.5

Stewart, S. The library 813

PICTURE BOOKS FOR CHILDREN

Abouraya, K. L. Hands around the library 962.055

Adler, D. A. Millions, billions & trillions E

Alber, M. And the tide comes in Fic

Allaire, C. Let's look at the rainforest close up 591.7

Altes, M. My grandpa E

Angleberger, T. Crankee Doodle E

Applesauce E

Arnosky, J. Shimmer & splash 591.77

Aronson, B. The chicken problem E

The art treasure hunt 701

Artist to artist 741.6

Ashman, L. Rain! E

Asper-Smith, S. I would tuck you in E

Aston, D. A butterfly is patient 595.78

Baines, B. Everything dogs 636.7

Baker-Smith, G. Farther Fic

Barber, N. Lost cities 930.1

Barnett, M. Oh no! Not again! E

Bateman, D. M. Out on the prairie 577.4

Bauer, M. D. Little dog, lost Fic

Beach feet E

Bean, J. Building our house E

Becoming a ballerina 792.8

Benjamin Bear in "Bright ideas!" 741.5

Berger, G. 101 animal records 590

Berger, L. Dream dog E

Birthday suit E

The Black rabbit E

Blechman, N. Night light E

Bloom, S. Oh! what a surprise! E

Bodden, V. Cockroaches 595.7

Bodden, V. Slugs 594

Bodden, V. Termites 595.7

Bodden, V. Ticks 595.4

Boldt, C. Odd dog E

Boy and Bot Fic

(il) Ravishankar, A. Elephants never forget   E
Pierce, Elijah, 1892-1984
Fiction
Rosen, M. J. Elijah's angel   813
Pierce, Roxanne Heide
Heide, F. P. Always listen to your mother   E
Pierce, Tamora
Magic steps   Fic
Pierpont, James, 1822-1893
About
Jingle bells   E
Pierre. Sendak, M.   E
Pierre in love. Pennypacker, S.   E
Pierre Le Poof! Beck, A.   E
Pierre the penguin. Marzollo, J.   598
Pierre's friends. Beck, A.   E
Pierre-Auguste Renoir. Somervill, B. A.   92
PIES
Ehlert, L. Pie in the sky   E
Lindsey, K. Sweet potato pie   E
PIES
See also Baking; Cooking
PIES -- FICTION
Best, C. Easy as pie   E
Ehlert, L. Pie in the sky   E
Freeman, M. Who stole Grandma's million-dollar pumpkin pie?   Fic
Lindsey, K. Sweet potato pie   E
Murray, A. Apple pie ABC   E
Parish, H. Amelia Bedelia's first apple pie   E
Sierra, J. Thelonius Monster's sky-high fly pie   E
Thompson, L. The apple pie that Papa baked   E
Weeks, S. Pie   Fic
Wheeler, L. Ugly Pie   E
Pietrzyk, Leslie
Maryland   975.2
Pig kahuna. Sattler, J.   E
A **pig** parade is a terrible idea. Black, M. I.   E
Pig Pig meets the lion. McPhail, D.   E
Pig Pig returns. McPhail, D. M.   E
The **pig** scramble. Kinney, J.   E
Pig-Boy. McDermott, G.   398.2
Pigeon and Pigeonette. Derom, D.   E
Pigeons. Patent, D. H.   598.6
PIGEONS
Burleigh, R. Fly, Cher Ami, fly!   940.4
Patent, D. H. Pigeons   598.6
Piehl, J. Let's look at pigeons   598
PIGEONS -- FICTION
The duckling gets a cookie!?   E
O'Connor, B. On the road to Mr. Mineo's   Fic
Piggie pie! Palatini, M.   E
Piggies. Wood, D.   E
Piggies in pajamas.   E
Piggies in the kitchen. Meadows, M.   E
Piggy and Dad go fishing. Martin, D.   E
Piggy Pie Po. Wood, A.   E
Piggybook. Browne, A.   E
Piglet and Mama. Wild, M.   E
Pigmares. Cushman, D.   E
Pigs. Minden, C.   636.4
PIGS
Falconer, I. Olivia   E
Gibbons, G. Pigs   636.4
Ichikawa, S. My pig Amarillo   E
Kasza, K. My lucky day   E
King-Smith, D. All pigs are beautiful   636.4
King-Smith, D. Lady Lollipop   Fic

Lin, G. Olvina flies   E
Marshall, J. Swine Lake   E
Minden, C. Pigs   636.4
Rockwood, L. Pigs are smart!   636.4
Van Leeuwen, J. Amanda Pig and the awful, scary monster E
Van Leeuwen, J. Oliver the Mighty Pig   E
Whatley, B. Wait! No paint!   E
Wiesner, D. The three pigs   E
PIGS
See also Domestic animals; Mammals
Pigs. Gibbons, G.   636.4
PIGS -- FICTION
Falconer, I. Olivia and the fairy princesses   E
Gal, S. Day by day   E
I know a wee piggy   E
PIGS -- JUVENILE FICTION
Gravett, E. Wolf won't bite!   E
Kurtz, C. The adventures of a South Pole pig   Fic
Piggies in pajamas   E
The princess and the pig   E
PIGS -- POETRY
Cushman, D. Pigmares   E
Pigs aplenty, pigs galore! McPhail, D. M.   813
Pigs are smart! Rockwood, L.   636.4
Pigs from 1 to 10. Geisert, A.   813
Pigs love potatoes. Denise, A.   E
Pigs, cows, and probability. Aboff, M.   519.2
Pigsty. Teague, M.   E
Pika. Bill, T.   599.35
PIKAS
Bill, T. Pika   599.35
Pike, Lip, 1845-1893
About
Michelson, R. Lipman Pike   92
Pike, Zebulon Montgomery, 1779-1813 -- Juvenile literature
About
Green, C. R. Zebulon Pike   978
PILATES METHOD
Aikman, L. Pilates step-by-step   613.7
PILATES METHOD
See also Exercise
Pilates step-by-step. Aikman, L.   613.7
PILGRIM FATHERS
Harness, C. The adventurous life of Myles Standish   92
PILGRIMS (NEW ENGLAND COLONISTS)
Grace, C. O. 1621   394.264
Harness, C. The adventurous life of Myles Standish   92
Sewall, M. The pilgrims of Plimoth   974.4
Waters, K. Sarah Morton's day   974.4
PILGRIMS (NEW ENGLAND COLONISTS) -- FICTION
Bruchac, J. Squanto's journey   Fic
PILGRIMS (NEW ENGLAND COLONISTS) -- JUVE-NILE LITERATURE
Sewall, M. The pilgrims of Plimoth   974.4
Waters, K. Sarah Morton's day   974.4
PILGRIMS (NEW PLYMOUTH COLONY) -- FICTION
Bruchac, J. Squanto's journey   Fic
PILGRIMS AND PILGRIMAGES
See also Voyages and travels
The **pilgrims** of Plimoth. Sewall, M.   974.4
Pilkey, Dav
The adventures of Ook and Gluk   741.5
The Hallo-wiener   813
The paperboy   E
Pilot & Huxley: the first adventure. McGuiness, D.   741.5
Pilot & Huxley: the next adventure. McGuiness, D.   741.5
PILOT GUIDES
See also Navigation

Pinter, Jason
  Zeke Bartholomew, superspy   **Fic**
Pinto, Sara
  Colin, B. My invisible sister   **Fic**
  (il) Gold, R. Kids cook 1-2-3   **641.5**
Pinwheel days. Tarlow, E.   **E**
Pio peep!   **398.8**
PIONEER CHILDREN -- WEST (U.S.) -- HISTORY --
   19TH CENTURY -- JUVENILE LITERATURE
  Calabro, M. The perilous journey of the Donner Party   **979.4**
Pioneer days. King, D. C.   **978**
Pioneer girl. Warren, A.   **92**
Pioneer girl: the story of Laura Ingalls Wilder. Anderson, W.
  T.   **92**
PIONEER LIFE *See* Frontier and pioneer life
A **pioneer** sampler. Greenwood, B.   **971**
PIONEERS
  Hailstone, R. The white ox   **92**
  Harness, C. The tragic tale of Narcissa Whitman and a faithful
    history of the Oregon Trail   **92**
  Kellogg, S. Johnny Appleseed   **634**
  Kellogg, S. Mike Fink   **398.22**
  Lowery, L. Aunt Clara Brown   **978.8**
  Lunn, J. L. S. Laura Secord: a story of courage   **Fic**
  Moses, W. Johnny Appleseed   **634**
  Rabin, S. Mr. Lincoln's boys   **92**
  Spradlin, M. P. Daniel Boone's great escape   **92**
  Worth, R. Johnny Appleseed   **92**
  Yolen, J. Johnny Appleseed   **92**
PIONEERS -- KENTUCKY -- BIOGRAPHY -- JUVENILE
   LITERATURE
  Green, C. R. Daniel Boone   **976.9**
PIONEERS -- TENNESSEE -- BIOGRAPHY -- JUVENILE
   LITERATURE
  Green, C. R. Davy Crockett   **976.8**
PIONEERS -- WEST (U.S.) -- BIOGRAPHY -- JUVENILE
   LITERATURE
  Green, C. R. Buffalo Bill Cody   **978**
  Green, C. R. Calamity Jane   **978**
Pip in the Grand Hotel. Hucke, J.   **E**
Pipe, Jim
  Swarms   **591.5**
PIPELINES
  See also Hydraulic structures; Transportation
Piper. Chichester-Clark, E.   **E**
Piper Reed gets a job. Holt, K. W.   **Fic**
Piper Reed, campfire girl. Holt, K. W.   **Fic**
Piper Reed, Navy brat. Holt, K. W.   **Fic**
Piper Reed, the great gypsy. Holt, K. W.   **Fic**
Piper, Sophie
  I can say a prayer   **242**
  Prayers for a better world   **242**
Piper, Watty
  The little engine that could   **E**
  The little engine that could   **E**
PIPIL INDIANS -- POETRY
  Argueta, J. Talking with Mother Earth   **811**
A **pipkin** of pepper. Cooper, H.   **E**
Pippa at the parade. Roosa, K.   **E**
Pippi in the South Seas. Lindgren, A.
Pippi Longstocking. Lindgren, A.   **Fic**
Pippin, Horace, 1888-1946
        About
  Venezia, M. Horace Pippin   **92**
Pippin, Horace, 1888-1946 -- Juvenile literature
        About
  Bryant, J. A splash of red   **759.13**
Pippo the Fool. Fern, T. E.   **E**

PIRACY *See* Pirates
Piranha. Ganeri, A.   **597**
Piranha pancakes. Friesen, R.   **741.5**
PIRANHAS
  Ganeri, A. Piranha   **597**
Pirate boy. Bunting, E.   **E**
Pirate nap. Smith, D.   **E**
The **pirate** of kindergarten. Lyon, G. E.   **E**
The **pirate** princess and other fairy tales. Philip, N.   **398.2**
Pirate vs. pirate. Quattlebaum, M.   **E**
The **pirate's** blood and other case files. Cheshire, S.   **Fic**
A **pirate's** guide to first grade. Preller, J.   **E**
Pirateria.   **E**
Pirates. Riggs, K.   **910.4**
PIRATES
  Clifford, B. Real pirates   **910.4**
  Lewis, J. P. Blackbeard, the pirate king   **811**
  Riggs, K. Pirates   **910.4**
Pirates & Princesses. Kargman, J.   **E**
PIRATES -- FICTION
  Lacey, J. Island of Thieves   **Fic**
  Leeds, C. The unfortunate son   **Fic**
  Pirateria   **E**
PIRATES -- GRAPHIC NOVELS
  Friesen, R. Cupcakes of doom!   **741.5**
PIRATES -- JUVENILE FICTION
  Flanagan, J. The hunters   **Fic**
  Flanagan, J. The invaders   **Fic**
  Horowitz, D. Twenty-six pirates   **E**
  Lucas, D. The Skeleton pirate   **E**
  Meisel, P. See me dig   **E**
PIRATES -- JUVENILE POETRY
  Florian, D. Shiver me timbers   **E**
  When you're a pirate dog and other pirate poems   **811**
PIRATES -- POETRY
  Florian, D. Shiver me timbers   **E**
  When you're a pirate dog and other pirate poems   **811**
Pirates don't take baths. Segal, J.   **E**
Pirates go to school. Demas, C.   **E**
The **pirates** of Crocodile Swamp. Arnosky, J.   **Fic**
Pirates, ho! Thomson, S. L.   **E**
Pirican Pic and Pirican Mor.   **398.2**
Pirner, Connie White
  Even little kids get diabetes   **616.4**
Pirotta, Saviour
  Children's stories from the Bible   **220.9**
  Firebird   **398.2**
  The McElderry book of Grimms' fairy tales   **398.2**
Pish and Posh wish for fairy wings. Bottner, B.   **E**
PIT BULL TERRIERS -- JUVENILE LITERATURE
  Patent, D. H. Saving Audie   **636.7**
Pitcairn, Ansel
  (il) Bolden, T. Portraits of African-American heroes   **920**
Pitcher. Glaser, J.   **796.357**
Pitcher, Molly, 1754-1832
        About
  Rockwell, A. F. They called her Molly Pitcher   **973.3**
Pitchford, Dean
  Captain Nobody   **Fic**
Pitching in for Eubie. Nolen, J.   **E**
Pittau, Francisco
  Out of sight   **590**
Piven, Hanoch
  My best friend is as sharp as a pencil   **E**
Piven, Hanoch
  My best friend is as sharp as a pencil   **E**
  My dog is as smelly as dirty socks   **E**
Pixar. Buckley, A. M.   **338.7**

Kenney, K. L. Super simple clay projects   **738.1**

Park, L. S. A single shard   **Fic**

POTTERY

    See also Ceramics; Clay industry; Decoration and ornament; Decorative arts; Tableware

POTTERY -- FICTION

Look, L. Polka Dot Penguin Pottery   **E**

Park, L. S. A single shard   **Fic**

POTTERY -- TECHNIQUE -- JUVENILE LITERATURE

Andrews-Goebel, N. The pot that Juan built   **738**

POTTERY, AMERICAN *See* American pottery

Potts, Aiden

The smash! smash! truck   **363.7**

Potty. Patricelli, L.   **E**

Potty animals. Vestergaard, H.   **E**

Pouch! Stein, D. E.   **E**

Poulsen, David A.

Old Man   **Fic**

POULTRY

    See also Birds; Domestic animals

The **pout-pout** fish. Diesen, D.   **E**

The **pout-pout** fish in the big-big dark. Diesen, D.   **E**

Poverty. Mason, P.   **362.5**

POVERTY

    See also Economic conditions; Social problems

POVERTY

Mason, P. Poverty   **362.5**

Tejubehan (Singer) Drawing from the City   **745**

POVERTY -- FICTION

Davis, A. A hen for Izzy Pippik   **Fic**

Jimmy the greatest!   **E**

Povey, Karen D.

Centipede   **595.6**

Pow, Tom

Tell me one thing, Dad   **E**

Powell, Ben

Stock, C. Skateboarding step-by-step   **796.22**

Powell, Consie

(il) Bevis, M. E. Wolf song   **E**

Powell, Eric

(il) Sniegoski, T. Billy Hooten, Owlboy   **Fic**

Powell, Jillian

Explaining cystic fibrosis   **616.3**

Fats for a healthy body   **613.2**

Powell, John Wesley, 1834-1902

         About

Waldman, S. The last river   **978**

Powell, John Wesley, 1834-1902

         About

Ray, D. K. Down the Colorado   **92**

Powell, Martin

The seven voyages of Sinbad   **741.5**

The tall tale of Paul Bunyan: the graphic novel   **741.5**

Powell, William J., 1916-

         About

Michelson, R. Twice as good   **796.352**

POWER (MECHANICS)

Claybourne, A. Pushes and pulls   **531**

Hillman, B. How strong is it?   **620.1**

Spilsbury, R. What is energy?   **621**

POWER (SOCIAL SCIENCES)

    See also Political science

POWER (SOCIAL SCIENCES) -- FICTION

Demi The greatest power   **E**

POWER OF ATTORNEY

    See also Law

The **power** of cute. Harper, C. M.   **E**

The **power** of energy. Weber, R.   **531**

The **power** of Un. Etchemendy, N.   **Fic**

POWER PLANTS, NUCLEAR *See* Nuclear power plants

Power play. O'Donnell, L.   **741.5**

POWER POLITICS *See* Balance of power; Cold war

POWER RESOURCES

Bradley, K. B. Energy makes things happen   **531**

POWER RESOURCES *See* Energy resources

POWER RESOURCES -- JUVENILE LITERATURE

Rau, D. M. Alternative energy beyond fossil fuels   **333.79**

POWER RESOURCES CONSERVATION *See* Energy conservation

POWER RESOURCES DEVELOPMENT *See* Energy development

POWER SUPPLY *See* Energy resources

POWER TOOLS

    See also Tools

POWER TRANSMISSION

    See also Mechanical engineering; Power (Mechanics)

POWER TRANSMISSION, ELECTRIC *See* Electric lines; Electric power distribution

Power up to fight pollution. Bullard, L.   **363.7**

Power up! Learn about energy. Vogel, J.   **333.79**

Powerful medicine

Markle, S. Bad burns   **617.1**

Markle, S. Faulty hearts   **612.1**

Markle, S. Leukemia   **616.99**

Markle, S. Lost sight   **617.7**

Markle, S. Shattered bones   **617.1**

Markle, S. Wounded brains   **617**

Powerful words. Hudson, W.   **081**

Powerless. Cody, M.   **Fic**

Powers, Don T.

(il) Hartnett, S. The silver donkey   **Fic**

The **Powhatan.** King, D. C.   **970.004**

POWHATAN INDIANS

Brimner, L. D. Pocahontas   **92**

King, D. C. The Powhatan   **970.004**

Krull, K. Pocahontas   **92**

POWHATAN INDIANS -- FICTION

Carbone, E. L. Blood on the river   **Fic**

Powwow. Ancona, G.   **394.2**

POWWOWS

    See also Festivals; Native Americans -- Rites and ceremonies; Native Americans -- Social life and customs

Poydar, Nancy

The biggest test in the universe   **E**

Fish school   **E**

No fair science fair   **E**

Poynter, Margaret

Doomsday rocks from space   **523.4**

PRACTICAL JOKES

    See also Jokes; Wit and humor

PRACTICAL JOKES -- FICTION

De Groat, D. April Fool! watch out at school!   **E**

PRACTICAL NURSES

    See also Nurses

PRACTICAL POLITICS *See* Politics

Practical puppetry A-Z. Exner, C. R.   **791.5**

PRACTICE TEACHING *See* Student teaching

PRAGMATISM

    See also Philosophy; Positivism; Realism; Theory of knowledge

PRAIRIE ANIMALS

Bateman, D. M. Out on the prairie   **577.4**

Pattison, D. Prairie storms   **577.4**

PRAIRIE ANIMALS -- SOUTH DAKOTA -- BADLANDS NATIONAL PARK

Bateman, D. M. Out on the prairie   **577.4**

Preddy, Leslie
Callison, D. The blue book on information age inquiry, instruction and literacy   **028.7**

PREDICTIONS *See* Forecasting; Prophecies

Preening, painting, and piercing. Bliss, J.   **391**

PREFABRICATED BUILDINGS
   See also Buildings

PREFABRICATED HOUSES
   See also Domestic architecture; House construction; Houses; Prefabricated buildings

Prefixes and suffixes. Heinrichs, A.   **428**

PREGNANCY
Butler, D. H. My mom's having a baby!   **612.6**
Cocovini, A. What's inside your tummy, Mommy?   **612.6**
Cole, J. How you were born   **612.6**
Cole, J. When you were inside Mommy   **612.6**
Harris, R. H. It's not the stork!   **612.6**
Harris, R. H. It's so amazing!   **612.6**
Pringle, L. P. Everybody has a bellybutton   **612.6**
Sears, W. Baby on the way   **612.6**

PREGNANCY
   See also Reproduction

PREGNANCY -- FICTION
Cadena, B. Supersister   **E**
Couloumbis, A. Love me tender   **Fic**
Pecan pie baby   **E**

PREGNANCY -- JUVENILE FICTION
Look, L. Alvin Ho   **Fic**

PREGNANCY -- JUVENILE LITERATURE
Pringle, L. P. Everybody has a bellybutton   **612.6**
Sears, W. Baby on the way   **612.6**

Prehistoric actual size. Jenkins, S.   **560**

PREHISTORIC ANIMALS
Arnold, C. Giant sea reptiles of the dinosaur age   **567.9**
Arnold, C. Giant shark: megalodon, prehistoric super predator   **567**
Arnold, C. Pterosaurs   **567.9**
Bonner, H. When bugs were big, plants were strange, and tetrapods stalked the earth   **560**
Bonner, H. When fish got feet, sharks got teeth, and bugs began to swarm   **560**
Bradley, T. J. Paleo bugs   **560**
Brown, C. L. Beyond the dinosaurs   **560**
Collard, S. B. Reign of the sea dragons   **567.9**
Dixon, D. Prehistoric skies   **567.9**
Eamer, C. Super crocs & monster wings   **591.3**
Jenkins, S. Prehistoric actual size   **560**
Leedy, L. My teacher is a dinosaur   **560**
Mehling, R. Great extinctions of the past   **576.8**
O'Brien, P. Megatooth!   **567**
Parker, S. Creatures of the sky   **560**
Parker, S. Sea monsters   **560**
Patkau, K. Creatures yesterday and today   **591.3**
Rushby, P. Discovering Supercroc   **567.9**
Sabuda, R. Sharks and other sea monsters   **560**

PREHISTORIC ANIMALS
   See also Animals; Fossils

PREHISTORIC ANIMALS -- FICTION
Cyrus, K. The voyage of Turtle Rex   **E**
Mason, T. The last synapsid   **Fic**
Rollins, J. Jake Ransom and the howling sphinx   **Fic**

PREHISTORIC ART
Discovery in the cave   **944**

PREHISTORIC ART
   See also Art

PREHISTORIC ART -- FICTION
McCully, E. A. The secret cave   **E**
Sloat, T. There was an old man who painted the sky   **E**

PREHISTORIC MAN *See* Fossil hominids; Prehistoric peoples

Prehistoric oceans. Dixon, D.   **567.9**

PREHISTORIC PEOPLES
Andryszewski, T. Walking the earth   **304.8**
Croy, A. Exploring the past   **930.1**
Deem, J. M. Bodies from the bog   **573.3**
Getz, D. Frozen man   **930.1**
Harrison, D. L. Mammoth bones and broken stones   **970.01**
Paver, M. Spirit walker   **Fic**

PREHISTORIC PEOPLES
   See also Antiquities; Archeology; Human beings

PREHISTORIC PEOPLES -- EUROPE -- JUVENILE LITERATURE
Deem, J. M. Bodies from the bog   **573.3**

PREHISTORIC PEOPLES -- FICTION
Winter, J. Kali's song   **E**

Prehistoric skies. Dixon, D.   **567.9**

PREHISTORY *See* Archeology; Fossil hominids; Prehistoric peoples

PREJUDICE *See* Prejudices

PREJUDICE-MOTIVATED CRIMES *See* Hate crimes

PREJUDICES
Haptie, C. Otto and the flying twins   **Fic**
Hesse, K. Witness   **Fic**
Lester, J. Let's talk about race   **305.8**
Marsden, C. The gold-threaded dress   **Fic**
Polacco, P. Mr. Lincoln's way   **E**
Schwartz, J. Short   **612.6**
Yep, L. The traitor   **Fic**

PREJUDICES
   See also Attitude (Psychology); Emotions; Interpersonal relations

PREJUDICES -- FICTION
Bunting, E. Walking to school   **E**
Conly, J. L. Crazy lady!   **Fic**
Curtis, C. P. The Watsons go to Birmingham--1963   **Fic**
Eversole, R. H. East Dragon, West Dragon   **E**
Frazier, S. T. The other half of my heart   **Fic**
Hesse, K. Witness   **Fic**
Hughes, S. The Christmas Eve ghost   **E**
Ketchum, L. Where the great hawk flies   **Fic**
Kurtz, J. The storyteller's beads   **Fic**
Levine, K. The best bad luck I ever had   **Fic**
Maclear, K. Spork   **E**
Magoon, K. Camo girl   **Fic**
Marsden, C. The gold-threaded dress   **Fic**
Miller, W. Night golf   **E**
Mochizuki, K. Baseball saved us   **E**
Mochizuki, K. Heroes   **E**
Mol, S. v. Meena   **E**
Noe, K. S. Something to hold   **Fic**
Polacco, P. Mr. Lincoln's way   **E**
Rahaman, V. Divali rose   **E**
Sherrard, V. The glory wind   **Fic**
Stanley, D. Saving Sky   **Fic**
Taylor, M. D. The gold Cadillac   **Fic**
Taylor, M. D. Mississippi bridge   **Fic**
Uchida, Y. A jar of dreams   **Fic**
Vernick, S. R. The blood lie   **Fic**
Whitaker, Z. Kali and the rat snake   **E**
Williams, L. E. Slant   **Fic**
Yep, L. The traitor   **Fic**

PREJUDICES -- JUVENILE LITERATURE
Lester, J. Let's talk about race   **305.8**

Preller, James
Justin Fisher declares war!   **Fic**
Mighty Casey   **E**

Louise the big cheese and the Ooh-la-la Charm School   E
Libby of High Hopes   Fic
Primavera, Elise
   (il) Fritz, J. Make way for Sam Houston   92
   Louise the big cheese: divine diva   E
   (il) Nolen, J. Raising dragons   E
   Louise the big cheese and the back-to-school smarty-pants   E
PRIME MINISTERS
   Blashfield, J. F. Golda Meir   92
   Franklin and Winston   940.53
   Krull, K. Lives of extraordinary women   920
   Naden, C. J. Benazir Bhutto   92
Prince of Dorkness. Collins, T.   Fic
The **Prince** of Fenway Park. Baggott, J.   Fic
The **prince** of the pond. Napoli, D. J.   Fic
Prince Puggly of Spud and the Kingdom of Spiff. Weston, R. P.   Fic
Prince William & Kate. Doeden, M.   92
The **prince** won't go to bed. Dodds, D. A.   E
The **Prince's** new pet. Anderson, B.   E
Prince, April Jones
   Twenty-one elephants and still standing   E
PRINCES
   Doeden, M. Prince William & Kate   92
   Fritz, J. Around the world in a hundred years   910.92
   McAlister, C. Brave Donatella and the Jasmine thief   E
   Saint-Exupery, A. d. The little prince   Fic
PRINCES
   See also Courts and courtiers
PRINCES -- FICTION
   Healy, C. The hero's guide to saving your kingdom   Fic
PRINCES AND PRINCESSES *See* Princes; Princesses
The **princess** and her panther. Orr, W.   E
The **princess** and the pea. Andersen, H. C.   Fic
The **princess** and the pea. Cech, J.   E
The **princess** and the pig.   E
Princess Baby. Katz, K.   E
Princess Bess gets dressed. Cuyler, M.   E
The **princess** curse. Haskell, M.   Fic
Princess for a week. Wright, B. R.   Fic
Princess Furball. Cinderella   398.2
The **princess** gown. Strauss, L. L.   E
Princess Hyacinth. Heide, F. P.   E
Princess K.I.M. and the lie that grew. Cocca-Leffler, M.   E
Princess Kim and too much truth. Cocca-Leffler, M.   E
The **princess** knight. Funke, C. C.   E
The **princess** mouse. Shepard, A.   398.2
The **Princess** of Borscht. Schubert, L.   E
The **princess** of Trelian. Knudsen, M.   Fic
Princess Peepers. Calvert, P.   E
Princess Peepers picks a pet. Calvert, P.   E
Princess Pigsty. Funke, C. C.   E
Princess Pigtoria and the pea. Edwards, P. D.   E
The **princess** plot. Boie, K.   Fic
Princess Posey and the first grade parade. Greene, S.   Fic
Princess Posey and the perfect present. Greene, S.   Fic
Princess says goodnight. Howland, N.   E
Princess stories.   398.2
Princess Super Kitty. Portis, A.   E
Princess Sylvie. Beskow, E.   E
The **princess** trap. Boie, K.   Fic
The **princess** who had almost everything. Levert, M.   E
PRINCESSES
   Brimner, L. D. Pocahontas   92
   Doeden, M. Prince William & Kate   92
   King-Smith, D. Lady Lollipop   Fic
   Krull, K. Pocahontas   92
   Levine, G. C. The two princesses of Bamarre   Fic

PRINCESSES
   See also Courts and courtiers
PRINCESSES -- FICTION
   Falconer, I. Olivia and the fairy princesses   E
PRINCESSES -- GRAPHIC NOVELS
   Alley, Z. B. There's a princess in the palace   398.2
   Espinosa, R. The courageous princess   741.5
PRINCESSES -- JUVENILE FICTION
   Knudsen, M. The princess of Trelian   Fic
   The princess and the pig   E
Principles and practice series
   Hughes-Hassell, S. School reform and the school library media specialist   027.8
Prineas, Sarah
   The magic thief   Fic
Prineas, Sarah
   The magic thief   Fic
   Found   Fic
   Lost   Fic
Pringle, Laurence
   Frogs!   597.8
   Ice!   621.5
Pringle, Laurence P.
   Billions of years, amazing changes   576.8
Pringle, Laurence P.
   Billions of years, amazing changes   576.8
   Alligators and crocodiles!   597.98
   American slave, American hero   92
   Cicadas!   595.7
   Come to the ocean's edge   577.7
   Everybody has a bellybutton   612.6
   Imagine a dragon   398.2
   Penguins! strange and wonderful   598
   Sharks!: strange and wonderful   597
The **printer.** Petersen, C.   686
PRINTERS
   Koscielniak, B. Johann Gutenberg and the amazing printing press   686.2
   Skelton, M. Endymion Spring   Fic
PRINTERS -- GERMANY -- BIOGRAPHY -- JUVENILE LITERATURE
   Rumford, J. From the good mountain   E
PRINTERS -- UNITED STATES -- BIOGRAPHY -- JUVENILE LITERATURE
   Adler, D. A. B. Franklin, printer   973.3
   Byrd, R. Electric Ben   973.309
   Freedman, R. Becoming Ben Franklin   973.309
PRINTING
   Hanson, A. Cool printmaking   760.2
   Luxbacher, I. 1 2 3 I can make prints!   760.2
PRINTING
   See also Bibliography; Book industry; Graphic arts; Industrial arts; Publishers and publishing
PRINTING -- HISTORY
   Rumford, J. From the good mountain   E
PRINTING -- HISTORY -- ORIGIN AND ANTECEDENTS -- JUVENILE LITERATURE
   Rumford, J. From the good mountain   E
PRINTING -- SPECIMENS
   See also Advertising; Initials
PRINTMAKERS
   Rivera, R. Arctic adventures   920
   Rubin, S. G. Whaam!: the art & life of Roy Lichtenstein   92
   Wing, N. An eye for color: the story of Josef Albers   92
PRINTMAKERS -- JAPAN -- BIOGRAPHY -- JUVENILE LITERATURE
   Ray, D. K. Hokusai   769.92
PRINTS

PUNS

    See also Wit and humor

PUNS -- FICTION

    Agee, J. Mr. Putney's quacking dog   **E**

PUNS -- JUVENILE LITERATURE

    Hall, M. Cat tale   **E**

Punxsutawney Phyllis. Hill, S. L.   **E**

Pup and Hound hatch an egg. Hood, S.   **E**

The **pup** who cried wolf. Kurtz, C.   **Fic**

Puppet magic. Lowe, J. L.   **027.62**

Puppet planet. Kennedy, J. E.   **791.5**

PUPPET THEATER IN EDUCATION

    Champlin, C. Storytelling with puppets   **372.66**

PUPPETEERS

    Jim Henson   **92**

    Sweet, M. Balloons over Broadway   **92**

PUPPETEERS -- FICTION

    Catmull, K. Summer and Bird   **Fic**

PUPPETS

    Bauer, C. F. Leading kids to books through puppets   **027.62**

    Champlin, C. Storytelling with puppets   **372.66**

PUPPETS -- FICTION

    Schlitz, L. A. Splendors and glooms   **Fic**

PUPPETS AND PUPPET PLAYS

    Bauer, C. F. Leading kids to books through puppets   **027.62**

    Champlin, C. Storytelling with puppets   **372.66**

    D'Cruz Make your own puppets   **791.5**

    Exner, C. R. Practical puppetry A-Z   **791.5**

    Jim Henson   **92**

    Kennedy, J. E. Puppet planet   **791.5**

    Lowe, J. L. Puppet magic   **027.62**

    Minkel, W. How to do The three bears with two hands   **791.5**

    Stanley, D. Mozart, the wonder child   **92**

    Sweet, M. Balloons over Broadway   **92**

PUPPETS AND PUPPET PLAYS

    See also Drama; Folk drama; Theater

PUPPETS AND PUPPET PLAYS -- FICTION

    Schlitz, L. A. Splendors and glooms   **Fic**

PUPPIES *See* Dogs

Puppies and piggies. Rylant, C.   **E**

Puppy power. Cox, J.   **Fic**

The **puppy** who wanted a boy. Thayer, J.   **E**

PURIM

    Kimmel, E. A. The story of Esther   **222**

PURIM -- FICTION

    Goldin, B. D. Cakes and miracles   **E**

PURITANS -- FICTION

    Speare, E. G. The witch of Blackbird Pond   **Fic**

Purmell, Ann

    Apple cider making days   **E**

    Christmas tree farm   **E**

    Maple syrup season   **E**

The **purple** balloon. Raschka, C.   **155.9**

The **purple** coat. Hest, A.   **E**

The **purple** kangaroo. Black, M. I.   **E**

Purple Little Bird. Foley, G.   **E**

The **purple** smurfs. Delporte, Y.   **741.5**

Push and pull! Learn about magnets. Vogel, J.   **538**

Push button. Aliki   **E**

The **pushcart** war. Merrill, J.   **Fic**

Pushes and pulls. Claybourne, A.   **531**

Pushing up the sky: seven Native American plays for children. Bruchac, J.   **812**

Puss in boots. Light, S.   **398.2**

Puss in boots. Puss in boots   **398.2**

Puss in boots. Puss in boots   **398.24**

Puss in boots. Cech, J.   **398.2**

PUSS IN BOOTS (TALE)

Light, S. Puss in boots   **398.2**

Put inclined planes to the test. Walker, S. M.   **621.8**

Put it all together. Cornwall, P.   **808**

Put it on the list. Darbyshire, K.   **E**

Put levers to the test. Walker, S. M.   **621.8**

Put pulleys to the test. Walker, S. M.   **621.8**

Put screws to the test. Walker, S. M.   **621.8**

Put wedges to the test. Walker, S. M.   **621.8**

Put wheels and axles to the test. Walker, S. M.   **621.8**

Putonti, Dorette

    Harker, C. Library research with emergent readers   **027.62**

Puttapipat, Niroot

    The musicians of Bremen   **398.2**

Putting on a play. Jacobs, P. D.   **792**

Puttock, Simon

    Little lost cowboy   **E**

Puybaret, Eric

    (il) Berne, J. Manfish: a story of Jacques Cousteau   **92**

    (il) Lipton, L. Puff, the magic dragon

Puybaret, Eric

    (il) Berne, J. Manfish: a story of Jacques Cousteau   **92**

    (il) Cech, J. The nutcracker   **E**

    (il) Harburg, E. Y. Over the rainbow   **782.42**

    (il) Lipton, L. Puff, the magic dragon

    (il) Moore, C. C. The night before Christmas   **811**

    (il) When you wish upon a star   **782.42**

    (il) Yarrow, P. Puff the magic dragon pop-up book   **E**

The **puzzle** of the platypus. Myers, J.   **590**

PUZZLES

    Carter, D. A. 600 black spots   **E**

    Carter, D. A. Blue 2   **E**

    Carter, D. A. One red dot   **E**

    Clark, D. C. A kid's guide to Washington, D.C.   **917**

    Hillenbrand, W. Mother Goose picture puzzles   **398.8**

    Horvath, D. What dat?   **E**

    Kidslabel (Firm) Spot 7 School   **793.73**

    Marzollo, J. I spy school days   **793.73**

    Munro, R. Circus   **E**

    Nickle, J. Alphabet explosion!   **793.73**

    Onishi, S. Who's hiding?   **E**

    Steiner, J. Look-alikes   **793.73**

    Steiner, J. Look-alikes around the world   **793.73**

    Steiner, J. Look-alikes Christmas   **793.73**

    Steiner, J. Look-alikes, jr.   **793.73**

    Wick, W. Can you see what I see?   **793.73**

    Wick, W. Can you see what I see? Cool collections   **793.73**

    Wick, W. Can you see what I see? Dream machine   **793.73**

    Wick, W. Can you see what I see? On a scary, scary night   **793.73**

    Wick, W. Can you see what I see? Seymour and the juice box boat   **793.73**

    Wick, W. Can you see what I see? toyland express   **793.73**

    Wick, W. Can you see what I see?: once upon a time   **793.73**

    Wick, W. Can you see what I see?: Treasure ship   **793.73**

    Wick, W. I spy   **793.73**

    Wick, W. I spy extreme challenger!   **793.73**

    Wick, W. I spy fantasy   **793.73**

    Wick, W. I spy gold challenger!   **793.73**

    Wick, W. I spy spooky night   **793.73**

    Wick, W. I spy super challenger!   **793.73**

    Wick, W. I spy treasure hunt   **793.73**

    Wick, W. I spy ultimate challenger!   **793.73**

PUZZLES

    See also Amusements

PUZZLES -- FICTION

    Beil, M. D. The Red Blazer Girls: the ring of Rocamadour   **Fic**

    Beil, M. The Red Blazer Girls: the mistaken masterpiece   **Fic**

    Berlin, E. The potato chip puzzles   **Fic**

What did the Vikings do for me? **948**

Rausch, Molly
My cold went on vacation **E**

Raut, Radhashyam
(il) Scott, N. K. The sacred banana leaf **398.2**

Rauzon, Mark J.
Water, water everywhere **551.48**

Raven. McDermott, G. **398.2**

Raven, Margot
Circle unbroken **E**
Happy birthday to you! **782.42**
Night boat to freedom **E**

The **Ravenmaster's** secret. Woodruff, E. **Fic**

Ravens. Webster, C. **598**

RAVENS
Aylesworth, J. Goldilocks and the three bears **398.2**
Webster, C. Ravens **598**

RAVENS -- FICTION
Bansch, H. Odd bird out **E**
George, J. C. Charlie's raven **Fic**
Woodruff, E. The Ravenmaster's secret **Fic**

Ravishankar, Anushka
Elephants never forget **E**
Tiger on a tree **E**

Rawlings, Marjorie Kinnan
The secret river **Fic**
The yearling **Fic**

Rawlins, Donna
(il) Whiting, S. The firefighters **E**

Rawlinson, Julia
Fletcher and the falling leaves **E**
Fletcher and the snowflake Christmas **E**

Rawls, Wilson
Where the red fern grows **Fic**

Ray & me. Gutman, D. **Fic**

Ray, Deborah Kogan
Paiute princess **979.004**

Ray, Deborah Kogan
(il) Bardhan-Quallen, S. Flying eagle **598**
(il) Herman, E. Hubknuckles **E**
Dinosaur mountain **567.9**
Down the Colorado **92**
Hokusai **769.92**
Wanda Gag **92**

Ray, Delia
Here lies Linc **Fic**

Ray, Delia
Ghost girl **Fic**
Here lies Linc **Fic**
Singing hands **Fic**

Ray, Jane
(il) Doherty, B. Fairy tales **398.2**
(il) Henderson, K. Lugalbanda **398.2**
Adam and Eve and the Garden of Eden **222**
Ahmed and the feather girl **E**
The apple-pip princess **E**
The dollhouse fairy **E**
Snow White **398.2**
The twelve days of Christmas **782.42**
(il) Steven, K. C. Stories for a fragile planet **398.2**

Ray, Mary Lyn
Stars **E**

Ray, Mary Lyn
Christmas farm **E**
Stars **E**

Ray, Virginia Lawrence
School wide book events **027.8**

Rayevsky, Robert

(il) Kimmel, E. A. Three sacks of truth **398.21**

Raymond and Graham rule the school. Knudson, M. **Fic**

Raymond and Nelda. Bottner, B. **E**

Rayner, Catherine
(il) Newbery, L. Posy! **E**
The bear who shared **E**
Ernest, the moose who doesn't fit **E**
Solomon Crocodile **E**

Rays. Walker, S. M. **597**

RAYS (FISHES)
Coldiron, D. Stingrays **597**
Sharks **597.3**
Walker, S. M. Rays **597**
Wearing, J. Manta rays **597**

Rayyan, Omar
(il) Cox, J. The case of the purloined professor **Fic**
Howe, P. Waggit again **Fic**
Howe, P. Waggit's tale **Fic**
(il) Kimmel, E. A. Joha makes a wish **E**
(il) Stewig, J. W. King Midas **398.209**
(il) Wagner, H. Nightshade City **Fic**

Reaching for the moon. Aldrin, B. **92**

REACTIONS, CHEMICAL *See* Chemical reactions

Read a rhyme, write a rhyme. **811**

Read and rise. Pinkney, S. L. **E**

Read and wonder [series]
King-Smith, D. All pigs are beautiful **636.4**

Read it, don't eat it! Schoenherr, I. **E**

Read to Tiger. Fore, S. J. **E**

Read to your bunny. Wells, R. **E**

Read, Leon
Keeping well **613**
My senses **612.8**

Read, Nicholas
(jt. auth) McAllister, I. The sea wolves **599.77**

Read, Nicholas
McAllister, I. Salmon bears **599.78**
(jt. auth) McAllister, I. The sea wolves **599.77**

Read, Tracy C.
Exploring the world of coyotes **599.77**
Exploring the world of eagles **598**
Exploring the world of seals and walruses **599.79**
Exploring the world of wolves **599.77**

The **read-aloud** handbook. Trelease, J. **028.5**

Read-aloud rhymes for the very young. **811**

Read-it! chapter books: historical tales [series]
Gunderson, J. Stranger on the silk road **Fic**

READER SERVICES (LIBRARIES) *See* Library services

READERS AND LIBRARIES *See* Library services

Readers theatre [series]
Black, A. N. Readers theatre for middle school boys **812**
Fredericks, A. D. African legends, myths, and folktales for readers theatre **812**

Readers theatre for middle school boys. Black, A. N. **812**

Readers' advisory for children and 'tweens. Peck, P. **025.5**

The **readers'** advisory guide to graphic novels. Goldsmith, F. **025.2**

READERS' THEATER
Black, A. N. Readers theatre for middle school boys **812**
Brill, M. T. Annie Shapiro and the clothing workers' strike **331.8**
Figley, M. R. John Greenwood's journey to Bunker Hill **973.3**
Fredericks, A. D. African legends, myths, and folktales for readers theatre **812**
Krensky, S. Lizzie Newton and the San Francisco earthquake **979.4**
Shepard, A. Stories on stage **812**

READERS' THEATER

Morgan, S. Waste and recycling — **363.7**

Murphy, S. J. Earth Day-hooray! — **513**

O'Neal, C. How to use waste energy to heat and light your home — **621.1**

Potts, A. The smash! smash! truck — **363.7**

Recycle this book — **333.72**

Ross, K. Earth-friendly crafts — **745.5**

Sirrine, C. Cool crafts with old jeans — **745.5**

Wolf, L. G. Recyclo-gami — **745.5**

Young, K. R. Junkyard science — **507.8**

RECYCLING

> *See also* Energy conservation; Pollution control industry; Salvage

RECYCLING (WASTE)

Martin, L. C. Recycled crafts box — **363.7**

Murphy, S. J. Earth Day-hooray! — **513**

RECYCLING (WASTE) -- FICTION

Messner, K. Marty McGuire digs worms! — **Fic**

RECYCLING (WASTE, ETC.) *See* Recycling

RECYCLING (WASTE, ETC.) -- JUVENILE LITERATURE

Enz, T. Repurpose it — **600**

Kroll, S. Stuff! — **E**

Martin, L. C. Recycled crafts box — **363.7**

McKay, K. True green kids — **333.72**

Murphy, S. J. Earth Day-hooray! — **513**

Reilly, K. M. Planet Earth — **333.72**

Walsh, M. 10 things I can do to help my world — **333.72**

RECYCLING -- FICTION

Messner, K. Marty McGuire digs worms! — **Fic**

RECYCLING -- GRAPHIC NOVELS

Sonishi, K. Leave it to PET!: the misadventures of a recycled super robot, vol. 1 — **741.5**

Recyclo-gami. Wolf, L. G. — **745.5**

Reczuch, Karen

(il) Vande Griek, S. Loon — **598**

RED

> *See also* Color

The **red** balloon. Lamorisse, A. — **E**

Red Bird sings: the story of Zitkala-Sa. — **92**

The **Red** Blazer Girls: the mistaken masterpiece. Beil, M. — **Fic**

The **Red** Blazer Girls: the ring of Rocamadour. Beil, M. D. — **Fic**

The **Red** Blazer Girls: The vanishing violin. Beil, M. D. — **Fic**

The **red** book. Lehman, B. — **E**

Red butterfly. Noyes, D. — **E**

Red Cloud, Sioux Chief, 1822-1909

> **About**

Ehrlich, A. Wounded Knee: an Indian history of the American West — **970.004**

Red Cloud, Sioux Chief, 1822-1909

> **About**

Freedman, R. Indian chiefs — **970.004**

RED CROSS OFFICIALS

Krensky, S. Clara Barton — **92**

Rosenberg, A. The Civil War — **920**

Somervill, B. A. Clara Barton — **92**

Wade, M. D. Amazing civil war nurse Clara Barton — **92**

The **red** dragon codex. Henham, R. D. — **Fic**

Red green blue. Jay, A. — **E**

Red hat. Judge, L. — **E**

The **red** hen. Emberley, E. — **398.2**

Red is a dragon. — **E**

Red Knit Cap Girl. Stoop, N. — **E**

Red knot. Willis, N. C. — **598**

RED KNOT -- JUVENILE LITERATURE

Hoose, P. Moonbird — **598.072**

Willis, N. C. Red knot — **598**

Red leaf, yellow leaf. Ehlert, L. — **582.16**

The **red** lemon. Staake, B. — **E**

Red light, green light. Suen, A. — **E**

The **red** piano. LeBlanc, A. — **92**

The **Red** Pyramid. Collar, O. — **741.5**

Red ridin' in the hood. Marcantonio, P. S. — **S**

Red Riding Hood. Little Red Riding Hood — **398.2**

Red River stallion. Harrison, T. — **Fic**

The **red** rose box. Woods, B. — **Fic**

The **red** scarf. Villeneuve, A. — **E**

Red scarf girl. Jiang — **951.05**

The **red** shoes. Glass, E. — **E**

Red sings from treetops. Sidman, J. — **E**

Red sled. Thomas, P. — **E**

Red sled. Judge, L. — **E**

Red Ted and the lost things. Rosen, M. — **E**

Red thread sisters. Peacock, C. A. — **Fic**

Red Truck. Hamilton, K. R. — **E**

Red wagon. Liwska, R. — **E**

The **red** wolf. Shannon, M. — **E**

Red wolves. Goldish, M. — **599.77**

Red, white, and boom! — **E**

Red, white, blue, and Uncle who? Bateman, T. — **929.9**

Red-eyed tree frog. Cowley, J. — **597.8**

RED-SIDED GARTER SNAKE -- JUVENILE LITERATURE

Montgomery, S. The snake scientist — **597.96**

RED-TAILED HAWK -- JUVENILE LITERATURE

Schulman, J. Pale Male — **598**

Winter, J. The tale of Pale Male — **598**

Redmond, Shirley-Raye

Tentacles! — **594**

Reduce, reuse, and recycle. Minden, C. — **363.7**

REDUCING *See* Weight loss

Redwall. Jacques, B. — **Fic**

REDWOOD

Chin, J. Redwoods — **585**

Redwoods. Chin, J. — **585**

REDWOODS -- JUVENILE LITERATURE

Chin, J. Redwoods — **585**

Reece, Florence

> **Juvenile literature**

Lyon, G. E. Which side are you on? — **782.42**

Reece, Florence -- Work -- Which side are you on?

> **About**

Lyon, G. E. Which side are you on? — **782.42**

Reed, Jennifer

Cape Hatteras National Seashore — **975.6**

Reed, Lynn Rowe

(il) Kanninen, B. J. A story with pictures — **E**

(il) Pulver, R. Happy endings — **E**

(il) Pulver, R. Nouns and verbs have a field day — **E**

(il) Pulver, R. Punctuation takes a vacation — **E**

(il) Pulver, R. Silent letters loud and clear — **E**

Basil's birds — **E**

Color chaos! — **E**

Roscoe and the pelican rescue — **E**

Reed, Mike

(il) Bollard, J. K. Scholastic children's thesaurus — **423**

(il) Clements, A. A million dots — **513**

(il) Nolan, L. A. Bad to the bone — **Fic**

(il) Nolan, L. A. Home on the range — **Fic**

(il) Nolan, L. A. On the road — **Fic**

(il) Nolan, L. A. Smarter than squirrels — **Fic**

Reeder, Carolyn

Across the lines — **Fic**

Reedy, Trent

Words in the dust — **Fic**

REEF ECOLOGY

Barshaw, R. M. Ellie McDoodle: best friends fur-ever Fic
Barshaw, R. M. Ellie McDoodle: new kid in school Fic
Baskin, N. R. Anything but typical Fic
Bauer, A. C. E. Come Fall Fic
Beaty, A. Firefighter Ted E
Becker, B. The magical Ms. Plum Fic
Beil, M. D. The Red Blazer Girls: the ring of Rocamadour Fic
Beil, M. The Red Blazer Girls: the mistaken masterpiece Fic
Bennett, O. The Allegra Biscotti collection Fic
Bergman, M. Lively Elizabeth! what happens when you push E
Berry, J. The colossal fossil freakout Fic
Berry, J. The rat brain fiasco Fic
Bertrand, D. G. Adelita and the veggie cousins E
Best, C. Shrinking Violet E
The big flush 741.5
Birney, B. G. Adventure according to Humphrey Fic
Birney, B. G. Friendship according to Humphrey Fic
Birney, B. G. Surprises according to Humphrey Fic
Birney, B. G. Trouble according to Humphrey Fic
Birney, B. G. The world according to Humphrey Fic
Blake, S. I don't want to go to school! E
Bliss, H. Bailey E
Bloch, S. Butterflies in my stomach and other school hazards E
Blume, J. Cool zone with the Pain and the Great One Fic
Blume, J. Friend or fiend? with the Pain & the Great One Fic
Blume, J. Going, going, gone! with the Pain and the Great One Fic
Bodeen, S. A. Elizabeti's school E
Boie, K. The princess trap Fic
Borden, L. The A+ custodian E
Borden, L. Good luck, Mrs. K! E
Borden, L. The John Hancock Club E
Borden, L. The last day of school Fic
Borden, L. The lost-and-found tooth Fic
Borden, L. Off to first grade E
Bottner, B. An annoying ABC E
Bottner, B. Miss Brooks loves books (and I don't) E
Bowe, J. My best frenemy Fic
Bowen, A. I know an old teacher E
Brand-new pencils, brand-new books E
Brennan, E. Dirtball Pete E
Brezenoff, S. The burglar who bit the Big Apple Fic
Brezenoff, S. The painting that wasn't there Fic
Brezenoff, S. The zombie who visited New Orleans Fic
Brisson, P. I remember Miss Perry E
Bromley, A. C. The lunch thief Fic
Bugs in my hair?! E
Bunting, E. Cheyenne again E
Bunting, E. My special day at Third Street School E
Bunting, E. One green apple E
Burnett, F. H. A little princess Fic
Burningham, J. John Patrick Norman McHennessy E
Butler, D. H. The case of the fire alarm Fic
Butler, D. H. The case of the library monster Fic
Butler, D. H. The truth about Truman School Fic
Buyea, R. Because of Mr. Terupt Fic
Buyea, R. Mr. Terupt falls again Fic
Buzzeo, T. Adventure Annie goes to kindergarten E
Byars, B. C. The SOS file Fic
Cabot, M. Allie Finkle's rules for girls: book two; The new girl Fic
Cabot, M. Best friends and drama queens Fic
Cabot, M. Blast from the past Fic
Cabot, M. Moving day Fic
Cabot, M. Stage fright Fic
Calmenson, S. Late for school! E

Carlson, N. L. Henry and the Valentine surprise E
Carlstrom, N. W. It's your first day of school, Annie Claire E
Catalanotto, P. No more pumpkins Fic
Catalanotto, P. The secret lunch special Fic
Charlie and Kiwi E
Chatterton, M. The Brain finds a leg Fic
Cheng, A. Where the steps were Fic
Cheshire, S. The pirate's blood and other case files Fic
Child, L. Clarice Bean, don't look now Fic
Child, L. I am too absolutely small for school Fic
Child, L. Utterly me, Clarice Bean Fic
Chodos-Irvine, M. Best best friends E
Choldenko, G. A giant crush E
Choldenko, G. If a tree falls at lunch period Fic
Choldenko, G. Louder, Lili E
Clark, C. G. Secrets of Greymoor Fic
Cleary, B. Dear Mr. Henshaw Fic
Cleary, B. Henry Huggins Fic
Cleary, B. Muggie Maggie Fic
Cleary, B. Ramona forever Fic
Cleary, B. Ramona Quimby, age 8 Fic
Cleary, B. Ramona the brave Fic
Cleary, B. Ramona the pest Fic
Cleary, B. Ramona's world Fic
Clements, A. The report card Fic
Clements, A. Fear itself Fic
Clements, A. Frindle Fic
Clements, A. Lost and found Fic
Clements, A. Lunch money Fic
Clements, A. No talking Fic
Clements, A. Room one Fic
Clements, A. We the children Fic
Cocca-Leffler, M. Princess Kim and too much truth E
Cody, M. Powerless Fic
Cohen, B. Molly's pilgrim E
Cohen, M. First grade takes a test E
Cohen, M. Will I have a friend? E
Colin, B. My invisible sister Fic
Comerford, L. B. Rissa Bartholomew's declaration of independence Fic
Conford, E. Jenny Archer, author Fic
Cooper, I. Angel in my pocket Fic
Cooper, I. Look at Lucy! Fic
Cornwell, N. Christophe's story Fic
Cousins, L. Maisy goes to preschool E
Cox, J. Butterfly buddies Fic
Cox, J. Carmen learns English E
Cox, J. Nora and the Texas terror Fic
Cox, J. Puppy power Fic
Coy, J. Love of the game Fic
Coy, J. Top of the order Fic
Creech, S. Bloomability Fic
Creech, S. Hate that cat Fic
Creech, S. Love that dog Fic
Crews, D. School bus E
Crummel, S. S. The Little Red Pen E
Cuyler, M. 100th day worries E
Cuyler, M. Hooray for Reading Day! E
Dahl, R. Matilda Fic
Daly, N. Bettina Valentino and the Picasso Club Fic
D'Amico, C. Ella sets the stage E
D'Amico, C. Ella the Elegant Elephant E
Daneshvari, G. Class is not dismissed! Fic
Daneshvari, G. School of Fear Fic
Danneberg, J. The big test E
Danziger, P. Amber Brown is not a crayon Fic
Danziger, P. Amber Brown sees red Fic
Danziger, P. Amber Brown wants extra credit Fic

AUTHOR, TITLE, AND SUBJECT INDEX
TWENTY-FIRST EDITION

SCHOOL STORIES -- GRAPHIC NOVELS

SCHOOL STORIES -- JUVENILE FICTION

SCHOOL SUPERVISION
    See also Schools -- Administration; Teaching
SCHOOL TEACHING *See* Teaching

Bardoe, C. Gregor Mendel — **92**
Barretta, G. Neo Leo — **609**
Barretta, G. Now & Ben — **609**
Before the World Was Ready — **509**
Benjamin Franklinstein meets the Fright brothers — **Fic**
Berne, J. Manfish: a story of Jacques Cousteau — **92**
Bolden, T. George Washington Carver — **92**
Cole, J. The magic school bus and the science fair expedition — **509**
Come see the Earth turn: the story of Leon Foucault — **92**
Dendy, L. A. Guinea pig scientists — **616**
Fleming, C. Ben Franklin's almanac — **92**
Fleming, C. The hatmaker's sign — **E**
Fortey, J. Great scientists — **920**
Fritz, J. Leonardo's horse — **730.92**
Fritz, J. What's the big idea, Ben Franklin? — **92**
Greenstein, E. The goose man — **92**
Harness, C. The groundbreaking, chance-taking life of George Washington Carver and science & invention in America — **92**
Harness, C. The remarkable Benjamin Franklin — **92**
Hodgkins, F. Champions of the ocean — **920**
Hollihan, K. L. Isaac Newton and physics for kids — **92**
Jackson, D. M. Extreme scientists — **509**
January, B. Science in colonial America — **509**
Kelsey, E. Strange new species — **578**
Knapp, R. Who stole Mona Lisa? — **E**
Krull, K. Isaac Newton — **92**
Krull, K. Leonardo da Vinci — **92**
Lawson, R. Ben and me — **Fic**
Lourie, P. The manatee scientists — **599.5**
MacDonald, B. The secret of the sealed room — **Fic**
Martin, J. B. Snowflake Bentley — **551.57**
McCutcheon, M. The kid who named Pluto — **509**
McElligott, M. Benjamin Franklinstein lives! — **Fic**
Meltzer, M. Albert Einstein — **92**
Miller, B. M. Benjamin Franklin, American genius — **92**
Ollhoff, J. The germ detectives — **616.9**
Phillips, J. Leonardo da Vinci — **92**
Reiche, D. Freddy in peril — **Fic**
Rushby, P. Ben Franklin — **92**
Saunders, B. R. Ivan Pavlov — **92**
Schroeder, A. Ben Franklin — **92**
Smith, L. John, Paul, George & Ben — **E**
Stanley, D. Leonardo da Vinci — **709.2**
Steele, P. Isaac Newton — **92**
Van Gorp, L. Gregor Mendel — **92**
Woodruff, E. George Washington's spy — **Fic**
Yaccarino, D. The fantastic undersea life of Jacques Cousteau — **92**
Zamosky, L. Louis Pasteur — **92**

SCIENTISTS -- FICTION
Benjamin Franklinstein meets the Fright brothers — **Fic**
Klages, E. The green glass sea — **Fic**
Klages, E. White sands, red menace — **Fic**

SCIENTISTS -- FRANCE -- BIOGRAPHY -- JUVENILE LITERATURE
Miles, L. Louis Pasteur — **509.2**

SCIENTISTS -- JUVENILE LITERATURE
Carson, M. K. Emi and the rhino scientist — **599.66**
Collard, S. B. Science warriors — **578.6**
Fortey, J. Great scientists — **920**
Jackson, D. M. Extreme scientists — **509**
Stronger Than Steel — **595.4**
Turner, P. S. The frog scientist — **597.8**

SCIENTISTS -- UNITED STATES -- BIOGRAPHY -- JUVENILE LITERATURE
Adler, D. A. B. Franklin, printer — **973.3**
Byrd, R. Electric Ben — **973.309**

Freedman, R. Becoming Ben Franklin — **973.309**
January, B. Science in colonial America — **509**

SCIENTISTS -- UNITED STATES -- BIOGRAPHY -- PICTORIAL WORKS -- JUVENILE LITERATURE
Martin, J. B. Snowflake Bentley — **551.57**

Scientists in the field [series]
Burns, L. G. The hive detectives — **638**
Burns, L. G. Tracking trash — **551.46**
Carson, M. K. The bat scientists — **599.4**
Carson, M. K. Emi and the rhino scientist — **599.66**
Collard, S. B. The prairie builders — **577.4**
Collard, S. B. Science warriors — **578.6**
Hodgkins, F. The whale scientists — **599.5**
Jackson, D. M. Extreme scientists — **509**
Jackson, E. B. The mysterious universe — **523.8**
Kramer, S. Hidden worlds: looking through a scientist's microscope — **502.8**
Lourie, P. The manatee scientists — **599.5**
Lourie, P. Whaling season — **599.5**
Mallory, K. Diving to a deep-sea volcano — **551.46**
Mallory, K. Swimming with hammerhead sharks — **597.3**
Montgomery, S. Kakapo rescue — **639.9**
Montgomery, S. Quest for the tree kangaroo — **599.2**
Montgomery, S. Saving the ghost of the mountain — **599.75**
Montgomery, S. The tarantula scientist — **595.4**
Sayre, A. P. Secrets of sound — **591.59**
Turner, P. S. The frog scientist — **597.8**
Turner, P. S. Project Seahorse — **597**

Scientists probe 11 animal mysteries [series]
Myers, J. The puzzle of the platypus — **590**

Scientists saving the earth [series]
Kushner, J. M. Who on earth is Dian Fossey? — **92**
Reichard, S. E. Who on earth is Sylvia Earle? — **92**
Scherer, G. Who on earth is Rachel Carson? — **92**

Scieszka, Jon
(ed) Guys read: funny business — **S**
Baloney (Henry P.) — **E**
Da wild, da crazy, da Vinci — **Fic**
Dizzy Izzy — **E**
The Frog Prince continued — **813**
The good, the bad, and the goofy — **Fic**
Guys read: thriller — **S**
Hey kid, want to buy a bridge? — **Fic**
It's all Greek to me — **Fic**
Kat's mystery gift — **E**
Knights of the kitchen table — **Fic**
Knucklehead — **92**
Marco? Polo! — **Fic**
Math curse — **793.7**
Me oh Maya! — **Fic**
Melvin's valentine — **E**
The not-so-jolly Roger — **Fic**
Oh say, I can't see — **Fic**
Pete's party — **E**
Robot Zot! — **E**
Sam Samurai — **Fic**
Science verse — **E**
See you later, gladiator — **Fic**
Seen Art? — **Fic**
Smash! crash! — **E**
Spaceheadz, book 2 — **Fic**
Spaceheadz, book 3 — **Fic**
The spooky tire — **E**
The Stinky Cheese Man and other fairly stupid tales — **398**
Summer reading is killing me! — **Fic**
Truckery rhymes — **811**
Tut, tut — **Fic**
Uh-oh Max — **E**

Seeger, Ruth Crawford
American folk songs for children in home, school, and nursery school   **782.42**

Seegert, Scott
How to grow up and rule the world   **Fic**

SEEING EYE DOGS *See* Guide dogs

Seeing red. Kyi, T. L.   **612.1**

Seeing symmetry. Leedy, L.   **516**

Seek & find [series]
Kidslabel (Firm) Spot 7 animals   **793.73**
Kidslabel (Firm) Spot 7 Christmas   **793.73**
Kidslabel (Firm) Spot 7 School   **793.73**
Kidslabel (Firm) Spot 7 spooky   **793.73**

Seeker of knowledge. Rumford, J.   **92**

Seeley, Tim
(il) Ross, M. E. Toy lab   **530**

The Seems [series]
Hulme, J. The glitch in sleep   **Fic**
Hulme, J. The split second   **Fic**

Seen Art? Scieszka, J.   **Fic**

Sees Behind Trees. Dorris, M.   **Fic**

Segal, John
Alistair and Kip's great adventure   **E**
Carrot soup   **E**
Far far away   **E**
Pirates don't take baths   **E**

Segal, Lore Groszmann
Morris the artist   **E**

Segovia, Carmen
(il) Blackaby, S. Brownie Groundhog and the February fox **E**

SEGREGATION
Woods, B. The red rose box   **Fic**

SEGREGATION
See also Race relations

SEGREGATION -- FICTION
Bandy, M. S. White water   **E**
Birtha, B. Grandmama's pride   **E**
Blue, R. Ron's big mission   **E**
McKissack, P. C. The clone codes   **Fic**
McKissack, P. C. Goin' someplace special   **E**
Mitchell, M. K. When grandmama sings   **E**
Ruth and the Green Book   **E**
Scattergood, A. Glory be   **Fic**

SEGREGATION -- LAW AND LEGISLATION
Russell, C. Complete copyright for K-12 librarians and educators   **346.730**

SEGREGATION IN EDUCATION
Walker, P. R. Remember Little Rock   **379**

SEGREGATION IN EDUCATION
See also Segregation

SEGREGATION IN EDUCATION -- FICTION
Conkling, W. Sylvia and Aki   **Fic**
Weatherford, C. B. Dear Mr. Rosenwald   **Fic**

SEGREGATION IN EDUCATION -- JUVENILE FICTION
Tuck, P. M. As fast as words could fly   **Fic**

Seguin, Juan Nepomuceno, 1806-1890 -- Juvenile literature
About
Chemerka, W. R. Juan Seguin   **976.4**

Seibold, J. Otto
(il) Edgemon, D. Seamore, the very forgetful porpoise   **E**
Olive the other reindeer   **E**
Other goose   **398.8**
(il) Sierra, J. Tell the truth, B.B. Wolf   **E**

Seidler, Tor
The dulcimer boy   **Fic**
Gully's travels   **Fic**
The Wainscott weasel   **Fic**

SEINEN

See also Manga

Seiple, Samantha
Ghosts in the fog   **940.54**

SEISMIC SEA WAVES *See* Tsunamis

SEISMOGRAPHY *See* Earthquakes

SEISMOLOGY *See* Earthquakes

Seki, Sunny
(il) Yuko-chan and the Daruma doll   **E**

Selbert, Kathryn
War dogs   **E**

Selden, George
Feldman, T. Harry Cat and Tucker Mouse: starring Harry **E**
The cricket in Times Square   **Fic**

The **seldom-ever-shady** glades. Van Wassenhove, S.   **811**

SELECTIVE MUTISM -- FICTION
Lean, S. A dog called Homeless   **Fic**

SELF
See also Consciousness; Individuality; Personality

SELF CONFIDENCE
Perez, L. K. First day in grapes   **E**

SELF HEALTH CARE *See* Health self-care

SELF IMAGE *See* Personal appearance

Self, David
Christianity   **230**

SELF-ACCEPTANCE
Henkes, K. The birthday room   **Fic**
Markes, J. Good thing you're not an octopus!   **E**
Spinelli, J. Loser   **Fic**

SELF-ACCEPTANCE
See also Psychology

SELF-ACCEPTANCE -- FICTION
Burn, D. Andrew Henry's meadow   **E**
Cavanaugh, N. J. This journal belongs to Ratchet   **Fic**
Garland, M. Fish had a wish   **E**
Howe, J. Addie on the inside   **Fic**
MacHale, D. J. The monster princess   **E**
The monster who lost his mean   **E**
Palacio, R. J. Wonder   **Fic**
Rosenthal, A. K. The OK book   **E**

SELF-ACCEPTANCE -- JUVENILE FICTION
Beiser, T. Miss Mousie's blind date   **E**
Exclamation mark   **E**

SELF-ACTUALIZATION *See* Self-realization

SELF-ACTUALIZATION (PSYCHOLOGY)
Marsden, C. Silk umbrellas   **Fic**

SELF-ACTUALIZATION (PSYCHOLOGY) -- FICTION
Brown, P. Mr. Tiger goes wild   **E**

SELF-ASSURANCE *See* Self-confidence; Self-reliance

SELF-AWARENESS *See* Self-perception

SELF-CARE, HEALTH *See* Health self-care

SELF-CARE, MEDICAL *See* Health self-care

SELF-CONCEPT *See* Self-perception

SELF-CONFIDENCE
Allen, D. Dancing in the wings   **E**
De Groat, D. Liar, liar, pants on fire   **E**
Levine, G. C. The two princesses of Bamarre   **Fic**
Moss, W. Being me   **158**
Reynolds, P. Ish   **E**
Simons, R. At home in your body   **613**

SELF-CONFIDENCE
See also Emotions

SELF-CONFIDENCE -- FICTION
Dowell, F. O. The second life of Abigail Walker   **Fic**

SELF-CONFIDENCE -- JUVENILE FICTION
Lewin, B. You can do it!   **E**

SELF-CONSCIOUSNESS
See also Psychology

SELF-CONTROL

See also Psychology

SELF-DEFENSE IN ANIMALS *See* Animal defenses

SELF-DESTRUCTIVE BEHAVIOR

   See also Psychology

SELF-EMPLOYED

   See also Businesspeople

SELF-ESTEEM

   Curtis, J. L. I'm gonna like me   E

   Moss, W. Being me   158

   Yep, L. When the circus came to town   Fic

SELF-ESTEEM

   See also Psychology

SELF-ESTEEM -- FICTION

   Danziger, P. I, Amber Brown   Fic

   Vawter, V. Paperboy   Fic

SELF-EXAMINATION, MEDICAL *See* Health self-care

SELF-EXPERIMENTATION IN MEDICINE

   Dendy, L. A. Guinea pig scientists   616

SELF-FULFILLMENT *See* Self-realization

SELF-GOVERNMENT *See* Democracy; Representative government and representation

SELF-HELP MEDICAL CARE *See* Health self-care

SELF-HELP TECHNIQUES

   See also Applied psychology; Life skills

SELF-IMPROVEMENT

   See also Life skills

SELF-INSTRUCTION

   See also Education; Study skills

SELF-LOVE (PSYCHOLOGY) *See* Self-acceptance; Self-esteem

SELF-MEDICATION *See* Health self-care

SELF-PERCEPTION

   Gantos, J. Jack on the tracks   Fic

   Van Draanen, W. Flipped   Fic

SELF-PERCEPTION

   See also Psychology

SELF-PERCEPTION -- FICTION

   Borden, L. A. Lincoln and me   E

   Docherty, T. Big scary monster   E

   Polacco, P. Thank you, Mr. Falker   E

Self-portrait with seven fingers. Lewis, J. P.   811

SELF-PORTRAITS

   Raczka, B. Here's looking at me   757

SELF-PORTRAITS -- JUVENILE LITERATURE

   Raczka, B. Here's looking at me   757

SELF-PROTECTION IN ANIMALS *See* Animal defenses

SELF-PUBLISHING

   See also Publishers and publishing

SELF-REALIZATION

   Arnold, M. D. Prancing, dancing Lily   E

SELF-REALIZATION

   See also Psychology

SELF-RELIANCE

   Horvath, P. Everything on a waffle   Fic

   Van Leeuwen, J. Cabin on Trouble Creek   Fic

   Wiles, D. Love, Ruby Lavender   Fic

SELF-RELIANCE -- FICTION

   Mister Max   Fic

SELF-RELIANCE -- PICTORIAL WORKS

   Aliki All by myself!   E

SELF-RESPECT *See* Self-esteem

Selfors, Suzanne

   Fortune's magic farm   Fic

   Smells like dog   Fic

   Smells like treasure   Fic

   To catch a mermaid   Fic

Selfridge, Benjamin

   A teen's guide to creating Web pages and blogs   006.7

Selfridge, Peter

   Selfridge, B. A teen's guide to creating Web pages and blogs   006.7

SELKIES -- FICTION

   Billingsley, F. The Folk Keeper   Fic

Selkirk, Alexander, 1676-1721

   About

   Kraske, R. Marooned   92

Sellier, Marie

   Renoir's colors   759.05

SELLING -- FICTION

   Watt, M. Have I got a book for you!   E

Selsam, Millicent Ellis

   Big tracks, little tracks   590

Selway, Martina

   Whitford, R. Little yoga   613.7

Selzer, Adam

   I put a spell on you   Fic

Selznick, Brian

   (il) Clements, A. Frindle   Fic

   (il) Clements, A. Lunch money   Fic

   (il) Conrad, P. Our house   S

   (il) The dulcimer boy   Fic

   (il) Kerley, B. The dinosaurs of Waterhouse Hawkins   567.9

   (il) Kerley, B. Walt Whitman   92

   (il) Martin, A. M. The doll people   Fic

   (il) Martin, A. M. The meanest doll in the world   Fic

   (il) Martin, A. M. The runaway dolls   Fic

   (il) Ryan, P. M. When Marian sang: the true recital of Marian Anderson, the voice of a century   92

   The Houdini box   Fic

   The invention of Hugo Cabret   Fic

   Wonderstruck   Fic

SEMICONDUCTORS

   See also Electric conductors; Electronics

The **Seminole.** King, D. C.   970.004

SEMINOLE INDIANS

   Annino, J. G. She sang promise: the story of Betty Mae Jumper, Seminole tribal leader   92

   King, D. C. The Seminole   970.004

SEMINOLE INDIANS -- FICTION

   Woods, B. My name is Sally Little Song   Fic

Semiprecious. Love, D. A.   Fic

Semmelweis, Ignaz Philipp, 1818-1865

   About

   Ollhoff, J. The germ detectives   616.9

Sempe

   Goscinny Nicholas   Fic

   Goscinny Nicholas on vacation   Fic

SENATORS

   Abramson, J. Obama   92

   Adler, D. A. A picture book of John F. Kennedy   973.922

   Aronson, B. Richard M. Nixon   92

   Blashfield, J. F. Hillary Clinton   92

   Bredeson, C. John Glenn returns to orbit   629.4

   Burgan, M. James Buchanan   92

   Feinstein, S. Barack Obama   92

   Fritz, J. Make way for Sam Houston   92

   Gold, S. D. Lyndon B. Johnson   92

   Grimes, N. Barack Obama   92

   Heiligman, D. High hopes   92

   Hopkinson, D. Michelle   92

   Kesselring, S. Barack Obama   92

   Krensky, S. Dangerous crossing   Fic

   Krull, K. The brothers Kennedy   920

   Mitchell, D. Liftoff   92

   Obama, B. Our enduring spirit   352.23

   Rappaport, D. Jack's path of courage   92

SINAI CAMPAIGN, 1956

See also Egypt -- History; Israel-Arab conflicts

Sing a song of sixpence. Chapman, J.   **398.8**

Sing down the moon. O'Dell, S.   **Fic**

Sing my song. Seskin, S.   **782.42**

Sing to the sun. Bryan, A.   **811**

Sing-along stories [series]

   Hoberman, M. A. Mary had a little lamb   **782.42**

Singapore. Layton, L.   **959.57**

SINGAPORE -- JUVENILE LITERATURE

   Layton, L. Singapore   **959.57**

Singer, Isaac Bashevis, 1904-1991

   Stories for children   **S**

   Zlateh the goat, and other stories   **398.2**

About

   Lives of the writers   **809**

Singer, Marilyn

   Caterpillars   **595.7**

   Central heating   **811**

   A dog's gotta do what a dog's gotta do   **636.7**

   Eggs   **591.4**

   First food fight this fall and other school poems   **811**

   Follow follow   **811**

   A full moon is rising   **811**

   I'm getting a checkup   **610**

   I'm your bus   **E**

   Mirror mirror   **811**

   Shoe bop!   **E**

   A stick is an excellent thing   **811**

   The superheroes' employment agency   **811**

   Tallulah's tutu   **E**

   What is your dog doing?   **E**

   (jt. auth) Singer, M. A strange place to call home   **571.1**

SINGERS

   Anderson, J. J. John Lennon   **92**

   Bieber, J. Justin Bieber: first step 2 forever   **92**

   Boynton, S. Sandra Boynton's One shoe blues   **782.42**

   Christensen, B. Woody Guthrie, poet of the people   **782.421**

   Collins, T. Elvis   **92**

   Golio, G. Jimi: sounds like a rainbow: a story of young Jimi Hendrix

   Greenfield, E. Paul Robeson   **92**

   Kimmel, E. A. A horn for Louis   **92**

   Krull, K. Lives of the musicians   **780.92**

   Medina, T. I and I   **92**

   Odetta, the queen of folk   **92**

   Orgill, R. Footwork   **92**

   Orgill, R. Skit-scat raggedy cat: Ella Fitzgerald   **92**

   Peck, R. Fair weather   **Fic**

   Pinkney, A. D. Ella Fitzgerald   **92**

   Prelutsky, J. Pizza, pigs, and poetry   **808.1**

   Rappaport, D. John's secret dreams   **92**

   Schroeder, A. Satchmo's blues   **E**

   Shange, N. Coretta Scott   **92**

   Stamaty, M. A. Shake, rattle & turn that noise down!   **781.66**

   Stauffacher, S. Bessie Smith and the night riders   **E**

   Weinstein, M. H. Play, Louis, play!   **92**

   Weinstein, M. H. When Louis Armstrong taught me scat   **E**

   Winter, J. Jazz age Josephine   **92**

   Yasuda, A. Justin Bieber   **92**

   Yasuda, A. Miranda Cosgrove   **92**

SINGERS

See also Musicians

SINGERS -- FICTION

   Alexander, C. Small Florence, piggy pop star   **E**

   Curry, J. L. The Black Canary   **Fic**

   Daly, N. A song for Jamela   **E**

   Mitchell, M. K. When grandmama sings   **E**

   Richardson, N. The pearl   **E**

SINGERS -- NEW YORK (STATE) -- NEW YORK -- BIOGRAPHY -- JUVENILE LITERATURE

   Harlem's little blackbird   **782.421**

Singh, Rina

   Nearly nonsense   **398.2**

Singh, Vandana

   Younguncle comes to town   **Fic**

Singing. Fishkin, R. L.   **783**

SINGING

See also Music

SINGING

   Fishkin, R. L. Singing   **783**

   Landau, E. Is singing for you?   **783**

SINGING -- FICTION

   Henkes, K. Penny and her song   **E**

SINGING GAMES

   Rueda, C. Let's play in the forest while the wolf is not around   **782.42**

   Sierra, J. Schoolyard rhymes   **398.8**

SINGING GAMES

See also Games

Singing hands. Ray, D.   **Fic**

SINGLE PARENT FAMILY *See* Single-parent families

SINGLE PARENT FAMILY -- FICTION

   Acampora, P. Rachel Spinelli punched me in the face   **Fic**

   Atkinson, E. J. I, Emma Freke   **Fic**

   Barrow, R. G. Saving Zasha   **Fic**

   Bateson, C. Magenta McPhee   **Fic**

   Bauer, J. Close to famous   **Fic**

   Birdsall, J. The Penderwicks   **Fic**

   Day, K. A million miles from Boston   **Fic**

   Fogelin, A. The sorta sisters   **Fic**

   Galante, C. Willowood   **Fic**

   Greenfield, E. Sister   **Fic**

   Horvath, P. My one hundred adventures   **Fic**

   Hughes, S. The Christmas Eve ghost   **E**

   Leal, A. H. A finders-keepers place   **Fic**

   Reinhardt, D. The summer I learned to fly   **Fic**

   Updale, E. Johnny Swanson   **Fic**

   Warner, S. Happily ever Emma   **Fic**

   Zolotow, C. A father like that   **E**

A **single** shard. Park, L. S.   **Fic**

SINGLE WOMEN

See also Single people; Women

SINGLE-PARENT FAMILIES

See also Family

SINGLE-PARENT FAMILIES -- FICTION

   Gantos, J. Joey Pigza swallowed the key   **Fic**

   Lean, S. A dog called Homeless   **Fic**

SINGLE-PARENT FAMILIES -- JUVENILE LITERATURE

   The great big book of families   **306.8**

SINGLE-SEX SCHOOLS

See also Schools

SINGULARITIES (MATHEMATICS)

See also Geometry

Siomades, Lorianne

   Katy did it!   **E**

Sioras, Efstathia

   Czech Republic   **943.7**

The **Sioux.** Cunningham, K.   **970.004**

Sipping spiders through a straw. DiPucchio, K. S.   **782.42**

Sir Charlie. Fleischman, S.   **92**

Sir Gawain and the Green Knight. Morpurgo, M.   **398.2**

Sir Reginald's logbook. Hammill, M.   **E**

The **sirens.** Orr, T.   **398.2**

SIRENS (MYTHOLOGY)

   Orr, T. The sirens   **398.2**

SNAKES -- STUDY AND TEACHING (ELEMENTARY) -- ACTIVITY PROGRAMS

Blobaum, C. Awesome snake science   597.960

SNAKES AS PETS

   See also Pets; Snakes

SNAKES AS PETS -- FICTION

Heilbroner, J. A pet named Sneaker   E
My snake Blake   E

SNAKES AS PETS -- JUVENILE FICTION

Heilbroner, J. A pet named Sneaker   E

Snakes! Stewart, M.   597.96
Snakey riddles. Hall, K.   793.73
Snap. McGhee, A.   Fic

Snap books [series]
   Alexander, C. Difficult origami   736
   Alexander, C. Sort-of-difficult origami   736
   Boonyadhistarn, T. Beading   745.58
   Meinking, M. Easy origami   736
   Meinking, M. Not-quite-so-easy origami   736

Snap books crafts [series]
   Hufford, D. Greeting card making   745.59

Snap books. Green crafts [series]
   Sirrine, C. Cool crafts with old CDs   745.58
   Sirrine, C. Cool crafts with old jeans   745.5
   Sirrine, C. Cool crafts with old t-shirts   745.5
   Sirrine, C. Cool crafts with old wrappers, cans and bottles   745.5

Snap! Manning, M.   E
Snapshots. Mannis, C. D.   591.7
Snarf attack, underfoodle, and the secret of life. Amato, M.   Fic
Sneakers. Cobb, V.   685

SNEAKERS

Blaxland, W. Sneakers   685
Cobb, V. Sneakers   685
Sneakers. Blaxland, W.   685

SNEAKERS -- JUVENILE LITERATURE

Cobb, V. Sneakers   685

Sneaking suspicions. Coman, C.   Fic
Sneaky art. Jocelyn, M.   745.5
Sneaky sheep. Monroe, C.   E
Sneaky weasel. Shaw, H.   E
Sneaky, spinning, baby spiders. Markle, S.   595.4

Snedden, Robert
   Earth's shifting surface   551.1
   Explaining autism   616.85
   Who invented the computer?   004

Sneed B. Collard III's most fun book ever about lizards. Collard S. B., III   597.95

Sneed, Dani
   Ferris wheel!: George Ferris and his amazing invention   92

SNEEZE -- JUVENILE LITERATURE

Siy, A. Sneeze!   612.2
Sneeze! Siy, A.   612.2
Sneeze, Big Bear, sneeze! Wright, M.   E
Sneezenesia. Lucke, D.   E

SNEEZING

Siy, A. Sneeze!   612.2

SNEEZING -- FICTION

Chu's day   E
Sneezy Louise. Breznak, I.   E

Snell, Gordon
   The King of Quizzical Island   E

Sneve, Virginia Driving Hawk
   The Christmas coat   92

Sneve, Virginia Driving Hawk
   The Christmas coat   92
   (comp) Dancing teepees: poems of American Indian youth   897

Lana's Lakota moons   Fic

About

The Christmas coat   92

Snicket, Lemony, 1970-
   13 words   E
   The bad beginning   Fic
   The composer is dead   E
   The dark   E
   The end   Fic
   The latke who couldn't stop screaming   E
   Lemony Snicket: the unauthorized autobiography   Fic
   Who could that be at this hour?   Fic

Snider, Jesse
   Toy Story   741.5

Sniegoski, Tom
   Quest for the Spark   Fic

Sniegoski, Tom
   Billy Hooten, Owlboy   Fic
   Quest for the spark   Fic

The **sniffles** for Bear. Becker, B.   E
Snip snap! Bergman, M.   E

Snir, Eleyor
   (il) Senir, M. When I first held you   E

Snook alone. Nelson, M.   E

SNORING -- FICTION

O'Hora, Z. Stop snoring, Bernard   E
Waber, B. The mouse that snored   E
Snoring Beauty. Hale, B.   E

SNORKELING See Skin diving

Snot, poop, vomit, and more. Silverstein, A.   612
A **snout** for chocolate. Cazet, D.   E
Snow. Rylant, C.   E
Snow. Shulevitz, U.   E

SNOW

Branley, F. M. Snow is falling   551.57
Cassino, M. The story of snow   551.57
Gibbons, G. It's snowing!   551.57
Johnson, D. Snow sounds   E
Kaner, E. Who likes the snow?   551.57
Lewis, J. P. The snowflake sisters   E
Libbrecht, K. G. The secret life of a snowflake   551.57
Marsico, K. Snowy weather days   551.57
Martin, J. B. Snowflake Bentley   551.57
McCully, E. A. First snow   E
Ralston, B. Snow play   796
Stewart, M. Under the snow   591.7
Waldman, N. The snowflake   551.48
Yee, W. H. Tracks in the snow   E

SNOW -- FICTION

April Fool, Phyllis!   E
Atinuke Have fun, Anna Hibiscus!   Fic
Berry, L. Duck skates   E
Bildner, P. Turkey Bowl   E
Briggs, R. The snowman   E
Buehner, C. Snowmen all year   E
Buehner, C. Snowmen at night   E
Burton, V. L. Katy and the big snow   E
Butler, M. C. The smiley snowman   E
Chessa, F. Holly's red boots   E
Child, L. Snow is my favorite and my best   E
Cole, H. Trudy   E
De Groat, D. Jingle bells, homework smells   E
Dunrea, O. It's snowing!   E
Ehlert, L. Snowballs   551.57
Ernst, L. C. Snow surprise   E
Fenner, C. Snowed in with Grandmother Silk   Fic
Fisher, C. The Snow Show   E
Fleming, D. The first day of winter   E

Ford, B. First snow   E
Garland, M. Super snow day: seek and find   E
Gore, L. Danny's first snow   E
Haas, R. d. Peter and the winter sleepers   E
Harper, L. Snow! Snow! Snow!   E
Hobbie, H. Toot & Puddle: let it snow   E
Hubbell, P. Snow happy!   E
Keats, E. J. The snowy day   E
Krupinski, L. Snow dog's journey   E
Lewis, J. P. The snowflake sisters   E
McCully, E. A. First snow   E
McDonald, M. Judy Moody & Stink: the holly joliday   Fic
McGhee, A. Making a friend   E
Meschenmoser, S. Waiting for winter   E
Moser, L. Perfect Soup   E
Mozelle, S. Zack's alligator and the first snow   E
Neitzel, S. The jacket I wear in the snow   646
Perkins, L. R. Snow music   E
Pfister, M. Snow puppy   E
Raczka, B. Snowy, blowy winter   E
Rawlinson, J. Fletcher and the snowflake Christmas   E
Reid, B. Perfect snow   E
Reynolds, A. Snowbots   E
Rohmann, E. A kitten tale   E
Roode, D. Little Bea and the snowy day   E
Rueda, C. No   E
Rylant, C. Henry and Mudge and the snowman plan   E
Rylant, C. Snow   E
Sakai, K. The snow day   E
Shulevitz, U. Snow   E
The Snow Blew Inn   E
Tresselt, A. R. White snow, bright snow   E
Waddell, M. Snow bears   E
Watts, B. The Smallest Snowflake   E
White, K. When will it snow?   E
Yee, W. H. Mouse and Mole, a winter wonderland   E
Yee, W. H. Tracks in the snow   E
Ziefert, H. Snow party   E
SNOW -- JUVENILE LITERATURE
Branley, F. M. Snow is falling   551.57
Ehlert, L. Snowballs   551.57
Fisher, C. The Snow Show   E
Rylant, C. Snow   E
Snow baby. Kirkpatrick, K. A.   92
Snow bears. Waddell, M.   E
The Snow Blew Inn.   E
SNOW BOARDING See Snowboarding
The snow day. Sakai, K.   E
Snow dog's journey. Krupinski, L.   E
Snow happy! Hubbell, P.   E
Snow in Summer. Yolen, J.   Fic
Snow is falling. Branley, F. M.   551.57
Snow is my favorite and my best. Child, L.   E
SNOW LEOPARD
Hatkoff, J. Leo the snow leopard   599.75
Montgomery, S. Saving the ghost of the mountain   599.75
Shores, E. L. Snow leopards   599.75
SNOW LEOPARD -- FICTION
McAllister, A. Little Mist   E
SNOW LEOPARD -- INFANCY -- JUVENILE LITERA-TURE
Markle, S. Snow school   E
SNOW LEOPARD -- JUVENILE LITERATURE
Markle, S. Snow school   E
Snow leopards. Shores, E. L.   599.75
Snow music. Perkins, L. R.   E
Snow party. Ziefert, H.   E
Snow play. Ralston, B.   796

Snow puppy. Pfister, M.   E
The Snow Queen. Ehrlich, A.   Fic
Snow rabbit, spring rabbit. Il Sung Na   E
Snow school. Markle, S.   E
The Snow Show. Fisher, C.   E
SNOW SKIING See Skiing
Snow sounds. Johnson, D.   E
The snow spider. Nimmo, J.   Fic
Snow surprise. Ernst, L. C.   E
Snow treasure. McSwigan, M.   Fic
Snow White. Grimm, J.   398.2
Snow White. Grimm, J.   398.2
Snow White. Ray, J.   398.2
Snow! Snow! Snow! Harper, L.   E
Snow, Alan
Here be monsters!   Fic
Snow, Maya
Sisters of the sword   Fic
Snow, Sarah
(il) Formento, A. These bees count!   E
Snow, Sarah
(il) Formento, A. This tree counts!   E
Snowball launchers, giant-pumpkin growers, and other cool contraptions. Fox, T.   745.5
Snowballs. Ehlert, L.   551.57
Snowboarding. Woods, B.   796.9
Snowboarding. Schwartz, H. E.   796.93
SNOWBOARDING
See also Winter sports
SNOWBOARDING
Kenney, K. L. Skiing & snowboarding   796.93
Schwartz, H. E. Snowboarding   796.93
Woods, B. Snowboarding   796.9
SNOWBOARDING -- FICTION
Ramthun, B. The White Gates   Fic
Snowbots. Reynolds, A.   E
Snowed in with Grandmother Silk. Fenner, C.   Fic
Snowed under and other Christmas confusions. Bloch, S.   E
The snowflake. Waldman, N.   551.48
Snowflake Bentley. Martin, J. B.   551.57
The snowflake sisters. Lewis, J. P.   E
SNOWFLAKES -- JUVENILE LITERATURE
Cassino, M. The story of snow   551.57
Libbrecht, K. G. The secret life of a snowflake   551.57
Waldman, N. The snowflake   551.48
SNOWFLAKES -- PICTORIAL WORKS -- JUVENILE LITERATURE
Martin, J. B. Snowflake Bentley   551.57
The snowman. Briggs, R.   E
SNOWMEN
Buehner, C. Snowmen at night   E
SNOWMEN -- FICTION
Rylant, C. Henry and Mudge and the snowman plan   E
Snowmen all year. Buehner, C.   E
Snowmen at night. Buehner, C.   E
Snowmobile racers. Woods, B.   796.94
SNOWMOBILES
Woods, B. Snowmobile racers   796.94
The snowshoeing adventure of Milton Daub, blizzard trekker. Wetterer, M. K.   741.5
SNOWSHOERS
Wetterer, M. K. The snowshoeing adventure of Milton Daub, blizzard trekker   741.5
The snowstorm. Riel, J.   Fic
The snowy day. Keats, E. J.   E
The snowy day and the art of Ezra Jack Keats. Nahson, C. J.   741.6
SNOWY OWL -- JUVENILE LITERATURE

Allen, J. The little rabbit who liked to say moo   E
Burleigh, R. Clang-clang! Beep-beep!   E
Carluccio, M. The sounds around town   E
Davies, J. The night is singing   E
Gershator, P. Listen, listen   E
Kato, Y. In the meadow   E
Listen to the silent night   E
Marsalis, W. Squeak! rumble! whomp! whomp! whomp!   E
O'Connell, R. The baby goes beep   E
Perkins, L. R. Snow music   E
Waring, G. Oscar and the bat   E
Wolff, F. It is the wind   E

SOUND -- JUVENILE FICTION
The Christmas quiet book   E
Marsalis, W. Squeak! rumble! whomp! whomp! whomp!   E

SOUND -- JUVENILE LITERATURE
Burleigh, R. Clang-clang! Beep-beep!   E
Sound and hearing. Farndon, J.   534
Sound and hearing. Veitch, C.   612.8

SOUND EFFECTS
See also Sound

SOUND EFFECTS BOOKS
Carle, E. The very clumsy click beetle   E

SOUND EFFECTS BOOKS -- SPECIMENS
Carle, E. The very clumsy click beetle   E
The **sound** of colors. Liao, J.   E
The **sound** of Kwanzaa. Tokunbo, D.   394.26
The **sound** of storytime. Dixon, T.   027.62
Sound off! Steinberg, D.   741.5

SOUND RECORDINGS
Crews, K. D. Copyright law for librarians and educators   346.04
Miles, L. Making a recording   781.49

SOUND WAVES
Guillain, C. Different sounds   534
Guillain, C. How do we hear?   612.8
Guillain, C. What is sound?   534
Spilsbury, R. What is sound?   534
Veitch, C. Sound and hearing   612.8

SOUND WAVES
See also Vibration; Waves
Sounder. Armstrong, W. H.   Fic

SOUNDPROOFING
See also Architectural acoustics; Sound

SOUNDS
Guillain, C. What is sound?   534
Hewitt, S. Hear this!   612.8

SOUNDS
See also Sound

SOUNDS -- FICTION
Alborough, J. The gobble gobble moooooo tractor book   E
Beaumont, K. No sleep for the sheep!   E
Bee, W. And the train goes. . .   E
Donaldson, J. What the ladybug heard   E
Garcia, E. Tap tap bang bang   E
Judge, L. Red sled   E
Krensky, S. Noah's bark   E
Krilanovich, N. Chicken, chicken, duck!   E
Macken, J. E. Baby says moo!   E
McCue, L. Quiet Bunny   E
Raschka, C. Farmy farm   E
Ruddell, D. Who said coo?   E
Schade, S. The noisy counting book   E
Stevens, A. Waking up Wendell   E
Symphony city   E

SOUNDS -- JUVENILE LITERATURE
Light, S. Trains go   E
Sounds all around us [series]

Guillain, C. Different sounds   534
Guillain, C. How do we hear?   612.8
Guillain, C. Making sounds   534
Guillain, C. What is sound?   534
Veitch, C. Sound and hearing   612.8
The **sounds** around town. Carluccio, M.   E
Soup day. Iwai, M.   E
Soup for breakfast. Brown, C.   811
Soup, Cuthbert
Another whole nother story   Fic
A whole nother story   Fic

SOUPS
See also Cooking

SOUPS -- FICTION
Iwai, M. Soup day   E
Moser, L. Perfect Soup   E
Rodman, M. A. Surprise soup   E
Schubert, L. The Princess of Borscht   E
Soupy Saturdays with The Pain and The Great One. Blume, J.   Fic

Souter, Gerry
Souter, J. War in Afghanistan and Iraq   355

Souter, Janet
War in Afghanistan and Iraq   355
South. McDonnell, P.   E
South Africa. Mace, V.   968

SOUTH AFRICA -- HISTORY
Nelson, K. Nelson Mandela   968.06

SOUTH AFRICA -- RACE RELATIONS
See also Race relations
South Africa in our world. Brownlie, A.   968.06

SOUTH AFRICAN COOKING
Cornell, K. A. Cooking the southern African way   641.5

SOUTH AMERICAN ART
See also Art
South by southeast. Horowitz, A.   Fic
South Carolina. Somervill, B. A.   975.7
South Carolina. Hoffman, N.   975.7
South Carolina. Harmon, D.   975.7
South Carolina, 1540-1776. Doak, R. S.   975.7
South Dakota. Petersen, C.   978.3
South Dakota. Burgan, M.   978.3

SOUTH POLE
Dowdeswell, E. Scott of the Antarctic   919.8

SOUTH POLE -- EXPLORATION -- JUVENILE LITERATURE
Bodden, V. To the South Pole   919.8
Southeast Asian Americans. Wachtel, A.   305.8

SOUTHERN COOKING
See also Cooking
Southern sea otters. Leardi, J.   599.7

SOUTHERN STATES -- AFRICAN AMERICANS *See* African Americans -- Southern States

SOUTHERN STATES -- HISTORY
See also United States -- History

SOUTHERN STATES -- RACE RELATIONS -- MISCELLANEA -- JUVENILE LITERATURE
Rappaport, D. Free at last!   305.8

SOUTHWEST, NEW -- HISTORY -- JUVENILE LITERATURE
Freedman, R. In the days of the vaqueros   636.2

SOUTHWEST, NEW -- SOCIAL LIFE AND CUSTOMS -- JUVENILE LITERATURE
Freedman, R. In the days of the vaqueros   636.2

SOUTHWESTERN STATES -- ANTIQUITIES
Croy, A. Ancient Pueblo   978

SOUTHWESTERN STATES -- HISTORY
Hernandez, R. E. Early explorations: the 1500s   970.01

Hernandez, R. E. New Spain: 1600-1760s   **973.1**

Souza, D. M.

Freaky flowers   **582.13**

Look what feet can do   **573.9**

Look what mouths can do   **573.9**

Look what tails can do   **573.9**

Plant invaders   **581.6**

SOVEREIGNS *See* Emperors; Kings and rulers; Monarchy;
Queens

SOVEREIGNTY

      See also International law; Political science

**SOVIET UNION -- HISTORY -- 1953-1991 -- GRAPHIC
NOVELS**

Abadzis, N. Laika   **741.5**

SOYBEAN

Bial, R. The super soybean   **633.3**

SOYBEAN -- JUVENILE LITERATURE

Bial, R. The super soybean   **633.3**

SOYBEAN PRODUCTS -- JUVENILE LITERATURE

Bial, R. The super soybean   **633.3**

Space. Riley, P. D.   **520**

Space and time.   **530.11**

SPACE AND TIME

Norton, M. Bed-knob and broomstick   **Fic**

Rand, C. Time   **530.1**

SPACE AND TIME

      See also Fourth dimension; Metaphysics; Space sci-
ences; Time

SPACE AND TIME -- FICTION

Asch, F. Time twister   **Fic**

Bransford, N. Jacob Wonderbar and the interstellar time
warp   **Fic**

Charlie and Kiwi   **E**

Choldenko, G. No passengers beyond this point   **Fic**

Colfer, E. Artemis Fowl   **Fic**

Colfer, E. Artemis Fowl: The Atlantis complex   **Fic**

Colfer, E. Artemis Fowl: the time paradox   **Fic**

Flavin, T. The Blackhope enigma   **Fic**

Flavin, T. The crimson shard   **Fic**

Haddix, M. P. Caught   **Fic**

Hahn, M. D. Time for Andrew   **Fic**

Lipsyte, R. The twinning project   **Fic**

Mason, T. The last synapsid   **Fic**

Messer, S. Windblowne   **Fic**

Mull, B. A world without heroes   **Fic**

Pearce, P. Tom's midnight garden   **Fic**

Snyder, L. Any which wall   **Fic**

Stead, R. When you reach me   **Fic**

Stephens, J. The emerald atlas   **Fic**

Stephens, J. The fire chronicle   **Fic**

Teague, M. The doom machine   **Fic**

Townley, R. The door in the forest   **Fic**

Webb, P. Six days   **Fic**

Wells, R. On the Blue Comet   **Fic**

West, J. The shadows   **Fic**

West, J. Spellbound   **Fic**

Wilson, N. D. The Chestnut King   **Fic**

Winterson, J. Tanglewreck   **Fic**

Wiseman, D. Jeremy Visick   **Fic**

SPACE AND TIME -- JUVENILE LITERATURE

Space and time   **530.11**

SPACE AND TIME IN ART

Meredith, S. What is space?   **701**

SPACE BIOLOGY

Bortz, A. B. Astrobiology   **576.8**

Turner, P. S. Life on earth--and beyond   **576.8**

SPACE BIOLOGY

      See also Biology; Space sciences

SPACE BIOLOGY -- JUVENILE LITERATURE

Turner, P. S. Life on earth--and beyond   **576.8**

Space boy. Landry, L.   **E**

Space case. Marshall, E.   **E**

SPACE CHEMISTRY

      See also Chemistry

SPACE DEBRIS

Silverman, B. Exploring dangers in space   **551.3**

SPACE DEBRIS

      See also Pollution; Space environment

Space emergency. Cole, M. D.   **629.45**

SPACE ENVIRONMENT

      See also Astronomy; Outer space

Space exploration. Stott, C.   **629.4**

Space exploration. Jankowski, C.   **520**

Space exploration. Harris, J.   **629.4**

SPACE EXPLORATION (ASTRONAUTICS) *See* Outer
space -- Exploration

SPACE FLIGHT

Aldrin, B. Look to the stars   **629.4**

Bredeson, C. John Glenn returns to orbit   **629.4**

Vogt, G. Spacewalks   **629.45**

Waxman, L. H. Exploring space travel   **629.45**

SPACE FLIGHT

      See also Aeronautics -- Flights; Astronautics

SPACE FLIGHT (FICTION) *See* Imaginary voyages; Science fiction

SPACE FLIGHT -- FICTION

Armstrong, A. Racing the moon   **Fic**

Arnold, T. Green Wilma, frog in space   **E**

Asch, F. Time twister   **Fic**

Hurd, T. Bongo fishing   **Fic**

Jeffers, O. The way back home   **E**

SPACE FLIGHT -- GRAPHIC NOVELS

Abadzis, N. Laika   **741.5**

Spires, A. Binky the space cat   **741.5**

**SPACE FLIGHT -- HISTORY -- JUVENILE LITERA-
TURE**

Benoit, P. The space race   **629.4**

SPACE FLIGHT -- JUVENILE LITERATURE

Benoit, P. The space race   **629.4**

Green, C. R. Spacewalk   **629.45**

Holden, H. M. The coolest job in the universe   **629.44**

SPACE FLIGHT TO MARS

Branley, F. M. Mission to Mars   **629.45**

Hartman, E. Mission to Mars   **629.45**

Leedy, L. Messages from Mars   **523.4**

SPACE FLIGHT TO MARS -- JUVENILE LITERATURE

Branley, F. M. Mission to Mars   **629.45**

Leedy, L. Messages from Mars   **523.4**

SPACE FLIGHT TO THE MOON

Bodden, V. Man walks on the Moon   **629.45**

Burleigh, R. One giant leap   **629.45**

Chaikin, A. Mission control, this is Apollo   **629.45**

Dyer, A. Mission to the moon   **629.45**

McNulty, F. If you decide to go to the moon   **629.45**

Moonshot   **629.45**

Platt, R. Moon landing   **629.45**

Ross, S. Moon: science, history, and mystery   **629.45**

Thimmesh, C. Team moon   **629.45**

Vogt, G. Apollo moonwalks   **629.45**

SPACE FLIGHT TO THE MOON

      See also Astronautics; Space flight

**SPACE FLIGHT TO THE MOON -- HISTORY -- JUVE-
NILE LITERATURE**

Bodden, V. To the moon   **629.45**

SPACE FLIGHT TO THE MOON -- FICTION

Aston, D. H. Moon over Star   **E**

Pimm, N. R. The Daytona 500 **796.72**

SPECTERS *See* Apparitions; Ghosts

SPECTRUM ANALYSIS

    See also Astronomy; Astrophysics; Chemistry; Optics; Radiation

SPEECH

    See also Language arts

SPEECH DISORDERS -- FICTION

  Lester, H. Hooway for Wodney Wat **E**

  Lester, H. Wodney Wat's wobot **E**

SPEECHES

  King, M. L. J. I have a dream **323.092**

SPEECHES

    See also Literature

SPEECHES, ADDRESSES, ETC

  Hudson, W. Powerful words **081**

SPEECHES, ADDRESSES, ETC. *See* Speeches

SPEECHES, ADDRESSES, ETC., AMERICAN *See* American speeches

SPEECHES, ADDRESSES, ETC., AMERICAN -- AFRICAN AMERICAN AUTHORS -- JUVENILE LITERATURE

  Hudson, W. Powerful words **081**

Speed. Sullivan, N. **531**

SPEED

    See also Motion

SPEED

  Gardner, R. Split-second science projects with speed **531**

  Hillman, B. How fast is it? **531**

  Mason, P. Improving speed **613.7**

  Smith, M. Speed machines **629.2**

  Somervill, B. A. Speed and acceleration **531**

  Sullivan, N. Speed **531**

SPEED -- EXPERIMENTS

  Gardner, R. Split-second science projects with speed **531**

SPEED -- EXPERIMENTS -- JUVENILE LITERATURE

  Gardner, R. Split-second science projects with speed **531**

SPEED -- FICTION

  McGrory, A. Quick, slow, mango! **E**

  Pearce, E. S. Slowpoke **E**

Speed and acceleration. Somervill, B. A. **531**

Speed machines. Smith, M. **629.2**

SPEED READING

    See also Reading

Speed skating. Marsico, K. **796.91**

Speir, Nancy

  (il) Hubbell, P. My first airplane ride **E**

  (il) McGinty, A. B. Eliza's kindergarten surprise **E**

Speirs, John

  (il) Murphy, S. J. It's about time! **529**

  (il) Myers, W. D. Three swords for Granada **Fic**

SPELEOLOGY *See* Caves

Spellbinder. Stringer, H. **Fic**

Spellbound. West, J. **Fic**

SPELLERS

  Terban, M. Scholastic dictionary of spelling **428**

SPELLERS

    See also English language -- Spelling

SPELLING -- JUVENILE FICTION

  Best, C. Beatrice spells some lulus and learns to write a letter **E**

SPELLING BEES -- FICTION

  Alter, A. Abigail spells **E**

  Selzer, A. I put a spell on you **Fic**

Spellman, David

  (jt. auth) Lutz, L. How to negotiate everything **302.3**

Spells. Gravett, E. **E**

SPELLS *See* Charms; Magic

Spelman, Lucy

  Animal encyclopedia **591.03**

SPELUNKERS

  Jackson, D. M. Extreme scientists **509**

Spencer, Britt

  (il) St. George, J. Make your mark, Franklin Roosevelt **92**

  (il) St. George, J. Zarafa **599.63**

  (il) Steig, J. Fleas **E**

Spencer, Russ

  Skateboarding **796.22**

Spengler, Margaret

  (il) Buzzeo, T. Ready or not, Dawdle Duckling **E**

  (il) Tekavec, H. Storm is coming! **E**

Spenser, Edmund

  Hodges, M. Saint George and the dragon **398.2**

SPERM WHALE -- PICTORIAL WORKS -- JUVENILE FICTION

  London, J. Baby whale's journey **E**

Sperring, Mark

  The sunflower sword **E**

Sperry, Armstrong

  Call it courage **Fic**

SPHDZ [series]

  Spaceheadz **Fic**

Spheres. Olson, N. **516**

SPHERES

  Olson, N. Spheres **516**

The **sphinx.** DiPrimio, P. **398.2**

The **sphinx.** Kallen, S. A. **398**

SPHINXES (MYTHOLOGY)

  DiPrimio, P. The sphinx **398.2**

  Hartland, J. How the sphinx got to the museum **932**

  Kallen, S. A. The sphinx **398**

SPHINXES (MYTHOLOGY) -- JUVENILE LITERATURE

  Hartland, J. How the sphinx got to the museum **932**

  Kallen, S. A. The sphinx **398**

SPICES

    See also Food

Spicy hot colors: colores picantes. Shahan, S. **E**

Spider. Lomberg, M. **639**

The **spider** and the fly. Howitt, M. B. **821**

SPIDER WEBS -- JUVENILE LITERATURE

  Murawski, D. Spiders and their webs **595.4**

  Stronger Than Steel **595.4**

SPIDER WEBS -- THERAPEUTIC USE -- JUVENILE LITERATURE

  Stronger Than Steel **595.4**

The **spider's** gift. Kimmel, E. A. **398.2**

SPIDER-MAN (FICTIONAL CHARACTER)

    See also Fictional characters; Superheroes

Spiders. Markle, S. **595.4**

Spiders. Bishop, N. **596**

Spiders. Simon, S. **595.4**

SPIDERS

  Berger, M. Spinning spiders **595.4**

  Bishop, N. Spiders **595.4**

  Dewey, J. Once I knew a spider **E**

  Johnson, J. Simon & Schuster children's guide to insects and spiders **595.7**

  Lomberg, M. Spider **639**

  Lunis, N. Deadly black widows **595.4**

  Markle, S. Black widows **595.4**

  Markle, S. Crab spiders **595.4**

  Markle, S. Fishing spiders **595.4**

  Markle, S. Harvestmen **595.4**

  Markle, S. Jumping spiders **595.4**

  Markle, S. Orb weavers **595.4**

  Markle, S. Sneaky, spinning, baby spiders **595.4**

Steinway family

About

VanHecke, S. Raggin', jazzin', rockin'   **784.19**

Stella, unleashed. Ashman, L.   **E**

Stellaluna. Cannon, J.   **E**

Stellar science projects about Earth's sky. Gardner, R.   **551.5**

STELLER'S SEA LION -- JUVENILE LITERATURE

Harvey, J. Astro the Steller sea lion   **599.79**

Stellings, Caroline

The contest   **Fic**

STEM CELL RESEARCH

Nardo, D. Cure quest   **616**

STEM CELL RESEARCH

    See also Medical technology; Medicine -- Research

Stemple, Adam

B.U.G.   **Fic**

Yolen, J. Apple for the teacher   **782.42**

Stemple, Heidi E. Y.

Yolen, J. The Barefoot book of dance stories   **398.2**

Yolen, J. Fairy tale feasts   **641.5**

Yolen, J. Not all princesses dress in pink   **E**

Yolen, J. Pretty princess pig   **E**

Yolen, J. Sleep, black bear, sleep   **E**

Stemple, Jason

(il) Birds of a feather   **811**

(il) Bug off!   **811.54**

(il) Yolen, J. An egret's day   **811**

(il) Yolen, J. A mirror to nature   **811**

Stems. Farndon, J.   **581.4**

STEMS (PLANTS)

Farndon, J. Stems   **581.4**

STENCIL WORK

    See also Decoration and ornament; Painting

STEP DANCING

    See also Dance

Step fourth, Mallory! Friedman, L. B.   **Fic**

Step gently out.

Step into reading [series]

Boelts, M. Dogerella   **E**

Bruchac, J. The Trail of Tears   **970.004**

Corey, S. Monster parade   **E**

Ghigna, C. Barn storm   **E**

Harrison, D. L. A monster is coming!   **E**

Hayes, G. A poor excuse for a dragon   **E**

Hays, A. J. Smarty Sara   **E**

Kohuth, J. Ducks go vroom   **E**

Redmond Tentacles!   **594**

Step into Reading. Step 1 [series]

Chicks!   **E**

Step into science [series]

Burns, K. What's going on?   **507.8**

Challen, P. C. What just happened?   **507.8**

Challen, P. C. What's going to happen?   **507.8**

Hyde, N. What's the plan?   **507.8**

Johnson, R. R. What do we know now?   **507.8**

Step-by-step science experiments in astronomy. VanCleave, J. P.   **520.78**

Step-by-step science experiments in biology. VanCleave, J. P.   **570**

Step-by-step science experiments in earth science. VanCleave, J. P.   **550.78**

Step-by-step science experiments in ecology. VanCleave, J. P.   **577.078**

Step-by-step science experiments in energy. VanCleave, J. P.   **531**

STEPCHILDREN

    See also Children; Parent-child relationship

STEPCHILDREN -- FICTION

Hahn, M. D. Wait till Helen comes   **Fic**

STEPFAMILIES

    See also Family

STEPFAMILIES -- FICTION

Clifton, L. Freaky Fast Frankie Joe   **Fic**

Cohn, R. The Steps   **Fic**

Cohn, R. Two steps forward   **Fic**

Deriso, C. H. The Right-Under Club   **Fic**

Grimes, N. Oh, brother!   **E**

Hicks, B. Out of order   **Fic**

Hoffman, M. Bravo Grace!   **Fic**

Jackson, A. Eggs over Evie   **Fic**

Kilworth, G. Attica   **Fic**

Luciani, B. A hubbub   **741.5**

Manley, C. Skeeter's dream   **Fic**

Sheinmel, C. All the things you are   **Fic**

Zimmer, T. V. Sketches from a spy tree   **Fic**

STEPFATHERS

Freeman, M. The trouble with cats   **Fic**

Salisbury, G. Lord of the deep   **Fic**

STEPFATHERS

    See also Fathers; Stepparents

STEPFATHERS -- FICTION

Bennett, K. Dad and Pop   **E**

Freeman, M. The trouble with cats   **Fic**

Hunt, L. M. One for the Murphys   **Fic**

Johnson, A. Bird   **Fic**

Salisbury, G. Lord of the deep   **Fic**

Stephen Hawking. Venezia, M.   **92**

Stephens, Claire Gatrell

(jt. auth) Franklin, P. School library collection development   **025.2**

Library 101   **027.8**

Stephens, Helen

The big adventure of the Smalls   **E**

Fleabag   **E**

Stephens, Jay

Heroes!   **741.5**

Monsters!   **741.5**

Robots!   **741.5**

Stephens, John

The emerald atlas   **Fic**

The fire chronicle   **Fic**

Stephens, Pat

(il) Hodge, D. Desert animals   **591.7**

(il) Hodge, D. Forest animals   **591.7**

(il) Hodge, D. Polar animals   **591.7**

(il) Hodge, D. Rain forest animals   **591.7**

(il) Hodge, D. Savanna animals   **591.7**

(il) Hodge, D. Wetland animals   **591.7**

Stephenson, Kristina

(il) Bauer, M. D. Thank you for me!   **E**

STEPMOTHERS

Bunting, E. The memory string   **E**

STEPMOTHERS -- FICTION

Bunting, E. The memory string   **E**

Grabenstein, C. The crossroads   **Fic**

Grabenstein, C. The Hanging Hill   **Fic**

Grabenstein, C. The smoky corridor   **Fic**

MacLachlan, P. Sarah, plain and tall   **Fic**

MacLachlan, P. Skylark   **Fic**

Yolen, J. Snow in Summer   **Fic**

Stepping on the cracks. Hahn, M. D.   **Fic**

Stepping stone book [series]

Kimmel, E. C. Balto and the great race   **636.73**

Penner, L. R. Dragons   **398.2**

The **Steps.** Cohn, R.   **Fic**

STEPSISTERS -- FICTION

Big or little? **E**
Stitchin' and pullin' McKissack, P. C. **Fic**
StJohn, Amanda, 1982-
   Bridget and Bo build a blog **Fic**
Stoberock, Martha
   (il) Pellowski, A. The storytelling handbook **372.64**
STOCK CAR RACING
     See also Automobile racing
STOCK EXCHANGE CRASHES *See* Financial crises
STOCK EXCHANGES
     See also Finance; Markets
STOCK MARKET PANICS *See* Financial crises
Stock, Catherine
   (il) Fitzgerald, D. Vinnie and Abraham **92**
   (il) Herold, M. R. A very important day **E**
   (il) Howe, J. Kaddish for Grandpa in Jesus' name, amen **E**
   (il) Lunde, D. After the kill **591.5**
   (il) Mills, C. Gus and Grandpa and the two-wheeled bike **E**
   Gugu's house **E**
   A porc in New York **E**
   (il) Walter, M. P. Justin and the best biscuits in the world **Fic**
   (il) Whitaker, S. The daring Miss Quimby **92**
   (il) Williams, K. L. Galimoto **E**
   (il) Williams, K. L. My name is Sangoel **E**
   (il) Williams, K. L. Painted dreams **E**
   (il) Wilson, S. The day we danced in underpants **E**
Stock, Charlotte
   Skateboarding step-by-step **796.22**
Stockdale, Susan
   Bring on the birds **598**
   Stripes of all types **591.47**
Stockdale, Susan
   Bring on the birds **598**
   Carry me! **591.56**
   Fabulous fishes **597**
Stockings of buttermilk: American folktales. **398.209**
STOCKS
     See also Commerce; Securities
STOCKS -- FICTION
   Weissman, E. B. The short seller **Fic**
Stockton, Frank
   The bee-man of Orn **Fic**
Stoeke, Janet Morgan
   The bus stop **E**
   A hat for Minerva Louise **E**
   It's library day **E**
   The Loopy Coop hens **E**
   Minerva Louise and the red truck **E**
   Waiting for May **E**
Stohner, Anu
   Brave Charlotte **E**
STOICS
     See also Ancient philosophy; Ethics
Stojic, Manya
   Hello world! **413**
   Rain **E**
STOMACH
   Cobb, V. Your body battles a stomachache **616.3**
   Guillain, C. Our stomachs **612.3**
   Korb, R. My stomach **612.3**
STOMACH
     See also Anatomy
STOMACH -- FICTION
   Harris, J. The belly book **E**
Stomp rockets, catapults, and kaleidoscopes. Gabrielson, C. **507.8**
Stompin' at the Savoy. Miller, N. **92**
Stompin' at the Savoy. Campbell, B. M. **E**

STONE AGE -- FICTION
   Kitamura, S. Stone Age boy **E**
Stone Age boy. Kitamura, S. **E**
Stone Arch readers [series]
   Hooks, G. Pet costume party **E**
The **stone** child. Poblocki, D. **Fic**
Stone Fox. Gardiner, J. R. **Fic**
Stone Rabbit [series]
   Craddock, E. BC mambo **741.5**
   Craddock, E. Night of the living dust bunnies **741.5**
   Craddock, E. Superhero stampede **741.5**
Stone rabbit #3: Deep-space disco. Craddock, E. **741.5**
Stone Rabbit: Pirate Palooza. Craddock, E. **741.5**
Stone soup. Muth, J. J. **398.2**
Stone soup. Soldier's soup **398.2**
Stone, Bryan
   (il) Explore water! **546**
Stone, Bryan
   (il) Yasuda, A. Explore simple machines **621.8**
Stone, Kate
   One spooky night **E**
Stone, Kazuko G.
   (il) Gollub, M. Cool melons--turn to frogs!: the life and poems of Issa **92**
Stone, Kyle M.
   (y) Esbaum, J. Tom's tweet **E**
   (il) Heide, F. P. Always listen to your mother **E**
   (il) Leuck, L. I love my pirate papa **E**
   (il) Lewis, J. P. Please bury me in the library **811**
Stone, Phoebe
   The boy on Cinnamon Street **Fic**
   Deep down popular **Fic**
   The Romeo and Juliet code **Fic**
   Romeo blue **Fic**
Stone, Tanya Lee
   Courage has no color, the true story of the Triple Nickles **940.54**
   Elizabeth leads the way: Elizabeth Cady Stanton and the right to vote **92**
   Sandy's circus **92**
   Who says women can't be doctors? **E**
Stone, Wendy
   (il) Williams, K. L. Beatrice's dream **967.62**
The **stone-faced** boy. Fox, P. **Fic**
STONECUTTERS -- FICTION
   Me and Momma and Big John **E**
STONECUTTING -- FICTION
   Daly, J. Sivu's six wishes **E**
Stoneheart. Fletcher, C. **Fic**
Stoneheart trilogy [series]
   Fletcher, C. Ironhand **Fic**
   Fletcher, C. Silvertongue **Fic**
   Fletcher, C. Stoneheart **Fic**
Stonehenge. Henzel, C. K. **936.2**
Stones in water. Napoli, D. J. **Fic**
Stonewall Hinkleman and the Battle of Bull Run. Hemphill, M. **Fic**
STONEWARE *See* Pottery
Stoop, Naoko
   Red Knit Cap Girl **E**
Stop and go, yes and no. Cleary, B. P. **428**
Stop snoring, Bernard. O'Hora, Z. **E**
Stop thief! Lane, A. J. B. **E**
Stop, drop, and roll. Cuyler, M. **E**
Storace, Patricia
   Sugar Cane **398.2**
Storad, Conrad J.
   Earth's crust **551.1**

Fox, M. Sleepy bears	E	Holub, J. Spring is here!	E
Fox, M. Ten little fingers and ten little toes	E	Hood, S. Pup and Hound hatch an egg	E
Fox, M. Where is the green sheep?	E	Howland, N. Princess says goodnight	E
Fox, M. Where the giant sleeps	E	Hubbell, P. Airplanes	E
Franco, B. Double play!	E	Hubbell, P. Boats	E
Frank, J. How to catch a fish	E	Hubbell, P. Cars	E
Frazier, C. Lots of dots	E	Hubbell, P. Firefighters! speeding! spraying! saving!	E
Frederick, H. V. Babyberry pie	E	Hubbell, P. Horses	E
Frederick, H. V. Hide-and-squeak	E	Hubbell, P. My first airplane ride	E
Fuge, C. Astonishing animal ABC	E	Hubbell, P. Police: hurrying! helping! saving!	E
Fuller, S. F. My cat, coon cat	E	Hubbell, P. Snow happy!	E
Fyleman, R. Mice	E	Hudes, Q. A. Welcome to my neighborhood!	E
Gaiman, N. Crazy hair	E	Hughes, T. My brother Bert	E
Gaiman, N. The dangerous alphabet	E	Hush, little horsie	E
Gall, C. Substitute Creacher	E	Hutchins, P. Ten red apples	E
George, K. O. Book!	811	I can be anything	E
George, K. O. Hummingbird nest	E	If all the animals came inside	E
George, K. O. Up!	E	Isop, L. How do you hug a porcupine?	E
Gershator, P. Listen, listen	E	Jacobs, P. D. Fire drill	E
Gershator, P. Moo, moo, brown cow, have you any milk?	E	Jane, P. Little goblins ten	E
Gershator, P. Who's awake in springtime?	E	Janovitz, M. Baby baby baby!	E
Gershator, P. Who's in the forest?	E	Javernick, E. The birthday pet	E
Ghigna, C. Barn storm	E	Jay, A. Red green blue	E
The gingerbread man loose in the school	E	Jocelyn, M. Ones and twos	E
Gliori, D. No matter what	E	Kalan, R. Jump, frog, jump!	E
Gliori, D. Stormy weather	E	Katz, A. Stalling	E
Gliori, D. The trouble with dragons	E	Katz, K. Ten tiny babies	E
Godwin, L. One moon, two cats	E	Kay, V. Covered wagons, bumpy trails	E
Goembel, P. Animal fair	E	Kay, V. Hornbooks and inkwells	E
Good night, world	E	Kelley, E. A. My life as a chicken	E
Goodhart, P. Three little ghosties	E	Kerr, J. One night in the zoo	E
Goodnight, goodnight, construction site	E	Ketteman, H. Goodnight, Little Monster	E
Gow, N. Ten big toes and a prince's nose	E	Ketteman, H. Swamp song	E
Gralley, J. The moon came down on Milk Street	E	Kimmelman, L. Everybody bonjours!	E
Granstrom, B. Baby knows best	E	Kinerk, R. Clorinda	E
Gravett, E. Dogs	E	The King of Quizzical Island	E
Greenberg, D. Crocs!	E	King, T. A Coyote solstice tale	Fic
Greenberg, D. Enchanted lions	E	Kirk, D. Honk honk! Beep beep!	E
Griffiths, A. The cat on the mat is flat	E	Kirk, D. Keisha Ann can!	E
Guarino, D. Is your mama a llama?	813	Kohuth, J. Duck sock hop	E
Guidone, T. Drum city	E	Kohuth, J. Ducks go vroom	E
Guinea pigs add up	E	Kraus, R. Whose mouse are you?	E
Guthrie, J. Last song	E	Krebs, L. The Beeman	E
Hajdusiewicz, B. B. Sputter, sputter, sput!	E	Kroll, V. L. Everybody has a teddy	E
Hall, M. My heart is like a zoo	E	Krull, K. Fartiste	Fic
Hamanaka, S. All the colors of the earth	813	Kumin, M. Oh, Harry!	E
Hamanaka, S. Grandparents song	E	Kuskin, K. A boy had a mother who bought him a hat	E
Hamilton, K. R. Police officers on patrol	E	Kuskin, K. Green as a bean	E
Hamilton, K. R. Red Truck	E	Lawrence, J. This little chick	E
Hanson, W. Bugtown Boogie	E	Lazo, C. E. Someday when my cat can talk	E
Harley, B. Dirty Joe, the pirate	E	Le Guin, U. K. Cat dreams	E
Harris, J. The belly book	E	Lendroth, S. Ocean wide, ocean deep	E
Harris, T. The clock struck one	E	Lester, A. Noni the pony	E
Harris, T. Tally cat keeps track	E	Leuck, L. One witch	E
Harvey, J. My hands sing the blues	E	Levine, A. A. Monday is one day	E
Harvey, M. Shopping with Dad	E	Lewin, B. Where is Tippy Toes?	E
Hays, A. J. Kindergarten countdown	E	Lewis, J. P. The Fantastic 5 & 10[cents] store	E
Hays, A. J. Smarty Sara	E	Lewis, J. P. The kindergarten cat	E
Heiligman, D. Cool dog, school dog	E	Lewis, J. P. The snowflake sisters	E
Hicks, B. J. Monsters don't eat broccoli	E	Lewis, K. Not inside this house!	E
Hindley, J. Baby talk	E	Light up the night	E
Hip hip hooray! it's Family Day!	E	Lindbergh, R. Homer, the library cat	E
Hip hop dog	E	Lindbergh, R. My hippie grandmother	E
Hoberman, M. A. The two sillies	E	Listen to the silent night	E
Hodgkinson, J. The talent show	E	Lithgow, J. Micawber	E
Hogwash	E	Lobel, A. On Market Street	E
Holub, J. Apple countdown	E	London, J. I'm a truck driver	E
Holub, J. The garden that we grew	E	London, J. A train goes clickety-clack	E

Stringer, Lauren

  (il) Ashman, L. Castles, caves, and honeycombs   **E**

  (il) Orr, W. The princess and her panther   **E**

  (il) Rylant, C. Snow   **E**

  When Stravinsky met Nijinsky   **781.5**

  Winter is the warmest season   **E**

STRIPES -- JUVENILE LITERATURE

  Stockdale, S. Stripes of all types   **591.47**

Stripes of all types. Stockdale, S.   **591.47**

STROKE -- FICTION

  Butler, D. H. My grandpa had a stroke   **E**

  De Paola, T. Now one foot, now the other   **E**

Stroll and walk, babble and talk. Cleary, B. P.   **428**

Strom, Kellie

  Sadie the air mail pilot   **E**

STRONG MEN

  Rubinstein, R. E. Zishe the strongman   **92**

A **strong** right arm: the story of Mamie Peanut Johnson. Green, M. Y.   **92**

Strong stuff. Harris, J.   **398.2**

Strong to the hoop. Coy, J.   **E**

Stronger Than Steel.   **595.4**

Strother, Ruth

  B is for blue planet   **550**

Strother, Scott

  The adventurous book of outdoor games   **796**

Stroud, Bettye

  Belle, the last mule at Gee's Bend   **E**

Stroud, Bettye

  Belle, the last mule at Gee's Bend   **E**

  The patchwork path   **E**

  The Reconstruction era   **973.8**

Struck by lightning! Person, S.   **551.56**

STRUCTURAL ANALYSIS (ENGINEERING)

  See also Structural engineering

STRUCTURAL DESIGN -- JUVENILE LITERATURE

  Fantastic feats and failures   **624**

STRUCTURAL ENGINEERING

  Mason, A. Build it!   **624.1**

STRUCTURAL ENGINEERING

  See also Civil engineering; Engineering

STRUCTURAL FAILURES -- JUVENILE LITERATURE

  Fantastic feats and failures   **624**

STRUCTURAL STEEL

  See also Building materials; Civil engineering; Steel

STRUCTURAL ZOOLOGY *See* Animals -- Anatomy

STRUCTURES *See* Buildings

Strugnell, Ann

  (il) Cameron, A. The stories Julian tells   **Fic**

Stryer, Andrea Stenn

  Kami and the yaks   **E**

Stuart Little. White, E. B.   **Fic**

Stuart-Clark, Christopher

  (ed) The Oxford book of story poems   **808.81**

Stuchner, Joan Betty

  Can hens give milk?   **E**

  Honey cake   **Fic**

Stuck. Jeffers, O.   **E**

Stuck in the mud. Clarke, J.   **E**

Stuck on Earth. Klass, D.   **Fic**

Stuck with the Blooz.   **E**

STUDENT ACHIEVEMENT *See* Academic achievement

STUDENT ACTIVITIES

  See also Students

Student atlas.   **912**

STUDENT GOVERNMENT

  See also School discipline; Schools -- Administration

STUDENT LIFE *See* College students; Students

STUDENT TEACHING

  McKeown, R. Into the classroom   **370.71**

STUDENT TEACHING

  See also Teachers -- Training; Teaching

STUDENT TEACHING -- UNITED STATES

  McKeown, R. Into the classroom   **370.71**

STUDENT VIOLENCE *See* School violence

STUDENTS

  Alexander, S. H. She touched the world: Laura Bridgman, deaf-blind pioneer   **92**

  Gladstone, V. A young dancer   **792.8**

  Glasser, D. New kid, new scene   **373.1**

  Hughes, S. Off to class   **371**

  Ruurs, M. My school in the rain forest   **370.9**

  Thimmesh, C. Girls think of everything   **920**

STUDENTS -- LIBRARY SERVICES

  See also Libraries and schools; Library services; School libraries

STUDENTS' SONGS

  See also Songs

STUDY GUIDES FOR EXAMINATIONS *See* Examinations -- Study guides

STUDY METHODS *See* Study skills

STUDY SKILLS

  Fox, J. S. Get organized without losing it   **371.3**

  Kraus, J. Annie's plan   **371.3**

STUDY SKILLS

  See also Education; Life skills; Teaching

Studying food webs [series]

  Hooks, G. Arctic appetizers   **577.5**

  Hooks, G. Freshwater feeders   **577.6**

  Hooks, G. Makers and takers   **577.7**

  Lundgren, J. K. Desert dinners   **577.5**

  Lundgren, J. K. Forest fare   **577.3**

  Lundgren, J. K. Grassland buffet   **577.4**

Stuey Lewis against all odds.   **Fic**

Stuff! Kroll, S.   **E**

STUFFED BEARS (TOYS) *See* Teddy bears

STUNT FLYING -- FICTION

  Tashjian, J. My life as a stuntboy   **Fic**

STUNT MEN *See* Stunt performers

STUNT PERFORMERS

  Cummins, J. Sam Patch   **92**

  Cummins, J. Women daredevils   **920**

  Van Allsburg, C. Queen of the Falls   **92**

STUNT PERFORMERS

  See also Actors

STUNTS

  Catel, P. Surviving stunts and other amazing feats   **613.6**

Sturges, Philemon

  Down to the sea in ships   **811**

  How do you make a baby smile?   **E**

  I love planes!   **E**

  I love school!   **E**

  I love trains!   **E**

  The Little Red Hen (makes a pizza)   **398.2**

Sturm, James

  Adventures in cartooning   **741.5**

Stutson, Caroline

  Cats' night out   **E**

Stutson, Caroline

  By the light of the Halloween moon   **E**

  Cats' night out   **E**

STUTTERING -- FICTION

  Vawter, V. Paperboy   **Fic**

STYLE IN DRESS *See* Clothing and dress; Costume; Fashion

Su Dongpo. Demi   **92**

Gibbons, G. Marshes & swamps | **577.68**

SWAMPS

   See also Wetlands

SWAMPS -- FICTION

Appelt, K. The true blue scouts of Sugarman Swamp | **Fic**

SWAMPS -- JUVENILE LITERATURE

Gibbons, G. Marshes & swamps | **577.68**

The swamps of Sleethe. Prelutsky, J. | **811**

Swan, Susan

   (il) Bateman, D. M. Out on the prairie | **577.4**

Swans. Helget, N. L. | **598**

SWANS

Helget, N. L. Swans | **598**

SWANS -- FICTION

Christopher, L. Flyaway | **Fic**

Swanson, Diane

   Animal aha! | **590**

   Bugs up close | **595.7**

   Nibbling on Einstein's brain | **500**

   You are weird | **612**

Swanson, Jennifer

   How hybrid cars work | **629.222**

Swanson, Susan Marie

   The first thing my mama told me | **E**

   The house in the night | **E**

   To be like the sun | **E**

Swarmed by bees. Hamilton, S. L. | **595.7**

Swarms. Pipe, J. | **591.5**

Swarner, Kristina

   Greenberg, D. Enchanted lions | **E**

   (il) Schwartz, H. Before you were born | **398.2**

   (il) Schwartz, H. Gathering sparks | **E**

Swartz, Daniel J.

   Bim and Bom | **E**

Swartz, Leslie

Simonds, N. Moonbeams, dumplings & dragon boats | **394.26**

SWASHBUCKLERS *See* Adventure fiction; Adventure films

Swearingen, Greg

   (il) Dakin, G. The Society of Unrelenting Vigilance | **Fic**

   (il) Easton, K. The outlandish adventures of Liberty Aimes | **Fic**

   (il) Williams, T. The dragons of Ordinary Farm | **Fic**

Sweat, Eddie, 1939-1998

         About

Scanlan, L. The big red horse | **798.4**

Sweat, Lynn

   (il) Parish, H. Amelia Bedelia bakes off | **E**

   (il) Parish, H. Go west, Amelia Bedelia! | **E**

   (il) Parish, P. An Amelia Bedelia celebration | **E**

Sweaters. Blaxland, W. | **746.9**

SWEATERS

Blaxland, W. Sweaters | **746.9**

SWEATERS -- FICTION

Jeffers, O. The Hueys in The new sweater | **E**

SWEATERS -- JUVENILE FICTION

Campbell, K. G. Lester's dreadful sweaters | **Fic**

Jeffers, O. The Hueys in The new sweater | **E**

Sweden. Phillips, C. | **948.5**

Sweden. Grahame, D. A. | **948.5**

Sweden. Docalavich, H. | **948.5**

SWEDEN -- JUVENILE LITERATURE

Docalavich, H. Sweden | **948.5**

SWEDISH AMERICANS -- FICTION

Sandin, J. At home in a new land | **E**

SWEDISH LITERATURE

   See also Literature; Scandinavian literature

Sweeney, Alyse

   Toads | **597.8**

Sweeping tsunamis. Spilsbury, L. | **551.46**

Sweet and sunny. Paratore, C. | **Fic**

Sweet Clara and the freedom quilt. Hopkinson, D. | **E**

Sweet dreams lullaby. Snyder, B. E. | **E**

Sweet eats. Dunnington, R. | **641.8**

Sweet land of liberty. Hopkinson, D. | **92**

Sweet music in Harlem. Taylor, D. A. | **E**

Sweet potato pie. Lindsey, K. | **E**

Sweet Thang. Whittenberg, A. | **Fic**

A **sweet** year. Podwal, M. H. | **296.4**

Sweet! Love, A. | **641.8**

Sweet, Melissa

   (il) Best, C. Easy as pie | **E**

   (il) Branzei, S. Adventurers | **920.72**

   (il) Branzei, S. Cowgirls | **920.720**

   (il) Bryant, J. A splash of red | **759.13**

   (il) Elya, S. M. Rubia and the three osos | **398.2**

   (il) Markel, M. Brave girl | **331.892**

Sweet, Melissa

   (il) Appelt, K. Bats around the clock | **E**

   (il) Best, C. Easy as pie | **E**

   (il) Bryant, J. A river of words: the story of William Carlos Williams | **92**

   (il) Choldenko, G. A giant crush | **E**

   (il) Davies, J. The boy who drew birds: a story of John James Audubon | **92**

   (il) Elya, S. M. Rubia and the three osos | **398.2**

   (il) Howe, J. Pinky and Rex | **E**

   (il) Knight, J. Charlotte in Giverny | **Fic**

   (il) Knight, J. Charlotte in London | **Fic**

   (il) Knight, J. Charlotte in New York | **Fic**

   (il) Knight, J. Charlotte in Paris | **Fic**

   (il) Logan, C. The 5,000-year-old puzzle | **932**

   (il) Martin, D. Christmas tree | **E**

   (il) Martin, D. Hanukkah lights | **E**

   (il) Moonlight: the Halloween cat | **E**

   (il) Rupp, R. Weather | **551.6**

   (il) Sierra, J. Schoolyard rhymes | **398.8**

   (il) Sierra, J. Sleepy little alphabet | **E**

Balloons over Broadway | **92**

Carmine | **E**

Tupelo rides the rails | **E**

   (il) Thimmesh, C. Girls think of everything | **920**

   (il) Thimmesh, C. The sky's the limit | **500.8**

   (il) Yolen, J. Baby Bear's books | **E**

The **sweetest** fig. Van Allsburg, C. | **E**

Sweethearts of rhythm. Nelson, M. | **811**

SWEETS *See* Candy; Confectionery

Swender, Jennifer

Jacobs, P. D. Fire drill | **E**

Jacobs, P. D. Putting on a play | **792**

Swerling, Lisa

   (il) Watts, C. The most explosive science book in the universe | **500**

Swett, Sarah

Kids weaving | **746.41**

Swiatkowska, Gabi

   (il) Hosford, K. Infinity and me | **E**

Swiatkowska, Gabriela

   (il) Banks, K. This baby | **E**

   (il) Cooper, I. The golden rule | **E**

   (il) Napoli, D. J. The Earth shook | **E**

   (il) Recorvits, H. My name is Yoon | **E**

   (il) Williams, C. K. A not scary story about big scary things | **E**

Swift, Hildegarde Hoyt

The little red lighthouse and the great gray bridge | **E**

Swifter, higher, stronger. Macy, S. | **796.48**

A **swiftly** tilting planet. L'Engle, M. | **Fic**

Aruego, J. Weird friends   **577.8**
SYMBOLIC LOGIC
    See also Logic; Mathematics
SYMBOLISM
    See also Art; Mythology
SYMBOLISM IN LITERATURE
    See also Literature; Symbolism
SYMBOLS *See* Signs and symbols
Symbols of American freedom [series]
    Staton, H. Ellis Island   **325**
    Staton, H. Independence Hall   **974.8**
    Thomas, W. Mount Rushmore   **978.3**
Symes, R. F.
    Rocks & minerals   **552**
Symes, Ruth
    Harriet dancing   **E**
SYMMETRY
    Kalman, B. What is symmetry in nature?   **570**
    Leedy, L. Seeing symmetry   **516**
    Murphy, S. J. Let's fly a kite   **516**
SYMMETRY -- JUVENILE LITERATURE
    Leedy, L. Seeing symmetry   **516**
    Murphy, S. J. Let's fly a kite   **516**
SYMPATHY
    See also Conduct of life; Emotions
Symphony city.   **E**
A **symphony** of whales. Schuch, S.   **E**
SYNAGOGUES
    Podwal, M. H. Built by angels   **296.4**
SYNAGOGUES
    See also Buildings; Religious institutions; Temples
SYNCHRONIZED SWIMMING
    See also Swimming
SYNESTHESIA -- FICTION
    Parkinson, S. Blue like Friday   **Fic**
Synonyms and antonyms. Heinrichs, A.   **428**
SYNTHETIC DRUGS OF ABUSE *See* Designer drugs
SYNTHETIC FABRICS
    See also Fabrics; Synthetic products
SYNTHETIC FUELS
    See also Fuel; Synthetic products
SYNTHETIC RUBBER
    See also Plastics; Synthetic products
Syren. Sage, A.   **Fic**
SYRUPS
    See also Sugar
SYSTEM THEORY
    See also Science
SYSTEMS ENGINEERING
    See also Automation; Cybernetics; Engineering; Industrial design; System analysis; System theory
Szpirglas, Jeff
    You just can't help it!   **599.9**
Szuc, Jeff
    (il) Kaner, E. Have you ever seen a hippo with sunscreen?   **591.4**

T

T is for terrible. McCarty, P.   **E**
T is for tugboat. Kirk, S.   **623.82**
T-Minus: the race to the moon. Ottaviani, J.   **629.45**
T-SHIRTS
    See also Clothing and dress
T. Rex. French, V.   **567.9**
T. rex and the great extinction. Bacchin, M.   **567.9**
T. Rex and the Mother's Day hug. Grambling, L. G.   **E**

Taback, Simms
    (il) Hall, K. Simms Taback's great big book of spacey, snakey, buggy riddles   **793.73**
    (il) Hall, K. Snakey riddles   **793.73**
    (il) McGovern, A. Too much noise   **398.2**
    I miss you every day   **E**
    Joseph had a little overcoat   **398.2**
    Kibitzers and fools   **398.2**
    Postcards from camp   **Fic**
    Simms Taback's big book of words   **E**
    Simms Taback's city animals   **E**
    Simms Taback's farm animals   **E**
    Simms Taback's Safari animals   **E**
    There was an old lady who swallowed a fly   **782.421**
    This is the house that Jack built   **398.8**
TABLE ETIQUETTE
    Lauber, P. What you never knew about fingers, forks, & chopsticks   **394.1**
TABLE ETIQUETTE
    See also Eating customs; Etiquette
TABLE TALK *See* Conversation
TABLE TENNIS
    See also Ball games
Tabletop scientist [series]
    Parker, S. The science of air   **533**
    Parker, S. The science of water   **532**
TABLEWARE
    Blaxland, W. Knives and forks   **683**
    Blaxland, W. Plates and mugs   **620.1**
    Lauber, P. What you never knew about fingers, forks, & chopsticks   **394.1**
TABLEWARE -- FICTION
    Grey, M. The adventures of the dish and the spoon   **E**
Tabori, Lena
    (ed) The big book for toddlers   **808.8**
Tacang, Brian
    Bully-be-gone   **Fic**
Tacky's Christmas. Lester, H.   **E**
TACTICS
    See also Military art and science; Strategy
Taddeo, John
    Chilman-Blair, K. Medikidz explain ADHD   **616.85**
    Chilman-Blair, K. Medikidz explain autism   **616.85**
    Chilman-Blair, K. Medikidz explain HIV   **616.97**
Tadgell, Nicole
    (il) Birtha, B. Lucky beans   **E**
    (il) Derby, S. No mush today   **E**
    (il) Elvgren, J. R. Josias, hold the book   **E**
    (il) Grigsby, S. In the garden with Dr. Carver   **E**
Tadjo, Veronique
    Talking drums   **808**
Tadpole Rex. Cyrus, K.   **E**
TADPOLES *See* Frogs
Tadpoles [series]
    Blackford, A. Bill's bike   **E**
    Blackford, A. The hungry little monkey   **E**
Tae kwon do. Haney-Withrow, A.   **796.8**
TAE KWON DO
    See also Karate; Martial arts; Self-defense
TAE KWON DO
    Haney-Withrow, A. Tae kwon do   **796.8**
Tafolla, Carmen
    Fiesta babies   **E**
    What can you do with a rebozo?   **E**
Tafuri, Nancy
    All kinds of kisses   **E**
    The big storm   **E**
    Blue Goose   **E**

Thayer, Ernest Lawrence
Gutman, D. Casey back at bat   811
Casey at the bat   811
Ernest L. Thayer's Casey at the bat   811
Thayer, Jane
The popcorn dragon   E
The puppy who wanted a boy   E
Thea's tree. Jackson, A.   E
THEATER
Amendola, D. A day at the New Amsterdam Theatre   792.6
Best, C. Shrinking Violet   E
Blackwood, G. L. Shakespeare's scribe   Fic
De Groat, D. Liar, liar, pants on fire   E
Kenney, K. L. Cool costumes   792
Korman, G. No more dead dogs   Fic
Schumacher, T. L. How does the show go on?   792
THEATER
     See also Amusements; Performing arts
THEATER -- ENGLAND -- LONDON -- HISTORY -- 16TH CENTURY -- JUVENILE LITERATURE
Aliki William Shakespeare & the Globe   792.09
THEATER -- ENGLAND -- LONDON -- HISTORY -- 17TH CENTURY -- JUVENILE LITERATURE
Chrisp, P. Welcome to the Globe   792
THEATER -- FICTION
Federle, T. Better Nate than ever   Fic
THEATER -- PRODUCTION AND DIRECTION
Cox, C. Shakespeare kids   792.9
Jacobs, P. D. Putting on a play   792
Kenney, K. L. Cool productions   792
Kenney, K. L. Cool scripts & acting   792
Underwood, D. Staging a play   792
THEATERS
     See also Buildings; Centers for the performing arts; Theaters
THEATERS -- ENGLAND -- LONDON -- JUVENILE LITERATURE
Chrisp, P. Welcome to the Globe   792
THEATERS -- ENGLAND -- LONDON -- RECONSTRUCTION -- JUVENILE LITERATURE
Aliki William Shakespeare & the Globe   792.09
THEATERS -- STAGE LIGHTING *See* Stage lighting
THEATERS -- STAGE SETTING AND SCENERY
Kenney, K. L. Cool sets & props   792
Kenney, K. L. Cool special effects   792
THEATRICAL COSTUME *See* Costume
THEATRICAL DIRECTORS
Krull, K. Lives of the musicians   780.92
Winter, J. The fabulous feud of Gilbert & Sullivan   E
THEATRICAL MAKEUP
Bliss, J. Preening, painting, and piercing   391
Kenney, K. L. Cool makeup   792
THEATRICAL MAKEUP
     See also Cosmetics; Costume
Thee, Hannah! De Angeli, M. L.   Fic
THEFT
     See also Crime; Offenses against property
THEFT -- FICTION
Amado, E. Tricycle   E
Bromley, A. C. The lunch thief   Fic
Cheshire, S. The pirate's blood and other case files   Fic
Hale, B. Hiss me deadly   Fic
Kelly, D. A. The L.A. Dodger   Fic
Korman, G. Framed   Fic
Korman, G. Zoobreak   Fic
MacDonald, M. R. Tunjur! Tunjur! Tunjur!   398.2
Santopolo, J. The Nina, the Pinta, and the vanishing treasure   Fic

Sheinmel, C. All the things you are   Fic
Teplin, S. The clock without a face   Fic
THEFT -- HISTORY
Guillain, C. Great art thefts   364.16
THEFT -- JUVENILE FICTION
Balliett, B. Hold fast   Fic
Donaldson, J. The Highway Rat   E
Doremus, G. Bear despair   E
Klassen, J. This is not my hat   E
THEISM
     See also Philosophy; Religion; Theology
Thelonious Mouse. Protopopescu, O.   E
Thelonius Monster's sky-high fly pie. Sierra, J.   E
Thematic inquiry through fiction and nonfiction, PreK to grade 6. MacDonell, C.   372
THEME PARKS *See* Amusement parks
THEOCRACY
     See also Church and state; Political science
Theodore. Keating, F.   92
Theodore Boone: kid lawyer. Grisham, J.   Fic
Theodore Boone: the abduction. Grisham, J.   Fic
Theodore Roosevelt. Elish, D.   92
Theodore Roosevelt for kids. Hollihan, K. L.   92
Theodosia and the eyes of Horus. La Fevers, R. L.   Fic
Theodosia and the last pharaoh. La Fevers, R. L.   Fic
Theodosia and the Serpents of Chaos. La Fevers, R. L.   Fic
Theodosia and the Staff of Osiris. La Fevers, R. L.   Fic
THEOLOGIANS
Ellis, S. From reader to writer   028
Jackson Issa, K. Howard Thurman's great hope   92
Michelson, R. As good as anybody: Martin Luther King Jr. and Abraham Joshua Heschel's amazing march toward freedom   92
THEORY OF KNOWLEDGE
     See also Consciousness; Logic; Metaphysics; Philosophy
THEOSOPHY
     See also Mysticism; Religions
THERAPEUTICS
Beccia, C. I feel better with a frog in my throat: history's strangest cures   615.8
THERAPEUTICS
     See also Medicine; Pathology
THERAPEUTICS -- JUVENILE LITERATURE
Beccia, C. I feel better with a frog in my throat: history's strangest cures   615.8
THERAPY *See* Therapeutics
Therapy dog heroes. Bozzo, L.   615.8
THERAPY, PSYCHOLOGICAL *See* Psychotherapy
There. Fitzpatrick   E
There are cats in this book. Schwarz, V.   E
There are no cats in this book! Schwarz, V.   E
There are no scary wolves. Yum, H.   E
There is a carrot in my ear, and other noodle tales. Schwartz, A.   398.2
There is a flower at the tip of my nose smelling me. Walker, A.   811
There was an old lady who swallowed Fly Guy. Arnold, T.   E
There was an old man who painted the sky. Sloat, T.   E
There was an old monster! Emberley, R.   E
There's a barnyard in my bedroom. Suzuki, D. T.   E
There's a frog in my throat. Leedy, L.   428
There's a girl in my hammerlock. Spinelli, J.   Fic
There's a nightmare in my closet. Mayer, M.   E
There's a princess in the palace. Alley, Z. B.   398.2
There's a wolf at the door. Alley, Z. B.   398.2
There's an owl in the shower. George, J. C.   Fic
There's going to be a baby. Burningham, J.   E

Ching, J. Jobs in green travel and tourism — **910.2**
TOURIST TRADE
    See also Commerce
TOURISTS *See* Tourist trade; Travelers
TOURNAMENTS *See* Medieval tournaments; Sports tournaments
Tourville, Amanda Doering
    Littlefield, H. The rooftop adventure of Minnie and Tessa, factory fire survivors — **741.5**
    Ransom, C. F. The lifesaving adventure of Sam Deal, shipwreck rescuer — **741.5**
    Roop, P. The stormy adventure of Abbie Burgess, lighthouse keeper — **741.5**
    Animal invaders — **591.6**
    Exploring the solar system — **523.2**
    A giraffe grows up — **599.63**
Toussaint Louverture, 1743?-1803
    About
    Rockwell, A. F. Open the door to liberty!: a biography of Toussaint L'Ouverture — **92**
Towell, Ann
    Grease town — **Fic**
Towell, Katy
    Skary childrin and the carousel of sorrow — **Fic**
TOWELS -- FICTION
    Mathers, P. Lottie's new beach towel — **E**
Tower of treasure. Chantler, S. — **741.5**
TOWN LIFE *See* City and town life
TOWN MEETING *See* Local government
The **town** mouse and the country mouse. Ward, H. — **E**
Town mouse, country mouse. Country mouse and the city mouse — **398.24**
Townley, Rod
    The blue shoe — **Fic**
    Townley, R. The door in the forest — **Fic**
Townley, Roderick
    The door in the forest — **Fic**
TOWNS *See* Cities and towns
Townsend, John
    Famous forensic cases — **363.2**
Townsend, Michael
    Billy Tartle in Say Cheese! — **E**
    Kit Feeny: on the move — **741.5**
    Kit Feeny: the ugly necklace — **741.5**
    Michael Townsend's amazing Greek myths of wonder and blunders — **292**
    Monkey & Elephant's worst fight ever! — **E**
Townsend, Wendy
    The sundown rule — **Fic**
TOWNSHIP GOVERNMENT *See* Local government
TOXIC PLANTS *See* Poisonous plants
TOXIC SUBSTANCES *See* Hazardous substances; Poisons and poisoning
TOXICOLOGY
    See also Medicine; Pharmacology
TOY AND MOVABLE BOOKS
    Bataille, M. ABC3D — **E**
    Brett, J. Gingerbread baby — **398.2**
    Carle, E. The very clumsy click beetle — **E**
    Carter, D. A. 600 black spots — **E**
    Dodds, D. A. Where's Pup? — **E**
    Ehlert, L. Hands — **E**
    The Enduring Ark — **222**
    Ernst, L. C. The turn-around upside-down alphabet book — **E**
    Horacek, P. One spotted giraffe — **E**
    Klausmeier, J. Open this little book — **E**
    Marceau, F. Panorama — **E**
    Press here — **E**

Sparrow, G. Cosmic! — **520**
Taback, S. Joseph had a little overcoat — **398.2**
Walsh, M. Living with mom and living with dad — **E**
Wickings, R. Pop-up — **070.5**
TOY AND MOVABLE BOOKS
    See also Picture books for children
TOY AND MOVABLE BOOKS -- SPECIMENS
    Brett, J. Gingerbread baby — **398.2**
    Dodds, D. A. Where's Pup? — **E**
    Ehlert, L. Hands — **E**
    Ernst, L. C. The turn-around upside-down alphabet book — **E**
    Greenwood, M. Amazing giant dinosaurs — **567.9**
    Klausmeier, J. Open this little book — **E**
    Taback, S. Joseph had a little overcoat — **398.2**
    What happens next? — **E**
    Who lives here? — **E**
The **toy** boat. De Seve, R. — **E**
Toy dance party. Jenkins, E. — **Fic**
Toy lab. Ross, M. E. — **530**
TOY MAKING
    See also Handicraft
Toy Story. Snider, J. — **741.5**
The **toymaker**. De Quidt, J. — **Fic**
TOYS
    Ehrlich, H. M. Louie's goose — **E**
    Gardner, R. Ace your science project using chemistry magic and toys — **540.7**
    Harbo, C. L. Easy origami toys — **736**
    Hirschmann, K. LEGO toys — **688.7**
    Jackson, P. Origami toys — **736**
    Lewis, K. Good night, Harry — **E**
    Rigsby, M. Amazing rubber band cars — **745.592**
    Ross, M. E. Toy lab — **530**
    Thomson, R. Toys and models — **745.592**
    Whybrow, I. Harry and the dinosaurs say Raahh! — **E**
    Wulffson, D. L. Toys! — **688.7**
TOYS
    See also Amusements
TOYS -- DESIGN AND CONSTRUCTION -- JUVENILE LITERATURE
    Oxlade, C. Gadgets and games — **688.7**
TOYS -- EXPERIMENTS
    Ross, M. E. Toy lab — **530**
TOYS -- FICTION
    Lucy rescued — **E**
    Rosenthal, E. I'll save you Bobo! — **E**
TOYS -- GRAPHIC NOVELS
    Snider, J. Toy Story — **741.5**
TOYS -- JUVENILE FICTION
    Grey, M. Traction Man and the beach odyssey — **E**
    Lane, A. J. B. Stop thief! — **E**
TOYS -- SONGS
    Paxton, T. The marvelous toy — **782.42**
Toys and models. Thomson, R. — **745.592**
Toys come home. Jenkins, E. — **Fic**
Toys go out. Jenkins, E. — **Fic**
Toys! Wulffson, D. L. — **688.7**
Traces. Fox, P. — **E**
Trachtenberg, Stanley
    The Elevator Man — **E**
Track & field. McDougall, C. — **796.42**
Track and field. Gifford, C. — **796.42**
TRACK AND FIELD *See* Track athletics
TRACK AND FIELD -- FICTION
    Cotler, S. Cheesie Mack is running like crazy! — **Fic**
TRACK AND FIELD ATHLETES -- UNITED STATES -- JUVENILE LITERATURE
    Malaspina, A. Touch the sky — **796.42**

Track athletics. Gifford, C. **796.42**

TRACK ATHLETICS
Adler, D. A. A picture book of Jesse Owens **796.42**
Gifford, C. Track and field **796.42**
Gifford, C. Track athletics **796.42**
Marsico, K. Running **796.42**
McDougall, C. Track & field **796.42**
Wade, M. D. Amazing Olympic athlete Wilma Rudolph **92**
Whitfield, S. Simon says gold: Simon Whitfield's pursuit of athletic excellence **92**

TRACK ATHLETICS
See also Athletics; Sports

TRACK ATHLETICS -- BIOGRAPHY
Krull, K. Wilma unlimited: how Wilma Rudolph became the world's fastest woman **92**

TRACK ATHLETICS -- FICTION
Hicks, B. Track attack **Fic**

TRACK ATHLETICS -- JUVENILE LITERATURE
Malaspina, A. Touch the sky **796.42**
Track attack. Hicks, B. **Fic**
Track that scat! **591.47**

TRACKING AND TRAILING
Johnson, J. Animal tracks & signs **590**
Selsam, M. E. Big tracks, little tracks **590**

TRACKING AND TRAILING
See also Hunting

TRACKING AND TRAILING -- JUVENILE LITERATURE
Selsam, M. E. Big tracks, little tracks **590**
Tracking trash. Burns, L. G. **551.46**
Tracks in the snow. Yee, W. H. **E**
Tracks of a panda. Dowson, N. **E**

TRACKS OF ANIMALS See Animal tracks

TRACTION ENGINES See Tractors
Traction Man and the beach odyssey. Grey, M. **E**
Traction Man is here! Grey, M. **E**
Tractors. Lindeen, M. **629.225**

TRACTORS
Lindeen, M. Tractors **629.225**

TRACTORS
See also Agricultural machinery

TRACTORS -- FICTION
Alborough, J. The gobble gobble moooooo tractor book **E**
Burton, V. L. Katy and the big snow **E**
Dobbins, J. Driving my tractor **E**
Long, L. Otis **E**
Long, L. Otis and the tornado **E**

Tracy, Kathleen
We visit Kuwait **953.67**
We visit Saudi Arabia **953.8**

Tracy, Kathleen
Cerberus **398.2**
We visit Cuba **972.91**

Tracy, Kristen
Bessica Lefter bites back **Fic**

Tracy, Kristen
Camille McPhee fell under the bus **Fic**
The reinvention of Bessica Lefter **Fic**

TRADE See Business; Commerce
Trade and commerce in the early Islamic world. Lassieur, A. **381.09**

TRADE ROUTES
See also Commerce; Commercial geography; Transportation

TRADE ROUTES -- FICTION
Kang, H. Chengli and the Silk Road caravan **Fic**

TRADE SECRETS
See also Right of privacy; Unfair competition

TRADE-UNIONS See Labor unions

TRADEMARKS
See also Commerce; Manufactures

TRADES See Industrial arts; Occupations

TRADITIONAL MEDICINE
See also Medicine; Popular medicine

TRADITIONS See Folklore; Legends; Manners and customs; Rites and ceremonies; Superstition

TRAFFIC ACCIDENTS -- FICTION
Newbery, L. Lost boy **Fic**
Pyron, B. A dog's way home **Fic**
Scieszka, J. Uh-oh Max **E**

TRAFFIC ENGINEERING
See also Engineering; Highway engineering; Transportation

Trafton, Jennifer
The rise and fall of Mount Majestic **Fic**
The tragic tale of Narcissa Whitman and a faithful history of the Oregon Trail. Harness, C. **92**
Trail. Pelham, D. **E**
The Trail of Tears. Bruchac, J. **970.004**
The Trail of Tears. Bjornlund, L. D. **970.004**

TRAIL OF TEARS, 1838
Bruchac, J. The Trail of Tears **970.004**

TRAIL RIDING
See also Horsemanship
Trailblazer biography [series]
Brill, M. T. Marshall Major Taylor **92**

TRAILER CAMPS -- FICTION
Ransom, C. Rebel McKenzie **Fic**

TRAILING See Tracking and trailing

TRAILS
See also Roads
A train goes clickety-clack. London, J. **E**
Train trip. Caswell, D. **E**
Training for sports [series]
Mason, P. Improving endurance **613.7**
Mason, P. Improving flexibility **613.7**
Mason, P. Improving speed **613.7**
Mason, P. Improving strength & power **613.7**
Trains. Lindeen, M. **625.1**
Trains. Curlee, L. **385**

TRAINS See Railroads
Trains. Barton, B. **625.1**
Trains go. Light, S. **E**
Trains on the move. Clark, W. **625.1**
Trains: a pop-up railroad book. Crowther, R. **625.1**
Trainstop. Lehman, B. **E**
The traitor. Yep, L. **Fic**
Traitor's gate. Avi **Fic**

TRAITORS -- FICTION
Avi Sophia's war **Fic**

Trammel, Howard K.
The solar system **523.2**
Wildfires **634.9**

TRAMPOLINES AND TRAMPOLINING -- FICTION
Brown, P. The fabulous bouncing Chowder **E**

TRAMPS
See also Homeless persons; Poor

TRAMPS -- FICTION
The family under the bridge **Fic**
Sweet, M. Tupelo rides the rails **E**

TRANSACTIONAL ANALYSIS
See also Psychotherapy

TRANSATLANTIC FLIGHTS See Aeronautics -- Flights

TRANSATLANTIC FLIGHTS -- JUVENILE LITERATURE
Burleigh, R. Night flight **629.13**

Jeffers, O. The great paper caper   **E**
Klise, K. Regarding the trees   **Fic**
Martin, D. Christmas tree   **E**
McMillan, B. How the ladies stopped the wind   **E**
Muldrow, D. We planted a tree   **E**
Obed, E. B. Who would like a Christmas tree?   **E**
Oldland, N. Big bear hug   **E**
Rawlinson, J. Fletcher and the falling leaves   **E**
Ray, M. L. Christmas farm   **E**
Reid, B. Picture a tree   **E**
Rocklin, J. One day and one amazing morning on Orange Street   **Fic**
Rodman, M. A. A tree for Emmy   **E**
Shelby, A. The man who lived in a hollow tree   **E**
Simpson, L. Yuvi's candy tree   **E**
Smith, L. The inside tree   **E**
Thompson, L. The apple pie that Papa baked   **E**
Udry, J. M. A tree is nice   **E**
Wahl, J. The golden Christmas tree   **E**
Ward, J. The busy tree   **E**
Zolotow, C. The beautiful Christmas tree   **E**
TREES -- JUVENILE FICTION
Arnold, T. Dirty Gert   **E**
De Lint, C. The tangled tale of a circle of cats   **Fic**
Happy birthday, Tree   **E**
Reid, B. Picture a tree   **E**
Yoon, S. Penguin and Pinecone   **E**
TREES -- JUVENILE LITERATURE
Florian, D. Poetrees   **811**
Gerber, C. Leaf jumpers   **E**
Preus, M. Celebritrees   **582.16**
TREES -- JUVENILE POETRY
George, K. O. Old Elm speaks   **811**
TREES -- POETRY
Florian, D. Poetrees   **811**
Frost, R. Birches   **811**
George, K. O. Old Elm speaks   **811**
The **trees** of the dancing goats. Polacco, P.   **E**
Trees, weeds, and vegetables--so many kinds of plants! Wade, M. D.   **580**
Trelease, Jim
(ed) Hey! listen to this   **028.5**
The read-aloud handbook   **028.5**
Tremaine, Jon
Magic with numbers   **793.8**
Magical illusions   **793.8**
Paper tricks   **793.8**
Pocket tricks   **793.8**
Tremendous tunnels. Graham, I.   **624.1**
TRENT AFFAIR, 1861
See also United States -- History -- 1861-1865, Civil War
TRENTON (N.J.), BATTLE OF, 1776
Murphy, J. The crossing   **973.3**
TRENTON (N.J.), BATTLE OF, 1776 -- FICTION
Scieszka, J. Oh say, I can't see   **Fic**
Tresselt, Alvin R.
Hide and seek fog   **E**
White snow, bright snow   **E**
Trevino, Elizabeth Borton de
I, Juan de Pareja   **Fic**
Trewin, Trudie
I lost my kisses   **E**
TRIALS (HOMICIDE)
Coleman, W. Racism on trial   **345**
TRIALS (MURDER) *See* Trials (Homicide)
TRIALS (POLITICAL CRIMES AND OFFENSES) -- NEW YORK (STATE) -- JUVENILE LITERATURE

Heart on fire   **E**
TRIALS -- FICTION
Buckley, M. Tales from the hood   **Fic**
Davies, J. The lemonade crime   **Fic**
Giovanni, N. The grasshopper's song   **E**
Thompson, P. B. The devil's door   **Fic**
TRIALS -- JUVENILE LITERATURE
Roach, M. K. In the days of the Salem witchcraft trials   **133.4**
TRIANGLE
See also Geometry; Shape
Triangles. Loughrey, A.   **516**
TRIASSIC PERIOD
Bonner, H. When dinos dawned, mammals got munched, and Pterosaurs took flight   **567.9**
TRIATHLETES
Whitfield, S. Simon says gold: Simon Whitfield's pursuit of athletic excellence   **92**
TRIATHLON
See also Sports
TRIBAL GOVERNMENT
See also Political science; Tribes
TRIBES
See also Clans; Family
TRICERATOPS
See also Dinosaurs
Trick of the eye. Vry, S.   **152.14**
Trick of the tale.   **398.2**
Trick or treat, Old Armadillo. Brimner, L. D.   **E**
Trick or treat, smell my feet. De Groat, D.   **E**
Trick or treat? Martin, B.   **E**
Tricking the Tallyman. Davies, J.   **E**
TRICKS
See also Amusements
Trickster: Native American tales.   **398.2**
TRICKSTERS
Aylesworth, J. The tale of Tricky Fox   **398.2**
TRICKSTERS -- FOLKLORE
Souhami, J. Foxy!   **E**
Tricky behavior. Pryor, K. J.   **591.47**
Tricky tree frogs. Lunis, N.   **597.8**
Tricycle. Amado, E.   **E**
TRICYCLES
See also Vehicles
TRIGONOMETRY
See also Geometry; Mathematics
TRILLION (THE NUMBER)
Schwartz, D. M. How much is a million?   **513**
TRILLION (THE NUMBER) -- JUVENILE LITERATURE
Adler, D. A. Millions, billions & trillions   **E**
Triple-dare to be scared. San Souci, R.   **S**
TRIPLETS
See also Multiple birth; Siblings
TRIPLETS -- FICTION
Jenkins, E. Daffodil, crocodile   **E**
Tripp, Irving
Stanley, J. Little Lulu, vol. 1: My dinner with Lulu   **741.5**
Tripp, Jenny
Pete & Fremont   **Fic**
Pete's disappearing act   **Fic**
Triumph on Everest: a photobiography of Sir Edmund Hillary. Coburn, B.   **92**
Trivas, Irene
(il) Blume, J. The Pain and the Great One   **E**
Trivas, Tracy
The wish stealers   **Fic**
TRIVIA *See* Curiosities and wonders; Questions and answers
Trivizas, Eugene
The three little wolves and the big bad pig   **398.24**

About

Krull, K. Lives of extraordinary women   **920**

U

U'Ren, Andrea
(il) DeFelice, C. C. One potato, two potato   **E**
(il) Kimmel, E. A. Stormy's hat   **E**
(il) Moss, M. The bravest woman in America   **92**
(il) Schubert, L. Feeding the sheep   **E**
Mary Smith

U.S. STATES -- MISCELLANEA -- JUVENILE LITERA-TURE
Leedy, L. Celebrate the 50 states   **973**

Ubiquitous.   **811**

Uchida, Yoshiko
The best bad thing   **Fic**
The bracelet   **E**
A jar of dreams   **Fic**
Journey to Topaz   **Fic**

Udry, Janice May
The moon jumpers   **E**
A tree is nice   **E**

Uegaki, Chieri
Rosie and Buttercup   **E**
Suki's kimono   **E**

Uff, Caroline
(il) Doyle, M. Get happy   **E**

Uganda. Barlas, R.   **967.61**

Ugliano, Natascia
(il) Jules, J. Abraham's search for God   **222**
(il) Jules, J. Benjamin and the silver goblet   **222**
(il) Jules, J. Miriam in the desert   **222**
(il) Jules, J. Sarah laughs   **222**

The uglified ducky. Claflin, W.   **E**
The ugly dinosaur. Bardoe, C.   **E**
The ugly duckling. Andersen, H. C.   **E**
The ugly duckling. Braun, S.   **E**
The ugly duckling. Isadora, R.   **E**
The ugly duckling. Mitchell, S.   **E**
The ugly duckling. Pinkney, J.   **E**
The ugly duckling. Watts, B.   **E**
Ugly Pie. Wheeler, L.   **E**

Uh-oh Cleo [series]
Harper, J. Underpants on my head   **Fic**

Uh-oh Max. Scieszka, J.   **E**
Uh-oh! DePalma, M. N.   **E**
Uh-oh! Isadora, R.   **E**
Uh-oh, Cleo. Harper, J.   **Fic**
Uh-oh, dodo!   **E**

Uhlberg, Myron
Dad, Jackie, and me   **E**
A storm called Katrina   **E**

Uhlich, Gerald R.
Hatkoff, J. Knut   **599.78**

Uhlman, Tom
(il) Carson, M. K. The bat scientists   **599.4**
(il) Carson, M. K. Emi and the rhino scientist   **599.66**
(il) Rusch, E. Eruption!   **363.34**

UIGHUR (TURKIC PEOPLE) -- FICTION
La Valley, J. The Vine basket   **Fic**

Ukraine. Bassis, V.   **947.7**

Ulmer, Wendy K.
A isn't for fox   **E**

Ulrich, George
(il) Murphy, S. J. Divide and ride   **513**

Ulriksen, Mark

(il) Winthrop, E. The biggest parade   **E**

The ultimate 10. Natural disasters [series]
Stewart, M. Blizzards and winter storms   **551.55**

The ultimate dinopedia. Lessem, D.   **567.9**
Ultimate fighting. Wiseman, B.   **796.8**
Ultimate guide to baseball. Buckley, J.   **796.357**
Ultimate guide to football. Buckley, J.   **796.332**
The ultimate guide to grandmas and grandpas. Jones, S. L.   **E**
The ultimate guide to your microscope. Levine, S.   **502.8**
The ultimate indoor games book. Gunter, V. A.   **793**
Ultimate trains. McMahon, P.   **385**

ULTRASONIC WAVES
See also Sound waves; Ultrasonics

ULTRASONICS
See also Sound

Uluru, Australia's Aboriginal heart. Arnold, C.   **994**

Ulysses Moore [series]
Baccalario, P. The door to time   **Fic**
Baccalario, P. The long-lost map   **Fic**

Uman, Jennifer
(il) Jemmy button   **E**

Umansky, Kaye
Clover Twig and the magical cottage   **Fic**
Solomon Snow and the stolen jewel   **Fic**

The umbrella. Schubert, I.   **E**
Umbrella. Iwamatsu, A. J.   **E**
The Umbrella Queen. Bridges, S. Y.   **E**
Umbrella summer. Graff, L.   **Fic**

UMBRELLAS AND PARASOLS
See also Clothing and dress

UMBRELLAS AND PARASOLS -- FICTION
Bridges, S. Y. The Umbrella Queen   **E**
Franson, S. E. Un-brella   **E**
Iwamatsu, A. J. Umbrella   **E**
Liu, J. S. Yellow umbrella   **E**
Na, I. S. The thingamabob   **E**
Schubert, I. The umbrella   **E**

Un-brella. Franson, S. E.   **E**
The un-forgotten coat. Cottrell Boyce, F.   **Fic**
UnBEElievables. Florian, D.   **811**
Unbored. Glenn, J.   **790**

UNBORN CHILD See Fetus

Unbuilding. Macaulay, D.   **690**
Uncle Andy's. Warhola, J.   **E**
Uncle Bobby's wedding. Brannen, S. S.   **E**
Uncle Elephant. Lobel, A.   **E**
Uncle Jed's barbershop. Mitchell, M. K.   **E**
Uncle monarch and the Day of the Dead. Goldman, J.   **E**
Uncle Montague's tales of terror. Priestley, C.   **S**
Uncle Nacho's hat. Rohmer, H.   **398.2**
Uncle Peter's amazing Chinese wedding. Look, L.   **E**
Uncle Pirate. Rees, D.   **Fic**
Uncle Pirate to the rescue. Rees, D.   **Fic**
Uncle Rain Cloud. Johnston, T.   **E**
Uncle Remus, the complete tales. Lester, J.   **398.2**
Uncle Wally's old brown shoe. Edwards, W.   **E**
Uncle Willie and the soup kitchen. DiSalvo, D.   **E**

UNCLES
Hartfield, C. Me and Uncle Romie   **E**
Henkes, K. The birthday room   **Fic**
Horvath, P. Everything on a waffle   **Fic**
Johnston, T. Uncle Rain Cloud   **E**

UNCLES
See also Family

UNCLES -- FICTION
Lacey, J. Island of Thieves   **Fic**

UNCLES -- JUVENILE FICTION
Schwartz, A. Willie and Uncle Bill   **E**

UNITED STATES -- HISTORY -- 1861-1865, CIVIL WAR -- BIOGRAPHY

Freedman, R. Abraham Lincoln and Frederick Douglass   **973.709**

UNITED STATES -- HISTORY -- 1861-1865, CIVIL WAR -- BIOGRAPHY

See also Biography

UNITED STATES -- HISTORY -- 1861-1865, CIVIL WAR -- HISTORIOGRAPHY

See also Historiography

UNITED STATES -- HISTORY -- 1861-1865, CIVIL WAR -- JUVENILE FICTION

Cole, H. Unspoken   **E**
Lyons, K. S. Hope's gift   **E**
Tarrant-Reid, L. Discovering Black America   **973**

UNITED STATES -- HISTORY -- 1861-1865, CIVIL WAR -- JUVENILE LITERATURE

Murphy, J. The boys' war   **973.7**

UNITED STATES -- HISTORY -- 1861-1865, CIVIL WAR -- MEDICAL CARE

See also Medical care

UNITED STATES -- HISTORY -- 1861-1865, CIVIL WAR -- PEACE -- JUVENILE LITERATURE

Benoit, P. The surrender at Appomattox   **973.7**

UNITED STATES -- HISTORY -- 1861-1865, CIVIL WAR -- PERSONAL NARRATIVES

See also Autobiographies; Biography

UNITED STATES -- HISTORY -- 1861-1865, CIVIL WAR -- RECONSTRUCTION *See* Reconstruction (1865-1876)

UNITED STATES -- HISTORY -- 18TH CENTURY -- FICTION

Bruchac, J. The arrow over the door   **Fic**

UNITED STATES -- HISTORY -- 19TH CENTURY

Explore the wild west!   **978**

UNITED STATES -- HISTORY -- JUVENILE LITERATURE

Rubel, D. Scholastic encyclopedia of the presidents and their times   **973**

UNITED STATES -- HISTORY -- MISCELLANEA -- JUVENILE LITERATURE

Leacock, E. Places in time   **911**

UNITED STATES -- HISTORY -- POETRY

I, too, am America   **811**

UNITED STATES -- HISTORY -- REVOLUTION, 1775-1783 -- BIOGRAPHY -- JUVENILE LITERATURE

Fritz, J. Why not, Lafayette?   **973.3**
Rockwell, A. F. They called her Molly Pitcher   **973.3**

UNITED STATES -- IMMIGRATION AND EMIGRATION

See also Americanization; Immigration and emigration

UNITED STATES -- IMMIGRATION AND EMIGRATION -- JUVENILE LITERATURE

I was dreaming to come to America   **304.8**
Murphy, J. Across America on an emigrant train   **385**

UNITED STATES -- JUVENILE POETRY

Bates, K. L. America the beautiful   **811**
My America   **811**
Myers, C. We are America   **811**

UNITED STATES -- MAPS

See also Atlases; Maps

UNITED STATES -- MILITARY HISTORY

See also Military history

UNITED STATES -- MISCELLANEA -- JUVENILE LITERATURE

Leedy, L. Celebrate the 50 states   **973**

UNITED STATES -- NATIONAL CHARACTERISTICS

See American national characteristics

UNITED STATES -- NATIONAL PARKS AND RESERVES

See National parks and reserves -- United States

UNITED STATES -- POLITICS AND GOVERNMENT

See also Political science; Politics; Public administration

UNITED STATES -- POPULATION

See also Population

UNITED STATES -- PRESIDENTS *See* Presidents -- United States

UNITED STATES -- RACE RELATIONS

See also Race relations

UNITED STATES -- RELIGION

See also Religion

UNITED STATES -- STATE GOVERNMENTS *See* State governments

UNITED STATES -- STATISTICS

See also Statistics

United States Holocaust Memorial Museum

Bachrach, S. D. Tell them we remember   **940.53**
Volavkova, H. --I never saw another butterfly--   **741.9**

UNITED STATES IN ART

Raczka, B. The art of freedom   **704.9**

UNITED STATES. ARMY

See also Armies; Military history; United States -- Armed forces

UNITED STATES. ARMY -- BIOGRAPHY

See also Biography

UNITED STATES. ARMY -- MILITARY LIFE

See also Military personnel; Soldiers

UNITED STATES. ARMY -- OFFICERS

See also Military personnel; Soldiers

UNITED STATES. ARMY -- PARACHUTE TROOPS

See also Parachute troops

UNITED STATES. ARMY -- SONGS

See also Songs

UNITED STATES. NAVY -- BIOGRAPHY

See also Biography

UNITED STATES. SUPREME COURT -- BIOGRAPHY

See also Biography

The United States: past and present [series]

Bailey, D. Kansas   **978.1**
Brezina, C. Arizona   **979.1**
Brezina, C. Indiana   **977.2**
Brezina, C. New Mexico   **978.9**
Bringle, J. Nebraska   **978.2**
Byers, A. West Virginia   **975.4**
Byers, A. Wyoming   **978.7**
Casil, A. S. Mississippi   **976.2**
Ching, J. Utah   **979.2**
Ciarleglio, L. New Hampshire   **974.2**
Cook, C. Kentucky   **976.9**
DaSilva-Gordon, M. Puerto Rico   **972.95**
Dorman, R. L. Oklahoma   **976.6**
Freedman, J. Iowa   **977.7**
Freedman, J. Louisiana   **976.3**
Freedman, J. Massachusetts   **974.4**
Furgang, A. Rhode Island   **974.5**
Harmon, D. Minnesota   **977.6**
Harmon, D. South Carolina   **975.7**
Harmon, D. Washington   **979.7**
Hasan, H. Pennsylvania   **974.8**
Heos, B. Alabama   **976.1**
Heos, B. Colorado   **978.8**
Heos, B. Wisconsin   **977.5**
La Bella, L. California   **979.4**
La Bella, L. Connecticut   **974.6**
Levy, J. Arkansas   **976.7**
Levy, J. Michigan   **977.4**
Lew, K. North Carolina   **975.6**
Lew, K. Ohio   **977.1**

Hound dog true **Fic**
Mouse was mad **E**

URBANIZATION

See also Cities and towns; Rural sociology; Social change; Social conditions; Urban sociology

Urbanovic, Jackie

(il) Kimmel, E. C. Glamsters **E**
(il) Prelutsky, J. I've lost my hippopotamus **811**
(il) Sayre, A. P. If you're hoppy **E**
Duck at the door **E**
Sitting duck **E**

Urberuaga, Emilio

(il) Lindo, E. Manolito Four-Eyes **Fic**

Urbigkit, Cat

Brave dogs, gentle dogs **636.7**
The guardian team **636.7**
Path of the pronghorn **599.65**
The shepherd's trail **636.3**
A young shepherd **636.3**

Urdahl, Catherine

Polka-dot fixes kindergarten **E**

URINARY ORGANS -- JUVENILE LITERATURE

Gold, S. D. Learning about the digestive and excretory systems **612.3**

URINE -- JUVENILE LITERATURE

The Scoop on Poop **E**

Urrutia, MarÃa Cristina

Who will save my planet? **304.2**

Ursell, Martin

(il) Lister, A. The Ice Age tracker's guide **569**

Ursu, Anne

Breadcrumbs **Fic**
The Real Boy **Fic**

Uruguay. Jermyn, L. **989.5**

The US Civil War and Reconstruction. Howell, B. **973.8**

USEFUL INSECTS *See* Beneficial insects

USER GENERATED CONTENT

Mills, J. E. Creating content **006.7**

Usher, Mark David

The golden ass of Lucius Apuleius **Fic**

Using alternative energies. Farrell, C. **333.79**

Using digital images. Rabbat, S. **775**

Using Earth's underground heat. White, N. **333.8**

Using energy. Hewitt, S. **333.79**

Using picture books to teach [series]

Hall, S. Using picture storybooks to teach literary devices **016**

Using picture storybooks to teach literary devices. Hall, S. **016**

Using poetry across the curriculum. Chatton, B. **372.6**

Using WEB 2.0 tools in the K-12 classroom. Crane, B. E. **371.3**

Using your research. Ollhoff, J. **929**

Utah. Stefoff, R. **979.2**

Utah. Ching, J. **979.2**

Utah. Kent, D. **979.2**

UTE INDIANS -- FICTION

Ramthun, B. The White Gates **Fic**
Wyss, T. H. Bear dancer **Fic**

UTE INDIANS -- FOLKLORE

Stevens, J. Coyote steals the blanket **398.2**

UTE INDIANS -- LEGENDS -- JUVENILE LITERATURE

Stevens, J. Coyote steals the blanket **398.2**

UTENSILS, KITCHEN *See* Kitchen utensils

UTILITARIANISM

See also Ethics

UTILITIES, PUBLIC *See* Public utilities

UTILIZATION OF WASTE *See* Salvage

UTOPIAN FICTION

See also Fantasy fiction; Science fiction

UTOPIAS

See also Political science; Socialism

Utterly me, Clarice Bean. Child, L. **Fic**
Utterly otterly day. Casanova, M. **E**
Utterly otterly night. Casanova, M. **E**

Uttley, Colin

Magnesium **546**

V

Vālmīki -- Adaptations

Arni, S. Sita's Ramayana **741.5**

Vacation. Harrison, D. L. **811**

A vacation for Pooch. Cocca-Leffler, M. **E**

VACATION HOMES

See also Houses

VACATIONS

Enright, E. Gone-Away Lake **Fic**

VACATIONS

See also Recreation

VACATIONS -- FICTION

Chitty Chitty Bang Bang flies again **Fic**

VACATIONS -- JUVENILE FICTION

Charlie Joe Jackson's guide to summer vacation **Fic**
Cocca-Leffler, M. A vacation for Pooch **E**
Lulu and the dog from the sea **Fic**

VACATIONS -- POETRY

Harrison, D. L. Vacation **811**

VACCINATION

See also Immunization; Preventive medicine; Public health

VACUUM TUBES

See also Electronic apparatus and appliances

Vail, Rachel

Avi Never mind! **Fic**
Jibberwillies at night **E**
Justin Case **Fic**
Righty & Lefty **E**
Sometimes I'm Bombaloo **E**

Vainio, Pirkko

(il) Andersen, H. C. The nightingale **E**
(il) Andersen, H. C. The ugly duckling **E**
Who hid the Easter eggs? **E**

Valat, Pierre-Marie

(il) Inside the body **611**

Valckx, Catharina

Lizette's green sock **E**

Valdivia, Paloma

Up above and down below **E**

Valente, Catherynne M.

The girl who circumnavigated Fairyland in a ship of her own making **Fic**
The girl who fell beneath Fairyland and led the revels there **Fic**

Valentine be mine. **E**

VALENTINE DECORATIONS -- JUVENILE LITERATURE

Owen, R. Valentine's Day origami **736**

Valentine surprise. Demas, C. **E**

VALENTINE'S DAY

McGee, R. Paper crafts for Valentine's Day **745.594**
Otto, C. Celebrate Valentine's Day **394.26**
The yuckiest, stinkiest, best Valentine ever **E**

VALENTINE'S DAY

See also Holidays

VALENTINE'S DAY -- FICTION

Carlson, N. L. Henry and the Valentine surprise **E**
Choldenko, G. A giant crush **E**
De Groat, D. Roses are pink, your feet really stink **E**

VAUDEVILLE
    See also Amusements; Theater

VAUDEVILLE -- FICTION
    Long, E. The Wing Wing brothers math spectacular! 372.7
    Phelan, M. Bluffton   Fic

Vaughan, Carolyn
    Invitation to ballet   792.8

Vaughan, Marcia
    Irena's jars of secrets   92

Vaughn, Jen
    (il) Mooney, C. The Industrial Revolution   330.9

Vaughn, Marcia
    Irena's jars of secrets   92

Vaupel, Robin
    The rules of the universe by Austin W. Hale   Fic

Vawter, Vince
    Paperboy   Fic

VEDANTA
    See also Hinduism; Theosophy

VEDAS
    See also Hinduism; Sacred books

VEGETABLE CARVING -- JUVENILE LITERATURE
    Freymann, S. How are you peeling?   152.4

VEGETABLE GARDENING
    Cherry, L. How Groundhog's garden grew   E
    Creasy, R. Blue potatoes, orange tomatoes   635
    First garden   712
    Grow it, cook it   635
    Hirsch, R. E. Growing your own garden   635
    Malam, J. Grow your own sandwich   635
    Malam, J. Grow your own smoothie   634
    Malam, J. Grow your own snack   641.3
    Malam, J. Grow your own soup   635

VEGETABLE GARDENING
    See also Gardening; Horticulture

VEGETABLE GARDENING -- FICTION
    Milway, K. S. The good garden   Fic

VEGETABLE GARDENING -- JUVENILE LITERATURE
    Creasy, R. Blue potatoes, orange tomatoes   635
    Ehlert, L. Growing vegetable soup   635
    What's in the garden?   635

VEGETABLE KINGDOM *See* Botany; Plants

VEGETABLE OILS *See* Essences and essential oils; Oils
    and fats

VEGETABLES
    Cleary, B. P. Green beans, potatoes, and even tomatoes 641.3
    Creasy, R. Blue potatoes, orange tomatoes   635
    Ehlert, L. Eating the alphabet   411
    Gibbons, G. The vegetables we eat   635
    Llewellyn, C. Cooking with fruits and vegetables   641.3
    McMillan, B. Growing colors   535.6
    Mora, P. Yum! mmmm! que rico!   811
    Sayre, A. P. Rah, rah, radishes!   641.3
    Siminovich, L. I like vegetables   E

VEGETABLES
    See also Food; Plants

VEGETABLES -- FICTION
    Kel Gilligan's daredevil stunt show   E
    Young, C. A few bites   E

VEGETABLES -- FOLKLORE
    Paye The talking vegetables   398.2

VEGETABLES -- JUVENILE LITERATURE
    Creasy, R. Blue potatoes, orange tomatoes   635
    Ehlert, L. Eating the alphabet   411
    McMillan, B. Growing colors   535.6
    The **vegetables** we eat. Gibbons, G.   635

VEGETARIAN COOKERY *See* Vegetarian cooking

VEGETARIAN COOKING

    Delicious vegetarian main dishes   641.5
    Katzen, M. Honest pretzels   641.5

VEGETARIAN COOKING
    See also Cooking

VEGETARIAN COOKING -- JUVENILE LITERATURE
    Delicious vegetarian main dishes   641.5

VEGETARIANISM
    See also Diet

VEHICLES
    Arlon, P. Emergency vehicles   629.04
    Biggs, B. Everything goes: On land   629
    Cooper, W. On the road   629.2
    Coppendale, J. The great big book of mighty machines 621.8
    Ganeri, A. Things that go   629
    Mortensen, D. D. Good night engines   E
    Parker, V. How heavy is heavy?   530.8
    Rex, M. Truck Duck   E
    Rockwell, A. F. Big wheels   E
    Smith, M. Speed machines   629.2
    Vetter, J. R. Down by the station   782.42

VEHICLES
    See also Transportation

VEHICLES -- FICTION
    Blechman, N. Night light   E
    Clement, N. Job site   E
    Dempsey, K. Mini racer   E
    Kirk, D. Honk honk! Beep beep!   E
    Mortensen, D. D. Good night engines   E
    Niemann, C. That's how!   E
    Rex, M. Truck Duck   E
    Sierra, J. Preschool to the rescue   E
    Stein, P. Cars galore   E
    Timmers, L. Who is driving?   E
    Wolf, S. Truck stuck   E

VEHICLES -- JUVENILE FICTION
    Low, W. Machines go to work in the city   E

VEHICLES -- JUVENILE LITERATURE
    Low, W. Machines go to work   621.8

VEHICLES IN ART
    Ames, L. J. Draw 50 boats, ships, trucks & trains   743

Veitch, Catherine
    Dancing   792.8
    Gymnastics   796.44
    Sound and hearing   612.8

Velasquez, Eric
    (il) Boswell, A. K. The rain stomper   E
    (il) Brewster, H. The other Mozart   92
    (il) Dant, T. Some kind of love   811
    (il) Fradin, D. B. The price of freedom   973.7
    (il) Krull, K. Houdini   92
    (il) Malaspina, A. Touch the sky   796.42
    (il) Michelson, R. Twice as good   796.352
    (il) My Uncle Martin's words of love for America   323.1
    (il) Naidoo, B. Journey to Jo'burg   Fic
    (il) Soto, G. The skirt   Fic
    Grandma's gift   E
    (il) Tuck, P. M. As fast as words could fly   Fic
    (il) Watkins, A. F. My Uncle Martin's big heart   92
    (il) Weatherford, C. B. Racing against the odds   92

Veláquez, Diego, 1599-1660
    Venezia, M. Diego Velazquez   92

Veláquez, Diego, 1599-1660
    Fiction
    Trevino, E. B. d. I, Juan de Pareja   Fic

Veldkamp, Tjibbe
    Tom the tamer   E

Velma Gratch & the way cool butterfly. Madison, A.   E

VELOCIRAPTORS

The tenth good thing about Barney   E

VIPERS *See* Snakes

Virgie goes to school with us boys. Howard, E. F.   E

Virginia. Kent, D.   **975.5**

Virginia. Porterfield, J.   **975.5**

Virginia. King, D. C.   **975.5**

Virginia Hamilton: speeches, essays, and conversations. Hamilton, V.   **813**

Virginia Shin-Mui Loh
   (jt. auth) James, H. F. Paper son   **Fic**

Virginia Wolf.   **Fic**

Virginia, 1607-1776. Pobst, S.   **975.5**

VIROLOGY
   See also Microbiology

VIRTUAL LIBRARIES *See* Digital libraries

VIRTUAL REALITY -- FICTION
   Cole, S. Z. Raptor   **Fic**
   Cole, S. Z. Rex   **Fic**

VIRTUE
   See also Conduct of life; Ethics; Human behavior

VIRUS DISEASES -- JUVENILE LITERATURE
   Faulk, M. The case of the flesh-eating bacteria   **616.5**
   Piddock, C. Outbreak   **614.4**

VIRUSES
   Berger, M. Germs make me sick!   **616.9**
   Ollhoff, J. The flu   **616.2**

VIRUSES
   See also Microorganisms

VIRUSES -- FICTION
   Alda, A. Iris has a virus   **E**
   Myklusch, M. The secret war   **Fic**

VIRUSES -- JUVENILE LITERATURE
   Berger, M. Germs make me sick!   **616.9**

Vischer, Frans
   Fuddles   **E**

The **Visconti** house. Edgar, E.   **Fic**

Visconti, Guido
   Clare and Francis   **271**

VISCOSITY
   See also Hydrodynamics; Mechanics

VISION
   Boothroyd, J. What is sight?   **612.8**
   Cobb, V. Open your eyes   **612.8**
   Hewitt, S. Look here!   **612.8**
   Markle, S. Lost sight   **617.7**
   Simon, S. Eyes and ears   **612.8**

VISION
   See also Optics; Senses and sensation

VISION -- FICTION
   Kostecki-Shaw, J. S. My travelin' eye   **E**

VISION DISORDERS
   Close, C. Chuck Close   **759.13**

VISION DISORDERS
   See also Vision

VISION DISORDERS -- FICTION
   Dorris, M. Sees Behind Trees   **Fic**
   Lyon, G. E. The pirate of kindergarten   **E**

Vision of beauty: the story of Sarah Breedlove Walker. Lasky, K.   **B**

VISIONS
   See also Parapsychology; Religion; Spiritual gifts

VISIONS -- FICTION
   O'Brien, A. Lara's gift   **Fic**

Visit to [series]
   Oxlade, C. A visit to England   **942**

A **visit** to England. Oxlade, C.   **942**

A **visit** to William Blake's inn. Willard, N.   **811**

VISITATION RIGHTS (DOMESTIC RELATIONS)

   See also Domestic relations

Visiting day. Woodson, J.   **E**

Visiting the dentist. Guillain, C.   **617.6**

A **visitor** for Bear. Becker, B.   **E**

VISUAL HANDICAPS *See* Vision disorders

VISUAL IMPAIRMENTS *See* Vision disorders

VISUAL INSTRUCTION *See* Audiovisual education

VISUAL LITERACY
   Marzollo, J. Help me learn subtraction   **513.2**

VISUAL LITERACY
   See also Arts; Literacy; Semiotics

VISUAL PERCEPTION -- JUVENILE LITERATURE
   McCarthy, M. A closer look   **E**
   Onishi, S. Who's hiding?   **E**

VISUAL POETRY
   Doodle dandies   **811**

VITAL STATISTICS
   See also Statistics

Vitale, Stefano
   (il) Bruchac, J. The girl who helped thunder and other Native American folktales   **398.2**
   (il) Franco, B. Pond circle   **E**
   (il) Sierra, J. Can you guess my name?   **398.2**
   (il) Sierra, J. Nursery tales around the world   **398.2**
   (il) Sloat, T. There was an old man who painted the sky   **E**
   (il) The story of Easter   **263**
   (il) Walker, A. There is a flower at the tip of my nose smelling me   **811**
   (il) Walker, A. Why war is never a good idea   **811**
   (il) When the wind stops   **E**

VITAMINS
   Royston, A. Vitamins and minerals for a healthy body   **613.2**

VITAMINS
   See also Food; Nutrition

Vitamins and minerals for a healthy body. Royston, A.   **613.2**

Viva, Frank
   Along a long road   **E**
   A long way away   **E**

Vivaldi, Antonio, 1678-1741
   About
   Krull, K. Lives of the musicians   **780.92**

Vivaldi, Antonio, 1678-1741
   About
   Shefelman, J. J. I, Vivaldi   **92**

Vivaldi, Antonio, 1678-1741
   About
   Shefelman, J. J. Anna Maria's gift   **Fic**

Vivaldi, Antonio, 1678-1741 -- Fiction
   About
   Shefelman, J. J. Anna Maria's gift   **Fic**

Vivas, Julie
   (il) Wild, M. Our granny   **E**
   (il) Wild, M. Puffling   **E**
   (il) Williams, S. Let's go visiting   **E**

VIVISECTION
   See also Animal experimentation; Surgery

Vizzini, Ned
   (jt. auth) Columbus, C. House of secrets   **Fic**

Voake, Charlotte
   Hello, twins   **E**

Voake, Charlotte
   (il) Richardson, J. Looking at pictures   **750.1**
   Ginger and the mystery visitor   **E**
   Hello, twins   **E**
   Tweedle dee dee   **782.42**
   (il) Voake, S. Insect detective   **595.7**

Voake, Steve
   Daisy Dawson is on her way!   **Fic**

Genes & DNA | **576.5**
Human body | **612**
Microscopic life | **579**
Ouch! | **612**

Walker, Rob D.
Mama says | **E**

Walker, Robert
Bar and bat mitzvahs | **296.4**

Walker, Robert
What is the theory of evolution? | **576.8**

Walker, Sally M.
Blizzard of glass | **971**
Druscilla's Halloween | **E**
Fireflies | **595.76**
Fossil fish found alive | **597.3**
Freedom song | **E**
Put inclined planes to the test | **621.8**
Put levers to the test | **621.8**
Put pulleys to the test | **621.8**
Put screws to the test | **621.8**
Put wedges to the test | **621.8**
Put wheels and axles to the test | **621.8**
Rays | **597**
The Vowel family | **E**

Walker, Steven
(il) The Stourbridge Lion | **625.26**

Walker, Steven
(il) Kittinger, J. S. Rosa's bus | **323.1**

WALKING
See also Aerobics; Athletics; Human locomotion

WALKING -- FICTION
Cooper, E. A good night walk | **E**
Frazee, M. Walk on! | **E**
Johnson, D. B. Henry hikes to Fitchburg | **E**
Walking catfish. Gray, S. H. | **597**

Walking Coyote
Juvenile literature
Bruchac, J. Buffalo song | **92**
Walking home to Rosie Lee. | **E**

WALKING IN SPACE *See* Extravehicular activity (Space flight)
Walking the Bible. Feiler, B. S. | **222**
Walking the earth. Andryszewski, T. | **304.8**
Walking to school. Bunting, E. | **E**
Walking to the bus-rider blues. Robinet, H. G. | **Fic**
The **wall.** Sis, P. | **92**
The **Wall.** Bunting, E. | **E**
The **Wall** and the Wing. Ruby, L. | **Fic**

WALL DECORATION *See* Mural painting and decoration
WALL PAINTING *See* Mural painting and decoration
Wall paintings. Harris, N. | **751.7**

Wall, Karen
(il) Helmore, J. Oh no, monster tomato! | **E**

Wallace, Bill
The legend of thunderfoot | **Fic**
Skinny-dipping at Monster Lake | **Fic**

Wallace, Carol
One nosy pup | **E**
The pumpkin mystery | **E**
The Santa secret | **E**
Turkeys together | **E**

Wallace, Chad
(il) Curtis, J. K. Seahorses | **597**

Wallace, Chad
(il) Guiberson, B. Z. Earth feeling the heat | **363.7**

Wallace, Ian
(il) Lightfoot, G. Canadian railroad trilogy | **782.42**

Wallace, John, 1966-

(il) Bauer, M. D. Wind | **551.51**

Wallace, Karen
Think of an eel | **597**

Wallace, Marianne D.
America's forests | **578.7**

Wallace, Mary
Inuksuk journey | **971**

Wallace, Nancy Elizabeth
(il) Friedlaender, L. K. Look! look! look! | **E**
Pond walk | **E**
Pumpkin day! | **E**
Ready! Set! 100th day! | **E**
Recycle every day! | **E**
Seeds! Seeds! Seeds! | **E**

Wallace, Rich
The ball hogs | **Fic**
Sports camp | **Fic**

Wallace, Sandra Neil
Little Joe | **Fic**

Walliams, David
The boy in the dress | **Fic**
Mr. Stink | **Fic**

Wallner, Alexandra
Susan B. Anthony | **324.6**

Wallner, Alexandra
(il) Adler, D. A. A picture book of Louis Braille | **686.2**
(il) Adler, D. A. A picture book of Thomas Jefferson | **973.4**
(il) The Farmer in the dell | **782.42**
Abigail Adams | **973.4**

Wallner, John C.
(il) Adler, D. A. A picture book of Louis Braille | **686.2**
(il) Adler, D. A. A picture book of Thomas Jefferson | **973.4**
(il) O'Neill, M. L. D. Hailstones and halibut bones | **811**

WALLPAPER
See also Interior design

WALLS
Knight, M. B. Talking walls | **721**

WALLS
See also Buildings; Civil engineering

WALLS -- FICTION
Dumont The chickens build a wall | **E**

WALLS -- JUVENILE LITERATURE
Knight, M. B. Talking walls | **721**
The **walls** of Cartagena. Durango, J. | **Fic**
Walls within walls. Sherry, M. | **Fic**
Wally and Mae. Kempter, C. | **E**

Walrod, Amy
(il) Howe, J. Horace and Morris but mostly Dolores | **E**
(il) Sturges, P. The Little Red Hen (makes a pizza) | **398.2**
A **walrus'** world. Arnold, C. | **599.79**
Walruses. Rebman, R. C. | **599.79**

WALRUSES
Arnold, C. A walrus' world | **599.79**
Malam, J. Pinnipeds | **599.79**
Marsh, L. Amazing animal journeys | **591.56**
Read, T. C. Exploring the world of seals and walruses | **599.79**
Rebman, R. C. Walruses | **599.79**

WALRUSES -- FICTION
Savage, S. Where's Walrus? | **E**

Walsh, Barbara
Sammy in the sky | **E**

Walsh, Danny
The cardboard box book | **745.54**

Walsh, Ellen Stoll
Balancing act | **E**
For Pete's sake | **E**
Mouse shapes | **E**

Walsh, Jake

The **wee** Christmas cabin. Hodges, M.   **E**
Wee little bunny. Thompson, L.   **E**
Wee little chick. Thompson, L.   **E**
Wee little lamb. Thompson, L.   **E**
Wee Winnie Witch's Skinny. Hamilton, V.   **E**
Wee, wee woman
   The teeny-tiny woman   **398.2**
Weedflower. Kadohata, C.   **Fic**
WEEDS
   See also Agricultural pests; Economic botany; Gardening; Plants
WEEK
   See also Calendars; Chronology
WEEK -- FICTION
   Alko, S. Every-day dress-up   **E**
   Darbyshire, K. Put it on the list   **E**
   Downing, J. No hugs till Saturday   **E**
   Glenn, S. M. Just what Mama needs   **E**
   Levine, A. A. Monday is one day   **E**
   Rosenstiehl, A. Silly Lilly in what will I be today?   **741.5**
WEEK -- SONGS -- JUVENILE LITERATURE
   Carle, E. Today is Monday   **782.421**
Weeks, Marcus
   Mozart   **92**
Weeks, Sarah
   Pie   **Fic**
Weeks, Sarah
   As simple as it seems   **Fic**
   Drip, drop   **E**
   Ella, of course!   **E**
   Guy wire   **Fic**
   Jumping the scratch   **Fic**
   Mac and Cheese   **E**
   Oggie Cooder   **Fic**
   Oggie Cooder, party animal   **Fic**
   Overboard!   **E**
   Pie   **Fic**
   Regular Guy   **Fic**
   So B. it   **Fic**
   Sophie Peterman tells the truth!   **E**
   Two eggs, please   **E**
   Woof   **E**
Weezer changes the world. McPhail, D. M.   **E**
Wegener, Alfred Lothar, 1880-1930
   About
   Saunders, C. What is the theory of plate tectonics?   **551.1**
Wehrman, Richard
   (il) Han, S. C. The rabbit's tail   **398.2**
Wehrman, Vicki
   (il) Lehman-Wilzig, T. Hanukkah around the world   **296.4**
Weigel, Jeff
   Atomic Ace   **E**
   Thunder from the sea   **741.5**
Weigelt, Udo
   Super Guinea Pig to the rescue   **E**
Weight. Sullivan, N.   **530**
WEIGHT
   See also Physics
WEIGHT (PHYSICS) -- EXPERIMENTS
   Gardner, R. Heavy-duty science projects with weight   **530.8**
WEIGHT (PHYSICS) -- EXPERIMENTS -- JUVENILE LITERATURE
   Gardner, R. Heavy-duty science projects with weight   **530.8**
WEIGHT (PHYSICS) -- MEASUREMENT
   Murphy, S. J. Mighty Maddie   **389**
WEIGHT (PHYSICS) -- MEASUREMENT -- JUVENILE LITERATURE
   Murphy, S. J. Mighty Maddie   **389**

WEIGHT CONTROL *See* Weight loss
WEIGHT LIFTING
   See also Athletics; Exercise
WEIGHT LOSS
   Edwards, H. Talking about your weight   **613.2**
   Hunt, J. The truth about diets   **613.2**
   Simons, R. I eat when I'm sad   **616.85**
   Zahensky, B. A. Diet fads   **613.2**
WEIGHT LOSS -- FICTION
   Bunting, E. My dog Jack is fat   **E**
The **Weight** of Water. Crossan, S.   **Fic**
Weighted down. Thompson, H.   **616.3**
WEIGHTS AND MEASURES
   Adamson, T. K. How do you measure weight?   **530.8**
   Cleary, B. P. On the scale   **530.8**
   Gardner, R. Ace your math and measuring science project   **530.8**
   Murphy, S. J. Mighty Maddie   **389**
   Parker, V. How big is big?   **530.8**
   Parker, V. How heavy is heavy?   **530.8**
   Parker, V. How small is small?   **591.4**
   Parker, V. How tall is tall?   **720**
   Schwartz, D. M. Millions to measure   **530.8**
   Somervill, B. A. Mass and weight   **530.8**
   Sullivan, N. Weight   **530**
WEIGHTS AND MEASURES
   See also Physics
WEIGHTS AND MEASURES -- JUVENILE LITERATURE
   Adler, D. A. Perimeter, area, and volume   **516**
   Robbins, K. For good measure   **530.8**
Weihs, Erika
   (il) Chaikin, M. Menorahs, mezuzas, and other Jewish symbols   **296.4**
Weihs, Jean
   (ed) Cataloging correctly for kids   **025.3**
Weill, Cynthia
   Count me in   **513.2**
Weiner, Miriam
   Shakespeare's Seasons   **822.3**
Weinhaus, Karen Ann
   (il) Schwartz, A. All of our noses are here, and other noodle tales   **398.2**
   (il) Schwartz, A. There is a carrot in my ear, and other noodle tales   **398.2**
Weinstein, Ellen
   Everywhere the cow says Moo!   **413**
Weinstein, Muriel Harris
   Play, Louis, play!   **92**
   When Louis Armstrong taught me scat   **E**
Weinstock, Robert
   (il) Smallcomb, P. I'm not   **E**
Weinstock, Robert
   (il) Smallcomb, P. I'm not   **E**
   Food hates you too   **811**
Weir, Jane
   Matter   **530**
   Max Planck   **92**
Weird animal sports. Watson, S. B.   **796**
Weird friends. Aruego, J.   **577.8**
Weird meat-eating plants. Aaseng, N.   **583**
Weird races. Kelley, K. C.   **796**
Weird sports [series]
   Kelley, K. C. Weird races   **796**
   Kelley, K. C. Weird sports moments   **796**
   Kelley, K. C. Weird water sports   **797**
   Watson, S. B. Weird animal sports   **796**
   Watson, S. B. Weird sports of the world   **796**

White fur flying. MacLachlan, P. — Fic
The **White** Gates. Ramthun, B. — Fic
The **white** giraffe. St. John, L. — Fic
The **White** House. Kenney, K. L. — 975.3
White House kids. — 973.09
White House Q & A. Rinaldo, D. — 975.3
White is for blueberry. Shannon, G. — E
The **White** Mountains. Christopher, J. — Fic
The **white** nights of Ramadan. Addasi, M. — E
White noise. Carter, D. A. — E
White on black. Hoban, T. — E
White owl, barn owl. Davies, N. — E
The **white** ox. Hailstone, R. — 92
The **white** ram. Gerstein, M. — E
White sands, red menace. Klages, E. — Fic
WHITE SHARK -- JUVENILE LITERATURE
  Markle, S. Great white sharks — 597
White snow, bright snow. Tresselt, A. R. — E
The **white** stag. Seredy, K. — Fic
WHITE SUPREMACISTS
  Coleman, W. Racism on trial — 345
WHITE SUPREMACY MOVEMENTS
  See also Race relations; Racism; Social movements
White tiger, blue serpent. Tseng, G. — 398.2
White water. Bandy, M. S. — E
White, Becky
  Betsy Ross — 92
White, David A.
  (il) Rotner, S. Body actions — 612
White, E. B.
  Charlotte's web — Fic
  Stuart Little — Fic
  The trumpet of the swan — Fic
White, E. B.
        About
  Lives of the writers — 809
White, Kathryn
  When will it snow? — E
White, Lee
  (il) Cannon, A. E. Sophie's fish — E
White, Lee
  (il) Nedwidek, J. Ducks don't wear socks — E
  (il) Odanaka, B. Crazy day at the Critter Cafe — E
  (il) Walker, S. M. Druscilla's Halloween — E
White, Linda
  I could do that! — 92
  Too many turkeys — E
White, Maureen
  Latrobe, K. H. The children's literature dictionary — 028.5
White, Mike
  Amity Blamity, book one — 741.5
White, Nancy
  Using Earth's underground heat — 333.8
White, Ruth
  You'll like it here (everybody does) — Fic
White, Ruth
  Belle Prater's boy — Fic
  Little Audrey — Fic
  Way Down Deep — Fic
  You'll like it here (everybody does) — Fic
White, T. H.
  The sword in the stone — Fic
White, Vicky
  (il) Jenkins, M. Can we save the tiger? — 591.68
White, Vicky
  (il) Jenkins, M. Ape — 599.8
  (il) Jenkins, M. Can we save the tiger? — 591.68
Whiteblack the penguin sees the world. Rey, M. — E

Whitehead, Jenny
  (il) Bruno, E. K. A punctuation celebration! — 428
  Holiday stew — 811
Whitehead, Kathy
  Art from her heart: folk artist Clementine Hunter — 92
Whitehead, Sarah
  How to speak cat — 636.8
  How to speak dog — 636.7
Whitehouse, Patricia
  Plants — 580.7
Whitfield, Simon
  Simon says gold: Simon Whitfield's pursuit of athletic excellence — 92
Whitfield, Simon, 1975-
        About
  Whitfield, S. Simon says gold: Simon Whitfield's pursuit of athletic excellence — 92
Whitfield, Susan
  Afghanistan — 958.1
Whitford, Rebecca
  Little yoga — 613.7
Whiting, Jim
  Space and time — 530.11
  The role of religion in the early Islamic world — 297.09
Whiting, Jim
  LeVert, S. Steroids — 362.29
  Frogs in danger — 597.8
  Threat to ancient Egyptian treasures — 932
  W.E.B. Du Bois — 92
Whiting, Sue
  The firefighters — E
Whitman, Candace
  Lines that wiggle — E
Whitman, Narcissa Prentiss, 1808-1847
        About
  Harness, C. The tragic tale of Narcissa Whitman and a faithful history of the Oregon Trail — 92
Whitman, Sylvia
  Under the Ramadan moon — 297.3
Whitman, Walt
  When I heard the learn'd astronomer — E
Whitman, Walt, 1819-1892
        About
  Kerley, B. Walt Whitman — 92
Whitt, Kelly Kizer
  Solar system forecast — 551.5
Whitt, Shannon
  (il) Weiner, M. Shakespeare's Seasons — 822.3
Whittemore, Jo
  Odd girl in — Fic
Whittenberg, Allison
  Hollywood & Maine — Fic
  Sweet Thang — Fic
Whittington. Armstrong, A. — Fic
Whittington, Richard, d. 1423
        About
  Hodges, M. Dick Whittington and his cat — 398.2
Whittington, Richard, d. 1423 -- Legends
        About
  Hodges, M. Dick Whittington and his cat — 398.2
Whitty, Hannah
  (il) Platt, C. A little bit of love — E
The **Whizz** Pop Chocolate Shop. Saunders, K. — Fic
Who ate all the cookie dough? Beaumont, K. — E
Who could that be at this hour? — Fic
Who discovered America? Wyatt, V. — 970.01
Who do I see? Yoon, S. — E
Who do you think you are? Waddell, D. — 929

Who eats what? Lauber, P.   **577**
Who feels scared? Graves, S.   **152.4**
Who has these feet?   **591.4**
Who has what? Harris, R. H.   **612.6**
Who hid the Easter eggs? Vainio, P.   **E**
Who invented the automobile? Williams, B.   **629.222**
Who invented the computer? Snedden, R.   **004**
Who is baseball's greatest pitcher? Kisseloff, J.   **796.357**
Who is driving? Timmers, L.   **E**
Who is stealing the 12 days of Christmas? Freeman, M.   **Fic**
Who likes rain? Yee, W. H.   **E**
Who likes the rain? Kaner, E.   **551.57**
Who likes the snow? Kaner, E.   **551.57**
Who likes the wind? Kaner, E.   **551.51**
Who lives here?   **E**
Who lives here? [series]
    Hodge, D. Desert animals   **591.7**
    Hodge, D. Forest animals   **591.7**
    Hodge, D. Polar animals   **591.7**
    Hodge, D. Rain forest animals   **591.7**
    Hodge, D. Savanna animals   **591.7**
    Hodge, D. Wetland animals   **591.7**
Who lives in a colorful coral reef? Lynette, R.   **591.7**
Who lives in a deep, dark cave? Lynette, R.   **591.7**
Who lives in a wet, wild rain forest? Lynette, R.   **591.7**
Who lives in an alligator hole? Rockwell, A. F.   **597.98**
Who lives on a towering mountain? Lynette, R.   **591.7**
Who lives on the icy, cold tundra. Lynette, R.   **591.7**
Who loves the fall? Raczka, B.   **E**
Who loves the little lamb? Evans, L.   **E**
Who made this cake? Nakagawa, C.   **E**
Who on earth is Dian Fossey? Kushner, J. M.   **92**
Who on earth is Rachel Carson? Scherer, G.   **92**
Who on earth is Sylvia Earle? Reichard, S. E.   **92**
Who said coo? Ruddell, D.   **E**
Who says women can't be doctors?   **E**
Who split the atom? Claybourne, A.   **539**
Who stole Grandma's million-dollar pumpkin pie? Freeman, M.   **Fic**
Who stole Halloween? Freeman, M.   **Fic**
Who stole Mona Lisa? Knapp, R.   **E**
Who stole Uncle Sam? Freeman, M.   **Fic**
Who took the farmer's [hat]? Lexau, J. M.   **E**
Who wants a cheap rhinoceros? Silverstein, S.   **E**
Who wants pizza? Thornhill, J.   **641.3**
Who wants to be a poodle I don't. Child, L.   **E**
Who was the woman who wore the hat? Patz, N.   **811**
Who what wear. Bennett, O.   **Fic**
Who will I be, Lord? Nelson, V. M.   **E**
Who will plant a tree? Pallotta, J.   **582.16**
Who will save my planet? Urrutia, M. C.   **304.2**
Who would like a Christmas tree? Obed, E. B.   **E**
Who wrote that? [series]
    Abrams, D. Gary Soto   **92**
Who's afraid of the dark? Bonsall, C. N.   **E**
Who's at the seashore? Himmelman, J.   **591.7**
Who's awake in springtime? Gershator, P.   **E**
Who's been here? Hodgkins, F.   **E**
Who's buying? Who's selling? Larson, J. S.   **381**
Who's hiding? Onishi, S.   **E**
Who's in charge?   **320.3**
Who's in my family? Harris, R. H.   **E**
Who's in Rabbit's house? Aardema, V.   **398.2**
Who's in the forest? Gershator, P.   **E**
Who's that knocking on Christmas Eve. Brett, J.   **398.2**
Who's that stepping on Plymouth Rock? Fritz, J.   **974.4**
Who's there?   **E**

WHODUNITS *See* Mystery and detective plays; Mystery fiction; Mystery films; Mystery radio programs; Mystery television programs
WHOLE LANGUAGE
    See also Education -- Experimental methods; Language arts
A **whole** nother story. Soup, C.   **Fic**
The **whole** story of half a girl. Hiranandani, V.   **Fic**
Whoo goes there?   **E**
Whooo's that? Winters, K.   **E**
Whooo's there? Serfozo, M.   **E**
WHOOPING CRANE -- JUVENILE LITERATURE
    Harkins, S. S. Threat to the whooping crane   **598**
Whooping cranes. Stearns, P. M.   **598**
Whoops-a-daisy world [series]
    Lloyd, S. Doctor Meow's big emergency   **E**
Whopper cake. Wilson, K.   **E**
Whose chick are you? Tafuri, N.   **E**
Whose mouse are you? Kraus, R.   **E**
Whose nest is this? Roemer, H. B.   **591.56**
Whose shoes? Swinburne, S. R.   **E**
Why are the ice caps melting? Rockwell, A. F.   **363.7**
Why are you picking on me? Burstein, J.   **302.3**
Why are you so scared? Andrews, B.   **616.85**
Why did the chicken cross the road? Agee, J.   **E**
Why did the chicken cross the road? and other riddles, old and new. Cole, J.   **793.73**
Why do birds sing? Holub, J.   **598**
Why do cats have whiskers? MacLeod, E.   **636.8**
Why do cats meow? Holub, J.   **636.8**
Why do dogs bark? Holub, J.   **636.7**
Why do dogs have wet noses? Coren, S.   **636.7**
Why do earthquakes happen? Mara, W.   **551.2**
Why do elephants need the sun? Wells, R. E.   **523.7**
Why do horses have manes? MacLeod, E.   **636.1**
Why do horses neigh? Holub, J.   **636.1**
Why do I brush my teeth? Royston, A.   **617.6**
Why do I burp? Thomas, I.   **612.3**
Why do I have to make my bed? Bradford, W.   **E**
Why do I run? Royston, A.   **613.7**
Why do I sleep? Royston, A.   **612.8**
Why do I wash my hands? Royston, A.   **613**
Why do leaves change color? Hicks, T. A.   **575**
Why do leaves change color? Maestro, B.   **582.16**
Why do rabbits hop? Holub, J.   **636.9**
Why do snakes hiss? Holub, J.   **597.96**
Why does it thunder and lightning? Bailer, D.   **551.55**
Why does the coqui sing? Polikoff, B. G.   **Fic**
Why does the moon change shape? Stewart, M.   **523.3**
Why don't you get a horse, Sam Adams? Fritz, J.   **92**
Why I sneeze, shiver, hiccup, and yawn. Berger, M.   **612.7**
Why Is Milk White? Coelho, A.   **540**
Why is snot green. Murphy, G.   **500**
Why is there life on Earth? Solway, A.   **576.8**
Why it works [series]
    Claybourne, A. Electricity   **537**
    Claybourne, A. Light and dark   **535**
    Claybourne, A. Materials   **620.1**
    Claybourne, A. Pushes and pulls   **531**
Why mosquitoes buzz in people's ears. Aardema, V.   **398.2**
Why not, Lafayette? Fritz, J.   **973.3**
Why pi. Ball, J.   **530.8**
Why the chicken crossed the road. Macaulay, D.   **E**
Why the sky is far away. Gerson   **398.2**
Why the Sun and the Moon live in the sky. Dayrell, E.   **398.2**
Why war is never a good idea. Walker, A.   **811**
Why? Torrey, R.   **E**
Why? De Paola, T.   **92**

Bidner, J. Is my dog a wolf? **636.7**
Brandenburg, J. Face to face with wolves **599.77**
Cohn, S. One wolf howls **599.77**
George, J. C. The wolves are back **599.77**
Gibbons, G. Wolves **599.74**
Goldish, M. Red wolves **599.77**
Markle, S. Wolves **599.77**
Marshall, J. Swine Lake **E**
McAllister, I. The sea wolves **599.77**
Patent, D. H. When the wolves returned **599.77**
Read, T. C. Exploring the world of wolves **599.77**
Riggs, K. Wolves **599.77**
Rutherford, C. A dog is a dog **636.7**
Slade, S. What if there were no gray wolves? **577.3**
Whatley, B. Wait! No paint! **E**
Wolves. Markle, S. **599.77**
Wolves. Gravett, E. **E**
WOLVES -- FICTION
　The unseen guest **Fic**
　Virginia Wolf **Fic**
WOLVES -- FOLKLORE -- GRAPHIC NOVELS
　Alley, Z. B. There's a wolf at the door **398.2**
WOLVES -- JUVENILE FICTION
　Gliori, D. What's the time, Mr. Wolf? **E**
　Gravett, E. Wolf won't bite! **E**
　Little Red Riding Hood **E**
　Brandenburg, J. Face to face with wolves **599.77**
　Cohn, S. One wolf howls **599.77**
　Gibbons, G. Wolves **599.74**
　Markle, S. Wolves **599.77**
　Patent, D. H. When the wolves returned **599.77**
WOLVES -- REINTRODUCTION -- JUVENILE LITERA-
　TURE
　George, J. C. The wolves are back **599.77**
WOLVES -- SONGS
　Rueda, C. Let's play in the forest while the wolf is not
　　around **782.42**
WOLVES -- YELLOWSTONE NATIONAL PARK -- JU-
　VENILE LITERATURE
　George, J. C. The wolves are back **599.77**
The **wolves** are back. George, J. C. **599.77**
The **wolves** in the walls. **E**
Wolves of the Beyond [series]
　Lasky, K. Frost wolf **Fic**
　Lasky, K. Lone wolf **Fic**
　Lasky, K. Shadow wolf **Fic**
Wolves of the beyond [series]
　Lasky, K. Watch wolf **Fic**
The **wolves** of Willoughby Chase. Aiken, J. **Fic**
WOMAN *See* Women
A **woman** for president. Krull, K. **92**
The **woman** who lived with wolves, & other stories from the
　tipi. Goble, P. **398.2**
The **woman** who married a bear. James, E. **398.2**
The **woman** who outshone the sun. Cruz, A. **398.21**
Wombat walkabout. Shields, C. D. **E**
A **wombat's** world. Arnold, C. **599.2**
WOMBATS
　Arnold, C. A wombat's world **599.2**
　French, J. How to scratch a wombat **599.2**
WOMBATS -- FICTION
　French, J. Christmas wombat **E**
　French, J. Diary of a baby wombat **E**
　French, J. Diary of a wombat **E**
　Shields, C. D. Wombat walkabout **E**
WOMBATS -- JUVENILE FICTION
　French, J. Christmas wombat **E**
WOMBATS -- JUVENILE LITERATURE

French, J. How to scratch a wombat **599.2**
WOMEN
　Branzei, S. Adventurers **920.72**
　Green, M. Y. A strong right arm: the story of Mamie Peanut
　　Johnson **92**
　Thimmesh, C. Girls think of everything **920**
　Yolen, J. Not one damsel in distress **398.22**
WOMEN -- BIBLIOGRAPHY
　Crew, H. S. Women engaged in war in literature for youth **016**
WOMEN -- BIOGRAPHY
　Hartland, J. Bon appetit! **641.509**
　McCann, M. R. Girls who rocked the world **920.72**
WOMEN -- BIOGRAPHY
　See also Biography
WOMEN -- BIOGRAPHY -- JUVENILE LITERATURE
　Branzei, S. Adventurers **920.72**
　Cummins, J. Women daredevils **920**
　León, V. Outrageous women of the Middle Ages **920.72**
WOMEN -- DISEASES
　See also Diseases
WOMEN -- EDUCATION -- AFGHANISTAN -- JUVE-
　NILE LITERATURE
　Winter, J. Nasreen's secret school **371.82**
WOMEN -- EMPLOYMENT
　Bingham, J. Women at war **305.4**
　Colman, P. Rosie the riveter **331.4**
WOMEN -- EMPLOYMENT -- JUVENILE LITERATURE
　Colman, P. Rosie the riveter **331.4**
WOMEN -- ENFRANCHISEMENT *See* Women -- Suffrage
WOMEN -- FICTION
　Alko, S. Every-day dress-up **E**
WOMEN -- FOLKLORE
　Clayton, S. P. Amazons! **398.2**
　San Souci, R. Cut from the same cloth **398.2**
　Tchana, K. H. The serpent slayer: and other stories of strong
　　women **398.2**
　Yolen, J. Not one damsel in distress **398.22**
WOMEN -- HEALTH AND HYGIENE
　See also Health; Hygiene
WOMEN -- HISTORY
　León, V. Outrageous women of the Middle Ages **920.72**
　McCann, M. R. Girls who rocked the world **920.72**
WOMEN -- HISTORY
　See also Feminism; History
WOMEN -- HISTORY -- JUVENILE LITERATURE
　Who says women can't be doctors? **E**
WOMEN -- INDIA
　Woog, A. Jyotirmayee Mohapatra **92**
WOMEN -- INDIA -- FICTION
　Whelan, G. Homeless bird **Fic**
WOMEN -- PHYSICAL FITNESS
　See also Physical fitness; Women -- Health and hygiene
WOMEN -- PSYCHOLOGY
　See also Psychology
WOMEN -- SOCIAL CONDITIONS
　Bingham, J. Women at war **305.4**
　Coster, P. A new deal for women **305.4**
　Gorman, J. L. The modern feminist movement **305.4**
　Stearman, K. Women of today **305.4**
WOMEN -- SOCIETIES
　See also Clubs; Societies
WOMEN -- SUFFRAGE
　Hollihan, K. L. Rightfully ours **324.6**
　Wallner, A. Susan B. Anthony **324.6**
WOMEN -- SUFFRAGE -- FICTION
　Beard, D. B. Operation Clean Sweep **Fic**
　Hurst, C. O. You come to Yokum **Fic**
　Murphy, C. R. Marching with Aunt Susan **E**

Matsen, B. The incredible record-setting deep-sea dive of the bathysphere **551.46**

McCully, E. A. Squirrel and John Muir **E**

McCurdy, M. Walden then & now **818**

McDonnell, P. Me . . . Jane **92**

Scherer, G. Who on earth is Rachel Carson? **92**

Sheldon, D. Into the deep **92**

Thomas, P. For the birds: the life of Roger Tory Peterson **92**

Wadsworth, G. Camping with the president **92**

Winter, J. The watcher: Jane Goodall's life with the chimps **92**

WRITERS ON POLITICS

Demi Gandhi **954.03**

Fritz, J. Why don't you get a horse, Sam Adams? **92**

Wilkinson, P. Gandhi **92**

WRITERS ON RELIGION

Avi Finding Providence: the story of Roger Williams **92**

De Paola, T. The song of Francis **E**

Demi Muhammad **297**

Egielski, R. Saint Francis and the wolf **398.2**

Gibfried, D. Brother Juniper **E**

Kennedy, R. F. Saint Francis of Assisi **271**

Langton, J. Saint Francis and the wolf **398.2**

Nobisso, J. Francis woke up early **E**

Norris, K. The holy twins: Benedict and Scholastica **271**

Visconti, G. Clare and Francis **271**

WRITERS ON SCIENCE

Adler, D. A. B. Franklin, printer **973.3**

Anderson, M. J. Carl Linnaeus **92**

Anderson, M. Amazing Leonardo da Vinci inventions you can build yourself **92**

Ashby, R. Young Charles Darwin and the voyage of the Beagle **92**

Balliett, B. The Danger Box **Fic**

Barretta, G. Neo Leo **609**

Barretta, G. Now & Ben **609**

Bausum, A. Dragon bones and dinosaur eggs: a photobiography of Roy Chapman Andrews **92**

Benjamin Franklinstein meets the Fright brothers **Fic**

Caper, W. American bison **599.64**

Cole, H. A nest for Celeste **Fic**

Conlan, K. Under the ice **578.7**

Davies, J. The boy who drew birds: a story of John James Audubon **92**

Ehrlich, A. Rachel **92**

Ellis, S. From reader to writer **028**

Fleming, C. Ben Franklin's almanac **92**

Fleming, C. The hatmaker's sign **E**

Fritz, J. Leonardo's horse **730.92**

Fritz, J. What's the big idea, Ben Franklin? **92**

Greenstein, E. The goose man **92**

Harness, C. The remarkable Benjamin Franklin **92**

Hightower, P. The greatest mathematician **92**

Hollihan, K. L. Isaac Newton and physics for kids **92**

Hopkinson, D. The humblebee hunter **E**

Hyde, N. What is germ theory? **615**

Knapp, R. Who stole Mona Lisa? **E**

Krull, K. Charles Darwin **92**

Krull, K. Isaac Newton **92**

Krull, K. Leonardo da Vinci **92**

Kushner, J. M. Who on earth is Dian Fossey? **92**

Lasky, K. One beetle too many: the extraordinary adventures of Charles Darwin **92**

Lawson, R. Ben and me **Fic**

The librarian who measured the earth **520**

MacDonald, B. The secret of the sealed room **Fic**

Macdonald, W. Galileo's leaning tower experiment **531**

Markle, S. Animals Charles Darwin saw **92**

Matsen, B. The incredible record-setting deep-sea dive of the

bathysphere **551.46**

McElligott, M. Benjamin Franklinstein lives! **Fic**

McGinty, A. B. Darwin **92**

McLean, A. What is atomic theory? **539.7**

Miller, B. M. Benjamin Franklin, American genius **92**

O'Leary, D. What are Newton's laws of motion? **531**

Ollhoff, J. The germ detectives **616.9**

Panchyk, R. Galileo for kids **92**

Phillips, J. Leonardo da Vinci **92**

Rushby, P. Ben Franklin **92**

Schanzer, R. What Darwin saw **92**

Scherer, G. Who on earth is Rachel Carson? **92**

Schroeder, A. Ben Franklin **92**

Scieszka, J. Da wild, da crazy, da Vinci **Fic**

Sheldon, D. Into the deep **92**

Sis, P. The tree of life: a book depicting the life of Charles Darwin, naturalist, geologist & thinker **92**

Sitarski, A. Cold light **572**

Smith, L. John, Paul, George & Ben **E**

Stanley, D. Leonardo da Vinci **709.2**

Starry messenger **520**

Steele, P. Galileo **92**

Steele, P. Isaac Newton **92**

Venezia, M. Stephen Hawking **92**

Walker, R. What is the theory of evolution? **576.8**

Weaver, A. H. The voyage of the beetle **576.8**

Wood, A. J. Charles Darwin and the Beagle adventure **508**

Woodruff, E. George Washington's spy **Fic**

Yount, L. William Harvey **92**

Zamosky, L. Louis Pasteur **92**

WRITING

Fletcher, R. Guy-write **808.06**

WRITING

See also Communication; Language and languages; Language arts

WRITING (AUTHORSHIP) See Authorship; Creative writing

WRITING -- FICTION

Dormer, F. W. The obstinate pen **E**

WRITING -- HISTORY

Donoughue, C. The story of writing **411**

Robb, D. Ox, house, stick **411**

WRITING -- JUVENILE LITERATURE

Lee, H. V. At the beach **495.1**

WRITING -- MATERIALS AND INSTRUMENTS -- FICTION

Yorinks, A. Homework **E**

Writing a screenplay. Miles, L. **808**

Writing and publishing. **808**

A **writing** kind of day. Fletcher, R. **811**

Writing magic. Levine, G. C. **808.3**

WRITING OF NUMERALS

See also Handwriting; Numerals; Writing

Writing the U.S. Constitution. Mortensen, L. **342**

WRITINGS OF TEENAGERS See Teenagers' writings

Wu, Daozi, 689-759 -- Fiction

About

Look, L. Brush of the gods **E**

Wu, Daozi, 689-759 -- Juvenile fiction

About

Look, L. Brush of the gods **E**

Wu, Donald

(il) Boelts, M. Dogerella **E**

(il) Fehler, G. Change-up **811**

(il) Hubbell, P. Shaggy dogs, waggy dogs **E**

Wu, Leslie

(il) Markle, S. Butterfly tree **E**

Wulffson, Don L.